P9-DCE-290

Presented to

BY

ON

Your word is a lamp to my feet and
a light for my path. Psalm 119:105

THIS CERTIFIES THAT

AND

WERE UNITED IN

HOLY MATRIMONY

ON THE

DAY OF A.D.

AT

IN ACCORDANCE WITH THE LAWS OF

OFFICIATING

WITNESS

WITNESS

A MAN WILL . . . BE UNITED TO HIS WIFE
AND THEY WILL BECOME ONE FLESH. GENESIS 2:24

MARRIAGES

HUSBAND

WIFE

PLACE DATE

HUSBAND

WIFE

PLACE DATE

HUSBAND

WIFE

PLACE DATE

HUSBAND

WIFE

PLACE DATE

HUSBAND

WIFE

PLACE DATE

HUSBAND

WIFE

PLACE DATE

LOVE IS PATIENT, LOVE IS KIND . . .
LOVE NEVER FAILS. 1 CORINTHIANS 13:4,8

BIRTHS

NAME

BORN TO DATE

NAME

BORN TO DATE

NAME

BORN TO DATE

NAME

BORN TO DATE

NAME

BORN TO DATE

NAME

BORN TO DATE

NAME

BORN TO DATE

NAME

BORN TO DATE

YOU KNIT ME TOGETHER IN MY MOTHER'S WOMB. PSALM 139:13

Baptisms

NAME

MINISTER

PLACE DATE

NAME

MINISTER

PLACE DATE

NAME

MINISTER

PLACE DATE

NAME

MINISTER

PLACE DATE

NAME

MINISTER

PLACE DATE

NAME

MINISTER

PLACE DATE

MAKE DISCIPLES OF ALL NATIONS,
BAPTIZING THEM. MATTHEW 28:19

SPECIAL EVENTS

EVENT

PLACE DATE

EVENT

PLACE DATE

EVENT

PLACE DATE

EVENT

PLACE DATE

EVENT

PLACE DATE

EVENT

PLACE DATE

THE LORD REIGNS,
LET THE EARTH BE GLAD. PSALM 97:1

Church Record

EVENT

MINISTER

CHURCH DATE

EVENT

MINISTER

CHURCH DATE

EVENT

MINISTER

CHURCH DATE

EVENT

MINISTER

CHURCH DATE

EVENT

MINISTER

CHURCH DATE

EVENT

MINISTER

CHURCH DATE

YOU ARE . . . MEMBERS OF GOD'S HOUSEHOLD. EPHESIANS 2:19

Deaths

NAME

DATE

NAME

DATE

NAME

DATE

NAME

DATE

NAME

DATE

NAME

DATE

NAME

DATE

NAME

DATE

For to me, to live is Christ
and to die is gain. Philippians 1:21

Old Testament Chronology

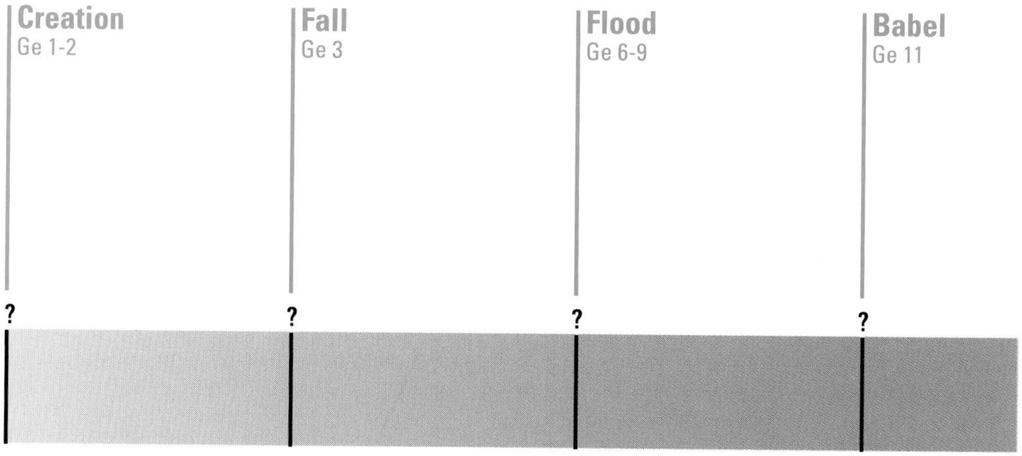

Creation Ge 1-2	Fall Ge 3	Flood Ge 6-9	Babel Ge 11
?	?	?	?

Old Testament Chronology

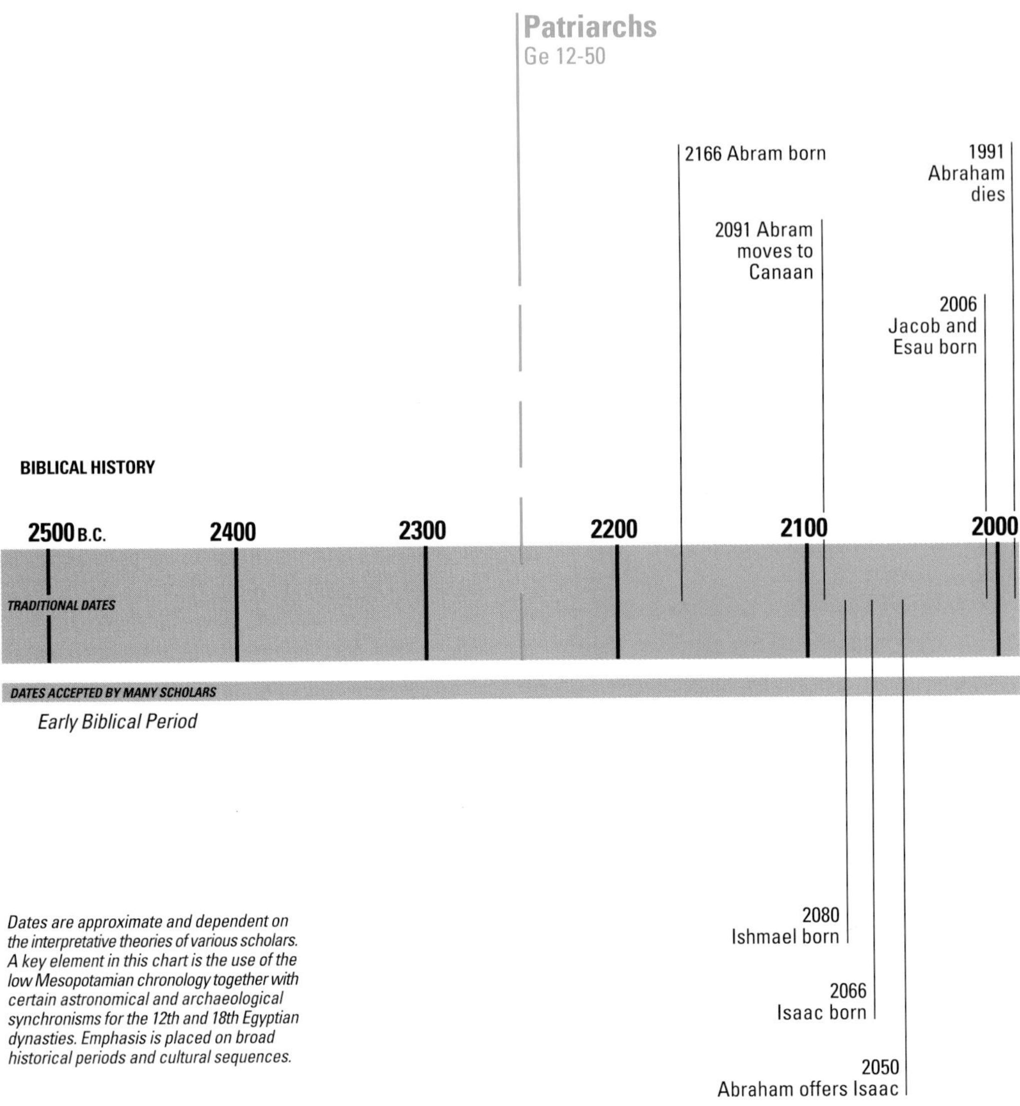

Dates are approximate and dependent on the interpretative theories of various scholars. A key element in this chart is the use of the low Mesopotamian chronology together with certain astronomical and archaeological synchronisms for the 12th and 18th Egyptian dynasties. Emphasis is placed on broad historical periods and cultural sequences.

WORLD HISTORY

	2500 B.C.	Ebla texts 2400	2300	2200	2100	Ur III texts 2000
S. MESOPOTAMIA / N. MESOPOTAMIA	Early Dynastic Period		Akkadian Period		Neo-Sumerian Period	
EGYPT		Old Kingdom			1st Intermediate Period	
SYRIA-PALESTINE		Ebla				
ANATOLIA				Hattian Kingdoms		
CRETE		Early Minoan Period				
PERSIA					Elamite Dynasties	
GREECE		Early Helladic Period				
ITALY						

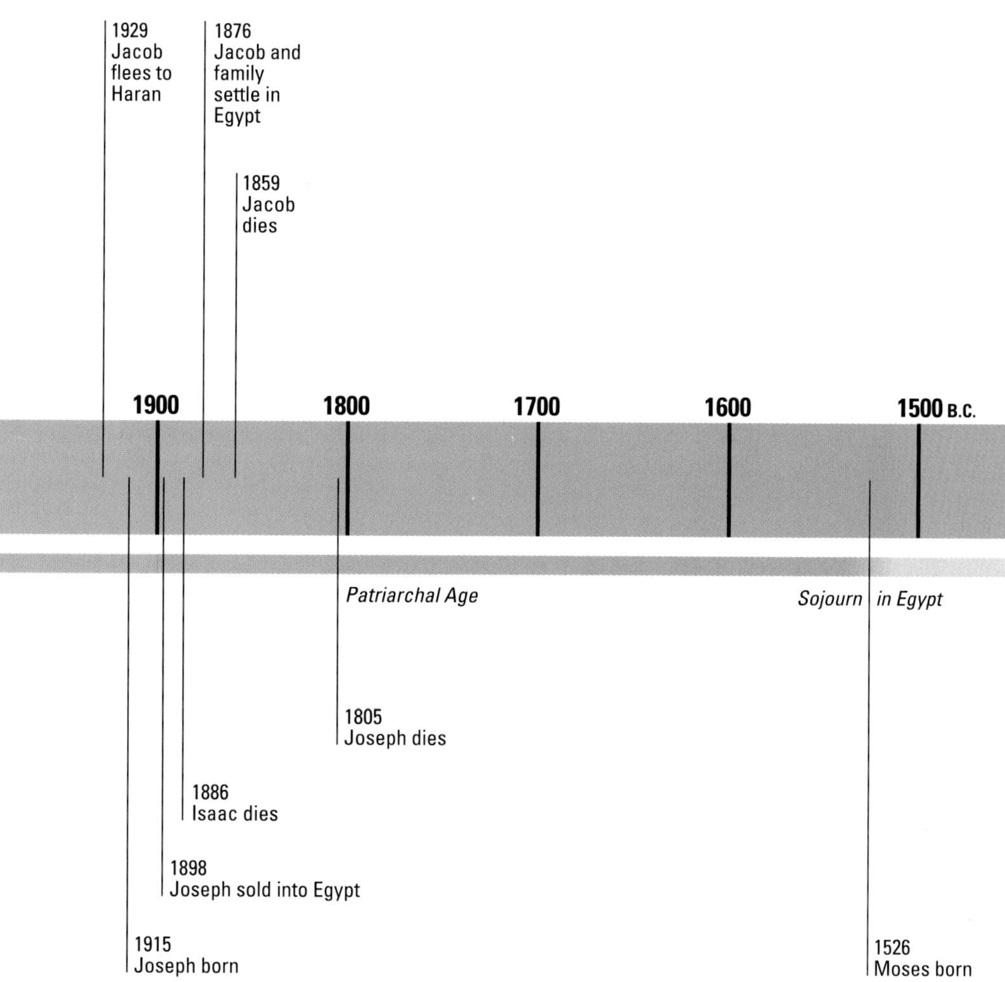

Cappadocian texts
Mari texts
Hammurapi texts

1900 1800 1700 1600 1500 B.C.

Isin-Larsa Period
Old Babylonian Period
Middle Kingdom
2nd Intermediate (Hyksos) Period
New Kingdom
Amorite Period
Hyksos Period
Late Canaanite Period
Hittite Old Kingdom
Middle Minoan Period
Middle Helladic Period

Old Testament Chronology

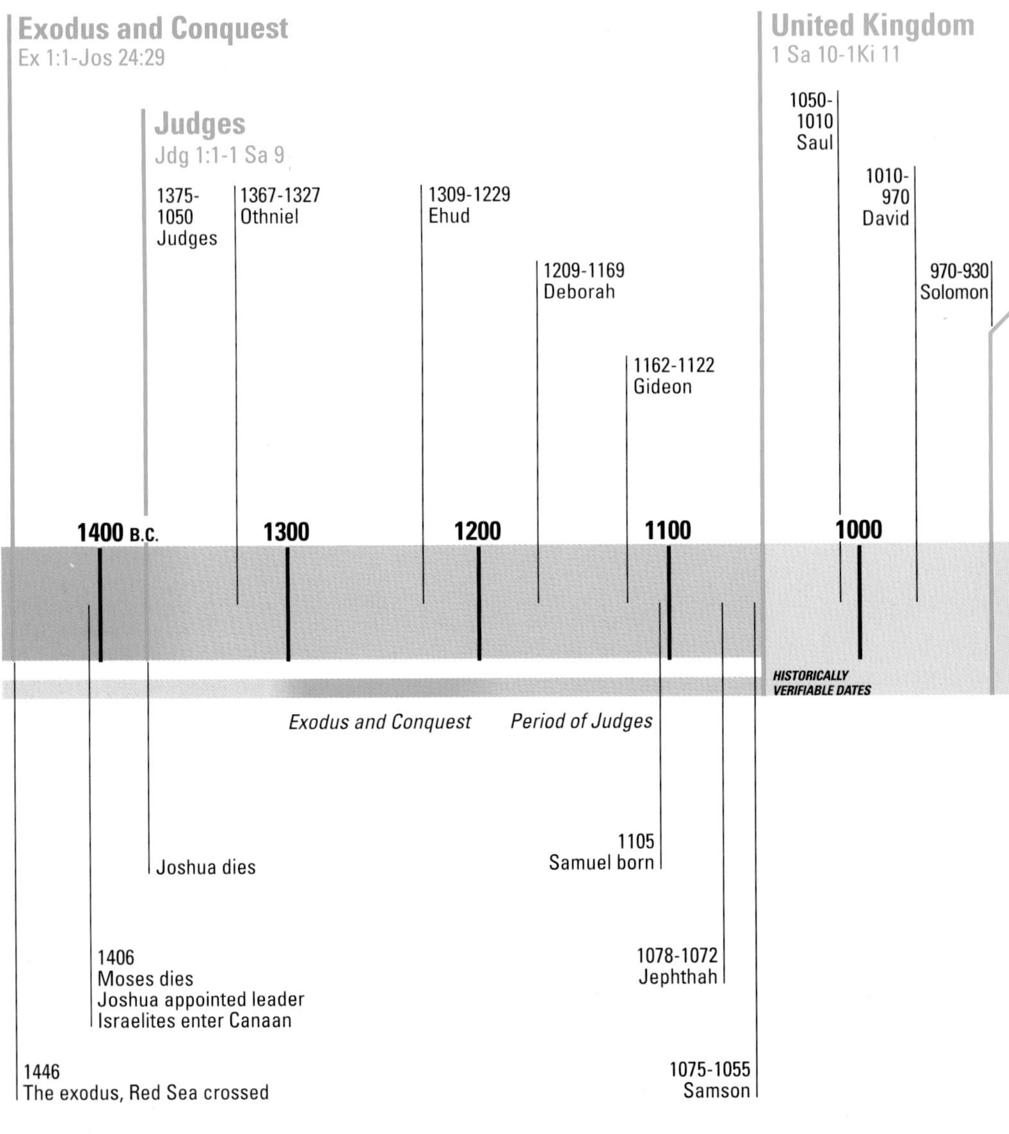

Nuzi texts · Ugaritic texts · Amarna texts · Merneptah inscription · Medinet Habu inscriptions · Shishak inscription

	1400 B.C. – 1300 – 1200 – 1100 – 1000
S. MESOPOTAMIA	Kassite Period
N. MESOPOTAMIA	← Mitannian Kingdom; Middle Assyrian Period
EGYPT	New Kingdom
SYRIA-PALESTINE	Late Canaanite Period; Sea Peoples; Phoenician,
ANATOLIA	Hittite Empire; Phrygian Period
CRETE	Late Minoan Period; Dorian States
PERSIA	
GREECE	Late Helladic (Mycenean) Period; Dorian States
ITALY	

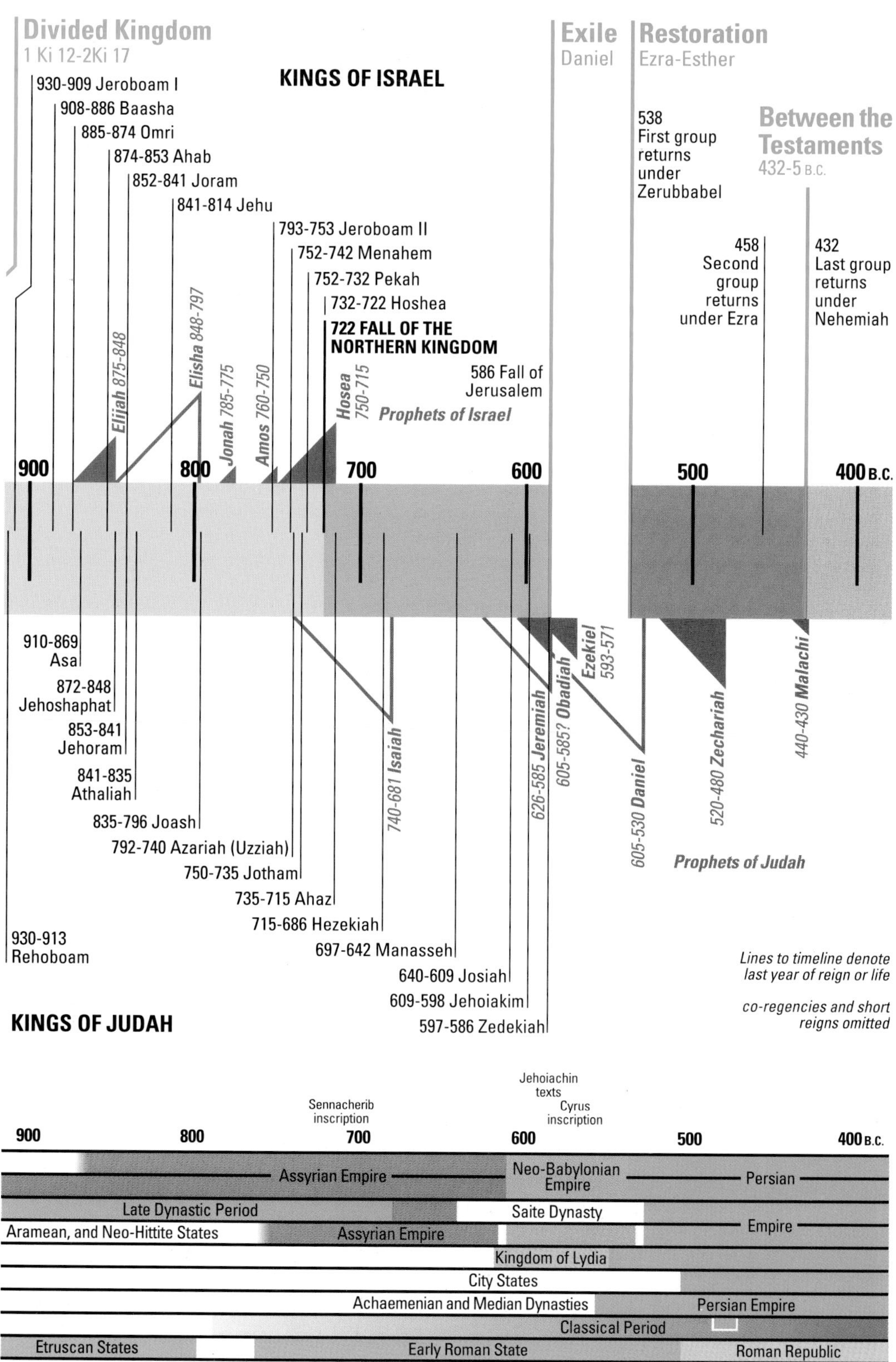

Divided Kingdom
1 Ki 12-2Ki 17
KINGS OF ISRAEL
930-909 Jeroboam I
908-886 Baasha
885-874 Omri
874-853 Ahab
852-841 Joram
841-814 Jehu
793-753 Jeroboam II
752-742 Menahem
752-732 Pekah
732-722 Hoshea
722 FALL OF THE NORTHERN KINGDOM
Exile
Daniel
Restoration
Ezra-Esther
538 First group returns under Zerubbabel
Between the Testaments
432-5 B.C.
458 Second group returns under Ezra
432 Last group returns under Nehemiah
586 Fall of Jerusalem
Elijah 875-848
Elisha 848-797
Jonah 785-775
Amos 760-750
Hosea 750-715
Prophets of Israel
900
800
700
600
500
400 B.C.
910-869 Asa
872-848 Jehoshaphat
853-841 Jehoram
841-835 Athaliah
835-796 Joash
792-740 Azariah (Uzziah)
750-735 Jotham
735-715 Ahaz
715-686 Hezekiah
697-642 Manasseh
640-609 Josiah
609-598 Jehoiakim
597-586 Zedekiah
930-913 Rehoboam
KINGS OF JUDAH
740-681 Isaiah
626-585 Jeremiah
605-585? Obadiah
Ezekiel 593-571
605-530 Daniel
520-480 Zechariah
440-430 Malachi
Prophets of Judah
Lines to timeline denote last year of reign or life
co-regencies and short reigns omitted
Sennacherib inscription
Jehoiachin texts
Cyrus inscription
900
800
700
600
500
400 B.C.
Assyrian Empire
Neo-Babylonian Empire
Persian
Late Dynastic Period
Saite Dynasty
Empire
Aramean, and Neo-Hittite States
Assyrian Empire
Kingdom of Lydia
City States
Achaemenian and Median Dynasties
Persian Empire
Classical Period
Etruscan States
Early Roman State
Roman Republic

New Testament Chronology

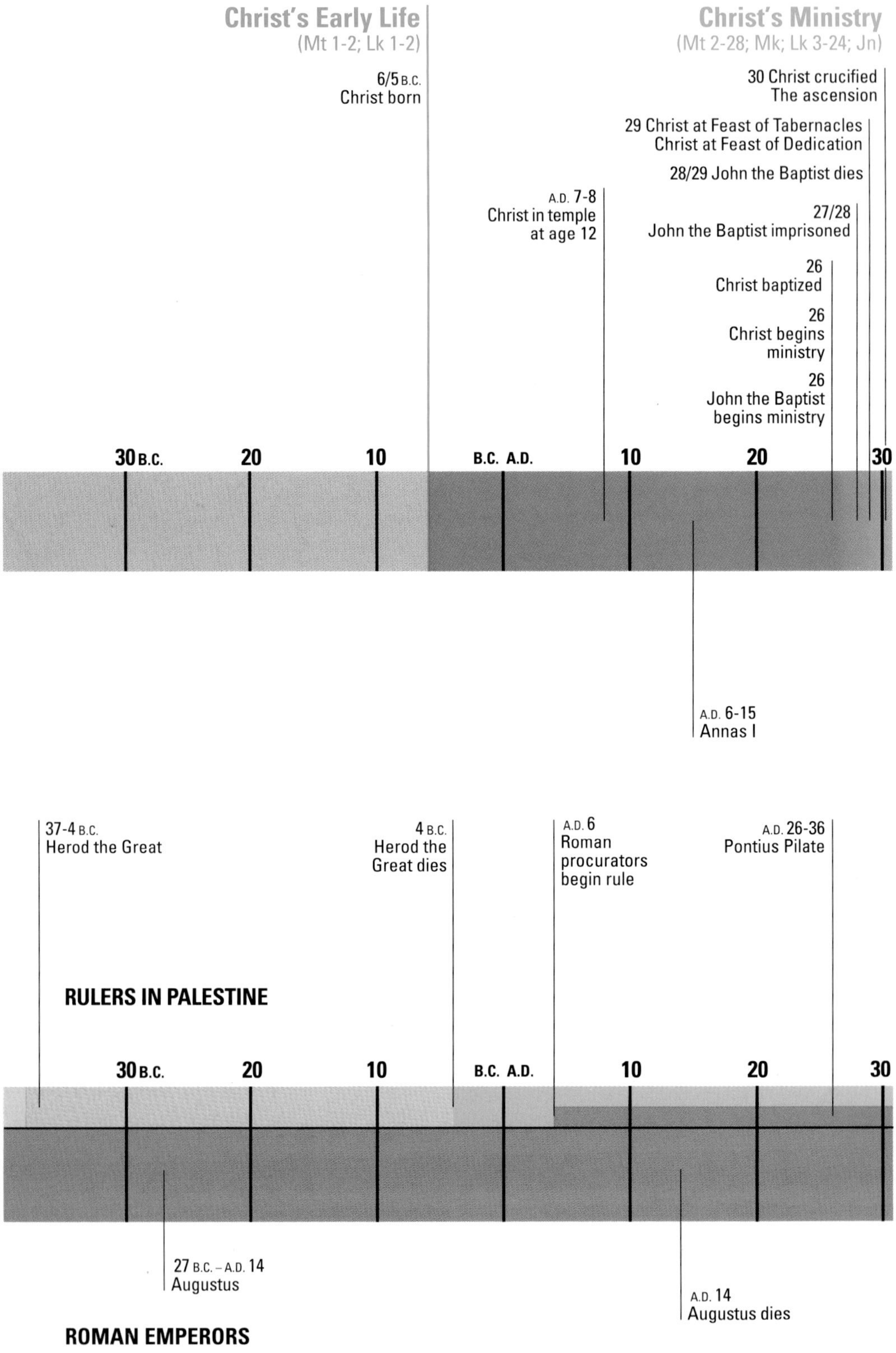

Christ's Early Life
(Mt 1-2; Lk 1-2)
6/5 B.C.
Christ born
Christ's Ministry
(Mt 2-28; Mk; Lk 3-24; Jn)
30 Christ crucified
The ascension
29 Christ at Feast of Tabernacles
Christ at Feast of Dedication
28/29 John the Baptist dies
A.D. 7-8
Christ in temple
at age 12
27/28
John the Baptist imprisoned
26
Christ baptized
26
Christ begins
ministry
26
John the Baptist
begins ministry
30 B.C.
20
10
B.C. A.D.
10
20
30
A.D. 6-15
Annas I
37-4 B.C.
Herod the Great
4 B.C.
Herod the
Great dies
A.D. 6
Roman
procurators
begin rule
A.D. 26-36
Pontius Pilate
RULERS IN PALESTINE
30 B.C.
20
10
B.C. A.D.
10
20
30
27 B.C. – A.D. 14
Augustus
A.D. 14
Augustus dies
ROMAN EMPERORS

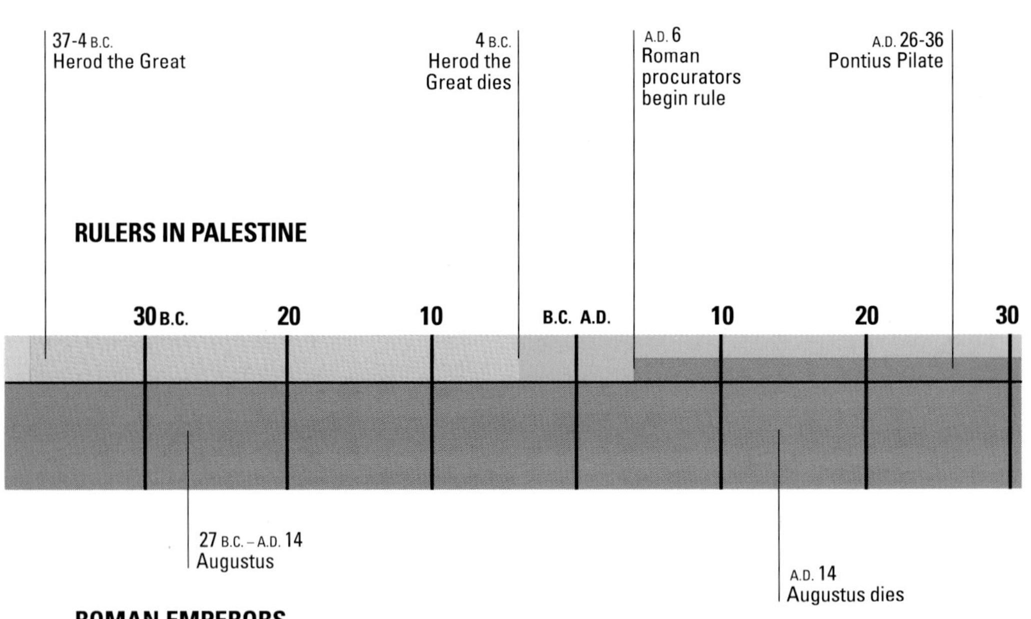

The Early Church
(Acts-Revelation)

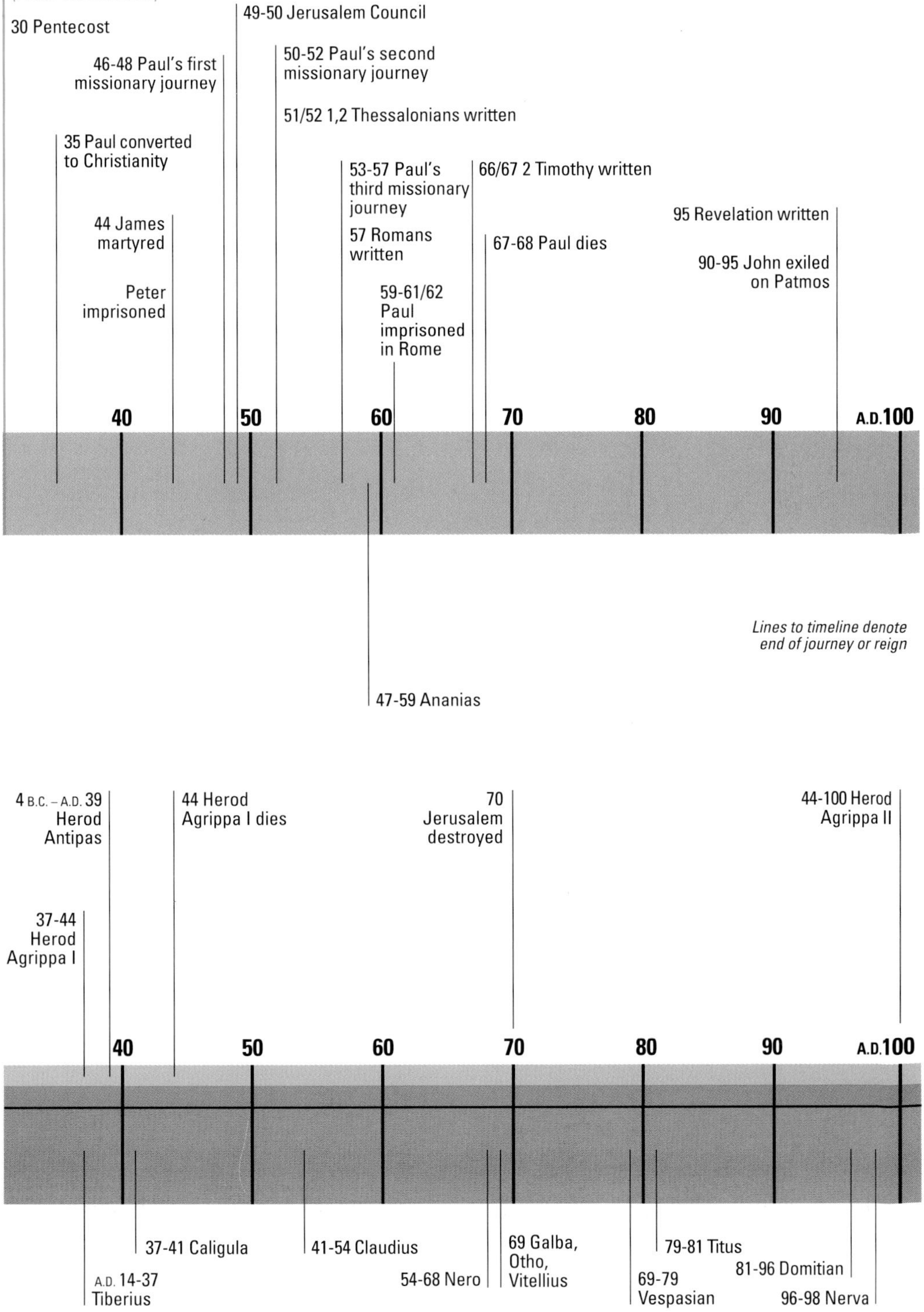

30 Pentecost
35 Paul converted to Christianity
44 James martyred
Peter imprisoned
46-48 Paul's first missionary journey
49-50 Jerusalem Council
50-52 Paul's second missionary journey
51/52 1,2 Thessalonians written
53-57 Paul's third missionary journey
57 Romans written
59-61/62 Paul imprisoned in Rome
66/67 2 Timothy written
67-68 Paul dies
95 Revelation written
90-95 John exiled on Patmos
40
50
60
70
80
90
A.D.100
Lines to timeline denote end of journey or reign
47-59 Ananias
4 B.C. – A.D. 39 Herod Antipas
37-44 Herod Agrippa I
44 Herod Agrippa I dies
70 Jerusalem destroyed
44-100 Herod Agrippa II
40
50
60
70
80
90
A.D.100
A.D. 14-37 Tiberius
37-41 Caligula
41-54 Claudius
54-68 Nero
69 Galba, Otho, Vitellius
69-79 Vespasian
79-81 Titus
81-96 Domitian
96-98 Nerva

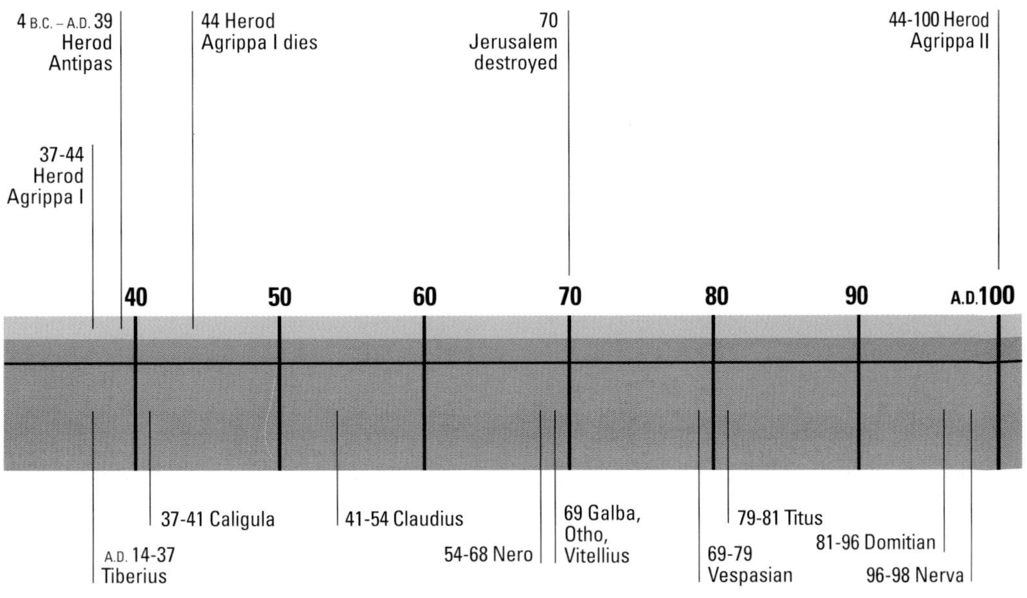

THE
LIVING
INSIGHTS
STUDY BIBLE

NEW

INTERNATIONAL

VERSION

CHARLES R. SWINDOLL

GENERAL EDITOR

Zondervan Publishing House
Grand Rapids, MI 49530, U.S.A.

Library of Congress Catalog Card Number 96-60770
Published by Zondervan Publishing House
Grand Rapids, Michigan 49530, U.S.A.
http://www.zondervan.com

Printed in the United States of America

96 97 98 99 00 01 02 8 7 6 5 4 3 2 1

Q

You will be pleased to know that a portion of the purchase price of your new NIV Bible has been provided to International Bible Society to help spread the gospel of Jesus Christ around the world!

The Living Insights Study Bible

General Editor's Preface

Dear Reader,

Throughout my ministry I have had no greater joy than to share the treasures of the Bible's wisdom and truth. This has caused me to realize there is no greater need than for people everywhere to immerse themselves in God's "library of living truth" and find the hope of salvation through this, the only trustworthy guide for living.

It is my heart's desire that *The Living Insights Study Bible* will warm your heart to these 66 books and provide you with the sturdy limbs to hold on to in your journey through the delightful forest of God's marvelous masterpiece—His inspired and inerrant Word.

Through a careful crafting of specific features contained within these pages, I have attempted to combine reliable scholarship with an "in-the-trenches" practicality so that you may be solidly grounded in the doctrines of the Christian faith and strongly encouraged in your Christian life. The ancillary material that accompanies the Bible text represents the distilling of a lifetime of preaching, teaching and reflecting on God's Word.

I pray that these insights will be helpful to you and lead to an enjoyment and excitement that perhaps you haven't experienced before in your study of the Scriptures. But I will have failed if in the end you read only the accompanying material and fail to read God's powerful and life-changing Word yourself, reverently reflecting on it and allowing Him to communicate to you what He would have you know and believe.

So let me express a word of thanks to you, my friend, for the privilege of accompanying you in this journey through the Book that is unlike any other book. I humbly offer you my insights gleaned from years of studying God's Word, with the prayer that you would have your faith energized and your understanding of God's truth deepened.

May our gracious Lord bless you and guide you, each one of you, as you draw closer to Him and as you grow deeper in love with Him and stronger in your love for one another.

Chuck Swindoll

Charles R. Swindoll

Abbreviations of the Books of the Bible

The following abbreviations are used in the end-of-paragraph reference system included in the text of the New International Version; the abbreviations are also used in the *Index to Subjects, Index to Living Insights* and *NIV Concordance* in the back of this Bible.

Genesis	*Ge*	Isaiah	*Isa*	Romans	*Ro*
Exodus	*Ex*	Jeremiah	*Jer*	1 Corinthians	*1Co*
Leviticus	*Lev*	Lamentations	*La*	2 Corinthians	*2Co*
Numbers	*Nu*	Ezekiel	*Eze*	Galatians	*Gal*
Deuteronomy	*Dt*	Daniel	*Da*	Ephesians	*Eph*
Joshua	*Jos*	Hosea	*Hos*	Philippians	*Php*
Judges	*Jdg*	Joel	*Joel*	Colossians	*Col*
Ruth	*Ru*	Amos	*Am*	1 Thessalonians	*1Th*
1 Samuel	*1Sa*	Obadiah	*Ob*	2 Thessalonians	*2Th*
2 Samuel	*2Sa*	Jonah	*Jnh*	1 Timothy	*1Ti*
1 Kings	*1Ki*	Micah	*Mic*	2 Timothy	*2Ti*
2 Kings	*2Ki*	Nahum	*Na*	Titus	*Tit*
1 Chronicles	*1Ch*	Habakkuk	*Hab*	Philemon	*Phm*
2 Chronicles	*2Ch*	Zephaniah	*Zep*	Hebrews	*Heb*
Ezra	*Ezr*	Haggai	*Hag*	James	*Jas*
Nehemiah	*Ne*	Zechariah	*Zec*	1 Peter	*1Pe*
Esther	*Est*	Malachi	*Mal*	2 Peter	*2Pe*
Job	*Job*	Matthew	*Mt*	1 John	*1Jn*
Psalms	*Ps*	Mark	*Mk*	2 John	*2Jn*
Proverbs	*Pr*	Luke	*Lk*	3 John	*3Jn*
Ecclesiastes	*Ecc*	John	*Jn*	Jude	*Jude*
Song of Songs	*SS*	Acts	*Ac*	Revelation	*Rev*

Contents: *Books of the Bible*

THE OLD TESTAMENT

THE NEW TESTAMENT

Contents: *Articles and Charts*

Articles are marked with ❖ and set in *italics.*

Contents: *Profiles*

The Living Insights Study Bible
Introduction

About The Living Insights Study Bible

The Living Insights Study Bible offers you an exciting opportunity to dig deeply into the text of God's Word in a fresh, new way. Now you can gain a clearer understanding of the truths of the Bible and grasp the wonder of God's great plan of salvation that fills the whole Bible from Genesis through Revelation. All the features of this special Bible edition are specially designed to help you hear God's voice speaking to you from His Word and drawing you closer to Him.

Features of The Living Insights Study Bible

The Living Insights Study Bible features the text of the New International Version, summary charts and articles at the beginning of each book of the Bible, in-depth articles on key doctrines of the Christian faith, character profiles, in-text charts, section summaries, "living insights," an end-of-paragraph cross-reference system, parallel passages in the Gospels, a glossary of doctrinal terms, comprehensive indexes and an NIV concordance.

The Bible Text

All of life must be guided by God's Word. In order for this to happen, there is no substitute for reading and studying the words of Scripture. Above all, enter Scripture's pages reverently and humbly, praying for divine illumination as the Lord speaks to you through His eternal Word.

Book Introductions

Page one of each book introduction contains a summary paragraph as well as basic information and a time line that will help you identify when some of the book's events took place. Each book introduction also has a unique chart giving a broad overview of the book's contents, followed by an extensive survey article that invites you into the drama of the Biblical story and draws out lessons for today.

In-depth Articles

The articles explore the themes and doctrines of the Christian faith in an accurate, clear and practical way. The material is covered in a broad-brush approach that is intended to whet your appetite for further study and reflection. See the table of Contents for Articles and Charts on page ix for a listing of the 14 articles.

Character Profiles

The character profiles provide biographical background and personal insight into the lives of some of the best-known, and even some of the least-known, men and women of the Bible. See the table of Contents for Profiles on page x for a listing of the 40 character profiles.

In-text Charts

The Living Insights Study Bible contains a number of charts designed to give important information at a glance. Two full-color time lines at the front of this Bible identify significant dates in the Old and New Testaments. Other charts can be found at selected locations throughout the text. See the table of Contents for Articles and Charts on page ix for a listing of the 20 charts.

Section Summaries

These summaries, located at the beginning of many chapters or sections in the Bible text, guide you to a clearer understanding of the main themes of each Bible book and enable you to grasp the big picture.

Living Insights

The "living insights," located near the Scripture verse or verses to which they relate, illuminate the truth of Scripture in fresh and inspiring ways. These nuggets of wisdom and encouragement will help you apply the Bible's teaching to your daily life.

Cross-Reference System

The end-of-paragraph cross-reference system is designed to help you connect one text of the Bible with others that have a similar theme. Cross references in *The Living Insights Study Bible* appear at the ends of paragraphs or following lines of poetry.

Parallel Passages

When two or more passages of Scripture are nearly identical or deal with the same event, this "parallel" is noted under the sectional headings in the Bible text. *The Living Insights Study Bible* employs this feature only in the four Gospels (Matthew, Mark, Luke and John).

Glossary of Doctrinal Terms

Located on page 1419 in the back of this Bible, the "glossary of doctrinal terms" will give you reader-friendly definitions of familiar and unfamiliar theological terms.

Indexes

The "Index to Subjects" on page 1425 contains references to key Biblical information and important topics. The "Index to Living Insights" on page 1443 lists major topics and gives you the location of the insights that relate to these topics. The "Index to Color Maps" on page 1603 helps in locating place-names on the 16-page color map set at the back of this Bible.

Concordance

The concordance on page 1449 will help you find Bible verses quickly and easily. By looking up key words, you can find verses for which you remember a word or two but not their location. For example, to find where the Bible states that the word of God "is sharper than any double-edged sword," you could look up "sharper," "double-edged" or "sword" and find the verse's location at Hebrews 4:12.

I hope that you will receive fresh and enriching insights as you read the words contained in *The Living Insights Study Bible*. I also hope that you will see God more clearly as the God of love who relentlessly pursues His people and seeks to reconcile us to Himself. And because God's revelation requires a response, I desire that you hear and heed the challenge to come to Him, to abide in Him and to walk with Him as you grow in grace and knowledge, applying His wisdom and truth.

ONE LIBRARY OF LIVING TRUTH

"He said to them, 'How foolish you are, and how slow of heart to believe all that the prophets have spoken! Did not the Christ have to suffer these things and then enter his glory?' And beginning with Moses and all the Prophets, he explained to them what was said in all the Scriptures concerning himself."

—LUKE 24:26–27

Have you ever considered how many hymns and songs have been written that refer to God's Word, the Bible? Note just three examples:

First, read these words from the hymn "How Firm a Foundation":

How firm a foundation,
Ye saints of the Lord,
Is laid for your faith
In His excellent Word!

Then, from the hymn "Holy Bible, Book Divine":

Holy Bible, book divine,
Precious treasure, thou art mine;
Mine to tell me whence I came;
Mine to teach me which I am;
Mine to tell of joys to come,
And the rebel sinner's doom;
O thou holy book divine,
Precious treasure, thou art mine.

Finally, from the hymn "O Word of God Incarnate":

O Word of God incarnate,
O wisdom from on high,
O truth unchanged, unchanging,
O light of our dark sky;
We praise Thee for the radiance
That from the hallowed page,
A lantern for our footsteps,
Shines on from age to age.

Picturesque, beautiful words and maybe a bit dated, but all of them vivid. The question is not, however, "Do you know the hymns well enough to sing them?" but *Do you know the Word well enough to use it?*

In order to become more familiar and more comfortable with the Bible (which continues, by the way, to be the most remarkable piece of literature that has ever graced the hands of humanity), it may be helpful to deal with some very basic issues in this brief survey article. Let me first observe that the Bible is not a collection of 66 independent books sewn together into one big book, but rather a library—a unit of books—that fits together into a perfectly harmonious system of thought revolving around a single theme: salvation through the Lord Jesus Christ. Like any library, it has certain divisions and sections and distinct topics, but everything fits into the central theme.

The Name: "The Bible"

The term "Bible" denotes the Holy Scriptures that were originally given by God, copies of which have been preserved down through the centuries. It may surprise you to know that the word "Bible" never once appears in the pages of Scripture. It derives from the Greek term *biblion*, or *biblos*, a name given to the fibrous coat or bark of the papyrus reed—a substance from which ancient scrolls were made. The plural form, *biblia*, came to mean "writings" or "rolls"—a designation for the rolled-up scrolls so common in ancient times. *Biblion* (used 34 times in the New Testament) is typically translated either "book(s)" or "scroll(s)."

Look at Luke's account of Jesus' rejection at Nazareth (Luke 4:17,20) for an example of how the term is used:

> *The scroll [*biblion*] of the prophet Isaiah was handed to him. Unrolling it, he found the place where it is written . . . Then he rolled up the scroll [*biblion*], gave it back to the attendant and sat down. The eyes of everyone in the synagogue were fastened on him.*

For other references, check Mark 12:26; John 20:30 and Acts 1:20. Each of these verses refers to a "book" of Holy Scripture, a "book" found in the Bible. In those days Scripture was written on scrolls and as they were read, they were rolled out of one hand and into the other. Scrolls measured up to thirty feet in length.

The Divisions

Although the Bible is one single unit of thought, a 66-book library with one central theme, God has wonderfully given us this Book in two divisions or "testaments." The term "testament" means "covenant, or arrangement, between two parties." God's old covenant was made with Moses and His people, the Jews (Exodus 24:7–8), and His new covenant with His family, the church (Hebrews 10:8–17).

The relationship between the two covenants is well summarized by the famous statement of Augustine: "the Old Testament revealed in the New, the New veiled in the Old," or by Graham Scroggie: "The New is in the Old contained, and the Old is in the New explained." While the Old gathers around Mount Sinai under the law, the New gathers around Calvary under grace. Another way to put it is this: The New is in the Old concealed and the Old is in the New revealed.

The English Bible

Have you ever wondered how this magnificent and priceless treasure, available to you in your own language, came into being? It's a surprise to some who haven't studied the subject to know that the English language wasn't even in existence when God gave His Word, when human writers were inspired to record without error the truths of God. And if God didn't originally communicate His Word to English-speaking people, how did we come to possess a Bible in our own language?

The Old Testament was originally written in Hebrew (and a very small section was written in Aramaic). In the New Testament God had His Word recorded in common Greek (known as *koine* Greek). Because that is true, what we have in our possession today is a copy, not only a copy of the original (the original manuscripts no longer exist) but a translation from another language. While it may bother us that we possess a copy that has been copied from other copies, a version that is in a language different from the one in which it was originally written, let me offer a word of reassurance about the complete reliability of God's Word.

Consider this illustration as a way to help us understand a little bit better what it is we now have: Let's imagine your father loved his grandfather very much. He may once have had an old photograph of that fine gentleman. The original photo began to yellow, fade and crack, so your dad had a copy made of that first photo due to the poor condition of the original. The picture you now have on the mantel at home, technically speaking, is *not* the actual photograph of your great-grandfather . . . it's a *copy* of the photograph. You have every reason to refer to it as a picture that was taken of your great-grandfather, for it is a duplicate, a copy of the original. It is a carefully made reproduction of the first photo. In the same way, our English Bible may be referred to as the book that was originally written hundreds of years ago by some forty human writers who wrote under the inspiration of the Holy Spirit. Technically, it is a copy but for all practical purposes, it is extremely similar to the original.

The process of copying was done with unbelievable patience and incredible accuracy, even though it was done *by hand* for centuries. Dr. Charles Ryrie summarized this in a vivid manner: "To guard against any errors slipping in, the one who was doing the copying carefully counted the number of letters and words on a page to be sure that every letter got into the new copy. He also counted to the middle letter of each page and each book, and then did the same on the new copy to double-check the accuracy of the copy. Try doing that with the page you are reading now, and then imagine doing it for an entire book of the Bible. That kind of painstaking care assured accurate copies."

One final comment—the copies we have today are in wonderful agreement with one another, even the early ones in comparison with the later ones. Aside from a few minor and insignificant disagreements, the copies dovetail perfectly. Not one major doctrine is affected.

Looking at the Old and New Testaments

There are thirty-nine Old Testament books and twenty-seven New Testament books. These books fall into eight sections, four in each Testament. (It may be helpful if you spend a moment with the table of contents at the front of this Bible to become familiar with the order of the books of the Bible.) The Old Testament can be divided as follows:

Section one: Genesis—Deuteronomy. This forms the LEGAL ("Law") section. (Note that this section is also called the Pentateuch, meaning "five-volumed book.") In these books Moses traces the beginning of all things, including the origins of the Jewish race and the first few centuries of the history of the nation of Israel.

Section two: Joshua—Esther. This is the HISTORICAL section, books that cover the history of the Israelites as they moved into the land of Canaan and took possession of it, through the days of the judges and the kings, and then into the experience of going into exile under foreign, pagan nations, and returning into the land under the leadership of Ezra and Nehemiah.

Section three: Job—Song of Songs. These five books form the POETICAL section. (Almost one-third of the Old Testament was originally written in poetry.) The name for this section is derived from the style of Hebrew text (poetry) used throughout these books. While David is thought to have written nearly half of the psalms, Solomon is considered to be the author of most of the proverbs, as well as the books of Ecclesiastes and Song of Songs.

Section four: Isaiah—Malachi. This section is made up of the PROPHETICAL books. Normally they are divided into two parts, the *major* prophets (Isaiah—Daniel) and the *minor* prophets (Hosea—Malachi). The titles are derived from the size of the books in each part, not the content. God spoke to His people through the prophets, calling His people back to Him as well as predicting future events.

The New Testament can be divided as follows:

Section one: Matthew—John. These books comprise the BIOGRAPHICAL section of the New Testament. They trace the life of Jesus Christ from His birth to His resurrection, covering the events from the unique viewpoint of each writer. Taken together, they give a complete picture of Jesus' life and teachings.

Section two: Acts. This is an HISTORICAL account of the growth of the church from the day of Pentecost to Paul's arrest in Rome. In chapters 1—12 Peter is the main character while Paul is the key character in chapters 13—28.

Section three: Romans—Jude. In the DOCTRINAL section, we find 21 letters from six different writers. The majority (the first 13, in fact), were written by Paul. The finer points of Christian doctrine, as well as outstanding practical counsel, are set forth in this section.

Section four: Revelation. This is the major PROPHETICAL book of the New Testament. It unveils and outlines God's plans for the future of this earth, Israel and the Gentile nations.

Central Theme of Scripture

The central theme of the Bible is the Lord Jesus Christ. The Old Testament looks forward to His birth, life and death as it prophetically pictures Him in shadows, types and pictures. The New Testament looks back and sets Him forth in reality, actuality and truth. The Old Testament *predicts* His arrival and His death, while the New Testament *portrays and explains* Him in complete fulfillment. Look carefully at the words of

Jesus recorded by Luke toward the end of His Gospel, where Jesus made it abundantly clear that He, the Messiah, was foretold in the whole Old Testament:

> *"How foolish you are, and how slow of heart to believe all that the prophets have spoken! Did not the Christ have to suffer these things and then enter his glory?" And beginning with Moses and all the Prophets, he explained to them what was said in all the Scriptures concerning himself (Luke 24:26–27).*

And then, a little later on, Jesus appeared to His disciples and told them this:

> *"This is what I told you while I was still with you: Everything must be fulfilled that is written about me in the Law of Moses, the Prophets and the Psalms." Then he opened their minds so they could understand the Scriptures. He told them, "This is what is written: The Christ will suffer and rise from the dead on the third day" (Luke 24:44–46).*

You may want to note one additional verse affirming that Jesus is the One to whom Scripture bears supreme testimony. Jesus Himself speaks these words to the Jewish leaders, who held the Scriptures in the highest regard:

> *You diligently study the Scriptures because you think that by them you possess eternal life. These are the Scriptures that testify about me, yet you refuse to come to me to have life (John 5:39–40).*

This removes all doubt. Jesus Christ is in all the Scriptures. Cut them any place and they bleed with the blood of God's Lamb. If you make a careful examination of the Scriptures, book by book, you will find the person of Christ enfolded into each in one form or another.

In Genesis, He is the woman's offspring (3:15)
In Exodus, He is the Passover lamb (12:1–14)
In Leviticus, He is the atoning sacrifice (17:11)
In Numbers, He is the bronze snake (21:8–9)
In Deuteronomy, He is the promised prophet (18:15)
In Joshua, He is the commander of the Lord's army (5:13–15)
In Judges, He is our deliverer
In Ruth, He is our heavenly kinsman-redeemer
In Samuel and Kings and Chronicles He is the promised king
In Ezra and Nehemiah, He is the restorer of the nation
In Esther, He is our advocate
In Job, He is our redeemer (19:25)
In Psalms, He is our all in all
In Proverbs, He is our pattern
In Ecclesiastes, He is our goal
In Song of Songs, He is our beloved
In the Prophets, He is the coming Prince of Peace
In Matthew, He is Christ: the King
In Mark, He is Christ: the Servant
In Luke, He is Christ: the Son of Man
In John, He is Christ: the Son of God
In Acts, He is Christ: risen, seated, sending
In the Letters, He is Christ: indwelling, filling
In Revelation, He is Christ: returning, reigning

Conclusion and Invitation

It isn't enough for us to understand with our minds that Jesus Christ is the central theme of Scripture. He longs to be the central theme of *our lives*—every section of it, from the legal section to the casual section, from the intellectual section to the intimate section. He wants to invade every area—the thought factory of our minds, our wills, our decisions, our businesses, our work, our play, our relationships, our home, our eyes, our hands and our hearts.

Have you allowed Him complete access to your life? Or are there a few locked doors that forbid His entrance? I plead with anyone who may have never asked Jesus Christ to come into his or her life and establish His control, to do that right now. He awaits your opening the door. He won't barge in uninvited. And if you *have* opened your heart to the Lord Jesus, let me simply remind you of the words of Paul: "Do you not know that your body is a temple of the Holy Spirit, who is in you, whom you have received from God? You are not your own; you were bought at a price. Therefore honor God with your body" (1 Corinthians 6:19–20). You belong to your Lord and Savior, not to yourself. The Holy Spirit desires *full* control of your will. As you walk step by step, moment by moment, in dependence on His power, you will experience Christ at the center of your life!

OLD TESTAMENT

GENESIS

No one would deny that of all of the 39 Old Testament books, Genesis is the most important. Being the foundation of all that follows, it is essential to the whole theme of Scripture. Remove this book, and we are immediately confused, completely at a loss to understand in which direction God is going. It is clear, therefore, why the book (like no other book in the Bible) is the target of constant criticism and attack. Disprove its validity, and we are well on our way to the destruction of our faith. But Genesis still stands! And it is . . . where it all begins.

WRITER: *Moses*

DATE: *c.1446–1406 B.C.*

PURPOSE: *To bring us back to our roots*

KEY VERSES: *1:1; 3:15*

KEY PHRASE: *"This is the account . . ."*

TIME LINE 2200BC 2100 2000 1900 1800 1700 1600 1500 1400

Creation, Fall

The Flood

The Tower of Babel

Abraham's life (c.2166–1991 B.C.)

Isaac's life (c.2066–1886 B.C.)

Jacob's life (c.2006–1859 B.C.)

Joseph's life (c.1915–1805 B.C.)

Book of Genesis written (c.1446–1406 B.C.)

Where It All Begins

	CREATION	FALL	FLOOD	NATIONS	ABRAHAM	ISAAC	JACOB	JOSEPH
	CHAPTERS 1–2	*CHAPTER 3*	*CHAPTERS 4–9*	*CHAPTERS 10–11*	*CHAPTERS 12–25*	*CHAPTERS 26–27*	*CHAPTERS 28–36*	*CHAPTERS 37–50*
BEGINNINGS	Beginning of the human race				Beginning of the chosen race			
RESULT	Confusion and scattering				Bondage in Egypt			
HISTORY	Primeval history				Patriarchal history			
CHRONOLOGY	Over 2,000 years				Approximately 300 years			
EMPHASIS	Four major events				Four important people			

There's something about going back to our beginnings that gives us a feeling of security and stability. I remember quite vividly the day my parents pointed out where I was born down in El Campo, Texas. I was sitting in the back seat of the car as my dad pointed over to a little garage apartment and said, "Charles, see that?" As I pressed my nose against the window and looked, he said, "That's where you were born, son." I can remember walking slowly up to that humble place where I was born and climbing the stairs to the second floor of that tiny apartment. In that strangely sacred moment all sorts of good feelings surrounded me; I was flooded with nostalgic memories . . . *these were my roots.*

As I look back, I have vivid memories of family reunions: crab gumbo, fishing, floundering with my dad and my granddad, outdoor barbecues and week-long mosquito fights down there in the South Texas area. That's where my roots are. I guess you could say that what South Texas means to me, the book of Genesis means to the Christian. It's all about beginnings!

Genesis is the book of our roots. Everything starts here. And everything that is significant in the balance of the Bible finds its foundation and meaning all the way back here in the book of our roots—the book of beginnings.

It may surprise you to know that critics have leveled all sorts of cannons and assaults against seven simple Hebrew words—*Bere'shith bara' 'Elohim 'eth ha-shamayim we'eth ha-'ahretz*—"In the beginning God created the heavens and the earth" (Genesis 1:1). If you can destroy this truth, you can destroy the whole Christian faith. The issue of our spiritual roots as recorded in Genesis has become the battlefield of the religious world today.

Where Do We Begin?

The name Genesis comes from the Greek verb *gennao*, which appears 97 times in the New Testament and is often translated as "to become the father of" or "to be born." The Greek noun *genesis* is found five times in the New Testament (three times in the Gospels). Matthew uses the term twice (translated "genealogy" in 1:1 and translated "birth" in 1:18—used in reference to the birth of Jesus of Nazareth); Luke uses the term once (translated "birth" in 1:14), in reference to the birth of John the Baptizer. The word "genesis" has the connotation of "origins," or "beginnings," as well as "birth." It communicates the idea of a starting point; of giving birth or begetting. It's a fitting title for the first book of the Bible.

The term "genesis" is traced through the entire scope of this book of Scripture. Let me give you several examples:

In Genesis 2:4 we find this word used in the *Septuagint* (the Greek translation of the Old Testament): "This is the account . . ." or, literally, "This is the 'genesis' . . . the beginning, the origin, the continuing story of the heavens and the earth."

In Genesis 5:1 we read of the beginning of man and his family, Adam's progeny.

In Genesis 6:9 we find the beginning of Noah's story, his genealogy (the tracing of his roots).

In Genesis 10:1 we discover that God records the lineage of Noah's sons. "This is the account ('genesis') of Shem, Ham and Japheth . . ."

In Genesis 11:10, right after work on the tower of Babel ceased, God observes: "This is the account ('genesis') of Shem . . . " One of Noah's three sons is highlighted, because from him the Jewish race, or the Jewish lineage, begins. The account of Shem leads to Terah (11:27), the father of Abram who in turn became the father of the Hebrew race. So, as you can see, we have the tracing of the origins and the continuing story of God's people—the "genesis" of the Jews. They would find their roots clearly described in Genesis 11.

In Genesis 25:12 there is yet another mention of this phrase "This is the account of" and then a reference to Abraham's son Ishmael. And a little further in Genesis 25 you will find these words: "This is the account ('genesis') of Abraham's son Isaac" (25:19). The last reference to this same phrase in Genesis is found in 37:2: "This is the account of Jacob."

Now, why go through this process of looking from one text to the next? Because I want you to see that the key phrase running through the book of Genesis is, "This is the *genesis* of, this is the *beginning* of, these are the *roots* of, this is *where it all begins*."

The book of Genesis is a book of beginnings. Whatever begins, begins here. The beginning of matter. The beginning of time. The beginning of mankind. The beginning of prophecy. The beginning of sin. The beginning of purpose and direction in the plan of God. The beginning of the Jews. The beginning of family. The beginning of the husband-and-wife relationship. The beginning of children. The beginning of life on this planet. The beginning of judgment. The beginning of the promise of the coming of the Messiah. All this, and so much more, starts in the book of Genesis.

About the Book

Moses is the author of Genesis. Because the history recorded here occurred before he was born, Moses must have received much of his revelation directly from God Himself. He also must have preserved information that was passed down from his parents and from their parents. By divine revelation, as well as by word of mouth, God preserved his inspired record of beginnings, the book of Genesis.

The book of Genesis can be divided into two sections: *chapters 1–11* and *chapters 12–50*. Now, these two sections stand in contrast to one another. Genesis 1–11 covers a period of thousands of years. It traces the human race, as it is set forth in Scripture in over two millennia from the beginning of humanity all the way to Abram. It's a primeval history. By contrast, in Genesis 12–50 we have about 300 years of history recorded, tracing the people of God from Abraham through Joseph. Here we find a patriarchal history.

The Beginning of the Human Race

The first 11 chapters of Genesis constitute the first major section of the book. We will call this "the beginning of the human race." It starts with eternity past, and it carries us right up to the beginning of God's work in the life of Abraham. In Genesis 1–11 the emphasis falls on four major events: the creation, the fall of humanity, the flood, and the record of the nations that came into existence after the flood.

The end results of the events of this first section were confusion and scattering. The people came to Babel and began to build a tower for their own glory, an edifice for the exaltation of humanity. Because of their pride, God stepped onto the scene, confused their language and scattered the people into many tribes, nations and languages.

The Beginning of the Chosen Race

The next 39 chapters of Genesis (12–50) contain the account of what we will call "the beginning of the Hebrew race." God focuses His attention on one people—the Jews. It's as though He snaps on the camera's zoom lens when He comes to chapter 12. From this point right through chapter 50, God is addressing the Hebrew people as He traces their history with careful detail beginning with Abraham. In Genesis 12–50 the spotlight shines on four people: Abraham; Abraham's son Isaac; Isaac's son Jacob; and Jacob's son Joseph.

The book of Genesis concludes with the life of Joseph, who, as the last verse of Genesis reveals, died at the age of 110. By the end of the final chapter of Genesis, the people of Israel were in Egypt—and the picture was not a pretty one . . . they were in bondage! At the conclusion of this book, God's people need redemption and release . . . they need a Deliverer!

Lessons of Life From the Beginning

Life is vividly illustrated in this great old book. Like the people whose stories are recorded in the book of Genesis, we have been created by God. In Psalm 139:14 we learn that we are "fearfully and wonderfully made" by God's own hand. We have been created by God, and His work is wonderful! We can look in the mirror each morning and behold the glorious creation of God . . . pretty amazing, isn't it?

We, like the people in this book, have chosen to leave the One who made us, and we have fallen. We were fallen at birth and have carried on what our parents and grandparents and great-grandparents passed down. It's called "sin." Our sin is an offense to the holiness of God and results in divine judgment (just like the flood) that has poured over the entire human race.

In the book of Genesis God enlisted a man as an instrument to preserve the human race; his name was Noah. In our lives God has also employed a man—not just any man, but One who is fully divine and fully human—as the One who would save us; His name is Jesus. God has given His one and only Son to be the One who would stand in our place and take the punishment for our sins. Jesus is the ark that gets us through the flood. We're safe on the inside and lost if we stay on the outside. Praise the Lord! By the grace of God, He has opened the door to eternal life for us through Jesus Christ.

Yet, let's be honest here. Some people are still trying to build towers—their own Babels—in their arrogant and futile attempts to make a name for themselves, to set a self-centered direction for their lives and to climb up to God in their own strength. It didn't work in the days of Genesis, and it doesn't work now. God is in the business of breaking down our towers and building bridges to draw us back to Him.

The End of the Beginning

So what about it? No matter where you are in your life's journey, the book of Genesis has a powerful message for you. And you have an important choice to make.

Just reflect for a moment, if you would, on how the book of Genesis ends. You might be surprised if you look closely. It ends where most men and women finish their lives: It comes to a close in a coffin.

> *So Joseph died at the age of a hundred and ten. And after they embalmed him, he was placed in a coffin in Egypt (50:26).*

Your life can end in a coffin. Period. End of story. Or it can begin at a cross. The place where Jesus died for the sins of the world. For your sin. The choice is yours. You can reject Him. You can run from Him. You can erect walls to keep Him out. Or you can accept His acceptance of you. You can run to Him. You can let Him tear down the walls. He wants to offer you a second birth, a fresh start, a new beginning.

Wherever your roots take you, they certainly have to go back somehow to Genesis. No matter what else you do, you've got to deal with what God says about our beginnings. You've got to see the account as recorded in Genesis as God's story in which *you* play an important role. You've got to own it as your account, your story—as the true account of the beginning of sin and the beginning of God's perfect plan for dealing with that sin. So as you think about the final words of the book of Genesis, remember: The only way to get beyond the coffin is through the cross. Genesis is the place of the first beginning, and Jesus Christ is the place of new beginnings!

The Creation Chapters 1–2

The first chapter of Genesis begins with the words, "In the beginning." What a fantastic concept! How profound! We can't fathom when there was an absence of matter and existence apart from time. For all eternity past there was nothing but the Godhead. No universe, nothing material—just infinity past. Out of this formlessness and emptiness God called forth everything we know: life, light, matter, land, sea, the heavens, vegetation, man, woman . . . everything. These two chapters chronicle the orderly creation of the heavens and the earth. God spoke, and it was so. When God finished all his wonderful work of creation, He made a final evaluation of his creative work and declared it to be "very good" (1:31).

The Beginning

1 In the beginning God created the heavens
and the earth. 2Now the earth was[a] formless
and empty, darkness was over the surface of
the deep, and the Spirit of God was hovering
over the waters. Jn 1:1-2; Isa 45:12,18

3And God said, "Let there be light," and there
was light. 4God saw that the light was good,
and he separated the light from the darkness.
5God called the light "day," and the darkness
he called "night." And there was evening, and
there was morning—the first day. 2Co 4:6

LIVING  INSIGHT

Why would intelligent men and women embrace human theories rather than the statement of God when it comes to the creation of a world and the origin of humanity? Perhaps it's just too simple for the sophisticated. Obviously it requires a belief in a supreme being greater than they. Yet, the existence of our world and humanity defies all mathematical calculations of chance!

(See Genesis 1:1–5.)

6And God said, "Let there be an expanse between
the waters to separate water from water." 7So
God made the expanse and separated the water
under the expanse from the water above it.
And it was so. 8God called the expanse "sky."
And there was evening, and there was morning—the
second day. Ps 148:4; Jer 10:12
9And God said, "Let the water under the sky be
gathered to one place, and let dry ground appear."
And it was so. 10God called the dry
ground "land," and the gathered waters he
called "seas." And God saw that it was good.
11Then God said, "Let the land produce
vegetation: seed-bearing plants and trees on
the land that bear fruit with seed in it, according
to their various kinds." And it was so.
12The land produced vegetation: plants bearing
seed according to their kinds and trees
bearing fruit with seed in it according to their
kinds. And God saw that it was good. 13And
there was evening, and there was morning—
the third day. Ps 65:9-13

LIVING  INSIGHT

In God's genius He put together form and order out of that which was formless and empty. He loves order—and He began to display the beauty of His handiwork. He called light in. He separated matter that was solid from matter that was space. He built the canvas of the universe above us. And He painted His world there—which still displays His glory. He put it all together so that humanity throughout time would see the glory of God.

(See Genesis 1:6–13.)

14And God said, "Let there be lights in the expanse
of the sky to separate the day from the
night, and let them serve as signs to mark
seasons and days and years, 15and let them be
lights in the expanse of the sky to give light on
the earth." And it was so. 16God made two
great lights—the greater light to govern the
day and the lesser light to govern the night. He
also made the stars. 17God set them in the
expanse of the sky to give light on the earth,
18to govern the day and the night, and to separate
light from darkness. And God saw that it
was good. 19And there was evening, and there
was morning—the fourth day. Ps 74:16; 104:19
20And God said, "Let the water teem with living
creatures, and let birds fly above the earth
across the expanse of the sky." 21So God created
the great creatures of the sea and every
living and moving thing with which the water
teems, according to their kinds, and every
winged bird according to its kind. And God
saw that it was good. 22God blessed them and
said, "Be fruitful and increase in number and
fill the water in the seas, and let the birds increase
on the earth." 23And there was evening,
and there was morning—the fifth day.
24And God said, "Let the land produce living creatures
according to their kinds: livestock, creatures
that move along the ground, and wild
animals, each according to its kind." And it
was so. 25God made the wild animals according
to their kinds, the livestock according to

[a]2 Or possibly *became*

their kinds, and all the creatures that move along the ground according to their kinds. And God saw that it was good.

26 Then God said, "Let us make man in our image, in our likeness, and let them rule over the fish of the sea and the birds of the air, over the livestock, over all the earth,[a] and over all the creatures that move along the ground."

27 So God created man in his own image, 1Co 11:7
in the image of God he created him;
male and female he created them. Ge 5:2

28 God blessed them and said to them, "Be fruitful and increase in number; fill the earth and subdue it. Rule over the fish of the sea and the birds of the air and over every living creature that moves on the ground." Ge 9:1,7

LIVING INSIGHT

Immediately after the Lord God created the first man and woman, He blessed them (placed His favor upon them), and then He spoke to them. In fact, the first command in all the Scriptures appears in this section. Interestingly, it had to do with the family.

(See Genesis 1:28.)

29 Then God said, "I give you every seed-bearing plant on the face of the whole earth and every tree that has fruit with seed in it. They will be yours for food. 30 And to all the beasts of the earth and all the birds of the air and all the creatures that move on the ground—everything that has the breath of life in it—I give every green plant for food." And it was so. Ps 104:14,27; 145:15

31 God saw all that he had made, and it was very good. And there was evening, and there was morning—the sixth day. Ps 104:24

2 Thus the heavens and the earth were completed in all their vast array. Isa 44:24

2 By the seventh day God had finished the work he had been doing; so on the seventh day he rested[b] from all his work. 3 And God blessed the seventh day and made it holy, because on it he rested from all the work of creating that he had done. Ex 20:11; Heb 4:4

Adam and Eve

4 This is the account of the heavens and the earth when they were created.

When the LORD God made the earth and the heavens— 5 and no shrub of the field had yet appeared on the earth[c] and no plant of the field had yet sprung up, for the LORD God had not sent rain on the earth[c] and there was no man to work the ground, 6 but streams[d] came up from the earth and watered the whole surface of the ground— 7 the LORD God formed the man[e] from the dust of the ground and breathed into his nostrils the breath of life, and the man became a living being.

LIVING INSIGHT

Following the sixth day of creation, the Lord God deliberately stopped working. He rested. It wasn't that there was nothing else He could have done. He could easily have made more worlds, created an infinite number of other forms of life and provided multiple millions of galaxies beyond what He did. But He didn't. He stopped. He spent an entire day resting. Sounds to me like He made the day on which He rested a "priority" period of time.

(See Genesis 2:2.)

8 Now the LORD God had planted a garden in the east, in Eden; and there he put the man he had formed. 9 And the LORD God made all kinds of trees grow out of the ground—trees that were pleasing to the eye and good for food. In the middle of the garden were the tree of life and the tree of the knowledge of good and evil. Ge 3:22,24

10 A river watering the garden flowed from Eden; from there it was separated into four headwaters. 11 The name of the first is the Pishon; it winds through the entire land of Havilah, where there is gold. 12 (The gold of that land is good; aromatic resin[f] and onyx are also there.) 13 The name of the second river is the Gihon; it winds through the entire land of Cush.[g] 14 The name of the third river is the Tigris; it runs along the east side of Asshur. And the fourth river is the Euphrates. Da 10:4

15 The LORD God took the man and put him in the Garden of Eden to work it and take care of it. 16 And the LORD God commanded the man, "You are free to eat from any tree in the garden; 17 but you must not eat from the tree of the knowledge of good and evil, for when you eat of it you will surely die." Ro 5:12; 6:23; Dt 30:15,19

18 The LORD God said, "It is not good for the man to be alone. I will make a helper suitable for him." 1Co 11:9

[a] 26 Hebrew; Syriac *all the wild animals* [b] 2 Or *ceased*; also in verse 3 [c] 5 Or *land*; also in verse 6 [d] 6 Or *mist*
[e] 7 The Hebrew for *man (adam)* sounds like and may be related to the Hebrew for *ground (adamah)*; it is also the name *Adam* (see Gen. 2:20). [f] 12 Or *good; pearls* [g] 13 Possibly southeast Mesopotamia

19Now the LORD God had formed out of the
ground all the beasts of the field and all the birds
of the air. He brought them to the man to see what
he would name them; and whatever the man called
each living creature, that was its name. 20So the
man gave names to all the livestock, the birds of
the air and all the beasts of the field. Ps 8:7
But for Adam[a] no suitable helper was found.
21So the LORD God caused the man to fall into a
deep sleep; and while he was sleeping, he took one
of the man's ribs[b] and closed up the place with
flesh. 22Then the LORD God made a woman from
the rib[c] he had taken out of the man, and he
brought her to the man. 1Co 11:8-9,12
23The man said,

"This is now bone of my bones
and flesh of my flesh; Eph 5:28-30
she shall be called 'woman,[d]'
for she was taken out of man."

24For this reason a man will leave his father and
mother and be united to his wife, and they will
become one flesh. Mt 19:5; Eph 5:31; Mal 2:15
25The man and his wife were both naked, and
they felt no shame. Ge 3:7,10-11

LIVING  **INSIGHT**

Here are four timeless one-word principles from Scripture that give a marriage (as well as a family) its strength:

SEVERANCE: ***"leave his father and . . . mother."***
PERMANENCE: ***"be united to his wife."***
UNITY: ***"they will become one flesh."***
INTIMACY: ***"both naked, and they felt no shame."***

(See Genesis 2:24–25.)

Paradise Lost **Chapters 3–5**

In all the beauty, delight and innocence of God's creation, we find the harmony of this pristine garden setting quickly broken. The devil, in the form of a serpent, came on the scene with deceitful intentions. The story, unfortunately, is all too familiar and heartbreaking. God had given the man and woman everything they needed. In all of His provision there was only one boundary, one nonnegotiable command: The man and woman were not to eat from the tree of the knowledge of good and evil (2:17). Adam and Eve, at the seductive leading of the serpent, decided to take what was forbidden. This act of willful rebellion led to judgment and expulsion from paradise. At the end of chapter 3, we find heavenly beings (cherubim) and a flaming sword to guard the garden from ever being entered again. The door to paradise was slammed shut. But the story of human sin and rebellion didn't end there; that was just the beginning. Chapter 4 chronicles the first murder in human history. Sin had taken root and was beginning to grow like a weed. Cain had killed his brother Abel, and following that ruthless act we witness the continued downward spiral into the costly consequences of human sinfulness.

The Fall of Man

3 Now the serpent was more crafty than any of
the wild animals the LORD God had made. He
said to the woman, "Did God really say, 'You must
not eat from any tree in the garden'?" 2Co 11:3
2The woman said to the serpent, "We may eat
fruit from the trees in the garden, 3but God did
say, 'You must not eat fruit from the tree that is in
the middle of the garden, and you must not touch
it, or you will die.'"

LIVING  **INSIGHT**

Adam's fall into sin left humanity without the hope of heaven apart from a new birth, made possible by the Savior's death and bodily resurrection.

(See Genesis 3:1–7.)

4"You will not surely die," the serpent said to
the woman. 5"For God knows that when you eat of
it your eyes will be opened, and you will be like
God, knowing good and evil." Jn 8:44; Isa 14:14
6When the woman saw that the fruit of the tree
was good for food and pleasing to the eye, and also
desirable for gaining wisdom, she took some and
ate it. She also gave some to her husband, who was
with her, and he ate it. 7Then the eyes of both of
them were opened, and they realized they were
naked; so they sewed fig leaves together and made
coverings for themselves. 1Ti 2:14; Jas 1:14-15; 1Jn 2:16
8Then the man and his wife heard the sound of
the LORD God as he was walking in the garden in
the cool of the day, and they hid from the LORD
God among the trees of the garden. 9But the LORD
God called to the man, "Where are you?"
10He answered, "I heard you in the garden, and
I was afraid because I was naked; so I hid."
11And he said, "Who told you that you were
naked? Have you eaten from the tree that I commanded you not to eat from?" Ge 2:17
12The man said, "The woman you put here with
me—she gave me some fruit from the tree, and I
ate it."
13Then the LORD God said to the woman, "What
is this you have done?"

[a]20 Or *the man* [b]21 Or *took part of the man's side* [c]22 Or *part* [d]23 The Hebrew for *woman* sounds like the Hebrew for *man.*

The woman said, "The serpent deceived me,
and I ate." 2Co 11:3; 1Ti 2:14
14So the LORD God said to the serpent, "Because
you have done this,

"Cursed are you above all the livestock
and all the wild animals!
You will crawl on your belly
and you will eat dust Isa 65:25
all the days of your life.
15And I will put enmity
between you and the woman,
and between your offspring[a] and hers;
he will crush[b] your head, Ro 16:20
and you will strike his heel."

16To the woman he said,

"I will greatly increase your pains in
childbearing;
with pain you will give birth to children.
Your desire will be for your husband,
and he will rule over you." 1Co 11:3

17To Adam he said, "Because you listened to
your wife and ate from the tree about which I
commanded you, 'You must not eat of it,'

"Cursed is the ground because of you;
through painful toil you will eat of it
all the days of your life. Job 5:7; Ecc 2:23
18It will produce thorns and thistles for you,
and you will eat the plants of the field.
19By the sweat of your brow
you will eat your food
until you return to the ground,
since from it you were taken;
for dust you are
and to dust you will return." Ge 2:7; Ps 90:3

20Adam[c] named his wife Eve,[d] because she
would become the mother of all the living.
21The LORD God made garments of skin for
Adam and his wife and clothed them. 22And the

LIVING  **INSIGHT**

From the Fall on through time, until this earth is no more, every human being born on this earth enters as a sinner. And that is why the story that unfolds is the story of redemption, bringing back into fellowship with God the men and women who once, in Adam and Eve, knew a fellowship that was unbroken and joyful and peaceful.

(See Genesis 3:21–24.)

LORD God said, "The man has now become like
one of us, knowing good and evil. He must not be
allowed to reach out his hand and take also from
the tree of life and eat, and live forever." 23So the
LORD God banished him from the Garden of Eden
to work the ground from which he had been taken.
24After he drove the man out, he placed on the east
side[e] of the Garden of Eden cherubim and a
flaming sword flashing back and forth to guard the
way to the tree of life. Ge 2:9; Rev 22:14; Ex 25:18-22

Cain and Abel

4 Adam[c] lay with his wife Eve, and she became pregnant and gave birth to Cain.[f] She
said, "With the help of the LORD I have brought
forth[g] a man." 2Later she gave birth to his brother
Abel. Lk 11:51
Now Abel kept flocks, and Cain worked the soil.
3In the course of time Cain brought some of the
fruits of the soil as an offering to the LORD. 4But
Abel brought fat portions from some of the firstborn of his flock. The LORD looked with favor on
Abel and his offering, 5but on Cain and his offering he did not look with favor. So Cain was very
angry, and his face was downcast. Heb 11:4; Ex 13:2,12
6Then the LORD said to Cain, "Why are you
angry? Why is your face downcast? 7If you do what
is right, will you not be accepted? But if you do not
do what is right, sin is crouching at your door; it
desires to have you, but you must master it."
8Now Cain said to his brother Abel, "Let's go
out to the field."[h] And while they were in the
field, Cain attacked his brother Abel and killed
him. Mt 23:35; 1Jn 3:12
9Then the LORD said to Cain, "Where is your
brother Abel?"
"I don't know," he replied. "Am I my brother's
keeper?"

LIVING  **INSIGHT**

When you don't concern yourself with being your brother's keeper, you don't have to get dirty anymore or take risks or lose your objectivity or run up against the thorny side of an issue that lacks easy answers.

(See Genesis 4:9.)

10The LORD said, "What have you done? Listen!
Your brother's blood cries out to me from the
ground. 11Now you are under a curse and driven
from the ground, which opened its mouth to receive your brother's blood from your hand.

[a]15 Or *seed* [b]15 Or *strike* [c]20,1 Or *The man* [d]20 *Eve* probably means *living.* [e]24 Or *placed in front*
[f]1 *Cain* sounds like the Hebrew for *brought forth* or *acquired.* [g]1 Or *have acquired* [h]8 Samaritan Pentateuch, Septuagint, Vulgate and Syriac; Masoretic Text does not have *"Let's go out to the field."*

CAIN

God's Mark of Grace

"Then the LORD put a mark on Cain so that no one who found him would kill him."
—GENESIS 4:15b

Cain and his brother Abel were born to Adam and Eve after the fall, following the curse. As the older son Cain grew, he chose to follow his dad's occupation—he became a farmer. Abel became a keeper of the flocks—a shepherd. As adults, these two young men brought their offerings to the Lord. I am confident that Adam and Eve had taught their sons the proper attitude with which to approach God—carefully and thoughtfully, out of a generous and grateful heart.

Now this is where the conflict began. This is where jealousy and deceitfully murderous thoughts began to express themselves in the human heart. Cain brought as his offering "some of the fruits of the soil." Abel brought "fat portions from some of the firstborn of his flock" (Genesis 4:3–4). Cain did it his own way, a way that proved to be unacceptable to God, and his offering was rejected. Abel did it God's way and found full acceptance because of his faith, as the letter to the Hebrews tells us (Hebrews 11:4).

God did not look with favor on Cain and his offering. Observe Cain's response carefully in verse 5 of Genesis 4. Cain became very angry. Interesting, isn't it? He knew what God expected, but he failed to do it. And when God responded in justice, Cain got angry. He was angry at God because He rejected his offering. He was jealous of Abel, plain and simple, because God accepted Abel's offering. God saw that the anger and the jealousy were consuming Cain and graciously gave him a warning. "Sin is crouching at your door; it desires to have you, but you must master it" (4:7). God said, in effect, "Don't let anger get the best of you. Your jealousy will subside if you will simply do what you know is right. If you continue to complicate the problem of this disobedient sacrifice, you will fall deeper into sin."

What happened next? The first murder. You want to know a chilling fact? The Hebrew word used here for "killed him" is used elsewhere for "sliced the throat." Through this monstrous act Cain said, in effect, "You want a sacrifice? Here's your sacrifice, God!" And the blood spilled onto the ground as Abel's lifeless body collapsed into Cain's arms. In a deed horrible beyond imagination, this young man killed his brother. And you know what the tragedy is? You don't read it here, but you feel it. It accompanies every consummated murder. It is the instantaneous, inhuman silence—a life that once breathed and laughed and talked and sang is snuffed out. But none of that humbled Cain. We picture him quickly burying Abel in the dirt and smacking his hands together, saying, "There. That's done. Mission accomplished."

But then God came along, asking a question He knew the answer to, a question designed to make Cain think deeply: "Where is your brother Abel?" Cain's impudent answer has lived on through the centuries: "Am I my brother's keeper?" (4:9). This was just moments after he had washed the blood off his hands! The man had done an unconscionable deed yet possessed absolutely no sense of guilt. He stood in the face of God with arms crossed, head unbowed and fists doubled up in defiance.

Only when God announced His judgment do we see a little emotion from Cain, even if it is self-seeking. God took away Cain's livelihood—his ability to produce crops. He was condemned to wander the earth. Listen to him: "My punishment is more than I can bear . . . I will be a restless wanderer on the earth, and whoever finds me will kill me" (4:13–14). He's afraid that others will treat him as he treated his brother.

Now watch for an incredible expression of grace. Had you or I been in charge of the case we very likely would have pounded down the gavel and said, "Next case. Serves you right, Cain." But God is gracious; He gave Cain a mark that warded people off, providing protection from any who would take revenge. What was that mark? We don't know. Whatever it was, I see it as an act of grace. I believe that in sparing Cain's life, God left a window of opportunity for Cain to repent. That mark was God's way of saying, "I'm ready to listen. I'm ready to accept you. Not even this murder can keep you from me permanently." That's a picture of God's amazing grace in the life of every one of us—descendants of Cain that we are.

12 When you work the ground, it will no longer yield its crops for you. You will be a restless wanderer on the earth." Heb 12:24; Rev 6:9-10

13 Cain said to the LORD, "My punishment is more than I can bear. 14 Today you are driving me from the land, and I will be hidden from your presence; I will be a restless wanderer on the earth, and whoever finds me will kill me." Ps 51:11

15 But the LORD said to him, "Not so[a]; if anyone kills Cain, he will suffer vengeance seven times over." Then the LORD put a mark on Cain so that no one who found him would kill him. 16 So Cain went out from the LORD's presence and lived in the land of Nod,[b] east of Eden. Eze 9:4,6; Ge 2:8

17 Cain lay with his wife, and she became pregnant and gave birth to Enoch. Cain was then building a city, and he named it after his son Enoch. 18 To Enoch was born Irad, and Irad was the father of Mehujael, and Mehujael was the father of Methushael, and Methushael was the father of Lamech. Ps 49:11

19 Lamech married two women, one named Adah and the other Zillah. 20 Adah gave birth to Jabal; he was the father of those who live in tents and raise livestock. 21 His brother's name was Jubal; he was the father of all who play the harp and flute. 22 Zillah also had a son, Tubal-Cain, who forged all kinds of tools out of[c] bronze and iron. Tubal-Cain's sister was Naamah. Ex 35:35

23 Lamech said to his wives,

"Adah and Zillah, listen to me;
  wives of Lamech, hear my words.
I have killed[d] a man for wounding me,
  a young man for injuring me.
24 If Cain is avenged seven times,
  then Lamech seventy-seven times." ver 15

25 Adam lay with his wife again, and she gave birth to a son and named him Seth,[e] saying, "God has granted me another child in place of Abel, since Cain killed him." 26 Seth also had a son, and he named him Enosh. Ge 5:3

At that time men began to call on[f] the name of the LORD. Ge 12:8; Joel 2:32; 1Co 1:2

From Adam to Noah

5 This is the written account of Adam's line.

When God created man, he made him in the likeness of God. 2 He created them male and female and blessed them. And when they were created, he called them "man.[g]" Ge 1:27; Eph 4:24; Col 3:10

3 When Adam had lived 130 years, he had a son in his own likeness, in his own image; and he named him Seth. 4 After Seth was born, Adam lived 800 years and had other sons and daughters. 5 Altogether, Adam lived 930 years, and then he died.

6 When Seth had lived 105 years, he became the father[h] of Enosh. 7 And after he became the father of Enosh, Seth lived 807 years and had other sons

LIVING  **INSIGHT**

When Eve gave birth, it was in Adam's likeness, not God's. Why? Because depravity had flooded humanity and polluted their innocence. Sin intercepted the pass, and it will never give the ball back—never! Not on this earth.

(See Genesis 5:1–3.)

and daughters. 8 Altogether, Seth lived 912 years, and then he died. Ge 4:26

9 When Enosh had lived 90 years, he became the father of Kenan. 10 And after he became the father of Kenan, Enosh lived 815 years and had other sons and daughters. 11 Altogether, Enosh lived 905 years, and then he died. 1Ch 1:2

12 When Kenan had lived 70 years, he became the father of Mahalalel. 13 And after he became the father of Mahalalel, Kenan lived 840 years and had other sons and daughters. 14 Altogether, Kenan lived 910 years, and then he died. Lk 3:37

15 When Mahalalel had lived 65 years, he became the father of Jared. 16 And after he became the father of Jared, Mahalalel lived 830 years and had other sons and daughters. 17 Altogether, Mahalalel lived 895 years, and then he died. 1Ch 1:2

18 When Jared had lived 162 years, he became the father of Enoch. 19 And after he became the father of Enoch, Jared lived 800 years and had other sons and daughters. 20 Altogether, Jared lived 962 years, and then he died. Jude 1:14

21 When Enoch had lived 65 years, he became the father of Methuselah. 22 And after he became the father of Methuselah, Enoch walked with God 300 years and had other sons and daughters. 23 Altogether, Enoch lived 365 years. 24 Enoch walked with God; then he was no more, because God took him away. Ge 6:9; Mic 6:8; Heb 11:5

25 When Methuselah had lived 187 years, he became the father of Lamech. 26 And after he became the father of Lamech, Methuselah lived 782 years and had other sons and daughters. 27 Altogether, Methuselah lived 969 years, and then he died.

28 When Lamech had lived 182 years, he had a son. 29 He named him Noah[i] and said, "He will comfort us in the labor and painful toil of our hands caused by the ground the LORD has cursed."

[a] 15 Septuagint, Vulgate and Syriac; Hebrew *Very well* [b] 16 *Nod* means *wandering* (see verses 12 and 14). [c] 22 Or *who instructed all who work in* [d] 23 Or *I will kill* [e] 25 *Seth* probably means *granted.* [f] 26 Or *to proclaim* [g] 2 Hebrew *adam* [h] 6 *Father* may mean *ancestor*; also in verses 7-26. [i] 29 *Noah* sounds like the Hebrew for *comfort.*

30After Noah was born, Lamech lived 595 years
and had other sons and daughters. 31Altogether,
Lamech lived 777 years, and then he died.
32After Noah was 500 years old, he became the
father of Shem, Ham and Japheth. Ge 10:1

From Bad to Worse **Chapters 6–9**

As we move through the opening chapters, life quickly degenerated from bad to unbearable. Sin and its destructive consequences had infected all of humanity; sin had begun to spread like wildfire. By chapter 6, God looked down on the earth and saw sin's widespread effects—and (humanly speaking) it tore Him apart. Listen: "The LORD was grieved that he had made man on the earth, and his heart was filled with pain" (6:6). With sorrow and sadness God looked at His creation and mourned their fallen condition. "I will blot them out," He said. "I will erase them from the face of the earth, along with every living thing" (6:7). But thanks be to God, there was someone who found favor in the eyes of the Lord (6:8)! His name was Noah. And that begins the whole story of the flood, which continues through chapter 9.

The Flood

6 When men began to increase in number on
the earth and daughters were born to them,
2the sons of God saw that the daughters of men
were beautiful, and they married any of them they
chose. 3Then the LORD said, "My Spirit will not
contend with[a] man forever, for he is mortal[b]; his
days will be a hundred and twenty years."
4The Nephilim were on the earth in those
days—and also afterward—when the sons of God
went to the daughters of men and had children by
them. They were the heroes of old, men of renown.
5The LORD saw how great man's wickedness on
the earth had become, and that every inclination of
the thoughts of his heart was only evil all the time.
6The LORD was grieved that he had made man on
the earth, and his heart was filled with pain. 7So the
LORD said, "I will wipe mankind, whom I have
created, from the face of the earth—men and animals, and creatures that move along the ground,
and birds of the air—for I am grieved that I have
made them." 8But Noah found favor in the eyes of
the LORD. Isa 63:10; Ge 8:21; 19:19

9This is the account of Noah.

Noah was a righteous man, blameless among
the people of his time, and he walked with God.
10Noah had three sons: Shem, Ham and Japheth.
11Now the earth was corrupt in God's sight and
was full of violence. 12God saw how corrupt the
earth had become, for all the people on earth had
corrupted their ways. 13So God said to Noah, "I
am going to put an end to all people, for the earth
is filled with violence because of them. I am surely
going to destroy both them and the earth. 14So
make yourself an ark of cypress[c] wood; make
rooms in it and coat it with pitch inside and out.
15This is how you are to build it: The ark is to be
450 feet long, 75 feet wide and 45 feet high.[d]
16Make a roof for it and finish[e] the ark to within
18 inches[f] of the top. Put a door in the side of the
ark and make lower, middle and upper decks. 17I
am going to bring floodwaters on the earth to
destroy all life under the heavens, every creature
that has the breath of life in it. Everything on earth
will perish. 18But I will establish my covenant with
you, and you will enter the ark—you and your
sons and your wife and your sons' wives with you.
19You are to bring into the ark two of all living
creatures, male and female, to keep them alive
with you. 20Two of every kind of bird, of every
kind of animal and of every kind of creature that
moves along the ground will come to you to be
kept alive. 21You are to take every kind of food that
is to be eaten and store it away as food for you and
for them." Ge 9:9-16; Ps 14:1-3; 2Pe 2:5
22Noah did everything just as God commanded
him. Ge 7:5,9,16

LIVING  **INSIGHT**

Why is it so hard for us today to believe that God can still do the seemingly impossible? When did He stop leading people down unusual paths? Did you ever notice that those in God's inspired Book who experienced the fullness of His power stepped in with total obedience.
(See Genesis 6:22.)

7 The LORD then said to Noah, "Go into the
ark, you and your whole family, because I
have found you righteous in this generation. 2Take
with you seven[g] of every kind of clean animal, a
male and its mate, and two of every kind of unclean animal, a male and its mate, 3and also seven
of every kind of bird, male and female, to keep
their various kinds alive throughout the earth.
4Seven days from now I will send rain on the earth
for forty days and forty nights, and I will wipe
from the face of the earth every living creature I
have made." Ge 6:9; Heb 11:7; Lev 10:10
5And Noah did all that the LORD commanded
him. Ge 6:22
6Noah was six hundred years old when the

[a] 3 Or *My spirit will not remain in* [b] 3 Or *corrupt* [c] 14 The meaning of the Hebrew for this word is uncertain.
[d] 15 Hebrew *300 cubits long, 50 cubits wide and 30 cubits high* (about 140 meters long, 23 meters wide and 13.5 meters high)
[e] 16 Or *Make an opening for light by finishing* [f] 16 Hebrew *a cubit* (about 0.5 meter) [g] 2 Or *seven pairs*; also in verse 3

THE BAD NEWS AND THE GOOD NEWS

"The LORD saw how great man's wickedness on the earth had become, and that every inclination of the thoughts of his heart was only evil all the time. The LORD was grieved that he had made man on the earth, and his heart was filled with pain."

—GENESIS 6:5–6

Let's be honest, no one likes bad news. We also tend to avoid the bearers of bad news. We view such folks as "prophets of doom." However, there are some things in life that must be said, even if they sound very much like bad news. Sin is one of those topics we would like to avoid but must learn to face and deal with honestly.

This is the reality: There is a terrible and inescapable condition in the human soul. The Bible calls it sin. It has been around almost as long as time. We all suffer from the same disease as did Adam, Eve, Cain—you name 'em. This Book called the Bible may be old, but it isn't out-of-date. It may relate our story in ancient terms, but its message is still true, still relevant. We've got the disease, the same root problem, as those who have gone before us. The best word for it is "depravity." And that root problem yields fruit: sinfulness . . . sinful thoughts, sinful words, sinful actions. There is nobody on earth who isn't affected. There is nobody on earth who can help us overcome our sin and depravity! That's really bad news.

Taking an Honest Look

The dictionary says *depraved* means "marked by corruption or evil; perverted, crooked." It's important that you understand this is an internal disease; you can't detect it from the outside. Most folks don't "look" depraved. Most of us do a masterful job of covering up. More often than not we don't even "act" depraved. But never doubt that underneath, deep down inside, there is this disease that eats away at us and pollutes our thoughts and our words (intellect), our feelings and relationships (emotions), and our actions (will).

The doctrine of depravity hasn't anything to do with our estimation of ourselves, but with *God's* estimation of us. We are the heirs of generations of the teachings of humanism, which sees humanity in an ever-ascending spiral, rising higher and higher from the depths from which we have sprung until finally we are able to reach stellar levels of goodness and greatness. So widely accepted is this concept that we have come to feel that there is so much good in the worst of us, humankind is really not so bad after all. When we measure ourselves by others around us, we can always find someone who is lower than we are on the moral or ethical scale, and the comparison gives us a feeling of self-satisfaction and pride. But the Scriptures do not measure us by those around us; they measure us by the God who has created us. The creature is measured by the Creator and is found wanting.

Someone once said it well when he suggested, "If depravity were blue, we'd be blue all over." Cut us anywhere and we'll bleed blue. Cut into our minds and you'll find blue thoughts. Cut into our vision and there are blue images full of envy and pride, greed and lust. Cut into our hearts and there are blue emotions of hatred, revenge and blame. Cut into our wills and you'll find blue decisions and responses.

But the fact is, we don't look blue! We look good, almost clean at times. We may even look better than our world has ever looked, physically. But there's something deep within us that is depraved. It's our nature. That's why we can't clean up our own act. That's why we can't handle our own lust. That's why we can't say no to certain temptations. That's why we become addicted to harmful habits. That's why we fight with each other and fight with God—even when we know we shouldn't. If we are going to gain control over sin, it must come from *outside* ourselves!

Exposing the Dark Side

I like good news. Therefore, I prefer to emphasize the happy, bright, cheerful, colorful side of life. But my problem with that emphasis is this: The good news is only *half* the message of Christianity. When we stop to think about it, we really cannot appreciate the bright and beautiful side of life until we know how dark and dismal the backdrop is. So to be true to my calling and to be complete in my presentation of Biblical doctrine, it is necessary to expose the dark side along with the bright side of life.

It was back in 1886 that Robert Louis Stevenson wrote a classic story that exposed everybody's life. He called it *Dr. Jekyll and Mr. Hyde*. Although a little older, Stevenson was a contemporary of Mark Twain, the American storyteller. Perhaps it was after reading that story that Twain came up with the statement so familiar to all of us: "Everyone is a moon, and has a dark side which he never shows to anybody." No one ever said it better than Jesus when He spoke so sternly against the hypocrisy of the Pharisees and teachers of the law:

> *Woe to you, teachers of the law and Pharisees, you hypocrites! You are like whitewashed tombs, which look beautiful on the outside but on the inside are full of dead men's bones and everything unclean. In the same way, on the outside you appear to people as righteous but on the inside you are full of hypocrisy and wickedness (Matthew 23:27–28).*

Lest you live under the delusion that the "dark side" was a problem only former generations struggled with, just think about your life over the past several days. Be sure to think inwardly as well as outwardly. More than likely you behaved reasonably well externally . . . but not from within! Call to mind the impulses, the drives, the secrets, the ugly thoughts, the hidden motives behind the actions you lived out. Perhaps a few of them did surface, but most of your dark side remained hidden to public scrutiny.

Depravity Defined and Explained

All I have said thus far has to do with the most ancient and all-pervasive disease that's ever plagued humanity. It's helpful to remember that the deadliest killer is not heart disease or cancer . . . it is depravity. Every last one of us has it. Every one of us suffers from its consequences. And to make matters even worse, we pass it on to each new generation.

One of the most sweeping, broad-brush statements in all of Scripture on the depravity of humanity is found in Genesis 6:5: "The LORD saw how great man's wickedness on the earth had become, and that every inclination of the thoughts of his heart was only evil all the time." Are you as gripped as I am when you read three prominent thoughts in that verse? Look at them again, and read them slowly, carefully: "every," "only," "all the time." The scene described in this verse is an inescapable, universal cesspool in the inner person of all humanity—a hidden source of pollution that lies at the root of evil.

Even from childhood this is true. A number of years ago the Minnesota Crime Commission released this statement: "Every baby starts life as a little savage. He is completely selfish and self-centered. He wants what he wants when he wants it—his bottle, his mother's attention, his playmate's toy, his uncle's watch. Deny him these once, and he seethes with rage and aggressiveness, which would be murderous were he not so helpless. He is, in fact, dirty. He has no morals, no knowledge, no skills. This means that all children—not just certain children—are born delinquent. If permitted to continue in the self-centered world of his infancy, given free reign to his impulsive actions to satisfy his wants, every child would grow up a criminal—a thief, a killer or a rapist."

Now that's reality. And if it's your tendency as a positive thinker to ignore it, it still won't go away. If it's your tendency as a parent to ignore it, that root of depravity will come back to haunt you in your home. A permissive, think-only-about-the-bright-side-of-life philosophy will be ripped to shreds by problems of depravity if your child grows up without restraints, boundaries and controls. Not even a kind and professional Dr. Jekyll could remove the savage-like Mr. Hyde from his own life. Face it, the dark side is permanently connected to us.

Psalm 51 is another section of Scripture worth examining as we come to terms with human depravity. It is the psalm David wrote following the prophet Nathan's confrontation after David's now famous adultery-murder-hypocrisy scandal. In the first five verses of this psalm, David penned these words:

Have mercy on me, O God,
according to your unfailing love;
according to your great compassion
blot out my transgressions.
Wash away all my iniquity
and cleanse me from my sin.
For I know my transgressions,
and my sin is always before me.
Against you, you only, have I sinned
and done what is evil in your sight,
so that you are proved right when you speak
and justified when you judge.
Surely I was sinful at birth,
sinful from the time my mother conceived me.

David began with a plea for grace, which shouldn't surprise us. The only way David could expect to survive would be by the grace of God. That's the only reason any of us survives! What is grace? How would you define it? Probably the most popular definition contains only two words: "unmerited favor." To amplify that a bit: Grace is what God does for human beings, which we do not deserve, cannot earn and will never be able to repay. Awash in our sinfulness, helpless to change on our own, polluted to the core with no possibility of cleaning ourselves up, we cry out for grace. It is our only hope. Our sinful natures cannot be improved, altered or removed. We came into this life sinful, and we continue on in a sinful state.

The One Great Exception

Jesus Christ is the one great exception. There is no grime in Him, only glory. No dark side, only light. No sinfulness, only righteousness. No blue, only spotless white. He is the great Good News. Scripture says three important things about Jesus. He *knew* no sin; He *had* no sin; He *did* no sin. Knowing no sin, having no sin, doing no sin, He qualified as the Lamb of God who took away the power of sin, the shame of guilt and the dread of death. Therefore, when we confess our sins, He hears us and cleanses us. What a relief! We make this honest confession, "Guilty as charged." He answers, "Heard and forgiven!" As Paul put it so powerfully in Romans 8:1: "Therefore, there is now no condemnation for those who are in Christ Jesus." Listen to the words of the apostle John as well:

This is the message we have heard from him and declare to you: God is light; in him there is no darkness at all. If we claim to have fellowship with him yet walk in the darkness, we lie and do not live by the truth. But if we walk in the light, as he is in the light, we have fellowship with one another, and the blood of Jesus, his Son, purifies us from all sin. If we claim to be without sin, we deceive ourselves and the truth is not in us. If we confess our sins, he is faithful and just and will forgive us our sins and purify us from all unrighteousness (1 John 1:5–9).

When we boil it all down, we really have two options. First of all, *we can choose to live according to our depravity* . . . for "evil is right there with me," as Paul wrote (Romans 7:21). Or second, *we can choose to live as victors through the power of Jesus Christ.* The last thing I desire to do is to leave in your mind the impression that you must spend your years as a helpless, depraved person. The redeemed have a better hope than that!

Remember, we never reach perfection while still on earth. There will always be some sin that lurks in the attics and basements of our lives, seeking to deceive and to devour and to divide us. But Jesus Christ has defeated sin, and we are made alive in Him (Romans 6:11). Therefore let me encourage you to live as a victor through the power of Jesus Christ. Start by coming to the cross, by faith. Ask Jesus Christ to come into your life. Then as you face evil, as you encounter it, as it rears its head in temptation, claim the power of God that Jesus offers, now that He's living within you through the indwelling presence of the Holy Spirit. And claim this powerful assurance as well, which the apostle Paul confidently proclaimed in his letter to the Romans:

> *For I am convinced that neither death nor life, neither angels nor demons, neither the present nor the future, nor any powers, neither height nor depth, nor anything else in all creation, will be able to separate us from the love of God that is in Christ Jesus our Lord (Romans 8:38–39).*

You can say, "Lord, right now, at this very moment, I am weak. You are strong. By Your strength I'm stepping away from this evil, and Your power is going to give me the grace to get through it victoriously. Take charge right now." And then walk away. Stand firm! Trust Jesus to meet your every need. He will.

Remember the old gospel song "Just As I Am"? While attending a Billy Graham crusade at the Anaheim Stadium some years ago, I listened to that song night after night as thousands of people poured onto the field to turn their lives over to Jesus Christ. Some were lost; some were saved. But every one of them sought help with the same problem—their sin. Only the spotless Lamb of God could solve that problem. And He can do it for you as well!

floodwaters came on the earth. 7And Noah and his
sons and his wife and his sons' wives entered the
ark to escape the waters of the flood. 8Pairs of
clean and unclean animals, of birds and of all creatures that move along the ground, 9male and female, came to Noah and entered the ark, as God
had commanded Noah. 10And after the seven days
the floodwaters came on the earth. Ge 5:32

11In the six hundredth year of Noah's life, on
the seventeenth day of the second month—on
that day all the springs of the great deep burst
forth, and the floodgates of the heavens were
opened. 12And rain fell on the earth forty days and
forty nights. Ge 8:2; Eze 26:19

13On that very day Noah and his sons, Shem,
Ham and Japheth, together with his wife and the
wives of his three sons, entered the ark. 14They had
with them every wild animal according to its kind,
all livestock according to their kinds, every creature that moves along the ground according to its
kind and every bird according to its kind, everything with wings. 15Pairs of all creatures that have
the breath of life in them came to Noah and entered the ark. 16The animals going in were male
and female of every living thing, as God had commanded Noah. Then the LORD shut him in.

17For forty days the flood kept coming on the
earth, and as the waters increased they lifted the
ark high above the earth. 18The waters rose and
increased greatly on the earth, and the ark floated
on the surface of the water. 19They rose greatly on
the earth, and all the high mountains under the
entire heavens were covered. 20The waters rose
and covered the mountains to a depth of more
than twenty feet.[a,b] 21Every living thing that
moved on the earth perished—birds, livestock,
wild animals, all the creatures that swarm over the
earth, and all mankind. 22Everything on dry land
that had the breath of life in its nostrils died. 23Ev-
ery living thing on the face of the earth was wiped
out; men and animals and the creatures that move
along the ground and the birds of the air were
wiped from the earth. Only Noah was left, and
those with him in the ark. 2Pe 2:5; Mt 24:39; Ge 1:30

24The waters flooded the earth for a hundred
and fifty days. Ge 8:3

8 But God remembered Noah and all the wild
animals and the livestock that were with him
in the ark, and he sent a wind over the earth, and
the waters receded. 2Now the springs of the deep
and the floodgates of the heavens had been closed,
and the rain had stopped falling from the sky.
3The water receded steadily from the earth. At
the end of the hundred and fifty days the water
had gone down, 4and on the seventeenth day of
the seventh month the ark came to rest on the
mountains of Ararat. 5The waters continued to re-
cede until the tenth month, and on the first day
of the tenth month the tops of the mountains
became visible.

6After forty days Noah opened the window he
had made in the ark 7and sent out a raven, and
it kept flying back and forth until the water had
dried up from the earth. 8Then he sent out a dove
to see if the water had receded from the surface of
the ground. 9But the dove could find no place to
set its feet because there was water over all the
surface of the earth; so it returned to Noah in the
ark. He reached out his hand and took the dove
and brought it back to himself in the ark. 10He
waited seven more days and again sent out the
dove from the ark. 11When the dove returned to
him in the evening, there in its beak was a freshly
plucked olive leaf! Then Noah knew that the water
had receded from the earth. 12He waited seven
more days and sent the dove out again, but this
time it did not return to him. Ge 7:12

13By the first day of the first month of Noah's
six hundred and first year, the water had dried up
from the earth. Noah then removed the covering
from the ark and saw that the surface of the
ground was dry. 14By the twenty-seventh day of
the second month the earth was completely dry.

15Then God said to Noah, 16"Come out of the
ark, you and your wife and your sons and their
wives. 17Bring out every kind of living creature that
is with you—the birds, the animals, and all the
creatures that move along the ground—so they
can multiply on the earth and be fruitful and increase in number upon it." Ge 1:22

18So Noah came out, together with his sons and
his wife and his sons' wives. 19All the animals and
all the creatures that move along the ground
and all the birds—everything that moves on the
earth—came out of the ark, one kind after another.

20Then Noah built an altar to the LORD and,
taking some of all the clean animals and clean
birds, he sacrificed burnt offerings on it. 21The
LORD smelled the pleasing aroma and said in his
heart: "Never again will I curse the ground because
of man, even though[c] every inclination of his
heart is evil from childhood. And never again will
I destroy all living creatures, as I have done.

22"As long as the earth endures,
seedtime and harvest,
cold and heat,
summer and winter,
day and night
will never cease." Jer 33:20,25; Ge 1:14

[a] 20 Hebrew *fifteen cubits* (about 6.9 meters) [b] 20 Or *rose more than twenty feet, and the mountains were covered*
[c] 21 Or *man, for*

God's Covenant With Noah

9 Then God blessed Noah and his sons, saying
to them, "Be fruitful and increase in number
and fill the earth. 2The fear and dread of you will
fall upon all the beasts of the earth and all the birds
of the air, upon every creature that moves along
the ground, and upon all the fish of the sea; they
are given into your hands. 3Everything that lives
and moves will be food for you. Just as I gave you
the green plants, I now give you everything.

4"But you must not eat meat that has its lifeblood still in it. 5And for your lifeblood I will
surely demand an accounting. I will demand an
accounting from every animal. And from each
man, too, I will demand an accounting for the life
of his fellow man. Ge 4:10; Lev 3:17; 17:10-14

6"Whoever sheds the blood of man,
by man shall his blood be shed; Ex 21:12,14
for in the image of God
has God made man. Ge 1:26

7As for you, be fruitful and increase in number;
multiply on the earth and increase upon it."

8Then God said to Noah and to his sons with
him: 9"I now establish my covenant with you and
with your descendants after you 10and with every
living creature that was with you—the birds, the
livestock and all the wild animals, all those that
came out of the ark with you—every living creature on earth. 11I establish my covenant with you:
Never again will all life be cut off by the waters of
a flood; never again will there be a flood to destroy
the earth." Ge 6:18; 8:21; Isa 54:9

12And God said, "This is the sign of the covenant I am making between me and you and every
living creature with you, a covenant for all generations to come: 13I have set my rainbow in the
clouds, and it will be the sign of the covenant
between me and the earth. 14Whenever I bring
clouds over the earth and the rainbow appears in
the clouds, 15I will remember my covenant between me and you and all living creatures of every
kind. Never again will the waters become a flood
to destroy all life. 16Whenever the rainbow appears
in the clouds, I will see it and remember the everlasting covenant between God and all living creatures of every kind on the earth." Ge 17:7,13,19

17So God said to Noah, "This is the sign of the
covenant I have established between me and all life
on the earth." ver 12; Ge 17:11

The Sons of Noah

18The sons of Noah who came out of the ark
were Shem, Ham and Japheth. (Ham was the father of Canaan.) 19These were the three sons of
Noah, and from them came the people who were
scattered over the earth. Ge 10:32

20Noah, a man of the soil, proceeded[a] to plant
a vineyard. 21When he drank some of its wine, he
became drunk and lay uncovered inside his tent.
22Ham, the father of Canaan, saw his father's na-

LIVING  **INSIGHT**

Learn a major lesson from the story of Noah: No one on earth deserves your worship. Try to remember that every person on earth is still a depraved human being. Some are being used by God in powerful ways, but in no way are they free from the disease. Example: Noah . . . a good man who distinguished himself in bad times . . . but was still imperfect.

(See Genesis 9:20–22.)

kedness and told his two brothers outside. 23But
Shem and Japheth took a garment and laid it
across their shoulders; then they walked in backward and covered their father's nakedness. Their
faces were turned the other way so that they would
not see their father's nakedness. Hab 2:15

24When Noah awoke from his wine and found
out what his youngest son had done to him, 25he
said,

"Cursed be Canaan! ver 18
The lowest of slaves
will he be to his brothers." Ge 25:23

26He also said,

"Blessed be the LORD, the God of Shem!
May Canaan be the slave of Shem.[b] 1Ki 9:21
27May God extend the territory of Japheth[c];
may Japheth live in the tents of Shem,
and may Canaan be his[d] slave."

28After the flood Noah lived 350 years. 29Alto-
gether, Noah lived 950 years, and then he died.

The Beginning of the Nations **Chapter 10**

This chapter may look like "Dull City," but in my opinion it is one of the most interesting in all of Genesis. It traces the origin, the "genesis," of the nations. In particular, it chronicles the family lineage of the three sons of Noah—Shem, Ham and Japheth. The Japhethites became the intellectuals and philosophers of the ancient world and settled much of what is now the Western Hemisphere. The Hamites populated what is modern Egypt, North Africa and Canaan and are characterized as ingenious, practical and creative people. The Shemites established many of the mideastern religions, and it is from this line that the family of Abraham would descend. We can learn much from tracing the branches on the family tree—as you will discover as you read this chapter.

[a]20 Or *soil, was the first* [b]26 Or *be his slave* [c]27 *Japheth* sounds like the Hebrew for *extend.* [d]27 Or *their*

The Table of Nations

10 This is the account of Shem, Ham and Japheth, Noah's sons, who themselves had
sons after the flood. Ge 2:4

The Japhethites

2The sons[a] of Japheth:
Gomer, Magog, Madai, Javan, Tubal,
Meshech and Tiras. Eze 38:2,6; Rev 20:8
3The sons of Gomer:
Ashkenaz, Riphath and Togarmah.
4The sons of Javan:
Elishah, Tarshish, the Kittim and the
Rodanim.[b] 5(From these the maritime
peoples spread out into their territories
by their clans within their nations, each
with its own language.) 1Ch 1:5-7; Jnh 1:3

The Hamites

6The sons of Ham:
Cush, Mizraim,[c] Put and Canaan.
7The sons of Cush:
Seba, Havilah, Sabtah, Raamah and Sab-
teca.
The sons of Raamah:
Sheba and Dedan.

8Cush was the father[d] of Nimrod, who grew to
be a mighty warrior on the earth. 9He was a mighty
hunter before the LORD; that is why it is said, "Like
Nimrod, a mighty hunter before the LORD." 10The
first centers of his kingdom were Babylon, Erech,
Akkad and Calneh, in[e] Shinar.[f] 11From that
land he went to Assyria, where he built Nineveh,
Rehoboth Ir,[g] Calah 12and Resen, which is between Nineveh and Calah; that is the great city.

13Mizraim was the father of
the Ludites, Anamites, Lehabites, Naph-
tuhites, 14Pathrusites, Casluhites (from
whom the Philistines came) and Caphtorites. Ge 21:32,34
15Canaan was the father of
Sidon his firstborn,[h] and of the Hittites,
16Jebusites, Amorites, Girgashites, 17Hi-
vites, Arkites, Sinites, 18Arvadites, Zema-
rites and Hamathites. Ge 9:18; Eze 28:21

Later the Canaanite clans scattered 19and the
borders of Canaan reached from Sidon toward Gerar as far as Gaza, and then toward Sodom, Gomorrah, Admah and Zeboiim, as far as Lasha.

20These are the sons of Ham by their clans and
languages, in their territories and nations.

The Semites

21Sons were also born to Shem, whose older
brother was[i] Japheth; Shem was the ancestor of
all the sons of Eber. Nu 24:24

22The sons of Shem:
Elam, Asshur, Arphaxad, Lud and Aram.
23The sons of Aram:
Uz, Hul, Gether and Meshech.[j] Job 1:1
24Arphaxad was the father of[k] Shelah,
and Shelah the father of Eber. Lk 3:35
25Two sons were born to Eber:
One was named Peleg,[l] because in his
time the earth was divided; his brother
was named Joktan.
26Joktan was the father of
Almodad, Sheleph, Hazarmaveth, Jerah,
27Hadoram, Uzal, Diklah, 28Obal, Abimael, Sheba, 29Ophir, Havilah and Jobab. All
these were sons of Joktan.

30The region where they lived stretched from Mesha toward Sephar, in the eastern hill country.
31These are the sons of Shem by their clans and
languages, in their territories and nations.

32These are the clans of Noah's sons, according
to their lines of descent, within their nations. From
these the nations spread out over the earth after
the flood. Ge 9:19

The Danger of Human Pride **Chapter 11**

The tower of Babel was a human attempt to reach God. As with all efforts to pull God down to our level, it failed miserably. When men and women, in their pride, sought to build a tower to God, He entered the picture and put an end to their construction project. He scattered the people and confused their language. From that time on there was an enlargement and multiplication of cultures . . . an alteration of life as they knew it. No longer would there be a unilingual human race but a multilingual world.

The Tower of Babel

11 Now the whole world had one language
and a common speech. 2As men moved
eastward,[m] they found a plain in Shinar[f] and
settled there. Ge 10:10

3They said to each other, "Come, let's make
bricks and bake them thoroughly." They used
brick instead of stone, and tar for mortar. 4Then

[a]2 *Sons* may mean *descendants* or *successors* or *nations*; also in verses 3, 4, 6, 7, 20-23, 29 and 31. [b]4 Some manuscripts of the Masoretic Text and Samaritan Pentateuch (see also Septuagint and 1 Chron. 1:7); most manuscripts of the Masoretic Text *Dodanim* [c]6 That is, Egypt; also in verse 13 [d]8 *Father* may mean *ancestor* or *predecessor* or *founder*; also in verses 13, 15, 24 and 26. [e]10 Or *Erech and Akkad—all of them in* [f]10,2 That is, Babylonia [g]11 Or *Nineveh with its city squares* [h]15 Or *of the Sidonians, the foremost* [i]21 Or *Shem, the older brother of* [j]23 See Septuagint and 1 Chron. 1:17; Hebrew *Mash* [k]24 Hebrew; Septuagint *father of Cainan, and Cainan was the father of* [l]25 *Peleg* means *division.* [m]2 Or *from the east*; or *in the east*

DISPENSATIONALISM

Dispensationalism is a theological system that helps us interpret the Bible with greater ease. Since this is true, we need to understand several things about it.

First, what dispensationalism is not:

Dispensationalism does not teach different ways of salvation in different ages.

Dispensationalism does not deny the importance of God's program for the church.

Dispensationalism does not minimize the centrality of Christ's death and resurrection in God's plan for the ages.

Second, what dispensationalism is:

Dispensationalism believes in interpreting the Bible as it is.

Dispensationalism sees a distinction between Israel and the church.

Dispensationalism anticipates a literal return of Jesus Christ to reign on earth.

Third, how dispensationalism unfolds in the Bible

Dispensationalism recognizes that God has administered His world in different ways during different periods of history. The specific number of dispensations is not important, but several major changes throughout God's program on earth can be identified. The following chart defines some of these periods.

Title	Time	Test	Termination
INNOCENCE	Garden of Eden *Genesis 1–3*	Obedience to God's revelation	Fall
CONSCIENCE	Expulsion from Garden *Genesis 4–8*	Obedience to God's revelation	Flood
HUMAN GOVERNMENT	Post-flood civilization *Genesis 9–11*	Obedience to God's revelation	Tower of Babel
ISRAEL	Call of Abraham *Genesis 12–Time of Christ*	Obedience to God's revelation	Death of Christ
CHURCH	Day of Pentecost *Acts 2–Today*	Obedience to God's revelation	Rapture of Church
KINGDOM	Second coming of Christ *Kingdom Age*	Obedience to God's revelation	Great White Throne Judgment

It is helpful to keep these different periods of time in mind as we read, study and teach Scripture. By doing so, we'll not only understand the context of each Bible passage more clearly, we'll guard against misinterpreting (and misapplying) the truth of God's Word. Let's never forget that God's program is a continual unfolding plan on this earth, culminating with an earthly kingdom where He fulfills His long-awaited promises to His people, the Jews.

they said, "Come, let us build ourselves a city, with
a tower that reaches to the heavens, so that we may
make a name for ourselves and not be scattered
over the face of the whole earth." Dt 1:28; Ge 6:4

LIVING  **INSIGHT**

What was it that was at the heart of all this building? I think it was something like this: Doing what I want to do will result in being what I ought to be. God stepped in and said, "There's no way." We cannot by our own human effort make ourselves be what we ought to be. And God stands ready to help us as we admit that we cannot help ourselves.

(See Genesis 11:1–9.)

5But the LORD came down to see the city and the
tower that the men were building. 6The LORD said,
"If as one people speaking the same language they
have begun to do this, then nothing they plan to
do will be impossible for them. 7Come, let us go
down and confuse their language so they will not
understand each other." Ge 18:21; 42:23
8So the LORD scattered them from there over all
the earth, and they stopped building the city. 9That
is why it was called Babel[a]—because there the
LORD confused the language of the whole world.
From there the LORD scattered them over the face
of the whole earth. Lk 1:51; Ge 10:10

From Shem to Abram

10This is the account of Shem.

Two years after the flood, when Shem was 100
years old, he became the father[b] of Arphaxad.
11And after he became the father of Arphaxad,
Shem lived 500 years and had other sons and
daughters.
12When Arphaxad had lived 35 years, he became the father of Shelah. 13And after he became
the father of Shelah, Arphaxad lived 403 years and
had other sons and daughters.[c] Lk 3:35
14When Shelah had lived 30 years, he became
the father of Eber. 15And after he became the father of Eber, Shelah lived 403 years and had other
sons and daughters. Lk 3:35
16When Eber had lived 34 years, he became the
father of Peleg. 17And after he became the father of
Peleg, Eber lived 430 years and had other sons and
daughters.
18When Peleg had lived 30 years, he became the
father of Reu. 19And after he became the father of
Reu, Peleg lived 209 years and had other sons and
daughters.
20When Reu had lived 32 years, he became the
father of Serug. 21And after he became the father
of Serug, Reu lived 207 years and had other sons
and daughters.
22When Serug had lived 30 years, he became the
father of Nahor. 23And after he became the father
of Nahor, Serug lived 200 years and had other sons
and daughters.
24When Nahor had lived 29 years, he became
the father of Terah. 25And after he became the
father of Terah, Nahor lived 119 years and had
other sons and daughters. Lk 3:34
26After Terah had lived 70 years, he became the
father of Abram, Nahor and Haran. Ge 10:21-31

27This is the account of Terah.

Terah became the father of Abram, Nahor and
Haran. And Haran became the father of Lot.
28While his father Terah was still alive, Haran died
in Ur of the Chaldeans, in the land of his birth.
29Abram and Nahor both married. The name of
Abram's wife was Sarai, and the name of Nahor's
wife was Milcah; she was the daughter of Haran,
the father of both Milcah and Iscah. 30Now Sarai
was barren; she had no children. Ge 12:4; 16:1; 17:15
31Terah took his son Abram, his grandson Lot
son of Haran, and his daughter-in-law Sarai, the
wife of his son Abram, and together they set out
from Ur of the Chaldeans to go to Canaan. But
when they came to Haran, they settled there.
32Terah lived 205 years, and he died in Haran.

The Beginning of a Nation **Chapters 12–20**

Chapter 12 introduces us to the beginning of the nation of Israel. At the outset we meet a man named Abram (meaning, "exalted father"), who would later be called Abraham ("father of many"). God made a promise to Abraham. He said he would make his name great and give him many descendants and provide a land for the great nation that would come from Abraham's descendants. This promise, or agreement, is called the Abrahamic Covenant. This covenant would never be forgotten; it was unconditional and binding throughout time. The sign of this covenant was circumcision. In his old age, Abraham finally received the promise of a son (15:4). When Sarah heard she would bear a child, even though she was past her childbearing years, she laughed at the idea (18:12).

[a] 9 That is, Babylon; *Babel* sounds like the Hebrew for *confused.* [b] 10 *Father* may mean *ancestor*; also in verses 11-25.
[c] 12,13 Hebrew; Septuagint (see also Luke 3:35, 36 and note at Gen. 10:24) *35 years, he became the father of Cainan. 13And after he became the father of Cainan, Arphaxad lived 430 years and had other sons and daughters, and then he died. When Cainan had lived 130 years, he became the father of Shelah. And after he became the father of Shelah, Cainan lived 330 years and had other sons and daughters*

The Call of Abram

12 The LORD had said to Abram, "Leave your
country, your people and your father's
household and go to the land I will show you.

2"I will make you into a great nation Ge 17:2,4
and I will bless you; Ge 24:1,35
I will make your name great,
and you will be a blessing.
3I will bless those who bless you,
and whoever curses you I will curse; Ge 27:29
and all peoples on earth
will be blessed through you." Ge 22:18; Ac 3:25

4So Abram left, as the LORD had told him; and
Lot went with him. Abram was seventy-five years

LIVING  **INSIGHT**

Abraham demonstrated faith by moving into an uncharted course with one guarantee—that God was with him. Think about this: Christianity is not complicated. The neglect of your walk is complicated. And the secret is to distill this walk through the filter of simplicity so that you come back to the basics, which is faith. Visit Abraham regarding faith. Learn from him.

(See Genesis 12:1–4.)

old when he set out from Haran. 5He took his wife
Sarai, his nephew Lot, all the possessions they had
accumulated and the people they had acquired in
Haran, and they set out for the land of Canaan,
and they arrived there. Ge 11:31; 14:14
6Abram traveled through the land as far as the
site of the great tree of Moreh at Shechem. At that
time the Canaanites were in the land. 7The LORD
appeared to Abram and said, "To your offspring[a]
I will give this land." So he built an altar there to
the LORD, who had appeared to him. Ge 13:15,17
8From there he went on toward the hills east of
Bethel and pitched his tent, with Bethel on the west
and Ai on the east. There he built an altar to the
LORD and called on the name of the LORD. 9Then
Abram set out and continued toward the Negev.

Abram in Egypt

10Now there was a famine in the land, and
Abram went down to Egypt to live there for a
while because the famine was severe. 11As he was
about to enter Egypt, he said to his wife Sarai, "I
know what a beautiful woman you are. 12When the
Egyptians see you, they will say, 'This is his wife.'
Then they will kill me but will let you live. 13Say
you are my sister, so that I will be treated well for
your sake and my life will be spared because of
you." Ge 20:2
14When Abram came to Egypt, the Egyptians
saw that she was a very beautiful woman. 15And
when Pharaoh's officials saw her, they praised her
to Pharaoh, and she was taken into his palace.
16He treated Abram well for her sake, and Abram
acquired sheep and cattle, male and female donkeys, menservants and maidservants, and camels.
17But the LORD inflicted serious diseases on
Pharaoh and his household because of Abram's
wife Sarai. 18So Pharaoh summoned Abram.
"What have you done to me?" he said. "Why
didn't you tell me she was your wife? 19Why did
you say, 'She is my sister,' so that I took her to be
my wife? Now then, here is your wife. Take her
and go!" 20Then Pharaoh gave orders about
Abram to his men, and they sent him on his way,
with his wife and everything he had. Ge 20:1-18

Abram and Lot Separate

13 So Abram went up from Egypt to the Negev, with his wife and everything he had,
and Lot went with him. 2Abram had become very
wealthy in livestock and in silver and gold.
3From the Negev he went from place to place
until he came to Bethel, to the place between Bethel and Ai where his tent had been earlier 4and
where he had first built an altar. There Abram
called on the name of the LORD. Ge 12:7-8
5Now Lot, who was moving about with Abram,
also had flocks and herds and tents. 6But the land
could not support them while they stayed together,
for their possessions were so great that they were
not able to stay together. 7And quarreling arose
between Abram's herdsmen and the herdsmen of
Lot. The Canaanites and Perizzites were also living
in the land at that time. Ge 26:20-21; 36:7; 12:6
8So Abram said to Lot, "Let's not have any
quarreling between you and me, or between your
herdsmen and mine, for we are brothers. 9Is not
the whole land before you? Let's part company. If
you go to the left, I'll go to the right; if you go to
the right, I'll go to the left." Ps 133:1; Pr 15:18
10Lot looked up and saw that the whole plain of
the Jordan was well watered, like the garden of the
LORD, like the land of Egypt, toward Zoar. (This
was before the LORD destroyed Sodom and Gomorrah.) 11So Lot chose for himself the whole
plain of the Jordan and set out toward the east.
The two men parted company: 12Abram lived in
the land of Canaan, while Lot lived among the
cities of the plain and pitched his tents near Sodom. 13Now the men of Sodom were wicked and
were sinning greatly against the LORD. Ge 18:20
14The LORD said to Abram after Lot had parted

[a]7 Or *seed*

from him, "Lift up your eyes from where you are and look north and south, east and west. 15All the land that you see I will give to you and your offspring[a] forever. 16I will make your offspring like the dust of the earth, so that if anyone could count the dust, then your offspring could be counted. 17Go, walk through the length and breadth of the land, for I am giving it to you." Ge 12:7; Nu 13:17-25

18So Abram moved his tents and went to live near the great trees of Mamre at Hebron, where he built an altar to the LORD. Ge 8:20; 14:13,24

Abram Rescues Lot

14 At this time Amraphel king of Shinar,[b] Arioch king of Ellasar, Kedorlaomer king of Elam and Tidal king of Goiim 2went to war against Bera king of Sodom, Birsha king of Gomorrah, Shinab king of Admah, Shemeber king of Zeboiim, and the king of Bela (that is, Zoar). 3All these latter kings joined forces in the Valley of Siddim (the Salt Sea[c]). 4For twelve years they had been subject to Kedorlaomer, but in the thirteenth year they rebelled. Nu 34:3,12; Jos 3:16

5In the fourteenth year, Kedorlaomer and the kings allied with him went out and defeated the Rephaites in Ashteroth Karnaim, the Zuzites in Ham, the Emites in Shaveh Kiriathaim 6and the Horites in the hill country of Seir, as far as El Paran near the desert. 7Then they turned back and went to En Mishpat (that is, Kadesh), and they conquered the whole territory of the Amalekites, as well as the Amorites who were living in Hazazon Tamar. Dt 2:12,22; Ge 21:21

8Then the king of Sodom, the king of Gomorrah, the king of Admah, the king of Zeboiim and the king of Bela (that is, Zoar) marched out and drew up their battle lines in the Valley of Siddim 9against Kedorlaomer king of Elam, Tidal king of Goiim, Amraphel king of Shinar and Arioch king of Ellasar—four kings against five. 10Now the Valley of Siddim was full of tar pits, and when the kings of Sodom and Gomorrah fled, some of the men fell into them and the rest fled to the hills. 11The four kings seized all the goods of Sodom and Gomorrah and all their food; then they went away. 12They also carried off Abram's nephew Lot and his possessions, since he was living in Sodom.

13One who had escaped came and reported this to Abram the Hebrew. Now Abram was living near the great trees of Mamre the Amorite, a brother[d] of Eshcol and Aner, all of whom were allied with Abram. 14When Abram heard that his relative had been taken captive, he called out the 318 trained men born in his household and went in pursuit as far as Dan. 15During the night Abram divided his men to attack them and he routed them, pursuing them as far as Hobah, north of Damascus. 16He recovered all the goods and brought back his relative Lot and his possessions, together with the women and the other people. Ge 13:18; 15:3

17After Abram returned from defeating Kedorlaomer and the kings allied with him, the king of Sodom came out to meet him in the Valley of Shaveh (that is, the King's Valley).

18Then Melchizedek king of Salem[e] brought out bread and wine. He was priest of God Most High, 19and he blessed Abram, saying, Ps 110:4

"Blessed be Abram by God Most High,
Creator[f] of heaven and earth.
20And blessed be[g] God Most High,
who delivered your enemies into your
hand." Ge 24:27

Then Abram gave him a tenth of everything.

21The king of Sodom said to Abram, "Give me the people and keep the goods for yourself."

22But Abram said to the king of Sodom, "I have raised my hand to the LORD, God Most High, Creator of heaven and earth, and have taken an oath 23that I will accept nothing belonging to you, not even a thread or the thong of a sandal, so that you will never be able to say, 'I made Abram rich.' 24I will accept nothing but what my men have eaten and the share that belongs to the men who went with me—to Aner, Eshcol and Mamre. Let them have their share." Ex 6:8; Rev 10:5-6

God's Covenant With Abram

15 After this, the word of the LORD came to Abram in a vision: Nu 12:6

"Do not be afraid, Abram. Ge 21:17; 26:24
I am your shield,[h] Dt 33:29
your very great reward.[i]"

2But Abram said, "O Sovereign LORD, what can you give me since I remain childless and the one who will inherit[j] my estate is Eliezer of Damascus?" 3And Abram said, "You have given me no children; so a servant in my household will be my heir." Ac 7:5; Ge 24:2,34

4Then the word of the LORD came to him: "This man will not be your heir, but a son coming from your own body will be your heir." 5He took him outside and said, "Look up at the heavens and count the stars—if indeed you can count them." Then he said to him, "So shall your offspring be."

6Abram believed the LORD, and he credited it to him as righteousness. Ro 4:3,20-24; Gal 3:6; Jas 2:23

7He also said to him, "I am the LORD, who brought you out of Ur of the Chaldeans to give you this land to take possession of it." Ge 13:17

[a]15 Or *seed*; also in verse 16 [b]1 That is, Babylonia; also in verse 9 [c]3 That is, the Dead Sea [d]13 Or *a relative*; or *an ally* [e]18 That is, Jerusalem [f]19 Or *Possessor*; also in verse 22 [g]20 Or *And praise be to* [h]1 Or *sovereign* [i]1 Or *shield; / your reward will be very great* [j]2 The meaning of the Hebrew for this phrase is uncertain.

8But Abram said, "O Sovereign LORD, how can
I know that I will gain possession of it?" Lk 1:18
9So the LORD said to him, "Bring me a heifer, a
goat and a ram, each three years old, along with a
dove and a young pigeon." Nu 19:2; Dt 21:3
10Abram brought all these to him, cut them in
two and arranged the halves opposite each other;
the birds, however, he did not cut in half. 11Then
birds of prey came down on the carcasses, but
Abram drove them away. Lev 1:17; Jer 34:18
12As the sun was setting, Abram fell into a deep
sleep, and a thick and dreadful darkness came over
him. 13Then the LORD said to him, "Know for certain that your descendants will be strangers in a
country not their own, and they will be enslaved
and mistreated four hundred years. 14But I will
punish the nation they serve as slaves, and afterward they will come out with great possessions.
15You, however, will go to your fathers in peace
and be buried at a good old age. 16In the fourth
generation your descendants will come back here,
for the sin of the Amorites has not yet reached its
full measure." Ex 12:32-38,40; Ge 25:8
17When the sun had set and darkness had fallen,
a smoking firepot with a blazing torch appeared
and passed between the pieces. 18On that day the
LORD made a covenant with Abram and said, "To
your descendants I give this land, from the river[a]
of Egypt to the great river, the Euphrates— 19the
land of the Kenites, Kenizzites, Kadmonites, 20Hit-
tites, Perizzites, Rephaites, 21Amorites, Canaanites,
Girgashites and Jebusites." Ge 17:2,4,7

Hagar and Ishmael

16 Now Sarai, Abram's wife, had borne him
no children. But she had an Egyptian
maidservant named Hagar; 2so she said to Abram,
"The LORD has kept me from having children. Go,
sleep with my maidservant; perhaps I can build a
family through her." Ge 11:30; 30:3-4,9-10; Gal 4:24-25
Abram agreed to what Sarai said. 3So after
Abram had been living in Canaan ten years, Sarai
his wife took her Egyptian maidservant Hagar and
gave her to her husband to be his wife. 4He slept
with Hagar, and she conceived. Ge 12:5
When she knew she was pregnant, she began to
despise her mistress. 5Then Sarai said to Abram,
"You are responsible for the wrong I am suffering.
I put my servant in your arms, and now that she
knows she is pregnant, she despises me. May the
LORD judge between you and me." Ge 31:53
6"Your servant is in your hands," Abram said.
"Do with her whatever you think best." Then Sarai
mistreated Hagar; so she fled from her. Jos 9:25
7The angel of the LORD found Hagar near a
spring in the desert; it was the spring that is beside
the road to Shur. 8And he said, "Hagar, servant of
Sarai, where have you come from, and where are
you going?" Ge 21:17; 22:11,15
"I'm running away from my mistress Sarai," she
answered.

LIVING  **INSIGHT**

Rationalization is what we do when we substitute false explanations for true reasons . . . when we cloud our actual motives with a smoke screen of nice-sounding excuses.

(See Genesis 16:5.)

9Then the angel of the LORD told her, "Go back
to your mistress and submit to her." 10The angel
added, "I will so increase your descendants that
they will be too numerous to count." Ge 13:16; 17:20
11The angel of the LORD also said to her:

"You are now with child
and you will have a son.
You shall name him Ishmael,[b]
for the LORD has heard of your misery.
12He will be a wild donkey of a man;
his hand will be against everyone
and everyone's hand against him,
and he will live in hostility
toward[c] all his brothers." Ge 25:18

13She gave this name to the LORD who spoke to
her: "You are the God who sees me," for she said,
"I have now seen[d] the One who sees me." 14That
is why the well was called Beer Lahai Roi[e]; it is
still there, between Kadesh and Bered. Ge 32:30
15So Hagar bore Abram a son, and Abram gave
the name Ishmael to the son she had borne.
16Abram was eighty-six years old when Hagar
bore him Ishmael. Gal 4:22

The Covenant of Circumcision

17 When Abram was ninety-nine years old,
the LORD appeared to him and said, "I am
God Almighty[f]; walk before me and be blameless. 2I will confirm my covenant between me and
you and will greatly increase your numbers."
3Abram fell facedown, and God said to him,
4"As for me, this is my covenant with you: You will
be the father of many nations. 5No longer will you
be called Abram[g]; your name will be Abraham,[h]
for I have made you a father of many nations. 6I
will make you very fruitful; I will make nations of
you, and kings will come from you. 7I will establish
my covenant as an everlasting covenant between

[a]18 Or *Wadi* [b]11 *Ishmael* means *God hears.* [c]12 Or *live to the east / of* [d]13 Or *seen the back of* [e]14 *Beer Lahai Roi* means *well of the Living One who sees me.* [f]1 Hebrew *El-Shaddai* [g]5 *Abram* means *exalted father.* [h]5 *Abraham* means *father of many.*

ABRAHAM

Pioneer of the Faith

"This is my covenant with you: You will be the father of many nations. No longer will you be called Abram; your name will be Abraham, for I have made you a father of many nations."

–GENESIS 17:4–5

Abraham was in many respects the pioneer of faith in God. At the age of 75, this man received God's call and pursued a life of faith that still seems amazing. He left everything that was familiar to him, and he and his wife started over! Where would he end up? Only God knew. Why should he go? Because God promised that he would be the one through whom all peoples on earth would be blessed (Genesis 12:3). Now, please remember: Abraham's wife Sarai was barren (11:30). But that didn't stop this man of faith. He demonstrated his great trust in God by moving into uncharted territory with only one guarantee in hand—that God would be with him.

Throughout his life, Abraham learned a lesson we would do well to learn: Following God doesn't have to be complicated. *Neglecting* to follow God is what complicates life. Through Abraham's willingness to follow God's leading Abraham demonstrated that walking with God is the only way to true blessing. Note these four characteristics of Abraham's life, distilled from Genesis 13 and 14.

First, *Abraham was genuinely unselfish*. He was a very rich man. However, he acknowledged the source. His heart was right before God. We read in verses 3 and 4 of chapter 13 that he spent time with God in prayer at Bethel, where he had earlier built an altar (12:8). So when the needs related to his prosperity clashed with those of his nephew Lot, Abraham didn't pull rank. Instead, he offered Canaan's choicest land to his nephew. He knew that the great wealth he possessed was not his own but was a gift from God. After Abraham released his hold on the land, God gave it all back to him (13:14–17).

Second, *Abraham was willing to sacrifice himself for the sake of others*. After Lot had moved to Sodom (13:12), a rebellion arose against the king of the region. When Abraham heard that Lot was in trouble, he could have reacted with indifference: "So what? I've got my own problems to deal with here." He could have been critical: "Well, he finally got what he had coming." Instead Abraham chose to lead the charge to rescue his nephew. With an army of just over three hundred men, Abraham won a battle that five other kings and all their forces hadn't been able to win (14:14–15)! When the battle was over, Abraham didn't accept one single thing as a reward; he chose instead to give God the glory (14:22).

Third, *Abraham acted out of pure motives*. I believe this truth is displayed in the words "I have raised my hand to the LORD . . . and have taken an oath" (14:22). Abraham's strong resolution went way back to the early days of his journey with the Lord. Long before there was a war, long before he assembled his troops together to carry out the raid, Abraham had gone to his altar (12:8) where he spent time with the Lord. He and God had gotten together, and Abraham had sorted out the motives for his actions. That's why, when tempted with the spoils of Sodom, he was able to stay true to his commitment to God.

Fourth, *Abraham demonstrated extraordinary restraint of power*. Even though he could have forced his commitments on others, he chose to keep them between himself and his God. Abraham was the boss. He could have required his "trained men" (14:14) to walk with God as he did. But in coming to terms with his own commitments, Abraham was openhanded enough to say, "Look, it's my choice, but it may not be someone else's." And by making that choice, he let his life serve as an outstanding example to others.

My dad used to say to me, "Son, always be sure you have more behind the counter than you put on display." In other words, be sure to work on your character. In our fast-paced world, our tendency is to pretty well display everything we've got and hope nobody asks for anything we have to go to the stock room to bring out. That wasn't Abraham. By faith he followed where God led, and chose to let Him manage the outcome.

me and you and your descendants after you for the
generations to come, to be your God and the God
of your descendants after you. 8The whole land of
Canaan, where you are now an alien, I will give as
an everlasting possession to you and your descendants after you; and I will be their God." Ge 12:2
9Then God said to Abraham, "As for you, you
must keep my covenant, you and your descendants after you for the generations to come. 10This
is my covenant with you and your descendants
after you, the covenant you are to keep: Every
male among you shall be circumcised. 11You are to
undergo circumcision, and it will be the sign of the
covenant between me and you. 12For the generations to come every male among you who is eight
days old must be circumcised, including those
born in your household or bought with money
from a foreigner—those who are not your offspring. 13Whether born in your household or
bought with your money, they must be circumcised. My covenant in your flesh is to be an everlasting covenant. 14Any uncircumcised male, who
has not been circumcised in the flesh, will be cut
off from his people; he has broken my covenant."
15God also said to Abraham, "As for Sarai your
wife, you are no longer to call her Sarai; her name
will be Sarah. 16I will bless her and will surely give
you a son by her. I will bless her so that she will be
the mother of nations; kings of peoples will come
from her." Ge 18:10; Gal 4:31
17Abraham fell facedown; he laughed and said
to himself, "Will a son be born to a man a hundred
years old? Will Sarah bear a child at the age of
ninety?" 18And Abraham said to God, "If only Ishmael might live under your blessing!" Ge 21:11
19Then God said, "Yes, but your wife Sarah will
bear you a son, and you will call him Isaac.[a] I will
establish my covenant with him as an everlasting
covenant for his descendants after him. 20And as
for Ishmael, I have heard you: I will surely bless
him; I will make him fruitful and will greatly increase his numbers. He will be the father of twelve
rulers, and I will make him into a great nation.
21But my covenant I will establish with Isaac,
whom Sarah will bear to you by this time next
year." 22When he had finished speaking with
Abraham, God went up from him. Ge 16:10; 21:18
23On that very day Abraham took his son Ishmael and all those born in his household or
bought with his money, every male in his household, and circumcised them, as God told him.
24Abraham was ninety-nine years old when he was
circumcised, 25and his son Ishmael was thirteen;
26Abraham and his son Ishmael were both circumcised on that same day. 27And every male in Abraham's household, including those born in his
household or bought from a foreigner, was circumcised with him. Ro 4:11

The Three Visitors

18 The LORD appeared to Abraham near the
great trees of Mamre while he was sitting at
the entrance to his tent in the heat of the day.
2Abraham looked up and saw three men standing
nearby. When he saw them, he hurried from the
entrance of his tent to meet them and bowed low
to the ground. ver 16,22; Heb 13:2
3He said, "If I have found favor in your eyes, my
lord,[b] do not pass your servant by. 4Let a little
water be brought, and then you may all wash your
feet and rest under this tree. 5Let me get you something to eat, so you can be refreshed and then go
on your way—now that you have come to your
servant." Ge 43:24; Jdg 13:15
"Very well," they answered, "do as you say."
6So Abraham hurried into the tent to Sarah.
"Quick," he said, "get three seahs[c] of fine flour
and knead it and bake some bread."
7Then he ran to the herd and selected a choice,
tender calf and gave it to a servant, who hurried to
prepare it. 8He then brought some curds and milk
and the calf that had been prepared, and set these
before them. While they ate, he stood near them
under a tree. Ge 19:3
9"Where is your wife Sarah?" they asked him.
"There, in the tent," he said.
10Then the LORD[d] said, "I will surely return to
you about this time next year, and Sarah your wife
will have a son." Ro 9:9
Now Sarah was listening at the entrance to the
tent, which was behind him. 11Abraham and Sarah
were already old and well advanced in years, and
Sarah was past the age of childbearing. 12So Sarah
laughed to herself as she thought, "After I am
worn out and my master[e] is old, will I now have
this pleasure?" Ge 17:17; Ro 4:19; 1Pe 3:6
13Then the LORD said to Abraham, "Why did
Sarah laugh and say, 'Will I really have a child,
now that I am old?' 14Is anything too hard for the
LORD? I will return to you at the appointed time
next year and Sarah will have a son." Jer 32:17,27
15Sarah was afraid, so she lied and said, "I did
not laugh."
But he said, "Yes, you did laugh."

Abraham Pleads for Sodom

16When the men got up to leave, they looked
down toward Sodom, and Abraham walked along
with them to see them on their way. 17Then the
LORD said, "Shall I hide from Abraham what I am
about to do? 18Abraham will surely become a great
and powerful nation, and all nations on earth will

[a] 19 *Isaac* means *he laughs.* [b] 3 Or *O Lord* [c] 6 That is, probably about 20 quarts (about 22 liters) [d] 10 Hebrew *Then he* [e] 12 Or *husband*

be blessed through him. 19For I have chosen him,
so that he will direct his children and his household after him to keep the way of the LORD by
doing what is right and just, so that the LORD will
bring about for Abraham what he has promised
him." Gal 3:8; Dt 4:9-10

LIVING  INSIGHT

The home is God's built-in training facility. The home is a laboratory where experiments are tried out. It is a place where life makes up its mind. It is a place where Biblical truth permeates everyday life and where children are taught to seek and to follow the way of the Lord.

(See Genesis 18:19.)

20Then the LORD said, "The outcry against Sodom and Gomorrah is so great and their sin so
grievous 21that I will go down and see if what they
have done is as bad as the outcry that has reached
me. If not, I will know." Ge 19:13; Eze 16:46
22The men turned away and went toward Sodom, but Abraham remained standing before the
LORD.[a] 23Then Abraham approached him and
said: "Will you sweep away the righteous with the
wicked? 24What if there are fifty righteous people
in the city? Will you really sweep it away and not
spare[b] the place for the sake of the fifty righteous
people in it? 25Far be it from you to do such a
thing—to kill the righteous with the wicked, treating the righteous and the wicked alike. Far be it
from you! Will not the Judge[c] of all the earth do
right?" Nu 16:22; Ro 3:6
26The LORD said, "If I find fifty righteous people
in the city of Sodom, I will spare the whole place
for their sake." Jer 5:1
27Then Abraham spoke up again: "Now that I
have been so bold as to speak to the Lord, though
I am nothing but dust and ashes, 28what if the
number of the righteous is five less than fifty? Will
you destroy the whole city because of five people?"
"If I find forty-five there," he said, "I will not
destroy it."
29Once again he spoke to him, "What if only
forty are found there?"
He said, "For the sake of forty, I will not do it."
30Then he said, "May the Lord not be angry, but
let me speak. What if only thirty can be found
there?"
He answered, "I will not do it if I find thirty
there."
31Abraham said, "Now that I have been so bold
as to speak to the Lord, what if only twenty can be
found there?"
He said, "For the sake of twenty, I will not
destroy it."
32Then he said, "May the Lord not be angry, but
let me speak just once more. What if only ten can
be found there?" Jdg 6:39
He answered, "For the sake of ten, I will not
destroy it."
33When the LORD had finished speaking with
Abraham, he left, and Abraham returned home.

Sodom and Gomorrah Destroyed

19 The two angels arrived at Sodom in the
evening, and Lot was sitting in the gateway
of the city. When he saw them, he got up to meet
them and bowed down with his face to the ground.
2"My lords," he said, "please turn aside to your
servant's house. You can wash your feet and spend
the night and then go on your way early in the
morning." Ge 18:22
"No," they answered, "we will spend the night
in the square." Jdg 19:15,20
3But he insisted so strongly that they did go
with him and entered his house. He prepared a
meal for them, baking bread without yeast, and
they ate. 4Before they had gone to bed, all the men
from every part of the city of Sodom—both young
and old—surrounded the house. 5They called to
Lot, "Where are the men who came to you tonight? Bring them out to us so that we can have sex
with them." Jdg 19:22; Ro 1:24-27
6Lot went outside to meet them and shut the
door behind him 7and said, "No, my friends.
Don't do this wicked thing. 8Look, I have two
daughters who have never slept with a man. Let
me bring them out to you, and you can do what
you like with them. But don't do anything to these
men, for they have come under the protection of
my roof." Jdg 19:24; 2Pe 2:7-8
9"Get out of our way," they replied. And they
said, "This fellow came here as an alien, and now
he wants to play the judge! We'll treat you worse
than them." They kept bringing pressure on Lot
and moved forward to break down the door.
10But the men inside reached out and pulled Lot
back into the house and shut the door. 11Then they
struck the men who were at the door of the house,
young and old, with blindness so that they could
not find the door. Dt 28:28-29; 2Ki 6:18; Ac 13:11
12The two men said to Lot, "Do you have anyone else here—sons-in-law, sons or daughters, or
anyone else in the city who belongs to you? Get
them out of here, 13because we are going to destroy this place. The outcry to the LORD against its
people is so great that he has sent us to destroy it."

[a]22 Masoretic Text; an ancient Hebrew scribal tradition *but the LORD remained standing before Abraham* [b]24 Or *forgive*; also in verse 26 [c]25 Or *Ruler*

14So Lot went out and spoke to his sons-in-law,
who were pledged to marry[a] his daughters. He
said, "Hurry and get out of this place, because the
LORD is about to destroy the city!" But his sons-in-
law thought he was joking. Nu 16:21
15With the coming of dawn, the angels urged
Lot, saying, "Hurry! Take your wife and your two
daughters who are here, or you will be swept away
when the city is punished." Nu 16:26; Rev 18:4
16When he hesitated, the men grasped his hand
and the hands of his wife and of his two daughters
and led them safely out of the city, for the LORD
was merciful to them. 17As soon as they had
brought them out, one of them said, "Flee for your
lives! Don't look back, and don't stop anywhere in
the plain! Flee to the mountains or you will be
swept away!" ver 26
18But Lot said to them, "No, my lords,[b] please!
19Your[c] servant has found favor in your[c] eyes,
and you[c] have shown great kindness to me in
sparing my life. But I can't flee to the mountains;
this disaster will overtake me, and I'll die. 20Look,
here is a town near enough to run to, and it is
small. Let me flee to it—it is very small, isn't it?
Then my life will be spared." Ge 6:8; 24:12
21He said to him, "Very well, I will grant this
request too; I will not overthrow the town you
speak of. 22But flee there quickly, because I cannot
do anything until you reach it." (That is why the
town was called Zoar.[d]) Ge 13:10
23By the time Lot reached Zoar, the sun had
risen over the land. 24Then the LORD rained down
burning sulfur on Sodom and Gomorrah—from
the LORD out of the heavens. 25Thus he overthrew
those cities and the entire plain, including all those
living in the cities—and also the vegetation in the
land. 26But Lot's wife looked back, and she became
a pillar of salt. ver 17; Lk 17:29,32
27Early the next morning Abraham got up and
returned to the place where he had stood before
the LORD. 28He looked down toward Sodom and
Gomorrah, toward all the land of the plain, and he
saw dense smoke rising from the land, like smoke
from a furnace. Ge 18:22; Rev 18:9
29So when God destroyed the cities of the plain,
he remembered Abraham, and he brought Lot out
of the catastrophe that overthrew the cities where
Lot had lived. 2Pe 2:7

Lot and His Daughters

30Lot and his two daughters left Zoar and settled
in the mountains, for he was afraid to stay in Zoar.
He and his two daughters lived in a cave. 31One
day the older daughter said to the younger, "Our
father is old, and there is no man around here to
lie with us, as is the custom all over the earth.
32Let's get our father to drink wine and then lie
with him and preserve our family line through our
father." Ge 14:10
33That night they got their father to drink wine,
and the older daughter went in and lay with him.
He was not aware of it when she lay down or when
she got up.
34The next day the older daughter said to the
younger, "Last night I lay with my father. Let's get
him to drink wine again tonight, and you go in
and lie with him so we can preserve our family line
through our father." 35So they got their father to
drink wine that night also, and the younger daughter went and lay with him. Again he was not aware
of it when she lay down or when she got up.
36So both of Lot's daughters became pregnant
by their father. 37The older daughter had a son,
and she named him Moab[e]; he is the father of the
Moabites of today. 38The younger daughter also
had a son, and she named him Ben-Ammi[f]; he is
the father of the Ammonites of today. Dt 2:9,19

Abraham and Abimelech

20 Now Abraham moved on from there into
the region of the Negev and lived between
Kadesh and Shur. For a while he stayed in Gerar,
2and there Abraham said of his wife Sarah, "She is
my sister." Then Abimelech king of Gerar sent for
Sarah and took her. ver 12; Ge 12:13; 26:7
3But God came to Abimelech in a dream one
night and said to him, "You are as good as dead
because of the woman you have taken; she is a
married woman." Ge 26:11
4Now Abimelech had not gone near her, so he
said, "Lord, will you destroy an innocent nation?
5Did he not say to me, 'She is my sister,' and didn't
she also say, 'He is my brother'? I have done this
with a clear conscience and clean hands."
6Then God said to him in the dream, "Yes, I
know you did this with a clear conscience, and so
I have kept you from sinning against me. That is
why I did not let you touch her. 7Now return the
man's wife, for he is a prophet, and he will pray for
you and you will live. But if you do not return her,
you may be sure that you and all yours will die."
8Early the next morning Abimelech summoned
all his officials, and when he told them all that had
happened, they were very much afraid. 9Then
Abimelech called Abraham in and said, "What
have you done to us? How have I wronged you
that you have brought such great guilt upon me
and my kingdom? You have done things to me
that should not be done." 10And Abimelech asked
Abraham, "What was your reason for doing this?"
11Abraham replied, "I said to myself, 'There is
surely no fear of God in this place, and they will

[a] 14 Or *were married to* [b] 18 Or *No, Lord*; or *No, my lord* [c] 19 The Hebrew is singular. [d] 22 *Zoar* means *small.*
[e] 37 *Moab* sounds like the Hebrew for *from father.* [f] 38 *Ben-Ammi* means *son of my people.*

kill me because of my wife.' 12Besides, she really is my sister, the daughter of my father though not of my mother; and she became my wife. 13And when God had me wander from my father's household, I said to her, 'This is how you can show your love to me: Everywhere we go, say of me, "He is my brother." ' " Ps 36:1; Ge 12:12; 26:7

14Then Abimelech brought sheep and cattle and male and female slaves and gave them to Abraham, and he returned Sarah his wife to him. 15And Abimelech said, "My land is before you; live wherever you like."

16To Sarah he said, "I am giving your brother a thousand shekels[a] of silver. This is to cover the offense against you before all who are with you; you are completely vindicated." Ge 12:16; 13:9

17Then Abraham prayed to God, and God healed Abimelech, his wife and his slave girls so they could have children again, 18for the LORD had closed up every womb in Abimelech's household because of Abraham's wife Sarah. Ge 12:10-20; 26:1-11

No Laughing Matter **Chapters 21–23**

Sarah, Abraham's wife, ultimately bore Abraham his beloved son (21:2). When the baby boy was born, he was given the appropriate name of Isaac, which means "he laughs." However, the most profound experience in Isaac's life was no laughing matter. His father Abraham took him to a mountain to offer a sacrifice to the Lord. To the surprise of young Isaac, Isaac himself ended up being placed on the altar as the sacrifice. This moment of truth and testing for Abraham must certainly have been a test for Isaac as well. The Lord stopped Abraham before any harm was done to his son and provided a more appropriate sacrifice . . . a ram (22:13).

The Birth of Isaac

21 Now the LORD was gracious to Sarah as he had said, and the LORD did for Sarah what he had promised. 2Sarah became pregnant and bore a son to Abraham in his old age, at the very time God had promised him. 3Abraham gave the name Isaac[b] to the son Sarah bore him. 4When his son Isaac was eight days old, Abraham circumcised him, as God commanded him. 5Abraham was a hundred years old when his son Isaac was born to him. Ge 17:10,12,19; Gal 4:22

6Sarah said, "God has brought me laughter, and everyone who hears about this will laugh with me." 7And she added, "Who would have said to Abraham that Sarah would nurse children? Yet I have borne him a son in his old age." Ge 17:17; Isa 54:1

Hagar and Ishmael Sent Away

8The child grew and was weaned, and on the day Isaac was weaned Abraham held a great feast. 9But Sarah saw that the son whom Hagar the Egyptian had borne to Abraham was mocking, 10and she said to Abraham, "Get rid of that slave woman and her son, for that slave woman's son will never share in the inheritance with my son Isaac." Gal 4:30; Ge 16:15

11The matter distressed Abraham greatly because it concerned his son. 12But God said to him, "Do not be so distressed about the boy and your maidservant. Listen to whatever Sarah tells you, because it is through Isaac that your offspring[c] will be reckoned. 13I will make the son of the maidservant into a nation also, because he is your offspring." Ro 9:7; Heb 11:18; Ge 17:18

14Early the next morning Abraham took some food and a skin of water and gave them to Hagar. He set them on her shoulders and then sent her off with the boy. She went on her way and wandered in the desert of Beersheba. ver 31,32

15When the water in the skin was gone, she put the boy under one of the bushes. 16Then she went off and sat down nearby, about a bowshot away, for she thought, "I cannot watch the boy die." And as she sat there nearby, she[d] began to sob.

17God heard the boy crying, and the angel of God called to Hagar from heaven and said to her, "What is the matter, Hagar? Do not be afraid; God has heard the boy crying as he lies there. 18Lift the boy up and take him by the hand, for I will make him into a great nation." Ge 17:20; Ex 3:7

19Then God opened her eyes and she saw a well of water. So she went and filled the skin with water and gave the boy a drink. Nu 22:31

20God was with the boy as he grew up. He lived in the desert and became an archer. 21While he was living in the Desert of Paran, his mother got a wife for him from Egypt. Ge 28:15; Lk 1:66; Ge 24:4,38

The Treaty at Beersheba

22At that time Abimelech and Phicol the commander of his forces said to Abraham, "God is with you in everything you do. 23Now swear to me here before God that you will not deal falsely with me or my children or my descendants. Show to me and the country where you are living as an alien the same kindness I have shown to you." Ge 26:28

24Abraham said, "I swear it."

25Then Abraham complained to Abimelech about a well of water that Abimelech's servants had seized. 26But Abimelech said, "I don't know who has done this. You did not tell me, and I heard about it only today." Ge 26:15,18,20-22

27So Abraham brought sheep and cattle and gave them to Abimelech, and the two men made a treaty. 28Abraham set apart seven ewe lambs from the flock, 29and Abimelech asked Abraham,

[a]*16* That is, about 25 pounds (about 11.5 kilograms) [b]*3* *Isaac* means *he laughs.* [c]*12* Or *seed* [d]*16* Hebrew; Septuagint *the child*

"What is the meaning of these seven ewe lambs you have set apart by themselves?" Ge 26:28,31

30He replied, "Accept these seven lambs from my hand as a witness that I dug this well."

31So that place was called Beersheba,[a] because the two men swore an oath there. Ge 26:33

32After the treaty had been made at Beersheba, Abimelech and Phicol the commander of his forces returned to the land of the Philistines. 33Abraham planted a tamarisk tree in Beersheba, and there he called upon the name of the LORD, the Eternal God. 34And Abraham stayed in the land of the Philistines for a long time. Ge 4:26; Dt 33:27

Abraham Tested

22 Some time later God tested Abraham. He said to him, "Abraham!" Dt 8:2,16; Heb 11:17

"Here I am," he replied.

2Then God said, "Take your son, your only son, Isaac, whom you love, and go to the region of Moriah. Sacrifice him there as a burnt offering on one of the mountains I will tell you about."

3Early the next morning Abraham got up and saddled his donkey. He took with him two of his servants and his son Isaac. When he had cut enough wood for the burnt offering, he set out for the place God had told him about. 4On the third day Abraham looked up and saw the place in the distance. 5He said to his servants, "Stay here with the donkey while I and the boy go over there. We will worship and then we will come back to you."

6Abraham took the wood for the burnt offering and placed it on his son Isaac, and he himself carried the fire and the knife. As the two of them went on together, 7Isaac spoke up and said to his father Abraham, "Father?" Jn 19:17

"Yes, my son?" Abraham replied.

"The fire and wood are here," Isaac said, "but where is the lamb for the burnt offering?"

8Abraham answered, "God himself will provide the lamb for the burnt offering, my son." And the two of them went on together. Jn 1:29

9When they reached the place God had told him about, Abraham built an altar there and arranged the wood on it. He bound his son Isaac and laid him on the altar, on top of the wood. 10Then he reached out his hand and took the knife to slay his son. 11But the angel of the LORD called out to him from heaven, "Abraham! Abraham!"

"Here I am," he replied.

12"Do not lay a hand on the boy," he said. "Do not do anything to him. Now I know that you fear God, because you have not withheld from me your son, your only son." 1Sa 15:22; Jn 3:16; 1Jn 4:9

13Abraham looked up and there in a thicket he saw a ram[b] caught by its horns. He went over and took the ram and sacrificed it as a burnt offering instead of his son. 14So Abraham called that place The LORD Will Provide. And to this day it is said, "On the mountain of the LORD it will be provided."

15The angel of the LORD called to Abraham from heaven a second time 16and said, "I swear by myself, declares the LORD, that because you have done this and have not withheld your son, your only son, 17I will surely bless you and make your descendants as numerous as the stars in the sky and as the sand on the seashore. Your descendants will take possession of the cities of their enemies, 18and through your offspring[c] all nations on earth will be blessed, because you have obeyed me." Ac 3:25; Heb 6:14

19Then Abraham returned to his servants, and they set off together for Beersheba. And Abraham stayed in Beersheba.

Nahor's Sons

20Some time later Abraham was told, "Milcah is also a mother; she has borne sons to your brother Nahor: 21Uz the firstborn, Buz his brother, Kemuel (the father of Aram), 22Kesed, Hazo, Pildash, Jidlaph and Bethuel." 23Bethuel became the father of Rebekah. Milcah bore these eight sons to Abraham's brother Nahor. 24His concubine, whose name was Reumah, also had sons: Tebah, Gaham, Tahash and Maacah. Ge 24:15

The Death of Sarah

23 Sarah lived to be a hundred and twenty-seven years old. 2She died at Kiriath Arba (that is, Hebron) in the land of Canaan, and Abraham went to mourn for Sarah and to weep over her. Ge 13:18; Jos 14:15

3Then Abraham rose from beside his dead wife and spoke to the Hittites.[d] He said, 4"I am an alien and a stranger among you. Sell me some property for a burial site here so I can bury my dead." Ps 105:12; Heb 11:9,13

5The Hittites replied to Abraham, 6"Sir, listen to us. You are a mighty prince among us. Bury your

LIVING  INSIGHT

God is pleased when we walk by faith. From cover to cover the Bible testifies to that fact. Nothing pleases the Lord more than when we walk by faith.

(See Genesis 22:8.)

[a] 31 *Beersheba* can mean *well of seven* or *well of the oath.* [b] 13 Many manuscripts of the Masoretic Text, Samaritan Pentateuch, Septuagint and Syriac; most manuscripts of the Masoretic Text *a ram behind ⌞him⌟* [c] 18 Or *seed* [d] 3 Or *the sons of Heth*; also in verses 5, 7, 10, 16, 18 and 20

ISAAC

Son of Promise, Son of Sacrifice

"When they reached the place God had told him about, Abraham built an altar there and arranged the wood on it. He bound his son Isaac and laid him on the altar, on top of the wood."

—GENESIS 22:9

Here are four words I hope we will never forget: *God keeps His promises*. God doesn't tell us one thing and do another. He doesn't string us along. We can trust Him, because He traffics in truthfulness.

Genesis 21 tells the story of how God kept His promises to Abraham and Sarah. For a quarter of a century God had been promising this couple that they would have a child. Abraham was a hundred years old and Sarah was ninety, but God hadn't let them forget His promise. And God keeps His promises: "The LORD did for Sarah what he had promised. Sarah became pregnant and bore a son to Abraham in his old age, at the very time God had promised him" (21:1–2).

Abraham and Sarah named their boy Isaac, which means "he laughs." And Isaac became the joy of Abraham and Sarah's life. In fact, I believe that Isaac became something of an idol of Abraham's heart. So serious to God was this adoration that He moved in on Abraham's life to put his relationship to Isaac into proper perspective. In so doing, He preserved the record to teach all of us something significant about giving back to God the things we hold dearest in this life. Look carefully at God's instructions to Abraham: "Take your son, your only son, Isaac, whom you love, and go to the region of Moriah. Sacrifice him there as a burnt offering" (22:2). Abraham wasted no time in following God's instructions, even though his heart must have been in anguish. First thing the next morning, he gathered his supplies, his son and his two servants, and headed for the mountains.

By this time in his life, Isaac had grown into a young man, strong enough to carry a load of firewood up the side of a mountain. As they continued on their uphill climb he may very well have begun to suspect what was happening on this trip. Now watch carefully: "When they reached the place God had told him about, Abraham built an altar there and arranged the wood on it" (22:9). And then he ran to find his son Isaac, because he had hidden himself? No. There was no hide-and-seek. Isaac didn't take off down Mount Moriah. He was right there with his dad. Trusting. Willing. Waiting to see what would happen: "He bound his son Isaac and laid him on the altar, on top of the wood."

I'm impressed with Isaac. He was the sacrifice, you see. And he crawled up onto the altar! This wasn't some kind of nightmare from which one could awaken in a cold sweat; no, this was real life. Isaac was lying on that altar, watching his father raise the knife to plunge it into his heart. Then, suddenly, out of nowhere came a voice: "Abraham! Abraham! . . . Do not lay a hand on the boy" (22:11–12). Try to imagine! Isaac had to have nearly passed out from relief, but no more so than Abraham himself. Both father and son had passed God's test. I have to believe that Abraham and Isaac must have just stood there in joyous embrace.

So Isaac stands along with Abraham as the heroes of this story. You know why he would get up on that altar? Because he had been trained by his dad to get up on altars. He had learned that when his dad said, "God himself will provide" (22:8), he meant it. So this son of Abraham was ready to trust God, to give his life in order to remain faithful.

Did you know that as the sands of time covered over this site, it was later rebuilt? Mount Moriah, where Abraham was called to sacrifice his son, later became known as Calvary. It was near this spot that God Himself did what He had earlier asked Abraham to do. Here God the Father willingly released Jesus Christ, His one and only Son, to be the once-for-all sacrifice for the sins of humanity.

dead in the choicest of our tombs. None of us will refuse you his tomb for burying your dead."

7Then Abraham rose and bowed down before the people of the land, the Hittites. 8He said to them, "If you are willing to let me bury my dead, then listen to me and intercede with Ephron son of Zohar on my behalf 9so he will sell me the cave of Machpelah, which belongs to him and is at the end of his field. Ask him to sell it to me for the full price as a burial site among you." Ge 25:9

10Ephron the Hittite was sitting among his people and he replied to Abraham in the hearing of all the Hittites who had come to the gate of his city. 11"No, my lord," he said. "Listen to me; I give[a] you the field, and I give[a] you the cave that is in it. I give[a] it to you in the presence of my people. Bury your dead." Ru 4:4

12Again Abraham bowed down before the people of the land 13and he said to Ephron in their hearing, "Listen to me, if you will. I will pay the price of the field. Accept it from me so I can bury my dead there."

14Ephron answered Abraham, 15"Listen to me, my lord; the land is worth four hundred shekels[b] of silver, but what is that between me and you? Bury your dead." Eze 45:12

16Abraham agreed to Ephron's terms and weighed out for him the price he had named in the hearing of the Hittites: four hundred shekels of silver, according to the weight current among the merchants. Jer 32:9

17So Ephron's field in Machpelah near Mamre—both the field and the cave in it, and all the trees within the borders of the field—was deeded 18to Abraham as his property in the presence of all the Hittites who had come to the gate of the city. 19Afterward Abraham buried his wife Sarah in the cave in the field of Machpelah near Mamre (which is at Hebron) in the land of Canaan. 20So the field and the cave in it were deeded to Abraham by the Hittites as a burial site. Ge 25:9; 50:13

A Legacy of Deceit **Chapters 24–36**

Isaac and Rebekah were the parents of the two most notorious twins in Biblical history. Esau, nicknamed "Red," was born first (25:25). Jacob was delivered second, and his name, appropriately, means "he deceives." His life history was marked by conflict, deceit and quick escapes in the night. Although God had promised to bless him, Jacob still took the initiative to trick his big brother out of the birthright (25:33) and out of the blessing traditionally reserved for the firstborn (27:27–29). Later in life, the deceiver received a dose of his own medicine after working seven years for his beloved Rachel—only to discover he must first marry her older sister Leah before marrying the younger (and, I might add, more attractive) sister (29:28). In a virtual battle of wives and maidservants, Jacob became the father of twelve sons who were to become the fathers of the twelve tribes of Israel. Later in life, Jacob's name was changed to Israel ("he struggles with God") after wrestling with an angel of the Lord and prevailing (32:28).

Isaac and Rebekah

24 Abraham was now old and well advanced in years, and the LORD had blessed him in every way. 2He said to the chief[c] servant in his household, the one in charge of all that he had, "Put your hand under my thigh. 3I want you to swear by the LORD, the God of heaven and the God of earth, that you will not get a wife for my son from the daughters of the Canaanites, among whom I am living, 4but will go to my country and my own relatives and get a wife for my son Isaac."

5The servant asked him, "What if the woman is unwilling to come back with me to this land? Shall I then take your son back to the country you came from?" Heb 11:15

6"Make sure that you do not take my son back there," Abraham said. 7"The LORD, the God of heaven, who brought me out of my father's household and my native land and who spoke to me and promised me on oath, saying, 'To your offspring[d] I will give this land'—he will send his angel before you so that you can get a wife for my son from there. 8If the woman is unwilling to come back with you, then you will be released from this oath of mine. Only do not take my son back there." 9So the servant put his hand under the thigh of his master Abraham and swore an oath to him concerning this matter. Ge 12:7; 13:15; Gal 3:16

10Then the servant took ten of his master's camels and left, taking with him all kinds of good things from his master. He set out for Aram Naharaim[e] and made his way to the town of Nahor. 11He had the camels kneel down near the well outside the town; it was toward evening, the time the women go out to draw water. 1Sa 9:11

12Then he prayed, "O LORD, God of my master Abraham, give me success today, and show kindness to my master Abraham. 13See, I am standing beside this spring, and the daughters of the townspeople are coming out to draw water. 14May it be that when I say to a girl, 'Please let down your jar that I may have a drink,' and she says, 'Drink, and I'll water your camels too'—let her be the one you have chosen for your servant Isaac. By this I will know that you have shown kindness to my master." Ge 26:24; Jdg 6:17,37

15Before he had finished praying, Rebekah came out with her jar on her shoulder. She was the daughter of Bethuel son of Milcah, who was the wife of Abraham's brother Nahor. 16The girl was

[a] *11* Or *sell* [b] *15* That is, about 10 pounds (about 4.5 kilograms) [c] *2* Or *oldest* [d] *7* Or *seed* [e] *10* That is, Northwest Mesopotamia

very beautiful, a virgin; no man had ever lain with
her. She went down to the spring, filled her jar and
came up again. Ge 22:23; 26:7
17The servant hurried to meet her and said,
"Please give me a little water from your jar."
18"Drink, my lord," she said, and quickly lowered the jar to her hands and gave him a drink.
19After she had given him a drink, she said, "I'll
draw water for your camels too, until they have
finished drinking." 20So she quickly emptied her
jar into the trough, ran back to the well to draw
more water, and drew enough for all his camels.
21Without saying a word, the man watched her
closely to learn whether or not the LORD had made
his journey successful. ver 12,14
22When the camels had finished drinking, the
man took out a gold nose ring weighing a beka[a]
and two gold bracelets weighing ten shekels.[b]
23Then he asked, "Whose daughter are you? Please
tell me, is there room in your father's house for us
to spend the night?" ver 47
24She answered him, "I am the daughter of Bethuel, the son that Milcah bore to Nahor." 25And
she added, "We have plenty of straw and fodder,
as well as room for you to spend the night."
26Then the man bowed down and worshiped
the LORD, 27saying, "Praise be to the LORD, the God
of my master Abraham, who has not abandoned
his kindness and faithfulness to my master. As for
me, the LORD has led me on the journey to the
house of my master's relatives." ver 48,52; Ge 32:10
28The girl ran and told her mother's household
about these things. 29Now Rebekah had a brother
named Laban, and he hurried out to the man at
the spring. 30As soon as he had seen the nose ring,
and the bracelets on his sister's arms, and had
heard Rebekah tell what the man said to her, he
went out to the man and found him standing by
the camels near the spring. 31"Come, you who are
blessed by the LORD," he said. "Why are you standing out here? I have prepared the house and a
place for the camels." Ge 26:29; 29:5,12,13
32So the man went to the house, and the camels
were unloaded. Straw and fodder were brought for
the camels, and water for him and his men to wash
their feet. 33Then food was set before him, but he
said, "I will not eat until I have told you what I
have to say." Ge 43:24
"Then tell us," ⌞Laban⌟ said.
34So he said, "I am Abraham's servant. 35The
LORD has blessed my master abundantly, and he
has become wealthy. He has given him sheep and
cattle, silver and gold, menservants and maidservants, and camels and donkeys. 36My master's wife
Sarah has borne him a son in her[c] old age, and he
has given him everything he owns. 37And my master made me swear an oath, and said, 'You must
not get a wife for my son from the daughters of the
Canaanites, in whose land I live, 38but go to my
father's family and to my own clan, and get a wife
for my son.' ver 1; Ge 25:5
39"Then I asked my master, 'What if the woman
will not come back with me?' ver 5
40"He replied, 'The LORD, before whom I have
walked, will send his angel with you and make
your journey a success, so that you can get a wife
for my son from my own clan and from my father's family. 41Then, when you go to my clan, you
will be released from my oath even if they refuse
to give her to you—you will be released from my
oath.' ver 7-8
42"When I came to the spring today, I said,
'O LORD, God of my master Abraham, if you will,
please grant success to the journey on which I have
come. 43See, I am standing beside this spring; if a
maiden comes out to draw water and I say to her,
"Please let me drink a little water from your jar,"
44and if she says to me, "Drink, and I'll draw water
for your camels too," let her be the one the LORD
has chosen for my master's son.' ver 12-14
45"Before I finished praying in my heart, Rebekah came out, with her jar on her shoulder. She
went down to the spring and drew water, and I
said to her, 'Please give me a drink.' 1Sa 1:13
46"She quickly lowered her jar from her shoulder and said, 'Drink, and I'll water your camels
too.' So I drank, and she watered the camels also.
47"I asked her, 'Whose daughter are you?'
"She said, 'The daughter of Bethuel son of Nahor, whom Milcah bore to him.' ver 24
"Then I put the ring in her nose and the bracelets on her arms, 48and I bowed down and worshiped the LORD. I praised the LORD, the God of my
master Abraham, who had led me on the right
road to get the granddaughter of my master's
brother for his son. 49Now if you will show kindness and faithfulness to my master, tell me; and if
not, tell me, so I may know which way to turn."
50Laban and Bethuel answered, "This is from
the LORD; we can say nothing to you one way or
the other. 51Here is Rebekah; take her and go, and
let her become the wife of your master's son, as the
LORD has directed." Ps 118:23; Ge 31:7,24,29,42
52When Abraham's servant heard what they
said, he bowed down to the ground before the
LORD. 53Then the servant brought out gold and
silver jewelry and articles of clothing and gave
them to Rebekah; he also gave costly gifts to her
brother and to her mother. 54Then he and the men
who were with him ate and drank and spent the
night there. ver 26
When they got up the next morning, he said,
"Send me on my way to my master." ver 56,59
55But her brother and her mother replied, "Let

[a]22 That is, about 1/5 ounce (about 5.5 grams) [b]22 That is, about 4 ounces (about 110 grams) [c]36 Or *his*

the girl remain with us ten days or so; then you[a]
may go." Jdg 19:4
56But he said to them, "Do not detain me, now
that the LORD has granted success to my journey.
Send me on my way so I may go to my master."
57Then they said, "Let's call the girl and ask her
about it." 58So they called Rebekah and asked her,
"Will you go with this man?"
"I will go," she said. Ru 1:16
59So they sent their sister Rebekah on her way,
along with her nurse and Abraham's servant and
his men. 60And they blessed Rebekah and said to
her, Ge 35:8

"Our sister, may you increase
to thousands upon thousands; Ge 17:16
may your offspring possess
the gates of their enemies." Ge 22:17

61Then Rebekah and her maids got ready and
mounted their camels and went back with the
man. So the servant took Rebekah and left.
62Now Isaac had come from Beer Lahai Roi, for
he was living in the Negev. 63He went out to the
field one evening to meditate,[b] and as he looked
up, he saw camels approaching. 64Rebekah also
looked up and saw Isaac. She got down from her
camel 65and asked the servant, "Who is that man
in the field coming to meet us?" Ps 1:2; Ge 16:14; 25:11
"He is my master," the servant answered. So she
took her veil and covered herself.
66Then the servant told Isaac all he had done.
67Isaac brought her into the tent of his mother
Sarah, and he married Rebekah. So she became his
wife, and he loved her; and Isaac was comforted
after his mother's death. Ge 25:20; 29:18,20

The Death of Abraham

25 Abraham took[c] another wife, whose
name was Keturah. 2She bore him Zimran,
Jokshan, Medan, Midian, Ishbak and Shuah. 3Jok-
shan was the father of Sheba and Dedan; the
descendants of Dedan were the Asshurites, the Le-
tushites and the Leummites. 4The sons of Midian
were Ephah, Epher, Hanoch, Abida and Eldaah.
All these were descendants of Keturah. 1Ch 1:32-33
5Abraham left everything he owned to Isaac.
6But while he was still living, he gave gifts to the
sons of his concubines and sent them away from
his son Isaac to the land of the east. Ge 24:36; 21:10
7Altogether, Abraham lived a hundred and seventy-five years. 8Then Abraham breathed his last
and died at a good old age, an old man and full of
years; and he was gathered to his people. 9His sons
Isaac and Ishmael buried him in the cave of Machpelah near Mamre, in the field of Ephron son of
Zohar the Hittite, 10the field Abraham had bought
from the Hittites.[d] There Abraham was buried
with his wife Sarah. 11After Abraham's death, God
blessed his son Isaac, who then lived near Beer
Lahai Roi. Ge 15:15; 23:16; 49:29,33

Ishmael's Sons

12This is the account of Abraham's son Ishmael,
whom Sarah's maidservant, Hagar the Egyptian,
bore to Abraham. Ge 16:15

13These are the names of the sons of Ishmael,
listed in the order of their birth: Nebaioth the firstborn of Ishmael, Kedar, Adbeel, Mibsam, 14Mish-
ma, Dumah, Massa, 15Hadad, Tema, Jetur, Naphish and Kedemah. 16These were the sons of
Ishmael, and these are the names of the twelve
tribal rulers according to their settlements and
camps. 17Altogether, Ishmael lived a hundred and
thirty-seven years. He breathed his last and died,
and he was gathered to his people. 18His descendants settled in the area from Havilah to Shur,
near the border of Egypt, as you go toward Asshur.
And they lived in hostility toward[e] all their brothers. 1Ch 1:29-31; Ge 16:12; 17:20

Jacob and Esau

19This is the account of Abraham's son Isaac.

Abraham became the father of Isaac, 20and
Isaac was forty years old when he married Rebekah daughter of Bethuel the Aramean from Paddan
Aram[f] and sister of Laban the Aramean.
21Isaac prayed to the LORD on behalf of his wife,
because she was barren. The LORD answered his
prayer, and his wife Rebekah became pregnant.
22The babies jostled each other within her, and she
said, "Why is this happening to me?" So she went
to inquire of the LORD. 1Ch 5:20; 1Sa 9:9
23The LORD said to her,

"Two nations are in your womb, Ge 17:4
and two peoples from within you will be
separated;
one people will be stronger than the other,
and the older will serve the younger."

24When the time came for her to give birth,
there were twin boys in her womb. 25The first to
come out was red, and his whole body was like a
hairy garment; so they named him Esau.[g] 26After
this, his brother came out, with his hand grasping
Esau's heel; so he was named Jacob.[h] Isaac was
sixty years old when Rebekah gave birth to them.
27The boys grew up, and Esau became a skillful
hunter, a man of the open country, while Jacob
was a quiet man, staying among the tents. 28Isaac,
who had a taste for wild game, loved Esau, but
Rebekah loved Jacob. Ge 27:3,5

[a] 55 Or *she* [b] 63 The meaning of the Hebrew for this word is uncertain. [c] 1 Or *had taken* [d] 10 Or *the sons of Heth*
[e] 18 Or *lived to the east of* [f] 20 That is, Northwest Mesopotamia [g] 25 *Esau* may mean *hairy*; he was also called Edom, which means *red.* [h] 26 *Jacob* means *he grasps the heel* (figuratively, *he deceives*).

[29]Once when Jacob was cooking some stew, Esau came in from the open country, famished. [30]He said to Jacob, "Quick, let me have some of that red stew! I'm famished!" (That is why he was also called Edom.[a]) Ge 32:3

[31]Jacob replied, "First sell me your birthright."

[32]"Look, I am about to die," Esau said. "What good is the birthright to me?"

[33]But Jacob said, "Swear to me first." So he swore an oath to him, selling his birthright to Jacob. Heb 12:16

[34]Then Jacob gave Esau some bread and some lentil stew. He ate and drank, and then got up and left.

So Esau despised his birthright.

Isaac and Abimelech

26 Now there was a famine in the land—besides the earlier famine of Abraham's time—and Isaac went to Abimelech king of the Philistines in Gerar. [2]The LORD appeared to Isaac and said, "Do not go down to Egypt; live in the land where I tell you to live. [3]Stay in this land for a while, and I will be with you and will bless you. For to you and your descendants I will give all these lands and will confirm the oath I swore to your father Abraham. [4]I will make your descendants as numerous as the stars in the sky and will give them all these lands, and through your offspring[b] all nations on earth will be blessed, [5]because Abraham obeyed me and kept my requirements, my commands, my decrees and my laws." [6]So Isaac stayed in Gerar. Ge 12:1,7,10

[7]When the men of that place asked him about his wife, he said, "She is my sister," because he was afraid to say, "She is my wife." He thought, "The men of this place might kill me on account of Rebekah, because she is beautiful." Ge 12:13; 20:2,12

[8]When Isaac had been there a long time, Abimelech king of the Philistines looked down from a window and saw Isaac caressing his wife Rebekah. [9]So Abimelech summoned Isaac and said, "She is really your wife! Why did you say, 'She is my sister'?"

Isaac answered him, "Because I thought I might lose my life on account of her."

[10]Then Abimelech said, "What is this you have done to us? One of the men might well have slept with your wife, and you would have brought guilt upon us." Ge 20:9

[11]So Abimelech gave orders to all the people: "Anyone who molests this man or his wife shall surely be put to death." Ge 12:10-20; 20:1-18

[12]Isaac planted crops in that land and the same year reaped a hundredfold, because the LORD blessed him. [13]The man became rich, and his wealth continued to grow until he became very wealthy. [14]He had so many flocks and herds and servants that the Philistines envied him. [15]So all the wells that his father's servants had dug in the time of his father Abraham, the Philistines stopped up, filling them with earth. ver 3; Ge 21:30

[16]Then Abimelech said to Isaac, "Move away from us; you have become too powerful for us."

[17]So Isaac moved away from there and encamped in the Valley of Gerar and settled there. [18]Isaac reopened the wells that had been dug in the time of his father Abraham, which the Philistines had stopped up after Abraham died, and he gave them the same names his father had given them.

[19]Isaac's servants dug in the valley and discovered a well of fresh water there. [20]But the herdsmen of Gerar quarreled with Isaac's herdsmen and said, "The water is ours!" So he named the well Esek,[c] because they disputed with him. [21]Then they dug another well, but they quarreled over that one also; so he named it Sitnah.[d] [22]He moved on from there and dug another well, and no one quarreled over it. He named it Rehoboth,[e] saying, "Now the LORD has given us room and we will flourish in the land." Ge 17:6

[23]From there he went up to Beersheba. [24]That night the LORD appeared to him and said, "I am the God of your father Abraham. Do not be afraid, for I am with you; I will bless you and will increase the number of your descendants for the sake of my servant Abraham." Ge 17:7; 24:12

[25]Isaac built an altar there and called on the name of the LORD. There he pitched his tent, and there his servants dug a well. Ge 12:7,8; 13:4,18

[26]Meanwhile, Abimelech had come to him from Gerar, with Ahuzzath his personal adviser and Phicol the commander of his forces. [27]Isaac asked them, "Why have you come to me, since you were hostile to me and sent me away?" Ge 21:22

[28]They answered, "We saw clearly that the LORD was with you; so we said, 'There ought to be a sworn agreement between us'—between us and you. Let us make a treaty with you [29]that you will do us no harm, just as we did not molest you but always treated you well and sent you away in peace. And now you are blessed by the LORD."

[30]Isaac then made a feast for them, and they ate and drank. [31]Early the next morning the men swore an oath to each other. Then Isaac sent them on their way, and they left him in peace. Ge 21:31

[32]That day Isaac's servants came and told him about the well they had dug. They said, "We've found water!" [33]He called it Shibah,[f] and to this day the name of the town has been Beersheba.[g]

[34]When Esau was forty years old, he married Judith daughter of Beeri the Hittite, and also Base-

[a]30 *Edom* means *red.* [b]4 Or *seed* [c]20 *Esek* means *dispute.* [d]21 *Sitnah* means *opposition.* [e]22 *Rehoboth* means *room.* [f]33 *Shibah* can mean *oath* or *seven.* [g]33 *Beersheba* can mean *well of the oath* or *well of seven.*

math daughter of Elon the Hittite. 35 They were a
source of grief to Isaac and Rebekah. Ge 27:46; 36:2

Jacob Gets Isaac's Blessing

27 When Isaac was old and his eyes were so
weak that he could no longer see, he called
for Esau his older son and said to him, "My son."
"Here I am," he answered.
2 Isaac said, "I am now an old man and don't
know the day of my death. 3 Now then, get your
weapons—your quiver and bow—and go out to
the open country to hunt some wild game for me.
4 Prepare me the kind of tasty food I like and bring
it to me to eat, so that I may give you my blessing
before I die." Ge 49:28; Dt 33:1; Heb 11:20
5 Now Rebekah was listening as Isaac spoke to
his son Esau. When Esau left for the open country
to hunt game and bring it back, 6 Rebekah said to
her son Jacob, "Look, I overheard your father say
to your brother Esau, 7 'Bring me some game and
prepare me some tasty food to eat, so that I may
give you my blessing in the presence of the LORD
before I die.' 8 Now, my son, listen carefully and do
what I tell you: 9 Go out to the flock and bring me
two choice young goats, so I can prepare some
tasty food for your father, just the way he likes it.
10 Then take it to your father to eat, so that he may
give you his blessing before he dies." ver 13,43
11 Jacob said to Rebekah his mother, "But my
brother Esau is a hairy man, and I'm a man with
smooth skin. 12 What if my father touches me? I
would appear to be tricking him and would bring
down a curse on myself rather than a blessing."

LIVING  **INSIGHT**

If you are in a position of authority, no matter how small or how large, the temptation to manipulate will never go away. You may have the authority to claim certain honors . . . to call attention to your right to be listened to. Don't yield. Resist at all costs!

(See Genesis 27:12.)

13 His mother said to him, "My son, let the curse
fall on me. Just do what I say; go and get them
for me." Mt 27:25
14 So he went and got them and brought them to
his mother, and she prepared some tasty food, just
the way his father liked it. 15 Then Rebekah took
the best clothes of Esau her older son, which she
had in the house, and put them on her younger
son Jacob. 16 She also covered his hands and the
smooth part of his neck with the goatskins. 17 Then
she handed to her son Jacob the tasty food and the
bread she had made. ver 27
18 He went to his father and said, "My father."
"Yes, my son," he answered. "Who is it?"
19 Jacob said to his father, "I am Esau your firstborn. I have done as you told me. Please sit up and
eat some of my game so that you may give me
your blessing." ver 4; Ge 25:28
20 Isaac asked his son, "How did you find it so
quickly, my son?"
"The LORD your God gave me success," he replied. Ge 24:12
21 Then Isaac said to Jacob, "Come near so I can
touch you, my son, to know whether you really are
my son Esau or not." ver 12
22 Jacob went close to his father Isaac, who
touched him and said, "The voice is the voice of
Jacob, but the hands are the hands of Esau." 23 He
did not recognize him, for his hands were hairy
like those of his brother Esau; so he blessed him.
24 "Are you really my son Esau?" he asked. ver 16
"I am," he replied.
25 Then he said, "My son, bring me some of your
game to eat, so that I may give you my blessing."
Jacob brought it to him and he ate; and he
brought some wine and he drank. 26 Then his father Isaac said to him, "Come here, my son, and
kiss me."
27 So he went to him and kissed him. When
Isaac caught the smell of his clothes, he blessed
him and said, Heb 11:20; SS 4:11

"Ah, the smell of my son
is like the smell of a field
that the LORD has blessed.
28 May God give you of heaven's dew Dt 33:13
and of earth's richness—
an abundance of grain and new wine.
29 May nations serve you Isa 49:7,23
and peoples bow down to you. Ge 9:25; 25:23
Be lord over your brothers,
and may the sons of your mother bow
down to you.
May those who curse you be cursed
and those who bless you be blessed." Ge 12:3

30 After Isaac finished blessing him and Jacob
had scarcely left his father's presence, his brother
Esau came in from hunting. 31 He too prepared
some tasty food and brought it to his father. Then
he said to him, "My father, sit up and eat some of
my game, so that you may give me your blessing."
32 His father Isaac asked him, "Who are you?"
"I am your son," he answered, "your firstborn,
Esau."
33 Isaac trembled violently and said, "Who was
it, then, that hunted game and brought it to me? I
ate it just before you came and I blessed him—
and indeed he will be blessed!" Ge 28:3,4; Ro 11:29
34 When Esau heard his father's words, he burst
out with a loud and bitter cry and said to his
father, "Bless me—me too, my father!" Heb 12:17

35But he said, "Your brother came deceitfully
and took your blessing." Jer 9:4
36Esau said, "Isn't he rightly named Jacob[a]?
He has deceived me these two times: He took my
birthright, and now he's taken my blessing!" Then
he asked, "Haven't you reserved any blessing
for me?" Ge 25:26,33
37Isaac answered Esau, "I have made him lord
over you and have made all his relatives his servants, and I have sustained him with grain and
new wine. So what can I possibly do for you, my
son?" ver 28
38Esau said to his father, "Do you have only one
blessing, my father? Bless me too, my father!"
Then Esau wept aloud. Heb 12:17
39His father Isaac answered him,

"Your dwelling will be
  away from the earth's richness,
  away from the dew of heaven above. ver 28
40You will live by the sword
  and you will serve your brother. Ge 25:23
But when you grow restless,
  you will throw his yoke
  from off your neck." 2Ki 8:20-22

Jacob Flees to Laban

41Esau held a grudge against Jacob because of
the blessing his father had given him. He said to
himself, "The days of mourning for my father are
near; then I will kill my brother Jacob." Ge 32:11

LIVING  **INSIGHT**

We who refuse to forgive—we who live in the gall of bitterness—will become victims of torture. If we nurture feelings of bitterness we are little better than inmates of an internal concentration camp. For your sake, let me urge you to put away all bitterness now. The escape route is clearly marked. It leads to the cross . . . where the only One who had a right to be bitter wasn't.

(See Genesis 27:41.)

42When Rebekah was told what her older son
Esau had said, she sent for her younger son Jacob
and said to him, "Your brother Esau is consoling
himself with the thought of killing you. 43Now
then, my son, do what I say: Flee at once to my
brother Laban in Haran. 44Stay with him for a
while until your brother's fury subsides. 45When
your brother is no longer angry with you and forgets what you did to him, I'll send word for you to
come back from there. Why should I lose both of
you in one day?" ver 8; Ge 11:31
46Then Rebekah said to Isaac, "I'm disgusted
with living because of these Hittite women. If Jacob takes a wife from among the women of this
land, from Hittite women like these, my life will
not be worth living." Ge 26:35

28 So Isaac called for Jacob and blessed[b] him
and commanded him: "Do not marry a
Canaanite woman. 2Go at once to Paddan Aram,[c]
to the house of your mother's father Bethuel. Take
a wife for yourself there, from among the daughters of Laban, your mother's brother. 3May God
Almighty[d] bless you and make you fruitful and
increase your numbers until you become a community of peoples. 4May he give you and your
descendants the blessing given to Abraham, so
that you may take possession of the land where
you now live as an alien, the land God gave to
Abraham." 5Then Isaac sent Jacob on his way, and
he went to Paddan Aram, to Laban son of Bethuel
the Aramean, the brother of Rebekah, who was the
mother of Jacob and Esau. Ge 12:2-3; 17:8; 24:3
6Now Esau learned that Isaac had blessed Jacob
and had sent him to Paddan Aram to take a wife
from there, and that when he blessed him he commanded him, "Do not marry a Canaanite woman," 7and that Jacob had obeyed his father and
mother and had gone to Paddan Aram. 8Esau then
realized how displeasing the Canaanite women
were to his father Isaac; 9so he went to Ishmael and
married Mahalath, the sister of Nebaioth and
daughter of Ishmael son of Abraham, in addition
to the wives he already had. Ge 26:34-35

Jacob's Dream at Bethel

10Jacob left Beersheba and set out for Haran.
11When he reached a certain place, he stopped for
the night because the sun had set. Taking one of
the stones there, he put it under his head and lay
down to sleep. 12He had a dream in which he saw
a stairway[e] resting on the earth, with its top
reaching to heaven, and the angels of God were
ascending and descending on it. 13There above it[f]
stood the LORD, and he said: "I am the LORD, the
God of your father Abraham and the God of Isaac.
I will give you and your descendants the land on
which you are lying. 14Your descendants will be
like the dust of the earth, and you will spread out
to the west and to the east, to the north and to the
south. All peoples on earth will be blessed through
you and your offspring. 15I am with you and will
watch over you wherever you go, and I will bring
you back to this land. I will not leave you until I
have done what I have promised you." Jn 1:51
16When Jacob awoke from his sleep, he

[a] 36 *Jacob* means *he grasps the heel* (figuratively, *he deceives*). [b] 1 Or *greeted* [c] 2 That is, Northwest Mesopotamia; also in verses 5, 6 and 7 [d] 3 Hebrew *El-Shaddai* [e] 12 Or *ladder* [f] 13 Or *There beside him*

thought, "Surely the LORD is in this place, and I was not aware of it." [17]He was afraid and said, "How awesome is this place! This is none other than the house of God; this is the gate of heaven."

[18]Early the next morning Jacob took the stone he had placed under his head and set it up as a pillar and poured oil on top of it. [19]He called that place Bethel,[a] though the city used to be called Luz. Jdg 1:23,26

[20]Then Jacob made a vow, saying, "If God will be with me and will watch over me on this journey I am taking and will give me food to eat and clothes to wear [21]so that I return safely to my father's house, then the LORD[b] will be my God [22]and[c] this stone that I have set up as a pillar will be God's house, and of all that you give me I will give you a tenth." Dt 26:17; Ge 14:20; 31:13

Jacob Arrives in Paddan Aram

29 Then Jacob continued on his journey and came to the land of the eastern peoples. [2]There he saw a well in the field, with three flocks of sheep lying near it because the flocks were watered from that well. The stone over the mouth of the well was large. [3]When all the flocks were gathered there, the shepherds would roll the stone away from the well's mouth and water the sheep. Then they would return the stone to its place over the mouth of the well. Jdg 6:3,33

[4]Jacob asked the shepherds, "My brothers, where are you from?"

"We're from Haran," they replied. Ge 28:10

[5]He said to them, "Do you know Laban, Nahor's grandson?"

"Yes, we know him," they answered. Ge 11:29

[6]Then Jacob asked them, "Is he well?"

"Yes, he is," they said, "and here comes his daughter Rachel with the sheep."

[7]"Look," he said, "the sun is still high; it is not time for the flocks to be gathered. Water the sheep and take them back to pasture." Ex 2:16

[8]"We can't," they replied, "until all the flocks are gathered and the stone has been rolled away from the mouth of the well. Then we will water the sheep." Ge 24:13

[9]While he was still talking with them, Rachel came with her father's sheep, for she was a shepherdess. [10]When Jacob saw Rachel daughter of Laban, his mother's brother, and Laban's sheep, he went over and rolled the stone away from the mouth of the well and watered his uncle's sheep. [11]Then Jacob kissed Rachel and began to weep aloud. [12]He had told Rachel that he was a relative of her father and a son of Rebekah. So she ran and told her father. Ge 24:28

[13]As soon as Laban heard the news about Jacob, his sister's son, he hurried to meet him. He embraced him and kissed him and brought him to his home, and there Jacob told him all these things. [14]Then Laban said to him, "You are my own flesh and blood." Ge 24:29; Jdg 9:2

Jacob Marries Leah and Rachel

After Jacob had stayed with him for a whole month, [15]Laban said to him, "Just because you are a relative of mine, should you work for me for nothing? Tell me what your wages should be."

[16]Now Laban had two daughters; the name of the older was Leah, and the name of the younger was Rachel. [17]Leah had weak[d] eyes, but Rachel was lovely in form, and beautiful. [18]Jacob was in love with Rachel and said, "I'll work for you seven years in return for your younger daughter Rachel."

[19]Laban said, "It's better that I give her to you than to some other man. Stay here with me." [20]So Jacob served seven years to get Rachel, but they seemed like only a few days to him because of his love for her. Ge 31:15; Hos 12:12

[21]Then Jacob said to Laban, "Give me my wife. My time is completed, and I want to lie with her."

[22]So Laban brought together all the people of the place and gave a feast. [23]But when evening came, he took his daughter Leah and gave her to Jacob, and Jacob lay with her. [24]And Laban gave his servant girl Zilpah to his daughter as her maidservant. Jdg 14:10; Jn 2:1-2

[25]When morning came, there was Leah! So Jacob said to Laban, "What is this you have done to me? I served you for Rachel, didn't I? Why have you deceived me?" Ge 12:18; 27:36

[26]Laban replied, "It is not our custom here to give the younger daughter in marriage before the older one. [27]Finish this daughter's bridal week; then we will give you the younger one also, in return for another seven years of work." Jdg 14:12

[28]And Jacob did so. He finished the week with Leah, and then Laban gave him his daughter Rachel to be his wife. [29]Laban gave his servant girl Bilhah to his daughter Rachel as her maidservant. [30]Jacob lay with Rachel also, and he loved Rachel more than Leah. And he worked for Laban another seven years. Ge 31:41

Jacob's Children

[31]When the LORD saw that Leah was not loved, he opened her womb, but Rachel was barren. [32]Leah became pregnant and gave birth to a son. She named him Reuben,[e] for she said, "It is because the LORD has seen my misery. Surely my husband will love me now." Dt 21:15-17; Ps 127:3

[33]She conceived again, and when she gave birth to a son she said, "Because the LORD heard that I

[a] 19 *Bethel* means *house of God.* [b] 20,21 Or *Since God . . . father's house, the LORD* [c] 21,22 Or *house, and the LORD will be my God,* [22]*then* [d] 17 Or *delicate* [e] 32 *Reuben* sounds like the Hebrew for *he has seen my misery*; the name means *see, a son.*

am not loved, he gave me this one too." So she
named him Simeon.[a] Ge 34:25
34Again she conceived, and when she gave birth
to a son she said, "Now at last my husband will
become attached to me, because I have borne him
three sons." So he was named Levi.[b] Ge 49:5-7
35She conceived again, and when she gave birth
to a son she said, "This time I will praise the
LORD." So she named him Judah.[c] Then she
stopped having children. Ge 49:8; Mt 1:2-3
30 When Rachel saw that she was not bearing
Jacob any children, she became jealous of
her sister. So she said to Jacob, "Give me children,
or I'll die!" Ge 29:31
2Jacob became angry with her and said, "Am I
in the place of God, who has kept you from having
children?" Ge 16:2
3Then she said, "Here is Bilhah, my maidservant. Sleep with her so that she can bear children
for me and that through her I too can build a
family." Ge 16:2
4So she gave him her servant Bilhah as a wife.
Jacob slept with her, 5and she became pregnant
and bore him a son. 6Then Rachel said, "God has
vindicated me; he has listened to my plea and
given me a son." Because of this she named him
Dan.[d] Ge 16:3-4; 49:16-17
7Rachel's servant Bilhah conceived again and
bore Jacob a second son. 8Then Rachel said, "I
have had a great struggle with my sister, and I have
won." So she named him Naphtali.[e] Ge 49:21
9When Leah saw that she had stopped having
children, she took her maidservant Zilpah and
gave her to Jacob as a wife. 10Leah's servant Zilpah
bore Jacob a son. 11Then Leah said, "What good
fortune!"[f] So she named him Gad.[g] ver 4
12Leah's servant Zilpah bore Jacob a second
son. 13Then Leah said, "How happy I am! The
women will call me happy." So she named him
Asher.[h] Lk 1:48; Ge 49:20
14During wheat harvest, Reuben went out into
the fields and found some mandrake plants, which
he brought to his mother Leah. Rachel said to
Leah, "Please give me some of your son's mandrakes." SS 7:13
15But she said to her, "Wasn't it enough that
you took away my husband? Will you take my
son's mandrakes too?" Nu 16:9,13
"Very well," Rachel said, "he can sleep with you
tonight in return for your son's mandrakes."
16So when Jacob came in from the fields that
evening, Leah went out to meet him. "You must
sleep with me," she said. "I have hired you with my
son's mandrakes." So he slept with her that night.
17God listened to Leah, and she became pregnant and bore Jacob a fifth son. 18Then Leah said,
"God has rewarded me for giving my maidservant
to my husband." So she named him Issachar.[i]
19Leah conceived again and bore Jacob a sixth
son. 20Then Leah said, "God has presented me
with a precious gift. This time my husband will
treat me with honor, because I have borne him six
sons." So she named him Zebulun.[j] 1Pe 3:7
21Some time later she gave birth to a daughter
and named her Dinah. Ge 34:1
22Then God remembered Rachel; he listened to
her and opened her womb. 23She became pregnant
and gave birth to a son and said, "God has taken
away my disgrace." 24She named him Joseph,[k]
and said, "May the LORD add to me another son."

Jacob's Flocks Increase

25After Rachel gave birth to Joseph, Jacob said
to Laban, "Send me on my way so I can go back
to my own homeland. 26Give me my wives and
children, for whom I have served you, and I will be
on my way. You know how much work I've done
for you." Ge 24:54; 29:20,30
27But Laban said to him, "If I have found favor
in your eyes, please stay. I have learned by divination that[l] the LORD has blessed me because of
you." 28He added, "Name your wages, and I will
pay them." Ge 26:24; 29:15; 39:3,5
29Jacob said to him, "You know how I have
worked for you and how your livestock has fared
under my care. 30The little you had before I came
has increased greatly, and the LORD has blessed
you wherever I have been. But now, when may I
do something for my own household?" Ge 31:38-40
31"What shall I give you?" he asked.
"Don't give me anything," Jacob replied. "But if
you will do this one thing for me, I will go on
tending your flocks and watching over them: 32Let
me go through all your flocks today and remove
from them every speckled or spotted sheep, every
dark-colored lamb and every spotted or speckled
goat. They will be my wages. 33And my honesty
will testify for me in the future, whenever you
check on the wages you have paid me. Any goat in
my possession that is not speckled or spotted, or
any lamb that is not dark-colored, will be considered stolen." Ge 31:8,12
34"Agreed," said Laban. "Let it be as you have
said." 35That same day he removed all the male
goats that were streaked or spotted, and all the
speckled or spotted female goats (all that had
white on them) and all the dark-colored lambs,
and he placed them in the care of his sons. 36Then

[a]33 *Simeon* probably means *one who hears.* [b]34 *Levi* sounds like and may be derived from the Hebrew for *attached.*
[c]35 *Judah* sounds like and may be derived from the Hebrew for *praise.* [d]6 *Dan* here means *he has vindicated.*
[e]8 *Naphtali* means *my struggle.* [f]11 Or *"A troop is coming!"* [g]11 *Gad* can mean *good fortune* or *a troop.*
[h]13 *Asher* means *happy.* [i]18 *Issachar* sounds like the Hebrew for *reward.* [j]20 *Zebulun* probably means *honor.*
[k]24 *Joseph* means *may he add.* [l]27 Or possibly *have become rich and*

he put a three-day journey between himself and Jacob, while Jacob continued to tend the rest of Laban's flocks. Ge 31:1

[37]Jacob, however, took fresh-cut branches from poplar, almond and plane trees and made white stripes on them by peeling the bark and exposing the white inner wood of the branches. [38]Then he placed the peeled branches in all the watering troughs, so that they would be directly in front of the flocks when they came to drink. When the flocks were in heat and came to drink, [39]they mated in front of the branches. And they bore young that were streaked or speckled or spotted. [40]Jacob set apart the young of the flock by themselves, but made the rest face the streaked and dark-colored animals that belonged to Laban. Thus he made separate flocks for himself and did not put them with Laban's animals. [41]Whenever the stronger females were in heat, Jacob would place the branches in the troughs in front of the animals so they would mate near the branches, [42]but if the animals were weak, he would not place them there. So the weak animals went to Laban and the strong ones to Jacob. [43]In this way the man grew exceedingly prosperous and came to own large flocks, and maidservants and menservants, and camels and donkeys. Ge 12:16; 13:2; 26:13-14

Jacob Flees From Laban

31 Jacob heard that Laban's sons were saying, "Jacob has taken everything our father owned and has gained all this wealth from what belonged to our father." [2]And Jacob noticed that Laban's attitude toward him was not what it had been. Ge 30:42

[3]Then the LORD said to Jacob, "Go back to the land of your fathers and to your relatives, and I will be with you." Ge 21:22; 26:3; 32:9

[4]So Jacob sent word to Rachel and Leah to come out to the fields where his flocks were. [5]He said to them, "I see that your father's attitude to ward me is not what it was before, but the God of my father has been with me. [6]You know that I've worked for your father with all my strength, [7]yet your father has cheated me by changing my wages ten times. However, God has not allowed him to harm me. [8]If he said, 'The speckled ones will be your wages,' then all the flocks gave birth to speckled young; and if he said, 'The streaked ones will be your wages,' then all the flocks bore streaked young. [9]So God has taken away your father's livestock and has given them to me. Ge 21:22; 30:32,42

[10]"In breeding season I once had a dream in which I looked up and saw that the male goats mating with the flock were streaked, speckled or spotted. [11]The angel of God said to me in the dream, 'Jacob.' I answered, 'Here I am.' [12]And he said, 'Look up and see that all the male goats mating with the flock are streaked, speckled or spotted, for I have seen all that Laban has been doing to you. [13]I am the God of Bethel, where you anointed a pillar and where you made a vow to me. Now leave this land at once and go back to your native land.'" Ge 28:10-22; Ex 3:7

[14]Then Rachel and Leah replied, "Do we still have any share in the inheritance of our father's estate? [15]Does he not regard us as foreigners? Not only has he sold us, but he has used up what was paid for us. [16]Surely all the wealth that God took away from our father belongs to us and our children. So do whatever God has told you." Ge 29:20

[17]Then Jacob put his children and his wives on camels, [18]and he drove all his livestock ahead of him, along with all the goods he had accumulated in Paddan Aram,[a] to go to his father Isaac in the land of Canaan. Ge 35:27

[19]When Laban had gone to shear his sheep, Rachel stole her father's household gods. [20]Moreover, Jacob deceived Laban the Aramean by not telling him he was running away. [21]So he fled with all he had, and crossing the River,[b] he headed for the hill country of Gilead. Ge 27:36; 35:2; Jdg 17:5

Laban Pursues Jacob

[22]On the third day Laban was told that Jacob had fled. [23]Taking his relatives with him, he pursued Jacob for seven days and caught up with him in the hill country of Gilead. [24]Then God came to Laban the Aramean in a dream at night and said to him, "Be careful not to say anything to Jacob, either good or bad." Ge 20:3; 24:50

[25]Jacob had pitched his tent in the hill country of Gilead when Laban overtook him, and Laban and his relatives camped there too. [26]Then Laban said to Jacob, "What have you done? You've deceived me, and you've carried off my daughters like captives in war. [27]Why did you run off secretly and deceive me? Why didn't you tell me, so I could send you away with joy and singing to the music of tambourines and harps? [28]You didn't even let me kiss my grandchildren and my daughters good-by. You have done a foolish thing. [29]I have the power to harm you; but last night the God of your father said to me, 'Be careful not to say anything to Jacob, either good or bad.' [30]Now you have gone off because you longed to return to your father's house. But why did you steal my gods?"

[31]Jacob answered Laban, "I was afraid, because I thought you would take your daughters away from me by force. [32]But if you find anyone who has your gods, he shall not live. In the presence of our relatives, see for yourself whether there is anything of yours here with me; and if so, take it."

[a] *18* That is, Northwest Mesopotamia [b] *21* That is, the Euphrates

Now Jacob did not know that Rachel had stolen the gods. Ge 44:9

33So Laban went into Jacob's tent and into Leah's tent and into the tent of the two maidservants, but he found nothing. After he came out of Leah's tent, he entered Rachel's tent. 34Now Rachel had taken the household gods and put them inside her camel's saddle and was sitting on them. Laban searched through everything in the tent but found nothing. ver 37; Ge 44:12

35Rachel said to her father, "Don't be angry, my lord, that I cannot stand up in your presence; I'm having my period." So he searched but could not find the household gods. Lev 19:3,32

36Jacob was angry and took Laban to task. "What is my crime?" he asked Laban. "What sin have I committed that you hunt me down? 37Now that you have searched through all my goods, what have you found that belongs to your household? Put it here in front of your relatives and mine, and let them judge between the two of us. ver 23

38"I have been with you for twenty years now. Your sheep and goats have not miscarried, nor have I eaten rams from your flocks. 39I did not bring you animals torn by wild beasts; I bore the loss myself. And you demanded payment from me for whatever was stolen by day or night. 40This was my situation: The heat consumed me in the daytime and the cold at night, and sleep fled from my eyes. 41It was like this for the twenty years I was in your household. I worked for you fourteen years for your two daughters and six years for your flocks, and you changed my wages ten times. 42If the God of my father, the God of Abraham and the Fear of Isaac, had not been with me, you would surely have sent me away empty-handed. But God has seen my hardship and the toil of my hands, and last night he rebuked you." Ge 29:30,32; Ex 22:13

43Laban answered Jacob, "The women are my daughters, the children are my children, and the flocks are my flocks. All you see is mine. Yet what can I do today about these daughters of mine, or about the children they have borne? 44Come now, let's make a covenant, you and I, and let it serve as a witness between us." Ge 21:27; Jos 24:27

45So Jacob took a stone and set it up as a pillar. 46He said to his relatives, "Gather some stones." So they took stones and piled them in a heap, and they ate there by the heap. 47Laban called it Jegar Sahadutha,[a] and Jacob called it Galeed.[b]

48Laban said, "This heap is a witness between you and me today." That is why it was called Galeed. 49It was also called Mizpah,[c] because he said, "May the LORD keep watch between you and me when we are away from each other. 50If you mistreat my daughters or if you take any wives besides my daughters, even though no one is with us, remember that God is a witness between you and me." Jdg 11:29; 1Sa 7:5-6; Jer 29:23

51Laban also said to Jacob, "Here is this heap, and here is this pillar I have set up between you and me. 52This heap is a witness, and this pillar is a witness, that I will not go past this heap to your side to harm you and that you will not go past this heap and pillar to my side to harm me. 53May the God of Abraham and the God of Nahor, the God of their father, judge between us." Ge 16:5

So Jacob took an oath in the name of the Fear of his father Isaac. 54He offered a sacrifice there in the hill country and invited his relatives to a meal. After they had eaten, they spent the night there.

55Early the next morning Laban kissed his grandchildren and his daughters and blessed them. Then he left and returned home. Ge 18:33

Jacob Prepares to Meet Esau

32 Jacob also went on his way, and the angels of God met him. 2When Jacob saw them, he said, "This is the camp of God!" So he named that place Mahanaim.[d] Ps 34:7; 91:11

3Jacob sent messengers ahead of him to his brother Esau in the land of Seir, the country of Edom. 4He instructed them: "This is what you are to say to my master Esau: 'Your servant Jacob says, I have been staying with Laban and have remained there till now. 5I have cattle and donkeys, sheep and goats, menservants and maidservants. Now I am sending this message to my lord, that I may find favor in your eyes.'" Ge 12:16; 33:8,10,15

6When the messengers returned to Jacob, they said, "We went to your brother Esau, and now he is coming to meet you, and four hundred men are with him." Ge 33:1

7In great fear and distress Jacob divided the people who were with him into two groups,[e] and the flocks and herds and camels as well. 8He thought, "If Esau comes and attacks one group,[f] the group[f] that is left may escape." ver 11

9Then Jacob prayed, "O God of my father Abraham, God of my father Isaac, O LORD, who said to me, 'Go back to your country and your relatives, and I will make you prosper,' 10I am unworthy of all the kindness and faithfulness you have shown your servant. I had only my staff when I crossed this Jordan, but now I have become two groups. 11Save me, I pray, from the hand of my brother Esau, for I am afraid he will come and attack me, and also the mothers with their children. 12But you have said, 'I will surely make you prosper and will make your descendants like the sand of the sea, which cannot be counted.'" Hos 1:10; Ge 24:27; 31:13

13He spent the night there, and from what he

[a]47 The Aramaic *Jegar Sahadutha* means *witness heap.* [b]47 The Hebrew *Galeed* means *witness heap.* [c]49 *Mizpah* means *watchtower.* [d]2 *Mahanaim* means *two camps.* [e]7 Or *camps*; also in verse 10 [f]8 Or *camp*

had with him he selected a gift for his brother
Esau: 14two hundred female goats and twenty male
goats, two hundred ewes and twenty rams, 15thirty
female camels with their young, forty cows and ten
bulls, and twenty female donkeys and ten male
donkeys. 16He put them in the care of his servants,
each herd by itself, and said to his servants, "Go
ahead of me, and keep some space between the
herds." Ge 43:11,15,25-26; Pr 18:16

17He instructed the one in the lead: "When my
brother Esau meets you and asks, 'To whom do
you belong, and where are you going, and who
owns all these animals in front of you?' 18then you
are to say, 'They belong to your servant Jacob.
They are a gift sent to my lord Esau, and he is
coming behind us.'" Ge 18:3

19He also instructed the second, the third and
all the others who followed the herds: "You are to
say the same thing to Esau when you meet him.
20And be sure to say, 'Your servant Jacob is coming behind us.'" For he thought, "I will pacify him
with these gifts I am sending on ahead; later, when
I see him, perhaps he will receive me." 21So Jacob's
gifts went on ahead of him, but he himself spent
the night in the camp. Ge 33:10; Pr 21:14

Jacob Wrestles With God

22That night Jacob got up and took his two
wives, his two maidservants and his eleven sons
and crossed the ford of the Jabbok. 23After he had
sent them across the stream, he sent over all his
possessions. 24So Jacob was left alone, and a man
wrestled with him till daybreak. 25When the man
saw that he could not overpower him, he touched
the socket of Jacob's hip so that his hip was
wrenched as he wrestled with the man. 26Then the
man said, "Let me go, for it is daybreak."

But Jacob replied, "I will not let you go unless
you bless me." Hos 12:4

27The man asked him, "What is your name?"

"Jacob," he answered.

28Then the man said, "Your name will no longer
be Jacob, but Israel,[a] because you have struggled
with God and with men and have overcome."

29Jacob said, "Please tell me your name."

But he replied, "Why do you ask my name?"
Then he blessed him there. Ge 35:9

30So Jacob called the place Peniel,[b] saying, "It
is because I saw God face to face, and yet my life
was spared." Ge 16:13; Ex 24:11; Jdg 6:22

31The sun rose above him as he passed Peniel,[c]
and he was limping because of his hip. 32Therefore
to this day the Israelites do not eat the tendon
attached to the socket of the hip, because the socket of Jacob's hip was touched near the tendon.

Jacob Meets Esau

33 Jacob looked up and there was Esau, coming with his four hundred men; so he divided the children among Leah, Rachel and the
two maidservants. 2He put the maidservants and
their children in front, Leah and her children next,
and Rachel and Joseph in the rear. 3He himself
went on ahead and bowed down to the ground
seven times as he approached his brother. Ge 32:6

4But Esau ran to meet Jacob and embraced him;
he threw his arms around his neck and kissed him.
And they wept. 5Then Esau looked up and saw the
women and children. "Who are these with you?"
he asked. Ge 45:14-15

Jacob answered, "They are the children God has
graciously given your servant." Ge 48:9; Ps 127:3

6Then the maidservants and their children approached and bowed down. 7Next, Leah and her
children came and bowed down. Last of all came
Joseph and Rachel, and they too bowed down.

8Esau asked, "What do you mean by all these
droves I met?" Ge 32:14-16

"To find favor in your eyes, my lord," he said.

9But Esau said, "I already have plenty, my
brother. Keep what you have for yourself."

10"No, please!" said Jacob. "If I have found favor in your eyes, accept this gift from me. For to
see your face is like seeing the face of God, now
that you have received me favorably. 11Please accept the present that was brought to you, for God
has been gracious to me and I have all I need."
And because Jacob insisted, Esau accepted it.

12Then Esau said, "Let us be on our way; I'll
accompany you."

13But Jacob said to him, "My lord knows that
the children are tender and that I must care for the
ewes and cows that are nursing their young. If they
are driven hard just one day, all the animals will
die. 14So let my lord go on ahead of his servant,
while I move along slowly at the pace of the droves
before me and that of the children, until I come to
my lord in Seir." Ge 32:3

15Esau said, "Then let me leave some of my men
with you."

"But why do that?" Jacob asked. "Just let me
find favor in the eyes of my lord." Ge 34:11

16So that day Esau started on his way back to
Seir. 17Jacob, however, went to Succoth, where he
built a place for himself and made shelters for his
livestock. That is why the place is called Succoth.[d]

18After Jacob came from Paddan Aram,[e] he
arrived safely at the[f] city of Shechem in Canaan
and camped within sight of the city. 19For a hundred pieces of silver,[g] he bought from the sons of
Hamor, the father of Shechem, the plot of ground

[a] 28 *Israel* means *he struggles with God.* [b] 30 *Peniel* means *face of God.* [c] 31 Hebrew *Penuel*, a variant of *Peniel*
[d] 17 *Succoth* means *shelters.* [e] 18 That is, Northwest Mesopotamia [f] 18 Or *arrived at Shalem, a* [g] 19 Hebrew *hundred kesitahs*; a kesitah was a unit of money of unknown weight and value.

where he pitched his tent. [20]There he set up an altar and called it El Elohe Israel.[a] Jos 24:1,32; Jn 4:5

Dinah and the Shechemites

34 Now Dinah, the daughter Leah had borne to Jacob, went out to visit the women of the land. [2]When Shechem son of Hamor the Hivite, the ruler of that area, saw her, he took her and violated her. [3]His heart was drawn to Dinah daughter of Jacob, and he loved the girl and spoke tenderly to her. [4]And Shechem said to his father Hamor, "Get me this girl as my wife." Ge 30:21

[5]When Jacob heard that his daughter Dinah had been defiled, his sons were in the fields with his livestock; so he kept quiet about it until they came home.

[6]Then Shechem's father Hamor went out to talk with Jacob. [7]Now Jacob's sons had come in from the fields as soon as they heard what had happened. They were filled with grief and fury, because Shechem had done a disgraceful thing in[b] Israel by lying with Jacob's daughter—a thing that should not be done. Dt 22:21; Jdg 20:6; 2Sa 13:12

[8]But Hamor said to them, "My son Shechem has his heart set on your daughter. Please give her to him as his wife. [9]Intermarry with us; give us your daughters and take our daughters for yourselves. [10]You can settle among us; the land is open to you. Live in it, trade[c] in it, and acquire property in it." Ge 13:9; 42:34; 47:6,27

[11]Then Shechem said to Dinah's father and brothers, "Let me find favor in your eyes, and I will give you whatever you ask. [12]Make the price for the bride and the gift I am to bring as great as you like, and I'll pay whatever you ask me. Only give me the girl as my wife." Ex 22:16; Dt 22:29

[13]Because their sister Dinah had been defiled, Jacob's sons replied deceitfully as they spoke to Shechem and his father Hamor. [14]They said to them, "We can't do such a thing; we can't give our sister to a man who is not circumcised. That would be a disgrace to us. [15]We will give our consent to you on one condition only: that you become like us by circumcising all your males. [16]Then we will give you our daughters and take your daughters for ourselves. We'll settle among you and become one people with you. [17]But if you will not agree to be circumcised, we'll take our sister[d] and go."

[18]Their proposal seemed good to Hamor and his son Shechem. [19]The young man, who was the most honored of all his father's household, lost no time in doing what they said, because he was delighted with Jacob's daughter. [20]So Hamor and his son Shechem went to the gate of their city to speak to their fellow townsmen. [21]"These men are friendly toward us," they said. "Let them live in our land and trade in it; the land has plenty of room for them. We can marry their daughters and they can marry ours. [22]But the men will consent to live with us as one people only on the condition that our males be circumcised, as they themselves are. [23]Won't their livestock, their property and all their other animals become ours? So let us give our consent to them, and they will settle among us."

[24]All the men who went out of the city gate agreed with Hamor and his son Shechem, and every male in the city was circumcised. Ge 23:10

[25]Three days later, while all of them were still in pain, two of Jacob's sons, Simeon and Levi, Dinah's brothers, took their swords and attacked the unsuspecting city, killing every male. [26]They put Hamor and his son Shechem to the sword and took Dinah from Shechem's house and left. [27]The sons of Jacob came upon the dead bodies and looted the city where[e] their sister had been defiled. [28]They seized their flocks and herds and donkeys and everything else of theirs in the city and out in the fields. [29]They carried off all their wealth and all their women and children, taking as plunder everything in the houses. Ge 49:5,7

[30]Then Jacob said to Simeon and Levi, "You have brought trouble on me by making me a stench to the Canaanites and Perizzites, the people living in this land. We are few in number, and if they join forces against me and attack me, I and my household will be destroyed." Ex 5:21; 1Ch 16:19

[31]But they replied, "Should he have treated our sister like a prostitute?"

Jacob Returns to Bethel

35 Then God said to Jacob, "Go up to Bethel and settle there, and build an altar there to God, who appeared to you when you were fleeing from your brother Esau." Ge 27:43; 28:19

[2]So Jacob said to his household and to all who were with him, "Get rid of the foreign gods you have with you, and purify yourselves and change your clothes. [3]Then come, let us go up to Bethel, where I will build an altar to God, who answered me in the day of my distress and who has been with me wherever I have gone." [4]So they gave Jacob all the foreign gods they had and the rings in their ears, and Jacob buried them under the oak at Shechem. [5]Then they set out, and the terror of God fell upon the towns all around them so that no one pursued them. Ge 28:15,20-22; 32:7; Ex 19:10,14

[6]Jacob and all the people with him came to Luz (that is, Bethel) in the land of Canaan. [7]There he built an altar, and he called the place El Bethel,[f] because it was there that God revealed himself to him when he was fleeing from his brother.

[8]Now Deborah, Rebekah's nurse, died and was

[a]*20 El Elohe Israel* can mean *God, the God of Israel* or *mighty is the God of Israel.* [b]*7* Or *against* [c]*10* Or *move about freely*; also in verse 21 [d]*17* Hebrew *daughter* [e]*27* Or *because* [f]*7 El Bethel* means *God of Bethel.*

buried under the oak below Bethel. So it was
named Allon Bacuth.[a] Ge 24:59
9After Jacob returned from Paddan Aram,[b]
God appeared to him again and blessed him.

LIVING INSIGHT

Waste no time in asking God to help you realize and remove any idols that are usurping His place in your heart. Use these verses as an example to guide you through the cleansing process.
(See Genesis 35:1–5.)

10God said to him, "Your name is Jacob,[c] but you
will no longer be called Jacob; your name will be
Israel.[d]" So he named him Israel. Ge 17:5; 32:29
11And God said to him, "I am God Almighty[e];
be fruitful and increase in number. A nation and
a community of nations will come from you, and
kings will come from your body. 12The land I gave
to Abraham and Isaac I also give to you, and I will
give this land to your descendants after you."
13Then God went up from him at the place where
he had talked with him. Ge 13:15; 17:6
14Jacob set up a stone pillar at the place where
God had talked with him, and he poured out a
drink offering on it; he also poured oil on it. 15Ja-
cob called the place where God had talked with
him Bethel.[f] Ge 28:18-19

The Deaths of Rachel and Isaac

16Then they moved on from Bethel. While they
were still some distance from Ephrath, Rachel began to give birth and had great difficulty. 17And as
she was having great difficulty in childbirth, the
midwife said to her, "Don't be afraid, for you have
another son." 18As she breathed her last—for she
was dying—she named her son Ben-Oni.[g] But
his father named him Benjamin.[h] Ge 30:24
19So Rachel died and was buried on the way to
Ephrath (that is, Bethlehem). 20Over her tomb Jacob set up a pillar, and to this day that pillar marks
Rachel's tomb. 1Sa 10:2
21Israel moved on again and pitched his tent
beyond Migdal Eder. 22While Israel was living in
that region, Reuben went in and slept with his
father's concubine Bilhah, and Israel heard of it.

Jacob had twelve sons:
23The sons of Leah:
Reuben the firstborn of Jacob, Ge 46:8
Simeon, Levi, Judah, Issachar and Zebulun. Ge 29:35
24The sons of Rachel:
Joseph and Benjamin. ver 18; Ge 30:24
25The sons of Rachel's maidservant Bilhah:
Dan and Naphtali.
26The sons of Leah's maidservant Zilpah:
Gad and Asher. Ge 30:11,13
These were the sons of Jacob, who were born to
him in Paddan Aram. 1Ch 2:1-2

27Jacob came home to his father Isaac in Mamre, near Kiriath Arba (that is, Hebron), where
Abraham and Isaac had stayed. 28Isaac lived a
hundred and eighty years. 29Then he breathed his
last and died and was gathered to his people, old
and full of years. And his sons Esau and Jacob
buried him. Ge 15:15; 25:8-9

Esau's Descendants

36 This is the account of Esau (that is, Edom).

2Esau took his wives from the women of
Canaan: Adah daughter of Elon the Hittite,
and Oholibamah daughter of Anah and
granddaughter of Zibeon the Hivite— 3also
Basemath daughter of Ishmael and sister of
Nebaioth. Ge 26:34; 28:8-9
4Adah bore Eliphaz to Esau, Basemath
bore Reuel, 5and Oholibamah bore Jeush, Jalam and Korah. These were the sons of Esau,
who were born to him in Canaan. 1Ch 1:35
6Esau took his wives and sons and daughters and all the members of his household, as
well as his livestock and all his other animals
and all the goods he had acquired in Canaan,
and moved to a land some distance from his
brother Jacob. 7Their possessions were too
great for them to remain together; the land
where they were staying could not support
them both because of their livestock. 8So
Esau (that is, Edom) settled in the hill country of Seir. Ge 13:6; 32:3

9This is the account of Esau the father of the
Edomites in the hill country of Seir.

10These are the names of Esau's sons:
Eliphaz, the son of Esau's wife Adah, and
Reuel, the son of Esau's wife Basemath.
11The sons of Eliphaz:
Teman, Omar, Zepho, Gatam and Kenaz.
12Esau's son Eliphaz also had a concubine
named Timna, who bore him Amalek.
These were grandsons of Esau's wife
Adah. Ex 17:8,16; Nu 24:20; 1Sa 15:2
13The sons of Reuel:
Nahath, Zerah, Shammah and Mizzah.

[a] 8 *Allon Bacuth* means *oak of weeping.* [b] 9 That is, Northwest Mesopotamia; also in verse 26 [c] 10 *Jacob* means *he grasps the heel* (figuratively, *he deceives*). [d] 10 *Israel* means *he struggles with God.* [e] 11 Hebrew *El-Shaddai*
[f] 15 *Bethel* means *house of God.* [g] 18 *Ben-Oni* means *son of my trouble.* [h] 18 *Benjamin* means *son of my right hand.*

These were grandsons of Esau's wife Basemath.
[14]The sons of Esau's wife Oholibamah daughter of Anah and granddaughter of Zibeon, whom she bore to Esau:
Jeush, Jalam and Korah. 1Ch 1:35-37

[15]These were the chiefs among Esau's descendants: Ex 15:15
The sons of Eliphaz the firstborn of Esau:
Chiefs Teman, Omar, Zepho, Kenaz,
[16]Korah,[a] Gatam and Amalek. These were the chiefs descended from Eliphaz in Edom; they were grandsons of Adah.
[17]The sons of Esau's son Reuel: 1Ch 1:37
Chiefs Nahath, Zerah, Shammah and Mizzah. These were the chiefs descended from Reuel in Edom; they were grandsons of Esau's wife Basemath.
[18]The sons of Esau's wife Oholibamah:
Chiefs Jeush, Jalam and Korah. These were the chiefs descended from Esau's wife Oholibamah daughter of Anah.
[19]These were the sons of Esau (that is, Edom),
and these were their chiefs. Ge 25:30

[20]These were the sons of Seir the Horite, who
were living in the region: Ge 14:6; Dt 2:12,22
Lotan, Shobal, Zibeon, Anah,
[21]Dishon, Ezer and Dishan. These sons of Seir in Edom were Horite chiefs.
[22]The sons of Lotan:
Hori and Homam.[b] Timna was Lotan's sister.
[23]The sons of Shobal:
Alvan, Manahath, Ebal, Shepho and Onam.
[24]The sons of Zibeon:
Aiah and Anah. This is the Anah who discovered the hot springs[c] in the desert while he was grazing the donkeys of his father Zibeon.
[25]The children of Anah:
Dishon and Oholibamah daughter of Anah.
[26]The sons of Dishon[d]:
Hemdan, Eshban, Ithran and Keran.
[27]The sons of Ezer:
Bilhan, Zaavan and Akan.
[28]The sons of Dishan:
Uz and Aran. 1Ch 1:38-42
[29]These were the Horite chiefs:
Lotan, Shobal, Zibeon, Anah,
[30]Dishon, Ezer and Dishan. These were the Horite chiefs, according to their divisions, in the land of Seir.

The Rulers of Edom

[31]These were the kings who reigned in Edom
before any Israelite king reigned[e]:
[32]Bela son of Beor became king of Edom. His city was named Dinhabah. 1Ch 1:43
[33]When Bela died, Jobab son of Zerah from Bozrah succeeded him as king.
[34]When Jobab died, Husham from the land of the Temanites succeeded him as king.
[35]When Husham died, Hadad son of Bedad, who defeated Midian in the country of Moab, succeeded him as king. His city was named Avith. Ge 19:37; Ru 1:1,6
[36]When Hadad died, Samlah from Masrekah succeeded him as king.
[37]When Samlah died, Shaul from Rehoboth on the river[f] succeeded him as king.
[38]When Shaul died, Baal-Hanan son of Acbor succeeded him as king.
[39]When Baal-Hanan son of Acbor died, Hadad[g] succeeded him as king. His city was named Pau, and his wife's name was Mehetabel daughter of Matred, the daughter of Me-Zahab.

[40]These were the chiefs descended from Esau,
by name, according to their clans and regions:
Timna, Alvah, Jetheth,
[41]Oholibamah, Elah, Pinon,
[42]Kenaz, Teman, Mibzar,
[43]Magdiel and Iram. These were the chiefs of Edom, according to their settlements in the land they occupied.

This was Esau the father of the Edomites.

A Colorful Personality — Chapters 37–50

Joseph had a colorful wardrobe; his many-colored coat is now almost legendary (37:3). However, even more colorful than his clothing was his personality. Although he was first hated by his brothers because of his dreams and the preferential treatment he received as the youngest son, he later became God's instrument to save his whole family and the nation of Israel. The same brothers who sold Joseph into slavery later bowed at his feet and sought his help. He was a shining light of integrity, faithfulness and forgiveness. By the end of his life, his whole family was living in the region of Goshen (46:34), and their presence in Egypt set the scene for what follows in the book of Exodus.

[a]16 Masoretic Text; Samaritan Pentateuch (see also Gen. 36:11 and 1 Chron. 1:36) does not have *Korah.* [b]22 Hebrew *Hemam,* a variant of *Homam* (see 1 Chron. 1:39) [c]24 Vulgate; Syriac *discovered water;* the meaning of the Hebrew for this word is uncertain. [d]26 Hebrew *Dishan,* a variant of *Dishon* [e]31 Or *before an Israelite king reigned over them* [f]37 Possibly the Euphrates [g]39 Many manuscripts of the Masoretic Text, Samaritan Pentateuch and Syriac (see also 1 Chron. 1:50); most manuscripts of the Masoretic Text *Hadar*

Joseph's Dreams

37 Jacob lived in the land where his father had
stayed, the land of Canaan. Ge 17:8

2This is the account of Jacob.

Joseph, a young man of seventeen, was tending
the flocks with his brothers, the sons of Bilhah and
the sons of Zilpah, his father's wives, and he
brought their father a bad report about them.
3Now Israel loved Joseph more than any of his
other sons, because he had been born to him in his
old age; and he made a richly ornamented[a] robe
for him. 4When his brothers saw that their father
loved him more than any of them, they hated him
and could not speak a kind word to him.
5Joseph had a dream, and when he told it to his
brothers, they hated him all the more. 6He said to
them, "Listen to this dream I had: 7We were binding sheaves of grain out in the field when suddenly
my sheaf rose and stood upright, while your
sheaves gathered around mine and bowed down
to it." Ge 42:6,9; 44:14; 50:18
8His brothers said to him, "Do you intend to
reign over us? Will you actually rule us?" And they
hated him all the more because of his dream and
what he had said. Ge 49:26
9Then he had another dream, and he told it
to his brothers. "Listen," he said, "I had another
dream, and this time the sun and moon and eleven
stars were bowing down to me." Ge 28:12
10When he told his father as well as his brothers,
his father rebuked him and said, "What is this
dream you had? Will your mother and I and your
brothers actually come and bow down to the
ground before you?" 11His brothers were jealous of
him, but his father kept the matter in mind.

Joseph Sold by His Brothers

12Now his brothers had gone to graze their father's flocks near Shechem, 13and Israel said to
Joseph, "As you know, your brothers are grazing
the flocks near Shechem. Come, I am going to
send you to them."
"Very well," he replied.
14So he said to him, "Go and see if all is well
with your brothers and with the flocks, and bring
word back to me." Then he sent him off from the
Valley of Hebron. Ge 13:18
When Joseph arrived at Shechem, 15a man
found him wandering around in the fields and
asked him, "What are you looking for?"
16He replied, "I'm looking for my brothers. Can
you tell me where they are grazing their flocks?"
17"They have moved on from here," the man
answered. "I heard them say, 'Let's go to Dothan.'" 2Ki 6:13
So Joseph went after his brothers and found
them near Dothan. 18But they saw him in the distance, and before he reached them, they plotted to
kill him. Mk 14:1
19"Here comes that dreamer!" they said to each
other. 20"Come now, let's kill him and throw him
into one of these cisterns and say that a ferocious
animal devoured him. Then we'll see what comes
of his dreams." Ge 50:20
21When Reuben heard this, he tried to rescue
him from their hands. "Let's not take his life," he
said. 22"Don't shed any blood. Throw him into this
cistern here in the desert, but don't lay a hand on
him." Reuben said this to rescue him from them
and take him back to his father. Ge 42:22
23So when Joseph came to his brothers, they
stripped him of his robe—the richly ornamented
robe he was wearing— 24and they took him and
threw him into the cistern. Now the cistern was
empty; there was no water in it. Jer 41:7
25As they sat down to eat their meal, they
looked up and saw a caravan of Ishmaelites coming from Gilead. Their camels were loaded with
spices, balm and myrrh, and they were on their
way to take them down to Egypt. ver 28
26Judah said to his brothers, "What will we gain
if we kill our brother and cover up his blood?
27Come, let's sell him to the Ishmaelites and not
lay our hands on him; after all, he is our brother,
our own flesh and blood." His brothers agreed.
28So when the Midianite merchants came by,
his brothers pulled Joseph up out of the cistern
and sold him for twenty shekels[b] of silver to the
Ishmaelites, who took him to Egypt. Ge 45:4-5
29When Reuben returned to the cistern and saw
that Joseph was not there, he tore his clothes. 30He
went back to his brothers and said, "The boy isn't
there! Where can I turn now?" ver 22; Ge 42:13,36
31Then they got Joseph's robe, slaughtered a
goat and dipped the robe in the blood. 32They took
the ornamented robe back to their father and said,
"We found this. Examine it to see whether it is
your son's robe." ver 3,23
33He recognized it and said, "It is my son's
robe! Some ferocious animal has devoured him.
Joseph has surely been torn to pieces." ver 20
34Then Jacob tore his clothes, put on sackcloth
and mourned for his son many days. 35All his sons
and daughters came to comfort him, but he refused to be comforted. "No," he said, "in mourning will I go down to the grave[c] to my son." So
his father wept for him. Ge 42:38; 44:22,29,31
36Meanwhile, the Midianites[d] sold Joseph in

[a]3 The meaning of the Hebrew for *richly ornamented* is uncertain; also in verses 23 and 32. [b]28 That is, about 8 ounces (about 0.2 kilogram) [c]35 Hebrew *Sheol* [d]36 Samaritan Pentateuch, Septuagint, Vulgate and Syriac (see also verse 28); Masoretic Text *Medanites*

Egypt to Potiphar, one of Pharaoh's officials, the captain of the guard. Ge 39:1

Judah and Tamar

38 At that time, Judah left his brothers and went down to stay with a man of Adullam named Hirah. 2There Judah met the daughter of a Canaanite man named Shua. He married her and lay with her; 3she became pregnant and gave birth to a son, who was named Er. 4She conceived again and gave birth to a son and named him Onan. 5She gave birth to still another son and named him Shelah. It was at Kezib that she gave birth to him.

6Judah got a wife for Er, his firstborn, and her name was Tamar. 7But Er, Judah's firstborn, was wicked in the LORD's sight; so the LORD put him to death. 1Ch 2:3

8Then Judah said to Onan, "Lie with your brother's wife and fulfill your duty to her as a brother-in-law to produce offspring for your brother." 9But Onan knew that the offspring would not be his; so whenever he lay with his brother's wife, he spilled his semen on the ground to keep from producing offspring for his brother. 10What he did was wicked in the LORD's sight; so he put him to death also. Dt 25:5-6; Mt 22:24-28; Ge 46:12

11Judah then said to his daughter-in-law Tamar, "Live as a widow in your father's house until my son Shelah grows up." For he thought, "He may die too, just like his brothers." So Tamar went to live in her father's house. Ru 1:13

12After a long time Judah's wife, the daughter of Shua, died. When Judah had recovered from his grief, he went up to Timnah, to the men who were shearing his sheep, and his friend Hirah the Adullamite went with him. Jos 15:10,57

13When Tamar was told, "Your father-in-law is on his way to Timnah to shear his sheep," 14she took off her widow's clothes, covered herself with a veil to disguise herself, and then sat down at the entrance to Enaim, which is on the road to Timnah. For she saw that, though Shelah had now grown up, she had not been given to him as his wife. Ge 31:19

15When Judah saw her, he thought she was a prostitute, for she had covered her face. 16Not realizing that she was his daughter-in-law, he went over to her by the roadside and said, "Come now, let me sleep with you." Lev 18:15; 20:12

"And what will you give me to sleep with you?" she asked.

17"I'll send you a young goat from my flock," he said. Eze 16:33

"Will you give me something as a pledge until you send it?" she asked.

18He said, "What pledge should I give you?"

"Your seal and its cord, and the staff in your hand," she answered. So he gave them to her and slept with her, and she became pregnant by him. 19After she left, she took off her veil and put on her widow's clothes again.

20Meanwhile Judah sent the young goat by his friend the Adullamite in order to get his pledge back from the woman, but he did not find her. 21He asked the men who lived there, "Where is the shrine prostitute who was beside the road at Enaim?" Lev 19:29; Hos 4:14

"There hasn't been any shrine prostitute here," they said.

22So he went back to Judah and said, "I didn't find her. Besides, the men who lived there said, 'There hasn't been any shrine prostitute here.' "

23Then Judah said, "Let her keep what she has, or we will become a laughingstock. After all, I did send her this young goat, but you didn't find her."

24About three months later Judah was told, "Your daughter-in-law Tamar is guilty of prostitution, and as a result she is now pregnant."

Judah said, "Bring her out and have her burned to death!" Lev 21:9; Dt 22:21,22

25As she was being brought out, she sent a message to her father-in-law. "I am pregnant by the man who owns these," she said. And she added, "See if you recognize whose seal and cord and staff these are." ver 18

26Judah recognized them and said, "She is more righteous than I, since I wouldn't give her to my son Shelah." And he did not sleep with her again.

27When the time came for her to give birth, there were twin boys in her womb. 28As she was giving birth, one of them put out his hand; so the midwife took a scarlet thread and tied it on his wrist and said, "This one came out first." 29But when he drew back his hand, his brother came out, and she said, "So this is how you have broken out!" And he was named Perez.[a] 30Then his brother, who had the scarlet thread on his wrist, came out and he was given the name Zerah.[b]

Joseph and Potiphar's Wife

39 Now Joseph had been taken down to Egypt. Potiphar, an Egyptian who was one of Pharaoh's officials, the captain of the guard, bought him from the Ishmaelites who had taken him there. Ge 37:25,36; Ps 105:17

2The LORD was with Joseph and he prospered, and he lived in the house of his Egyptian master. 3When his master saw that the LORD was with him and that the LORD gave him success in everything he did, 4Joseph found favor in his eyes and became his attendant. Potiphar put him in charge of his household, and he entrusted to his care everything he owned. 5From the time he put him in charge of his household and of all that he owned, the LORD

[a]29 *Perez* means *breaking out.* [b]30 *Zerah* can mean *scarlet* or *brightness.*

JOSEPH

Providence Made Personal

"The LORD was with Joseph and he prospered, and he lived in the house of his Egyptian master."
—GENESIS 39:2

The story of Joseph is the story of a boy who didn't ask for the trouble he got into—but he surely got into a peck of it. As we are introduced to Joseph, he was a "a young man of seventeen" (Genesis 37:2) who had a special place in his father's heart. He was much loved by Jacob, his father—in fact, he was loved "more than any of [Jacob's] other sons, because he had been born to him in his old age" (37:3).

It's not too difficult to see that there were some ominous storm clouds beginning to form overhead in the life of this boy who was the recipient of the special love of his aging father. You see, Joseph's brothers didn't take kindly to that kind of favoritism: "When his brothers saw that their father loved him more than any of them, they hated him and could not speak a kind word to him" (37:4). Joseph certainly didn't help matters. He tattled on his brothers (37:2) and gleefully recounted his dreams (37:5–9).

Can't you imagine these brothers lying awake at night plotting revenge? Looking for the right moment to give this spoiled brother of theirs exactly what he deserved? So one day when they saw him, alone and vulnerable, heading directly toward them in the open field, they huddled for one last strategy meeting and concocted the plan that they hastened to carry out. They captured him and threw him into a cistern, fully expecting, I suspect, that he would die there in due time. But a caravan of Ishmaelites on their way to Egypt came along. I can imagine Joseph's brothers thinking to themselves, "What a stroke of luck! We can at least earn a little something for our troubles." So they sold Joseph to them. They must have thought, "Good riddance. Now we can get on with our lives." They took the multicolored tunic and doused it with the blood of an animal—to use as the basis of their report to their father.

As time passed Joseph's brothers forgot about him. They wrote him off for good. But God didn't. While his brothers may not have known where he had ended up, God knew where he was. You see, Joseph was taken to Egypt, where he was sold to one of the pharaoh's officials. The Bible tells us that "the LORD was with Joseph and he prospered" (39:2)—to the point that Joseph was placed in charge of his master Potiphar's household. But he was set up for a fall by Potiphar's wife, who tried to seduce him. Joseph was thrown into prison, where he lived in undeserved punishment. Then, through a beautifully and divinely orchestrated chain of events (40:1–41:38), he regained the pharaoh's confidence and was promoted to the position of prime minister in the land (41:40).

Throughout this time Joseph's brothers didn't know what had become of him. Jacob, of course, thought his son was dead (37:33–34). But in Genesis 42 we have God's awesome "Plan B" set into motion when Joseph's brothers headed down to Egypt. It culminated in the ultimate family reunion in Genesis 45 and 46—the kind of family reunion that could never be forgotten: "Then Joseph said to his brothers, 'Come close to me.' When they had done so, he said, 'I am your brother, Joseph, the one you sold into Egypt! And now, do not be distressed and do not be angry with yourselves for selling me here, because it was to save lives that God sent me ahead of you' " (45:4–5).

Did Joseph have some kind of mental block? Had he forgotten that his brothers had done him such incredible wrong? No—he was realistic. He remembered being wrestled down, stripped of his tunic, thrown into the cistern and sold to the caravan. But Joseph had experienced growth since his childhood. Certainly he had struggled with anger and bitterness; surely he had savored thoughts of revenge. Yet he desperately wanted to reconcile with his brothers. And in the end, the Lord would have His way. Joseph knew it as he reflected on his life. He could see God's hand at work through the years. Ultimately that's how he could forgive his brothers. That's how he could sum it up in the end: "You intended to harm me, but God intended it for good to accomplish what is now being done, the saving of many lives" (50:20).

blessed the household of the Egyptian because of
Joseph. The blessing of the LORD was on everything Potiphar had, both in the house and in the
field. 6So he left in Joseph's care everything he had;
with Joseph in charge, he did not concern himself
with anything except the food he ate. Ge 21:22; 26:28
Now Joseph was well-built and handsome, 7and
after a while his master's wife took notice of Joseph
and said, "Come to bed with me!" Pr 7:15-18

LIVING  INSIGHT

Lust is no respecter of persons. No one is immune. You're not. I'm not. And beware—lust never gives up . . . it never runs out of ideas. How do you handle such an aggressive intruder? Try this: When lust suggests a rendezvous, send Jesus Christ as your representative.

(See Genesis 39:7.)

8But he refused. "With me in charge," he told
her, "my master does not concern himself with
anything in the house; everything he owns he has
entrusted to my care. 9No one is greater in this
house than I am. My master has withheld nothing
from me except you, because you are his wife.
How then could I do such a wicked thing and sin
against God?" 10And though she spoke to Joseph
day after day, he refused to go to bed with her or
even be with her. Ge 20:6; 42:18; Pr 6:23-24
11One day he went into the house to attend to
his duties, and none of the household servants was
inside. 12She caught him by his cloak and said,
"Come to bed with me!" But he left his cloak in her
hand and ran out of the house. Pr 7:13
13When she saw that he had left his cloak in her
hand and had run out of the house, 14she called
her household servants. "Look," she said to them,
"this Hebrew has been brought to us to make
sport of us! He came in here to sleep with me, but
I screamed. 15When he heard me scream for help,
he left his cloak beside me and ran out of the
house." Dt 22:24,27
16She kept his cloak beside her until his master
came home. 17Then she told him this story: "That
Hebrew slave you brought us came to me to make
sport of me. 18But as soon as I screamed for help,
he left his cloak beside me and ran out of the
house." Ex 23:1,7; Ps 101:5
19When his master heard the story his wife told
him, saying, "This is how your slave treated me,"
he burned with anger. 20Joseph's master took him
and put him in prison, the place where the king's
prisoners were confined. Ps 105:18
But while Joseph was there in the prison, 21the
LORD was with him; he showed him kindness and
granted him favor in the eyes of the prison warden. 22So the warden put Joseph in charge of all
those held in the prison, and he was made responsible for all that was done there. 23The warden paid
no attention to anything under Joseph's care, because the LORD was with Joseph and gave him
success in whatever he did. ver 3; Ex 3:21

The Cupbearer and the Baker

40 Some time later, the cupbearer and the
baker of the king of Egypt offended their
master, the king of Egypt. 2Pharaoh was angry
with his two officials, the chief cupbearer and the
chief baker, 3and put them in custody in the house
of the captain of the guard, in the same prison
where Joseph was confined. 4The captain of the
guard assigned them to Joseph, and he attended
them. Ge 39:4,20
After they had been in custody for some time,
5each of the two men—the cupbearer and the baker of the king of Egypt, who were being held in
prison—had a dream the same night, and each
dream had a meaning of its own. Ge 41:11
6When Joseph came to them the next morning,
he saw that they were dejected. 7So he asked Pharaoh's officials who were in custody with him in his
master's house, "Why are your faces so sad today?" Ne 2:2
8"We both had dreams," they answered, "but
there is no one to interpret them." Ge 41:8,15
Then Joseph said to them, "Do not interpretations belong to God? Tell me your dreams."
9So the chief cupbearer told Joseph his dream.
He said to him, "In my dream I saw a vine in front
of me, 10and on the vine were three branches. As
soon as it budded, it blossomed, and its clusters
ripened into grapes. 11Pharaoh's cup was in my
hand, and I took the grapes, squeezed them into
Pharaoh's cup and put the cup in his hand."
12"This is what it means," Joseph said to him.
"The three branches are three days. 13Within three
days Pharaoh will lift up your head and restore
you to your position, and you will put Pharaoh's
cup in his hand, just as you used to do when you
were his cupbearer. 14But when all goes well with
you, remember me and show me kindness; mention me to Pharaoh and get me out of this prison.
15For I was forcibly carried off from the land of the
Hebrews, and even here I have done nothing to
deserve being put in a dungeon." Da 2:36; 4:19
16When the chief baker saw that Joseph had
given a favorable interpretation, he said to Joseph,
"I too had a dream: On my head were three baskets of bread.[a] 17In the top basket were all kinds
of baked goods for Pharaoh, but the birds were
eating them out of the basket on my head."

[a] 16 Or *three wicker baskets*

18“This is what it means,” Joseph said. “The three baskets are three days. 19Within three days Pharaoh will lift off your head and hang you on a tree.[a] And the birds will eat away your flesh.”

20Now the third day was Pharaoh’s birthday, and he gave a feast for all his officials. He lifted up the heads of the chief cupbearer and the chief baker in the presence of his officials: 21He restored the chief cupbearer to his position, so that he once again put the cup into Pharaoh’s hand, 22but he hanged[b] the chief baker, just as Joseph had said to them in his interpretation. ver 13; Ps 105:19

23The chief cupbearer, however, did not remember Joseph; he forgot him. Job 19:14

Pharaoh’s Dreams

41 When two full years had passed, Pharaoh had a dream: He was standing by the Nile, 2when out of the river there came up seven cows, sleek and fat, and they grazed among the reeds. 3After them, seven other cows, ugly and gaunt, came up out of the Nile and stood beside those on the riverbank. 4And the cows that were ugly and gaunt ate up the seven sleek, fat cows. Then Pharaoh woke up. Ge 20:3; Isa 19:6

5He fell asleep again and had a second dream: Seven heads of grain, healthy and good, were growing on a single stalk. 6After them, seven other heads of grain sprouted—thin and scorched by the east wind. 7The thin heads of grain swallowed up the seven healthy, full heads. Then Pharaoh woke up; it had been a dream.

8In the morning his mind was troubled, so he sent for all the magicians and wise men of Egypt. Pharaoh told them his dreams, but no one could interpret them for him. Da 2:1,3; 4:5,19; Ex 7:11,22

9Then the chief cupbearer said to Pharaoh, “Today I am reminded of my shortcomings. 10Pharaoh was once angry with his servants, and he imprisoned me and the chief baker in the house of the captain of the guard. 11Each of us had a dream the same night, and each dream had a meaning of its own. 12Now a young Hebrew was there with us, a servant of the captain of the guard. We told him our dreams, and he interpreted them for us, giving each man the interpretation of his dream. 13And things turned out exactly as he interpreted them to us: I was restored to my position, and the other man was hanged.[b]” Ge 40:2,5,12,22

14So Pharaoh sent for Joseph, and he was quickly brought from the dungeon. When he had shaved and changed his clothes, he came before Pharaoh. Ps 105:20; Da 2:25

15Pharaoh said to Joseph, “I had a dream, and no one can interpret it. But I have heard it said of you that when you hear a dream you can interpret it.” Da 15:16

16“I cannot do it,” Joseph replied to Pharaoh, “but God will give Pharaoh the answer he desires.”

17Then Pharaoh said to Joseph, “In my dream I was standing on the bank of the Nile, 18when out of the river there came up seven cows, fat and sleek, and they grazed among the reeds. 19After them, seven other cows came up—scrawny and very ugly and lean. I had never seen such ugly cows in all the land of Egypt. 20The lean, ugly cows ate up the seven fat cows that came up first. 21But even after they ate them, no one could tell that they had done so; they looked just as ugly as before. Then I woke up.

22“In my dreams I also saw seven heads of grain, full and good, growing on a single stalk. 23After them, seven other heads sprouted—withered and thin and scorched by the east wind. 24The thin heads of grain swallowed up the seven good heads. I told this to the magicians, but none could explain it to me.” ver 8

25Then Joseph said to Pharaoh, “The dreams of Pharaoh are one and the same. God has revealed to Pharaoh what he is about to do. 26The seven good cows are seven years, and the seven good heads of grain are seven years; it is one and the same dream. 27The seven lean, ugly cows that came up afterward are seven years, and so are the seven worthless heads of grain scorched by the east wind: They are seven years of famine. Da 2:45

28“It is just as I said to Pharaoh: God has shown Pharaoh what he is about to do. 29Seven years of great abundance are coming throughout the land of Egypt, 30but seven years of famine will follow them. Then all the abundance in Egypt will be forgotten, and the famine will ravage the land. 31The abundance in the land will not be remembered, because the famine that follows it will be so severe. 32The reason the dream was given to Pharaoh in two forms is that the matter has been firmly decided by God, and God will do it soon.

33“And now let Pharaoh look for a discerning and wise man and put him in charge of the land of Egypt. 34Let Pharaoh appoint commissioners over the land to take a fifth of the harvest of Egypt during the seven years of abundance. 35They should collect all the food of these good years that are coming and store up the grain under the authority of Pharaoh, to be kept in the cities for food. 36This food should be held in reserve for the country, to be used during the seven years of famine that will come upon Egypt, so that the country may not be ruined by the famine.” ver 48,56

37The plan seemed good to Pharaoh and to all his officials. 38So Pharaoh asked them, “Can we find anyone like this man, one in whom is the spirit of God[c]?” Nu 27:18; Da 4:8-9,18; 5:11,14

39Then Pharaoh said to Joseph, “Since God has

[a] 19 Or *and impale you on a pole* [b] 22,13 Or *impaled* [c] 38 Or *of the gods*

made all this known to you, there is no one so discerning and wise as you. 40You shall be in charge of my palace, and all my people are to submit to your orders. Only with respect to the throne will I be greater than you." Ps 105:21-22

Joseph in Charge of Egypt

41So Pharaoh said to Joseph, "I hereby put you in charge of the whole land of Egypt." 42Then Pharaoh took his signet ring from his finger and put it on Joseph's finger. He dressed him in robes of fine linen and put a gold chain around his neck. 43He had him ride in a chariot as his second-in-command,[a] and men shouted before him, "Make way[b]!" Thus he put him in charge of the whole land of Egypt. Ge 42:6; Est 3:10; Da 5:7,16,29

44Then Pharaoh said to Joseph, "I am Pharaoh, but without your word no one will lift hand or foot in all Egypt." 45Pharaoh gave Joseph the name Zaphenath-Paneah and gave him Asenath daughter of Potiphera, priest of On,[c] to be his wife. And Joseph went throughout the land of Egypt.

46Joseph was thirty years old when he entered the service of Pharaoh king of Egypt. And Joseph went out from Pharaoh's presence and traveled throughout Egypt. 47During the seven years of abundance the land produced plentifully. 48Joseph collected all the food produced in those seven years of abundance in Egypt and stored it in the cities. In each city he put the food grown in the fields surrounding it. 49Joseph stored up huge quantities of grain, like the sand of the sea; it was so much that he stopped keeping records because it was beyond measure. Da 1:19

50Before the years of famine came, two sons were born to Joseph by Asenath daughter of Potiphera, priest of On. 51Joseph named his firstborn Manasseh[d] and said, "It is because God has made me forget all my trouble and all my father's household." 52The second son he named Ephraim[e] and said, "It is because God has made me fruitful in the land of my suffering." Ge 17:6; 49:22

53The seven years of abundance in Egypt came to an end, 54and the seven years of famine began, just as Joseph had said. There was famine in all the other lands, but in the whole land of Egypt there was food. 55When all Egypt began to feel the famine, the people cried to Pharaoh for food. Then Pharaoh told all the Egyptians, "Go to Joseph and do what he tells you." ver 30; Ps 105:11; Ac 7:11

56When the famine had spread over the whole country, Joseph opened the storehouses and sold grain to the Egyptians, for the famine was severe throughout Egypt. 57And all the countries came to Egypt to buy grain from Joseph, because the famine was severe in all the world. Ge 12:10; 42:5

Joseph's Brothers Go to Egypt

42 When Jacob learned that there was grain in Egypt, he said to his sons, "Why do you just keep looking at each other?" 2He continued, "I have heard that there is grain in Egypt. Go down there and buy some for us, so that we may live and not die." Ge 43:8; Ac 7:12

3Then ten of Joseph's brothers went down to buy grain from Egypt. 4But Jacob did not send Benjamin, Joseph's brother, with the others, because he was afraid that harm might come to him. 5So Israel's sons were among those who went to buy grain, for the famine was in the land of Canaan also. ver 38; Ac 7:11

6Now Joseph was the governor of the land, the one who sold grain to all its people. So when Joseph's brothers arrived, they bowed down to him with their faces to the ground. 7As soon as Joseph saw his brothers, he recognized them, but he pretended to be a stranger and spoke harshly to them. "Where do you come from?" he asked. Ge 37:7-10

"From the land of Canaan," they replied, "to buy food."

8Although Joseph recognized his brothers, they did not recognize him. 9Then he remembered his dreams about them and said to them, "You are spies! You have come to see where our land is unprotected." Ge 37:7

10"No, my lord," they answered. "Your servants have come to buy food. 11We are all the sons of one man. Your servants are honest men, not spies."

12"No!" he said to them. "You have come to see where our land is unprotected."

13But they replied, "Your servants were twelve brothers, the sons of one man, who lives in the land of Canaan. The youngest is now with our father, and one is no more." Ge 37:30,33; 44:20

14Joseph said to them, "It is just as I told you: You are spies! 15And this is how you will be tested: As surely as Pharaoh lives, you will not leave this place unless your youngest brother comes here. 16Send one of your number to get your brother; the rest of you will be kept in prison, so that your words may be tested to see if you are telling the truth. If you are not, then as surely as Pharaoh lives, you are spies!" 17And he put them all in custody for three days. Ge 40:4; 1Sa 17:55

18On the third day, Joseph said to them, "Do this and you will live, for I fear God: 19If you are honest men, let one of your brothers stay here in prison, while the rest of you go and take grain back for your starving households. 20But you must bring your youngest brother to me, so that your

[a]43 Or *in the chariot of his second-in-command*; or *in his second chariot* [b]43 Or *Bow down* [c]45 That is, Heliopolis; also in verse 50 [d]51 *Manasseh* sounds like and may be derived from the Hebrew for *forget.* [e]52 *Ephraim* sounds like the Hebrew for *twice fruitful.*

words may be verified and that you may not die." This they proceeded to do. ver 15,34; Ge 43:5; Lev 25:43

21They said to one another, "Surely we are being punished because of our brother. We saw how distressed he was when he pleaded with us for his life, but we would not listen; that's why this distress has come upon us." Hos 5:15

22Reuben replied, "Didn't I tell you not to sin against the boy? But you wouldn't listen! Now we must give an accounting for his blood." 23They did not realize that Joseph could understand them, since he was using an interpreter. Ge 9:5; 37:21-22

24He turned away from them and began to weep, but then turned back and spoke to them again. He had Simeon taken from them and bound before their eyes. Ge 45:14-15

25Joseph gave orders to fill their bags with grain, to put each man's silver back in his sack, and to give them provisions for their journey. After this was done for them, 26they loaded their grain on their donkeys and left. Ro 12:17,20-21

27At the place where they stopped for the night one of them opened his sack to get feed for his donkey, and he saw his silver in the mouth of his sack. 28"My silver has been returned," he said to his brothers. "Here it is in my sack." Ge 43:21-22

Their hearts sank and they turned to each other trembling and said, "What is this that God has done to us?" Ge 43:23

29When they came to their father Jacob in the land of Canaan, they told him all that had happened to them. They said, 30"The man who is lord over the land spoke harshly to us and treated us as though we were spying on the land. 31But we said to him, 'We are honest men; we are not spies. 32We were twelve brothers, sons of one father. One is no more, and the youngest is now with our father in Canaan.' ver 7

33"Then the man who is lord over the land said to us, 'This is how I will know whether you are honest men: Leave one of your brothers here with me, and take food for your starving households and go. 34But bring your youngest brother to me so I will know that you are not spies but honest men. Then I will give your brother back to you, and you can trade[a] in the land.'" Ge 34:10

35As they were emptying their sacks, there in each man's sack was his pouch of silver! When they and their father saw the money pouches, they were frightened. 36Their father Jacob said to them, "You have deprived me of my children. Joseph is no more and Simeon is no more, and now you want to take Benjamin. Everything is against me!"

37Then Reuben said to his father, "You may put both of my sons to death if I do not bring him back to you. Entrust him to my care, and I will bring him back."

38But Jacob said, "My son will not go down there with you; his brother is dead and he is the only one left. If harm comes to him on the journey you are taking, you will bring my gray head down to the grave[b] in sorrow." Ge 37:33,35

The Second Journey to Egypt

43 Now the famine was still severe in the land. 2So when they had eaten all the grain they had brought from Egypt, their father said to them, "Go back and buy us a little more food." Ge 12:10

3But Judah said to him, "The man warned us solemnly, 'You will not see my face again unless your brother is with you.' 4If you will send our brother along with us, we will go down and buy food for you. 5But if you will not send him, we will not go down, because the man said to us, 'You will not see my face again unless your brother is with you.'" Ge 42:15

6Israel asked, "Why did you bring this trouble on me by telling the man you had another brother?"

7They replied, "The man questioned us closely about ourselves and our family. 'Is your father still living?' he asked us. 'Do you have another brother?' We simply answered his questions. How were we to know he would say, 'Bring your brother down here'?" Ge 42:13

8Then Judah said to Israel his father, "Send the boy along with me and we will go at once, so that we and you and our children may live and not die. 9I myself will guarantee his safety; you can hold me personally responsible for him. If I do not bring him back to you and set him here before you, I will bear the blame before you all my life. 10As it is, if we had not delayed, we could have gone and returned twice." Ge 42:37; 44:32; Phm 1:18-19

11Then their father Israel said to them, "If it must be, then do this: Put some of the best products of the land in your bags and take them down to the man as a gift—a little balm and a little honey, some spices and myrrh, some pistachio nuts and almonds. 12Take double the amount of silver with you, for you must return the silver that was put back into the mouths of your sacks. Perhaps it was a mistake. 13Take your brother also and go back to the man at once. 14And may God Almighty[c] grant you mercy before the man so that he will let your other brother and Benjamin come back with you. As for me, if I am bereaved, I am bereaved." Ge 32:20; 37:25; 42:25

15So the men took the gifts and double the amount of silver, and Benjamin also. They hurried down to Egypt and presented themselves to Joseph. 16When Joseph saw Benjamin with them, he said to the steward of his house, "Take these men

[a]34 Or *move about freely* [b]38 Hebrew *Sheol* [c]14 Hebrew *El-Shaddai*

to my house, slaughter an animal and prepare dinner; they are to eat with me at noon." Ge 44:1,4,12

17The man did as Joseph told him and took the men to Joseph's house. 18Now the men were frightened when they were taken to his house. They thought, "We were brought here because of the silver that was put back into our sacks the first time. He wants to attack us and overpower us and seize us as slaves and take our donkeys."

19So they went up to Joseph's steward and spoke to him at the entrance to the house. 20"Please, sir," they said, "we came down here the first time to buy food. 21But at the place where we stopped for the night we opened our sacks and each of us found his silver—the exact weight—in the mouth of his sack. So we have brought it back with us. 22We have also brought additional silver with us to buy food. We don't know who put our silver in our sacks." ver 15; Ge 42:27,35

23"It's all right," he said. "Don't be afraid. Your God, the God of your father, has given you treasure in your sacks; I received your silver." Then he brought Simeon out to them. Ge 42:28

24The steward took the men into Joseph's house, gave them water to wash their feet and provided fodder for their donkeys. 25They prepared their gifts for Joseph's arrival at noon, because they had heard that they were to eat there.

26When Joseph came home, they presented to him the gifts they had brought into the house, and they bowed down before him to the ground. 27He asked them how they were, and then he said, "How is your aged father you told me about? Is he still living?" Ge 37:7,10; Mt 2:11

28They replied, "Your servant our father is still alive and well." And they bowed low to pay him honor. Ge 37:7

29As he looked about and saw his brother Benjamin, his own mother's son, he asked, "Is this your youngest brother, the one you told me about?" And he said, "God be gracious to you, my son." 30Deeply moved at the sight of his brother, Joseph hurried out and looked for a place to weep. He went into his private room and wept there.

31After he had washed his face, he came out and, controlling himself, said, "Serve the food."

32They served him by himself, the brothers by themselves, and the Egyptians who ate with him by themselves, because Egyptians could not eat with Hebrews, for that is detestable to Egyptians. 33The men had been seated before him in the order of their ages, from the firstborn to the youngest; and they looked at each other in astonishment. 34When portions were served to them from Joseph's table, Benjamin's portion was five times as much as anyone else's. So they feasted and drank freely with him. Ge 37:3; 45:22; 46:34

A Silver Cup in a Sack

44 Now Joseph gave these instructions to the steward of his house: "Fill the men's sacks with as much food as they can carry, and put each man's silver in the mouth of his sack. 2Then put my cup, the silver one, in the mouth of the youngest one's sack, along with the silver for his grain." And he did as Joseph said. Ge 42:25

3As morning dawned, the men were sent on their way with their donkeys. 4They had not gone far from the city when Joseph said to his steward, "Go after those men at once, and when you catch up with them, say to them, 'Why have you repaid good with evil? 5Isn't this the cup my master drinks from and also uses for divination? This is a wicked thing you have done.'" Ge 30:27; Ps 35:12

6When he caught up with them, he repeated these words to them. 7But they said to him, "Why does my lord say such things? Far be it from your servants to do anything like that! 8We even brought back to you from the land of Canaan the silver we found inside the mouths of our sacks. So why would we steal silver or gold from your master's house? 9If any of your servants is found to have it, he will die; and the rest of us will become my lord's slaves." Ge 31:32; 42:25; 43:21

10"Very well, then," he said, "let it be as you say. Whoever is found to have it will become my slave; the rest of you will be free from blame."

11Each of them quickly lowered his sack to the ground and opened it. 12Then the steward proceeded to search, beginning with the oldest and ending with the youngest. And the cup was found in Benjamin's sack. 13At this, they tore their clothes. Then they all loaded their donkeys and returned to the city. Ge 37:29; Nu 14:6

14Joseph was still in the house when Judah and his brothers came in, and they threw themselves to the ground before him. 15Joseph said to them, "What is this you have done? Don't you know that a man like me can find things out by divination?"

16"What can we say to my lord?" Judah replied. "What can we say? How can we prove our innocence? God has uncovered your servants' guilt. We are now my lord's slaves—we ourselves and the one who was found to have the cup." ver 9

17But Joseph said, "Far be it from me to do such a thing! Only the man who was found to have the cup will become my slave. The rest of you, go back to your father in peace."

18Then Judah went up to him and said: "Please, my lord, let your servant speak a word to my lord. Do not be angry with your servant, though you are equal to Pharaoh himself. 19My lord asked his servants, 'Do you have a father or a brother?' 20And we answered, 'We have an aged father, and there is a young son born to him in his old age. His brother is dead, and he is the only one of his mother's sons left, and his father loves him.'

21“Then you said to your servants, ‘Bring him
down to me so I can see him for myself.’ 22And we
said to my lord, ‘The boy cannot leave his father;
if he leaves him, his father will die.’ 23But you told
your servants, ‘Unless your youngest brother
comes down with you, you will not see my face
again.’ 24When we went back to your servant my
father, we told him what my lord had said.
25“Then our father said, ‘Go back and buy a
little more food.’ 26But we said, ‘We cannot go
down. Only if our youngest brother is with us will
we go. We cannot see the man’s face unless our
youngest brother is with us.’ Ge 43:2
27“Your servant my father said to us, ‘You know
that my wife bore me two sons. 28One of them
went away from me, and I said, “He has surely
been torn to pieces.” And I have not seen him
since. 29If you take this one from me too and harm
comes to him, you will bring my gray head down
to the grave[a] in misery.’ Ge 37:33; 42:38; 46:19
30“So now, if the boy is not with us when I go
back to your servant my father and if my father,
whose life is closely bound up with the boy’s life,
31sees that the boy isn’t there, he will die. Your
servants will bring the gray head of our father
down to the grave in sorrow. 32Your servant guaranteed the boy’s safety to my father. I said, ‘If I do
not bring him back to you, I will bear the blame
before you, my father, all my life!’ Ge 43:9; 1Sa 18:1
33“Now then, please let your servant remain
here as my lord’s slave in place of the boy, and let
the boy return with his brothers. 34How can I go
back to my father if the boy is not with me? No!
Do not let me see the misery that would come
upon my father.” Jn 15:13

Joseph Makes Himself Known

45 Then Joseph could no longer control himself before all his attendants, and he cried
out, “Have everyone leave my presence!” So there
was no one with Joseph when he made himself
known to his brothers. 2And he wept so loudly
that the Egyptians heard him, and Pharaoh’s
household heard about it. Ge 29:11
3Joseph said to his brothers, “I am Joseph! Is my
father still living?” But his brothers were not able
to answer him, because they were terrified at his
presence. Ac 7:13
4Then Joseph said to his brothers, “Come close
to me.” When they had done so, he said, “I am
your brother Joseph, the one you sold into Egypt!
5And now, do not be distressed and do not be
angry with yourselves for selling me here, because
it was to save lives that God sent me ahead of you.
6For two years now there has been famine in the
land, and for the next five years there will not be
plowing and reaping. 7But God sent me ahead of
you to preserve for you a remnant on earth and to
save your lives by a great deliverance.[b] Ge 37:28
8“So then, it was not you who sent me here, but
God. He made me father to Pharaoh, lord of his
entire household and ruler of all Egypt. 9Now hurry back to my father and say to him, ‘This is what
your son Joseph says: God has made me lord of all
Egypt. Come down to me; don’t delay. 10You shall
live in the region of Goshen and be near me—you,
your children and grandchildren, your flocks and
herds, and all you have. 11I will provide for you
there, because five years of famine are still to
come. Otherwise you and your household and all
who belong to you will become destitute.’
12“You can see for yourselves, and so can my
brother Benjamin, that it is really I who am speaking to you. 13Tell my father about all the honor
accorded me in Egypt and about everything you
have seen. And bring my father down here
quickly.” Ac 7:14
14Then he threw his arms around his brother
Benjamin and wept, and Benjamin embraced him,
weeping. 15And he kissed all his brothers and wept
over them. Afterward his brothers talked with him.
16When the news reached Pharaoh’s palace that
Joseph’s brothers had come, Pharaoh and all his
officials were pleased. 17Pharaoh said to Joseph,
“Tell your brothers, ‘Do this: Load your animals
and return to the land of Canaan, 18and bring your
father and your families back to me. I will give you
the best of the land of Egypt and you can enjoy the
fat of the land.’ Ge 27:28; 46:34; 47:6,11,27
19“You are also directed to tell them, ‘Do this:
Take some carts from Egypt for your children and
your wives, and get your father and come. 20Never
mind about your belongings, because the best of
all Egypt will be yours.’ ” Ge 46:5
21So the sons of Israel did this. Joseph gave
them carts, as Pharaoh had commanded, and he
also gave them provisions for their journey. 22To
each of them he gave new clothing, but to Benjamin he gave three hundred shekels[c] of silver and
five sets of clothes. 23And this is what he sent to his
father: ten donkeys loaded with the best things of

LIVING  **INSIGHT**

Nothing, absolutely nothing, on this earth is more important to us when the chips are down than the members of our family. Do everything possible to cultivate those relationships.

(See Genesis 45:1.)

[a] 29 Hebrew *Sheol*; also in verse 31
[b] 7 Or *save you as a great band of survivors*
[c] 22 That is, about 7 1/2 pounds (about 3.5 kilograms)

Egypt, and ten female donkeys loaded with grain and bread and other provisions for his journey. 24Then he sent his brothers away, and as they were leaving he said to them, "Don't quarrel on the way!" Ge 42:21-22

25So they went up out of Egypt and came to their father Jacob in the land of Canaan. 26They told him, "Joseph is still alive! In fact, he is ruler of all Egypt." Jacob was stunned; he did not believe them. 27But when they told him everything Joseph had said to them, and when he saw the carts Joseph had sent to carry him back, the spirit of their father Jacob revived. 28And Israel said, "I'm convinced! My son Joseph is still alive. I will go and see him before I die." ver 19; Ge 44:28

Jacob Goes to Egypt

46 So Israel set out with all that was his, and when he reached Beersheba, he offered sacrifices to the God of his father Isaac. Ge 31:42

2And God spoke to Israel in a vision at night and said, "Jacob! Jacob!" Ge 15:1; Job 33:14-15

"Here I am," he replied. Ge 22:1

3"I am God, the God of your father," he said. "Do not be afraid to go down to Egypt, for I will make you into a great nation there. 4I will go down to Egypt with you, and I will surely bring you back again. And Joseph's own hand will close your eyes." Ge 12:2; 50:1,24

5Then Jacob left Beersheba, and Israel's sons took their father Jacob and their children and their wives in the carts that Pharaoh had sent to transport him. 6They also took with them their livestock and the possessions they had acquired in Canaan, and Jacob and all his offspring went to Egypt. 7He took with him to Egypt his sons and grandsons and his daughters and granddaughters—all his offspring. Dt 26:5; Jos 24:4

8These are the names of the sons of Israel (Jacob and his descendants) who went to Egypt: Ex 1:1

Reuben the firstborn of Jacob.

9The sons of Reuben: 1Ch 5:3
Hanoch, Pallu, Hezron and Carmi.

10The sons of Simeon: Ge 29:33
Jemuel, Jamin, Ohad, Jakin, Zohar and Shaul the son of a Canaanite woman.

11The sons of Levi: Ge 29:34
Gershon, Kohath and Merari.

12The sons of Judah: Ge 29:35
Er, Onan, Shelah, Perez and Zerah (but Er and Onan had died in the land of Canaan).
The sons of Perez: 1Ch 2:5
Hezron and Hamul.

13The sons of Issachar: Ge 30:18
Tola, Puah,[a] Jashub[b] and Shimron.

14The sons of Zebulun: Ge 30:20
Sered, Elon and Jahleel.

15These were the sons Leah bore to Jacob in Paddan Aram,[c] besides his daughter Dinah. These sons and daughters of his were thirty-three in all.

16The sons of Gad: Ge 30:11
Zephon,[d] Haggi, Shuni, Ezbon, Eri, Arodi and Areli. Nu 26:15

17The sons of Asher: Ge 30:13
Imnah, Ishvah, Ishvi and Beriah.
Their sister was Serah.
The sons of Beriah:
Heber and Malkiel.

18These were the children born to Jacob by Zilpah, whom Laban had given to his daughter Leah—sixteen in all.

19The sons of Jacob's wife Rachel:
Joseph and Benjamin. 20In Egypt, Manasseh and Ephraim were born to Joseph by Asenath daughter of Potiphera, priest of On.[e] Ge 41:51-52; 44:27

21The sons of Benjamin: 1Ch 7:6-12
Bela, Beker, Ashbel, Gera, Naaman, Ehi, Rosh, Muppim, Huppim and Ard.

22These were the sons of Rachel who were born to Jacob—fourteen in all.

23The son of Dan:
Hushim.

24The sons of Naphtali:
Jahziel, Guni, Jezer and Shillem.

25These were the sons born to Jacob by Bilhah, whom Laban had given to his daughter Rachel—seven in all. Ge 29:29; 30:8

26All those who went to Egypt with Jacob—those who were his direct descendants, not counting his sons' wives—numbered sixty-six persons. 27With the two sons[f] who had been born to Joseph in Egypt, the members of Jacob's family, which went to Egypt, were seventy[g] in all.

28Now Jacob sent Judah ahead of him to Joseph to get directions to Goshen. When they arrived in the region of Goshen, 29Joseph had his chariot made ready and went to Goshen to meet his father Israel. As soon as Joseph appeared before him, he threw his arms around his father[h] and wept for a long time. Ge 45:14-15

30Israel said to Joseph, "Now I am ready to die,

[a] 13 Samaritan Pentateuch and Syriac (see also 1 Chron. 7:1); Masoretic Text *Puvah*
[b] 13 Samaritan Pentateuch and some Septuagint manuscripts (see also Num. 26:24 and 1 Chron. 7:1); Masoretic Text *Iob*
[c] 15 That is, Northwest Mesopotamia
[d] 16 Samaritan Pentateuch and Septuagint (see also Num. 26:15); Masoretic Text *Ziphion*
[e] 20 That is, Heliopolis
[f] 27 Hebrew; Septuagint *the nine children*
[g] 27 Hebrew (see also Exodus 1:5 and footnote); Septuagint (see also Acts 7:14) *seventy-five*
[h] 29 Hebrew *around him*

since I have seen for myself that you are still alive."

31 Then Joseph said to his brothers and to his father's household, "I will go up and speak to Pharaoh and will say to him, 'My brothers and my father's household, who were living in the land of Canaan, have come to me. 32 The men are shepherds; they tend livestock, and they have brought along their flocks and herds and everything they own.' 33 When Pharaoh calls you in and asks, 'What is your occupation?' 34 you should answer, 'Your servants have tended livestock from our boyhood on, just as our fathers did.' Then you will be allowed to settle in the region of Goshen, for all shepherds are detestable to the Egyptians."

47 Joseph went and told Pharaoh, "My father and brothers, with their flocks and herds and everything they own, have come from the land of Canaan and are now in Goshen." 2 He chose five of his brothers and presented them before Pharaoh. Ge 46:31

3 Pharaoh asked the brothers, "What is your occupation?" Ge 46:33

"Your servants are shepherds," they replied to Pharaoh, "just as our fathers were." 4 They also said to him, "We have come to live here awhile, because the famine is severe in Canaan and your servants' flocks have no pasture. So now, please let your servants settle in Goshen." Ge 46:34

5 Pharaoh said to Joseph, "Your father and your brothers have come to you, 6 and the land of Egypt is before you; settle your father and your brothers in the best part of the land. Let them live in Goshen. And if you know of any among them with special ability, put them in charge of my own livestock." Ge 45:18; Ex 18:21,25

7 Then Joseph brought his father Jacob in and presented him before Pharaoh. After Jacob blessed[a] Pharaoh, 8 Pharaoh asked him, "How old are you?"

9 And Jacob said to Pharaoh, "The years of my pilgrimage are a hundred and thirty. My years have been few and difficult, and they do not equal the years of the pilgrimage of my fathers." 10 Then Jacob blessed[b] Pharaoh and went out from his presence. ver 7; Ge 25:7; 35:28

11 So Joseph settled his father and his brothers in Egypt and gave them property in the best part of the land, the district of Rameses, as Pharaoh directed. 12 Joseph also provided his father and his brothers and all his father's household with food, according to the number of their children.

Joseph and the Famine

13 There was no food, however, in the whole region because the famine was severe; both Egypt and Canaan wasted away because of the famine. 14 Joseph collected all the money that was to be found in Egypt and Canaan in payment for the grain they were buying, and he brought it to Pharaoh's palace. 15 When the money of the people of Egypt and Canaan was gone, all Egypt came to Joseph and said, "Give us food. Why should we die before your eyes? Our money is used up."

16 "Then bring your livestock," said Joseph. "I will sell you food in exchange for your livestock, since your money is gone." 17 So they brought their livestock to Joseph, and he gave them food in exchange for their horses, their sheep and goats, their cattle and donkeys. And he brought them through that year with food in exchange for all their livestock. Ex 14:9

18 When that year was over, they came to him the following year and said, "We cannot hide from our lord the fact that since our money is gone and our livestock belongs to you, there is nothing left for our lord except our bodies and our land. 19 Why should we perish before your eyes—we and our land as well? Buy us and our land in exchange for food, and we with our land will be in bondage to Pharaoh. Give us seed so that we may live and not die, and that the land may not become desolate." Ge 42:2

20 So Joseph bought all the land in Egypt for Pharaoh. The Egyptians, one and all, sold their fields, because the famine was too severe for them. The land became Pharaoh's, 21 and Joseph reduced the people to servitude,[c] from one end of Egypt to the other. 22 However, he did not buy the land of the priests, because they received a regular allotment from Pharaoh and had food enough from the allotment Pharaoh gave them. That is why they did not sell their land. Dt 14:28-29; Ezr 7:24

23 Joseph said to the people, "Now that I have bought you and your land today for Pharaoh, here is seed for you so you can plant the ground. 24 But when the crop comes in, give a fifth of it to Pharaoh. The other four-fifths you may keep as seed for the fields and as food for yourselves and your households and your children." Ge 41:34

25 "You have saved our lives," they said. "May we find favor in the eyes of our lord; we will be in bondage to Pharaoh." Ge 32:5

26 So Joseph established it as a law concerning land in Egypt—still in force today—that a fifth of the produce belongs to Pharaoh. It was only the land of the priests that did not become Pharaoh's.

27 Now the Israelites settled in Egypt in the region of Goshen. They acquired property there and were fruitful and increased greatly in number.

28 Jacob lived in Egypt seventeen years, and the years of his life were a hundred and forty-seven. 29 When the time drew near for Israel to die, he

[a] 7 Or *greeted* [b] 10 Or *said farewell to* [c] 21 Samaritan Pentateuch and Septuagint (see also Vulgate); Masoretic Text *and he moved the people into the cities*

called for his son Joseph and said to him, "If I have found favor in your eyes, put your hand under my thigh and promise that you will show me kindness and faithfulness. Do not bury me in Egypt, 30but when I rest with my fathers, carry me out of Egypt and bury me where they are buried." Ge 49:29-32

"I will do as you say," he said.

31"Swear to me," he said. Then Joseph swore to him, and Israel worshiped as he leaned on the top of his staff.[a] Heb 11:21

Manasseh and Ephraim

48 Some time later Joseph was told, "Your father is ill." So he took his two sons Manasseh and Ephraim along with him. 2When Jacob was told, "Your son Joseph has come to you," Israel rallied his strength and sat up on the bed.

3Jacob said to Joseph, "God Almighty[b] appeared to me at Luz in the land of Canaan, and there he blessed me 4and said to me, 'I am going to make you fruitful and will increase your numbers. I will make you a community of peoples, and I will give this land as an everlasting possession to your descendants after you.' Ge 28:13,19; 35:9-12

5"Now then, your two sons born to you in Egypt before I came to you here will be reckoned as mine; Ephraim and Manasseh will be mine, just as Reuben and Simeon are mine. 6Any children born to you after them will be yours; in the territory they inherit they will be reckoned under the names of their brothers. 7As I was returning from Paddan,[c] to my sorrow Rachel died in the land of Canaan while we were still on the way, a little distance from Ephrath. So I buried her there beside the road to Ephrath" (that is, Bethlehem).

8When Israel saw the sons of Joseph, he asked, "Who are these?"

9"They are the sons God has given me here," Joseph said to his father. Ge 33:5

Then Israel said, "Bring them to me so I may bless them." Ge 27:4

10Now Israel's eyes were failing because of old age, and he could hardly see. So Joseph brought his sons close to him, and his father kissed them and embraced them. Ge 27:1,27

11Israel said to Joseph, "I never expected to see your face again, and now God has allowed me to see your children too."

12Then Joseph removed them from Israel's knees and bowed down with his face to the ground. 13And Joseph took both of them, Ephraim on his right toward Israel's left hand and Manasseh on his left toward Israel's right hand, and brought them close to him. 14But Israel reached out his right hand and put it on Ephraim's head, though he was the younger, and crossing his arms, he put his left hand on Manasseh's head, even though Manasseh was the firstborn. Ge 41:51

15Then he blessed Joseph and said, Ge 17:1

"May the God before whom my fathers
Abraham and Isaac walked,
the God who has been my shepherd Ge 49:24
all my life to this day,
16the Angel who has delivered me from all harm
—may he bless these boys. Heb 11:21
May they be called by my name
and the names of my fathers Abraham and
Isaac, Ge 28:13
and may they increase greatly
upon the earth."

17When Joseph saw his father placing his right hand on Ephraim's head he was displeased; so he took hold of his father's hand to move it from Ephraim's head to Manasseh's head. 18Joseph said to him, "No, my father, this one is the firstborn; put your right hand on his head." ver 14; Ge 25:23

19But his father refused and said, "I know, my son, I know. He too will become a people, and he too will become great. Nevertheless, his younger brother will be greater than he, and his descendants will become a group of nations." 20He blessed them that day and said,

"In your[d] name will Israel pronounce this
blessing:
'May God make you like Ephraim and
Manasseh.' " Nu 2:20; Ru 4:11

So he put Ephraim ahead of Manasseh.

21Then Israel said to Joseph, "I am about to die, but God will be with you[e] and take you[e] back to the land of your[e] fathers. 22And to you, as one who is over your brothers, I give the ridge of land[f] I took from the Amorites with my sword and my bow." Jn 4:5; Ge 26:3; 28:13

Jacob Blesses His Sons

49 Then Jacob called for his sons and said: "Gather around so I can tell you what will happen to you in days to come. Nu 24:14

2"Assemble and listen, sons of Jacob;
listen to your father Israel.

3"Reuben, you are my firstborn, Ge 29:32
my might, the first sign of my strength,
excelling in honor, excelling in power.
4Turbulent as the waters, you will no longer
excel,
for you went up onto your father's bed,
onto my couch and defiled it. Ge 35:22; Dt 27:20

5"Simeon and Levi are brothers—

[a] 31 Or *Israel bowed down at the head of his bed* [b] 3 Hebrew *El-Shaddai* [c] 7 That is, Northwest Mesopotamia
[d] 20 The Hebrew is singular. [e] 21 The Hebrew is plural. [f] 22 Or *And to you I give one portion more than to your brothers — the portion*

their swords[a] are weapons of violence.
6 Let me not enter their council,
let me not join their assembly, Pr 1:15; Eph 5:11
for they have killed men in their anger Ge 34:26
and hamstrung oxen as they pleased.
7 Cursed be their anger, so fierce,
and their fury, so cruel!
I will scatter them in Jacob
and disperse them in Israel. Jos 19:1,9

8 "Judah,[b] your brothers will praise you;
your hand will be on the neck of your
enemies;
your father's sons will bow down to you.
9 You are a lion's cub, O Judah; Nu 24:9
you return from the prey, my son.
Like a lion he crouches and lies down,
like a lioness—who dares to rouse him?
10 The scepter will not depart from Judah,
nor the ruler's staff from between his feet,
until he comes to whom it belongs[c]
and the obedience of the nations is his.
11 He will tether his donkey to a vine,
his colt to the choicest branch;
he will wash his garments in wine,
his robes in the blood of grapes.
12 His eyes will be darker than wine,
his teeth whiter than milk.[d]

13 "Zebulun will live by the seashore Dt 33:18-19
and become a haven for ships;
his border will extend toward Sidon.

14 "Issachar is a rawboned[e] donkey
lying down between two saddlebags.[f]
15 When he sees how good is his resting place
and how pleasant is his land,
he will bend his shoulder to the burden
and submit to forced labor.

16 "Dan[g] will provide justice for his people
as one of the tribes of Israel.
17 Dan will be a serpent by the roadside, Jdg 18:27
a viper along the path,
that bites the horse's heels
so that its rider tumbles backward.

18 "I look for your deliverance, O LORD.

19 "Gad[h] will be attacked by a band of raiders,
but he will attack them at their heels.

20 "Asher's food will be rich; Dt 33:24
he will provide delicacies fit for a king.

21 "Naphtali is a doe set free Dt 33:23
that bears beautiful fawns.[i]

22 "Joseph is a fruitful vine, Dt 33:13-17
a fruitful vine near a spring,
whose branches climb over a wall.[j]
23 With bitterness archers attacked him;
they shot at him with hostility.
24 But his bow remained steady,
his strong arms stayed[k] limber, Ps 18:34
because of the hand of the Mighty One of
Jacob, Ps 132:2,5; Isa 1:24
because of the Shepherd, the Rock of Israel,
25 because of your father's God, who helps you,
because of the Almighty,[l] who blesses you
with blessings of the heavens above,
blessings of the deep that lies below,
blessings of the breast and womb.
26 Your father's blessings are greater
than the blessings of the ancient mountains,
than[m] the bounty of the age-old hills.
Let all these rest on the head of Joseph,
on the brow of the prince among[n] his
brothers. Dt 33:15-16

27 "Benjamin is a ravenous wolf;
in the morning he devours the prey,
in the evening he divides the plunder."

28 All these are the twelve tribes of Israel, and
this is what their father said to them when he
blessed them, giving each the blessing appropriate
to him. Dt 33:1-29

The Death of Jacob

29 Then he gave them these instructions: "I am
about to be gathered to my people. Bury me with
my fathers in the cave in the field of Ephron the
Hittite, 30 the cave in the field of Machpelah, near
Mamre in Canaan, which Abraham bought as a
burial place from Ephron the Hittite, along with
the field. 31 There Abraham and his wife Sarah were
buried, there Isaac and his wife Rebekah were buried, and there I buried Leah. 32 The field and the
cave in it were bought from the Hittites.[o]"
33 When Jacob had finished giving instructions
to his sons, he drew his feet up into the bed,
breathed his last and was gathered to his people.
50 Joseph threw himself upon his father and
wept over him and kissed him. 2 Then Joseph directed the physicians in his service to em-
balm his father Israel. So the physicians embalmed
him, 3 taking a full forty days, for that was the

[a] 5 The meaning of the Hebrew for this word is uncertain. [b] 8 *Judah* sounds like and may be derived from the Hebrew for *praise.* [c] 10 Or *until Shiloh comes*; or *until he comes to whom tribute belongs* [d] 12 Or *will be dull from wine, / his teeth white from milk* [e] 14 Or *strong* [f] 14 Or *campfires* [g] 16 *Dan* here means *he provides justice.* [h] 19 *Gad* can mean *attack* and *band of raiders.* [i] 21 Or *free; / he utters beautiful words* [j] 22 Or *Joseph is a wild colt, / a wild colt near a spring, / a wild donkey on a terraced hill* [k] 23,24 Or *archers will attack . . . will shoot . . . will remain . . . will stay* [l] 25 Hebrew *Shaddai* [m] 26 Or *of my progenitors, / as great as* [n] 26 Or *the one separated from* [o] 32 Or *the sons of Heth*

time required for embalming. And the Egyptians
mourned for him seventy days. Ge 46:4; 2Ch 16:14
4When the days of mourning had passed, Joseph said to Pharaoh's court, "If I have found
favor in your eyes, speak to Pharaoh for me. Tell
him, 5'My father made me swear an oath and said,
"I am about to die; bury me in the tomb I dug for
myself in the land of Canaan." Now let me go up
and bury my father; then I will return.'" Ge 47:31
6Pharaoh said, "Go up and bury your father, as
he made you swear to do."
7So Joseph went up to bury his father. All Pharaoh's officials accompanied him—the dignitaries
of his court and all the dignitaries of Egypt—
8besides all the members of Joseph's household
and his brothers and those belonging to his father's household. Only their children and their
flocks and herds were left in Goshen. 9Chariots
and horsemen[a] also went up with him. It was a
very large company.
10When they reached the threshing floor of
Atad, near the Jordan, they lamented loudly and
bitterly; and there Joseph observed a seven-day
period of mourning for his father. 11When the
Canaanites who lived there saw the mourning at
the threshing floor of Atad, they said, "The Egyptians are holding a solemn ceremony of mourning." That is why that place near the Jordan is
called Abel Mizraim.[b] 1Sa 31:13; Job 2:13; Ac 8:2
12So Jacob's sons did as he had commanded
them: 13They carried him to the land of Canaan
and buried him in the cave in the field of Machpelah, near Mamre, which Abraham had bought as a
burial place from Ephron the Hittite, along with
the field. 14After burying his father, Joseph returned to Egypt, together with his brothers and all
the others who had gone with him to bury his
father. Ge 23:20; Ac 7:16

Joseph Reassures His Brothers

15When Joseph's brothers saw that their father
was dead, they said, "What if Joseph holds a
grudge against us and pays us back for all the
wrongs we did to him?" 16So they sent word to
Joseph, saying, "Your father left these instructions
before he died: 17'This is what you are to say to
Joseph: I ask you to forgive your brothers the sins
and the wrongs they committed in treating you so
badly.' Now please forgive the sins of the servants
of the God of your father." When their message
came to him, Joseph wept. Ge 37:28
18His brothers then came and threw themselves
down before him. "We are your slaves," they said.
19But Joseph said to them, "Don't be afraid.
Am I in the place of God? 20You intended to harm
me, but God intended it for good to accomplish
what is now being done, the saving of many lives.
21So then, don't be afraid. I will provide for you
and your children." And he reassured them and
spoke kindly to them. Ro 8:28; 12:19; Ge 45:5

LIVING  **INSIGHT**

It is not the circumstance itself but our reaction to it that makes any event a tragedy or a triumph. Instead of nursing old, bitter wounds, Joseph freely extended grace from an open hand.

(See Genesis 50:20.)

The Death of Joseph

22Joseph stayed in Egypt, along with all his father's family. He lived a hundred and ten years
23and saw the third generation of Ephraim's children. Also the children of Makir son of Manasseh
were placed at birth on Joseph's knees.[c]
24Then Joseph said to his brothers, "I am about
to die. But God will surely come to your aid and
take you up out of this land to the land he promised on oath to Abraham, Isaac and Jacob." 25And
Joseph made the sons of Israel swear an oath and
said, "God will surely come to your aid, and then
you must carry my bones up from this place."
26So Joseph died at the age of a hundred and
ten. And after they embalmed him, he was placed
in a coffin in Egypt.

a9 Or *charioteers* b11 *Abel Mizraim* means *mourning of the Egyptians.* c23 That is, were counted as his

EXODUS

As the book of Genesis ended, the Israelites were in Egypt. A famine in Canaan had forced the journey, and Joseph's assistance had made it possible for them to live there. The book of Exodus records the situation that arose after Joseph's death—as the Israelites became victims of bondage rather than visitors in Egypt. This book is the account of how God miraculously delivered His people and then began to train them in a walk of faith. He provided a set of written instructions for them to follow and a place of meeting for worship. The book begins with a "groan" . . . and ends in glory—the incomparable glory of the Lord!

WRITER: *Moses*

DATE: *c.1440 B.C.*

KEY VERSES: *12:40-42*

KEY PHRASE: *"Brought (or bring) out"*

TIME LINE — 2200BC 2100 2000 1900 1800 1700 1600 1500 1400

Moses' birth (c.1526 B.C.)

The plagues; The Passover (c.1446 B.C.)

The exodus (c.1446 B.C.)

Desert wanderings (c.1446-1406 B.C.)

The Ten Commandments (c.1445 B.C.)

Book of Exodus written (c.1440 B.C.)

Moses dies; Joshua becomes leader (c.1406 B.C.)

Israelites enter Canaan (c.1406 B.C.)

The Story of a Miraculous Freedom

GENESIS — 350 YEARS — GROAN OF THE ISRAELITES

BONDAGE	DELIVERANCE	JOURNEY	LAW	TABERNACLE
Israelites became numerous	Blood, Frogs, Gnats, Flies, Livestock, Boils, Hail, Locusts, Darkness, Death	Cloud and fire	Moral	Outer court 150′ x 75′
New pharaoh	Passover	Red Sea	Civil	Inner court 45′ x 15′
Plan to destroy Israelites	Exodus	Grumbling	Social	
Moses				
CHAPTERS 1–2	*CHAPTERS 3–12*	*CHAPTERS 13–18*	*CHAPTERS 19–24*	*CHAPTERS 25–40*

GLORY OF THE LORD

	BONDAGE / DELIVERANCE	JOURNEY	LAW / TABERNACLE
PLACE	**Egypt**	**En route**	**Mount Sinai**
TIME	**430 years**	**3 months**	**1 year**
THEME	**Suffering and liberation of people of God**	**Guidance of God**	**Worship of God**
CHRIST	**Passover Lamb**	**Sacrificial offerings and furniture**	

There's nothing better than being completely free. Free from the bondage of things that ensnare us, trip us up and trap us. The going word of our day is "liberation." It is a great, pulsating theme in the human heart. "I want to be free" can be heard from every continent.

When you look at a world map of the 1960s and then compare it to one that was printed this year, you'll see countries now that weren't even in existence then. Why? Because countries are crying for liberation from the bondage of control over them. There is literally nothing people won't do to get the freedom they long for. Deep down in the heart of mankind is the gnawing, clawing, unceasing hunger to be free—free at last.

It stands to reason that in God's compiling His list of inspired books of Scripture, He would include in the list a book on freedom. That's the book of Exodus. It's the book of deliverance. A book that says to God's people, "You are free to enter the land I've promised you. You are no longer under bondage."

The name, "Exodus," means "departure; going out, or going forth." When you refer to an exodus, you speak of leaving, getting away from something, departing.

The background of this word is Greek. It's from the *Septuagint* (the translation of the Hebrew Old Testament into Greek). The Greeks chose the word because they believed it was the major theme of the book. When the Hebrews were delivered from the tyranny of Egyptian rule, they experienced an "exodus."

The Burdens of Bondage

Between the end of the book of Genesis and the beginning of the time of the exodus, 350 years have passed. Not only did Joseph die, but his sons died and their sons died, and there were new generations that followed. Furthermore, the long line of the pharaohs in Egypt passed down from one to the next to the next—until finally we have a completely new scene in the land of Goshen.

When you open the book of Exodus, you encounter a setting potentially very threatening to the Egyptians. There are at least two important reasons for concern:

First, *the Israelites had become numerous*: "Now Joseph and all his brothers and all that generation died, but the Israelites were fruitful and multiplied greatly and became exceedingly numerous, so that the land was filled with them" (1:6–7).

The Israelites were a very prolific people, and they had grown to 600,000 men—not counting women and children—totaling approximately two million in number in Goshen. Not only were they large in number, but they also were viewed as a threat to the Egyptians. So one thing to remember as Exodus begins is that we have a large number of Israelites living under a foreign flag. In fact, some believe that the Israelites were approaching the time when they would outnumber the Egyptians. God reminded those Israelites of the promise He had made to their forefather Abraham: "I will make you into a great nation . . . and all peoples on earth will be blessed through you" (Genesis 12:2–3). Understand, the pharaoh didn't know that, but the people of God knew it as they began to grow in number.

The second fact to remember is that *a new pharaoh had come on the scene*: "Then a new king, who did not know about Joseph, came to power in Egypt" (1:8).

The Israelites found they were serving a pharaoh who didn't care about their welfare. In fact, Pharaoh viewed them as a potential threat. Because he feared that the Israelites had become much too numerous, he set up a plan of extermination, or at least partial extermination. The king of Egypt told the Hebrew midwives to kill every boy who was born. Now, even though we're thousands of years removed from that time, there is not a mother alive today who can't identify with the pressure of that extermination plan. The Hebrew midwives did not cooperate—at least initially they didn't, which prompted the ire of Pharaoh, and his plan became increasingly intense. He was determined to stamp out those Hebrew boys.

The first major section of the book of Exodus, chapters 1–2, focuses on *bondage*. The scene is set for this great drama. There's a plan to exterminate part of the Hebrew people. There's a pharaoh who didn't know about Joseph and didn't care for the people of God. And there's a large number of Hebrews who pose a threat to the nation of Egypt. As this is going on, all of a sudden, as the Spirit of God can do, He snaps a zoom lens on the camera and comes right down into the tribe of Levi and brings into view a couple by the name of Amram (the dad) and Jochebed (the mom). They have a little baby boy, Moses. Why would the Spirit of God, in the movement of time covering so many years in the second book of the Bible, take time to focus in on one little family? The reason, of course, is to emphasize the birth and the preparation of the deliverer. Here was a man who would ultimately lead the people to freedom. The Spirit of God put His hand on an unknown couple, and He pulled from that life one little boy and prepared him in an incredible way.

The Hope of Deliverance

The man who was to deliver Israel from Egypt needed to know all about Egypt—and to make that happen, God got Moses right into the court of the king and then gave him a forty-year education in Egyptian culture free of charge. Pharaoh's daughter's adopted son was perfect for the job of liberator. And that's exactly what happened—in God's perfect timing. Although Moses was a Hebrew baby, he received all the privileges of an Egyptian prince. Although no one but God knew it, Moses was being prepared by God to deliver his people from their bondage.

In forty years of training he learned science, medicine, astronomy and mathematics. He learned the ingenious language of hieroglyphs—a fascinating pictorial language. He was mighty in word and deed, and quite bright . . . superior qualities for one who was to be the deliverer. Stay alert now, as the plot thickens. Even though Moses knew the role God had given him, he decided to take things into his own hands. When he saw an Egyptian taskmaster beating a Hebrew slave (one of Moses' people), Moses responded with violence and killed the Egyptian. Moses had decided to do God's will his own way—and that led him into the desert.

Like Moses, we have times in our lives when we try to do God's will *our* way. God gives us direction and we say, "Great! Get out of the way. I'll take care of it from here. If I need you, I'll whistle. Right now I'm gonna get it done on my own." When we rush ahead on our own, we may very well find ourselves in the same place as Moses . . . the desert.

After murdering the Egyptian and escaping to the Midian desert, Moses married a Hebrew woman, Zipporah, and worked for her father as a shepherd for forty years. At the end of that extended period of isolation and anonymity, we find a highly educated shepherd schooled in the courts of Pharaoh but now seasoned in the classroom of the desert. At the ripe age of eighty, Moses was, at last, ready to be used by God.

Exodus 3 begins the next major section, which is the story of deliverance. If the first section focused on bondage, the second (chapters 3–12) certainly has to do with *deliverance*.

As chapter 3 begins, Moses was in the desert, staring at the burning bush as God spoke to him: "So now, go. I am sending you to Pharaoh to bring my people the Israelites out of Egypt" (3:10).

Take note of the words "bring" and "out"; and remember the meaning of "exodus"—"bring out." The Lord had a message for Moses—a message that was to change his life. "Moses, you're going to lead an exodus. Through your leadership, Moses, My people will be free!"

Moses responded to this startling news with a profound, one-word response: "Mmmm-m-me?" The response of Moses is much like our initial response often is when the Lord calls us to do his work. God says, "You're the one." And we respond, "Who am I, that I should do that?" Do you realize how many of us are a Moses in the making? We may have an arsenal of responses and excuses: "I'm too young," or "I'm too old." Or, "I don't have a college degree," or "I've never been to seminary." Or "I simply cannot do it. You've got the wrong person." But God won't give up. He sees you not as who you are but as who you are to become.

Moses was arguing and resisting, but he finally gave in. Like Moses, we need to learn a simple lesson: Don't fight with the living God . . . He will win every time!

Moving from chapter 4 to chapter 12, we quickly pass over the ten plagues. Just picture what it must have been like as God marshaled a variety of forces against Pharaoh to let the people go. The Nile was turned to blood. There were frogs in the land. There were gnats everywhere. There were flies. There was a disease that killed the livestock. There were boils. There was hail. There were locusts. There was gross darkness that light could not penetrate. And finally, the angel of death. All of that took a devastating toll on Pharaoh and his leadership. At last, the people of Israel heard those long-awaited words, "Get out!" Pharaoh finally said to Moses and Aaron, "Up! Leave my people, you and the Israelites!" (12:31).

At the beginning of chapter 12 we find a record of the Passover. God told the Israelites how they could be protected from the final plague, the angel of death. The angel was to come and kill all of the firstborn males. Every home in Egypt would soon be struck with the death of their firstborn. In effect, God gave these instructions: "Now here's the way to miss it . . . sacrifice a spotless lamb. Take the blood, as you kill the lamb, and smear it on the side of your doors and above your door, and when that angel of death comes in the night, he will pass by your home. He'll overlook it—literally, pass over it." That night became a memorial for the Jews from generation to generation—the Biblical basis of *Passover*. In Exodus 12:40–42, the people of God left the land of Egypt in a mass exodus.

Joy on the Journey

Chapters 13–18 record the account of a journey. That's the third word to remember: first, *bondage*, next, *deliverance* . . . now, *journey*. God led the people out. They were going from Egypt to the Desert of Sinai as God miraculously led them every day:

> *By day the* L*ORD* *went ahead of them in a pillar of cloud to guide them on their way and by night in a pillar of fire to give them light, so that they could travel by day or night. Neither the pillar of cloud by day nor the pillar of fire by night left its place in front of the people (13:21–22).*

The pillar of cloud by day and the pillar of fire by night were always before the Hebrews. God never removed either. The cloud led them right out to the Red Sea (chapters 14–15)—with the Egyptians right behind them. Miraculously, the sea opened up. They walked through and got to the other side. Just as soon as the Egyptians entered the sea, the water rushed back over them. God proved Himself faithful.

The Israelites responded by praising God through song. It was a glorious moment in their pilgrimage, but it didn't last long. Not many days later the people began to grumble about their hunger. God heard their grumbling and provided manna. Three months passed, and they arrived at Sinai. Moses met with God on Mount Sinai, and God wrote His Word for Moses to record and bring to the people. For the first time in all of time, God actually wrote down His revelation. God put His truth in stone with His own finger.

Think of it! God gave Moses a written document—the Law. The Law simply told the people how holy God was, how sinful they were, and how there could be nothing but obedience if they intended to walk with Him. The Law spelled out God's standard, the stick by which people could measure their lives. In chapter 20 we find the Ten Commandments, followed in chapters 21–23 by laws expanding on and explaining the Ten Commandments.

This wandering and worshiping people needed a place to meet with God. For the next number of chapters, in fact, the last 16 chapters in Exodus, we read of plans for the building of the tabernacle. This was the beautiful Tent of Meeting where God would now meet with His people in the holiest of all places, that little inner sanctum behind the curtain where the high priest would come annually to offer the sacrificial blood to atone for the sins of the Hebrews (see Leviticus 16 for a detailed description of the Day of Atonement). The curtain was pulled back once a year, as the high priest walked in and poured out the sacrificial blood—in the place where the very holiness of God was said to dwell . . . on the mercy seat! In the last scene in the book, the glory of the Lord filled the tabernacle. Inside that place was the blinding, splendid, pure light of God—the God who would accompany the people on their journey, who would tent among them and lead them to the land of fulfilled promises.

Final Reflections

As I reflect on the book of Exodus, three thoughts stand out in my mind. First, *lasting freedom is a direct result of God's intervention.* Unless God intervenes, we will never know freedom. Second, *when God brings deliverance, He uses choice instruments in the process.* We should give God thanks for the people like Moses in our lives. Each of us has a few—those unique persons God uses to bring deliverance to us. Third, *freedom must be balanced with submission to God's authority.* When He delivers us, He does so in order that we may follow Him.

Although we may feel trapped in bondage, God is ready to deliver us. Our Savior waits with open hands, ready to part the seas, provide the manna and lead us across the desert to the promised land. The journey may not be easy, but the Lord promises to be with us every step of the way. Our Lord is a faithful deliverer. The freedom of the exodus can be experienced today, if we are willing to depend on Him and follow His plan. As the old gospel song puts it, "Trust and obey, for there's no other way . . ."

The Burden of Bondage — Chapter 1

The book of Exodus is a book of deliverance. The big question is—deliverance from what? Clearly, deliverance from bondage. This book tells us that the small band of Jacob's descendants who were brought to Egypt by Joseph were now a great and mighty nation. Over the course of four centuries the promise to Abraham of numerous descendants had come true in a big way. There were now over 600,000 men of Israel and quite probably a total of over two million Hebrews living in Egypt. The pharaoh of Egypt became fearful of the sheer numbers of the Hebrews and began seeking to subdue them by using them as slave labor. The threat and fear grew to such proportions that the Egyptians instituted a systematic execution of all newborn Israelite boys. As Exodus begins, the people of Israel were in the most severe bondage imaginable: They were being used as slaves, they were being abused and they were facing possible genocide.

The Israelites Oppressed

1 These are the names of the sons of Israel who went to Egypt with Jacob, each with his family: 2Reuben, Simeon, Levi and Judah; 3Issachar, Zebulun and Benjamin; 4Dan and Naphtali; Gad and Asher. 5The descendants of Jacob numbered seventy[a] in all; Joseph was already in Egypt.

6Now Joseph and all his brothers and all that generation died, 7but the Israelites were fruitful and multiplied greatly and became exceedingly numerous, so that the land was filled with them.

8Then a new king, who did not know about Joseph, came to power in Egypt. 9"Look," he said to his people, "the Israelites have become much too numerous for us. 10Come, we must deal shrewdly with them or they will become even more numerous and, if war breaks out, will join our enemies, fight against us and leave the country." Ps 105:24-25; Ac 7:17-19

11So they put slave masters over them to oppress them with forced labor, and they built Pithom and Rameses as store cities for Pharaoh. 12But the more they were oppressed, the more they multiplied and spread; so the Egyptians came to dread the Israelites 13and worked them ruthlessly. 14They made their lives bitter with hard labor in brick and mortar and with all kinds of work in the fields; in all their hard labor the Egyptians used them ruthlessly. Ex 3:7; 2:23; Nu 20:15

15The king of Egypt said to the Hebrew midwives, whose names were Shiphrah and Puah, 16"When you help the Hebrew women in childbirth and observe them on the delivery stool, if it is a boy, kill him; but if it is a girl, let her live." 17The midwives, however, feared God and did not do what the king of Egypt had told them to do; they let the boys live. 18Then the king of Egypt summoned the midwives and asked them, "Why have you done this? Why have you let the boys live?" ver 21; Pr 16:6

19The midwives answered Pharaoh, "Hebrew women are not like Egyptian women; they are vigorous and give birth before the midwives arrive."

20So God was kind to the midwives and the people increased and became even more numerous. 21And because the midwives feared God, he gave them families of their own. 1Sa 2:35

22Then Pharaoh gave this order to all his people: "Every boy that is born[b] you must throw into the Nile, but let every girl live." Ac 7:19

God's Hand of Deliverance — Chapters 2–12

God began his plan of deliverance with the birth of a little baby Jewish boy (does that sound at all familiar?). After an effort to protect her newborn child, Jochebed, Moses' mother, set him afloat in a basket in the Nile in hopes of sparing his life from the Egyptian executioners. In God's providence, not only was the baby spared but he was returned to his mother's arms to raise him until he was weaned. The baby Moses was reared in his own home during that time, and then he was turned over to the court of Egypt where he was to be reared as Pharaoh's grandson.

As a young man, Moses made the mistake of trying to hurry God's will in his own strength. The attempt failed and led to Moses running from Egypt as a fugitive. Moses spent forty years in the desert until he was called by God to return to Egypt when he was eighty years old. Moses, at God's leading, asked Pharaoh if the Israelites could go to the desert to worship. Because Pharaoh's heart was hard, the Egyptians faced a series of ten plagues, which devastated land, livestock, crops and finally the families of Egypt whose firstborn sons died. At long last, in the high point of the history of the Hebrews, the people were freed from bondage and relieved from the harsh grip of Pharaoh.

The Birth of Moses

2 Now a man of the house of Levi married a Levite woman, 2and she became pregnant and gave birth to a son. When she saw that he was a fine child, she hid him for three months. 3But when she could hide him no longer, she got a papyrus basket for him and coated it with tar and pitch. Then she placed the child in it and put it among the reeds along the bank of the Nile. 4His sister stood at a distance to see what would happen to him. Heb 11:23; Ex 15:20; 6:20

5Then Pharaoh's daughter went down to the Nile to bathe, and her attendants were walking along the river bank. She saw the basket among the reeds and sent her slave girl to get it. 6She opened it and saw the baby. He was crying, and she felt sorry for him. "This is one of the Hebrew babies," she said. Ex 7:15

[a]5 Masoretic Text (see also Gen. 46:27); Dead Sea Scrolls and Septuagint (see also Acts 7:14 and note at Gen. 46:27) *seventy-five*
[b]22 Masoretic Text; Samaritan Pentateuch, Septuagint and Targums *born to the Hebrews*

7Then his sister asked Pharaoh's daughter, "Shall I go and get one of the Hebrew women to nurse the baby for you?"

8"Yes, go," she answered. And the girl went and got the baby's mother. 9Pharaoh's daughter said to her, "Take this baby and nurse him for me, and I will pay you." So the woman took the baby and nursed him. 10When the child grew older, she took him to Pharaoh's daughter and he became her son. She named him Moses,[a] saying, "I drew him out of the water."

Moses Flees to Midian

11One day, after Moses had grown up, he went out to where his own people were and watched them at their hard labor. He saw an Egyptian beating a Hebrew, one of his own people. 12Glancing this way and that and seeing no one, he killed the Egyptian and hid him in the sand. 13The next day he went out and saw two Hebrews fighting. He asked the one in the wrong, "Why are you hitting your fellow Hebrew?" Ac 7:23; Heb 11:24-26

14The man said, "Who made you ruler and judge over us? Are you thinking of killing me as you killed the Egyptian?" Then Moses was afraid and thought, "What I did must have become known." Ac 7:27

15When Pharaoh heard of this, he tried to kill Moses, but Moses fled from Pharaoh and went to live in Midian, where he sat down by a well. 16Now a priest of Midian had seven daughters, and they came to draw water and fill the troughs to water their father's flock. 17Some shepherds came along and drove them away, but Moses got up and came to their rescue and watered their flock. Ex 3:1

18When the girls returned to Reuel their father, he asked them, "Why have you returned so early today?" Nu 10:29

19They answered, "An Egyptian rescued us from the shepherds. He even drew water for us and watered the flock."

20"And where is he?" he asked his daughters. "Why did you leave him? Invite him to have something to eat." Ge 31:54

21Moses agreed to stay with the man, who gave his daughter Zipporah to Moses in marriage. 22Zipporah gave birth to a son, and Moses named him Gershom,[b] saying, "I have become an alien in a foreign land." Ex 18:2; Heb 11:13

23During that long period, the king of Egypt died. The Israelites groaned in their slavery and cried out, and their cry for help because of their slavery went up to God. 24God heard their groaning and he remembered his covenant with Abraham, with Isaac and with Jacob. 25So God looked on the Israelites and was concerned about them.

Moses and the Burning Bush

3 Now Moses was tending the flock of Jethro his father-in-law, the priest of Midian, and he led the flock to the far side of the desert and came to Horeb, the mountain of God. 2There the angel of the LORD appeared to him in flames of fire from within a bush. Moses saw that though the bush was on fire it did not burn up. 3So Moses thought, "I will go over and see this strange sight—why the bush does not burn up." Dt 33:16

4When the LORD saw that he had gone over to look, God called to him from within the bush, "Moses! Moses!"

And Moses said, "Here I am." Ge 31:11

5"Do not come any closer," God said. "Take off your sandals, for the place where you are standing is holy ground." 6Then he said, "I am the God of your father, the God of Abraham, the God of Isaac and the God of Jacob." At this, Moses hid his face, because he was afraid to look at God. Ac 7:32-33

7The LORD said, "I have indeed seen the misery of my people in Egypt. I have heard them crying out because of their slave drivers, and I am concerned about their suffering. 8So I have come down to rescue them from the hand of the Egyptians and to bring them up out of that land into a good and spacious land, a land flowing with milk and honey—the home of the Canaanites, Hittites, Amorites, Perizzites, Hivites and Jebusites. 9And now the cry of the Israelites has reached me, and I have seen the way the Egyptians are oppressing them. 10So now, go. I am sending you to Pharaoh to bring my people the Israelites out of Egypt."

11But Moses said to God, "Who am I, that I should go to Pharaoh and bring the Israelites out of Egypt?" Ex 6:12,30; 1Sa 18:18

12And God said, "I will be with you. And this will be the sign to you that it is I who have sent you: When you have brought the people out of Egypt, you[c] will worship God on this mountain."

13Moses said to God, "Suppose I go to the Isra-

LIVING  **INSIGHT**

The Lord uses our "desert" experiences to peel away our masks so that we may discover who we really are. With our strengths and weaknesses vividly exposed, we are more prepared to stand humbly before God than we otherwise would. It is at this stage of nakedness that the Lord performs some of His best refining work in our lives.

(See Exodus 2:21–22.)

[a] 10 *Moses* sounds like the Hebrew for *draw out.*
[b] 22 *Gershom* sounds like the Hebrew for *an alien there.*
[c] 12 The Hebrew is plural.

MOSES

God's Man for a Crisis

"So now, go. I am sending you to Pharaoh to bring my people the Israelites out of Egypt."
—EXODUS 3:10

Moses' life, according to Acts 7, can be divided into three forty-year segments. The first forty years he spent in Egypt, where he was nurtured by his mother and taught in Egyptian schools. The second forty years he spent alone in the desert, where he was nurtured by solitude and taught by God. The third forty years he spent with the Hebrew people in the desert, where he was nurtured by trials, discouragements and tests and taught by the Law he had personally received from God.

Ponder for a moment, if you would, Moses' incredible birth. He was born in the darkest moment in Israel's history—the time of slavery in Egypt. But Moses' parents were people of faith. Commanded by the pharaoh to drown any male child that was born to them, they refused. Moses' mother Jochebed placed her newborn son in a waterproof basket and put it in the Nile River, right under the nose of the pharaoh's daughter. The princess took the baby and brought him up in the ways and customs of the Egyptians, giving Moses a free forty-year education that at the time was the best in the world. Josephus the historian tells us that Moses was being trained as the next pharaoh-elect!

One day Moses decided to go back to his roots—to pay a visit to his people. When he saw an Egyptian beating a Hebrew, he decided to take matters into his own hands. In the words of Scripture, "He killed the Egyptian and hid him in the sand" (Exodus 2:12). Moses fled to Midian where he took a job as a sheep herder for the next four decades.

This greatly gifted man turned out to be a failure. A murderer. A man with a criminal record. Because he ran ahead of God's plan, this man who might have been a ruler in Egypt spent forty years in a hot, dry, barren desert with a herd of bleating sheep. But do you know what? God had Moses right where he wanted him. An eighty-year old shepherd with a useless education? No!—a man who had been broken and was now ready to be used. In that unforgettable scene in Exodus 3, God spoke to Moses out of the burning bush: "I am sending you to Pharaoh to bring my people the Israelites out of Egypt" (3:10). Those were the last words Moses wanted to hear! But God wanted to use Moses, and He was going to—no matter what. And when muleheaded Moses complained about his inadequacy, God gave Moses all the assurance he needed: "I will be with you" (3:12). In effect God said, "Wait a minute Moses. You didn't get the plan. All you have to do is be at the right place at the right time and watch Me work. Simply prepare your heart and be sure you're walking in obedience with Me, and *I'll* deliver the Israelites out of Egypt."

After he left the site of the burning bush, Moses often looked to God for help. During the remaining forty years of his life, he was God's representative to His people on earth. He led the Hebrews out of Egypt. He trusted God to deliver His people as they stood on the shore of the Red Sea. He brought God's law to the people in the desert. He brought them, after another forty years, to the edge of the promised land. And even though God didn't allow him to enter Canaan, He blessed Moses in his death as one who had faithfully served the Lord through it all (Deuteronomy 34:5–12).

What a servant of God! As we consider his life, there are at least three truths we can apply to our lives. First, *the secret of fulfillment in life is involvement*. Moses never retired from serving people or learning God's Word. He stayed in touch with those things that are eternal. Second, *the secret of authenticity in life is humility*. Moses never became enthralled with his own track record. His humility made him believable and vulnerable. Third, *the secret of happiness in life is perspective*. Surely Moses faced many situations that could have led to despair. In those times he turned to the Lord and drew his strength from God's unlimited resources.

Dwight L. Moody summed up Moses' life in this memorable way. "He spent his first forty years thinking he was somebody. He spent his second forty years learning he was a nobody. He spent his third forty years discovering what God can do with a nobody."

elites and say to them, 'The God of your fathers
has sent me to you,' and they ask me, 'What is his
name?' Then what shall I tell them?"
[14]God said to Moses, "I AM WHO I AM.[a] This is
what you are to say to the Israelites: 'I AM has sent
me to you.'" Ex 6:2-3; Jn 8:58; Heb 13:8
[15]God also said to Moses, "Say to the Israelites,
'The LORD,[b] the God of your fathers—the God of
Abraham, the God of Isaac and the God of Jacob—has sent me to you.' This is my name forever, the name by which I am to be remembered
from generation to generation. Ps 135:13

LIVING  **INSIGHT**

The divine name "I AM" is a declaration of God's eternal and immutable self-existence. He is pure being. Nothing has brought or could bring Him into existence. Nor could anything ever cause Him to cease to be. He has always existed and will always exist because He is existence. There is no other attribute of God that better stands as a summation of His nature than this one.

(See Exodus 3:13–15.)

[16]"Go, assemble the elders of Israel and say to
them, 'The LORD, the God of your fathers—the
God of Abraham, Isaac and Jacob—appeared to
me and said: I have watched over you and have
seen what has been done to you in Egypt. [17]And I
have promised to bring you up out of your misery
in Egypt into the land of the Canaanites, Hittites,
Amorites, Perizzites, Hivites and Jebusites—a
land flowing with milk and honey.' Ge 15:16
[18]"The elders of Israel will listen to you. Then
you and the elders are to go to the king of Egypt
and say to him, 'The LORD, the God of the Hebrews, has met with us. Let us take a three-day
journey into the desert to offer sacrifices to the
LORD our God.' [19]But I know that the king of Egypt
will not let you go unless a mighty hand compels
him. [20]So I will stretch out my hand and strike the
Egyptians with all the wonders that I will perform
among them. After that, he will let you go.
[21]"And I will make the Egyptians favorably
disposed toward this people, so that when you
leave you will not go empty-handed. [22]Every
woman is to ask her neighbor and any woman
living in her house for articles of silver and gold
and for clothing, which you will put on your
sons and daughters. And so you will plunder the
Egyptians."

Signs for Moses

4 Moses answered, "What if they do not believe
me or listen to me and say, 'The LORD did not
appear to you'?" Ex 3:18
[2]Then the LORD said to him, "What is that in
your hand?"
"A staff," he replied. ver 17,20
[3]The LORD said, "Throw it on the ground."
Moses threw it on the ground and it became a
snake, and he ran from it. [4]Then the LORD said to
him, "Reach out your hand and take it by the tail."
So Moses reached out and took hold of the snake
and it turned back into a staff in his hand. [5]"This,"
said the LORD, "is so that they may believe that the
LORD, the God of their fathers—the God of Abraham, the God of Isaac and the God of Jacob—has
appeared to you." Ex 19:9
[6]Then the LORD said, "Put your hand inside
your cloak." So Moses put his hand into his cloak,
and when he took it out, it was leprous,[c] like
snow. Nu 12:10; 2Ki 5:1,27
[7]"Now put it back into your cloak," he said. So
Moses put his hand back into his cloak, and when
he took it out, it was restored, like the rest of his
flesh. Nu 12:13-15
[8]Then the LORD said, "If they do not believe you
or pay attention to the first miraculous sign, they
may believe the second. [9]But if they do not believe
these two signs or listen to you, take some water
from the Nile and pour it on the dry ground. The
water you take from the river will become blood
on the ground." Ex 7:17-21
[10]Moses said to the LORD, "O Lord, I have never
been eloquent, neither in the past nor since you
have spoken to your servant. I am slow of speech
and tongue." Ex 6:12; Jer 1:6
[11]The LORD said to him, "Who gave man his
mouth? Who makes him deaf or mute? Who gives
him sight or makes him blind? Is it not I, the LORD?
[12]Now go; I will help you speak and will teach you
what to say." Isa 50:4; Jer 1:9; Lk 12:12
[13]But Moses said, "O Lord, please send someone else to do it." Jnh 1:1-3
[14]Then the LORD's anger burned against Moses
and he said, "What about your brother, Aaron
the Levite? I know he can speak well. He is already on his way to meet you, and his heart will
be glad when he sees you. [15]You shall speak to
him and put words in his mouth; I will help
both of you speak and will teach you what to
do. [16]He will speak to the people for you, and
it will be as if he were your mouth and as if
you were God to him. [17]But take this staff in
your hand so you can perform miraculous signs
with it." Ex 7:1-2,9-21

[a]*14* Or *I WILL BE WHAT I WILL BE* [b]*15* The Hebrew for *LORD* sounds like and may be derived from the Hebrew for *I AM* in verse 14. [c]*6* The Hebrew word was used for various diseases affecting the skin—not necessarily leprosy.

Moses Returns to Egypt

18 Then Moses went back to Jethro his father-in-law and said to him, "Let me go back to my own people in Egypt to see if any of them are still alive."

Jethro said, "Go, and I wish you well."

19 Now the LORD had said to Moses in Midian, "Go back to Egypt, for all the men who wanted to kill you are dead." 20 So Moses took his wife and sons, put them on a donkey and started back to Egypt. And he took the staff of God in his hand.

21 The LORD said to Moses, "When you return to Egypt, see that you perform before Pharaoh all the wonders I have given you the power to do. But I will harden his heart so that he will not let the people go. 22 Then say to Pharaoh, 'This is what the LORD says: Israel is my firstborn son, 23 and I told you, "Let my son go, so he may worship me." But you refused to let him go; so I will kill your firstborn son.'" Ex 12:12,29; Jer 31:9

24 At a lodging place on the way, the LORD met ⌞Moses⌟[a] and was about to kill him. 25 But Zipporah took a flint knife, cut off her son's foreskin and touched ⌞Moses'⌟ feet with it.[b] "Surely you are a bridegroom of blood to me," she said. 26 So the LORD let him alone. (At that time she said "bridegroom of blood," referring to circumcision.)

27 The LORD said to Aaron, "Go into the desert to meet Moses." So he met Moses at the mountain of God and kissed him. 28 Then Moses told Aaron everything the LORD had sent him to say, and also about all the miraculous signs he had commanded him to perform. Ex 3:1

29 Moses and Aaron brought together all the elders of the Israelites, 30 and Aaron told them everything the LORD had said to Moses. He also performed the signs before the people, 31 and they believed. And when they heard that the LORD was concerned about them and had seen their misery, they bowed down and worshiped. Ex 3:16,18

Bricks Without Straw

5 Afterward Moses and Aaron went to Pharaoh and said, "This is what the LORD, the God of Israel, says: 'Let my people go, so that they may hold a festival to me in the desert.'" Ex 4:23

2 Pharaoh said, "Who is the LORD, that I should obey him and let Israel go? I do not know the LORD and I will not let Israel go." Ex 3:19; Job 21:15

3 Then they said, "The God of the Hebrews has met with us. Now let us take a three-day journey into the desert to offer sacrifices to the LORD our God, or he may strike us with plagues or with the sword." Ex 3:18-19; Job 21:15

4 But the king of Egypt said, "Moses and Aaron, why are you taking the people away from their labor? Get back to your work!" 5 Then Pharaoh said, "Look, the people of the land are now numerous, and you are stopping them from working." Ex 1:11

6 That same day Pharaoh gave this order to the slave drivers and foremen in charge of the people: 7 "You are no longer to supply the people with straw for making bricks; let them go and gather their own straw. 8 But require them to make the same number of bricks as before; don't reduce the quota. They are lazy; that is why they are crying out, 'Let us go and sacrifice to our God.' 9 Make the work harder for the men so that they keep working and pay no attention to lies." Ge 15:13

10 Then the slave drivers and the foremen went out and said to the people, "This is what Pharaoh says: 'I will not give you any more straw. 11 Go and get your own straw wherever you can find it, but your work will not be reduced at all.'" 12 So the people scattered all over Egypt to gather stubble to use for straw. 13 The slave drivers kept pressing them, saying, "Complete the work required of you for each day, just as when you had straw." 14 The Israelite foremen appointed by Pharaoh's slave drivers were beaten and were asked, "Why didn't you meet your quota of bricks yesterday or today, as before?" Isa 10:24

15 Then the Israelite foremen went and appealed to Pharaoh: "Why have you treated your servants this way? 16 Your servants are given no straw, yet we are told, 'Make bricks!' Your servants are being beaten, but the fault is with your own people."

17 Pharaoh said, "Lazy, that's what you are—lazy! That is why you keep saying, 'Let us go and sacrifice to the LORD.' 18 Now get to work. You will not be given any straw, yet you must produce your full quota of bricks."

19 The Israelite foremen realized they were in trouble when they were told, "You are not to reduce the number of bricks required of you for each day." 20 When they left Pharaoh, they found Moses and Aaron waiting to meet them, 21 and they said, "May the LORD look upon you and judge you! You have made us a stench to Pharaoh and his officials and have put a sword in their hand to kill us." Ge 34:30; Ex 14:11

God Promises Deliverance

22 Moses returned to the LORD and said, "O Lord, why have you brought trouble upon this people? Is this why you sent me? 23 Ever since I went to Pharaoh to speak in your name, he has brought trouble upon this people, and you have not rescued your people at all." Jer 4:10

6 Then the LORD said to Moses, "Now you will see what I will do to Pharaoh: Because of my mighty hand he will let them go; because of my mighty hand he will drive them out of his country." Ex 3:19; 12:31,33,39

[a] 24 Or ⌞*Moses' son*⌟; Hebrew *him* [b] 25 Or *and drew near* ⌞*Moses'*⌟ *feet*

2God also said to Moses, "I am the LORD. 3I appeared to Abraham, to Isaac and to Jacob as God Almighty,[a] but by my name the LORD[b] I did not make myself known to them.[c] 4I also established my covenant with them to give them the land of Canaan, where they lived as aliens. 5Moreover, I have heard the groaning of the Israelites, whom the Egyptians are enslaving, and I have remembered my covenant. Ex 2:23; 3:14; Ge 15:18

6"Therefore, say to the Israelites: 'I am the LORD, and I will bring you out from under the yoke of the Egyptians. I will free you from being slaves to them, and I will redeem you with an outstretched arm and with mighty acts of judgment. 7I will take you as my own people, and I will be your God. Then you will know that I am the LORD your God, who brought you out from under the yoke of the Egyptians. 8And I will bring you to the land I swore with uplifted hand to give to Abraham, to Isaac and to Jacob. I will give it to you as a possession. I am the LORD.'" Ge 15:18; Dt 7:8; Ps 136:21-22

LIVING  **INSIGHT**

We cannot endure those times that go from bad to worse until we rivet our attention on the Lord. We must contemplate His sovereignty, goodness, power, justice, compassion, love and wisdom—especially when we find ourselves sinking in treacherous waters. Because of who God is, we can be confident that He is in control of our circumstances and we can look to Him for strength and victory.

(See Exodus 6:2–8.)

9Moses reported this to the Israelites, but they did not listen to him because of their discouragement and cruel bondage.

10Then the LORD said to Moses, 11"Go, tell Pharaoh king of Egypt to let the Israelites go out of his country."

12But Moses said to the LORD, "If the Israelites will not listen to me, why would Pharaoh listen to me, since I speak with faltering lips[d]?" Ex 4:10

Family Record of Moses and Aaron

13Now the LORD spoke to Moses and Aaron about the Israelites and Pharaoh king of Egypt, and he commanded them to bring the Israelites out of Egypt. Ex 3:10

14These were the heads of their families[e]:

The sons of Reuben the firstborn son of Israel were Hanoch and Pallu, Hezron and Carmi. These were the clans of Reuben.

15The sons of Simeon were Jemuel, Jamin, Ohad, Jakin, Zohar and Shaul the son of a Canaanite woman. These were the clans of Simeon. 1Ch 4:24

16These were the names of the sons of Levi according to their records: Gershon, Kohath and Merari. Levi lived 137 years. Ge 46:11

17The sons of Gershon, by clans, were Libni and Shimei. 1Ch 6:17

18The sons of Kohath were Amram, Izhar, Hebron and Uzziel. Kohath lived 133 years.

19The sons of Merari were Mahli and Mushi. 1Ch 6:19

These were the clans of Levi according to their records.

20Amram married his father's sister Jochebed, who bore him Aaron and Moses. Amram lived 137 years. Ex 2:1-2

21The sons of Izhar were Korah, Nepheg and Zicri. 1Ch 6:38

22The sons of Uzziel were Mishael, Elzaphan and Sithri. Lev 10:4

23Aaron married Elisheba, daughter of Amminadab and sister of Nahshon, and she bore him Nadab and Abihu, Eleazar and Ithamar. Lev 10:1; Nu 3:2,32

24The sons of Korah were Assir, Elkanah and Abiasaph. These were the Korahite clans. Nu 26:11

25Eleazar son of Aaron married one of the daughters of Putiel, and she bore him Phinehas. Nu 25:7,11; Jos 24:33

These were the heads of the Levite families, clan by clan.

26It was this same Aaron and Moses to whom the LORD said, "Bring the Israelites out of Egypt by their divisions." 27They were the ones who spoke to Pharaoh king of Egypt about bringing the Israelites out of Egypt. It was the same Moses and Aaron. Ex 7:4

Aaron to Speak for Moses

28Now when the LORD spoke to Moses in Egypt, 29he said to him, "I am the LORD. Tell Pharaoh king of Egypt everything I tell you." ver 2,11

30But Moses said to the LORD, "Since I speak with faltering lips, why would Pharaoh listen to me?" ver 12

7 Then the LORD said to Moses, "See, I have made you like God to Pharaoh, and your brother Aaron will be your prophet. 2You are to say everything I command you, and your brother Aaron is to tell Pharaoh to let the Israelites go out

[a]3 Hebrew *El-Shaddai* [b]3 See note at Exodus 3:15. [c]3 Or *Almighty, and by my name the LORD did I not let myself be known to them?* [d]12 Hebrew *I am uncircumcised of lips*; also in verse 30 [e]14 The Hebrew for *families* here and in verse 25 refers to units larger than clans.

of his country. 3But I will harden Pharaoh's heart, and though I multiply my miraculous signs and wonders in Egypt, 4he will not listen to you. Then I will lay my hand on Egypt and with mighty acts of judgment I will bring out my divisions, my people the Israelites. 5And the Egyptians will know that I am the LORD when I stretch out my hand against Egypt and bring the Israelites out of it."

6Moses and Aaron did just as the LORD commanded them. 7Moses was eighty years old and Aaron eighty-three when they spoke to Pharaoh.

Aaron's Staff Becomes a Snake

8The LORD said to Moses and Aaron, 9"When Pharaoh says to you, 'Perform a miracle,' then say to Aaron, 'Take your staff and throw it down before Pharaoh,' and it will become a snake."

10So Moses and Aaron went to Pharaoh and did just as the LORD commanded. Aaron threw his staff down in front of Pharaoh and his officials, and it became a snake. 11Pharaoh then summoned wise men and sorcerers, and the Egyptian magicians also did the same things by their secret arts: 12Each one threw down his staff and it became a snake. But Aaron's staff swallowed up their staffs. 13Yet Pharaoh's heart became hard and he would not listen to them, just as the LORD had said. Ge 41:8

The Plague of Blood

14Then the LORD said to Moses, "Pharaoh's heart is unyielding; he refuses to let the people go. 15Go to Pharaoh in the morning as he goes out to the water. Wait on the bank of the Nile to meet him, and take in your hand the staff that was changed into a snake. 16Then say to him, 'The LORD, the God of the Hebrews, has sent me to say to you: Let my people go, so that they may worship me in the desert. But until now you have not listened. 17This is what the LORD says: By this you will know that I am the LORD: With the staff that is in my hand I will strike the water of the Nile, and it will be changed into blood. 18The fish in the Nile will die, and the river will stink; the Egyptians will not be able to drink its water.'" Ex 3:18; 4:9; Rev 16:4

19The LORD said to Moses, "Tell Aaron, 'Take your staff and stretch out your hand over the waters of Egypt—over the streams and canals, over the ponds and all the reservoirs'—and they will turn to blood. Blood will be everywhere in Egypt, even in the wooden buckets and stone jars."

20Moses and Aaron did just as the LORD had commanded. He raised his staff in the presence of Pharaoh and his officials and struck the water of the Nile, and all the water was changed into blood. 21The fish in the Nile died, and the river smelled so bad that the Egyptians could not drink its water. Blood was everywhere in Egypt. Ps 78:44; 105:29

22But the Egyptian magicians did the same things by their secret arts, and Pharaoh's heart became hard; he would not listen to Moses and Aaron, just as the LORD had said. 23Instead, he turned and went into his palace, and did not take even this to heart. 24And all the Egyptians dug along the Nile to get drinking water, because they could not drink the water of the river. ver 11

The Plague of Frogs

25Seven days passed after the LORD struck the Nile.

8 1Then the LORD said to Moses, "Go to Pharaoh and say to him, 'This is what the LORD says: Let my people go, so that they may worship me. 2If you refuse to let them go, I will plague your whole country with frogs. 3The Nile will teem with frogs. They will come up into your palace and your bedroom and onto your bed, into the houses of your officials and on your people, and into your ovens and kneading troughs. 4The frogs will go up on you and your people and all your officials.'" Ex 3:12,18; 10:6

5Then the LORD said to Moses, "Tell Aaron, 'Stretch out your hand with your staff over the streams and canals and ponds, and make frogs come up on the land of Egypt.'" Ex 7:19

6So Aaron stretched out his hand over the waters of Egypt, and the frogs came up and covered the land. 7But the magicians did the same things by their secret arts; they also made frogs come up on the land of Egypt. Ex 7:11; Ps 78:45

8Pharaoh summoned Moses and Aaron and said, "Pray to the LORD to take the frogs away from me and my people, and I will let your people go to offer sacrifices to the LORD." Ex 9:28; 10:17

9Moses said to Pharaoh, "I leave to you the honor of setting the time for me to pray for you and your officials and your people that you and your houses may be rid of the frogs, except for those that remain in the Nile."

10"Tomorrow," Pharaoh said.

Moses replied, "It will be as you say, so that you may know there is no one like the LORD our God. 11The frogs will leave you and your houses, your officials and your people; they will remain only in the Nile." Ex 9:14; Dt 33:26

12After Moses and Aaron left Pharaoh, Moses cried out to the LORD about the frogs he had brought on Pharaoh. 13And the LORD did what Moses asked. The frogs died in the houses, in the courtyards and in the fields. 14They were piled into heaps, and the land reeked of them. 15But when Pharaoh saw that there was relief, he hardened his heart and would not listen to Moses and Aaron, just as the LORD had said. Ex 7:14

The Plague of Gnats

16Then the LORD said to Moses, "Tell Aaron, 'Stretch out your staff and strike the dust of the ground,' and throughout the land of Egypt the dust will become gnats." 17They did this, and when

Aaron stretched out his hand with the staff and struck the dust of the ground, gnats came upon men and animals. All the dust throughout the land of Egypt became gnats. 18But when the magicians tried to produce gnats by their secret arts, they could not. And the gnats were on men and animals. Ex 9:11; Ps 105:31

19The magicians said to Pharaoh, "This is the finger of God." But Pharaoh's heart was hard and he would not listen, just as the LORD had said.

The Plague of Flies

20Then the LORD said to Moses, "Get up early in the morning and confront Pharaoh as he goes to the water and say to him, 'This is what the LORD says: Let my people go, so that they may worship me. 21If you do not let my people go, I will send swarms of flies on you and your officials, on your people and into your houses. The houses of the Egyptians will be full of flies, and even the ground where they are. Ex 3:18; 7:15

22" 'But on that day I will deal differently with the land of Goshen, where my people live; no swarms of flies will be there, so that you will know that I, the LORD, am in this land. 23I will make a distinction[a] between my people and your people. This miraculous sign will occur tomorrow.' "

24And the LORD did this. Dense swarms of flies poured into Pharaoh's palace and into the houses of his officials, and throughout Egypt the land was ruined by the flies. Ps 78:45; 105:31

25Then Pharaoh summoned Moses and Aaron and said, "Go, sacrifice to your God here in the land." Ex 9:27; 10:16

26But Moses said, "That would not be right. The sacrifices we offer the LORD our God would be detestable to the Egyptians. And if we offer sacrifices that are detestable in their eyes, will they not stone us? 27We must take a three-day journey into the desert to offer sacrifices to the LORD our God, as he commands us." Ge 43:32; Ex 3:18

28Pharaoh said, "I will let you go to offer sacrifices to the LORD your God in the desert, but you must not go very far. Now pray for me." ver 8

29Moses answered, "As soon as I leave you, I will pray to the LORD, and tomorrow the flies will leave Pharaoh and his officials and his people. Only be sure that Pharaoh does not act deceitfully again by not letting the people go to offer sacrifices to the LORD."

30Then Moses left Pharaoh and prayed to the LORD, 31and the LORD did what Moses asked: The flies left Pharaoh and his officials and his people; not a fly remained. 32But this time also Pharaoh hardened his heart and would not let the people go. ver 12; Ex 4:21

The Plague on Livestock

9 Then the LORD said to Moses, "Go to Pharaoh and say to him, 'This is what the LORD, the God of the Hebrews, says: "Let my people go, so that they may worship me." 2If you refuse to let them go and continue to hold them back, 3the hand of the LORD will bring a terrible plague on your livestock in the field—on your horses and donkeys and camels and on your cattle and sheep and goats. 4But the LORD will make a distinction between the livestock of Israel and that of Egypt, so that no animal belonging to the Israelites will die.' " Ex 8:1,22

5The LORD set a time and said, "Tomorrow the LORD will do this in the land." 6And the next day the LORD did it: All the livestock of the Egyptians died, but not one animal belonging to the Israelites died. 7Pharaoh sent men to investigate and found that not even one of the animals of the Israelites had died. Yet his heart was unyielding and he would not let the people go. Ex 7:14; 8:32

The Plague of Boils

8Then the LORD said to Moses and Aaron, "Take handfuls of soot from a furnace and have Moses toss it into the air in the presence of Pharaoh. 9It will become fine dust over the whole land of Egypt, and festering boils will break out on men and animals throughout the land." Rev 16:2

10So they took soot from a furnace and stood before Pharaoh. Moses tossed it into the air, and festering boils broke out on men and animals. 11The magicians could not stand before Moses because of the boils that were on them and on all the Egyptians. 12But the LORD hardened Pharaoh's heart and he would not listen to Moses and Aaron, just as the LORD had said to Moses. Ex 4:21

The Plague of Hail

13Then the LORD said to Moses, "Get up early in the morning, confront Pharaoh and say to him, 'This is what the LORD, the God of the Hebrews, says: Let my people go, so that they may worship me, 14or this time I will send the full force of my plagues against you and against your officials and your people, so you may know that there is no one like me in all the earth. 15For by now I could have stretched out my hand and struck you and your people with a plague that would have wiped you off the earth. 16But I have raised you up[b] for this very purpose, that I might show you my power and that my name might be proclaimed in all the earth. 17You still set yourself against my people and will not let them go. 18Therefore, at this time tomorrow I will send the worst hailstorm that has ever fallen on Egypt, from the day it was founded till now. 19Give an order now to bring your live-

[a] 23 Septuagint and Vulgate; Hebrew *will put a deliverance*

[b] 16 Or *have spared you*

stock and everything you have in the field to a place of shelter, because the hail will fall on every man and animal that has not been brought in and is still out in the field, and they will die.'" Ro 9:17

20Those officials of Pharaoh who feared the word of the LORD hurried to bring their slaves and their livestock inside. 21But those who ignored the word of the LORD left their slaves and livestock in the field. Pr 13:13

22Then the LORD said to Moses, "Stretch out your hand toward the sky so that hail will fall all over Egypt—on men and animals and on everything growing in the fields of Egypt." 23When Moses stretched out his staff toward the sky, the LORD sent thunder and hail, and lightning flashed down to the ground. So the LORD rained hail on the land of Egypt; 24hail fell and lightning flashed back and forth. It was the worst storm in all the land of Egypt since it had become a nation. 25Throughout Egypt hail struck everything in the fields—both men and animals; it beat down everything growing in the fields and stripped every tree. 26The only place it did not hail was the land of Goshen, where the Israelites were. ver 4; Ps 105:32-33; Jos 10:11

27Then Pharaoh summoned Moses and Aaron. "This time I have sinned," he said to them. "The LORD is in the right, and I and my people are in the wrong. 28Pray to the LORD, for we have had enough thunder and hail. I will let you go; you don't have to stay any longer." Ex 8:8; 10:16; 2Ch 12:6

29Moses replied, "When I have gone out of the city, I will spread out my hands in prayer to the LORD. The thunder will stop and there will be no more hail, so you may know that the earth is the LORD's. 30But I know that you and your officials still do not fear the LORD God." 1Ki 8:22,38; Ps 24:1

31(The flax and barley were destroyed, since the barley had headed and the flax was in bloom. 32The wheat and spelt, however, were not destroyed, because they ripen later.) Ru 1:22

33Then Moses left Pharaoh and went out of the city. He spread out his hands toward the LORD; the thunder and hail stopped, and the rain no longer poured down on the land. 34When Pharaoh saw that the rain and hail and thunder had stopped, he sinned again: He and his officials hardened their hearts. 35So Pharaoh's heart was hard and he would not let the Israelites go, just as the LORD had said through Moses. Ex 4:21

The Plague of Locusts

10 Then the LORD said to Moses, "Go to Pharaoh, for I have hardened his heart and the hearts of his officials so that I may perform these miraculous signs of mine among them 2that you may tell your children and grandchildren how I dealt harshly with the Egyptians and how I performed my signs among them, and that you may know that I am the LORD." Dt 4:9; Ps 44:1

3So Moses and Aaron went to Pharaoh and said to him, "This is what the LORD, the God of the Hebrews, says: 'How long will you refuse to humble yourself before me? Let my people go, so that they may worship me. 4If you refuse to let them go, I will bring locusts into your country tomorrow. 5They will cover the face of the ground so that it cannot be seen. They will devour what little you have left after the hail, including every tree that is growing in your fields. 6They will fill your houses and those of all your officials and all the Egyptians—something neither your fathers nor your forefathers have ever seen from the day they settled in this land till now.'" Then Moses turned and left Pharaoh. Joel 1:4; Jas 4:10

7Pharaoh's officials said to him, "How long will this man be a snare to us? Let the people go, so that they may worship the LORD their God. Do you not yet realize that Egypt is ruined?" Ex 8:19; 23:33

8Then Moses and Aaron were brought back to Pharaoh. "Go, worship the LORD your God," he said. "But just who will be going?" Ex 8:8

9Moses answered, "We will go with our young and old, with our sons and daughters, and with our flocks and herds, because we are to celebrate a festival to the LORD."

10Pharaoh said, "The LORD be with you—if I let you go, along with your women and children! Clearly you are bent on evil.[a] 11No! Have only the men go; and worship the LORD, since that's what you have been asking for." Then Moses and Aaron were driven out of Pharaoh's presence.

12And the LORD said to Moses, "Stretch out your hand over Egypt so that locusts will swarm over the land and devour everything growing in the fields, everything left by the hail." Ex 7:19

13So Moses stretched out his staff over Egypt, and the LORD made an east wind blow across the land all that day and all that night. By morning the wind had brought the locusts; 14they invaded all Egypt and settled down in every area of the country in great numbers. Never before had there been such a plague of locusts, nor will there ever be again. 15They covered all the ground until it was black. They devoured all that was left after the hail—everything growing in the fields and the fruit on the trees. Nothing green remained on tree or plant in all the land of Egypt. Joel 2:1-11,25

16Pharaoh quickly summoned Moses and Aaron and said, "I have sinned against the LORD your God and against you. 17Now forgive my sin once more and pray to the LORD your God to take this deadly plague away from me." Ex 9:27

18Moses then left Pharaoh and prayed to the LORD. 19And the LORD changed the wind to a very

[a]10 Or *Be careful, trouble is in store for you!*

strong west wind, which caught up the locusts and carried them into the Red Sea.[a] Not a locust was left anywhere in Egypt. 20But the LORD hardened Pharaoh's heart, and he would not let the Israelites go. Ex 4:21

The Plague of Darkness

21Then the LORD said to Moses, "Stretch out your hand toward the sky so that darkness will spread over Egypt—darkness that can be felt." 22So Moses stretched out his hand toward the sky, and total darkness covered all Egypt for three days. 23No one could see anyone else or leave his place for three days. Yet all the Israelites had light in the places where they lived. Ps 105:28; Rev 16:10

24Then Pharaoh summoned Moses and said, "Go, worship the LORD. Even your women and children may go with you; only leave your flocks and herds behind." ver 8-10

25But Moses said, "You must allow us to have sacrifices and burnt offerings to present to the LORD our God. 26Our livestock too must go with us; not a hoof is to be left behind. We have to use some of them in worshiping the LORD our God, and until we get there we will not know what we are to use to worship the LORD."

27But the LORD hardened Pharaoh's heart, and he was not willing to let them go. 28Pharaoh said to Moses, "Get out of my sight! Make sure you do not appear before me again! The day you see my face you will die."

29"Just as you say," Moses replied, "I will never appear before you again." Heb 11:27

The Plague on the Firstborn

11 Now the LORD had said to Moses, "I will bring one more plague on Pharaoh and on Egypt. After that, he will let you go from here, and when he does, he will drive you out completely. 2Tell the people that men and women alike are to ask their neighbors for articles of silver and gold." 3(The LORD made the Egyptians favorably disposed toward the people, and Moses himself was highly regarded in Egypt by Pharaoh's officials and by the people.) Dt 34:11; Ex 3:21-22

4So Moses said, "This is what the LORD says: 'About midnight I will go throughout Egypt. 5Every firstborn son in Egypt will die, from the firstborn son of Pharaoh, who sits on the throne, to the firstborn son of the slave girl, who is at her hand mill, and all the firstborn of the cattle as well. 6There will be loud wailing throughout Egypt—worse than there has ever been or ever will be again. 7But among the Israelites not a dog will bark at any man or animal.' Then you will know that the LORD makes a distinction between Egypt and Israel. 8All these officials of yours will come to me, bowing down before me and saying, 'Go, you and all the people who follow you!' After that I will leave." Then Moses, hot with anger, left Pharaoh.

9The LORD had said to Moses, "Pharaoh will refuse to listen to you—so that my wonders may be multiplied in Egypt." 10Moses and Aaron performed all these wonders before Pharaoh, but the LORD hardened Pharaoh's heart, and he would not let the Israelites go out of his country. Ex 4:21; 7:4

The Passover

12 The LORD said to Moses and Aaron in Egypt, 2"This month is to be for you the first month, the first month of your year. 3Tell the whole community of Israel that on the tenth day of this month each man is to take a lamb[b] for his family, one for each household. 4If any household is too small for a whole lamb, they must share one with their nearest neighbor, having taken into account the number of people there are. You are to determine the amount of lamb needed in accordance with what each person will eat. 5The animals you choose must be year-old males without defect, and you may take them from the sheep or the goats. 6Take care of them until the fourteenth day of the month, when all the people of the community of Israel must slaughter them at twilight. 7Then they are to take some of the blood and put it on the sides and tops of the doorframes of the houses where they eat the lambs. 8That same night they are to eat the meat roasted over the fire, along with bitter herbs, and bread made without yeast. 9Do not eat the meat raw or cooked in water, but roast it over the fire—head, legs and inner parts. 10Do not leave any of it till morning; if some is left till morning, you must burn it. 11This is how you are to eat it: with your cloak tucked into your belt, your sandals on your feet and your staff in your hand. Eat it in haste; it is the LORD's Passover.

12"On that same night I will pass through Egypt and strike down every firstborn—both men and animals—and I will bring judgment on all the gods of Egypt. I am the LORD. 13The blood will be a sign for you on the houses where you are; and when I see the blood, I will pass over you. No destructive plague will touch you when I strike Egypt. Nu 33:4; Heb 11:28

14"This is a day you are to commemorate; for the generations to come you shall celebrate it as a festival to the LORD—a lasting ordinance. 15For seven days you are to eat bread made without yeast. On the first day remove the yeast from your houses, for whoever eats anything with yeast in it from the first day through the seventh must be cut off from Israel. 16On the first day hold a sacred assembly, and another one on the seventh day. Do no work at all on these days, except to prepare

[a] 19 Hebrew *Yam Suph*; that is, Sea of Reeds [b] 3 The Hebrew word can mean *lamb* or *kid*; also in verse 4.

food for everyone to eat—that is all you may do.
17“Celebrate the Feast of Unleavened Bread, because it was on this very day that I brought your
divisions out of Egypt. Celebrate this day as a lasting ordinance for the generations to come. 18In the
first month you are to eat bread made without
yeast, from the evening of the fourteenth day until
the evening of the twenty-first day. 19For seven
days no yeast is to be found in your houses. And
whoever eats anything with yeast in it must be cut
off from the community of Israel, whether he is an
alien or native-born. 20Eat nothing made with
yeast. Wherever you live, you must eat unleavened
bread.” Lev 23:4-8; Nu 28:16-25; Dt 16:1-8
21Then Moses summoned all the elders of Israel
and said to them, “Go at once and select the animals for your families and slaughter the Passover
lamb. 22Take a bunch of hyssop, dip it into the
blood in the basin and put some of the blood on
the top and on both sides of the doorframe. Not
one of you shall go out the door of his house until
morning. 23When the LORD goes through the land
to strike down the Egyptians, he will see the blood
on the top and sides of the doorframe and will pass
over that doorway, and he will not permit the
destroyer to enter your houses and strike you
down. Mk 14:12-16; 1Co 10:10
24“Obey these instructions as a lasting ordinance for you and your descendants. 25When you
enter the land that the LORD will give you as he
promised, observe this ceremony. 26And when
your children ask you, ‘What does this ceremony
mean to you?’ 27then tell them, ‘It is the Passover
sacrifice to the LORD, who passed over the houses
of the Israelites in Egypt and spared our homes
when he struck down the Egyptians.’ ” Then the
people bowed down and worshiped. 28The Israelites did just what the LORD commanded Moses and
Aaron. ver 11; Jos 4:6
29At midnight the LORD struck down all the
firstborn in Egypt, from the firstborn of Pharaoh,
who sat on the throne, to the firstborn of the prisoner, who was in the dungeon, and the firstborn of
all the livestock as well. 30Pharaoh and all his officials and all the Egyptians got up during the night,
and there was loud wailing in Egypt, for there was
not a house without someone dead. Ex 4:23; 11:4,6

The Exodus

31During the night Pharaoh summoned Moses
and Aaron and said, “Up! Leave my people, you
and the Israelites! Go, worship the LORD as you
have requested. 32Take your flocks and herds, as
you have said, and go. And also bless me.”
33The Egyptians urged the people to hurry and
leave the country. “For otherwise,” they said, “we
will all die!” 34So the people took their dough before the yeast was added, and carried it on their
shoulders in kneading troughs wrapped in clothing. 35The Israelites did as Moses instructed and
asked the Egyptians for articles of silver and gold
and for clothing. 36The LORD had made the Egyptians favorably disposed toward the people, and
they gave them what they asked for; so they plundered the Egyptians. Ex 3:22
37The Israelites journeyed from Rameses to
Succoth. There were about six hundred thousand
men on foot, besides women and children. 38Many
other people went up with them, as well as large
droves of livestock, both flocks and herds. 39With
the dough they had brought from Egypt, they
baked cakes of unleavened bread. The dough was
without yeast because they had been driven out of
Egypt and did not have time to prepare food for
themselves. Nu 11:13,21; 33:3-5
40Now the length of time the Israelite people
lived in Egypt[a] was 430 years. 41At the end of the
430 years, to the very day, all the LORD’s divisions
left Egypt. 42Because the LORD kept vigil that night
to bring them out of Egypt, on this night all the
Israelites are to keep vigil to honor the LORD for
the generations to come. Dt 16:1,6; Ac 7:6

Passover Restrictions

43The LORD said to Moses and Aaron, “These
are the regulations for the Passover: ver 11
“No foreigner is to eat of it. 44Any slave you
have bought may eat of it after you have circumcised him, 45but a temporary resident and a hired
worker may not eat of it. Ge 17:12-13
46“It must be eaten inside one house; take none
of the meat outside the house. Do not break any of
the bones. 47The whole community of Israel must
celebrate it. Nu 9:12; Jn 19:36
48“An alien living among you who wants to celebrate the LORD’s Passover must have all the males
in his household circumcised; then he may take
part like one born in the land. No uncircumcised

LIVING  **INSIGHT**

As we see God's awesome power at work, we discover afresh that doing God's will God's way demands both our availability and our obedience. Are you prepared to respond obediently to God's will as revealed in Scripture? And are you willing and ready to move from the familiar to the unfamiliar at the moment God tells you to go? Will you be available and obedient when He calls?

(See Exodus 12:24–28.)

[a]40 Masoretic Text; Samaritan Pentateuch and Septuagint *Egypt and Canaan*

male may eat of it. 49The same law applies to the native-born and to the alien living among you."

50All the Israelites did just what the LORD had commanded Moses and Aaron. 51And on that very day the LORD brought the Israelites out of Egypt by their divisions. Ex 6:26

Provisions on the Journey **Chapters 13–18**

In this section we see the people of Israel moving forward on a journey of faith. With a cloud by day and a column of fire illuminating their way by night, God's people marched onward. What a beautiful picture! They left Egypt on foot and walked confidently into the desert. The familiarities of Goshen were behind them and the scorching heat of the desert was ahead of them, but they continued onward. To the surprise of the Hebrews, the divine cloud brought them to the edge of the Red Sea. With mountains to the north, desert sands to the south and the sea in front of them, they would be trapped—should anyone be chasing them. Guess what? Pharaoh and his army *were* hot on their trail; the king of Egypt had begun to have second thoughts about letting the people go. God, in his love and mercy, parted the Red Sea and led His people across on dry land. The Egyptians were not as successful in their attempt to cross the sea.

Following that amazing deliverance, the Lord provided all His people needed. When they were hungry, He gave them manna—bread from heaven—to satisfy their hunger. When they were thirsty, He gave them pure, clean water from the rock. Yet, even with the Lord's provision the people continued to grumble and complain. If truth be told, we can all be like that at times, can't we? The Lord provides all we really need, and we still find something to complain about. Maybe, just maybe, as we listen to the voices of the Israelites we'll look carefully at our own attitudes as we continue our own journey.

Consecration of the Firstborn

13 The LORD said to Moses, 2"Consecrate to me every firstborn male. The first offspring of every womb among the Israelites belongs to me, whether man or animal." Lk 2:23

3Then Moses said to the people, "Commemorate this day, the day you came out of Egypt, out of the land of slavery, because the LORD brought you out of it with a mighty hand. Eat nothing containing yeast. 4Today, in the month of Abib, you are leaving. 5When the LORD brings you into the land of the Canaanites, Hittites, Amorites, Hivites and Jebusites—the land he swore to your forefathers to give you, a land flowing with milk and honey—you are to observe this ceremony in this month: 6For seven days eat bread made without yeast and on the seventh day hold a festival to the LORD. 7Eat unleavened bread during those seven days; nothing with yeast in it is to be seen among you, nor shall any yeast be seen anywhere within your borders. 8On that day tell your son, 'I do this because of what the LORD did for me when I came out of Egypt.' 9This observance will be for you like a sign on your hand and a reminder on your forehead that the law of the LORD is to be on your lips. For the LORD brought you out of Egypt with his mighty hand. 10You must keep this ordinance at the appointed time year after year.

11"After the LORD brings you into the land of the Canaanites and gives it to you, as he promised on oath to you and your forefathers, 12you are to give over to the LORD the first offspring of every womb. All the firstborn males of your livestock belong to the LORD. 13Redeem with a lamb every firstborn donkey, but if you do not redeem it, break its neck. Redeem every firstborn among your sons.

14"In days to come, when your son asks you, 'What does this mean?' say to him, 'With a mighty hand the LORD brought us out of Egypt, out of the land of slavery. 15When Pharaoh stubbornly refused to let us go, the LORD killed every firstborn in Egypt, both man and animal. This is why I sacrifice to the LORD the first male offspring of every womb and redeem each of my firstborn sons.' 16And it will be like a sign on your hand and a symbol on your forehead that the LORD brought us out of Egypt with his mighty hand." Ex 12:29

Crossing the Sea

17When Pharaoh let the people go, God did not lead them on the road through the Philistine country, though that was shorter. For God said, "If they face war, they might change their minds and return to Egypt." 18So God led the people around by the desert road toward the Red Sea.[a] The Israelites went up out of Egypt armed for battle.

19Moses took the bones of Joseph with him because Joseph had made the sons of Israel swear an oath. He had said, "God will surely come to your aid, and then you must carry my bones up with you from this place."[b] Ge 50:24-25; Jos 24:32

20After leaving Succoth they camped at Etham on the edge of the desert. 21By day the LORD went ahead of them in a pillar of cloud to guide them on their way and by night in a pillar of fire to give them light, so that they could travel by day or night. 22Neither the pillar of cloud by day nor the pillar of fire by night left its place in front of the people. Ex 14:19,24; Ps 78:14; 1Co 10:1

14 Then the LORD said to Moses, 2"Tell the Israelites to turn back and encamp near Pi Hahiroth, between Migdol and the sea. They are to encamp by the sea, directly opposite Baal Zephon. 3Pharaoh will think, 'The Israelites are wandering around the land in confusion, hemmed in by the desert.' 4And I will harden Pharaoh's heart, and he will pursue them. But I will gain glory for myself

[a] 18 Hebrew *Yam Suph*; that is, Sea of Reeds [b] 19 See Gen. 50:25.

THE EXODUS

The exodus and conquest narratives form the classic historical and spiritual drama of Old Testament times. Subsequent ages looked back to this period as one of obedient and victorious living under divine guidance. Close examination of the environment and circumstances also reveals the strenuous exertions, human sin and bloody conflicts of the era.

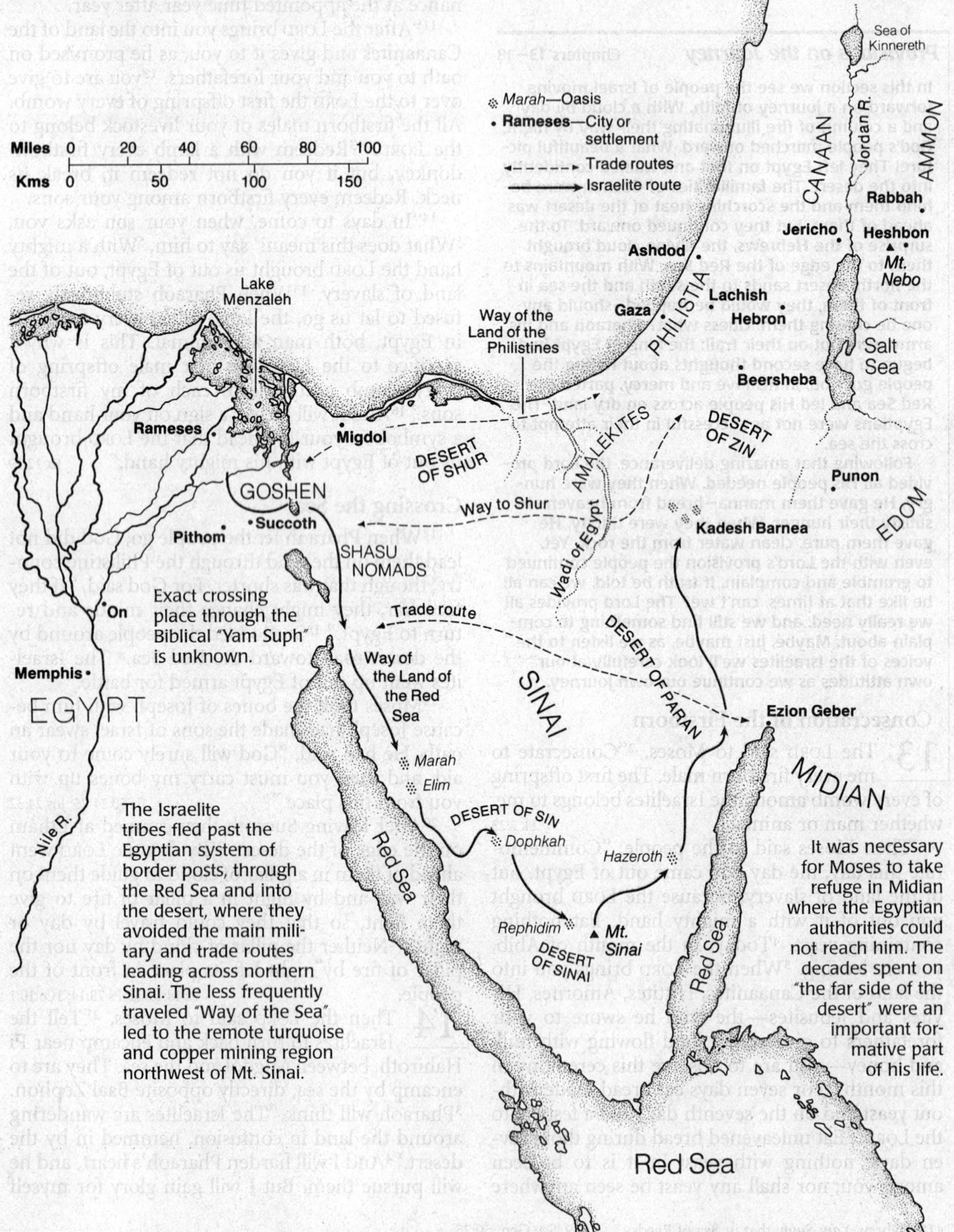

through Pharaoh and all his army, and the Egyptians will know that I am the LORD." So the Israelites did this. Ro 9:17,22-23; Ex 4:21

[5]When the king of Egypt was told that the people had fled, Pharaoh and his officials changed their minds about them and said, "What have we done? We have let the Israelites go and have lost their services!" [6]So he had his chariot made ready and took his army with him. [7]He took six hundred of the best chariots, along with all the other chariots of Egypt, with officers over all of them. [8]The LORD hardened the heart of Pharaoh king of Egypt, so that he pursued the Israelites, who were marching out boldly. [9]The Egyptians—all Pharaoh's horses and chariots, horsemen[a] and troops—pursued the Israelites and overtook them as they camped by the sea near Pi Hahiroth, opposite Baal Zephon. Ex 15:9; Nu 33:3

[10]As Pharaoh approached, the Israelites looked up, and there were the Egyptians, marching after them. They were terrified and cried out to the LORD. [11]They said to Moses, "Was it because there were no graves in Egypt that you brought us to the desert to die? What have you done to us by bringing us out of Egypt? [12]Didn't we say to you in Egypt, 'Leave us alone; let us serve the Egyptians'? It would have been better for us to serve the Egyptians than to die in the desert!" Ne 9:9; Ps 34:17

[13]Moses answered the people, "Do not be afraid. Stand firm and you will see the deliverance the LORD will bring you today. The Egyptians you see today you will never see again. [14]The LORD will fight for you; you need only to be still." Ps 46:10

[15]Then the LORD said to Moses, "Why are you crying out to me? Tell the Israelites to move on. [16]Raise your staff and stretch out your hand over the sea to divide the water so that the Israelites can go through the sea on dry ground. [17]I will harden the hearts of the Egyptians so that they will go in after them. And I will gain glory through Pharaoh and all his army, through his chariots and his horsemen. [18]The Egyptians will know that I am the LORD when I gain glory through Pharaoh, his chariots and his horsemen." Ex 4:17; Isa 10:26

[19]Then the angel of God, who had been traveling in front of Israel's army, withdrew and went behind them. The pillar of cloud also moved from in front and stood behind them, [20]coming between the armies of Egypt and Israel. Throughout the night the cloud brought darkness to the one side and light to the other side; so neither went near the other all night long. Ex 13:21

[21]Then Moses stretched out his hand over the sea, and all that night the LORD drove the sea back with a strong east wind and turned it into dry land. The waters were divided, [22]and the Israelites went through the sea on dry ground, with a wall of water on their right and on their left. Heb 11:29

[23]The Egyptians pursued them, and all Pharaoh's horses and chariots and horsemen followed

LIVING  **INSIGHT**

Take heart. When God is involved, anything can happen. The One who split the Red Sea down the middle and leveled the wall around Jericho and brought His Son back from the dead takes delight in the incredible!

(See Exodus 14:21–22.)

them into the sea. [24]During the last watch of the night the LORD looked down from the pillar of fire and cloud at the Egyptian army and threw it into confusion. [25]He made the wheels of their chariots come off[b] so that they had difficulty driving. And the Egyptians said, "Let's get away from the Israelites! The LORD is fighting for them against Egypt."

[26]Then the LORD said to Moses, "Stretch out your hand over the sea so that the waters may flow back over the Egyptians and their chariots and horsemen." [27]Moses stretched out his hand over the sea, and at daybreak the sea went back to its place. The Egyptians were fleeing toward[c] it, and the LORD swept them into the sea. [28]The water flowed back and covered the chariots and horsemen—the entire army of Pharaoh that had followed the Israelites into the sea. Not one of them survived. Ex 15:1,21; Ps 106:11

[29]But the Israelites went through the sea on dry ground, with a wall of water on their right and on their left. [30]That day the LORD saved Israel from the hands of the Egyptians, and Israel saw the Egyptians lying dead on the shore. [31]And when the Israelites saw the great power the LORD displayed against the Egyptians, the people feared the LORD and put their trust in him and in Moses his servant. Jn 2:11; Ps 106:8,10,21

The Song of Moses and Miriam

15 Then Moses and the Israelites sang this song to the LORD: Rev 15:3

"I will sing to the LORD, Ps 106:12
  for he is highly exalted.
The horse and its rider
  he has hurled into the sea.
[2]The LORD is my strength and my song; Ps 59:17
  he has become my salvation. Ps 18:2,46; Hab 3:18
He is my God, and I will praise him,
  my father's God, and I will exalt him.
[3]The LORD is a warrior; Rev 19:11

[a]9 Or *charioteers*; also in verses 17, 18, 23, 26 and 28 [b]25 Or *He jammed the wheels of their chariots* (see Samaritan Pentateuch, Septuagint and Syriac) [c]27 Or *from*

the LORD is his name.
4Pharaoh's chariots and his army
he has hurled into the sea.
The best of Pharaoh's officers
are drowned in the Red Sea.[a]
5The deep waters have covered them;
they sank to the depths like a stone. Ne 9:11

6"Your right hand, O LORD, Ps 118:15
was majestic in power.
Your right hand, O LORD,
shattered the enemy.
7In the greatness of your majesty
you threw down those who opposed you.
You unleashed your burning anger;
it consumed them like stubble.
8By the blast of your nostrils
the waters piled up. Ps 78:13
The surging waters stood firm like a wall;
the deep waters congealed in the heart of
the sea.
9"The enemy boasted,
'I will pursue, I will overtake them. Ex 14:5-9
I will divide the spoils;
I will gorge myself on them.
I will draw my sword
and my hand will destroy them.'
10But you blew with your breath,
and the sea covered them.
They sank like lead
in the mighty waters.
11"Who among the gods is like you, O LORD?
Who is like you—
majestic in holiness, Isa 6:3
awesome in glory, Ps 18:1
working wonders?
12You stretched out your right hand
and the earth swallowed them.
13"In your unfailing love you will lead Ne 9:12
the people you have redeemed.
In your strength you will guide them
to your holy dwelling. Ps 78:54

LIVING  **INSIGHT**

God never gives a goal that we cannot accomplish in His strength. I want to assure you that you can glorify God, you must glorify God. But you have to determine deep within your heart that you're going to do it His way. That's right—His way.

(See Exodus 15:2–13.)

14The nations will hear and tremble;
anguish will grip the people of Philistia.
15The chiefs of Edom will be terrified,
the leaders of Moab will be seized with
trembling, Nu 22:3
the people[b] of Canaan will melt away;
16 terror and dread will fall upon them.
By the power of your arm
they will be as still as a stone—
until your people pass by, O LORD,
until the people you bought[c] pass by.
17You will bring them in and plant them Ps 44:2
on the mountain of your inheritance—
the place, O LORD, you made for your
dwelling,
the sanctuary, O Lord, your hands
established.
18The LORD will reign
for ever and ever."

19When Pharaoh's horses, chariots and horsemen[d] went into the sea, the LORD brought the
waters of the sea back over them, but the Israelites
walked through the sea on dry ground. 20Then
Miriam the prophetess, Aaron's sister, took a tambourine in her hand, and all the women followed
her, with tambourines and dancing. 21Miriam sang
to them: Ex 14:28; Nu 26:59; 1Sa 18:6

"Sing to the LORD,
for he is highly exalted.
The horse and its rider
he has hurled into the sea."

The Waters of Marah and Elim

22Then Moses led Israel from the Red Sea and
they went into the Desert of Shur. For three days
they traveled in the desert without finding water.
23When they came to Marah, they could not drink
its water because it was bitter. (That is why the
place is called Marah.[e]) 24So the people grumbled
against Moses, saying, "What are we to drink?"
25Then Moses cried out to the LORD, and the
LORD showed him a piece of wood. He threw it
into the water, and the water became sweet.

There the LORD made a decree and a law for
them, and there he tested them. 26He said, "If you
listen carefully to the voice of the LORD your God
and do what is right in his eyes, if you pay attention to his commands and keep all his decrees, I
will not bring on you any of the diseases I brought
on the Egyptians, for I am the LORD, who heals
you." Ex 23:25-26; Dt 28:27,58-60

27Then they came to Elim, where there were
twelve springs and seventy palm trees, and they
camped there near the water. Nu 33:9

[a]4 Hebrew *Yam Suph*; that is, Sea of Reeds; also in verse 22 [b]15 Or *rulers* [c]16 Or *created* [d]19 Or *charioteers*
[e]23 *Marah* means *bitter*.

Manna and Quail

16 The whole Israelite community set out from Elim and came to the Desert of Sin, which is between Elim and Sinai, on the fifteenth day of the second month after they had come out of Egypt. [2]In the desert the whole community grumbled against Moses and Aaron. [3]The Israelites said to them, "If only we had died by the LORD's hand in Egypt! There we sat around pots of meat and ate all the food we wanted, but you have brought us out into this desert to starve this entire assembly to death." Nu 11:4,34; 1Co 10:10

[4]Then the LORD said to Moses, "I will rain down bread from heaven for you. The people are to go out each day and gather enough for that day. In this way I will test them and see whether they will follow my instructions. [5]On the sixth day they are to prepare what they bring in, and that is to be twice as much as they gather on the other days."

[6]So Moses and Aaron said to all the Israelites, "In the evening you will know that it was the LORD who brought you out of Egypt, [7]and in the morning you will see the glory of the LORD, because he has heard your grumbling against him. Who are we, that you should grumble against us?" [8]Moses also said, "You will know that it was the LORD when he gives you meat to eat in the evening and all the bread you want in the morning, because he has heard your grumbling against him. Who are we? You are not grumbling against us, but against the LORD." Nu 16:11; Ro 13:2

[9]Then Moses told Aaron, "Say to the entire Israelite community, 'Come before the LORD, for he has heard your grumbling.' "

[10]While Aaron was speaking to the whole Israelite community, they looked toward the desert, and there was the glory of the LORD appearing in the cloud. Ex 13:21; 1Ki 8:10

[11]The LORD said to Moses, [12]"I have heard the grumbling of the Israelites. Tell them, 'At twilight you will eat meat, and in the morning you will be filled with bread. Then you will know that I am the LORD your God.' "

[13]That evening quail came and covered the camp, and in the morning there was a layer of dew around the camp. [14]When the dew was gone, thin flakes like frost on the ground appeared on the desert floor. [15]When the Israelites saw it, they said to each other, "What is it?" For they did not know what it was. Nu 11:7-9,31; Ps 78:27-28

Moses said to them, "It is the bread the LORD has given you to eat. [16]This is what the LORD has commanded: 'Each one is to gather as much as he needs. Take an omer[a] for each person you have in your tent.' "

[17]The Israelites did as they were told; some gathered much, some little. [18]And when they measured it by the omer, he who gathered much did not have too much, and he who gathered little did not have too little. Each one gathered as much as he needed. 2Co 8:15

[19]Then Moses said to them, "No one is to keep any of it until morning." Ex 12:10

[20]However, some of them paid no attention to Moses; they kept part of it until morning, but it was full of maggots and began to smell. So Moses was angry with them.

[21]Each morning everyone gathered as much as he needed, and when the sun grew hot, it melted away. [22]On the sixth day, they gathered twice as much—two omers[b] for each person—and the leaders of the community came and reported this to Moses. [23]He said to them, "This is what the LORD commanded: 'Tomorrow is to be a day of rest, a holy Sabbath to the LORD. So bake what you want to bake and boil what you want to boil. Save whatever is left and keep it until morning.' "

[24]So they saved it until morning, as Moses commanded, and it did not stink or get maggots in it. [25]"Eat it today," Moses said, "because today is a Sabbath to the LORD. You will not find any of it on the ground today. [26]Six days you are to gather it, but on the seventh day, the Sabbath, there will not be any." Ge 2:3; Ex 20:8

[27]Nevertheless, some of the people went out on the seventh day to gather it, but they found none. [28]Then the LORD said to Moses, "How long will you[c] refuse to keep my commands and my instructions? [29]Bear in mind that the LORD has given you the Sabbath; that is why on the sixth day he gives you bread for two days. Everyone is to stay where he is on the seventh day; no one is to go out." [30]So the people rested on the seventh day.

[31]The people of Israel called the bread manna.[d] It was white like coriander seed and tasted like wafers made with honey. [32]Moses said, "This is what the LORD has commanded: 'Take an omer of manna and keep it for the generations to come, so they can see the bread I gave you to eat in the desert when I brought you out of Egypt.' "

[33]So Moses said to Aaron, "Take a jar and put an omer of manna in it. Then place it before the LORD to be kept for the generations to come."

[34]As the LORD commanded Moses, Aaron put the manna in front of the Testimony, that it might be kept. [35]The Israelites ate manna forty years, until they came to a land that was settled; they ate manna until they reached the border of Canaan.

[36](An omer is one tenth of an ephah.)

[a] *16* That is, probably about 2 quarts (about 2 liters); also in verses 18, 32, 33 and 36 [b] *22* That is, probably about 4 quarts (about 4.5 liters) [c] *28* The Hebrew is plural. [d] *31 Manna* means *What is it?* (see verse 15).

Water From the Rock

17 The whole Israelite community set out
from the Desert of Sin, traveling from
place to place as the LORD commanded. They
camped at Rephidim, but there was no water for
the people to drink. 2So they quarreled with Moses
and said, "Give us water to drink." Nu 20:2
Moses replied, "Why do you quarrel with me?
Why do you put the LORD to the test?" Dt 6:16
3But the people were thirsty for water there, and
they grumbled against Moses. They said, "Why
did you bring us up out of Egypt to make us and
our children and livestock die of thirst?" Ex 15:24
4Then Moses cried out to the LORD, "What am
I to do with these people? They are almost ready
to stone me." Nu 14:10
5The LORD answered Moses, "Walk on ahead of
the people. Take with you some of the elders of
Israel and take in your hand the staff with which
you struck the Nile, and go. 6I will stand there
before you by the rock at Horeb. Strike the rock,
and water will come out of it for the people to
drink." So Moses did this in the sight of the elders
of Israel. 7And he called the place Massah[a] and
Meribah[b] because the Israelites quarreled and because they tested the LORD saying, "Is the LORD
among us or not?" Nu 20:11; 1Co 10:4

The Amalekites Defeated

8The Amalekites came and attacked the Israelites at Rephidim. 9Moses said to Joshua, "Choose
some of our men and go out to fight the Amalekites. Tomorrow I will stand on top of the hill with
the staff of God in my hands." Dt 25:17-19
10So Joshua fought the Amalekites as Moses had
ordered, and Moses, Aaron and Hur went to the
top of the hill. 11As long as Moses held up his
hands, the Israelites were winning, but whenever
he lowered his hands, the Amalekites were winning. 12When Moses' hands grew tired, they took
a stone and put it under him and he sat on it.
Aaron and Hur held his hands up—one on one
side, one on the other—so that his hands remained steady till sunset. 13So Joshua overcame
the Amalekite army with the sword. Jas 5:16
14Then the LORD said to Moses, "Write this on
a scroll as something to be remembered and make
sure that Joshua hears it, because I will completely
blot out the memory of Amalek from under
heaven." Ex 34:27
15Moses built an altar and called it The LORD is
my Banner. 16He said, "For hands were lifted up to
the throne of the LORD. The[c] LORD will be at war
against the Amalekites from generation to generation." Ge 22:14; Nu 24:7

Jethro Visits Moses

18 Now Jethro, the priest of Midian and father-in-law of Moses, heard of everything
God had done for Moses and for his people Israel,
and how the LORD had brought Israel out of Egypt.
2After Moses had sent away his wife Zipporah,
his father-in-law Jethro received her 3and her two
sons. One son was named Gershom,[d] for Moses
said, "I have become an alien in a foreign land";
4and the other was named Eliezer,[e] for he said,
"My father's God was my helper; he saved me
from the sword of Pharaoh." Ex 2:22; 4:25; Ac 7:29
5Jethro, Moses' father-in-law, together with
Moses' sons and wife, came to him in the desert,
where he was camped near the mountain of God.
6Jethro had sent word to him, "I, your father-in-
law Jethro, am coming to you with your wife and
her two sons." Ex 3:1
7So Moses went out to meet his father-in-law
and bowed down and kissed him. They greeted
each other and then went into the tent. 8Moses
told his father-in-law about everything the LORD
had done to Pharaoh and the Egyptians for Israel's
sake and about all the hardships they had met
along the way and how the LORD had saved them.
9Jethro was delighted to hear about all the good
things the LORD had done for Israel in rescuing
them from the hand of the Egyptians. 10He said,
"Praise be to the LORD, who rescued you from the
hand of the Egyptians and of Pharaoh, and who
rescued the people from the hand of the Egyptians.
11Now I know that the LORD is greater than all
other gods, for he did this to those who had treated Israel arrogantly." 12Then Jethro, Moses' father-in-law, brought a burnt offering and other
sacrifices to God, and Aaron came with all the
elders of Israel to eat bread with Moses' father-in-
law in the presence of God. Lk 1:51; Ps 68:19-20
13The next day Moses took his seat to serve as
judge for the people, and they stood around him
from morning till evening. 14When his father-in-
law saw all that Moses was doing for the people, he
said, "What is this you are doing for the people?
Why do you alone sit as judge, while all these
people stand around you from morning till evening?"
15Moses answered him, "Because the people
come to me to seek God's will. 16Whenever they
have a dispute, it is brought to me, and I decide
between the parties and inform them of God's
decrees and laws." Nu 9:6,8; Dt 17:8-13
17Moses' father-in-law replied, "What you are
doing is not good. 18You and these people who
come to you will only wear yourselves out. The
work is too heavy for you; you cannot handle it
alone. 19Listen now to me and I will give you some

[a]7 *Massah* means *testing.* [b]7 *Meribah* means *quarreling.* [c]16 Or *"Because a hand was against the throne of the LORD, the*
[d]3 *Gershom* sounds like the Hebrew for *an alien there.* [e]4 *Eliezer* means *my God is helper.*

advice, and may God be with you. You must be the people's representative before God and bring their disputes to him. 20Teach them the decrees and laws, and show them the way to live and the duties

LIVING INSIGHT

Asking for help is smart. It's also the answer to fatigue and the "I'm indispensable" attitude. But something keeps us from this wise course of action, and that something is pride. Plain, stubborn unwillingness to admit need. The greatest battle many believers fight today is not with inefficiency, but with super efficiency.

(See Exodus 18:13–23.)

they are to perform. 21But select capable men from all the people—men who fear God, trustworthy men who hate dishonest gain—and appoint them as officials over thousands, hundreds, fifties and tens. 22Have them serve as judges for the people at all times, but have them bring every difficult case to you; the simple cases they can decide themselves. That will make your load lighter, because they will share it with you. 23If you do this and God so commands, you will be able to stand the strain, and all these people will go home satisfied."

24Moses listened to his father-in-law and did everything he said. 25He chose capable men from all Israel and made them leaders of the people, officials over thousands, hundreds, fifties and tens. 26They served as judges for the people at all times. The difficult cases they brought to Moses, but the simple ones they decided themselves. ver 22

27Then Moses sent his father-in-law on his way, and Jethro returned to his own country.

God's Law Revealed **Chapters 19–24**

After all of his travels, Moses returned to Mount Sinai. He had left alone and now he returned with about two million family members. Talk about a family reunion! The Lord called Moses up the mountain to record His Word and then to bring it to the people. For the first time God wrote down His revelation. The living God wrote His truth on tablets of stone for all to see. In this section, we find one of the most famous passages in the whole Bible . . . the Ten Commandments. Knowing what is best for humanity, God saw the need to reveal His law—not His suggestions, not options, but God's law for the people of Israel—and for us.

At Mount Sinai

19 In the third month after the Israelites left Egypt—on the very day—they came to the Desert of Sinai. 2After they set out from Rephidim, they entered the Desert of Sinai, and Israel camped there in the desert in front of the mountain. Ex 17:1

3Then Moses went up to God, and the LORD called to him from the mountain and said, "This is what you are to say to the house of Jacob and what you are to tell the people of Israel: 4'You yourselves have seen what I did to Egypt, and how I carried you on eagles' wings and brought you to myself. 5Now if you obey me fully and keep my covenant, then out of all nations you will be my treasured possession. Although the whole earth is mine, 6you[a] will be for me a kingdom of priests and a holy nation.' These are the words you are to speak to the Israelites." Dt 7:6; 1Pe 2:5

7So Moses went back and summoned the elders of the people and set before them all the words the LORD had commanded him to speak. 8The people all responded together, "We will do everything the LORD has said." So Moses brought their answer back to the LORD. Ex 24:3,7; Dt 5:27

9The LORD said to Moses, "I am going to come to you in a dense cloud, so that the people will hear me speaking with you and will always put their trust in you." Then Moses told the LORD what the people had said. ver 16; Ex 24:15-16

10And the LORD said to Moses, "Go to the people and consecrate them today and tomorrow. Have them wash their clothes 11and be ready by the third day, because on that day the LORD will come down on Mount Sinai in the sight of all the people. 12Put limits for the people around the mountain and tell them, 'Be careful that you do not go up the mountain or touch the foot of it. Whoever touches the mountain shall surely be put to death. 13He shall surely be stoned or shot with arrows; not a hand is to be laid on him. Whether man or animal, he shall not be permitted to live.' Only when the ram's horn sounds a long blast may they go up to the mountain." Lev 11:44; Heb 12:20

14After Moses had gone down the mountain to the people, he consecrated them, and they washed

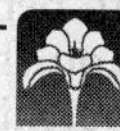

LIVING INSIGHT

Do you have a shallow concept of God? Almighty God is not a kindly grandfather or a neighborhood buddy. He is the Creator, Sustainer, Redeemer and Judge of the entire universe. He deserves—indeed demands—our utmost reverence and ultimate obedience. And He expects nothing less.

(See Exodus 19:10–13.)

[a]5,6 Or *possession, for the whole earth is mine.* 6*You*

their clothes. 15Then he said to the people, "Prepare yourselves for the third day. Abstain from
sexual relations." Ge 35:2; 1Sa 21:4
16On the morning of the third day there was
thunder and lightning, with a thick cloud over the
mountain, and a very loud trumpet blast. Everyone in the camp trembled. 17Then Moses led the
people out of the camp to meet with God, and they
stood at the foot of the mountain. 18Mount Sinai
was covered with smoke, because the LORD descended on it in fire. The smoke billowed up from
it like smoke from a furnace, the whole mountain[a] trembled violently, 19and the sound of the
trumpet grew louder and louder. Then Moses
spoke and the voice of God answered him.[b]
20The LORD descended to the top of Mount Sinai and called Moses to the top of the mountain.
So Moses went up 21and the LORD said to him, "Go
down and warn the people so they do not force
their way through to see the LORD and many of
them perish. 22Even the priests, who approach the
LORD, must consecrate themselves, or the LORD will
break out against them." Lev 10:3; 1Sa 6:19
23Moses said to the LORD, "The people cannot
come up Mount Sinai, because you yourself
warned us, 'Put limits around the mountain and
set it apart as holy.'" ver 12
24The LORD replied, "Go down and bring Aaron
up with you. But the priests and the people must
not force their way through to come up to the
LORD, or he will break out against them."
25So Moses went down to the people and told
them.

The Ten Commandments

20 And God spoke all these words:

2"I am the LORD your God, who
brought you out of Egypt, out of the
land of slavery. Ex 13:3
3"You shall have no other gods before[c] me.
4"You shall not make for yourself an idol in
the form of anything in heaven above
or on the earth beneath or in the waters below. 5You shall not bow down
to them or worship them; for I, the
LORD your God, am a jealous God,
punishing the children for the sin of
the fathers to the third and fourth generation of those who hate me, 6but
showing love to a thousand ⌞genera-
tions⌟ of those who love me and keep
my commandments. Dt 4:24; 7:9; Jer 32:18
7"You shall not misuse the name of the LORD
your God, for the LORD will not hold
anyone guiltless who misuses his
name. Lev 19:12
8"Remember the Sabbath day by keeping it
holy. 9Six days you shall labor and do
all your work, 10but the seventh day is
a Sabbath to the LORD your God. On
it you shall not do any work, neither
you, nor your son or daughter, nor
your manservant or maidservant, nor
your animals, nor the alien within
your gates. 11For in six days the LORD
made the heavens and the earth, the
sea, and all that is in them, but he
rested on the seventh day. Therefore
the LORD blessed the Sabbath day and
made it holy. Ex 31:13-16; Ge 2:2
12"Honor your father and your mother, so
that you may live long in the land the
LORD your God is giving you. Mt 15:4
13"You shall not murder. Ro 13:9
14"You shall not commit adultery. Mt 19:18
15"You shall not steal. Lev 19:11,13; Mt 19:18
16"You shall not give false testimony against
your neighbor. Ex 23:1,7
17"You shall not covet your neighbor's house.
You shall not covet your neighbor's
wife, or his manservant or maidservant, his ox or donkey, or anything
that belongs to your neighbor."

LIVING  **INSIGHT**

In the ancient days of Moses, God was so concerned that His people know His truth that He, with His finger as it were, wrote His laws into stone. Moses brought the stone tablets down from a mountain in his arms. God wanted His people to know His truth.

(See Exodus 20:1–17.)

18When the people saw the thunder and lightning and heard the trumpet and saw the mountain
in smoke, they trembled with fear. They stayed at
a distance 19and said to Moses, "Speak to us yourself and we will listen. But do not have God speak
to us or we will die." Dt 5:5,23-27; Ex 19:16-19
20Moses said to the people, "Do not be afraid.
God has come to test you, so that the fear of God
will be with you to keep you from sinning."
21The people remained at a distance, while Moses approached the thick darkness where God was.

Idols and Altars

22Then the LORD said to Moses, "Tell the Israel-

[a]18 Most Hebrew manuscripts; a few Hebrew manuscripts and Septuagint *all the people* [b]19 Or *and God answered him with thunder* [c]3 Or *besides*

ites this: 'You have seen for yourselves that I have spoken to you from heaven: 23Do not make any gods to be alongside me; do not make for yourselves gods of silver or gods of gold. ver 3

24" 'Make an altar of earth for me and sacrifice on it your burnt offerings and fellowship offerings,[a] your sheep and goats and your cattle. Wherever I cause my name to be honored, I will come to you and bless you. 25If you make an altar of stones for me, do not build it with dressed stones, for you will defile it if you use a tool on it. 26And do not go up to my altar on steps, lest your nakedness be exposed on it.' Ge 12:2; Dt 27:5-6

21 "These are the laws you are to set before them: Dt 4:14

Hebrew Servants

2"If you buy a Hebrew servant, he is to serve you for six years. But in the seventh year, he shall go free, without paying anything. 3If he comes alone, he is to go free alone; but if he has a wife when he comes, she is to go with him. 4If his master gives him a wife and she bears him sons or daughters, the woman and her children shall belong to her master, and only the man shall go free.

5"But if the servant declares, 'I love my master and my wife and children and do not want to go free,' 6then his master must take him before the judges.[b] He shall take him to the door or the doorpost and pierce his ear with an awl. Then he will be his servant for life. Dt 15:12-18

7"If a man sells his daughter as a servant, she is not to go free as menservants do. 8If she does not please the master who has selected her for himself,[c] he must let her be redeemed. He has no right to sell her to foreigners, because he has broken faith with her. 9If he selects her for his son, he must grant her the rights of a daughter. 10If he marries another woman, he must not deprive the first one of her food, clothing and marital rights. 11If he does not provide her with these three things, she is to go free, without any payment of money. Lev 25:39-55; 1Co 7:3-5

Personal Injuries

12"Anyone who strikes a man and kills him shall surely be put to death. 13However, if he does not do it intentionally, but God lets it happen, he is to flee to a place I will designate. 14But if a man schemes and kills another man deliberately, take him away from my altar and put him to death.

15"Anyone who attacks[d] his father or his mother must be put to death.

16"Anyone who kidnaps another and either sells him or still has him when he is caught must be put to death. Dt 24:7

17"Anyone who curses his father or mother must be put to death. Mk 7:10

18"If men quarrel and one hits the other with a stone or with his fist[e] and he does not die but is confined to bed, 19the one who struck the blow will not be held responsible if the other gets up and walks around outside with his staff; however, he must pay the injured man for the loss of his time and see that he is completely healed.

20"If a man beats his male or female slave with a rod and the slave dies as a direct result, he must be punished, 21but he is not to be punished if the slave gets up after a day or two, since the slave is his property. Lev 25:44-46

22"If men who are fighting hit a pregnant woman and she gives birth prematurely[f] but there is no serious injury, the offender must be fined whatever the woman's husband demands and the court allows. 23But if there is serious injury, you are to take life for life, 24eye for eye, tooth for tooth, hand for hand, foot for foot, 25burn for burn, wound for wound, bruise for bruise. Mt 5:38

26"If a man hits a manservant or maidservant in the eye and destroys it, he must let the servant go free to compensate for the eye. 27And if he knocks out the tooth of a manservant or maidservant, he must let the servant go free to compensate for the tooth.

28"If a bull gores a man or a woman to death, the bull must be stoned to death, and its meat must not be eaten. But the owner of the bull will not be held responsible. 29If, however, the bull has had the habit of goring and the owner has been warned but has not kept it penned up and it kills a man or woman, the bull must be stoned and the owner also must be put to death. 30However, if payment is demanded of him, he may redeem his life by paying whatever is demanded. 31This law also applies if the bull gores a son or daughter. 32If the bull gores a male or female slave, the owner must pay thirty shekels[g] of silver to the master of the slave, and the bull must be stoned. Zec 11:12-13

33"If a man uncovers a pit or digs one and fails to cover it and an ox or a donkey falls into it, 34the owner of the pit must pay for the loss; he must pay its owner, and the dead animal will be his.

35"If a man's bull injures the bull of another and it dies, they are to sell the live one and divide both the money and the dead animal equally. 36However, if it was known that the bull had the habit of goring, yet the owner did not keep it penned up, the owner must pay, animal for animal, and the dead animal will be his.

[a] 24 Traditionally *peace offerings* [b] 6 Or *before God* [c] 8 Or *master so that he does not choose her* [d] 15 Or *kills* [e] 18 Or *with a tool* [f] 22 Or *she has a miscarriage* [g] 32 That is, about 12 ounces (about 0.3 kilogram)

Protection of Property

22 “If a man steals an ox or a sheep and slaughters it or sells it, he must pay back five head of cattle for the ox and four sheep for the sheep. 2Sa 12:6

2“If a thief is caught breaking in and is struck so that he dies, the defender is not guilty of bloodshed; 3but if it happens[a] after sunrise, he is guilty of bloodshed. Mt 24:43

“A thief must certainly make restitution, but if he has nothing, he must be sold to pay for his theft. Ex 21:2

4“If the stolen animal is found alive in his possession—whether ox or donkey or sheep—he must pay back double. Ge 43:12

5“If a man grazes his livestock in a field or vineyard and lets them stray and they graze in another man’s field, he must make restitution from the best of his own field or vineyard. ver 1

6“If a fire breaks out and spreads into thornbushes so that it burns shocks of grain or standing grain or the whole field, the one who started the fire must make restitution. Jdg 15:5

7“If a man gives his neighbor silver or goods for safekeeping and they are stolen from the neighbor’s house, the thief, if he is caught, must pay back double. 8But if the thief is not found, the owner of the house must appear before the judges[b] to determine whether he has laid his hands on the other man’s property. 9In all cases of illegal possession of an ox, a donkey, a sheep, a garment, or any other lost property about which somebody says, ‘This is mine,’ both parties are to bring their cases before the judges. The one whom the judges declare[c] guilty must pay back double to his neighbor. Dt 25:1

10“If a man gives a donkey, an ox, a sheep or any other animal to his neighbor for safekeeping and it dies or is injured or is taken away while no one is looking, 11the issue between them will be settled by the taking of an oath before the LORD that the neighbor did not lay hands on the other person’s property. The owner is to accept this, and no restitution is required. 12But if the animal was stolen from the neighbor, he must make restitution to the owner. 13If it was torn to pieces by a wild animal, he shall bring in the remains as evidence and he will not be required to pay for the torn animal. Ge 31:39; Heb 6:16

14“If a man borrows an animal from his neighbor and it is injured or dies while the owner is not present, he must make restitution. 15But if the owner is with the animal, the borrower will not have to pay. If the animal was hired, the money paid for the hire covers the loss. Lev 19:13

Social Responsibility

16“If a man seduces a virgin who is not pledged to be married and sleeps with her, he must pay the bride-price, and she shall be his wife. 17If her father absolutely refuses to give her to him, he must still pay the bride-price for virgins. Dt 22:28

18“Do not allow a sorceress to live. Lev 20:27

19“Anyone who has sexual relations with an animal must be put to death. Lev 18:23

20“Whoever sacrifices to any god other than the LORD must be destroyed.[d] Dt 17:2-5

21“Do not mistreat an alien or oppress him, for you were aliens in Egypt. Dt 10:19

22“Do not take advantage of a widow or an orphan. 23If you do and they cry out to me, I will certainly hear their cry. 24My anger will be aroused, and I will kill you with the sword; your wives will become widows and your children fatherless. Ps 18:6; 109:9; Lk 18:7

25“If you lend money to one of my people among you who is needy, do not be like a moneylender; charge him no interest.[e] 26If you take your neighbor’s cloak as a pledge, return it to him by sunset, 27because his cloak is the only covering he has for his body. What else will he sleep in? When he cries out to me, I will hear, for I am compassionate. Ex 34:6; Lev 25:35-37

28“Do not blaspheme God[f] or curse the ruler of your people. Ac 23:5; Lev 24:11,16

29“Do not hold back offerings from your granaries or your vats.[g] Ex 23:15-16,19

“You must give me the firstborn of your sons. 30Do the same with your cattle and your sheep. Let them stay with their mothers for seven days, but give them to me on the eighth day. Ex 13:2; Lev 22:27

31“You are to be my holy people. So do not eat the meat of an animal torn by wild beasts; throw it to the dogs. Lev 19:2

Laws of Justice and Mercy

23 “Do not spread false reports. Do not help a wicked man by being a malicious witness.

2“Do not follow the crowd in doing wrong. When you give testimony in a lawsuit, do not pervert justice by siding with the crowd, 3and do not show favoritism to a poor man in his lawsuit.

4“If you come across your enemy’s ox or donkey wandering off, be sure to take it back to him. 5If you see the donkey of someone who hates you fallen down under its load, do not leave it there; be sure you help him with it. Dt 22:4

6“Do not deny justice to your poor people in their lawsuits. 7Have nothing to do with a false charge and do not put an innocent or honest person to death, for I will not acquit the guilty.

a3 Or *if he strikes him* b8 Or *before God*; also in verse 9 c9 Or *whom God declares* d20 The Hebrew term refers to the irrevocable giving over of things or persons to the LORD, often by totally destroying them. e25 Or *excessive interest* f28 Or *Do not revile the judges* g29 The meaning of the Hebrew for this phrase is uncertain.

8"Do not accept a bribe, for a bribe blinds those
who see and twists the words of the righteous.
9"Do not oppress an alien; you yourselves know
how it feels to be aliens, because you were aliens in
Egypt. Ex 22:21

Sabbath Laws

10"For six years you are to sow your fields and
harvest the crops, 11but during the seventh year let
the land lie unplowed and unused. Then the poor
among your people may get food from it, and the
wild animals may eat what they leave. Do the same
with your vineyard and your olive grove.
12"Six days do your work, but on the seventh
day do not work, so that your ox and your donkey
may rest and the slave born in your household,
and the alien as well, may be refreshed. Ex 20:9
13"Be careful to do everything I have said to
you. Do not invoke the names of other gods; do
not let them be heard on your lips. 1Ti 4:16

The Three Annual Festivals

14"Three times a year you are to celebrate a
festival to me. Ex 34:23-24
15"Celebrate the Feast of Unleavened Bread; for
seven days eat bread made without yeast, as I commanded
you. Do this at the appointed time in the
month of Abib, for in that month you came out of
Egypt. Ex 12:17
"No one is to appear before me empty-handed.
16"Celebrate the Feast of Harvest with the firstfruits
of the crops you sow in your field. Ex 34:22
"Celebrate the Feast of Ingathering at the end of
the year, when you gather in your crops from the
field. Dt 16:13
17"Three times a year all the men are to appear
before the Sovereign LORD. Dt 16:16
18"Do not offer the blood of a sacrifice to me
along with anything containing yeast. Ex 34:25
"The fat of my festival offerings must not be
kept until morning. Dt 16:4
19"Bring the best of the firstfruits of your soil to
the house of the LORD your God. Dt 26:2,10
"Do not cook a young goat in its mother's milk.

God's Angel to Prepare the Way

20"See, I am sending an angel ahead of you to
guard you along the way and to bring you to the
place I have prepared. 21Pay attention to him and
listen to what he says. Do not rebel against him; he
will not forgive your rebellion, since my Name is
in him. 22If you listen carefully to what he says and
do all that I say, I will be an enemy to your enemies
and will oppose those who oppose you. 23My
angel will go ahead of you and bring you into the
land of the Amorites, Hittites, Perizzites, Canaanites,
Hivites and Jebusites, and I will wipe them
out. 24Do not bow down before their gods or worship
them or follow their practices. You must demolish
them and break their sacred stones to
pieces. 25Worship the LORD your God, and his
blessing will be on your food and water. I will take
away sickness from among you, 26and none will
miscarry or be barren in your land. I will give you
a full life span. Dt 12:30-31; Ps 78:8,40,56; Mt 4:10
27"I will send my terror ahead of you and throw
into confusion every nation you encounter. I will
make all your enemies turn their backs and run.
28I will send the hornet ahead of you to drive the
Hivites, Canaanites and Hittites out of your way.
29But I will not drive them out in a single year,
because the land would become desolate and the
wild animals too numerous for you. 30Little by
little I will drive them out before you, until you
have increased enough to take possession of the
land. Dt 7:23; Jos 24:12
31"I will establish your borders from the Red
Sea[a] to the Sea of the Philistines,[b] and from the
desert to the River.[c] I will hand over to you the
people who live in the land and you will drive
them out before you. 32Do not make a covenant
with them or with their gods. 33Do not let them
live in your land, or they will cause you to sin
against me, because the worship of their gods will
certainly be a snare to you." Dt 7:16; Jos 21:44

The Covenant Confirmed

24 Then he said to Moses, "Come up to the
LORD, you and Aaron, Nadab and Abihu,
and seventy of the elders of Israel. You are to
worship at a distance, 2but Moses alone is to approach
the LORD; the others must not come near.
And the people may not come up with him."
3When Moses went and told the people all the
LORD's words and laws, they responded with one
voice, "Everything the LORD has said we will do."
4Moses then wrote down everything the LORD had
said. Ex 19:8; Dt 31:9
He got up early the next morning and built an
altar at the foot of the mountain and set up twelve
stone pillars representing the twelve tribes of Israel.
5Then he sent young Israelite men, and they
offered burnt offerings and sacrificed young bulls
as fellowship offerings[d] to the LORD. 6Moses took
half of the blood and put it in bowls, and the other
half he sprinkled on the altar. 7Then he took the
Book of the Covenant and read it to the people.
They responded, "We will do everything the LORD
has said; we will obey." Heb 9:19; Ex 19:8
8Moses then took the blood, sprinkled it on the
people and said, "This is the blood of the covenant

[a]31 Hebrew *Yam Suph*; that is, Sea of Reeds [b]31 That is, the Mediterranean [c]31 That is, the Euphrates
[d]5 Traditionally *peace offerings*

that the LORD has made with you in accordance with all these words." Heb 9:20; 1Pe 1:2

9Moses and Aaron, Nadab and Abihu, and the seventy elders of Israel went up 10and saw the God of Israel. Under his feet was something like a pavement made of sapphire,[a] clear as the sky itself. 11But God did not raise his hand against these leaders of the Israelites; they saw God, and they ate and drank. Ge 32:30; Eze 1:26; Rev 4:3

12The LORD said to Moses, "Come up to me on the mountain and stay here, and I will give you the tablets of stone, with the law and commands I have written for their instruction." Ex 32:15-16

13Then Moses set out with Joshua his aide, and Moses went up on the mountain of God. 14He said to the elders, "Wait here for us until we come back to you. Aaron and Hur are with you, and anyone involved in a dispute can go to them." Ex 3:1; 17:9

15When Moses went up on the mountain, the cloud covered it, 16and the glory of the LORD settled on Mount Sinai. For six days the cloud covered the mountain, and on the seventh day the LORD called to Moses from within the cloud. 17To the Israelites the glory of the LORD looked like a consuming fire on top of the mountain. 18Then Moses entered the cloud as he went on up the mountain. And he stayed on the mountain forty days and forty nights. Heb 12:18,29; Ex 19:9

A Place to Worship **Chapters 25–40**

Now that the people of Israel were delivered from Egypt they needed a place where they could worship the Lord. The remaining chapters of Exodus are devoted, therefore, to specific instructions for building the tabernacle. This portable sanctuary was not a large structure. The outer court was only 150 feet long and 75 feet wide. Inside this area was the Tent of Meeting, which was only 45 feet long and 15 feet wide. Inside the tabernacle were many articles devoted for the worship of God: a bronze altar, a basin, a golden lampstand, a table for bread, an altar for incense and the ark of the covenant. The very presence of God was said to dwell over the atonement cover, which was on top of the ark. This portable tabernacle was central in the community life of the nation. After it was set up, the glory of the Lord flooded the holy place. What a wonderful reminder of the Lord's presence with the people wherever they went!

Offerings for the Tabernacle

25 The LORD said to Moses, 2"Tell the Israelites to bring me an offering. You are to receive the offering for me from each man whose heart prompts him to give. 3These are the offerings you are to receive from them: gold, silver and bronze; 4blue, purple and scarlet yarn and fine linen; goat hair; 5ram skins dyed red and hides of sea cows[b]; acacia wood; 6olive oil for the light; spices for the anointing oil and for the fragrant incense; 7and onyx stones and other gems to be mounted on the ephod and breastpiece. Ex 35:4-9

8"Then have them make a sanctuary for me, and I will dwell among them. 9Make this tabernacle and all its furnishings exactly like the pattern I will show you. Ex 29:45; Rev 21:3

The Ark

10"Have them make a chest of acacia wood—two and a half cubits long, a cubit and a half wide, and a cubit and a half high.[c] 11Overlay it with pure gold, both inside and out, and make a gold molding around it. 12Cast four gold rings for it and fasten them to its four feet, with two rings on one side and two rings on the other. 13Then make poles of acacia wood and overlay them with gold. 14Insert the poles into the rings on the sides of the chest to carry it. 15The poles are to remain in the rings of this ark; they are not to be removed. 16Then put in the ark the Testimony, which I will give you. Dt 31:26; Heb 9:4

17"Make an atonement cover[d] of pure gold—two and a half cubits long and a cubit and a half wide.[e] 18And make two cherubim out of hammered gold at the ends of the cover. 19Make one cherub on one end and the second cherub on the other; make the cherubim of one piece with the cover, at the two ends. 20The cherubim are to have their wings spread upward, overshadowing the cover with them. The cherubim are to face each other, looking toward the cover. 21Place the cover on top of the ark and put in the ark the Testimony, which I will give you. 22There, above the cover between the two cherubim that are over the ark of the Testimony, I will meet with you and give you all my commands for the Israelites. Ex 37:1-9

The Table

23"Make a table of acacia wood—two cubits long, a cubit wide and a cubit and a half high.[f] 24Overlay it with pure gold and make a gold molding around it. 25Also make around it a rim a handbreadth[g] wide and put a gold molding on the rim. 26Make four gold rings for the table and fasten them to the four corners, where the four legs are. 27The rings are to be close to the rim to hold the poles used in carrying the table. 28Make the poles of acacia wood, overlay them with gold and carry the table with them. 29And make its plates and dishes of pure gold, as well as its pitchers and bowls for the pouring out of offerings. 30Put the

[a] 10 Or *lapis lazuli* [b] 5 That is, dugongs [c] 10 That is, about 3 3/4 feet (about 1.1 meters) long and 2 1/4 feet (about 0.7 meter) wide and high [d] 17 Traditionally *a mercy seat* [e] 17 That is, about 3 3/4 feet (about 1.1 meters) long and 2 1/4 feet (about 0.7 meter) wide [f] 23 That is, about 3 feet (about 0.9 meter) long and 1 1/2 feet (about 0.5 meter) wide and 2 1/4 feet (about 0.7 meter) high [g] 25 That is, about 3 inches (about 8 centimeters)

bread of the Presence on this table to be before me at all times. Ex 37:10-16; Nu 4:7

The Lampstand

31“Make a lampstand of pure gold and hammer it out, base and shaft; its flowerlike cups, buds and blossoms shall be of one piece with it. 32Six branches are to extend from the sides of the lampstand—three on one side and three on the other. 33Three cups shaped like almond flowers with buds and blossoms are to be on one branch, three on the next branch, and the same for all six branches extending from the lampstand. 34And on the lampstand there are to be four cups shaped like almond flowers with buds and blossoms. 35One bud shall be under the first pair of branches extending from the lampstand, a second bud under the second pair, and a third bud under the third pair—six branches in all. 36The buds and branches shall all be of one piece with the lampstand, hammered out of pure gold. Zec 4:2; Rev 1:12

37“Then make its seven lamps and set them up on it so that they light the space in front of it. 38Its wick trimmers and trays are to be of pure gold. 39A talent[a] of pure gold is to be used for the lampstand and all these accessories. 40See that you make them according to the pattern shown you on the mountain. Ex 37:17-24; Ac 7:44; Heb 8:5

The Tabernacle

26 “Make the tabernacle with ten curtains of finely twisted linen and blue, purple and scarlet yarn, with cherubim worked into them by a skilled craftsman. 2All the curtains are to be the same size—twenty-eight cubits long and four cubits wide.[b] 3Join five of the curtains together, and do the same with the other five. 4Make loops of blue material along the edge of the end curtain in one set, and do the same with the end curtain in the other set. 5Make fifty loops on one curtain and fifty loops on the end curtain of the other set, with the loops opposite each other. 6Then make fifty gold clasps and use them to fasten the curtains together so that the tabernacle is a unit. Ex 36:8-13

7“Make curtains of goat hair for the tent over the tabernacle—eleven altogether. 8All eleven curtains are to be the same size—thirty cubits long and four cubits wide.[c] 9Join five of the curtains together into one set and the other six into another set. Fold the sixth curtain double at the front of the tent. 10Make fifty loops along the edge of the end curtain in one set and also along the edge of the end curtain in the other set. 11Then make fifty bronze clasps and put them in the loops to fasten the tent together as a unit. 12As for the additional length of the tent curtains, the half curtain that is left over is to hang down at the rear of the tabernacle. 13The tent curtains will be a cubit[d] longer on both sides; what is left will hang over the sides of the tabernacle so as to cover it. 14Make for the tent a covering of ram skins dyed red, and over that a covering of hides of sea cows.[e] Ex 36:14-19

15“Make upright frames of acacia wood for the tabernacle. 16Each frame is to be ten cubits long and a cubit and a half wide,[f] 17with two projections set parallel to each other. Make all the frames of the tabernacle in this way. 18Make twenty frames for the south side of the tabernacle 19and make forty silver bases to go under them—two bases for each frame, one under each projection. 20For the other side, the north side of the tabernacle, make twenty frames 21and forty silver bases—two under each frame. 22Make six frames for the far end, that is, the west end of the tabernacle, 23and make two frames for the corners at the far end. 24At these two corners they must be double from the bottom all the way to the top, and fitted into a single ring; both shall be like that. 25So there will be eight frames and sixteen silver bases—two under each frame. Ex 36:20-30

26“Also make crossbars of acacia wood: five for the frames on one side of the tabernacle, 27five for those on the other side, and five for the frames on the west, at the far end of the tabernacle. 28The center crossbar is to extend from end to end at the middle of the frames. 29Overlay the frames with gold and make gold rings to hold the crossbars. Also overlay the crossbars with gold. Ex 36:31-34

30“Set up the tabernacle according to the plan shown you on the mountain. Ex 25:9,40; Ac 7:44; Heb 8:5

31“Make a curtain of blue, purple and scarlet yarn and finely twisted linen, with cherubim worked into it by a skilled craftsman. 32Hang it with gold hooks on four posts of acacia wood overlaid with gold and standing on four silver bases. 33Hang the curtain from the clasps and place the ark of the Testimony behind the curtain. The curtain will separate the Holy Place from the Most Holy Place. 34Put the atonement cover on the ark of the Testimony in the Most Holy Place. 35Place the table outside the curtain on the north side of the tabernacle and put the lampstand opposite it on the south side. Ex 36:35-36; Heb 9:2-3

36“For the entrance to the tent make a curtain of blue, purple and scarlet yarn and finely twisted linen—the work of an embroiderer. 37Make gold hooks for this curtain and five posts of acacia wood overlaid with gold. And cast five bronze bases for them. Ex 36:37-38

[a] *39* That is, about 75 pounds (about 34 kilograms) [b] *2* That is, about 42 feet (about 12.5 meters) long and 6 feet (about 1.8 meters) wide [c] *8* That is, about 45 feet (about 13.5 meters) long and 6 feet (about 1.8 meters) wide [d] *13* That is, about 1 1/2 feet (about 0.5 meter) [e] *14* That is, dugongs [f] *16* That is, about 15 feet (about 4.5 meters) long and 2 1/4 feet (about 0.7 meter) wide

The Altar of Burnt Offering

27 "Build an altar of acacia wood, three cubits[a] high; it is to be square, five cubits long and five cubits wide.[b] 2Make a horn at each of the four corners, so that the horns and the altar are of one piece, and overlay the altar with bronze. 3Make all its utensils of bronze—its pots to remove the ashes, and its shovels, sprinkling bowls, meat forks and firepans. 4Make a grating for it, a bronze network, and make a bronze ring at each of the four corners of the network. 5Put it under the ledge of the altar so that it is halfway up the altar. 6Make poles of acacia wood for the altar and overlay them with bronze. 7The poles are to be inserted into the rings so they will be on two sides of the altar when it is carried. 8Make the altar hollow, out of boards. It is to be made just as you were shown on the mountain. Ex 38:1-7

The Courtyard

9"Make a courtyard for the tabernacle. The south side shall be a hundred cubits[c] long and is to have curtains of finely twisted linen, 10with twenty posts and twenty bronze bases and with silver hooks and bands on the posts. 11The north side shall also be a hundred cubits long and is to have curtains, with twenty posts and twenty bronze bases and with silver hooks and bands on the posts.

12"The west end of the courtyard shall be fifty cubits[d] wide and have curtains, with ten posts and ten bases. 13On the east end, toward the sunrise, the courtyard shall also be fifty cubits wide. 14Curtains fifteen cubits[e] long are to be on one side of the entrance, with three posts and three bases, 15and curtains fifteen cubits long are to be on the other side, with three posts and three bases.

16"For the entrance to the courtyard, provide a curtain twenty cubits[f] long, of blue, purple and scarlet yarn and finely twisted linen—the work of an embroiderer—with four posts and four bases. 17All the posts around the courtyard are to have silver bands and hooks, and bronze bases. 18The courtyard shall be a hundred cubits long and fifty cubits wide,[g] with curtains of finely twisted linen five cubits[h] high, and with bronze bases. 19All the other articles used in the service of the tabernacle, whatever their function, including all the tent pegs for it and those for the courtyard, are to be of bronze. Ex 38:9-20

Oil for the Lampstand

20"Command the Israelites to bring you clear oil of pressed olives for the light so that the lamps may be kept burning. 21In the Tent of Meeting, outside the curtain that is in front of the Testimony, Aaron and his sons are to keep the lamps burning before the LORD from evening till morning. This is to be a lasting ordinance among the Israelites for the generations to come. Lev 24:1-3

The Priestly Garments

28 "Have Aaron your brother brought to you from among the Israelites, along with his sons Nadab and Abihu, Eleazar and Ithamar, so they may serve me as priests. 2Make sacred garments for your brother Aaron, to give him dignity and honor. 3Tell all the skilled men to whom I have given wisdom in such matters that they are to make garments for Aaron, for his consecration, so he may serve me as priest. 4These are the garments they are to make: a breastpiece, an ephod, a robe, a woven tunic, a turban and a sash. They are to make these sacred garments for your brother Aaron and his sons, so they may serve me as priests. 5Have them use gold, and blue, purple and scarlet yarn, and fine linen. Ex 31:3,6

The Ephod

6"Make the ephod of gold, and of blue, purple and scarlet yarn, and of finely twisted linen—the work of a skilled craftsman. 7It is to have two shoulder pieces attached to two of its corners, so it can be fastened. 8Its skillfully woven waistband is to be like it—of one piece with the ephod and made with gold, and with blue, purple and scarlet yarn, and with finely twisted linen.

9"Take two onyx stones and engrave on them the names of the sons of Israel 10in the order of their birth—six names on one stone and the remaining six on the other. 11Engrave the names of the sons of Israel on the two stones the way a gem cutter engraves a seal. Then mount the stones in gold filigree settings 12and fasten them on the shoulder pieces of the ephod as memorial stones for the sons of Israel. Aaron is to bear the names on his shoulders as a memorial before the LORD. 13Make gold filigree settings 14and two braided chains of pure gold, like a rope, and attach the chains to the settings. Ex 39:2-7

The Breastpiece

15"Fashion a breastpiece for making decisions—the work of a skilled craftsman. Make it like the ephod: of gold, and of blue, purple and scarlet yarn, and of finely twisted linen. 16It is to be square—a span[i] long and a span wide—and folded double. 17Then mount four rows of pre-

[a] *1* That is, about 4 1/2 feet (about 1.3 meters) [b] *1* That is, about 7 1/2 feet (about 2.3 meters) long and wide [c] *9* That is, about 150 feet (about 46 meters); also in verse 11 [d] *12* That is, about 75 feet (about 23 meters); also in verse 13 [e] *14* That is, about 22 1/2 feet (about 6.9 meters); also in verse 15 [f] *16* That is, about 30 feet (about 9 meters) [g] *18* That is, about 150 feet (about 46 meters) long and 75 feet (about 23 meters) wide [h] *18* That is, about 7 1/2 feet (about 2.3 meters) [i] *16* That is, about 9 inches (about 22 centimeters)

cious stones on it. In the first row there shall be a ruby, a topaz and a beryl; 18in the second row a turquoise, a sapphire[a] and an emerald; 19in the third row a jacinth, an agate and an amethyst; 20in the fourth row a chrysolite, an onyx and a jasper.[b] Mount them in gold filigree settings. 21There are to be twelve stones, one for each of the names of the sons of Israel, each engraved like a seal with the name of one of the twelve tribes. Rev 21:12

22"For the breastpiece make braided chains of pure gold, like a rope. 23Make two gold rings for it and fasten them to two corners of the breastpiece. 24Fasten the two gold chains to the rings at the corners of the breastpiece, 25and the other ends of the chains to the two settings, attaching them to the shoulder pieces of the ephod at the front. 26Make two gold rings and attach them to the other two corners of the breastpiece on the inside edge next to the ephod. 27Make two more gold rings and attach them to the bottom of the shoulder pieces on the front of the ephod, close to the seam just above the waistband of the ephod. 28The rings of the breastpiece are to be tied to the rings of the ephod with blue cord, connecting it to the waistband, so that the breastpiece will not swing out from the ephod. Ex 39:8-21

29"Whenever Aaron enters the Holy Place, he will bear the names of the sons of Israel over his heart on the breastpiece of decision as a continuing memorial before the LORD. 30Also put the Urim and the Thummim in the breastpiece, so they may be over Aaron's heart whenever he enters the presence of the LORD. Thus Aaron will always bear the means of making decisions for the Israelites over his heart before the LORD. Lev 8:8; Nu 27:21

Other Priestly Garments

31"Make the robe of the ephod entirely of blue cloth, 32with an opening for the head in its center. There shall be a woven edge like a collar[c] around this opening, so that it will not tear. 33Make pomegranates of blue, purple and scarlet yarn around the hem of the robe, with gold bells between them. 34The gold bells and the pomegranates are to alternate around the hem of the robe. 35Aaron must wear it when he ministers. The sound of the bells will be heard when he enters the Holy Place before the LORD and when he comes out, so that he will not die.

36"Make a plate of pure gold and engrave on it as on a seal: HOLY TO THE LORD. 37Fasten a blue cord to it to attach it to the turban; it is to be on the front of the turban. 38It will be on Aaron's forehead, and he will bear the guilt involved in the sacred gifts the Israelites consecrate, whatever their gifts may be. It will be on Aaron's forehead continually so that they will be acceptable to the LORD.

39"Weave the tunic of fine linen and make the turban of fine linen. The sash is to be the work of an embroiderer. 40Make tunics, sashes and headbands for Aaron's sons, to give them dignity and honor. 41After you put these clothes on your brother Aaron and his sons, anoint and ordain them. Consecrate them so they may serve me as priests. Ex 29:7-9; Lev 18:1-36

42"Make linen undergarments as a covering for the body, reaching from the waist to the thigh. 43Aaron and his sons must wear them whenever they enter the Tent of Meeting or approach the altar to minister in the Holy Place, so that they will not incur guilt and die. Ex 20:26

"This is to be a lasting ordinance for Aaron and his descendants. Ex 39:22-31

Consecration of the Priests

29 "This is what you are to do to consecrate them, so they may serve me as priests: Take a young bull and two rams without defect. 2And from fine wheat flour, without yeast, make bread, and cakes mixed with oil, and wafers spread with oil. 3Put them in a basket and present them in it—along with the bull and the two rams. 4Then bring Aaron and his sons to the entrance to the Tent of Meeting and wash them with water. 5Take the garments and dress Aaron with the tunic, the robe of the ephod, the ephod itself and the breastpiece. Fasten the ephod on him by its skillfully woven waistband. 6Put the turban on his head and attach the sacred diadem to the turban. 7Take the anointing oil and anoint him by pouring it on his head. 8Bring his sons and dress them in tunics 9and put headbands on them. Then tie sashes on Aaron and his sons.[d] The priesthood is theirs by a lasting ordinance. In this way you shall ordain Aaron and his sons. Nu 18:7; Ex 30:25,30-31; Lev 21:10

10"Bring the bull to the front of the Tent of Meeting, and Aaron and his sons shall lay their hands on its head. 11Slaughter it in the LORD's presence at the entrance to the Tent of Meeting. 12Take some of the bull's blood and put it on the horns of the altar with your finger, and pour out the rest of it at the base of the altar. 13Then take all the fat around the inner parts, the covering of the liver, and both kidneys with the fat on them, and burn them on the altar. 14But burn the bull's flesh and its hide and its offal outside the camp. It is a sin offering. Lev 1:4; Heb 13:11

15"Take one of the rams, and Aaron and his sons shall lay their hands on its head. 16Slaughter it and take the blood and sprinkle it against the altar on all sides. 17Cut the ram into pieces and wash the inner parts and the legs, putting them

[a] 18 Or *lapis lazuli* [b] 20 The precise identification of some of these precious stones is uncertain. [c] 32 The meaning of the Hebrew for this word is uncertain. [d] 9 Hebrew; Septuagint *on them*

with the head and the other pieces. [18]Then burn the entire ram on the altar. It is a burnt offering to the LORD, a pleasing aroma, an offering made to the LORD by fire. Ge 8:21

[19]"Take the other ram, and Aaron and his sons shall lay their hands on its head. [20]Slaughter it, take some of its blood and put it on the lobes of the right ears of Aaron and his sons, on the thumbs of their right hands, and on the big toes of their right feet. Then sprinkle blood against the altar on all sides. [21]And take some of the blood on the altar and some of the anointing oil and sprinkle it on Aaron and his garments and on his sons and their garments. Then he and his sons and their garments will be consecrated. Heb 9:22

[22]"Take from this ram the fat, the fat tail, the fat around the inner parts, the covering of the liver, both kidneys with the fat on them, and the right thigh. (This is the ram for the ordination.) [23]From the basket of bread made without yeast, which is before the LORD, take a loaf, and a cake made with oil, and a wafer. [24]Put all these in the hands of Aaron and his sons and wave them before the LORD as a wave offering. [25]Then take them from their hands and burn them on the altar along with the burnt offering for a pleasing aroma to the LORD, an offering made to the LORD by fire. [26]After you take the breast of the ram for Aaron's ordination, wave it before the LORD as a wave offering, and it will be your share. Lev 7:30

[27]"Consecrate those parts of the ordination ram that belong to Aaron and his sons: the breast that was waved and the thigh that was presented. [28]This is always to be the regular share from the Israelites for Aaron and his sons. It is the contribution the Israelites are to make to the LORD from their fellowship offerings.[a] Lev 7:31,34

[29]"Aaron's sacred garments will belong to his descendants so that they can be anointed and ordained in them. [30]The son who succeeds him as priest and comes to the Tent of Meeting to minister in the Holy Place is to wear them seven days.

[31]"Take the ram for the ordination and cook the meat in a sacred place. [32]At the entrance to the Tent of Meeting, Aaron and his sons are to eat the meat of the ram and the bread that is in the basket. [33]They are to eat these offerings by which atonement was made for their ordination and consecration. But no one else may eat them, because they are sacred. [34]And if any of the meat of the ordination ram or any bread is left over till morning, burn it up. It must not be eaten, because it is sacred. Lev 22:10,13

[35]"Do for Aaron and his sons everything I have commanded you, taking seven days to ordain them. [36]Sacrifice a bull each day as a sin offering to make atonement. Purify the altar by making atonement for it, and anoint it to consecrate it. [37]For seven days make atonement for the altar and consecrate it. Then the altar will be most holy, and whatever touches it will be holy. Lev 8:1-36

[38]"This is what you are to offer on the altar regularly each day: two lambs a year old. [39]Offer one in the morning and the other at twilight. [40]With the first lamb offer a tenth of an ephah[b] of fine flour mixed with a quarter of a hin[c] of oil from pressed olives, and a quarter of a hin of wine as a drink offering. [41]Sacrifice the other lamb at twilight with the same grain offering and its drink offering as in the morning—a pleasing aroma, an offering made to the LORD by fire. Nu 28:3-8

[42]"For the generations to come this burnt offering is to be made regularly at the entrance to the Tent of Meeting before the LORD. There I will meet you and speak to you; [43]there also I will meet with the Israelites, and the place will be consecrated by my glory. Ex 25:22; 1Ki 8:11

[44]"So I will consecrate the Tent of Meeting and the altar and will consecrate Aaron and his sons to serve me as priests. [45]Then I will dwell among the Israelites and be their God. [46]They will know that I am the LORD their God, who brought them out of Egypt so that I might dwell among them. I am the LORD their God. Ex 25:8; 2Co 6:16; Rev 21:3

The Altar of Incense

30 "Make an altar of acacia wood for burning incense. [2]It is to be square, a cubit long and a cubit wide, and two cubits high[d]—its horns of one piece with it. [3]Overlay the top and all the sides and the horns with pure gold, and make a gold molding around it. [4]Make two gold rings for the altar below the molding—two on opposite sides—to hold the poles used to carry it. [5]Make the poles of acacia wood and overlay them with gold. [6]Put the altar in front of the curtain that is before the ark of the Testimony—before the atonement cover that is over the Testimony—where I will meet with you. Ex 37:25-28

[7]"Aaron must burn fragrant incense on the altar every morning when he tends the lamps. [8]He must burn incense again when he lights the lamps at twilight so incense will burn regularly before the LORD for the generations to come. [9]Do not offer on this altar any other incense or any burnt offering or grain offering, and do not pour a drink offering on it. [10]Once a year Aaron shall make atonement on its horns. This annual atonement must be made with the blood of the atoning sin offering for the generations to come. It is most holy to the LORD." Lev 16:18-19,30

[a]28 Traditionally *peace offerings* [b]40 That is, probably about 2 quarts (about 2 liters) [c]40 That is, probably about 1 quart (about 1 liter) [d]2 That is, about 1 1/2 feet (about 0.5 meter) long and wide and about 3 feet (about 0.9 meter) high

Atonement Money

11Then the LORD said to Moses, 12“When you take a census of the Israelites to count them, each one must pay the LORD a ransom for his life at the time he is counted. Then no plague will come on them when you number them. 13Each one who crosses over to those already counted is to give a half shekel,[a] according to the sanctuary shekel, which weighs twenty gerahs. This half shekel is an offering to the LORD. 14All who cross over, those twenty years old or more, are to give an offering to the LORD. 15The rich are not to give more than a half shekel and the poor are not to give less when you make the offering to the LORD to atone for your lives. 16Receive the atonement money from the Israelites and use it for the service of the Tent of Meeting. It will be a memorial for the Israelites before the LORD, making atonement for your lives.” Nu 1:2,49; 31:50

Basin for Washing

17Then the LORD said to Moses, 18“Make a bronze basin, with its bronze stand, for washing. Place it between the Tent of Meeting and the altar, and put water in it. 19Aaron and his sons are to wash their hands and feet with water from it. 20Whenever they enter the Tent of Meeting, they shall wash with water so that they will not die. Also, when they approach the altar to minister by presenting an offering made to the LORD by fire, 21they shall wash their hands and feet so that they will not die. This is to be a lasting ordinance for Aaron and his descendants for the generations to come.” Ex 27:21; 40:31-32

Anointing Oil

22Then the LORD said to Moses, 23“Take the following fine spices: 500 shekels[b] of liquid myrrh, half as much (that is, 250 shekels) of fragrant cinnamon, 250 shekels of fragrant cane, 24500 shekels of cassia—all according to the sanctuary shekel—and a hin[c] of olive oil. 25Make these into a sacred anointing oil, a fragrant blend, the work of a perfumer. It will be the sacred anointing oil. 26Then use it to anoint the Tent of Meeting, the ark of the Testimony, 27the table and all its articles, the lampstand and its accessories, the altar of incense, 28the altar of burnt offering and all its utensils, and the basin with its stand. 29You shall consecrate them so they will be most holy, and whatever touches them will be holy. Ex 37:29; Lev 8:10

30“Anoint Aaron and his sons and consecrate them so they may serve me as priests. 31Say to the Israelites, ‘This is to be my sacred anointing oil for the generations to come. 32Do not pour it on men’s bodies and do not make any oil with the same formula. It is sacred, and you are to consider it sacred. 33Whoever makes perfume like it and whoever puts it on anyone other than a priest must be cut off from his people.’ ” Lev 8:2,12,30

Incense

34Then the LORD said to Moses, “Take fragrant spices—gum resin, onycha and galbanum—and pure frankincense, all in equal amounts, 35and make a fragrant blend of incense, the work of a perfumer. It is to be salted and pure and sacred. 36Grind some of it to powder and place it in front of the Testimony in the Tent of Meeting, where I will meet with you. It shall be most holy to you. 37Do not make any incense with this formula for yourselves; consider it holy to the LORD. 38Whoever makes any like it to enjoy its fragrance must be cut off from his people.” Ex 29:37; Lev 2:3

Bezalel and Oholiab

31 Then the LORD said to Moses, 2“See, I have chosen Bezalel son of Uri, the son of Hur, of the tribe of Judah, 3and I have filled him with the Spirit of God, with skill, ability and knowledge in all kinds of crafts— 4to make artistic designs for work in gold, silver and bronze, 5to cut and set stones, to work in wood, and to engage in all kinds of craftsmanship. 6Moreover, I have appointed Oholiab son of Ahisamach, of the tribe of Dan, to help him. Also I have given skill to all the craftsmen to make everything I have commanded you: 7the Tent of Meeting, the ark of the Testimony with the atonement cover on it, and all the other furnishings of the tent— 8the table and its articles, the pure gold lampstand and all its accessories, the altar of incense, 9the altar of burnt offering and all its utensils, the basin with its stand— 10and also the woven garments, both the sacred garments for Aaron the priest and the garments for his sons when they serve as priests, 11and the anointing oil and fragrant incense for the Holy Place. They are to make them just as I commanded you.”

The Sabbath

12Then the LORD said to Moses, 13“Say to the Israelites, ‘You must observe my Sabbaths. This will be a sign between me and you for the generations to come, so you may know that I am the LORD, who makes you holy.[d] Eze 20:12,20

14“ ‘Observe the Sabbath, because it is holy to you. Anyone who desecrates it must be put to death; whoever does any work on that day must be cut off from his people. 15For six days, work is to be done, but the seventh day is a Sabbath of rest, holy to the LORD. Whoever does any work on the Sabbath day must be put to death. 16The Israelites

[a] 13 That is, about 1/5 ounce (about 6 grams); also in verse 15
[b] 23 That is, about 12 1/2 pounds (about 6 kilograms)
[c] 24 That is, probably about 4 quarts (about 4 liters)
[d] 13 Or *who sanctifies you*; or *who sets you apart as holy*

are to observe the Sabbath, celebrating it for the generations to come as a lasting covenant. [17]It will be a sign between me and the Israelites forever, for in six days the LORD made the heavens and the earth, and on the seventh day he abstained from work and rested.'" Ex 20:8-11

[18]When the LORD finished speaking to Moses on Mount Sinai, he gave him the two tablets of the Testimony, the tablets of stone inscribed by the finger of God. Ex 32:15-16

The Golden Calf

32 When the people saw that Moses was so long in coming down from the mountain, they gathered around Aaron and said, "Come, make us gods[a] who will go before us. As for this fellow Moses who brought us up out of Egypt, we don't know what has happened to him." Ac 7:40

> **LIVING**  **INSIGHT**
>
> ***Defiance is frequently permitted by us and sometimes totally ignored, leaving others in the wake of its serious consequences. God never overlooks or winks at defiance. He deals with it, and we are to take our cues from our Lord.***
>
> **(See Exodus 32:1.)**

[2]Aaron answered them, "Take off the gold earrings that your wives, your sons and your daughters are wearing, and bring them to me." [3]So all the people took off their earrings and brought them to Aaron. [4]He took what they handed him and made it into an idol cast in the shape of a calf, fashioning it with a tool. Then they said, "These are your gods,[b] O Israel, who brought you up out of Egypt." Dt 9:16

[5]When Aaron saw this, he built an altar in front of the calf and announced, "Tomorrow there will be a festival to the LORD." [6]So the next day the people rose early and sacrificed burnt offerings and presented fellowship offerings.[c] Afterward they sat down to eat and drink and got up to indulge in revelry. 1Co 10:7

[7]Then the LORD said to Moses, "Go down, because your people, whom you brought up out of Egypt, have become corrupt. [8]They have been quick to turn away from what I commanded them and have made themselves an idol cast in the shape of a calf. They have bowed down to it and sacrificed to it and have said, 'These are your gods, O Israel, who brought you up out of Egypt.'

[9]"I have seen these people," the LORD said to Moses, "and they are a stiff-necked people. [10]Now leave me alone so that my anger may burn against them and that I may destroy them. Then I will make you into a great nation." Ex 33:3,5; Isa 48:4

[11]But Moses sought the favor of the LORD his God. "O LORD," he said, "why should your anger burn against your people, whom you brought out of Egypt with great power and a mighty hand? [12]Why should the Egyptians say, 'It was with evil intent that he brought them out, to kill them in the mountains and to wipe them off the face of the earth'? Turn from your fierce anger; relent and do not bring disaster on your people. [13]Remember your servants Abraham, Isaac and Israel, to whom you swore by your own self: 'I will make your descendants as numerous as the stars in the sky and I will give your descendants all this land I promised them, and it will be their inheritance forever.'" [14]Then the LORD relented and did not bring on his people the disaster he had threatened.

[15]Moses turned and went down the mountain with the two tablets of the Testimony in his hands. They were inscribed on both sides, front and back. [16]The tablets were the work of God; the writing was the writing of God, engraved on the tablets.

[17]When Joshua heard the noise of the people shouting, he said to Moses, "There is the sound of war in the camp."

[18]Moses replied:

"It is not the sound of victory,
  it is not the sound of defeat;
  it is the sound of singing that I hear."

[19]When Moses approached the camp and saw the calf and the dancing, his anger burned and he threw the tablets out of his hands, breaking them to pieces at the foot of the mountain. [20]And he took the calf they had made and burned it in the fire; then he ground it to powder, scattered it on the water and made the Israelites drink it.

[21]He said to Aaron, "What did these people do to you, that you led them into such great sin?"

[22]"Do not be angry, my lord," Aaron answered. "You know how prone these people are to evil. [23]They said to me, 'Make us gods who will go before us. As for this fellow Moses who brought us up out of Egypt, we don't know what has happened to him.' [24]So I told them, 'Whoever has any gold jewelry, take it off.' Then they gave me the gold, and I threw it into the fire, and out came this calf!" Dt 9:24

[25]Moses saw that the people were running wild and that Aaron had let them get out of control and so become a laughingstock to their enemies. [26]So he stood at the entrance to the camp and said, "Whoever is for the LORD, come to me." And all the Levites rallied to him.

[27]Then he said to them, "This is what the LORD, the God of Israel, says: 'Each man strap a sword to

[a]1 Or *a god*; also in verses 23 and 31 [b]4 Or *This is your god*; also in verse 8 [c]6 Traditionally *peace offerings*

his side. Go back and forth through the camp from
one end to the other, each killing his brother and
friend and neighbor.' " 28The Levites did as Moses
commanded, and that day about three thousand of
the people died. 29Then Moses said, "You have
been set apart to the LORD today, for you were
against your own sons and brothers, and he has
blessed you this day." Nu 25:3,5; Dt 33:9
30The next day Moses said to the people, "You
have committed a great sin. But now I will go up
to the LORD; perhaps I can make atonement for
your sin." Lev 1:4; Nu 25:13
31So Moses went back to the LORD and said,
"Oh, what a great sin these people have committed! They have made themselves gods of gold.
32But now, please forgive their sin—but if not,
then blot me out of the book you have written."
33The LORD replied to Moses, "Whoever has
sinned against me I will blot out of my book.
34Now go, lead the people to the place I spoke of,
and my angel will go before you. However, when
the time comes for me to punish, I will punish
them for their sin." Dt 29:20; 32:35; Ps 99:8
35And the LORD struck the people with a plague
because of what they did with the calf Aaron had
made.

33 Then the LORD said to Moses, "Leave this
place, you and the people you brought up
out of Egypt, and go up to the land I promised on
oath to Abraham, Isaac and Jacob, saying, 'I will
give it to your descendants.' 2I will send an angel
before you and drive out the Canaanites, Amorites, Hittites, Perizzites, Hivites and Jebusites. 3Go
up to the land flowing with milk and honey. But
I will not go with you, because you are a stiff-
necked people and I might destroy you on the
way." Ex 3:8; 32:10
4When the people heard these distressing
words, they began to mourn and no one put on
any ornaments. 5For the LORD had said to Moses,
"Tell the Israelites, 'You are a stiff-necked people.
If I were to go with you even for a moment, I
might destroy you. Now take off your ornaments
and I will decide what to do with you.' " 6So the
Israelites stripped off their ornaments at Mount
Horeb. Nu 14:39

The Tent of Meeting

7Now Moses used to take a tent and pitch it
outside the camp some distance away, calling it the
"tent of meeting." Anyone inquiring of the LORD
would go to the tent of meeting outside the camp.
8And whenever Moses went out to the tent, all the
people rose and stood at the entrances to their
tents, watching Moses until he entered the tent.
9As Moses went into the tent, the pillar of cloud
would come down and stay at the entrance, while
the LORD spoke with Moses. 10Whenever the people saw the pillar of cloud standing at the entrance
to the tent, they all stood and worshiped, each at
the entrance to his tent. 11The LORD would speak
to Moses face to face, as a man speaks with his
friend. Then Moses would return to the camp, but
his young aide Joshua son of Nun did not leave the
tent. Nu 12:8; Dt 34:10; Ps 99:7

Moses and the Glory of the LORD

12Moses said to the LORD, "You have been telling me, 'Lead these people,' but you have not let
me know whom you will send with me. You have
said, 'I know you by name and you have found
favor with me.' 13If you are pleased with me, teach
me your ways so I may know you and continue to
find favor with you. Remember that this nation is
your people." Dt 9:26,29; Ps 25:4
14The LORD replied, "My Presence will go with
you, and I will give you rest." Jos 21:44; Isa 63:9

LIVING  **INSIGHT**

God does not dispense strength and encouragement like a druggist who fills your prescription. The Lord doesn't promise to give us something to take so we can handle our weary moments. He promises us* Himself. *That is all. And that is enough.

(See Exodus 33:14.)

15Then Moses said to him, "If your Presence
does not go with us, do not send us up from here.
16How will anyone know that you are pleased with
me and with your people unless you go with us?
What else will distinguish me and your people
from all the other people on the face of the earth?"
17And the LORD said to Moses, "I will do the
very thing you have asked, because I am pleased
with you and I know you by name." Jas 5:16
18Then Moses said, "Now show me your glory."
19And the LORD said, "I will cause all my goodness to pass in front of you, and I will proclaim my
name, the LORD, in your presence. I will have mercy on whom I will have mercy, and I will have
compassion on whom I will have compassion.
20But," he said, "you cannot see my face, for no
one may see me and live." Ro 9:15
21Then the LORD said, "There is a place near me
where you may stand on a rock. 22When my glory
passes by, I will put you in a cleft in the rock and
cover you with my hand until I have passed by.
23Then I will remove my hand and you will see my
back; but my face must not be seen." Ps 91:4

The New Stone Tablets

34 The LORD said to Moses, "Chisel out two
stone tablets like the first ones, and I will
write on them the words that were on the first

tablets, which you broke. 2Be ready in the morning, and then come up on Mount Sinai. Present
yourself to me there on top of the mountain. 3No
one is to come with you or be seen anywhere on
the mountain; not even the flocks and herds may
graze in front of the mountain." Ex 19:11; 32:19

4So Moses chiseled out two stone tablets like the
first ones and went up Mount Sinai early in the
morning, as the LORD had commanded him; and
he carried the two stone tablets in his hands. 5Then
the LORD came down in the cloud and stood there
with him and proclaimed his name, the LORD.
6And he passed in front of Moses, proclaiming,
"The LORD, the LORD, the compassionate and gracious God, slow to anger, abounding in love and
faithfulness, 7maintaining love to thousands, and
forgiving wickedness, rebellion and sin. Yet he
does not leave the guilty unpunished; he punishes
the children and their children for the sin of the
fathers to the third and fourth generation."

8Moses bowed to the ground at once and worshiped. 9"O Lord, if I have found favor in your
eyes," he said, "then let the Lord go with us. Although this is a stiff-necked people, forgive our
wickedness and our sin, and take us as your inheritance." Ps 33:12

10Then the LORD said: "I am making a covenant
with you. Before all your people I will do wonders
never before done in any nation in all the world.
The people you live among will see how awesome
is the work that I, the LORD, will do for you. 11Obey
what I command you today. I will drive out before
you the Amorites, Canaanites, Hittites, Perizzites,
Hivites and Jebusites. 12Be careful not to make a
treaty with those who live in the land where you
are going, or they will be a snare among you.
13Break down their altars, smash their sacred
stones and cut down their Asherah poles.[a] 14Do
not worship any other god, for the LORD, whose
name is Jealous, is a jealous God. Ex 33:2; Dt 5:2-3

15"Be careful not to make a treaty with those
who live in the land; for when they prostitute
themselves to their gods and sacrifice to them, they
will invite you and you will eat their sacrifices.
16And when you choose some of their daughters as
wives for your sons and those daughters prostitute
themselves to their gods, they will lead your sons
to do the same. Nu 25:2; Dt 7:3

17"Do not make cast idols. Ex 32:8

18"Celebrate the Feast of Unleavened Bread. For
seven days eat bread made without yeast, as I commanded you. Do this at the appointed time in the
month of Abib, for in that month you came out of
Egypt. Ex 12:2,15,17

19"The first offspring of every womb belongs to
me, including all the firstborn males of your livestock, whether from herd or flock. 20Redeem the
firstborn donkey with a lamb, but if you do not
redeem it, break its neck. Redeem all your firstborn sons. Ex 13:2

"No one is to appear before me empty-handed.
21"Six days you shall labor, but on the seventh
day you shall rest; even during the plowing season
and harvest you must rest. Ex 20:9

22"Celebrate the Feast of Weeks with the firstfruits of the wheat harvest, and the Feast of Ingathering at the turn of the year.[b] 23Three times a year
all your men are to appear before the Sovereign
LORD, the God of Israel. 24I will drive out nations
before you and enlarge your territory, and no one
will covet your land when you go up three times
each year to appear before the LORD your God.

25"Do not offer the blood of a sacrifice to me
along with anything containing yeast, and do not
let any of the sacrifice from the Passover Feast
remain until morning. Ex 23:18

26"Bring the best of the firstfruits of your soil to
the house of the LORD your God. Ex 22:29

"Do not cook a young goat in its mother's
milk." Ex 23:19

27Then the LORD said to Moses, "Write down
these words, for in accordance with these words I
have made a covenant with you and with Israel."
28Moses was there with the LORD forty days and
forty nights without eating bread or drinking water. And he wrote on the tablets the words of the
covenant—the Ten Commandments. Dt 4:13; 10:4

The Radiant Face of Moses

29When Moses came down from Mount Sinai
with the two tablets of the Testimony in his hands,
he was not aware that his face was radiant because
he had spoken with the LORD. 30When Aaron and
all the Israelites saw Moses, his face was radiant,
and they were afraid to come near him. 31But Moses called to them; so Aaron and all the leaders of
the community came back to him, and he spoke to
them. 32Afterward all the Israelites came near him,
and he gave them all the commands the LORD had
given him on Mount Sinai. Mt 17:2; 2Co 3:7,13

33When Moses finished speaking to them, he
put a veil over his face. 34But whenever he entered
the LORD's presence to speak with him, he removed the veil until he came out. And when he
came out and told the Israelites what he had been
commanded, 35they saw that his face was radiant.
Then Moses would put the veil back over his face
until he went in to speak with the LORD. 2Co 3:13

Sabbath Regulations

35 Moses assembled the whole Israelite community and said to them, "These are the
things the LORD has commanded you to do: 2For
six days, work is to be done, but the seventh day

[a]13 That is, symbols of the goddess Asherah [b]22 That is, in the fall

shall be your holy day, a Sabbath of rest to the LORD. Whoever does any work on it must be put to death. 3Do not light a fire in any of your dwellings on the Sabbath day." Ex 16:23

Materials for the Tabernacle

4Moses said to the whole Israelite community, "This is what the LORD has commanded: 5From what you have, take an offering for the LORD. Everyone who is willing is to bring to the LORD an offering of gold, silver and bronze; 6blue, purple and scarlet yarn and fine linen; goat hair; 7ram skins dyed red and hides of sea cows[a]; acacia wood; 8olive oil for the light; spices for the anointing oil and for the fragrant incense; 9and onyx stones and other gems to be mounted on the ephod and breastpiece. Ex 25:1-7

10"All who are skilled among you are to come and make everything the LORD has commanded: 11the tabernacle with its tent and its covering, clasps, frames, crossbars, posts and bases; 12the ark with its poles and the atonement cover and the curtain that shields it; 13the table with its poles and all its articles and the bread of the Presence; 14the lampstand that is for light with its accessories, lamps and oil for the light; 15the altar of incense with its poles, the anointing oil and the fragrant incense; the curtain for the doorway at the entrance to the tabernacle; 16the altar of burnt offering with its bronze grating, its poles and all its utensils; the bronze basin with its stand; 17the curtains of the courtyard with its posts and bases, and the curtain for the entrance to the courtyard; 18the tent pegs for the tabernacle and for the courtyard, and their ropes; 19the woven garments worn for ministering in the sanctuary—both the sacred garments for Aaron the priest and the garments for his sons when they serve as priests."

20Then the whole Israelite community withdrew from Moses' presence, 21and everyone who was willing and whose heart moved him came and brought an offering to the LORD for the work on the Tent of Meeting, for all its service, and for the sacred garments. 22All who were willing, men and women alike, came and brought gold jewelry of all kinds: brooches, earrings, rings and ornaments. They all presented their gold as a wave offering to the LORD. 23Everyone who had blue, purple or scarlet yarn or fine linen, or goat hair, ram skins dyed red or hides of sea cows brought them. 24Those presenting an offering of silver or bronze brought it as an offering to the LORD, and everyone who had acacia wood for any part of the work brought it. 25Every skilled woman spun with her hands and brought what she had spun—blue, purple or scarlet yarn or fine linen. 26And all the women who were willing and had the skill spun the goat hair. 27The leaders brought onyx stones and other gems to be mounted on the ephod and breastpiece. 28They also brought spices and olive oil for the light and for the anointing oil and for the fragrant incense. 29All the Israelite men and women who were willing brought to the LORD freewill offerings for all the work the LORD through Moses had commanded them to do. ver 4-9

Bezalel and Oholiab

30Then Moses said to the Israelites, "See, the LORD has chosen Bezalel son of Uri, the son of Hur, of the tribe of Judah, 31and he has filled him with the Spirit of God, with skill, ability and knowledge in all kinds of crafts— 32to make artistic designs for work in gold, silver and bronze, 33to cut and set stones, to work in wood and to engage in all kinds of artistic craftsmanship. 34And he has given both him and Oholiab son of Ahisamach, of the tribe of Dan, the ability to teach others. 35He has filled them with skill to do all kinds of work as craftsmen, designers, embroiderers in blue, purple and scarlet yarn and fine linen, and weavers—all

36 of them master craftsmen and designers. 1So Bezalel, Oholiab and every skilled person to whom the LORD has given skill and ability to know how to carry out all the work of constructing the sanctuary are to do the work just as the Lord has commanded." Ex 21:2-6

2Then Moses summoned Bezalel and Oholiab and every skilled person to whom the LORD had given ability and who was willing to come and do the work. 3They received from Moses all the offerings the Israelites had brought to carry out the work of constructing the sanctuary. And the people continued to bring freewill offerings morning after morning. 4So all the skilled craftsmen who were doing all the work on the sanctuary left their work 5and said to Moses, "The people are bringing more than enough for doing the work the LORD commanded to be done." 2Ch 24:14; 2Co 8:2-3

LIVING  **INSIGHT**

Four simple suggestions for giving with gusto: Reflect on God's gifts to you. Remind yourself of His promises regarding generosity. Examine your heart, and ask yourself, "Is my giving proportionate to my income? Am I motivated by guilt . . . or by contagious joy? If someone else knew the level of my giving, would I be a model to follow?" Finally, trust God to honor consistent generosity.

(See Exodus 35:20–21.)

[a]7 That is, dugongs; also in verse 23

6Then Moses gave an order and they sent this word throughout the camp: "No man or woman is to make anything else as an offering for the sanctuary." And so the people were restrained from bringing more, 7because what they already had was more than enough to do all the work.

The Tabernacle

8All the skilled men among the workmen made the tabernacle with ten curtains of finely twisted linen and blue, purple and scarlet yarn, with cherubim worked into them by a skilled craftsman. 9All the curtains were the same size—twenty-eight cubits long and four cubits wide.[a] 10They joined five of the curtains together and did the same with the other five. 11Then they made loops of blue material along the edge of the end curtain in one set, and the same was done with the end curtain in the other set. 12They also made fifty loops on one curtain and fifty loops on the end curtain of the other set, with the loops opposite each other. 13Then they made fifty gold clasps and used them to fasten the two sets of curtains together so that the tabernacle was a unit.

14They made curtains of goat hair for the tent over the tabernacle—eleven altogether. 15All eleven curtains were the same size—thirty cubits long and four cubits wide.[b] 16They joined five of the curtains into one set and the other six into another set. 17Then they made fifty loops along the edge of the end curtain in one set and also along the edge of the end curtain in the other set. 18They made fifty bronze clasps to fasten the tent together as a unit. 19Then they made for the tent a covering of ram skins dyed red, and over that a covering of hides of sea cows.[c]

20They made upright frames of acacia wood for the tabernacle. 21Each frame was ten cubits long and a cubit and a half wide,[d] 22with two projections set parallel to each other. They made all the frames of the tabernacle in this way. 23They made twenty frames for the south side of the tabernacle 24and made forty silver bases to go under them—two bases for each frame, one under each projection. 25For the other side, the north side of the tabernacle, they made twenty frames 26and forty silver bases—two under each frame. 27They made six frames for the far end, that is, the west end of the tabernacle, 28and two frames were made for the corners of the tabernacle at the far end. 29At these two corners the frames were double from the bottom all the way to the top and fitted into a single ring; both were made alike. 30So there were eight frames and sixteen silver bases—two under each frame.

31They also made crossbars of acacia wood: five for the frames on one side of the tabernacle, 32five for those on the other side, and five for the frames on the west, at the far end of the tabernacle. 33They made the center crossbar so that it extended from end to end at the middle of the frames. 34They overlaid the frames with gold and made gold rings to hold the crossbars. They also overlaid the crossbars with gold.

35They made the curtain of blue, purple and scarlet yarn and finely twisted linen, with cherubim worked into it by a skilled craftsman. 36They made four posts of acacia wood for it and overlaid them with gold. They made gold hooks for them and cast their four silver bases. 37For the entrance to the tent they made a curtain of blue, purple and scarlet yarn and finely twisted linen—the work of an embroiderer; 38and they made five posts with hooks for them. They overlaid the tops of the posts and their bands with gold and made their five bases of bronze. Ex 26:1-37

The Ark

37 Bezalel made the ark of acacia wood—two and a half cubits long, a cubit and a half wide, and a cubit and a half high.[e] 2He overlaid it with pure gold, both inside and out, and made a gold molding around it. 3He cast four gold rings for it and fastened them to its four feet, with two rings on one side and two rings on the other. 4Then he made poles of acacia wood and overlaid them with gold. 5And he inserted the poles into the rings on the sides of the ark to carry it. ver 11,26

6He made the atonement cover of pure gold—two and a half cubits long and a cubit and a half wide.[f] 7Then he made two cherubim out of hammered gold at the ends of the cover. 8He made one cherub on one end and the second cherub on the other; at the two ends he made them of one piece with the cover. 9The cherubim had their wings spread upward, overshadowing the cover with them. The cherubim faced each other, looking toward the cover. Ex 25:10-20

The Table

10They[g] made the table of acacia wood—two cubits long, a cubit wide, and a cubit and a half high.[h] 11Then they overlaid it with pure gold and made a gold molding around it. 12They also made around it a rim a handbreadth[i] wide and put a gold molding on the rim. 13They cast four gold

[a] 9 That is, about 42 feet (about 12.5 meters) long and 6 feet (about 1.8 meters) wide [b] 15 That is, about 45 feet (about 13.5 meters) long and 6 feet (about 1.8 meters) wide [c] 19 That is, dugongs [d] 21 That is, about 15 feet (about 4.5 meters) long and 2 1/4 feet (about 0.7 meter) wide [e] 1 That is, about 3 3/4 feet (about 1.1 meters) long and 2 1/4 feet (about 0.7 meter) wide and high [f] 6 That is, about 3 3/4 feet (about 1.1 meters) long and 2 1/4 feet (about 0.7 meter) wide [g] 10 Or *He*; also in verses 11-29 [h] 10 That is, about 3 feet (about 0.9 meter) long, 1 1/2 feet (about 0.5 meter) wide, and 2 1/4 feet (about 0.7 meter) high [i] 12 That is, about 3 inches (about 8 centimeters)

rings for the table and fastened them to the four corners, where the four legs were. 14The rings were put close to the rim to hold the poles used in carrying the table. 15The poles for carrying the table were made of acacia wood and were overlaid with gold. 16And they made from pure gold the articles for the table—its plates and dishes and bowls and its pitchers for the pouring out of drink offerings. Ex 25:23-29

The Lampstand

17They made the lampstand of pure gold and hammered it out, base and shaft; its flowerlike cups, buds and blossoms were of one piece with it. 18Six branches extended from the sides of the lampstand—three on one side and three on the other. 19Three cups shaped like almond flowers with buds and blossoms were on one branch, three on the next branch and the same for all six branches extending from the lampstand. 20And on the lampstand were four cups shaped like almond flowers with buds and blossoms. 21One bud was under the first pair of branches extending from the lampstand, a second bud under the second pair, and a third bud under the third pair—six branches in all. 22The buds and the branches were all of one piece with the lampstand, hammered out of pure gold. Heb 9:2; Rev 1:12

23They made its seven lamps, as well as its wick trimmers and trays, of pure gold. 24They made the lampstand and all its accessories from one talent[a] of pure gold. Ex 25:31-39

The Altar of Incense

25They made the altar of incense out of acacia wood. It was square, a cubit long and a cubit wide, and two cubits high[b]—its horns of one piece with it. 26They overlaid the top and all the sides and the horns with pure gold, and made a gold molding around it. 27They made two gold rings below the molding—two on opposite sides—to hold the poles used to carry it. 28They made the poles of acacia wood and overlaid them with gold.

29They also made the sacred anointing oil and the pure, fragrant incense—the work of a perfumer. Ex 30:1,25; 31:11

The Altar of Burnt Offering

38 They[c] built the altar of burnt offering of acacia wood, three cubits[d] high; it was square, five cubits long and five cubits wide.[e] 2They made a horn at each of the four corners, so that the horns and the altar were of one piece, and they overlaid the altar with bronze. 3They made all its utensils of bronze—its pots, shovels, sprinkling bowls, meat forks and firepans. 4They made a grating for the altar, a bronze network, to be under its ledge, halfway up the altar. 5They cast bronze rings to hold the poles for the four corners of the bronze grating. 6They made the poles of acacia wood and overlaid them with bronze. 7They inserted the poles into the rings so they would be on the sides of the altar for carrying it. They made it hollow, out of boards. Ex 27:1-8

Basin for Washing

8They made the bronze basin and its bronze stand from the mirrors of the women who served at the entrance to the Tent of Meeting. Dt 23:17

The Courtyard

9Next they made the courtyard. The south side was a hundred cubits[f] long and had curtains of finely twisted linen, 10with twenty posts and twenty bronze bases, and with silver hooks and bands on the posts. 11The north side was also a hundred cubits long and had twenty posts and twenty bronze bases, with silver hooks and bands on the posts.

12The west end was fifty cubits[g] wide and had curtains, with ten posts and ten bases, with silver hooks and bands on the posts. 13The east end, toward the sunrise, was also fifty cubits wide. 14Curtains fifteen cubits[h] long were on one side of the entrance, with three posts and three bases, 15and curtains fifteen cubits long were on the other side of the entrance to the courtyard, with three posts and three bases. 16All the curtains around the courtyard were of finely twisted linen. 17The bases for the posts were bronze. The hooks and bands on the posts were silver, and their tops were overlaid with silver; so all the posts of the courtyard had silver bands.

18The curtain for the entrance to the courtyard was of blue, purple and scarlet yarn and finely twisted linen—the work of an embroiderer. It was twenty cubits[i] long and, like the curtains of the courtyard, five cubits[j] high, 19with four posts and four bronze bases. Their hooks and bands were silver, and their tops were overlaid with silver. 20All the tent pegs of the tabernacle and of the surrounding courtyard were bronze. Ex 27:9-19

The Materials Used

21These are the amounts of the materials used for the tabernacle, the tabernacle of the Testimony, which were recorded at Moses' command by the Levites under the direction of Ithamar son of Aar-

[a] *24* That is, about 75 pounds (about 34 kilograms) [b] *25* That is, about 1 1/2 feet (about 0.5 meter) long and wide, and about 3 feet (about 0.9 meter) high [c] *1* Or *He*; also in verses 2-9 [d] *1* That is, about 4 1/2 feet (about 1.3 meters) [e] *1* That is, about 7 1/2 feet (about 2.3 meters) long and wide [f] *9* That is, about 150 feet (about 46 meters) [g] *12* That is, about 75 feet (about 23 meters) [h] *14* That is, about 22 1/2 feet (about 6.9 meters) [i] *18* That is, about 30 feet (about 9 meters) [j] *18* That is, about 7 1/2 feet (about 2.3 meters)

on, the priest. 22(Bezalel son of Uri, the son of Hur, of the tribe of Judah, made everything the LORD commanded Moses; 23with him was Oholiab son of Ahisamach, of the tribe of Dan—a craftsman and designer, and an embroiderer in blue, purple and scarlet yarn and fine linen.) 24The total amount of the gold from the wave offering used for all the work on the sanctuary was 29 talents and 730 shekels,[a] according to the sanctuary shekel. Nu 1:50,53; 9:15

25The silver obtained from those of the community who were counted in the census was 100 talents and 1,775 shekels,[b] according to the sanctuary shekel— 26one beka per person, that is, half a shekel,[c] according to the sanctuary shekel, from everyone who had crossed over to those counted, twenty years old or more, a total of 603,550 men. 27The 100 talents[d] of silver were used to cast the bases for the sanctuary and for the curtain—100 bases from the 100 talents, one talent for each base. 28They used the 1,775 shekels[e] to make the hooks for the posts, to overlay the tops of the posts, and to make their bands. Ex 30:12-14

29The bronze from the wave offering was 70 talents and 2,400 shekels.[f] 30They used it to make the bases for the entrance to the Tent of Meeting, the bronze altar with its bronze grating and all its utensils, 31the bases for the surrounding courtyard and those for its entrance and all the tent pegs for the tabernacle and those for the surrounding courtyard.

The Priestly Garments

39 From the blue, purple and scarlet yarn they made woven garments for ministering in the sanctuary. They also made sacred garments for Aaron, as the LORD commanded Moses.

The Ephod

2They[g] made the ephod of gold, and of blue, purple and scarlet yarn, and of finely twisted linen. 3They hammered out thin sheets of gold and cut strands to be worked into the blue, purple and scarlet yarn and fine linen—the work of a skilled craftsman. 4They made shoulder pieces for the ephod, which were attached to two of its corners, so it could be fastened. 5Its skillfully woven waistband was like it—of one piece with the ephod and made with gold, and with blue, purple and scarlet yarn, and with finely twisted linen, as the LORD commanded Moses.

6They mounted the onyx stones in gold filigree settings and engraved them like a seal with the names of the sons of Israel. 7Then they fastened them on the shoulder pieces of the ephod as memorial stones for the sons of Israel, as the LORD commanded Moses. Ex 28:6-14

The Breastpiece

8They fashioned the breastpiece—the work of a skilled craftsman. They made it like the ephod: of gold, and of blue, purple and scarlet yarn, and of finely twisted linen. 9It was square—a span[h] long and a span wide—and folded double. 10Then they mounted four rows of precious stones on it. In the first row there was a ruby, a topaz and a beryl; 11in the second row a turquoise, a sapphire[i] and an emerald; 12in the third row a jacinth, an agate and an amethyst; 13in the fourth row a chrysolite, an onyx and a jasper.[j] They were mounted in gold filigree settings. 14There were twelve stones, one for each of the names of the sons of Israel, each engraved like a seal with the name of one of the twelve tribes.

15For the breastpiece they made braided chains of pure gold, like a rope. 16They made two gold filigree settings and two gold rings, and fastened the rings to two of the corners of the breastpiece. 17They fastened the two gold chains to the rings at the corners of the breastpiece, 18and the other ends of the chains to the two settings, attaching them to the shoulder pieces of the ephod at the front. 19They made two gold rings and attached them to the other two corners of the breastpiece on the inside edge next to the ephod. 20Then they made two more gold rings and attached them to the bottom of the shoulder pieces on the front of the ephod, close to the seam just above the waistband of the ephod. 21They tied the rings of the breastpiece to the rings of the ephod with blue cord, connecting it to the waistband so that the breastpiece would not swing out from the ephod—as the LORD commanded Moses. Ex 28:15-28

Other Priestly Garments

22They made the robe of the ephod entirely of blue cloth—the work of a weaver— 23with an opening in the center of the robe like the opening of a collar,[k] and a band around this opening, so that it would not tear. 24They made pomegranates of blue, purple and scarlet yarn and finely twisted linen around the hem of the robe. 25And they made bells of pure gold and attached them around the hem between the pomegranates. 26The bells and pomegranates alternated around the hem of

[a] *24* The weight of the gold was a little over one ton (about 1 metric ton). [b] *25* The weight of the silver was a little over 3 3/4 tons (about 3.4 metric tons). [c] *26* That is, about 1/5 ounce (about 5.5 grams) [d] *27* That is, about 3 3/4 tons (about 3.4 metric tons) [e] *28* That is, about 45 pounds (about 20 kilograms) [f] *29* The weight of the bronze was about 2 1/2 tons (about 2.4 metric tons). [g] *2* Or *He*; also in verses 7, 8 and 22 [h] *9* That is, about 9 inches (about 22 centimeters) [i] *11* Or *lapis lazuli* [j] *13* The precise identification of some of these precious stones is uncertain. [k] *23* The meaning of the Hebrew for this word is uncertain.

the robe to be worn for ministering, as the LORD commanded Moses.

[27]For Aaron and his sons, they made tunics of fine linen—the work of a weaver— [28]and the turban of fine linen, the linen headbands and the undergarments of finely twisted linen. [29]The sash was of finely twisted linen and blue, purple and scarlet yarn—the work of an embroiderer—as the LORD commanded Moses. Ex 28:4; Lev 6:10

[30]They made the plate, the sacred diadem, out of pure gold and engraved on it, like an inscription on a seal: HOLY TO THE LORD. [31]Then they fastened a blue cord to it to attach it to the turban, as the LORD commanded Moses. Ex 28:31-43

Moses Inspects the Tabernacle

[32]So all the work on the tabernacle, the Tent of Meeting, was completed. The Israelites did everything just as the LORD commanded Moses. [33]Then they brought the tabernacle to Moses: the tent and all its furnishings, its clasps, frames, crossbars, posts and bases; [34]the covering of ram skins dyed red, the covering of hides of sea cows[a] and the shielding curtain; [35]the ark of the Testimony with its poles and the atonement cover; [36]the table with all its articles and the bread of the Presence; [37]the pure gold lampstand with its row of lamps and all its accessories, and the oil for the light; [38]the gold altar, the anointing oil, the fragrant incense, and the curtain for the entrance to the tent; [39]the bronze altar with its bronze grating, its poles and all its utensils; the basin with its stand; [40]the curtains of the courtyard with its posts and bases, and the curtain for the entrance to the courtyard; the ropes and tent pegs for the courtyard; all the furnishings for the tabernacle, the Tent of Meeting; [41]and the woven garments worn for ministering in the sanctuary, both the sacred garments for Aaron the priest and the garments for his sons when serving as priests. Ex 35:10-19

[42]The Israelites had done all the work just as the LORD had commanded Moses. [43]Moses inspected the work and saw that they had done it just as the LORD had commanded. So Moses blessed them.

Setting Up the Tabernacle

40 Then the LORD said to Moses: [2]"Set up the tabernacle, the Tent of Meeting, on the first day of the first month. [3]Place the ark of the Testimony in it and shield the ark with the curtain. [4]Bring in the table and set out what belongs on it. Then bring in the lampstand and set up its lamps. [5]Place the gold altar of incense in front of the ark of the Testimony and put the curtain at the entrance to the tabernacle. Ex 26:33; Nu 1:1

[6]"Place the altar of burnt offering in front of the entrance to the tabernacle, the Tent of Meeting; [7]place the basin between the Tent of Meeting and the altar and put water in it. [8]Set up the courtyard around it and put the curtain at the entrance to the courtyard. Ex 30:18; 2Ki 16:14

[9]"Take the anointing oil and anoint the tabernacle and everything in it; consecrate it and all its furnishings, and it will be holy. [10]Then anoint the altar of burnt offering and all its utensils; consecrate the altar, and it will be most holy. [11]Anoint the basin and its stand and consecrate them.

[12]"Bring Aaron and his sons to the entrance to the Tent of Meeting and wash them with water. [13]Then dress Aaron in the sacred garments, anoint him and consecrate him so he may serve me as priest. [14]Bring his sons and dress them in tunics. [15]Anoint them just as you anointed their father, so they may serve me as priests. Their anointing will be to a priesthood that will continue for all generations to come." [16]Moses did everything just as the LORD commanded him. Ex 29:9; Nu 25:13

[17]So the tabernacle was set up on the first day of the first month in the second year. [18]When Moses set up the tabernacle, he put the bases in place, erected the frames, inserted the crossbars and set up the posts. [19]Then he spread the tent over the tabernacle and put the covering over the tent, as the LORD commanded him. Nu 7:1; 2Ch 1:3

[20]He took the Testimony and placed it in the ark, attached the poles to the ark and put the atonement cover over it. [21]Then he brought the ark into the tabernacle and hung the shielding curtain and shielded the ark of the Testimony, as the LORD commanded him. Ex 16:34; Heb 9:4

[22]Moses placed the table in the Tent of Meeting on the north side of the tabernacle outside the curtain [23]and set out the bread on it before the LORD, as the LORD commanded him. Ex 26:35

[24]He placed the lampstand in the Tent of Meeting opposite the table on the south side of the tabernacle [25]and set up the lamps before the LORD, as the LORD commanded him. Ex 26:35

[26]Moses placed the gold altar in the Tent of Meeting in front of the curtain [27]and burned fragrant incense on it, as the LORD commanded him. [28]Then he put up the curtain at the entrance to the tabernacle. Ex 30:6

[29]He set the altar of burnt offering near the entrance to the tabernacle, the Tent of Meeting, and offered on it burnt offerings and grain offerings, as the LORD commanded him. ver 6; Ex 29:38-42

[30]He placed the basin between the Tent of Meeting and the altar and put water in it for washing, [31]and Moses and Aaron and his sons used it to wash their hands and feet. [32]They washed whenever they entered the Tent of Meeting or approached the altar, as the LORD commanded Moses. Ex 30:20

[a] *34* That is, dugongs

33Then Moses set up the courtyard around the
tabernacle and altar and put up the curtain at the
entrance to the courtyard. And so Moses finished
the work. ver 8; Ex 27:9

The Glory of the LORD

34Then the cloud covered the Tent of Meeting,
and the glory of the LORD filled the tabernacle.
35Moses could not enter the Tent of Meeting because the cloud had settled upon it, and the glory
of the LORD filled the tabernacle. Nu 9:15-23
36In all the travels of the Israelites, whenever the
cloud lifted from above the tabernacle, they would
set out; 37but if the cloud did not lift, they did not
set out—until the day it lifted. 38So the cloud of
the LORD was over the tabernacle by day, and fire
was in the cloud by night, in the sight of all the
house of Israel during all their travels. Nu 9:17-23

INTRODUCTION

LEVITICUS God's Picture Book on Worship

In the book of Genesis we saw humanity ruined by the fall. In Exodus we saw God's chosen people redeemed from bondage. In the book called Leviticus, God's people are revived through worship. Although frequently dismissed as an unimportant document of out-of-date details, this book has been preserved by God for a particular purpose. Like no other Old Testament book, it is filled with pictures of the Lord Jesus Christ. Without exception, every offering and every feast provides another vivid portrait of Jesus, God's sacrificial Lamb "who takes away the sin of the world" (John 1:29).

WRITER: *Moses*

DATE: *c.1440 B.C.*

KEY QUESTION: *How can sinful humans worship a holy God?*

KEY VERSES: *17:11; 19:2; 20:7-8*

KEY TERM: *"Holy" (occurs 74 times)*

TIME LINE 2200BC 2100 2000 1900 1800 1700 1600 1500 1400

- **Moses' birth (c.1526 B.C.)**
- **The plagues; The Passover (c.1446 B.C.)**
- **The exodus (c.1446 B.C.)**
- **Desert wanderings (c.1446-1406 B.C.)**
- **The Ten Commandments (c.1445 B.C.)**
- **Book of Leviticus written (c.1440 B.C.)**
- **Moses dies; Joshua becomes leader (c.1406 B.C.)**
- **Israelites enter Canaan (c.1406 B.C.)**

God's Picture Book on Worship

	THE WAY TO GOD	THE WALK WITH GOD
	Access	**Lifestyle**
	The approach: Offerings	Practical guidelines
	The representative: Priest	Chronological observances
	The laws: Cleansing *Physically* *Spiritually*	Severe consequences Verbal promises
	CHAPTERS 1–17	***CHAPTERS 18–27***
EMPHASIS	**Ritual (for worship)**	**Practical (for living)**
LOCATION	**Mount Sinai . . . one full year**	
CHRIST	**Pictured in each sacrifice and ritual**	

If you have ever set out to read through the Bible, you probably got bogged down in the book of Leviticus. Whatever else you might say about the book, it is not your basic "bedside reading material." Although some of it is interesting and insightful, much of it, quite frankly, is tedious and difficult to read (I'm trying hard not to write "boring"). This is not only true of Leviticus but of other sections of Scripture as well. God never promised His Word would be interesting from cover to cover, but *all of it* is inspired. Inerrancy makes no claim on easy reading. The simple truth is that some portions of Scripture are downright tough to read.

Let me give you a couple of insights that will help you appreciate tough sections of Scripture like Leviticus. These thoughts may help you understand why we may find these sections so uninteresting. First, *this book's primary purpose was never intended for us.* When God recorded and preserved the book of Leviticus, He did not have in mind twentieth-century folks living in our culture who worshiped in permanent buildings, who drove automobiles and did not raise sheep. God wrote it to Israelites who worshiped in a portable tabernacle and who could not come to God without a sacrificial offering of a lamb, goat, bird or some other animal.

Designed Obsolescence and Eternal Relevance

Because Jesus Christ has come, we no longer need animal sacrifices. Jesus was, once for all, offered up on our behalf because of our sins. When Jesus came, the book of Leviticus lost much of its relevance and impact. It was designed to be that way.

This raises a second thought about Leviticus: *Its significance was designed to become obsolete*. That's not heresy. That's good, solid truth. I suppose we could say that God designed the book of Leviticus to go out of date. Once Jesus came and said, "It is finished," at least part of what He meant was finished was the whole Levitical system, including the need for priests to be the mediators between God and humanity. All of that Old Testament ritual was fulfilled. It is now set aside, and the believer-priest can come, through Jesus, directly to God. We have an inside channel. We have direct access. So, Leviticus was designed to become obsolete.

I should clarify that Leviticus is *not* obsolete in its application. None of Scripture is obsolete in its application. But in its basic impact and interpretation for today, the saint in the body of Christ does not need the book of Leviticus to gain access to God in the way the Israelites needed this book's directions centuries ago.

A Look at Leviticus

Let's begin our study by uncovering the meaning of the name "Leviticus." You don't need to be a Bible scholar to see the root word in "Leviticus." Obviously, it is "Levite." The name means "pertaining to the Levites."

Who were the Levites? Think of them as the ancient ministers. They were the priests, the mediators. When you think of priest in the Old Testament, think of a mediator. Every time you read the word "priest" in your Old Testament, substitute the word "mediator," and you'll have its basic meaning.

In those days, for the Israelites to approach the Lord God, they had to go through a mediator. He was called a "priest." He was from the tribe of Levi, which means he was a Levite. Leviticus is an instructional handbook for the priests who were set apart to provide leadership among the people of God in their worship.

For a full year the Israelites pitched their tents at the foot of Mount Sinai. While they were there they received two directives from the Lord; He gave them His Word, which was the written Law of Moses, and He also gave them a blueprint for their place of worship. The tabernacle gave them a place of meeting, while the law declared what was expected of them in their relationships—to God and to each other. Both the law and the tabernacle were given from the hand of God, through Moses, to the Israelites.

Leviticus falls neatly into two parts. The first 17 chapters teach us about *the way to God*. The way to approach God was by blood sacrifice. That was God's design; He deliberately planned it that way. If you, the sinner, wanted to come to God, the Holy One, the only way was through that God-honored detergent—the blood of sacrificed animals. It washed away sin. God honored it. And so for 17 chapters, the Lord spells out how sinners could reach God, how they could find cleansing from sin and be right with Him. In the last section of this book, chapters 18–27, we have directions for *the walk with God*. This portion of Leviticus teaches how sinners can stay in touch with a holy God.

Leviticus is a picture book, portraying ancient predictions of Jesus Christ in the form of pen portraits. The book of Leviticus is directly linked in the New Testament to the book of Hebrews. Hebrews makes Leviticus come alive. G. Campbell Morgan, a fine British Bible teacher for many years, agreed. He once wrote these words: "Leviticus and Hebrews are always to be kept together in your Bible study. I say, frankly, to anyone who thinks he is studying Hebrews, if he does not study Leviticus, he does not know Hebrews. Hebrews shows a fulfilling of everything suggested in Leviticus."

The literal interpretation of Leviticus may seem uninteresting and irrelevant to us. However, it is vital to a proper understanding of the letter to the Hebrews and of other parts of the New Testament—and when we read it with open hearts, we will be challenged to a closer walk with our holy God.

Images of the Savior

Many people have snubbed Leviticus, saying, "It just doesn't have much to offer." While Leviticus appears to be irrelevant and out of touch, it is neither . . . not really. When you see it in the light of all God's plan, it becomes much more significant. For example, in the first five chapters there are five offerings presented—and they're all different. Interestingly, each one portrays Jesus Christ from a different perspective.

In chapter 1 we have the *burnt offering*. This offering was laid on an altar and was completely consumed in fire and smoke. As I study this chapter, I find it to be a vivid picture of the complete dedication of Jesus Christ—the total consecration of His life. Jesus could come before the Father at the time of death and, in effect, say, "Nothing is left undone. All that I have done has been for Your glory, and as a whole burnt offering, I offer Myself at the Tent of Meeting." Jesus Christ, our sacrifice, was offered, once for all, as our whole burnt offering.

In chapter 2 we find another kind of offering—a *grain offering*. As I study this chapter, it speaks to me of the service of Jesus Christ. The grain was grown by the people. It was ground up into fine flour by the people—the work of their own hands. It was the service of their lives to God. So it is with Jesus. Our Lord performed all of His works for the Father's glory and came to the cross as our ultimate, final, eternal grain offering. He offered up His life as a fine flour, and it was perfectly accepted—never to be offered again.

The third offering, described in chapter 3, is the *fellowship offering*, also known as the *peace offering*. The peace offering speaks of Jesus Christ, who is our peace. You don't have to work hard to gain peace with God. Jesus has already won your peace.

Chapter 4 describes the *sin offering*, which applies in the case of sins that were committed unintentionally. Jesus Christ, in his perfect nature, offered the sin offering to God. He came as the spotless Lamb who took away the sin of the world and reconciled us to God. Once He came, the price never had to be paid again.

Chapter 5 records one more offering—the *guilt offering*, which applies in the case of sins committed unintentionally but where restitution was possible. Jesus Christ not only paid the payment for our sinful nature, but He also paid the payment for our intentional and unintentional actions of sin. He brought the guilt offering to God at the cross of Calvary, and the Father honored and accepted it once for all.

The Way to God

Chapters 6 and 7 give specific instructions regarding the details of offering up the sacrifices. From chapters 8–10 we gain information about the priests—vital information to those mediators of that day. In chapters 11–17 we read of laws for cleansing. Here we find information on diet and foods that were considered clean and unclean by God. Issues of hygiene are addressed, including how to take care of a mother at the time of birth and shortly after the time of her delivery. Subsequent chapters talk about the treatment of diseases. Throughout this section the priests were given divine insight and warnings and wisdom so that the Hebrews might stay healthy and be preserved.

Finally, in chapters 16 and 17, we are given information about the Day of Atonement. Once a year the priest would come with blood and, on behalf of the entire nation, would offer up the blood to make atonement. Do you want to see how God views blood? Look closely at 17:11—one of the key verses in the book of Leviticus.

> *For the life of a creature is in the blood, and I have given it to you to make atonement for yourselves on the altar; it is the blood that makes atonement for one's life.*

Remember that old gospel song?

> *What can wash away my sin? Nothing but the blood of Jesus;*
> *What can make me whole again? Nothing but the blood of Jesus.*
> *O! precious is the flow That makes me white as snow;*
> *No other fount I know, Nothing but the blood of Jesus.*

In order for sinful people to approach a holy God, blood is essential. When Jesus gave Himself on the cross, when the blood was spilled, God saw the sacrificial offering and was immediately and perpetually satisfied. Sins are covered only through the blood of Jesus Christ, the Lamb of God, sacrificed for the sins of the world. Leviticus takes this truth and advertises it on a neon sign with bold letters so we will never forget! THE WAY YOU COME TO GOD IS THROUGH THE BLOOD OF JESUS' PERFECT OFFERING.

The Walk With God

From chapter 18 to the end of the book we are given some practical guidelines by which to live. Chapters 18–22 contain truth about holy living. Chapters 23–26 describe sacred celebrations in which the Hebrew calendar was designed around the number seven. Godliness was never intended to be "tacked on" in Israelite homes. It was woven into the very fabric of the people. These celebrations were a vital part of the Israelite lifestyle. Here is a list of the Old Testament feasts (see also the chart on page 126):

Sabbath
Sabbath Year
Year of Jubilee

Passover
Firstfruits
Weeks (Pentecost)
Trumpets
Day of Atonement
Tabernacles (Booths)

Leviticus ends with holy vows (chapter 27)—where God commanded the people to refrain from speaking lies. When the people spoke vows to God, they were to keep them—an expectation God communicated in no uncertain terms.

A helpful way to conclude our study of Leviticus is by comparing its teachings to the teachings of a wonderful passage of Scripture in the New Testament, Hebrews 9:6–14. Here is a clear, concise contrast that we should never forget:

Leviticus Says:	*Hebrews Says:*
There are many priests.	There is only one Savior-Priest.
There is only a temporary removal of sin.	There is an eternal erasing of sin.
There is a long list of continual regulations.	There is a once-for-all act of salvation.
There is a requirement to be satisfied.	There is a payment that has been made, God's satisfaction guaranteed.
There is work *I* must continue to do.	There is hope in what *He* has done.

The Offerings **Chapters 1–7**

The book of Leviticus explained how the people of Israel were to approach the living God and relate to him through blood sacrifice. Why would God require the shedding of blood as part of the process for people to draw near to Him? It is a picture of the coming Messiah who would pour out his blood for the world. In the opening seven chapters we read of five distinct offerings. As we have seen in the book introduction, each offering has a spiritual meaning that relates to the person and/or work of Jesus Christ. The *Burnt Offering* reminds us of the complete dedication of Jesus to the Father (chapter 1). The *Grain Offering* reflects the service of the Lord and the works He performed for the Father's glory (chapter 2). The *Fellowship Offering* (or *Peace Offering*) brings to mind the peace we receive through the blood of Jesus on the cross (chapter 3). The *Sin Offering* portrays the giving of Jesus' whole life to cover our sinful life and lifestyle (chapter 4). The *Guilt Offering* reminds us that Jesus' death pays the price for our sins that were not intentionally committed (chapter 5). Embedded in the ritual sacrifices of Israel is a picture of the final sacrifice God has given us through the death of Jesus Christ on the cross.

The Burnt Offering

1 The LORD called to Moses and spoke to him
from the Tent of Meeting. He said, 2"Speak to
the Israelites and say to them: 'When any of you
brings an offering to the LORD, bring as your offering an animal from either the herd or the flock.
3" 'If the offering is a burnt offering from the
herd, he is to offer a male without defect. He must
present it at the entrance to the Tent of Meeting so
that it[a] will be acceptable to the LORD. 4He is to
lay his hand on the head of the burnt offering, and
it will be accepted on his behalf to make atonement for him. 5He is to slaughter the young bull
before the LORD, and then Aaron's sons the priests
shall bring the blood and sprinkle it against the
altar on all sides at the entrance to the Tent of
Meeting. 6He is to skin the burnt offering and cut
it into pieces. 7The sons of Aaron the priest are to
put fire on the altar and arrange wood on the fire.
8Then Aaron's sons the priests shall arrange the
pieces, including the head and the fat, on the burning wood that is on the altar. 9He is to wash the
inner parts and the legs with water, and the priest
is to burn all of it on the altar. It is a burnt offering,
an offering made by fire, an aroma pleasing to the
LORD. Ge 8:21; Eph 5:2
10" 'If the offering is a burnt offering from the
flock, from either the sheep or the goats, he is to
offer a male without defect. 11He is to slaughter it
at the north side of the altar before the LORD, and
Aaron's sons the priests shall sprinkle its blood
against the altar on all sides. 12He is to cut it into
pieces, and the priest shall arrange them, including
the head and the fat, on the burning wood that is
on the altar. 13He is to wash the inner parts and the
legs with water, and the priest is to bring all of it
and burn it on the altar. It is a burnt offering, an
offering made by fire, an aroma pleasing to the
LORD.
14" 'If the offering to the LORD is a burnt offering
of birds, he is to offer a dove or a young pigeon.
15The priest shall bring it to the altar, wring off the
head and burn it on the altar; its blood shall be
drained out on the side of the altar. 16He is to
remove the crop with its contents[b] and throw it
to the east side of the altar, where the ashes are.
17He shall tear it open by the wings, not severing
it completely, and then the priest shall burn it on
the wood that is on the fire on the altar. It is a
burnt offering, an offering made by fire, an aroma
pleasing to the LORD. Lev 5:7; 6:10

The Grain Offering

2 " 'When someone brings a grain offering to
the LORD, his offering is to be of fine flour. He
is to pour oil on it, put incense on it 2and take it
to Aaron's sons the priests. The priest shall take a
handful of the fine flour and oil, together with all
the incense, and burn this as a memorial portion
on the altar, an offering made by fire, an aroma
pleasing to the LORD. 3The rest of the grain offering
belongs to Aaron and his sons; it is a most holy
part of the offerings made to the LORD by fire.
4" 'If you bring a grain offering baked in an
oven, it is to consist of fine flour: cakes made
without yeast and mixed with oil, or[c] wafers
made without yeast and spread with oil. 5If your
grain offering is prepared on a griddle, it is to be
made of fine flour mixed with oil, and without
yeast. 6Crumble it and pour oil on it; it is a grain
offering. 7If your grain offering is cooked in a pan,
it is to be made of fine flour and oil. 8Bring the
grain offering made of these things to the LORD;
present it to the priest, who shall take it to the
altar. 9He shall take out the memorial portion
from the grain offering and burn it on the altar as
an offering made by fire, an aroma pleasing to the
LORD. 10The rest of the grain offering belongs to
Aaron and his sons; it is a most holy part of the
offerings made to the LORD by fire. Ex 29:2; Lev 7:9
11" 'Every grain offering you bring to the LORD
must be made without yeast, for you are not to
burn any yeast or honey in an offering made to the
LORD by fire. 12You may bring them to the LORD as
an offering of the firstfruits, but they are not to be
offered on the altar as a pleasing aroma. 13Season
all your grain offerings with salt. Do not leave the
salt of the covenant of your God out of your grain
offerings; add salt to all your offerings. Nu 18:19
14" 'If you bring a grain offering of firstfruits to
the LORD, offer crushed heads of new grain roasted

[a] 3 Or *he* [b] 16 Or *crop and the feathers*; the meaning of the Hebrew for this word is uncertain. [c] 4 Or *and*

in the fire. 15Put oil and incense on it; it is a grain offering. 16The priest shall burn the memorial portion of the crushed grain and the oil, together with all the incense, as an offering made to the LORD by fire. Lev 23:10

The Fellowship Offering

3 “‘If someone’s offering is a fellowship offering,[a] and he offers an animal from the herd, whether male or female, he is to present before the LORD an animal without defect. 2He is to lay his hand on the head of his offering and slaughter it at the entrance to the Tent of Meeting. Then Aaron’s sons the priests shall sprinkle the blood against the altar on all sides. 3From the fellowship offering he is to bring a sacrifice made to the LORD by fire: all the fat that covers the inner parts or is connected to them, 4both kidneys with the fat on them near the loins, and the covering of the liver, which he will remove with the kidneys. 5Then Aaron’s sons are to burn it on the altar on top of the burnt offering that is on the burning wood, as an offering made by fire, an aroma pleasing to the LORD. Lev 7:11-34; 22:21

6“‘If he offers an animal from the flock as a fellowship offering to the LORD, he is to offer a male or female without defect. 7If he offers a lamb, he is to present it before the LORD. 8He is to lay his hand on the head of his offering and slaughter it in front of the Tent of Meeting. Then Aaron’s sons shall sprinkle its blood against the altar on all sides. 9From the fellowship offering he is to bring a sacrifice made to the LORD by fire: its fat, the entire fat tail cut off close to the backbone, all the fat that covers the inner parts or is connected to them, 10both kidneys with the fat on them near the loins, and the covering of the liver, which he will remove with the kidneys. 11The priest shall burn them on the altar as food, an offering made to the LORD by fire. Lev 21:6,17

12“‘If his offering is a goat, he is to present it before the LORD. 13He is to lay his hand on its head and slaughter it in front of the Tent of Meeting. Then Aaron’s sons shall sprinkle its blood against the altar on all sides. 14From what he offers he is to make this offering to the LORD by fire: all the fat that covers the inner parts or is connected to them, 15both kidneys with the fat on them near the loins, and the covering of the liver, which he will remove with the kidneys. 16The priest shall burn them on the altar as food, an offering made by fire, a pleasing aroma. All the fat is the LORD’s. Lev 1:9; 1Sa 2:16

17“‘This is a lasting ordinance for the generations to come, wherever you live: You must not eat any fat or any blood.’”

The Sin Offering

4 The LORD said to Moses, 2“Say to the Israelites: ‘When anyone sins unintentionally and does what is forbidden in any of the LORD’s commands— Lev 5:15-18; Heb 9:7

3“‘If the anointed priest sins, bringing guilt on the people, he must bring to the LORD a young bull without defect as a sin offering for the sin he has committed. 4He is to present the bull at the entrance to the Tent of Meeting before the LORD. He is to lay his hand on its head and slaughter it before the LORD. 5Then the anointed priest shall take some of the bull’s blood and carry it into the Tent of Meeting. 6He is to dip his finger into the blood and sprinkle some of it seven times before the LORD, in front of the curtain of the sanctuary. 7The priest shall then put some of the blood on the horns of the altar of fragrant incense that is before the LORD in the Tent of Meeting. The rest of the bull’s blood he shall pour out at the base of the altar of burnt offering at the entrance to the Tent of Meeting. 8He shall remove all the fat from the bull of the sin offering—the fat that covers the inner parts or is connected to them, 9both kidneys with the fat on them near the loins, and the covering of the liver, which he will remove with the kidneys— 10just as the fat is removed from the ox[b] sacrificed as a fellowship offering.[c] Then the priest shall burn them on the altar of burnt offering. 11But the hide of the bull and all its flesh, as well as the head and legs, the inner parts and offal— 12that is, all the rest of the bull—he must take outside the camp to a place ceremonially clean, where the ashes are thrown, and burn it in a wood fire on the ash heap. Lev 5:9; Heb 13:11

13“‘If the whole Israelite community sins unintentionally and does what is forbidden in any of the LORD’s commands, even though the community is unaware of the matter, they are guilty. 14When they become aware of the sin they committed, the assembly must bring a young bull as a sin offering and present it before the Tent of Meeting. 15The elders of the community are to lay their hands on the bull’s head before the LORD, and the bull shall be slaughtered before the LORD. 16Then the anointed priest is to take some of the bull’s blood into the Tent of Meeting. 17He shall dip his finger into the blood and sprinkle it before the LORD seven times in front of the curtain. 18He is to put some of the blood on the horns of the altar that is before the LORD in the Tent of Meeting. The rest of the blood he shall pour out at the base of the altar of burnt offering at the entrance to the Tent of Meeting. 19He shall remove all the fat from it and burn it on the altar, 20and do with this bull just as he did with

[a] *1* Traditionally *peace offering*; also in verses 3, 6 and 9
[b] *10* The Hebrew word can include both male and female.
[c] *10* Traditionally *peace offering*; also in verses 26, 31 and 35

OLD TESTAMENT SACRIFICES

Sacrifice	Old Testament References	Elements	Purpose
BURNT OFFERING	*Leviticus 1; 6:8-13; 8:18-21; 16:24*	Bull, ram or male bird (dove or young pigeon for the poor); wholly consumed; no defect	Voluntary act of worship; atonement for unintentional sin in general; expression of devotion, commitment and complete surrender to God
GRAIN OFFERING	*Leviticus 2; 6:14-23*	Grain, fine flour, olive oil, incense, baked bread (cakes or wafers), salt; no yeast or honey; accompanied burnt offering and fellowship offering (along with drink offering)	Voluntary act of worship; recognition of God's goodness and provisions; devotion to God
FELLOWSHIP OFFERING	*Leviticus 3; 7:11-34*	Any animal without defect from herd or flock; variety of breads	Voluntary act of worship; thanksgiving and fellowship (it included a communal meal)
SIN OFFERING	*Leviticus 4:1–5:13; 6:24-30; 8:14-17; 16:3-22*	1. Young bull: for high priest and congregation 2. Male goat: for leader 3. Female goat or lamb: for common person 4. Dove or pigeon: for the poor 5. Tenth of an ephah of fine flour: for the very poor	Mandatory atonement for specific unintentional sin; confession of sin; forgiveness of sin; cleansing from defilement
GUILT OFFERING	*Leviticus 5:14–6:7; 7:1-6*	Ram or lamb	Mandatory atonement for unintentional sin requiring restitution; cleansing from defilement; make restitution; pay 20% fine

When more than one kind of offering was presented (as in Numbers 7:16,17), the procedure was usually as follows: (1) sin offering or guilt offering, (2) burnt offering, (3) fellowship offering and grain offering (along with a drink offering). This sequence furnishes part of the spiritual significance of the sacrificial system. First, sin had to be dealt with (sin offering or guilt offering). Second, the worshiper committed himself completely to God (burnt offering and grain offering). Third, fellowship or communion between the Lord, the priest and the worshiper was established (fellowship offering).

the bull for the sin offering. In this way the priest will make atonement for them, and they will be forgiven. 21Then he shall take the bull outside the camp and burn it as he burned the first bull. This is the sin offering for the community. ver 3

22" 'When a leader sins unintentionally and does what is forbidden in any of the commands of the LORD his God, he is guilty. 23When he is made aware of the sin he committed, he must bring as his offering a male goat without defect. 24He is to lay his hand on the goat's head and slaughter it at the place where the burnt offering is slaughtered before the LORD. It is a sin offering. 25Then the priest shall take some of the blood of the sin offering with his finger and put it on the horns of the altar of burnt offering and pour out the rest of the blood at the base of the altar. 26He shall burn all the fat on the altar as he burned the fat of the fellowship offering. In this way the priest will make atonement for the man's sin, and he will be forgiven. Lev 9:9; Nu 31:13

27" 'If a member of the community sins unintentionally and does what is forbidden in any of the LORD's commands, he is guilty. 28When he is made aware of the sin he committed, he must bring as his offering for the sin he committed a female goat without defect. 29He is to lay his hand on the head of the sin offering and slaughter it at the place of the burnt offering. 30Then the priest is to take some of the blood with his finger and put it on the horns of the altar of burnt offering and pour out the rest of the blood at the base of the altar. 31He shall remove all the fat, just as the fat is removed from the fellowship offering, and the priest shall burn it on the altar as an aroma pleasing to the LORD. In this way the priest will make atonement for him, and he will be forgiven.

32" 'If he brings a lamb as his sin offering, he is to bring a female without defect. 33He is to lay his hand on its head and slaughter it for a sin offering at the place where the burnt offering is slaughtered. 34Then the priest shall take some of the blood of the sin offering with his finger and put it on the horns of the altar of burnt offering and pour out the rest of the blood at the base of the altar. 35He shall remove all the fat, just as the fat is removed from the lamb of the fellowship offering, and the priest shall burn it on the altar on top of the offerings made to the LORD by fire. In this way the priest will make atonement for him for the sin he has committed, and he will be forgiven.

5 " 'If a person sins because he does not speak up when he hears a public charge to testify regarding something he has seen or learned about, he will be held responsible. Pr 29:24

2" 'Or if a person touches anything ceremonially unclean—whether the carcasses of unclean wild animals or of unclean livestock or of unclean creatures that move along the ground—even though he is unaware of it, he has become unclean and is guilty. Lev 11:11,24-40

3" 'Or if he touches human uncleanness—anything that would make him unclean—even though he is unaware of it, when he learns of it he will be guilty. Nu 19:11-16

4" 'Or if a person thoughtlessly takes an oath to do anything, whether good or evil—in any matter one might carelessly swear about—even though he is unaware of it, in any case when he learns of it he will be guilty. Nu 30:6,8

5" 'When anyone is guilty in any of these ways, he must confess in what way he has sinned 6and, as a penalty for the sin he has committed, he must bring to the LORD a female lamb or goat from the flock as a sin offering; and the priest shall make atonement for him for his sin. Lev 16:21; 26:40

7" 'If he cannot afford a lamb, he is to bring two doves or two young pigeons to the LORD as a penalty for his sin—one for a sin offering and the other for a burnt offering. 8He is to bring them to the priest, who shall first offer the one for the sin offering. He is to wring its head from its neck, not severing it completely, 9and is to sprinkle some of the blood of the sin offering against the side of the altar; the rest of the blood must be drained out at the base of the altar. It is a sin offering. 10The priest shall then offer the other as a burnt offering in the prescribed way and make atonement for him for the sin he has committed, and he will be forgiven.

11" 'If, however, he cannot afford two doves or two young pigeons, he is to bring as an offering for his sin a tenth of an ephah[a] of fine flour for a sin offering. He must not put oil or incense on it, because it is a sin offering. 12He is to bring it to the priest, who shall take a handful of it as a memorial portion and burn it on the altar on top of the offerings made to the LORD by fire. It is a sin offering. 13In this way the priest will make atonement for him for any of these sins he has committed, and he will be forgiven. The rest of the offering will belong to the priest, as in the case of the grain offering.' " Lev 2:1,3; 4:26

The Guilt Offering

14The LORD said to Moses: 15"When a person commits a violation and sins unintentionally in regard to any of the LORD's holy things, he is to bring to the LORD as a penalty a ram from the flock, one without defect and of the proper value in silver, according to the sanctuary shekel.[b] It is a guilt offering. 16He must make restitution for what he has failed to do in regard to the holy things, add a fifth of the value to that and give it

[a] 11 That is, probably about 2 quarts (about 2 liters)
[b] 15 That is, about 2/5 ounce (about 11.5 grams)

all to the priest, who will make atonement for him with the ram as a guilt offering, and he will be forgiven. Lev 6:4; 22:14; Nu 5:7

17“If a person sins and does what is forbidden in any of the LORD’s commands, even though he does not know it, he is guilty and will be held responsible. 18He is to bring to the priest as a guilt offering a ram from the flock, one without defect and of the proper value. In this way the priest will make atonement for him for the wrong he has committed unintentionally, and he will be forgiven. 19It is a guilt offering; he has been guilty of[a] wrongdoing against the LORD.” Lev 6:6; 14:12

6 The LORD said to Moses: 2“If anyone sins and is unfaithful to the LORD by deceiving his neighbor about something entrusted to him or left in his care or stolen, or if he cheats him, 3or if he finds lost property and lies about it, or if he swears falsely, or if he commits any such sin that people may do— 4when he thus sins and becomes guilty, he must return what he has stolen or taken by extortion, or what was entrusted to him, or the lost property he found, 5or whatever it was he swore falsely about. He must make restitution in full, add a fifth of the value to it and give it all to the owner on the day he presents his guilt offering. 6And as a penalty he must bring to the priest, that is, to the LORD, his guilt offering, a ram from the flock, one without defect and of the proper value. 7In this way the priest will make atonement for him before the LORD, and he will be forgiven for any of these things he did that made him guilty.” Lev 5:15

The Burnt Offering

8The LORD said to Moses: 9“Give Aaron and his sons this command: ‘These are the regulations for the burnt offering: The burnt offering is to remain on the altar hearth throughout the night, till morning, and the fire must be kept burning on the altar. 10The priest shall then put on his linen clothes, with linen undergarments next to his body, and shall remove the ashes of the burnt offering that the fire has consumed on the altar and place them beside the altar. 11Then he is to take off these clothes and put on others, and carry the ashes outside the camp to a place that is ceremonially clean. 12The fire on the altar must be kept burning; it must not go out. Every morning the priest is to add firewood and arrange the burnt offering on the fire and burn the fat of the fellowship offerings[b] on it. 13The fire must be kept burning on the altar continuously; it must not go out.

The Grain Offering

14“ ‘These are the regulations for the grain offering: Aaron’s sons are to bring it before the LORD, in front of the altar. 15The priest is to take a handful of fine flour and oil, together with all the incense on the grain offering, and burn the memorial portion on the altar as an aroma pleasing to the LORD. 16Aaron and his sons shall eat the rest of it, but it is to be eaten without yeast in a holy place; they are to eat it in the courtyard of the Tent of Meeting. 17It must not be baked with yeast; I have given it as their share of the offerings made to me by fire. Like the sin offering and the guilt offering, it is most holy. 18Any male descendant of Aaron may eat it. It is his regular share of the offerings made to the LORD by fire for the generations to come. Whatever touches them will become holy.[c] ’ ” Lev 2:3; Eze 44:29

19The LORD also said to Moses, 20“This is the offering Aaron and his sons are to bring to the LORD on the day he[d] is anointed: a tenth of an ephah[e] of fine flour as a regular grain offering, half of it in the morning and half in the evening. 21Prepare it with oil on a griddle; bring it well-mixed and present the grain offering broken[f] in pieces as an aroma pleasing to the LORD. 22The son who is to succeed him as anointed priest shall prepare it. It is the LORD’s regular share and is to be burned completely. 23Every grain offering of a priest shall be burned completely; it must not be eaten.” Ex 29:2; Lev 2:5

The Sin Offering

24The LORD said to Moses, 25“Say to Aaron and his sons: ‘These are the regulations for the sin offering: The sin offering is to be slaughtered before the LORD in the place the burnt offering is slaughtered; it is most holy. 26The priest who offers it shall eat it; it is to be eaten in a holy place, in the courtyard of the Tent of Meeting. 27Whatever touches any of the flesh will become holy, and if any of the blood is spattered on a garment, you must wash it in a holy place. 28The clay pot the meat is cooked in must be broken; but if it is cooked in a bronze pot, the pot is to be scoured and rinsed with water. 29Any male in a priest’s family may eat it; it is most holy. 30But any sin offering whose blood is brought into the Tent of Meeting to make atonement in the Holy Place must not be eaten; it must be burned. Ex 29:37

The Guilt Offering

7 “ ‘These are the regulations for the guilt offering, which is most holy: 2The guilt offering is to be slaughtered in the place where the burnt offering is slaughtered, and its blood is to be sprinkled against the altar on all sides. 3All its fat shall be offered: the fat tail and the fat that covers the

[a] 19 Or *has made full expiation for his* [b] 12 Traditionally *peace offerings* [c] 18 Or *Whoever touches them must be holy*; similarly in verse 27 [d] 20 Or *each* [e] 20 That is, probably about 2 quarts (about 2 liters) [f] 21 The meaning of the Hebrew for this word is uncertain.

inner parts, 4both kidneys with the fat on them near the loins, and the covering of the liver, which is to be removed with the kidneys. 5The priest shall burn them on the altar as an offering made to the LORD by fire. It is a guilt offering. 6Any male in a priest's family may eat it, but it must be eaten in a holy place; it is most holy. Ex 29:13; Lev 6:18

7" 'The same law applies to both the sin offering and the guilt offering: They belong to the priest who makes atonement with them. 8The priest who offers a burnt offering for anyone may keep its hide for himself. 9Every grain offering baked in an oven or cooked in a pan or on a griddle belongs to the priest who offers it, 10and every grain offering, whether mixed with oil or dry, belongs equally to all the sons of Aaron. Lev 2:5; 16:17,26

The Fellowship Offering

11" 'These are the regulations for the fellowship offering[a] a person may present to the LORD:

12" 'If he offers it as an expression of thankfulness, then along with this thank offering he is to offer cakes of bread made without yeast and mixed with oil, wafers made without yeast and spread with oil, and cakes of fine flour well-kneaded and mixed with oil. 13Along with his fellowship offering of thanksgiving he is to present an offering with cakes of bread made with yeast. 14He is to bring one of each kind as an offering, a contribution to the LORD; it belongs to the priest who sprinkles the blood of the fellowship offerings. 15The meat of his fellowship offering of thanksgiving must be eaten on the day it is offered; he must leave none of it till morning. Lev 22:30; Am 4:5

16" 'If, however, his offering is the result of a vow or is a freewill offering, the sacrifice shall be eaten on the day he offers it, but anything left over may be eaten on the next day. 17Any meat of the sacrifice left over till the third day must be burned up. 18If any meat of the fellowship offering is eaten on the third day, it will not be accepted. It will not be credited to the one who offered it, for it is impure; the person who eats any of it will be held responsible. Lev 19:5-8; Nu 18:27

19" 'Meat that touches anything ceremonially unclean must not be eaten; it must be burned up. As for other meat, anyone ceremonially clean may eat it. 20But if anyone who is unclean eats any meat of the fellowship offering belonging to the LORD, that person must be cut off from his people. 21If anyone touches something unclean—whether human uncleanness or an unclean animal or any unclean, detestable thing—and then eats any of the meat of the fellowship offering belonging to the LORD, that person must be cut off from his people.' " Lev 22:3-7

Eating Fat and Blood Forbidden

22The LORD said to Moses, 23"Say to the Israelites: 'Do not eat any of the fat of cattle, sheep or goats. 24The fat of an animal found dead or torn by wild animals may be used for any other purpose, but you must not eat it. 25Anyone who eats the fat of an animal from which an offering by fire may be[b] made to the LORD must be cut off from his people. 26And wherever you live, you must not eat the blood of any bird or animal. 27If anyone eats blood, that person must be cut off from his people.' " Ge 9:4; Lev 17:10-24

The Priests' Share

28The LORD said to Moses, 29"Say to the Israelites: 'Anyone who brings a fellowship offering to the LORD is to bring part of it as his sacrifice to the LORD. 30With his own hands he is to bring the offering made to the LORD by fire; he is to bring the fat, together with the breast, and wave the breast before the LORD as a wave offering. 31The priest shall burn the fat on the altar, but the breast belongs to Aaron and his sons. 32You are to give the right thigh of your fellowship offerings to the priest as a contribution. 33The son of Aaron who offers the blood and the fat of the fellowship offering shall have the right thigh as his share. 34From the fellowship offerings of the Israelites, I have taken the breast that is waved and the thigh that is presented and have given them to Aaron the priest and his sons as their regular share from the Israelites.' " Ex 29:27; Nu 18:18-19

35This is the portion of the offerings made to the LORD by fire that were allotted to Aaron and his sons on the day they were presented to serve the LORD as priests. 36On the day they were anointed, the LORD commanded that the Israelites give this to them as their regular share for the generations to come. Lev 8:12,30

37These, then, are the regulations for the burnt offering, the grain offering, the sin offering, the guilt offering, the ordination offering and the fellowship offering, 38which the LORD gave Moses on Mount Sinai on the day he commanded the Israelites to bring their offerings to the LORD, in the Desert of Sinai. Lev 1:2; 6:9

The Plan for the Priesthood **Chapters 8–10**

In these chapters the priests received specific and minute details on how they were to dress, live and conduct their ministry. As Levites, their lives were ordered very clearly. From their daily acts of service to their personal hygiene and cleansing, there was no detail left unclear or unstated. As you read these chapters, you may begin to feel the binding confinement of the law. (If you don't, you may not be

[a] *11* Traditionally *peace offering*; also in verses 13-37 [b] *25* Or *fire is*

paying close enough attention!) The law spelled out every single detail for the life of a priest, and there were never other options or suggestions for alternate actions. The path was narrow. The commands were very clear: "Do this, and you will live." Sometimes the opposite was stated: "If you don't do this, you will die."

The Ordination of Aaron and His Sons

8 The LORD said to Moses, 2"Bring Aaron and his sons, their garments, the anointing oil, the bull for the sin offering, the two rams and the basket containing bread made without yeast, 3and gather the entire assembly at the entrance to the Tent of Meeting." 4Moses did as the LORD commanded him, and the assembly gathered at the entrance to the Tent of Meeting. Ex 29:2-3; 30:23-25,30

5Moses said to the assembly, "This is what the LORD has commanded to be done." 6Then Moses brought Aaron and his sons forward and washed them with water. 7He put the tunic on Aaron, tied the sash around him, clothed him with the robe and put the ephod on him. He also tied the ephod to him by its skillfully woven waistband; so it was fastened on him. 8He placed the breastpiece on him and put the Urim and Thummim in the breastpiece. 9Then he placed the turban on Aaron's head and set the gold plate, the sacred diadem, on the front of it, as the LORD commanded Moses. Ex 28:30,36; Ac 22:16

10Then Moses took the anointing oil and anointed the tabernacle and everything in it, and so consecrated them. 11He sprinkled some of the oil on the altar seven times, anointing the altar and all its utensils and the basin with its stand, to consecrate them. 12He poured some of the anointing oil on Aaron's head and anointed him to consecrate him. 13Then he brought Aaron's sons forward, put tunics on them, tied sashes around them and put headbands on them, as the LORD commanded Moses. Ex 30:26,30

14He then presented the bull for the sin offering, and Aaron and his sons laid their hands on its head. 15Moses slaughtered the bull and took some of the blood, and with his finger he put it on all the horns of the altar to purify the altar. He poured out the rest of the blood at the base of the altar. So he consecrated it to make atonement for it. 16Moses also took all the fat around the inner parts, the covering of the liver, and both kidneys and their fat, and burned it on the altar. 17But the bull with its hide and its flesh and its offal he burned up outside the camp, as the LORD commanded Moses.

18He then presented the ram for the burnt offering, and Aaron and his sons laid their hands on its head. 19Then Moses slaughtered the ram and sprinkled the blood against the altar on all sides. 20He cut the ram into pieces and burned the head, the pieces and the fat. 21He washed the inner parts and the legs with water and burned the whole ram on the altar as a burnt offering, a pleasing aroma, an offering made to the LORD by fire, as the LORD commanded Moses.

22He then presented the other ram, the ram for the ordination, and Aaron and his sons laid their hands on its head. 23Moses slaughtered the ram and took some of its blood and put it on the lobe of Aaron's right ear, on the thumb of his right hand and on the big toe of his right foot. 24Moses also brought Aaron's sons forward and put some of the blood on the lobes of their right ears, on the thumbs of their right hands and on the big toes of their right feet. Then he sprinkled blood against the altar on all sides. 25He took the fat, the fat tail, all the fat around the inner parts, the covering of the liver, both kidneys and their fat and the right thigh. 26Then from the basket of bread made without yeast, which was before the LORD, he took a cake of bread, and one made with oil, and a wafer; he put these on the fat portions and on the right thigh. 27He put all these in the hands of Aaron and his sons and waved them before the LORD as a wave offering. 28Then Moses took them from their hands and burned them on the altar on top of the burnt offering as an ordination offering, a pleasing aroma, an offering made to the LORD by fire. 29He also took the breast—Moses' share of the ordination ram—and waved it before the LORD as a wave offering, as the LORD commanded Moses.

30Then Moses took some of the anointing oil and some of the blood from the altar and sprinkled them on Aaron and his garments and on his sons and their garments. So he consecrated Aaron and his garments and his sons and their garments.

31Moses then said to Aaron and his sons, "Cook the meat at the entrance to the Tent of Meeting and eat it there with the bread from the basket of ordination offerings, as I commanded, saying,[a] 'Aaron and his sons are to eat it.' 32Then burn up the rest of the meat and the bread. 33Do not leave the entrance to the Tent of Meeting for seven days, until the days of your ordination are completed, for your ordination will last seven days. 34What has been done today was commanded by the LORD to make atonement for you. 35You must stay at the entrance to the Tent of Meeting day and night for seven days and do what the LORD requires, so you will not die; for that is what I have been commanded." 36So Aaron and his sons did everything the LORD commanded through Moses. Ex 29:1-37; Dt 11:1

The Priests Begin Their Ministry

9 On the eighth day Moses summoned Aaron and his sons and the elders of Israel. 2He said to Aaron, "Take a bull calf for your sin offering

[a]31 Or *I was commanded:*

and a ram for your burnt offering, both without defect, and present them before the LORD. [3]Then say to the Israelites: 'Take a male goat for a sin offering, a calf and a lamb—both a year old and without defect—for a burnt offering, [4]and an ox[a] and a ram for a fellowship offering[b] to sacrifice before the LORD, together with a grain offering mixed with oil. For today the LORD will appear to you.' " Ex 29:43; Eze 43:27

[5]They took the things Moses commanded to the front of the Tent of Meeting, and the entire assembly came near and stood before the LORD. [6]Then Moses said, "This is what the LORD has commanded you to do, so that the glory of the LORD may appear to you." Ex 24:16

[7]Moses said to Aaron, "Come to the altar and sacrifice your sin offering and your burnt offering and make atonement for yourself and the people; sacrifice the offering that is for the people and make atonement for them, as the LORD has commanded." Heb 5:1,3; 7:27

[8]So Aaron came to the altar and slaughtered the calf as a sin offering for himself. [9]His sons brought the blood to him, and he dipped his finger into the blood and put it on the horns of the altar; the rest of the blood he poured out at the base of the altar. [10]On the altar he burned the fat, the kidneys and the covering of the liver from the sin offering, as the LORD commanded Moses; [11]the flesh and the hide he burned up outside the camp. Lev 4:1-12

[12]Then he slaughtered the burnt offering. His sons handed him the blood, and he sprinkled it against the altar on all sides. [13]They handed him the burnt offering piece by piece, including the head, and he burned them on the altar. [14]He washed the inner parts and the legs and burned them on top of the burnt offering on the altar.

[15]Aaron then brought the offering that was for the people. He took the goat for the people's sin offering and slaughtered it and offered it for a sin offering as he did with the first one. Lev 4:27-31

[16]He brought the burnt offering and offered it in the prescribed way. [17]He also brought the grain offering, took a handful of it and burned it on the altar in addition to the morning's burnt offering.

[18]He slaughtered the ox and the ram as the fellowship offering for the people. His sons handed him the blood, and he sprinkled it against the altar on all sides. [19]But the fat portions of the ox and the ram—the fat tail, the layer of fat, the kidneys and the covering of the liver— [20]these they laid on the breasts, and then Aaron burned the fat on the altar. [21]Aaron waved the breasts and the right thigh before the LORD as a wave offering, as Moses commanded. Lev 3:1-11; 7:30-34

[22]Then Aaron lifted his hands toward the people and blessed them. And having sacrificed the sin offering, the burnt offering and the fellowship offering, he stepped down. Nu 6:23; Lk 24:50

[23]Moses and Aaron then went into the Tent of Meeting. When they came out, they blessed the people; and the glory of the LORD appeared to all the people. [24]Fire came out from the presence of the LORD and consumed the burnt offering and the fat portions on the altar. And when all the people saw it, they shouted for joy and fell facedown.

The Death of Nadab and Abihu

10 Aaron's sons Nadab and Abihu took their censers, put fire in them and added incense; and they offered unauthorized fire before the LORD, contrary to his command. [2]So fire came out from the presence of the LORD and consumed them, and they died before the LORD. [3]Moses then said to Aaron, "This is what the LORD spoke of when he said: Lev 16:12; Nu 3:2-4

" 'Among those who approach me
I will show myself holy; Ex 30:29; Eze 28:22
in the sight of all the people
I will be honored.' " Isa 49:3

Aaron remained silent.

[4]Moses summoned Mishael and Elzaphan, sons of Aaron's uncle Uzziel, and said to them, "Come here; carry your cousins outside the camp, away from the front of the sanctuary." [5]So they came and carried them, still in their tunics, outside the camp, as Moses ordered. Ex 6:22

[6]Then Moses said to Aaron and his sons Eleazar and Ithamar, "Do not let your hair become unkempt,[c] and do not tear your clothes, or you will die and the LORD will be angry with the whole community. But your relatives, all the house of Israel, may mourn for those the LORD has destroyed by fire. [7]Do not leave the entrance to the Tent of Meeting or you will die, because the LORD's anointing oil is on you." So they did as Moses said.

[8]Then the LORD said to Aaron, [9]"You and your sons are not to drink wine or other fermented drink whenever you go into the Tent of Meeting, or you will die. This is a lasting ordinance for the generations to come. [10]You must distinguish between the holy and the common, between the unclean and the clean, [11]and you must teach the Israelites all the decrees the LORD has given them through Moses." Lev 20:25; Eze 44:21

[12]Moses said to Aaron and his remaining sons, Eleazar and Ithamar, "Take the grain offering left over from the offerings made to the LORD by fire and eat it prepared without yeast beside the altar, for it is most holy. [13]Eat it in a holy place, because it is your share and your sons' share of the offer-

[a]4 The Hebrew word can include both male and female; also in verses 18 and 19. [b]4 Traditionally *peace offering*; also in verses 18 and 22 [c]6 Or *Do not uncover your heads*

ings made to the LORD by fire; for so I have been commanded. 14But you and your sons and your daughters may eat the breast that was waved and the thigh that was presented. Eat them in a ceremonially clean place; they have been given to you and your children as your share of the Israelites' fellowship offerings.[a] 15The thigh that was presented and the breast that was waved must be brought with the fat portions of the offerings made by fire, to be waved before the LORD as a wave offering. This will be the regular share for you and your children, as the LORD has commanded."

16When Moses inquired about the goat of the sin offering and found that it had been burned up, he was angry with Eleazar and Ithamar, Aaron's remaining sons, and asked, 17"Why didn't you eat the sin offering in the sanctuary area? It is most holy; it was given to you to take away the guilt of the community by making atonement for them before the LORD. 18Since its blood was not taken into the Holy Place, you should have eaten the goat in the sanctuary area, as I commanded."

19Aaron replied to Moses, "Today they sacrificed their sin offering and their burnt offering before the LORD, but such things as this have happened to me. Would the LORD have been pleased if I had eaten the sin offering today?" 20When Moses heard this, he was satisfied. Lev 9:12

The Laws for Cleansing **Chapters 11–17**

In these seven chapters God covers the basic regulations for cleansing in the following areas: *food* or *diet* (chapter 11), *hygiene* (chapter 12), treating *diseases* (chapters 13–15) and *atonement* (chapters 16–17). Because God is holy, the people needed to be clean as they approached him in worship. These chapters help us understand how the people of Israel experienced cleansing in their personal and community life. The centrality of blood in cleansing is also emphasized in this section. In order for sinful humanity to approach a perfectly holy God, there must be inward cleansing. Leviticus made it clear that blood was the essential ingredient in this cleansing process (see 17:11).

Clean and Unclean Food

11 The LORD said to Moses and Aaron, 2"Say to the Israelites: 'Of all the animals that live on land, these are the ones you may eat: 3You may eat any animal that has a split hoof completely divided and that chews the cud. Ac 10:12-14

4" 'There are some that only chew the cud or only have a split hoof, but you must not eat them. The camel, though it chews the cud, does not have a split hoof; it is ceremonially unclean for you. 5The coney,[b] though it chews the cud, does not have a split hoof; it is unclean for you. 6The rabbit, though it chews the cud, does not have a split hoof; it is unclean for you. 7And the pig, though it has a split hoof completely divided, does not chew the cud; it is unclean for you. 8You must not eat their meat or touch their carcasses; they are unclean for you. Isa 65:4; Heb 9:10

9" 'Of all the creatures living in the water of the seas and the streams, you may eat any that have fins and scales. 10But all creatures in the seas or streams that do not have fins and scales—whether among all the swarming things or among all the other living creatures in the water—you are to detest. 11And since you are to detest them, you must not eat their meat and you must detest their carcasses. 12Anything living in the water that does not have fins and scales is to be detestable to you.

13" 'These are the birds you are to detest and not eat because they are detestable: the eagle, the vulture, the black vulture, 14the red kite, any kind of black kite, 15any kind of raven, 16the horned owl, the screech owl, the gull, any kind of hawk, 17the little owl, the cormorant, the great owl, 18the white owl, the desert owl, the osprey, 19the stork, any kind of heron, the hoopoe and the bat.[c]

20" 'All flying insects that walk on all fours are to be detestable to you. 21There are, however, some winged creatures that walk on all fours that you may eat: those that have jointed legs for hopping on the ground. 22Of these you may eat any kind of locust, katydid, cricket or grasshopper. 23But all other winged creatures that have four legs you are to detest. Dt 14:3-20; Mt 3:4

24" 'You will make yourselves unclean by these; whoever touches their carcasses will be unclean till evening. 25Whoever picks up one of their carcasses must wash his clothes, and he will be unclean till evening. Lev 14:8,47; 15:5; Nu 31:24

26" 'Every animal that has a split hoof not completely divided or that does not chew the cud is unclean for you; whoever touches ⌊the carcass of⌋ any of them will be unclean. 27Of all the animals that walk on all fours, those that walk on their paws are unclean for you; whoever touches their carcasses will be unclean till evening. 28Anyone who picks up their carcasses must wash his clothes, and he will be unclean till evening. They are unclean for you.

29" 'Of the animals that move about on the ground, these are unclean for you: the weasel, the rat, any kind of great lizard, 30the gecko, the monitor lizard, the wall lizard, the skink and the chameleon. 31Of all those that move along the ground, these are unclean for you. Whoever touches them when they are dead will be unclean till evening. 32When one of them dies and falls on something,

[a] *14* Traditionally *peace offerings* [b] *5* That is, the hyrax or rock badger [c] *19* The precise identification of some of the birds, insects and animals in this chapter is uncertain.

that article, whatever its use, will be unclean,
whether it is made of wood, cloth, hide or sackcloth. Put it in water; it will be unclean till evening,
and then it will be clean. 33If one of them falls into
a clay pot, everything in it will be unclean, and you
must break the pot. 34Any food that could be eaten
but has water on it from such a pot is unclean, and
any liquid that could be drunk from it is unclean.
35Anything that one of their carcasses falls on becomes unclean; an oven or cooking pot must be
broken up. They are unclean, and you are to regard them as unclean. 36A spring, however, or a
cistern for collecting water remains clean, but anyone who touches one of these carcasses is unclean.
37If a carcass falls on any seeds that are to be
planted, they remain clean. 38But if water has been
put on the seed and a carcass falls on it, it is
unclean for you. Lev 15:12

39"'If an animal that you are allowed to eat dies,
anyone who touches the carcass will be unclean till
evening. 40Anyone who eats some of the carcass
must wash his clothes, and he will be unclean till
evening. Anyone who picks up the carcass must
wash his clothes, and he will be unclean till evening. Lev 17:15; 22:8

41"'Every creature that moves about on the
ground is detestable; it is not to be eaten. 42You are
not to eat any creature that moves about on the
ground, whether it moves on its belly or walks on
all fours or on many feet; it is detestable. 43Do not
defile yourselves by any of these creatures. Do not
make yourselves unclean by means of them or be
made unclean by them. 44I am the LORD your God;
consecrate yourselves and be holy, because I am
holy. Do not make yourselves unclean by any

LIVING  **INSIGHT**

The more I get to know my God, the more I become like Him. I discover He's holy; I want to be holy. I discover He's good; I want to be better. I discover He's in control; I don't want to panic my way through life. I want to be like my Father. And in order to be like Him, I need to know what He is like.

(See Leviticus 11:44–45.)

creature that moves about on the ground. 45I am
the LORD who brought you up out of Egypt to be
your God; therefore be holy, because I am holy.

46"'These are the regulations concerning animals, birds, every living thing that moves in the
water and every creature that moves about on the
ground. 47You must distinguish between the unclean and the clean, between living creatures that
may be eaten and those that may not be eaten.'"

Purification After Childbirth

12 The LORD said to Moses, 2"Say to the Israelites: 'A woman who becomes pregnant
and gives birth to a son will be ceremonially unclean for seven days, just as she is unclean during
her monthly period. 3On the eighth day the boy is
to be circumcised. 4Then the woman must wait
thirty-three days to be purified from her bleeding.
She must not touch anything sacred or go to the
sanctuary until the days of her purification are
over. 5If she gives birth to a daughter, for two
weeks the woman will be unclean, as during her
period. Then she must wait sixty-six days to be
purified from her bleeding. Ge 17:12; Lk 1:59

6"'When the days of her purification for a son
or daughter are over, she is to bring to the priest
at the entrance to the Tent of Meeting a year-old
lamb for a burnt offering and a young pigeon or
a dove for a sin offering. 7He shall offer them
before the LORD to make atonement for her, and
then she will be ceremonially clean from her flow
of blood.

"'These are the regulations for the woman who
gives birth to a boy or a girl. 8If she cannot afford
a lamb, she is to bring two doves or two young
pigeons, one for a burnt offering and the other for
a sin offering. In this way the priest will make
atonement for her, and she will be clean.'"

Regulations About Infectious Skin Diseases

13 The LORD said to Moses and Aaron,
2"When anyone has a swelling or a rash or
a bright spot on his skin that may become an
infectious skin disease,[a] he must be brought to
Aaron the priest or to one of his sons[b] who is a
priest. 3The priest is to examine the sore on his
skin, and if the hair in the sore has turned white
and the sore appears to be more than skin deep,[c]
it is an infectious skin disease. When the priest
examines him, he shall pronounce him ceremonially unclean. 4If the spot on his skin is white but
does not appear to be more than skin deep and the
hair in it has not turned white, the priest is to put
the infected person in isolation for seven days. 5On
the seventh day the priest is to examine him, and
if he sees that the sore is unchanged and has not
spread in the skin, he is to keep him in isolation
another seven days. 6On the seventh day the priest
is to examine him again, and if the sore has faded
and has not spread in the skin, the priest shall
pronounce him clean; it is only a rash. The man
must wash his clothes, and he will be clean. 7But if
the rash does spread in his skin after he has shown

[a]2 Traditionally *leprosy*; the Hebrew word was used for various diseases affecting the skin—not necessarily leprosy; also elsewhere in this chapter. [b]2 Or *descendants* [c]3 Or *be lower than the rest of the skin*; also elsewhere in this chapter

himself to the priest to be pronounced clean, he must appear before the priest again. [8]The priest is to examine him, and if the rash has spread in the skin, he shall pronounce him unclean; it is an infectious disease. Lev 11:25; Dt 24:8

[9]"When anyone has an infectious skin disease, he must be brought to the priest. [10]The priest is to examine him, and if there is a white swelling in the skin that has turned the hair white and if there is raw flesh in the swelling, [11]it is a chronic skin disease and the priest shall pronounce him unclean. He is not to put him in isolation, because he is already unclean. Lev 14:8; Nu 12:10

[12]"If the disease breaks out all over his skin and, so far as the priest can see, it covers all the skin of the infected person from head to foot, [13]the priest is to examine him, and if the disease has covered his whole body, he shall pronounce that person clean. Since it has all turned white, he is clean. [14]But whenever raw flesh appears on him, he will be unclean. [15]When the priest sees the raw flesh, he shall pronounce him unclean. The raw flesh is unclean; he has an infectious disease. [16]Should the raw flesh change and turn white, he must go to the priest. [17]The priest is to examine him, and if the sores have turned white, the priest shall pronounce the infected person clean; then he will be clean. ver 2,6

[18]"When someone has a boil on his skin and it heals, [19]and in the place where the boil was, a white swelling or reddish-white spot appears, he must present himself to the priest. [20]The priest is to examine it, and if it appears to be more than skin deep and the hair in it has turned white, the priest shall pronounce him unclean. It is an infectious skin disease that has broken out where the boil was. [21]But if, when the priest examines it, there is no white hair in it and it is not more than skin deep and has faded, then the priest is to put him in isolation for seven days. [22]If it is spreading in the skin, the priest shall pronounce him unclean; it is infectious. [23]But if the spot is unchanged and has not spread, it is only a scar from the boil, and the priest shall pronounce him clean. Ex 9:9

[24]"When someone has a burn on his skin and a reddish-white or white spot appears in the raw flesh of the burn, [25]the priest is to examine the spot, and if the hair in it has turned white, and it appears to be more than skin deep, it is an infectious disease that has broken out in the burn. The priest shall pronounce him unclean; it is an infectious skin disease. [26]But if the priest examines it and there is no white hair in the spot and if it is not more than skin deep and has faded, then the priest is to put him in isolation for seven days. [27]On the seventh day the priest is to examine him, and if it is spreading in the skin, the priest shall pronounce him unclean; it is an infectious skin disease. [28]If, however, the spot is unchanged and has not spread in the skin but has faded, it is a swelling from the burn, and the priest shall pronounce him clean; it is only a scar from the burn. ver 4-5

[29]"If a man or woman has a sore on the head or on the chin, [30]the priest is to examine the sore, and if it appears to be more than skin deep and the hair in it is yellow and thin, the priest shall pronounce that person unclean; it is an itch, an infectious disease of the head or chin. [31]But if, when the priest examines this kind of sore, it does not seem to be more than skin deep and there is no black hair in it, then the priest is to put the infected person in isolation for seven days. [32]On the seventh day the priest is to examine the sore, and if the itch has not spread and there is no yellow hair in it and it does not appear to be more than skin deep, [33]he must be shaved except for the diseased area, and the priest is to keep him in isolation another seven days. [34]On the seventh day the priest is to examine the itch, and if it has not spread in the skin and appears to be no more than skin deep, the priest shall pronounce him clean. He must wash his clothes, and he will be clean. [35]But if the itch does spread in the skin after he is pronounced clean, [36]the priest is to examine him, and if the itch has spread in the skin, the priest does not need to look for yellow hair; the person is unclean. [37]If, however, in his judgment it is unchanged and black hair has grown in it, the itch is healed. He is clean, and the priest shall pronounce him clean. Lev 11:25

[38]"When a man or woman has white spots on the skin, [39]the priest is to examine them, and if the spots are dull white, it is a harmless rash that has broken out on the skin; that person is clean.

[40]"When a man has lost his hair and is bald, he is clean. [41]If he has lost his hair from the front of his scalp and has a bald forehead, he is clean. [42]But if he has a reddish-white sore on his bald head or forehead, it is an infectious disease breaking out on his head or forehead. [43]The priest is to examine him, and if the swollen sore on his head or forehead is reddish-white like an infectious skin disease, [44]the man is diseased and is unclean. The priest shall pronounce him unclean because of the sore on his head. 2Ki 2:23; Eze 29:18

[45]"The person with such an infectious disease must wear torn clothes, let his hair be unkempt,[a] cover the lower part of his face and cry out, 'Unclean! Unclean!' [46]As long as he has the infection he remains unclean. He must live alone; he must live outside the camp. Nu 5:1-4; La 4:15; Lk 17:12

Regulations About Mildew

[47]"If any clothing is contaminated with mil-

[a]45 Or *clothes, uncover his head*

dew—any woolen or linen clothing, 48any woven or knitted material of linen or wool, any leather or anything made of leather— 49and if the contamination in the clothing, or leather, or woven or knitted material, or any leather article, is greenish or reddish, it is a spreading mildew and must be shown to the priest. 50The priest is to examine the mildew and isolate the affected article for seven days. 51On the seventh day he is to examine it, and if the mildew has spread in the clothing, or the woven or knitted material, or the leather, whatever its use, it is a destructive mildew; the article is unclean. 52He must burn up the clothing, or the woven or knitted material of wool or linen, or any leather article that has the contamination in it, because the mildew is destructive; the article must be burned up. Mk 1:44; Lev 14:44

53"But if, when the priest examines it, the mildew has not spread in the clothing, or the woven or knitted material, or the leather article, 54he shall order that the contaminated article be washed. Then he is to isolate it for another seven days. 55After the affected article has been washed, the priest is to examine it, and if the mildew has not changed its appearance, even though it has not spread, it is unclean. Burn it with fire, whether the mildew has affected one side or the other. 56If, when the priest examines it, the mildew has faded after the article has been washed, he is to tear the contaminated part out of the clothing, or the leather, or the woven or knitted material. 57But if it reappears in the clothing, or in the woven or knitted material, or in the leather article, it is spreading, and whatever has the mildew must be burned with fire. 58The clothing, or the woven or knitted material, or any leather article that has been washed and is rid of the mildew, must be washed again, and it will be clean."

59These are the regulations concerning contamination by mildew in woolen or linen clothing, woven or knitted material, or any leather article, for pronouncing them clean or unclean.

Cleansing From Infectious Skin Diseases

14 The LORD said to Moses, 2"These are the regulations for the diseased person at the time of his ceremonial cleansing, when he is brought to the priest: 3The priest is to go outside the camp and examine him. If the person has been healed of his infectious skin disease,[a] 4the priest shall order that two live clean birds and some cedar wood, scarlet yarn and hyssop be brought for the one to be cleansed. 5Then the priest shall order that one of the birds be killed over fresh water in a clay pot. 6He is then to take the live bird and dip it, together with the cedar wood, the scarlet yarn and the hyssop, into the blood of the bird that was killed over the fresh water. 7Seven times he shall sprinkle the one to be cleansed of the infectious disease and pronounce him clean. Then he is to release the live bird in the open fields. Mt 8:2-4

8"The person to be cleansed must wash his clothes, shave off all his hair and bathe with water; then he will be ceremonially clean. After this he may come into the camp, but he must stay outside his tent for seven days. 9On the seventh day he must shave off all his hair; he must shave his head, his beard, his eyebrows and the rest of his hair. He must wash his clothes and bathe himself with water, and he will be clean. Lev 11:25; 13:6

10"On the eighth day he must bring two male lambs and one ewe lamb a year old, each without defect, along with three-tenths of an ephah[b] of fine flour mixed with oil for a grain offering, and one log[c] of oil. 11The priest who pronounces him clean shall present both the one to be cleansed and his offerings before the LORD at the entrance to the Tent of Meeting. Mt 8:4

12"Then the priest is to take one of the male lambs and offer it as a guilt offering, along with the log of oil; he shall wave them before the LORD as a wave offering. 13He is to slaughter the lamb in the holy place where the sin offering and the burnt offering are slaughtered. Like the sin offering, the guilt offering belongs to the priest; it is most holy. 14The priest is to take some of the blood of the guilt offering and put it on the lobe of the right ear of the one to be cleansed, on the thumb of his right hand and on the big toe of his right foot. 15The priest shall then take some of the log of oil, pour it in the palm of his own left hand, 16dip his right forefinger into the oil in his palm, and with his finger sprinkle some of it before the LORD seven times. 17The priest is to put some of the oil remaining in his palm on the lobe of the right ear of the one to be cleansed, on the thumb of his right hand and on the big toe of his right foot, on top of the blood of the guilt offering. 18The rest of the oil in his palm the priest shall put on the head of the one to be cleansed and make atonement for him before the LORD. Ex 29:11; Lev 5:18

19"Then the priest is to sacrifice the sin offering and make atonement for the one to be cleansed from his uncleanness. After that, the priest shall slaughter the burnt offering 20and offer it on the altar, together with the grain offering, and make atonement for him, and he will be clean.

21"If, however, he is poor and cannot afford these, he must take one male lamb as a guilt offering to be waved to make atonement for him, together with a tenth of an ephah[d] of fine flour mixed with oil for a grain offering, a log of oil,

[a] *3* Traditionally *leprosy*; the Hebrew word was used for various diseases affecting the skin—not necessarily leprosy; also elsewhere in this chapter. [b] *10* That is, probably about 6 quarts (about 6.5 liters) [c] *10* That is, probably about 2/3 pint (about 0.3 liter); also in verses 12, 15, 21 and 24 [d] *21* That is, probably about 2 quarts (about 2 liters)

22 and two doves or two young pigeons, which he can afford, one for a sin offering and the other for a burnt offering. Lev 5:7; 12:8

23 "On the eighth day he must bring them for his cleansing to the priest at the entrance to the Tent of Meeting, before the LORD. 24 The priest is to take the lamb for the guilt offering, together with the log of oil, and wave them before the LORD as a wave offering. 25 He shall slaughter the lamb for the guilt offering and take some of its blood and put it on the lobe of the right ear of the one to be cleansed, on the thumb of his right hand and on the big toe of his right foot. 26 The priest is to pour some of the oil into the palm of his own left hand, 27 and with his right forefinger sprinkle some of the oil from his palm seven times before the LORD. 28 Some of the oil in his palm he is to put on the same places he put the blood of the guilt offering—on the lobe of the right ear of the one to be cleansed, on the thumb of his right hand and on the big toe of his right foot. 29 The rest of the oil in his palm the priest shall put on the head of the one to be cleansed, to make atonement for him before the LORD. 30 Then he shall sacrifice the doves or the young pigeons, which the person can afford, 31 one[a] as a sin offering and the other as a burnt offering, together with the grain offering. In this way the priest will make atonement before the LORD on behalf of the one to be cleansed."

32 These are the regulations for anyone who has an infectious skin disease and who cannot afford the regular offerings for his cleansing. Lev 5:7; 13:2

Cleansing From Mildew

33 The LORD said to Moses and Aaron, 34 "When you enter the land of Canaan, which I am giving you as your possession, and I put a spreading mildew in a house in that land, 35 the owner of the house must go and tell the priest, 'I have seen something that looks like mildew in my house.' 36 The priest is to order the house to be emptied before he goes in to examine the mildew, so that nothing in the house will be pronounced unclean. After this the priest is to go in and inspect the house. 37 He is to examine the mildew on the walls, and if it has greenish or reddish depressions that appear to be deeper than the surface of the wall, 38 the priest shall go out the doorway of the house and close it up for seven days. 39 On the seventh day the priest shall return to inspect the house. If the mildew has spread on the walls, 40 he is to order that the contaminated stones be torn out and thrown into an unclean place outside the town. 41 He must have all the inside walls of the house scraped and the material that is scraped off dumped into an unclean place outside the town. 42 Then they are to take other stones to replace these and take new clay and plaster the house.

43 "If the mildew reappears in the house after the stones have been torn out and the house scraped and plastered, 44 the priest is to go and examine it and, if the mildew has spread in the house, it is a destructive mildew; the house is unclean. 45 It must be torn down—its stones, timbers and all the plaster—and taken out of the town to an unclean place. Lev 13:51

46 "Anyone who goes into the house while it is closed up will be unclean till evening. 47 Anyone who sleeps or eats in the house must wash his clothes. Lev 11:24-25

48 "But if the priest comes to examine it and the mildew has not spread after the house has been plastered, he shall pronounce the house clean, because the mildew is gone. 49 To purify the house he is to take two birds and some cedar wood, scarlet yarn and hyssop. 50 He shall kill one of the birds over fresh water in a clay pot. 51 Then he is to take the cedar wood, the hyssop, the scarlet yarn and the live bird, dip them into the blood of the dead bird and the fresh water, and sprinkle the house seven times. 52 He shall purify the house with the bird's blood, the fresh water, the live bird, the cedar wood, the hyssop and the scarlet yarn. 53 Then he is to release the live bird in the open fields outside the town. In this way he will make atonement for the house, and it will be clean."

54 These are the regulations for any infectious skin disease, for an itch, 55 for mildew in clothing or in a house, 56 and for a swelling, a rash or a bright spot, 57 to determine when something is clean or unclean. Lev 13:2,47-52

These are the regulations for infectious skin diseases and mildew. Lev 10:10

Discharges Causing Uncleanness

15 The LORD said to Moses and Aaron, 2 "Speak to the Israelites and say to them: 'When any man has a bodily discharge, the discharge is unclean. 3 Whether it continues flowing from his body or is blocked, it will make him unclean. This is how his discharge will bring about uncleanness: Lev 22:4; Mt 9:20

4 " 'Any bed the man with a discharge lies on will be unclean, and anything he sits on will be unclean. 5 Anyone who touches his bed must wash his clothes and bathe with water, and he will be unclean till evening. 6 Whoever sits on anything that the man with a discharge sat on must wash his clothes and bathe with water, and he will be unclean till evening. Lev 11:25; 14:8

7 " 'Whoever touches the man who has a discharge must wash his clothes and bathe with water, and he will be unclean till evening. Lev 22:5

[a] 31 Septuagint and Syriac; Hebrew 31 *such as the person can afford, one*

8“ ‘If the man with the discharge spits on someone who is clean, that person must wash his clothes and bathe with water, and he will be unclean till evening. Nu 12:14

9“ ‘Everything the man sits on when riding will be unclean, 10and whoever touches any of the things that were under him will be unclean till evening; whoever picks up those things must wash his clothes and bathe with water, and he will be unclean till evening. Nu 19:10

11“ ‘Anyone the man with a discharge touches without rinsing his hands with water must wash his clothes and bathe with water, and he will be unclean till evening.

12“ ‘A clay pot that the man touches must be broken, and any wooden article is to be rinsed with water. Lev 6:28

13“ ‘When a man is cleansed from his discharge, he is to count off seven days for his ceremonial cleansing; he must wash his clothes and bathe himself with fresh water, and he will be clean. 14On the eighth day he must take two doves or two young pigeons and come before the LORD to the entrance to the Tent of Meeting and give them to the priest. 15The priest is to sacrifice them, the one for a sin offering and the other for a burnt offering. In this way he will make atonement before the LORD for the man because of his discharge.

16“ ‘When a man has an emission of semen, he must bathe his whole body with water, and he will be unclean till evening. 17Any clothing or leather that has semen on it must be washed with water, and it will be unclean till evening. 18When a man lies with a woman and there is an emission of semen, both must bathe with water, and they will be unclean till evening. Lev 22:4; Dt 23:10

19“ ‘When a woman has her regular flow of blood, the impurity of her monthly period will last seven days, and anyone who touches her will be unclean till evening. Lev 12:2

20“ ‘Anything she lies on during her period will be unclean, and anything she sits on will be unclean. 21Whoever touches her bed must wash his clothes and bathe with water, and he will be unclean till evening. 22Whoever touches anything she sits on must wash his clothes and bathe with water, and he will be unclean till evening. 23Whether it is the bed or anything she was sitting on, when anyone touches it, he will be unclean till evening.

24“ ‘If a man lies with her and her monthly flow touches him, he will be unclean for seven days; any bed he lies on will be unclean. Lev 12:2; 18:19

25“ ‘When a woman has a discharge of blood for many days at a time other than her monthly period or has a discharge that continues beyond her period, she will be unclean as long as she has the discharge, just as in the days of her period. 26Any bed she lies on while her discharge continues will be unclean, as is her bed during her monthly period, and anything she sits on will be unclean, as during her period. 27Whoever touches them will be unclean; he must wash his clothes and bathe with water, and he will be unclean till evening.

28“ ‘When she is cleansed from her discharge, she must count off seven days, and after that she will be ceremonially clean. 29On the eighth day she must take two doves or two young pigeons and bring them to the priest at the entrance to the Tent of Meeting. 30The priest is to sacrifice one for a sin offering and the other for a burnt offering. In this way he will make atonement for her before the LORD for the uncleanness of her discharge.

31“ ‘You must keep the Israelites separate from things that make them unclean, so they will not die in their uncleanness for defiling my dwelling place,[a] which is among them.’ ” Nu 19:13,20; Eze 5:11

32These are the regulations for a man with a discharge, for anyone made unclean by an emission of semen, 33for a woman in her monthly period, for a man or a woman with a discharge, and for a man who lies with a woman who is ceremonially unclean. ver 2

The Day of Atonement

16 The LORD spoke to Moses after the death of the two sons of Aaron who died when they approached the LORD. 2The LORD said to Moses: “Tell your brother Aaron not to come whenever he chooses into the Most Holy Place behind the curtain in front of the atonement cover on the ark, or else he will die, because I appear in the cloud over the atonement cover. Ex 25:22; Lev 10:1

3“This is how Aaron is to enter the sanctuary area: with a young bull for a sin offering and a ram for a burnt offering. 4He is to put on the sacred linen tunic, with linen undergarments next to his body; he is to tie the linen sash around him and put on the linen turban. These are sacred garments; so he must bathe himself with water before he puts them on. 5From the Israelite community he is to take two male goats for a sin offering and a ram for a burnt offering. Lev 4:13-21; 2Ch 29:23

6“Aaron is to offer the bull for his own sin offering to make atonement for himself and his household. 7Then he is to take the two goats and present them before the LORD at the entrance to the Tent of Meeting. 8He is to cast lots for the two goats—one lot for the LORD and the other for the scapegoat.[b] 9Aaron shall bring the goat whose lot falls to the LORD and sacrifice it for a sin offering. 10But the goat chosen by lot as the scapegoat shall be presented alive before the LORD to be used for making atonement by sending it into the desert as a scapegoat. Lev 9:7; Heb 7:27; 9:7,12

[a] 31 Or *my tabernacle* [b] 8 That is, the goat of removal; Hebrew *azazel*; also in verses 10 and 26

11“Aaron shall bring the bull for his own sin
offering to make atonement for himself and his
household, and he is to slaughter the bull for his
own sin offering. 12He is to take a censer full of
burning coals from the altar before the LORD and
two handfuls of finely ground fragrant incense and
take them behind the curtain. 13He is to put the
incense on the fire before the LORD, and the smoke
of the incense will conceal the atonement cover
above the Testimony, so that he will not die. 14He
is to take some of the bull’s blood and with his
finger sprinkle it on the front of the atonement
cover; then he shall sprinkle some of it with his
finger seven times before the atonement cover.

15“He shall then slaughter the goat for the sin
offering for the people and take its blood behind
the curtain and do with it as he did with the bull’s
blood: He shall sprinkle it on the atonement cover
and in front of it. 16In this way he will make atonement for the Most Holy Place because of the uncleanness and rebellion of the Israelites, whatever
their sins have been. He is to do the same for the
Tent of Meeting, which is among them in the
midst of their uncleanness. 17No one is to be in
the Tent of Meeting from the time Aaron goes in
to make atonement in the Most Holy Place until
he comes out, having made atonement for himself,
his household and the whole community of Israel.

18“Then he shall come out to the altar that is
before the LORD and make atonement for it. He
shall take some of the bull’s blood and some of the
goat’s blood and put it on all the horns of the altar.
19He shall sprinkle some of the blood on it with his
finger seven times to cleanse it and to consecrate
it from the uncleanness of the Israelites. Lev 4:7,25

20“When Aaron has finished making atonement
for the Most Holy Place, the Tent of Meeting and
the altar, he shall bring forward the live goat. 21He
is to lay both hands on the head of the live goat
and confess over it all the wickedness and rebellion
of the Israelites—all their sins—and put them on
the goat’s head. He shall send the goat away into
the desert in the care of a man appointed for the
task. 22The goat will carry on itself all their sins to
a solitary place; and the man shall release it in the
desert. Lev 5:5; Isa 53:12

23“Then Aaron is to go into the Tent of Meeting
and take off the linen garments he put on before
he entered the Most Holy Place, and he is to leave
them there. 24He shall bathe himself with water in
a holy place and put on his regular garments. Then
he shall come out and sacrifice the burnt offering
for himself and the burnt offering for the people,
to make atonement for himself and for the people.
25He shall also burn the fat of the sin offering on
the altar. Eze 42:14; 44:19

26“The man who releases the goat as a scapegoat
must wash his clothes and bathe himself with water; afterward he may come into the camp. 27The
bull and the goat for the sin offerings, whose blood
was brought into the Most Holy Place to make
atonement, must be taken outside the camp; their
hides, flesh and offal are to be burned up. 28The
man who burns them must wash his clothes and
bathe himself with water; afterward he may come
into the camp. Lev 11:25; Heb 13:11

29“This is to be a lasting ordinance for you: On
the tenth day of the seventh month you must deny
yourselves[a] and not do any work—whether native-born or an alien living among you— 30be-
cause on this day atonement will be made for you,
to cleanse you. Then, before the LORD, you will be
clean from all your sins. 31It is a sabbath of rest,
and you must deny yourselves; it is a lasting ordinance. 32The priest who is anointed and ordained
to succeed his father as high priest is to make
atonement. He is to put on the sacred linen garments 33and make atonement for the Most Holy
Place, for the Tent of Meeting and the altar, and
for the priests and all the people of the community. Nu 29:7; Eph 5:26

34“This is to be a lasting ordinance for you:
Atonement is to be made once a year for all the
sins of the Israelites.” Heb 9:7,25

And it was done, as the LORD commanded Moses. Lev 23:26-32; Nu 29:7-11

Eating Blood Forbidden

17 The LORD said to Moses, 2“Speak to Aaron
and his sons and to all the Israelites and
say to them: ‘This is what the LORD has commanded: 3Any Israelite who sacrifices an ox,[b] a lamb or
a goat in the camp or outside of it 4instead of
bringing it to the entrance to the Tent of Meeting
to present it as an offering to the LORD in front of
the tabernacle of the LORD—that man shall be
considered guilty of bloodshed; he has shed blood
and must be cut off from his people. 5This is so the
Israelites will bring to the LORD the sacrifices they
are now making in the open fields. They must
bring them to the priest, that is, to the LORD, at the
entrance to the Tent of Meeting and sacrifice them
as fellowship offerings.[c] 6The priest is to sprinkle
the blood against the altar of the LORD at the entrance to the Tent of Meeting and burn the fat as
an aroma pleasing to the LORD. 7They must no
longer offer any of their sacrifices to the goat
idols[d] to whom they prostitute themselves. This is
to be a lasting ordinance for them and for the
generations to come.’ Ex 34:15; 1Co 10:20

8“Say to them: ‘Any Israelite or any alien living
among them who offers a burnt offering or sacri-

[a] 29 Or *must fast*; also in verse 31 [b] 3 The Hebrew word can include both male and female. [c] 5 Traditionally *peace offerings* [d] 7 Or *demons*

fice 9and does not bring it to the entrance to the
Tent of Meeting to sacrifice it to the LORD—that
man must be cut off from his people. Lev 1:3; 3:7
10" 'Any Israelite or any alien living among
them who eats any blood—I will set my face
against that person who eats blood and will cut
him off from his people. 11For the life of a creature
is in the blood, and I have given it to you to make
atonement for yourselves on the altar; it is the
blood that makes atonement for one's life.

LIVING  **INSIGHT**

Do you realize that the animal sacrifices never permanently took away sins? Never! The people found momentary relief from their guilt. They found temporary forgiveness. They went on their way rejoicing, which lasted for a while . . . but they'd soon be back carrying still another animal, atoning for still more sins. It is only the blood of Jesus that can wash away our sins—once for all (read Hebrews 9:11–10:18).

(See Leviticus 17:11.)

12Therefore I say to the Israelites, "None of you
may eat blood, nor may an alien living among you
eat blood." Ge 9:4; Heb 9:22
13" 'Any Israelite or any alien living among you
who hunts any animal or bird that may be eaten
must drain out the blood and cover it with earth,
14because the life of every creature is its blood.
That is why I have said to the Israelites, "You must
not eat the blood of any creature, because the life
of every creature is its blood; anyone who eats it
must be cut off." Ge 9:4; Dt 12:16
15" 'Anyone, whether native-born or alien, who
eats anything found dead or torn by wild animals
must wash his clothes and bathe with water, and
he will be ceremonially unclean till evening; then
he will be clean. 16But if he does not wash his
clothes and bathe himself, he will be held responsible.' " Ex 22:31; Dt 14:21

Holy Living **Chapters 18–27**

Chapters 18–22 focus on the need for holy living. Holy living was never an afterthought in God's plan for His people; it was woven into the very fabric of their lives and faith. This call is best summarized when the Lord declared, "Be holy because I, the LORD your God, am holy" (19:2).

Chapters 23–25 record the Lord's appointed feasts. Look for the number seven—the number signifying completeness or totality—as you read through these chapters. The Passover lasted seven days. The Feast of Weeks (Pentecost) fell seven weeks after Passover and lasted seven days. In the seventh month the people celebrated the Feasts of Trumpets, Tabernacles and Atonement. Every seventh day was a Sabbath and every seventh year was a Sabbath Year. Also, after seven sets of seven years had passed, forty-nine years, the people celebrated the freedom and joy of the Year of Jubilee—a sort of religious Emancipation Proclamation when slaves were set free, land was returned to its original owner and everything had a new beginning.

The last two chapters of Leviticus summarize rewards for obedience and punishment for disobedience, as well as regulations for offerings vowed to the Lord.

Unlawful Sexual Relations

18 The LORD said to Moses, 2"Speak to the
Israelites and say to them: 'I am the LORD
your God. 3You must not do as they do in Egypt,
where you used to live, and you must not do as
they do in the land of Canaan, where I am bringing you. Do not follow their practices. 4You must
obey my laws and be careful to follow my decrees.
I am the LORD your God. 5Keep my decrees and
laws, for the man who obeys them will live by
them. I am the LORD. Eze 20:11; Ro 10:5; Gal 3:12
6" 'No one is to approach any close relative to
have sexual relations. I am the LORD.
7" 'Do not dishonor your father by having sexual relations with your mother. She is your mother;
do not have relations with her. Lev 20:11
8" 'Do not have sexual relations with your father's wife; that would dishonor your father.
9" 'Do not have sexual relations with your sister,
either your father's daughter or your mother's
daughter, whether she was born in the same home
or elsewhere. Lev 20:17
10" 'Do not have sexual relations with your son's
daughter or your daughter's daughter; that would
dishonor you.
11" 'Do not have sexual relations with the
daughter of your father's wife, born to your father;
she is your sister.
12" 'Do not have sexual relations with your father's sister; she is your father's close relative.
13" 'Do not have sexual relations with your
mother's sister, because she is your mother's close
relative.
14" 'Do not dishonor your father's brother by
approaching his wife to have sexual relations; she
is your aunt. Lev 20:20
15" 'Do not have sexual relations with your
daughter-in-law. She is your son's wife; do not
have relations with her. Lev 20:12
16" 'Do not have sexual relations with your
brother's wife; that would dishonor your brother.
17" 'Do not have sexual relations with both a
woman and her daughter. Do not have sexual relations with either her son's daughter or her daughter's daughter; they are her close relatives. That is
wickedness. Lev 20:14
18" 'Do not take your wife's sister as a rival wife

and have sexual relations with her while your wife is living.

19“ ‘Do not approach a woman to have sexual relations during the uncleanness of her monthly period. Lev 15:24

20“ ‘Do not have sexual relations with your neighbor’s wife and defile yourself with her.

21“ ‘Do not give any of your children to be sacrificed[a] to Molech, for you must not profane the name of your God. I am the LORD. Lev 19:12; 20:2-5

22“ ‘Do not lie with a man as one lies with a woman; that is detestable. Lev 20:13; Ro 1:27

23“ ‘Do not have sexual relations with an animal and defile yourself with it. A woman must not present herself to an animal to have sexual relations with it; that is a perversion. Lev 20:15

24“ ‘Do not defile yourselves in any of these ways, because this is how the nations that I am going to drive out before you became defiled. 25Even the land was defiled; so I punished it for its sin, and the land vomited out its inhabitants. 26But you must keep my decrees and my laws. The native-born and the aliens living among you must not do any of these detestable things, 27for all these things were done by the people who lived in the land before you, and the land became defiled. 28And if you defile the land, it will vomit you out as it vomited out the nations that were before you.

29“ ‘Everyone who does any of these detestable things—such persons must be cut off from their people. 30Keep my requirements and do not follow any of the detestable customs that were practiced before you came and do not defile yourselves with them. I am the LORD your God.’ ” Dt 11:1

Various Laws

19 The LORD said to Moses, 2“Speak to the entire assembly of Israel and say to them: ‘Be holy because I, the LORD your God, am holy.

3“ ‘Each of you must respect his mother and father, and you must observe my Sabbaths. I am the LORD your God. Ex 20:12

4“ ‘Do not turn to idols or make gods of cast metal for yourselves. I am the LORD your God.

5“ ‘When you sacrifice a fellowship offering[b] to the LORD, sacrifice it in such a way that it will be accepted on your behalf. 6It shall be eaten on the day you sacrifice it or on the next day; anything left over until the third day must be burned up. 7If any of it is eaten on the third day, it is impure and will not be accepted. 8Whoever eats it will be held responsible because he has desecrated what is holy to the LORD; that person must be cut off from his people. Lev 7:16-17

9“ ‘When you reap the harvest of your land, do not reap to the very edges of your field or gather the gleanings of your harvest. 10Do not go over your vineyard a second time or pick up the grapes that have fallen. Leave them for the poor and the alien. I am the LORD your God. Dt 24:19-22

11“ ‘Do not steal. Ex 20:15

“ ‘Do not lie. Eph 4:25

“ ‘Do not deceive one another. Lev 6:2

12“ ‘Do not swear falsely by my name and so profane the name of your God. I am the LORD.

13“ ‘Do not defraud your neighbor or rob him.

“ ‘Do not hold back the wages of a hired man overnight. Dt 24:15; Jas 5:4

14“ ‘Do not curse the deaf or put a stumbling block in front of the blind, but fear your God. I am the LORD. Dt 27:18

15“ ‘Do not pervert justice; do not show partiality to the poor or favoritism to the great, but judge your neighbor fairly. Ex 23:2,6; Dt 1:17

16“ ‘Do not go about spreading slander among your people. Ps 15:3; Eze 22:9

“ ‘Do not do anything that endangers your neighbor’s life. I am the LORD. Ex 23:7

17“ ‘Do not hate your brother in your heart. Rebuke your neighbor frankly so you will not share in his guilt. Jn 2:9; Mt 18:15

18“ ‘Do not seek revenge or bear a grudge against one of your people, but love your neighbor as yourself. I am the LORD. Mt 5:43; Gal 5:14; Ro 12:19

LIVING  **INSIGHT**

Involved in a lot of activities? In a hurry most of the time? Seldom pausing to ask why? Still substituting doing for being? It will never satisfy. What does God suggest? Having a heart of compassion, being kind, tender, transparent, gentle, patient, forgiving, loving and lovable. All those things spell R-E-A-L.

(See Leviticus 19:18.)

19“ ‘Keep my decrees.

“ ‘Do not mate different kinds of animals.

“ ‘Do not plant your field with two kinds of seed.

“ ‘Do not wear clothing woven of two kinds of material. Dt 22:9,11

20“ ‘If a man sleeps with a woman who is a slave girl promised to another man but who has not been ransomed or given her freedom, there must be due punishment. Yet they are not to be put to death, because she had not been freed. 21The man, however, must bring a ram to the entrance to the Tent of Meeting for a guilt offering to the LORD. 22With the ram of the guilt offering the priest is to make atonement for him before the LORD for the sin he has committed, and his sin will be forgiven.

[a]21 Or *to be passed through* ⌞*the fire*⌟ [b]5 Traditionally *peace offering*

23“ ‘When you enter the land and plant any kind
of fruit tree, regard its fruit as forbidden.[a] For
three years you are to consider it forbidden[a]; it
must not be eaten. 24In the fourth year all its fruit
will be holy, an offering of praise to the LORD.
25But in the fifth year you may eat its fruit. In this
way your harvest will be increased. I am the LORD
your God. Pr 3:9
26“ ‘Do not eat any meat with the blood still
in it. Lev 17:10
“ ‘Do not practice divination or sorcery.
27“ ‘Do not cut the hair at the sides of your head
or clip off the edges of your beard. Lev 21:5
28“ ‘Do not cut your bodies for the dead or put
tattoo marks on yourselves. I am the LORD.
29“ ‘Do not degrade your daughter by making
her a prostitute, or the land will turn to prostitution and be filled with wickedness. Dt 23:18
30“ ‘Observe my Sabbaths and have reverence
for my sanctuary. I am the LORD. Lev 26:2
31“ ‘Do not turn to mediums or seek out spiritists, for you will be defiled by them. I am the LORD
your God. Lev 20:6; Isa 8:19
32“ ‘Rise in the presence of the aged, show respect for the elderly and revere your God. I am the
LORD. Job 32:4; 1Ti 5:1
33“ ‘When an alien lives with you in your land,
do not mistreat him. 34The alien living with you
must be treated as one of your native-born. Love
him as yourself, for you were aliens in Egypt. I am
the LORD your God. ver 18; Ex 12:48; Dt 10:19
35“ ‘Do not use dishonest standards when measuring length, weight or quantity. 36Use honest
scales and honest weights, an honest ephah[b] and
an honest hin.[c] I am the LORD your God, who
brought you out of Egypt. Dt 25:13-15
37“ ‘Keep all my decrees and all my laws and
follow them. I am the LORD.’ ” 2Ki 17:37

Punishments for Sin

20 The LORD said to Moses, 2“Say to the Israelites: ‘Any Israelite or any alien living in
Israel who gives[d] any of his children to Molech
must be put to death. The people of the community are to stone him. 3I will set my face against that
man and I will cut him off from his people; for by
giving his children to Molech, he has defiled my
sanctuary and profaned my holy name. 4If the
people of the community close their eyes when
that man gives one of his children to Molech and
they fail to put him to death, 5I will set my face
against that man and his family and will cut off
from their people both him and all who follow him
in prostituting themselves to Molech. Lev 18:21
6“ ‘I will set my face against the person who
turns to mediums and spiritists to prostitute himself by following them, and I will cut him off from
his people. Lev 19:31
7“ ‘Consecrate yourselves and be holy, because I
am the LORD your God. 8Keep my decrees and
follow them. I am the LORD, who makes you
holy.[e] Eph 1:4; 1Pe 1:16
9“ ‘If anyone curses his father or mother, he
must be put to death. He has cursed his father or
his mother, and his blood will be on his own head.
10“ ‘If a man commits adultery with another
man’s wife—with the wife of his neighbor—both
the adulterer and the adulteress must be put to
death. Ex 20:14
11“ ‘If a man sleeps with his father’s wife, he has
dishonored his father. Both the man and the woman must be put to death; their blood will be on
their own heads. Lev 18:7
12“ ‘If a man sleeps with his daughter-in-law,
both of them must be put to death. What they
have done is a perversion; their blood will be on
their own heads. Lev 18:15
13“ ‘If a man lies with a man as one lies with a
woman, both of them have done what is detestable. They must be put to death; their blood will be
on their own heads. Lev 18:22
14“ ‘If a man marries both a woman and her
mother, it is wicked. Both he and they must be
burned in the fire, so that no wickedness will be
among you. Dt 27:23
15“ ‘If a man has sexual relations with an animal,
he must be put to death, and you must kill the
animal. Lev 18:23
16“ ‘If a woman approaches an animal to have
sexual relations with it, kill both the woman and
the animal. They must be put to death; their blood
will be on their own heads.
17“ ‘If a man marries his sister, the daughter of
either his father or his mother, and they have sexual relations, it is a disgrace. They must be cut off
before the eyes of their people. He has dishonored
his sister and will be held responsible. Lev 18:9
18“ ‘If a man lies with a woman during her
monthly period and has sexual relations with her,
he has exposed the source of her flow, and she has
also uncovered it. Both of them must be cut off
from their people. Lev 15:24; 18:19
19“ ‘Do not have sexual relations with the sister
of either your mother or your father, for that
would dishonor a close relative; both of you would
be held responsible. Lev 18:12-13
20“ ‘If a man sleeps with his aunt, he has dishonored his uncle. They will be held responsible; they
will die childless. Lev 18:14
21“ ‘If a man marries his brother’s wife, it is an
act of impurity; he has dishonored his brother.
They will be childless. Lev 18:16

[a]23 Hebrew *uncircumcised* also in verses 3 and 4 [b]36 An ephah was a dry measure. [c]36 A hin was a liquid measure. [d]2 Or *sacrifices*; [e]8 Or *who sanctifies you*; or *who sets you apart as holy*

22“ ‘Keep all my decrees and laws and follow them, so that the land where I am bringing you to live may not vomit you out. 23You must not live according to the customs of the nations I am going to drive out before you. Because they did all these things, I abhorred them. 24But I said to you, “You will possess their land; I will give it to you as an inheritance, a land flowing with milk and honey.” I am the LORD your God, who has set you apart from the nations. Ex 33:16; Lev 18:3,25-28

25“ ‘You must therefore make a distinction between clean and unclean animals and between unclean and clean birds. Do not defile yourselves by any animal or bird or anything that moves along the ground—those which I have set apart as unclean for you. 26You are to be holy to me[a] because I, the LORD, am holy, and I have set you apart from the nations to be my own. Dt 14:3-21

27“ ‘A man or woman who is a medium or spiritist among you must be put to death. You are to stone them; their blood will be on their own heads.’ ” Lev 19:31

Rules for Priests

21 The LORD said to Moses, “Speak to the priests, the sons of Aaron, and say to them: ‘A priest must not make himself ceremonially unclean for any of his people who die, 2except for a close relative, such as his mother or father, his son or daughter, his brother, 3or an unmarried sister who is dependent on him since she has no husband—for her he may make himself unclean. 4He must not make himself unclean for people related to him by marriage,[b] and so defile himself.

5“ ‘Priests must not shave their heads or shave off the edges of their beards or cut their bodies. 6They must be holy to their God and must not profane the name of their God. Because they present the offerings made to the LORD by fire, the food of their God, they are to be holy. Lev 18:21

7“ ‘They must not marry women defiled by prostitution or divorced from their husbands, because priests are holy to their God. 8Regard them as holy, because they offer up the food of your God. Consider them holy, because I the LORD am holy—I who make you holy.[c] Eze 44:22

9“ ‘If a priest’s daughter defiles herself by becoming a prostitute, she disgraces her father; she must be burned in the fire. Ge 38:24; Lev 19:29

10“ ‘The high priest, the one among his brothers who has had the anointing oil poured on his head and who has been ordained to wear the priestly garments, must not let his hair become unkempt[d] or tear his clothes. 11He must not enter a place where there is a dead body. He must not make himself unclean, even for his father or mother, 12nor leave the sanctuary of his God or desecrate it, because he has been dedicated by the anointing oil of his God. I am the LORD. Lev 10:6-7

13“ ‘The woman he marries must be a virgin. 14He must not marry a widow, a divorced woman, or a woman defiled by prostitution, but only a virgin from his own people, 15so he will not defile his offspring among his people. I am the LORD, who makes him holy.[e]’ ” Eze 44:22

16The LORD said to Moses, 17“Say to Aaron: ‘For the generations to come none of your descendants who has a defect may come near to offer the food of his God. 18No man who has any defect may come near: no man who is blind or lame, disfigured or deformed; 19no man with a crippled foot or hand, 20or who is hunchbacked or dwarfed, or who has any eye defect, or who has festering or running sores or damaged testicles. 21No descendant of Aaron the priest who has any defect is to come near to present the offerings made to the LORD by fire. He has a defect; he must not come near to offer the food of his God. 22He may eat the most holy food of his God, as well as the holy food; 23yet because of his defect, he must not go near the curtain or approach the altar, and so desecrate my sanctuary. I am the LORD, who makes them holy.[f]’ ” Lev 22:19-25; Dt 23:1

24So Moses told this to Aaron and his sons and to all the Israelites.

22 The LORD said to Moses, 2“Tell Aaron and his sons to treat with respect the sacred offerings the Israelites consecrate to me, so they will not profane my holy name. I am the LORD.

3“Say to them: ‘For the generations to come, if any of your descendants is ceremonially unclean and yet comes near the sacred offerings that the Israelites consecrate to the LORD, that person must be cut off from my presence. I am the LORD.

4“ ‘If a descendant of Aaron has an infectious skin disease[g] or a bodily discharge, he may not eat the sacred offerings until he is cleansed. He will also be unclean if he touches something defiled by a corpse or by anyone who has an emission of semen, 5or if he touches any crawling thing that makes him unclean, or any person who makes him unclean, whatever the uncleanness may be. 6The one who touches any such thing will be unclean till evening. He must not eat any of the sacred offerings unless he has bathed himself with water. 7When the sun goes down, he will be clean, and after that he may eat the sacred offerings, for they are his food. 8He must not eat anything found dead or torn by wild animals, and so become unclean through it. I am the LORD. Lev 11:24-28,39

[a]26 Or *be my holy ones* [b]4 Or *unclean as a leader among his people* [c]8 Or *who sanctify you*; or *who set you apart as holy* [d]10 Or *not uncover his head* [e]15 Or *who sanctifies him*; or *who sets him apart as holy* [f]23 Or *who sanctifies them*; or *who sets them apart as holy* [g]4 Traditionally *leprosy*; the Hebrew word was used for various diseases affecting the skin—not necessarily leprosy.

9“ ‘The priests are to keep my requirements so
that they do not become guilty and die for treating
them with contempt. I am the LORD, who makes
them holy.[a] Ex 28:43
10“ ‘No one outside a priest’s family may eat the
sacred offering, nor may the guest of a priest or his
hired worker eat it. 11But if a priest buys a slave
with money, or if a slave is born in his household,
that slave may eat his food. 12If a priest’s daughter
marries anyone other than a priest, she may not
eat any of the sacred contributions. 13But if a
priest’s daughter becomes a widow or is divorced,
yet has no children, and she returns to live in her
father’s house as in her youth, she may eat of her
father’s food. No unauthorized person, however,
may eat any of it. Ge 17:13; Ex 12:44
14“ ‘If anyone eats a sacred offering by mistake,
he must make restitution to the priest for the offering and add a fifth of the value to it. 15The priests
must not desecrate the sacred offerings the Israelites present to the LORD 16by allowing them to eat
the sacred offerings and so bring upon them guilt
requiring payment. I am the LORD, who makes
them holy.’ ” Lev 5:15

Unacceptable Sacrifices

17The LORD said to Moses, 18“Speak to Aaron
and his sons and to all the Israelites and say to
them: ‘If any of you—either an Israelite or an alien
living in Israel—presents a gift for a burnt offering
to the LORD, either to fulfill a vow or as a freewill
offering, 19you must present a male without defect
from the cattle, sheep or goats in order that it may
be accepted on your behalf. 20Do not bring anything with a defect, because it will not be accepted
on your behalf. 21When anyone brings from the
herd or flock a fellowship offering[b] to the LORD to
fulfill a special vow or as a freewill offering, it must
be without defect or blemish to be acceptable.
22Do not offer to the LORD the blind, the injured or
the maimed, or anything with warts or festering or
running sores. Do not place any of these on the
altar as an offering made to the LORD by fire. 23You
may, however, present as a freewill offering an
ox[c] or a sheep that is deformed or stunted, but it
will not be accepted in fulfillment of a vow. 24You
must not offer to the LORD an animal whose testicles are bruised, crushed, torn or cut. You must
not do this in your own land, 25and you must not
accept such animals from the hand of a foreigner
and offer them as the food of your God. They will
not be accepted on your behalf, because they are
deformed and have defects.’ ” Lev 3:6; Dt 15:21
26The LORD said to Moses, 27“When a calf, a
lamb or a goat is born, it is to remain with its
mother for seven days. From the eighth day on, it
will be acceptable as an offering made to the LORD
by fire. 28Do not slaughter a cow or a sheep and its
young on the same day. Ex 22:30; Dt 22:6-7
29“When you sacrifice a thank offering to the
LORD, sacrifice it in such a way that it will be accepted on your behalf. 30It must be eaten that same
day; leave none of it till morning. I am the LORD.
31“Keep my commands and follow them. I am
the LORD. 32Do not profane my holy name. I must
be acknowledged as holy by the Israelites. I am the
LORD, who makes[d] you holy[e] 33and who brought
you out of Egypt to be your God. I am the LORD.”

23 The LORD said to Moses, 2“Speak to the
Israelites and say to them: ‘These are my
appointed feasts, the appointed feasts of the LORD,
which you are to proclaim as sacred assemblies.

The Sabbath

3“ ‘There are six days when you may work, but
the seventh day is a Sabbath of rest, a day of sacred
assembly. You are not to do any work; wherever
you live, it is a Sabbath to the LORD. Ex 20:9-10

LIVING  **INSIGHT**

Constant production without restoration depletes resources and, in fact, diminishes the quality of what is produced. We can learn a lesson from nature. A period of rest always follows a harvest; the land must be allowed time to renew itself.

(See Leviticus 23:3.)

The Passover and Unleavened Bread

4“ ‘These are the LORD’s appointed feasts, the
sacred assemblies you are to proclaim at their appointed times: 5The LORD’s Passover begins at twilight on the fourteenth day of the first month. 6On
the fifteenth day of that month the LORD’s Feast of
Unleavened Bread begins; for seven days you must
eat bread made without yeast. 7On the first day
hold a sacred assembly and do no regular work.
8For seven days present an offering made to the
LORD by fire. And on the seventh day hold a sacred
assembly and do no regular work.’ ” Ex 12:14-20

Firstfruits

9The LORD said to Moses, 10“Speak to the Israelites and say to them: ‘When you enter the land I
am going to give you and you reap its harvest,
bring to the priest a sheaf of the first grain you
harvest. 11He is to wave the sheaf before the LORD

[a]9 Or *who sanctifies them*; or *who sets them apart as holy*; also in verse 16 [b]21 Traditionally *peace offering* [c]23 The Hebrew word can include both male and female. [d]32 Or *made* [e]32 Or *who sanctifies you*; or *who sets you apart as holy*

OLD TESTAMENT FEASTS

Name	Old Testament References	Time	Description	New Testament References
SABBATH	*Exodus 20:8-11; 31:12-17; Leviticus 23:3; Deuteronomy 5:12-15*	7th day	Day of rest; no work	*Matthew 12:1-14; Mark 2:23–3:5; Luke 4:16-30; 6:1-10; 13:10-16; 14:1-5; John 5:1-15; 9:1-34; Acts 13:14-48; 17:2; 18:4; Hebrews 4:1-11*
SABBATH YEAR	*Exodus 23:10-11; Leviticus 25:1-7*	7th year	Year of rest; fallow fields	
YEAR OF JUBILEE	*Leviticus 25:8-55; 27:17-24; Numbers 36:4*	50th year	Canceled debts; liberation of slaves and indentured servants; land returned to original family owners	
PASSOVER	*Exodus 12:1-14; Leviticus 23:5; Numbers 9:1-14; 28:16; Deuteronomy 16:1-7*	1st month (Abib) 14	Slaying and eating a lamb, together with bitter herbs and bread made without yeast in every household	*Matthew 26:1-2,17-29; Mark 14:12-26; Luke 22:7-38; John 2:13-25; 11:55-56; 13:1-30; 1 Corinthians 5:7*
UNLEAVENED BREAD	*Exodus 12:15-20; 13:3-10; 23:15; Leviticus 23:6-8; Numbers 28:17-25; Deuteronomy 16:3-4,8*	1st month (Abib) 15-21	Eating bread made without yeast; holding several assemblies; making designated offerings	*Matthew 26:17; Mark 14:1,12; Luke 22:1,7; Acts 12:3; 20:6; 1 Corinthians 5:6-8*
FIRSTFRUITS	*Leviticus 23:9-14*	1st month (Abib) 16	Presenting a sheaf of the first of the barley harvest as a wave offering; making a burnt offering and a grain offering	*Romans 8:23; 1 Corinthians 15:20-23*
WEEKS (Pentecost) (Harvest)	*Exodus 23:16a; 34:22a; Leviticus 23:15-21; Numbers 28:26-31; Deuteronomy 16:9-12*	3rd month (Sivan) 6	A festival of joy; mandatory and voluntary offerings, including the firstfruits of the wheat harvest	*Acts 2:1-41; 20:16; 1 Corinthians 16:8*
TRUMPETS (Later: Rosh Hashanah—New Year's Day)	*Leviticus 23:23-25; Numbers 29:1-6*	7th month (Tishri) 1	An assembly on a day of rest commemorated with trumpet blasts and sacrifices	
DAY OF ATONEMENT (Yom Kippur)	*Leviticus 16; 23:26-32; Numbers 29:7-11*	7th month (Tishri) 10	A day of rest, fasting and and sacrifices of atonement for priests and people and atonement for the tabernacle and altar	*Acts 27:9; Romans 3:24-26; Hebrews 9:1-14,23-26; 10:19-22*
TABERNACLES (Booths) (Ingathering)	*Exodus 23:16b; 34:22b; Leviticus 23:33-36,39-43; Numbers 29:12-34; Deuteronomy 16:13-15*	7th month (Tishri) 15-21	A week of celebration for the harvest; living in booths and offering sacrifices	*John 7:2-37*
SACRED ASSEMBLY	*Leviticus 23:36; Numbers 29:35-38*	7th month (Tishri) 22	A day of convocation, rest and offering sacrifices	*John 7:37-44*
DEDICATION		9th month	A commemoration of the purification of the temple in the Maccabean era (166-160 B.C.)	*John 10:22-39*
PURIM	*Esther 9:18-32*	12th month (Adar) 14,15	A day of joy and feasting and giving presents	

so it will be accepted on your behalf; the priest is to wave it on the day after the Sabbath. 12On the day you wave the sheaf, you must sacrifice as a burnt offering to the LORD a lamb a year old without defect, 13together with its grain offering of two-tenths of an ephah[a] of fine flour mixed with oil—an offering made to the LORD by fire, a pleasing aroma—and its drink offering of a quarter of a hin[b] of wine. 14You must not eat any bread, or roasted or new grain, until the very day you bring this offering to your God. This is to be a lasting ordinance for the generations to come, wherever you live. Ex 23:16,19; Ro 11:16

Feast of Weeks

15" 'From the day after the Sabbath, the day you brought the sheaf of the wave offering, count off seven full weeks. 16Count off fifty days up to the day after the seventh Sabbath, and then present an offering of new grain to the LORD. 17From wherever you live, bring two loaves made of two-tenths of an ephah of fine flour, baked with yeast, as a wave offering of firstfruits to the LORD. 18Present with this bread seven male lambs, each a year old and without defect, one young bull and two rams. They will be a burnt offering to the LORD, together with their grain offerings and drink offerings—an offering made by fire, an aroma pleasing to the LORD. 19Then sacrifice one male goat for a sin offering and two lambs, each a year old, for a fellowship offering.[c] 20The priest is to wave the two lambs before the LORD as a wave offering, together with the bread of the firstfruits. They are a sacred offering to the LORD for the priest. 21On that same day you are to proclaim a sacred assembly and do no regular work. This is to be a lasting ordinance for the generations to come, wherever you live.

22" 'When you reap the harvest of your land, do not reap to the very edges of your field or gather the gleanings of your harvest. Leave them for the poor and the alien. I am the LORD your God.' "

Feast of Trumpets

23The LORD said to Moses, 24"Say to the Israelites: 'On the first day of the seventh month you are to have a day of rest, a sacred assembly commemorated with trumpet blasts. 25Do no regular work, but present an offering made to the LORD by fire.' "

Day of Atonement

26The LORD said to Moses, 27"The tenth day of this seventh month is the Day of Atonement. Hold a sacred assembly and deny yourselves,[d] and present an offering made to the LORD by fire. 28Do no work on that day, because it is the Day of Atonement, when atonement is made for you before the LORD your God. 29Anyone who does not deny himself on that day must be cut off from his people. 30I will destroy from among his people anyone who does any work on that day. 31You shall do no work at all. This is to be a lasting ordinance for the generations to come, wherever you live. 32It is a sabbath of rest for you, and you must deny yourselves. From the evening of the ninth day of the month until the following evening you are to observe your sabbath." Lev 16:2-34

Feast of Tabernacles

33The LORD said to Moses, 34"Say to the Israelites: 'On the fifteenth day of the seventh month the LORD's Feast of Tabernacles begins, and it lasts for seven days. 35The first day is a sacred assembly; do no regular work. 36For seven days present offerings made to the LORD by fire, and on the eighth day hold a sacred assembly and present an offering made to the LORD by fire. It is the closing assembly; do no regular work. Ex 23:16; Dt 16:13; Jn 7:2

37(" 'These are the LORD's appointed feasts, which you are to proclaim as sacred assemblies for bringing offerings made to the LORD by fire—the burnt offerings and grain offerings, sacrifices and drink offerings required for each day. 38These offerings are in addition to those for the LORD's Sabbaths and[e] in addition to your gifts and whatever you have vowed and all the freewill offerings you give to the LORD.) ver 2,4; Eze 45:17

39" 'So beginning with the fifteenth day of the seventh month, after you have gathered the crops of the land, celebrate the festival to the LORD for seven days; the first day is a day of rest, and the eighth day also is a day of rest. 40On the first day you are to take choice fruit from the trees, and palm fronds, leafy branches and poplars, and rejoice before the LORD your God for seven days. 41Celebrate this as a festival to the LORD for seven days each year. This is to be a lasting ordinance for the generations to come; celebrate it in the seventh month. 42Live in booths for seven days: All native-born Israelites are to live in booths 43so your descendants will know that I had the Israelites live in booths when I brought them out of Egypt. I am the LORD your God.' " Nu 29:12-39; Dt 16:13-17

44So Moses announced to the Israelites the appointed feasts of the LORD.

Oil and Bread Set Before the LORD

24 The LORD said to Moses, 2"Command the Israelites to bring you clear oil of pressed olives for the light so that the lamps may be kept burning continually. 3Outside the curtain of the Testimony in the Tent of Meeting, Aaron is to tend the lamps before the LORD from evening till

[a] 13 That is, probably about 4 quarts (about 4.5 liters); also in verse 17 [b] 13 That is, probably about 1 quart (about 1 liter) [c] 19 Traditionally *peace offering* [d] 27 Or *and fast*; also in verses 29 and 32 [e] 38 Or *These feasts are in addition to the LORD's Sabbaths, and these offerings are*

morning, continually. This is to be a lasting ordinance for the generations to come. 4The lamps on the pure gold lampstand before the LORD must be tended continually. Ex 27:20-21

5"Take fine flour and bake twelve loaves of bread, using two-tenths of an ephah[a] for each loaf. 6Set them in two rows, six in each row, on the table of pure gold before the LORD. 7Along each row put some pure incense as a memorial portion to represent the bread and to be an offering made to the LORD by fire. 8This bread is to be set out before the LORD regularly, Sabbath after Sabbath, on behalf of the Israelites, as a lasting covenant. 9It belongs to Aaron and his sons, who are to eat it in a holy place, because it is a most holy part of their regular share of the offerings made to the LORD by fire." Mt 12:4; Nu 4:7; 2Ch 2:4

A Blasphemer Stoned

10Now the son of an Israelite mother and an Egyptian father went out among the Israelites, and a fight broke out in the camp between him and an Israelite. 11The son of the Israelite woman blasphemed the Name with a curse; so they brought him to Moses. (His mother's name was Shelomith, the daughter of Dibri the Danite.) 12They put him in custody until the will of the LORD should be made clear to them. Ex 18:16; Nu 15:34

13Then the LORD said to Moses: 14"Take the blasphemer outside the camp. All those who heard him are to lay their hands on his head, and the entire assembly is to stone him. 15Say to the Israelites: 'If anyone curses his God, he will be held responsible; 16anyone who blasphemes the name of the LORD must be put to death. The entire assembly must stone him. Whether an alien or native-born, when he blasphemes the Name, he must be put to death. Dt 13:9; 1Ki 21:10,13

17" 'If anyone takes the life of a human being, he must be put to death. 18Anyone who takes the life of someone's animal must make restitution—life for life. 19If anyone injures his neighbor, whatever he has done must be done to him: 20fracture for fracture, eye for eye, tooth for tooth. As he has injured the other, so he is to be injured. 21Whoever kills an animal must make restitution, but whoever kills a man must be put to death. 22You are to have the same law for the alien and the native-born. I am the LORD your God.' " Ex 21:12; Mt 5:38

23Then Moses spoke to the Israelites, and they took the blasphemer outside the camp and stoned him. The Israelites did as the LORD commanded Moses.

The Sabbath Year

25 The LORD said to Moses on Mount Sinai, 2"Speak to the Israelites and say to them: 'When you enter the land I am going to give you, the land itself must observe a sabbath to the LORD. 3For six years sow your fields, and for six years prune your vineyards and gather their crops. 4But in the seventh year the land is to have a sabbath of rest, a sabbath to the LORD. Do not sow your fields or prune your vineyards. 5Do not reap what grows of itself or harvest the grapes of your untended vines. The land is to have a year of rest. 6Whatever the land yields during the sabbath year will be food for you—for yourself, your manservant and maidservant, and the hired worker and temporary resident who live among you, 7as well as for your livestock and the wild animals in your land. Whatever the land produces may be eaten. Ex 23:10

The Year of Jubilee

8" 'Count off seven sabbaths of years—seven times seven years—so that the seven sabbaths of years amount to a period of forty-nine years. 9Then have the trumpet sounded everywhere on the tenth day of the seventh month; on the Day of Atonement sound the trumpet throughout your land. 10Consecrate the fiftieth year and proclaim liberty throughout the land to all its inhabitants. It shall be a jubilee for you; each one of you is to return to his family property and each to his own clan. 11The fiftieth year shall be a jubilee for you; do not sow and do not reap what grows of itself or harvest the untended vines. 12For it is a jubilee and is to be holy for you; eat only what is taken directly from the fields. Jer 34:8,15,17; Lk 4:19

13" 'In this Year of Jubilee everyone is to return to his own property. ver 10

14" 'If you sell land to one of your countrymen or buy any from him, do not take advantage of each other. 15You are to buy from your countryman on the basis of the number of years since the Jubilee. And he is to sell to you on the basis of the number of years left for harvesting crops. 16When the years are many, you are to increase the price, and when the years are few, you are to decrease the price, because what he is really selling you is the number of crops. 17Do not take advantage of each other, but fear your God. I am the LORD your God.

18" 'Follow my decrees and be careful to obey my laws, and you will live safely in the land. 19Then the land will yield its fruit, and you will eat your fill and live there in safety. 20You may ask, "What will we eat in the seventh year if we do not plant or harvest our crops?" 21I will send you such a blessing in the sixth year that the land will yield enough for three years. 22While you plant during the eighth year, you will eat from the old crop and will continue to eat from it until the harvest of the ninth year comes in. Lev 26:10; Hag 2:19

23" 'The land must not be sold permanently, be-

[a]5 That is, probably about 4 quarts (about 4.5 liters)

cause the land is mine and you are but aliens and my tenants. [24]Throughout the country that you hold as a possession, you must provide for the redemption of the land. Ge 23:4; Ex 19:5; 1Pe 2:11

[25]" 'If one of your countrymen becomes poor and sells some of his property, his nearest relative is to come and redeem what his countryman has sold. [26]If, however, a man has no one to redeem it for him but he himself prospers and acquires sufficient means to redeem it, [27]he is to determine the value for the years since he sold it and refund the balance to the man to whom he sold it; he can then go back to his own property. [28]But if he does not acquire the means to repay him, what he sold will remain in the possession of the buyer until the Year of Jubilee. It will be returned in the Jubilee, and he can then go back to his property.

[29]" 'If a man sells a house in a walled city, he retains the right of redemption a full year after its sale. During that time he may redeem it. [30]If it is not redeemed before a full year has passed, the house in the walled city shall belong permanently to the buyer and his descendants. It is not to be returned in the Jubilee. [31]But houses in villages without walls around them are to be considered as open country. They can be redeemed, and they are to be returned in the Jubilee.

[32]" 'The Levites always have the right to redeem their houses in the Levitical towns, which they possess. [33]So the property of the Levites is redeemable—that is, a house sold in any town they hold—and is to be returned in the Jubilee, because the houses in the towns of the Levites are their property among the Israelites. [34]But the pastureland belonging to their towns must not be sold; it is their permanent possession. Nu 35:1-8

[35]" 'If one of your countrymen becomes poor and is unable to support himself among you, help him as you would an alien or a temporary resident, so he can continue to live among you. [36]Do not take interest of any kind[a] from him, but fear your God, so that your countryman may continue to live among you. [37]You must not lend him money at interest or sell him food at a profit. [38]I am the LORD your God, who brought you out of Egypt to give you the land of Canaan and to be your God.

[39]" 'If one of your countrymen becomes poor among you and sells himself to you, do not make him work as a slave. [40]He is to be treated as a hired worker or a temporary resident among you; he is to work for you until the Year of Jubilee. [41]Then he and his children are to be released, and he will go back to his own clan and to the property of his forefathers. [42]Because the Israelites are my servants, whom I brought out of Egypt, they must not be sold as slaves. [43]Do not rule over them ruthlessly, but fear your God. 1Ki 9:22; Eze 34:4; Col 4:1

[44]" 'Your male and female slaves are to come from the nations around you; from them you may buy slaves. [45]You may also buy some of the temporary residents living among you and members of their clans born in your country, and they will become your property. [46]You can will them to your children as inherited property and can make them slaves for life, but you must not rule over your fellow Israelites ruthlessly.

[47]" 'If an alien or a temporary resident among you becomes rich and one of your countrymen becomes poor and sells himself to the alien living among you or to a member of the alien's clan, [48]he retains the right of redemption after he has sold himself. One of his relatives may redeem him: [49]An uncle or a cousin or any blood relative in his clan may redeem him. Or if he prospers, he may redeem himself. [50]He and his buyer are to count the time from the year he sold himself up to the Year of Jubilee. The price for his release is to be based on the rate paid to a hired man for that number of years. [51]If many years remain, he must pay for his redemption a larger share of the price paid for him. [52]If only a few years remain until the Year of Jubilee, he is to compute that and pay for his redemption accordingly. [53]He is to be treated as a man hired from year to year; you must see to it that his owner does not rule over him ruthlessly.

[54]" 'Even if he is not redeemed in any of these ways, he and his children are to be released in the Year of Jubilee, [55]for the Israelites belong to me as servants. They are my servants, whom I brought out of Egypt. I am the LORD your God.

Reward for Obedience

26 " 'Do not make idols or set up an image or a sacred stone for yourselves, and do not place a carved stone in your land to bow down before it. I am the LORD your God. Ex 20:4; Dt 5:8

[2]" 'Observe my Sabbaths and have reverence for my sanctuary. I am the LORD. Lev 19:30

[3]" 'If you follow my decrees and are careful to obey my commands, [4]I will send you rain in its season, and the ground will yield its crops and the trees of the field their fruit. [5]Your threshing will continue until grape harvest and the grape harvest will continue until planting, and you will eat all the food you want and live in safety in your land.

[6]" 'I will grant peace in the land, and you will lie down and no one will make you afraid. I will remove savage beasts from the land, and the sword will not pass through your country. [7]You will pursue your enemies, and they will fall by the sword before you. [8]Five of you will chase a hundred, and a hundred of you will chase ten thousand, and your enemies will fall by the sword before you.

[9]" 'I will look on you with favor and make you

[a] *36* Or *take excessive interest*; similarly in verse 37

fruitful and increase your numbers, and I will keep my covenant with you. [10]You will still be eating last year's harvest when you will have to move it out to make room for the new. [11]I will put my dwelling place[a] among you, and I will not abhor you. [12]I will walk among you and be your God, and you will be my people. [13]I am the LORD your God, who brought you out of Egypt so that you would no longer be slaves to the Egyptians; I broke the bars of your yoke and enabled you to walk with heads held high. Ge 17:6; 2Co 6:16

Punishment for Disobedience

[14]" 'But if you will not listen to me and carry out all these commands, [15]and if you reject my decrees and abhor my laws and fail to carry out all my commands and so violate my covenant, [16]then I will do this to you: I will bring upon you sudden terror, wasting diseases and fever that will destroy your sight and drain away your life. You will plant seed in vain, because your enemies will eat it. [17]I will set my face against you so that you will be defeated by your enemies; those who hate you will rule over you, and you will flee even when no one is pursuing you. Dt 28:15-68; Mal 2:2

[18]" 'If after all this you will not listen to me, I will punish you for your sins seven times over. [19]I will break down your stubborn pride and make the sky above you like iron and the ground beneath you like bronze. [20]Your strength will be spent in vain, because your soil will not yield its crops, nor will the trees of the land yield their fruit. Dt 28:23

[21]" 'If you remain hostile toward me and refuse to listen to me, I will multiply your afflictions seven times over, as your sins deserve. [22]I will send wild animals against you, and they will rob you of your children, destroy your cattle and make you so few in number that your roads will be deserted.

[23]" 'If in spite of these things you do not accept my correction but continue to be hostile toward me, [24]I myself will be hostile toward you and will afflict you for your sins seven times over. [25]And I will bring the sword upon you to avenge the breaking of the covenant. When you withdraw into your cities, I will send a plague among you, and you will be given into enemy hands. [26]When I cut off your supply of bread, ten women will be able to bake your bread in one oven, and they will dole out the bread by weight. You will eat, but you will not be satisfied. Ps 105:16; Jer 2:30

[27]" 'If in spite of this you still do not listen to me but continue to be hostile toward me, [28]then in my anger I will be hostile toward you, and I myself will punish you for your sins seven times over. [29]You will eat the flesh of your sons and the flesh of your daughters. [30]I will destroy your high places, cut down your incense altars and pile your dead bodies on the lifeless forms of your idols, and I will abhor you. [31]I will turn your cities into ruins and lay waste your sanctuaries, and I will take no delight in the pleasing aroma of your offerings. [32]I will lay waste the land, so that your enemies who live there will be appalled. [33]I will scatter you among the nations and will draw out my sword and pursue you. Your land will be laid waste, and your cities will lie in ruins. [34]Then the land will enjoy its sabbath years all the time that it lies desolate and you are in the country of your enemies; then the land will rest and enjoy its sabbaths. [35]All the time that it lies desolate, the land will have the rest it did not have during the sabbaths you lived in it. Dt 4:27; Ps 74:3-7; Jer 9:11

[36]" 'As for those of you who are left, I will make their hearts so fearful in the lands of their enemies that the sound of a windblown leaf will put them to flight. They will run as though fleeing from the sword, and they will fall, even though no one is pursuing them. [37]They will stumble over one another as though fleeing from the sword, even though no one is pursuing them. So you will not be able to stand before your enemies. [38]You will perish among the nations; the land of your enemies will devour you. [39]Those of you who are left will waste away in the lands of their enemies because of their sins; also because of their fathers' sins they will waste away. Eze 21:7

[40]" 'But if they will confess their sins and the sins of their fathers—their treachery against me and their hostility toward me, [41]which made me hostile toward them so that I sent them into the land of their enemies—then when their uncircumcised hearts are humbled and they pay for their sin, [42]I will remember my covenant with Jacob and my covenant with Isaac and my covenant with Abraham, and I will remember the land. [43]For the land will be deserted by them and will enjoy its sabbaths while it lies desolate without them. They will pay for their sins because they rejected my laws and

LIVING  **INSIGHT**

A problem we all have at one time or another is allowing unconfessed sin to build up in our lives—cutting us off from fellowship with our Lord and generally making us miserable. Think of at least one practical way you might remind yourself to keep short accounts with God—that is, coming to Him in confession* immediately *after you become aware of sin in your life.

(See Leviticus 26:40–45.)

[a]11 Or *my tabernacle*

abhorred my decrees. 44Yet in spite of this, when they are in the land of their enemies, I will not reject them or abhor them so as to destroy them completely, breaking my covenant with them. I am the LORD their God. 45But for their sake I will remember the covenant with their ancestors whom I brought out of Egypt in the sight of the nations to be their God. I am the LORD.' " Dt 4:31

46These are the decrees, the laws and the regulations that the LORD established on Mount Sinai between himself and the Israelites through Moses.

Redeeming What Is the LORD's

27 The LORD said to Moses, 2"Speak to the Israelites and say to them: 'If anyone makes a special vow to dedicate persons to the LORD by giving equivalent values, 3set the value of a male between the ages of twenty and sixty at fifty shekels[a] of silver, according to the sanctuary shekel[b]; 4and if it is a female, set her value at thirty shekels.[c] 5If it is a person between the ages of five and twenty, set the value of a male at twenty shekels[d] and of a female at ten shekels.[e] 6If it is a person between one month and five years, set the value of a male at five shekels[f] of silver and that of a female at three shekels[g] of silver. 7If it is a person sixty years old or more, set the value of a male at fifteen shekels[h] and of a female at ten shekels. 8If anyone making the vow is too poor to pay the specified amount, he is to present the person to the priest, who will set the value for him according to what the man making the vow can afford. Ex 30;13; Nu 18:16

9" 'If what he vowed is an animal that is acceptable as an offering to the LORD, such an animal given to the LORD becomes holy. 10He must not exchange it or substitute a good one for a bad one, or a bad one for a good one; if he should substitute one animal for another, both it and the substitute become holy. 11If what he vowed is a ceremonially unclean animal—one that is not acceptable as an offering to the LORD—the animal must be presented to the priest, 12who will judge its quality as good or bad. Whatever value the priest then sets, that is what it will be. 13If the owner wishes to redeem the animal, he must add a fifth to its value. Lev 25:25

14" 'If a man dedicates his house as something holy to the LORD, the priest will judge its quality as good or bad. Whatever value the priest then sets, so it will remain. 15If the man who dedicates his house redeems it, he must add a fifth to its value, and the house will again become his. ver 13,20

16" 'If a man dedicates to the LORD part of his family land, its value is to be set according to the amount of seed required for it—fifty shekels of silver to a homer[i] of barley seed. 17If he dedicates his field during the Year of Jubilee, the value that has been set remains. 18But if he dedicates his field after the Jubilee, the priest will determine the value according to the number of years that remain until the next Year of Jubilee, and its set value will be reduced. 19If the man who dedicates the field wishes to redeem it, he must add a fifth to its value, and the field will again become his. 20If, however, he does not redeem the field, or if he has sold it to someone else, it can never be redeemed. 21When the field is released in the Jubilee, it will become holy, like a field devoted to the LORD; it will become the property of the priests.[j] Nu 18:14

22" 'If a man dedicates to the LORD a field he has bought, which is not part of his family land, 23the priest will determine its value up to the Year of Jubilee, and the man must pay its value on that day as something holy to the LORD. 24In the Year of Jubilee the field will revert to the person from whom he bought it, the one whose land it was. 25Every value is to be set according to the sanctuary shekel, twenty gerahs to the shekel. Ex 30:13

26" 'No one, however, may dedicate the firstborn of an animal, since the firstborn already belongs to the LORD; whether an ox[k] or a sheep, it is the LORD's. 27If it is one of the unclean animals, he may buy it back at its set value, adding a fifth of the value to it. If he does not redeem it, it is to be sold at its set value. Ex 13:2,12

28" 'But nothing that a man owns and devotes[l] to the LORD—whether man or animal or family land—may be sold or redeemed; everything so devoted is most holy to the LORD. Jos 6:17-19

29" 'No person devoted to destruction[m] may be ransomed; he must be put to death.

30" 'A tithe of everything from the land, whether grain from the soil or fruit from the trees, belongs to the LORD; it is holy to the LORD. 31If a man redeems any of his tithe, he must add a fifth of the value to it. 32The entire tithe of the herd and flock—every tenth animal that passes under the shepherd's rod—will be holy to the LORD. 33He must not pick out the good from the bad or make any substitution. If he does make a substitution, both the animal and its substitute become holy and cannot be redeemed.' " Ge 28:22; Mal 3:8

34These are the commands the LORD gave Moses on Mount Sinai for the Israelites. Lev 26:46

[a]3 That is, about 1 1/4 pounds (about 0.6 kilogram); also in verse 16 [b]3 That is, about 2/5 ounce (about 11.5 grams); also in verse 25 [c]4 That is, about 12 ounces (about 0.3 kilogram) [d]5 That is, about 8 ounces (about 0.2 kilogram) [e]5 That is, about 4 ounces (about 110 grams); also in verse 7 [f]6 That is, about 2 ounces (about 55 grams) [g]6 That is, about 1 1/4 ounces (about 35 grams) [h]7 That is, about 6 ounces (about 170 grams) [i]16 That is, probably about 6 bushels (about 220 liters) [j]21 Or *priest* [k]26 The Hebrew word can include both male and female. [l]28 The Hebrew term refers to the irrevocable giving over of things or persons to the LORD. [m]29 The Hebrew term refers to the irrevocable giving over of things or persons to the LORD, often by totally destroying them.

INTRODUCTION

NUMBERS

The promised land! If it was mentioned once, it must have been mentioned a dozen times a day as the time grew closer for the Israelites to leave Mount Sinai. There was no doubt now of God's promise. The heaven-sent cloud by day and fire by night. Moses' reliable leadership. Divine protection from enemy attack and other hindrances. But then tragedy struck. At a *crucial* juncture, the people doubted God's promise and retreated in unbelief. The result? Monotonous wandering in circles for almost forty years as all those individuals twenty years and older died off, leaving a new generation to enter Canaan, the land of promise. The Old Testament book of Numbers is an historical account of those events surrounding the tragic pilgrimage of the Israelites between Sinai and Canaan.

WRITER: *Moses*

DATE: *c.1406* B.C.

PURPOSE: *To show God's judgment and His faithfulness*

KEY MESSAGE: *God's redemptive purpose will not be thwarted*

TIME LINE 2200BC 2100 2000 1900 1800 1700 1600 1500 1400

Moses' birth (c.1526 B.C.)

The plagues; The Passover (c.1446)

The exodus (c.1446 B.C.)

Desert wanderings (c.1446-1406 B.C.)

Exploration of Canaan (c.1443 B.C.)

Book of Numbers written (c.1406 B.C.)

Moses dies; Joshua becomes leader (c.1406 B.C.)

Israelites enter Canaan (c.1406 B.C.)

A Tragic Pilgrimage

AT MOUNT SINAI	GREAT EXPECTATIONS *CHAPTERS 1–9*	DASHED DREAMS *CHAPTERS 10–14*	RENEWED HOPES *CHAPTERS 15–36*	ON THE EDGE OF THE PROMISED LAND
GEOGRAPHICALLY	**Mount Sinai**	**On the way to Kadesh**	**Wandering in the desert**	
CHRONOLOGICALLY	**Several weeks**	**Several days**	**Over 38 years**	
HISTORICALLY	**Preparation for the pilgrimage**	**Rebellion and judgment**	**Passing of the old guard Anticipation of conquest**	
PRACTICALLY	**Anticipating/Dreaming**	**Unbelieving/Complaining**	**Listening/Trusting**	

Every Christian who reads these words at this very moment is on a "pilgrimage." By that I mean a journey toward maturity, a course of life. For some of you this pilgrimage is, thus far, rather pleasurable, exciting and fulfilling. But I rather suspect that for many of you it is a pilgrimage that has been marked by pain, a measure of disappointment and even periods of doubt, disillusionment and deep struggle. Because so many of us have difficult pilgrimages rather than easy, pleasant ones, I am not surprised to discover that God has recorded for us an entire book on that very subject.

Numbers is a book about a tragic pilgrimage where a group of people who knew better did not live better. They suffered the consequences of a bad decision they made at a crossroads of paramount importance in their lives.

The book of Numbers begins at Mount Sinai. The exodus has already occurred. The Israelites have remained at Mount Sinai for thirteen months. At the beginning of that fourteenth month we find the people waiting on God for His directions. He is about to tell them that they are going to begin an important journey . . . a pilgrimage that will lead them up into the land of Canaan, which He had promised to give them as their own. And so, in the beginning of Numbers God is preparing the people for their journey. He is leading them back to the promised land where their forefathers had lived.

Preparation for the Journey

The Israelites were ready to establish themselves as a nation of distinct people. To do this required a great deal of organization—not the least of which was the need to "number," or take a census of, the Hebrews at Sinai. Numbers begins with the account of God telling Moses to number the people. Everyone was counted except the tribe of the Levites. The Levites serviced the tabernacle of God, so they were not included in the count. In this book we have two censuses. The second numbering takes place 38 years after the first. More on this later.

Numbers falls rather naturally into three sections: chapters 1–9; chapters 10–14; and chapters 15–36. For each section I want to make observations centering around four areas: geographical, chronological, historical and practical.

In the first section of Numbers (chapters 1–9) . . .

Geographically, the Israelites were at Mount Sinai.

Chronologically, they were there for several weeks.

Historically, they were preparing for the pilgrimage.

Practically, it was a time of excitement and anticipation, of dreaming, of hoping and of being filled with great delight. It was a thrilling period of time.

During this time the people were given specific instructions on how to conduct themselves by faith. They were engaged in learning how to worship. They were told how to remain pure. They were taught how to prepare for battle and how to fight. They were told how to maintain the tabernacle and how they should walk with the Lord during those years they'd be in the desert. They were given all this instruction as the Lord laid the foundation for what was to come. In short, God was putting them through basic training to get them in shape for the journey ahead.

Grumbling Pilgrims

In the middle section of Numbers (chapters 10–14) we have a whole new setting and situation:

Geographically, the Israelites were on a journey to Kadesh Barnea.

Chronologically, they were there several days. They were traveling from Mount Sinai to Kadesh Barnea in the first journey. And it would bring them right to the edge of the promised land. As chapter 10 begins we find the people of Israel ready to go. They were standing near the tabernacle, waiting to depart for the land of Canaan. The sense of anticipation and excitement stayed with them as they traveled.

Historically, God said, "I'll give you the land. Trust Me. It's yours." With God leading them during the day by the cloud and at night by fire, they never had to question the presence of their God. When the cloud was lifted from above the tent, they would set out; and when the cloud stopped and settled, they would stop and stay there.

Practically, the people of Israel should have been walking in confident faith but instead they were stumbling along in fear and a lack of faith.

In spite of the guidance of the cloud and the fire, they failed. You don't need a cloud, and you don't need a fire. You need faith! And that's where they faltered. And isn't that so often where we fail as well? Let's look more closely at the events of chapters 10–14 to see what we can learn about walking in faith.

Verse 11 of chapter 10 tells us that the Israelites were ready to set out twenty days after God's conversation with Moses recorded in chapter 1. On the twentieth day the cloud lifted from above the tabernacle, and God's people were on their way. Verse 12 reports that the cloud settled in the Desert of Paran. Now, if you have ever been to the Desert of Paran or read about it or seen pictures of it, it is not a very pretty site. It is rough, rugged, barren, stony, dry, harsh and demanding. What was the response of these people who are anticipating the walk of faith? They began to complain and grumble about the way the Lord had led them.

Ever had that happen? Sure you have! "Lord, you just lead me in Your will and I'll be pleased. I just want to know Your will." The Lord shows you the direction He wants you to go and your response is, "Well, now wait a minute, Lord. I didn't anticipate *that* direction. That isn't exactly what I had in mind." If you're not careful, having said all those great and glowing words, you begin to grumble and you begin to cry out and ask all kinds of questions. Do any of these questions sound familiar? "Why now, Lord?" "Why me, God?" "Are you sure you want me to go in that direction?" "Lord, can't you use someone else to do your will in this situation?"

When the journey gets tough, sometimes we just want to turn our backs and run. That's how the Israelites felt when their pilgrimage got tough. Look at their response. They began to grumble about the food the Lord had provided for them. They were fed up with the manna God had provided and complained about the way He was taking care of them. God heard their plea for meat (11:4) and granted their request, but it was not without consequences. The Israelites really wanted their own way; they wanted a little bit of Egypt, mixed with a little bit of Sinai and a little bit of Kadesh Barnea and a pinch of Canaan. In the end, they got what they wanted—but it came at a price (11:33–34).

Stopping on the Edge of the Promise

Finally the people of God came to Kadesh Barnea. God gave Moses a directive to send spies into the land of Canaan to investigate the land He was going to give them. Twelve spies were sent into the land; they looked it over closely and returned back with their report. With the exception of two men, Joshua and Caleb, these spies informed the people that there was *no way* they could possess the land. The people panicked because of the pessimistic report, and, in unbelief, they blamed Moses. With fear in their hearts, they refused to enter into the promised land. After all of the Lord's great miracles and wonderful provision, they refused to believe He could take them the final few steps into the land of Canaan. The result of this decision brought judgment from God.

Moses interceded for the people and in humble prayer asked the Lord to judge them with compassion—to spare the rebellious Israelites and to forgive them. God responded with his promise of pardon (14:20) *and* punishment (14:29–30):

> *In this desert your bodies will fall—every one of you twenty years old or more who was counted in the census and who has grumbled against me. Not one of you will enter the land I swore with uplifted hand to make your home, except Caleb son of Jephunneh and Joshua son of Nun.*

Hope on the Journey

In the next section of Numbers (chapters 15–20), we see the Israelites reaping the fruit of their hard-heartedness and stubborn spirit. God had led them on the pilgrimage all the way to the promised land. They stood on the border, looked across, became fearful and refused to take the final step of faith. The decision was theirs to make, and the consequences of their choice lasted four decades. Think of it . . . an entire generation! Here's the situation in this section:

Geographically, the Israelites were wandering around a massive cul-de-sac in the desert.
Chronologically, the people of God spent over 38 years in the desert wasteland.
Historically, the journey was strewn with the bodies of a generation of a people caught in unbelief.
Practically, the people of God had stopped believing, and in their refusal to follow the Lord, they condemned themselves to incarceration in the desert. They learned about the cost of not trusting God—and (as is often the case) they learned it the hard way!

Before you get too discouraged or disheartened, you need to know that *there is hope at the end of the journey*. It was true for the Israelites, and it is true for us. Chapters 21–36 depict the new generation of people about to enter the land. By the end of Numbers the Israelites have grown in trust and are ready to enter the promised land. They had learned their lesson, and they were anxious to follow in faith.

Lessons From a Fellow Traveler

Moses traveled the hard road of a pilgrim seeking to follow the Lord. Everyone who seeks to follow God down the winding path of this life will know the temptation to grumble, complain and even quit. If Moses were here today, I think he would offer this counsel as we continue our journey of faith.

First, *complaining is usually contagious*. If you are a grumbler, you will infect others with the same disease. Hold your tongue. Think about your words before speaking them; be very careful what you say. A complaining spirit is not pleasing to the Lord. A negative attitude is infectious!

Second, *doubting can be disastrous*. When you find yourself doubting the Lord's ability to get you through, look back on the miles you have already traveled. He has never left you, and He has never failed you. Trust Him for today. He will prove Himself faithful!

Third, *wandering is always humbling*. Along this pilgrimage of faith there will be times of wandering, times of darkness, times of fear, times of uncertainty. In these fearful moments, fall to your knees and cry out to the Lord who ultimately led the people of Israel to their promised land. In your confusion, lift up a weary hand and ask the Lord to lead you. Humbly seek Him. You will feel His mighty hand lift you and lead you onward. And let this be your assurance: You may sometimes feel lonely on your journey of faith, but you are never alone. The same Almighty God who walked with the Israelites through the desert will be with you every step of the way.

Preparing for the Pilgrimage Chapters 1–9

If truth be told, we are all on a pilgrimage. For some the journey leads through the hot and sandy paths of the desert, and the road seems poorly marked. For others, the path feels smooth and the signs on the way are well posted and clear . . . the journey is easy and the direction is clear. For most, however, our adventure of faith takes us through *both* the arid desert and the lush, green pastures. The book of Numbers tells the story of the desert wandering of the people of Israel. The first nine chapters take place at Mount Sinai and cover a time span of several weeks. The people were being prepared to begin their journey. In this section we find the first census, or numbering, of the people. Also, the opening chapters clarify the order of worship the Lord established for the people, including the laws for priests, the instructions for Nazirites, the use of the tabernacle and the observance of Passover. Finally, we witness the wondrous presence of the Lord filling the tabernacle like a blinding, brilliant light. As the Israelites prepared for their pilgrimage, it was clear for everyone to see—the Lord was with them.

The Census

1 The LORD spoke to Moses in the Tent of Meeting in the Desert of Sinai on the first day of the second month of the second year after the Israelites came out of Egypt. He said: [2]"Take a census of the whole Israelite community by their clans and families, listing every man by name, one by one. [3]You and Aaron are to number by their divisions all the men in Israel twenty years old or more who are able to serve in the army. [4]One man from each tribe, each the head of his family, is to help you. [5]These are the names of the men who are to assist you: Ex 30:11-16; Dt 1:15

from Reuben, Elizur son of Shedeur;
[6]from Simeon, Shelumiel son of Zurishaddai;
[7]from Judah, Nahshon son of Amminadab;
[8]from Issachar, Nethanel son of Zuar;
[9]from Zebulun, Eliab son of Helon; Nu 10:16
[10]from the sons of Joseph:
from Ephraim, Elishama son of Ammihud; Nu 2:18
from Manasseh, Gamaliel son of Pedahzur; Nu 10:23
[11]from Benjamin, Abidan son of Gideoni;
[12]from Dan, Ahiezer son of Ammishaddai;
[13]from Asher, Pagiel son of Ocran; Nu 2:27
[14]from Gad, Eliasaph son of Deuel; Nu 2:14
[15]from Naphtali, Ahira son of Enan." Nu 2:29

[16]These were the men appointed from the community, the leaders of their ancestral tribes. They were the heads of the clans of Israel. Ex 18:25

[17]Moses and Aaron took these men whose names had been given, [18]and they called the whole community together on the first day of the second month. The people indicated their ancestry by their clans and families, and the men twenty years old or more were listed by name, one by one, [19]as the LORD commanded Moses. And so he counted them in the Desert of Sinai: Ezr 2:59; Heb 7:3

[20]From the descendants of Reuben the firstborn son of Israel: Nu 26:5-11; Rev 7:5
All the men twenty years old or more who were able to serve in the army were listed by name, one by one, according to the records of their clans and families. [21]The number from the tribe of Reuben was 46,500.

[22]From the descendants of Simeon: Nu 26:12-14
All the men twenty years old or more who were able to serve in the army were counted and listed by name, one by one, according to the records of their clans and families. [23]The number from the tribe of Simeon was 59,300.

[24]From the descendants of Gad: Nu 26:15-18; Rev 7:5
All the men twenty years old or more who were able to serve in the army were listed by name, according to the records of their clans and families. [25]The number from the tribe of Gad was 45,650.

[26]From the descendants of Judah: Nu 26:19-22; Mt 1:2
All the men twenty years old or more who were able to serve in the army were listed by name, according to the records of their clans and families. [27]The number from the tribe of Judah was 74,600.

[28]From the descendants of Issachar: Nu 26:23-25
All the men twenty years old or more who were able to serve in the army were listed by name, according to the records of their clans and families. [29]The number from the tribe of Issachar was 54,400.

[30]From the descendants of Zebulun: Nu 26:26-27
All the men twenty years old or more who were able to serve in the army were listed by name, according to the records of their clans and families. [31]The number from the tribe of Zebulun was 57,400.

[32]From the sons of Joseph:
From the descendants of Ephraim: Nu 26:35-37
All the men twenty years old or more who were able to serve in the army were listed by name, according to the records of their clans and families. [33]The number from the tribe of Ephraim was 40,500.

[34]From the descendants of Manasseh: Nu 26:28-34
All the men twenty years old or more who were able to serve in the army were listed by name, according to the records of their clans and families. [35]The number from the tribe of Manasseh was 32,200.

[36]From the descendants of Benjamin: Nu 26:38-41
All the men twenty years old or more who were able to serve in the army were listed by name, according to the records of their clans and families. [37]The number from the tribe of Benjamin was 35,400.

[38]From the descendants of Dan: Nu 26:42-43
All the men twenty years old or more who were able to serve in the army were listed by name, according to the records of their clans and families. [39]The number from the tribe of Dan was 62,700.

[40]From the descendants of Asher: Nu 26:44-47
All the men twenty years old or more who were able to serve in the army were listed by name, according to the records of their clans and families. [41]The number from the tribe of Asher was 41,500.

[42]From the descendants of Naphtali: Nu 26:48-50
All the men twenty years old or more who were able to serve in the army were listed by name, according to the records of their clans and families. [43]The number from the tribe of Naphtali was 53,400.

[44]These were the men counted by Moses and Aaron and the twelve leaders of Israel, each one representing his family. [45]All the Israelites twenty years old or more who were able to serve in Israel's army were counted according to their families. [46]The total number was 603,550. Nu 2:32; 26:64

[47]The families of the tribe of Levi, however, were not counted along with the others. [48]The LORD had said to Moses: [49]"You must not count the tribe of Levi or include them in the census of the other Israelites. [50]Instead, appoint the Levites to be in charge of the tabernacle of the Testimony—over all its furnishings and everything belonging to it. They are to carry the tabernacle and all its furnishings; they are to take care of it and encamp around it. [51]Whenever the tabernacle is to move, the Levites are to take it down, and whenever the tabernacle is to be set up, the Levites shall do it. Anyone else who goes near it shall be put to death. [52]The Israelites are to set up their tents by divisions, each man in his own camp under his own standard. [53]The Levites, however, are to set up their tents around the tabernacle of the Testimony so that wrath will not fall on the Israelite community. The Levites are to be responsible for the care of the tabernacle of the Testimony."

[54]The Israelites did all this just as the LORD commanded Moses.

The Arrangement of the Tribal Camps

2 The LORD said to Moses and Aaron: [2]"The Israelites are to camp around the Tent of Meeting some distance from it, each man under his standard with the banners of his family."

[3]On the east, toward the sunrise, the divisions of the camp of Judah are to encamp under their standard. The leader of the people of Judah is Nahshon son of Amminadab. [4]His division numbers 74,600. Nu 10:14

[5]The tribe of Issachar will camp next to them. The leader of the people of Issachar is Nethanel son of Zuar. [6]His division numbers 54,400. Nu 1:8; 10:15

[7]The tribe of Zebulun will be next. The leader of the people of Zebulun is Eliab son of Helon. [8]His division numbers 57,400.

[9]All the men assigned to the camp of Judah, according to their divisions, number 186,400. They will set out first. Nu 10:14

[10]On the south will be the divisions of the camp of Reuben under their standard. The leader of the people of Reuben is Elizur son of Shedeur. [11]His division numbers 46,500.

[12]The tribe of Simeon will camp next to them. The leader of the people of Simeon is Shelumiel son of Zurishaddai. [13]His division numbers 59,300. Nu 1:6

[14]The tribe of Gad will be next. The leader of the people of Gad is Eliasaph son of Deuel.[a] [15]His division numbers 45,650. Nu 1:14

[16]All the men assigned to the camp of Reuben, according to their divisions, number 151,450. They will set out second.

[17]Then the Tent of Meeting and the camp of the Levites will set out in the middle of the camps. They will set out in the same order as they encamp, each in his own place under his standard. Nu 10:21

[18]On the west will be the divisions of the camp of Ephraim under their standard. The leader of the people of Ephraim is Elishama son of Ammihud. [19]His division numbers 40,500. Ge 48:20; Nu 1:10

[20]The tribe of Manasseh will be next to them. The leader of the people of Manasseh is Gamaliel son of Pedahzur. [21]His division numbers 32,200. Nu 1:10

[22]The tribe of Benjamin will be next. The leader of the people of Benjamin is Abidan son of Gideoni. [23]His division numbers 35,400. Nu 1:11; Ps 68:27

[24]All the men assigned to the camp of

[a] *14* Many manuscripts of the Masoretic Text, Samaritan Pentateuch and Vulgate (see also Num. 1:14); most manuscripts of the Masoretic Text *Reuel*

Ephraim, according to their divisions, number 108,100. They will set out third. Nu 10:22

[25]On the north will be the divisions of the camp of Dan, under their standard. The leader of the people of Dan is Ahiezer son of Ammishaddai. [26]His division numbers 62,700. Nu 1:12

[27]The tribe of Asher will camp next to them. The leader of the people of Asher is Pagiel son of Ocran. [28]His division numbers 41,500. Nu 1:13

[29]The tribe of Naphtali will be next. The leader of the people of Naphtali is Ahira son of Enan. [30]His division numbers 53,400.

[31]All the men assigned to the camp of Dan number 157,600. They will set out last, under their standards. Nu 10:25

[32]These are the Israelites, counted according to their families. All those in the camps, by their divisions, number 603,550. [33]The Levites, however, were not counted along with the other Israelites, as the LORD commanded Moses.

[34]So the Israelites did everything the LORD commanded Moses; that is the way they encamped under their standards, and that is the way they set out, each with his clan and family. Ex 38:26

The Levites

3 This is the account of the family of Aaron and Moses at the time the LORD talked with Moses on Mount Sinai. Ex 6:27

[2]The names of the sons of Aaron were Nadab the firstborn and Abihu, Eleazar and Ithamar. [3]Those were the names of Aaron's sons, the anointed priests, who were ordained to serve as priests. [4]Nadab and Abihu, however, fell dead before the LORD when they made an offering with unauthorized fire before him in the Desert of Sinai. They had no sons; so only Eleazar and Ithamar served as priests during the lifetime of their father Aaron. Ex 6:23; Lev 10:1-2

[5]The LORD said to Moses, [6]"Bring the tribe of Levi and present them to Aaron the priest to assist him. [7]They are to perform duties for him and for the whole community at the Tent of Meeting by doing the work of the tabernacle. [8]They are to take care of all the furnishings of the Tent of Meeting, fulfilling the obligations of the Israelites by doing the work of the tabernacle. [9]Give the Levites to Aaron and his sons; they are the Israelites who are to be given wholly to him.[a] [10]Appoint Aaron and his sons to serve as priests; anyone else who approaches the sanctuary must be put to death."

[11]The LORD also said to Moses, [12]"I have taken the Levites from among the Israelites in place of the first male offspring of every Israelite woman. The Levites are mine, [13]for all the firstborn are mine. When I struck down all the firstborn in Egypt, I set apart for myself every firstborn in Israel, whether man or animal. They are to be mine. I am the LORD." Ex 13:12; Nu 8:16,18

[14]The LORD said to Moses in the Desert of Sinai, [15]"Count the Levites by their families and clans. Count every male a month old or more." [16]So Moses counted them, as he was commanded by the word of the LORD. Nu 26:62

[17]These were the names of the sons of Levi:

Gershon, Kohath and Merari. Ex 6:16

[18]These were the names of the Gershonite clans:

Libni and Shimei. Ex 6:17

[19]The Kohathite clans:

Amram, Izhar, Hebron and Uzziel.

[20]The Merarite clans:

Mahli and Mushi. Ex 6:19

These were the Levite clans, according to their families.

[21]To Gershon belonged the clans of the Libnites and Shimeites; these were the Gershonite clans. [22]The number of all the males a month old or more who were counted was 7,500. [23]The Gershonite clans were to camp on the west, behind the tabernacle. [24]The leader of the families of the Gershonites was Eliasaph son of Lael. [25]At the Tent of Meeting the Gershonites were responsible for the care of the tabernacle and tent, its coverings, the curtain at the entrance to the Tent of Meeting, [26]the curtains of the courtyard, the curtain at the entrance to the courtyard surrounding the tabernacle and altar, and the ropes—and everything related to their use. Ex 6:17; 25:9; Nu 4:25

[27]To Kohath belonged the clans of the Amramites, Izharites, Hebronites and Uzzielites; these were the Kohathite clans. [28]The number of all the males a month old or more was 8,600.[b] The Kohathites were responsible for the care of the sanctuary. [29]The Kohathite clans were to camp on the south side of the tabernacle. [30]The leader of the families of the Kohathite clans was Elizaphan son of Uzziel. [31]They were responsible for the care of the ark, the table, the lampstand, the altars, the articles of the sanctuary used in ministering, the curtain, and everything related to their use. [32]The chief leader of the Levites was Eleazar son of Aaron, the priest. He was appointed over those who were responsible for the care of the sanctuary.

[33]To Merari belonged the clans of the Mahlites

[a]9 Most manuscripts of the Masoretic Text; some manuscripts of the Masoretic Text, Samaritan Pentateuch and Septuagint (see also Num. 8:16) *to me* [b]28 Hebrew; some Septuagint manuscripts *8,300*

and the Mushites; these were the Merarite clans. 34The number of all the males a month old or more who were counted was 6,200. 35The leader of the families of the Merarite clans was Zuriel son of Abihail; they were to camp on the north side of the tabernacle. 36The Merarites were appointed to take care of the frames of the tabernacle, its crossbars, posts, bases, all its equipment, and everything related to their use, 37as well as the posts of the surrounding courtyard with their bases, tent pegs and ropes. Ex 6:19; Nu 4:32

38Moses and Aaron and his sons were to camp to the east of the tabernacle, toward the sunrise, in front of the Tent of Meeting. They were responsible for the care of the sanctuary on behalf of the Israelites. Anyone else who approached the sanctuary was to be put to death. Nu 18:5

39The total number of Levites counted at the LORD's command by Moses and Aaron according to their clans, including every male a month old or more, was 22,000. Nu 26:62

40The LORD said to Moses, "Count all the firstborn Israelite males who are a month old or more and make a list of their names. 41Take the Levites for me in place of all the firstborn of the Israelites, and the livestock of the Levites in place of all the firstborn of the livestock of the Israelites. I am the LORD." ver 12,15

42So Moses counted all the firstborn of the Israelites, as the LORD commanded him. 43The total number of firstborn males a month old or more, listed by name, was 22,273.

44The LORD also said to Moses, 45"Take the Levites in place of all the firstborn of Israel, and the livestock of the Levites in place of their livestock. The Levites are to be mine. I am the LORD. 46To redeem the 273 firstborn Israelites who exceed the number of the Levites, 47collect five shekels[a] for each one, according to the sanctuary shekel, which weighs twenty gerahs. 48Give the money for the redemption of the additional Israelites to Aaron and his sons." Ex 13:13; Nu 18:15

49So Moses collected the redemption money from those who exceeded the number redeemed by the Levites. 50From the firstborn of the Israelites he collected silver weighing 1,365 shekels,[b] according to the sanctuary shekel. 51Moses gave the redemption money to Aaron and his sons, as he was commanded by the word of the LORD.

The Kohathites

4 The LORD said to Moses and Aaron: 2"Take a census of the Kohathite branch of the Levites by their clans and families. 3Count all the men from thirty to fifty years of age who come to serve in the work in the Tent of Meeting. Ex 30:12; Nu 8:25

4"This is the work of the Kohathites in the Tent of Meeting: the care of the most holy things. 5When the camp is to move, Aaron and his sons are to go in and take down the shielding curtain and cover the ark of the Testimony with it. 6Then they are to cover this with hides of sea cows,[c] spread a cloth of solid blue over that and put the poles in place. Ex 25:10,16; 26:31,33

7"Over the table of the Presence they are to spread a blue cloth and put on it the plates, dishes and bowls, and the jars for drink offerings; the bread that is continually there is to remain on it. 8Over these they are to spread a scarlet cloth, cover that with hides of sea cows and put its poles in place. Ex 25:30; Lev 24:6

9"They are to take a blue cloth and cover the lampstand that is for light, together with its lamps, its wick trimmers and trays, and all its jars for the oil used to supply it. 10Then they are to wrap it and all its accessories in a covering of hides of sea cows and put it on a carrying frame. Ex 25:31,37-38

11"Over the gold altar they are to spread a blue cloth and cover that with hides of sea cows and put its poles in place. Ex 30:1

12"They are to take all the articles used for ministering in the sanctuary, wrap them in a blue cloth, cover that with hides of sea cows and put them on a carrying frame.

13"They are to remove the ashes from the bronze altar and spread a purple cloth over it. 14Then they are to place on it all the utensils used for ministering at the altar, including the firepans, meat forks, shovels and sprinkling bowls. Over it they are to spread a covering of hides of sea cows and put its poles in place. Ex 27:1-8

15"After Aaron and his sons have finished covering the holy furnishings and all the holy articles, and when the camp is ready to move, the Kohathites are to come to do the carrying. But they must not touch the holy things or they will die. The Kohathites are to carry those things that are in the Tent of Meeting. Nu 1:51; 2Sa 6:6-7

16"Eleazar son of Aaron, the priest, is to have charge of the oil for the light, the fragrant incense, the regular grain offering and the anointing oil. He is to be in charge of the entire tabernacle and everything in it, including its holy furnishings and articles." Ex 25:6; 29:41

17The LORD said to Moses and Aaron, 18"See that the Kohathite tribal clans are not cut off from the Levites. 19So that they may live and not die when they come near the most holy things, do this for them: Aaron and his sons are to go into the

[a] *47* That is, about 2 ounces (about 55 grams) [b] *50* That is, about 35 pounds (about 15.5 kilograms) [c] *6* That is, dugongs; also in verses 8, 10, 11, 12, 14 and 25

sanctuary and assign to each man his work and what he is to carry. [20]But the Kohathites must not go in to look at the holy things, even for a moment, or they will die." Ex 19:21; 1Sa 6:19

The Gershonites

[21]The LORD said to Moses, [22]"Take a census also of the Gershonites by their families and clans. [23]Count all the men from thirty to fifty years of age who come to serve in the work at the Tent of Meeting.

[24]"This is the service of the Gershonite clans as they work and carry burdens: [25]They are to carry the curtains of the tabernacle, the Tent of Meeting, its covering and the outer covering of hides of sea cows, the curtains for the entrance to the Tent of Meeting, [26]the curtains of the courtyard surrounding the tabernacle and altar, the curtain for the entrance, the ropes and all the equipment used in its service. The Gershonites are to do all that needs to be done with these things. [27]All their service, whether carrying or doing other work, is to be done under the direction of Aaron and his sons. You shall assign to them as their responsibility all they are to carry. [28]This is the service of the Gershonite clans at the Tent of Meeting. Their duties are to be under the direction of Ithamar son of Aaron, the priest. Ex 27:10-18; Nu 3:25-26

The Merarites

[29]"Count the Merarites by their clans and families. [30]Count all the men from thirty to fifty years of age who come to serve in the work at the Tent of Meeting. [31]This is their duty as they perform service at the Tent of Meeting: to carry the frames of the tabernacle, its crossbars, posts and bases, [32]as well as the posts of the surrounding courtyard with their bases, tent pegs, ropes, all their equipment and everything related to their use. Assign to each man the specific things he is to carry. [33]This is the service of the Merarite clans as they work at the Tent of Meeting under the direction of Ithamar son of Aaron, the priest." Ge 46:11; Nu 3:36

The Numbering of the Levite Clans

[34]Moses, Aaron and the leaders of the community counted the Kohathites by their clans and families. [35]All the men from thirty to fifty years of age who came to serve in the work in the Tent of Meeting, [36]counted by clans, were 2,750. [37]This was the total of all those in the Kohathite clans who served in the Tent of Meeting. Moses and Aaron counted them according to the LORD's command through Moses. Nu 3:27

[38]The Gershonites were counted by their clans and families. [39]All the men from thirty to fifty years of age who came to serve in the work at the Tent of Meeting, [40]counted by their clans and families, were 2,630. [41]This was the total of those in the Gershonite clans who served at the Tent of Meeting. Moses and Aaron counted them according to the LORD's command. Ge 46:11

[42]The Merarites were counted by their clans and families. [43]All the men from thirty to fifty years of age who came to serve in the work at the Tent of Meeting, [44]counted by their clans, were 3,200. [45]This was the total of those in the Merarite clans. Moses and Aaron counted them according to the LORD's command through Moses. ver 29

[46]So Moses, Aaron and the leaders of Israel counted all the Levites by their clans and families. [47]All the men from thirty to fifty years of age who came to do the work of serving and carrying the Tent of Meeting [48]numbered 8,580. [49]At the LORD's command through Moses, each was assigned his work and told what to carry. Nu 3:39

Thus they were counted, as the LORD commanded Moses. Nu 1:47

The Purity of the Camp

5 The LORD said to Moses, [2]"Command the Israelites to send away from the camp anyone who has an infectious skin disease[a] or a discharge of any kind, or who is ceremonially unclean because of a dead body. [3]Send away male and female alike; send them outside the camp so they will not defile their camp, where I dwell among them." [4]The Israelites did this; they sent them outside the camp. They did just as the LORD had instructed Moses. Lev 26:12; 2Co 6:16

Restitution for Wrongs

[5]The LORD said to Moses, [6]"Say to the Israelites: 'When a man or woman wrongs another in any way[b] and so is unfaithful to the LORD, that person is guilty [7]and must confess the sin he has committed. He must make full restitution for his wrong, add one fifth to it and give it all to the person he has wronged. [8]But if that person has no close relative to whom restitution can be made for the wrong, the restitution belongs to the LORD and must be given to the priest, along with the ram with which atonement is made for him. [9]All the sacred contributions the Israelites bring to a priest will belong to him. [10]Each man's sacred gifts are his own, but what he gives to the priest will belong to the priest.'" Lev 5:5; 6:2; Lk 19:8

The Test for an Unfaithful Wife

[11]Then the LORD said to Moses, [12]"Speak to the Israelites and say to them: 'If a man's wife goes astray and is unfaithful to him [13]by sleeping with

[a]2 Traditionally *leprosy*; the Hebrew word was used for various diseases affecting the skin—not necessarily leprosy.
[b]6 Or *woman commits any wrong common to mankind*

another man, and this is hidden from her husband and her impurity is undetected (since there is no witness against her and she has not been caught in the act), 14and if feelings of jealousy come over her husband and he suspects his wife and she is impure—or if he is jealous and suspects her even though she is not impure— 15then he is to take his wife to the priest. He must also take an offering of a tenth of an ephah[a] of barley flour on her behalf. He must not pour oil on it or put incense on it, because it is a grain offering for jealousy, a reminder offering to draw attention to guilt.

16" 'The priest shall bring her and have her stand before the LORD. 17Then he shall take some holy water in a clay jar and put some dust from the tabernacle floor into the water. 18After the priest has had the woman stand before the LORD, he shall loosen her hair and place in her hands the reminder offering, the grain offering for jealousy, while he himself holds the bitter water that brings a curse. 19Then the priest shall put the woman under oath and say to her, "If no other man has slept with you and you have not gone astray and become impure while married to your husband, may this bitter water that brings a curse not harm you. 20But if you have gone astray while married to your husband and you have defiled yourself by sleeping with a man other than your husband"— 21here the priest is to put the woman under this curse of the oath—"may the LORD cause your people to curse and denounce you when he causes your thigh to waste away and your abdomen to swell.[b] 22May this water that brings a curse enter your body so that your abdomen swells and your thigh wastes away.[c]" Jos 6:26; Ps 109:18

" 'Then the woman is to say, "Amen. So be it."

23" 'The priest is to write these curses on a scroll and then wash them off into the bitter water. 24He shall have the woman drink the bitter water that brings a curse, and this water will enter her and cause bitter suffering. 25The priest is to take from her hands the grain offering for jealousy, wave it before the LORD and bring it to the altar. 26The priest is then to take a handful of the grain offering as a memorial offering and burn it on the altar; after that, he is to have the woman drink the water. 27If she has defiled herself and been unfaithful to her husband, then when she is made to drink the water that brings a curse, it will go into her and cause bitter suffering; her abdomen will swell and her thigh waste away,[d] and she will become accursed among her people. 28If, however, the woman has not defiled herself and is free from impurity, she will be cleared of guilt and will be able to have children. Jer 29:18; 42:18

29" 'This, then, is the law of jealousy when a woman goes astray and defiles herself while married to her husband, 30or when feelings of jealousy come over a man because he suspects his wife. The priest is to have her stand before the LORD and is to apply this entire law to her. 31The husband will be innocent of any wrongdoing, but the woman will bear the consequences of her sin.' " Lev 5:1

The Nazirite

6 The LORD said to Moses, 2"Speak to the Israelites and say to them: 'If a man or woman wants to make a special vow, a vow of separation to the LORD as a Nazirite, 3he must abstain from wine and other fermented drink and must not drink vinegar made from wine or from other fermented drink. He must not drink grape juice or eat grapes or raisins. 4As long as he is a Nazirite, he must not eat anything that comes from the grapevine, not even the seeds or skins. Jdg 13:5

5" 'During the entire period of his vow of separation no razor may be used on his head. He must be holy until the period of his separation to the LORD is over; he must let the hair of his head grow long. 6Throughout the period of his separation to the LORD he must not go near a dead body. 7Even if his own father or mother or brother or sister dies, he must not make himself ceremonially unclean on account of them, because the symbol of his separation to God is on his head. 8Throughout the period of his separation he is consecrated to the LORD. Nu 9:6; 1Sa 1:11

9" 'If someone dies suddenly in his presence, thus defiling the hair he has dedicated, he must shave his head on the day of his cleansing—the seventh day. 10Then on the eighth day he must bring two doves or two young pigeons to the priest at the entrance to the Tent of Meeting. 11The priest is to offer one as a sin offering and the other as a burnt offering to make atonement for him because he sinned by being in the presence of the dead body. That same day he is to consecrate his head. 12He must dedicate himself to the LORD for the period of his separation and must bring a year-old male lamb as a guilt offering. The previous days do not count, because he became defiled during his separation. Lev 5:7; 14:22

13" 'Now this is the law for the Nazirite when the period of his separation is over. He is to be brought to the entrance to the Tent of Meeting. 14There he is to present his offerings to the LORD: a year-old male lamb without defect for a burnt offering, a year-old ewe lamb without defect for a sin offering, a ram without defect for a fellowship

[a] 15 That is, probably about 2 quarts (about 2 liters) [b] 21 Or *causes you to have a miscarrying womb and barrenness* [c] 22 Or *body and cause you to be barren and have a miscarrying womb* [d] 27 Or *suffering; she will have barrenness and a miscarrying womb*

offering,[a] 15together with their grain offerings
and drink offerings, and a basket of bread made
without yeast—cakes made of fine flour mixed
with oil, and wafers spread with oil. Lev 14:10
16" 'The priest is to present them before the
LORD and make the sin offering and the burnt
offering. 17He is to present the basket of unleavened bread and is to sacrifice the ram as a fellowship offering to the LORD, together with its grain
offering and drink offering. Lev 1:3; 23:13
18" 'Then at the entrance to the Tent of Meeting,
the Nazirite must shave off the hair that he dedicated. He is to take the hair and put it in the fire
that is under the sacrifice of the fellowship offering. ver 9; Ac 21:24
19" 'After the Nazirite has shaved off the hair of
his dedication, the priest is to place in his hands a
boiled shoulder of the ram, and a cake and a wafer
from the basket, both made without yeast. 20The
priest shall then wave them before the LORD as a
wave offering; they are holy and belong to the
priest, together with the breast that was waved and
the thigh that was presented. After that, the Nazirite may drink wine. Ecc 9:7
21" 'This is the law of the Nazirite who vows his
offering to the LORD in accordance with his separation, in addition to whatever else he can afford. He
must fulfill the vow he has made, according to the
law of the Nazirite.' " ver 2,13

The Priestly Blessing

22The LORD said to Moses, 23"Tell Aaron and his
sons, 'This is how you are to bless the Israelites.
Say to them: 1Ch 23:13

24" ' "The LORD bless you Dt 28:3-6
and keep you;
25the LORD make his face shine upon you Ps 80:3
and be gracious to you; Ge 43:29; Ps 25:16
26the LORD turn his face toward you Ps 4:6; 44:3
and give you peace." ' Ps 29:11

27"So they will put my name on the Israelites,
and I will bless them." Dt 28:10; 2Ch 7:14

LIVING  **INSIGHT**

God continues to hold out to all His children a peaceful, worry-free lifestyle that we can enter into on a moment-by-moment basis.

(See Numbers 6:24–26.)

Offerings at the Dedication of the Tabernacle

7 When Moses finished setting up the tabernacle, he anointed it and consecrated it and all
its furnishings. He also anointed and consecrated
the altar and all its utensils. 2Then the leaders of
Israel, the heads of families who were the tribal
leaders in charge of those who were counted, made
offerings. 3They brought as their gifts before the
LORD six covered carts and twelve oxen—an ox
from each leader and a cart from every two. These
they presented before the tabernacle. Ex 40:9,17
4The LORD said to Moses, 5"Accept these from
them, that they may be used in the work at the
Tent of Meeting. Give them to the Levites as each
man's work requires."
6So Moses took the carts and oxen and gave
them to the Levites. 7He gave two carts and four
oxen to the Gershonites, as their work required,
8and he gave four carts and eight oxen to the Merarites, as their work required. They were all under
the direction of Ithamar son of Aaron, the priest.
9But Moses did not give any to the Kohathites,
because they were to carry on their shoulders the
holy things, for which they were responsible.
10When the altar was anointed, the leaders
brought their offerings for its dedication and presented them before the altar. 11For the LORD had
said to Moses, "Each day one leader is to bring his
offering for the dedication of the altar." 2Ch 7:9

12The one who brought his offering on the first day
was Nahshon son of Amminadab of the tribe of
Judah.
13His offering was one silver plate weighing a
hundred and thirty shekels,[b] and one silver
sprinkling bowl weighing seventy shekels,[c]
both according to the sanctuary shekel, each
filled with fine flour mixed with oil as a grain
offering; 14one gold dish weighing ten shekels,[d] filled with incense; 15one young bull,
one ram and one male lamb a year old, for a
burnt offering; 16one male goat for a sin offering; 17and two oxen, five rams, five male
goats and five male lambs a year old, to be
sacrificed as a fellowship offering.[e] This was
the offering of Nahshon son of Amminadab.

18On the second day Nethanel son of Zuar, the
leader of Issachar, brought his offering. Nu 1:8
19The offering he brought was one silver
plate weighing a hundred and thirty shekels,
and one silver sprinkling bowl weighing seventy shekels, both according to the sanctuary
shekel, each filled with fine flour mixed with
oil as a grain offering; 20one gold dish weigh-

[a] 14 Traditionally *peace offering*; also in verses 17 and 18
[b] 13 That is, about 3 1/4 pounds (about 1.5 kilograms); also elsewhere in this chapter
[c] 13 That is, about 1 3/4 pounds (about 0.8 kilogram); also elsewhere in this chapter
[d] 14 That is, about 4 ounces (about 110 grams); also elsewhere in this chapter
[e] 17 Traditionally *peace offering*; also elsewhere in this chapter

ing ten shekels, filled with incense; 21one
young bull, one ram and one male lamb a
year old, for a burnt offering; 22one male goat
for a sin offering; 23and two oxen, five rams,
five male goats and five male lambs a year
old, to be sacrificed as a fellowship offering.
This was the offering of Nethanel son of
Zuar.

24On the third day, Eliab son of Helon, the leader
of the people of Zebulun, brought his offering.
25His offering was one silver plate weighing a
hundred and thirty shekels, and one silver
sprinkling bowl weighing seventy shekels,
both according to the sanctuary shekel, each
filled with fine flour mixed with oil as a grain
offering; 26one gold dish weighing ten shekels, filled with incense; 27one young bull, one
ram and one male lamb a year old, for a
burnt offering; 28one male goat for a sin offering; 29and two oxen, five rams, five male
goats and five male lambs a year old, to be
sacrificed as a fellowship offering. This was
the offering of Eliab son of Helon.

30On the fourth day Elizur son of Shedeur, the
leader of the people of Reuben, brought his offering. Nu 1:5
31His offering was one silver plate weighing a
hundred and thirty shekels, and one silver
sprinkling bowl weighing seventy shekels,
both according to the sanctuary shekel, each
filled with fine flour mixed with oil as a grain
offering; 32one gold dish weighing ten shekels, filled with incense; 33one young bull, one
ram and one male lamb a year old, for a
burnt offering; 34one male goat for a sin offering; 35and two oxen, five rams, five male
goats and five male lambs a year old, to be
sacrificed as a fellowship offering. This was
the offering of Elizur son of Shedeur.

36On the fifth day Shelumiel son of Zurishaddai,
the leader of the people of Simeon, brought his
offering. Nu 1:6
37His offering was one silver plate weighing a
hundred and thirty shekels, and one silver
sprinkling bowl weighing seventy shekels,
both according to the sanctuary shekel, each
filled with fine flour mixed with oil as a grain
offering; 38one gold dish weighing ten shekels, filled with incense; 39one young bull, one
ram and one male lamb a year old, for a
burnt offering; 40one male goat for a sin offering; 41and two oxen, five rams, five male
goats and five male lambs a year old, to be
sacrificed as a fellowship offering. This was
the offering of Shelumiel son of Zurishaddai.

42On the sixth day Eliasaph son of Deuel, the leader of the people of Gad, brought his offering.
43His offering was one silver plate weighing a
hundred and thirty shekels, and one silver
sprinkling bowl weighing seventy shekels,
both according to the sanctuary shekel, each
filled with fine flour mixed with oil as a grain
offering; 44one gold dish weighing ten shekels, filled with incense; 45one young bull, one
ram and one male lamb a year old, for a
burnt offering; 46one male goat for a sin offering; 47and two oxen, five rams, five male
goats and five male lambs a year old, to be
sacrificed as a fellowship offering. This was
the offering of Eliasaph son of Deuel.

48On the seventh day Elishama son of Ammihud,
the leader of the people of Ephraim, brought his
offering. Nu 1:10
49His offering was one silver plate weighing a
hundred and thirty shekels, and one silver
sprinkling bowl weighing seventy shekels,
both according to the sanctuary shekel, each
filled with fine flour mixed with oil as a grain
offering; 50one gold dish weighing ten shekels, filled with incense; 51one young bull, one
ram and one male lamb a year old, for a
burnt offering; 52one male goat for a sin offering; 53and two oxen, five rams, five male
goats and five male lambs a year old, to be
sacrificed as a fellowship offering. This was
the offering of Elishama son of Ammihud.

54On the eighth day Gamaliel son of Pedahzur, the
leader of the people of Manasseh, brought his offering. Nu 1:10; 2:20
55His offering was one silver plate weighing a
hundred and thirty shekels, and one silver
sprinkling bowl weighing seventy shekels,
both according to the sanctuary shekel, each
filled with fine flour mixed with oil as a grain
offering; 56one gold dish weighing ten shekels, filled with incense; 57one young bull, one
ram and one male lamb a year old, for a
burnt offering; 58one male goat for a sin offering; 59and two oxen, five rams, five male
goats and five male lambs a year old, to be
sacrificed as a fellowship offering. This was
the offering of Gamaliel son of Pedahzur.

60On the ninth day Abidan son of Gideoni, the
leader of the people of Benjamin, brought his offering. Nu 1:11
61His offering was one silver plate weighing a
hundred and thirty shekels, and one silver
sprinkling bowl weighing seventy shekels,
both according to the sanctuary shekel, each
filled with fine flour mixed with oil as a grain
offering; 62one gold dish weighing ten shekels, filled with incense; 63one young bull, one
ram and one male lamb a year old, for a
burnt offering; 64one male goat for a sin of-

fering; 65and two oxen, five rams, five male
goats and five male lambs a year old, to be
sacrificed as a fellowship offering. This was
the offering of Abidan son of Gideoni.

66On the tenth day Ahiezer son of Ammishaddai,
the leader of the people of Dan, brought his offering. Nu 1:12; 2:25

67His offering was one silver plate weighing a
hundred and thirty shekels, and one silver
sprinkling bowl weighing seventy shekels,
both according to the sanctuary shekel, each
filled with fine flour mixed with oil as a grain
offering; 68one gold dish weighing ten shekels, filled with incense; 69one young bull, one
ram and one male lamb a year old, for a
burnt offering; 70one male goat for a sin offering; 71and two oxen, five rams, five male
goats and five male lambs a year old, to be
sacrificed as a fellowship offering. This was
the offering of Ahiezer son of Ammishaddai.

72On the eleventh day Pagiel son of Ocran, the
leader of the people of Asher, brought his offering.

73His offering was one silver plate weighing a
hundred and thirty shekels, and one silver
sprinkling bowl weighing seventy shekels,
both according to the sanctuary shekel, each
filled with fine flour mixed with oil as a grain
offering; 74one gold dish weighing ten shekels, filled with incense; 75one young bull, one
ram and one male lamb a year old, for a
burnt offering; 76one male goat for a sin offering; 77and two oxen, five rams, five male
goats and five male lambs a year old, to be
sacrificed as a fellowship offering. This was
the offering of Pagiel son of Ocran.

78On the twelfth day Ahira son of Enan, the leader
of the people of Naphtali, brought his offering.

79His offering was one silver plate weighing a
hundred and thirty shekels, and one silver
sprinkling bowl weighing seventy shekels,
both according to the sanctuary shekel, each
filled with fine flour mixed with oil as a grain
offering; 80one gold dish weighing ten shekels, filled with incense; 81one young bull, one
ram and one male lamb a year old, for a
burnt offering; 82one male goat for a sin offering; 83and two oxen, five rams, five male
goats and five male lambs a year old, to be
sacrificed as a fellowship offering. This was
the offering of Ahira son of Enan.

84These were the offerings of the Israelite leaders for the dedication of the altar when it was
anointed: twelve silver plates, twelve silver sprinkling bowls and twelve gold dishes. 85Each silver
plate weighed a hundred and thirty shekels, and
each sprinkling bowl seventy shekels. Altogether,
the silver dishes weighed two thousand four hundred shekels,[a] according to the sanctuary shekel.
86The twelve gold dishes filled with incense
weighed ten shekels each, according to the sanctuary shekel. Altogether, the gold dishes weighed a
hundred and twenty shekels.[b] 87The total number
of animals for the burnt offering came to twelve
young bulls, twelve rams and twelve male lambs a
year old, together with their grain offering. Twelve
male goats were used for the sin offering. 88The
total number of animals for the sacrifice of the
fellowship offering came to twenty-four oxen, sixty rams, sixty male goats and sixty male lambs a
year old. These were the offerings for the dedication of the altar after it was anointed. ver 1,10

89When Moses entered the Tent of Meeting to
speak with the LORD, he heard the voice speaking
to him from between the two cherubim above the
atonement cover on the ark of the Testimony. And
he spoke with him. Ex 25:21-22; Ps 80:1; 99:1

Setting Up the Lamps

8 The LORD said to Moses, 2"Speak to Aaron
and say to him, 'When you set up the seven
lamps, they are to light the area in front of the
lampstand.' "

3Aaron did so; he set up the lamps so that they
faced forward on the lampstand, just as the LORD
commanded Moses. 4This is how the lampstand
was made: It was made of hammered gold—from
its base to its blossoms. The lampstand was made
exactly like the pattern the LORD had shown Moses. Ex 25:36-37

The Setting Apart of the Levites

5The LORD said to Moses: 6"Take the Levites
from among the other Israelites and make them
ceremonially clean. 7To purify them, do this:
Sprinkle the water of cleansing on them; then have
them shave their whole bodies and wash their
clothes, and so purify themselves. 8Have them take
a young bull with its grain offering of fine flour
mixed with oil; then you are to take a second
young bull for a sin offering. 9Bring the Levites to
the front of the Tent of Meeting and assemble the
whole Israelite community. 10You are to bring the
Levites before the LORD, and the Israelites are to
lay their hands on them. 11Aaron is to present the
Levites before the LORD as a wave offering from the
Israelites, so that they may be ready to do the work
of the LORD. Lev 8:3; Isa 52:11; Ac 6:6

12"After the Levites lay their hands on the heads

[a]85 That is, about 60 pounds (about 28 kilograms) [b]86 That is, about 3 pounds (about 1.4 kilograms)

of the bulls, use the one for a sin offering to the LORD and the other for a burnt offering, to make atonement for the Levites. [13]Have the Levites stand in front of Aaron and his sons and then present them as a wave offering to the LORD. [14]In this way you are to set the Levites apart from the other Israelites, and the Levites will be mine. Nu 3:12

[15]"After you have purified the Levites and presented them as a wave offering, they are to come to do their work at the Tent of Meeting. [16]They are the Israelites who are to be given wholly to me. I have taken them as my own in place of the firstborn, the first male offspring from every Israelite woman. [17]Every firstborn male in Israel, whether man or animal, is mine. When I struck down all the firstborn in Egypt, I set them apart for myself. [18]And I have taken the Levites in place of all the firstborn sons in Israel. [19]Of all the Israelites, I have given the Levites as gifts to Aaron and his sons to do the work at the Tent of Meeting on behalf of the Israelites and to make atonement for them so that no plague will strike the Israelites when they go near the sanctuary." Ex 13:2; Nu 3:12

[20]Moses, Aaron and the whole Israelite community did with the Levites just as the LORD commanded Moses. [21]The Levites purified themselves and washed their clothes. Then Aaron presented them as a wave offering before the LORD and made atonement for them to purify them. [22]After that, the Levites came to do their work at the Tent of Meeting under the supervision of Aaron and his sons. They did with the Levites just as the LORD commanded Moses. Ge 35:2; Nu 16:47

[23]The LORD said to Moses, [24]"This applies to the Levites: Men twenty-five years old or more shall come to take part in the work at the Tent of Meeting, [25]but at the age of fifty, they must retire from their regular service and work no longer. [26]They may assist their brothers in performing their duties at the Tent of Meeting, but they themselves must not do the work. This, then, is how you are to assign the responsibilities of the Levites."

The Passover

9 The LORD spoke to Moses in the Desert of Sinai in the first month of the second year after they came out of Egypt. He said, [2]"Have the Israelites celebrate the Passover at the appointed time. [3]Celebrate it at the appointed time, at twilight on the fourteenth day of this month, in accordance with all its rules and regulations."

[4]So Moses told the Israelites to celebrate the Passover, [5]and they did so in the Desert of Sinai at twilight on the fourteenth day of the first month. The Israelites did everything just as the LORD commanded Moses. Ex 12:1-13; Jos 5:10

[6]But some of them could not celebrate the Passover on that day because they were ceremonially unclean on account of a dead body. So they came to Moses and Aaron that same day [7]and said to Moses, "We have become unclean because of a dead body, but why should we be kept from presenting the LORD's offering with the other Israelites at the appointed time?" Ex 18:15; Nu 27:2

[8]Moses answered them, "Wait until I find out what the LORD commands concerning you."

[9]Then the LORD said to Moses, [10]"Tell the Israelites: 'When any of you or your descendants are unclean because of a dead body or are away on a journey, they may still celebrate the LORD's Passover. [11]They are to celebrate it on the fourteenth day of the second month at twilight. They are to eat the lamb, together with unleavened bread and bitter herbs. [12]They must not leave any of it till morning or break any of its bones. When they celebrate the Passover, they must follow all the regulations. [13]But if a man who is ceremonially clean and not on a journey fails to celebrate the Passover, that person must be cut off from his people because he did not present the LORD's offering at the appointed time. That man will bear the consequences of his sin. Ge 17:14; Ex 12:8,15,46

[14]" 'An alien living among you who wants to celebrate the LORD's Passover must do so in accordance with its rules and regulations. You must have the same regulations for the alien and the native-born.' " Ex 12:48-49

The Cloud Above the Tabernacle

[15]On the day the tabernacle, the Tent of the Testimony, was set up, the cloud covered it. From evening till morning the cloud above the tabernacle looked like fire. [16]That is how it continued to be; the cloud covered it, and at night it looked like fire. [17]Whenever the cloud lifted from above the Tent, the Israelites set out; wherever the cloud settled, the Israelites encamped. [18]At the LORD's command the Israelites set out, and at his command they encamped. As long as the cloud stayed over the tabernacle, they remained in camp. [19]When the cloud remained over the tabernacle a long time, the Israelites obeyed the LORD's order and did not set out. [20]Sometimes the cloud was over the tabernacle only a few days; at the LORD's command they would encamp, and then at his command they would set out. [21]Sometimes the cloud stayed only from evening till morning, and when it lifted in the morning, they set out. Whether by day or by night, whenever the cloud lifted, they set out. [22]Whether the cloud stayed over the tabernacle for two days or a month or a year, the Israelites would remain in camp and not set out; but when it lifted, they would set out. [23]At the LORD's command they encamped, and at the LORD's command they set out. They obeyed the LORD's order, in accordance with his command through Moses.

The Chorus of Grumbling **Chapters 10–12**

The Israelites were living with a constant visual reminder of the Lord's presence. At any time during the night they could simply look toward the center of the camp and see this awesome pillar of fire rising up into the sky from the tabernacle. All day, every day, a clearly visible cloud was there to guide them on. Talk about a confidence builder! We might think these powerful reminders of the Lord's presence would guarantee absolute faithfulness and confidence to move forward and follow God's leading. Not so! As a matter of fact, this central section of Numbers is filled with accounts of rebellion and resistance. The people complained about the manna the Lord had provided . . . now they wanted meat along with the manna! Well, God gave them quail to eat, and I mean a lot of quail! They were up to their waists in quail. They got what they asked for, but it did not satisfy. Next, Miriam and Aaron rose up and opposed Moses. Even his adult siblings joined in the community chorus of grumbling.

The Silver Trumpets

10 The LORD said to Moses: 2"Make two trumpets of hammered silver, and use them for calling the community together and for having the camps set out. 3When both are sounded, the whole community is to assemble before you at the entrance to the Tent of Meeting. 4If only one is sounded, the leaders—the heads of the clans of Israel—are to assemble before you. 5When a trumpet blast is sounded, the tribes camping on the east are to set out. 6At the sounding of a second blast, the camps on the south are to set out. The blast will be the signal for setting out. 7To gather the assembly, blow the trumpets, but not with the same signal. Ps 47:5; Jer 4:5,19

8"The sons of Aaron, the priests, are to blow the trumpets. This is to be a lasting ordinance for you and the generations to come. 9When you go into battle in your own land against an enemy who is oppressing you, sound a blast on the trumpets. Then you will be remembered by the LORD your God and rescued from your enemies. 10Also at your times of rejoicing—your appointed feasts and New Moon festivals—you are to sound the trumpets over your burnt offerings and fellowship offerings,[a] and they will be a memorial for you before your God. I am the LORD your God."

The Israelites Leave Sinai

11On the twentieth day of the second month of the second year, the cloud lifted from above the tabernacle of the Testimony. 12Then the Israelites set out from the Desert of Sinai and traveled from place to place until the cloud came to rest in the Desert of Paran. 13They set out, this first time, at the LORD's command through Moses. Nu 9:17; Dt 1:6

14The divisions of the camp of Judah went first, under their standard. Nahshon son of Amminadab was in command. 15Nethanel son of Zuar was over the division of the tribe of Issachar, 16and Eliab son of Helon was over the division of the tribe of Zebulun. 17Then the tabernacle was taken down, and the Gershonites and Merarites, who carried it, set out. Nu 2:3-9; 4:21-32

18The divisions of the camp of Reuben went next, under their standard. Elizur son of Shedeur was in command. 19Shelumiel son of Zurishaddai was over the division of the tribe of Simeon, 20and Eliasaph son of Deuel was over the division of the tribe of Gad. 21Then the Kohathites set out, carrying the holy things. The tabernacle was to be set up before they arrived. Nu 2:10-16; 4:20

22The divisions of the camp of Ephraim went next, under their standard. Elishama son of Ammihud was in command. 23Gamaliel son of Pedahzur was over the division of the tribe of Manasseh, 24and Abidan son of Gideoni was over the division of the tribe of Benjamin. Nu 1:10-11; 2:24

25Finally, as the rear guard for all the units, the divisions of the camp of Dan set out, under their standard. Ahiezer son of Ammishaddai was in command. 26Pagiel son of Ocran was over the division of the tribe of Asher, 27and Ahira son of Enan was over the division of the tribe of Naphtali. 28This was the order of march for the Israelite divisions as they set out. Nu 2:31; Jos 6:9

29Now Moses said to Hobab son of Reuel the Midianite, Moses' father-in-law, "We are setting out for the place about which the LORD said, 'I will give it to you.' Come with us and we will treat you well, for the LORD has promised good things to Israel." Ge 12:7; Ex 2:18

30He answered, "No, I will not go; I am going back to my own land and my own people."

31But Moses said, "Please do not leave us. You know where we should camp in the desert, and you can be our eyes. 32If you come with us, we will share with you whatever good things the LORD gives us." Dt 10:18; Ps 22:27-31

33So they set out from the mountain of the LORD and traveled for three days. The ark of the covenant of the LORD went before them during those three days to find them a place to rest. 34The cloud of the LORD was over them by day when they set out from the camp. Nu 9:15-23; Jos 3:3

35Whenever the ark set out, Moses said,

"Rise up, O LORD!
May your enemies be scattered; Ps 68:1
may your foes flee before you." Dt 7:10; 32:41

36Whenever it came to rest, he said,

"Return, O LORD,
to the countless thousands of Israel." Dt 1:10

[a]10 Traditionally *peace offerings*

Fire From the LORD

11 Now the people complained about their hardships in the hearing of the LORD, and when he heard them his anger was aroused. Then fire from the LORD burned among them and consumed some of the outskirts of the camp. 2When the people cried out to Moses, he prayed to the LORD and the fire died down. 3So that place was called Taberah,[a] because fire from the LORD had burned among them. Lev 10:2; Nu 21:7

Quail From the LORD

4The rabble with them began to crave other food, and again the Israelites started wailing and said, "If only we had meat to eat! 5We remember the fish we ate in Egypt at no cost—also the cucumbers, melons, leeks, onions and garlic. 6But now we have lost our appetite; we never see anything but this manna!" Ex 16:3; Ps 78:18

7The manna was like coriander seed and looked like resin. 8The people went around gathering it, and then ground it in a handmill or crushed it in a mortar. They cooked it in a pot or made it into cakes. And it tasted like something made with olive oil. 9When the dew settled on the camp at night, the manna also came down. Ex 16:13,31

10Moses heard the people of every family wailing, each at the entrance to his tent. The LORD became exceedingly angry, and Moses was troubled. 11He asked the LORD, "Why have you brought this trouble on your servant? What have I done to displease you that you put the burden of all these people on me? 12Did I conceive all these people? Did I give them birth? Why do you tell me to carry them in my arms, as a nurse carries an infant, to the land you promised on oath to their forefathers? 13Where can I get meat for all these people? They keep wailing to me, 'Give us meat to eat!' 14I cannot carry all these people by myself; the burden is too heavy for me. 15If this is how you are going to treat me, put me to death right now—if I have found favor in your eyes—and do not let me face my own ruin." Ex 5:22; 18:18; 1Ki 19:4

16The LORD said to Moses: "Bring me seventy of Israel's elders who are known to you as leaders and officials among the people. Have them come to the Tent of Meeting, that they may stand there with you. 17I will come down and speak with you there, and I will take of the Spirit that is on you and put the Spirit on them. They will help you carry the burden of the people so that you will not have to carry it alone. Ex 18:18; 1Sa 10:6

18"Tell the people: 'Consecrate yourselves in preparation for tomorrow, when you will eat meat. The LORD heard you when you wailed, "If only we had meat to eat! We were better off in Egypt!" Now the LORD will give you meat, and you will eat it. 19You will not eat it for just one day, or two days, or five, ten or twenty days, 20but for a whole month—until it comes out of your nostrils and you loathe it—because you have rejected the LORD, who is among you, and have wailed before him, saying, "Why did we ever leave Egypt?" ' "

21But Moses said, "Here I am among six hundred thousand men on foot, and you say, 'I will give them meat to eat for a whole month!' 22Would they have enough if flocks and herds were slaughtered for them? Would they have enough if all the fish in the sea were caught for them?" Mt 15:33

23The LORD answered Moses, "Is the LORD's arm too short? You will now see whether or not what I say will come true for you." Isa 50:2; 59:1

24So Moses went out and told the people what the LORD had said. He brought together seventy of their elders and had them stand around the Tent. 25Then the LORD came down in the cloud and spoke with him, and he took of the Spirit that was on him and put the Spirit on the seventy elders. When the Spirit rested on them, they prophesied, but they did not do so again.[b] Nu 12:5; 1Sa 10:10

26However, two men, whose names were Eldad and Medad, had remained in the camp. They were listed among the elders, but did not go out to the Tent. Yet the Spirit also rested on them, and they prophesied in the camp. 27A young man ran and told Moses, "Eldad and Medad are prophesying in the camp."

28Joshua son of Nun, who had been Moses' aide since youth, spoke up and said, "Moses, my lord, stop them!" Mk 9:38-40

29But Moses replied, "Are you jealous for my sake? I wish that all the LORD's people were prophets and that the LORD would put his Spirit on them!" 30Then Moses and the elders of Israel returned to the camp. 1Co 14:5

31Now a wind went out from the LORD and drove quail in from the sea. It brought them[c] down all around the camp to about three feet[d] above the ground, as far as a day's walk in any direction. 32All that day and night and all the next day the people went out and gathered quail. No one gathered less than ten homers.[e] Then they spread them out all around the camp. 33But while the meat was still between their teeth and before it could be consumed, the anger of the LORD burned against the people, and he struck them with a severe plague. 34Therefore the place was named Kibroth Hattaavah,[f] because there they buried the people who had craved other food. Ex 16:13; Ps 78:30

35From Kibroth Hattaavah the people traveled to Hazeroth and stayed there. Nu 33:17

[a]3 *Taberah* means *burning*. [b]25 Or *prophesied and continued to do so* [c]31 Or *They flew* [d]31 Hebrew *two cubits* (about 1 meter) [e]32 That is, probably about 60 bushels (about 2.2 kiloliters) [f]34 *Kibroth Hattaavah* means *graves of craving*.

Miriam and Aaron Oppose Moses

12 Miriam and Aaron began to talk against Moses because of his Cushite wife, for he had married a Cushite. 2"Has the LORD spoken only through Moses?" they asked. "Hasn't he also spoken through us?" And the LORD heard this.

3(Now Moses was a very humble man, more humble than anyone else on the face of the earth.)

4At once the LORD said to Moses, Aaron and Miriam, "Come out to the Tent of Meeting, all three of you." So the three of them came out. 5Then the LORD came down in a pillar of cloud; he stood at the entrance to the Tent and summoned Aaron and Miriam. When both of them stepped forward, 6he said, "Listen to my words: Nu 11:25

"When a prophet of the LORD is among you,
 I reveal myself to him in visions, Ge 15:1; 46:2
 I speak to him in dreams. Ge 31:10; Heb 1:1
7But this is not true of my servant Moses;
 he is faithful in all my house. Heb 3:2,5
8With him I speak face to face,
 clearly and not in riddles; Dt 34:10
 he sees the form of the LORD. Ps 17:15
Why then were you not afraid
 to speak against my servant Moses?"

9The anger of the LORD burned against them, and he left them. Ge 17:22

10When the cloud lifted from above the Tent, there stood Miriam—leprous,[a] like snow. Aaron turned toward her and saw that she had leprosy; 11and he said to Moses, "Please, my lord, do not hold against us the sin we have so foolishly committed. 12Do not let her be like a stillborn infant coming from its mother's womb with its flesh half eaten away." Dt 24:9; 2Sa 19:19; 2Ki 5:1,27

13So Moses cried out to the LORD, "O God, please heal her!" Isa 30:26; Jer 17:14

14The LORD replied to Moses, "If her father had spit in her face, would she not have been in disgrace for seven days? Confine her outside the camp for seven days; after that she can be brought back." 15So Miriam was confined outside the camp for seven days, and the people did not move on till she was brought back. Lev 13:46; Nu 5:2-3

16After that, the people left Hazeroth and encamped in the Desert of Paran. Nu 11:35

The High Cost of Rebellion **Chapters 13–14**

After investigating the land of Canaan, twelve Hebrew spies came back with their report. The land was perfect and plentiful, with fruit trees, fertile fields and everything the people could dream of. Everything looked great—except for one little detail. There were these people called "the Nephilim." These guys looked like defensive linemen on a professional football team—except they were larger and more intimidating! Most of the spies said that the Israelites were like tiny grasshoppers compared to the giants in the land. They cast a vote, and the spies were split, ten against entering the land and only two in favor of following God's direction. While the people should have been looking at the greatness of their God, they were focusing on the size of their enemy. The rest of the story is a tragedy in the history of God's people. The people were sentenced to wander in the desert for almost four decades. Only Joshua and Caleb, the two spies with the favorable report and positive vote, would ever see the promised land; the rest would die in the desert. In this section we see the people's unbelieving hearts, complaining spirits, grumbling mouths and rebellious attitudes. Numbers reminds us of the painfully high cost of rebellion.

Exploring Canaan

13 The LORD said to Moses, 2"Send some men to explore the land of Canaan, which I am giving to the Israelites. From each ancestral tribe send one of its leaders." Dt 1:22

3So at the LORD's command Moses sent them out from the Desert of Paran. All of them were leaders of the Israelites. 4These are their names:

from the tribe of Reuben, Shammua son of Zaccur;
5from the tribe of Simeon, Shaphat son of Hori;
6from the tribe of Judah, Caleb son of Jephunneh; Nu 14:6,24; Jdg 1:12-15
7from the tribe of Issachar, Igal son of Joseph;
8from the tribe of Ephraim, Hoshea son of Nun; Nu 11:28
9from the tribe of Benjamin, Palti son of Raphu;
10from the tribe of Zebulun, Gaddiel son of Sodi;
11from the tribe of Manasseh (a tribe of Joseph), Gaddi son of Susi;
12from the tribe of Dan, Ammiel son of Gemalli;
13from the tribe of Asher, Sethur son of Michael;
14from the tribe of Naphtali, Nahbi son of Vophsi;
15from the tribe of Gad, Geuel son of Maki.

16These are the names of the men Moses sent to explore the land. (Moses gave Hoshea son of Nun the name Joshua.) Dt 32:44

17When Moses sent them to explore Canaan, he said, "Go up through the Negev and on into the hill country. 18See what the land is like and whether the people who live there are strong or weak, few or many. 19What kind of land do they live in? Is it good or bad? What kind of towns do they live

[a] 10 The Hebrew word was used for various diseases affecting the skin—not necessarily leprosy.

in? Are they unwalled or fortified? [20]How is the soil? Is it fertile or poor? Are there trees on it or not? Do your best to bring back some of the fruit of the land." (It was the season for the first ripe grapes.) Ge 12:9; Dt 1:25

[21]So they went up and explored the land from the Desert of Zin as far as Rehob, toward Lebo[a] Hamath. [22]They went up through the Negev and came to Hebron, where Ahiman, Sheshai and Talmai, the descendants of Anak, lived. (Hebron had been built seven years before Zoan in Egypt.) [23]When they reached the Valley of Eshcol,[b] they cut off a branch bearing a single cluster of grapes. Two of them carried it on a pole between them, along with some pomegranates and figs. [24]That place was called the Valley of Eshcol because of the cluster of grapes the Israelites cut off there. [25]At the end of forty days they returned from exploring the land. Jos 15:13-14; Ps 78:12,43

Report on the Exploration

[26]They came back to Moses and Aaron and the whole Israelite community at Kadesh in the Desert of Paran. There they reported to them and to the whole assembly and showed them the fruit of the land. [27]They gave Moses this account: "We went into the land to which you sent us, and it does flow with milk and honey! Here is its fruit. [28]But the people who live there are powerful, and the cities are fortified and very large. We even saw descendants of Anak there. [29]The Amalekites live in the Negev; the Hittites, Jebusites and Amorites live in the hill country; and the Canaanites live near the sea and along the Jordan." Ex 3:8; Dt 1:25,28

[30]Then Caleb silenced the people before Moses and said, "We should go up and take possession of the land, for we can certainly do it."

[31]But the men who had gone up with him said, "We can't attack those people; they are stronger than we are." [32]And they spread among the Israelites a bad report about the land they had explored. They said, "The land we explored devours those living in it. All the people we saw there are of great size. [33]We saw the Nephilim there (the descendants of Anak come from the Nephilim). We seemed like grasshoppers in our own eyes, and we looked the same to them." Dt 1:28; 9:1; Jos 14:8

The People Rebel

14 That night all the people of the community raised their voices and wept aloud. [2]All the Israelites grumbled against Moses and Aaron, and the whole assembly said to them, "If only we had died in Egypt! Or in this desert! [3]Why is the LORD bringing us to this land only to let us fall by the sword? Our wives and children will be taken as plunder. Wouldn't it be better for us to go back to Egypt?" [4]And they said to each other, "We should choose a leader and go back to Egypt." Nu 11:1

[5]Then Moses and Aaron fell facedown in front of the whole Israelite assembly gathered there. [6]Joshua son of Nun and Caleb son of Jephunneh, who were among those who had explored the land, tore their clothes [7]and said to the entire Israelite assembly, "The land we passed through and explored is exceedingly good. [8]If the LORD is pleased with us, he will lead us into that land, a land flowing with milk and honey, and will give it to us. [9]Only do not rebel against the LORD. And do not be afraid of the people of the land, because we will swallow them up. Their protection is gone, but the LORD is with us. Do not be afraid of them."

[10]But the whole assembly talked about stoning them. Then the glory of the LORD appeared at the Tent of Meeting to all the Israelites. [11]The LORD said to Moses, "How long will these people treat me with contempt? How long will they refuse to believe in me, in spite of all the miraculous signs I have performed among them? [12]I will strike them down with a plague and destroy them, but I will make you into a nation greater and stronger than they." Ex 32:10; Lev 9:23

[13]Moses said to the LORD, "Then the Egyptians will hear about it! By your power you brought these people up from among them. [14]And they will tell the inhabitants of this land about it. They have already heard that you, O LORD, are with these people and that you, O LORD, have been seen face to face, that your cloud stays over them, and that you go before them in a pillar of cloud by day and a pillar of fire by night. [15]If you put these people to death all at one time, the nations who have heard this report about you will say, [16]'The LORD was not able to bring these people into the land he promised them on oath; so he slaughtered them in the desert.' Ex 13:21; 15:14; 32:11-14

[17]"Now may the Lord's strength be displayed, just as you have declared: [18]'The LORD is slow to anger, abounding in love and forgiving sin and rebellion. Yet he does not leave the guilty unpunished; he punishes the children for the sin of the fathers to the third and fourth generation.' [19]In accordance with your great love, forgive the sin of these people, just as you have pardoned them from the time they left Egypt until now." Ex 20:5; 34:6,9

[20]The LORD replied, "I have forgiven them, as you asked. [21]Nevertheless, as surely as I live and as surely as the glory of the LORD fills the whole earth, [22]not one of the men who saw my glory and the miraculous signs I performed in Egypt and in the desert but who disobeyed me and tested me ten times— [23]not one of them will ever see the land I promised on oath to their forefathers. No one who has treated me with contempt will ever see it. [24]But

[a]21 Or *toward the entrance to* [b]23 *Eshcol* means *cluster*; also in verse 24.

CALEB

Determined to Hang Tough

"But because my servant Caleb has a different spirit and follows me wholeheartedly, I will bring him into the land he went to, and his descendants will inherit it."
–NUMBERS 14:24

One thing that makes for greatness is determination, a willingness to persist in the same direction over the long haul, to stay at the task, whatever the cost. Former United States president Calvin Coolidge once said, "Nothing in the world can take the place of persistence. Talent will not—nothing is more common than unsuccessful men with talent. Genius will not—unrewarded genius is almost a proverb. Education will not—the world is full of educated derelicts. Persistence and determination alone are important." The first important trait that characterized Caleb was this: *He was a man who possessed this dogged determination, this consistent obedience to God over the years.*

Second, *Caleb was a man who was gifted with vision.* He had the ability to see above and beyond the majority. He looked at life through a different lens and read the scene that stretched out in front of him—with God in sharp focus. He was committed to living his life from a God-centered, eternal perspective, which is something that doesn't come naturally. It takes hard work. It takes commitment. It takes courage. It takes a death of sorts—a death to self and an awakening to a life that puts God in first place.

Finally, *Caleb was a man who had a dream.* He had a God-given agenda that led to God-honoring results. The individual who cultivates God's lordship in his or her life has these dreams. Not the kind of dreams that come to a person at night. These dreams are specific and personal. They're often accompanied by a strong desire to fulfill them. To the public, these dreams may seem extreme or even illogical; they are always outside the realm of the expected. Caleb's dreams allowed him to lead. They gave direction to his determination to serve God and his vision for God's direction in the life of Israel and in his own life.

After their forty-day reconnaissance mission (see Numbers 13:25–31), Caleb and Joshua came back full of confidence. "No doubt about it, we should go up and possess the land," was the essence of Caleb's message. But these two men were surrounded by ten others who said, "No, we can't do it." They were surrounded by a congregation who said, in effect, "Thumbs down. It's impossible. Let's go back to Egypt."

How can people look at a situation so differently? One group has determination, vision, dreams; the other does not. It's that simple. The problem is that the latter group always seems to be in the majority. They'll always carry the vote. They live by sight, not by faith. In this story, ten men saw the obstacles; two saw the answers. Ten men focused on what could not be accomplished; two focused on what could easily be accomplished by God's power. Ten were impressed with the size of their enemies; two were impressed with the size of their God. And for the unbelief of the majority, the Lord exacted His punishment: "In this desert your bodies will fall—every one of you twenty years old or more who was counted in the census and who has grumbled against me" (Numbers 14:29).

Caleb certainly began well. The work he carried out for God began with courage and commitment. But did he end well? The answer can be found in Joshua 14. Caleb was forty years old when he was sent to spy out the land of Canaan (see Joshua 14:7). Now, at age 85, Joshua records Caleb's request to be sent back into battle, to lay claim to another section of the land. What a man! Did you catch the special quality of his stalwart spirit, as he said, in effect, "Whatever life throws at me, I'm ready. I'm still as strong now as I was 45 years ago. Let me at 'em"? That's one of the last scenes we have of Caleb. He is trudging up the mountain, rolling up his sleeves, ready to take on those giants.

Caleb had determination. He had vision. He had a dream. Joshua tells us that Caleb took that land as his inheritance "because he followed the LORD, the God of Israel, wholeheartedly" (14:14). In other words, Caleb was marked by his determination to hang tough with his God his whole life long. Are you?

because my servant Caleb has a different spirit and follows me wholeheartedly, I will bring him into the land he went to, and his descendants will inherit it. 25Since the Amalekites and Canaanites are living in the valleys, turn back tomorrow and set out toward the desert along the route to the Red Sea.[a]"
Nu 32:12; Jos 14:8,14; Heb 3:18

LIVING  **INSIGHT**

Every one of us was poured into a mold . . . but some are "moldier" than others. If you are determined and work quickly, you can keep the concrete of predictability from setting rock-hard up to your ears. Why not broaden yourself in some new way to the greater glory of God?

(See Numbers 14:24.)

26The LORD said to Moses and Aaron: 27"How long will this wicked community grumble against me? I have heard the complaints of these grumbling Israelites. 28So tell them, 'As surely as I live, declares the LORD, I will do to you the very things I heard you say: 29In this desert your bodies will fall—every one of you twenty years old or more who was counted in the census and who has grumbled against me. 30Not one of you will enter the land I swore with uplifted hand to make your home, except Caleb son of Jephunnch and Joshua son of Nun. 31As for your children that you said would be taken as plunder, I will bring them in to enjoy the land you have rejected. 32But you—your bodies will fall in this desert. 33Your children will be shepherds here for forty years, suffering for your unfaithfulness, until the last of your bodies lies in the desert. 34For forty years—one year for each of the forty days you explored the land—you will suffer for your sins and know what it is like to have me against you.' 35I, the LORD, have spoken, and I will surely do these things to this whole wicked community, which has banded together against me. They will meet their end in this desert; here they will die."
Nu 13:25; 23:19; 1Co 10:5

36So the men Moses had sent to explore the land, who returned and made the whole community grumble against him by spreading a bad report about it— 37these men responsible for spreading the bad report about the land were struck down and died of a plague before the LORD. 38Of the men who went to explore the land, only Joshua son of Nun and Caleb son of Jephunneh survived.
Nu 13:32; 1Co 10:10

39When Moses reported this to all the Israelites, they mourned bitterly. 40Early the next morning they went up toward the high hill country. "We have sinned," they said. "We will go up to the place the LORD promised."
Dt 1:41

41But Moses said, "Why are you disobeying the LORD's command? This will not succeed! 42Do not go up, because the LORD is not with you. You will be defeated by your enemies, 43for the Amalekites and Canaanites will face you there. Because you have turned away from the LORD, he will not be with you and you will fall by the sword."
Dt 1:42

44Nevertheless, in their presumption they went up toward the high hill country, though neither Moses nor the ark of the LORD's covenant moved from the camp. 45Then the Amalekites and Canaanites who lived in that hill country came down and attacked them and beat them down all the way to Hormah.
Nu 21:3; Dt 1:43-44

Desert Wandering **Chapters 15–36**

As we come to the last chapters, a significant period of time has passed. By the time we get to chapter 26, over 38 years have transpired. It is important to know that the trip from Sinai to the promised land should have taken only 11 days by foot. The wandering of the Israelites had caused them to take almost forty years for an 11-day trip. We all know what it is like to get lost and arrive at our destination late, but 38 years late seems rather outrageous! As is always true, sin slows us down and delays us from reaching the destination the Lord has put before us.

Note also that not a single person over 57 years old (except Joshua and Caleb) would enter the promised land. As a matter of fact, *not even Moses* would enter the land. The record of his exclusion from the land of Canaan is found in chapter 20. Moses decided to do things his way instead of God's way . . . always a mistake. God told Moses to speak gently to the rock (the people's source of water), but Moses struck the rock in anger. Because Moses was the model, and he had disobeyed God's plan, God told him he would never set foot in the holy land. Through all of their grumbling and complaining, the people were finally starting to learn their lesson; at last they appeared ready to follow the Lord into the land He had promised them. They were learning that they would walk by faith—or they would not walk at all.

Supplementary Offerings

15 The LORD said to Moses, 2"Speak to the Israelites and say to them: 'After you enter the land I am giving you as a home 3and you present to the LORD offerings made by fire, from the herd or the flock, as an aroma pleasing to the LORD—whether burnt offerings or sacrifices, for special vows or freewill offerings or festival offerings— 4then the one who brings his offering shall present to the LORD a grain offering of a tenth of an ephah[b] of fine flour mixed with a quarter of a

[a]25 Hebrew *Yam Suph*; that is, Sea of Reeds [b]4 That is, probably about 2 quarts (about 2 liters)

hin[a] of oil. 5With each lamb for the burnt offering or the sacrifice, prepare a quarter of a hin of wine as a drink offering. Lev 1:2; 6:14; 23:1-44

6" 'With a ram prepare a grain offering of two-tenths of an ephah[b] of fine flour mixed with a third of a hin[c] of oil, 7and a third of a hin of wine as a drink offering. Offer it as an aroma pleasing to the LORD. Nu 28:12

8" 'When you prepare a young bull as a burnt offering or sacrifice, for a special vow or a fellowship offering[d] to the LORD, 9bring with the bull a grain offering of three-tenths of an ephah[e] of fine flour mixed with half a hin[f] of oil. 10Also bring half a hin of wine as a drink offering. It will be an offering made by fire, an aroma pleasing to the LORD. 11Each bull or ram, each lamb or young goat, is to be prepared in this manner. 12Do this for each one, for as many as you prepare. Lev 1:3

13" 'Everyone who is native-born must do these things in this way when he brings an offering made by fire as an aroma pleasing to the LORD. 14For the generations to come, whenever an alien or anyone else living among you presents an offering made by fire as an aroma pleasing to the LORD, he must do exactly as you do. 15The community is to have the same rules for you and for the alien living among you; this is a lasting ordinance for the generations to come. You and the alien shall be the same before the LORD: 16The same laws and regulations will apply both to you and to the alien living among you.' " ver 29; Nu 9:14

17The LORD said to Moses, 18"Speak to the Israelites and say to them: 'When you enter the land to which I am taking you 19and you eat the food of the land, present a portion as an offering to the LORD. 20Present a cake from the first of your ground meal and present it as an offering from the threshing floor. 21Throughout the generations to come you are to give this offering to the LORD from the first of your ground meal. Jos 5:11-12; Ro 11:16

Offerings for Unintentional Sins

22" 'Now if you unintentionally fail to keep any of these commands the LORD gave Moses— 23any of the LORD's commands to you through him, from the day the LORD gave them and continuing through the generations to come— 24and if this is done unintentionally without the community being aware of it, then the whole community is to offer a young bull for a burnt offering as an aroma pleasing to the LORD, along with its prescribed grain offering and drink offering, and a male goat for a sin offering. 25The priest is to make atonement for the whole Israelite community, and they will be forgiven, for it was not intentional and they have brought to the LORD for their wrong an offering made by fire and a sin offering. 26The whole Israelite community and the aliens living among them will be forgiven, because all the people were involved in the unintentional wrong. Lev 4:2,14,20

27" 'But if just one person sins unintentionally, he must bring a year-old female goat for a sin offering. 28The priest is to make atonement before the LORD for the one who erred by sinning unintentionally, and when atonement has been made for him, he will be forgiven. 29One and the same law applies to everyone who sins unintentionally, whether he is a native-born Israelite or an alien.

30" 'But anyone who sins defiantly, whether native-born or alien, blasphemes the LORD, and that person must be cut off from his people. 31Because he has despised the LORD's word and broken his commands, that person must surely be cut off; his guilt remains on him.' " Lev 5:1; Dt 17:13; 2Sa 12:9

The Sabbath-Breaker Put to Death

32While the Israelites were in the desert, a man was found gathering wood on the Sabbath day. 33Those who found him gathering wood brought him to Moses and Aaron and the whole assembly, 34and they kept him in custody, because it was not clear what should be done to him. 35Then the LORD said to Moses, "The man must die. The whole assembly must stone him outside the camp." 36So the assembly took him outside the camp and stoned him to death, as the LORD commanded Moses. Ex 31:14-15; Lev 24:14

Tassels on Garments

37The LORD said to Moses, 38"Speak to the Israelites and say to them: 'Throughout the generations to come you are to make tassels on the corners of your garments, with a blue cord on each tassel. 39You will have these tassels to look at and so you will remember all the commands of the LORD, that you may obey them and not prostitute yourselves by going after the lusts of your own hearts and eyes. 40Then you will remember to obey all my commands and will be consecrated to your God. 41I am the LORD your God, who brought you out of Egypt to be your God. I am the LORD your God.' " Lev 11:44; Ro 12:1; Col 1:22

Korah, Dathan and Abiram

16 Korah son of Izhar, the son of Kohath, the son of Levi, and certain Reubenites—Dathan and Abiram, sons of Eliab, and On son of Peleth—became insolent[g] 2and rose up against Moses. With them were 250 Israelite men, well-known community leaders who had been appoint-

[a] 4 That is, probably about 1 quart (about 1 liter); also in verse 5 [b] 6 That is, probably about 4 quarts (about 4.5 liters) [c] 6 That is, probably about 1 1/4 quarts (about 1.2 liters); also in verse 7 [d] 8 Traditionally *peace offering* [e] 9 That is, probably about 6 quarts (about 6.5 liters) [f] 9 That is, probably about 2 quarts (about 2 liters); also in verse 10 [g] 1 Or *Peleth—took* ⌞*men*⌟

ed members of the council. [3]They came as a group to oppose Moses and Aaron and said to them, "You have gone too far! The whole community is holy, every one of them, and the LORD is with them. Why then do you set yourselves above the LORD's assembly?" Ex 19:6; Ps 106:16

[4]When Moses heard this, he fell facedown. [5]Then he said to Korah and all his followers: "In the morning the LORD will show who belongs to him and who is holy, and he will have that person come near him. The man he chooses he will cause to come near him. [6]You, Korah, and all your followers are to do this: Take censers [7]and tomorrow put fire and incense in them before the LORD. The man the LORD chooses will be the one who is holy. You Levites have gone too far!" Nu 14:5; 17:5

[8]Moses also said to Korah, "Now listen, you Levites! [9]Isn't it enough for you that the God of Israel has separated you from the rest of the Israelite community and brought you near himself to do the work at the LORD's tabernacle and to stand before the community and minister to them? [10]He has brought you and all your fellow Levites near himself, but now you are trying to get the priesthood too. [11]It is against the LORD that you and all your followers have banded together. Who is Aaron that you should grumble against him?" Dt 10:8

[12]Then Moses summoned Dathan and Abiram, the sons of Eliab. But they said, "We will not come! [13]Isn't it enough that you have brought us up out of a land flowing with milk and honey to kill us in the desert? And now you also want to lord it over us? [14]Moreover, you haven't brought us into a land flowing with milk and honey or given us an inheritance of fields and vineyards. Will you gouge out the eyes of[a] these men? No, we will not come!" Lev 20:24; Ac 7:27,35

[15]Then Moses became very angry and said to the LORD, "Do not accept their offering. I have not taken so much as a donkey from them, nor have I wronged any of them." 1Sa 12:3

[16]Moses said to Korah, "You and all your followers are to appear before the LORD tomorrow—you and they and Aaron. [17]Each man is to take his censer and put incense in it—250 censers in all—and present it before the LORD. You and Aaron are to present your censers also." [18]So each man took his censer, put fire and incense in it, and stood with Moses and Aaron at the entrance to the Tent of Meeting. [19]When Korah had gathered all his followers in opposition to them at the entrance to the Tent of Meeting, the glory of the LORD appeared to the entire assembly. [20]The LORD said to Moses and Aaron, [21]"Separate yourselves from this assembly so I can put an end to them at once."

[22]But Moses and Aaron fell facedown and cried out, "O God, God of the spirits of all mankind, will you be angry with the entire assembly when only one man sins?" Ge 18:23; Job 21:20

[23]Then the LORD said to Moses, [24]"Say to the assembly, 'Move away from the tents of Korah, Dathan and Abiram.'"

[25]Moses got up and went to Dathan and Abiram, and the elders of Israel followed him. [26]He warned the assembly, "Move back from the tents of these wicked men! Do not touch anything belonging to them, or you will be swept away because of all their sins." [27]So they moved away from the tents of Korah, Dathan and Abiram. Dathan and Abiram had come out and were standing with their wives, children and little ones at the entrances to their tents. Ge 19:15; Isa 52:11

[28]Then Moses said, "This is how you will know that the LORD has sent me to do all these things and that it was not my idea: [29]If these men die a natural death and experience only what usually happens to men, then the LORD has not sent me. [30]But if the LORD brings about something totally new, and the earth opens its mouth and swallows them, with everything that belongs to them, and they go down alive into the grave,[b] then you will know that these men have treated the LORD with contempt." Ex 3:12; Jn 5:36; 6:38

[31]As soon as he finished saying all this, the ground under them split apart [32]and the earth opened its mouth and swallowed them, with their households and all Korah's men and all their possessions. [33]They went down alive into the grave, with everything they owned; the earth closed over them, and they perished and were gone from the community. [34]At their cries, all the Israelites around them fled, shouting, "The earth is going to swallow us too!" Nu 26:11; Mic 1:3-4

[35]And fire came out from the LORD and consumed the 250 men who were offering the incense.

[36]The LORD said to Moses, [37]"Tell Eleazar son of Aaron, the priest, to take the censers out of the smoldering remains and scatter the coals some distance away, for the censers are holy— [38]the censers of the men who sinned at the cost of their lives. Hammer the censers into sheets to overlay the altar, for they were presented before the LORD and have become holy. Let them be a sign to the Israelites." Nu 26:10; Pr 20:2; Eze 14:8

[39]So Eleazar the priest collected the bronze censers brought by those who had been burned up, and he had them hammered out to overlay the altar, [40]as the LORD directed him through Moses. This was to remind the Israelites that no one except a descendant of Aaron should come to burn incense before the LORD, or he would become like Korah and his followers. Nu 3:10; 2Ch 26:18; Ex 30:7-10

[41]The next day the whole Israelite community

[a]14 Or *you make slaves of*; or *you deceive* [b]30 Hebrew *Sheol*; also in verse 33

grumbled against Moses and Aaron. "You have killed the LORD's people," they said.

42But when the assembly gathered in opposition to Moses and Aaron and turned toward the Tent of Meeting, suddenly the cloud covered it and the glory of the LORD appeared. 43Then Moses and Aaron went to the front of the Tent of Meeting, 44and the LORD said to Moses, 45"Get away from this assembly so I can put an end to them at once." And they fell facedown. ver 19; Nu 20:6

46Then Moses said to Aaron, "Take your censer and put incense in it, along with fire from the altar, and hurry to the assembly to make atonement for them. Wrath has come out from the LORD; the plague has started." 47So Aaron did as Moses said, and ran into the midst of the assembly. The plague had already started among the people, but Aaron offered the incense and made atonement for them. 48He stood between the living and the dead, and the plague stopped. 49But 14,700 people died from the plague, in addition to those who had died because of Korah. 50Then Aaron returned to Moses at the entrance to the Tent of Meeting, for the plague had stopped. Ps 106:30; Nu 8:19; 25:13

The Budding of Aaron's Staff

17 The LORD said to Moses, 2"Speak to the Israelites and get twelve staffs from them, one from the leader of each of their ancestral tribes. Write the name of each man on his staff. 3On the staff of Levi write Aaron's name, for there must be one staff for the head of each ancestral tribe. 4Place them in the Tent of Meeting in front of the Testimony, where I meet with you. 5The staff belonging to the man I choose will sprout, and I will rid myself of this constant grumbling against you by the Israelites." Nu 16:5; Ex 16:7; 25:22

6So Moses spoke to the Israelites, and their leaders gave him twelve staffs, one for the leader of each of their ancestral tribes, and Aaron's staff was among them. 7Moses placed the staffs before the LORD in the Tent of the Testimony. Ex 38:21; Ac 7:44

8The next day Moses entered the Tent of the Testimony and saw that Aaron's staff, which represented the house of Levi, had not only sprouted but had budded, blossomed and produced almonds. 9Then Moses brought out all the staffs from the LORD's presence to all the Israelites. They looked at them, and each man took his own staff.

10The LORD said to Moses, "Put back Aaron's staff in front of the Testimony, to be kept as a sign to the rebellious. This will put an end to their grumbling against me, so that they will not die." 11Moses did just as the LORD commanded him.

12The Israelites said to Moses, "We will die! We are lost, we are all lost! 13Anyone who even comes near the tabernacle of the LORD will die. Are we all going to die?" Nu 1:51

Duties of Priests and Levites

18 The LORD said to Aaron, "You, your sons and your father's family are to bear the responsibility for offenses against the sanctuary, and you and your sons alone are to bear the responsibility for offenses against the priesthood. 2Bring your fellow Levites from your ancestral tribe to join you and assist you when you and your sons minister before the Tent of the Testimony. 3They are to be responsible to you and are to perform all the duties of the Tent, but they must not go near the furnishings of the sanctuary or the altar, or both they and you will die. 4They are to join you and be responsible for the care of the Tent of Meeting—all the work at the Tent—and no one else may come near where you are. Nu 3:10

5"You are to be responsible for the care of the sanctuary and the altar, so that wrath will not fall on the Israelites again. 6I myself have selected your fellow Levites from among the Israelites as a gift to you, dedicated to the LORD to do the work at the Tent of Meeting. 7But only you and your sons may serve as priests in connection with everything at the altar and inside the curtain. I am giving you the service of the priesthood as a gift. Anyone else who comes near the sanctuary must be put to death." Ex 29:9; Nu 3:9; Heb 9:3,6

Offerings for Priests and Levites

8Then the LORD said to Aaron, "I myself have put you in charge of the offerings presented to me; all the holy offerings the Israelites give me I give to you and your sons as your portion and regular share. 9You are to have the part of the most holy offerings that is kept from the fire. From all the gifts they bring me as most holy offerings, whether grain or sin or guilt offerings, that part belongs to you and your sons. 10Eat it as something most holy; every male shall eat it. You must regard it as holy. Lev 6:16,25

11"This also is yours: whatever is set aside from the gifts of all the wave offerings of the Israelites. I give this to you and your sons and daughters as your regular share. Everyone in your household who is ceremonially clean may eat it. Ex 29:26

12"I give you all the finest olive oil and all the finest new wine and grain they give the LORD as the firstfruits of their harvest. 13All the land's firstfruits that they bring to the LORD will be yours. Everyone in your household who is ceremonially clean may eat it. Ex 23:19; Ne 10:35

14"Everything in Israel that is devoted[a] to the LORD is yours. 15The first offspring of every womb, both man and animal, that is offered to the LORD

[a] *14* The Hebrew term refers to the irrevocable giving over of things or persons to the LORD.

is yours. But you must redeem every firstborn son and every firstborn male of unclean animals. 16When they are a month old, you must redeem them at the redemption price set at five shekels[a] of silver, according to the sanctuary shekel, which weighs twenty gerahs. Ex 13:2; Lev 27:6,28

17"But you must not redeem the firstborn of an ox, a sheep or a goat; they are holy. Sprinkle their blood on the altar and burn their fat as an offering made by fire, an aroma pleasing to the LORD. 18Their meat is to be yours, just as the breast of the wave offering and the right thigh are yours. 19Whatever is set aside from the holy offerings the Israelites present to the LORD I give to you and your sons and daughters as your regular share. It is an everlasting covenant of salt before the LORD for both you and your offspring." 2Ch 13:5; Lev 3:2

20The LORD said to Aaron, "You will have no inheritance in their land, nor will you have any share among them; I am your share and your inheritance among the Israelites. Dt 10:9; 18:1-2; Jos 13:33

21"I give to the Levites all the tithes in Israel as their inheritance in return for the work they do while serving at the Tent of Meeting. 22From now on the Israelites must not go near the Tent of Meeting, or they will bear the consequences of their sin and will die. 23It is the Levites who are to do the work at the Tent of Meeting and bear the responsibility for offenses against it. This is a lasting ordinance for the generations to come. They will receive no inheritance among the Israelites. 24Instead, I give to the Levites as their inheritance the tithes that the Israelites present as an offering to the LORD. That is why I said concerning them: 'They will have no inheritance among the Israelites.'" Lev 27:30-33; Nu 1:51

25The LORD said to Moses, 26"Speak to the Levites and say to them: 'When you receive from the Israelites the tithe I give you as your inheritance, you must present a tenth of that tithe as the LORD's offering. 27Your offering will be reckoned to you as grain from the threshing floor or juice from the winepress. 28In this way you also will present an offering to the LORD from all the tithes you receive from the Israelites. From these tithes you must give the LORD's portion to Aaron the priest. 29You must present as the LORD's portion the best and holiest part of everything given to you.' Ne 10:38

30"Say to the Levites: 'When you present the best part, it will be reckoned to you as the product of the threshing floor or the winepress. 31You and your households may eat the rest of it anywhere, for it is your wages for your work at the Tent of Meeting. 32By presenting the best part of it you will not be guilty in this matter; then you will not defile the holy offerings of the Israelites, and you will not die.'" Lev 19:8; 22:15

[a]16 That is, about 2 ounces (about 55 grams)

The Water of Cleansing

19 The LORD said to Moses and Aaron: 2"This is a requirement of the law that the LORD has commanded: Tell the Israelites to bring you a red heifer without defect or blemish and that has never been under a yoke. 3Give it to Eleazar the priest; it is to be taken outside the camp and slaughtered in his presence. 4Then Eleazar the priest is to take some of its blood on his finger and sprinkle it seven times toward the front of the Tent of Meeting. 5While he watches, the heifer is to be burned—its hide, flesh, blood and offal. 6The priest is to take some cedar wood, hyssop and scarlet wool and throw them onto the burning heifer. 7After that, the priest must wash his clothes and bathe himself with water. He may then come into the camp, but he will be ceremonially unclean till evening. 8The man who burns it must also wash his clothes and bathe with water, and he too will be unclean till evening. Ex 29:14; Lev 4:12,21; Dt 21:3

9"A man who is clean shall gather up the ashes of the heifer and put them in a ceremonially clean place outside the camp. They shall be kept by the Israelite community for use in the water of cleansing; it is for purification from sin. 10The man who gathers up the ashes of the heifer must also wash his clothes, and he too will be unclean till evening. This will be a lasting ordinance both for the Israelites and for the aliens living among them. ver 13

11"Whoever touches the dead body of anyone will be unclean for seven days. 12He must purify himself with the water on the third day and on the seventh day; then he will be clean. But if he does not purify himself on the third and seventh days, he will not be clean. 13Whoever touches the dead body of anyone and fails to purify himself defiles the LORD's tabernacle. That person must be cut off from Israel. Because the water of cleansing has not been sprinkled on him, he is unclean; his uncleanness remains on him. Lev 7:20; 21:1; Nu 31:19

14"This is the law that applies when a person dies in a tent: Anyone who enters the tent and anyone who is in it will be unclean for seven days, 15and every open container without a lid fastened on it will be unclean.

16"Anyone out in the open who touches someone who has been killed with a sword or someone who has died a natural death, or anyone who touches a human bone or a grave, will be unclean for seven days. Nu 31:19; Mt 23:27

17"For the unclean person, put some ashes from the burned purification offering into a jar and pour fresh water over them. 18Then a man who is ceremonially clean is to take some hyssop, dip it in the water and sprinkle the tent and all the furnishings and the people who were there. He must also sprinkle anyone who has touched a human bone

or a grave or someone who has been killed or
someone who has died a natural death. 19The man
who is clean is to sprinkle the unclean person on
the third and seventh days, and on the seventh day
he is to purify him. The person being cleansed
must wash his clothes and bathe with water, and
that evening he will be clean. 20But if a person who
is unclean does not purify himself, he must be cut
off from the community, because he has defiled
the sanctuary of the LORD. The water of cleansing
has not been sprinkled on him, and he is unclean.
21This is a lasting ordinance for them. Eze 36:25

"The man who sprinkles the water of cleansing
must also wash his clothes, and anyone who
touches the water of cleansing will be unclean till
evening. 22Anything that an unclean person touches
becomes unclean, and anyone who touches it
becomes unclean till evening." Lev 5:2

Water From the Rock

20 In the first month the whole Israelite community arrived at the Desert of Zin, and
they stayed at Kadesh. There Miriam died and was
buried. Ex 15:20; Nu 33:36

2Now there was no water for the community,
and the people gathered in opposition to Moses
and Aaron. 3They quarreled with Moses and said,
"If only we had died when our brothers fell dead
before the LORD! 4Why did you bring the LORD's
community into this desert, that we and our livestock should die here? 5Why did you bring us up
out of Egypt to this terrible place? It has no grain
or figs, grapevines or pomegranates. And there is
no water to drink!" Ex 14:11; 17:1-2

6Moses and Aaron went from the assembly to
the entrance to the Tent of Meeting and fell facedown, and the glory of the LORD appeared to them.
7The LORD said to Moses, 8"Take the staff, and you
and your brother Aaron gather the assembly together. Speak to that rock before their eyes and it
will pour out its water. You will bring water out of
the rock for the community so they and their livestock can drink." Ex 17:6; Isa 43:20; Nu 14:5

9So Moses took the staff from the LORD's presence, just as he commanded him. 10He and Aaron
gathered the assembly together in front of the rock
and Moses said to them, "Listen, you rebels, must
we bring you water out of this rock?" 11Then Moses raised his arm and struck the rock twice with
his staff. Water gushed out, and the community
and their livestock drank. Ex 17:6; Nu 17:10; Ps 106:32-33

12But the LORD said to Moses and Aaron, "Because you did not trust in me enough to honor me
as holy in the sight of the Israelites, you will not
bring this community into the land I give them."
13These were the waters of Meribah,[a] where
the Israelites quarreled with the LORD and where
he showed himself holy among them. Ex 17:7

Edom Denies Israel Passage

14Moses sent messengers from Kadesh to the
king of Edom, saying: Dt 2:4; Jdg 11:16-17

"This is what your brother Israel says: You
know about all the hardships that have come
upon us. 15Our forefathers went down into
Egypt, and we lived there many years. The
Egyptians mistreated us and our fathers,
16but when we cried out to the LORD, he
heard our cry and sent an angel and brought
us out of Egypt. Ex 2:23; 14:19

"Now we are here at Kadesh, a town on
the edge of your territory. 17Please let us pass
through your country. We will not go
through any field or vineyard, or drink water
from any well. We will travel along the king's
highway and not turn to the right or to the
left until we have passed through your territory." Nu 21:22

18But Edom answered:

"You may not pass through here; if you
try, we will march out and attack you with
the sword." Nu 21:23

19The Israelites replied:

"We will go along the main road, and if
we or our livestock drink any of your water,
we will pay for it. We only want to pass
through on foot—nothing else." Dt 2:6,28

20Again they answered:

"You may not pass through."

Then Edom came out against them with a large
and powerful army. 21Since Edom refused to let
them go through their territory, Israel turned away
from them. Dt 2:8; Jdg 11:18

The Death of Aaron

22The whole Israelite community set out from
Kadesh and came to Mount Hor. 23At Mount Hor,
near the border of Edom, the LORD said to Moses
and Aaron, 24"Aaron will be gathered to his people. He will not enter the land I give the Israelites,
because both of you rebelled against my command
at the waters of Meribah. 25Get Aaron and his son
Eleazar and take them up Mount Hor. 26Remove
Aaron's garments and put them on his son Eleazar, for Aaron will be gathered to his people; he
will die there." ver 10; Ge 25:8

27Moses did as the LORD commanded: They
went up Mount Hor in the sight of the whole
community. 28Moses removed Aaron's garments

[a] 13 *Meribah* means *quarreling.*

and put them on his son Eleazar. And Aaron died
there on top of the mountain. Then Moses and
Eleazar came down from the mountain, 29and
when the whole community learned that Aaron
had died, the entire house of Israel mourned for
him thirty days. Ex 29:29; Nu 33:38; Dt 34:8

Arad Destroyed

21 When the Canaanite king of Arad, who
lived in the Negev, heard that Israel was
coming along the road to Atharim, he attacked the
Israelites and captured some of them. 2Then Israel
made this vow to the LORD: "If you will deliver
these people into our hands, we will totally destroy[a] their cities." 3The LORD listened to Israel's
plea and gave the Canaanites over to them. They
completely destroyed them and their towns; so the
place was named Hormah.[b] Ex 22:20; Nu 33:40

The Bronze Snake

4They traveled from Mount Hor along the route
to the Red Sea,[c] to go around Edom. But the
people grew impatient on the way; 5they spoke
against God and against Moses, and said, "Why
have you brought us up out of Egypt to die in the
desert? There is no bread! There is no water! And
we detest this miserable food!" Ps 78:19; Nu 20:22

6Then the LORD sent venomous snakes among
them; they bit the people and many Israelites died.
7The people came to Moses and said, "We sinned
when we spoke against the LORD and against you.
Pray that the LORD will take the snakes away from
us." So Moses prayed for the people. Dt 8:15

8The LORD said to Moses, "Make a snake and
put it up on a pole; anyone who is bitten can look
at it and live." 9So Moses made a bronze snake and
put it up on a pole. Then when anyone was bitten
by a snake and looked at the bronze snake, he
lived. Jn 3:14-15; 2Ki 18:4

The Journey to Moab

10The Israelites moved on and camped at
Oboth. 11Then they set out from Oboth and
camped in Iye Abarim, in the desert that faces
Moab toward the sunrise. 12From there they
moved on and camped in the Zered Valley. 13They
set out from there and camped alongside the Arnon, which is in the desert extending into Amorite
territory. The Arnon is the border of Moab, between Moab and the Amorites. 14That is why the
Book of the Wars of the LORD says: Nu 33:44

"... Waheb in Suphah[d] and the ravines,
the Arnon 15and[e] the slopes of the ravines
that lead to the site of Ar Dt 2:9,18
and lie along the border of Moab."

16From there they continued on to Beer, the well
where the LORD said to Moses, "Gather the people
together and I will give them water."

17Then Israel sang this song: Ex 15:1

"Spring up, O well!
Sing about it,
18about the well that the princes dug,
that the nobles of the people sank—
the nobles with scepters and staffs."

Then they went from the desert to Mattanah,
19from Mattanah to Nahaliel, from Nahaliel to Bamoth, 20and from Bamoth to the valley in Moab
where the top of Pisgah overlooks the wasteland.

Defeat of Sihon and Og

21Israel sent messengers to say to Sihon king of
the Amorites: Dt 1:4; Jdg 11:19-21

22"Let us pass through your country. We
will not turn aside into any field or vineyard,
or drink water from any well. We will travel
along the king's highway until we have
passed through your territory." Nu 20:17

23But Sihon would not let Israel pass through
his territory. He mustered his entire army and
marched out into the desert against Israel. When
he reached Jahaz, he fought with Israel. 24Israel,
however, put him to the sword and took over his
land from the Arnon to the Jabbok, but only as far
as the Ammonites, because their border was fortified. 25Israel captured all the cities of the Amorites
and occupied them, including Heshbon and all its
surrounding settlements. 26Heshbon was the city
of Sihon king of the Amorites, who had fought
against the former king of Moab and had taken
from him all his land as far as the Arnon. Dt 2:32

27That is why the poets say:

"Come to Heshbon and let it be rebuilt;
let Sihon's city be restored.

28"Fire went out from Heshbon,
a blaze from the city of Sihon. Jer 48:45
It consumed Ar of Moab,
the citizens of Arnon's heights. Isa 15:2
29Woe to you, O Moab!
You are destroyed, O people of Chemosh!
He has given up his sons as fugitives
and his daughters as captives
to Sihon king of the Amorites.

30"But we have overthrown them;
Heshbon is destroyed all the way to Dibon.
We have demolished them as far as Nophah,
which extends to Medeba."

31So Israel settled in the land of the Amorites.

[a] *2* The Hebrew term refers to the irrevocable giving over of things or persons to the LORD, often by totally destroying them; also in verse 3. [b] *3* *Hormah* means *destruction.* [c] *4* Hebrew *Yam Suph*; that is, Sea of Reeds [d] *14* The meaning of the Hebrew for this phrase is uncertain. [e] *14,15* Or *"I have been given from Suphah and the ravines / of the Arnon* 15*to*

32After Moses had sent spies to Jazer, the Israelites captured its surrounding settlements and drove out the Amorites who were there. 33Then they turned and went up along the road toward Bashan, and Og king of Bashan and his whole army marched out to meet them in battle at Edrei.

34The LORD said to Moses, "Do not be afraid of him, for I have handed him over to you, with his whole army and his land. Do to him what you did to Sihon king of the Amorites, who reigned in Heshbon." Dt 3:2

35So they struck him down, together with his sons and his whole army, leaving them no survivors. And they took possession of his land.

Balak Summons Balaam

22 Then the Israelites traveled to the plains of Moab and camped along the Jordan across from Jericho.[a] Nu 33:48

2Now Balak son of Zippor saw all that Israel had done to the Amorites, 3and Moab was terrified because there were so many people. Indeed, Moab was filled with dread because of the Israelites.

4The Moabites said to the elders of Midian, "This horde is going to lick up everything around us, as an ox licks up the grass of the field."

So Balak son of Zippor, who was king of Moab at that time, 5sent messengers to summon Balaam son of Beor, who was at Pethor, near the River,[b] in his native land. Balak said: Dt 23:4; 2Pe 2:15

> "A people has come out of Egypt; they cover the face of the land and have settled next to me. 6Now come and put a curse on these people, because they are too powerful for me. Perhaps then I will be able to defeat them and drive them out of the country. For I know that those you bless are blessed, and those you curse are cursed." Nu 23:7,11,13

7The elders of Moab and Midian left, taking with them the fee for divination. When they came to Balaam, they told him what Balak had said.

8"Spend the night here," Balaam said to them, "and I will bring you back the answer the LORD gives me." So the Moabite princes stayed with him.

9God came to Balaam and asked, "Who are these men with you?" Ge 20:3

10Balaam said to God, "Balak son of Zippor, king of Moab, sent me this message: 11'A people that has come out of Egypt covers the face of the land. Now come and put a curse on them for me. Perhaps then I will be able to fight them and drive them away.'"

12But God said to Balaam, "Do not go with them. You must not put a curse on those people, because they are blessed." Ge 12:2; 22:17

13The next morning Balaam got up and said to Balak's princes, "Go back to your own country, for the LORD has refused to let me go with you."

14So the Moabite princes returned to Balak and said, "Balaam refused to come with us."

15Then Balak sent other princes, more numerous and more distinguished than the first. 16They came to Balaam and said:

> "This is what Balak son of Zippor says: Do not let anything keep you from coming to me, 17because I will reward you handsomely and do whatever you say. Come and put a curse on these people for me."

18But Balaam answered them, "Even if Balak gave me his palace filled with silver and gold, I could not do anything great or small to go beyond the command of the LORD my God. 19Now stay here tonight as the others did, and I will find out what else the LORD will tell me." Nu 24:13; 1Ki 22:14

20That night God came to Balaam and said, "Since these men have come to summon you, go with them, but do only what I tell you."

Balaam's Donkey

21Balaam got up in the morning, saddled his donkey and went with the princes of Moab. 22But God was very angry when he went, and the angel of the LORD stood in the road to oppose him. Balaam was riding on his donkey, and his two servants were with him. 23When the donkey saw the angel of the LORD standing in the road with a drawn sword in his hand, she turned off the road into a field. Balaam beat her to get her back on the road. Ex 23:20

24Then the angel of the LORD stood in a narrow path between two vineyards, with walls on both sides. 25When the donkey saw the angel of the LORD, she pressed close to the wall, crushing Balaam's foot against it. So he beat her again.

26Then the angel of the LORD moved on ahead and stood in a narrow place where there was no room to turn, either to the right or to the left. 27When the donkey saw the angel of the LORD, she lay down under Balaam, and he was angry and beat her with his staff. 28Then the LORD opened the donkey's mouth, and she said to Balaam, "What have I done to you to make you beat me these three times?" Jas 1:19; 2Pe 2:16

29Balaam answered the donkey, "You have made a fool of me! If I had a sword in my hand, I would kill you right now." Pr 12:10; Mt 15:19

30The donkey said to Balaam, "Am I not your own donkey, which you have always ridden, to this day? Have I been in the habit of doing this to you?"

"No," he said.

31Then the LORD opened Balaam's eyes, and he

[a] 1 Hebrew *Jordan of Jericho*; possibly an ancient name for the Jordan River [b] 5 That is, the Euphrates

saw the angel of the LORD standing in the road with
his sword drawn. So he bowed low and fell facedown. Ge 21:19
32The angel of the LORD asked him, "Why have
you beaten your donkey these three times? I have
come here to oppose you because your path is a
reckless one before me.[a] 33The donkey saw me
and turned away from me these three times. If she
had not turned away, I would certainly have killed
you by now, but I would have spared her."
34Balaam said to the angel of the LORD, "I have
sinned. I did not realize you were standing in the
road to oppose me. Now if you are displeased, I
will go back." Nu 14:40
35The angel of the LORD said to Balaam, "Go
with the men, but speak only what I tell you." So
Balaam went with the princes of Balak.
36When Balak heard that Balaam was coming,
he went out to meet him at the Moabite town on
the Arnon border, at the edge of his territory. 37Ba-
lak said to Balaam, "Did I not send you an urgent
summons? Why didn't you come to me? Am I
really not able to reward you?" Nu 21:13
38"Well, I have come to you now," Balaam replied. "But can I say just anything? I must speak
only what God puts in my mouth." Nu 23:5,16,26
39Then Balaam went with Balak to Kiriath Hu-
zoth. 40Balak sacrificed cattle and sheep, and gave
some to Balaam and the princes who were with
him. 41The next morning Balak took Balaam up to
Bamoth Baal, and from there he saw part of the
people. Nu 21:28; 23:13

Balaam's First Oracle

23 Balaam said, "Build me seven altars here,
and prepare seven bulls and seven rams for
me." 2Balak did as Balaam said, and the two of
them offered a bull and a ram on each altar.
3Then Balaam said to Balak, "Stay here beside
your offering while I go aside. Perhaps the LORD
will come to meet with me. Whatever he reveals to
me I will tell you." Then he went off to a barren
height. ver 15
4God met with him, and Balaam said, "I have
prepared seven altars, and on each altar I have
offered a bull and a ram."
5The LORD put a message in Balaam's mouth
and said, "Go back to Balak and give him this
message." Dt 18:18; Jer 1:9
6So he went back to him and found him standing beside his offering, with all the princes of
Moab. 7Then Balaam uttered his oracle: ver 18

"Balak brought me from Aram,
the king of Moab from the eastern mountains.
'Come,' he said, 'curse Jacob for me;
come, denounce Israel.' Nu 22:6
8How can I curse
those whom God has not cursed? Nu 22:12
How can I denounce
those whom the LORD has not denounced?
9From the rocky peaks I see them,
from the heights I view them.
I see a people who live apart
and do not consider themselves one of the
nations. Dt 32:8; 33:28
10Who can count the dust of Jacob
or number the fourth part of Israel?
Let me die the death of the righteous,
and may my end be like theirs!" Ps 37:37

11Balak said to Balaam, "What have you done to
me? I brought you to curse my enemies, but you
have done nothing but bless them!" Nu 24:10
12He answered, "Must I not speak what the
LORD puts in my mouth?" Nu 22:20,38

Balaam's Second Oracle

13Then Balak said to him, "Come with me to
another place where you can see them; you will see
only a part but not all of them. And from there,
curse them for me." 14So he took him to the field
of Zophim on the top of Pisgah, and there he built
seven altars and offered a bull and a ram on each
altar.
15Balaam said to Balak, "Stay here beside your
offering while I meet with him over there."
16The LORD met with Balaam and put a message
in his mouth and said, "Go back to Balak and give
him this message." Nu 22:38
17So he went to him and found him standing
beside his offering, with the princes of Moab. Balak asked him, "What did the LORD say?"
18Then he uttered his oracle:

"Arise, Balak, and listen;
hear me, son of Zippor.
19God is not a man, that he should lie, Isa 55:9
nor a son of man, that he should change
his mind. 1Sa 15:29; Mal 3:6; Jas 1:17
Does he speak and then not act?
Does he promise and not fulfill?
20I have received a command to bless;
he has blessed, and I cannot change it.

21"No misfortune is seen in Jacob, Ps 32:2,5; Ro 4:7-8
no misery observed in Israel.[b]
The LORD their God is with them;
the shout of the King is among them.
22God brought them out of Egypt;
they have the strength of a wild ox. Nu 24:8
23There is no sorcery against Jacob,
no divination against Israel. Nu 24:1; Jos 13:22
It will now be said of Jacob

[a] 32 The meaning of the Hebrew for this clause is uncertain. [b] 21 Or *He has not looked on Jacob's offenses / or on the wrongs found in Israel.*

and of Israel, 'See what God has done!'
24The people rise like a lioness;
they rouse themselves like a lion Ge 49:9
that does not rest till he devours his prey
and drinks the blood of his victims."

25Then Balak said to Balaam, "Neither curse
them at all nor bless them at all!"
26Balaam answered, "Did I not tell you I must
do whatever the LORD says?"

Balaam's Third Oracle

27Then Balak said to Balaam, "Come, let me
take you to another place. Perhaps it will please
God to let you curse them for me from there."
28And Balak took Balaam to the top of Peor, overlooking the wasteland. Ps 106:28
29Balaam said, "Build me seven altars here, and
prepare seven bulls and seven rams for me." 30Ba-
lak did as Balaam had said, and offered a bull and
a ram on each altar.

24 Now when Balaam saw that it pleased the
LORD to bless Israel, he did not resort to
sorcery as at other times, but turned his face toward the desert. 2When Balaam looked out and
saw Israel encamped tribe by tribe, the Spirit of
God came upon him 3and he uttered his oracle:

"The oracle of Balaam son of Beor,
the oracle of one whose eye sees clearly,
4the oracle of one who hears the words of God,
who sees a vision from the Almighty,[a]
who falls prostrate, and whose eyes are
opened:

5"How beautiful are your tents, O Jacob,
your dwelling places, O Israel!

6"Like valleys they spread out,
like gardens beside a river,
like aloes planted by the LORD,
like cedars beside the waters. Ps 1:3; 104:16
7Water will flow from their buckets;
their seed will have abundant water.

"Their king will be greater than Agag;
their kingdom will be exalted. 2Sa 5:12; 1Ch 14:2

8"God brought them out of Egypt;
they have the strength of a wild ox.
They devour hostile nations
and break their bones in pieces; Ps 2:9; Jer 50:17
with their arrows they pierce them. Ps 45:5
9Like a lion they crouch and lie down,
like a lioness—who dares to rouse them?

"May those who bless you be blessed
and those who curse you be cursed!" Ge 12:3

10Then Balak's anger burned against Balaam.
He struck his hands together and said to him, "I
summoned you to curse my enemies, but you have
blessed them these three times. 11Now leave at
once and go home! I said I would reward you
handsomely, but the LORD has kept you from being rewarded." Nu 22:17; 23:11
12Balaam answered Balak, "Did I not tell the
messengers you sent me, 13'Even if Balak gave me
his palace filled with silver and gold, I could not do
anything of my own accord, good or bad, to go
beyond the command of the LORD—and I must
say only what the LORD says'? 14Now I am going
back to my people, but come, let me warn you of
what this people will do to your people in days to
come." Nu 22:18,20; Mic 6:5

Balaam's Fourth Oracle

15Then he uttered his oracle:

"The oracle of Balaam son of Beor,
the oracle of one whose eye sees clearly,
16the oracle of one who hears the words of God,
who has knowledge from the Most High,
who sees a vision from the Almighty,
who falls prostrate, and whose eyes are
opened:

17"I see him, but not now;
I behold him, but not near. Rev 1:7
A star will come out of Jacob; Mt 2:2
a scepter will rise out of Israel. Ge 49:10
He will crush the foreheads of Moab,
the skulls[b] of[c] all the sons of Sheth.[d]
18Edom will be conquered;
Seir, his enemy, will be conquered,
but Israel will grow strong.
19A ruler will come out of Jacob
and destroy the survivors of the city."

Balaam's Final Oracles

20Then Balaam saw Amalek and uttered his oracle:

"Amalek was first among the nations,
but he will come to ruin at last." Dt 25:19

21Then he saw the Kenites and uttered his oracle:

"Your dwelling place is secure,
your nest is set in a rock;
22yet you Kenites will be destroyed
when Asshur takes you captive." Ge 10:22

23Then he uttered his oracle:

"Ah, who can live when God does this?[e]

[a]4 Hebrew *Shaddai*; also in verse 16 [b]17 Samaritan Pentateuch (see also Jer. 48:45); the meaning of the word in the Masoretic Text is uncertain. [c]17 Or possibly *Moab, / batter* [d]17 Or *all the noisy boasters* [e]23 Masoretic Text; with a different word division of the Hebrew *A people will gather from the north.*

24 Ships will come from the shores of Kittim;
they will subdue Asshur and Eber,
but they too will come to ruin." Ge 10:4,21

25Then Balaam got up and returned home and Balak went his own way. Nu 31:8

Moab Seduces Israel

25 While Israel was staying in Shittim, the men began to indulge in sexual immorality with Moabite women, 2who invited them to the sacrifices to their gods. The people ate and bowed down before these gods. 3So Israel joined in worshiping the Baal of Peor. And the LORD's anger burned against them. Ex 20:5; Nu 31:16; Ps 106:28

4The LORD said to Moses, "Take all the leaders of these people, kill them and expose them in broad daylight before the LORD, so that the LORD's fierce anger may turn away from Israel." Dt 4:3

5So Moses said to Israel's judges, "Each of you must put to death those of your men who have joined in worshiping the Baal of Peor."

6Then an Israelite man brought to his family a Midianite woman right before the eyes of Moses and the whole assembly of Israel while they were weeping at the entrance to the Tent of Meeting. 7When Phinehas son of Eleazar, the son of Aaron, the priest, saw this, he left the assembly, took a spear in his hand 8and followed the Israelite into the tent. He drove the spear through both of them—through the Israelite and into the woman's body. Then the plague against the Israelites was stopped; 9but those who died in the plague numbered 24,000. Nu 14:37; 1Co 10:8

10The LORD said to Moses, 11"Phinehas son of Eleazar, the son of Aaron, the priest, has turned my anger away from the Israelites; for he was as zealous as I am for my honor among them, so that in my zeal I did not put an end to them. 12Therefore tell him I am making my covenant of peace with him. 13He and his descendants will have a covenant of a lasting priesthood, because he was zealous for the honor of his God and made atonement for the Israelites." Isa 54:10; Mal 2:4-5; Ex 20:5

14The name of the Israelite who was killed with the Midianite woman was Zimri son of Salu, the leader of a Simeonite family. 15And the name of the Midianite woman who was put to death was Cozbi daughter of Zur, a tribal chief of a Midianite family. Nu 31:8; Jos 13:21

16The LORD said to Moses, 17"Treat the Midianites as enemies and kill them, 18because they treated you as enemies when they deceived you in the affair of Peor and their sister Cozbi, the daughter of a Midianite leader, the woman who was killed when the plague came as a result of Peor."

The Second Census

26 After the plague the LORD said to Moses and Eleazar son of Aaron, the priest, 2"Take a census of the whole Israelite community by families—all those twenty years old or more who are able to serve in the army of Israel." 3So on the plains of Moab by the Jordan across from Jericho,[a] Moses and Eleazar the priest spoke with them and said, 4"Take a census of the men twenty years old or more, as the LORD commanded Moses." Ex 30:11-16; Nu 22:1

These were the Israelites who came out of Egypt:

5The descendants of Reuben, the firstborn son of Israel, were:
through Hanoch, the Hanochite clan;
through Pallu, the Palluite clan;
6through Hezron, the Hezronite clan;
through Carmi, the Carmite clan. Nu 1:20
7These were the clans of Reuben; those numbered were 43,730.

8The son of Pallu was Eliab, 9and the sons of Eliab were Nemuel, Dathan and Abiram. The same Dathan and Abiram were the community officials who rebelled against Moses and Aaron and were among Korah's followers when they rebelled against the LORD. 10The earth opened its mouth and swallowed them along with Korah, whose followers died when the fire devoured the 250 men. And they served as a warning sign. 11The line of Korah, however, did not die out. Ex 6:24; Nu 16:2

12The descendants of Simeon by their clans were:
through Nemuel, the Nemuelite clan;
through Jamin, the Jaminite clan; 1Ch 4:24
through Jakin, the Jakinite clan;
13through Zerah, the Zerahite clan; Ge 46:10
through Shaul, the Shaulite clan.
14These were the clans of Simeon; there were 22,200 men.

15The descendants of Gad by their clans were:
through Zephon, the Zephonite clan;
through Haggi, the Haggite clan;
through Shuni, the Shunite clan;
16through Ozni, the Oznite clan;
through Eri, the Erite clan;
17through Arodi,[b] the Arodite clan;
through Areli, the Arelite clan.
18These were the clans of Gad; those numbered were 40,500. Nu 1:25; Jos 13:24-28

19Er and Onan were sons of Judah, but they died in Canaan. Ge 38:2-10; 46:12
20The descendants of Judah by their clans were:
through Shelah, the Shelanite clan; 1Ch 2:3

[a]3 Hebrew *Jordan of Jericho*; possibly an ancient name for the Jordan River; also in verse 63 [b]17 Samaritan Pentateuch and Syriac (see also Gen. 46:16); Masoretic Text *Arod*

through Perez, the Perezite clan;
through Zerah, the Zerahite clan.
21 The descendants of Perez were:
through Hezron, the Hezronite clan;
through Hamul, the Hamulite clan.
22 These were the clans of Judah; those numbered
were 76,500. Nu 1:27

23 The descendants of Issachar by their clans were:
through Tola, the Tolaite clan; Ge 46:13
through Puah, the Puite[a] clan;
24 through Jashub, the Jashubite clan;
through Shimron, the Shimronite clan.
25 These were the clans of Issachar; those numbered
were 64,300. Nu 1:29

26 The descendants of Zebulun by their clans were:
through Sered, the Seredite clan;
through Elon, the Elonite clan;
through Jahleel, the Jahleelite clan.
27 These were the clans of Zebulun; those numbered
were 60,500. Nu 1:31

28 The descendants of Joseph by their clans through
Manasseh and Ephraim were:

29 The descendants of Manasseh:
through Makir, the Makirite clan (Makir
was the father of Gilead); Jos 17:1
through Gilead, the Gileadite clan.
30 These were the descendants of Gilead:
through Iezer, the Iezerite clan; Jos 17:2
through Helek, the Helekite clan;
31 through Asriel, the Asrielite clan;
through Shechem, the Shechemite clan;
32 through Shemida, the Shemidaite clan;
through Hepher, the Hepherite clan.
33 (Zelophehad son of Hepher had no sons;
he had only daughters, whose names
were Mahlah, Noah, Hoglah, Milcah and
Tirzah.) Nu 27:1; 36:11
34 These were the clans of Manasseh; those numbered
were 52,700.

35 These were the descendants of Ephraim by their
clans:
through Shuthelah, the Shuthelahite clan;
through Beker, the Bekerite clan;
through Tahan, the Tahanite clan.
36 These were the descendants of Shuthelah:
through Eran, the Eranite clan.
37 These were the clans of Ephraim; those numbered
were 32,500. Nu 1:33

These were the descendants of Joseph by their
clans.

38 The descendants of Benjamin by their clans
were: Ge 46:21
through Bela, the Belaite clan;
through Ashbel, the Ashbelite clan;
through Ahiram, the Ahiramite clan;
39 through Shupham,[b] the Shuphamite clan;
through Hupham, the Huphamite clan.
40 The descendants of Bela through Ard and
Naaman were:
through Ard,[c] the Ardite clan;
through Naaman, the Naamite clan.
41 These were the clans of Benjamin; those numbered
were 45,600. Nu 1:37

42 These were the descendants of Dan by their
clans:
through Shuham, the Shuhamite clan.
These were the clans of Dan: 43 All of them were
Shuhamite clans; and those numbered were
64,400.

44 The descendants of Asher by their clans were:
through Imnah, the Imnite clan;
through Ishvi, the Ishvite clan;
through Beriah, the Beriite clan;
45 and through the descendants of Beriah:
through Heber, the Heberite clan;
through Malkiel, the Malkielite clan.
46 (Asher had a daughter named Serah.)
47 These were the clans of Asher; those numbered
were 53,400. Nu 1:41

48 The descendants of Naphtali by their clans were:
through Jahzeel, the Jahzeelite clan;
through Guni, the Gunite clan;
49 through Jezer, the Jezerite clan;
through Shillem, the Shillemite clan.
50 These were the clans of Naphtali; those numbered
were 45,400.

51 The total number of the men of Israel was
601,730. Ex 12:37; 38:26

52 The LORD said to Moses, 53 "The land is to be
allotted to them as an inheritance based on the
number of names. 54 To a larger group give a larger
inheritance, and to a smaller group a smaller one;
each is to receive its inheritance according to the
number of those listed. 55 Be sure that the land is
distributed by lot. What each group inherits will
be according to the names for its ancestral tribe.
56 Each inheritance is to be distributed by lot
among the larger and smaller groups." Nu 33:54

57 These were the Levites who were counted by
their clans: Ge 46:11
through Gershon, the Gershonite clan;

[a] 23 Samaritan Pentateuch, Septuagint, Vulgate and Syriac (see also 1 Chron. 7:1); Masoretic Text *through Puvah, the Punite*
[b] 39 A few manuscripts of the Masoretic Text, Samaritan Pentateuch, Vulgate and Syriac (see also Septuagint); most manuscripts of the Masoretic Text *Shephupham*
[c] 40 Samaritan Pentateuch and Vulgate (see also Septuagint); Masoretic Text does not have *through Ard.*

through Kohath, the Kohathite clan;
through Merari, the Merarite clan.
58These also were Levite clans:
the Libnite clan,
the Hebronite clan,
the Mahlite clan,
the Mushite clan,
the Korahite clan.
(Kohath was the forefather of Amram; 59the name of Amram's wife was Jochebed, a descendant of Levi, who was born to the Levites[a] in Egypt. To Amram she bore Aaron, Moses and their sister Miriam. 60Aaron was the father of Nadab and Abihu, Eleazar and Ithamar. 61But Nadab and Abihu died when they made an offering before the LORD with unauthorized fire.) Ex 6:20; Lev 10:1-2; Nu 3:2

62All the male Levites a month old or more numbered 23,000. They were not counted along with the other Israelites because they received no inheritance among them. Nu 1:47; 18:23

63These are the ones counted by Moses and Eleazar the priest when they counted the Israelites on the plains of Moab by the Jordan across from Jericho. 64Not one of them was among those counted by Moses and Aaron the priest when they counted the Israelites in the Desert of Sinai. 65For the LORD had told those Israelites they would surely die in the desert, and not one of them was left except Caleb son of Jephunneh and Joshua son of Nun. Nu 14:28; Dt 2:14-15; Heb 3:17

Zelophehad's Daughters

27 The daughters of Zelophehad son of Hepher, the son of Gilead, the son of Makir, the son of Manasseh, belonged to the clans of Manasseh son of Joseph. The names of the daughters were Mahlah, Noah, Hoglah, Milcah and Tirzah. They approached 2the entrance to the Tent of Meeting and stood before Moses, Eleazar the priest, the leaders and the whole assembly, and said, 3"Our father died in the desert. He was not among Korah's followers, who banded together against the LORD, but he died for his own sin and left no sons. 4Why should our father's name disappear from his clan because he had no son? Give us property among our father's relatives." Nu 16:2

5So Moses brought their case before the LORD 6and the LORD said to him, 7"What Zelophehad's daughters are saying is right. You must certainly give them property as an inheritance among their father's relatives and turn their father's inheritance over to them. Nu 9:8; Jos 17:4

8"Say to the Israelites, 'If a man dies and leaves no son, turn his inheritance over to his daughter. 9If he has no daughter, give his inheritance to his brothers. 10If he has no brothers, give his inheritance to his father's brothers. 11If his father had no brothers, give his inheritance to the nearest relative in his clan, that he may possess it. This is to be a legal requirement for the Israelites, as the LORD commanded Moses.'" Nu 36:1-12

Joshua to Succeed Moses

12Then the LORD said to Moses, "Go up this mountain in the Abarim range and see the land I have given the Israelites. 13After you have seen it, you too will be gathered to your people, as your brother Aaron was, 14for when the community rebelled at the waters in the Desert of Zin, both of you disobeyed my command to honor me as holy before their eyes." (These were the waters of Meribah Kadesh, in the Desert of Zin.) Nu 20:12; 33:47

15Moses said to the LORD, 16"May the LORD, the God of the spirits of all mankind, appoint a man over this community 17to go out and come in before them, one who will lead them out and bring them in, so the LORD's people will not be like sheep without a shepherd." Nu 16:22; Dt 31:2; Mt 9:36

18So the LORD said to Moses, "Take Joshua son of Nun, a man in whom is the spirit,[b] and lay your hand on him. 19Have him stand before Eleazar the priest and the entire assembly and commission him in their presence. 20Give him some of your authority so the whole Israelite community will obey him. 21He is to stand before Eleazar the priest, who will obtain decisions for him by inquiring of the Urim before the LORD. At his command he and the entire community of the Israelites will go out, and at his command they will come in."

22Moses did as the LORD commanded him. He took Joshua and had him stand before Eleazar the priest and the whole assembly. 23Then he laid his hands on him and commissioned him, as the LORD instructed through Moses.

Daily Offerings

28 The LORD said to Moses, 2"Give this command to the Israelites and say to them: 'See that you present to me at the appointed time the food for my offerings made by fire, as an aroma pleasing to me.' 3Say to them: 'This is the offering made by fire that you are to present to the LORD: two lambs a year old without defect, as a regular burnt offering each day. 4Prepare one lamb in the morning and the other at twilight, 5together with a grain offering of a tenth of an ephah[c] of fine flour mixed with a quarter of a hin[d] of oil from pressed olives. 6This is the regular burnt offering instituted at Mount Sinai as a pleasing aroma, an offering made to the LORD by fire. 7The accompa-

[a] 59 Or *Jochebed, a daughter of Levi, who was born to Levi* [b] 18 Or *Spirit* [c] 5 That is, probably about 2 quarts (about 2 liters); also in verses 13, 21 and 29 [d] 5 That is, probably about 1 quart (about 1 liter); also in verses 7 and 14

nying drink offering is to be a quarter of a hin of fermented drink with each lamb. Pour out the drink offering to the LORD at the sanctuary. 8Prepare the second lamb at twilight, along with the same kind of grain offering and drink offering that you prepare in the morning. This is an offering made by fire, an aroma pleasing to the LORD.

Sabbath Offerings

9" 'On the Sabbath day, make an offering of two lambs a year old without defect, together with its drink offering and a grain offering of two-tenths of an ephah[a] of fine flour mixed with oil. 10This is the burnt offering for every Sabbath, in addition to the regular burnt offering and its drink offering.

Monthly Offerings

11" 'On the first of every month, present to the LORD a burnt offering of two young bulls, one ram and seven male lambs a year old, all without defect. 12With each bull there is to be a grain offering of three-tenths of an ephah[b] of fine flour mixed with oil; with the ram, a grain offering of two-tenths of an ephah of fine flour mixed with oil; 13and with each lamb, a grain offering of a tenth of an ephah of fine flour mixed with oil. This is for a burnt offering, a pleasing aroma, an offering made to the LORD by fire. 14With each bull there is to be a drink offering of half a hin[c] of wine; with the ram, a third of a hin[d]; and with each lamb, a quarter of a hin. This is the monthly burnt offering to be made at each new moon during the year. 15Besides the regular burnt offering with its drink offering, one male goat is to be presented to the LORD as a sin offering. Lev 4:3; Nu 10:10

The Passover

16" 'On the fourteenth day of the first month the LORD's Passover is to be held. 17On the fifteenth day of this month there is to be a festival; for seven days eat bread made without yeast. 18On the first day hold a sacred assembly and do no regular work. 19Present to the LORD an offering made by fire, a burnt offering of two young bulls, one ram and seven male lambs a year old, all without defect. 20With each bull prepare a grain offering of three-tenths of an ephah of fine flour mixed with oil; with the ram, two-tenths; 21and with each of the seven lambs, one-tenth. 22Include one male goat as a sin offering to make atonement for you. 23Prepare these in addition to the regular morning burnt offering. 24In this way prepare the food for the offering made by fire every day for seven days as an aroma pleasing to the LORD; it is to be prepared in addition to the regular burnt offering and its drink offering. 25On the seventh day hold a sacred assembly and do no regular work.

Feast of Weeks

26" 'On the day of firstfruits, when you present to the LORD an offering of new grain during the Feast of Weeks, hold a sacred assembly and do no regular work. 27Present a burnt offering of two young bulls, one ram and seven male lambs a year old as an aroma pleasing to the LORD. 28With each bull there is to be a grain offering of three-tenths of an ephah of fine flour mixed with oil; with the ram, two-tenths; 29and with each of the seven lambs, one-tenth. 30Include one male goat to make atonement for you. 31Prepare these together with their drink offerings, in addition to the regular burnt offering and its grain offering. Be sure the animals are without defect. Lev 23:15-22; Dt 16:9-12

Feast of Trumpets

29 " 'On the first day of the seventh month hold a sacred assembly and do no regular work. It is a day for you to sound the trumpets. 2As an aroma pleasing to the LORD, prepare a burnt offering of one young bull, one ram and seven male lambs a year old, all without defect. 3With the bull prepare a grain offering of three-tenths of an ephah[e] of fine flour mixed with oil; with the ram, two-tenths[f]; 4and with each of the seven lambs, one-tenth.[g] 5Include one male goat as a sin offering to make atonement for you. 6These are in addition to the monthly and daily burnt offerings with their grain offerings and drink offerings as specified. They are offerings made to the LORD by fire—a pleasing aroma. Lev 23:23-25

Day of Atonement

7" 'On the tenth day of this seventh month hold a sacred assembly. You must deny yourselves[h] and do no work. 8Present as an aroma pleasing to the LORD a burnt offering of one young bull, one ram and seven male lambs a year old, all without defect. 9With the bull prepare a grain offering of three-tenths of an ephah of fine flour mixed with oil; with the ram, two-tenths; 10and with each of the seven lambs, one-tenth. 11Include one male goat as a sin offering, in addition to the sin offering for atonement and the regular burnt offering with its grain offering, and their drink offerings.

Feast of Tabernacles

12" 'On the fifteenth day of the seventh month, hold a sacred assembly and do no regular work.

[a]9 That is, probably about 4 quarts (about 4.5 liters); also in verses 12, 20 and 28 [b]12 That is, probably about 6 quarts (about 6.5 liters); also in verses 20 and 28 [c]14 That is, probably about 2 quarts (about 2 liters) [d]14 That is, probably about 1 1/4 quarts (about 1.2 liters) [e]3 That is, probably about 6 quarts (about 6.5 liters); also in verses 9 and 14 [f]3 That is, probably about 4 quarts (about 4.5 liters); also in verses 9 and 14 [g]4 That is, probably about 2 quarts (about 2 liters); also in verses 10 and 15 [h]7 Or *must fast*

Celebrate a festival to the LORD for seven days.
13Present an offering made by fire as an aroma
pleasing to the LORD, a burnt offering of thirteen
young bulls, two rams and fourteen male lambs a
year old, all without defect. 14With each of the
thirteen bulls prepare a grain offering of three-
tenths of an ephah of fine flour mixed with oil;
with each of the two rams, two-tenths; 15and with
each of the fourteen lambs, one-tenth. 16Include
one male goat as a sin offering, in addition to the
regular burnt offering with its grain offering and
drink offering. Lev 23:24; 1Ki 8:2

17" 'On the second day prepare twelve young
bulls, two rams and fourteen male lambs a year
old, all without defect. 18With the bulls, rams and
lambs, prepare their grain offerings and drink offerings according to the number specified. 19In-
clude one male goat as a sin offering, in addition
to the regular burnt offering with its grain offering,
and their drink offerings. Nu 28:3,15

20" 'On the third day prepare eleven bulls, two
rams and fourteen male lambs a year old, all without defect. 21With the bulls, rams and lambs, prepare their grain offerings and drink offerings according to the number specified. 22Include one
male goat as a sin offering, in addition to the regular burnt offering with its grain offering and drink
offering.

23" 'On the fourth day prepare ten bulls, two
rams and fourteen male lambs a year old, all without defect. 24With the bulls, rams and lambs, prepare their grain offerings and drink offerings according to the number specified. 25Include one
male goat as a sin offering, in addition to the regular burnt offering with its grain offering and drink
offering.

26" 'On the fifth day prepare nine bulls, two
rams and fourteen male lambs a year old, all without defect. 27With the bulls, rams and lambs, prepare their grain offerings and drink offerings according to the number specified. 28Include one
male goat as a sin offering, in addition to the regular burnt offering with its grain offering and drink
offering.

29" 'On the sixth day prepare eight bulls, two
rams and fourteen male lambs a year old, all without defect. 30With the bulls, rams and lambs, prepare their grain offerings and drink offerings according to the number specified. 31Include one
male goat as a sin offering, in addition to the regular burnt offering with its grain offering and drink
offering.

32" 'On the seventh day prepare seven bulls, two
rams and fourteen male lambs a year old, all without defect. 33With the bulls, rams and lambs, prepare their grain offerings and drink offerings according to the number specified. 34Include one
male goat as a sin offering, in addition to the regular burnt offering with its grain offering and drink
offering.

35" 'On the eighth day hold an assembly and do
no regular work. 36Present an offering made by fire
as an aroma pleasing to the LORD, a burnt offering
of one bull, one ram and seven male lambs a year
old, all without defect. 37With the bull, the ram
and the lambs, prepare their grain offerings and
drink offerings according to the number specified.
38Include one male goat as a sin offering, in addition to the regular burnt offering with its grain
offering and drink offering. Lev 1:9; 23:36

39" 'In addition to what you vow and your freewill offerings, prepare these for the LORD at your
appointed feasts: your burnt offerings, grain offerings, drink offerings and fellowship offerings.[a]' "

40Moses told the Israelites all that the LORD
commanded him.

Vows

30 Moses said to the heads of the tribes of
Israel: "This is what the LORD commands:
2When a man makes a vow to the LORD or takes an
oath to obligate himself by a pledge, he must not
break his word but must do everything he said.

LIVING 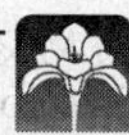 INSIGHT

Judging yourself on this matter of keeping your word, are you bridging or widening the credibility gap? Are you encouraging or discouraging others? Let God's Word motivate you today to the highest standard—God's standard—of integrity.

(See Numbers 30:2.)

3"When a young woman still living in her father's house makes a vow to the LORD or obligates
herself by a pledge 4and her father hears about her
vow or pledge but says nothing to her, then all her
vows and every pledge by which she obligated herself will stand. 5But if her father forbids her when
he hears about it, none of her vows or the pledges
by which she obligated herself will stand; the LORD
will release her because her father has forbidden
her.

6"If she marries after she makes a vow or after
her lips utter a rash promise by which she obligates
herself 7and her husband hears about it but says
nothing to her, then her vows or the pledges by
which she obligated herself will stand. 8But if her
husband forbids her when he hears about it, he
nullifies the vow that obligates her or the rash

[a]39 Traditionally *peace offerings*

promise by which she obligates herself, and the LORD will release her. Ge 3:16; Lev 5:4

9“Any vow or obligation taken by a widow or divorced woman will be binding on her.

10“If a woman living with her husband makes a vow or obligates herself by a pledge under oath 11and her husband hears about it but says nothing to her and does not forbid her, then all her vows or the pledges by which she obligated herself will stand. 12But if her husband nullifies them when he hears about them, then none of the vows or pledges that came from her lips will stand. Her husband has nullified them, and the LORD will release her. 13Her husband may confirm or nullify any vow she makes or any sworn pledge to deny herself. 14But if her husband says nothing to her about it from day to day, then he confirms all her vows or the pledges binding on her. He confirms them by saying nothing to her when he hears about them. 15If, however, he nullifies them some time after he hears about them, then he is responsible for her guilt.” Eph 5:22; Col 3:18

16These are the regulations the LORD gave Moses concerning relationships between a man and his wife, and between a father and his young daughter still living in his house.

Vengeance on the Midianites

31 The LORD said to Moses, 2“Take vengeance on the Midianites for the Israelites. After that, you will be gathered to your people.”

3So Moses said to the people, “Arm some of your men to go to war against the Midianites and to carry out the LORD’s vengeance on them. 4Send into battle a thousand men from each of the tribes of Israel.” 5So twelve thousand men armed for battle, a thousand from each tribe, were supplied from the clans of Israel. 6Moses sent them into battle, a thousand from each tribe, along with Phinehas son of Eleazar, the priest, who took with him articles from the sanctuary and the trumpets for signaling. Nu 10:9; Jdg 11:36; Ps 94:1

7They fought against Midian, as the LORD commanded Moses, and killed every man. 8Among their victims were Evi, Rekem, Zur, Hur and Reba—the five kings of Midian. They also killed Balaam son of Beor with the sword. 9The Israelites captured the Midianite women and children and took all the Midianite herds, flocks and goods as plunder. 10They burned all the towns where the Midianites had settled, as well as all their camps. 11They took all the plunder and spoils, including the people and animals, 12and brought the captives, spoils and plunder to Moses and Eleazar the priest and the Israelite assembly at their camp on the plains of Moab, by the Jordan across from Jericho.[a] Dt 20:13; Jdg 21:11; Jos 13:21-22

13Moses, Eleazar the priest and all the leaders of the community went to meet them outside the camp. 14Moses was angry with the officers of the army—the commanders of thousands and commanders of hundreds—who returned from the battle. Ex 18:21; Dt 1:15

15“Have you allowed all the women to live?” he asked them. 16“They were the ones who followed Balaam’s advice and were the means of turning the Israelites away from the LORD in what happened at Peor, so that a plague struck the LORD’s people. 17Now kill all the boys. And kill every woman who has slept with a man, 18but save for yourselves every girl who has never slept with a man.

19“All of you who have killed anyone or touched anyone who was killed must stay outside the camp seven days. On the third and seventh days you must purify yourselves and your captives. 20Purify every garment as well as everything made of leather, goat hair or wood.” Nu 19:12,16

21Then Eleazar the priest said to the soldiers who had gone into battle, “This is the requirement of the law that the LORD gave Moses: 22Gold, silver, bronze, iron, tin, lead 23and anything else that can withstand fire must be put through the fire, and then it will be clean. But it must also be purified with the water of cleansing. And whatever cannot withstand fire must be put through that water. 24On the seventh day wash your clothes and you will be clean. Then you may come into the camp.”

Dividing the Spoils

25The LORD said to Moses, 26“You and Eleazar the priest and the family heads of the community are to count all the people and animals that were captured. 27Divide the spoils between the soldiers who took part in the battle and the rest of the community. 28From the soldiers who fought in the battle, set apart as tribute for the LORD one out of every five hundred, whether persons, cattle, donkeys, sheep or goats. 29Take this tribute from their half share and give it to Eleazar the priest as the LORD’s part. 30From the Israelites’ half, select one out of every fifty, whether persons, cattle, donkeys, sheep, goats or other animals. Give them to the Levites, who are responsible for the care of the LORD’s tabernacle.” 31So Moses and Eleazar the priest did as the LORD commanded Moses.

32The plunder remaining from the spoils that the soldiers took was 675,000 sheep, 3372,000 cattle, 3461,000 donkeys 35and 32,000 women who had never slept with a man.

36The half share of those who fought in the battle was:

337,500 sheep, 37of which the tribute for the LORD was 675;

[a] 12 Hebrew *Jordan of Jericho*; possibly an ancient name for the Jordan River

38 36,000 cattle, of which the tribute for the
LORD was 72;
39 30,500 donkeys, of which the tribute for the
LORD was 61;
40 16,000 people, of which the tribute for the
LORD was 32.

41 Moses gave the tribute to Eleazar the priest as
the LORD's part, as the LORD commanded Moses.
42 The half belonging to the Israelites, which
Moses set apart from that of the fighting men—
43 the community's half—was 337,500 sheep,
44 36,000 cattle, 45 30,500 donkeys 46 and 16,000 people. 47 From the Israelites' half, Moses selected one
out of every fifty persons and animals, as the LORD
commanded him, and gave them to the Levites,
who were responsible for the care of the LORD's
tabernacle.
48 Then the officers who were over the units of
the army—the commanders of thousands and
commanders of hundreds—went to Moses 49 and
said to him, "Your servants have counted the soldiers under our command, and not one is missing.
50 So we have brought as an offering to the LORD
the gold articles each of us acquired—armlets,
bracelets, signet rings, earrings and necklaces—to
make atonement for ourselves before the LORD."
51 Moses and Eleazar the priest accepted from
them the gold—all the crafted articles. 52 All the
gold from the commanders of thousands and
commanders of hundreds that Moses and Eleazar
presented as a gift to the LORD weighed 16,750
shekels.[a] 53 Each soldier had taken plunder for
himself. 54 Moses and Eleazar the priest accepted
the gold from the commanders of thousands and
commanders of hundreds and brought it into the
Tent of Meeting as a memorial for the Israelites
before the LORD. Ex 28:12; Dt 20:14

The Transjordan Tribes

32 The Reubenites and Gadites, who had very
large herds and flocks, saw that the lands of
Jazer and Gilead were suitable for livestock. 2 So
they came to Moses and Eleazar the priest and to
the leaders of the community, and said, 3 "Ataroth,
Dibon, Jazer, Nimrah, Heshbon, Elealeh, Sebam,
Nebo and Beon— 4 the land the LORD subdued
before the people of Israel—are suitable for livestock, and your servants have livestock. 5 If we have
found favor in your eyes," they said, "let this land
be given to your servants as our possession. Do
not make us cross the Jordan." Ex 12:38; Nu 21:32,34
6 Moses said to the Gadites and Reubenites,
"Shall your countrymen go to war while you sit
here? 7 Why do you discourage the Israelites from
going over into the land the LORD has given them?
8 This is what your fathers did when I sent them
from Kadesh Barnea to look over the land. 9 After
they went up to the Valley of Eshcol and viewed
the land, they discouraged the Israelites from entering the land the LORD had given them. 10 The
LORD's anger was aroused that day and he swore
this oath: 11 'Because they have not followed me
wholeheartedly, not one of the men twenty years
old or more who came up out of Egypt will see the
land I promised on oath to Abraham, Isaac and
Jacob— 12 not one except Caleb son of Jephunneh
the Kenizzite and Joshua son of Nun, for they
followed the LORD wholeheartedly.' 13 The LORD's
anger burned against Israel and he made them
wander in the desert forty years, until the whole
generation of those who had done evil in his sight
was gone. Nu 13:27-14:4; Dt 1:19-25; Ps 63:8
14 "And here you are, a brood of sinners, standing in the place of your fathers and making the
LORD even more angry with Israel. 15 If you turn
away from following him, he will again leave all
this people in the desert, and you will be the cause
of their destruction." Dt 30:17-18; 2Ch 7:20
16 Then they came up to him and said, "We
would like to build pens here for our livestock and
cities for our women and children. 17 But we are
ready to arm ourselves and go ahead of the Israelites until we have brought them to their place.
Meanwhile our women and children will live in
fortified cities, for protection from the inhabitants
of the land. 18 We will not return to our homes
until every Israelite has received his inheritance.
19 We will not receive any inheritance with them on
the other side of the Jordan, because our inheritance has come to us on the east side of the Jordan." Jos 4:12-13; 12:1; 22:1-4
20 Then Moses said to them, "If you will do
this—if you will arm yourselves before the LORD
for battle, 21 and if all of you will go armed over the
Jordan before the LORD until he has driven his
enemies out before him— 22 then when the land is
subdued before the LORD, you may return and be
free from your obligation to the LORD and to Israel.
And this land will be your possession before the
LORD. Dt 3:18-20
23 "But if you fail to do this, you will be sinning
against the LORD; and you may be sure that your
sin will find you out. 24 Build cities for your women
and children, and pens for your flocks, but do
what you have promised." Ge 4:7
25 The Gadites and Reubenites said to Moses,
"We your servants will do as our lord commands.
26 Our children and wives, our flocks and herds will
remain here in the cities of Gilead. 27 But your
servants, every man armed for battle, will cross
over to fight before the LORD, just as our lord
says." Jos 1:14
28 Then Moses gave orders about them to Eleazar the priest and Joshua son of Nun and to the

[a] *52* That is, about 420 pounds (about 190 kilograms)

family heads of the Israelite tribes. 29He said to them, "If the Gadites and Reubenites, every man armed for battle, cross over the Jordan with you before the LORD, then when the land is subdued before you, give them the land of Gilead as their possession. 30But if they do not cross over with you armed, they must accept their possession with you in Canaan." Dt 3:18-20; Jos 1:13

31The Gadites and Reubenites answered, "Your servants will do what the LORD has said. 32We will cross over before the LORD into Canaan armed, but the property we inherit will be on this side of the Jordan."

33Then Moses gave to the Gadites, the Reubenites and the half-tribe of Manasseh son of Joseph the kingdom of Sihon king of the Amorites and the kingdom of Og king of Bashan—the whole land with its cities and the territory around them.

34The Gadites built up Dibon, Ataroth, Aroer, 35Atroth Shophan, Jazer, Jogbehah, 36Beth Nimrah and Beth Haran as fortified cities, and built pens for their flocks. 37And the Reubenites rebuilt Heshbon, Elealeh and Kiriathaim, 38as well as Nebo and Baal Meon (these names were changed) and Sibmah. They gave names to the cities they rebuilt. ver 3; Dt 2:36

39The descendants of Makir son of Manasseh went to Gilead, captured it and drove out the Amorites who were there. 40So Moses gave Gilead to the Makirites, the descendants of Manasseh, and they settled there. 41Jair, a descendant of Manasseh, captured their settlements and called them Havvoth Jair.[a] 42And Nobah captured Kenath and its surrounding settlements and called it Nobah after himself. Ge 50:23; Dt 3:14; 2Sa 18:18

Stages in Israel's Journey

33 Here are the stages in the journey of the Israelites when they came out of Egypt by divisions under the leadership of Moses and Aaron. 2At the LORD's command Moses recorded the stages in their journey. This is their journey by stages: Ps 77:20; Mic 6:4

3The Israelites set out from Rameses on
the fifteenth day of the first month, the day
after the Passover. They marched out boldly
in full view of all the Egyptians, 4who were
burying all their firstborn, whom the LORD
had struck down among them; for the LORD
had brought judgment on their gods.

5The Israelites left Rameses and camped at
Succoth.

6They left Succoth and camped at Etham,
on the edge of the desert. Ex 13:20

7They left Etham, turned back to Pi Hahiroth, to the east of Baal Zephon, and camped near Migdol. Ex 14:2

8They left Pi Hahiroth[b] and passed through the sea into the desert, and when they had traveled for three days in the Desert of Etham, they camped at Marah. Ex 14:22

9They left Marah and went to Elim, where there were twelve springs and seventy palm trees, and they camped there. Ex 15:27

10They left Elim and camped by the Red Sea.[c]

11They left the Red Sea and camped in the Desert of Sin. Ex 16:1

12They left the Desert of Sin and camped at Dophkah.

13They left Dophkah and camped at Alush.

14They left Alush and camped at Rephidim, where there was no water for the people to drink.

15They left Rephidim and camped in the Desert of Sinai. Ex 17:1; 19:1

16They left the Desert of Sinai and camped at Kibroth Hattaavah. Nu 11:34

17They left Kibroth Hattaavah and camped at Hazeroth. Nu 11:35

18They left Hazeroth and camped at Rithmah.

19They left Rithmah and camped at Rimmon Perez.

20They left Rimmon Perez and camped at Libnah. Jos 10:29

21They left Libnah and camped at Rissah.

22They left Rissah and camped at Kehelathah.

23They left Kehelathah and camped at Mount Shepher.

24They left Mount Shepher and camped at Haradah.

25They left Haradah and camped at Makheloth.

26They left Makheloth and camped at Tahath.

27They left Tahath and camped at Terah.

28They left Terah and camped at Mithcah.

29They left Mithcah and camped at Hashmonah.

30They left Hashmonah and camped at Moseroth. Dt 10:6

31They left Moseroth and camped at Bene Jaakan.

32They left Bene Jaakan and camped at Hor Haggidgad.

33They left Hor Haggidgad and camped at Jotbathah.

[a] 41 Or *them the settlements of Jair* [b] 8 Many manuscripts of the Masoretic Text, Samaritan Pentateuch and Vulgate; most manuscripts of the Masoretic Text *left from before Hahiroth* [c] 10 Hebrew *Yam Suph*; that is, Sea of Reeds; also in verse 11

34They left Jotbathah and camped at
Abronah.
35They left Abronah and camped at Ezion
Geber. Dt 2:8
36They left Ezion Geber and camped at
Kadesh, in the Desert of Zin. Nu 20:1
37They left Kadesh and camped at Mount
Hor, on the border of Edom. 38At the LORD's
command Aaron the priest went up Mount
Hor, where he died on the first day of the
fifth month of the fortieth year after the Israelites came out of Egypt. 39Aaron was a hundred and twenty-three years old when he
died on Mount Hor. Nu 20:22,25-28; Dt 10:6
40The Canaanite king of Arad, who lived
in the Negev of Canaan, heard that the Israelites were coming. Nu 21:1
41They left Mount Hor and camped at
Zalmonah.
42They left Zalmonah and camped at Punon.
43They left Punon and camped at Oboth.
44They left Oboth and camped at Iye Abarim, on the border of Moab.
45They left Iyim[a] and camped at Dibon
Gad.
46They left Dibon Gad and camped at Almon Diblathaim.
47They left Almon Diblathaim and
camped in the mountains of Abarim, near
Nebo.
48They left the mountains of Abarim and
camped on the plains of Moab by the Jordan
across from Jericho.[b] 49There on the plains
of Moab they camped along the Jordan from
Beth Jeshimoth to Abel Shittim. Nu 22:1; 25:1

50On the plains of Moab by the Jordan across
from Jericho the LORD said to Moses, 51"Speak to
the Israelites and say to them: 'When you cross the
Jordan into Canaan, 52drive out all the inhabitants
of the land before you. Destroy all their carved
images and their cast idols, and demolish all their
high places. 53Take possession of the land and settle in it, for I have given you the land to possess.
54Distribute the land by lot, according to your
clans. To a larger group give a larger inheritance,
and to a smaller group a smaller one. Whatever
falls to them by lot will be theirs. Distribute it
according to your ancestral tribes. Ex 23:24
55" 'But if you do not drive out the inhabitants
of the land, those you allow to remain will become
barbs in your eyes and thorns in your sides. They
will give you trouble in the land where you will
live. 56And then I will do to you what I plan to do
to them.' " Jos 23:13; Jdg 2:3; Ps 106:36

Boundaries of Canaan

34 The LORD said to Moses, 2"Command the
Israelites and say to them: 'When you enter
Canaan, the land that will be allotted to you as an
inheritance will have these boundaries: Ge 17:8

3" 'Your southern side will include some of the
Desert of Zin along the border of Edom. On the
east, your southern boundary will start from
the end of the Salt Sea,[c] 4cross south of Scorpion[d] Pass, continue on to Zin and go south of
Kadesh Barnea. Then it will go to Hazar Addar
and over to Azmon, 5where it will turn, join the
Wadi of Egypt and end at the Sea.[e] Ge 15:18
6" 'Your western boundary will be the coast of
the Great Sea. This will be your boundary on the
west.
7" 'For your northern boundary, run a line from
the Great Sea to Mount Hor 8and from Mount
Hor to Lebo[f] Hamath. Then the boundary will
go to Zedad, 9continue to Ziphron and end at
Hazar Enan. This will be your boundary on the
north.
10" 'For your eastern boundary, run a line from
Hazar Enan to Shepham. 11The boundary will go
down from Shepham to Riblah on the east side of
Ain and continue along the slopes east of the Sea
of Kinnereth.[g] 12Then the boundary will go down
along the Jordan and end at the Salt Sea. Dt 3:17
" 'This will be your land, with its boundaries on
every side.' "
13Moses commanded the Israelites: "Assign this
land by lot as an inheritance. The LORD has ordered that it be given to the nine and a half tribes,
14because the families of the tribe of Reuben, the
tribe of Gad and the half-tribe of Manasseh have
received their inheritance. 15These two and a half
tribes have received their inheritance on the east
side of the Jordan of Jericho,[h] toward the sunrise." Nu 32:33; Jos 14:1-5
16The LORD said to Moses, 17"These are the
names of the men who are to assign the land for
you as an inheritance: Eleazar the priest and Joshua son of Nun. 18And appoint one leader from
each tribe to help assign the land. 19These are their
names: Nu 1:4,16; Jos 14:1

Caleb son of Jephunneh,
from the tribe of Judah; Ge 29:35; Nu 26:65
20Shemuel son of Ammihud,
from the tribe of Simeon; Ge 49:5
21Elidad son of Kislon,
from the tribe of Benjamin; Ge 49:27
22Bukki son of Jogli,
the leader from the tribe of Dan;
23Hanniel son of Ephod,

[a]45 That is, Iye Abarim [b]48 Hebrew *Jordan of Jericho*; possibly an ancient name for the Jordan River; also in verse 50
[c]3 That is, the Dead Sea; also in verse 12 [d]4 Hebrew *Akrabbim* [e]5 That is, the Mediterranean; also in verses 6 and 7
[f]8 Or *to the entrance to* [g]11 That is, Galilee [h]15 *Jordan of Jericho* was possibly an ancient name for the Jordan River.

the leader from the tribe of Manasseh son of Joseph;
24 Kemuel son of Shiphtan,
the leader from the tribe of Ephraim son of Joseph; Nu 1:32,34
25 Elizaphan son of Parnach,
the leader from the tribe of Zebulun;
26 Paltiel son of Azzan,
the leader from the tribe of Issachar;
27 Ahihud son of Shelomi,
the leader from the tribe of Asher;
28 Pedahel son of Ammihud,
the leader from the tribe of Naphtali."

29 These are the men the LORD commanded to assign the inheritance to the Israelites in the land of Canaan.

Towns for the Levites

35 On the plains of Moab by the Jordan across from Jericho,[a] the LORD said to Moses, 2 "Command the Israelites to give the Levites towns to live in from the inheritance the Israelites will possess. And give them pasturelands around the towns. 3 Then they will have towns to live in and pasturelands for their cattle, flocks and all their other livestock. Lev 25:32-34; Jos 14:3-4

4 "The pasturelands around the towns that you give the Levites will extend out fifteen hundred feet[b] from the town wall. 5 Outside the town, measure three thousand feet[c] on the east side, three thousand on the south side, three thousand on the west and three thousand on the north, with the town in the center. They will have this area as pastureland for the towns.

Cities of Refuge

6 "Six of the towns you give the Levites will be cities of refuge, to which a person who has killed someone may flee. In addition, give them forty-two other towns. 7 In all you must give the Levites forty-eight towns, together with their pasturelands. 8 The towns you give the Levites from the land the Israelites possess are to be given in proportion to the inheritance of each tribe: Take many towns from a tribe that has many, but few from one that has few." Nu 26:54; Jos 20:7-9

9 Then the LORD said to Moses: 10 "Speak to the Israelites and say to them: 'When you cross the Jordan into Canaan, 11 select some towns to be your cities of refuge, to which a person who has killed someone accidentally may flee. 12 They will be places of refuge from the avenger, so that a person accused of murder may not die before he stands trial before the assembly. 13 These six towns you give will be your cities of refuge. 14 Give three on this side of the Jordan and three in Canaan as cities of refuge. 15 These six towns will be a place of refuge for Israelites, aliens and any other people living among them, so that anyone who has killed another accidentally can flee there. Ex 21:13; Jos 20:3

16 " 'If a man strikes someone with an iron object so that he dies, he is a murderer; the murderer shall be put to death. 17 Or if anyone has a stone in his hand that could kill, and he strikes someone so that he dies, he is a murderer; the murderer shall be put to death. 18 Or if anyone has a wooden object in his hand that could kill, and he hits someone so that he dies, he is a murderer; the murderer shall be put to death. 19 The avenger of blood shall put the murderer to death; when he meets him, he shall put him to death. 20 If anyone with malice aforethought shoves another or throws something at him intentionally so that he dies 21 or if in hostility he hits him with his fist so that he dies, that person shall be put to death; he is a murderer. The avenger of blood shall put the murderer to death when he meets him. Ex 21:12,14

22 " 'But if without hostility someone suddenly shoves another or throws something at him unintentionally 23 or, without seeing him, drops a stone on him that could kill him, and he dies, then since he was not his enemy and he did not intend to harm him, 24 the assembly must judge between him and the avenger of blood according to these regulations. 25 The assembly must protect the one accused of murder from the avenger of blood and send him back to the city of refuge to which he fled. He must stay there until the death of the high priest, who was anointed with the holy oil.

26 " 'But if the accused ever goes outside the limits of the city of refuge to which he has fled 27 and the avenger of blood finds him outside the city, the avenger of blood may kill the accused without being guilty of murder. 28 The accused must stay in his city of refuge until the death of the high priest; only after the death of the high priest may he return to his own property.

29 " 'These are to be legal requirements for you throughout the generations to come, wherever you live.

30 " 'Anyone who kills a person is to be put to death as a murderer only on the testimony of witnesses. But no one is to be put to death on the testimony of only one witness. Dt 17:6; Mt 18:16

31 " 'Do not accept a ransom for the life of a murderer, who deserves to die. He must surely be put to death.

32 " 'Do not accept a ransom for anyone who has fled to a city of refuge and so allow him to go back and live on his own land before the death of the high priest.

33 " 'Do not pollute the land where you are.

[a] 1 Hebrew *Jordan of Jericho*; possibly an ancient name for the Jordan River [b] 4 Hebrew *a thousand cubits* (about 450 meters) [c] 5 Hebrew *two thousand cubits* (about 900 meters)

Bloodshed pollutes the land, and atonement cannot be made for the land on which blood has been
shed, except by the blood of the one who shed it.
[34]Do not defile the land where you live and where
I dwell, for I, the LORD, dwell among the Israelites.'" Dt 4:41-43; 19:1-14; Jos 20:1-9

Inheritance of Zelophehad's Daughters

36 The family heads of the clan of Gilead son
of Makir, the son of Manasseh, who were
from the clans of the descendants of Joseph, came
and spoke before Moses and the leaders, the heads
of the Israelite families. [2]They said, "When the
LORD commanded my lord to give the land as an
inheritance to the Israelites by lot, he ordered you
to give the inheritance of our brother Zelophehad
to his daughters. [3]Now suppose they marry men
from other Israelite tribes; then their inheritance
will be taken from our ancestral inheritance and
added to that of the tribe they marry into. And so
part of the inheritance allotted to us will be taken
away. [4]When the Year of Jubilee for the Israelites
comes, their inheritance will be added to that of
the tribe into which they marry, and their property
will be taken from the tribal inheritance of our
forefathers." Lev 25:10; Nu 26:33; 26:29

[5]Then at the LORD's command Moses gave this
order to the Israelites: "What the tribe of the
descendants of Joseph is saying is right. [6]This is
what the LORD commands for Zelophehad's
daughters: They may marry anyone they please as
long as they marry within the tribal clan of their
father. [7]No inheritance in Israel is to pass from
tribe to tribe, for every Israelite shall keep the tribal land inherited from his forefathers. [8]Every
daughter who inherits land in any Israelite tribe
must marry someone in her father's tribal clan, so
that every Israelite will possess the inheritance of
his fathers. [9]No inheritance may pass from tribe to
tribe, for each Israelite tribe is to keep the land it
inherits." 1Ki 21:3; 1Ch 23:22

[10]So Zelophehad's daughters did as the LORD
commanded Moses. [11]Zelophehad's daughters—
Mahlah, Tirzah, Hoglah, Milcah and Noah—married their cousins on their father's side. [12]They
married within the clans of the descendants of
Manasseh son of Joseph, and their inheritance remained in their father's clan and tribe. Nu 27:1-11

[13]These are the commands and regulations the
LORD gave through Moses to the Israelites on the
plains of Moab by the Jordan across from Jericho.[a] Lev 26:46; Nu 22:1

[a] 13 Hebrew *Jordan of Jericho*; possibly an ancient name for the Jordan River

INTRODUCTION

DEUTERONOMY

The desert wanderings were, at last, over. A new generation was on the scene. Canaan—the "promised land"—was just across the border. The Israelites were anxious to invade and claim the territory. For almost 500 years they had lived away from home, like fugitives. They longed to settle down and deepen their roots once again. But a strategic matter had to be settled beforehand. This vast multitude of people needed to be instructed and warned. Once they moved into Canaan, it would be easy to forget many of those hard-learned lessons from the desert. With the possibility of becoming fat and presumptuous in Canaan, the Israelites could easily drift into moral compromise and direct disobedience. So God pulled them aside and directed Moses to speak, to challenge, to warn and to remind.

WRITER: *Moses*

DATE: *c.1406 B.C.*

PURPOSE: *To give counsel to people about to make a great transition*

KEY MESSAGE: *Devote yourself wholeheartedly to Almighty God*

KEY TERM: *"Remember"*

TIME LINE

	2200BC	2100	2000	1900	1800	1700	1600	1500	1400
Moses' birth (c.1526 B.C.)									
The plagues; The Passover (c.1446 B.C.)									
The exodus (c.1446 B.C.)									
Desert wanderings (c.1446-1406 B.C.)									
The Ten Commandments (c.1445 B.C.)									
Book of Deuteronomy written (c.1406 B.C.)									
Moses dies; Joshua becomes leader (c.1406 B.C.)									
Israelites enter Canaan (c.1406 B.C.)									

Remember! Remember! Remember!

	LOOKING BACK	LOOKING UP	LOOKING AHEAD	
DESERT WANDERING	REMEMBER! Failure at Kadesh Faithfulness of God	REMEMBER! Blessings accompany obedience Compromises weaken distinctives Consequences follow disobedience	REMEMBER! The land is yours, possess it! The Lord is holy, obey Him!	CONQUERING CANAAN
	CHAPTERS 1–4	*CHAPTERS 5–26*	*CHAPTERS 27–34*	

LOCATION	**Everything occurs on the edge of the promised land of Canaan**
LEADERSHIP	**At the beginning of the book MOSES is the leader *(34:5)* . . . . . . by the end of the book JOSHUA is the leader *(1:38; 34:9)***
TIME	**The events recorded in Deuteronomy were first spoken *(1:6)* then written *(31:24)* during a period of forty days. Compare Deuteronomy 1:3; 34:8; and Joshua 4:19.**

There are certain junctures in our lives where we need counsel or advice. Often those times of counsel are related to transitional periods. In other words, when we are about to enter a new phase of life's experiences, it is wise to get counsel and straightforward advice from those who possess wisdom and spiritual maturity. At major transitions in life, advice is needed more than most of us realize.

Deuteronomy is a book of counsel given to people who were about to make a great transition in their lives. It is addressed to the people of Israel at a vital time in their experience as a nation and as God's people. They have just finished forty hot and miserable years walking in circles in the desert. They've never had the experience of entering the promised land.

Deuteronomy takes us from the generation of wanderings and brings the people of God right back to the edge of Canaan. Here they are, at the edge of the promised land once again. Forty years earlier they had refused to enter the land because of their fear and lack of faith. Now Moses calls them aside and gives them counsel and advice to prepare them for their next big step of faith. God is about to have them take a leap of faith, and they have some lessons to learn before they will be ready to move forward.

The Law . . . Take Two

As we look at Deuteronomy, let's begin with the name. It's a difficult name to pronounce. Part of the reason is that it's a Greek word. "Deuteros" means "second." "Nomos" means "law." When you put "deuteros" and "nomos" together, you get "Deuteronomy"—the "second law."

This title, however, doesn't merely refer to a repetition of the same law that was given earlier in the Pentateuch. This term means "a summary, a reminder, a repeating of God's law." As the Israelites stood at the edge of the promised land, Moses told the people to look back and to remember God's law. So here in Deuteronomy we have a reaffirming, a reemphasizing of the law.

Deuteronomy seeks to revisit the truth the Israelites already knew. They knew these teachings, but they needed to hear them again. All of us need to go back to those basic truths of the faith at important times in our lives. We need to rehearse them in our minds and let them fill our hearts again. In the same way, the Israelites needed to hear God's law in a new and fresh way as they prepared to embark on a whole new chapter in their national history.

On the Edge of the Promise . . . Again

As Deuteronomy begins we find the Israelites in the land of Moab. They were on the other side of the Jordan River—just about to cross over, then invade and conquer the land of Canaan in God's power. The location is significant because they've been there before. Back in the book of Numbers they came right up to the land of Moab before sending in the twelve spies. Because they were paralyzed by fear and refused to enter the land, they ended up wandering in the desert for forty years. Now they were right back where they started.

The timing of God's instruction and teaching in this book can be determined by looking at three Scriptural references:

Deuteronomy 1:3 opens with the first day of the eleventh month in the fortieth year. The exodus is the point of reference for this dating. So forty years after the exodus, Moses began to instruct and warn the people.

In *Joshua 4:19* we read that the Israelites crossed the Jordan on the tenth day of the first month in the next year. If you figure thirty days per month, you come up with seventy days in between. But this doesn't mean that it took seventy days for God to give the teaching in the book of Deuteronomy to the people. It didn't take quite that long.

Deuteronomy 34:8 records that the people mourned for Moses for thirty days after his death. When you subtract thirty from seventy, you come up with a final tally of forty days of instruction. Over the course of this time, God instructed the Israelites so they would be prepared to enter the land and remain faithful to Him.

A Single-minded Loyalty

The purpose of these messages given by Moses was to arouse Israel's loyalty to God. If I were to select a key section for the entire book, it would be Deuteronomy 6:4–7:

> *Hear, O Israel: The Lord our God, the Lord is one. Love the Lord your God with all your heart and with all your soul and with all your strength. These commandments that I give you today are to be upon your hearts. Impress them on your children. Talk about them when you sit at home and when you walk along the road, when you lie down and when you get up.*

Moses instructed the people to love God "with all your heart and with all your soul and with all your strength." It is rare to find someone who loves God that much. We may say we do, but it's difficult to find someone that serious in their walk with God—so serious that from the moment you wake up until you fall asleep at night, throughout the whole day God is central in all you think, say and do. That kind of commitment means you evaluate everything with God's will in mind. Your value judgments are determined by His will and law. Your character is formed and shaped on the basis of His character and attributes. Direction in life is established on His plan for you. That's loving Him with heart and soul and strength. He's not playing around with those words. These words are to mark your life and your children's lives and are to characterize life in your home.

As we hear these exhortations, we need to keep in mind that this is a second generation of people who have been wandering in the desert. A significant number of them had been born during the desert wanderings, and they needed to know the Lord's laws and teachings if they were to faithfully uphold His will and represent His name.

Three Things to Remember

As we read the book of Deuteronomy, we soon discover that Moses directed the Israelites to learn three important lessons. First, *remember the faithfulness of God in the past.* In the first four chapters, Moses retraced their past forty years. Moses wanted the Israelites to remember their failure at Kadesh Barnea and their tendency toward unbelief. He wanted them to remember their days in the desert. If nothing more, to keep this in mind would serve as a motivation never to go back. He wanted them to remember that, in spite of their failure at Kadesh Barnea and their frequent unbelief, God always proved Himself faithful.

When we look back in our own lives, we can see that in our times of failure and unbelief, God never left us. He reproved us. He disciplined us. He may even have scarred us so we'd never forget it, but He never left us. God has been faithful. Never forget it! One of the motivating factors of living for God in the future is the reminder of those days in the past when we didn't live for Him and the terrible consequences that occurred. It is a good discipline to pause and look back. To think about your past. To recall your times of failure, wandering, blessing, learning, pain, pleasure, disappointment and joy.

The theme changes when we get to chapters 5–26. In this next section the emphasis is not on God's faithfulness, but on His holiness. And so the second imperative is: *remember the holiness of God in the present*. Let me summarize these chapters by making three statements.

First, *blessings accompany obedience*. When we consider the holiness of God, then God says, "Obey Me." If we faithfully obey, God blesses. Second, *compromises weaken distinctives*. When the Lord gives us a standard and we begin to compromise, our distinctive as His children begins to weaken. Third, *consequences follow disobedience*. It was true for Israel, and it is just as true for us today. When we walk in the presence of a holy God, the sin of disobedience will always carry a steep price.

The last section of Deuteronomy (chapters 27–34) contains the third command: *remember the warnings of God for the future*. Before the book came to an end, Moses reminded the people: "Listen to God's warnings for the future." God proclaimed two things to Moses in this last section. First, *the land is yours . . . possess it*. The people must not doubt. They must believe in God's promises. Second, *the Lord is God . . . obey Him*. Their parents and grandparents had died in the desert because they did not have the faith to possess the land. It was this generation's turn to obey God and step into the future with confidence in God's power and the assurance of His faithfulness.

I challenge you today to *look back* and thank God for His faithfulness. Also, take some time to *look at today*. Examine your life and consider it in light of His holiness. Finally, *look ahead* and listen to the warnings God gives you. Learn from the experiences of the Israelites, and let the word of God dwell in your heart richly. This personal exercise will liberate and strengthen you for the journey ahead.

Remembering God's Faithfulness Chapters 1–4

The time had finally come. After wandering in the desert for four decades, the people received their marching orders. It was time to enter the land of Canaan. As God prepared the people to move onward, He had them pause and look back. God had His people remember their experience forty years earlier. Although this memory may have been painful, it was necessary. The Lord had said, "The land is yours," but they refused to take it. They needed to remember their rebellion, their wandering in the desert and God's faithfulness to care for them even when they were hardhearted. Just as the Israelites had to look back and remember their Lord's provision, leading and love, we must also reflect on how God has led and cared for us. The discipline of remembering God's faithfulness in the past will strengthen us for our journey in the present.

The Command to Leave Horeb

1 These are the words Moses spoke to all Israel in the desert east of the Jordan—that is, in the Arabah—opposite Suph, between Paran and Tophel, Laban, Hazeroth and Dizahab. 2(It takes eleven days to go from Horeb to Kadesh Barnea by the Mount Seir road.) Dt 19:23

3In the fortieth year, on the first day of the eleventh month, Moses proclaimed to the Israelites all that the LORD had commanded him concerning them. 4This was after he had defeated Sihon king of the Amorites, who reigned in Heshbon, and at Edrei had defeated Og king of Bashan, who reigned in Ashtaroth. Nu 21:33-35; 33:38

5East of the Jordan in the territory of Moab, Moses began to expound this law, saying:

6The LORD our God said to us at Horeb, "You have stayed long enough at this mountain. 7Break camp and advance into the hill country of the Amorites; go to all the neighboring peoples in the Arabah, in the mountains, in the western foothills, in the Negev and along the coast, to the land of the Canaanites and to Lebanon, as far as the great river, the Euphrates. 8See, I have given you this land. Go in and take possession of the land that the LORD swore he would give to your fathers—to Abraham, Isaac and Jacob—and to their descendants after them." Ge 12:7; Dt 11:24; Nu 10:13

The Appointment of Leaders

9At that time I said to you, "You are too heavy a burden for me to carry alone. 10The LORD your God has increased your numbers so that today you are as many as the stars in the sky. 11May the LORD, the God of your fathers, increase you a thousand times and bless you as he has promised! 12But how can I bear your problems and your burdens and your disputes all by myself? 13Choose some wise, understanding and respected men from each of your tribes, and I will set them over you."

14You answered me, "What you propose to do is good."

15So I took the leading men of your tribes, wise and respected men, and appointed them to have authority over you—as commanders of thousands, of hundreds, of fifties and of tens and as tribal officials. 16And I charged your judges at that time: Hear the disputes between your brothers and judge fairly, whether the case is between brother Israelites or between one of them and an alien. 17Do not show partiality in judging; hear both small and great alike. Do not be afraid of any man, for judgment belongs to God. Bring me any case too hard for you, and I will hear it. 18And at that time I told you everything you were to do.

Spies Sent Out

19Then, as the LORD our God commanded us, we set out from Horeb and went toward the hill country of the Amorites through all that vast and dreadful desert that you have seen, and so we reached Kadesh Barnea. 20Then I said to you, "You have reached the hill country of the Amorites, which the LORD our God is giving us. 21See, the LORD your God has given you the land. Go up and take possession of it as the LORD, the God of your fathers, told you. Do not be afraid; do not be discouraged." Jos 1:6,9,18; Dt 8:15

LIVING  INSIGHT

Want to know the shortest route to ineffectiveness? Start running scared. Try to cover every base at all times. Take no chances. Say no to courage and yes to caution. Expect the worst. Keep yourself safely tucked away in the secure nest of inaction. And before you know it, loneliness and isolation will set in.

(See Deuteronomy 1:21.)

22Then all of you came to me and said, "Let us send men ahead to spy out the land for us and bring back a report about the route we are to take and the towns we will come to." Nu 13:1-3

23The idea seemed good to me; so I selected twelve of you, one man from each tribe. 24They left and went up into the hill country, and came to the Valley of Eshcol and explored it. 25Taking with them some of the fruit of the land, they brought it down to us and reported, "It is a good land that the LORD our God is giving us." Nu 13:21-25

Rebellion Against the LORD

26But you were unwilling to go up; you rebelled against the command of the LORD your God. 27You grumbled in your tents and said, "The LORD hates us; so he brought us out of Egypt to deliver us into

the hands of the Amorites to destroy us. [28]Where
can we go? Our brothers have made us lose heart.
They say, 'The people are stronger and taller than
we are; the cities are large, with walls up to the sky.
We even saw the Anakites there.'" Nu 14:1-4; Dt 9:28
[29]Then I said to you, "Do not be terrified; do
not be afraid of them. [30]The LORD your God, who
is going before you, will fight for you, as he did for
you in Egypt, before your very eyes, [31]and in the
desert. There you saw how the LORD your God
carried you, as a father carries his son, all the way
you went until you reached this place." Dt 32:10-12
[32]In spite of this, you did not trust in the LORD
your God, [33]who went ahead of you on your journey, in fire by night and in a cloud by day, to
search out places for you to camp and to show you
the way you should go. Ps 106:24; Ex 13:21
[34]When the LORD heard what you said, he was
angry and solemnly swore: [35]"Not a man of this
evil generation shall see the good land I swore to
give your forefathers, [36]except Caleb son of Jephunneh. He will see it, and I will give him and his
descendants the land he set his feet on, because he
followed the LORD wholeheartedly." Nu 14:23,28-30
[37]Because of you the LORD became angry with
me also and said, "You shall not enter it, either.
[38]But your assistant, Joshua son of Nun, will enter
it. Encourage him, because he will lead Israel to
inherit it. [39]And the little ones that you said would
be taken captive, your children who do not yet
know good from bad—they will enter the land. I
will give it to them and they will take possession of
it. [40]But as for you, turn around and set out toward
the desert along the route to the Red Sea.[a]"
[41]Then you replied, "We have sinned against
the LORD. We will go up and fight, as the LORD our
God commanded us." So every one of you put on
his weapons, thinking it easy to go up into the hill
country.
[42]But the LORD said to me, "Tell them, 'Do not
go up and fight, because I will not be with you.
You will be defeated by your enemies.'"
[43]So I told you, but you would not listen. You
rebelled against the LORD's command and in your
arrogance you marched up into the hill country.
[44]The Amorites who lived in those hills came out
against you; they chased you like a swarm of bees
and beat you down from Seir all the way to Hormah. [45]You came back and wept before the LORD,
but he paid no attention to your weeping and
turned a deaf ear to you. [46]And so you stayed in
Kadesh many days—all the time you spent there.

Wanderings in the Desert

2 Then we turned back and set out toward the
desert along the route to the Red Sea,[a] as the
LORD had directed me. For a long time we made
our way around the hill country of Seir.
[2]Then the LORD said to me, [3]"You have made
your way around this hill country long enough;
now turn north. [4]Give the people these orders:
'You are about to pass through the territory of
your brothers the descendants of Esau, who live in
Seir. They will be afraid of you, but be very careful.
[5]Do not provoke them to war, for I will not give
you any of their land, not even enough to put your
foot on. I have given Esau the hill country of Seir
as his own. [6]You are to pay them in silver for the
food you eat and the water you drink.'" Jos 24:4
[7]The LORD your God has blessed you in all the
work of your hands. He has watched over your
journey through this vast desert. These forty years
the LORD your God has been with you, and you
have not lacked anything. Dt 8:2-4
[8]So we went on past our brothers the descendants of Esau, who live in Seir. We turned from
the Arabah road, which comes up from Elath and
Ezion Geber, and traveled along the desert road of
Moab. 1Ki 9:26; Dt 1:1
[9]Then the LORD said to me, "Do not harass the
Moabites or provoke them to war, for I will not
give you any part of their land. I have given Ar to
the descendants of Lot as a possession."
[10](The Emites used to live there—a people
strong and numerous, and as tall as the Anakites.
[11]Like the Anakites, they too were considered
Rephaites, but the Moabites called them Emites.
[12]Horites used to live in Seir, but the descendants
of Esau drove them out. They destroyed the Horites from before them and settled in their place,
just as Israel did in the land the LORD gave them as
their possession.) ver 22; Ge 14:5
[13]And the LORD said, "Now get up and cross the
Zered Valley." So we crossed the valley.
[14]Thirty-eight years passed from the time we
left Kadesh Barnea until we crossed the Zered Valley. By then, that entire generation of fighting men
had perished from the camp, as the LORD had
sworn to them. [15]The LORD's hand was against
them until he had completely eliminated them
from the camp. Nu 14:29-35; Dt 1:34-35; Ps 106:26
[16]Now when the last of these fighting men
among the people had died, [17]the LORD said to me,
[18]"Today you are to pass by the region of Moab at
Ar. [19]When you come to the Ammonites, do not
harass them or provoke them to war, for I will not
give you possession of any land belonging to the
Ammonites. I have given it as a possession to the
descendants of Lot." ver 9; Ge 19:38
[20](That too was considered a land of the Rephaites, who used to live there; but the Ammonites
called them Zamzummites. [21]They were a people
strong and numerous, and as tall as the Anakites.

[a]40,1 Hebrew *Yam Suph*; that is, Sea of Reeds

The LORD destroyed them from before the Ammonites, who drove them out and settled in their
place. 22The LORD had done the same for the
descendants of Esau, who lived in Seir, when he
destroyed the Horites from before them. They
drove them out and have lived in their place to this
day. 23And as for the Avvites who lived in villages
as far as Gaza, the Caphtorites coming out from
Caphtor[a] destroyed them and settled in their
place.) Ge 10:14; Jos 13:3; Am 9:7

Defeat of Sihon King of Heshbon

24"Set out now and cross the Arnon Gorge. See,
I have given into your hand Sihon the Amorite,
king of Heshbon, and his country. Begin to take
possession of it and engage him in battle. 25This
very day I will begin to put the terror and fear of
you on all the nations under heaven. They will
hear reports of you and will tremble and be in
anguish because of you." Ex 15:14-16; Dt 11:25

26From the desert of Kedemoth I sent messengers to Sihon king of Heshbon offering peace and
saying, 27"Let us pass through your country. We
will stay on the main road; we will not turn aside
to the right or to the left. 28Sell us food to eat and
water to drink for their price in silver. Only let us
pass through on foot— 29as the descendants of
Esau, who live in Seir, and the Moabites, who live
in Ar, did for us—until we cross the Jordan into
the land the LORD our God is giving us." 30But
Sihon king of Heshbon refused to let us pass
through. For the LORD your God had made his
spirit stubborn and his heart obstinate in order to
give him into your hands, as he has now done.

31The LORD said to me, "See, I have begun to
deliver Sihon and his country over to you. Now
begin to conquer and possess his land." Dt 1:8

32When Sihon and all his army came out to
meet us in battle at Jahaz, 33the LORD our God
delivered him over to us and we struck him down,
together with his sons and his whole army. 34At
that time we took all his towns and completely
destroyed[b] them—men, women and children.
We left no survivors. 35But the livestock and the
plunder from the towns we had captured we carried off for ourselves. 36From Aroer on the rim of
the Arnon Gorge, and from the town in the gorge,
even as far as Gilead, not one town was too strong
for us. The LORD our God gave us all of them.
37But in accordance with the command of the
LORD our God, you did not encroach on any of the
land of the Ammonites, neither the land along
the course of the Jabbok nor that around the
towns in the hills. Dt 3:6; 7:2; Ge 32:22

Defeat of Og King of Bashan

3 Next we turned and went up along the road
toward Bashan, and Og king of Bashan with
his whole army marched out to meet us in battle
at Edrei. 2The LORD said to me, "Do not be afraid
of him, for I have handed him over to you with his
whole army and his land. Do to him what you did
to Sihon king of the Amorites, who reigned in
Heshbon." Nu 21:33

3So the LORD our God also gave into our hands
Og king of Bashan and all his army. We struck
them down, leaving no survivors. 4At that time we
took all his cities. There was not one of the sixty
cities that we did not take from them—the whole
region of Argob, Og's kingdom in Bashan. 5All
these cities were fortified with high walls and with
gates and bars, and there were also a great many
unwalled villages. 6We completely destroyed[b]
them, as we had done with Sihon king of Heshbon,
destroying[b] every city—men, women and children. 7But all the livestock and the plunder from
their cities we carried off for ourselves. Dt 2:24,34

8So at that time we took from these two kings
of the Amorites the territory east of the Jordan,
from the Arnon Gorge as far as Mount Hermon.
9(Hermon is called Sirion by the Sidonians; the
Amorites call it Senir.) 10We took all the towns on
the plateau, and all Gilead, and all Bashan as far as
Salecah and Edrei, towns of Og's kingdom in Bashan. 11(Only Og king of Bashan was left of the
remnant of the Rephaites. His bed[c] was made of
iron and was more than thirteen feet long and six
feet wide.[d] It is still in Rabbah of the Ammonites.) Ge 14:5; 2Sa 12:26; Ps 29:6

Division of the Land

12Of the land that we took over at that time, I
gave the Reubenites and the Gadites the territory
north of Aroer by the Arnon Gorge, including half
the hill country of Gilead, together with its towns.
13The rest of Gilead and also all of Bashan, the
kingdom of Og, I gave to the half tribe of Manasseh. (The whole region of Argob in Bashan used
to be known as a land of the Rephaites. 14Jair, a
descendant of Manasseh, took the whole region of
Argob as far as the border of the Geshurites and
the Maacathites; it was named after him, so that to
this day Bashan is called Havvoth Jair.[e]) 15And I
gave Gilead to Makir. 16But to the Reubenites and
the Gadites I gave the territory extending from
Gilead down to the Arnon Gorge (the middle of
the gorge being the border) and out to the Jabbok
River, which is the border of the Ammonites. 17Its
western border was the Jordan in the Arabah, from

[a] 23 That is, Crete [b] 34,6 The Hebrew term refers to the irrevocable giving over of things or persons to the LORD, often by totally destroying them. [c] 11 Or *sarcophagus* [d] 11 Hebrew *nine cubits long and four cubits wide* (about 4 meters long and 1.8 meters wide) [e] 14 Or *called the settlements of Jair*

Kinnereth to the Sea of the Arabah (the Salt
Sea[a]), below the slopes of Pisgah. Nu 32:32-38
18I commanded you at that time: "The LORD
your God has given you this land to take possession of it. But all your able-bodied men, armed for
battle, must cross over ahead of your brother Israelites. 19However, your wives, your children and
your livestock (I know you have much livestock)
may stay in the towns I have given you, 20until the
LORD gives rest to your brothers as he has to you,
and they too have taken over the land that the
LORD your God is giving them, across the Jordan.
After that, each of you may go back to the possession I have given you." Nu 32:17; Jos 1:14

Moses Forbidden to Cross the Jordan

21At that time I commanded Joshua: "You have
seen with your own eyes all that the LORD your
God has done to these two kings. The LORD will do
the same to all the kingdoms over there where you
are going. 22Do not be afraid of them; the LORD
your God himself will fight for you." Ex 14:14
23At that time I pleaded with the LORD: 24"O
Sovereign LORD, you have begun to show to your
servant your greatness and your strong hand. For
what god is there in heaven or on earth who can
do the deeds and mighty works you do? 25Let me
go over and see the good land beyond the Jordan—that fine hill country and Lebanon."
26But because of you the LORD was angry with
me and would not listen to me. "That is enough,"
the LORD said. "Do not speak to me anymore
about this matter. 27Go up to the top of Pisgah and
look west and north and south and east. Look at
the land with your own eyes, since you are not
going to cross this Jordan. 28But commission Joshua, and encourage and strengthen him, for he will
lead this people across and will cause them to inherit the land that you will see." 29So we stayed in
the valley near Beth Peor. Dt 1:37; Nu 27:12; Dt 34:6

Obedience Commanded

4 Hear now, O Israel, the decrees and laws I am
about to teach you. Follow them so that you
may live and may go in and take possession of the
land that the LORD, the God of your fathers, is
giving you. 2Do not add to what I command you
and do not subtract from it, but keep the commands of the LORD your God that I give you.
3You saw with your own eyes what the LORD did
at Baal Peor. The LORD your God destroyed from
among you everyone who followed the Baal of
Peor, 4but all of you who held fast to the LORD your
God are still alive today. Ps 106:28
5See, I have taught you decrees and laws as the
LORD my God commanded me, so that you may
follow them in the land you are entering to take
possession of it. 6Observe them carefully, for this
will show your wisdom and understanding to the
nations, who will hear about all these decrees and
say, "Surely this great nation is a wise and understanding people." 7What other nation is so great as
to have their gods near them the way the LORD our
God is near us whenever we pray to him? 8And
what other nation is so great as to have such righteous decrees and laws as this body of laws I am
setting before you today? 2Sa 7:23; Isa 55:6; 2Ti 3:15
9Only be careful, and watch yourselves closely
so that you do not forget the things your eyes have
seen or let them slip from your heart as long as
you live. Teach them to your children and to their

LIVING  **INSIGHT**

The task of "indoctrinating" children was a responsibility of the home, not of some institution or the combined efforts of a group of professionals. And the teaching was to be deliberate. The Hebrew term translated "teach" suggests "repeating," telling over and over again as well as modeling a consistent message.

(See Deuteronomy 4:9.)

children after them. 10Remember the day you
stood before the LORD your God at Horeb, when
he said to me, "Assemble the people before me to
hear my words so that they may learn to revere me
as long as they live in the land and may teach them
to their children." 11You came near and stood at
the foot of the mountain while it blazed with fire
to the very heavens, with black clouds and deep
darkness. 12Then the LORD spoke to you out of the
fire. You heard the sound of words but saw no
form; there was only a voice. 13He declared to you
his covenant, the Ten Commandments, which he
commanded you to follow and then wrote them
on two stone tablets. 14And the LORD directed me
at that time to teach you the decrees and laws you
are to follow in the land that you are crossing the
Jordan to possess. Pr 4:23; Eph 6:4; Ex 34:28

Idolatry Forbidden

15You saw no form of any kind the day the LORD
spoke to you at Horeb out of the fire. Therefore
watch yourselves very carefully, 16so that you do
not become corrupt and make for yourselves an
idol, an image of any shape, whether formed like
a man or a woman, 17or like any animal on earth
or any bird that flies in the air, 18or like any creature that moves along the ground or any fish in the
waters below. 19And when you look up to the sky
and see the sun, the moon and the stars—all the

[a] 17 That is, the Dead Sea

heavenly array—do not be enticed into bowing down to them and worshiping things the LORD your God has apportioned to all the nations under heaven. 20But as for you, the LORD took you and brought you out of the iron-smelting furnace, out of Egypt, to be the people of his inheritance, as you now are. Ex 20:4-5; Dt 5:8; 1Ki 8:51

21The LORD was angry with me because of you, and he solemnly swore that I would not cross the Jordan and enter the good land the LORD your God is giving you as your inheritance. 22I will die in this land; I will not cross the Jordan; but you are about to cross over and take possession of that good land. 23Be careful not to forget the covenant of the LORD your God that he made with you; do not make for yourselves an idol in the form of anything the LORD your God has forbidden. 24For the LORD your God is a consuming fire, a jealous God.

25After you have had children and grandchildren and have lived in the land a long time—if you then become corrupt and make any kind of idol, doing evil in the eyes of the LORD your God and provoking him to anger, 26I call heaven and earth as witnesses against you this day that you will quickly perish from the land that you are crossing the Jordan to possess. You will not live there long but will certainly be destroyed. 27The LORD will scatter you among the peoples, and only a few of you will survive among the nations to which the LORD will drive you. 28There you will worship man-made gods of wood and stone, which cannot see or hear or eat or smell. 29But if from there you seek the LORD your God, you will find him if you look for him with all your heart and with all your soul. 30When you are in distress and all these things have happened to you, then in later days you will return to the LORD your God and obey him. 31For the LORD your God is a merciful God; he will not abandon or destroy you or forget the covenant with your forefathers, which he confirmed to them by oath. Dt 30:18-19; 2Ki 17:2,17; 2Ch 15:4

The LORD Is God

32Ask now about the former days, long before your time, from the day God created man on the earth; ask from one end of the heavens to the other. Has anything so great as this ever happened, or has anything like it ever been heard of? 33Has any other people heard the voice of God[a] speaking out of fire, as you have, and lived? 34Has any god ever tried to take for himself one nation out of another nation, by testings, by miraculous signs and wonders, by war, by a mighty hand and an outstretched arm, or by great and awesome deeds, like all the things the LORD your God did for you in Egypt before your very eyes? Dt 5:24-26; 7:19

35You were shown these things so that you might know that the LORD is God; besides him there is no other. 36From heaven he made you hear his voice to discipline you. On earth he showed you his great fire, and you heard his words from out of the fire. 37Because he loved your forefathers and chose their descendants after them, he brought you out of Egypt by his Presence and his great strength, 38to drive out before you nations greater and stronger than you and to bring you into their land to give it to you for your inheritance, as it is today. Ex 19:9,19; Dt 10:15; 1Sa 2:2

39Acknowledge and take to heart this day that the LORD is God in heaven above and on the earth below. There is no other. 40Keep his decrees and commands, which I am giving you today, so that it may go well with you and your children after you and that you may live long in the land the LORD your God gives you for all time. Jos 2:11

Cities of Refuge

41Then Moses set aside three cities east of the Jordan, 42to which anyone who had killed a person could flee if he had unintentionally killed his neighbor without malice aforethought. He could flee into one of these cities and save his life. 43The cities were these: Bezer in the desert plateau, for the Reubenites; Ramoth in Gilead, for the Gadites; and Golan in Bashan, for the Manassites.

Introduction to the Law

44This is the law Moses set before the Israelites. 45These are the stipulations, decrees and laws Moses gave them when they came out of Egypt 46and were in the valley near Beth Peor east of the Jordan, in the land of Sihon king of the Amorites, who reigned in Heshbon and was defeated by Moses and the Israelites as they came out of Egypt. 47They took possession of his land and the land of Og king of Bashan, the two Amorite kings east of the Jordan. 48This land extended from Aroer on the rim of the Arnon Gorge to Mount Siyon[b] (that is, Hermon), 49and included all the Arabah east of the Jordan, as far as the Sea of the Arabah,[c] below the slopes of Pisgah. Nu 21:26

Experiencing God's Holiness **Chapters 5–26**

The people had come to the place they had been forty years before. As they prepared to enter the promised land, they needed to focus on the character of their God. Deuteronomy 5 records the second giving of the law. After the Israelites looked back at their own legacy of weakness and rebellion, they were reminded again of the holiness of the God they served. What a dramatic contrast! The same holy God who had given the Ten Commandments was still with them, and His law had not changed. As the people prepared to move forward in God's plan, they needed to hear the call to seek His holiness

[a]33 Or *of a god* [b]48 Hebrew; Syriac (see also Deut. 3:9) *Sirion* [c]49 That is, the Dead Sea

above the seductions of the nations around them. Although the world offered fortune, fame, power and pleasure, God's people were to seek God above all else. Although there were many gods and idols they would be tempted to worship and follow, they were to follow only the Lord their God. Only as their eyes were fixed on the holy and true God could the people resist all of the temptations and attractions of the world around them. Some things never change!

The Ten Commandments

5 Moses summoned all Israel and said:
Hear, O Israel, the decrees and laws I declare
in your hearing today. Learn them and be sure to
follow them. 2The LORD our God made a covenant
with us at Horeb. 3It was not with our fathers that
the LORD made this covenant, but with us, with all
of us who are alive here today. 4The LORD spoke to
you face to face out of the fire on the mountain.
5(At that time I stood between the LORD and you
to declare to you the word of the LORD, because
you were afraid of the fire and did not go up the
mountain.) And he said: Ex 19:5; 20:18,21; Dt 4:12,33,36

6"I am the LORD your God, who
brought you out of Egypt, out of the
land of slavery. Lev 26:1
7"You shall have no other gods before[a] me.
8"You shall not make for yourself an idol in
the form of anything in heaven above
or on the earth beneath or in the waters
below. 9You shall not bow down
to them or worship them; for I, the
LORD your God, am a jealous God,
punishing the children for the sin of
the fathers to the third and fourth generation
of those who hate me, 10but
showing love to a thousand ⌞generations⌟
of those who love me and keep
my commandments. Ex 34:7; Jer 32:18
11"You shall not misuse the name of the LORD
your God, for the LORD will not hold
anyone guiltless who misuses his
name. Lev 19:12
12"Observe the Sabbath day by keeping it
holy, as the LORD your God has commanded
you. 13Six days you shall labor
and do all your work, 14but the seventh
day is a Sabbath to the LORD your
God. On it you shall not do any work,
neither you, nor your son or daughter,
nor your manservant or maidservant,
nor your ox, your donkey or any of
your animals, nor the alien within
your gates, so that your manservant
and maidservant may rest, as you do.
15Remember that you were slaves in
Egypt and that the LORD your God
brought you out of there with a mighty
hand and an outstretched arm. Therefore
the LORD your God has commanded
you to observe the Sabbath
day. Ge 2:2; Heb 4:4; Mk 2:27
16"Honor your father and your mother, as the
LORD your God has commanded you,
so that you may live long and that it
may go well with you in the land the
LORD your God is giving you. Lev 19:3
17"You shall not murder. Ge 9:6; Mt 5:21-22
18"You shall not commit adultery. Mt 5:27-30
19"You shall not steal. Lev 19:11; Mt 19:19
20"You shall not give false testimony against
your neighbor. Mk 10:19
21"You shall not covet your neighbor's wife.
You shall not set your desire on your
neighbor's house or land, his manservant
or maidservant, his ox or donkey,
or anything that belongs to your
neighbor." Ex 20:1-17; Ro 7:7

22These are the commandments the LORD proclaimed
in a loud voice to your whole assembly
there on the mountain from out of the fire, the
cloud and the deep darkness; and he added nothing
more. Then he wrote them on two stone tablets
and gave them to me. Ex 31:18; Dt 4:13
23When you heard the voice out of the darkness,
while the mountain was ablaze with fire, all
the leading men of your tribes and your elders
came to me. 24And you said, "The LORD our God
has shown us his glory and his majesty, and we
have heard his voice from the fire. Today we have
seen that a man can live even if God speaks with
him. 25But now, why should we die? This great fire
will consume us, and we will die if we hear the
voice of the LORD our God any longer. 26For what
mortal man has ever heard the voice of the living
God speaking out of fire, as we have, and survived?
27Go near and listen to all that the LORD our God
says. Then tell us whatever the LORD our God tells
you. We will listen and obey." Dt 4:33; 18:16; Ex 19:19
28The LORD heard you when you spoke to me
and the LORD said to me, "I have heard what this
people said to you. Everything they said was good.
29Oh, that their hearts would be inclined to fear me
and keep all my commands always, so that it might
go well with them and their children forever!
30"Go, tell them to return to their tents. 31But
you stay here with me so that I may give you all the
commands, decrees and laws you are to teach
them to follow in the land I am giving them to
possess." Ex 24:12
32So be careful to do what the LORD your God
has commanded you; do not turn aside to the right
or to the left. 33Walk in all the way that the LORD
your God has commanded you, so that you may

[a] 7 Or *besides*

live and prosper and prolong your days in the land
that you will possess. Dt 17:11,20; Jos 1:7; Jer 7:23

Love the LORD Your God

6 These are the commands, decrees and laws
the LORD your God directed me to teach you
to observe in the land that you are crossing the
Jordan to possess, 2so that you, your children and
their children after them may fear the LORD your
God as long as you live by keeping all his decrees
and commands that I give you, and so that you
may enjoy long life. 3Hear, O Israel, and be careful
to obey so that it may go well with you and that
you may increase greatly in a land flowing with
milk and honey, just as the LORD, the God of your
fathers, promised you. Ex 3:8; 20:20; Dt 10:12-13
4Hear, O Israel: The LORD our God, the LORD is

LIVING  **INSIGHT**

Notice what formed the foundation of the faith of the Hebrews. Two primary truths: First, the Lord (Yahweh) is unique, unlike any and all other deities, and second, He is unity. One in essence, one in harmony.

(See Deuteronomy 6:4.)

one.[a] 5Love the LORD your God with all your
heart and with all your soul and with all your
strength. 6These commandments that I give you
today are to be upon your hearts. 7Impress them
on your children. Talk about them when you sit at
home and when you walk along the road, when
you lie down and when you get up. 8Tie them as
symbols on your hands and bind them on your
foreheads. 9Write them on the doorframes of your
houses and on your gates. Mt 22:37; Dt 11:18; Eph 6:4

LIVING  **INSIGHT**

Home is indeed where life makes up its mind. It is there—with fellow family members—we hammer out our convictions on the anvil of relationships. It is there we cultivate the valuable things in life, like attitudes, memories, beliefs and, most of all, character. Give God thanks today for His help in using your home to develop these all-important essentials.

(See Deuteronomy 6:6–9.)

10When the LORD your God brings you into the
land he swore to your fathers, to Abraham, Isaac
and Jacob, to give you—a land with large, flourishing cities you did not build, 11houses filled with
all kinds of good things you did not provide, wells
you did not dig, and vineyards and olive groves
you did not plant—then when you eat and are
satisfied, 12be careful that you do not forget the
LORD, who brought you out of Egypt, out of the
land of slavery. Dt 8:10; Jos 24:13; Ps 103:2
13Fear the LORD your God, serve him only and
take your oaths in his name. 14Do not follow other
gods, the gods of the peoples around you; 15for the
LORD your God, who is among you, is a jealous
God and his anger will burn against you, and he
will destroy you from the face of the land. 16Do not
test the LORD your God as you did at Massah. 17Be
sure to keep the commands of the LORD your God
and the stipulations and decrees he has given you.
18Do what is right and good in the LORD's sight, so
that it may go well with you and you may go in
and take over the good land that the LORD promised on oath to your forefathers, 19thrusting out all
your enemies before you, as the LORD said.
20In the future, when your son asks you, "What
is the meaning of the stipulations, decrees and laws
the LORD our God has commanded you?" 21tell
him: "We were slaves of Pharaoh in Egypt, but the
LORD brought us out of Egypt with a mighty hand.
22Before our eyes the LORD sent miraculous signs
and wonders—great and terrible—upon Egypt
and Pharaoh and his whole household. 23But he
brought us out from there to bring us in and give
us the land that he promised on oath to our forefathers. 24The LORD commanded us to obey all these
decrees and to fear the LORD our God, so that we
might always prosper and be kept alive, as is the
case today. 25And if we are careful to obey all this
law before the LORD our God, as he has commanded us, that will be our righteousness." Ex 13:14

Driving Out the Nations

7 When the LORD your God brings you into the
land you are entering to possess and drives
out before you many nations—the Hittites, Girgashites, Amorites, Canaanites, Perizzites, Hivites
and Jebusites, seven nations larger and stronger
than you— 2and when the LORD your God has
delivered them over to you and you have defeated
them, then you must destroy them totally.[b] Make
no treaty with them, and show them no mercy.
3Do not intermarry with them. Do not give your
daughters to their sons or take their daughters for
your sons, 4for they will turn your sons away from
following me to serve other gods, and the LORD's

[a]4 Or *The LORD our God is one LORD*; or *The LORD is our God, the LORD is one*; or *The LORD is our God, the LORD alone*
[b]2 The Hebrew term refers to the irrevocable giving over of things or persons to the LORD, often by totally destroying them; also in verse 26.

anger will burn against you and will quickly destroy you. [5]This is what you are to do to them: Break down their altars, smash their sacred stones, cut down their Asherah poles[a] and burn their idols in the fire. [6]For you are a people holy to the LORD your God. The LORD your God has chosen you out of all the peoples on the face of the earth to be his people, his treasured possession.

[7]The LORD did not set his affection on you and choose you because you were more numerous than other peoples, for you were the fewest of all peoples. [8]But it was because the LORD loved you and kept the oath he swore to your forefathers that he brought you out with a mighty hand and redeemed you from the land of slavery, from the power of Pharaoh king of Egypt. [9]Know therefore that the LORD your God is God; he is the faithful God, keeping his covenant of love to a thousand generations of those who love him and keep his commands. [10]But

those who hate him he will repay to their face
by destruction;
he will not be slow to repay to their face
those who hate him.

[11]Therefore, take care to follow the commands, decrees and laws I give you today.

[12]If you pay attention to these laws and are careful to follow them, then the LORD your God will keep his covenant of love with you, as he swore to your forefathers. [13]He will love you and bless you and increase your numbers. He will bless the fruit of your womb, the crops of your land—your grain, new wine and oil—the calves of your herds and the lambs of your flocks in the land that he swore to your forefathers to give you. [14]You will be blessed more than any other people; none of your men or women will be childless, nor any of your livestock without young. [15]The LORD will keep you free from every disease. He will not inflict on you the horrible diseases you knew in Egypt, but he will inflict them on all who hate you. [16]You must destroy all the peoples the LORD your God gives over to you. Do not look on them with pity and do not serve their gods, for that will be a snare to you. Dt 28:1-14; Ex 23:26; 15:26

[17]You may say to yourselves, "These nations are stronger than we are. How can we drive them out?" [18]But do not be afraid of them; remember well what the LORD your God did to Pharaoh and to all Egypt. [19]You saw with your own eyes the great trials, the miraculous signs and wonders, the mighty hand and outstretched arm, with which the LORD your God brought you out. The LORD your God will do the same to all the peoples you now fear. [20]Moreover, the LORD your God will send the hornet among them until even the survivors who hide from you have perished. [21]Do not be terrified by them, for the LORD your God, who is among you, is a great and awesome God. [22]The LORD your God will drive out those nations before you, little by little. You will not be allowed to eliminate them all at once, or the wild animals will multiply around you. [23]But the LORD your God will deliver them over to you, throwing them into great confusion until they are destroyed. [24]He will give their kings into your hand, and you will wipe out their names from under heaven. No one will be able to stand up against you; you will destroy them. [25]The images of their gods you are to burn in the fire. Do not covet the silver and gold on them, and do not take it for yourselves, or you will be ensnared by it, for it is detestable to the LORD your God. [26]Do not bring a detestable thing into your house or you, like it, will be set apart for destruction. Utterly abhor and detest it, for it is set apart for destruction. Dt 4:34; Ex 23:28-30; Ps 105:5

Do Not Forget the LORD

8 Be careful to follow every command I am giving you today, so that you may live and increase and may enter and possess the land that the LORD promised on oath to your forefathers. [2]Remember how the LORD your God led you all the way in the desert these forty years, to humble you and to test you in order to know what was in your heart, whether or not you would keep his commands. [3]He humbled you, causing you to hunger and then feeding you with manna, which neither you nor your fathers had known, to teach you that man does not live on bread alone but on every word that comes from the mouth of the LORD. [4]Your clothes did not wear out and your feet did not swell during these forty years. [5]Know then in your heart that as a man disciplines his son, so the LORD your God disciplines you. Dt 4:1; Mt 4:4

[6]Observe the commands of the LORD your God, walking in his ways and revering him. [7]For the LORD your God is bringing you into a good land—a land with streams and pools of water, with springs flowing in the valleys and hills; [8]a land with wheat and barley, vines and fig trees, pomegranates, olive oil and honey; [9]a land where bread will not be scarce and you will lack nothing; a land where the rocks are iron and you can dig copper out of the hills. Dt 11:9-12; Jer 2:7

[10]When you have eaten and are satisfied, praise the LORD your God for the good land he has given you. [11]Be careful that you do not forget the LORD your God, failing to observe his commands, his laws and his decrees that I am giving you this day. [12]Otherwise, when you eat and are satisfied, when you build fine houses and settle down, [13]and when your herds and flocks grow large and your silver

[a]5 That is, symbols of the goddess Asherah; here and elsewhere in Deuteronomy

and gold increase and all you have is multiplied, 14then your heart will become proud and you will forget the LORD your God, who brought you out of Egypt, out of the land of slavery. 15He led you

LIVING  **INSIGHT**

Adversity or prosperity, both are tough tests on our balance. To stay balanced through prosperity—ah, that demands* integrity. *The swift wind of compromise is a lot more devastating than the sudden jolt of misfortune.

(See Deuteronomy 8:10–14.)

through the vast and dreadful desert, that thirsty and waterless land, with its venomous snakes and scorpions. He brought you water out of hard rock. 16He gave you manna to eat in the desert, something your fathers had never known, to humble and to test you so that in the end it might go well with you. 17You may say to yourself, "My power and the strength of my hands have produced this wealth for me." 18But remember the LORD your God, for it is he who gives you the ability to produce wealth, and so confirms his covenant, which he swore to your forefathers, as it is today.

19If you ever forget the LORD your God and follow other gods and worship and bow down to them, I testify against you today that you will surely be destroyed. 20Like the nations the LORD destroyed before you, so you will be destroyed for not obeying the LORD your God. Dt 4:26; 30:18

Not Because of Israel's Righteousness

9 Hear, O Israel. You are now about to cross the Jordan to go in and dispossess nations greater and stronger than you, with large cities that have walls up to the sky. 2The people are strong and tall—Anakites! You know about them and have heard it said: "Who can stand up against the Anakites?" 3But be assured today that the LORD your God is the one who goes across ahead of you like a devouring fire. He will destroy them; he will subdue them before you. And you will drive them out and annihilate them quickly, as the LORD has promised you. Nu 13:22,28,32-33; Dt 7:23-24; 31:3

4After the LORD your God has driven them out before you, do not say to yourself, "The LORD has brought me here to take possession of this land because of my righteousness." No, it is on account of the wickedness of these nations that the LORD is going to drive them out before you. 5It is not because of your righteousness or your integrity that you are going in to take possession of their land; but on account of the wickedness of these nations, the LORD your God will drive them out before you, to accomplish what he swore to your fathers, to Abraham, Isaac and Jacob. 6Understand, then, that it is not because of your righteousness that the LORD your God is giving you this good land to possess, for you are a stiff-necked people. Ge 12:7; Lev 18:21,24-30; Dt 8:17

The Golden Calf

7Remember this and never forget how you provoked the LORD your God to anger in the desert. From the day you left Egypt until you arrived here, you have been rebellious against the LORD. 8At Horeb you aroused the LORD's wrath so that he was angry enough to destroy you. 9When I went up on the mountain to receive the tablets of stone, the tablets of the covenant that the LORD had made with you, I stayed on the mountain forty days and forty nights; I ate no bread and drank no water. 10The LORD gave me two stone tablets inscribed by the finger of God. On them were all the commandments the LORD proclaimed to you on the mountain out of the fire, on the day of the assembly.

11At the end of the forty days and forty nights, the LORD gave me the two stone tablets, the tablets of the covenant. 12Then the LORD told me, "Go down from here at once, because your people whom you brought out of Egypt have become corrupt. They have turned away quickly from what I commanded them and have made a cast idol for themselves." Ex 32:7-8; Jdg 2:17

13And the LORD said to me, "I have seen this people, and they are a stiff-necked people indeed! 14Let me alone, so that I may destroy them and blot out their name from under heaven. And I will make you into a nation stronger and more numerous than they." Ex 32:10

15So I turned and went down from the mountain while it was ablaze with fire. And the two tablets of the covenant were in my hands.[a] 16When I looked, I saw that you had sinned against the LORD your God; you had made for yourselves an idol cast in the shape of a calf. You had turned aside quickly from the way that the LORD had commanded you. 17So I took the two tablets and threw them out of my hands, breaking them to pieces before your eyes. Ex 32:15

18Then once again I fell prostrate before the LORD for forty days and forty nights; I ate no bread and drank no water, because of all the sin you had committed, doing what was evil in the LORD's sight and so provoking him to anger. 19I feared the anger and wrath of the LORD, for he was angry enough with you to destroy you. But again the LORD listened to me. 20And the LORD was angry enough with Aaron to destroy him, but at that time I prayed for Aaron too. 21Also I took that

[a] 15 Or *And I had the two tablets of the covenant with me, one in each hand*

sinful thing of yours, the calf you had made, and burned it in the fire. Then I crushed it and ground it to powder as fine as dust and threw the dust into a stream that flowed down the mountain. Ex 34:28

22You also made the LORD angry at Taberah, at Massah and at Kibroth Hattaavah. Nu 11:3; Ex 17:7

23And when the LORD sent you out from Kadesh Barnea, he said, "Go up and take possession of the land I have given you." But you rebelled against the command of the LORD your God. You did not trust him or obey him. 24You have been rebellious against the LORD ever since I have known you.

25I lay prostrate before the LORD those forty days and forty nights because the LORD had said he would destroy you. 26I prayed to the LORD and said, "O Sovereign LORD, do not destroy your people, your own inheritance that you redeemed by your great power and brought out of Egypt with a mighty hand. 27Remember your servants Abraham, Isaac and Jacob. Overlook the stubbornness of this people, their wickedness and their sin. 28Otherwise, the country from which you brought us will say, 'Because the LORD was not able to take them into the land he had promised them, and because he hated them, he brought them out to put them to death in the desert.' 29But they are your people, your inheritance that you brought out by your great power and your outstretched arm." Ex 32:11; Dt 4:20; 1Ki 8:51

Tablets Like the First Ones

10 At that time the LORD said to me, "Chisel out two stone tablets like the first ones and come up to me on the mountain. Also make a wooden chest.[a] 2I will write on the tablets the words that were on the first tablets, which you broke. Then you are to put them in the chest."

3So I made the ark out of acacia wood and chiseled out two stone tablets like the first ones, and I went up on the mountain with the two tablets in my hands. 4The LORD wrote on these tablets what he had written before, the Ten Commandments he had proclaimed to you on the mountain, out of the fire, on the day of the assembly. And the LORD gave them to me. 5Then I came back down the mountain and put the tablets in the ark I had made, as the LORD commanded me, and they are there now. Ex 20:1; 40:20

6(The Israelites traveled from the wells of the Jaakanites to Moserah. There Aaron died and was buried, and Eleazar his son succeeded him as priest. 7From there they traveled to Gudgodah and on to Jotbathah, a land with streams of water. 8At that time the LORD set apart the tribe of Levi to carry the ark of the covenant of the LORD, to stand before the LORD to minister and to pronounce blessings in his name, as they still do today. 9That is why the Levites have no share or inheritance among their brothers; the LORD is their inheritance, as the LORD your God told them.)

10Now I had stayed on the mountain forty days and nights, as I did the first time, and the LORD listened to me at this time also. It was not his will to destroy you. 11"Go," the LORD said to me, "and lead the people on their way, so that they may enter and possess the land that I swore to their fathers to give them." Ex 34:28; Dt 9:18-19,25

Fear the LORD

12And now, O Israel, what does the LORD your God ask of you but to fear the LORD your God, to walk in all his ways, to love him, to serve the LORD your God with all your heart and with all your soul, 13and to observe the LORD's commands and decrees that I am giving you today for your own good? Mic 6:8; Dt 6:5

14To the LORD your God belong the heavens, even the highest heavens, the earth and everything in it. 15Yet the LORD set his affection on your forefathers and loved them, and he chose you, their descendants, above all the nations, as it is today. 16Circumcise your hearts, therefore, and do not be stiff-necked any longer. 17For the LORD your God is God of gods and Lord of lords, the great God, mighty and awesome, who shows no partiality and accepts no bribes. 18He defends the cause of the fatherless and the widow, and loves the alien, giving him food and clothing. 19And you are to love those who are aliens, for you yourselves were aliens in Egypt. 20Fear the LORD your God and serve him. Hold fast to him and take your oaths in his name. 21He is your praise; he is your God, who performed for you those great and awesome wonders you saw with your own eyes. 22Your forefathers who went down into Egypt were seventy in all, and now the LORD your God has made you as numerous as the stars in the sky. Lev 19:34; Dt 4:37

Love and Obey the LORD

11 Love the LORD your God and keep his requirements, his decrees, his laws and his commands always. 2Remember today that your children were not the ones who saw and experienced the discipline of the LORD your God: his majesty, his mighty hand, his outstretched arm; 3the signs he performed and the things he did in the heart of Egypt, both to Pharaoh king of Egypt and to his whole country; 4what he did to the Egyptian army, to its horses and chariots, how he overwhelmed them with the waters of the Red Sea[b] as they were pursuing you, and how the LORD brought lasting ruin on them. 5It was not your children who saw what he did for you in the desert until you arrived at this place, 6and what he

[a] *1* That is, an ark [b] *4* Hebrew *Yam Suph*; that is, Sea of Reeds

did to Dathan and Abiram, sons of Eliab the Reubenite, when the earth opened its mouth right in
the middle of all Israel and swallowed them up
with their households, their tents and every living
thing that belonged to them. 7But it was your own
eyes that saw all these great things the LORD has
done. Nu 16:1-35; Dt 5:24; 10:12
8Observe therefore all the commands I am giving you today, so that you may have the strength
to go in and take over the land that you are crossing the Jordan to possess, 9and so that you may
live long in the land that the LORD swore to your
forefathers to give to them and their descendants,
a land flowing with milk and honey. 10The land
you are entering to take over is not like the land
of Egypt, from which you have come, where you
planted your seed and irrigated it by foot as in a
vegetable garden. 11But the land you are crossing
the Jordan to take possession of is a land of mountains and valleys that drinks rain from heaven. 12It
is a land the LORD your God cares for; the eyes of
the LORD your God are continually on it from the
beginning of the year to its end. Jos 1:7; Dt 4:40; 8:7
13So if you faithfully obey the commands I am
giving you today—to love the LORD your God and
to serve him with all your heart and with all your
soul— 14then I will send rain on your land in its
season, both autumn and spring rains, so that you
may gather in your grain, new wine and oil. 15I will
provide grass in the fields for your cattle, and you
will eat and be satisfied. Dt 4:29; Joel 2:23; Ps 104:14
16Be careful, or you will be enticed to turn away
and worship other gods and bow down to them.
17Then the LORD's anger will burn against you, and
he will shut the heavens so that it will not rain and
the ground will yield no produce, and you will
soon perish from the good land the LORD is giving
you. 18Fix these words of mine in your hearts and
minds; tie them as symbols on your hands and
bind them on your foreheads. 19Teach them to
your children, talking about them when you sit at
home and when you walk along the road, when
you lie down and when you get up. 20Write them
on the doorframes of your houses and on your

LIVING  **INSIGHT**

Christianity is designed for everyday living. Society has often made it out to be a "Sunday religion." But true-to-life Christianity is designed for Tuesday afternoon just as beautifully as Saturday morning or Sunday evening.

(See Deuteronomy 11:19.)

gates, 21so that your days and the days of your
children may be many in the land that the LORD
swore to give your forefathers, as many as the days
that the heavens are above the earth. Dt 4:9-10; 6:6-8
22If you carefully observe all these commands I
am giving you to follow—to love the LORD your
God, to walk in all his ways and to hold fast to
him— 23then the LORD will drive out all these
nations before you, and you will dispossess nations larger and stronger than you. 24Every place
where you set your foot will be yours: Your territory will extend from the desert to Lebanon, and
from the Euphrates River to the western sea.[a]
25No man will be able to stand against you. The
LORD your God, as he promised you, will put the
terror and fear of you on the whole land, wherever
you go. Ge 15:18; Dt 7:24; 9:1
26See, I am setting before you today a blessing
and a curse— 27the blessing if you obey the commands of the LORD your God that I am giving you
today; 28the curse if you disobey the commands of
the LORD your God and turn from the way that
I command you today by following other gods,
which you have not known. 29When the LORD your
God has brought you into the land you are entering to possess, you are to proclaim on Mount Gerizim the blessings, and on Mount Ebal the curses.
30As you know, these mountains are across the
Jordan, west of the road,[b] toward the setting sun,
near the great trees of Moreh, in the territory of
those Canaanites living in the Arabah in the vicinity of Gilgal. 31You are about to cross the Jordan to
enter and take possession of the land the LORD
your God is giving you. When you have taken it
over and are living there, 32be sure that you obey
all the decrees and laws I am setting before you
today. Dt 28:1-14; 30:1,15,19; 27:12-13

The One Place of Worship

12 These are the decrees and laws you must be
careful to follow in the land that the LORD,
the God of your fathers, has given you to possess—as long as you live in the land. 2Destroy
completely all the places on the high mountains
and on the hills and under every spreading tree
where the nations you are dispossessing worship
their gods. 3Break down their altars, smash their
sacred stones and burn their Asherah poles in the
fire; cut down the idols of their gods and wipe out
their names from those places. Dt 4:9-10; Nu 33:52
4You must not worship the LORD your God in
their way. 5But you are to seek the place the LORD
your God will choose from among all your tribes
to put his Name there for his dwelling. To that
place you must go; 6there bring your burnt offerings and sacrifices, your tithes and special gifts,
what you have vowed to give and your freewill

[a] 24 That is, the Mediterranean [b] 30 Or *Jordan, westward*

offerings, and the firstborn of your herds and flocks. [7]There, in the presence of the LORD your God, you and your families shall eat and shall rejoice in everything you have put your hand to, because the LORD your God has blessed you.

[8]You are not to do as we do here today, everyone as he sees fit, [9]since you have not yet reached the resting place and the inheritance the LORD your God is giving you. [10]But you will cross the Jordan and settle in the land the LORD your God is giving you as an inheritance, and he will give you rest from all your enemies around you so that you will live in safety. [11]Then to the place the LORD your God will choose as a dwelling for his Name—there you are to bring everything I command you: your burnt offerings and sacrifices, your tithes and special gifts, and all the choice possessions you have vowed to the LORD. [12]And there rejoice before the LORD your God, you, your sons and daughters, your menservants and maidservants, and the Levites from your towns, who have no allotment or inheritance of their own. [13]Be careful not to sacrifice your burnt offerings anywhere you please. [14]Offer them only at the place the LORD will choose in one of your tribes, and there observe everything I command you. Dt 10:9; 15:20; 3:20

[15]Nevertheless, you may slaughter your animals in any of your towns and eat as much of the meat as you want, as if it were gazelle or deer, according to the blessing the LORD your God gives you. Both the ceremonially unclean and the clean may eat it. [16]But you must not eat the blood; pour it out on the ground like water. [17]You must not eat in your own towns the tithe of your grain and new wine and oil, or the firstborn of your herds and flocks, or whatever you have vowed to give, or your freewill offerings or special gifts. [18]Instead, you are to eat them in the presence of the LORD your God at the place the LORD your God will choose—you, your sons and daughters, your menservants and maidservants, and the Levites from your towns—and you are to rejoice before the LORD your God in everything you put your hand to. [19]Be careful not to neglect the Levites as long as you live in your land. Lev 17:10-12; Dt 14:5,27

[20]When the LORD your God has enlarged your territory as he promised you, and you crave meat and say, "I would like some meat," then you may eat as much of it as you want. [21]If the place where the LORD your God chooses to put his Name is too far away from you, you may slaughter animals from the herds and flocks the LORD has given you, as I have commanded you, and in your own towns you may eat as much of them as you want. [22]Eat them as you would gazelle or deer. Both the ceremonially unclean and the clean may eat. [23]But be sure you do not eat the blood, because the blood is the life, and you must not eat the life with the meat. [24]You must not eat the blood; pour it out on the ground like water. [25]Do not eat it, so that it may go well with you and your children after you, because you will be doing what is right in the eyes of the LORD. Ge 15:18; Lev 17:11,14; Dt 4:40

[26]But take your consecrated things and whatever you have vowed to give, and go to the place the LORD will choose. [27]Present your burnt offerings on the altar of the LORD your God, both the meat and the blood. The blood of your sacrifices must be poured beside the altar of the LORD your God, but you may eat the meat. [28]Be careful to obey all these regulations I am giving you, so that it may always go well with you and your children after you, because you will be doing what is good and right in the eyes of the LORD your God.

[29]The LORD your God will cut off before you the nations you are about to invade and dispossess. But when you have driven them out and settled in their land, [30]and after they have been destroyed before you, be careful not to be ensnared by inquiring about their gods, saying, "How do these nations serve their gods? We will do the same." [31]You must not worship the LORD your God in their way, because in worshiping their gods, they do all kinds of detestable things the LORD hates. They even burn their sons and daughters in the fire as sacrifices to their gods. Dt 9:5; 18:10

[32]See that you do all I command you; do not add to it or take away from it. Dt 4:2

Worshiping Other Gods

13 If a prophet, or one who foretells by dreams, appears among you and announces to you a miraculous sign or wonder, [2]and if the sign or wonder of which he has spoken takes place, and he says, "Let us follow other gods" (gods you have not known) "and let us worship them," [3]you must not listen to the words of that prophet or dreamer. The LORD your God is testing you to find out whether you love him with all your heart and with all your soul. [4]It is the LORD your God you must follow, and him you must revere. Keep his commands and obey him; serve him and hold fast to him. [5]That prophet or dreamer must be put to death, because he preached rebellion against the LORD your God, who brought you out of Egypt and redeemed you from the land of slavery; he has tried to turn you from the way the LORD your God commanded you to follow. You must purge the evil from among you. Dt 8:2,16; 2Ki 23:3

[6]If your very own brother, or your son or daughter, or the wife you love, or your closest friend secretly entices you, saying, "Let us go and worship other gods" (gods that neither you nor your fathers have known, [7]gods of the peoples around you, whether near or far, from one end of the land to the other), [8]do not yield to him or listen to him. Show him no pity. Do not spare him or shield him. [9]You must certainly put him to

death. Your hand must be the first in putting him to death, and then the hands of all the people. [10]Stone him to death, because he tried to turn you away from the LORD your God, who brought you out of Egypt, out of the land of slavery. [11]Then all Israel will hear and be afraid, and no one among you will do such an evil thing again. Dt 17:2-7; 17:13

[12]If you hear it said about one of the towns the LORD your God is giving you to live in [13]that wicked men have arisen among you and have led the people of their town astray, saying, "Let us go and worship other gods" (gods you have not known), [14]then you must inquire, probe and investigate it thoroughly. And if it is true and it has been proved that this detestable thing has been done among you, [15]you must certainly put to the sword all who live in that town. Destroy it completely,[a] both its people and its livestock. [16]Gather all the plunder of the town into the middle of the public square and completely burn the town and all its plunder as a whole burnt offering to the LORD your God. It is to remain a ruin forever, never to be rebuilt. [17]None of those condemned things[a] shall be found in your hands, so that the LORD will turn from his fierce anger; he will show you mercy, have compassion on you, and increase your numbers, as he promised on oath to your forefathers, [18]because you obey the LORD your God, keeping all his commands that I am giving you today and doing what is right in his eyes. Jos 8:28; Nu 25:4; Dt 7:25-26

Clean and Unclean Food

14 You are the children of the LORD your God. Do not cut yourselves or shave the front of your heads for the dead, [2]for you are a people holy to the LORD your God. Out of all the peoples on the face of the earth, the LORD has chosen you to be his treasured possession. Lev 21:5; Ro 8:14; Dt 7:6

[3]Do not eat any detestable thing. [4]These are the animals you may eat: the ox, the sheep, the goat, [5]the deer, the gazelle, the roe deer, the wild goat, the ibex, the antelope and the mountain sheep.[b] [6]You may eat any animal that has a split hoof divided in two and that chews the cud. [7]However, of those that chew the cud or that have a split hoof completely divided you may not eat the camel, the rabbit or the coney.[c] Although they chew the cud, they do not have a split hoof; they are ceremonially unclean for you. [8]The pig is also unclean; although it has a split hoof, it does not chew the cud. You are not to eat their meat or touch their carcasses.

[9]Of all the creatures living in the water, you may eat any that has fins and scales. [10]But anything that does not have fins and scales you may not eat; for you it is unclean.

[11]You may eat any clean bird. [12]But these you may not eat: the eagle, the vulture, the black vulture, [13]the red kite, the black kite, any kind of falcon, [14]any kind of raven, [15]the horned owl, the screech owl, the gull, any kind of hawk, [16]the little owl, the great owl, the white owl, [17]the desert owl, the osprey, the cormorant, [18]the stork, any kind of heron, the hoopoe and the bat.

[19]All flying insects that swarm are unclean to you; do not eat them. [20]But any winged creature that is clean you may eat. Lev 11:1-23

[21]Do not eat anything you find already dead. You may give it to an alien living in any of your towns, and he may eat it, or you may sell it to a foreigner. But you are a people holy to the LORD your God. Lev 17:15

Do not cook a young goat in its mother's milk.

Tithes

[22]Be sure to set aside a tenth of all that your fields produce each year. [23]Eat the tithe of your grain, new wine and oil, and the firstborn of your herds and flocks in the presence of the LORD your God at the place he will choose as a dwelling for his Name, so that you may learn to revere the LORD your God always. [24]But if that place is too distant and you have been blessed by the LORD your God and cannot carry your tithe (because the place where the LORD will choose to put his Name is so far away), [25]then exchange your tithe for silver, and take the silver with you and go to the place the LORD your God will choose. [26]Use the silver to buy whatever you like: cattle, sheep, wine or other fermented drink, or anything you wish. Then you and your household shall eat there in the presence of the LORD your God and rejoice. [27]And do not neglect the Levites living in your towns, for they have no allotment or inheritance of their own.

[28]At the end of every three years, bring all the tithes of that year's produce and store it in your towns, [29]so that the Levites (who have no allotment or inheritance of their own) and the aliens, the fatherless and the widows who live in your towns may come and eat and be satisfied, and so that the LORD your God may bless you in all the work of your hands. Dt 15:10; 26:12

The Year for Canceling Debts

15 At the end of every seven years you must cancel debts. [2]This is how it is to be done: Every creditor shall cancel the loan he has made to his fellow Israelite. He shall not require payment from his fellow Israelite or brother, because the LORD's time for canceling debts has been proclaimed. [3]You may require payment from a foreigner, but you must cancel any debt your brother owes you. [4]However, there should be no poor

[a]*15,17* The Hebrew term refers to the irrevocable giving over of things or persons to the LORD, often by totally destroying them.
[b]*5* The precise identification of some of the birds and animals in this chapter is uncertain. [c]*7* That is, the hyrax or rock badger

among you, for in the land the LORD your God is giving you to possess as your inheritance, he will richly bless you, 5if only you fully obey the LORD your God and are careful to follow all these commands I am giving you today. 6For the LORD your God will bless you as he has promised, and you will lend to many nations but will borrow from none. You will rule over many nations but none will rule over you. Dt 31:10; 23:20; 28:12-13,44

7If there is a poor man among your brothers in any of the towns of the land that the LORD your God is giving you, do not be hardhearted or tightfisted toward your poor brother. 8Rather be openhanded and freely lend him whatever he needs. 9Be careful not to harbor this wicked thought: "The seventh year, the year for canceling debts, is near," so that you do not show ill will toward your needy brother and give him nothing. He may then appeal to the LORD against you, and you will be found guilty of sin. 10Give generously to him and do so without a grudging heart; then because of this the LORD your God will bless you in all your work and in everything you put your hand to. 11There will always be poor people in the land. Therefore I command you to be openhanded toward your brothers and toward the poor and needy in your land. Lev 25:8-38; Mt 26:11; 1Jn 3:17

Freeing Servants

12If a fellow Hebrew, a man or a woman, sells himself to you and serves you six years, in the seventh year you must let him go free. 13And when you release him, do not send him away empty-handed. 14Supply him liberally from your flock, your threshing floor and your winepress. Give to him as the LORD your God has blessed you. 15Remember that you were slaves in Egypt and the LORD your God redeemed you. That is why I give you this command today. Ex 21:2-6; Lev 25:38-55

16But if your servant says to you, "I do not want to leave you," because he loves you and your family and is well off with you, 17then take an awl and push it through his ear lobe into the door, and he will become your servant for life. Do the same for your maidservant.

18Do not consider it a hardship to set your servant free, because his service to you these six years has been worth twice as much as that of a hired hand. And the LORD your God will bless you in everything you do.

The Firstborn Animals

19Set apart for the LORD your God every firstborn male of your herds and flocks. Do not put the firstborn of your oxen to work, and do not shear the firstborn of your sheep. 20Each year you and your family are to eat them in the presence of the LORD your God at the place he will choose. 21If an animal has a defect, is lame or blind, or has any serious flaw, you must not sacrifice it to the LORD your God. 22You are to eat it in your own towns. Both the ceremonially unclean and the clean may eat it, as if it were gazelle or deer. 23But you must not eat the blood; pour it out on the ground like water. Ex 13:2; Lev 22:19-25; Dt 12:5-7,17-18

Passover

16 Observe the month of Abib and celebrate the Passover of the LORD your God, because in the month of Abib he brought you out of Egypt by night. 2Sacrifice as the Passover to the LORD your God an animal from your flock or herd at the place the LORD will choose as a dwelling for his Name. 3Do not eat it with bread made with yeast, but for seven days eat unleavened bread, the bread of affliction, because you left Egypt in haste—so that all the days of your life you may remember the time of your departure from Egypt. 4Let no yeast be found in your possession in all your land for seven days. Do not let any of the meat you sacrifice on the evening of the first day remain until morning. Ex 12:2; 34:25

5You must not sacrifice the Passover in any town the LORD your God gives you 6except in the place he will choose as a dwelling for his Name. There you must sacrifice the Passover in the evening, when the sun goes down, on the anniversary[a] of your departure from Egypt. 7Roast it and eat it at the place the LORD your God will choose. Then in the morning return to your tents. 8For six days eat unleavened bread and on the seventh day hold an assembly to the LORD your God and do no work. Ex 12:14-20; Lev 23:4-8; Nu 28:16-25

Feast of Weeks

9Count off seven weeks from the time you begin to put the sickle to the standing grain. 10Then celebrate the Feast of Weeks to the LORD your God by giving a freewill offering in proportion to the blessings the LORD your God has given you. 11And rejoice before the LORD your God at the place he will choose as a dwelling for his Name—you, your sons and daughters, your menservants and maidservants, the Levites in your towns, and the aliens, the fatherless and the widows living among you. 12Remember that you were slaves in Egypt, and follow carefully these decrees. Lev 23:15-22; Nu 28:26-31

Feast of Tabernacles

13Celebrate the Feast of Tabernacles for seven days after you have gathered the produce of your threshing floor and your winepress. 14Be joyful at your Feast—you, your sons and daughters, your menservants and maidservants, and the Levites,

[a]6 Or *down, at the time of day*

the aliens, the fatherless and the widows who live in your towns. 15For seven days celebrate the Feast to the LORD your God at the place the LORD will choose. For the LORD your God will bless you in all your harvest and in all the work of your hands, and your joy will be complete. Lev 23:34

16Three times a year all your men must appear before the LORD your God at the place he will choose: at the Feast of Unleavened Bread, the Feast of Weeks and the Feast of Tabernacles. No man should appear before the LORD empty-handed: 17Each of you must bring a gift in proportion to the way the LORD your God has blessed you.

Judges

18Appoint judges and officials for each of your tribes in every town the LORD your God is giving you, and they shall judge the people fairly. 19Do not pervert justice or show partiality. Do not accept a bribe, for a bribe blinds the eyes of the wise and twists the words of the righteous. 20Follow justice and justice alone, so that you may live and possess the land the LORD your God is giving you.

Worshiping Other Gods

21Do not set up any wooden Asherah pole[a] beside the altar you build to the LORD your God, 22and do not erect a sacred stone, for these the LORD your God hates. Lev 26:1

17 Do not sacrifice to the LORD your God an ox or a sheep that has any defect or flaw in it, for that would be detestable to him. Dt 15:21

2If a man or woman living among you in one of the towns the LORD gives you is found doing evil in the eyes of the LORD your God in violation of his covenant, 3and contrary to my command has worshiped other gods, bowing down to them or to the sun or the moon or the stars of the sky, 4and this has been brought to your attention, then you must investigate it thoroughly. If it is true and it has been proved that this detestable thing has been done in Israel, 5take the man or woman who has done this evil deed to your city gate and stone that person to death. 6On the testimony of two or three witnesses a man shall be put to death, but no one shall be put to death on the testimony of only one witness. 7The hands of the witnesses must be the first in putting him to death, and then the hands of all the people. You must purge the evil from among you. Nu 35:30; Dt 13:6-11; Mt 18:16

Law Courts

8If cases come before your courts that are too difficult for you to judge—whether bloodshed, lawsuits or assaults—take them to the place the LORD your God will choose. 9Go to the priests, who are Levites, and to the judge who is in office at that time. Inquire of them and they will give you the verdict. 10You must act according to the decisions they give you at the place the LORD will choose. Be careful to do everything they direct you to do. 11Act according to the law they teach you and the decisions they give you. Do not turn aside from what they tell you, to the right or to the left. 12The man who shows contempt for the judge or for the priest who stands ministering there to the LORD your God must be put to death. You must purge the evil from Israel. 13All the people will hear and be afraid, and will not be contemptuous again.

The King

14When you enter the land the LORD your God is giving you and have taken possession of it and settled in it, and you say, "Let us set a king over us like all the nations around us," 15be sure to appoint over you the king the LORD your God chooses. He must be from among your own brothers. Do not place a foreigner over you, one who is not a brother Israelite. 16The king, moreover, must not acquire great numbers of horses for himself or make the people return to Egypt to get more of them, for the LORD has told you, "You are not to go back that way again." 17He must not take many wives, or his heart will be led astray. He must not accumulate large amounts of silver and gold.

18When he takes the throne of his kingdom, he is to write for himself on a scroll a copy of this law, taken from that of the priests, who are Levites. 19It is to be with him, and he is to read it all the days of his life so that he may learn to revere the LORD his God and follow carefully all the words of this law and these decrees 20and not consider himself better than his brothers and turn from the law to the right or to the left. Then he and his descendants will reign a long time over his kingdom in Israel. Jos 1:8; 1Ki 15:5

Offerings for Priests and Levites

18 The priests, who are Levites—indeed the whole tribe of Levi—are to have no allotment or inheritance with Israel. They shall live on the offerings made to the LORD by fire, for that is their inheritance. 2They shall have no inheritance among their brothers; the LORD is their inheritance, as he promised them. Dt 10:9; 1Co 9:13

3This is the share due the priests from the people who sacrifice a bull or a sheep: the shoulder, the jowls and the inner parts. 4You are to give them the firstfruits of your grain, new wine and oil, and the first wool from the shearing of your sheep, 5for the LORD your God has chosen them and their descendants out of all your tribes to stand and minister in the LORD's name always. Lev 7:28-34

6If a Levite moves from one of your towns any-

[a]21 Or *Do not plant any tree dedicated to Asherah*

where in Israel where he is living, and comes in all
earnestness to the place the LORD will choose, 7he
may minister in the name of the LORD his God like
all his fellow Levites who serve there in the presence of the LORD. 8He is to share equally in their
benefits, even though he has received money from
the sale of family possessions. Ne 12:44,47

Detestable Practices

9When you enter the land the LORD your God is
giving you, do not learn to imitate the detestable
ways of the nations there. 10Let no one be found
among you who sacrifices his son or daughter in[a]
the fire, who practices divination or sorcery, interprets omens, engages in witchcraft, 11or casts
spells, or who is a medium or spiritist or who
consults the dead. 12Anyone who does these things
is detestable to the LORD, and because of these
detestable practices the LORD your God will drive
out those nations before you. 13You must be
blameless before the LORD your God. Dt 12:31

The Prophet

14The nations you will dispossess listen to those
who practice sorcery or divination. But as for you,
the LORD your God has not permitted you to do
so. 15The LORD your God will raise up for you a
prophet like me from among your own brothers.
You must listen to him. 16For this is what you
asked of the LORD your God at Horeb on the day
of the assembly when you said, "Let us not hear
the voice of the LORD our God nor see this great
fire anymore, or we will die." Ex 20:19; Jn 1:21; Ac 3:22
17The LORD said to me: "What they say is good.
18I will raise up for them a prophet like you from
among their brothers; I will put my words in his
mouth, and he will tell them everything I command him. 19If anyone does not listen to my words
that the prophet speaks in my name, I myself will
call him to account. 20But a prophet who presumes
to speak in my name anything I have not commanded him to say, or a prophet who speaks in
the name of other gods, must be put to death."
21You may say to yourselves, "How can we
know when a message has not been spoken by the
LORD?" 22If what a prophet proclaims in the name
of the LORD does not take place or come true, that
is a message the LORD has not spoken. That prophet has spoken presumptuously. Do not be afraid of
him. Jer 28:9

Cities of Refuge

19 When the LORD your God has destroyed
the nations whose land he is giving you,
and when you have driven them out and settled in
their towns and houses, 2then set aside for yourselves three cities centrally located in the land the
LORD your God is giving you to possess. 3Build
roads to them and divide into three parts the land
the LORD your God is giving you as an inheritance,
so that anyone who kills a man may flee there.
4This is the rule concerning the man who kills
another and flees there to save his life—one who
kills his neighbor unintentionally, without malice
aforethought. 5For instance, a man may go into
the forest with his neighbor to cut wood, and as he
swings his ax to fell a tree, the head may fly off and
hit his neighbor and kill him. That man may flee
to one of these cities and save his life. 6Otherwise,
the avenger of blood might pursue him in a rage,
overtake him if the distance is too great, and kill
him even though he is not deserving of death,
since he did it to his neighbor without malice
aforethought. 7This is why I command you to set
aside for yourselves three cities.
8If the LORD your God enlarges your territory,
as he promised on oath to your forefathers, and
gives you the whole land he promised them, 9be-
cause you carefully follow all these laws I command you today—to love the LORD your God and
to walk always in his ways—then you are to set
aside three more cities. 10Do this so that innocent
blood will not be shed in your land, which the
LORD your God is giving you as your inheritance,
and so that you will not be guilty of bloodshed.
11But if a man hates his neighbor and lies in wait
for him, assaults and kills him, and then flees to
one of these cities, 12the elders of his town shall
send for him, bring him back from the city, and
hand him over to the avenger of blood to die.
13Show him no pity. You must purge from Israel
the guilt of shedding innocent blood, so that it
may go well with you.
14Do not move your neighbor's boundary stone
set up by your predecessors in the inheritance you
receive in the land the LORD your God is giving
you to possess. Nu 35:6-34; Dt 4:41-43; Jos 20:1-9

Witnesses

15One witness is not enough to convict a man
accused of any crime or offense he may have committed. A matter must be established by the testimony of two or three witnesses.
16If a malicious witness takes the stand to accuse
a man of a crime, 17the two men involved in the
dispute must stand in the presence of the LORD
before the priests and the judges who are in office
at the time. 18The judges must make a thorough
investigation, and if the witness proves to be a liar,
giving false testimony against his brother, 19then
do to him as he intended to do to his brother. You
must purge the evil from among you. 20The rest of
the people will hear of this and be afraid, and
never again will such an evil thing be done among

[a]10 Or *who makes his son or daughter pass through*

you. 21Show no pity: life for life, eye for eye, tooth for tooth, hand for hand, foot for foot. Mt 5:38

Going to War

20 When you go to war against your enemies and see horses and chariots and an army greater than yours, do not be afraid of them, because the LORD your God, who brought you up out of Egypt, will be with you. 2When you are about to go into battle, the priest shall come forward and address the army. 3He shall say: "Hear, O Israel, today you are going into battle against your enemies. Do not be fainthearted or afraid; do not be terrified or give way to panic before them. 4For the LORD your God is the one who goes with you to fight for you against your enemies to give you victory." Dt 1:30; 31:6,8; 2Ch 32:7-8

5The officers shall say to the army: "Has anyone built a new house and not dedicated it? Let him go home, or he may die in battle and someone else may dedicate it. 6Has anyone planted a vineyard and not begun to enjoy it? Let him go home, or he may die in battle and someone else enjoy it. 7Has anyone become pledged to a woman and not married her? Let him go home, or he may die in battle and someone else marry her." 8Then the officers shall add, "Is any man afraid or fainthearted? Let him go home so that his brothers will not become disheartened too." 9When the officers have finished speaking to the army, they shall appoint commanders over it. Dt 24:5; Jdg 7:3

10When you march up to attack a city, make its people an offer of peace. 11If they accept and open their gates, all the people in it shall be subject to forced labor and shall work for you. 12If they refuse to make peace and they engage you in battle, lay siege to that city. 13When the LORD your God delivers it into your hand, put to the sword all the men in it. 14As for the women, the children, the livestock and everything else in the city, you may take these as plunder for yourselves. And you may use the plunder the LORD your God gives you from your enemies. 15This is how you are to treat all the cities that are at a distance from you and do not belong to the nations nearby. Nu 31:7; Jos 8:2; 1Ki 9:21

16However, in the cities of the nations the LORD your God is giving you as an inheritance, do not leave alive anything that breathes. 17Completely destroy[a] them—the Hittites, Amorites, Canaanites, Perizzites, Hivites and Jebusites—as the LORD your God has commanded you. 18Otherwise, they will teach you to follow all the detestable things they do in worshiping their gods, and you will sin against the LORD your God. Ex 23:33; Dt 7:2; Jos 11:14

19When you lay siege to a city for a long time, fighting against it to capture it, do not destroy its trees by putting an ax to them, because you can eat their fruit. Do not cut them down. Are the trees of the field people, that you should besiege them?[b] 20However, you may cut down trees that you know are not fruit trees and use them to build siege works until the city at war with you falls.

Atonement for an Unsolved Murder

21 If a man is found slain, lying in a field in the land the LORD your God is giving you to possess, and it is not known who killed him, 2your elders and judges shall go out and measure the distance from the body to the neighboring towns. 3Then the elders of the town nearest the body shall take a heifer that has never been worked and has never worn a yoke 4and lead her down to a valley that has not been plowed or planted and where there is a flowing stream. There in the valley they are to break the heifer's neck. 5The priests, the sons of Levi, shall step forward, for the LORD your God has chosen them to minister and to pronounce blessings in the name of the LORD and to decide all cases of dispute and assault. 6Then all the elders of the town nearest the body shall wash their hands over the heifer whose neck was broken in the valley, 7and they shall declare: "Our hands did not shed this blood, nor did our eyes see it done. 8Accept this atonement for your people Israel, whom you have redeemed, O LORD, and do not hold your people guilty of the blood of an innocent man." And the bloodshed will be atoned for. 9So you will purge from yourselves the guilt of shedding innocent blood, since you have done what is right in the eyes of the LORD. Dt 17:8-11

Marrying a Captive Woman

10When you go to war against your enemies and the LORD your God delivers them into your hands and you take captives, 11if you notice among the captives a beautiful woman and are attracted to her, you may take her as your wife. 12Bring her into your home and have her shave her head, trim her nails 13and put aside the clothes she was wearing when captured. After she has lived in your house and mourned her father and mother for a full month, then you may go to her and be her husband and she shall be your wife. 14If you are not pleased with her, let her go wherever she wishes. You must not sell her or treat her as a slave, since you have dishonored her. Lev 14:9

The Right of the Firstborn

15If a man has two wives, and he loves one but not the other, and both bear him sons but the firstborn is the son of the wife he does not love, 16when he wills his property to his sons, he must

[a] 17 The Hebrew term refers to the irrevocable giving over of things or persons to the LORD, often by totally destroying them.
[b] 19 Or *down to use in the siege, for the fruit trees are for the benefit of man.*

not give the rights of the firstborn to the son of the wife he loves in preference to his actual firstborn, the son of the wife he does not love. 17He must acknowledge the son of his unloved wife as the firstborn by giving him a double share of all he has. That son is the first sign of his father's strength. The right of the firstborn belongs to him.

A Rebellious Son

18If a man has a stubborn and rebellious son who does not obey his father and mother and will not listen to them when they discipline him, 19his father and mother shall take hold of him and bring him to the elders at the gate of his town. 20They shall say to the elders, "This son of ours is stubborn and rebellious. He will not obey us. He is a profligate and a drunkard." 21Then all the men of his town shall stone him to death. You must purge the evil from among you. All Israel will hear of it and be afraid. Dt 13:11; Eph 6:1-3

Various Laws

22If a man guilty of a capital offense is put to death and his body is hung on a tree, 23you must not leave his body on the tree overnight. Be sure to bury him that same day, because anyone who is hung on a tree is under God's curse. You must not desecrate the land the LORD your God is giving you as an inheritance. Gal 3:13; Jos 8:29; Jn 19:31

22 If you see your brother's ox or sheep straying, do not ignore it but be sure to take it back to him. 2If the brother does not live near you or if you do not know who he is, take it home with you and keep it until he comes looking for it. Then give it back to him. 3Do the same if you find your brother's donkey or his cloak or anything he loses. Do not ignore it. Ex 23:4-5

4If you see your brother's donkey or his ox fallen on the road, do not ignore it. Help him get it to its feet.

5A woman must not wear men's clothing, nor a man wear women's clothing, for the LORD your God detests anyone who does this.

6If you come across a bird's nest beside the road, either in a tree or on the ground, and the mother is sitting on the young or on the eggs, do not take the mother with the young. 7You may take the young, but be sure to let the mother go, so that it may go well with you and you may have a long life. Lev 22:28; Dt 4:40

8When you build a new house, make a parapet around your roof so that you may not bring the guilt of bloodshed on your house if someone falls from the roof.

9Do not plant two kinds of seed in your vineyard; if you do, not only the crops you plant but also the fruit of the vineyard will be defiled.[a]

10Do not plow with an ox and a donkey yoked together. 2Co 6:14

11Do not wear clothes of wool and linen woven together.

12Make tassels on the four corners of the cloak you wear. Nu 15:37-41; Mt 23:5

Marriage Violations

13If a man takes a wife and, after lying with her, dislikes her 14and slanders her and gives her a bad name, saying, "I married this woman, but when I approached her, I did not find proof of her virginity," 15then the girl's father and mother shall bring proof that she was a virgin to the town elders at the gate. 16The girl's father will say to the elders, "I gave my daughter in marriage to this man, but he dislikes her. 17Now he has slandered her and said, 'I did not find your daughter to be a virgin.' But here is the proof of my daughter's virginity." Then her parents shall display the cloth before the elders of the town, 18and the elders shall take the man and punish him. 19They shall fine him a hundred shekels of silver[b] and give them to the girl's father, because this man has given an Israelite virgin a bad name. She shall continue to be his wife; he must not divorce her as long as he lives. Ex 18:21

20If, however, the charge is true and no proof of the girl's virginity can be found, 21she shall be brought to the door of her father's house and there the men of her town shall stone her to death. She has done a disgraceful thing in Israel by being promiscuous while still in her father's house. You must purge the evil from among you. Ge 34:7

22If a man is found sleeping with another man's wife, both the man who slept with her and the woman must die. You must purge the evil from Israel. Lev 20:10; Jn 8:5

23If a man happens to meet in a town a virgin pledged to be married and he sleeps with her, 24you shall take both of them to the gate of that town and stone them to death—the girl because she was in a town and did not scream for help, and the man because he violated another man's wife. You must purge the evil from among you.

25But if out in the country a man happens to meet a girl pledged to be married and rapes her, only the man who has done this shall die. 26Do nothing to the girl; she has committed no sin deserving death. This case is like that of someone who attacks and murders his neighbor, 27for the man found the girl out in the country, and though the betrothed girl screamed, there was no one to rescue her.

28If a man happens to meet a virgin who is not pledged to be married and rapes her and they are discovered, 29he shall pay the girl's father fifty

[a] 9 Or *be forfeited to the sanctuary*

[b] 19 That is, about 2 1/2 pounds (about 1 kilogram)

shekels of silver.[a] He must marry the girl, for he
has violated her. He can never divorce her as long
as he lives. Ex 22:16
30A man is not to marry his father's wife; he
must not dishonor his father's bed. Lev 18:8; Dt 27:20

Exclusion From the Assembly

23 No one who has been emasculated by
crushing or cutting may enter the assembly
of the LORD.
2No one born of a forbidden marriage[b] nor
any of his descendants may enter the assembly of
the LORD, even down to the tenth generation.
3No Ammonite or Moabite or any of his
descendants may enter the assembly of the LORD,
even down to the tenth generation. 4For they did
not come to meet you with bread and water on
your way when you came out of Egypt, and they
hired Balaam son of Beor from Pethor in Aram
Naharaim[c] to pronounce a curse on you. 5How-
ever, the LORD your God would not listen to Balaam but turned the curse into a blessing for you,
because the LORD your God loves you. 6Do not
seek a treaty of friendship with them as long as you
live. Nu 22:5-6; Ezr 9:12; Ne 13:2
7Do not abhor an Edomite, for he is your brother. Do not abhor an Egyptian, because you lived as
an alien in his country. 8The third generation of
children born to them may enter the assembly of
the LORD. Ge 25:26; Ex 22:21

Uncleanness in the Camp

9When you are encamped against your enemies, keep away from everything impure. 10If one
of your men is unclean because of a nocturnal
emission, he is to go outside the camp and stay
there. 11But as evening approaches he is to wash
himself, and at sunset he may return to the camp.
12Designate a place outside the camp where you
can go to relieve yourself. 13As part of your equipment have something to dig with, and when you
relieve yourself, dig a hole and cover up your excrement. 14For the LORD your God moves about in
your camp to protect you and to deliver your enemies to you. Your camp must be holy, so that he
will not see among you anything indecent and
turn away from you. Lev 26:12

Miscellaneous Laws

15If a slave has taken refuge with you, do not
hand him over to his master. 16Let him live among
you wherever he likes and in whatever town he
chooses. Do not oppress him. 1Sa 30:15
17No Israelite man or woman is to become a
shrine prostitute. 18You must not bring the earnings of a female prostitute or of a male prostitute[d]
into the house of the LORD your God to pay any
vow, because the LORD your God detests them
both. Lev 19:29; 20:13
19Do not charge your brother interest, whether
on money or food or anything else that may earn
interest. 20You may charge a foreigner interest, but
not a brother Israelite, so that the LORD your God
may bless you in everything you put your hand to
in the land you are entering to possess. Ex 22:25
21If you make a vow to the LORD your God, do
not be slow to pay it, for the LORD your God will
certainly demand it of you and you will be guilty
of sin. 22But if you refrain from making a vow, you
will not be guilty. 23Whatever your lips utter you
must be sure to do, because you made your vow
freely to the LORD your God with your own mouth.
24If you enter your neighbor's vineyard, you
may eat all the grapes you want, but do not put
any in your basket. 25If you enter your neighbor's
grainfield, you may pick kernels with your hands,
but you must not put a sickle to his standing grain.

24 If a man marries a woman who becomes
displeasing to him because he finds something indecent about her, and he writes her a certificate of divorce, gives it to her and sends her
from his house, 2and if after she leaves his house
she becomes the wife of another man, 3and her
second husband dislikes her and writes her a certificate of divorce, gives it to her and sends her
from his house, or if he dies, 4then her first husband, who divorced her, is not allowed to marry
her again after she has been defiled. That would be
detestable in the eyes of the LORD. Do not bring sin
upon the land the LORD your God is giving you as
an inheritance. Jer 3:1; Mt 5:31; 19:7-9
5If a man has recently married, he must not be
sent to war or have any other duty laid on him. For

LIVING  **INSIGHT**

The disease of sin affected everything and everyone. Conflict replaced harmony. Sorrow replaced joy. And things like disobedience and rebellion became the status quo. In nations. In cities. And in homes as well. Unlike the original match, husbands and wives became selfish and unfaithful and hateful. Because of the rebellious will of sinful people, divorce evolved. But remember, it was not desired or designed in God's original arrangement for marriage. Sin polluted the plan.

(See Deuteronomy 24:1–4.)

[a]29 That is, about 1 1/4 pounds (about 0.6 kilogram) [b]2 Or *one of illegitimate birth* [c]4 That is, Northwest Mesopotamia [d]18 Hebrew *of a dog*

MAJOR SOCIAL CONCERNS IN THE COVENANT

PERSONHOOD	Everyone's person is to be secure	*Exodus 20:13; Deuteronomy 5:17; Exodus 21:16-21,26-31; Leviticus 19:14; Deuteronomy 24:7; 27:18*
FALSE ACCUSATION	Everyone is to be secure against slander and false accusation	*Exodus 20:16; Deuteronomy 5:20; Exodus 23:1-3; Leviticus 19:16; Deuteronomy 19:15-21*
WOMAN	No woman is to be taken advantage of within her subordinate status in society	*Exodus 21:7-11,20,26-32; 22:16-17; Deuteronomy 21:10-14; 22:13-30; 24:1-5*
PUNISHMENT	Punishment for wrongdoing shall not be excessive so that the culprit is dehumanized	*Deuteronomy 25:1-5*
DIGNITY	Every Israelite's dignity and right to be God's freedman and servant are to be honored and safeguarded	*Exodus 21:2,5-6; Leviticus 25; Deuteronomy 15:12-18*
INHERITANCE	Every Israelite's inheritance in the promised land is to be secure	*Leviticus 25; Numbers 27:5-7; 36:1-9; Deuteronomy 25:5-10*
PROPERTY	Everyone's property is to be secure	*Exodus 20:15; Deuteronomy 5:19; Exodus 21:33-36; 22:1-15; 23:4-5; Leviticus 19:35-36; Deuteronomy 22:1-4; 25:13-15*
FRUIT OF LABOR	Everyone is to receive the fruit of his labors	*Leviticus 19:13; Deuteronomy 24:14; 25:4*
FRUIT OF THE GROUND	Everyone is to share the fruit of the ground	*Exodus 23:10-11; Leviticus 19:9-10; 23:22; 25:3-55; Deuteronomy 14:28-29; 24:19-21*
REST ON SABBATH	Everyone, down to the humblest servant and the resident alien, is to share in the weekly rest of God's Sabbath	*Exodus 20:8-11; Deuteronomy 5:12-15; Exodus 23:12*
MARRIAGE	The marriage relationship is to be kept inviolate	*Exodus 20:14; Deuteronomy 5:18;* see also *Leviticus 18:6-23; 20:10-21; Deuteronomy 22:13-30*
EXPLOITATION	No one, however disabled, impoverished or powerless, is to be oppressed or exploited	*Exodus 22:21-27; Leviticus 19:14,33-34; 25:35-36; Deuteronomy 23:19; 24:6,12-15,17; 27:18*
FAIR TRIAL	Everyone is to have free access to the courts and is to be afforded a fair trial	*Exodus 23:6,8; Leviticus 19:15; Deuteronomy 1:17; 10:17-18; 16:18-20; 17:8-13; 19:15-21*
SOCIAL ORDER	Every person's God-given place in the social order is to be honored	*Exodus 20:12; Deuteronomy 5:16; Exodus 21:15,17; 22:28; Leviticus 19:3,32; 20:9; Deuteronomy 17:8-13; 21:15-21; 27:16*
LAW	No one shall be above the law, not even the king	*Deuteronomy 17:18-20*
ANIMALS	Concern for the welfare of other creatures is to be extended to the animal world	*Exodus 23:5,11; Leviticus 25:7; Deuteronomy 22:4,6-7; 25:4*

one year he is to be free to stay at home and bring happiness to the wife he has married. Dt 20:7

6Do not take a pair of millstones—not even the upper one—as security for a debt, because that would be taking a man's livelihood as security.

7If a man is caught kidnapping one of his brother Israelites and treats him as a slave or sells him, the kidnapper must die. You must purge the evil from among you. Ex 21:16

8In cases of leprous[a] diseases be very careful to do exactly as the priests, who are Levites, instruct you. You must follow carefully what I have commanded them. 9Remember what the LORD your God did to Miriam along the way after you came out of Egypt. Lev 13:1-46; Nu 12:10

10When you make a loan of any kind to your neighbor, do not go into his house to get what he is offering as a pledge. 11Stay outside and let the man to whom you are making the loan bring the pledge out to you. 12If the man is poor, do not go to sleep with his pledge in your possession. 13Return his cloak to him by sunset so that he may sleep in it. Then he will thank you, and it will be regarded as a righteous act in the sight of the LORD your God. Ex 22:26; Dt 6:25; Da 4:27

14Do not take advantage of a hired man who is poor and needy, whether he is a brother Israelite or an alien living in one of your towns. 15Pay him his wages each day before sunset, because he is poor and is counting on it. Otherwise he may cry to the LORD against you, and you will be guilty of sin. Lev 19:13; Jas 5:4

16Fathers shall not be put to death for their children, nor children put to death for their fathers; each is to die for his own sin. Jer 31:29-30

17Do not deprive the alien or the fatherless of justice, or take the cloak of the widow as a pledge. 18Remember that you were slaves in Egypt and the LORD your God redeemed you from there. That is why I command you to do this.

19When you are harvesting in your field and you overlook a sheaf, do not go back to get it. Leave it for the alien, the fatherless and the widow, so that the LORD your God may bless you in all the work of your hands. 20When you beat the olives from your trees, do not go over the branches a second time. Leave what remains for the alien, the fatherless and the widow. 21When you harvest the grapes in your vineyard, do not go over the vines again. Leave what remains for the alien, the fatherless and the widow. 22Remember that you were slaves in Egypt. That is why I command you to do this. Lev 19:9; 23:22

25 When men have a dispute, they are to take it to court and the judges will decide the case, acquitting the innocent and condemning the guilty. 2If the guilty man deserves to be beaten, the judge shall make him lie down and have him flogged in his presence with the number of lashes his crime deserves, 3but he must not give him more than forty lashes. If he is flogged more than that, your brother will be degraded in your eyes.

4Do not muzzle an ox while it is treading out the grain. 1Ti 5:18

5If brothers are living together and one of them dies without a son, his widow must not marry outside the family. Her husband's brother shall take her and marry her and fulfill the duty of a brother-in-law to her. 6The first son she bears shall carry on the name of the dead brother so that his name will not be blotted out from Israel.

7However, if a man does not want to marry his brother's wife, she shall go to the elders at the town gate and say, "My husband's brother refuses to carry on his brother's name in Israel. He will not fulfill the duty of a brother-in-law to me." 8Then the elders of his town shall summon him and talk to him. If he persists in saying, "I do not want to marry her," 9his brother's widow shall go up to him in the presence of the elders, take off one of his sandals, spit in his face and say, "This is what is done to the man who will not build up his brother's family line." 10That man's line shall be known in Israel as The Family of the Unsandaled.

11If two men are fighting and the wife of one of them comes to rescue her husband from his assailant, and she reaches out and seizes him by his private parts, 12you shall cut off her hand. Show her no pity.

13Do not have two differing weights in your bag—one heavy, one light. 14Do not have two differing measures in your house—one large, one small. 15You must have accurate and honest weights and measures, so that you may live long in the land the LORD your God is giving you. 16For the LORD your God detests anyone who does these things, anyone who deals dishonestly. Lev 19:35-37

17Remember what the Amalekites did to you along the way when you came out of Egypt. 18When you were weary and worn out, they met you on your journey and cut off all who were lagging behind; they had no fear of God. 19When the LORD your God gives you rest from all the enemies around you in the land he is giving you to possess as an inheritance, you shall blot out the memory of Amalek from under heaven. Do not forget! Ex 17:8; Ps 36:1; 1Sa 15:2-3

Firstfruits and Tithes

26 When you have entered the land the LORD your God is giving you as an inheritance and have taken possession of it and settled in it, 2take some of the firstfruits of all that you produce from the soil of the land the LORD your God is

[a]8 The Hebrew word was used for various diseases affecting the skin—not necessarily leprosy.

giving you and put them in a basket. Then go
to the place the LORD your God will choose as a
dwelling for his Name 3and say to the priest in
office at the time, "I declare today to the LORD your
God that I have come to the land the LORD swore
to our forefathers to give us." 4The priest shall take
the basket from your hands and set it down in
front of the altar of the LORD your God. 5Then you
shall declare before the LORD your God: "My father
was a wandering Aramean, and he went down into
Egypt with a few people and lived there and became a great nation, powerful and numerous. 6But
the Egyptians mistreated us and made us suffer,
putting us to hard labor. 7Then we cried out to the
LORD, the God of our fathers, and the LORD heard
our voice and saw our misery, toil and oppression.
8So the LORD brought us out of Egypt with a
mighty hand and an outstretched arm, with great
terror and with miraculous signs and wonders.
9He brought us to this place and gave us this land,
a land flowing with milk and honey; 10and now I
bring the firstfruits of the soil that you, O LORD,
have given me." Place the basket before the LORD
your God and bow down before him. 11And you
and the Levites and the aliens among you shall
rejoice in all the good things the LORD your God
has given to you and your household. Ex 3:8

12When you have finished setting aside a tenth
of all your produce in the third year, the year of
the tithe, you shall give it to the Levite, the alien,
the fatherless and the widow, so that they may eat
in your towns and be satisfied. 13Then say to the
LORD your God: "I have removed from my house
the sacred portion and have given it to the Levite,
the alien, the fatherless and the widow, according
to all you commanded. I have not turned aside
from your commands nor have I forgotten any of
them. 14I have not eaten any of the sacred portion
while I was in mourning, nor have I removed any
of it while I was unclean, nor have I offered any of
it to the dead. I have obeyed the LORD my God; I
have done everything you commanded me. 15Look
down from heaven, your holy dwelling place, and
bless your people Israel and the land you have
given us as you promised on oath to our forefathers, a land flowing with milk and honey."

Follow the LORD's Commands

16The LORD your God commands you this day
to follow these decrees and laws; carefully observe
them with all your heart and with all your soul.
17You have declared this day that the LORD is your
God and that you will walk in his ways, that you
will keep his decrees, commands and laws, and
that you will obey him. 18And the LORD has declared this day that you are his people, his treasured possession as he promised, and that you are
to keep all his commands. 19He has declared that
he will set you in praise, fame and honor high
above all the nations he has made and that you will
be a people holy to the LORD your God, as he
promised. Dt 7:6; 28:1,13,44; 4:7-8

Heeding God's Warning — Chapters 27–34

Before Deuteronomy concluded, Moses called the people to listen to God's warnings for the future. In chapter 28 one of the strongest warnings in all of Scripture is recorded. The first 14 verses contain wonderful promises for obedience. However, the more than fifty verses that follow chronicle the consequences of walking in disobedience. As we read these chapters, we should experience a sober desire to examine our lives to be sure we are being shaped by God's Word and by the leading of His Spirit. Verses 15–18 of chapter 30 record a sort of finale to God's exhortations. Reflect on these words that are as powerful today as they were when God first inspired them: "See, I set before you today life and prosperity, death and destruction. For I command you today to love the LORD your God, to walk in his ways, and to keep his commands, decrees and laws; then you will live and increase, and the LORD your God will bless you in the land you are entering to possess. But if your heart turns away and you are not obedient, and if you are drawn away to bow down to other gods and worship them, I declare to you this day that you will certainly be destroyed."

God's warnings still apply today. In His love He has recorded these words to help us choose the path of obedience and blessing. The choice is still ours. If we remember His faithfulness in the past, experience His holiness in the present and heed His warnings for the future, we will be well on our way to walking in obedience to His call in our lives. We will also have taken to heart the powerful message of the book of Deuteronomy.

The Altar on Mount Ebal

27 Moses and the elders of Israel commanded
the people: "Keep all these commands that
I give you today. 2When you have crossed the
Jordan into the land the LORD your God is giving
you, set up some large stones and coat them with
plaster. 3Write on them all the words of this law
when you have crossed over to enter the land the
LORD your God is giving you, a land flowing with
milk and honey, just as the LORD, the God of your
fathers, promised you. 4And when you have
crossed the Jordan, set up these stones on Mount
Ebal, as I command you today, and coat them with
plaster. 5Build there an altar to the LORD your God,
an altar of stones. Do not use any iron tool upon
them. 6Build the altar of the LORD your God with
fieldstones and offer burnt offerings on it to the
LORD your God. 7Sacrifice fellowship offerings[a]
there, eating them and rejoicing in the presence of
the LORD your God. 8And you shall write very

[a]7 Traditionally *peace offerings*

clearly all the words of this law on these stones you
have set up." Ex 20:25; Dt 26:9; Jos 8:31

Curses From Mount Ebal

9Then Moses and the priests, who are Levites,
said to all Israel, "Be silent, O Israel, and listen!
You have now become the people of the LORD your
God. 10Obey the LORD your God and follow his
commands and decrees that I give you today."

11On the same day Moses commanded the people:

12When you have crossed the Jordan, these
tribes shall stand on Mount Gerizim to bless the
people: Simeon, Levi, Judah, Issachar, Joseph and
Benjamin. 13And these tribes shall stand on Mount
Ebal to pronounce curses: Reuben, Gad, Asher,
Zebulun, Dan and Naphtali. Jos 8:35

14The Levites shall recite to all the people of
Israel in a loud voice:

15"Cursed is the man who carves an image
or casts an idol—a thing detestable to the
LORD, the work of the craftsman's hands—
and sets it up in secret." Ex 20:4; 34:17

Then all the people shall say, "Amen!"

16"Cursed is the man who dishonors his
father or his mother." Ex 21:17

Then all the people shall say, "Amen!"

17"Cursed is the man who moves his
neighbor's boundary stone." Pr 22:28

Then all the people shall say, "Amen!"

18"Cursed is the man who leads the blind
astray on the road." Lev 19:14

Then all the people shall say, "Amen!"

19"Cursed is the man who withholds justice from the alien, the fatherless or the
widow." Dt 10:18; 24:19

Then all the people shall say, "Amen!"

20"Cursed is the man who sleeps with his
father's wife, for he dishonors his father's
bed." Lev 18:7; Dt 22:30

Then all the people shall say, "Amen!"

21"Cursed is the man who has sexual relations with any animal." Lev 18:23

Then all the people shall say, "Amen!"

22"Cursed is the man who sleeps with his
sister, the daughter of his father or the
daughter of his mother."

Then all the people shall say, "Amen!"

23"Cursed is the man who sleeps with his
mother-in-law."

Then all the people shall say, "Amen!"

24"Cursed is the man who kills his neighbor secretly." Nu 35:31

Then all the people shall say, "Amen!"

25"Cursed is the man who accepts a bribe
to kill an innocent person." Ex 23:7-8

Then all the people shall say, "Amen!"

26"Cursed is the man who does not uphold the words of this law by carrying them
out." Gal 3:10

Then all the people shall say, "Amen!"

Blessings for Obedience

28 If you fully obey the LORD your God and
carefully follow all his commands I give
you today, the LORD your God will set you high
above all the nations on earth. 2All these blessings
will come upon you and accompany you if you
obey the LORD your God: Dt 26:19; Lev 26:3

3You will be blessed in the city and blessed
in the country. Ge 39:5

4The fruit of your womb will be blessed,
and the crops of your land and the young of
your livestock—the calves of your herds and
the lambs of your flocks. Ge 49:25

5Your basket and your kneading trough
will be blessed.

6You will be blessed when you come in
and blessed when you go out. Ps 121:8

7The LORD will grant that the enemies who rise
up against you will be defeated before you. They
will come at you from one direction but flee from
you in seven. Lev 26:8,17

8The LORD will send a blessing on your barns
and on everything you put your hand to. The LORD
your God will bless you in the land he is giving
you.

9The LORD will establish you as his holy people,
as he promised you on oath, if you keep the commands of the LORD your God and walk in his ways.
10Then all the peoples on earth will see that you are
called by the name of the LORD, and they will fear
you. 11The LORD will grant you abundant prosperity—in the fruit of your womb, the young of your
livestock and the crops of your ground—in the
land he swore to your forefathers to give you.
12The LORD will open the heavens, the storehouse of his bounty, to send rain on your land in
season and to bless all the work of your hands.
You will lend to many nations but will borrow
from none. 13The LORD will make you the head,
not the tail. If you pay attention to the commands
of the LORD your God that I give you this day and
carefully follow them, you will always be at the top,
never at the bottom. 14Do not turn aside from any
of the commands I give you today, to the right or
to the left, following other gods and serving them.

Curses for Disobedience

15However, if you do not obey the LORD your
God and do not carefully follow all his commands
and decrees I am giving you today, all these curses
will come upon you and overtake you: Lev 26:14

16You will be cursed in the city and cursed
in the country.

17 Your basket and your kneading trough
will be cursed.
18 The fruit of your womb will be cursed,
and the crops of your land, and the calves of
your herds and the lambs of your flocks.
19 You will be cursed when you come in
and cursed when you go out.

20 The LORD will send on you curses, confusion
and rebuke in everything you put your hand to,
until you are destroyed and come to sudden ruin
because of the evil you have done in forsaking
him.[a] 21 The LORD will plague you with diseases
until he has destroyed you from the land you are
entering to possess. 22 The LORD will strike you with
wasting disease, with fever and inflammation, with
scorching heat and drought, with blight and mildew, which will plague you until you perish. 23 The
sky over your head will be bronze, the ground
beneath you iron. 24 The LORD will turn the rain of
your country into dust and powder; it will come
down from the skies until you are destroyed.
25 The LORD will cause you to be defeated before
your enemies. You will come at them from one
direction but flee from them in seven, and you will
become a thing of horror to all the kingdoms on
earth. 26 Your carcasses will be food for all the birds
of the air and the beasts of the earth, and there will
be no one to frighten them away. 27 The LORD will
afflict you with the boils of Egypt and with tumors,
festering sores and the itch, from which you cannot be cured. 28 The LORD will afflict you with madness, blindness and confusion of mind. 29 At midday you will grope about like a blind man in the
dark. You will be unsuccessful in everything you
do; day after day you will be oppressed and
robbed, with no one to rescue you. Jer 15:4; 7:33
30 You will be pledged to be married to a woman, but another will take her and ravish her. You
will build a house, but you will not live in it. You
will plant a vineyard, but you will not even begin
to enjoy its fruit. 31 Your ox will be slaughtered
before your eyes, but you will eat none of it. Your
donkey will be forcibly taken from you and will
not be returned. Your sheep will be given to your
enemies, and no one will rescue them. 32 Your sons
and daughters will be given to another nation, and
you will wear out your eyes watching for them day
after day, powerless to lift a hand. 33 A people that
you do not know will eat what your land and labor
produce, and you will have nothing but cruel oppression all your days. 34 The sights you see will
drive you mad. 35 The LORD will afflict your knees
and legs with painful boils that cannot be cured,
spreading from the soles of your feet to the top of
your head. Jer 5:15-17; 8:10; Am 5:11
36 The LORD will drive you and the king you set
over you to a nation unknown to you or your
fathers. There you will worship other gods, gods of
wood and stone. 37 You will become a thing of
horror and an object of scorn and ridicule to all
the nations where the LORD will drive you.
38 You will sow much seed in the field but you
will harvest little, because locusts will devour it.
39 You will plant vineyards and cultivate them but
you will not drink the wine or gather the grapes,
because worms will eat them. 40 You will have olive
trees throughout your country but you will not use
the oil, because the olives will drop off. 41 You will
have sons and daughters but you will not keep
them, because they will go into captivity. 42 Swarms
of locusts will take over all your trees and the crops
of your land. Joel 1:4; Mic 6:15; Hag 1:6,9
43 The alien who lives among you will rise above
you higher and higher, but you will sink lower and
lower. 44 He will lend to you, but you will not lend
to him. He will be the head, but you will be the tail.
45 All these curses will come upon you. They will
pursue you and overtake you until you are destroyed, because you did not obey the LORD your
God and observe the commands and decrees he
gave you. 46 They will be a sign and a wonder to
you and your descendants forever. 47 Because you
did not serve the LORD your God joyfully and gladly in the time of prosperity, 48 therefore in hunger
and thirst, in nakedness and dire poverty, you will
serve the enemies the LORD sends against you. He
will put an iron yoke on your neck until he has
destroyed you. Ne 9:35; Isa 8:18; Jer 28:13-14
49 The LORD will bring a nation against you from
far away, from the ends of the earth, like an eagle
swooping down, a nation whose language you will
not understand, 50 a fierce-looking nation without
respect for the old or pity for the young. 51 They
will devour the young of your livestock and the
crops of your land until you are destroyed. They
will leave you no grain, new wine or oil, nor any
calves of your herds or lambs of your flocks until
you are ruined. 52 They will lay siege to all the cities
throughout your land until the high fortified walls
in which you trust fall down. They will besiege all
the cities throughout the land the LORD your God
is giving you. Isa 47:6; Jer 48:40; Zep 1:14-17
53 Because of the suffering that your enemy will
inflict on you during the siege, you will eat the fruit
of the womb, the flesh of the sons and daughters
the LORD your God has given you. 54 Even the most
gentle and sensitive man among you will have no
compassion on his own brother or the wife he
loves or his surviving children, 55 and he will not
give to one of them any of the flesh of his children
that he is eating. It will be all he has left because of
the suffering your enemy will inflict on you during
the siege of all your cities. 56 The most gentle and
sensitive woman among you—so sensitive and

[a]20 Hebrew *me*

gentle that she would not venture to touch the ground with the sole of her foot—will begrudge the husband she loves and her own son or daughter 57the afterbirth from her womb and the children she bears. For she intends to eat them secretly during the siege and in the distress that your enemy will inflict on you in your cities. Lev 26:29

58If you do not carefully follow all the words of this law, which are written in this book, and do not revere this glorious and awesome name—the LORD your God— 59the LORD will send fearful plagues on you and your descendants, harsh and prolonged disasters, and severe and lingering illnesses. 60He will bring upon you all the diseases of Egypt that you dreaded, and they will cling to you. 61The LORD will also bring on you every kind of sickness and disaster not recorded in this Book of the Law, until you are destroyed. 62You who were as numerous as the stars in the sky will be left but few in number, because you did not obey the LORD your God. 63Just as it pleased the LORD to make you prosper and increase in number, so it will please him to ruin and destroy you. You will be uprooted from the land you are entering to possess. Dt 10:22; Ne 9:23; Pr 1:26

64Then the LORD will scatter you among all nations, from one end of the earth to the other. There you will worship other gods—gods of wood and stone, which neither you nor your fathers have known. 65Among those nations you will find no repose, no resting place for the sole of your foot. There the LORD will give you an anxious mind, eyes weary with longing, and a despairing heart. 66You will live in constant suspense, filled with dread both night and day, never sure of your life. 67In the morning you will say, "If only it were evening!" and in the evening, "If only it were morning!"—because of the terror that will fill your hearts and the sights that your eyes will see. 68The LORD will send you back in ships to Egypt on a journey I said you should never make again. There you will offer yourselves for sale to your enemies as male and female slaves, but no one will buy you. Dt 4:27; Lev 26:16,36; Job 7:4

Renewal of the Covenant

29 These are the terms of the covenant the LORD commanded Moses to make with the Israelites in Moab, in addition to the covenant he had made with them at Horeb. Dt 5:2-3

2Moses summoned all the Israelites and said to them:

Your eyes have seen all that the LORD did in Egypt to Pharaoh, to all his officials and to all his land. 3With your own eyes you saw those great trials, those miraculous signs and great wonders. 4But to this day the LORD has not given you a mind that understands or eyes that see or ears that hear. 5During the forty years that I led you through the desert, your clothes did not wear out, nor did the sandals on your feet. 6You ate no bread and drank no wine or other fermented drink. I did this so that you might know that I am the LORD your God.

7When you reached this place, Sihon king of Heshbon and Og king of Bashan came out to fight against us, but we defeated them. 8We took their land and gave it as an inheritance to the Reubenites, the Gadites and the half-tribe of Manasseh.

9Carefully follow the terms of this covenant, so that you may prosper in everything you do. 10All of you are standing today in the presence of the LORD your God—your leaders and chief men, your elders and officials, and all the other men of Israel, 11together with your children and your wives, and the aliens living in your camps who chop your wood and carry your water. 12You are standing here in order to enter into a covenant with the LORD your God, a covenant the LORD is making with you this day and sealing with an oath, 13to confirm you this day as his people, that he may be your God as he promised you and as he swore to your fathers, Abraham, Isaac and Jacob. 14I am making this covenant, with its oath, not only with you 15who are standing here with us today in the presence of the LORD our God but also with those who are not here today. Ge 17:7; Jos 1:7

16You yourselves know how we lived in Egypt and how we passed through the countries on the way here. 17You saw among them their detestable images and idols of wood and stone, of silver and gold. 18Make sure there is no man or woman, clan or tribe among you today whose heart turns away from the LORD our God to go and worship the gods of those nations; make sure there is no root among you that produces such bitter poison.

19When such a person hears the words of this oath, he invokes a blessing on himself and therefore thinks, "I will be safe, even though I persist in going my own way." This will bring disaster on the watered land as well as the dry.[a] 20The LORD will never be willing to forgive him; his wrath and zeal will burn against that man. All the curses written in this book will fall upon him, and the LORD will blot out his name from under heaven. 21The LORD will single him out from all the tribes of Israel for disaster, according to all the curses of the covenant written in this Book of the Law. Dt 9:14; Ps 74:1; 79:5

22Your children who follow you in later generations and foreigners who come from distant lands will see the calamities that have fallen on the land and the diseases with which the LORD has afflicted it. 23The whole land will be a burning waste of salt and sulfur—nothing planted, nothing sprouting, no vegetation growing on it. It will be like the

[a] 19 Or *way, in order to add drunkenness to thirst."*

destruction of Sodom and Gomorrah, Admah and
Zeboiim, which the LORD overthrew in fierce anger. 24All the nations will ask: "Why has the LORD
done this to this land? Why this fierce, burning
anger?" Jer 19:8; 22:8-9; Zep 2:9
25And the answer will be: "It is because this
people abandoned the covenant of the LORD, the
God of their fathers, the covenant he made with
them when he brought them out of Egypt. 26They
went off and worshiped other gods and bowed
down to them, gods they did not know, gods he
had not given them. 27Therefore the LORD's anger
burned against this land, so that he brought on it
all the curses written in this book. 28In furious
anger and in great wrath the LORD uprooted them
from their land and thrust them into another land,
as it is now." 1Ki 14:15; 2Ki 17:23; Da 9:11,13-14
29The secret things belong to the LORD our God,
but the things revealed belong to us and to our
children forever, that we may follow all the words
of this law. 2Ti 3:16

Prosperity After Turning to the LORD

30 When all these blessings and curses I have
set before you come upon you and you
take them to heart wherever the LORD your God
disperses you among the nations, 2and when you
and your children return to the LORD your God
and obey him with all your heart and with all your
soul according to everything I command you today, 3then the LORD your God will restore your
fortunes[a] and have compassion on you and gather you again from all the nations where he scattered you. 4Even if you have been banished to the
most distant land under the heavens, from there
the LORD your God will gather you and bring you
back. 5He will bring you to the land that belonged
to your fathers, and you will take possession of it.
He will make you more prosperous and numerous
than your fathers. 6The LORD your God will circumcise your hearts and the hearts of your descendants, so that you may love him with all your heart
and with all your soul, and live. 7The LORD your
God will put all these curses on your enemies who
hate and persecute you. 8You will again obey the
LORD and follow all his commands I am giving you
today. 9Then the LORD your God will make you
most prosperous in all the work of your hands and
in the fruit of your womb, the young of your livestock and the crops of your land. The LORD will
again delight in you and make you prosperous,
just as he delighted in your fathers, 10if you obey
the LORD your God and keep his commands and
decrees that are written in this Book of the Law
and turn to the LORD your God with all your heart
and with all your soul. Dt 11:26; Ps 126:4; Jer 32:39

The Offer of Life or Death

11Now what I am commanding you today is not
too difficult for you or beyond your reach. 12It is
not up in heaven, so that you have to ask, "Who
will ascend into heaven to get it and proclaim it to
us so we may obey it?" 13Nor is it beyond the sea,
so that you have to ask, "Who will cross the sea to
get it and proclaim it to us so we may obey it?"
14No, the word is very near you; it is in your
mouth and in your heart so you may obey it.

LIVING  **INSIGHT**

Who can possibly measure the lasting impact of the Word of God? In a world without standards, where everything is relative, where the pace is maddening and prices are soaring, there is great security in opening God's timeless Book and hearing His voice. It calms our fears. It clears our heads. It comforts our walk. It confirms our commitment.

(See Deuteronomy 30:14.)

15See, I set before you today life and prosperity,
death and destruction. 16For I command you today to love the LORD your God, to walk in his ways,
and to keep his commands, decrees and laws; then
you will live and increase, and the LORD your God
will bless you in the land you are entering to possess. Dt 4:1; 11:26
17But if your heart turns away and you are not
obedient, and if you are drawn away to bow down
to other gods and worship them, 18I declare to you
this day that you will certainly be destroyed. You
will not live long in the land you are crossing the
Jordan to enter and possess. Dt 8:19
19This day I call heaven and earth as witnesses
against you that I have set before you life and
death, blessings and curses. Now choose life, so
that you and your children may live 20and that you
may love the LORD your God, listen to his voice,
and hold fast to him. For the LORD is your life, and
he will give you many years in the land he swore
to give to your fathers, Abraham, Isaac and Jacob.

Joshua to Succeed Moses

31 Then Moses went out and spoke these
words to all Israel: 2"I am now a hundred
and twenty years old and I am no longer able to
lead you. The LORD has said to me, 'You shall not
cross the Jordan.' 3The LORD your God himself will
cross over ahead of you. He will destroy these
nations before you, and you will take possession of
their land. Joshua also will cross over ahead of you,

[a]3 Or *will bring you back from captivity*

as the LORD said. 4And the LORD will do to them
what he did to Sihon and Og, the kings of the
Amorites, whom he destroyed along with their
land. 5The LORD will deliver them to you, and you
must do to them all that I have commanded you.
6Be strong and courageous. Do not be afraid or
terrified because of them, for the LORD your God
goes with you; he will never leave you nor forsake
you." Dt 3:23,26; 7:2; Jos 10:25

7Then Moses summoned Joshua and said to
him in the presence of all Israel, "Be strong and
courageous, for you must go with this people into
the land that the LORD swore to their forefathers to
give them, and you must divide it among them as
their inheritance. 8The LORD himself goes before
you and will be with you; he will never leave you
nor forsake you. Do not be afraid; do not be discouraged." Dt 1:38; 3:28; Ex 13:21

The Reading of the Law

9So Moses wrote down this law and gave it to
the priests, the sons of Levi, who carried the ark of
the covenant of the LORD, and to all the elders of
Israel. 10Then Moses commanded them: "At the
end of every seven years, in the year for canceling
debts, during the Feast of Tabernacles, 11when all
Israel comes to appear before the LORD your God
at the place he will choose, you shall read this law
before them in their hearing. 12Assemble the people—men, women and children, and the aliens
living in your towns—so they can listen and learn
to fear the LORD your God and follow carefully all
the words of this law. 13Their children, who do not
know this law, must hear it and learn to fear the
LORD your God as long as you live in the land you
are crossing the Jordan to possess." Nu 4:15; Dt 15:1

Israel's Rebellion Predicted

14The LORD said to Moses, "Now the day of your
death is near. Call Joshua and present yourselves
at the Tent of Meeting, where I will commission
him." So Moses and Joshua came and presented
themselves at the Tent of Meeting. Nu 27:13

15Then the LORD appeared at the Tent in a pillar
of cloud, and the cloud stood over the entrance to
the Tent. 16And the LORD said to Moses: "You are
going to rest with your fathers, and these people
will soon prostitute themselves to the foreign gods
of the land they are entering. They will forsake me
and break the covenant I made with them. 17On
that day I will become angry with them and forsake them; I will hide my face from them, and they
will be destroyed. Many disasters and difficulties
will come upon them, and on that day they will
ask, 'Have not these disasters come upon us because our God is not with us?' 18And I will certainly hide my face on that day because of all their
wickedness in turning to other gods. Ex 33:9

19"Now write down for yourselves this song and
teach it to the Israelites and have them sing it,
so that it may be a witness for me against them.
20When I have brought them into the land flowing
with milk and honey, the land I promised on oath
to their forefathers, and when they eat their fill and
thrive, they will turn to other gods and worship
them, rejecting me and breaking my covenant.
21And when many disasters and difficulties come
upon them, this song will testify against them, because it will not be forgotten by their descendants.
I know what they are disposed to do, even before
I bring them into the land I promised them on
oath." 22So Moses wrote down this song that day
and taught it to the Israelites. Dt 32:15-17; Jn 2:24-25

23The LORD gave this command to Joshua son
of Nun: "Be strong and courageous, for you will
bring the Israelites into the land I promised them
on oath, and I myself will be with you." Jos 1:6

24After Moses finished writing in a book the
words of this law from beginning to end, 25he gave
this command to the Levites who carried the ark
of the covenant of the LORD: 26"Take this Book of
the Law and place it beside the ark of the covenant
of the LORD your God. There it will remain as a
witness against you. 27For I know how rebellious
and stiff-necked you are. If you have been rebellious against the LORD while I am still alive and
with you, how much more will you rebel after I
die! 28Assemble before me all the elders of your
tribes and all your officials, so that I can speak
these words in their hearing and call heaven and
earth to testify against them. 29For I know that
after my death you are sure to become utterly
corrupt and to turn from the way I have commanded you. In days to come, disaster will fall
upon you because you will do evil in the sight of
the LORD and provoke him to anger by what your
hands have made." Dt 4:26; 9:6,24; 32:1

The Song of Moses

30And Moses recited the words of this song
from beginning to end in the hearing of the whole
assembly of Israel:

32 Listen, O heavens, and I will speak;
hear, O earth, the words of my mouth.

2Let my teaching fall like rain
and my words descend like dew,
like showers on new grass,
like abundant rain on tender plants. Isa 55:11

3I will proclaim the name of the LORD. Ex 33:19
Oh, praise the greatness of our God! Dt 3:24
4He is the Rock, his works are perfect, 2Sa 22:31
and all his ways are just.
A faithful God who does no wrong,
upright and just is he. Dt 7:9

5They have acted corruptly toward him;

to their shame they are no longer his
children,
but a warped and crooked generation.[a]
6Is this the way you repay the LORD,
O foolish and unwise people? Ps 74:2; 116:12
Is he not your Father, your Creator,[b]
who made you and formed you? Dt 1:31

7Remember the days of old;
consider the generations long past. Ps 44:1
Ask your father and he will tell you,
your elders, and they will explain to you.
8When the Most High gave the nations their
inheritance,
when he divided all mankind,
he set up boundaries for the peoples
according to the number of the sons of
Israel.[c] Ge 11:8; Ac 17:26
9For the LORD's portion is his people,
Jacob his allotted inheritance. Jer 10:16

10In a desert land he found him,
in a barren and howling waste. Jer 2:6
He shielded him and cared for him;
he guarded him as the apple of his eye,
11like an eagle that stirs up its nest
and hovers over its young,
that spreads its wings to catch them
and carries them on its pinions. Ex 19:4
12The LORD alone led him;
no foreign god was with him. Dt 4:35; Isa 43:12

13He made him ride on the heights of the land
and fed him with the fruit of the fields.
He nourished him with honey from the rock,
and with oil from the flinty crag, Dt 8:8
14with curds and milk from herd and flock
and with fattened lambs and goats,
with choice rams of Bashan
and the finest kernels of wheat.
You drank the foaming blood of the grape.

15Jeshurun[d] grew fat and kicked;
filled with food, he became heavy and sleek.
He abandoned the God who made him
and rejected the Rock his Savior. Isa 1:4,28
16They made him jealous with their foreign gods
and angered him with their detestable idols.
17They sacrificed to demons, which are not
God—
gods they had not known,
gods that recently appeared,
gods your fathers did not fear. Dt 28:64; Jdg 5:8
18You deserted the Rock, who fathered you;
you forgot the God who gave you birth.

19The LORD saw this and rejected them Jer 44:21-23
because he was angered by his sons and
daughters. Ps 106:40
20"I will hide my face from them," he said,
"and see what their end will be;
for they are a perverse generation,
children who are unfaithful.
21They made me jealous by what is no god
and angered me with their worthless idols.
I will make them envious by those who are
not a people;
I will make them angry by a nation that
has no understanding. Ro 10:19
22For a fire has been kindled by my wrath,
one that burns to the realm of death[e]
below.
It will devour the earth and its harvests
and set afire the foundations of the
mountains. Jer 15:14; La 4:11

23"I will heap calamities upon them
and spend my arrows against them. Dt 29:21
24I will send wasting famine against them,
consuming pestilence and deadly plague;
I will send against them the fangs of wild
beasts, Lev 26:22
the venom of vipers that glide in the dust.
25In the street the sword will make them
childless;
in their homes terror will reign.
Young men and young women will perish,
infants and gray-haired men. 2Ch 36:17; Eze 7:15
26I said I would scatter them
and blot out their memory from mankind,
27but I dreaded the taunt of the enemy,
lest the adversary misunderstand
and say, 'Our hand has triumphed;
the LORD has not done all this.'" Isa 10:13

28They are a nation without sense,
there is no discernment in them. Isa 1:3; 27:11
29If only they were wise and would understand
this
and discern what their end will be! Ps 81:13
30How could one man chase a thousand,
or two put ten thousand to flight,
unless their Rock had sold them,
unless the LORD had given them up? Lev 26:8
31For their rock is not like our Rock,
as even our enemies concede. Ge 49:24
32Their vine comes from the vine of Sodom
and from the fields of Gomorrah.
Their grapes are filled with poison,
and their clusters with bitterness. Dt 29:18
33Their wine is the venom of serpents,
the deadly poison of cobras. Ps 58:4

34"Have I not kept this in reserve

[a]5 Or *Corrupt are they and not his children, / a generation warped and twisted to their shame* [b]6 Or *Father, who bought you*
[c]8 Masoretic Text; Dead Sea Scrolls (see also Septuagint) *sons of God* [d]15 *Jeshurun* means *the upright one*, that is, Israel.
[e]22 Hebrew *to Sheol*

and sealed it in my vaults?
35It is mine to avenge; I will repay.
In due time their foot will slip;
their day of disaster is near
and their doom rushes upon them." Ro 12:19

36The LORD will judge his people
and have compassion on his servants
when he sees their strength is gone
and no one is left, slave or free. Ps 135:14
37He will say: "Now where are their gods,
the rock they took refuge in, Jdg 10:14; Jer 2:28
38the gods who ate the fat of their sacrifices
and drank the wine of their drink offerings?
Let them rise up to help you!
Let them give you shelter!

39"See now that I myself am He!
There is no god besides me. Isa 41:4; 45:5
I put to death and I bring to life,
I have wounded and I will heal,
and no one can deliver out of my hand.
40I lift my hand to heaven and declare:
As surely as I live forever,
41when I sharpen my flashing sword
and my hand grasps it in judgment, Isa 66:16
I will take vengeance on my adversaries
and repay those who hate me. Jer 50:29
42I will make my arrows drunk with blood,
while my sword devours flesh:
the blood of the slain and the captives,
the heads of the enemy leaders." Jer 12:12

43Rejoice, O nations, with his people,[a, b]
for he will avenge the blood of his servants;
he will take vengeance on his enemies
and make atonement for his land and
people. Ps 85:1; Rev 19:2

44Moses came with Joshua[c] son of Nun and
spoke all the words of this song in the hearing
of the people. 45When Moses finished reciting all
these words to all Israel, 46he said to them, "Take
to heart all the words I have solemnly declared to
you this day, so that you may command your
children to obey carefully all the words of this law.
47They are not just idle words for you—they are
your life. By them you will live long in the land you
are crossing the Jordan to possess." Eze 40:4; Dt 30:20

Moses to Die on Mount Nebo

48On that same day the LORD told Moses, 49"Go
up into the Abarim Range to Mount Nebo in
Moab, across from Jericho, and view Canaan, the
land I am giving the Israelites as their own possession. 50There on the mountain that you have
climbed you will die and be gathered to your people, just as your brother Aaron died on Mount
Hor and was gathered to his people. 51This is because both of you broke faith with me in the presence of the Israelites at the waters of Meribah Kadesh in the Desert of Zin and because you did not
uphold my holiness among the Israelites. 52There-
fore, you will see the land only from a distance;
you will not enter the land I am giving to the
people of Israel." Ge 25:8; Nu 20:11-13; 27:12

Moses Blesses the Tribes

33 This is the blessing that Moses the man of
God pronounced on the Israelites before
his death. 2He said: Jos 14:6

"The LORD came from Sinai
and dawned over them from Seir;
he shone forth from Mount Paran. Ps 50:2
He came with[d] myriads of holy ones
from the south, from his mountain
slopes.[e] Da 17:10; Rev 5:11
3Surely it is you who love the people;
all the holy ones are in your hand.
At your feet they all bow down,
and from you receive instruction, Lk 10:39
4the law that Moses gave us,
the possession of the assembly of Jacob.
5He was king over Jeshurun[f]
when the leaders of the people assembled,
along with the tribes of Israel. Nu 23:21

6"Let Reuben live and not die,
nor[g] his men be few."

7And this he said about Judah:

"Hear, O LORD, the cry of Judah;
bring him to his people.
With his own hands he defends his cause.
Oh, be his help against his foes!" Ge 49:10

8About Levi he said:

"Your Thummim and Urim belong
to the man you favored. Ex 28:30
You tested him at Massah;
you contended with him at the waters of
Meribah. Ex 17:7
9He said of his father and mother,
'I have no regard for them.'
He did not recognize his brothers
or acknowledge his own children,
but he watched over your word
and guarded your covenant. Ex 32:26-29; Mal 2:5
10He teaches your precepts to Jacob
and your law to Israel.
He offers incense before you
and whole burnt offerings on your altar.
11Bless all his skills, O LORD,
and be pleased with the work of his hands.

[a]43 Or *Make his people rejoice, O nations* [b]43 Masoretic Text; Dead Sea Scrolls (see also Septuagint) *people, / and let all the angels worship him /* [c]44 Hebrew *Hoshea,* a variant of *Joshua* [d]2 Or *from* [e]2 The meaning of the Hebrew for this phrase is uncertain. [f]5 *Jeshurun* means *the upright one,* that is, Israel; also in verse 26. [g]6 Or *but let*

Smite the loins of those who rise up against him;
strike his foes till they rise no more."

[12]About Benjamin he said:

"Let the beloved of the LORD rest secure in him,
for he shields him all day long,
and the one the LORD loves rests between his shoulders." Ex 28:12; Dt 12:10

[13]About Joseph he said:

"May the LORD bless his land
with the precious dew from heaven above
and with the deep waters that lie below;
[14]with the best the sun brings forth
and the finest the moon can yield;
[15]with the choicest gifts of the ancient mountains
and the fruitfulness of the everlasting hills;
[16]with the best gifts of the earth and its fullness
and the favor of him who dwelt in the burning bush.
Let all these rest on the head of Joseph,
on the brow of the prince among[a] his brothers. Ex 3:2
[17]In majesty he is like a firstborn bull;
his horns are the horns of a wild ox.
With them he will gore the nations,
even those at the ends of the earth. Nu 23:22
Such are the ten thousands of Ephraim;
such are the thousands of Manasseh."

[18]About Zebulun he said:

"Rejoice, Zebulun, in your going out,
and you, Issachar, in your tents. Ge 49:13-15
[19]They will summon peoples to the mountain
and there offer sacrifices of righteousness;
they will feast on the abundance of the seas,
on the treasures hidden in the sand."

[20]About Gad he said:

"Blessed is he who enlarges Gad's domain!
Gad lives there like a lion,
tearing at arm or head. Ge 30:11; 49:19
[21]He chose the best land for himself;
the leader's portion was kept for him.
When the heads of the people assembled,
he carried out the LORD's righteous will,
and his judgments concerning Israel."

[22]About Dan he said:

"Dan is a lion's cub,
springing out of Bashan." Ge 49:16

[23]About Naphtali he said:

"Naphtali is abounding with the favor of the LORD
and is full of his blessing;
he will inherit southward to the lake."

[24]About Asher he said:

"Most blessed of sons is Asher;
let him be favored by his brothers,
and let him bathe his feet in oil. Ge 49:21
[25]The bolts of your gates will be iron and bronze, Ne 3:3
and your strength will equal your days.

[26]"There is no one like the God of Jeshurun,
who rides on the heavens to help you
and on the clouds in his majesty. Ex 15:11
[27]The eternal God is your refuge,
and underneath are the everlasting arms.
He will drive out your enemy before you,
saying, 'Destroy him!' Dt 7:2; Jos 24:18
[28]So Israel will live in safety alone;
Jacob's spring is secure
in a land of grain and new wine,
where the heavens drop dew. Ge 27:28; Jer 23:6
[29]Blessed are you, O Israel!
Who is like you,
a people saved by the LORD? 2Sa 7:23; Ps 144:15
He is your shield and helper
and your glorious sword.
Your enemies will cower before you,
and you will trample down their high places.[b]" Ex 18:4; Ps 115:9-11

The Death of Moses

34 Then Moses climbed Mount Nebo from
the plains of Moab to the top of Pisgah,
across from Jericho. There the LORD showed him
the whole land—from Gilead to Dan, [2]all of
Naphtali, the territory of Ephraim and Manasseh,
all the land of Judah as far as the western sea,[c]
[3]the Negev and the whole region from the Valley
of Jericho, the City of Palms, as far as Zoar. [4]Then
the LORD said to him, "This is the land I promised
on oath to Abraham, Isaac and Jacob when I said,
'I will give it to your descendants.' I have let you
see it with your eyes, but you will not cross over
into it." Ge 12:7; Dt 32:52; 2Ch 28:15
[5]And Moses the servant of the LORD died there
in Moab, as the LORD had said. [6]He buried him[d]
in Moab, in the valley opposite Beth Peor, but to
this day no one knows where his grave is. [7]Moses
was a hundred and twenty years old when he died,
yet his eyes were not weak nor his strength gone.
[8]The Israelites grieved for Moses in the plains of
Moab thirty days, until the time of weeping and
mourning was over. Jos 1:1-2; Jude 1:9; Ge 27:1

[a]16 Or *of the one separated from* [b]29 Or *will tread upon their bodies* [c]2 That is, the Mediterranean [d]6 Or *He was buried*

[9]Now Joshua son of Nun was filled with the spirit[a] of wisdom because Moses had laid his hands on him. So the Israelites listened to him and did what the LORD had commanded Moses.

[10]Since then, no prophet has risen in Israel like Moses, whom the LORD knew face to face, [11]who did all those miraculous signs and wonders the LORD sent him to do in Egypt—to Pharaoh and to all his officials and to his whole land. [12]For no one has ever shown the mighty power or performed the awesome deeds that Moses did in the sight of all Israel. Dt 18:15,18; Ex 33:11; Nu 12:6,8

[a]9 Or *Spirit*

JOSHUA

The book of Joshua brings us into the historical section of the Old Testament, the first part of which can be called the period of the rise of the nation. This era is covered in five books—Joshua, Judges, Ruth, 1 Samuel and 2 Samuel. In the book of Joshua, the Israelites invade, conquer, distribute and settle down in the land of Canaan. The events recorded in Joshua took place during a span of approximately 25 years. All the way through, one person stands out as God's appointed leader and shining example—the man chosen to bring Moses' work to completion and establish Israel in the promised land. Joshua was God's man at God's time to be a part of God's work of bringing triumph after tragedy.

WRITER: *Joshua*

DATE: *c.1390 B.C.*

PURPOSE: *To reassure people that what God promises . . . God accomplishes*

KEY MESSAGE: *Faith is the victory*

KEY TERM: *"Possession"*

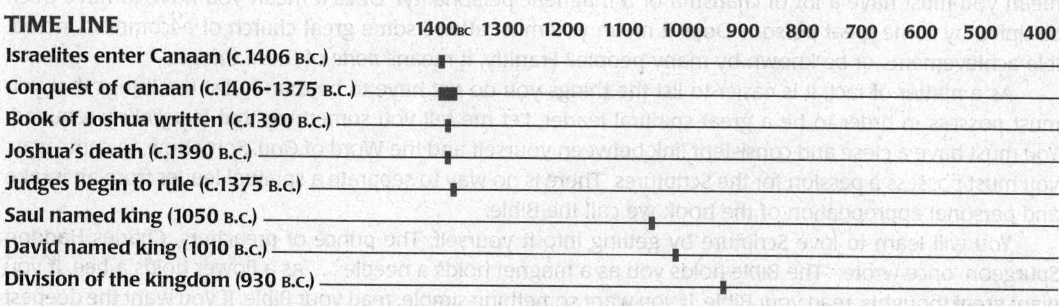

Triumph After Tragedy

OUTSIDE CANAAN / PROMISES GIVEN

COMMISSIONING THE LEADER PREPARING THE PEOPLE	CONQUERING THE ENEMY		DIVIDING THE SPOIL				WARNING THE VICTORS
Invasion of Land	Subjection of Land		Distribution of Land				The Conclusion
	CENTRAL CAMPAIGN		PHASE ONE	PHASE TWO	PHASE THREE		
The commission *(1)* The spying *(2)* The Jordan *(3)* The memorials *(4)* The consecration *(5)*	Jericho *(6)* Ai (Defeat) *(7)* Ai (Victory) *(8)* Gibeonites *(9)*	Southern Campaign *(10)* Northern Campaign (and survey) *(11)* Summary by kings *(12)*	Reuben, Gad, ½ Manasseh *(13)* Caleb's auto-biography *(14)* Judah *(15)* Ephraim *(16)* ½ Manasseh *(17)*	Benjamin *(18)* Simeon, Zebulun, Issachar, Asher, Naphtali, Dan, Joshua *(19)*	Man-slaughter refuge *(20)* Levites (48 towns) *(21)*	Civil war threat *(22)*	Separation *(23)* Service *(24)*
CHAPTERS 1–5	***CHAPTERS 6–9***	***CHAPTERS 10–12***	***CHAPTERS 13–17***	***CHAPTERS 18–19***	***CHAPTERS 20–21***	***CHAPTER 22***	***CHAPTERS 23–24***

INSIDE CANAAN / PROMISES FULFILLED

What does it mean to be a spiritual leader? Does it mean you must have your life all together? Does it mean you must have a lot of charisma or a magnetic personality? Does it mean you have to have been discipled by some great person? Does it mean you must attend some great church or accomplish incredible achievements or be known by many people? Frankly, it means *none* of these things.

As a matter of fact, it is easier to list the things you do *not* have to be than to list the things that you must possess in order to be a great spiritual leader. Let me tell you something that is *definitely* required: You must have a close and consistent link between yourself and the Word of God. Somehow, in some way, you must possess a passion for the Scriptures. There is no way to separate a spiritual leader from an intake and personal appropriation of the book we call the Bible.

You will learn to love Scripture by getting into it yourself. The prince of preachers, Charles Haddon Spurgeon, once wrote: "The Bible holds you as a magnet holds a needle . . . as a flower holds a bee. If you want great thoughts, read your Bible. If you want something simple, read your Bible. If you want the deepest and highest truth that ever was, read your Bible." What can I add to these wonderful words except a hearty, "Amen!" Leaders must love the Word of God and keep it close to their hearts and ever on their lips. Furthermore, spiritual leaders must walk in obedience to God's Word and His will.

A Leader Called by God

Joshua was just such a leader . . . a man who loved God and obeyed His Word. The book named after Joshua is an account of warfare, of conquest, and of a great triumph following the tragedy of a forty-year period when the people of Israel wandered in the desert. In Joshua you will read of the invasion, subjection and ultimately the distribution of the land of Canaan. Joshua was called by God to be the man to lead God's people into the promised land. What a responsibility!

There is no specific verse in the Bible that clearly states that Joshua wrote this book. But tradition, logic and the accepted title of the book all point to Joshua as the author. I suggest that this book is the result of a "journal" kept on a regular basis—either by Joshua himself or by someone who was very close to the events recorded in the book. Some of what is written in the book of Joshua is too detailed not to have been the result of an eyewitness account. There is no place in the book that dates its contents, but when you do your figuring from the exodus and add the forty years for the desert wanderings you come up with a date of about 1400 B.C.

Speaking of Journals . . .

I have often encouraged people to keep a journal. This is a discipline I have practiced for many years. A journal is different from a diary. A diary is a record of what you do. A journal is a record of what God is doing in your life and through you. If you want to get a handle on your life and begin to track the spiritual growth in your life, start a journal. You don't have to write in your journal every day but only at those junctures when God reveals some insight to you or teaches you during a time of trial or provides you with some blessing. Make a record of it. Write down your thoughts. Keep a journal of *His* hand in *your* life.

The Value of Good Examples

Joshua was born in a slave camp in Egypt. In the earliest record of Joshua, he was called "Moses' aide." This means he was trained at the feet of Moses. Today we might use the term, "intern." The man who spoke with God face to face trained and discipled Joshua. He was Joshua's mentor. There was an historic link between the lives of Moses and Joshua.

You want to be a man or a woman of God? Spend time up close and personal with godly people—preferably one or two you greatly respect. Learn their ways. Learn the techniques and the character development that have made them great. Observe and follow their example . . . you won't regret it.

Joshua was also Moses' close companion (Exodus 24:13). He was tutored and shaped by Moses (Exodus 33:11). It stood to reason that Joshua would become God's choice as Moses' replacement. When Moses died, Joshua took up right where the mourning left off in the history of the Hebrews (Deuteronomy 31:14,23). When we come to the end of Moses' life, we find Joshua stepping into a big pair of sandals. He was ready for the task, however, because he had learned from the man who once wore them.

Stop Mourning and Start Moving

Chapter 1 begins with the Lord's speaking to Joshua after a time of mourning over the death of Moses. God let Joshua know that the time for mourning was over; it was time for him and for all the Hebrews to move ahead. Joshua was reminded that Moses was dead. He was gone. Joshua could no longer live in Moses' shadow. God promised Joshua that He alone would be the One to whom Joshua must look as he led the people. Look at the awesome promise God gave Joshua:

> *I will give you every place where you set your foot, as I promised Moses . . . No one will be able to stand up against you all the days of your life. As I was with Moses, so I will be with you; I will never leave you nor forsake you (Joshua 1:3,5).*

What courage that must have given Joshua! I wonder if he returned to these words in his mind again and again. Probably so.

Faith Is the Victory

The theme of the book of Joshua is this: *Faith is the victory*. God had promised the Israelites the land. As they believed Him, obeyed Him and lived by faith, God gave them the fulfillment of His promises.

Let's scan the book's chapters and note the occasions when the people were faithful—and therefore victorious. In chapter 1 we read of the commissioning of their new leader. Try to put yourself in Joshua's place . . . his longtime friend, mentor and leader was now dead. All the load Moses once carried appears to be placed squarely on his shoulders. It is easy to understand his fear. It makes a lot of sense that God gave Joshua the same command three times in the first nine verses of the book, "Be strong and (very) courageous." The Lord wanted Joshua to realize that the full weight of responsibility rested *not on him*, but *on the Lord God*. In chapters 2–5 we find the preparation of the Israelites. Here, the people were mobilized and then brought into Canaan. If they were faithful to obey and march forward, the Lord would give them the victory.

In chapters 6–12 we read about the subjection of the promised land. A close examination reveals that the central campaign started at Jericho. The people of God were at a very strategic city. They had come up across the Jordan—think of it as the first Normandy . . . the first "D day." Their plan was to invade Jericho and weaken the troops. Once they had made that strategic inroad there, they would sweep to the south and annihilate their enemies and then go to the north to take the major forces away. Jericho was strategic for the maneuver. As the Israelites came across the Jordan River, they must have viewed the wall of Jericho from a distance and thought, "How in the world can we possibly scale that wall?" Joshua and his troops probably began to think about ladders, ropes, spears, swords . . .

That's so often what we do, isn't it? When we come across a large obstacle, we begin to use our own ingenuity. But the Lord let Joshua know He had a plan. I suggest to you that the strategy given for fighting the battle at Jericho was the strangest strategy any warrior ever received from a commanding officer! But in this seemingly impossible situation, God said, "Faith is the victory. Trust Me. Just believe Me." The Israelites followed God's unusual plan and experienced victory through their faith in the Lord. The wall around Jericho collapsed.

The Israelites didn't permanently learn that lesson, because in the very next chapter after the fall of Jericho we read the story of a defeat (see chapter 7). In a little suburb of Ai, they sent a few troops down to overtake the city. The results this time were quite different. They failed miserably because they weren't walking by faith. One of the troops, Achan by name, picked up a Babylonian robe (7:21) and said to himself, "Ah, that would look nice," and so he tucked it away even though God had told the people not to take *any* of their enemies' garments. But Achan didn't listen; he failed to obey and walk by faith. He did things his own way. As a result, the people of Israel learned a very important lesson: You can never presume on the victory that God promises. It requires obedience *every step of the way*. God doesn't give His answers on credit; it's a day-by-day process.

By driving a wedge into the central section of the land of Canaan, the Israelites divided the power of the Canaanites. They severed their enemies' sense of military strength. Then they moved south (chapter 10), and then they moved north (chapter 11). When you get to Joshua 11:16, you will see that Joshua did exactly what God led him to do. When God said, "Joshua, do this," he did it. That's wise leadership. True spiritual leaders demonstrate complete reliance on the Lord.

In Joshua we learn a couple of powerful principles that live on to this very day. First, *what God promises, God accomplishes*. Now we need to be careful with this principle. God's provision may not come when we expect it, or just as we envisioned it, or because we are worthy, or according to our logic, but just because the Lord is God. Don't forget: The Lord accomplishes His will and brings victory in His time and for *His* glory, not ours. Second, *God's abundant provisions do not nullify the need to obey*. All the way throughout the book of Joshua, the Israelites had to be reminded to obey. God's abundant provisions were always connected to the faithful obedience of His people.

Joshua is a great book on the subject of victory. If you want to use a book in the Bible to teach about leadership or the victorious life or a life of obedience that is honored with victory, this is a great book to study. This is a book that will build up faith to the point of invincibility. Joshua is a book that promises . . . and delivers.

Commissioning the Leader — Chapter 1

Joshua had many years of training for leadership. He studied under one of the best-known leaders in all the Bible . . . a man named Moses. Now his friend and mentor was gone. Here stood Joshua, with an entire nation looking to him. He had the training, the gifts and the people who were ready to follow. Now he heard the voice of God commissioning him to be the leader of this great nation. The Lord urged him to be "strong and courageous" (1:6) as he took on this monumental task.

Joshua accepted this high calling. His example stands before believers of all times. God can use ordinary people for extraordinary purposes. Joshua had always been the follower; Moses had been the leader. But during those years of preparation, Joshua watched his mentor and learned vital principles he would one day employ. Now it was time for Joshua to step forward and be the leader God had prepared him to be.

The LORD Commands Joshua

1 After the death of Moses the servant of the
LORD, the LORD said to Joshua son of Nun,
Moses' aide: 2"Moses my servant is dead. Now
then, you and all these people, get ready to cross
the Jordan River into the land I am about to give
to them—to the Israelites. 3I will give you every
place where you set your foot, as I promised Moses. 4Your territory will extend from the desert to
Lebanon, and from the great river, the Euphrates—all the Hittite country—to the Great Sea[a]
on the west. 5No one will be able to stand up
against you all the days of your life. As I was with
Moses, so I will be with you; I will never leave you
nor forsake you. Dt 7:24; 11:24; 31:6-8

LIVING  **INSIGHT**

God may be invisible, but He's in touch. You may not be able to see Him, but He is in control. And that includes you—and all your circumstances. That includes what you've just lost. That includes what you've just gained. That includes all of life . . . past, present and future.

(See Joshua 1:5.)

6"Be strong and courageous, because you will
lead these people to inherit the land I swore to
their forefathers to give them. 7Be strong and very
courageous. Be careful to obey all the law my servant Moses gave you; do not turn from it to the
right or to the left, that you may be successful
wherever you go. 8Do not let this Book of the Law
depart from your mouth; meditate on it day and
night, so that you may be careful to do everything
written in it. Then you will be prosperous and
successful. 9Have I not commanded you? Be
strong and courageous. Do not be terrified; do not
be discouraged, for the LORD your God will be with
you wherever you go." Dt 31:23; Ps 1:1-3; Jer 1:8

LIVING  **INSIGHT**

It's impossible to live victoriously for Jesus Christ without courage! That's why God's thrice-spoken command to Joshua is as timeless as it is true.

(See Joshua 1:9.)

10So Joshua ordered the officers of the people:
11"Go through the camp and tell the people, 'Get
your supplies ready. Three days from now you will
cross the Jordan here to go in and take possession
of the land the LORD your God is giving you for
your own.' " Jos 3:2; Joel 3:2
12But to the Reubenites, the Gadites and the
half-tribe of Manasseh, Joshua said, 13"Remember
the command that Moses the servant of the LORD
gave you: 'The LORD your God is giving you rest
and has granted you this land.' 14Your wives, your
children and your livestock may stay in the land
that Moses gave you east of the Jordan, but all
your fighting men, fully armed, must cross over
ahead of your brothers. You are to help your
brothers 15until the LORD gives them rest, as he has
done for you, and until they too have taken possession of the land that the LORD your God is
giving them. After that, you may go back and occupy your own land, which Moses the servant of
the LORD gave you east of the Jordan toward the
sunrise." Nu 32:20-22; Jos 22:1-4; Dt 3:18-20
16Then they answered Joshua, "Whatever you
have commanded us we will do, and wherever you
send us we will go. 17Just as we fully obeyed Moses,
so we will obey you. Only may the LORD your God
be with you as he was with Moses. 18Whoever
rebels against your word and does not obey your
words, whatever you may command them, will be
put to death. Only be strong and courageous!"

Preparing the People — Chapters 2–5

Once Joshua had his commission, he was ready to move. Like any good military commander, he surveyed the land and sized up the enemy. He sent spies into the land to help determine the best point of entry and attack. Remember, the Lord promised the people they would possess the promised land, but He also told them they would have to fight for it. The people of Israel needed to position themselves in the right place. As you read this account, you will see how the Lord again parted waters so

[a]4 That is, the Mediterranean

JOSHUA

Moving Forward in God's Power

"Be strong and courageous. Do not be terrified; do not be discouraged, for the LORD your God will be with you wherever you go."
—JOSHUA 1:9

"Moses my servant is dead" (Joshua 1:2). With those words we begin the book of Joshua knowing that an era has come to an end. But this opening chapter also gives us a sense of God's realism. If the people of Israel had been given their way, they very likely would have stood by that memorial the rest of their days—unwilling and unable to move. But God is always on the move, always looking ahead, always leading us forward. Yes, a great man was no longer there to provide leadership. But as A.W. Tozer once wrote, "When a man of God dies, nothing of God dies." So God spoke directly and frankly to a man named Joshua, Moses' successor, encouraging him to move the people forward into Canaan and reassuring him of His presence.

Put yourself in Joshua's sandals for a moment. He had seen Moses at his best and at his worst. He had seen the miracles that flowed from Moses' staff year after year. To Joshua, the man Moses and the God of Moses were so interconnected that they seemed almost inseparable. Now Joshua heard that same God assuring him with words to this effect: "As I was with Moses, so I will be with you. Nothing of Me died when Moses died. This is all part of My plan. Now, Joshua, go and take the land."

At this point you can almost hear Joshua's knees knocking under his robe. He'd begun to listen to God's plan, and he got scared. So God reassured Joshua in the strongest possible terms: "Be strong and courageous" (1:6). And in case Joshua missed it, God said it again in verses 7 and 9. Finally, the people themselves echoed the refrain in verse 18. They were a unified group, and they were ready to accept God's challenge to take the land of Canaan with all fear of failure banished from their minds and hearts.

Joshua 6 lets us in on one of this great leader's finest moments. God brought Joshua to a powerfully fortified city, saying, "See, I have delivered Jericho into your hands, along with its king and its fighting men" (6:2). Okay, let's assess what we have here: a ragtag band of nomads who don't know much about fighting; a thirty-foot-high wall, incredibly thick, made of solid stone. Now put yourself in Joshua's shoes, and leave the halo and wings off, okay? Remember, he's just one solitary person, just one ordinary human being. He had never seen walls crumble before. Joshua glanced up at the wall, then glanced back at his people. Can you imagine what was going through his head? Utter, complete confidence that God would make true on His promise? Maybe. But don't you think it was a bit more likely that Joshua muttered under his breath, "Yeah, right. How in the world do you expect us to pull *this* one off?"

How *could* the Israelites win this victory? Joshua stood ready for a great military strategy. "You got your boots tightened? Got your swords sharpened? Got your bows and arrows ready? Throw them away. You're not going to need them," God told him, in effect. "I'm moving you forward in My power, not your own." Then Joshua took this plan to the people. The beautiful part of this chapter is that we do not hear one word of resistance or reluctance from the Israelites. They were unified. Remarkable! After Joshua laid out the plan, the people strapped on their sandals, polished their trumpets and prepared for war. They waited to see what God would do, and those walls came crashing down, just as He had promised.

Our last glimpse of Joshua shows him reviewing some history for the people of Israel (chapter 24). The land of Canaan was now theirs. The people were enjoying the riches of the land. In this context, Joshua recounted how God's hand had been working in their lives in the years since the exodus from Egypt. He began with Abraham, their most distant ancestor, and showed how God had moved them forward in the intervening years, all the way to the present. Joshua then gave the people of Israel a choice, realizing that they now had a tantalizing menu of gods and religions to choose from. But there was no doubt where Joshua stood: "As for me and my household, we will serve the LORD" (24:15).

that His people could pass over on dry ground. What a confirmation for Joshua! The same God who had parted the Red Sea when Moses led the people now drew back the waters of the Jordan River. God was still leading the people of Israel!

There was one more detail of preparation. During their forty years in the desert the people had stopped circumcising their sons. The sign God had given to Abraham was no longer being observed. The sign of circumcision carried deep spiritual meaning. Before the people could take over the land, all the men needed to be circumcised (5:3). This act was a dramatic reaffirmation of the covenant—the final preparation for God's people to enter the promised land. At last they were ready to move forward!

Rahab and the Spies

2 Then Joshua son of Nun secretly sent two
spies from Shittim. "Go, look over the land,"
he said, "especially Jericho." So they went and entered the house of a prostitute[a] named Rahab and
stayed there. Heb 11:31; Jas 2:25
2The king of Jericho was told, "Look! Some of
the Israelites have come here tonight to spy out the
land." 3So the king of Jericho sent this message to
Rahab: "Bring out the men who came to you and
entered your house, because they have come to
spy out the whole land."
4But the woman had taken the two men and
hidden them. She said, "Yes, the men came to me,
but I did not know where they had come from. 5At
dusk, when it was time to close the city gate, the
men left. I don't know which way they went. Go
after them quickly. You may catch up with them."
6(But she had taken them up to the roof and hidden them under the stalks of flax she had laid out
on the roof.) 7So the men set out in pursuit of the
spies on the road that leads to the fords of the
Jordan, and as soon as the pursuers had gone out,
the gate was shut. 2Sa 17:19-20; Nu 22:1; Jos 6:22
8Before the spies lay down for the night, she
went up on the roof 9and said to them, "I know
that the LORD has given this land to you and that
a great fear of you has fallen on us, so that all who
live in this country are melting in fear because of
you. 10We have heard how the LORD dried up the
water of the Red Sea[b] for you when you came out
of Egypt, and what you did to Sihon and Og, the
two kings of the Amorites east of the Jordan,
whom you completely destroyed.[c] 11When we
heard of it, our hearts melted and everyone's courage failed because of you, for the LORD your God
is God in heaven above and on the earth below.
12Now then, please swear to me by the LORD that
you will show kindness to my family, because I
have shown kindness to you. Give me a sure sign
13that you will spare the lives of my father and
mother, my brothers and sisters, and all who belong to them, and that you will save us from
death." Ex 14:21; 23:27; Nu 21:21,24,34-35
14"Our lives for your lives!" the men assured
her. "If you don't tell what we are doing, we will
treat you kindly and faithfully when the LORD gives
us the land." Jdg 1:24; Mt 5:7
15So she let them down by a rope through the
window, for the house she lived in was part of the
city wall. 16Now she had said to them, "Go to
the hills so the pursuers will not find you. Hide
yourselves there three days until they return, and
then go on your way." Ac 9:25; Jer 38:6,11
17The men said to her, "This oath you made us
swear will not be binding on us 18unless, when we
enter the land, you have tied this scarlet cord in the
window through which you let us down, and unless you have brought your father and mother,
your brothers and all your family into your house.
19If anyone goes outside your house into the street,
his blood will be on his own head; we will not be
responsible. As for anyone who is in the house
with you, his blood will be on our head if a hand
is laid on him. 20But if you tell what we are doing,
we will be released from the oath you made us
swear." Ge 24:8; Mt 27:25; Eze 33:4
21"Agreed," she replied. "Let it be as you say."
So she sent them away and they departed. And she
tied the scarlet cord in the window.
22When they left, they went into the hills and
stayed there three days, until the pursuers had
searched all along the road and returned without
finding them. 23Then the two men started back.
They went down out of the hills, forded the river
and came to Joshua son of Nun and told him
everything that had happened to them. 24They said
to Joshua, "The LORD has surely given the whole
land into our hands; all the people are melting in
fear because of us." ver 9

Crossing the Jordan

3 Early in the morning Joshua and all the Israelites set out from Shittim and went to the
Jordan, where they camped before crossing over.
2After three days the officers went throughout the
camp, 3giving orders to the people: "When you see
the ark of the covenant of the LORD your God, and
the priests, who are Levites, carrying it, you are to
move out from your positions and follow it. 4Then
you will know which way to go, since you have
never been this way before. But keep a distance of
about a thousand yards[d] between you and the
ark; do not go near it." Dt 31:9; Jos 2:1; 1:11
5Joshua told the people, "Consecrate your-

[a] 1 Or possibly *an innkeeper* [b] 10 Hebrew *Yam Suph*; that is, Sea of Reeds [c] 10 The Hebrew term refers to the irrevocable giving over of things or persons to the LORD, often by totally destroying them. [d] 4 Hebrew *about two thousand cubits* (about 900 meters)

selves, for tomorrow the LORD will do amazing things among you." Ex 19:10,14; Jos 7:13

6Joshua said to the priests, "Take up the ark of the covenant and pass on ahead of the people." So they took it up and went ahead of them.

7And the LORD said to Joshua, "Today I will begin to exalt you in the eyes of all Israel, so they may know that I am with you as I was with Moses. 8Tell the priests who carry the ark of the covenant: 'When you reach the edge of the Jordan's waters, go and stand in the river.'" Jos 1:5; 1Ch 29:25

9Joshua said to the Israelites, "Come here and listen to the words of the LORD your God. 10This is how you will know that the living God is among you and that he will certainly drive out before you the Canaanites, Hittites, Hivites, Perizzites, Girgashites, Amorites and Jebusites. 11See, the ark of the covenant of the Lord of all the earth will go into the Jordan ahead of you. 12Now then, choose twelve men from the tribes of Israel, one from each tribe. 13And as soon as the priests who carry the ark of the LORD—the Lord of all the earth—set foot in the Jordan, its waters flowing downstream will be cut off and stand up in a heap." Dt 5:26

14So when the people broke camp to cross the Jordan, the priests carrying the ark of the covenant went ahead of them. 15Now the Jordan is at flood stage all during harvest. Yet as soon as the priests who carried the ark reached the Jordan and their feet touched the water's edge, 16the water from upstream stopped flowing. It piled up in a heap a great distance away, at a town called Adam in the vicinity of Zarethan, while the water flowing down to the Sea of the Arabah (the Salt Sea[a]) was completely cut off. So the people crossed over opposite Jericho. 17The priests who carried the ark of the covenant of the LORD stood firm on dry ground in the middle of the Jordan, while all Israel passed by until the whole nation had completed the crossing on dry ground. Ex 14:22,29; Jos 4:18; Ac 7:44-45

4 When the whole nation had finished crossing the Jordan, the LORD said to Joshua, 2"Choose twelve men from among the people, one from each tribe, 3and tell them to take up twelve stones from the middle of the Jordan from right where the priests stood and to carry them over with you and put them down at the place where you stay tonight." Dt 27:2; Jos 3:12; ver 20

4So Joshua called together the twelve men he had appointed from the Israelites, one from each tribe, 5and said to them, "Go over before the ark of the LORD your God into the middle of the Jordan. Each of you is to take up a stone on his shoulder, according to the number of the tribes of the Israelites, 6to serve as a sign among you. In the future, when your children ask you, 'What do these stones mean?' 7tell them that the flow of the Jordan was cut off before the ark of the covenant of the LORD. When it crossed the Jordan, the waters of the Jordan were cut off. These stones are to be a memorial to the people of Israel forever."

8So the Israelites did as Joshua commanded them. They took twelve stones from the middle of the Jordan, according to the number of the tribes of the Israelites, as the LORD had told Joshua; and they carried them over with them to their camp, where they put them down. 9Joshua set up the twelve stones that had been[b] in the middle of the Jordan at the spot where the priests who carried the ark of the covenant had stood. And they are there to this day. Ex 28:21; 1Sa 7:12

10Now the priests who carried the ark remained standing in the middle of the Jordan until everything the LORD had commanded Joshua was done by the people, just as Moses had directed Joshua. The people hurried over, 11and as soon as all of them had crossed, the ark of the LORD and the priests came to the other side while the people watched. 12The men of Reuben, Gad and the half-tribe of Manasseh crossed over, armed, in front of the Israelites, as Moses had directed them. 13About forty thousand armed for battle crossed over before the LORD to the plains of Jericho for war.

14That day the LORD exalted Joshua in the sight of all Israel; and they revered him all the days of his life, just as they had revered Moses. Jos 3:7

15Then the LORD said to Joshua, 16"Command the priests carrying the ark of the Testimony to come up out of the Jordan." Ex 25:22

17So Joshua commanded the priests, "Come up out of the Jordan."

18And the priests came up out of the river carrying the ark of the covenant of the LORD. No sooner had they set their feet on the dry ground than the waters of the Jordan returned to their place and ran at flood stage as before. Jos 3:15

19On the tenth day of the first month the people went up from the Jordan and camped at Gilgal on the eastern border of Jericho. 20And Joshua set up at Gilgal the twelve stones they had taken out of the Jordan. 21He said to the Israelites, "In the future when your descendants ask their fathers, 'What do these stones mean?' 22tell them, 'Israel crossed the Jordan on dry ground.' 23For the LORD your God dried up the Jordan before you until you had crossed over. The LORD your God did to the Jordan just what he had done to the Red Sea[c] when he dried it up before us until we had crossed over. 24He did this so that all the peoples of the earth might know that the hand of the LORD is powerful and so that you might always fear the LORD your God." Ex 15:16; 1Ki 8:42-43; Ps 106:8

[a] 16 That is, the Dead Sea [b] 9 Or *Joshua also set up twelve stones* [c] 23 Hebrew *Yam Suph*; that is, Sea of Reeds

Circumcision at Gilgal

5 Now when all the Amorite kings west of the Jordan and all the Canaanite kings along the coast heard how the LORD had dried up the Jordan before the Israelites until we had crossed over, their hearts melted and they no longer had the courage to face the Israelites. Nu 13:29; Jos 2:9-11

2At that time the LORD said to Joshua, "Make flint knives and circumcise the Israelites again." 3So Joshua made flint knives and circumcised the Israelites at Gibeath Haaraloth.[a] Ex 4:25

4Now this is why he did so: All those who came out of Egypt—all the men of military age—died in the desert on the way after leaving Egypt. 5All the people that came out had been circumcised, but all the people born in the desert during the journey from Egypt had not. 6The Israelites had moved about in the desert forty years until all the men who were of military age when they left Egypt had died, since they had not obeyed the LORD. For the LORD had sworn to them that they would not see the land that he had solemnly promised their fathers to give us, a land flowing with milk and honey. 7So he raised up their sons in their place, and these were the ones Joshua circumcised. They were still uncircumcised because they had not been circumcised on the way. 8And after the whole nation had been circumcised, they remained where they were in camp until they were healed.

9Then the LORD said to Joshua, "Today I have rolled away the reproach of Egypt from you." So the place has been called Gilgal[b] to this day.

10On the evening of the fourteenth day of the month, while camped at Gilgal on the plains of Jericho, the Israelites celebrated the Passover. 11The day after the Passover, that very day, they ate some of the produce of the land: unleavened bread and roasted grain. 12The manna stopped the day after[c] they ate this food from the land; there was no longer any manna for the Israelites, but that year they ate of the produce of Canaan. Ex 12:6

The Fall of Jericho

13Now when Joshua was near Jericho, he looked up and saw a man standing in front of him with a drawn sword in his hand. Joshua went up to him and asked, "Are you for us or for our enemies?"

14"Neither," he replied, "but as commander of the army of the LORD I have now come." Then Joshua fell facedown to the ground in reverence, and asked him, "What message does my Lord[d] have for his servant?" Ge 17:3; 19:1

15The commander of the LORD's army replied, "Take off your sandals, for the place where you are standing is holy." And Joshua did so. Ex 3:5; Ac 7:33

Conquering the Enemy — Chapters 6–12

As the Israelites invaded the land, Joshua had a plan of attack. First, the people would take the city of Jericho. Once they had made strategic inroads, they would sweep south and then north to destroy the Canaanites. When they had conquered the majority of their enemies, they would settle the land little by little with small mopping-up skirmishes. Joshua may even have thought, "God has promised to give us the land. How hard could it be?" However, Jericho was strongly fortified and secure. From a human perspective, there was no way to defeat and destroy this great fortress. In one of the Bible's most familiar stories, God called Joshua and the Israelites to overcome the city of Jericho through some highly unusual methods of warfare (chapter 6). Isn't that just like our God? Human wisdom would indicate one path, but divine instruction sends us down an entirely different road . . . and at the end of the journey, we look back and realize the great wisdom and powerful leading of our God.

These chapters record other victories and even a few defeats. Along the way the people discovered that the victory belonged to the Lord. They also learned that the only way to victory was to do the *Lord's will* the *Lord's way*. Deviation from God's instruction led to serious consequences for those who strayed. Obedience to the call led to victory and the conquest of the land.

6 Now Jericho was tightly shut up because of the Israelites. No one went out and no one came in. Jos 24:11

2Then the LORD said to Joshua, "See, I have delivered Jericho into your hands, along with its king and its fighting men. 3March around the city once with all the armed men. Do this for six days. 4Have seven priests carry trumpets of rams' horns in front of the ark. On the seventh day, march around the city seven times, with the priests blowing the trumpets. 5When you hear them sound a long blast on the trumpets, have all the people give a loud shout; then the wall of the city will collapse and the people will go up, every man straight in."

6So Joshua son of Nun called the priests and said to them, "Take up the ark of the covenant of the LORD and have seven priests carry trumpets in front of it." 7And he ordered the people, "Advance! March around the city, with the armed guard going ahead of the ark of the LORD."

8When Joshua had spoken to the people, the seven priests carrying the seven trumpets before the LORD went forward, blowing their trumpets, and the ark of the LORD's covenant followed them. 9The armed guard marched ahead of the priests who blew the trumpets, and the rear guard followed the ark. All this time the trumpets were sounding. 10But Joshua had commanded the people, "Do not give a war cry, do not raise your voices, do not say a word until the day I tell you

[a] 3 *Gibeath Haaraloth* means *hill of foreskins.* [b] 9 *Gilgal* sounds like the Hebrew for *roll.* [c] 12 Or *the day*
[d] 14 Or *lord*

to shout. Then shout!" 11So he had the ark of the LORD carried around the city, circling it once. Then the people returned to camp and spent the night there. Isa 52:12

12Joshua got up early the next morning and the priests took up the ark of the LORD. 13The seven priests carrying the seven trumpets went forward, marching before the ark of the LORD and blowing the trumpets. The armed men went ahead of them and the rear guard followed the ark of the LORD, while the trumpets kept sounding. 14So on the second day they marched around the city once and returned to the camp. They did this for six days.

15On the seventh day, they got up at daybreak and marched around the city seven times in the same manner, except that on that day they circled the city seven times. 16The seventh time around, when the priests sounded the trumpet blast, Joshua commanded the people, "Shout! For the LORD has given you the city! 17The city and all that is in it are to be devoted[a] to the LORD. Only Rahab the prostitute[b] and all who are with her in her house shall be spared, because she hid the spies we sent. 18But keep away from the devoted things, so that you will not bring about your own destruction by taking any of them. Otherwise you will make the camp of Israel liable to destruction and bring trouble on it. 19All the silver and gold and the articles of bronze and iron are sacred to the LORD and must go into his treasury." Lev 27:28; Jos 2:4; 7:1

20When the trumpets sounded, the people shouted, and at the sound of the trumpet, when the people gave a loud shout, the wall collapsed; so every man charged straight in, and they took the

LIVING  **INSIGHT**

Take heart. When God is involved, anything can happen. The One who split the Red Sea down the middle and leveled the wall around Jericho and brought His Son back from the dead takes delight in the incredible!

(See Joshua 6:20–21.)

city. 21They devoted the city to the LORD and destroyed with the sword every living thing in it—men and women, young and old, cattle, sheep and donkeys. Dt 20:16; Am 2:2

22Joshua said to the two men who had spied out the land, "Go into the prostitute's house and bring her out and all who belong to her, in accordance with your oath to her." 23So the young men who had done the spying went in and brought out Rahab, her father and mother and brothers and all who belonged to her. They brought out her entire family and put them in a place outside the camp of Israel. Jos 2:14; Heb 11:31

24Then they burned the whole city and everything in it, but they put the silver and gold and the articles of bronze and iron into the treasury of the LORD's house. 25But Joshua spared Rahab the prostitute, with her family and all who belonged to her, because she hid the men Joshua had sent as spies to Jericho—and she lives among the Israelites to this day. Jdg 1:25

26At that time Joshua pronounced this solemn oath: "Cursed before the LORD is the man who undertakes to rebuild this city, Jericho:

"At the cost of his firstborn son
  will he lay its foundations;
at the cost of his youngest
  will he set up its gates." 1Ki 16:34

27So the LORD was with Joshua, and his fame spread throughout the land. Jos 1:5; 9:1

Achan's Sin

7 But the Israelites acted unfaithfully in regard to the devoted things[c]; Achan son of Carmi, the son of Zimri,[d] the son of Zerah, of the tribe of Judah, took some of them. So the LORD's anger burned against Israel. Jos 6:18

2Now Joshua sent men from Jericho to Ai, which is near Beth Aven to the east of Bethel, and told them, "Go up and spy out the region." So the men went up and spied out Ai. Jos 18:12

3When they returned to Joshua, they said, "Not all the people will have to go up against Ai. Send two or three thousand men to take it and do not weary all the people, for only a few men are there." 4So about three thousand men went up; but they were routed by the men of Ai, 5who killed about thirty-six of them. They chased the Israelites from the city gate as far as the stone quarries[e] and struck them down on the slopes. At this the hearts of the people melted and became like water.

6Then Joshua tore his clothes and fell facedown to the ground before the ark of the LORD, remaining there till evening. The elders of Israel did the same, and sprinkled dust on their heads. 7And Joshua said, "Ah, Sovereign LORD, why did you ever bring this people across the Jordan to deliver us into the hands of the Amorites to destroy us? If only we had been content to stay on the other side of the Jordan! 8O Lord, what can I say, now that Israel has been routed by its enemies? 9The Canaanites and the other people of the country will hear about this and they will surround us and wipe

[a]17 The Hebrew term refers to the irrevocable giving over of things or persons to the LORD, often by totally destroying them; also in verses 18 and 21. [b]17 Or possibly *innkeeper*; also in verses 22 and 25 [c]1 The Hebrew term refers to the irrevocable giving over of things or persons to the LORD, often by totally destroying them; also in verses 11, 12, 13 and 15. [d]1 See Septuagint and 1 Chron. 2:6; Hebrew *Zabdi*; also in verses 17 and 18. [e]5 Or *as far as Shebarim*

out our name from the earth. What then will you do for your own great name?" Ex 32:12; Job 2:12

10The LORD said to Joshua, "Stand up! What are you doing down on your face? 11Israel has sinned; they have violated my covenant, which I commanded them to keep. They have taken some of the devoted things; they have stolen, they have lied, they have put them with their own possessions. 12That is why the Israelites cannot stand against their enemies; they turn their backs and run because they have been made liable to destruction. I will not be with you anymore unless you destroy whatever among you is devoted to destruction. Jos 6:17-19; Ac 5:1-2; Dt 29:27

13"Go, consecrate the people. Tell them, 'Consecrate yourselves in preparation for tomorrow; for this is what the LORD, the God of Israel, says: That which is devoted is among you, O Israel. You cannot stand against your enemies until you remove it. Jos 3:5; 6:18

14" 'In the morning, present yourselves tribe by tribe. The tribe that the LORD takes shall come forward clan by clan; the clan that the LORD takes shall come forward family by family; and the family that the LORD takes shall come forward man by man. 15He who is caught with the devoted things shall be destroyed by fire, along with all that belongs to him. He has violated the covenant of the LORD and has done a disgraceful thing in Israel!' "

16Early the next morning Joshua had Israel come forward by tribes, and Judah was taken. 17The clans of Judah came forward, and he took the Zerahites. He had the clan of the Zerahites come forward by families, and Zimri was taken. 18Joshua had his family come forward man by man, and Achan son of Carmi, the son of Zimri, the son of Zerah, of the tribe of Judah, was taken.

19Then Joshua said to Achan, "My son, give glory to the LORD,[a] the God of Israel, and give him the praise.[b] Tell me what you have done; do not hide it from me." Jer 13:16; Jn 9:24; 1Sa 6:5

20Achan replied, "It is true! I have sinned against the LORD, the God of Israel. This is what I have done: 21When I saw in the plunder a beautiful robe from Babylonia,[c] two hundred shekels[d] of silver and a wedge of gold weighing fifty shekels,[e] I coveted them and took them. They are hidden in the ground inside my tent, with the silver underneath." Eph 5:5; 1Ti 6:10

22So Joshua sent messengers, and they ran to the tent, and there it was, hidden in his tent, with the silver underneath. 23They took the things from the tent, brought them to Joshua and all the Israelites and spread them out before the LORD.

24Then Joshua, together with all Israel, took Achan son of Zerah, the silver, the robe, the gold wedge, his sons and daughters, his cattle, donkeys and sheep, his tent and all that he had, to the Valley of Achor. 25Joshua said, "Why have you brought this trouble on us? The LORD will bring trouble on you today." Jos 6:18; 15:7

Then all Israel stoned him, and after they had stoned the rest, they burned them. 26Over Achan they heaped up a large pile of rocks, which remains to this day. Then the LORD turned from his fierce anger. Therefore that place has been called the Valley of Achor[f] ever since. Dt 13:17; 17:5

Ai Destroyed

8 Then the LORD said to Joshua, "Do not be afraid; do not be discouraged. Take the whole army with you, and go up and attack Ai. For I have delivered into your hands the king of Ai, his people, his city and his land. 2You shall do to Ai and its king as you did to Jericho and its king, except that you may carry off their plunder and livestock for yourselves. Set an ambush behind the city."

3So Joshua and the whole army moved out to attack Ai. He chose thirty thousand of his best fighting men and sent them out at night 4with these orders: "Listen carefully. You are to set an ambush behind the city. Don't go very far from it. All of you be on the alert. 5I and all those with me will advance on the city, and when the men come out against us, as they did before, we will flee from them. 6They will pursue us until we have lured them away from the city, for they will say, 'They are running away from us as they did before.' So when we flee from them, 7you are to rise up from ambush and take the city. The LORD your God will give it into your hand. 8When you have taken the city, set it on fire. Do what the LORD has commanded. See to it; you have my orders." Jdg 7:7

9Then Joshua sent them off, and they went to the place of ambush and lay in wait between Bethel and Ai, to the west of Ai—but Joshua spent that night with the people. 2Ch 13:13

10Early the next morning Joshua mustered his men, and he and the leaders of Israel marched before them to Ai. 11The entire force that was with him marched up and approached the city and arrived in front of it. They set up camp north of Ai, with the valley between them and the city. 12Joshua had taken about five thousand men and set them in ambush between Bethel and Ai, to the west of the city. 13They had the soldiers take up their positions—all those in the camp to the north of the city and the ambush to the west of it. That night Joshua went into the valley. Ge 22:3

14When the king of Ai saw this, he and all the men of the city hurried out early in the morning to meet Israel in battle at a certain place overlook-

[a] *19* A solemn charge to tell the truth [b] *19* Or *and confess to him* [c] *21* Hebrew *Shinar* [d] *21* That is, about 5 pounds (about 2.3 kilograms) [e] *21* That is, about 1 1/4 pounds (about 0.6 kilogram) [f] *26* *Achor* means *trouble.*

ing the Arabah. But he did not know that an ambush had been set against him behind the city.
15Joshua and all Israel let themselves be driven
back before them, and they fled toward the desert.
16All the men of Ai were called to pursue them,
and they pursued Joshua and were lured away
from the city. 17Not a man remained in Ai or
Bethel who did not go after Israel. They left the city
open and went in pursuit of Israel. Jos 15:61; 18:12
18Then the LORD said to Joshua, "Hold out toward Ai the javelin that is in your hand, for into
your hand I will deliver the city." So Joshua held
out his javelin toward Ai. 19As soon as he did this,
the men in the ambush rose quickly from their
position and rushed forward. They entered the city
and captured it and quickly set it on fire. Ex 14:16
20The men of Ai looked back and saw the
smoke of the city rising against the sky, but they
had no chance to escape in any direction, for the
Israelites who had been fleeing toward the desert
had turned back against their pursuers. 21For when
Joshua and all Israel saw that the ambush had
taken the city and that smoke was going up from
the city, they turned around and attacked the men
of Ai. 22The men of the ambush also came out of
the city against them, so that they were caught in
the middle, with Israelites on both sides. Israel cut
them down, leaving them neither survivors nor
fugitives. 23But they took the king of Ai alive and
brought him to Joshua. Dt 7:2; 1Sa 15:8
24When Israel had finished killing all the men of
Ai in the fields and in the desert where they had
chased them, and when every one of them had
been put to the sword, all the Israelites returned to
Ai and killed those who were in it. 25Twelve thousand men and women fell that day—all the people
of Ai. 26For Joshua did not draw back the hand
that held out his javelin until he had destroyed[a]
all who lived in Ai. 27But Israel did carry off for
themselves the livestock and plunder of this city,
as the LORD had instructed Joshua. Ex 17:12
28So Joshua burned Ai and made it a permanent
heap of ruins, a desolate place to this day. 29He
hung the king of Ai on a tree and left him there
until evening. At sunset, Joshua ordered them to
take his body from the tree and throw it down at
the entrance of the city gate. And they raised a
large pile of rocks over it, which remains to this
day. Dt 13:16; 21:23; Jn 19:31

The Covenant Renewed at Mount Ebal

30Then Joshua built on Mount Ebal an altar to
the LORD, the God of Israel, 31as Moses the servant
of the LORD had commanded the Israelites. He
built it according to what is written in the Book of
the Law of Moses—an altar of uncut stones, on
which no iron tool had been used. On it they
offered to the LORD burnt offerings and sacrificed
fellowship offerings.[b] 32There, in the presence of
the Israelites, Joshua copied on stones the law of
Moses, which he had written. 33All Israel, aliens
and citizens alike, with their elders, officials and
judges, were standing on both sides of the ark of
the covenant of the LORD, facing those who carried
it—the priests, who were Levites. Half of the people stood in front of Mount Gerizim and half of
them in front of Mount Ebal, as Moses the servant
of the LORD had formerly commanded when he
gave instructions to bless the people of Israel.
34Afterward, Joshua read all the words of the
law—the blessings and the curses—just as it is
written in the Book of the Law. 35There was not a
word of all that Moses had commanded that Joshua did not read to the whole assembly of Israel,
including the women and children, and the aliens
who lived among them. Dt 31:12; Jos 1:8

The Gibeonite Deception

9 Now when all the kings west of the Jordan
heard about these things—those in the hill
country, in the western foothills, and along the
entire coast of the Great Sea[c] as far as Lebanon
(the kings of the Hittites, Amorites, Canaanites,
Perizzites, Hivites and Jebusites)— 2they came together to make war against Joshua and Israel.
3However, when the people of Gibeon heard
what Joshua had done to Jericho and Ai, 4they
resorted to a ruse: They went as a delegation
whose donkeys were loaded[d] with worn-out
sacks and old wineskins, cracked and mended.
5The men put worn and patched sandals on their
feet and wore old clothes. All the bread of their
food supply was dry and moldy. 6Then they went
to Joshua in the camp at Gilgal and said to him
and the men of Israel, "We have come from a
distant country; make a treaty with us." Jos 5:10
7The men of Israel said to the Hivites, "But
perhaps you live near us. How then can we make
a treaty with you?" Ex 23:32; Jos 11:19
8"We are your servants," they said to Joshua.
But Joshua asked, "Who are you and where do
you come from?"
9They answered: "Your servants have come
from a very distant country because of the fame of
the LORD your God. For we have heard reports of
him: all that he did in Egypt, 10and all that he did
to the two kings of the Amorites east of the Jordan—Sihon king of Heshbon, and Og king of
Bashan, who reigned in Ashtaroth. 11And our elders and all those living in our country said to us,
'Take provisions for your journey; go and meet
them and say to them, "We are your servants;

[a]26 The Hebrew term refers to the irrevocable giving over of things or persons to the LORD, often by totally destroying them.
[b]31 Traditionally *peace offerings* [c]1 That is, the Mediterranean [d]4 Most Hebrew manuscripts; some Hebrew
manuscripts, Vulgate and Syriac (see also Septuagint) *They prepared provisions and loaded their donkeys*

make a treaty with us." ' 12This bread of ours was warm when we packed it at home on the day we left to come to you. But now see how dry and moldy it is. 13And these wineskins that we filled were new, but see how cracked they are. And our clothes and sandals are worn out by the very long journey." Dt 20:15; Jos 2:9; Nu 21:24,35

14The men of Israel sampled their provisions but did not inquire of the LORD. 15Then Joshua made a treaty of peace with them to let them live, and the leaders of the assembly ratified it by oath.

16Three days after they made the treaty with the Gibeonites, the Israelites heard that they were neighbors, living near them. 17So the Israelites set out and on the third day came to their cities: Gibeon, Kephirah, Beeroth and Kiriath Jearim. 18But the Israelites did not attack them, because the leaders of the assembly had sworn an oath to them by the LORD, the God of Israel. Jos 18:25; Ps 15:4

The whole assembly grumbled against the leaders, 19but all the leaders answered, "We have given them our oath by the LORD, the God of Israel, and we cannot touch them now. 20This is what we will do to them: We will let them live, so that wrath will not fall on us for breaking the oath we swore to them." 21They continued, "Let them live, but let them be woodcutters and water carriers for the entire community." So the leaders' promise to them was kept. Ex 15:24; Dt 29:11

22Then Joshua summoned the Gibeonites and said, "Why did you deceive us by saying, 'We live a long way from you,' while actually you live near us? 23You are now under a curse: You will never cease to serve as woodcutters and water carriers for the house of my God." Ge 9:25

24They answered Joshua, "Your servants were clearly told how the LORD your God had commanded his servant Moses to give you the whole land and to wipe out all its inhabitants from before you. So we feared for our lives because of you, and that is why we did this. 25We are now in your hands. Do to us whatever seems good and right to you." Ge 16:6; Jer 26:14

26So Joshua saved them from the Israelites, and they did not kill them. 27That day he made the Gibeonites woodcutters and water carriers for the community and for the altar of the LORD at the place the LORD would choose. And that is what they are to this day. Dt 12:5

The Sun Stands Still

10 Now Adoni-Zedek king of Jerusalem heard that Joshua had taken Ai and totally destroyed[a] it, doing to Ai and its king as he had done to Jericho and its king, and that the people of Gibeon had made a treaty of peace with Israel and were living near them. 2He and his people were very much alarmed at this, because Gibeon was an important city, like one of the royal cities; it was larger than Ai, and all its men were good fighters. 3So Adoni-Zedek king of Jerusalem appealed to Hoham king of Hebron, Piram king of Jarmuth, Japhia king of Lachish and Debir king of Eglon. 4"Come up and help me attack Gibeon," he said, "because it has made peace with Joshua and the Israelites." Ge 13:18; Jos 8:22; Jdg 1:7

5Then the five kings of the Amorites—the kings of Jerusalem, Hebron, Jarmuth, Lachish and Eglon—joined forces. They moved up with all their troops and took up positions against Gibeon and attacked it. Nu 13:29

6The Gibeonites then sent word to Joshua in the camp at Gilgal: "Do not abandon your servants. Come up to us quickly and save us! Help us, because all the Amorite kings from the hill country have joined forces against us."

7So Joshua marched up from Gilgal with his entire army, including all the best fighting men. 8The LORD said to Joshua, "Do not be afraid of them; I have given them into your hand. Not one of them will be able to withstand you." Jos 1:9; 8:1

9After an all-night march from Gilgal, Joshua took them by surprise. 10The LORD threw them into confusion before Israel, who defeated them in a great victory at Gibeon. Israel pursued them along the road going up to Beth Horon and cut them down all the way to Azekah and Makkedah. 11As they fled before Israel on the road down from Beth Horon to Azekah, the LORD hurled large hailstones down on them from the sky, and more of them died from the hailstones than were killed by the swords of the Israelites. Dt 7:23; Jdg 5:20; Ps 18:12

12On the day the LORD gave the Amorites over to Israel, Joshua said to the LORD in the presence of Israel:

"O sun, stand still over Gibeon,
O moon, over the Valley of Aijalon." Am 2:9
13So the sun stood still,
and the moon stopped,
till the nation avenged itself on[b] its enemies,

as it is written in the Book of Jashar. 2Sa 1:18

The sun stopped in the middle of the sky and delayed going down about a full day. 14There has never been a day like it before or since, a day when the LORD listened to a man. Surely the LORD was fighting for Israel! Ex 14:14; Isa 38:8

15Then Joshua returned with all Israel to the camp at Gilgal. ver 43

[a] *1* The Hebrew term refers to the irrevocable giving over of things or persons to the LORD, often by totally destroying them; also in verses 28, 35, 37, 39 and 40. [b] *13* Or *nation triumphed over*

Five Amorite Kings Killed

16Now the five kings had fled and hidden in the cave at Makkedah. 17When Joshua was told that the five kings had been found hiding in the cave at Makkedah, 18he said, "Roll large rocks up to the mouth of the cave, and post some men there to guard it. 19But don't stop! Pursue your enemies, attack them from the rear and don't let them reach their cities, for the LORD your God has given them into your hand."

20So Joshua and the Israelites destroyed them completely—almost to a man—but the few who were left reached their fortified cities. 21The whole army then returned safely to Joshua in the camp at Makkedah, and no one uttered a word against the Israelites. Dt 20:16

22Joshua said, "Open the mouth of the cave and bring those five kings out to me." 23So they brought the five kings out of the cave—the kings of Jerusalem, Hebron, Jarmuth, Lachish and Eglon. 24When they had brought these kings to Joshua, he summoned all the men of Israel and said to the army commanders who had come with him, "Come here and put your feet on the necks of these kings." So they came forward and placed their feet on their necks. Dt 7:24; Mal 4:3

25Joshua said to them, "Do not be afraid; do not be discouraged. Be strong and courageous. This is what the LORD will do to all the enemies you are going to fight." 26Then Joshua struck and killed the kings and hung them on five trees, and they were left hanging on the trees until evening.

27At sunset Joshua gave the order and they took them down from the trees and threw them into the cave where they had been hiding. At the mouth of the cave they placed large rocks, which are there to this day. Dt 21:23

28That day Joshua took Makkedah. He put the city and its king to the sword and totally destroyed everyone in it. He left no survivors. And he did to the king of Makkedah as he had done to the king of Jericho. Dt 20:16; Jos 6:21

Southern Cities Conquered

29Then Joshua and all Israel with him moved on from Makkedah to Libnah and attacked it. 30The LORD also gave that city and its king into Israel's hand. The city and everyone in it Joshua put to the sword. He left no survivors there. And he did to its king as he had done to the king of Jericho.

31Then Joshua and all Israel with him moved on from Libnah to Lachish; he took up positions against it and attacked it. 32The LORD handed Lachish over to Israel, and Joshua took it on the second day. The city and everyone in it he put to the sword, just as he had done to Libnah. 33Meanwhile, Horam king of Gezer had come up to help Lachish, but Joshua defeated him and his army—until no survivors were left.

34Then Joshua and all Israel with him moved on from Lachish to Eglon; they took up positions against it and attacked it. 35They captured it that same day and put it to the sword and totally destroyed everyone in it, just as they had done to Lachish.

36Then Joshua and all Israel with him went up from Eglon to Hebron and attacked it. 37They took the city and put it to the sword, together with its king, its villages and everyone in it. They left no survivors. Just as at Eglon, they totally destroyed it and everyone in it. Jos 14:13; 15:13; Jdg 1:10

38Then Joshua and all Israel with him turned around and attacked Debir. 39They took the city, its king and its villages, and put them to the sword. Everyone in it they totally destroyed. They left no survivors. They did to Debir and its king as they had done to Libnah and its king and to Hebron.

40So Joshua subdued the whole region, including the hill country, the Negev, the western foothills and the mountain slopes, together with all their kings. He left no survivors. He totally destroyed all who breathed, just as the LORD, the God of Israel, had commanded. 41Joshua subdued them from Kadesh Barnea to Gaza and from the whole region of Goshen to Gibeon. 42All these kings and their lands Joshua conquered in one campaign, because the LORD, the God of Israel, fought for Israel. Dt 7:24; Jos 11:16; ver 14

43Then Joshua returned with all Israel to the camp at Gilgal.

Northern Kings Defeated

11 When Jabin king of Hazor heard of this, he sent word to Jobab king of Madon, to the kings of Shimron and Acshaph, 2and to the northern kings who were in the mountains, in the Arabah south of Kinnereth, in the western foothills and in Naphoth Dor[a] on the west; 3to the Canaanites in the east and west; to the Amorites, Hittites, Perizzites and Jebusites in the hill country; and to the Hivites below Hermon in the region of Mizpah. 4They came out with all their troops and a large number of horses and chariots—a huge army, as numerous as the sand on the seashore. 5All these kings joined forces and made camp together at the Waters of Merom, to fight against Israel. Jdg 7:12; Jos 12:3; Dt 7:1

6The LORD said to Joshua, "Do not be afraid of them, because by this time tomorrow I will hand all of them over to Israel, slain. You are to hamstring their horses and burn their chariots."

7So Joshua and his whole army came against them suddenly at the Waters of Merom and attacked them, 8and the LORD gave them into the

[a]2 Or *in the heights of Dor*

hand of Israel. They defeated them and pursued
them all the way to Greater Sidon, to Misrephoth
Maim, and to the Valley of Mizpah on the east,
until no survivors were left. 9Joshua did to them as
the LORD had directed: He hamstrung their horses
and burned their chariots. Jos 13:6

10At that time Joshua turned back and captured
Hazor and put its king to the sword. (Hazor had
been the head of all these kingdoms.) 11Everyone
in it they put to the sword. They totally destroyed[a] them, not sparing anything that breathed,
and he burned up Hazor itself.

12Joshua took all these royal cities and their
kings and put them to the sword. He totally destroyed them, as Moses the servant of the LORD
had commanded. 13Yet Israel did not burn any of
the cities built on their mounds—except Hazor,
which Joshua burned. 14The Israelites carried off
for themselves all the plunder and livestock of
these cities, but all the people they put to the sword
until they completely destroyed them, not sparing
anyone that breathed. 15As the LORD commanded
his servant Moses, so Moses commanded Joshua,
and Joshua did it; he left nothing undone of all
that the LORD commanded Moses. Ex 34:11

16So Joshua took this entire land: the hill country, all the Negev, the whole region of Goshen, the
western foothills, the Arabah and the mountains of
Israel with their foothills, 17from Mount Halak,
which rises toward Seir, to Baal Gad in the Valley
of Lebanon below Mount Hermon. He captured
all their kings and struck them down, putting them
to death. 18Joshua waged war against all these
kings for a long time. 19Except for the Hivites living in Gibeon, not one city made a treaty of peace
with the Israelites, who took them all in battle.
20For it was the LORD himself who hardened their
hearts to wage war against Israel, so that he might
destroy them totally, exterminating them without
mercy, as the LORD had commanded Moses.

21At that time Joshua went and destroyed the
Anakites from the hill country: from Hebron, Debir and Anab, from all the hill country of Judah,
and from all the hill country of Israel. Joshua totally destroyed them and their towns. 22No Anakites
were left in Israelite territory; only in Gaza, Gath
and Ashdod did any survive. 23So Joshua took the
entire land, just as the LORD had directed Moses,
and he gave it as an inheritance to Israel according
to their tribal divisions. Nu 13:22,33; Jos 21:43-45; 1Sa 17:4

Then the land had rest from war. Ex 33:14

List of Defeated Kings

12 These are the kings of the land whom the
Israelites had defeated and whose territory
they took over east of the Jordan, from the Arnon
Gorge to Mount Hermon, including all the eastern
side of the Arabah: Dt 3:8

2Sihon king of the Amorites,
who reigned in Heshbon. He ruled from
Aroer on the rim of the Arnon Gorge—from
the middle of the gorge—to the Jabbok River, which is the border of the Ammonites.
This included half of Gilead. 3He also ruled
over the eastern Arabah from the Sea of Kinnereth[b] to the Sea of the Arabah (the Salt
Sea[c]), to Beth Jeshimoth, and then southward below the slopes of Pisgah. Jos 11:2

4And the territory of Og king of Bashan,
one of the last of the Rephaites, who reigned
in Ashtaroth and Edrei. 5He ruled over
Mount Hermon, Salecah, all of Bashan to the
border of the people of Geshur and Maacah,
and half of Gilead to the border of Sihon
king of Heshbon. Nu 21:21,33; Dt 1:4; 3:10

6Moses, the servant of the LORD, and the Israelites conquered them. And Moses the servant of the
LORD gave their land to the Reubenites, the Gadites
and the half-tribe of Manasseh to be their possession. Nu 32:29,33

7These are the kings of the land that Joshua and
the Israelites conquered on the west side of the
Jordan, from Baal Gad in the Valley of Lebanon to
Mount Halak, which rises toward Seir (their lands
Joshua gave as an inheritance to the tribes of Israel
according to their tribal divisions— 8the hill
country, the western foothills, the Arabah, the
mountain slopes, the desert and the Negev—the
lands of the Hittites, Amorites, Canaanites, Perizzites, Hivites and Jebusites): Jos 11:17; Ezr 9:1

9the king of Jericho one
the king of Ai (near Bethel) one
10the king of Jerusalem one
the king of Hebron one
11the king of Jarmuth one
the king of Lachish one
12the king of Eglon one
the king of Gezer one
13the king of Debir one
the king of Geder one
14the king of Hormah one
the king of Arad one
15the king of Libnah one
the king of Adullam one
16the king of Makkedah one
the king of Bethel one
17the king of Tappuah one
the king of Hepher one
18the king of Aphek one
the king of Lasharon one

[a]11 The Hebrew term refers to the irrevocable giving over of things or persons to the LORD, often by totally destroying them; also in verses 12, 20 and 21. [b]3 That is, Galilee [c]3 That is, the Dead Sea

19the king of Madon one
the king of Hazor one
20the king of Shimron Meron one
the king of Acshaph one
21the king of Taanach one
the king of Megiddo one
22the king of Kedesh one
the king of Jokneam in Carmel one
23the king of Dor (in Naphoth Dor[a]) one
the king of Goyim in Gilgal one
24the king of Tirzah one
thirty-one kings in all. Jos 6:2; 10:33; Ps 135:11

Dividing the Spoil **Chapters 13–22**

In these chapters we find the record of where the people of Israel were told to settle in the promised land. Each tribe was given a place to establish roots and make their home. In the midst of this account we find a wonderful and ageless elderly gentleman named Caleb (14:6–15). You may remember him as one of the two spies who had given a good report of the land more than forty years earlier. He supported Joshua as the leader without a trace of jealousy. His desire was to see God's will accomplished among the people. He depended on the Lord's strength to uphold him, not his own powers or abilities. Caleb's example is an encouraging one for all who are establishing roots wherever the Lord has planted them on this earth.

Land Still to Be Taken

13 When Joshua was old and well advanced in years, the LORD said to him, "You are very old, and there are still very large areas of land to be taken over. Jos 14:10

2"This is the land that remains: all the regions of the Philistines and Geshurites: 3from
the Shihor River on the east of Egypt to the
territory of Ekron on the north, all of it
counted as Canaanite (the territory of the
five Philistine rulers in Gaza, Ashdod, Ashkelon, Gath and Ekron—that of the Avvites); 4from the south, all the land of the
Canaanites, from Arah of the Sidonians as
far as Aphek, the region of the Amorites, 5the
area of the Gebalites[b]; and all Lebanon to
the east, from Baal Gad below Mount Hermon to Lebo[c] Hamath. Dt 2:23; Jdg 3:3; Am 2:10

6"As for all the inhabitants of the mountain
regions from Lebanon to Misrephoth Maim, that
is, all the Sidonians, I myself will drive them out
before the Israelites. Be sure to allocate this land to
Israel for an inheritance, as I have instructed you,
7and divide it as an inheritance among the nine
tribes and half of the tribe of Manasseh." Jos 11:8

Division of the Land East of the Jordan

8The other half of Manasseh,[d] the Reubenites and the Gadites had received the inheritance that Moses had given them east of the Jordan, as he, the servant of the LORD, had assigned it to them.

9It extended from Aroer on the rim of the
Arnon Gorge, and from the town in the middle of the gorge, and included the whole plateau of Medeba as far as Dibon, 10and all the
towns of Sihon king of the Amorites, who
ruled in Heshbon, out to the border of the
Ammonites. 11It also included Gilead, the
territory of the people of Geshur and Maacah, all of Mount Hermon and all Bashan as
far as Salecah— 12that is, the whole kingdom
of Og in Bashan, who had reigned in Ashtaroth and Edrei and had survived as one of
the last of the Rephaites. Moses had defeated
them and taken over their land. 13But the
Israelites did not drive out the people of Geshur and Maacah, so they continue to live
among the Israelites to this day. Dt 2:36; 3:11

14But to the tribe of Levi he gave no inheritance, since the offerings made by fire to the LORD, the God of Israel, are their inheritance, as he promised them. Dt 18:1-2

15This is what Moses had given to the tribe of Reuben, clan by clan:

16The territory from Aroer on the rim of the
Arnon Gorge, and from the town in the mid-
dle of the gorge, and the whole plateau past
Medeba 17to Heshbon and all its towns on
the plateau, including Dibon, Bamoth Baal,
Beth Baal Meon, 18Jahaz, Kedemoth, Mephaath, 19Kiriathaim, Sibmah, Zereth Shahar on
the hill in the valley, 20Beth Peor, the slopes
of Pisgah, and Beth Jeshimoth 21—all the
towns on the plateau and the entire realm of
Sihon king of the Amorites, who ruled at
Heshbon. Moses had defeated him and the
Midianite chiefs, Evi, Rekem, Zur, Hur and
Reba—princes allied with Sihon—who lived
in that country. 22In addition to those slain in
battle, the Israelites had put to the sword
Balaam son of Beor, who practiced divination. 23The boundary of the Reubenites was
the bank of the Jordan. These towns and
their villages were the inheritance of the Reubenites, clan by clan. Nu 21:23; 31:8; 32:37

24This is what Moses had given to the tribe of Gad, clan by clan:

25The territory of Jazer, all the towns of Gilead and half the Ammonite country as far as

[a]23 Or *in the heights of Dor* [b]5 That is, the area of Byblos [c]5 Or *to the entrance to* [d]8 Hebrew *With it* (that is, with the other half of Manasseh)

Aroer, near Rabbah; 26and from Heshbon to Ramath Mizpah and Betonim, and from Mahanaim to the territory of Debir; 27and in the valley, Beth Haram, Beth Nimrah, Succoth and Zaphon with the rest of the realm of Sihon king of Heshbon (the east side of the Jordan, the territory up to the end of the Sea of Kinnereth[a]). 28These towns and their villages were the inheritance of the Gadites, clan by clan. Nu 21:32; 34:11

29This is what Moses had given to the half-tribe of Manasseh, that is, to half the family of the descendants of Manasseh, clan by clan:

30The territory extending from Mahanaim and including all of Bashan, the entire realm of Og king of Bashan—all the settlements of Jair in Bashan, sixty towns, 31half of Gilead, and Ashtaroth and Edrei (the royal cities of Og in Bashan). This was for the descendants of Makir son of Manasseh—for half of the sons of Makir, clan by clan. Nu 32:41; Jos 12:4

32This is the inheritance Moses had given when he was in the plains of Moab across the Jordan east of Jericho. 33But to the tribe of Levi, Moses had given no inheritance; the LORD, the God of Israel, is their inheritance, as he promised them.

Division of the Land West of the Jordan

14 Now these are the areas the Israelites received as an inheritance in the land of Canaan, which Eleazar the priest, Joshua son of Nun and the heads of the tribal clans of Israel allotted to them. 2Their inheritances were assigned by lot to the nine-and-a-half tribes, as the LORD had commanded through Moses. 3Moses had granted the two-and-a-half tribes their inheritance east of the Jordan but had not granted the Levites an inheritance among the rest, 4for the sons of Joseph had become two tribes—Manasseh and Ephraim. The Levites received no share of the land but only towns to live in, with pasturelands for their flocks and herds. 5So the Israelites divided the land, just as the LORD had commanded Moses. Nu 32:33

Hebron Given to Caleb

6Now the men of Judah approached Joshua at Gilgal, and Caleb son of Jephunneh the Kenizzite said to him, "You know what the LORD said to Moses the man of God at Kadesh Barnea about you and me. 7I was forty years old when Moses the servant of the LORD sent me from Kadesh Barnea to explore the land. And I brought him back a report according to my convictions, 8but my brothers who went up with me made the hearts of the people melt with fear. I, however, followed the LORD my God wholeheartedly. 9So on that day Moses swore to me, 'The land on which your feet have walked will be your inheritance and that of your children forever, because you have followed the LORD my God wholeheartedly.'[b] Nu 13:30

10"Now then, just as the LORD promised, he has kept me alive for forty-five years since the time he said this to Moses, while Israel moved about in the desert. So here I am today, eighty-five years old! 11I am still as strong today as the day Moses sent me out; I'm just as vigorous to go out to battle now as I was then. 12Now give me this hill country that the LORD promised me that day. You yourself heard then that the Anakites were there and their cities were large and fortified, but, the LORD helping me, I will drive them out just as he said."

13Then Joshua blessed Caleb son of Jephunneh and gave him Hebron as his inheritance. 14So Hebron has belonged to Caleb son of Jephunneh the Kenizzite ever since, because he followed the LORD, the God of Israel, wholeheartedly. 15(Hebron used to be called Kiriath Arba after Arba, who was the greatest man among the Anakites.) Jos 22:6-7

LIVING 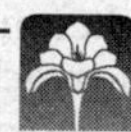 **INSIGHT**

The thing that makes for greatness is determination, persisting in the same direction over the long haul, staying at the task. Determination is applying the discipline to remain consistent regardless of the obstacles. It is faith in the long haul.

(See Joshua 14:6–14.)

Then the land had rest from war. Jos 11:23

Allotment for Judah

15 The allotment for the tribe of Judah, clan by clan, extended down to the territory of Edom, to the Desert of Zin in the extreme south.

2Their southern boundary started from the bay at the southern end of the Salt Sea,[c] 3crossed south of Scorpion[d] Pass, continued on to Zin and went over to the south of Kadesh Barnea. Then it ran past Hezron up to Addar and curved around to Karka. 4It then passed along to Azmon and joined the Wadi of Egypt, ending at the sea. This is their[e] southern boundary.

5The eastern boundary is the Salt Sea as far as the mouth of the Jordan. Ge 14:3

The northern boundary started from the bay of the sea at the mouth of the Jordan, 6went up to Beth Hoglah and continued

[a]27 That is, Galilee [b]9 Deut. 1:36 [c]2 That is, the Dead Sea; also in verse 5 [d]3 Hebrew *Akrabbim* [e]4 Hebrew *your*

north of Beth Arabah to the Stone of Bohan son of Reuben. 7The boundary then went up to Debir from the Valley of Achor and turned north to Gilgal, which faces the Pass of Adummim south of the gorge. It continued along to the waters of En Shemesh and came out at En Rogel. 8Then it ran up the Valley of Ben Hinnom along the southern slope of the Jebusite city (that is, Jerusalem). From there it climbed to the top of the hill west of the Hinnom Valley at the northern end of the Valley of Rephaim. 9From the hilltop the boundary headed toward the spring of the waters of Nephtoah, came out at the towns of Mount Ephron and went down toward Baalah (that is, Kiriath Jearim). 10Then it curved westward from Baalah to Mount Seir, ran along the northern slope of Mount Jearim (that is, Kesalon), continued down to Beth Shemesh and crossed to Timnah. 11It went to the northern slope of Ekron, turned toward Shikkeron, passed along to Mount Baalah and reached Jabneel. The boundary ended at the sea. Jos 7:24; 18:17

12The western boundary is the coastline of the Great Sea.[a] Nu 34:6

These are the boundaries around the people of Judah by their clans.

13In accordance with the LORD's command to him, Joshua gave to Caleb son of Jephunneh a portion in Judah—Kiriath Arba, that is, Hebron. (Arba was the forefather of Anak.) 14From Hebron Caleb drove out the three Anakites—Sheshai, Ahiman and Talmai—descendants of Anak. 15From there he marched against the people living in Debir (formerly called Kiriath Sepher). 16And Caleb said, "I will give my daughter Acsah in marriage to the man who attacks and captures Kiriath Sepher." 17Othniel son of Kenaz, Caleb's brother, took it; so Caleb gave his daughter Acsah to him in marriage.

18One day when she came to Othniel, she urged him[b] to ask her father for a field. When she got off her donkey, Caleb asked her, "What can I do for you?" Jos 14:13-15; Jdg 1:12; 3:9,11

19She replied, "Do me a special favor. Since you have given me land in the Negev, give me also springs of water." So Caleb gave her the upper and lower springs. Jdg 1:11-15

20This is the inheritance of the tribe of Judah, clan by clan:

21The southernmost towns of the tribe of Judah in the Negev toward the boundary of Edom were:

Kabzeel, Eder, Jagur, 22Kinah, Dimonah, Adadah, 23Kedesh, Hazor, Ithnan, 24Ziph, Telem, Bealoth, 25Hazor Hadattah, Kerioth Hezron (that is, Hazor), 26Amam, Shema, Moladah, 27Hazar Gaddah, Heshmon, Beth Pelet, 28Hazar Shual, Beersheba, Biziothiah, 29Baalah, Iim, Ezem, 30Eltolad, Kesil, Hormah, 31Ziklag, Madmannah, Sansannah, 32Lebaoth, Shilhim, Ain and Rimmon—a total of twenty-nine towns and their villages.

33In the western foothills:

Eshtaol, Zorah, Ashnah, 34Zanoah, En Gannim, Tappuah, Enam, 35Jarmuth, Adullam, Socoh, Azekah, 36Shaaraim, Adithaim and Gederah (or Gederothaim)[c]—fourteen towns and their villages. Jdg 13:25; 16:31; 1Sa 22:1

37Zenan, Hadashah, Migdal Gad, 38Dilean, Mizpah, Joktheel, 39Lachish, Bozkath, Eglon, 40Cabbon, Lahmas, Kitlish, 41Gederoth, Beth Dagon, Naamah and Makkedah—sixteen towns and their villages. Jos 10:3; 2Ki 14:7,19

42Libnah, Ether, Ashan, 43Iphtah, Ashnah, Nezib, 44Keilah, Aczib and Mareshah—nine towns and their villages. 1Ch 6:59

45Ekron, with its surrounding settlements and villages; 46west of Ekron, all that were in the vicinity of Ashdod, together with their villages; 47Ashdod, its surrounding settlements and villages; and Gaza, its settlements and villages, as far as the Wadi of Egypt and the coastline of the Great Sea. Nu 34:6

48In the hill country:

Shamir, Jattir, Socoh, 49Dannah, Kiriath Sannah (that is, Debir), 50Anab, Eshtemoh, Anim, 51Goshen, Holon and Giloh—eleven towns and their villages. Jos 10:41; Jdg 10:1

52Arab, Dumah, Eshan, 53Janim, Beth Tappuah, Aphekah, 54Humtah, Kiriath Arba (that is, Hebron) and Zior—nine towns and their villages. Ge 25:14

55Maon, Carmel, Ziph, Juttah, 56Jezreel, Jokdeam, Zanoah, 57Kain, Gibeah and Timnah—ten towns and their villages. Jdg 10:12

58Halhul, Beth Zur, Gedor, 59Maarath, Beth Anoth and Eltekon—six towns and their villages.

60Kiriath Baal (that is, Kiriath Jearim) and Rabbah—two towns and their villages.

61In the desert:

Beth Arabah, Middin, Secacah, 62Nibshan, the City of Salt and En Gedi—six towns and their villages. Jos 8:15; Eze 47:10

63Judah could not dislodge the Jebusites, who were living in Jerusalem; to this day the Jebusites live there with the people of Judah. Jdg 1:21; 2Sa 5:6

[a] *12* That is, the Mediterranean; also in verse 47 [b] *18* Hebrew and some Septuagint manuscripts; other Septuagint manuscripts (see also note at Judges 1:14) *Othniel, he urged her* [c] *36* Or *Gederah and Gederothaim*

Allotment for Ephraim and Manasseh

16 The allotment for Joseph began at the Jordan of Jericho,[a] east of the waters of Jericho, and went up from there through the desert into the hill country of Bethel. [2]It went on from Bethel (that is, Luz),[b] crossed over to the territory of the Arkites in Ataroth, [3]descended westward to the territory of the Japhletites as far as the region of Lower Beth Horon and on to Gezer, ending at the sea.

[4]So Manasseh and Ephraim, the descendants of Joseph, received their inheritance. Jos 18:5

[5]This was the territory of Ephraim, clan by clan:

The boundary of their inheritance went from Ataroth Addar in the east to Upper Beth Horon [6]and continued to the sea. From Micmethath on the north it curved eastward to Taanath Shiloh, passing by it to Janoah on the east. [7]Then it went down from Janoah to Ataroth and Naarah, touched Jericho and came out at the Jordan. [8]From Tappuah the border went west to the Kanah Ravine and ended at the sea. This was the inheritance of the tribe of the Ephraimites, clan by clan. [9]It also included all the towns and their villages that were set aside for the Ephraimites within the inheritance of the Manassites. Jos 17:7,9

[10]They did not dislodge the Canaanites living in Gezer; to this day the Canaanites live among the people of Ephraim but are required to do forced labor. Jos 17:13; Jdg 1:28-29; 1Ki 9:16

17 This was the allotment for the tribe of Manasseh as Joseph's firstborn, that is, for Makir, Manasseh's firstborn. Makir was the ancestor of the Gileadites, who had received Gilead and Bashan because the Makirites were great soldiers. [2]So this allotment was for the rest of the people of Manasseh—the clans of Abiezer, Helek, Asriel, Shechem, Hepher and Shemida. These are the other male descendants of Manasseh son of Joseph by their clans. Ge 41:51; 50:23; Nu 26:30

[3]Now Zelophehad son of Hepher, the son of Gilead, the son of Makir, the son of Manasseh, had no sons but only daughters, whose names were Mahlah, Noah, Hoglah, Milcah and Tirzah. [4]They went to Eleazar the priest, Joshua son of Nun, and the leaders and said, "The LORD commanded Moses to give us an inheritance among our brothers." So Joshua gave them an inheritance along with the brothers of their father, according to the LORD's command. [5]Manasseh's share consisted of ten tracts of land besides Gilead and Bashan east of the Jordan, [6]because the daughters of the tribe of Manasseh received an inheritance among the sons. The land of Gilead belonged to the rest of the descendants of Manasseh. Nu 27:1,5-7; Jos 13:30-31

[7]The territory of Manasseh extended from Asher to Micmethath east of Shechem. The boundary ran southward from there to include the people living at En Tappuah. [8](Manasseh had the land of Tappuah, but Tappuah itself, on the boundary of Manasseh, belonged to the Ephraimites.) [9]Then the boundary continued south to the Kanah Ravine. There were towns belonging to Ephraim lying among the towns of Manasseh, but the boundary of Manasseh was the northern side of the ravine and ended at the sea. [10]On the south the land belonged to Ephraim, on the north to Manasseh. The territory of Manasseh reached the sea and bordered Asher on the north and Issachar on the east.

[11]Within Issachar and Asher, Manasseh also had Beth Shan, Ibleam and the people of Dor, Endor, Taanach and Megiddo, together with their surrounding settlements (the third in the list is Naphoth[c]). Jos 11:2; 1Sa 31:10

[12]Yet the Manassites were not able to occupy these towns, for the Canaanites were determined to live in that region. [13]However, when the Israelites grew stronger, they subjected the Canaanites to forced labor but did not drive them out completely.

[14]The people of Joseph said to Joshua, "Why have you given us only one allotment and one portion for an inheritance? We are a numerous people and the LORD has blessed us abundantly."

[15]"If you are so numerous," Joshua answered, "and if the hill country of Ephraim is too small for you, go up into the forest and clear land for yourselves there in the land of the Perizzites and Rephaites."

[16]The people of Joseph replied, "The hill country is not enough for us, and all the Canaanites who live in the plain have iron chariots, both those in Beth Shan and its settlements and those in the Valley of Jezreel." Jdg 1:19; 1Sa 29:1

[17]But Joshua said to the house of Joseph—to Ephraim and Manasseh—"You are numerous and very powerful. You will have not only one allotment [18]but the forested hill country as well. Clear it, and its farthest limits will be yours; though the Canaanites have iron chariots and though they are strong, you can drive them out."

Division of the Rest of the Land

18 The whole assembly of the Israelites gathered at Shiloh and set up the Tent of Meeting there. The country was brought under their control, [2]but there were still seven Israelite tribes who had not yet received their inheritance.

[a]*1 Jordan of Jericho* was possibly an ancient name for the Jordan River. [b]*2* Septuagint; Hebrew *Bethel to Luz*
[c]*11* That is, Naphoth Dor

3So Joshua said to the Israelites: "How long will
you wait before you begin to take possession of the
land that the LORD, the God of your fathers, has
given you? 4Appoint three men from each tribe. I
will send them out to make a survey of the land
and to write a description of it, according to the
inheritance of each. Then they will return to me.
5You are to divide the land into seven parts. Judah
is to remain in its territory on the south and the
house of Joseph in its territory on the north. 6After
you have written descriptions of the seven parts of
the land, bring them here to me and I will cast lots
for you in the presence of the LORD our God. 7The
Levites, however, do not get a portion among you,
because the priestly service of the LORD is their
inheritance. And Gad, Reuben and the half-tribe
of Manasseh have already received their inheritance on the east side of the Jordan. Moses the
servant of the LORD gave it to them." Jos 13:33; 15:1
8As the men started on their way to map out the
land, Joshua instructed them, "Go and make a
survey of the land and write a description of it.
Then return to me, and I will cast lots for you here
at Shiloh in the presence of the LORD." 9So the men
left and went through the land. They wrote its
description on a scroll, town by town, in seven
parts, and returned to Joshua in the camp at Shiloh. 10Joshua then cast lots for them in Shiloh in
the presence of the LORD, and there he distributed
the land to the Israelites according to their tribal
divisions. Jos 19:51; Jer 7:12

Allotment for Benjamin

11The lot came up for the tribe of Benjamin, clan
by clan. Their allotted territory lay between the
tribes of Judah and Joseph:

12On the north side their boundary began
at the Jordan, passed the northern slope of
Jericho and headed west into the hill country,
coming out at the desert of Beth Aven.
13From there it crossed to the south slope of
Luz (that is, Bethel) and went down to Ataroth Addar on the hill south of Lower Beth
Horon. Ge 28:19; Jos 16:1; Jdg 1:23

14From the hill facing Beth Horon on the
south the boundary turned south along the
western side and came out at Kiriath Baal
(that is, Kiriath Jearim), a town of the people
of Judah. This was the western side.

15The southern side began at the outskirts
of Kiriath Jearim on the west, and the
boundary came out at the spring of the waters of Nephtoah. 16The boundary went
down to the foot of the hill facing the Valley
of Ben Hinnom, north of the Valley of Rephaim. It continued down the Hinnom Valley
along the southern slope of the Jebusite city
and so to En Rogel. 17It then curved north,
went to En Shemesh, continued to Geliloth,
which faces the Pass of Adummim, and ran
down to the Stone of Bohan son of Reuben.
18It continued to the northern slope of Beth
Arabah[a] and on down into the Arabah. 19It
then went to the northern slope of Beth Hoglah and came out at the northern bay of the
Salt Sea,[b] at the mouth of the Jordan in the
south. This was the southern boundary.

20The Jordan formed the boundary on the
eastern side.

These were the boundaries that marked out the
inheritance of the clans of Benjamin on all sides.

21The tribe of Benjamin, clan by clan, had the
following cities:

Jericho, Beth Hoglah, Emek Keziz, 22Beth
Arabah, Zemaraim, Bethel, 23Avvim, Parah,
Ophrah, 24Kephar Ammoni, Ophni and
Geba—twelve towns and their villages.

25Gibeon, Ramah, Beeroth, 26Mizpah, Kephirah, Mozah, 27Rekem, Irpeel, Taralah,
28Zelah, Haeleph, the Jebusite city (that is,
Jerusalem), Gibeah and Kiriath—fourteen
towns and their villages. Jos 15:8; Jdg 4:5; 2Sa 21:14

This was the inheritance of Benjamin for its clans.

Allotment for Simeon

19 The second lot came out for the tribe of
Simeon, clan by clan. Their inheritance lay
within the territory of Judah. 2It included: Ge 49:7

Beersheba (or Sheba),[c] Moladah, 3Hazar
Shual, Balah, Ezem, 4Eltolad, Bethul, Hormah, 5Ziklag, Beth Marcaboth, Hazar Susah,
6Beth Lebaoth and Sharuhen—thirteen
towns and their villages; Ge 21:14

7Ain, Rimmon, Ether and Ashan—four
towns and their villages— 8and all the villages around these towns as far as Baalath
Beer (Ramah in the Negev). Jos 15:32

This was the inheritance of the tribe of the Simeonites, clan by clan. 9The inheritance of the Simeonites was taken from the share of Judah, because
Judah's portion was more than they needed. So the
Simeonites received their inheritance within the
territory of Judah. Ge 49:7

Allotment for Zebulun

10The third lot came up for Zebulun, clan by clan:

The boundary of their inheritance went as
far as Sarid. 11Going west it ran to Maralah,
touched Dabbesheth, and extended to the ravine near Jokneam. 12It turned east from Sarid toward the sunrise to the territory of Kis-
loth Tabor and went on to Daberath and up

[a] 18 Septuagint; Hebrew *slope facing the Arabah* [b] 19 That is, the Dead Sea [c] 2 Or *Beersheba, Sheba*; 1 Chron. 4:28 does not have *Sheba.*

to Japhia. [13]Then it continued eastward to
Gath Hepher and Eth Kazin; it came out at
Rimmon and turned toward Neah. [14]There
the boundary went around on the north to
Hannathon and ended at the Valley of Iph-
tah El. [15]Included were Kattath, Nahalal,
Shimron, Idalah and Bethlehem. There were
twelve towns and their villages. Ge 35:19
[16]These towns and their villages were the inheritance of Zebulun, clan by clan. Eze 48:26

Allotment for Issachar

[17]The fourth lot came out for Issachar, clan by
clan. [18]Their territory included: Ge 30:18
Jezreel, Kesulloth, Shunem, [19]Hapharaim,
Shion, Anaharath, [20]Rabbith, Kishion, Ebez,
[21]Remeth, En Gannim, En Haddah and Beth
Pazzez. [22]The boundary touched Tabor, Sha-
hazumah and Beth Shemesh, and ended at
the Jordan. There were sixteen towns and
their villages. 1Sa 28:4; 2Ki 4:8; Ps 89:12
[23]These towns and their villages were the inheritance of the tribe of Issachar, clan by clan.

Allotment for Asher

[24]The fifth lot came out for the tribe of Asher, clan
by clan. [25]Their territory included: Jos 17:7
Helkath, Hali, Beten, Acshaph, [26]Allam-
melech, Amad and Mishal. On the west the
boundary touched Carmel and Shihor Lib-
nath. [27]It then turned east toward Beth Dagon, touched Zebulun and the Valley of Iph-
tah El, and went north to Beth Emek and
Neiel, passing Cabul on the left. [28]It went to
Abdon,[a] Rehob, Hammon and Kanah, as
far as Greater Sidon. [29]The boundary then
turned back toward Ramah and went to the
fortified city of Tyre, turned toward Hosah
and came out at the sea in the region of
Aczib, [30]Ummah, Aphek and Rehob. There
were twenty-two towns and their villages.
[31]These towns and their villages were the inheritance of the tribe of Asher, clan by clan. Ge 30:13

Allotment for Naphtali

[32]The sixth lot came out for Naphtali, clan by clan:
[33]Their boundary went from Heleph and
the large tree in Zaanannim, passing Adami
Nekeb and Jabneel to Lakkum and ending at
the Jordan. [34]The boundary ran west through
Aznoth Tabor and came out at Hukkok. It
touched Zebulun on the south, Asher on the
west and the Jordan[b] on the east. [35]The fortified cities were Ziddim, Zer, Hammath,
Rakkath, Kinnereth, [36]Adamah, Ramah, Hazor, [37]Kedesh, Edrei, En Hazor, [38]Iron, Migdal El, Horem, Beth Anath and Beth Shemesh. There were nineteen towns and their
villages. Jos 11:1; Jdg 4:11
[39]These towns and their villages were the inheritance of the tribe of Naphtali, clan by clan.

Allotment for Dan

[40]The seventh lot came out for the tribe of Dan,
clan by clan. [41]The territory of their inheritance
included:
Zorah, Eshtaol, Ir Shemesh, [42]Shaalabbin,
Aijalon, Ithlah, [43]Elon, Timnah, Ekron, [44]El-
tekeh, Gibbethon, Baalath, [45]Jehud, Bene Be-
rak, Gath Rimmon, [46]Me Jarkon and Rak-
kon, with the area facing Joppa. Jdg 1:35
[47](But the Danites had difficulty taking possession of their territory, so they went up and attacked Leshem, took it, put it to the sword and
occupied it. They settled in Leshem and named it
Dan after their forefather.) Jdg 18:1,27,29
[48]These towns and their villages were the inheritance of the tribe of Dan, clan by clan.

Allotment for Joshua

[49]When they had finished dividing the land into
its allotted portions, the Israelites gave Joshua son
of Nun an inheritance among them, [50]as the LORD
had commanded. They gave him the town he
asked for—Timnath Serah[c] in the hill country of
Ephraim. And he built up the town and settled
there. Jos 24:30
[51]These are the territories that Eleazar the priest,
Joshua son of Nun and the heads of the tribal clans
of Israel assigned by lot at Shiloh in the presence
of the LORD at the entrance to the Tent of Meeting.
And so they finished dividing the land. Jos 14:1

Cities of Refuge

20 Then the LORD said to Joshua: [2]"Tell the
Israelites to designate the cities of refuge,
as I instructed you through Moses, [3]so that anyone
who kills a person accidentally and unintentionally
may flee there and find protection from the avenger of blood. Lev 4:2
[4]"When he flees to one of these cities, he is to
stand in the entrance of the city gate and state his
case before the elders of that city. Then they are to
admit him into their city and give him a place to
live with them. [5]If the avenger of blood pursues
him, they must not surrender the one accused,
because he killed his neighbor unintentionally and
without malice aforethought. [6]He is to stay in that
city until he has stood trial before the assembly
and until the death of the high priest who is serving at that time. Then he may go back to his own
home in the town from which he fled." Nu 35:12

[a]28 Some Hebrew manuscripts (see also Joshua 21:30); most Hebrew manuscripts *Ebron* [b]34 Septuagint; Hebrew *west, and Judah, the Jordan,* [c]50 Also known as *Timnath Heres* (see Judges 2:9)

7So they set apart Kedesh in Galilee in the hill
country of Naphtali, Shechem in the hill country
of Ephraim, and Kiriath Arba (that is, Hebron) in
the hill country of Judah. 8On the east side of the

LIVING  **INSIGHT**

We do not in this day and age establish cities of refuge, but we are to be people of refuge, shelters for storm victims. People of refuge are willing to go the distance for someone in trouble. People of refuge exhibit an attitude of loving compassion for those in need. And people of refuge make themselves available to help in practical, tangible ways.

(See Joshua 20:4.)

Jordan of Jericho[a] they designated Bezer in the
desert on the plateau in the tribe of Reuben, Ramoth in Gilead in the tribe of Gad, and Golan in
Bashan in the tribe of Manasseh. 9Any of the Israelites or any alien living among them who killed
someone accidentally could flee to these designated cities and not be killed by the avenger of blood
prior to standing trial before the assembly.

Towns for the Levites

21 Now the family heads of the Levites approached Eleazar the priest, Joshua son of
Nun, and the heads of the other tribal families of
Israel 2at Shiloh in Canaan and said to them, "The
LORD commanded through Moses that you give us
towns to live in, with pasturelands for our livestock." 3So, as the LORD had commanded, the Israelites gave the Levites the following towns and pasturelands out of their own inheritance: Nu 35:2-3
4The first lot came out for the Kohathites, clan
by clan. The Levites who were descendants of Aaron the priest were allotted thirteen towns from the
tribes of Judah, Simeon and Benjamin. 5The rest
of Kohath's descendants were allotted ten towns
from the clans of the tribes of Ephraim, Dan and
half of Manasseh. Nu 3:17
6The descendants of Gershon were allotted thirteen towns from the clans of the tribes of Issachar,
Asher, Naphtali and the half-tribe of Manasseh in
Bashan. Ge 30:18
7The descendants of Merari, clan by clan, received twelve towns from the tribes of Reuben,
Gad and Zebulun. Ex 6:16
8So the Israelites allotted to the Levites these
towns and their pasturelands, as the LORD had
commanded through Moses.
9From the tribes of Judah and Simeon they allotted
the following towns by name 10(these towns were
assigned to the descendants of Aaron who were
from the Kohathite clans of the Levites, because
the first lot fell to them):
11They gave them Kiriath Arba (that is,
Hebron), with its surrounding pastureland,
in the hill country of Judah. (Arba was the
forefather of Anak.) 12But the fields and villages around the city they had given to Caleb
son of Jephunneh as his possession. Jos 15:13
13So to the descendants of Aaron the
priest they gave Hebron (a city of refuge for
one accused of murder), Libnah, 14Jattir,
Eshtemoa, 15Holon, Debir, 16Ain, Juttah and
Beth Shemesh, together with their pasturelands—nine towns from these two tribes.
17And from the tribe of Benjamin they
gave them Gibeon, Geba, 18Anathoth and Almon, together with their pasturelands—four
towns. Jos 18:24; Ne 11:32; Jer 32:7
19All the towns for the priests, the descendants of
Aaron, were thirteen, together with their pasturelands. 2Ch 31:15

20The rest of the Kohathite clans of the Levites
were allotted towns from the tribe of Ephraim:
21In the hill country of Ephraim they were
given Shechem (a city of refuge for one accused of murder) and Gezer, 22Kibzaim and
Beth Horon, together with their pasturelands—four towns. Jos 20:7; 1Sa 1:1
23Also from the tribe of Dan they received
Eltekeh, Gibbethon, 24Aijalon and Gath Rimmon, together with their pasturelands—four
towns. Jos 19:44
25From half the tribe of Manasseh they
received Taanach and Gath Rimmon, together with their pasturelands—two towns.
26All these ten towns and their pasturelands were
given to the rest of the Kohathite clans.

27The Levite clans of the Gershonites were given:
from the half-tribe of Manasseh,
Golan in Bashan (a city of refuge for one
accused of murder) and Be Eshtarah, together with their pasturelands—two towns;
28from the tribe of Issachar,
Kishion, Daberath, 29Jarmuth and En Gannim, together with their pasturelands—four
towns; Ge 30:18
30from the tribe of Asher,
Mishal, Abdon, 31Helkath and Rehob, together with their pasturelands—four towns;
32from the tribe of Naphtali,
Kedesh in Galilee (a city of refuge for one
accused of murder), Hammoth Dor and
Kartan, together with their pasturelands—
three towns. Jos 20:7; Nu 35:6

[a]8 *Jordan of Jericho* was possibly an ancient name for the Jordan River.

[33]All the towns of the Gershonite clans were thirteen, together with their pasturelands.

[34]The Merarite clans (the rest of the Levites) were given:

from the tribe of Zebulun,
Jokneam, Kartah, [35]Dimnah and Nahalal, together with their pasturelands—four towns;
[36]from the tribe of Reuben,
Bezer, Jahaz, [37]Kedemoth and Mephaath, together with their pasturelands—four towns;
[38]from the tribe of Gad,
Ramoth in Gilead (a city of refuge for one accused of murder), Mahanaim, [39]Heshbon and Jazer, together with their pasturelands—four towns in all. 1Ch 6:54-80; Dt 4:43

[40]All the towns allotted to the Merarite clans, who were the rest of the Levites, were twelve.

[41]The towns of the Levites in the territory held by the Israelites were forty-eight in all, together with their pasturelands. [42]Each of these towns had pasturelands surrounding it; this was true for all these towns. Nu 35:7

[43]So the LORD gave Israel all the land he had sworn to give their forefathers, and they took possession of it and settled there. [44]The LORD gave them rest on every side, just as he had sworn to their forefathers. Not one of their enemies withstood them; the LORD handed all their enemies over to them. [45]Not one of all the LORD's good promises to the house of Israel failed; every one was fulfilled. Dt 11:31; Jos 1:13; 23:14

Eastern Tribes Return Home

22 Then Joshua summoned the Reubenites, the Gadites and the half-tribe of Manasseh [2]and said to them, "You have done all that Moses the servant of the LORD commanded, and you have obeyed me in everything I commanded. [3]For a long time now—to this very day—you have not deserted your brothers but have carried out the mission the LORD your God gave you. [4]Now that the LORD your God has given your brothers rest as he promised, return to your homes in the land that Moses the servant of the LORD gave you on the other side of the Jordan. [5]But be very careful to keep the commandment and the law that Moses the servant of the LORD gave you: to love the LORD your God, to walk in all his ways, to obey his commands, to hold fast to him and to serve him with all your heart and all your soul." Dt 3:20; 5:29

[6]Then Joshua blessed them and sent them away, and they went to their homes. [7](To the half-tribe of Manasseh Moses had given land in Bashan, and to the other half of the tribe Joshua gave land on the west side of the Jordan with their brothers.) When Joshua sent them home, he blessed them, [8]saying, "Return to your homes with your great wealth—with large herds of livestock, with silver, gold, bronze and iron, and a great quantity of clothing—and divide with your brothers the plunder from your enemies." Ex 39:43; Nu 31:27; 1Sa 30:16

[9]So the Reubenites, the Gadites and the half-tribe of Manasseh left the Israelites at Shiloh in Canaan to return to Gilead, their own land, which they had acquired in accordance with the command of the LORD through Moses. Nu 32:26,29

[10]When they came to Geliloth near the Jordan in the land of Canaan, the Reubenites, the Gadites and the half-tribe of Manasseh built an imposing altar there by the Jordan. [11]And when the Israelites heard that they had built the altar on the border of Canaan at Geliloth near the Jordan on the Israelite side, [12]the whole assembly of Israel gathered at Shiloh to go to war against them. Jos 18:1

[13]So the Israelites sent Phinehas son of Eleazar, the priest, to the land of Gilead—to Reuben, Gad and the half-tribe of Manasseh. [14]With him they sent ten of the chief men, one for each of the tribes of Israel, each the head of a family division among the Israelite clans. Nu 1:4; 25:7

[15]When they went to Gilead—to Reuben, Gad and the half-tribe of Manasseh—they said to them: [16]"The whole assembly of the LORD says: 'How could you break faith with the God of Israel like this? How could you turn away from the LORD and build yourselves an altar in rebellion against him now? [17]Was not the sin of Peor enough for us? Up to this very day we have not cleansed ourselves from that sin, even though a plague fell on the community of the LORD! [18]And are you now turning away from the LORD? Nu 25:1-9; Dt 12:13-14

"'If you rebel against the LORD today, tomorrow he will be angry with the whole community of Israel. [19]If the land you possess is defiled, come over to the LORD's land, where the LORD's tabernacle stands, and share the land with us. But do not rebel against the LORD or against us by building an altar for yourselves, other than the altar of the LORD our God. [20]When Achan son of Zerah acted unfaithfully regarding the devoted things,[a] did not wrath come upon the whole community of Israel? He was not the only one who died for his sin.'" Nu 16:22; Jos 7:1

[21]Then Reuben, Gad and the half-tribe of Manasseh replied to the heads of the clans of Israel: [22]"The Mighty One, God, the LORD! The Mighty One, God, the LORD! He knows! And let Israel know! If this has been in rebellion or disobedience to the LORD, do not spare us this day. [23]If we have built our own altar to turn away from the LORD and to offer burnt offerings and grain offerings, or

[a]20 The Hebrew term refers to the irrevocable giving over of things or persons to the LORD, often by totally destroying them.

to sacrifice fellowship offerings[a] on it, may the
LORD himself call us to account. Dt 10:17; 18:19
24“No! We did it for fear that some day your
descendants might say to ours, ‘What do you have
to do with the LORD, the God of Israel? 25The LORD
has made the Jordan a boundary between us and
you—you Reubenites and Gadites! You have no
share in the LORD.’ So your descendants might
cause ours to stop fearing the LORD.
26“That is why we said, ‘Let us get ready and
build an altar—but not for burnt offerings or sacrifices.’ 27On the contrary, it is to be a witness
between us and you and the generations that follow, that we will worship the LORD at his sanctuary
with our burnt offerings, sacrifices and fellowship
offerings. Then in the future your descendants will
not be able to say to ours, ‘You have no share in
the LORD.’ Dt 12:6; Jos 24:27
28“And we said, ‘If they ever say this to us, or to
our descendants, we will answer: Look at the repli-
ca of the LORD’s altar, which our fathers built, not
for burnt offerings and sacrifices, but as a witness
between us and you.’
29“Far be it from us to rebel against the LORD
and turn away from him today by building an altar
for burnt offerings, grain offerings and sacrifices,
other than the altar of the LORD our God that
stands before his tabernacle.” Dt 12:13-14; Jos 24:16
30When Phinehas the priest and the leaders of
the community—the heads of the clans of the Israelites—heard what Reuben, Gad and Manasseh
had to say, they were pleased. 31And Phinehas son
of Eleazar, the priest, said to Reuben, Gad and
Manasseh, “Today we know that the LORD is with
us, because you have not acted unfaithfully toward
the LORD in this matter. Now you have rescued the
Israelites from the LORD’s hand.” Lev 26:11-12
32Then Phinehas son of Eleazar, the priest, and
the leaders returned to Canaan from their meeting
with the Reubenites and Gadites in Gilead and
reported to the Israelites. 33They were glad to hear
the report and praised God. And they talked no
more about going to war against them to devastate
the country where the Reubenites and the Gadites
lived. 1Ch 29:20; Da 2:19
34And the Reubenites and the Gadites gave the
altar this name: A Witness Between Us that the
LORD is God. Ge 21:30

Warning the Victors **Chapters 23–24**

As Joshua drew near to the end of his life, he issued strong warnings to the people of Israel. After reminding them of all the great works and wonders of the Lord, he called them to hold firm to God's law and to keep the covenant God had established with them. If they followed the Lord, they would experience His blessing; if they rebelled, they would lose the blessing He would otherwise have poured out on them. Some of Joshua's final words were offered as a testimony and example for the believers of his day—and for all who would follow: "But as for me and my household, we will serve the LORD" (24:15). May this be our declaration and the living testimony of our lives!

Joshua's Farewell to the Leaders

23 After a long time had passed and the LORD
had given Israel rest from all their enemies
around them, Joshua, by then old and well advanced in years, 2summoned all Israel—their elders, leaders, judges and officials—and said to
them: “I am old and well advanced in years. 3You
yourselves have seen everything the LORD your
God has done to all these nations for your sake; it
was the LORD your God who fought for you. 4Re-
member how I have allotted as an inheritance for
your tribes all the land of the nations that remain—the nations I conquered—between the
Jordan and the Great Sea[b] in the west. 5The LORD
your God himself will drive them out of your way.
He will push them out before you, and you will
take possession of their land, as the LORD your
God promised you. Jos 13:1; 21:44; Nu 33:53
6“Be very strong; be careful to obey all that is
written in the Book of the Law of Moses, without
turning aside to the right or to the left. 7Do not
associate with these nations that remain among
you; do not invoke the names of their gods or
swear by them. You must not serve them or bow
down to them. 8But you are to hold fast to the
LORD your God, as you have until now. Ex 23:13
9“The LORD has driven out before you great and
powerful nations; to this day no one has been able
to withstand you. 10One of you routs a thousand,
because the LORD your God fights for you, just as
he promised. 11So be very careful to love the LORD
your God. Dt 3:22; 11:23; Lev 26:8
12“But if you turn away and ally yourselves with
the survivors of these nations that remain among
you and if you intermarry with them and associate
with them, 13then you may be sure that the LORD
your God will no longer drive out these nations
before you. Instead, they will become snares and
traps for you, whips on your backs and thorns in
your eyes, until you perish from this good land,
which the LORD your God has given you. Ex 34:16
14“Now I am about to go the way of all the
earth. You know with all your heart and soul that
not one of all the good promises the LORD your
God gave you has failed. Every promise has been
fulfilled; not one has failed. 15But just as every
good promise of the LORD your God has come
true, so the LORD will bring on you all the evil he
has threatened, until he has destroyed you from
this good land he has given you. 16If you violate

[a]23 Traditionally *peace offerings*; also in verse 27
[b]4 That is, the Mediterranean

the covenant of the LORD your God, which he
commanded you, and go and serve other gods and
bow down to them, the LORD's anger will burn
against you, and you will quickly perish from the
good land he has given you." Dt 28:15; Jos 21:45; 1Ki 2:2

LIVING  **INSIGHT**

In an impersonal, fast-moving world where we feel more like a number than a person, it is easy to believe that our vertical relationship is much the same. Nameless faces before a preoccupied God; busy people involved in meaningless, futile activity. Not so. God's Word assures us of an identity and promises us that our lives have order, reason and purpose. God knows what He is about.

(See Joshua 23:14–16.)

The Covenant Renewed at Shechem

24 Then Joshua assembled all the tribes of Israel at Shechem. He summoned the elders,
leaders, judges and officials of Israel, and they presented themselves before God. Jos 23:2
2Joshua said to all the people, "This is what the
LORD, the God of Israel, says: 'Long ago your forefathers, including Terah the father of Abraham
and Nahor, lived beyond the River[a] and worshiped other gods. 3But I took your father Abraham from the land beyond the River and led
him throughout Canaan and gave him many descendants. I gave him Isaac, 4and to Isaac I gave
Jacob and Esau. I assigned the hill country of
Seir to Esau, but Jacob and his sons went down
to Egypt.
5" 'Then I sent Moses and Aaron, and I afflicted
the Egyptians by what I did there, and I brought
you out. 6When I brought your fathers out of
Egypt, you came to the sea, and the Egyptians
pursued them with chariots and horsemen[b] as far
as the Red Sea.[c] 7But they cried to the LORD for
help, and he put darkness between you and the
Egyptians; he brought the sea over them and covered them. You saw with your own eyes what I did
to the Egyptians. Then you lived in the desert for
a long time. Ex 3:10; 14:9; Dt 1:46
8" 'I brought you to the land of the Amorites
who lived east of the Jordan. They fought against
you, but I gave them into your hands. I destroyed
them from before you, and you took possession of
their land. 9When Balak son of Zippor, the king of
Moab, prepared to fight against Israel, he sent for
Balaam son of Beor to put a curse on you. 10But
I would not listen to Balaam, so he blessed you
again and again, and I delivered you out of his
hand. Ex 23:23; Nu 22:2; Dt 23:5
11" 'Then you crossed the Jordan and came to
Jericho. The citizens of Jericho fought against you,
as did also the Amorites, Perizzites, Canaanites,
Hittites, Girgashites, Hivites and Jebusites, but I
gave them into your hands. 12I sent the hornet
ahead of you, which drove them out before you—
also the two Amorite kings. You did not do it with
your own sword and bow. 13So I gave you a land
on which you did not toil and cities you did not
build; and you live in them and eat from vineyards
and olive groves that you did not plant.'
14"Now fear the LORD and serve him with all
faithfulness. Throw away the gods your forefathers
worshiped beyond the River and in Egypt, and
serve the LORD. 15But if serving the LORD seems
undesirable to you, then choose for yourselves this
day whom you will serve, whether the gods your
forefathers served beyond the River, or the gods of
the Amorites, in whose land you are living. But as
for me and my household, we will serve the LORD."

LIVING  **INSIGHT**

Joshua was a strong leader who knew where he was going, but he gave others the space they needed to choose for themselves. That's not only smart; it's an evidence of two admirable virtues: first, a security in self that comes from resting in God's will and second, a genuine respect for others.

(See Joshua 24:15.)

16Then the people answered, "Far be it from us
to forsake the LORD to serve other gods! 17It was
the LORD our God himself who brought us and our
fathers up out of Egypt, from that land of slavery,
and performed those great signs before our eyes.
He protected us on our entire journey and among
all the nations through which we traveled. 18And
the LORD drove out before us all the nations, including the Amorites, who lived in the land. We
too will serve the LORD, because he is our God."
19Joshua said to the people, "You are not able to
serve the LORD. He is a holy God; he is a jealous
God. He will not forgive your rebellion and your
sins. 20If you forsake the LORD and serve foreign
gods, he will turn and bring disaster on you and
make an end of you, after he has been good to
you." Ex 23:21; Jos 23:15; 1Ch 28:9,20

[a]2 That is, the Euphrates; also in verses 3, 14 and 15 [b]6 Or *charioteers* [c]6 Hebrew *Yam Suph*; that is, Sea of Reeds

[21]But the people said to Joshua, "No! We will serve the LORD."

[22]Then Joshua said, "You are witnesses against yourselves that you have chosen to serve the LORD." Ru 4:10; Ps 119:30,173

"Yes, we are witnesses," they replied. Dt 25:9

[23]"Now then," said Joshua, "throw away the foreign gods that are among you and yield your hearts to the LORD, the God of Israel." 1Ki 8:58

[24]And the people said to Joshua, "We will serve the LORD our God and obey him." Ex 19:8; 24:3,7

[25]On that day Joshua made a covenant for the people, and there at Shechem he drew up for them
decrees and laws. [26]And Joshua recorded these
things in the Book of the Law of God. Then he took a large stone and set it up there under the oak near the holy place of the LORD. Ex 24:8; Dt 31:24

[27]"See!" he said to all the people. "This stone will be a witness against us. It has heard all the words the LORD has said to us. It will be a witness against you if you are untrue to your God."

Buried in the Promised Land

[28]Then Joshua sent the people away, each to his own inheritance. Jdg 21:23-24

[29]After these things, Joshua son of Nun, the servant of the LORD, died at the age of a hundred
and ten. [30]And they buried him in the land of his
inheritance, at Timnath Serah[a] in the hill country of Ephraim, north of Mount Gaash. Jos 19:50; Jdg 1:1

[31]Israel served the LORD throughout the lifetime of Joshua and of the elders who outlived him and who had experienced everything the LORD had done for Israel. Jdg 2:6-9

[32]And Joseph's bones, which the Israelites had brought up from Egypt, were buried at Shechem in the tract of land that Jacob bought for a hundred pieces of silver[b] from the sons of Hamor, the father of Shechem. This became the inheritance of Joseph's descendants. Ge 33:19; 50:25; Ex 13:19

[33]And Eleazar son of Aaron died and was buried at Gibeah, which had been allotted to his son Phinehas in the hill country of Ephraim. Jos 22:13

[a] *30* Also known as *Timnath Heres* (see Judges 2:9) unknown weight and value.

[b] *32* Hebrew *hundred kesitahs*; a kesitah was a unit of money of

INTRODUCTION

JUDGES

It's difficult for a modern nation like the United States or Canada to pull itself out of the swamp of political scandal and public distrust . . . but to do so several times in a row is unheard of. Or is it? If we think we have a hard time recovering from times of political and social misery, consider the Israelites after they entered the land of Canaan under Joshua's leadership. Although clearly instructed to drive out the inhabitants who remained in the land, the Israelites compromised and dragged their feet, and they ultimately ignored God's direct command. The result of this disobedience: a cycle repeated several times in the book. As God heard their cry for deliverance, He graciously sent a deliverer (a "judge"). Victory came, the judge died, and the nation again compromised and fell under the rule of godless people . . . resulting in another cry for deliverance . . . Recycled misery—and through it all, God's incredible faithfulness.

WRITER: *Unknown, possibly Samuel*

DATE: *c.1000 B.C.*

PURPOSE: *To describe human depravity at its worst—and God's unrelenting love*

KEY THEME: *Failure through compromise*

KEY VERSE: *21:25*

DISTINCTIVES: *Two commencements (1:1; 2:6); oldest known parable (9:8-15); the greatest and grandest battle song (chapter 5); the first record of a woman heading a nation (Deborah—chapter 4)*

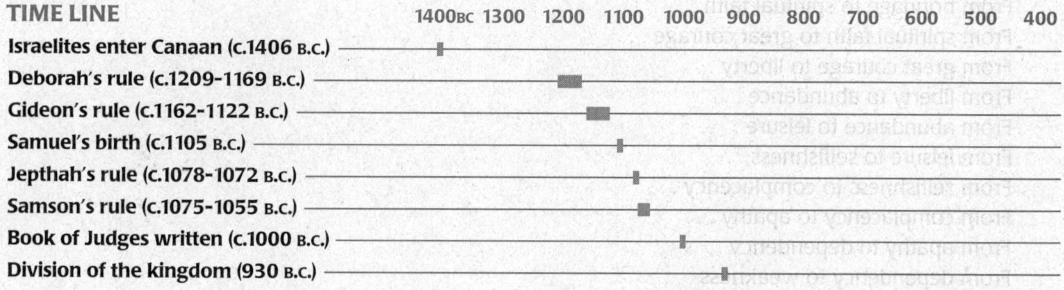

Recycled Misery

JOSHUA c. 1375 B.C.

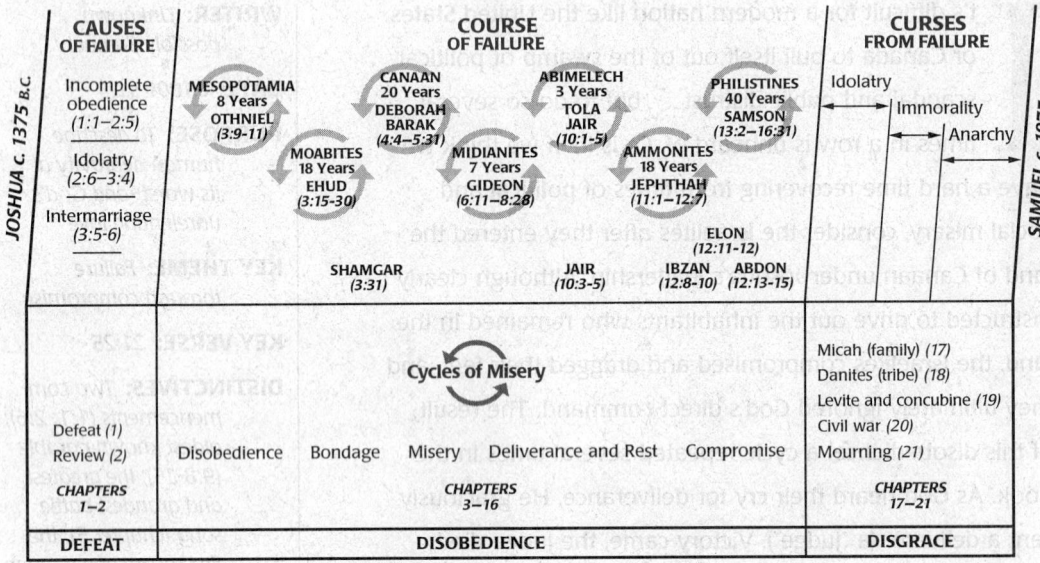

CAUSES OF FAILURE

Incomplete obedience *(1:1–2:5)*

Idolatry *(2:6–3:4)*

Intermarriage *(3:5-6)*

COURSE OF FAILURE

MESOPOTAMIA 8 Years OTHNIEL *(3:9-11)*

MOABITES 18 Years EHUD *(3:15-30)*

CANAAN 20 Years DEBORAH BARAK *(4:4–5:31)*

MIDIANITES 7 Years GIDEON *(6:11–8:28)*

ABIMELECH 3 Years TOLA JAIR *(10:1-5)*

AMMONITES 18 Years JEPHTHAH *(11:1–12:7)*

PHILISTINES 40 Years SAMSON *(13:2–16:31)*

SHAMGAR *(3:31)*

JAIR *(10:3-5)*

ELON *(12:11-12)*

IBZAN *(12:8-10)*

ABDON *(12:13-15)*

CURSES FROM FAILURE

Idolatry

Immorality

Anarchy

SAMUEL c. 1075 B.C.

Defeat *(1)*

Review *(2)*

CHAPTERS 1–2

Disobedience

Bondage

Cycles of Misery

Misery

Deliverance and Rest

Compromise

CHAPTERS 3–16

Micah (family) *(17)*

Danites (tribe) *(18)*

Levite and concubine *(19)*

Civil war *(20)*

Mourning *(21)*

CHAPTERS 17–21

DEFEAT | **DISOBEDIENCE** | **DISGRACE**

The history of great civilizations reminds me of a giant, revolving door that turns on the axis of depravity. The outside perimeter is the passing of time. It is one monotonous, repetitive revolution after another—a process leading to a cycle of misery that repeats itself generation after generation.

I was interested to discover from one historian that the average age of most world civilizations is a duration of about 200 years. Almost without exception, each civilization passed through a similar sequence of events:

From bondage to spiritual faith . . .
From spiritual faith to great courage . . .
From great courage to liberty . . .
From liberty to abundance . . .
From abundance to leisure . . .
From leisure to selfishness . . .
From selfishness to complacency . . .
From complacency to apathy . . .
From apathy to dependency . . .
From dependency to weakness . . .
From weakness BACK TO BONDAGE . . .

This "revolving door" cycle has not only been true in secular history, but it was also true in the sacred history of God's people. We find this to be the case as far back as the ancient people of Israel and never more obviously described than in the book of Judges. If ever we'd want to erase from our minds an era of time in Jewish history, it would be the time covered in this old book! This is the book that portrays most vividly the downward, repetitive spiral of human depravity.

These Judges Carried Swords, Not Gavels!

Now when you think of a judge, if you're like me, you think of a dignified-looking person who's robed, sits behind a desk and makes judgments on legal matters. In Bible times, however, a judge was more a warrior in the open field than a person of legal proceedings. At times, a judge was a counselor, a priest or a prophet—but at no time was the judge a theorizing individual who would oversee litigation.

Often the judge was simply a strong leader God raised up during a time of great crisis to bring His people back to Himself. So the "judge" was a "deliverer"; in fact, that's exactly what the name means.

The book of Judges covers about 300 years of Hebrew history—from 1375 all the way down to 1075 B.C. Those 300 years were three centuries of misery, where seven separate cycles ran their miserable course. Even though God was seeking to bring the nation back to Him, the people chose to run away from Him . . . again and again and again.

An End and a New Beginning

There's a contrast I want to emphasize as we view the books of Joshua and Judges back to back. Both books begin with an obituary, and the obituary is exceedingly important—not particularly because of who is present, but because of who has just died: Joshua 1:1—"After the death of Moses . . ." and Judges 1:1—"After the death of Joshua . . ." So the book of Joshua begins with the death of Moses. In the same way, the book of Judges notes the death of Joshua in its opening verse.

When a man or woman of God dies, nothing of God dies. Never forget that principle! When a person God has used to influence other people's lives passes from this earth, nothing of God's impact passes away. As a matter of fact, those men and women who are used by God in our lives often prompt us to take charge in an even better way *after* their death.

Compare and Contrast

While both Joshua and Judges begin in a similar manner with an obituary, the remainder of the books are in strong contrast to one another. Notice the stark differences:

In Joshua the People Experience:	*In Judges the People Experience:*
Joy and Achievement	Sorrow and Suffering
Strength	Weakness
Victory	Defeat
Unity—Determination	Disunity—Anarchy
Freedom	Bondage
Obedient Following of God	Disobedient Running From God
Mobilization to Fight	Fruitless Maintaining of Mediocrity

Where Did We Go Wrong?

The theme of Judges is *failure through compromise.* The book is about failure, failure and more failure. It's a monotonous message of depravity: Depravity on display—constantly waving its hand in the reader's face all through the book.

We ask the question, "How could it be, on the heels of such remarkable victories won through Joshua's leadership? How could the same nation regress to such an extent?" In the early part of Joshua, three reasons are listed: *lack of total obedience*, a *fondness for idolatry* and *intermarriage with foreign peoples.* It was all this that set in motion the cycle of misery that ran its course for three tragic centuries.

The Cycle of Misery

There were five significant factors that made up this cycle of misery. First, *disobedience* (2:11–13). God said, "Drive the Canaanites out," but the Israelites didn't. Second, *bondage* (2:14). Don't think for a moment that getting your own way, running your own life, building your own lifestyle on a foundation of disobedience will set you free. It will put you in bondage every time—as it certainly did to the Israelites. Bondage leads to the third factor: *misery* (2:15). At this stage you may be asking, "Where's the happy lifestyle?" It just isn't there. As Solomon wrote, "The way of the unfaithful is hard" (Proverbs 13:15). As a child of God I say, "Yes," to my Lord. My Lord replies, "Then walk with Me." And if I say back to Him, "I know there are some things you don't want for me, but I am going to seek them anyway," God says, "I understand that the road is tough at times, but you must keep following Me!" If your response is, "But I don't want to do that," then you will spend sleepless nights and will be hard-pressed to know where to find peace. It will flee from you. Just read the book of Judges, and you will find tragic examples of the misery that came on a people who refused to follow their Lord. Fourth, God's grace entered in for His people through *deliverance and rest* (2:18)—sometimes a rest as long as eighty years and sometimes as short as twenty years. When a judge was called forth and deliverance was experienced, then there was rest in the land. Fifth, and finally, the time came when the judge would die and the people of God would once again *compromise* (2:19)—and the process would start all over again. It was a long process of repeated violations. From one judge to the next the same cycle repeated itself. You'd think they would have learned their lesson the first time.

Chapters 3–16 show us what happens in a society where compromise continues and sin dominates. Here we read of the depths of disgrace to which God's people had fallen. In chapters 17–21 we see the horrible results of a sick and disgraceful society. This final section portrays three forms of disgraceful lifestyles highlighted in Judges: idolatry, immorality and anarchy.

Breaking the Cycle

What can we learn from the book of Judges? Several practical truths come to mind—truths that live on:

First, *depravity results in permissiveness when righteousness is ignored*. Second, *permissiveness leads to rationalization when holiness is ignored*. In other words, in a time such as ours, it is no longer vogue for someone to refer to something as "bad, sinful and wrong." Such appraisals mark us in the eyes of many as rather ignorant or ill-informed, because moral absolutes and ethical values are now redefined. Rationalization has become a way of life in this generation. Finally, *rationalization encourages rebellion when repentance is ignored*. This all happens so slowly, like an erosion that, though silent, causes immeasurable damage over time.

Some of you are right at that crucial juncture in your life. You may be making some tough, gut-level decisions, and if you're honest with yourself, you have to admit that you're dangerously close to the edge. I plead with you as a friend: Be different. Be distinctive. How patient is our Lord! How graciously merciful He is toward us! Don't make His patience your license to continue in sin.

The book of Judges is in many ways a case study in futility. As we read Judges we may find ourselves saying, "When will they ever learn?" But a better question to ask is, "When will *we* ever learn?" How many times must we compromise before we finally fall on our knees and say, "O God, help us out of this mess we've made."

Before you and I get too critical of the Israelites in the days of the judges, we need to take a look at our own history and read our own autobiography a little more closely. Wise are the people who read such stories and say, "That's enough for me. My walk will be a walk of obedience and righteousness." *It pays to listen to and obey God.* If I learn nothing else from Judges, I want to learn this life-changing lesson.

Downward Cycle of Disobedience **Chapters 1–3**

Over the three centuries of the judges we find God's people caught in a vicious cycle of disobedience and rebellion. When the people entered the land and settled it, they initially experienced rest and a time of prosperity—which didn't last. The warnings Joshua spoke at the end of his life were quickly forgotten.

The cycle began with *disobedience.* The people embraced the pagan gods of the nations they had conquered and began to turn away from the one true God. This disobedience led to a time of *bondage* to the pagan people who surrounded God's people. *Misery* was experienced in the constant oppression by other nations and even in the hand of the Lord being lifted against the people of Israel. When the Israelites recognized the evil of their ways and the consequences they were reaping, they cried out to the Lord for help, and He sent them *deliverance and rest.* This help came in the form of a political and military leader called a "judge." After a time of rest in the land (and the death or departure of the judge), the people's hearts started to wander, and they began to *compromise* and fall into sin and rebellion all over again. When disobedience began to reign, the same cycle repeated itself. This process is clearly illustrated throughout Judges. In the early chapters of Judges we are introduced to the first three men who were called to lead Israel as its judges: Othniel, then Ehud, followed by Shamgar. As you read their stories you will see how this cycle unfolded.

Israel Fights the Remaining Canaanites

1 After the death of Joshua, the Israelites asked the LORD, "Who will be the first to go up and fight for us against the Canaanites?" Nu 27:21

2The LORD answered, "Judah is to go; I have given the land into their hands." Ge 49:8

3Then the men of Judah said to the Simeonites their brothers, "Come up with us into the territory allotted to us, to fight against the Canaanites. We in turn will go with you into yours." So the Simeonites went with them.

4When Judah attacked, the LORD gave the Canaanites and Perizzites into their hands and they struck down ten thousand men at Bezek. 5It was there that they found Adoni-Bezek and fought against him, putting to rout the Canaanites and Perizzites. 6Adoni-Bezek fled, but they chased him and caught him, and cut off his thumbs and big toes. Ge 13:7; Jos 3:10

7Then Adoni-Bezek said, "Seventy kings with their thumbs and big toes cut off have picked up scraps under my table. Now God has paid me back for what I did to them." They brought him to Jerusalem, and he died there. Lev 24:19

8The men of Judah attacked Jerusalem also and took it. They put the city to the sword and set it on fire. Jos 15:63

9After that, the men of Judah went down to fight against the Canaanites living in the hill country, the Negev and the western foothills. 10They advanced against the Canaanites living in Hebron (formerly called Kiriath Arba) and defeated Sheshai, Ahiman and Talmai. Nu 13:17; Jos 15:14

11From there they advanced against the people living in Debir (formerly called Kiriath Sepher). 12And Caleb said, "I will give my daughter Acsah in marriage to the man who attacks and captures Kiriath Sepher." 13Othniel son of Kenaz, Caleb's younger brother, took it; so Caleb gave his daughter Acsah to him in marriage.

14One day when she came to Othniel, she urged him[a] to ask her father for a field. When she got off her donkey, Caleb asked her, "What can I do for you?"

15She replied, "Do me a special favor. Since you have given me land in the Negev, give me also springs of water." Then Caleb gave her the upper and lower springs. Jos 15:15-19

16The descendants of Moses' father-in-law, the Kenite, went up from the City of Palms[b] with the men of Judah to live among the people of the Desert of Judah in the Negev near Arad.

17Then the men of Judah went with the Simeonites their brothers and attacked the Canaanites living in Zephath, and they totally destroyed[c] the city. Therefore it was called Hormah.[d] 18The men of Judah also took[e] Gaza, Ashkelon and Ekron—each city with its territory. Nu 21:3; Jos 11:22

19The LORD was with the men of Judah. They took possession of the hill country, but they were unable to drive the people from the plains, because they had iron chariots. 20As Moses had promised, Hebron was given to Caleb, who drove from it the three sons of Anak. 21The Benjamites, however, failed to dislodge the Jebusites, who were living in Jerusalem; to this day the Jebusites live there with the Benjamites. Jos 14:9; 15:63; 17:16

22Now the house of Joseph attacked Bethel, and the LORD was with them. 23When they sent men to spy out Bethel (formerly called Luz), 24the spies saw a man coming out of the city and they said to him, "Show us how to get into the city and we will see that you are treated well." 25So he showed them, and they put the city to the sword but spared the man and his whole family. 26He then went to the land of the Hittites, where he built a city and called it Luz, which is its name to this day.

27But Manasseh did not drive out the people of Beth Shan or Taanach or Dor or Ibleam or Megiddo and their surrounding settlements, for the Canaanites were determined to live in that land. 28When Israel became strong, they pressed the Canaanites into forced labor but never drove them

[a] 14 Hebrew; Septuagint and Vulgate *Othniel, he urged her* [b] 16 That is, Jericho [c] 17 The Hebrew term refers to the irrevocable giving over of things or persons to the LORD, often by totally destroying them. [d] 17 *Hormah* means *destruction.* [e] 18 Hebrew; Septuagint *Judah did not take*

out completely. [29]Nor did Ephraim drive out the Canaanites living in Gezer, but the Canaanites continued to live there among them. [30]Neither did Zebulun drive out the Canaanites living in Kitron or Nahalol, who remained among them; but they did subject them to forced labor. [31]Nor did Asher drive out those living in Acco or Sidon or Ahlab or Aczib or Helbah or Aphek or Rehob, [32]and because of this the people of Asher lived among the Canaanite inhabitants of the land. [33]Neither did Naphtali drive out those living in Beth Shemesh or Beth Anath; but the Naphtalites too lived among the Canaanite inhabitants of the land, and those living in Beth Shemesh and Beth Anath became forced laborers for them. [34]The Amorites confined the Danites to the hill country, not allowing them to come down into the plain. [35]And the Amorites were determined also to hold out in Mount Heres, Aijalon and Shaalbim, but when the power of the house of Joseph increased, they too were pressed into forced labor. [36]The boundary of the Amorites was from Scorpion[a] Pass to Sela and beyond.

The Angel of the LORD at Bokim

2 The angel of the LORD went up from Gilgal to Bokim and said, "I brought you up out of Egypt and led you into the land that I swore to give to your forefathers. I said, 'I will never break my covenant with you, [2]and you shall not make a covenant with the people of this land, but you shall break down their altars.' Yet you have disobeyed me. Why have you done this? [3]Now therefore I tell you that I will not drive them out before you; they will be ⌞thorns⌟ in your sides and their gods will be a snare to you." Ex 20:2; Jos 23:13; Ps 106:36

[4]When the angel of the LORD had spoken these things to all the Israelites, the people wept aloud, [5]and they called that place Bokim.[b] There they offered sacrifices to the LORD.

Disobedience and Defeat

[6]After Joshua had dismissed the Israelites, they went to take possession of the land, each to his own inheritance. [7]The people served the LORD throughout the lifetime of Joshua and of the elders who outlived him and who had seen all the great things the LORD had done for Israel.

[8]Joshua son of Nun, the servant of the LORD, died at the age of a hundred and ten. [9]And they buried him in the land of his inheritance, at Timnath Heres[c] in the hill country of Ephraim, north of Mount Gaash. Jos 24:29-31; 19:50

[10]After that whole generation had been gathered to their fathers, another generation grew up, who knew neither the LORD nor what he had done for Israel. [11]Then the Israelites did evil in the eyes of the LORD and served the Baals. [12]They forsook the LORD, the God of their fathers, who had brought them out of Egypt. They followed and worshiped various gods of the peoples around them. They provoked the LORD to anger [13]because they forsook him and served Baal and the Ashtoreths. [14]In his anger against Israel the LORD handed them over to raiders who plundered them. He sold them to their enemies all around, whom they were no longer able to resist. [15]Whenever Israel went out to fight, the hand of the LORD was against them to defeat them, just as he had sworn to them. They were in great distress. Dt 28:25; 31:16; 1 Sa 2:12

[16]Then the LORD raised up judges,[d] who saved them out of the hands of these raiders. [17]Yet they would not listen to their judges but prostituted themselves to other gods and worshiped them. Unlike their fathers, they quickly turned from the way in which their fathers had walked, the way of obedience to the LORD's commands. [18]Whenever the LORD raised up a judge for them, he was with the judge and saved them out of the hands of their enemies as long as the judge lived; for the LORD had compassion on them as they groaned under those who oppressed and afflicted them. [19]But when the judge died, the people returned to ways even more corrupt than those of their fathers, following other gods and serving and worshiping them. They refused to give up their evil practices and stubborn ways. Jos 1:5; Jdg 3:12; Ac 13:20

[20]Therefore the LORD was very angry with Israel and said, "Because this nation has violated the covenant that I laid down for their forefathers and has not listened to me, [21]I will no longer drive out before them any of the nations Joshua left when he died. [22]I will use them to test Israel and see whether they will keep the way of the LORD and walk in it as their forefathers did." [23]The LORD had allowed those nations to remain; he did not drive them out at once by giving them into the hands of Joshua.

3 These are the nations the LORD left to test all those Israelites who had not experienced any of the wars in Canaan [2](he did this only to teach warfare to the descendants of the Israelites who had not had previous battle experience): [3]the five rulers of the Philistines, all the Canaanites, the Sidonians, and the Hivites living in the Lebanon mountains from Mount Baal Hermon to Lebo[e] Hamath. [4]They were left to test the Israelites to see whether they would obey the LORD's commands, which he had given their forefathers through Moses. Ex 15:25; Jos 13:3; Jdg 2:21-22

[5]The Israelites lived among the Canaanites, Hittites, Amorites, Perizzites, Hivites and Jebusites. [6]They took their daughters in marriage and gave

[a]36 Hebrew *Akrabbim* [b]5 *Bokim* means *weepers.* [c]9 Also known as *Timnath Serah* (see Joshua 19:50 and 24:30)
[d]16 Or *leaders*; similarly in verses 17-19 [e]3 Or *to the entrance to*

their own daughters to their sons, and served their gods. Ex 34:16; Dt 7:3-4; Ps 106:35

Othniel

7 The Israelites did evil in the eyes of the LORD; they forgot the LORD their God and served the Baals and the Asherahs. 8 The anger of the LORD burned against Israel so that he sold them into the hands of Cushan-Rishathaim king of Aram Naharaim,[a] to whom the Israelites were subject for eight years. 9 But when they cried out to the LORD, he raised up for them a deliverer, Othniel son of Kenaz, Caleb's younger brother, who saved them. 10 The Spirit of the LORD came upon him, so that he became Israel's judge[b] and went to war. The LORD gave Cushan-Rishathaim king of Aram into the hands of Othniel, who overpowered him. 11 So the land had peace for forty years, until Othniel son of Kenaz died. Nu 11:25,29; Dt 4:9; Jdg 6:34

Ehud

12 Once again the Israelites did evil in the eyes of the LORD, and because they did this evil the LORD gave Eglon king of Moab power over Israel. 13 Getting the Ammonites and Amalekites to join him, Eglon came and attacked Israel, and they took possession of the City of Palms.[c] 14 The Israelites were subject to Eglon king of Moab for eighteen years. Jdg 1:16; 2:11,14

15 Again the Israelites cried out to the LORD, and he gave them a deliverer—Ehud, a left-handed man, the son of Gera the Benjamite. The Israelites sent him with tribute to Eglon king of Moab. 16 Now Ehud had made a double-edged sword about a foot and a half[d] long, which he strapped to his right thigh under his clothing. 17 He presented the tribute to Eglon king of Moab, who was a very fat man. 18 After Ehud had presented the tribute, he sent on their way the men who had carried it. 19 At the idols[e] near Gilgal he himself turned back and said, "I have a secret message for you, O king." 1Ch 12:2; Ps 78:34

The king said, "Quiet!" And all his attendants left him.

20 Ehud then approached him while he was sitting alone in the upper room of his summer palace[f] and said, "I have a message from God for you." As the king rose from his seat, 21 Ehud reached with his left hand, drew the sword from his right thigh and plunged it into the king's belly. 22 Even the handle sank in after the blade, which came out his back. Ehud did not pull the sword out, and the fat closed in over it. 23 Then Ehud went out to the porch[g]; he shut the doors of the upper room behind him and locked them.

24 After he had gone, the servants came and found the doors of the upper room locked. They said, "He must be relieving himself in the inner room of the house." 25 They waited to the point of embarrassment, but when he did not open the doors of the room, they took a key and unlocked them. There they saw their lord fallen to the floor, dead. 1Sa 24:3; 2Ki 2:17

26 While they waited, Ehud got away. He passed by the idols and escaped to Seirah. 27 When he arrived there, he blew a trumpet in the hill country of Ephraim, and the Israelites went down with him from the hills, with him leading them. Jdg 6:34

28 "Follow me," he ordered, "for the LORD has given Moab, your enemy, into your hands." So they followed him down and, taking possession of the fords of the Jordan that led to Moab, they allowed no one to cross over. 29 At that time they struck down about ten thousand Moabites, all vigorous and strong; not a man escaped. 30 That day Moab was made subject to Israel, and the land had peace for eighty years. Jdg 7:9,15,24; 12:5

Shamgar

31 After Ehud came Shamgar son of Anath, who struck down six hundred Philistines with an oxgoad. He too saved Israel. Jdg 5:6

Unexpected Leadership — Chapters 4–5

God will use whomever God chooses to do God's willl Sometimes we try to put God in a box and predict how He will act. This is impossible! He is God. He can't be limited, analyzed or pinned down that easily. In this critical time in Israel's history, God lifted up a woman by the name of Deborah to serve as the judge of His people. The choice of a woman for this task might not seem strange to us today, but try to imagine the response of the people thousands of years ago in a culture that left very little room for women in community leadership of any kind. It is safe to say that Deborah was an unexpected leader. However, she was the right person at the right time to do the work of the Lord.

Deborah

4 After Ehud died, the Israelites once again did evil in the eyes of the LORD. 2 So the LORD sold them into the hands of Jabin, a king of Canaan, who reigned in Hazor. The commander of his army was Sisera, who lived in Harosheth Haggoyim. 3 Because he had nine hundred iron chariots and had cruelly oppressed the Israelites for twenty years, they cried to the LORD for help.

4 Deborah, a prophetess, the wife of Lappidoth, was leading[h] Israel at that time. 5 She held court under the Palm of Deborah between Ramah and Bethel in the hill country of Ephraim, and the

[a] 8 That is, Northwest Mesopotamia [b] 10 Or *leader* [c] 13 That is, Jericho [d] 16 Hebrew *a cubit* (about 0.5 meter) [e] 19 Or *the stone quarries*; also in verse 26 [f] 20 The meaning of the Hebrew for this phrase is uncertain. [g] 23 The meaning of the Hebrew for this word is uncertain. [h] 4 Traditionally *judging*

Israelites came to her to have their disputes decided. 6She sent for Barak son of Abinoam from Kedesh in Naphtali and said to him, "The LORD, the
God of Israel, commands you: 'Go, take with you
ten thousand men of Naphtali and Zebulun and
lead the way to Mount Tabor. 7I will lure Sisera,
the commander of Jabin's army, with his chariots
and his troops to the Kishon River and give him
into your hands.'" Heb 11:32; Ps 83:9; Ge 35:8
8Barak said to her, "If you go with me, I will go;
but if you don't go with me, I won't go."
9"Very well," Deborah said, "I will go with you.
But because of the way you are going about this,[a]
the honor will not be yours, for the LORD will hand
Sisera over to a woman." So Deborah went with
Barak to Kedesh, 10where he summoned Zebulun
and Naphtali. Ten thousand men followed him,
and Deborah also went with him. Jdg 5:15,18
11Now Heber the Kenite had left the other Kenites, the descendants of Hobab, Moses' brother-
in-law,[b] and pitched his tent by the great tree in
Zaanannim near Kedesh. Jdg 1:16
12When they told Sisera that Barak son of Abinoam had gone up to Mount Tabor, 13Sisera gathered together his nine hundred iron chariots and
all the men with him, from Harosheth Haggoyim
to the Kishon River.
14Then Deborah said to Barak, "Go! This is the
day the LORD has given Sisera into your hands. Has
not the LORD gone ahead of you?" So Barak went
down Mount Tabor, followed by ten thousand
men. 15At Barak's advance, the LORD routed Sisera
and all his chariots and army by the sword, and
Sisera abandoned his chariot and fled on foot.
16But Barak pursued the chariots and army as far
as Harosheth Haggoyim. All the troops of Sisera
fell by the sword; not a man was left. Dt 9:3
17Sisera, however, fled on foot to the tent of Jael,
the wife of Heber the Kenite, because there were
friendly relations between Jabin king of Hazor and
the clan of Heber the Kenite.
18Jael went out to meet Sisera and said to him,
"Come, my lord, come right in. Don't be afraid."
So he entered her tent, and she put a covering over
him.
19"I'm thirsty," he said. "Please give me some
water." She opened a skin of milk, gave him a
drink, and covered him up. Jdg 5:25
20"Stand in the doorway of the tent," he told
her. "If someone comes by and asks you, 'Is anyone here?' say 'No.'"
21But Jael, Heber's wife, picked up a tent peg
and a hammer and went quietly to him while he
lay fast asleep, exhausted. She drove the peg
through his temple into the ground, and he died.
22Barak came by in pursuit of Sisera, and Jael
went out to meet him. "Come," she said, "I will
show you the man you're looking for." So he went
in with her, and there lay Sisera with the tent peg
through his temple—dead.
23On that day God subdued Jabin, the Canaanite king, before the Israelites. 24And the hand of the
Israelites grew stronger and stronger against Jabin,
the Canaanite king, until they destroyed him.

The Song of Deborah

5 On that day Deborah and Barak son of Abinoam sang this song: Ex 15:1

2"When the princes in Israel take the lead,
when the people willingly offer
themselves— 2Ch 17:16
praise the LORD!

3"Hear this, you kings! Listen, you rulers!
I will sing to[c] the LORD, I will sing;
I will make music to[d] the LORD, the God
of Israel. Ps 27:6

LIVING  **INSIGHT**

The Spirit-filled saint is a song-filled saint! Animals can't sing. Neither can pews or pulpits or Bibles or buildings. Only you. And your melody is broadcast right into heaven—live—where God's antenna is always receptive . . . where the soothing strains of your song are always appreciated.

(See Judges 5:3.)

4"O LORD, when you went out from Seir,
when you marched from the land of Edom,
the earth shook, the heavens poured,
the clouds poured down water. Ps 68:8
5The mountains quaked before the LORD, the
One of Sinai,
before the LORD, the God of Israel. Ex 19:18

6"In the days of Shamgar son of Anath, Jdg 3:31
in the days of Jael, the roads were
abandoned; Jdg 4:17
travelers took to winding paths.
7Village life[e] in Israel ceased,
ceased until I,[f] Deborah, arose,
arose a mother in Israel.
8When they chose new gods, Dt 32:17
war came to the city gates,
and not a shield or spear was seen
among forty thousand in Israel.
9My heart is with Israel's princes,

[a]9 Or *But on the expedition you are undertaking* [b]11 Or *father-in-law* [c]3 Or *of* [d]3 Or / *with song I will praise*
[e]7 Or *Warriors* [f]7 Or *you*

DEBORAH

Judge and Mother in Israel

"Village life in Israel ceased,
ceased until I, Deborah, arose,
arose a mother in Israel."
–JUDGES 5:7

Deborah was a mother and a prophetess. She also became a judge in Israel—a responsible and respected woman. And people from all over Israel came to receive her judgment regarding their disputes. She lived in the days when Israel had no king, when no one gave the orders, when no one was in control (Judges 17:6). Throughout this time, Deborah was a powerful instrument in God's hands to receive His words of instruction and declare them to the people as she encouraged them to trust God completely and obey Him faithfully. She was God's courageous mouthpiece in a dark and dismal time in Israel's history.

There are several traits that stand out in my mind when I study Deborah's life. First, *Deborah had a great heart of compassion when she heard the cries of anguish and need.* Deborah saw the suffering the Israelites had experienced at the hands of King Jabin and his army commander Sisera. This wonderful servant of God named Deborah summoned Barak and told him to mobilize an army, because the time had come for God to deliver His people. She later reflected on this call in her victory song: "My heart is with Israel's princes, with the willing volunteers among the people" (5:9). Deborah was no cold-hearted ruler. She was a woman of compassion—surely one of her great contributions as a woman in God's service.

Second, *Deborah had superb leadership ability when the time came for decisive action.* Deborah motivated a people who had previously been paralyzed by fear and hopelessness. At her command, Barak enlisted ten thousand men to go into battle against Sisera's troops. Now note carefully Barak's response to Deborah. He recognized Deborah's leadership abilities openly. In effect, he told her, "If you want to go into battle, then you come along with me. You seem to have the courage and insight that I need" (see 4:8). And through the mouth of Deborah, God told Barak the precise moment to make their move against Sisera and his army: "Go! This is the day the LORD has given Sisera into your hands . . . At Barak's advance, the LORD routed Sisera and all his chariots and army by the sword" (4:14–15).

Third, *Deborah had a charitable spirit when others served well in the Lord's service.* During the rout of his armies, Sisera escaped on foot. Just as Deborah had predicted (4:9), this military commander fell at the hands of a woman. But that woman wasn't Deborah; it was Jael (her story is found in verses 17–22 of Judges 4). Jael's courage and resourcefulness stand out among all the warriors in the battle, and Deborah celebrated her great act of bravery in her victory song: "Most blessed of women be Jael . . . Her hand reached for the tent peg, her right hand for the workman's hammer. She struck Sisera, she crushed his head, she shattered and pierced his temple. At her feet he sank, he fell; there he lay" (5:24–27). I'm sure Barak must have thought, as he reflected on the accomplishments of Deborah and Jael, "What manner of women are these?" The fact is, they were great women mightily used by the Lord, just as there are today compassionate, wise women who make themselves available to God to accomplish great things for His glory.

Fourth, *Deborah had an enduring commitment to the Lord when life returned to normal.* After the joyous and artistically colorful celebration as expressed in Deborah's victory song, Judges 5 ends on a quiet note: "Then the land had peace forty years." When the battle was over, Deborah didn't search for a name for herself. She didn't greedily grab for power. She just went on doing what the Lord told her to do.

Deborah was a wonderfully gifted woman and a mighty servant of the Lord. The worst thing we can do is to present Deborah as though she were some kind of super saint who lived in the celestial castles of heaven saying, "Oh, bless you, bless you" to whomever passed her way. That wasn't Deborah. Deborah was a real woman, a wise and capable leader who undoubtedly had more than her share of exhausting and irritating moments. But she stood out like a rose blooming above a cesspool. And if we bless Deborah today, it is only right to bless today's Deborah. Only God knows how many of us have had Deborahs for mothers and sisters and grandmothers—and how many of those Deborahs serve God to this day!

with the willing volunteers among the
people.
Praise the LORD!

10"You who ride on white donkeys, Jdg 10:4
sitting on your saddle blankets,
and you who walk along the road,
consider 11the voice of the singers[a] at the
watering places.
They recite the righteous acts of the LORD,
the righteous acts of his warriors[b] in Israel.

"Then the people of the LORD
went down to the city gates.
12'Wake up, wake up, Deborah! Ps 57:8
Wake up, wake up, break out in song!
Arise, O Barak!
Take captive your captives, O son of
Abinoam.' Ps 68:18; Eph 4:8

13"Then the men who were left
came down to the nobles;
the people of the LORD
came to me with the mighty.
14Some came from Ephraim, whose roots were
in Amalek;
Benjamin was with the people who followed
you.
From Makir captains came down,
from Zebulun those who bear a
commander's staff.
15The princes of Issachar were with Deborah;
yes, Issachar was with Barak,
rushing after him into the valley.
In the districts of Reuben
there was much searching of heart.
16Why did you stay among the campfires[c]
to hear the whistling for the flocks? Nu 32:1
In the districts of Reuben
there was much searching of heart.
17Gilead stayed beyond the Jordan.
And Dan, why did he linger by the ships?
Asher remained on the coast
and stayed in his coves. Jos 19:29
18The people of Zebulun risked their very lives;
so did Naphtali on the heights of the field.

19"Kings came, they fought; Jos 11:5
the kings of Canaan fought
at Taanach by the waters of Megiddo, Jdg 1:27
but they carried off no silver, no plunder.
20From the heavens the stars fought,
from their courses they fought against
Sisera. Jos 10:11
21The river Kishon swept them away,
the age-old river, the river Kishon.
March on, my soul; be strong!
22Then thundered the horses' hoofs—
galloping, galloping go his mighty steeds.

23'Curse Meroz,' said the angel of the LORD.
'Curse its people bitterly,
because they did not come to help the LORD,
to help the LORD against the mighty.'

24"Most blessed of women be Jael, Jdg 4:17
the wife of Heber the Kenite,
most blessed of tent-dwelling women.
25He asked for water, and she gave him milk;
in a bowl fit for nobles she brought him
curdled milk.
26Her hand reached for the tent peg,
her right hand for the workman's hammer.
She struck Sisera, she crushed his head,
she shattered and pierced his temple.
27At her feet he sank,
he fell; there he lay.
At her feet he sank, he fell;
where he sank, there he fell—dead.

28"Through the window peered Sisera's mother;
behind the lattice she cried out, Pr 7:6
'Why is his chariot so long in coming?
Why is the clatter of his chariots delayed?'
29The wisest of her ladies answer her;
indeed, she keeps saying to herself,
30'Are they not finding and dividing the spoils:
a girl or two for each man,
colorful garments as plunder for Sisera,
colorful garments embroidered,
highly embroidered garments for my
neck—
all this as plunder?'

31"So may all your enemies perish, O LORD!
But may they who love you be like the sun
when it rises in its strength."
Then the land had peace forty years. Jdg 3:11

Reluctant Leadership **Chapters 6–9**

There are people who follow God's leading with unquestioning obedience. When God calls them, they jump into His work with both feet. There are people of faith in every generation who are ready to follow wherever the Lord leads, even without a clear road map of what lies ahead. There are those who possess an unwavering integrity and confidence as they boldly serve the Lord . . . and then there's Gideon. He was a man who had a whole list of reasons why he should not be a leader. Gideon tried to resist God's calling; he asked for signs every step of the way to be sure that God was still leading. To call Gideon a "reluctant leader" is to put it mildly! However, he was called by God, and with great prompting and many assurances, he led God's people to freedom. God still calls those who may be reluctant and who may lack personal confidence. If you fall

[a] 11 Or *archers*; the meaning of the Hebrew for this word is uncertain. [b] 11 Or *villagers* [c] 16 Or *saddlebags*

into that category, remember Gideon. God can do amazing things through those who would never dream that the Lord could use them.

Gideon

6 Again the Israelites did evil in the eyes of the LORD, and for seven years he gave them into the hands of the Midianites. [2]Because the power of Midian was so oppressive, the Israelites prepared shelters for themselves in mountain clefts, caves and strongholds. [3]Whenever the Israelites planted their crops, the Midianites, Amalekites and other eastern peoples invaded the country. [4]They camped on the land and ruined the crops all the way to Gaza and did not spare a living thing for Israel, neither sheep nor cattle nor donkeys. [5]They came up with their livestock and their tents like swarms of locusts. It was impossible to count the men and their camels; they invaded the land to ravage it. [6]Midian so impoverished the Israelites that they cried out to the LORD for help. Lev 26:16

[7]When the Israelites cried to the LORD because of Midian, [8]he sent them a prophet, who said, "This is what the LORD, the God of Israel, says: I brought you up out of Egypt, out of the land of slavery. [9]I snatched you from the power of Egypt and from the hand of all your oppressors. I drove them from before you and gave you their land. [10]I said to you, 'I am the LORD your God; do not worship the gods of the Amorites, in whose land you live.' But you have not listened to me."

[11]The angel of the LORD came and sat down under the oak in Ophrah that belonged to Joash the Abiezrite, where his son Gideon was threshing wheat in a winepress to keep it from the Midianites. [12]When the angel of the LORD appeared to Gideon, he said, "The LORD is with you, mighty warrior." Jos 1:5; Heb 11:32

[13]"But sir," Gideon replied, "if the LORD is with us, why has all this happened to us? Where are all his wonders that our fathers told us about when they said, 'Did not the LORD bring us up out of Egypt?' But now the LORD has abandoned us and put us into the hand of Midian." Ps 44:1

[14]The LORD turned to him and said, "Go in the strength you have and save Israel out of Midian's hand. Am I not sending you?" Heb 11:34

[15]"But Lord,[a]" Gideon asked, "how can I save Israel? My clan is the weakest in Manasseh, and I am the least in my family." 1Sa 9:21

[16]The LORD answered, "I will be with you, and you will strike down all the Midianites together."

[17]Gideon replied, "If now I have found favor in your eyes, give me a sign that it is really you talking to me. [18]Please do not go away until I come back and bring my offering and set it before you."

And the LORD said, "I will wait until you return."

[19]Gideon went in, prepared a young goat, and from an ephah[b] of flour he made bread without yeast. Putting the meat in a basket and its broth in a pot, he brought them out and offered them to him under the oak. Ge 18:7-8

[20]The angel of God said to him, "Take the meat and the unleavened bread, place them on this rock, and pour out the broth." And Gideon did so. [21]With the tip of the staff that was in his hand, the angel of the LORD touched the meat and the unleavened bread. Fire flared from the rock, consuming the meat and the bread. And the angel of the LORD disappeared. [22]When Gideon realized that it was the angel of the LORD, he exclaimed, "Ah, Sovereign LORD! I have seen the angel of the LORD face to face!" Jdg 13:16,19,21; Lev 9:24; Ge 32:30

[23]But the LORD said to him, "Peace! Do not be afraid. You are not going to die." Da 10:19

[24]So Gideon built an altar to the LORD there and called it The LORD is Peace. To this day it stands in Ophrah of the Abiezrites. Jdg 8:32

[25]That same night the LORD said to him, "Take the second bull from your father's herd, the one seven years old.[c] Tear down your father's altar to Baal and cut down the Asherah pole[d] beside it. [26]Then build a proper kind of[e] altar to the LORD your God on the top of this height. Using the wood of the Asherah pole that you cut down, offer the second[f] bull as a burnt offering." Ex 34:13

[27]So Gideon took ten of his servants and did as the LORD told him. But because he was afraid of his family and the men of the town, he did it at night rather than in the daytime.

[28]In the morning when the men of the town got up, there was Baal's altar, demolished, with the Asherah pole beside it cut down and the second bull sacrificed on the newly built altar! 1Ki 16:32

[29]They asked each other, "Who did this?"

When they carefully investigated, they were told, "Gideon son of Joash did it."

[30]The men of the town demanded of Joash, "Bring out your son. He must die, because he has broken down Baal's altar and cut down the Asherah pole beside it."

[31]But Joash replied to the hostile crowd around him, "Are you going to plead Baal's cause? Are you trying to save him? Whoever fights for him shall be put to death by morning! If Baal really is a god, he can defend himself when someone breaks down his altar." [32]So that day they called Gideon "Jerub-Baal,[g]" saying, "Let Baal contend with him," because he broke down Baal's altar. Jdg 7:1; 1Sa 12:11

[33]Now all the Midianites, Amalekites and other eastern peoples joined forces and crossed over the

[a] 15 Or *sir*
[b] 19 That is, probably about 3/5 bushel (about 22 liters)
[c] 25 Or *Take a full-grown, mature bull from your father's herd*
[d] 25 That is, a symbol of the goddess Asherah; here and elsewhere in Judges
[e] 26 Or *build with layers of stone an*
[f] 26 Or *full-grown*; also in verse 28
[g] 32 *Jerub-Baal* means *let Baal contend.*

Jordan and camped in the Valley of Jezreel. [34]Then
the Spirit of the LORD came upon Gideon, and he
blew a trumpet, summoning the Abiezrites to follow him. [35]He sent messengers throughout Manasseh, calling them to arms, and also into Asher,
Zebulun and Naphtali, so that they too went up to
meet them. Jos 17:16; Jdg 3:10,27; 4:6
[36]Gideon said to God, "If you will save Israel by
my hand as you have promised— [37]look, I will
place a wool fleece on the threshing floor. If there
is dew only on the fleece and all the ground is dry,
then I will know that you will save Israel by my
hand, as you said." [38]And that is what happened.
Gideon rose early the next day; he squeezed the
fleece and wrung out the dew—a bowlful of water.
[39]Then Gideon said to God, "Do not be angry
with me. Let me make just one more request. Allow me one more test with the fleece. This time
make the fleece dry and the ground covered with
dew." [40]That night God did so. Only the fleece was
dry; all the ground was covered with dew.

Gideon Defeats the Midianites

7 Early in the morning, Jerub-Baal (that is,
Gideon) and all his men camped at the spring
of Harod. The camp of Midian was north of them
in the valley near the hill of Moreh. [2]The LORD said
to Gideon, "You have too many men for me to
deliver Midian into their hands. In order that Israel may not boast against me that her own strength
has saved her, [3]announce now to the people, 'Anyone who trembles with fear may turn back and
leave Mount Gilead.'" So twenty-two thousand
men left, while ten thousand remained. Dt 8:17
[4]But the LORD said to Gideon, "There are still
too many men. Take them down to the water, and
I will sift them for you there. If I say, 'This one
shall go with you,' he shall go; but if I say, 'This
one shall not go with you,' he shall not go."
[5]So Gideon took the men down to the water.
There the LORD told him, "Separate those who lap
the water with their tongues like a dog from those
who kneel down to drink." [6]Three hundred men
lapped with their hands to their mouths. All the
rest got down on their knees to drink.
[7]The LORD said to Gideon, "With the three hundred men that lapped I will save you and give the
Midianites into your hands. Let all the other men
go, each to his own place." [8]So Gideon sent the
rest of the Israelites to their tents but kept the three
hundred, who took over the provisions and trumpets of the others. Jos 8:7
Now the camp of Midian lay below him in the
valley. [9]During that night the LORD said to Gideon,
"Get up, go down against the camp, because I am
going to give it into your hands. [10]If you are afraid
to attack, go down to the camp with your servant
Purah [11]and listen to what they are saying. Afterward, you will be encouraged to attack the camp."
So he and Purah his servant went down to the
outposts of the camp. [12]The Midianites, the Amalekites and all the other eastern peoples had settled
in the valley, thick as locusts. Their camels could
no more be counted than the sand on the seashore. Jos 2:24; 11:4; Jdg 8:10
[13]Gideon arrived just as a man was telling a
friend his dream. "I had a dream," he was saying.
"A round loaf of barley bread came tumbling into
the Midianite camp. It struck the tent with such
force that the tent overturned and collapsed."
[14]His friend responded, "This can be nothing
other than the sword of Gideon son of Joash, the
Israelite. God has given the Midianites and the
whole camp into his hands."
[15]When Gideon heard the dream and its interpretation, he worshiped God. He returned to the
camp of Israel and called out, "Get up! The LORD
has given the Midianite camp into your hands."
[16]Dividing the three hundred men into three companies, he placed trumpets and empty jars in the
hands of all of them, with torches inside.
[17]"Watch me," he told them. "Follow my lead.
When I get to the edge of the camp, do exactly as
I do. [18]When I and all who are with me blow our
trumpets, then from all around the camp blow
yours and shout, 'For the LORD and for Gideon.'"
[19]Gideon and the hundred men with him
reached the edge of the camp at the beginning of
the middle watch, just after they had changed the
guard. They blew their trumpets and broke the jars

LIVING  INSIGHT

When we make the Lord alone our single source of protection or solitary refuge, He shows Himself strong, doesn't He? And then who gets the glory? When He comes through, all you can do is say, "Praise be to the Lord . . . He did it again!"

(See Judges 7:19–22.)

that were in their hands. [20]The three companies
blew the trumpets and smashed the jars. Grasping
the torches in their left hands and holding in their
right hands the trumpets they were to blow, they
shouted, "A sword for the LORD and for Gideon!"
[21]While each man held his position around the
camp, all the Midianites ran, crying out as they
fled. 2Ki 7:7
[22]When the three hundred trumpets sounded,
the LORD caused the men throughout the camp to
turn on each other with their swords. The army
fled to Beth Shittah toward Zererah as far as the
border of Abel Meholah near Tabbath. [23]Israelites
from Naphtali, Asher and all Manasseh were called
out, and they pursued the Midianites. [24]Gideon

sent messengers throughout the hill country of Ephraim, saying, "Come down against the Midianites and seize the waters of the Jordan ahead of them as far as Beth Barah." Jdg 3:28; 6:35; 1Sa 14:20

So all the men of Ephraim were called out and they took the waters of the Jordan as far as Beth Barah. 25They also captured two of the Midianite leaders, Oreb and Zeeb. They killed Oreb at the rock of Oreb, and Zeeb at the winepress of Zeeb. They pursued the Midianites and brought the heads of Oreb and Zeeb to Gideon, who was by the Jordan. Jdg 8:4; Ps 83:11; Isa 10:26

Zebah and Zalmunna

8 Now the Ephraimites asked Gideon, "Why have you treated us like this? Why didn't you call us when you went to fight Midian?" And they criticized him sharply. Jdg 12:1

2But he answered them, "What have I accomplished compared to you? Aren't the gleanings of Ephraim's grapes better than the full grape harvest of Abiezer? 3God gave Oreb and Zeeb, the Midianite leaders, into your hands. What was I able to do compared to you?" At this, their resentment against him subsided. Jdg 7:25; Pr 15:1

4Gideon and his three hundred men, exhausted yet keeping up the pursuit, came to the Jordan and crossed it. 5He said to the men of Succoth, "Give my troops some bread; they are worn out, and I am still pursuing Zebah and Zalmunna, the kings of Midian." Ge 33:17

6But the officials of Succoth said, "Do you already have the hands of Zebah and Zalmunna in your possession? Why should we give bread to your troops?" 1Sa 25:11

7Then Gideon replied, "Just for that, when the LORD has given Zebah and Zalmunna into my hand, I will tear your flesh with desert thorns and briers." Jdg 7:15

8From there he went up to Peniel[a] and made the same request of them, but they answered as the men of Succoth had. 9So he said to the men of Peniel, "When I return in triumph, I will tear down this tower." Ge 32:30; 1Ki 12:25

10Now Zebah and Zalmunna were in Karkor with a force of about fifteen thousand men, all that were left of the armies of the eastern peoples; a hundred and twenty thousand swordsmen had fallen. 11Gideon went up by the route of the nomads east of Nobah and Jogbehah and fell upon the unsuspecting army. 12Zebah and Zalmunna, the two kings of Midian, fled, but he pursued them and captured them, routing their entire army.

13Gideon son of Joash then returned from the battle by the Pass of Heres. 14He caught a young man of Succoth and questioned him, and the young man wrote down for him the names of the seventy-seven officials of Succoth, the elders of the town. 15Then Gideon came and said to the men of Succoth, "Here are Zebah and Zalmunna, about whom you taunted me by saying, 'Do you already have the hands of Zebah and Zalmunna in your possession? Why should we give bread to your exhausted men?'" 16He took the elders of the town and taught the men of Succoth a lesson by punishing them with desert thorns and briers. 17He also pulled down the tower of Peniel and killed the men of the town. Jdg 6:11

18Then he asked Zebah and Zalmunna, "What kind of men did you kill at Tabor?" Jdg 4:6

"Men like you," they answered, "each one with the bearing of a prince."

19Gideon replied, "Those were my brothers, the sons of my own mother. As surely as the LORD lives, if you had spared their lives, I would not kill you." 20Turning to Jether, his oldest son, he said, "Kill them!" But Jether did not draw his sword, because he was only a boy and was afraid.

21Zebah and Zalmunna said, "Come, do it yourself. 'As is the man, so is his strength.'" So Gideon stepped forward and killed them, and took the ornaments off their camels' necks. Ps 83:11

Gideon's Ephod

22The Israelites said to Gideon, "Rule over us—you, your son and your grandson—because you have saved us out of the hand of Midian."

23But Gideon told them, "I will not rule over you, nor will my son rule over you. The LORD will rule over you." 24And he said, "I do have one request, that each of you give me an earring from your share of the plunder." (It was the custom of the Ishmaelites to wear gold earrings.) 1Sa 8:7; 12:12

25They answered, "We'll be glad to give them." So they spread out a garment, and each man threw a ring from his plunder onto it. 26The weight of the gold rings he asked for came to seventeen hundred shekels,[b] not counting the ornaments, the pendants and the purple garments worn by the kings of Midian or the chains that were on their camels' necks. 27Gideon made the gold into an ephod, which he placed in Ophrah, his town. All Israel prostituted themselves by worshiping it there, and it became a snare to Gideon and his family.

Gideon's Death

28Thus Midian was subdued before the Israelites and did not raise its head again. During Gideon's lifetime, the land enjoyed peace forty years.

29Jerub-Baal son of Joash went back home to live. 30He had seventy sons of his own, for he had many wives. 31His concubine, who lived in Shechem, also bore him a son, whom he named Abimelech. 32Gideon son of Joash died at a good

[a] 8 Hebrew *Penuel*, a variant of *Peniel*; also in verses 9 and 17

[b] 26 That is, about 43 pounds (about 19.5 kilograms)

old age and was buried in the tomb of his father Joash in Ophrah of the Abiezrites. Jdg 7:1; 9:2,5,18,24

[33]No sooner had Gideon died than the Israelites again prostituted themselves to the Baals. They set up Baal-Berith as their god and [34]did not remember the LORD their God, who had rescued them from the hands of all their enemies on every side. [35]They also failed to show kindness to the family of Jerub-Baal (that is, Gideon) for all the good things he had done for them. Jdg 2:11,13,19; 9:16; Dt 4:9

Abimelech

9 Abimelech son of Jerub-Baal went to his mother's brothers in Shechem and said to them and to all his mother's clan, [2]"Ask all the citizens of Shechem, 'Which is better for you: to have all seventy of Jerub-Baal's sons rule over you, or just one man?' Remember, I am your flesh and blood." Ge 29:14; Jdg 8:31

[3]When the brothers repeated all this to the citizens of Shechem, they were inclined to follow Abimelech, for they said, "He is our brother." [4]They gave him seventy shekels[a] of silver from the temple of Baal-Berith, and Abimelech used it to hire reckless adventurers, who became his followers. [5]He went to his father's home in Ophrah and on one stone murdered his seventy brothers, the sons of Jerub-Baal. But Jotham, the youngest son of Jerub-Baal, escaped by hiding. [6]Then all the citizens of Shechem and Beth Millo gathered beside the great tree at the pillar in Shechem to crown Abimelech king. Jdg 8:33; 2Ki 11:2

[7]When Jotham was told about this, he climbed up on the top of Mount Gerizim and shouted to them, "Listen to me, citizens of Shechem, so that God may listen to you. [8]One day the trees went out to anoint a king for themselves. They said to the olive tree, 'Be our king.' Dt 11:29; Jn 4:20

[9]"But the olive tree answered, 'Should I give up my oil, by which both gods and men are honored, to hold sway over the trees?'

[10]"Next, the trees said to the fig tree, 'Come and be our king.'

[11]"But the fig tree replied, 'Should I give up my fruit, so good and sweet, to hold sway over the trees?'

[12]"Then the trees said to the vine, 'Come and be our king.'

[13]"But the vine answered, 'Should I give up my wine, which cheers both gods and men, to hold sway over the trees?' Ecc 2:3

[14]"Finally all the trees said to the thornbush, 'Come and be our king.'

[15]"The thornbush said to the trees, 'If you really want to anoint me king over you, come and take refuge in my shade; but if not, then let fire come out of the thornbush and consume the cedars of Lebanon!' Isa 30:2

[16]"Now if you have acted honorably and in good faith when you made Abimelech king, and if you have been fair to Jerub-Baal and his family, and if you have treated him as he deserves— [17]and to think that my father fought for you, risked his life to rescue you from the hand of Midian [18](but today you have revolted against my father's family, murdered his seventy sons on a single stone, and made Abimelech, the son of his slave girl, king over the citizens of Shechem because he is your brother)— [19]if then you have acted honorably and in good faith toward Jerub-Baal and his family today, may Abimelech be your joy, and may you be his, too! [20]But if you have not, let fire come out from Abimelech and consume you, citizens of Shechem and Beth Millo, and let fire come out from you, citizens of Shechem and Beth Millo, and consume Abimelech!" Jdg 8:30

[21]Then Jotham fled, escaping to Beer, and he lived there because he was afraid of his brother Abimelech.

[22]After Abimelech had governed Israel three years, [23]God sent an evil spirit between Abimelech and the citizens of Shechem, who acted treacherously against Abimelech. [24]God did this in order that the crime against Jerub-Baal's seventy sons, the shedding of their blood, might be avenged on their brother Abimelech and on the citizens of Shechem, who had helped him murder his brothers. [25]In opposition to him these citizens of Shechem set men on the hilltops to ambush and rob everyone who passed by, and this was reported to Abimelech. Nu 35:33; Dt 27:25; 1Sa 16:14,23

[26]Now Gaal son of Ebed moved with his brothers into Shechem, and its citizens put their confidence in him. [27]After they had gone out into the fields and gathered the grapes and trodden them, they held a festival in the temple of their god. While they were eating and drinking, they cursed Abimelech. [28]Then Gaal son of Ebed said, "Who is Abimelech, and who is Shechem, that we should be subject to him? Isn't he Jerub-Baal's son, and isn't Zebul his deputy? Serve the men of Hamor, Shechem's father! Why should we serve Abimelech? [29]If only this people were under my command! Then I would get rid of him. I would say to Abimelech, 'Call out your whole army!' "[b]

[30]When Zebul the governor of the city heard what Gaal son of Ebed said, he was very angry. [31]Under cover he sent messengers to Abimelech, saying, "Gaal son of Ebed and his brothers have come to Shechem and are stirring up the city against you. [32]Now then, during the night you and your men should come and lie in wait in the fields.

[a]4 That is, about 1 3/4 pounds (about 0.8 kilogram)

[b]29 Septuagint; Hebrew *him." Then he said to Abimelech, "Call out your whole army!"*

33In the morning at sunrise, advance against the
city. When Gaal and his men come out against
you, do whatever your hand finds to do."
34So Abimelech and all his troops set out by
night and took up concealed positions near Shechem in four companies. 35Now Gaal son of Ebed
had gone out and was standing at the entrance to
the city gate just as Abimelech and his soldiers
came out from their hiding place. Ps 32:7; Jer 49:10
36When Gaal saw them, he said to Zebul, "Look,
people are coming down from the tops of the
mountains!"

Zebul replied, "You mistake the shadows of the
mountains for men."

37But Gaal spoke up again: "Look, people are
coming down from the center of the land, and a
company is coming from the direction of the
soothsayers' tree."
38Then Zebul said to him, "Where is your big
talk now, you who said, 'Who is Abimelech that
we should be subject to him?' Aren't these the men
you ridiculed? Go out and fight them!"
39So Gaal led out[a] the citizens of Shechem and
fought Abimelech. 40Abimelech chased him, and
many fell wounded in the flight—all the way to
the entrance to the gate. 41Abimelech stayed in
Arumah, and Zebul drove Gaal and his brothers
out of Shechem.
42The next day the people of Shechem went out
to the fields, and this was reported to Abimelech.
43So he took his men, divided them into three
companies and set an ambush in the fields. When
he saw the people coming out of the city, he rose
to attack them. 44Abimelech and the companies
with him rushed forward to a position at the entrance to the city gate. Then two companies rushed
upon those in the fields and struck them down.
45All that day Abimelech pressed his attack against
the city until he had captured it and killed its
people. Then he destroyed the city and scattered
salt over it. Dt 29:23; 2Ki 3:25
46On hearing this, the citizens in the tower of
Shechem went into the stronghold of the temple of
El-Berith. 47When Abimelech heard that they had
assembled there, 48he and all his men went up
Mount Zalmon. He took an ax and cut off some
branches, which he lifted to his shoulders. He ordered the men with him, "Quick! Do what you
have seen me do!" 49So all the men cut branches
and followed Abimelech. They piled them against
the stronghold and set it on fire over the people
inside. So all the people in the tower of Shechem,
about a thousand men and women, also died.
50Next Abimelech went to Thebez and besieged
it and captured it. 51Inside the city, however, was
a strong tower, to which all the men and women—
all the people of the city—fled. They locked themselves in and climbed up on the tower roof.
52Abimelech went to the tower and stormed it. But
as he approached the entrance to the tower to set
it on fire, 53a woman dropped an upper millstone
on his head and cracked his skull. 2Sa 11:21
54Hurriedly he called to his armor-bearer,
"Draw your sword and kill me, so that they can't
say, 'A woman killed him.'" So his servant ran him
through, and he died. 55When the Israelites saw
that Abimelech was dead, they went home.
56Thus God repaid the wickedness that Abimelech had done to his father by murdering his seventy brothers. 57God also made the men of Shechem pay for all their wickedness. The curse of
Jotham son of Jerub-Baal came on them.

The Cycle Continues — Chapters 10–12

As the generations passed, the Hebrew people continued to disobey the Lord. With each rebellion came oppression and misery and finally another judge to save the people from their enemies. The Lord used Tola, Jair, Jephthah, Ibzan, Elon and Abdon, each in turn, to lead His people. When the people were delivered, they experienced peace for a time but again fell into disobedience. The cycle went on and on. During this time, one judge stood out—his name was Jephthah. Before he ever came to the plate, Jephthah had three strikes against him. He was an illegitimate child. (Strike one.) He was the son of a barmaid and a brute. (Strike two.) He was raised in an atmosphere of hatred and hostility. (Strike three.) Kicked out of his home before reaching young manhood, he adopted the lifestyle of a rebel among a bunch of thugs who hung out in a place called Tob. When the people of Israel encountered a barrage of hostilities from their not-so-friendly neighbors to the east (the Ammonites), they needed a leader with guts to stand up to their fiery foes. Guess who they thought of? Right! They figured that only a guy with his record would qualify for the job, so they called the man from Tob. Predictably, Jephthah annihilated the Ammonites in short order. I can just imagine the following scene—the Tob Evening News rolling off the presses with the headline: "Hoodlum Becomes Hero—Ex-Con Elected Judge!"

Such a radical transformation seems impossible. That would have been true—except for one thing: God's grace. Never, ever forget: *God is the One who builds trophies from the scrap pile.*

Tola

10 After the time of Abimelech a man of Issachar, Tola son of Puah, the son of Dodo,
rose to save Israel. He lived in Shamir, in the hill
country of Ephraim. 2He led[b] Israel twenty-three
years; then he died, and was buried in Shamir.

Jair

3He was followed by Jair of Gilead, who led
Israel twenty-two years. 4He had thirty sons, who

[a]39 Or *Gaal went out in the sight of*

[b]2 Traditionally *judged*; also in verse 3

rode thirty donkeys. They controlled thirty towns
in Gilead, which to this day are called Havvoth
Jair.[a] 5When Jair died, he was buried in Kamon.

Jephthah

6Again the Israelites did evil in the eyes of the
LORD. They served the Baals and the Ashtoreths,
and the gods of Aram, the gods of Sidon, the gods
of Moab, the gods of the Ammonites and the gods
of the Philistines. And because the Israelites forsook the LORD and no longer served him, 7he became angry with them. He sold them into the
hands of the Philistines and the Ammonites, 8who
that year shattered and crushed them. For eighteen
years they oppressed all the Israelites on the east
side of the Jordan in Gilead, the land of the Amorites. 9The Ammonites also crossed the Jordan to
fight against Judah, Benjamin and the house of
Ephraim; and Israel was in great distress. 10Then
the Israelites cried out to the LORD, "We have
sinned against you, forsaking our God and serving
the Baals." Jdg 2:13; Dt 31:17; 1Sa 12:10

11The LORD replied, "When the Egyptians, the
Amorites, the Ammonites, the Philistines, 12the Sidonians, the Amalekites and the Maonites[b] oppressed you and you cried to me for help, did I not
save you from their hands? 13But you have forsak-
en me and served other gods, so I will no longer
save you. 14Go and cry out to the gods you have
chosen. Let them save you when you are in trouble!" Dt 32:37; Jdg 3:13; Ps 106:42

15But the Israelites said to the LORD, "We have
sinned. Do with us whatever you think best, but
please rescue us now." 16Then they got rid of the
foreign gods among them and served the LORD.
And he could bear Israel's misery no longer.

17When the Ammonites were called to arms and
camped in Gilead, the Israelites assembled and
camped at Mizpah. 18The leaders of the people of
Gilead said to each other, "Whoever will launch
the attack against the Ammonites will be the head
of all those living in Gilead." Jdg 11:8,9,29

11 Jephthah the Gileadite was a mighty warrior. His father was Gilead; his mother was
a prostitute. 2Gilead's wife also bore him sons, and
when they were grown up, they drove Jephthah
away. "You are not going to get any inheritance in
our family," they said, "because you are the son
of another woman." 3So Jephthah fled from his
brothers and settled in the land of Tob, where a
group of adventurers gathered around him and
followed him. Heb 11:32; 2Sa 10:6,8

4Some time later, when the Ammonites made
war on Israel, 5the elders of Gilead went to get
Jephthah from the land of Tob. 6"Come," they
said, "be our commander, so we can fight the Ammonites." Jdg 10:9

7Jephthah said to them, "Didn't you hate me
and drive me from my father's house? Why do you
come to me now, when you're in trouble?"

8The elders of Gilead said to him, "Nevertheless, we are turning to you now; come with us to
fight the Ammonites, and you will be our head
over all who live in Gilead." Jdg 10:18

9Jephthah answered, "Suppose you take me
back to fight the Ammonites and the LORD gives
them to me—will I really be your head?"

10The elders of Gilead replied, "The LORD is our
witness; we will certainly do as you say." 11So Jephthah went with the elders of Gilead, and the people
made him head and commander over them. And
he repeated all his words before the LORD in Mizpah. Jer 42:5

12Then Jephthah sent messengers to the Ammonite king with the question: "What do you have
against us that you have attacked our country?"

13The king of the Ammonites answered Jephthah's messengers, "When Israel came up out of
Egypt, they took away my land from the Arnon to
the Jabbok, all the way to the Jordan. Now give it
back peaceably." Nu 21:24

14Jephthah sent back messengers to the Ammonite king, 15saying:

"This is what Jephthah says: Israel did not
take the land of Moab or the land of the
Ammonites. 16But when they came up out of
Egypt, Israel went through the desert to the
Red Sea[c] and on to Kadesh. 17Then Israel
sent messengers to the king of Edom, saying,
'Give us permission to go through your
country,' but the king of Edom would not
listen. They sent also to the king of Moab,
and he refused. So Israel stayed at Kadesh.

18"Next they traveled through the desert,
skirted the lands of Edom and Moab, passed
along the eastern side of the country of
Moab, and camped on the other side of the
Arnon. They did not enter the territory of
Moab, for the Arnon was its border. Nu 21:4

19"Then Israel sent messengers to Sihon
king of the Amorites, who ruled in Heshbon,

LIVING  **INSIGHT**

One of the wonderful things about the Bible, which only adds to its credibility, is that it tells us the truth, the whole truth and nothing but the truth regarding its characters.

(See Judges 11:1–3.)

[a] 4 Or *called the settlements of Jair* [b] 12 Hebrew; some Septuagint manuscripts *Midianites* [c] 16 Hebrew *Yam Suph*; that is, Sea of Reeds

and said to him, 'Let us pass through your
country to our own place.' 20Sihon, however,
did not trust Israel[a] to pass through his territory. He mustered all his men and encamped at Jahaz and fought with Israel.

21"Then the LORD, the God of Israel, gave
Sihon and all his men into Israel's hands, and
they defeated them. Israel took over all the
land of the Amorites who lived in that country, 22capturing all of it from the Arnon to
the Jabbok and from the desert to the Jordan.

23"Now since the LORD, the God of Israel,
has driven the Amorites out before his people Israel, what right have you to take it over?
24Will you not take what your god Chemosh
gives you? Likewise, whatever the LORD our
God has given us, we will possess. 25Are you
better than Balak son of Zippor, king of
Moab? Did he ever quarrel with Israel or
fight with them? 26For three hundred years
Israel occupied Heshbon, Aroer, the surrounding settlements and all the towns along
the Arnon. Why didn't you retake them during that time? 27I have not wronged you, but
you are doing me wrong by waging war
against me. Let the LORD, the Judge,[b] decide
the dispute this day between the Israelites
and the Ammonites." Ge 16:5; 18:25; 1Ki 11:7

28The king of Ammon, however, paid no attention
to the message Jephthah sent him.

29Then the Spirit of the LORD came upon Jephthah. He crossed Gilead and Manasseh, passed
through Mizpah of Gilead, and from there he advanced against the Ammonites. 30And Jephthah
made a vow to the LORD: "If you give the Ammonites into my hands, 31whatever comes out of the
door of my house to meet me when I return in
triumph from the Ammonites will be the LORD's,
and I will sacrifice it as a burnt offering." Jdg 3:10

32Then Jephthah went over to fight the Ammonites, and the LORD gave them into his hands.
33He devastated twenty towns from Aroer to the
vicinity of Minnith, as far as Abel Keramim. Thus
Israel subdued Ammon. Eze 27:17

34When Jephthah returned to his home in Mizpah, who should come out to meet him but his
daughter, dancing to the sound of tambourines!
She was an only child. Except for her he had neither son nor daughter. 35When he saw her, he tore
his clothes and cried, "Oh! My daughter! You have
made me miserable and wretched, because I have
made a vow to the LORD that I cannot break."

36"My father," she replied, "you have given your
word to the LORD. Do to me just as you promised,
now that the LORD has avenged you of your enemies, the Ammonites. 37But grant me this one request," she said. "Give me two months to roam the
hills and weep with my friends, because I will never marry."

38"You may go," he said. And he let her go for
two months. She and the girls went into the hills
and wept because she would never marry. 39After
the two months, she returned to her father and he
did to her as he had vowed. And she was a virgin.

From this comes the Israelite custom 40that
each year the young women of Israel go out for
four days to commemorate the daughter of Jephthah the Gileadite.

Jephthah and Ephraim

12 The men of Ephraim called out their
forces, crossed over to Zaphon and said to
Jephthah, "Why did you go to fight the Ammonites without calling us to go with you? We're going
to burn down your house over your head."

2Jephthah answered, "I and my people were engaged in a great struggle with the Ammonites, and
although I called, you didn't save me out of their
hands. 3When I saw that you wouldn't help, I took
my life in my hands and crossed over to fight the
Ammonites, and the LORD gave me the victory
over them. Now why have you come up today to
fight me?" 1Sa 19:5

4Jephthah then called together the men of Gilead and fought against Ephraim. The Gileadites
struck them down because the Ephraimites had
said, "You Gileadites are renegades from Ephraim
and Manasseh." 5The Gileadites captured the fords
of the Jordan leading to Ephraim, and whenever a
survivor of Ephraim said, "Let me cross over," the
men of Gilead asked him, "Are you an Ephraimite?" If he replied, "No," 6they said, "All right, say
'Shibboleth.'" If he said, "Sibboleth," because he
could not pronounce the word correctly, they
seized him and killed him at the fords of the Jordan. Forty-two thousand Ephraimites were killed
at that time. Jdg 3:28

7Jephthah led[c] Israel six years. Then Jephthah
the Gileadite died, and was buried in a town in
Gilead.

Ibzan, Elon and Abdon

8After him, Ibzan of Bethlehem led Israel. 9He
had thirty sons and thirty daughters. He gave his
daughters away in marriage to those outside his
clan, and for his sons he brought in thirty young
women as wives from outside his clan. Ibzan led
Israel seven years. 10Then Ibzan died, and was buried in Bethlehem. Ge 35:19

11After him, Elon the Zebulunite led Israel ten
years. 12Then Elon died, and was buried in Aijalon
in the land of Zebulun. Jos 10:12

13After him, Abdon son of Hillel, from Pirathon, led Israel. 14He had forty sons and thirty

[a] 20 Or *however, would not make an agreement for Israel* [b] 27 Or *Ruler* [c] 7 Traditionally *judged*; also in verses 8-14

grandsons, who rode on seventy donkeys. He led Israel eight years. 15Then Abdon son of Hillel died, and was buried at Pirathon in Ephraim, in the hill country of the Amalekites. Jdg 5:10,14

Unbridled Passions **Chapters 13–16**

To put it bluntly, Samson was a he-man with a she-weakness. In spite of the fact that he was born of godly parents, set apart from birth to be a Nazirite and elevated to the enviable position of judge in Israel, he never conquered his tendency toward lust. On the contrary, it conquered him. Several examples of his lustful bent may be observed from the record of his life. Look at his first recorded words, indicative of his attraction to the outward appearance of the other sex: "I have seen a Philistine woman . . . Now get her for me" (14:2). Second, after judging Israel for twenty years, Samson went right back to his old habit of chasing women—a prostitute in Gaza, and finally Delilah (15:20–16:4). And third, he became so preoccupied with his lustful passions that he didn't even know that the Lord had left him (16:20).

The results of Samson's illicit affairs are familiar to many of us. The strong man from the tribe of Dan was taken captive and became a slave, his eyes were gouged out of his head, and he was appointed to be a grinder in a Philistine prison. Lust binds and blinds and grinds. The swarthy pride of Israel, once the holder of the highest office in the land, was now the bald-headed clown of Philistia. His eyes would never wander again. His life, once filled with promise and dignity, was now a portrait of helpless, hopeless despair.

The Birth of Samson

13 Again the Israelites did evil in the eyes of the LORD, so the LORD delivered them into the hands of the Philistines for forty years.

2A certain man of Zorah, named Manoah, from the clan of the Danites, had a wife who was sterile and remained childless. 3The angel of the LORD appeared to her and said, "You are sterile and childless, but you are going to conceive and have a son. 4Now see to it that you drink no wine or other fermented drink and that you do not eat anything unclean, 5because you will conceive and give birth to a son. No razor may be used on his head, because the boy is to be a Nazirite, set apart to God from birth, and he will begin the deliverance of Israel from the hands of the Philistines."

6Then the woman went to her husband and told him, "A man of God came to me. He looked like an angel of God, very awesome. I didn't ask him where he came from, and he didn't tell me his name. 7But he said to me, 'You will conceive and give birth to a son. Now then, drink no wine or other fermented drink and do not eat anything unclean, because the boy will be a Nazirite of God from birth until the day of his death.'"

8Then Manoah prayed to the LORD: "O Lord, I beg you, let the man of God you sent to us come again to teach us how to bring up the boy who is to be born."

9God heard Manoah, and the angel of God came again to the woman while she was out in the field; but her husband Manoah was not with her. 10The woman hurried to tell her husband, "He's here! The man who appeared to me the other day!"

11Manoah got up and followed his wife. When he came to the man, he said, "Are you the one who talked to my wife?"

"I am," he said.

12So Manoah asked him, "When your words are fulfilled, what is to be the rule for the boy's life and work?"

13The angel of the LORD answered, "Your wife must do all that I have told her. 14She must not eat anything that comes from the grapevine, nor drink any wine or other fermented drink nor eat anything unclean. She must do everything I have commanded her." Nu 6:4

15Manoah said to the angel of the LORD, "We would like you to stay until we prepare a young goat for you." Jdg 6:19

16The angel of the LORD replied, "Even though you detain me, I will not eat any of your food. But if you prepare a burnt offering, offer it to the LORD." (Manoah did not realize that it was the angel of the LORD.)

17Then Manoah inquired of the angel of the LORD, "What is your name, so that we may honor you when your word comes true?" Ge 32:29

18He replied, "Why do you ask my name? It is beyond understanding.[a]" 19Then Manoah took a young goat, together with the grain offering, and sacrificed it on a rock to the LORD. And the LORD did an amazing thing while Manoah and his wife watched: 20As the flame blazed up from the altar toward heaven, the angel of the LORD ascended in the flame. Seeing this, Manoah and his wife fell with their faces to the ground. 21When the angel of the LORD did not show himself again to Manoah and his wife, Manoah realized that it was the angel of the LORD. Lev 9:24; 1Ch 21:16

22"We are doomed to die!" he said to his wife. "We have seen God!" Dt 5:26

23But his wife answered, "If the LORD had meant to kill us, he would not have accepted a burnt offering and grain offering from our hands, nor shown us all these things or now told us this."

24The woman gave birth to a boy and named him Samson. He grew and the LORD blessed him, 25and the Spirit of the LORD began to stir him while he was in Mahaneh Dan, between Zorah and Eshtaol. 1Sa 3:19; Heb 11:32; Jdg 18:12

[a] 18 Or *is wonderful*

Samson's Marriage

14 Samson went down to Timnah and saw
there a young Philistine woman. 2When he
returned, he said to his father and mother, "I have
seen a Philistine woman in Timnah; now get her
for me as my wife." Ge 21:21; 34:4
3His father and mother replied, "Isn't there an
acceptable woman among your relatives or among
all our people? Must you go to the uncircumcised
Philistines to get a wife?" Ge 24:4; Ex 34:16
But Samson said to his father, "Get her for me.
She's the right one for me." 4(His parents did not
know that this was from the LORD, who was seeking an occasion to confront the Philistines; for at
that time they were ruling over Israel.) 5Samson
went down to Timnah together with his father and
mother. As they approached the vineyards of Timnah, suddenly a young lion came roaring toward
him. 6The Spirit of the LORD came upon him in
power so that he tore the lion apart with his bare
hands as he might have torn a young goat. But he
told neither his father nor his mother what he had
done. 7Then he went down and talked with the
woman, and he liked her. Jos 11:20; Jdg 3:10; 13:1
8Some time later, when he went back to marry
her, he turned aside to look at the lion's carcass. In
it was a swarm of bees and some honey, 9which he
scooped out with his hands and ate as he went
along. When he rejoined his parents, he gave them
some, and they too ate it. But he did not tell them
that he had taken the honey from the lion's carcass.
10Now his father went down to see the woman.
And Samson made a feast there, as was customary
for bridegrooms. 11When he appeared, he was giv-
en thirty companions.
12"Let me tell you a riddle," Samson said to
them. "If you can give me the answer within the
seven days of the feast, I will give you thirty linen
garments and thirty sets of clothes. 13If you can't
tell me the answer, you must give me thirty linen
garments and thirty sets of clothes." Eze 17:2
"Tell us your riddle," they said. "Let's hear it."
14He replied,

"Out of the eater, something to eat;
out of the strong, something sweet."

For three days they could not give the answer.
15On the fourth[a] day, they said to Samson's
wife, "Coax your husband into explaining the riddle for us, or we will burn you and your father's
household to death. Did you invite us here to
rob us?" Jdg 15:6; 16:5; Ecc 7:26
16Then Samson's wife threw herself on him,
sobbing, "You hate me! You don't really love me.
You've given my people a riddle, but you haven't
told me the answer." Jdg 16:15
"I haven't even explained it to my father or
mother," he replied, "so why should I explain it to
you?" 17She cried the whole seven days of the feast.
So on the seventh day he finally told her, because
she continued to press him. She in turn explained
the riddle to her people.
18Before sunset on the seventh day the men of
the town said to him,

"What is sweeter than honey?
What is stronger than a lion?"

Samson said to them,

"If you had not plowed with my heifer,
you would not have solved my riddle."

19Then the Spirit of the LORD came upon him in
power. He went down to Ashkelon, struck down
thirty of their men, stripped them of their belongings and gave their clothes to those who had explained the riddle. Burning with anger, he went up
to his father's house. 20And Samson's wife was
given to the friend who had attended him at his
wedding. Jdg 6:34; 1Sa 11:6; Isa 11:2

Samson's Vengeance on the Philistines

15 Later on, at the time of wheat harvest,
Samson took a young goat and went to
visit his wife. He said, "I'm going to my wife's
room." But her father would not let him go in.
2"I was so sure you thoroughly hated her," he
said, "that I gave her to your friend. Isn't her
younger sister more attractive? Take her instead."
3Samson said to them, "This time I have a right
to get even with the Philistines; I will really harm
them." 4So he went out and caught three hundred
foxes and tied them tail to tail in pairs. He then
fastened a torch to every pair of tails, 5lit the
torches and let the foxes loose in the standing
grain of the Philistines. He burned up the shocks
and standing grain, together with the vineyards
and olive groves.
6When the Philistines asked, "Who did this?"
they were told, "Samson, the Timnite's son-in-
law, because his wife was given to his friend."
So the Philistines went up and burned her and
her father to death. 7Samson said to them, "Since
you've acted like this, I won't stop until I get my
revenge on you." 8He attacked them viciously and
slaughtered many of them. Then he went down
and stayed in a cave in the rock of Etam.
9The Philistines went up and camped in Judah,
spreading out near Lehi. 10The men of Judah
asked, "Why have you come to fight us?"
"We have come to take Samson prisoner," they
answered, "to do to him as he did to us."
11Then three thousand men from Judah went
down to the cave in the rock of Etam and said to

[a] 15 Some Septuagint manuscripts and Syriac; Hebrew *seventh*

SAMSON

A He-Man With a She-Weakness

"Samson went down to Timnah and saw there a young Philistine woman."
—JUDGES 14:1

I remember as a boy having a Bible with pictures sprinkled throughout its pages. The most dog-eared page was the one with the picture of Samson—muscular, tall, with hair flowing down his back, pushing against two big pillars just beginning to crack. And I remember thinking, "What a he-man! He must have been the luckiest guy in the world." As the years passed, however, I've come to realize that Samson was not very strong at all. On the outside he had flashes of great strength, to be sure. But on the inside he was a pitiful pawn of his own passions.

Samson was born following a dramatic announcement from God's angel. His mother received the visitation and the message: "You will conceive and give birth to a son" (Judges 13:7). Samson's father prayed that God would send this messenger back with further instructions on how to raise the child (13:8). He was to be a Nazirite, so the angel had said—a person whose entire life was devoted to God (Numbers 6). His purpose in life was clearly laid out: "He will begin the deliverance of Israel from the hands of the Philistines" (13:5). So God's hand was on Samson even before his birth.

As it turned out, it seemed that Samson could be all too easily sidetracked. Unfortunately, he spent very little time delivering Israel and a great deal of time pleasing himself. How telling that the first recorded words of Samson were this: "I have seen a Philistine woman . . ." (14:2).

Here was a man who had a bent toward the sensuous side of life. He gazed at this woman from Timnah and liked the way she looked. He focused on physical appearance only. Now when you combine *liking* what he saw with *wanting* what he saw, you have the ingredients for trouble. "She looks good to me. Get her for me," he told his godly parents, in effect. And if you read the story of the wedding party in Judges 14, you'll find out what Samson discovered—focusing on the sensual side of life will bring one anxiety, one heartache, after another. Through the treachery of his new bride his marriage failed. The revenge he took against the Philistines incited them to an intense hatred in return.

God didn't just leave Samson to his own pathetic devices. He turned cursing into blessing. When the Philistines came to take Samson prisoner, "the Spirit of the LORD came upon him in power" (15:14). God gave him the strength to defeat these men with only a donkey's jawbone as a weapon. And God's purposes were fulfilled. After this massacre Samson led Israel for the next twenty years (15:20).

Be assured of this: The sensuous lifestyle may lie dormant for a time, but it never completely dies. Enter Delilah, a Philistine prostitute who caught Samson's eye as he strolled through the streets of Gaza. While Samson should have been about the business of protecting Israel, he was busy tempting fate.

You've got to believe that the Philistines recognized Samson's weakness. They came to Delilah and put a little bug in her ear that went something like this: "Entice him, Delilah. He's a pushover for a woman like you. When you do, find out the secret of his strength." Delilah begged to learn the secret of his strength, and Samson toyed with her. Three times he lied to her about that secret, but with each lie he let himself be pushed a little closer toward revealing the true source of his strength. By the time he gave in to Delilah's incessant pleading and told her the truth, he was in too deep. He'd thrown off his devotion to God, replacing it with devotion to this Philistine prostitute. Delilah's cohorts came on him in a flash, and before he knew it he was a slave in a filth-ridden dungeon. Ironically, his eyes—the very instrument that led him into sin—were the first thing his captors took away from him.

Samson was a he-man with a she-weakness. And he never did learn how to handle that passion. He wrestled with it, to be sure, but never walked in victory because, frankly, he loved his addiction. He carefully cultivated the sensuous lifestyle, and it marked him for the rest of his days. His death was a terrible price to pay for the ultimately unsatisfying thrill of a season of sensuality.

Samson, "Don't you realize that the Philistines are
rulers over us? What have you done to us?"
He answered, "I merely did to them what they
did to me."
12They said to him, "We've come to tie you up
and hand you over to the Philistines."
Samson said, "Swear to me that you won't kill
me yourselves." Ge 47:31
13"Agreed," they answered. "We will only tie
you up and hand you over to them. We will not
kill you." So they bound him with two new ropes
and led him up from the rock. 14As he approached
Lehi, the Philistines came toward him shouting.
The Spirit of the LORD came upon him in power.
The ropes on his arms became like charred flax,
and the bindings dropped from his hands. 15Find-
ing a fresh jawbone of a donkey, he grabbed it and
struck down a thousand men. Lev 26:8; Jos 23:10
16Then Samson said,

"With a donkey's jawbone
  I have made donkeys of them.[a]
With a donkey's jawbone
  I have killed a thousand men."

17When he finished speaking, he threw away the
jawbone; and the place was called Ramath Lehi.[b]
18Because he was very thirsty, he cried out to the
LORD, "You have given your servant this great victory. Must I now die of thirst and fall into the
hands of the uncircumcised?" 19Then God opened
up the hollow place in Lehi, and water came out of
it. When Samson drank, his strength returned and
he revived. So the spring was called En Hakkore,[c]
and it is still there in Lehi. Ge 45:27; Jdg 16:28; Isa 40:29
20Samson led[d] Israel for twenty years in the
days of the Philistines. Jdg 13:1; 16:31

Samson and Delilah

16 One day Samson went to Gaza, where he
saw a prostitute. He went in to spend the
night with her. 2The people of Gaza were told,
"Samson is here!" So they surrounded the place
and lay in wait for him all night at the city gate.
They made no move during the night, saying, "At
dawn we'll kill him." 1Sa 19:11; Ps 118:10-12
3But Samson lay there only until the middle of
the night. Then he got up and took hold of the
doors of the city gate, together with the two posts,
and tore them loose, bar and all. He lifted them to
his shoulders and carried them to the top of the
hill that faces Hebron.
4Some time later, he fell in love with a woman
in the Valley of Sorek whose name was Delilah.
5The rulers of the Philistines went to her and said,
"See if you can lure him into showing you the
secret of his great strength and how we can overpower him so we may tie him up and subdue him.
Each one of us will give you eleven hundred shekels[e] of silver." Ge 24:67; Jos 13:3; Jdg 14:15
6So Delilah said to Samson, "Tell me the secret
of your great strength and how you can be tied up
and subdued."
7Samson answered her, "If anyone ties me with
seven fresh thongs[f] that have not been dried, I'll
become as weak as any other man."
8Then the rulers of the Philistines brought her
seven fresh thongs that had not been dried, and
she tied him with them. 9With men hidden in the
room, she called to him, "Samson, the Philistines
are upon you!" But he snapped the thongs as easily
as a piece of string snaps when it comes close to a
flame. So the secret of his strength was not discovered.
10Then Delilah said to Samson, "You have
made a fool of me; you lied to me. Come now, tell
me how you can be tied."
11He said, "If anyone ties me securely with new
ropes that have never been used, I'll become as
weak as any other man." Jdg 15:13
12So Delilah took new ropes and tied him with
them. Then, with men hidden in the room, she
called to him, "Samson, the Philistines are upon
you!" But he snapped the ropes off his arms as if
they were threads.
13Delilah then said to Samson, "Until now, you
have been making a fool of me and lying to me.
Tell me how you can be tied."
He replied, "If you weave the seven braids of
my head into the fabric ⌞on the loom⌟ and tighten
it with the pin, I'll become as weak as any other
man." So while he was sleeping, Delilah took the
seven braids of his head, wove them into the fabric
14and[g] tightened it with the pin.
Again she called to him, "Samson, the Philistines are upon you!" He awoke from his sleep and
pulled up the pin and the loom, with the fabric.
15Then she said to him, "How can you say, 'I
love you,' when you won't confide in me? This is
the third time you have made a fool of me and
haven't told me the secret of your great strength."

LIVING  **INSIGHT**

Lust is one flame you dare not fan. You'll get burned if you do.
(See Judges 16:1.)

[a]16 Or *made a heap or two*; the Hebrew for *donkey* sounds like the Hebrew for *heap*. [b]17 *Ramath Lehi* means *jawbone hill.*
[c]19 *En Hakkore* means *caller's spring.* [d]20 Traditionally *judged* [e]5 That is, about 28 pounds (about 13 kilograms)
[f]7 Or *bowstrings*; also in verses 8 and 9 [g]13,14 Some Septuagint manuscripts; Hebrew "⌞*I can*⌟ *if you weave the seven braids of my head into the fabric* ⌞*on the loom*⌟." [14]*So she*

16With such nagging she prodded him day after
day until he was tired to death. Jdg 14:16
17So he told her everything. "No razor has ever
been used on my head," he said, "because I have
been a Nazirite set apart to God since birth. If my
head were shaved, my strength would leave me,
and I would become as weak as any other man."
18When Delilah saw that he had told her everything, she sent word to the rulers of the Philistines,
"Come back once more; he has told me everything." So the rulers of the Philistines returned
with the silver in their hands. 19Having put him to
sleep on her lap, she called a man to shave off the
seven braids of his hair, and so began to subdue
him.[a] And his strength left him. Pr 7:26-27
20Then she called, "Samson, the Philistines are
upon you!"

He awoke from his sleep and thought, "I'll go out as before and shake myself free." But he did not know that the LORD had left him. Nu 14:42

21Then the Philistines seized him, gouged out
his eyes and took him down to Gaza. Binding him
with bronze shackles, they set him to grinding in
the prison. 22But the hair on his head began to
grow again after it had been shaved. Jer 47:1

The Death of Samson

23Now the rulers of the Philistines assembled to
offer a great sacrifice to Dagon their god and to
celebrate, saying, "Our god has delivered Samson,
our enemy, into our hands." 1Sa 5:2
24When the people saw him, they praised their
god, saying, Da 5:4

"Our god has delivered our enemy
into our hands, 1Sa 31:9; 1Ch 10:9
the one who laid waste our land
and multiplied our slain."

25While they were in high spirits, they shouted,
"Bring out Samson to entertain us." So they called
Samson out of the prison, and he performed for
them. Jdg 9:27; Ru 3:7
When they stood him among the pillars, 26Sam-
son said to the servant who held his hand, "Put me
where I can feel the pillars that support the temple,
so that I may lean against them." 27Now the temple
was crowded with men and women; all the rulers
of the Philistines were there, and on the roof were
about three thousand men and women watching
Samson perform. 28Then Samson prayed to the
LORD, "O Sovereign LORD, remember me. O God,
please strengthen me just once more, and let me
with one blow get revenge on the Philistines for
my two eyes." 29Then Samson reached toward the
two central pillars on which the temple stood.
Bracing himself against them, his right hand on
the one and his left hand on the other, 30Samson
said, "Let me die with the Philistines!" Then he
pushed with all his might, and down came the
temple on the rulers and all the people in it. Thus
he killed many more when he died than while he
lived. Jdg 15:18; Jer 15:15
31Then his brothers and his father's whole family went down to get him. They brought him back
and buried him between Zorah and Eshtaol in the
tomb of Manoah his father. He had led[b] Israel
twenty years. Jdg 13:2; Ru 1:1

Disobedience and Disgrace **Chapters 17–21**

In the days of the judges the hearts of God's people continued to turn away from the Lord. In their rebellion and disobedience the people of Israel grieved God's heart and brought disgrace on their nation. In their religious expressions they wandered from the one true God to worship man-made idols. In their personal lives they practiced immorality and other behaviors that clearly went against the will of their God. In their community life there was anarchy, as the people sought what was right in their own eyes rather than what was right in the eyes of the Lord. The axiom remains forever true: *Disobedience will lead to disgrace every time.*

Micah's Idols

17 Now a man named Micah from the hill
country of Ephraim 2said to his mother,
"The eleven hundred shekels[c] of silver that were
taken from you and about which I heard you utter
a curse—I have that silver with me; I took it."
Then his mother said, "The LORD bless you, my
son!" Ru 2:20
3When he returned the eleven hundred shekels
of silver to his mother, she said, "I solemnly consecrate my silver to the LORD for my son to make a
carved image and a cast idol. I will give it back to
you." Ex 20:4,23
4So he returned the silver to his mother, and she
took two hundred shekels[d] of silver and gave
them to a silversmith, who made them into the
image and the idol. And they were put in Micah's
house. Ex 32:4; Isa 17:8
5Now this man Micah had a shrine, and he
made an ephod and some idols and installed one
of his sons as his priest. 6In those days Israel had
no king; everyone did as he saw fit. Dt 12:8; Jdg 8:27
7A young Levite from Bethlehem in Judah, who
had been living within the clan of Judah, 8left that
town in search of some other place to stay. On his
way[e] he came to Micah's house in the hill country
of Ephraim. Jdg 19:1; Mic 5:2; Mt 2:1
9Micah asked him, "Where are you from?"
"I'm a Levite from Bethlehem in Judah," he
said, "and I'm looking for a place to stay."

[a] 19 Hebrew; some Septuagint manuscripts *and he began to weaken* [b] 31 Traditionally *judged* [c] 2 That is, about 28 pounds (about 13 kilograms) [d] 4 That is, about 5 pounds (about 2.3 kilograms) [e] 8 Or *To carry on his profession*

10 Then Micah said to him, "Live with me and be my father and priest, and I'll give you ten shekels[a] of silver a year, your clothes and your food." 11 So the Levite agreed to live with him, and the young man was to him like one of his sons. 12 Then Micah installed the Levite, and the young man became his priest and lived in his house. 13 And Micah said, "Now I know that the LORD will be good to me, since this Levite has become my priest." Nu 18:7

Danites Settle in Laish

18 In those days Israel had no king. Jdg 17:6

And in those days the tribe of the Danites was seeking a place of their own where they might settle, because they had not yet come into an inheritance among the tribes of Israel. 2 So the Danites sent five warriors from Zorah and Eshtaol to spy out the land and explore it. These men represented all their clans. They told them, "Go, explore the land." Jos 2:1; 19:47; Jdg 13:25

The men entered the hill country of Ephraim and came to the house of Micah, where they spent the night. 3 When they were near Micah's house, they recognized the voice of the young Levite; so they turned in there and asked him, "Who brought you here? What are you doing in this place? Why are you here?" Jdg 17:1

4 He told them what Micah had done for him, and said, "He has hired me and I am his priest."

5 Then they said to him, "Please inquire of God to learn whether our journey will be successful."

6 The priest answered them, "Go in peace. Your journey has the LORD's approval."

7 So the five men left and came to Laish, where they saw that the people were living in safety, like the Sidonians, unsuspecting and secure. And since their land lacked nothing, they were prosperous.[b] Also, they lived a long way from the Sidonians and had no relationship with anyone else.[c] Ge 34:25

8 When they returned to Zorah and Eshtaol, their brothers asked them, "How did you find things?"

9 They answered, "Come on, let's attack them! We have seen that the land is very good. Aren't you going to do something? Don't hesitate to go there and take it over. 10 When you get there, you will find an unsuspecting people and a spacious land that God has put into your hands, a land that lacks nothing whatever." Nu 13:30; Dt 8:9; 1Ki 22:3

11 Then six hundred men from the clan of the Danites, armed for battle, set out from Zorah and Eshtaol. 12 On their way they set up camp near Kiriath Jearim in Judah. This is why the place west of Kiriath Jearim is called Mahaneh Dan[d] to this day. 13 From there they went on to the hill country of Ephraim and came to Micah's house. Jdg 13:25

14 Then the five men who had spied out the land of Laish said to their brothers, "Do you know that one of these houses has an ephod, other household gods, a carved image and a cast idol? Now you know what to do." 15 So they turned in there and went to the house of the young Levite at Micah's place and greeted him. 16 The six hundred Danites, armed for battle, stood at the entrance to the gate. 17 The five men who had spied out the land went inside and took the carved image, the ephod, the other household gods and the cast idol while the priest and the six hundred armed men stood at the entrance to the gate. Ge 31:19; Jdg 17:5; Mic 5:13

18 When these men went into Micah's house and took the carved image, the ephod, the other household gods and the cast idol, the priest said to them, "What are you doing?"

19 They answered him, "Be quiet! Don't say a word. Come with us, and be our father and priest. Isn't it better that you serve a tribe and clan in Israel as priest rather than just one man's household?" 20 Then the priest was glad. He took the ephod, the other household gods and the carved image and went along with the people. 21 Putting their little children, their livestock and their possessions in front of them, they turned away and left. Jdg 17:10; Job 21:5; 29:9

22 When they had gone some distance from Micah's house, the men who lived near Micah were called together and overtook the Danites. 23 As they shouted after them, the Danites turned and said to Micah, "What's the matter with you that you called out your men to fight?"

24 He replied, "You took the gods I made, and my priest, and went away. What else do I have? How can you ask, 'What's the matter with you?' "

25 The Danites answered, "Don't argue with us, or some hot-tempered men will attack you, and you and your family will lose your lives." 26 So the Danites went their way, and Micah, seeing that they were too strong for him, turned around and went back home. Ps 18:17

27 Then they took what Micah had made, and his priest, and went on to Laish, against a peaceful and unsuspecting people. They attacked them with the sword and burned down their city. 28 There was no one to rescue them because they lived a long way from Sidon and had no relationship with anyone else. The city was in a valley near Beth Rehob.

The Danites rebuilt the city and settled there. 29 They named it Dan after their forefather Dan, who was born to Israel—though the city used to be called Laish. 30 There the Danites set up for themselves the idols, and Jonathan son of Gershom, the son of Moses,[e] and his sons were priests for the tribe of Dan until the time of the

[a] *10* That is, about 4 ounces (about 110 grams) [b] *7* The meaning of the Hebrew for this clause is uncertain. [c] *7* Hebrew; some Septuagint manuscripts *with the Arameans* [d] *12 Mahaneh Dan* means *Dan's camp.* [e] *30* An ancient Hebrew scribal tradition, some Septuagint manuscripts and Vulgate; Masoretic Text *Manasseh*

captivity of the land. 31They continued to use the idols Micah had made, all the time the house of God was in Shiloh. Ex 2:22; Jos 19:47; 18:1

A Levite and His Concubine

19 In those days Israel had no king.

Now a Levite who lived in a remote area in the hill country of Ephraim took a concubine from Bethlehem in Judah. 2But she was unfaithful to him. She left him and went back to her father's house in Bethlehem, Judah. After she had been there four months, 3her husband went to her to persuade her to return. He had with him his servant and two donkeys. She took him into her father's house, and when her father saw him, he gladly welcomed him. 4His father-in-law, the girl's father, prevailed upon him to stay; so he remained with him three days, eating and drinking, and sleeping there. Ex 32:6

5On the fourth day they got up early and he prepared to leave, but the girl's father said to his son-in-law, "Refresh yourself with something to eat; then you can go." 6So the two of them sat down to eat and drink together. Afterward the girl's father said, "Please stay tonight and enjoy yourself." 7And when the man got up to go, his father-in-law persuaded him, so he stayed there that night. 8On the morning of the fifth day, when he rose to go, the girl's father said, "Refresh yourself. Wait till afternoon!" So the two of them ate together.

9Then when the man, with his concubine and his servant, got up to leave, his father-in-law, the girl's father, said, "Now look, it's almost evening. Spend the night here; the day is nearly over. Stay and enjoy yourself. Early tomorrow morning you can get up and be on your way home." 10But, unwilling to stay another night, the man left and went toward Jebus (that is, Jerusalem), with his two saddled donkeys and his concubine.

11When they were near Jebus and the day was almost gone, the servant said to his master, "Come, let's stop at this city of the Jebusites and spend the night."

12His master replied, "No. We won't go into an alien city, whose people are not Israelites. We will go on to Gibeah." 13He added, "Come, let's try to reach Gibeah or Ramah and spend the night in one of those places." 14So they went on, and the sun set as they neared Gibeah in Benjamin. 15There they stopped to spend the night. They went and sat in the city square, but no one took them into his home for the night. Ge 19:2; 1Sa 10:26

16That evening an old man from the hill country of Ephraim, who was living in Gibeah (the men of the place were Benjamites), came in from his work in the fields. 17When he looked and saw the traveler in the city square, the old man asked, "Where are you going? Where did you come from?"

18He answered, "We are on our way from Bethlehem in Judah to a remote area in the hill country of Ephraim where I live. I have been to Bethlehem in Judah and now I am going to the house of the LORD. No one has taken me into his house. 19We have both straw and fodder for our donkeys and bread and wine for ourselves your servants—me, your maidservant, and the young man with us. We don't need anything." Jdg 18:31

20"You are welcome at my house," the old man said. "Let me supply whatever you need. Only don't spend the night in the square." 21So he took him into his house and fed his donkeys. After they had washed their feet, they had something to eat and drink. Ge 24:32-33; Lk 7:44

22While they were enjoying themselves, some of the wicked men of the city surrounded the house. Pounding on the door, they shouted to the old man who owned the house, "Bring out the man who came to your house so we can have sex with him." Ge 19:4-5; Dt 13:13; Ro 1:26-27

23The owner of the house went outside and said to them, "No, my friends, don't be so vile. Since this man is my guest, don't do this disgraceful thing. 24Look, here is my virgin daughter, and his concubine. I will bring them out to you now, and you can use them and do to them whatever you wish. But to this man, don't do such a disgraceful thing." Ge 34:7; Dt 22:21; 2Sa 13:12

25But the men would not listen to him. So the man took his concubine and sent her outside to them, and they raped her and abused her throughout the night, and at dawn they let her go. 26At daybreak the woman went back to the house where her master was staying, fell down at the door and lay there until daylight. Jdg 20:5; 1Sa 31:4

27When her master got up in the morning and opened the door of the house and stepped out to continue on his way, there lay his concubine, fallen in the doorway of the house, with her hands on the threshold. 28He said to her, "Get up; let's go." But there was no answer. Then the man put her on his donkey and set out for home.

29When he reached home, he took a knife and cut up his concubine, limb by limb, into twelve parts and sent them into all the areas of Israel. 30Everyone who saw it said, "Such a thing has never been seen or done, not since the day the Israelites came up out of Egypt. Think about it! Consider it! Tell us what to do!" Jdg 20:7; 1Sa 11:7

Israelites Fight the Benjamites

20 Then all the Israelites from Dan to Beersheba and from the land of Gilead came out as one man and assembled before the LORD in Mizpah. 2The leaders of all the people of the tribes of Israel took their places in the assembly of the people of God, four hundred thousand soldiers armed with swords. 3(The Benjamites heard that

the Israelites had gone up to Mizpah.) Then the Israelites said, "Tell us how this awful thing happened." Jdg 8:10; 21:5; 1Sa 7:5

[4]So the Levite, the husband of the murdered woman, said, "I and my concubine came to Gibeah in Benjamin to spend the night. [5]During the night the men of Gibeah came after me and surrounded the house, intending to kill me. They raped my concubine, and she died. [6]I took my concubine, cut her into pieces and sent one piece to each region of Israel's inheritance, because they committed this lewd and disgraceful act in Israel. [7]Now, all you Israelites, speak up and give your verdict." Jos 7:15; Jdg 19:25-26

[8]All the people rose as one man, saying, "None of us will go home. No, not one of us will return to his house. [9]But now this is what we'll do to Gibeah: We'll go up against it as the lot directs. [10]We'll take ten men out of every hundred from all the tribes of Israel, and a hundred from a thousand, and a thousand from ten thousand, to get provisions for the army. Then, when the army arrives at Gibeah[a] in Benjamin, it can give them what they deserve for all this vileness done in Israel." [11]So all the men of Israel got together and united as one man against the city.

[12]The tribes of Israel sent men throughout the tribe of Benjamin, saying, "What about this awful crime that was committed among you? [13]Now surrender those wicked men of Gibeah so that we may put them to death and purge the evil from Israel." Dt 13:13

But the Benjamites would not listen to their fellow Israelites. [14]From their towns they came together at Gibeah to fight against the Israelites. [15]At once the Benjamites mobilized twenty-six thousand swordsmen from their towns, in addition to seven hundred chosen men from those living in Gibeah. [16]Among all these soldiers there were seven hundred chosen men who were left-handed, each of whom could sling a stone at a hair and not miss. Jdg 3:15; 1Ch 12:2

[17]Israel, apart from Benjamin, mustered four hundred thousand swordsmen, all of them fighting men.

[18]The Israelites went up to Bethel[b] and inquired of God. They said, "Who of us shall go first to fight against the Benjamites?" Jos 12:9; Jdg 18:5

The LORD replied, "Judah shall go first."

[19]The next morning the Israelites got up and pitched camp near Gibeah. [20]The men of Israel went out to fight the Benjamites and took up battle positions against them at Gibeah. [21]The Benjamites came out of Gibeah and cut down twenty-two thousand Israelites on the battlefield that day. [22]But the men of Israel encouraged one another and again took up their positions where they had stationed themselves the first day. [23]The Israelites went up and wept before the LORD until evening, and they inquired of the LORD. They said, "Shall we go up again to battle against the Benjamites, our brothers?" Nu 14:1; Jos 7:6

The LORD answered, "Go up against them."

[24]Then the Israelites drew near to Benjamin the second day. [25]This time, when the Benjamites came out from Gibeah to oppose them, they cut down another eighteen thousand Israelites, all of them armed with swords.

[26]Then the Israelites, all the people, went up to Bethel, and there they sat weeping before the LORD. They fasted that day until evening and presented burnt offerings and fellowship offerings[c] to the LORD. [27]And the Israelites inquired of the LORD. (In those days the ark of the covenant of God was there, [28]with Phinehas son of Eleazar, the son of Aaron, ministering before it.) They asked, "Shall we go up again to battle with Benjamin our brother, or not?" Dt 18:5; Jdg 21:4

The LORD responded, "Go, for tomorrow I will give them into your hands." Jdg 7:9

[29]Then Israel set an ambush around Gibeah. [30]They went up against the Benjamites on the third day and took up positions against Gibeah as they had done before. [31]The Benjamites came out to meet them and were drawn away from the city. They began to inflict casualties on the Israelites as before, so that about thirty men fell in the open field and on the roads—the one leading to Bethel and the other to Gibeah. Jos 8:2,4

[32]While the Benjamites were saying, "We are defeating them as before," the Israelites were saying, "Let's retreat and draw them away from the city to the roads."

[33]All the men of Israel moved from their places and took up positions at Baal Tamar, and the Israelite ambush charged out of its place on the west[d] of Gibeah.[e] [34]Then ten thousand of Israel's finest men made a frontal attack on Gibeah. The fighting was so heavy that the Benjamites did not realize how near disaster was. [35]The LORD defeated Benjamin before Israel, and on that day the Israelites struck down 25,100 Benjamites, all armed with swords. [36]Then the Benjamites saw that they were beaten. Jos 8:19; 1Sa 9:21

Now the men of Israel had given way before Benjamin, because they relied on the ambush they had set near Gibeah. [37]The men who had been in ambush made a sudden dash into Gibeah, spread out and put the whole city to the sword. [38]The men of Israel had arranged with the ambush that they should send up a great cloud of smoke from the

[a] *10* One Hebrew manuscript; most Hebrew manuscripts *Geba,* a variant of *Gibeah* [b] *18* Or *to the house of God*; also in verse 26 [c] *26* Traditionally *peace offerings* [d] *33* Some Septuagint manuscripts and Vulgate; the meaning of the Hebrew for this word is uncertain. [e] *33* Hebrew *Geba,* a variant of *Gibeah*

city, 39and then the men of Israel would turn in the battle. Jos 8:15

The Benjamites had begun to inflict casualties on the men of Israel (about thirty), and they said, "We are defeating them as in the first battle." 40But when the column of smoke began to rise from the city, the Benjamites turned and saw the smoke of the whole city going up into the sky. 41Then the men of Israel turned on them, and the men of Benjamin were terrified, because they realized that disaster had come upon them. 42So they fled before the Israelites in the direction of the desert, but they could not escape the battle. And the men of Israel who came out of the towns cut them down there. 43They surrounded the Benjamites, chased them and easily[a] overran them in the vicinity of Gibeah on the east. 44Eighteen thousand Benjamites fell, all of them valiant fighters. 45As they turned and fled toward the desert to the rock of Rimmon, the Israelites cut down five thousand men along the roads. They kept pressing after the Benjamites as far as Gidom and struck down two thousand more. Jos 15:32; Jdg 21:13

46On that day twenty-five thousand Benjamite swordsmen fell, all of them valiant fighters. 47But six hundred men turned and fled into the desert to the rock of Rimmon, where they stayed four months. 48The men of Israel went back to Benjamin and put all the towns to the sword, including the animals and everything else they found. All the towns they came across they set on fire. 1Sa 9:21

Wives for the Benjamites

21 The men of Israel had taken an oath at Mizpah: "Not one of us will give his daughter in marriage to a Benjamite." Jos 9:18

2The people went to Bethel,[b] where they sat before God until evening, raising their voices and weeping bitterly. 3"O LORD, the God of Israel," they cried, "why has this happened to Israel? Why should one tribe be missing from Israel today?"

4Early the next day the people built an altar and presented burnt offerings and fellowship offerings.[c] Jdg 20:26; 2Sa 24:25

5Then the Israelites asked, "Who from all the tribes of Israel has failed to assemble before the LORD?" For they had taken a solemn oath that anyone who failed to assemble before the LORD at Mizpah should certainly be put to death. Jdg 5:23

6Now the Israelites grieved for their brothers, the Benjamites. "Today one tribe is cut off from Israel," they said. 7"How can we provide wives for those who are left, since we have taken an oath by the LORD not to give them any of our daughters in marriage?" 8Then they asked, "Which one of the tribes of Israel failed to assemble before the LORD at Mizpah?" They discovered that no one from Jabesh Gilead had come to the camp for the assembly. 9For when they counted the people, they found that none of the people of Jabesh Gilead were there. 1Sa 11:1

10So the assembly sent twelve thousand fighting men with instructions to go to Jabesh Gilead and put to the sword those living there, including the women and children. 11"This is what you are to do," they said. "Kill every male and every woman who is not a virgin." 12They found among the people living in Jabesh Gilead four hundred young women who had never slept with a man, and they took them to the camp at Shiloh in Canaan.

13Then the whole assembly sent an offer of peace to the Benjamites at the rock of Rimmon. 14So the Benjamites returned at that time and were given the women of Jabesh Gilead who had been spared. But there were not enough for all of them.

15The people grieved for Benjamin, because the LORD had made a gap in the tribes of Israel. 16And the elders of the assembly said, "With the women of Benjamin destroyed, how shall we provide wives for the men who are left? 17The Benjamite survivors must have heirs," they said, "so that a tribe of Israel will not be wiped out. 18We can't give them our daughters as wives, since we Israelites have taken this oath: 'Cursed be anyone who gives a wife to a Benjamite.' 19But look, there is the annual festival of the LORD in Shiloh, to the north of Bethel, and east of the road that goes from Bethel to Shechem, and to the south of Lebonah." Jos 16:1

20So they instructed the Benjamites, saying, "Go and hide in the vineyards 21and watch. When the girls of Shiloh come out to join in the dancing, then rush from the vineyards and each of you seize a wife from the girls of Shiloh and go to the land of Benjamin. 22When their fathers or brothers complain to us, we will say to them, 'Do us a kindness by helping them, because we did not get wives for them during the war, and you are innocent, since you did not give your daughters to them.'" Ex 15:20; Jdg 11:34

23So that is what the Benjamites did. While the girls were dancing, each man caught one and carried her off to be his wife. Then they returned to their inheritance and rebuilt the towns and settled in them. Jdg 20:48

24At that time the Israelites left that place and went home to their tribes and clans, each to his own inheritance.

25In those days Israel had no king; everyone did as he saw fit. Jdg 17:6; 18:1; 19:1

[a]43 The meaning of the Hebrew for this word is uncertain. [b]2 Or *to the house of God* [c]4 Traditionally *peace offerings*

INTRODUCTION

RUTH

"Priceless gems have often been found in unlikely places. Many a choice flower has been found blooming in a rocky crevice. Rainbow artistries have suddenly lit up the drabbest skies. Beauty spots have charmed the traveler at surprise turns on the least-promising road. It is even so with the superbly beautiful little idyll, the book of Ruth." So writes the eloquent J. Sidlow Baxter in *Explore the Book*. And he is correct. Like an exquisite rose blooming in a foul garbage dump, the story of Ruth adds elegance, grace and charm to an otherwise depressing scene . . . especially when we realize it took place "in the days when the judges ruled" and when "there was a famine in the land" (Ruth 1:1). What hope this affords us! In spite of depravity's depths and our bleak surroundings, God still has His choice instruments, His unique and lovely vessels, to bring us reminders of His presence and care.

WRITER: *Unknown*

DATE: *c.1000 B.C.*

KEY THEME: *Redemption*

KEY MESSAGE: *God doesn't leave us in hard times*

NEW TESTAMENT COUNTERPART: *"Humble yourselves, therefore, under God's mighty hand, that he may lift you up in due time. Cast all your anxiety on him because he cares for you" (1 Peter 5:6-7).*

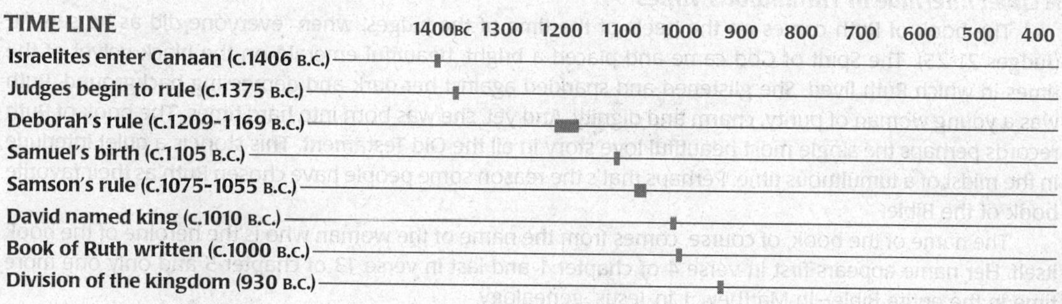

Interlude of Love

JUDGES Turbulent Times	CHOICE OF RUTH	OCCUPATION OF RUTH	CLAIM OF RUTH	MARRIAGE OF RUTH	1 SAMUEL Changing Times
	NAOMI AND RUTH (Mutual grief)	RUTH AND NAOMI AND BOAZ (Mutual pursuit)		BOAZ AND RUTH (Mutual love)	
	"May the LORD grant that each of you will find rest."	*"Naomi had a relative . . . whose name was Boaz."*	*"Wait . . . until you find out what happens."*	*"Boaz took Ruth and she became his wife."*	*"Praise be to the LORD, who this day has not left you . . ."*
	CHAPTER 1	*CHAPTER 2*	*CHAPTER 3*	*CHAPTER 4*	
	GEOGRAPHICAL	**CHRONOLOGICAL**		**PERSONAL**	
SETTING	***"In the days when the judges ruled, there was a famine in the land."***				
CIRCUMSTANCE	**Loss—deeper commitment**		**Gain—deeper love**		
EMOTION	**Grief**	**Loneliness**	**Companionship**	**Rejoicing**	

In many dramatic performances like a play, a movie or a television production, there is often a story within a story. Frequently, these are in strong contrast to one another. For example, there may be a story about revolution and violence, but behind the scenes there is a love relationship between two rather insignificant people. All of this is interwoven as part of the plot.

What is true in those dramas is also true in the Bible. For example, in the early part of Exodus we read of Pharaoh and the slave masters bringing all kinds of wrong and hardship on the Hebrews. But over in the little hut of Amram and Jochebed a baby is born and nurtured. That love relationship between mother and Moses stands in bold relief against the dark backdrop of mistreatment and misery. It's remarkable!

A Quiet Interlude in Tumultuous Times

The book of Ruth comes on the heels of the time of the judges, when "everyone did as he saw fit" (Judges 21:25). The Spirit of God came and placed a bright, beautiful emerald on the black velvet of the times in which Ruth lived. She glistened and sparkled against her dark and depressing background. Ruth was a young woman of purity, charm and dignity. And yet, she was born into hard times. The book of Ruth records perhaps the single most beautiful love story in all the Old Testament. This story is a quiet interlude in the midst of a tumultuous time. Perhaps that's the reason some people have chosen Ruth as their favorite book of the Bible.

The name of the book, of course, comes from the name of the woman who is the heroine of the book itself. Her name appears first in verse 4 of chapter 1 and last in verse 13 of chapter 5 and only one more time in the entire Bible—in Matthew 1 in Jesus' genealogy.

Ruth is a young widow when we first meet her. She has a mother-in-law named Naomi, whom she loves dearly. Naomi is also a widow. It's beautiful how God ties their lives together. Ruth emerges on the scene as an encouragement to her mother-in-law. They become more than family; they are intimate friends.

God Never Leaves Us

There's one significant message that comes through in the book of Ruth: *God doesn't leave us in hard times.* Occasionally, when we are going through tough times in our lives, we may question this truth. When times are troubled and the rug is pulled out from under us, we may begin to question God's goodness. However, it is at just these times that the Lord is the nearest—right when you and I question it the most.

During hard times our heavenly Father comes close and stays near. When we doubt the most, God cares the greatest! When I am ready to shake my fist in His face, He stands with arms outstretched. If you've lost someone near and dear or if you have suddenly found yourself losing hope, I want to assure you, as a child of God, those are the times when the Father is touched with our feelings of infirmity—even though we may not feel it at that moment.

The major characters of the book of Ruth are three in number: *Naomi*, the mother-in-law; *Ruth*, one of the daughters-in-law; and *Boaz*, who comes along later in the book. Just when Ruth was expecting a life of widowhood, God sent her this man Boaz, ready, waiting and anxious to get acquainted. It's beautiful how the Lord wove their lives together!

Ruth Makes a Choice

Even though Ruth lost someone very valuable to her, she reacted in a way that was pleasing to God. Ruth accepted the fact that her husband was dead and didn't lash out in anger or bitterness toward God. The tendency on our part might be to wonder about God's goodness in allowing this to happen. Not this woman. Instead, she committed herself to staying beside Naomi, who was also alone and grieving. Ruth loved her mother-in-law very much. Even though Naomi very graciously urged her to return to her homeland, Ruth chose to remain by her mother-in-law's side. In Ruth 1:16–17 we read Ruth's reply:

> *Don't urge me to leave you or to turn back from you. Where you go I will go, and where you stay I will stay. Your people will be my people and your God my God. Where you die I will die, and there I will be buried. May the Lord deal with me, be it ever so severely, if anything but death separates you and me.*

Now that's commitment! Those words must have been overwhelming for Naomi to hear. Ruth truly was a remarkable young woman.

Ruth Gets an Occupation

Ruth knew life had to continue, so she went to work. In chapter 2 we find her gleaning in the fields. One of the least helpful things that you can do after grieving the loss of someone close to you is to keep on lingering month after month over the loss. You will become useless to yourself and to others. Ruth, in spite of her grief and loneliness, got back to work. While Ruth was gleaning, the owner of the field greeted the harvesters and spotted Ruth in the fields. He asked, "Whose young woman is that?" (2:5). After being told who she was, he approached her. He told Ruth to remain in his fields and offered her protection. Ruth was surprised by his kindness and asked why she had found favor in his eyes even though she was a foreigner. Boaz replied by telling her that he had heard about her commitment to her mother-in-law, and he desired that she would be rewarded for her kindness. When Ruth returned home, she found out that Boaz was a close relative of theirs, one of their "kinsman-redeemers."

You can't appreciate the term "kinsman-redeemer" unless you understand the ancient Hebrew law of the kinsman. In those days there was an interesting law established to help widows who were bereft of assistance. The kinsman was the widow's closest living relative. It was his obligation to first avenge any violence done against his brothers. Second, he was to manage his brother's estate if the brother had died, and third, if it was appropriate and necessary, he could marry the widow and thereby deliver her from widowhood. That was the law of the kinsman-redeemer.

Ruth Stakes Her Claim

In chapter 3 Boaz and Ruth got to know each other. Ruth was available, but careful. She was responsive, but pure. She did just what the custom allowed and nothing more. Both Boaz and Ruth were interested, but patient. However, Boaz seemed reluctant. One of the reasons for this reluctance was a legal one; he wasn't the closest kinsman. In this case, Boaz was the nephew of Elimelech (Naomi's deceased husband)—and as it turned out, not his closest relative. Elimelech had a brother who had the first right to redeem Ruth. It is essential to keep this in mind. Boaz and Ruth were in love, but you get the distinct impression that both wanted the Lord's will to be the single most important factor in their companionship. They had the right attitude toward companionship. No one forced anything. In a romantic courtship, when the Lord is allowed to lead, it flows. God is able to open the doors. He knows what He's doing. Boaz realized that he wasn't the closest relative and that this relationship couldn't be from God unless he got the green light on this issue. Ruth didn't argue.

Ruth Gets Married

Chapter 4 outlines the right approach to marriage. Ruth waited as Boaz tracked down the real kinsman, the closest relative. Boaz was ready to relinquish Ruth if he himself was not the appropriate kinsman. Boaz found out that the closest kinsman was not available to redeem Ruth, so Boaz had the right of redemption. Wow! Can you imagine how Boaz must have felt? As the last door was flung open by the Lord, Boaz and Ruth got married. God enabled Ruth to conceive, and she gave birth to a son, Obed. The moment Ruth became a mother, Naomi became a grandmother. What an unexpected surprise for Naomi in her old age. There's nothing like grandchildren to sustain a person in the later years of life. Grandchildren become like little fountains of youth to the aging!

Thanks to this love story, we have recorded three generations that we would otherwise not be able to trace. Isn't that beautiful! Here's Boaz, who marries Ruth, and they have Obed. Obed became the father of Jesse, the father of David. By the way, just in case you want to know who Boaz's mother was, read Matthew 1:5. She was a former prostitute named Rahab from the ancient city of Jericho. *God never runs out of possibilities.* He can use any of us. Grace! Amazing grace!

Ruth Opens Our Eyes to Truth

There are at least three lessons we learn from the book of Ruth. Lesson one: *Even in the worst of times God still has His choice instruments.* Some of you are God's choicest instruments in the worst of times. Don't miss that opportunity. Continue to walk with God in those difficult times. You are among the rare ones. Keep doing it! Lesson two: *In spite of our natural desires, God is still to be glorified and placed before everything else.* When it comes to contemplating marriage and planning your future, be sure to ask God if it's His plan for you to be married or single. Seek His leading and follow His direction. Lesson three: *Being a grandparent is a great blessing.* What a joy to hold those little ones in your arms! What a joy to see those children grow! If you are a grandparent, be sure to thank the Lord for the precious gift of grandchildren.

One final observation as we look at the book of Ruth: Boaz was Ruth's kinsman-redeemer. He purchased her and made her his own. *We also have a Kinsman-Redeemer who has bought us at immeasurable cost and who has called us His beloved.* His name is Jesus Christ. He is the nearest relative to the Father. He came to buy us back—even those of us who are bereft, confused, lost, unsure of our way. What a blessing to know that while we were lost and wandering the Lord gave His own life so that we could have eternal life. What a mighty God we serve!

Reacting to Loss Chapter 1

As we meet Ruth, we encounter a woman in a painful and difficult time of life. There had been three deaths in her family: her husband, her brother-in-law and her father-in-law. This was clearly a time of great pain as well as deep concern for the future. In the midst of this time of grief, Ruth revealed that she had a heart filled with love and concern for others rather than bitterness and self-pity. She stands as a powerful example of strength in the midst of the storm.

Naomi and Ruth

1 In the days when the judges ruled,[a] there was a famine in the land, and a man from Bethlehem in Judah, together with his wife and two sons, went to live for a while in the country of Moab. 2The man's name was Elimelech, his wife's name Naomi, and the names of his two sons were Mahlon and Kilion. They were Ephrathites from Bethlehem, Judah. And they went to Moab and lived there. Ge 35:19; Jdg 2:16-18; 3:30

3Now Elimelech, Naomi's husband, died, and she was left with her two sons. 4They married Moabite women, one named Orpah and the other Ruth. After they had lived there about ten years, 5both Mahlon and Kilion also died, and Naomi was left without her two sons and her husband.

6When she heard in Moab that the LORD had come to the aid of his people by providing food for them, Naomi and her daughters-in-law prepared to return home from there. 7With her two daughters-in-law she left the place where she had been living and set out on the road that would take them back to the land of Judah. Ex 4:31; Mt 6:11

8Then Naomi said to her two daughters-in-law, "Go back, each of you, to your mother's home. May the LORD show kindness to you, as you have shown to your dead and to me. 9May the LORD grant that each of you will find rest in the home of another husband." Ru 2:20 3:1; 2Ti 1:16

Then she kissed them and they wept aloud 10and said to her, "We will go back with you to your people."

11But Naomi said, "Return home, my daughters. Why would you come with me? Am I going to have any more sons, who could become your husbands? 12Return home, my daughters; I am too old to have another husband. Even if I thought there was still hope for me—even if I had a husband tonight and then gave birth to sons—13would you wait until they grew up? Would you remain unmarried for them? No, my daughters. It is more bitter for me than for you, because the LORD's hand has gone out against me!" Ge 38:11

14At this they wept again. Then Orpah kissed her mother-in-law good-by, but Ruth clung to her. Pr 17:17; 18:24

15"Look," said Naomi, "your sister-in-law is going back to her people and her gods. Go back with her." Jos 24:14; Jdg 11:24

16But Ruth replied, "Don't urge me to leave you or to turn back from you. Where you go I will go, and where you stay I will stay. Your people will be my people and your God my God. 17Where you die I will die, and there I will be buried. May the LORD deal with me, be it ever so severely, if anything but death separates you and me." 18When Naomi realized that Ruth was determined to go with her, she stopped urging her. 1Sa 3:17; 2Ki 2:2

19So the two women went on until they came to Bethlehem. When they arrived in Bethlehem, the whole town was stirred because of them, and the women exclaimed, "Can this be Naomi?" Mt 21:10

20"Don't call me Naomi,[b]" she told them. "Call me Mara,[c] because the Almighty[d] has made my life very bitter. 21I went away full, but the LORD has brought me back empty. Why call me Naomi? The LORD has afflicted[e] me; the Almighty has brought misfortune upon me." Job 1:21

22So Naomi returned from Moab accompanied by Ruth the Moabitess, her daughter-in-law, arriving in Bethlehem as the barley harvest was beginning. Ex 9:31

Responding to Loneliness Chapter 2

Although Ruth was lonely, she did not allow herself to cut off other relationships and live alone. She soon found herself working in the fields among the other gleaners. Along the way, the Lord brought Boaz into contact with Ruth. There was a spark between these two people. It is important to remember that those who are spiritually minded can be romantically minded as well.

Ruth Meets Boaz

2 Now Naomi had a relative on her husband's side, from the clan of Elimelech, a man of standing, whose name was Boaz. Ru 1:2; 3:2,12

2And Ruth the Moabitess said to Naomi, "Let me go to the fields and pick up the leftover grain behind anyone in whose eyes I find favor."

Naomi said to her, "Go ahead, my daughter." 3So she went out and began to glean in the fields behind the harvesters. As it turned out, she found herself working in a field belonging to Boaz, who was from the clan of Elimelech.

4Just then Boaz arrived from Bethlehem and greeted the harvesters, "The LORD be with you!"

"The LORD bless you!" they called back.

5Boaz asked the foreman of his harvesters, "Whose young woman is that?"

[a]*1* Traditionally *judged* [b]*20 Naomi* means *pleasant*; also in verse 21. [c]*20 Mara* means *bitter.* [d]*20* Hebrew *Shaddai*; also in verse 21 [e]*21* Or *has testified against*

6The foreman replied, "She is the Moabitess who came back from Moab with Naomi. 7She said, 'Please let me glean and gather among the sheaves behind the harvesters.' She went into the field and has worked steadily from morning till now, except for a short rest in the shelter." Ru 1:22

8So Boaz said to Ruth, "My daughter, listen to me. Don't go and glean in another field and don't go away from here. Stay here with my servant girls. 9Watch the field where the men are harvesting, and follow along after the girls. I have told the men not to touch you. And whenever you are thirsty, go and get a drink from the water jars the men have filled."

10At this, she bowed down with her face to the ground. She exclaimed, "Why have I found such favor in your eyes that you notice me—a foreigner?" 1Sa 25:23

11Boaz replied, "I've been told all about what you have done for your mother-in-law since the death of your husband—how you left your father and mother and your homeland and came to live with a people you did not know before. 12May the LORD repay you for what you have done. May you be richly rewarded by the LORD, the God of Israel, under whose wings you have come to take refuge."

13"May I continue to find favor in your eyes, my lord," she said. "You have given me comfort and have spoken kindly to your servant—though I do not have the standing of one of your servant girls."

14At mealtime Boaz said to her, "Come over here. Have some bread and dip it in the wine vinegar."

When she sat down with the harvesters, he offered her some roasted grain. She ate all she wanted and had some left over. 15As she got up to glean, Boaz gave orders to his men, "Even if she gathers among the sheaves, don't embarrass her. 16Rather, pull out some stalks for her from the bundles and leave them for her to pick up, and don't rebuke her."

17So Ruth gleaned in the field until evening. Then she threshed the barley she had gathered, and it amounted to about an ephah.[a] 18She carried it back to town, and her mother-in-law saw how much she had gathered. Ruth also brought out and gave her what she had left over after she had eaten enough.

19Her mother-in-law asked her, "Where did you glean today? Where did you work? Blessed be the man who took notice of you!" Ps 41:1

Then Ruth told her mother-in-law about the one at whose place she had been working. "The name of the man I worked with today is Boaz," she said.

20"The LORD bless him!" Naomi said to her daughter-in-law. "He has not stopped showing his kindness to the living and the dead." She added, "That man is our close relative; he is one of our kinsman-redeemers." Ru 3:10

21Then Ruth the Moabitess said, "He even said to me, 'Stay with my workers until they finish harvesting all my grain.' "

22Naomi said to Ruth her daughter-in-law, "It will be good for you, my daughter, to go with his girls, because in someone else's field you might be harmed."

23So Ruth stayed close to the servant girls of Boaz to glean until the barley and wheat harvests were finished. And she lived with her mother-in-law. Dt 16:9

Regarding Companionship **Chapter 3**

Boaz had to fulfill specific legal requirements before he could marry Ruth. There was an attraction and a desire for romance between Boaz and Ruth, but neither would let their desire for companionship force them to do something that might have been wrong in God's sight. They restrained themselves until the law had been fulfilled. What an encouraging example in a day when unbridled passion often runs wild. Ruth's life story is a helpful reminder to be keenly aware of the Lord's leading in the midst of our natural tendency to fulfill our own desires for companionship in our own way.

Ruth and Boaz at the Threshing Floor

3 One day Naomi her mother-in-law said to her, "My daughter, should I not try to find a home[b] for you, where you will be well provided for? 2Is not Boaz, with whose servant girls you have been, a kinsman of ours? Tonight he will be winnowing barley on the threshing floor. 3Wash and perfume yourself, and put on your best clothes. Then go down to the threshing floor, but don't let him know you are there until he has finished eating and drinking. 4When he lies down, note the place where he is lying. Then go and uncover his feet and lie down. He will tell you what to do." Ru 2:1; 2Sa 14:2

5"I will do whatever you say," Ruth answered. 6So she went down to the threshing floor and did everything her mother-in-law told her to do.

7When Boaz had finished eating and drinking and was in good spirits, he went over to lie down at the far end of the grain pile. Ruth approached quietly, uncovered his feet and lay down. 8In the middle of the night something startled the man, and he turned and discovered a woman lying at his feet. Jdg 19:6,9,22; 2Sa 13:28; 1Ki 21:7

9"Who are you?" he asked.

"I am your servant Ruth," she said. "Spread the corner of your garment over me, since you are a kinsman-redeemer." Ru 2:20

10"The LORD bless you, my daughter," he re-

[a] *17* That is, probably about 3/5 bushel (about 22 liters)

[b] *1* Hebrew *find rest* (see Ruth 1:9)

plied. "This kindness is greater than that which
you showed earlier: You have not run after the
younger men, whether rich or poor. 11And now,
my daughter, don't be afraid. I will do for you all
you ask. All my fellow townsmen know that you
are a woman of noble character. 12Although it is
true that I am near of kin, there is a kinsman-
redeemer nearer than I. 13Stay here for the night,
and in the morning if he wants to redeem, good;
let him redeem. But if he is not willing, as surely
as the LORD lives I will do it. Lie here until morning."

14So she lay at his feet until morning, but got up
before anyone could be recognized; and he said,
"Don't let it be known that a woman came to the
threshing floor." Ro 14:16; 2Co 8:21

15He also said, "Bring me the shawl you are
wearing and hold it out." When she did so, he
poured into it six measures of barley and put it on
her. Then he[a] went back to town.

16When Ruth came to her mother-in-law, Naomi asked, "How did it go, my daughter?"

Then she told her everything Boaz had done for
her 17and added, "He gave me these six measures
of barley, saying, 'Don't go back to your mother-
in-law empty-handed.'"

18Then Naomi said, "Wait, my daughter, until
you find out what happens. For the man will not
rest until the matter is settled today." Ps 37:3-5

Reflecting on Marriage **Chapter 4**

When it comes to contemplating marriage, many of us respond in one of two ways. Sometimes we knock the door in and rush into a relationship without taking time for prayer and reflection. At other times we slam the door shut and refuse to open our hearts to a person the Lord may want us to get to know better. Ruth and Boaz are wonderful examples of a couple who allowed *the Lord* to open and close doors in their relationship. They neither knocked the door in nor slammed it shut; they waited on the Lord.

Boaz Marries Ruth

4 Meanwhile Boaz went up to the town gate
and sat there. When the kinsman-redeemer
he had mentioned came along, Boaz said, "Come
over here, my friend, and sit down." So he went
over and sat down. Ru 3:12

2Boaz took ten of the elders of the town and
said, "Sit here," and they did so. 3Then he said to
the kinsman-redeemer, "Naomi, who has come
back from Moab, is selling the piece of land that
belonged to our brother Elimelech. 4I thought I
should bring the matter to your attention and suggest that you buy it in the presence of these seated
here and in the presence of the elders of my people. If you will redeem it, do so. But if you[b] will
not, tell me, so I will know. For no one has the
right to do it except you, and I am next in line."

"I will redeem it," he said.

5Then Boaz said, "On the day you buy the land
from Naomi and from Ruth the Moabitess, you
acquire[c] the dead man's widow, in order to
maintain the name of the dead with his property."

6At this, the kinsman-redeemer said, "Then I
cannot redeem it because I might endanger my
own estate. You redeem it yourself. I cannot
do it." Ru 3:13

7(Now in earlier times in Israel, for the redemption and transfer of property to become final, one
party took off his sandal and gave it to the other.
This was the method of legalizing transactions in
Israel.) Dt 25:7-9

8So the kinsman-redeemer said to Boaz, "Buy it
yourself." And he removed his sandal.

9Then Boaz announced to the elders and all
the people, "Today you are witnesses that I have
bought from Naomi all the property of Elimelech,
Kilion and Mahlon. 10I have also acquired Ruth
the Moabitess, Mahlon's widow, as my wife, in
order to maintain the name of the dead with his
property, so that his name will not disappear from
among his family or from the town records. Today
you are witnesses!"

11Then the elders and all those at the gate said,
"We are witnesses. May the LORD make the woman
who is coming into your home like Rachel and
Leah, who together built up the house of Israel.
May you have standing in Ephrathah and be fa-
mous in Bethlehem. 12Through the offspring the
LORD gives you by this young woman, may your
family be like that of Perez, whom Tamar bore to
Judah." Ps 127:3; 128:3; Ge 38:29

The Genealogy of David

13So Boaz took Ruth and she became his wife.

LIVING  **INSIGHT**

You will discover in life, if you haven't already, that in all things God works for the good of those who love Him (see Romans 8:28). This searing pain, this blinding loss . . . by and by God begins to unveil a new plan you never would have imagined. And you look back and say, "God was so faithful."

(See Ruth 4:13–22.)

[a] *15* Most Hebrew manuscripts; many Hebrew manuscripts, Vulgate and Syriac *she*

[b] *4* Many Hebrew manuscripts, Septuagint, Vulgate and Syriac; most Hebrew manuscripts *he*

[c] *5* Hebrew; Vulgate and Syriac *Naomi, you acquire Ruth the Moabitess,*

Then he went to her, and the LORD enabled her to
conceive, and she gave birth to a son. [14]The wom-
en said to Naomi: "Praise be to the LORD, who this
day has not left you without a kinsman-redeemer.
May he become famous throughout Israel! [15]He
will renew your life and sustain you in your old
age. For your daughter-in-law, who loves you and
who is better to you than seven sons, has given
him birth." Ge 29:31; Ru 1:16-17; 1Sa 1:8
[16]Then Naomi took the child, laid him in her
lap and cared for him. [17]The women living there
said, "Naomi has a son." And they named him
Obed. He was the father of Jesse, the father of
David. 1Sa 16:1,18
[18]This, then, is the family line of Perez:

Perez was the father of Hezron,
[19]Hezron the father of Ram,
Ram the father of Amminadab,
[20]Amminadab the father of Nahshon,
Nahshon the father of Salmon,[a]
[21]Salmon the father of Boaz,
Boaz the father of Obed,
[22]Obed the father of Jesse,
and Jesse the father of David. 1Ch 2:5-15

[a]20 A few Hebrew manuscripts, some Septuagint manuscripts and Vulgate (see also verse 21 and Septuagint of 1 Chron. 2:11); most Hebrew manuscripts *Salma*

1 SAMUEL

Transitional times can be disconcerting. Those who have gone through the remodeling of a home can testify to that! Likewise, changes in leadership in a place of employment or moving across the country or setting into motion new procedures and policies bring the need to adapt and change. Being creatures of habit, we are often disturbed by these changes. What is true of us as individuals is equally true on a national level. Presidential and governmental changes affect our feelings just as much as they alter the stock market. For centuries God personally governed His people Israel. Throughout this theocratic rule, God used *His* anointed leaders to govern His people; the last leaders were called judges. But with the last judge, Samuel, a whole new dynamic was experienced—the people's choice. A king—King Saul. This book records the beginnings of the changes that occurred during the transition from a theocracy to a monarchy... from God's anointed servants to Israel's appointed king.

WRITER: *Unknown*

DATE: *c.925 B.C.*

PURPOSE: *To record the establishment of kingship in Israel*

KEY THEME: *Transition*

KEY CHAPTERS: *8, 16, 17, 28, 31*

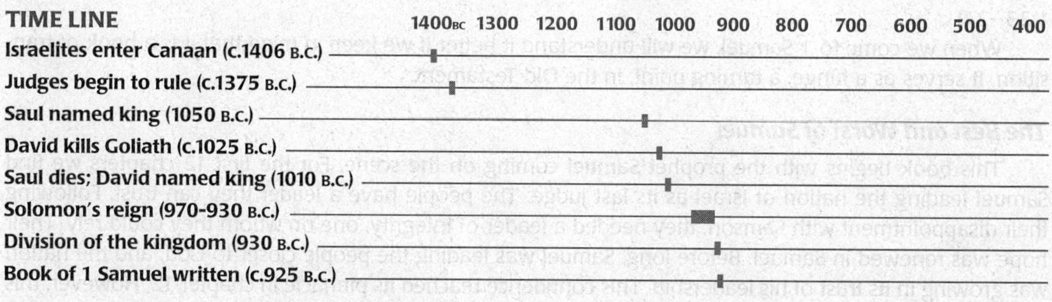

Nation in Transition

BEGINNING
Samuel's godliness
National hope
Motivation
Purity

SAMUEL
The Last Judge

SAUL
The First King

BIRTH	GROWTH AND CALL	MINISTRY	CHANGE	REJECTION BY GOD	REBELLION AGAINST GOD
				Impatient Rash Disobedient "Insane" Jealous Murderous	DAVID chosen, trained, tested, protected . . .
CHAPTER 1	*CHAPTERS 2–3*	*CHAPTERS 4–7*	*CHAPTERS 8–12*	*CHAPTERS 13–16*	*CHAPTERS 17–31*

ENDING
Saul's suicide
Personal despair
Depression
Apostasy

DEMONIC INVOLVEMENT AND CARNALITY

PUBLIC TRUST AND CONFIDENCE

The entire Christian life is made up of one transition after another. Romans 8:29 says that God the Father is committed to conforming us to the likeness of His Son. This transformation occurs in the realm of our character. God the Father is concerned that we bear the image of His Son. Just as God is committed to our change in character, so we must be seeking changes in our attitudes and behavior.

The apostle Peter reminds us that we are aliens and strangers on this earth (1 Peter 2:11). We are, spiritually speaking, foreigners on this earth and citizens of heaven. We are awaiting the fulfillment of our hope in Jesus Christ our Redeemer. As the old gospel song says, "This world is not my home, I'm just a'passin through."

We live in a transitional time. It's hard to operate in transition. It's sometimes very confusing and occasionally downright irritating. We are like Paul, who said, "I am torn between the two: I desire to depart and be with Christ, which is better by far; but it is more necessary for you that I remain in the body" (Philippians 1:23–24).

When we come to 1 Samuel, we will understand it better if we keep in mind that it is a book of transition. It serves as a hinge, a turning point, in the Old Testament.

The Best and Worst of Samuel

This book begins with the prophet Samuel coming on the scene. For the first 12 chapters we find Samuel leading the nation of Israel as its last judge. The people have a leader they can trust. Following their disappointment with Samson, they needed a leader of integrity, one on whom they could rely. Their hope was renewed in Samuel. Before long, Samuel was leading the people closer to God, and the nation was growing in its trust of his leadership. This confidence reached its pinnacle in chapter 12. However, this chapter also records the end of Samuel's ministry. At this time Saul entered the scene, and it wasn't long before we see public trust and confidence begin to decline. Saul remained the king of Israel throughout the rest of this book of Scripture . . . and each chapter takes us lower and lower in our opinion of Saul—who in the end took his own life. What a study in tragedy!

First, let's look at Samuel. His birth was unique. His mother's name was Hannah; the name means "grace." Hannah was a woman of deep faith. She was barren, which was just about the worst stigma a Hebrew wife could live with. Hannah made a promise to God that if He would give her a son, she would consecrate that child to holy service all the days of his life. God honored her prayer, and she literally gave her son back to God.

Those parents who have the greatest difficulty letting go of their children are often the ones who have never surrendered their children to God. Please understand that this doesn't mean we release the responsibility of rearing, discipling, training, educating, and all the other responsibilities that God calls us to undertake as parents. It means that throughout the process we realize that *our children are the Lord's.*

When Hannah had weaned Samuel, she took him to the house of the Lord and placed him in the care of Eli. You might imagine, "What a terrific place to grow up . . . living with a great priest and his family!" But it wasn't such an ideal place after all. There was a scandalous problem of immorality that grew to embarrassing extremes in the lives of Eli's sons. Eli responded passively to his sons' evil ways. He did little to correct their rebellious lives. God spoke to Samuel and told him what He was going to do to the family of Eli. Ultimately He brought judgment to Eli's family for the wickedness of his sons and for Eli's unwillingness to discipline them.

Parents who read these words, take heart. Keep setting the standard of godliness for your children. Continue to stand your ground on issues of right and wrong. How you administer discipline will certainly need to flex as your children grow older. But always remember this: *Just as you need to love and affirm your children, you must also discipline your children.* They need to know you love them enough to set clear boundaries. It will give them security. Tremendous insecurity grows in the lives of children who grow up without boundaries that are firmly and consistently respected.

In spite of the unhealthy environment in which Samuel found himself, he remained pure. Be sure to note, however, the area of weakness that had crept into Samuel's life (see chapter 8). When Samuel was old, he appointed his sons as judges over Israel. Samuel hoped that his boys would carry on the priestly ministry in his place. His sons, however, were not that different from Eli's. They did not walk in God's ways either. The people, therefore, did not want Samuel's sons to lead the nation, because they did not walk with God as their father Samuel had. Instead, they wanted Samuel to appoint a king over Israel. And so . . . the transition from judges to kings took place.

From Judges to Kings

If we look discerningly at verses 4 and 5 of chapter 8, we find three distinct reasons why the people demanded the change in national leadership from a judge to a king:

> *So all the elders of Israel gathered together and came to Samuel at Ramah. They said to him, "You are old, and your sons do not walk in your ways; now appoint a king to lead us, such as all the other nations have."*

First reason: *Samuel was old, so he couldn't carry on the work of ministry.* Second reason: *Samuel's sons were corrupt, and therefore they were disqualified from priestly service.* Third reason: *The people wanted to be like all the other nations.*

Samuel was deeply disappointed with their request, so he brought it before the Lord. The Lord responded with these words: "Listen to all that the people are saying to you; it is not you they have rejected, but they have rejected me as their king" (8:7).

In the next several verses Samuel spoke to the people of Israel. In today's terms, he said, in effect, "All right. You want a king? Number one: He'll rip you off. Number two: He'll take the best of your sons and daughters and put them into slavery to feather his own nest. Number three: He will tax you to ten, twelve, fifteen, twenty percent of your income. Number four: You will live to regret the day you asked for a king. But you may have a king if you really want one. Are you really sure you want a king?" The speech didn't change their mind, so God allowed the people to have their way. They chose to be led by an earthly king rather than by a judge whom God would choose and send to them.

The Israelites chose a very impressive man. If you want to judge only by externals, Saul was the guy for the job. He had all the markings of greatness. Impressed by externals, the people were convinced that Saul was the man for the job. With a broken heart, Samuel put a crown on Saul's head and then backed away after delivering his swan song in chapter 12.

The transition was complete. Saul was now king. As he began his reign, national trust was at its highest level—not because of the new king, but because of the old judge Samuel, who had done his job faithfully. But slowly things began to change. Something like an erosion happened in the life of Saul. He couldn't handle this level of leadership. When the lights are out and nobody's around checking the books or holding a leader accountable for his or her private life—that's when character reveals itself. And guess what . . . that's where Saul blew it.

The Fall of a King

In chapters 13—15 Saul showed his true colors. He made three major mistakes. Like a batter at the plate, Saul struck out:

Saul was supposed to wait for Samuel to come as the priest and offer the sacrifice. He didn't want to wait; he was impulsive. Samuel reminded him that he was a king—not a priest. Offering the sacrifice was not for him to do. In prideful rebellion he rushed in and overstepped his bounds (13:9). *Strike one!*

A war broke out and things went badly for Israel. In the heat of the battle, *Saul made a rash vow*. You know what he said? "No one is to eat until we win the victory." Saul found out later that his son Jonathan had eaten (14:27), and so Saul prepared to kill his own son! Fortunately someone wiser than Saul restrained him and spared Jonathan's life. How would you like a leader like that? He makes a rash vow, and it almost costs the life of his own son! *Strike two!*

A short time later *Saul ignored God's command to destroy the Amalekites completely*. Saul fought the nation, but he spared the king and some of the animals and attempted to justify his disobedience (15:20—21). By the time you get to chapter 15, things had deteriorated so far that the Lord had rejected Saul as king. *Strike three . . . you're out!* When he heard God's words of rejection, Saul knew that his days were numbered. In the very next chapter God chose David to succeed Saul as king.

The sands of time have covered over this ancient scene, but our bent to disobey is still present. With this in mind, ask yourself three questions Saul should have asked before he decided to disobey the Lord: First, *has the Lord clearly led you to do something and yet you are saying "No" or "Not now"*? Maybe you're trying to bargain with Him, substituting something else in place of His clear and direct advice—like Saul did. WAIT NO LONGER—OBEY! Second, *is there within you a stubborn spirit that causes you to rebel, argue and fight back, even though you know it's against God's leading*? Perhaps you've bragged about your strong will or have cultivated the habit of resistance—like Saul did. REBEL NO MORE—OBEY! Third, *have you developed the deceitful technique of hiding your disobedience behind the human masks of lies or rationalization or manipulation or blame—like Saul did*? DECEIVE NO FURTHER—OBEY! The very best proof of your love for your Lord is obedience . . . nothing more, nothing less, nothing else.

God's Shepherd King

God called young David from tending sheep to lead His nation. David may have come from obscurity, but he had integrity. Just a country kid raised with the sheep—but he had character . . . he could be trusted. The Lord brought David to play music and help Saul out of his deep depression. While David was encouraging Saul with his music, he was also learning what it meant to be king.

Isn't it great how God can mold and shape a person? God prepared David for leadership in the kingdom by placing him in the palace where he could watch, listen and learn. He had been with the sheep all his life; he had been out in the fields since his childhood. Now he was brought into the kingdom setting for a time of preparation and training.

As recorded in chapter 17, David won a mighty victory over Goliath. Following that remarkable victory, David was instantly famous. Saul overheard the song written for David's victory. Out of jealousy, Saul tried to kill the young hero. For the remainder of 1 Samuel David showed himself strong and proved himself faithful to Saul, even though Saul tried to murder him. For years David ran from Saul. Every time Saul threw a spear at David or pursued him, David ducked, ran and hid. What he refused to do was retaliate. Again and again, David passed the integrity test with flying colors.

When Saul set his army against David and drove him into the bush like an animal, David used this time to write some of his best material. David's expression of his pain, loneliness and struggle would one day fill large sections of the book of Psalms. It is usually during the hardest times of life that we produce our best work. It is at these moments that we are most dependent on our God.

Life Lessons From 1 Samuel

Two lingering lessons live on as we compare and contrast the lives of Samuel and Saul. Lesson one: *No environmental handicap can cripple anyone whose life is touched by the hand of God.* If you have come from the lowest of the low, from the pit from which you have been dug, and have been lifted to the place where God is using you, praise God. Lesson two: *No amount of lofty, impressive qualifications can preserve anyone who willfully rejects the Word of God.* Such willful rebellion, like Saul's, results in horrible consequences.

I want to underscore this truth with absolute clarity: No amount of giftedness, training, intellectual capability, scholarship or any other human accomplishment will preserve you if you willfully reject the truth of God. It is only a matter of time before your inner erosion will lead to complete and total disarray. Let's learn from Saul what *not* to do, and let's learn from David what *to* do, as we forsake a life of pursuing our own desires and turn to a life of trusting God completely and serving Him gladly.

Birth and Call of Samuel **Chapters 1–7**

These chapters paint a beautiful picture of commitment and devotion. A godly couple named Elkanah and Hannah longed for a child, but Hannah had remained barren. In a passionate prayer of commitment, Hannah promised to give her firstborn son to the Lord for all the days of his life if only the Lord would bless her and allow her to conceive. Her prayer was answered. By and by their little boy Samuel was placed in the care of Eli, the priest of God. While Samuel was still a young boy, the Lord spoke to him and called him to a prophetic ministry. Samuel was a unique character in this time of Israel's history because he functioned in the role of judge and priest. Along the way, the Lord began to show Samuel that judgment was coming on the house of Eli because of the sin and rebellion of Eli's sons.

These chapters stand as a firm reminder that the Lord will use anyone he chooses to do His will. Although Samuel was very young, the Lord began speaking to him and leading his life. Let's remember this as we pray for our children and grandchildren. God can speak to the little ones with just as much power (sometimes more!) as when He speaks to those who are grown up. Young or old, God desires to call and lead each of us in His ways.

The Birth of Samuel

1 There was a certain man from Ramathaim, a Zuphite[a] from the hill country of Ephraim, whose name was Elkanah son of Jeroham, the son of Elihu, the son of Tohu, the son of Zuph, an Ephraimite. 2He had two wives; one was called Hannah and the other Peninnah. Peninnah had children, but Hannah had none. 1Ch 6:27,34

3Year after year this man went up from his town to worship and sacrifice to the LORD Almighty at Shiloh, where Hophni and Phinehas, the two sons of Eli, were priests of the LORD. 4Whenever the day came for Elkanah to sacrifice, he would give portions of the meat to his wife Peninnah and to all her sons and daughters. 5But to Hannah he gave a double portion because he loved her, and the LORD had closed her womb. 6And because the LORD had closed her womb, her rival kept provoking her in order to irritate her. 7This went on year after year. Whenever Hannah went up to the house of the LORD, her rival provoked her till she wept and would not eat. 8Elkanah her husband would say to her, "Hannah, why are you weeping? Why don't you eat? Why are you downhearted? Don't I mean more to you than ten sons?" Ge 16:1; Ru 4:15; Job 24:21

9Once when they had finished eating and drinking in Shiloh, Hannah stood up. Now Eli the priest was sitting on a chair by the doorpost of the LORD's temple.[b] 10In bitterness of soul Hannah wept much and prayed to the LORD. 11And she made a vow, saying, "O LORD Almighty, if you will only look upon your servant's misery and remember me, and not forget your servant but give her a son, then I will give him to the LORD for all the days of his life, and no razor will ever be used on his head." Nu 6:1-21; Jdg 13:5; 1Sa 3:3

12As she kept on praying to the LORD, Eli observed her mouth. 13Hannah was praying in her heart, and her lips were moving but her voice was not heard. Eli thought she was drunk 14and said to her, "How long will you keep on getting drunk? Get rid of your wine."

15"Not so, my lord," Hannah replied, "I am a woman who is deeply troubled. I have not been drinking wine or beer; I was pouring out my soul to the LORD. 16Do not take your servant for a wicked woman; I have been praying here out of my great anguish and grief." Ps 42:4; 62:8

17Eli answered, "Go in peace, and may the God of Israel grant you what you have asked of him."

18She said, "May your servant find favor in your eyes." Then she went her way and ate something, and her face was no longer downcast. Ru 2:13

19Early the next morning they arose and worshiped before the LORD and then went back to their home at Ramah. Elkanah lay with Hannah his wife, and the LORD remembered her. 20So in the course of time Hannah conceived and gave birth to a son. She named him Samuel,[c] saying, "Because I asked the LORD for him." Ge 30:22; Ex 2:10,22

Hannah Dedicates Samuel

21When the man Elkanah went up with all his family to offer the annual sacrifice to the LORD and to fulfill his vow, 22Hannah did not go. She said to her husband, "After the boy is weaned, I will take him and present him before the LORD, and he will live there always." Dt 12:11; Lk 2:22

23"Do what seems best to you," Elkanah her husband told her. "Stay here until you have weaned him; only may the LORD make good his[d] word." So the woman stayed at home and nursed her son until she had weaned him. Nu 30:7

24After he was weaned, she took the boy with her, young as he was, along with a three-year-old bull,[e] an ephah[f] of flour and a skin of wine, and brought him to the house of the LORD at Shiloh. 25When they had slaughtered the bull, they brought the boy to Eli, 26and she said to him, "As surely as you live, my lord, I am the woman who stood here beside you praying to the LORD. 27I prayed for this child, and the LORD has granted me what I asked of him. 28So now I give him to the LORD. For his whole life he will be given over to the LORD." And he worshiped the LORD there.

[a] *1* Or *from Ramathaim Zuphim* [b] *9* That is, tabernacle [c] *20* *Samuel* sounds like the Hebrew for *heard of God.* [d] *23* Masoretic Text; Dead Sea Scrolls, Septuagint and Syriac *your* [e] *24* Dead Sea Scrolls, Septuagint and Syriac; Masoretic Text *with three bulls* [f] *24* That is, probably about 3/5 bushel (about 22 liters)

HANNAH

A Mother, A Baby and God's Plan

"So in the course of time Hannah conceived and gave birth to a son. She named him Samuel, saying, 'Because I asked the LORD for him.'"
—1 SAMUEL 1:20

What in the world could an ancient Jewish book out of an ancient Bible have to do with life in our modern era? You may be surprised. The similarities are nothing short of amazing, and they are no more pronounced than in this first chapter of 1 Samuel. How many couples don't pray as Hannah did—that the Lord would provide them a child? Their desire comes, as did Hannah's, from the deepest places of the heart.

Hannah was the wife of a man named Elkanah. Actually she was the first of two wives, if they are named in the order of marriage. She shared her husband with a woman named Peninnah, a woman who "had children, but Hannah had none" (1 Samuel 1:2). Why? Because "the LORD had closed her womb" (1:5). Who or what is responsible for the conception of a child? Two individuals? A biological process? A sudden burst of passion? No. The writer stated it twice (verses 5 and 6): God is the One who's responsible.

In Hannah's day the stigma of childlessness was next to adultery—it was, simply stated, one of the worst afflictions a Jewish woman could bear. And Peninnah made sure Hannah recalled that pain on a regular basis. Perhaps it was because she saw that Hannah had a happy and harmonious relationship with Elkanah. Perhaps she was jealous. Whatever the reason, the constant provocation took its toll on Hannah.

I'm impressed with Hannah's response to her distress. Look carefully: "In bitterness of soul Hannah wept much and prayed to the LORD" (1:10). And her constant prayer was one of submission to God's mercy, pleading with Him and trusting in His sovereign plan for her life.

Read on and pause at verse 20 of chapter 1. It's awe-inspiring: "In the course of time Hannah conceived and gave birth to a son." That's another way of saying, "In God's time." Is God aware of seemingly insignificant things like this one barren woman's plight? Does He know about unhappy home situations? Does He hear when people cry out to Him for help? Yes. Yes, He does! The Lord hears. At the time, whatever we are enduring is so painful, so inconvenient. Why would Hannah have to wait and look on in regret and shame while Peninnah conceived and gave birth to child after child? Good question. But remember this: The Lord was responsible for what happened in Hannah's life—*and God's timing is perfect*!

Hannah named her son Samuel, meaning literally, "heard of God." What a perfect name for this child! Through God's gift to her of that precious son, Hannah testified that God hears and answers prayer. Then she lived up to her promise, bringing Samuel to the temple and giving him to another to raise. She passed the boy into the hands of Eli, the priest (1:24–28).

Have you been able to follow the pattern of response modeled in Hannah's life? First, she poured out her heart to the Lord. Second, she waited on the Lord to work. Third, she accepted this child as a gift from the Lord. Fourth, she gave the boy a name that reflected the joy brought about by his conception and subsequent birth. Finally, she dedicated him for lifelong service to God (1:22); she gave him back to God.

As you consider Hannah's experience, remember and give thanks for another birth that surprised all the world—and still surprises people today. This One who was born nearly 2,000 years ago was conceived by the Holy Spirit in the womb of a virgin (see Matthew 1:20–22). Most of the critics of His day saw Him as nothing but an illegitimate child; yet that miraculous conception protected Him from the stain of sin. Isn't it interesting that Jesus, the Savior of the world, was born in that most unexpected manner? This God-Man, who to this day captures the hearts of more people than anyone who has ever lived, came to the world in God's perfect timing—to restore us to right relationship with Him (see Galatians 4:4–5).

Hannah's Prayer

2 Then Hannah prayed and said: Lk 1:46-55

"My heart rejoices in the LORD;
in the LORD my horn[a] is lifted high.
My mouth boasts over my enemies,
for I delight in your deliverance.

2"There is no one holy[b] like the LORD; Ex 15:11
there is no one besides you;
there is no Rock like our God. Dt 32:30-31

3"Do not keep talking so proudly
or let your mouth speak such arrogance,
for the LORD is a God who knows,
and by him deeds are weighed. 1Sa 16:7
4"The bows of the warriors are broken, Ps 37:15
but those who stumbled are armed with
strength.
5Those who were full hire themselves out for
food,
but those who were hungry hunger no
more.
She who was barren has borne seven children,
but she who has had many sons pines
away. Ps 113:9; Jer 15:9
6"The LORD brings death and makes alive;
he brings down to the grave[c] and raises
up.
7The LORD sends poverty and wealth;
he humbles and he exalts. Ps 75:7
8He raises the poor from the dust
and lifts the needy from the ash heap;
he seats them with princes
and has them inherit a throne of honor.
"For the foundations of the earth are the
LORD's;
upon them he has set the world. Job 38:4
9He will guard the feet of his saints, Ps 91:12
but the wicked will be silenced in darkness.

"It is not by strength that one prevails;
10 those who oppose the LORD will be
shattered. Ex 15:6; Ps 2:9
He will thunder against them from heaven;
the LORD will judge the ends of the earth.

"He will give strength to his king
and exalt the horn of his anointed." Ps 89:24

11Then Elkanah went home to Ramah, but the
boy ministered before the LORD under Eli the
priest. 1Sa 3:1

Eli's Wicked Sons

12Eli's sons were wicked men; they had no regard for the LORD. 13Now it was the practice of the
priests with the people that whenever anyone offered a sacrifice and while the meat was being
boiled, the servant of the priest would come with
a three-pronged fork in his hand. 14He would
plunge it into the pan or kettle or caldron or pot,
and the priest would take for himself whatever the
fork brought up. This is how they treated all the
Israelites who came to Shiloh. 15But even before
the fat was burned, the servant of the priest would
come and say to the man who was sacrificing,
"Give the priest some meat to roast; he won't accept boiled meat from you, but only raw."
16If the man said to him, "Let the fat be burned
up first, and then take whatever you want," the
servant would then answer, "No, hand it over now;
if you don't, I'll take it by force."
17This sin of the young men was very great in
the LORD's sight, for they[d] were treating the
LORD's offering with contempt. Mal 2:7-9
18But Samuel was ministering before the
LORD—a boy wearing a linen ephod. 19Each year
his mother made him a little robe and took it to
him when she went up with her husband to offer
the annual sacrifice. 20Eli would bless Elkanah and
his wife, saying, "May the LORD give you children
by this woman to take the place of the one she
prayed for and gave to the LORD." Then they
would go home. 21And the LORD was gracious to
Hannah; she conceived and gave birth to three
sons and two daughters. Meanwhile, the boy Samuel grew up in the presence of the LORD. Ge 21:1
22Now Eli, who was very old, heard about everything his sons were doing to all Israel and how
they slept with the women who served at the entrance to the Tent of Meeting. 23So he said to them,
"Why do you do such things? I hear from all the
people about these wicked deeds of yours. 24No,
my sons; it is not a good report that I hear spreading among the LORD's people. 25If a man sins
against another man, God[e] may mediate for him;
but if a man sins against the LORD, who will intercede for him?" His sons, however, did not listen to
their father's rebuke, for it was the LORD's will to
put them to death. Ex 38:8; Nu 15:30; Jos 11:20
26And the boy Samuel continued to grow in
stature and in favor with the LORD and with men.

Prophecy Against the House of Eli

27Now a man of God came to Eli and said to
him, "This is what the LORD says: 'Did I not clearly
reveal myself to your father's house when they
were in Egypt under Pharaoh? 28I chose your father out of all the tribes of Israel to be my priest,
to go up to my altar, to burn incense, and to wear
an ephod in my presence. I also gave your father's
house all the offerings made with fire by the Israel-

[a] 1 *Horn* here symbolizes strength; also in verse 10. [b] 2 Or *no Holy One* [c] 6 Hebrew *Sheol* [d] 17 Or *men*
[e] 25 Or *the judges*

ites. 29Why do you[a] scorn my sacrifice and offering that I prescribed for my dwelling? Why do you honor your sons more than me by fattening yourselves on the choice parts of every offering made by my people Israel?' Ex 4:14-16; 28:1; Dt 12:5

30"Therefore the LORD, the God of Israel, declares: 'I promised that your house and your father's house would minister before me forever.' But now the LORD declares: 'Far be it from me! Those who honor me I will honor, but those who despise me will be disdained. 31The time is coming when I will cut short your strength and the strength of your father's house, so that there will not be an old man in your family line 32and you will see distress in my dwelling. Although good will be done to Israel, in your family line there will never be an old man. 33Every one of you that I do not cut off from my altar will be spared only to blind your eyes with tears and to grieve your heart, and all your descendants will die in the prime of life. Ex 29:9; 1Sa 4:11-18; Zec 8:4

34" 'And what happens to your two sons, Hophni and Phinehas, will be a sign to you—they will both die on the same day. 35I will raise up for myself a faithful priest, who will do according to what is in my heart and mind. I will firmly establish his house, and he will minister before my anointed one always. 36Then everyone left in your family line will come and bow down before him for a piece of silver and a crust of bread and plead, "Appoint me to some priestly office so I can have food to eat." ' " 1Sa 4:11; 2Sa 7:11,27; 1Ki 11:38

The LORD Calls Samuel

3 The boy Samuel ministered before the LORD under Eli. In those days the word of the LORD was rare; there were not many visions. Ps 74:9

2One night Eli, whose eyes were becoming so weak that he could barely see, was lying down in his usual place. 3The lamp of God had not yet gone out, and Samuel was lying down in the temple[b] of the LORD, where the ark of God was. 4Then the LORD called Samuel. Lev 24:1-4; 1Sa 4:15

Samuel answered, "Here I am." 5And he ran to Eli and said, "Here I am; you called me." Isa 6:8

But Eli said, "I did not call; go back and lie down." So he went and lay down.

6Again the LORD called, "Samuel!" And Samuel got up and went to Eli and said, "Here I am; you called me."

"My son," Eli said, "I did not call; go back and lie down."

7Now Samuel did not yet know the LORD: The word of the LORD had not yet been revealed to him. Ac 19:12

8The LORD called Samuel a third time, and Samuel got up and went to Eli and said, "Here I am; you called me."

Then Eli realized that the LORD was calling the boy. 9So Eli told Samuel, "Go and lie down, and if he calls you, say, 'Speak, LORD, for your servant is listening.' " So Samuel went and lay down in his place.

10The LORD came and stood there, calling as at the other times, "Samuel! Samuel!"

Then Samuel said, "Speak, for your servant is listening."

11And the LORD said to Samuel: "See, I am about to do something in Israel that will make the ears of everyone who hears of it tingle. 12At that time I will carry out against Eli everything I spoke against his family—from beginning to end. 13For I told him that I would judge his family forever because of the sin he knew about; his sons made themselves contemptible,[c] and he failed to restrain them. 14Therefore, I swore to the house of Eli, 'The guilt of Eli's house will never be atoned for by sacrifice or offering.' " 1Sa 2:27-36; 2Ki 21:12

15Samuel lay down until morning and then opened the doors of the house of the LORD. He was afraid to tell Eli the vision, 16but Eli called him and said, "Samuel, my son."

Samuel answered, "Here I am."

17"What was it he said to you?" Eli asked. "Do not hide it from me. May God deal with you, be it ever so severely, if you hide from me anything he told you." 18So Samuel told him everything, hiding nothing from him. Then Eli said, "He is the LORD; let him do what is good in his eyes." 2Sa 3:35

19The LORD was with Samuel as he grew up, and he let none of his words fall to the ground. 20And all Israel from Dan to Beersheba recognized that Samuel was attested as a prophet of the LORD. 21The LORD continued to appear at Shiloh, and there he revealed himself to Samuel through his word. Ge 39:2; 1Sa 9:6; 2:21

4 And Samuel's word came to all Israel.

The Philistines Capture the Ark

Now the Israelites went out to fight against the Philistines. The Israelites camped at Ebenezer, and the Philistines at Aphek. 2The Philistines deployed their forces to meet Israel, and as the battle spread, Israel was defeated by the Philistines, who killed about four thousand of them on the battlefield. 3When the soldiers returned to camp, the elders of Israel asked, "Why did the LORD bring defeat upon us today before the Philistines? Let us bring the ark of the LORD's covenant from Shiloh, so that it[d] may go with us and save us from the hand of our enemies." Nu 10:35; Jos 7:7; 1Sa 7:12

4So the people sent men to Shiloh, and they

[a]29 The Hebrew is plural. [b]3 That is, tabernacle [c]13 Masoretic Text; an ancient Hebrew scribal tradition and Septuagint *sons blasphemed God* [d]3 Or *he*

brought back the ark of the covenant of the LORD Almighty, who is enthroned between the cherubim. And Eli's two sons, Hophni and Phinehas, were there with the ark of the covenant of God.

5When the ark of the LORD's covenant came into the camp, all Israel raised such a great shout that the ground shook. 6Hearing the uproar, the Philistines asked, "What's all this shouting in the Hebrew camp?" Jos 6:5,10

When they learned that the ark of the LORD had come into the camp, 7the Philistines were afraid. "A god has come into the camp," they said. "We're in trouble! Nothing like this has happened before. 8Woe to us! Who will deliver us from the hand of these mighty gods? They are the gods who struck the Egyptians with all kinds of plagues in the desert. 9Be strong, Philistines! Be men, or you will be subject to the Hebrews, as they have been to you. Be men, and fight!" Ex 15:14; Jdg 13:1; 1Co 16:13

10So the Philistines fought, and the Israelites were defeated and every man fled to his tent. The slaughter was very great; Israel lost thirty thousand foot soldiers. 11The ark of God was captured, and Eli's two sons, Hophni and Phinehas, died.

Death of Eli

12That same day a Benjamite ran from the battle line and went to Shiloh, his clothes torn and dust on his head. 13When he arrived, there was Eli sitting on his chair by the side of the road, watching, because his heart feared for the ark of God. When the man entered the town and told what had happened, the whole town sent up a cry. Jos 7:6; 2Sa 1:2

14Eli heard the outcry and asked, "What is the meaning of this uproar?"

The man hurried over to Eli, 15who was ninety-eight years old and whose eyes were set so that he could not see. 16He told Eli, "I have just come from the battle line; I fled from it this very day."

Eli asked, "What happened, my son?"

17The man who brought the news replied, "Israel fled before the Philistines, and the army has suffered heavy losses. Also your two sons, Hophni and Phinehas, are dead, and the ark of God has been captured."

18When he mentioned the ark of God, Eli fell backward off his chair by the side of the gate. His neck was broken and he died, for he was an old man and heavy. He had led[a] Israel forty years.

19His daughter-in-law, the wife of Phinehas, was pregnant and near the time of delivery. When she heard the news that the ark of God had been captured and that her father-in-law and her husband were dead, she went into labor and gave birth, but was overcome by her labor pains. 20As she was dying, the women attending her said, "Don't despair; you have given birth to a son." But she did not respond or pay any attention.

21She named the boy Ichabod,[b] saying, "The glory has departed from Israel"—because of the capture of the ark of God and the deaths of her father-in-law and her husband. 22She said, "The glory has departed from Israel, for the ark of God has been captured." Ps 106:20

The Ark in Ashdod and Ekron

5 After the Philistines had captured the ark of God, they took it from Ebenezer to Ashdod. 2Then they carried the ark into Dagon's temple and set it beside Dagon. 3When the people of Ashdod rose early the next day, there was Dagon, fallen on his face on the ground before the ark of the LORD! They took Dagon and put him back in his place. 4But the following morning when they rose, there was Dagon, fallen on his face on the ground before the ark of the LORD! His head and hands had been broken off and were lying on the threshold; only his body remained. 5That is why to this day neither the priests of Dagon nor any others who enter Dagon's temple at Ashdod step on the threshold. Jdg 16:23; Isa 46:7; Eze 6:6

6The LORD's hand was heavy upon the people of Ashdod and its vicinity; he brought devastation upon them and afflicted them with tumors.[c] 7When the men of Ashdod saw what was happening, they said, "The ark of the god of Israel must not stay here with us, because his hand is heavy upon us and upon Dagon our god." 8So they called together all the rulers of the Philistines and asked them, "What shall we do with the ark of the god of Israel?" Ex 9:3; Ps 78:66; 1Sa 6:5

They answered, "Have the ark of the god of Israel moved to Gath." So they moved the ark of the God of Israel.

9But after they had moved it, the LORD's hand was against that city, throwing it into a great panic. He afflicted the people of the city, both young and old, with an outbreak of tumors.[d] 10So they sent the ark of God to Ekron. 1Sa 7:13

As the ark of God was entering Ekron, the people of Ekron cried out, "They have brought the ark of the god of Israel around to us to kill us and our people." 11So they called together all the rulers of the Philistines and said, "Send the ark of the god of Israel away; let it go back to its own place, or it[e] will kill us and our people." For death had filled the city with panic; God's hand was very heavy upon it. 12Those who did not die were afflicted with tumors, and the outcry of the city went up to heaven. 1Sa 4:8

[a] 18 Traditionally *judged* [b] 21 *Ichabod* means *no glory.* [c] 6 Hebrew; Septuagint and Vulgate *tumors. And rats appeared in their land, and death and destruction were throughout the city* [d] 9 Or *with tumors in the groin* (see Septuagint) [e] 11 Or *he*

The Ark Returned to Israel

6 When the ark of the LORD had been in Philistine territory seven months, 2the Philistines called for the priests and the diviners and said, "What shall we do with the ark of the LORD? Tell us how we should send it back to its place."

3They answered, "If you return the ark of the god of Israel, do not send it away empty, but by all means send a guilt offering to him. Then you will be healed, and you will know why his hand has not been lifted from you." Ex 23:15; Lev 5:15; Dt 16:16

4The Philistines asked, "What guilt offering should we send to him?"

They replied, "Five gold tumors and five gold rats, according to the number of the Philistine rulers, because the same plague has struck both you and your rulers. 5Make models of the tumors and of the rats that are destroying the country, and pay honor to Israel's god. Perhaps he will lift his hand from you and your gods and your land. 6Why do you harden your hearts as the Egyptians and Pharaoh did? When he[a] treated them harshly, did they not send the Israelites out so they could go on their way? Ex 12:31,33; Jos 7:19; 13:3

7"Now then, get a new cart ready, with two cows that have calved and have never been yoked. Hitch the cows to the cart, but take their calves away and pen them up. 8Take the ark of the LORD and put it on the cart, and in a chest beside it put the gold objects you are sending back to him as a guilt offering. Send it on its way, 9but keep watching it. If it goes up to its own territory, toward Beth Shemesh, then the LORD has brought this great disaster on us. But if it does not, then we will know that it was not his hand that struck us and that it happened to us by chance." 2Sa 6:3; Nu 19:2; Jos 15:10

10So they did this. They took two such cows and hitched them to the cart and penned up their calves. 11They placed the ark of the LORD on the cart and along with it the chest containing the gold rats and the models of the tumors. 12Then the cows went straight up toward Beth Shemesh, keeping on the road and lowing all the way; they did not turn to the right or to the left. The rulers of the Philistines followed them as far as the border of Beth Shemesh.

13Now the people of Beth Shemesh were harvesting their wheat in the valley, and when they looked up and saw the ark, they rejoiced at the sight. 14The cart came to the field of Joshua of Beth Shemesh, and there it stopped beside a large rock. The people chopped up the wood of the cart and sacrificed the cows as a burnt offering to the LORD. 15The Levites took down the ark of the LORD, together with the chest containing the gold objects, and placed them on the large rock. On that day the people of Beth Shemesh offered burnt offerings and made sacrifices to the LORD. 16The five rulers of the Philistines saw all this and then returned that same day to Ekron. 2Sa 24:22; 1Ki 19:21

17These are the gold tumors the Philistines sent as a guilt offering to the LORD—one each for Ashdod, Gaza, Ashkelon, Gath and Ekron. 18And the number of the gold rats was according to the number of Philistine towns belonging to the five rulers—the fortified towns with their country villages. The large rock, on which[b] they set the ark of the LORD, is a witness to this day in the field of Joshua of Beth Shemesh.

19But God struck down some of the men of Beth Shemesh, putting seventy[c] of them to death because they had looked into the ark of the LORD. The people mourned because of the heavy blow the LORD had dealt them, 20and the men of Beth Shemesh asked, "Who can stand in the presence of the LORD, this holy God? To whom will the ark go up from here?" Ex 19:21; Lev 11:45; Mal 3:2

21Then they sent messengers to the people of Kiriath Jearim, saying, "The Philistines have returned the ark of the LORD. Come down and take

7 it up to your place." 1So the men of Kiriath Jearim came and took up the ark of the LORD. They took it to Abinadab's house on the hill and consecrated Eleazar his son to guard the ark of the LORD. 2Sa 6:3

Samuel Subdues the Philistines at Mizpah

2It was a long time, twenty years in all, that the ark remained at Kiriath Jearim, and all the people of Israel mourned and sought after the LORD. 3And Samuel said to the whole house of Israel, "If you are returning to the LORD with all your hearts, then rid yourselves of the foreign gods and the Ashtoreths and commit yourselves to the LORD and serve him only, and he will deliver you out of the hand of the Philistines." 4So the Israelites put away their Baals and Ashtoreths, and served the LORD only.

5Then Samuel said, "Assemble all Israel at Mizpah and I will intercede with the LORD for you." 6When they had assembled at Mizpah, they drew water and poured it out before the LORD. On that day they fasted and there they confessed, "We have sinned against the LORD." And Samuel was leader[d] of Israel at Mizpah. Jdg 10:10; Ne 9:1; La 2:19

7When the Philistines heard that Israel had assembled at Mizpah, the rulers of the Philistines came up to attack them. And when the Israelites heard of it, they were afraid because of the Philistines. 8They said to Samuel, "Do not stop crying out to the LORD our God for us, that he may rescue us from the hand of the Philistines." 9Then Samuel took a suckling lamb and offered it up as a whole

[a] 6 That is, God
[b] 18 A few Hebrew manuscripts (see also Septuagint); most Hebrew manuscripts *villages as far as Greater Abel, where*
[c] 19 A few Hebrew manuscripts; most Hebrew manuscripts and Septuagint *50,070*
[d] 6 Traditionally *judge*

burnt offering to the LORD. He cried out to the LORD on Israel's behalf, and the LORD answered him. 1Sa 17:11; Isa 37:4; Ps 99:6

10While Samuel was sacrificing the burnt offering, the Philistines drew near to engage Israel in battle. But that day the LORD thundered with loud thunder against the Philistines and threw them into such a panic that they were routed before the Israelites. 11The men of Israel rushed out of Mizpah and pursued the Philistines, slaughtering them along the way to a point below Beth Car.

12Then Samuel took a stone and set it up between Mizpah and Shen. He named it Ebenezer,[a] saying, "Thus far has the LORD helped us." 13So the Philistines were subdued and did not invade Israelite territory again. Jos 4:9; Jdg 13:1,5; 1Sa 13:5

Throughout Samuel's lifetime, the hand of the LORD was against the Philistines. 14The towns from Ekron to Gath that the Philistines had captured from Israel were restored to her, and Israel delivered the neighboring territory from the power of the Philistines. And there was peace between Israel and the Amorites.

15Samuel continued as judge over Israel all the days of his life. 16From year to year he went on a circuit from Bethel to Gilgal to Mizpah, judging Israel in all those places. 17But he always went back to Ramah, where his home was, and there he also judged Israel. And he built an altar there to the LORD. 1Sa 12:11; Jdg 21:4

Israel's First King **Chapters 8–11**

As Samuel grew older, the people of Israel became determined that he anoint a king to rule over them. They wanted a king like all the other nations had. They desired a leader who could wear a crown and sit on a throne. It seemed like the right thing to do . . . after all, everyone else had a king! Samuel did everything he could to discourage the people from this course of action. As they insisted, the Lord told Samuel to offer them what they wanted but also to warn them about the consequences that would accompany their decision to enthrone a human king. In spite of those warnings, their voices prevailed; Saul was anointed as the first king of Israel. He was a full head taller than anyone else, and he appeared to have all the essential requirements to rule the nation. He was your basic "tall, dark and handsome" ruler. But, as we learn with time, looks can be deceiving.

Israel Asks for a King

8 When Samuel grew old, he appointed his sons as judges for Israel. 2The name of his firstborn was Joel and the name of his second was Abijah, and they served at Beersheba. 3But his sons did not walk in his ways. They turned aside after dishonest gain and accepted bribes and perverted justice. Dt 16:18-19; Ps 15:5

4So all the elders of Israel gathered together and came to Samuel at Ramah. 5They said to him, "You are old, and your sons do not walk in your ways; now appoint a king to lead[b] us, such as all the other nations have." Dt 17:14-20; 1Sa 7:17

6But when they said, "Give us a king to lead us," this displeased Samuel; so he prayed to the LORD. 7And the LORD told him: "Listen to all that the people are saying to you; it is not you they have rejected, but they have rejected me as their king. 8As they have done from the day I brought them up out of Egypt until this day, forsaking me and serving other gods, so they are doing to you. 9Now listen to them; but warn them solemnly and let them know what the king who will reign over them will do." Ex 16:8; 1Sa 10:19; 15:11

10Samuel told all the words of the LORD to the people who were asking him for a king. 11He said, "This is what the king who will reign over you will do: He will take your sons and make them serve with his chariots and horses, and they will run in front of his chariots. 12Some he will assign to be commanders of thousands and commanders of fifties, and others to plow his ground and reap his harvest, and still others to make weapons of war and equipment for his chariots. 13He will take your daughters to be perfumers and cooks and bakers. 14He will take the best of your fields and vineyards and olive groves and give them to his attendants. 15He will take a tenth of your grain and of your vintage and give it to his officials and attendants. 16Your menservants and maidservants and the best of your cattle[c] and donkeys he will take for his own use. 17He will take a tenth of your flocks, and you yourselves will become his slaves. 18When that day comes, you will cry out for relief from the king you have chosen, and the LORD will not answer you in that day." 1Sa 14:52; 1Ki 21:7,15; Mic 3:4

19But the people refused to listen to Samuel. "No!" they said. "We want a king over us. 20Then we will be like all the other nations, with a king to lead us and to go out before us and fight our battles." Isa 66:4; Jer 44:16

21When Samuel heard all that the people said, he repeated it before the LORD. 22The LORD answered, "Listen to them and give them a king."

Then Samuel said to the men of Israel, "Everyone go back to his town."

Samuel Anoints Saul

9 There was a Benjamite, a man of standing, whose name was Kish son of Abiel, the son of Zeror, the son of Becorath, the son of Aphiah of Benjamin. 2He had a son named Saul, an impressive young man without equal among the Israelites—a head taller than any of the others.

3Now the donkeys belonging to Saul's father

[a] 12 *Ebenezer* means *stone of help.* [b] 5 Traditionally *judge*; also in verses 6 and 20 [c] 16 Septuagint; Hebrew *young men*

Kish were lost, and Kish said to his son Saul, "Take
one of the servants with you and go and look for
the donkeys." 4So he passed through the hill country of Ephraim and through the area around Shali-
sha, but they did not find them. They went on into
the district of Shaalim, but the donkeys were not
there. Then he passed through the territory of
Benjamin, but they did not find them. Jos 24:33
5When they reached the district of Zuph, Saul
said to the servant who was with him, "Come, let's
go back, or my father will stop thinking about the
donkeys and start worrying about us." 1Sa 10:2
6But the servant replied, "Look, in this town
there is a man of God; he is highly respected, and
everything he says comes true. Let's go there now.
Perhaps he will tell us what way to take." Dt 33:1
7Saul said to his servant, "If we go, what can we
give the man? The food in our sacks is gone. We
have no gift to take to the man of God. What do
we have?" 1Ki 14:3; 2Ki 8:8
8The servant answered him again. "Look," he
said, "I have a quarter of a shekel[a] of silver. I will
give it to the man of God so that he will tell us what
way to take." 9(Formerly in Israel, if a man went to
inquire of God, he would say, "Come, let us go to
the seer," because the prophet of today used to be
called a seer.) 2Sa 24:11; 1Ch 26:28; Isa 30:10
10"Good," Saul said to his servant. "Come, let's
go." So they set out for the town where the man of
God was.
11As they were going up the hill to the town,
they met some girls coming out to draw water, and
they asked them, "Is the seer here?"
12"He is," they answered. "He's ahead of you.
Hurry now; he has just come to our town today,
for the people have a sacrifice at the high place.
13As soon as you enter the town, you will find him
before he goes up to the high place to eat. The
people will not begin eating until he comes, because he must bless the sacrifice; afterward, those
who are invited will eat. Go up now; you should
find him about this time." Ge 31:54; Nu 28:11-15; Mt 14:19
14They went up to the town, and as they were
entering it, there was Samuel, coming toward them
on his way up to the high place.
15Now the day before Saul came, the LORD had
revealed this to Samuel: 16"About this time tomorrow I will send you a man from the land of Benjamin. Anoint him leader over my people Israel; he
will deliver my people from the hand of the Philistines. I have looked upon my people, for their cry
has reached me." Ex 3:7-9; 1Sa 10:1
17When Samuel caught sight of Saul, the LORD
said to him, "This is the man I spoke to you about;
he will govern my people." 1Sa 16:12
18Saul approached Samuel in the gateway and
asked, "Would you please tell me where the seer's
house is?"
19"I am the seer," Samuel replied. "Go up ahead
of me to the high place, for today you are to eat
with me, and in the morning I will let you go and
will tell you all that is in your heart. 20As for the
donkeys you lost three days ago, do not worry
about them; they have been found. And to whom
is all the desire of Israel turned, if not to you and
all your father's family?" 1Sa 8:5; 12:13; Ezr 6:8
21Saul answered, "But am I not a Benjamite,
from the smallest tribe of Israel, and is not my clan
the least of all the clans of the tribe of Benjamin?
Why do you say such a thing to me?" Jdg 20:35,46
22Then Samuel brought Saul and his servant
into the hall and seated them at the head of those
who were invited—about thirty in number.
23Samuel said to the cook, "Bring the piece of meat
I gave you, the one I told you to lay aside."
24So the cook took up the leg with what was on
it and set it in front of Saul. Samuel said, "Here is
what has been kept for you. Eat, because it was set
aside for you for this occasion, from the time I
said, 'I have invited guests.'" And Saul dined with
Samuel that day.
25After they came down from the high place to
the town, Samuel talked with Saul on the roof of
his house. 26They rose about daybreak and Samuel
called to Saul on the roof, "Get ready, and I will
send you on your way." When Saul got ready, he
and Samuel went outside together. 27As they were
going down to the edge of the town, Samuel said
to Saul, "Tell the servant to go on ahead of us"—
and the servant did so—"but you stay here awhile,
so that I may give you a message from God."
10 Then Samuel took a flask of oil and poured
it on Saul's head and kissed him, saying,
"Has not the LORD anointed you leader over his
inheritance?[b] 2When you leave me today, you will
meet two men near Rachel's tomb, at Zelzah on
the border of Benjamin. They will say to you, 'The
donkeys you set out to look for have been found.
And now your father has stopped thinking about
them and is worried about you. He is asking,
"What shall I do about my son?"' 2Ki 9:1,3,6; Dt 32:9
3"Then you will go on from there until you
reach the great tree of Tabor. Three men going up
to God at Bethel will meet you there. One will be
carrying three young goats, another three loaves of
bread, and another a skin of wine. 4They will greet
you and offer you two loaves of bread, which you
will accept from them. Ge 35:7-8; Pr 18:16
5"After that you will go to Gibeah of God, where
there is a Philistine outpost. As you approach the
town, you will meet a procession of prophets coming down from the high place with lyres, tambou-

[a]8 That is, about 1/10 ounce (about 3 grams) [b]1 Hebrew; Septuagint and Vulgate *over his people Israel? You will reign over the LORD's people and save them from the power of their enemies round about. And this will be a sign to you that the LORD has anointed you leader over his inheritance:*

KING SAUL

Failing to Take God Seriously

"Then Samuel took a flask of oil and poured it on Saul's head and kissed him, saying, 'Has not the LORD anointed you leader over his inheritance?' "
—1 SAMUEL 10:1

Saul is a tragic example of a man who started well but finished poorly. Like a man on a rooftop, Saul came from obscurity, reached a peak and then slid down the other side, ending his own life in misery.

When the people of Israel asked for a king, Saul seemed like a perfect fit. Saul was tall, and he was handsome. There was a mystique about him that appealed to the people. They wanted to see impressive size, good looks and outstanding image in their first king. And Saul ranked high in those areas. On top of that, he was genuinely modest (1 Samuel 9:21). So Samuel anointed Saul as king. By chapter 13 of 1 Samuel, Saul had come to the peak of the roof. He had won the people's vote. He had fought and defeated the Philistines. He had shown himself a capable warrior. Public opinion ran high—probably an 85 to 90 percent favorability rating. But as we all know, people who hold such high positions run the enormous risk of a fall. A spirit of pride, impatience, jealousy and rebellion can cause such people to defeat themselves and cause untold suffering for themselves and for those around them. Three things happened in Saul's life that halted his ascent to success and started him on the descent to failure.

First, *Saul took his circumstances seriously, but he didn't take God seriously*. Chapter 13 tells us of an irreverent act of presumption. Samuel had told King Saul to go to Gilgal and wait for him to come and sacrifice offerings to the Lord (10:8). But with the Philistines perched menacingly all around them, Saul took it upon himself to offer the sacrifice (13:9). Saul was a king, remember, not a priest. Kings had no right to offer sacrifices. But isn't it true that when you're on the downside of pride and arrogance, driven by fear and worry, you care little about roles and realms of responsibility? After all, *you're* in charge of everything! So Saul roared out his command, saying in effect, "Bring the sacrifices to me. I'll offer them on the altar."

Second, *Saul took himself seriously, but he didn't take God seriously*. Chapter 14 demonstrates how Saul's erosion continued unabated. Jonathan, Saul's son, was the one responsible for victory over the Philistines (14:14). In the heat and confusion of battle, Saul made an unwise oath: "Cursed be any man who eats food before evening comes, before I have avenged myself on my enemies!" (14:24). Why would he make such a statement? For a fairly simple reason: When you're on the downside of life, you tend to make statements that are foolish, irresponsible, and sometimes even downright dangerous. Saul refused to renounce his vow even when his own son was the one who violated his command (14:43–45). Saul let his growing ego get in the way of his devotion to his son and to his God.

Third, *Saul took the people seriously, but he didn't take God seriously*. Chapter 15 shows us the true colors of Saul's character. Saul took his army into battle against the Amalekites. But in an action completely contrary to Samuel's direct marching orders, Saul spared Agag, the king of the Amalekites, along with the best of the plunder (15:8–9). The Israelites had been commanded to leave only corpses on the ground in obedience to God. Now watch carefully: When Samuel confronted Saul, Saul passed the buck and blamed the soldiers (15:21). But Saul later admitted, "I was afraid of the people and so I gave in to them" (15:24). Saul's loyalty to God's commands had given way to shallow rationalizations.

Toward the end of his life Saul careened even further out of control. And when his life had reached the lowest point, as he lay wounded on the battlefield, he drew his sword and ended his life, the culmination of a long process of self-destruction (31:4). This man who was once mighty in battle and strong in leadership finally turned against everything he had been appointed to represent. King Saul was a man who started strong, but ended poorly. Without knowing it, this man spoke the words that could serve as his own epitaph: "Surely I have acted like a fool and have erred greatly" (26:21).

rines, flutes and harps being played before them, and they will be prophesying. 6The Spirit of the LORD will come upon you in power, and you will prophesy with them; and you will be changed into a different person. 7Once these signs are fulfilled, do whatever your hand finds to do, for God is with you. Nu 11:25; 1Sa 19:23-24; Jdg 6:12

8"Go down ahead of me to Gilgal. I will surely come down to you to sacrifice burnt offerings and fellowship offerings,[a] but you must wait seven days until I come to you and tell you what you are to do." 1Sa 11:14-15; 13:8

Saul Made King

9As Saul turned to leave Samuel, God changed Saul's heart, and all these signs were fulfilled that day. 10When they arrived at Gibeah, a procession of prophets met him; the Spirit of God came upon him in power, and he joined in their prophesying. 11When all those who had formerly known him saw him prophesying with the prophets, they asked each other, "What is this that has happened to the son of Kish? Is Saul also among the prophets?" 1Sa 19:20,24; Mt 13:54

LIVING  **INSIGHT**

God's specialty is changing people. He shapes us and changes us whichever way He pleases. When God is ready to change a heart, it gets changed, whether it's a proud king, a stubborn husband, a strong-willed athlete, one of your own family members, or you. He turns it wherever . . . wherever He wishes.

(See 1 Samuel 10:5–11.)

12A man who lived there answered, "And who is their father?" So it became a saying: "Is Saul also among the prophets?" 13After Saul stopped prophesying, he went to the high place.

14Now Saul's uncle asked him and his servant, "Where have you been?" 1Sa 14:50

"Looking for the donkeys," he said. "But when we saw they were not to be found, we went to Samuel."

15Saul's uncle said, "Tell me what Samuel said to you."

16Saul replied, "He assured us that the donkeys had been found." But he did not tell his uncle what Samuel had said about the kingship. 1Sa 9:20

17Samuel summoned the people of Israel to the LORD at Mizpah 18and said to them, "This is what the LORD, the God of Israel, says: 'I brought Israel up out of Egypt, and I delivered you from the power of Egypt and all the kingdoms that oppressed you.' 19But you have now rejected your God, who saves you out of all your calamities and distresses. And you have said, 'No, set a king over us.' So now present yourselves before the LORD by your tribes and clans." Jdg 6:8-9; 1Sa 7:5; 8:5-7

20When Samuel brought all the tribes of Israel near, the tribe of Benjamin was chosen. 21Then he brought forward the tribe of Benjamin, clan by clan, and Matri's clan was chosen. Finally Saul son of Kish was chosen. But when they looked for him, he was not to be found. 22So they inquired further of the LORD, "Has the man come here yet?"

And the LORD said, "Yes, he has hidden himself among the baggage."

23They ran and brought him out, and as he stood among the people he was a head taller than any of the others. 24Samuel said to all the people, "Do you see the man the LORD has chosen? There is no one like him among all the people."

Then the people shouted, "Long live the king!"

25Samuel explained to the people the regulations of the kingship. He wrote them down on a scroll and deposited it before the LORD. Then Samuel dismissed the people, each to his own home. 26Saul also went to his home in Gibeah, accompanied by valiant men whose hearts God had touched. 27But some troublemakers said, "How can this fellow save us?" They despised him and brought him no gifts. But Saul kept silent.

Saul Rescues the City of Jabesh

11 Nahash the Ammonite went up and besieged Jabesh Gilead. And all the men of Jabesh said to him, "Make a treaty with us, and we will be subject to you." Jdg 21:8; 1Sa 12:12

2But Nahash the Ammonite replied, "I will make a treaty with you only on the condition that I gouge out the right eye of every one of you and so bring disgrace on all Israel." Nu 16:14; 1Sa 17:26

3The elders of Jabesh said to him, "Give us seven days so we can send messengers throughout Israel; if no one comes to rescue us, we will surrender to you." 1Sa 8:4

4When the messengers came to Gibeah of Saul and reported these terms to the people, they all wept aloud. 5Just then Saul was returning from the fields, behind his oxen, and he asked, "What is wrong with the people? Why are they weeping?" Then they repeated to him what the men of Jabesh had said. 1Sa 10:5,26; Jdg 2:4; 1Sa 30:4

6When Saul heard their words, the Spirit of God came upon him in power, and he burned with anger. 7He took a pair of oxen, cut them into pieces, and sent the pieces by messengers throughout Israel, proclaiming, "This is what will be done to the oxen of anyone who does not follow Saul and Samuel." Then the terror of the LORD fell on

[a]8 Traditionally *peace offerings*

the people, and they turned out as one man. 8When Saul mustered them at Bezek, the men of Israel numbered three hundred thousand and the men of Judah thirty thousand. Jdg 3:10; 19:29; 21:5

9They told the messengers who had come, "Say to the men of Jabesh Gilead, 'By the time the sun is hot tomorrow, you will be delivered.'" When the messengers went and reported this to the men of Jabesh, they were elated. 10They said to the Ammonites, "Tomorrow we will surrender to you, and you can do to us whatever seems good to you."

11The next day Saul separated his men into three divisions; during the last watch of the night they broke into the camp of the Ammonites and slaughtered them until the heat of the day. Those who survived were scattered, so that no two of them were left together. Jdg 7:16

Saul Confirmed as King

12The people then said to Samuel, "Who was it that asked, 'Shall Saul reign over us?' Bring these men to us and we will put them to death."

13But Saul said, "No one shall be put to death today, for this day the LORD has rescued Israel."

14Then Samuel said to the people, "Come, let us go to Gilgal and there reaffirm the kingship." 15So all the people went to Gilgal and confirmed Saul as king in the presence of the LORD. There they sacrificed fellowship offerings[a] before the LORD, and Saul and all the Israelites held a great celebration.

Rebuke and Conflict — Chapters 12–14

Here the nation was enduring a tough, unstable transitional period. They had pressed for a king and had gotten their way. It became Samuel's lot to confront them—to spell out the lack of wisdom in their stubborn urgency to be like "all the other nations." They saw the foolishness in their decision after the fact (isn't that usually the way it is?). On top of dealing with their own guilt, they witnessed the Lord's sending thunder and rain that same day (12:18), which only intensified their fears.

What next? Could they go on, having blown it so badly? Wisely, they made the right request of Samuel and asked him to pray for God's mercy (12:19). There is no more significant involvement in another's life than a commitment to prevailing, consistent prayer. It is more helpful than a gift of money, more encouraging than a strong sermon, more effective than a compliment, more reassuring than a physical embrace. In the midst of national conflict and struggle, the people finally fell to their knees.

Samuel's Farewell Speech

12 Samuel said to all Israel, "I have listened to everything you said to me and have set a king over you. 2Now you have a king as your leader. As for me, I am old and gray, and my sons are here with you. I have been your leader from my youth until this day. 3Here I stand. Testify against me in the presence of the LORD and his anointed. Whose ox have I taken? Whose donkey have I taken? Whom have I cheated? Whom have I oppressed? From whose hand have I accepted a bribe to make me shut my eyes? If I have done any of these, I will make it right." 1Sa 8:7; 24:6; 2Sa 1:14

4"You have not cheated or oppressed us," they replied. "You have not taken anything from anyone's hand." Ex 22:4; Ac 23:9

5Samuel said to them, "The LORD is witness against you, and also his anointed is witness this day, that you have not found anything in my hand."

"He is witness," they said.

6Then Samuel said to the people, "It is the LORD who appointed Moses and Aaron and brought your forefathers up out of Egypt. 7Now then, stand here, because I am going to confront you with evidence before the LORD as to all the righteous acts performed by the LORD for you and your fathers. Ex 6:26; Eze 20:35; Mic 6:1-5

8"After Jacob entered Egypt, they cried to the LORD for help, and the LORD sent Moses and Aaron, who brought your forefathers out of Egypt and settled them in this place. Ex 2:23; 3:10; 4:16

9"But they forgot the LORD their God; so he sold them into the hand of Sisera, the commander of the army of Hazor, and into the hands of the Philistines and the king of Moab, who fought against them. 10They cried out to the LORD and said, 'We have sinned; we have forsaken the LORD and served the Baals and the Ashtoreths. But now deliver us from the hands of our enemies, and we will serve you.' 11Then the LORD sent Jerub-Baal,[b] Barak,[c] Jephthah and Samuel,[d] and he delivered you from the hands of your enemies on every side, so that you lived securely. Jdg 3:7; 4:2; 6:14,32

12"But when you saw that Nahash king of the Ammonites was moving against you, you said to me, 'No, we want a king to rule over us'—even though the LORD your God was your king. 13Now here is the king you have chosen, the one you asked for; see, the LORD has set a king over you. 14If you fear the LORD and serve and obey him and do not rebel against his commands, and if both you and the king who reigns over you follow the LORD your God—good! 15But if you do not obey the LORD, and if you rebel against his commands, his hand will be against you, as it was against your fathers. Jdg 8:23; Jos 24:14; Hos 13:11

16"Now then, stand still and see this great thing the LORD is about to do before your eyes! 17Is it not wheat harvest now? I will call upon the LORD to

[a] 15 Traditionally *peace offerings* [b] 11 Also called *Gideon* [d] 11 Hebrew; some Septuagint manuscripts and Syriac *Samson* [c] 11 Some Septuagint manuscripts and Syriac; Hebrew *Bedan*

send thunder and rain. And you will realize what an evil thing you did in the eyes of the LORD when you asked for a king." Ex 14:13; 1Sa 8:6-7; Pr 26:1

[18]Then Samuel called upon the LORD, and that same day the LORD sent thunder and rain. So all the people stood in awe of the LORD and of Samuel.

[19]The people all said to Samuel, "Pray to the LORD your God for your servants so that we will not die, for we have added to all our other sins the evil of asking for a king." Ex 9:28

LIVING  **INSIGHT**

When we pray for someone, we intercede. That means we mentally get involved in their world as we deliberately make contact with God on their behalf. This, admittedly, is only one aspect of prayer, but it's a mighty important one!

(See 1 Samuel 12:19.)

[20]"Do not be afraid," Samuel replied. "You have done all this evil; yet do not turn away from the LORD, but serve the LORD with all your heart. [21]Do not turn away after useless idols. They can do you no good, nor can they rescue you, because they are useless. [22]For the sake of his great name the LORD will not reject his people, because the LORD was pleased to make you his own. [23]As for me, far be it from me that I should sin against the LORD by failing to pray for you. And I will teach you the way that is good and right. [24]But be sure to fear the LORD and serve him faithfully with all your heart; consider what great things he has done for you. [25]Yet if you persist in doing evil, both you and your king will be swept away." Dt 31:6; Hab 2:18

Samuel Rebukes Saul

13 Saul was ⌞thirty⌟[a] years old when he became king, and he reigned over Israel ⌞forty-⌟[b] two years.

[2]Saul[c] chose three thousand men from Israel; two thousand were with him at Micmash and in the hill country of Bethel, and a thousand were with Jonathan at Gibeah in Benjamin. The rest of the men he sent back to their homes.

[3]Jonathan attacked the Philistine outpost at Geba, and the Philistines heard about it. Then Saul had the trumpet blown throughout the land and said, "Let the Hebrews hear!" [4]So all Israel heard the news: "Saul has attacked the Philistine outpost, and now Israel has become a stench to the Philistines." And the people were summoned to join Saul at Gilgal. 1Sa 10:5; Jdg 3:27

[5]The Philistines assembled to fight Israel, with three thousand[d] chariots, six thousand charioteers, and soldiers as numerous as the sand on the seashore. They went up and camped at Micmash, east of Beth Aven. [6]When the men of Israel saw that their situation was critical and that their army was hard pressed, they hid in caves and thickets, among the rocks, and in pits and cisterns. [7]Some Hebrews even crossed the Jordan to the land of Gad and Gilead. Jos 11:4; Jdg 6:2; Nu 32:33

Saul remained at Gilgal, and all the troops with him were quaking with fear. [8]He waited seven days, the time set by Samuel; but Samuel did not come to Gilgal, and Saul's men began to scatter. [9]So he said, "Bring me the burnt offering and the fellowship offerings.[e]" And Saul offered up the burnt offering. [10]Just as he finished making the offering, Samuel arrived, and Saul went out to greet him. 1Sa 10:8; 15:13; 2Sa 24:25

[11]"What have you done?" asked Samuel.

Saul replied, "When I saw that the men were scattering, and that you did not come at the set time, and that the Philistines were assembling at Micmash, [12]I thought, 'Now the Philistines will come down against me at Gilgal, and I have not sought the LORD's favor.' So I felt compelled to offer the burnt offering."

[13]"You acted foolishly," Samuel said. "You have not kept the command the LORD your God gave you; if you had, he would have established your kingdom over Israel for all time. [14]But now your kingdom will not endure; the LORD has sought out a man after his own heart and appointed him leader of his people, because you have not kept the LORD's command." 2Ch 16:9; Ac 7:46; 13:22

[15]Then Samuel left Gilgal[f] and went up to Gibeah in Benjamin, and Saul counted the men who were with him. They numbered about six hundred. 1Sa 14:2

Israel Without Weapons

[16]Saul and his son Jonathan and the men with them were staying in Gibeah[g] in Benjamin, while the Philistines camped at Micmash. [17]Raiding parties went out from the Philistine camp in three detachments. One turned toward Ophrah in the vicinity of Shual, [18]another toward Beth Horon, and the third toward the borderland overlooking the Valley of Zeboim facing the desert. Jos 18:23

[19]Not a blacksmith could be found in the whole land of Israel, because the Philistines had said, "Otherwise the Hebrews will make swords or

[a]1 A few late manuscripts of the Septuagint; Hebrew does not have *thirty*. [b]1 See the round number in Acts 13:21; Hebrew does not have *forty-*. [c]1,2 Or *and when he had reigned over Israel two years,* [2]*he* [d]5 Some Septuagint manuscripts and Syriac; Hebrew *thirty thousand* [e]9 Traditionally *peace offerings* [f]15 Hebrew; Septuagint *Gilgal and went his way; the rest of the people went after Saul to meet the army, and they went out of Gilgal* [g]16 Two Hebrew manuscripts; most Hebrew manuscripts *Geba,* a variant of *Gibeah*

spears!" 20So all Israel went down to the Philistines to have their plowshares, mattocks, axes and sickles[a] sharpened. 21The price was two thirds of a shekel[b] for sharpening plowshares and mattocks, and a third of a shekel[c] for sharpening forks and axes and for repointing goads. 2Ki 24:14

22So on the day of the battle not a soldier with Saul and Jonathan had a sword or spear in his hand; only Saul and his son Jonathan had them.

Jonathan Attacks the Philistines

23Now a detachment of Philistines had gone out

14 to the pass at Micmash. 1One day Jonathan son of Saul said to the young man bearing his armor, "Come, let's go over to the Philistine outpost on the other side." But he did not tell his father.

2Saul was staying on the outskirts of Gibeah under a pomegranate tree in Migron. With him were about six hundred men, 3among whom was Ahijah, who was wearing an ephod. He was a son of Ichabod's brother Ahitub son of Phinehas, the son of Eli, the LORD's priest in Shiloh. No one was aware that Jonathan had left. 1Sa 4:21; 13:15; 22:11,20

4On each side of the pass that Jonathan intended to cross to reach the Philistine outpost was a cliff; one was called Bozez, and the other Seneh. 5One cliff stood to the north toward Micmash, the other to the south toward Geba. 1Sa 13:23

6Jonathan said to his young armor-bearer, "Come, let's go over to the outpost of those uncircumcised fellows. Perhaps the LORD will act in our behalf. Nothing can hinder the LORD from saving, whether by many or by few." Jdg 7:4; 1Sa 17:46-47

7"Do all that you have in mind," his armor-bearer said. "Go ahead; I am with you heart and soul."

8Jonathan said, "Come, then; we will cross over toward the men and let them see us. 9If they say to us, 'Wait there until we come to you,' we will stay where we are and not go up to them. 10But if they say, 'Come up to us,' we will climb up, because that will be our sign that the LORD has given them into our hands." Ge 24:14; Jdg 6:36-37

11So both of them showed themselves to the Philistine outpost. "Look!" said the Philistines. "The Hebrews are crawling out of the holes they were hiding in." 12The men of the outpost shouted to Jonathan and his armor-bearer, "Come up to us and we'll teach you a lesson." 1Sa 13:6; 17:43-44

So Jonathan said to his armor-bearer, "Climb up after me; the LORD has given them into the hand of Israel." 2Sa 5:24

13Jonathan climbed up, using his hands and feet, with his armor-bearer right behind him. The Philistines fell before Jonathan, and his armor-bearer followed and killed behind him. 14In that first attack Jonathan and his armor-bearer killed some twenty men in an area of about half an acre.[d]

Israel Routs the Philistines

15Then panic struck the whole army—those in the camp and field, and those in the outposts and raiding parties—and the ground shook. It was a panic sent by God.[e] Ge 35:5; 2Ki 7:5-7; 1Sa 13:17

16Saul's lookouts at Gibeah in Benjamin saw the army melting away in all directions. 17Then Saul said to the men who were with him, "Muster the forces and see who has left us." When they did, it was Jonathan and his armor-bearer who were not there.

18Saul said to Ahijah, "Bring the ark of God." (At that time it was with the Israelites.)[f] 19While Saul was talking to the priest, the tumult in the Philistine camp increased more and more. So Saul said to the priest, "Withdraw your hand."

20Then Saul and all his men assembled and went to the battle. They found the Philistines in total confusion, striking each other with their swords. 21Those Hebrews who had previously been with the Philistines and had gone up with them to their camp went over to the Israelites who were with Saul and Jonathan. 22When all the Israelites who had hidden in the hill country of Ephraim heard that the Philistines were on the run, they joined the battle in hot pursuit. 23So the LORD rescued Israel that day, and the battle moved on beyond Beth Aven. Ex 14:30; Jdg 7:22; 1Sa 13:6

Jonathan Eats Honey

24Now the men of Israel were in distress that day, because Saul had bound the people under an oath, saying, "Cursed be any man who eats food before evening comes, before I have avenged myself on my enemies!" So none of the troops tasted food. Jos 6:26

25The entire army[g] entered the woods, and there was honey on the ground. 26When they went into the woods, they saw the honey oozing out, yet no one put his hand to his mouth, because they feared the oath. 27But Jonathan had not heard that his father had bound the people with the oath, so he reached out the end of the staff that was in his hand and dipped it into the honeycomb. He raised his hand to his mouth, and his eyes brightened.[h] 28Then one of the soldiers told him, "Your father bound the army under a strict oath, saying, 'Cursed be any man who eats food today!' That is why the men are faint." 1Sa 30:12; Ps 19:10; Pr 16:24

[a] *20* Septuagint; Hebrew *plowshares* [b] *21* Hebrew *pim*; that is, about 1/4 ounce (about 8 grams) [c] *21* That is, about 1/8 ounce (about 4 grams) [d] *14* Hebrew *half a yoke*; a "yoke" was the land plowed by a yoke of oxen in one day. [e] *15* Or *a terrible panic* [f] *18* Hebrew; Septuagint *"Bring the ephod." (At that time he wore the ephod before the Israelites.)* [g] *25* Or *Now all the people of the land* [h] *27* Or *his strength was renewed*

29Jonathan said, "My father has made trouble for the country. See how my eyes brightened[a] when I tasted a little of this honey. 30How much better it would have been if the men had eaten today some of the plunder they took from their enemies. Would not the slaughter of the Philistines have been even greater?" 1Ki 18:18

31That day, after the Israelites had struck down the Philistines from Micmash to Aijalon, they were exhausted. 32They pounced on the plunder and, taking sheep, cattle and calves, they butchered them on the ground and ate them, together with the blood. 33Then someone said to Saul, "Look, the men are sinning against the LORD by eating meat that has blood in it." Ge 9:4; Lev 17:10-14; 1Sa 15:19

"You have broken faith," he said. "Roll a large stone over here at once." 34Then he said, "Go out among the men and tell them, 'Each of you bring me your cattle and sheep, and slaughter them here and eat them. Do not sin against the LORD by eating meat with blood still in it.' "

So everyone brought his ox that night and slaughtered it there. 35Then Saul built an altar to the LORD; it was the first time he had done this.

36Saul said, "Let us go down after the Philistines by night and plunder them till dawn, and let us not leave one of them alive."

"Do whatever seems best to you," they replied.

But the priest said, "Let us inquire of God here."

37So Saul asked God, "Shall I go down after the Philistines? Will you give them into Israel's hand?" But God did not answer him that day. 1Sa 10:22

38Saul therefore said, "Come here, all you who are leaders of the army, and let us find out what sin has been committed today. 39As surely as the LORD who rescues Israel lives, even if it lies with my son Jonathan, he must die." But not one of the men said a word. 2Sa 12:5

40Saul then said to all the Israelites, "You stand over there; I and Jonathan my son will stand over here."

"Do what seems best to you," the men replied.

41Then Saul prayed to the LORD, the God of Israel, "Give me the right answer."[b] And Jonathan and Saul were taken by lot, and the men were cleared. 42Saul said, "Cast the lot between me and Jonathan my son." And Jonathan was taken.

43Then Saul said to Jonathan, "Tell me what you have done." Jos 7:19

So Jonathan told him, "I merely tasted a little honey with the end of my staff. And now must I die?"

44Saul said, "May God deal with me, be it ever so severely, if you do not die, Jonathan." Ru 1:17

45But the men said to Saul, "Should Jonathan die—he who has brought about this great deliverance in Israel? Never! As surely as the LORD lives, not a hair of his head will fall to the ground, for he did this today with God's help." So the men rescued Jonathan, and he was not put to death.

46Then Saul stopped pursuing the Philistines, and they withdrew to their own land.

47After Saul had assumed rule over Israel, he fought against their enemies on every side: Moab, the Ammonites, Edom, the kings[c] of Zobah, and the Philistines. Wherever he turned, he inflicted punishment on them.[d] 48He fought valiantly and defeated the Amalekites, delivering Israel from the hands of those who had plundered them.

Saul's Family

49Saul's sons were Jonathan, Ishvi and Malki-Shua. The name of his older daughter was Merab, and that of the younger was Michal. 50His wife's name was Ahinoam daughter of Ahimaaz. The name of the commander of Saul's army was Abner son of Ner, and Ner was Saul's uncle. 51Saul's father Kish and Abner's father Ner were sons of Abiel. 1Sa 9:1; 18:17-20; 31:2

52All the days of Saul there was bitter war with the Philistines, and whenever Saul saw a mighty or brave man, he took him into his service. 1Sa 8:11

Saul's Rejection **Chapter 15**

Plain and simple, King Saul was to carry out God's plans. He didn't. It was an open-and-shut case of divine extermination that God had laid out for Saul to accomplish. The Sovereign Lord of heaven and earth had spoken . . . and there was to be absolute, instant obedience by King Saul. There wasn't. And so? Not surprisingly, the Lord rejected Saul as king.

The LORD Rejects Saul as King

15 Samuel said to Saul, "I am the one the LORD sent to anoint you king over his people Israel; so listen now to the message from the LORD. 2This is what the LORD Almighty says: 'I will punish the Amalekites for what they did to Israel when they waylaid them as they came up from Egypt. 3Now go, attack the Amalekites and totally destroy[e] everything that belongs to them. Do not spare them; put to death men and women, children and infants, cattle and sheep, camels and donkeys.' " Ex 17:8-14; Nu 24:20; 1Sa 9:16

4So Saul summoned the men and mustered them at Telaim—two hundred thousand foot sol-

[a] 29 Or *my strength was renewed* [b] 41 Hebrew; Septuagint *"Why have you not answered your servant today? If the fault is in me or my son Jonathan, respond with Urim, but if the men of Israel are at fault, respond with Thummim."* [c] 47 Masoretic Text; Dead Sea Scrolls and Septuagint *king* [d] 47 Hebrew; Septuagint *he was victorious* [e] 3 The Hebrew term refers to the irrevocable giving over of things or persons to the LORD, often by totally destroying them; also in verses 8, 9, 15, 18, 20 and 21.

diers and ten thousand men from Judah. 5Saul
went to the city of Amalek and set an ambush in
the ravine. 6Then he said to the Kenites, "Go away,
leave the Amalekites so that I do not destroy you
along with them; for you showed kindness to all
the Israelites when they came up out of Egypt." So
the Kenites moved away from the Amalekites.

7Then Saul attacked the Amalekites all the way
from Havilah to Shur, to the east of Egypt. 8He
took Agag king of the Amalekites alive, and all his
people he totally destroyed with the sword. 9But
Saul and the army spared Agag and the best of the
sheep and cattle, the fat calves[a] and lambs—everything that was good. These they were unwilling
to destroy completely, but everything that was despised and weak they totally destroyed. Ge 16:7

10Then the word of the LORD came to Samuel:
11"I am grieved that I have made Saul king, because he has turned away from me and has not
carried out my instructions." Samuel was troubled, and he cried out to the LORD all that night.

12Early in the morning Samuel got up and went
to meet Saul, but he was told, "Saul has gone to
Carmel. There he has set up a monument in his
own honor and has turned and gone on down to
Gilgal." Jos 15:55

13When Samuel reached him, Saul said, "The
LORD bless you! I have carried out the LORD's instructions."

14But Samuel said, "What then is this bleating of
sheep in my ears? What is this lowing of cattle that
I hear?"

15Saul answered, "The soldiers brought them
from the Amalekites; they spared the best of the
sheep and cattle to sacrifice to the LORD your God,
but we totally destroyed the rest."

16"Stop!" Samuel said to Saul. "Let me tell you
what the LORD said to me last night."

"Tell me," Saul replied.

17Samuel said, "Although you were once small
in your own eyes, did you not become the head of
the tribes of Israel? The LORD anointed you king

LIVING  INSIGHT

I don't care how gifted, how capable, how eloquent you may be, how widely used in your ministry; you can always benefit from the help of someone else—to hone you, to sharpen you. Leadership requires accountability.

(See 1 Samuel 15:17–23.)

over Israel. 18And he sent you on a mission, saying, 'Go and completely destroy those wicked people, the Amalekites; make war on them until you
have wiped them out.' 19Why did you not obey the
LORD? Why did you pounce on the plunder and do
evil in the eyes of the LORD?" 1Sa 9:21; 14:32

20"But I did obey the LORD," Saul said. "I went
on the mission the LORD assigned me. I completely
destroyed the Amalekites and brought back Agag
their king. 21The soldiers took sheep and cattle
from the plunder, the best of what was devoted to
God, in order to sacrifice them to the LORD your
God at Gilgal."

22But Samuel replied:

"Does the LORD delight in burnt offerings and
sacrifices
as much as in obeying the voice of the
LORD?
To obey is better than sacrifice,
and to heed is better than the fat of rams.
23For rebellion is like the sin of divination,
and arrogance like the evil of idolatry.
Because you have rejected the word of the
LORD,
he has rejected you as king." 1Sa 13:13

24Then Saul said to Samuel, "I have sinned. I
violated the LORD's command and your instructions. I was afraid of the people and so I gave in to
them. 25Now I beg you, forgive my sin and come
back with me, so that I may worship the LORD."

26But Samuel said to him, "I will not go back
with you. You have rejected the word of the LORD,
and the LORD has rejected you as king over Israel!"

27As Samuel turned to leave, Saul caught hold of
the hem of his robe, and it tore. 28Samuel said to
him, "The LORD has torn the kingdom of Israel
from you today and has given it to one of your
neighbors—to one better than you. 29He who is
the Glory of Israel does not lie or change his mind;
for he is not a man, that he should change his
mind." Eze 24:14; 1Sa 28:17; 1Ki 11:11,31

30Saul replied, "I have sinned. But please honor
me before the elders of my people and before Israel; come back with me, so that I may worship the
LORD your God." 31So Samuel went back with Saul,
and Saul worshiped the LORD. Jn 12:43

32Then Samuel said, "Bring me Agag king of the
Amalekites."

Agag came to him confidently,[b] thinking,
"Surely the bitterness of death is past."

33But Samuel said,

"As your sword has made women childless,
so will your mother be childless among
women." Ge 9:6; Jdg 1:7

And Samuel put Agag to death before the LORD at
Gilgal.

34Then Samuel left for Ramah, but Saul went up
to his home in Gibeah of Saul. 35Until the day

[a]9 Or *the grown bulls*; the meaning of the Hebrew for this phrase is uncertain. [b]32 Or *him trembling, yet*

Samuel died, he did not go to see Saul again, though Samuel mourned for him. And the LORD was grieved that he had made Saul king over Israel.

David's Rise to Fame — Chapters 16–21

Although there were a number of events that led up to David's fame and popularity, there is one story that defined his whole life. It is the story of David's battle with a giant named Goliath. You know the outcome. With a well-worn leather sling and a smooth stone (not to mention an unbending confidence in his mighty God!), David introduced Goliath and all the Philistine hordes to the Lord of hosts, whose name they had blasphemed long enough.

To this day two timeless truths of giant warfare live on. Both are as appropriate today as they were in the days of David and Goliath. First, *prevailing over giants isn't accomplished by using our own techniques.* David's greatest piece of armor, the lethal weapon that made him unique and gave him victory, was his inner shield of faith. It kept him free from fear; it made him hard of hearing when it came to Goliath's intimidating threats; it gave him cool composure amid chaos; it cleared his vision. Second, *conquering giants isn't accomplished without great skill and discipline.* To be God's warrior, to fight according to His will and way, demands much more expertise and control than one can imagine. Using the sling and stone of the Spirit is a far more delicate thing than swinging the club of the flesh. But oh, how sweet is the victory when the stone finds its mark . . . and how complete!

Samuel Anoints David

16 The LORD said to Samuel, "How long will you mourn for Saul, since I have rejected him as king over Israel? Fill your horn with oil and be on your way; I am sending you to Jesse of Bethlehem. I have chosen one of his sons to be king." Ac 13:22; Ru 4:17; 1Sa 15:23

2But Samuel said, "How can I go? Saul will hear about it and kill me."

The LORD said, "Take a heifer with you and say, 'I have come to sacrifice to the LORD.' 3Invite Jesse to the sacrifice, and I will show you what to do. You are to anoint for me the one I indicate."

4Samuel did what the LORD said. When he arrived at Bethlehem, the elders of the town trembled when they met him. They asked, "Do you come in peace?" 1Ki 2:13; 2Ki 9:17

5Samuel replied, "Yes, in peace; I have come to sacrifice to the LORD. Consecrate yourselves and come to the sacrifice with me." Then he consecrated Jesse and his sons and invited them to the sacrifice. Ex 19:10,22

6When they arrived, Samuel saw Eliab and thought, "Surely the LORD's anointed stands here before the LORD." 1Sa 17:13

7But the LORD said to Samuel, "Do not consider his appearance or his height, for I have rejected him. The LORD does not look at the things man looks at. Man looks at the outward appearance, but the LORD looks at the heart." 1Ki 8:39; 1Ch 28:9

8Then Jesse called Abinadab and had him pass in front of Samuel. But Samuel said, "The LORD has not chosen this one either." 9Jesse then had Shammah pass by, but Samuel said, "Nor has the LORD chosen this one." 10Jesse had seven of his sons pass before Samuel, but Samuel said to him, "The LORD has not chosen these." 11So he asked Jesse, "Are these all the sons you have?" 1Sa 17:12

"There is still the youngest," Jesse answered, "but he is tending the sheep."

Samuel said, "Send for him; we will not sit down[a] until he arrives."

12So he sent and had him brought in. He was ruddy, with a fine appearance and handsome features. Ge 39:6; 1Sa 9:17

Then the LORD said, "Rise and anoint him; he is the one."

13So Samuel took the horn of oil and anointed him in the presence of his brothers, and from that day on the Spirit of the LORD came upon David in power. Samuel then went to Ramah. 1Sa 10:1,6,9-10

David in Saul's Service

14Now the Spirit of the LORD had departed from Saul, and an evil[b] spirit from the LORD tormented him. Jdg 16:20; 9:23

15Saul's attendants said to him, "See, an evil spirit from God is tormenting you. 16Let our lord command his servants here to search for someone who can play the harp. He will play when the evil spirit from God comes upon you, and you will feel better." 1Sa 18:10; 2Ki 3:15

17So Saul said to his attendants, "Find someone who plays well and bring him to me."

18One of the servants answered, "I have seen a son of Jesse of Bethlehem who knows how to play the harp. He is a brave man and a warrior. He speaks well and is a fine-looking man. And the LORD is with him." 1Sa 3:19; 17:32-37

19Then Saul sent messengers to Jesse and said, "Send me your son David, who is with the sheep." 20So Jesse took a donkey loaded with bread, a skin of wine and a young goat and sent them with his son David to Saul. 1Sa 10:27; Pr 18:16

21David came to Saul and entered his service. Saul liked him very much, and David became one of his armor-bearers. 22Then Saul sent word to Jesse, saying, "Allow David to remain in my service, for I am pleased with him." Ge 41:46; Pr 22:29

23Whenever the spirit from God came upon Saul, David would take his harp and play. Then relief would come to Saul; he would feel better, and the evil spirit would leave him. Jdg 9:23

[a] 11 Some Septuagint manuscripts; Hebrew *not gather around*

[b] 14 Or *injurious*; also in verses 15, 16 and 23

David and Goliath

17 Now the Philistines gathered their forces for war and assembled at Socoh in Judah. They pitched camp at Ephes Dammim, between Socoh and Azekah. 2Saul and the Israelites assembled and camped in the Valley of Elah and drew up their battle line to meet the Philistines. 3The Philistines occupied one hill and the Israelites another, with the valley between them. 1Sa 13:5

4A champion named Goliath, who was from Gath, came out of the Philistine camp. He was over nine feet[a] tall. 5He had a bronze helmet on his head and wore a coat of scale armor of bronze weighing five thousand shekels[b]; 6on his legs he wore bronze greaves, and a bronze javelin was slung on his back. 7His spear shaft was like a weaver's rod, and its iron point weighed six hundred shekels.[c] His shield bearer went ahead of him.

8Goliath stood and shouted to the ranks of Israel, "Why do you come out and line up for battle? Am I not a Philistine, and are you not the servants of Saul? Choose a man and have him come down to me. 9If he is able to fight and kill me, we will become your subjects; but if I overcome him and kill him, you will become our subjects and serve us." 10Then the Philistine said, "This day I defy the ranks of Israel! Give me a man and let us fight each other." 11On hearing the Philistine's words, Saul and all the Israelites were dismayed and terrified.

12Now David was the son of an Ephrathite named Jesse, who was from Bethlehem in Judah. Jesse had eight sons, and in Saul's time he was old and well advanced in years. 13Jesse's three oldest sons had followed Saul to the war: The firstborn was Eliab; the second, Abinadab; and the third, Shammah. 14David was the youngest. The three oldest followed Saul, 15but David went back and forth from Saul to tend his father's sheep at Bethlehem. 1Ch 2:13-15; Ge 35:19; 1Sa 16:6

16For forty days the Philistine came forward every morning and evening and took his stand.

17Now Jesse said to his son David, "Take this ephah[d] of roasted grain and these ten loaves of bread for your brothers and hurry to their camp. 18Take along these ten cheeses to the commander of their unit.[e] See how your brothers are and bring back some assurance[f] from them. 19They are with Saul and all the men of Israel in the Valley of Elah, fighting against the Philistines." Ge 37:14

20Early in the morning David left the flock with a shepherd, loaded up and set out, as Jesse had directed. He reached the camp as the army was going out to its battle positions, shouting the war cry. 21Israel and the Philistines were drawing up their lines facing each other. 22David left his things with the keeper of supplies, ran to the battle lines and greeted his brothers. 23As he was talking with them, Goliath, the Philistine champion from Gath, stepped out from his lines and shouted his usual defiance, and David heard it. 24When the Israelites saw the man, they all ran from him in great fear.

25Now the Israelites had been saying, "Do you see how this man keeps coming out? He comes out to defy Israel. The king will give great wealth to the man who kills him. He will also give him his daughter in marriage and will exempt his father's family from taxes in Israel." Jos 15:16; 1Sa 18:17

26David asked the men standing near him, "What will be done for the man who kills this Philistine and removes this disgrace from Israel? Who is this uncircumcised Philistine that he should defy the armies of the living God?"

27They repeated to him what they had been saying and told him, "This is what will be done for the man who kills him."

28When Eliab, David's oldest brother, heard him speaking with the men, he burned with anger at him and asked, "Why have you come down here? And with whom did you leave those few sheep in the desert? I know how conceited you are and how wicked your heart is; you came down only to watch the battle." Ge 37:4,8,11; Pr 18:19

29"Now what have I done?" said David. "Can't I even speak?" 30He then turned away to someone else and brought up the same matter, and the men answered him as before. 31What David said was overheard and reported to Saul, and Saul sent for him.

32David said to Saul, "Let no one lose heart on account of this Philistine; your servant will go and fight him." Dt 20:3; 1Sa 16:18

33Saul replied, "You are not able to go out against this Philistine and fight him; you are only a boy, and he has been a fighting man from his youth." Nu 13:31

34But David said to Saul, "Your servant has been keeping his father's sheep. When a lion or a bear came and carried off a sheep from the flock, 35I went after it, struck it and rescued the sheep from its mouth. When it turned on me, I seized it by its hair, struck it and killed it. 36Your servant has killed both the lion and the bear; this uncircumcised Philistine will be like one of them, because he has defied the armies of the living God. 37The LORD who delivered me from the paw of the lion and the paw of the bear will deliver me from the hand of this Philistine." Jer 49:19; 2Co 1:10; 2Ti 4:17

Saul said to David, "Go, and the LORD be with you." 1Sa 20:13; 1Ch 22:11,16

38Then Saul dressed David in his own tunic. He put a coat of armor on him and a bronze helmet

[a] 4 Hebrew *was six cubits and a span* (about 3 meters) [b] 5 That is, about 125 pounds (about 57 kilograms) [c] 7 That is, about 15 pounds (about 7 kilograms) [d] 17 That is, probably about 3/5 bushel (about 22 liters) [e] 18 Hebrew *thousand* [f] 18 Or *some token*; or *some pledge of spoils*

on his head. 39David fastened on his sword over the tunic and tried walking around, because he was not used to them. Ge 41:42

"I cannot go in these," he said to Saul, "because I am not used to them." So he took them off. 40Then he took his staff in his hand, chose five smooth stones from the stream, put them in the pouch of his shepherd's bag and, with his sling in his hand, approached the Philistine.

41Meanwhile, the Philistine, with his shield bearer in front of him, kept coming closer to David. 42He looked David over and saw that he was only a boy, ruddy and handsome, and he despised him. 43He said to David, "Am I a dog, that you come at me with sticks?" And the Philistine cursed David by his gods. 44"Come here," he said, "and I'll give your flesh to the birds of the air and the beasts of the field!" 1Sa 24:14; 1Ki 20:10-11; Pr 16:18

45David said to the Philistine, "You come against me with sword and spear and javelin, but I come against you in the name of the LORD Almighty, the God of the armies of Israel, whom you have defied. 46This day the LORD will hand you over to me, and I'll strike you down and cut off your head. Today I will give the carcasses of the Philistine army to the birds of the air and the beasts of the earth, and the whole world will know that there is a God in Israel. 47All those gathered here will know that it is not by sword or spear that the LORD saves; for the battle is the LORD's, and he will give all of you into our hands." 1Ki 18:36

48As the Philistine moved closer to attack him, David ran quickly toward the battle line to meet him. 49Reaching into his bag and taking out a stone, he slung it and struck the Philistine on the forehead. The stone sank into his forehead, and he fell facedown on the ground.

LIVING 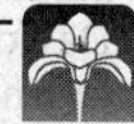 **INSIGHT**

Take heart. When God is involved, anything can happen. The One who directed that stone in between Goliath's eyes and divided the Red Sea and brought His Son back from the dead takes delight in the incredible!

(See 1 Samuel 17:49.)

50So David triumphed over the Philistine with a sling and a stone; without a sword in his hand he struck down the Philistine and killed him.

51David ran and stood over him. He took hold of the Philistine's sword and drew it from the scabbard. After he killed him, he cut off his head with the sword. Heb 11:34

When the Philistines saw that their hero was dead, they turned and ran. 52Then the men of Israel and Judah surged forward with a shout and pursued the Philistines to the entrance of Gath[a] and to the gates of Ekron. Their dead were strewn along the Shaaraim road to Gath and Ekron. 53When the Israelites returned from chasing the Philistines, they plundered their camp. 54David took the Philistine's head and brought it to Jerusalem, and he put the Philistine's weapons in his own tent. Jos 15:36

55As Saul watched David going out to meet the Philistine, he said to Abner, commander of the army, "Abner, whose son is that young man?"

Abner replied, "As surely as you live, O king, I don't know."

56The king said, "Find out whose son this young man is."

57As soon as David returned from killing the Philistine, Abner took him and brought him before Saul, with David still holding the Philistine's head.

58"Whose son are you, young man?" Saul asked him.

David said, "I am the son of your servant Jesse of Bethlehem." Ru 4:17

Saul's Jealousy of David

18 After David had finished talking with Saul, Jonathan became one in spirit with David, and he loved him as himself. 2From that day Saul kept David with him and did not let him return to his father's house. 3And Jonathan made a covenant with David because he loved him as himself. 4Jonathan took off the robe he was wearing and gave it to David, along with his tunic, and even his sword, his bow and his belt. Ge 41:42; 44:30; 2Sa 1:26

5Whatever Saul sent him to do, David did it so successfully[b] that Saul gave him a high rank in the army. This pleased all the people, and Saul's officers as well.

6When the men were returning home after David had killed the Philistine, the women came out from all the towns of Israel to meet King Saul with singing and dancing, with joyful songs and with tambourines and lutes. 7As they danced, they sang:

"Saul has slain his thousands,
and David his tens of thousands." 1Sa 21:11

8Saul was very angry; this refrain galled him. "They have credited David with tens of thousands," he thought, "but me with only thousands. What more can he get but the kingdom?" 9And from that time on Saul kept a jealous eye on David. 1Sa 15:8

10The next day an evil[c] spirit from God came forcefully upon Saul. He was prophesying in his house, while David was playing the harp, as he

[a]52 Some Septuagint manuscripts; Hebrew *a valley* [b]5 Or *wisely* [c]10 Or *injurious*

usually did. Saul had a spear in his hand 11and he hurled it, saying to himself, "I'll pin David to the wall." But David eluded him twice. 1Sa 16:14; 19:7

12Saul was afraid of David, because the LORD was with David but had left Saul. 13So he sent David away from him and gave him command over a thousand men, and David led the troops in their campaigns. 14In everything he did he had great success,[a] because the LORD was with him. 15When Saul saw how successful[b] he was, he was afraid of him. 16But all Israel and Judah loved David, because he led them in their campaigns.

17Saul said to David, "Here is my older daughter Merab. I will give her to you in marriage; only serve me bravely and fight the battles of the LORD." For Saul said to himself, "I will not raise a hand against him. Let the Philistines do that!" 1Sa 17:25

18But David said to Saul, "Who am I, and what is my family or my father's clan in Israel, that I should become the king's son-in-law?" 19So[c] when the time came for Merab, Saul's daughter, to be given to David, she was given in marriage to Adriel of Meholah. 2Sa 7:18; 21:8; Jdg 7:22

20Now Saul's daughter Michal was in love with David, and when they told Saul about it, he was pleased. 21"I will give her to him," he thought, "so that she may be a snare to him and so that the hand of the Philistines may be against him." So Saul said to David, "Now you have a second opportunity to become my son-in-law."

22Then Saul ordered his attendants: "Speak to David privately and say, 'Look, the king is pleased with you, and his attendants all like you; now become his son-in-law.'"

23They repeated these words to David. But David said, "Do you think it is a small matter to become the king's son-in-law? I'm only a poor man and little known."

24When Saul's servants told him what David had said, 25Saul replied, "Say to David, 'The king wants no other price for the bride than a hundred Philistine foreskins, to take revenge on his enemies.'" Saul's plan was to have David fall by the hands of the Philistines. Ex 22:17; Jer 20:10

26When the attendants told David these things, he was pleased to become the king's son-in-law. So before the allotted time elapsed, 27David and his men went out and killed two hundred Philistines. He brought their foreskins and presented the full number to the king so that he might become the king's son-in-law. Then Saul gave him his daughter Michal in marriage. 2Sa 3:14

28When Saul realized that the LORD was with David and that his daughter Michal loved David, 29Saul became still more afraid of him, and he remained his enemy the rest of his days.

30The Philistine commanders continued to go out to battle, and as often as they did, David met with more success[d] than the rest of Saul's officers, and his name became well known.

Saul Tries to Kill David

19 Saul told his son Jonathan and all the attendants to kill David. But Jonathan was very fond of David 2and warned him, "My father Saul is looking for a chance to kill you. Be on your guard tomorrow morning; go into hiding and stay there. 3I will go out and stand with my father in the field where you are. I'll speak to him about you and will tell you what I find out." 1Sa 18:9; 20:12

4Jonathan spoke well of David to Saul his father and said to him, "Let not the king do wrong to his servant David; he has not wronged you, and what he has done has benefited you greatly. 5He took his life in his hands when he killed the Philistine. The LORD won a great victory for all Israel, and you saw it and were glad. Why then would you do wrong to an innocent man like David by killing him for no reason?" Ge 42:22; 1Sa 11:13; Mt 27:4

6Saul listened to Jonathan and took this oath: "As surely as the LORD lives, David will not be put to death."

7So Jonathan called David and told him the whole conversation. He brought him to Saul, and David was with Saul as before. 1Sa 16:21

8Once more war broke out, and David went out and fought the Philistines. He struck them with such force that they fled before him.

9But an evil[e] spirit from the LORD came upon Saul as he was sitting in his house with his spear in his hand. While David was playing the harp, 10Saul tried to pin him to the wall with his spear, but David eluded him as Saul drove the spear into the wall. That night David made good his escape.

11Saul sent men to David's house to watch it and to kill him in the morning. But Michal, David's wife, warned him, "If you don't run for your life tonight, tomorrow you'll be killed." 12So Michal let David down through a window, and he fled and escaped. 13Then Michal took an idol[f] and laid it on the bed, covering it with a garment and putting some goats' hair at the head. Jos 2:15

14When Saul sent the men to capture David, Michal said, "He is ill." Jos 2:4

15Then Saul sent the men back to see David and told them, "Bring him up to me in his bed so that I may kill him." 16But when the men entered, there was the idol in the bed, and at the head was some goats' hair.

17Saul said to Michal, "Why did you deceive me like this and send my enemy away so that he escaped?"

[a]14 Or *he was very wise* [b]15 Or *wise* [c]19 Or *However,* [d]30 Or *David acted more wisely* [e]9 Or *injurious* [f]13 Hebrew *teraphim*; also in verse 16

Michal told him, "He said to me, 'Let me get away. Why should I kill you?' "

18When David had fled and made his escape, he went to Samuel at Ramah and told him all that Saul had done to him. Then he and Samuel went to Naioth and stayed there. 19Word came to Saul: "David is in Naioth at Ramah"; 20so he sent men to capture him. But when they saw a group of prophets prophesying, with Samuel standing there as their leader, the Spirit of God came upon Saul's men and they also prophesied. 21Saul was told about it, and he sent more men, and they prophesied too. Saul sent men a third time, and they also prophesied. 22Finally, he himself left for Ramah and went to the great cistern at Secu. And he asked, "Where are Samuel and David?" Nu 11:25

"Over in Naioth at Ramah," they said.

23So Saul went to Naioth at Ramah. But the Spirit of God came even upon him, and he walked along prophesying until he came to Naioth. 24He stripped off his robes and also prophesied in Samuel's presence. He lay that way all that day and night. This is why people say, "Is Saul also among the prophets?" 1Sa 15:35; Isa 20:2; Mic 1:8

David and Jonathan

20 Then David fled from Naioth at Ramah and went to Jonathan and asked, "What have I done? What is my crime? How have I wronged your father, that he is trying to take my life?" 1Sa 24:9

2"Never!" Jonathan replied. "You are not going to die! Look, my father doesn't do anything, great or small, without confiding in me. Why would he hide this from me? It's not so!"

3But David took an oath and said, "Your father knows very well that I have found favor in your eyes, and he has said to himself, 'Jonathan must not know this or he will be grieved.' Yet as surely as the LORD lives and as you live, there is only a step between me and death." Dt 6:13

4Jonathan said to David, "Whatever you want me to do, I'll do for you."

5So David said, "Look, tomorrow is the New Moon festival, and I am supposed to dine with the king; but let me go and hide in the field until the evening of the day after tomorrow. 6If your father misses me at all, tell him, 'David earnestly asked my permission to hurry to Bethlehem, his hometown, because an annual sacrifice is being made there for his whole clan.' 7If he says, 'Very well,' then your servant is safe. But if he loses his temper, you can be sure that he is determined to harm me. 8As for you, show kindness to your servant, for you have brought him into a covenant with you before the LORD. If I am guilty, then kill me yourself! Why hand me over to your father?" 1Sa 18:3

9"Never!" Jonathan said. "If I had the least inkling that my father was determined to harm you, wouldn't I tell you?"

10David asked, "Who will tell me if your father answers you harshly?"

11"Come," Jonathan said, "let's go out into the field." So they went there together.

12Then Jonathan said to David: "By the LORD, the God of Israel, I will surely sound out my father by this time the day after tomorrow! If he is favorably disposed toward you, will I not send you word and let you know? 13But if my father is inclined to harm you, may the LORD deal with me, be it ever so severely, if I do not let you know and send you away safely. May the LORD be with you as he has been with my father. 14But show me unfailing kindness like that of the LORD as long as I live, so that I may not be killed, 15and do not ever cut off your kindness from my family—not even when the LORD has cut off every one of David's enemies from the face of the earth." Ru 1:17

16So Jonathan made a covenant with the house of David, saying, "May the LORD call David's enemies to account." 17And Jonathan had David reaffirm his oath out of love for him, because he loved him as he loved himself. 1Sa 25:22

LIVING 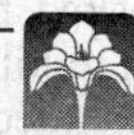 **INSIGHT**

When the searing rays of adversity's sun burn their way into our day, there's nothing quite like a sheltering tree—a true friend—to give us relief in its cool shade. Its massive trunk of understanding gives security as its thick leaves of love wash our face and wipe our brow. Beneath its branches have rested many a discouraged soul.

(See 1 Samuel 20:17.)

18Then Jonathan said to David: "Tomorrow is the New Moon festival. You will be missed, because your seat will be empty. 19The day after tomorrow, toward evening, go to the place where you hid when this trouble began, and wait by the stone Ezel. 20I will shoot three arrows to the side of it, as though I were shooting at a target. 21Then I will send a boy and say, 'Go, find the arrows.' If I say to him, 'Look, the arrows are on this side of you; bring them here,' then come, because, as surely as the LORD lives, you are safe; there is no danger. 22But if I say to the boy, 'Look, the arrows are beyond you,' then you must go, because the LORD has sent you away. 23And about the matter you and I discussed—remember, the LORD is witness between you and me forever." Ge 31:50; 1Sa 19:2

24So David hid in the field, and when the New Moon festival came, the king sat down to eat. 25He sat in his customary place by the wall, opposite

Jonathan,[a] and Abner sat next to Saul, but David's place was empty. 26Saul said nothing that day,
for he thought, "Something must have happened
to David to make him ceremonially unclean—
surely he is unclean." 27But the next day, the second day of the month, David's place was empty
again. Then Saul said to his son Jonathan, "Why
hasn't the son of Jesse come to the meal, either
yesterday or today?" Lev 7:20-21; 15:5; 1Sa 16:5

28Jonathan answered, "David earnestly asked
me for permission to go to Bethlehem. 29He said,
'Let me go, because our family is observing a sacrifice in the town and my brother has ordered me to
be there. If I have found favor in your eyes, let me
get away to see my brothers.' That is why he has
not come to the king's table."

30Saul's anger flared up at Jonathan and he said
to him, "You son of a perverse and rebellious
woman! Don't I know that you have sided with the
son of Jesse to your own shame and to the shame
of the mother who bore you? 31As long as the son
of Jesse lives on this earth, neither you nor your
kingdom will be established. Now send and bring
him to me, for he must die!"

32"Why should he be put to death? What has
he done?" Jonathan asked his father. 33But Saul
hurled his spear at him to kill him. Then Jonathan
knew that his father intended to kill David.

34Jonathan got up from the table in fierce anger;
on that second day of the month he did not eat,
because he was grieved at his father's shameful
treatment of David.

35In the morning Jonathan went out to the field
for his meeting with David. He had a small boy
with him, 36and he said to the boy, "Run and find
the arrows I shoot." As the boy ran, he shot an
arrow beyond him. 37When the boy came to the
place where Jonathan's arrow had fallen, Jonathan
called out after him, "Isn't the arrow beyond you?"
38Then he shouted, "Hurry! Go quickly! Don't
stop!" The boy picked up the arrow and returned
to his master. 39(The boy knew nothing of all this;
only Jonathan and David knew.) 40Then Jonathan
gave his weapons to the boy and said, "Go, carry
them back to town."

41After the boy had gone, David got up from the
south side ⌞of the stone⌟ and bowed down before
Jonathan three times, with his face to the ground.
Then they kissed each other and wept together—
but David wept the most.

42Jonathan said to David, "Go in peace, for we
have sworn friendship with each other in the name
of the LORD, saying, 'The LORD is witness between
you and me, and between your descendants and
my descendants forever.'" Then David left, and
Jonathan went back to the town. 1Sa 1:17; 2Sa 1:26

David at Nob

21 David went to Nob, to Ahimelech the
priest. Ahimelech trembled when he met
him, and asked, "Why are you alone? Why is no
one with you?" 1Sa 14:3; 16:4

2David answered Ahimelech the priest, "The
king charged me with a certain matter and said to
me, 'No one is to know anything about your mission and your instructions.' As for my men, I have
told them to meet me at a certain place. 3Now
then, what do you have on hand? Give me five
loaves of bread, or whatever you can find."

4But the priest answered David, "I don't have
any ordinary bread on hand; however, there is
some consecrated bread here—provided the men
have kept themselves from women." Mt 12:4

5David replied, "Indeed women have been kept
from us, as usual whenever[b] I set out. The men's
things[c] are holy even on missions that are not
holy. How much more so today!" 6So the priest
gave him the consecrated bread, since there was no
bread there except the bread of the Presence that
had been removed from before the LORD and replaced by hot bread on the day it was taken away.

7Now one of Saul's servants was there that day,
detained before the LORD; he was Doeg the Edomite, Saul's head shepherd. 1Sa 22:9,22

8David asked Ahimelech, "Don't you have a
spear or a sword here? I haven't brought my sword
or any other weapon, because the king's business
was urgent."

9The priest replied, "The sword of Goliath the
Philistine, whom you killed in the Valley of Elah,
is here; it is wrapped in a cloth behind the ephod.
If you want it, take it; there is no sword here but
that one." 1Sa 17:51

David said, "There is none like it; give it to me."

David at Gath

10That day David fled from Saul and went to
Achish king of Gath. 11But the servants of Achish
said to him, "Isn't this David, the king of the land?
Isn't he the one they sing about in their dances:

"'Saul has slain his thousands,
and David his tens of thousands'?" 1Sa 18:7

12David took these words to heart and was very
much afraid of Achish king of Gath. 13So he pretended to be insane in their presence; and while he
was in their hands he acted like a madman, making marks on the doors of the gate and letting
saliva run down his beard.

14Achish said to his servants, "Look at the man!
He is insane! Why bring him to me? 15Am I so
short of madmen that you have to bring this fellow
here to carry on like this in front of me? Must this
man come into my house?"

[a] 25 Septuagint; Hebrew *wall. Jonathan arose* [b] 5 Or *from us in the past few days since* [c] 5 Or *bodies*

On the Run but Not Alone **Chapters 22–31**

David continued to run from a mad king who wanted him dead. Although his life was threatened time after time, David would not retaliate. During these days, David's home became caves and other rugged hillside hiding places. While on the run, a group of outcasts began to follow David. It became his responsibility to turn that mob into an organized, well-disciplined fighting force . . . mighty men of valor. Talk about a challenge! These weren't the filthy five, or the nasty nine, or the dirty dozen. These were 400 hard-luck hooligans in "the cave of Adullam" (22:1), whose ranks quickly swelled to 600.

Did David pull it off? Could a shepherd from Bethlehem assume command of such a nefarious band of ne'er-do-wells? Did he meet the challenge? Indeed! In a brief period of time he had the troops in shape—combat ready. Incredible as it seems, he was doing battle against enemy forces before the year was up. These very men who fought loyally by David's side gave him strong support when he became the king of Israel. They were later named "the mighty men" (2 Samuel 23:8), and many of their names are listed later in the Bible as examples of heroism and dedication.

Be encouraged! If David could handle that cave full of malcontents, you can take on the challenge in your cave. Do you need strength? Peace? Wisdom? Direction? Discipline? A strategy for victory? Ask for it! God will hear you. He gives special attention to cries when they come out of caves.

David at Adullam and Mizpah

22 David left Gath and escaped to the cave of
Adullam. When his brothers and his father's household heard about it, they went down
to him there. [2]All those who were in distress or in
debt or discontented gathered around him, and he
became their leader. About four hundred men
were with him. 1Sa 25:13; 2Sa 23:13; Ps 57 Title
[3]From there David went to Mizpah in Moab
and said to the king of Moab, "Would you let my
father and mother come and stay with you until I
learn what God will do for me?" [4]So he left them
with the king of Moab, and they stayed with him
as long as David was in the stronghold.
[5]But the prophet Gad said to David, "Do not
stay in the stronghold. Go into the land of Judah."
So David left and went to the forest of Hereth.

Saul Kills the Priests of Nob

[6]Now Saul heard that David and his men had
been discovered. And Saul, spear in hand, was
seated under the tamarisk tree on the hill at Gibeah, with all his officials standing around him. [7]Saul
said to them, "Listen, men of Benjamin! Will the
son of Jesse give all of you fields and vineyards?
Will he make all of you commanders of thousands
and commanders of hundreds? [8]Is that why you
have all conspired against me? No one tells me
when my son makes a covenant with the son of
Jesse. None of you is concerned about me or tells
me that my son has incited my servant to lie in
wait for me, as he does today." 1Sa 8:14; 18:3; Jdg 4:5
[9]But Doeg the Edomite, who was standing with
Saul's officials, said, "I saw the son of Jesse come
to Ahimelech son of Ahitub at Nob. [10]Ahimelech
inquired of the LORD for him; he also gave him
provisions and the sword of Goliath the Philistine." 1Sa 17:51; 21:7; Nu 27:21
[11]Then the king sent for the priest Ahimelech
son of Ahitub and his father's whole family, who
were the priests at Nob, and they all came to the
king. [12]Saul said, "Listen now, son of Ahitub."
"Yes, my lord," he answered.
[13]Saul said to him, "Why have you conspired
against me, you and the son of Jesse, giving him
bread and a sword and inquiring of God for him,
so that he has rebelled against me and lies in wait
for me, as he does today?"
[14]Ahimelech answered the king, "Who of all
your servants is as loyal as David, the king's son-in-law, captain of your bodyguard and highly respected in your household? [15]Was that day the first
time I inquired of God for him? Of course not! Let
not the king accuse your servant or any of his
father's family, for your servant knows nothing at
all about this whole affair."
[16]But the king said, "You will surely die, Ahimelech, you and your father's whole family."
[17]Then the king ordered the guards at his side:
"Turn and kill the priests of the LORD, because they
too have sided with David. They knew he was
fleeing, yet they did not tell me."
But the king's officials were not willing to raise
a hand to strike the priests of the LORD. Ex 1:17
[18]The king then ordered Doeg, "You turn and
strike down the priests." So Doeg the Edomite
turned and struck them down. That day he killed
eighty-five men who wore the linen ephod. [19]He
also put to the sword Nob, the town of the priests,
with its men and women, its children and infants,
and its cattle, donkeys and sheep. 1Sa 2:18,31; 15:3
[20]But Abiathar, a son of Ahimelech son of Ahitub, escaped and fled to join David. [21]He told David that Saul had killed the priests of the LORD.
[22]Then David said to Abiathar: "That day, when
Doeg the Edomite was there, I knew he would be
sure to tell Saul. I am responsible for the death of
your father's whole family. [23]Stay with me; don't
be afraid; the man who is seeking your life is seeking mine also. You will be safe with me." 1Sa 2:32

David Saves Keilah

23 When David was told, "Look, the Philistines are fighting against Keilah and are
looting the threshing floors," [2]he inquired of the
LORD, saying, "Shall I go and attack these Philistines?" Jos 15:44; 1Sa 30:8
The LORD answered him, "Go, attack the Philistines and save Keilah."

3But David's men said to him, "Here in Judah we are afraid. How much more, then, if we go to Keilah against the Philistine forces!"

4Once again David inquired of the LORD, and the LORD answered him, "Go down to Keilah, for I am going to give the Philistines into your hand." 5So David and his men went to Keilah, fought the Philistines and carried off their livestock. He inflicted heavy losses on the Philistines and saved the people of Keilah. 6(Now Abiathar son of Ahimelech had brought the ephod down with him when he fled to David at Keilah.) Jos 8:7; Jdg 7:7; 1Sa 22:20

Saul Pursues David

7Saul was told that David had gone to Keilah, and he said, "God has handed him over to me, for David has imprisoned himself by entering a town with gates and bars." 8And Saul called up all his forces for battle, to go down to Keilah to besiege David and his men.

9When David learned that Saul was plotting against him, he said to Abiathar the priest, "Bring the ephod." 10David said, "O LORD, God of Israel, your servant has heard definitely that Saul plans to come to Keilah and destroy the town on account of me. 11Will the citizens of Keilah surrender me to him? Will Saul come down, as your servant has heard? O LORD, God of Israel, tell your servant."

And the LORD said, "He will."

12Again David asked, "Will the citizens of Keilah surrender me and my men to Saul?"

And the LORD said, "They will."

13So David and his men, about six hundred in number, left Keilah and kept moving from place to place. When Saul was told that David had escaped from Keilah, he did not go there. 1Sa 22:2; 25:13

14David stayed in the desert strongholds and in the hills of the Desert of Ziph. Day after day Saul searched for him, but God did not give David into his hands. Ps 32:7; 54:3-4

15While David was at Horesh in the Desert of Ziph, he learned that Saul had come out to take his life. 16And Saul's son Jonathan went to David at Horesh and helped him find strength in God. 17"Don't be afraid," he said. "My father Saul will not lay a hand on you. You will be king over Israel, and I will be second to you. Even my father Saul knows this." 18The two of them made a covenant before the LORD. Then Jonathan went home, but David remained at Horesh. 1Sa 20:16,42; 24:20; 2 Sa 21:7

19The Ziphites went up to Saul at Gibeah and said, "Is not David hiding among us in the strongholds at Horesh, on the hill of Hakilah, south of Jeshimon? 20Now, O king, come down whenever it pleases you to do so, and we will be responsible for handing him over to the king." 1Sa 26:1

21Saul replied, "The LORD bless you for your concern for me. 22Go and make further preparation. Find out where David usually goes and who has seen him there. They tell me he is very crafty. 23Find out about all the hiding places he uses and come back to me with definite information.[a] Then I will go with you; if he is in the area, I will track him down among all the clans of Judah."

24So they set out and went to Ziph ahead of Saul. Now David and his men were in the Desert of Maon, in the Arabah south of Jeshimon. 25Saul and his men began the search, and when David was told about it, he went down to the rock and stayed in the Desert of Maon. When Saul heard this, he went into the Desert of Maon in pursuit of David. Jos 15:55; 1Sa 25:2

26Saul was going along one side of the mountain, and David and his men were on the other side, hurrying to get away from Saul. As Saul and his forces were closing in on David and his men to capture them, 27a messenger came to Saul, saying, "Come quickly! The Philistines are raiding the land." 28Then Saul broke off his pursuit of David and went to meet the Philistines. That is why they call this place Sela Hammahlekoth.[b] 29And David went up from there and lived in the strongholds of En Gedi. 1Sa 24:22; Ps 17:9; 2Ch 20:2

David Spares Saul's Life

24 After Saul returned from pursuing the Philistines, he was told, "David is in the Desert of En Gedi." 2So Saul took three thousand chosen men from all Israel and set out to look for David and his men near the Crags of the Wild Goats.

3He came to the sheep pens along the way; a cave was there, and Saul went in to relieve himself. David and his men were far back in the cave. 4The men said, "This is the day the LORD spoke of when he said[c] to you, 'I will give your enemy into your hands for you to deal with as you wish.'" Then David crept up unnoticed and cut off a corner of Saul's robe. 1Sa 25:28-30; Jdg 3:24

5Afterward, David was conscience-stricken for having cut off a corner of his robe. 6He said to his men, "The LORD forbid that I should do such a thing to my master, the LORD's anointed, or lift my hand against him; for he is the anointed of the LORD." 7With these words David rebuked his men and did not allow them to attack Saul. And Saul left the cave and went his way. 1Sa 26:11; 2Sa 24:10

8Then David went out of the cave and called out to Saul, "My lord the king!" When Saul looked behind him, David bowed down and prostrated himself with his face to the ground. 9He said to Saul, "Why do you listen when men say, 'David is bent on harming you'? 10This day you have seen with your own eyes how the LORD delivered you into my hands in the cave. Some urged me to kill

[a] 23 Or *me at Nacon* [b] 28 *Sela Hammahlekoth* means *rock of parting.* [c] 4 Or *"Today the LORD is saying*

you, but I spared you; I said, 'I will not lift my
hand against my master, because he is the LORD's
anointed.' 11See, my father, look at this piece of
your robe in my hand! I cut off the corner of your
robe but did not kill you. Now understand and
recognize that I am not guilty of wrongdoing or
rebellion. I have not wronged you, but you are
hunting me down to take my life. 12May the LORD
judge between you and me. And may the LORD
avenge the wrongs you have done to me, but my
hand will not touch you. 13As the old saying goes,
'From evildoers come evil deeds,' so my hand will
not touch you. Ge 16:5; Jdg 11:27; Mt 7:20

14"Against whom has the king of Israel come
out? Whom are you pursuing? A dead dog? A flea?
15May the LORD be our judge and decide between
us. May he consider my cause and uphold it; may
he vindicate me by delivering me from your
hand." 1Sa 17:43; Ps 35:1,23; Mic 7:9

16When David finished saying this, Saul asked,
"Is that your voice, David my son?" And he wept
aloud. 17"You are more righteous than I," he said.
"You have treated me well, but I have treated you
badly. 18You have just now told me of the good
you did to me; the LORD delivered me into your
hands, but you did not kill me. 19When a man
finds his enemy, does he let him get away unharmed? May the LORD reward you well for the
way you treated me today. 20I know that you will
surely be king and that the kingdom of Israel will
be established in your hands. 21Now swear to me
by the LORD that you will not cut off my descendants or wipe out my name from my father's family." Ge 38:26; 2Sa 21:1-9; Mt 5:44

22So David gave his oath to Saul. Then Saul
returned home, but David and his men went up to
the stronghold. 1Sa 23:29

David, Nabal and Abigail

25 Now Samuel died, and all Israel assembled
and mourned for him; and they buried
him at his home in Ramah. Dt 34:8; 1Sa 28:3; Ge 21:21

Then David moved down into the Desert of
Maon.[a] 2A certain man in Maon, who had property there at Carmel, was very wealthy. He had a
thousand goats and three thousand sheep, which
he was shearing in Carmel. 3His name was Nabal
and his wife's name was Abigail. She was an intelligent and beautiful woman, but her husband, a
Calebite, was surly and mean in his dealings.

4While David was in the desert, he heard that
Nabal was shearing sheep. 5So he sent ten young
men and said to them, "Go up to Nabal at Carmel
and greet him in my name. 6Say to him: 'Long life
to you! Good health to you and your household!
And good health to all that is yours! 1Ch 12:18

7"'Now I hear that it is sheep-shearing time.
When your shepherds were with us, we did not
mistreat them, and the whole time they were at
Carmel nothing of theirs was missing. 8Ask your
own servants and they will tell you. Therefore be
favorable toward my young men, since we come at
a festive time. Please give your servants and your
son David whatever you can find for them.'"

9When David's men arrived, they gave Nabal
this message in David's name. Then they waited.

10Nabal answered David's servants, "Who is
this David? Who is this son of Jesse? Many servants are breaking away from their masters these
days. 11Why should I take my bread and water,
and the meat I have slaughtered for my shearers,
and give it to men coming from who knows
where?" Jdg 8:6; 9:28

12David's men turned around and went back.
When they arrived, they reported every word.
13David said to his men, "Put on your swords!" So
they put on their swords, and David put on his.
About four hundred men went up with David,
while two hundred stayed with the supplies.

14One of the servants told Nabal's wife Abigail:
"David sent messengers from the desert to give
our master his greetings, but he hurled insults at
them. 15Yet these men were very good to us. They
did not mistreat us, and the whole time we were
out in the fields near them nothing was missing.
16Night and day they were a wall around us all the
time we were herding our sheep near them. 17Now
think it over and see what you can do, because
disaster is hanging over our master and his whole
household. He is such a wicked man that no one
can talk to him." Ex 14:22; 1Sa 20:7; Job 1:10

18Abigail lost no time. She took two hundred
loaves of bread, two skins of wine, five dressed
sheep, five seahs[b] of roasted grain, a hundred
cakes of raisins and two hundred cakes of pressed
figs, and loaded them on donkeys. 19Then she told
her servants, "Go on ahead; I'll follow you." But
she did not tell her husband Nabal. Ge 32:20

20As she came riding her donkey into a mountain ravine, there were David and his men descending toward her, and she met them. 21David
had just said, "It's been useless—all my watching
over this fellow's property in the desert so that
nothing of his was missing. He has paid me back
evil for good. 22May God deal with David,[c] be it
ever so severely, if by morning I leave alive one
male of all who belong to him!" 1Sa 3:17; 1Ki 14:10

23When Abigail saw David, she quickly got off
her donkey and bowed down before David with
her face to the ground. 24She fell at his feet and
said: "My lord, let the blame be on me alone.
Please let your servant speak to you; hear what

[a] 1 Some Septuagint manuscripts; Hebrew *Paran* [b] 18 That is, probably about a bushel (about 37 liters) [c] 22 Some Septuagint manuscripts; Hebrew *with David's enemies*

ABIGAIL

A Woman of Discernment

"His wife's name was Abigail. She was an intelligent and beautiful woman."

–1 SAMUEL 25:3

I often think of the story of Abigail in terms of a play. To appreciate the play, you need some background on the main characters and an understanding of the story line.

First, we have David, the king-elect of Israel. At this point in life, however, he was not on the throne—far from it, in fact. As this scene unfolds David was a fugitive, running from the murderous threats of King Saul, who had been pursuing David for the last dozen or so years. David surrounded himself with six hundred men (1 Samuel 23:13)—malcontents and outlaws (22:2)—and had turned them into a fighting force. He and his men acted as a type of police force, protecting the flocks of wealthy livestock owners from raiders and wild animals. In those days the custom was that when the sheep were sheared, these "protectors" would be paid a gratuity, something like a tip you would pay to a server in a restaurant. Sheep-shearing time had arrived (25:7). David and his men had been protecting the flocks of a man named Nabal (25:15–16).

Let's get better acquainted with Nabal. First of all, his name meant "Fool" (see 25:25)—not in the sense that he was dull or unintelligent, but more in the sense that he was belligerent, obstinate, arrogant, ill-mannered, rude. The Bible calls him "surly and mean" (25:3). He was bigoted. He was disrespectful. He was stingy. He was all of these things—even though he was a man who enjoyed many material blessings (25:2), and he was married to "an intelligent and beautiful woman" named Abigail (25:3).

Abigail, to put it bluntly, was the total opposite of her husband. She was wise, prudent, sensible, gracious, generous. She not only planned, she also planned ahead. She was a woman of discernment. On top of all that, she was beautiful in appearance. She was wise on the inside and beautiful on the outside. She was a rare treasure indeed—a diamond in comparison with her surly husband.

The conflict began when Nabal decided not to pay David and his men for their services. David's men respectfully requested what was their due (25:6–8), but Nabal responded in what seems to have been his typical fashion, with words to this effect: "Why should I give any of my wealth to you? I don't know David, and I don't know where he comes from. For all I know, he's an escaped convict" (25:10–11). So the plot has been set: a band of men who have more than earned their pay, and an ornery, coarse tightwad of a sheep owner who isn't about to pay them one red shekel.

But then Abigail hurried into the fray. She called on all her powers of discernment to bring calm to the tense situation. Can you imagine how quickly her mind must have leaped into action to find a way to appease David and to protect Nabal? How could she keep David from carrying out revenge with his own hands? How could she leave room for God to move in the life of Nabal, her husband, in God's own way and in His own time? What would most honor God? Although she may not have known the exact answers to all those questions, she knew she had to act, and act quickly. So she had her servants whip out the cooking pot and prepare a feast fit for a king. She sent her servants on ahead as she followed close behind, undoubtedly rehearsing what she would say to God's anointed.

When she went out to meet David and his band of angry men, she did more than just appeal to their stomachs. She deflected the blame from Nabal: "My lord, let the blame be on me alone" (25:24). What a sensitive, gentle spirit! She knew her husband deserved everything he had coming to him. But in this simple, beautiful way, Abigail resolved the situation. She wasn't thinking about herself. She was thinking about David's future. She was thinking about her husband and about the innocent family members whose lives were in grave danger. Abigail's actions prove that a person who has discernment can serve in a quiet, peace-promoting way that sees beyond himself or herself to look out for the interests of others. This "play" has a happy ending (see verses 32–42). What a testament to the rewards of noble character and godly insight in the face of a crisis!

your servant has to say. 25 May my lord pay no attention to that wicked man Nabal. He is just like his name—his name is Fool, and folly goes with him. But as for me, your servant, I did not see the men my master sent. 1Sa 20:41; Pr 14:16; 17:12

26 "Now since the LORD has kept you, my master, from bloodshed and from avenging yourself with your own hands, as surely as the LORD lives and as you live, may your enemies and all who intend to harm my master be like Nabal. 27 And let this gift, which your servant has brought to my master, be given to the men who follow you. 28 Please forgive your servant's offense, for the LORD will certainly make a lasting dynasty for my master, because he fights the LORD's battles. Let no wrongdoing be found in you as long as you live. 29 Even though someone is pursuing you to take your life, the life of my master will be bound securely in the bundle of the living by the LORD your God. But the lives of your enemies he will hurl away as from the pocket of a sling. 30 When the LORD has done for my master every good thing he promised concerning him and has appointed him leader over Israel, 31 my master will not have on his conscience the staggering burden of needless bloodshed or of having avenged himself. And when the LORD has brought my master success, remember your servant." 2Sa 7:11,26; 18:32; Jer 10:18

32 David said to Abigail, "Praise be to the LORD, the God of Israel, who has sent you today to meet me. 33 May you be blessed for your good judgment and for keeping me from bloodshed this day and from avenging myself with my own hands. 34 Otherwise, as surely as the LORD, the God of Israel, lives, who has kept me from harming you, if you had not come quickly to meet me, not one male belonging to Nabal would have been left alive by daybreak." Ge 24:27; Ex 18:10; Lk 1:68

35 Then David accepted from her hand what she had brought him and said, "Go home in peace. I have heard your words and granted your request."

36 When Abigail went to Nabal, he was in the house holding a banquet like that of a king. He was in high spirits and very drunk. So she told him nothing until daybreak. 37 Then in the morning, when Nabal was sober, his wife told him all these things, and his heart failed him and he became like a stone. 38 About ten days later, the LORD struck Nabal and he died. Pr 20:1; Ecc 10:17; 1Sa 26:10

39 When David heard that Nabal was dead, he said, "Praise be to the LORD, who has upheld my cause against Nabal for treating me with contempt. He has kept his servant from doing wrong and has brought Nabal's wrongdoing down on his own head."

Then David sent word to Abigail, asking her to become his wife. 40 His servants went to Carmel and said to Abigail, "David has sent us to you to take you to become his wife."

41 She bowed down with her face to the ground and said, "Here is your maidservant, ready to serve you and wash the feet of my master's servants." 42 Abigail quickly got on a donkey and, attended by her five maids, went with David's messengers and became his wife. 43 David had also married Ahinoam of Jezreel, and they both were his wives. 44 But Saul had given his daughter Michal, David's wife, to Paltiel[a] son of Laish, who was from Gallim. Ge 24:61-67; Jos 15:56; 2Sa 3:15

David Again Spares Saul's Life

26 The Ziphites went to Saul at Gibeah and said, "Is not David hiding on the hill of Hakilah, which faces Jeshimon?" 1Sa 23:19; Ps 54 Title

2 So Saul went down to the Desert of Ziph, with his three thousand chosen men of Israel, to search there for David. 3 Saul made his camp beside the road on the hill of Hakilah facing Jeshimon, but David stayed in the desert. When he saw that Saul had followed him there, 4 he sent out scouts and learned that Saul had definitely arrived.[b] 1Sa 24:2

5 Then David set out and went to the place where Saul had camped. He saw where Saul and Abner son of Ner, the commander of the army, had lain down. Saul was lying inside the camp, with the army encamped around him. 1Sa 17:55

6 David then asked Ahimelech the Hittite and Abishai son of Zeruiah, Joab's brother, "Who will go down into the camp with me to Saul?"

"I'll go with you," said Abishai.

7 So David and Abishai went to the army by night, and there was Saul, lying asleep inside the camp with his spear stuck in the ground near his head. Abner and the soldiers were lying around him.

8 Abishai said to David, "Today God has delivered your enemy into your hands. Now let me pin him to the ground with one thrust of my spear; I won't strike him twice."

9 But David said to Abishai, "Don't destroy him! Who can lay a hand on the LORD's anointed and be guiltless? 10 As surely as the LORD lives," he said, "the LORD himself will strike him; either his time will come and he will die, or he will go into battle and perish. 11 But the LORD forbid that I should lay a hand on the LORD's anointed. Now get the spear and water jug that are near his head, and let's go."

12 So David took the spear and water jug near Saul's head, and they left. No one saw or knew about it, nor did anyone wake up. They were all sleeping, because the LORD had put them into a deep sleep. Ge 2:21; 15:12

13 Then David crossed over to the other side and stood on top of the hill some distance away; there

[a] *44* Hebrew *Palti,* a variant of *Paltiel* [b] *4* Or *had come to Nacon*

was a wide space between them. [14]He called out to the army and to Abner son of Ner, "Aren't you going to answer me, Abner?"

Abner replied, "Who are you who calls to the king?"

[15]David said, "You're a man, aren't you? And who is like you in Israel? Why didn't you guard your lord the king? Someone came to destroy your lord the king. [16]What you have done is not good. As surely as the LORD lives, you and your men deserve to die, because you did not guard your master, the LORD's anointed. Look around you. Where are the king's spear and water jug that were near his head?"

[17]Saul recognized David's voice and said, "Is that your voice, David my son?" 1Sa 24:16

David replied, "Yes it is, my lord the king." [18]And he added, "Why is my lord pursuing his servant? What have I done, and what wrong am I guilty of? [19]Now let my lord the king listen to his servant's words. If the LORD has incited you against me, then may he accept an offering. If, however, men have done it, may they be cursed before the LORD! They have now driven me from my share in the LORD's inheritance and have said, 'Go, serve other gods.' [20]Now do not let my blood fall to the ground far from the presence of the LORD. The king of Israel has come out to look for a flea—as one hunts a partridge in the mountains."

[21]Then Saul said, "I have sinned. Come back, David my son. Because you considered my life precious today, I will not try to harm you again. Surely I have acted like a fool and have erred greatly." Ex 9:27; 1Sa 15:24; 24:17

[22]"Here is the king's spear," David answered. "Let one of your young men come over and get it. [23]The LORD rewards every man for his righteousness and faithfulness. The LORD delivered you into my hands today, but I would not lay a hand on the LORD's anointed. [24]As surely as I valued your life today, so may the LORD value my life and deliver me from all trouble." Ps 7:8; 54:7; 62:12

[25]Then Saul said to David, "May you be blessed, my son David; you will do great things and surely triumph."

So David went on his way, and Saul returned home.

David Among the Philistines

27 But David thought to himself, "One of these days I will be destroyed by the hand of Saul. The best thing I can do is to escape to the land of the Philistines. Then Saul will give up searching for me anywhere in Israel, and I will slip out of his hand."

[2]So David and the six hundred men with him left and went over to Achish son of Maoch king of Gath. [3]David and his men settled in Gath with Achish. Each man had his family with him, and David had his two wives: Ahinoam of Jezreel and Abigail of Carmel, the widow of Nabal. [4]When Saul was told that David had fled to Gath, he no longer searched for him. 1Sa 25:13; 21:10; 1Ki 2:39

[5]Then David said to Achish, "If I have found favor in your eyes, let a place be assigned to me in one of the country towns, that I may live there. Why should your servant live in the royal city with you?"

[6]So on that day Achish gave him Ziklag, and it has belonged to the kings of Judah ever since. [7]David lived in Philistine territory a year and four months. Jos 15:31; 19:5; 1Sa 29:3

[8]Now David and his men went up and raided the Geshurites, the Girzites and the Amalekites. (From ancient times these peoples had lived in the land extending to Shur and Egypt.) [9]Whenever David attacked an area, he did not leave a man or woman alive, but took sheep and cattle, donkeys and camels, and clothes. Then he returned to Achish. Jos 13:2,13; Ex 17:8; 1Sa 15:3

[10]When Achish asked, "Where did you go raiding today?" David would say, "Against the Negev of Judah" or "Against the Negev of Jerahmeel" or "Against the Negev of the Kenites." [11]He did not leave a man or woman alive to be brought to Gath, for he thought, "They might inform on us and say, 'This is what David did.'" And such was his practice as long as he lived in Philistine territory. [12]Achish trusted David and said to himself, "He has become so odious to his people, the Israelites, that he will be my servant forever." Jdg 1:16

Saul and the Witch of Endor

28 In those days the Philistines gathered their forces to fight against Israel. Achish said to David, "You must understand that you and your men will accompany me in the army." 1Sa 29:1

[2]David said, "Then you will see for yourself what your servant can do."

Achish replied, "Very well, I will make you my bodyguard for life."

[3]Now Samuel was dead, and all Israel had mourned for him and buried him in his own town of Ramah. Saul had expelled the mediums and spiritists from the land. Lev 19:31; Dt 18:10-11

[4]The Philistines assembled and came and set up camp at Shunem, while Saul gathered all the Israelites and set up camp at Gilboa. [5]When Saul saw the Philistine army, he was afraid; terror filled his heart. [6]He inquired of the LORD, but the LORD did not answer him by dreams or Urim or prophets. [7]Saul then said to his attendants, "Find me a woman who is a medium, so I may go and inquire of her." Ex 28:30; 1Ch 10:13-14; 2Ki 4:8

"There is one in Endor," they said. Jos 17:11

[8]So Saul disguised himself, putting on other clothes, and at night he and two men went to the

woman. "Consult a spirit for me," he said, "and
bring up for me the one I name." Dt 18:10-11
9But the woman said to him, "Surely you know
what Saul has done. He has cut off the mediums
and spiritists from the land. Why have you set a
trap for my life to bring about my death?"
10Saul swore to her by the LORD, "As surely as
the LORD lives, you will not be punished for this."
11Then the woman asked, "Whom shall I bring
up for you?"
"Bring up Samuel," he said.
12When the woman saw Samuel, she cried out
at the top of her voice and said to Saul, "Why have
you deceived me? You are Saul!"
13The king said to her, "Don't be afraid. What
do you see?"
The woman said, "I see a spirit[a] coming up out
of the ground."
14"What does he look like?" he asked.
"An old man wearing a robe is coming up," she
said. 1Sa 15:27
Then Saul knew it was Samuel, and he bowed
down and prostrated himself with his face to the
ground.
15Samuel said to Saul, "Why have you disturbed
me by bringing me up?"
"I am in great distress," Saul said. "The Philistines are fighting against me, and God has turned
away from me. He no longer answers me, either by
prophets or by dreams. So I have called on you to
tell me what to do." 1Sa 18:12
16Samuel said, "Why do you consult me, now
that the LORD has turned away from you and become your enemy? 17The LORD has done what he
predicted through me. The LORD has torn the
kingdom out of your hands and given it to one of
your neighbors—to David. 18Because you did not
obey the LORD or carry out his fierce wrath against
the Amalekites, the LORD has done this to you
today. 19The LORD will hand over both Israel and
you to the Philistines, and tomorrow you and your
sons will be with me. The LORD will also hand over
the army of Israel to the Philistines." 1Sa 15:28; 31:2
20Immediately Saul fell full length on the
ground, filled with fear because of Samuel's words.
His strength was gone, for he had eaten nothing all
that day and night.
21When the woman came to Saul and saw that
he was greatly shaken, she said, "Look, your maidservant has obeyed you. I took my life in my hands
and did what you told me to do. 22Now please
listen to your servant and let me give you some
food so you may eat and have the strength to go
on your way." Jdg 12:3; 1Sa 19:5
23He refused and said, "I will not eat."
But his men joined the woman in urging him,
and he listened to them. He got up from the
ground and sat on the couch. 2Ki 5:13
24The woman had a fattened calf at the house,
which she butchered at once. She took some flour,
kneaded it and baked bread without yeast. 25Then
she set it before Saul and his men, and they ate.
That same night they got up and left.

Achish Sends David Back to Ziklag

29 The Philistines gathered all their forces at
Aphek, and Israel camped by the spring in
Jezreel. 2As the Philistine rulers marched with their
units of hundreds and thousands, David and his
men were marching at the rear with Achish. 3The
commanders of the Philistines asked, "What about
these Hebrews?" 1Sa 4:1; 28:1; 2Ki 9:30
Achish replied, "Is this not David, who was an
officer of Saul king of Israel? He has already been
with me for over a year, and from the day he left
Saul until now, I have found no fault in him."
4But the Philistine commanders were angry
with him and said, "Send the man back, that he
may return to the place you assigned him. He
must not go with us into battle, or he will turn
against us during the fighting. How better could he
regain his master's favor than by taking the heads
of our own men? 5Isn't this the David they sang
about in their dances: 1Sa 14:21; 1Ch 12:19

"'Saul has slain his thousands,
and David his tens of thousands'?" 1Sa 18:7

6So Achish called David and said to him, "As
surely as the LORD lives, you have been reliable,
and I would be pleased to have you serve with me
in the army. From the day you came to me until
now, I have found no fault in you, but the rulers
don't approve of you. 7Turn back and go in peace;
do nothing to displease the Philistine rulers."
8"But what have I done?" asked David. "What
have you found against your servant from the day
I came to you until now? Why can't I go and fight
against the enemies of my lord the king?"
9Achish answered, "I know that you have been
as pleasing in my eyes as an angel of God; nevertheless, the Philistine commanders have said, 'He
must not go up with us into battle.' 10Now get up
early, along with your master's servants who have
come with you, and leave in the morning as soon
as it is light." 2Sa 14:17,20; 19:27; 1Ch 12:19
11So David and his men got up early in the
morning to go back to the land of the Philistines,
and the Philistines went up to Jezreel.

David Destroys the Amalekites

30 David and his men reached Ziklag on the
third day. Now the Amalekites had raided
the Negev and Ziklag. They had attacked Ziklag

[a]13 Or *see spirits*; or *see gods*

and burned it, 2and had taken captive the women
and all who were in it, both young and old. They
killed none of them, but carried them off as they
went on their way. 1Sa 15:7; 27:8

3When David and his men came to Ziklag, they
found it destroyed by fire and their wives and sons
and daughters taken captive. 4So David and his
men wept aloud until they had no strength left to
weep. 5David's two wives had been captured—
Ahinoam of Jezreel and Abigail, the widow of Nabal of Carmel. 6David was greatly distressed because the men were talking of stoning him; each
one was bitter in spirit because of his sons and
daughters. But David found strength in the LORD
his God. Ex 17:4; Ps 56:3-4,11

7Then David said to Abiathar the priest, the son
of Ahimelech, "Bring me the ephod." Abiathar
brought it to him, 8and David inquired of the
LORD, "Shall I pursue this raiding party? Will I
overtake them?" 1Sa 22:20; 23:2

"Pursue them," he answered. "You will certainly overtake them and succeed in the rescue."

9David and the six hundred men with him came
to the Besor Ravine, where some stayed behind,
10for two hundred men were too exhausted to
cross the ravine. But David and four hundred men
continued the pursuit. 1Sa 27:2

11They found an Egyptian in a field and brought
him to David. They gave him water to drink and
food to eat— 12part of a cake of pressed figs and
two cakes of raisins. He ate and was revived, for he
had not eaten any food or drunk any water for
three days and three nights. Jdg 15:19

13David asked him, "To whom do you belong,
and where do you come from?"

He said, "I am an Egyptian, the slave of an
Amalekite. My master abandoned me when I became ill three days ago. 14We raided the Negev of
the Kerethites and the territory belonging to Judah
and the Negev of Caleb. And we burned Ziklag."

15David asked him, "Can you lead me down to
this raiding party?"

He answered, "Swear to me before God that
you will not kill me or hand me over to my master,
and I will take you down to them."

16He led David down, and there they were, scattered over the countryside, eating, drinking and
reveling because of the great amount of plunder
they had taken from the land of the Philistines and
from Judah. 17David fought them from dusk until
the evening of the next day, and none of them got
away, except four hundred young men who rode
off on camels and fled. 18David recovered everything the Amalekites had taken, including his two
wives. 19Nothing was missing: young or old, boy
or girl, plunder or anything else they had taken.
David brought everything back. 20He took all the
flocks and herds, and his men drove them ahead
of the other livestock, saying, "This is David's
plunder." Ge 14:16; 1Sa 15:3; Lk 12:19

21Then David came to the two hundred men
who had been too exhausted to follow him and
who were left behind at the Besor Ravine. They
came out to meet David and the people with him.
As David and his men approached, he greeted
them. 22But all the evil men and troublemakers
among David's followers said, "Because they did
not go out with us, we will not share with them the
plunder we recovered. However, each man may
take his wife and children and go."

23David replied, "No, my brothers, you must
not do that with what the LORD has given us. He
has protected us and handed over to us the forces
that came against us. 24Who will listen to what you
say? The share of the man who stayed with the
supplies is to be the same as that of him who went
down to the battle. All will share alike." 25David
made this a statute and ordinance for Israel from
that day to this. Nu 31:27; Jos 22:8

26When David arrived in Ziklag, he sent some
of the plunder to the elders of Judah, who were his
friends, saying, "Here is a present for you from the
plunder of the LORD's enemies." Ge 33:11

27He sent it to those who were in Bethel, Ramoth Negev and Jattir; 28to those in Aroer, Siph-
moth, Eshtemoa 29and Racal; to those in the towns
of the Jerahmeelites and the Kenites; 30to those in
Hormah, Bor Ashan, Athach 31and Hebron; and to
those in all the other places where David and his
men had roamed. Jos 13:16; 14:13; Jdg 1:17

Saul Takes His Life

31 Now the Philistines fought against Israel;
the Israelites fled before them, and many
fell slain on Mount Gilboa. 2The Philistines
pressed hard after Saul and his sons, and they
killed his sons Jonathan, Abinadab and Malki-
Shua. 3The fighting grew fierce around Saul, and
when the archers overtook him, they wounded
him critically. 1Sa 28:4; 2Sa 1:6; 1Ch 10:1-12

4Saul said to his armor-bearer, "Draw your
sword and run me through, or these uncircumcised fellows will come and run me through and
abuse me." Jdg 9:54; 1Sa 14:6

But his armor-bearer was terrified and would
not do it; so Saul took his own sword and fell on
it. 5When the armor-bearer saw that Saul was
dead, he too fell on his sword and died with him.
6So Saul and his three sons and his armor-bearer
and all his men died together that same day.

7When the Israelites along the valley and those
across the Jordan saw that the Israelite army had
fled and that Saul and his sons had died, they
abandoned their towns and fled. And the Philistines came and occupied them.

8The next day, when the Philistines came to

strip the dead, they found Saul and his three sons
fallen on Mount Gilboa. 9They cut off his head and
stripped off his armor, and they sent messengers
throughout the land of the Philistines to proclaim
the news in the temple of their idols and among
their people. 10They put his armor in the temple of
the Ashtoreths and fastened his body to the wall of
Beth Shan. Jos 17:11; Jdg 2:12-13; 2Sa 1:20

11When the people of Jabesh Gilead heard of
what the Philistines had done to Saul, 12all their
valiant men journeyed through the night to Beth
Shan. They took down the bodies of Saul and his
sons from the wall of Beth Shan and went to Jabesh, where they burned them. 13Then they took
their bones and buried them under a tamarisk tree
at Jabesh, and they fasted seven days. 1Ch 10:1-12

INTRODUCTION

2 SAMUEL

"So long as time lasts, David must always enlist affection and command respect." So wrote F.B. Meyer, the British biographer. No question about it—King David remains among the brightest lights of the Bible. So significant was he that God set aside an entire book of the Old Testament to cover his forty-year reign . . . his highest pinnacle of achievement down to his lowest valley of misery and defeat. Without sparing many details of either extreme, the Spirit of God records (with admiration as well as with grief) the things that made David great and the things that led to his agony of soul. The book of 2 Samuel, tracing forty years of a colorful as well as a contrasting life, holds several lessons that live on to this very day.

WRITER: *Unknown*

DATE: *c.925* B.C.

PURPOSE: *To trace Israel's history from Saul's death to the end of David's reign*

KEY PERSON: *David*

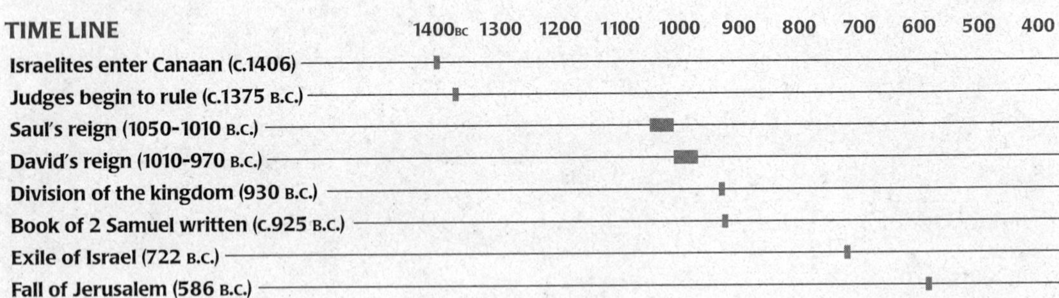

Ecstasy and Agony of a King

DAVID'S TRIUMPHS		DAVID'S TROUBLES			APPENDIX
Reigning in Hebron Over Judah	**Reigning in Jerusalem Over All Israel**	**With Himself**	**With His Family**	**With His Nation**	**Miscellaneous Narratives**
David's lament *(1)* David's crowning *(2)* David's increase *(3–4)*	A new capital *(5)* A new worship center *(6)* A new dynasty *(7)* A new boundary *(8)* A new son *(9)* A new boundary *(10)*	David's sin *(11)* Nathan's denunciation *(12)*	Amnon's immorality *(13)* Absalom's crime and flight *(14)* Absalom's revolt *(15)* Absalom's counselors *(16–17)* Absalom's death *(18)*	David's return *(19)* Sheba's revolt *(20)*	A famine *(21)* A song *(22)* A prophecy *(23)* A failure *(24)*
CHAPTERS 1–4	***CHAPTERS 5–10***	***CHAPTERS 11–12***	***CHAPTERS 13–18***	***CHAPTERS 19–20***	***CHAPTERS 21–24***

At times I try to imagine what it would be like if God were still writing His Book, the Bible. It makes me wonder which events in our lifetime He would choose to include. I wonder which people He would highlight, considering them significant enough to be included in His Word. When the Bible was written and compiled, there was one man so significant that God set aside an entire book and a half of the Bible to tell us about his life. God picked out a young man who became so important that 62 chapters of the Bible mention some segment of his life. Furthermore, when the New Testament was written, he was referred to more than any other man or woman from the entire Old Testament. It's no wonder he was called "a man after God's heart" two different times (1 Samuel 13 and Acts 13). His name, of course, was David.

David is in focus the entire book of 2 Samuel. This portion of Scripture portrays David's life during his highest delights to his lowest days. It covers David's life for more than forty years. Stop and think of all the things connected with David's name: the City of David, the star of David, the lineage of David, the seed of David, the key of David, the house of David, the tower of David, the throne of David, the Offspring of David and the Root of David.

A History of the Kings

You might find it interesting that when the books of the Bible were originally put together, 1 and 2 Samuel and 1 and 2 Kings were first named "1, 2, 3 and 4 Kings." Until the *Septuagint* (the Greek rendering of the Hebrew Old Testament) was written, these books remained 1, 2, 3 and 4 Kings. These four books contain the history and story of the monarchs who led the Hebrew people in ancient times.

The book of 1 Samuel records the stories of Samuel and Saul. Woven into the account of Saul's life is the beginning of David's story. This young shepherd boy came on the scene as the anointed king elect. However, David doesn't take the throne until we get to 2 Samuel. Remember, God had been preparing him for over 15 years. He had learned how to "take it" in the rugged, lonely hills of Judea as a young shepherd.

He had learned how to "king it" in the throne room of Saul. The death of Saul (1 Samuel 31) brought David out of hiding and paved the way for David's ascent to the throne.

God never employs useless afflictions. He never wastes those training years. He never wastes a grief, a disappointment, a disillusionment, a sorrow or a period of pain. All of that is part of His training program. That was surely true for David. At last, after more than a decade and a half of training, David took the throne and began to reign. *What a day that must have been*!

Historically, 2 Samuel can be divided into two sections: Chapters 1–4 cover David's limited reign over the house of Judah for seven and a half years. Chapters 5–24 record David's unlimited reign over all Israel for over three decades. You will gain a good overall view of the book of 2 Samuel if you remember that.

Years of Blessing and Years of Agony

If you were to outline the book of 2 Samuel, it would take the shape of a rooftop. It would go up, hit the pinnacle, and then it would slide down. For the first 10 chapters David could do no wrong. He was never defeated in battle. He unified the nation. He obtained a royal capital. He expanded the nation's boundaries. He brought prosperity. Everybody was feeling secure. There was positive public opinion that soared right up to the top of the chart! For 17 years David enjoyed uninterrupted and incredible blessings from the Lord in his life. His wealth and popularity multiplied. Wisdom and courage, integrity and humility, vision and determination marked his steps. But suddenly everything came to a screeching halt.

In an unguarded moment David succumbed to the flesh—a lustful thought bore fruit and several sins occurred back to back in rapid succession: adultery, deception, hypocrisy, murder, and finally a wholesale cover-up. No one is immune to the enemy's assaults and schemes—not even a godly king named David! After this whole episode David began to slide further down the roof, losing his family as well as his nation and ultimately his life. In the book of 2 Samuel we find a tragic study in contrasts.

In chapters 11 and 12 we read about David and Bathsheba. Next to David's victory over Goliath, this is probably the most familiar story about David. Unfortunately, this event in his life is notorious rather than victorious. David committed adultery with Bathsheba and then proceeded to deceive, lie and finally commit murder to cover his sinful tracks. Just when he thought he had gotten away with his evil deeds, the Lord sent the prophet Nathan to confront David with his sins. After being confronted, David said, "I have sinned against the LORD" (12:13), and Nathan responded with, "The LORD has taken away your sin." There were, however, consequences that no repentance could erase. Carnal sowing invariably reaps a horrible harvest of heartaches.

This series of events marked a turning point in the life of David. From this time on things seemed to go from bad to worse. In chapter 13 one of David's sons, Amnon, raped his half-sister, Tamar. Absalom, Tamar's full brother, heard about this and murdered Amnon. Absalom then planned a military takeover and drove his father, David, from the throne and out of Jerusalem. For five chapters (14–18), Absalom ruled Israel while his father was in humiliating exile. David kept running from his own son until finally Joab, the commander of the army of Israel, murdered Absalom. All of these troubles came upon the family of David. At this point David had hit rock bottom.

Here's the scene beyond the peak of the roof . . . the consequences of carnality: the death of the newborn baby of David and Bathsheba (12:18), the rape of Tamar (13:14), the murder of Amnon (13:29), the rebellion of Absalom (15:10), and David running for his life (15:14). It was Absalom's death (18:14) that finally put David down on his face:

> *The king was shaken. He went up to the room over the gateway and wept. As he went, he said: "O my son Absalom! My son, my son Absalom! If only I had died instead of you—O Absalom, my son, my son!"(18:33).*

No more vivid scene of heartache mixed with guilt and grief can be found in the pages of the Old Testament. The man had absolutely hit bottom. His sin had found him out. He had "sown the wind" and now was "reaping the whirlwind" (see Hosea 8:7).

Bible commentator F.B. Meyer wrote, "This is the bitterest of all: to know that suffering need not have been; that it has resulted from indiscretion and inconsistency; that it is the harvest of one's own sowing; that the vulture which feeds on the vitals is a nestling of one's own rearing. Ah, me! This is pain."

Beware the Beast of Lust

Are you allowing the beast of lust to grow up in your life? Do you entertain and secretly enjoy those little wicked thoughts that "won't hurt anyone"? Maybe you think, "What's a little wicked thought in the privacy of my own secret world?" It won't be long before the monster will rear its ugly head and stand up at full height. No one is immune! We need to remember that no person is so great that the enemy is not greater still. If the devil can win a victory over an influential Christian, then he's won a victory over all those whose lives have been touched by that Christian.

Learning From Others' Mistakes

The book of 2 Samuel yields three lessons. First, *prosperity and ease can be perilous at times and not necessarily a blessing*. Second, *gross sin is often the culmination of a process, not a sudden act*. Way back in chapter 3, David was already adding to his fortune a number of wives. Why in the world would he reach down and take some other man's ewe lamb when he had a whole harem full of them? That was the prophet Nathan's point! Question: You have a harem full of them and you're still not satisfied—why not? Simple answer: Because you're driven by lust, and lust is *never* satisfied. It grows slowly . . . but one day, like a hungry beast in the wild, it consumes its victim. Third, *confession and repentance help heal a wound but will never erase the scars*. If we're honest enough to admit it, there are times when we enter into willful sin saying to ourselves, "Well, if I confess and repent later, God will forgive me." Ah! But don't forget the scar. He'll heal the wound, but many of the scars will remain for a lifetime. And speaking of that, let's be reminded that there will also be times our children will suffer the fallout of the consequences . . . and their children after them. That's one of the biggest heartaches of all. Our sins affect more people than we would ever dream.

The only hope we have is in daily dependence on the living Lord. Yes, *daily*! It's the only way we'll make it. God is touched by our infirmities, our weaknesses, our inability in the dark and lonely times to say "No." He is touched by our struggles, and He says, "I'm ready with the power. Call on Me, and I'll give you what you need."

Let me simply remind you to look at the ultimate end of sinful acts, not just the beginning. See the consequences, not just the fun and games. See the heartache, not just the ecstasy. Be honest and look at the agony and misery you will be inviting into your life and the lives of those you love. Remember David's experiences in 2 Samuel, and ask yourself this hard question: "Is it really worth it?" Then answer that question with all the honesty you can muster.

David's Triumphs **Chapters 1–10**

The first ten chapters of 2 Samuel record the golden years of David's kingship. He was God's man of the year . . . year after year. Everyone loved David and everything seemed to go his way. There are no less than 11 different military victories recorded in these chapters. The empire was growing, the nation was prosperous and powerful, and everything seemed perfect . . . not only a "chicken in every pot" but grapes on every vine! Israel was blessed by God as David walked with the Lord. It was a time of triumph, victory and uninterrupted blessing for the nation of Israel and their shepherd-king.

David Hears of Saul's Death

1 After the death of Saul, David returned from defeating the Amalekites and stayed in Ziklag two days. 2On the third day a man arrived from Saul's camp, with his clothes torn and with dust on his head. When he came to David, he fell to the ground to pay him honor. 1Sa 4:12; 30:17; 31:6

3"Where have you come from?" David asked him.

He answered, "I have escaped from the Israelite camp."

4"What happened?" David asked. "Tell me."

He said, "The men fled from the battle. Many of them fell and died. And Saul and his son Jonathan are dead."

5Then David said to the young man who brought him the report, "How do you know that Saul and his son Jonathan are dead?"

6"I happened to be on Mount Gilboa," the young man said, "and there was Saul, leaning on his spear, with the chariots and riders almost upon him. 7When he turned around and saw me, he called out to me, and I said, 'What can I do?'

8"He asked me, 'Who are you?'

"'An Amalekite,' I answered. 1Sa 15:2

9"Then he said to me, 'Stand over me and kill me! I am in the throes of death, but I'm still alive.'

10"So I stood over him and killed him, because I knew that after he had fallen he could not survive. And I took the crown that was on his head and the band on his arm and have brought them here to my lord." Jdg 9:54; 2Ki 11:12

11Then David and all the men with him took hold of their clothes and tore them. 12They mourned and wept and fasted till evening for Saul and his son Jonathan, and for the army of the LORD and the house of Israel, because they had fallen by the sword. 1Sa 31:1-13; 1Ch 10:1-12; Ge 37:29

13David said to the young man who brought him the report, "Where are you from?"

"I am the son of an alien, an Amalekite," he answered.

14David asked him, "Why were you not afraid to lift your hand to destroy the LORD's anointed?"

15Then David called one of his men and said, "Go, strike him down!" So he struck him down, and he died. 16For David had said to him, "Your blood be on your own head. Your own mouth testified against you when you said, 'I killed the LORD's anointed.'" 2Sa 4:10; Lev 20:9; Mt 27:24-25

David's Lament for Saul and Jonathan

17David took up this lament concerning Saul and his son Jonathan, 18and ordered that the men of Judah be taught this lament of the bow (it is written in the Book of Jashar): Jos 10:13; 2Ch 35:25

19"Your glory, O Israel, lies slain on your
heights.
How the mighty have fallen! 2Sa 3:38

20"Tell it not in Gath, Mic 1:10
proclaim it not in the streets of Ashkelon,
lest the daughters of the Philistines be glad,
lest the daughters of the uncircumcised
rejoice. Ex 15:20; 1Sa 18:6; 31:8

21"O mountains of Gilboa, 1Sa 31:1
may you have neither dew nor rain,
nor fields that yield offerings ⌞of grain⌟.
For there the shield of the mighty was defiled,
the shield of Saul—no longer rubbed with
oil. Isa 21:5

22From the blood of the slain,
from the flesh of the mighty, Isa 34:3,7
the bow of Jonathan did not turn back,
the sword of Saul did not return
unsatisfied. 1Sa 18:4

23"Saul and Jonathan—
in life they were loved and gracious,
and in death they were not parted.
They were swifter than eagles, Jer 4:13
they were stronger than lions. Jdg 14:18

24"O daughters of Israel,
weep for Saul,
who clothed you in scarlet and finery,
who adorned your garments with
ornaments of gold.

25"How the mighty have fallen in battle!
Jonathan lies slain on your heights.
26I grieve for you, Jonathan my brother; 1Sa 20:42
you were very dear to me.
Your love for me was wonderful,
more wonderful than that of women.

27"How the mighty have fallen!
The weapons of war have perished!"

David Anointed King Over Judah

2 In the course of time, David inquired of the LORD. "Shall I go up to one of the towns of Judah?" he asked. 1Sa 23:2,11-12

The LORD said, "Go up."

David asked, "Where shall I go?"

"To Hebron," the LORD answered. Ge 13:18

2So David went up there with his two wives, Ahinoam of Jezreel and Abigail, the widow of Nabal of Carmel. 3David also took the men who were with him, each with his family, and they settled in Hebron and its towns. 4Then the men of Judah came to Hebron and there they anointed David king over the house of Judah. 1Sa 25:42; 27:2; 2Sa 5:3-5

When David was told that it was the men of Jabesh Gilead who had buried Saul, 5he sent messengers to the men of Jabesh Gilead to say to them, "The LORD bless you for showing this kindness to Saul your master by burying him. 6May the LORD now show you kindness and faithfulness, and I too will show you the same favor because you have done this. 7Now then, be strong and brave, for Saul your master is dead, and the house of Judah has anointed me king over them." Ex 34:6; 1Sa 23:21

War Between the Houses of David and Saul

8Meanwhile, Abner son of Ner, the commander of Saul's army, had taken Ish-Bosheth son of Saul and brought him over to Mahanaim. 9He made him king over Gilead, Ashuri[a] and Jezreel, and also over Ephraim, Benjamin and all Israel.

10Ish-Bosheth son of Saul was forty years old when he became king over Israel, and he reigned two years. The house of Judah, however, followed David. 11The length of time David was king in Hebron over the house of Judah was seven years and six months. 2Sa 5:5

12Abner son of Ner, together with the men of Ish-Bosheth son of Saul, left Mahanaim and went to Gibeon. 13Joab son of Zeruiah and David's men went out and met them at the pool of Gibeon. One group sat down on one side of the pool and one group on the other side. Jos 18:25; 2Sa 8:16; 1Ch 2:16

14Then Abner said to Joab, "Let's have some of the young men get up and fight hand to hand in front of us."

"All right, let them do it," Joab said.

15So they stood up and were counted off—twelve men for Benjamin and Ish-Bosheth son of Saul, and twelve for David. 16Then each man grabbed his opponent by the head and thrust his dagger into his opponent's side, and they fell down together. So that place in Gibeon was called Helkath Hazzurim.[b]

17The battle that day was very fierce, and Abner and the men of Israel were defeated by David's men. 2Sa 3:1

18The three sons of Zeruiah were there: Joab, Abishai and Asahel. Now Asahel was as fleet-footed as a wild gazelle. 19He chased Abner, turning neither to the right nor to the left as he pursued him. 20Abner looked behind him and asked, "Is that you, Asahel?" 1Ch 2:16; 12:8

"It is," he answered.

21Then Abner said to him, "Turn aside to the right or to the left; take on one of the young men and strip him of his weapons." But Asahel would not stop chasing him.

22Again Abner warned Asahel, "Stop chasing me! Why should I strike you down? How could I look your brother Joab in the face?" 2Sa 3:27

23But Asahel refused to give up the pursuit; so Abner thrust the butt of his spear into Asahel's stomach, and the spear came out through his back. He fell there and died on the spot. And every man stopped when he came to the place where Asahel had fallen and died. 2Sa 3:27; 20:12

24But Joab and Abishai pursued Abner, and as the sun was setting, they came to the hill of Ammah, near Giah on the way to the wasteland of Gibeon. 25Then the men of Benjamin rallied behind Abner. They formed themselves into a group and took their stand on top of a hill.

26Abner called out to Joab, "Must the sword devour forever? Don't you realize that this will end in bitterness? How long before you order your men to stop pursuing their brothers?" Dt 32:42

27Joab answered, "As surely as God lives, if you had not spoken, the men would have continued the pursuit of their brothers until morning.[c]"

28So Joab blew the trumpet, and all the men came to a halt; they no longer pursued Israel, nor did they fight anymore. 2Sa 18:16; Jdg 3:27

29All that night Abner and his men marched through the Arabah. They crossed the Jordan, continued through the whole Bithron[d] and came to Mahanaim.

30Then Joab returned from pursuing Abner and assembled all his men. Besides Asahel, nineteen of David's men were found missing. 31But David's men had killed three hundred and sixty Benjamites who were with Abner. 32They took Asahel and buried him in his father's tomb at Bethlehem. Then Joab and his men marched all night and arrived at Hebron by daybreak. Ge 49:29

3 The war between the house of Saul and the house of David lasted a long time. David grew stronger and stronger, while the house of Saul grew weaker and weaker. 2Sa 2:17; 5:10; 1Ki 14:30

2Sons were born to David in Hebron:

His firstborn was Amnon the son of Ahinoam of Jezreel; 1Sa 25:43; 1Ch 3:1-3
3his second, Kileab the son of Abigail the widow of Nabal of Carmel; 1Sa 25:42
the third, Absalom the son of Maacah daughter of Talmai king of Geshur;
4the fourth, Adonijah the son of Haggith;

[a] 9 Or *Asher* [b] 16 *Helkath Hazzurim* means *field of daggers* or *field of hostilities.* [c] 27 Or *spoken this morning, the men would not have taken up the pursuit of their brothers*; or *spoken, the men would have given up the pursuit of their brothers by morning* [d] 29 Or *morning*; or *ravine*; the meaning of the Hebrew for this word is uncertain.

the fifth, Shephatiah the son of Abital;
5and the sixth, Ithream the son of David's
wife Eglah.
These were born to David in Hebron.

Abner Goes Over to David

6During the war between the house of Saul and the house of David, Abner had been strengthening his own position in the house of Saul. 7Now Saul had had a concubine named Rizpah daughter of Aiah. And Ish-Bosheth said to Abner, "Why did you sleep with my father's concubine?"

8Abner was very angry because of what Ish-Bosheth said and he answered, "Am I a dog's head—on Judah's side? This very day I am loyal to the house of your father Saul and to his family and friends. I haven't handed you over to David. Yet now you accuse me of an offense involving this woman! 9May God deal with Abner, be it ever so severely, if I do not do for David what the LORD promised him on oath 10and transfer the kingdom from the house of Saul and establish David's throne over Israel and Judah from Dan to Beersheba." 11Ish-Bosheth did not dare to say another word to Abner, because he was afraid of him.

12Then Abner sent messengers on his behalf to say to David, "Whose land is it? Make an agreement with me, and I will help you bring all Israel over to you."

13"Good," said David. "I will make an agreement with you. But I demand one thing of you: Do not come into my presence unless you bring Michal daughter of Saul when you come to see me." 14Then David sent messengers to Ish-Bosheth son of Saul, demanding, "Give me my wife Michal, whom I betrothed to myself for the price of a hundred Philistine foreskins." Ge 43:5; 1Sa 18:27

15So Ish-Bosheth gave orders and had her taken away from her husband Paltiel son of Laish. 16Her husband, however, went with her, weeping behind her all the way to Bahurim. Then Abner said to him, "Go back home!" So he went back. Dt 24:1-4

17Abner conferred with the elders of Israel and said, "For some time you have wanted to make David your king. 18Now do it! For the LORD promised David, 'By my servant David I will rescue my people Israel from the hand of the Philistines and from the hand of all their enemies.'" Jdg 11:11

19Abner also spoke to the Benjamites in person. Then he went to Hebron to tell David everything that Israel and the whole house of Benjamin wanted to do. 20When Abner, who had twenty men with him, came to David at Hebron, David prepared a feast for him and his men. 21Then Abner said to David, "Let me go at once and assemble all Israel for my lord the king, so that they may make a compact with you, and that you may rule over all that your heart desires." So David sent Abner away, and he went in peace. 1Sa 10:20-21; 1Ki 11:37

Joab Murders Abner

22Just then David's men and Joab returned from a raid and brought with them a great deal of plunder. But Abner was no longer with David in Hebron, because David had sent him away, and he had gone in peace. 23When Joab and all the soldiers with him arrived, he was told that Abner son of Ner had come to the king and that the king had sent him away and that he had gone in peace.

24So Joab went to the king and said, "What have you done? Look, Abner came to you. Why did you let him go? Now he is gone! 25You know Abner son of Ner; he came to deceive you and observe your movements and find out everything you are doing."

26Joab then left David and sent messengers after Abner, and they brought him back from the well of Sirah. But David did not know it. 27Now when Abner returned to Hebron, Joab took him aside into the gateway, as though to speak with him privately. And there, to avenge the blood of his brother Asahel, Joab stabbed him in the stomach, and he died. 2Sa 2:22; 20:9-10; 1Ki 2:5

28Later, when David heard about this, he said, "I and my kingdom are forever innocent before the LORD concerning the blood of Abner son of Ner. 29May his blood fall upon the head of Joab and upon all his father's house! May Joab's house never be without someone who has a running sore or leprosy[a] or who leans on a crutch or who falls by the sword or who lacks food." Dt 21:9; Lev 15:2

30(Joab and his brother Abishai murdered Abner because he had killed their brother Asahel in the battle at Gibeon.)

31Then David said to Joab and all the people with him, "Tear your clothes and put on sackcloth and walk in mourning in front of Abner." King David himself walked behind the bier. 32They buried Abner in Hebron, and the king wept aloud at Abner's tomb. All the people wept also. Ge 37:34

33The king sang this lament for Abner: 2Sa 1:17

"Should Abner have died as the lawless die?
34 Your hands were not bound,
your feet were not fettered.
You fell as one falls before wicked men."

And all the people wept over him again.

35Then they all came and urged David to eat something while it was still day; but David took an oath, saying, "May God deal with me, be it ever so severely, if I taste bread or anything else before the sun sets!" Ru 1:17; 2Sa 1:12; 12:17

36All the people took note and were pleased; indeed, everything the king did pleased them. 37So

[a]29 The Hebrew word was used for various diseases affecting the skin—not necessarily leprosy.

on that day all the people and all Israel knew that the king had no part in the murder of Abner son of Ner.

[38]Then the king said to his men, "Do you not realize that a prince and a great man has fallen in Israel this day? [39]And today, though I am the anointed king, I am weak, and these sons of Zeruiah are too strong for me. May the LORD repay the evildoer according to his evil deeds!" 2Sa 19:5-7

Ish-Bosheth Murdered

4 When Ish-Bosheth son of Saul heard that Abner had died in Hebron, he lost courage, and all Israel became alarmed. [2]Now Saul's son had two men who were leaders of raiding bands. One was named Baanah and the other Recab; they were sons of Rimmon the Beerothite from the tribe of Benjamin—Beeroth is considered part of Benjamin, [3]because the people of Beeroth fled to Gittaim and have lived there as aliens to this day.

[4](Jonathan son of Saul had a son who was lame in both feet. He was five years old when the news about Saul and Jonathan came from Jezreel. His nurse picked him up and fled, but as she hurried to leave, he fell and became crippled. His name was Mephibosheth.) 1Sa 18:1; 2Sa 9:3,6; 1Ch 8:34

[5]Now Recab and Baanah, the sons of Rimmon the Beerothite, set out for the house of Ish-Bosheth, and they arrived there in the heat of the day while he was taking his noonday rest. [6]They went into the inner part of the house as if to get some wheat, and they stabbed him in the stomach. Then Recab and his brother Baanah slipped away.

[7]They had gone into the house while he was lying on the bed in his bedroom. After they stabbed and killed him, they cut off his head. Taking it with them, they traveled all night by way of the Arabah. [8]They brought the head of Ish-Bosheth to David at Hebron and said to the king, "Here is the head of Ish-Bosheth son of Saul, your enemy, who tried to take your life. This day the LORD has avenged my lord the king against Saul and his offspring." 1Sa 24:4; 25:29

[9]David answered Recab and his brother Baanah, the sons of Rimmon the Beerothite, "As surely as the LORD lives, who has delivered me out of all trouble, [10]when a man told me, 'Saul is dead,' and thought he was bringing good news, I seized him and put him to death in Ziklag. That was the reward I gave him for his news! [11]How much more—when wicked men have killed an innocent man in his own house and on his own bed—should I not now demand his blood from your hand and rid the earth of you!" 1Ki 1:29; 2Sa 1:2-16

[12]So David gave an order to his men, and they killed them. They cut off their hands and feet and hung the bodies by the pool in Hebron. But they took the head of Ish-Bosheth and buried it in Abner's tomb at Hebron. 2Sa 1:15

David Becomes King Over Israel

5 All the tribes of Israel came to David at Hebron and said, "We are your own flesh and blood. [2]In the past, while Saul was king over us, you were the one who led Israel on their military campaigns. And the LORD said to you, 'You will shepherd my people Israel, and you will become their ruler.'" 1Sa 16:1; 18:5,13,16

[3]When all the elders of Israel had come to King David at Hebron, the king made a compact with them at Hebron before the LORD, and they anointed David king over Israel. 1Ch 11:1-3; 2Sa 2:4; 3:21

[4]David was thirty years old when he became king, and he reigned forty years. [5]In Hebron he reigned over Judah seven years and six months, and in Jerusalem he reigned over all Israel and Judah thirty-three years. Lk 3:23; 1Ch 3:4; 26:31

David Conquers Jerusalem

[6]The king and his men marched to Jerusalem to attack the Jebusites, who lived there. The Jebusites said to David, "You will not get in here; even the blind and the lame can ward you off." They thought, "David cannot get in here." [7]Nevertheless, David captured the fortress of Zion, the City of David. Jos 15:8; Jdg 1:8; 1Ki 2:10

[8]On that day, David said, "Anyone who conquers the Jebusites will have to use the water shaft[a] to reach those 'lame and blind' who are David's enemies.[b]" That is why they say, "The 'blind and lame' will not enter the palace."

[9]David then took up residence in the fortress and called it the City of David. He built up the area around it, from the supporting terraces[c] inward. [10]And he became more and more powerful, because the LORD God Almighty was with him.

[11]Now Hiram king of Tyre sent messengers to David, along with cedar logs and carpenters and stonemasons, and they built a palace for David. [12]And David knew that the LORD had established him as king over Israel and had exalted his kingdom for the sake of his people Israel. 1Ki 5:1,18

[13]After he left Hebron, David took more concubines and wives in Jerusalem, and more sons and daughters were born to him. [14]These are the names of the children born to him there: Shammua, Shobab, Nathan, Solomon, [15]Ibhar, Elishua, Nepheg, Japhia, [16]Elishama, Eliada and Eliphelet.

David Defeats the Philistines

[17]When the Philistines heard that David had been anointed king over Israel, they went up in full force to search for him, but David heard about it and went down to the stronghold. [18]Now the Phi-

[a]8 Or *use scaling hooks* [b]8 Or *are hated by David* [c]9 Or *the Millo*

listines had come and spread out in the Valley of Rephaim; [19]so David inquired of the LORD, "Shall I go and attack the Philistines? Will you hand them over to me?" 1Sa 23:2; 2Sa 23:14; Jos 15:8

The LORD answered him, "Go, for I will surely hand the Philistines over to you."

[20]So David went to Baal Perazim, and there he defeated them. He said, "As waters break out, the LORD has broken out against my enemies before me." So that place was called Baal Perazim.[a] [21]The Philistines abandoned their idols there, and David and his men carried them off. 1Ch 14:12

[22]Once more the Philistines came up and spread out in the Valley of Rephaim; [23]so David inquired of the LORD, and he answered, "Do not go straight up, but circle around behind them and attack them in front of the balsam trees. [24]As soon as you hear the sound of marching in the tops of the balsam trees, move quickly, because that will mean the LORD has gone out in front of you to strike the Philistine army." [25]So David did as the LORD commanded him, and he struck down the Philistines all the way from Gibeon[b] to Gezer. 1Ch 14:8-17

The Ark Brought to Jerusalem

6 David again brought together out of Israel chosen men, thirty thousand in all. [2]He and all his men set out from Baalah of Judah[c] to bring up from there the ark of God, which is called by the Name,[d] the name of the LORD Almighty, who is enthroned between the cherubim that are on the ark. [3]They set the ark of God on a new cart and brought it from the house of Abinadab, which was on the hill. Uzzah and Ahio, sons of Abinadab, were guiding the new cart [4]with the ark of God on it,[e] and Ahio was walking in front of it. [5]David and the whole house of Israel were celebrating with all their might before the LORD, with songs[f] and with harps, lyres, tambourines, sistrums and cymbals. Lev 24:16; 1Sa 4:4; 6:7

[6]When they came to the threshing floor of Nacon, Uzzah reached out and took hold of the ark of God, because the oxen stumbled. [7]The LORD's anger burned against Uzzah because of his irreverent act; therefore God struck him down and he died there beside the ark of God. Ex 19:22

[8]Then David was angry because the LORD's wrath had broken out against Uzzah, and to this day that place is called Perez Uzzah.[g] Ps 7:11

[9]David was afraid of the LORD that day and said, "How can the ark of the LORD ever come to me?" [10]He was not willing to take the ark of the LORD to be with him in the City of David. Instead, he took it aside to the house of Obed-Edom the Gittite. [11]The ark of the LORD remained in the house of Obed-Edom the Gittite for three months, and the LORD blessed him and his entire household.

[12]Now King David was told, "The LORD has blessed the household of Obed-Edom and everything he has, because of the ark of God." So David went down and brought up the ark of God from the house of Obed-Edom to the City of David with rejoicing. [13]When those who were carrying the ark of the LORD had taken six steps, he sacrificed a bull and a fattened calf. [14]David, wearing a linen ephod, danced before the LORD with all his might, [15]while he and the entire house of Israel brought up the ark of the LORD with shouts and the sound of trumpets. Ex 15:20; 1Ki 8:1,5,62; 1Ch 15:25

[16]As the ark of the LORD was entering the City of David, Michal daughter of Saul watched from a window. And when she saw King David leaping and dancing before the LORD, she despised him in her heart.

[17]They brought the ark of the LORD and set it in its place inside the tent that David had pitched for it, and David sacrificed burnt offerings and fellowship offerings[h] before the LORD. [18]After he had finished sacrificing the burnt offerings and fellowship offerings, he blessed the people in the name of the LORD Almighty. [19]Then he gave a loaf of bread, a cake of dates and a cake of raisins to each person in the whole crowd of Israelites, both men and women. And all the people went to their homes.

[20]When David returned home to bless his household, Michal daughter of Saul came out to meet him and said, "How the king of Israel has distinguished himself today, disrobing in the sight of the slave girls of his servants as any vulgar fellow would!"

[21]David said to Michal, "It was before the LORD, who chose me rather than your father or anyone from his house when he appointed me ruler over the LORD's people Israel—I will celebrate before the LORD. [22]I will become even more undignified than this, and I will be humiliated in my own eyes. But by these slave girls you spoke of, I will be held in honor." 1Sa 13:14

[23]And Michal daughter of Saul had no children to the day of her death.

God's Promise to David

7 After the king was settled in his palace and the LORD had given him rest from all his enemies around him, [2]he said to Nathan the prophet,

[a]20 *Baal Perazim* means *the lord who breaks out.* [b]25 Septuagint (see also 1 Chron. 14:16); Hebrew *Geba* [c]2 That is, Kiriath Jearim; Hebrew *Baale Judah,* a variant of *Baalah of Judah* [d]2 Hebrew; Septuagint and Vulgate do not have *the Name.* [e]3,4 Dead Sea Scrolls and some Septuagint manuscripts; Masoretic Text *cart* [4]*and they brought it with the ark of God from the house of Abinadab, which was on the hill* [f]5 See Dead Sea Scrolls, Septuagint and 1 Chronicles 13:8; Masoretic Text *celebrating before the LORD with all kinds of instruments made of pine.* [g]8 *Perez Uzzah* means *outbreak against Uzzah.* [h]17 Traditionally *peace offerings*; also in verse 18

"Here I am, living in a palace of cedar, while the ark of God remains in a tent." Ex 26:1; 2Sa 5:11

[3]Nathan replied to the king, "Whatever you have in mind, go ahead and do it, for the LORD is with you."

[4]That night the word of the LORD came to Nathan, saying:

[5]"Go and tell my servant David, 'This is what the LORD says: Are you the one to build me a house to dwell in? [6]I have not dwelt in a house from the day I brought the Israelites up out of Egypt to this day. I have been moving from place to place with a tent as my dwelling. [7]Wherever I have moved with all the Israelites, did I ever say to any of their rulers whom I commanded to shepherd my people Israel, "Why have you not built me a house of cedar?"' Ex 40:18,34; Lev 26:11-12; 1Ki 5:3-5

[8]"Now then, tell my servant David, 'This is what the LORD Almighty says: I took you from the pasture and from following the flock to be ruler over my people Israel. [9]I have been with you wherever you have gone, and I have cut off all your enemies from before you. Now I will make your name great, like the names of the greatest men of the earth. [10]And I will provide a place for my people Israel and will plant them so that they can have a home of their own and no longer be disturbed. Wicked people will not oppress them anymore, as they did at the beginning [11]and have done ever since the time I appointed leaders[a] over my people Israel. I will also give you rest from all your enemies.

"'The LORD declares to you that the LORD himself will establish a house for you: [12]When your days are over and you rest with your fathers, I will raise up your offspring to succeed you, who will come from your own body, and I will establish his kingdom. [13]He is the one who will build a house for my Name, and I will establish the throne of his kingdom forever. [14]I will be his father, and he will be my son. When he does wrong, I will punish him with the rod of men, with floggings inflicted by men. [15]But my love will never be taken away from him, as I took it away from Saul, whom I removed from before you. [16]Your house and your kingdom will endure forever before me[b]; your throne will be established forever.'" 1Ch 17:1-15

[17]Nathan reported to David all the words of this entire revelation.

David's Prayer

[18]Then King David went in and sat before the LORD, and he said:

"Who am I, O Sovereign LORD, and what is my family, that you have brought me this far? [19]And as if this were not enough in your sight, O Sovereign LORD, you have also spoken about the future of the house of your servant. Is this your usual way of dealing with man, O Sovereign LORD? 1Sa 18:18

[20]"What more can David say to you? For you know your servant, O Sovereign LORD. [21]For the sake of your word and according to your will, you have done this great thing and made it known to your servant. 1Sa 16:7

[22]"How great you are, O Sovereign LORD! There is no one like you, and there is no God but you, as we have heard with our own ears. [23]And who is like your people Israel—the one nation on earth that God went out to redeem as a people for himself, and to make a name for himself, and to perform great and awesome wonders by driving out nations and their gods from before your people, whom you redeemed from Egypt?[c] [24]You have established your people Israel as your very own forever, and you, O LORD, have become their God. Dt 3:24; 4:32-38; 26:18

[25]"And now, LORD God, keep forever the promise you have made concerning your servant and his house. Do as you promised, [26]so that your name will be great forever. Then men will say, 'The LORD Almighty is God over Israel!' And the house of your servant David will be established before you.

[27]"O LORD Almighty, God of Israel, you have revealed this to your servant, saying, 'I will build a house for you.' So your servant has found courage to offer you this prayer. [28]O Sovereign LORD, you are God! Your words are trustworthy, and you have promised these good things to your servant. [29]Now be pleased to bless the house of your servant, that it may continue forever in your sight; for you, O Sovereign LORD, have spoken, and with your blessing the house of your servant will be blessed forever."

David's Victories

8 In the course of time, David defeated the Philistines and subdued them, and he took Metheg Ammah from the control of the Philistines.

[2]David also defeated the Moabites. He made

[a]*11* Traditionally *judges* [b]*16* Some Hebrew manuscripts and Septuagint; most Hebrew manuscripts *you* [c]*23* See Septuagint and 1 Chron. 17:21; Hebrew *wonders for your land and before your people, whom you redeemed from Egypt, from the nations and their gods.*

them lie down on the ground and measured them off with a length of cord. Every two lengths of them were put to death, and the third length was allowed to live. So the Moabites became subject to David and brought tribute. Nu 24:17

3Moreover, David fought Hadadezer son of Rehob, king of Zobah, when he went to restore his control along the Euphrates River. 4David captured a thousand of his chariots, seven thousand charioteers[a] and twenty thousand foot soldiers. He hamstrung all but a hundred of the chariot horses. Jos 11:9; 1Sa 14:47; 2Sa 10:16,19

5When the Arameans of Damascus came to help Hadadezer king of Zobah, David struck down twenty-two thousand of them. 6He put garrisons in the Aramean kingdom of Damascus, and the Arameans became subject to him and brought tribute. The LORD gave David victory wherever he went. 2Sa 3:18; 1Ki 11:24

7David took the gold shields that belonged to the officers of Hadadezer and brought them to Jerusalem. 8From Tebah[b] and Berothai, towns that belonged to Hadadezer, King David took a great quantity of bronze. 1Ki 10:16; Eze 47:16

9When Tou[c] king of Hamath heard that David had defeated the entire army of Hadadezer, 10he sent his son Joram[d] to King David to greet him and congratulate him on his victory in battle over Hadadezer, who had been at war with Tou. Joram brought with him articles of silver and gold and bronze.

11King David dedicated these articles to the LORD, as he had done with the silver and gold from all the nations he had subdued: 12Edom[e] and Moab, the Ammonites and the Philistines, and Amalek. He also dedicated the plunder taken from Hadadezer son of Rehob, king of Zobah. 1Ki 7:51

13And David became famous after he returned from striking down eighteen thousand Edomites[f] in the Valley of Salt. 2Ki 14:7

14He put garrisons throughout Edom, and all the Edomites became subject to David. The LORD gave David victory wherever he went. 1Ch 18:1-13

David's Officials

15David reigned over all Israel, doing what was just and right for all his people. 16Joab son of Zeruiah was over the army; Jehoshaphat son of Ahilud was recorder; 17Zadok son of Ahitub and Ahimelech son of Abiathar were priests; Seraiah was secretary; 18Benaiah son of Jehoiada was over the Kerethites and Pelethites; and David's sons were royal advisers.[g] Ge 18:19; 1Sa 30:14; 1Ch 24:3

David and Mephibosheth

9 David asked, "Is there anyone still left of the house of Saul to whom I can show kindness for Jonathan's sake?" 1Sa 20:14-17,42

2Now there was a servant of Saul's household named Ziba. They called him to appear before David, and the king said to him, "Are you Ziba?"

"Your servant," he replied.

3The king asked, "Is there no one still left of the house of Saul to whom I can show God's kindness?"

Ziba answered the king, "There is still a son of Jonathan; he is crippled in both feet." 2Sa 4:4

4"Where is he?" the king asked.

Ziba answered, "He is at the house of Makir son of Ammiel in Lo Debar." 2Sa 17:27-29

5So King David had him brought from Lo Debar, from the house of Makir son of Ammiel.

6When Mephibosheth son of Jonathan, the son of Saul, came to David, he bowed down to pay him honor.

David said, "Mephibosheth!"

"Your servant," he replied.

7"Don't be afraid," David said to him, "for I will surely show you kindness for the sake of your father Jonathan. I will restore to you all the land that belonged to your grandfather Saul, and you will always eat at my table." 1Ki 2:7; 2Ki 25:29

8Mephibosheth bowed down and said, "What is your servant, that you should notice a dead dog like me?" 2Sa 16:9

9Then the king summoned Ziba, Saul's servant, and said to him, "I have given your master's grandson everything that belonged to Saul and his family. 10You and your sons and your servants are to farm the land for him and bring in the crops, so that your master's grandson may be provided for. And Mephibosheth, grandson of your master, will always eat at my table." (Now Ziba had fifteen sons and twenty servants.)

11Then Ziba said to the king, "Your servant will do whatever my lord the king commands his servant to do." So Mephibosheth ate at David's[h] table like one of the king's sons.

12Mephibosheth had a young son named Mica, and all the members of Ziba's household were servants of Mephibosheth. 13And Mephibosheth lived in Jerusalem, because he always ate at the king's table, and he was crippled in both feet. 1Ch 8:34

David Defeats the Ammonites

10 In the course of time, the king of the Ammonites died, and his son Hanun succeeded him as king. 2David thought, "I will show kind-

[a]4 Septuagint (see also Dead Sea Scrolls and 1 Chron. 18:4); Masoretic Text *captured seventeen hundred of his charioteers*
[b]8 See some Septuagint manuscripts (see also 1 Chron. 18:8); Hebrew *Betah.*
[c]9 Hebrew *Toi*, a variant of *Tou*; also in verse 10
[d]10 A variant of *Hadoram*
[e]12 Some Hebrew manuscripts, Septuagint and Syriac (see also 1 Chron. 18:11); most Hebrew manuscripts *Aram*
[f]13 A few Hebrew manuscripts, Septuagint and Syriac (see also 1 Chron. 18:12); most Hebrew manuscripts *Aram* (that is, Arameans)
[g]18 Or *were priests*
[h]11 Septuagint; Hebrew *my*

ness to Hanun son of Nahash, just as his father
showed kindness to me." So David sent a delegation to express his sympathy to Hanun concerning
his father. 1Sa 11:1
When David's men came to the land of the
Ammonites, 3the Ammonite nobles said to Hanun
their lord, "Do you think David is honoring your
father by sending men to you to express sympathy? Hasn't David sent them to you to explore the
city and spy it out and overthrow it?" 4So Hanun
seized David's men, shaved off half of each man's
beard, cut off their garments in the middle at the
buttocks, and sent them away. Isa 15:2; 20:4
5When David was told about this, he sent messengers to meet the men, for they were greatly
humiliated. The king said, "Stay at Jericho till your
beards have grown, and then come back."
6When the Ammonites realized that they had
become a stench in David's nostrils, they hired
twenty thousand Aramean foot soldiers from Beth
Rehob and Zobah, as well as the king of Maacah
with a thousand men, and also twelve thousand
men from Tob. Ge 34:30; 2Sa 8:5; Jdg 18:28
7On hearing this, David sent Joab out with the
entire army of fighting men. 8The Ammonites
came out and drew up in battle formation at the
entrance to their city gate, while the Arameans of
Zobah and Rehob and the men of Tob and Maacah were by themselves in the open country.
9Joab saw that there were battle lines in front of
him and behind him; so he selected some of the
best troops in Israel and deployed them against the
Arameans. 10He put the rest of the men under
the command of Abishai his brother and deployed
them against the Ammonites. 11Joab said, "If the
Arameans are too strong for me, then you are to
come to my rescue; but if the Ammonites are too
strong for you, then I will come to rescue you. 12Be
strong and let us fight bravely for our people and
the cities of our God. The LORD will do what is
good in his sight." Dt 31:6; 1Sa 3:18; 1Co 16:13
13Then Joab and the troops with him advanced
to fight the Arameans, and they fled before him.
14When the Ammonites saw that the Arameans
were fleeing, they fled before Abishai and went
inside the city. So Joab returned from fighting the
Ammonites and came to Jerusalem.
15After the Arameans saw that they had been
routed by Israel, they regrouped. 16Hadadezer had
Arameans brought from beyond the River[a]; they
went to Helam, with Shobach the commander of
Hadadezer's army leading them.
17When David was told of this, he gathered all
Israel, crossed the Jordan and went to Helam. The
Arameans formed their battle lines to meet David
and fought against him. 18But they fled before Israel, and David killed seven hundred of their charioteers and forty thousand of their foot soldiers.[b]
He also struck down Shobach the commander of
their army, and he died there. 19When all the kings
who were vassals of Hadadezer saw that they had
been defeated by Israel, they made peace with the
Israelites and became subject to them. 2Sa 8:6
So the Arameans were afraid to help the Ammonites anymore. 1Ch 19:1-19; 1Ki 11:25

David's Turning Point **Chapters 11–12**

The next two chapters of this book record the turning point in David's kingship. Talk about a transition! The story of David's adultery with Bathsheba is a prime example of the way sin tends to snowball and get bigger and bigger as it rolls downhill. It all began with an innocent glance over the edge of David's palace roof. One look turned into a stare as lust began to fill the heart of David. Lust led to an invitation for Bathsheba to come to the king's chambers in the palace. This meeting led to the overpowering allurement of lust—and finally to the act of adultery; David had sexual relations with a married woman. This sin led to an immediate cover-up of deception and finally to the murder of Bathsheba's husband. Each act of sin led to another until the whole situation had careened out of control.

David and Bathsheba

11 In the spring, at the time when kings go off
to war, David sent Joab out with the king's
men and the whole Israelite army. They destroyed
the Ammonites and besieged Rabbah. But David
remained in Jerusalem. 1Ki 20:22,26; 1Ch 20:1
2One evening David got up from his bed and
walked around on the roof of the palace. From the
roof he saw a woman bathing. The woman was
very beautiful, 3and David sent someone to find
out about her. The man said, "Isn't this Bathsheba,
the daughter of Eliam and the wife of Uriah the
Hittite?" 4Then David sent messengers to get her.
She came to him, and he slept with her. (She had
purified herself from her uncleanness.) Then[c] she

LIVING  INSIGHT

It is terribly important, especially in the area of personal morality, that we keep a safe distance when there is the temptation to be involved in illicit activity. Most of us have been down the pike far enough to know that we cannot trust our sinful nature. Heed this word of counsel: **Don't get yourself in a situation where your nature takes charge.**

(See 2 Samuel 11:2–5.)

[a]16 That is, the Euphrates [b]18 Some Septuagint manuscripts (see also 1 Chron. 19:18); Hebrew *horsemen* [c]4 Or *with her. When she purified herself from her uncleanness,*

went back home. 5The woman conceived and sent
word to David, saying, "I am pregnant."
6So David sent this word to Joab: "Send me
Uriah the Hittite." And Joab sent him to David.
7When Uriah came to him, David asked him how
Joab was, how the soldiers were and how the war
was going. 8Then David said to Uriah, "Go down
to your house and wash your feet." So Uriah left
the palace, and a gift from the king was sent after
him. 9But Uriah slept at the entrance to the palace
with all his master's servants and did not go down
to his house. 1Ch 11:41
10When David was told, "Uriah did not go
home," he asked him, "Haven't you just come
from a distance? Why didn't you go home?"
11Uriah said to David, "The ark and Israel and
Judah are staying in tents, and my master Joab and
my lord's men are camped in the open fields. How
could I go to my house to eat and drink and lie
with my wife? As surely as you live, I will not do
such a thing!" 2Sa 7:2
12Then David said to him, "Stay here one more
day, and tomorrow I will send you back." So Uriah
remained in Jerusalem that day and the next. 13At
David's invitation, he ate and drank with him, and
David made him drunk. But in the evening Uriah
went out to sleep on his mat among his master's
servants; he did not go home.
14In the morning David wrote a letter to Joab
and sent it with Uriah. 15In it he wrote, "Put Uriah
in the front line where the fighting is fiercest. Then
withdraw from him so he will be struck down and
die." 1Ki 21:8; 2Sa 12:12
16So while Joab had the city under siege, he put
Uriah at a place where he knew the strongest de-
fenders were. 17When the men of the city came out
and fought against Joab, some of the men in David's army fell; moreover, Uriah the Hittite died.
18Joab sent David a full account of the battle.
19He instructed the messenger: "When you have
finished giving the king this account of the battle,
20the king's anger may flare up, and he may ask
you, 'Why did you get so close to the city to fight?
Didn't you know they would shoot arrows from
the wall? 21Who killed Abimelech son of Jerub-
Besheth[a]? Didn't a woman throw an upper millstone on him from the wall, so that he died in
Thebez? Why did you get so close to the wall?' If
he asks you this, then say to him, 'Also, your servant Uriah the Hittite is dead.'" Jdg 9:50-54
22The messenger set out, and when he arrived
he told David everything Joab had sent him to say.
23The messenger said to David, "The men overpowered us and came out against us in the open,
but we drove them back to the entrance to the city
gate. 24Then the archers shot arrows at your servants from the wall, and some of the king's men
died. Moreover, your servant Uriah the Hittite is
dead."
25David told the messenger, "Say this to Joab:
'Don't let this upset you; the sword devours one as
well as another. Press the attack against the city
and destroy it.' Say this to encourage Joab."
26When Uriah's wife heard that her husband
was dead, she mourned for him. 27After the time
of mourning was over, David had her brought to
his house, and she became his wife and bore him
a son. But the thing David had done displeased the
LORD. 2Sa 12:9; Ps 51:4-5

Nathan Rebukes David

12 The LORD sent Nathan to David. When he
came to him, he said, "There were two men
in a certain town, one rich and the other poor.
2The rich man had a very large number of sheep
and cattle, 3but the poor man had nothing except
one little ewe lamb he had bought. He raised it,
and it grew up with him and his children. It shared
his food, drank from his cup and even slept in his
arms. It was like a daughter to him. 2Sa 14:4
4"Now a traveler came to the rich man, but the
rich man refrained from taking one of his own
sheep or cattle to prepare a meal for the traveler
who had come to him. Instead, he took the ewe
lamb that belonged to the poor man and prepared
it for the one who had come to him."
5David burned with anger against the man and
said to Nathan, "As surely as the LORD lives, the
man who did this deserves to die! 6He must pay
for that lamb four times over, because he did such
a thing and had no pity." Ex 22:1; Lk 19:8
7Then Nathan said to David, "You are the man!
This is what the LORD, the God of Israel, says: 'I
anointed you king over Israel, and I delivered you
from the hand of Saul. 8I gave your master's house
to you, and your master's wives into your arms. I
gave you the house of Israel and Judah. And if all
this had been too little, I would have given you
even more. 9Why did you despise the word of the
LORD by doing what is evil in his eyes? You struck
down Uriah the Hittite with the sword and took
his wife to be your own. You killed him with the
sword of the Ammonites. 10Now, therefore, the
sword will never depart from your house, because
you despised me and took the wife of Uriah the
Hittite to be your own.' 2Sa 11:15; 13:28; 1Ki 20:42
11"This is what the LORD says: 'Out of your own
household I am going to bring calamity upon you.
Before your very eyes I will take your wives and
give them to one who is close to you, and he will
lie with your wives in broad daylight. 12You did it

[a] 21 Also known as *Jerub-Baal* (that is, Gideon)

in secret, but I will do this thing in broad daylight before all Israel.' " Dt 28:30; 2Sa 11:4-15; 16:21-22

13Then David said to Nathan, "I have sinned against the LORD." 1Sa 15:24; 2Sa 24:10

Nathan replied, "The LORD has taken away your sin. You are not going to die. 14But because by doing this you have made the enemies of the LORD show utter contempt,[a] the son born to you will die." Pr 28:13; Isa 52:5; Mic 7:18-19

15After Nathan had gone home, the LORD struck the child that Uriah's wife had borne to David, and he became ill. 16David pleaded with God for the child. He fasted and went into his house and spent the nights lying on the ground. 17The elders of his household stood beside him to get him up from the ground, but he refused, and he would not eat any food with them. 1Sa 25:38; 2Sa 13:31; Ps 5:7

18On the seventh day the child died. David's servants were afraid to tell him that the child was dead, for they thought, "While the child was still living, we spoke to David but he would not listen to us. How can we tell him the child is dead? He may do something desperate."

19David noticed that his servants were whispering among themselves and he realized the child was dead. "Is the child dead?" he asked.

"Yes," they replied, "he is dead."

20Then David got up from the ground. After he had washed, put on lotions and changed his clothes, he went into the house of the LORD and worshiped. Then he went to his own house, and at his request they served him food, and he ate.

21His servants asked him, "Why are you acting this way? While the child was alive, you fasted and wept, but now that the child is dead, you get up and eat!" Jdg 20:26

22He answered, "While the child was still alive, I fasted and wept. I thought, 'Who knows? The LORD may be gracious to me and let the child live.' 23But now that he is dead, why should I fast? Can I bring him back again? I will go to him, but he will not return to me." Jnh 3:9; Ge 37:35; Isa 38:1-5

24Then David comforted his wife Bathsheba, and he went to her and lay with her. She gave birth to a son, and they named him Solomon. The LORD loved him; 25and because the LORD loved him, he sent word through Nathan the prophet to name him Jedidiah.[b] 1Ki 1:11; 1Ch 22:9; Mt 1:6

26Meanwhile Joab fought against Rabbah of the Ammonites and captured the royal citadel. 27Joab then sent messengers to David, saying, "I have fought against Rabbah and taken its water supply. 28Now muster the rest of the troops and besiege the city and capture it. Otherwise I will take the city, and it will be named after me." Dt 3:11

29So David mustered the entire army and went to Rabbah, and attacked and captured it. 30He took the crown from the head of their king[c]—its weight was a talent[d] of gold, and it was set with precious stones—and it was placed on David's head. He took a great quantity of plunder from the city 31and brought out the people who were there, consigning them to labor with saws and with iron picks and axes, and he made them work at brickmaking.[e] He did this to all the Ammonite towns. Then David and his entire army returned to Jerusalem. 1Ch 20:1-3; 1Sa 14:47

David's Troubles **Chapters 13–24**

The final section of 2 Samuel tells the heartbreaking story of David's kingdom in turmoil. Chapters 13–18 chronicle the deterioration of David's family. Rape, incest, murder and betrayal all entered the home of David. His heart was broken as he saw his children rebel and not only turn from the Lord but also against each other. Just like any father, David grieved as he saw conflict tearing his family apart. His grief was intensified by guilt, as he knew in his heart that he had started the whole nasty mess.

At the same time the kingdom and nation began to face its own set of problems. In chapters 19–24 we read the record of the political turmoil faced by David later in his life. After a civil uprising and military confrontation led by his own son, David faced public abuse, a famine in the land and God's judgment for the numbering of Israel. Also, the tide of military victories that had marked the early years of David's reign now turned, and the army of Israel faced defeat rather than victory. If ever a life modeled the truth of Galatians 6:7–8, David's did: "Do not be deceived: God cannot be mocked. A man reaps what he sows. The one who sows to please his sinful nature, from that nature will reap destruction; the one who sows to please the Spirit, from the Spirit will reap eternal life."

Amnon and Tamar

13 In the course of time, Amnon son of David fell in love with Tamar, the beautiful sister of Absalom son of David. 2Sa 3:2; 1Ch 3:9

2Amnon became frustrated to the point of illness on account of his sister Tamar, for she was a virgin, and it seemed impossible for him to do anything to her.

3Now Amnon had a friend named Jonadab son of Shimeah, David's brother. Jonadab was a very shrewd man. 4He asked Amnon, "Why do you, the king's son, look so haggard morning after morning? Won't you tell me?" 1Sa 16:9

Amnon said to him, "I'm in love with Tamar, my brother Absalom's sister."

5"Go to bed and pretend to be ill," Jonadab said. "When your father comes to see you, say to him, 'I would like my sister Tamar to come and

[a] 14 Masoretic Text; an ancient Hebrew scribal tradition *this you have shown utter contempt for the LORD* [b] 25 *Jedidiah* means *loved by the LORD.* [c] 30 Or *of Milcom* (that is, Molech) [d] 30 That is, about 75 pounds (about 34 kilograms) [e] 31 The meaning of the Hebrew for this clause is uncertain.

give me something to eat. Let her prepare the food
in my sight so I may watch her and then eat it from
her hand.' "
6So Amnon lay down and pretended to be ill.
When the king came to see him, Amnon said to
him, "I would like my sister Tamar to come and
make some special bread in my sight, so I may eat
from her hand."
7David sent word to Tamar at the palace: "Go to
the house of your brother Amnon and prepare
some food for him." 8So Tamar went to the house
of her brother Amnon, who was lying down. She
took some dough, kneaded it, made the bread in
his sight and baked it. 9Then she took the pan and
served him the bread, but he refused to eat.
"Send everyone out of here," Amnon said. So
everyone left him. 10Then Amnon said to Tamar,
"Bring the food here into my bedroom so I may
eat from your hand." And Tamar took the bread
she had prepared and brought it to her brother
Amnon in his bedroom. 11But when she took it to
him to eat, he grabbed her and said, "Come to bed
with me, my sister." Ge 39:12; 45:1
12"Don't, my brother!" she said to him. "Don't
force me. Such a thing should not be done in
Israel! Don't do this wicked thing. 13What about
me? Where could I get rid of my disgrace? And
what about you? You would be like one of the
wicked fools in Israel. Please speak to the king; he
will not keep me from being married to you."
14But he refused to listen to her, and since he was
stronger than she, he raped her. Lev 18:9; Dt 22:25
15Then Amnon hated her with intense hatred.
In fact, he hated her more than he had loved her.
Amnon said to her, "Get up and get out!"
16"No!" she said to him. "Sending me away
would be a greater wrong than what you have
already done to me."
But he refused to listen to her. 17He called his
personal servant and said, "Get this woman out of
here and bolt the door after her." 18So his servant
put her out and bolted the door after her. She was
wearing a richly ornamented[a] robe, for this was
the kind of garment the virgin daughters of the
king wore. 19Tamar put ashes on her head and tore
the ornamented[b] robe she was wearing. She put
her hand on her head and went away, weeping
aloud as she went. Ge 37:23; Jos 7:6; Est 4:1
20Her brother Absalom said to her, "Has that
Amnon, your brother, been with you? Be quiet
now, my sister; he is your brother. Don't take this
thing to heart." And Tamar lived in her brother
Absalom's house, a desolate woman.
21When King David heard all this, he was furi-

[a] 18 The meaning of the Hebrew for this phrase is uncertain.

[b] 19 The meaning of the Hebrew for this word is uncertain.

PARABLES OF THE OLD TESTAMENT

Parable	Reference
The trees	*Judges 9:7-15*
The ewe lamb	*2 Samuel 12:1-4*
Two sons	*2 Samuel 14:1-24*
Thistle and cedar	*2 Kings 14:8-14*
The vineyard	*Isaiah 5:1-7*
Almond rod and boiling pot	*Jeremiah 1:11-19*
Linen belt	*Jeremiah 13:1-11*
Wineskins	*Jeremiah 13:12-14*
Potter and clay	*Jeremiah 18:1-10*
Two baskets of figs	*Jeremiah 24:1-10*
Cup of God's wrath	*Jeremiah 25:15-38*
Useless vine	*Ezekiel 15:1-8*
Cooking pot	*Ezekiel 24:1-4*
Valley of dry bones	*Ezekiel 37:1-14*
Measuring line	*Zechariah 2:1-13*
Gold lampstand and two olive trees	*Zechariah 4:1-14*
Flying scroll	*Zechariah 5:1-4*

ous. 22Absalom never said a word to Amnon, either good or bad; he hated Amnon because he had disgraced his sister Tamar. Ge 31:24; Lev 19:17-18

Absalom Kills Amnon

23Two years later, when Absalom's sheepshearers were at Baal Hazor near the border of Ephraim, he invited all the king's sons to come there. 24Absalom went to the king and said, "Your servant has had shearers come. Will the king and his officials please join me?" 1Sa 25:7

25"No, my son," the king replied. "All of us should not go; we would only be a burden to you." Although Absalom urged him, he still refused to go, but gave him his blessing.

26Then Absalom said, "If not, please let my brother Amnon come with us."

The king asked him, "Why should he go with you?" 27But Absalom urged him, so he sent with him Amnon and the rest of the king's sons.

28Absalom ordered his men, "Listen! When Amnon is in high spirits from drinking wine and I say to you, 'Strike Amnon down,' then kill him. Don't be afraid. Have not I given you this order? Be strong and brave." 29So Absalom's men did to Amnon what Absalom had ordered. Then all the king's sons got up, mounted their mules and fled.

30While they were on their way, the report came to David: "Absalom has struck down all the king's sons; not one of them is left." 31The king stood up, tore his clothes and lay down on the ground; and all his servants stood by with their clothes torn.

32But Jonadab son of Shimeah, David's brother, said, "My lord should not think that they killed all the princes; only Amnon is dead. This has been Absalom's expressed intention ever since the day Amnon raped his sister Tamar. 33My lord the king should not be concerned about the report that all the king's sons are dead. Only Amnon is dead."

34Meanwhile, Absalom had fled.

Now the man standing watch looked up and saw many people on the road west of him, coming down the side of the hill. The watchman went and told the king, "I see men in the direction of Horonaim, on the side of the hill."[a]

35Jonadab said to the king, "See, the king's sons are here; it has happened just as your servant said."

36As he finished speaking, the king's sons came in, wailing loudly. The king, too, and all his servants wept very bitterly.

37Absalom fled and went to Talmai son of Ammihud, the king of Geshur. But King David mourned for his son every day. 2Sa 3:3; 14:23,32

38After Absalom fled and went to Geshur, he stayed there three years. 39And the spirit of the king[b] longed to go to Absalom, for he was consoled concerning Amnon's death. 2Sa 12:19-23

Absalom Returns to Jerusalem

14 Joab son of Zeruiah knew that the king's heart longed for Absalom. 2So Joab sent someone to Tekoa and had a wise woman brought from there. He said to her, "Pretend you are in mourning. Dress in mourning clothes, and don't use any cosmetic lotions. Act like a woman who has spent many days grieving for the dead. 3Then go to the king and speak these words to him." And Joab put the words in her mouth. 2Sa 12:20; 20:16

4When the woman from Tekoa went[c] to the king, she fell with her face to the ground to pay him honor, and she said, "Help me, O king!"

5The king asked her, "What is troubling you?"

She said, "I am indeed a widow; my husband is dead. 6I your servant had two sons. They got into a fight with each other in the field, and no one was there to separate them. One struck the other and killed him. 7Now the whole clan has risen up against your servant; they say, 'Hand over the one who struck his brother down, so that we may put him to death for the life of his brother whom he killed; then we will get rid of the heir as well.' They would put out the only burning coal I have left, leaving my husband neither name nor descendant on the face of the earth." Dt 19:10-13; Nu 35:19; Mt 21:38

8The king said to the woman, "Go home, and I will issue an order in your behalf." 1Sa 25:35

9But the woman from Tekoa said to him, "My lord the king, let the blame rest on me and on my father's family, and let the king and his throne be without guilt." 1Sa 25:24; 1Ki 2:33; Mt 27:25

10The king replied, "If anyone says anything to you, bring him to me, and he will not bother you again."

11She said, "Then let the king invoke the LORD his God to prevent the avenger of blood from adding to the destruction, so that my son will not be destroyed." Nu 35:12,21

"As surely as the LORD lives," he said, "not one hair of your son's head will fall to the ground."

12Then the woman said, "Let your servant speak a word to my lord the king."

"Speak," he replied.

13The woman said, "Why then have you devised a thing like this against the people of God? When the king says this, does he not convict himself, for the king has not brought back his banished son? 14Like water spilled on the ground, which cannot be recovered, so we must die. But God does not take away life; instead, he devises ways so that a banished person may not remain estranged from him. 2Sa 12:7; Nu 35:15,25-28; Heb 9:27

[a] 34 Septuagint; Hebrew does not have this sentence. [b] 39 Dead Sea Scrolls and some Septuagint manuscripts; Masoretic Text *But* ⌊*the spirit of*⌋ *David the king* [c] 4 Many Hebrew manuscripts, Septuagint, Vulgate and Syriac; most Hebrew manuscripts *spoke*

15“And now I have come to say this to my lord
the king because the people have made me afraid.
Your servant thought, ‘I will speak to the king;
perhaps he will do what his servant asks. 16Perhaps
the king will agree to deliver his servant from
the hand of the man who is trying to cut off
both me and my son from the inheritance God
gave us.’

17“And now your servant says, ‘May the word of
my lord the king bring me rest, for my lord the
king is like an angel of God in discerning good and
evil. May the LORD your God be with you.’”

18Then the king said to the woman, “Do not
keep from me the answer to what I am going to
ask you.”

“Let my lord the king speak,” the woman said.

19The king asked, “Isn’t the hand of Joab with
you in all this?”

The woman answered, “As surely as you live,
my lord the king, no one can turn to the right or
to the left from anything my lord the king says.
Yes, it was your servant Joab who instructed me to
do this and who put all these words into the mouth
of your servant. 20Your servant Joab did this to
change the present situation. My lord has wisdom
like that of an angel of God—he knows everything
that happens in the land.” 2Sa 18:13; Isa 28:6

21The king said to Joab, “Very well, I will do it.
Go, bring back the young man Absalom.”

22Joab fell with his face to the ground to pay
him honor, and he blessed the king. Joab said,
“Today your servant knows that he has found favor in your eyes, my lord the king, because the
king has granted his servant’s request.” Ge 47:7

23Then Joab went to Geshur and brought Absalom back to Jerusalem. 24But the king said, “He
must go to his own house; he must not see my
face.” So Absalom went to his own house and did
not see the face of the king.

25In all Israel there was not a man so highly
praised for his handsome appearance as Absalom.
From the top of his head to the sole of his foot
there was no blemish in him. 26Whenever he cut
the hair of his head—he used to cut his hair from
time to time when it became too heavy for him—
he would weigh it, and its weight was two hundred
shekels[a] by the royal standard. Eze 44:20

27Three sons and a daughter were born to Absalom. The daughter’s name was Tamar, and she
became a beautiful woman. 2Sa 13:1; 18:18

28Absalom lived two years in Jerusalem without
seeing the king’s face. 29Then Absalom sent for
Joab in order to send him to the king, but Joab
refused to come to him. So he sent a second time,
but he refused to come. 30Then he said to his servants, “Look, Joab’s field is next to mine, and he
has barley there. Go and set it on fire.” So Absalom’s servants set the field on fire.

31Then Joab did go to Absalom’s house and he
said to him, “Why have your servants set my field
on fire?” Jdg 15:5

32Absalom said to Joab, “Look, I sent word to
you and said, ‘Come here so I can send you to the
king to ask, “Why have I come from Geshur? It
would be better for me if I were still there!” ’ Now
then, I want to see the king’s face, and if I am
guilty of anything, let him put me to death.”

33So Joab went to the king and told him this.
Then the king summoned Absalom, and he came
in and bowed down with his face to the ground
before the king. And the king kissed Absalom.

Absalom’s Conspiracy

15 In the course of time, Absalom provided
himself with a chariot and horses and with
fifty men to run ahead of him. 2He would get up
early and stand by the side of the road leading to
the city gate. Whenever anyone came with a complaint to be placed before the king for a decision,
Absalom would call out to him, “What town are
you from?” He would answer, “Your servant is
from one of the tribes of Israel.” 3Then Absalom
would say to him, “Look, your claims are valid and
proper, but there is no representative of the king
to hear you.” 4And Absalom would add, “If only
I were appointed judge in the land! Then everyone
who has a complaint or case could come to me and
I would see that he gets justice.” Jdg 9:29; 2Sa 19:8

5Also, whenever anyone approached him to
bow down before him, Absalom would reach out
his hand, take hold of him and kiss him. 6Absalom
behaved in this way toward all the Israelites who
came to the king asking for justice, and so he stole
the hearts of the men of Israel. Ro 16:18

7At the end of four[b] years, Absalom said to the
king, “Let me go to Hebron and fulfill a vow I
made to the LORD. 8While your servant was living
at Geshur in Aram, I made this vow: ‘If the LORD
takes me back to Jerusalem, I will worship the
LORD in Hebron.[c]’” Ge 28:20; 2Sa 13:37-38

9The king said to him, “Go in peace.” So he
went to Hebron.

10Then Absalom sent secret messengers
throughout the tribes of Israel to say, “As soon as
you hear the sound of the trumpets, then say, ‘Absalom is king in Hebron.’” 11Two hundred men
from Jerusalem had accompanied Absalom. They
had been invited as guests and went quite inno-
cently, knowing nothing about the matter. 12While
Absalom was offering sacrifices, he also sent for
Ahithophel the Gilonite, David’s counselor, to
come from Giloh, his hometown. And so the con-

[a]26 That is, about 5 pounds (about 2.3 kilograms) [b]7 Some Septuagint manuscripts, Syriac and Josephus; Hebrew *forty*
[c]8 Some Septuagint manuscripts; Hebrew does not have *in Hebron.*

ABSALOM

The Rebel Prince Charming

"A messenger came and told David, 'The hearts of the men of Israel are with Absalom.'"

—2 SAMUEL 15:13

The story of Absalom, the handsome rebel dripping with charisma, hinges on two key factors—David's failure as a father and the violation of Absalom's sister Tamar.

Absalom was born to David's third wife, Maacah (2 Samuel 3:3). Now, the Bible never flatters its heroes. It tells us flat out that David was a polygamist. Over the years these wives produced over twenty offspring (not to mention the children from his concubines), all of whom lived in the palace. Absalom was raised, no doubt, in a home of incessant bickering, hatred and jealousy. To make matters worse, his father, King David, appeared to have had a habit of making himself scarce. The only one close to Absalom among blood relatives was his sister Tamar, whom he loved dearly.

If I read it right, Absalom was a teenager when David committed adultery with Bathsheba (see 2 Samuel 11). Therefore he very likely already had resentment built up against his father that was now turning into disillusionment as news of the scandal spread like wildfire in a wheat field. And Absalom was caught in the middle, hanging on to what he could of a strained respect for his father.

Adding to his disillusionment with his father was David's lack of appropriate action when Absalom's older half brother, Amnon, violated Absalom's beautiful sister Tamar (see 2 Samuel 13). She was utterly crushed—her life virtually ruined by this lustful half brother. But Amnon knew his father David only too well; he knew he could get away with the wicked deed. True to form, we read that David was "furious" (13:21), but that was as far as his response went. He didn't do a thing. Perhaps Amnon's sin reminded David of his own hideous failures. So Absalom's hatred for Amnon mixed with contempt for David began to boil, as he quietly bided his time. Two years later, Absalom carried out his revenge. He masterminded the killing of his brother Amnon and fled, leaving the murdered body in a pool of blood (13:28–29).

Three years passed, during which time David's "spirit . . . longed to go to Absalom" (13:39). David loved his son; he missed his boy. But he wasn't about to offer forgiveness and restoration. Absalom's return to Jerusalem was quite a bit different than the New Testament story of the prodigal son (see Luke 15:20). In 2 Samuel 14:24 David said, in effect, "Absalom can come back to the city, but I don't want to see him. I want nothing to do with him." Another abdication of his role as Absalom's father.

Now, Absalom was popular for various reasons. First, he was extraordinarily handsome (14:25–26). Not a blemish from head to toe. Long, flowing hair that was the envy of many. Second, after his return to Jerusalem, he set out to promote his own interests (15:2–4). He was a smooth talker who knew how to push all the right buttons. Within a short period of time, Absalom "stole the hearts of the men of Israel" (15:6). Ultimately Absalom's conniving work paid off. He took over the throne for a period of time (15:10–18:13)—that is, until some of David's faithful soldiers took it upon themselves to kill Absalom as he hung entangled in a tree, snagged by the long hair that had helped him gain his popularity (18:14–15).

Absalom's story was not dreamed up by some creative screenplay writer. This is inspired Scripture from God, placed within the Bible to teach us how *not* to relate to our family members. David may have been a man after God's own heart (see Acts 13:22); he may have been Israel's greatest king. But he failed miserably when it came to his own family. He set a deplorable example for his sons, left them woefully undisciplined and steadfastly refused to correct the damage he'd done. As a result, the words of Nathan the prophet tragically came true in the case of Absalom, this gifted yet fatally flawed son of David: "Now, therefore, the sword will never depart from your house . . ." (2 Samuel 12:10).

spiracy gained strength, and Absalom's following
kept on increasing. 2Sa 16:15,23; 1Ki 1:34,39; Ps 3:1

David Flees

13A messenger came and told David, "The
hearts of the men of Israel are with Absalom."
14Then David said to all his officials who were
with him in Jerusalem, "Come! We must flee, or
none of us will escape from Absalom. We must
leave immediately, or he will move quickly to
overtake us and bring ruin upon us and put the
city to the sword." 2Sa 19:9; 1Ki 2:26
15The king's officials answered him, "Your servants are ready to do whatever our lord the king
chooses."
16The king set out, with his entire household
following him; but he left ten concubines to take
care of the palace. 17So the king set out, with all the
people following him, and they halted at a place
some distance away. 18All his men marched past
him, along with all the Kerethites and Pelethites;
and all the six hundred Gittites who had accompanied him from Gath marched before the king.
19The king said to Ittai the Gittite, "Why should
you come along with us? Go back and stay with
King Absalom. You are a foreigner, an exile from
your homeland. 20You came only yesterday. And
today shall I make you wander about with us,
when I do not know where I am going? Go back,
and take your countrymen. May kindness and
faithfulness be with you." 1Sa 23:13; 2Sa 2:6; 18:2
21But Ittai replied to the king, "As surely as the
LORD lives, and as my lord the king lives, wherever
my lord the king may be, whether it means life or
death, there will your servant be." Ru 1:16-17
22David said to Ittai, "Go ahead, march on." So
Ittai the Gittite marched on with all his men and
the families that were with him.
23The whole countryside wept aloud as all the
people passed by. The king also crossed the Kidron Valley, and all the people moved on toward
the desert. 1Sa 11:4
24Zadok was there, too, and all the Levites who
were with him were carrying the ark of the covenant of God. They set down the ark of God, and
Abiathar offered sacrifices[a] until all the people
had finished leaving the city. Nu 4:15; 1Sa 22:20; 2Sa 8:17
25Then the king said to Zadok, "Take the ark of
God back into the city. If I find favor in the LORD's
eyes, he will bring me back and let me see it and
his dwelling place again. 26But if he says, 'I am not
pleased with you,' then I am ready; let him do to
me whatever seems good to him." Ex 15:13; 1Sa 3:18
27The king also said to Zadok the priest, "Aren't
you a seer? Go back to the city in peace, with your
son Ahimaaz and Jonathan son of Abiathar. You
and Abiathar take your two sons with you. 28I will
wait at the fords in the desert until word comes
from you to inform me." 29So Zadok and Abiathar
took the ark of God back to Jerusalem and stayed
there. 1Sa 9:9; 2Sa 17:17
30But David continued up the Mount of Olives,
weeping as he went; his head was covered and he
was barefoot. All the people with him covered
their heads too and were weeping as they went up.
31Now David had been told, "Ahithophel is among
the conspirators with Absalom." So David prayed,
"O LORD, turn Ahithophel's counsel into foolishness." 2Sa 16:23; Est 6:12; Isa 20:2-4
32When David arrived at the summit, where
people used to worship God, Hushai the Arkite
was there to meet him, his robe torn and dust on
his head. 33David said to him, "If you go with me,
you will be a burden to me. 34But if you return to
the city and say to Absalom, 'I will be your servant,
O king; I was your father's servant in the past, but
now I will be your servant,' then you can help me
by frustrating Ahithophel's advice. 35Won't the
priests Zadok and Abiathar be there with you? Tell
them anything you hear in the king's palace.
36Their two sons, Ahimaaz son of Zadok and Jonathan son of Abiathar, are there with them. Send
them to me with anything you hear." 2Sa 17:15-16
37So David's friend Hushai arrived at Jerusalem
as Absalom was entering the city. 1Ch 27:33

David and Ziba

16 When David had gone a short distance beyond the summit, there was Ziba, the steward of Mephibosheth, waiting to meet him. He had
a string of donkeys saddled and loaded with two
hundred loaves of bread, a hundred cakes of raisins, a hundred cakes of figs and a skin of wine.
2The king asked Ziba, "Why have you brought
these?"
Ziba answered, "The donkeys are for the king's
household to ride on, the bread and fruit are for
the men to eat, and the wine is to refresh those
who become exhausted in the desert." 2Sa 17:27-29
3The king then asked, "Where is your master's
grandson?" 2Sa 19:26-27
Ziba said to him, "He is staying in Jerusalem,
because he thinks, 'Today the house of Israel will
give me back my grandfather's kingdom.'"
4Then the king said to Ziba, "All that belonged
to Mephibosheth is now yours."
"I humbly bow," Ziba said. "May I find favor in
your eyes, my lord the king."

Shimei Curses David

5As King David approached Bahurim, a man
from the same clan as Saul's family came out from
there. His name was Shimei son of Gera, and he
cursed as he came out. 6He pelted David and all

[a]24 Or *Abiathar went up*

the king's officials with stones, though all the troops and the special guard were on David's right and left. 7As he cursed, Shimei said, "Get out, get out, you man of blood, you scoundrel! 8The LORD has repaid you for all the blood you shed in the household of Saul, in whose place you have reigned. The LORD has handed the kingdom over to your son Absalom. You have come to ruin because you are a man of blood!" 2Sa 19:16-23

9Then Abishai son of Zeruiah said to the king, "Why should this dead dog curse my lord the king? Let me go over and cut off his head."

10But the king said, "What do you and I have in common, you sons of Zeruiah? If he is cursing because the LORD said to him, 'Curse David,' who can ask, 'Why do you do this?' " 2Sa 19:22; Ro 9:20

11David then said to Abishai and all his officials, "My son, who is of my own flesh, is trying to take my life. How much more, then, this Benjamite! Leave him alone; let him curse, for the LORD has told him to. 12It may be that the LORD will see my distress and repay me with good for the cursing I am receiving today." Dt 23:5; 2Sa 12:11; Ro 8:28

13So David and his men continued along the road while Shimei was going along the hillside opposite him, cursing as he went and throwing stones at him and showering him with dirt. 14The king and all the people with him arrived at their destination exhausted. And there he refreshed himself. 2Sa 17:2

The Advice of Hushai and Ahithophel

15Meanwhile, Absalom and all the men of Israel came to Jerusalem, and Ahithophel was with him. 16Then Hushai the Arkite, David's friend, went to Absalom and said to him, "Long live the king! Long live the king!" 2Sa 15:37

17Absalom asked Hushai, "Is this the love you show your friend? Why didn't you go with your friend?" 2Sa 19:25

18Hushai said to Absalom, "No, the one chosen by the LORD, by these people, and by all the men of Israel—his I will be, and I will remain with him. 19Furthermore, whom should I serve? Should I not serve the son? Just as I served your father, so I will serve you." 2Sa 15:34

20Absalom said to Ahithophel, "Give us your advice. What should we do?"

21Ahithophel answered, "Lie with your father's concubines whom he left to take care of the palace. Then all Israel will hear that you have made yourself a stench in your father's nostrils, and the hands of everyone with you will be strengthened." 22So they pitched a tent for Absalom on the roof, and he lay with his father's concubines in the sight of all Israel. 2Sa 12:11-12

23Now in those days the advice Ahithophel gave was like that of one who inquires of God. That was how both David and Absalom regarded all of Ahithophel's advice. 2Sa 15:12; 17:14,23

17 Ahithophel said to Absalom, "I would[a] choose twelve thousand men and set out tonight in pursuit of David. 2I would[b] attack him while he is weary and weak. I would[b] strike him with terror, and then all the people with him will flee. I would[b] strike down only the king 3and bring all the people back to you. The death of the man you seek will mean the return of all; all the people will be unharmed." 4This plan seemed good to Absalom and to all the elders of Israel.

5But Absalom said, "Summon also Hushai the Arkite, so we can hear what he has to say." 6When Hushai came to him, Absalom said, "Ahithophel has given this advice. Should we do what he says? If not, give us your opinion." 2Sa 15:32

7Hushai replied to Absalom, "The advice Ahithophel has given is not good this time. 8You know your father and his men; they are fighters, and as fierce as a wild bear robbed of her cubs. Besides, your father is an experienced fighter; he will not spend the night with the troops. 9Even now, he is hidden in a cave or some other place. If he should attack your troops first,[c] whoever hears about it will say, 'There has been a slaughter among the troops who follow Absalom.' 10Then even the bravest soldier, whose heart is like the heart of a lion, will melt with fear, for all Israel knows that your father is a fighter and that those with him are brave. Jos 2:9,11; 1Sa 16:18; Hos 13:8

11"So I advise you: Let all Israel, from Dan to Beersheba—as numerous as the sand on the seashore—be gathered to you, with you yourself leading them into battle. 12Then we will attack him wherever he may be found, and we will fall on him as dew settles on the ground. Neither he nor any of his men will be left alive. 13If he withdraws into a city, then all Israel will bring ropes to that city, and we will drag it down to the valley until not even a piece of it can be found." Ge 12:2; 22:17

14Absalom and all the men of Israel said, "The advice of Hushai the Arkite is better than that of Ahithophel." For the LORD had determined to frustrate the good advice of Ahithophel in order to bring disaster on Absalom. 2Sa 15:34; Ne 4:15; Ps 9:16

15Hushai told Zadok and Abiathar, the priests, "Ahithophel has advised Absalom and the elders of Israel to do such and such, but I have advised them to do so and so. 16Now send a message immediately and tell David, 'Do not spend the night at the fords in the desert; cross over without fail, or the king and all the people with him will be swallowed up.' "

17Jonathan and Ahimaaz were staying at En Rogel. A servant girl was to go and inform them, and

[a]1 Or *Let me* [b]2 Or *will* [c]9 Or *When some of the men fall at the first attack*

they were to go and tell King David, for they could not risk being seen entering the city. 18But a young man saw them and told Absalom. So the two of them left quickly and went to the house of a man in Bahurim. He had a well in his courtyard, and they climbed down into it. 19His wife took a covering and spread it out over the opening of the well and scattered grain over it. No one knew anything about it. Jos 2:6; 15:7; 2Sa 3:16

20When Absalom's men came to the woman at the house, they asked, "Where are Ahimaaz and Jonathan?"

The woman answered them, "They crossed over the brook."[a] The men searched but found no one, so they returned to Jerusalem. Ex 1:19; Jos 2:3-5

21After the men had gone, the two climbed out of the well and went to inform King David. They said to him, "Set out and cross the river at once; Ahithophel has advised such and such against you." 22So David and all the people with him set out and crossed the Jordan. By daybreak, no one was left who had not crossed the Jordan.

23When Ahithophel saw that his advice had not been followed, he saddled his donkey and set out for his house in his hometown. He put his house in order and then hanged himself. So he died and was buried in his father's tomb. 2Sa 15:12; Mt 27:5

24David went to Mahanaim, and Absalom crossed the Jordan with all the men of Israel. 25Absalom had appointed Amasa over the army in place of Joab. Amasa was the son of a man named Jether,[b] an Israelite[c] who had married Abigail,[d] the daughter of Nahash and sister of Zeruiah the mother of Joab. 26The Israelites and Absalom camped in the land of Gilead. Ge 32:2; 2Sa 19:13

27When David came to Mahanaim, Shobi son of Nahash from Rabbah of the Ammonites, and Makir son of Ammiel from Lo Debar, and Barzillai the Gileadite from Rogelim 28brought bedding and bowls and articles of pottery. They also brought wheat and barley, flour and roasted grain, beans and lentils,[e] 29honey and curds, sheep, and cheese from cows' milk for David and his people to eat. For they said, "The people have become hungry and tired and thirsty in the desert." 2Sa 10:1-2; 16:2

Absalom's Death

18 David mustered the men who were with him and appointed over them commanders of thousands and commanders of hundreds. 2David sent the troops out—a third under the command of Joab, a third under Joab's brother Abishai son of Zeruiah, and a third under Ittai the Gittite. The king told the troops, "I myself will surely march out with you." 1Sa 11:11; 26:6; 2Sa 15:19

3But the men said, "You must not go out; if we are forced to flee, they won't care about us. Even if half of us die, they won't care; but you are worth ten thousand of us.[f] It would be better now for you to give us support from the city." 1Sa 18:7

4The king answered, "I will do whatever seems best to you."

So the king stood beside the gate while all the men marched out in units of hundreds and of thousands. 5The king commanded Joab, Abishai and Ittai, "Be gentle with the young man Absalom for my sake." And all the troops heard the king giving orders concerning Absalom to each of the commanders.

6The army marched into the field to fight Israel, and the battle took place in the forest of Ephraim. 7There the army of Israel was defeated by David's men, and the casualties that day were great—twenty thousand men. 8The battle spread out over the whole countryside, and the forest claimed more lives that day than the sword. Jos 17:18

9Now Absalom happened to meet David's men. He was riding his mule, and as the mule went under the thick branches of a large oak, Absalom's head got caught in the tree. He was left hanging in midair, while the mule he was riding kept on going. 2Sa 14:26

10When one of the men saw this, he told Joab, "I just saw Absalom hanging in an oak tree."

11Joab said to the man who had told him this, "What! You saw him? Why didn't you strike him to the ground right there? Then I would have had to give you ten shekels[g] of silver and a warrior's belt."

12But the man replied, "Even if a thousand shekels[h] were weighed out into my hands, I would not lift my hand against the king's son. In our hearing the king commanded you and Abishai and Ittai, 'Protect the young man Absalom for my sake.[i]' 13And if I had put my life in jeopardy[j]—and nothing is hidden from the king—you would have kept your distance from me." 2Sa 14:19-20

14Joab said, "I'm not going to wait like this for you." So he took three javelins in his hand and plunged them into Absalom's heart while Absalom was still alive in the oak tree. 15And ten of Joab's armor-bearers surrounded Absalom, struck him and killed him. 2Sa 14:30; 12:10

16Then Joab sounded the trumpet, and the

[a]20 Or *"They passed by the sheep pen toward the water."* [b]25 Hebrew *Ithra,* a variant of *Jether* [c]25 Hebrew and some Septuagint manuscripts; other Septuagint manuscripts (see also 1 Chron. 2:17) *Ishmaelite* or *Jezreelite* [d]25 Hebrew *Abigal,* a variant of *Abigail* [e]28 Most Septuagint manuscripts and Syriac; Hebrew *lentils, and roasted grain* [f]3 Two Hebrew manuscripts, some Septuagint manuscripts and Vulgate; most Hebrew manuscripts *care; for now there are ten thousand like us* [g]11 That is, about 4 ounces (about 115 grams) [h]12 That is, about 25 pounds (about 11 kilograms) [i]12 A few Hebrew manuscripts, Septuagint, Vulgate and Syriac; most Hebrew manuscripts may be translated *Absalom, whoever you may be.* [j]13 Or *Otherwise, if I had acted treacherously toward him*

troops stopped pursuing Israel, for Joab halted
them. 17They took Absalom, threw him into a big
pit in the forest and piled up a large heap of rocks
over him. Meanwhile, all the Israelites fled to their
homes. 2Sa 2:28; 20:22; Jos 7:26
18During his lifetime Absalom had taken a pillar
and erected it in the King's Valley as a monument
to himself, for he thought, "I have no son to carry
on the memory of my name." He named the pillar
after himself, and it is called Absalom's Monument
to this day. Ge 14:17; 1Sa 15:12; 2Sa 14:27

David Mourns

19Now Ahimaaz son of Zadok said, "Let me run
and take the news to the king that the LORD has
delivered him from the hand of his enemies."
20"You are not the one to take the news today,"
Joab told him. "You may take the news another
time, but you must not do so today, because the
king's son is dead."
21Then Joab said to a Cushite, "Go, tell the king
what you have seen." The Cushite bowed down
before Joab and ran off.
22Ahimaaz son of Zadok again said to Joab,
"Come what may, please let me run behind the
Cushite."
But Joab replied, "My son, why do you want to
go? You don't have any news that will bring you a
reward."
23He said, "Come what may, I want to run."
So Joab said, "Run!" Then Ahimaaz ran by way
of the plain[a] and outran the Cushite.
24While David was sitting between the inner
and outer gates, the watchman went up to the roof
of the gateway by the wall. As he looked out, he
saw a man running alone. 25The watchman called
out to the king and reported it. 2Sa 19:8; 2Ki 9:17
The king said, "If he is alone, he must have
good news." And the man came closer and closer.
26Then the watchman saw another man running, and he called down to the gatekeeper, "Look,
another man running alone!"
The king said, "He must be bringing good
news, too." 1Ki 1:42
27The watchman said, "It seems to me that the
first one runs like Ahimaaz son of Zadok."
"He's a good man," the king said. "He comes
with good news."
28Then Ahimaaz called out to the king, "All is
well!" He bowed down before the king with his
face to the ground and said, "Praise be to the LORD
your God! He has delivered up the men who lifted
their hands against my lord the king."
29The king asked, "Is the young man Absalom
safe?"
Ahimaaz answered, "I saw great confusion just
as Joab was about to send the king's servant and
me, your servant, but I don't know what it was."
30The king said, "Stand aside and wait here." So
he stepped aside and stood there.
31Then the Cushite arrived and said, "My lord
the king, hear the good news! The LORD has delivered you today from all who rose up against you."
32The king asked the Cushite, "Is the young
man Absalom safe?"
The Cushite replied, "May the enemies of my
lord the king and all who rise up to harm you be
like that young man." Jdg 5:31; 1Sa 25:26
33The king was shaken. He went up to the room
over the gateway and wept. As he went, he said:
"O my son Absalom! My son, my son Absalom! If
only I had died instead of you—O Absalom, my
son, my son!" Ex 32:32; Ro 9:3

19 Joab was told, "The king is weeping and
mourning for Absalom." 2And for the
whole army the victory that day was turned into
mourning, because on that day the troops heard it
said, "The king is grieving for his son." 3The men
stole into the city that day as men steal in who are
ashamed when they flee from battle. 4The king
covered his face and cried aloud, "O my son Absalom! O Absalom, my son, my son!"
5Then Joab went into the house to the king and
said, "Today you have humiliated all your men,
who have just saved your life and the lives of your
sons and daughters and the lives of your wives and
concubines. 6You love those who hate you and
hate those who love you. You have made it clear
today that the commanders and their men mean
nothing to you. I see that you would be pleased if
Absalom were alive today and all of us were dead.
7Now go out and encourage your men. I swear by
the LORD that if you don't go out, not a man will
be left with you by nightfall. This will be worse for
you than all the calamities that have come upon
you from your youth till now." Pr 14:28
8So the king got up and took his seat in the
gateway. When the men were told, "The king is
sitting in the gateway," they all came before him.

David Returns to Jerusalem

Meanwhile, the Israelites had fled to their
homes. 9Throughout the tribes of Israel, the people were all arguing with each other, saying, "The
king delivered us from the hand of our enemies; he
is the one who rescued us from the hand of the
Philistines. But now he has fled the country because of Absalom; 10and Absalom, whom we
anointed to rule over us, has died in battle. So why
do you say nothing about bringing the king back?"
11King David sent this message to Zadok and
Abiathar, the priests: "Ask the elders of Judah,
'Why should you be the last to bring the king back

[a]23 That is, the plain of the Jordan

to his palace, since what is being said throughout Israel has reached the king at his quarters? 12You are my brothers, my own flesh and blood. So why should you be the last to bring back the king?' 13And say to Amasa, 'Are you not my own flesh and blood? May God deal with me, be it ever so severely, if from now on you are not the commander of my army in place of Joab.' " Ge 29:14

14He won over the hearts of all the men of Judah as though they were one man. They sent word to the king, "Return, you and all your men." 15Then the king returned and went as far as the Jordan.

Now the men of Judah had come to Gilgal to go out and meet the king and bring him across the Jordan. 16Shimei son of Gera, the Benjamite from Bahurim, hurried down with the men of Judah to meet King David. 17With him were a thousand Benjamites, along with Ziba, the steward of Saul's household, and his fifteen sons and twenty servants. They rushed to the Jordan, where the king was. 18They crossed at the ford to take the king's household over and to do whatever he wished.

When Shimei son of Gera crossed the Jordan, he fell prostrate before the king 19and said to him, "May my lord not hold me guilty. Do not remember how your servant did wrong on the day my lord the king left Jerusalem. May the king put it out of his mind. 20For I your servant know that I have sinned, but today I have come here as the first of the whole house of Joseph to come down and meet my lord the king." 1Sa 22:15; 2Sa 16:6-8

21Then Abishai son of Zeruiah said, "Shouldn't Shimei be put to death for this? He cursed the LORD's anointed." Ex 22:28

22David replied, "What do you and I have in common, you sons of Zeruiah? This day you have become my adversaries! Should anyone be put to death in Israel today? Do I not know that today I am king over Israel?" 23So the king said to Shimei, "You shall not die." And the king promised him on oath. 1Sa 11:13; 2Sa 16:10; 1Ki 2:8,42

24Mephibosheth, Saul's grandson, also went down to meet the king. He had not taken care of his feet or trimmed his mustache or washed his clothes from the day the king left until the day he returned safely. 25When he came from Jerusalem to meet the king, the king asked him, "Why didn't you go with me, Mephibosheth?" 2Sa 4:4; 9:6-10

26He said, "My lord the king, since I your servant am lame, I said, 'I will have my donkey saddled and will ride on it, so I can go with the king.' But Ziba my servant betrayed me. 27And he has slandered your servant to my lord the king. My lord the king is like an angel of God; so do whatever pleases you. 28All my grandfather's descendants deserved nothing but death from my lord the king, but you gave your servant a place among those who eat at your table. So what right do I have to make any more appeals to the king?"

29The king said to him, "Why say more? I order you and Ziba to divide the fields."

30Mephibosheth said to the king, "Let him take everything, now that my lord the king has arrived home safely."

31Barzillai the Gileadite also came down from Rogelim to cross the Jordan with the king and to send him on his way from there. 32Now Barzillai was a very old man, eighty years of age. He had provided for the king during his stay in Mahanaim, for he was a very wealthy man. 33The king said to Barzillai, "Cross over with me and stay with me in Jerusalem, and I will provide for you."

34But Barzillai answered the king, "How many more years will I live, that I should go up to Jerusalem with the king? 35I am now eighty years old. Can I tell the difference between what is good and what is not? Can your servant taste what he eats and drinks? Can I still hear the voices of men and women singers? Why should your servant be an added burden to my lord the king? 36Your servant will cross over the Jordan with the king for a short distance, but why should the king reward me in this way? 37Let your servant return, that I may die in my own town near the tomb of my father and mother. But here is your servant Kimham. Let him cross over with my lord the king. Do for him whatever pleases you." 1Ki 2:7; Ps 90:10; Jer 41:17

38The king said, "Kimham shall cross over with me, and I will do for him whatever pleases you. And anything you desire from me I will do for you."

39So all the people crossed the Jordan, and then the king crossed over. The king kissed Barzillai and gave him his blessing, and Barzillai returned to his home. Ge 31:55

40When the king crossed over to Gilgal, Kimham crossed with him. All the troops of Judah and half the troops of Israel had taken the king over.

41Soon all the men of Israel were coming to the king and saying to him, "Why did our brothers, the men of Judah, steal the king away and bring him and his household across the Jordan, together with all his men?" Jdg 8:1; 12:1

42All the men of Judah answered the men of Israel, "We did this because the king is closely related to us. Why are you angry about it? Have we eaten any of the king's provisions? Have we taken anything for ourselves?"

43Then the men of Israel answered the men of Judah, "We have ten shares in the king; and besides, we have a greater claim on David than you have. So why do you treat us with contempt? Were we not the first to speak of bringing back our king?"

But the men of Judah responded even more harshly than the men of Israel.

Sheba Rebels Against David

20 Now a troublemaker named Sheba son of Bicri, a Benjamite, happened to be there. He sounded the trumpet and shouted,

"We have no share in David,
no part in Jesse's son! 1Ki 12:16; 2Ch 10:16
Every man to his tent, O Israel!"

2So all the men of Israel deserted David to follow Sheba son of Bicri. But the men of Judah stayed by their king all the way from the Jordan to Jerusalem.

3When David returned to his palace in Jerusalem, he took the ten concubines he had left to take care of the palace and put them in a house under guard. He provided for them, but did not lie with them. They were kept in confinement till the day of their death, living as widows. 2Sa 15:16; 16:21-22

4Then the king said to Amasa, "Summon the men of Judah to come to me within three days, and be here yourself." 5But when Amasa went to summon Judah, he took longer than the time the king had set for him. 2Sa 19:13

6David said to Abishai, "Now Sheba son of Bicri will do us more harm than Absalom did. Take your master's men and pursue him, or he will find fortified cities and escape from us." 7So Joab's men and the Kerethites and Pelethites and all the mighty warriors went out under the command of Abishai. They marched out from Jerusalem to pursue Sheba son of Bicri. 2Sa 8:18; 1Ki 1:38

8While they were at the great rock in Gibeon, Amasa came to meet them. Joab was wearing his military tunic, and strapped over it at his waist was a belt with a dagger in its sheath. As he stepped forward, it dropped out of its sheath. Jos 9:3

9Joab said to Amasa, "How are you, my brother?" Then Joab took Amasa by the beard with his right hand to kiss him. 10Amasa was not on his guard against the dagger in Joab's hand, and Joab plunged it into his belly, and his intestines spilled out on the ground. Without being stabbed again, Amasa died. Then Joab and his brother Abishai pursued Sheba son of Bicri. 2Sa 2:23

11One of Joab's men stood beside Amasa and said, "Whoever favors Joab, and whoever is for David, let him follow Joab!" 12Amasa lay wallowing in his blood in the middle of the road, and the man saw that all the troops came to a halt there. When he realized that everyone who came up to Amasa stopped, he dragged him from the road into a field and threw a garment over him. 13After Amasa had been removed from the road, all the men went on with Joab to pursue Sheba son of Bicri. 2Sa 2:23

14Sheba passed through all the tribes of Israel to Abel Beth Maacah[a] and through the entire region of the Berites, who gathered together and followed him. 15All the troops with Joab came and besieged Sheba in Abel Beth Maacah. They built a siege ramp up to the city, and it stood against the outer fortifications. While they were battering the wall to bring it down, 16a wise woman called from the city, "Listen! Listen! Tell Joab to come here so I can speak to him." 17He went toward her, and she asked, "Are you Joab?" 2Sa 14:2; 2Ki 19:32; 1Ki 15:20

"I am," he answered.

She said, "Listen to what your servant has to say."

"I'm listening," he said.

18She continued, "Long ago they used to say, 'Get your answer at Abel,' and that settled it. 19We are the peaceful and faithful in Israel. You are trying to destroy a city that is a mother in Israel. Why do you want to swallow up the LORD's inheritance?" Dt 2:26; 1Sa 26:19; 2Sa 21:3

20"Far be it from me!" Joab replied, "Far be it from me to swallow up or destroy! 21That is not the case. A man named Sheba son of Bicri, from the hill country of Ephraim, has lifted up his hand against the king, against David. Hand over this one man, and I'll withdraw from the city."

The woman said to Joab, "His head will be thrown to you from the wall." 2Sa 4:8

22Then the woman went to all the people with her wise advice, and they cut off the head of Sheba son of Bicri and threw it to Joab. So he sounded the trumpet, and his men dispersed from the city, each returning to his home. And Joab went back to the king in Jerusalem. Ecc 9:13

23Joab was over Israel's entire army; Benaiah son of Jehoiada was over the Kerethites and Pelethites; 24Adoniram[b] was in charge of forced labor; Jehoshaphat son of Ahilud was recorder; 25Sheva was secretary; Zadok and Abiathar were priests; 26and Ira the Jairite was David's priest. 2Sa 8:16-18

The Gibeonites Avenged

21 During the reign of David, there was a famine for three successive years; so David sought the face of the LORD. The LORD said, "It is on account of Saul and his blood-stained house; it is because he put the Gibeonites to death."

2The king summoned the Gibeonites and spoke to them. (Now the Gibeonites were not a part of Israel but were survivors of the Amorites; the Israelites had sworn to ⌞spare⌟ them, but Saul in his zeal for Israel and Judah had tried to annihilate them.) 3David asked the Gibeonites, "What shall I do for you? How shall I make amends so that you will bless the LORD's inheritance?" Jos 9:15; 1Sa 26:19

4The Gibeonites answered him, "We have no

[a]14 Or *Abel, even Beth Maacah*; also in verse 15 [b]24 Some Septuagint manuscripts (see also 1 Kings 4:6 and 5:14); Hebrew *Adoram*

right to demand silver or gold from Saul or his
family, nor do we have the right to put anyone in
Israel to death." Nu 35:33-34
"What do you want me to do for you?" David
asked.
5They answered the king, "As for the man who
destroyed us and plotted against us so that we have
been decimated and have no place anywhere in
Israel, 6let seven of his male descendants be given
to us to be killed and exposed before the LORD at
Gibeah of Saul—the LORD's chosen one." Nu 25:4
So the king said, "I will give them to you."
7The king spared Mephibosheth son of Jonathan, the son of Saul, because of the oath before
the LORD between David and Jonathan son of Saul.
8But the king took Armoni and Mephibosheth, the
two sons of Aiah's daughter Rizpah, whom she
had borne to Saul, together with the five sons of
Saul's daughter Merab,[a] whom she had borne to
Adriel son of Barzillai the Meholathite. 9He handed them over to the Gibeonites, who killed and
exposed them on a hill before the LORD. All seven
of them fell together; they were put to death during the first days of the harvest, just as the barley
harvest was beginning. 1Sa 20:8,15; 2Sa 3:7; 4:4
10Rizpah daughter of Aiah took sackcloth and
spread it out for herself on a rock. From the beginning of the harvest till the rain poured down from
the heavens on the bodies, she did not let the birds
of the air touch them by day or the wild animals
by night. 11When David was told what Aiah's
daughter Rizpah, Saul's concubine, had done, 12he
went and took the bones of Saul and his son Jonathan from the citizens of Jabesh Gilead. (They had
taken them secretly from the public square at Beth
Shan, where the Philistines had hung them after
they struck Saul down on Gilboa.) 13David
brought the bones of Saul and his son Jonathan
from there, and the bones of those who had been
killed and exposed were gathered up. Dt 21:23
14They buried the bones of Saul and his son
Jonathan in the tomb of Saul's father Kish, at Zela
in Benjamin, and did everything the king commanded. After that, God answered prayer in behalf
of the land. Jos 7:26; 18:28; 2Sa 24:25

Wars Against the Philistines

15Once again there was a battle between the
Philistines and Israel. David went down with his
men to fight against the Philistines, and he became
exhausted. 16And Ishbi-Benob, one of the descendants of Rapha, whose bronze spearhead weighed
three hundred shekels[b] and who was armed with
a new ⌞sword⌟, said he would kill David. 17But
Abishai son of Zeruiah came to David's rescue; he
struck the Philistine down and killed him. Then
David's men swore to him, saying, "Never again
will you go out with us to battle, so that the lamp
of Israel will not be extinguished." 2Sa 18:3; 20:6
18In the course of time, there was another battle
with the Philistines, at Gob. At that time Sibbecai
the Hushathite killed Saph, one of the descendants
of Rapha. 1Ch 11:29; 20:4
19In another battle with the Philistines at Gob,
Elhanan son of Jaare-Oregim[c] the Bethlehemite
killed Goliath[d] the Gittite, who had a spear with
a shaft like a weaver's rod. 1Sa 17:7
20In still another battle, which took place at
Gath, there was a huge man with six fingers on
each hand and six toes on each foot—twenty-four
in all. He also was descended from Rapha. 21When
he taunted Israel, Jonathan son of Shimeah, David's brother, killed him. 1Ch 20:4-8; 1Sa 16:9
22These four were descendants of Rapha in
Gath, and they fell at the hands of David and his
men.

David's Song of Praise

22 David sang to the LORD the words of this
song when the LORD delivered him from
the hand of all his enemies and from the hand of
Saul. 2He said: Ex 15:1; Jdg 5:1

"The LORD is my rock, my fortress and my
deliverer; Dt 32:4; Ps 31:3; 144:2
3 my God is my rock, in whom I take refuge,
my shield and the horn[e] of my salvation.
He is my stronghold, my refuge and my
savior— Ps 9:9
from violent men you save me.
4I call to the LORD, who is worthy of praise,
and I am saved from my enemies.

5"The waves of death swirled about me;
the torrents of destruction overwhelmed
me.
6The cords of the grave[f] coiled around me;
the snares of death confronted me.
7In my distress I called to the LORD;
I called out to my God. Ps 116:4; 120:1
From his temple he heard my voice;
my cry came to his ears.

8"The earth trembled and quaked, Jdg 5:4; Ps 77:18
the foundations of the heavens[g] shook;
they trembled because he was angry.
9Smoke rose from his nostrils;
consuming fire came from his mouth,
burning coals blazed out of it.
10He parted the heavens and came down;
dark clouds were under his feet. 1Ki 8:12; Na 1:3

[a]8 Two Hebrew manuscripts, some Septuagint manuscripts and Syriac (see also 1 Samuel 18:19); most Hebrew and Septuagint manuscripts *Michal* [b]16 That is, about 7 1/2 pounds (about 3.5 kilograms) [c]19 Or *son of Jair the weaver*
[d]19 Hebrew and Septuagint; 1 Chron. 20:5 *son of Jair killed Lahmi the brother of Goliath* [e]3 *Horn* here symbolizes strength.
[f]6 Hebrew *Sheol* [g]8 Hebrew; Vulgate and Syriac (see also Psalm 18:7) *mountains*

[11]He mounted the cherubim and flew;
he soared[a] on the wings of the wind.
[12]He made darkness his canopy around him—
the dark[b] rain clouds of the sky.
[13]Out of the brightness of his presence
bolts of lightning blazed forth. ver 9
[14]The LORD thundered from heaven; 1Sa 2:10
the voice of the Most High resounded.
[15]He shot arrows and scattered ⌊the enemies⌋,
bolts of lightning and routed them.
[16]The valleys of the sea were exposed
and the foundations of the earth laid bare
at the rebuke of the LORD, Na 1:4
at the blast of breath from his nostrils.

[17]"He reached down from on high and took
hold of me; Ps 144:7
he drew me out of deep waters. Ex 2:10
[18]He rescued me from my powerful enemy,
from my foes, who were too strong for me.
[19]They confronted me in the day of my disaster,
but the LORD was my support. Ps 23:4
[20]He brought me out into a spacious place;
he rescued me because he delighted in me.

[21]"The LORD has dealt with me according to my
righteousness; 1Sa 26:23
according to the cleanness of my hands he
has rewarded me. Ps 24:4
[22]For I have kept the ways of the LORD; Ge 18:19
I have not done evil by turning from my
God.
[23]All his laws are before me; Dt 6:4-9; Ps 119:30-32
I have not turned away from his decrees.
[24]I have been blameless before him Ge 6:9; Eph 1:4
and have kept myself from sin.
[25]The LORD has rewarded me according to my
righteousness, ver 21
according to my cleanness[c] in his sight.

[26]"To the faithful you show yourself faithful,
to the blameless you show yourself
blameless,
[27]to the pure you show yourself pure, Mt 5:8
but to the crooked you show yourself
shrewd. Lev 26:23-24
[28]You save the humble, Ps 72:12-13
but your eyes are on the haughty to bring
them low. Isa 2:12,17; 5:15
[29]You are my lamp, O LORD; Ps 27:1
the LORD turns my darkness into light.
[30]With your help I can advance against a
troop[d];
with my God I can scale a wall.

[31]"As for God, his way is perfect; Dt 32:4; Mt 5:48
the word of the LORD is flawless. Ps 12:6
He is a shield Ge 15:1
for all who take refuge in him.
[32]For who is God besides the LORD?
And who is the Rock except our God?
[33]It is God who arms me with strength[e]
and makes my way perfect.
[34]He makes my feet like the feet of a deer;
he enables me to stand on the heights.

LIVING  INSIGHT

Knowledge stabilizes us during times of testing. When we know what God has said, and then we go through a period of pain where the bottom virtually drops out of our life, we don't panic, we don't doubt, we don't ship out the faith. The knowledge we have gained stabilizes us and equips us with essential, calming fortitude when the tests come.

(See 2 Samuel 22:31–34.)

[35]He trains my hands for battle; Ps 144:1
my arms can bend a bow of bronze.
[36]You give me your shield of victory; Eph 6:16
you stoop down to make me great.
[37]You broaden the path beneath me, Pr 4:11
so that my ankles do not turn.

[38]"I pursued my enemies and crushed them;
I did not turn back till they were destroyed.
[39]I crushed them completely, and they could
not rise; Mal 4:3
they fell beneath my feet.
[40]You armed me with strength for battle;
you made my adversaries bow at my feet.
[41]You made my enemies turn their backs in
flight, Ex 23:27
and I destroyed my foes.
[42]They cried for help, but there was no one to
save them— Ps 50:22; Isa 1:15
to the LORD, but he did not answer.
[43]I beat them as fine as the dust of the earth;
I pounded and trampled them like mud in
the streets. Isa 10:6; Mic 7:10

[44]"You have delivered me from the attacks of
my people; 2Sa 3:1
you have preserved me as the head of
nations. Dt 28:13
People I did not know are subject to me,
[45] and foreigners come cringing to me; Ps 66:3
as soon as they hear me, they obey me.
[46]They all lose heart;

[a]*11* Many Hebrew manuscripts (see also Psalm 18:10); most Hebrew manuscripts *appeared* [b]*12* Septuagint and Vulgate (see also Psalm 18:11); Hebrew *massed* [c]*25* Hebrew; Septuagint and Vulgate (see also Psalm 18:24) *to the cleanness of my hands* [d]*30* Or *can run through a barricade* [e]*33* Dead Sea Scrolls, some Septuagint manuscripts, Vulgate and Syriac (see also Psalm 18:32); Masoretic Text *who is my strong refuge*

they come trembling[a] from their
strongholds. Mic 7:17

47 “The LORD lives! Praise be to my Rock!
Exalted be God, the Rock, my Savior!
48 He is the God who avenges me,
who puts the nations under me, Ps 144:2
49 who sets me free from my enemies. Ps 140:1,4
You exalted me above my foes;
from violent men you rescued me.
50 Therefore I will praise you, O LORD, among
the nations;
I will sing praises to your name. Ro 15:9
51 He gives his king great victories; Ps 144:9-10
he shows unfailing kindness to his
anointed, Ps 89:20
to David and his descendants forever.”

The Last Words of David

23 These are the last words of David:

“The oracle of David son of Jesse,
the oracle of the man exalted by the Most
High, Ps 78:70-71; 89:27
the man anointed by the God of Jacob,
Israel’s singer of songs[b]:

2 “The Spirit of the LORD spoke through me;
his word was on my tongue.
3 The God of Israel spoke,
the Rock of Israel said to me: Dt 32:4; 2Sa 22:2,32
‘When one rules over men in righteousness,
when he rules in the fear of God, 2Ch 19:7,9
4 he is like the light of morning at sunrise
on a cloudless morning,
like the brightness after rain
that brings the grass from the earth.’

5 “Is not my house right with God?
Has he not made with me an everlasting
covenant, Ps 89:29; Isa 55:3
arranged and secured in every part?
Will he not bring to fruition my salvation
and grant me my every desire?
6 But evil men are all to be cast aside like
thorns, Mt 13:40-41
which are not gathered with the hand.
7 Whoever touches thorns
uses a tool of iron or the shaft of a spear;
they are burned up where they lie.”

David’s Mighty Men

8 These are the names of David’s mighty men:
Josheb-Basshebeth,[c] a Tahkemonite,[d] was chief
of the Three; he raised his spear against eight
hundred men, whom he killed[e] in one encounter.
9 Next to him was Eleazar son of Dodai the Ahohite. As one of the three mighty men, he was with
David when they taunted the Philistines gathered
⌞at Pas Dammim⌟[f] for battle. Then the men of
Israel retreated, 10 but he stood his ground and
struck down the Philistines till his hand grew tired
and froze to the sword. The LORD brought about a
great victory that day. The troops returned to Eleazar, but only to strip the dead. 1Ch 8:4; 27:4
11 Next to him was Shammah son of Agee the
Hararite. When the Philistines banded together at
a place where there was a field full of lentils, Israel’s troops fled from them. 12 But Shammah took
his stand in the middle of the field. He defended
it and struck the Philistines down, and the LORD
brought about a great victory.
13 During harvest time, three of the thirty chief
men came down to David at the cave of Adullam,
while a band of Philistines was encamped in the
Valley of Rephaim. 14 At that time David was in the
stronghold, and the Philistine garrison was at
Bethlehem. 15 David longed for water and said,
“Oh, that someone would get me a drink of water
from the well near the gate of Bethlehem!” 16 So the
three mighty men broke through the Philistine
lines, drew water from the well near the gate of
Bethlehem and carried it back to David. But he
refused to drink it; instead, he poured it out before
the LORD. 17 “Far be it from me, O LORD, to do
this!” he said. “Is it not the blood of men who went
at the risk of their lives?” And David would not
drink it. 1Sa 22:4-5; 2Sa 5:18; Ge 35:14
Such were the exploits of the three mighty men.
18 Abishai the brother of Joab son of Zeruiah
was chief of the Three.[g] He raised his spear
against three hundred men, whom he killed, and
so he became as famous as the Three. 19 Was he not
held in greater honor than the Three? He became
their commander, even though he was not included among them. 2Sa 10:10,14; 1Ch 11:20
20 Benaiah son of Jehoiada was a valiant fighter
from Kabzeel, who performed great exploits. He
struck down two of Moab’s best men. He also
went down into a pit on a snowy day and killed a
lion. 21 And he struck down a huge Egyptian. Although the Egyptian had a spear in his hand, Benaiah went against him with a club. He snatched
the spear from the Egyptian’s hand and killed him
with his own spear. 22 Such were the exploits of
Benaiah son of Jehoiada; he too was as famous as
the three mighty men. 23 He was held in greater
honor than any of the Thirty, but he was not in-

[a] *46* Some Septuagint manuscripts and Vulgate (see also Psalm 18:45); Masoretic Text *they arm themselves.* [b] *1* Or *Israel’s beloved singer* [c] *8* Hebrew; some Septuagint manuscripts suggest *Ish-Bosheth,* that is, *Esh-Baal* (see also 1 Chron. 11:11 *Jashobeam*). [d] *8* Probably a variant of *Hacmonite* (see 1 Chron. 11:11) [e] *8* Some Septuagint manuscripts (see also 1 Chron. 11:11); Hebrew and other Septuagint manuscripts *Three; it was Adino the Eznite who killed eight hundred men* [f] *9* See 1 Chron. 11:13; Hebrew *gathered there.* [g] *18* Most Hebrew manuscripts (see also 1 Chron. 11:20); two Hebrew manuscripts and Syriac *Thirty*

cluded among the Three. And David put him in charge of his bodyguard. 2Sa 8:18; Jos 15:21

[24]Among the Thirty were:
Asahel the brother of Joab, 2Sa 2:18
Elhanan son of Dodo from Bethlehem,
[25]Shammah the Harodite, Jdg 7:1; 1Ch 11:27
Elika the Harodite,
[26]Helez the Paltite, 1Ch 27:10
Ira son of Ikkesh from Tekoa,
[27]Abiezer from Anathoth, Jos 21:18
Mebunnai[a] the Hushathite,
[28]Zalmon the Ahohite,
Maharai the Netophathite, 2Ki 25:23; Ne 7:26
[29]Heled[b] son of Baanah the Netophathite,
Ithai son of Ribai from Gibeah in Benjamin, Jos 15:57
[30]Benaiah the Pirathonite, Jdg 12:13
Hiddai[c] from the ravines of Gaash,
[31]Abi-Albon the Arbathite,
Azmaveth the Barhumite, 2Sa 3:16
[32]Eliahba the Shaalbonite,
the sons of Jashen,
Jonathan [33]son of[d] Shammah the Hararite,
Ahiam son of Sharar[e] the Hararite,
[34]Eliphelet son of Ahasbai the Maacathite,
Eliam son of Ahithophel the Gilonite,
[35]Hezro the Carmelite,
Paarai the Arbite,
[36]Igal son of Nathan from Zobah, 1Sa 14:47
the son of Hagri,[f]
[37]Zelek the Ammonite,
Naharai the Beerothite, the armor-bearer of Joab son of Zeruiah,
[38]Ira the Ithrite, 1Ch 2:53
Gareb the Ithrite
[39]and Uriah the Hittite. 2Sa 11:3
There were thirty-seven in all.

David Counts the Fighting Men

24 Again the anger of the LORD burned
against Israel, and he incited David against
them, saying, "Go and take a census of Israel and
Judah." Jos 9:15; 1Ch 27:23
[2]So the king said to Joab and the army commanders[g] with him, "Go throughout the tribes of
Israel from Dan to Beersheba and enroll the fighting men, so that I may know how many there are."
[3]But Joab replied to the king, "May the LORD
your God multiply the troops a hundred times
over, and may the eyes of my lord the king see it.
But why does my lord the king want to do such a
thing?" Dt 1:11
[4]The king's word, however, overruled Joab
and the army commanders; so they left the presence of the king to enroll the fighting men of Israel.
[5]After crossing the Jordan, they camped near
Aroer, south of the town in the gorge, and then
went through Gad and on to Jazer. [6]They went to
Gilead and the region of Tahtim Hodshi, and on
to Dan Jaan and around toward Sidon. [7]Then they
went toward the fortress of Tyre and all the towns
of the Hivites and Canaanites. Finally, they went
on to Beersheba in the Negev of Judah. Jos 13:9
[8]After they had gone through the entire land,
they came back to Jerusalem at the end of nine
months and twenty days.
[9]Joab reported the number of the fighting men
to the king: In Israel there were eight hundred
thousand able-bodied men who could handle a
sword, and in Judah five hundred thousand.
[10]David was conscience-stricken after he had
counted the fighting men, and he said to the LORD,
"I have sinned greatly in what I have done. Now,
O LORD, I beg you, take away the guilt of your
servant. I have done a very foolish thing."
[11]Before David got up the next morning, the
word of the LORD had come to Gad the prophet,
David's seer: [12]"Go and tell David, 'This is what
the LORD says: I am giving you three options.
Choose one of them for me to carry out against
you.'" 1Sa 9:9; 22:5; 1Ch 29:29
[13]So Gad went to David and said to him, "Shall
there come upon you three[h] years of famine in
your land? Or three months of fleeing from your
enemies while they pursue you? Or three days of
plague in your land? Now then, think it over and
decide how I should answer the one who
sent me." Eze 14:21; Lev 26:25
[14]David said to Gad, "I am in deep distress. Let
us fall into the hands of the LORD, for his mercy is
great; but do not let me fall into the hands of
men." Ps 51:1; 103:8,13
[15]So the LORD sent a plague on Israel from that
morning until the end of the time designated, and
seventy thousand of the people from Dan to Beersheba died. [16]When the angel stretched out his
hand to destroy Jerusalem, the LORD was grieved
because of the calamity and said to the angel who
was afflicting the people, "Enough! Withdraw your
hand." The angel of the LORD was then at the
threshing floor of Araunah the Jebusite. Ge 6:6
[17]When David saw the angel who was striking
down the people, he said to the LORD, "I am the
one who has sinned and done wrong. These are

[a]27 Hebrew; some Septuagint manuscripts (see also 1 Chron. 11:29) *Sibbecai* [b]29 Some Hebrew manuscripts and Vulgate (see also 1 Chron. 11:30); most Hebrew manuscripts *Heleb* [c]30 Hebrew; some Septuagint manuscripts (see also 1 Chron. 11:32) *Hurai* [d]33 Some Septuagint manuscripts (see also 1 Chron. 11:34); Hebrew does not have *son of.* [e]33 Hebrew; some Septuagint manuscripts (see also 1 Chron. 11:35) *Sacar* [f]36 Some Septuagint manuscripts (see also 1 Chron. 11:38); Hebrew *Haggadi* [g]2 Septuagint (see also verse 4 and 1 Chron. 21:2); Hebrew *Joab the army commander* [h]13 Septuagint (see also 1 Chron. 21:12); Hebrew *seven*

but sheep. What have they done? Let your hand
fall upon me and my family." 1Ch 21:1-17; Ps 74:1

David Builds an Altar

18On that day Gad went to David and said to
him, "Go up and build an altar to the LORD on the
threshing floor of Araunah the Jebusite." 19So David went up, as the LORD had commanded through
Gad. 20When Araunah looked and saw the king
and his men coming toward him, he went out and
bowed down before the king with his face to the
ground.

21Araunah said, "Why has my lord the king
come to his servant?"

"To buy your threshing floor," David answered,
"so I can build an altar to the LORD, that the plague
on the people may be stopped." Nu 16:44-50

22Araunah said to David, "Let my lord the king
take whatever pleases him and offer it up. Here are
oxen for the burnt offering, and here are threshing
sledges and ox yokes for the wood. 23O king,
Araunah gives all this to the king." Araunah
also said to him, "May the LORD your God accept
you."

24But the king replied to Araunah, "No, I
insist on paying you for it. I will not sacrifice to
the LORD my God burnt offerings that cost me
nothing."

So David bought the threshing floor and the
oxen and paid fifty shekels[a] of silver for them.
25David built an altar to the LORD there and sacrificed burnt offerings and fellowship offerings.[b]
Then the LORD answered prayer in behalf of the
land, and the plague on Israel was stopped.

[a] 24 That is, about 1 1/4 pounds (about 0.6 kilogram) [b] 25 Traditionally *peace offerings*

Introduction

1 KINGS

Defining moments. Into every life there comes one—at least one. So it was for Solomon. As the book of 1 Kings begins, King David was in the last days of his life, and Solomon was anointed to take the throne as ruler of the united kingdom of Israel. The first ten chapters of 1 Kings describe the "glory years" of Solomon's forty-year reign. There he was, a man endowed with great wisdom, tremendous gifts, incomparable fame. His kingdom was securely established, and the beautiful temple of God was built and dedicated. For all intents and purposes Solomon had it all—money, fame, power, possessions. And then, that defining moment. What do you do when you have it all? Chapter 11 of 1 Kings tells us how Solomon answered the question. He took his eyes off the Lord . . . and the rest, as they say, is history. Disruption. A divided kingdom. A civil war. All because of a defining moment . . . squandered!

WRITER: *Unknown*

DATE: *c.560–550 B.C.*

PURPOSE: *To describe the movement from a united kingdom to a divided kingdom*

KEY VERSES: *9:4-5; 22:53*

TURNING POINT: *11:11*

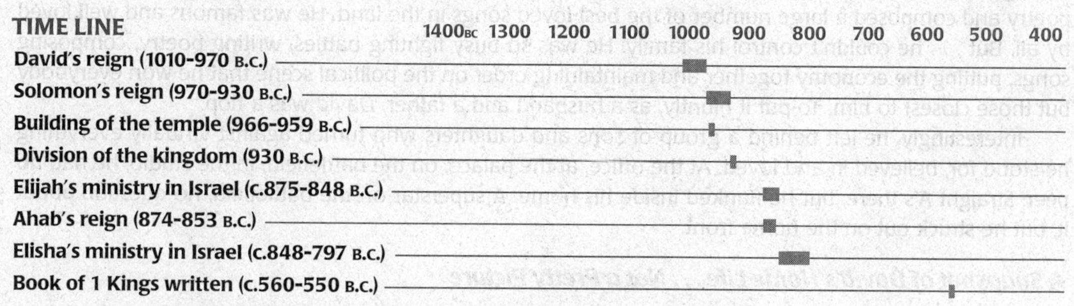

Solomon and a Civil War

	SOLOMON	DECLINE AND DEMISE	DISRUPTION	
	"In all his splendor"		*"A kingdom divided against itself"*	
POLITICALLY David succeeded by Solomon **NATIONALLY** Kingdom united **ECONOMICALLY** Solid and secure **SPIRITUALLY** "Shaky"	Crowned and inaugurated *(1–2)* Married and exalted *(3–4)* Temple erected and dedicated *(5–8)* Warned and blessed *(9–10)*		Internal conflict and hostility *(12–14)* Civil war and idolatry *(15–16)* A king and a prophet *(17–22)* **Key Verse–*22:53*** *"He served and worshiped Baal and provoked the LORD, the God of Israel, to anger, just as his father had done."*	**POLITICALLY** King after king **NATIONALLY** Kingdom divided **ECONOMICALLY** Unstable **SPIRITUALLY** Empty
	CHAPTERS 1–10	***CHAPTER 11***	***CHAPTERS 12–22***	

TIME	**Forty years**	**Eighty years**
KINGDOM	**United and strong**	**Divided and weak**
PEOPLE	**Solomon**	**Jeroboam to Ahaziah** **Rehoboam to Jehoshaphat**
IDENTITY	***"All Israel . . . sons of Israel"***	**NORTH: Israel; Samaria; Ephraim** **SOUTH: Judah; Jerusalem**

One of the haunting perils of leadership often is the great divorce between what happens at the office and what happens at home. Many a business/professional man and many a career woman may hit a home run in the workplace, but what good is it if they strike out at home? Admittedly, it can be a little confusing, because the world will call that kind of person a success. In fact, what happens at home is often considered of such insignificant value that it's not even mentioned in a progress report or any other written analysis of success from the world's perspective.

Israel's greatest king was a success if you viewed him from the eyes of the world. On the battlefield, David was undefeated. In the area of export and import, he was unsurpassed up to his day. As a man of courage, determination and clearheaded military leadership, he never met his equal. He wrote insightful poetry and composed a large number of the best-loved songs in the land. He was famous and well loved by all. But . . . he couldn't control his family. He was so busy fighting battles, writing poetry, composing songs, putting the economy together and maintaining order on the political scene that he won everybody but those closest to him. To put it bluntly, as a husband and a father, David was a flop.

Interestingly, he left behind a group of sons and daughters who turned against virtually everything he stood for, believed in and loved. At the office, at the palace, on the battlefield, in the studio, he had no peer. Straight A's there, but he flunked inside his home. A superstar on the battlefield, no question about it, but he struck out on the home front.

A Snapshot of David's Home Life . . . Not a Pretty Picture

As we undertake a survey of 1 Kings, let's understand that the roots of these 22 chapters go back into the life of David, the father of Solomon. In fact, it was from his famous father that Solomon got his first and most lasting impressions of leadership. At home, David's polygamy, hypocrisy and struggles with guilt led to a permissiveness that spawned a rebellious spirit in the lives of several of his children. If you look at 1 Kings 1:5–6 as a vignette in the life of David, you get a picture of what life must have been like at home. We are given a brief biographical snapshot of one of his sons named Adonijah:

> *Now Adonijah, whose mother was Haggith, put himself forward and said, "I will be king." So he got chariots and horses ready, with fifty men to run ahead of him. (His father had never interfered with him by asking, "Why do you behave as you do?" He was also very handsome and was born next after Absalom.)*

What an eloquent statement from Scripture! Here was a boy who had often *longed* for time with his daddy, only to receive a promise here and a wishful hope there—but rarely any significant attention. David was too busy. Too busy to be a father—and therefore too busy to confront his son with the words he really needed to hear: "Why do you behave as you do?" I suggest that Adonijah hardly knew right from wrong. Children learn that from their parents, early on. Adonijah didn't know the scoop, because David hadn't taken the time to nurture him, to train him, to warn him with such counsel as, "That's wrong, son." And what's worse, he hadn't done it with Solomon either. And so Solomon came to the throne unconfronted. Untrained. Small wonder that later on his life careened out of control!

The Best Investment of All

If you are a parent reading these words, I want to remind you that there is no greater investment than the investment you make in the lives of your children. As a minister of the gospel, I am involved in a career that has sufficient time demands to destroy a family if I give myself to it with all of the expectations that accompany the job. I can be involved in giving people the best of information from the living Book, the Bible, and at the same time my family can disintegrate before my unseeing eyes. Strange irony, isn't it? David, the man mentioned more times in the New Testament than any other Bible character from the Old Testament, experienced just that! This man literally watched the disintegration of his family. Parents, don't forget this: *You cannot spend time any more effectively than training and rearing your young children.* Be careful, because life in the fast lane can cause you to forget this. (So can too many hours at the church!)

Advice From a Deathbed

It was out of his experience of an undisciplined childhood that Solomon came onto the pages of 1 Kings at the young age of 20. In the first couple of chapters, Solomon was appointed as the next king of Israel. There was that poignant moment where David, on his deathbed, pulled his son aside and gave him some good advice. Sadly, we wish he had done this many years earlier. Look at what David said:

> *"I am about to go the way of all the earth," he said. "So be strong, show yourself a man, and observe what the LORD your God requires: Walk in his ways, and keep his decrees and commands, his laws and requirements, as written in the Law of Moses, so that you may prosper in all you do and wherever you go, and that the LORD may keep his promise to me: 'If your descendants watch how they live, and if they walk faithfully before me with all their heart and soul, you will never fail to have a man on the throne of Israel' " (2:2–4).*

With David's death, Solomon took the throne of his father. This transfer of authority marked the beginning of a new era. Solomon began to experience unrestrained blessings from the hand of God, according to the early record of 1 Kings.

The book can be divided into two distinct sections. The first 11 chapters show a united and strong kingdom of Israel under the leadership of Solomon. Halfway through the book 1 Kings turns like a door on its hinges. The final 11 chapters uncover a divided and weakened kingdom—now split into a northern and southern kingdom under separate leaders, most of them wicked. Chapters 1–11 span a period of forty years; chapters 12–22 cover about eighty or ninety years—including the sad record of a civil war that broke out and divided the nation.

Solomon in All His Glory

Three separate times in 1 Kings the Lord appeared to Solomon (see 3:4–5; 9:1–9; 11:9–13). In chapter 3 we read of *the Lord's first appearance to Solomon*. In a dream at night God said, "Ask for whatever you want me to give you" (3:5). Solomon responded: "So give your servant a discerning heart to govern your people and to distinguish between right and wrong" (3:9).

Some people think Solomon was being modest and humble when he prayed these words. They believe he already possessed great wisdom and was only asking for more of what he already had in abundance. I don't agree. The way he was raised signifies to me that he may have had a head full of knowledge but realized, due to his upbringing and young age, that he lacked wisdom. He knew he needed God's wisdom, so he asked for it with an honest view of his own limitations. His request pleased the Lord. Not only did God give him great discernment but riches and fame on top of that.

Solomon undertook the work of building a temple, and by the end of chapter 8, the work was completed and the dedication of the temple had taken place. His prayer (8:23–53) was the longest recorded prayer of dedication in all the Old Testament. Let me add at this point, Solomon was never more famous or revered or loved than he was at this time. It was a time of beautiful prosperity. Now, at the height of Solomon's reign, God came *and appeared to him a second time*. God promised to establish the throne of his kingdom over Israel forever, but He also gave a warning to Solomon (9:6–7). He had never warned Solomon before. Why now? Probably because we are at our most vulnerable when we're sailing through life on the calm seas of success. When everything is going in our favor and when there are very few struggles, that is precisely the time we need to be on our guard. When life is a bowl of cherries, we're not always aware of the pits. So it was for Solomon. His prosperity made him extremely vulnerable—and so the Lord gave him a sobering warning.

Solomon's Compromise and Failure

How could it have happened? How could a man with so much promise hit the skids so dramatically? You see, it's extremely difficult to shake off the impact of our home . . . the way we were brought up—especially if we were given free reign. The time may come, later on, when life loses its challenge and boredom sets in, often when enjoying mid-life prosperity. At the height of Solomon's career, I believe he became bored. It's difficult to imagine Solomon going down the wrong path with such a clear leading from God, twenty years on the throne, the heritage of David and the whole nation hanging in the balance. However, with the words of God still ringing in his ears, Solomon "loved many foreign women" (11:1) from the very nations with which God had told him *not* to associate. All his pagan wives brought with them all of the gods of their pagan roots. Influenced by their background in high-level idolatry and low-level morality, Solomon began to traffic in the most incredible extremes of immorality we could ever imagine.

The Lord was angry, and *He appeared to him a third time*. At this point, God said, "I will most certainly tear the kingdom away from you and give it to one of your subordinates. Nevertheless, for the sake of David your father, I will not do it during your lifetime. I will tear it out of the hand of your son" (11:11b–12). The demise of Solomon set in motion the fulfillment of the Lord's prediction.

The Divided Kingdom

As Solomon's life came to an end, his son Rehoboam succeeded him on the throne. A man named Jeroboam, who had been one of Solomon's officials (11:26), stepped to the forefront. He was an aggressive young man, and he wanted the throne. Just as God had warned Solomon when describing the consequences of straying from a righteous lifestyle, a civil war did in fact take place. The group that went to the north came to be known as *Israel*, and the group that remained in the south came to be known as *Judah*. *Note well: When reading Kings and Chronicles, always remember, when you see the name "Judah," it's south; when you see "Israel," it's north.*

The final 11 chapters of 1 Kings contain the tragic account of war, threats, revolutions, assassinations, as well as gross idolatry and unashamed immorality. It was a time of national compromise and failure. While Jeroboam was reigning in the north, Judah went through a succession of three separate kings down south: Rehoboam, Abijah and Asa. As you near the end of 1 Kings, you meet a man named Jehoshaphat, who was the king of Judah in the south. Also, you meet a man named Ahaziah, who was the king of Israel in the north.

The Sin of Idolatry

Before we look at the last verse in the book, which, by the way, nicely summarizes 1 Kings, I want to take a quick glance at chapter 17. It's a breath of fresh air in an otherwise stale environment. While Ahab was king over Israel and did evil in the sight of the Lord (more than all the other kings who were before him!), God sent a stronghearted prophet on the scene named Elijah. What a courageous, uncompromising, fearless man of God! This was a man with a mission. Elijah was suddenly in King Ahab's face, confronting him with all of his sins. In the midst of this whole mess, God placed His man Elijah right in the middle of Ahab's life to challenge him. Isn't that just like the Lord? When things look so bad you become convinced there will never be a way out, along comes an Elijah. When things are the darkest, it seems as though the Lord brings out of the woodwork just the right kind of person perfectly suited for that hour. Even though Ahab did not change, he was nonetheless continually confronted with the truth. God does not force us to accept the truth, but He will send His messengers to be sure we hear it and, hopefully, come to terms with it.

Learning From the Kings

Here are four areas of application that come to mind as I meditate on the message of this book:

First, *unchecked sinful behaviors are usually passed from parent to child.* If sinful behaviors aren't dealt with, they may very well corrupt the next generation in that same family. If a child isn't instructed contrary to what may be the evil lifestyle of his or her parents, that child very likely will begin to practice it, a la Solomon, a la Rehoboam and right on down in the manner of Ahab and later kings.

Second, *we are most vulnerable when we least expect the temptation.* When our guard is down, we leave ourselves open to the uppercut of sin to deal us a knockout blow!

Third, *God always has the right person to match the hour.* When the hour calls for it, He has a way of bringing just the right person who offers the support we need. God is gracious and uses His people to encourage and bless, as well as to confront and convict—all of it done because of His great love and out of deep concern for His children.

Fourth, *when life seems especially dark, God comes especially close.* Some of the most precious times with the living Lord are recorded in the last part of 1 Kings, as Elijah, in the darkness of that era, walked closely with God. It was in *that* era that miracles often occurred to remind the people of the Lord's presence and power. When life seems dark, God makes His presence known, reminding us that He cares for us with tenderness and compassion.

Solomon in All His Splendor — Chapters 1–10

The opening chapters paint a picture of unity, strength and political prosperity. Solomon was ruling the kingdom in all of his glory and splendor. The first two chapters record his inauguration as he followed his father David in becoming the sovereign king of Israel . . . God's nation. He then set his attention to building the temple as a place for the worship of *Yahweh*, the God of Israel. Once the temple was dedicated, Solomon was given a warning to follow the Lord, to exalt His name, uphold His reputation and obey His ways. Everything seemed to be going well in Solomon's life as these chapters drew to a close. The meaning of his name (*Shalom*—Peace) was personified in his rule.

Not only was the picture rosy for Solomon, but the whole nation appeared to be thriving and healthy. The tribes of Israel were united, standing together as God's people. The people were prosperous, and the Lord was providing all they needed for a healthy and growing economy. During those forty years everything seemed to be going well in the promised land—but there was a growing sense of a spiritual erosion taking place behind the scenes in the palace as well as throughout the nation of Israel.

Adonijah Sets Himself Up as King

1 When King David was old and well advanced in years, he could not keep warm even when they put covers over him. [2]So his servants said to him, "Let us look for a young virgin to attend the king and take care of him. She can lie beside him so that our lord the king may keep warm."

[3]Then they searched throughout Israel for a beautiful girl and found Abishag, a Shunammite, and brought her to the king. [4]The girl was very beautiful; she took care of the king and waited on him, but the king had no intimate relations with her.

[5]Now Adonijah, whose mother was Haggith, put himself forward and said, "I will be king." So he got chariots and horses[a] ready, with fifty men to run ahead of him. [6](His father had never interfered with him by asking, "Why do you behave as you do?" He was also very handsome and was born next after Absalom.) 2Sa 3:4; 15:1

[7]Adonijah conferred with Joab son of Zeruiah and with Abiathar the priest, and they gave him their support. [8]But Zadok the priest, Benaiah son of Jehoiada, Nathan the prophet, Shimei and Rei[b] and David's special guard did not join Adonijah.

[9]Adonijah then sacrificed sheep, cattle and fattened calves at the Stone of Zoheleth near En Rogel. He invited all his brothers, the king's sons, and all the men of Judah who were royal officials, [10]but he did not invite Nathan the prophet or Benaiah or the special guard or his brother Solomon.

[11]Then Nathan asked Bathsheba, Solomon's mother, "Have you not heard that Adonijah, the son of Haggith, has become king without our lord David's knowing it? [12]Now then, let me advise you how you can save your own life and the life of your son Solomon. [13]Go in to King David and say to him, 'My lord the king, did you not swear to me your servant: "Surely Solomon your son shall be king after me, and he will sit on my throne"? Why then has Adonijah become king?' [14]While you are still there talking to the king, I will come in and confirm what you have said." 2Sa 3:4; 1Ch 22:9-13

[15]So Bathsheba went to see the aged king in his room, where Abishag the Shunammite was attending him. [16]Bathsheba bowed low and knelt before the king. ver 1

"What is it you want?" the king asked.

[17]She said to him, "My lord, you yourself swore to me your servant by the LORD your God: 'Solomon your son shall be king after me, and he will sit on my throne.' [18]But now Adonijah has become king, and you, my lord the king, do not know about it. [19]He has sacrificed great numbers of cattle, fattened calves, and sheep, and has invited all the king's sons, Abiathar the priest and Joab the commander of the army, but he has not invited Solomon your servant. [20]My lord the king, the eyes of all Israel are on you, to learn from you who will sit on the throne of my lord the king after him. [21]Otherwise, as soon as my lord the king is laid to rest with his fathers, I and my son Solomon will be treated as criminals." ver 13,30; Dt 31:16; 1Ki 2:10

[22]While she was still speaking with the king, Nathan the prophet arrived. [23]And they told the king, "Nathan the prophet is here." So he went before the king and bowed with his face to the ground.

[24]Nathan said, "Have you, my lord the king, declared that Adonijah shall be king after you, and that he will sit on your throne? [25]Today he has gone down and sacrificed great numbers of cattle, fattened calves, and sheep. He has invited all the king's sons, the commanders of the army and Abiathar the priest. Right now they are eating and drinking with him and saying, 'Long live King Adonijah!' [26]But me your servant, and Zadok the priest, and Benaiah son of Jehoiada, and your servant Solomon he did not invite. [27]Is this something my lord the king has done without letting his servants know who should sit on the throne of my lord the king after him?"

David Makes Solomon King

[28]Then King David said, "Call in Bathsheba." So she came into the king's presence and stood before him.

[29]The king then took an oath: "As surely as the LORD lives, who has delivered me out of every trouble, [30]I will surely carry out today what I swore to you by the LORD, the God of Israel: Solomon

[a]5 Or *charioteers* [b]8 Or *and his friends*

your son shall be king after me, and he will sit on
my throne in my place." ver 13,17; 2Sa 4:9
[31]Then Bathsheba bowed low with her face to
the ground and, kneeling before the king, said,
"May my lord King David live forever!"
[32]King David said, "Call in Zadok the priest,
Nathan the prophet and Benaiah son of Jehoiada."
When they came before the king, [33]he said to
them: "Take your lord's servants with you and set
Solomon my son on my own mule and take him
down to Gihon. [34]There have Zadok the priest and
Nathan the prophet anoint him king over Israel.
Blow the trumpet and shout, 'Long live King Solomon!' [35]Then you are to go up with him, and he
is to come and sit on my throne and reign in my
place. I have appointed him ruler over Israel and
Judah." 1Sa 10:1; 2Sa 15:10; 20:6-7
[36]Benaiah son of Jehoiada answered the king,
"Amen! May the LORD, the God of my lord the
king, so declare it. [37]As the LORD was with my lord
the king, so may he be with Solomon to make his
throne even greater than the throne of my lord
King David!" ver 47; Jos 1:5,17; 1Sa 20:13
[38]So Zadok the priest, Nathan the prophet, Benaiah son of Jehoiada, the Kerethites and the Pelethites went down and put Solomon on King David's mule and escorted him to Gihon. [39]Zadok the
priest took the horn of oil from the sacred tent and
anointed Solomon. Then they sounded the trumpet and all the people shouted, "Long live King
Solomon!" [40]And all the people went up after him,
playing flutes and rejoicing greatly, so that the
ground shook with the sound. 1Sa 10:24; 2Sa 8:18
[41]Adonijah and all the guests who were with
him heard it as they were finishing their feast. On
hearing the sound of the trumpet, Joab asked,
"What's the meaning of all the noise in the city?"
[42]Even as he was speaking, Jonathan son of Abiathar the priest arrived. Adonijah said, "Come in.
A worthy man like you must be bringing good
news." 2Sa 18:26
[43]"Not at all!" Jonathan answered. "Our lord
King David has made Solomon king. [44]The king
has sent with him Zadok the priest, Nathan the
prophet, Benaiah son of Jehoiada, the Kerethites
and the Pelethites, and they have put him on the
king's mule, [45]and Zadok the priest and Nathan
the prophet have anointed him king at Gihon.
From there they have gone up cheering, and the
city resounds with it. That's the noise you hear.
[46]Moreover, Solomon has taken his seat on the
royal throne. [47]Also, the royal officials have come
to congratulate our lord King David, saying, 'May
your God make Solomon's name more famous
than yours and his throne greater than yours!' And
the king bowed in worship on his bed [48]and said,
'Praise be to the LORD, the God of Israel, who has
allowed my eyes to see a successor on my throne
today.'" ver 37; 1Ki 3:6
[49]At this, all Adonijah's guests rose in alarm and
dispersed. [50]But Adonijah, in fear of Solomon,
went and took hold of the horns of the altar.
[51]Then Solomon was told, "Adonijah is afraid of
King Solomon and is clinging to the horns of the
altar. He says, 'Let King Solomon swear to me
today that he will not put his servant to death with
the sword.'" 1Ki 2:28
[52]Solomon replied, "If he shows himself to be a
worthy man, not a hair of his head will fall to the
ground; but if evil is found in him, he will die."
[53]Then King Solomon sent men, and they brought
him down from the altar. And Adonijah came and
bowed down to King Solomon, and Solomon said,
"Go to your home." 1Ch 29:21-25; 1Sa 14:45

David's Charge to Solomon

2 When the time drew near for David to die, he
gave a charge to Solomon his son.
[2]"I am about to go the way of all the earth," he
said. "So be strong, show yourself a man, [3]and
observe what the LORD your God requires: Walk in
his ways, and keep his decrees and commands, his
laws and requirements, as written in the Law of
Moses, so that you may prosper in all you do and

LIVING  **INSIGHT**

Let us never forget that our Lord's goal for us is that we become people who obey, not merely study . . . disciples of Jesus Christ who yield our wills in greater obedience, not merely expand our minds for greater intelligence.

(See 1 Kings 2:3.)

wherever you go, [4]and that the LORD may keep his
promise to me: 'If your descendants watch how
they live, and if they walk faithfully before me with
all their heart and soul, you will never fail to have
a man on the throne of Israel.' 2Sa 7:13,25; 2Ki 20:3
[5]"Now you yourself know what Joab son of Zeruiah did to me—what he did to the two commanders of Israel's armies, Abner son of Ner and
Amasa son of Jether. He killed them, shedding
their blood in peacetime as if in battle, and with
that blood stained the belt around his waist and
the sandals on his feet. [6]Deal with him according
to your wisdom, but do not let his gray head go
down to the grave[a] in peace. 2Sa 2:18; 20:10
[7]"But show kindness to the sons of Barzillai of
Gilead and let them be among those who eat at
your table. They stood by me when I fled from
your brother Absalom. 2Sa 9:7; 17:27; 19:31-39

[a]6 Hebrew *Sheol*; also in verse 9

8“And remember, you have with you Shimei son of Gera, the Benjamite from Bahurim, who called down bitter curses on me the day I went to Mahanaim. When he came down to meet me at the Jordan, I swore to him by the LORD: ‘I will not put you to death by the sword.’ 9But now, do not consider him innocent. You are a man of wisdom; you will know what to do to him. Bring his gray head down to the grave in blood.” 2Sa 16:5-13

10Then David rested with his fathers and was buried in the City of David. 11He had reigned forty years over Israel—seven years in Hebron and thirty-three in Jerusalem. 12So Solomon sat on the throne of his father David, and his rule was firmly established. 1Ch 29:26-28; 2Ch 1:1; 2Sa 5:7

Solomon’s Throne Established

13Now Adonijah, the son of Haggith, went to Bathsheba, Solomon’s mother. Bathsheba asked him, “Do you come peacefully?” 1Sa 16:4

He answered, “Yes, peacefully.” 14Then he added, “I have something to say to you.”

“You may say it,” she replied.

15“As you know,” he said, “the kingdom was mine. All Israel looked to me as their king. But things changed, and the kingdom has gone to my brother; for it has come to him from the LORD. 16Now I have one request to make of you. Do not refuse me.”

“You may make it,” she said.

17So he continued, “Please ask King Solomon—he will not refuse you—to give me Abishag the Shunammite as my wife.” 1Ki 1:3

18“Very well,” Bathsheba replied, “I will speak to the king for you.”

19When Bathsheba went to King Solomon to speak to him for Adonijah, the king stood up to meet her, bowed down to her and sat down on his throne. He had a throne brought for the king’s mother, and she sat down at his right hand.

20“I have one small request to make of you,” she said. “Do not refuse me.”

The king replied, “Make it, my mother; I will not refuse you.”

21So she said, “Let Abishag the Shunammite be given in marriage to your brother Adonijah.”

22King Solomon answered his mother, “Why do you request Abishag the Shunammite for Adonijah? You might as well request the kingdom for him—after all, he is my older brother—yes, for him and for Abiathar the priest and Joab son of Zeruiah!” 2Sa 12:8; 1Ki 1:3; 1Ch 3:2

23Then King Solomon swore by the LORD: “May God deal with me, be it ever so severely, if Adonijah does not pay with his life for this request! 24And now, as surely as the LORD lives—he who has established me securely on the throne of my father David and has founded a dynasty for me as he promised—Adonijah shall be put to death today!” 25So King Solomon gave orders to Benaiah son of Jehoiada, and he struck down Adonijah and he died. 2Sa 7:11; 8:18; Ru 1:17

26To Abiathar the priest the king said, “Go back to your fields in Anathoth. You deserve to die, but I will not put you to death now, because you carried the ark of the Sovereign LORD before my father David and shared all my father’s hardships.” 27So Solomon removed Abiathar from the priesthood of the LORD, fulfilling the word the LORD had spoken at Shiloh about the house of Eli.

28When the news reached Joab, who had conspired with Adonijah though not with Absalom, he fled to the tent of the LORD and took hold of the horns of the altar. 29King Solomon was told that Joab had fled to the tent of the LORD and was beside the altar. Then Solomon ordered Benaiah son of Jehoiada, “Go, strike him down!” ver 25

30So Benaiah entered the tent of the LORD and said to Joab, “The king says, ‘Come out!’ ”

But he answered, “No, I will die here.”

Benaiah reported to the king, “This is how Joab answered me.”

31Then the king commanded Benaiah, “Do as he says. Strike him down and bury him, and so clear me and my father’s house of the guilt of the innocent blood that Joab shed. 32The LORD will repay him for the blood he shed, because without the knowledge of my father David he attacked two men and killed them with the sword. Both of them—Abner son of Ner, commander of Israel’s army, and Amasa son of Jether, commander of Judah’s army—were better men and more upright than he. 33May the guilt of their blood rest on the head of Joab and his descendants forever. But on David and his descendants, his house and his throne, may there be the LORD’s peace forever.”

34So Benaiah son of Jehoiada went up and struck down Joab and killed him, and he was buried on his own land[a] in the desert. 35The king put Benaiah son of Jehoiada over the army in Joab’s position and replaced Abiathar with Zadok the priest. 1Ki 4:4; 1Ch 29:22

36Then the king sent for Shimei and said to him, “Build yourself a house in Jerusalem and live there, but do not go anywhere else. 37The day you leave and cross the Kidron Valley, you can be sure you will die; your blood will be on your own head.”

38Shimei answered the king, “What you say is good. Your servant will do as my lord the king has said.” And Shimei stayed in Jerusalem for a long time.

39But three years later, two of Shimei’s slaves ran off to Achish son of Maacah, king of Gath, and Shimei was told, “Your slaves are in Gath.” 40At

[a]34 Or *buried in his tomb*

this, he saddled his donkey and went to Achish at Gath in search of his slaves. So Shimei went away and brought the slaves back from Gath. 1Sa 27:2

41When Solomon was told that Shimei had gone from Jerusalem to Gath and had returned, 42the king summoned Shimei and said to him, "Did I not make you swear by the LORD and warn you, 'On the day you leave to go anywhere else, you can be sure you will die'? At that time you said to me, 'What you say is good. I will obey.' 43Why then did you not keep your oath to the LORD and obey the command I gave you?"

44The king also said to Shimei, "You know in your heart all the wrong you did to my father David. Now the LORD will repay you for your wrongdoing. 45But King Solomon will be blessed, and David's throne will remain secure before the LORD forever." 2Sa 7:13; 16:5-13; Pr 25:5

46Then the king gave the order to Benaiah son of Jehoiada, and he went out and struck Shimei down and killed him.

The kingdom was now firmly established in Solomon's hands. ver 12; 2Ch 1:1

Solomon Asks for Wisdom

3 Solomon made an alliance with Pharaoh king of Egypt and married his daughter. He brought her to the City of David until he finished building his palace and the temple of the LORD, and the wall around Jerusalem. 2The people, however, were still sacrificing at the high places, because a temple had not yet been built for the Name of the LORD. 3Solomon showed his love for the LORD by walking according to the statutes of his father David, except that he offered sacrifices and burned incense on the high places. Dt 6:5; 12:2,4-5

4The king went to Gibeon to offer sacrifices, for that was the most important high place, and Solomon offered a thousand burnt offerings on that altar. 5At Gibeon the LORD appeared to Solomon during the night in a dream, and God said, "Ask for whatever you want me to give you." Nu 12:6

6Solomon answered, "You have shown great kindness to your servant, my father David, because he was faithful to you and righteous and upright in heart. You have continued this great kindness to him and have given him a son to sit on his throne this very day. 1Ki 1:48; 2:4; 9:4

7"Now, O LORD my God, you have made your servant king in place of my father David. But I am only a little child and do not know how to carry out my duties. 8Your servant is here among the people you have chosen, a great people, too numerous to count or number. 9So give your servant a discerning heart to govern your people and to distinguish between right and wrong. For who is able to govern this great people of yours?"

10The Lord was pleased that Solomon had asked for this. 11So God said to him, "Since you have asked for this and not for long life or wealth for yourself, nor have asked for the death of your enemies but for discernment in administering justice, 12I will do what you have asked. I will give you

LIVING  INSIGHT

Discernment gives us a proper frame of reference, a definite line separating good and evil. It acts as an umpire in life and blows the whistle on the spurious. It's as particular as a pathologist peering into a microscope. Discernment picks and chooses its dates with great care. It doesn't fall for fakes . . . or flirt with phonies . . . or dance with deceivers . . . or kiss counterfeits good night.

(See 1 Kings 3:9.)

a wise and discerning heart, so that there will never have been anyone like you, nor will there ever be. 13Moreover, I will give you what you have not asked for—both riches and honor—so that in your lifetime you will have no equal among kings. 14And if you walk in my ways and obey my statutes and commands as David your father did, I will give you a long life." 15Then Solomon awoke—and he realized it had been a dream.

He returned to Jerusalem, stood before the ark of the Lord's covenant and sacrificed burnt offerings and fellowship offerings.[a] Then he gave a feast for all his court. 2Ch 1:2-13; 1Ki 8:65

A Wise Ruling

16Now two prostitutes came to the king and stood before him. 17One of them said, "My lord, this woman and I live in the same house. I had a baby while she was there with me. 18The third day after my child was born, this woman also had a baby. We were alone; there was no one in the house but the two of us.

19"During the night this woman's son died because she lay on him. 20So she got up in the middle of the night and took my son from my side while I your servant was asleep. She put him by her breast and put her dead son by my breast. 21The next morning, I got up to nurse my son—and he was dead! But when I looked at him closely in the morning light, I saw that it wasn't the son I had borne."

22The other woman said, "No! The living one is my son; the dead one is yours."

But the first one insisted, "No! The dead one is

[a]15 Traditionally *peace offerings*

yours; the living one is mine." And so they argued before the king.

23The king said, "This one says, 'My son is alive and your son is dead,' while that one says, 'No! Your son is dead and mine is alive.'"

24Then the king said, "Bring me a sword." So they brought a sword for the king. 25He then gave an order: "Cut the living child in two and give half to one and half to the other."

26The woman whose son was alive was filled with compassion for her son and said to the king, "Please, my lord, give her the living baby! Don't kill him!" Ge 43:30; Isa 49:15; Jer 31:20

But the other said, "Neither I nor you shall have him. Cut him in two!"

27Then the king gave his ruling: "Give the living baby to the first woman. Do not kill him; she is his mother."

28When all Israel heard the verdict the king had given, they held the king in awe, because they saw that he had wisdom from God to administer justice. ver 9,11-12; Col 2:3

Solomon's Officials and Governors

4 So King Solomon ruled over all Israel. 2And these were his chief officials:

Azariah son of Zadok—the priest; 1Ch 6:10
3Elihoreph and Ahijah, sons of Shisha—secretaries;
Jehoshaphat son of Ahilud—recorder;
4Benaiah son of Jehoiada—commander in chief; 1Ki 2:35
Zadok and Abiathar—priests; 1Ki 2:27
5Azariah son of Nathan—in charge of the district officers;
Zabud son of Nathan—a priest and personal adviser to the king;
6Ahishar—in charge of the palace;
Adoniram son of Abda—in charge of forced labor.

7Solomon also had twelve district governors over all Israel, who supplied provisions for the king and the royal household. Each one had to provide supplies for one month in the year. 8These are their names:

Ben-Hur—in the hill country of Ephraim;
9Ben-Deker—in Makaz, Shaalbim, Beth Shemesh and Elon Bethhanan; Jdg 1:35
10Ben-Hesed—in Arubboth (Socoh and all the land of Hepher were his); Jos 12:17
11Ben-Abinadab—in Naphoth Dor[a] (he was married to Taphath daughter of Solomon); Jos 11:2
12Baana son of Ahilud—in Taanach and Megiddo, and in all of Beth Shan next to Zarethan below Jezreel, from Beth Shan to Abel Meholah across to Jokmeam;
13Ben-Geber—in Ramoth Gilead (the settlements of Jair son of Manasseh in Gilead were his, as well as the district of Argob in Bashan and its sixty large walled cities with bronze gate bars); Nu 32:41; Dt 3:4
14Ahinadab son of Iddo—in Mahanaim;
15Ahimaaz—in Naphtali (he had married Basemath daughter of Solomon);
16Baana son of Hushai—in Asher and in Aloth; 2Sa 15:32
17Jehoshaphat son of Paruah—in Issachar;
18Shimei son of Ela—in Benjamin; 1Ki 1:8
19Geber son of Uri—in Gilead (the country of Sihon king of the Amorites and the country of Og king of Bashan). He was the only governor over the district. Dt 3:8-10

Solomon's Daily Provisions

20The people of Judah and Israel were as numerous as the sand on the seashore; they ate, they drank and they were happy. 21And Solomon ruled over all the kingdoms from the River[b] to the land of the Philistines, as far as the border of Egypt. These countries brought tribute and were Solomon's subjects all his life. 2Ch 9:26; Ps 72:8; Ge 15:18

22Solomon's daily provisions were thirty cors[c] of fine flour and sixty cors[d] of meal, 23ten head of stall-fed cattle, twenty of pasture-fed cattle and a hundred sheep and goats, as well as deer, gazelles, roebucks and choice fowl. 24For he ruled over all the kingdoms west of the River, from Tiphsah to Gaza, and had peace on all sides. 25During Solomon's lifetime Judah and Israel, from Dan to Beersheba, lived in safety, each man under his own vine and fig tree. Jer 23:6; Mic 4:4; Zec 3:10

26Solomon had four[e] thousand stalls for chariot horses, and twelve thousand horses.[f] 1Ki 10:26

27The district officers, each in his month, supplied provisions for King Solomon and all who came to the king's table. They saw to it that nothing was lacking. 28They also brought to the proper place their quotas of barley and straw for the chariot horses and the other horses.

Solomon's Wisdom

29God gave Solomon wisdom and very great insight, and a breadth of understanding as measureless as the sand on the seashore. 30Solomon's wisdom was greater than the wisdom of all the men of the East, and greater than all the wisdom of Egypt. 31He was wiser than any other man, including Ethan the Ezrahite—wiser than Heman, Calcol and Darda, the sons of Mahol. And his

[a] *11* Or *in the heights of Dor* [b] *21* That is, the Euphrates; also in verse 24 [c] *22* That is, probably about 185 bushels (about 6.6 kiloliters) [d] *22* That is, probably about 375 bushels (about 13.2 kiloliters) [e] *26* Some Septuagint manuscripts (see also 2 Chron. 9:25); Hebrew *forty* [f] *26* Or *charioteers*

fame spread to all the surrounding nations. 32He spoke three thousand proverbs and his songs numbered a thousand and five. 33He described plant life, from the cedar of Lebanon to the hyssop that grows out of walls. He also taught about animals and birds, reptiles and fish. 34Men of all nations came to listen to Solomon's wisdom, sent by all the kings of the world, who had heard of his wisdom. 1Ki 3:12; Pr 1:1; 2Ch 9:23

Preparations for Building the Temple

5 When Hiram king of Tyre heard that Solomon had been anointed king to succeed his father David, he sent his envoys to Solomon, because he had always been on friendly terms with David. 2Solomon sent back this message to Hiram:

> 3"You know that because of the wars waged against my father David from all sides, he could not build a temple for the Name of the LORD his God until the LORD put his enemies under his feet. 4But now the LORD my God has given me rest on every side, and there is no adversary or disaster. 5I intend, therefore, to build a temple for the Name of the LORD my God, as the LORD told my father David, when he said, 'Your son whom I will put on the throne in your place will build the temple for my Name.' 2Sa 7:13; 1Ch 17:12; 22:9
>
> 6"So give orders that cedars of Lebanon be cut for me. My men will work with yours, and I will pay you for your men whatever wages you set. You know that we have no one so skilled in felling timber as the Sidonians."

7When Hiram heard Solomon's message, he was greatly pleased and said, "Praise be to the LORD today, for he has given David a wise son to rule over this great nation."

8So Hiram sent word to Solomon:

> "I have received the message you sent me and will do all you want in providing the cedar and pine logs. 9My men will haul them down from Lebanon to the sea, and I will float them in rafts by sea to the place you specify. There I will separate them and you can take them away. And you are to grant my wish by providing food for my royal household." Ezr 3:7; Eze 27:17; Ac 12:20

10In this way Hiram kept Solomon supplied with all the cedar and pine logs he wanted, 11and Solomon gave Hiram twenty thousand cors[a] of wheat as food for his household, in addition to twenty thousand baths[b,c] of pressed olive oil. Solomon continued to do this for Hiram year after year. 12The LORD gave Solomon wisdom, just as he had promised him. There were peaceful relations between Hiram and Solomon, and the two of them made a treaty. 1Ki 3:12; Am 1:9

13King Solomon conscripted laborers from all Israel—thirty thousand men. 14He sent them off to Lebanon in shifts of ten thousand a month, so that they spent one month in Lebanon and two months at home. Adoniram was in charge of the forced labor. 15Solomon had seventy thousand carriers and eighty thousand stonecutters in the hills, 16as well as thirty-three hundred[d] foremen who supervised the project and directed the workmen. 17At the king's command they removed from the quarry large blocks of quality stone to provide a foundation of dressed stone for the temple. 18The craftsmen of Solomon and Hiram and the men of Gebal[e] cut and prepared the timber and stone for the building of the temple. 1Ki 4:6; 1Ch 22:2

Solomon Builds the Temple

6 In the four hundred and eightieth[f] year after the Israelites had come out of Egypt, in the fourth year of Solomon's reign over Israel, in the month of Ziv, the second month, he began to build the temple of the LORD. Ac 7:47

2The temple that King Solomon built for the LORD was sixty cubits long, twenty wide and thirty high.[g] 3The portico at the front of the main hall of the temple extended the width of the temple, that is twenty cubits,[h] and projected ten cubits[i] from the front of the temple. 4He made narrow clerestory windows in the temple. 5Against the walls of the main hall and inner sanctuary he built a structure around the building, in which there were side rooms. 6The lowest floor was five cubits[j] wide, the middle floor six cubits[k] and the third floor seven.[l] He made offset ledges around the outside of the temple so that nothing would be inserted into the temple walls. Eze 40:16; 41:5-6

7In building the temple, only blocks dressed at the quarry were used, and no hammer, chisel or any other iron tool was heard at the temple site while it was being built. Ex 20:25; Dt 27:5

8The entrance to the lowest[m] floor was on the south side of the temple; a stairway led up to the middle level and from there to the third. 9So he built the temple and completed it, roofing it with

[a] 11 That is, probably about 125,000 bushels (about 4,400 kiloliters) [b] 11 Septuagint (see also 2 Chron. 2:10); Hebrew *twenty cors* [c] 11 That is, about 115,000 gallons (about 440 kiloliters) [d] 16 Hebrew; some Septuagint manuscripts (see also 2 Chron. 2:2, 18) *thirty-six hundred* [e] 18 That is, Byblos [f] 1 Hebrew; Septuagint *four hundred and fortieth* [g] 2 That is, about 90 feet (about 27 meters) long and 30 feet (about 9 meters) wide and 45 feet (about 13.5 meters) high [h] 3 That is, about 30 feet (about 9 meters) [i] 3 That is, about 15 feet (about 4.5 meters) [j] 6 That is, about 7 1/2 feet (about 2.3 meters); also in verses 10 and 24 [k] 6 That is, about 9 feet (about 2.7 meters) [l] 6 That is, about 10 1/2 feet (about 3.1 meters) [m] 8 Septuagint; Hebrew *middle*

beams and cedar planks. 10And he built the side
rooms all along the temple. The height of each was
five cubits, and they were attached to the temple
by beams of cedar. ver 14,38

11The word of the LORD came to Solomon: 12"As
for this temple you are building, if you follow my
decrees, carry out my regulations and keep all my
commands and obey them, I will fulfill through
you the promise I gave to David your father. 13And
I will live among the Israelites and will not abandon my people Israel." Dt 31:6; 2Sa 7:12-16; 1Ki 9:5

14So Solomon built the temple and completed
it. 15He lined its interior walls with cedar boards,
paneling them from the floor of the temple to the
ceiling, and covered the floor of the temple with
planks of pine. 16He partitioned off twenty cubits[a] at the rear of the temple with cedar boards
from floor to ceiling to form within the temple an
inner sanctuary, the Most Holy Place. 17The main
hall in front of this room was forty cubits[b] long.
18The inside of the temple was cedar, carved with
gourds and open flowers. Everything was cedar;
no stone was to be seen. Ex 26:33; Ps 74:6

19He prepared the inner sanctuary within the
temple to set the ark of the covenant of the LORD
there. 20The inner sanctuary was twenty cubits
long, twenty wide and twenty high.[c] He overlaid
the inside with pure gold, and he also overlaid the
altar of cedar. 21Solomon covered the inside of the
temple with pure gold, and he extended gold
chains across the front of the inner sanctuary,
which was overlaid with gold. 22So he overlaid the
whole interior with gold. He also overlaid with
gold the altar that belonged to the inner sanctuary.

23In the inner sanctuary he made a pair of cherubim of olive wood, each ten cubits[d] high. 24One
wing of the first cherub was five cubits long, and
the other wing five cubits—ten cubits from wing
tip to wing tip. 25The second cherub also measured
ten cubits, for the two cherubim were identical in
size and shape. 26The height of each cherub was
ten cubits. 27He placed the cherubim inside the
innermost room of the temple, with their wings
spread out. The wing of one cherub touched one
wall, while the wing of the other touched the other
wall, and their wings touched each other in the
middle of the room. 28He overlaid the cherubim
with gold. Ex 25:20; 37:1-9

29On the walls all around the temple, in both the
inner and outer rooms, he carved cherubim, palm
trees and open flowers. 30He also covered the
floors of both the inner and outer rooms of the
temple with gold. 2Ch 3:1-14

31For the entrance of the inner sanctuary he
made doors of olive wood with five-sided jambs.
32And on the two olive wood doors he carved
cherubim, palm trees and open flowers, and overlaid the cherubim and palm trees with beaten gold.
33In the same way he made four-sided jambs of
olive wood for the entrance to the main hall. 34He
also made two pine doors, each having two leaves
that turned in sockets. 35He carved cherubim,
palm trees and open flowers on them and overlaid
them with gold hammered evenly over the carv-
ings.

36And he built the inner courtyard of three
courses of dressed stone and one course of
trimmed cedar beams. 1Ki 7:12; Ezr 6:4

37The foundation of the temple of the LORD was
laid in the fourth year, in the month of Ziv. 38In
the eleventh year in the month of Bul, the eighth
month, the temple was finished in all its details
according to its specifications. He had spent seven
years building it. Heb 8:5

Solomon Builds His Palace

7 It took Solomon thirteen years, however, to
complete the construction of his palace. 2He
built the Palace of the Forest of Lebanon a hundred cubits long, fifty wide and thirty high,[e] with
four rows of cedar columns supporting trimmed
cedar beams. 3It was roofed with cedar above the
beams that rested on the columns—forty-five
beams, fifteen to a row. 4Its windows were placed
high in sets of three, facing each other. 5All the
doorways had rectangular frames; they were in the
front part in sets of three, facing each other.[f]

6He made a colonnade fifty cubits long and
thirty wide.[g] In front of it was a portico, and in
front of that were pillars and an overhanging roof.

7He built the throne hall, the Hall of Justice,
where he was to judge, and he covered it with
cedar from floor to ceiling.[h] 8And the palace in
which he was to live, set farther back, was similar
in design. Solomon also made a palace like this
hall for Pharaoh's daughter, whom he had married. 1Ki 3:1; 6:15; 2Ch 8:11

9All these structures, from the outside to the
great courtyard and from foundation to eaves,
were made of blocks of high-grade stone cut to
size and trimmed with a saw on their inner and
outer faces. 10The foundations were laid with large
stones of good quality, some measuring ten cubits[d] and some eight.[i] 11Above were high-grade
stones, cut to size, and cedar beams. 12The great
courtyard was surrounded by a wall of three
courses of dressed stone and one course of

[a] *16* That is, about 30 feet (about 9 meters) [b] *17* That is, about 60 feet (about 18 meters) [c] *20* That is, about 30 feet (about 9 meters) long, wide and high [d] *23,10* That is, about 15 feet (about 4.5 meters) [e] *2* That is, about 150 feet (about 46 meters) long, 75 feet (about 23 meters) wide and 45 feet (about 13.5 meters) high [f] *5* The meaning of the Hebrew for this verse is uncertain. [g] *6* That is, about 75 feet (about 23 meters) long and 45 feet (about 13.5 meters) wide [h] *7* Vulgate and Syriac; Hebrew *floor* [i] *10* That is, about 12 feet (about 3.6 meters)

trimmed cedar beams, as was the inner courtyard of the temple of the LORD with its portico.

The Temple's Furnishings

13King Solomon sent to Tyre and brought Huram,[a] 14whose mother was a widow from the tribe of Naphtali and whose father was a man of Tyre and a craftsman in bronze. Huram was highly skilled and experienced in all kinds of bronze work. He came to King Solomon and did all the work assigned to him. Ex 31:2-5; 2Ch 2:14; 4:11-16

15He cast two bronze pillars, each eighteen cubits high and twelve cubits around,[b] by line. 16He also made two capitals of cast bronze to set on the tops of the pillars; each capital was five cubits[c] high. 17A network of interwoven chains festooned the capitals on top of the pillars, seven for each capital. 18He made pomegranates in two rows[d] encircling each network to decorate the capitals on top of the pillars.[e] He did the same for each capital. 19The capitals on top of the pillars in the portico were in the shape of lilies, four cubits[f] high. 20On the capitals of both pillars, above the bowl-shaped part next to the network, were the two hundred pomegranates in rows all around. 21He erected the pillars at the portico of the temple. The pillar to the south he named Jakin[g] and the one to the north Boaz.[h] 22The capitals on top were in the shape of lilies. And so the work on the pillars was completed. 2Ki 25:17; 2Ch 3:16-17; 4:13

23He made the Sea of cast metal, circular in shape, measuring ten cubits[i] from rim to rim and five cubits high. It took a line of thirty cubits[j] to measure around it. 24Below the rim, gourds encircled it—ten to a cubit. The gourds were cast in two rows in one piece with the Sea. 2Ki 25:13

25The Sea stood on twelve bulls, three facing north, three facing west, three facing south and three facing east. The Sea rested on top of them, and their hindquarters were toward the center. 26It was a handbreadth[k] in thickness, and its rim was like the rim of a cup, like a lily blossom. It held two thousand baths.[l] 2Ch 4:2-5; Jer 52:20

27He also made ten movable stands of bronze; each was four cubits long, four wide and three high.[m] 28This is how the stands were made: They had side panels attached to uprights. 29On the panels between the uprights were lions, bulls and cherubim—and on the uprights as well. Above and below the lions and bulls were wreaths of hammered work. 30Each stand had four bronze wheels with bronze axles, and each had a basin resting on four supports, cast with wreaths on each side. 31On the inside of the stand there was an opening that had a circular frame one cubit[n] deep. This opening was round, and with its basework it measured a cubit and a half.[o] Around its opening there was engraving. The panels of the stands were square, not round. 32The four wheels were under the panels, and the axles of the wheels were attached to the stand. The diameter of each wheel was a cubit and a half. 33The wheels were made like chariot wheels; the axles, rims, spokes and hubs were all of cast metal. 2Ki 16:17; 2Ch 4:14

34Each stand had four handles, one on each corner, projecting from the stand. 35At the top of the stand there was a circular band half a cubit[p] deep. The supports and panels were attached to the top of the stand. 36He engraved cherubim, lions and palm trees on the surfaces of the supports and on the panels, in every available space, with wreaths all around. 37This is the way he made the ten stands. They were all cast in the same molds and were identical in size and shape.

38He then made ten bronze basins, each holding forty baths[q] and measuring four cubits across, one basin to go on each of the ten stands. 39He placed five of the stands on the south side of the temple and five on the north. He placed the Sea on the south side, at the southeast corner of the temple. 40He also made the basins and shovels and sprinkling bowls. 2Ch 4:6

So Huram finished all the work he had undertaken for King Solomon in the temple of the LORD:

41the two pillars;
the two bowl-shaped capitals on top of the pillars;
the two sets of network decorating the two bowl-shaped capitals on top of the pillars;
42the four hundred pomegranates for the two sets of network (two rows of pomegranates for each network, decorating the bowl-shaped capitals on top of the pillars); ver 20
43the ten stands with their ten basins;
44the Sea and the twelve bulls under it;
45the pots, shovels and sprinkling bowls.

All these objects that Huram made for King

[a] 13 Hebrew *Hiram*, a variant of *Huram*; also in verses 40 and 45 [b] 15 That is, about 27 feet (about 8.1 meters) high and 18 feet (about 5.4 meters) around [c] 16 That is, about 7 1/2 feet (about 2.3 meters); also in verse 23 [d] 18 Two Hebrew manuscripts and Septuagint; most Hebrew manuscripts *made the pillars, and there were two rows* [e] 18 Many Hebrew manuscripts and Syriac; most Hebrew manuscripts *pomegranates* [f] 19 That is, about 6 feet (about 1.8 meters); also in verse 38 [g] 21 *Jakin* probably means *he establishes.* [h] 21 *Boaz* probably means *in him is strength.* [i] 23 That is, about 15 feet (about 4.5 meters) [j] 23 That is, about 45 feet (about 13.5 meters) [k] 26 That is, about 3 inches (about 8 centimeters) [l] 26 That is, probably about 11,500 gallons (about 44 kiloliters); the Septuagint does not have this sentence. [m] 27 That is, about 6 feet (about 1.8 meters) long and wide and about 4 1/2 feet (about 1.3 meters) high [n] 31 That is, about 1 1/2 feet (about 0.5 meter) [o] 31 That is, about 2 1/4 feet (about 0.7 meter); also in verse 32 [p] 35 That is, about 3/4 foot (about 0.2 meter) [q] 38 That is, about 230 gallons (about 880 liters)

Solomon for the temple of the LORD were of burnished bronze. [46]The king had them cast in clay molds in the plain of the Jordan between Succoth and Zarethan. [47]Solomon left all these things unweighed, because there were so many; the weight of the bronze was not determined. 1Ch 22:3

[48]Solomon also made all the furnishings that were in the LORD's temple:

the golden altar;
the golden table on which the bread of the Presence; Ex 25:30; 37:10
[49]the lampstands of pure gold (five on the right and five on the left, in front of the inner sanctuary); Ex 25:31-38
the gold floral work and lamps and tongs;
[50]the pure gold basins, wick trimmers, sprinkling bowls, dishes and censers; 2Ki 25:13
and the gold sockets for the doors of the innermost room, the Most Holy Place, and also for the doors of the main hall of the temple.

[51]When all the work King Solomon had done for the temple of the LORD was finished, he brought in the things his father David had dedicated—the silver and gold and the furnishings—and he placed them in the treasuries of the LORD's temple. 2Ch 4:6,10-5:1; 2Sa 8:11

The Ark Brought to the Temple

8 Then King Solomon summoned into his presence at Jerusalem the elders of Israel, all the heads of the tribes and the chiefs of the Israelite families, to bring up the ark of the LORD's covenant from Zion, the City of David. [2]All the men of Israel came together to King Solomon at the time of the festival in the month of Ethanim, the seventh month. Lev 23:34; 2Sa 5:7; 6:17

[3]When all the elders of Israel had arrived, the priests took up the ark, [4]and they brought up the ark of the LORD and the Tent of Meeting and all the sacred furnishings in it. The priests and Levites carried them up, [5]and King Solomon and the entire assembly of Israel that had gathered about him were before the ark, sacrificing so many sheep and cattle that they could not be recorded or counted.

[6]The priests then brought the ark of the LORD's covenant to its place in the inner sanctuary of the temple, the Most Holy Place, and put it beneath the wings of the cherubim. [7]The cherubim spread their wings over the place of the ark and overshadowed the ark and its carrying poles. [8]These poles were so long that their ends could be seen from the Holy Place in front of the inner sanctuary, but not from outside the Holy Place; and they are still there today. [9]There was nothing in the ark except the two stone tablets that Moses had placed in it at Horeb, where the LORD made a covenant with the Israelites after they came out of Egypt.

[10]When the priests withdrew from the Holy Place, the cloud filled the temple of the LORD. [11]And the priests could not perform their service because of the cloud, for the glory of the LORD filled his temple. Ex 40:34-35

[12]Then Solomon said, "The LORD has said that he would dwell in a dark cloud; [13]I have indeed built a magnificent temple for you, a place for you to dwell forever." Ps 132:13

[14]While the whole assembly of Israel was standing there, the king turned around and blessed them. [15]Then he said:

"Praise be to the LORD, the God of Israel, who with his own hand has fulfilled what he promised with his own mouth to my father David. For he said, [16]'Since the day I brought my people Israel out of Egypt, I have not chosen a city in any tribe of Israel to have a temple built for my Name to be there, but I have chosen David to rule my people Israel.' 2Sa 6:18

[17]"My father David had it in his heart to build a temple for the Name of the LORD, the God of Israel. [18]But the LORD said to my father David, 'Because it was in your heart to build a temple for my Name, you did well to have this in your heart. [19]Nevertheless, you are not the one to build the temple, but your son, who is your own flesh and blood—he is the one who will build the temple for my Name.' 2Sa 7:2,5,13; 1Ki 5:3,5

[20]"The LORD has kept the promise he made: I have succeeded David my father and now I sit on the throne of Israel, just as the LORD promised, and I have built the temple for the Name of the LORD, the God of Israel. [21]I have provided a place there for the ark, in which is the covenant of the LORD that he made with our fathers when he brought them out of Egypt." 1Ch 28:6

Solomon's Prayer of Dedication

[22]Then Solomon stood before the altar of the LORD in front of the whole assembly of Israel, spread out his hands toward heaven [23]and said:

"O LORD, God of Israel, there is no God like you in heaven above or on earth below—you who keep your covenant of love with your servants who continue wholeheartedly in your way. [24]You have kept your promise to your servant David my father; with your mouth you have promised and with your hand you have fulfilled it—as it is today. Dt 7:9,12; Ne 1:5; 9:32

[25]"Now LORD, God of Israel, keep for your servant David my father the promises you made to him when you said, 'You shall never fail to have a man to sit before me on the throne of Israel, if only your sons are careful

in all they do to walk before me as you have done.' 26And now, O God of Israel, let your word that you promised your servant David my father come true. 2Sa 7:25; 1Ki 2:4

27"But will God really dwell on earth? The heavens, even the highest heaven, cannot contain you. How much less this temple I have built! 28Yet give attention to your servant's prayer and his plea for mercy, O LORD my God. Hear the cry and the prayer that your servant is praying in your presence this day. 29May your eyes be open toward this temple night and day, this place of which you said, 'My Name shall be there,' so that you will hear the prayer your servant prays toward this place. 30Hear the supplication of your servant and of your people Israel when they pray toward this place. Hear from heaven, your dwelling place, and when you hear, forgive. Dt 12:11; 2Ch 2:6; Isa 66:1

31"When a man wrongs his neighbor and is required to take an oath and he comes and swears the oath before your altar in this temple, 32then hear from heaven and act. Judge between your servants, condemning the guilty and bringing down on his own head what he has done. Declare the innocent not guilty, and so establish his innocence.

33"When your people Israel have been defeated by an enemy because they have sinned against you, and when they turn back to you and confess your name, praying and making supplication to you in this temple, 34then hear from heaven and forgive the sin of your people Israel and bring them back to the land you gave to their fathers. Lev 26:17; Dt 28:25

35"When the heavens are shut up and there is no rain because your people have sinned against you, and when they pray toward this place and confess your name and turn from their sin because you have afflicted them, 36then hear from heaven and forgive the sin of your servants, your people Israel. Teach them the right way to live, and send rain on the land you gave your people for an inheritance. Lev 26:19; 1Sa 12:23; Ps 27:11

37"When famine or plague comes to the land, or blight or mildew, locusts or grasshoppers, or when an enemy besieges them in any of their cities, whatever disaster or disease may come, 38and when a prayer or plea is made by any of your people Israel—each one aware of the afflictions of his own heart, and spreading out his hands toward this temple— 39then hear from heaven, your dwelling place. Forgive and act; deal with each man according to all he does, since you know his heart (for you alone know the hearts of all men), 40so that they will fear you all the time they live in the land you gave our fathers. 1Sa 16:7; 1Ch 28:9; Ps 11:4

41"As for the foreigner who does not belong to your people Israel but has come from a distant land because of your name— 42for men will hear of your great name and your mighty hand and your outstretched arm—when he comes and prays toward this temple, 43then hear from heaven, your dwelling place, and do whatever the foreigner asks of you, so that all the peoples of the earth may know your name and fear you, as do your own people Israel, and may know that this house I have built bears your Name. Dt 3:24

44"When your people go to war against their enemies, wherever you send them, and when they pray to the LORD toward the city you have chosen and the temple I have built for your Name, 45then hear from heaven their prayer and their plea, and uphold their cause. Ps 9:4; 140:12

46"When they sin against you—for there is no one who does not sin—and you become angry with them and give them over to the enemy, who takes them captive to his own land, far away or near; 47and if they have a change of heart in the land where they are held captive, and repent and plead with you in the land of their conquerors and say, 'We have sinned, we have done wrong, we have acted wickedly'; 48and if they turn back to you with all their heart and soul in the land of their enemies who took them captive, and pray to you toward the land you gave their fathers, toward the city you have chosen and the temple I have built for your Name; 49then from heaven, your dwelling place, hear their prayer and their plea, and uphold their cause. 50And forgive your people, who have sinned against you; forgive all the offenses they have committed against you, and cause their conquerors to show them mercy; 51for they are your people and your inheritance, whom you brought out of Egypt, out of that iron-smelting furnace. Dt 9:29; Ps 106:6; Da 6:10

52"May your eyes be open to your servant's plea and to the plea of your people Israel, and may you listen to them whenever they cry out to you. 53For you singled them out from all the nations of the world to be your own inheritance, just as you declared through your servant Moses when you, O Sovereign LORD, brought our fathers out of Egypt." 2Ch 6:12-40; Ex 19:5

54When Solomon had finished all these prayers and supplications to the LORD, he rose from before the altar of the LORD, where he had been kneeling with his hands spread out toward heaven. 55He

stood and blessed the whole assembly of Israel in
a loud voice, saying: ver 14; 2Sa 6:18

56"Praise be to the LORD, who has given
rest to his people Israel just as he promised.
Not one word has failed of all the good
promises he gave through his servant Moses.
57May the LORD our God be with us as he was
with our fathers; may he never leave us nor
forsake us. 58May he turn our hearts to him,
to walk in all his ways and to keep the commands, decrees and regulations he gave our
fathers. 59And may these words of mine,
which I have prayed before the LORD, be near
to the LORD our God day and night, that he
may uphold the cause of his servant and the
cause of his people Israel according to each
day's need, 60so that all the peoples of the
earth may know that the LORD is God and
that there is no other. 61But your hearts must
be fully committed to the LORD our God, to
live by his decrees and obey his commands,
as at this time." 1Ki 11:4; Ps 119:36; Heb 13:5

The Dedication of the Temple

62Then the king and all Israel with him offered
sacrifices before the LORD. 63Solomon offered a
sacrifice of fellowship offerings[a] to the LORD:
twenty-two thousand cattle and a hundred and
twenty thousand sheep and goats. So the king and
all the Israelites dedicated the temple of the LORD.
64On that same day the king consecrated the
middle part of the courtyard in front of the temple
of the LORD, and there he offered burnt offerings,
grain offerings and the fat of the fellowship offerings, because the bronze altar before the LORD was
too small to hold the burnt offerings, the grain
offerings and the fat of the fellowship offerings.
65So Solomon observed the festival at that time,
and all Israel with him—a vast assembly, people
from Lebo[b] Hamath to the Wadi of Egypt. They
celebrated it before the LORD our God for seven
days and seven days more, fourteen days in all.
66On the following day he sent the people away.
They blessed the king and then went home, joyful
and glad in heart for all the good things the LORD
had done for his servant David and his people
Israel. 2Ch 7:1-10; Ge 15:18; Nu 34:8

The LORD Appears to Solomon

9 When Solomon had finished building the
temple of the LORD and the royal palace, and
had achieved all he had desired to do, 2the LORD
appeared to him a second time, as he had appeared to him at Gibeon. 3The LORD said to him:

"I have heard the prayer and plea you
have made before me; I have consecrated this
temple, which you have built, by putting my
Name there forever. My eyes and my heart
will always be there. Dt 11:12; 1Ki 8:29; 2Ki 20:5
4"As for you, if you walk before me in
integrity of heart and uprightness, as David
your father did, and do all I command and
observe my decrees and laws, 5I will establish
your royal throne over Israel forever, as I
promised David your father when I said,
'You shall never fail to have a man on the
throne of Israel.' 1Ki 2:4; 15:5; 1Ch 22:10
6"But if you[c] or your sons turn away
from me and do not observe the commands
and decrees I have given you[c] and go off to
serve other gods and worship them, 7then I
will cut off Israel from the land I have given
them and will reject this temple I have consecrated for my Name. Israel will then become
a byword and an object of ridicule among all
peoples. 8And though this temple is now imposing, all who pass by will be appalled and
will scoff and say, 'Why has the LORD done
such a thing to this land and to this temple?'
9People will answer, 'Because they have forsaken the LORD their God, who brought their
fathers out of Egypt, and have embraced other gods, worshiping and serving them—that
is why the LORD brought all this disaster on
them.'" 2Ch 7:11-22; 2Ki 17:23; Jer 7:14

LIVING  **INSIGHT**

You cannot handle the honors in life nor can you handle the attacks if your walk with God is inconsistent. You will begin to think you really are deserving of honor or you will begin to doubt in the midst of a trial because you think you are deserving of something else. If you genuinely desire to be different, God can lead you to a life of integrity.

(See 1 Kings 9:4.)

Solomon's Other Activities

10At the end of twenty years, during which Solomon built these two buildings—the temple of the
LORD and the royal palace— 11King Solomon gave
twenty towns in Galilee to Hiram king of Tyre,
because Hiram had supplied him with all the cedar
and pine and gold he wanted. 12But when Hiram
went from Tyre to see the towns that Solomon had
given him, he was not pleased with them. 13"What
kind of towns are these you have given me, my
brother?" he asked. And he called them the Land

[a]63 Traditionally *peace offerings*; also in verse 64 [b]65 Or *from the entrance to* [c]6 The Hebrew is plural.

of Cabul,[a] a name they have to this day. 14Now Hiram had sent to the king 120 talents[b] of gold.

15Here is the account of the forced labor King Solomon conscripted to build the LORD's temple, his own palace, the supporting terraces,[c] the wall of Jerusalem, and Hazor, Megiddo and Gezer. 16(Pharaoh king of Egypt had attacked and captured Gezer. He had set it on fire. He killed its Canaanite inhabitants and then gave it as a wedding gift to his daughter, Solomon's wife. 17And Solomon rebuilt Gezer.) He built up Lower Beth Horon, 18Baalath, and Tadmor[d] in the desert, within his land, 19as well as all his store cities and the towns for his chariots and for his horses[e]—whatever he desired to build in Jerusalem, in Lebanon and throughout all the territory he ruled.

20All the people left from the Amorites, Hittites, Perizzites, Hivites and Jebusites (these peoples were not Israelites), 21that is, their descendants remaining in the land, whom the Israelites could not exterminate[f]—these Solomon conscripted for his slave labor force, as it is to this day. 22But Solomon did not make slaves of any of the Israelites; they were his fighting men, his government officials, his officers, his captains, and the commanders of his chariots and charioteers. 23They were also the chief officials in charge of Solomon's projects—550 officials supervising the men who did the work. Lev 25:39; Jos 15:63; Ezr 2:55,58

24After Pharaoh's daughter had come up from the City of David to the palace Solomon had built for her, he constructed the supporting terraces.

25Three times a year Solomon sacrificed burnt offerings and fellowship offerings[g] on the altar he had built for the LORD, burning incense before the LORD along with them, and so fulfilled the temple obligations. Ex 23:14; 2Ch 8:12-13,16

26King Solomon also built ships at Ezion Geber, which is near Elath in Edom, on the shore of the Red Sea.[h] 27And Hiram sent his men—sailors who knew the sea—to serve in the fleet with Solomon's men. 28They sailed to Ophir and brought back 420 talents[i] of gold, which they delivered to King Solomon. Nu 33:35; 1Ki 10:11; 22:48

The Queen of Sheba Visits Solomon

10 When the queen of Sheba heard about the fame of Solomon and his relation to the name of the LORD, she came to test him with hard questions. 2Arriving at Jerusalem with a very great caravan—with camels carrying spices, large quantities of gold, and precious stones—she came to Solomon and talked with him about all that she had on her mind. 3Solomon answered all her questions; nothing was too hard for the king to explain to her. 4When the queen of Sheba saw all the wisdom of Solomon and the palace he had built, 5the food on his table, the seating of his officials, the attending servants in their robes, his cupbearers, and the burnt offerings he made at[j] the temple of the LORD, she was overwhelmed. Mt 12:42; Jdg 14:12

6She said to the king, "The report I heard in my own country about your achievements and your wisdom is true. 7But I did not believe these things until I came and saw with my own eyes. Indeed, not even half was told me; in wisdom and wealth you have far exceeded the report I heard. 8How happy your men must be! How happy your officials, who continually stand before you and hear your wisdom! 9Praise be to the LORD your God, who has delighted in you and placed you on the throne of Israel. Because of the LORD's eternal love for Israel, he has made you king, to maintain justice and righteousness." 2Sa 8:15; Ps 72:2; Pr 8:34

10And she gave the king 120 talents[b] of gold, large quantities of spices, and precious stones. Never again were so many spices brought in as those the queen of Sheba gave to King Solomon.

11(Hiram's ships brought gold from Ophir; and from there they brought great cargoes of almugwood[k] and precious stones. 12The king used the almugwood to make supports for the temple of the LORD and for the royal palace, and to make harps and lyres for the musicians. So much almugwood has never been imported or seen since that day.)

13King Solomon gave the queen of Sheba all she desired and asked for, besides what he had given her out of his royal bounty. Then she left and returned with her retinue to her own country.

Solomon's Splendor

14The weight of the gold that Solomon received yearly was 666 talents,[l] 15not including the revenues from merchants and traders and from all the Arabian kings and the governors of the land.

16King Solomon made two hundred large shields of hammered gold; six hundred bekas[m] of gold went into each shield. 17He also made three hundred small shields of hammered gold, with three minas[n] of gold in each shield. The king put them in the Palace of the Forest of Lebanon.

18Then the king made a great throne inlaid with ivory and overlaid with fine gold. 19The throne had six steps, and its back had a rounded top. On both

[a] 13 *Cabul* sounds like the Hebrew for *good-for-nothing.* [b] 14,10 That is, about 4 1/2 tons (about 4 metric tons) [c] 15 Or *the Millo;* also in verse 24 [d] 18 The Hebrew may also be read *Tamar.* [e] 19 Or *charioteers* [f] 21 The Hebrew term refers to the irrevocable giving over of things or persons to the LORD, often by totally destroying them. [g] 25 Traditionally *peace offerings* [h] 26 Hebrew *Yam Suph;* that is, Sea of Reeds [i] 28 That is, about 16 tons (about 14.5 metric tons) [j] 5 Or *the ascent by which he went up to* [k] 11 Probably a variant of *algumwood;* also in verse 12 [l] 14 That is, about 25 tons (about 23 metric tons) [m] 16 That is, about 7 1/2 pounds (about 3.5 kilograms) [n] 17 That is, about 3 3/4 pounds (about 1.7 kilograms)

sides of the seat were armrests, with a lion standing beside each of them. 20Twelve lions stood on the six steps, one at either end of each step. Nothing like it had ever been made for any other kingdom. 21All King Solomon's goblets were gold, and all the household articles in the Palace of the Forest of Lebanon were pure gold. Nothing was made of silver, because silver was considered of little value in Solomon's days. 22The king had a fleet of trading ships[a] at sea along with the ships of Hiram. Once every three years it returned, carrying gold, silver and ivory, and apes and baboons. 1Ki 9:26

23King Solomon was greater in riches and wisdom than all the other kings of the earth. 24The whole world sought audience with Solomon to hear the wisdom God had put in his heart. 25Year after year, everyone who came brought a gift—articles of silver and gold, robes, weapons and spices, and horses and mules. 1Ki 3:13; 4:30

26Solomon accumulated chariots and horses; he had fourteen hundred chariots and twelve thousand horses,[b] which he kept in the chariot cities and also with him in Jerusalem. 27The king made silver as common in Jerusalem as stones, and cedar as plentiful as sycamore-fig trees in the foothills. 28Solomon's horses were imported from Egypt[c] and from Kue[d]—the royal merchants purchased them from Kue. 29They imported a chariot from Egypt for six hundred shekels[e] of silver, and a horse for a hundred and fifty.[f] They also exported them to all the kings of the Hittites and of the Arameans. 2Ch 1:14-17; 9:13-28; 1Ki 4:26

Decline and Demise **Chapter 11**

We see the picture start to change for Israel. In the opening verses of chapter 11 we read of Solomon's compromise, failure and rebellion against the ways of the Lord. As I mentioned in the book introduction, chapter 11 becomes a hinge on which the direction of this book turns. After Solomon married numerous foreign wives and permitted pagan worship to enter Israel, a poison began to spread through the kingdom. Like his father David, Solomon's moral compromise eroded his life and his kingdom from the inside out. Like father . . . like son!

Solomon's Wives

11 King Solomon, however, loved many foreign women besides Pharaoh's daughter—Moabites, Ammonites, Edomites, Sidonians and Hittites. 2They were from nations about which the LORD had told the Israelites, "You must not intermarry with them, because they will surely turn your hearts after their gods." Nevertheless, Solomon held fast to them in love. 3He had seven hundred wives of royal birth and three hundred concubines, and his wives led him astray. 4As Solomon grew old, his wives turned his heart after other gods, and his heart was not fully devoted to the LORD his God, as the heart of David his father had been. 5He followed Ashtoreth the goddess of the Sidonians, and Molech[g] the detestable god of the Ammonites. 6So Solomon did evil in the eyes of the LORD; he did not follow the LORD completely, as David his father had done. Ne 13:26; Dt 7:3-4

7On a hill east of Jerusalem, Solomon built a high place for Chemosh the detestable god of Moab, and for Molech the detestable god of the Ammonites. 8He did the same for all his foreign wives, who burned incense and offered sacrifices to their gods. Nu 21:29; Jdg 11:24; 2Ki 23:13

9The LORD became angry with Solomon because his heart had turned away from the LORD, the God of Israel, who had appeared to him twice. 10Although he had forbidden Solomon to follow other gods, Solomon did not keep the LORD's command. 11So the LORD said to Solomon, "Since this is your attitude and you have not kept my covenant and my decrees, which I commanded you, I will most certainly tear the kingdom away from you and give it to one of your subordinates. 12Nevertheless, for the sake of David your father, I will not do it during your lifetime. I will tear it out of the hand of your son. 13Yet I will not tear the whole kingdom from him, but will give him one tribe for the sake of David my servant and for the sake of Jerusalem, which I have chosen." 2Sa 7:15; 1Ki 12:15-16

Solomon's Adversaries

14Then the LORD raised up against Solomon an adversary, Hadad the Edomite, from the royal line of Edom. 15Earlier when David was fighting with Edom, Joab the commander of the army, who had gone up to bury the dead, had struck down all the men in Edom. 16Joab and all the Israelites stayed there for six months, until they had destroyed all the men in Edom. 17But Hadad, still only a boy, fled to Egypt with some Edomite officials who had served his father. 18They set out from Midian and went to Paran. Then taking men from Paran with them, they went to Egypt, to Pharaoh king of Egypt, who gave Hadad a house and land and provided him with food. 2Sa 8:14; 1Ch 18:12

19Pharaoh was so pleased with Hadad that he gave him a sister of his own wife, Queen Tahpenes, in marriage. 20The sister of Tahpenes bore him a son named Genubath, whom Tahpenes brought up in the royal palace. There Genubath lived with Pharaoh's own children.

21While he was in Egypt, Hadad heard that David rested with his fathers and that Joab the commander of the army was also dead. Then Hadad

[a]22 Hebrew *of ships of Tarshish* [b]26 Or *charioteers* [c]28 Or possibly *Muzur*, a region in Cilicia; also in verse 29 [d]28 Probably *Cilicia* [e]29 That is, about 15 pounds (about 7 kilograms) [f]29 That is, about 3 3/4 pounds (about 1.7 kilograms) [g]5 Hebrew *Milcom*; also in verse 33

said to Pharaoh, “Let me go, that I may return to
my own country.”
22“What have you lacked here that you want to
go back to your own country?” Pharaoh asked.
“Nothing,” Hadad replied, “but do let me go!”
23And God raised up against Solomon another
adversary, Rezon son of Eliada, who had fled from
his master, Hadadezer king of Zobah. 24He gathered men around him and became the leader of a
band of rebels when David destroyed the forces[a]
⌞of Zobah⌟; the rebels went to Damascus, where
they settled and took control. 25Rezon was Israel’s
adversary as long as Solomon lived, adding to the
trouble caused by Hadad. So Rezon ruled in Aram
and was hostile toward Israel. 2Sa 8:3; 10:8,18-19

Jeroboam Rebels Against Solomon

26Also, Jeroboam son of Nebat rebelled against
the king. He was one of Solomon’s officials, an
Ephraimite from Zeredah, and his mother was a
widow named Zeruah. 2Sa 20:21; 1Ki 12:2; 2Ch 13:6
27Here is the account of how he rebelled against
the king: Solomon had built the supporting terraces[b] and had filled in the gap in the wall of the
city of David his father. 28Now Jeroboam was a
man of standing, and when Solomon saw how well
the young man did his work, he put him in charge
of the whole labor force of the house of Joseph.
29About that time Jeroboam was going out of
Jerusalem, and Ahijah the prophet of Shiloh met
him on the way, wearing a new cloak. The two of
them were alone out in the country, 30and Ahijah
took hold of the new cloak he was wearing and
tore it into twelve pieces. 31Then he said to Jeroboam, “Take ten pieces for yourself, for this is what
the LORD, the God of Israel, says: ‘See, I am going
to tear the kingdom out of Solomon’s hand and
give you ten tribes. 32But for the sake of my servant
David and the city of Jerusalem, which I have chosen out of all the tribes of Israel, he will have one
tribe. 33I will do this because they have[c] forsaken
me and worshiped Ashtoreth the goddess of the
Sidonians, Chemosh the god of the Moabites, and
Molech the god of the Ammonites, and have not
walked in my ways, nor done what is right in my
eyes, nor kept my statutes and laws as David, Solomon’s father, did. 1Sa 15:27; 1Ki 3:3; 14:2
34“ ‘But I will not take the whole kingdom out of
Solomon’s hand; I have made him ruler all the
days of his life for the sake of David my servant,
whom I chose and who observed my commands
and statutes. 35I will take the kingdom from his
son’s hands and give you ten tribes. 36I will give
one tribe to his son so that David my servant may
always have a lamp before me in Jerusalem, the
city where I chose to put my Name. 37However, as
for you, I will take you, and you will rule over all
that your heart desires; you will be king over Israel.
38If you do whatever I command you and walk in
my ways and do what is right in my eyes by keeping my statutes and commands, as David my servant did, I will be with you. I will build you a
dynasty as enduring as the one I built for David
and will give Israel to you. 39I will humble David’s
descendants because of this, but not forever.’ ”
40Solomon tried to kill Jeroboam, but Jeroboam
fled to Egypt, to Shishak the king, and stayed there
until Solomon’s death. 2Ch 12:2

Solomon’s Death

41As for the other events of Solomon’s reign—
all he did and the wisdom he displayed—are they
not written in the book of the annals of Solomon?
42Solomon reigned in Jerusalem over all Israel forty years. 43Then he rested with his fathers and was
buried in the city of David his father. And Rehoboam his son succeeded him as king. 2Ch 9:29-31

A Kingdom Divided — Chapters 12–22

In the final 11 chapters we uncover the sordid details of war, threats, revolutions, assassinations, idolatry and immorality. The kingdom was divided and fragmented. Jeroboam led ten of the tribes as they broke from their brothers and formed a new kingdom to the north. From this time on they were called *Israel*, and Samaria was their capital. Rehoboam, the son of Solomon, led the two remaining tribes in forming a new kingdom to the south. Their capital was Jerusalem, and they were called *Judah*. During these years the kingdom was torn by division, the economic picture was dismal and the spiritual picture was dark. No one could tell by looking at them that these were “God’s chosen people.” The final verse of the book provides a fitting summary of the times. Note this dismal reference to King Ahab’s son Ahaziah and the tragic course of his life: “He served and worshiped Baal and provoked the LORD, the God of Israel, to anger, just as his father had done” (22:53).

Israel Rebels Against Rehoboam

12 Rehoboam went to Shechem, for all the
Israelites had gone there to make him king.
2When Jeroboam son of Nebat heard this (he was
still in Egypt, where he had fled from King Solomon), he returned from[d] Egypt. 3So they sent for
Jeroboam, and he and the whole assembly of Israel
went to Rehoboam and said to him: 4“Your father
put a heavy yoke on us, but now lighten the harsh
labor and the heavy yoke he put on us, and we will
serve you.” 1Sa 8:11-18; 1Ki 4:20-28; 11:40
5Rehoboam answered, “Go away for three days
and then come back to me.” So the people went
away.

[a]24 Hebrew *destroyed them* [b]27 Or *the Millo* [c]33 Hebrew; Septuagint, Vulgate and Syriac *because he has*
[d]2 Or *he remained in*

6 Then King Rehoboam consulted the elders
who had served his father Solomon during his
lifetime. "How would you advise me to answer
these people?" he asked. 1Ki 4:2
7 They replied, "If today you will be a servant to
these people and serve them and give them a favorable answer, they will always be your servants."
8 But Rehoboam rejected the advice the elders
gave him and consulted the young men who had
grown up with him and were serving him. 9 He
asked them, "What is your advice? How should we
answer these people who say to me, 'Lighten the
yoke your father put on us'?"
10 The young men who had grown up with him
replied, "Tell these people who have said to you,
'Your father put a heavy yoke on us, but make our
yoke lighter'—tell them, 'My little finger is thicker
than my father's waist. 11 My father laid on you a
heavy yoke; I will make it even heavier. My father
scourged you with whips; I will scourge you with
scorpions.'"
12 Three days later Jeroboam and all the people
returned to Rehoboam, as the king had said,
"Come back to me in three days." 13 The king answered the people harshly. Rejecting the advice
given him by the elders, 14 he followed the advice of
the young men and said, "My father made your
yoke heavy; I will make it even heavier. My father
scourged you with whips; I will scourge you with
scorpions." 15 So the king did not listen to the people, for this turn of events was from the LORD, to
fulfill the word the LORD had spoken to Jeroboam
son of Nebat through Ahijah the Shilonite.
16 When all Israel saw that the king refused to
listen to them, they answered the king:

"What share do we have in David,
what part in Jesse's son?
To your tents, O Israel! 2Sa 20:1
Look after your own house, O David!"

So the Israelites went home. 17 But as for the Israelites who were living in the towns of Judah, Rehoboam still ruled over them. 1Ki 11:13,36
18 King Rehoboam sent out Adoniram,[a] who
was in charge of forced labor, but all Israel stoned
him to death. King Rehoboam, however, managed
to get into his chariot and escape to Jerusalem.
19 So Israel has been in rebellion against the house
of David to this day. 1Ki 4:6; 5:14; 2Ki 17:21
20 When all the Israelites heard that Jeroboam
had returned, they sent and called him to the assembly and made him king over all Israel. Only the
tribe of Judah remained loyal to the house of David. 1Ki 11:13,32
21 When Rehoboam arrived in Jerusalem, he
mustered the whole house of Judah and the tribe
of Benjamin—a hundred and eighty thousand
fighting men—to make war against the house of
Israel and to regain the kingdom for Rehoboam
son of Solomon. 2Ch 11:1

[a] 18 Some Septuagint manuscripts and Syriac (see also 1 Kings 4:6 and 5:14); Hebrew *Adoram*

THE KINGS OF ISRAEL AND JUDAH

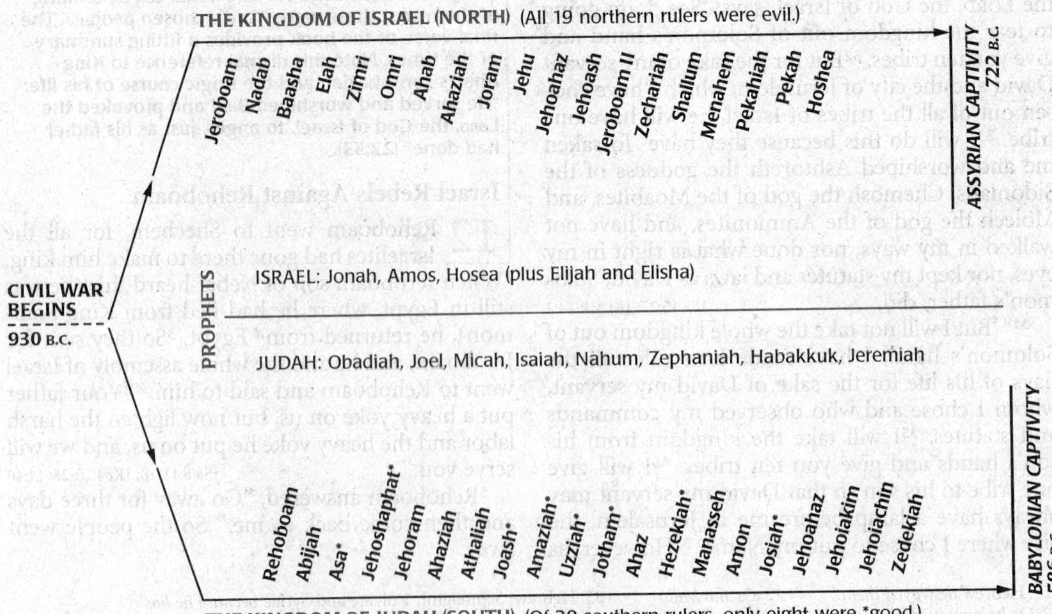

22But this word of God came to Shemaiah the man of God: 23"Say to Rehoboam son of Solomon king of Judah, to the whole house of Judah and Benjamin, and to the rest of the people, 24'This is what the LORD says: Do not go up to fight against your brothers, the Israelites. Go home, every one of you, for this is my doing.'" So they obeyed the word of the LORD and went home again, as the LORD had ordered. 2Ch 10:1-11:4

Golden Calves at Bethel and Dan

25Then Jeroboam fortified Shechem in the hill country of Ephraim and lived there. From there he went out and built up Peniel.[a] Jdg 8:8,17; 9:45

26Jeroboam thought to himself, "The kingdom will now likely revert to the house of David. 27If these people go up to offer sacrifices at the temple of the LORD in Jerusalem, they will again give their allegiance to their lord, Rehoboam king of Judah. They will kill me and return to King Rehoboam."

28After seeking advice, the king made two golden calves. He said to the people, "It is too much for you to go up to Jerusalem. Here are your gods, O Israel, who brought you up out of Egypt." 29One he set up in Bethel, and the other in Dan. 30And this thing became a sin; the people went even as far as Dan to worship the one there.

31Jeroboam built shrines on high places and appointed priests from all sorts of people, even though they were not Levites. 32He instituted a festival on the fifteenth day of the eighth month, like the festival held in Judah, and offered sacrifices on the altar. This he did in Bethel, sacrificing to the calves he had made. And at Bethel he also installed priests at the high places he had made. 33On the fifteenth day of the eighth month, a month of his own choosing, he offered sacrifices on the altar he had built at Bethel. So he instituted the festival for the Israelites and went up to the altar to make offerings. Nu 29:12; 1Ki 13:32; 2Ki 17:32

The Man of God From Judah

13 By the word of the LORD a man of God came from Judah to Bethel, as Jeroboam was standing by the altar to make an offering. 2He cried out against the altar by the word of the LORD: "O altar, altar! This is what the LORD says: 'A son named Josiah will be born to the house of David. On you he will sacrifice the priests of the high places who now make offerings here, and human bones will be burned on you.'" 3That same day the man of God gave a sign: "This is the sign the LORD has declared: The altar will be split apart and the ashes on it will be poured out." 2Ki 23:15-16,20; Jn 2:11

4When King Jeroboam heard what the man of God cried out against the altar at Bethel, he stretched out his hand from the altar and said, "Seize him!" But the hand he stretched out toward the man shriveled up, so that he could not pull it back. 5Also, the altar was split apart and its ashes poured out according to the sign given by the man of God by the word of the LORD.

6Then the king said to the man of God, "Intercede with the LORD your God and pray for me that my hand may be restored." So the man of God interceded with the LORD, and the king's hand was restored and became as it was before. Ex 8:8

7The king said to the man of God, "Come home with me and have something to eat, and I will give you a gift." 1Sa 9:7; 2Ki 5:15

8But the man of God answered the king, "Even if you were to give me half your possessions, I would not go with you, nor would I eat bread or drink water here. 9For I was commanded by the word of the LORD: 'You must not eat bread or drink water or return by the way you came.'" 10So he took another road and did not return by the way he had come to Bethel. Nu 22:18; 24:13

11Now there was a certain old prophet living in Bethel, whose sons came and told him all that the man of God had done there that day. They also told their father what he had said to the king. 12Their father asked them, "Which way did he go?" And his sons showed him which road the man of God from Judah had taken. 13So he said to his sons, "Saddle the donkey for me." And when they had saddled the donkey for him, he mounted it 14and rode after the man of God. He found him sitting under an oak tree and asked, "Are you the man of God who came from Judah?"

"I am," he replied.

15So the prophet said to him, "Come home with me and eat."

16The man of God said, "I cannot turn back and go with you, nor can I eat bread or drink water with you in this place. 17I have been told by the word of the LORD: 'You must not eat bread or drink water there or return by the way you came.'"

18The old prophet answered, "I too am a prophet, as you are. And an angel said to me by the word of the LORD: 'Bring him back with you to your house so that he may eat bread and drink water.'" (But he was lying to him.) 19So the man of God returned with him and ate and drank in his house.

20While they were sitting at the table, the word of the LORD came to the old prophet who had brought him back. 21He cried out to the man of God who had come from Judah, "This is what the LORD says: 'You have defied the word of the LORD and have not kept the command the LORD your God gave you. 22You came back and ate bread and drank water in the place where he told you not to

[a]25 Hebrew *Penuel,* a variant of *Peniel*

eat or drink. Therefore your body will not be buried in the tomb of your fathers.' " ver 26; 1Ki 20:35

23When the man of God had finished eating and drinking, the prophet who had brought him back saddled his donkey for him. 24As he went on his way, a lion met him on the road and killed him, and his body was thrown down on the road, with both the donkey and the lion standing beside it. 25Some people who passed by saw the body thrown down there, with the lion standing beside the body, and they went and reported it in the city where the old prophet lived. 1Ki 20:36

26When the prophet who had brought him back from his journey heard of it, he said, "It is the man of God who defied the word of the LORD. The LORD has given him over to the lion, which has mauled him and killed him, as the word of the LORD had warned him."

27The prophet said to his sons, "Saddle the donkey for me," and they did so. 28Then he went out and found the body thrown down on the road, with the donkey and the lion standing beside it. The lion had neither eaten the body nor mauled the donkey. 29So the prophet picked up the body of the man of God, laid it on the donkey, and brought it back to his own city to mourn for him and bury him. 30Then he laid the body in his own tomb, and they mourned over him and said, "Oh, my brother!" Jer 22:18

31After burying him, he said to his sons, "When I die, bury me in the grave where the man of God is buried; lay my bones beside his bones. 32For the message he declared by the word of the LORD against the altar in Bethel and against all the shrines on the high places in the towns of Samaria will certainly come true." Lev 26:30; 1Ki 16:24,28

33Even after this, Jeroboam did not change his evil ways, but once more appointed priests for the high places from all sorts of people. Anyone who wanted to become a priest he consecrated for the high places. 34This was the sin of the house of Jeroboam that led to its downfall and to its destruction from the face of the earth. 1Ki 12:30-31

Ahijah's Prophecy Against Jeroboam

14 At that time Abijah son of Jeroboam became ill, 2and Jeroboam said to his wife, "Go, disguise yourself, so you won't be recognized as the wife of Jeroboam. Then go to Shiloh. Ahijah the prophet is there—the one who told me I would be king over this people. 3Take ten loaves of bread with you, some cakes and a jar of honey, and go to him. He will tell you what will happen to the boy." 4So Jeroboam's wife did what he said and went to Ahijah's house in Shiloh. 1Sa 9:7

Now Ahijah could not see; his sight was gone because of his age. 5But the LORD had told Ahijah, "Jeroboam's wife is coming to ask you about her son, for he is ill, and you are to give her such and such an answer. When she arrives, she will pretend to be someone else."

6So when Ahijah heard the sound of her footsteps at the door, he said, "Come in, wife of Jeroboam. Why this pretense? I have been sent to you with bad news. 7Go, tell Jeroboam that this is what the LORD, the God of Israel, says: 'I raised you up from among the people and made you a leader over my people Israel. 8I tore the kingdom away from the house of David and gave it to you, but you have not been like my servant David, who kept my commands and followed me with all his heart, doing only what was right in my eyes. 9You have done more evil than all who lived before you. You have made for yourself other gods, idols made of metal; you have provoked me to anger and thrust me behind your back. 1Ki 11:31,33,38; 2Ch 11:15

10" 'Because of this, I am going to bring disaster on the house of Jeroboam. I will cut off from Jeroboam every last male in Israel—slave or free. I will burn up the house of Jeroboam as one burns dung, until it is all gone. 11Dogs will eat those belonging to Jeroboam who die in the city, and the birds of the air will feed on those who die in the country. The LORD has spoken!' 1Ki 15:29; 16:4; 21:24

12"As for you, go back home. When you set foot in your city, the boy will die. 13All Israel will mourn for him and bury him. He is the only one belonging to Jeroboam who will be buried, because he is the only one in the house of Jeroboam in whom the LORD, the God of Israel, has found anything good. 2Ch 12:12; 19:3

14"The LORD will raise up for himself a king over Israel who will cut off the family of Jeroboam. This is the day! What? Yes, even now.[a] 15And the LORD will strike Israel, so that it will be like a reed swaying in the water. He will uproot Israel from this good land that he gave to their forefathers and scatter them beyond the River,[b] because they provoked the LORD to anger by making Asherah poles.[c] 16And he will give Israel up because of the sins Jeroboam has committed and has caused Israel to commit." Dt 12:3; Jos 23:15-16; 1Ki 12:30

17Then Jeroboam's wife got up and left and went to Tirzah. As soon as she stepped over the threshold of the house, the boy died. 18They buried him, and all Israel mourned for him, as the LORD had said through his servant the prophet Ahijah.

19The other events of Jeroboam's reign, his wars and how he ruled, are written in the book of the annals of the kings of Israel. 20He reigned for twenty-two years and then rested with his fathers. And Nadab his son succeeded him as king.

[a] 14 The meaning of the Hebrew for this sentence is uncertain. [b] 15 That is, the Euphrates [c] 15 That is, symbols of the goddess Asherah; here and elsewhere in 1 Kings

Rehoboam King of Judah

21Rehoboam son of Solomon was king in Judah.
He was forty-one years old when he became king,
and he reigned seventeen years in Jerusalem, the
city the LORD had chosen out of all the tribes of
Israel in which to put his Name. His mother's
name was Naamah; she was an Ammonite.
22Judah did evil in the eyes of the LORD. By the
sins they committed they stirred up his jealous
anger more than their fathers had done. 23They
also set up for themselves high places, sacred
stones and Asherah poles on every high hill and
under every spreading tree. 24There were even
male shrine prostitutes in the land; the people engaged in all the detestable practices of the nations
the LORD had driven out before the Israelites.
25In the fifth year of King Rehoboam, Shishak
king of Egypt attacked Jerusalem. 26He carried off
the treasures of the temple of the LORD and the
treasures of the royal palace. He took everything,
including all the gold shields Solomon had made.
27So King Rehoboam made bronze shields to replace them and assigned these to the commanders
of the guard on duty at the entrance to the royal
palace. 28Whenever the king went to the LORD's
temple, the guards bore the shields, and afterward
they returned them to the guardroom. 1Ki 10:17
29As for the other events of Rehoboam's reign,
and all he did, are they not written in the book of
the annals of the kings of Judah? 30There was continual warfare between Rehoboam and Jeroboam.
31And Rehoboam rested with his fathers and was
buried with them in the City of David. His mother's name was Naamah; she was an Ammonite.
And Abijah[a] his son succeeded him as king.

Abijah King of Judah

15 In the eighteenth year of the reign of Jeroboam son of Nebat, Abijah[b] became king
of Judah, 2and he reigned in Jerusalem three years.
His mother's name was Maacah daughter of
Abishalom.[c] 2Ch 11:20; 13:2
3He committed all the sins his father had done
before him; his heart was not fully devoted to the
LORD his God, as the heart of David his forefather
had been. 4Nevertheless, for David's sake the LORD
his God gave him a lamp in Jerusalem by raising
up a son to succeed him and by making Jerusalem
strong. 5For David had done what was right in the
eyes of the LORD and had not failed to keep any of
the LORD's commands all the days of his life—except in the case of Uriah the Hittite. 2Sa 11:2-27
6There was war between Rehoboam[d] and Jeroboam throughout ⌊Abijah's⌋ lifetime. 7As for the
other events of Abijah's reign, and all he did, are
they not written in the book of the annals of the
kings of Judah? There was war between Abijah and
Jeroboam. 8And Abijah rested with his fathers and
was buried in the City of David. And Asa his son
succeeded him as king. 2Ch 13:1-2,22-14:1

Asa King of Judah

9In the twentieth year of Jeroboam king of Israel, Asa became king of Judah, 10and he reigned
in Jerusalem forty-one years. His grandmother's
name was Maacah daughter of Abishalom. ver 2
11Asa did what was right in the eyes of the LORD,
as his father David had done. 12He expelled the
male shrine prostitutes from the land and got rid
of all the idols his fathers had made. 13He even
deposed his grandmother Maacah from her position as queen mother, because she had made a
repulsive Asherah pole. Asa cut the pole down and
burned it in the Kidron Valley. 14Although he did
not remove the high places, Asa's heart was fully
committed to the LORD all his life. 15He brought
into the temple of the LORD the silver and gold and
the articles that he and his father had dedicated.
16There was war between Asa and Baasha king
of Israel throughout their reigns. 17Baasha king of
Israel went up against Judah and fortified Ramah
to prevent anyone from leaving or entering the
territory of Asa king of Judah. Jos 18:25; 1Ki 12:27
18Asa then took all the silver and gold that was
left in the treasuries of the LORD's temple and of his
own palace. He entrusted it to his officials and sent
them to Ben-Hadad son of Tabrimmon, the son of
Hezion, the king of Aram, who was ruling in Damascus. 19"Let there be a treaty between me and
you," he said, "as there was between my father and
your father. See, I am sending you a gift of silver
and gold. Now break your treaty with Baasha king
of Israel so he will withdraw from me."
20Ben-Hadad agreed with King Asa and sent
the commanders of his forces against the towns of
Israel. He conquered Ijon, Dan, Abel Beth Maacah
and all Kinnereth in addition to Naphtali. 21When
Baasha heard this, he stopped building Ramah and
withdrew to Tirzah. 22Then King Asa issued an
order to all Judah—no one was exempt—and
they carried away from Ramah the stones and timber Baasha had been using there. With them King
Asa built up Geba in Benjamin, and also Mizpah.
23As for all the other events of Asa's reign, all his
achievements, all he did and the cities he built, are
they not written in the book of the annals of the
kings of Judah? In his old age, however, his feet
became diseased. 24Then Asa rested with his fathers and was buried with them in the city of his

[a] 31 Some Hebrew manuscripts and Septuagint (see also 2 Chron. 12:16); most Hebrew manuscripts *Abijam* [b] 1 Some Hebrew manuscripts and Septuagint (see also 2 Chron. 12:16); most Hebrew manuscripts *Abijam*; also in verses 7 and 8 [c] 2 A variant of *Absalom*; also in verse 10 [d] 6 Most Hebrew manuscripts; some Hebrew manuscripts and Syriac *Abijam* (that is, Abijah)

father David. And Jehoshaphat his son succeeded
him as king. Mt 1:8

Nadab King of Israel

25Nadab son of Jeroboam became king of Israel
in the second year of Asa king of Judah, and he
reigned over Israel two years. 26He did evil in the
eyes of the LORD, walking in the ways of his father
and in his sin, which he had caused Israel to commit. 1Ki 12:30

27Baasha son of Ahijah of the house of Issachar
plotted against him, and he struck him down at
Gibbethon, a Philistine town, while Nadab and all
Israel were besieging it. 28Baasha killed Nadab in
the third year of Asa king of Judah and succeeded
him as king. Jos 19:44; 1Ki 14:14

29As soon as he began to reign, he killed Jeroboam's whole family. He did not leave Jeroboam
anyone that breathed, but destroyed them all, according to the word of the LORD given through his
servant Ahijah the Shilonite— 30because of the
sins Jeroboam had committed and had caused Israel to commit, and because he provoked the
LORD, the God of Israel, to anger. 1Ki 14:9-10,14,16

31As for the other events of Nadab's reign, and
all he did, are they not written in the book of the
annals of the kings of Israel? 32There was war between Asa and Baasha king of Israel throughout
their reigns. ver 16

Baasha King of Israel

33In the third year of Asa king of Judah, Baasha
son of Ahijah became king of all Israel in Tirzah,
and he reigned twenty-four years. 34He did evil in
the eyes of the LORD, walking in the ways of Jeroboam and in his sin, which he had caused Israel to
commit.

16 Then the word of the LORD came to Jehu
son of Hanani against Baasha: 2"I lifted
you up from the dust and made you leader of my
people Israel, but you walked in the ways of Jeroboam and caused my people Israel to sin and to
provoke me to anger by their sins. 3So I am about
to consume Baasha and his house, and I will make
your house like that of Jeroboam son of Nebat.
4Dogs will eat those belonging to Baasha who die
in the city, and the birds of the air will feed on
those who die in the country." 1Ki 14:7-11

5As for the other events of Baasha's reign, what
he did and his achievements, are they not written
in the book of the annals of the kings of Israel?
6Baasha rested with his fathers and was buried in
Tirzah. And Elah his son succeeded him as king.

7Moreover, the word of the LORD came through
the prophet Jehu son of Hanani to Baasha and his
house, because of all the evil he had done in the
eyes of the LORD, provoking him to anger by the
things he did, and becoming like the house of
Jeroboam—and also because he destroyed it.

Elah King of Israel

8In the twenty-sixth year of Asa king of Judah,
Elah son of Baasha became king of Israel, and he
reigned in Tirzah two years.

9Zimri, one of his officials, who had command
of half his chariots, plotted against him. Elah was
in Tirzah at the time, getting drunk in the home of
Arza, the man in charge of the palace at Tirzah.
10Zimri came in, struck him down and killed him
in the twenty-seventh year of Asa king of Judah.
Then he succeeded him as king. 1Ki 18:3; 2Ki 9:30-33

11As soon as he began to reign and was seated
on the throne, he killed off Baasha's whole family.
He did not spare a single male, whether relative or
friend. 12So Zimri destroyed the whole family of
Baasha, in accordance with the word of the LORD
spoken against Baasha through the prophet
Jehu— 13because of all the sins Baasha and his son
Elah had committed and had caused Israel to com-
mit, so that they provoked the LORD, the God of
Israel, to anger by their worthless idols. Dt 32:21

14As for the other events of Elah's reign, and all
he did, are they not written in the book of the
annals of the kings of Israel?

Zimri King of Israel

15In the twenty-seventh year of Asa king of Judah, Zimri reigned in Tirzah seven days. The army
was encamped near Gibbethon, a Philistine town.
16When the Israelites in the camp heard that Zimri
had plotted against the king and murdered him,
they proclaimed Omri, the commander of the
army, king over Israel that very day there in the
camp. 17Then Omri and all the Israelites with him
withdrew from Gibbethon and laid siege to Tirzah.
18When Zimri saw that the city was taken, he went
into the citadel of the royal palace and set the
palace on fire around him. So he died, 19because of
the sins he had committed, doing evil in the eyes
of the LORD and walking in the ways of Jeroboam
and in the sin he had committed and had caused
Israel to commit. Jos 19:44; 1Ki 15:27

20As for the other events of Zimri's reign, and
the rebellion he carried out, are they not written in
the book of the annals of the kings of Israel?

Omri King of Israel

21Then the people of Israel were split into two
factions; half supported Tibni son of Ginath for
king, and the other half supported Omri. 22But
Omri's followers proved stronger than those of
Tibni son of Ginath. So Tibni died and Omri became king.

23In the thirty-first year of Asa king of Judah,
Omri became king of Israel, and he reigned twelve
years, six of them in Tirzah. 24He bought the hill

of Samaria from Shemer for two talents[a] of silver and built a city on the hill, calling it Samaria, after Shemer, the name of the former owner of the hill.

25But Omri did evil in the eyes of the LORD and sinned more than all those before him. 26He walked in all the ways of Jeroboam son of Nebat and in his sin, which he had caused Israel to commit, so that they provoked the LORD, the God of Israel, to anger by their worthless idols. Dt 4:25

27As for the other events of Omri's reign, what he did and the things he achieved, are they not written in the book of the annals of the kings of Israel? 28Omri rested with his fathers and was buried in Samaria. And Ahab his son succeeded him as king.

Ahab Becomes King of Israel

29In the thirty-eighth year of Asa king of Judah, Ahab son of Omri became king of Israel, and he reigned in Samaria over Israel twenty-two years. 30Ahab son of Omri did more evil in the eyes of the LORD than any of those before him. 31He not only considered it trivial to commit the sins of Jeroboam son of Nebat, but he also married Jezebel daughter of Ethbaal king of the Sidonians, and began to serve Baal and worship him. 32He set up an altar for Baal in the temple of Baal that he built in Samaria. 33Ahab also made an Asherah pole and did more to provoke the LORD, the God of Israel, to anger than did all the kings of Israel before him.

34In Ahab's time, Hiel of Bethel rebuilt Jericho. He laid its foundations at the cost of his firstborn son Abiram, and he set up its gates at the cost of his youngest son Segub, in accordance with the word of the LORD spoken by Joshua son of Nun.

Elijah Fed by Ravens

17 Now Elijah the Tishbite, from Tishbe[b] in Gilead, said to Ahab, "As the LORD, the God of Israel, lives, whom I serve, there will be neither dew nor rain in the next few years except at my word." 2Ki 3:14; Lk 4:25; Jas 5:17

2Then the word of the LORD came to Elijah: 3"Leave here, turn eastward and hide in the Kerith Ravine, east of the Jordan. 4You will drink from the brook, and I have ordered the ravens to feed you there." Ge 8:7

5So he did what the LORD had told him. He went to the Kerith Ravine, east of the Jordan, and stayed there. 6The ravens brought him bread and meat in the morning and bread and meat in the evening, and he drank from the brook. Ex 16:8

The Widow at Zarephath

7Some time later the brook dried up because there had been no rain in the land. 8Then the word of the LORD came to him: 9"Go at once to Zarephath of Sidon and stay there. I have commanded a widow in that place to supply you with food." 10So he went to Zarephath. When he came to the town gate, a widow was there gathering sticks. He called to her and asked, "Would you bring me a little water in a jar so I may have a drink?" 11As she was going to get it, he called, "And bring me, please, a piece of bread." Ge 24:17; Ob 1:20; Lk 4:26

12"As surely as the LORD your God lives," she replied, "I don't have any bread—only a handful of flour in a jar and a little oil in a jug. I am gathering a few sticks to take home and make a meal for myself and my son, that we may eat it—and die." 2Ki 4:2

13Elijah said to her, "Don't be afraid. Go home and do as you have said. But first make a small cake of bread for me from what you have and bring it to me, and then make something for yourself and your son. 14For this is what the LORD, the God of Israel, says: 'The jar of flour will not be used up and the jug of oil will not run dry until the day the LORD gives rain on the land.' "

15She went away and did as Elijah had told her. So there was food every day for Elijah and for the woman and her family. 16For the jar of flour was not used up and the jug of oil did not run dry, in keeping with the word of the LORD spoken by Elijah.

17Some time later the son of the woman who owned the house became ill. He grew worse and worse, and finally stopped breathing. 18She said to Elijah, "What do you have against me, man of God? Did you come to remind me of my sin and kill my son?" 2Ki 3:13; Lk 5:8

19"Give me your son," Elijah replied. He took him from her arms, carried him to the upper room where he was staying, and laid him on his bed. 20Then he cried out to the LORD, "O LORD my God, have you brought tragedy also upon this widow I am staying with, by causing her son to die?" 21Then he stretched himself out on the boy three times and cried to the LORD, "O LORD my God, let this boy's life return to him!" 2Ki 4:34; Ac 20:10

22The LORD heard Elijah's cry, and the boy's life returned to him, and he lived. 23Elijah picked up the child and carried him down from the room into the house. He gave him to his mother and said, "Look, your son is alive!"

24Then the woman said to Elijah, "Now I know that you are a man of God and that the word of the LORD from your mouth is the truth." Jn 3:2; 16:30

Elijah and Obadiah

18 After a long time, in the third year, the word of the LORD came to Elijah: "Go and present yourself to Ahab, and I will send rain on

[a]24 That is, about 150 pounds (about 70 kilograms) [b]1 Or *Tishbite, of the settlers*

ELIJAH

Standing Alone in the Gap

"Then the word of the LORD came to Elijah . . . So he did what the LORD had told him."
—1 KINGS 17:2,5a

Elijah prophesied to Israel during a time of rampant idolatry and rebellion against God at the highest levels. The Bible goes into some depth in its account of wicked King Ahab's reign (beginning at 1 Kings 16:29)—more than six decades of bloodshed, conspiracy, deception, idolatry and immorality. When Ahab married Jezebel, they almost made the evil kings who went before them appear like amateurs. Take note of these words from 1 Kings 16:32–33: "He set up an altar for Baal in the temple of Baal that he built in Samaria. Ahab . . . did more to provoke the LORD, the God of Israel, to anger than did all the kings of Israel before him." This understated expression of complete despair is like a sigh in the narrative. If you miss it, you miss the whole impact of Elijah's stunning arrival on the scene.

The name Elijah means "My God is the LORD." Elijah's very name spoke of his character. He stood alone in the midst of an idolatrous society, proclaiming boldly, fearlessly, this essential message: "I have one God. His name is the LORD. He is the only One I serve."

Elijah was from Tishbe, a place about which very little is known. But historians have pieced together, with the help of the archaeologist's spade, these details. Tishbe was a place of solitude and outdoor life. It was apparently not a place of high polish or great sophistication. Elijah seemed to be very much like the land from which he came. He came close to being coarse and crude; certainly he was a prophet of God who pulled no punches in his mission to rescue Israel from its spiritual and moral decay.

It was this man who came to Ahab and confidently stated, "As the LORD, the God of Israel, lives, whom I serve, there will be neither dew nor rain in the next few years except at my word" (1 Kings 17:1). That was the beginning of Elijah's ministry—this rugged stranger making a pronouncement in front of Israel's king. From then on, Elijah became King Ahab's and Queen Jezebel's "public enemy number one."

After Elijah's bold proclamation, God sent him out to boot camp in a place called the Kerith Ravine—in order to accomplish two purposes: first, to provide protection from Ahab; second, to provide a period of training. There God promised him that he would have enough water to drink and food miraculously supplied by ravens. What a fabulous catering service! So Elijah stepped out of the limelight for a time, communicating a message to God that went something like this: "Lord, if you want me standing in Ahab's presence, I'm there. If you want me by the brook, I'm there. I'll serve you there, in public, or here in silence." It was in the place of solitude Elijah learned that when God leads, He always provides.

When we get to 1 Kings 19, however, we see a man who had forgotten that principle. Here we find Elijah, just coming off the greatest victory of his career in which he represented the all-powerful God in a showdown with the prophets of Baal on Mount Carmel, running in fear from the wicked Queen Jezebel's death threat. Take a good look at Elijah: He had lost his ability to think clearly. His physical and emotional exhaustion had overwhelmed him. He caved in to self-pity. He took his eyes off God and focused on his own immediate situation of despair and apparent defeat. He even asked God to take his life (19:4). Yet even there, in that place of dark and desperate discouragement, God provided. No preaching, no lecturing—just another miraculous catering service from heaven. God graciously allowed him rest and refreshment.

Then God put some flesh on His provision. He assured Elijah that he wasn't alone, then gave him some wise counsel. First He appeared to Elijah—not in the wind, not in the earthquake, not in the fire, but in a gentle whisper (19:12). Then He gave Elijah a glimpse of the work he was going to do in the future (19:15–17) and told him of seven thousand other people in Israel who had not bowed the knee to Baal (19:18). Finally, God provided Elijah with an intimate, personal friend who loved him and ministered to him—Elisha, the one who would replace Elijah as God's prophet. What a beautiful picture of God's encouraging work in our lives! You can count on Him to be there for you and with you, no matter what.

the land." 2So Elijah went to present himself to Ahab. Dt 28:12; Lk 4:25; Jas 5:17

Now the famine was severe in Samaria, 3and Ahab had summoned Obadiah, who was in charge of his palace. (Obadiah was a devout believer in the LORD. 4While Jezebel was killing off the LORD's prophets, Obadiah had taken a hundred prophets and hidden them in two caves, fifty in each, and had supplied them with food and water.) 5Ahab had said to Obadiah, "Go through the land to all the springs and valleys. Maybe we can find some grass to keep the horses and mules alive so we will not have to kill any of our animals." 6So they divided the land they were to cover, Ahab going in one direction and Obadiah in another. 2Ki 9:7

7As Obadiah was walking along, Elijah met him. Obadiah recognized him, bowed down to the ground, and said, "Is it really you, my lord Elijah?"

8"Yes," he replied. "Go tell your master, 'Elijah is here.' "

9"What have I done wrong," asked Obadiah, "that you are handing your servant over to Ahab to be put to death? 10As surely as the LORD your God lives, there is not a nation or kingdom where my master has not sent someone to look for you. And whenever a nation or kingdom claimed you were not there, he made them swear they could not find you. 11But now you tell me to go to my master and say, 'Elijah is here.' 12I don't know where the Spirit of the LORD may carry you when I leave you. If I go and tell Ahab and he doesn't find you, he will kill me. Yet I your servant have worshiped the LORD since my youth. 13Haven't you heard, my lord, what I did while Jezebel was killing the prophets of the LORD? I hid a hundred of the LORD's prophets in two caves, fifty in each, and supplied them with food and water. 14And now you tell me to go to my master and say, 'Elijah is here.' He will kill me!" 2Ki 2:16; Eze 3:14; Ac 8:39

15Elijah said, "As the LORD Almighty lives, whom I serve, I will surely present myself to Ahab today." 1Ki 17:1

Elijah on Mount Carmel

16So Obadiah went to meet Ahab and told him, and Ahab went to meet Elijah. 17When he saw Elijah, he said to him, "Is that you, you troubler of Israel?" Jos 7:25; 1Ki 21:20

18"I have not made trouble for Israel," Elijah replied. "But you and your father's family have. You have abandoned the LORD's commands and have followed the Baals. 19Now summon the people from all over Israel to meet me on Mount Carmel. And bring the four hundred and fifty prophets of Baal and the four hundred prophets of Asherah, who eat at Jezebel's table." Jos 19:26

20So Ahab sent word throughout all Israel and assembled the prophets on Mount Carmel. 21Elijah went before the people and said, "How long will you waver between two opinions? If the LORD is God, follow him; but if Baal is God, follow him."

But the people said nothing.

22Then Elijah said to them, "I am the only one of the LORD's prophets left, but Baal has four hundred and fifty prophets. 23Get two bulls for us. Let them choose one for themselves, and let them cut it into pieces and put it on the wood but not set fire to it. I will prepare the other bull and put it on the wood but not set fire to it. 24Then you call on the name of your god, and I will call on the name of the LORD. The god who answers by fire—he is God." 1Ki 19:10; 1Ch 21:26

LIVING  **INSIGHT**

Are you an eagle-type, soaring to heights beyond your peers? Don't expect pats on the back or great waves of applause. Mavericks who don't color within the lines are also notorious for not staying within the fences. Many an alleged heretic today will be a hero tomorrow. Which is another way of saying, "first the cross, then the crown."

(See 1 Kings 18:16–17.)

Then all the people said, "What you say is good."

25Elijah said to the prophets of Baal, "Choose one of the bulls and prepare it first, since there are so many of you. Call on the name of your god, but do not light the fire." 26So they took the bull given them and prepared it.

Then they called on the name of Baal from morning till noon. "O Baal, answer us!" they shouted. But there was no response; no one answered. And they danced around the altar they had made. Ps 115:4-5; Jer 10:5; 1Co 8:4

27At noon Elijah began to taunt them. "Shout louder!" he said. "Surely he is a god! Perhaps he is deep in thought, or busy, or traveling. Maybe he is sleeping and must be awakened." 28So they shouted louder and slashed themselves with swords and spears, as was their custom, until their blood flowed. 29Midday passed, and they continued their frantic prophesying until the time for the evening sacrifice. But there was no response, no one answered, no one paid attention. Lev 19:28; Hab 2:19

30Then Elijah said to all the people, "Come here to me." They came to him, and he repaired the altar of the LORD, which was in ruins. 31Elijah took twelve stones, one for each of the tribes descended from Jacob, to whom the word of the LORD had come, saying, "Your name shall be Israel." 32With the stones he built an altar in the name of the LORD, and he dug a trench around it large enough

to hold two seahs[a] of seed. 33He arranged the
wood, cut the bull into pieces and laid it on the
wood. Then he said to them, "Fill four large jars
with water and pour it on the offering and on the
wood." 1Ki 19:10; 2Ki 17:34; Col 3:17
34"Do it again," he said, and they did it again.
"Do it a third time," he ordered, and they did
it the third time. 35The water ran down around the
altar and even filled the trench.
36At the time of sacrifice, the prophet Elijah
stepped forward and prayed: "O LORD, God of
Abraham, Isaac and Israel, let it be known today
that you are God in Israel and that I am your
servant and have done all these things at your
command. 37Answer me, O LORD, answer me, so
these people will know that you, O LORD, are God,
and that you are turning their hearts back again."
38Then the fire of the LORD fell and burned up
the sacrifice, the wood, the stones and the soil, and
also licked up the water in the trench. Lev 9:24
39When all the people saw this, they fell prostrate and cried, "The LORD—he is God! The
LORD—he is God!" ver 24; Ps 46:10
40Then Elijah commanded them, "Seize the
prophets of Baal. Don't let anyone get away!" They
seized them, and Elijah had them brought down to
the Kishon Valley and slaughtered there. Dt 13:5
41And Elijah said to Ahab, "Go, eat and drink,
for there is the sound of a heavy rain." 42So Ahab
went off to eat and drink, but Elijah climbed to the
top of Carmel, bent down to the ground and put
his face between his knees. Jas 5:18
43"Go and look toward the sea," he told his
servant. And he went up and looked.
"There is nothing there," he said.
Seven times Elijah said, "Go back."
44The seventh time the servant reported, "A
cloud as small as a man's hand is rising from the
sea." Lk 12:54
So Elijah said, "Go and tell Ahab, 'Hitch up
your chariot and go down before the rain stops
you.'"
45Meanwhile, the sky grew black with clouds,
the wind rose, a heavy rain came on and Ahab
rode off to Jezreel. 46The power of the LORD came
upon Elijah and, tucking his cloak into his belt, he
ran ahead of Ahab all the way to Jezreel. 2Ki 3:15

Elijah Flees to Horeb

19 Now Ahab told Jezebel everything Elijah
had done and how he had killed all the
prophets with the sword. 2So Jezebel sent a messenger to Elijah to say, "May the gods deal with
me, be it ever so severely, if by this time tomorrow
I do not make your life like that of one of them."
3Elijah was afraid[b] and ran for his life. When
he came to Beersheba in Judah, he left his servant
there, 4while he himself went a day's journey into
the desert. He came to a broom tree, sat down
under it and prayed that he might die. "I have had
enough, LORD," he said. "Take my life; I am no

LIVING  **INSIGHT**

The most damaging impact of self-pity is its ultimate end. Cuddle and nurse it as an infant, and you'll have on your hands in a brief period of time a beast, a monster, a raging, coarse brute that will spread the poison of bitterness and paranoia throughout your system. You will soon discover that the sea of self-pity has brought with it prickly urchins of doubt, despair, and even the desire to die.

(See 1 Kings 19:4.)

better than my ancestors." 5Then he lay down under the tree and fell asleep. Nu 11:15; Jnh 4:8; Ge 31:21
All at once an angel touched him and said, "Get
up and eat." 6He looked around, and there by his
head was a cake of bread baked over hot coals, and
a jar of water. He ate and drank and then lay down
again. Ge 16:7
7The angel of the LORD came back a second time
and touched him and said, "Get up and eat, for the
journey is too much for you." 8So he got up and
ate and drank. Strengthened by that food, he traveled forty days and forty nights until he reached
Horeb, the mountain of God. 9There he went into
a cave and spent the night. Ex 3:1; 34:28; Mt 4:2

The LORD Appears to Elijah

And the word of the LORD came to him: "What
are you doing here, Elijah?"
10He replied, "I have been very zealous for the
LORD God Almighty. The Israelites have rejected
your covenant, broken down your altars, and put
your prophets to death with the sword. I am the
only one left, and now they are trying to kill me
too." 1Ki 18:4,22; Ro 11:3*
11The LORD said, "Go out and stand on the
mountain in the presence of the LORD, for the
LORD is about to pass by." Ex 24:12
Then a great and powerful wind tore the mountains apart and shattered the rocks before the
LORD, but the LORD was not in the wind. After the
wind there was an earthquake, but the LORD was
not in the earthquake. 12After the earthquake came
a fire, but the LORD was not in the fire. And after
the fire came a gentle whisper. 13When Elijah
heard it, he pulled his cloak over his face and went
out and stood at the mouth of the cave. Zec 4:6

[a] 32 That is, probably about 13 quarts (about 15 liters) [b] 3 Or *Elijah saw*

Then a voice said to him, "What are you doing here, Elijah?"

14He replied, "I have been very zealous for the LORD God Almighty. The Israelites have rejected your covenant, broken down your altars, and put your prophets to death with the sword. I am the only one left, and now they are trying to kill me too." Ro 11:3*

15The LORD said to him, "Go back the way you came, and go to the Desert of Damascus. When you get there, anoint Hazael king over Aram. 16Also, anoint Jehu son of Nimshi king over Israel, and anoint Elisha son of Shaphat from Abel Meholah to succeed you as prophet. 17Jehu will put to death any who escape the sword of Hazael, and Elisha will put to death any who escape the sword of Jehu. 18Yet I reserve seven thousand in Israel—all whose knees have not bowed down to Baal and all whose mouths have not kissed him." Ro 11:4*

The Call of Elisha

19So Elijah went from there and found Elisha son of Shaphat. He was plowing with twelve yoke of oxen, and he himself was driving the twelfth pair. Elijah went up to him and threw his cloak around him. 20Elisha then left his oxen and ran after Elijah. "Let me kiss my father and mother good-by," he said, "and then I will come with you." 2Ki 2:8,14; Mt 8:21-22; Lk 9:61

"Go back," Elijah replied. "What have I done to you?"

21So Elisha left him and went back. He took his yoke of oxen and slaughtered them. He burned the plowing equipment to cook the meat and gave it to the people, and they ate. Then he set out to follow Elijah and became his attendant. 2Sa 24:22

Ben-Hadad Attacks Samaria

20 Now Ben-Hadad king of Aram mustered his entire army. Accompanied by thirty-two kings with their horses and chariots, he went up and besieged Samaria and attacked it. 2He sent messengers into the city to Ahab king of Israel, saying, "This is what Ben-Hadad says: 3'Your silver and gold are mine, and the best of your wives and children are mine.'" 1Ki 15:18; 22:31; 2Ki 6:24

4The king of Israel answered, "Just as you say, my lord the king. I and all I have are yours."

5The messengers came again and said, "This is what Ben-Hadad says: 'I sent to demand your silver and gold, your wives and your children. 6But about this time tomorrow I am going to send my officials to search your palace and the houses of your officials. They will seize everything you value and carry it away.'"

7The king of Israel summoned all the elders of the land and said to them, "See how this man is looking for trouble! When he sent for my wives and my children, my silver and my gold, I did not refuse him." 2Ki 5:7

8The elders and the people all answered, "Don't listen to him or agree to his demands."

9So he replied to Ben-Hadad's messengers, "Tell my lord the king, 'Your servant will do all you demanded the first time, but this demand I cannot meet.'" They left and took the answer back to Ben-Hadad.

10Then Ben-Hadad sent another message to Ahab: "May the gods deal with me, be it ever so severely, if enough dust remains in Samaria to give each of my men a handful." 1Ki 19:2

11The king of Israel answered, "Tell him: 'One who puts on his armor should not boast like one who takes it off.'" Pr 27:1

12Ben-Hadad heard this message while he and the kings were drinking in their tents,[a] and he ordered his men: "Prepare to attack." So they prepared to attack the city. 1Ki 16:9

Ahab Defeats Ben-Hadad

13Meanwhile a prophet came to Ahab king of Israel and announced, "This is what the LORD says: 'Do you see this vast army? I will give it into your hand today, and then you will know that I am the LORD.'" ver 28; Ex 6:7

14"But who will do this?" asked Ahab.

The prophet replied, "This is what the LORD says: 'The young officers of the provincial commanders will do it.'"

"And who will start the battle?" he asked.

The prophet answered, "You will."

15So Ahab summoned the young officers of the provincial commanders, 232 men. Then he assembled the rest of the Israelites, 7,000 in all. 16They set out at noon while Ben-Hadad and the 32 kings allied with him were in their tents getting drunk. 17The young officers of the provincial commanders went out first. ver 12; 1Ki 16:9

Now Ben-Hadad had dispatched scouts, who reported, "Men are advancing from Samaria."

18He said, "If they have come out for peace, take them alive; if they have come out for war, take them alive."

19The young officers of the provincial commanders marched out of the city with the army behind them 20and each one struck down his opponent. At that, the Arameans fled, with the Israelites in pursuit. But Ben-Hadad king of Aram escaped on horseback with some of his horsemen. 21The king of Israel advanced and overpowered the horses and chariots and inflicted heavy losses on the Arameans.

22Afterward, the prophet came to the king of Israel and said, "Strengthen your position and see

[a] 12 Or *in Succoth*; also in verse 16

what must be done, because next spring the king
of Aram will attack you again." 2Sa 11:1
23Meanwhile, the officials of the king of Aram
advised him, "Their gods are gods of the hills. That
is why they were too strong for us. But if we fight
them on the plains, surely we will be stronger than
they. 24Do this: Remove all the kings from their
commands and replace them with other officers.
25You must also raise an army like the one you
lost—horse for horse and chariot for chariot—so
we can fight Israel on the plains. Then surely we
will be stronger than they." He agreed with them
and acted accordingly. 1Ki 14:23; Ro 1:21-23
26The next spring Ben-Hadad mustered the Arameans and went up to Aphek to fight against
Israel. 27When the Israelites were also mustered
and given provisions, they marched out to meet
them. The Israelites camped opposite them like
two small flocks of goats, while the Arameans covered the countryside. Jdg 6:6; 1Sa 13:6; 2Ki 13:17
28The man of God came up and told the king of
Israel, "This is what the LORD says: 'Because the
Arameans think the LORD is a god of the hills and
not a god of the valleys, I will deliver this vast army
into your hands, and you will know that I am the
LORD.'" ver 13
29For seven days they camped opposite each
other, and on the seventh day the battle was
joined. The Israelites inflicted a hundred thousand
casualties on the Aramean foot soldiers in one day.
30The rest of them escaped to the city of Aphek,
where the wall collapsed on twenty-seven thousand of them. And Ben-Hadad fled to the city and
hid in an inner room. 1Ki 22:25; 2Ch 18:24
31His officials said to him, "Look, we have heard
that the kings of the house of Israel are merciful.
Let us go to the king of Israel with sackcloth
around our waists and ropes around our heads.
Perhaps he will spare your life." Ge 37:34
32Wearing sackcloth around their waists and
ropes around their heads, they went to the king of
Israel and said, "Your servant Ben-Hadad says:
'Please let me live.'"
The king answered, "Is he still alive? He is my
brother."
33The men took this as a good sign and were
quick to pick up his word. "Yes, your brother
Ben-Hadad!" they said.
"Go and get him," the king said. When Ben-
Hadad came out, Ahab had him come up into his
chariot.
34"I will return the cities my father took from
your father," Ben-Hadad offered. "You may set up
your own market areas in Damascus, as my father
did in Samaria." 1Ki 15:20; Jer 49:23-27

⌞Ahab said,⌟ "On the basis of a treaty I will set
you free." So he made a treaty with him, and let
him go. Ex 23:32

A Prophet Condemns Ahab

35By the word of the LORD one of the sons of the
prophets said to his companion, "Strike me with
your weapon," but the man refused. 1Ki 13:20
36So the prophet said, "Because you have not
obeyed the LORD, as soon as you leave me a lion
will kill you." And after the man went away, a lion
found him and killed him. 1Ki 13:24
37The prophet found another man and said,
"Strike me, please." So the man struck him and
wounded him. 38Then the prophet went and stood
by the road waiting for the king. He disguised
himself with his headband down over his eyes.
39As the king passed by, the prophet called out to
him, "Your servant went into the thick of the battle, and someone came to me with a captive and
said, 'Guard this man. If he is missing, it will be
your life for his life, or you must pay a talent[a] of
silver.' 40While your servant was busy here and
there, the man disappeared." 2Ki 10:24
"That is your sentence," the king of Israel said.
"You have pronounced it yourself."
41Then the prophet quickly removed the headband from his eyes, and the king of Israel recognized him as one of the prophets. 42He said to the
king, "This is what the LORD says: 'You have set
free a man I had determined should die.[b] Therefore it is your life for his life, your people for his
people.'" 43Sullen and angry, the king of Israel
went to his palace in Samaria. 1Ki 21:4; 22:31-37

Naboth's Vineyard

21 Some time later there was an incident involving a vineyard belonging to Naboth
the Jezreelite. The vineyard was in Jezreel, close to
the palace of Ahab king of Samaria. 2Ahab said to
Naboth, "Let me have your vineyard to use for a
vegetable garden, since it is close to my palace. In
exchange I will give you a better vineyard or, if you
prefer, I will pay you whatever it is worth."
3But Naboth replied, "The LORD forbid that I
should give you the inheritance of my fathers."
4So Ahab went home, sullen and angry because
Naboth the Jezreelite had said, "I will not give you
the inheritance of my fathers." He lay on his bed
sulking and refused to eat. 1Ki 20:43
5His wife Jezebel came in and asked him, "Why
are you so sullen? Why won't you eat?"
6He answered her, "Because I said to Naboth
the Jezreelite, 'Sell me your vineyard; or if you
prefer, I will give you another vineyard in its

[a]39 That is, about 75 pounds (about 34 kilograms) [b]42 The Hebrew term refers to the irrevocable giving over of things or persons to the LORD, often by totally destroying them.

AHAB AND JEZEBEL

When God Says, "That's Enough!"

"There was never a man like Ahab, who sold himself to do evil in the eyes of the Lord, urged on by Jezebel his wife."

—1 KINGS 21:25

"A scoundrel and villain, who goes about with a corrupt mouth . . . who plots evil with deceit in his heart—he always stirs up dissension. Therefore disaster will overtake him in an instant; he will suddenly be destroyed—without remedy" (Proverbs 6:12,14). In 1 Kings 19 and 21 we have two stories in which the truth of this proverb is played out in the lives of a husband and wife who were partners in sin—Ahab and Jezebel.

Ahab was the classic weak-willed, dependent husband. You may think that's a harsh thing for me to write, but in both of these stories, Ahab acted out the part nearly to perfection. In chapter 19 he told Jezebel everything that happened in that dramatic confrontation at Mount Carmel where Elijah single-handedly killed hundreds of the prophets of Baal (19:1). In chapter 21 Ahab pouted like a child when he couldn't lay his hands on Naboth's vineyard—that little plot of land next to the palace where Ahab wanted to plant a garden (21:2).

I call him a weak-willed husband because he fit the mold in both stories. First, he fell apart under pressure and leaned on Jezebel to help him get through it. Now, there's nothing wrong with being vulnerable with your spouse or with a close friend, but it's another thing entirely to look to another person to provide the strength you ought to have within yourself. In both of these stories, Ahab looked to Jezebel to do his work for him. So it was that Jezebel took over, almost with a sense of glee, one might think. She fit to a "T" the classic image of a domineering person. First, she took matters into her own hands quickly. Second, she did Ahab's job her way. Third, she relied on underhanded schemes that exploited her husband's weakness in order to accomplish her own purposes.

Look at how Jezebel used these situations to her own advantage. In chapter 19, Jezebel sent a messenger to Elijah to deliver her threat of vengeance. It wasn't her role to send messengers to God's prophets—that was the king's role. But in this case, she took charge. The result was a dire threat on the life of God's prophet (19:2). No one messed with this mighty queen!—or so Jezebel thought.

Chapter 21 records another instance of Jezebel's power mongering. When she saw her husband sullen and sulking on his bed, refusing to eat, she said, in effect, "What's the matter with you, Ahab? Don't you know you can have anything you want. Awww, get out of my way, I'll handle it." Like a child, Ahab blinked from underneath his bed linens, never lifting a finger to stop the murder of Naboth, an innocent man. And when the deed was done, Ahab arose unashamedly to claim what wasn't his.

Observe God's response at this juncture in the lives of Ahab and Jezebel. He had seen enough. It was time to put a halt to this madness. Through the mouth of the prophet Elijah, God declared his intentions for this wicked couple; He uttered prophecies that would surely be fulfilled: "I am going to bring disaster on you. I will consume your descendants and cut off from Ahab every last male in Israel . . . And also concerning Jezebel the Lord says: 'Dogs will devour Jezebel by the wall of Jezreel' " (21:21,23).

Often in Scripture we find humans embraced in God's grace. As the psalmist wrote, God "knows how we are formed, he remembers that we are dust" (Psalm 103:14). He knows that we are imperfect. In light of that, He stands always ready to forgive, to reinstate, to reinvest in the relationship. But these stories of wicked King Ahab and Queen Jezebel tell us that there is a point at which God will allow evil to go no further, and no human being knows what that point is. The wisdom of Solomon with which we began this profile on Ahab and Jezebel is wisdom for us: Those who stubbornly refuse to listen to God's voice *will* meet with God's judgment. It's a warning all of us would do well to heed.

place.' But he said, 'I will not give you my vineyard.'"

7 Jezebel his wife said, "Is this how you act as king over Israel? Get up and eat! Cheer up. I'll get you the vineyard of Naboth the Jezreelite."

8 So she wrote letters in Ahab's name, placed his seal on them, and sent them to the elders and nobles who lived in Naboth's city with him. 9 In those letters she wrote: Ge 38:18; Est 3:12; 8:8,10

> "Proclaim a day of fasting and seat Naboth in a prominent place among the people. 10 But seat two scoundrels opposite him and have them testify that he has cursed both God and the king. Then take him out and stone him to death." Ac 6:11; Ex 22:28; Lev 24:15-16

11 So the elders and nobles who lived in Naboth's city did as Jezebel directed in the letters she had written to them. 12 They proclaimed a fast and seated Naboth in a prominent place among the people. 13 Then two scoundrels came and sat opposite him and brought charges against Naboth before the people, saying, "Naboth has cursed both God and the king." So they took him outside the city and stoned him to death. 14 Then they sent word to Jezebel: "Naboth has been stoned and is dead." 2Ki 9:26; Isa 58:4

15 As soon as Jezebel heard that Naboth had been stoned to death, she said to Ahab, "Get up and take possession of the vineyard of Naboth the Jezreelite that he refused to sell you. He is no longer alive, but dead." 16 When Ahab heard that Naboth was dead, he got up and went down to take possession of Naboth's vineyard. 1Sa 8:14

17 Then the word of the LORD came to Elijah the Tishbite: 18 "Go down to meet Ahab king of Israel, who rules in Samaria. He is now in Naboth's vineyard, where he has gone to take possession of it. 19 Say to him, 'This is what the LORD says: Have you not murdered a man and seized his property?' Then say to him, 'This is what the LORD says: In the place where dogs licked up Naboth's blood, dogs will lick up your blood—yes, yours!'" 1Ki 22:38

20 Ahab said to Elijah, "So you have found me, my enemy!" 1Ki 18:17

"I have found you," he answered, "because you have sold yourself to do evil in the eyes of the LORD. 21 'I am going to bring disaster on you. I will consume your descendants and cut off from Ahab every last male in Israel—slave or free. 22 I will make your house like that of Jeroboam son of Nebat and that of Baasha son of Ahijah, because you have provoked me to anger and have caused Israel to sin.' 1Ki 12:30; 14:10; 15:29

23 "And also concerning Jezebel the LORD says: 'Dogs will devour Jezebel by the wall of[a] Jezreel.'

24 "Dogs will eat those belonging to Ahab who die in the city, and the birds of the air will feed on those who die in the country." 1Ki 14:11; 16:4

25 (There was never a man like Ahab, who sold himself to do evil in the eyes of the LORD, urged on by Jezebel his wife. 26 He behaved in the vilest manner by going after idols, like the Amorites the LORD drove out before Israel.) Ge 15:16; 1Ki 16:33

27 When Ahab heard these words, he tore his clothes, put on sackcloth and fasted. He lay in sackcloth and went around meekly. Ge 37:34; 2Sa 3:31

28 Then the word of the LORD came to Elijah the Tishbite: 29 "Have you noticed how Ahab has humbled himself before me? Because he has humbled himself, I will not bring this disaster in his day, but I will bring it on his house in the days of his son."

Micaiah Prophesies Against Ahab

22 For three years there was no war between Aram and Israel. 2 But in the third year Jehoshaphat king of Judah went down to see the king of Israel. 3 The king of Israel had said to his officials, "Don't you know that Ramoth Gilead belongs to us and yet we are doing nothing to retake it from the king of Aram?" Dt 4:43; Jos 21:38

4 So he asked Jehoshaphat, "Will you go with me to fight against Ramoth Gilead?" 2Ki 3:7

Jehoshaphat replied to the king of Israel, "I am as you are, my people as your people, my horses as your horses." 5 But Jehoshaphat also said to the king of Israel, "First seek the counsel of the LORD."

6 So the king of Israel brought together the prophets—about four hundred men—and asked them, "Shall I go to war against Ramoth Gilead, or shall I refrain?"

"Go," they answered, "for the Lord will give it into the king's hand." 1Ki 18:19

7 But Jehoshaphat asked, "Is there not a prophet of the LORD here whom we can inquire of?"

8 The king of Israel answered Jehoshaphat, "There is still one man through whom we can inquire of the LORD, but I hate him because he never prophesies anything good about me, but always bad. He is Micaiah son of Imlah." Isa 5:20

"The king should not say that," Jehoshaphat replied.

9 So the king of Israel called one of his officials and said, "Bring Micaiah son of Imlah at once."

10 Dressed in their royal robes, the king of Israel and Jehoshaphat king of Judah were sitting on their thrones at the threshing floor by the entrance of the gate of Samaria, with all the prophets prophesying before them. 11 Now Zedekiah son of Kenaanah had made iron horns and he declared, "This is what the LORD says: 'With these you will gore the Arameans until they are destroyed.'" Dt 33:17

[a] *23* Most Hebrew manuscripts; a few Hebrew manuscripts, Vulgate and Syriac (see also 2 Kings 9:26) *the plot of ground at*

12 All the other prophets were prophesying the same thing. "Attack Ramoth Gilead and be victorious," they said, "for the LORD will give it into the king's hand."

13 The messenger who had gone to summon Micaiah said to him, "Look, as one man the other prophets are predicting success for the king. Let your word agree with theirs, and speak favorably."

14 But Micaiah said, "As surely as the LORD lives, I can tell him only what the LORD tells me."

15 When he arrived, the king asked him, "Micaiah, shall we go to war against Ramoth Gilead, or shall I refrain?"

"Attack and be victorious," he answered, "for the LORD will give it into the king's hand."

16 The king said to him, "How many times must I make you swear to tell me nothing but the truth in the name of the LORD?"

17 Then Micaiah answered, "I saw all Israel scattered on the hills like sheep without a shepherd, and the LORD said, 'These people have no master. Let each one go home in peace.'" Nu 27:17; Mt 9:36

18 The king of Israel said to Jehoshaphat, "Didn't I tell you that he never prophesies anything good about me, but only bad?"

19 Micaiah continued, "Therefore hear the word of the LORD: I saw the LORD sitting on his throne with all the host of heaven standing around him on his right and on his left. 20 And the LORD said, 'Who will entice Ahab into attacking Ramoth Gilead and going to his death there?' Job 1:6; Isa 6:1

"One suggested this, and another that. 21 Finally, a spirit came forward, stood before the LORD and said, 'I will entice him.'

22 " 'By what means?' the LORD asked.

" 'I will go out and be a lying spirit in the mouths of all his prophets,' he said. Jdg 9:23

" 'You will succeed in enticing him,' said the LORD. 'Go and do it.'

23 "So now the LORD has put a lying spirit in the mouths of all these prophets of yours. The LORD has decreed disaster for you." Eze 14:9

24 Then Zedekiah son of Kenaanah went up and slapped Micaiah in the face. "Which way did the spirit from[a] the LORD go when he went from me to speak to you?" he asked. ver 11; Ac 23:2

25 Micaiah replied, "You will find out on the day you go to hide in an inner room." 1Ki 20:30

26 The king of Israel then ordered, "Take Micaiah and send him back to Amon the ruler of the city and to Joash the king's son 27 and say, 'This is what the king says: Put this fellow in prison and give him nothing but bread and water until I return safely.'" 2Ch 16:10

28 Micaiah declared, "If you ever return safely, the LORD has not spoken through me." Then he added, "Mark my words, all you people!"

Ahab Killed at Ramoth Gilead

29 So the king of Israel and Jehoshaphat king of Judah went up to Ramoth Gilead. 30 The king of Israel said to Jehoshaphat, "I will enter the battle in disguise, but you wear your royal robes." So the king of Israel disguised himself and went into battle. 2Ch 35:32

31 Now the king of Aram had ordered his thirty-two chariot commanders, "Do not fight with anyone, small or great, except the king of Israel." 32 When the chariot commanders saw Jehoshaphat, they thought, "Surely this is the king of Israel." So they turned to attack him, but when Jehoshaphat cried out, 33 the chariot commanders saw that he was not the king of Israel and stopped pursuing him. 2Sa 17:2

34 But someone drew his bow at random and hit the king of Israel between the sections of his armor. The king told his chariot driver, "Wheel around and get me out of the fighting. I've been wounded." 35 All day long the battle raged, and the king was propped up in his chariot facing the Arameans. The blood from his wound ran onto the floor of the chariot, and that evening he died. 36 As the sun was setting, a cry spread through the army: "Every man to his town; everyone to his land!"

37 So the king died and was brought to Samaria, and they buried him there. 38 They washed the chariot at a pool in Samaria (where the prostitutes bathed),[b] and the dogs licked up his blood, as the word of the LORD had declared. 1Ki 21:19

39 As for the other events of Ahab's reign, including all he did, the palace he built and inlaid with ivory, and the cities he fortified, are they not written in the book of the annals of the kings of Israel? 40 Ahab rested with his fathers. And Ahaziah his son succeeded him as king. 2Ch 9:17; Am 3:15

Jehoshaphat King of Judah

41 Jehoshaphat son of Asa became king of Judah in the fourth year of Ahab king of Israel. 42 Jehoshaphat was thirty-five years old when he became king, and he reigned in Jerusalem twenty-five years. His mother's name was Azubah daughter of Shilhi. 43 In everything he walked in the ways of his father Asa and did not stray from them; he did what was right in the eyes of the LORD. The high places, however, were not removed, and the people continued to offer sacrifices and burn incense there. 44 Jehoshaphat was also at peace with the king of Israel. 1Ki 15:14; 2Ki 12:3; 2Ch 17:3

45 As for the other events of Jehoshaphat's reign,

[a] 24 Or *Spirit of* [b] 38 Or *Samaria and cleaned the weapons*

the things he achieved and his military exploits,
are they not written in the book of the annals of
the kings of Judah? 46He rid the land of the rest of
the male shrine prostitutes who remained there
even after the reign of his father Asa. 47There was
then no king in Edom; a deputy ruled. 2Sa 8:14

48Now Jehoshaphat built a fleet of trading
ships[a] to go to Ophir for gold, but they never set
sail—they were wrecked at Ezion Geber. 49At that
time Ahaziah son of Ahab said to Jehoshaphat,
"Let my men sail with your men," but Jehoshaphat
refused. 1Ki 9:26

50Then Jehoshaphat rested with his fathers and
was buried with them in the city of David his
father. And Jehoram his son succeeded him.

Ahaziah King of Israel

51Ahaziah son of Ahab became king of Israel in
Samaria in the seventeenth year of Jehoshaphat
king of Judah, and he reigned over Israel two
years. 52He did evil in the eyes of the LORD, because
he walked in the ways of his father and mother and
in the ways of Jeroboam son of Nebat, who caused
Israel to sin. 53He served and worshiped Baal and
provoked the LORD, the God of Israel, to anger,
just as his father had done. 1Ki 15:26; 16:30-32

[a]48 Hebrew *of ships of Tarshish*

INTRODUCTION

2 KINGS

Rough Road Ahead! Have you ever come across that sign on the side of the road? Very likely there were potholes and craters ahead—perhaps the result of a slow, silent, steady process of erosion and inattention. That destruction didn't happen overnight—and neither did the destruction of the kingdoms whose histories are recorded in the book of 2 Kings. Erosion in the form of rebellion and disobedience was doing its dastardly deed to the people of God. Underneath the surface of their daily lives, look at what was forming: potholes of idolatry and pride; ever-widening cracks of immorality; and finally collapse and captivity. The tragic story of the decline and fall of the northern kingdom of Israel and the southern kingdom of Judah—it's all here in the book of 2 Kings. By the three-quarter mark in the book the northern kingdom had fallen, and as the book ends, the people of Judah were carried off to foreign lands. The effect of erosion had run its course—from compromise to captivity.

WRITER: *Unknown*

DATE: *c.560–550 B.C.*

PURPOSE: *To record the downfall of the northern and southern kingdoms*

KEY MESSAGE: *Persistent sin may be forgiven, but its consequences can't be erased*

KEY VERSES: *17:1-18; 25:1-11*

TIME LINE 1400BC 1300 1200 1100 1000 900 800 700 600 500 400

Division of the kingdom (930 B.C.)

Elijah's ministry in Israel (c.875-848 B.C.)

Elisha's ministry in Israel (c.848-797 B.C.)

Exile of Israel (722 B.C.)

Hezekiah's reign (715-686 B.C.)

Fall of Jerusalem (586 B.C.)

King Jehoiachin released from prison (c.561 B.C.)

Book of 2 Kings written (c.560-550 B.C.)

Compromise to Captivity

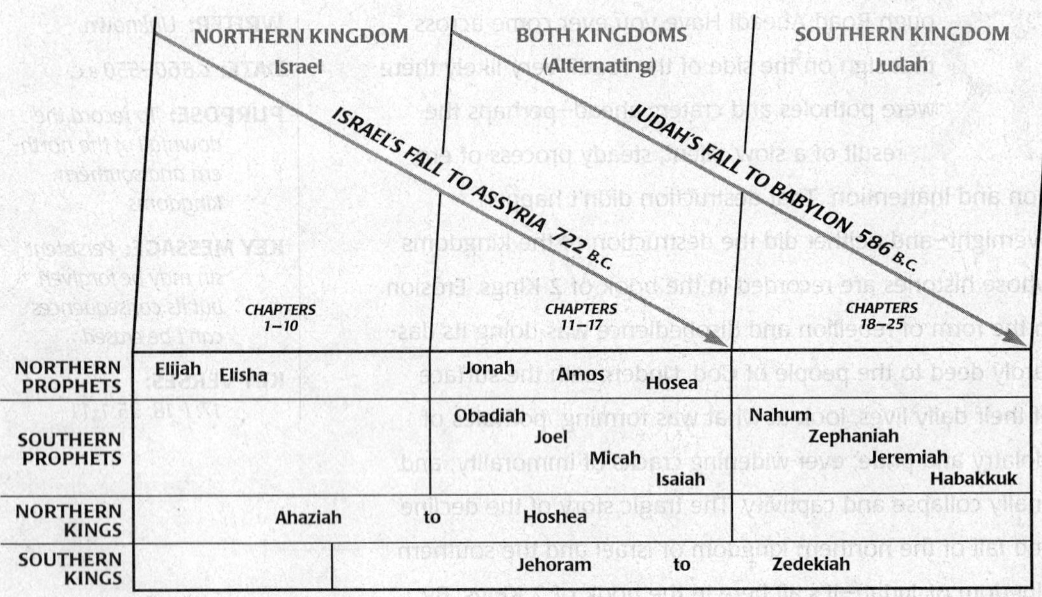

NORTHERN KINGDOM
Israel
BOTH KINGDOMS
(Alternating)
SOUTHERN KINGDOM
Judah
ISRAEL'S FALL TO ASSYRIA 722 B.C.
JUDAH'S FALL TO BABYLON 586 B.C.
CHAPTERS 1–10
CHAPTERS 11–17
CHAPTERS 18–25
NORTHERN PROPHETS
Elijah
Elisha
Jonah
Amos
Hosea
SOUTHERN PROPHETS
Obadiah
Joel
Micah
Isaiah
Nahum
Zephaniah
Jeremiah
Habakkuk
NORTHERN KINGS
Ahaziah
to
Hoshea
SOUTHERN KINGS
Jehoram
to
Zedekiah

The book of 2 Kings revolves around a principle in life that God Himself will not violate. Even though it's a principle consistently in operation, we tend to ignore it; even though it is painful to endure its application, we tend to deny it. It is this: *Persistent sin may be forgiven, but its consequences will not be erased*. Spiritually, our sins may be washed away, but often we continue to bear the earthly and painful reminder of those sins.

Let's hear from the lips of a man named Eliphaz in Job 4:8, who stated this principle succinctly and scrupulously: "As I have observed, those who plow evil and those who sow trouble reap it." Note the application of the language of agriculture to the actions of our lives. It's the planting of a different kind of seed that is in view here—the sowing of the seed of habitual, perpetual sin. The one who sows it and irrigates it is the same one who will harvest it. It's one of those laws of the harvest you cannot ignore or erase. Make a mental note of Eliphaz's words, and then look to see it illustrated in a prolonged and potent fashion in 2 Kings—a book about the consequences of sin.

A Tragedy of Biblical Proportions

In the book of 2 Kings we should not be surprised to find calamity, tragedy, demonism, death, heartache, sorrow, desolation, compromise and, ultimately, the decline of two great powers that should never been divided in the first place. In 2 Kings we pick up the story midstream.

If we want to read a couple of verses to give the feeling of the book, we do well to pause at the first two verses in the book:

After Ahab's death, Moab rebelled against Israel. Now Ahaziah had fallen through the lattice of his upper room in Samaria and injured himself. So he sent messengers, saying to them, "Go and consult Baal-Zebub, the god of Ekron, to see if I will recover from this injury"(1:1–2).

We're hardly into the book before we're encountering rebellion, spiritism, demonism, death and calamity. Unfortunately, it's only a preview of coming attractions.

Warning Signs

By turning back to 1 Kings 11:9–11 we discover what will await us in 2 Kings. Here is the record of God's judgment against Solomon: "Since this is your attitude and you have not kept my covenant and my decrees, which I commanded you, I will most certainly tear the kingdom away from you and give it to one of your subordinates" (11:11). A little later in that chapter we read of God's intention to create a divided kingdom. As we read in 1 Kings, a civil war did in fact split the nation. Some of the tribes went up to the north and established a headquarters in the place called Samaria. This capital of Israel stood for 208 years, until 722 B.C., when the kingdom fell into the hands of the Assyrians.

Take special note of the fact that in over 200 years of the northern kingdom's existence, *not one* of the 19 monarchs was godly. And in the more than 340 years of the southern kingdom's existence, *only eight* rulers walked with God, some of those inconsistently. The book of 2 Kings is a visible and tangible reminder that God meant what He said when He spoke of punishing the children for the sin of the fathers to the third and fourth generation (see Deuteronomy 5:9).

Two Kingdoms and Two Prophets

The structure of 2 Kings is rather complicated for two reasons: First, the book traces two kingdoms without clearly announcing which one is being referred to, and second, it includes the ministry of prophets intermingled with the account of the kings. I have, however, identified three rather evenly divided sections. *Chapters 1–10* seem to emphasize the northern kingdom and its decline. In *chapters 11–17* the writer alternates between the two kingdoms—and by the end of chapter 17 we read of the demise of the northern kingdom. In *chapters 18–25* we find a record of the demise of the southern kingdom.

It is important to note that 2 Kings begins with an extended emphasis on two prophets. First, 2 Kings continues the record of Elijah's ministry, and second, the book chronicles Elisha's ministry. (Try not to confuse the two prophets. Their names are similar . . . but Elijah came first, then Elisha.) Very early in the book, Elijah concluded his work among the people of the northern kingdom. After Elijah was caught up into heaven (2:11), Elisha carried on the work of a prophet, remaining a thorn in the side of the kings as he called the people back to the worship of the one true God. Elisha's death is recorded in chapter 13.

As this first two sections of 2 Kings unfold, listen for the steady drumbeat of decline in both northern and southern kingdoms. As we read its pages, we note a constant theme of murder, deceit, intrigue, idolatry and total insensitivity toward the Lord. There were no bright spots on the canvas of the northern kingdom—and only an occasional stroke of light penetrating the gloom in the southern kingdom. God's people were in trouble—and they seemed not to notice . . . or to care. A note of interest: even though they are not mentioned in this book, there were three other prophets of significance during the dreadful years described in 2 Kings: Jonah, Amos and Hosea. The Bible books that bear their names tell their stories.

In chapters 18–25 the focus became riveted on Judah. As chapter 18 began, there was a whiff of hope in the air. Reform under Hezekiah looked promising. But look a little more closely at what happened. It is important to study the three generations of kings described in this section: First, *Ahaz* was 20 years old when he became king. He reigned for 16 years. Ahaz did evil in the eyes of the Lord (16:2). Second, *Hezekiah* was 25 years old when he became king, and he reigned for 29 years. He did what was right in the eyes of the Lord (18:5). Ever since the age of nine he had been under the influence of an ungodly father. But nonetheless, he led a reformation. He was an unparalleled godly model. Third, *Manasseh* was only 12 when he took the throne. He became the antithesis, the direct opposite, of his father. He was permitted to outlive all other kings of Judah. He reigned as king for 55 years (21:1–2).

No Promises

I'm going to make a statement that may disturb some who prefer strict, predictable, hard-and-fast formulas for living: *There is no absolute guarantee when it comes to rearing a child.* Prodigals with bents toward evil are born into godly families, just as children with a love for spiritual things are born into godless families. How else could anyone explain Hezekiah coming from a father like Ahaz? Or Manasseh coming from a father like Hezekiah? As much as we would love to have airtight assurance that if we only use this or that parenting method, everything will turn out right—we simply cannot have that assurance. I can't tell you why prodigals are, on occasion, the products of godly parents—just as I cannot explain how children who love the Lord sometimes come from homes that are woefully weak spiritually. This reality makes us all the more dependent on the Lord for His grace and power to work in the lives of our children.

Some have come from homes that didn't provide helpful, solid models of what the Christian life is all about. And the only thing you can claim, since you didn't learn it from your parents, was that your faith in Jesus Christ came by the sovereign and gracious hand of your heavenly Father, who overruled the odds. That reality may explain why it happens in some families that two of the four children can be bent in the direction of rejection of faith in Jesus, and two of them love Jesus and desire to walk in His ways. It may explain why your brothers and sisters are different from you. It is the mix of bents that has been given to each. If you are a parent, let me simply encourage you to do all in your power to battle the wrong and cultivate the right. Do all you can to point your children in the direction of Jesus Christ. Let your love and your faith be evident to them. Walk your talk . . . and then leave the results to God.

The Fall of the Southern Kingdom

Finally, according to chapter 25, the kingdom of Judah fell into the hands of the Babylonians. In spite of the faithful ministries of men like Obadiah, Joel, Isaiah, Micah, Habakkuk, Nahum, Zephaniah and Jeremiah (for a fascinating account of the times described in 2 Kings, read the Bible books that bear their names), the nation fell to Babylon. How the mighty had fallen! One of the psalms describes the awful scene of a captured people (take a good look at Psalm 137:1–3):

> *By the rivers of Babylon we sat and wept*
> *when we remembered Zion.*
> *There on the poplars*
> *we hung our harps,*
> *for there our captors asked us for songs,*
> *our tormentors demanded songs of joy;*
> *they said, "Sing us one of the songs of Zion!"*

And so it was . . . a living, vivid reminder that persistent sin pays a dreadful wage. Sins may be forgiven, but their consequences are not easily erased!

United They Stood, Divided They Fell

The Israelites were never stronger than when they comprised a united kingdom under David's rule and then during the early reign of Solomon. The slide down the slippery slope toward destruction began when they selfishly and stubbornly took up arms against themselves and split the kingdom with a civil war. The rest, as they say, is history. The northern tribes fell first to Assyria in 722 B.C. Later, the southern kingdom fell into Babylonian hands in 586 B.C.

J. Sidlow Baxter's words are sad, but true: "We cannot read 2 Kings without thinking of Solomon's proverb: 'The way of the unfaithful is hard' [Proverbs 13:15]. Paul's words, 'the wages of sin is death' [Romans 6:23], are here demonstrated on a national scale and clearly declared in terms of poetic justice for all to see and heed. Sinning despite warning brings ruin without remedy. Inexcusable wrong brings inescapable wrath. Abused privilege incurs increased penalty. The deeper the guilt the heavier the stroke. Correction may be resisted, but retribution cannot be evaded. All these thoughts crowd into our minds when we read 2 Kings—as we see the battered, broken tribes of Israel and Judah dragged behind the chariots of their pagan conquerors. We cannot fail to see the book's central message: Willful sin brings a woeful end."

Viewing the Northern Kingdom Chapters 1–10

Although 2 Kings focuses on both the northern and southern kingdoms, the first ten chapters zoom in primarily on the nation of Israel and the ten tribes that had made Samaria their new capital to the north. Note that the opening chapters of this dismal book emphasize two prophets: Elijah, and his successor, Elisha. Elijah prophesied to the northern kingdom and in many ways was a pain in the neck of the rulers of Israel. Elisha took up the mantle and carried on the prophetic work of calling the nation back to God. These chapters record many powerful miracles of God and chronicle His constant efforts to win back the hearts of His people and save them from the imminent disaster that would result from their rebellious ways.

The LORD's Judgment on Ahaziah

1 After Ahab's death, Moab rebelled against Israel. [2]Now Ahaziah had fallen through the
lattice of his upper room in Samaria and injured
himself. So he sent messengers, saying to them,
"Go and consult Baal-Zebub, the god of Ekron, to
see if I will recover from this injury." 2Sa 8:2
[3]But the angel of the LORD said to Elijah the
Tishbite, "Go up and meet the messengers of the
king of Samaria and ask them, 'Is it because there
is no God in Israel that you are going off to consult
Baal-Zebub, the god of Ekron?' [4]Therefore this is
what the LORD says: 'You will not leave the bed you
are lying on. You will certainly die!' " So Elijah
went. Ge 16:7; 1Ki 17:1
[5]When the messengers returned to the king, he
asked them, "Why have you come back?"
[6]"A man came to meet us," they replied. "And
he said to us, 'Go back to the king who sent you
and tell him, "This is what the LORD says: Is it
because there is no God in Israel that you are
sending men to consult Baal-Zebub, the god of
Ekron? Therefore you will not leave the bed you
are lying on. You will certainly die!" ' "
[7]The king asked them, "What kind of man was
it who came to meet you and told you this?"
[8]They replied, "He was a man with a garment of
hair and with a leather belt around his waist."
The king said, "That was Elijah the Tishbite."
[9]Then he sent to Elijah a captain with his company of fifty men. The captain went up to Elijah,
who was sitting on the top of a hill, and said to
him, "Man of God, the king says, 'Come down!' "
[10]Elijah answered the captain, "If I am a man of
God, may fire come down from heaven and consume you and your fifty men!" Then fire fell from
heaven and consumed the captain and his men.
[11]At this the king sent to Elijah another captain
with his fifty men. The captain said to him, "Man
of God, this is what the king says, 'Come down at
once!' "
[12]"If I am a man of God," Elijah replied, "may
fire come down from heaven and consume you
and your fifty men!" Then the fire of God fell from
heaven and consumed him and his fifty men.
[13]So the king sent a third captain with his fifty
men. This third captain went up and fell on his
knees before Elijah. "Man of God," he begged,
"please have respect for my life and the lives of
these fifty men, your servants! [14]See, fire has fallen
from heaven and consumed the first two captains
and all their men. But now have respect for my
life!" 1Sa 26:21; Ps 72:14
[15]The angel of the LORD said to Elijah, "Go
down with him; do not be afraid of him." So Elijah
got up and went down with him to the king.
[16]He told the king, "This is what the LORD says:
Is it because there is no God in Israel for you to
consult that you have sent messengers to consult
Baal-Zebub, the god of Ekron? Because you have
done this, you will never leave the bed you are
lying on. You will certainly die!" [17]So he died,
according to the word of the LORD that Elijah had
spoken. 2Ki 8:15; Jer 20:6; 28:17
Because Ahaziah had no son, Joram[a] succeeded him as king in the second year of Jehoram son
of Jehoshaphat king of Judah. [18]As for all the other
events of Ahaziah's reign, and what he did, are
they not written in the book of the annals of the
kings of Israel? 2Ki 3:1; 8:16

Elijah Taken Up to Heaven

2 When the LORD was about to take Elijah up to
heaven in a whirlwind, Elijah and Elisha were
on their way from Gilgal. [2]Elijah said to Elisha,
"Stay here; the LORD has sent me to Bethel."
But Elisha said, "As surely as the LORD lives and
as you live, I will not leave you." So they went
down to Bethel. Ru 1:16; 1Sa 1:26
[3]The company of the prophets at Bethel came
out to Elisha and asked, "Do you know that the
LORD is going to take your master from you today?" 1Sa 10:5; 2Ki 4:1,38
"Yes, I know," Elisha replied, "but do not speak
of it."
[4]Then Elijah said to him, "Stay here, Elisha; the
LORD has sent me to Jericho." Jos 3:16; 6:26
And he replied, "As surely as the LORD lives and
as you live, I will not leave you." So they went to
Jericho.
[5]The company of the prophets at Jericho went
up to Elisha and asked him, "Do you know that
the LORD is going to take your master from you
today?"
"Yes, I know," he replied, "but do not speak
of it."
[6]Then Elijah said to him, "Stay here; the LORD
has sent me to the Jordan." Jos 3:15
And he replied, "As surely as the LORD lives and

[a]17 Hebrew *Jehoram,* a variant of *Joram*

as you live, I will not leave you." So the two of them walked on. Ru 1:16

7Fifty men of the company of the prophets went and stood at a distance, facing the place where Elijah and Elisha had stopped at the Jordan. 8Elijah took his cloak, rolled it up and struck the water with it. The water divided to the right and to the left, and the two of them crossed over on dry ground. Ex 14:21-22,29; 1Ki 19:19

9When they had crossed, Elijah said to Elisha, "Tell me, what can I do for you before I am taken from you?"

"Let me inherit a double portion of your spirit," Elisha replied. Nu 11:17; Dt 21:17

10"You have asked a difficult thing," Elijah said, "yet if you see me when I am taken from you, it will be yours—otherwise not."

11As they were walking along and talking together, suddenly a chariot of fire and horses of fire appeared and separated the two of them, and Elijah went up to heaven in a whirlwind. 12Elisha saw this and cried out, "My father! My father! The chariots and horsemen of Israel!" And Elisha saw him no more. Then he took hold of his own clothes and tore them apart. Ge 5:24; 2Ki 13:14

13He picked up the cloak that had fallen from Elijah and went back and stood on the bank of the Jordan. 14Then he took the cloak that had fallen from him and struck the water with it. "Where now is the LORD, the God of Elijah?" he asked. When he struck the water, it divided to the right and to the left, and he crossed over. 1Ki 19:19

15The company of the prophets from Jericho, who were watching, said, "The spirit of Elijah is resting on Elisha." And they went to meet him and bowed to the ground before him. 16"Look," they said, "we your servants have fifty able men. Let them go and look for your master. Perhaps the Spirit of the LORD has picked him up and set him down on some mountain or in some valley."

"No," Elisha replied, "do not send them."

17But they persisted until he was too ashamed to refuse. So he said, "Send them." And they sent fifty men, who searched for three days but did not find him. 18When they returned to Elisha, who was staying in Jericho, he said to them, "Didn't I tell you not to go?" 2Ki 8:11

Healing of the Water

19The men of the city said to Elisha, "Look, our lord, this town is well situated, as you can see, but the water is bad and the land is unproductive."

20"Bring me a new bowl," he said, "and put salt in it." So they brought it to him.

21Then he went out to the spring and threw the salt into it, saying, "This is what the LORD says: 'I have healed this water. Never again will it cause death or make the land unproductive.'" 22And the water has remained wholesome to this day, according to the word Elisha had spoken. Ex 15:25

Elisha Is Jeered

23From there Elisha went up to Bethel. As he was walking along the road, some youths came out of the town and jeered at him. "Go on up, you baldhead!" they said. "Go on up, you baldhead!" 24He turned around, looked at them and called down a curse on them in the name of the LORD. Then two bears came out of the woods and mauled forty-two of the youths. 25And he went on to Mount Carmel and from there returned to Samaria. 1Ki 18:20; Ge 4:11; Ne 13:25-27

Moab Revolts

3 Joram[a] son of Ahab became king of Israel in Samaria in the eighteenth year of Jehoshaphat king of Judah, and he reigned twelve years. 2He did evil in the eyes of the LORD, but not as his father and mother had done. He got rid of the sacred stone of Baal that his father had made. 3Nevertheless he clung to the sins of Jeroboam son of Nebat, which he had caused Israel to commit; he did not turn away from them. 1Ki 12:28-32; 14:9,16

4Now Mesha king of Moab raised sheep, and he had to supply the king of Israel with a hundred thousand lambs and with the wool of a hundred thousand rams. 5But after Ahab died, the king of Moab rebelled against the king of Israel. 6So at that time King Joram set out from Samaria and mobilized all Israel. 7He also sent this message to Jehoshaphat king of Judah: "The king of Moab has rebelled against me. Will you go with me to fight against Moab?" 1Ki 22:4; 2Ki 1:1; Isa 16:1

"I will go with you," he replied. "I am as you are, my people as your people, my horses as your horses."

8"By what route shall we attack?" he asked.

"Through the Desert of Edom," he answered.

9So the king of Israel set out with the king of Judah and the king of Edom. After a roundabout march of seven days, the army had no more water for themselves or for the animals with them.

10"What!" exclaimed the king of Israel. "Has the LORD called us three kings together only to hand us over to Moab?"

11But Jehoshaphat asked, "Is there no prophet of the LORD here, that we may inquire of the LORD through him?" 1Ki 22:7

An officer of the king of Israel answered, "Elisha son of Shaphat is here. He used to pour water on the hands of Elijah.[b]" Ge 20:7; 1Ki 19:16

12Jehoshaphat said, "The word of the LORD is with him." So the king of Israel and Jehoshaphat and the king of Edom went down to him.

[a] 1 Hebrew *Jehoram,* a variant of *Joram;* also in verse 6

[b] 11 That is, he was Elijah's personal servant.

13Elisha said to the king of Israel, "What do we have to do with each other? Go to the prophets of your father and the prophets of your mother."

"No," the king of Israel answered, "because it was the LORD who called us three kings together to hand us over to Moab."

14Elisha said, "As surely as the LORD Almighty lives, whom I serve, if I did not have respect for the presence of Jehoshaphat king of Judah, I would not look at you or even notice you. 15But now bring me a harpist." 1Sa 16:23

While the harpist was playing, the hand of the LORD came upon Elisha 16and he said, "This is what the LORD says: Make this valley full of ditches. 17For this is what the LORD says: You will see neither wind nor rain, yet this valley will be filled with water, and you, your cattle and your other animals will drink. 18This is an easy thing in the eyes of the LORD; he will also hand Moab over to you. 19You will overthrow every fortified city and every major town. You will cut down every good tree, stop up all the springs, and ruin every good field with stones." Ge 18:14; Jer 32:17,27

20The next morning, about the time for offering the sacrifice, there it was—water flowing from the direction of Edom! And the land was filled with water. Ex 29:39-40

21Now all the Moabites had heard that the kings had come to fight against them; so every man, young and old, who could bear arms was called up and stationed on the border. 22When they got up early in the morning, the sun was shining on the water. To the Moabites across the way, the water looked red—like blood. 23"That's blood!" they said. "Those kings must have fought and slaughtered each other. Now to the plunder, Moab!"

24But when the Moabites came to the camp of Israel, the Israelites rose up and fought them until they fled. And the Israelites invaded the land and slaughtered the Moabites. 25They destroyed the towns, and each man threw a stone on every good field until it was covered. They stopped up all the springs and cut down every good tree. Only Kir Hareseth was left with its stones in place, but men armed with slings surrounded it and attacked it as well. Isa 16:7; Jer 48:31,36; Eze 1:3

26When the king of Moab saw that the battle had gone against him, he took with him seven hundred swordsmen to break through to the king of Edom, but they failed. 27Then he took his firstborn son, who was to succeed him as king, and offered him as a sacrifice on the city wall. The fury against Israel was great; they withdrew and returned to their own land. Am 2:1; Mic 6:7

The Widow's Oil

4 The wife of a man from the company of the prophets cried out to Elisha, "Your servant my husband is dead, and you know that he revered the LORD. But now his creditor is coming to take my two boys as his slaves." Lev 25:39-43; Ne 5:3-5

2Elisha replied to her, "How can I help you? Tell me, what do you have in your house?"

"Your servant has nothing there at all," she said, "except a little oil." 1Ki 17:12

3Elisha said, "Go around and ask all your neighbors for empty jars. Don't ask for just a few. 4Then go inside and shut the door behind you and your sons. Pour oil into all the jars, and as each is filled, put it to one side."

5She left him and afterward shut the door behind her and her sons. They brought the jars to her and she kept pouring. 6When all the jars were full, she said to her son, "Bring me another one."

But he replied, "There is not a jar left." Then the oil stopped flowing.

7She went and told the man of God, and he said, "Go, sell the oil and pay your debts. You and your sons can live on what is left." 1Ki 12:22

The Shunammite's Son Restored to Life

8One day Elisha went to Shunem. And a well-to-do woman was there, who urged him to stay for a meal. So whenever he came by, he stopped there to eat. 9She said to her husband, "I know that this man who often comes our way is a holy man of God. 10Let's make a small room on the roof and put in it a bed and a table, a chair and a lamp for him. Then he can stay there whenever he comes to us." Jos 19:18; Mt 10:41; Ro 12:13

11One day when Elisha came, he went up to his room and lay down there. 12He said to his servant Gehazi, "Call the Shunammite." So he called her, and she stood before him. 13Elisha said to him, "Tell her, 'You have gone to all this trouble for us. Now what can be done for you? Can we speak on your behalf to the king or the commander of the army?'" 2Ki 8:1

She replied, "I have a home among my own people."

14"What can be done for her?" Elisha asked.

Gehazi said, "Well, she has no son and her husband is old."

15Then Elisha said, "Call her." So he called her, and she stood in the doorway. 16"About this time next year," Elisha said, "you will hold a son in your arms." Ge 18:10

"No, my lord," she objected. "Don't mislead your servant, O man of God!"

17But the woman became pregnant, and the next year about that same time she gave birth to a son, just as Elisha had told her.

18The child grew, and one day he went out to his father, who was with the reapers. 19"My head! My head!" he said to his father. Ru 2:3

His father told a servant, "Carry him to his mother." 20After the servant had lifted him up and

MIRACLES OF THE OLD TESTAMENT

Miracle	Reference
Burning bush	*Exodus 3:1-14*
Rod becoming a snake	*Exodus 4:1-5; 7:8-13*
Leprous hand	*Exodus 4:6-12*
Ten plagues	*Exodus 7:14–12:30*
Dividing of the Red Sea	*Exodus 14:21-31*
Water from the rock	*Exodus 17:1-9*
Destruction of Korah	*Numbers 16:31-35*
Aaron's staff budding	*Numbers 17:1-19*
Water from the rock in Kadesh	*Numbers 20:9-11*
Bronze snake	*Numbers 21:4-9*
Balaam's donkey	*Numbers 22:20-35*
The Jordan divided	*Joshua 3:7-17*
Fall of Jericho	*Joshua 6:1-20*
Sun standing still	*Joshua 10:1-14*
Slain lion	*Judges 14:5-10*
Dagon's temple pulled down	*Judges 16:23-30*
Thunder and rain	*1 Samuel 12:16-18*
Jeroboam's hand withered and restored	*1 Kings 13:16*
Elijah fed by ravens	*1 Kings 17:1-6*
Widow's flour and oil	*1 Kings 17:8-16*
Widow's son raised from the dead	*1 Kings 17:17-24*
Sacrifice consumed by fire	*1 Kings 18:30-39*
Rain in answer to prayer	*1 Kings 18:41-45*
The Jordan divided	*2 Kings 2:1-8*
Waters sweetened	*2 Kings 2:19-22*
Widow's oil multiplied	*2 Kings 4:1-7*
Shunammite's son restored to life	*2 Kings 4:8-37*
Poison stew rendered harmless	*2 Kings 4:38-41*
Feeding of one hundred men	*2 Kings 4:42-44*
Naaman healed of leprosy	*2 Kings 5:1-19*
Floating axhead	*2 Kings 6:1-7*
Blinded eyes	*2 Kings 6:8-23*
Dead man restored to life	*2 Kings 13:21*
Hezekiah healed	*2 Kings 20:1-7*
Three men delivered from blazing furnace	*Daniel 3:23-27*
Daniel delivered from the den of lions	*Daniel 6:10-23*
Sea stilled when Jonah cast in	*Jonah 1:15*
Jonah delivered from fish's mouth	*Jonah 2:10*
Withering of the vine	*Jonah 4:6-7*

carried him to his mother, the boy sat on her lap
until noon, and then he died. 21She went up and
laid him on the bed of the man of God, then shut
the door and went out. ver 32
22She called her husband and said, "Please send
me one of the servants and a donkey so I can go
to the man of God quickly and return."
23"Why go to him today?" he asked. "It's not
the New Moon or the Sabbath." Nu 10:10; 1Ch 23:31
"It's all right," she said.
24She saddled the donkey and said to her servant, "Lead on; don't slow down for me unless I
tell you." 25So she set out and came to the man of
God at Mount Carmel. 1Ki 18:20; 2Ki 2:25
When he saw her in the distance, the man of
God said to his servant Gehazi, "Look! There's the
Shunammite! 26Run to meet her and ask her, 'Are
you all right? Is your husband all right? Is your
child all right?'"
"Everything is all right," she said.
27When she reached the man of God at the
mountain, she took hold of his feet. Gehazi came
over to push her away, but the man of God said,
"Leave her alone! She is in bitter distress, but the
LORD has hidden it from me and has not told me
why." 1Sa 1:15
28"Did I ask you for a son, my lord?" she said.
"Didn't I tell you, 'Don't raise my hopes'?"
29Elisha said to Gehazi, "Tuck your cloak into
your belt, take my staff in your hand and run. If
you meet anyone, do not greet him, and if anyone
greets you, do not answer. Lay my staff on the
boy's face." Ex 7:19; 1Ki 18:46
30But the child's mother said, "As surely as the
LORD lives and as you live, I will not leave you." So
he got up and followed her.
31Gehazi went on ahead and laid the staff on the
boy's face, but there was no sound or response. So
Gehazi went back to meet Elisha and told him,
"The boy has not awakened."
32When Elisha reached the house, there was the
boy lying dead on his couch. 33He went in, shut the
door on the two of them and prayed to the LORD.
34Then he got on the bed and lay upon the boy,
mouth to mouth, eyes to eyes, hands to hands. As
he stretched himself out upon him, the boy's body
grew warm. 35Elisha turned away and walked back
and forth in the room and then got on the bed and
stretched out upon him once more. The boy
sneezed seven times and opened his eyes.
36Elisha summoned Gehazi and said, "Call the
Shunammite." And he did. When she came, he
said, "Take your son." 37She came in, fell at his feet
and bowed to the ground. Then she took her son
and went out. Heb 11:35

Death in the Pot

38Elisha returned to Gilgal and there was a famine in that region. While the company of the
prophets was meeting with him, he said to his
servant, "Put on the large pot and cook some stew
for these men." 2Ki 2:1; 8:1
39One of them went out into the fields to gather
herbs and found a wild vine. He gathered some of
its gourds and filled the fold of his cloak. When he
returned, he cut them up into the pot of stew,
though no one knew what they were. 40The stew
was poured out for the men, but as they began to
eat it, they cried out, "O man of God, there is
death in the pot!" And they could not eat it.
41Elisha said, "Get some flour." He put it into
the pot and said, "Serve it to the people to eat."
And there was nothing harmful in the pot.

Feeding of a Hundred

42A man came from Baal Shalishah, bringing
the man of God twenty loaves of barley bread
baked from the first ripe grain, along with some
heads of new grain. "Give it to the people to eat,"
Elisha said. 1Sa 9:4,7; Mt 14:17; 15:36
43"How can I set this before a hundred men?"
his servant asked.
But Elisha answered, "Give it to the people to
eat. For this is what the LORD says: 'They will eat
and have some left over.'" 44Then he set it before
them, and they ate and had some left over, according to the word of the LORD. Lk 9:13; Jn 6:12

Naaman Healed of Leprosy

5 Now Naaman was commander of the army of
the king of Aram. He was a great man in the
sight of his master and highly regarded, because
through him the LORD had given victory to Aram.
He was a valiant soldier, but he had leprosy.[a]
2Now bands from Aram had gone out and had
taken captive a young girl from Israel, and she
served Naaman's wife. 3She said to her mistress,
"If only my master would see the prophet who is
in Samaria! He would cure him of his leprosy."
4Naaman went to his master and told him what
the girl from Israel had said. 5"By all means, go,"
the king of Aram replied. "I will send a letter to the
king of Israel." So Naaman left, taking with him
ten talents[b] of silver, six thousand shekels[c] of
gold and ten sets of clothing. 6The letter that he
took to the king of Israel read: "With this letter I
am sending my servant Naaman to you so that you
may cure him of his leprosy." 1Sa 9:7
7As soon as the king of Israel read the letter, he
tore his robes and said, "Am I God? Can I kill and
bring back to life? Why does this fellow send

[a] 1 The Hebrew word was used for various diseases affecting the skin—not necessarily leprosy; also in verses 3, 6, 7, 11 and 27.
[b] 5 That is, about 750 pounds (about 340 kilograms) [c] 5 That is, about 150 pounds (about 70 kilograms)

NAAMAN

Taking the Plunge

"Now Naaman was commander of the army of the king of Aram. He was a great man in the sight of his master and highly regarded, because through him the LORD had given victory to Aram."

—2 KINGS 5:1

Naaman was a commander in the army of Aram, who served under the direction of his commander-in-chief, the king. He enjoyed the respect of his master, his peers and his subordinates. The Lord had given victory to the nation of Aram through this man (2 Kings 5:1). Now Naaman may not have known the Lord, the God of Israel, but God still had His hand on him. He was using this commander for some future plan. Yet Naaman's brilliant résumé shriveled under the blast of the last phrase of verse 1: "He was a valiant soldier, *but* he had leprosy" (emphasis added). This man lived the terrible "living death" of his day.

Enter a young slave girl from Israel, who had been taken captive when Naaman's army raided her land. She saw Naaman's distress. She was aware of the awful nature of his disease. And one day she came to her mistress, Naaman's wife, and told her of a prophet in Samaria who could give Naaman relief.

Naaman got the word. He was eager to go. And there's where his sin came in, the besetting sin of the unbeliever. Naaman's first thought went something like this: "I'll need to buy this cleansing." He took with him the equivalent of about $20,000 in silver and about $60,000 in gold. He also took ten sets of beautiful clothing, right from the best shops in Aram (see 5:5). *Naaman tried to do God's will his own way.*

So Naaman took his entourage—horses, chariots, foot soldiers—right to Elisha's hut in Samaria. And in all his authority and glory he hammered on the door, expecting this prophet to bow at his feet. You know, "Here's eighty grand, prophet. Do your thing. Make me clean." The prophet didn't even bother to open the door. He simply sent him a message that said, "Go, wash yourself seven times in the Jordan, and your flesh will be restored and you will be cleansed" (5:10). No purchase necessary, Naaman.

That can be a very hard pill to swallow for someone who doesn't know the Lord. After all, we buy everything else in life, why can't we buy salvation? How many people today are so tied to the commercial enterprise of buying and selling that they simply cannot seem to realize that God's gift of cleansing, of salvation, is *free*? Free! No money can purchase it. The debt has already been paid in full by Christ.

Watch carefully Naaman's reaction. He heard Elijah's message, and he threw a fit (5:11). He thought about all the power and respect that he had as a commander in the army of Aram, yet this foolish little prophet wouldn't even show his face! Then he tipped his hand: "I thought . . ." (5:11). He had it all planned out. When he spoke, people jumped! He was Naaman, after all! But God isn't impressed by human pride. God's instructions through Elisha were crystal-clear—they weren't up for debate. But Naaman wanted to change the plan—to do God's will his way. "If water is all it takes," Naaman must have thought, "then why not take a dip in our own clean, pure, beautiful rivers" (see 5:12).

It strikes me that the unbeliever lives in a world something like that. God tells him or her that there is one way to salvation, and that it comes through faith in the Lord Jesus Christ (Acts 16:31; Ephesians 2:8). But the unbeliever struggles to understand: "There must be something I can do. I earn everything else in life, after all." Follow this through now. Naaman had stalked off in a rage. But the Lord pursued him through Naaman's servants, who broke through that barrier he had erected. "The prophet's instructions are so simple," they said, in effect. "Why not just accept them?" Naaman did, and was cleansed.

If you've not yet accepted the salvation freely offered to you in Jesus Christ, this message is for you. It's a matter of joyful acceptance. And if you're a believer, never underestimate your role in the life of your seeking friends. It was, after all, an unnamed servant girl and a few anonymous servants who convinced Naaman to take the plunge. They became God's instructions who helped change his life forever.

someone to me to be cured of his leprosy? See how
he is trying to pick a quarrel with me!" Ge 30:2
8When Elisha the man of God heard that the
king of Israel had torn his robes, he sent him this
message: "Why have you torn your robes? Have
the man come to me and he will know that there
is a prophet in Israel." 9So Naaman went with his
horses and chariots and stopped at the door of
Elisha's house. 10Elisha sent a messenger to say to
him, "Go, wash yourself seven times in the Jordan,
and your flesh will be restored and you will be
cleansed." Jn 9:7; Lev 14:7; 1Ki 22:7
11But Naaman went away angry and said, "I
thought that he would surely come out to me and
stand and call on the name of the LORD his God,
wave his hand over the spot and cure me of my
leprosy. 12Are not Abana and Pharpar, the rivers
of Damascus, better than any of the waters of Israel? Couldn't I wash in them and be cleansed?" So
he turned and went off in a rage. Pr 14:17,29; 19:11
13Naaman's servants went to him and said, "My
father, if the prophet had told you to do some
great thing, would you not have done it? How
much more, then, when he tells you, 'Wash and be
cleansed'!" 14So he went down and dipped himself
in the Jordan seven times, as the man of God had
told him, and his flesh was restored and became
clean like that of a young boy. Jos 6:15; Job 33:25
15Then Naaman and all his attendants went
back to the man of God. He stood before him and
said, "Now I know that there is no God in all the
world except in Israel. Please accept now a gift
from your servant." Jos 4:24; 1Sa 17:46
16The prophet answered, "As surely as the LORD
lives, whom I serve, I will not accept a thing." And
even though Naaman urged him, he refused.
17"If you will not," said Naaman, "please let me,
your servant, be given as much earth as a pair of
mules can carry, for your servant will never again
make burnt offerings and sacrifices to any other
god but the LORD. 18But may the LORD forgive your
servant for this one thing: When my master enters
the temple of Rimmon to bow down and he is
leaning on my arm and I bow there also—when I
bow down in the temple of Rimmon, may the
LORD forgive your servant for this." Ex 20:24; 2Ki 7:2
19"Go in peace," Elisha said. 1Sa 1:17; Ac 15:33
After Naaman had traveled some distance,
20Gehazi, the servant of Elisha the man of God,
said to himself, "My master was too easy on Naaman, this Aramean, by not accepting from him
what he brought. As surely as the LORD lives, I will
run after him and get something from him."
21So Gehazi hurried after Naaman. When Naaman saw him running toward him, he got down
from the chariot to meet him. "Is everything all
right?" he asked.
22"Everything is all right," Gehazi answered.
"My master sent me to say, 'Two young men from
the company of the prophets have just come to me
from the hill country of Ephraim. Please give them
a talent[a] of silver and two sets of clothing.'"
23"By all means, take two talents," said Naaman.
He urged Gehazi to accept them, and then tied up
the two talents of silver in two bags, with two sets
of clothing. He gave them to two of his servants,
and they carried them ahead of Gehazi. 24When
Gehazi came to the hill, he took the things from
the servants and put them away in the house. He
sent the men away and they left. 25Then he went in
and stood before his master Elisha.
"Where have you been, Gehazi?" Elisha asked.
"Your servant didn't go anywhere," Gehazi answered.
26But Elisha said to him, "Was not my spirit
with you when the man got down from his chariot
to meet you? Is this the time to take money, or
to accept clothes, olive groves, vineyards, flocks,
herds, or menservants and maidservants? 27Naa-
man's leprosy will cling to you and to your descendants forever." Then Gehazi went from Elisha's
presence and he was leprous, as white as snow.

An Axhead Floats

6 The company of the prophets said to Elisha,
"Look, the place where we meet with you is
too small for us. 2Let us go to the Jordan, where
each of us can get a pole; and let us build a place
there for us to live." 1Sa 10:5; 2Ki 4:38
And he said, "Go."
3Then one of them said, "Won't you please
come with your servants?"
"I will," Elisha replied. 4And he went with them.
They went to the Jordan and began to cut down
trees. 5As one of them was cutting down a tree, the
iron axhead fell into the water. "Oh, my lord," he
cried out, "it was borrowed!"
6The man of God asked, "Where did it fall?"
When he showed him the place, Elisha cut a stick
and threw it there, and made the iron float. 7"Lift
it out," he said. Then the man reached out his
hand and took it. Ex 15:25; 2Ki 2:21

Elisha Traps Blinded Arameans

8Now the king of Aram was at war with Israel.
After conferring with his officers, he said, "I will
set up my camp in such and such a place."
9The man of God sent word to the king of Israel: "Beware of passing that place, because the Arameans are going down there." 10So the king of
Israel checked on the place indicated by the man
of God. Time and again Elisha warned the king, so
that he was on his guard in such places. ver 12
11This enraged the king of Aram. He sum-

[a] 22 That is, about 75 pounds (about 34 kilograms)

moned his officers and demanded of them, “Will you not tell me which of us is on the side of the king of Israel?”

12“None of us, my lord the king,” said one of his officers, “but Elisha, the prophet who is in Israel, tells the king of Israel the very words you speak in your bedroom.”

13“Go, find out where he is,” the king ordered, “so I can send men and capture him.” The report came back: “He is in Dothan.” 14Then he sent horses and chariots and a strong force there. They went by night and surrounded the city. Ge 37:17

15When the servant of the man of God got up and went out early the next morning, an army with horses and chariots had surrounded the city. “Oh, my lord, what shall we do?” the servant asked.

16“Don't be afraid,” the prophet answered. “Those who are with us are more than those who are with them.” 2Ch 32:7; Ps 55:18; 1Jn 4:4

LIVING  **INSIGHT**

What we think about God gives us strength when we are tempted. What we think about God keeps us faithful and courageous when we are outnumbered. What we think about God sensitizes our conscience and creates the desire to be obedient.

(See 2 Kings 6:16–17.)

17And Elisha prayed, “O LORD, open his eyes so he may see.” Then the LORD opened the servant's eyes, and he looked and saw the hills full of horses and chariots of fire all around Elisha. 2Ki 2:11-12

18As the enemy came down toward him, Elisha prayed to the LORD, “Strike these people with blindness.” So he struck them with blindness, as Elisha had asked. Ge 19:11; Ac 13:11

19Elisha told them, “This is not the road and this is not the city. Follow me, and I will lead you to the man you are looking for.” And he led them to Samaria.

20After they entered the city, Elisha said, “LORD, open the eyes of these men so they can see.” Then the LORD opened their eyes and they looked, and there they were, inside Samaria.

21When the king of Israel saw them, he asked Elisha, “Shall I kill them, my father? Shall I kill them?” 2Ki 5:13

22“Do not kill them,” he answered. “Would you kill men you have captured with your own sword or bow? Set food and water before them so that they may eat and drink and then go back to their master.” 23So he prepared a great feast for them, and after they had finished eating and drinking, he sent them away, and they returned to their master. So the bands from Aram stopped raiding Israel's territory. Dt 20:11; 2Ki 5:2; Ro 12:20

Famine in Besieged Samaria

24Some time later, Ben-Hadad king of Aram mobilized his entire army and marched up and laid siege to Samaria. 25There was a great famine in the city; the siege lasted so long that a donkey's head sold for eighty shekels[a] of silver, and a quarter of a cab[b] of seed pods[c] for five shekels.[d]

26As the king of Israel was passing by on the wall, a woman cried to him, “Help me, my lord the king!”

27The king replied, “If the LORD does not help you, where can I get help for you? From the threshing floor? From the winepress?” 28Then he asked her, “What's the matter?”

She answered, “This woman said to me, ‘Give up your son so we may eat him today, and tomorrow we'll eat my son.’ 29So we cooked my son and ate him. The next day I said to her, ‘Give up your son so we may eat him,’ but she had hidden him.”

30When the king heard the woman's words, he tore his robes. As he went along the wall, the people looked, and there, underneath, he had sackcloth on his body. 31He said, “May God deal with me, be it ever so severely, if the head of Elisha son of Shaphat remains on his shoulders today!”

32Now Elisha was sitting in his house, and the elders were sitting with him. The king sent a messenger ahead, but before he arrived, Elisha said to the elders, “Don't you see how this murderer is sending someone to cut off my head? Look, when the messenger comes, shut the door and hold it shut against him. Is not the sound of his master's footsteps behind him?” 1Ki 18:4; Eze 8:1

33While he was still talking to them, the messenger came down to him. And ⌞the king⌟ said, “This disaster is from the LORD. Why should I wait for the LORD any longer?” Job 2:9; 14:14; Isa 40:31

7 Elisha said, “Hear the word of the LORD. This is what the LORD says: About this time tomorrow, a seah[e] of flour will sell for a shekel[f] and two seahs[g] of barley for a shekel at the gate of Samaria.” ver 16

2The officer on whose arm the king was leaning said to the man of God, “Look, even if the LORD should open the floodgates of the heavens, could this happen?” 2Ki 5:18; Mal 3:10

“You will see it with your own eyes,” answered Elisha, “but you will not eat any of it!” ver 17

[a]25 That is, about 2 pounds (about 1 kilogram) [b]25 That is, probably about 1/2 pint (about 0.3 liter) [c]25 Or *of dove's dung* [d]25 That is, about 2 ounces (about 55 grams) [e]1 That is, probably about 7 quarts (about 7.3 liters); also in verses 16 and 18 [f]1 That is, about 2/5 ounce (about 11 grams); also in verses 16 and 18 [g]1 That is, probably about 13 quarts (about 15 liters); also in verses 16 and 18

The Siege Lifted

3Now there were four men with leprosy[a] at the entrance of the city gate. They said to each other, "Why stay here until we die? 4If we say, 'We'll go into the city'—the famine is there, and we will die. And if we stay here, we will die. So let's go over to the camp of the Arameans and surrender. If they spare us, we live; if they kill us, then we die."

5At dusk they got up and went to the camp of the Arameans. When they reached the edge of the camp, not a man was there, 6for the Lord had caused the Arameans to hear the sound of chariots and horses and a great army, so that they said to one another, "Look, the king of Israel has hired the Hittite and Egyptian kings to attack us!" 7So they got up and fled in the dusk and abandoned their tents and their horses and donkeys. They left the camp as it was and ran for their lives. 2Sa 5:24

8The men who had leprosy reached the edge of the camp and entered one of the tents. They ate and drank, and carried away silver, gold and clothes, and went off and hid them. They returned and entered another tent and took some things from it and hid them also. Isa 33:23; 35:6

9Then they said to each other, "We're not doing right. This is a day of good news and we are keeping it to ourselves. If we wait until daylight, punishment will overtake us. Let's go at once and report this to the royal palace."

10So they went and called out to the city gatekeepers and told them, "We went into the Aramean camp and not a man was there—not a sound of anyone—only tethered horses and donkeys, and the tents left just as they were." 11The gatekeepers shouted the news, and it was reported within the palace.

12The king got up in the night and said to his officers, "I will tell you what the Arameans have done to us. They know we are starving; so they have left the camp to hide in the countryside, thinking, 'They will surely come out, and then we will take them alive and get into the city.'"

13One of his officers answered, "Have some men take five of the horses that are left in the city. Their plight will be like that of all the Israelites left here—yes, they will only be like all these Israelites who are doomed. So let us send them to find out what happened."

14So they selected two chariots with their horses, and the king sent them after the Aramean army. He commanded the drivers, "Go and find out what has happened." 15They followed them as far as the Jordan, and they found the whole road strewn with the clothing and equipment the Arameans had thrown away in their headlong flight. So the messengers returned and reported to the king. 16Then the people went out and plundered the camp of the Arameans. So a seah of flour sold for a shekel, and two seahs of barley sold for a shekel, as the LORD had said. ver 1; Isa 33:4,23

17Now the king had put the officer on whose arm he leaned in charge of the gate, and the people trampled him in the gateway, and he died, just as the man of God had foretold when the king came down to his house. 18It happened as the man of God had said to the king: "About this time tomorrow, a seah of flour will sell for a shekel and two seahs of barley for a shekel at the gate of Samaria." 19The officer had said to the man of God, "Look, even if the LORD should open the floodgates of the heavens, could this happen?" The man of God had replied, "You will see it with your own eyes, but you will not eat any of it!" 20And that is exactly what happened to him, for the people trampled him in the gateway, and he died. ver 2

The Shunammite's Land Restored

8 Now Elisha had said to the woman whose son he had restored to life, "Go away with your family and stay for a while wherever you can, because the LORD has decreed a famine in the land that will last seven years." 2The woman proceeded to do as the man of God said. She and her family went away and stayed in the land of the Philistines seven years. 2Ki 4:8-37; Ps 105:16; Hag 1:11

3At the end of the seven years she came back from the land of the Philistines and went to the king to beg for her house and land. 4The king was talking to Gehazi, the servant of the man of God, and had said, "Tell me about all the great things Elisha has done." 5Just as Gehazi was telling the king how Elisha had restored the dead to life, the woman whose son Elisha had brought back to life came to beg the king for her house and land.

Gehazi said, "This is the woman, my lord the king, and this is her son whom Elisha restored to life." 6The king asked the woman about it, and she told him.

Then he assigned an official to her case and said to him, "Give back everything that belonged to her, including all the income from her land from the day she left the country until now."

Hazael Murders Ben-Hadad

7Elisha went to Damascus, and Ben-Hadad king of Aram was ill. When the king was told, "The man of God has come all the way up here," 8he said to Hazael, "Take a gift with you and go to meet the man of God. Consult the LORD through him; ask him, 'Will I recover from this illness?'"

9Hazael went to meet Elisha, taking with him as a gift forty camel-loads of all the finest wares of Damascus. He went in and stood before him, and

a3 The Hebrew word is used for various diseases affecting the skin—not necessarily leprosy; also in verse 8.

said, "Your son Ben-Hadad king of Aram has sent me to ask, 'Will I recover from this illness?'"

10Elisha answered, "Go and say to him, 'You will certainly recover'; but[a] the LORD has revealed to me that he will in fact die." 11He stared at him with a fixed gaze until Hazael felt ashamed. Then the man of God began to weep. Jdg 3:25; Isa 38:1

12"Why is my lord weeping?" asked Hazael.

"Because I know the harm you will do to the Israelites," he answered. "You will set fire to their fortified places, kill their young men with the sword, dash their little children to the ground, and rip open their pregnant women." 2Ki 10:32; 12:17

13Hazael said, "How could your servant, a mere dog, accomplish such a feat?" 1Sa 17:43; 2Sa 3:8

"The LORD has shown me that you will become king of Aram," answered Elisha. 1Ki 19:15

14Then Hazael left Elisha and returned to his master. When Ben-Hadad asked, "What did Elisha say to you?" Hazael replied, "He told me that you would certainly recover." 15But the next day he took a thick cloth, soaked it in water and spread it over the king's face, so that he died. Then Hazael succeeded him as king. 2Ki 1:17

Jehoram King of Judah

16In the fifth year of Joram son of Ahab king of Israel, when Jehoshaphat was king of Judah, Jehoram son of Jehoshaphat began his reign as king of Judah. 17He was thirty-two years old when he became king, and he reigned in Jerusalem eight years. 18He walked in the ways of the kings of Israel, as the house of Ahab had done, for he married a daughter of Ahab. He did evil in the eyes of the LORD. 19Nevertheless, for the sake of his servant David, the LORD was not willing to destroy Judah. He had promised to maintain a lamp for David and his descendants forever. 2Sa 7:13; 2Ki 1:17

20In the time of Jehoram, Edom rebelled against Judah and set up its own king. 21So Jehoram[b] went to Zair with all his chariots. The Edomites surrounded him and his chariot commanders, but he rose up and broke through by night; his army, however, fled back home. 22To this day Edom has been in rebellion against Judah. Libnah revolted at the same time. Ge 27:40; Jos 21:13; 1Ki 22:47

23As for the other events of Jehoram's reign, and all he did, are they not written in the book of the annals of the kings of Judah? 24Jehoram rested with his fathers and was buried with them in the City of David. And Ahaziah his son succeeded him as king. 2Ch 21:5-10,20

Ahaziah King of Judah

25In the twelfth year of Joram son of Ahab king of Israel, Ahaziah son of Jehoram king of Judah began to reign. 26Ahaziah was twenty-two years old when he became king, and he reigned in Jerusalem one year. His mother's name was Athaliah, a granddaughter of Omri king of Israel. 27He walked in the ways of the house of Ahab and did evil in the eyes of the LORD, as the house of Ahab had done, for he was related by marriage to Ahab's family. 1Ki 15:26; 16:23,30

28Ahaziah went with Joram son of Ahab to war against Hazael king of Aram at Ramoth Gilead. The Arameans wounded Joram; 29so King Joram returned to Jezreel to recover from the wounds the Arameans had inflicted on him at Ramoth[c] in his battle with Hazael king of Aram. 1Ki 19:15,17; 22:3,29

Then Ahaziah son of Jehoram king of Judah went down to Jezreel to see Joram son of Ahab, because he had been wounded. 2Ch 22:1-6

Jehu Anointed King of Israel

9 The prophet Elisha summoned a man from the company of the prophets and said to him, "Tuck your cloak into your belt, take this flask of oil with you and go to Ramoth Gilead. 2When you get there, look for Jehu son of Jehoshaphat, the son of Nimshi. Go to him, get him away from his companions and take him into an inner room. 3Then take the flask and pour the oil on his head and declare, 'This is what the LORD says: I anoint you king over Israel.' Then open the door and run; don't delay!" 1Ki 19:16; 2Ki 4:29; 8:28

4So the young man, the prophet, went to Ramoth Gilead. 5When he arrived, he found the army officers sitting together. "I have a message for you, commander," he said.

"For which of us?" asked Jehu.

"For you, commander," he replied.

6Jehu got up and went into the house. Then the prophet poured the oil on Jehu's head and declared, "This is what the LORD, the God of Israel, says: 'I anoint you king over the LORD's people Israel. 7You are to destroy the house of Ahab your master, and I will avenge the blood of my servants the prophets and the blood of all the LORD's servants shed by Jezebel. 8The whole house of Ahab will perish. I will cut off from Ahab every last male in Israel—slave or free. 9I will make the house of Ahab like the house of Jeroboam son of Nebat and like the house of Baasha son of Ahijah. 10As for Jezebel, dogs will devour her on the plot of ground at Jezreel, and no one will bury her.'" Then he opened the door and ran. 1Ki 14:10; 15:29; 21:23

11When Jehu went out to his fellow officers, one of them asked him, "Is everything all right? Why did this madman come to you?" Jer 29:26; Jn 10:20

"You know the man and the sort of things he says," Jehu replied.

[a] *10* The Hebrew may also be read *Go and say, 'You will certainly not recover,' for.* [b] *21* Hebrew *Joram,* a variant of *Jehoram;* also in verses 23 and 24 [c] *29* Hebrew *Ramah,* a variant of *Ramoth*

12“That’s not true!” they said. “Tell us.”
Jehu said, “Here is what he told me: ‘This is
what the LORD says: I anoint you king over Israel.’ ”
13They hurried and took their cloaks and spread
them under him on the bare steps. Then they blew
the trumpet and shouted, “Jehu is king!” Mt 21:8

Jehu Kills Joram and Ahaziah

14So Jehu son of Jehoshaphat, the son of Nimshi, conspired against Joram. (Now Joram and all
Israel had been defending Ramoth Gilead against
Hazael king of Aram, 15but King Joram[a] had returned to Jezreel to recover from the wounds the
Arameans had inflicted on him in the battle with
Hazael king of Aram.) Jehu said, “If this is the way
you feel, don’t let anyone slip out of the city to go
and tell the news in Jezreel.” 16Then he got into his
chariot and rode to Jezreel, because Joram was
resting there and Ahaziah king of Judah had gone
down to see him. 2Ki 8:28-29; 2Ch 22:7
17When the lookout standing on the tower in
Jezreel saw Jehu’s troops approaching, he called
out, “I see some troops coming.” Isa 21:6
“Get a horseman,” Joram ordered. “Send him
to meet them and ask, ‘Do you come in peace?’ ”
18The horseman rode off to meet Jehu and said,
“This is what the king says: ‘Do you come in
peace?’ ”
“What do you have to do with peace?” Jehu
replied. “Fall in behind me.”
The lookout reported, “The messenger has
reached them, but he isn’t coming back.”
19So the king sent out a second horseman.
When he came to them he said, “This is what the
king says: ‘Do you come in peace?’ ”
Jehu replied, “What do you have to do with
peace? Fall in behind me.”
20The lookout reported, “He has reached them,
but he isn’t coming back either. The driving is like
that of Jehu son of Nimshi—he drives like a madman.” 2Sa 18:27
21“Hitch up my chariot,” Joram ordered. And
when it was hitched up, Joram king of Israel and
Ahaziah king of Judah rode out, each in his own
chariot, to meet Jehu. They met him at the plot of
ground that had belonged to Naboth the Jezreelite.
22When Joram saw Jehu he asked, “Have you
come in peace, Jehu?” 1Ki 21:1-7,15-19
“How can there be peace,” Jehu replied, “as
long as all the idolatry and witchcraft of your
mother Jezebel abound?” 1Ki 18:19; 2Ch 21:13; Rev 2:20
23Joram turned about and fled, calling out to
Ahaziah, “Treachery, Ahaziah!” 2Ki 11:14
24Then Jehu drew his bow and shot Joram between the shoulders. The arrow pierced his heart
and he slumped down in his chariot. 25Jehu said to
Bidkar, his chariot officer, “Pick him up and throw
him on the field that belonged to Naboth the Jezreelite. Remember how you and I were riding together in chariots behind Ahab his father when the
LORD made this prophecy about him: 26‘Yesterday
I saw the blood of Naboth and the blood of his
sons, declares the LORD, and I will surely make you
pay for it on this plot of ground, declares the
LORD.’[b] Now then, pick him up and throw him
on that plot, in accordance with the word of the
LORD.” 1Ki 21:19-22,24-29; 22:34
27When Ahaziah king of Judah saw what had
happened, he fled up the road to Beth Haggan.[c]
Jehu chased him, shouting, “Kill him too!” They
wounded him in his chariot on the way up to Gur
near Ibleam, but he escaped to Megiddo and died
there. 28His servants took him by chariot to Jerusalem and buried him with his fathers in his tomb in
the City of David. 29(In the eleventh year of Joram
son of Ahab, Ahaziah had become king of Judah.)

Jezebel Killed

30Then Jehu went to Jezreel. When Jezebel
heard about it, she painted her eyes, arranged her
hair and looked out of a window. 31As Jehu entered the gate, she asked, “Have you come in
peace, Zimri, you murderer of your master?”[d]
32He looked up at the window and called out,
“Who is on my side? Who?” Two or three eunuchs
looked down at him. 33“Throw her down!” Jehu
said. So they threw her down, and some of her
blood spattered the wall and the horses as they
trampled her underfoot. Ps 7:5
34Jehu went in and ate and drank. “Take care of
that cursed woman,” he said, “and bury her, for
she was a king’s daughter.” 35But when they went
out to bury her, they found nothing except her
skull, her feet and her hands. 36They went back
and told Jehu, who said, “This is the word of the
LORD that he spoke through his servant Elijah the
Tishbite: On the plot of ground at Jezreel dogs will
devour Jezebel’s flesh.[e] 37Jezebel’s body will be

LIVING  **INSIGHT**

God’s work of grace often moves downward, have you noticed? Sometimes, the last part of us to experience full salvation is our right foot, which can be filled with the sinew of selfishness. The way we act behind the wheel is often far more indicative of our walk with God than the way we act praying in a pew.

(See 2 Kings 9:20.)

[a] 15 Hebrew *Jehoram,* a variant of *Joram;* also in verses 17 and 21-24 [b] 26 See 1 Kings 21:19. [c] 27 Or *fled by way of the garden house* [d] 31 Or *“Did Zimri have peace, who murdered his master?”* [e] 36 See 1 Kings 21:23.

like refuse on the ground in the plot at Jezreel, so
that no one will be able to say, 'This is Jezebel.'"

Ahab's Family Killed

10 Now there were in Samaria seventy sons of
the house of Ahab. So Jehu wrote letters
and sent them to Samaria: to the officials of Jezreel,[a] to the elders and to the guardians of Ahab's
children. He said, 2"As soon as this letter reaches
you, since your master's sons are with you and you
have chariots and horses, a fortified city and weapons, 3choose the best and most worthy of your
master's sons and set him on his father's throne.
Then fight for your master's house." 1Ki 13:32; 21:1
4But they were terrified and said, "If two kings
could not resist him, how can we?"
5So the palace administrator, the city governor,
the elders and the guardians sent this message to
Jehu: "We are your servants and we will do anything you say. We will not appoint anyone as king;
you do whatever you think best." Jos 9:8; 1Ki 20:4,32
6Then Jehu wrote them a second letter, saying,
"If you are on my side and will obey me, take the
heads of your master's sons and come to me in
Jezreel by this time tomorrow."
Now the royal princes, seventy of them, were
with the leading men of the city, who were rearing
them. 7When the letter arrived, these men took the
princes and slaughtered all seventy of them. They
put their heads in baskets and sent them to Jehu
in Jezreel. 8When the messenger arrived, he told
Jehu, "They have brought the heads of the
princes." 2Sa 4:8; 1Ki 21:21
Then Jehu ordered, "Put them in two piles at
the entrance of the city gate until morning."
9The next morning Jehu went out. He stood
before all the people and said, "You are innocent.
It was I who conspired against my master and
killed him, but who killed all these? 10Know then,
that not a word the LORD has spoken against the
house of Ahab will fail. The LORD has done what he
promised through his servant Elijah." 11So Jehu
killed everyone in Jezreel who remained of the
house of Ahab, as well as all his chief men, his
close friends and his priests, leaving him no survivor. 1Ki 21:29; 2Ki 9:7-10
12Jehu then set out and went toward Samaria.
At Beth Eked of the Shepherds, 13he met some
relatives of Ahaziah king of Judah and asked,
"Who are you?"
They said, "We are relatives of Ahaziah, and we
have come down to greet the families of the king
and of the queen mother." 2Ki 8:24,29; 2Ch 22:8
14"Take them alive!" he ordered. So they took
them alive and slaughtered them by the well of
Beth Eked—forty-two men. He left no survivor.
15After he left there, he came upon Jehonadab
son of Recab, who was on his way to meet him.
Jehu greeted him and said, "Are you in accord
with me, as I am with you?" 1Ch 2:55; Jer 35:6,14-19
"I am," Jehonadab answered.
"If so," said Jehu, "give me your hand." So he
did, and Jehu helped him up into the chariot.
16Jehu said, "Come with me and see my zeal for
the LORD." Then he had him ride along in his
chariot. 1Ki 19:10; Ezr 10:19; Eze 17:18
17When Jehu came to Samaria, he killed all who
were left there of Ahab's family; he destroyed
them, according to the word of the LORD spoken to
Elijah. 2Ki 9:8

Ministers of Baal Killed

18Then Jehu brought all the people together and
said to them, "Ahab served Baal a little; Jehu will
serve him much. 19Now summon all the prophets
of Baal, all his ministers and all his priests. See that
no one is missing, because I am going to hold a
great sacrifice for Baal. Anyone who fails to come
will no longer live." But Jehu was acting deceptive-
ly in order to destroy the ministers of Baal.
20Jehu said, "Call an assembly in honor of Baal."
So they proclaimed it. 21Then he sent word
throughout Israel, and all the ministers of Baal
came; not one stayed away. They crowded into the
temple of Baal until it was full from one end to the
other. 22And Jehu said to the keeper of the wardrobe, "Bring robes for all the ministers of Baal." So
he brought out robes for them. Ex 32:5; Joel 1:14
23Then Jehu and Jehonadab son of Recab went
into the temple of Baal. Jehu said to the ministers
of Baal, "Look around and see that no servants of
the LORD are here with you—only ministers of
Baal." 24So they went in to make sacrifices and
burnt offerings. Now Jehu had posted eighty men
outside with this warning: "If one of you lets any
of the men I am placing in your hands escape, it
will be your life for his life." 1Ki 20:39
25As soon as Jehu had finished making the
burnt offering, he ordered the guards and officers:
"Go in and kill them; let no one escape." So they
cut them down with the sword. The guards and
officers threw the bodies out and then entered the
inner shrine of the temple of Baal. 26They brought
the sacred stone out of the temple of Baal and
burned it. 27They demolished the sacred stone of
Baal and tore down the temple of Baal, and people
have used it for a latrine to this day. 1Ki 14:23; 18:40
28So Jehu destroyed Baal worship in Israel.
29However, he did not turn away from the sins of
Jeroboam son of Nebat, which he had caused Israel to commit—the worship of the golden calves at
Bethel and Dan. 1Ki 12:28-29; 19:17
30The LORD said to Jehu, "Because you have
done well in accomplishing what is right in my

a1 Hebrew; some Septuagint manuscripts and Vulgate *of the city*

eyes and have done to the house of Ahab all I had
in mind to do, your descendants will sit on the
throne of Israel to the fourth generation." [31]Yet
Jehu was not careful to keep the law of the LORD,
the God of Israel, with all his heart. He did not
turn away from the sins of Jeroboam, which he
had caused Israel to commit. 2Ki 15:12; Pr 4:23

[32]In those days the LORD began to reduce the
size of Israel. Hazael overpowered the Israelites
throughout their territory [33]east of the Jordan in
all the land of Gilead (the region of Gad, Reuben
and Manasseh), from Aroer by the Arnon Gorge
through Gilead to Bashan. 2Ki 8:12; 13:25

[34]As for the other events of Jehu's reign, all he
did, and all his achievements, are they not written
in the book of the annals of the kings of Israel?

[35]Jehu rested with his fathers and was buried in
Samaria. And Jehoahaz his son succeeded him as
king. [36]The time that Jehu reigned over Israel in
Samaria was twenty-eight years.

Kingdoms in Conflict **Chapters 11–17**

These chapters move back and forth between the two kingdoms. At times the writer does not clearly explain which kingdom is being presented, so read closely and note if you are reading about the southern or northern kingdom. Each king is introduced briefly, and we learn only a little about their reign. In each case their kingship is summarized in a few words. Either they "did what was right in the eyes of the LORD," or they "did evil in the eyes of the LORD." Unfortunately, there were more kings who did evil than there were those who did good. This section closes with the heartbreaking account of the fall of the northern kingdom to Assyria.

Athaliah and Joash

11 When Athaliah the mother of Ahaziah saw
that her son was dead, she proceeded to
destroy the whole royal family. [2]But Jehosheba, the
daughter of King Jehoram[a] and sister of Ahaziah,
took Joash son of Ahaziah and stole him away
from among the royal princes, who were about to
be murdered. She put him and his nurse in a bedroom to hide him from Athaliah; so he was not
killed. [3]He remained hidden with his nurse at the
temple of the LORD for six years while Athaliah
ruled the land. 2Ki 12:1; Jdg 9:5

[4]In the seventh year Jehoiada sent for the commanders of units of a hundred, the Carites and the
guards and had them brought to him at the temple
of the LORD. He made a covenant with them and
put them under oath at the temple of the LORD.
Then he showed them the king's son. [5]He commanded them, saying, "This is what you are to do:
You who are in the three companies that are going
on duty on the Sabbath—a third of you guarding
the royal palace, [6]a third at the Sur Gate, and a
third at the gate behind the guard, who take turns
guarding the temple— [7]and you who are in the
other two companies that normally go off Sabbath
duty are all to guard the temple for the king. [8]Station yourselves around the king, each man with his
weapon in his hand. Anyone who approaches your
ranks[b] must be put to death. Stay close to the
king wherever he goes." 1Ch 9:25

[9]The commanders of units of a hundred did
just as Jehoiada the priest ordered. Each one took
his men—those who were going on duty on the
Sabbath and those who were going off duty—and
came to Jehoiada the priest. [10]Then he gave the
commanders the spears and shields that had belonged to King David and that were in the temple
of the LORD. [11]The guards, each with his weapon in
his hand, stationed themselves around the king—
near the altar and the temple, from the south side
to the north side of the temple. 2Sa 8:7; 1Ch 18:7

[12]Jehoiada brought out the king's son and put
the crown on him; he presented him with a copy
of the covenant and proclaimed him king. They
anointed him, and the people clapped their hands
and shouted, "Long live the king!" Ex 25:16; 1Sa 10:24

[13]When Athaliah heard the noise made by the
guards and the people, she went to the people at
the temple of the LORD. [14]She looked and there was
the king, standing by the pillar, as the custom was.
The officers and the trumpeters were beside the
king, and all the people of the land were rejoicing
and blowing trumpets. Then Athaliah tore her
robes and called out, "Treason! Treason!"

[15]Jehoiada the priest ordered the commanders
of units of a hundred, who were in charge of the
troops: "Bring her out between the ranks[c] and
put to the sword anyone who follows her." For the
priest had said, "She must not be put to death in
the temple of the LORD." [16]So they seized her as she
reached the place where the horses enter the palace
grounds, and there she was put to death. Ge 4:14

[17]Jehoiada then made a covenant between the
LORD and the king and people that they would be
the LORD's people. He also made a covenant between the king and the people. [18]All the people of
the land went to the temple of Baal and tore it
down. They smashed the altars and idols to pieces
and killed Mattan the priest of Baal in front of the
altars. 1Ki 18:40; 2Ki 10:25; 23:3

Then Jehoiada the priest posted guards at the
temple of the LORD. [19]He took with him the commanders of hundreds, the Carites, the guards and
all the people of the land, and together they
brought the king down from the temple of the
LORD and went into the palace, entering by way of
the gate of the guards. The king then took his place
on the royal throne, [20]and all the people of the land

[a]2 Hebrew *Joram,* a variant of *Jehoram* [b]8 Or *approaches the precincts* [c]15 Or *out from the precincts*

rejoiced. And the city was quiet, because Athaliah had been slain with the sword at the palace.

[21]Joash[a] was seven years old when he began to reign. 2Ch 22:10-23:21

Joash Repairs the Temple

12 In the seventh year of Jehu, Joash[b] became king, and he reigned in Jerusalem forty years. His mother's name was Zibiah; she was from Beersheba. [2]Joash did what was right in the eyes of the LORD all the years Jehoiada the priest instructed him. [3]The high places, however, were not removed; the people continued to offer sacrifices and burn incense there. 2Ki 14:4; 15:35; 18:4

[4]Joash said to the priests, "Collect all the money that is brought as sacred offerings to the temple of the LORD—the money collected in the census, the money received from personal vows and the money brought voluntarily to the temple. [5]Let every priest receive the money from one of the treasurers, and let it be used to repair whatever damage is found in the temple." Ex 35:5; 2Ki 22:4; 1Ch 29:3-9

[6]But by the twenty-third year of King Joash the priests still had not repaired the temple. [7]Therefore King Joash summoned Jehoiada the priest and the other priests and asked them, "Why aren't you repairing the damage done to the temple? Take no more money from your treasurers, but hand it over for repairing the temple." [8]The priests agreed that they would not collect any more money from the people and that they would not repair the temple themselves.

[9]Jehoiada the priest took a chest and bored a hole in its lid. He placed it beside the altar, on the right side as one enters the temple of the LORD. The priests who guarded the entrance put into the chest all the money that was brought to the temple of the LORD. [10]Whenever they saw that there was a large amount of money in the chest, the royal secretary and the high priest came, counted the money that had been brought into the temple of the LORD and put it into bags. [11]When the amount had been determined, they gave the money to the men appointed to supervise the work on the temple. With it they paid those who worked on the temple of the LORD—the carpenters and builders, [12]the masons and stonecutters. They purchased timber and dressed stone for the repair of the temple of the LORD, and met all the other expenses of restoring the temple. Mk 12:41; Lk 21:1

[13]The money brought into the temple was not spent for making silver basins, wick trimmers, sprinkling bowls, trumpets or any other articles of gold or silver for the temple of the LORD; [14]it was paid to the workmen, who used it to repair the temple. [15]They did not require an accounting from those to whom they gave the money to pay the workers, because they acted with complete honesty. [16]The money from the guilt offerings and sin offerings was not brought into the temple of the LORD; it belonged to the priests. Lev 7:7; 2Ki 22:7

[17]About this time Hazael king of Aram went up and attacked Gath and captured it. Then he turned to attack Jerusalem. [18]But Joash king of Judah took all the sacred objects dedicated by his fathers—Jehoshaphat, Jehoram and Ahaziah, the kings of Judah—and the gifts he himself had dedicated and all the gold found in the treasuries of the temple of the LORD and of the royal palace, and he sent them to Hazael king of Aram, who then withdrew from Jerusalem. 1Ki 15:18; 2Ki 8:12

[19]As for the other events of the reign of Joash, and all he did, are they not written in the book of the annals of the kings of Judah? [20]His officials conspired against him and assassinated him at Beth Millo, on the road down to Silla. [21]The officials who murdered him were Jozabad son of Shimeath and Jehozabad son of Shomer. He died and was buried with his fathers in the City of David. And Amaziah his son succeeded him as king. 2Ch 24:1-14; 24:23-27

Jehoahaz King of Israel

13 In the twenty-third year of Joash son of Ahaziah king of Judah, Jehoahaz son of Jehu became king of Israel in Samaria, and he reigned seventeen years. [2]He did evil in the eyes of the LORD by following the sins of Jeroboam son of Nebat, which he had caused Israel to commit, and he did not turn away from them. [3]So the LORD's anger burned against Israel, and for a long time he kept them under the power of Hazael king of Aram and Ben-Hadad his son. Jdg 2:14; 1Ki 12:26-33

[4]Then Jehoahaz sought the LORD's favor, and the LORD listened to him, for he saw how severely the king of Aram was oppressing Israel. [5]The LORD provided a deliverer for Israel, and they escaped from the power of Aram. So the Israelites lived in their own homes as they had before. [6]But they did not turn away from the sins of the house of Jeroboam, which he had caused Israel to commit; they continued in them. Also, the Asherah pole[c] remained standing in Samaria. 1Ki 16:33; 2Ki 14:26

[7]Nothing had been left of the army of Jehoahaz except fifty horsemen, ten chariots and ten thousand foot soldiers, for the king of Aram had destroyed the rest and made them like the dust at threshing time. 2Ki 10:32-33

[8]As for the other events of the reign of Jehoahaz, all he did and his achievements, are they not written in the book of the annals of the kings of Israel? [9]Jehoahaz rested with his fathers and was

[a] *21* Hebrew *Jehoash,* a variant of *Joash* [b] *1* Hebrew *Jehoash,* a variant of *Joash*; also in verses 2, 4, 6, 7 and 18
[c] *6* That is, a symbol of the goddess Asherah; here and elsewhere in 2 Kings

buried in Samaria. And Jehoash[a] his son succeeded him as king.

Jehoash King of Israel

10 In the thirty-seventh year of Joash king of Judah, Jehoash son of Jehoahaz became king of Israel in Samaria, and he reigned sixteen years. 11 He did evil in the eyes of the LORD and did not turn away from any of the sins of Jeroboam son of Nebat, which he had caused Israel to commit; he continued in them.

12 As for the other events of the reign of Jehoash, all he did and his achievements, including his war against Amaziah king of Judah, are they not written in the book of the annals of the kings of Israel? 13 Jehoash rested with his fathers, and Jeroboam succeeded him on the throne. Jehoash was buried in Samaria with the kings of Israel. 2Ki 14:15,23

14 Now Elisha was suffering from the illness from which he died. Jehoash king of Israel went down to see him and wept over him. "My father! My father!" he cried. "The chariots and horsemen of Israel!" 2Ki 2:12

15 Elisha said, "Get a bow and some arrows," and he did so. 16 "Take the bow in your hands," he said to the king of Israel. When he had taken it, Elisha put his hands on the king's hands.

17 "Open the east window," he said, and he opened it. "Shoot!" Elisha said, and he shot. "The LORD's arrow of victory, the arrow of victory over Aram!" Elisha declared. "You will completely destroy the Arameans at Aphek." 1Ki 20:26

18 Then he said, "Take the arrows," and the king took them. Elisha told him, "Strike the ground." He struck it three times and stopped. 19 The man of God was angry with him and said, "You should have struck the ground five or six times; then you would have defeated Aram and completely destroyed it. But now you will defeat it only three times." ver 25

20 Elisha died and was buried.

Now Moabite raiders used to enter the country every spring. 21 Once while some Israelites were burying a man, suddenly they saw a band of raiders; so they threw the man's body into Elisha's tomb. When the body touched Elisha's bones, the man came to life and stood up on his feet.

22 Hazael king of Aram oppressed Israel throughout the reign of Jehoahaz. 23 But the LORD was gracious to them and had compassion and showed concern for them because of his covenant with Abraham, Isaac and Jacob. To this day he has been unwilling to destroy them or banish them from his presence. Ex 2:24; 1Ki 19:17; 2Ki 8:12

24 Hazael king of Aram died, and Ben-Hadad his son succeeded him as king. 25 Then Jehoash son of Jehoahaz recaptured from Ben-Hadad son of Hazael the towns he had taken in battle from his father Jehoahaz. Three times Jehoash defeated him, and so he recovered the Israelite towns.

Amaziah King of Judah

14 In the second year of Jehoash[b] son of Jehoahaz king of Israel, Amaziah son of Joash king of Judah began to reign. 2 He was twenty-five years old when he became king, and he reigned in Jerusalem twenty-nine years. His mother's name was Jehoaddin; she was from Jerusalem. 3 He did what was right in the eyes of the LORD, but not as his father David had done. In everything he followed the example of his father Joash. 4 The high places, however, were not removed; the people continued to offer sacrifices and burn incense there.

5 After the kingdom was firmly in his grasp, he executed the officials who had murdered his father the king. 6 Yet he did not put the sons of the assassins to death, in accordance with what is written in the Book of the Law of Moses where the LORD commanded: "Fathers shall not be put to death for their children, nor children put to death for their fathers; each is to die for his own sins."[c]

7 He was the one who defeated ten thousand Edomites in the Valley of Salt and captured Sela in battle, calling it Joktheel, the name it has to this day. 2Ch 25:1-4,11-12

8 Then Amaziah sent messengers to Jehoash son of Jehoahaz, the son of Jehu, king of Israel, with the challenge: "Come, meet me face to face."

9 But Jehoash king of Israel replied to Amaziah king of Judah: "A thistle in Lebanon sent a message to a cedar in Lebanon, 'Give your daughter to my son in marriage.' Then a wild beast in Lebanon came along and trampled the thistle underfoot. 10 You have indeed defeated Edom and now you are arrogant. Glory in your victory, but stay at home! Why ask for trouble and cause your own downfall and that of Judah also?" Dt 8:14; Jdg 9:8-15

11 Amaziah, however, would not listen, so Jehoash king of Israel attacked. He and Amaziah king of Judah faced each other at Beth Shemesh in Judah. 12 Judah was routed by Israel, and every man fled to his home. 13 Jehoash king of Israel captured Amaziah king of Judah, the son of Joash, the son of Ahaziah, at Beth Shemesh. Then Jehoash went to Jerusalem and broke down the wall of Jerusalem from the Ephraim Gate to the Corner Gate—a section about six hundred feet long.[d] 14 He took all the gold and silver and all the articles found in the temple of the LORD and in the treasuries of the royal palace. He also took hostages and returned to Samaria. Jos 15:10; Jer 31:38; Zec 14:10

[a] *9* Hebrew *Joash,* a variant of *Jehoash;* also in verses 12-14 and 25 [b] *1* Hebrew *Joash,* a variant of *Jehoash;* also in verses 13, 23 and 27 [c] *6* Deut. 24:16 [d] *13* Hebrew *four hundred cubits* (about 180 meters)

RULERS OF THE DIVIDED KINGDOM OF ISRAEL AND JUDAH

This chart depicts the reigns of the kings of Israel and Judah from Jeroboam of Israel and Rehoboam of Judah until the fall of Jerusalem. As best can be determined, the dates reflect the official reign of each king and not any years of his co-regency with another king. The center column is divided into increments of twenty years; the outside columns give the passages in 1 and 2 Kings and 2 Chronicles where the reign of each king is described. By using this chart, you can see at a glance both the length of each reign and the kings in Israel and Judah who were contemporaries. The final column depicts when the major prophets lived and ministered.

PASSAGES	KINGS OF ISRAEL	DATE B.C.	KINGS OF JUDAH	PASSAGES		PROPHETS
1 Kings				*1 Kings*	*2 Chronicles*	
12:25–14:20	JEROBOAM I	**930**	REHOBOAM	*12:1-24; 14:21-31*	*10:1–12:16*	
			ABIJAH	*15:1-8*	*13:1–14:1*	
15:25-31	NADAB	**910**	ASA	*15:9-24*	*14:2–16:14*	
15:32–16:7	BAASHA					
		890				
16:8-14	ELAH					
16:15-22	ZIMRI, TIBNI/OMRI					
16:23-28	OMRI					
						Elijah
16:29–22:40	AHAB					
		870	JEHOSHAPHAT	*22:41-50*	*17:1–21:3*	
2 Kings						
1:1-18	AHAZIAH					
3:1–8:15	JORAM	**850**				**Elisha**

RULERS OF THE DIVIDED KINGDOM OF ISRAEL AND JUDAH (CONTINUED)

PASSAGES	KINGS OF ISRAEL	DATE B.C.	KINGS OF JUDAH	PASSAGES		PROPHETS
2 Kings				*2 Kings*	*2 Chronicles*	
		850				**Elisha** (cont.)
			JEHORAM	*8:16-24*	*21:4-20*	
9:30–10:36	**JEHU**		**AHAZIAH**	*8:25-29*	*22:1-9*	
			ATHALIAH	*11:1-21*	*22:10–23:21*	
			JOASH	*12:1-21*	*24:1-27*	
		830				
13:1-9	**JEHOAHAZ**					
		810				
13:10-25	**JEHOASH**					
			AMAZIAH	*14:1-22*	*25:1-28*	
		790				
						Jonah
14:23-29	**JEROBOAM II**					
		770				
			AZARIAH (UZZIAH)	*15:1-7*	*26:1-23*	
						Amos
15:8-15	**ZECHARIAH, SHALLUM**					
						Hosea
15:16-22	**MENAHEM**					
		750				

RULERS OF THE DIVIDED KINGDOM OF ISRAEL AND JUDAH (CONTINUED)

PASSAGES	KINGS OF ISRAEL	DATE B.C.	KINGS OF JUDAH	PASSAGES		PROPHETS
2 Kings		**750**		*2 Kings*	*2 Chronicles*	Hosea (cont.)
						Micah
15:23-26	PEKAHIAH					Isaiah
15:27-31	PEKAH		JOTHAM	*15:32-38*	*27:1-8*	
17:1-6	HOSHEA		AHAZ	*16:1-20*	*28:1-27*	
		730				
	FALL OF SAMARIA					
		722				
			HEZEKIAH	*18:1–20:21*	*29:1–32:33*	
		710				
		690				
			MANASSEH	*21:1-18*	*33:1-20*	
		670				
						Nahum
		650				

RULERS OF THE DIVIDED KINGDOM OF ISRAEL AND JUDAH (CONTINUED)

PASSAGES	KINGS OF ISRAEL	DATE B.C.	KINGS OF JUDAH	PASSAGES		PROPHETS
		650		*2 Kings*	*2 Chronicles*	Nahum (cont.)
			AMON	*21:19-26*	*33:21-25*	Zephaniah
			JOSIAH	*22:1–23:30*	*34:1–35:27*	
		630				
						Jeremiah
						Habakkuk
		610				
			JEHOAHAZ	*23:31-33*	*36:1-4*	
			JEHOIAKIM	*23:36–24:7*	*36:5-8*	Daniel
			JEHOIACHIN	*24:8-17*	*36:9-10*	
			ZEDEKIAH	*24:18–25:21*	*36:11-21*	Ezekiel
		590				
		586	FALL OF JERUSALEM	*25:8-17*	*36:15-19*	
		570				
		550				

15 As for the other events of the reign of Jehoash,
what he did and his achievements, including his
war against Amaziah king of Judah, are they not
written in the book of the annals of the kings of
Israel? 16 Jehoash rested with his fathers and was
buried in Samaria with the kings of Israel. And
Jeroboam his son succeeded him as king.
17 Amaziah son of Joash king of Judah lived for
fifteen years after the death of Jehoash son of Jehoahaz king of Israel. 18 As for the other events of
Amaziah's reign, are they not written in the book
of the annals of the kings of Judah?
19 They conspired against him in Jerusalem, and
he fled to Lachish, but they sent men after him to
Lachish and killed him there. 20 He was brought
back by horse and was buried in Jerusalem with
his fathers, in the City of David. 2Ki 9:28; 18:14,17
21 Then all the people of Judah took Azariah,[a]
who was sixteen years old, and made him king in
place of his father Amaziah. 22 He was the one who
rebuilt Elath and restored it to Judah after Amaziah rested with his fathers. 2Ch 25:17-26:2

Jeroboam II King of Israel

23 In the fifteenth year of Amaziah son of Joash
king of Judah, Jeroboam son of Jehoash king of
Israel became king in Samaria, and he reigned
forty-one years. 24 He did evil in the eyes of the
LORD and did not turn away from any of the sins
of Jeroboam son of Nebat, which he had caused
Israel to commit. 25 He was the one who restored
the boundaries of Israel from Lebo[b] Hamath to
the Sea of the Arabah,[c] in accordance with the
word of the LORD, the God of Israel, spoken
through his servant Jonah son of Amittai, the
prophet from Gath Hepher. Jnh 1:1; Mt 12:39; Dt 3:17
26 The LORD had seen how bitterly everyone in
Israel, whether slave or free, was suffering; there
was no one to help them. 27 And since the LORD
had not said he would blot out the name of Israel
from under heaven, he saved them by the hand of
Jeroboam son of Jehoash. 2Ki 13:4; Ps 18:41; Dt 32:36
28 As for the other events of Jeroboam's reign, all
he did, and his military achievements, including
how he recovered for Israel both Damascus and
Hamath, which had belonged to Yaudi,[d] are they
not written in the book of the annals of the kings
of Israel? 29 Jeroboam rested with his fathers, the
kings of Israel. And Zechariah his son succeeded
him as king. 2Sa 8:5; 1Ki 11:24; 2Ch 8:3

Azariah King of Judah

15 In the twenty-seventh year of Jeroboam
king of Israel, Azariah son of Amaziah
king of Judah began to reign. 2 He was sixteen years
old when he became king, and he reigned in Jerusalem fifty-two years. His mother's name was Jecoliah; she was from Jerusalem. 3 He did what was
right in the eyes of the LORD, just as his father
Amaziah had done. 4 The high places, however,
were not removed; the people continued to offer
sacrifices and burn incense there. 2Ki 14:21
5 The LORD afflicted the king with leprosy[e] until
the day he died, and he lived in a separate house.[f]
Jotham the king's son had charge of the palace and
governed the people of the land. Lev 13:46; 2Ch 27:1
6 As for the other events of Azariah's reign, and
all he did, are they not written in the book of the
annals of the kings of Judah? 7 Azariah rested with
his fathers and was buried near them in the City of
David. And Jotham his son succeeded him as king.

Zechariah King of Israel

8 In the thirty-eighth year of Azariah king of
Judah, Zechariah son of Jeroboam became king of
Israel in Samaria, and he reigned six months. 9 He
did evil in the eyes of the LORD, as his fathers had
done. He did not turn away from the sins of Jeroboam son of Nebat, which he had caused Israel to
commit. 1Ki 15:26
10 Shallum son of Jabesh conspired against
Zechariah. He attacked him in front of the people,[g] assassinated him and succeeded him as
king. 11 The other events of Zechariah's reign are
written in the book of the annals of the kings of
Israel. 12 So the word of the LORD spoken to Jehu
was fulfilled: "Your descendants will sit on the
throne of Israel to the fourth generation."[h]

Shallum King of Israel

13 Shallum son of Jabesh became king in the
thirty-ninth year of Uzziah king of Judah, and he
reigned in Samaria one month. 14 Then Menahem
son of Gadi went from Tirzah up to Samaria. He
attacked Shallum son of Jabesh in Samaria, assassinated him and succeeded him as king. 1Ki 14:17
15 The other events of Shallum's reign, and the
conspiracy he led, are written in the book of the
annals of the kings of Israel. 1Ki 15:31
16 At that time Menahem, starting out from Tirzah, attacked Tiphsah and everyone in the city and
its vicinity, because they refused to open their
gates. He sacked Tiphsah and ripped open all the
pregnant women. 1Ki 4:24; 2Ki 8:12; Hos 13:16

Menahem King of Israel

17 In the thirty-ninth year of Azariah king of
Judah, Menahem son of Gadi became king of Israel, and he reigned in Samaria ten years. 18 He did
evil in the eyes of the LORD. During his entire reign
he did not turn away from the sins of Jeroboam

[a] 21 Also called *Uzziah* [b] 25 Or *from the entrance to* [c] 25 That is, the Dead Sea [d] 28 Or *Judah* [e] 5 The Hebrew word was used for various diseases affecting the skin—not necessarily leprosy. [f] 5 Or *in a house where he was relieved of responsibility* [g] 10 Hebrew; some Septuagint manuscripts *in Ibleam* [h] 12 2 Kings 10:30

son of Nebat, which he had caused Israel to commit.

19Then Pul[a] king of Assyria invaded the land, and Menahem gave him a thousand talents[b] of silver to gain his support and strengthen his own hold on the kingdom. 20Menahem exacted this money from Israel. Every wealthy man had to contribute fifty shekels[c] of silver to be given to the king of Assyria. So the king of Assyria withdrew and stayed in the land no longer. 2Ki 12:18; 1Ch 5:6,26

21As for the other events of Menahem's reign, and all he did, are they not written in the book of the annals of the kings of Israel? 22Menahem rested with his fathers. And Pekahiah his son succeeded him as king.

Pekahiah King of Israel

23In the fiftieth year of Azariah king of Judah, Pekahiah son of Menahem became king of Israel in Samaria, and he reigned two years. 24Pekahiah did evil in the eyes of the LORD. He did not turn away from the sins of Jeroboam son of Nebat, which he had caused Israel to commit. 25One of his chief officers, Pekah son of Remaliah, conspired against him. Taking fifty men of Gilead with him, he assassinated Pekahiah, along with Argob and Arieh, in the citadel of the royal palace at Samaria. So Pekah killed Pekahiah and succeeded him as king. 2Ki 12:20; 2Ch 28:6; Isa 7:1,4

26The other events of Pekahiah's reign, and all he did, are written in the book of the annals of the kings of Israel.

Pekah King of Israel

27In the fifty-second year of Azariah king of Judah, Pekah son of Remaliah became king of Israel in Samaria, and he reigned twenty years. 28He did evil in the eyes of the LORD. He did not turn away from the sins of Jeroboam son of Nebat, which he had caused Israel to commit. 2Ch 28:6

29In the time of Pekah king of Israel, Tiglath-Pileser king of Assyria came and took Ijon, Abel Beth Maacah, Janoah, Kedesh and Hazor. He took Gilead and Galilee, including all the land of Naphtali, and deported the people to Assyria. 30Then Hoshea son of Elah conspired against Pekah son of Remaliah. He attacked and assassinated him, and then succeeded him as king in the twentieth year of Jotham son of Uzziah. 2Ki 16:9; 17:1,6

31As for the other events of Pekah's reign, and all he did, are they not written in the book of the annals of the kings of Israel?

Jotham King of Judah

32In the second year of Pekah son of Remaliah king of Israel, Jotham son of Uzziah king of Judah began to reign. 33He was twenty-five years old when he became king, and he reigned in Jerusalem sixteen years. His mother's name was Jerusha daughter of Zadok. 34He did what was right in the eyes of the LORD, just as his father Uzziah had done. 35The high places, however, were not removed; the people continued to offer sacrifices and burn incense there. Jotham rebuilt the Upper Gate of the temple of the LORD. ver 3; 2Ch 26:4-5

36As for the other events of Jotham's reign, and what he did, are they not written in the book of the annals of the kings of Judah? 37(In those days the LORD began to send Rezin king of Aram and Pekah son of Remaliah against Judah.) 38Jotham rested with his fathers and was buried with them in the City of David, the city of his father. And Ahaz his son succeeded him as king. 2Ch 27:1-4,7-9

Ahaz King of Judah

16 In the seventeenth year of Pekah son of Remaliah, Ahaz son of Jotham king of Judah began to reign. 2Ahaz was twenty years old when he became king, and he reigned in Jerusalem sixteen years. Unlike David his father, he did not do what was right in the eyes of the LORD his God. 3He walked in the ways of the kings of Israel and even sacrificed his son in[d] the fire, following the detestable ways of the nations the LORD had driven out before the Israelites. 4He offered sacrifices and burned incense at the high places, on the hilltops and under every spreading tree. Lev 18:21; Dt 12:2,31

5Then Rezin king of Aram and Pekah son of Remaliah king of Israel marched up to fight against Jerusalem and besieged Ahaz, but they could not overpower him. 6At that time, Rezin king of Aram recovered Elath for Aram by driving out the men of Judah. Edomites then moved into Elath and have lived there to this day. 2Ki 14:22

7Ahaz sent messengers to say to Tiglath-Pileser king of Assyria, "I am your servant and vassal. Come up and save me out of the hand of the king of Aram and of the king of Israel, who are attacking me." 8And Ahaz took the silver and gold found in the temple of the LORD and in the treasuries of the royal palace and sent it as a gift to the king of Assyria. 9The king of Assyria complied by attacking Damascus and capturing it. He deported its inhabitants to Kir and put Rezin to death.

10Then King Ahaz went to Damascus to meet Tiglath-Pileser king of Assyria. He saw an altar in Damascus and sent to Uriah the priest a sketch of the altar, with detailed plans for its construction. 11So Uriah the priest built an altar in accordance with all the plans that King Ahaz had sent from Damascus and finished it before King Ahaz returned. 12When the king came back from Damas-

[a] 19 Also called *Tiglath-Pileser* [b] 19 That is, about 37 tons (about 34 metric tons) [c] 20 That is, about 1 1/4 pounds (about 0.6 kilogram) [d] 3 Or *even made his son pass through*

cus and saw the altar, he approached it and presented offerings[a] on it. 13He offered up his burnt offering and grain offering, poured out his drink offering, and sprinkled the blood of his fellowship offerings[b] on the altar. 14The bronze altar that stood before the LORD he brought from the front of the temple—from between the new altar and the temple of the LORD—and put it on the north side of the new altar. 2Ch 4:1; 26:16; Isa 8:2

15King Ahaz then gave these orders to Uriah the priest: "On the large new altar, offer the morning burnt offering and the evening grain offering, the king's burnt offering and his grain offering, and the burnt offering of all the people of the land, and their grain offering and their drink offering. Sprinkle on the altar all the blood of the burnt offerings and sacrifices. But I will use the bronze altar for seeking guidance." 16And Uriah the priest did just as King Ahaz had ordered. Ex 29:38-41; 1Sa 9:9

17King Ahaz took away the side panels and removed the basins from the movable stands. He removed the Sea from the bronze bulls that supported it and set it on a stone base. 18He took away the Sabbath canopy[c] that had been built at the temple and removed the royal entryway outside the temple of the LORD, in deference to the king of Assyria. 1Ki 7:27; Eze 16:28

19As for the other events of the reign of Ahaz, and what he did, are they not written in the book of the annals of the kings of Judah? 20Ahaz rested with his fathers and was buried with them in the City of David. And Hezekiah his son succeeded him as king. 2Ch 28:1-27

Hoshea Last King of Israel

17 In the twelfth year of Ahaz king of Judah, Hoshea son of Elah became king of Israel in Samaria, and he reigned nine years. 2He did evil in the eyes of the LORD, but not like the kings of Israel who preceded him.

3Shalmaneser king of Assyria came up to attack Hoshea, who had been Shalmaneser's vassal and had paid him tribute. 4But the king of Assyria discovered that Hoshea was a traitor, for he had sent envoys to So[d] king of Egypt, and he no longer paid tribute to the king of Assyria, as he had done year by year. Therefore Shalmaneser seized him and put him in prison. 5The king of Assyria invaded the entire land, marched against Samaria and laid siege to it for three years. 6In the ninth year of Hoshea, the king of Assyria captured Samaria and deported the Israelites to Assyria. He settled them in Halah, in Gozan on the Habor River and in the towns of the Medes. 2Ki 18:9-12

Israel Exiled Because of Sin

7All this took place because the Israelites had sinned against the LORD their God, who had brought them up out of Egypt from under the power of Pharaoh king of Egypt. They worshiped other gods 8and followed the practices of the nations the LORD had driven out before them, as well as the practices that the kings of Israel had introduced. 9The Israelites secretly did things against the LORD their God that were not right. From watchtower to fortified city they built themselves high places in all their towns. 10They set up sacred stones and Asherah poles on every high hill and under every spreading tree. 11At every high place they burned incense, as the nations whom the LORD had driven out before them had done. They did wicked things that provoked the LORD to anger. 12They worshiped idols, though the LORD had said, "You shall not do this."[e] 13The LORD warned Israel and Judah through all his prophets and seers: "Turn from your evil ways. Observe my commands and decrees, in accordance with the entire Law that I commanded your fathers to obey and that I delivered to you through my servants the prophets." 1Sa 9:9; Jer 18:11

14But they would not listen and were as stiff-necked as their fathers, who did not trust in the LORD their God. 15They rejected his decrees and the covenant he had made with their fathers and the warnings he had given them. They followed worthless idols and themselves became worthless. They imitated the nations around them although the LORD had ordered them, "Do not do as they do," and they did the things the LORD had forbidden them to do. Dt 12:30-31; 29:25; 32:21

16They forsook all the commands of the LORD their God and made for themselves two idols cast in the shape of calves, and an Asherah pole. They bowed down to all the starry hosts, and they worshiped Baal. 17They sacrificed their sons and daughters in[f] the fire. They practiced divination and sorcery and sold themselves to do evil in the eyes of the LORD, provoking him to anger.

18So the LORD was very angry with Israel and removed them from his presence. Only the tribe of Judah was left, 19and even Judah did not keep the commands of the LORD their God. They followed the practices Israel had introduced. 20Therefore the LORD rejected all the people of Israel; he afflicted them and gave them into the hands of plunderers, until he thrust them from his presence.

21When he tore Israel away from the house of David, they made Jeroboam son of Nebat their king. Jeroboam enticed Israel away from following the LORD and caused them to commit a great sin.

[a] 12 Or *and went up to the*; [b] 13 Traditionally *peace offerings* [c] 18 Or *the dais of his throne* (see Septuagint) [d] 4 Or *to Sais, to the*; *So* is possibly an abbreviation for *Osorkon*. [e] 12 Exodus 20:4, 5 [f] 17 Or *They made their sons and daughters pass through*

22The Israelites persisted in all the sins of Jeroboam and did not turn away from them 23until the
LORD removed them from his presence, as he had
warned through all his servants the prophets. So
the people of Israel were taken from their homeland into exile in Assyria, and they are still there.

Samaria Resettled

24The king of Assyria brought people from Babylon, Cuthah, Avva, Hamath and Sepharvaim and
settled them in the towns of Samaria to replace the
Israelites. They took over Samaria and lived in its
towns. 25When they first lived there, they did not
worship the LORD; so he sent lions among them
and they killed some of the people. 26It was reported to the king of Assyria: "The people you deported and resettled in the towns of Samaria do not
know what the god of that country requires. He
has sent lions among them, which are killing them
off, because the people do not know what he requires." Ge 37:20; 2Ki 18:34; Ezr 4:2,10

27Then the king of Assyria gave this order:
"Have one of the priests you took captive from
Samaria go back to live there and teach the people
what the god of the land requires." 28So one of the
priests who had been exiled from Samaria came to
live in Bethel and taught them how to worship the
LORD.

29Nevertheless, each national group made its
own gods in the several towns where they settled,
and set them up in the shrines the people of Samaria had made at the high places. 30The men
from Babylon made Succoth Benoth, the men
from Cuthah made Nergal, and the men from Hamath made Ashima; 31the Avvites made Nibhaz
and Tartak, and the Sepharvites burned their children in the fire as sacrifices to Adrammelech and
Anammelech, the gods of Sepharvaim. 32They
worshiped the LORD, but they also appointed all
sorts of their own people to officiate for them as
priests in the shrines at the high places. 33They
worshiped the LORD, but they also served their
own gods in accordance with the customs of the
nations from which they had been brought.

34To this day they persist in their former practices. They neither worship the LORD nor adhere to
the decrees and ordinances, the laws and commands that the LORD gave the descendants of Jacob, whom he named Israel. 35When the LORD
made a covenant with the Israelites, he commanded them: "Do not worship any other gods or bow
down to them, serve them or sacrifice to them.
36But the LORD, who brought you up out of Egypt
with mighty power and outstretched arm, is the
one you must worship. To him you shall bow
down and to him offer sacrifices. 37You must always be careful to keep the decrees and ordinances, the laws and commands he wrote for you.
Do not worship other gods. 38Do not forget the
covenant I have made with you, and do not worship other gods. 39Rather, worship the LORD your
God; it is he who will deliver you from the hand of
all your enemies." Dt 44:23; 5:32

40They would not listen, however, but persisted
in their former practices. 41Even while these people
were worshiping the LORD, they were serving their
idols. To this day their children and grandchildren
continue to do as their fathers did. 1Ki 18:21; Mt 6:24

Viewing the Southern Kingdom **Chapters 18–25**

In the remaining chapters the spotlight shines on the southern kingdom. We read accounts of the reigns of various kings—some who did what was right and others who did evil. Hezekiah was a bright light on the landscape as he did what was pleasing in God's sight during his reign of 29 years (chapters 18–20). Although his father Ahaz had been ungodly, Hezekiah lived a righteous and holy life. In contrast, Hezekiah's son Manasseh turned from the Lord and did evil in His sight (chapter 21). Take note also of the reign of young Josiah, who began his rule at eight years of age and followed the Lord and purged the land of idolatry (chapters 22–23). This boy used the position the Lord gave him to call a nation back to its spiritual roots. During the reigns of the four kings who followed Josiah, the kingdom of Judah regressed spiritually and finally fell to the army of Babylon (chapters 24–25). Jerusalem was destroyed, and the people were taken into exile. It must have been with a heavy sigh that the writer of 2 Kings included this statement near the end of the book: "So Judah went into captivity, away from her land" (25:21b).

Hezekiah King of Judah

18 In the third year of Hoshea son of Elah
king of Israel, Hezekiah son of Ahaz king
of Judah began to reign. 2He was twenty-five years
old when he became king, and he reigned in Jerusalem twenty-nine years. His mother's name was
Abijah[a] daughter of Zechariah. 3He did what was
right in the eyes of the LORD, just as his father
David had done. 4He removed the high places,
smashed the sacred stones and cut down the Asherah poles. He broke into pieces the bronze snake
Moses had made, for up to that time the Israelites
had been burning incense to it. (It was called[b]
Nehushtan.[c]) 2Ch 29:1-2; 31:1

5Hezekiah trusted in the LORD, the God of Israel. There was no one like him among all the kings
of Judah, either before him or after him. 6He held
fast to the LORD and did not cease to follow him;
he kept the commands the LORD had given Moses.
7And the LORD was with him; he was successful in
whatever he undertook. He rebelled against the

[a]2 Hebrew *Abi,* a variant of *Abijah* [b]4 Or *He called it* [c]4 *Nehushtan* sounds like the Hebrew for *bronze* and *snake* and *unclean thing.*

king of Assyria and did not serve him. 8From watchtower to fortified city, he defeated the Philistines, as far as Gaza and its territory. 2Ch 31:20-21

9In King Hezekiah's fourth year, which was the seventh year of Hoshea son of Elah king of Israel, Shalmaneser king of Assyria marched against Samaria and laid siege to it. 10At the end of three years the Assyrians took it. So Samaria was captured in Hezekiah's sixth year, which was the ninth year of Hoshea king of Israel. 11The king of Assyria deported Israel to Assyria and settled them in Halah, in Gozan on the Habor River and in towns of the Medes. 12This happened because they had not obeyed the LORD their God, but had violated his covenant—all that Moses the servant of the LORD commanded. They neither listened to the commands nor carried them out. 2Ki 17:3-7; Da 9:6,10

13In the fourteenth year of King Hezekiah's reign, Sennacherib king of Assyria attacked all the fortified cities of Judah and captured them. 14So Hezekiah king of Judah sent this message to the king of Assyria at Lachish: "I have done wrong. Withdraw from me, and I will pay whatever you demand of me." The king of Assyria exacted from Hezekiah king of Judah three hundred talents[a] of silver and thirty talents[b] of gold. 15So Hezekiah gave him all the silver that was found in the temple of the LORD and in the treasuries of the royal palace. 1Ki 15:18; 2Ki 16:8

16At this time Hezekiah king of Judah stripped off the gold with which he had covered the doors and doorposts of the temple of the LORD, and gave it to the king of Assyria.

Sennacherib Threatens Jerusalem

17The king of Assyria sent his supreme commander, his chief officer and his field commander with a large army, from Lachish to King Hezekiah at Jerusalem. They came up to Jerusalem and stopped at the aqueduct of the Upper Pool, on the road to the Washerman's Field. 18They called for the king; and Eliakim son of Hilkiah the palace administrator, Shebna the secretary, and Joah son of Asaph the recorder went out to them. 2Ki 19:2

19The field commander said to them, "Tell Hezekiah:

"'This is what the great king, the king of Assyria, says: On what are you basing this confidence of yours? 20You say you have strategy and military strength—but you speak only empty words. On whom are you depending, that you rebel against me? 21Look now, you are depending on Egypt, that splintered reed of a staff, which pierces a man's hand and wounds him if he leans on it! Such is Pharaoh king of Egypt to all who depend on him. 22And if you say to me, "We are depending on the LORD our God"—isn't he the one whose high places and altars Hezekiah removed, saying to Judah and Jerusalem, "You must worship before this altar in Jerusalem"? Isa 30:5,7; Eze 29:6

23"'Come now, make a bargain with my master, the king of Assyria: I will give you two thousand horses—if you can put riders on them! 24How can you repulse one officer of the least of my master's officials, even though you are depending on Egypt for chariots and horsemen[c]? 25Furthermore, have I come to attack and destroy this place without word from the LORD? The LORD himself told me to march against this country and destroy it.'" 2Ki 19:6,22

26Then Eliakim son of Hilkiah, and Shebna and Joah said to the field commander, "Please speak to your servants in Aramaic, since we understand it. Don't speak to us in Hebrew in the hearing of the people on the wall." Ezr 4:7

27But the commander replied, "Was it only to your master and you that my master sent me to say these things, and not to the men sitting on the wall—who, like you, will have to eat their own filth and drink their own urine?"

28Then the commander stood and called out in Hebrew: "Hear the word of the great king, the king of Assyria! 29This is what the king says: Do not let Hezekiah deceive you. He cannot deliver you from my hand. 30Do not let Hezekiah persuade you to trust in the LORD when he says, 'The LORD will surely deliver us; this city will not be given into the hand of the king of Assyria.'

31"Do not listen to Hezekiah. This is what the king of Assyria says: Make peace with me and come out to me. Then every one of you will eat from his own vine and fig tree and drink water from his own cistern, 32until I come and take you to a land like your own, a land of grain and new wine, a land of bread and vineyards, a land of olive trees and honey. Choose life and not death!

"Do not listen to Hezekiah, for he is misleading you when he says, 'The LORD will deliver us.' 33Has the god of any nation ever delivered his land from the hand of the king of Assyria? 34Where are the gods of Hamath and Arpad? Where are the gods of Sepharvaim, Hena and Ivvah? Have they rescued Samaria from my hand? 35Who of all the gods of these countries has been able to save his land from me? How then can the LORD deliver Jerusalem from my hand?" 2Ch 32:9-19

36But the people remained silent and said nothing in reply, because the king had commanded, "Do not answer him."

37Then Eliakim son of Hilkiah the palace administrator, Shebna the secretary and Joah son of

[a] 14 That is, about 11 tons (about 10 metric tons) [b] 14 That is, about 1 ton (about 1 metric ton) [c] 24 Or *charioteers*

Asaph the recorder went to Hezekiah, with their
clothes torn, and told him what the field commander had said. Isa 36:1-22

Jerusalem's Deliverance Foretold

19 When King Hezekiah heard this, he tore
his clothes and put on sackcloth and went
into the temple of the LORD. 2He sent Eliakim the
palace administrator, Shebna the secretary and the
leading priests, all wearing sackcloth, to the prophet Isaiah son of Amoz. 3They told him, "This is
what Hezekiah says: This day is a day of distress
and rebuke and disgrace, as when children come
to the point of birth and there is no strength to
deliver them. 4It may be that the LORD your God
will hear all the words of the field commander,
whom his master, the king of Assyria, has sent to
ridicule the living God, and that he will rebuke
him for the words the LORD your God has heard.
Therefore pray for the remnant that still survives."
5When King Hezekiah's officials came to Isaiah,
6Isaiah said to them, "Tell your master, 'This is
what the LORD says: Do not be afraid of what you
have heard—those words with which the underlings of the king of Assyria have blasphemed me.
7Listen! I am going to put such a spirit in him that
when he hears a certain report, he will return to his
own country, and there I will have him cut down
with the sword.'" ver 37; 2Ki 18:25
8When the field commander heard that the king
of Assyria had left Lachish, he withdrew and found
the king fighting against Libnah. 2Ki 18:14
9Now Sennacherib received a report that Tirhakah, the Cushite[a] king ⌊of Egypt⌋, was marching
out to fight against him. So he again sent messengers to Hezekiah with this word: 10"Say to Hezekiah king of Judah: Do not let the god you depend
on deceive you when he says, 'Jerusalem will not
be handed over to the king of Assyria.' 11Surely
you have heard what the kings of Assyria have
done to all the countries, destroying them completely. And will you be delivered? 12Did the gods
of the nations that were destroyed by my forefathers deliver them: the gods of Gozan, Haran, Rezeph and the people of Eden who were in Tel
Assar? 13Where is the king of Hamath, the king of
Arpad, the king of the city of Sepharvaim, or of
Hena or Ivvah?" Isa 37:1-13

Hezekiah's Prayer

14Hezekiah received the letter from the messengers and read it. Then he went up to the temple of
the LORD and spread it out before the LORD. 15And
Hezekiah prayed to the LORD: "O LORD, God of
Israel, enthroned between the cherubim, you alone
are God over all the kingdoms of the earth. You
have made heaven and earth. 16Give ear, O LORD,
and hear; open your eyes, O LORD, and see; listen
to the words Sennacherib has sent to insult the
living God.
17"It is true, O LORD, that the Assyrian kings
have laid waste these nations and their lands.
18They have thrown their gods into the fire and
destroyed them, for they were not gods but only
wood and stone, fashioned by men's hands.
19Now, O LORD our God, deliver us from his hand,
so that all kingdoms on earth may know that you
alone, O LORD, are God." Isa 37:14-20; Ps 83:18

Isaiah Prophesies Sennacherib's Fall

20Then Isaiah son of Amoz sent a message to
Hezekiah: "This is what the LORD, the God of Israel, says: I have heard your prayer concerning Sennacherib king of Assyria. 21This is the word that
the LORD has spoken against him: 2Ki 20:5; Isa 10:5

"'The Virgin Daughter of Zion La 2:13
despises you and mocks you. Ps 22:7-8
The Daughter of Jerusalem
tosses her head as you flee. Ps 109:25
22Who is it you have insulted and blasphemed?
Against whom have you raised your voice
and lifted your eyes in pride?
Against the Holy One of Israel! Ps 71:22
23By your messengers
you have heaped insults on the Lord.
And you have said, Isa 10:18
"With my many chariots Ps 20:7
I have ascended the heights of the mountains,
the utmost heights of Lebanon.
I have cut down its tallest cedars, Isa 10:34
the choicest of its pines.
I have reached its remotest parts,
the finest of its forests.
24I have dug wells in foreign lands
and drunk the water there.
With the soles of my feet
I have dried up all the streams of Egypt."

25"'Have you not heard? Isa 40:21,28
Long ago I ordained it.
In days of old I planned it; Isa 10:5; 45:7
now I have brought it to pass,
that you have turned fortified cities
into piles of stone. Mic 1:6
26Their people, drained of power,
are dismayed and put to shame. Ps 6:10
They are like plants in the field,
like tender green shoots, Isa 4:2
like grass sprouting on the roof,
scorched before it grows up. Ps 129:6

27"'But I know where you stay Ps 139:1-4
and when you come and go
and how you rage against me.
28Because you rage against me

[a]9 That is, from the upper Nile region

and your insolence has reached my ears,
I will put my hook in your nose Eze 29:4
and my bit in your mouth,
and I will make you return ver 33
by the way you came.’

29“This will be the sign for you, O Hezekiah:

“This year you will eat what grows by itself,
and the second year what springs from that.
But in the third year sow and reap,
plant vineyards and eat their fruit. Ps 107:37
30Once more a remnant of the house of Judah
will take root below and bear fruit above.
31For out of Jerusalem will come a remnant,
and out of Mount Zion a band of
survivors. Isa 66:19

The zeal of the LORD Almighty will accomplish
this. Isa 9:7

32“Therefore this is what the LORD says concerning the king of Assyria:

“He will not enter this city
or shoot an arrow here.
He will not come before it with shield
or build a siege ramp against it.
33By the way that he came he will return; ver 28
he will not enter this city,
declares the LORD.
34I will defend this city and save it, 2Ki 20:6
for my sake and for the sake of David my
servant.” 1Ki 11:12-13

35That night the angel of the LORD went out and
put to death a hundred and eighty-five thousand
men in the Assyrian camp. When the people got
up the next morning—there were all the dead
bodies! 36So Sennacherib king of Assyria broke
camp and withdrew. He returned to Nineveh and
stayed there. Ex 12:23; Job 24:24; Jnh 1:2
37One day, while he was worshiping in the temple of his god Nisroch, his sons Adrammelech and
Sharezer cut him down with the sword, and they
escaped to the land of Ararat. And Esarhaddon his
son succeeded him as king. 2Ch 32:20-21; Isa 37:21-38

Hezekiah’s Illness

20 In those days Hezekiah became ill and was
at the point of death. The prophet Isaiah
son of Amoz went to him and said, “This is what
the LORD says: Put your house in order, because
you are going to die; you will not recover.”
2Hezekiah turned his face to the wall and
prayed to the LORD, 3“Remember, O LORD, how I
have walked before you faithfully and with wholehearted devotion and have done what is good in
your eyes.” And Hezekiah wept bitterly. 2Ki 18:3-6
4Before Isaiah had left the middle court, the
word of the LORD came to him: 5“Go back and tell
Hezekiah, the leader of my people, ‘This is what
the LORD, the God of your father David, says: I
have heard your prayer and seen your tears; I will
heal you. On the third day from now you will go
up to the temple of the LORD. 6I will add fifteen
years to your life. And I will deliver you and this
city from the hand of the king of Assyria. I will
defend this city for my sake and for the sake of my
servant David.’ ” 2Ki 19:20,34; Ps 39:12
7Then Isaiah said, “Prepare a poultice of figs.”
They did so and applied it to the boil, and he
recovered. Isa 38:21
8Hezekiah had asked Isaiah, “What will be the
sign that the LORD will heal me and that I will go
up to the temple of the LORD on the third day from
now?”
9Isaiah answered, “This is the LORD’s sign to you
that the LORD will do what he has promised: Shall
the shadow go forward ten steps, or shall it go back
ten steps?” Dt 13:2; Jer 44:29
10“It is a simple matter for the shadow to go
forward ten steps,” said Hezekiah. “Rather, have it
go back ten steps.”
11Then the prophet Isaiah called upon the LORD,
and the LORD made the shadow go back the ten
steps it had gone down on the stairway of Ahaz.

Envoys From Babylon

12At that time Merodach-Baladan son of Baladan king of Babylon sent Hezekiah letters and a
gift, because he had heard of Hezekiah’s illness.
13Hezekiah received the messengers and showed
them all that was in his storehouses—the silver,
the gold, the spices and the fine oil—his armory
and everything found among his treasures. There
was nothing in his palace or in all his kingdom that
Hezekiah did not show them.
14Then Isaiah the prophet went to King Hezekiah and asked, “What did those men say, and
where did they come from?”
“From a distant land,” Hezekiah replied. “They
came from Babylon.”
15The prophet asked, “What did they see in
your palace?”
“They saw everything in my palace,” Hezekiah
said. “There is nothing among my treasures that I
did not show them.”
16Then Isaiah said to Hezekiah, “Hear the word
of the LORD: 17The time will surely come when
everything in your palace, and all that your fathers
have stored up until this day, will be carried off to
Babylon. Nothing will be left, says the LORD. 18And
some of your descendants, your own flesh and
blood, that will be born to you, will be taken away,
and they will become eunuchs in the palace of the
king of Babylon.” 2Ki 24:15; 2Ch 33:11
19“The word of the LORD you have spoken is
good,” Hezekiah replied. For he thought, “Will
there not be peace and security in my lifetime?”
20As for the other events of Hezekiah’s reign, all

his achievements and how he made the pool and the tunnel by which he brought water into the city, are they not written in the book of the annals of the kings of Judah? [21]Hezekiah rested with his fathers. And Manasseh his son succeeded him as king. Ne 3:16

Manasseh King of Judah

21 Manasseh was twelve years old when he became king, and he reigned in Jerusalem fifty-five years. His mother's name was Hephzibah. [2]He did evil in the eyes of the LORD, following the detestable practices of the nations the LORD had driven out before the Israelites. [3]He rebuilt the high places his father Hezekiah had destroyed; he also erected altars to Baal and made an Asherah pole, as Ahab king of Israel had done. He bowed down to all the starry hosts and worshiped them. [4]He built altars in the temple of the LORD, of which the LORD had said, "In Jerusalem I will put my Name." [5]In both courts of the temple of the LORD, he built altars to all the starry hosts. [6]He sacrificed his own son in[a] the fire, practiced sorcery and divination, and consulted mediums and spiritists. He did much evil in the eyes of the LORD, provoking him to anger. Jer 15:4; Lev 18:21; 19:31

[7]He took the carved Asherah pole he had made and put it in the temple, of which the LORD had said to David and to his son Solomon, "In this temple and in Jerusalem, which I have chosen out of all the tribes of Israel, I will put my Name forever. [8]I will not again make the feet of the Israelites wander from the land I gave their forefathers, if only they will be careful to do everything I commanded them and will keep the whole Law that my servant Moses gave them." [9]But the people did not listen. Manasseh led them astray, so that they did more evil than the nations the LORD had destroyed before the Israelites. 2Ch 33:1-10

[10]The LORD said through his servants the prophets: [11]"Manasseh king of Judah has committed these detestable sins. He has done more evil than the Amorites who preceded him and has led Judah into sin with his idols. [12]Therefore this is what the LORD, the God of Israel, says: I am going to bring such disaster on Jerusalem and Judah that the ears of everyone who hears of it will tingle. [13]I will stretch out over Jerusalem the measuring line used against Samaria and the plumb line used against the house of Ahab. I will wipe out Jerusalem as one wipes a dish, wiping it and turning it upside down. [14]I will forsake the remnant of my inheritance and hand them over to their enemies. They will be looted and plundered by all their foes, [15]because they have done evil in my eyes and have provoked me to anger from the day their forefathers came out of Egypt until this day." 2Ki 19:4

[16]Moreover, Manasseh also shed so much innocent blood that he filled Jerusalem from end to end—besides the sin that he had caused Judah to commit, so that they did evil in the eyes of the LORD. 2Ki 24:4

[17]As for the other events of Manasseh's reign, and all he did, including the sin he committed, are they not written in the book of the annals of the kings of Judah? [18]Manasseh rested with his fathers and was buried in his palace garden, the garden of Uzza. And Amon his son succeeded him as king.

Amon King of Judah

[19]Amon was twenty-two years old when he became king, and he reigned in Jerusalem two years. His mother's name was Meshullemeth daughter of Haruz; she was from Jotbah. [20]He did evil in the eyes of the LORD, as his father Manasseh had done. [21]He walked in all the ways of his father; he worshiped the idols his father had worshiped, and bowed down to them. [22]He forsook the LORD, the God of his fathers, and did not walk in the way of the LORD. ver 2-6; 1Ki 11:33

[23]Amon's officials conspired against him and assassinated the king in his palace. [24]Then the people of the land killed all who had plotted against King Amon, and they made Josiah his son king in his place. 2Ch 33:21-25

[25]As for the other events of Amon's reign, and what he did, are they not written in the book of the annals of the kings of Judah? [26]He was buried in his grave in the garden of Uzza. And Josiah his son succeeded him as king.

The Book of the Law Found

22 Josiah was eight years old when he became king, and he reigned in Jerusalem thirty-one years. His mother's name was Jedidah daughter of Adaiah; she was from Bozkath. [2]He did what was right in the eyes of the LORD and walked in all the ways of his father David, not turning aside to the right or to the left. Dt 5:32; 17:19; Jos 15:39

[3]In the eighteenth year of his reign, King Josiah sent the secretary, Shaphan son of Azaliah, the son of Meshullam, to the temple of the LORD. He said: [4]"Go up to Hilkiah the high priest and have him get ready the money that has been brought into the temple of the LORD, which the doorkeepers have collected from the people. [5]Have them entrust it to the men appointed to supervise the work on the temple. And have these men pay the workers who repair the temple of the LORD— [6]the carpenters, the builders and the masons. Also have them purchase timber and dressed stone to repair the temple. [7]But they need not account for the money entrusted to them, because they are acting faithfully." 2Ki 12:4-5,11-15

[a]6 Or *He made his own son pass through*

8Hilkiah the high priest said to Shaphan the secretary, "I have found the Book of the Law in the temple of the LORD." He gave it to Shaphan, who read it. 9Then Shaphan the secretary went to the king and reported to him: "Your officials have paid out the money that was in the temple of the LORD and have entrusted it to the workers and supervisors at the temple." 10Then Shaphan the secretary informed the king, "Hilkiah the priest has given me a book." And Shaphan read from it in the presence of the king. Dt 31:24; Jer 36:21

11When the king heard the words of the Book of the Law, he tore his robes. 12He gave these orders to Hilkiah the priest, Ahikam son of Shaphan, Acbor son of Micaiah, Shaphan the secretary and Asaiah the king's attendant: 13"Go and inquire of the LORD for me and for the people and for all Judah about what is written in this book that has been found. Great is the LORD's anger that burns against us because our fathers have not obeyed the words of this book; they have not acted in accordance with all that is written there concerning us."

14Hilkiah the priest, Ahikam, Acbor, Shaphan and Asaiah went to speak to the prophetess Huldah, who was the wife of Shallum son of Tikvah, the son of Harhas, keeper of the wardrobe. She lived in Jerusalem, in the Second District.

15She said to them, "This is what the LORD, the God of Israel, says: Tell the man who sent you to me, 16'This is what the LORD says: I am going to bring disaster on this place and its people, according to everything written in the book the king of Judah has read. 17Because they have forsaken me and burned incense to other gods and provoked me to anger by all the idols their hands have made,[a] my anger will burn against this place and will not be quenched.' 18Tell the king of Judah, who sent you to inquire of the LORD, 'This is what the LORD, the God of Israel, says concerning the words you heard: 19Because your heart was responsive and you humbled yourself before the LORD when you heard what I have spoken against this place and its people, that they would become accursed and laid waste, and because you tore your robes and wept in my presence, I have heard you, declares the LORD. 20Therefore I will gather you to your fathers, and you will be buried in peace. Your eyes will not see all the disaster I am going to bring on this place.'" 2Ch 34:1-2,8-28

So they took her answer back to the king.

Josiah Renews the Covenant

23 Then the king called together all the elders of Judah and Jerusalem. 2He went up to the temple of the LORD with the men of Judah, the people of Jerusalem, the priests and the prophets—all the people from the least to the greatest. He read in their hearing all the words of the Book of the Covenant, which had been found in the temple of the LORD. 3The king stood by the pillar and renewed the covenant in the presence of the LORD—to follow the LORD and keep his commands, regulations and decrees with all his heart and all his soul, thus confirming the words of the covenant written in this book. Then all the people pledged themselves to the covenant. 2Ch 34:29-32

> **LIVING**  **INSIGHT**
>
> ***There can be no more reliable authority on earth than God's Word, the Bible. This timeless, trustworthy source of truth holds the key that unlocks life's mysteries. It alone provides us with the shelter we need in times of storm.***
>
> **(See 2 Kings 23:1–3.)**

4The king ordered Hilkiah the high priest, the priests next in rank and the doorkeepers to remove from the temple of the LORD all the articles made for Baal and Asherah and all the starry hosts. He burned them outside Jerusalem in the fields of the Kidron Valley and took the ashes to Bethel. 5He did away with the pagan priests appointed by the kings of Judah to burn incense on the high places of the towns of Judah and on those around Jerusalem—those who burned incense to Baal, to the sun and moon, to the constellations and to all the starry hosts. 6He took the Asherah pole from the temple of the LORD to the Kidron Valley outside Jerusalem and burned it there. He ground it to powder and scattered the dust over the graves of the common people. 7He also tore down the quarters of the male shrine prostitutes, which were in the temple of the LORD and where women did weaving for Asherah. 1Ki 14:24; 15:12; Eze 16:16

8Josiah brought all the priests from the towns of Judah and desecrated the high places, from Geba to Beersheba, where the priests had burned incense. He broke down the shrines[b] at the gates—at the entrance to the Gate of Joshua, the city governor, which is on the left of the city gate. 9Although the priests of the high places did not serve at the altar of the LORD in Jerusalem, they ate unleavened bread with their fellow priests.

10He desecrated Topheth, which was in the Valley of Ben Hinnom, so no one could use it to sacrifice his son or daughter in[c] the fire to Molech. 11He removed from the entrance to the temple of the LORD the horses that the kings of Judah had dedicated to the sun. They were in the court near the room of an official named Nathan-

[a]17 Or *by everything they have done* [b]8 Or *high places* [c]10 Or *to make his son or daughter pass through*

Melech. Josiah then burned the chariots dedicated
to the sun. Isa 30:33; Jer 7:31-32; 19:6
12He pulled down the altars the kings of Judah
had erected on the roof near the upper room of
Ahaz, and the altars Manasseh had built in the two
courts of the temple of the LORD. He removed
them from there, smashed them to pieces and
threw the rubble into the Kidron Valley. 13The
king also desecrated the high places that were east
of Jerusalem on the south of the Hill of Corruption—the ones Solomon king of Israel had built
for Ashtoreth the vile goddess of the Sidonians, for
Chemosh the vile god of Moab, and for Molech[a]
the detestable god of the people of Ammon. 14Josi-
ah smashed the sacred stones and cut down the
Asherah poles and covered the sites with human
bones. Dt 7:5,25; 1Ki 11:7
15Even the altar at Bethel, the high place made
by Jeroboam son of Nebat, who had caused Israel
to sin—even that altar and high place he demolished. He burned the high place and ground it to
powder, and burned the Asherah pole also. 16Then
Josiah looked around, and when he saw the tombs
that were there on the hillside, he had the bones
removed from them and burned on the altar to
defile it, in accordance with the word of the LORD
proclaimed by the man of God who foretold these
things. 1Ki 13:2
17The king asked, "What is that tombstone I
see?"

The men of the city said, "It marks the tomb of
the man of God who came from Judah and pronounced against the altar of Bethel the very things
you have done to it."
18"Leave it alone," he said. "Don't let anyone
disturb his bones." So they spared his bones and
those of the prophet who had come from Samaria.
19Just as he had done at Bethel, Josiah removed
and defiled all the shrines at the high places that
the kings of Israel had built in the towns of Samaria that had provoked the LORD to anger. 20Josiah
slaughtered all the priests of those high places on
the altars and burned human bones on them.
Then he went back to Jerusalem. 2Ch 34:3-7,33
21The king gave this order to all the people:
"Celebrate the Passover to the LORD your God, as
it is written in this Book of the Covenant." 22Not
since the days of the judges who led Israel, nor
throughout the days of the kings of Israel and the
kings of Judah, had any such Passover been observed. 23But in the eighteenth year of King Josiah,
this Passover was celebrated to the LORD in Jerusalem. 2Ch 35:1,18-19
24Furthermore, Josiah got rid of the mediums
and spiritists, the household gods, the idols and all
the other detestable things seen in Judah and Jerusalem. This he did to fulfill the requirements of the
law written in the book that Hilkiah the priest had
discovered in the temple of the LORD. 25Neither
before nor after Josiah was there a king like him
who turned to the LORD as he did—with all his
heart and with all his soul and with all his strength,
in accordance with all the Law of Moses. Dt 18:11
26Nevertheless, the LORD did not turn away
from the heat of his fierce anger, which burned
against Judah because of all that Manasseh had
done to provoke him to anger. 27So the LORD said,
"I will remove Judah also from my presence as I
removed Israel, and I will reject Jerusalem, the city
I chose, and this temple, about which I said, 'There
shall my Name be.'[b]" 2Ki 18:11; 21:13
28As for the other events of Josiah's reign, and
all he did, are they not written in the book of the
annals of the kings of Judah?
29While Josiah was king, Pharaoh Neco king of
Egypt went up to the Euphrates River to help the
king of Assyria. King Josiah marched out to meet
him in battle, but Neco faced him and killed him
at Megiddo. 30Josiah's servants brought his body
in a chariot from Megiddo to Jerusalem and buried him in his own tomb. And the people of the
land took Jehoahaz son of Josiah and anointed
him and made him king in place of his father.

Jehoahaz King of Judah

31Jehoahaz was twenty-three years old when he
became king, and he reigned in Jerusalem three
months. His mother's name was Hamutal daughter of Jeremiah; she was from Libnah. 32He did evil
in the eyes of the LORD, just as his fathers had
done. 33Pharaoh Neco put him in chains at Riblah
in the land of Hamath[c] so that he might not reign
in Jerusalem, and he imposed on Judah a levy of
a hundred talents[d] of silver and a talent[e] of gold.
34Pharaoh Neco made Eliakim son of Josiah king
in place of his father Josiah and changed Eliakim's
name to Jehoiakim. But he took Jehoahaz and carried him off to Egypt, and there he died. 35Jehoia-
kim paid Pharaoh Neco the silver and gold he
demanded. In order to do so, he taxed the land
and exacted the silver and gold from the people of
the land according to their assessments. 2Ch 36:2-4

Jehoiakim King of Judah

36Jehoiakim was twenty-five years old when he
became king, and he reigned in Jerusalem eleven
years. His mother's name was Zebidah daughter of
Pedaiah; she was from Rumah. 37And he did evil
in the eyes of the LORD, just as his fathers had
done. Jer 26:1

24 During Jehoiakim's reign, Nebuchadnezzar king of Babylon invaded the land, and

[a] 13 Hebrew *Milcom* [b] 27 1 Kings 8:29 [c] 33 Hebrew; Septuagint (see also 2 Chron. 36:3) *Neco at Riblah in Hamath removed him* [d] 33 That is, about 3 3/4 tons (about 3.4 metric tons) [e] 33 That is, about 75 pounds (about 34 kilograms)

Jehoiakim became his vassal for three years. But then he changed his mind and rebelled against Nebuchadnezzar. 2The LORD sent Babylonian,[a] Aramean, Moabite and Ammonite raiders against him. He sent them to destroy Judah, in accordance with the word of the LORD proclaimed by his servants the prophets. 3Surely these things happened to Judah according to the LORD's command, in order to remove them from his presence because of the sins of Manasseh and all he had done, 4including the shedding of innocent blood. For he had filled Jerusalem with innocent blood, and the LORD was not willing to forgive. 2Ki 21:16; 23:26

5As for the other events of Jehoiakim's reign, and all he did, are they not written in the book of the annals of the kings of Judah? 6Jehoiakim rested with his fathers. And Jehoiachin his son succeeded him as king. 2Ch 36:5-8; Jer 22:19

7The king of Egypt did not march out from his own country again, because the king of Babylon had taken all his territory, from the Wadi of Egypt to the Euphrates River. Jer 37:5-7; 46:2

Jehoiachin King of Judah

8Jehoiachin was eighteen years old when he became king, and he reigned in Jerusalem three months. His mother's name was Nehushta daughter of Elnathan; she was from Jerusalem. 9He did evil in the eyes of the LORD, just as his father had done. 1Ch 3:16

10At that time the officers of Nebuchadnezzar king of Babylon advanced on Jerusalem and laid siege to it, 11and Nebuchadnezzar himself came up to the city while his officers were besieging it. 12Jehoiachin king of Judah, his mother, his attendants, his nobles and his officials all surrendered to him.

In the eighth year of the reign of the king of Babylon, he took Jehoiachin prisoner. 13As the LORD had declared, Nebuchadnezzar removed all the treasures from the temple of the LORD and from the royal palace, and took away all the gold articles that Solomon king of Israel had made for the temple of the LORD. 14He carried into exile all Jerusalem: all the officers and fighting men, and all the craftsmen and artisans—a total of ten thousand. Only the poorest people of the land were left.

15Nebuchadnezzar took Jehoiachin captive to Babylon. He also took from Jerusalem to Babylon the king's mother, his wives, his officials and the leading men of the land. 16The king of Babylon also deported to Babylon the entire force of seven thousand fighting men, strong and fit for war, and a thousand craftsmen and artisans. 17He made Mattaniah, Jehoiachin's uncle, king in his place and changed his name to Zedekiah. 2Ch 36:9-10

Zedekiah King of Judah

18Zedekiah was twenty-one years old when he became king, and he reigned in Jerusalem eleven years. His mother's name was Hamutal daughter of Jeremiah; she was from Libnah. 19He did evil in the eyes of the LORD, just as Jehoiakim had done. 20It was because of the LORD's anger that all this happened to Jerusalem and Judah, and in the end he thrust them from his presence. 2Ch 36:11-16

The Fall of Jerusalem

Now Zedekiah rebelled against the king of Babylon.

25 So in the ninth year of Zedekiah's reign, on the tenth day of the tenth month, Nebuchadnezzar king of Babylon marched against Jerusalem with his whole army. He encamped outside the city and built siege works all around it. 2The city was kept under siege until the eleventh year of King Zedekiah. 3By the ninth day of the ⌞fourth⌟[b] month the famine in the city had become so severe that there was no food for the people to eat. 4Then the city wall was broken through, and the whole army fled at night through the gate between the two walls near the king's garden, though the Babylonians[c] were surrounding the city. They fled toward the Arabah,[d] 5but the Babylonian[e] army pursued the king and overtook him in the plains of Jericho. All his soldiers were separated from him and scattered, 6and he was captured. He was taken to the king of Babylon at Riblah, where sentence was pronounced on him. 7They killed the sons of Zedekiah before his eyes. Then they put out his eyes, bound him with bronze shackles and took him to Babylon. 2Ki 23:33; Jer 34:21-22; Eze 33:21

8On the seventh day of the fifth month, in the nineteenth year of Nebuchadnezzar king of Babylon, Nebuzaradan commander of the imperial guard, an official of the king of Babylon, came to Jerusalem. 9He set fire to the temple of the LORD, the royal palace and all the houses of Jerusalem. Every important building he burned down. 10The whole Babylonian army, under the commander of the imperial guard, broke down the walls around Jerusalem. 11Nebuzaradan the commander of the guard carried into exile the people who remained in the city, along with the rest of the populace and those who had gone over to the king of Babylon. 12But the commander left behind some of the poorest people of the land to work the vineyards and fields. Jer 39:1-10; 2Ki 24:14

13The Babylonians broke up the bronze pillars, the movable stands and the bronze Sea that were at the temple of the LORD and they carried the bronze to Babylon. 14They also took away the pots, shovels, wick trimmers, dishes and all the bronze

[a]2 Or *Chaldean* [b]3 See Jer. 52:6. [c]4 Or *Chaldeans*; also in verses 13, 25 and 26 [d]4 Or *the Jordan Valley*
[e]5 Or *Chaldean*; also in verses 10 and 24

articles used in the temple service. 15The commander of the imperial guard took away the censers and sprinkling bowls—all that were made of
pure gold or silver. Ex 27:3; 1Ki 7:47-50

16The bronze from the two pillars, the Sea and
the movable stands, which Solomon had made for
the temple of the LORD, was more than could be
weighed. 17Each pillar was twenty-seven feet[a]
high. The bronze capital on top of one pillar was
four and a half feet[b] high and was decorated with
a network and pomegranates of bronze all around.
The other pillar, with its network, was similar.

18The commander of the guard took as prisoners Seraiah the chief priest, Zephaniah the priest
next in rank and the three doorkeepers. 19Of those
still in the city, he took the officer in charge of the
fighting men and five royal advisers. He also took
the secretary who was chief officer in charge of
conscripting the people of the land and sixty of his
men who were found in the city. 20Nebuzaradan
the commander took them all and brought them
to the king of Babylon at Riblah. 21There at Riblah,
in the land of Hamath, the king had them executed. Jer 21:1; 29:25

So Judah went into captivity, away from her
land. 2Ch 36:17-20; Jer 52:4-27

22Nebuchadnezzar king of Babylon appointed
Gedaliah son of Ahikam, the son of Shaphan, to
be over the people he had left behind in Judah.
23When all the army officers and their men heard
that the king of Babylon had appointed Gedaliah
as governor, they came to Gedaliah at Mizpah—
Ishmael son of Nethaniah, Johanan son of Kareah,
Seraiah son of Tanhumeth the Netophathite, Jaazaniah the son of the Maacathite, and their men.
24Gedaliah took an oath to reassure them and their
men. "Do not be afraid of the Babylonian officials," he said. "Settle down in the land and serve
the king of Babylon, and it will go well with you."

25In the seventh month, however, Ishmael son
of Nethaniah, the son of Elishama, who was of
royal blood, came with ten men and assassinated
Gedaliah and also the men of Judah and the Babylonians who were with him at Mizpah. 26At this,
all the people from the least to the greatest, together with the army officers, fled to Egypt for fear of
the Babylonians. Jer 40:7-9; 41:1-3,16-18

Jehoiachin Released

27In the thirty-seventh year of the exile of Jehoiachin king of Judah, in the year Evil-Merodach[c]
became king of Babylon, he released Jehoiachin
from prison on the twenty-seventh day of the
twelfth month. 28He spoke kindly to him and gave
him a seat of honor higher than those of the other
kings who were with him in Babylon. 29So Jehoiachin put aside his prison clothes and for the rest of
his life ate regularly at the king's table. 30Day by
day the king gave Jehoiachin a regular allowance as
long as he lived. Jer 52:31-34

[a] 17 Hebrew *eighteen cubits* (about 8.1 meters) [b] 17 Hebrew *three cubits* (about 1.3 meters) [c] 27 Also called *Amel-Marduk*

INTRODUCTION

1 CHRONICLES

What a waste! That is a common response when a novice opens the book of 1 Chronicles. At first glance, this book, as well as its sequel called 2 Chronicles, seems boring, tedious and pointless. Even after wading through nine chapters of genealogies, the remaining sections appear to be redundant and dry—a little like spending the afternoon in the telephone book or the card catalog at a public library. But God preserved these books of 1 and 2 Chronicles. He watched over their composition and cared for their preservation. To what end? To bore us? Never! He is pleased to have this account on record for reasons not immediately obvious to many of us. But as you read, you may begin to understand. Pay attention, if you would, as we discover how essential these "incidentals" really are.

WRITER: *Possibly Ezra*

DATE: *c.450–400 B.C.*

PURPOSE: *To show the Israelites how they fit into God's plan*

GOAL: *That God's people would recognize their godly roots and rediscover their heritage*

KEY VERSES: *29:10-13*

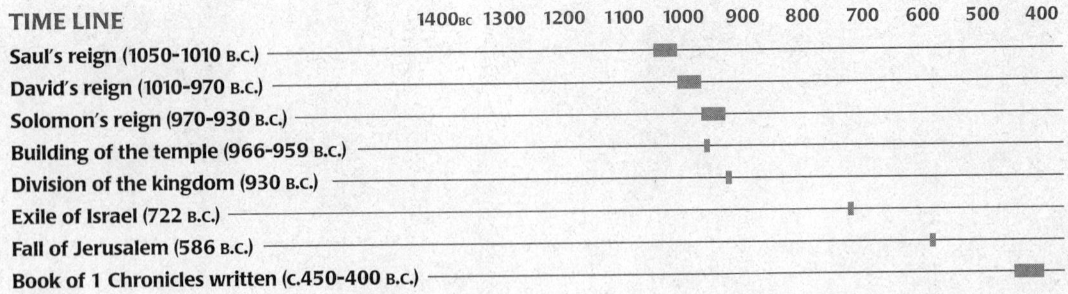

Essential Incidentals

1 CHRONICLES

God's View: *"From Nothingness to Greatness"*

GENEALOGIES — SAUL — DAVID — TEMPLE

CHAPTERS 1–9 — ***CHAPTER 10*** — ***CHAPTERS 11–21*** — ***CHAPTERS 22–29***

2 CHRONICLES

". . . From Greatness to Nothingness"

SOLOMON The King — JUDAH The Nation

GLORY — MISERY — REVIVAL — REJECTION

CHAPTERS 1–9 — ***CHAPTERS 10–36***

CONSECRATION — ***CAPTIVITY***

	1 Chronicles	2 Chronicles
PROCESS	**Little made great**	**Great becoming little**
EMPHASIS	**Personal determination**	**National deterioration**
KEY	***1 Chronicles 29:10-13***	***2 Chronicles 7:12-18***

Reading through the Bible is a little like driving across America coast to coast. It's one thing to plan an extensive trip like this, but it is something entirely different to actually do it.

Before the journey you sit down in your family room or around the kitchen table with a large map to plan the trip. At that time everything seems exciting. You can envision the desert scenes across Arizona, including the Grand Canyon, the majestic mountains of Colorado, the rolling hills of Utah and the green forests of Illinois. The anticipation of these noteworthy places presses you on to plan the rest of your lengthy trip. The excitement grows as you plan to see a few of the lakes of Minnesota, the lush countryside of Pennsylvania, the splendor of upstate New York, the stately scenes of Virginia, the monuments of Washington, D.C., the fall colors of New Hampshire and the breathtaking coastline of Maine—it all seems so fabulous!

However, when you actually set out on your journey from the west coast, it isn't too long before you are driving across a section you had not planned to travel. When we plan a more than 3,000-mile trip, we often forget how long and hot the trip through a place like the Mojave Desert will be. No matter how many wonderful sights we will see along the way, there will always be those long and arid sections of our trip. There's no escaping it: Traveling west to east includes several hours in the barren desert.

What is true of a trip across the country is also true of a journey through the Bible. As you read through God's Word, you eagerly anticipate meeting men like Noah, Abraham, Moses, Jacob, Joseph, Nehemiah, David, the kings, the prophets, Peter, Paul and many others. You also look forward to learning about women like Miriam, Sarah, Deborah, Ruth, Esther, Elizabeth, Mary and many others. It is easy to forget, however, that you also must travel through places like 1 and 2 Chronicles. There's no escaping the Chronicles!

Inspiration Does Not Necessarily Equal Excitement

In one of his devotional booklets, Bruce Wilkinson says, "Some sections of Chronicles may *not* be a candidate for 'Favorite Devotional Passage of the Year,' but they are certainly a cure for insomnia." There are large portions of Chronicles that do not strike the interest of most people. If this is true for you, let me put your mind at ease—much of what you will read here isn't supposed to be interesting! But it is, nevertheless, *inspired*.

To say that the books of Chronicles aren't supposed to be interesting neither calls into question the inspiration of Chronicles nor the importance of these books of Scripture. It is the simple truth. The fact is, *these books are an obituary*! They are a record of those who have gone before and have now died—and, at least to the vast majority of us, obituaries aren't stimulating reading.

I have had people, many people, say to me, "Hey, did you read the editorial in yesterday's paper?" Or, "Did you see what the sports section said about this athlete or that game?" I've even had people search me out just to tell me about something funny from the comics section of the paper. But I have never had anyone say, "Did you read the obituaries yesterday? They were so interesting I just couldn't put them down!" You get the point.

God knew he was not whipping up a best seller when he inspired the books of Chronicles—but he never intended to. Look at it this way: 1 and 2 Chronicles may not be terribly exciting, but they are *absolutely essential*. For God's Book to be complete, it must include the record of the Chronicles. It is to our faith what the telephone book is to communication or what the dictionary is to the English language. These are great resources, but they were never meant to be read in one sitting.

A Journal of God's People

The Hebrew title *dibre hayyamin* means "the words of the days." It is a term referring to the diaries and journals of the times. Originally 1 and 2 Chronicles were only one book . . . one long scroll called "the diary of the days." The Greek title (*paraleipomena*) in the *Septuagint* (the Greek translation of the Old Testament) is interesting. It means "the things omitted," or "the things remaining." The books of Chronicles cover the events already recorded in 2 Samuel, 1 Kings and 2 Kings—but 1 and 2 Chronicles add things these three books omitted.

The word "Chronicles" is from the Latin *chronicoram*. This word literally conveys this idea: "A continuous detailed account of events arranged chronologically and without analysis or interpretation." In other words, the books of Chronicles simply tell us what happened. A modern-day analogy would be our encyclopedia or a trustworthy history book of a nation.

The author of 1 and 2 Chronicles was probably Ezra. He was a scribe and a careful student of the Bible. We can learn a great deal about this man through a close study of the Bible book that bears his name—the book of Ezra (see "True Man of the Word" on page 470).

Ezra wrote from a specific perspective and vantage point. He was looking back on the history of his people after their spiritual erosion, fall and captivity. When you write something from hindsight, you have a lot of insight, and that is what Ezra brought to the record contained in the Chronicles.

History From Behind Bars

The Chronicles of Israel are important because they were written out of something like a concentration camp experience. Reading Chronicles would be somewhat akin to reading a history written from Dachau during the reign of Hitler. It is the writer's way of saying, "Let's never forget *God's* hand on our nation now that we have been under another's regime." This section of Scripture was written after Israel had been under the oppressive hand of the Babylonian government.

After listing one name after another for eight chapters, Ezra penned these words: "All Israel was listed in the genealogies recorded in the book of the kings of Israel. The people of Judah were taken captive to Babylon because of their unfaithfulness" (9:1). Ezra wanted his readers to know that he was writing out of the experience of exile and captivity and return from exile. Although his words might seem boring or difficult to comprehend, Ezra wrote this record with a fair amount of pathos and passion.

The Glory Years

The bulk of the history in 1 Chronicles is devoted to the reign of David. Chapter 10 records the death of Israel's first king, Saul, who died "because he was unfaithful to the LORD" (10:13), while chapters 11–21 paint a portrait of David's reign that glows with glory. Anything that might diminish the glory of David's reign was omitted in this history book—things like David's sin with Bathsheba and the tragic stories of David's sons Amnon and Absalom. To a community coming out of years of exile, a view of history that offered hope for the future was desperately needed—and graciously provided in the book of 1 Chronicles. Even in judgment, even in exile, even in restoration, God was in control. He was at work, throughout the years of David's reign, to preserve His people and to sustain Israel's hope for the promised Messiah. Furthermore, He could be trusted to carry His people through as they returned to their homeland. The reality of *God's faithfulness* was carefully depicted in 1 Chronicles.

The final chapters (22–29) detail preparations and plans for the building of the temple as the place where God's Name would be present among His people. Writing for a generation coming out of captivity, Ezra took great pains to show that the temple of the Lord and its service (described in depth in chapters 23–26) were preeminent gifts of God given to Israel through the dynasty of David. As the book ends, David's death is recorded with this summary statement: "He died at a good old age, having enjoyed long life, wealth and honor" (29:28). David's son Solomon stood ready to follow in his father's footsteps—and chapters 1–9 of 2 Chronicles tell the story of his reign.

The Period at the End of the Old Testament

The two books of Chronicles are actually found at the end of the Hebrew Bible. The Jews concluded the Old Testament with these four books: Daniel, Ezra, Nehemiah and the Chronicles. One way to put it is this: Chronicles is the period at the end of the Old Testament "sentence." Note that on one occasion in the New Testament Jesus spoke these serious and severe words to the Pharisees and the teachers of the law:

> *Therefore this generation will be held responsible for the blood of all the prophets that has been shed since the beginning of the world, from the blood of Abel to the blood of Zechariah, who was killed between the altar and the sanctuary. Yes, I tell you this generation will be held responsible for it all (Luke 11:50–51).*

In effect, Jesus was saying, "From Genesis to 2 Chronicles the blood of the prophets that has been shed will be held against this generation." From Abel to Zechariah . . . From A to Z, if you please. Here is a clear reference to the first and last of the 39 books of the Old Testament as arranged in the Hebrew canon. These final books of the Old Testament Bible (1 and 2 Chronicles) record God's hand on His people from beginning to end.

Essential Incidentals

The details of Chronicles may not seem very important to us. Names we have never heard of, places we have never been, and practices that we have not participated in are not very exciting. However, these incidental details are absolutely essential in God's sight. The little details matter to God, and therefore they should matter to us. In a sense, our names, our lives, and the places we travel might seem unimportant to those who live generations after we have departed this earth. And yet, we can be so thankful that the details of our lives matter to God. The incidentals of our lives are essentials in God's sight—because He loves us and because His plan encompasses everything and everyone. That fact assures us that He is involved in *all of life*, including the boring, the tedious, and that which seems, at the time, absolutely unimportant. Bottom line: God cares about us! We matter to Him!

Names, Names, Names — Chapters 1–9

Just open the book of 1 Chronicles anywhere in the first nine chapters and drop your finger onto the page. Go ahead . . . do it. I know exactly what you're going to find. Names! Names, names and then some more names. In these chapters you will find the names of kings, leaders of Israel, descendants of the tribes of Israel, musicians and priests . . . the lists go on and on. In these chapters we find hundreds upon hundreds of names—records that helped the Israelites remember their position as members of God's family.

Reading through these lists of names may seem to us like a dusty, monotonous drive through the desert. To God, these were the names of his children, his servants, his friends. Although these names may not seem very important to us, we can be thankful that they are important to God. The truth is, *names are important to God.* The Bible tells us that he knows each of us *by name* (see Isaiah 43:1). If we know the Savior, then our names are written in the book of life (Revelation 21:27). Before we dismiss this collection of names as boring or irrelevant, let's remember that the God of heaven knows us by name. Names really do matter to God . . . yours included!

Historical Records From Adam to Abraham

To Noah's Sons

1 Adam, Seth, Enosh, 2Kenan, Mahalalel, Jared,
3Enoch, Methuselah, Lamech, Noah.

4The sons of Noah:[a]
Shem, Ham and Japheth. Ge 5:32; 6:10

The Japhethites

5The sons[b] of Japheth:
Gomer, Magog, Madai, Javan, Tubal,
Meshech and Tiras.
6The sons of Gomer:
Ashkenaz, Riphath[c] and Togarmah.
7The sons of Javan:
Elishah, Tarshish, the Kittim and the
Rodanim. Ge 10:2-5

The Hamites

8The sons of Ham:
Cush, Mizraim,[d] Put and Canaan.
9The sons of Cush:
Seba, Havilah, Sabta, Raamah and Sab-
teca.
The sons of Raamah:
Sheba and Dedan.
10Cush was the father[e] of
Nimrod, who grew to be a mighty warrior on earth.
11Mizraim was the father of
the Ludites, Anamites, Lehabites, Naph-
tuhites, 12Pathrusites, Casluhites (from
whom the Philistines came) and Caphtorites.
13Canaan was the father of
Sidon his firstborn,[f] and of the Hittites,
14Jebusites, Amorites, Girgashites, 15Hi-
vites, Arkites, Sinites, 16Arvadites, Zema-
rites and Hamathites. Ge 10:6-20

The Semites

17The sons of Shem:
Elam, Asshur, Arphaxad, Lud and Aram.
The sons of Aram[g]:
Uz, Hul, Gether and Meshech.
18Arphaxad was the father of Shelah,
and Shelah the father of Eber.
19Two sons were born to Eber:
One was named Peleg,[h] because in his
time the earth was divided; his brother
was named Joktan.
20Joktan was the father of
Almodad, Sheleph, Hazarmaveth, Jerah,
21Hadoram, Uzal, Diklah, 22Obal,[i]
Abimael, Sheba, 23Ophir, Havilah and Jobab. All these were sons of Joktan.

24Shem, Arphaxad,[j] Shelah, Lk 3:34-36
25Eber, Peleg, Reu,
26Serug, Nahor, Terah
27and Abram (that is, Abraham).

The Family of Abraham

28The sons of Abraham:
Isaac and Ishmael.

Descendants of Hagar

29These were their descendants:
Nebaioth the firstborn of Ishmael, Kedar,
Adbeel, Mibsam, 30Mishma, Dumah,
Massa, Hadad, Tema, 31Jetur, Naphish
and Kedemah. These were the sons of
Ishmael. Ge 25:12-16

Descendants of Keturah

32The sons born to Keturah, Abraham's concubine: Ge 22:24
Zimran, Jokshan, Medan, Midian, Ishbak
and Shuah.
The sons of Jokshan:

[a]4 Septuagint; Hebrew does not have *The sons of Noah:* [b]5 *Sons* may mean *descendants* or *successors* or *nations*; also in verses 6-10, 17 and 20. [c]6 Many Hebrew manuscripts and Vulgate (see also Septuagint and Gen. 10:3); most Hebrew manuscripts *Diphath* [d]8 That is, Egypt; also in verse 11 [e]10 *Father* may mean *ancestor* or *predecessor* or *founder*; also in verses 11, 13, 18 and 20. [f]13 Or *of the Sidonians, the foremost* [g]17 One Hebrew manuscript and some Septuagint manuscripts (see also Gen. 10:23); most Hebrew manuscripts do not have this line. [h]19 *Peleg* means *division.* [i]22 Some Hebrew manuscripts and Syriac (see also Gen. 10:28); most Hebrew manuscripts *Ebal* [j]24 Hebrew; some Septuagint manuscripts *Arphaxad, Cainan* (see also note at Gen. 11:10)

Sheba and Dedan. Ge 10:7
33The sons of Midian:
Ephah, Epher, Hanoch, Abida and Eldaah.
All these were descendants of Keturah.

Descendants of Sarah

34Abraham was the father of Isaac. Ge 21:2-3
The sons of Isaac:
Esau and Israel. Ge 17:5; 25:25-26

Esau's Sons

35The sons of Esau: Ge 36:19
Eliphaz, Reuel, Jeush, Jalam and Korah.
36The sons of Eliphaz:
Teman, Omar, Zepho,[a] Gatam and Kenaz;
by Timna: Amalek.[b] Ex 17:14
37The sons of Reuel: Ge 36:17
Nahath, Zerah, Shammah and Mizzah.

The People of Seir in Edom

38The sons of Seir:
Lotan, Shobal, Zibeon, Anah, Dishon, Ezer and Dishan.
39The sons of Lotan:
Hori and Homam. Timna was Lotan's sister.
40The sons of Shobal:
Alvan,[c] Manahath, Ebal, Shepho and Onam.
The sons of Zibeon:
Aiah and Anah. Ge 36:2
41The son of Anah:
Dishon.
The sons of Dishon:
Hemdan,[d] Eshban, Ithran and Keran.
42The sons of Ezer:
Bilhan, Zaavan and Akan.[e]
The sons of Dishan[f]:
Uz and Aran. Ge 36:20-28

The Rulers of Edom

43These were the kings who reigned in Edom before any Israelite king reigned[g]:
Bela son of Beor, whose city was named Dinhabah.
44When Bela died, Jobab son of Zerah from Bozrah succeeded him as king.
45When Jobab died, Husham from the land of the Temanites succeeded him as king.
46When Husham died, Hadad son of Bedad, who defeated Midian in the country of Moab, succeeded him as king. His city was named Avith.
47When Hadad died, Samlah from Masrekah succeeded him as king.
48When Samlah died, Shaul from Rehoboth on the river[h] succeeded him as king.
49When Shaul died, Baal-Hanan son of Acbor succeeded him as king.
50When Baal-Hanan died, Hadad succeeded him as king. His city was named Pau,[i] and his wife's name was Mehetabel daughter of Matred, the daughter of Me-Zahab. 51Hadad also died.

The chiefs of Edom were:
Timna, Alvah, Jetheth, 52Oholibamah, Elah, Pinon, 53Kenaz, Teman, Mibzar, 54Magdiel and Iram. These were the chiefs of Edom. Ge 36:31-43

Israel's Sons

2 These were the sons of Israel:
Reuben, Simeon, Levi, Judah, Issachar, Zebulun, 2Dan, Joseph, Benjamin, Naphtali, Gad and Asher. Ge 35:23-26

Judah

To Hezron's Sons

3The sons of Judah: Ge 38:2-10
Er, Onan and Shelah. These three were born to him by a Canaanite woman, the daughter of Shua. Er, Judah's firstborn, was wicked in the LORD's sight; so the LORD put him to death. 4Tamar, Judah's daughter-in-law, bore him Perez and Zerah. Judah had five sons in all.

5The sons of Perez: Ge 46:12
Hezron and Hamul. Nu 26:21
6The sons of Zerah:
Zimri, Ethan, Heman, Calcol and Darda[j]—five in all.
7The son of Carmi:
Achar,[k] who brought trouble on Israel by violating the ban on taking devoted things.[l] Jos 6:18; 7:1

[a] 36 Many Hebrew manuscripts, some Septuagint manuscripts and Syriac (see also Gen. 36:11); most Hebrew manuscripts *Zephi* [b] 36 Some Septuagint manuscripts (see also Gen. 36:12); Hebrew *Gatam, Kenaz, Timna and Amalek* [c] 40 Many Hebrew manuscripts and some Septuagint manuscripts (see also Gen. 36:23); most Hebrew manuscripts *Alian* [d] 41 Many Hebrew manuscripts and some Septuagint manuscripts (see also Gen. 36:26); most Hebrew manuscripts *Hamran* [e] 42 Many Hebrew and Septuagint manuscripts (see also Gen. 36:27); most Hebrew manuscripts *Zaavan, Jaakan* [f] 42 Hebrew *Dishon,* a variant of *Dishan* [g] 43 Or *before an Israelite king reigned over them* [h] 48 Possibly the Euphrates [i] 50 Many Hebrew manuscripts, some Septuagint manuscripts, Vulgate and Syriac (see also Gen. 36:39); most Hebrew manuscripts *Pai*
[j] 6 Many Hebrew manuscripts, some Septuagint manuscripts and Syriac (see also 1 Kings 4:31); most Hebrew manuscripts *Dara*
[k] 7 *Achar* means *trouble*; *Achar* is called *Achan* in Joshua. [l] 7 The Hebrew term refers to the irrevocable giving over of things or persons to the LORD, often by totally destroying them.

8The son of Ethan:
Azariah.
9The sons born to Hezron were:
Jerahmeel, Ram and Caleb.[a] Nu 26:21

From Ram Son of Hezron

10Ram was the father of Lk 3:32-33
Amminadab, and Amminadab the father
of Nahshon, the leader of the people of
Judah. 11Nahshon was the father of Salmon,[b] Salmon the father of Boaz, 12Boaz
the father of Obed and Obed the father of
Jesse. Ru 2:1; 4:17
13Jesse was the father of Ru 4:17
Eliab his firstborn; the second son was
Abinadab, the third Shimea, 14the fourth
Nethanel, the fifth Raddai, 15the sixth
Ozem and the seventh David. 16Their sisters were Zeruiah and Abigail. Zeruiah's
three sons were Abishai, Joab and Asahel.
17Abigail was the mother of Amasa,
whose father was Jether the Ishmaelite.

Caleb Son of Hezron

18Caleb son of Hezron had children by his
wife Azubah (and by Jerioth). These were
her sons: Jesher, Shobab and Ardon.
19When Azubah died, Caleb married
Ephrath, who bore him Hur. 20Hur was
the father of Uri, and Uri the father of
Bezalel. ver 42,50; Ex 31:2
21Later, Hezron lay with the daughter of Makir the father of Gilead (he had married
her when he was sixty years old), and she
bore him Segub. 22Segub was the father of
Jair, who controlled twenty-three towns
in Gilead. 23(But Geshur and Aram captured Havvoth Jair,[c] as well as Kenath
with its surrounding settlements—sixty
towns.) All these were descendants of
Makir the father of Gilead. Nu 32:41; Dt 3:14

24After Hezron died in Caleb Ephrathah, Abijah the wife of Hezron bore him Ashhur
the father[d] of Tekoa. 1Ch 4:5

Jerahmeel Son of Hezron

25The sons of Jerahmeel the firstborn of Hezron:
Ram his firstborn, Bunah, Oren, Ozem
and[e] Ahijah. 26Jerahmeel had another
wife, whose name was Atarah; she was
the mother of Onam.
27The sons of Ram the firstborn of Jerahmeel:
Maaz, Jamin and Eker.
28The sons of Onam:
Shammai and Jada.
The sons of Shammai:
Nadab and Abishur.
29Abishur's wife was named Abihail, who
bore him Ahban and Molid.
30The sons of Nadab:
Seled and Appaim. Seled died without
children.
31The son of Appaim:
Ishi, who was the father of Sheshan.
Sheshan was the father of Ahlai.
32The sons of Jada, Shammai's brother:
Jether and Jonathan. Jether died without
children.
33The sons of Jonathan:
Peleth and Zaza.
These were the descendants of Jerahmeel.
34Sheshan had no sons—only daughters.
He had an Egyptian servant named Jarha.
35Sheshan gave his daughter in marriage
to his servant Jarha, and she bore him
Attai.
36Attai was the father of Nathan,
Nathan the father of Zabad, 1Ch 11:41
37Zabad the father of Ephlal,
Ephlal the father of Obed,
38Obed the father of Jehu,
Jehu the father of Azariah,
39Azariah the father of Helez,
Helez the father of Eleasah,
40Eleasah the father of Sismai,
Sismai the father of Shallum,
41Shallum the father of Jekamiah,
and Jekamiah the father of Elishama.

The Clans of Caleb

42The sons of Caleb the brother of Jerahmeel:
Mesha his firstborn, who was the father
of Ziph, and his son Mareshah,[f] who
was the father of Hebron.
43The sons of Hebron:
Korah, Tappuah, Rekem and Shema.
44Shema was the father of Raham, and
Raham the father of Jorkeam. Rekem was
the father of Shammai. 45The son of
Shammai was Maon, and Maon was the
father of Beth Zur. Jos 15:55,58
46Caleb's concubine Ephah was the mother of
Haran, Moza and Gazez. Haran was the
father of Gazez.
47The sons of Jahdai:
Regem, Jotham, Geshan, Pelet, Ephah
and Shaaph.
48Caleb's concubine Maacah was the mother
of Sheber and Tirhanah. 49She also gave
birth to Shaaph the father of Madman-

[a]9 Hebrew *Kelubai,* a variant of *Caleb* [b]11 Septuagint (see also Ruth 4:21); Hebrew *Salma* [c]23 Or *captured the settlements of Jair* [d]24 *Father* may mean *civic leader* or *military leader*; also in verses 42, 45, 49-52 and possibly elsewhere. [e]25 Or *Oren and Ozem, by* [f]42 The meaning of the Hebrew for this phrase is uncertain.

nah and to Sheva the father of Macbenah
and Gibea. Caleb's daughter was Acsah.
50 These were the descendants of Caleb.

The sons of Hur the firstborn of Ephrathah:
Shobal the father of Kiriath Jearim, 51 Salma the father of Bethlehem, and Hareph
the father of Beth Gader. ver 19
52 The descendants of Shobal the father of Kiriath Jearim were:
Haroeh, half the Manahathites, 53 and the
clans of Kiriath Jearim: the Ithrites, Pu-
thites, Shumathites and Mishraites. From
these descended the Zorathites and Esh-
taolites. 2Sa 23:38
54 The descendants of Salma:
Bethlehem, the Netophathites, Atroth
Beth Joab, half the Manahathites, the Zo-
rites, 55 and the clans of scribes[a] who
lived at Jabez: the Tirathites, Shimeathites
and Sucathites. These are the Kenites
who came from Hammath, the father of
the house of Recab.[b] Jdg 1:16; Jer 35:2-19

The Sons of David

3 These were the sons of David born to him in
Hebron: 1Ch 14:3; 28:5
The firstborn was Amnon the son of
Ahinoam of Jezreel; Jos 15:56
the second, Daniel the son of Abigail of
Carmel; 1Sa 25:42
2 the third, Absalom the son of Maacah
daughter of Talmai king of Geshur;
the fourth, Adonijah the son of Haggith;
3 the fifth, Shephatiah the son of Abital;
and the sixth, Ithream, by his wife Eglah.
4 These six were born to David in Hebron,
where he reigned seven years and six
months. 2Sa 3:2-5
David reigned in Jerusalem thirty-three years,
5 and these were the children born to him there:
Shammua,[c] Shobab, Nathan and Solo-
mon. These four were by Bathsheba[d]
daughter of Ammiel. 6 There were also Ib-
har, Elishua,[e] Eliphelet, 7 Nogah, Nepheg, Japhia, 8 Elishama, Eliada and
Eliphelet—nine in all. 9 All these were the
sons of David, besides his sons by his
concubines. And Tamar was their sister.

The Kings of Judah

10 Solomon's son was Rehoboam, 1Ki 11:43
Abijah his son,
Asa his son,
Jehoshaphat his son, 2Ch 17:1-21:3
11 Jehoram[f] his son, 2Ki 8:16-24; 2Ch 21:1
Ahaziah his son, 2Ch 22:1-10
Joash his son, 2Ki 11:1-12:21
12 Amaziah his son, 2Ki 14:1-22
Azariah his son,
Jotham his son, Isa 1:1; Hos 1:1
13 Ahaz his son, Isa 7:1
Hezekiah his son, Jer 26:19
Manasseh his son, 2Ch 33:1
14 Amon his son, 2Ki 21:19-26
Josiah his son. Jer 1:2; 25:3
15 The sons of Josiah:
Johanan the firstborn,
Jehoiakim the second son, 2Ki 23:34
Zedekiah the third, Jer 37:1
Shallum the fourth. 2Ki 23:31
16 The successors of Jehoiakim:
Jehoiachin[g] his son, Mt 1:11
and Zedekiah. 2Ki 24:18

The Royal Line After the Exile

17 The descendants of Jehoiachin the captive:
Shealtiel his son, 18 Malkiram, Pedaiah,
Shenazzar, Jekamiah, Hoshama and
Nedabiah. Ezr 1:8; 5:14; Jer 22:30
19 The sons of Pedaiah:
Zerubbabel and Shimei. Ezr 5:2; Ne 7:7
The sons of Zerubbabel:
Meshullam and Hananiah.
Shelomith was their sister.
20 There were also five others:
Hashubah, Ohel, Berekiah, Hasadiah and
Jushab-Hesed.
21 The descendants of Hananiah:
Pelatiah and Jeshaiah, and the sons of
Rephaiah, of Arnan, of Obadiah and of
Shecaniah.
22 The descendants of Shecaniah:
Shemaiah and his sons:
Hattush, Igal, Bariah, Neariah and Sha-
phat—six in all. Ezr 8:2-3
23 The sons of Neariah:
Elioenai, Hizkiah and Azrikam—three in
all.
24 The sons of Elioenai:
Hodaviah, Eliashib, Pelaiah, Akkub, Jo-
hanan, Delaiah and Anani—seven in all.

Other Clans of Judah

4 The descendants of Judah: Ge 46:12; 1Ch 2:3
Perez, Hezron, Carmi, Hur and Shobal.
2 Reaiah son of Shobal was the father of Jahath, and Jahath the father of Ahumai
and Lahad. These were the clans of the
Zorathites.

[a] 55 Or *of the Sopherites* [b] 55 Or *father of Beth Recab* [c] 5 Hebrew *Shimea,* a variant of *Shammua* [d] 5 One Hebrew manuscript and Vulgate (see also Septuagint and 2 Samuel 11:3); most Hebrew manuscripts *Bathshua* [e] 6 Two Hebrew manuscripts (see also 2 Samuel 5:15 and 1 Chron. 14:5); most Hebrew manuscripts *Elishama* [f] 11 Hebrew *Joram,* a variant of *Jehoram* [g] 16 Hebrew *Jeconiah,* a variant of *Jehoiachin*; also in verse 17

[3]These were the sons[a] of Etam:
Jezreel, Ishma and Idbash. Their sister
was named Hazzelelponi. [4]Penuel was the
father of Gedor, and Ezer the father of
Hushah.
These were the descendants of Hur, the
firstborn of Ephrathah and father[b] of
Bethlehem. Ru 1:19; 1Ch 2:50
[5]Ashhur the father of Tekoa had two wives,
Helah and Naarah. 1Ch 2:24
[6]Naarah bore him Ahuzzam, Hepher, Temeni and Haahashtari. These were the
descendants of Naarah.
[7]The sons of Helah:
Zereth, Zohar, Ethnan, [8]and Koz, who
was the father of Anub and Hazzobebah
and of the clans of Aharhel son of Harum.

[9]Jabez was more honorable than his brothers.
His mother had named him Jabez,[c] saying, "I
gave birth to him in pain." [10]Jabez cried out to the
God of Israel, "Oh, that you would bless me and
enlarge my territory! Let your hand be with me,
and keep me from harm so that I will be free from
pain." And God granted his request.

[11]Kelub, Shuhah's brother, was the father of
Mehir, who was the father of Eshton.
[12]Eshton was the father of Beth Rapha,
Paseah and Tehinnah the father of Ir Nahash.[d] These were the men of Recah.

[13]The sons of Kenaz:
Othniel and Seraiah. Jos 15:17
The sons of Othniel:
Hathath and Meonothai.[e] [14]Meonothai
was the father of Ophrah.
Seraiah was the father of Joab,
the father of Ge Harashim.[f] It was called
this because its people were craftsmen.
[15]The sons of Caleb son of Jephunneh:
Iru, Elah and Naam.
The son of Elah:
Kenaz.
[16]The sons of Jehallelel:
Ziph, Ziphah, Tiria and Asarel.
[17]The sons of Ezrah:
Jether, Mered, Epher and Jalon. One of
Mered's wives gave birth to Miriam,
Shammai and Ishbah the father of Eshtemoa. [18](His Judean wife gave birth to Jered the father of Gedor, Heber the father
of Soco, and Jekuthiel the father of Zanoah.) These were the children of Pharaoh's
daughter Bithiah, whom Mered had married. Ex 15:20; Jos 15:34
[19]The sons of Hodiah's wife, the sister of Naham:
the father of Keilah the Garmite, and
Eshtemoa the Maacathite. Dt 3:14; Jos 15:44
[20]The sons of Shimon:
Amnon, Rinnah, Ben-Hanan and Tilon.
The descendants of Ishi:
Zoheth and Ben-Zoheth.
[21]The sons of Shelah son of Judah:
Er the father of Lecah, Laadah the father
of Mareshah and the clans of the linen
workers at Beth Ashbea, [22]Jokim, the
men of Cozeba, and Joash and Saraph,
who ruled in Moab and Jashubi Lehem.
(These records are from ancient times.)
[23]They were the potters who lived at Netaim and Gederah; they stayed there and
worked for the king. Ge 38:5

Simeon

[24]The descendants of Simeon: Ge 29:33
Nemuel, Jamin, Jarib, Zerah and Shaul;
[25]Shallum was Shaul's son, Mibsam his son
and Mishma his son.
[26]The descendants of Mishma:
Hammuel his son, Zaccur his son and
Shimei his son.

[27]Shimei had sixteen sons and six daughters,
but his brothers did not have many children; so
their entire clan did not become as numerous as
the people of Judah. [28]They lived in Beersheba,
Moladah, Hazar Shual, [29]Bilhah, Ezem, Tolad,
[30]Bethuel, Hormah, Ziklag, [31]Beth Marcaboth, Hazar Susim, Beth Biri and Shaaraim. These were
their towns until the reign of David. [32]Their surrounding villages were Etam, Ain, Rimmon, Token and Ashan—five towns— [33]and all the villages around these towns as far as Baalath.[g] These
were their settlements. And they kept a genealogical record. Jos 19:2-10

[34]Meshobab, Jamlech, Joshah son of Amaziah, [35]Joel, Jehu son of Joshibiah, the son of
Seraiah, the son of Asiel, [36]also Elioenai, Jaakobah, Jeshohaiah, Asaiah, Adiel, Jesimiel,
Benaiah, [37]and Ziza son of Shiphi, the son of
Allon, the son of Jedaiah, the son of Shimri,
the son of Shemaiah.

[38]The men listed above by name were leaders of
their clans. Their families increased greatly, [39]and
they went to the outskirts of Gedor to the east
of the valley in search of pasture for their flocks.
[40]They found rich, good pasture, and the land was

[a] 3 Some Septuagint manuscripts (see also Vulgate); Hebrew *father* [b] 4 *Father* may mean *civic leader* or *military leader*; also in verses 12, 14, 17, 18 and possibly elsewhere. [c] 9 *Jabez* sounds like the Hebrew for *pain.* [d] 12 Or *of the city of Nahash* [e] 13 Some Septuagint manuscripts and Vulgate; Hebrew does not have *and Meonothai.* [f] 14 *Ge Harashim* means *valley of craftsmen.* [g] 33 Some Septuagint manuscripts (see also Joshua 19:8); Hebrew *Baal*

A Man Named "Pain"

"Jabez cried out to the God of Israel, 'Oh, that you would bless me and enlarge my territory!'"
– 1 CHRONICLES 4:10a

The name Jabez stands out in one of the most ancient obituaries in the history of literature. In the middle of a series of genealogies of people whose names you can hardly pronounce, most of which you've never heard before, God lingered over this name for two verses. When God purposely singles out one person in a myriad of other names that get no attention, it's worth the time we might take to ponder that life.

This mother named her baby "Jabez"—a descriptive title. His name sounds like the Hebrew word for "pain" or "suffering." Now why would a mother name a baby "pain"? Jabez came into the world under distressing circumstances. There was something agonizing about the times in which he was born and the manner in which he was born. I take it his mother was at the height of despair.

Perhaps you know what it's like to be unwanted. Maybe you were born into a home already filled with children, and you weren't wanted. Perhaps you have lived with the sneaking suspicion, or maybe the stark statement, that you were an "accident." If so, you can begin to appreciate how Jabez must have felt about the label that followed him throughout his life.

There is a shaft of light that penetrates the cloud of pessimism that seemed to surround Jabez's entrance into this world. The Bible records this testimony about Jabez's character: "Jabez was more honorable than his brothers" (1 Chronicles 4:9). Jabez had distinguished himself within his family circle; he stood out as a man of integrity, as a man worthy of a high reputation. Fascinating! Here was a man who began his life under the most difficult of circumstances. He lived with that reminder every time he heard his name spoken. In the minds of those around him he may very well have been thought of as a "born loser." But observe this: He may have entered the world in pain, but he was not pushed aside.

It gets better the deeper you dig. In verse 10 of chapter 4, this "honorable" man approached God in prayer. He prayed with courage, presenting his optimistic requests to God: "Oh, that you would bless me . . ." Jabez seemed to be saying to God, "I've been Jabez long enough. I've lived my life in pain and dishonor. Please give me your blessing now, and turn my life around." Jabez continued to pour out his heart to God: " . . . and enlarge my territory." Many people have prayed that God would bless them, but Jabez prayed with sanctioned ambition. He wasn't content just to survive; he wanted to thrive. He had big dreams.

And then Jabez concluded his prayer with these words: "Let your hand be with me, and keep me from harm so that I will be free from pain." You see, Jabez was very wise. He realized that if God's answer to this prayer was "yes," then he would need to have God's hand on his life, guiding him and protecting him. It's a simple fact that there are very few people who can handle God's abundant blessings; there are dozens of people who handle poverty with uncommon grace for every one person who can properly deal with prosperity. And in the midst of making his requests Jabez remembered to ask for God's hand to be active in his life, saying, in effect, "I want to go out trusting You to do great things, Lord. And when You do them, I just want to walk with You, to be Your man. Keep Your hand on my life."

Did you catch the pattern? First he prayed for God's blessing; then he asked for God's cooperation; finally, he prayed for God's protection. "Lord, I'm Jabez by name. I know what pain is like. But I'm weary of that kind of lifestyle. I pray that You might turn my life around and stop the hurtful patterns. As I come out from under the cloud of difficulty, I pray that You would make of me a man altogether unique, because I don't want to live up to my name." And the best part of this story is that "God granted his request." Jabez, the man named "Pain," was honored because of his relationship with God.

Are you ready to ask God to do a major work in your life? Take a cue from Jabez. God answers us when we pray with courage, with determination, with boldness—in a spirit of vulnerability before Him.

spacious, peaceful and quiet. Some Hamites had
lived there formerly. Jdg 18:7-10

41 The men whose names were listed came in the
days of Hezekiah king of Judah. They attacked the
Hamites in their dwellings and also the Meunites
who were there and completely destroyed[a] them,
as is evident to this day. Then they settled in their
place, because there was pasture for their flocks.
42 And five hundred of these Simeonites, led by
Pelatiah, Neariah, Rephaiah and Uzziel, the sons of
Ishi, invaded the hill country of Seir. 43 They killed
the remaining Amalekites who had escaped, and
they have lived there to this day. 1Sa 15:8; 30:17

Reuben

5 The sons of Reuben the firstborn of Israel (he
was the firstborn, but when he defiled his
father's marriage bed, his rights as firstborn were
given to the sons of Joseph son of Israel; so he
could not be listed in the genealogical record in
accordance with his birthright, 2 and though Judah
was the strongest of his brothers and a ruler came
from him, the rights of the firstborn belonged to
Joseph)— 3 the sons of Reuben the firstborn of
Israel: Ps 60:7; Mic 5:2; Mt 2:6

Hanoch, Pallu, Hezron and Carmi. Nu 26:5

4 The descendants of Joel:
Shemaiah his son, Gog his son,
Shimei his son, 5 Micah his son,
Reaiah his son, Baal his son,
6 and Beerah his son, whom Tiglath-Pileser[b] king of Assyria took into exile. Beerah was a leader of the Reubenites.

7 Their relatives by clans, listed according to
their genealogical records: ver 17
Jeiel the chief, Zechariah, 8 and Bela son
of Azaz, the son of Shema, the son of Joel.
They settled in the area from Aroer to
Nebo and Baal Meon. 9 To the east they
occupied the land up to the edge of the
desert that extends to the Euphrates River, because their livestock had increased
in Gilead. Nu 32:26; Jos 22:9

10 During Saul's reign they waged war
against the Hagrites, who were defeated at
their hands; they occupied the dwellings of
the Hagrites throughout the entire region
east of Gilead. ver 18-21

Gad

11 The Gadites lived next to them in Bashan, as
far as Salecah: Jos 13:11,24-28

12 Joel was the chief, Shapham the second,
then Janai and Shaphat, in Bashan.

13 Their relatives, by families, were:
Michael, Meshullam, Sheba, Jorai, Jacan,
Zia and Eber—seven in all.

14 These were the sons of Abihail son of
Huri, the son of Jaroah, the son of Gilead,
the son of Michael, the son of Jeshishai,
the son of Jahdo, the son of Buz.

15 Ahi son of Abdiel, the son of Guni, was
head of their family.

16 The Gadites lived in Gilead, in Bashan and
its outlying villages, and on all the pasturelands of Sharon as far as they extended.

17 All these were entered in the genealogical
records during the reigns of Jotham king of Judah
and Jeroboam king of Israel. 2Ki 14:16,28; 15:32

18 The Reubenites, the Gadites and the half-tribe
of Manasseh had 44,760 men ready for military
service—able-bodied men who could handle
shield and sword, who could use a bow, and who
were trained for battle. 19 They waged war against
the Hagrites, Jetur, Naphish and Nodab. 20 They
were helped in fighting them, and God handed the
Hagrites and all their allies over to them, because
they cried out to him during the battle. He answered their prayers, because they trusted in him.
21 They seized the livestock of the Hagrites—fifty
thousand camels, two hundred fifty thousand
sheep and two thousand donkeys. They also took
one hundred thousand people captive, 22 and many
others fell slain, because the battle was God's. And
they occupied the land until the exile. 2Ki 15:29

The Half-Tribe of Manasseh

23 The people of the half-tribe of Manasseh were
numerous; they settled in the land from Bashan to
Baal Hermon, that is, to Senir (Mount Hermon).

24 These were the heads of their families: Epher,
Ishi, Eliel, Azriel, Jeremiah, Hodaviah and Jahdiel.
They were brave warriors, famous men, and heads
of their families. 25 But they were unfaithful to the
God of their fathers and prostituted themselves to
the gods of the peoples of the land, whom God had
destroyed before them. 26 So the God of Israel
stirred up the spirit of Pul king of Assyria (that
is, Tiglath-Pileser king of Assyria), who took the
Reubenites, the Gadites and the half-tribe of Manasseh into exile. He took them to Halah, Habor,
Hara and the river of Gozan, where they are to this
day. 2Ki 15:29; 17:6; 18:11

Levi

6 The sons of Levi: Ge 46:11; Ex 6:16; Nu 26:57
Gershon, Kohath and Merari.

2 The sons of Kohath:
Amram, Izhar, Hebron and Uzziel.

3 The children of Amram:

[a] 41 The Hebrew term refers to the irrevocable giving over of things or persons to the LORD, often by totally destroying them.
[b] 6 Hebrew *Tilgath-Pilneser*, a variant of *Tiglath-Pileser*; also in verse 26

Aaron, Moses and Miriam.
The sons of Aaron:
Nadab, Abihu, Eleazar and Ithamar.
[4]Eleazar was the father of Phinehas,
Phinehas the father of Abishua,
[5]Abishua the father of Bukki,
Bukki the father of Uzzi,
[6]Uzzi the father of Zerahiah,
Zerahiah the father of Meraioth,
[7]Meraioth the father of Amariah,
Amariah the father of Ahitub,
[8]Ahitub the father of Zadok, 2Sa 8:17; 15:27
Zadok the father of Ahimaaz,
[9]Ahimaaz the father of Azariah,
Azariah the father of Johanan,
[10]Johanan the father of Azariah (it was he who served as priest in the temple Solomon built in Jerusalem), 1Ki 6:1; 2Ch 3:1
[11]Azariah the father of Amariah,
Amariah the father of Ahitub,
[12]Ahitub the father of Zadok,
Zadok the father of Shallum,
[13]Shallum the father of Hilkiah, 2Ki 22:1-20
Hilkiah the father of Azariah,
[14]Azariah the father of Seraiah,
and Seraiah the father of Jehozadak.
[15]Jehozadak was deported when the LORD sent Judah and Jerusalem into exile by the hand of Nebuchadnezzar. 2Ki 25:18; Hag 1:1,14; Zec 6:11

[16]The sons of Levi: Ge 29:34; Ex 6:16
Gershon,[a] Kohath and Merari. Nu 26:57
[17]These are the names of the sons of Gershon:
Libni and Shimei.
[18]The sons of Kohath:
Amram, Izhar, Hebron and Uzziel.
[19]The sons of Merari: 1Ch 23:21; 24:26
Mahli and Mushi.
These are the clans of the Levites listed according to their fathers:
[20]Of Gershon:
Libni his son, Jehath his son,
Zimmah his son, [21]Joah his son,
Iddo his son, Zerah his son
and Jeatherai his son.
[22]The descendants of Kohath:
Amminadab his son, Korah his son,
Assir his son, [23]Elkanah his son,
Ebiasaph his son, Assir his son,
[24]Tahath his son, Uriel his son, 1Ch 15:5
Uzziah his son and Shaul his son.
[25]The descendants of Elkanah:
Amasai, Ahimoth,
[26]Elkanah his son,[b] Zophai his son,
Nahath his son, [27]Eliab his son,
Jeroham his son, Elkanah his son 1Sa 1:1
and Samuel his son.[c] 1Sa 1:20
[28]The sons of Samuel:
Joel[d] the firstborn ver 33; 1Sa 8:2
and Abijah the second son.
[29]The descendants of Merari:
Mahli, Libni his son,
Shimei his son, Uzzah his son,
[30]Shimea his son, Haggiah his son
and Asaiah his son.

The Temple Musicians

[31]These are the men David put in charge of the
music in the house of the LORD after the ark came
to rest there. [32]They ministered with music before
the tabernacle, the Tent of Meeting, until Solomon
built the temple of the LORD in Jerusalem. They
performed their duties according to the regulations laid down for them. 1Ch 15:19; Ezr 3:10; Ps 68:25
[33]Here are the men who served, together with
their sons:
From the Kohathites:
Heman, the musician, 1Ki 4:31; 1Ch 15:17
the son of Joel, the son of Samuel,
[34]the son of Elkanah, the son of Jeroham,
the son of Eliel, the son of Toah,
[35]the son of Zuph, the son of Elkanah,
the son of Mahath, the son of Amasai,
[36]the son of Elkanah, the son of Joel,
the son of Azariah, the son of Zephaniah,
[37]the son of Tahath, the son of Assir,
the son of Ebiasaph, the son of Korah,
[38]the son of Izhar, the son of Kohath,
the son of Levi, the son of Israel;
[39]and Heman's associate Asaph, who served at his right hand: 1Ch 25:1,9; 2Ch 29:13
Asaph son of Berekiah, the son of Shimea, 1Ch 15:17
[40]the son of Michael, the son of Baaseiah,[e]
the son of Malkijah, [41]the son of Ethni,
the son of Zerah, the son of Adaiah,
[42]the son of Ethan, the son of Zimmah,
the son of Shimei, [43]the son of Jahath,
the son of Gershon, the son of Levi;
[44]and from their associates, the Merarites, at his left hand:
Ethan son of Kishi, the son of Abdi,
the son of Malluch, [45]the son of Hashabiah,
the son of Amaziah, the son of Hilkiah,
[46]the son of Amzi, the son of Bani,
the son of Shemer, [47]the son of Mahli,

[a] *16* Hebrew *Gershom*, a variant of *Gershon*; also in verses 17, 20, 43, 62 and 71 [b] *26* Some Hebrew manuscripts, Septuagint and Syriac; most Hebrew manuscripts *Ahimoth* [26]*and Elkanah. The sons of Elkanah:* [c] *27* Some Septuagint manuscripts (see also 1 Samuel 1:19,20 and 1 Chron. 6:33,34); Hebrew does not have *and Samuel his son.* [d] *28* Some Septuagint manuscripts and Syriac (see also 1 Samuel 8:2 and 1 Chron. 6:33); Hebrew does not have *Joel.* [e] *40* Most Hebrew manuscripts; some Hebrew manuscripts, one Septuagint manuscript and Syriac *Maaseiah*

the son of Mushi, the son of Merari,
the son of Levi.

48 Their fellow Levites were assigned to all the
other duties of the tabernacle, the house of God.
49 But Aaron and his descendants were the ones
who presented offerings on the altar of burnt offering and on the altar of incense in connection
with all that was done in the Most Holy Place,
making atonement for Israel, in accordance with
all that Moses the servant of God had commanded. Ex 27:1-8; 30:1-7,10; 1Ch 23:32

50 These were the descendants of Aaron:
Eleazar his son, Phinehas his son,
Abishua his son, 51 Bukki his son,
Uzzi his son, Zerahiah his son,
52 Meraioth his son, Amariah his son,
Ahitub his son, 53 Zadok his son 2Sa 8:17
and Ahimaaz his son.

54 These were the locations of their settlements
allotted as their territory (they were assigned to the
descendants of Aaron who were from the Kohathite clan, because the first lot was for them):
55 They were given Hebron in Judah with
its surrounding pasturelands. 56 But the fields
and villages around the city were given to
Caleb son of Jephunneh. Jos 14:13; 15:13
57 So the descendants of Aaron were given
Hebron (a city of refuge), and Libnah,[a] Jattir, Eshtemoa, 58 Hilen, Debir, 59 Ashan, Juttah[b] and Beth Shemesh, together with their
pasturelands. 60 And from the tribe of Benjamin they were given Gibeon,[c] Geba, Alemeth and Anathoth, together with their pasturelands. Jos 10:3; Jer 1:1
These towns, which were distributed among
the Kohathite clans, were thirteen in all.
61 The rest of Kohath's descendants were allotted ten towns from the clans of half the tribe of
Manasseh.
62 The descendants of Gershon, clan by clan,
were allotted thirteen towns from the tribes of Issachar, Asher and Naphtali, and from the part of
the tribe of Manasseh that is in Bashan.
63 The descendants of Merari, clan by clan, were
allotted twelve towns from the tribes of Reuben,
Gad and Zebulun.
64 So the Israelites gave the Levites these towns
and their pasturelands. 65 From the tribes of Judah,
Simeon and Benjamin they allotted the previously
named towns. Nu 35:1-8; Jos 21:3,41-42
66 Some of the Kohathite clans were given as
their territory towns from the tribe of Ephraim.
67 In the hill country of Ephraim they were
given Shechem (a city of refuge), and Gezer,[d] 68 Jokmeam, Beth Horon, 69 Aijalon and
Gath Rimmon, together with their pasturelands. Jos 10:10,12; 19:45
70 And from half the tribe of Manasseh the
Israelites gave Aner and Bileam, together
with their pasturelands, to the rest of the Kohathite clans.

71 The Gershonites received the following:
From the clan of the half-tribe of Manasseh
they received Golan in Bashan and also
Ashtaroth, together with their pasturelands; Jos 20:8
72 from the tribe of Issachar
they received Kedesh, Daberath, 73 Ramoth and Anem, together with their pasturelands; Jos 19:12
74 from the tribe of Asher
they received Mashal, Abdon, 75 Hukok
and Rehob, together with their pasturelands; Nu 13:21; Jos 19:28,34
76 and from the tribe of Naphtali
they received Kedesh in Galilee, Hammon and Kiriathaim, together with their
pasturelands. Nu 32:37; Jos 19:28

77 The Merarites (the rest of the Levites) received the following:
From the tribe of Zebulun
they received Jokneam, Kartah,[e] Rim-
mono and Tabor, together with their pasturelands;
78 from the tribe of Reuben across the Jordan
east of Jericho
they received Bezer in the desert, Jahzah,
79 Kedemoth and Mephaath, together
with their pasturelands; Dt 2:26; Jos 20:8
80 and from the tribe of Gad
they received Ramoth in Gilead, Mahanaim, 81 Heshbon and Jazer, together with
their pasturelands. Jos 21:4-39; 2Ch 11:14

Issachar

7 The sons of Issachar: Nu 26:23
Tola, Puah, Jashub and Shimron—four
in all. Ge 46:13
2 The sons of Tola:
Uzzi, Rephaiah, Jeriel, Jahmai, Ibsam and
Samuel—heads of their families. During
the reign of David, the descendants of
Tola listed as fighting men in their gene-
alogy numbered 22,600.
3 The son of Uzzi:
Izrahiah.
The sons of Izrahiah:
Michael, Obadiah, Joel and Isshiah. All
five of them were chiefs. 4 According to

[a] 57 See Joshua 21:13; Hebrew *given the cities of refuge: Hebron, Libnah.* [b] 59 Syriac (see also Septuagint and Joshua 21:16); Hebrew does not have *Juttah.* [c] 60 See Joshua 21:17; Hebrew does not have *Gibeon.* [d] 67 See Joshua 21:21; Hebrew *given the cities of refuge: Shechem, Gezer.* [e] 77 See Septuagint and Joshua 21:34; Hebrew does not have *Jokneam, Kartah.*

their family genealogy, they had 36,000 men ready for battle, for they had many wives and children.

5The relatives who were fighting men belonging to all the clans of Issachar, as listed in their genealogy, were 87,000 in all.

Benjamin

6Three sons of Benjamin: Ge 46:21; Nu 26:38
Bela, Beker and Jediael.
7The sons of Bela:
Ezbon, Uzzi, Uzziel, Jerimoth and Iri, heads of families—five in all. Their genealogical record listed 22,034 fighting men.
8The sons of Beker:
Zemirah, Joash, Eliezer, Elioenai, Omri, Jeremoth, Abijah, Anathoth and Alemeth. All these were the sons of Beker.
9Their genealogical record listed the heads of families and 20,200 fighting men.
10The son of Jediael:
Bilhan.
The sons of Bilhan:
Jeush, Benjamin, Ehud, Kenaanah, Zethan, Tarshish and Ahishahar.
11All these sons of Jediael were heads of families. There were 17,200 fighting men ready to go out to war.
12The Shuppites and Huppites were the descendants of Ir, and the Hushites the descendants of Aher.

Naphtali

13The sons of Naphtali: Ge 30:8; 46:24
Jahziel, Guni, Jezer and Shillem[a]—the descendants of Bilhah.

Manasseh

14The descendants of Manasseh: Ge 41:51
Asriel was his descendant through his Aramean concubine. She gave birth to Makir the father of Gilead.
15Makir took a wife from among the Huppites and Shuppites. His sister's name was Maacah. Nu 26:30
Another descendant was named Zelophehad, who had only daughters. Nu 36:1-12
16Makir's wife Maacah gave birth to a son and named him Peresh. His brother was named Sheresh, and his sons were Ulam and Rakem.
17The son of Ulam:
Bedan.
These were the sons of Gilead son of Makir, the son of Manasseh.
18His sister Hammoleketh gave birth to Ishhod, Abiezer and Mahlah. 1Sa 12:11; Jos 17:2
19The sons of Shemida were:
Ahian, Shechem, Likhi and Aniam.

Ephraim

20The descendants of Ephraim: Nu 1:33; 26:35
Shuthelah, Bered his son,
Tahath his son, Eleadah his son,
Tahath his son,
21Zabad his son
and Shuthelah his son.
Ezer and Elead were killed by the native-born men of Gath, when they went down to seize their livestock.
22Their father Ephraim mourned for them many days, and his relatives came to comfort him.
23Then he lay with his wife again, and she became pregnant and gave birth to a son. He named him Beriah,[b] because there had been misfortune in his family.
24His daughter was Sheerah, who built Lower and Upper Beth Horon as well as Uzzen Sheerah. Jos 16:3,5
25Rephah was his son, Resheph his son,[c]
Telah his son, Tahan his son,
26Ladan his son, Ammihud his son,
Elishama his son,
27Nun his son
and Joshua his son.
28Their lands and settlements included Bethel
and its surrounding villages, Naaran to the east,
Gezer and its villages to the west, and Shechem
and its villages all the way to Ayyah and its villages.
29Along the borders of Manasseh were Beth Shan,
Taanach, Megiddo and Dor, together with their
villages. The descendants of Joseph son of Israel
lived in these towns. Jos 16:7; 17:11

Asher

30The sons of Asher: Ge 46:17; Nu 26:44
Imnah, Ishvah, Ishvi and Beriah. Their sister was Serah.
31The sons of Beriah:
Heber and Malkiel, who was the father of Birzaith.
32Heber was the father of Japhlet, Shomer and Hotham and of their sister Shua.
33The sons of Japhlet:
Pasach, Bimhal and Ashvath.
These were Japhlet's sons.
34The sons of Shomer:
Ahi, Rohgah,[d] Hubbah and Aram.
35The sons of his brother Helem:
Zophah, Imna, Shelesh and Amal.
36The sons of Zophah:
Suah, Harnepher, Shual, Beri, Imrah,
37Bezer, Hod, Shamma, Shilshah, Ithran[e] and Beera.

[a] *13* Some Hebrew and Septuagint manuscripts (see also Gen. 46:24 and Num. 26:49); most Hebrew manuscripts *Shallum*
[b] *23* *Beriah* sounds like the Hebrew for *misfortune.*
[c] *25* Some Septuagint manuscripts; Hebrew does not have *his son.*
[d] *34* Or *of his brother Shomer: Rohgah*
[e] *37* Possibly a variant of *Jether*

38The sons of Jether:
Jephunneh, Pispah and Ara.
39The sons of Ulla:
Arah, Hanniel and Rizia.
40All these were descendants of Asher—heads
of families, choice men, brave warriors and outstanding leaders. The number of men ready for
battle, as listed in their genealogy, was 26,000.

The Genealogy of Saul the Benjamite

8 Benjamin was the father of Bela his firstborn,
Ashbel the second son, Aharah the third,
2Nohah the fourth and Rapha the fifth.
3The sons of Bela were:
Addar, Gera, Abihud,[a] 4Abishua, Naaman, Ahoah, 5Gera, Shephuphan and
Huram. 2Sa 23:9
6These were the descendants of Ehud, who
were heads of families of those living in
Geba and were deported to Manahath:
7Naaman, Ahijah, and Gera, who deported them and who was the father of Uzza
and Ahihud.
8Sons were born to Shaharaim in Moab after
he had divorced his wives Hushim and
Baara. 9By his wife Hodesh he had Jobab,
Zibia, Mesha, Malcam, 10Jeuz, Sakia and
Mirmah. These were his sons, heads of
families. 11By Hushim he had Abitub and
Elpaal.
12The sons of Elpaal:
Eber, Misham, Shemed (who built Ono
and Lod with its surrounding villages),
13and Beriah and Shema, who were heads
of families of those living in Aijalon and
who drove out the inhabitants of Gath.
14Ahio, Shashak, Jeremoth, 15Zebadiah, Arad,
Eder, 16Michael, Ishpah and Joha were
the sons of Beriah.
17Zebadiah, Meshullam, Hizki, Heber, 18Ish-
merai, Izliah and Jobab were the sons of
Elpaal.
19Jakim, Zicri, Zabdi, 20Elienai, Zillethai, Eliel,
21Adaiah, Beraiah and Shimrath were the
sons of Shimei.
22Ishpan, Eber, Eliel, 23Abdon, Zicri, Hanan,
24Hananiah, Elam, Anthothijah, 25Iphde-
iah and Penuel were the sons of Shashak.
26Shamsherai, Shehariah, Athaliah, 27Jaareshi-
ah, Elijah and Zicri were the sons of Jeroham.
28All these were heads of families, chiefs as listed
in their genealogy, and they lived in Jerusalem.
29Jeiel[b] the father[c] of Gibeon lived in Gibeon.
His wife's name was Maacah, 30and his
firstborn son was Abdon, followed by
Zur, Kish, Baal, Ner,[d] Nadab, 31Gedor,
Ahio, Zeker 32and Mikloth, who was the
father of Shimeah. They too lived near
their relatives in Jerusalem.
33Ner was the father of Kish, Kish the father of
Saul, and Saul the father of Jonathan,
Malki-Shua, Abinadab and Esh-Baal.[e]
34The son of Jonathan: 2Sa 9:12
Merib-Baal,[f] who was the father of Micah. 2Sa 4:4
35The sons of Micah:
Pithon, Melech, Tarea and Ahaz.
36Ahaz was the father of Jehoaddah, Jehoaddah was the father of Alemeth, Azmaveth and Zimri, and Zimri was the father
of Moza. 37Moza was the father of Binea;
Raphah was his son, Eleasah his son and
Azel his son.
38Azel had six sons, and these were their
names:
Azrikam, Bokeru, Ishmael, Sheariah,
Obadiah and Hanan. All these were the
sons of Azel. 1Ch 9:34-44
39The sons of his brother Eshek:
Ulam his firstborn, Jeush the second son
and Eliphelet the third. 40The sons of
Ulam were brave warriors who could
handle the bow. They had many sons and
grandsons—150 in all.
All these were the descendants of Benjamin.

9 All Israel was listed in the genealogies recorded in the book of the kings of Israel.

The People in Jerusalem

The people of Judah were taken captive to Babylon because of their unfaithfulness. 2Now the first
to resettle on their own property in their own
towns were some Israelites, priests, Levites and
temple servants. 1Ch 5:25; Ezr 2:43,58,70
3Those from Judah, from Benjamin, and from
Ephraim and Manasseh who lived in Jerusalem
were:
4Uthai son of Ammihud, the son of Omri,
the son of Imri, the son of Bani, a descendant of Perez son of Judah. Ge 46:12
5Of the Shilonites:
Asaiah the firstborn and his sons.
6Of the Zerahites:
Jeuel.
The people from Judah numbered 690.
7Of the Benjamites:
Sallu son of Meshullam, the son of Hodaviah, the son of Hassenuah;

[a]3 Or *Gera the father of Ehud* [b]29 Some Septuagint manuscripts (see also 1 Chron. 9:35); Hebrew does not have *Jeiel.* [c]29 *Father* may mean *civic leader* or *military leader.* [d]30 Some Septuagint manuscripts (see also 1 Chron. 9:36); Hebrew does not have *Ner.* [e]33 Also known as *Ish-Bosheth* [f]34 Also known as *Mephibosheth*

8 Ibneiah son of Jeroham; Elah son of Uzzi,
the son of Micri; and Meshullam son of
Shephatiah, the son of Reuel, the son of
Ibnijah.
9 The people from Benjamin, as listed in
their genealogy, numbered 956. All these
men were heads of their families.
10 Of the priests:
Jedaiah; Jehoiarib; Jakin;
11 Azariah son of Hilkiah, the son of Meshullam, the son of Zadok, the son of
Meraioth, the son of Ahitub, the official
in charge of the house of God;
12 Adaiah son of Jeroham, the son of Pashhur, the son of Malkijah; and Maasai son
of Adiel, the son of Jahzerah, the son of
Meshullam, the son of Meshillemith, the
son of Immer. Ezr 2:38; 10:22; Ne 10:3
13 The priests, who were heads of families,
numbered 1,760. They were able men, responsible for ministering in the house of
God.
14 Of the Levites:
Shemaiah son of Hasshub, the son of Azrikam, the son of Hashabiah, a Merarite;
15 Bakbakkar, Heresh, Galal and Mattaniah son of Mica, the son of Zicri, the son
of Asaph; 16 Obadiah son of Shemaiah,
the son of Galal, the son of Jeduthun; and
Berekiah son of Asa, the son of Elkanah,
who lived in the villages of the Netophathites. 2Ch 20:14; Ne 11:22; 12:28
17 The gatekeepers: ver 22; 1Ch 26:1
Shallum, Akkub, Talmon, Ahiman and
their brothers, Shallum their chief 18 being
stationed at the King's Gate on the east,
up to the present time. These were the
gatekeepers belonging to the camp of the
Levites. 19 Shallum son of Kore, the son of
Ebiasaph, the son of Korah, and his fellow gatekeepers from his family (the Korahites) were responsible for guarding
the thresholds of the Tent[a] just as their
fathers had been responsible for guarding
the entrance to the dwelling of the LORD.
20 In earlier times Phinehas son of Eleazar
was in charge of the gatekeepers, and the
LORD was with him. 21 Zechariah son of
Meshelemiah was the gatekeeper at the
entrance to the Tent of Meeting.
22 Altogether, those chosen to be gatekeepers at
the thresholds numbered 212. They were registered by genealogy in their villages. The gatekeepers had been assigned to their positions of trust
by David and Samuel the seer. 23 They and their
descendants were in charge of guarding the gates
of the house of the LORD—the house called the
Tent. 24 The gatekeepers were on the four sides:
east, west, north and south. 25 Their brothers in
their villages had to come from time to time and
share their duties for seven-day periods. 26 But the
four principal gatekeepers, who were Levites, were
entrusted with the responsibility for the rooms and
treasuries in the house of God. 27 They would
spend the night stationed around the house of
God, because they had to guard it; and they had
charge of the key for opening it each morning.
28 Some of them were in charge of the articles
used in the temple service; they counted them
when they were brought in and when they were
taken out. 29 Others were assigned to take care of
the furnishings and all the other articles of the
sanctuary, as well as the flour and wine, and the
oil, incense and spices. 30 But some of the priests
took care of mixing the spices. 31 A Levite named
Mattithiah, the firstborn son of Shallum the Korahite, was entrusted with the responsibility for
baking the offering bread. 32 Some of their Kohathite brothers were in charge of preparing for every
Sabbath the bread set out on the table. Lev 24:5-8
33 Those who were musicians, heads of Levite
families, stayed in the rooms of the temple and
were exempt from other duties because they were
responsible for the work day and night. 1Ch 6:31
34 All these were heads of Levite families, chiefs
as listed in their genealogy, and they lived in Jerusalem.

The Genealogy of Saul

35 Jeiel the father[b] of Gibeon lived in Gibeon.
His wife's name was Maacah, 36 and his
firstborn son was Abdon, followed by
Zur, Kish, Baal, Ner, Nadab, 37 Gedor,
Ahio, Zechariah and Mikloth. 38 Mikloth
was the father of Shimeam. They too
lived near their relatives in Jerusalem.
39 Ner was the father of Kish, Kish the father of
Saul, and Saul the father of Jonathan,
Malki-Shua, Abinadab and Esh-Baal.[c]
40 The son of Jonathan:
Merib-Baal,[d] who was the father of Micah. 2Sa 4:4
41 The sons of Micah:
Pithon, Melech, Tahrea and Ahaz.[e]
42 Ahaz was the father of Jadah, Jadah[f] was
the father of Alemeth, Azmaveth and
Zimri, and Zimri was the father of Moza.
43 Moza was the father of Binea; Rephaiah
was his son, Eleasah his son and Azel his
son.

[a] *19* That is, the temple; also in verses 21 and 23 [b] *35* *Father* may mean *civic leader* or *military leader.* [c] *39* Also known as *Ish-Bosheth* [d] *40* Also known as *Mephibosheth* [e] *41* Vulgate and Syriac (see also Septuagint and 1 Chron. 8:35); Hebrew does not have *and Ahaz.* [f] *42* Some Hebrew manuscripts and Septuagint (see also 1 Chron. 8:36); most Hebrew manuscripts *Jarah, Jarah*

44Azel had six sons, and these were their names:
Azrikam, Bokeru, Ishmael, Sheariah, Obadiah and Hanan. These were the sons of Azel. 1Ch 8:28-38

The Story of David **Chapters 10–21**

These chapters record the rise and growth of David's kingdom. After Saul died (chapter 10), David stepped into his rightful place as the anointed ruler of Israel. However, as became evident to David, following God's will isn't always easy. Although he was now the king, he still had to conquer Jerusalem and take up his throne. Joab stepped forward to lead the battle and became David's commander-in-chief over the armies of Israel (11:6).

In these chapters we read of David's mighty men and those who joined the king as he began his rule. The ark of the covenant played an important role here as David brought it into Jerusalem. With the ark came a symbolic image of God's presence among the people of Israel. Chapter 16 records a glorious psalm of praise David was inspired to write as the ark was brought into Jerusalem; chapter 17 contains the Lord's pledge to David, as well as David's poignant and powerful prayer of response to the Lord his God. What a beautiful example of devotion and commitment! The rest of this section records David's victories on the battlefield and the growing prosperity of his kingdom.

Saul Takes His Life

10 Now the Philistines fought against Israel; the Israelites fled before them, and many fell slain on Mount Gilboa. 2The Philistines pressed hard after Saul and his sons, and they killed his sons Jonathan, Abinadab and Malki-Shua. 3The fighting grew fierce around Saul, and when the archers overtook him, they wounded him.

4Saul said to his armor-bearer, "Draw your sword and run me through, or these uncircumcised fellows will come and abuse me."

But his armor-bearer was terrified and would not do it; so Saul took his own sword and fell on it. 5When the armor-bearer saw that Saul was dead, he too fell on his sword and died. 6So Saul and his three sons died, and all his house died together.

7When all the Israelites in the valley saw that the army had fled and that Saul and his sons had died, they abandoned their towns and fled. And the Philistines came and occupied them.

8The next day, when the Philistines came to strip the dead, they found Saul and his sons fallen on Mount Gilboa. 9They stripped him and took his head and his armor, and sent messengers throughout the land of the Philistines to proclaim the news among their idols and their people. 10They put his armor in the temple of their gods and hung up his head in the temple of Dagon.

11When all the inhabitants of Jabesh Gilead heard of everything the Philistines had done to Saul, 12all their valiant men went and took the bodies of Saul and his sons and brought them to Jabesh. Then they buried their bones under the great tree in Jabesh, and they fasted seven days.

13Saul died because he was unfaithful to the LORD; he did not keep the word of the LORD and even consulted a medium for guidance, 14and did not inquire of the LORD. So the LORD put him to death and turned the kingdom over to David son of Jesse. 1Sa 15:28; 2Sa 1:1; 1Ch 12:23

David Becomes King Over Israel

11 All Israel came together to David at Hebron and said, "We are your own flesh and blood. 2In the past, even while Saul was king, you were the one who led Israel on their military campaigns. And the LORD your God said to you, 'You will shepherd my people Israel, and you will become their ruler.'" 1Sa 18:5,16; 1Ch 5:2; Mt 2:6

3When all the elders of Israel had come to King David at Hebron, he made a compact with them at Hebron before the LORD, and they anointed David king over Israel, as the LORD had promised through Samuel. 2Sa 5:1-3; 1Sa 16:1-13

David Conquers Jerusalem

4David and all the Israelites marched to Jerusalem (that is, Jebus). The Jebusites who lived there 5said to David, "You will not get in here." Nevertheless, David captured the fortress of Zion, the City of David. Jdg 1:21; 19:10

6David had said, "Whoever leads the attack on the Jebusites will become commander-in-chief." Joab son of Zeruiah went up first, and so he received the command. 2Sa 8:16

7David then took up residence in the fortress, and so it was called the City of David. 8He built up the city around it, from the supporting terraces[a] to the surrounding wall, while Joab restored the rest of the city. 9And David became more and more powerful, because the LORD Almighty was with him. 2Sa 3:1; 4:6-10

David's Mighty Men

10These were the chiefs of David's mighty men—they, together with all Israel, gave his kingship strong support to extend it over the whole land, as the LORD had promised— 11this is the list of David's mighty men: ver 3; 2Sa 17:10

Jashobeam,[b] a Hacmonite, was chief of the officers[c]; he raised his spear against three hundred men, whom he killed in one encounter.

[a]8 Or *the Millo* [b]11 Possibly a variant of *Jashob-Baal* [c]11 Or *Thirty*; some Septuagint manuscripts *Three* (see also 2 Samuel 23:8)

DAVID

A Man After God's Own Heart

"And David became more and more powerful, because the LORD Almighty was with him."
—1 CHRONICLES 11:9

When we hear the name David, different images come to mind. Some remember David as the shepherd boy anointed as king over all Israel. Some remember David as the great giant-killing warrior-king. Some remember David as the one who slept with another man's wife and then engineered a cover-up that included a murder. Others remember him as the great poet, the composer of many of the psalms. But none of those things describes what God remembers about His man, Israel's greatest king, the one whose name would be forever linked with the Messiah, "the son of David" (Matthew 1:1). To find out what God remembers, turn to Acts 13:22. In the process of retelling the history of the Jews for his audience, Paul wrote, "[God] testified concerning him: 'I have found David son of Jesse a man after my own heart; he will do everything I want him to do.' "

What an epitaph! Not "I have found David a great warrior"; or "I have found David a faithful shepherd"; or "I have found David a gifted and creative poet"—none of those things. God said, in effect, "I have found David a man who cared about the things I care about. He was a man whose heart beat in sync with mine. When I looked to the right, David looked to the right. When I looked to the left, David looked to the left." That's what it means to be a person who is "after God's own heart."

When God chose David over his seven brothers to be king, He saw a person of integrity and character. God knew that this man's heart was in harmony with His own. He could see David's humility, cultivated as a lowly shepherd while his brothers pursued success in the military. He knew that David remained faithful in his tasks when nobody was looking, during the nights and days spent in obscurity in the fields. It was during those times, those solitary, even mundane times, that God was at work in David's life, preparing him, training him and building character into his life.

That character shone through when David faced off against Goliath, the Philistine giant. When David volunteered to fight Goliath, Saul looked only at the externals, mocking David with words to this effect: "You're just a little tyke. Look at that giant!" I imagine David thinking, "What giant? The only giant in my life is God! That's just a dwarf over there." Listen to his words: "I come against you in the name of the LORD Almighty . . . This day the LORD will hand you over to me, and I'll strike you down and cut off your head" (1 Samuel 17:45–46). Truly this was a man after God's own heart.

Still, this man of God was not perfect. When he was about fifty years old, in the prime of his life and his reign, he committed adultery with a married woman named Bathsheba. To make matters worse, he had Bathsheba's husband Uriah murdered to cover up his act. During the months David spent covering up his sin, he knew he'd done wrong. Read Psalms 32 and 51 to get a picture of his intense suffering. He had sleepless nights and guilt-ridden days. And when Nathan the prophet confronted him with his sin (2 Samuel 12:7), David was brought to his knees before God. He freely and fully acknowledged his sin. A gush of relief must have swept over David as the pain of his sin drained out when he confessed and heard Nathan's assurance of the Lord's pardon: "The LORD has taken away your sin" (2 Samuel 12:13).

Chapters 28 and 29 of 1 Chronicles record David's final reflections on a life lived for God. Here David gave Solomon the kind of advice (28:9) every Christian parent should emulate: "Acknowledge the God of your father, and serve him with wholehearted devotion and with a willing mind, for the LORD searches every heart and understands every motive behind the thoughts . . ." Sound advice from one who had experienced this truth firsthand: "If you seek him, he will be found by you; but if you forsake him, he will reject you forever" (28:9).

12Next to him was Eleazar son of Dodai the
Ahohite, one of the three mighty men. 13He was
with David at Pas Dammim when the Philistines
gathered there for battle. At a place where there
was a field full of barley, the troops fled from the
Philistines. 14But they took their stand in the middle of the field. They defended it and struck the
Philistines down, and the LORD brought about a
great victory. Ex 14:30; 1Sa 11:13

15Three of the thirty chiefs came down to David
to the rock at the cave of Adullam, while a band of
Philistines was encamped in the Valley of Rephaim. 16At that time David was in the stronghold,
and the Philistine garrison was at Bethlehem.
17David longed for water and said, "Oh, that
someone would get me a drink of water from the
well near the gate of Bethlehem!" 18So the Three
broke through the Philistine lines, drew water
from the well near the gate of Bethlehem and carried it back to David. But he refused to drink it;
instead, he poured it out before the LORD. 19"God
forbid that I should do this!" he said. "Should I
drink the blood of these men who went at the risk
of their lives?" Because they risked their lives to
bring it back, David would not drink it. 2Sa 5:17

Such were the exploits of the three mighty men.

20Abishai the brother of Joab was chief of the
Three. He raised his spear against three hundred
men, whom he killed, and so he became as famous
as the Three. 21He was doubly honored above the
Three and became their commander, even though
he was not included among them. 1Sa 26:6

22Benaiah son of Jehoiada was a valiant fighter
from Kabzeel, who performed great exploits. He
struck down two of Moab's best men. He also
went down into a pit on a snowy day and killed a
lion. 23And he struck down an Egyptian who was
seven and a half feet[a] tall. Although the Egyptian
had a spear like a weaver's rod in his hand, Benaiah went against him with a club. He snatched the
spear from the Egyptian's hand and killed him
with his own spear. 24Such were the exploits of
Benaiah son of Jehoiada; he too was as famous as
the three mighty men. 25He was held in greater
honor than any of the Thirty, but he was not included among the Three. And David put him in
charge of his bodyguard. 1Sa 17:7,36; Jos 15:21

26The mighty men were:
Asahel the brother of Joab, 2Sa 2:18
Elhanan son of Dodo from Bethlehem,
27Shammoth the Harorite, 1Ch 27:8
Helez the Pelonite,
28Ira son of Ikkesh from Tekoa,
Abiezer from Anathoth, 1Ch 27:12
29Sibbecai the Hushathite, 2Sa 21:18
Ilai the Ahohite,
30Maharai the Netophathite,
Heled son of Baanah the Netophathite,
31Ithai son of Ribai from Gibeah in Benjamin,
Benaiah the Pirathonite, Jdg 12:13; 1Ch 27:14
32Hurai from the ravines of Gaash,
Abiel the Arbathite,
33Azmaveth the Baharumite,
Eliahba the Shaalbonite,
34the sons of Hashem the Gizonite,
Jonathan son of Shagee the Hararite,
35Ahiam son of Sacar the Hararite,
Eliphal son of Ur,
36Hepher the Mekerathite,
Ahijah the Pelonite,
37Hezro the Carmelite,
Naarai son of Ezbai,
38Joel the brother of Nathan,
Mibhar son of Hagri,
39Zelek the Ammonite,
Naharai the Berothite, the armor-bearer
of Joab son of Zeruiah,
40Ira the Ithrite,
Gareb the Ithrite,
41Uriah the Hittite, 2Sa 11:6
Zabad son of Ahlai, 2Sa 23:8-39
42Adina son of Shiza the Reubenite, who
was chief of the Reubenites, and the thirty with him,
43Hanan son of Maacah,
Joshaphat the Mithnite,
44Uzzia the Ashterathite, Dt 1:4
Shama and Jeiel the sons of Hotham the
Aroerite,
45Jediael son of Shimri,
his brother Joha the Tizite,
46Eliel the Mahavite,
Jeribai and Joshaviah the sons of Elnaam,
Ithmah the Moabite,
47Eliel, Obed and Jaasiel the Mezobaite.

Warriors Join David

12 These were the men who came to David at
Ziklag, while he was banished from the
presence of Saul son of Kish (they were among the
warriors who helped him in battle; 2they were
armed with bows and were able to shoot arrows or
to sling stones right-handed or left-handed; they
were kinsmen of Saul from the tribe of Benjamin):
3Ahiezer their chief and Joash the sons of
Shemaah the Gibeathite; Jeziel and Pelet the
sons of Azmaveth; Beracah, Jehu the Anathothite, 4and Ishmaiah the Gibeonite, a
mighty man among the Thirty, who was a
leader of the Thirty; Jeremiah, Jahaziel, Johanan, Jozabad the Gederathite, 5Eluzai, Jerimoth, Bealiah, Shemariah and Shephatiah
the Haruphite; 6Elkanah, Isshiah, Azarel, Jo-

[a] 23 Hebrew *five cubits* (about 2.3 meters)

ezer and Jashobeam the Korahites; 7and Joe-
lah and Zebadiah the sons of Jeroham from
Gedor. Jos 15:36,58

8Some Gadites defected to David at his stronghold in the desert. They were brave warriors, ready
for battle and able to handle the shield and spear.
Their faces were the faces of lions, and they were
as swift as gazelles in the mountains. 2Sa 2:18; 17:10

9Ezer was the chief,
Obadiah the second in command, Eliab the third,
10Mishmannah the fourth, Jeremiah the fifth,
11Attai the sixth, Eliel the seventh,
12Johanan the eighth, Elzabad the ninth,
13Jeremiah the tenth and Macbannai the eleventh.

14These Gadites were army commanders; the
least was a match for a hundred, and the greatest
for a thousand. 15It was they who crossed the Jordan in the first month when it was overflowing all
its banks, and they put to flight everyone living in
the valleys, to the east and to the west. Dt 32:30

16Other Benjamites and some men from Judah
also came to David in his stronghold. 17David went
out to meet them and said to them, "If you have
come to me in peace, to help me, I am ready to
have you unite with me. But if you have come to
betray me to my enemies when my hands are free
from violence, may the God of our fathers see it
and judge you." 2Sa 3:19

18Then the Spirit came upon Amasai, chief of
the Thirty, and he said: Jdg 6:34; 2Sa 17:25

"We are yours, O David!
We are with you, O son of Jesse!
Success, success to you, 1Sa 25:5-6
and success to those who help you,
for your God will help you."

So David received them and made them leaders
of his raiding bands.

19Some of the men of Manasseh defected to
David when he went with the Philistines to fight
against Saul. (He and his men did not help the
Philistines because, after consultation, their rulers
sent him away. They said, "It will cost us our heads
if he deserts to his master Saul.") 20When David
went to Ziklag, these were the men of Manasseh
who defected to him: Adnah, Jozabad, Jediael, Michael, Jozabad, Elihu and Zillethai, leaders of units
of a thousand in Manasseh. 21They helped David
against raiding bands, for all of them were brave
warriors, and they were commanders in his army.
22Day after day men came to help David, until he
had a great army, like the army of God.[a]

Others Join David at Hebron

23These are the numbers of the men armed for
battle who came to David at Hebron to turn Saul's
kingdom over to him, as the LORD had said:

24men of Judah, carrying shield and spear—6,800 armed for battle;
25men of Simeon, warriors ready for battle—7,100;
26men of Levi—4,600, 27including Jehoiada,
leader of the family of Aaron, with 3,700 men, 28and Zadok, a brave young warrior, with 22 officers from his family;
29men of Benjamin, Saul's kinsmen—3,000, most of whom had remained loyal to Saul's house until then; 2Sa 2:8-9; 3:19
30men of Ephraim, brave warriors, famous in their own clans—20,800;
31men of half the tribe of Manasseh, designated by name to come and make David king—18,000;
32men of Issachar, who understood the times and knew what Israel should do—200 chiefs, with all their relatives under their command; Est 1:13
33men of Zebulun, experienced soldiers prepared for battle with every type of weapon, to help David with undivided loyalty—50,000;
34men of Naphtali—1,000 officers, together with 37,000 men carrying shields and spears;
35men of Dan, ready for battle—28,600;
36men of Asher, experienced soldiers prepared for battle—40,000;
37and from east of the Jordan, men of Reuben, Gad and the half-tribe of Manasseh, armed with every type of weapon—120,000.

38All these were fighting men who volunteered
to serve in the ranks. They came to Hebron fully
determined to make David king over all Israel. All
the rest of the Israelites were also of one mind
to make David king. 39The men spent three days
there with David, eating and drinking, for their
families had supplied provisions for them. 40Also,
their neighbors from as far away as Issachar, Zebulun and Naphtali came bringing food on donkeys,
camels, mules and oxen. There were plentiful supplies of flour, fig cakes, raisin cakes, wine, oil, cattle and sheep, for there was joy in Israel. 1Sa 25:18

Bringing Back the Ark

13 David conferred with each of his officers,
the commanders of thousands and commanders of hundreds. 2He then said to the whole
assembly of Israel, "If it seems good to you and if
it is the will of the LORD our God, let us send word
far and wide to the rest of our brothers throughout
the territories of Israel, and also to the priests and

[a]22 Or *a great and mighty army*

Levites who are with them in their towns and pasturelands, to come and join us. 3Let us bring the ark of our God back to us, for we did not inquire of[a] it[b] during the reign of Saul." 4The whole assembly agreed to do this, because it seemed right to all the people. 1Sa 7:1-2; 2Ch 1:5

5So David assembled all the Israelites, from the Shihor River in Egypt to Lebo[c] Hamath, to bring the ark of God from Kiriath Jearim. 6David and all the Israelites with him went to Baalah of Judah (Kiriath Jearim) to bring up from there the ark of God the LORD, who is enthroned between the cherubim—the ark that is called by the Name.

7They moved the ark of God from Abinadab's house on a new cart, with Uzzah and Ahio guiding it. 8David and all the Israelites were celebrating with all their might before God, with songs and with harps, lyres, tambourines, cymbals and trumpets. Nu 4:15; 1Sa 7:1; 2Sa 6:5

9When they came to the threshing floor of Kidon, Uzzah reached out his hand to steady the ark, because the oxen stumbled. 10The LORD's anger burned against Uzzah, and he struck him down because he had put his hand on the ark. So he died there before God. Lev 10:2; 1Ch 15:13,15

11Then David was angry because the LORD's wrath had broken out against Uzzah, and to this day that place is called Perez Uzzah.[d] 1Ch 15:13

12David was afraid of God that day and asked, "How can I ever bring the ark of God to me?" 13He did not take the ark to be with him in the City of David. Instead, he took it aside to the house of Obed-Edom the Gittite. 14The ark of God remained with the family of Obed-Edom in his house for three months, and the LORD blessed his household and everything he had. 2Sa 6:1-11

David's House and Family

14 Now Hiram king of Tyre sent messengers to David, along with cedar logs, stonemasons and carpenters to build a palace for him. 2And David knew that the LORD had established him as king over Israel and that his kingdom had been highly exalted for the sake of his people Israel. Nu 24:7; Dt 26:19

3In Jerusalem David took more wives and became the father of more sons and daughters. 4These are the names of the children born to him there: Shammua, Shobab, Nathan, Solomon, 5Ibhar, Elishua, Elpelet, 6Nogah, Nepheg, Japhia, 7Elishama, Beeliada[e] and Eliphelet. 2Sa 5:11-16

David Defeats the Philistines

8When the Philistines heard that David had been anointed king over all Israel, they went up in full force to search for him, but David heard about it and went out to meet them. 9Now the Philistines had come and raided the Valley of Rephaim; 10so David inquired of God: "Shall I go and attack the Philistines? Will you hand them over to me?"

The LORD answered him, "Go, I will hand them over to you."

11So David and his men went up to Baal Perazim, and there he defeated them. He said, "As waters break out, God has broken out against my enemies by my hand." So that place was called Baal Perazim.[f] 12The Philistines had abandoned their gods there, and David gave orders to burn them in the fire. Ex 32:20; Jos 7:15; Isa 28:21

13Once more the Philistines raided the valley; 14so David inquired of God again, and God answered him, "Do not go straight up, but circle around them and attack them in front of the balsam trees. 15As soon as you hear the sound of marching in the tops of the balsam trees, move out to battle, because that will mean God has gone out in front of you to strike the Philistine army." 16So David did as God commanded him, and they struck down the Philistine army, all the way from Gibeon to Gezer. ver 9; Jos 9:3; 10:33

17So David's fame spread throughout every land, and the LORD made all the nations fear him.

The Ark Brought to Jerusalem

15 After David had constructed buildings for himself in the City of David, he prepared a place for the ark of God and pitched a tent for it. 2Then David said, "No one but the Levites may carry the ark of God, because the LORD chose them to carry the ark of the LORD and to minister before him forever." Nu 4:15; Dt 10:8; 1Ch 16:1

3David assembled all Israel in Jerusalem to bring up the ark of the LORD to the place he had prepared for it. 4He called together the descendants of Aaron and the Levites: 1Ki 8:1; 1Ch 13:5

5From the descendants of Kohath,
Uriel the leader and 120 relatives;
6from the descendants of Merari,
Asaiah the leader and 220 relatives;
7from the descendants of Gershon,[g]
Joel the leader and 130 relatives;
8from the descendants of Elizaphan, Ex 6:22
Shemaiah the leader and 200 relatives;
9from the descendants of Hebron, Ex 6:18
Eliel the leader and 80 relatives;
10from the descendants of Uzziel,
Amminadab the leader and 112 relatives.

11Then David summoned Zadok and Abiathar the priests, and Uriel, Asaiah, Joel, Shemaiah, Eliel and Amminadab the Levites. 12He said to them, "You are the heads of the Levitical families; you and your fellow Levites are to consecrate your-

a3 Or *we neglected* b3 Or *him* c5 Or *to the entrance to* d11 *Perez Uzzah* means *outbreak against Uzzah.*
e7 A variant of *Eliada* f11 *Baal Perazim* means *the lord who breaks out.* g7 Hebrew *Gershom,* a variant of *Gershon*

selves and bring up the ark of the LORD, the God
of Israel, to the place I have prepared for it. 13It
was because you, the Levites, did not bring it up
the first time that the LORD our God broke out in
anger against us. We did not inquire of him about
how to do it in the prescribed way." 14So the
priests and Levites consecrated themselves in order to bring up the ark of the LORD, the God of
Israel. 15And the Levites carried the ark of God
with the poles on their shoulders, as Moses had
commanded in accordance with the word of the
LORD. Ex 25:14; 2Sa 6:3; 1Ch 13:7-10

16David told the leaders of the Levites to appoint their brothers as singers to sing joyful songs,
accompanied by musical instruments: lyres, harps
and cymbals. 1Ch 25:1; Ne 12:27,36; Ps 68:25

17So the Levites appointed Heman son of Joel;
from his brothers, Asaph son of Berekiah; and
from their brothers the Merarites, Ethan son of
Kushaiah; 18and with them their brothers next in
rank: Zechariah,[a] Jaaziel, Shemiramoth, Jehiel,
Unni, Eliab, Benaiah, Maaseiah, Mattithiah, Eliphelehu, Mikneiah, Obed-Edom and Jeiel,[b] the
gatekeepers. 1Ch 6:33,39,44; 26:4-5

19The musicians Heman, Asaph and Ethan were
to sound the bronze cymbals; 20Zechariah, Aziel,
Shemiramoth, Jehiel, Unni, Eliab, Maaseiah and
Benaiah were to play the lyres according to *alamoth*,[c] 21and Mattithiah, Eliphelehu, Mikneiah,
Obed-Edom, Jeiel and Azaziah were to play the
harps, directing according to *sheminith*.[c] 22Kena-
niah the head Levite was in charge of the singing;
that was his responsibility because he was skillful
at it. 1Ch 25:6

23Berekiah and Elkanah were to be doorkeepers
for the ark. 24Shebaniah, Joshaphat, Nethanel,
Amasai, Zechariah, Benaiah and Eliezer the priests
were to blow trumpets before the ark of God.
Obed-Edom and Jehiah were also to be doorkeepers for the ark. ver 28; 1Ch 16:6

25So David and the elders of Israel and the commanders of units of a thousand went to bring up
the ark of the covenant of the LORD from the house
of Obed-Edom, with rejoicing. 26Because God had
helped the Levites who were carrying the ark of the
covenant of the LORD, seven bulls and seven rams
were sacrificed. 27Now David was clothed in a robe
of fine linen, as were all the Levites who were
carrying the ark, and as were the singers, and Kenaniah, who was in charge of the singing of the
choirs. David also wore a linen ephod. 28So all
Israel brought up the ark of the covenant of the
LORD with shouts, with the sounding of rams'
horns and trumpets, and of cymbals, and the playing of lyres and harps. 1Ch 13:8,13; 2Ch 1:4

29As the ark of the covenant of the LORD was
entering the City of David, Michal daughter of
Saul watched from a window. And when she saw
King David dancing and celebrating, she despised
him in her heart.

16 They brought the ark of God and set it
inside the tent that David had pitched for
it, and they presented burnt offerings and fellowship offerings[d] before God. 2After David had finished sacrificing the burnt offerings and fellowship
offerings, he blessed the people in the name of the
LORD. 3Then he gave a loaf of bread, a cake of dates
and a cake of raisins to each Israelite man and
woman. 2Sa 6:12-19; 1Ch 15:1

4He appointed some of the Levites to minister
before the ark of the LORD, to make petition, to
give thanks, and to praise the LORD, the God of
Israel: 5Asaph was the chief, Zechariah second,
then Jeiel, Shemiramoth, Jehiel, Mattithiah, Eliab,
Benaiah, Obed-Edom and Jeiel. They were to play
the lyres and harps, Asaph was to sound the cymbals, 6and Benaiah and Jahaziel the priests were to
blow the trumpets regularly before the ark of the
covenant of God. 1Ch 15:2

David's Psalm of Thanks

7That day David first committed to Asaph and
his associates this psalm of thanks to the LORD:

8Give thanks to the LORD, call on his name;
make known among the nations what he
has done. 2Ki 19:19
9Sing to him, sing praise to him;
tell of all his wonderful acts. Ex 15:1
10Glory in his holy name;
let the hearts of those who seek the LORD
rejoice.
11Look to the LORD and his strength;
seek his face always. Ps 24:6; 119:2,58
12Remember the wonders he has done, Ps 77:11
his miracles, and the judgments he
pronounced, Ps 78:43
13O descendants of Israel his servant,
O sons of Jacob, his chosen ones.
14He is the LORD our God;
his judgments are in all the earth. Isa 26:9
15He remembers[e] his covenant forever,
the word he commanded, for a thousand
generations,
16the covenant he made with Abraham, Ge 17:2
the oath he swore to Isaac.
17He confirmed it to Jacob as a decree, Ge 35:9-12
to Israel as an everlasting covenant:
18"To you I will give the land of Canaan
as the portion you will inherit."

[a] *18* Three Hebrew manuscripts and most Septuagint manuscripts (see also verse 20 and 1 Chron. 16:5); most Hebrew manuscripts *Zechariah son and* or *Zechariah, Ben and* [b] *18* Hebrew; Septuagint (see also verse 21) *Jeiel and Azaziah* [c] *20,21* Probably a musical term [d] *1* Traditionally *peace offerings*; also in verse 2 [e] *15* Some Septuagint manuscripts (see also Psalm 105:8); Hebrew *Remember*

[19]When they were but few in number, Ge 34:30
few indeed, and strangers in it,
[20]they[a] wandered from nation to nation,
from one kingdom to another.
[21]He allowed no man to oppress them;
for their sake he rebuked kings: Ge 12:17; 20:3
[22]"Do not touch my anointed ones;
do my prophets no harm." Ps 105:1-15; Ge 20:7

[23]Sing to the LORD, all the earth;
proclaim his salvation day after day.

LIVING  **INSIGHT**

God is glorified when we worship in truth. When I come across something that I can't handle or explain, He's pleased when I trust Him to get me through it. And when I gather with other believers—or all alone—and I worship my God, He's glorified in it.
(See 1 Chronicles 16:23–36.)

[24]Declare his glory among the nations,
his marvelous deeds among all peoples.
[25]For great is the LORD and most worthy of
praise; Ps 48:1
he is to be feared above all gods. Ps 89:7
[26]For all the gods of the nations are idols,
but the LORD made the heavens. Lev 19:4
[27]Splendor and majesty are before him;
strength and joy in his dwelling place.
[28]Ascribe to the LORD, O families of nations,
ascribe to the LORD glory and strength,
[29] ascribe to the LORD the glory due his name.
Bring an offering and come before him;
worship the LORD in the splendor of his[b]
holiness.
[30]Tremble before him, all the earth! Ps 114:7
The world is firmly established; it cannot be
moved.
[31]Let the heavens rejoice, let the earth be glad;
let them say among the nations, "The LORD
reigns!" Ps 93:1
[32]Let the sea resound, and all that is in it; Ps 98:7
let the fields be jubilant, and everything in
them!
[33]Then the trees of the forest will sing,
they will sing for joy before the LORD,
for he comes to judge the earth. Ps 96:1-13
[34]Give thanks to the LORD, for he is good;
his love endures forever. Ezr 3:11; Ps 136:1-26
[35]Cry out, "Save us, O God our Savior; Mic 7:7
gather us and deliver us from the nations,
that we may give thanks to your holy name,
that we may glory in your praise."
[36]Praise be to the LORD, the God of Israel,
from everlasting to everlasting.

Then all the people said "Amen" and "Praise the
LORD." Ps 106:1,47-48
[37]David left Asaph and his associates before the
ark of the covenant of the LORD to minister there
regularly, according to each day's requirements.
[38]He also left Obed-Edom and his sixty-eight associates to minister with them. Obed-Edom son of
Jeduthun, and also Hosah, were gatekeepers.
[39]David left Zadok the priest and his fellow
priests before the tabernacle of the LORD at the
high place in Gibeon [40]to present burnt offerings
to the LORD on the altar of burnt offering regularly,
morning and evening, in accordance with everything written in the Law of the LORD, which he had
given Israel. [41]With them were Heman and Jeduthun and the rest of those chosen and designated
by name to give thanks to the LORD, "for his love
endures forever." [42]Heman and Jeduthun were responsible for the sounding of the trumpets and
cymbals and for the playing of the other instruments for sacred song. The sons of Jeduthun were
stationed at the gate. Ex 29:38; 2Ch 5:13; 7:6
[43]Then all the people left, each for his own
home, and David returned home to bless his
family.

God's Promise to David

17 After David was settled in his palace, he
said to Nathan the prophet, "Here I am,
living in a palace of cedar, while the ark of the
covenant of the LORD is under a tent." 1Ch 15:1
[2]Nathan replied to David, "Whatever you have
in mind, do it, for God is with you." 2Ch 6:7
[3]That night the word of God came to Nathan,
saying:
[4]"Go and tell my servant David, 'This is
what the LORD says: You are not the one to
build me a house to dwell in. [5]I have not
dwelt in a house from the day I brought Israel up out of Egypt to this day. I have moved
from one tent site to another, from one
dwelling place to another. [6]Wherever I have
moved with all the Israelites, did I ever say to
any of their leaders[c] whom I commanded to
shepherd my people, "Why have you not
built me a house of cedar?" ' 1Ch 28:3
[7]"Now then, tell my servant David, 'This is
what the LORD Almighty says: I took you
from the pasture and from following the
flock, to be ruler over my people Israel. [8]I

[a] *18-20* One Hebrew manuscript, Septuagint and Vulgate (see also Psalm 105:12); most Hebrew manuscripts *inherit, / [19]though you are but few in number, / few indeed, and strangers in it." / [20]They* [b] *29* Or *LORD with the splendor of*
[c] *6* Traditionally *judges*; also in verse 10

have been with you wherever you have gone, and I have cut off all your enemies from before you. Now I will make your name like the names of the greatest men of the earth.
9And I will provide a place for my people Israel and will plant them so that they can have a home of their own and no longer be disturbed. Wicked people will not oppress them anymore, as they did at the beginning
10and have done ever since the time I appointed leaders over my people Israel. I will also subdue all your enemies. Jdg 2:16; 2Sa 6:21
"'I declare to you that the LORD will build a house for you: 11When your days are over and you go to be with your fathers, I will raise up your offspring to succeed you, one of your own sons, and I will establish his kingdom. 12He is the one who will build a house for me, and I will establish his throne forever. 13I will be his father, and he will be my son. I will never take my love away from him, as I took it away from your predecessor.
14I will set him over my house and my kingdom forever; his throne will be established forever.'" 1Ki 2:12; Jer 33:17; 2Ch 6:18

15Nathan reported to David all the words of this entire revelation. 2Sa 7:1-17

David's Prayer

16Then King David went in and sat before the LORD, and he said:

"Who am I, O LORD God, and what is my family, that you have brought me this far?
17And as if this were not enough in your sight, O God, you have spoken about the future of the house of your servant. You have looked on me as though I were the most exalted of men, O LORD God.
18"What more can David say to you for honoring your servant? For you know your servant, 19O LORD. For the sake of your servant and according to your will, you have done this great thing and made known all these great promises.
20"There is no one like you, O LORD, and there is no God but you, as we have heard with our own ears. 21And who is like your people Israel—the one nation on earth whose God went out to redeem a people for himself, and to make a name for yourself, and to perform great and awesome wonders by driving out nations from before your people, whom you redeemed from Egypt? 22You made your people Israel your very own forever, and you, O LORD, have become their God. Ex 9:14; 19:5-6; Isa 44:6

23"And now, LORD, let the promise you have made concerning your servant and his house be established forever. Do as you promised, 24so that it will be established and that your name will be great forever. Then men will say, 'The LORD Almighty, the God over Israel, is Israel's God!' And the house of your servant David will be established before you. 1Ki 8:25
25"You, my God, have revealed to your servant that you will build a house for him. So your servant has found courage to pray to you. 26O LORD, you are God! You have promised these good things to your servant.
27Now you have been pleased to bless the house of your servant, that it may continue forever in your sight; for you, O LORD, have blessed it, and it will be blessed forever."

David's Victories

18 In the course of time, David defeated the Philistines and subdued them, and he took Gath and its surrounding villages from the control of the Philistines.

2David also defeated the Moabites, and they became subject to him and brought tribute.
3Moreover, David fought Hadadezer king of Zobah, as far as Hamath, when he went to establish his control along the Euphrates River. 4David captured a thousand of his chariots, seven thousand charioteers and twenty thousand foot soldiers. He hamstrung all but a hundred of the chariot horses. Ge 2:14; 49:6; 1Ch 19:6
5When the Arameans of Damascus came to help Hadadezer king of Zobah, David struck down twenty-two thousand of them. 6He put garrisons in the Aramean kingdom of Damascus, and the Arameans became subject to him and brought tribute. The LORD gave David victory everywhere he went. 1Ch 19:6
7David took the gold shields carried by the officers of Hadadezer and brought them to Jerusalem.
8From Tebah[a] and Cun, towns that belonged to Hadadezer, David took a great quantity of bronze, which Solomon used to make the bronze Sea, the pillars and various bronze articles. 1Ki 7:23
9When Tou king of Hamath heard that David had defeated the entire army of Hadadezer king of Zobah, 10he sent his son Hadoram to King David to greet him and congratulate him on his victory in battle over Hadadezer, who had been at war with Tou. Hadoram brought all kinds of articles of gold and silver and bronze.
11King David dedicated these articles to the LORD, as he had done with the silver and gold he had taken from all these nations: Edom and Moab, the Ammonites and the Philistines, and Amalek.

[a]8 Hebrew *Tibhath*, a variant of *Tebah*

12 Abishai son of Zeruiah struck down eighteen thousand Edomites in the Valley of Salt. 13 He put garrisons in Edom, and all the Edomites became subject to David. The LORD gave David victory everywhere he went. 2Sa 8:1-14; 1Ki 11:15

David's Officials

14 David reigned over all Israel, doing what was just and right for all his people. 15 Joab son of Zeruiah was over the army; Jehoshaphat son of Ahilud was recorder; 16 Zadok son of Ahitub and Ahimelech[a] son of Abiathar were priests; Shavsha was secretary; 17 Benaiah son of Jehoiada was over the Kerethites and Pelethites; and David's sons were chief officials at the king's side. 2Sa 8:15-18; 1Ch 29:26

The Battle Against the Ammonites

19 In the course of time, Nahash king of the Ammonites died, and his son succeeded him as king. 2 David thought, "I will show kindness to Hanun son of Nahash, because his father showed kindness to me." So David sent a delegation to express his sympathy to Hanun concerning his father. Ge 19:38; Jdg 10:17-11:33

When David's men came to Hanun in the land of the Ammonites to express sympathy to him, 3 the Ammonite nobles said to Hanun, "Do you think David is honoring your father by sending men to you to express sympathy? Haven't his men come to you to explore and spy out the country and overthrow it?" 4 So Hanun seized David's men, shaved them, cut off their garments in the middle at the buttocks, and sent them away. Nu 21:32

5 When someone came and told David about the men, he sent messengers to meet them, for they were greatly humiliated. The king said, "Stay at Jericho till your beards have grown, and then come back."

6 When the Ammonites realized that they had become a stench in David's nostrils, Hanun and the Ammonites sent a thousand talents[b] of silver to hire chariots and charioteers from Aram Naharaim,[c] Aram Maacah and Zobah. 7 They hired thirty-two thousand chariots and charioteers, as well as the king of Maacah with his troops, who came and camped near Medeba, while the Ammonites were mustered from their towns and moved out for battle. Jos 13:9,16; 1Ch 18:3,5,9

8 On hearing this, David sent Joab out with the entire army of fighting men. 9 The Ammonites came out and drew up in battle formation at the entrance to their city, while the kings who had come were by themselves in the open country.

10 Joab saw that there were battle lines in front of him and behind him; so he selected some of the best troops in Israel and deployed them against the Arameans. 11 He put the rest of the men under the command of Abishai his brother, and they were deployed against the Ammonites. 12 Joab said, "If the Arameans are too strong for me, then you are to rescue me; but if the Ammonites are too strong for you, then I will rescue you. 13 Be strong and let us fight bravely for our people and the cities of our God. The LORD will do what is good in his sight." 1Sa 26:6

14 Then Joab and the troops with him advanced to fight the Arameans, and they fled before him. 15 When the Ammonites saw that the Arameans were fleeing, they too fled before his brother Abishai and went inside the city. So Joab went back to Jerusalem.

16 After the Arameans saw that they had been routed by Israel, they sent messengers and had Arameans brought from beyond the River,[d] with Shophach the commander of Hadadezer's army leading them.

17 When David was told of this, he gathered all Israel and crossed the Jordan; he advanced against them and formed his battle lines opposite them. David formed his lines to meet the Arameans in battle, and they fought against him. 18 But they fled before Israel, and David killed seven thousand of their charioteers and forty thousand of their foot soldiers. He also killed Shophach the commander of their army.

19 When the vassals of Hadadezer saw that they had been defeated by Israel, they made peace with David and became subject to him.

So the Arameans were not willing to help the Ammonites anymore. 2Sa 10:1-19

The Capture of Rabbah

20 In the spring, at the time when kings go off to war, Joab led out the armed forces. He laid waste the land of the Ammonites and went to Rabbah and besieged it, but David remained in Jerusalem. Joab attacked Rabbah and left it in ruins. 2 David took the crown from the head of their king[e]—its weight was found to be a talent[f] of gold, and it was set with precious stones—and it was placed on David's head. He took a great quantity of plunder from the city 3 and brought out the people who were there, consigning them to labor with saws and with iron picks and axes. David did this to all the Ammonite towns. Then David and his entire army returned to Jerusalem. 2Sa 11:1

War With the Philistines

4 In the course of time, war broke out with the Philistines, at Gezer. At that time Sibbecai the Hushathite killed Sippai, one of the descendants of the Rephaites, and the Philistines were subjugated.

[a] *16* Some Hebrew manuscripts, Vulgate and Syriac (see also 2 Samuel 8:17); most Hebrew manuscripts *Abimelech* [b] *6* That is, about 37 tons (about 34 metric tons) [c] *6* That is, Northwest Mesopotamia [d] *16* That is, the Euphrates [e] *2* Or *of Milcom,* that is, Molech [f] *2* That is, about 75 pounds (about 34 kilograms)

5In another battle with the Philistines, Elhanan son of Jair killed Lahmi the brother of Goliath the Gittite, who had a spear with a shaft like a weaver's rod.

6In still another battle, which took place at Gath, there was a huge man with six fingers on each hand and six toes on each foot—twenty-four in all. He also was descended from Rapha. 7When he taunted Israel, Jonathan son of Shimea, David's brother, killed him.

8These were descendants of Rapha in Gath, and they fell at the hands of David and his men.

David Numbers the Fighting Men

21 Satan rose up against Israel and incited David to take a census of Israel. 2So David said to Joab and the commanders of the troops, "Go and count the Israelites from Beersheba to Dan. Then report back to me so that I may know how many there are." 1Ch 27:23-24; 2Ch 18:21

3But Joab replied, "May the LORD multiply his troops a hundred times over. My lord the king, are they not all my lord's subjects? Why does my lord want to do this? Why should he bring guilt on Israel?" Dt 1:11

4The king's word, however, overruled Joab; so Joab left and went throughout Israel and then came back to Jerusalem. 5Joab reported the number of the fighting men to David: In all Israel there were one million one hundred thousand men who could handle a sword, including four hundred and seventy thousand in Judah. 1Ch 9:1

6But Joab did not include Levi and Benjamin in the numbering, because the king's command was repulsive to him. 7This command was also evil in the sight of God; so he punished Israel.

8Then David said to God, "I have sinned greatly by doing this. Now, I beg you, take away the guilt of your servant. I have done a very foolish thing."

9The LORD said to Gad, David's seer, 10"Go and tell David, 'This is what the LORD says: I am giving you three options. Choose one of them for me to carry out against you.'" 1Sa 9:9; 22:5

11So Gad went to David and said to him, "This is what the LORD says: 'Take your choice: 12three years of famine, three months of being swept away[a] before your enemies, with their swords overtaking you, or three days of the sword of the LORD—days of plague in the land, with the angel of the LORD ravaging every part of Israel.' Now then, decide how I should answer the one who sent me." Dt 32:24; Eze 30:25

13David said to Gad, "I am in deep distress. Let me fall into the hands of the LORD, for his mercy is very great; but do not let me fall into the hands of men." Ps 130:4,7

14So the LORD sent a plague on Israel, and seventy thousand men of Israel fell dead. 15And God sent an angel to destroy Jerusalem. But as the angel was doing so, the LORD saw it and was grieved because of the calamity and said to the angel who was destroying the people, "Enough! Withdraw your hand." The angel of the LORD was then standing at the threshing floor of Araunah[b] the Jebusite. Ge 6:6; Ex 32:14; 1Ch 27:24

16David looked up and saw the angel of the LORD standing between heaven and earth, with a drawn sword in his hand extended over Jerusalem. Then David and the elders, clothed in sackcloth, fell facedown. Nu 14:5; Jos 7:6

17David said to God, "Was it not I who ordered the fighting men to be counted? I am the one who has sinned and done wrong. These are but sheep. What have they done? O LORD my God, let your hand fall upon me and my family, but do not let this plague remain on your people." 2Sa 7:8; Ps 74:1

18Then the angel of the LORD ordered Gad to tell David to go up and build an altar to the LORD on the threshing floor of Araunah the Jebusite. 19So David went up in obedience to the word that Gad had spoken in the name of the LORD. 2Ch 3:1

20While Araunah was threshing wheat, he turned and saw the angel; his four sons who were with him hid themselves. 21Then David approached, and when Araunah looked and saw him, he left the threshing floor and bowed down before David with his face to the ground. Jdg 6:11

22David said to him, "Let me have the site of your threshing floor so I can build an altar to the LORD, that the plague on the people may be stopped. Sell it to me at the full price."

23Araunah said to David, "Take it! Let my lord the king do whatever pleases him. Look, I will give the oxen for the burnt offerings, the threshing sledges for the wood, and the wheat for the grain offering. I will give all this."

24But King David replied to Araunah, "No, I insist on paying the full price. I will not take for the LORD what is yours, or sacrifice a burnt offering that costs me nothing."

25So David paid Araunah six hundred shekels[c] of gold for the site. 26David built an altar to the LORD there and sacrificed burnt offerings and fellowship offerings.[d] He called on the LORD, and the LORD answered him with fire from heaven on the altar of burnt offering. 2Sa 24:1-25

27Then the LORD spoke to the angel, and he put his sword back into its sheath. 28At that time, when David saw that the LORD had answered him on the threshing floor of Araunah the Jebusite, he offered sacrifices there. 29The tabernacle of the LORD, which Moses had made in the desert, and the altar

[a] 12 Hebrew; Septuagint and Vulgate (see also 2 Samuel 24:13) *of fleeing* [b] 15 Hebrew *Ornan*, a variant of *Araunah*; also in verses 18-28 [c] 25 That is, about 15 pounds (about 7 kilograms) [d] 26 Traditionally *peace offerings*

of burnt offering were at that time on the high place at Gibeon. [30]But David could not go before it to inquire of God, because he was afraid of the sword of the angel of the LORD. 1Ki 3:4; 1Ch 16:39

The Glory of the Temple **Chapters 22–29**

The book's final section chronicles the preparations for the building of the temple and the worship of God. Although David knew he would not build the temple, he charged his son Solomon to take up the task and therefore helped prepare the way for this monumental undertaking. Provisions were made for priests, singers, gatekeepers and all those who would serve to make worship in the temple possible. These chapters record David's efforts to plan and accomplish all he could before his death. The book closes with David's prayer of praise—followed by the record of his death.

22 Then David said, "The house of the LORD God is to be here, and also the altar of burnt offering for Israel." 1Ch 21:18-29; 2Ch 3:1

Preparations for the Temple

[2]So David gave orders to assemble the aliens living in Israel, and from among them he appointed stonecutters to prepare dressed stone for building the house of God. [3]He provided a large amount of iron to make nails for the doors of the gateways and for the fittings, and more bronze than could be weighed. [4]He also provided more cedar logs than could be counted, for the Sidonians and Tyrians had brought large numbers of them to David. 1Ki 5:6; 9:21

[5]David said, "My son Solomon is young and inexperienced, and the house to be built for the LORD should be of great magnificence and fame and splendor in the sight of all the nations. Therefore I will make preparations for it." So David made extensive preparations before his death.

[6]Then he called for his son Solomon and charged him to build a house for the LORD, the God of Israel. [7]David said to Solomon: "My son, I had it in my heart to build a house for the Name of the LORD my God. [8]But this word of the LORD came to me: 'You have shed much blood and have fought many wars. You are not to build a house for my Name, because you have shed much blood on the earth in my sight. [9]But you will have a son who will be a man of peace and rest, and I will give him rest from all his enemies on every side. His name will be Solomon,[a] and I will grant Israel peace and quiet during his reign. [10]He is the one who will build a house for my Name. He will be my son, and I will be his father. And I will establish the throne of his kingdom over Israel forever.'

[11]"Now, my son, the LORD be with you, and may you have success and build the house of the LORD your God, as he said you would. [12]May the LORD give you discretion and understanding when he puts you in command over Israel, so that you may keep the law of the LORD your God. [13]Then you will have success if you are careful to observe the decrees and laws that the LORD gave Moses for Israel. Be strong and courageous. Do not be afraid or discouraged. Jos 1:6-9; 1Ki 3:9-12; 1Ch 28:7

LIVING  INSIGHT

If I've counted correctly, there are over 350 "fear nots" in the Bible. Think of them as God's one-a-day vitamins.

(See 1 Chronicles 22:13.)

[14]"I have taken great pains to provide for the temple of the LORD a hundred thousand talents[b] of gold, a million talents[c] of silver, quantities of bronze and iron too great to be weighed, and wood and stone. And you may add to them. [15]You have many workmen: stonecutters, masons and carpenters, as well as men skilled in every kind of work [16]in gold and silver, bronze and iron—craftsmen beyond number. Now begin the work, and the LORD be with you." ver 11; 2Ch 2:7

[17]Then David ordered all the leaders of Israel to help his son Solomon. [18]He said to them, "Is not the LORD your God with you? And has he not granted you rest on every side? For he has handed the inhabitants of the land over to me, and the land is subject to the LORD and to his people. [19]Now devote your heart and soul to seeking the LORD your God. Begin to build the sanctuary of the LORD God, so that you may bring the ark of the covenant of the LORD and the sacred articles belonging to God into the temple that will be built for the Name of the LORD." 2Ch 5:7; 1Ch 23:25; 28:1-6

The Levites

23 When David was old and full of years, he made his son Solomon king over Israel.

[2]He also gathered together all the leaders of Israel, as well as the priests and Levites. [3]The Levites thirty years old or more were counted, and the total number of men was thirty-eight thousand. [4]David said, "Of these, twenty-four thousand are to supervise the work of the temple of the LORD and six thousand are to be officials and judges. [5]Four thousand are to be gatekeepers and four thousand are to praise the LORD with the musical instruments I have provided for that purpose." 1Ch 15:16; 2Ch 19:8

[a]9 *Solomon* sounds like and may be derived from the Hebrew for *peace.* [b]14 That is, about 3,750 tons (about 3,450 metric tons) [c]14 That is, about 37,500 tons (about 34,500 metric tons)

[6]David divided the Levites into groups corresponding to the sons of Levi: Gershon, Kohath and Merari. 2Ch 8:14; 29:25

Gershonites

[7]Belonging to the Gershonites:
Ladan and Shimei.
[8]The sons of Ladan:
Jehiel the first, Zetham and Joel—three in all.
[9]The sons of Shimei:
Shelomoth, Haziel and Haran—three in all.
These were the heads of the families of Ladan.
[10]And the sons of Shimei:
Jahath, Ziza,[a] Jeush and Beriah.
These were the sons of Shimei—four in all.
[11]Jahath was the first and Ziza the second, but Jeush and Beriah did not have many sons; so they were counted as one family with one assignment.

Kohathites

[12]The sons of Kohath:
Amram, Izhar, Hebron and Uzziel—four in all. Ex 6:18
[13]The sons of Amram: Ex 6:20; 28:1
Aaron and Moses.
Aaron was set apart, he and his descendants forever, to consecrate the most holy things, to offer sacrifices before the LORD, to minister before him and to pronounce blessings in his name forever.
[14]The sons of Moses the man of God were counted as part of the tribe of Levi.
[15]The sons of Moses:
Gershom and Eliezer. Ex 18:4
[16]The descendants of Gershom: 1Ch 26:24-28
Shubael was the first.
[17]The descendants of Eliezer:
Rehabiah was the first.
Eliezer had no other sons, but the sons of Rehabiah were very numerous.
[18]The sons of Izhar:
Shelomith was the first.
[19]The sons of Hebron: 1Ch 24:23
Jeriah the first, Amariah the second, Jahaziel the third and Jekameam the fourth.
[20]The sons of Uzziel:
Micah the first and Isshiah the second.

Merarites

[21]The sons of Merari: 1Ch 24:26
Mahli and Mushi.
The sons of Mahli:
Eleazar and Kish.
[22]Eleazar died without having sons: he had only daughters. Their cousins, the sons of Kish, married them.
[23]The sons of Mushi:
Mahli, Eder and Jerimoth—three in all.

[24]These were the descendants of Levi by their
families—the heads of families as they were registered under their names and counted individually,
that is, the workers twenty years old or more who
served in the temple of the LORD. [25]For David had
said, "Since the LORD, the God of Israel, has granted rest to his people and has come to dwell in
Jerusalem forever, [26]the Levites no longer need to
carry the tabernacle or any of the articles used in
its service." [27]According to the last instructions of
David, the Levites were counted from those twenty
years old or more. Nu 4:5,15; Dt 10:8
[28]The duty of the Levites was to help Aaron's
descendants in the service of the temple of the
LORD: to be in charge of the courtyards, the side
rooms, the purification of all sacred things and the
performance of other duties at the house of God.
[29]They were in charge of the bread set out on the
table, the flour for the grain offerings, the unleavened wafers, the baking and the mixing, and all
measurements of quantity and size. [30]They were
also to stand every morning to thank and praise
the LORD. They were to do the same in the evening
[31]and whenever burnt offerings were presented to
the LORD on Sabbaths and at New Moon festivals
and at appointed feasts. They were to serve before
the LORD regularly in the proper number and in
the way prescribed for them. Ex 25:30; Lev 19:35-36; 23:4
[32]And so the Levites carried out their responsibilities for the Tent of Meeting, for the Holy
Place and, under their brothers the descendants of
Aaron, for the service of the temple of the LORD.

The Divisions of Priests

24 These were the divisions of the sons of Aaron: Nu 3:2-4; 1Ch 23:6
The sons of Aaron were Nadab, Abihu, Eleazar
and Ithamar. [2]But Nadab and Abihu died before
their father did, and they had no sons; so Eleazar
and Ithamar served as the priests. [3]With the help
of Zadok a descendant of Eleazar and Ahimelech
a descendant of Ithamar, David separated them
into divisions for their appointed order of ministering. [4]A larger number of leaders were found
among Eleazar's descendants than among Ithamar's, and they were divided accordingly: sixteen
heads of families from Eleazar's descendants and
eight heads of families from Ithamar's descendants. [5]They divided them impartially by drawing
lots, for there were officials of the sanctuary and

[a] *10* One Hebrew manuscript, Septuagint and Vulgate (see also verse 11); most Hebrew manuscripts *Zina*

officials of God among the descendants of both
Eleazar and Ithamar. Ex 6:23; Lev 10:1-2; Nu 3:4
6The scribe Shemaiah son of Nethanel, a Levite,
recorded their names in the presence of the king
and of the officials: Zadok the priest, Ahimelech
son of Abiathar and the heads of families of the
priests and of the Levites—one family being taken
from Eleazar and then one from Ithamar.

7The first lot fell to Jehoiarib,
the second to Jedaiah, Ezr 2:36; Ne 12:6
8the third to Harim, Ezr 2:39; Ne 10:5
the fourth to Seorim,
9the fifth to Malkijah,
the sixth to Mijamin,
10the seventh to Hakkoz,
the eighth to Abijah, Ne 12:4,17; Lk 1:5
11the ninth to Jeshua,
the tenth to Shecaniah,
12the eleventh to Eliashib,
the twelfth to Jakim,
13the thirteenth to Huppah,
the fourteenth to Jeshebeab,
14the fifteenth to Bilgah,
the sixteenth to Immer, Jer 20:1
15the seventeenth to Hezir,
the eighteenth to Happizzez,
16the nineteenth to Pethahiah,
the twentieth to Jehezkel,
17the twenty-first to Jakin,
the twenty-second to Gamul,
18the twenty-third to Delaiah
and the twenty-fourth to Maaziah.

19This was their appointed order of ministering
when they entered the temple of the LORD, according to the regulations prescribed for them by their
forefather Aaron, as the LORD, the God of Israel,
had commanded him.

The Rest of the Levites

20As for the rest of the descendants of Levi:
from the sons of Amram: Shubael;
from the sons of Shubael: Jehdeiah.
21As for Rehabiah, from his sons: 1Ch 23:17
Isshiah was the first.
22From the Izharites: Shelomoth;
from the sons of Shelomoth: Jahath.
23The sons of Hebron: Jeriah the first,[a] Amariah the second, Jahaziel the third and
Jekameam the fourth. 1Ch 23:19
24The son of Uzziel: Micah;
from the sons of Micah: Shamir.
25The brother of Micah: Isshiah;
from the sons of Isshiah: Zechariah.
26The sons of Merari: Mahli and Mushi.
The son of Jaaziah: Beno.
27The sons of Merari:
from Jaaziah: Beno, Shoham, Zaccur and Ibri.
28From Mahli: Eleazar, who had no sons.
29From Kish: the son of Kish:
Jerahmeel.
30And the sons of Mushi: Mahli, Eder and
Jerimoth.

These were the Levites, according to their families.
31They also cast lots, just as their brothers the
descendants of Aaron did, in the presence of King
David and of Zadok, Ahimelech, and the heads of
families of the priests and of the Levites. The families of the oldest brother were treated the same as
those of the youngest.

The Singers

25 David, together with the commanders of the army, set apart some of the sons of
Asaph, Heman and Jeduthun for the ministry
of prophesying, accompanied by harps, lyres and
cymbals. Here is the list of the men who performed this service: 1Sa 10:5; 1Ch 6:33,39; 15:16

2From the sons of Asaph:
Zaccur, Joseph, Nethaniah and Asarelah. The sons of Asaph were under the supervision of Asaph, who prophesied under the king's supervision.
3As for Jeduthun, from his sons:
Gedaliah, Zeri, Jeshaiah, Shimei,[b] Hashabiah and Mattithiah, six in all, under the supervision of their father Jeduthun, who prophesied, using the harp in thanking and praising the LORD. Ge 4:21; Ps 33:2
4As for Heman, from his sons:
Bukkiah, Mattaniah, Uzziel, Shubael and Jerimoth; Hananiah, Hanani, Eliathah, Giddalti and Romamti-Ezer; Joshbekashah, Mallothi,
Hothir and Mahazioth. 5All these were sons
of Heman the king's seer. They were given him through the promises of God to exalt him.[c] God gave Heman fourteen sons and three daughters.

6All these men were under the supervision of
their fathers for the music of the temple of the
LORD, with cymbals, lyres and harps, for the ministry at the house of God. Asaph, Jeduthun and
Heman were under the supervision of the king.
7Along with their relatives—all of them trained
and skilled in music for the LORD—they numbered 288.
8Young and old alike, teacher as well as
student, cast lots for their duties. 1Ch 15:16,19; 26:13

9The first lot, which was for Asaph, fell to
Joseph,

[a] 23 Two Hebrew manuscripts and some Septuagint manuscripts (see also 1 Chron. 23:19); most Hebrew manuscripts *The sons of Jeriah:* [b] 3 One Hebrew manuscript and some Septuagint manuscripts (see also verse 17); most Hebrew manuscripts do not have *Shimei.* [c] 5 Hebrew *exalt the horn*

his sons and relatives,[a] 12[b]
the second to Gedaliah,
he and his relatives and sons, 12
10the third to Zaccur,
his sons and relatives, 12
11the fourth to Izri,[c]
his sons and relatives, 12
12the fifth to Nethaniah,
his sons and relatives, 12
13the sixth to Bukkiah,
his sons and relatives, 12
14the seventh to Jesarelah,[d]
his sons and relatives, 12
15the eighth to Jeshaiah,
his sons and relatives, 12
16the ninth to Mattaniah,
his sons and relatives, 12
17the tenth to Shimei,
his sons and relatives, 12
18the eleventh to Azarel,[e]
his sons and relatives, 12
19the twelfth to Hashabiah,
his sons and relatives, 12
20the thirteenth to Shubael,
his sons and relatives, 12
21the fourteenth to Mattithiah,
his sons and relatives, 12
22the fifteenth to Jerimoth,
his sons and relatives, 12
23the sixteenth to Hananiah,
his sons and relatives, 12
24the seventeenth to Joshbekashah,
his sons and relatives, 12
25the eighteenth to Hanani,
his sons and relatives, 12
26the nineteenth to Mallothi,
his sons and relatives, 12
27the twentieth to Eliathah,
his sons and relatives, 12
28the twenty-first to Hothir,
his sons and relatives, 12
29the twenty-second to Giddalti,
his sons and relatives, 12
30the twenty-third to Mahazioth,
his sons and relatives, 12
31the twenty-fourth to Romamti-Ezer,
his sons and relatives, 12

The Gatekeepers

26 The divisions of the gatekeepers: 1Ch 9:17

From the Korahites: Meshelemiah son of
Kore, one of the sons of Asaph.
2Meshelemiah had sons:
Zechariah the firstborn, 1Ch 9:21
Jediael the second,
Zebadiah the third,
Jathniel the fourth,
3Elam the fifth,
Jehohanan the sixth
and Eliehoenai the seventh.
4Obed-Edom also had sons:
Shemaiah the firstborn,
Jehozabad the second,
Joah the third,
Sacar the fourth,
Nethanel the fifth,
5Ammiel the sixth,
Issachar the seventh
and Peullethai the eighth.
(For God had blessed Obed-Edom.)
6His son Shemaiah also had sons, who were
leaders in their father's family because
they were very capable men. 7The sons of
Shemaiah: Othni, Rephael, Obed and Elzabad; his relatives Elihu and Semakiah
were also able men. 8All these were
descendants of Obed-Edom; they and
their sons and their relatives were capable
men with the strength to do the work—
descendants of Obed-Edom, 62 in all.
9Meshelemiah had sons and relatives, who
were able men—18 in all.
10Hosah the Merarite had sons: Shimri the
first (although he was not the firstborn,
his father had appointed him the first),
11Hilkiah the second, Tabaliah the third
and Zechariah the fourth. The sons and
relatives of Hosah were 13 in all.
12These divisions of the gatekeepers, through
their chief men, had duties for ministering in the
temple of the LORD, just as their relatives had.
13Lots were cast for each gate, according to their
families, young and old alike. 1Ch 24:5,31; 25:8
14The lot for the East Gate fell to Shelemiah.[f]
Then lots were cast for his son Zechariah, a wise
counselor, and the lot for the North Gate fell
to him. 15The lot for the South Gate fell to Obed-
Edom, and the lot for the storehouse fell to his
sons. 16The lots for the West Gate and the Shalle-
keth Gate on the upper road fell to Shuppim and
Hosah. 1Ch 9:18,21; 13:13
Guard was alongside of guard: 17There were six
Levites a day on the east, four a day on the north,
four a day on the south and two at a time at the
storehouse. 18As for the court to the west, there
were four at the road and two at the court itself.
19These were the divisions of the gatekeepers
who were descendants of Korah and Merari.

[a] 9 See Septuagint; Hebrew does not have *his sons and relatives.* [b] 9 See the total in verse 7; Hebrew does not have *twelve.* [c] 11 A variant of *Zeri* [d] 14 A variant of *Asarelah* [e] 18 A variant of *Uzziel* [f] 14 A variant of *Meshelemiah*

The Treasurers and Other Officials

[20]Their fellow Levites were[a] in charge of the
treasuries of the house of God and the treasuries
for the dedicated things. 1Ch 28:12; 2Ch 24:5
[21]The descendants of Ladan, who were Gershonites through Ladan and who were heads of
families belonging to Ladan the Gershonite, were
Jehieli, [22]the sons of Jehieli, Zetham and his brother Joel. They were in charge of the treasuries of the
temple of the LORD. 1Ch 23:7; 29:8
[23]From the Amramites, the Izharites, the Hebronites and the Uzzielites: Nu 3:27

[24]Shubael, a descendant of Gershom son of
Moses, was the officer in charge of the
treasuries. [25]His relatives through Eliezer:
Rehabiah his son, Jeshaiah his son, Joram
his son, Zicri his son and Shelomith his
son. [26]Shelomith and his relatives were in
charge of all the treasuries for the things
dedicated by King David, by the heads of
families who were the commanders of
thousands and commanders of hundreds, and by the other army commanders. [27]Some of the plunder taken in battle
they dedicated for the repair of the temple of the LORD. [28]And everything dedicated by Samuel the seer and by Saul son
of Kish, Abner son of Ner and Joab son
of Zeruiah, and all the other dedicated
things were in the care of Shelomith and
his relatives. 1Sa 9:9; 2Sa 8:11; 1Ch 23:18
[29]From the Izharites: Kenaniah and his sons
were assigned duties away from the temple, as officials and judges over Israel.
[30]From the Hebronites: Hashabiah and his
relatives—seventeen hundred able
men—were responsible in Israel west of
the Jordan for all the work of the LORD
and for the king's service. [31]As for the
Hebronites, Jeriah was their chief according to the genealogical records of their
families. In the fortieth year of David's
reign a search was made in the records,
and capable men among the Hebronites
were found at Jazer in Gilead. [32]Jeriah
had twenty-seven hundred relatives, who
were able men and heads of families, and
King David put them in charge of the
Reubenites, the Gadites and the half-
tribe of Manasseh for every matter pertaining to God and for the affairs of the
king. 1Ch 23:19; 27:17

Army Divisions

27 This is the list of the Israelites—heads of
families, commanders of thousands and
commanders of hundreds, and their officers, who
served the king in all that concerned the army
divisions that were on duty month by month
throughout the year. Each division consisted of
24,000 men.

[2]In charge of the first division, for the first
month, was Jashobeam son of Zabdiel. There
were 24,000 men in his division. [3]He was a
descendant of Perez and chief of all the army
officers for the first month. 2Sa 23:8; 1Ch 11:11
[4]In charge of the division for the second month
was Dodai the Ahohite; Mikloth was the leader
of his division. There were 24,000 men in his
division. 2Sa 23:9
[5]The third army commander, for the third
month, was Benaiah son of Jehoiada the priest.
He was chief and there were 24,000 men in his
division. [6]This was the Benaiah who was a
mighty man among the Thirty and was over
the Thirty. His son Ammizabad was in charge
of his division.
[7]The fourth, for the fourth month, was Asahel the
brother of Joab; his son Zebadiah was his successor. There were 24,000 men in his division.
[8]The fifth, for the fifth month, was the commander Shamhuth the Izrahite. There were
24,000 men in his division. 1Ch 11:27
[9]The sixth, for the sixth month, was Ira the son
of Ikkesh the Tekoite. There were 24,000 men
in his division. 2Sa 23:26; 1Ch 11:28
[10]The seventh, for the seventh month, was Helez
the Pelonite, an Ephraimite. There were 24,000
men in his division. 2Sa 23:26; 1Ch 11:27
[11]The eighth, for the eighth month, was Sibbecai
the Hushathite, a Zerahite. There were 24,000
men in his division. 2Sa 21:18
[12]The ninth, for the ninth month, was Abiezer the
Anathothite, a Benjamite. There were 24,000
men in his division. 2Sa 23:27; 1Ch 11:28
[13]The tenth, for the tenth month, was Maharai the
Netophathite, a Zerahite. There were 24,000
men in his division. 2Sa 23:28; 1Ch 11:30
[14]The eleventh, for the eleventh month, was Benaiah the Pirathonite, an Ephraimite. There were
24,000 men in his division. 1Ch 11:31
[15]The twelfth, for the twelfth month, was Heldai
the Netophathite, from the family of Othniel.
There were 24,000 men in his division.

Officers of the Tribes

[16]The officers over the tribes of Israel:

over the Reubenites: Eliezer son of Zicri;
over the Simeonites: Shephatiah son of Maacah;
[17]over Levi: Hashabiah son of Kemuel;
over Aaron: Zadok; 1Ch 12:28

[a] 20 Septuagint; Hebrew *As for the Levites, Ahijah was*

[18]over Judah: Elihu, a brother of David;
over Issachar: Omri son of Michael;
[19]over Zebulun: Ishmaiah son of Obadiah;
over Naphtali: Jerimoth son of Azriel;
[20]over the Ephraimites: Hoshea son of Azaziah;
over half the tribe of Manasseh: Joel son of Pedaiah;
[21]over the half-tribe of Manasseh in Gilead: Iddo son of Zechariah;
over Benjamin: Jaasiel son of Abner;
[22]over Dan: Azarel son of Jeroham.
These were the officers over the tribes of Israel.

[23]David did not take the number of the men
twenty years old or less, because the LORD had
promised to make Israel as numerous as the stars
in the sky. [24]Joab son of Zeruiah began to count
the men but did not finish. Wrath came on Israel
on account of this numbering, and the number
was not entered in the book[a] of the annals of
King David. Ge 15:5; 2Sa 24:15

The King's Overseers

[25]Azmaveth son of Adiel was in charge of the royal storehouses.

Jonathan son of Uzziah was in charge of the storehouses in the outlying districts, in the towns, the villages and the watchtowers.

[26]Ezri son of Kelub was in charge of the field workers who farmed the land.

[27]Shimei the Ramathite was in charge of the vineyards.

Zabdi the Shiphmite was in charge of the produce of the vineyards for the wine vats.

[28]Baal-Hanan the Gederite was in charge of the olive and sycamore-fig trees in the western foothills. 1Ki 10:27

Joash was in charge of the supplies of olive oil.

[29]Shitrai the Sharonite was in charge of the herds grazing in Sharon.

Shaphat son of Adlai was in charge of the herds in the valleys.

[30]Obil the Ishmaelite was in charge of the camels.

Jehdeiah the Meronothite was in charge of the donkeys.

[31]Jaziz the Hagrite was in charge of the flocks.

All these were the officials in charge of King David's property.

[32]Jonathan, David's uncle, was a counselor, a man of insight and a scribe. Jehiel son of Hacmoni took care of the king's sons.

[33]Ahithophel was the king's counselor.

Hushai the Arkite was the king's friend.

[34]Ahithophel was succeeded by Jehoiada son of Benaiah and by Abiathar. 2Sa 15:37; 1Ki 1:7

Joab was the commander of the royal army.

David's Plans for the Temple

28 David summoned all the officials of Israel
to assemble at Jerusalem: the officers over
the tribes, the commanders of the divisions in the
service of the king, the commanders of thousands
and commanders of hundreds, and the officials in
charge of all the property and livestock belonging
to the king and his sons, together with the palace
officials, the mighty men and all the brave warriors. 1Ch 27:1-31
[2]King David rose to his feet and said: "Listen to
me, my brothers and my people. I had it in my
heart to build a house as a place of rest for the ark
of the covenant of the LORD, for the footstool of
our God, and I made plans to build it. [3]But God
said to me, 'You are not to build a house for my
Name, because you are a warrior and have shed
blood.' 1Ch 22:8; Ps 132:7
[4]"Yet the LORD, the God of Israel, chose me
from my whole family to be king over Israel forever. He chose Judah as leader, and from the house
of Judah he chose my family, and from my father's
sons he was pleased to make me king over all
Israel. [5]Of all my sons—and the LORD has given
me many—he has chosen my son Solomon to sit
on the throne of the kingdom of the LORD over
Israel. [6]He said to me: 'Solomon your son is the
one who will build my house and my courts, for I
have chosen him to be my son, and I will be his
father. [7]I will establish his kingdom forever if he is
unswerving in carrying out my commands and
laws, as is being done at this time.' 2Sa 7:13
[8]"So now I charge you in the sight of all Israel
and of the assembly of the LORD, and in the hearing of our God: Be careful to follow all the commands of the LORD your God, that you may possess this good land and pass it on as an inheritance
to your descendants forever. Dt 4:1; 6:1
[9]"And you, my son Solomon, acknowledge the
God of your father, and serve him with wholehearted devotion and with a willing mind, for the
LORD searches every heart and understands every
motive behind the thoughts. If you seek him, he
will be found by you; but if you forsake him, he
will reject you forever. [10]Consider now, for the
LORD has chosen you to build a temple as a sanctuary. Be strong and do the work." 1Sa 16:7; 2Ch 15:2
[11]Then David gave his son Solomon the plans
for the portico of the temple, its buildings, its
storerooms, its upper parts, its inner rooms and
the place of atonement. [12]He gave him the plans of
all that the Spirit had put in his mind for the courts
of the temple of the LORD and all the surrounding

[a]24 Septuagint; Hebrew *number*

rooms, for the treasuries of the temple of God and for the treasuries for the dedicated things. 13He gave him instructions for the divisions of the priests and Levites, and for all the work of serving in the temple of the LORD, as well as for all the articles to be used in its service. 14He designated the weight of gold for all the gold articles to be used in various kinds of service, and the weight of silver for all the silver articles to be used in various kinds of service: 15the weight of gold for the gold lampstands and their lamps, with the weight for each lampstand and its lamps; and the weight of silver for each silver lampstand and its lamps, according to the use of each lampstand; 16the weight of gold for each table for consecrated bread; the weight of silver for the silver tables; 17the weight of pure gold for the forks, sprinkling bowls and pitchers; the weight of gold for each gold dish; the weight of silver for each silver dish; 18and the weight of the refined gold for the altar of incense. He also gave him the plan for the chariot, that is, the cherubim of gold that spread their wings and shelter the ark of the covenant of the LORD.

19"All this," David said, "I have in writing from the hand of the LORD upon me, and he gave me understanding in all the details of the plan."

20David also said to Solomon his son, "Be strong and courageous, and do the work. Do not be afraid or discouraged, for the LORD God, my God, is with you. He will not fail you or forsake you until all the work for the service of the temple of the LORD is finished. 21The divisions of the priests and Levites are ready for all the work on the temple of God, and every willing man skilled in any craft will help you in all the work. The officials and all the people will obey your every command."

Gifts for Building the Temple

29 Then King David said to the whole assembly: "My son Solomon, the one whom God has chosen, is young and inexperienced. The task is great, because this palatial structure is not for man but for the LORD God. 2With all my resources I have provided for the temple of my God—gold for the gold work, silver for the silver, bronze for the bronze, iron for the iron and wood for the wood, as well as onyx for the settings, turquoise,[a] stones of various colors, and all kinds of fine stone and marble—all of these in large quantities. 3Besides, in my devotion to the temple of my God I now give my personal treasures of gold and silver for the temple of my God, over and above everything I have provided for this holy temple: 4three thousand talents[b] of gold (gold of Ophir) and seven thousand talents[c] of refined silver, for the overlaying of the walls of the buildings, 5for the gold work and the silver work, and for all the work to be done by the craftsmen. Now, who is willing to consecrate himself today to the LORD?"

6Then the leaders of families, the officers of the tribes of Israel, the commanders of thousands and commanders of hundreds, and the officials in charge of the king's work gave willingly. 7They gave toward the work on the temple of God five thousand talents[d] and ten thousand darics[e] of gold, ten thousand talents[f] of silver, eighteen thousand talents[g] of bronze and a hundred thousand talents[h] of iron. 8Any who had precious stones gave them to the treasury of the temple of the LORD in the custody of Jehiel the Gershonite. 9The people rejoiced at the willing response of their leaders, for they had given freely and wholeheartedly to the LORD. David the king also rejoiced greatly. 1Ki 8:61; 1Ch 26:21; 2Co 9:7

David's Prayer

10David praised the LORD in the presence of the whole assembly, saying,

"Praise be to you, O LORD,
God of our father Israel,
from everlasting to everlasting.
11Yours, O LORD, is the greatness and the power
and the glory and the majesty and the splendor,
for everything in heaven and earth is yours.
Yours, O LORD, is the kingdom;
you are exalted as head over all. Rev 5:12-13
12Wealth and honor come from you; 2Ch 1:12
you are the ruler of all things. 2Ch 20:6; Ro 11:36
In your hands are strength and power
to exalt and give strength to all.
13Now, our God, we give you thanks,
and praise your glorious name.

14"But who am I, and who are my people, that we should be able to give as generously as this? Everything comes from you, and we have given you only what comes from your hand. 15We are aliens and strangers in your sight, as were all our forefathers. Our days on earth are like a shadow, without hope. 16O LORD our God, as for all this abundance that we have provided for building you a temple for your Holy Name, it comes from your hand, and all of it belongs to you. 17I know, my God, that you test the heart and are pleased with integrity. All these things have I given willingly and with honest intent. And now I have seen with joy how willingly your people who are here have given to you. 18O LORD, God of our fathers Abraham, Isaac and Israel, keep this desire in the hearts

[a] 2 The meaning of the Hebrew for this word is uncertain. [b] 4 That is, about 110 tons (about 100 metric tons) [c] 4 That is, about 260 tons (about 240 metric tons) [d] 7 That is, about 190 tons (about 170 metric tons) [e] 7 That is, about 185 pounds (about 84 kilograms) [f] 7 That is, about 375 tons (about 345 metric tons) [g] 7 That is, about 675 tons (about 610 metric tons) [h] 7 That is, about 3,750 tons (about 3,450 metric tons)

of your people forever, and keep their hearts loyal
to you. 19And give my son Solomon the wholehearted devotion to keep your commands, requirements and decrees and to do everything to

LIVING  **INSIGHT**

Want a challenge? Start modeling the truth . . . Think truth. Confess truth. Face truth. Love truth. Pursue truth. Walk truth. Talk truth. Ah, that last one! That is a good place to start. From this day forward, deliberately and conscientiously speak the truth. Start practicing gut-level authenticity.

(See 1 Chronicles 29:17.)

build the palatial structure for which I have provided." 1Ch 22:14; 28:9; Ps 72:1

20Then David said to the whole assembly,
"Praise the LORD your God." So they all praised the
LORD, the God of their fathers; they bowed low and
fell prostrate before the LORD and the king.

Solomon Acknowledged as King

21The next day they made sacrifices to the LORD
and presented burnt offerings to him: a thousand
bulls, a thousand rams and a thousand male
lambs, together with their drink offerings, and
other sacrifices in abundance for all Israel. 22They
ate and drank with great joy in the presence of the
LORD that day. 1Ki 8:62; 1Ch 23:1

Then they acknowledged Solomon son of David
as king a second time, anointing him before the
LORD to be ruler and Zadok to be priest. 23So Solomon sat on the throne of the LORD as king in place
of his father David. He prospered and all Israel
obeyed him. 24All the officers and mighty men, as
well as all of King David's sons, pledged their submission to King Solomon. 1Ki 1:33-39; 2:12

25The LORD highly exalted Solomon in the sight
of all Israel and bestowed on him royal splendor
such as no king over Israel ever had before.

The Death of David

26David son of Jesse was king over all Israel.
27He ruled over Israel forty years—seven in Hebron and thirty-three in Jerusalem. 28He died at a
good old age, having enjoyed long life, wealth and
honor. His son Solomon succeeded him as king.

29As for the events of King David's reign, from
beginning to end, they are written in the records of
Samuel the seer, the records of Nathan the prophet
and the records of Gad the seer, 30together with the
details of his reign and power, and the circumstances that surrounded him and Israel and the
kingdoms of all the other lands. 1Sa 9:9; 22:5; 2Sa 7:2

INTRODUCTION

2 CHRONICLES

Hindsight! Yes, it is, as the old saying goes, "20/20." How often haven't we said it—"if only we had known then what we know now. If only we'd had a perspective different from the one we had then. Oh, what might have been!" The book of 2 Chronicles provides such a perspective. Written to a people resettling in Judah, about to start over, 2 Chronicles is a remarkable account of *God's* view of all that has happened to the people of Judah from the time of Solomon until the time of captivity. To those who stepped back to survey the painful and poignant scene of national deterioration, 2 Chronicles spoke a powerful reminder: "Remember what made your nation great, and remember what brought your nation down. You have the advantage of hindsight—so learn your lessons well."

WRITER: *Possibly Ezra*

DATE: *c.450–400* B.C.

PURPOSE: *To encourage obedience and warn against disobedience*

KEY MESSAGE: *A nation that honors God will see success*

KEY VERSES: 7:12-22

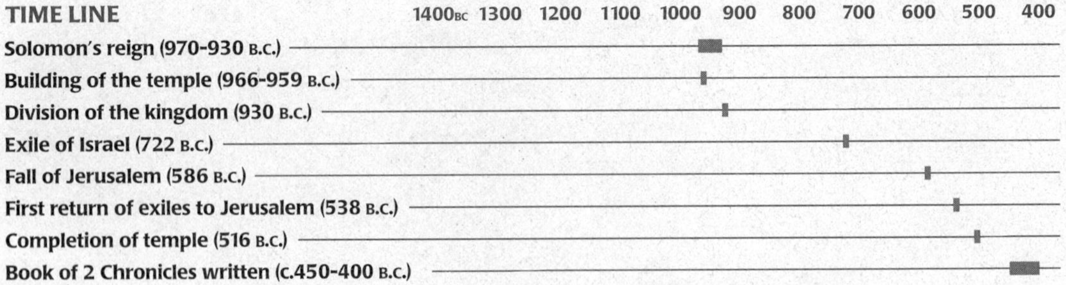

From Greatness to Nothingness

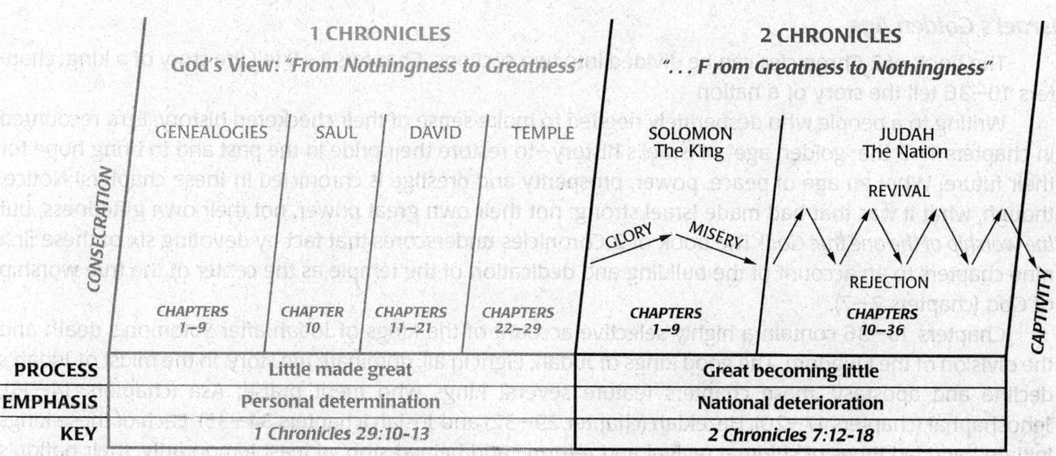

In the book of 1 Chronicles we saw a movement from nothingness to greatness; in the book of 2 Chronicles we see a movement from greatness back to nothingness. These two books, originally one in the Hebrew canon, form a cycle. Perhaps a better analogy would be an arrow that shoots straight up, hits a peak in elevation, then turns and plunges straight down. In these books we see the people of God moving from obscurity to the zenith of their history—only to wind up in defeat and captivity.

These books start with consecration and end with captivity. As we read 1 and 2 Chronicles we detect an unusual contrast. In the first book little things become great; in the second book great things become little.

Give God the Glory

The key theme in the Chronicles is found in David's last words as recorded in verses 10 and 11 of 1 Chronicles 29. Reflect carefully on these words recorded for us as a legacy. They form a literary segue from 1 Chronicles to 2 Chronicles:

David praised the Lord in the presence of the whole assembly, saying,

Praise be to you, O Lord,
God of our father Israel,
from everlasting to everlasting.
Yours, O Lord, is the greatness and the power
and the glory and the majesty and the splendor,
for everything in heaven and earth is yours.
Yours, O Lord, is the kingdom;
you are exalted as head over all.

It's as if we can feel David's view of his God oozing off the page. As you read these words, do you begin to grasp the greatness of the God we worship? As Christians, let's never forget that the Lord is to be exalted. He is to receive all glory. From the songs lifted from the lips of little children, to the trained voices filling a choir, to the ministry of a church, to the work of a denomination, to the message that goes out across the media . . . God should always receive the glory!

When we are blessed by God, when the Lord God uses us, when He allows us to become well educated or ascend to places of significance and prominence, it may be easy for us to try to steal the glory that is His alone. We may forget the very One who gave us all we have. When we're tempted to forget, God points us to the example of David. At the end of his life, in the light of all of his successes and failures, David had learned this all-important lesson. After forty years of reigning over Israel, even to this final scene as he lay on his deathbed, David was able to declare his view of life in but a few words . . . God gets all the glory.

Israel's Golden Age

The book of 2 Chronicles can be divided into two sections. Chapters 1–9 tell the story of a king; chapters 10–36 tell the story of a nation.

Writing to a people who desperately needed to make sense of their checkered history, Ezra recounted in chapters 1–9 the "golden age" of Israel's history—to restore their pride in the past and to bring hope for their future. What an age of peace, power, prosperity and prestige is chronicled in these chapters! Notice, though, what it was that had made Israel strong: not their own great power, not their own giftedness, but *the worship of the one true God*! The book of 2 Chronicles underscores that fact by devoting six of these first nine chapters to an account of the building and dedication of the temple as the center of the true worship of God (chapters 2–7).

Chapters 10–36 contain a highly selective account of the kings of Judah after Solomon's death and the division of the kingdom. The good kings of Judah, eight in all, dominate the story. In the midst of Judah's decline and apostasy, these chapters feature several kings who merit praise: Asa (chapters 14–15), Jehoshaphat (chapters 17–20), Hezekiah (chapter 29–32) and Josiah (chapters 34–35). Each of these kings initiated and led times of spiritual revival and reform—and helped stop, at least temporarily, their nation's slide away from God.

As 2 Chronicles comes to a close, however, the momentum of reform had reversed. Quickly, with very little comment, Ezra summarized the reigns of Judah's final four kings and brought the book to an end with his account of the fall of Jerusalem and, following the years of captivity, the decree of King Cyrus of Persia permitting the exiles to return.

Lessons From Chronicles

The first major lesson from the books of Chronicles reveals this: *The compassion of God and the rebellion of humanity are two powers that oppose one another.* In His great faithfulness God never stopped expressing compassion to His children. The people, on the other hand, continually mocked their Maker, disobeyed Him and despised Him. The compassion of God and the rebellion of humans are constantly in tension. Lest we lose heart, remember this: God's compassion and mercy are greater than our sins. He has provided the way through the coming of the Messiah, the Promised One—God's one and only Son, Jesus Christ, the One who came "to seek and to save what was lost" (Luke 19:10).

The second lesson should cause us to pause for serious reflection: *Being the recipient of God's judgment is a fearful experience.* We don't like to think about judgment, and so we rarely discuss this topic. However, the writer of 2 Chronicles will not let us forget the reality and severity of it.

The third lesson is also sobering: *Living outside of the blessings of God can be described in one word: desolation.* The Chronicles remind us that life beyond the boundaries of God's will is not a walk in the park; as a matter of fact, it is more like a walk across the Sahara Desert. A dry soul, a parched heart and an empty life await those who choose to live outside the blessings of God. The word is *desolation*.

The fourth lesson reminds us: *Never forget the past.* Even though our consciences may say, "Forget what has happened," 2 Chronicles says, "Remember it!" The writer calls us to remember the failings of God's people in the past and to learn from their mistakes. When we remember the past, we decrease the likelihood of repeating the same mistakes over and over again. And, on a more positive note, Chronicles prompts us to remember this essential truth about the way we ought to live our lives: *Only God gets the glory*!

Remember, Remember, Remember

I would take issue with those who say that to spend time reading the books of 1 and 2 Chronicles is a waste of time. I am grateful that these books call us to remember, remember, remember. We dare not forget! When we remember, then God will get the glory. When we forget, we will begin to give ourselves the glory. When we remember, we will repeat behavior that makes us more like Jesus Christ. When we forget, we will find ourselves bogged down in the mire of sins that we keep repeating over and over again. When we remember, we will learn from the Lord as His Holy Word teaches us profound lessons from the past that still hold powerful truths for us today. God uses the books of Chronicles to call us to *remember, remember, remember*. The question is a searching one: Do we hear the call?

The Story of a King **Chapters 1–9**

These chapters contain the colorful story of King Solomon. The opening chapter paints an exciting picture of a ruler who humbly sought the Lord's wisdom and leading. Next, we see the glory and splendor of Solomon's temple as plans were made and the construction begun (chapters 2–4). The temple was to be the central place of worship for the Israelite people, a place where all the nations of the world could come to worship *Yahweh,* the Lord God of Israel. Once the temple was completed, the ark of the covenant was brought in (chapter 5) and the glory of the Lord so filled the temple that the priests could not even enter to perform their duties (5:14). In a climax of pomp and dedication, Solomon lifted up his prayer to the Lord and consecrated that holy place (chapters 6–7). What wonderful reading where we can let our imaginations run free!

In chapters 8–9, Solomon's other accomplishments and exploits are listed. We read of his building projects, material wealth, unsurpassed wisdom and his glorious reign. These chapters paint a very positive picture of Solomon's life and reign. However, this pretty picture of a united kingdom was about to shatter. From a pinnacle of prosperity, the nation of Israel was about to fall. After the death of Solomon, the situation quickly disintegrated.

Solomon Asks for Wisdom

1 Solomon son of David established himself firmly over his kingdom, for the LORD his God was with him and made him exceedingly great. Ge 39:2; 1Ki 2:12,26; 1Ch 29:25

2Then Solomon spoke to all Israel—to the commanders of thousands and commanders of hundreds, to the judges and to all the leaders in Israel, the heads of families— 3and Solomon and the whole assembly went to the high place at Gibeon, for God's Tent of Meeting was there, which Moses the LORD's servant had made in the desert. 4Now David had brought up the ark of God from Kiriath Jearim to the place he had prepared for it, because he had pitched a tent for it in Jerusalem. 5But the bronze altar that Bezalel son of Uri, the son of Hur, had made was in Gibeon in front of the tabernacle of the LORD; so Solomon and the assembly inquired of him there. 6Solomon went up to the bronze altar before the LORD in the Tent of Meeting and offered a thousand burnt offerings on it. Ex 36:8; 38:2; 2Sa 6:17

7That night God appeared to Solomon and said to him, "Ask for whatever you want me to give you." 2Ch 7:12

8Solomon answered God, "You have shown great kindness to David my father and have made me king in his place. 9Now, LORD God, let your promise to my father David be confirmed, for you have made me king over a people who are as numerous as the dust of the earth. 10Give me wisdom and knowledge, that I may lead this people, for who is able to govern this great people of yours?"

11God said to Solomon, "Since this is your heart's desire and you have not asked for wealth, riches or honor, nor for the death of your enemies, and since you have not asked for a long life but for wisdom and knowledge to govern my people over whom I have made you king, 12therefore wisdom and knowledge will be given you. And I will also give you wealth, riches and honor, such as no king who was before you ever had and none after you will have." 1Ch 29:25; 2Ch 9:22; Ne 13:26

13Then Solomon went to Jerusalem from the high place at Gibeon, from before the Tent of Meeting. And he reigned over Israel.

14Solomon accumulated chariots and horses; he had fourteen hundred chariots and twelve thousand horses,[a] which he kept in the chariot cities and also with him in Jerusalem. 15The king made silver and gold as common in Jerusalem as stones, and cedar as plentiful as sycamore-fig trees in the foothills. 16Solomon's horses were imported from Egypt[b] and from Kue[c]—the royal merchants purchased them from Kue. 17They imported a chariot from Egypt for six hundred shekels[d] of silver, and a horse for a hundred and fifty.[e] They also exported them to all the kings of the Hittites and of the Arameans. 1Ki 3:4,15; 10:26-29; 2Ch 9:25-28

Preparations for Building the Temple

2 Solomon gave orders to build a temple for the Name of the LORD and a royal palace for himself. 2He conscripted seventy thousand men as carriers and eighty thousand as stonecutters in the hills and thirty-six hundred as foremen over them.

3Solomon sent this message to Hiram[f] king of Tyre:

"Send me cedar logs as you did for my father David when you sent him cedar to build a palace to live in. 4Now I am about to build a temple for the Name of the LORD my God and to dedicate it to him for burning fragrant incense before him, for setting out the consecrated bread regularly, and for making burnt offerings every morning and evening and on Sabbaths and New Moons and at the appointed feasts of the LORD our God. This is a lasting ordinance for Israel.

5"The temple I am going to build will be great, because our God is greater than all other gods. 6But who is able to build a temple for him, since the heavens, even the highest heavens, cannot contain him? Who then am I to build a temple for him, except as a place to burn sacrifices before him? 1Ki 8:27

[a]14 Or *charioteers* [b]16 Or possibly *Muzur,* a region in Cilicia; also in verse 17 [c]16 Probably Cilicia [d]17 That is, about 15 pounds (about 7 kilograms) [e]17 That is, about 3 3/4 pounds (about 1.7 kilograms) [f]3 Hebrew *Huram,* a variant of *Hiram;* also in verses 11 and 12

SOLOMON

The King Who Had Everything

"Solomon son of David established himself firmly over his kingdom, for the LORD his God was with him and made him exceedingly great."

—2 CHRONICLES 1:1

Solomon was a man who had so much to begin with and lost it all as his life drew to a close. But we can't let what we know about this man's failures color our impressions of his life as a whole. Scripture's account of Solomon's life reveals at least four ways in which the Lord "was with him and made him exceedingly great" (2 Chronicles 1:1).

First, *God gave Solomon wisdom and knowledge.* After Solomon's inauguration as king, he went to the tabernacle to worship. There God spoke to him and said, "Ask for whatever you want me to give you" (2 Chronicles 1:7). Now that's not bad, is it? You're alone with God, and He gives you essentially a blank check and says, "I've signed it. You fill it in." Read Solomon's answer in verse 10: "Give me wisdom and knowledge, that I may lead this people, for who is able to govern this great people of yours?" How impressive! Solomon began his reign recognizing his need for wisdom above all else.

Second, *God gave Solomon the ability to put his wisdom into action*—and people noticed, both near and far. The author of 1 Kings records the memorable story of Solomon's wise ruling in the dispute between two women—a classic example of Solomon's wisdom applied to life. Note the reaction of the people: "When all Israel heard the verdict the king had given, they held the king in awe, because they saw he had wisdom from God to administer justice" (1 Kings 3:28). And Solomon's reputation spread throughout the world in such a way that Israel and Israel's God became known among the nations (see 2 Chronicles 9:23).

Third, *God gave Solomon riches and fame as well as prosperity and contentment to the nation.* "The people of Judah and Israel were as numerous as the sand on the seashore; they ate, they drank and they were happy" (1 Kings 4:20). That's what happened during his reign. The people enjoyed incredible peace and prosperity while Solomon ruled. And Solomon himself amassed wealth and honor beyond compare.

Fourth, *God gave Solomon the ability to impart his wisdom in creative and lasting ways.* What a talent this man had! He was a student of the life sciences and natural history (1 Kings 4:33); he had an astounding gift for writing—beautiful songs as well as those pithy, power-packed nuggets of wisdom called proverbs. Many of his writings have been preserved in the books of Proverbs, Ecclesiastes and Song of Songs.

But like the proverbial frog that dies in a kettle of water slowly heated until boiling, Solomon let a series of compromises get in the way of his relationship with God. First, he allied himself with unbelievers in an attempt to smooth out international relations. He married the daughter of the Egyptian pharaoh (1 Kings 3:1) and the princesses of many other nations (1 Kings 11:1). Second, he tolerated the idolatry of the Israelites and of his many wives (11:7–8), an abomination in the eyes of a holy God. Third, he had an extravagant love life. In spite of the Lord's clear warning against intermarriage, Solomon would not be restrained: "King Solomon, however, loved many foreign women . . . He had seven hundred wives of royal birth and three hundred concubines, and his wives led him astray" (11:1–3).

By this time the pan of water in which Solomon sat was in full boil: "Solomon did evil in the eyes of the LORD; he did not follow the LORD completely, as David his father had done" (11:6). In anger God came to him and said, "Since this is your attitude and you have not kept my covenant and decrees, which I commanded you, I will most certainly tear the kingdom away from you . . ." (11:11).

Solomon started so well, yet ended so tragically. The man who had everything failed so miserably in the end. Solomon had wanted to live his life his own way, but he found himself ensnared by the trappings of his own desires. As it was in Solomon's day, so it is today: An arrogant attitude of defiance against God leads to personal misery.

7"Send me, therefore, a man skilled to work in gold and silver, bronze and iron, and in purple, crimson and blue yarn, and experienced in the art of engraving, to work in Judah and Jerusalem with my skilled craftsmen, whom my father David provided.

8"Send me also cedar, pine and algum[a] logs from Lebanon, for I know that your men are skilled in cutting timber there. My men will work with yours 9to provide me with plenty of lumber, because the temple I build must be large and magnificent. 10I will give your servants, the woodsmen who cut the timber, twenty thousand cors[b] of ground wheat, twenty thousand cors of barley, twenty thousand baths[c] of wine and twenty thousand baths of olive oil." Ezr 3:7

11Hiram king of Tyre replied by letter to Solomon:

"Because the LORD loves his people, he has made you their king." 1Ki 10:9; 2Ch 9:8

12And Hiram added:

"Praise be to the LORD, the God of Israel, who made heaven and earth! He has given King David a wise son, endowed with intelligence and discernment, who will build a temple for the LORD and a palace for himself.

13"I am sending you Huram-Abi, a man of great skill, 14whose mother was from Dan and whose father was from Tyre. He is trained to work in gold and silver, bronze and iron, stone and wood, and with purple and blue and crimson yarn and fine linen. He is experienced in all kinds of engraving and can execute any design given to him. He will work with your craftsmen and with those of my lord, David your father. Ex 31:6; 1Ki 7:13

15"Now let my lord send his servants the wheat and barley and the olive oil and wine he promised, 16and we will cut all the logs from Lebanon that you need and will float them in rafts by sea down to Joppa. You can then take them up to Jerusalem." Jos 19:46

17Solomon took a census of all the aliens who were in Israel, after the census his father David had taken; and they were found to be 153,600. 18He assigned 70,000 of them to be carriers and 80,000 to be stonecutters in the hills, with 3,600 foremen over them to keep the people working. 1Ki 5:1-16

Solomon Builds the Temple

3 Then Solomon began to build the temple of the LORD in Jerusalem on Mount Moriah, where the LORD had appeared to his father David. It was on the threshing floor of Araunah[d] the Jebusite, the place provided by David. 2He began building on the second day of the second month in the fourth year of his reign. 1Ch 21:18; Ac 7:47

3The foundation Solomon laid for building the temple of God was sixty cubits long and twenty cubits wide[e] (using the cubit of the old standard). 4The portico at the front of the temple was twenty cubits[f] long across the width of the building and twenty cubits[g] high. Eze 41:2

He overlaid the inside with pure gold. 5He paneled the main hall with pine and covered it with fine gold and decorated it with palm tree and chain designs. 6He adorned the temple with precious stones. And the gold he used was gold of Parvaim. 7He overlaid the ceiling beams, doorframes, walls and doors of the temple with gold, and he carved cherubim on the walls. Ge 3:24

8He built the Most Holy Place, its length corresponding to the width of the temple—twenty cubits long and twenty cubits wide. He overlaid the inside with six hundred talents[h] of fine gold. 9The gold nails weighed fifty shekels.[i] He also overlaid the upper parts with gold. Ex 26:32-33

10In the Most Holy Place he made a pair of sculptured cherubim and overlaid them with gold. 11The total wingspan of the cherubim was twenty cubits. One wing of the first cherub was five cubits[j] long and touched the temple wall, while its other wing, also five cubits long, touched the wing of the other cherub. 12Similarly one wing of the second cherub was five cubits long and touched the other temple wall, and its other wing, also five cubits long, touched the wing of the first cherub. 13The wings of these cherubim extended twenty cubits. They stood on their feet, facing the main hall.[k] Ex 25:18

14He made the curtain of blue, purple and crimson yarn and fine linen, with cherubim worked into it. 1Ki 6:1-29

15In the front of the temple he made two pillars, which ⌞together⌟ were thirty-five cubits[l] long, each with a capital on top measuring five cubits. 16He made interwoven chains[m] and put them on top of the pillars. He also made a hundred pomegranates and attached them to the chains. 17He erected the pillars in the front of the temple, one to the south and one to the north. The one to the

[a]8 Probably a variant of *almug*; possibly juniper [b]10 That is, probably about 125,000 bushels (about 4,400 kiloliters) [c]10 That is, probably about 115,000 gallons (about 440 kiloliters) [d]1 Hebrew *Ornan*, a variant of *Araunah* [e]3 That is, about 90 feet (about 27 meters) long and 30 feet (about 9 meters) wide [f]4 That is, about 30 feet (about 9 meters); also in verses 8, 11 and 13 [g]4 Some Septuagint and Syriac manuscripts; Hebrew *and a hundred and twenty* [h]8 That is, about 23 tons (about 21 metric tons) [i]9 That is, about 1 1/4 pounds (about 0.6 kilogram) [j]11 That is, about 7 1/2 feet (about 2.3 meters); also in verse 15 [k]13 Or *facing inward* [l]15 That is, about 52 feet (about 16 meters) [m]16 Or possibly *made chains in the inner sanctuary*; the meaning of the Hebrew for this phrase is uncertain.

south he named Jakin[a] and the one to the north Boaz.[b] 1Ki 7:15,17,20

The Temple's Furnishings

4 He made a bronze altar twenty cubits long, twenty cubits wide and ten cubits high.[c] 2He made the Sea of cast metal, circular in shape, measuring ten cubits from rim to rim and five cubits[d] high. It took a line of thirty cubits[e] to measure around it. 3Below the rim, figures of bulls encircled it—ten to a cubit.[f] The bulls were cast in two rows in one piece with the Sea. Ex 27:1-2; 2Ki 16:14

4The Sea stood on twelve bulls, three facing north, three facing west, three facing south and three facing east. The Sea rested on top of them, and their hindquarters were toward the center. 5It was a handbreadth[g] in thickness, and its rim was like the rim of a cup, like a lily blossom. It held three thousand baths.[h]

6He then made ten basins for washing and placed five on the south side and five on the north. In them the things to be used for the burnt offerings were rinsed, but the Sea was to be used by the priests for washing. 1Ki 7:23-26,38-51

7He made ten gold lampstands according to the specifications for them and placed them in the temple, five on the south side and five on the north. Ex 25:31,40

8He made ten tables and placed them in the temple, five on the south side and five on the north. He also made a hundred gold sprinkling bowls. Ex 25:23; Nu 4:14

9He made the courtyard of the priests, and the large court and the doors for the court, and overlaid the doors with bronze. 10He placed the Sea on the south side, at the southeast corner. 1Ki 6:36

11He also made the pots and shovels and sprinkling bowls.

So Huram finished the work he had undertaken for King Solomon in the temple of God: 1Ki 7:14

12the two pillars;
the two bowl-shaped capitals on top of the pillars;
the two sets of network decorating the two bowl-shaped capitals on top of the pillars;
13the four hundred pomegranates for the two sets of network (two rows of pomegranates for each network, decorating the bowl-shaped capitals on top of the pillars);
14the stands with their basins; 1Ki 7:27-30
15the Sea and the twelve bulls under it;
16the pots, shovels, meat forks and all related articles.

All the objects that Huram-Abi made for King Solomon for the temple of the LORD were of polished bronze. 17The king had them cast in clay molds in the plain of the Jordan between Succoth and Zarethan.[i] 18All these things that Solomon made amounted to so much that the weight of the bronze was not determined. 1Ki 7:13,23

19Solomon also made all the furnishings that were in God's temple:

the golden altar;
the tables on which was the bread of the Presence; Ex 25:23,30
20the lampstands of pure gold with their lamps, to burn in front of the inner sanctuary as prescribed; Ex 25:31
21the gold floral work and lamps and tongs (they were solid gold);
22the pure gold wick trimmers, sprinkling bowls, dishes and censers; and the gold doors of the temple: the inner doors to the Most Holy Place and the doors of the main hall. Lev 10:1; Nu 7:14

5 When all the work Solomon had done for the temple of the LORD was finished, he brought in the things his father David had dedicated—the silver and gold and all the furnishings—and he placed them in the treasuries of God's temple.

The Ark Brought to the Temple

2Then Solomon summoned to Jerusalem the elders of Israel, all the heads of the tribes and the chiefs of the Israelite families, to bring up the ark of the LORD's covenant from Zion, the City of David. 3And all the men of Israel came together to the king at the time of the festival in the seventh month. 2Sa 6:12; 1Ch 9:1; 15:25

4When all the elders of Israel had arrived, the Levites took up the ark, 5and they brought up the ark and the Tent of Meeting and all the sacred furnishings in it. The priests, who were Levites, carried them up; 6and King Solomon and the entire assembly of Israel that had gathered about him were before the ark, sacrificing so many sheep and cattle that they could not be recorded or counted.

7The priests then brought the ark of the LORD's covenant to its place in the inner sanctuary of the temple, the Most Holy Place, and put it beneath the wings of the cherubim. 8The cherubim spread their wings over the place of the ark and covered the ark and its carrying poles. 9These poles were so

[a] 17 *Jakin* probably means *he establishes.* [b] 17 *Boaz* probably means *in him is strength.* [c] 1 That is, about 30 feet (about 9 meters) long and wide, and about 15 feet (about 4.5 meters) high [d] 2 That is, about 7 1/2 feet (about 2.3 meters) [e] 2 That is, about 45 feet (about 13.5 meters) [f] 3 That is, about 1 1/2 feet (about 0.5 meter) [g] 5 That is, about 3 inches (about 8 centimeters) [h] 5 That is, about 17,500 gallons (about 66 kiloliters) [i] 17 Hebrew *Zeredatha,* a variant of *Zarethan*

long that their ends, extending from the ark, could
be seen from in front of the inner sanctuary, but
not from outside the Holy Place; and they are still
there today. 10There was nothing in the ark except
the two tablets that Moses had placed in it at Horeb, where the LORD made a covenant with the
Israelites after they came out of Egypt. Dt 10:2
11The priests then withdrew from the Holy
Place. All the priests who were there had consecrated themselves, regardless of their divisions.
12All the Levites who were musicians—Asaph, Heman, Jeduthun and their sons and relatives—
stood on the east side of the altar, dressed in fine
linen and playing cymbals, harps and lyres. They
were accompanied by 120 priests sounding trumpets. 13The trumpeters and singers joined in unison, as with one voice, to give praise and thanks to
the LORD. Accompanied by trumpets, cymbals and
other instruments, they raised their voices in
praise to the LORD and sang: 1Ch 15:24; 25:1

"He is good;
his love endures forever." 1Ch 16:34,41; 2Ch 7:3

Then the temple of the LORD was filled with a
cloud, 14and the priests could not perform their
service because of the cloud, for the glory of the
LORD filled the temple of God. Ex 29:43; 2Ch 7:2

6 Then Solomon said, "The LORD has said that
he would dwell in a dark cloud; 2I have built
a magnificent temple for you, a place for you to
dwell forever." 1Ki 8:12-50; Ps 135:21
3While the whole assembly of Israel was standing there, the king turned around and blessed
them. 4Then he said:

"Praise be to the LORD, the God of Israel,
who with his hands has fulfilled what he
promised with his mouth to my father David. For he said, 5'Since the day I brought my
people out of Egypt, I have not chosen a city
in any tribe of Israel to have a temple built
for my Name to be there, nor have I chosen
anyone to be the leader over my people Israel. 6But now I have chosen Jerusalem for my
Name to be there, and I have chosen David
to rule my people Israel.' 1Ch 28:4; 2Ch 12:13
7"My father David had it in his heart to
build a temple for the Name of the LORD, the
God of Israel. 8But the LORD said to my father
David, 'Because it was in your heart to build
a temple for my Name, you did well to have
this in your heart. 9Nevertheless, you are not
the one to build the temple, but your son,
who is your own flesh and blood—he is the
one who will build the temple for my Name.'
10"The LORD has kept the promise he
made. I have succeeded David my father and
now I sit on the throne of Israel, just as the
LORD promised, and I have built the temple
for the Name of the LORD, the God of Israel.
11There I have placed the ark, in which is the
covenant of the LORD that he made with the
people of Israel." 1Ki 8:1-21; 2Ch 5:10

Solomon's Prayer of Dedication

12Then Solomon stood before the altar of the
LORD in front of the whole assembly of Israel and
spread out his hands. 13Now he had made a bronze
platform, five cubits[a] long, five cubits wide and
three cubits[b] high, and had placed it in the center
of the outer court. He stood on the platform and
then knelt down before the whole assembly of Israel and spread out his hands toward heaven. 14He
said: Ne 8:4; Ps 95:6

"O LORD, God of Israel, there is no God
like you in heaven or on earth—you who
keep your covenant of love with your servants who continue wholeheartedly in your
way. 15You have kept your promise to your
servant David my father; with your mouth
you have promised and with your hand you
have fulfilled it—as it is today. Dt 7:9
16"Now LORD, God of Israel, keep for your
servant David my father the promises you
made to him when you said, 'You shall never
fail to have a man to sit before me on the
throne of Israel, if only your sons are careful
in all they do to walk before me according
to my law, as you have done.' 17And now,
O LORD, God of Israel, let your word that
you promised your servant David come true.
18"But will God really dwell on earth with
men? The heavens, even the highest heavens,
cannot contain you. How much less this
temple I have built! 19Yet give attention to
your servant's prayer and his plea for mercy,
O LORD my God. Hear the cry and the prayer
that your servant is praying in your presence.
20May your eyes be open toward this temple
day and night, this place of which you said
you would put your Name there. May you
hear the prayer your servant prays toward
this place. 21Hear the supplications of your
servant and of your people Israel when they
pray toward this place. Hear from heaven,
your dwelling place; and when you hear, forgive. Isa 43:25; Mic 7:18
22"When a man wrongs his neighbor and
is required to take an oath and he comes and
swears the oath before your altar in this temple, 23then hear from heaven and act. Judge
between your servants, repaying the guilty by
bringing down on his own head what he has
done. Declare the innocent not guilty and so
establish his innocence. Ex 22:11; Isa 3:11

[a] 13 That is, about 7 1/2 feet (about 2.3 meters) [b] 13 That is, about 4 1/2 feet (about 1.3 meters)

24“When your people Israel have been defeated by an enemy because they have sinned
against you and when they turn back and
confess your name, praying and making supplication before you in this temple, 25then
hear from heaven and forgive the sin of your
people Israel and bring them back to the land
you gave to them and their fathers. Lev 26:17
26“When the heavens are shut up and
there is no rain because your people have
sinned against you, and when they pray toward this place and confess your name and
turn from their sin because you have afflicted
them, 27then hear from heaven and forgive
the sin of your servants, your people Israel.
Teach them the right way to live, and send
rain on the land you gave your people for an
inheritance. 1Ki 17:1
28“When famine or plague comes to the
land, or blight or mildew, locusts or grasshoppers, or when enemies besiege them in
any of their cities, whatever disaster or disease may come, 29and when a prayer or plea
is made by any of your people Israel—each
one aware of his afflictions and pains, and
spreading out his hands toward this temple— 30then hear from heaven, your dwelling place. Forgive, and deal with each man
according to all he does, since you know
his heart (for you alone know the hearts of
men), 31so that they will fear you and walk in
your ways all the time they live in the land
you gave our fathers. 1Sa 16:7; 1Ch 28:9; 2Ch 20:9
32“As for the foreigner who does not belong to your people Israel but has come from
a distant land because of your great name
and your mighty hand and your outstretched
arm—when he comes and prays toward this
temple, 33then hear from heaven, your dwelling place, and do whatever the foreigner asks
of you, so that all the peoples of the earth
may know your name and fear you, as do
your own people Israel, and may know that
this house I have built bears your Name.
34“When your people go to war against
their enemies, wherever you send them, and
when they pray to you toward this city you
have chosen and the temple I have built for
your Name, 35then hear from heaven their
prayer and their plea, and uphold their
cause. Dt 28:7; 1Ch 5:20
36“When they sin against you—for there
is no one who does not sin—and you become angry with them and give them over to
the enemy, who takes them captive to a land
far away or near; 37and if they have a change
of heart in the land where they are held captive, and repent and plead with you in the
land of their captivity and say, ‘We have
sinned, we have done wrong and acted wickedly’; 38and if they turn back to you with all
their heart and soul in the land of their captivity where they were taken, and pray toward the land you gave their fathers, toward
the city you have chosen and toward the
temple I have built for your Name; 39then
from heaven, your dwelling place, hear their
prayer and their pleas, and uphold their
cause. And forgive your people, who have
sinned against you. Job 15:14; Jas 3:1; 1Jn 1:8-10
40“Now, my God, may your eyes be open
and your ears attentive to the prayers offered
in this place. 1Ki 8:22-53

41“Now arise, O LORD God, and come to
your resting place, 1Ch 28:2; Isa 33:10
you and the ark of your might.
May your priests, O LORD God, be
clothed with salvation, Ps 132:16
may your saints rejoice in your
goodness. Ps 116:12
42O LORD God, do not reject your
anointed one.
Remember the great love promised to
David your servant.” Ps 132:8-10

The Dedication of the Temple

7 When Solomon finished praying, fire came
down from heaven and consumed the burnt
offering and the sacrifices, and the glory of the
LORD filled the temple. 2The priests could not enter
the temple of the LORD because the glory of the
LORD filled it. 3When all the Israelites saw the fire
coming down and the glory of the LORD above the
temple, they knelt on the pavement with their
faces to the ground, and they worshiped and gave
thanks to the LORD, saying, Ex 29:43; 40:35; 2Ch 5:14

“He is good;
his love endures forever.”

LIVING  **INSIGHT**

Thanksgiving prompts the spirit of humility. What a delight it is to show genuine gratitude to God for His mercy, His abundance, His protection, His smile of favor, His love that never ends.

(See 2 Chronicles 7:3.)

4Then the king and all the people offered sacrifices
before the LORD. 5And King Solomon offered a
sacrifice of twenty-two thousand head of cattle
and a hundred and twenty thousand sheep and
goats. So the king and all the people dedicated the
temple of God. 6The priests took their positions, as
did the Levites with the LORD’s musical instru-

ments, which King David had made for praising
the LORD and which were used when he gave
thanks, saying, "His love endures forever." Opposite the Levites, the priests blew their trumpets,
and all the Israelites were standing. 1Ch 15:16
7Solomon consecrated the middle part of the
courtyard in front of the temple of the LORD, and
there he offered burnt offerings and the fat of the
fellowship offerings,[a] because the bronze altar he
had made could not hold the burnt offerings, the
grain offerings and the fat portions.
8So Solomon observed the festival at that time
for seven days, and all Israel with him—a vast
assembly, people from Lebo[b] Hamath to the
Wadi of Egypt. 9On the eighth day they held an
assembly, for they had celebrated the dedication of
the altar for seven days and the festival for seven
days more. 10On the twenty-third day of the seventh month he sent the people to their homes,
joyful and glad in heart for the good things the
LORD had done for David and Solomon and for his
people Israel. Lev 23:36; 2Ch 30:26

The LORD Appears to Solomon

11When Solomon had finished the temple of the
LORD and the royal palace, and had succeeded in
carrying out all he had in mind to do in the temple
of the LORD and in his own palace, 12the LORD
appeared to him at night and said:

"I have heard your prayer and have chosen this place for myself as a temple for sacrifices. Dt 12:5
13"When I shut up the heavens so that
there is no rain, or command locusts to devour the land or send a plague among my
people, 14if my people, who are called by my
name, will humble themselves and pray and
seek my face and turn from their wicked
ways, then will I hear from heaven and will
forgive their sin and will heal their land.
15Now my eyes will be open and my ears
attentive to the prayers offered in this place.
16I have chosen and consecrated this temple
so that my Name may be there forever. My
eyes and my heart will always be there.
17"As for you, if you walk before me as
David your father did, and do all I command, and observe my decrees and laws, 18I
will establish your royal throne, as I covenanted with David your father when I said,
'You shall never fail to have a man to rule
over Israel.' 1Ki 9:4; 2Ch 6:16
19"But if you[c] turn away and forsake the
decrees and commands I have given you[c]
and go off to serve other gods and worship
them, 20then I will uproot Israel from my
land, which I have given them, and will reject
this temple I have consecrated for my Name.
I will make it a byword and an object of
ridicule among all peoples. 21And though
this temple is now so imposing, all who pass
by will be appalled and say, 'Why has the
LORD done such a thing to this land and to
this temple?' 22People will answer, 'Because
they have forsaken the LORD, the God of their
fathers, who brought them out of Egypt, and
have embraced other gods, worshiping and
serving them—that is why he brought all this
disaster on them.'" 1Ki 9:1-9; Dt 29:24

Solomon's Other Activities

8 At the end of twenty years, during which Solomon built the temple of the LORD and his
own palace, 2Solomon rebuilt the villages that Hiram[d] had given him, and settled Israelites in
them. 3Solomon then went to Hamath Zobah and
captured it. 4He also built up Tadmor in the desert
and all the store cities he had built in Hamath. 5He
rebuilt Upper Beth Horon and Lower Beth Horon
as fortified cities, with walls and with gates and
bars, 6as well as Baalath and all his store cities, and
all the cities for his chariots and for his horses[e]—
whatever he desired to build in Jerusalem, in Lebanon and throughout all the territory he ruled.
7All the people left from the Hittites, Amorites,
Perizzites, Hivites and Jebusites (these peoples
were not Israelites), 8that is, their descendants remaining in the land, whom the Israelites had not
destroyed—these Solomon conscripted for his
slave labor force, as it is to this day. 9But Solomon
did not make slaves of the Israelites for his work;
they were his fighting men, commanders of his
captains, and commanders of his chariots and
charioteers. 10They were also King Solomon's chief
officials—two hundred and fifty officials supervising the men. Ge 10:16; 1Ki 4:6; 9:21
11Solomon brought Pharaoh's daughter up
from the City of David to the palace he had built
for her, for he said, "My wife must not live in the
palace of David king of Israel, because the places
the ark of the LORD has entered are holy." 1Ki 3:1
12On the altar of the LORD that he had built in
front of the portico, Solomon sacrificed burnt offerings to the LORD, 13according to the daily requirement for offerings commanded by Moses for
Sabbaths, New Moons and the three annual
feasts—the Feast of Unleavened Bread, the Feast
of Weeks and the Feast of Tabernacles. 14In keeping with the ordinance of his father David, he appointed the divisions of the priests for their duties,
and the Levites to lead the praise and to assist the
priests according to each day's requirement. He

[a] 7 Traditionally *peace offerings* [b] 8 Or *from the entrance to* [c] 19 The Hebrew is plural. [d] 2 Hebrew *Huram,* a variant of *Hiram;* also in verse 18 [e] 6 Or *charioteers*

also appointed the gatekeepers by divisions for the
various gates, because this was what David the
man of God had ordered. 15They did not deviate
from the king's commands to the priests or to the
Levites in any matter, including that of the treasuries. Nu 28:3; 1Ch 25:1; Ne 12:24,36
16All Solomon's work was carried out, from the
day the foundation of the temple of the LORD was
laid until its completion. So the temple of the LORD
was finished.
17Then Solomon went to Ezion Geber and Elath
on the coast of Edom. 18And Hiram sent him ships
commanded by his own officers, men who knew
the sea. These, with Solomon's men, sailed to
Ophir and brought back four hundred and fifty
talents[a] of gold, which they delivered to King
Solomon. 1Ki 9:10-28; 2Ch 9:9

The Queen of Sheba Visits Solomon

9 When the queen of Sheba heard of Solomon's
fame, she came to Jerusalem to test him with
hard questions. Arriving with a very great caravan—with camels carrying spices, large quantities
of gold, and precious stones—she came to Solomon and talked with him about all she had on her
mind. 2Solomon answered all her questions; nothing was too hard for him to explain to her. 3When
the queen of Sheba saw the wisdom of Solomon, as
well as the palace he had built, 4the food on his
table, the seating of his officials, the attending servants in their robes, the cupbearers in their robes
and the burnt offerings he made at[b] the temple of
the LORD, she was overwhelmed. 1Ki 5:12; Mt 12:42
5She said to the king, "The report I heard in my
own country about your achievements and your
wisdom is true. 6But I did not believe what they
said until I came and saw with my own eyes. Indeed, not even half the greatness of your wisdom
was told me; you have far exceeded the report I
heard. 7How happy your men must be! How happy your officials, who continually stand before you
and hear your wisdom! 8Praise be to the LORD your
God, who has delighted in you and placed you on
his throne as king to rule for the LORD your God.
Because of the love of your God for Israel and his
desire to uphold them forever, he has made you
king over them, to maintain justice and righteousness." 1Ch 28:5; 29:23; 2Ch 2:11
9Then she gave the king 120 talents[c] of gold,
large quantities of spices, and precious stones.
There had never been such spices as those the
queen of Sheba gave to King Solomon. 2Ch 8:18
10(The men of Hiram and the men of Solomon
brought gold from Ophir; they also brought algumwood[d] and precious stones. 11The king used
the algumwood to make steps for the temple of the
LORD and for the royal palace, and to make harps
and lyres for the musicians. Nothing like them had
ever been seen in Judah.) 2Ch 8:18
12King Solomon gave the queen of Sheba all she
desired and asked for; he gave her more than she
had brought to him. Then she left and returned
with her retinue to her own country. 1Ki 10:1-13

Solomon's Splendor

13The weight of the gold that Solomon received
yearly was 666 talents,[e] 14not including the revenues brought in by merchants and traders. Also all
the kings of Arabia and the governors of the land
brought gold and silver to Solomon. 2Ch 17:11
15King Solomon made two hundred large
shields of hammered gold; six hundred bekas[f] of
hammered gold went into each shield. 16He also
made three hundred small shields of hammered
gold, with three hundred bekas[g] of gold in each
shield. The king put them in the Palace of the
Forest of Lebanon. 1Ki 7:2; 2Ch 12:9
17Then the king made a great throne inlaid with
ivory and overlaid with pure gold. 18The throne
had six steps, and a footstool of gold was attached
to it. On both sides of the seat were armrests, with
a lion standing beside each of them. 19Twelve lions
stood on the six steps, one at either end of each
step. Nothing like it had ever been made for any
other kingdom. 20All King Solomon's goblets were
gold, and all the household articles in the Palace of
the Forest of Lebanon were pure gold. Nothing
was made of silver, because silver was considered
of little value in Solomon's day. 21The king had a
fleet of trading ships[h] manned by Hiram's[i] men.
Once every three years it returned, carrying gold,
silver and ivory, and apes and baboons. 1Ki 22:39
22King Solomon was greater in riches and wisdom than all the other kings of the earth. 23All the
kings of the earth sought audience with Solomon
to hear the wisdom God had put in his heart.
24Year after year, everyone who came brought a
gift—articles of silver and gold, and robes, weapons and spices, and horses and mules. 1Ki 3:13
25Solomon had four thousand stalls for horses
and chariots, and twelve thousand horses,[j] which
he kept in the chariot cities and also with him in
Jerusalem. 26He ruled over all the kings from the
River[k] to the land of the Philistines, as far as the
border of Egypt. 27The king made silver as common in Jerusalem as stones, and cedar as plentiful
as sycamore-fig trees in the foothills. 28Solomon's

[a] 18 That is, about 17 tons (about 16 metric tons) [b] 4 Or *the ascent by which he went up to* [c] 9 That is, about 4 1/2 tons (about 4 metric tons) [d] 10 Probably a variant of *almugwood* [e] 13 That is, about 25 tons (about 23 metric tons) [f] 15 That is, about 7 1/2 pounds (about 3.5 kilograms) [g] 16 That is, about 3 3/4 pounds (about 1.7 kilograms) [h] 21 Hebrew *of ships that could go to Tarshish* [i] 21 Hebrew *Huram,* a variant of *Hiram* [j] 25 Or *charioteers* [k] 26 That is, the Euphrates

horses were imported from Egypt[a] and from all other countries. 1Ki 10:14-29; 2Ch 1:14-17

Solomon's Death

29As for the other events of Solomon's reign, from beginning to end, are they not written in the records of Nathan the prophet, in the prophecy of Ahijah the Shilonite and in the visions of Iddo the seer concerning Jeroboam son of Nebat? 30Solomon reigned in Jerusalem over all Israel forty years. 31Then he rested with his fathers and was buried in the city of David his father. And Rehoboam his son succeeded him as king. 1Ki 2:10

The Story of a Nation — Chapters 10–36

These chapters record the history of the southern kingdom, the nation of Judah. They chronicle the names and acts of the kings who reigned in Jerusalem. Ezra must have recorded these events with a sense of sadness and sorrow. There was a fatal flaw leading to deterioration in the very fabric of the kingdom. Great things of former years had become little. Unity had become disunity. Faithfulness to the one true God had been supplanted by idolatry and apostasy. The picture turned dark and grim as the nation spiraled downward and the people drifted away from the Lord.

Although there were four revivals in the land during these years, the people, as a whole, were determined to walk away from the Lord. Some of the kings tried to call them back to God, but the people kept backsliding, intent on serving the idols of the foreign nations that surrounded them. The end result, as foretold by the Lord earlier (7:19–20), was the demise of the nation.

Israel Rebels Against Rehoboam

10 Rehoboam went to Shechem, for all the Israelites had gone there to make him king. 2When Jeroboam son of Nebat heard this (he was in Egypt, where he had fled from King Solomon), he returned from Egypt. 3So they sent for Jeroboam, and he and all Israel went to Rehoboam and said to him: 4"Your father put a heavy yoke on us, but now lighten the harsh labor and the heavy yoke he put on us, and we will serve you."

5Rehoboam answered, "Come back to me in three days." So the people went away.

6Then King Rehoboam consulted the elders who had served his father Solomon during his lifetime. "How would you advise me to answer these people?" he asked. Job 8:8-9; 12:12

7They replied, "If you will be kind to these people and please them and give them a favorable answer, they will always be your servants."

8But Rehoboam rejected the advice the elders gave him and consulted the young men who had grown up with him and were serving him. 9He asked them, "What is your advice? How should we answer these people who say to me, 'Lighten the yoke your father put on us'?" 2Sa 17:14; Pr 13:20

10The young men who had grown up with him replied, "Tell the people who have said to you, 'Your father put a heavy yoke on us, but make our yoke lighter'—tell them, 'My little finger is thicker than my father's waist. 11My father laid on you a heavy yoke; I will make it even heavier. My father scourged you with whips; I will scourge you with scorpions.'"

12Three days later Jeroboam and all the people returned to Rehoboam, as the king had said, "Come back to me in three days." 13The king answered them harshly. Rejecting the advice of the elders, 14he followed the advice of the young men and said, "My father made your yoke heavy; I will make it even heavier. My father scourged you with whips; I will scourge you with scorpions." 15So the king did not listen to the people, for this turn of events was from God, to fulfill the word the LORD had spoken to Jeroboam son of Nebat through Ahijah the Shilonite. 1Ki 11:29; 2Ch 25:16-20

16When all Israel saw that the king refused to listen to them, they answered the king: 1Ch 9:1

"What share do we have in David, 2Sa 20:1
  what part in Jesse's son?
To your tents, O Israel!
  Look after your own house, O David!"

So all the Israelites went home. 17But as for the Israelites who were living in the towns of Judah, Rehoboam still ruled over them.

18King Rehoboam sent out Adoniram,[b] who was in charge of forced labor, but the Israelites stoned him to death. King Rehoboam, however, managed to get into his chariot and escape to Jerusalem. 19So Israel has been in rebellion against the house of David to this day. 1Ki 5:14

11 When Rehoboam arrived in Jerusalem, he mustered the house of Judah and Benjamin—a hundred and eighty thousand fighting men—to make war against Israel and to regain the kingdom for Rehoboam. 1Ki 12:21

2But this word of the LORD came to Shemaiah the man of God: 3"Say to Rehoboam son of Solomon king of Judah and to all the Israelites in Judah and Benjamin, 4'This is what the LORD says: Do not go up to fight against your brothers. Go home, every one of you, for this is my doing.'" So they obeyed the words of the LORD and turned back from marching against Jeroboam. 1Ki 12:1-24

Rehoboam Fortifies Judah

5Rehoboam lived in Jerusalem and built up towns for defense in Judah: 6Bethlehem, Etam, Tekoa, 7Beth Zur, Soco, Adullam, 8Gath, Mareshah, Ziph, 9Adoraim, Lachish, Azekah, 10Zorah, Aijalon

[a] 28 Or possibly *Muzur,* a region in Cilicia [b] 18 Hebrew *Hadoram,* a variant of *Adoniram*

and Hebron. These were fortified cities in Judah and Benjamin. 11He strengthened their defenses and put commanders in them, with supplies of food, olive oil and wine. 12He put shields and spears in all the cities, and made them very strong. So Judah and Benjamin were his.

13The priests and Levites from all their districts throughout Israel sided with him. 14The Levites even abandoned their pasturelands and property, and came to Judah and Jerusalem because Jeroboam and his sons had rejected them as priests of the LORD. 15And he appointed his own priests for the high places and for the goat and calf idols he had made. 16Those from every tribe of Israel who set their hearts on seeking the LORD, the God of Israel, followed the Levites to Jerusalem to offer sacrifices to the LORD, the God of their fathers. 17They strengthened the kingdom of Judah and supported Rehoboam son of Solomon three years, walking in the ways of David and Solomon during this time.

Rehoboam's Family

18Rehoboam married Mahalath, who was the daughter of David's son Jerimoth and of Abihail, the daughter of Jesse's son Eliab. 19She bore him sons: Jeush, Shemariah and Zaham. 20Then he married Maacah daughter of Absalom, who bore him Abijah, Attai, Ziza and Shelomith. 21Rehoboam loved Maacah daughter of Absalom more than any of his other wives and concubines. In all, he had eighteen wives and sixty concubines, twenty-eight sons and sixty daughters. Dt 17:17; 1Ki 15:2

22Rehoboam appointed Abijah son of Maacah to be the chief prince among his brothers, in order to make him king. 23He acted wisely, dispersing some of his sons throughout the districts of Judah and Benjamin, and to all the fortified cities. He gave them abundant provisions and took many wives for them. Dt 21:15-17

Shishak Attacks Jerusalem

12 After Rehoboam's position as king was established and he had become strong, he and all Israel[a] with him abandoned the law of the LORD. 2Because they had been unfaithful to the LORD, Shishak king of Egypt attacked Jerusalem in the fifth year of King Rehoboam. 3With twelve hundred chariots and sixty thousand horsemen and the innumerable troops of Libyans, Sukkites and Cushites[b] that came with him from Egypt, 4he captured the fortified cities of Judah and came as far as Jerusalem. 2Ch 11:10; 16:8

5Then the prophet Shemaiah came to Rehoboam and to the leaders of Judah who had assembled in Jerusalem for fear of Shishak, and he said to them, "This is what the LORD says, 'You have abandoned me; therefore, I now abandon you to Shishak.'" 2Ch 11:2; 15:2

6The leaders of Israel and the king humbled themselves and said, "The LORD is just." Ex 9:27

7When the LORD saw that they humbled themselves, this word of the LORD came to Shemaiah: "Since they have humbled themselves, I will not destroy them but will soon give them deliverance. My wrath will not be poured out on Jerusalem through Shishak. 8They will, however, become subject to him, so that they may learn the difference between serving me and serving the kings of other lands." Dt 28:48; 1Ki 21:29; Ps 78:38

9When Shishak king of Egypt attacked Jerusalem, he carried off the treasures of the temple of the LORD and the treasures of the royal palace. He took everything, including the gold shields Solomon had made. 10So King Rehoboam made bronze shields to replace them and assigned these to the commanders of the guard on duty at the entrance to the royal palace. 11Whenever the king went to the LORD's temple, the guards went with him, bearing the shields, and afterward they returned them to the guardroom. 2Ch 9:16

12Because Rehoboam humbled himself, the LORD's anger turned from him, and he was not totally destroyed. Indeed, there was some good in Judah. 2Ch 19:3

13King Rehoboam established himself firmly in Jerusalem and continued as king. He was forty-one years old when he became king, and he reigned seventeen years in Jerusalem, the city the LORD had chosen out of all the tribes of Israel in which to put his Name. His mother's name was Naamah; she was an Ammonite. 14He did evil because he had not set his heart on seeking the LORD.

15As for the events of Rehoboam's reign, from beginning to end, are they not written in the records of Shemaiah the prophet and of Iddo the seer that deal with genealogies? There was continual warfare between Rehoboam and Jeroboam. 16Rehoboam rested with his fathers and was buried in the City of David. And Abijah his son succeeded him as king. 1Ki 14:21,25-31; 2Ch 9:29

Abijah King of Judah

13 In the eighteenth year of the reign of Jeroboam, Abijah became king of Judah, 2and he reigned in Jerusalem three years. His mother's name was Maacah,[c] a daughter[d] of Uriel of Gibeah.

There was war between Abijah and Jeroboam. 3Abijah went into battle with a force of four hundred thousand able fighting men, and Jeroboam drew up a battle line against him with eight hundred thousand able troops. 1Ki 15:6; 2Ch 11:20

[a] *1* That is, Judah, as frequently in 2 Chronicles [b] *3* That is, people from the upper Nile region [c] *2* Most Septuagint manuscripts and Syriac (see also 2 Chron. 11:20 and 1 Kings 15:2); Hebrew *Micaiah* [d] *2* Or *granddaughter*

4Abijah stood on Mount Zemaraim, in the hill country of Ephraim, and said, "Jeroboam and all Israel, listen to me! 5Don't you know that the LORD, the God of Israel, has given the kingship of Israel to David and his descendants forever by a covenant of salt? 6Yet Jeroboam son of Nebat, an official of Solomon son of David, rebelled against his master. 7Some worthless scoundrels gathered around him and opposed Rehoboam son of Solomon when he was young and indecisive and not strong enough to resist them. Nu 18:19; 1Ki 11:26

8"And now you plan to resist the kingdom of the LORD, which is in the hands of David's descendants. You are indeed a vast army and have with you the golden calves that Jeroboam made to be your gods. 9But didn't you drive out the priests of the LORD, the sons of Aaron, and the Levites, and make priests of your own as the peoples of other lands do? Whoever comes to consecrate himself with a young bull and seven rams may become a priest of what are not gods. 1Ki 12:28; 2Ch 11:15; Jer 2:11

10"As for us, the LORD is our God, and we have not forsaken him. The priests who serve the LORD are sons of Aaron, and the Levites assist them. 11Every morning and evening they present burnt offerings and fragrant incense to the LORD. They set out the bread on the ceremonially clean table and light the lamps on the gold lampstand every evening. We are observing the requirements of the LORD our God. But you have forsaken him. 12God is with us; he is our leader. His priests with their trumpets will sound the battle cry against you. Men of Israel, do not fight against the LORD, the God of your fathers, for you will not succeed."

13Now Jeroboam had sent troops around to the rear, so that while he was in front of Judah the ambush was behind them. 14Judah turned and saw that they were being attacked at both front and rear. Then they cried out to the LORD. The priests blew their trumpets 15and the men of Judah raised the battle cry. At the sound of their battle cry, God routed Jeroboam and all Israel before Abijah and Judah. 16The Israelites fled before Judah, and God delivered them into their hands. 17Abijah and his men inflicted heavy losses on them, so that there were five hundred thousand casualties among Israel's able men. 18The men of Israel were subdued on that occasion, and the men of Judah were victorious because they relied on the LORD, the God of their fathers. 2Ch 14:11; 16:8; Ps 22:5

19Abijah pursued Jeroboam and took from him the towns of Bethel, Jeshanah and Ephron, with their surrounding villages. 20Jeroboam did not regain power during the time of Abijah. And the LORD struck him down and he died.

21But Abijah grew in strength. He married fourteen wives and had twenty-two sons and sixteen daughters.

22The other events of Abijah's reign, what he did and what he said, are written in the annotations of the prophet Iddo.

14 And Abijah rested with his fathers and was buried in the City of David. Asa his son succeeded him as king, and in his days the country was at peace for ten years. 1Ki 15:1-2,6-8

Asa King of Judah

2Asa did what was good and right in the eyes of the LORD his God. 3He removed the foreign altars and the high places, smashed the sacred stones and cut down the Asherah poles.[a] 4He commanded Judah to seek the LORD, the God of their fathers, and to obey his laws and commands. 5He removed the high places and incense altars in every town in Judah, and the kingdom was at peace under him. 6He built up the fortified cities of Judah, since the land was at peace. No one was at war with him during those years, for the LORD gave him rest.

7"Let us build up these towns," he said to Judah, "and put walls around them, with towers, gates and bars. The land is still ours, because we have sought the LORD our God; we sought him and he has given us rest on every side." So they built and prospered.

8Asa had an army of three hundred thousand men from Judah, equipped with large shields and with spears, and two hundred and eighty thousand from Benjamin, armed with small shields and with bows. All these were brave fighting men.

9Zerah the Cushite marched out against them with a vast army[b] and three hundred chariots, and came as far as Mareshah. 10Asa went out to meet him, and they took up battle positions in the Valley of Zephathah near Mareshah. 2Ch 11:8; 16:8

11Then Asa called to the LORD his God and said, "LORD, there is no one like you to help the powerless against the mighty. Help us, O LORD our God, for we rely on you, and in your name we have come against this vast army. O LORD, you are our God; do not let man prevail against you."

12The LORD struck down the Cushites before Asa and Judah. The Cushites fled, 13and Asa and his army pursued them as far as Gerar. Such a great number of Cushites fell that they could not recover; they were crushed before the LORD and his forces. The men of Judah carried off a large amount of plunder. 14They destroyed all the villages around Gerar, for the terror of the LORD had fallen upon them. They plundered all these villages, since there was much booty there. 15They also attacked the camps of the herdsmen and car-

[a]3 That is, symbols of the goddess Asherah; here and elsewhere in 2 Chronicles [b]9 Hebrew *with an army of a thousand thousands* or *with an army of thousands upon thousands*

ried off droves of sheep and goats and camels.
Then they returned to Jerusalem. Ge 10:19; 35:5

Asa's Reform

15 The Spirit of God came upon Azariah son
of Oded. 2He went out to meet Asa and
said to him, "Listen to me, Asa and all Judah and
Benjamin. The LORD is with you when you are with
him. If you seek him, he will be found by you, but
if you forsake him, he will forsake you. 3For a long
time Israel was without the true God, without a
priest to teach and without the law. 4But in their
distress they turned to the LORD, the God of Israel,
and sought him, and he was found by them. 5In
those days it was not safe to travel about, for all the
inhabitants of the lands were in great turmoil.
6One nation was being crushed by another and
one city by another, because God was troubling
them with every kind of distress. 7But as for you,
be strong and do not give up, for your work will
be rewarded." Jos 1:7,9; Jas 4:8
8When Asa heard these words and the prophecy
of Azariah son of[a] Oded the prophet, he took
courage. He removed the detestable idols from the
whole land of Judah and Benjamin and from the
towns he had captured in the hills of Ephraim. He
repaired the altar of the LORD that was in front of
the portico of the LORD's temple. 2Ch 13:19
9Then he assembled all Judah and Benjamin
and the people from Ephraim, Manasseh and Simeon who had settled among them, for large numbers had come over to him from Israel when they
saw that the LORD his God was with him.
10They assembled at Jerusalem in the third
month of the fifteenth year of Asa's reign. 11At that
time they sacrificed to the LORD seven hundred
head of cattle and seven thousand sheep and goats
from the plunder they had brought back. 12They
entered into a covenant to seek the LORD, the God
of their fathers, with all their heart and soul. 13All
who would not seek the LORD, the God of Israel,
were to be put to death, whether small or great,
man or woman. 14They took an oath to the LORD
with loud acclamation, with shouting and with
trumpets and horns. 15All Judah rejoiced about the
oath because they had sworn it wholeheartedly.
They sought God eagerly, and he was found by
them. So the LORD gave them rest on every side.
16King Asa also deposed his grandmother Maacah from her position as queen mother, because
she had made a repulsive Asherah pole. Asa cut
the pole down, broke it up and burned it in the
Kidron Valley. 17Although he did not remove the
high places from Israel, Asa's heart was fully committed ⌊to the LORD⌋ all his life. 18He brought into
the temple of God the silver and gold and the
articles that he and his father had dedicated.
19There was no more war until the thirty-fifth
year of Asa's reign. 1Ki 15:13-16

Asa's Last Years

16 In the thirty-sixth year of Asa's reign Baasha king of Israel went up against Judah
and fortified Ramah to prevent anyone from leaving or entering the territory of Asa king of Judah.
2Asa then took the silver and gold out of the
treasuries of the LORD's temple and of his own
palace and sent it to Ben-Hadad king of Aram,
who was ruling in Damascus. 3"Let there be a treaty between me and you," he said, "as there was
between my father and your father. See, I am sending you silver and gold. Now break your treaty
with Baasha king of Israel so he will withdraw
from me." 2Ch 20:35
4Ben-Hadad agreed with King Asa and sent the
commanders of his forces against the towns of
Israel. They conquered Ijon, Dan, Abel Maim[b]
and all the store cities of Naphtali. 5When Baasha
heard this, he stopped building Ramah and abandoned his work. 6Then King Asa brought all the
men of Judah, and they carried away from Ramah
the stones and timber Baasha had been using.
With them he built up Geba and Mizpah.
7At that time Hanani the seer came to Asa king
of Judah and said to him: "Because you relied on
the king of Aram and not on the LORD your God,
the army of the king of Aram has escaped from
your hand. 8Were not the Cushites[c] and Libyans
a mighty army with great numbers of chariots and
horsemen[d]? Yet when you relied on the LORD, he
delivered them into your hand. 9For the eyes of the
LORD range throughout the earth to strengthen
those whose hearts are fully committed to him.
You have done a foolish thing, and from now on
you will be at war." 1Sa 13:13; Pr 15:3; Zec 4:10

LIVING 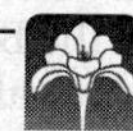 **INSIGHT**

Many things happen when we set our hearts to seek God, including personal evaluation. Is your heart "fully committed to him"? Choose one area of reservation and invite the Spirit of God to break through, to dig up, to conquer and to create something new in your life. Turn your prayers today in the direction of surrender rather than defense. God will "strengthen" you in that attitude.

(See 2 Chronicles 16:9.)

[a]8 Vulgate and Syriac (see also Septuagint and verse 1); Hebrew does not have *Azariah son of.* [b]4 Also known as *Abel Beth Maacah* [c]8 That is, people from the upper Nile region [d]8 Or *charioteers*

10Asa was angry with the seer because of this; he
was so enraged that he put him in prison. At the
same time Asa brutally oppressed some of the people.
11The events of Asa's reign, from beginning to
end, are written in the book of the kings of Judah
and Israel. 12In the thirty-ninth year of his reign
Asa was afflicted with a disease in his feet. Though
his disease was severe, even in his illness he did not
seek help from the LORD, but only from the physicians. 13Then in the forty-first year of his reign Asa
died and rested with his fathers. 14They buried him
in the tomb that he had cut out for himself in the
City of David. They laid him on a bier covered
with spices and various blended perfumes, and
they made a huge fire in his honor. Ge 50:2

Jehoshaphat King of Judah

17 Jehoshaphat his son succeeded him as king
and strengthened himself against Israel.
2He stationed troops in all the fortified cities of
Judah and put garrisons in Judah and in the towns
of Ephraim that his father Asa had captured.
3The LORD was with Jehoshaphat because in his
early years he walked in the ways his father David
had followed. He did not consult the Baals 4but
sought the God of his father and followed his commands rather than the practices of Israel. 5The
LORD established the kingdom under his control;
and all Judah brought gifts to Jehoshaphat, so that
he had great wealth and honor. 6His heart was
devoted to the ways of the LORD; furthermore, he
removed the high places and the Asherah poles
from Judah. 2Ch 15:17; 19:3; 22:9
7In the third year of his reign he sent his officials
Ben-Hail, Obadiah, Zechariah, Nethanel and Micaiah to teach in the towns of Judah. 8With them
were certain Levites—Shemaiah, Nethaniah, Zebadiah, Asahel, Shemiramoth, Jehonathan, Adonijah, Tobijah and Tob-Adonijah—and the priests
Elishama and Jehoram. 9They taught throughout
Judah, taking with them the Book of the Law of the
LORD; they went around to all the towns of Judah
and taught the people. Dt 6:4-9; 2Ch 15:3; 19:8
10The fear of the LORD fell on all the kingdoms
of the lands surrounding Judah, so that they did
not make war with Jehoshaphat. 11Some Philistines brought Jehoshaphat gifts and silver as tribute, and the Arabs brought him flocks: seven thousand seven hundred rams and seven thousand
seven hundred goats. Ge 35:5; 2Ch 9:14; 26:8
12Jehoshaphat became more and more powerful; he built forts and store cities in Judah 13and
had large supplies in the towns of Judah. He also
kept experienced fighting men in Jerusalem.
14Their enrollment by families was as follows:

From Judah, commanders of units of 1,000:
Adnah the commander, with 300,000
fighting men;
15next, Jehohanan the commander, with
280,000;
16next, Amasiah son of Zicri, who volunteered himself for the service of the
LORD, with 200,000. Jdg 5:9; 1Ch 29:9
17From Benjamin: Nu 1:36
Eliada, a valiant soldier, with 200,000 men
armed with bows and shields;
18next, Jehozabad, with 180,000 men armed
for battle.

19These were the men who served the king, besides
those he stationed in the fortified cities throughout
Judah. 2Ch 11:10; 25:5

Micaiah Prophesies Against Ahab

18 Now Jehoshaphat had great wealth and
honor, and he allied himself with Ahab by
marriage. 2Some years later he went down to visit
Ahab in Samaria. Ahab slaughtered many sheep
and cattle for him and the people with him and
urged him to attack Ramoth Gilead. 3Ahab king of
Israel asked Jehoshaphat king of Judah, "Will you
go with me against Ramoth Gilead?" 2Ch 17:5; 21:6
Jehoshaphat replied, "I am as you are, and my
people as your people; we will join you in the war."
4But Jehoshaphat also said to the king of Israel,
"First seek the counsel of the LORD."
5So the king of Israel brought together the
prophets—four hundred men—and asked them,
"Shall we go to war against Ramoth Gilead, or
shall I refrain?"
"Go," they answered, "for God will give it into
the king's hand."
6But Jehoshaphat asked, "Is there not a prophet
of the LORD here whom we can inquire of?"
7The king of Israel answered Jehoshaphat,
"There is still one man through whom we can
inquire of the LORD, but I hate him because he
never prophesies anything good about me, but always bad. He is Micaiah son of Imlah."
"The king should not say that," Jehoshaphat
replied.
8So the king of Israel called one of his officials
and said, "Bring Micaiah son of Imlah at once."
9Dressed in their royal robes, the king of Israel
and Jehoshaphat king of Judah were sitting on
their thrones at the threshing floor by the entrance
to the gate of Samaria, with all the prophets
prophesying before them. 10Now Zedekiah son of
Kenaanah had made iron horns, and he declared,
"This is what the LORD says: 'With these you will
gore the Arameans until they are destroyed.'"
11All the other prophets were prophesying the
same thing. "Attack Ramoth Gilead and be victorious," they said, "for the LORD will give it into the
king's hand." 2Ch 22:5

12The messenger who had gone to summon Micaiah said to him, "Look, as one man the other prophets are predicting success for the king. Let your word agree with theirs, and speak favorably."

13But Micaiah said, "As surely as the LORD lives, I can tell him only what my God says."

14When he arrived, the king asked him, "Micaiah, shall we go to war against Ramoth Gilead, or shall I refrain?"

"Attack and be victorious," he answered, "for they will be given into your hand."

15The king said to him, "How many times must I make you swear to tell me nothing but the truth in the name of the LORD?"

16Then Micaiah answered, "I saw all Israel scattered on the hills like sheep without a shepherd, and the LORD said, 'These people have no master. Let each one go home in peace.'" Nu 27:17; Eze 34:5-8

17The king of Israel said to Jehoshaphat, "Didn't I tell you that he never prophesies anything good about me, but only bad?"

18Micaiah continued, "Therefore hear the word of the LORD: I saw the LORD sitting on his throne with all the host of heaven standing on his right and on his left. 19And the LORD said, 'Who will entice Ahab king of Israel into attacking Ramoth Gilead and going to his death there?' Da 7:9

"One suggested this, and another that. 20Finally, a spirit came forward, stood before the LORD and said, 'I will entice him.'

"'By what means?' the LORD asked.

21"'I will go and be a lying spirit in the mouths of all his prophets,' he said. Job 1:6; Jn 8:44

"'You will succeed in enticing him,' said the LORD. 'Go and do it.'

22"So now the LORD has put a lying spirit in the mouths of these prophets of yours. The LORD has decreed disaster for you." Job 12:16; Eze 14:9

23Then Zedekiah son of Kenaanah went up and slapped Micaiah in the face. "Which way did the spirit from[a] the LORD go when he went from me to speak to you?" he asked. Jer 20:2; Mk 14:65; Ac 23:2

24Micaiah replied, "You will find out on the day you go to hide in an inner room."

25The king of Israel then ordered, "Take Micaiah and send him back to Amon the ruler of the city and to Joash the king's son, 26and say, 'This is what the king says: Put this fellow in prison and give him nothing but bread and water until I return safely.'" 2Ch 16:10; Heb 11:36

27Micaiah declared, "If you ever return safely, the LORD has not spoken through me." Then he added, "Mark my words, all you people!"

Ahab Killed at Ramoth Gilead

28So the king of Israel and Jehoshaphat king of Judah went up to Ramoth Gilead. 29The king of Israel said to Jehoshaphat, "I will enter the battle in disguise, but you wear your royal robes." So the king of Israel disguised himself and went into battle.

30Now the king of Aram had ordered his chariot commanders, "Do not fight with anyone, small or great, except the king of Israel." 31When the chariot commanders saw Jehoshaphat, they thought, "This is the king of Israel." So they turned to attack him, but Jehoshaphat cried out, and the LORD helped him. God drew them away from him, 32for when the chariot commanders saw that he was not the king of Israel, they stopped pursuing him.

33But someone drew his bow at random and hit the king of Israel between the sections of his armor. The king told the chariot driver, "Wheel around and get me out of the fighting. I've been wounded." 34All day long the battle raged, and the king of Israel propped himself up in his chariot facing the Arameans until evening. Then at sunset he died. 1Ki 22:29-36; 2Ch 13:14

19 When Jehoshaphat king of Judah returned safely to his palace in Jerusalem, 2Jehu the seer, the son of Hanani, went out to meet him and said to the king, "Should you help the wicked and love[b] those who hate the LORD? Because of this, the wrath of the LORD is upon you. 3There is, however, some good in you, for you have rid the land of the Asherah poles and have set your heart on seeking God." 2Ch 17:6; 32:25; Ps 139:21-22

Jehoshaphat Appoints Judges

4Jehoshaphat lived in Jerusalem, and he went out again among the people from Beersheba to the hill country of Ephraim and turned them back to the LORD, the God of their fathers. 5He appointed judges in the land, in each of the fortified cities of Judah. 6He told them, "Consider carefully what you do, because you are not judging for man but for the LORD, who is with you whenever you give a verdict. 7Now let the fear of the LORD be upon you. Judge carefully, for with the LORD our God there is no injustice or partiality or bribery."

8In Jerusalem also, Jehoshaphat appointed some of the Levites, priests and heads of Israelite families to administer the law of the LORD and to settle disputes. And they lived in Jerusalem. 9He gave them these orders: "You must serve faithfully and wholeheartedly in the fear of the LORD. 10In every case that comes before you from your fellow countrymen who live in the cities—whether bloodshed or other concerns of the law, commands, decrees or ordinances—you are to warn them not to sin against the LORD; otherwise his wrath will come on you and your brothers. Do this, and you will not sin. Dt 17:8-13; 2Ch 17:8-9

11"Amariah the chief priest will be over you in

[a]23 Or *Spirit of* [b]2 Or *and make alliances with*

any matter concerning the LORD, and Zebadiah son of Ishmael, the leader of the tribe of Judah, will be over you in any matter concerning the king, and the Levites will serve as officials before you. Act with courage, and may the LORD be with those who do well." 1Ch 28:20

Jehoshaphat Defeats Moab and Ammon

20 After this, the Moabites and Ammonites with some of the Meunites[a] came to make war on Jehoshaphat. 1Ch 4:41

2Some men came and told Jehoshaphat, "A vast army is coming against you from Edom,[b] from the other side of the Sea.[c] It is already in Hazazon Tamar" (that is, En Gedi). 3Alarmed, Jehoshaphat resolved to inquire of the LORD, and he proclaimed a fast for all Judah. 4The people of Judah came together to seek help from the LORD; indeed, they came from every town in Judah to seek him.

5Then Jehoshaphat stood up in the assembly of Judah and Jerusalem at the temple of the LORD in the front of the new courtyard 6and said:

"O LORD, God of our fathers, are you not the God who is in heaven? You rule over all the kingdoms of the nations. Power and might are in your hand, and no one can withstand you. 7O our God, did you not drive out the inhabitants of this land before your people Israel and give it forever to the descendants of Abraham your friend? 8They have lived in it and have built in it a sanctuary for your Name, saying, 9'If calamity comes upon us, whether the sword of judgment, or plague or famine, we will stand in your presence before this temple that bears your Name and will cry out to you in our distress, and you will hear us and save us.'

10"But now here are men from Ammon, Moab and Mount Seir, whose territory you would not allow Israel to invade when they came from Egypt; so they turned away from them and did not destroy them. 11See how they are repaying us by coming to drive us out of the possession you gave us as an inheritance. 12O our God, will you not judge them? For we have no power to face this vast army that is attacking us. We do not know what to do, but our eyes are upon you."

13All the men of Judah, with their wives and children and little ones, stood there before the LORD.

14Then the Spirit of the LORD came upon Jahaziel son of Zechariah, the son of Benaiah, the son of Jeiel, the son of Mattaniah, a Levite and descendant of Asaph, as he stood in the assembly.

15He said: "Listen, King Jehoshaphat and all who live in Judah and Jerusalem! This is what the LORD says to you: 'Do not be afraid or discouraged because of this vast army. For the battle is not

LIVING  **INSIGHT**

Are you facing some difficult battle today? Don't run! Stand still . . . and refuse to retreat. Look at it as God looks at it and draw on His power to hold up under the blast. Sure, it's tough. Nobody ever said the Christian life was easy. He offers something better— His own sustaining presence through any trouble we may encounter.

(See 2 Chronicles 20:15–17.)

yours, but God's. 16Tomorrow march down against them. They will be climbing up by the Pass of Ziz, and you will find them at the end of the gorge in the Desert of Jeruel. 17You will not have to fight this battle. Take up your positions; stand firm and see the deliverance the LORD will give you, O Judah and Jerusalem. Do not be afraid; do not be discouraged. Go out to face them tomorrow, and the LORD will be with you.'" Ex 14:13

18Jehoshaphat bowed with his face to the ground, and all the people of Judah and Jerusalem fell down in worship before the LORD. 19Then some Levites from the Kohathites and Korahites stood up and praised the LORD, the God of Israel, with very loud voice. Ex 4:31

20Early in the morning they left for the Desert of Tekoa. As they set out, Jehoshaphat stood and said, "Listen to me, Judah and people of Jerusalem! Have faith in the LORD your God and you will be upheld; have faith in his prophets and you will be successful." 21After consulting the people, Jehoshaphat appointed men to sing to the LORD and to praise him for the splendor of his[d] holiness as they went out at the head of the army, saying:

"Give thanks to the LORD,
for his love endures forever." 2Ch 5:13; Ps 136:1

22As they began to sing and praise, the LORD set ambushes against the men of Ammon and Moab and Mount Seir who were invading Judah, and they were defeated. 23The men of Ammon and Moab rose up against the men from Mount Seir to destroy and annihilate them. After they finished slaughtering the men from Seir, they helped to destroy one another. Jdg 7:22; 1Sa 14:20; 2Ch 23:13

24When the men of Judah came to the place that overlooks the desert and looked toward the vast

[a] *1* Some Septuagint manuscripts; Hebrew *Ammonites* [b] *2* One Hebrew manuscript; most Hebrew manuscripts, Septuagint and Vulgate *Aram* [c] *2* That is, the Dead Sea [d] *21* Or *him with the splendor of*

army, they saw only dead bodies lying on the ground; no one had escaped. 25So Jehoshaphat and his men went to carry off their plunder, and they found among them a great amount of equipment and clothing[a] and also articles of value—more than they could take away. There was so much plunder that it took three days to collect it. 26On the fourth day they assembled in the Valley of Beracah, where they praised the LORD. This is why it is called the Valley of Beracah[b] to this day.

27Then, led by Jehoshaphat, all the men of Judah and Jerusalem returned joyfully to Jerusalem, for the LORD had given them cause to rejoice over their enemies. 28They entered Jerusalem and went to the temple of the LORD with harps and lutes and trumpets.

29The fear of God came upon all the kingdoms of the countries when they heard how the LORD had fought against the enemies of Israel. 30And the kingdom of Jehoshaphat was at peace, for his God had given him rest on every side. 2Ch 15:15; 17:10

The End of Jehoshaphat's Reign

31So Jehoshaphat reigned over Judah. He was thirty-five years old when he became king of Judah, and he reigned in Jerusalem twenty-five years. His mother's name was Azubah daughter of Shilhi. 32He walked in the ways of his father Asa and did not stray from them; he did what was right in the eyes of the LORD. 33The high places, however, were not removed, and the people still had not set their hearts on the God of their fathers.

34The other events of Jehoshaphat's reign, from beginning to end, are written in the annals of Jehu son of Hanani, which are recorded in the book of the kings of Israel. 1Ki 16:1

35Later, Jehoshaphat king of Judah made an alliance with Ahaziah king of Israel, who was guilty of wickedness. 36He agreed with him to construct a fleet of trading ships.[c] After these were built at Ezion Geber, 37Eliezer son of Dodavahu of Mareshah prophesied against Jehoshaphat, saying, "Because you have made an alliance with Ahaziah, the LORD will destroy what you have made." The ships were wrecked and were not able to set sail to trade.[d]

21 Then Jehoshaphat rested with his fathers and was buried with them in the City of David. And Jehoram his son succeeded him as king. 2Jehoram's brothers, the sons of Jehoshaphat, were Azariah, Jehiel, Zechariah, Azariahu, Michael and Shephatiah. All these were sons of Jehoshaphat king of Israel.[e] 3Their father had given them many gifts of silver and gold and articles of value, as well as fortified cities in Judah, but he had given the kingdom to Jehoram because he was his firstborn son. 2Ch 9:21; 11:10

Jehoram King of Judah

4When Jehoram established himself firmly over his father's kingdom, he put all his brothers to the sword along with some of the princes of Israel. 5Jehoram was thirty-two years old when he became king, and he reigned in Jerusalem eight years. 6He walked in the ways of the kings of Israel, as the house of Ahab had done, for he married a daughter of Ahab. He did evil in the eyes of the LORD. 7Nevertheless, because of the covenant the LORD had made with David, the LORD was not willing to destroy the house of David. He had promised to maintain a lamp for him and his descendants forever.

8In the time of Jehoram, Edom rebelled against Judah and set up its own king. 9So Jehoram went there with his officers and all his chariots. The Edomites surrounded him and his chariot commanders, but he rose up and broke through by night. 10To this day Edom has been in rebellion against Judah.

Libnah revolted at the same time, because Jehoram had forsaken the LORD, the God of his fathers. 11He had also built high places on the hills of Judah and had caused the people of Jerusalem to prostitute themselves and had led Judah astray.

12Jehoram received a letter from Elijah the prophet, which said: 2Ki 1:16-17

> "This is what the LORD, the God of your father David, says: 'You have not walked in the ways of your father Jehoshaphat or of Asa king of Judah. 13But you have walked in the ways of the kings of Israel, and you have led Judah and the people of Jerusalem to prostitute themselves, just as the house of Ahab did. You have also murdered your own brothers, members of your father's house, men who were better than you. 14So now the LORD is about to strike your people, your sons, your wives and everything that is yours, with a heavy blow. 15You yourself will be very ill with a lingering disease of the bowels, until the disease causes your bowels to come out.'" 1Ki 16:29-33; 2Ch 17:3-6

16The LORD aroused against Jehoram the hostility of the Philistines and of the Arabs who lived near the Cushites. 17They attacked Judah, invaded it and carried off all the goods found in the king's palace, together with his sons and wives. Not a son was left to him except Ahaziah,[f] the youngest.

18After all this, the LORD afflicted Jehoram with an incurable disease of the bowels. 19In the course

[a] 25 Some Hebrew manuscripts and Vulgate; most Hebrew manuscripts *corpses* [b] 26 *Beracah* means *praise.* [c] 36 Hebrew *of ships that could go to Tarshish* [d] 37 Hebrew *sail for Tarshish* [e] 2 That is, Judah, as frequently in 2 Chronicles [f] 17 Hebrew *Jehoahaz,* a variant of *Ahaziah*

of time, at the end of the second year, his bowels came out because of the disease, and he died in great pain. His people made no fire in his honor, as they had for his fathers. 2Ch 16:14

20Jehoram was thirty-two years old when he became king, and he reigned in Jerusalem eight years. He passed away, to no one's regret, and was buried in the City of David, but not in the tombs of the kings. 2Ki 8:16-24; 2Ch 24:25

Ahaziah King of Judah

22 The people of Jerusalem made Ahaziah, Jehoram's youngest son, king in his place, since the raiders, who came with the Arabs into the camp, had killed all the older sons. So Ahaziah son of Jehoram king of Judah began to reign.

2Ahaziah was twenty-two[a] years old when he became king, and he reigned in Jerusalem one year. His mother's name was Athaliah, a granddaughter of Omri.

3He too walked in the ways of the house of Ahab, for his mother encouraged him in doing wrong. 4He did evil in the eyes of the LORD, as the house of Ahab had done, for after his father's death they became his advisers, to his undoing. 5He also followed their counsel when he went with Joram[b] son of Ahab king of Israel to war against Hazael king of Aram at Ramoth Gilead. The Arameans wounded Joram; 6so he returned to Jezreel to recover from the wounds they had inflicted on him at Ramoth[c] in his battle with Hazael king of Aram. 2Ch 18:1; 21:6

Then Ahaziah[d] son of Jehoram king of Judah went down to Jezreel to see Joram son of Ahab because he had been wounded. 2Ki 8:25-29

7Through Ahaziah's visit to Joram, God brought about Ahaziah's downfall. When Ahaziah arrived, he went out with Joram to meet Jehu son of Nimshi, whom the LORD had anointed to destroy the house of Ahab. 8While Jehu was executing judgment on the house of Ahab, he found the princes of Judah and the sons of Ahaziah's relatives, who had been attending Ahaziah, and he killed them. 9He then went in search of Ahaziah, and his men captured him while he was hiding in Samaria. He was brought to Jehu and put to death. They buried him, for they said, "He was a son of Jehoshaphat, who sought the LORD with all his heart." So there was no one in the house of Ahaziah powerful enough to retain the kingdom.

Athaliah and Joash

10When Athaliah the mother of Ahaziah saw that her son was dead, she proceeded to destroy the whole royal family of the house of Judah. 11But Jehosheba,[e] the daughter of King Jehoram, took Joash son of Ahaziah and stole him away from among the royal princes who were about to be murdered and put him and his nurse in a bedroom. Because Jehosheba,[e] the daughter of King Jehoram and wife of the priest Jehoiada, was Ahaziah's sister, she hid the child from Athaliah so she could not kill him. 12He remained hidden with them at the temple of God for six years while Athaliah ruled the land.

23 In the seventh year Jehoiada showed his strength. He made a covenant with the commanders of units of a hundred: Azariah son of Jeroham, Ishmael son of Jehohanan, Azariah son of Obed, Maaseiah son of Adaiah, and Elishaphat son of Zicri. 2They went throughout Judah and gathered the Levites and the heads of Israelite families from all the towns. When they came to Jerusalem, 3the whole assembly made a covenant with the king at the temple of God. Nu 35:2-5; 2Ki 11:17

Jehoiada said to them, "The king's son shall reign, as the LORD promised concerning the descendants of David. 4Now this is what you are to do: A third of you priests and Levites who are going on duty on the Sabbath are to keep watch at the doors, 5a third of you at the royal palace and a third at the Foundation Gate, and all the other men are to be in the courtyards of the temple of the LORD. 6No one is to enter the temple of the LORD except the priests and Levites on duty; they may enter because they are consecrated, but all the other men are to guard what the LORD has assigned to them.[f] 7The Levites are to station themselves around the king, each man with his weapons in his hand. Anyone who enters the temple must be put to death. Stay close to the king wherever he goes."

8The Levites and all the men of Judah did just as Jehoiada the priest ordered. Each one took his men—those who were going on duty on the Sabbath and those who were going off duty—for Jehoiada the priest had not released any of the divisions. 9Then he gave the commanders of units of a hundred the spears and the large and small shields that had belonged to King David and that were in the temple of God. 10He stationed all the men, each with his weapon in his hand, around the king—near the altar and the temple, from the south side to the north side of the temple.

11Jehoiada and his sons brought out the king's son and put the crown on him; they presented him with a copy of the covenant and proclaimed him king. They anointed him and shouted, "Long live the king!" Dt 17:18; 1Sa 10:24

12When Athaliah heard the noise of the people running and cheering the king, she went to them

[a]2 Some Septuagint manuscripts and Syriac (see also 2 Kings 8:26); Hebrew *forty-two* [b]5 Hebrew *Jehoram,* a variant of *Joram;* also in verses 6 and 7 [c]6 Hebrew *Ramah,* a variant of *Ramoth* [d]6 Some Hebrew manuscripts, Septuagint, Vulgate and Syriac (see also 2 Kings 8:29); most Hebrew manuscripts *Azariah* [e]11 Hebrew *Jehoshabeath,* a variant of *Jehosheba* [f]6 Or *to observe the LORD's command ⌊not to enter⌋*

at the temple of the LORD. 13She looked, and there was the king, standing by his pillar at the entrance. The officers and the trumpeters were beside the king, and all the people of the land were rejoicing and blowing trumpets, and singers with musical instruments were leading the praises. Then Athaliah tore her robes and shouted, "Treason! Treason!" 1Ki 1:41; 7:15

14Jehoiada the priest sent out the commanders of units of a hundred, who were in charge of the troops, and said to them: "Bring her out between the ranks[a] and put to the sword anyone who follows her." For the priest had said, "Do not put her to death at the temple of the LORD." 15So they seized her as she reached the entrance of the Horse Gate on the palace grounds, and there they put her to death. Ne 3:28; Jer 31:40

16Jehoiada then made a covenant that he and the people and the king[b] would be the LORD's people. 17All the people went to the temple of Baal and tore it down. They smashed the altars and idols and killed Mattan the priest of Baal in front of the altars. Dt 13:6-9; 2Ch 29:10

18Then Jehoiada placed the oversight of the temple of the LORD in the hands of the priests, who were Levites, to whom David had made assignments in the temple, to present the burnt offerings of the LORD as written in the Law of Moses, with rejoicing and singing, as David had ordered. 19He also stationed doorkeepers at the gates of the LORD's temple so that no one who was in any way unclean might enter. 1Ch 9:22; 23:6,28-32

20He took with him the commanders of hundreds, the nobles, the rulers of the people and all the people of the land and brought the king down from the temple of the LORD. They went into the palace through the Upper Gate and seated the king on the royal throne, 21and all the people of the land rejoiced. And the city was quiet, because Athaliah had been slain with the sword. 2Ki 11:1-21; 15:35

Joash Repairs the Temple

24 Joash was seven years old when he became king, and he reigned in Jerusalem forty years. His mother's name was Zibiah; she was from Beersheba. 2Joash did what was right in the eyes of the LORD all the years of Jehoiada the priest. 3Jehoiada chose two wives for him, and he had sons and daughters. 2Ch 26:5

4Some time later Joash decided to restore the temple of the LORD. 5He called together the priests and Levites and said to them, "Go to the towns of Judah and collect the money due annually from all Israel, to repair the temple of your God. Do it now." But the Levites did not act at once.

6Therefore the king summoned Jehoiada the chief priest and said to him, "Why haven't you required the Levites to bring in from Judah and Jerusalem the tax imposed by Moses the servant of the LORD and by the assembly of Israel for the Tent of the Testimony?" Ex 30:12-16; Nu 1:50

7Now the sons of that wicked woman Athaliah had broken into the temple of God and had used even its sacred objects for the Baals.

8At the king's command, a chest was made and placed outside, at the gate of the temple of the LORD. 9A proclamation was then issued in Judah and Jerusalem that they should bring to the LORD the tax that Moses the servant of God had required of Israel in the desert. 10All the officials and all the people brought their contributions gladly, dropping them into the chest until it was full. 11Whenever the chest was brought in by the Levites to the king's officials and they saw that there was a large amount of money, the royal secretary and the officer of the chief priest would come and empty the chest and carry it back to its place. They did this regularly and collected a great amount of money. 12The king and Jehoiada gave it to the men who carried out the work required for the temple of the LORD. They hired masons and carpenters to restore the LORD's temple, and also workers in iron and bronze to repair the temple.

13The men in charge of the work were diligent, and the repairs progressed under them. They rebuilt the temple of God according to its original design and reinforced it. 14When they had finished, they brought the rest of the money to the king and Jehoiada, and with it were made articles for the LORD's temple: articles for the service and for the burnt offerings, and also dishes and other objects of gold and silver. As long as Jehoiada lived, burnt offerings were presented continually in the temple of the LORD. 2Ki 12:1-16; 1Ch 29:3,6,9

15Now Jehoiada was old and full of years, and he died at the age of a hundred and thirty. 16He was buried with the kings in the City of David, because of the good he had done in Israel for God and his temple.

The Wickedness of Joash

17After the death of Jehoiada, the officials of Judah came and paid homage to the king, and he listened to them. 18They abandoned the temple of the LORD, the God of their fathers, and worshiped Asherah poles and idols. Because of their guilt, God's anger came upon Judah and Jerusalem. 19Although the LORD sent prophets to the people to bring them back to him, and though they testified against them, they would not listen. Ex 34:13

20Then the Spirit of God came upon Zechariah son of Jehoiada the priest. He stood before the people and said, "This is what God says: 'Why do you disobey the LORD's commands? You will not

[a]14 Or *out from the precincts* [b]16 Or *covenant between ⌞the LORD⌟ and the people and the king that they* (see 2 Kings 11:17)

prosper. Because you have forsaken the LORD, he has forsaken you.' " Nu 14:41; 2Ch 15:2; 20:14

21But they plotted against him, and by order of the king they stoned him to death in the courtyard of the LORD's temple. 22King Joash did not remember the kindness Zechariah's father Jehoiada had shown him but killed his son, who said as he lay dying, "May the LORD see this and call you to account." Ge 9:5; Ne 9:26; Ac 7:58-59

23At the turn of the year,[a] the army of Aram marched against Joash; it invaded Judah and Jerusalem and killed all the leaders of the people. They sent all the plunder to their king in Damascus. 24Although the Aramean army had come with only a few men, the LORD delivered into their hands a much larger army. Because Judah had forsaken the LORD, the God of their fathers, judgment was executed on Joash. 25When the Arameans withdrew, they left Joash severely wounded. His officials conspired against him for murdering the son of Jehoiada the priest, and they killed him in his bed. So he died and was buried in the City of David, but not in the tombs of the kings. Lev 26:23-25

26Those who conspired against him were Zabad,[b] son of Shimeath an Ammonite woman, and Jehozabad, son of Shimrith[c] a Moabite woman. 27The account of his sons, the many prophecies about him, and the record of the restoration of the temple of God are written in the annotations on the book of the kings. And Amaziah his son succeeded him as king. 2Ki 12:17-21

Amaziah King of Judah

25 Amaziah was twenty-five years old when he became king, and he reigned in Jerusalem twenty-nine years. His mother's name was Jehoaddin[d]; she was from Jerusalem. 2He did what was right in the eyes of the LORD, but not wholeheartedly. 3After the kingdom was firmly in his control, he executed the officials who had murdered his father the king. 4Yet he did not put their sons to death, but acted in accordance with what is written in the Law, in the Book of Moses, where the LORD commanded: "Fathers shall not be put to death for their children, nor children put to death for their fathers; each is to die for his own sins."[e]

5Amaziah called the people of Judah together and assigned them according to their families to commanders of thousands and commanders of hundreds for all Judah and Benjamin. He then mustered those twenty years old or more and found that there were three hundred thousand men ready for military service, able to handle the spear and shield. 6He also hired a hundred thousand fighting men from Israel for a hundred talents[f] of silver. Nu 1:3; 1Ch 21:1

7But a man of God came to him and said, "O king, these troops from Israel must not march with you, for the LORD is not with Israel—not with any of the people of Ephraim. 8Even if you go and fight courageously in battle, God will overthrow you before the enemy, for God has the power to help or to overthrow." 2Ch 14:11; 20:6

9Amaziah asked the man of God, "But what about the hundred talents I paid for these Israelite troops?"

The man of God replied, "The LORD can give you much more than that." Dt 8:18; Pr 10:22

10So Amaziah dismissed the troops who had come to him from Ephraim and sent them home. They were furious with Judah and left for home in a great rage.

11Amaziah then marshaled his strength and led his army to the Valley of Salt, where he killed ten thousand men of Seir. 12The army of Judah also captured ten thousand men alive, took them to the top of a cliff and threw them down so that all were dashed to pieces. 2Ki 14:7; Ps 141:6

13Meanwhile the troops that Amaziah had sent back and had not allowed to take part in the war raided Judean towns from Samaria to Beth Horon. They killed three thousand people and carried off great quantities of plunder.

14When Amaziah returned from slaughtering the Edomites, he brought back the gods of the people of Seir. He set them up as his own gods, bowed down to them and burned sacrifices to them. 15The anger of the LORD burned against Amaziah, and he sent a prophet to him, who said, "Why do you consult this people's gods, which could not save their own people from your hand?"

16While he was still speaking, the king said to him, "Have we appointed you an adviser to the king? Stop! Why be struck down?"

So the prophet stopped but said, "I know that God has determined to destroy you, because you have done this and have not listened to my counsel."

17After Amaziah king of Judah consulted his advisers, he sent this challenge to Jehoash[g] son of Jehoahaz, the son of Jehu, king of Israel: "Come, meet me face to face."

18But Jehoash king of Israel replied to Amaziah king of Judah: "A thistle in Lebanon sent a message to a cedar in Lebanon, 'Give your daughter to my son in marriage.' Then a wild beast in Lebanon came along and trampled the thistle underfoot. 19You say to yourself that you have defeated Edom, and now you are arrogant and proud. But stay at home! Why ask for trouble and cause your own downfall and that of Judah also?" Jdg 9:8-15

20Amaziah, however, would not listen, for God

[a] *23* Probably in the spring [b] *26* A variant of *Jozabad* [c] *26* A variant of *Shomer* [d] *1* Hebrew *Jehoaddan,* a variant of *Jehoaddin* [e] *4* Deut. 24:16 [f] *6* That is, about 3 3/4 tons (about 3.4 metric tons); also in verse 9 [g] *17* Hebrew *Joash,* a variant of *Jehoash*; also in verses 18, 21, 23 and 25

so worked that he might hand them over to ⌊Jeho-
ash⌋, because they sought the gods of Edom. 21So
Jehoash king of Israel attacked. He and Amaziah
king of Judah faced each other at Beth Shemesh in
Judah. 22Judah was routed by Israel, and every
man fled to his home. 23Jehoash king of Israel
captured Amaziah king of Judah, the son of Joash,
the son of Ahaziah,[a] at Beth Shemesh. Then Jehoash brought him to Jerusalem and broke down the
wall of Jerusalem from the Ephraim Gate to the
Corner Gate—a section about six hundred feet[b]
long. 24He took all the gold and silver and all the
articles found in the temple of God that had been
in the care of Obed-Edom, together with the palace treasures and the hostages, and returned to
Samaria. 1Ki 12:15; 2Ch 22:7; Jer 31:38

25Amaziah son of Joash king of Judah lived for
fifteen years after the death of Jehoash son of Jehoahaz king of Israel. 26As for the other events of
Amaziah's reign, from beginning to end, are they
not written in the book of the kings of Judah and
Israel? 27From the time that Amaziah turned away
from following the LORD, they conspired against
him in Jerusalem and he fled to Lachish, but they
sent men after him to Lachish and killed him
there. 28He was brought back by horse and was
buried with his fathers in the City of Judah.

Uzziah King of Judah

26 Then all the people of Judah took Uzziah,[c] who was sixteen years old, and made
him king in place of his father Amaziah. 2He was
the one who rebuilt Elath and restored it to Judah
after Amaziah rested with his fathers.

3Uzziah was sixteen years old when he became
king, and he reigned in Jerusalem fifty-two years.
His mother's name was Jecoliah; she was from
Jerusalem. 4He did what was right in the eyes of
the LORD, just as his father Amaziah had done. 5He
sought God during the days of Zechariah, who
instructed him in the fear[d] of God. As long as he
sought the LORD, God gave him success.

6He went to war against the Philistines and
broke down the walls of Gath, Jabneh and Ashdod.
He then rebuilt towns near Ashdod and elsewhere
among the Philistines. 7God helped him against
the Philistines and against the Arabs who lived in
Gur Baal and against the Meunites. 8The Ammonites brought tribute to Uzziah, and his fame spread
as far as the border of Egypt, because he had become very powerful. 2Ch 17:11; 21:16; Isa 14:29

9Uzziah built towers in Jerusalem at the Corner
Gate, at the Valley Gate and at the angle of the
wall, and he fortified them. 10He also built towers
in the desert and dug many cisterns, because he
had much livestock in the foothills and in the
plain. He had people working his fields and vineyards in the hills and in the fertile lands, for he
loved the soil. 2Ch 25:23; Ne 3:13

11Uzziah had a well-trained army, ready to go
out by divisions according to their numbers as
mustered by Jeiel the secretary and Maaseiah the
officer under the direction of Hananiah, one of the
royal officials. 12The total number of family leaders
over the fighting men was 2,600. 13Under their
command was an army of 307,500 men trained for
war, a powerful force to support the king against
his enemies. 14Uzziah provided shields, spears,
helmets, coats of armor, bows and slingstones for
the entire army. 15In Jerusalem he made machines
designed by skillful men for use on the towers and
on the corner defenses to shoot arrows and hurl
large stones. His fame spread far and wide, for he
was greatly helped until he became powerful.

16But after Uzziah became powerful, his pride
led to his downfall. He was unfaithful to the LORD
his God, and entered the temple of the LORD to

LIVING  **INSIGHT**

Check your "pride quotient" by listening and counting how many times you talk about yourself today. Whenever you hear the word "I," it's a clue that you're patting yourself on the back.

(See 2 Chronicles 26:16.)

burn incense on the altar of incense. 17Azariah the
priest with eighty other courageous priests of the
LORD followed him in. 18They confronted him and
said, "It is not right for you, Uzziah, to burn incense to the LORD. That is for the priests, the
descendants of Aaron, who have been consecrated
to burn incense. Leave the sanctuary, for you have
been unfaithful; and you will not be honored by
the LORD God." Ex 30:7; Dt 32:15; 1Ch 6:10

19Uzziah, who had a censer in his hand ready to
burn incense, became angry. While he was raging
at the priests in their presence before the incense
altar in the LORD's temple, leprosy[e] broke out on
his forehead. 20When Azariah the chief priest and
all the other priests looked at him, they saw that he
had leprosy on his forehead, so they hurried him
out. Indeed, he himself was eager to leave, because
the LORD had afflicted him. 2Ki 5:25-27

21King Uzziah had leprosy until the day he died.
He lived in a separate house[f]—leprous, and excluded from the temple of the LORD. Jotham his

[a]23 Hebrew *Jehoahaz,* a variant of *Ahaziah* [b]23 Hebrew *four hundred cubits* (about 180 meters) [c]1 Also called *Azariah* [d]5 Many Hebrew manuscripts, Septuagint and Syriac; other Hebrew manuscripts *vision* [e]19 The Hebrew word was used for various diseases affecting the skin—not necessarily leprosy; also in verses 20, 21 and 23. [f]21 Or *in a house where he was relieved of responsibilities*

UZZIAH

Epitaph: "He Had Leprosy"

"But after Uzziah became powerful, his pride led to his downfall."
—2 CHRONICLES 26:16a

Uzziah began his reign as king of Judah at the tender age of sixteen. Listen to Scripture's account of the early years of Uzziah's rule: "He did what was right in the eyes of the LORD, just as his father Amaziah had done" (2 Chronicles 26:4). How? Uzziah spent time in prayer. He walked humbly with God. He was a man who exercised his authority with great care. Zechariah, his mentor (26:5), undoubtedly reminded him continually of the respect he needed to maintain for the God who had placed him in his high position.

Look at what Uzziah achieved under God's direction. Verses 6–16 of 2 Chronicles 26 make for one incredible biography. Uzziah fought against the Philistines, the ancient enemies of Judah. He beat them at their own game on their own turf. Uzziah was also a master builder, a man of vision and progress. He built towers around Jerusalem and fortified the city. And verse 10 tells us that he was a farmer at heart: "He loved the soil." And if that wasn't enough, through it all he maintained a strong army and gathered highly skilled people around him to create ingenious machines for war.

Uzziah was a man eminently gifted and blessed of God. Under Uzziah's creative, strong, strategic and sensitive rule, Jerusalem became a citadel of military might. Uzziah grew in confidence. He increased in strength. His fame began to spread. As far away as Egypt, people talked about him (26:8). The flags flew. The parades were held. The people sang their joy-filled songs, and all eyes were turned to Uzziah.

And then one day Uzziah began to believe what people were saying about him. His favorite piece of furniture in the palace became a mirror. And that was precisely when he began his descent down the slippery slope of his own self-satisfaction. The Bible describes it sadly and succinctly: "But after Uzziah became powerful, his pride led to his downfall" (26:16). Egotism such as Uzziah had is nothing but the anesthetic that dulls the pain of stupidity. In his stupid pride, Uzziah began to believe in himself rather than in God. And no one had enough courage to tell him, "You're arrogant. The glory has departed from your leadership." Let me say it straight—pride stinks! The problem is, the proud person is the only one who can't smell it.

Pay careful attention now as we read on: "He was unfaithful to the LORD his God, and entered the temple of the LORD to burn incense on the altar of incense" (26:16). Not the temple! The unfathomable glory of Almighty God was in there! But when you're afflicted with pride, no place is off limits. And so Uzziah arrogantly ambled into the place reserved for priests and grabbed articles that were to be handled with reverence, with humility, with the utmost of care. When confronted with his sin, Uzziah burned with anger. Oppose a proud person in an area where he or she has gone too far, and that's the reaction you're apt to get. The Bible tells us that he raged at the priests (26:19).

Pause for a moment to see in your mind's eye what happened next: There Uzziah stood in all of his glory, dressed in flowing kingly garments, censer in hand—showering the priests with angry shouts, cursing anyone who would have the gall to oppose him. As the beads of sweat formed on his brow, leprosy broke out. And then it began to spread. From that moment on, Uzziah lived as an outcast. The God he had failed to credit for his success struck him for his unfaithfulness and his pride. How is Uzziah remembered? Not as a great and powerful king. No, his place in history sifts down to this concluding statement: "Uzziah rested with his fathers and was buried near them in a field for burial that belonged to the kings, for people said, 'He had leprosy' " (26:23). What a sad epitaph!

You're gifted? That's terrific! Don't become impressed with yourself. You're blessed of God? Give Him *every bit* of the praise. Thank Him for the breath in your lungs and for the beating of your heart and for the voice in your vocal chords. Thank Him for your mind, and make sure it's always at His disposal. To live any other way is to tempt pride, and pride leads in the end to destruction.

son had charge of the palace and governed the people of the land.

22The other events of Uzziah's reign, from beginning to end, are recorded by the prophet Isaiah son of Amoz. 23Uzziah rested with his fathers and was buried near them in a field for burial that belonged to the kings, for people said, "He had leprosy." And Jotham his son succeeded him as king. 2Ki 15:5-7; Isa 6:1

Jotham King of Judah

27 Jotham was twenty-five years old when he became king, and he reigned in Jerusalem sixteen years. His mother's name was Jerusha daughter of Zadok. 2He did what was right in the eyes of the LORD, just as his father Uzziah had done, but unlike him he did not enter the temple of the LORD. The people, however, continued their corrupt practices. 3Jotham rebuilt the Upper Gate of the temple of the LORD and did extensive work on the wall at the hill of Ophel. 4He built towns in the Judean hills and forts and towers in the wooded areas. 2Ch 33:14; Ne 3:26; 1Ch 3:12

5Jotham made war on the king of the Ammonites and conquered them. That year the Ammonites paid him a hundred talents[a] of silver, ten thousand cors[b] of wheat and ten thousand cors of barley. The Ammonites brought him the same amount also in the second and third years.

6Jotham grew powerful because he walked steadfastly before the LORD his God. 2Ch 26:5

7The other events in Jotham's reign, including all his wars and the other things he did, are written in the book of the kings of Israel and Judah. 8He was twenty-five years old when he became king, and he reigned in Jerusalem sixteen years. 9Jotham rested with his fathers and was buried in the City of David. And Ahaz his son succeeded him as king. 2Ki 15:33-38

Ahaz King of Judah

28 Ahaz was twenty years old when he became king, and he reigned in Jerusalem sixteen years. Unlike David his father, he did not do what was right in the eyes of the LORD. 2He walked in the ways of the kings of Israel and also made cast idols for worshiping the Baals. 3He burned sacrifices in the Valley of Ben Hinnom and sacrificed his sons in the fire, following the detestable ways of the nations the LORD had driven out before the Israelites. 4He offered sacrifices and burned incense at the high places, on the hilltops and under every spreading tree. Lev 18:21; 2Ch 33:2,6

5Therefore the LORD his God handed him over to the king of Aram. The Arameans defeated him and took many of his people as prisoners and brought them to Damascus. Isa 7:1

He was also given into the hands of the king of Israel, who inflicted heavy casualties on him. 6In one day Pekah son of Remaliah killed a hundred and twenty thousand soldiers in Judah—because Judah had forsaken the LORD, the God of their fathers. 7Zicri, an Ephraimite warrior, killed Maaseiah the king's son, Azrikam the officer in charge of the palace, and Elkanah, second to the king. 8The Israelites took captive from their kinsmen two hundred thousand wives, sons and daughters. They also took a great deal of plunder, which they carried back to Samaria. 2Ki 15:25,27; 2Ch 11:4

9But a prophet of the LORD named Oded was there, and he went out to meet the army when it returned to Samaria. He said to them, "Because the LORD, the God of your fathers, was angry with Judah, he gave them into your hand. But you have slaughtered them in a rage that reaches to heaven. 10And now you intend to make the men and women of Judah and Jerusalem your slaves. But aren't you also guilty of sins against the LORD your God? 11Now listen to me! Send back your fellow countrymen you have taken as prisoners, for the LORD's fierce anger rests on you." Lev 25:39-46; Ezr 9:6; Isa 47:6

12Then some of the leaders in Ephraim—Azariah son of Jehohanan, Berekiah son of Meshillemoth, Jehizkiah son of Shallum, and Amasa son of Hadlai—confronted those who were arriving from the war. 13"You must not bring those prisoners here," they said, "or we will be guilty before the LORD. Do you intend to add to our sin and guilt? For our guilt is already great, and his fierce anger rests on Israel."

14So the soldiers gave up the prisoners and plunder in the presence of the officials and all the assembly. 15The men designated by name took the prisoners, and from the plunder they clothed all who were naked. They provided them with clothes and sandals, food and drink, and healing balm. All those who were weak they put on donkeys. So they took them back to their fellow countrymen at Jericho, the City of Palms, and returned to Samaria.

16At that time King Ahaz sent to the king[c] of Assyria for help. 17The Edomites had again come and attacked Judah and carried away prisoners, 18while the Philistines had raided towns in the foothills and in the Negev of Judah. They captured and occupied Beth Shemesh, Aijalon and Gederoth, as well as Soco, Timnah and Gimzo, with their surrounding villages. 19The LORD had humbled Judah because of Ahaz king of Israel,[d] for he had promoted wickedness in Judah and had been most unfaithful to the LORD. 20Tiglath-Pileser[e] king of Assyria came to him, but he gave him

[a] 5 That is, about 3 3/4 tons (about 3.4 metric tons) [b] 5 That is, probably about 62,000 bushels (about 2,200 kiloliters)
[c] 16 One Hebrew manuscript, Septuagint and Vulgate (see also 2 Kings 16:7); most Hebrew manuscripts *kings* [d] 19 That is, Judah, as frequently in 2 Chronicles [e] 20 Hebrew *Tilgath-Pilneser,* a variant of *Tiglath-Pileser*

trouble instead of help. [21]Ahaz took some of the
things from the temple of the LORD and from the
royal palace and from the princes and presented
them to the king of Assyria, but that did not help
him. 2Ki 16:7; 2Ch 21:2; Eze 16:27,57

[22]In his time of trouble King Ahaz became even
more unfaithful to the LORD. [23]He offered sacrifices to the gods of Damascus, who had defeated
him; for he thought, "Since the gods of the kings
of Aram have helped them, I will sacrifice to them
so they will help me." But they were his downfall
and the downfall of all Israel. 2Ch 25:14; Jer 44:17-18

[24]Ahaz gathered together the furnishings from
the temple of God and took them away.[a] He shut
the doors of the LORD's temple and set up altars at
every street corner in Jerusalem. [25]In every town in
Judah he built high places to burn sacrifices to
other gods and provoked the LORD, the God of his
fathers, to anger. 2Ki 16:18; 2Ch 29:7

[26]The other events of his reign and all his ways,
from beginning to end, are written in the book of
the kings of Judah and Israel. [27]Ahaz rested with
his fathers and was buried in the city of Jerusalem,
but he was not placed in the tombs of the kings of
Israel. And Hezekiah his son succeeded him as
king. 2Ki 16:1-20

Hezekiah Purifies the Temple

29 Hezekiah was twenty-five years old when
he became king, and he reigned in Jerusalem twenty-nine years. His mother's name was
Abijah daughter of Zechariah. [2]He did what was
right in the eyes of the LORD, just as his father
David had done. 2Ki 18:1-3; 2Ch 34:2

[3]In the first month of the first year of his reign,
he opened the doors of the temple of the LORD and
repaired them. [4]He brought in the priests and the
Levites, assembled them in the square on the east
side [5]and said: "Listen to me, Levites! Consecrate
yourselves now and consecrate the temple of the
LORD, the God of your fathers. Remove all defilement from the sanctuary. [6]Our fathers were unfaithful; they did evil in the eyes of the LORD our
God and forsook him. They turned their faces
away from the LORD's dwelling place and turned
their backs on him. [7]They also shut the doors of
the portico and put out the lamps. They did not
burn incense or present any burnt offerings at the
sanctuary to the God of Israel. [8]Therefore, the anger of the LORD has fallen on Judah and Jerusalem;
he has made them an object of dread and horror
and scorn, as you can see with your own eyes.
[9]This is why our fathers have fallen by the sword
and why our sons and daughters and our wives are
in captivity. [10]Now I intend to make a covenant
with the LORD, the God of Israel, so that his fierce
anger will turn away from us. [11]My sons, do not be
negligent now, for the LORD has chosen you to
stand before him and serve him, to minister before
him and to burn incense." Nu 3:6; 2Ch 23:16; Jer 25:9,18

[12]Then these Levites set to work: Nu 3:17-20
from the Kohathites,
Mahath son of Amasai and Joel son of
Azariah;
from the Merarites,
Kish son of Abdi and Azariah son of Je-
hallelel;
from the Gershonites,
Joah son of Zimmah and Eden son of
Joah; 2Ch 31:15
[13]from the descendants of Elizaphan,
Shimri and Jeiel;
from the descendants of Asaph, 1Ch 6:39
Zechariah and Mattaniah;
[14]from the descendants of Heman,
Jehiel and Shimei;
from the descendants of Jeduthun,
Shemaiah and Uzziel.

[15]When they had assembled their brothers and
consecrated themselves, they went in to purify the
temple of the LORD, as the king had ordered, following the word of the LORD. [16]The priests went
into the sanctuary of the LORD to purify it. They
brought out to the courtyard of the LORD's temple
everything unclean that they found in the temple
of the LORD. The Levites took it and carried it out
to the Kidron Valley. [17]They began the consecration on the first day of the first month, and by the
eighth day of the month they reached the portico
of the LORD. For eight more days they consecrated
the temple of the LORD itself, finishing on the sixteenth day of the first month. 1Ch 23:28; 2Ch 30:12

[18]Then they went in to King Hezekiah and reported: "We have purified the entire temple of the
LORD, the altar of burnt offering with all its utensils, and the table for setting out the consecrated
bread, with all its articles. [19]We have prepared and
consecrated all the articles that King Ahaz removed in his unfaithfulness while he was king.
They are now in front of the LORD's altar."

[20]Early the next morning King Hezekiah gathered the city officials together and went up to the
temple of the LORD. [21]They brought seven bulls,
seven rams, seven male lambs and seven male
goats as a sin offering for the kingdom, for the
sanctuary and for Judah. The king commanded
the priests, the descendants of Aaron, to offer
these on the altar of the LORD. [22]So they slaughtered the bulls, and the priests took the blood and
sprinkled it on the altar; next they slaughtered the
rams and sprinkled their blood on the altar; then
they slaughtered the lambs and sprinkled their
blood on the altar. [23]The goats for the sin offering
were brought before the king and the assembly,

[a]24 Or *and cut them up*

and they laid their hands on them. 24The priests then slaughtered the goats and presented their blood on the altar for a sin offering to atone for all Israel, because the king had ordered the burnt offering and the sin offering for all Israel.

25He stationed the Levites in the temple of the LORD with cymbals, harps and lyres in the way prescribed by David and Gad the king's seer and Nathan the prophet; this was commanded by the LORD through his prophets. 26So the Levites stood ready with David's instruments, and the priests with their trumpets. 1Ch 15:24; 23:5; 25:6

27Hezekiah gave the order to sacrifice the burnt offering on the altar. As the offering began, singing to the LORD began also, accompanied by trumpets and the instruments of David king of Israel. 28The whole assembly bowed in worship, while the singers sang and the trumpeters played. All this continued until the sacrifice of the burnt offering was completed. 2Ch 23:18

29When the offerings were finished, the king and everyone present with him knelt down and worshiped. 30King Hezekiah and his officials ordered the Levites to praise the LORD with the words of David and of Asaph the seer. So they sang praises with gladness and bowed their heads and worshiped. 2Ch 20:18

31Then Hezekiah said, "You have now dedicated yourselves to the LORD. Come and bring sacrifices and thank offerings to the temple of the LORD." So the assembly brought sacrifices and thank offerings, and all whose hearts were willing brought burnt offerings. Ex 35:22; Heb 13:15-16

32The number of burnt offerings the assembly brought was seventy bulls, a hundred rams and two hundred male lambs—all of them for burnt offerings to the LORD. 33The animals consecrated as sacrifices amounted to six hundred bulls and three thousand sheep and goats. 34The priests, however, were too few to skin all the burnt offerings; so their kinsmen the Levites helped them until the task was finished and until other priests had been consecrated, for the Levites had been more conscientious in consecrating themselves than the priests had been. 35There were burnt offerings in abundance, together with the fat of the fellowship offerings[a] and the drink offerings that accompanied the burnt offerings. Lev 3:16; Nu 15:5-10

So the service of the temple of the LORD was reestablished. 36Hezekiah and all the people rejoiced at what God had brought about for his people, because it was done so quickly.

Hezekiah Celebrates the Passover

30 Hezekiah sent word to all Israel and Judah and also wrote letters to Ephraim and Manasseh, inviting them to come to the temple of the LORD in Jerusalem and celebrate the Passover to the LORD, the God of Israel. 2The king and his officials and the whole assembly in Jerusalem decided to celebrate the Passover in the second month. 3They had not been able to celebrate it at the regular time because not enough priests had consecrated themselves and the people had not assembled in Jerusalem. 4The plan seemed right both to the king and to the whole assembly. 5They decided to send a proclamation throughout Israel, from Beersheba to Dan, calling the people to come to Jerusalem and celebrate the Passover to the LORD, the God of Israel. It had not been celebrated in large numbers according to what was written.

6At the king's command, couriers went throughout Israel and Judah with letters from the king and from his officials, which read:

> "People of Israel, return to the LORD, the God of Abraham, Isaac and Israel, that he may return to you who are left, who have escaped from the hand of the kings of Assyria. 7Do not be like your fathers and brothers, who were unfaithful to the LORD, the God of their fathers, so that he made them an object of horror, as you see. 8Do not be stiff-necked, as your fathers were; submit to the LORD. Come to the sanctuary, which he has consecrated forever. Serve the LORD your God, so that his fierce anger will turn away from you. 9If you return to the LORD, then your brothers and your children will be shown compassion by their captors and will come back to this land, for the LORD your God is gracious and compassionate. He will not turn his face from you if you return to him." Dt 30:2-5; Mic 7:18

10The couriers went from town to town in Ephraim and Manasseh, as far as Zebulun, but the people scorned and ridiculed them. 11Nevertheless, some men of Asher, Manasseh and Zebulun humbled themselves and went to Jerusalem. 12Also in Judah the hand of God was on the people to give them unity of mind to carry out what the king and his officials had ordered, following the word of the LORD. 2Ch 36:16; Jer 32:39

13A very large crowd of people assembled in Jerusalem to celebrate the Feast of Unleavened Bread in the second month. 14They removed the altars in Jerusalem and cleared away the incense altars and threw them into the Kidron Valley.

15They slaughtered the Passover lamb on the fourteenth day of the second month. The priests and the Levites were ashamed and consecrated themselves and brought burnt offerings to the temple of the LORD. 16Then they took up their regular positions as prescribed in the Law of Mo-

[a]35 Traditionally *peace offerings*

ses the man of God. The priests sprinkled the blood handed to them by the Levites. 17Since many in the crowd had not consecrated themselves, the Levites had to kill the Passover lambs for all those who were not ceremonially clean and could not consecrate ⌊their lambs⌋ to the LORD. 18Although most of the many people who came from Ephraim, Manasseh, Issachar and Zebulun had not purified themselves, yet they ate the Passover, contrary to what was written. But Hezekiah prayed for them, saying, "May the LORD, who is good, pardon everyone 19who sets his heart on seeking God—the LORD, the God of his fathers—even if he is not clean according to the rules of the sanctuary." 20And the LORD heard Hezekiah and healed the people. 2Ch 7:14; Mal 4:2; Jas 5:16

21The Israelites who were present in Jerusalem celebrated the Feast of Unleavened Bread for seven days with great rejoicing, while the Levites and priests sang to the LORD every day, accompanied by the LORD's instruments of praise.[a]

22Hezekiah spoke encouragingly to all the Levites, who showed good understanding of the service of the LORD. For the seven days they ate their assigned portion and offered fellowship offerings[b] and praised the LORD, the God of their fathers. Ex 12:15,17; 13:6

23The whole assembly then agreed to celebrate the festival seven more days; so for another seven days they celebrated joyfully. 24Hezekiah king of Judah provided a thousand bulls and seven thousand sheep and goats for the assembly, and the officials provided them with a thousand bulls and ten thousand sheep and goats. A great number of priests consecrated themselves. 25The entire assembly of Judah rejoiced, along with the priests and Levites and all who had assembled from Israel, including the aliens who had come from Israel and those who lived in Judah. 26There was great joy in Jerusalem, for since the days of Solomon son of David king of Israel there had been nothing like this in Jerusalem. 27The priests and the Levites stood to bless the people, and God heard them, for their prayer reached heaven, his holy dwelling place. Nu 6:23; Dt 26:15; 2Ch 23:18

31 When all this had ended, the Israelites who were there went out to the towns of Judah, smashed the sacred stones and cut down the Asherah poles. They destroyed the high places and the altars throughout Judah and Benjamin and in Ephraim and Manasseh. After they had destroyed all of them, the Israelites returned to their own towns and to their own property. 2Ki 18:4; 2Ch 32:12

Contributions for Worship

2Hezekiah assigned the priests and Levites to divisions—each of them according to their duties as priests or Levites—to offer burnt offerings and fellowship offerings,[b] to minister, to give thanks and to sing praises at the gates of the LORD's dwelling. 3The king contributed from his own possessions for the morning and evening burnt offerings and for the burnt offerings on the Sabbaths, New Moons and appointed feasts as written in the Law of the LORD. 4He ordered the people living in Jerusalem to give the portion due the priests and Levites so they could devote themselves to the Law of the LORD. 5As soon as the order went out, the Israelites generously gave the firstfruits of their grain, new wine, oil and honey and all that the fields produced. They brought a great amount, a tithe of everything. 6The men of Israel and Judah who lived in the towns of Judah also brought a tithe of their herds and flocks and a tithe of the holy things dedicated to the LORD their God, and they piled them in heaps. 7They began doing this in the third month and finished in the seventh month. 8When Hezekiah and his officials came and saw the heaps, they praised the LORD and blessed his people Israel. Dt 14:28; Ps 144:13-15

9Hezekiah asked the priests and Levites about the heaps; 10and Azariah the chief priest, from the family of Zadok, answered, "Since the people began to bring their contributions to the temple of the LORD, we have had enough to eat and plenty to spare, because the LORD has blessed his people, and this great amount is left over." Mal 3:10-12

11Hezekiah gave orders to prepare storerooms in the temple of the LORD, and this was done. 12Then they faithfully brought in the contributions, tithes and dedicated gifts. Conaniah, a Levite, was in charge of these things, and his brother Shimei was next in rank. 13Jehiel, Azaziah, Nahath, Asahel, Jerimoth, Jozabad, Eliel, Ismakiah, Mahath and Benaiah were supervisors under Conaniah and Shimei his brother, by appointment of King Hezekiah and Azariah the official in charge of the temple of God. 2Ch 35:9

14Kore son of Imnah the Levite, keeper of the East Gate, was in charge of the freewill offerings given to God, distributing the contributions made to the LORD and also the consecrated gifts. 15Eden, Miniamin, Jeshua, Shemaiah, Amariah and Shecaniah assisted him faithfully in the towns of the priests, distributing to their fellow priests according to their divisions, old and young alike.

16In addition, they distributed to the males three years old or more whose names were in the genealogical records—all who would enter the temple of the LORD to perform the daily duties of their various tasks, according to their responsibilities and their divisions. 17And they distributed to

[a] 21 Or *priests praised the LORD every day with resounding instruments belonging to the LORD* [b] 22,2 Traditionally *peace offerings*

the priests enrolled by their families in the genealogical records and likewise to the Levites twenty
years old or more, according to their responsibilities and their divisions. 18They included all the
little ones, the wives, and the sons and daughters
of the whole community listed in these genealogical records. For they were faithful in consecrating
themselves. 1Ch 23:3; Ezr 3:4
19As for the priests, the descendants of Aaron,
who lived on the farm lands around their towns or
in any other towns, men were designated by name
to distribute portions to every male among them
and to all who were recorded in the genealogies of
the Levites.
20This is what Hezekiah did throughout Judah,
doing what was good and right and faithful before
the LORD his God. 21In everything that he undertook in the service of God's temple and in obedience to the law and the commands, he sought his
God and worked wholeheartedly. And so he prospered. 2Ki 18:5-7

LIVING  **INSIGHT**

Rather than live with reluctance, let's live with exuberance. Instead of fearing what's ahead, let's face it head-on, with enthusiasm. And because life is so terribly short, let's do everything we can to make it sweet.

(See 2 Chronicles 31:20–21.)

Sennacherib Threatens Jerusalem

32 After all that Hezekiah had so faithfully
done, Sennacherib king of Assyria came
and invaded Judah. He laid siege to the fortified
cities, thinking to conquer them for himself.
2When Hezekiah saw that Sennacherib had come
and that he intended to make war on Jerusalem,
3he consulted with his officials and military staff
about blocking off the water from the springs outside the city, and they helped him. 4A large force
of men assembled, and they blocked all the springs
and the stream that flowed through the land.
"Why should the kings[a] of Assyria come and find
plenty of water?" they said. 5Then he worked hard
repairing all the broken sections of the wall and
building towers on it. He built another wall outside that one and reinforced the supporting terraces[b] of the City of David. He also made large
numbers of weapons and shields. 1Ki 9:24; 1Ch 11:8
6He appointed military officers over the people
and assembled them before him in the square at
the city gate and encouraged them with these
words: 7"Be strong and courageous. Do not be
afraid or discouraged because of the king of Assyria and the vast army with him, for there is a greater
power with us than with him. 8With him is only
the arm of flesh, but with us is the LORD our God
to help us and to fight our battles." And the people
gained confidence from what Hezekiah the king of
Judah said. 2Ki 6:16; 2Ch 20:17; Jer 17:5
9Later, when Sennacherib king of Assyria and
all his forces were laying siege to Lachish, he sent
his officers to Jerusalem with this message for Hezekiah king of Judah and for all the people of Judah
who were there: Jos 10:3,31

10"This is what Sennacherib king of Assyria says: On what are you basing your confidence, that you remain in Jerusalem under
siege? 11When Hezekiah says, 'The LORD our
God will save us from the hand of the king of
Assyria,' he is misleading you, to let you die
of hunger and thirst. 12Did not Hezekiah
himself remove this god's high places and
altars, saying to Judah and Jerusalem, 'You
must worship before one altar and burn sacrifices on it'? 2Ch 31:1; Isa 37:10; Eze 29:16
13"Do you not know what I and my fathers have done to all the peoples of the other
lands? Were the gods of those nations ever
able to deliver their land from my hand?
14Who of all the gods of these nations that
my fathers destroyed has been able to save
his people from me? How then can your god
deliver you from my hand? 15Now do not let
Hezekiah deceive you and mislead you like
this. Do not believe him, for no god of any
nation or kingdom has been able to deliver
his people from my hand or the hand of my
fathers. How much less will your god deliver
you from my hand!" Ex 5:2; Da 3:15

16Sennacherib's officers spoke further against
the LORD God and against his servant Hezekiah.
17The king also wrote letters insulting the LORD,
the God of Israel, and saying this against him:
"Just as the gods of the peoples of the other lands
did not rescue their people from my hand, so the
god of Hezekiah will not rescue his people from
my hand." 18Then they called out in Hebrew to the
people of Jerusalem who were on the wall, to terrify them and make them afraid in order to capture
the city. 19They spoke about the God of Jerusalem
as they did about the gods of the other peoples of
the world—the work of men's hands. 2Ki 18:17-35
20King Hezekiah and the prophet Isaiah son of
Amoz cried out in prayer to heaven about this.
21And the LORD sent an angel, who annihilated all
the fighting men and the leaders and officers in the
camp of the Assyrian king. So he withdrew to his
own land in disgrace. And when he went into the

[a]4 Hebrew; Septuagint and Syriac *king* [b]5 Or *the Millo*

temple of his god, some of his sons cut him down with the sword. 2Ki 19:35-37; Isa 37:36-38

[22]So the LORD saved Hezekiah and the people of Jerusalem from the hand of Sennacherib king of Assyria and from the hand of all others. He took care of them[a] on every side. [23]Many brought offerings to Jerusalem for the LORD and valuable gifts for Hezekiah king of Judah. From then on he was highly regarded by all the nations. 2Ch 17:5; Isa 45:14

Hezekiah's Pride, Success and Death

[24]In those days Hezekiah became ill and was at the point of death. He prayed to the LORD, who answered him and gave him a miraculous sign. [25]But Hezekiah's heart was proud and he did not respond to the kindness shown him; therefore the LORD's wrath was on him and on Judah and Jerusalem. [26]Then Hezekiah repented of the pride of his heart, as did the people of Jerusalem; therefore the LORD's wrath did not come upon them during the days of Hezekiah. 2Ch 26:16; Jer 26:18-19

[27]Hezekiah had very great riches and honor, and he made treasuries for his silver and gold and for his precious stones, spices, shields and all kinds of valuables. [28]He also made buildings to store the harvest of grain, new wine and oil; and he made stalls for various kinds of cattle, and pens for the flocks. [29]He built villages and acquired great numbers of flocks and herds, for God had given him very great riches. 1Ch 29:12

[30]It was Hezekiah who blocked the upper outlet of the Gihon spring and channeled the water down to the west side of the City of David. He succeeded in everything he undertook. [31]But when envoys were sent by the rulers of Babylon to ask him about the miraculous sign that had occurred in the land, God left him to test him and to know everything that was in his heart. Dt 8:16; Isa 39:1

[32]The other events of Hezekiah's reign and his acts of devotion are written in the vision of the prophet Isaiah son of Amoz in the book of the kings of Judah and Israel. [33]Hezekiah rested with his fathers and was buried on the hill where the tombs of David's descendants are. All Judah and the people of Jerusalem honored him when he died. And Manasseh his son succeeded him as king. 2Ki 20:1-21; Isa 37:21-38; 38:1-8

Manasseh King of Judah

33 Manasseh was twelve years old when he became king, and he reigned in Jerusalem fifty-five years. [2]He did evil in the eyes of the LORD, following the detestable practices of the nations the LORD had driven out before the Israelites. [3]He rebuilt the high places his father Hezekiah had demolished; he also erected altars to the Baals and made Asherah poles. He bowed down to all the starry hosts and worshiped them. [4]He built altars in the temple of the LORD, of which the LORD had said, "My Name will remain in Jerusalem forever." [5]In both courts of the temple of the LORD, he built altars to all the starry hosts. [6]He sacrificed his sons in[b] the fire in the Valley of Ben Hinnom, practiced sorcery, divination and witchcraft, and consulted mediums and spiritists. He did much evil in the eyes of the LORD, provoking him to anger.

[7]He took the carved image he had made and put it in God's temple, of which God had said to David and to his son Solomon, "In this temple and in Jerusalem, which I have chosen out of all the tribes of Israel, I will put my Name forever. [8]I will not again make the feet of the Israelites leave the land I assigned to your forefathers, if only they will be careful to do everything I commanded them concerning all the laws, decrees and ordinances given through Moses." [9]But Manasseh led Judah and the people of Jerusalem astray, so that they did more evil than the nations the LORD had destroyed before the Israelites. 2Ki 21:1-10; Jer 15:4

[10]The LORD spoke to Manasseh and his people, but they paid no attention. [11]So the LORD brought against them the army commanders of the king of Assyria, who took Manasseh prisoner, put a hook in his nose, bound him with bronze shackles and took him to Babylon. [12]In his distress he sought the favor of the LORD his God and humbled himself greatly before the God of his fathers. [13]And when he prayed to him, the LORD was moved by his entreaty and listened to his plea; so he brought him back to Jerusalem and to his kingdom. Then Manasseh knew that the LORD is God. 2Ch 32:26

[14]Afterward he rebuilt the outer wall of the City of David, west of the Gihon spring in the valley, as far as the entrance of the Fish Gate and encircling the hill of Ophel; he also made it much higher. He stationed military commanders in all the fortified cities in Judah. 1Ki 1:33; 2Ch 27:3

[15]He got rid of the foreign gods and removed the image from the temple of the LORD, as well as all the altars he had built on the temple hill and in Jerusalem; and he threw them out of the city. [16]Then he restored the altar of the LORD and sacrificed fellowship offerings[c] and thank offerings on it, and told Judah to serve the LORD, the God of Israel. [17]The people, however, continued to sacrifice at the high places, but only to the LORD their God. ver 3-7; Lev 7:11-18

[18]The other events of Manasseh's reign, including his prayer to his God and the words the seers spoke to him in the name of the LORD, the God of Israel, are written in the annals of the kings of Israel.[d] [19]His prayer and how God was moved by

[a] 22 Hebrew; Septuagint and Vulgate *He gave them rest* [b] 6 Or *He made his sons pass through* [c] 16 Traditionally *peace offerings* [d] 18 That is, Judah, as frequently in 2 Chronicles

his entreaty, as well as all his sins and unfaithfulness, and the sites where he built high places and set up Asherah poles and idols before he humbled himself—all are written in the records of the seers.[a] 20Manasseh rested with his fathers and was buried in his palace. And Amon his son succeeded him as king. 2Ki 21:17-18

Amon King of Judah

21Amon was twenty-two years old when he became king, and he reigned in Jerusalem two years. 22He did evil in the eyes of the LORD, as his father Manasseh had done. Amon worshiped and offered sacrifices to all the idols Manasseh had made. 23But unlike his father Manasseh, he did not humble himself before the LORD; Amon increased his guilt.

24Amon's officials conspired against him and assassinated him in his palace. 25Then the people of the land killed all who had plotted against King Amon, and they made Josiah his son king in his place. 2Ki 21:19-24

Josiah's Reforms

34 Josiah was eight years old when he became king, and he reigned in Jerusalem thirty-one years. 2He did what was right in the eyes of the LORD and walked in the ways of his father David, not turning aside to the right or to the left.

3In the eighth year of his reign, while he was still young, he began to seek the God of his father David. In his twelfth year he began to purge Judah and Jerusalem of high places, Asherah poles, carved idols and cast images. 4Under his direction the altars of the Baals were torn down; he cut to pieces the incense altars that were above them, and smashed the Asherah poles, the idols and the images. These he broke to pieces and scattered over the graves of those who had sacrificed to them. 5He burned the bones of the priests on their altars, and so he purged Judah and Jerusalem. 6In the towns of Manasseh, Ephraim and Simeon, as far as Naphtali, and in the ruins around them, 7he tore down the altars and the Asherah poles and crushed the idols to powder and cut to pieces all the incense altars throughout Israel. Then he went back to Jerusalem. Lev 26:30; 1Ki 13:2; 2Ch 31:1

8In the eighteenth year of Josiah's reign, to purify the land and the temple, he sent Shaphan son of Azaliah and Maaseiah the ruler of the city, with Joah son of Joahaz, the recorder, to repair the temple of the LORD his God.

9They went to Hilkiah the high priest and gave him the money that had been brought into the temple of God, which the Levites who were the doorkeepers had collected from the people of Manasseh, Ephraim and the entire remnant of Israel and from all the people of Judah and Benjamin and the inhabitants of Jerusalem. 10Then they entrusted it to the men appointed to supervise the work on the LORD's temple. These men paid the workers who repaired and restored the temple. 11They also gave money to the carpenters and builders to purchase dressed stone, and timber for joists and beams for the buildings that the kings of Judah had allowed to fall into ruin. 2Ch 33:4-7; 35:8

12The men did the work faithfully. Over them to direct them were Jahath and Obadiah, Levites descended from Merari, and Zechariah and Meshullam, descended from Kohath. The Levites—all who were skilled in playing musical instruments—13had charge of the laborers and supervised all the workers from job to job. Some of the Levites were secretaries, scribes and doorkeepers. 2Ki 12:15

The Book of the Law Found

14While they were bringing out the money that had been taken into the temple of the LORD, Hilkiah the priest found the Book of the Law of the LORD that had been given through Moses. 15Hilkiah said to Shaphan the secretary, "I have found the Book of the Law in the temple of the LORD." He gave it to Shaphan. 2Ki 22:8; Ezr 7:6; Ne 8:1

16Then Shaphan took the book to the king and reported to him: "Your officials are doing everything that has been committed to them. 17They have paid out the money that was in the temple of the LORD and have entrusted it to the supervisors and workers." 18Then Shaphan the secretary informed the king, "Hilkiah the priest has given me a book." And Shaphan read from it in the presence of the king.

19When the king heard the words of the Law, he tore his robes. 20He gave these orders to Hilkiah, Ahikam son of Shaphan, Abdon son of Micah,[b] Shaphan the secretary and Asaiah the king's attendant: 21"Go and inquire of the LORD for me and for the remnant in Israel and Judah about what is written in this book that has been found. Great is the LORD's anger that is poured out on us because our fathers have not kept the word of the LORD; they have not acted in accordance with all that is written in this book." 2Ch 29:8; La 2:4; Eze 36:18

22Hilkiah and those the king had sent with him[c] went to speak to the prophetess Huldah, who was the wife of Shallum son of Tokhath,[d] the son of Hasrah,[e] keeper of the wardrobe. She lived in Jerusalem, in the Second District. Ex 15:20

23She said to them, "This is what the LORD, the God of Israel, says: Tell the man who sent you to

[a] *19* One Hebrew manuscript and Septuagint; most Hebrew manuscripts *of Hozai* [b] *20* Also called *Acbor son of Micaiah* [c] *22* One Hebrew manuscript, Vulgate and Syriac; most Hebrew manuscripts do not have *had sent with him.* [d] *22* Also called *Tikvah* [e] *22* Also called *Harhas*

me, 24"This is what the LORD says: I am going to
bring disaster on this place and its people—all the
curses written in the book that has been read in the
presence of the king of Judah. 25Because they have
forsaken me and burned incense to other gods and
provoked me to anger by all that their hands have
made,[a] my anger will be poured out on this place
and will not be quenched.' 26Tell the king of Judah,
who sent you to inquire of the LORD, 'This is what
the LORD, the God of Israel, says concerning the
words you heard: 27Because your heart was responsive and you humbled yourself before God
when you heard what he spoke against this place
and its people, and because you humbled yourself
before me and tore your robes and wept in my
presence, I have heard you, declares the LORD.
28Now I will gather you to your fathers, and you
will be buried in peace. Your eyes will not see all
the disaster I am going to bring on this place and
on those who live here.' " 2Ch 12:7; 32:26; 35:20-25

So they took her answer back to the king.
29Then the king called together all the elders of
Judah and Jerusalem. 30He went up to the temple
of the LORD with the men of Judah, the people
of Jerusalem, the priests and the Levites—all the
people from the least to the greatest. He read in
their hearing all the words of the Book of the
Covenant, which had been found in the temple of
the LORD. 31The king stood by his pillar and renewed the covenant in the presence of the LORD—
to follow the LORD and keep his commands, regulations and decrees with all his heart and all his
soul, and to obey the words of the covenant written in this book.

LIVING  **INSIGHT**

Do you want to know what influenced Josiah to be such a contrast to his times? It was the Word of God, which Josiah found and followed, and it was a tender heart, which the young man nourished. He embraced Scripture without reservation, and he cultivated a heart for God.

(See 2 Chronicles 34:29–33.)

32Then he had everyone in Jerusalem and Benjamin pledge themselves to it; the people of Jerusalem did this in accordance with the covenant of
God, the God of their fathers. 2Ki 23:1-3; 2Ch 23:16
33Josiah removed all the detestable idols from
all the territory belonging to the Israelites, and he
had all who were present in Israel serve the LORD
their God. As long as he lived, they did not fail to
follow the LORD, the God of their fathers. ver 3-7

Josiah Celebrates the Passover

35 Josiah celebrated the Passover to the LORD
in Jerusalem, and the Passover lamb was
slaughtered on the fourteenth day of the first
month. 2He appointed the priests to their duties
and encouraged them in the service of the LORD's
temple. 3He said to the Levites, who instructed all
Israel and who had been consecrated to the LORD:
"Put the sacred ark in the temple that Solomon
son of David king of Israel built. It is not to be
carried about on your shoulders. Now serve the
LORD your God and his people Israel. 4Prepare
yourselves by families in your divisions, according
to the directions written by David king of Israel
and by his son Solomon. Ex 12:1-30; 2Ch 17:7; Ezr 6:18

5"Stand in the holy place with a group of Levites
for each subdivision of the families of your fellow
countrymen, the lay people. 6Slaughter the Passover lambs, consecrate yourselves and prepare ⌊the
lambs⌋ for your fellow countrymen, doing what
the LORD commanded through Moses." Lev 11:44

7Josiah provided for all the lay people who were
there a total of thirty thousand sheep and goats for
the Passover offerings, and also three thousand
cattle—all from the king's own possessions.

8His officials also contributed voluntarily to the
people and the priests and Levites. Hilkiah, Zechariah and Jehiel, the administrators of God's temple, gave the priests twenty-six hundred Passover
offerings and three hundred cattle. 9Also Conaniah along with Shemaiah and Nethanel, his brothers, and Hashabiah, Jeiel and Jozabad, the leaders
of the Levites, provided five thousand Passover
offerings and five hundred head of cattle for the
Levites. 2Ch 31:12-13

10The service was arranged and the priests stood
in their places with the Levites in their divisions as
the king had ordered. 11The Passover lambs were
slaughtered, and the priests sprinkled the blood
handed to them, while the Levites skinned the animals. 12They set aside the burnt offerings to give
them to the subdivisions of the families of the
people to offer to the LORD, as is written in the
Book of Moses. They did the same with the cattle.
13They roasted the Passover animals over the fire
as prescribed, and boiled the holy offerings in
pots, caldrons and pans and served them quickly
to all the people. 14After this, they made preparations for themselves and for the priests, because
the priests, the descendants of Aaron, were sacrificing the burnt offerings and the fat portions until
nightfall. So the Levites made preparations for
themselves and for the Aaronic priests. Ex 12:2-11

15The musicians, the descendants of Asaph,
were in the places prescribed by David, Asaph,
Heman and Jeduthun the king's seer. The gatekeepers at each gate did not need to leave their

[a]25 Or *by everything they have done*

posts, because their fellow Levites made the preparations for them. 1Ch 25:1; 26:12-19; 2Ch 29:30
[16]So at that time the entire service of the LORD
was carried out for the celebration of the Passover
and the offering of burnt offerings on the altar of
the LORD, as King Josiah had ordered. [17]The Israelites who were present celebrated the Passover at
that time and observed the Feast of Unleavened
Bread for seven days. [18]The Passover had not been
observed like this in Israel since the days of the
prophet Samuel; and none of the kings of Israel
had ever celebrated such a Passover as did Josiah,
with the priests, the Levites and all Judah and Israel who were there with the people of Jerusalem.
[19]This Passover was celebrated in the eighteenth
year of Josiah's reign. 2Ki 23:21-23

The Death of Josiah

[20]After all this, when Josiah had set the temple
in order, Neco king of Egypt went up to fight at
Carchemish on the Euphrates, and Josiah marched
out to meet him in battle. [21]But Neco sent messengers to him, saying, "What quarrel is there between you and me, O king of Judah? It is not you
I am attacking at this time, but the house with
which I am at war. God has told me to hurry; so
stop opposing God, who is with me, or he will
destroy you." 1Ki 13:18; Isa 10:9
[22]Josiah, however, would not turn away from
him, but disguised himself to engage him in battle.
He would not listen to what Neco had said at
God's command but went to fight him on the
plain of Megiddo. 1Sa 28:8; 2Ch 18:29
[23]Archers shot King Josiah, and he told his officers, "Take me away; I am badly wounded." [24]So
they took him out of his chariot, put him in the
other chariot he had and brought him to Jerusalem, where he died. He was buried in the tombs of
his fathers, and all Judah and Jerusalem mourned
for him. 1Ki 22:34
[25]Jeremiah composed laments for Josiah, and to
this day all the men and women singers commemorate Josiah in the laments. These became a tradition in Israel and are written in the Laments.
[26]The other events of Josiah's reign and his acts
of devotion, according to what is written in the
Law of the LORD— [27]all the events, from beginning
to end, are written in the book of the kings of
36 Israel and Judah. [1]And the people of the
land took Jehoahaz son of Josiah and made
him king in Jerusalem in place of his father.

Jehoahaz King of Judah

[2]Jehoahaz[a] was twenty-three years old when
he became king, and he reigned in Jerusalem three
months. [3]The king of Egypt dethroned him in Jerusalem and imposed on Judah a levy of a hundred talents[b] of silver and a talent[c] of gold. [4]The
king of Egypt made Eliakim, a brother of Jehoahaz, king over Judah and Jerusalem and changed
Eliakim's name to Jehoiakim. But Neco took Eliakim's brother Jehoahaz and carried him off to
Egypt. 2Ki 23:31-34

Jehoiakim King of Judah

[5]Jehoiakim was twenty-five years old when he
became king, and he reigned in Jerusalem eleven
years. He did evil in the eyes of the LORD his God.
[6]Nebuchadnezzar king of Babylon attacked him
and bound him with bronze shackles to take him
to Babylon. [7]Nebuchadnezzar also took to Babylon articles from the temple of the LORD and put
them in his temple[d] there. 2Ki 24:13; Jer 26:1; 35:1
[8]The other events of Jehoiakim's reign, the detestable things he did and all that was found
against him, are written in the book of the kings of
Israel and Judah. And Jehoiachin his son succeeded him as king. 2Ki 23:36-24:6

Jehoiachin King of Judah

[9]Jehoiachin was eighteen[e] years old when he
became king, and he reigned in Jerusalem three
months and ten days. He did evil in the eyes of the
LORD. [10]In the spring, King Nebuchadnezzar sent
for him and brought him to Babylon, together
with articles of value from the temple of the LORD,
and he made Jehoiachin's uncle,[f] Zedekiah, king
over Judah and Jerusalem. Jer 22:25; 37:1; Eze 17:12

Zedekiah King of Judah

[11]Zedekiah was twenty-one years old when he
became king, and he reigned in Jerusalem eleven
years. [12]He did evil in the eyes of the LORD his God
and did not humble himself before Jeremiah the
prophet, who spoke the word of the LORD. [13]He
also rebelled against King Nebuchadnezzar, who
had made him take an oath in God's name. He
became stiff-necked and hardened his heart and
would not turn to the LORD, the God of Israel.
[14]Furthermore, all the leaders of the priests and the
people became more and more unfaithful, following all the detestable practices of the nations and
defiling the temple of the LORD, which he had consecrated in Jerusalem. 2Ki 24:18-20; Jer 52:1-3

The Fall of Jerusalem

[15]The LORD, the God of their fathers, sent word
to them through his messengers again and again,
because he had pity on his people and on his
dwelling place. [16]But they mocked God's messengers, despised his words and scoffed at his prophets until the wrath of the LORD was aroused against

[a]2 Hebrew *Joahaz,* a variant of *Jehoahaz;* also in verse 4
[b]3 That is, about 3 3/4 tons (about 3.4 metric tons)
[c]3 That is, about 75 pounds (about 34 kilograms)
[d]7 Or *palace*
[e]9 One Hebrew manuscript, some Septuagint manuscripts and Syriac (see also 2 Kings 24:8); most Hebrew manuscripts *eight*
[f]10 Hebrew *brother,* that is, relative (see 2 Kings 24:17)

his people and there was no remedy. 17He brought
up against them the king of the Babylonians,[a]
who killed their young men with the sword in the
sanctuary, and spared neither young man nor
young woman, old man or aged. God handed all
of them over to Nebuchadnezzar. 18He carried to
Babylon all the articles from the temple of God,
both large and small, and the treasures of the
LORD's temple and the treasures of the king and his
officials. 19They set fire to God's temple and broke
down the wall of Jerusalem; they burned all the
palaces and destroyed everything of value there.

20He carried into exile to Babylon the remnant,
who escaped from the sword, and they became
servants to him and his sons until the kingdom of
Persia came to power. 21The land enjoyed its sabbath rests; all the time of its desolation it rested,
until the seventy years were completed in fulfillment of the word of the LORD spoken by Jeremiah.

22In the first year of Cyrus king of Persia, in
order to fulfill the word of the LORD spoken by
Jeremiah, the LORD moved the heart of Cyrus king
of Persia to make a proclamation throughout his
realm and to put it in writing: Isa 44:28; Jer 25:12; 29:10

23"This is what Cyrus king of Persia says:

"'The LORD, the God of heaven, has given
me all the kingdoms of the earth and he has
appointed me to build a temple for him at
Jerusalem in Judah. Anyone of his people
among you—may the LORD his God be with
him, and let him go up.'" Jdg 4:10

[a] 17 Or *Chaldeans*

EZRA

Ordinary people, hoping that our lives will count for something in the end. Isn't that what most of us are—ordinary people? No big superhero. No colorful, charismatic leader. Just plain you. Just plain me. And isn't it true that all we really want is to know that we've made a difference? That the world is maybe just a little bit different, a little bit better, because we were here? Here, in this book of the Bible, is the man for us. We can learn from him. Ezra, true man of the Word. A man with a passion. A man with a heart for God, A man who walked hand in hand with God. And he made a difference in his day, as an instrument of revival, as not only a hearer but also a doer of the Word, as one who lived what he believed and taught. Ezra—true man of the Word.

WRITER: *Ezra*

DATE: *c.440 B.C.*

PURPOSE: *To show God as the power behind earthly events*

KEY THEME: *Revival and reformation*

KEY VERSE: *7:10*

TIME LINE

1400BC 1300 1200 1100 1000 900 800 700 600 500 400

Fall of Jerusalem (586 B.C.)
Persia's conquest of Babylon (539 B.C.)
First return of exiles to Jerusalem (538 B.C.)
Ministries of Haggai and Zechariah (c.520-480 B.C.)
Completion of temple (516 B.C.)
Second return to Jerusalem under Ezra (458 B.C.)
Third return to Jerusalem under Nehemiah (445 B.C.)
Book of Ezra written (c.440 B.C.)

True Man of the Word

	CHRONICLES	CONSTRUCTION Leader: Zerubbabel		ESTHER	REFORMATION Leader: Ezra		NEHEMIAH
		CENSUS AND JOURNEY	TEMPLE Foundation Opposition Determination Completion		CENSUS AND JOURNEY	REVIVAL Condition Confession Covenant Cleansing	
		CHAPTERS 1–2	*CHAPTERS 3–6*		*CHAPTERS 7–8*	*CHAPTERS 9–10*	
EMPHASIS		**Construction of the temple**		XERXES	**Reformation of the people**		
PERSIAN KING		**Cyrus**	**Darius**		**Artaxerxes**		
SCOPE		**National**	**General**		**Personal**	**Specific**	

In every great movement there are always great people involved. Within the ranks of those great people there also seem to be at least two types. Type "A" people would be those who are the greater lights—people who are up-front, stronghearted, visionary, the leader-types—people who have what it takes to capture the big picture and to rally others around a cause.

But then there are always the type "B" folks who work behind the scenes—and who are just as important, just as crucial. They're often the quiet, lesser lights. They are the ones who are usually contemplative and studious. Often they are people of detail and scholarship. They never seem to get any of the public attention and applause, but they are just as important as the greater lights.

To me, Ezra was one of those quiet "B" type personalities who served God at one of the most vulnerable periods of time in Jewish history. It would not be surprising if we have never given Ezra a passing thought, even though we really owe him so much when it comes to worship today. Ezra was the Thomas Jefferson of his time—laying the constitutional foundation of the future and instituting the system of synagogue worship so closely akin to our style today. His passion for God's Word still inspires us today, particularly if it is true, as some believe, that he wrote Psalm 119—the greatest of all the psalms about the Word of God.

Some of you are called to be the Ezras of this day. You may not have a great deal of public charisma. You may not have the qualities necessary to be a person in an up-front type of ministry. But don't misunderstand your role. Don't belittle what you can do—and don't be discouraged. The Ezras of our day are absolutely essential!

Understanding the Times

To appreciate Ezra you have to understand his times, which can prove a little complicated. Some history will help. The book of Ezra is placed in our Bible just after the book of 2 Chronicles. Toward the end of 2 Chronicles, verses 15–16 of chapter 36, we see why those were vulnerable days for the Jews:

> *The* Lord*, the God of their fathers, sent word to them through his messengers again and again, because he had pity on his people and on his dwelling place. But they mocked God's messengers, despised his words and scoffed at his prophets until the wrath of the* Lord *was aroused against his people and there was no remedy.*

God had looked on His people, the Jews, with a heart of compassion year after disobedient year. He continued to pour out His grace and patience. In effect He kept on saying, "Come along now. Straighten up. Walk with Me. Obey My word." But they didn't. There finally came a time when He was patient no longer. That's not an uncommon scene in the home of many a parent, when the parent says, "You've crossed the line. That's enough." (And children shudder when those words are uttered.) That's what God said to His people. In today's terms, "That's it! You've gone far enough. *There's no remedy*. The only thing that will turn you around is a period of captivity." God raised up against them the king of the Babylonians—which led to a wholesale plundering of Jerusalem. The temple was left in ruins; the wall that once surrounded the holy city was totally destroyed. Many of the people were killed. Some, however, were taken away, as the darkest era in the history of the Hebrews unfolded.

Three Steps to Getting Home

Following a full seventy years of captivity, the Jews were set free to return to Jerusalem. They didn't leave all at once, please understand. The people didn't all of a sudden, en masse, start making their way back to their homeland. They went in three groups. It may help to call them companies. It is interesting to note that each "company" returned under a different leader, or commander.

"Company A" went back under the leadership of Zerubbabel. "Company B" returned about 80 years later, under the command of Ezra. Finally, "Company C" came home 12 years after that, led by Nehemiah. The book of Ezra covers the return of the first two groups.

It's also helpful to remember that each group returned with a distinct mission. The first group came back to *rebuild the temple*, the second to *reestablish worship* in the holy city and the third to *rebuild the wall* around the city for protection. Zerubbabel led the rebuilding of the temple. Ezra, with a passionate heart for God, led the reorganization of formal worship, and Nehemiah headed up the effort to rebuild the wall around the city. How beautifully it all fits together in Scripture, one, two, three . . . just the way God directed it!

The Centrality of the Temple

In our time our worship centers around the person of Jesus Christ, not a building. But back in the days of the returned exiles, the building was central because God had promised that a representation of His presence would dwell in His temple. Therefore, when the temple had been destroyed, there was a distinct sense of the loss of God's presence. With all this in mind, the people knew the importance of rebuilding the temple so that the glory of the Lord could return. It was that task to which Zerubbabel and his colleagues applied themselves (chapters 3–6), beginning their work in 536 B.C. and completing their work in 516 B.C.

The Passion of Ezra's Life

In chapter 7 we read three times that God's hand was on Ezra (verses 6,9,28). You might be wondering why. What set *him* apart for special recognition? There were many others who were scribes and priests. The answer to this question is at the core of this entire book. What was the secret of Ezra's life? When we look closely at verse 10 of chapter 7, we discover the heartbeat of this man of God:

> *For Ezra had devoted himself to the study and observance of the Law of the* Lord*, and to teaching its decrees and laws in Israel.*

I find in these words the master passion of Ezra's life. Clearly, his life revolved around the Word of God.

Pay close attention to the words, "Ezra had devoted himself." The verb is a very colorful term. The original word meant "to be firm, to direct, to arrange something." It carried the idea of establishing top priority and fixing something as the central passion of one's life. Ezra set his heart toward something—something that was his fervent objective and his heart's longing. For Ezra, his heart's desire was first to study the Law of the Lord. To know God's Word the best he could. He was devoted to seeking, to consulting God's Word.

Ezra had made a decision early in his life. He would be, if nothing else, a careful and consistent student of the Torah . . . God's Law, God's Word. That would be the characteristic mark of his life. He was, therefore, a "scribe"—which is another way of saying a "careful teacher of the Bible." People in Ezra's day knew they would get sound Biblical counsel when they went to him for advice. He made God's Word his guide.

I love the balance in Ezra 7:10, because Ezra also set his heart on *observing* what the Law of the Lord taught. The principles he discovered there would guide his life. He yielded his heart to God's divine directions. To remove this ingredient is to make one's life fall flat. Without a commitment to orienting our lives around God's Word, we start to become heady. We may become conceited. We may also become severe. Without that commitment, we may lose touch with people. If we study the Bible for the sake of study only, we are in danger of becoming aloof scholars. But Ezra set his heart on studying so as to carry out and put to use what he learned from God's Word. He kept asking, "So what? How does this apply? Where does this truth touch me and the world around me?" He looked for ways to implement, to put into practice, the teachings of the Scriptures.

When it's all said and done, isn't that exactly the goal of our study . . . *to have one's life changed*? We cannot, we must not, study the Bible for the simple sake of study. The Word of God was not given to satisfy idle, intellectual curiosity. It was given to change lives, influence homes, alter business practices, heal relationships and, in the final analysis, to make us more like the Savior.

What Is the Passion of Your Life?

What about you? What is your objective as you come to God's Word? Do you hunger to know the Scriptures and to practice what they teach? Learn a lifelong lesson from Ezra. Become a careful student of the Bible. Devote yourself to this discipline as long as the Lord gives you life. Carry God's Word with you so that in your leisure moments you can open it and continue reading its life-changing truths. Think deeply about the lessons God is teaching you through His Word, take notes, compare passage with passage and book with book. Study the Bible as a lover of God and as a serious student of His Word.

And then follow God's teaching. Adjust your life to His Word. Obey His truth. Practice what you learn from the Book of God. I'll tell you without hesitation, as you become a student of the Bible you will be a person in demand in your neighborhood, as well as with friends and even with strangers. People long to be around those who know and obey the teachings of Scripture. We all know how rare those individuals are who can open the Word and give help and hope to the hurting. That was the desire and vision of Ezra's life. May it become the passion of your life as well!

The Census **Chapters 1–2**

The opening verse of this book gives us a perfect example of how God uses the unsaved. Did you know that God often works through unbelievers to accomplish His will? Remember, *He is God*, and He can use whomever He wants to use whenever He wants to use them! In this case the Lord employed a man named Cyrus, the king of Persia, to release the Jews from captivity. Read the opening verses closely. *It was God* who moved in the heart of this ruler to achieve God's purpose of bringing His people back to their homeland.

These chapters also record the census figures of how many Israelites returned to Jerusalem under the leadership of Zerubbabel. Why so many numbers? Why so many names? Simply a reminder . . . people matter to God! He knew their names, just as He knows your name.

Cyrus Helps the Exiles to Return

1 In the first year of Cyrus king of Persia, in
order to fulfill the word of the LORD spoken
by Jeremiah, the LORD moved the heart of Cyrus
king of Persia to make a proclamation throughout
his realm and to put it in writing: Jer 25:11-12

2"This is what Cyrus king of Persia says:
"'The LORD, the God of heaven, has given
me all the kingdoms of the earth and he has
appointed me to build a temple for him at
Jerusalem in Judah. 3Anyone of his people
among you—may his God be with him, and
let him go up to Jerusalem in Judah and
build the temple of the LORD, the God of
Israel, the God who is in Jerusalem. 4And the
people of any place where survivors may
now be living are to provide him with silver
and gold, with goods and livestock, and with
freewill offerings for the temple of God in
Jerusalem.'" Ezr 4:3; 5:13; 6:3,14

5Then the family heads of Judah and Benjamin,
and the priests and Levites—everyone whose
heart God had moved—prepared to go up and
build the house of the LORD in Jerusalem. 6All their
neighbors assisted them with articles of silver and
gold, with goods and livestock, and with valuable
gifts, in addition to all the freewill offerings.
7Moreover, King Cyrus brought out the articles
belonging to the temple of the LORD, which Nebuchadnezzar had carried away from Jerusalem and
had placed in the temple of his god.[a] 8Cyrus king
of Persia had them brought by Mithredath the
treasurer, who counted them out to Sheshbazzar
the prince of Judah. 2Ki 24:13; Ezr 5:14
9This was the inventory:

gold dishes	30
silver dishes	1,000
silver pans[b]	29
10gold bowls	30
matching silver bowls	410
other articles	1,000

11In all, there were 5,400 articles of gold and of
silver. Sheshbazzar brought all these along when
the exiles came up from Babylon to Jerusalem.

The List of the Exiles Who Returned

2 Now these are the people of the province who
came up from the captivity of the exiles,
whom Nebuchadnezzar king of Babylon had taken
captive to Babylon (they returned to Jerusalem
and Judah, each to his own town, 2in company
with Zerubbabel, Jeshua, Nehemiah, Seraiah, Reel-
aiah, Mordecai, Bilshan, Mispar, Bigvai, Rehum
and Baanah): 2Ch 36:20; Ne 7:6,73

The list of the men of the people of Israel:

3the descendants of Parosh	2,172
4of Shephatiah	372
5of Arah	775
6of Pahath-Moab (through the line of Jeshua and Joab)	2,812
7of Elam	1,254
8of Zattu	945
9of Zaccai	760
10of Bani	642
11of Bebai	623
12of Azgad	1,222
13of Adonikam	666
14of Bigvai	2,056

[a]7 Or *gods* [b]9 The meaning of the Hebrew for this word is uncertain.

EZRA: CHRONOLOGY OF EVENTS

Three Returns to Jerusalem

BABYLONIAN CAPTIVITY
70 years
Jeremiah 29:10

PERSIA
2 Chronicles 36:20

COMPANY "A" → Commander: **Zerubbabel** ***(Ezra 2:2)***

COMPANY "B" → Commander: **Ezra** ***(Ezra 7:6-10)***

COMPANY "C" → Commander: **Nehemiah** ***(Nehemiah 2:4-11)***

[15]of Adin 454
[16]of Ater (through Hezekiah) 98
[17]of Bezai 323
[18]of Jorah 112
[19]of Hashum 223
[20]of Gibbar 95

[21]the men of Bethlehem 123
[22]of Netophah 56
[23]of Anathoth 128
[24]of Azmaveth 42
[25]of Kiriath Jearim,[a] Kephirah and Beeroth 743
[26]of Ramah and Geba 621
[27]of Micmash 122
[28]of Bethel and Ai 223
[29]of Nebo 52
[30]of Magbish 156
[31]of the other Elam 1,254
[32]of Harim 320
[33]of Lod, Hadid and Ono 725
[34]of Jericho 345
[35]of Senaah 3,630

[36]The priests:

the descendants of Jedaiah (through the family of Jeshua) 973
[37]of Immer 1,052
[38]of Pashhur 1,247
[39]of Harim 1,017

[40]The Levites: Ge 29:34; Nu 3:9; Dt 18:6-7

the descendants of Jeshua and Kadmiel (through the line of Hodaviah) 74

[41]The singers: 1Ch 15:16

the descendants of Asaph 128

[42]The gatekeepers of the temple: 1Sa 3:15

the descendants of
Shallum, Ater, Talmon,
Akkub, Hatita and Shobai 139

[43]The temple servants: 1Ch 9:2; Ne 11:21

the descendants of
Ziha, Hasupha, Tabbaoth,
[44]Keros, Siaha, Padon,
[45]Lebanah, Hagabah, Akkub,
[46]Hagab, Shalmai, Hanan,
[47]Giddel, Gahar, Reaiah,
[48]Rezin, Nekoda, Gazzam,
[49]Uzza, Paseah, Besai,
[50]Asnah, Meunim, Nephussim,
[51]Bakbuk, Hakupha, Harhur,
[52]Bazluth, Mehida, Harsha,
[53]Barkos, Sisera, Temah,
[54]Neziah and Hatipha

[55]The descendants of the servants of Solomon:

the descendants of
Sotai, Hassophereth, Peruda,
[56]Jaala, Darkon, Giddel,
[57]Shephatiah, Hattil,
Pokereth-Hazzebaim and Ami

[58]The temple servants and the descendants of the servants of Solomon 392

[59]The following came up from the towns
of Tel Melah, Tel Harsha, Kerub, Addon and
Immer, but they could not show that their
families were descended from Israel: Nu 1:18

[60]The descendants of
Delaiah, Tobiah and Nekoda 652

[61]And from among the priests:

The descendants of
Hobaiah, Hakkoz and Barzillai (a man who had married a daughter of Barzillai the Gileadite and was called by that name). 2Sa 17:27

[62]These searched for their family records,
but they could not find them and so were
excluded from the priesthood as unclean.
[63]The governor ordered them not to eat any
of the most sacred food until there was a
priest ministering with the Urim and Thummim. Ex 28:30; Lev 2:3,10

[64]The whole company numbered 42,360,
[65]besides their 7,337 menservants and maidservants; and they also had 200 men and
women singers. [66]They had 736 horses, 245
mules, [67]435 camels and 6,720 donkeys.

[68]When they arrived at the house of the LORD in
Jerusalem, some of the heads of the families gave
freewill offerings toward the rebuilding of the
house of God on its site. [69]According to their ability they gave to the treasury for this work 61,000
drachmas[b] of gold, 5,000 minas[c] of silver and
100 priestly garments. Ex 25:2

[70]The priests, the Levites, the singers, the gatekeepers and the temple servants settled in their
own towns, along with some of the other people,
and the rest of the Israelites settled in their towns.

Temple Construction **Chapters 3–6**

It was Zerubbabel's job to oversee the rebuilding of the temple and the beginning of the reestablishment of worship in the land. When the Babylonians took the Israelites captive, the beautiful temple built by Solomon had been destroyed. God called Sheshbazzar (1:11), Zerubbabel and Jeshua (2:2) to lead the

[a] *25* See Septuagint (see also Neh. 7:29); Hebrew *Kiriath Arim.*
[b] *69* That is, about 1,100 pounds (about 500 kilograms)
[c] *69* That is, about 3 tons (about 2.9 metric tons)

first group of exiles back to undertake the task of rebuilding the temple of the Lord. While they were working at this task, there were other godly men ministering to the nation. Haggai, Zechariah (see 5:1) and Malachi were speaking the word of the Lord to the people. You might find it interesting and helpful, while you are studying Ezra, to read the records of these three prophets in the books that bear their names.

In these chapters we meet another king whom the Lord used to accomplish His will among the returned exiles. King Darius went out of his way to help the Jews reestablish their roots and rebuild the temple. By the end of these chapters the temple was complete, the dedication had been celebrated and the Passover had been observed. What a joy it must have been to celebrate that first Passover upon completion of the temple!

Rebuilding the Altar

3 When the seventh month came and the Israelites had settled in their towns, the people assembled as one man in Jerusalem. 2Then Jeshua son of Jozadak and his fellow priests and Zerubbabel son of Shealtiel and his associates began to build the altar of the God of Israel to sacrifice burnt offerings on it, in accordance with what is written in the Law of Moses the man of God. 3Despite their fear of the peoples around them, they built the altar on its foundation and sacrificed burnt offerings on it to the LORD, both the morning and evening sacrifices. 4Then in accordance with what is written, they celebrated the Feast of Tabernacles with the required number of burnt offerings prescribed for each day. 5After that, they presented the regular burnt offerings, the New Moon sacrifices and the sacrifices for all the appointed sacred feasts of the LORD, as well as those brought as freewill offerings to the LORD. 6On the first day of the seventh month they began to offer burnt offerings to the LORD, though the foundation of the LORD's temple had not yet been laid.

Rebuilding the Temple

7Then they gave money to the masons and carpenters, and gave food and drink and oil to the people of Sidon and Tyre, so that they would bring cedar logs by sea from Lebanon to Joppa, as authorized by Cyrus king of Persia. Ezr 1:2-4; 6:3

8In the second month of the second year after their arrival at the house of God in Jerusalem, Zerubbabel son of Shealtiel, Jeshua son of Jozadak and the rest of their brothers (the priests and the Levites and all who had returned from the captivity to Jerusalem) began the work, appointing Levites twenty years of age and older to supervise the building of the house of the LORD. 9Jeshua and his sons and brothers and Kadmiel and his sons (descendants of Hodaviah[a]) and the sons of Henadad and their sons and brothers—all Levites—joined together in supervising those working on the house of God. 1Ch 23:24; Ezr 2:40

10When the builders laid the foundation of the temple of the LORD, the priests in their vestments and with trumpets, and the Levites (the sons of Asaph) with cymbals, took their places to praise the LORD, as prescribed by David king of Israel. 11With praise and thanksgiving they sang to the LORD: 1Ch 6:31; 25:1; Zec 6:12

"He is good;
his love to Israel endures forever."

And all the people gave a great shout of praise to the LORD, because the foundation of the house of the LORD was laid. 12But many of the older priests and Levites and family heads, who had seen the former temple, wept aloud when they saw the foundation of this temple being laid, while many others shouted for joy. 13No one could distinguish the sound of the shouts of joy from the sound of weeping, because the people made so much noise. And the sound was heard far away. Ne 12:24; Isa 16:9

Opposition to the Rebuilding

4 When the enemies of Judah and Benjamin heard that the exiles were building a temple for the LORD, the God of Israel, 2they came to Zerubbabel and to the heads of the families and said, "Let us help you build because, like you, we seek your God and have been sacrificing to him since the time of Esarhaddon king of Assyria, who brought us here." 2Ki 17:24,41

3But Zerubbabel, Jeshua and the rest of the heads of the families of Israel answered, "You have no part with us in building a temple to our God. We alone will build it for the LORD, the God of Israel, as King Cyrus, the king of Persia, commanded us." Ezr 1:1-4; Ne 2:20

4Then the peoples around them set out to discourage the people of Judah and make them afraid to go on building.[b] 5They hired counselors to work against them and frustrate their plans during the entire reign of Cyrus king of Persia and down to the reign of Darius king of Persia. Ezr 3:3

Later Opposition Under Xerxes and Artaxerxes

6At the beginning of the reign of Xerxes,[c] they lodged an accusation against the people of Judah and Jerusalem. Est 1:1; Da 9:1

7And in the days of Artaxerxes king of Persia, Bishlam, Mithredath, Tabeel and the rest of his associates wrote a letter to Artaxerxes. The letter was written in Aramaic script and in the Aramaic language.[d,e] 2Ki 18:26; Da 2:4

[a]9 Hebrew *Yehudah,* probably a variant of *Hodaviah* [b]4 Or *and troubled them as they built* [c]6 Hebrew *Ahasuerus,* a variant of Xerxes' Persian name [d]7 Or *written in Aramaic and translated* [e]7 The text of Ezra 4:8—6:18 is in Aramaic.

[8]Rehum the commanding officer and Shimshai
the secretary wrote a letter against Jerusalem to
Artaxerxes the king as follows:

[9]Rehum the commanding officer and Shimshai the secretary, together with the rest of
their associates—the judges and officials
over the men from Tripolis, Persia,[a] Erech
and Babylon, the Elamites of Susa, [10]and the
other people whom the great and honorable
Ashurbanipal[b] deported and settled in the
city of Samaria and elsewhere in Trans-Euphrates. Ezr 5:6; Ne 4:2

[11](This is a copy of the letter they sent him.)

To King Artaxerxes,

From your servants, the men of Trans-Euphrates:

[12]The king should know that the Jews who
came up to us from you have gone to Jerusalem and are rebuilding that rebellious and
wicked city. They are restoring the walls and
repairing the foundations. Ezr 5:3,9
[13]Furthermore, the king should know that
if this city is built and its walls are restored,
no more taxes, tribute or duty will be paid,
and the royal revenues will suffer. [14]Now
since we are under obligation to the palace
and it is not proper for us to see the king
dishonored, we are sending this message to
inform the king, [15]so that a search may be
made in the archives of your predecessors. In
these records you will find that this city is
a rebellious city, troublesome to kings and
provinces, a place of rebellion from ancient
times. That is why this city was destroyed.
[16]We inform the king that if this city is built
and its walls are restored, you will be left with
nothing in Trans-Euphrates. Ezr 7:24; Ne 5:4

[17]The king sent this reply:

To Rehum the commanding officer, Shimshai the secretary and the rest of their associates living in Samaria and elsewhere in
Trans-Euphrates:

Greetings.

[18]The letter you sent us has been read and
translated in my presence. [19]I issued an order
and a search was made, and it was found that
this city has a long history of revolt against
kings and has been a place of rebellion and
sedition. [20]Jerusalem has had powerful kings
ruling over the whole of Trans-Euphrates,
and taxes, tribute and duty were paid to
them. [21]Now issue an order to these men to
stop work, so that this city will not be rebuilt
until I so order. [22]Be careful not to neglect
this matter. Why let this threat grow, to the
detriment of the royal interests? 1Ki 4:21

[23]As soon as the copy of the letter of King Artaxerxes was read to Rehum and Shimshai the secretary and their associates, they went immediately
to the Jews in Jerusalem and compelled them by
force to stop.

[24]Thus the work on the house of God in Jerusalem came to a standstill until the second year of
the reign of Darius king of Persia. Ne 2:1-8; Da 9:25

Tattenai's Letter to Darius

5 Now Haggai the prophet and Zechariah the
prophet, a descendant of Iddo, prophesied to
the Jews in Judah and Jerusalem in the name of the
God of Israel, who was over them. [2]Then Zerubbabel son of Shealtiel and Jeshua son of Jozadak set
to work to rebuild the house of God in Jerusalem.
And the prophets of God were with them, helping
them. Ezr 3:2; Zec 1:1
[3]At that time Tattenai, governor of Trans-Euphrates, and Shethar-Bozenai and their associates
went to them and asked, "Who authorized you to
rebuild this temple and restore this structure?"
[4]They also asked, "What are the names of the men
constructing this building?"[c] [5]But the eye of their
God was watching over the elders of the Jews, and
they were not stopped until a report could go to
Darius and his written reply be received. Ezr 1:3
[6]This is a copy of the letter that Tattenai, governor of Trans-Euphrates, and Shethar-Bozenai and
their associates, the officials of Trans-Euphrates,
sent to King Darius. [7]The report they sent him
read as follows:

To King Darius:

Cordial greetings.

[8]The king should know that we went to
the district of Judah, to the temple of the
great God. The people are building it with
large stones and placing the timbers in the
walls. The work is being carried on with diligence and is making rapid progress under
their direction.
[9]We questioned the elders and asked
them, "Who authorized you to rebuild this
temple and restore this structure?" [10]We also
asked them their names, so that we could
write down the names of their leaders for
your information. Ezr 4:12
[11]This is the answer they gave us:

[a]9 Or *officials, magistrates and governors over the men from* [b]10 Aramaic *Osnappar,* a variant of *Ashurbanipal*
[c]4 See Septuagint; Aramaic [4]*We told them the names of the men constructing this building.*

"We are the servants of the God of heaven
and earth, and we are rebuilding the temple
that was built many years ago, one that a
great king of Israel built and finished. 12But
because our fathers angered the God of heav-
en, he handed them over to Nebuchadnezzar
the Chaldean, king of Babylon, who destroyed this temple and deported the people
to Babylon. 2Ki 24:1; 25:8-9,11; 2Ch 36:16
13"However, in the first year of Cyrus king
of Babylon, King Cyrus issued a decree to
rebuild this house of God. 14He even removed from the temple[a] of Babylon the
gold and silver articles of the house of God,
which Nebuchadnezzar had taken from the
temple in Jerusalem and brought to the temple[a] in Babylon. Ezr 1:7; 6:5
"Then King Cyrus gave them to a man
named Sheshbazzar, whom he had appointed governor, 15and he told him, 'Take these
articles and go and deposit them in the temple in Jerusalem. And rebuild the house of
God on its site.' 16So this Sheshbazzar came
and laid the foundations of the house of God
in Jerusalem. From that day to the present it
has been under construction but is not yet
finished." Ezr 3:10; 6:15

17Now if it pleases the king, let a search be
made in the royal archives of Babylon to see
if King Cyrus did in fact issue a decree to
rebuild this house of God in Jerusalem. Then
let the king send us his decision in this matter. Ezr 4:15; 6:1-2

The Decree of Darius

6 King Darius then issued an order, and they
searched in the archives stored in the treasury
at Babylon. 2A scroll was found in the citadel of
Ecbatana in the province of Media, and this was
written on it: Ezr 5:17

Memorandum:

3In the first year of King Cyrus, the king
issued a decree concerning the temple of
God in Jerusalem:

Let the temple be rebuilt as a place to
present sacrifices, and let its foundations be
laid. It is to be ninety feet[b] high and ninety
feet wide, 4with three courses of large stones
and one of timbers. The costs are to be paid
by the royal treasury. 5Also, the gold and
silver articles of the house of God, which
Nebuchadnezzar took from the temple in Jerusalem and brought to Babylon, are to be
returned to their places in the temple in Jerusalem; they are to be deposited in the house
of God. Ezr 1:7; 5:14

6Now then, Tattenai, governor of Trans-
Euphrates, and Shethar-Bozenai and you,
their fellow officials of that province, stay
away from there. 7Do not interfere with the
work on this temple of God. Let the governor
of the Jews and the Jewish elders rebuild this
house of God on its site. Ezr 5:3
8Moreover, I hereby decree what you are
to do for these elders of the Jews in the construction of this house of God:

The expenses of these men are to be fully
paid out of the royal treasury, from the revenues of Trans-Euphrates, so that the work
will not stop. 9Whatever is needed—young
bulls, rams, male lambs for burnt offerings to
the God of heaven, and wheat, salt, wine and
oil, as requested by the priests in Jerusalem—must be given them daily without fail,
10so that they may offer sacrifices pleasing to
the God of heaven and pray for the well-being of the king and his sons. Ezr 7:23; 1Ti 2:1-2
11Furthermore, I decree that if anyone
changes this edict, a beam is to be pulled
from his house and he is to be lifted up and
impaled on it. And for this crime his house
is to be made a pile of rubble. 12May God,
who has caused his Name to dwell there,
overthrow any king or people who lifts a
hand to change this decree or to destroy this
temple in Jerusalem. Dt 12:5; Ezr 7:26; Da 2:5
I Darius have decreed it. Let it be carried
out with diligence.

Completion and Dedication of the Temple

13Then, because of the decree King Darius had
sent, Tattenai, governor of Trans-Euphrates, and
Shethar-Bozenai and their associates carried it out
with diligence. 14So the elders of the Jews continued to build and prosper under the preaching of
Haggai the prophet and Zechariah, a descendant
of Iddo. They finished building the temple according to the command of the God of Israel and the
decrees of Cyrus, Darius and Artaxerxes, kings of
Persia. 15The temple was completed on the third
day of the month Adar, in the sixth year of the
reign of King Darius. Ezr 5:1; 7:1; Zec 1:1
16Then the people of Israel—the priests, the
Levites and the rest of the exiles—celebrated the
dedication of the house of God with joy. 17For
the dedication of this house of God they offered a
hundred bulls, two hundred rams, four hundred
male lambs and, as a sin offering for all Israel,
twelve male goats, one for each of the tribes of
Israel. 18And they installed the priests in their divisions and the Levites in their groups for the service

[a] *14* Or *palace* [b] *3* Aramaic *sixty cubits* (about 27 meters)

of God at Jerusalem, according to what is written in the Book of Moses. 1Ki 8:63; 2Ch 7:5; 35:4

The Passover

[19]On the fourteenth day of the first month, the
exiles celebrated the Passover. [20]The priests and
Levites had purified themselves and were all ceremonially clean. The Levites slaughtered the Passover lamb for all the exiles, for their brothers the
priests and for themselves. [21]So the Israelites who
had returned from the exile ate it, together with all who had separated themselves from the unclean practices of their Gentile neighbors in order to
seek the LORD, the God of Israel. [22]For seven days
they celebrated with joy the Feast of Unleavened Bread, because the LORD had filled them with joy by changing the attitude of the king of Assyria, so that he assisted them in the work on the house of God, the God of Israel. Ex 12:11; Ezr 1:1

Census and Journey — Chapters 7–8

God used Artaxerxes, the king of Persia, to set free another group of Jews who desired to return to their homeland. Ezra was given authority to appoint leaders among the people. And so a new wave of Jews returned to the city of Jerusalem, and through Ezra's leadership, a new commitment to God's Word was encouraged. Through a foreign king, the Lord once again provided what was needed for the Jews to return home. Their exile was coming to an end, and their homeland was beckoning them.

Ezra Comes to Jerusalem

7 After these things, during the reign of Artaxerxes king of Persia, Ezra son of Seraiah, the son of Azariah, the son of Hilkiah, [2]the son of
Shallum, the son of Zadok, the son of Ahitub, [3]the
son of Amariah, the son of Azariah, the son of
Meraioth, [4]the son of Zerahiah, the son of Uzzi,
the son of Bukki, [5]the son of Abishua, the son of
Phinehas, the son of Eleazar, the son of Aaron the
chief priest— [6]this Ezra came up from Babylon.
He was a teacher well versed in the Law of Moses, which the LORD, the God of Israel, had given. The king had granted him everything he asked, for the
hand of the LORD his God was on him. [7]Some of
the Israelites, including priests, Levites, singers, gatekeepers and temple servants, also came up to Jerusalem in the seventh year of King Artaxerxes.
[8]Ezra arrived in Jerusalem in the fifth month of
the seventh year of the king. [9]He had begun his
journey from Babylon on the first day of the first month, and he arrived in Jerusalem on the first day of the fifth month, for the gracious hand of his
God was on him. [10]For Ezra had devoted himself
to the study and observance of the Law of the LORD, and to teaching its decrees and laws in Israel. Dt 33:10; Ne 8:1-8

LIVING  INSIGHT

Never stop studying. Never stop reading. Never stop learning. Don't believe something just because someone says it. Check it out for yourself. Dig into God's Word, for it is our authority, the final resting place of all our cares, our worries, our sorrows and our surprises. It is the final answer to our questions, our search. Turning to the Scriptures will provide something that nothing else on the entire earth will provide.

(See Ezra 7:10.)

King Artaxerxes' Letter to Ezra

[11]This is a copy of the letter King Artaxerxes
had given to Ezra the priest and teacher, a man learned in matters concerning the commands and decrees of the LORD for Israel:

[12][a]Artaxerxes, king of kings, Eze 26:7; Da 2:37

To Ezra the priest, a teacher of the Law of the God of heaven:

Greetings.

[13]Now I decree that any of the Israelites in
my kingdom, including priests and Levites, who wish to go to Jerusalem with you, may
go. [14]You are sent by the king and his seven
advisers to inquire about Judah and Jerusalem with regard to the Law of your God,
which is in your hand. [15]Moreover, you are
to take with you the silver and gold that the king and his advisers have freely given to the God of Israel, whose dwelling is in Jerusalem,
[16]together with all the silver and gold you
may obtain from the province of Babylon, as well as the freewill offerings of the people and priests for the temple of their God in Jerusalem. [17]With this money be sure to buy bulls,
rams and male lambs, together with their grain offerings and drink offerings, and sacrifice them on the altar of the temple of your God in Jerusalem. 2Ch 6:2; Zec 6:10; Dt 12:5-11

[18]You and your brother Jews may then do
whatever seems best with the rest of the silver and gold, in accordance with the will of your
God. [19]Deliver to the God of Jerusalem all the
articles entrusted to you for worship in the
temple of your God. [20]And anything else

[a] 12 The text of Ezra 7:12-26 is in Aramaic.

needed for the temple of your God that you
may have occasion to supply, you may provide from the royal treasury. Ezr 6:4; Jer 27:22
21Now I, King Artaxerxes, order all the
treasurers of Trans-Euphrates to provide
with diligence whatever Ezra the priest, a
teacher of the Law of the God of heaven, may
ask of you— 22up to a hundred talents[a] of
silver, a hundred cors[b] of wheat, a hundred
baths[c] of wine, a hundred baths[c] of olive
oil, and salt without limit. 23Whatever the
God of heaven has prescribed, let it be done
with diligence for the temple of the God of
heaven. Why should there be wrath against
the realm of the king and of his sons? 24You
are also to know that you have no authority
to impose taxes, tribute or duty on any of the
priests, Levites, singers, gatekeepers, temple
servants or other workers at this house of
God. Ezr 6:10; 8:36
25And you, Ezra, in accordance with the
wisdom of your God, which you possess, appoint magistrates and judges to administer
justice to all the people of Trans-Euphrates—all who know the laws of your God.
And you are to teach any who do not know
them. 26Whoever does not obey the law of
your God and the law of the king must surely
be punished by death, banishment, confiscation of property, or imprisonment.

27Praise be to the LORD, the God of our fathers,
who has put it into the king's heart to bring honor
to the house of the LORD in Jerusalem in this way
28and who has extended his good favor to me before the king and his advisers and all the king's
powerful officials. Because the hand of the LORD
my God was on me, I took courage and gathered
leading men from Israel to go up with me.

List of the Family Heads Returning With Ezra

8 These are the family heads and those registered with them who came up with me from
Babylon during the reign of King Artaxerxes:

2of the descendants of Phinehas, Gershom;
of the descendants of Ithamar, Daniel;
of the descendants of David, Hattush 3of the
descendants of Shecaniah; 1Ch 3:22

of the descendants of Parosh, Zechariah,
and with him were registered 150 men;
4of the descendants of Pahath-Moab, Eliehoenai son of Zerahiah, and with him 200
men; Ezr 2:6
5of the descendants of Zattu,[d] Shecaniah
son of Jahaziel, and with him 300 men;
6of the descendants of Adin, Ebed son of
Jonathan, and with him 50 men; Ezr 2:15
7of the descendants of Elam, Jeshaiah son of
Athaliah, and with him 70 men;
8of the descendants of Shephatiah, Zebadiah
son of Michael, and with him 80 men;
9of the descendants of Joab, Obadiah son of
Jehiel, and with him 218 men;
10of the descendants of Bani,[e] Shelomith son
of Josiphiah, and with him 160 men;
11of the descendants of Bebai, Zechariah son
of Bebai, and with him 28 men;
12of the descendants of Azgad, Johanan son of
Hakkatan, and with him 110 men;
13of the descendants of Adonikam, the last
ones, whose names were Eliphelet, Jeuel
and Shemaiah, and with them 60 men;
14of the descendants of Bigvai, Uthai and Zaccur, and with them 70 men.

The Return to Jerusalem

15I assembled them at the canal that flows toward Ahava, and we camped there three days.
When I checked among the people and the priests,
I found no Levites there. 16So I summoned Eliezer,
Ariel, Shemaiah, Elnathan, Jarib, Elnathan, Nathan, Zechariah and Meshullam, who were leaders,
and Joiarib and Elnathan, who were men of learning, 17and I sent them to Iddo, the leader in Casiphia. I told them what to say to Iddo and his
kinsmen, the temple servants in Casiphia, so that
they might bring attendants to us for the house of
our God. 18Because the gracious hand of our God
was on us, they brought us Sherebiah, a capable
man, from the descendants of Mahli son of Levi,
the son of Israel, and Sherebiah's sons and brothers, 18 men; 19and Hashabiah, together with Jeshaiah from the descendants of Merari, and his brothers and nephews, 20 men. 20They also brought 220
of the temple servants—a body that David and the
officials had established to assist the Levites. All
were registered by name. Ezr 2:43; 5:5
21There, by the Ahava Canal, I proclaimed a
fast, so that we might humble ourselves before our
God and ask him for a safe journey for us and our
children, with all our possessions. 22I was ashamed
to ask the king for soldiers and horsemen to protect us from enemies on the road, because we had
told the king, "The gracious hand of our God is on
everyone who looks to him, but his great anger is
against all who forsake him." 23So we fasted and
petitioned our God about this, and he answered
our prayer. 2Ch 33:13; Ezr 7:6,9,28
24Then I set apart twelve of the leading priests,
together with Sherebiah, Hashabiah and ten of
their brothers, 25and I weighed out to them the

[a] 22 That is, about 3 3/4 tons (about 3.4 metric tons) [b] 22 That is, probably about 600 bushels (about 22 kiloliters) [c] 22 That is, probably about 600 gallons (about 2.2 kiloliters) [d] 5 Some Septuagint manuscripts (also 1 Esdras 8:32); Hebrew does not have *Zattu.* [e] 10 Some Septuagint manuscripts (also 1 Esdras 8:36); Hebrew does not have *Bani.*

offering of silver and gold and the articles that the
king, his advisers, his officials and all Israel present
there had donated for the house of our God. [26]I
weighed out to them 650 talents[a] of silver, silver
articles weighing 100 talents,[b] 100 talents[b] of
gold, [27]20 bowls of gold valued at 1,000 darics,[c]
and two fine articles of polished bronze, as precious as gold. Ezr 7:15-16

[28]I said to them, "You as well as these articles
are consecrated to the LORD. The silver and gold
are a freewill offering to the LORD, the God of your
fathers. [29]Guard them carefully until you weigh
them out in the chambers of the house of the LORD
in Jerusalem before the leading priests and the
Levites and the family heads of Israel." [30]Then the
priests and Levites received the silver and gold and
sacred articles that had been weighed out to be
taken to the house of our God in Jerusalem.

[31]On the twelfth day of the first month we set
out from the Ahava Canal to go to Jerusalem. The
hand of our God was on us, and he protected us
from enemies and bandits along the way. [32]So we
arrived in Jerusalem, where we rested three days.

[33]On the fourth day, in the house of our God,
we weighed out the silver and gold and the sacred
articles into the hands of Meremoth son of Uriah,
the priest. Eleazar son of Phinehas was with him,
and so were the Levites Jozabad son of Jeshua and
Noadiah son of Binnui. [34]Everything was account-
ed for by number and weight, and the entire
weight was recorded at that time. Ne 3:4,21,24

[35]Then the exiles who had returned from captivity sacrificed burnt offerings to the God of Israel: twelve bulls for all Israel, ninety-six rams, seventy-seven male lambs and, as a sin offering,
twelve male goats. All this was a burnt offering to
the LORD. [36]They also delivered the king's orders to
the royal satraps and to the governors of Trans-
Euphrates, who then gave assistance to the people
and to the house of God. Ezr 7:21-24; Est 9:3

Revival in the Land **Chapters 9–10**

When the Jews returned home, they must have pondered why they had been exiled in the first place. They needed to bring to mind the idolatry and unfaithfulness of those who had gone before them. They needed to learn from the past so that they would not follow in the footsteps of their ancestors and return someday to exile. With that danger in mind, Ezra warned the people not to marry foreign people who worshiped pagan gods—lest the Jews be drawn away from the worship of the one true God. In response to Ezra's convicting words, the people repented and committed themselves to walk in the ways of the Lord and turn away from false religion and idolatry. In short, there was a revival in the land!

Ezra's Prayer About Intermarriage

9 After these things had been done, the leaders
came to me and said, "The people of Israel,
including the priests and the Levites, have not kept
themselves separate from the neighboring peoples
with their detestable practices, like those of the
Canaanites, Hittites, Perizzites, Jebusites, Ammonites, Moabites, Egyptians and Amorites. [2]They
have taken some of their daughters as wives for
themselves and their sons, and have mingled the
holy race with the peoples around them. And the
leaders and officials have led the way in this unfaithfulness." Ex 22:31; 34:16; Ezr 10:2

[3]When I heard this, I tore my tunic and cloak,
pulled hair from my head and beard and sat down
appalled. [4]Then everyone who trembled at the
words of the God of Israel gathered around me
because of this unfaithfulness of the exiles. And I
sat there appalled until the evening sacrifice.

[5]Then, at the evening sacrifice, I rose from my
self-abasement, with my tunic and cloak torn, and
fell on my knees with my hands spread out to the
LORD my God [6]and prayed: Ex 29:41

"O my God, I am too ashamed and disgraced to lift up my face to you, my God,
because our sins are higher than our heads
and our guilt has reached to the heavens.
[7]From the days of our forefathers until now,
our guilt has been great. Because of our sins,
we and our kings and our priests have been
subjected to the sword and captivity, to pillage and humiliation at the hand of foreign
kings, as it is today. Dt 28:37; 2Ch 28:9; Rev 18:5

[8]"But now, for a brief moment, the LORD
our God has been gracious in leaving us a
remnant and giving us a firm place in his
sanctuary, and so our God gives light to our
eyes and a little relief in our bondage.
[9]Though we are slaves, our God has not deserted us in our bondage. He has shown us
kindness in the sight of the kings of Persia:
He has granted us new life to rebuild the
house of our God and repair its ruins, and he
has given us a wall of protection in Judah and
Jerusalem. Ne 9:36; Ps 13:3; Isa 22:23

[10]"But now, O our God, what can we say
after this? For we have disregarded the commands [11]you gave through your servants the
prophets when you said: 'The land you are
entering to possess is a land polluted by the
corruption of its peoples. By their detestable
practices they have filled it with their impurity from one end to the other. [12]Therefore, do
not give your daughters in marriage to their
sons or take their daughters for your sons.

[a]26 That is, about 25 tons (about 22 metric tons) [b]26 That is, about 3 3/4 tons (about 3.4 metric tons) [c]27 That is, about 19 pounds (about 8.5 kilograms)

Do not seek a treaty of friendship with them at any time, that you may be strong and eat the good things of the land and leave it to your children as an everlasting inheritance.’

13“What has happened to us is a result of our evil deeds and our great guilt, and yet, our God, you have punished us less than our sins have deserved and have given us a remnant like this. 14Shall we again break your commands and intermarry with the peoples who commit such detestable practices? Would you not be angry enough with us to destroy us, leaving us no remnant or survivor? 15O LORD, God of Israel, you are righteous! We are left this day as a remnant. Here we are before you in our guilt, though because of it not one of us can stand in your presence.” 1Ki 8:47; Ps 130:3

The People’s Confession of Sin

10 While Ezra was praying and confessing, weeping and throwing himself down before the house of God, a large crowd of Israelites—men, women and children—gathered around him. They too wept bitterly. 2Then Shecaniah son of Jehiel, one of the descendants of Elam, said to Ezra, “We have been unfaithful to our God by marrying foreign women from the peoples around us. But in spite of this, there is still hope for Israel. 3Now let us make a covenant before our God to send away all these women and their children, in accordance with the counsel of my lord and of those who fear the commands of our God. Let it be done according to the Law. 4Rise up; this matter is in your hands. We will support you, so take courage and do it.” Dt 7:2-3; Ezr 9:4

5So Ezra rose up and put the leading priests and Levites and all Israel under oath to do what had been suggested. And they took the oath. 6Then Ezra withdrew from before the house of God and went to the room of Jehohanan son of Eliashib. While he was there, he ate no food and drank no water, because he continued to mourn over the unfaithfulness of the exiles. Dt 9:18; Ne 5:12; 13:25

7A proclamation was then issued throughout Judah and Jerusalem for all the exiles to assemble in Jerusalem. 8Anyone who failed to appear within three days would forfeit all his property, in accordance with the decision of the officials and elders, and would himself be expelled from the assembly of the exiles.

9Within the three days, all the men of Judah and Benjamin had gathered in Jerusalem. And on the twentieth day of the ninth month, all the people were sitting in the square before the house of God, greatly distressed by the occasion and because of the rain. 10Then Ezra the priest stood up and said to them, “You have been unfaithful; you have married foreign women, adding to Israel’s guilt. 11Now make confession to the LORD, the God of your fathers, and do his will. Separate yourselves from the peoples around you and from your foreign wives.” Dt 24:1; Mal 2:10-16

12The whole assembly responded with a loud voice: “You are right! We must do as you say. 13But there are many people here and it is the rainy season; so we cannot stand outside. Besides, this matter cannot be taken care of in a day or two, because we have sinned greatly in this thing. 14Let our officials act for the whole assembly. Then let everyone in our towns who has married a foreign woman come at a set time, along with the elders and judges of each town, until the fierce anger of our God in this matter is turned away from us.” 15Only Jonathan son of Asahel and Jahzeiah son of Tikvah, supported by Meshullam and Shabbethai the Levite, opposed this. 2Ch 29:10; 30:8; Ne 11:16

16So the exiles did as was proposed. Ezra the priest selected men who were family heads, one from each family division, and all of them designated by name. On the first day of the tenth month they sat down to investigate the cases, 17and by the first day of the first month they finished dealing with all the men who had married foreign women.

Those Guilty of Intermarriage

18Among the descendants of the priests, the following had married foreign women:

From the descendants of Jeshua son of Jozadak, and his brothers: Maaseiah, Eliezer, Jarib and Gedaliah. 19(They all gave their hands in pledge to put away their wives, and for their guilt they each presented a ram from the flock as a guilt offering.)

20From the descendants of Immer: 1Ch 24:14
Hanani and Zebadiah.

21From the descendants of Harim: 1Ch 24:8
Maaseiah, Elijah, Shemaiah, Jehiel and Uzziah.

22From the descendants of Pashhur: 1Ch 9:12
Elioenai, Maaseiah, Ishmael, Nethanel, Jozabad and Elasah.

23Among the Levites: Ne 8:7; 9:4

Jozabad, Shimei, Kelaiah (that is, Kelita), Pethahiah, Judah and Eliezer.

24From the singers:
Eliashib. Ne 3:1; 12:10; 13:7,28

From the gatekeepers:
Shallum, Telem and Uri.

25And among the other Israelites:

From the descendants of Parosh: Ezr 2:3
Ramiah, Izziah, Malkijah, Mijamin, Eleazar, Malkijah and Benaiah.

26From the descendants of Elam:

Mattaniah, Zechariah, Jehiel, Abdi, Jeremoth and Elijah.

[27]From the descendants of Zattu:
Elioenai, Eliashib, Mattaniah, Jeremoth, Zabad and Aziza.

[28]From the descendants of Bebai:
Jehohanan, Hananiah, Zabbai and Athlai.

[29]From the descendants of Bani:
Meshullam, Malluch, Adaiah, Jashub, Sheal and Jeremoth.

[30]From the descendants of Pahath-Moab:
Adna, Kelal, Benaiah, Maaseiah, Mattaniah, Bezalel, Binnui and Manasseh.

[31]From the descendants of Harim:
Eliezer, Ishijah, Malkijah, Shemaiah, Shimeon, [32]Benjamin, Malluch and Shemariah.

[33]From the descendants of Hashum:
Mattenai, Mattattah, Zabad, Eliphelet, Jeremai, Manasseh and Shimei.

[34]From the descendants of Bani:
Maadai, Amram, Uel, [35]Benaiah, Bedeiah, Keluhi, [36]Vaniah, Meremoth, Eliashib, [37]Mattaniah, Mattenai and Jaasu.

[38]From the descendants of Binnui:[a]
Shimei, [39]Shelemiah, Nathan, Adaiah, [40]Macnadebai, Shashai, Sharai, [41]Azarel, Shelemiah, Shemariah, [42]Shallum, Amariah and Joseph.

[43]From the descendants of Nebo:
Jeiel, Mattithiah, Zabad, Zebina, Jaddai, Joel and Benaiah.

[44]All these had married foreign women, and some of them had children by these wives.[b]

[a] 37,38 See Septuagint (also 1 Esdras 9:34); Hebrew *Jaasu* [38]*and Bani and Binnui,* [b] 44 Or *and they sent them away with their children*

INTRODUCTION

NEHEMIAH

Do you ever feel like you've just got too many hats to wear? Spouse. Parent. Child. Employee. Church member. Community volunteer. Over the course of a lifetime we wear many different hats. That was true for a man in Bible times, a man for whom a Bible book is named. Nehemiah was the man of the hour for the people who had returned to Jerusalem, and to be that kind of man he had to be ready to put on the hats the Lord had prepared for him. As the book begins, he is the cupbearer to the king of Persia, but before long he dons the hard hat of the builder—commissioned to rebuild the broken-down walls of Jerusalem. That task completed, he accepts the hat of governor of the people. Nehemiah—the right man for the right time for the right job. Nehemiah—the man of many hats . . . and a single heart, devoted to God!

WRITER: *Possibly Ezra and Nehemiah*

DATE: *c.430 B.C.*

PURPOSE: *To remind the returned exiles of their spiritual heritage*

KEY THEME: *God's power and a nation's determination*

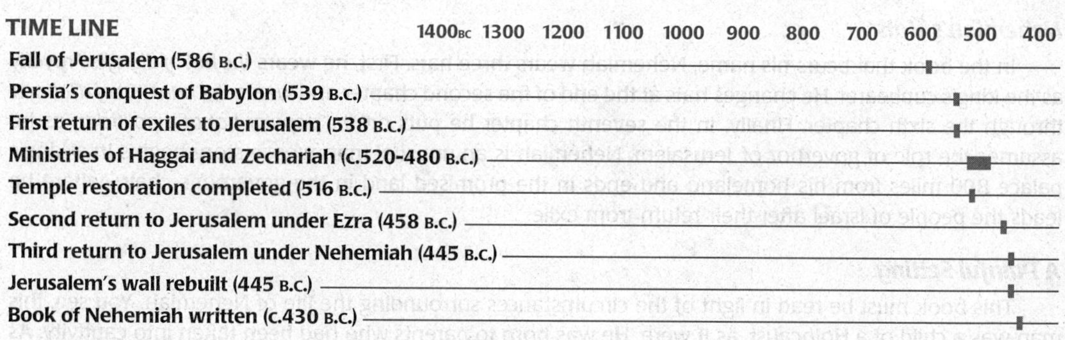

Softhearted Hard Hat

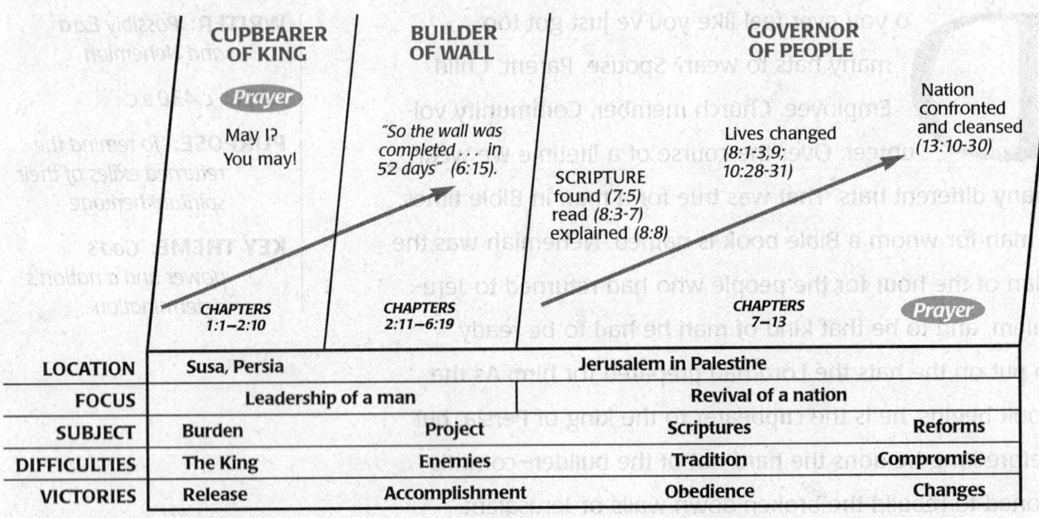

LOCATION	Susa, Persia	Jerusalem in Palestine		
FOCUS	Leadership of a man		Revival of a nation	
SUBJECT	Burden	Project	Scriptures	Reforms
DIFFICULTIES	The King	Enemies	Tradition	Compromise
VICTORIES	Release	Accomplishment	Obedience	Changes

I think of Nehemiah as a guy similar to the late John Wayne. Nehemiah was a man who loved his country. He was also a man who didn't mind standing alone and who didn't mince words. He had a tough hide but a tender heart. Down underneath all the zeal and conviction, Nehemiah had a soft place in his heart for the living God.

I would have to say he is within the circle of my favorite Bible characters. Part of the reason is that he is so thoroughly masculine and yet at the same time so tender in his relationship to God. I find him extremely appealing.

Nehemiah's Hats

In the book that bears his name, Nehemiah wears three hats. First, he wears *the hat of dignified royalty* as the king's cupbearer. He changes hats at the end of the second chapter and wears *the hard hat of a laborer* through the sixth chapter. Finally, in the seventh chapter he puts on *the popular hat of a politician* as he assumes the role of governor of Jerusalem. Nehemiah is an unusual man whose story begins in a king's palace 800 miles from his homeland and ends in the promised land in the governor's chair—where he leads the people of Israel after their return from exile.

A Painful Setting

This book must be read in light of the circumstances surrounding the life of Nehemiah. You see, this man was a child of a Holocaust, as it were. He was born to parents who had been taken into captivity. As a result, he never knew what it was like to live as a free man until his adult years. He would likely have suffered some of the same things as those who were born into the more familiar Holocaust of the World War II generation.

Nehemiah was a man who had been deeply scarred, and yet had emerged beautifully. He had been a choice man in the eyes of the king—so much so that he was given a prized position in the very palace and private chamber of the king. He was the cupbearer, which meant that he tasted the king's food and wine before it ever came to the lips of the king. His was a position of great responsibility. His was a place of trust. The cupbearer of that day was thought to be the person, like no other except perhaps the king's wife, who had the closest communion with the king.

Nehemiah may have been living in a foreign country, but his heart was beating for Zion. He and his people had been under Babylonian rule for years, but they were now under the rule of the Persians. Two groups of exiles had already been allowed to return to their homeland and had rebuilt the temple and begun to reestablish formal worship. But now, about seventy years after the temple rebuilding had been completed, reports were coming to Nehemiah about the depressing condition of the holy city, Jerusalem. He couldn't escape the fact that Zion, the city of God, lay in ruins while he was living in luxury. His people may have had a temple in which to worship, but they had no wall to protect it.

Carrying a Burden

The news of the city's condition created a burden deep in Nehemiah's heart. He wanted to become part of the answer. As soon as Nehemiah heard about the lack of a city wall, he brought that burden to God in prayer. Nehemiah *wept* and *mourned* for days. See his tenderness? He *wept*. He was *burdened*. He *fasted* and *prayed* before the God of heaven. The balance of chapter 1 records his passionate prayer for his homeland (verses 5–11). The prayer, put in summary form, was simply this: "Lord God, if it is possible, use me to build the wall around the city I love, Jerusalem, to help protect the people who are the apple of Your eye." Nehemiah pleaded the case of a city that had been in ruins for almost three-quarters of a century.

And so Nehemiah, being a man of strength and determination, began to carry the burden in his heart for rebuilding the wall. He was a pragmatic kind of man. He pondered the situation, evaluating the vulnerability of a city without walls, knowing the need for protection. In Bible times, a city was not complete until a wall of protection was erected. It was only after the wall was built that people could occupy the city with any sense of security—because physical protection had been provided. Without walls, the people were defenseless against their enemies.

Waiting for an Open Door

Nehemiah lived with this burden for months. He was waiting for God to open the doors. Nothing changed. The situation remained the same. Have you ever had that happen? You see a need. You feel the need. You get concerned about it and you pray. You pray with such fervency that you think perhaps the situation will change tomorrow. But not only does it *not* change tomorrow, it doesn't change in a week. It doesn't change in a month. It doesn't change in three months. And after a while your patience begins to wear thin. That's what happened to Nehemiah. The strain began to show on his face. The king noticed and asked him why his face wore such a sad look. Finally! His moment had arrived. He had waited so long for the Lord to give him the open door. He had been determined not to push it open on his own. He had waited patiently for God—and now the day of opportunity had come. Nehemiah silently prayed to the God of heaven and responded to the king's question with these words: "If it pleases the king and if your servant has found favor in his sight, let him send me to the city in Judah where my fathers are buried so that I can rebuild it" (2:5).

And God answered Nehemiah's prayer! God moved in the heart of King Artaxerxes, who gave Nehemiah permission to go.

Nehemiah began the work of rebuilding the walls, but it was not without obstacles. During the process of rebuilding, Nehemiah experienced the full spectrum of all you could possibly imagine when it comes to dealing with people. In spite of opposition from without and conflict from within, Nehemiah got the job done; his faithful leadership bore fruit, and his burden was lifted. The wall was completed in less than two months after the work started (6:15). Amazing!

A Dream Becomes a Reality

Nehemiah had served as both cupbearer and builder, and as the book reaches its final chapters, his attention turned to the work of governing the people. As governor, he supported the efforts of Ezra the scribe to reestablish the worship of the true God. At the heart of the spiritual restoration was the public reading of the Book of the Law (chapter 8), a commitment to praise (9:5), confession of national sin and prayers for God's grace (chapter 9), and a new resolve to obey God's commands (chapter 10). In chapters 11–13 Nehemiah addressed certain national issues. The wall of Jerusalem was dedicated with a tremendous sense of celebration (12:27). The clanging of cymbals, the strumming of various instruments and the melodious strains of people singing at the top of their voices all joined in praise and thanksgiving to God because the wall had been built and the enemy silenced. God inhabited their praise, and the dedication was marvelous!

Lessons From Nehemiah

Three lessons linger as we look at the book of Nehemiah. First, *honest observation is the beginning of dealing with a problem*. Before there can ever be a solution, there must be detection. We have to diagnose what's wrong before it can be addressed. Nehemiah never lost the sensitivity to see things as they were. He looked around and saw compromising alliances, appalling financial habits, ill-advised friendships that would ultimately take their toll, and a general failure to obey the Word of God. Nehemiah just rolled up his sleeves and took each one on, one after another.

Nehemiah knew, and I think many of us, if we're honest, would admit, that long-standing wrongs are not easily or quickly removed. It takes time, and it usually involves a struggle to uproot them from our lives. Often our parents are the first to point out those areas of sin and weakness and immaturity in our lives that need attention. If we don't begin to address those areas, and our offensive behavior continues, then our roommate, colleague or friend may point them out again. If I may make a gentle suggestion to all of us: Let's be open to what the Lord may be trying to teach us. He may be using the tongue of another person to point out sin and weakness in our lives so we might get with it and make some changes. Change typically will not happen until the problem is detected, until it is honestly seen and confronted.

The second lesson from Nehemiah is this: *Correcting what is wrong demands fearless conviction*. I am thinking mainly of our own conviction, our own determination to change whatever needs changing in our lives. Nehemiah gives us a wonderful example of holding on to God's leading in his life, no matter what the cost or the obstacles encountered. We can learn from his example as we live for the Lord.

If we are going to make a difference in our homes, workplace, community and world, it will require a fearless commitment to the truth. We need to seek the Lord's strength, set aside personal pride and serve the Lord with passion. By means of intense prayer, sincere fasting, strong determination and unyielding commitment we must stick to the task at hand. When we do, God can and will use us to make a greater difference than we ever dreamed.

Third, and finally, *honest observation and fearless conviction must be tempered with authentic devotion*. Nehemiah had a heart for God. He didn't go running around the king's court demanding to be sent to Jerusalem. He simply got on his knees, sought the face of God and waited for Him to open a door. He knew the work would only be finished if God's hand were leading. Therefore, Nehemiah waited on God every step of the way. He was a worker, no question about that—but first and foremost, he was a man of prayer. Devotion to God first, service for God second.

Can the same be said of you?

Cupbearer to the King — Chapters 1:1–2:10

Nehemiah, like Ezra, was a child of the captivity. He was born into the home of parents who had known the horrors of exile. He had lived with the reality of being a Jewish stranger in a strange Gentile land. In these opening chapters we meet a man who had risen to a place of prominence in a foreign land, but his heart still yearned for Jerusalem—the city of God.

Nehemiah held a position of great honor and respectability. His place was one of royal stature. As cupbearer to the king he had access to the most powerful man in the kingdom. At the same time, he was a man of prayer and was deeply committed to his God. In reading these opening chapters we quickly begin to see the hand of God at work, placing the right person in the right place at the right time. Isn't that just like our Lord!

Nehemiah's Prayer

1 The words of Nehemiah son of Hacaliah:

In the month of Kislev in the twentieth year, while I was in the citadel of Susa, 2Hanani, one of my brothers, came from Judah with some other men, and I questioned them about the Jewish remnant that survived the exile, and also about Jerusalem. Ne 10:1; Zec 7:1

3They said to me, "Those who survived the exile and are back in the province are in great trouble and disgrace. The wall of Jerusalem is broken down, and its gates have been burned with fire."

4When I heard these things, I sat down and wept. For some days I mourned and fasted and prayed before the God of heaven. 5Then I said:

"O LORD, God of heaven, the great and awesome God, who keeps his covenant of love with those who love him and obey his commands, 6let your ear be attentive and your eyes open to hear the prayer your servant is praying before you day and night for your servants, the people of Israel. I confess the sins we Israelites, including myself and my father's house, have committed against you. 7We have acted very wickedly toward you. We have not obeyed the commands, decrees and laws you gave your servant Moses. Dt 28:14-15; Ne 4:14; Da 9:17

8"Remember the instruction you gave your servant Moses, saying, 'If you are unfaithful, I will scatter you among the nations, 9but if you return to me and obey my commands, then even if your exiled people are at the farthest horizon, I will gather them from there and bring them to the place I have chosen as a dwelling for my Name.'

10"They are your servants and your people, whom you redeemed by your great strength and your mighty hand. 11O Lord, let your ear be attentive to the prayer of this your servant and to the prayer of your servants who delight in revering your name. Give your servant success today by granting him favor in the presence of this man."

I was cupbearer to the king. Ge 40:1

Artaxerxes Sends Nehemiah to Jerusalem

2 In the month of Nisan in the twentieth year of King Artaxerxes, when wine was brought for him, I took the wine and gave it to the king. I had not been sad in his presence before; 2so the king asked me, "Why does your face look so sad when you are not ill? This can be nothing but sadness of heart." Ezr 7:1

I was very much afraid, 3but I said to the king, "May the king live forever! Why should my face not look sad when the city where my fathers are buried lies in ruins, and its gates have been destroyed by fire?" Ne 1:3; Da 2:4

4The king said to me, "What is it you want?"

Then I prayed to the God of heaven, 5and I answered the king, "If it pleases the king and if your servant has found favor in his sight, let him send me to the city in Judah where my fathers are buried so that I can rebuild it."

6Then the king, with the queen sitting beside him, asked me, "How long will your journey take, and when will you get back?" It pleased the king to send me; so I set a time. Ne 5:14; 13:6

7I also said to him, "If it pleases the king, may I have letters to the governors of Trans-Euphrates, so that they will provide me safe-conduct until I arrive in Judah? 8And may I have a letter to Asaph, keeper of the king's forest, so he will give me timber to make beams for the gates of the citadel by the temple and for the city wall and for the residence I will occupy?" And because the gracious hand of my God was upon me, the king granted my requests. 9So I went to the governors of Trans-Euphrates and gave them the king's letters. The king had also sent army officers and cavalry with me. Ezr 7:6; 8:22,36

10When Sanballat the Horonite and Tobiah the Ammonite official heard about this, they were very much disturbed that someone had come to promote the welfare of the Israelites. Ne 4:3; 13:4-7

Builder of the Wall — Chapters 2:11–6:19

In these chapters Nehemiah filled a new role. The splendor, comfort and privilege of the royal palace were behind him. His attire was that of a laborer and his hat was the hard hat of a construction worker. He was now in charge of the rebuilding of the wall around Jerusalem. These chapters are filled with intrigue, conflict, commitment, and finally accomplishment and victory! Along the way there were times when the workers carried out their task with trowel in hand and with swords strapped to their side because the resistance was so strong and

NEHEMIAH

The Prayer-filled Leader

"When I heard these things, I sat down and wept. For some days I mourned and fasted and prayed before the God of heaven."

—NEHEMIAH 1:4

Nehemiah's story may not be one of the most familiar in the Bible, but it is a great story nonetheless. It's about a man who heartily loved his God and his country, who courageously spoke his mind, who fearlessly stood against opposition, and who carried out a most incredible task. He did it all without fanfare, all for the purpose of sustaining his beloved nation of Israel and especially the city of Jerusalem.

When we look closely at the story of Nehemiah, we see a picture of a leader who sought *God's* leadership in his life. From him we learn four important lessons about leadership: First, *expect opposition*; second, *keep a positive perspective*; third, *fight your battles with prayer*; and fourth, *stay close to others.*

Nehemiah had a wall to build. After gaining permission from the king of Persia to go to Jerusalem, Nehemiah started his project the right way: with careful planning. He went out at night—surveying the walls, envisioning what the finished product would look like. Then he went about gathering people to help him rebuild the ruined wall that surrounded the once-great city (Nehemiah 2:18). That's when the opposition came. There were people who didn't want the wall rebuilt, because a broken-down wall gave them free access to loot the city whenever they pleased. The same group showed up again and again, causing trouble wherever they went. Sanballat, Tobiah and Geshem started small—trying to demoralize Nehemiah's crew of volunteer workers by planting seeds of doubt in their minds: "What are those feeble Jews doing? Will they restore their wall? Will they offer sacrifices? Will they finish in a day? Can they bring the stones back to life from those heaps of rubble—burned as they are?" (4:2). Later the opposition became more intense; it took the form of an open letter to the community, spreading lies about Nehemiah's motives for rebuilding the wall. And when the threats came, Nehemiah combined prayers to God with preparations to defend himself and his workers (4:9). *Nehemiah expected opposition*, and when it came, he was prepared.

Throughout this opposition phase, Nehemiah never lost his motivation or his confidence in his powerful God. *He maintained a positive perspective.* And before his enemies knew it, the job was moving along quickly: "So we rebuilt the wall till all of it reached half its height, for the people worked with all their heart" (4:6). How's that for a positive attitude? Not, "Hey, we're only half done," but "Praise God! We're done halfway!" That's the way people act who are positive and who have a perspective from God.

From the time he requested leave from the king, his former employer, *Nehemiah bathed this work in prayer.* Woven throughout this personal journal are brief prayers: "Then I prayed to the God of heaven . . ." (2:4); "Hear us, O our God, for we are despised . . ." (4:4); "Remember Tobiah and Sanballat, O my God, because of what they have done . . ." (6:14). Nehemiah's prayers turn this book into a beautifully woven tapestry of intercession before God. He fought his battles on his knees.

Finally, *Nehemiah stayed close to others.* After he inspired his cadre of volunteers with his vision for the new wall, he stayed close to them. As Solomon wrote so many years ago, "Two are better than one, because they have a good return for their work: If one falls down, his friend can help him up" (Ecclesiastes 4:9–10a). Nehemiah's friends were with him to lift him up when the opposition became intense. They worked with him and prayed with him and stood guard with him during the construction process.

Perhaps you've heard the old joke—Question: Who holds the honor of being the shortest person in the Bible? Answer: Knee-high-miah. Strangely enough, however, that tired old joke identifies the very part of Nehemiah's body that was most effective throughout his life—his knees. Nehemiah was a man who fought his battles in humility. At the times when most people would have fought back or sought to make their own way through opposition, this man fell to his knees in prayer. In that sense, he was one of the "tallest" men who ever stood on the face of the earth.

the danger of attack so close. However, through their faithful commitment and Nehemiah's determined leadership, the labor of love was completed.

Nehemiah Inspects Jerusalem's Walls

11 I went to Jerusalem, and after staying there three days 12 I set out during the night with a few men. I had not told anyone what my God had put in my heart to do for Jerusalem. There were no mounts with me except the one I was riding on.

13 By night I went out through the Valley Gate toward the Jackal[a] Well and the Dung Gate, examining the walls of Jerusalem, which had been broken down, and its gates, which had been destroyed by fire. 14 Then I moved on toward the Fountain Gate and the King's Pool, but there was not enough room for my mount to get through; 15 so I went up the valley by night, examining the wall. Finally, I turned back and reentered through the Valley Gate. 16 The officials did not know where I had gone or what I was doing, because as yet I had said nothing to the Jews or the priests or nobles or officials or any others who would be doing the work. Ne 1:3; 3:13,15

LIVING  **INSIGHT**

Looking for a role model on how to handle criticism? Check out the book of Nehemiah. On several occasions this greathearted statesman was openly criticized, falsely accused and grossly misunderstood. Each time he kept his cool, he rolled with the punch, he considered the source, he refused to get discouraged, he went to God in prayer, he kept on rebuilding the wall.

(See Nehemiah 2:11–20.)

17 Then I said to them, "You see the trouble we are in: Jerusalem lies in ruins, and its gates have been burned with fire. Come, let us rebuild the wall of Jerusalem, and we will no longer be in disgrace." 18 I also told them about the gracious hand of my God upon me and what the king had said to me. 2Sa 2:7; Ne 1:3

They replied, "Let us start rebuilding." So they began this good work.

19 But when Sanballat the Horonite, Tobiah the Ammonite official and Geshem the Arab heard about it, they mocked and ridiculed us. "What is this you are doing?" they asked. "Are you rebelling against the king?" Ps 44:13-16

20 I answered them by saying, "The God of heaven will give us success. We his servants will start rebuilding, but as for you, you have no share in Jerusalem or any claim or historic right to it."

Builders of the Wall

3 Eliashib the high priest and his fellow priests went to work and rebuilt the Sheep Gate. They dedicated it and set its doors in place, building as far as the Tower of the Hundred, which they dedicated, and as far as the Tower of Hananel. 2 The men of Jericho built the adjoining section, and Zaccur son of Imri built next to them.

3 The Fish Gate was rebuilt by the sons of Hassenaah. They laid its beams and put its doors and bolts and bars in place. 4 Meremoth son of Uriah, the son of Hakkoz, repaired the next section. Next to him Meshullam son of Berekiah, the son of Meshezabel, made repairs, and next to him Zadok son of Baana also made repairs. 5 The next section was repaired by the men of Tekoa, but their nobles would not put their shoulders to the work under their supervisors.[b] 2Sa 14:2; Ne 12:39

6 The Jeshanah[c] Gate was repaired by Joiada son of Paseah and Meshullam son of Besodeiah. They laid its beams and put its doors and bolts and bars in place. 7 Next to them, repairs were made by men from Gibeon and Mizpah—Melatiah of Gibeon and Jadon of Meronoth—places under the authority of the governor of Trans-Euphrates. 8 Uzziel son of Harhaiah, one of the goldsmiths, repaired the next section; and Hananiah, one of the perfume-makers, made repairs next to that. They restored[d] Jerusalem as far as the Broad Wall. 9 Rephaiah son of Hur, ruler of a half-district of Jerusalem, repaired the next section. 10 Adjoining this, Jedaiah son of Harumaph made repairs opposite his house, and Hattush son of Hashabneiah made repairs next to him. 11 Malkijah son of Harim and Hasshub son of Pahath-Moab repaired another section and the Tower of the Ovens. 12 Shallum son of Hallohesh, ruler of a half-district of Jerusalem, repaired the next section with the help of his daughters. Ne 2:7; 12:38-39

13 The Valley Gate was repaired by Hanun and the residents of Zanoah. They rebuilt it and put its doors and bolts and bars in place. They also repaired five hundred yards[e] of the wall as far as the Dung Gate. Ne 2:13; 2Ch 26:9

14 The Dung Gate was repaired by Malkijah son of Recab, ruler of the district of Beth Hakkerem. He rebuilt it and put its doors and bolts and bars in place. Jer 6:1

15 The Fountain Gate was repaired by Shallun son of Col-Hozeh, ruler of the district of Mizpah. He rebuilt it, roofing it over and putting its doors

[a] 13 Or *Serpent* or *Fig* [b] 5 Or *their Lord* or *the governor* [c] 6 Or *Old* [d] 8 Or *They left out part of* [e] 13 Hebrew *a thousand cubits* (about 450 meters)

and bolts and bars in place. He also repaired the wall of the Pool of Siloam,[a] by the King's Garden, as far as the steps going down from the City of David. [16]Beyond him, Nehemiah son of Azbuk, ruler of a half-district of Beth Zur, made repairs up to a point opposite the tombs[b] of David, as far as the artificial pool and the House of the Heroes.

[17]Next to him, the repairs were made by the Levites under Rehum son of Bani. Beside him, Hashabiah, ruler of half the district of Keilah, carried out repairs for his district. [18]Next to him, the repairs were made by their countrymen under Binnui[c] son of Henadad, ruler of the other half-district of Keilah. [19]Next to him, Ezer son of Jeshua, ruler of Mizpah, repaired another section, from a point facing the ascent to the armory as far as the angle. [20]Next to him, Baruch son of Zabbai zealously repaired another section, from the angle to the entrance of the house of Eliashib the high priest. [21]Next to him, Meremoth son of Uriah, the son of Hakkoz, repaired another section, from the entrance of Eliashib's house to the end of it.

[22]The repairs next to him were made by the priests from the surrounding region. [23]Beyond them, Benjamin and Hasshub made repairs in front of their house; and next to them, Azariah son of Maaseiah, the son of Ananiah, made repairs beside his house. [24]Next to him, Binnui son of Henadad repaired another section, from Azariah's house to the angle and the corner, [25]and Palal son of Uzai worked opposite the angle and the tower projecting from the upper palace near the court of the guard. Next to him, Pedaiah son of Parosh [26]and the temple servants living on the hill of Ophel made repairs up to a point opposite the Water Gate toward the east and the projecting tower. [27]Next to them, the men of Tekoa repaired another section, from the great projecting tower to the wall of Ophel. Ne 8:1,3,16; Jer 32:2

[28]Above the Horse Gate, the priests made repairs, each in front of his own house. [29]Next to them, Zadok son of Immer made repairs opposite his house. Next to him, Shemaiah son of Shecaniah, the guard at the East Gate, made repairs. [30]Next to him, Hananiah son of Shelemiah, and Hanun, the sixth son of Zalaph, repaired another section. Next to them, Meshullam son of Berekiah made repairs opposite his living quarters. [31]Next to him, Malkijah, one of the goldsmiths, made repairs as far as the house of the temple servants and the merchants, opposite the Inspection Gate, and as far as the room above the corner; [32]and between the room above the corner and the Sheep Gate the goldsmiths and merchants made repairs.

Opposition to the Rebuilding

4 When Sanballat heard that we were rebuilding the wall, he became angry and was greatly incensed. He ridiculed the Jews, [2]and in the presence of his associates and the army of Samaria, he said, "What are those feeble Jews doing? Will they restore their wall? Will they offer sacrifices? Will they finish in a day? Can they bring the stones back to life from those heaps of rubble—burned as they are?" Ne 2:10; Ps 79:1

[3]Tobiah the Ammonite, who was at his side, said, "What they are building—if even a fox climbed up on it, he would break down their wall of stones!" Ne 2:10; Job 13:12

[4]Hear us, O our God, for we are despised. Turn their insults back on their own heads. Give them over as plunder in a land of captivity. [5]Do not cover up their guilt or blot out their sins from your sight, for they have thrown insults in the face of[d] the builders. Ps 69:27-28; Jer 18:23

[6]So we rebuilt the wall till all of it reached half its height, for the people worked with all their heart.

[7]But when Sanballat, Tobiah, the Arabs, the Ammonites and the men of Ashdod heard that the repairs to Jerusalem's walls had gone ahead and that the gaps were being closed, they were very angry. [8]They all plotted together to come and fight against Jerusalem and stir up trouble against it. [9]But we prayed to our God and posted a guard day and night to meet this threat. Ps 2:2; 83:1-18

[10]Meanwhile, the people in Judah said, "The strength of the laborers is giving out, and there is so much rubble that we cannot rebuild the wall."

[11]Also our enemies said, "Before they know it or see us, we will be right there among them and will kill them and put an end to the work."

[12]Then the Jews who lived near them came and told us ten times over, "Wherever you turn, they will attack us."

[13]Therefore I stationed some of the people behind the lowest points of the wall at the exposed places, posting them by families, with their swords, spears and bows. [14]After I looked things over, I stood up and said to the nobles, the officials and the rest of the people, "Don't be afraid of them. Remember the Lord, who is great and awesome, and fight for your brothers, your sons and your daughters, your wives and your homes." Nu 14:9

[15]When our enemies heard that we were aware of their plot and that God had frustrated it, we all returned to the wall, each to his own work.

[16]From that day on, half of my men did the work, while the other half were equipped with

[a]15 Hebrew *Shelah,* a variant of *Shiloah,* that is, Siloam [b]16 Hebrew; Septuagint, some Vulgate manuscripts and Syriac *tomb* [c]18 Two Hebrew manuscripts and Syriac (see also Septuagint and verse 24); most Hebrew manuscripts *Bavvai*
[d]5 Or *have provoked you to anger before*

spears, shields, bows and armor. The officers posted themselves behind all the people of Judah [17]who were building the wall. Those who carried materials did their work with one hand and held a weapon in the other, [18]and each of the builders wore his sword at his side as he worked. But the man who sounded the trumpet stayed with me. Nu 10:2

[19]Then I said to the nobles, the officials and the rest of the people, "The work is extensive and spread out, and we are widely separated from each other along the wall. [20]Wherever you hear the sound of the trumpet, join us there. Our God will fight for us!" Ex 14:14; Dt 1:30; 20:4

[21]So we continued the work with half the men holding spears, from the first light of dawn till the stars came out. [22]At that time I also said to the people, "Have every man and his helper stay inside Jerusalem at night, so they can serve us as guards by night and workmen by day." [23]Neither I nor my brothers nor my men nor the guards with me took off our clothes; each had his weapon, even when he went for water.[a]

LIVING  INSIGHT

People who are in great demand today are those who can see an "end result" in their imaginations—then pull it off. Those who can think—and then follow through. Those who dress their daring dreams in practical denim work clothes. That takes a measure of gift, a pinch of skill and a ton of discipline!

(See Nehemiah 4:21–23.)

Nehemiah Helps the Poor

5 Now the men and their wives raised a great outcry against their Jewish brothers. [2]Some were saying, "We and our sons and daughters are numerous; in order for us to eat and stay alive, we must get grain."

[3]Others were saying, "We are mortgaging our fields, our vineyards and our homes to get grain during the famine." Ge 47:23; Ps 109:11

[4]Still others were saying, "We have had to borrow money to pay the king's tax on our fields and vineyards. [5]Although we are of the same flesh and blood as our countrymen and though our sons are as good as theirs, yet we have to subject our sons and daughters to slavery. Some of our daughters have already been enslaved, but we are powerless, because our fields and our vineyards belong to others." Lev 25:39-43,47; Ezr 4:13

[6]When I heard their outcry and these charges, I was very angry. [7]I pondered them in my mind and then accused the nobles and officials. I told them, "You are exacting usury from your own countrymen!" So I called together a large meeting to deal with them [8]and said: "As far as possible, we have bought back our Jewish brothers who were sold to the Gentiles. Now you are selling your brothers, only for them to be sold back to us!" They kept quiet, because they could find nothing to say. Ex 22:25-27; Lev 25:35-37,47

[9]So I continued, "What you are doing is not right. Shouldn't you walk in the fear of our God to avoid the reproach of our Gentile enemies? [10]I and my brothers and my men are also lending the people money and grain. But let the exacting of usury stop! [11]Give back to them immediately their fields, vineyards, olive groves and houses, and also the usury you are charging them—the hundredth part of the money, grain, new wine and oil."

[12]"We will give it back," they said. "And we will not demand anything more from them. We will do as you say."

Then I summoned the priests and made the nobles and officials take an oath to do what they had promised. [13]I also shook out the folds of my robe and said, "In this way may God shake out of his house and possessions every man who does not keep this promise. So may such a man be shaken out and emptied!"

At this the whole assembly said, "Amen," and praised the LORD. And the people did as they had promised. Ezr 10:5; Mt 10:14; Ac 18:6

[14]Moreover, from the twentieth year of King Artaxerxes, when I was appointed to be their governor in the land of Judah, until his thirty-second year—twelve years—neither I nor my brothers ate the food allotted to the governor. [15]But the earlier governors—those preceding me—placed a heavy burden on the people and took forty shekels[b] of silver from them in addition to food and wine. Their assistants also lorded it over the people. But out of reverence for God I did not act like that. [16]Instead, I devoted myself to the work on this wall. All my men were assembled there for the work; we[c] did not acquire any land. Ne 13:6

[17]Furthermore, a hundred and fifty Jews and officials ate at my table, as well as those who came to us from the surrounding nations. [18]Each day one ox, six choice sheep and some poultry were prepared for me, and every ten days an abundant supply of wine of all kinds. In spite of all this, I never demanded the food allotted to the governor, because the demands were heavy on these people.

[19]Remember me with favor, O my God, for all I have done for these people. Ge 8:1; Ne 1:8; 13:14,22,31

[a] *23* The meaning of the Hebrew for this clause is uncertain. [b] *15* That is, about 1 pound (about 0.5 kilogram)
[c] *16* Most Hebrew manuscripts; some Hebrew manuscripts, Septuagint, Vulgate and Syriac *I*

Further Opposition to the Rebuilding

6 When word came to Sanballat, Tobiah, Geshem the Arab and the rest of our enemies that I had rebuilt the wall and not a gap was left in it—though up to that time I had not set the doors in the gates— 2Sanballat and Geshem sent me this message: "Come, let us meet together in one of the villages[a] on the plain of Ono." 1Ch 8:12; Ne 2:10,19

But they were scheming to harm me; 3so I sent messengers to them with this reply: "I am carrying on a great project and cannot go down. Why should the work stop while I leave it and go down to you?" 4Four times they sent me the same message, and each time I gave them the same answer.

5Then, the fifth time, Sanballat sent his aide to me with the same message, and in his hand was an unsealed letter 6in which was written: Ne 2:10

"It is reported among the nations—and Geshem[b] says it is true—that you and the Jews are plotting to revolt, and therefore you are building the wall. Moreover, according to these reports you are about to become their king 7and have even appointed prophets to make this proclamation about you in Jerusalem: 'There is a king in Judah!' Now this report will get back to the king; so come, let us confer together." Ne 2:19

8I sent him this reply: "Nothing like what you are saying is happening; you are just making it up out of your head."

9They were all trying to frighten us, thinking, "Their hands will get too weak for the work, and it will not be completed."

⌊But I prayed,⌋ "Now strengthen my hands."

10One day I went to the house of Shemaiah son of Delaiah, the son of Mehetabel, who was shut in at his home. He said, "Let us meet in the house of God, inside the temple, and let us close the temple doors, because men are coming to kill you—by night they are coming to kill you." Nu 18:7

11But I said, "Should a man like me run away? Or should one like me go into the temple to save his life? I will not go!" 12I realized that God had not sent him, but that he had prophesied against me because Tobiah and Sanballat had hired him. 13He had been hired to intimidate me so that I would commit a sin by doing this, and then they would give me a bad name to discredit me. Ne 2:10

14Remember Tobiah and Sanballat, O my God, because of what they have done; remember also the prophetess Noadiah and the rest of the prophets who have been trying to intimidate me.

The Completion of the Wall

15So the wall was completed on the twenty-fifth of Elul, in fifty-two days. 16When all our enemies heard about this, all the surrounding nations were afraid and lost their self-confidence, because they realized that this work had been done with the help of our God.

17Also, in those days the nobles of Judah were sending many letters to Tobiah, and replies from Tobiah kept coming to them. 18For many in Judah were under oath to him, since he was son-in-law to Shecaniah son of Arah, and his son Jehohanan had married the daughter of Meshullam son of Berekiah. 19Moreover, they kept reporting to me his good deeds and then telling him what I said. And Tobiah sent letters to intimidate me.

Governor of the People — Chapters 7–13

Once the wall was rebuilt and the city secure, the people celebrated and dedicated themselves to the Lord. Their celebration was unique because of the way it began. First, before the food, drink, songs and dancing . . . *they read the Word of the Lord.* Through the leadership of Nehemiah and Ezra, the people gathered together to hear God's Holy Word read in their presence. This focus on God's truth brought tears (8:9) and joy (8:12)—the hearts of the people were visibly moved. After the reading of the Law, the governor, Nehemiah, invited the people to eat choice food and to enjoy sweet drinks (8:10). First, they feasted on the sweet fruits of heavenly food . . . God's Word, and then they partook of the goodness of earthly foods. What a picture of celebration!

In a spirit of humility and contrition, the people experienced revival as they recommitted their lives to obeying God's Word and seeking His will (chapters 9–10). The final chapters (11–13) record certain national issues addressed by Nehemiah.

7 After the wall had been rebuilt and I had set the doors in place, the gatekeepers and the singers and the Levites were appointed. 2I put in charge of Jerusalem my brother Hanani, along with[c] Hananiah the commander of the citadel, because he was a man of integrity and feared God

LIVING  INSIGHT

True integrity implies you do what is right when no one is looking or when everyone is compromising.

(See Nehemiah 7:2.)

more than most men do. 3I said to them, "The gates of Jerusalem are not to be opened until the sun is hot. While the gatekeepers are still on duty, have them shut the doors and bar them. Also appoint residents of Jerusalem as guards, some at their posts and some near their own houses."

[a]2 Or *in Kephirim* [b]6 Hebrew *Gashmu,* a variant of *Geshem* [c]2 Or *Hanani, that is,*

The List of the Exiles Who Returned

[4]Now the city was large and spacious, but there
were few people in it, and the houses had not yet
been rebuilt. [5]So my God put it into my heart to
assemble the nobles, the officials and the common
people for registration by families. I found the
genealogical record of those who had been the first
to return. This is what I found written there:

[6]These are the people of the province who
came up from the captivity of the exiles
whom Nebuchadnezzar king of Babylon had
taken captive (they returned to Jerusalem
and Judah, each to his own town, [7]in company with Zerubbabel, Jeshua, Nehemiah, Azariah, Raamiah, Nahamani, Mordecai, Bilshan, Mispereth, Bigvai, Nehum and
Baanah): Ezr 2:1-70; Ne 1:2

The list of the men of Israel:

[8]the descendants of Parosh 2,172
[9]of Shephatiah 372
[10]of Arah 652
[11]of Pahath-Moab (through the line of Jeshua and Joab) 2,818
[12]of Elam 1,254
[13]of Zattu 845
[14]of Zaccai 760
[15]of Binnui 648
[16]of Bebai 628
[17]of Azgad 2,322
[18]of Adonikam 667
[19]of Bigvai 2,067
[20]of Adin 655
[21]of Ater (through Hezekiah) 98
[22]of Hashum 328
[23]of Bezai 324
[24]of Hariph 112
[25]of Gibeon 95
[26]the men of Bethlehem and Netophah 188
[27]of Anathoth 128
[28]of Beth Azmaveth 42
[29]of Kiriath Jearim, Kephirah and Beeroth 743
[30]of Ramah and Geba 621
[31]of Micmash 122
[32]of Bethel and Ai 123
[33]of the other Nebo 52
[34]of the other Elam 1,254
[35]of Harim 320
[36]of Jericho 345
[37]of Lod, Hadid and Ono 721
[38]of Senaah 3,930

[39]The priests:

the descendants of Jedaiah (through the family of Jeshua) 973
[40]of Immer 1,052
[41]of Pashhur 1,247
[42]of Harim 1,017

[43]The Levites:

the descendants of Jeshua (through Kadmiel through the line of Hodaviah) 74

[44]The singers:

the descendants of Asaph 148

[45]The gatekeepers:

the descendants of Shallum, Ater, Talmon, Akkub, Hatita and Shobai 138

[46]The temple servants:

the descendants of
Ziha, Hasupha, Tabbaoth,
[47]Keros, Sia, Padon,
[48]Lebana, Hagaba, Shalmai,
[49]Hanan, Giddel, Gahar,
[50]Reaiah, Rezin, Nekoda,
[51]Gazzam, Uzza, Paseah,
[52]Besai, Meunim, Nephussim,
[53]Bakbuk, Hakupha, Harhur,
[54]Bazluth, Mehida, Harsha,
[55]Barkos, Sisera, Temah,
[56]Neziah and Hatipha

[57]The descendants of the servants of Solomon:

the descendants of
Sotai, Sophereth, Perida,
[58]Jaala, Darkon, Giddel,
[59]Shephatiah, Hattil,
Pokereth-Hazzebaim and Amon

[60]The temple servants and the descendants of the servants of Solomon 392

[61]The following came up from the towns
of Tel Melah, Tel Harsha, Kerub, Addon and
Immer, but they could not show that their
families were descended from Israel:

[62]the descendants of
Delaiah, Tobiah and Nekoda 642

[63]And from among the priests:

the descendants of
Hobaiah, Hakkoz and Barzillai (a man who had married a daughter of Barzillai the Gileadite and was called by that name).

[64]These searched for their family records,
but they could not find them and so were
excluded from the priesthood as unclean.
[65]The governor, therefore, ordered them not
to eat any of the most sacred food until there

should be a priest ministering with the Urim and Thummim. Ex 28:30; Ne 8:9

66 The whole company numbered 42,360, 67 besides their 7,337 menservants and maidservants; and they also had 245 men and women singers. 68 There were 736 horses, 245 mules,[a] 69 435 camels and 6,720 donkeys.

70 Some of the heads of the families contributed to the work. The governor gave to the treasury 1,000 drachmas[b] of gold, 50 bowls and 530 garments for priests. 71 Some of the heads of the families gave to the treasury for the work 20,000 drachmas[c] of gold and 2,200 minas[d] of silver. 72 The total given by the rest of the people was 20,000 drachmas of gold, 2,000 minas[e] of silver and 67 garments for priests. Ex 25:2; 1Ch 29:7

73 The priests, the Levites, the gatekeepers, the singers and the temple servants, along with certain of the people and the rest of the Israelites, settled in their own towns. Ezr 3:1

Ezra Reads the Law

When the seventh month came and the Israelites had settled in their towns, 8 1 all the people assembled as one man in the square before the Water Gate. They told Ezra the scribe to bring out the Book of the Law of Moses, which the LORD had commanded for Israel. Dt 28:61; Ne 3:26; Ezr 7:6

LIVING  **INSIGHT**

If I could have only one wish for God's people, it would be that all of us would return to the Word of God, that we would realize once and for all that His Book has the answers to life's deepest and most important questions.

(See Nehemiah 8:1–3.)

2 So on the first day of the seventh month Ezra the priest brought the Law before the assembly, which was made up of men and women and all who were able to understand. 3 He read it aloud from daybreak till noon as he faced the square before the Water Gate in the presence of the men, women and others who could understand. And all the people listened attentively to the Book of the Law. Lev 23:23-25; Dt 31:11; Ne 3:26

4 Ezra the scribe stood on a high wooden platform built for the occasion. Beside him on his right stood Mattithiah, Shema, Anaiah, Uriah, Hilkiah and Maaseiah; and on his left were Pedaiah, Mishael, Malkijah, Hashum, Hashbaddanah, Zechariah and Meshullam. 2Ch 6:13

5 Ezra opened the book. All the people could see him because he was standing above them; and as he opened it, the people all stood up. 6 Ezra praised the LORD, the great God; and all the people lifted their hands and responded, "Amen! Amen!" Then they bowed down and worshiped the LORD with their faces to the ground. Ex 4:31; Ezr 9:5; 1Ti 2:8

7 The Levites—Jeshua, Bani, Sherebiah, Jamin, Akkub, Shabbethai, Hodiah, Maaseiah, Kelita, Azariah, Jozabad, Hanan and Pelaiah—instructed the people in the Law while the people were standing there. 8 They read from the Book of the Law of God, making it clear[f] and giving the meaning so that the people could understand what was being read. Lev 10:11; 2Ch 17:7

9 Then Nehemiah the governor, Ezra the priest and scribe, and the Levites who were instructing the people said to them all, "This day is sacred to the LORD your God. Do not mourn or weep." For all the people had been weeping as they listened to the words of the Law. Ne 7:1,65,70; Dt 12:7,12; 16:14-15

10 Nehemiah said, "Go and enjoy choice food and sweet drinks, and send some to those who have nothing prepared. This day is sacred to our Lord. Do not grieve, for the joy of the LORD is your strength." Lev 23:40; Dt 12:18; Lk 14:12-14

11 The Levites calmed all the people, saying, "Be still, for this is a sacred day. Do not grieve."

12 Then all the people went away to eat and drink, to send portions of food and to celebrate with great joy, because they now understood the words that had been made known to them.

13 On the second day of the month, the heads of all the families, along with the priests and the Levites, gathered around Ezra the scribe to give attention to the words of the Law. 14 They found written in the Law, which the LORD had commanded through Moses, that the Israelites were to live in booths during the feast of the seventh month 15 and that they should proclaim this word and spread it throughout their towns and in Jerusalem: "Go out into the hill country and bring back branches from olive and wild olive trees, and from myrtles, palms and shade trees, to make booths"—as it is written.[g]

16 So the people went out and brought back branches and built themselves booths on their own roofs, in their courtyards, in the courts of the house of God and in the square by the Water Gate and the one by the Gate of Ephraim. 17 The whole company that had returned from exile built booths and lived in them. From the days of Joshua son of

[a] *68* Some Hebrew manuscripts (see also Ezra 2:66); most Hebrew manuscripts do not have this verse. [b] *70* That is, about 19 pounds (about 8.5 kilograms) [c] *71* That is, about 375 pounds (about 170 kilograms); also in verse 72 [d] *71* That is, about 1 1/3 tons (about 1.2 metric tons) [e] *72* That is, about 1 1/4 tons (about 1.1 metric tons) [f] *8* Or *God, translating it* [g] *15* See Lev. 23:37-40.

Let It Shine! Let It Shine!

*"Ezra opened the book. All the people could see him because
he was standing above them; and as he opened it, the people all stood up.
Ezra praised the LORD, the great God; and all the people lifted their hands
and responded, 'Amen! Amen!' Then they bowed down
and worshiped the LORD with their faces to the ground."*
—NEHEMIAH 8:5–6

A.W. Tozer once said, "Worship is the missing jewel of the evangelical church." Even though decades have passed since Tozer first said it, I'm afraid the jewel, in most places of our world, is still missing. And the tragedy is intensified by the fact that there don't seem to be many in the church who are looking very hard for it. The jewel, most unfortunately, often remains hidden.

Stop and think. You may have walked through the doors and sat in the pews of lots of churches, as I have. There are formal churches, casual churches, Bible-teaching churches, evangelistic churches, beautiful churches, small, lovely and even quaint churches. We have seen discipling churches, growing churches, dying churches, busy churches, renewal churches, denominational churches, liturgical churches, independent churches; yes, even a few that call themselves "New Testament churches." But chances are we can count on both hands (with fingers left over) the churches we attended that were *worshiping* churches . . . places where we genuinely sensed the awesome presence of Almighty God . . . where we left wholly absorbed in the greatness and glory of God.

When I think of a worshiping church, I envision a place where there is balance. A solid message from the Scriptures, as well as an accompanying blend of music and prayer with sufficient quietness that exalts the living God whom you came to worship. And along with all that, appropriate, distinct themes of careful thought conveyed through well-chosen words—freedom from clichés, without all the inane side comments and program hype that seem, without fail, to interrupt true worship. I am envisioning, in short, those settings where we encounter the presence of the living God and find ourselves, as Charles Wesley expressed it, "lost in wonder, love and praise." These are settings where we can catch a glimpse of the Lord as Isaiah saw Him: "high and exalted" (Isaiah 6:1). When we find such places of worship, we truly have rediscovered a missing jewel.

Entering into Worship

How am I to enter into the experience of worship? How am I to let it shine in my life and in the corporate life of my church family? I think I have found something of the answer, thanks to God's Book. At the center of our English Bible, in the hymnbook known as the book of Psalms, is a grand statement of invitation found in Psalm 95. I'd like us to think about that ancient hymn—to ponder the truth that has been preserved for centuries.

If we sometimes struggle with worship as something "too elusive," we must be equally concerned about making it too mechanical. I deliberately resist suggesting something like "Five Simple Steps to Worship," or "Worship Made Easy—Here's How!" I have no plan to package it so that you are able, after reading this article, to pass along several "transferable concepts" of worship. But perhaps you will grasp what I'm driving at as you digest these thoughts. Like the Scottish people say, "Some things are better felt than telt."

The Identity and Meaning of Worship

I'd like you to "feel" what worship is—by way of Psalm 95. I'd like you to experience the emotions flowing from the psalmist's pen as you read this passage. Let's see if an age-old hymn can help us get a handle on this jewel called worship:

Come, let us sing for joy to the LORD;
let us shout aloud to the Rock of our salvation.
Let us come before him with thanksgiving
and extol him with music and song.
For the LORD is the great God,
the great King above all gods.
In his hand are the depths of the earth,
and the mountain peaks belong to him.
The sea is his, for he made it,
and his hands formed the dry land.
Come, let us bow down in worship,
let us kneel before the LORD our Maker;
for he is our God
and we are the people of his pasture,
the flock under his care.

Why should we come before our God with thanksgiving and joyful shouts? Why take the psalmist up on his invitation? Because our God is great. He deserves our highest praise. From the deepest place on earth, which would be in the bottom of the sea, to the highest peak in the Himalayan mountain range—earth's highest spot—from depth to height, our God is above and over all things. And Someone that awesome, that great, is deserving of our awe-filled, silent praise as well as our exuberantly vocal, melodious praise. Our God is great! He is above *all* other gods; He is great . . . greater than the ear-splitting depths and the dizzy, towering heights.

Did you know that the most basic meaning of worship is the thought of being on one's face—as if to kiss the feet of the one you worship. And to intensify such a position of abject submission, ancient worshipers would kneel, place the palms of their hands on the ground, and remain in the prone position, with their faces hidden before God. Try *that* sometime!

In worship we become preoccupied with the Lord. We don't watch something happen; we *participate* in it. It isn't like going to a football game and seeing a few players knocking themselves out on a field. It's coming to a place in one's life, either alone, with a few, or with many, where one "connects" with the living God. It is almost as though we could reach out and touch Him as we draw near to the God who, in reality, draws near to us.

The most succinct definition I can come up with is this: *Worship is a human response to a divine revelation.* God has said something, and we respond to it. God is doing things, and we respond to what He is doing. On occasion, the most appropriate response may be absolute silence as we meditate on the awesome power and love of our God. On other occasions, the best response may be in the loudest possible voice of praise. An amazing reality about worship is that you don't care what anybody else thinks as your heart is lifted up in profound awe and penetrating gratitude. It's as if everything else is blocked out as you are being "touched" by God. Yes, touched—not literally, but symbolically, figuratively. Although this touch is intangible, it is more powerful than the touch of any other human being. In essence, our worship is an active, open, unguarded response to God, whereby we declare His worth in an intimate, spontaneous manner, leaving Him room to touch us and to flood us with His glorious and life-transforming presence.

The Significance and Purpose of Worship

What happens when this spiritual "connection" occurs? Whether it's in a gathering of thousands, or when I'm alone in a closet of prayer and communion with Him, what happens? First, *worship magnifies our God*. He is "the great God, the great King above all gods" (Psalm 95:3). He is the only One who is worthy of our worship. All else is eclipsed in His presence and becomes less significant as we stand in awe at His glory and His grace.

Second, *worship enlarges our horizons and changes our perspective.* We begin to see beyond the self-imposed fences of our own limitations. We begin to look at life through a new set of lenses. We employ a different paradigm. It is nothing short of remarkable. An attitude on Friday is frequently different than on a Monday, because sandwiched between a Friday and a Monday is a worship service in which our whole perspective undergoes change.

Third, *worship eclipses our fears and refreshes our spirit.* We soon forget those things that gnaw at us, claw at our minds and preoccupy our thoughts. A bold confidence grows in our hearts as the Almighty God surrounds and fills us. How can we possibly describe this? Like a drink of cool water filling a parched and dry soul, we are renewed again!

Fourth, *worship enhances our work.* When we put worship to work in our lives, when we see worship as a response to God woven through the fabric of our day, it's amazing how our attitude toward tasks changes. Life takes on a melodious dimension that sets our hearts to singing. At this point I have to say more about music. Few things bring out the beauty and luster of worship like music. God gave us a song to sing! His longest book in Scripture is the ancient Psalter—the collection of psalms. Then why do we so often resist giving music a prominent place, especially music that is so fundamentally centered around the Word of God? Music is not simply a "preliminary." Music is not something that is tacked on at the end or slipped in at the beginning. Nor is it a "filler." It's not something we do while getting ready for the "important" part. A worshiping church is a singing church, because music is vital to worship. And I'm including here the grand hymns, the stately songs, as well as the newer choruses of worship and praise.

I wonder why it is that the song has dried up in our hearts? Why are there so few who sing, including the pastors . . . I mean who really sing heartily to the Lord with full and unrestrained voice. Stop and consider. I wouldn't doubt if fewer people than ever sing in the shower any more. How many of you in a business or profession hear your partner humming a song? How many do you see singing out joyfully on a freeway? No wonder our singing is so restrained and puny on the Lord's Day . . . most don't sing much the rest of the week. It's time to bring back this God-given expression of adoration. Let us sing, sing, sing!

Overlooked Facets of the Jewel

There are at least three facets of the missing jewel of worship that are easily overlooked. As I mention them, perhaps you will find fresh motivation to cultivate a greater love for worship.

First, *worship is sought by God.* Listen to the words Jesus spoke to the Samaritan woman at the well: "Yet a time is coming and has now come when the true worshipers will worship the Father in spirit and truth, for they are the kind of worshipers the Father seeks. God is spirit, and his worshipers must worship in spirit and in truth" (John 4:23–24).

Our worship *must* be in keeping with the revealed Word of God. The Bible is God's Book of truth. And our worship must be in spirit, which expresses the depth of our emotions and our love for God. True, healthy worship, the worship God desires, combines both our heads and our hearts. Until we integrate both, we aren't worshiping as God intends. Our heavenly Father *seeks* worshipers who blend spirit and truth.

Second, *worship has been practiced in the past.* If I had the time to trace where worship occurs in history, according to Scripture, I could literally take you from Genesis to Revelation. Do you know the first appearance of worship in the Bible? It will surprise you. The first act of worship is mentioned in verses 3 and 4 of Genesis 4, when Cain and Abel brought their gifts to God. God looked with favor on Abel's offering, because it reflected a gift from his heart, while the offering of Cain lacked the same depth of love and sacrifice. The first time the *word* "worship" is mentioned is in verse 5 of Genesis 22, when Abraham is about to sacrifice his son Isaac on the altar. The old patriarch said to his friends: "Stay here with the donkey while I and the boy go over there. We will worship and then we will come back to you."

And then there's Job, that great suffering saint from the time of the patriarchs, who engaged in worship after he had lost everything. Sitting bankrupt, grieved and humiliated in sackcloth and ashes he said, "Naked I came from my mother's womb, and naked I will depart. The LORD gave and the LORD has taken away; may the name of the LORD be praised" (Job 1:21).

It's possible to worship anywhere . . . even on a hospital bed! It is possible to worship when bankrupt, bruised and beaten. Worship doesn't require comfortable surroundings, organ music or synthesizer, or padded seats on a church pew. You don't have to have beautiful music or an orchestra or the words of songs projected onto a screen. Those things may help enhance it, but worship is more a matter of our hearts—as it was for Abel and for Abraham and for Job.

Third, *worship requires our participation today*. Worship is not merely something to be enjoyed as a spectator, but more important, it is something to *do as a participant*. Worship is not dreamy and passive. Worship is something we *do*. We need to be energetically involved in the corporate acts of singing, praying, listening, offering our hearts and gifts, confessing our sins, and so forth. But worship also has a personal dimension: "Therefore, I urge you, brothers, in view of God's mercy, to offer your bodies as living sacrifices holy and pleasing to God—this is your spiritual act of worship" (Romans 12:1).

Do you serve on a board or on a committee in your church? Believe it or not, that's to be an experience of worship. Do you teach a class of children or teenagers or adults? That is your worship . . . "your spiritual act of worship." Do you sing in a choir? Do you play an instrument in the church orchestra or praise team? Do you sing as a soloist or as a part of an ensemble? *Whatever* it is you do is a statement of worship as you proclaim the gospel to others. Do you work behind the scenes, outside of the public eye, as you give time to young people or to adults or to children? That is your worship. Do you give regularly and sacrificially to the work of God? Do you realize that God calls your sacrificial giving your "spiritual act of worship"—whether it be corporate (with others) or personal (by yourself)? Giving is worship! It will revolutionize your whole concept of Christian service if you think of all your involvements as acts of worship.

Sparkling Beauty of the Jewel

A. W. Tozer was right. Worship has been the missing jewel of the evangelical church. But I would like to add: It need not *remain* missing. Let's make a difference! Let's risk being innovative . . . let's cultivate a renewed appreciation for and participation in active, fulfilling worship. In brief, let's celebrate God!

There are three important questions to ask yourself about worship. First, *does your public worship sparkle with a sense of expectancy and an openness to a variety of ways to worship God*? If you want that to happen, start letting the hymns and choruses speak to you. Allow your mind to meditate on the significance of each act of worship, even the music being played as you enter and as you leave. Let the sparkle of genuine worship return. Let it shine!

Second, *does your personal worship sparkle with quality and consistency*? Years ago, during my months as a Marine in Southeast Asia, I was working closely with a man who was trying to help me understand personal worship. He was going through a very, very low time in his life. I went by his home one afternoon to find him, and he wasn't there. His wife said, "I think he's down at his office." It had begun to rain. By the time I got to his office down in the center of town, it was pouring. I made my way around the corner to this little, inauspicious office where he met with God. Before I saw him, I could hear him. I could hear him singing the lines from that great hymn, "Come, Thou Fount of Every Blessing." I stood alone in the darkness and the rain, listening . . . pondering the truth I heard expressed so beautifully from the man's lips:

> *Prone to wander, Lord, I feel it, Prone to leave the God I love:*
> *Here's my heart, O take and seal it, Seal it for Thy courts above.*

As I stood outside that simple little room, I felt I was standing on sacred soil. His personal worship was obvious to me. And I walked away having learned more in that brief moment than I could have learned in a year of instruction. He worshiped publicly, because he had first worshiped personally.

Third, and finally, *has something taken the sparkle out of your worship*? If so, it's time to do some soul-searching. Probe deeply. Whatever it is that is stealing your joy and sucking the life out of your worship must be removed. Yes, it must! Until that happens, I must warn you, you will continue to do little more than "play church" on the day set aside for worship.

If you love God, if you love His Word, if you love the doctrines revealed in His Word, if you love to express it in song and in reverent silence, then I encourage you to become an active participant in worship. Find the jewel, and let it shine! Let it shine!

Nun until that day, the Israelites had not celebrated it like this. And their joy was very great.
18Day after day, from the first day to the last,
Ezra read from the Book of the Law of God. They
celebrated the feast for seven days, and on the
eighth day, in accordance with the regulation,
there was an assembly. Nu 29:35; Dt 31:11

The Israelites Confess Their Sins

9 On the twenty-fourth day of the same month,
the Israelites gathered together, fasting and
wearing sackcloth and having dust on their heads.
2Those of Israelite descent had separated themselves from all foreigners. They stood in their
places and confessed their sins and the wickedness
of their fathers. 3They stood where they were and
read from the Book of the Law of the LORD their
God for a quarter of the day, and spent another
quarter in confession and in worshiping the LORD
their God. 4Standing on the stairs were the Levites—Jeshua, Bani, Kadmiel, Shebaniah, Bunni,
Sherebiah, Bani and Kenani—who called with
loud voices to the LORD their God. 5And the Levites—Jeshua, Kadmiel, Bani, Hashabneiah, Sherebiah, Hodiah, Shebaniah and Pethahiah—said:
"Stand up and praise the LORD your God, who is
from everlasting to everlasting.[a]" 1Sa 4:12; Ezr 10:11

"Blessed be your glorious name, and may
it be exalted above all blessing and praise.
6You alone are the LORD. You made the
heavens, even the highest heavens, and all
their starry host, the earth and all that is on
it, the seas and all that is in them. You give
life to everything, and the multitudes of
heaven worship you. Ge 1:1; 2Ki 19:15; Ps 95:5
7"You are the LORD God, who chose
Abram and brought him out of Ur of the
Chaldeans and named him Abraham. 8You
found his heart faithful to you, and you made
a covenant with him to give to his descendants the land of the Canaanites, Hittites,
Amorites, Perizzites, Jebusites and Girgashites. You have kept your promise because
you are righteous. Ge 15:6,18-21; Ezr 9;15
9"You saw the suffering of our forefathers
in Egypt; you heard their cry at the Red
Sea.[b] 10You sent miraculous signs and wonders against Pharaoh, against all his officials
and all the people of his land, for you knew
how arrogantly the Egyptians treated them.
You made a name for yourself, which remains to this day. 11You divided the sea before them, so that they passed through it on
dry ground, but you hurled their pursuers
into the depths, like a stone into mighty waters. 12By day you led them with a pillar of
cloud, and by night with a pillar of fire to
give them light on the way they were to take.
13"You came down on Mount Sinai; you
spoke to them from heaven. You gave them
regulations and laws that are just and right,
and decrees and commands that are good.
14You made known to them your holy Sabbath and gave them commands, decrees and
laws through your servant Moses. 15In their
hunger you gave them bread from heaven
and in their thirst you brought them water
from the rock; you told them to go in and
take possession of the land you had sworn
with uplifted hand to give them. Ex 16:4; 17:6
16"But they, our forefathers, became arrogant and stiff-necked, and did not obey your
commands. 17They refused to listen and
failed to remember the miracles you performed among them. They became stiff-
necked and in their rebellion appointed a
leader in order to return to their slavery. But
you are a forgiving God, gracious and compassionate, slow to anger and abounding in
love. Therefore you did not desert them,
18even when they cast for themselves an image of a calf and said, 'This is your god, who
brought you up out of Egypt,' or when they
committed awful blasphemies. Ex 32:4
19"Because of your great compassion you
did not abandon them in the desert. By day
the pillar of cloud did not cease to guide
them on their path, nor the pillar of fire by
night to shine on the way they were to take.
20You gave your good Spirit to instruct them.
You did not withhold your manna from their
mouths, and you gave them water for their
thirst. 21For forty years you sustained them
in the desert; they lacked nothing, their
clothes did not wear out nor did their feet
become swollen. Nu 11:17; Dt 2:7; Isa 63:11,14
22"You gave them kingdoms and nations,
allotting to them even the remotest frontiers.
They took over the country of Sihon[c] king
of Heshbon and the country of Og king of
Bashan. 23You made their sons as numerous
as the stars in the sky, and you brought them
into the land that you told their fathers to
enter and possess. 24Their sons went in and
took possession of the land. You subdued
before them the Canaanites, who lived in the
land; you handed the Canaanites over to
them, along with their kings and the peoples
of the land, to deal with them as they pleased.
25They captured fortified cities and fertile
land; they took possession of houses filled
with all kinds of good things, wells already

[a]5 Or *God for ever and ever* [b]9 Hebrew *Yam Suph*; that is, Sea of Reeds [c]22 One Hebrew manuscript and Septuagint; most Hebrew manuscripts *Sihon, that is, the country of the*

dug, vineyards, olive groves and fruit trees in
abundance. They ate to the full and were
well-nourished; they reveled in your great
goodness. Dt 6:10-12; 32:12-15
26"But they were disobedient and rebelled
against you; they put your law behind their
backs. They killed your prophets, who had
admonished them in order to turn them
back to you; they committed awful blasphemies. 27So you handed them over to their
enemies, who oppressed them. But when
they were oppressed they cried out to you.
From heaven you heard them, and in your
great compassion you gave them deliverers,
who rescued them from the hand of their
enemies. Jdg 2:12-14; 1Ki 14:9
28"But as soon as they were at rest, they
again did what was evil in your sight. Then
you abandoned them to the hand of their
enemies so that they ruled over them. And
when they cried out to you again, you heard
from heaven, and in your compassion you
delivered them time after time. Ps 106:43
29"You warned them to return to your
law, but they became arrogant and disobeyed
your commands. They sinned against your
ordinances, by which a man will live if he
obeys them. Stubbornly they turned their
backs on you, became stiff-necked and refused to listen. 30For many years you were
patient with them. By your Spirit you admonished them through your prophets. Yet
they paid no attention, so you handed them
over to the neighboring peoples. 31But in
your great mercy you did not put an end to
them or abandon them, for you are a gracious and merciful God. Dt 30:16; 2Ki 17:13-18
32"Now therefore, O our God, the great,
mighty and awesome God, who keeps his
covenant of love, do not let all this hardship
seem trifling in your eyes—the hardship that
has come upon us, upon our kings and leaders, upon our priests and prophets, upon our
fathers and all your people, from the days of
the kings of Assyria until today. 33In all that
has happened to us, you have been just; you
have acted faithfully, while we did wrong.
34Our kings, our leaders, our priests and our
fathers did not follow your law; they did not
pay attention to your commands or the
warnings you gave them. 35Even while they
were in their kingdom, enjoying your great
goodness to them in the spacious and fertile
land you gave them, they did not serve you
or turn from their evil ways. Ge 18:25
36"But see, we are slaves today, slaves in
the land you gave our forefathers so they
could eat its fruit and the other good things
it produces. 37Because of our sins, its abundant harvest goes to the kings you have
placed over us. They rule over our bodies
and our cattle as they please. We are in great
distress. Dt 28:33,48; Ezr 9:9

The Agreement of the People

38"In view of all this, we are making a binding
agreement, putting it in writing, and our leaders,
our Levites and our priests are affixing their seals
to it." 2Ch 23:16; Isa 44:5

10 Those who sealed it were:

Nehemiah the governor, the son of Hacaliah.

Zedekiah, 2Seraiah, Azariah, Jeremiah,
3Pashhur, Amariah, Malkijah, 1Ch 9:12
4Hattush, Shebaniah, Malluch,
5Harim, Meremoth, Obadiah, 1Ch 24:8
6Daniel, Ginnethon, Baruch,
7Meshullam, Abijah, Mijamin,
8Maaziah, Bilgai and Shemaiah.
These were the priests.

9The Levites: Ne 12:1

Jeshua son of Azaniah, Binnui of the sons of Henadad, Kadmiel,
10and their associates: Shebaniah,
Hodiah, Kelita, Pelaiah, Hanan,
11Mica, Rehob, Hashabiah,
12Zaccur, Sherebiah, Shebaniah,
13Hodiah, Bani and Beninu.

14The leaders of the people:

Parosh, Pahath-Moab, Elam, Zattu, Bani,
15Bunni, Azgad, Bebai,
16Adonijah, Bigvai, Adin, Ezr 8:6
17Ater, Hezekiah, Azzur,
18Hodiah, Hashum, Bezai,
19Hariph, Anathoth, Nebai,
20Magpiash, Meshullam, Hezir, 1Ch 24:15
21Meshezabel, Zadok, Jaddua,
22Pelatiah, Hanan, Anaiah,
23Hoshea, Hananiah, Hasshub,
24Hallohesh, Pilha, Shobek,
25Rehum, Hashabnah, Maaseiah,
26Ahiah, Hanan, Anan,
27Malluch, Harim and Baanah.

28"The rest of the people—priests, Levites,
gatekeepers, singers, temple servants and all
who separated themselves from the neighboring peoples for the sake of the Law of
God, together with their wives and all their
sons and daughters who are able to understand— 29all these now join their brothers
the nobles, and bind themselves with a curse
and an oath to follow the Law of God given
through Moses the servant of God and to

obey carefully all the commands, regulations
and decrees of the LORD our Lord. Ne 9:2
30“We promise not to give our daughters
in marriage to the peoples around us or take
their daughters for our sons. Ex 34:16; Dt 7:3
31“When the neighboring peoples bring
merchandise or grain to sell on the Sabbath,
we will not buy from them on the Sabbath or
on any holy day. Every seventh year we will
forgo working the land and will cancel all
debts. Ex 23:11; Dt 15:1; Ne 13:16,18
32“We assume the responsibility for carrying out the commands to give a third of a
shekel[a] each year for the service of the
house of our God: 33for the bread set out on
the table; for the regular grain offerings and
burnt offerings; for the offerings on the Sabbaths, New Moon festivals and appointed
feasts; for the holy offerings; for sin offerings
to make atonement for Israel; and for all the
duties of the house of our God. Lev 24:6
34“We—the priests, the Levites and the
people—have cast lots to determine when
each of our families is to bring to the house
of our God at set times each year a contribution of wood to burn on the altar of the LORD
our God, as it is written in the Law.
35“We also assume responsibility for
bringing to the house of the LORD each year
the firstfruits of our crops and of every fruit
tree. Ex 23:19; Nu 18:12
36“As it is also written in the Law, we will
bring the firstborn of our sons and of our
cattle, of our herds and of our flocks to the
house of our God, to the priests ministering
there. Ex 13:2; Nu 18:14-16
37“Moreover, we will bring to the storerooms of the house of our God, to the
priests, the first of our ground meal, of our
⌞grain⌟ offerings, of the fruit of all our trees
and of our new wine and oil. And we will
bring a tithe of our crops to the Levites, for
it is the Levites who collect the tithes in all the
towns where we work. 38A priest descended
from Aaron is to accompany the Levites
when they receive the tithes, and the Levites
are to bring a tenth of the tithes up to the
house of our God, to the storerooms of the
treasury. 39The people of Israel, including
the Levites, are to bring their contributions
of grain, new wine and oil to the storerooms
where the articles for the sanctuary are kept
and where the ministering priests, the gatekeepers and the singers stay. Lev 23:17
“We will not neglect the house of our
God.” Dt 12:6; Ne 13:11-12

The New Residents of Jerusalem

11 Now the leaders of the people settled in
Jerusalem, and the rest of the people cast
lots to bring one out of every ten to live in Jerusalem, the holy city, while the remaining nine were
to stay in their own towns. 2The people commended all the men who volunteered to live in Jerusalem. Ne 7:4,73; Isa 48:2
3These are the provincial leaders who settled in
Jerusalem (now some Israelites, priests, Levites,
temple servants and descendants of Solomon's
servants lived in the towns of Judah, each on his
own property in the various towns, 4while other
people from both Judah and Benjamin lived in
Jerusalem): 1Ch 9:2-3; Ezr 2:1

From the descendants of Judah:

Athaiah son of Uzziah, the son of Zechariah,
the son of Amariah, the son of Shephatiah,
the son of Mahalalel, a descendant of Perez;
5and Maaseiah son of Baruch, the son of Col-
Hozeh, the son of Hazaiah, the son of Adaiah, the son of Joiarib, the son of Zechariah,
a descendant of Shelah. 6The descendants of
Perez who lived in Jerusalem totaled 468 able
men.

7From the descendants of Benjamin:

Sallu son of Meshullam, the son of Joed, the
son of Pedaiah, the son of Kolaiah, the son of
Maaseiah, the son of Ithiel, the son of Jeshaiah, 8and his followers, Gabbai and Sallai—
928 men. 9Joel son of Zicri was their chief
officer, and Judah son of Hassenuah was
over the Second District of the city.

10From the priests:

Jedaiah; the son of Joiarib; Jakin; 11Seraiah
son of Hilkiah, the son of Meshullam, the
son of Zadok, the son of Meraioth, the son
of Ahitub, supervisor in the house of God,
12and their associates, who carried on work
for the temple—822 men; Adaiah son of Jeroham, the son of Pelaliah, the son of Amzi,
the son of Zechariah, the son of Pashhur, the
son of Malkijah, 13and his associates, who
were heads of families—242 men; Amashsai
son of Azarel, the son of Ahzai, the son of
Meshillemoth, the son of Immer, 14and his[b]
associates, who were able men—128. Their
chief officer was Zabdiel son of Haggedolim.

15From the Levites:

Shemaiah son of Hasshub, the son of Azrikam, the son of Hashabiah, the son of Bunni;
16Shabbethai and Jozabad, two of the heads
of the Levites, who had charge of the outside

[a] *32* That is, about 1/8 ounce (about 4 grams) [b] *14* Most Septuagint manuscripts; Hebrew *their*

work of the house of God; 17Mattaniah son of Mica, the son of Zabdi, the son of Asaph, the director who led in thanksgiving and prayer; Bakbukiah, second among his associates; and Abda son of Shammua, the son of Galal, the son of Jeduthun. 18The Levites in the holy city totaled 284. 1Ch 9:15; 25:1; Rev 21:2

19The gatekeepers:

Akkub, Talmon and their associates, who kept watch at the gates—172 men.

20The rest of the Israelites, with the priests and Levites, were in all the towns of Judah, each on his ancestral property.

21The temple servants lived on the hill of Ophel, and Ziha and Gishpa were in charge of them.

22The chief officer of the Levites in Jerusalem was Uzzi son of Bani, the son of Hashabiah, the son of Mattaniah, the son of Mica. Uzzi was one of Asaph's descendants, who were the singers responsible for the service of the house of God. 23The singers were under the king's orders, which regulated their daily activity. 1Ch 9:15; Ne 7:44

24Pethahiah son of Meshezabel, one of the descendants of Zerah son of Judah, was the king's agent in all affairs relating to the people. Ge 38:30

25As for the villages with their fields, some of the people of Judah lived in Kiriath Arba and its surrounding settlements, in Dibon and its settlements, in Jekabzeel and its villages, 26in Jeshua, in Moladah, in Beth Pelet, 27in Hazar Shual, in Beersheba and its settlements, 28in Ziklag, in Meconah and its settlements, 29in En Rimmon, in Zorah, in Jarmuth, 30Zanoah, Adullam and their villages, in Lachish and its fields, and in Azekah and its settlements. So they were living all the way from Beersheba to the Valley of Hinnom. Ge 21:14; Jos 10:3

31The descendants of the Benjamites from Geba lived in Micmash, Aija, Bethel and its settlements, 32in Anathoth, Nob and Ananiah, 33in Hazor, Ramah and Gittaim, 34in Hadid, Zeboim and Neballat, 35in Lod and Ono, and in the Valley of the Craftsmen. Jos 11:1; 21:17; 1Sa 13:18

36Some of the divisions of the Levites of Judah settled in Benjamin.

Priests and Levites

12 These were the priests and Levites who returned with Zerubbabel son of Shealtiel and with Jeshua: 1Ch 3:19; Ezr 2:2

Seraiah, Jeremiah, Ezra, Ezr 2:2
2Amariah, Malluch, Hattush,
3Shecaniah, Rehum, Meremoth,
4Iddo, Ginnethon,[a] Abijah, Lk 1:5; Zec 1:1
5Mijamin,[b] Moadiah, Bilgah,
6Shemaiah, Joiarib, Jedaiah, 1Ch 24:7
7Sallu, Amok, Hilkiah and Jedaiah.

These were the leaders of the priests and their associates in the days of Jeshua.

8The Levites were Jeshua, Binnui, Kadmiel, Sherebiah, Judah, and also Mattaniah, who, together with his associates, was in charge of the songs of thanksgiving. 9Bakbukiah and Unni, their associates, stood opposite them in the services.

10Jeshua was the father of Joiakim, Joiakim the father of Eliashib, Eliashib the father of Joiada, 11Joiada the father of Jonathan, and Jonathan the father of Jaddua. Ezr 10:24

12In the days of Joiakim, these were the heads of the priestly families:

of Seraiah's family, Meraiah;
of Jeremiah's, Hananiah;
13of Ezra's, Meshullam;
of Amariah's, Jehohanan;
14of Malluch's, Jonathan;
of Shecaniah's,[c] Joseph;
15of Harim's, Adna;
of Meremoth's,[d] Helkai;
16of Iddo's, Zechariah;
of Ginnethon's, Meshullam;
17of Abijah's, Zicri;
of Miniamin's and of Moadiah's, Piltai;
18of Bilgah's, Shammua;
of Shemaiah's, Jehonathan;
19of Joiarib's, Mattenai;
of Jedaiah's, Uzzi;
20of Sallu's, Kallai;
of Amok's, Eber;
21of Hilkiah's, Hashabiah;
of Jedaiah's, Nethanel.

22The family heads of the Levites in the days of Eliashib, Joiada, Johanan and Jaddua, as well as those of the priests, were recorded in the reign of Darius the Persian. 23The family heads among the descendants of Levi up to the time of Johanan son of Eliashib were recorded in the book of the annals. 24And the leaders of the Levites were Hashabiah, Sherebiah, Jeshua son of Kadmiel, and their associates, who stood opposite them to give praise and thanksgiving, one section responding to the other, as prescribed by David the man of God.

25Mattaniah, Bakbukiah, Obadiah, Meshullam, Talmon and Akkub were gatekeepers who guarded the storerooms at the gates. 26They served in the days of Joiakim son of Jeshua, the son of Jozadak, and in the days of Nehemiah the governor and of Ezra the priest and scribe.

Dedication of the Wall of Jerusalem

27At the dedication of the wall of Jerusalem, the Levites were sought out from where they lived and

[a]4 Many Hebrew manuscripts and Vulgate (see also Neh. 12:16); most Hebrew manuscripts *Ginnethoi* [b]5 A variant of *Miniamin* [c]14 Very many Hebrew manuscripts, some Septuagint manuscripts and Syriac (see also Neh. 12:3); most Hebrew manuscripts *Shebaniah's* [d]15 Some Septuagint manuscripts (see also Neh. 12:3); Hebrew *Meraioth's*

were brought to Jerusalem to celebrate joyfully the dedication with songs of thanksgiving and with the music of cymbals, harps and lyres. 28The singers also were brought together from the region around Jerusalem—from the villages of the Netophathites, 29from Beth Gilgal, and from the area of Geba and Azmaveth, for the singers had built villages for themselves around Jerusalem. 30When the priests and Levites had purified themselves ceremonially, they purified the people, the gates and the wall. 1Ch 25:6; Ps 92:3

31I had the leaders of Judah go up on top[a] of the wall. I also assigned two large choirs to give thanks. One was to proceed on top[b] of the wall to

LIVING  INSIGHT

Thanksgiving is good for our roots. It deepens them and strengthens them and thickens them, making our trunks and limbs more secure in spite of the threatening gales of our times.

(See Nehemiah 12:31.)

the right, toward the Dung Gate. 32Hoshaiah and half the leaders of Judah followed them, 33along with Azariah, Ezra, Meshullam, 34Judah, Benjamin, Shemaiah, Jeremiah, 35as well as some priests with trumpets, and also Zechariah son of Jonathan, the son of Shemaiah, the son of Mattaniah, the son of Micaiah, the son of Zaccur, the son of Asaph, 36and his associates—Shemaiah, Azarel, Milalai, Gilalai, Maai, Nethanel, Judah and Hanani—with musical instruments ⌞prescribed by⌟ David the man of God. Ezra the scribe led the procession. 37At the Fountain Gate they continued directly up the steps of the City of David on the ascent to the wall and passed above the house of David to the Water Gate on the east. Ne 2:13-14

38The second choir proceeded in the opposite direction. I followed them on top[c] of the wall, together with half the people—past the Tower of the Ovens to the Broad Wall, 39over the Gate of Ephraim, the Jeshanah[d] Gate, the Fish Gate, the Tower of Hananel and the Tower of the Hundred, as far as the Sheep Gate. At the Gate of the Guard they stopped. Ne 3:1,3,8,11; 8:16

40The two choirs that gave thanks then took their places in the house of God; so did I, together with half the officials, 41as well as the priests—Eliakim, Maaseiah, Miniamin, Micaiah, Elioenai, Zechariah and Hananiah with their trumpets—42and also Maaseiah, Shemaiah, Eleazar, Uzzi, Jehohanan, Malkijah, Elam and Ezer. The choirs sang under the direction of Jezrahiah. 43And on that day they offered great sacrifices, rejoicing because God had given them great joy. The women and children also rejoiced. The sound of rejoicing in Jerusalem could be heard far away.

44At that time men were appointed to be in charge of the storerooms for the contributions, firstfruits and tithes. From the fields around the towns they were to bring into the storerooms the portions required by the Law for the priests and the Levites, for Judah was pleased with the ministering priests and Levites. 45They performed the service of their God and the service of purification, as did also the singers and gatekeepers, according to the commands of David and his son Solomon. 46For long ago, in the days of David and Asaph, there had been directors for the singers and for the songs of praise and thanksgiving to God. 47So in the days of Zerubbabel and of Nehemiah, all Israel contributed the daily portions for the singers and gatekeepers. They also set aside the portion for the other Levites, and the Levites set aside the portion for the descendants of Aaron. Nu 18:21; Dt 18:8

Nehemiah's Final Reforms

13 On that day the Book of Moses was read aloud in the hearing of the people and there it was found written that no Ammonite or Moabite should ever be admitted into the assembly of God, 2because they had not met the Israelites with food and water but had hired Balaam to call a curse down on them. (Our God, however, turned the curse into a blessing.) 3When the people heard this law, they excluded from Israel all who were of foreign descent. Dt 23:3; Nu 22:3-11; 23:11

4Before this, Eliashib the priest had been put in charge of the storerooms of the house of our God. He was closely associated with Tobiah, 5and he had provided him with a large room formerly used to store the grain offerings and incense and temple articles, and also the tithes of grain, new wine and oil prescribed for the Levites, singers and gatekeepers, as well as the contributions for the priests.

6But while all this was going on, I was not in Jerusalem, for in the thirty-second year of Artaxerxes king of Babylon I had returned to the king. Some time later I asked his permission 7and came back to Jerusalem. Here I learned about the evil thing Eliashib had done in providing Tobiah a room in the courts of the house of God. 8I was greatly displeased and threw all Tobiah's household goods out of the room. 9I gave orders to purify the rooms, and then I put back into them the equipment of the house of God, with the grain offerings and the incense. 2Ch 29:5; Ne 5:14; Mt 21:12-13

10I also learned that the portions assigned to the Levites had not been given to them, and that all the Levites and singers responsible for the service had

[a]31 Or *go alongside* [b]31 Or *proceed alongside* [c]38 Or *them alongside* [d]39 Or *Old*

gone back to their own fields. [11]So I rebuked the officials and asked them, "Why is the house of God neglected?" Then I called them together and stationed them at their posts. Ne 10:37-39; Hag 1:1-9

[12]All Judah brought the tithes of grain, new wine and oil into the storerooms. [13]I put Shelemiah the priest, Zadok the scribe, and a Levite named Pedaiah in charge of the storerooms and made Hanan son of Zaccur, the son of Mattaniah, their assistant, because these men were considered trustworthy. They were made responsible for distributing the supplies to their brothers. Ne 10:37-39

[14]Remember me for this, O my God, and do not blot out what I have so faithfully done for the house of my God and its services. Ge 8:1

[15]In those days I saw men in Judah treading winepresses on the Sabbath and bringing in grain and loading it on donkeys, together with wine, grapes, figs and all other kinds of loads. And they were bringing all this into Jerusalem on the Sabbath. Therefore I warned them against selling food on that day. [16]Men from Tyre who lived in Jerusalem were bringing in fish and all kinds of merchandise and selling them in Jerusalem on the Sabbath to the people of Judah. [17]I rebuked the nobles of Judah and said to them, "What is this wicked thing you are doing—desecrating the Sabbath day? [18]Didn't your forefathers do the same things, so that our God brought all this calamity upon us and upon this city? Now you are stirring up more wrath against Israel by desecrating the Sabbath."

[19]When evening shadows fell on the gates of Jerusalem before the Sabbath, I ordered the doors to be shut and not opened until the Sabbath was over. I stationed some of my own men at the gates so that no load could be brought in on the Sabbath day. [20]Once or twice the merchants and sellers of all kinds of goods spent the night outside Jerusalem. [21]But I warned them and said, "Why do you spend the night by the wall? If you do this again, I will lay hands on you." From that time on they no longer came on the Sabbath. [22]Then I commanded the Levites to purify themselves and go and guard the gates in order to keep the Sabbath day holy. Lev 23:32; Ne 12:30

Remember me for this also, O my God, and show mercy to me according to your great love.

[23]Moreover, in those days I saw men of Judah who had married women from Ashdod, Ammon and Moab. [24]Half of their children spoke the language of Ashdod or the language of one of the other peoples, and did not know how to speak the language of Judah. [25]I rebuked them and called curses down on them. I beat some of the men and pulled out their hair. I made them take an oath in God's name and said: "You are not to give your daughters in marriage to their sons, nor are you to take their daughters in marriage for your sons or for yourselves. [26]Was it not because of marriages like these that Solomon king of Israel sinned? Among the many nations there was no king like him. He was loved by his God, and God made him king over all Israel, but even he was led into sin by foreign women. [27]Must we hear now that you too are doing all this terrible wickedness and are being unfaithful to our God by marrying foreign women?" 1Ki 11:3; 2Ch 1:12; Ezr 10:2

[28]One of the sons of Joiada son of Eliashib the high priest was son-in-law to Sanballat the Horonite. And I drove him away from me. Ezr 10:24

[29]Remember them, O my God, because they defiled the priestly office and the covenant of the priesthood and of the Levites. Ne 6:14

[30]So I purified the priests and the Levites of everything foreign, and assigned them duties, each to his own task. [31]I also made provision for contributions of wood at designated times, and for the firstfruits. Ne 10:30,34-36

Remember me with favor, O my God. ver 14,22

INTRODUCTION

ESTHER

Bible commentator J. Sidlow Baxter has called the book of Esther "a crisis book." The book could appear, at first glance, to be a fictional account, because it bears all the marks of the standard short story: a dramatic plot, a villain, a hero, a damsel in distress . . . and a surprising climax, followed by everyone living "happily ever after." But it is absolutely authentic, bearing all the marks of inspired literature. It is, in fact, a vital link in the chain of Jewish history as it reveals what neither the book of Ezra nor the book of Nehemiah includes—crucial experiences of the Jews who remained in Persia. As we lay bare the account, it will not be difficult to see why there are those who have called Esther "a crisis book" in which God was at work behind the scenes to preserve His people.

WRITER: *Unknown*

DATE: *c.460–350 B.C.*

PURPOSE: *To keep alive the memory of the preservation of the Jewish people*

KEY THEME: *God at work behind the scenes*

KEY VERSES: *4:14-16*

KEY TERM: *"Jew(s)"*

TIME LINE 1400BC 1300 1200 1100 1000 900 800 700 600 500 400

Fall of Jerusalem (586 B.C.)
Persia's conquest of Babylon (539 B.C.)
First return of exiles to Jerusalem (538 B.C.)
Xerxes' reign in Persia (486-465 B.C.)
Esther's reign in Persia (479 B.C.)
Second return to Jerusalem under Ezra (458 B.C.)
Third return to Jerusalem under Nehemiah (445 B.C.)
Jerusalem's wall rebuilt (445 B.C.)
Book of Esther written (c.460-350 B.C.)

Beauty and the Best

GOD'S PROVIDENCE AMONG HIS PEOPLE DURING . . .

	. . . Hard Times				. . . Happy Times		
	KING'S BANQUET	HAMAN'S EDICT	QUEEN'S OBEDIENCE	GOD'S DELIVERANCE	MORDECAI'S EDICT	JEWS' REJOICING	SHALOM!
	Honoring the kingdom		To her God	Esther honored		Enemies destroyed	
	Honoring the queen		To herself	Haman hanged		Feast established	
	CHAPTERS 1–2	*CHAPTER 3*	*CHAPTERS 4–5*	*CHAPTERS 6–7*	*CHAPTER 8*	*CHAPTER 9*	*CHAPTER 10*
CIRCUMSTANCE	Threat and trust				Deliverance and praise		
FEASTS	of the king	of the queen			of the nation		
DATES	483 B.C.						473 B.C.

Every once in a while we come across a man or a woman who casts an extremely significant shadow across this earth. Often he or she receives a great deal of power, authority and clout from God without even asking for it. Esther was just such a person.

She was a remarkable person. Without losing dignity, purity, character or identity, Esther stood alone against the rising tide of wrong. She even broke with her cultural moorings to be God's woman of the century in which she lived! Unfortunately, most Christians today would be hard-pressed to give even the gist of the book of Esther in a few sentences—to say nothing of relating the story chapter by chapter. Even though it's dated as an ancient book of the Bible, it has an incredibly relevant ring to it, especially for women today who have lost their sense of direction. Esther will help you know how to address the times in which you live. Esther stands as a wonderful model, worthy of serious study and certainly worthy of emulating her depth of character.

The book begins almost like a fairy tale. It takes place in the days of the kings. There is a beautiful queen. There is an evil villain. At the crux of the story there is the age-old conflict between good and evil. But it isn't a fairy tale. It is an inspired, true account of a remarkable woman who saved her nation. She stood alone at a crucial time, and, as a result, the Jews survived. Even though we may not be very well acquainted with Esther, believe me, the Jews will never forget her!

Five Characters in the Drama

To understand this drama it will help to identify the five major characters in the story. First, there's a king named *Ahasuerus* (in the Hebrew), or *Xerxes* if you prefer (see 1:1). Xerxes was the king of 127 provinces that stretched from India to Ethiopia. His kingdom was the ancient kingdom of the Persians. He was the most significant man in the world. His reign took place during the era of the laws of the Medes and Persians—a time of unprecedented dictatorship. Whatever the king said was law; his word was never questioned.

Onto this scene came a woman named *Vashti*. She was the king's first wife, the queen of the Persians. She was a beautiful woman—and is revealed as such in the Scriptures (1:11). She was also a woman of principle who ended up losing her crown because she would not compromise her integrity.

After Vashti we meet a man named *Haman*. He was an anti-Semitic Persian who was promoted to a place of influential authority in the court of the king (3:1). He was a conceited, money-hungry individual always looking out for no one except himself.

The story includes another man, who was Haman's antithesis. He was a Jew named *Mordecai* (2:5)—a man who stood apart as a righteous person. He had the difficult job of rearing his uncle's daughter, whose parents had died. This orphan girl's Hebrew name was Hadassah (2:7). We know her best as Esther—a name that is likely derived from the Persian word *Ester*, meaning "star; dazzling or brilliant one." She was a very beautiful Jewess who eventually became the queen of Persia. *Esther* is the fifth character in this compelling story.

Strangers in a Strange Land

The events recorded in the book of Esther took place during the zenith of the Persian empire. Let me give a little history lesson. There was a time when the Jews went into captivity under the Babylonians (see the end of 2 Kings and the end of 2 Chronicles). For seventy years the Babylonians (also called Chaldeans in the Old Testament) ruled over the Jews. The Babylonians were finally overthrown by the Persians as the Medes and the Persians joined forces and swept the Babylonian empire off the earth and took charge of the spoil. Interestingly, the Persians chose to be kind toward the Jews, and the king of Persia declared that the Jews could go back to their land if they so desired. Many of the people did. Some went back under Zerubbabel, you may recall. Others went back under Ezra. And a third group went back under Nehemiah. (See the books of Ezra, page 469, and Nehemiah, page 483.) However, many of the Jews chose to stay in Persia. The events in Esther took place among the Jews who remained in Persia.

In Esther's book we learn of the lifestyle of those who remained in Persia under the rule of a monarch named Xerxes, or Ahasuerus. A period of ten years (483–473 B.C.) is covered in the book of Esther—a decade of time in which God preserved the Jews in Persia, thanks to Esther.

The Finger of God

The book of Esther is unlike any other book in the Bible. The name of God is never mentioned within its pages. Furthermore, Esther is never once quoted in the New Testament—which has led some Bible scholars to question whether it should even be included in the sacred canon. However, Matthew Henry once wrote, "If the name of God is not here, His finger certainly is"—and he is assuredly correct.

Though silent and unannounced, God's providence was surely at work behind the scenes. That's often the way it is with God. He doesn't get top billing. He doesn't make the headlines. But God was at work in and through the lives of Mordecai and Esther. As we read about their lives, we sense God's invisible yet invincible fingerprint all through this book. We see His mighty hand moving the affairs of human life. That's what is meant by *providence*: God quietly but sovereignly at work in the lives of men and women.

God Is at Work

Esther can be divided into two major sections: *the providence of God in the hard times* (chapters 1–6) and *the providence of God in the happy times* (chapters 7–10).

The book of Esther begins with a banquet for the king. After a great deal of drinking and celebrating, King Xerxes called for Queen Vashti to be brought in and paraded before his drunken guests. She refused to participate. As a result, she lost her throne, which left the king in need of a new queen. In response to this need, Xerxes put on a national beauty contest to seek his new bride. God's hand was clearly at work on the landscape of the royal palace: Esther, a beautiful and godly Jewess, won the contest.

At the same time an influential leader in the king's court was growing in power. His name was Haman. He was a wealthy, power-hungry, jealous person who hated the Jews. He hated Mordecai most of all, because this Jew would not bow down to him and give him the respect he believed was due him. In his anger, Haman began to plot the destruction of the Jews.

He might have gotten away with his evil plan if it hadn't been for the hand of God at work among His people. You see, the new queen was not only a Jew, but she had been brought up by the man Haman hated the most—her uncle, Mordecai. Through a divinely planned series of events, Mordecai was publicly honored and Haman was humiliated! In fact, the king commanded Haman to escort Mordecai through the streets, declaring Mordecai's greatness before the eyes of all the people. This infuriated Haman and intensified his determination to exterminate the Jews.

But life really fell apart for Haman when Esther entered the scene. Her uncle Mordecai had informed her of Haman's wicked scheme. With Mordecai's encouragement, she planned a dinner with the king at which she would make an appeal for the lives of her people. Haman was also invited—and again we see the Lord at work! Haman's plot was exposed; he lost his place of honor and ultimately his life. The Jews were given permission from the king to defend themselves against any who would participate in Haman's plan to destroy their people.

Again and again though the book of Esther we see the Lord's working. As you read Esther, take note of how many times God worked in the little things of life. From a beauty contest to a king who suffered from insomnia, He was there, accomplishing His purposes. Isn't it good to know that our God has not changed? He is still at work in the smallest details of our lives. May I suggest that right now you slow down and think back. I dare say you will be amazed as you realize how often the Lord has worked out the details in your life. If He did it back then . . . He is still doing so today . . . and He will continue to do the same every step of your way!

Courage to Stand

There are times in our lives when we make a decision, and we must stand all alone in our commitment. You may be at that place as you read this now. If that's where you find yourself right now, you are experiencing one of the greatest tests of individual courage—and your struggle to maintain the courage of your convictions doesn't necessarily happen in front of people. As it turns out, it often happens when we are alone.

At times, it may seem that God is doing strange things in our lives. He maneuvers and changes and alters and shifts various events. And we may wonder at the time, "Why in the world is this such a low tide when I expected it to be high tide? Why is it that this is such a difficult time when it looked like it was going to be easy?" You ask agonizing questions—only to realize when it is all over that God clearly was leading every step of the way.

At this time in your life, which for some of you may not be your all-time favorite period, you might feel that God is coming down hard on you, or perhaps even that He has forsaken you. If nothing more, I hope you will learn from your study of Esther that God is sovereign. He is in charge even when things seem out of control. Remember: When He is in control, nothing is ever *out* of control!

Learning From Esther

As I read the book of Esther, a couple of lessons stay with me. First, *the providence of God doesn't require high visibility*. God's name isn't mentioned once in Esther—but He's there. God's best moves are not made by shouting. God isn't hiding in the corner at the end of our day, saying, "Hey, did you see Me at work today?" No. As a matter of fact, as C.S. Lewis put it so well, "It is His silence that is often the most frustrating. He whispers in our pleasures and He shouts in our pain." It takes the Hamans of this world to make us appreciate the Mordecais. Are you learning that sometimes the people who give you the greatest trouble are the people you need the most? It may be that in those very situations God comes the nearest in order to do His work of healing and renewal in your life.

Second, *a commitment to obedience doesn't oblige low self-esteem*. Esther is a beautiful illustration of someone who willingly submitted to following God's will—no matter what. Her commitment to God's will included times when she had to be very decisive and strong-minded, and God honored her actions and attitudes. Her obedience was first of all to God. Though wonderfully submissive to her uncle Mordecai as well as to her husband Xerxes, her self-esteem was upheld. May the Lord raise up many such women of God (and men of God as well) who humbly obey Him and see His will accomplished in their lives—to the praise of His glorious grace!

From Vashti to Esther Chapters 1–3

In the first two chapters, the ruling queen (Vashti) was removed from the throne and a new queen (Esther) was crowned. The unique part of the story is that a Jew—a foreigner, an otherwise unknown Jewess—became the new "First Lady" of the Medes and the Persians. Isn't God's plan astonishing? The tension mounts when we get to chapter 3. Haman, a key leader in the king's cabinet, was plotting to have the Jews exterminated and forever removed from the Persian empire. Haman was not aware of Esther's heritage as he moved forward with a plot to destroy the Jews. As humans plot their wicked plans, the awesome God of heaven is at work setting the scene for His will to overrule.

Queen Vashti Deposed

1 This is what happened during the time of Xerxes,[a] the Xerxes who ruled over 127 provinces stretching from India to Cush[b]: [2]At that time King Xerxes reigned from his royal throne in the citadel of Susa, [3]and in the third year of his reign he gave a banquet for all his nobles and officials. The military leaders of Persia and Media, the princes, and the nobles of the provinces were present. Est 8:9; 9:30; Da 9:1

[4]For a full 180 days he displayed the vast wealth of his kingdom and the splendor and glory of his majesty. [5]When these days were over, the king gave a banquet, lasting seven days, in the enclosed garden of the king's palace, for all the people from the least to the greatest, who were in the citadel of Susa. [6]The garden had hangings of white and blue linen, fastened with cords of white linen and purple material to silver rings on marble pillars. There were couches of gold and silver on a mosaic pavement of porphyry, marble, mother-of-pearl and other costly stones. [7]Wine was served in goblets of gold, each one different from the other, and the royal wine was abundant, in keeping with the king's liberality. [8]By the king's command each guest was allowed to drink in his own way, for the king instructed all the wine stewards to serve each man what he wished. Est 2:18; 7:7-8; Eze 23:41

[9]Queen Vashti also gave a banquet for the women in the royal palace of King Xerxes.

[10]On the seventh day, when King Xerxes was in high spirits from wine, he commanded the seven eunuchs who served him—Mehuman, Biztha, Harbona, Bigtha, Abagtha, Zethar and Carcas—[11]to bring before him Queen Vashti, wearing her royal crown, in order to display her beauty to the people and nobles, for she was lovely to look at. [12]But when the attendants delivered the king's command, Queen Vashti refused to come. Then the king became furious and burned with anger.

[13]Since it was customary for the king to consult experts in matters of law and justice, he spoke with the wise men who understood the times [14]and were closest to the king—Carshena, Shethar, Admatha, Tarshish, Meres, Marsena and Memucan, the seven nobles of Persia and Media who had special access to the king and were highest in the kingdom. 2Ki 25:19; 1Ch 12:32; Jer 10:7

[15]"According to law, what must be done to Queen Vashti?" he asked. "She has not obeyed the command of King Xerxes that the eunuchs have taken to her."

[16]Then Memucan replied in the presence of the king and the nobles, "Queen Vashti has done wrong, not only against the king but also against all the nobles and the peoples of all the provinces of King Xerxes. [17]For the queen's conduct will become known to all the women, and so they will despise their husbands and say, 'King Xerxes commanded Queen Vashti to be brought before him, but she would not come.' [18]This very day the Persian and Median women of the nobility who have heard about the queen's conduct will respond to all the king's nobles in the same way. There will be no end of disrespect and discord. Pr 19:13; 27:15

[19]"Therefore, if it pleases the king, let him issue a royal decree and let it be written in the laws of Persia and Media, which cannot be repealed, that Vashti is never again to enter the presence of King Xerxes. Also let the king give her royal position to someone else who is better than she. [20]Then when the king's edict is proclaimed throughout all his vast realm, all the women will respect their husbands, from the least to the greatest." Est 8:8

[21]The king and his nobles were pleased with this advice, so the king did as Memucan proposed. [22]He sent dispatches to all parts of the kingdom, to each province in its own script and to each people in its own language, proclaiming in each people's tongue that every man should be ruler over his own household. Ne 13:24; Eph 5:22-24

Esther Made Queen

2 Later when the anger of King Xerxes had subsided, he remembered Vashti and what she had done and what he had decreed about her. [2]Then the king's personal attendants proposed, "Let a search be made for beautiful young virgins for the king. [3]Let the king appoint commissioners in every province of his realm to bring all these beautiful girls into the harem at the citadel of Susa. Let them be placed under the care of Hegai, the king's eunuch, who is in charge of the women; and let beauty treatments be given to them. [4]Then let the girl who pleases the king be queen instead of Vashti." This advice appealed to the king, and he followed it. Est 1:19-20; 7:10

[5]Now there was in the citadel of Susa a Jew of the tribe of Benjamin, named Mordecai son of Jair,

[a]1 Hebrew *Ahasuerus*, a variant of Xerxes' Persian name; here and throughout Esther [b]1 That is, the upper Nile region

the son of Shimei, the son of Kish, 6who had been
carried into exile from Jerusalem by Nebuchadnezzar king of Babylon, among those taken captive
with Jehoiachin[a] king of Judah. 7Mordecai had a
cousin named Hadassah, whom he had brought
up because she had neither father nor mother.
This girl, who was also known as Esther, was lovely
in form and features, and Mordecai had taken her
as his own daughter when her father and mother
died. 2Ki 24:6,15; 2Ch 36:10,20; Est 3:2

8When the king's order and edict had been proclaimed, many girls were brought to the citadel of
Susa and put under the care of Hegai. Esther also
was taken to the king's palace and entrusted to
Hegai, who had charge of the harem. 9The girl
pleased him and won his favor. Immediately he
provided her with her beauty treatments and special food. He assigned to her seven maids selected
from the king's palace and moved her and her
maids into the best place in the harem. 2Ki 25:30

10Esther had not revealed her nationality and
family background, because Mordecai had forbidden her to do so. 11Every day he walked back and
forth near the courtyard of the harem to find out
how Esther was and what was happening to her.

12Before a girl's turn came to go in to King
Xerxes, she had to complete twelve months of
beauty treatments prescribed for the women, six
months with oil of myrrh and six with perfumes
and cosmetics. 13And this is how she would go to
the king: Anything she wanted was given her to
take with her from the harem to the king's palace.
14In the evening she would go there and in the
morning return to another part of the harem to
the care of Shaashgaz, the king's eunuch who was
in charge of the concubines. She would not return
to the king unless he was pleased with her and
summoned her by name. 1Ki 11:3; Est 4:11; Pr 27:9

15When the turn came for Esther (the girl Mordecai had adopted, the daughter of his uncle Abihail) to go to the king, she asked for nothing other
than what Hegai, the king's eunuch who was in
charge of the harem, suggested. And Esther won
the favor of everyone who saw her. 16She was taken
to King Xerxes in the royal residence in the tenth
month, the month of Tebeth, in the seventh year
of his reign. Est 9:29; Ps 45:14

17Now the king was attracted to Esther more
than to any of the other women, and she won his
favor and approval more than any of the other
virgins. So he set a royal crown on her head and
made her queen instead of Vashti. 18And the king
gave a great banquet, Esther's banquet, for all his
nobles and officials. He proclaimed a holiday
throughout the provinces and distributed gifts
with royal liberality. Est 1:3,7,11

Mordecai Uncovers a Conspiracy

19When the virgins were assembled a second
time, Mordecai was sitting at the king's gate. 20But
Esther had kept secret her family background and
nationality just as Mordecai had told her to do, for
she continued to follow Mordecai's instructions as
she had done when he was bringing her up.

21During the time Mordecai was sitting at the
king's gate, Bigthana[b] and Teresh, two of the
king's officers who guarded the doorway, became
angry and conspired to assassinate King Xerxes.
22But Mordecai found out about the plot and told
Queen Esther, who in turn reported it to the king,
giving credit to Mordecai. 23And when the report
was investigated and found to be true, the two
officials were hanged on a gallows.[c] All this was
recorded in the book of the annals in the presence
of the king. Est 6:1-2; Ps 7:14-16

Haman's Plot to Destroy the Jews

3 After these events, King Xerxes honored Haman son of Hammedatha, the Agagite, ele-
vating him and giving him a seat of honor higher
than that of all the other nobles. 2All the royal
officials at the king's gate knelt down and paid
honor to Haman, for the king had commanded
this concerning him. But Mordecai would not
kneel down or pay him honor. Nu 24:7; Dt 25:17-19

3Then the royal officials at the king's gate asked
Mordecai, "Why do you disobey the king's command?" 4Day after day they spoke to him but he
refused to comply. Therefore they told Haman
about it to see whether Mordecai's behavior would
be tolerated, for he had told them he was a Jew.

5When Haman saw that Mordecai would not
kneel down or pay him honor, he was enraged.
6Yet having learned who Mordecai's people were,
he scorned the idea of killing only Mordecai. Instead Haman looked for a way to destroy all Mordecai's people, the Jews, throughout the whole
kingdom of Xerxes. Est 5:9; Ps 83:4

7In the twelfth year of King Xerxes, in the first
month, the month of Nisan, they cast the *pur* (that
is, the lot) in the presence of Haman to select a
day and month. And the lot fell on[d] the twelfth
month, the month of Adar. Est 9:24,26

8Then Haman said to King Xerxes, "There is a
certain people dispersed and scattered among the
peoples in all the provinces of your kingdom
whose customs are different from those of all other
people and who do not obey the king's laws; it is
not in the king's best interest to tolerate them. 9If
it pleases the king, let a decree be issued to destroy
them, and I will put ten thousand talents[e] of sil-

[a]6 Hebrew *Jeconiah,* a variant of *Jehoiachin* [b]21 Hebrew *Bigthan,* a variant of *Bigthana* [c]23 Or *were hung* (or *impaled*) *on poles*; similarly elsewhere in Esther [d]7 Septuagint; Hebrew does not have *And the lot fell on.* [e]9 That is, about 375 tons (about 345 metric tons)

ver into the royal treasury for the men who carry
out this business." Ezr 4:15; Ac 16:20-21
10So the king took his signet ring from his finger
and gave it to Haman son of Hammedatha, the
Agagite, the enemy of the Jews. 11"Keep the money," the king said to Haman, "and do with the
people as you please." Ge 41:42; Est 7:6; 8:2
12Then on the thirteenth day of the first month
the royal secretaries were summoned. They wrote
out in the script of each province and in the language of each people all Haman's orders to the
king's satraps, the governors of the various provinces and the nobles of the various peoples. These
were written in the name of King Xerxes himself
and sealed with his own ring. 13Dispatches were
sent by couriers to all the king's provinces with the
order to destroy, kill and annihilate all the Jews—
young and old, women and little children—on a
single day, the thirteenth day of the twelfth month,
the month of Adar, and to plunder their goods.
14A copy of the text of the edict was to be issued
as law in every province and made known to the
people of every nationality so they would be ready
for that day. 1Ki 21:8; Est 8:10-14; 9:10
15Spurred on by the king's command, the couriers went out, and the edict was issued in the citadel
of Susa. The king and Haman sat down to drink,
but the city of Susa was bewildered. Est 1:10; 8:15

The Queen's Disobedience **Chapters 4–5**

Haman's anger and hatred were directed toward all the Jews, but specifically toward Mordecai. This stronghearted Jewish gentleman refused to bow down in Haman's presence. It just so happened that Esther and Mordecai were related . . . she had been raised by this godly man. When Mordecai heard of Haman's plot to have the Jews destroyed, he went to Esther for help. He urged her to use the position the Lord had placed her in to speak to the king on behalf of the Jews. Esther honored Mordecai's request and began to plan how she would approach the king with her request.

Mordecai Persuades Esther to Help

4 When Mordecai learned of all that had been
done, he tore his clothes, put on sackcloth
and ashes, and went out into the city, wailing loudly and bitterly. 2But he went only as far as the
king's gate, because no one clothed in sackcloth
was allowed to enter it. 3In every province to
which the edict and order of the king came, there
was great mourning among the Jews, with fasting,
weeping and wailing. Many lay in sackcloth and
ashes. Nu 14:6; Est 2:19; Eze 27:30-31
4When Esther's maids and eunuchs came and
told her about Mordecai, she was in great distress.
She sent clothes for him to put on instead of his
sackcloth, but he would not accept them. 5Then
Esther summoned Hathach, one of the king's eunuchs assigned to attend her, and ordered him to
find out what was troubling Mordecai and why.
6So Hathach went out to Mordecai in the open
square of the city in front of the king's gate. 7Mor-
decai told him everything that had happened to
him, including the exact amount of money Haman
had promised to pay into the royal treasury for the
destruction of the Jews. 8He also gave him a copy
of the text of the edict for their annihilation, which
had been published in Susa, to show to Esther and
explain it to her, and he told him to urge her to
go into the king's presence to beg for mercy and
plead with him for her people. Est 3:9; 7:4
9Hathach went back and reported to Esther
what Mordecai had said. 10Then she instructed
him to say to Mordecai, 11"All the king's officials
and the people of the royal provinces know that
for any man or woman who approaches the king
in the inner court without being summoned the
king has but one law: that he be put to death. The
only exception to this is for the king to extend the
gold scepter to him and spare his life. But thirty
days have passed since I was called to go to the
king." Da 2:9; Est 5:1-2; 8:4
12When Esther's words were reported to Mordecai, 13he sent back this answer: "Do not think
that because you are in the king's house you alone
of all the Jews will escape. 14For if you remain
silent at this time, relief and deliverance for the
Jews will arise from another place, but you and
your father's family will perish. And who knows
but that you have come to royal position for such
a time as this?" Ge 50:20; Dt 28:29; Am 5:13
15Then Esther sent this reply to Mordecai:
16"Go, gather together all the Jews who are in Susa,
and fast for me. Do not eat or drink for three days,
night or day. I and my maids will fast as you do.
When this is done, I will go to the king, even
though it is against the law. And if I perish, I
perish." Ge 43:14; 2Ch 20:3; Est 9:31

LIVING  **INSIGHT**

How rare are those who live differently! Ask God to do a new work in you this day, to lift your sights above the expected, to develop in you the qualities that make for excellence. As He lifts your sights, watch for those who may be struggling in their quest . . . perhaps dangerously near giving up. May He grant you a sensitive heart and a ready word of encouragement.

(See Esther 4:9–16.)

ESTHER

A Woman for Such a Time as This

"Who knows but that you have come to royal position for such a time as this?"
—ESTHER 4:14b

The story of Esther is in some respects one of the least known (and perhaps one of the least popular) in all the Bible, largely because the name "God" is never mentioned in the book. Yet God's fingerprint, if you will, His hand, is seen moving all the way throughout these chapters as an independent, strong-minded woman named Esther emerged and played an unforgettable role in the history of the Jews.

The Bible tells us that Esther was an orphan, raised in the care of her relative Mordecai in the kingdom of Persia. She grew up to be a beautiful woman, "lovely in form and features" (Esther 2:7), which proved to serve Esther well when King Xerxes announced his search for a new queen. Mordecai entered her name in this Persian beauty contest to see who would become the next queen, and Esther won. Imagine . . . this orphaned Jewess, in God's incredible providence, became the queen of Persia!

Enter Haman, the king's right-hand man. His was a position of maximum power in the kingdom—"all the royal officials at the king's gate knelt down and paid honor to Haman" (3:2). All of them, that is, except Mordecai. Why? Because Mordecai was a Jew, and Haman was an Amalekite. And there was a history of bad blood between the Amalekites and the Jews. Finding out that Mordecai was a Jew ignited a deep hatred in Haman, one he had undoubtedly been nursing since childhood. Now he was in a position to do something about those hated Jews. So instead of simply eliminating Mordecai, he hatched a plan to exterminate Mordecai's entire race (3:5–6). He wanted to kill *all* of the Jews! Then he came up with a skillful and sly blend of truth and falsehood to sell his boss on the idea (3:8–9).

When Mordecai learned what had happened, he had but one hope. Can't you just imagine what he must have been thinking: "I've got to get to Esther. She's the queen!"? Esther, who had been unaware of the cruel edict against her people, listened to Mordecai's passionate plea that went something like this: "This is it, Esther! This is your moment! This is why God had me take you in as a little girl and bring you up His way. Don't be silent, Esther! Use your influence now, Esther, while there's still time."

Esther got the message. And something incredibly significant happened in the time that elapsed between her receiving the message of 4:14 and her responding to the message as recorded in 4:15. Esther evaluated, she counted the cost, she sought to discern God's will, and the result was an eloquence that went beyond what we read in print. What was it that spoke so eloquently? It was Esther's courageous and committed character, demonstrated by her brave actions throughout the rest of the book.

Notice the strategy that Esther chose to carry out. She planned a banquet for Haman and King Xerxes. And there she extended an invitation for them to come to another banquet the following day. Esther planned to confront the king with her identity as a Jewess and plead the cause of her people. Keep your eyes open as a series of divine "coincidences" begin to unfold. The king couldn't sleep that night (6:1), which set into motion a series of events that culminated in the lifting up of Mordecai and the bringing down of Haman and the ultimate protection and deliverance of the Jews. These "coincidences" were not mere coincidences. No, they were God's hand sovereignly directing His plan for His people.

Only God could have brought about an ending like this one. Who would have thought that God would place His hand on a humble orphan girl and her faithful relative? Who would have expected that Mordecai's work to rear Esther as a young woman of God would lead to her being such a vital link to the survival of the Jews? Without question, the story in this book is an image of God's handiwork. The events of Esther's life were like a pile of pearls—beautiful, but seemingly disconnected and disjointed. Then God took the string and the clasp in His own hands. He did a marvelous work in Esther's life to make it a necklace of beauty, perfectly designed to suit His purposes and reflect His glory.

[17]So Mordecai went away and carried out all of Esther's instructions.

Esther's Request to the King

5 On the third day Esther put on her royal robes and stood in the inner court of the palace, in front of the king's hall. The king was sitting on his royal throne in the hall, facing the entrance. [2]When he saw Queen Esther standing in the court, he was pleased with her and held out to her the gold scepter that was in his hand. So Esther approached and touched the tip of the scepter.

[3]Then the king asked, "What is it, Queen Esther? What is your request? Even up to half the kingdom, it will be given you." Est 7:2; Mk 6:23

[4]"If it pleases the king," replied Esther, "let the king, together with Haman, come today to a banquet I have prepared for him."

[5]"Bring Haman at once," the king said, "so that we may do what Esther asks."

So the king and Haman went to the banquet Esther had prepared. [6]As they were drinking wine, the king again asked Esther, "Now what is your petition? It will be given you. And what is your request? Even up to half the kingdom, it will be granted." Est 7:2; 9:12

[7]Esther replied, "My petition and my request is this: [8]If the king regards me with favor and if it pleases the king to grant my petition and fulfill my request, let the king and Haman come tomorrow to the banquet I will prepare for them. Then I will answer the king's question." Est 2:15; 6:14

Haman's Rage Against Mordecai

[9]Haman went out that day happy and in high spirits. But when he saw Mordecai at the king's gate and observed that he neither rose nor showed fear in his presence, he was filled with rage against Mordecai. [10]Nevertheless, Haman restrained himself and went home. Est 2:21; 3:3,5; Pr 14:17

Calling together his friends and Zeresh, his wife, [11]Haman boasted to them about his vast wealth, his many sons, and all the ways the king had honored him and how he had elevated him above the other nobles and officials. [12]"And that's not all," Haman added. "I'm the only person Queen Esther invited to accompany the king to the banquet she gave. And she has invited me along with the king tomorrow. [13]But all this gives me no satisfaction as long as I see that Jew Mordecai sitting at the king's gate." Est 6:13; 9:7-10,13

[14]His wife Zeresh and all his friends said to him, "Have a gallows built, seventy-five feet[a] high, and ask the king in the morning to have Mordecai hanged on it. Then go with the king to the dinner and be happy." This suggestion delighted Haman, and he had the gallows built. Est 6:4; 7:9

[a]14 Hebrew *fifty cubits* (about 23 meters)

God's Deliverance **Chapters 6–8**

These chapters record a wonderful twist of events. Haman, who was plotting the death of the Jews, was forced to honor Mordecai, his greatest enemy. Haman's pride and arrogance led to his downfall. In a panic, Haman tried to turn the tide that was pressing against him, but it ended up costing him his own life. God's hand worked against the forces of evil. As a result the Jews were given permission, by royal declaration, to defend themselves against any attack.

Mordecai Honored

6 That night the king could not sleep; so he ordered the book of the chronicles, the record of his reign, to be brought in and read to him. [2]It was found recorded there that Mordecai had exposed Bigthana and Teresh, two of the king's officers who guarded the doorway, who had conspired to assassinate King Xerxes. Est 2:23

[3]"What honor and recognition has Mordecai received for this?" the king asked.

"Nothing has been done for him," his attendants answered.

[4]The king said, "Who is in the court?" Now Haman had just entered the outer court of the palace to speak to the king about hanging Mordecai on the gallows he had erected for him.

[5]His attendants answered, "Haman is standing in the court."

"Bring him in," the king ordered.

[6]When Haman entered, the king asked him, "What should be done for the man the king delights to honor?"

Now Haman thought to himself, "Who is there that the king would rather honor than me?" [7]So he answered the king, "For the man the king delights to honor, [8]have them bring a royal robe the king has worn and a horse the king has ridden, one with a royal crest placed on its head. [9]Then let the robe and horse be entrusted to one of the king's most noble princes. Let them robe the man the king delights to honor, and lead him on the horse through the city streets, proclaiming before him, 'This is what is done for the man the king delights to honor!'" Ge 41:43; 1Ki 1:33

[10]"Go at once," the king commanded Haman. "Get the robe and the horse and do just as you have suggested for Mordecai the Jew, who sits at the king's gate. Do not neglect anything you have recommended."

[11]So Haman got the robe and the horse. He robed Mordecai, and led him on horseback through the city streets, proclaiming before him, "This is what is done for the man the king delights to honor!" Ge 41:42

[12]Afterward Mordecai returned to the king's gate. But Haman rushed home, with his head cov-

ered in grief, 13and told Zeresh his wife and all his
friends everything that had happened to him.
His advisers and his wife Zeresh said to him,
"Since Mordecai, before whom your downfall has
started, is of Jewish origin, you cannot stand
against him—you will surely come to ruin!"
14While they were still talking with him, the king's
eunuchs arrived and hurried Haman away to the
banquet Esther had prepared. 1Ki 3:15; Est 5:8

Haman Hanged

7 So the king and Haman went to dine with
Queen Esther, 2and as they were drinking
wine on that second day, the king again asked,
"Queen Esther, what is your petition? It will be
given you. What is your request? Even up to half
the kingdom, it will be granted." Est 5:3; 9:12
3Then Queen Esther answered, "If I have found
favor with you, O king, and if it pleases your majesty, grant me my life—this is my petition. And
spare my people—this is my request. 4For I and
my people have been sold for destruction and
slaughter and annihilation. If we had merely been
sold as male and female slaves, I would have kept
quiet, because no such distress would justify disturbing the king.[a]" Est 2:15; 3:9
5King Xerxes asked Queen Esther, "Who is he?
Where is the man who has dared to do such a
thing?"
6Esther said, "The adversary and enemy is this
vile Haman."
Then Haman was terrified before the king and
queen. 7The king got up in a rage, left his wine and
went out into the palace garden. But Haman, realizing that the king had already decided his fate,
stayed behind to beg Queen Esther for his life.
8Just as the king returned from the palace garden to the banquet hall, Haman was falling on the
couch where Esther was reclining. Est 1:6
The king exclaimed, "Will he even molest the
queen while she is with me in the house?" Ge 34:7
As soon as the word left the king's mouth, they
covered Haman's face. 9Then Harbona, one of the
eunuchs attending the king, said, "A gallows seventy-five feet[b] high stands by Haman's house. He
had it made for Mordecai, who spoke up to help
the king." Est 1:10; 5:14
The king said, "Hang him on it!" 10So they
hanged Haman on the gallows he had prepared for
Mordecai. Then the king's fury subsided.

The King's Edict in Behalf of the Jews

8 That same day King Xerxes gave Queen Esther the estate of Haman, the enemy of the
Jews. And Mordecai came into the presence of the
king, for Esther had told how he was related to her.
2The king took off his signet ring, which he had
reclaimed from Haman, and presented it to Mordecai. And Esther appointed him over Haman's
estate. Est 2:7; 3:10; Pr 13:22
3Esther again pleaded with the king, falling at
his feet and weeping. She begged him to put an
end to the evil plan of Haman the Agagite, which
he had devised against the Jews. 4Then the king
extended the gold scepter to Esther and she arose
and stood before him. Est 4:11; 5:2
5"If it pleases the king," she said, "and if he
regards me with favor and thinks it the right thing
to do, and if he is pleased with me, let an order be
written overruling the dispatches that Haman son
of Hammedatha, the Agagite, devised and wrote to
destroy the Jews in all the king's provinces. 6For
how can I bear to see disaster fall on my people?
How can I bear to see the destruction of my family?" Est 7:4; 9:1
7King Xerxes replied to Queen Esther and to
Mordecai the Jew, "Because Haman attacked the
Jews, I have given his estate to Esther, and they
have hanged him on the gallows. 8Now write another decree in the king's name in behalf of the
Jews as seems best to you, and seal it with the
king's signet ring—for no document written in
the king's name and sealed with his ring can be
revoked." Est 1:19; 3:12-14; Da 6:15
9At once the royal secretaries were summoned—on the twenty-third day of the third
month, the month of Sivan. They wrote out all
Mordecai's orders to the Jews, and to the satraps,
governors and nobles of the 127 provinces stretching from India to Cush.[c] These orders were written in the script of each province and the language
of each people and also to the Jews in their own
script and language. 10Mordecai wrote in the name
of King Xerxes, sealed the dispatches with the
king's signet ring, and sent them by mounted couriers, who rode fast horses especially bred for the
king. Est 1:1,22
11The king's edict granted the Jews in every city
the right to assemble and protect themselves; to
destroy, kill and annihilate any armed force of any
nationality or province that might attack them and
their women and children; and to plunder the
property of their enemies. 12The day appointed for
the Jews to do this in all the provinces of King
Xerxes was the thirteenth day of the twelfth
month, the month of Adar. 13A copy of the text of
the edict was to be issued as law in every province
and made known to the people of every nationality
so that the Jews would be ready on that day to
avenge themselves on their enemies. Est 3:14
14The couriers, riding the royal horses, raced

[a]4 Or *quiet, but the compensation our adversary offers cannot be compared with the loss the king would suffer* [b]9 Hebrew *fifty cubits* (about 23 meters) [c]9 That is, the upper Nile region

out, spurred on by the king's command. And the edict was also issued in the citadel of Susa.

15Mordecai left the king's presence wearing royal garments of blue and white, a large crown of gold and a purple robe of fine linen. And the city of Susa held a joyous celebration. 16For the Jews it was a time of happiness and joy, gladness and honor. 17In every province and in every city, wherever the edict of the king went, there was joy and gladness among the Jews, with feasting and celebrating. And many people of other nationalities became Jews because fear of the Jews had seized them. Est 9:3; Ps 97:10-12

A Happy Ending **Chapters 9–10**

The book of Esther ends on a joyous note. Those who hated the Jews began to carry out their attack according to the plan laid out by Haman. However, instead of destroying a helpless enemy, they ended up being conquered by the Jews. The tables were turned and the Israelites vanquished their enemy. In celebration, the Jews had a time of feasting and joy. This commemoration became a regular observance of the Jews. *Purim* remains a time of Jewish celebration to this very day.

Triumph of the Jews

9 On the thirteenth day of the twelfth month, the month of Adar, the edict commanded by the king was to be carried out. On this day the enemies of the Jews had hoped to overpower them, but now the tables were turned and the Jews got the upper hand over those who hated them. 2The Jews assembled in their cities in all the provinces of King Xerxes to attack those seeking their destruction. No one could stand against them, because the people of all the other nationalities were afraid of them. 3And all the nobles of the provinces, the satraps, the governors and the king's administrators helped the Jews, because fear of Mordecai had seized them. 4Mordecai was prominent in the palace; his reputation spread throughout the provinces, and he became more and more powerful. 2Sa 3:1; Est 3:12-14; Pr 22:22-23

5The Jews struck down all their enemies with the sword, killing and destroying them, and they did what they pleased to those who hated them. 6In the citadel of Susa, the Jews killed and destroyed five hundred men. 7They also killed Parshandatha, Dalphon, Aspatha, 8Poratha, Adalia, Aridatha, 9Parmashta, Arisai, Aridai and Vaizatha, 10the ten sons of Haman son of Hammedatha, the enemy of the Jews. But they did not lay their hands on the plunder. Est 5:11; 8:11

11The number of those slain in the citadel of Susa was reported to the king that same day. 12The king said to Queen Esther, "The Jews have killed and destroyed five hundred men and the ten sons of Haman in the citadel of Susa. What have they done in the rest of the king's provinces? Now what is your petition? It will be given you. What is your request? It will also be granted." Est 5:6; 7:2

13"If it pleases the king," Esther answered, "give the Jews in Susa permission to carry out this day's edict tomorrow also, and let Haman's ten sons be hanged on gallows." Dt 21:22-23; Est 5:11

14So the king commanded that this be done. An edict was issued in Susa, and they hanged the ten sons of Haman. 15The Jews in Susa came together on the fourteenth day of the month of Adar, and they put to death in Susa three hundred men, but they did not lay their hands on the plunder.

16Meanwhile, the remainder of the Jews who were in the king's provinces also assembled to protect themselves and get relief from their enemies. They killed seventy-five thousand of them but did not lay their hands on the plunder. 17This happened on the thirteenth day of the month of Adar, and on the fourteenth they rested and made it a day of feasting and joy. Dt 25:19; 1Ki 3:15; 1Ch 4:43

Purim Celebrated

18The Jews in Susa, however, had assembled on the thirteenth and fourteenth, and then on the fifteenth they rested and made it a day of feasting and joy.

19That is why rural Jews—those living in villages—observe the fourteenth of the month of Adar as a day of joy and feasting, a day for giving presents to each other. ver 22; Dt 16:11,14; Ne 8:10,12

20Mordecai recorded these events, and he sent letters to all the Jews throughout the provinces of King Xerxes, near and far, 21to have them celebrate annually the fourteenth and fifteenth days of the month of Adar 22as the time when the Jews got relief from their enemies, and as the month when their sorrow was turned into joy and their mourning into a day of celebration. He wrote them to observe the days as days of feasting and joy and giving presents of food to one another and gifts to the poor. Ne 8:12; Ps 30:11-12

23So the Jews agreed to continue the celebration they had begun, doing what Mordecai had written to them. 24For Haman son of Hammedatha, the Agagite, the enemy of all the Jews, had plotted against the Jews to destroy them and had cast the *pur* (that is, the lot) for their ruin and destruction. 25But when the plot came to the king's attention,[a] he issued written orders that the evil scheme Haman had devised against the Jews should come back onto his own head, and that he and his sons should be hanged on the gallows. 26(Therefore these days were called Purim, from the word *pur.*) Because of everything written in this letter and

[a]25 Or *when Esther came before the king*

because of what they had seen and what had happened to them, 27the Jews took it upon themselves
to establish the custom that they and their descendants and all who join them should without fail
observe these two days every year, in the way prescribed and at the time appointed. 28These days
should be remembered and observed in every generation by every family, and in every province and
in every city. And these days of Purim should
never cease to be celebrated by the Jews, nor
should the memory of them die out among their
descendants. Est 3:7; 7:10; Ps 7:16
29So Queen Esther, daughter of Abihail, along
with Mordecai the Jew, wrote with full authority
to confirm this second letter concerning Purim.
30And Mordecai sent letters to all the Jews in the
127 provinces of the kingdom of Xerxes—words
of goodwill and assurance— 31to establish these
days of Purim at their designated times, as Mordecai the Jew and Queen Esther had decreed for
them, and as they had established for themselves
and their descendants in regard to their times of
fasting and lamentation. 32Esther's decree confirmed these regulations about Purim, and it was
written down in the records. Est 4:1-3,16

The Greatness of Mordecai

10 King Xerxes imposed tribute throughout
the empire, to its distant shores. 2And all
his acts of power and might, together with a full
account of the greatness of Mordecai to which the
king had raised him, are they not written in the
book of the annals of the kings of Media and Persia? 3Mordecai the Jew was second in rank to King
Xerxes, preeminent among the Jews, and held in
high esteem by his many fellow Jews, because he
worked for the good of his people and spoke up
for the welfare of all the Jews. Ne 2:10; Jer 29:4-7; Da 6:3

INTRODUCTION

JOB

The mystery of suffering! It is one of life's most perplexing mysteries. "How could a God who is by His very nature considered to be loving allow His people to suffer—some of them in such horrible ways?" is often how the question is framed. Stated another way, "Why do bad things happen to good people?" The hero of this book, Job by name, was a good man who suffered shocking emotional and physical agony. He struggled to do what we try to do in the midst of our suffering—yet what seems almost impossible to do: maintain faith in a loving God even when all evidence seems to point against it. Let's learn from Job, this magnificent man of misery, who found out in the end that although he didn't find answers to all his questions, he could know this one thing beyond the shadow of a doubt: God still speaks to us in the midst of our pain; He is still in control!

WRITER: *Unknown*

DATE OF STORY: *The patriarchal period (c.1900–1700 B.C.)*

PURPOSE: *To illustrate God's sovereign permission of suffering*

KEY THEME: *The mystery of suffering*

KEY VERSE: *1:9 "Does Job fear God for nothing?"*

TIME LINE

2200BC 2100 2000 1900 1800 1700 1600 1500 1400

Creation, Fall, Flood

Abraham's life (c.2166-1991 B.C.)

Isaac's life (c.2066-1886 B.C.)

Jacob's life (c.2006-1859 B.C.)

Joseph's life (c.1915-1805 B.C.)

Historical setting of Job (c.1900-1700 B.C.)

Moses' life (c.1526-1406 B.C.)

Magnificent Man of Misery

	INTRODUCTION TO THE SUFFERING	DISCUSSION OF THE SUFFERING				SOLUTION TO THE SUFFERING		SUBMISSION UNDER THE SUFFERING	RESTORATION FROM THE SUFFERING
	SCENE 1 Job's purity and prosperity SCENE 2 Satan's proposition and Yahweh's permission SCENE 3 Satan's persecution and Job's patience SCENE 4 Satan's persistence and Yahweh's permission SCENE 5 Poverty and plagues	**Words of Job (Eyes on Self)** Curses birth Curses life	**Words of Three Friends (Eyes on Humanity)** ELIPHAZ JOB ZOPHAR BILDAD	ELIPHAZ JOB ZOPHAR BILDAD	ELIPHAZ JOB BILDAD	**Words of Elihu (Eyes on Yahweh)** To Job To three friends To Job	**Words of Yahweh (Emphasis on Power)**	Job's admission Job's confession	Yahweh's wrath on the three friends Yahweh's blessing on Job
	CHAPTERS 1–2	*CHAPTER 3*	*CHAPTERS 4–14*	*CHAPTERS 15–21*	*CHAPTERS 22–31*	*CHAPTERS 32–37*	*CHAPTERS 38–41*	*CHAPTER 42:1-6*	*CHAPTER 42:7-17*
KEY SECTIONS	Historical	Philosophical				Practical	Doctrinal	Devotional	Historical
KEY SUBJECTS	Job, Yahweh (the LORD) and Satan	Job, Eliphaz, Bildad, Zophar				Elihu	Yahweh	Job	Yahweh, Job and the three friends
KEY SAYINGS	*"Have you considered my servant Job?" (1:8)*	*". . . then Job . . . Eliphaz . . . Bildad . . . Zophar replied"*				God *"does great things beyond our understanding" (37:5)*	*"Everything under heaven belongs to me" (41:11)*	*"Therefore I despise myself and repent in dust and ashes" (42:6)*	*"The LORD blessed the latter part of Job's life more than the first" (42:12)*

The topic of pain, suffering or affliction is popular for one simple reason: We humans experience a lot of it. We characteristically enter this life kicking and screaming and crying at the top of our lungs. Tragically, that's the way some of us leave this life as well. Within the parentheses between birth and death, heartaches are common and pain is universal. There's not a person reading these words who has completely escaped its grip within the past 12 months.

Suffering is never out of date. A man once wrote: "Man is born to trouble as surely as sparks fly upward." This pithy statement didn't come from a local police chief or a newspaper editor. This wise observation came from an ancient sufferer, whose mind and body had endured what most of us would call the maximum grief and pain any one person could experience. These words of lament came from one of the ancient writers of Scripture. He wrote those words in verse 7 of chapter 5 of a book called by his name. His name . . . was Job.

Job was a man of practicality, and not a theorizer. He was an authentic sufferer, a magnificent man of misery. He did not write a philosophical treatise on the dynamics of human suffering. He simply recorded the pain and the misery of his own suffering. These are not words written from an ivory tower; they are anguished cries from an ash heap.

A Drama in Five Parts

To give some structure to the study of the book of Job, I have divided this chronicle of suffering into five sections: Chapters 1–2 provide an *introduction* to suffering. Chapters 3–31, the bulk of the book, cover a *discussion* of suffering itself. Chapters 32–41 present a *solution* to the suffering of Job. Chapter 46:1–6 show us Job's *submission* under the authority of the suffering. Finally, in chapter 42:7–17 we read of *restoration* from the suffering, as provided by God's grace.

Job is a book of intense passion. You can hardly read this book without shaking your head and even at times weeping. You may find yourself nodding in understanding because you have been there; you may find yourself standing by, not knowing what to say in the face of the enormity of human suffering—because you've been there too. But certainly this truth remains: You will appreciate the depth of this book every time you return to it.

The Question Facing Job

Please keep in mind, we're not talking about affliction that is deserved. When we have done what is wrong, we may expect to suffer some sense of consequence. But when we have done what is right—and we have done it for the right motives—and then we suffer, you and I may very well have difficulty reconciling that with a God we call "just and righteous." And that introduces us to the weighty question that weaves its way through the book of Job: *"How can God be just and still allow a righteous child of His to suffer so terribly?"*

Living the Fairy Tale Life

Job's story begins almost like a timeworn fairy tale. You might be tempted to add, "Once upon a time," as you start reading:

> *In the land of Uz there lived a man whose name was Job. This man was blameless and upright; he feared God and shunned evil (1:1).*

What a remarkable biography in one verse! Job was, according to the verses that follow, an extraordinary, righteous man, more famous than any in the ancient East. It is believed by most Old Testament evangelical scholars that the story of Job ranks in age alongside the history of the patriarchs recorded in Genesis. Job is believed by many to have lived during the time of the patriarchs, like Abraham and Jacob and Joseph.

Job had seven sons and three daughters. He also had many possessions. If he were alive today we would call him a "wealthy rancher." He had landholdings, he had livestock, and he had the best of this world's goods. Chapter 1 tells us that he held the lives of his children very close to his heart. He would remember each one of them in prayer (1:5). What a father! Job wasn't satisfied simply to rear his children God's way; even after they reached adulthood he remembered them in his prayers daily. To Job, parenting was a lifelong commitment. He cared deeply about the spiritual welfare of his children and did all he could to encourage their faith. Whoever said that it's impossible to be rich and still have integrity? Job was a man whom God could trust!

By the way, if you have, or had, a godly parent like Job, you are of all people most blessed. Give God thanks for your parents (or for you it may be only one parent) who care about you and your spiritual life. Give thanks for their spiritual commitment to you. Take the time this week to express your gratitude to them. If their earthly pilgrimage is over, why not say a prayer in which you thank God for the influence they had in your life.

A Scene From the Heavens

Just six verses into the book of Job we are suddenly transported to heaven. In this unusual scene, we are permitted to witness something found nowhere else in Scripture: A dialogue between God and Satan regarding a righteous man on earth . . . the subject is Job. Do not think for a moment that Satan is sort of strolling around casually in heaven. Not on your life! He is there like one of lesser rank who stands in front of an officer. God is clearly and absolutely in charge. Watch what transpired! After God pointed to Job as a blameless and upright man, Satan made this observation:

> *"Does Job fear God for nothing?" Satan replied. "Have you not put a hedge around him and his household and everything he has? You have blessed the work of his hands, so that his flocks and herds are spread throughout the land. But stretch out your hand and strike everything he has, and he will surely curse you to your face" (1:9–11).*

God granted Satan permission to test Job. Why did He do that? I do not know. We're never specifically told why God allowed such a thing. The sovereign God is not obliged to tell us His reasons. He does not ask our permission when He is ready to act. He doesn't knock on our doors three days in advance and say, "It's coming. Get your act together." No, God's will prevails, and occasionally it entails pain in our lives. And when it does, we may find ourselves asking these questions: "Why me?" "How long is this going to continue?" "Why this?" "Why now?" Those questions frequently go unanswered.

What Can We Expect From God?

As you read the book of Job, you will discover what terrible suffering this man endured. After losing all of his earthly pleasures and possessions, he also lost all ten of his children. Following that, the man lost his health. After experiencing suffering beyond what you and I will ever face, his wife confronted Job with these piercing words: "Are you still holding on to your integrity? Curse God and die!" (2:9). Now note very carefully Job's response:

> *He replied, "You are talking like a foolish woman. Shall we accept good from God, and not trouble?" In all this, Job did not sin in what he said (2:10).*

What a question Job asked his wife! That question came from a godly man—a question that, in today's terms, might go something like this: "Who are we to think that we have some kind of corner on God's goodness, to be so presumptuous as to think that He is obligated to bless us. Shall we accept year after year of blessings and never think He has the right to put us through hard times as well? Is there something different about God when adversity strikes? He is sovereign! His character hasn't changed."

We hear a lot of shallow, strange theology these days telling us that God is only a God of love, a God of uninterrupted goodness, a God who only hands out gifts, a God of grace and, therefore, obliged to keep us healthy, happy, smiling and prosperous at all times. The Bible does not support a "Santa Claus" concept of God. It does not teach about a God who promises unceasing blessing every moment of life. He is *indeed* a God of love and goodness and grace . . . but He is also engaged in conforming us to the likeness of His Son (Romans 8:29). Cultivating such character includes tests that are painful and sometimes extremely hard to endure.

In the Bible we read of a faithful God. We read of a balanced God. We read of a sovereign God who, without explaining His reasons, gives as well as takes; blesses as well as tests. During such occasions, without explanation He often removes from us the very things we have treasured. When Job was confronted with this truth, he asked the right question: "Shall we accept good from God, and not trouble?" (2:10).

Support in the Midst of Suffering?

As time went on, Job became a human scab. His whole body was covered with sores and boils. He sat on an ash heap and suffered alone (2:8). One day, three friends came to give him support and counsel (2:11). Try to imagine how Job must have looked as his friends approached. As they came close and looked at him, they may very well have thought to themselves, "He doesn't even look like the same man we knew only a few months ago; look at this calamity that has struck him!"

Job's condition sketched a horrible picture of anguished humanity. As the three friends approached, they were at a loss to know what to say. As a matter of fact, for the first seven days they did not say a word; they simply sat in silence with their suffering friend. And you know, that was the most valuable thing they could have done, because when they started talking, whatever compassion they may have felt earlier vanished into thin air.

After their week-long silence, these so-called counselors began to preach to, argue with, blame, harass and antagonize Job. They put his life under a microscope and concluded that he must be suffering because of some hidden sin. They dug into Job's life and probed all around. They were relentless. They were cruel. They were bloodthirsty. They didn't let up!

Finally, Job reached the end of his rope; he leveled with his counselors, telling them in effect, "You men are not counselors; in fact, you don't know the first thing about counseling. You're worthless when it comes to providing help; you're miserable counselors, my friends, but you certainly have a gift for being mockers. I don't need that!" (see 13:4; 16:2; 17:2). The point is: There is no easy, simple, quick answer when this kind of calamity strikes, this kind of suffering comes. There wasn't one back then . . . there isn't one today.

God was not pleased with the counsel of Job's friends. Even though they mouthed a number of correct and often eloquent statements (at least on the surface), they charged in where sensitive souls fear to tread—the realm of human suffering. In the end, God responded to these false counselors with a severe rebuke (42:7–9), and Job was commended and restored. And so at the end of the book of Job we find God providing the ultimate comfort to Job. God doesn't give him answers to all of his questions, but *He gives Himself*.

No Simple Answers

Some who read these words have not yet gone through deep valleys. If that is true of you, learn a lesson from Job. When you come alongside those who have suffered, those who have lost a loved one, for example, say little. Just be there. Don't feel you have to give reasons or answers. Don't try to rationalize. Their loved one is gone. The grief is great. The loss is real. And the horror of death is not yet finished. People do not get over grief until they have expressed it fully. We need to give them the freedom to do that. Our presence alone is an eloquent statement that we care.

May I offer a few words of advice for you sensitive souls who deal with the reality of human suffering day in and day out? Be very compassionate and pay close attention to the words you use when you come alongside the grieving and the hurting. Be tactful and thoughtful as you select your words. If you are not absolutely certain your words are coming from God, *stay quiet*. Grief is a deep river, a strong current, pulling many people under. Your fellow sufferers need a lifeline to draw them into the arms of God. In His time, God will give you the right words to say; in the meantime, when the words won't come, be available, be honest, be willing to help carry the burden. Be willing simply to comfort with the comfort we've received from God (see 2 Corinthians 1:3–7).

The great theologian Charles Hodge once said, "If anyone thinks he has a simple solution to the problem of pain and suffering he should hold a tiny infant screaming with pain. And as he holds that baby in his arms, any simple solution will fly out the window."

If you're a parent and you have little ones and they scream with pain and they're too young to understand, you just hold them and pray, walk, think, sing, talk—and then pray some more. All the time you are wondering, "Why?" But the fact is, even if you had the answer, try to explain it to that little suffering child and all you would hear is their tormented crying right back at you.

There is no simple, quick, easy solution. Wherever human suffering is found, the anguished questions remain. In the end, the reason for our suffering may lie hidden deep within the mystery of God's divine purpose. We may never know in this life why we suffer, but for each of us the ultimate question must be faced: "Will we trust Him as the God who does only what is right? Will we accept His plan for our lives?"

Introduction to Suffering Chapters 1–2

If there was one person in the Old Testament who typified suffering, it was Job. When he woke up that fateful morning (1:13), he had no idea of what awaited him. He did not know about the dialogue in heaven. He did not know about the permission granted to Satan to torment him. All he knew was that he loved the Lord and that he was blessed with a wonderful family, good health and a vast supply of earthly goods. To all appearances, Job was leading the ideal life.

Before the day was over, he had lost all his earthly wealth and then his grown children—each of them. Within a short time he had also lost his health. It seems the only thing he did not lose was his faith in God (2:10). At this point, some of Job's friends arrived to comfort him. They sat with him in silence for a whole week. Their silence and presence was all the comfort Job needed. Later, when they began to speak, the comfort ceased.

Prologue

1 In the land of Uz there lived a man whose
name was Job. This man was blameless and
upright; he feared God and shunned evil. 2He had
seven sons and three daughters, 3and he owned
seven thousand sheep, three thousand camels, five
hundred yoke of oxen and five hundred donkeys,
and had a large number of servants. He was the
greatest man among all the people of the East.

4His sons used to take turns holding feasts in
their homes, and they would invite their three sisters to eat and drink with them. 5When a period of
feasting had run its course, Job would send and
have them purified. Early in the morning he would
sacrifice a burnt offering for each of them, thinking, "Perhaps my children have sinned and cursed
God in their hearts." This was Job's regular custom. Ge 8:20; 1Ki 21:10,13

Job's First Test

6One day the angels[a] came to present themselves before the LORD, and Satan[b] also came with
them. 7The LORD said to Satan, "Where have you
come from?" Job 2:1; 38:7

Satan answered the LORD, "From roaming
through the earth and going back and forth in it."

8Then the LORD said to Satan, "Have you considered my servant Job? There is no one on earth
like him; he is blameless and upright, a man who
fears God and shuns evil." Jos 1:7; Job 42:7-8

9"Does Job fear God for nothing?" Satan replied. 10"Have you not put a hedge around him
and his household and everything he has? You
have blessed the work of his hands, so that his
flocks and herds are spread throughout the land.
11But stretch out your hand and strike everything
he has, and he will surely curse you to your face."

12The LORD said to Satan, "Very well, then, everything he has is in your hands, but on the man
himself do not lay a finger."

Then Satan went out from the presence of the
LORD.

13One day when Job's sons and daughters were
feasting and drinking wine at the oldest brother's
house, 14a messenger came to Job and said, "The
oxen were plowing and the donkeys were grazing
nearby, 15and the Sabeans attacked and carried
them off. They put the servants to the sword, and
I am the only one who has escaped to tell you!"

16While he was still speaking, another messenger came and said, "The fire of God fell from the
sky and burned up the sheep and the servants, and
I am the only one who has escaped to tell you!"

17While he was still speaking, another messenger came and said, "The Chaldeans formed three
raiding parties and swept down on your camels
and carried them off. They put the servants to the
sword, and I am the only one who has escaped to
tell you!" Ge 11:28,31

18While he was still speaking, yet another messenger came and said, "Your sons and daughters
were feasting and drinking wine at the oldest
brother's house, 19when suddenly a mighty wind
swept in from the desert and struck the four corners of the house. It collapsed on them and they
are dead, and I am the only one who has escaped
to tell you!" Jer 4:11; 13:24

20At this, Job got up and tore his robe and
shaved his head. Then he fell to the ground in
worship 21and said: Ge 37:29; 1Pe 5:6

"Naked I came from my mother's womb,
and naked I will depart.[c] Ecc 5:15; 1Ti 6:7
The LORD gave and the LORD has taken away;
may the name of the LORD be praised."

22In all this, Job did not sin by charging God
with wrongdoing. Job 2:10

LIVING  **INSIGHT**

Job uttered these words as he grieved and looked to God for strength in his worship. There is no sin in his honest, passionate expressions of grief.

(See Job 1:20–22.)

Job's Second Test

2 On another day the angels[a] came to present
themselves before the LORD, and Satan also
came with them to present himself before him.
2And the LORD said to Satan, "Where have you
come from?" Job 1:6

Satan answered the LORD, "From roaming

[a]6,1 Hebrew *the sons of God* [b]6 *Satan* means *accuser.* [c]21 Or *will return there*

JOB

Patience in the Face of Calamity

"In the land of Uz there lived a man whose name was Job. This man was blameless and upright; he feared God and shunned evil."

—JOB 1:1

If you or I had been looking for an ideal family back in the old days, we very likely would have stopped dead in our tracks when we came to the residence of Mr. and Mrs. Job, who lived in the land of Uz. Job was a model father, wholly dedicated to God and to his children. His family got along well. They laughed together and shared meals together. And Job was consistent in remembering his children in prayer to God (1:5). Job's family was also very affluent—with servants, perhaps, to wait upon their every need. Sounds nice, doesn't it? A fully functioning family with plenty of love to go around and plenty of cash to spare. Living in this kind of environment, it's easy to see why Job was dedicated to God, right? Who wouldn't be happy and content in this situation? Make no mistake, Job *was* happy, and God was happy with Job.

Suddenly, without warning, Job's life flipped completely upside-down. Verse 13 of chapter 1 begins with the words "One day," which gives us an ominous introduction to the sudden nature of the hellish calamity that came upon Job, orchestrated by Satan himself. Job awoke one morning, expecting a day just like any other. But by sundown he had lost everything. Four messengers entered his house virtually in lightning-flash fashion, one right after the other. Desperate and panicked, each one declared to Job the loss of everything tangible in his life. First the oxen, then the sheep, then the camels, along with the faithful employees who had attended the herds. What shocking material and human loss! And then, the most unspeakable horror of all—all ten of Job's precious children, gone in an instant!

If we live to be a hundred years old, we will never be able to enter into the grief of this man at this point in his life. He had lost his livestock, his servants, his entire base of financial security. And before he could even begin to digest what had happened, he was standing beside ten fresh graves on a windswept hill in the land of Uz. That's how tragedy usually happens in this life. That's how grief comes.

Job could have reacted in anger. He could have shaken his fist at God and cursed Him, raging against the injustice of his losses. Instead, he worshiped the God he had walked with for years and would continue to walk with, no matter what. Interestingly, the *first word* we hear from this man, who just moments before had a large family and great wealth, is "naked": "Naked I came from my mother's womb, and naked I will depart. The LORD gave and the LORD has taken away; may the name of the LORD be praised" (1:21). He admitted that he was unabashedly open-handed, completely dependent, possessing nothing in himself. His head was shaved. His robe was torn. He was completely bankrupt before the Lord, able by the grace of God to avoid sinning (1:22) in his reaction to the train wreck his life had become.

The most telling picture of Job's faithfulness came as he sat among the ashes, an ancient symbol of mourning, scraping his sores with a piece of broken pottery. His wife, who had experienced the same gut-wrenching losses as Job, gave him some profoundly unpalatable counsel. In a fit of rage, she spat out advice that went something like this: "Why not just end it all, Job? Just curse God and die" (2:9). But Job's soul was healthy. His faith didn't depend on possessions or, for that matter, even his family or even his own physical health. He knew that the Ruler of his life had every right to allow such afflictions. He had taken a step deeper than most of us ever do: "Shall we accept good from God, and not trouble?" (2:10).

Amen! Job's God is not some doting, gracious creature who sits on the edge of heaven dropping good little gifts wrapped in ribbons. That's not the God of heaven! Our sovereign God dispenses what brings glory to Him. God's great goal for us is not that we be rich and successful and smiling and happy at all times. God's goal is that we glorify Him no matter what our circumstances (see 1 Corinthians 10:31). Job put it in a nutshell: "But he knows the way that I take; when he has tested me, I will come forth as gold" (23:10). That's trust. That's faith. That's the source of Job's legendary patience.

through the earth and going back and forth in it."
3Then the LORD said to Satan, "Have you considered my servant Job? There is no one on earth
like him; he is blameless and upright, a man who
fears God and shuns evil. And he still maintains
his integrity, though you incited me against him to
ruin him without any reason." Job 9:17; 27:6
4"Skin for skin!" Satan replied. "A man will give
all he has for his own life. 5But stretch out your
hand and strike his flesh and bones, and he will
surely curse you to your face." Job 1:11; 19:20
6The LORD said to Satan, "Very well, then, he is
in your hands; but you must spare his life."
7So Satan went out from the presence of the
LORD and afflicted Job with painful sores from the
soles of his feet to the top of his head. 8Then Job
took a piece of broken pottery and scraped himself
with it as he sat among the ashes. Job 42:6; Eze 27:30
9His wife said to him, "Are you still holding on
to your integrity? Curse God and die!"
10He replied, "You are talking like a foolish[a]
woman. Shall we accept good from God, and not
trouble?" Job 1:21
In all this, Job did not sin in what he said.

LIVING  INSIGHT

One of the most important questions we can ask when some unforeseen tragedy brings us pain and suffering is whom we will permit it to serve—God or the devil? Will it cause us to become alive in wisdom or paralyzed by bitterness?

(See Job 2:10.)

Job's Three Friends

11When Job's three friends, Eliphaz the Temanite, Bildad the Shuhite and Zophar the Naamathite, heard about all the troubles that had come
upon him, they set out from their homes and met
together by agreement to go and sympathize with
him and comfort him. 12When they saw him from
a distance, they could hardly recognize him; they
began to weep aloud, and they tore their robes and
sprinkled dust on their heads. 13Then they sat on
the ground with him for seven days and seven
nights. No one said a word to him, because they
saw how great his suffering was. Ge 50:10; Pr 17:28

A Discussion of Suffering **Chapters 3–31**

This significant section records a series of speeches offered by each of Job's "friends." The three main speakers here, in addition to Job, were Eliphaz, Bildad and Zophar. Each one, in turn, gave his own theory on why Job was suffering. After each spoke, Job responded and sought to defend himself. This cycle was repeated three times. Job's friends appeared certain that their friend *must* have done something terrible to warrant this kind of "punishment" from God. Job stood by his belief that he had not wronged or offended God. At the end of their lengthy debate, they appeared no closer to solving the mystery of suffering than they were when they had begun to speak.

Job Speaks

3 After this, Job opened his mouth and cursed
the day of his birth. 2He said:

3"May the day of my birth perish,
and the night it was said, 'A boy is born!'
4That day—may it turn to darkness;
may God above not care about it;
may no light shine upon it.
5May darkness and deep shadow[b] claim it
once more; Job 10:21-22; Jer 2:6; 13:16
may a cloud settle over it;
may blackness overwhelm its light.
6That night—may thick darkness seize it;
may it not be included among the days of
the year
nor be entered in any of the months.
7May that night be barren;
may no shout of joy be heard in it.
8May those who curse days[c] curse that day,
those who are ready to rouse Leviathan.
9May its morning stars become dark;
may it wait for daylight in vain
and not see the first rays of dawn, Job 41:18
10for it did not shut the doors of the womb on
me
to hide trouble from my eyes.

11"Why did I not perish at birth,
and die as I came from the womb? Job 10:18
12Why were there knees to receive me Ge 30:3
and breasts that I might be nursed?
13For now I would be lying down in peace;
I would be asleep and at rest Job 7:8-10,21
14with kings and counselors of the earth, Job 12:17
who built for themselves places now lying
in ruins, Job 15:28
15with rulers who had gold, Job 12:21
who filled their houses with silver. Job 27:17
16Or why was I not hidden in the ground like a
stillborn child, Ps 58:8; Ecc 6:3
like an infant who never saw the light of
day?
17There the wicked cease from turmoil,
and there the weary are at rest. Job 17:16
18Captives also enjoy their ease;
they no longer hear the slave driver's shout.
19The small and the great are there,
and the slave is freed from his master.

[a] *10* The Hebrew word rendered *foolish* denotes moral deficiency. [b] *5* Or *and the shadow of death* [c] *8* Or *the sea*

[20]"Why is light given to those in misery,
and life to the bitter of soul, 1Sa 1:10; Jer 20:18
[21]to those who long for death that does not come, Rev 9:6
who search for it more than for hidden treasure, Pr 2:4
[22]who are filled with gladness
and rejoice when they reach the grave?
[23]Why is life given to a man
whose way is hidden,
whom God has hedged in? Job 19:6,8,12; La 3:7
[24]For sighing comes to me instead of food;
my groans pour out like water. Ps 42:3-4
[25]What I feared has come upon me;
what I dreaded has happened to me.
[26]I have no peace, no quietness;
I have no rest, but only turmoil." Job 7:4,14

LIVING  **INSIGHT**

It has been said that humans are the only creatures who run faster when they lose their way. The result? Increased irritability. Frayed nerves. Impatience. Shorter fuses. Preoccupation. Procrastination when it comes to choosing the right priorities.

(See Job 3:26.)

Eliphaz

4 Then Eliphaz the Temanite replied:

[2]"If someone ventures a word with you, will you be impatient?
But who can keep from speaking? Job 32:20
[3]Think how you have instructed many,
how you have strengthened feeble hands.
[4]Your words have supported those who stumbled;
you have strengthened faltering knees.
[5]But now trouble comes to you, and you are discouraged;
it strikes you, and you are dismayed. Job 6:14
[6]Should not your piety be your confidence
and your blameless ways your hope? Job 1:1

[7]"Consider now: Who, being innocent, has ever perished? Job 36:7
Where were the upright ever destroyed?
[8]As I have observed, those who plow evil
and those who sow trouble reap it. Pr 22:8
[9]At the breath of God they are destroyed;
at the blast of his anger they perish. Job 40:13
[10]The lions may roar and growl,
yet the teeth of the great lions are broken.
[11]The lion perishes for lack of prey, Ps 34:10
and the cubs of the lioness are scattered.

[12]"A word was secretly brought to me,
my ears caught a whisper of it. Job 26:14; 33:14
[13]Amid disquieting dreams in the night,
when deep sleep falls on men, Job 33:15
[14]fear and trembling seized me
and made all my bones shake. Jer 23:9; Hab 3:16
[15]A spirit glided past my face,
and the hair on my body stood on end.
[16]It stopped,
but I could not tell what it was.
A form stood before my eyes,
and I heard a hushed voice:
[17]'Can a mortal be more righteous than God?
Can a man be more pure than his Maker?
[18]If God places no trust in his servants,
if he charges his angels with error, Job 15:15
[19]how much more those who live in houses of clay, Job 10:9
whose foundations are in the dust, Ge 2:7
who are crushed more readily than a moth!
[20]Between dawn and dusk they are broken to pieces;
unnoticed, they perish forever. Job 20:7
[21]Are not the cords of their tent pulled up,
so that they die without wisdom?'[a] Job 36:12

5 "Call if you will, but who will answer you?
To which of the holy ones will you turn?
[2]Resentment kills a fool,
and envy slays the simple. Pr 12:16
[3]I myself have seen a fool taking root, Jer 12:2
but suddenly his house was cursed. Job 24:18
[4]His children are far from safety, Job 4:11
crushed in court without a defender. Am 5:12
[5]The hungry consume his harvest, Job 18:8-10
taking it even from among thorns,
and the thirsty pant after his wealth.
[6]For hardship does not spring from the soil,
nor does trouble sprout from the ground.
[7]Yet man is born to trouble Job 14:1
as surely as sparks fly upward.

[8]"But if it were I, I would appeal to God;
I would lay my cause before him. Ps 35:23
[9]He performs wonders that cannot be fathomed, Job 42:3; Ps 40:5
miracles that cannot be counted.
[10]He bestows rain on the earth;
he sends water upon the countryside.
[11]The lowly he sets on high, Ps 113:7-8
and those who mourn are lifted to safety.
[12]He thwarts the plans of the crafty, Ne 4:15
so that their hands achieve no success.
[13]He catches the wise in their craftiness, 1Co 3:19
and the schemes of the wily are swept away.

[a] 21 Some interpreters end the quotation after verse 17.

14Darkness comes upon them in the daytime;
at noon they grope as in the night. Dt 28:29
15He saves the needy from the sword in their
mouth; Ps 35:10
he saves them from the clutches of the
powerful. Job 4:10
16So the poor have hope,
and injustice shuts its mouth. Ps 107:42

17"Blessed is the man whom God corrects;
so do not despise the discipline of the
Almighty.[a] Ps 94:12; Pr 3:11; Heb 12:5-11
18For he wounds, but he also binds up; Isa 30:26
he injures, but his hands also heal. 1Sa 2:6
19From six calamities he will rescue you;
in seven no harm will befall you. Ps 34:19
20In famine he will ransom you from death,
and in battle from the stroke of the sword.
21You will be protected from the lash of the
tongue, Ps 31:20
and need not fear when destruction comes.
22You will laugh at destruction and famine,
and need not fear the beasts of the earth.
23For you will have a covenant with the stones
of the field, Ps 91:12
and the wild animals will be at peace with
you. Isa 11:6-9
24You will know that your tent is secure;
you will take stock of your property and
find nothing missing. Job 8:6
25You will know that your children will be
many, Ps 112:2
and your descendants like the grass of the
earth. Ps 72:16; Isa 44:3-4
26You will come to the grave in full vigor,
like sheaves gathered in season.

27"We have examined this, and it is true.
So hear it and apply it to yourself." Job 8:5

Job

6 Then Job replied:

2"If only my anguish could be weighed
and all my misery be placed on the scales!
3It would surely outweigh the sand of the
seas— Pr 27:3
no wonder my words have been impetuous.
4The arrows of the Almighty are in me,
my spirit drinks in their poison; Job 21:20
God's terrors are marshaled against me.
5Does a wild donkey bray when it has grass,
or an ox bellow when it has fodder?
6Is tasteless food eaten without salt,
or is there flavor in the white of an egg[b]?
7I refuse to touch it;
such food makes me ill. Job 3:24

8"Oh, that I might have my request,
that God would grant what I hope for,
9that God would be willing to crush me,
to let loose his hand and cut me off!
10Then I would still have this consolation—
my joy in unrelenting pain—
that I had not denied the words of the
Holy One. Job 23:12

11"What strength do I have, that I should still
hope?
What prospects, that I should be patient?
12Do I have the strength of stone?
Is my flesh bronze?
13Do I have any power to help myself, Job 26:2
now that success has been driven from me?

14"A despairing man should have the devotion
of his friends, Job 4:5; 15:4
even though he forsakes the fear of the
Almighty.
15But my brothers are as undependable as
intermittent streams, Ps 38:11; Jer 15:18
as the streams that overflow
16when darkened by thawing ice
and swollen with melting snow,
17but that cease to flow in the dry season,
and in the heat vanish from their channels.
18Caravans turn aside from their routes;
they go up into the wasteland and perish.
19The caravans of Tema look for water, Ge 25:15
the traveling merchants of Sheba look in
hope.
20They are distressed, because they had been
confident;
they arrive there, only to be disappointed.
21Now you too have proved to be of no help;
you see something dreadful and are afraid.
22Have I ever said, 'Give something on my
behalf,
pay a ransom for me from your wealth,
23deliver me from the hand of the enemy,
ransom me from the clutches of the
ruthless'?

24"Teach me, and I will be quiet; Ps 39:1
show me where I have been wrong.
25How painful are honest words! Ecc 12:11
But what do your arguments prove?
26Do you mean to correct what I say,
and treat the words of a despairing man as
wind? Job 8:2; 15:3
27You would even cast lots for the fatherless
and barter away your friend.

28"But now be so kind as to look at me.
Would I lie to your face? Job 27:4
29Relent, do not be unjust;

[a] 17 Hebrew *Shaddai*; here and throughout Job [b] 6 The meaning of the Hebrew for this phrase is uncertain.

reconsider, for my integrity is at stake.[a]
30 Is there any wickedness on my lips? Job 27:4
Can my mouth not discern malice? Job 12:11

7 "Does not man have hard service on earth?
Are not his days like those of a hired man?
2 Like a slave longing for the evening shadows,
or a hired man waiting eagerly for his
wages, Lev 19:13
3 so I have been allotted months of futility,
and nights of misery have been assigned to
me. Job 16:7; Ps 6:6
4 When I lie down I think, 'How long before I
get up?' Dt 28:67
The night drags on, and I toss till dawn.
5 My body is clothed with worms and scabs,
my skin is broken and festering.

6 "My days are swifter than a weaver's shuttle,
and they come to an end without hope.
7 Remember, O God, that my life is but a
breath; Ps 78:39; Jas 4:14
my eyes will never see happiness again.
8 The eye that now sees me will see me no
longer;
you will look for me, but I will be no more.
9 As a cloud vanishes and is gone,
so he who goes down to the grave[b] does
not return. 2Sa 12:23; Job 11:8
10 He will never come to his house again;
his place will know him no more. Job 8:18
11 "Therefore I will not keep silent; Ps 40:9
I will speak out in the anguish of my spirit,
I will complain in the bitterness of my soul.
12 Am I the sea, or the monster of the deep,
that you put me under guard?
13 When I think my bed will comfort me
and my couch will ease my complaint,
14 even then you frighten me with dreams
and terrify me with visions, Job 9:34
15 so that I prefer strangling and death, 1Ki 19:4
rather than this body of mine.
16 I despise my life; I would not live forever.
Let me alone; my days have no meaning.

17 "What is man that you make so much of him,
that you give him so much attention, Ps 8:4
18 that you examine him every morning
and test him every moment? Job 14:3
19 Will you never look away from me,
or let me alone even for an instant? Job 9:18
20 If I have sinned, what have I done to you,
O watcher of men?
Why have you made me your target? Job 16:12
Have I become a burden to you?[c]
21 Why do you not pardon my offenses
and forgive my sins? Job 10:14
For I will soon lie down in the dust; Ps 104:29
you will search for me, but I will be no
more."

Bildad

8 Then Bildad the Shuhite replied:

2 "How long will you say such things?
Your words are a blustering wind. Job 6:26
3 Does God pervert justice? Dt 32:4; Ro 3:5
Does the Almighty pervert what is right?
4 When your children sinned against him,
he gave them over to the penalty of their
sin. Job 1:19
5 But if you will look to God
and plead with the Almighty, Job 11:13
6 if you are pure and upright,
even now he will rouse himself on your
behalf Ps 7:6
and restore you to your rightful place.
7 Your beginnings will seem humble,
so prosperous will your future be. Job 42:12

8 "Ask the former generations Dt 32:7; Job 15:18
and find out what their fathers learned,
9 for we were born only yesterday and know
nothing, Ge 47:9
and our days on earth are but a shadow.
10 Will they not instruct you and tell you?
Will they not bring forth words from their
understanding? Pr 4:1
11 Can papyrus grow tall where there is no
marsh?
Can reeds thrive without water?
12 While still growing and uncut,
they wither more quickly than grass. Ps 129:6
13 Such is the destiny of all who forget God;
so perishes the hope of the godless. Job 11:20
14 What he trusts in is fragile[d];
what he relies on is a spider's web. Isa 59:5
15 He leans on his web, but it gives way; Job 27:18
he clings to it, but it does not hold. Ps 49:11
16 He is like a well-watered plant in the
sunshine,
spreading its shoots over the garden; Ps 37:35
17 it entwines its roots around a pile of rocks
and looks for a place among the stones.
18 But when it is torn from its spot,
that place disowns it and says, 'I never saw
you.' Job 7:8; Ps 37:36
19 Surely its life withers away, Job 20:5
and[e] from the soil other plants grow.

20 "Surely God does not reject a blameless man
or strengthen the hands of evildoers.
21 He will yet fill your mouth with laughter
and your lips with shouts of joy. Ps 126:2

[a]29 Or *my righteousness still stands* [b]9 Hebrew *Sheol* [c]20 A few manuscripts of the Masoretic Text, an ancient Hebrew scribal tradition and Septuagint; most manuscripts of the Masoretic Text *I have become a burden to myself.* [d]14 The meaning of the Hebrew for this word is uncertain. [e]19 Or *Surely all the joy it has / is that*

22 Your enemies will be clothed in shame, Ps 35:26
and the tents of the wicked will be no
more." Job 18:6,14,21

Job

9 Then Job replied:

2 "Indeed, I know that this is true.
But how can a mortal be righteous before
God? Ro 3:20
3 Though one wished to dispute with him,
he could not answer him one time out of a
thousand. Job 10:2
4 His wisdom is profound, his power is vast.
Who has resisted him and come out
unscathed? 2Ch 13:12
5 He moves mountains without their knowing it
and overturns them in his anger. Mic 1:4
6 He shakes the earth from its place Isa 2:21
and makes its pillars tremble. Job 26:11
7 He speaks to the sun and it does not shine;
he seals off the light of the stars. Isa 13:10
8 He alone stretches out the heavens Ge 1:6
and treads on the waves of the sea. Job 38:16
9 He is the Maker of the Bear and Orion,
the Pleiades and the constellations of the
south. Ge 1:16; Job 38:31
10 He performs wonders that cannot be
fathomed, Ps 71:15
miracles that cannot be counted. Job 5:9
11 When he passes me, I cannot see him;
when he goes by, I cannot perceive him.
12 If he snatches away, who can stop him?
Who can say to him, 'What are you doing?'
13 God does not restrain his anger;
even the cohorts of Rahab cowered at his
feet. Job 26:12; Isa 30:7
14 "How then can I dispute with him?
How can I find words to argue with him?
15 Though I were innocent, I could not answer
him; Job 10:15
I could only plead with my Judge for
mercy. Job 8:5
16 Even if I summoned him and he responded,
I do not believe he would give me a
hearing.
17 He would crush me with a storm Job 16:12; 30:22
and multiply my wounds for no reason.
18 He would not let me regain my breath
but would overwhelm me with misery.
19 If it is a matter of strength, he is mighty!
And if it is a matter of justice, who will
summon him[a]?
20 Even if I were innocent, my mouth would
condemn me;
if I were blameless, it would pronounce me
guilty.

21 "Although I am blameless, Job 1:1
I have no concern for myself;
I despise my own life. Job 7:16
22 It is all the same; that is why I say,
'He destroys both the blameless and the
wicked.' Ecc 9:2-3; Eze 21:3
23 When a scourge brings sudden death, Heb 11:36
he mocks the despair of the innocent.
24 When a land falls into the hands of the
wicked, Job 10:3
he blindfolds its judges. Job 12:6
If it is not he, then who is it?

25 "My days are swifter than a runner; Job 7:6
they fly away without a glimpse of joy.
26 They skim past like boats of papyrus, Isa 18:2
like eagles swooping down on their prey.
27 If I say, 'I will forget my complaint, Job 7:11
I will change my expression, and smile,'
28 I still dread all my sufferings, Ps 119:120
for I know you will not hold me innocent.
29 Since I am already found guilty,
why should I struggle in vain? Ps 37:33
30 Even if I washed myself with soap[b]
and my hands with washing soda, Jer 2:22
31 you would plunge me into a slime pit
so that even my clothes would detest me.

32 "He is not a man like me that I might answer
him, Ro 9:20
that we might confront each other in court.
33 If only there were someone to arbitrate
between us, 1Sa 2:25
to lay his hand upon us both,
34 someone to remove God's rod from me,
so that his terror would frighten me no
more.
35 Then I would speak up without fear of him,
but as it now stands with me, I cannot.

10 "I loathe my very life; 1Ki 19:4
therefore I will give free rein to my
complaint
and speak out in the bitterness of my soul.
2 I will say to God: Do not condemn me,
but tell me what charges you have against
me. Job 9:29
3 Does it please you to oppress me, Job 9:22
to spurn the work of your hands, Job 14:15
while you smile on the schemes of the
wicked? Job 21:16; 22:18
4 Do you have eyes of flesh?
Do you see as a mortal sees? 1Sa 16:7
5 Are your days like those of a mortal
or your years like those of a man, Ps 90:2,4
6 that you must search out my faults
and probe after my sin— Job 14:16
7 though you know that I am not guilty

[a] 19 See Septuagint; Hebrew *me.*
[b] 30 Or *snow*

and that no one can rescue me from your
hand?
8"Your hands shaped me and made me.
Will you now turn and destroy me?
9Remember that you molded me like clay.
Will you now turn me to dust again? Ge 2:7
10Did you not pour me out like milk
and curdle me like cheese,
11clothe me with skin and flesh
and knit me together with bones and
sinews? Ps 139:13,15
12You gave me life and showed me kindness,
and in your providence watched over my
spirit.

13"But this is what you concealed in your heart,
and I know that this was in your mind:
14If I sinned, you would be watching me
and would not let my offense go
unpunished. Job 7:21
15If I am guilty—woe to me! Job 9:13
Even if I am innocent, I cannot lift my
head, Job 9:15
for I am full of shame
and drowned in[a] my affliction.
16If I hold my head high, you stalk me like a
lion Isa 38:13; La 3:10
and again display your awesome power
against me.
17You bring new witnesses against me Job 16:8
and increase your anger toward me; Ru 1:21
your forces come against me wave upon
wave.

18"Why then did you bring me out of the
womb? Job 3:11
I wish I had died before any eye saw me.
19If only I had never come into being,
or had been carried straight from the
womb to the grave!
20Are not my few days almost over? Job 7:19; 14:1
Turn away from me so I can have a
moment's joy Job 7:16
21before I go to the place of no return, Job 3:13
to the land of gloom and deep shadow,[b]
22to the land of deepest night,
of deep shadow and disorder,
where even the light is like darkness."

Zophar

11 Then Zophar the Naamathite replied:

2"Are all these words to go unanswered? Job 8:2
Is this talker to be vindicated?
3Will your idle talk reduce men to silence?
Will no one rebuke you when you mock?
4You say to God, 'My beliefs are flawless
and I am pure in your sight.' Job 10:7
5Oh, how I wish that God would speak,
that he would open his lips against you
6and disclose to you the secrets of wisdom,
for true wisdom has two sides.
Know this: God has even forgotten some of
your sin. Ezr 9:13; Job 15:5

7"Can you fathom the mysteries of God?
Can you probe the limits of the Almighty?
8They are higher than the heavens—what can
you do? Job 22:12
They are deeper than the depths of the
grave[c]—what can you know? Ps 139:8
9Their measure is longer than the earth
and wider than the sea. Isa 40:26

10"If he comes along and confines you in prison
and convenes a court, who can oppose
him? Job 9:12; Rev 3:7
11Surely he recognizes deceitful men;
and when he sees evil, does he not take
note? Job 34:21-25; Ps 10:14
12But a witless man can no more become wise
than a wild donkey's colt can be born a
man.[d]

13"Yet if you devote your heart to him 1Sa 7:3
and stretch out your hands to him, Ps 88:9
14if you put away the sin that is in your hand
and allow no evil to dwell in your tent,
15then you will lift up your face without shame;
you will stand firm and without fear.
16You will surely forget your trouble, Isa 65:16
recalling it only as waters gone by. Job 22:11
17Life will be brighter than noonday, Ps 37:6
and darkness will become like morning.
18You will be secure, because there is hope;
you will look about you and take your rest
in safety. Lev 26:6; Ps 3:5; Pr 3:24
19You will lie down, with no one to make you
afraid, Lev 26:6
and many will court your favor. Isa 45:14
20But the eyes of the wicked will fail, Dt 28:65
and escape will elude them;
their hope will become a dying gasp."

Job

12 Then Job replied:

2"Doubtless you are the people,
and wisdom will die with you! Job 17:10
3But I have a mind as well as you;
I am not inferior to you.
Who does not know all these things? Job 13:2

4"I have become a laughingstock to my friends,

[a]15 Or *and aware of* [b]21 Or *and the shadow of death*; also in verse 22 [c]8 Hebrew *than Sheol* [d]12 Or *wild donkey can be born tame*

though I called upon God and he
answered— Ps 91:15
a mere laughingstock, though righteous and
blameless! Job 6:29
5Men at ease have contempt for misfortune
as the fate of those whose feet are slipping.
6The tents of marauders are undisturbed,
and those who provoke God are secure—
those who carry their god in their hands.[a]
7"But ask the animals, and they will teach you,
or the birds of the air, and they will tell
you; Mt 6:26
8or speak to the earth, and it will teach you,
or let the fish of the sea inform you.
9Which of all these does not know
that the hand of the LORD has done this?
10In his hand is the life of every creature
and the breath of all mankind. Job 27:3; 33:4
11Does not the ear test words
as the tongue tastes food? Job 34:3
12Is not wisdom found among the aged? Job 15:10
Does not long life bring understanding?

13"To God belong wisdom and power; Job 9:4
counsel and understanding are his. Job 32:8
14What he tears down cannot be rebuilt; Job 19:10
the man he imprisons cannot be released.
15If he holds back the waters, there is drought;
if he lets them loose, they devastate the
land. Ge 7:11
16To him belong strength and victory;
both deceived and deceiver are his. Job 13:7,9
17He leads counselors away stripped Job 19:9
and makes fools of judges. Job 3:14
18He takes off the shackles put on by kings
and ties a loincloth[b] around their waist.
19He leads priests away stripped
and overthrows men long established.
20He silences the lips of trusted advisers
and takes away the discernment of elders.
21He pours contempt on nobles
and disarms the mighty.
22He reveals the deep things of darkness 1Co 4:5
and brings deep shadows into the light.
23He makes nations great, and destroys them;
he enlarges nations, and disperses them.
24He deprives the leaders of the earth of their
reason;
he sends them wandering through a
trackless waste.
25They grope in darkness with no light; Job 5:14
he makes them stagger like drunkards.

13 "My eyes have seen all this,
my ears have heard and understood it.
2What you know, I also know;
I am not inferior to you. Job 12:3
3But I desire to speak to the Almighty
and to argue my case with God. Job 23:3-4
4You, however, smear me with lies; Ps 119:69
you are worthless physicians, all of you!
5If only you would be altogether silent!
For you, that would be wisdom. Pr 17:28

LIVING  **INSIGHT**

The way to show yourself wise is not so much by speech but by silence.

(See Job 13:5.)

6Hear now my argument;
listen to the plea of my lips.
7Will you speak wickedly on God's behalf?
Will you speak deceitfully for him? Job 36:4
8Will you show him partiality? Lev 19:15
Will you argue the case for God?
9Would it turn out well if he examined you?
Could you deceive him as you might
deceive men? Job 12:16; Gal 6:7
10He would surely rebuke you
if you secretly showed partiality.
11Would not his splendor terrify you? Job 31:23
Would not the dread of him fall on you?
12Your maxims are proverbs of ashes;
your defenses are defenses of clay.
13"Keep silent and let me speak;
then let come to me what may. Job 9:21
14Why do I put myself in jeopardy
and take my life in my hands?
15Though he slay me, yet will I hope in him;
I will surely[c] defend my ways to his face.
16Indeed, this will turn out for my deliverance,
for no godless man would dare come
before him!
17Listen carefully to my words; Job 21:2
let your ears take in what I say.
18Now that I have prepared my case, Job 23:4
I know I will be vindicated.
19Can anyone bring charges against me? Isa 50:8
If so, I will be silent and die. Job 10:8
20"Only grant me these two things, O God,
and then I will not hide from you:
21Withdraw your hand far from me, Ps 39:10
and stop frightening me with your terrors.
22Then summon me and I will answer, Job 14:15
or let me speak, and you reply. Job 9:16
23How many wrongs and sins have I
committed? 1Sa 26:18
Show me my offense and my sin.
24Why do you hide your face Dt 32:20; Ps 13:1; Isa 8:17

[a]6 Or *secure / in what God's hand brings them* [b]18 Or *shackles of kings / and ties a belt* [c]15 Or *He will surely slay me; I have no hope — / yet I will*

and consider me your enemy? Job 19:11; La 2:5
25Will you torment a windblown leaf?
Will you chase after dry chaff? Job 21:18
26For you write down bitter things against me
and make me inherit the sins of my youth.
27You fasten my feet in shackles; Job 33:11
you keep close watch on all my paths
by putting marks on the soles of my feet.

28"So man wastes away like something rotten,
like a garment eaten by moths. Isa 50:9; Jas 5:2

14 "Man born of woman
is of few days and full of trouble. Job 5:7
2He springs up like a flower and withers away;
like a fleeting shadow, he does not endure.
3Do you fix your eye on such a one? Ps 144:3
Will you bring him[a] before you for
judgment? Ps 143:2
4Who can bring what is pure from the impure?
No one! Jn 3:6; Ro 5:12
5Man's days are determined;
you have decreed the number of his
months Job 21:21
and have set limits he cannot exceed.
6So look away from him and let him alone,
till he has put in his time like a hired man.

7"At least there is hope for a tree:
If it is cut down, it will sprout again,
and its new shoots will not fail.
8Its roots may grow old in the ground
and its stump die in the soil, Isa 6:13
9yet at the scent of water it will bud
and put forth shoots like a plant. Lev 26:4
10But man dies and is laid low;
he breathes his last and is no more. Job 13:19
11As water disappears from the sea
or a riverbed becomes parched and dry,
12so man lies down and does not rise;
till the heavens are no more, men will not
awake Rev 20:11; 21:1
or be roused from their sleep. Ac 3:21

13"If only you would hide me in the grave[b]
and conceal me till your anger has passed!
If only you would set me a time
and then remember me!
14If a man dies, will he live again?
All the days of my hard service
I will wait for my renewal[c] to come.
15You will call and I will answer you; Job 13:22
you will long for the creature your hands
have made.
16Surely then you will count my steps Pr 5:21
but not keep track of my sin. Job 10:6
17My offenses will be sealed up in a bag; Dt 32:34
you will cover over my sin. Hos 13:12

18"But as a mountain erodes and crumbles
and as a rock is moved from its place,
19as water wears away stones
and torrents wash away the soil, Job 7:6
so you destroy man's hope.
20You overpower him once for all, and he is
gone;
you change his countenance and send him
away. Job 12:19; Jas 1:10
21If his sons are honored, he does not know it;
if they are brought low, he does not see it.
22He feels but the pain of his own body
and mourns only for himself." Job 21:21

Eliphaz

15 Then Eliphaz the Temanite replied:

2"Would a wise man answer with empty
notions
or fill his belly with the hot east wind?
3Would he argue with useless words,
with speeches that have no value?
4But you even undermine piety
and hinder devotion to God.
5Your sin prompts your mouth; Pr 16:23
you adopt the tongue of the crafty. Job 5:13
6Your own mouth condemns you, not mine;
your own lips testify against you. Lk 19:22

7"Are you the first man ever born? Job 38:21
Were you brought forth before the hills?
8Do you listen in on God's council? Ro 11:34
Do you limit wisdom to yourself?
9What do you know that we do not know?
What insights do you have that we do not
have? Job 13:2
10The gray-haired and the aged are on our side,
men even older than your father.
11Are God's consolations not enough for you,
words spoken gently to you? Job 36:16
12Why has your heart carried you away, Job 11:13
and why do your eyes flash,
13so that you vent your rage against God Pr 29:11
and pour out such words from your
mouth?

14"What is man, that he could be pure,
or one born of woman, that he could be
righteous? Job 14:4; Pr 20:9; Ecc 7:20
15If God places no trust in his holy ones,
if even the heavens are not pure in his eyes,
16how much less man, who is vile and corrupt,
who drinks up evil like water! Job 34:7; Pr 19:28

17"Listen to me and I will explain to you;
let me tell you what I have seen,
18what wise men have declared,
hiding nothing received from their fathers
19(to whom alone the land was given
when no alien passed among them):

[a] 3 Septuagint, Vulgate and Syriac; Hebrew *me* [b] 13 Hebrew *Sheol* [c] 14 Or *release*

20 All his days the wicked man suffers torment,
the ruthless through all the years stored up
for him. Job 24:1; 27:13-23
21 Terrifying sounds fill his ears; Job 18:11; 20:25
when all seems well, marauders attack him.
22 He despairs of escaping the darkness;
he is marked for the sword. Job 27:14
23 He wanders about—food for vultures[a];
he knows the day of darkness is at hand.
24 Distress and anguish fill him with terror;
they overwhelm him, like a king poised to
attack,
25 because he shakes his fist at God
and vaunts himself against the Almighty,
26 defiantly charging against him
with a thick, strong shield.

27 "Though his face is covered with fat
and his waist bulges with flesh, Ps 17:10
28 he will inhabit ruined towns
and houses where no one lives, Isa 5:9
houses crumbling to rubble. Job 3:14
29 He will no longer be rich and his wealth will
not endure, Job 27:16-17
nor will his possessions spread over the
land.
30 He will not escape the darkness; Job 5:14
a flame will wither his shoots, Job 22:20
and the breath of God's mouth will carry
him away. Job 4:9
31 Let him not deceive himself by trusting what
is worthless, Isa 59:4
for he will get nothing in return.
32 Before his time he will be paid in full, Job 22:16
and his branches will not flourish. Job 18:16
33 He will be like a vine stripped of its unripe
grapes, Hab 3:17
like an olive tree shedding its blossoms.
34 For the company of the godless will be barren,
and fire will consume the tents of those
who love bribes. Job 8:22
35 They conceive trouble and give birth to evil;
their womb fashions deceit."

Job

16 Then Job replied:

2 "I have heard many things like these;
miserable comforters are you all! Job 13:4
3 Will your long-winded speeches never end?
What ails you that you keep on arguing?
4 I also could speak like you,
if you were in my place;
I could make fine speeches against you
and shake my head at you. Ps 22:7; 109:25
5 But my mouth would encourage you;
comfort from my lips would bring you
relief.

6 "Yet if I speak, my pain is not relieved;
and if I refrain, it does not go away.
7 Surely, O God, you have worn me out; Job 7:3
you have devastated my entire household.
8 You have bound me—and it has become a
witness;
my gauntness rises up and testifies against
me. Job 10:17; 19:20
9 God assails me and tears me in his anger
and gnashes his teeth at me; Ps 35:16; La 2:16
my opponent fastens on me his piercing
eyes. Job 13:24
10 Men open their mouths to jeer at me; Ps 22:13
they strike my cheek in scorn La 3:30; Mic 5:1
and unite together against me. Ps 35:15
11 God has turned me over to evil men
and thrown me into the clutches of the
wicked. Job 1:15,17
12 All was well with me, but he shattered me;
he seized me by the neck and crushed me.
He has made me his target; La 3:12
13 his archers surround me.
Without pity, he pierces my kidneys Job 20:24
and spills my gall on the ground.
14 Again and again he bursts upon me; Job 9:17
he rushes at me like a warrior. Joel 2:7

15 "I have sewed sackcloth over my skin Ge 37:34
and buried my brow in the dust.
16 My face is red with weeping,
deep shadows ring my eyes;
17 yet my hands have been free of violence
and my prayer is pure.

18 "O earth, do not cover my blood; Isa 26:21
may my cry never be laid to rest! Ps 66:18-19
19 Even now my witness is in heaven; Ro 1:9; 1Th 2:5
my advocate is on high.
20 My intercessor is my friend[b]
as my eyes pour out tears to God; La 2:19
21 on behalf of a man he pleads with God Ps 9:4
as a man pleads for his friend.

22 "Only a few years will pass
before I go on the journey of no return.

17 1 My spirit is broken, Ps 143:4
my days are cut short,
the grave awaits me. Ps 88:3-4
2 Surely mockers surround me; 1Sa 1:6-7
my eyes must dwell on their hostility.

3 "Give me, O God, the pledge you demand.
Who else will put up security for me?
4 You have closed their minds to understanding;
therefore you will not let them triumph.
5 If a man denounces his friends for reward,
the eyes of his children will fail. Job 11:20

6 "God has made me a byword to everyone,
a man in whose face people spit.

[a] 23 Or *about, looking for food* [b] 20 Or *My friends treat me with scorn*

7 My eyes have grown dim with grief; Job 16:8
my whole frame is but a shadow.
8 Upright men are appalled at this;
the innocent are aroused against the
ungodly. Job 22:19
9 Nevertheless, the righteous will hold to their
ways, Pr 4:18
and those with clean hands will grow
stronger. Job 22:30

10 "But come on, all of you, try again!
I will not find a wise man among you.
11 My days have passed, my plans are shattered,
and so are the desires of my heart. Job 7:6
12 These men turn night into day;
in the face of darkness they say, 'Light is
near.'
13 If the only home I hope for is the grave,[a]
if I spread out my bed in darkness,
14 if I say to corruption, 'You are my father,'
and to the worm, 'My mother' or 'My
sister,' Job 21:26
15 where then is my hope? Job 7:6
Who can see any hope for me?
16 Will it go down to the gates of death[a]?
Will we descend together into the dust?"

Bildad

18 Then Bildad the Shuhite replied:

2 "When will you end these speeches? Job 16:3
Be sensible, and then we can talk.
3 Why are we regarded as cattle
and considered stupid in your sight? Ps 73:22
4 You who tear yourself to pieces in your anger,
is the earth to be abandoned for your sake?
Or must the rocks be moved from their
place?

5 "The lamp of the wicked is snuffed out; Pr 13:9
the flame of his fire stops burning.
6 The light in his tent becomes dark;
the lamp beside him goes out. Job 11:17
7 The vigor of his step is weakened; Pr 4:12
his own schemes throw him down. Job 5:13
8 His feet thrust him into a net Job 22:10; Ps 9:15; 35:7
and he wanders into its mesh.
9 A trap seizes him by the heel; Pr 5:22
a snare holds him fast.
10 A noose is hidden for him on the ground;
a trap lies in his path.
11 Terrors startle him on every side Job 15:21
and dog his every step. Job 20:8
12 Calamity is hungry for him; Isa 8:21
disaster is ready for him when he falls.
13 It eats away parts of his skin;
death's firstborn devours his limbs. Zec 14:12
14 He is torn from the security of his tent Job 8:22
and marched off to the king of terrors.
15 Fire resides[b] in his tent;
burning sulfur is scattered over his
dwelling. Ps 11:6
16 His roots dry up below Isa 5:24; Am 2:9
and his branches wither above. Mal 4:1
17 The memory of him perishes from the earth;
he has no name in the land. Ps 34:16; Pr 10:7
18 He is driven from light into darkness Job 5:14
and is banished from the world.
19 He has no offspring or descendants among his
people, Isa 14:22; Jer 22:30
no survivor where once he lived.
20 Men of the west are appalled at his fate;
men of the east are seized with horror.
21 Surely such is the dwelling of an evil man;
such is the place of one who knows not
God." 1Th 4:5

Job

19 Then Job replied:

2 "How long will you torment me Job 13:25
and crush me with words?
3 Ten times now you have reproached me;
shamelessly you attack me.
4 If it is true that I have gone astray,
my error remains my concern alone. Job 6:24
5 If indeed you would exalt yourselves above me
and use my humiliation against me,
6 then know that God has wronged me Job 27:2
and drawn his net around me. Job 18:8

7 "Though I cry, 'I've been wronged!' I get no
response; Job 30:20
though I call for help, there is no justice.
8 He has blocked my way so I cannot pass;
he has shrouded my paths in darkness.
9 He has stripped me of my honor Job 12:17
and removed the crown from my head.
10 He tears me down on every side till I am
gone; Job 12:14
he uproots my hope like a tree. Job 7:6; 24:20
11 His anger burns against me; Job 16:9
he counts me among his enemies. Job 13:24
12 His troops advance in force; Job 16:13
they build a siege ramp against me Job 30:12
and encamp around my tent.

13 "He has alienated my brothers from me;
my acquaintances are completely estranged
from me. Job 16:7; Ps 88:8
14 My kinsmen have gone away;
my friends have forgotten me. Ps 88:18
15 My guests and my maidservants count me a
stranger;
they look upon me as an alien.

[a] *13,16* Hebrew *Sheol* [b] *15* Or *Nothing he had remains*

[16]I summon my servant, but he does not answer,
though I beg him with my own mouth.
[17]My breath is offensive to my wife;
I am loathsome to my own brothers.
[18]Even the little boys scorn me; 2Ki 2:23
when I appear, they ridicule me.
[19]All my intimate friends detest me; Ps 38:11
those I love have turned against me. Jn 13:18
[20]I am nothing but skin and bones; Job 33:21
I have escaped with only the skin of my teeth.[a]

[21]"Have pity on me, my friends, have pity,
for the hand of God has struck me.
[22]Why do you pursue me as God does? Job 13:25
Will you never get enough of my flesh?

[23]"Oh, that my words were recorded,
that they were written on a scroll, Isa 30:8
[24]that they were inscribed with an iron tool on[b] lead,
or engraved in rock forever!
[25]I know that my Redeemer[c] lives, Job 16:19
and that in the end he will stand upon the earth.[d]
[26]And after my skin has been destroyed,
yet[e] in[f] my flesh I will see God; Mt 5:8
[27]I myself will see him
with my own eyes—I, and not another.
How my heart yearns within me! Ps 73:26

LIVING  **INSIGHT**

What an encouragement to hang on to! In a context of perfect peace, physically and personally, all Christians will enjoy the presence of our Lord forever and ever and ever. Every believer in Jesus Christ who goes home to be with the Lord has a marvelous future in front of him or her. What a future God has planned for those who love Him! The old gospel song says it well: "Oh, that will be glory for me!"

(See Job 19:25–27.)

[28]"If you say, 'How we will hound him, Job 13:25
since the root of the trouble lies in him,[g]'
[29]you should fear the sword yourselves;
for wrath will bring punishment by the sword, Job 15:22
and then you will know that there is judgment.[h]" Job 22:4; Ps 1:5

Zophar

20 Then Zophar the Naamathite replied:

[2]"My troubled thoughts prompt me to answer
because I am greatly disturbed. Ps 42:5
[3]I hear a rebuke that dishonors me, Job 19:3
and my understanding inspires me to reply.

[4]"Surely you know how it has been from of old, Dt 4:32
ever since man[i] was placed on the earth,
[5]that the mirth of the wicked is brief,
the joy of the godless lasts but a moment.
[6]Though his pride reaches to the heavens
and his head touches the clouds, Isa 14:13-14
[7]he will perish forever, like his own dung;
those who have seen him will say, 'Where is he?'
[8]Like a dream he flies away, no more to be found, Ps 73:20
banished like a vision of the night. Ps 90:5
[9]The eye that saw him will not see him again;
his place will look on him no more. Job 7:8
[10]His children must make amends to the poor;
his own hands must give back his wealth.
[11]The youthful vigor that fills his bones Job 13:26
will lie with him in the dust.

[12]"Though evil is sweet in his mouth
and he hides it under his tongue,
[13]though he cannot bear to let it go
and keeps it in his mouth, Nu 11:18-20
[14]yet his food will turn sour in his stomach;
it will become the venom of serpents within him.
[15]He will spit out the riches he swallowed;
God will make his stomach vomit them up.
[16]He will suck the poison of serpents; Dt 32:32
the fangs of an adder will kill him.
[17]He will not enjoy the streams,
the rivers flowing with honey and cream.
[18]What he toiled for he must give back uneaten;
he will not enjoy the profit from his trading.
[19]For he has oppressed the poor and left them destitute; Job 24:4,14; 35:9
he has seized houses he did not build.

[20]"Surely he will have no respite from his craving; Ecc 5:12-14
he cannot save himself by his treasure.
[21]Nothing is left for him to devour;
his prosperity will not endure. Job 15:29
[22]In the midst of his plenty, distress will overtake him;
the full force of misery will come upon him.

[a]20 Or *only my gums* [b]24 Or *and* [c]25 Or *defender* [d]25 Or *upon my grave* [e]26 Or *And after I awake, / though this ⌞body⌟ has been destroyed, / then* [f]26 Or */ apart from* [g]28 Many Hebrew manuscripts, Septuagint and Vulgate; most Hebrew manuscripts *me* [h]29 Or */ that you may come to know the Almighty* [i]4 Or *Adam*

23 When he has filled his belly,
God will vent his burning anger against him
and rain down his blows upon him.
24 Though he flees from an iron weapon, Isa 24:18
a bronze-tipped arrow pierces him.
25 He pulls it out of his back,
the gleaming point out of his liver.
Terrors will come over him; Job 16:13; 18:11
26 total darkness lies in wait for his treasures.
A fire unfanned will consume him Ps 21:9
and devour what is left in his tent.
27 The heavens will expose his guilt;
the earth will rise up against him.
28 A flood will carry off his house, Dt 28:31
rushing waters[a] on the day of God's wrath. Job 21:17,20,30
29 Such is the fate God allots the wicked,
the heritage appointed for them by God."

Job

21

Then Job replied:

2 "Listen carefully to my words; Job 13:17
let this be the consolation you give me.
3 Bear with me while I speak,
and after I have spoken, mock on. Job 16:10

4 "Is my complaint directed to man?
Why should I not be impatient? Job 6:11
5 Look at me and be astonished;
clap your hand over your mouth. Jdg 18:19
6 When I think about this, I am terrified;
trembling seizes my body.
7 Why do the wicked live on,
growing old and increasing in power? Ps 73:3
8 They see their children established around them,
their offspring before their eyes. Ps 17:14
9 Their homes are safe and free from fear;
the rod of God is not upon them.
10 Their bulls never fail to breed;
their cows calve and do not miscarry.
11 They send forth their children as a flock;
their little ones dance about.
12 They sing to the music of tambourine and harp; Ps 33:2
they make merry to the sound of the flute.
13 They spend their years in prosperity Job 36:11
and go down to the grave[b] in peace.[c]
14 Yet they say to God, 'Leave us alone! Job 22:17
We have no desire to know your ways.
15 Who is the Almighty, that we should serve him?
What would we gain by praying to him?'
16 But their prosperity is not in their own hands,
so I stand aloof from the counsel of the wicked.

17 "Yet how often is the lamp of the wicked snuffed out? Job 18:5
How often does calamity come upon them,
the fate God allots in his anger?
18 How often are they like straw before the wind,
like chaff swept away by a gale? Ps 1:4
19 ⌞It is said,⌟ 'God stores up a man's punishment for his sons.' Ex 20:5
Let him repay the man himself, so that he will know it!
20 Let his own eyes see his destruction;
let him drink of the wrath of the Almighty.[d] Isa 51:17; Jer 25:15; Rev 14:10
21 For what does he care about the family he leaves behind
when his allotted months come to an end?

22 "Can anyone teach knowledge to God,
since he judges even the highest? Ps 82:1
23 One man dies in full vigor,
completely secure and at ease,
24 his body[e] well nourished,
his bones rich with marrow. Pr 3:8
25 Another man dies in bitterness of soul,
never having enjoyed anything good.
26 Side by side they lie in the dust,
and worms cover them both. Job 24:20; Ecc 9:2-3

27 "I know full well what you are thinking,
the schemes by which you would wrong me.
28 You say, 'Where now is the great man's house, Job 1:3; 12:21
the tents where wicked men lived?' Job 8:22
29 Have you never questioned those who travel?
Have you paid no regard to their accounts—
30 that the evil man is spared from the day of calamity, Pr 16:4
that he is delivered from[f] the day of wrath? Job 20:22,28; 2Pe 2:9
31 Who denounces his conduct to his face?
Who repays him for what he has done?
32 He is carried to the grave,
and watch is kept over his tomb.
33 The soil in the valley is sweet to him; Job 3:22
all men follow after him,
and a countless throng goes[g] before him.

34 "So how can you console me with your nonsense? Job 16:2
Nothing is left of your answers but falsehood!"

[a] 28 Or *The possessions in his house will be carried off, / washed away* [b] 13 Hebrew *Sheol* [c] 13 Or *in an instant* [d] 17-20 Verses 17 and 18 may be taken as exclamations and 19 and 20 as declarations. [e] 24 The meaning of the Hebrew for this word is uncertain. [f] 30 Or *man is reserved for the day of calamity, / that he is brought forth to* [g] 33 Or */ as a countless throng went*

Eliphaz

22 Then Eliphaz the Temanite replied:

2"Can a man be of benefit to God? Lk 17:10
Can even a wise man benefit him?
3What pleasure would it give the Almighty if
you were righteous? Isa 1:11
What would he gain if your ways were
blameless?

4"Is it for your piety that he rebukes you
and brings charges against you? Job 14:3; 19:29
5Is not your wickedness great?
Are not your sins endless? Job 11:6
6You demanded security from your brothers
for no reason; Ex 22:26
you stripped men of their clothing, leaving
them naked.
7You gave no water to the weary
and you withheld food from the hungry,
8though you were a powerful man, owning
land—
an honored man, living on it. Isa 3:3
9And you sent widows away empty-handed
and broke the strength of the fatherless.
10That is why snares are all around you,
why sudden peril terrifies you,
11why it is so dark you cannot see, Job 5:14
and why a flood of water covers you.

12"Is not God in the heights of heaven? Job 11:8
And see how lofty are the highest stars!
13Yet you say, 'What does God know? Ps 10:11
Does he judge through such darkness?
14Thick clouds veil him, so he does not see us
as he goes about in the vaulted heavens.'
15Will you keep to the old path
that evil men have trod?
16They were carried off before their time,
their foundations washed away by a flood.
17They said to God, 'Leave us alone!
What can the Almighty do to us?'
18Yet it was he who filled their houses with
good things, Job 12:6
so I stand aloof from the counsel of the
wicked.

19"The righteous see their ruin and rejoice;
the innocent mock them, saying, Ps 52:6
20'Surely our foes are destroyed,
and fire devours their wealth.' Job 15:30

21"Submit to God and be at peace with him;
in this way prosperity will come to you.
22Accept instruction from his mouth
and lay up his words in your heart.
23If you return to the Almighty, you will be
restored: Isa 19:22; Ac 20:32
If you remove wickedness far from your
tent Job 11:14
24and assign your nuggets to the dust,
your gold of Ophir to the rocks in the
ravines, Job 31:25
25then the Almighty will be your gold,
the choicest silver for you. Isa 33:6
26Surely then you will find delight in the
Almighty Job 27:10; Isa 58:14
and will lift up your face to God.
27You will pray to him, and he will hear you,
and you will fulfill your vows.
28What you decide on will be done,
and light will shine on your ways.
29When men are brought low and you say, 'Lift
them up!'
then he will save the downcast. Mt 23:12; 1Pe 5:5
30He will deliver even one who is not innocent,
who will be delivered through the cleanness
of your hands." Job 42:7-8

Job

23 Then Job replied:

2"Even today my complaint is bitter; Job 6:3
his hand[a] is heavy in spite of[b] my
groaning. Ps 6:6
3If only I knew where to find him;
if only I could go to his dwelling!
4I would state my case before him Job 13:18
and fill my mouth with arguments.
5I would find out what he would answer me,
and consider what he would say.
6Would he oppose me with great power? Job 9:4
No, he would not press charges against me.
7There an upright man could present his case
before him, Job 13:3
and I would be delivered forever from my
judge.

8"But if I go to the east, he is not there;
if I go to the west, I do not find him.
9When he is at work in the north, I do not see
him;
when he turns to the south, I catch no
glimpse of him. Job 9:11
10But he knows the way that I take;
when he has tested me, I will come forth as
gold. Ps 139:1-3; 1Pe 1:7
11My feet have closely followed his steps;
I have kept to his way without turning
aside. Ps 44:18
12I have not departed from the commands of
his lips; Job 6:10
I have treasured the words of his mouth
more than my daily bread. Jn 4:32,34

[a]2 Septuagint and Syriac; Hebrew / *the hand on me* [b]2 Or *heavy on me in*

[13]"But he stands alone, and who can oppose
him?
He does whatever he pleases. Ps 115:3
[14]He carries out his decree against me,
and many such plans he still has in store.
[15]That is why I am terrified before him;
when I think of all this, I fear him.
[16]God has made my heart faint; Ps 22:14; Jer 51:46
the Almighty has terrified me.
[17]Yet I am not silenced by the darkness, Job 19:8
by the thick darkness that covers my face.

24 "Why does the Almighty not set times
for judgment? Jer 46:10
Why must those who know him look in
vain for such days? Ac 1:7
[2]Men move boundary stones; Dt 19:14; 27:17
they pasture flocks they have stolen.
[3]They drive away the orphan's donkey
and take the widow's ox in pledge. Job 22:6
[4]They thrust the needy from the path
and force all the poor of the land into
hiding. Pr 28:28
[5]Like wild donkeys in the desert,
the poor go about their labor of foraging
food; Ps 104:23
the wasteland provides food for their
children.
[6]They gather fodder in the fields
and glean in the vineyards of the wicked.
[7]Lacking clothes, they spend the night naked;
they have nothing to cover themselves in
the cold. Ex 22:27; Job 22:6
[8]They are drenched by mountain rains
and hug the rocks for lack of shelter. La 4:5
[9]The fatherless child is snatched from the
breast; Dt 24:17
the infant of the poor is seized for a debt.
[10]Lacking clothes, they go about naked;
they carry the sheaves, but still go hungry.
[11]They crush olives among the terraces[a];
they tread the winepresses, yet suffer thirst.
[12]The groans of the dying rise from the city,
and the souls of the wounded cry out for
help. Eze 26:15
But God charges no one with wrongdoing.

[13]"There are those who rebel against the light,
who do not know its ways
or stay in its paths. Isa 5:20
[14]When daylight is gone, the murderer rises up
and kills the poor and needy;
in the night he steals forth like a thief.
[15]The eye of the adulterer watches for dusk;
he thinks, 'No eye will see me,' Ps 10:11
and he keeps his face concealed.
[16]In the dark, men break into houses, Ex 22:2
but by day they shut themselves in;
they want nothing to do with the light.
[17]For all of them, deep darkness is their
morning[b];
they make friends with the terrors of
darkness.[c]

[18]"Yet they are foam on the surface of the
water; Job 9:26; 22:16
their portion of the land is cursed,
so that no one goes to the vineyards.
[19]As heat and drought snatch away the melted
snow, Job 6:17
so the grave[d] snatches away those who
have sinned.
[20]The womb forgets them,
the worm feasts on them;
evil men are no longer remembered Pr 10:7
but are broken like a tree. Ps 31:12
[21]They prey on the barren and childless woman,
and to the widow show no kindness. Job 22:9
[22]But God drags away the mighty by his power;
though they become established, they have
no assurance of life. Dt 28:66
[23]He may let them rest in a feeling of security,
but his eyes are on their ways. Job 12:6
[24]For a little while they are exalted, and then
they are gone; Ps 37:10
they are brought low and gathered up like
all others;
they are cut off like heads of grain. Isa 17:5

[25]"If this is not so, who can prove me false
and reduce my words to nothing?" Job 6:28

Bildad

25 Then Bildad the Shuhite replied:

[2]"Dominion and awe belong to God; Job 9:4
he establishes order in the heights of
heaven.
[3]Can his forces be numbered?
Upon whom does his light not rise? Jas 1:17
[4]How then can a man be righteous before
God?
How can one born of woman be pure?
[5]If even the moon is not bright
and the stars are not pure in his eyes,
[6]how much less man, who is but a maggot—
a son of man, who is only a worm!" Ps 22:6

Job

26 Then Job replied:

[2]"How you have helped the powerless! Job 6:12
How you have saved the arm that is feeble!

[a] 11 Or *olives between the millstones*; the meaning of the Hebrew for this word is uncertain. [b] 17 Or *them, their morning is like the shadow of death* [c] 17 Or *of the shadow of death* [d] 19 Hebrew *Sheol*

3What advice you have offered to one without
wisdom!
And what great insight you have displayed!
4Who has helped you utter these words?
And whose spirit spoke from your mouth?

5"The dead are in deep anguish, Ps 88:10
those beneath the waters and all that live in
them.
6Death[a] is naked before God; Ps 139:8
Destruction[b] lies uncovered. Heb 4:13
7He spreads out the northern ⌊skies⌋ over
empty space; Job 9:8
he suspends the earth over nothing.
8He wraps up the waters in his clouds, Pr 30:4
yet the clouds do not burst under their
weight.
9He covers the face of the full moon,
spreading his clouds over it.
10He marks out the horizon on the face of the
waters
for a boundary between light and darkness.
11The pillars of the heavens quake,
aghast at his rebuke.
12By his power he churned up the sea; Isa 51:15
by his wisdom he cut Rahab to pieces.
13By his breath the skies became fair;
his hand pierced the gliding serpent. Isa 27:1
14And these are but the outer fringe of his
works;
how faint the whisper we hear of him!
Who then can understand the thunder of
his power?" Job 36:29

27

And Job continued his discourse:

2"As surely as God lives, who has denied me
justice, Job 34:5
the Almighty, who has made me taste
bitterness of soul, Job 9:18
3as long as I have life within me,
the breath of God in my nostrils, Job 32:8; 33:4
4my lips will not speak wickedness,
and my tongue will utter no deceit. Job 6:28
5I will never admit you are in the right;
till I die, I will not deny my integrity. Job 2:9
6I will maintain my righteousness and never let
go of it;
my conscience will not reproach me as long
as I live. Job 2:3

7"May my enemies be like the wicked,
my adversaries like the unjust!
8For what hope has the godless when he is cut
off, Job 8:13
when God takes away his life? Job 11:20; Lk 12:20
9Does God listen to his cry
when distress comes upon him? Job 35:12
10Will he find delight in the Almighty? Job 22:26
Will he call upon God at all times?

11"I will teach you about the power of God;
the ways of the Almighty I will not conceal.
12You have all seen this yourselves.
Why then this meaningless talk?

13"Here is the fate God allots to the wicked,
the heritage a ruthless man receives from
the Almighty: Job 20:29
14However many his children, their fate is the
sword; Dt 28:41; Hos 9:13
his offspring will never have enough to eat.
15The plague will bury those who survive him,
and their widows will not weep for them.
16Though he heaps up silver like dust
and clothes like piles of clay, Zec 9:3
17what he lays up the righteous will wear, Pr 28:8
and the innocent will divide his silver.
18The house he builds is like a moth's cocoon,
like a hut made by a watchman. Isa 1:8
19He lies down wealthy, but will do so no more;
when he opens his eyes, all is gone.
20Terrors overtake him like a flood; Job 15:21
a tempest snatches him away in the night.
21The east wind carries him off, and he is gone;
it sweeps him out of his place. Job 7:10
22It hurls itself against him without mercy
as he flees headlong from its power.
23It claps its hands in derision
and hisses him out of his place. Job 18:18

28

"There is a mine for silver
and a place where gold is refined. Ps 12:6
2Iron is taken from the earth,
and copper is smelted from ore. Dt 8:9
3Man puts an end to the darkness; Ecc 1:13
he searches the farthest recesses
for ore in the blackest darkness. Job 26:10
4Far from where people dwell he cuts a shaft,
in places forgotten by the foot of man;
far from men he dangles and sways.
5The earth, from which food comes, Ps 104:14
is transformed below as by fire;
6sapphires[c] come from its rocks, Isa 54:11
and its dust contains nuggets of gold.
7No bird of prey knows that hidden path,
no falcon's eye has seen it.
8Proud beasts do not set foot on it, Job 41:34
and no lion prowls there.
9Man's hand assaults the flinty rock Dt 8:15
and lays bare the roots of the mountains.
10He tunnels through the rock;
his eyes see all its treasures.
11He searches[d] the sources of the rivers Ge 7:11
and brings hidden things to light. Isa 48:6

[a]6 Hebrew *Sheol* [b]6 Hebrew *Abaddon* [c]6 Or *lapis lazuli*; also in verse 16 [d]*11* Septuagint, Aquila and Vulgate; Hebrew *He dams up*

12"But where can wisdom be found? Pr 1:20; 8:1
Where does understanding dwell?
13Man does not comprehend its worth; Pr 3:15
it cannot be found in the land of the living.
14The deep says, 'It is not in me'; Ps 42:7
the sea says, 'It is not with me.' Dt 30:13
15It cannot be bought with the finest gold,
nor can its price be weighed in silver.
16It cannot be bought with the gold of Ophir,
with precious onyx or sapphires. Ex 24:10
17Neither gold nor crystal can compare with it,
nor can it be had for jewels of gold. Pr 16:16
18Coral and jasper are not worthy of mention;
the price of wisdom is beyond rubies. Pr 3:15
19The topaz of Cush cannot compare with it;
it cannot be bought with pure gold. Pr 8:19

20"Where then does wisdom come from?
Where does understanding dwell? ver 23,28
21It is hidden from the eyes of every living thing,
concealed even from the birds of the air.
22Destruction[a] and Death say, Job 26:6
'Only a rumor of it has reached our ears.'
23God understands the way to it
and he alone knows where it dwells,
24for he views the ends of the earth Ps 33:13-14
and sees everything under the heavens.
25When he established the force of the wind
and measured out the waters, Job 12:15; Ps 135:7
26when he made a decree for the rain
and a path for the thunderstorm, Job 37:3,8,11
27then he looked at wisdom and appraised it;
he confirmed it and tested it. Pr 3:19; 8:22-31
28And he said to man,
'The fear of the Lord—that is wisdom,
and to shun evil is understanding.'" Dt 4:6

29 Job continued his discourse: Job 13:12

2"How I long for the months gone by,
for the days when God watched over me,
3when his lamp shone upon my head
and by his light I walked through darkness!
4Oh, for the days when I was in my prime,
when God's intimate friendship blessed my house, Ps 25:14
5when the Almighty was still with me
and my children were around me,
6when my path was drenched with cream
and the rock poured out for me streams of olive oil. Dt 32:13; Ps 81:16

7"When I went to the gate of the city Job 31:21
and took my seat in the public square,
8the young men saw me and stepped aside
and the old men rose to their feet;
9the chief men refrained from speaking
and covered their mouths with their hands;
10the voices of the nobles were hushed,
and their tongues stuck to the roof of their mouths. Ps 137:6
11Whoever heard me spoke well of me,
and those who saw me commended me,
12because I rescued the poor who cried for help,
and the fatherless who had none to assist him. Job 31:17,21; Ps 72:12; Pr 21:13
13The man who was dying blessed me;
I made the widow's heart sing. Job 22:9
14I put on righteousness as my clothing; Isa 59:17
justice was my robe and my turban.
15I was eyes to the blind Nu 10:31
and feet to the lame.
16I was a father to the needy; Pr 29:7
I took up the case of the stranger.
17I broke the fangs of the wicked
and snatched the victims from their teeth.

18"I thought, 'I will die in my own house,
my days as numerous as the grains of sand.
19My roots will reach to the water, Jer 17:8
and the dew will lie all night on my branches.
20My glory will remain fresh in me,
the bow ever new in my hand.' Ge 49:24

21"Men listened to me expectantly,
waiting in silence for my counsel.
22After I had spoken, they spoke no more;
my words fell gently on their ears. Dt 32:2
23They waited for me as for showers
and drank in my words as the spring rain.
24When I smiled at them, they scarcely believed it;
the light of my face was precious to them.[b]
25I chose the way for them and sat as their chief;
I dwelt as a king among his troops; Job 1:3
I was like one who comforts mourners.

30 "But now they mock me, Job 12:4
men younger than I,
whose fathers I would have disdained
to put with my sheep dogs.
2Of what use was the strength of their hands to me,
since their vigor had gone from them?
3Haggard from want and hunger,
they roamed[c] the parched land Isa 8:21
in desolate wastelands at night. Job 24:5
4In the brush they gathered salt herbs, Job 39:6
and their food[d] was the root of the broom tree. 1Ki 19:4
5They were banished from their fellow men,
shouted at as if they were thieves.
6They were forced to live in the dry stream beds,

[a]22 Hebrew *Abaddon* [b]24 The meaning of the Hebrew for this clause is uncertain. [c]3 Or *gnawed* [d]4 Or *fuel*

among the rocks and in holes in the
ground.
7They brayed among the bushes Job 39:5-6
and huddled in the undergrowth.
8A base and nameless brood,
they were driven out of the land. Job 18:18

9"And now their sons mock me in song; Job 12:4
I have become a byword among them.
10They detest me and keep their distance;
they do not hesitate to spit in my face.
11Now that God has unstrung my bow and
afflicted me, Ru 1:21
they throw off restraint in my presence.
12On my right the tribe[a] attacks;
they lay snares for my feet, Ps 140:4-5
they build their siege ramps against me.
13They break up my road; Isa 3:12
they succeed in destroying me—
without anyone's helping them.[b]
14They advance as through a gaping breach;
amid the ruins they come rolling in.
15Terrors overwhelm me; Ps 55:4-5
my dignity is driven away as by the wind,
my safety vanishes like a cloud. Job 3:25

16"And now my life ebbs away; Ps 42:4
days of suffering grip me.
17Night pierces my bones;
my gnawing pains never rest.
18In his great power ⌞God⌟ becomes like
clothing to me[c];
he binds me like the neck of my garment.
19He throws me into the mud, Ps 69:2,14
and I am reduced to dust and ashes.

20"I cry out to you, O God, but you do not
answer; Job 19:7
I stand up, but you merely look at me.
21You turn on me ruthlessly; Job 19:6,22
with the might of your hand you attack me.
22You snatch me up and drive me before the
wind; Job 27:21
you toss me about in the storm. Job 9:17
23I know you will bring me down to death,
to the place appointed for all the living.

24"Surely no one lays a hand on a broken man
when he cries for help in his distress.
25Have I not wept for those in trouble?
Has not my soul grieved for the poor?
26Yet when I hoped for good, evil came;
when I looked for light, then came
darkness. Jer 8:15
27The churning inside me never stops; La 2:11
days of suffering confront me.
28I go about blackened, but not by the sun;
I stand up in the assembly and cry for help.
29I have become a brother of jackals, Ps 44:19
a companion of owls. Mic 1:8
30My skin grows black and peels; La 4:8
my body burns with fever. Ps 102:3
31My harp is tuned to mourning, Isa 24:8
and my flute to the sound of wailing.

31 "I made a covenant with my eyes
not to look lustfully at a girl. Mt 5:28
2For what is man's lot from God above,
his heritage from the Almighty on high?
3Is it not ruin for the wicked, Job 21:30
disaster for those who do wrong? Job 34:22
4Does he not see my ways 2Ch 16:9
and count my every step? Pr 5:21

5"If I have walked in falsehood
or my foot has hurried after deceit—
6let God weigh me in honest scales Job 6:2
and he will know that I am blameless—
7if my steps have turned from the path, Job 23:11
if my heart has been led by my eyes,
or if my hands have been defiled, Job 9:30
8then may others eat what I have sown, Lev 26:16
and may my crops be uprooted. Mic 6:15

9"If my heart has been enticed by a woman,
or if I have lurked at my neighbor's door,
10then may my wife grind another man's grain,
and may other men sleep with her. Jer 8:10
11For that would have been shameful,
a sin to be judged. Ge 38:24
12It is a fire that burns to Destruction[d]; Job 15:30
it would have uprooted my harvest. Job 20:28

13"If I have denied justice to my menservants
and maidservants
when they had a grievance against me,
14what will I do when God confronts me?
What will I answer when called to account?
15Did not he who made me in the womb make
them?
Did not the same one form us both within
our mothers? Job 10:3

16"If I have denied the desires of the poor
or let the eyes of the widow grow weary,
17if I have kept my bread to myself,
not sharing it with the fatherless— Job 22:7
18but from my youth I reared him as would a
father,
and from my birth I guided the widow—
19if I have seen anyone perishing for lack of
clothing, Job 22:6
or a needy man without a garment, Job 24:4
20and his heart did not bless me

[a] 12 The meaning of the Hebrew for this word is uncertain. [b] 13 Or *me.* / *'No one can help him,'* ⌞*they say*⌟
[c] 18 Hebrew; Septuagint ⌞*God*⌟ *grasps my clothing* [d] 12 Hebrew *Abaddon*

for warming him with the fleece from my
sheep,
[21]if I have raised my hand against the fatherless,
knowing that I had influence in court,
[22]then let my arm fall from the shoulder,
let it be broken off at the joint. Job 38:15
[23]For I dreaded destruction from God,
and for fear of his splendor I could not do
such things. Job 13:11
[24]"If I have put my trust in gold Job 22:25
or said to pure gold, 'You are my security,'
[25]if I have rejoiced over my great wealth, Ps 62:10
the fortune my hands had gained,
[26]if I have regarded the sun in its radiance
or the moon moving in splendor,
[27]so that my heart was secretly enticed
and my hand offered them a kiss of
homage,
[28]then these also would be sins to be judged,
for I would have been unfaithful to God on
high.

[29]"If I have rejoiced at my enemy's misfortune
or gloated over the trouble that came to
him— Pr 17:5; 24:17-18
[30]I have not allowed my mouth to sin
by invoking a curse against his life—
[31]if the men of my household have never said,
'Who has not had his fill of Job's meat?'—
[32]but no stranger had to spend the night in the
street,
for my door was always open to the
traveler— Ge 19:2-3; Ro 12:13
[33]if I have concealed my sin as men do,[a]
by hiding my guilt in my heart Ge 3:8
[34]because I so feared the crowd Ex 23:2
and so dreaded the contempt of the clans
that I kept silent and would not go outside

[35]("Oh, that I had someone to hear me! Job 19:7
I sign now my defense—let the Almighty
answer me;
let my accuser put his indictment in
writing. Job 35:14
[36]Surely I would wear it on my shoulder,
I would put it on like a crown.
[37]I would give him an account of my every step;
like a prince I would approach him.)—

[38]"if my land cries out against me Ge 4:10
and all its furrows are wet with tears,
[39]if I have devoured its yield without payment
or broken the spirit of its tenants, Jas 5:4
[40]then let briers come up instead of wheat
and weeds instead of barley."

The words of Job are ended. Ps 72:20

The Solution to Suffering — Chapters 32–41

Finally, a fourth man, younger than the others, spoke up. His name was Elihu. It seems Elihu had been sitting and listening to the dialogue, but he had refrained from saying a word because of his age. Out of respect for the years of experience of the other men, he patiently listened to their counsel. Now, frustrated with their inability to bring any wisdom to bear on Job's situation, he invited himself into the fray. Elihu urged Job, in the midst of his excruciating suffering, to turn his eyes upward and set his attention on the God of heaven—to focus on God's wonders and majesty.

When Elihu finished his speech, Job didn't have opportunity to respond, as he did with his other friends—for it was the Lord who spoke out of the storm (38:1). Chapters 38–41 are a record of God's counsel and wisdom declared to Job in the midst of his pain. In these chapters the Lord reminded Job who made and sustains all of creation. God put Job through a battery of intense questioning, wanting to know exactly why Job felt adequate to put the Almighty on the witness stand. These four chapters are absolutely wonderful! Read them carefully. Think them through.

Elihu

32 So these three men stopped answering Job,
because he was righteous in his own eyes.
[2]But Elihu son of Barakel the Buzite, of the family
of Ram, became very angry with Job for justifying
himself rather than God. [3]He was also angry with
the three friends, because they had found no way
to refute Job, and yet had condemned him.[b]
[4]Now Elihu had waited before speaking to Job
because they were older than he. [5]But when he saw
that the three men had nothing more to say, his
anger was aroused. Ge 22:21; Job 33:9
[6]So Elihu son of Barakel the Buzite said:

"I am young in years,
and you are old; Job 15:10
that is why I was fearful,
not daring to tell you what I know.
[7]I thought, 'Age should speak;
advanced years should teach wisdom.'
[8]But it is the spirit[c] in a man,
the breath of the Almighty, that gives him
understanding. Job 27:3; Pr 2:6
[9]It is not only the old[d] who are wise, 1Co 1:26
not only the aged who understand what is
right. Job 12:12,20; Lk 2:47

[10]"Therefore I say: Listen to me;
I too will tell you what I know. Job 5:27
[11]I waited while you spoke,
I listened to your reasoning;
while you were searching for words,
[12] I gave you my full attention.
But not one of you has proved Job wrong;

[a]33 Or *as Adam did* [b]3 Masoretic Text; an ancient Hebrew scribal tradition *Job, and so had condemned God*
[c]8 Or *Spirit*; also in verse 18 [d]9 Or *many*; or *great*

none of you has answered his arguments.
13Do not say, 'We have found wisdom; Jer 9:23
let God refute him, not man.'
14But Job has not marshaled his words against me, Job 23:4
and I will not answer him with your arguments.

15"They are dismayed and have no more to say;
words have failed them.
16Must I wait, now that they are silent,
now that they stand there with no reply?
17I too will have my say;
I too will tell what I know. Job 33:3
18For I am full of words,
and the spirit within me compels me; Ac 4:20
19inside I am like bottled-up wine,
like new wineskins ready to burst.
20I must speak and find relief;
I must open my lips and reply.
21I will show partiality to no one, Lev 19:15; Mt 22:16
nor will I flatter any man;
22for if I were skilled in flattery,
my Maker would soon take me away.

33 "But now, Job, listen to my words;
pay attention to everything I say. Job 13:6
2I am about to open my mouth;
my words are on the tip of my tongue.
3My words come from an upright heart;
my lips sincerely speak what I know. Job 6:28
4The Spirit of God has made me; Ge 2:7
the breath of the Almighty gives me life.
5Answer me then, if you can;
prepare yourself and confront me. Job 13:18
6I am just like you before God;
I too have been taken from clay. Job 4:19
7No fear of me should alarm you,
nor should my hand be heavy upon you.

8"But you have said in my hearing—
I heard the very words—
9'I am pure and without sin; Job 10:7
I am clean and free from guilt.
10Yet God has found fault with me;
he considers me his enemy. Job 13:24
11He fastens my feet in shackles; Job 13:27
he keeps close watch on all my paths.'

12"But I tell you, in this you are not right,
for God is greater than man. Ecc 7:20
13Why do you complain to him Isa 45:9
that he answers none of man's words[a]?
14For God does speak—now one way, now another— Ps 62:11
though man may not perceive it.
15In a dream, in a vision of the night, Job 4:13
when deep sleep falls on men
as they slumber in their beds,
16he may speak in their ears Job 36:10,15
and terrify them with warnings,
17to turn man from wrongdoing
and keep him from pride,
18to preserve his soul from the pit,[b]
his life from perishing by the sword.[c]
19Or a man may be chastened on a bed of pain
with constant distress in his bones,
20so that his very being finds food repulsive
and his soul loathes the choicest meal.
21His flesh wastes away to nothing,
and his bones, once hidden, now stick out.
22His soul draws near to the pit,[d]
and his life to the messengers of death.[e]

23"Yet if there is an angel on his side
as a mediator, one out of a thousand,
to tell a man what is right for him, Mic 6:8
24to be gracious to him and say,
'Spare him from going down to the pit[f];
I have found a ransom for him'—
25then his flesh is renewed like a child's;
it is restored as in the days of his youth.
26He prays to God and finds favor with him,
he sees God's face and shouts for joy;
he is restored by God to his righteous state.
27Then he comes to men and says,
'I sinned, and perverted what was right,
but I did not get what I deserved. Ro 6:21
28He redeemed my soul from going down to the pit,[g]
and I will live to enjoy the light.' Job 22:28

29"God does all these things to a man— Eph 1:11
twice, even three times—
30to turn back his soul from the pit,[h]
that the light of life may shine on him.

31"Pay attention, Job, and listen to me;
be silent, and I will speak.
32If you have anything to say, answer me;
speak up, for I want you to be cleared.
33But if not, then listen to me;
be silent, and I will teach you wisdom."

34 Then Elihu said:

2"Hear my words, you wise men;
listen to me, you men of learning.
3For the ear tests words
as the tongue tastes food. Job 12:11
4Let us discern for ourselves what is right;
let us learn together what is good. 1Th 5:21

5"Job says, 'I am innocent, Job 33:9
but God denies me justice. Job 27:2
6Although I am right,

[a]13 Or *that he does not answer for any of his actions* [b]18 Or *preserve him from the grave* [c]18 Or *from crossing the River* [d]22 Or *He draws near to the grave* [e]22 Or *to the dead* [f]24 Or *grave* [g]28 Or *redeemed me from going down to the grave* [h]30 Or *turn him back from the grave*

I am considered a liar;
although I am guiltless,
his arrow inflicts an incurable wound.'
7 What man is like Job,
who drinks scorn like water? Job 15:16
8 He keeps company with evildoers;
he associates with wicked men. Ps 50:18
9 For he says, 'It profits a man nothing
when he tries to please God.' Job 21:15

10 "So listen to me, you men of understanding.
Far be it from God to do evil, Ge 18:25
from the Almighty to do wrong. Dt 32:4; Job 8:3
11 He repays a man for what he has done;
he brings upon him what his conduct
deserves. Jer 32:19; Eze 33:20
12 It is unthinkable that God would do wrong,
that the Almighty would pervert justice.
13 Who appointed him over the earth?
Who put him in charge of the whole world?
14 If it were his intention
and he withdrew his spirit[a] and breath,
15 all mankind would perish together
and man would return to the dust. Ge 3:19

16 "If you have understanding, hear this;
listen to what I say.
17 Can he who hates justice govern? 2Sa 23:3-4
Will you condemn the just and mighty
One? Job 40:8
18 Is he not the One who says to kings, 'You are
worthless,'
and to nobles, 'You are wicked,' Ex 22:28
19 who shows no partiality to princes Dt 10:17
and does not favor the rich over the poor,
for they are all the work of his hands?
20 They die in an instant, in the middle of the
night; Ex 12:29
the people are shaken and they pass away;
the mighty are removed without human
hand.
21 "His eyes are on the ways of men;
he sees their every step. Job 31:4
22 There is no dark place, no deep shadow,
where evildoers can hide.
23 God has no need to examine men further,
that they should come before him for
judgment. Job 11:11
24 Without inquiry he shatters the mighty
and sets up others in their place. Da 2:21
25 Because he takes note of their deeds,
he overthrows them in the night and they
are crushed. Pr 5:21-23
26 He punishes them for their wickedness
where everyone can see them,
27 because they turned from following him Ps 28:5
and had no regard for any of his ways.
28 They caused the cry of the poor to come
before him,
so that he heard the cry of the needy.
29 But if he remains silent, who can condemn
him?
If he hides his face, who can see him?
Yet he is over man and nation alike,
30 to keep a godless man from ruling,
from laying snares for the people. Pr 29:2-12

31 "Suppose a man says to God,
'I am guilty but will offend no more.
32 Teach me what I cannot see; Job 35:11; Ps 25:4
if I have done wrong, I will not do so
again.' Job 33:27
33 Should God then reward you on your terms,
when you refuse to repent? Job 41:11
You must decide, not I;
so tell me what you know.

34 "Men of understanding declare,
wise men who hear me say to me,
35 'Job speaks without knowledge; Job 35:16
his words lack insight.'
36 Oh, that Job might be tested to the utmost
for answering like a wicked man! Job 22:15
37 To his sin he adds rebellion;
scornfully he claps his hands among us
and multiplies his words against God."

35

Then Elihu said:

2 "Do you think this is just?
You say, 'I will be cleared by God.[b]'
3 Yet you ask him, 'What profit is it to me,[c]
and what do I gain by not sinning?'

4 "I would like to reply to you
and to your friends with you.
5 Look up at the heavens and see; Ge 15:5
gaze at the clouds so high above you.
6 If you sin, how does that affect him?
If your sins are many, what does that do to
him? Pr 8:36
7 If you are righteous, what do you give to him,
or what does he receive from your hand?
8 Your wickedness affects only a man like
yourself,
and your righteousness only the sons of
men.

9 "Men cry out under a load of oppression;
they plead for relief from the arm of the
powerful. Job 12:19
10 But no one says, 'Where is God my Maker,
who gives songs in the night, Ps 42:8; Ac 16:25
11 who teaches more to us than to[d] the beasts
of the earth Ps 94:12

[a] 14 Or *Spirit* [b] 2 Or *My righteousness is more than God's* [c] 3 Or *you* [d] 11 Or *teaches us by*

and makes us wiser than[a] the birds of the air?'

12He does not answer when men cry out Pr 1:28
because of the arrogance of the wicked.
13Indeed, God does not listen to their empty plea;
the Almighty pays no attention to it. Isa 1:15
14How much less, then, will he listen
when you say that you do not see him,
that your case is before him Ps 37:6
and you must wait for him,
15and further, that his anger never punishes
and he does not take the least notice of wickedness.[b] Ps 10:11
16So Job opens his mouth with empty talk;
without knowledge he multiplies words."

36

Elihu continued:

2"Bear with me a little longer and I will show you
that there is more to be said in God's behalf.
3I get my knowledge from afar;
I will ascribe justice to my Maker. Job 8:3
4Be assured that my words are not false; Job 33:3
one perfect in knowledge is with you.

5"God is mighty, but does not despise men;
he is mighty, and firm in his purpose.
6He does not keep the wicked alive Job 8:22
but gives the afflicted their rights. Job 5:15
7He does not take his eyes off the righteous;
he enthrones them with kings Ps 113:8
and exalts them forever.
8But if men are bound in chains, Ps 107:10,14
held fast by cords of affliction,
9he tells them what they have done—
that they have sinned arrogantly. Job 15:25
10He makes them listen to correction Job 33:16
and commands them to repent of their evil.
11If they obey and serve him, Isa 1:19
they will spend the rest of their days in prosperity
and their years in contentment.
12But if they do not listen,
they will perish by the sword[c] Job 15:22
and die without knowledge. Job 4:21

13"The godless in heart harbor resentment;
even when he fetters them, they do not cry for help.
14They die in their youth,
among male prostitutes of the shrines.
15But those who suffer he delivers in their suffering;
he speaks to them in their affliction.
16"He is wooing you from the jaws of distress
to a spacious place free from restriction,
to the comfort of your table laden with
choice food. Ps 23:5

LIVING  **INSIGHT**

The answer to resentment isn't complicated, it's just painful. It requires honesty. You must first admit that resentment is there. It then requires humility. You must confess it before the One who died for such sins. Finally, it requires vulnerability—a willingness to keep that tendency submissive to God's regular reproof and to hold to a genuinely teachable, unguarded attitude.

(See Job 36:13.)

17But now you are laden with the judgment due the wicked;
judgment and justice have taken hold of you. Job 22:11
18Be careful that no one entices you by riches;
do not let a large bribe turn you aside.
19Would your wealth
or even all your mighty efforts
sustain you so you would not be in distress?
20Do not long for the night, Job 34:20,25
to drag people away from their homes.[d]
21Beware of turning to evil, Ps 66:18
which you seem to prefer to affliction.

22"God is exalted in his power.
Who is a teacher like him? Isa 40:13
23Who has prescribed his ways for him, Job 34:13
or said to him, 'You have done wrong'?
24Remember to extol his work, Ps 92:5
which men have praised in song. Rev 15:3
25All mankind has seen it;
men gaze on it from afar.
26How great is God—beyond our understanding! 1Co 13:12
The number of his years is past finding out.

27"He draws up the drops of water,
which distill as rain to the streams[e];
28the clouds pour down their moisture
and abundant showers fall on mankind.
29Who can understand how he spreads out the clouds,
how he thunders from his pavilion? Job 37:16
30See how he scatters his lightning about him,
bathing the depths of the sea.

[a] *11* Or *us wise by* [b] *15* Symmachus, Theodotion and Vulgate; the meaning of the Hebrew for this word is uncertain. [c] *12* Or *will cross the River* [d] *20* The meaning of the Hebrew for verses 18-20 is uncertain. [e] *27* Or *distill from the mist as rain*

[31]This is the way he governs[a] the nations
and provides food in abundance. Ac 14:17
[32]He fills his hands with lightning
and commands it to strike its mark.
[33]His thunder announces the coming storm;
even the cattle make known its approach.[b]

37 "At this my heart pounds Ps 38:10
and leaps from its place.
[2]Listen! Listen to the roar of his voice, Job 32:10
to the rumbling that comes from his
mouth. Ps 29:3-9
[3]He unleashes his lightning beneath the whole
heaven
and sends it to the ends of the earth.
[4]After that comes the sound of his roar;
he thunders with his majestic voice. Ex 20:19
When his voice resounds,
he holds nothing back.
[5]God's voice thunders in marvelous ways;
he does great things beyond our
understanding. Job 5:9
[6]He says to the snow, 'Fall on the earth,'
and to the rain shower, 'Be a mighty
downpour.' Job 36:27
[7]So that all men he has made may know his
work,
he stops every man from his labor.[c]
[8]The animals take cover;
they remain in their dens. Ps 104:22
[9]The tempest comes out from its chamber,
the cold from the driving winds.
[10]The breath of God produces ice,
and the broad waters become frozen.
[11]He loads the clouds with moisture;
he scatters his lightning through them.
[12]At his direction they swirl around
over the face of the whole earth
to do whatever he commands them. Ps 148:8
[13]He brings the clouds to punish men, 1Sa 12:17
or to water his earth[d] and show his love.

[14]"Listen to this, Job; Job 32:10
stop and consider God's wonders. Job 5:9
[15]Do you know how God controls the clouds
and makes his lightning flash? Job 36:30,32
[16]Do you know how the clouds hang poised,
those wonders of him who is perfect in
knowledge? Job 36:4
[17]You who swelter in your clothes
when the land lies hushed under the south
wind,
[18]can you join him in spreading out the skies,
hard as a mirror of cast bronze? Dt 28:23

[19]"Tell us what we should say to him; Ro 8:26
we cannot draw up our case because of our
darkness.
[20]Should he be told that I want to speak?
Would any man ask to be swallowed up?
[21]Now no one can look at the sun, Jdg 5:31
bright as it is in the skies
after the wind has swept them clean.
[22]Out of the north he comes in golden
splendor; Ps 19:5
God comes in awesome majesty.
[23]The Almighty is beyond our reach and exalted
in power; Job 9:4; 1Ti 6:16
in his justice and great righteousness, he
does not oppress. Isa 63:9; Eze 18:23,32
[24]Therefore, men revere him, Mt 10:28
for does he not have regard for all the wise
in heart?[e]" Mt 11:25

The LORD Speaks

38 Then the LORD answered Job out of the
storm. He said: Job 40:6

[2]"Who is this that darkens my counsel
with words without knowledge? 1Ti 1:7
[3]Brace yourself like a man;
I will question you,
and you shall answer me. Job 40:7

[4]"Where were you when I laid the earth's
foundation? Ps 104:5; Pr 8:29
Tell me, if you understand.
[5]Who marked off its dimensions? Surely you
know! Pr 8:29; Isa 40:12
Who stretched a measuring line across it?
[6]On what were its footings set,
or who laid its cornerstone— Job 26:7
[7]while the morning stars sang together
and all the angels[f] shouted for joy?

[8]"Who shut up the sea behind doors Jer 5:22
when it burst forth from the womb, Ge 1:9-10
[9]when I made the clouds its garment
and wrapped it in thick darkness,
[10]when I fixed limits for it Ps 33:7; 104:9
and set its doors and bars in place, Job 26:10
[11]when I said, 'This far you may come and no
farther;
here is where your proud waves halt'?

[12]"Have you ever given orders to the morning,
or shown the dawn its place,
[13]that it might take the earth by the edges
and shake the wicked out of it? Ps 104:35
[14]The earth takes shape like clay under a seal;
its features stand out like those of a
garment.
[15]The wicked are denied their light, Job 18:5
and their upraised arm is broken. Ps 10:15

[a]31 Or *nourishes* [b]33 Or *announces his coming— / the One zealous against evil* [c]7 Or / *he fills all men with fear by his power* [d]13 Or *to favor them* [e]24 Or *for he does not have regard for any who think they are wise.* [f]7 Hebrew *the sons of God*

16"Have you journeyed to the springs of the sea
or walked in the recesses of the deep?
17Have the gates of death been shown to you?
Have you seen the gates of the shadow of death[a]?
18Have you comprehended the vast expanses of the earth? Job 28:24
Tell me, if you know all this.

19"What is the way to the abode of light?
And where does darkness reside?
20Can you take them to their places?
Do you know the paths to their dwellings?
21Surely you know, for you were already born!
You have lived so many years!

22"Have you entered the storehouses of the snow Job 37:6
or seen the storehouses of the hail,
23which I reserve for times of trouble, Isa 30:30
for days of war and battle? Ex 9:18; Jos 10:11
24What is the way to the place where the lightning is dispersed,
or the place where the east winds are scattered over the earth?
25Who cuts a channel for the torrents of rain,
and a path for the thunderstorm, Job 28:26
26to water a land where no man lives, Job 36:27
a desert with no one in it,
27to satisfy a desolate wasteland
and make it sprout with grass? Ps 104:14
28Does the rain have a father? Ps 147:8; Jer 14:22
Who fathers the drops of dew?
29From whose womb comes the ice?
Who gives birth to the frost from the heavens Ps 147:16-17
30when the waters become hard as stone,
when the surface of the deep is frozen?

31"Can you bind the beautiful[b] Pleiades?
Can you loose the cords of Orion? Job 9:9
32Can you bring forth the constellations in their seasons[c]
or lead out the Bear[d] with its cubs?
33Do you know the laws of the heavens? Ps 148:6
Can you set up ⌞God's[e]⌟ dominion over the earth?

34"Can you raise your voice to the clouds
and cover yourself with a flood of water?
35Do you send the lightning bolts on their way?
Do they report to you, 'Here we are'?
36Who endowed the heart[f] with wisdom Job 9:4
or gave understanding to the mind[f]?
37Who has the wisdom to count the clouds?
Who can tip over the water jars of the heavens Jos 3:16
38when the dust becomes hard
and the clods of earth stick together?

39"Do you hunt the prey for the lioness
and satisfy the hunger of the lions Ps 104:21
40when they crouch in their dens Job 37:8
or lie in wait in a thicket?
41Who provides food for the raven Lk 12:24
when its young cry out to God
and wander about for lack of food? Ps 147:9

39

"Do you know when the mountain goats give birth? Dt 14:5
Do you watch when the doe bears her fawn?
2Do you count the months till they bear?
Do you know the time they give birth?
3They crouch down and bring forth their young;
their labor pains are ended.
4Their young thrive and grow strong in the wilds;
they leave and do not return.

5"Who let the wild donkey go free? Job 6:5
Who untied his ropes?
6I gave him the wasteland as his home, Job 24:5
the salt flats as his habitat. Hos 8:9
7He laughs at the commotion in the town;
he does not hear a driver's shout. Job 3:18
8He ranges the hills for his pasture
and searches for any green thing.

9"Will the wild ox consent to serve you?
Will he stay by your manger at night?
10Can you hold him to the furrow with a harness?
Will he till the valleys behind you?
11Will you rely on him for his great strength?
Will you leave your heavy work to him?
12Can you trust him to bring in your grain
and gather it to your threshing floor?

13"The wings of the ostrich flap joyfully,
but they cannot compare with the pinions and feathers of the stork. Zec 5:9
14She lays her eggs on the ground
and lets them warm in the sand,
15unmindful that a foot may crush them,
that some wild animal may trample them.
16She treats her young harshly, as if they were not hers; La 4:3
she cares not that her labor was in vain,
17for God did not endow her with wisdom
or give her a share of good sense. Job 35:11
18Yet when she spreads her feathers to run,
she laughs at horse and rider.

19"Do you give the horse his strength

[a]17 Or *gates of deep shadows* [b]31 Or *the twinkling*; or *the chains of the* [c]32 Or *the morning star in its season* [d]32 Or *out Leo* [e]33 Or *his*; or *their* [f]36 The meaning of the Hebrew for this word is uncertain.

or clothe his neck with a flowing mane?
20 Do you make him leap like a locust, Joel 2:4-5
striking terror with his proud snorting?
21 He paws fiercely, rejoicing in his strength,
and charges into the fray. Jer 8:6
22 He laughs at fear, afraid of nothing;
he does not shy away from the sword.
23 The quiver rattles against his side,
along with the flashing spear and lance.
24 In frenzied excitement he eats up the ground;
he cannot stand still when the trumpet
sounds. Jer 4:5,19; Eze 7:14
25 At the blast of the trumpet he snorts, 'Aha!'
He catches the scent of battle from afar,
the shout of commanders and the battle
cry. Am 1:14; 2:2
26 "Does the hawk take flight by your wisdom
and spread his wings toward the south?
27 Does the eagle soar at your command
and build his nest on high? Ob 1:4
28 He dwells on a cliff and stays there at night;
a rocky crag is his stronghold.
29 From there he seeks out his food; Job 9:26
his eyes detect it from afar.
30 His young ones feast on blood,
and where the slain are, there is he."

40 The LORD said to Job: Job 33:13

2 "Will the one who contends with the
Almighty correct him? Job 9:15
Let him who accuses God answer him!"

3 Then Job answered the LORD:

4 "I am unworthy—how can I reply to you?
I put my hand over my mouth. Job 29:9
5 I spoke once, but I have no answer— Job 9:3
twice, but I will say no more."

6 Then the LORD spoke to Job out of the storm:

7 "Brace yourself like a man;
I will question you,
and you shall answer me. Job 42:4
8 "Would you discredit my justice? Ro 3:3
Would you condemn me to justify
yourself?
9 Do you have an arm like God's, 2Ch 32:8
and can your voice thunder like his? Job 37:5
10 Then adorn yourself with glory and splendor,
and clothe yourself in honor and majesty.
11 Unleash the fury of your wrath, Isa 42:25; Na 1:6
look at every proud man and bring him
low, Isa 2:11-12,17; Da 4:37
12 look at every proud man and humble him,
crush the wicked where they stand. Isa 13:11
13 Bury them all in the dust together;
shroud their faces in the grave.
14 Then I myself will admit to you
that your own right hand can save you.

15 "Look at the behemoth,[a]
which I made along with you Job 9:9
and which feeds on grass like an ox. Isa 11:7
16 What strength he has in his loins, Job 39:11
what power in the muscles of his belly!
17 His tail[b] sways like a cedar;
the sinews of his thighs are close-knit.
18 His bones are tubes of bronze,
his limbs like rods of iron.
19 He ranks first among the works of God,
yet his Maker can approach him with his
sword.
20 The hills bring him their produce, Ps 104:14
and all the wild animals play nearby.
21 Under the lotus plants he lies,
hidden among the reeds in the marsh.
22 The lotuses conceal him in their shadow;
the poplars by the stream surround him.
23 When the river rages, he is not alarmed; Isa 8:7
he is secure, though the Jordan should
surge against his mouth. Jos 3:1
24 Can anyone capture him by the eyes,[c]
or trap him and pierce his nose? Job 41:2,7,26

41 "Can you pull in the leviathan[d] with a
fishhook Ps 104:26; Isa 27:1
or tie down his tongue with a rope?
2 Can you put a cord through his nose
or pierce his jaw with a hook? Isa 37:29
3 Will he keep begging you for mercy?
Will he speak to you with gentle words?
4 Will he make an agreement with you
for you to take him as your slave for life?
5 Can you make a pet of him like a bird
or put him on a leash for your girls?
6 Will traders barter for him?
Will they divide him up among the
merchants?
7 Can you fill his hide with harpoons
or his head with fishing spears? Job 40:24
8 If you lay a hand on him,
you will remember the struggle and never
do it again! Job 3:8
9 Any hope of subduing him is false;
the mere sight of him is overpowering.
10 No one is fierce enough to rouse him. Job 3:8
Who then is able to stand against me?
11 Who has a claim against me that I must pay?
Everything under heaven belongs to me.

12 "I will not fail to speak of his limbs, Job 40:18
his strength and his graceful form. Job 39:11
13 Who can strip off his outer coat?

[a] 15 Possibly the hippopotamus or the elephant
[b] 17 Possibly trunk
[c] 24 Or *by a water hole*
[d] 1 Possibly the crocodile

Who would approach him with a bridle?
14Who dares open the doors of his mouth,
ringed about with his fearsome teeth?
15His back has[a] rows of shields
tightly sealed together; Job 40:17
16each is so close to the next
that no air can pass between.
17They are joined fast to one another;
they cling together and cannot be parted.
18His snorting throws out flashes of light;
his eyes are like the rays of dawn. Job 3:9
19Firebrands stream from his mouth; Da 10:6
sparks of fire shoot out.
20Smoke pours from his nostrils Ps 18:8
as from a boiling pot over a fire of reeds.
21His breath sets coals ablaze, Isa 40:7
and flames dart from his mouth. Ps 18:8
22Strength resides in his neck;
dismay goes before him.
23The folds of his flesh are tightly joined;
they are firm and immovable.
24His chest is hard as rock,
hard as a lower millstone.
25When he rises up, the mighty are terrified;
they retreat before his thrashing. Job 3:8
26The sword that reaches him has no effect,
nor does the spear or the dart or the
javelin. Jos 8:18
27Iron he treats like straw
and bronze like rotten wood.
28Arrows do not make him flee; Ps 91:5
slingstones are like chaff to him.
29A club seems to him but a piece of straw;
he laughs at the rattling of the lance. Job 5:22
30His undersides are jagged potsherds,
leaving a trail in the mud like a threshing
sledge. Isa 41:15
31He makes the depths churn like a boiling
caldron
and stirs up the sea like a pot of ointment.
32Behind him he leaves a glistening wake;
one would think the deep had white hair.
33Nothing on earth is his equal— Job 40:19
a creature without fear.
34He looks down on all that are haughty;
he is king over all that are proud." Job 28:8

Submission and Restoration **Chapter 42**

Job responded to the Lord's words with humility and a deepened understanding. By the end of all his suffering, he finally looked to the Lord and openly declared his repentance. Job also prayed for his friends to experience the mercy and grace of the Lord. Finally, Job received back all he had lost—and more. The blessing Job experienced is summarized in these words: "The LORD blessed the latter part of Job's life more than the first" (42:12).

Job

42 Then Job replied to the LORD:

2"I know that you can do all things; Ge 18:14
no plan of yours can be thwarted. 2Ch 20:6
3⌞You asked,⌟ 'Who is this that obscures my
counsel without knowledge?' Job 38:2
Surely I spoke of things I did not
understand,
things too wonderful for me to know.

LIVING  **INSIGHT**

Job confessed his own lack of understanding. What a relief that brought! Job didn't feel obligated to explain the "whys" of his situation. He confessed his inability to put it all together. Resting his case with the righteous Judge, Job did not feel compelled to answer all the questions or unravel all the burning riddles. God would judge. And the Judge would be right.
(See Job 42:3.)

4⌞"You said,⌟ 'Listen now, and I will speak;
I will question you,
and you shall answer me.' Job 38:3; 40:7
5My ears had heard of you Job 26:14; Ro 10:17
but now my eyes have seen you. Jdg 13:22
6Therefore I despise myself
and repent in dust and ashes." Job 40:4; Ro 12:3

Epilogue

7After the LORD had said these things to Job, he
said to Eliphaz the Temanite, "I am angry with you
and your two friends, because you have not spoken of me what is right, as my servant Job has. 8So
now take seven bulls and seven rams and go to my
servant Job and sacrifice a burnt offering for yourselves. My servant Job will pray for you, and I will
accept his prayer and not deal with you according
to your folly. You have not spoken of me what is
right, as my servant Job has." 9So Eliphaz the Temanite, Bildad the Shuhite and Zophar the Naamathite did what the LORD told them; and the
LORD accepted Job's prayer. Job 22:30; Jas 5:15-16
10After Job had prayed for his friends, the LORD
made him prosperous again and gave him twice as
much as he had before. 11All his brothers and sisters and everyone who had known him before
came and ate with him in his house. They comforted and consoled him over all the trouble the
LORD had brought upon him, and each one gave
him a piece of silver[b] and a gold ring. Dt 30:3

[a] 15 Or *His pride is his*
[b] 11 Hebrew *him a kesitah*; a kesitah was a unit of money of unknown weight and value.

12The LORD blessed the latter part of Job's life
more than the first. He had fourteen thousand
sheep, six thousand camels, a thousand yoke of
oxen and a thousand donkeys. 13And he also had
seven sons and three daughters. 14The first daughter he named Jemimah, the second Keziah and the
third Keren-Happuch. 15Nowhere in all the land
were there found women as beautiful as Job's
daughters, and their father granted them an inheritance along with their brothers.

16After this, Job lived a hundred and forty
years; he saw his children and their children to the
fourth generation. 17And so he died, old and full
of years.

INTRODUCTION

PSALMS

Every emotion that has ever swept across the keyboard of the human soul is here recorded in the book of Psalms. This book is the epitome, the very nucleus, of worship . . . and yet it drips with the whole range of human feeling—from joy and love and ecstasy to anger, fear, hurt and sadness. The psalms address the full spectrum of human needs. More than any other book in the Old Testament, we turn to this one that contains the collection of psalms in order to find direction for our lives and to be lifted up by its comfort and encouragement. Read the psalms with an open heart, and God will speak to you in ways you have never experienced before.

WRITERS: *David, Asaph and others*

DATE: *c.1490–444 B.C.*

PURPOSE: *To reflect in a myriad of ways the reality of a loving and strong God who cares for His people*

KEY THEMES: *The character of God; the person of the Messiah; the triumphs and trials of humanity*

KEY MESSAGE: *Giving God praise*

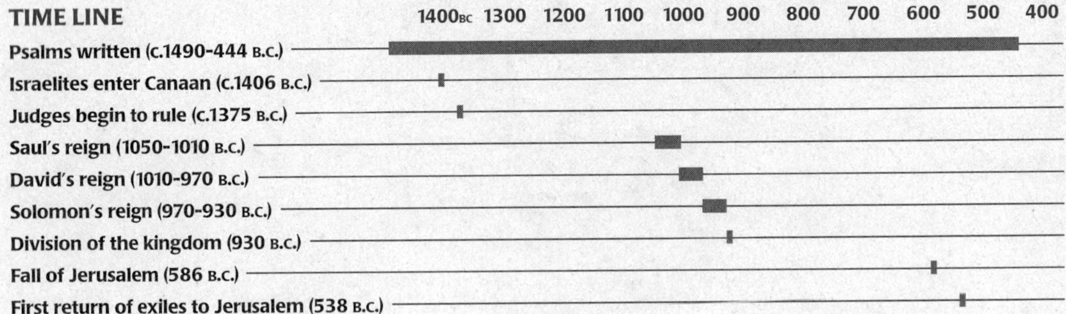

Ancient Hymnal of Praise

1490 B.C. DAYS OF MOSES	BOOK ONE	BOOK TWO	BOOK THREE	BOOK FOUR	BOOK FIVE	444 B.C. DAYS OF EZRA
	41 Hymns	31 Hymns	17 Hymns	17 Hymns	44 Hymns	
	HUMANITY	DELIVERANCE	SANCTUARY	GOD'S REIGN OVER THE EARTH	WORD OF GOD	
	PSALMS 1–41	*PSALMS 42–72*	*PSALMS 73–89*	*PSALMS 90–106*	*PSALMS 107–150*	
ANALOGY	**Genesis**	**Exodus**	**Leviticus**	**Numbers**	**Deuteronomy**	
CONTENT	**Personal**	**Devotional**	**Liturgical, Historical**	**General**	**Prophetical, Natural**	
DOXOLOGY	***Psalm 41:13***	***Psalm 72:18-19***	***Psalm 89:52***	***Psalm 106:48***	***Psalm 150:6***	

The German reformer Martin Luther believed that the Protestant Reformation would not be complete until the saints of God had two books in their possession. First, *they needed a Bible in their own language* that could lead them to a greater understanding of God's will and His ways. Second, *they needed a hymnal*, a "Psalter," from which they could praise their God and declare the heart of their faith. This companion volume to the Bible would help them as they expressed their faith through songs.

Down through the centuries, God's Word and hymns, or songs, of faith have played a central role in every revival. However, I have observed a curious phenomenon in evangelical churches. Many modern churches have fabricated a strange tension between these two. On the one hand, you will rarely find anyone who would diminish the value of the Bible. God's Word is upheld. It is loved. It is often passionately defended. On the other hand, it is becoming more common to encounter those who would belittle the need for music. It concerns me that these folks do not seem to understand the importance of expressing our faith in song. I'm concerned because I believe that worship through song means a great deal to our God. I greatly suspect that genuine worship cannot exist without these two elements blending together.

Music From Start to Finish

When you stop to think about it, long before the voice of humanity was heard on the earth, there was music. The book of Job tells us that at the time of creation "the morning stars sang together" (Job 38:7). Now either the stars in the sky had voices back then, or the angelic host sang praises to God. I believe it was the latter. The angels of heaven surrounded the throne in antiphonal voice and sang praises to the Creator. It must have been some kind of harmony! I also read, if I understand Revelation correctly, that when we gather around our Lord's throne in eternity, our purest expression of praise and worship will come in song. We will sing unto Him, "Worthy is the Lamb, who was slain" (Revelation 5:12). If it is true that there was singing *before the earth* and there will be singing *after this life*, it stands to reason there should be a lot of singing *while we are on the earth*.

Getting the Facts Straight

Let me give some introductory facts worth considering as we study the book of Psalms. Allow me to introduce you to the earliest hymnal that was ever put into print—"The Psalter." In fact, it was the only hymnal the early church had available. The Hebrew title for Psalms (which is *tehillim*) simply means "praises." This is a book of praises directed to God. Interestingly, in both the Hebrew and the Greek, the terms used in the title of the book have the same root meaning: "playing an instrumental piece of music."

As time passed, the name "Psalms" came to mean "songs sung to musical accompaniment." Over the centuries it was the singing to musical accompaniment that came more sharply into focus. If you pay close attention in your reading of the psalms you'll notice musical notations sprinkled throughout the book. Note the word "Selah," for example—which possibly means "pause," or "think on that." If you are involved in public speaking, or in composing instrumental music, you know there are times when a pause is just as significant as the loudest crescendo. "Pause and think on that."

Heights, Depths and Everywhere In-between

One of the beautiful facets of the psalms is that each one is born out of its own unique context. The diverse settings add an exquisite variety to the book unlike any other book of the Bible. It's a book of broad experiences—and deep experiences. You will scale the heights of celebration and ecstasy and you will plumb the depths of conflict and agony. You will walk with David, Asaph, Solomon and Moses through the joys of healing and deliverance, as well as through the heartache of despair and guilt. Psalms is, of course, the most emotional of all the books of the Bible. Each psalm adds it own matchless contribution to the whole collection.

Authors and Dates

We often refer to this book as "The Psalms of David"—even though we're not sure that he wrote even half of them. We are quite certain he wrote more psalms than anyone else—at least 73 of them. Asaph was credited with 12 psalms. Solomon wrote two. Moses wrote at least one. Heman and Ethan, who were "Ezrahites," were credited with writing one each. About forty of the psalms are anonymous—some have called them "orphan psalms." In other words, they were born but no one knows who the parents were.

Let me point out that the sweep of time covered in the book of Psalms is very broad. If we go all the way back to a psalm Moses is credited as writing (see Psalm 90), that would take us back to about 1490 B.C. And if we move all the way forward to the people of Ezra (the Ezrahites; see Psalms 88—89), it would bring us to about 444 B.C. The psalms reflect different kinds of experiences spanning at least ten centuries.

Watch for Details

In order to read the psalms correctly, we want to heed two technical hints. First: *Read the superscriptions.* Superscriptions are the words that appear just beneath the titles of many psalms. You may be surprised to hear this, but these words are also inspired. They are just as much a part of the psalm as any of its verses. Look, for example, at Psalm 3, which begins, "A psalm of David. When he fled from his son Absalom." In the psalm David went on to describe the situation ("O LORD, how many are my foes!") and his emotions as he fled from Absalom.

Now here's the point: When we pay close attention to the superscription, we gain a feel for the psalm. If you have a son or a daughter who is going through a time of rebellion, Psalm 3 is for you. It was composed in a time of extremely difficult conflict in David's home. These words of introduction to many of the psalms give us the setting and spirit of what is to follow. So read these words carefully and let them help the message of the psalm come alive in your heart.

The second hint is this: *Read the psalms the way an artist views his or her work.* If you tend to look at things literally, you may have trouble getting into the spirit of the psalms. If you are a person who loves the arts, you may very well find depths of truth in the psalms that you will find nowhere else in Scripture. Why? Simply because they were written by artists. The authors were gifted in music and/or poetry; they have expressed a series of profound truths that are not meant so much to be analyzed as to be felt and experienced.

When you read the psalms, it is not like reading a text merely to be put in the correct sentence structure and objectively analyzed. It's like reading a person's prayer; it's like hearing a heartfelt song of praise or a moving lament of sorrow. There are depths and heights that you dare not miss. As you read, use your *eyes* to see the words and your *mind* to understand God's revelation, but do not forget to let your *heart* feel the passion and pulse of each inspired artist.

Putting It All Together

The psalms are divided into five books. *Humanity* is the emphasis in Book I (Psalms 1–41). Many of these psalms describe humans as blessed, fallen and redeemed by God. David wrote most of these psalms; they are very personal in nature.

Deliverance is the theme of the second set of psalms (42–72). These 31 songs have much to say about trouble—and God's power to deliver us from that trouble. They have much to say about discouragement—and God's power to lift our hearts from the depths of despair. In these psalms we find encouragement and strength for all who are in the midst of struggles.

The *sanctuary*, God's "dwelling place," is the focus of Book III (Psalms 73–89). Many of the psalms were originally sung in the temple as the people worshiped. The psalms in this section, many of which are attributed to Asaph, leader of one of David's Levitical choirs (Psalms 73–83), contain prayers of the ancient Israelites as they drew near to their Lord in worship.

God's righteous reign over all the earth is in view in Book IV (Psalms 90–106). The power of the everlasting God is celebrated in the context of all the experiences of humanity—a power demonstrated in God's anger as well as in His unfailing love (see Psalm 90). *The Lord reigns*—that is the truth that rings throughout this section of the book of Psalms. His reign is eternal, universal and invincible!

The *revelation of God through His works and His Word* is the emphasis in Book V (Psalms 107–150). The last 44 hymns in the collection of psalms celebrate the greatness of God and His revelation—particularly as it is given to us in His Word. Certainly Psalm 119 is the most famous of these psalms.

Five Exclamation Marks

Each of the five books of Psalms ends with a doxology. A doxology is an expression of jubilant praise, and in the book of Psalms is often accompanied by a "double Amen." As each section within the book of Psalms comes to a close, the people are expected to respond with voices raised in praise, with their unambiguous "Amen" to the contents of each book. As Psalm 41 ends, these words are found: "Praise be to the LORD, the God of Israel, from everlasting to everlasting. Amen and Amen" (41:13). What a powerful crescendo of praise and affirmation marking the end of the first book of Psalms! Then, 31 hymns later, this doxology appears: "Praise be to the LORD God, the God of Israel, who alone does marvelous deeds. Praise be to his glorious name forever; may the whole earth be filled with his glory. Amen and Amen" (72:18–19).

Do you see the consistent pattern at the end of each section? A series of songs focusing on a theme and then a response of loudest praise and a chorus of "Amens." God has collected 150 songs inspired over a millennium in a format that still calls for our response of loudest praise and affirmation.

Where the Psalms Meet Life

Let me suggest two practical principles. First, *the psalms are designed to meet our needs immediately*. We don't have to wait three days for God's medication to enter our bloodstream. It works instantly. God gives us precise assurance when we read His Word. When we're feeling low, the psalms lift us up. When we're lonely and confused, they comfort us. When we're afraid, they embrace us and pacify us. When we're discouraged, they encourage us. The psalms will provide assistance—whatever your most pressing need may be.

Second, *the psalms afford profound insight*. Do you need insight? Do you want practical wisdom for living? You've got it right here in this book. Those who become keen students of God's truth are equipped to deal with whatever life throws at them. No degree in the highest educational system will give you the wisdom and insight and understanding that this book will give you. Read the psalms with an open heart, and God will come close and speak to you in ways you have never experienced before.

BOOK I

Psalms 1–41

Psalms of Humanity — **Psalms 1–41**

The book of Psalms is divided into five sections, or books. Interestingly, these five books find some parallel in the themes of the Pentateuch—the first five books of the Old Testament. This first section, like the book of Genesis, follows the development of our understanding of humanity. These psalms move through humanity's state of blessedness, fall and recovery. Because David wrote most of these psalms, they are very personal and passionate. They plumb the depths of human suffering and sorrow as well as explore the heights of human ecstasy and joy.

Psalm 1

1Blessed is the man
who does not walk in the counsel of the wicked Pr 4:14
or stand in the way of sinners
or sit in the seat of mockers. Ps 26:4; Jer 15:17
2But his delight is in the law of the LORD,
and on his law he meditates day and night.
3He is like a tree planted by streams of water,
which yields its fruit in season
and whose leaf does not wither.
Whatever he does prospers. Ge 39:3

LIVING  INSIGHT

Whatever your circumstances may be, no matter how long your tough times may have lasted, wherever you may be today, I bring you this reminder: the stronger the winds . . . the deeper the roots, and the longer the winds . . . the more beautiful the tree.

(See Psalm 1:3.)

4Not so the wicked!
They are like chaff
that the wind blows away. Job 21:18; Isa 17:13
5Therefore the wicked will not stand in the judgment,
nor sinners in the assembly of the righteous.

6For the LORD watches over the way of the righteous, Ps 37:18; 2Ti 2:19
but the way of the wicked will perish.

Psalm 2

1Why do the nations conspire[a]
and the peoples plot in vain? Ps 21:11
2The kings of the earth take their stand
and the rulers gather together
against the LORD
and against his Anointed One.[b] Jn 1:41
3"Let us break their chains," they say,
"and throw off their fetters."

4The One enthroned in heaven laughs;
the Lord scoffs at them. Ps 37:13
5Then he rebukes them in his anger
and terrifies them in his wrath, saying,
6"I have installed my King[c]
on Zion, my holy hill." Ex 15:17

7I will proclaim the decree of the LORD:

He said to me, "You are my Son[d];
today I have become your Father.[e] Ac 13:33*
8Ask of me,
and I will make the nations your inheritance,
the ends of the earth your possession.
9You will rule them with an iron scepter[f];
you will dash them to pieces like pottery."

10Therefore, you kings, be wise;
be warned, you rulers of the earth.
11Serve the LORD with fear
and rejoice with trembling. Heb 12:28
12Kiss the Son, lest he be angry
and you be destroyed in your way,
for his wrath can flare up in a moment.
Blessed are all who take refuge in him.

Psalm 3

A psalm of David. When he fled from his son Absalom.

1O LORD, how many are my foes!
How many rise up against me!
2Many are saying of me,
"God will not deliver him." *Selah*[g]

3But you are a shield around me, O LORD;
you bestow glory on me and lift[h] up my head. Ps 27:6
4To the LORD I cry aloud,
and he answers me from his holy hill. *Selah*

5I lie down and sleep; Lev 26:6
I wake again, because the LORD sustains me.
6I will not fear the tens of thousands
drawn up against me on every side. Ps 27:3
7Arise, O LORD!

[a] *1* Hebrew; Septuagint *rage* [b] *2* Or *anointed one* [c] *6* Or *king* [d] *7* Or *son*; also in verse 12 [e] *7* Or *have begotten you* [f] *9* Or *will break them with a rod of iron* [g] *2* A word of uncertain meaning, occurring frequently in the Psalms; possibly a musical term [h] *3* Or *LORD, / my Glorious One, who lifts*

Deliver me, O my God!
Strike all my enemies on the jaw;
break the teeth of the wicked. Job 16:10

8 From the LORD comes deliverance. Isa 43:3,11
May your blessing be on your people. *Selah*

Psalm 4

For the director of music. With stringed instruments. A psalm of David.

1 Answer me when I call to you,
O my righteous God.
Give me relief from my distress;
be merciful to me and hear my prayer.

2 How long, O men, will you turn my glory
into shame[a]?
How long will you love delusions and seek
false gods[b]? *Selah*
3 Know that the LORD has set apart the godly
for himself; Ps 31:23
the LORD will hear when I call to him. Ps 6:8

4 In your anger do not sin; Eph 4:26*
when you are on your beds, Ps 77:6
search your hearts and be silent. *Selah*
5 Offer right sacrifices
and trust in the LORD. Dt 33:19; Ps 37:3

LIVING  INSIGHT

God wants my unreserved love, my unqualified devotion, my undaunted trust—not my unenlightened analysis of His impenetrable ways.

(See Psalm 4:5.)

6 Many are asking, "Who can show us any
good?"
Let the light of your face shine upon us,
O LORD. Nu 6:25
7 You have filled my heart with greater joy
than when their grain and new wine
abound.
8 I will lie down and sleep in peace, Ps 3:5
for you alone, O LORD,
make me dwell in safety. Lev 25:18

Psalm 5

For the director of music. For flutes. A psalm of David.

1 Give ear to my words, O LORD,
consider my sighing.
2 Listen to my cry for help, Ps 3:4
my King and my God, Ps 84:3
for to you I pray.
3 In the morning, O LORD, you hear my voice;
in the morning I lay my requests before
you
and wait in expectation.

4 You are not a God who takes pleasure in evil;
with you the wicked cannot dwell. Ps 11:5
5 The arrogant cannot stand in your presence;
you hate all who do wrong. Ps 11:5
6 You destroy those who tell lies; Ps 55:23
bloodthirsty and deceitful men
the LORD abhors.

7 But I, by your great mercy,
will come into your house;
in reverence will I bow down
toward your holy temple. Ps 138:2
8 Lead me, O LORD, in your righteousness Ps 31:1
because of my enemies—
make straight your way before me. Ps 27:11

9 Not a word from their mouth can be trusted;
their heart is filled with destruction.
Their throat is an open grave; Lk 11:44
with their tongue they speak deceit. Ro 3:13*
10 Declare them guilty, O God!
Let their intrigues be their downfall.
Banish them for their many sins, Ps 9:16
for they have rebelled against you. Ps 107:11

11 But let all who take refuge in you be glad;
let them ever sing for joy. Ps 2:12
Spread your protection over them,
that those who love your name may rejoice
in you. Ps 69:36; Isa 65:13
12 For surely, O LORD, you bless the righteous;
you surround them with your favor as with
a shield. Ps 32:7

Psalm 6

For the director of music. With stringed instruments. According to *sheminith*.[c] A psalm of David.

1 O LORD, do not rebuke me in your anger
or discipline me in your wrath.
2 Be merciful to me, LORD, for I am faint;
O LORD, heal me, for my bones are in
agony. Ps 22:14
3 My soul is in anguish. Jn 12:27
How long, O LORD, how long?
4 Turn, O LORD, and deliver me;
save me because of your unfailing love.
5 No one remembers you when he is dead.
Who praises you from the grave[d]? Ps 30:9

[a] 2 Or *you dishonor my Glorious One* [b] 2 Or *seek lies* [c] Title: Probably a musical term [d] 5 Hebrew *Sheol*

6 I am worn out from groaning;
all night long I flood my bed with weeping
and drench my couch with tears. Ps 42:3
7 My eyes grow weak with sorrow; Ps 31:9
they fail because of all my foes.

8 Away from me, all you who do evil, Ps 119:115
for the LORD has heard my weeping.
9 The LORD has heard my cry for mercy; Ps 116:1
the LORD accepts my prayer.
10 All my enemies will be ashamed and
dismayed;
they will turn back in sudden disgrace.

Psalm 7

A *shiggaion*[a] of David, which he sang to the LORD concerning Cush, a Benjamite.

1 O LORD my God, I take refuge in you;
save and deliver me from all who pursue
me, Ps 31:15
2 or they will tear me like a lion
and rip me to pieces with no one to rescue
me.

3 O LORD my God, if I have done this
and there is guilt on my hands— 1Sa 24:11
4 if I have done evil to him who is at peace
with me
or without cause have robbed my foe—
5 then let my enemy pursue and overtake me;
let him trample my life to the ground
and make me sleep in the dust. *Selah*

6 Arise, O LORD, in your anger; Ps 94:2
rise up against the rage of my enemies.
Awake, my God; decree justice. Ps 44:23
7 Let the assembled peoples gather around you.
Rule over them from on high;
8 let the LORD judge the peoples.
Judge me, O LORD, according to my
righteousness, Ps 18:20
according to my integrity, O Most High.
9 O righteous God, Jer 11:20
who searches minds and hearts, Rev 2:23
bring to an end the violence of the wicked
and make the righteous secure.

10 My shield[b] is God Most High,
who saves the upright in heart. Ps 125:4
11 God is a righteous judge,
a God who expresses his wrath every day.
12 If he does not relent,
he[c] will sharpen his sword; Dt 32:41
he will bend and string his bow.
13 He has prepared his deadly weapons;
he makes ready his flaming arrows.
14 He who is pregnant with evil
and conceives trouble gives birth to
disillusionment. Isa 59:4; Jas 1:15
15 He who digs a hole and scoops it out
falls into the pit he has made. Job 4:8
16 The trouble he causes recoils on himself;
his violence comes down on his own head.

17 I will give thanks to the LORD because of his
righteousness Ps 71:15-16
and will sing praise to the name of the
LORD Most High.

Psalm 8

For the director of music. According to *gittith.*[d] A psalm of David.

1 O LORD, our Lord,
how majestic is your name in all the earth!

You have set your glory
above the heavens. Ps 113:4; 148:13
2 From the lips of children and infants
you have ordained praise[e] Mt 21:16*
because of your enemies,
to silence the foe and the avenger. Ps 44:16

3 When I consider your heavens, Ps 89:11
the work of your fingers,
the moon and the stars,
which you have set in place,
4 what is man that you are mindful of him,
the son of man that you care for him?
5 You made him a little lower than the heavenly
beings[f]
and crowned him with glory and honor.

LIVING  **INSIGHT**

Ask the Lord to help you catch a new vision of who He is . . . what He demands . . . and what He can accomplish in and through your life as you trust in Him. Isn't it astonishing that God cares for us so much that He crowns us with glory and honor? It calls for our response of loudest praise!

(See Psalm 8:1–9.)

6 You made him ruler over the works of your
hands;
you put everything under his feet: Heb 2:6-8*
7 all flocks and herds,
and the beasts of the field,
8 the birds of the air,

[a]Title: Probably a literary or musical term [b]10 Or *sovereign* [c]12 Or *If a man does not repent, / God*
[d]Title: Probably a musical term [e]2 Or *strength* [f]5 Or *than God*

and the fish of the sea,
all that swim the paths of the seas. Ge 1:26

9O LORD, our Lord,
how majestic is your name in all the earth!

Psalm 9[a]

For the director of music. To ⌞the tune of⌟ "The Death of the Son." A psalm of David.

1I will praise you, O LORD, with all my heart;
I will tell of all your wonders.
2I will be glad and rejoice in you; Ps 5:11
I will sing praise to your name, O Most High. Ps 83:18

3My enemies turn back;
they stumble and perish before you.
4For you have upheld my right and my cause;
you have sat on your throne, judging righteously. 1Pe 2:23
5You have rebuked the nations and destroyed the wicked;
you have blotted out their name for ever and ever. Pr 10:7
6Endless ruin has overtaken the enemy,
you have uprooted their cities;
even the memory of them has perished.

7The LORD reigns forever;
he has established his throne for judgment.
8He will judge the world in righteousness;
he will govern the peoples with justice.
9The LORD is a refuge for the oppressed,
a stronghold in times of trouble. Ps 32:7
10Those who know your name will trust in you,
for you, LORD, have never forsaken those who seek you.

11Sing praises to the LORD, enthroned in Zion;
proclaim among the nations what he has done. Ps 105:1
12For he who avenges blood remembers; Ge 9:5
he does not ignore the cry of the afflicted.

13O LORD, see how my enemies persecute me!
Have mercy and lift me up from the gates of death,
14that I may declare your praises Ps 106:2
in the gates of the Daughter of Zion
and there rejoice in your salvation. Ps 13:5
15The nations have fallen into the pit they have dug; Ps 7:15-16
their feet are caught in the net they have hidden.
16The LORD is known by his justice;
the wicked are ensnared by the work of their hands. *Higgaion.*[b] *Selah*
17The wicked return to the grave,[c]
all the nations that forget God. Job 8:13
18But the needy will not always be forgotten,
nor the hope of the afflicted ever perish.
19Arise, O LORD, let not man triumph;
let the nations be judged in your presence.
20Strike them with terror, O LORD;
let the nations know they are but men. *Selah*

Psalm 10[a]

1Why, O LORD, do you stand far off? Ps 22:1,11
Why do you hide yourself in times of trouble? Ps 13:1

2In his arrogance the wicked man hunts down the weak,
who are caught in the schemes he devises.
3He boasts of the cravings of his heart; Ps 94:4
he blesses the greedy and reviles the LORD.
4In his pride the wicked does not seek him;
in all his thoughts there is no room for God. Ps 14:1; 36:1
5His ways are always prosperous;
he is haughty and your laws are far from him;
he sneers at all his enemies.
6He says to himself, "Nothing will shake me;
I'll always be happy and never have trouble." Rev 18:7
7His mouth is full of curses and lies and threats; Ro 3:14*
trouble and evil are under his tongue.
8He lies in wait near the villages;
from ambush he murders the innocent,
watching in secret for his victims.
9He lies in wait like a lion in cover;
he lies in wait to catch the helpless; Ps 17:12
he catches the helpless and drags them off in his net.
10His victims are crushed, they collapse;
they fall under his strength.
11He says to himself, "God has forgotten;
he covers his face and never sees."

12Arise, LORD! Lift up your hand, O God. Mic 5:9
Do not forget the helpless. Ps 9:12
13Why does the wicked man revile God?
Why does he say to himself,
"He won't call me to account"?
14But you, O God, do see trouble and grief;
you consider it to take it in hand.
The victim commits himself to you;

[a]Psalms 9 and 10 may have been originally a single acrostic poem, the stanzas of which begin with the successive letters of the Hebrew alphabet. In the Septuagint they constitute one psalm. [b]16 Or *Meditation*; possibly a musical notation [c]17 Hebrew *Sheol*

you are the helper of the fatherless. Ps 68:5
[15]Break the arm of the wicked and evil man;
call him to account for his wickedness
that would not be found out.

[16]The LORD is King for ever and ever; Ps 29:10
the nations will perish from his land. Dt 8:20
[17]You hear, O LORD, the desire of the afflicted;
you encourage them, and you listen to their
cry, Ps 34:15
[18]defending the fatherless and the oppressed,
in order that man, who is of the earth, may
terrify no more.

Psalm 11

For the director of music. Of David.

[1]In the LORD I take refuge. Ps 56:11
How then can you say to me:
"Flee like a bird to your mountain.
[2]For look, the wicked bend their bows;
they set their arrows against the strings
to shoot from the shadows
at the upright in heart. Ps 64:3-4
[3]When the foundations are being destroyed,
what can the righteous do[a]?"

[4]The LORD is in his holy temple; Ps 18:6
the LORD is on his heavenly throne.
He observes the sons of men;
his eyes examine them. Ps 34:15-16
[5]The LORD examines the righteous, Ge 22:1
but the wicked[b] and those who love
violence
his soul hates. Ps 5:5
[6]On the wicked he will rain
fiery coals and burning sulfur; Eze 38:22
a scorching wind will be their lot. Jer 4:11-12

[7]For the LORD is righteous,
he loves justice;
upright men will see his face. Ps 17:15

Psalm 12

For the director of music. According to *sheminith.*[c] A psalm of David.

[1]Help, LORD, for the godly are no more; Isa 57:1
the faithful have vanished from among
men.
[2]Everyone lies to his neighbor;
their flattering lips speak with deception.

[3]May the LORD cut off all flattering lips
and every boastful tongue Da 7:8; Rev 13:5
[4]that says, "We will triumph with our tongues;
we own our lips[d]—who is our master?"

[5]"Because of the oppression of the weak
and the groaning of the needy,
I will now arise," says the LORD.
"I will protect them from those who malign
them." Ps 10:18; 34:6
[6]And the words of the LORD are flawless,
like silver refined in a furnace of clay,
purified seven times.

[7]O LORD, you will keep us safe
and protect us from such people forever.
[8]The wicked freely strut about
when what is vile is honored among men.

Psalm 13

For the director of music. A psalm of David.

[1]How long, O LORD? Will you forget me
forever?
How long will you hide your face from me?
[2]How long must I wrestle with my thoughts
and every day have sorrow in my heart?
How long will my enemy triumph over me?

[3]Look on me and answer, O LORD my God.
Give light to my eyes, or I will sleep in
death; Ezr 9:8; Jer 51:39
[4]my enemy will say, "I have overcome him,"
and my foes will rejoice when I fall.

[5]But I trust in your unfailing love;
my heart rejoices in your salvation. Ps 9:14
[6]I will sing to the LORD,
for he has been good to me. Ps 116:7

Psalm 14

For the director of music. Of David.

[1]The fool[e] says in his heart,
"There is no God." Ps 10:4
They are corrupt, their deeds are vile;
there is no one who does good.

[2]The LORD looks down from heaven Ps 33:13
on the sons of men
to see if there are any who understand, Ps 92:6
any who seek God.
[3]All have turned aside,
they have together become corrupt; Ps 58:3
there is no one who does good,
not even one. Ro 3:10-12*

[4]Will evildoers never learn—

[a]3 Or *what is the Righteous One doing* [b]5 Or *The LORD, the Righteous One, examines the wicked, /* [c]Title: Probably a musical term [d]4 Or */ our lips are our plowshares* [e]1 The Hebrew words rendered *fool* in Psalms denote one who is morally deficient.

those who devour my people as men eat
bread
and who do not call on the LORD? Isa 64:7
5There they are, overwhelmed with dread,
for God is present in the company of the
righteous.
6You evildoers frustrate the plans of the poor,
but the LORD is their refuge. Ps 9:9
7Oh, that salvation for Israel would come out
of Zion!
When the LORD restores the fortunes of his
people, Ps 53:6
let Jacob rejoice and Israel be glad!

Psalm 15

A psalm of David.

1LORD, who may dwell in your sanctuary?
Who may live on your holy hill? Ps 24:3-5
2He whose walk is blameless
and who does what is righteous,
who speaks the truth from his heart Eph 4:25
3 and has no slander on his tongue, Ex 23:1
who does his neighbor no wrong
and casts no slur on his fellowman,
4who despises a vile man
but honors those who fear the LORD, Ac 28:10
who keeps his oath
even when it hurts,
5who lends his money without usury Ex 22:25
and does not accept a bribe against the
innocent.

He who does these things
will never be shaken. 2Pe 1:10

Psalm 16

A *miktam*[a] of David.

1Keep me safe, O God,
for in you I take refuge. Ps 7:1
2I said to the LORD, "You are my Lord;
apart from you I have no good thing."
3As for the saints who are in the land,
they are the glorious ones in whom is all
my delight.[b] Ps 101:6
4The sorrows of those will increase
who run after other gods. Ps 32:10
I will not pour out their libations of blood
or take up their names on my lips. Ex 23:13
5LORD, you have assigned me my portion and
my cup; Ps 23:5
you have made my lot secure.
6The boundary lines have fallen for me in
pleasant places;
surely I have a delightful inheritance. Ps 78:55
7I will praise the LORD, who counsels me;
even at night my heart instructs me.
8I have set the LORD always before me.
Because he is at my right hand, Ps 73:23
I will not be shaken.
9Therefore my heart is glad and my tongue
rejoices; Ps 4:7
my body also will rest secure,
10because you will not abandon me to the
grave,[c]
nor will you let your Holy One[d] see decay.
11You have made[e] known to me the path of
life; Mt 7:14
you will fill me with joy in your presence,
with eternal pleasures at your right hand.

Psalm 17

A prayer of David.

1Hear, O LORD, my righteous plea;
listen to my cry. Ps 61:1
Give ear to my prayer—
it does not rise from deceitful lips. Isa 29:13
2May my vindication come from you;
may your eyes see what is right.
3Though you probe my heart and examine me
at night,
though you test me, you will find nothing;
I have resolved that my mouth will not sin.
4As for the deeds of men—
by the word of your lips
I have kept myself
from the ways of the violent.
5My steps have held to your paths; Ps 44:18
my feet have not slipped.
6I call on you, O God, for you will answer me;
give ear to me and hear my prayer. Ps 116:2
7Show the wonder of your great love, Ps 31:21
you who save by your right hand
those who take refuge in you from their
foes.
8Keep me as the apple of your eye; Dt 32:10
hide me in the shadow of your wings
9from the wicked who assail me,
from my mortal enemies who surround me.
10They close up their callous hearts, Ps 73:7
and their mouths speak with arrogance.
11They have tracked me down, they now
surround me, Ps 88:17
with eyes alert, to throw me to the ground.

[a]Title: Probably a literary or musical term [b]3 Or *As for the pagan priests who are in the land / and the nobles in whom all delight, I said:* [c]10 Hebrew *Sheol* [d]10 Or *your faithful one* [e]11 Or *You will make*

12They are like a lion hungry for prey, Ps 7:2
like a great lion crouching in cover.
13Rise up, O LORD, confront them, bring them down; Ps 73:18
rescue me from the wicked by your sword.
14O LORD, by your hand save me from such men,
from men of this world whose reward is in this life. Lk 16:8
You still the hunger of those you cherish;
their sons have plenty,
and they store up wealth for their children.
15And I—in righteousness I will see your face;
when I awake, I will be satisfied with seeing your likeness. Ps 4:6-7; 16:11; 1Jn 3:2

Psalm 18

For the director of music. Of David the servant of the LORD. He sang to the LORD the words of this song when the LORD delivered him from the hand of all his enemies and from the hand of Saul. He said:

1I love you, O LORD, my strength. Ex 15:2
2The LORD is my rock, my fortress and my deliverer; Ps 19:14
my God is my rock, in whom I take refuge.
He is my shield and the horn[a] of my salvation, my stronghold. Ps 59:11; 75:10
3I call to the LORD, who is worthy of praise,
and I am saved from my enemies.
4The cords of death entangled me; Ps 116:3
the torrents of destruction overwhelmed me. Ps 124:4
5The cords of the grave[b] coiled around me;
the snares of death confronted me. Ps 116:3
6In my distress I called to the LORD;
I cried to my God for help.
From his temple he heard my voice; Ps 34:15
my cry came before him, into his ears.
7The earth trembled and quaked, Jdg 5:4
and the foundations of the mountains shook;
they trembled because he was angry.
8Smoke rose from his nostrils;
consuming fire came from his mouth,
burning coals blazed out of it.
9He parted the heavens and came down; Ps 144:5
dark clouds were under his feet.
10He mounted the cherubim and flew;
he soared on the wings of the wind. Ps 104:3
11He made darkness his covering, his canopy around him—
the dark rain clouds of the sky. Ps 97:2
12Out of the brightness of his presence clouds advanced, Ps 104:2
with hailstones and bolts of lightning.
13The LORD thundered from heaven;
the voice of the Most High resounded.[c]
14He shot his arrows and scattered ⌊the enemies⌋,
great bolts of lightning and routed them.
15The valleys of the sea were exposed
and the foundations of the earth laid bare
at your rebuke, O LORD, Ps 76:6; 106:9
at the blast of breath from your nostrils.

16He reached down from on high and took hold of me;
he drew me out of deep waters. Ps 144:7
17He rescued me from my powerful enemy,
from my foes, who were too strong for me.
18They confronted me in the day of my disaster,
but the LORD was my support. Ps 59:16
19He brought me out into a spacious place;
he rescued me because he delighted in me.

20The LORD has dealt with me according to my righteousness;
according to the cleanness of my hands he has rewarded me. Ps 24:4
21For I have kept the ways of the LORD; 2Ch 34:33
I have not done evil by turning from my God.
22All his laws are before me;
I have not turned away from his decrees.
23I have been blameless before him
and have kept myself from sin.
24The LORD has rewarded me according to my righteousness, 1Sa 26:23
according to the cleanness of my hands in his sight.

25To the faithful you show yourself faithful,
to the blameless you show yourself blameless,
26to the pure you show yourself pure, Mt 5:8
but to the crooked you show yourself shrewd. Pr 3:34
27You save the humble
but bring low those whose eyes are haughty. Pr 6:17
28You, O LORD, keep my lamp burning;
my God turns my darkness into light.
29With your help I can advance against a troop[d]; Heb 11:34
with my God I can scale a wall.
30As for God, his way is perfect; Dt 32:4
the word of the LORD is flawless. Ps 12:6
He is a shield
for all who take refuge in him.

[a]2 *Horn* here symbolizes strength. [b]5 Hebrew *Sheol* [c]13 Some Hebrew manuscripts and Septuagint (see also 2 Samuel 22:14); most Hebrew manuscripts *resounded, / amid hailstones and bolts of lightning* [d]29 Or *can run through a barricade*

[31]For who is God besides the LORD? Dt 32:39; Ps 86:8
And who is the Rock except our God?
[32]It is God who arms me with strength
and makes my way perfect.

LIVING  INSIGHT

Feeling the pressure today? Beginning to get the "under the pile" blues? Shift the load from your shoulders to God's. He can handle it. He cares about you!
(See Psalm 18:25–36.)

[33]He makes my feet like the feet of a deer;
he enables me to stand on the heights.
[34]He trains my hands for battle; Ps 144:1
my arms can bend a bow of bronze.
[35]You give me your shield of victory,
and your right hand sustains me; Ps 119:116
you stoop down to make me great.
[36]You broaden the path beneath me,
so that my ankles do not turn.

[37]I pursued my enemies and overtook them;
I did not turn back till they were destroyed.
[38]I crushed them so that they could not rise;
they fell beneath my feet.
[39]You armed me with strength for battle;
you made my adversaries bow at my feet.
[40]You made my enemies turn their backs in
flight, Ps 21:12
and I destroyed my foes.
[41]They cried for help, but there was no one to
save them— Ps 50:22
to the LORD, but he did not answer. Pr 1:28
[42]I beat them as fine as dust borne on the wind;
I poured them out like mud in the streets.

[43]You have delivered me from the attacks of the
people;
you have made me the head of nations;
people I did not know are subject to me.
[44]As soon as they hear me, they obey me;
foreigners cringe before me. Ps 66:3
[45]They all lose heart;
they come trembling from their
strongholds. Mic 7:17

[46]The LORD lives! Praise be to my Rock!
Exalted be God my Savior! Ps 51:14
[47]He is the God who avenges me,
who subdues nations under me, Ps 47:3
[48] who saves me from my enemies. Ps 59:1
You exalted me above my foes;
from violent men you rescued me.
[49]Therefore I will praise you among the nations,
O LORD;
I will sing praises to your name. Ps 108:1
[50]He gives his king great victories;
he shows unfailing kindness to his
anointed,
to David and his descendants forever.

Psalm 19

For the director of music. A psalm of David.

[1]The heavens declare the glory of God; Isa 40:22
the skies proclaim the work of his hands.
[2]Day after day they pour forth speech;
night after night they display knowledge.
[3]There is no speech or language
where their voice is not heard.[a]
[4]Their voice[b] goes out into all the earth,
their words to the ends of the world.
In the heavens he has pitched a tent for the
sun, Ps 104:2

LIVING  INSIGHT

God has given us a **general revelation** ***of Himself in the heavens. He has written His handiwork in the heavens for all to see.***
(See Psalm 19:1–4.)

[5] which is like a bridegroom coming forth
from his pavilion,
like a champion rejoicing to run his course.
[6]It rises at one end of the heavens
and makes its circuit to the other; Ps 113:3
nothing is hidden from its heat.

[7]The law of the LORD is perfect,
reviving the soul. Ps 23:3
The statutes of the LORD are trustworthy,
making wise the simple. Ps 119:98-100
[8]The precepts of the LORD are right, Ps 119:128
giving joy to the heart.
The commands of the LORD are radiant,
giving light to the eyes.
[9]The fear of the LORD is pure,
enduring forever.
The ordinances of the LORD are sure
and altogether righteous. Ps 119:138,142
[10]They are more precious than gold, Pr 8:10
than much pure gold;
they are sweeter than honey,
than honey from the comb.
[11]By them is your servant warned;
in keeping them there is great reward.

[a]3 Or *They have no speech, there are no words; / no sound is heard from them* [b]4 Septuagint, Jerome and Syriac; Hebrew *line*

[12]Who can discern his errors?
Forgive my hidden faults. Ps 51:2; 90:8
[13]Keep your servant also from willful sins;
may they not rule over me.
Then will I be blameless,
innocent of great transgression.

[14]May the words of my mouth and the meditation of my heart
be pleasing in your sight, Ps 104:34
O LORD, my Rock and my Redeemer. Ps 18:2

Psalm 20

For the director of music. A psalm of David.

[1]May the LORD answer you when you are in distress;
may the name of the God of Jacob protect you. Ps 91:14
[2]May he send you help from the sanctuary
and grant you support from Zion.
[3]May he remember all your sacrifices Ac 10:4
and accept your burnt offerings. *Selah*
[4]May he give you the desire of your heart
and make all your plans succeed.
[5]We will shout for joy when you are victorious
and will lift up our banners in the name of our God. Ps 59:14; 60:4
May the LORD grant all your requests. 1Sa 1:17

[6]Now I know that the LORD saves his anointed;
he answers him from his holy heaven
with the saving power of his right hand.
[7]Some trust in chariots and some in horses,
but we trust in the name of the LORD our God. 2Ch 32:8
[8]They are brought to their knees and fall,
but we rise up and stand firm. Ps 37:23

[9]O LORD, save the king!
Answer[a] us when we call! Ps 17:6

Psalm 21

For the director of music. A psalm of David.

[1]O LORD, the king rejoices in your strength.
How great is his joy in the victories you give! Ps 59:16-17
[2]You have granted him the desire of his heart
and have not withheld the request of his lips. *Selah*
[3]You welcomed him with rich blessings
and placed a crown of pure gold on his head. 2Sa 12:30
[4]He asked you for life, and you gave it to him—
length of days, for ever and ever. Ps 133:3
[5]Through the victories you gave, his glory is great; Ps 18:50
you have bestowed on him splendor and majesty.
[6]Surely you have granted him eternal blessings
and made him glad with the joy of your presence. 1Ch 17:27
[7]For the king trusts in the LORD;
through the unfailing love of the Most High
he will not be shaken. Ps 15:5

[8]Your hand will lay hold on all your enemies;
your right hand will seize your foes. Isa 10:10
[9]At the time of your appearing
you will make them like a fiery furnace.
In his wrath the LORD will swallow them up,
and his fire will consume them.
[10]You will destroy their descendants from the earth,
their posterity from mankind. Dt 28:18
[11]Though they plot evil against you Ps 2:1
and devise wicked schemes, they cannot succeed; Ps 10:2
[12]for you will make them turn their backs
when you aim at them with drawn bow.

[13]Be exalted, O LORD, in your strength; Ps 18:46
we will sing and praise your might.

Psalm 22

For the director of music. To ⌞the tune of⌟ "The Doe of the Morning." A psalm of David.

[1]My God, my God, why have you forsaken me?
Why are you so far from saving me,
so far from the words of my groaning?
[2]O my God, I cry out by day, but you do not answer,
by night, and am not silent. Ps 42:3

[3]Yet you are enthroned as the Holy One; Ps 99:9
you are the praise of Israel.[b] Dt 10:21
[4]In you our fathers put their trust;
they trusted and you delivered them.
[5]They cried to you and were saved;
in you they trusted and were not disappointed. Isa 49:23

[6]But I am a worm and not a man, Job 25:6
scorned by men and despised by the people. Ps 31:11
[7]All who see me mock me;
they hurl insults, shaking their heads:
[8]"He trusts in the LORD;
let the LORD rescue him. Ps 91:14
Let him deliver him,
since he delights in him." Mt 27:43
[9]Yet you brought me out of the womb; Ps 71:6

[a]9 Or *save! / O King, answer* [b]3 Or *Yet you are holy, / enthroned on the praises of Israel*

you made me trust in you
even at my mother's breast.
10From birth I was cast upon you; Isa 46:3
from my mother's womb you have been my God.
11Do not be far from me,
for trouble is near
and there is no one to help. Ps 72:12
12Many bulls surround me; Ps 68:30
strong bulls of Bashan encircle me.
13Roaring lions tearing their prey Ps 17:12
open their mouths wide against me.
14I am poured out like water,
and all my bones are out of joint.
My heart has turned to wax;
it has melted away within me. Da 5:6
15My strength is dried up like a potsherd,
and my tongue sticks to the roof of my mouth;
you lay me[a] in the dust of death. Ps 104:29
16Dogs have surrounded me;
a band of evil men has encircled me,
they have pierced[b] my hands and my feet.
17I can count all my bones;
people stare and gloat over me. Lk 23:35
18They divide my garments among them
and cast lots for my clothing. Jn 19:24*
19But you, O LORD, be not far off;
O my Strength, come quickly to help me.
20Deliver my life from the sword,
my precious life from the power of the dogs. Ps 35:17
21Rescue me from the mouth of the lions;
save[c] me from the horns of the wild oxen.
22I will declare your name to my brothers;
in the congregation I will praise you.
23You who fear the LORD, praise him! Ps 135:19
All you descendants of Jacob, honor him!
Revere him, all you descendants of Israel!
24For he has not despised or disdained
the suffering of the afflicted one;
he has not hidden his face from him Ps 69:17
but has listened to his cry for help. Heb 5:7
25From you comes the theme of my praise in the great assembly; Ps 35:18
before those who fear you[d] will I fulfill my vows.
26The poor will eat and be satisfied; Ps 107:9
they who seek the LORD will praise him—
may your hearts live forever!
27All the ends of the earth Ps 2:8
will remember and turn to the LORD,
and all the families of the nations
will bow down before him, Ps 86:9
28for dominion belongs to the LORD
and he rules over the nations. Ps 47:7-8
29All the rich of the earth will feast and worship; Ps 45:12
all who go down to the dust will kneel before him— Isa 26:19
those who cannot keep themselves alive.
30Posterity will serve him; Ps 102:28
future generations will be told about the Lord.
31They will proclaim his righteousness
to a people yet unborn— Ps 78:6
for he has done it.

Psalm 23

A psalm of David.

1The LORD is my shepherd, I shall not be in want. Isa 40:11; Jn 10:11; Php 4:19
2 He makes me lie down in green pastures,
he leads me beside quiet waters, Eze 34:14; Rev 7:17
3 he restores my soul.
He guides me in paths of righteousness Ps 5:8
for his name's sake.
4Even though I walk
through the valley of the shadow of death,[e] Job 10:21-22
I will fear no evil, Ps 3:6; 27:1
for you are with me; Isa 43:2
your rod and your staff,
they comfort me.

LIVING  INSIGHT

Drink in the stillness! Linger as long as you can in the presence of your loving Shepherd. His word will restore you as the "paths of righteousness" become clear. Even if this day is shadowed by fear or uncertainty, He is with you . . . as close as your heartbeat, as close as your next breath. Sing your praise to Him! The worship of God anoints our days and causes dry cups to overflow.

(See Psalm 23:1–6.)

5You prepare a table before me
in the presence of my enemies.
You anoint my head with oil; Ps 92:10
my cup overflows. Ps 16:5
6Surely goodness and love will follow me
all the days of my life,
and I will dwell in the house of the LORD
forever.

[a]15 Or / *I am laid* [b]16 Some Hebrew manuscripts, Septuagint and Syriac; most Hebrew manuscripts / *like the lion,*
[c]21 Or / *you have heard* [d]25 Hebrew *him* [e]4 Or *through the darkest valley*

Psalm 24

Of David. A psalm.

1The earth is the LORD's, and everything in it,
the world, and all who live in it; 1Co 10:26
2for he founded it upon the seas
and established it upon the waters.

3Who may ascend the hill of the LORD?
Who may stand in his holy place? Ps 15:1
4He who has clean hands and a pure heart,
who does not lift up his soul to an idol
or swear by what is false.[a]
5He will receive blessing from the LORD
and vindication from God his Savior. Ps 17:2
6Such is the generation of those who seek him,
who seek your face, O God of Jacob.[b]
Selah

7Lift up your heads, O you gates; Isa 26:2
be lifted up, you ancient doors,
that the King of glory may come in. Ps 97:6
8Who is this King of glory?
The LORD strong and mighty,
the LORD mighty in battle. Ps 76:3-6
9Lift up your heads, O you gates;
lift them up, you ancient doors,
that the King of glory may come in.
10Who is he, this King of glory?
The LORD Almighty— 1Sa 1:11
he is the King of glory. *Selah*

Psalm 25[c]

Of David.

1To you, O LORD, I lift up my soul; Ps 86:4
2 in you I trust, O my God.
Do not let me be put to shame,
nor let my enemies triumph over me.
3No one whose hope is in you
will ever be put to shame, Isa 49:23
but they will be put to shame
who are treacherous without excuse.

4Show me your ways, O LORD,
teach me your paths; Ex 33:13
5guide me in your truth and teach me,
for you are God my Savior,
and my hope is in you all day long.
6Remember, O LORD, your great mercy and love, Ps 103:17; Isa 63:7,15
for they are from of old.
7Remember not the sins of my youth Job 13:26
and my rebellious ways;
according to your love remember me, Ps 51:1
for you are good, O LORD.

8Good and upright is the LORD; Ps 92:15
therefore he instructs sinners in his ways.
9He guides the humble in what is right Ps 23:3
and teaches them his way.
10All the ways of the LORD are loving and faithful
for those who keep the demands of his covenant. Ps 103:18
11For the sake of your name, O LORD, Ps 31:3; 79:9
forgive my iniquity, though it is great.
12Who, then, is the man that fears the LORD?
He will instruct him in the way chosen for him. Ps 37:23
13He will spend his days in prosperity, Pr 19:23
and his descendants will inherit the land.
14The LORD confides in those who fear him;
he makes his covenant known to them.
15My eyes are ever on the LORD, Ps 141:8
for only he will release my feet from the snare.

16Turn to me and be gracious to me, Ps 69:16
for I am lonely and afflicted.
17The troubles of my heart have multiplied;
free me from my anguish. Ps 107:6
18Look upon my affliction and my distress
and take away all my sins.
19See how my enemies have increased Ps 3:1
and how fiercely they hate me!
20Guard my life and rescue me; Ps 86:2
let me not be put to shame,
for I take refuge in you.
21May integrity and uprightness protect me,
because my hope is in you.

22Redeem Israel, O God,
from all their troubles! Ps 130:8

Psalm 26

Of David.

1Vindicate me, O LORD,
for I have led a blameless life; Ps 7:8
I have trusted in the LORD
without wavering. 2Ki 20:3; Heb 10:23
2Test me, O LORD, and try me,
examine my heart and my mind; Ps 7:9
3for your love is ever before me,
and I walk continually in your truth. 2Ki 20:3
4I do not sit with deceitful men, Ps 1:1
nor do I consort with hypocrites;
5I abhor the assembly of evildoers Ps 139:21
and refuse to sit with the wicked.
6I wash my hands in innocence, Ps 73:13
and go about your altar, O LORD,
7proclaiming aloud your praise
and telling of all your wonderful deeds.

[a]4 Or *swear falsely* [b]6 Two Hebrew manuscripts and Syriac (see also Septuagint); most Hebrew manuscripts *face, Jacob*
[c]This psalm is an acrostic poem, the verses of which begin with the successive letters of the Hebrew alphabet.

8 I love the house where you live, O LORD,
the place where your glory dwells.

9 Do not take away my soul along with sinners,
my life with bloodthirsty men, Ps 28:3
10 in whose hands are wicked schemes,
whose right hands are full of bribes. 1Sa 8:3
11 But I lead a blameless life;
redeem me and be merciful to me. Ps 69:18

12 My feet stand on level ground; Ps 27:11; 40:2
in the great assembly I will praise the LORD.

Psalm 27

Of David.

1 The LORD is my light and my salvation—
whom shall I fear?
The LORD is the stronghold of my life—
of whom shall I be afraid? Ps 118:6
2 When evil men advance against me
to devour my flesh,[a]
when my enemies and my foes attack me,
they will stumble and fall. Ps 14:4
3 Though an army besiege me,
my heart will not fear; Ps 3:6
though war break out against me,
even then will I be confident.

4 One thing I ask of the LORD, Ps 90:17
this is what I seek:
that I may dwell in the house of the LORD
all the days of my life, Ps 26:8
to gaze upon the beauty of the LORD
and to seek him in his temple.
5 For in the day of trouble
he will keep me safe in his dwelling;
he will hide me in the shelter of his tabernacle
and set me high upon a rock. Ps 40:2
6 Then my head will be exalted Ps 3:3
above the enemies who surround me;
at his tabernacle will I sacrifice with shouts of
joy; Ps 107:22
I will sing and make music to the LORD.

7 Hear my voice when I call, O LORD;
be merciful to me and answer me. Ps 13:3
8 My heart says of you, "Seek his[b] face!"
Your face, LORD, I will seek.
9 Do not hide your face from me, Ps 69:17
do not turn your servant away in anger;
you have been my helper.
Do not reject me or forsake me,
O God my Savior.
10 Though my father and mother forsake me,
the LORD will receive me.
11 Teach me your way, O LORD;
lead me in a straight path Ps 25:4
because of my oppressors.
12 Do not turn me over to the desire of my foes,
for false witnesses rise up against me,
breathing out violence.

13 I am still confident of this:
I will see the goodness of the LORD Ps 31:19
in the land of the living. Jer 11:19; Eze 26:20
14 Wait for the LORD;
be strong and take heart
and wait for the LORD. Ps 40:1

Psalm 28

Of David.

1 To you I call, O LORD my Rock;
do not turn a deaf ear to me.
For if you remain silent, Ps 83:1
I will be like those who have gone down to
the pit. Ps 88:4
2 Hear my cry for mercy Ps 138:2
as I call to you for help,
as I lift up my hands
toward your Most Holy Place. Ps 5:7

LIVING  **INSIGHT**

Do you need strength? Peace? Wisdom? Direction? Discipline? Whatever your need is, ask for it. God will surely hear you!

(See Psalm 28:1–2.)

3 Do not drag me away with the wicked,
with those who do evil,
who speak cordially with their neighbors
but harbor malice in their hearts. Ps 12:2
4 Repay them for their deeds
and for their evil work;
repay them for what their hands have done
and bring back upon them what they
deserve. Rev 18:6
5 Since they show no regard for the works of
the LORD
and what his hands have done, Isa 5:12
he will tear them down
and never build them up again.

6 Praise be to the LORD,
for he has heard my cry for mercy.
7 The LORD is my strength and my shield; Ps 18:1
my heart trusts in him, and I am helped.
My heart leaps for joy
and I will give thanks to him in song.
8 The LORD is the strength of his people,
a fortress of salvation for his anointed one.

[a]2 Or *to slander me* [b]8 Or *To you, O my heart, he has said, "Seek my*

[9]Save your people and bless your inheritance;
be their shepherd and carry them forever.

Psalm 29

A psalm of David.

[1]Ascribe to the LORD, O mighty ones, 1Ch 16:28
ascribe to the LORD glory and strength.
[2]Ascribe to the LORD the glory due his name;
worship the LORD in the splendor of his[a]
holiness. 2Ch 20:21

[3]The voice of the LORD is over the waters;
the God of glory thunders,
the LORD thunders over the mighty waters.
[4]The voice of the LORD is powerful; Ps 68:33
the voice of the LORD is majestic.
[5]The voice of the LORD breaks the cedars;
the LORD breaks in pieces the cedars of
Lebanon. Jdg 9:15
[6]He makes Lebanon skip like a calf, Ps 114:4
Sirion[b] like a young wild ox. Dt 3:9
[7]The voice of the LORD strikes
with flashes of lightning.
[8]The voice of the LORD shakes the desert;
the LORD shakes the Desert of Kadesh.
[9]The voice of the LORD twists the oaks[c]
and strips the forests bare.
And in his temple all cry, "Glory!" Ps 26:8

LIVING  **INSIGHT**

What comes from the Lord because it is impossible for humans to manufacture it? Wisdom. What comes from humans because it is impossible for the Lord to experience it? Worry. And what is it that brings wisdom and dispels worry? Worship.
(See Psalm 29:1–11.)

[10]The LORD sits[d] enthroned over the flood;
the LORD is enthroned as King forever.
[11]The LORD gives strength to his people; Ps 28:8
the LORD blesses his people with peace.

Psalm 30

A psalm. A song. For the dedication
of the temple.[e] Of David.

[1]I will exalt you, O LORD,
for you lifted me out of the depths
and did not let my enemies gloat over me.
[2]O LORD my God, I called to you for help
and you healed me. Ps 6:2
[3]O LORD, you brought me up from the grave[f];
you spared me from going down into the
pit. Ps 86:13
[4]Sing to the LORD, you saints of his; Ps 149:1
praise his holy name.
[5]For his anger lasts only a moment, Ps 103:9
but his favor lasts a lifetime;
weeping may remain for a night,
but rejoicing comes in the morning. 2Co 4:17

LIVING  **INSIGHT**

Sorrow and her grim family of sighs and tears may drop by for a visit, but they won't stay long when they realize that faith got there first . . . and doesn't plan to leave.
(See Psalm 30:4–5.)

[6]When I felt secure, I said,
"I will never be shaken."
[7]O LORD, when you favored me,
you made my mountain[g] stand firm;
but when you hid your face,
I was dismayed. Ps 104:29

[8]To you, O LORD, I called;
to the Lord I cried for mercy:
[9]"What gain is there in my destruction,[h]
in my going down into the pit?
Will the dust praise you?
Will it proclaim your faithfulness? Ps 6:5
[10]Hear, O LORD, and be merciful to me; Ps 4:1
O LORD, be my help."

[11]You turned my wailing into dancing;
you removed my sackcloth and clothed me
with joy, Ps 4:7; Jer 31:4,13
[12]that my heart may sing to you and not be
silent.
O LORD my God, I will give you thanks
forever. Ps 16:9; 44:8

Psalm 31

For the director of music. A psalm of David.

[1]In you, O LORD, I have taken refuge; Ps 7:1
let me never be put to shame;
deliver me in your righteousness.
[2]Turn your ear to me,
come quickly to my rescue;
be my rock of refuge,
a strong fortress to save me.
[3]Since you are my rock and my fortress, Ps 18:2

[a]2 Or *LORD with the splendor of* [b]6 That is, Mount Hermon [c]9 Or *LORD makes the deer give birth* [d]10 Or *sat*
[e]Title: Or *palace* [f]3 Hebrew *Sheol* [g]7 Or *hill country* [h]9 Or *there if I am silenced*

for the sake of your name lead and guide
me. Ps 23:3
[4]Free me from the trap that is set for me,
for you are my refuge. Ps 71:1-3
[5]Into your hands I commit my spirit; Lk 23:46
redeem me, O LORD, the God of truth.

[6]I hate those who cling to worthless idols;
I trust in the LORD. Jnh 2:8
[7]I will be glad and rejoice in your love,
for you saw my affliction
and knew the anguish of my soul. Ps 10:14
[8]You have not handed me over to the enemy
but have set my feet in a spacious place.

[9]Be merciful to me, O LORD, for I am in
distress;
my eyes grow weak with sorrow, Ps 6:7
my soul and my body with grief.
[10]My life is consumed by anguish
and my years by groaning;
my strength fails because of my affliction,[a]
and my bones grow weak. Ps 38:3; 39:11
[11]Because of all my enemies,
I am the utter contempt of my neighbors;
I am a dread to my friends—
those who see me on the street flee from
me.
[12]I am forgotten by them as though I were
dead; Ps 88:4
I have become like broken pottery.
[13]For I hear the slander of many;
there is terror on every side; Jer 20:3,10
they conspire against me
and plot to take my life. Mt 27:1

[14]But I trust in you, O LORD; Ps 140:6
I say, "You are my God."
[15]My times are in your hands;
deliver me from my enemies
and from those who pursue me.
[16]Let your face shine on your servant; Ps 4:6
save me in your unfailing love.
[17]Let me not be put to shame, O LORD, Ps 25:2-3
for I have cried out to you;
but let the wicked be put to shame
and lie silent in the grave.[b]
[18]Let their lying lips be silenced, Ps 120:2
for with pride and contempt
they speak arrogantly against the righteous.

[19]How great is your goodness,
which you have stored up for those who
fear you,
which you bestow in the sight of men Isa 64:4
on those who take refuge in you.
[20]In the shelter of your presence you hide them
from the intrigues of men; Job 5:21
in your dwelling you keep them safe
from accusing tongues.

[21]Praise be to the LORD,
for he showed his wonderful love to me
when I was in a besieged city. 1Sa 23:7
[22]In my alarm I said, Ps 116:11
"I am cut off from your sight!"
Yet you heard my cry for mercy
when I called to you for help. Ps 145:19

[23]Love the LORD, all his saints! Ps 34:9
The LORD preserves the faithful,
but the proud he pays back in full. Ps 94:2
[24]Be strong and take heart, Ps 27:14
all you who hope in the LORD.

Psalm 32

Of David. A *maskil*.[c]

[1]Blessed is he
whose transgressions are forgiven,
whose sins are covered. Ps 85:2
[2]Blessed is the man
whose sin the LORD does not count against
him 2Co 5:19
and in whose spirit is no deceit. Jn 1:47

[3]When I kept silent,
my bones wasted away Ps 31:10
through my groaning all day long.
[4]For day and night
your hand was heavy upon me; Job 33:7
my strength was sapped
as in the heat of summer. *Selah*
[5]Then I acknowledged my sin to you
and did not cover up my iniquity.
I said, "I will confess Pr 28:13
my transgressions to the LORD"—
and you forgave
the guilt of my sin. *Selah*

[6]Therefore let everyone who is godly pray to
you
while you may be found; Ps 69:13
surely when the mighty waters rise,
they will not reach him.
[7]You are my hiding place;
you will protect me from trouble Ps 9:9
and surround me with songs of deliverance.
Selah

[8]I will instruct you and teach you in the way
you should go;
I will counsel you and watch over you.
[9]Do not be like the horse or the mule,
which have no understanding
but must be controlled by bit and bridle
or they will not come to you. Pr 26:3

[a]10 Or *guilt* [b]17 Hebrew *Sheol* [c]Title: Probably a literary or musical term

10Many are the woes of the wicked, Ro 2:9
but the LORD's unfailing love
surrounds the man who trusts in him.

11Rejoice in the LORD and be glad, you
righteous; Ps 64:10
sing, all you who are upright in heart!

Psalm 33

1Sing joyfully to the LORD, you righteous;
it is fitting for the upright to praise him.
2Praise the LORD with the harp;
make music to him on the ten-stringed
lyre.
3Sing to him a new song; Ps 96:1
play skillfully, and shout for joy.

4For the word of the LORD is right and true;
he is faithful in all he does.
5The LORD loves righteousness and justice;
the earth is full of his unfailing love.

6By the word of the LORD were the heavens
made, Heb 11:3
their starry host by the breath of his
mouth.
7He gathers the waters of the sea into jars[a];
he puts the deep into storehouses.
8Let all the earth fear the LORD;
let all the people of the world revere him.
9For he spoke, and it came to be;
he commanded, and it stood firm. Ge 1:3
10The LORD foils the plans of the nations; Isa 8:10
he thwarts the purposes of the peoples.
11But the plans of the LORD stand firm forever,
the purposes of his heart through all
generations. Job 23:13

LIVING  **INSIGHT**

It's awesome to realize that today was in God's mind and plan long before this earth was created. He knew you would be where you are at this very moment, living in your present circumstances. Turn over the controls of your life to Him. Admit your weakness, your hypocrisy, your tendency to worry, your deep need of His presence and His counsel in your life.

(See Psalm 33:6–11.)

12Blessed is the nation whose God is the LORD,
the people he chose for his inheritance.
13From heaven the LORD looks down
and sees all mankind; Job 28:24; Ps 11:4
14from his dwelling place he watches
all who live on earth—
15he who forms the hearts of all,
who considers everything they do. Jer 32:19
16No king is saved by the size of his army;
no warrior escapes by his great strength.
17A horse is a vain hope for deliverance; Ps 20:7
despite all its great strength it cannot save.
18But the eyes of the LORD are on those who
fear him, Ps 34:15
on those whose hope is in his unfailing
love, Ps 147:11
19to deliver them from death
and keep them alive in famine. Job 5:20
20We wait in hope for the LORD; Ps 130:6
he is our help and our shield.
21In him our hearts rejoice, Jn 16:22
for we trust in his holy name.
22May your unfailing love rest upon us, O LORD,
even as we put our hope in you. Ps 6:4

Psalm 34[b]

Of David. When he pretended to be insane before Abimelech, who drove him away, and he left.

1I will extol the LORD at all times;
his praise will always be on my lips. Ps 71:6
2My soul will boast in the LORD; Jer 9:24
let the afflicted hear and rejoice.
3Glorify the LORD with me;
let us exalt his name together. Lk 1:46

LIVING  **INSIGHT**

As you glorify the Lord God, you'll be glorified in Him. You will find that your attitude is contagious. When you glorify God, it has a healthy impact on others. They will see your example and want to glorify Him as well.

(See Psalm 34:1–3.)

4I sought the LORD, and he answered me; Mt 7:7
he delivered me from all my fears.
5Those who look to him are radiant; Ps 36:9
their faces are never covered with shame.
6This poor man called, and the LORD heard
him;
he saved him out of all his troubles. Ps 25:17
7The angel of the LORD encamps around those
who fear him, Da 6:22
and he delivers them.

8Taste and see that the LORD is good; 1Pe 2:3
blessed is the man who takes refuge in him.

[a]7 Or *sea as into a heap* [b]This psalm is an acrostic poem, the verses of which begin with the successive letters of the Hebrew alphabet.

[9]Fear the LORD, you his saints,
for those who fear him lack nothing. Ps 23:1
[10]The lions may grow weak and hungry,
but those who seek the LORD lack no good thing. Ps 84:11

[11]Come, my children, listen to me;
I will teach you the fear of the LORD.
[12]Whoever of you loves life 1Pe 3:10
and desires to see many good days,
[13]keep your tongue from evil
and your lips from speaking lies.
[14]Turn from evil and do good; Ps 37:27
seek peace and pursue it. Heb 12:14

[15]The eyes of the LORD are on the righteous
and his ears are attentive to their cry;
[16]the face of the LORD is against those who do evil,
to cut off the memory of them from the earth. Pr 10:7

[17]The righteous cry out, and the LORD hears them; Ps 145:19
he delivers them from all their troubles.
[18]The LORD is close to the brokenhearted Isa 57:15
and saves those who are crushed in spirit.

[19]A righteous man may have many troubles,
but the LORD delivers him from them all;
[20]he protects all his bones,
not one of them will be broken. Jn 19:36

[21]Evil will slay the wicked; Ps 94:23
the foes of the righteous will be condemned.
[22]The LORD redeems his servants; 1Ki 1:29
no one will be condemned who takes refuge in him.

Psalm 35

Of David.

[1]Contend, O LORD, with those who contend with me;
fight against those who fight against me.
[2]Take up shield and buckler;
arise and come to my aid. Ps 62:2
[3]Brandish spear and javelin[a]
against those who pursue me.
Say to my soul,
"I am your salvation."

[4]May those who seek my life
be disgraced and put to shame; Ps 70:2
may those who plot my ruin
be turned back in dismay.
[5]May they be like chaff before the wind,
with the angel of the LORD driving them away;
[6]may their path be dark and slippery,
with the angel of the LORD pursuing them.
[7]Since they hid their net for me without cause
and without cause dug a pit for me, Ps 7:4
[8]may ruin overtake them by surprise— 1Th 5:3
may the net they hid entangle them,
may they fall into the pit, to their ruin.
[9]Then my soul will rejoice in the LORD Lk 1:47
and delight in his salvation. Isa 61:10
[10]My whole being will exclaim,
"Who is like you, O LORD? Ex 15:11
You rescue the poor from those too strong for them,
the poor and needy from those who rob them." Ps 37:14

[11]Ruthless witnesses come forward;
they question me on things I know nothing about.
[12]They repay me evil for good Jn 10:32
and leave my soul forlorn.
[13]Yet when they were ill, I put on sackcloth
and humbled myself with fasting. Job 30:25
When my prayers returned to me unanswered,
[14]I went about mourning Ps 38:6
as though for my friend or brother.
I bowed my head in grief
as though weeping for my mother.
[15]But when I stumbled, they gathered in glee;
attackers gathered against me when I was unaware.
They slandered me without ceasing. Job 30:1,8
[16]Like the ungodly they maliciously mocked[b];
they gnashed their teeth at me. La 2:16
[17]O Lord, how long will you look on? Hab 1:13
Rescue my life from their ravages,
my precious life from these lions. Ps 22:20
[18]I will give you thanks in the great assembly;
among throngs of people I will praise you.

[19]Let not those gloat over me
who are my enemies without cause;
let not those who hate me without reason
maliciously wink the eye. Ps 13:4
[20]They do not speak peaceably,
but devise false accusations
against those who live quietly in the land.
[21]They gape at me and say, "Aha! Aha! Ps 22:13
With our own eyes we have seen it."
[22]O LORD, you have seen this; be not silent.
Do not be far from me, O Lord. Ps 10:1
[23]Awake, and rise to my defense! Ps 44:23
Contend for me, my God and Lord.
[24]Vindicate me in your righteousness, O LORD my God;
do not let them gloat over me. Ps 22:17

[a] 3 Or *and block the way* [b] 16 Septuagint; Hebrew may mean *ungodly circle of mockers.*

25Do not let them think, "Aha, just what we
wanted!"
or say, "We have swallowed him up." La 2:16

26May all who gloat over my distress
be put to shame and confusion; Ps 40:14; 109:29
may all who exalt themselves over me
be clothed with shame and disgrace.
27May those who delight in my vindication
shout for joy and gladness;
may they always say, "The LORD be exalted,
who delights in the well-being of his
servant." Ps 147:11
28My tongue will speak of your righteousness
and of your praises all day long.

Psalm 36

For the director of music. Of David the servant of the LORD.

1An oracle is within my heart
concerning the sinfulness of the wicked:[a]
There is no fear of God
before his eyes. Ro 3:18*
2For in his own eyes he flatters himself
too much to detect or hate his sin.
3The words of his mouth are wicked and
deceitful; Ps 10:7
he has ceased to be wise and to do good.
4Even on his bed he plots evil; Pr 4:16
he commits himself to a sinful course
and does not reject what is wrong.

5Your love, O LORD, reaches to the heavens,
your faithfulness to the skies. Ps 57:10
6Your righteousness is like the mighty
mountains,
your justice like the great deep. Ro 11:33
O LORD, you preserve both man and beast.
7 How priceless is your unfailing love!
Both high and low among men
find[b] refuge in the shadow of your wings.
8They feast on the abundance of your house;
you give them drink from your river of
delights. Job 20:17; Rev 22:1
9For with you is the fountain of life; Jer 2:13
in your light we see light. 1Pe 2:9

10Continue your love to those who know you,
your righteousness to the upright in heart.
11May the foot of the proud not come against
me,
nor the hand of the wicked drive me away.
12See how the evildoers lie fallen—
thrown down, not able to rise! Ps 140:10

Psalm 37[c]

Of David.

1Do not fret because of evil men
or be envious of those who do wrong;
2for like the grass they will soon wither,
like green plants they will soon die away.

3Trust in the LORD and do good;
dwell in the land and enjoy safe pasture.
4Delight yourself in the LORD Isa 58:14
and he will give you the desires of your
heart.

LIVING  INSIGHT

Our God knows us so well. When we begin to fret because of one who prospers in wickedness, then anger replaces peace. That anger boils over, and wrath begins to consume us. How much better to focus on letting God do our defending.
(See Psalm 37:1–4.)

5Commit your way to the LORD;
trust in him and he will do this: Ps 55:22
6He will make your righteousness shine like the
dawn, Job 11:17
the justice of your cause like the noonday
sun.

7Be still before the LORD and wait patiently for
him;
do not fret when men succeed in their
ways,
when they carry out their wicked schemes.

8Refrain from anger and turn from wrath;
do not fret—it leads only to evil.
9For evil men will be cut off,
but those who hope in the LORD will inherit
the land. Isa 57:13; 60:21

10A little while, and the wicked will be no more;
though you look for them, they will not be
found.
11But the meek will inherit the land Mt 5:5
and enjoy great peace.

12The wicked plot against the righteous
and gnash their teeth at them; Ps 35:16
13but the Lord laughs at the wicked,
for he knows their day is coming. 1Sa 26:10

14The wicked draw the sword
and bend the bow Ps 11:2

[a] 1 Or *heart: / Sin proceeds from the wicked.* [b] 7 Or *love, O God! / Men find*; or *love! / Both heavenly beings and men / find*
[c] This psalm is an acrostic poem, the stanzas of which begin with the successive letters of the Hebrew alphabet.

to bring down the poor and needy, Ps 35:10
to slay those whose ways are upright.
15 But their swords will pierce their own hearts,
and their bows will be broken.

16 Better the little that the righteous have
than the wealth of many wicked; Pr 15:16
17 for the power of the wicked will be broken,
but the LORD upholds the righteous.

18 The days of the blameless are known to the LORD, Ps 1:6
and their inheritance will endure forever.
19 In times of disaster they will not wither;
in days of famine they will enjoy plenty.

20 But the wicked will perish: Ps 34:21
The LORD's enemies will be like the beauty of the fields,
they will vanish—vanish like smoke. Ps 102:3

21 The wicked borrow and do not repay,
but the righteous give generously; Ps 112:5
22 those the LORD blesses will inherit the land,
but those he curses will be cut off. Pr 3:33

23 If the LORD delights in a man's way,
he makes his steps firm; 1Sa 2:9
24 though he stumble, he will not fall, Pr 24:16
for the LORD upholds him with his hand.

25 I was young and now I am old,
yet I have never seen the righteous forsaken
or their children begging bread.
26 They are always generous and lend freely;
their children will be blessed. Ps 147:13

27 Turn from evil and do good; Ps 34:14
then you will dwell in the land forever.
28 For the LORD loves the just
and will not forsake his faithful ones.

They will be protected forever,
but the offspring of the wicked will be cut off;
29 the righteous will inherit the land
and dwell in it forever.

30 The mouth of the righteous man utters wisdom,
and his tongue speaks what is just.
31 The law of his God is in his heart; Dt 6:6; Ps 40:8
his feet do not slip.

32 The wicked lie in wait for the righteous, Ps 10:8
seeking their very lives;
33 but the LORD will not leave them in their power
or let them be condemned when brought to trial. Ps 109:31; 2Pe 2:9

34 Wait for the LORD Ps 27:14
and keep his way.
He will exalt you to inherit the land;
when the wicked are cut off, you will see it.

35 I have seen a wicked and ruthless man
flourishing like a green tree in its native soil, Job 5:3
36 but he soon passed away and was no more;
though I looked for him, he could not be found. Job 20:5

37 Consider the blameless, observe the upright;
there is a future[a] for the man of peace.
38 But all sinners will be destroyed;
the future[b] of the wicked will be cut off.

39 The salvation of the righteous comes from the LORD; Ps 3:8
he is their stronghold in time of trouble.
40 The LORD helps them and delivers them;
he delivers them from the wicked and saves them,
because they take refuge in him.

Psalm 38

A psalm of David. A petition.

1 O LORD, do not rebuke me in your anger
or discipline me in your wrath. Ps 6:1
2 For your arrows have pierced me, Job 6:4; Ps 32:4
and your hand has come down upon me.
3 Because of your wrath there is no health in my body;
my bones have no soundness because of my sin. Ps 6:2; Isa 1:6
4 My guilt has overwhelmed me
like a burden too heavy to bear. Ezr 9:6

5 My wounds fester and are loathsome
because of my sinful folly. Ps 69:5
6 I am bowed down and brought very low;
all day long I go about mourning. Ps 35:14
7 My back is filled with searing pain;
there is no health in my body.
8 I am feeble and utterly crushed;
I groan in anguish of heart. Ps 22:1

9 All my longings lie open before you, O Lord;
my sighing is not hidden from you. Job 3:24
10 My heart pounds, my strength fails me;
even the light has gone from my eyes. Ps 6:7
11 My friends and companions avoid me because of my wounds;
my neighbors stay far away. Ps 31:11
12 Those who seek my life set their traps, Ps 140:5
those who would harm me talk of my ruin;
all day long they plot deception. Ps 35:20

13 I am like a deaf man, who cannot hear,
like a mute, who cannot open his mouth;

[a] 37 Or *there will be posterity* [b] 38 Or *posterity*

14 I have become like a man who does not hear,
whose mouth can offer no reply.
15 I wait for you, O LORD; Ps 39:7
you will answer, O Lord my God.
16 For I said, "Do not let them gloat Ps 35:26
or exalt themselves over me when my foot
slips."
17 For I am about to fall,
and my pain is ever with me.
18 I confess my iniquity; Ps 32:5
I am troubled by my sin.
19 Many are those who are my vigorous enemies;
those who hate me without reason are
numerous. Ps 35:19
20 Those who repay my good with evil Ps 35:12
slander me when I pursue what is good.

21 O LORD, do not forsake me;
be not far from me, O my God. Ps 35:22
22 Come quickly to help me,
O Lord my Savior. Ps 27:1

Psalm 39

For the director of music. For Jeduthun. A psalm of David.

1 I said, "I will watch my ways 1Ki 2:4
and keep my tongue from sin;
I will put a muzzle on my mouth
as long as the wicked are in my presence."
2 But when I was silent and still, Ps 38:13
not even saying anything good,
my anguish increased.
3 My heart grew hot within me,
and as I meditated, the fire burned; Jer 20:9
then I spoke with my tongue:

4 "Show me, O LORD, my life's end
and the number of my days; Ps 90:12
let me know how fleeting is my life. Ps 103:14
5 You have made my days a mere handbreadth;
the span of my years is as nothing before
you.
Each man's life is but a breath. *Selah*
6 Man is a mere phantom as he goes to and fro:
He bustles about, but only in vain; Ps 127:2
he heaps up wealth, not knowing who will
get it. Lk 12:20

7 "But now, Lord, what do I look for?
My hope is in you.
8 Save me from all my transgressions; Ps 44:13
do not make me the scorn of fools.
9 I was silent; I would not open my mouth,
for you are the one who has done this.
10 Remove your scourge from me;
I am overcome by the blow of your hand.
11 You rebuke and discipline men for their sin;
you consume their wealth like a moth—
each man is but a breath. *Selah*

12 "Hear my prayer, O LORD,
listen to my cry for help;
be not deaf to my weeping.
For I dwell with you as an alien, 1Pe 2:11
a stranger, as all my fathers were. Heb 11:13
13 Look away from me, that I may rejoice again
before I depart and am no more." Job 10:21

Psalm 40

For the director of music. Of David. A psalm.

1 I waited patiently for the LORD; Ps 27:14
he turned to me and heard my cry.
2 He lifted me out of the slimy pit,
out of the mud and mire; Ps 69:14
he set my feet on a rock Ps 27:5
and gave me a firm place to stand.
3 He put a new song in my mouth, Ps 33:3
a hymn of praise to our God.
Many will see and fear
and put their trust in the LORD.

4 Blessed is the man
who makes the LORD his trust, Ps 84:12
who does not look to the proud,
to those who turn aside to false gods.[a]
5 Many, O LORD my God,
are the wonders you have done. Ps 136:4
The things you planned for us
no one can recount to you; Isa 55:8
were I to speak and tell of them,
they would be too many to declare.

6 Sacrifice and offering you did not desire,
but my ears you have pierced[b,c];
burnt offerings and sin offerings
you did not require. Isa 1:11
7 Then I said, "Here I am, I have come—
it is written about me in the scroll.[d]
8 I desire to do your will, O my God; Jn 4:34
your law is within my heart." Ps 37:31

9 I proclaim righteousness in the great assembly;
I do not seal my lips,
as you know, O LORD. Ps 119:13
10 I do not hide your righteousness in my heart;
I speak of your faithfulness and salvation.
I do not conceal your love and your truth
from the great assembly. Ac 20:20

11 Do not withhold your mercy from me,
O LORD;
may your love and your truth always
protect me. Ps 43:3

[a]4 Or *to falsehood* [b]6 Hebrew; Septuagint *but a body you have prepared for me* (see also Symmachus and Theodotion)
[c]6 Or *opened* [d]7 Or *come / with the scroll written for me*

[12]For troubles without number surround me;
my sins have overtaken me, and I cannot see. Ps 38:4
They are more than the hairs of my head,
and my heart fails within me. Ps 73:26

[13]Be pleased, O LORD, to save me;
O LORD, come quickly to help me. Ps 70:1
[14]May all who seek to take my life
be put to shame and confusion;
may all who desire my ruin
be turned back in disgrace. Ps 35:4
[15]May those who say to me, "Aha! Aha!"
be appalled at their own shame.
[16]But may all who seek you Ps 9:10
rejoice and be glad in you;
may those who love your salvation always say,
"The LORD be exalted!" Ps 35:27
[17]Yet I am poor and needy;
may the Lord think of me. Ps 144:3
You are my help and my deliverer;
O my God, do not delay. Ps 70:5

Psalm 41

For the director of music. A psalm of David.

[1]Blessed is he who has regard for the weak;
the LORD delivers him in times of trouble.
[2]The LORD will protect him and preserve his life;
he will bless him in the land Ps 37:22
and not surrender him to the desire of his foes. Ps 27:12
[3]The LORD will sustain him on his sickbed
and restore him from his bed of illness.

[4]I said, "O LORD, have mercy on me; Ps 6:2
heal me, for I have sinned against you."
[5]My enemies say of me in malice,
"When will he die and his name perish?"
[6]Whenever one comes to see me,
he speaks falsely, while his heart gathers slander; Ps 12:2; Pr 26:24
then he goes out and spreads it abroad.

[7]All my enemies whisper together against me;
they imagine the worst for me, saying,
[8]"A vile disease has beset him;
he will never get up from the place where he lies." 2Ki 1:4
[9]Even my close friend, whom I trusted, Ps 55:12
he who shared my bread,
has lifted up his heel against me. Job 19:19

[10]But you, O LORD, have mercy on me;
raise me up, that I may repay them. Ps 3:3
[11]I know that you are pleased with me, Ps 147:11
for my enemy does not triumph over me.
[12]In my integrity you uphold me Ps 37:17
and set me in your presence forever. Job 36:7

[13]Praise be to the LORD, the God of Israel,
from everlasting to everlasting.
Amen and Amen.

BOOK II

Psalms 42–72

Psalms of Deliverance **Psalms 42–72**

In these 31 psalms the theme of deliverance is highlighted. The "Exodus" theme of God's powerful hand at work to set His people free from enemies and from danger saturates this section of psalms. This God is our Savior; He is our Stronghold; He is our *only* Deliverer! In these psalms you will find the gracious hand of God leading His people from the pits of despair to the mountain peaks of freedom and maximum safety in His arms.

Psalm 42[a]

For the director of music. A *maskil*[b] of the Sons of Korah.

[1]As the deer pants for streams of water,
so my soul pants for you, O God. Ps 119:131
[2]My soul thirsts for God, for the living God.
When can I go and meet with God?
[3]My tears have been my food
day and night, Ps 80:5
while men say to me all day long,
"Where is your God?"
[4]These things I remember
as I pour out my soul:
how I used to go with the multitude,
leading the procession to the house of God,
with shouts of joy and thanksgiving Ps 100:4
among the festive throng.

[5]Why are you downcast, O my soul? Ps 38:6; 77:3
Why so disturbed within me?
Put your hope in God, La 3:24
for I will yet praise him,
my Savior and [6]my God. Ps 44:3

My[c] soul is downcast within me;
therefore I will remember you
from the land of the Jordan,
the heights of Hermon—from Mount Mizar.
[7]Deep calls to deep
in the roar of your waterfalls;

[a]In many Hebrew manuscripts Psalms 42 and 43 constitute one psalm. [b]Title: Probably a literary or musical term
[c]5,6 A few Hebrew manuscripts, Septuagint and Syriac; most Hebrew manuscripts *praise him for his saving help. / [6]O my God, my*

all your waves and breakers
have swept over me. Ps 88:7

8By day the LORD directs his love,
at night his song is with me— Job 35:10
a prayer to the God of my life.

9I say to God my Rock,
"Why have you forgotten me?
Why must I go about mourning, Ps 38:6
oppressed by the enemy?"
10My bones suffer mortal agony Ps 6:2
as my foes taunt me,
saying to me all day long,
"Where is your God?"

11Why are you downcast, O my soul?
Why so disturbed within me?
Put your hope in God,
for I will yet praise him,
my Savior and my God. Ps 43:5

Psalm 43[a]

1Vindicate me, O God,
and plead my cause against an ungodly
nation; Ps 26:1
rescue me from deceitful and wicked
men.
2You are God my stronghold.
Why have you rejected me?
Why must I go about mourning,
oppressed by the enemy? Ps 42:9
3Send forth your light and your truth, Ps 36:9
let them guide me;
let them bring me to your holy mountain,
to the place where you dwell. Ps 84:1
4Then will I go to the altar of God, Ps 26:6
to God, my joy and my delight.
I will praise you with the harp,
O God, my God. Ps 33:2

5Why are you downcast, O my soul?
Why so disturbed within me?
Put your hope in God,
for I will yet praise him,
my Savior and my God. Ps 42:6

Psalm 44

For the director of music. Of the Sons of Korah.
A *maskil*.[b]

1We have heard with our ears, O God;
our fathers have told us Ex 12:26; Ps 78:3
what you did in their days,
in days long ago.
2With your hand you drove out the nations
and planted our fathers; Ex 15:17
you crushed the peoples
and made our fathers flourish. Ps 80:9
3It was not by their sword that they won the
land, Jos 24:12
nor did their arm bring them victory;
it was your right hand, your arm,
and the light of your face, for you loved
them. Dt 7:7-8

4You are my King and my God, Ps 74:12
who decrees[c] victories for Jacob.
5Through you we push back our enemies;
through your name we trample our foes.
6I do not trust in my bow, Ps 33:16
my sword does not bring me victory;
7but you give us victory over our enemies,
you put our adversaries to shame. Ps 53:5
8In God we make our boast all day long, Ps 34:2
and we will praise your name forever. *Selah*

9But now you have rejected and humbled us;
you no longer go out with our armies.
10You made us retreat before the enemy,
and our adversaries have plundered us.
11You gave us up to be devoured like sheep
and have scattered us among the nations.
12You sold your people for a pittance, Isa 52:3
gaining nothing from their sale.

13You have made us a reproach to our
neighbors,
the scorn and derision of those around us.
14You have made us a byword among the
nations;
the peoples shake their heads at us. Jer 24:9
15My disgrace is before me all day long,
and my face is covered with shame
16at the taunts of those who reproach and revile
me, Ps 74:10
because of the enemy, who is bent on
revenge.

17All this happened to us,
though we had not forgotten you Ps 78:7,57
or been false to your covenant.
18Our hearts had not turned back; Job 23:11
our feet had not strayed from your path.
19But you crushed us and made us a haunt for
jackals Ps 51:8
and covered us over with deep darkness.

20If we had forgotten the name of our God
or spread out our hands to a foreign god,
21would not God have discovered it,
since he knows the secrets of the heart?

[a]In many Hebrew manuscripts Psalms 42 and 43 constitute one psalm. [b]Title: Probably a literary or musical term
[c]4 Septuagint, Aquila and Syriac; Hebrew *King, O God; / command*

[22]Yet for your sake we face death all day long;
we are considered as sheep to be
slaughtered. Ro 8:36*

[23]Awake, O Lord! Why do you sleep? Ps 7:6
Rouse yourself! Do not reject us forever.
[24]Why do you hide your face Job 13:24
and forget our misery and oppression?

[25]We are brought down to the dust; Ps 119:25
our bodies cling to the ground.
[26]Rise up and help us;
redeem us because of your unfailing love.

Psalm 45

For the director of music. To ˪the tune of˩ "Lilies." Of the Sons of Korah. A *maskil.*[a] A wedding song.

[1]My heart is stirred by a noble theme
as I recite my verses for the king;
my tongue is the pen of a skillful writer.

[2]You are the most excellent of men
and your lips have been anointed with
grace, Lk 4:22
since God has blessed you forever.
[3]Gird your sword upon your side, O mighty
one; Isa 9:6
clothe yourself with splendor and majesty.
[4]In your majesty ride forth victoriously Rev 6:2
in behalf of truth, humility and
righteousness;
let your right hand display awesome deeds.
[5]Let your sharp arrows pierce the hearts of the
king's enemies;
let the nations fall beneath your feet.
[6]Your throne, O God, will last for ever and
ever; Ps 93:2
a scepter of justice will be the scepter of
your kingdom.
[7]You love righteousness and hate wickedness;
therefore God, your God, has set you above
your companions
by anointing you with the oil of joy.
[8]All your robes are fragrant with myrrh and
aloes and cassia; SS 1:3
from palaces adorned with ivory
the music of the strings makes you glad.
[9]Daughters of kings are among your honored
women;
at your right hand is the royal bride in gold
of Ophir. 1Ki 2:19

[10]Listen, O daughter, consider and give ear:
Forget your people and your father's house.
[11]The king is enthralled by your beauty;
honor him, for he is your lord. Ps 95:6; Isa 54:5
[12]The Daughter of Tyre will come with a gift,[b]
men of wealth will seek your favor. Ps 22:29

[13]All glorious is the princess within ˪her
chamber˩; Isa 61:10
her gown is interwoven with gold.
[14]In embroidered garments she is led to the
king; SS 1:4
her virgin companions follow her
and are brought to you.
[15]They are led in with joy and gladness;
they enter the palace of the king.

[16]Your sons will take the place of your fathers;
you will make them princes throughout the
land. Ps 68:27
[17]I will perpetuate your memory through all
generations; Mal 1:11
therefore the nations will praise you for
ever and ever. Ps 138:4

Psalm 46

For the director of music. Of the Sons of Korah. According to *alamoth.*[c] A song.

[1]God is our refuge and strength,
an ever-present help in trouble. Dt 4:7
[2]Therefore we will not fear, though the earth
give way Ps 23:4; 82:5
and the mountains fall into the heart of the
sea, Ps 18:7
[3]though its waters roar and foam Ps 93:3
and the mountains quake with their
surging. *Selah*

[4]There is a river whose streams make glad the
city of God, Ps 48:1,8; Isa 60:14
the holy place where the Most High dwells.
[5]God is within her, she will not fall; Isa 12:6
God will help her at break of day.
[6]Nations are in uproar, kingdoms fall; Ps 2:1
he lifts his voice, the earth melts.

LIVING  INSIGHT

I am desperately concerned that we slow down so that each week we carve out time for quietness, solitude, thought, prayer, meditation and soul-searching. Oh, how much agitation will begin to fade away, how insignificant petty differences will seem, how big God will become and how small our troubles will seem. Security, peace and confidence will move right in.

(See Psalm 46:10.)

[a]Title: Probably a literary or musical term [b]12 Or *A Tyrian robe is among the gifts* [c]Title: Probably a musical term

[7]The LORD Almighty is with us;
the God of Jacob is our fortress. *Selah*

[8]Come and see the works of the LORD, Ps 66:5
the desolations he has brought on the earth.
[9]He makes wars cease to the ends of the earth;
he breaks the bow and shatters the spear,
he burns the shields[a] with fire. Eze 39:9
[10]"Be still, and know that I am God; Ps 100:3
I will be exalted among the nations,
I will be exalted in the earth." Isa 2:11

[11]The LORD Almighty is with us;
the God of Jacob is our fortress. *Selah*

Psalm 47

For the director of music. Of the Sons of Korah.
A psalm.

[1]Clap your hands, all you nations; Ps 98:8; Isa 55:12
shout to God with cries of joy.
[2]How awesome is the LORD Most High, Dt 7:21
the great King over all the earth!
[3]He subdued nations under us,
peoples under our feet. Ps 18:39,47
[4]He chose our inheritance for us, 1Pe 1:4
the pride of Jacob, whom he loved. *Selah*

[5]God has ascended amid shouts of joy,
the LORD amid the sounding of trumpets.
[6]Sing praises to God, sing praises;
sing praises to our King, sing praises. Ps 68:4

[7]For God is the King of all the earth;
sing to him a psalm[b] of praise. Col 3:16
[8]God reigns over the nations; 1Ch 16:31
God is seated on his holy throne.
[9]The nobles of the nations assemble
as the people of the God of Abraham,
for the kings[c] of the earth belong to God;
he is greatly exalted.

Psalm 48

A song. A psalm of the Sons of Korah.

[1]Great is the LORD, and most worthy of praise,
in the city of our God, his holy mountain.
[2]It is beautiful in its loftiness, Ps 50:2
the joy of the whole earth.
Like the utmost heights of Zaphon[d] is Mount Zion,
the[e] city of the Great King. Mt 5:35
[3]God is in her citadels;
he has shown himself to be her fortress.
[4]When the kings joined forces,
when they advanced together, 2Sa 10:1-19
[5]they saw ⌞her⌟ and were astounded;
they fled in terror. Ex 15:16
[6]Trembling seized them there,
pain like that of a woman in labor.
[7]You destroyed them like ships of Tarshish
shattered by an east wind. Jer 18:17

[8]As we have heard,
so have we seen
in the city of the LORD Almighty,
in the city of our God:
God makes her secure forever. *Selah*

[9]Within your temple, O God,
we meditate on your unfailing love. Ps 26:3
[10]Like your name, O God, Jos 7:9
your praise reaches to the ends of the earth;
your right hand is filled with righteousness.
[11]Mount Zion rejoices,
the villages of Judah are glad
because of your judgments. Ps 97:8

[12]Walk about Zion, go around her,
count her towers,
[13]consider well her ramparts,
view her citadels, Ps 122:7
that you may tell of them to the next generation. Ps 78:6
[14]For this God is our God for ever and ever;
he will be our guide even to the end. Ps 23:4

Psalm 49

For the director of music. Of the Sons of Korah.
A psalm.

[1]Hear this, all you peoples; Ps 78:1
listen, all who live in this world, Ps 33:8
[2]both low and high,
rich and poor alike:
[3]My mouth will speak words of wisdom;
the utterance from my heart will give understanding.
[4]I will turn my ear to a proverb; Ps 78:2
with the harp I will expound my riddle:
[5]Why should I fear when evil days come, Ps 23:4
when wicked deceivers surround me—
[6]those who trust in their wealth Job 31:24
and boast of their great riches?
[7]No man can redeem the life of another
or give to God a ransom for him—
[8]the ransom for a life is costly,
no payment is ever enough— Mt 16:26
[9]that he should live on forever
and not see decay. Ps 89:48

[a]9 Or *chariots* [b]7 Or *a maskil* (probably a literary or musical term) [c]9 Or *shields* [d]2 *Zaphon* can refer to a sacred mountain or the direction north. [e]2 Or *earth, / Mount Zion, on the northern side / of the*

10 For all can see that wise men die; Ecc 2:16
the foolish and the senseless alike perish
and leave their wealth to others. Ecc 2:18,21
11 Their tombs will remain their houses[a]
forever,
their dwellings for endless generations,
though they had[b] named lands after
themselves. Ge 4:17; Dt 3:14

12 But man, despite his riches, does not endure;
he is[c] like the beasts that perish.

13 This is the fate of those who trust in
themselves, Lk 12:20
and of their followers, who approve their
sayings. *Selah*
14 Like sheep they are destined for the grave,[d]
and death will feed on them.
The upright will rule over them in the
morning; Da 7:18; Mal 4:3
their forms will decay in the grave,[d]
far from their princely mansions.
15 But God will redeem my life[e] from the grave;
he will surely take me to himself. *Selah*

16 Do not be overawed when a man grows rich,
when the splendor of his house increases;
17 for he will take nothing with him when he
dies,
his splendor will not descend with him.
18 Though while he lived he counted himself
blessed— Lk 12:19
and men praise you when you prosper—
19 he will join the generation of his fathers,
who will never see the light ⌞of life⌟. Job 33:30

20 A man who has riches without understanding
is like the beasts that perish. Ecc 3:19

Psalm 50

A psalm of Asaph.

1 The Mighty One, God, the LORD,
speaks and summons the earth
from the rising of the sun to the place
where it sets. Ps 113:3
2 From Zion, perfect in beauty,
God shines forth. Dt 33:2; Ps 80:1
3 Our God comes and will not be silent;
a fire devours before him, Ps 97:3; Da 7:10
and around him a tempest rages.
4 He summons the heavens above,
and the earth, that he may judge his
people: Dt 4:26
5 "Gather to me my consecrated ones,
who made a covenant with me by
sacrifice." Ex 24:7
6 And the heavens proclaim his righteousness,
for God himself is judge. *Selah*

7 "Hear, O my people, and I will speak,
O Israel, and I will testify against you:
I am God, your God. Ex 20:2
8 I do not rebuke you for your sacrifices
or your burnt offerings, which are ever
before me. Hos 6:6
9 I have no need of a bull from your stall
or of goats from your pens,
10 for every animal of the forest is mine,
and the cattle on a thousand hills. Ps 104:24
11 I know every bird in the mountains, Mt 6:26
and the creatures of the field are mine.
12 If I were hungry I would not tell you,
for the world is mine, and all that is in it.
13 Do I eat the flesh of bulls
or drink the blood of goats?
14 Sacrifice thank offerings to God, Heb 13:15
fulfill your vows to the Most High, Dt 23:21
15 and call upon me in the day of trouble;
I will deliver you, and you will honor me."

16 But to the wicked, God says:

"What right have you to recite my laws
or take my covenant on your lips? Isa 29:13
17 You hate my instruction
and cast my words behind you. Ne 9:26
18 When you see a thief, you join with him;
you throw in your lot with adulterers.
19 You use your mouth for evil
and harness your tongue to deceit. Ps 52:2
20 You speak continually against your brother
and slander your own mother's son.
21 These things you have done and I kept silent;
you thought I was altogether[f] like you.
But I will rebuke you
and accuse you to your face. Ps 90:8

22 "Consider this, you who forget God, Job 8:13
or I will tear you to pieces, with none to
rescue:
23 He who sacrifices thank offerings honors me,
and he prepares the way Ps 85:13
so that I may show him[g] the salvation of
God." Ps 91:16

Psalm 51

For the director of music. A psalm of David.
When the prophet Nathan came to him after
David had committed adultery with Bathsheba.

1 Have mercy on me, O God,
according to your unfailing love;
according to your great compassion

[a] 11 Septuagint and Syriac; Hebrew *In their thoughts their houses will remain* [b] 11 Or / *for they have* [c] 12 Hebrew; Septuagint and Syriac read verse 12 the same as verse 20. [d] 14 Hebrew *Sheol*; also in verse 15 [e] 15 Or *soul* [f] 21 Or *thought the 'I AM' was* [g] 23 Or *and to him who considers his way / I will show*

blot out my transgressions. Isa 43:25; Ac 3:19
2Wash away all my iniquity
and cleanse me from my sin. Heb 9:14

3For I know my transgressions,
and my sin is always before me. Isa 59:12
4Against you, you only, have I sinned
and done what is evil in your sight, Ge 20:6
so that you are proved right when you speak
and justified when you judge. Ro 3:4
5Surely I was sinful at birth, Job 14:4
sinful from the time my mother conceived
me.
6Surely you desire truth in the inner parts[a];
you teach[b] me wisdom in the inmost
place. Ps 15:2; Pr 2:6

7Cleanse me with hyssop, and I will be clean;
wash me, and I will be whiter than snow.
8Let me hear joy and gladness; Isa 35:10
let the bones you have crushed rejoice.
9Hide your face from my sins Jer 16:17
and blot out all my iniquity.

10Create in me a pure heart, O God, Ac 15:9
and renew a steadfast spirit within me.
11Do not cast me from your presence
or take your Holy Spirit from me. Eph 4:30
12Restore to me the joy of your salvation Ps 13:5
and grant me a willing spirit, to sustain me.

LIVING  INSIGHT

When the Spirit of God is in control, it is nothing short of awesome. And when He is absent, it is dreadful.
(See Psalm 51:10–12.)

13Then I will teach transgressors your ways,
and sinners will turn back to you.
14Save me from bloodguilt, O God, 2Sa 12:9
the God who saves me,
and my tongue will sing of your
righteousness. Ps 35:28
15O Lord, open my lips, Ps 9:14
and my mouth will declare your praise.
16You do not delight in sacrifice, or I would
bring it; 1Sa 15:22; Ps 40:6
you do not take pleasure in burnt offerings.
17The sacrifices of God are[c] a broken spirit;
a broken and contrite heart, Ps 34:18
O God, you will not despise.

18In your good pleasure make Zion prosper;
build up the walls of Jerusalem.
19Then there will be righteous sacrifices, Ps 4:5
whole burnt offerings to delight you;
then bulls will be offered on your altar.

Psalm 52

For the director of music. A *maskil*[d] of David. When Doeg the Edomite had gone to Saul and told him: "David has gone to the house of Ahimelech."

1Why do you boast of evil, you mighty man?
Why do you boast all day long, Ps 94:4
you who are a disgrace in the eyes of God?
2Your tongue plots destruction;
it is like a sharpened razor, Ps 57:4
you who practice deceit.
3You love evil rather than good,
falsehood rather than speaking the truth.
Selah
4You love every harmful word,
O you deceitful tongue! Ps 120:2-3

5Surely God will bring you down to everlasting
ruin:
He will snatch you up and tear you from
your tent; Isa 22:19
he will uproot you from the land of the
living. *Selah*
6The righteous will see and fear;
they will laugh at him, saying, Job 22:19; Ps 37:34
7"Here now is the man
who did not make God his stronghold
but trusted in his great wealth Ps 49:6
and grew strong by destroying others!"
8But I am like an olive tree Jer 11:16
flourishing in the house of God;
I trust in God's unfailing love
for ever and ever.
9I will praise you forever for what you have
done; Ps 30:12
in your name I will hope, for your name is
good. Ps 54:6
I will praise you in the presence of your
saints.

Psalm 53

For the director of music. According to *mahalath*.[e] A *maskil*[d] of David.

1The fool says in his heart, Ro 3:10
"There is no God." Ps 10:4
They are corrupt, and their ways are vile;
there is no one who does good.

2God looks down from heaven Ps 33:13
on the sons of men
to see if there are any who understand,

[a]6 The meaning of the Hebrew for this phrase is uncertain. [b]6 Or *you desired . . . ; / you taught* [c]17 Or *My sacrifice, O God, is* [d]Title: Probably a literary or musical term [e]Title: Probably a musical term

any who seek God. 2Ch 15:2
[3]Everyone has turned away,
they have together become corrupt;
there is no one who does good,
not even one. Ro 3:10-12*
[4]Will the evildoers never learn—
those who devour my people as men eat bread
and who do not call on God?
[5]There they were, overwhelmed with dread,
where there was nothing to dread. Lev 26:17
God scattered the bones of those who attacked you; Eze 6:5
you put them to shame, for God despised them.

[6]Oh, that salvation for Israel would come out of Zion!
When God restores the fortunes of his people,
let Jacob rejoice and Israel be glad!

Psalm 54

For the director of music. With stringed instruments. A *maskil*[a] of David. When the Ziphites had gone to Saul and said, "Is not David hiding among us?"

[1]Save me, O God, by your name; Ps 20:1
vindicate me by your might. 2Ch 20:6
[2]Hear my prayer, O God;
listen to the words of my mouth. Ps 5:1; 55:1
[3]Strangers are attacking me; Ps 86:14
ruthless men seek my life—
men without regard for God. *Selah*

[4]Surely God is my help; Ps 118:7
the Lord is the one who sustains me.

[5]Let evil recoil on those who slander me;
in your faithfulness destroy them. Ps 89:49

[6]I will sacrifice a freewill offering to you;
I will praise your name, O LORD,
for it is good. Ps 52:9
[7]For he has delivered me from all my troubles,
and my eyes have looked in triumph on my foes. Ps 59:10

Psalm 55

For the director of music. With stringed instruments. A *maskil*[a] of David.

[1]Listen to my prayer, O God,
do not ignore my plea; Ps 27:9
[2] hear me and answer me.
My thoughts trouble me and I am distraught
[3] at the voice of the enemy,
at the stares of the wicked;
for they bring down suffering upon me
and revile me in their anger.

[4]My heart is in anguish within me;
the terrors of death assail me. Ps 116:3
[5]Fear and trembling have beset me; Job 21:6
horror has overwhelmed me.
[6]I said, "Oh, that I had the wings of a dove!
I would fly away and be at rest—
[7]I would flee far away
and stay in the desert; *Selah*
[8]I would hurry to my place of shelter,
far from the tempest and storm." Isa 4:6

[9]Confuse the wicked, O Lord, confound their speech,
for I see violence and strife in the city.
[10]Day and night they prowl about on its walls;
malice and abuse are within it.
[11]Destructive forces are at work in the city;
threats and lies never leave its streets. Ps 10:7

[12]If an enemy were insulting me,
I could endure it;
if a foe were raising himself against me,
I could hide from him.
[13]But it is you, a man like myself,
my companion, my close friend, Ps 41:9
[14]with whom I once enjoyed sweet fellowship
as we walked with the throng at the house of God. Ps 42:4

[15]Let death take my enemies by surprise;
let them go down alive to the grave,[b]
for evil finds lodging among them.
[16]But I call to God,
and the LORD saves me.
[17]Evening, morning and noon Ps 5:3; 141:2
I cry out in distress,
and he hears my voice.
[18]He ransoms me unharmed
from the battle waged against me,
even though many oppose me.
[19]God, who is enthroned forever, Dt 33:27
will hear them and afflict them— *Selah*
men who never change their ways
and have no fear of God. Ps 36:1

[20]My companion attacks his friends; Ps 7:4
he violates his covenant.
[21]His speech is smooth as butter,
yet war is in his heart;
his words are more soothing than oil,
yet they are drawn swords. Ps 28:3

[22]Cast your cares on the LORD
and he will sustain you; Ps 37:5
he will never let the righteous fall. Ps 37:24

[a]Title: Probably a literary or musical term [b]15 Hebrew *Sheol*

[23]But you, O God, will bring down the wicked
into the pit of corruption;
bloodthirsty and deceitful men Ps 5:6
will not live out half their days. Job 15:32

But as for me, I trust in you. Ps 25:2

LIVING INSIGHT

God is longing to take your burden and carry it for you, but He won't force you to let go of it. You must do that yourself. You must take the risk and, in faith, entrust it all into His care. He says to you, "Then, and only then, will you know that I am God."

(See Psalm 55:22–23.)

Psalm 56

For the director of music. To ⌞the tune of⌟ "A Dove on Distant Oaks." Of David. A *miktam.*[a] When the Philistines had seized him in Gath.

[1]Be merciful to me, O God, for men hotly
pursue me; Ps 57:1-3
all day long they press their attack.
[2]My slanderers pursue me all day long; Ps 57:3
many are attacking me in their pride.

[3]When I am afraid, Ps 55:4-5
I will trust in you.
[4]In God, whose word I praise,
in God I trust; I will not be afraid.
What can mortal man do to me? Ps 118:6

LIVING INSIGHT

Ask the Lord for deliverance, safety, stability and great grace to see you through, to settle your fears and to calm your spirit so you can think and act responsibly.

(See Psalm 56:3–4.)

[5]All day long they twist my words; Ps 41:7
they are always plotting to harm me.
[6]They conspire, they lurk, Ps 59:3
they watch my steps,
eager to take my life.

[7]On no account let them escape;
in your anger, O God, bring down the
nations. Ps 36:12; 55:23
[8]Record my lament;
list my tears on your scroll[b]—
are they not in your record? Mal 3:16

[9]Then my enemies will turn back Ps 9:3
when I call for help. Ps 102:2
By this I will know that God is for me.
[10]In God, whose word I praise,
in the LORD, whose word I praise—
[11]in God I trust; I will not be afraid.
What can man do to me?

[12]I am under vows to you, O God; Ps 50:14
I will present my thank offerings to you.
[13]For you have delivered me[c] from death
and my feet from stumbling,
that I may walk before God
in the light of life.[d] Job 33:30

Psalm 57

For the director of music. ⌞To the tune of⌟ "Do Not Destroy." Of David. A *miktam.*[a] When he had fled from Saul into the cave.

[1]Have mercy on me, O God, have mercy on
me,
for in you my soul takes refuge. Ps 2:12
I will take refuge in the shadow of your wings
until the disaster has passed. Isa 26:20

[2]I cry out to God Most High,
to God, who fulfills ⌞his purpose⌟ for me.
[3]He sends from heaven and saves me, Ps 18:9,16
rebuking those who hotly pursue me; *Selah*
God sends his love and his faithfulness.

[4]I am in the midst of lions; Ps 35:17
I lie among ravenous beasts—
men whose teeth are spears and arrows,
whose tongues are sharp swords. Pr 30:14

[5]Be exalted, O God, above the heavens;
let your glory be over all the earth. Ps 108:5

[6]They spread a net for my feet—
I was bowed down in distress. Ps 145:14
They dug a pit in my path—
but they have fallen into it themselves.
Selah

[7]My heart is steadfast, O God,
my heart is steadfast; Ps 108:1
I will sing and make music.
[8]Awake, my soul!
Awake, harp and lyre! Ps 16:9
I will awaken the dawn.

[9]I will praise you, O Lord, among the nations;
I will sing of you among the peoples.

[a]Title: Probably a literary or musical term [b]8 Or / *put my tears in your wineskin* [c]13 Or *my soul* [d]13 Or *the land of the living*

[10]For great is your love, reaching to the
heavens;
your faithfulness reaches to the skies. Ps 36:5
[11]Be exalted, O God, above the heavens;
let your glory be over all the earth. ver 5

Psalm 58

For the director of music. ⌞To the tune of⌟ "Do Not Destroy." Of David. A *miktam*.[a]

[1]Do you rulers indeed speak justly? Ps 82:2
Do you judge uprightly among men?
[2]No, in your heart you devise injustice,
and your hands mete out violence on the
earth. Ps 94:20
[3]Even from birth the wicked go astray;
from the womb they are wayward and
speak lies.
[4]Their venom is like the venom of a snake,
like that of a cobra that has stopped its
ears,
[5]that will not heed the tune of the charmer,
however skillful the enchanter may be.

[6]Break the teeth in their mouths, O God;
tear out, O LORD, the fangs of the lions!
[7]Let them vanish like water that flows away;
when they draw the bow, let their arrows
be blunted.
[8]Like a slug melting away as it moves along,
like a stillborn child, may they not see the
sun. Job 3:16

[9]Before your pots can feel ⌞the heat of⌟ the
thorns—
whether they be green or dry—the wicked
will be swept away.[b] Pr 10:25
[10]The righteous will be glad when they are
avenged,
when they bathe their feet in the blood of
the wicked. Ps 68:23
[11]Then men will say,
"Surely the righteous still are rewarded;
surely there is a God who judges the earth."

Psalm 59

For the director of music. ⌞To the tune of⌟ "Do Not Destroy." Of David. A *miktam*.[a] When Saul had sent men to watch David's house in order to kill him.

[1]Deliver me from my enemies, O God; Ps 143:9
protect me from those who rise up
against me.
[2]Deliver me from evildoers
and save me from bloodthirsty men.
[3]See how they lie in wait for me!
Fierce men conspire against me Ps 56:6
for no offense or sin of mine, O LORD.
[4]I have done no wrong, yet they are ready to
attack me. Ps 35:19,23
Arise to help me; look on my plight!
[5]O LORD God Almighty, the God of Israel,
rouse yourself to punish all the nations;
show no mercy to wicked traitors. *Selah*

[6]They return at evening,
snarling like dogs, ver 14
and prowl about the city.
[7]See what they spew from their mouths—
they spew out swords from their lips, Ps 57:4
and they say, "Who can hear us?" Ps 10:11
[8]But you, O LORD, laugh at them; Ps 37:13
you scoff at all those nations. Ps 2:4

[9]O my Strength, I watch for you;
you, O God, are my fortress, [10]my loving
God. Ps 62:2

God will go before me
and will let me gloat over those who
slander me.
[11]But do not kill them, O Lord our shield,[c]
or my people will forget. Dt 4:9
In your might make them wander about,
and bring them down.
[12]For the sins of their mouths,
for the words of their lips, Pr 12:13
let them be caught in their pride.
For the curses and lies they utter,
[13] consume them in wrath,
consume them till they are no more.
Then it will be known to the ends of the
earth
that God rules over Jacob. *Selah*

[14]They return at evening,
snarling like dogs,
and prowl about the city.
[15]They wander about for food Job 15:23
and howl if not satisfied.
[16]But I will sing of your strength,
in the morning I will sing of your love;
for you are my fortress,
my refuge in times of trouble. Ps 46:1

[17]O my Strength, I sing praise to you;
you, O God, are my fortress, my loving
God. ver 10

[a]Title: Probably a literary or musical term [b]9 The meaning of the Hebrew for this verse is uncertain. [c]11 Or *sovereign*

Psalm 60

For the director of music. To ⌊the tune of⌋ "The Lily of the Covenant." A *miktam*[a] of David. For teaching. When he fought Aram Naharaim[b] and Aram Zobah,[c] and when Joab returned and struck down twelve thousand Edomites in the Valley of Salt.

1You have rejected us, O God, and burst forth
upon us; Ps 44:9
you have been angry—now restore us!
2You have shaken the land and torn it open;
mend its fractures, for it is quaking. 2Ch 7:14
3You have shown your people desperate times;
you have given us wine that makes us
stagger.

4But for those who fear you, you have raised a
banner Isa 11:10,12
to be unfurled against the bow. *Selah*
5Save us and help us with your right hand,
that those you love may be delivered.
6God has spoken from his sanctuary:
"In triumph I will parcel out Shechem
and measure off the Valley of Succoth.
7Gilead is mine, and Manasseh is mine; Jos 13:31
Ephraim is my helmet,
Judah my scepter. Ge 49:10; Dt 33:17
8Moab is my washbasin,
upon Edom I toss my sandal;
over Philistia I shout in triumph." 2Sa 8:1
9Who will bring me to the fortified city?
Who will lead me to Edom?
10Is it not you, O God, you who have rejected
us
and no longer go out with our armies?
11Give us aid against the enemy,
for the help of man is worthless. Ps 146:3
12With God we will gain the victory,
and he will trample down our enemies.

Psalm 61

For the director of music. With stringed instruments. Of David.

1Hear my cry, O God; Ps 64:1
listen to my prayer.

2From the ends of the earth I call to you,
I call as my heart grows faint; Ps 77:3
lead me to the rock that is higher than I.
3For you have been my refuge,
a strong tower against the foe. Pr 18:10

4I long to dwell in your tent forever
and take refuge in the shelter of your
wings. *Selah*
5For you have heard my vows, O God; Ps 56:12
you have given me the heritage of those
who fear your name. Ps 86:11

6Increase the days of the king's life,
his years for many generations. Ps 21:4
7May he be enthroned in God's presence
forever; Ps 41:12
appoint your love and faithfulness to
protect him.

8Then will I ever sing praise to your name
and fulfill my vows day after day.

Psalm 62

For the director of music. For Jeduthun. A psalm of David.

1My soul finds rest in God alone; Dt 23:21
my salvation comes from him.
2He alone is my rock and my salvation; Ps 89:26
he is my fortress, I will never be shaken.

3How long will you assault a man?
Would all of you throw him down—
this leaning wall, this tottering fence?
4They fully intend to topple him
from his lofty place;
they take delight in lies.
With their mouths they bless,
but in their hearts they curse. *Selah*

5Find rest, O my soul, in God alone;
my hope comes from him.
6He alone is my rock and my salvation;
he is my fortress, I will not be shaken.
7My salvation and my honor depend on
God[d];
he is my mighty rock, my refuge. Ps 46:1; 85:9
8Trust in him at all times, O people;
pour out your hearts to him, 1Sa 1:15; La 2:19
for God is our refuge. *Selah*

9Lowborn men are but a breath, Ps 39:5,11
the highborn are but a lie;
if weighed on a balance, they are nothing;
together they are only a breath.
10Do not trust in extortion
or take pride in stolen goods;
though your riches increase,
do not set your heart on them. Job 31:25

11One thing God has spoken,
two things have I heard:
that you, O God, are strong, 1Ch 29:11
12 and that you, O Lord, are loving. Ps 86:5

[a]Title: Probably a literary or musical term [b]Title: That is, Arameans of Northwest Mesopotamia [c]Title: That is, Arameans of central Syria [d]7 Or / *God Most High is my salvation and my honor*

Surely you will reward each person
according to what he has done. Mt 16:27

Psalm 63

A psalm of David. When he was in the Desert of Judah.

[1]O God, you are my God,
earnestly I seek you;
my soul thirsts for you, Ps 42:2
my body longs for you,
in a dry and weary land
where there is no water. Ps 143:6
[2]I have seen you in the sanctuary Ps 27:4
and beheld your power and your glory.
[3]Because your love is better than life, Ps 69:16
my lips will glorify you.
[4]I will praise you as long as I live, Ps 104:33
and in your name I will lift up my hands.
[5]My soul will be satisfied as with the richest of foods; Ps 36:8
with singing lips my mouth will praise you.

[6]On my bed I remember you;
I think of you through the watches of the night. Ps 42:8
[7]Because you are my help, Ps 27:9
I sing in the shadow of your wings.
[8]My soul clings to you;
your right hand upholds me. Ps 18:35
[9]They who seek my life will be destroyed;
they will go down to the depths of the earth. Ps 55:15
[10]They will be given over to the sword
and become food for jackals.
[11]But the king will rejoice in God;
all who swear by God's name will praise him, Dt 6:13; Isa 45:23
while the mouths of liars will be silenced.

Psalm 64

For the director of music. A psalm of David.

[1]Hear me, O God, as I voice my complaint;
protect my life from the threat of the enemy. Ps 140:1
[2]Hide me from the conspiracy of the wicked,
from that noisy crowd of evildoers.

[3]They sharpen their tongues like swords
and aim their words like deadly arrows.
[4]They shoot from ambush at the innocent man; Ps 11:2
they shoot at him suddenly, without fear.
[5]They encourage each other in evil plans,
they talk about hiding their snares;
they say, "Who will see them[a]?" Ps 10:11
[6]They plot injustice and say,
"We have devised a perfect plan!"
Surely the mind and heart of man are cunning.

[7]But God will shoot them with arrows;
suddenly they will be struck down.
[8]He will turn their own tongues against them
and bring them to ruin;
all who see them will shake their heads in scorn. Ps 22:7
[9]All mankind will fear;
they will proclaim the works of God
and ponder what he has done. Jer 51:10
[10]Let the righteous rejoice in the LORD
and take refuge in him; Ps 25:20
let all the upright in heart praise him!

Psalm 65

For the director of music. A psalm of David. A song.

[1]Praise awaits[b] you, O God, in Zion;
to you our vows will be fulfilled. Ps 116:18
[2]O you who hear prayer,
to you all men will come. Isa 66:23
[3]When we were overwhelmed by sins, Ps 38:4
you forgave[c] our transgressions. Heb 9:14
[4]Blessed are those you choose Ps 33:12
and bring near to live in your courts!
We are filled with the good things of your house, Ps 36:8
of your holy temple.

[5]You answer us with awesome deeds of righteousness,
O God our Savior, Ps 85:4
the hope of all the ends of the earth
and of the farthest seas, Ps 107:23
[6]who formed the mountains by your power,
having armed yourself with strength, Ps 93:1
[7]who stilled the roaring of the seas, Mt 8:26
the roaring of their waves,
and the turmoil of the nations. Isa 17:12-13
[8]Those living far away fear your wonders;
where morning dawns and evening fades
you call forth songs of joy.
[9]You care for the land and water it; Ps 68:9-10
you enrich it abundantly.
The streams of God are filled with water
to provide the people with grain, Ps 46:4
for so you have ordained it.[d]
[10]You drench its furrows

[a]5 Or *us* [b]1 Or *befits*; the meaning of the Hebrew for this word is uncertain. [c]3 Or *made atonement for*
[d]9 Or *for that is how you prepare the land*

and level its ridges;
you soften it with showers
and bless its crops.
11You crown the year with your bounty,
and your carts overflow with abundance.
12The grasslands of the desert overflow; Job 28:26
the hills are clothed with gladness.
13The meadows are covered with flocks Ps 144:13
and the valleys are mantled with grain;
they shout for joy and sing. Ps 98:8; Isa 55:12

Psalm 66

For the director of music. A song. A psalm.

1Shout with joy to God, all the earth! Ps 100:1
2 Sing the glory of his name;
make his praise glorious!
3Say to God, "How awesome are your deeds!
So great is your power
that your enemies cringe before you. Ps 18:44
4All the earth bows down to you;
they sing praise to you,
they sing praise to your name." *Selah*

5Come and see what God has done,
how awesome his works in man's behalf!
6He turned the sea into dry land, Ex 14:22
they passed through the waters on foot—
come, let us rejoice in him.
7He rules forever by his power, Ps 145:13
his eyes watch the nations—
let not the rebellious rise up against him.
Selah

8Praise our God, O peoples, Ps 98:4
let the sound of his praise be heard;
9he has preserved our lives
and kept our feet from slipping. Ps 121:3
10For you, O God, tested us;
you refined us like silver. Ps 17:3; 1Pe 1:6-7
11You brought us into prison
and laid burdens on our backs. La 1:13
12You let men ride over our heads; Isa 51:23
we went through fire and water,
but you brought us to a place of
abundance. Isa 43:2

13I will come to your temple with burnt
offerings
and fulfill my vows to you— Ecc 5:4
14vows my lips promised and my mouth spoke
when I was in trouble.
15I will sacrifice fat animals to you
and an offering of rams;
I will offer bulls and goats. *Selah*

16Come and listen, all you who fear God;
let me tell you what he has done for me.
17I cried out to him with my mouth;
his praise was on my tongue.
18If I had cherished sin in my heart,
the Lord would not have listened; Jas 4:3
19but God has surely listened
and heard my voice in prayer. Ps 116:1-2
20Praise be to God,
who has not rejected my prayer Ps 22:24; 68:35
or withheld his love from me!

LIVING  **INSIGHT**

Do you have needs today? Are you backed against the wall? Disturbed and disquieted? Uncertain about your future? Anxious over a strained relationship? Needing extra strength, new hope or greater wisdom? Your solution can be found in one word: prayer. Tell God every detail. Call on the only One who can help. He awaits your request.
(See Psalm 66:16–20.)

Psalm 67

For the director of music. With stringed instruments. A psalm. A song.

1May God be gracious to us and bless us
and make his face shine upon us, *Selah*
2that your ways may be known on earth,
your salvation among all nations. Tit 2:11

3May the peoples praise you, O God;
may all the peoples praise you.
4May the nations be glad and sing for joy,
for you rule the peoples justly Ps 96:10-13
and guide the nations of the earth. *Selah*
5May the peoples praise you, O God;
may all the peoples praise you.

6Then the land will yield its harvest, Lev 26:4
and God, our God, will bless us.
7God will bless us,
and all the ends of the earth will fear him.

Psalm 68

For the director of music. Of David. A psalm. A song.

1May God arise, may his enemies be scattered;
may his foes flee before him. Nu 10:35
2As smoke is blown away by the wind, Hos 13:3
may you blow them away;
as wax melts before the fire, Isa 9:18; Mic 1:4
may the wicked perish before God.
3But may the righteous be glad
and rejoice before God; Ps 32:11
may they be happy and joyful.

4 Sing to God, sing praise to his name, Ps 66:2
extol him who rides on the clouds[a]—
his name is the LORD— Ex 6:3; Ps 83:18
and rejoice before him.
5 A father to the fatherless, a defender of
widows, Ps 10:14
is God in his holy dwelling. Dt 26:15
6 God sets the lonely in families,[b] Ps 113:9
he leads forth the prisoners with singing;
but the rebellious live in a sun-scorched
land. Ps 107:34

7 When you went out before your people,
O God, Ex 13:21
when you marched through the wasteland,
Selah
8 the earth shook,
the heavens poured down rain,
before God, the One of Sinai,
before God, the God of Israel.
9 You gave abundant showers, O God; Dt 11:11
you refreshed your weary inheritance.
10 Your people settled in it,
and from your bounty, O God, you
provided for the poor. Ps 74:19

11 The Lord announced the word,
and great was the company of those who
proclaimed it:
12 "Kings and armies flee in haste; Jos 10:16
in the camps men divide the plunder.
13 Even while you sleep among the campfires,[c]
the wings of ⌞my⌟ dove are sheathed with
silver,
its feathers with shining gold."
14 When the Almighty[d] scattered the kings in
the land, Jos 10:10
it was like snow fallen on Zalmon.

15 The mountains of Bashan are majestic
mountains; ver 22; Nu 21:33
rugged are the mountains of Bashan.
16 Why gaze in envy, O rugged mountains,
at the mountain where God chooses to
reign, Dt 12:5
where the LORD himself will dwell forever?
17 The chariots of God are tens of thousands
and thousands of thousands; Dt 33:2
the Lord ⌞has come⌟ from Sinai into his
sanctuary.
18 When you ascended on high,
you led captives in your train; Jdg 5:12
you received gifts from men, Eph 4:8
even from[e] the rebellious—
that you,[f] O LORD God, might dwell there.

19 Praise be to the Lord, to God our Savior,
who daily bears our burdens. *Selah*
20 Our God is a God who saves;
from the Sovereign LORD comes escape
from death. Ps 56:13

21 Surely God will crush the heads of his
enemies,
the hairy crowns of those who go on in
their sins.
22 The Lord says, "I will bring them from
Bashan;
I will bring them from the depths of the
sea, Nu 21:33
23 that you may plunge your feet in the blood of
your foes, Ps 58:10
while the tongues of your dogs have their
share." 1Ki 21:19

24 Your procession has come into view, O God,
the procession of my God and King into
the sanctuary. Ps 63:2
25 In front are the singers, after them the
musicians;
with them are the maidens playing
tambourines. 1Ch 13:8
26 Praise God in the great congregation;
praise the LORD in the assembly of Israel.
27 There is the little tribe of Benjamin, leading
them, 1Sa 9:21
there the great throng of Judah's princes,
and there the princes of Zebulun and of
Naphtali. Jdg 5:18

28 Summon your power, O God[g];
show us your strength, O God, as you have
done before.
29 Because of your temple at Jerusalem
kings will bring you gifts. Ps 72:10
30 Rebuke the beast among the reeds,
the herd of bulls among the calves of the
nations. Ps 22:12
Humbled, may it bring bars of silver.
Scatter the nations who delight in war.
31 Envoys will come from Egypt; Isa 45:14
Cush[h] will submit herself to God.

32 Sing to God, O kingdoms of the earth,
sing praise to the Lord, *Selah*
33 to him who rides the ancient skies above,
who thunders with mighty voice.
34 Proclaim the power of God, Ps 29:1
whose majesty is over Israel,
whose power is in the skies.
35 You are awesome, O God, in your sanctuary;
the God of Israel gives power and strength
to his people. Ps 29:11

Praise be to God! Ps 66:20

[a] 4 Or / *prepare the way for him who rides through the deserts* [b] 6 Or *the desolate in a homeland* [c] 13 Or *saddlebags* [d] 14 Hebrew *Shaddai* [e] 18 Or *gifts for men, / even* [f] 18 Or *they* [g] 28 Many Hebrew manuscripts, Septuagint and Syriac; most Hebrew manuscripts *Your God has summoned power for you* [h] 31 That is, the upper Nile region

Psalm 69

For the director of music. To ⌊the tune of⌋ "Lilies." Of David.

[1]Save me, O God,
for the waters have come up to my neck.
[2]I sink in the miry depths, Ps 40:2
where there is no foothold.
I have come into the deep waters;
the floods engulf me.
[3]I am worn out calling for help; Ps 6:6
my throat is parched.
My eyes fail, Ps 119:82; Isa 38:14
looking for my God.
[4]Those who hate me without reason Jn 15:25*
outnumber the hairs of my head;
many are my enemies without cause, Ps 35:19
those who seek to destroy me.
I am forced to restore
what I did not steal.

[5]You know my folly, O God; Ps 38:5
my guilt is not hidden from you. Ps 44:21

[6]May those who hope in you
not be disgraced because of me,
O Lord, the LORD Almighty;
may those who seek you
not be put to shame because of me,
O God of Israel.
[7]For I endure scorn for your sake, Jer 15:15
and shame covers my face. Ps 44:15
[8]I am a stranger to my brothers,
an alien to my own mother's sons; Ps 31:11
[9]for zeal for your house consumes me, Jn 2:17
and the insults of those who insult you fall
on me.
[10]When I weep and fast, Ps 35:13
I must endure scorn;
[11]when I put on sackcloth,
people make sport of me.
[12]Those who sit at the gate mock me,
and I am the song of the drunkards. Job 30:9

[13]But I pray to you, O LORD,
in the time of your favor; Isa 49:8
in your great love, O God,
answer me with your sure salvation.
[14]Rescue me from the mire,
do not let me sink;
deliver me from those who hate me,
from the deep waters. Ps 144:7
[15]Do not let the floodwaters engulf me
or the depths swallow me up Nu 16:33
or the pit close its mouth over me.
[16]Answer me, O LORD, out of the goodness of
your love; Ps 63:3
in your great mercy turn to me.
[17]Do not hide your face from your servant;
answer me quickly, for I am in trouble.
[18]Come near and rescue me;
redeem me because of my foes.

[19]You know how I am scorned, disgraced and
shamed; Ps 22:6
all my enemies are before you.
[20]Scorn has broken my heart
and has left me helpless;
I looked for sympathy, but there was none,
for comforters, but I found none. Job 16:2
[21]They put gall in my food
and gave me vinegar for my thirst. Jn 19:28-30

[22]May the table set before them become a snare;
may it become retribution and[a] a trap.
[23]May their eyes be darkened so they cannot
see,
and their backs be bent forever. Ro 11:9-10*
[24]Pour out your wrath on them;
let your fierce anger overtake them.
[25]May their place be deserted; Mt 23:38
let there be no one to dwell in their tents.
[26]For they persecute those you wound
and talk about the pain of those you hurt.
[27]Charge them with crime upon crime;
do not let them share in your salvation.
[28]May they be blotted out of the book of life
and not be listed with the righteous.

[29]I am in pain and distress;
may your salvation, O God, protect me.

[30]I will praise God's name in song Ps 28:7
and glorify him with thanksgiving.
[31]This will please the LORD more than an ox,
more than a bull with its horns and hoofs.
[32]The poor will see and be glad— Ps 34:2
you who seek God, may your hearts live!
[33]The LORD hears the needy
and does not despise his captive people.

[34]Let heaven and earth praise him,
the seas and all that move in them, Ps 96:11
[35]for God will save Zion
and rebuild the cities of Judah. Ps 51:18
Then people will settle there and possess it;
[36] the children of his servants will inherit it,
and those who love his name will dwell
there. Ps 102:28

Psalm 70

For the director of music. Of David. A petition.

[1]Hasten, O God, to save me;
O LORD, come quickly to help me. Ps 40:13
[2]May those who seek my life Ps 35:4
be put to shame and confusion;

[a]22 Or *snare / and their fellowship become*

may all who desire my ruin
be turned back in disgrace. Ps 35:26
[3]May those who say to me, "Aha! Aha!"
turn back because of their shame.
[4]But may all who seek you Ps 9:10
rejoice and be glad in you;
may those who love your salvation always say,
"Let God be exalted!" Ps 35:27

[5]Yet I am poor and needy; Ps 40:17
come quickly to me, O God.
You are my help and my deliverer; Ps 18:2
O LORD, do not delay.

Psalm 71

[1]In you, O LORD, I have taken refuge;
let me never be put to shame. Ps 25:2-3; 31:1
[2]Rescue me and deliver me in your
righteousness;
turn your ear to me and save me. Ps 17:6
[3]Be my rock of refuge,
to which I can always go;
give the command to save me,
for you are my rock and my fortress. Ps 18:2
[4]Deliver me, O my God, from the hand of the
wicked, Ps 140:4
from the grasp of evil and cruel men.

[5]For you have been my hope, O Sovereign
LORD,
my confidence since my youth. Jer 17:7
[6]From birth I have relied on you; Ps 22:10
you brought me forth from my mother's
womb. Isa 46:3
I will ever praise you. Ps 34:1
[7]I have become like a portent to many, Isa 8:18
but you are my strong refuge. Ps 61:3
[8]My mouth is filled with your praise,
declaring your splendor all day long. Ps 35:28

[9]Do not cast me away when I am old; ver 18
do not forsake me when my strength is
gone.
[10]For my enemies speak against me;
those who wait to kill me conspire together.
[11]They say, "God has forsaken him;
pursue him and seize him,
for no one will rescue him." Ps 7:2
[12]Be not far from me, O God; Ps 35:22
come quickly, O my God, to help me.
[13]May my accusers perish in shame;
may those who want to harm me
be covered with scorn and disgrace. ver 24

[14]But as for me, I will always have hope; Ps 130:7
I will praise you more and more.
[15]My mouth will tell of your righteousness,
of your salvation all day long,
though I know not its measure.
[16]I will come and proclaim your mighty acts,
O Sovereign LORD; Ps 106:2
I will proclaim your righteousness, yours
alone.
[17]Since my youth, O God, you have taught me,
and to this day I declare your marvelous
deeds. Ps 26:7
[18]Even when I am old and gray,
do not forsake me, O God,
till I declare your power to the next
generation,
your might to all who are to come.

[19]Your righteousness reaches to the skies,
O God, Ps 57:10
you who have done great things.
Who, O God, is like you? Ps 35:10
[20]Though you have made me see troubles, many
and bitter, Ps 60:3
you will restore my life again; Hos 6:2
from the depths of the earth
you will again bring me up.
[21]You will increase my honor Ps 18:35
and comfort me once again. Ps 23:4

[22]I will praise you with the harp
for your faithfulness, O my God;
I will sing praise to you with the lyre,
O Holy One of Israel. 2Ki 19:22
[23]My lips will shout for joy
when I sing praise to you—
I, whom you have redeemed. Ps 103:4
[24]My tongue will tell of your righteous acts
all day long, Ps 35:28
for those who wanted to harm me
have been put to shame and confusion.

Psalm 72

Of Solomon.

[1]Endow the king with your justice, O God,
the royal son with your righteousness.
[2]He will[a] judge your people in righteousness,
your afflicted ones with justice.
[3]The mountains will bring prosperity to the
people,
the hills the fruit of righteousness.
[4]He will defend the afflicted among the people
and save the children of the needy; Isa 11:4
he will crush the oppressor.

[5]He will endure[b] as long as the sun,
as long as the moon, through all
generations.
[6]He will be like rain falling on a mown field,
like showers watering the earth.
[7]In his days the righteous will flourish; Ps 92:12

[a]2 Or *May he*; similarly in verses 3-11 and 17 [b]5 Septuagint; Hebrew *You will be feared*

prosperity will abound till the moon is no
more.

8He will rule from sea to sea
and from the River[a] to the ends of the
earth.[b] Ex 23:31; Zec 9:10
9The desert tribes will bow before him
and his enemies will lick the dust.
10The kings of Tarshish and of distant shores
will bring tribute to him;
the kings of Sheba and Seba Ge 10:7
will present him gifts. 2Ch 9:24
11All kings will bow down to him
and all nations will serve him.

12For he will deliver the needy who cry out,
the afflicted who have no one to help.
13He will take pity on the weak and the needy
and save the needy from death.
14He will rescue them from oppression and
violence, Ps 69:18
for precious is their blood in his sight.

15Long may he live!
May gold from Sheba be given him. Isa 60:6
May people ever pray for him
and bless him all day long.
16Let grain abound throughout the land;
on the tops of the hills may it sway.
Let its fruit flourish like Lebanon; Ps 104:16
let it thrive like the grass of the field.
17May his name endure forever; Ex 3:15
may it continue as long as the sun. Ps 89:36

All nations will be blessed through him,
and they will call him blessed. Ge 12:3; Lk 1:48

18Praise be to the LORD God, the God of Israel,
who alone does marvelous deeds.
19Praise be to his glorious name forever;
may the whole earth be filled with his glory.
Amen and Amen.

20This concludes the prayers of David son of
Jesse.

BOOK III

Psalms 73–89

Psalms of the Sanctuary Psalms 73–89

If you enjoy liturgy and the expressions of "high church" worship, you will love these psalms. The focus of these songs of praise is the sanctuary of God. In this section we find 17 great hymns of worship for God's people as they gathered in the temple of the Lord. It was not the building itself, however, that was of central importance to God's people, but the presence of the majestic God dwelling in the temple. These songs reflect the formal worship and temple-centered celebration of God's people; therefore, there are parallels to the themes of the book of Leviticus.

Psalm 73

A psalm of Asaph.

1Surely God is good to Israel,
to those who are pure in heart. Mt 5:8

2But as for me, my feet had almost slipped;
I had nearly lost my foothold.
3For I envied the arrogant Ps 37:1
when I saw the prosperity of the wicked.

4They have no struggles;
their bodies are healthy and strong.[c]
5They are free from the burdens common to
man; Job 21:9
they are not plagued by human ills.
6Therefore pride is their necklace;
they clothe themselves with violence.
7From their callous hearts comes iniquity[d];
the evil conceits of their minds know no
limits.
8They scoff, and speak with malice;
in their arrogance they threaten oppression.
9Their mouths lay claim to heaven,
and their tongues take possession of the
earth.
10Therefore their people turn to them
and drink up waters in abundance.[e]
11They say, "How can God know?
Does the Most High have knowledge?"

12This is what the wicked are like—
always carefree, they increase in wealth.

13Surely in vain have I kept my heart pure;
in vain have I washed my hands in
innocence. Ps 26:6
14All day long I have been plagued;
I have been punished every morning.

15If I had said, "I will speak thus,"
I would have betrayed your children.
16When I tried to understand all this,
it was oppressive to me Ecc 8:17
17till I entered the sanctuary of God; Ps 77:13
then I understood their final destiny. Ps 37:38

18Surely you place them on slippery ground;
you cast them down to ruin.
19How suddenly are they destroyed, Isa 47:11
completely swept away by terrors!
20As a dream when one awakes, Job 20:8

[a]8 That is, the Euphrates [b]8 Or *the end of the land* [c]4 With a different word division of the Hebrew; Masoretic Text *struggles at their death; / their bodies are healthy* [d]7 Syriac (see also Septuagint); Hebrew *Their eyes bulge with fat* [e]10 The meaning of the Hebrew for this verse is uncertain.

so when you arise, O Lord,
you will despise them as fantasies.

21When my heart was grieved
and my spirit embittered,
22I was senseless and ignorant; Ps 49:10
I was a brute beast before you. Ecc 3:18

23Yet I am always with you;
you hold me by my right hand.
24You guide me with your counsel, Ps 32:8; 48:14
and afterward you will take me into glory.
25Whom have I in heaven but you?
And earth has nothing I desire besides you.
26My flesh and my heart may fail, Ps 84:2
but God is the strength of my heart
and my portion forever.

27Those who are far from you will perish;
you destroy all who are unfaithful to you.
28But as for me, it is good to be near God.
I have made the Sovereign LORD my refuge;
I will tell of all your deeds. Ps 40:5

Psalm 74

A *maskil*[a] of Asaph.

1Why have you rejected us forever, O God?
Why does your anger smolder against the
sheep of your pasture? Ps 95:7
2Remember the people you purchased of old,
the tribe of your inheritance, whom you
redeemed—
Mount Zion, where you dwelt. Ps 68:16
3Turn your steps toward these everlasting
ruins,
all this destruction the enemy has brought
on the sanctuary.

4Your foes roared in the place where you met
with us; La 2:7
they set up their standards as signs.
5They behaved like men wielding axes
to cut through a thicket of trees. Jer 46:22
6They smashed all the carved paneling
with their axes and hatchets.
7They burned your sanctuary to the ground;
they defiled the dwelling place of your
Name. Ps 75:1
8They said in their hearts, "We will crush them
completely!" Ps 83:4
They burned every place where God was
worshiped in the land.
9We are given no miraculous signs;
no prophets are left, 1Sa 3:1
and none of us knows how long this
will be.

10How long will the enemy mock you, O God?
Will the foe revile your name forever?
11Why do you hold back your hand, your right
hand? La 2:3
Take it from the folds of your garment and
destroy them!

12But you, O God, are my king from of old;
you bring salvation upon the earth.
13It was you who split open the sea by your
power; Ex 14:21
you broke the heads of the monster in the
waters. Isa 51:9
14It was you who crushed the heads of
Leviathan
and gave him as food to the creatures of
the desert.
15It was you who opened up springs and
streams; Ex 17:6; Nu 20:11
you dried up the ever flowing rivers.
16The day is yours, and yours also the night;
you established the sun and moon. Ge 1:16
17It was you who set all the boundaries of the
earth;
you made both summer and winter. Ge 8:22

18Remember how the enemy has mocked you,
O LORD,
how foolish people have reviled your name.
19Do not hand over the life of your dove to
wild beasts;
do not forget the lives of your afflicted
people forever. Ps 9:18
20Have regard for your covenant, Ge 17:7; Ps 106:45
because haunts of violence fill the dark
places of the land.
21Do not let the oppressed retreat in disgrace;
may the poor and needy praise your name.

22Rise up, O God, and defend your cause;
remember how fools mock you all day
long. Ps 53:1
23Do not ignore the clamor of your adversaries,
the uproar of your enemies, which rises
continually.

Psalm 75

For the director of music. ⌊To the tune of⌋ "Do Not Destroy." A psalm of Asaph. A song.

1We give thanks to you, O God,
we give thanks, for your Name is near;
men tell of your wonderful deeds. Ps 44:1

2You say, "I choose the appointed time;
it is I who judge uprightly. Ps 7:11
3When the earth and all its people quake,
it is I who hold its pillars firm. *Selah*
4To the arrogant I say, 'Boast no more,'

[a]Title: Probably a literary or musical term

and to the wicked, 'Do not lift up your
horns. Zec 1:21
5Do not lift your horns against heaven;
do not speak with outstretched neck.'"

6No one from the east or the west
or from the desert can exalt a man.
7But it is God who judges: Ps 50:6
He brings one down, he exalts another.
8In the hand of the LORD is a cup
full of foaming wine mixed with spices;
he pours it out, and all the wicked of the
earth
drink it down to its very dregs. Jer 25:15

9As for me, I will declare this forever; Ps 40:10
I will sing praise to the God of Jacob.
10I will cut off the horns of all the wicked,
but the horns of the righteous will be
lifted up. Ps 89:17; 148:14

Psalm 76

For the director of music. With stringed instruments. A psalm of Asaph. A song.

1In Judah God is known;
his name is great in Israel. Ps 99:3
2His tent is in Salem, Ge 14:18
his dwelling place in Zion.
3There he broke the flashing arrows,
the shields and the swords, the weapons of
war. *Selah*

4You are resplendent with light, Ps 36:9
more majestic than mountains rich with
game.
5Valiant men lie plundered,
they sleep their last sleep; Ps 13:3
not one of the warriors
can lift his hands.
6At your rebuke, O God of Jacob,
both horse and chariot lie still. Ex 15:1
7You alone are to be feared.
Who can stand before you when you are
angry? Na 1:6
8From heaven you pronounced judgment,
and the land feared and was quiet—
9when you, O God, rose up to judge, Ps 9:8
to save all the afflicted of the land. *Selah*
10Surely your wrath against men brings you
praise, Ex 9:16; Ro 9:17
and the survivors of your wrath are
restrained.[a]

11Make vows to the LORD your God and fulfill
them; Ps 50:14; Ecc 5:4-5
let all the neighboring lands
bring gifts to the One to be feared. Ps 68:29
12He breaks the spirit of rulers;
he is feared by the kings of the earth.

Psalm 77

For the director of music. For Jeduthun. Of Asaph. A psalm.

1I cried out to God for help; Ps 3:4
I cried out to God to hear me.
2When I was in distress, I sought the Lord;
at night I stretched out untiring hands
and my soul refused to be comforted.

3I remembered you, O God, and I groaned;
I mused, and my spirit grew faint. *Selah*
4You kept my eyes from closing;
I was too troubled to speak.
5I thought about the former days, Dt 32:7; Ps 143:5
the years of long ago;
6I remembered my songs in the night.
My heart mused and my spirit inquired:

7"Will the Lord reject forever?
Will he never show his favor again? Ps 85:1
8Has his unfailing love vanished forever?
Has his promise failed for all time? 2Pe 3:9
9Has God forgotten to be merciful?
Has he in anger withheld his compassion?"
Selah

10Then I thought, "To this I will appeal:
the years of the right hand of the Most
High." Ps 31:22
11I will remember the deeds of the LORD;
yes, I will remember your miracles of long
ago. Ps 143:5
12I will meditate on all your works
and consider all your mighty deeds.

13Your ways, O God, are holy.
What god is so great as our God? Ex 15:11
14You are the God who performs miracles;
you display your power among the peoples.
15With your mighty arm you redeemed your
people, Ex 6:6; Dt 9:29
the descendants of Jacob and Joseph. *Selah*

16The waters saw you, O God, Ex 14:21,28
the waters saw you and writhed; Ps 114:4
the very depths were convulsed.
17The clouds poured down water, Jdg 5:4
the skies resounded with thunder;
your arrows flashed back and forth.
18Your thunder was heard in the whirlwind,
your lightning lit up the world;
the earth trembled and quaked. Jdg 5:4
19Your path led through the sea, Hab 3:15
your way through the mighty waters,
though your footprints were not seen.

[a] 10 Or *Surely the wrath of men brings you praise, / and with the remainder of wrath you arm yourself*

[20]You led your people like a flock Ex 13:21; Isa 63:11
by the hand of Moses and Aaron.

Psalm 78

A *maskil*[a] of Asaph.

[1]O my people, hear my teaching; Isa 51:4
listen to the words of my mouth.
[2]I will open my mouth in parables, Mt 13:35*
I will utter hidden things, things from of old—
[3]what we have heard and known,
what our fathers have told us. Ps 44:1
[4]We will not hide them from their children;
we will tell the next generation
the praiseworthy deeds of the LORD, Ps 26:7; 71:17
his power, and the wonders he has done.
[5]He decreed statutes for Jacob Ps 147:19
and established the law in Israel,
which he commanded our forefathers
to teach their children,
[6]so the next generation would know them,
even the children yet to be born, Ps 102:18
and they in turn would tell their children.
[7]Then they would put their trust in God
and would not forget his deeds
but would keep his commands.
[8]They would not be like their forefathers—
a stubborn and rebellious generation, Ex 32:9
whose hearts were not loyal to God,
whose spirits were not faithful to him.

LIVING  **INSIGHT**

Strong families survive from generation to generation because diligence is applied to the teaching process. And remember, the teaching weaves very naturally and comfortably into the fabric of everyday life.

(See Psalm 78:1–8.)

[9]The men of Ephraim, though armed with bows,
turned back on the day of battle; Jdg 20:39
[10]they did not keep God's covenant 2Ki 17:15
and refused to live by his law.
[11]They forgot what he had done, Ps 106:13
the wonders he had shown them.
[12]He did miracles in the sight of their fathers
in the land of Egypt, in the region of Zoan.
[13]He divided the sea and led them through;
he made the water stand firm like a wall.
[14]He guided them with the cloud by day
and with light from the fire all night.
[15]He split the rocks in the desert Nu 20:11
and gave them water as abundant as the seas;
[16]he brought streams out of a rocky crag
and made water flow down like rivers.
[17]But they continued to sin against him, Heb 3:16
rebelling in the desert against the Most High.
[18]They willfully put God to the test 1Co 10:9
by demanding the food they craved. Nu 11:4
[19]They spoke against God, saying, Nu 21:5
"Can God spread a table in the desert?
[20]When he struck the rock, water gushed out,
and streams flowed abundantly.
But can he also give us food?
Can he supply meat for his people?" Nu 11:18
[21]When the LORD heard them, he was very angry;
his fire broke out against Jacob, Nu 11:1
and his wrath rose against Israel,
[22]for they did not believe in God
or trust in his deliverance. Heb 3:19
[23]Yet he gave a command to the skies above
and opened the doors of the heavens;
[24]he rained down manna for the people to eat,
he gave them the grain of heaven.
[25]Men ate the bread of angels;
he sent them all the food they could eat.
[26]He let loose the east wind from the heavens
and led forth the south wind by his power.
[27]He rained meat down on them like dust,
flying birds like sand on the seashore.
[28]He made them come down inside their camp,
all around their tents.
[29]They ate till they had more than enough,
for he had given them what they craved.
[30]But before they turned from the food they craved,
even while it was still in their mouths,
[31]God's anger rose against them;
he put to death the sturdiest among them,
cutting down the young men of Israel.
[32]In spite of all this, they kept on sinning;
in spite of his wonders, they did not believe. ver 11,22
[33]So he ended their days in futility Nu 14:29,35
and their years in terror.
[34]Whenever God slew them, they would seek him; Hos 5:15
they eagerly turned to him again.
[35]They remembered that God was their Rock,
that God Most High was their Redeemer.
[36]But then they would flatter him with their mouths, Eze 33:31
lying to him with their tongues;
[37]their hearts were not loyal to him,

[a]Title: Probably a literary or musical term

they were not faithful to his covenant.
38 Yet he was merciful; Ex 34:6
he forgave their iniquities Isa 48:10
and did not destroy them.
Time after time he restrained his anger
and did not stir up his full wrath.
39 He remembered that they were but flesh,
a passing breeze that does not return. Job 7:7

40 How often they rebelled against him in the
desert
and grieved him in the wasteland! Ps 95:8
41 Again and again they put God to the test;
they vexed the Holy One of Israel. Ps 89:18
42 They did not remember his power—
the day he redeemed them from the
oppressor,
43 the day he displayed his miraculous signs in
Egypt,
his wonders in the region of Zoan.
44 He turned their rivers to blood; Ex 7:20-21
they could not drink from their streams.
45 He sent swarms of flies that devoured them,
and frogs that devastated them. Ex 8:2,6
46 He gave their crops to the grasshopper,
their produce to the locust.
47 He destroyed their vines with hail Ex 9:23
and their sycamore-figs with sleet.
48 He gave over their cattle to the hail,
their livestock to bolts of lightning.
49 He unleashed against them his hot anger,
his wrath, indignation and hostility—
a band of destroying angels.
50 He prepared a path for his anger;
he did not spare them from death
but gave them over to the plague.
51 He struck down all the firstborn of Egypt,
the firstfruits of manhood in the tents of
Ham.
52 But he brought his people out like a flock;
he led them like sheep through the desert.
53 He guided them safely, so they were unafraid;
but the sea engulfed their enemies. Ex 14:28
54 Thus he brought them to the border of his
holy land,
to the hill country his right hand had taken.
55 He drove out nations before them Ps 44:2
and allotted their lands to them as an
inheritance;
he settled the tribes of Israel in their
homes.

56 But they put God to the test
and rebelled against the Most High;
they did not keep his statutes.
57 Like their fathers they were disloyal and
faithless, Eze 20:27
as unreliable as a faulty bow.
58 They angered him with their high places;
they aroused his jealousy with their idols.
59 When God heard them, he was very angry;
he rejected Israel completely. Dt 32:19
60 He abandoned the tabernacle of Shiloh, Jos 18:1
the tent he had set up among men.
61 He sent ⌊the ark of⌋ his might into captivity,
his splendor into the hands of the enemy.
62 He gave his people over to the sword;
he was very angry with his inheritance.
63 Fire consumed their young men, Nu 11:1
and their maidens had no wedding songs;
64 their priests were put to the sword, 1Sa 22:18
and their widows could not weep.

65 Then the Lord awoke as from sleep,
as a man wakes from the stupor of wine.
66 He beat back his enemies;
he put them to everlasting shame. 1Sa 5:6
67 Then he rejected the tents of Joseph,
he did not choose the tribe of Ephraim;
68 but he chose the tribe of Judah,
Mount Zion, which he loved. Ps 87:2
69 He built his sanctuary like the heights,
like the earth that he established forever.
70 He chose David his servant 1Sa 16:1
and took him from the sheep pens;
71 from tending the sheep he brought him
to be the shepherd of his people Jacob,
of Israel his inheritance.
72 And David shepherded them with integrity of
heart; 1Ki 9:4
with skillful hands he led them.

Psalm 79

A psalm of Asaph.

1 O God, the nations have invaded your
inheritance; Ps 74:2
they have defiled your holy temple,
they have reduced Jerusalem to rubble.
2 They have given the dead bodies of your
servants
as food to the birds of the air,
the flesh of your saints to the beasts of the
earth. Jer 7:33
3 They have poured out blood like water
all around Jerusalem,
and there is no one to bury the dead.
4 We are objects of reproach to our neighbors,
of scorn and derision to those around us.

5 How long, O LORD? Will you be angry
forever? Ps 74:1,10
How long will your jealousy burn like fire?
6 Pour out your wrath on the nations
that do not acknowledge you, Jer 10:25; 2Th 1:8
on the kingdoms
that do not call on your name; Ps 14:4
7 for they have devoured Jacob
and destroyed his homeland.

[8]Do not hold against us the sins of the fathers;
may your mercy come quickly to meet us,
for we are in desperate need. Ps 116:6; 142:6

[9]Help us, O God our Savior,
for the glory of your name;
deliver us and forgive our sins
for your name's sake. Jer 14:7
[10]Why should the nations say,
"Where is their God?" Ps 42:10
Before our eyes, make known among the nations
that you avenge the outpoured blood of your servants. Ps 94:1
[11]May the groans of the prisoners come before you;
by the strength of your arm
preserve those condemned to die.

[12]Pay back into the laps of our neighbors seven times Ge 4:15; Isa 65:6; Jer 32:18
the reproach they have hurled at you, O Lord.
[13]Then we your people, the sheep of your pasture, Ps 74:1; 95:7
will praise you forever;
from generation to generation
we will recount your praise.

Psalm 80

For the director of music. To ⌊the tune of⌋ "The Lilies of the Covenant." Of Asaph. A psalm.

[1]Hear us, O Shepherd of Israel,
you who lead Joseph like a flock; Ps 77:20
you who sit enthroned between the cherubim,
shine forth Ex 25:22
[2] before Ephraim, Benjamin and Manasseh.
Awaken your might;
come and save us.

[3]Restore us, O God; Nu 6:25; La 5:21
make your face shine upon us,
that we may be saved.

[4]O LORD God Almighty,
how long will your anger smolder Dt 29:20
against the prayers of your people?
[5]You have fed them with the bread of tears;
you have made them drink tears by the bowlful. Ps 42:3
[6]You have made us a source of contention to our neighbors,
and our enemies mock us. Ps 79:4

[7]Restore us, O God Almighty;
make your face shine upon us,
that we may be saved.

[8]You brought a vine out of Egypt; Isa 5:1-2
you drove out the nations and planted it.
[9]You cleared the ground for it,
and it took root and filled the land.
[10]The mountains were covered with its shade,
the mighty cedars with its branches.
[11]It sent out its boughs to the Sea,[a]
its shoots as far as the River.[b] Ps 72:8

[12]Why have you broken down its walls
so that all who pass by pick its grapes?
[13]Boars from the forest ravage it Jer 5:6
and the creatures of the field feed on it.
[14]Return to us, O God Almighty!
Look down from heaven and see! Isa 63:15
Watch over this vine,
[15] the root your right hand has planted,
the son[c] you have raised up for yourself.
[16]Your vine is cut down, it is burned with fire;
at your rebuke your people perish. Ps 39:11
[17]Let your hand rest on the man at your right hand,
the son of man you have raised up for yourself.
[18]Then we will not turn away from you;
revive us, and we will call on your name.

[19]Restore us, O LORD God Almighty;
make your face shine upon us,
that we may be saved.

Psalm 81

For the director of music. According to *gittith*.[d] Of Asaph.

[1]Sing for joy to God our strength;
shout aloud to the God of Jacob! Ps 66:1
[2]Begin the music, strike the tambourine,
play the melodious harp and lyre. Ps 92:3

[3]Sound the ram's horn at the New Moon,
and when the moon is full, on the day of our Feast;
[4]this is a decree for Israel,
an ordinance of the God of Jacob.
[5]He established it as a statute for Joseph
when he went out against Egypt, Ex 11:4

LIVING  **INSIGHT**

The Good Shepherd cares for His sheep! How He loves us and rescues us! How often He lifts us when we are low and supports us when we are weak! As long as we rely on Him, He keeps us from falling.
(See Psalm 80:1–3.)

[a]11 Probably the Mediterranean [b]11 That is, the Euphrates [c]15 Or *branch* [d]Title: Probably a musical term

where we heard a language we did not
understand.[a] Ps 114:1

6He says, "I removed the burden from their
shoulders; Isa 9:4
their hands were set free from the basket.
7In your distress you called and I rescued you,
I answered you out of a thundercloud;
I tested you at the waters of Meribah. *Selah*

8"Hear, O my people, and I will warn you—
if you would but listen to me, O Israel!
9You shall have no foreign god among you;
you shall not bow down to an alien god.
10I am the LORD your God,
who brought you up out of Egypt. Ex 20:2
Open wide your mouth and I will fill it.

11"But my people would not listen to me;
Israel would not submit to me.
12So I gave them over to their stubborn hearts
to follow their own devices.

13"If my people would but listen to me, Dt 5:29
if Israel would follow my ways,
14how quickly would I subdue their enemies
and turn my hand against their foes! Am 1:8
15Those who hate the LORD would cringe before
him,
and their punishment would last forever.
16But you would be fed with the finest of wheat;
with honey from the rock I would satisfy
you."

Psalm 82

A psalm of Asaph.

1God presides in the great assembly;
he gives judgment among the "gods":

2"How long will you[b] defend the unjust
and show partiality to the wicked? *Selah*
3Defend the cause of the weak and fatherless;
maintain the rights of the poor and
oppressed.
4Rescue the weak and needy;
deliver them from the hand of the wicked.

5"They know nothing, they understand
nothing. Mic 3:1
They walk about in darkness;
all the foundations of the earth are shaken.

6"I said, 'You are "gods";
you are all sons of the Most High.' Jn 10:34*
7But you will die like mere men; Ps 49:12
you will fall like every other ruler."

8Rise up, O God, judge the earth,
for all the nations are your inheritance.

Psalm 83

A song. A psalm of Asaph.

1O God, do not keep silent; Ps 28:1
be not quiet, O God, be not still.
2See how your enemies are astir, Ps 2:1
how your foes rear their heads. Ps 81:15
3With cunning they conspire against your
people; Ps 31:13
they plot against those you cherish.
4"Come," they say, "let us destroy them as a
nation, Est 3:6
that the name of Israel be remembered no
more."

5With one mind they plot together; Ps 2:2
they form an alliance against you—
6the tents of Edom and the Ishmaelites,
of Moab and the Hagrites, 2Ch 20:1
7Gebal,[c] Ammon and Amalek, Jos 13:5
Philistia, with the people of Tyre.
8Even Assyria has joined them
to lend strength to the descendants of Lot.
Selah

9Do to them as you did to Midian, Jdg 7:1-23
as you did to Sisera and Jabin at the river
Kishon, Jdg 4:23-24
10who perished at Endor
and became like refuse on the ground.
11Make their nobles like Oreb and Zeeb,
all their princes like Zebah and Zalmunna,
12who said, "Let us take possession
of the pasturelands of God."

13Make them like tumbleweed, O my God,
like chaff before the wind. Ps 35:5; Isa 17:13
14As fire consumes the forest
or a flame sets the mountains ablaze,
15so pursue them with your tempest
and terrify them with your storm.
16Cover their faces with shame Ps 109:29; 132:18
so that men will seek your name, O LORD.

17May they ever be ashamed and dismayed;
may they perish in disgrace. Ps 35:4
18Let them know that you, whose name is the
LORD—
that you alone are the Most High over all
the earth. Ps 59:13

Psalm 84

For the director of music. According to *gittith*.[d]
Of the Sons of Korah. A psalm.

1How lovely is your dwelling place, Ps 27:4
O LORD Almighty!

[a]5 Or / *and we heard a voice we had not known* [b]2 The Hebrew is plural. [c]7 That is, Byblos [d]Title: Probably a musical term

2 My soul yearns, even faints, Ps 42:1-2
for the courts of the LORD;
my heart and my flesh cry out
for the living God. Jos 3:10

3 Even the sparrow has found a home,
and the swallow a nest for herself,
where she may have her young—
a place near your altar, Ps 43:4
O LORD Almighty, my King and my God.
4 Blessed are those who dwell in your house;
they are ever praising you. *Selah*

5 Blessed are those whose strength is in you,
who have set their hearts on pilgrimage.
6 As they pass through the Valley of Baca,
they make it a place of springs;
the autumn rains also cover it with pools.[a]
7 They go from strength to strength, Pr 4:18
till each appears before God in Zion. Dt 16:16

8 Hear my prayer, O LORD God Almighty;
listen to me, O God of Jacob. *Selah*
9 Look upon our shield,[b] O God; Ps 59:11
look with favor on your anointed one.

10 Better is one day in your courts
than a thousand elsewhere;
I would rather be a doorkeeper in the house
of my God 1Ch 23:5
than dwell in the tents of the wicked.
11 For the LORD God is a sun and shield; Isa 60:19
the LORD bestows favor and honor;
no good thing does he withhold Ps 34:10
from those whose walk is blameless.

12 O LORD Almighty,
blessed is the man who trusts in you. Ps 2:12

Psalm 85

For the director of music. Of the Sons of Korah.
A psalm.

1 You showed favor to your land, O LORD;
you restored the fortunes of Jacob. Jer 30:18
2 You forgave the iniquity of your people
and covered all their sins. *Selah*
3 You set aside all your wrath
and turned from your fierce anger. Dt 13:17

4 Restore us again, O God our Savior, Ps 80:3,7
and put away your displeasure toward us.
5 Will you be angry with us forever? Ps 79:5
Will you prolong your anger through all
generations?
6 Will you not revive us again, Ps 80:18; Hab 3:2
that your people may rejoice in you?
7 Show us your unfailing love, O LORD,
and grant us your salvation.

8 I will listen to what God the LORD will say;
he promises peace to his people, his
saints— Zec 9:10
but let them not return to folly.
9 Surely his salvation is near those who fear
him, Isa 46:13
that his glory may dwell in our land. Zec 2:5

10 Love and faithfulness meet together;
righteousness and peace kiss each other.
11 Faithfulness springs forth from the earth,
and righteousness looks down from heaven.
12 The LORD will indeed give what is good,
and our land will yield its harvest. Ps 67:6
13 Righteousness goes before him
and prepares the way for his steps.

Psalm 86

A prayer of David.

1 Hear, O LORD, and answer me, Ps 17:6
for I am poor and needy.
2 Guard my life, for I am devoted to you.
You are my God; save your servant
who trusts in you.
3 Have mercy on me, O Lord, Ps 57:1
for I call to you all day long.
4 Bring joy to your servant,
for to you, O Lord,
I lift up my soul. Ps 143:8

5 You are forgiving and good, O Lord,
abounding in love to all who call to you.
6 Hear my prayer, O LORD;
listen to my cry for mercy.
7 In the day of my trouble I will call to you,
for you will answer me.

8 Among the gods there is none like you,
O Lord; Ex 15:11; Dt 3:24; Ps 89:6
no deeds can compare with yours.
9 All the nations you have made
will come and worship before you, O Lord;
they will bring glory to your name.
10 For you are great and do marvelous deeds;
you alone are God. Dt 6:4; Mk 12:29

11 Teach me your way, O LORD, Ps 25:5
and I will walk in your truth;
give me an undivided heart, Jer 32:39
that I may fear your name.
12 I will praise you, O Lord my God, with all my
heart; Ps 9:1
I will glorify your name forever.
13 For great is your love toward me;
you have delivered me from the depths of
the grave.[c] Ps 16:10

14 The arrogant are attacking me, O God;

[a] 6 Or *blessings* [b] 9 Or *sovereign* [c] 13 Hebrew *Sheol*

a band of ruthless men seeks my life—
men without regard for you. Ps 54:3
15 But you, O Lord, are a compassionate and
gracious God, Ps 103:8
slow to anger, abounding in love and
faithfulness. Ex 34:6; Ne 9:17; Joel 2:13
16 Turn to me and have mercy on me;
grant your strength to your servant
and save the son of your maidservant.[a]
17 Give me a sign of your goodness,
that my enemies may see it and be put to
shame,
for you, O LORD, have helped me and
comforted me.

Psalm 87

Of the Sons of Korah. A psalm. A song.

1 He has set his foundation on the holy
mountain; Ps 48:1
2 the LORD loves the gates of Zion Ps 78:68
more than all the dwellings of Jacob.
3 Glorious things are said of you,
O city of God: *Selah*
4 "I will record Rahab[b] and Babylon Job 9:13
among those who acknowledge me—
Philistia too, and Tyre, along with Cush[c]—
and will say, 'This[d] one was born in
Zion.'" Isa 19:25
5 Indeed, of Zion it will be said,
"This one and that one were born in her,
and the Most High himself will establish
her."
6 The LORD will write in the register of the
peoples: Eze 13:9
"This one was born in Zion." *Selah*
7 As they make music they will sing,
"All my fountains are in you." Ps 36:9

Psalm 88

A song. A psalm of the Sons of Korah. For the director of music. According to *mahalath leannoth.*[e] A *maskil*[f] of Heman the Ezrahite.

1 O LORD, the God who saves me, Ps 51:14
day and night I cry out before you. Ps 22:2
2 May my prayer come before you;
turn your ear to my cry.
3 For my soul is full of trouble
and my life draws near the grave.[g]
4 I am counted among those who go down to
the pit; Ps 28:1
I am like a man without strength.
5 I am set apart with the dead,
like the slain who lie in the grave,
whom you remember no more,
who are cut off from your care. Isa 53:8
6 You have put me in the lowest pit,
in the darkest depths. Ps 69:15; La 3:55
7 Your wrath lies heavily upon me;
you have overwhelmed me with all your
waves. *Selah*
8 You have taken from me my closest friends
and have made me repulsive to them.
I am confined and cannot escape;
9 my eyes are dim with grief. Ps 38:10
I call to you, O LORD, every day; Ps 86:3
I spread out my hands to you. Ps 143:6
10 Do you show your wonders to the dead?
Do those who are dead rise up and praise
you? *Selah*
11 Is your love declared in the grave,
your faithfulness in Destruction[h]? Ps 30:9
12 Are your wonders known in the place of
darkness,
or your righteous deeds in the land of
oblivion?
13 But I cry to you for help, O LORD; Ps 30:2
in the morning my prayer comes before
you. Ps 5:3
14 Why, O LORD, do you reject me
and hide your face from me? Job 13:24; Ps 13:1
15 From my youth I have been afflicted and close
to death;
I have suffered your terrors and am in
despair. Job 6:4
16 Your wrath has swept over me;
your terrors have destroyed me.
17 All day long they surround me like a flood;
they have completely engulfed me.
18 You have taken my companions and loved
ones from me; Job 19:13
the darkness is my closest friend.

Psalm 89

A *maskil*[f] of Ethan the Ezrahite.

1 I will sing of the LORD's great love forever;
with my mouth I will make your
faithfulness known through all
generations. Ps 36:5
2 I will declare that your love stands firm
forever,
that you established your faithfulness in
heaven itself. Ps 36:5

[a] 16 Or *save your faithful son* [b] 4 A poetic name for Egypt [c] 4 That is, the upper Nile region [d] 4 Or *"O Rahab and Babylon, / Philistia, Tyre and Cush, / I will record concerning those who acknowledge me: / 'This* [e] Title: Possibly a tune, "The Suffering of Affliction" [f] Title: Probably a literary or musical term [g] 3 Hebrew *Sheol* [h] 11 Hebrew *Abaddon*

[3]You said, "I have made a covenant with my chosen one,
I have sworn to David my servant,
[4]'I will establish your line forever
and make your throne firm through all generations.'" *Selah*

[5]The heavens praise your wonders, O LORD,
your faithfulness too, in the assembly of the holy ones.
[6]For who in the skies above can compare with the LORD?
Who is like the LORD among the heavenly beings? Ps 113:5
[7]In the council of the holy ones God is greatly feared;
he is more awesome than all who surround him. Ps 47:2
[8]O LORD God Almighty, who is like you?
You are mighty, O LORD, and your faithfulness surrounds you.

[9]You rule over the surging sea;
when its waves mount up, you still them.
[10]You crushed Rahab like one of the slain;
with your strong arm you scattered your enemies.
[11]The heavens are yours, and yours also the earth; 1Ch 29:11; Ps 24:1
you founded the world and all that is in it.
[12]You created the north and the south;
Tabor and Hermon sing for joy at your name. Jos 12:1; 19:22
[13]Your arm is endued with power;
your hand is strong, your right hand exalted.

[14]Righteousness and justice are the foundation of your throne;
love and faithfulness go before you. Ps 97:2
[15]Blessed are those who have learned to acclaim you,
who walk in the light of your presence, O LORD. Ps 44:3
[16]They rejoice in your name all day long;
they exult in your righteousness.
[17]For you are their glory and strength,
and by your favor you exalt our horn.[a]
[18]Indeed, our shield[b] belongs to the LORD,
our king to the Holy One of Israel. Ps 47:9

[19]Once you spoke in a vision,
to your faithful people you said:
"I have bestowed strength on a warrior;
I have exalted a young man from among the people.
[20]I have found David my servant; Ac 13:22
with my sacred oil I have anointed him.
[21]My hand will sustain him;
surely my arm will strengthen him. Ps 18:35
[22]No enemy will subject him to tribute;
no wicked man will oppress him. 2Sa 7:10
[23]I will crush his foes before him
and strike down his adversaries. 2Sa 7:9
[24]My faithful love will be with him,
and through my name his horn[c] will be exalted.
[25]I will set his hand over the sea,
his right hand over the rivers. Ps 72:8
[26]He will call out to me, 'You are my Father,
my God, the Rock my Savior.' 2Sa 22:47
[27]I will also appoint him my firstborn,
the most exalted of the kings of the earth.
[28]I will maintain my love to him forever,
and my covenant with him will never fail.
[29]I will establish his line forever,
his throne as long as the heavens endure.

[30]"If his sons forsake my law
and do not follow my statutes,
[31]if they violate my decrees
and fail to keep my commands,
[32]I will punish their sin with the rod,
their iniquity with flogging;
[33]but I will not take my love from him, 2Sa 7:15
nor will I ever betray my faithfulness.
[34]I will not violate my covenant
or alter what my lips have uttered. Nu 23:19
[35]Once for all, I have sworn by my holiness—
and I will not lie to David—
[36]that his line will continue forever
and his throne endure before me like the sun;
[37]it will be established forever like the moon,
the faithful witness in the sky." *Selah*

[38]But you have rejected, you have spurned,
you have been very angry with your anointed one.
[39]You have renounced the covenant with your servant
and have defiled his crown in the dust.
[40]You have broken through all his walls
and reduced his strongholds to ruins. La 2:2
[41]All who pass by have plundered him;
he has become the scorn of his neighbors.
[42]You have exalted the right hand of his foes;
you have made all his enemies rejoice.
[43]You have turned back the edge of his sword
and have not supported him in battle.
[44]You have put an end to his splendor
and cast his throne to the ground.
[45]You have cut short the days of his youth;
you have covered him with a mantle of shame. *Selah*

[46]How long, O LORD? Will you hide yourself forever?

[a]17 *Horn* here symbolizes strong one. [b]18 Or *sovereign* [c]24 *Horn* here symbolizes strength.

How long will your wrath burn like fire?
47Remember how fleeting is my life. Job 7:7
For what futility you have created all men!
48What man can live and not see death,
or save himself from the power of the grave[a]? *Selah*
49O Lord, where is your former great love,
which in your faithfulness you swore to David?
50Remember, Lord, how your servant has[b] been mocked, Ps 69:19
how I bear in my heart the taunts of all the nations,
51the taunts with which your enemies have mocked, O LORD,
with which they have mocked every step of your anointed one. Ps 74:10

52Praise be to the LORD forever!
Amen and Amen.

BOOK IV
Psalms 90–106

Psalms of the Earth **Psalms 90–106**

The themes found in this section revolve around God's ruling power and our capacity to resist His power and wander from His care. We desperately need a place of refuge and relief in this life—even if we rigorously deny it. These hymns remind us of our wanderings and the Lord's leading in the midst of this journey on earth. As the book of Numbers teaches us, the only way to find our way through the desert of life is through the trustworthy leading of our God.

Psalm 90

A prayer of Moses the man of God.

1Lord, you have been our dwelling place
throughout all generations.
2Before the mountains were born Pr 8:25
or you brought forth the earth and the world,
from everlasting to everlasting you are God.

3You turn men back to dust,
saying, "Return to dust, O sons of men."
4For a thousand years in your sight
are like a day that has just gone by,
or like a watch in the night. 2Pe 3:8
5You sweep men away in the sleep of death;
they are like the new grass of the morning—
6though in the morning it springs up new,
by evening it is dry and withered. Mt 6:30
7We are consumed by your anger
and terrified by your indignation.
8You have set our iniquities before you,
our secret sins in the light of your presence.
9All our days pass away under your wrath;
we finish our years with a moan. Ps 78:33
10The length of our days is seventy years—
or eighty, if we have the strength;
yet their span[c] is but trouble and sorrow,
for they quickly pass, and we fly away.

11Who knows the power of your anger?
For your wrath is as great as the fear that is due you. Ps 76:7
12Teach us to number our days aright, Ps 39:4
that we may gain a heart of wisdom.

LIVING  **INSIGHT**

What is today? A day the Lord has made. A twenty-four hour segment of time never lived before and never to be repeated. You may never live to see another day like this one. You may never be closer to a decision you need to make, a step you need to take, a sin you need to forsake, a choice you need to determine. So do so today—before tomorrow's demands eclipse today's desires.
(See Psalm 90:12.)

13Relent, O LORD! How long will it be?
Have compassion on your servants. Dt 32:36
14Satisfy us in the morning with your unfailing love, Ps 103:5
that we may sing for joy and be glad all our days. Ps 85:6
15Make us glad for as many days as you have afflicted us,
for as many years as we have seen trouble.
16May your deeds be shown to your servants,
your splendor to their children. Hab 3:2

17May the favor[d] of the Lord our God rest upon us; Isa 26:12
establish the work of our hands for us—
yes, establish the work of our hands.

Psalm 91

1He who dwells in the shelter of the Most High
will rest in the shadow of the Almighty.[e]
2I will say[f] of the LORD, "He is my refuge and my fortress, Ps 142:5
my God, in whom I trust."

[a]48 Hebrew *Sheol* [b]50 Or *your servants have* [c]10 Or *yet the best of them* [d]17 Or *beauty* [e]1 Hebrew *Shaddai* [f]2 Or *He says*

[3]Surely he will save you from the fowler's snare
and from the deadly pestilence. 1Ki 8:37
[4]He will cover you with his feathers,
and under his wings you will find refuge;
his faithfulness will be your shield and
rampart. Ps 35:2

LIVING  **INSIGHT**

Do you need a refuge? A willing, caring, available "someone." A trusted confidant and comrade-at-arms. Can't find one? Why not share David's shelter? The One he called my Strength, Mighty Rock, Fortress, Stronghold and High Tower. David's Refuge never failed him. Not even once. And David never regretted the times he dropped his heavy load and ran for cover. Neither will you.

(See Psalm 91:1–2.)

[5]You will not fear the terror of night, Job 5:21
nor the arrow that flies by day,
[6]nor the pestilence that stalks in the darkness,
nor the plague that destroys at midday.
[7]A thousand may fall at your side,
ten thousand at your right hand,
but it will not come near you.
[8]You will only observe with your eyes
and see the punishment of the wicked.

[9]If you make the Most High your dwelling—
even the LORD, who is my refuge—
[10]then no harm will befall you, Pr 12:21
no disaster will come near your tent.
[11]For he will command his angels concerning
you Heb 1:14
to guard you in all your ways; Ps 34:7
[12]they will lift you up in their hands,
so that you will not strike your foot against
a stone. Mt 4:6*; Lk 4:10-11*
[13]You will tread upon the lion and the cobra;
you will trample the great lion and the
serpent. Da 6:22; Lk 10:19

[14]"Because he loves me," says the LORD, "I will
rescue him;
I will protect him, for he acknowledges my
name.
[15]He will call upon me, and I will answer him;
I will be with him in trouble,
I will deliver him and honor him. 1Sa 2:30
[16]With long life will I satisfy him Dt 6:2; Ps 21:4
and show him my salvation." Ps 50:23

Psalm 92

A psalm. A song. For the Sabbath day.

[1]It is good to praise the LORD
and make music to your name, O Most
High, Ps 147:1
[2]to proclaim your love in the morning
and your faithfulness at night, Ps 89:1
[3]to the music of the ten-stringed lyre
and the melody of the harp. Ps 33:2

[4]For you make me glad by your deeds,
O LORD;
I sing for joy at the works of your hands.
[5]How great are your works, O LORD,
how profound your thoughts! Ps 40:5; Ro 11:33
[6]The senseless man does not know, Ps 73:22
fools do not understand,
[7]that though the wicked spring up like grass
and all evildoers flourish,
they will be forever destroyed. Ps 37:2
[8]But you, O LORD, are exalted forever.

[9]For surely your enemies, O LORD,
surely your enemies will perish;
all evildoers will be scattered. Ps 68:1
[10]You have exalted my horn[a] like that of a
wild ox; Ps 89:17
fine oils have been poured upon me. Ps 23:5
[11]My eyes have seen the defeat of my
adversaries;
my ears have heard the rout of my wicked
foes. Ps 54:7

[12]The righteous will flourish like a palm tree,
they will grow like a cedar of Lebanon;

LIVING  **INSIGHT**

No one fails to see that growing old has its difficulties and heartaches. It does, indeed. But to see only the hot sands of your desert experience and miss the lovely oasis here and there (though they may be few) is to turn the latter part of your journey through life into an arid, tasteless endurance contest that makes everyone miserable.

(See Psalm 92:12–15.)

[13]planted in the house of the LORD,
they will flourish in the courts of our God.
[14]They will still bear fruit in old age, Jn 15:2
they will stay fresh and green,
[15]proclaiming, "The LORD is upright;

[a]10 *Horn* here symbolizes strength.

he is my Rock, and there is no wickedness
in him." Job 34:10

Psalm 93

1The LORD reigns, he is robed in majesty; Ps 97:1
the LORD is robed in majesty
and is armed with strength. Ps 65:6
The world is firmly established;
it cannot be moved. Ps 96:10
2Your throne was established long ago;
you are from all eternity. Ps 45:6

3The seas have lifted up, O LORD, Ps 96:11
the seas have lifted up their voice;
the seas have lifted up their pounding
waves.
4Mightier than the thunder of the great waters,
mightier than the breakers of the sea—
the LORD on high is mighty.

5Your statutes stand firm;
holiness adorns your house Ps 29:2
for endless days, O LORD.

Psalm 94

1O LORD, the God who avenges, Na 1:2
O God who avenges, shine forth.
2Rise up, O Judge of the earth; Ge 18:25
pay back to the proud what they deserve.
3How long will the wicked, O LORD,
how long will the wicked be jubilant? Ps 13:2

4They pour out arrogant words; Ps 31:18
all the evildoers are full of boasting.
5They crush your people, O LORD; Isa 3:15
they oppress your inheritance.
6They slay the widow and the alien;
they murder the fatherless.
7They say, "The LORD does not see; Ps 10:11
the God of Jacob pays no heed."

8Take heed, you senseless ones among the
people; Ps 92:6
you fools, when will you become wise?
9Does he who implanted the ear not hear?
Does he who formed the eye not see? Ex 4:11
10Does he who disciplines nations not punish?
Does he who teaches man lack knowledge?
11The LORD knows the thoughts of man;
he knows that they are futile. 1Co 3:20*

12Blessed is the man you discipline, O LORD,
the man you teach from your law;
13you grant him relief from days of trouble,
till a pit is dug for the wicked. Ps 55:23
14For the LORD will not reject his people;
he will never forsake his inheritance.

15Judgment will again be founded on
righteousness, Ps 97:2
and all the upright in heart will follow it.

16Who will rise up for me against the wicked?
Who will take a stand for me against
evildoers? Ps 59:2
17Unless the LORD had given me help, Ps 124:2
I would soon have dwelt in the silence of
death.
18When I said, "My foot is slipping," Ps 38:16
your love, O LORD, supported me.
19When anxiety was great within me, Ecc 11:10
your consolation brought joy to my soul.

20Can a corrupt throne be allied with you—
one that brings on misery by its decrees?
21They band together against the righteous
and condemn the innocent to death.
22But the LORD has become my fortress,
and my God the rock in whom I take
refuge. Ps 59:9
23He will repay them for their sins Ps 7:16
and destroy them for their wickedness;
the LORD our God will destroy them.

Psalm 95

1Come, let us sing for joy to the LORD; Ps 5:11
let us shout aloud to the Rock of our
salvation. 2Sa 22:47; Ps 81:1
2Let us come before him with thanksgiving
and extol him with music and song. Ps 81:2

3For the LORD is the great God,
the great King above all gods. Ps 96:4
4In his hand are the depths of the earth,
and the mountain peaks belong to him.
5The sea is his, for he made it,
and his hands formed the dry land. Ge 1:9

6Come, let us bow down in worship, Php 2:10
let us kneel before the LORD our Maker;
7for he is our God
and we are the people of his pasture,
the flock under his care.

Today, if you hear his voice,
8 do not harden your hearts as you did at
Meribah,[a] Ex 17:7
as you did that day at Massah[b] in the
desert,
9where your fathers tested and tried me, Ps 78:18
though they had seen what I did.
10For forty years I was angry with that
generation;
I said, "They are a people whose hearts go
astray, Ps 119:67,176

[a]8 *Meribah* means *quarreling.* [b]8 *Massah* means *testing.*

and they have not known my ways." Dt 8:6
[11]So I declared on oath in my anger,
"They shall never enter my rest." Heb 4:3*

LIVING  **INSIGHT**

We are to be diligent to enter into rest. That doesn't mean we adopt a lazy, irresponsible lifestyle full of indolence and inactivity. No, this is first and foremost a mental rest, a quiet confidence in the living Lord. A refusal to churn, to fret, to strive.
(See Psalm 95:11.)

Psalm 96

[1]Sing to the LORD a new song; 1Ch 16:23
sing to the LORD, all the earth.
[2]Sing to the LORD, praise his name;
proclaim his salvation day after day. Ps 71:15
[3]Declare his glory among the nations, Ps 8:1
his marvelous deeds among all peoples.

[4]For great is the LORD and most worthy of
praise; Ps 18:3; 145:3
he is to be feared above all gods. Ps 95:3
[5]For all the gods of the nations are idols,
but the LORD made the heavens. Ps 115:15
[6]Splendor and majesty are before him;
strength and glory are in his sanctuary.

[7]Ascribe to the LORD, O families of nations,
ascribe to the LORD glory and strength.
[8]Ascribe to the LORD the glory due his name;
bring an offering and come into his courts.
[9]Worship the LORD in the splendor of his[a]
holiness; Ps 29:2
tremble before him, all the earth.

LIVING  **INSIGHT**

There's one fundamental answer to why the church, the body of believers, exists. The church's primary purpose is to glorify the Lord our God.
(See Psalm 96:4–9.)

[10]Say among the nations, "The LORD reigns."
The world is firmly established, it cannot be
moved; Ps 93:1
he will judge the peoples with equity. Ps 67:4
[11]Let the heavens rejoice, let the earth be glad;
let the sea resound, and all that is in it;
[12]let the fields be jubilant, and everything in
them.
Then all the trees of the forest will sing for
joy; Ps 65:13
[13]they will sing before the LORD, for he
comes,
he comes to judge the earth. Rev 19:11
He will judge the world in righteousness
and the peoples in his truth. Ps 86:11

Psalm 97

[1]The LORD reigns, let the earth be glad; Ps 96:10
let the distant shores rejoice.

[2]Clouds and thick darkness surround him;
righteousness and justice are the foundation
of his throne. Ps 89:14
[3]Fire goes before him
and consumes his foes on every side. Ps 18:8
[4]His lightning lights up the world;
the earth sees and trembles.
[5]The mountains melt like wax before the LORD,
before the Lord of all the earth.
[6]The heavens proclaim his righteousness, Ps 50:6
and all the peoples see his glory. Ps 19:1

[7]All who worship images are put to shame,
those who boast in idols—
worship him, all you gods! Heb 1:6

[8]Zion hears and rejoices
and the villages of Judah are glad
because of your judgments, O LORD. Ps 48:11
[9]For you, O LORD, are the Most High over all
the earth; Ps 83:18; 95:3
you are exalted far above all gods. Ex 18:11

[10]Let those who love the LORD hate evil, Ps 34:14
for he guards the lives of his faithful ones
and delivers them from the hand of the
wicked. Ps 37:40; Da 3:28
[11]Light is shed upon the righteous Job 22:28
and joy on the upright in heart.
[12]Rejoice in the LORD, you who are righteous,
and praise his holy name. Ps 30:4

Psalm 98

A psalm.

[1]Sing to the LORD a new song, Ps 96:1
for he has done marvelous things;
his right hand and his holy arm Ex 15:6; Isa 52:10
have worked salvation for him.
[2]The LORD has made his salvation known
and revealed his righteousness to the
nations.

[a]9 Or *LORD with the splendor of*

3He has remembered his love Lk 1:54
and his faithfulness to the house of Israel;
all the ends of the earth have seen
the salvation of our God. Ps 50:23

4Shout for joy to the LORD, all the earth,
burst into jubilant song with music;
5make music to the LORD with the harp, Ps 92:3
with the harp and the sound of singing,
6with trumpets and the blast of the ram's
horn— Nu 10:10
shout for joy before the LORD, the King.

7Let the sea resound, and everything in it,
the world, and all who live in it. Ps 24:1
8Let the rivers clap their hands,
let the mountains sing together for joy;
9let them sing before the LORD,
for he comes to judge the earth.
He will judge the world in righteousness
and the peoples with equity. Ps 96:10

Psalm 99

1The LORD reigns, Ps 97:1
let the nations tremble;
he sits enthroned between the cherubim,
let the earth shake.
2Great is the LORD in Zion;
he is exalted over all the nations. Ps 97:9
3Let them praise your great and awesome
name— Ps 76:1
he is holy.

4The King is mighty, he loves justice— Ps 11:7
you have established equity; Ps 98:9
in Jacob you have done
what is just and right.
5Exalt the LORD our God Ps 132:7
and worship at his footstool;
he is holy.

6Moses and Aaron were among his priests,
Samuel was among those who called on his
name; Jer 15:1
they called on the LORD
and he answered them. 1Sa 7:9
7He spoke to them from the pillar of cloud;
they kept his statutes and the decrees he
gave them.

8O LORD our God,
you answered them;
you were to Israel[a] a forgiving God, Nu 14:20
though you punished their misdeeds.[b]
9Exalt the LORD our God
and worship at his holy mountain,
for the LORD our God is holy.

Psalm 100

A psalm. For giving thanks.

1Shout for joy to the LORD, all the earth. Ps 98:4
2 Worship the LORD with gladness;
come before him with joyful songs. Ps 95:2
3Know that the LORD is God. Ps 46:10
It is he who made us, and we are his[c];
we are his people, the sheep of his pasture.

4Enter his gates with thanksgiving
and his courts with praise;
give thanks to him and praise his name.
5For the LORD is good and his love endures
forever; Ps 25:8
his faithfulness continues through all
generations. Ps 119:90

Psalm 101

Of David. A psalm.

1I will sing of your love and justice; Ps 89:1
to you, O LORD, I will sing praise.
2I will be careful to lead a blameless life—
when will you come to me?

I will walk in my house
with blameless heart.
3I will set before my eyes
no vile thing. Dt 15:9

The deeds of faithless men I hate; Ps 40:4
they will not cling to me.
4Men of perverse heart shall be far from me;
I will have nothing to do with evil.

5Whoever slanders his neighbor in secret,
him will I put to silence;
whoever has haughty eyes and a proud heart,
him will I not endure.

6My eyes will be on the faithful in the land,
that they may dwell with me;
he whose walk is blameless Ps 119:1
will minister to me.

7No one who practices deceit
will dwell in my house;
no one who speaks falsely
will stand in my presence.

8Every morning I will put to silence Jer 21:12
all the wicked in the land; Ps 75:10
I will cut off every evildoer Ps 118:10-12
from the city of the LORD.

[a]8 Hebrew *them* [b]8 Or / *an avenger of the wrongs done to them* [c]3 Or *and not we ourselves*

Psalm 102

A prayer of an afflicted man. When he is faint and pours out his lament before the LORD.

[1]Hear my prayer, O LORD;
let my cry for help come to you. Ex 2:23
[2]Do not hide your face from me Ps 69:17
when I am in distress.
Turn your ear to me; 2Ki 19:16
when I call, answer me quickly.

LIVING  **INSIGHT**

Some situations cannot be solved by a person or through some nice-sounding principle; they must be endured until God steps in and brings relief.
(See Psalm 102:1–2.)

[3]For my days vanish like smoke; Jas 4:14
my bones burn like glowing embers.
[4]My heart is blighted and withered like grass;
I forget to eat my food.
[5]Because of my loud groaning
I am reduced to skin and bones.
[6]I am like a desert owl, Isa 34:11
like an owl among the ruins.
[7]I lie awake; I have become Ps 77:4
like a bird alone on a roof.
[8]All day long my enemies taunt me; Ps 42:10
those who rail against me use my name as a curse.
[9]For I eat ashes as my food
and mingle my drink with tears Ps 42:3
[10]because of your great wrath,
for you have taken me up and thrown me aside.
[11]My days are like the evening shadow; Job 14:2
I wither away like grass.

[12]But you, O LORD, sit enthroned forever; Ps 9:7
your renown endures through all generations. Ps 135:13
[13]You will arise and have compassion on Zion,
for it is time to show favor to her;
the appointed time has come. Ex 13:10
[14]For her stones are dear to your servants;
her very dust moves them to pity.
[15]The nations will fear the name of the LORD,
all the kings of the earth will revere your glory.
[16]For the LORD will rebuild Zion
and appear in his glory. Isa 60:1-2
[17]He will respond to the prayer of the destitute;
he will not despise their plea.

[18]Let this be written for a future generation,
that a people not yet created may praise the LORD: Ps 22:31
[19]"The LORD looked down from his sanctuary on high, Dt 26:15
from heaven he viewed the earth,
[20]to hear the groans of the prisoners
and release those condemned to death."
[21]So the name of the LORD will be declared in Zion Ps 22:22
and his praise in Jerusalem
[22]when the peoples and the kingdoms
assemble to worship the LORD. Ps 22:27

[23]In the course of my life[a] he broke my strength;
he cut short my days. Ps 39:5
[24]So I said:
"Do not take me away, O my God, in the midst of my days;
your years go on through all generations.
[25]In the beginning you laid the foundations of the earth, Heb 1:10-12*
and the heavens are the work of your hands.
[26]They will perish, but you remain; Isa 34:4
they will all wear out like a garment.
Like clothing you will change them
and they will be discarded.
[27]But you remain the same, Mal 3:6
and your years will never end.
[28]The children of your servants will live in your presence; Ps 69:36
their descendants will be established before you." Ps 89:4

Psalm 103

Of David.

[1]Praise the LORD, O my soul; Ps 104:1
all my inmost being, praise his holy name.
[2]Praise the LORD, O my soul, Ps 106:1
and forget not all his benefits—
[3]who forgives all your sins Ps 130:8
and heals all your diseases, Ex 15:26
[4]who redeems your life from the pit Ps 34:22
and crowns you with love and compassion,
[5]who satisfies your desires with good things
so that your youth is renewed like the eagle's. Isa 40:31

[6]The LORD works righteousness
and justice for all the oppressed. Ps 74:21

[7]He made known his ways to Moses, Ex 33:13
his deeds to the people of Israel: Ps 106:22
[8]The LORD is compassionate and gracious,
slow to anger, abounding in love.

[a] 23 Or *By his power*

[9]He will not always accuse,
nor will he harbor his anger forever; Ps 30:5
[10]he does not treat us as our sins deserve Ezr 9:13
or repay us according to our iniquities.
[11]For as high as the heavens are above the earth,
so great is his love for those who fear him;
[12]as far as the east is from the west,
so far has he removed our transgressions from us. 2Sa 12:13

LIVING  **INSIGHT**

You who truly love God have received His peace and forgiveness, so your guilt has been relieved. And what a relief it is! You don't spend your days wallowing around in how wrong or how badly you feel. You have claimed His mercy. You're free of guilt. You're free to respond in unrestrained praise!

(See Psalm 103:8–12.)

[13]As a father has compassion on his children,
so the LORD has compassion on those who fear him;
[14]for he knows how we are formed, Isa 29:16
he remembers that we are dust.
[15]As for man, his days are like grass,
he flourishes like a flower of the field;
[16]the wind blows over it and it is gone, Isa 40:7
and its place remembers it no more. Job 7:10
[17]But from everlasting to everlasting
the LORD's love is with those who fear him,
and his righteousness with their children's children— Ge 48:11
[18]with those who keep his covenant Dt 29:9
and remember to obey his precepts. Dt 7:9

[19]The LORD has established his throne in heaven,
and his kingdom rules over all. Ps 47:2

[20]Praise the LORD, you his angels, Ps 148:2; Heb 1:14
you mighty ones who do his bidding,
who obey his word.
[21]Praise the LORD, all his heavenly hosts, 1Ki 22:19
you his servants who do his will.
[22]Praise the LORD, all his works Ps 145:10
everywhere in his dominion.

Praise the LORD, O my soul. ver 1; Ps 104:1

Psalm 104

[1]Praise the LORD, O my soul. Ps 103:22

O LORD my God, you are very great;
you are clothed with splendor and majesty.
[2]He wraps himself in light as with a garment;
he stretches out the heavens like a tent
[3] and lays the beams of his upper chambers on their waters. Am 9:6
He makes the clouds his chariot Isa 19:1
and rides on the wings of the wind. Ps 18:10
[4]He makes winds his messengers,[a] Heb 1:7*
flames of fire his servants.

[5]He set the earth on its foundations; Job 26:7
it can never be moved.
[6]You covered it with the deep as with a garment; Ge 1:2; 7:19
the waters stood above the mountains.
[7]But at your rebuke the waters fled, Ps 18:15
at the sound of your thunder they took to flight; Ex 9:23
[8]they flowed over the mountains,
they went down into the valleys,
to the place you assigned for them. Ps 33:7
[9]You set a boundary they cannot cross;
never again will they cover the earth.

[10]He makes springs pour water into the ravines;
it flows between the mountains.
[11]They give water to all the beasts of the field;
the wild donkeys quench their thirst. Ge 16:12
[12]The birds of the air nest by the waters; Mt 8:20
they sing among the branches.
[13]He waters the mountains from his upper chambers; Ps 147:8; Jer 10:13
the earth is satisfied by the fruit of his work.
[14]He makes grass grow for the cattle, Job 38:27
and plants for man to cultivate—
bringing forth food from the earth: Ge 1:30
[15]wine that gladdens the heart of man, Jdg 9:13
oil to make his face shine, Ps 23:5; 92:10; Lk 7:46
and bread that sustains his heart.
[16]The trees of the LORD are well watered,
the cedars of Lebanon that he planted.
[17]There the birds make their nests; ver 12
the stork has its home in the pine trees.
[18]The high mountains belong to the wild goats;
the crags are a refuge for the coneys.[b]

[19]The moon marks off the seasons, Ge 1:14
and the sun knows when to go down.
[20]You bring darkness, it becomes night, Isa 45:7
and all the beasts of the forest prowl.
[21]The lions roar for their prey
and seek their food from God. Job 38:39
[22]The sun rises, and they steal away;
they return and lie down in their dens.
[23]Then man goes out to his work, Ge 3:19
to his labor until evening.

[24]How many are your works, O LORD!

[a]4 Or *angels* [b]18 That is, the hyrax or rock badger

In wisdom you made them all; Pr 3:19
the earth is full of your creatures.
25There is the sea, vast and spacious, Ps 69:34
teeming with creatures beyond number—
living things both large and small.
26There the ships go to and fro,
and the leviathan, which you formed to
frolic there. Job 41:1

27These all look to you
to give them their food at the proper time.
28When you give it to them,
they gather it up;
when you open your hand,
they are satisfied with good things. Ps 145:16
29When you hide your face,
they are terrified; Dt 31:17
when you take away their breath,
they die and return to the dust. Job 34:14
30When you send your Spirit, Ge 1:2
they are created,
and you renew the face of the earth.

31May the glory of the LORD endure forever;
may the LORD rejoice in his works— Ge 1:31
32he who looks at the earth, and it trembles,
who touches the mountains, and they
smoke. Ps 144:5

33I will sing to the LORD all my life; Ps 63:4
I will sing praise to my God as long as I
live.
34May my meditation be pleasing to him, Ps 9:2
as I rejoice in the LORD.
35But may sinners vanish from the earth Ps 37:38
and the wicked be no more.

Praise the LORD, O my soul.

Praise the LORD.[a] Ps 105:45; 106:48

Psalm 105

1Give thanks to the LORD, call on his name;
make known among the nations what he
has done.
2Sing to him, sing praise to him; Ps 96:1
tell of all his wonderful acts.
3Glory in his holy name;
let the hearts of those who seek the LORD
rejoice.
4Look to the LORD and his strength;
seek his face always. Ps 27:8

5Remember the wonders he has done, Ps 40:5
his miracles, and the judgments he
pronounced, Ps 77:11
6O descendants of Abraham his servant,
O sons of Jacob, his chosen ones. Ps 106:5
7He is the LORD our God;
his judgments are in all the earth.

8He remembers his covenant forever, Lk 1:72
the word he commanded, for a thousand
generations,
9the covenant he made with Abraham, Ge 17:2
the oath he swore to Isaac.
10He confirmed it to Jacob as a decree, Ge 28:13-15
to Israel as an everlasting covenant:
11"To you I will give the land of Canaan Ge 13:15
as the portion you will inherit." Nu 34:2

12When they were but few in number, Ge 34:30
few indeed, and strangers in it, Heb 11:9
13they wandered from nation to nation,
from one kingdom to another.
14He allowed no one to oppress them; Ge 35:5
for their sake he rebuked kings: Ge 12:17-20
15"Do not touch my anointed ones;
do my prophets no harm."

16He called down famine on the land Lev 26:26
and destroyed all their supplies of food;
17and he sent a man before them—
Joseph, sold as a slave. Ge 37:28
18They bruised his feet with shackles,
his neck was put in irons,
19till what he foretold came to pass, Ge 40:20-22
till the word of the LORD proved him true.
20The king sent and released him,
the ruler of peoples set him free. Ge 41:14
21He made him master of his household,
ruler over all he possessed,
22to instruct his princes as he pleased Ge 41:43-44
and teach his elders wisdom.

23Then Israel entered Egypt; Ge 46:6
Jacob lived as an alien in the land of Ham.
24The LORD made his people very fruitful;
he made them too numerous for their foes,
25whose hearts he turned to hate his people,
to conspire against his servants.
26He sent Moses his servant, Ex 3:10
and Aaron, whom he had chosen.
27They performed his miraculous signs among
them, Ex 7:8-12:51
his wonders in the land of Ham.
28He sent darkness and made the land dark—
for had they not rebelled against his words?
29He turned their waters into blood,
causing their fish to die. Ex 7:21
30Their land teemed with frogs, Ex 8:2,6
which went up into the bedrooms of their
rulers.
31He spoke, and there came swarms of flies,
and gnats throughout their country.
32He turned their rain into hail, Ex 9:22-25
with lightning throughout their land;
33he struck down their vines and fig trees
and shattered the trees of their country.
34He spoke, and the locusts came, Ex 10:4,12-15

[a] *35* Hebrew *Hallelu Yah*; in the Septuagint this line stands at the beginning of Psalm 105.

grasshoppers without number;
35they ate up every green thing in their land,
ate up the produce of their soil.
36Then he struck down all the firstborn in their
land, Ex 12:29
the firstfruits of all their manhood.

37He brought out Israel, laden with silver and
gold, Ex 12:35
and from among their tribes no one
faltered.
38Egypt was glad when they left,
because dread of Israel had fallen on them.
39He spread out a cloud as a covering, Ex 13:21
and a fire to give light at night.
40They asked, and he brought them quail Ex 16:13
and satisfied them with the bread of
heaven.
41He opened the rock, and water gushed out;
like a river it flowed in the desert.

42For he remembered his holy promise Ge 15:13-16
given to his servant Abraham.
43He brought out his people with rejoicing,
his chosen ones with shouts of joy;
44he gave them the lands of the nations, Jos 13:6-7
and they fell heir to what others had toiled
for—
45that they might keep his precepts
and observe his laws. Dt 4:40; 6:21-24

Praise the LORD.[a] Ps 104:35

Psalm 106

1Praise the LORD.[b] Ps 22:23

Give thanks to the LORD, for he is good;
his love endures forever. Jer 33:11
2Who can proclaim the mighty acts of the
LORD Ps 145:4,12
or fully declare his praise?
3Blessed are they who maintain justice,
who constantly do what is right. Ps 15:2
4Remember me, O LORD, when you show favor
to your people, Ps 119:132
come to my aid when you save them,
5that I may enjoy the prosperity of your
chosen ones, Ps 1:3
that I may share in the joy of your nation
and join your inheritance in giving praise.

6We have sinned, even as our fathers did; Da 9:5
we have done wrong and acted wickedly.
7When our fathers were in Egypt,
they gave no thought to your miracles;
they did not remember your many kindnesses,
and they rebelled by the sea, the Red Sea.[c]
8Yet he saved them for his name's sake, Ex 9:16
to make his mighty power known.
9He rebuked the Red Sea, and it dried up;
he led them through the depths as through
a desert. Isa 63:11-14
10He saved them from the hand of the foe;
from the hand of the enemy he redeemed
them.
11The waters covered their adversaries; Ex 14:28
not one of them survived.
12Then they believed his promises
and sang his praise.

13But they soon forgot what he had done Ex 15:24
and did not wait for his counsel.
14In the desert they gave in to their craving;
in the wasteland they put God to the test.
15So he gave them what they asked for, Nu 11:31
but sent a wasting disease upon them.

16In the camp they grew envious of Moses
and of Aaron, who was consecrated to the
LORD.
17The earth opened up and swallowed Dathan;
it buried the company of Abiram.
18Fire blazed among their followers;
a flame consumed the wicked. Nu 16:35

19At Horeb they made a calf Ex 32:4
and worshiped an idol cast from metal.
20They exchanged their Glory Jer 2:11; Ro 1:23
for an image of a bull, which eats grass.
21They forgot the God who saved them, Ps 78:11
who had done great things in Egypt,
22miracles in the land of Ham Ps 105:27
and awesome deeds by the Red Sea.
23So he said he would destroy them— Ex 32:10
had not Moses, his chosen one,
stood in the breach before him
to keep his wrath from destroying them.

24Then they despised the pleasant land; Dt 8:7
they did not believe his promise. Heb 3:18-19
25They grumbled in their tents Nu 14:2
and did not obey the LORD.
26So he swore to them with uplifted hand
that he would make them fall in the desert,
27make their descendants fall among the nations
and scatter them throughout the lands.

28They yoked themselves to the Baal of Peor
and ate sacrifices offered to lifeless gods;
29they provoked the LORD to anger by their
wicked deeds,
and a plague broke out among them.
30But Phinehas stood up and intervened,
and the plague was checked. Nu 25:8
31This was credited to him as righteousness
for endless generations to come.

[a]45 Hebrew *Hallelu Yah* [b]1 Hebrew *Hallelu Yah*; also in verse 48 [c]7 Hebrew *Yam Suph*; that is, Sea of Reeds; also in verses 9 and 22

[32]By the waters of Meribah they angered the LORD, Nu 20:2-13
and trouble came to Moses because of them;
[33]for they rebelled against the Spirit of God,
and rash words came from Moses' lips.[a]

[34]They did not destroy the peoples Jdg 1:21
as the LORD had commanded them, Dt 7:16
[35]but they mingled with the nations Jdg 3:5-6
and adopted their customs.
[36]They worshiped their idols, Jdg 2:12
which became a snare to them.
[37]They sacrificed their sons
and their daughters to demons.
[38]They shed innocent blood,
the blood of their sons and daughters,
whom they sacrificed to the idols of Canaan,
and the land was desecrated by their blood.
[39]They defiled themselves by what they did;
by their deeds they prostituted themselves.

[40]Therefore the LORD was angry with his people
and abhorred his inheritance.
[41]He handed them over to the nations, Jdg 2:14
and their foes ruled over them.
[42]Their enemies oppressed them
and subjected them to their power.
[43]Many times he delivered them,
but they were bent on rebellion Jdg 2:16-19
and they wasted away in their sin.

[44]But he took note of their distress
when he heard their cry; Jdg 10:10
[45]for their sake he remembered his covenant
and out of his great love he relented. Jdg 2:18
[46]He caused them to be pitied Ezr 9:9; Jer 42:12
by all who held them captive.

[47]Save us, O LORD our God,
and gather us from the nations, Ps 147:2
that we may give thanks to your holy name
and glory in your praise.

[48]Praise be to the LORD, the God of Israel,
from everlasting to everlasting.
Let all the people say, "Amen!" Ps 41:13

Praise the LORD.

BOOK V

Psalms 107–150

Psalms of God's Word Psalms 107–150

The final 44 hymns revolve around the power, blessing and importance of God's Holy Word. It is in this final book that we find the longest psalm in the Bible—Psalm 119. The praise of God's Word goes on for an astounding 176 verses. As you read this song you will find no less than 174 references to the beauty and greatness of Scripture. That's what I call getting the point across! This section of psalms praises the wonderful works of God and His wonderful Word, just as the book of Deuteronomy reviews God's mighty acts and outlines His life-giving laws for godly living. As in the days of old, the best sacrifice we can offer to God is an obedient and faithful life that resounds with glorious praise to Him.

Psalm 107

[1]Give thanks to the LORD, for he is good;
his love endures forever.
[2]Let the redeemed of the LORD say this—
those he redeemed from the hand of the foe,
[3]those he gathered from the lands, Ps 106:47
from east and west, from north and south.[b]

[4]Some wandered in desert wastelands, Nu 14:33
finding no way to a city where they could settle.
[5]They were hungry and thirsty, Ex 15:22
and their lives ebbed away.
[6]Then they cried out to the LORD in their trouble, Ps 50:15
and he delivered them from their distress.
[7]He led them by a straight way Ezr 8:21
to a city where they could settle.
[8]Let them give thanks to the LORD for his unfailing love Ps 6:4
and his wonderful deeds for men, Ps 75:1
[9]for he satisfies the thirsty Lk 1:53
and fills the hungry with good things.

[10]Some sat in darkness and the deepest gloom,
prisoners suffering in iron chains, Job 36:8
[11]for they had rebelled against the words of God
and despised the counsel of the Most High.
[12]So he subjected them to bitter labor;
they stumbled, and there was no one to help. Ps 22:11
[13]Then they cried to the LORD in their trouble,
and he saved them from their distress.
[14]He brought them out of darkness and the deepest gloom
and broke away their chains. Ac 12:7
[15]Let them give thanks to the LORD for his unfailing love Ps 105:1
and his wonderful deeds for men, Ps 75:1
[16]for he breaks down gates of bronze
and cuts through bars of iron.

[17]Some became fools through their rebellious ways
and suffered affliction because of their iniquities. Isa 65:6-7; La 3:39
[18]They loathed all food

[a]33 Or *against his spirit, / and rash words came from his lips*

[b]3 Hebrew *north and the sea*

and drew near the gates of death. Ps 9:13
19Then they cried to the LORD in their trouble,
and he saved them from their distress.
20He sent forth his word and healed them;
he rescued them from the grave. Ps 30:3
21Let them give thanks to the LORD for his
unfailing love
and his wonderful deeds for men.
22Let them sacrifice thank offerings Lev 7:12
and tell of his works with songs of joy.

23Others went out on the sea in ships;
they were merchants on the mighty waters.
24They saw the works of the LORD, Ps 64:9
his wonderful deeds in the deep.
25For he spoke and stirred up a tempest Jnh 1:4
that lifted high the waves. Ps 93:3
26They mounted up to the heavens and went
down to the depths;
in their peril their courage melted away.
27They reeled and staggered like drunken men;
they were at their wits' end.
28Then they cried out to the LORD in their
trouble,
and he brought them out of their distress.
29He stilled the storm to a whisper; Mt 8:26
the waves of the sea were hushed. Ps 89:9
30They were glad when it grew calm,
and he guided them to their desired haven.
31Let them give thanks to the LORD for his
unfailing love Ps 6:4
and his wonderful deeds for men.
32Let them exalt him in the assembly of the
people Ps 22:22,25; 35:18
and praise him in the council of the elders.

33He turned rivers into a desert, 1Ki 17:1; Ps 74:15
flowing springs into thirsty ground,
34and fruitful land into a salt waste, Ge 13:10
because of the wickedness of those who
lived there.
35He turned the desert into pools of water
and the parched ground into flowing
springs;
36there he brought the hungry to live,
and they founded a city where they could
settle.
37They sowed fields and planted vineyards
that yielded a fruitful harvest;
38he blessed them, and their numbers greatly
increased, Ge 12:2
and he did not let their herds diminish.

39Then their numbers decreased, and they were
humbled 2Ki 10:32; Eze 5:12
by oppression, calamity and sorrow;
40he who pours contempt on nobles Job 12:21
made them wander in a trackless waste.
41But he lifted the needy out of their affliction
and increased their families like flocks.
42The upright see and rejoice, Job 22:19
but all the wicked shut their mouths. Job 5:16

43Whoever is wise, let him heed these things
and consider the great love of the LORD.

Psalm 108

A song. A psalm of David.

1My heart is steadfast, O God;
I will sing and make music with all my
soul. Ps 18:49
2Awake, harp and lyre! Job 21:12
I will awaken the dawn.
3I will praise you, O LORD, among the nations;
I will sing of you among the peoples.
4For great is your love, higher than the
heavens;
your faithfulness reaches to the skies. Ps 36:5
5Be exalted, O God, above the heavens, Ps 8:1
and let your glory be over all the earth.
6Save us and help us with your right hand,
that those you love may be delivered.
7God has spoken from his sanctuary: Ps 68:35
"In triumph I will parcel out Shechem
and measure off the Valley of Succoth.
8Gilead is mine, Manasseh is mine;
Ephraim is my helmet,
Judah my scepter. Ge 49:10
9Moab is my washbasin,
upon Edom I toss my sandal; 2Sa 8:13-14
over Philistia I shout in triumph." 2Sa 8:1
10Who will bring me to the fortified city?
Who will lead me to Edom?
11Is it not you, O God, you who have rejected
us
and no longer go out with our armies?
12Give us aid against the enemy,
for the help of man is worthless. Ps 118:8
13With God we will gain the victory,
and he will trample down our enemies.

Psalm 109

For the director of music. Of David. A psalm.

1O God, whom I praise,
do not remain silent, Ps 83:1
2for wicked and deceitful men Ps 43:1
have opened their mouths against me;
they have spoken against me with lying
tongues. Ps 120:2
3With words of hatred they surround me;
they attack me without cause.
4In return for my friendship they accuse me,
but I am a man of prayer.
5They repay me evil for good, Ps 35:12; 38:20
and hatred for my friendship.

[6]Appoint[a] an evil man[b] to oppose him;
let an accuser[c] stand at his right hand.
[7]When he is tried, let him be found guilty,
and may his prayers condemn him. Pr 28:9
[8]May his days be few;
may another take his place of leadership.
[9]May his children be fatherless
and his wife a widow. Ex 22:24
[10]May his children be wandering beggars;
may they be driven[d] from their ruined homes.
[11]May a creditor seize all he has;
may strangers plunder the fruits of his labor. Job 5:5
[12]May no one extend kindness to him
or take pity on his fatherless children.
[13]May his descendants be cut off, Ps 37:28
their names blotted out from the next generation. Pr 10:7
[14]May the iniquity of his fathers be remembered
before the LORD; Ex 20:5; Ne 4:5; Jer 18:23
may the sin of his mother never be blotted out.
[15]May their sins always remain before the LORD,
that he may cut off the memory of them
from the earth. Ps 34:16

[16]For he never thought of doing a kindness,
but hounded to death the poor
and the needy and the brokenhearted.
[17]He loved to pronounce a curse—
may it[e] come on him; Pr 14:14
he found no pleasure in blessing—
may it be[f] far from him.
[18]He wore cursing as his garment;
it entered into his body like water, Nu 5:22
into his bones like oil.
[19]May it be like a cloak wrapped about him,
like a belt tied forever around him.
[20]May this be the LORD's payment to my
accusers, Ps 94:23; 2Ti 4:14
to those who speak evil of me. Ps 71:10

[21]But you, O Sovereign LORD,
deal well with me for your name's sake;
out of the goodness of your love, deliver
me. Ps 69:16
[22]For I am poor and needy,
and my heart is wounded within me.
[23]I fade away like an evening shadow; Ps 102:11
I am shaken off like a locust.
[24]My knees give way from fasting; Heb 12:12
my body is thin and gaunt.
[25]I am an object of scorn to my accusers; Ps 22:6
when they see me, they shake their heads.

[26]Help me, O LORD my God;
save me in accordance with your love.
[27]Let them know that it is your hand, Job 37:7
that you, O LORD, have done it.
[28]They may curse, but you will bless; 2Sa 16:12
when they attack they will be put to shame,
but your servant will rejoice. Isa 65:14
[29]My accusers will be clothed with disgrace
and wrapped in shame as in a cloak. Ps 35:26

[30]With my mouth I will greatly extol the LORD;
in the great throng I will praise him.
[31]For he stands at the right hand of the needy
one, Ps 16:8
to save his life from those who condemn
him.

Psalm 110

Of David. A psalm.

[1]The LORD says to my Lord: Mt 22:44*; Ac 2:34*
"Sit at my right hand
until I make your enemies
a footstool for your feet." 1Co 15:25

[2]The LORD will extend your mighty scepter
from Zion; Ps 45:6
you will rule in the midst of your enemies.
[3]Your troops will be willing
on your day of battle.
Arrayed in holy majesty, Jdg 5:2; Ps 96:9
from the womb of the dawn
you will receive the dew of your youth.[g]

[4]The LORD has sworn
and will not change his mind: Nu 23:19
"You are a priest forever, Heb 5:6*; 7:21*
in the order of Melchizedek." Heb 7:15-17*

[5]The Lord is at your right hand; Ps 16:8
he will crush kings on the day of his wrath.
[6]He will judge the nations, heaping up the
dead Isa 2:4
and crushing the rulers of the whole earth.
[7]He will drink from a brook beside the way[h];
therefore he will lift up his head. Ps 27:6

Psalm 111

[1]Praise the LORD.[j]

I will extol the LORD with all my heart Ps 34:1
in the council of the upright and in the
assembly.

[2]Great are the works of the LORD; Ps 92:5

[a]6 Or ⌊They say:⌋ "Appoint (with quotation marks at the end of verse 19) [b]6 Or *the Evil One* [c]6 Or *let Satan* [d]10 Septuagint; Hebrew *sought* [e]17 Or *curse, / and it has* [f]17 Or *blessing, / and it is* [g]3 Or */ your young men will come to you like the dew* [h]7 Or */ The One who grants succession will set him in authority* [i]This psalm is an acrostic poem, the lines of which begin with the successive letters of the Hebrew alphabet. [j]1 Hebrew *Hallelu Yah*

they are pondered by all who delight in
them.
[3]Glorious and majestic are his deeds,
and his righteousness endures forever.
[4]He has caused his wonders to be remembered;
the LORD is gracious and compassionate.
[5]He provides food for those who fear him;
he remembers his covenant forever.
[6]He has shown his people the power of his
works,
giving them the lands of other nations.
[7]The works of his hands are faithful and just;
all his precepts are trustworthy. Ps 19:7
[8]They are steadfast for ever and ever,
done in faithfulness and uprightness.
[9]He provided redemption for his people; Lk 1:68
he ordained his covenant forever—
holy and awesome is his name. Ps 99:3

[10]The fear of the LORD is the beginning of
wisdom; Pr 9:10
all who follow his precepts have good
understanding. Ecc 12:13
To him belongs eternal praise. Ps 145:2

Psalm 112[a]

[1]Praise the LORD.[b] Ps 33:2

Blessed is the man who fears the LORD, Ps 128:1
who finds great delight in his commands.

[2]His children will be mighty in the land; Ps 25:13
the generation of the upright will be
blessed.
[3]Wealth and riches are in his house, Dt 8:18
and his righteousness endures forever.
[4]Even in darkness light dawns for the upright,
for the gracious and compassionate and
righteous man.[c] Ps 97:11
[5]Good will come to him who is generous and
lends freely, Ps 37:21,26
who conducts his affairs with justice.
[6]Surely he will never be shaken;
a righteous man will be remembered
forever. Pr 10:7
[7]He will have no fear of bad news;
his heart is steadfast, trusting in the LORD.
[8]His heart is secure, he will have no fear;
in the end he will look in triumph on his
foes.
[9]He has scattered abroad his gifts to the poor,
his righteousness endures forever;
his horn[d] will be lifted high in honor.

[10]The wicked man will see and be vexed,
he will gnash his teeth and waste away;
the longings of the wicked will come to
nothing. Pr 11:7

Psalm 113

[1]Praise the LORD.[e]

Praise, O servants of the LORD, Ps 135:1
praise the name of the LORD.
[2]Let the name of the LORD be praised,
both now and forevermore. Da 2:20
[3]From the rising of the sun to the place where
it sets, Isa 59:19; Mal 1:11
the name of the LORD is to be praised.

[4]The LORD is exalted over all the nations, Ps 99:2
his glory above the heavens. Ps 8:1
[5]Who is like the LORD our God,
the One who sits enthroned on high,
[6]who stoops down to look Ps 11:4; 138:6; Isa 57:15
on the heavens and the earth?

[7]He raises the poor from the dust 1Sa 2:8
and lifts the needy from the ash heap;
[8]he seats them with princes,
with the princes of their people.
[9]He settles the barren woman in her home
as a happy mother of children.

Praise the LORD.

Psalm 114

[1]When Israel came out of Egypt, Ex 13:3
the house of Jacob from a people of foreign
tongue,
[2]Judah became God's sanctuary, Ex 15:17
Israel his dominion.

[3]The sea looked and fled, Ex 14:21
the Jordan turned back;
[4]the mountains skipped like rams,
the hills like lambs.

[5]Why was it, O sea, that you fled, Ex 14:21
O Jordan, that you turned back,
[6]you mountains, that you skipped like rams,
you hills, like lambs?

[7]Tremble, O earth, at the presence of the Lord,
at the presence of the God of Jacob,
[8]who turned the rock into a pool,
the hard rock into springs of water. Ex 17:6

Psalm 115

[1]Not to us, O LORD, not to us
but to your name be the glory, Ps 96:8
because of your love and faithfulness. Ex 34:6

[a]This psalm is an acrostic poem, the lines of which begin with the successive letters of the Hebrew alphabet. [b]*1* Hebrew *Hallelu Yah* [c]*4* Or / *for* ⌞*the LORD*⌟ *is gracious and compassionate and righteous* [d]*9* *Horn* here symbolizes dignity.
[e]*1* Hebrew *Hallelu Yah*; also in verse 9

[2]Why do the nations say,
"Where is their God?" Ps 42:3
[3]Our God is in heaven;
he does whatever pleases him. Ps 103:19; Ps 135:6

LIVING  INSIGHT

Do you want to learn a verse of Scripture that will save you from months, if not years, of discouragement and bitterness. Learn Psalm 115:3. "Our God is in heaven; he does whatever pleases him." Nothing, nothing, has happened on this earth that has not passed through His permissive and directed will. This truth will change your perspective on life's heartaches, disappointments and losses.

(See Psalm 115:1–3.)

[4]But their idols are silver and gold,
made by the hands of men. Jer 10:3-5
[5]They have mouths, but cannot speak, Jer 10:5
eyes, but they cannot see;
[6]they have ears, but cannot hear,
noses, but they cannot smell;
[7]they have hands, but cannot feel,
feet, but they cannot walk;
nor can they utter a sound with their throats.
[8]Those who make them will be like them,
and so will all who trust in them.

[9]O house of Israel, trust in the LORD— Ps 37:3
he is their help and shield.
[10]O house of Aaron, trust in the LORD— Ps 118:3
he is their help and shield.
[11]You who fear him, trust in the LORD— Ps 22:23
he is their help and shield.

[12]The LORD remembers us and will bless us:
He will bless the house of Israel,
he will bless the house of Aaron,
[13]he will bless those who fear the LORD—
small and great alike.

[14]May the LORD make you increase,
both you and your children.
[15]May you be blessed by the LORD,
the Maker of heaven and earth. Ps 96:5

[16]The highest heavens belong to the LORD,
but the earth he has given to man.
[17]It is not the dead who praise the LORD, Ps 6:5
those who go down to silence;
[18]it is we who extol the LORD,
both now and forevermore. Ps 113:2

Praise the LORD.[a] Ps 28:6

Psalm 116

[1]I love the LORD, for he heard my voice; Ps 18:1
he heard my cry for mercy. Ps 66:19
[2]Because he turned his ear to me, Ps 40:1
I will call on him as long as I live.

[3]The cords of death entangled me, Ps 18:4-5
the anguish of the grave[b] came upon me;
I was overcome by trouble and sorrow.
[4]Then I called on the name of the LORD: Ps 118:5
"O LORD, save me!" Ps 22:20

[5]The LORD is gracious and righteous; Ezr 9:15
our God is full of compassion.
[6]The LORD protects the simplehearted;
when I was in great need, he saved me.

[7]Be at rest once more, O my soul, Mt 11:29
for the LORD has been good to you. Ps 13:6

[8]For you, O LORD, have delivered my soul from
death, Ps 56:13
my eyes from tears,
my feet from stumbling,
[9]that I may walk before the LORD
in the land of the living. Ps 27:13
[10]I believed; therefore[c] I said, 2Co 4:13*
"I am greatly afflicted."
[11]And in my dismay I said,
"All men are liars." Ro 3:4

[12]How can I repay the LORD
for all his goodness to me?
[13]I will lift up the cup of salvation
and call on the name of the LORD.
[14]I will fulfill my vows to the LORD Ps 22:25
in the presence of all his people.

[15]Precious in the sight of the LORD Ps 72:14
is the death of his saints.
[16]O LORD, truly I am your servant; Ps 119:125; 143:12

LIVING  INSIGHT

Every believer in Jesus Christ who goes home to be with the Lord has this unshakable and marvelous future in front of him or her. Every burial is a reminder that life is merely a temporary abode for this body. Never, ever doubt it: This body will be raised and will be changed. What a future God has planned for those who love Him and live lives pleasing to Him!

(See Psalm 116:15.)

[a]18 Hebrew *Hallelu Yah* [b]3 Hebrew *Sheol* [c]10 Or *believed even when*

I am your servant, the son of your
maidservant[a]; Ps 86:16
you have freed me from my chains.
17 I will sacrifice a thank offering to you Ps 50:14
and call on the name of the LORD.
18 I will fulfill my vows to the LORD
in the presence of all his people,
19 in the courts of the house of the LORD—
in your midst, O Jerusalem.

Praise the LORD.[b]

Psalm 117

1 Praise the LORD, all you nations; Ro 15:11*
extol him, all you peoples.
2 For great is his love toward us,
and the faithfulness of the LORD endures
forever. Ps 100:5

Praise the LORD.[b]

Psalm 118

1 Give thanks to the LORD, for he is good;
his love endures forever. Ps 106:1; 136:1

2 Let Israel say: Ps 115:9
"His love endures forever."
3 Let the house of Aaron say:
"His love endures forever."
4 Let those who fear the LORD say: Ps 115:11
"His love endures forever."

5 In my anguish I cried to the LORD, Ps 120:1
and he answered by setting me free.
6 The LORD is with me; I will not be afraid.
What can man do to me? Ps 56:4
7 The LORD is with me; he is my helper.
I will look in triumph on my enemies.

8 It is better to take refuge in the LORD
than to trust in man. Ps 40:4
9 It is better to take refuge in the LORD
than to trust in princes. Ps 146:3

10 All the nations surrounded me,
but in the name of the LORD I cut them off.
11 They surrounded me on every side, Ps 3:6; 88:17
but in the name of the LORD I cut them off.
12 They swarmed around me like bees, Dt 1:44
but they died out as quickly as burning
thorns;
in the name of the LORD I cut them off.

13 I was pushed back and about to fall,
but the LORD helped me.
14 The LORD is my strength and my song; Ex 15:2
he has become my salvation. Isa 12:2

15 Shouts of joy and victory
resound in the tents of the righteous:
"The LORD's right hand has done mighty
things! Ps 89:13
16 The LORD's right hand is lifted high;
the LORD's right hand has done mighty
things!"

17 I will not die but live, Hab 1:12
and will proclaim what the LORD has
done.
18 The LORD has chastened me severely,
but he has not given me over to death.
19 Open for me the gates of righteousness; Isa 26:2
I will enter and give thanks to the LORD.
20 This is the gate of the LORD
through which the righteous may enter.
21 I will give you thanks, for you answered
me;
you have become my salvation.

22 The stone the builders rejected
has become the capstone; Mt 21:42; Lk 20:17*
23 the LORD has done this,
and it is marvelous in our eyes. Mt 21:42*
24 This is the day the LORD has made;
let us rejoice and be glad in it. Ps 70:4

LIVING  **INSIGHT**

Times may be hard and people may be demanding, but never forget that life is special. All of life. The pleasurable days as well as the painful ones. The Wednesdays as well as the weekends. Every single day is a special day. God is at work in us!

(See Psalm 118:24.)

25 O LORD, save us;
O LORD, grant us success.
26 Blessed is he who comes in the name of the
LORD. Mt 21:9*; Jn 12:13*
From the house of the LORD we bless you.[c]
27 The LORD is God,
and he has made his light shine upon us.
With boughs in hand, join in the festal
procession
up[d] to the horns of the altar. Ex 27:2

28 You are my God, and I will give you thanks;
you are my God, and I will exalt you.

29 Give thanks to the LORD, for he is good;
his love endures forever.

[a] 16 Or *servant, your faithful son* [b] 19,2 Hebrew *Hallelu Yah* [c] 26 The Hebrew is plural. [d] 27 Or *Bind the festal sacrifice with ropes / and take it*

Psalm 119[a]

א Aleph

1Blessed are they whose ways are blameless,
who walk according to the law of the LORD.
2Blessed are they who keep his statutes
and seek him with all their heart. Dt 6:5
3They do nothing wrong; Jn 3:9; 5:18
they walk in his ways. Ps 128:1
4You have laid down precepts Ps 103:18
that are to be fully obeyed. Dt 6:17
5Oh, that my ways were steadfast
in obeying your decrees! Lev 19:37
6Then I would not be put to shame
when I consider all your commands. ver 117
7I will praise you with an upright heart
as I learn your righteous laws. Dt 4:8
8I will obey your decrees;
do not utterly forsake me. Ps 38:21

ב Beth

9How can a young man keep his way pure?
By living according to your word. 2Ch 6:16
10I seek you with all my heart; 2Ch 15:15
do not let me stray from your commands.
11I have hidden your word in my heart Ps 37:31
that I might not sin against you.
12Praise be to you, O LORD;
teach me your decrees.
13With my lips I recount
all the laws that come from your mouth.
14I rejoice in following your statutes
as one rejoices in great riches.
15I meditate on your precepts Ps 1:2
and consider your ways.
16I delight in your decrees; Ps 1:2
I will not neglect your word.

LIVING  **INSIGHT**

Scripture memory gives you a firm grasp of the Word—and allows the Word to get a firm grasp of you.
(See Psalm 119:9–16.)

ג Gimel

17Do good to your servant, and I will live;
I will obey your word.
18Open my eyes that I may see
wonderful things in your law.
19I am a stranger on earth; 1Ch 29:15; Ps 39:12; Heb 11:13
do not hide your commands from me.
20My soul is consumed with longing Ps 42:2; 84:2
for your laws at all times. Ps 63:1
21You rebuke the arrogant, who are cursed
and who stray from your commands. ver 10
22Remove from me scorn and contempt, Ps 39:8
for I keep your statutes.
23Though rulers sit together and slander me,
your servant will meditate on your decrees.
24Your statutes are my delight;
they are my counselors.

ד Daleth

25I am laid low in the dust; Ps 44:25
preserve my life according to your word.
26I recounted my ways and you answered me;
teach me your decrees. Ps 25:4
27Let me understand the teaching of your
precepts;
then I will meditate on your wonders.
28My soul is weary with sorrow; Ps 107:26
strengthen me according to your word.
29Keep me from deceitful ways; Ps 26:4
be gracious to me through your law. Nu 6:25
30I have chosen the way of truth; Ps 26:3
I have set my heart on your laws. Ps 108:1
31I hold fast to your statutes, O LORD; Dt 10:20
do not let me be put to shame.
32I run in the path of your commands,
for you have set my heart free.

ה He

33Teach me, O LORD, to follow your decrees;
then I will keep them to the end.
34Give me understanding, and I will keep your
law Dt 6:25
and obey it with all my heart.
35Direct me in the path of your commands,
for there I find delight. Ps 1:2
36Turn my heart toward your statutes
and not toward selfish gain. Lk 12:15; Heb 13:5
37Turn my eyes away from worthless things;
preserve my life according to your word.[b]
38Fulfill your promise to your servant, 2Sa 7:25
so that you may be feared.
39Take away the disgrace I dread, Ps 69:9
for your laws are good.
40How I long for your precepts! ver 20
Preserve my life in your righteousness.

ו Waw

41May your unfailing love come to me, O LORD,
your salvation according to your promise;
42then I will answer the one who taunts me,
for I trust in your word.
43Do not snatch the word of truth from my
mouth,
for I have put my hope in your laws.
44I will always obey your law, Dt 6:25

[a]This psalm is an acrostic poem; the verses of each stanza begin with the same letter of the Hebrew alphabet. [b]*37* Two manuscripts of the Masoretic Text and Dead Sea Scrolls; most manuscripts of the Masoretic Text *life in your way*

for ever and ever.
45I will walk about in freedom,
for I have sought out your precepts.
46I will speak of your statutes before kings
and will not be put to shame,
47for I delight in your commands Ps 112:1
because I love them.
48I lift up my hands to[a] your commands,
which I love,
and I meditate on your decrees. Ge 24:63

ז Zayin

49Remember your word to your servant,
for you have given me hope. ver 43
50My comfort in my suffering is this:
Your promise preserves my life. Ro 15:4
51The arrogant mock me without restraint,
but I do not turn from your law. Job 23:11
52I remember your ancient laws, O LORD,
and I find comfort in them.
53Indignation grips me because of the wicked,
who have forsaken your law. Ps 89:30
54Your decrees are the theme of my song
wherever I lodge.
55In the night I remember your name, O LORD,
and I will keep your law.
56This has been my practice:
I obey your precepts. Nu 15:40

ח Heth

57You are my portion, O LORD; Ps 16:5; La 3:24
I have promised to obey your words.
58I have sought your face with all my heart;
be gracious to me according to your
promise. 1Ki 13:6
59I have considered my ways Lk 15:17-18
and have turned my steps to your statutes.
60I will hasten and not delay
to obey your commands.
61Though the wicked bind me with ropes,
I will not forget your law. Ps 140:5
62At midnight I rise to give you thanks Ac 16:25
for your righteous laws.
63I am a friend to all who fear you, Ps 101:6-7
to all who follow your precepts.
64The earth is filled with your love, O LORD;
teach me your decrees.

ט Teth

65Do good to your servant
according to your word, O LORD. Ps 125:4
66Teach me knowledge and good judgment,
for I believe in your commands.
67Before I was afflicted I went astray, Jer 31:18-19
but now I obey your word.
68You are good, and what you do is good;
teach me your decrees.
69Though the arrogant have smeared me with
lies, Job 13:4
I keep your precepts with all my heart.
70Their hearts are callous and unfeeling, Ps 17:10
but I delight in your law.
71It was good for me to be afflicted ver 67,75
so that I might learn your decrees.
72The law from your mouth is more precious to
me
than thousands of pieces of silver and gold.

י Yodh

73Your hands made me and formed me; Job 10:8
give me understanding to learn your
commands.
74May those who fear you rejoice when they see
me, Ps 34:2
for I have put my hope in your word.
75I know, O LORD, that your laws are righteous,
and in faithfulness you have afflicted me.
76May your unfailing love be my comfort,
according to your promise to your servant.
77Let your compassion come to me that I may
live, ver 41; Ps 90:13
for your law is my delight.
78May the arrogant be put to shame for
wronging me without cause; ver 86,161
but I will meditate on your precepts.
79May those who fear you turn to me,
those who understand your statutes.
80May my heart be blameless toward your
decrees, Ge 26:5
that I may not be put to shame.

כ Kaph

81My soul faints with longing for your salvation,
but I have put my hope in your word.
82My eyes fail, looking for your promise; Ps 69:3
I say, "When will you comfort me?"
83Though I am like a wineskin in the smoke,
I do not forget your decrees.
84How long must your servant wait? Ps 39:4
When will you punish my persecutors?
85The arrogant dig pitfalls for me, Ps 35:7
contrary to your law.
86All your commands are trustworthy; Ps 35:19
help me, for men persecute me without
cause. Ps 109:26
87They almost wiped me from the earth,
but I have not forsaken your precepts.
88Preserve my life according to your love,
and I will obey the statutes of your mouth.

ל Lamedh

89Your word, O LORD, is eternal; Mt 24:34-35; 1Pe 1:25
it stands firm in the heavens.

[a]48 Or *for*

[90]Your faithfulness continues through all
generations;
you established the earth, and it endures.
[91]Your laws endure to this day, Jer 33:25
for all things serve you.
[92]If your law had not been my delight, Ps 37:4
I would have perished in my affliction.
[93]I will never forget your precepts,
for by them you have preserved my life.
[94]Save me, for I am yours;
I have sought out your precepts.
[95]The wicked are waiting to destroy me, Ps 69:4
but I will ponder your statutes.
[96]To all perfection I see a limit;
but your commands are boundless. Ps 19:7

LIVING  INSIGHT

The Scriptures give us our standard. That's a given. The truths of God are our sure foundation.
(See Psalm 119:89–96.)

מ Mem

[97]Oh, how I love your law!
I meditate on it all day long. Ps 1:2
[98]Your commands make me wiser than my
enemies, Dt 4:6
for they are ever with me.
[99]I have more insight than all my teachers,
for I meditate on your statutes. ver 15
[100]I have more understanding than the elders,
for I obey your precepts. Job 32:7-9
[101]I have kept my feet from every evil path
so that I might obey your word.
[102]I have not departed from your laws,
for you yourself have taught me.
[103]How sweet are your words to my taste,
sweeter than honey to my mouth! Ps 19:10
[104]I gain understanding from your precepts;
therefore I hate every wrong path. ver 128

נ Nun

[105]Your word is a lamp to my feet
and a light for my path. Pr 6:23
[106]I have taken an oath and confirmed it,
that I will follow your righteous laws.
[107]I have suffered much;
preserve my life, O LORD, according to your
word. ver 25
[108]Accept, O LORD, the willing praise of my
mouth, Hos 14:2; Heb 13:15
and teach me your laws.
[109]Though I constantly take my life in my
hands, Jdg 12:3; Job 13:14
I will not forget your law.
[110]The wicked have set a snare for me, Ps 140:5
but I have not strayed from your precepts.
[111]Your statutes are my heritage forever;
they are the joy of my heart.

LIVING  INSIGHT

The Bible is the authority, the final resting place of our cares, our worries, our griefs, our tragedies, our sorrows and our surprises. It is the final answer to our questions, our search. Turning back to the Scriptures will provide something that nothing else can provide: light to keep us from groping about in the darkness.
(See Psalm 119:105.)

[112]My heart is set on keeping your decrees
to the very end.

ס Samekh

[113]I hate double-minded men, Jas 1:8
but I love your law.
[114]You are my refuge and my shield; Ps 32:7; 91:1
I have put my hope in your word.
[115]Away from me, you evildoers, Ps 6:8; Mt 7:23
that I may keep the commands of my God!
[116]Sustain me according to your promise, and I
will live; Ps 54:4
do not let my hopes be dashed. Ps 25:2; Ro 5:5
[117]Uphold me, and I will be delivered; Isa 41:10
I will always have regard for your decrees.
[118]You reject all who stray from your decrees,
for their deceitfulness is in vain.
[119]All the wicked of the earth you discard like
dross; Eze 22:18-19
therefore I love your statutes.
[120]My flesh trembles in fear of you; Hab 3:16
I stand in awe of your laws.

ע Ayin

[121]I have done what is righteous and just;
do not leave me to my oppressors.
[122]Ensure your servant's well-being; Job 17:3
let not the arrogant oppress me.
[123]My eyes fail, looking for your salvation,
looking for your righteous promise. ver 82
[124]Deal with your servant according to your
love
and teach me your decrees. ver 12
[125]I am your servant; give me discernment
that I may understand your statutes.
[126]It is time for you to act, O LORD;
your law is being broken.
[127]Because I love your commands
more than gold, more than pure gold,

128and because I consider all your precepts
right,
I hate every wrong path. ver 104,163

פ Pe

129Your statutes are wonderful; ver 18
therefore I obey them.
130The unfolding of your words gives light;
it gives understanding to the simple. Ps 19:7
131I open my mouth and pant, Ps 42:1
longing for your commands.
132Turn to me and have mercy on me, Ps 25:16
as you always do to those who love your
name.
133Direct my footsteps according to your word;
let no sin rule over me. Ps 19:13; Ro 6:12
134Redeem me from the oppression of men,
that I may obey your precepts.
135Make your face shine upon your servant
and teach me your decrees.
136Streams of tears flow from my eyes, Jer 9:1,18
for your law is not obeyed. Eze 9:4

צ Tsadhe

137Righteous are you, O LORD, Ezr 9:15; Jer 12:1
and your laws are right. Ne 9:13
138The statutes you have laid down are
righteous; Ps 19:7
they are fully trustworthy.
139My zeal wears me out, Ps 69:9; Jn 2:17
for my enemies ignore your words.
140Your promises have been thoroughly tested,
and your servant loves them.
141Though I am lowly and despised, Ps 22:6
I do not forget your precepts.
142Your righteousness is everlasting
and your law is true. Ps 19:7
143Trouble and distress have come upon me,
but your commands are my delight.
144Your statutes are forever right;
give me understanding that I may live.

ק Qoph

145I call with all my heart; answer me, O LORD,
and I will obey your decrees. ver 22,55
146I call out to you; save me
and I will keep your statutes.
147I rise before dawn and cry for help; Ps 5:3; 57:8
I have put my hope in your word.
148My eyes stay open through the watches of the
night, Ps 63:6
that I may meditate on your promises.
149Hear my voice in accordance with your love;
preserve my life, O LORD, according to your
laws.
150Those who devise wicked schemes are near,
but they are far from your law.
151Yet you are near, O LORD, Ps 145:18
and all your commands are true. ver 142
152Long ago I learned from your statutes
that you established them to last forever.

ר Resh

153Look upon my suffering and deliver me,
for I have not forgotten your law. Pr 3:1
154Defend my cause and redeem me; 1Sa 24:15
preserve my life according to your promise.
155Salvation is far from the wicked,
for they do not seek out your decrees.
156Your compassion is great, O LORD;
preserve my life according to your laws.
157Many are the foes who persecute me, Ps 7:1
but I have not turned from your statutes.
158I look on the faithless with loathing, Ps 139:21
for they do not obey your word.
159See how I love your precepts;
preserve my life, O LORD, according to your
love. Ps 41:2
160All your words are true;
all your righteous laws are eternal. ver 89

ש Sin and Shin

161Rulers persecute me without cause, 1Sa 24:11
but my heart trembles at your word.
162I rejoice in your promise
like one who finds great spoil. 1Sa 30:16
163I hate and abhor falsehood
but I love your law. ver 47
164Seven times a day I praise you
for your righteous laws.
165Great peace have they who love your law,
and nothing can make them stumble.
166I wait for your salvation, O LORD, Ge 49:18
and I follow your commands.
167I obey your statutes,
for I love them greatly.
168I obey your precepts and your statutes,
for all my ways are known to you. Pr 5:21

ת Taw

169May my cry come before you, O LORD; Ps 18:6
give me understanding according to your
word.
170May my supplication come before you; Ps 28:2
deliver me according to your promise.
171May my lips overflow with praise, Ps 51:15
for you teach me your decrees.
172May my tongue sing of your word,
for all your commands are righteous.
173May your hand be ready to help me, Ps 37:24
for I have chosen your precepts. Jos 24:22
174I long for your salvation, O LORD,
and your law is my delight.
175Let me live that I may praise you, Isa 55:3
and may your laws sustain me.
176I have strayed like a lost sheep. Isa 53:6
Seek your servant,
for I have not forgotten your commands.

THREE GATES THAT OPEN SCRIPTURE

"The unfolding of your words gives light;
it gives understanding to the simple."
—PSALM 119:130

There are many Christians today who know more than a few things about the Bible, God's precious Word. Most anyone can bring to mind several Old Testament stories or a few memorized verses of Scripture. At times you are able to find a believer who can do a good job of explaining the contents of a chapter here and there or even be able to summarize an entire book found in the Bible. However, many of us must admit that it is a different story when we are asked to fit the books of the Bible together and explain how they are arranged and what they are communicating in their overall scope.

In this article we want to get a good look at the Biblical forest without getting too intricately involved with each tree. We want to back off and get an overall perspective that we can so easily miss in a more detailed study of the Scriptures. By taking the time to examine carefully the gates through which we must pass in order to undertake a journey through the 66 books of Scripture, we will be better equipped to see the details with greater understanding and appreciation. It is my hope that we will find ourselves putting together pieces of the Biblical puzzle that perhaps have never fallen into place before.

Doctrinal Foundation

In order for us to grasp the contents of the entire Word of God and gain confidence in its integrity and its power, it is essential that we understand the three major doctrines related to the Scriptures, the three "gates," if you will, that open up God's Word to us. Our belief about these three doctrines will determine our belief about the Bible. These doctrines, therefore, are *crucial*. Let me urge you to commit the definition of each one to memory, for you will find yourself coming back to them time and again.

The Doctrine of Revelation

"Revelation" can be defined as follows: the supernatural act of God by which He communicated divine truth to humans that they would otherwise not know. God chose to communicate His truth in three key ways. First, *He revealed Himself through oral communication*. He spoke His Word to humanity. This is the testimony of Scripture: "The LORD spoke to Moses in the Tent of Meeting . . ." (Numbers 1:1); "After the death of Moses the servant of the LORD, the LORD said to Joshua son of Nun, Moses' aide . . ." (Joshua 1:1); "So the LORD said to Solomon . . ." (1 Kings 11:11). God spoke His truths to His people.

Second, *God revealed Himself through visible communication*. He illustrated, or visually demonstrated, His Word to humanity—through nature, the mountains, the heavens that declare His glory. As Paul wrote in Romans 1:19–20, "What may be known about God is plain to them, because God has made it plain to them. For since the creation of the world God's invisible qualities—his eternal power and divine nature—have been clearly seen, being understood from what has been made, so that men are without excuse."

Third, *God revealed Himself through written communication*. He personally wrote His Word. Look at the words of Moses: "These are the commandments the LORD proclaimed in a loud voice to your whole assembly there on the mountain from out of the fire, the cloud and the deep darkness; and he added nothing more. Then he wrote them on two stone tablets and gave them to me" (Deuteronomy 5:22).

Furthermore, there are occasions in Scripture where the *fact* of revelation is presented, but not the method. On such occasions we do not know *how* God communicated His truths. Galatians 1:11–12 is an example: "I want you to know, brothers, that the gospel I preached is not something that man made up. I did not receive it from any man, nor was I taught it; rather, I received it by revelation from Jesus Christ."

God also employed human beings as His instruments in communicating His revelation to humanity. Those who were called to proclaim the divine revelation were commonly called prophets (*prophetes*, from *propheteuo* meaning "to speak forth a revelation" in the Greek). Those who were called to write down the revelation became the chosen human writers of the Scriptures.

God's written revelation is a finished revelation. In the written Word of God we have 66 books of God's truths. It is in some sense God's "last will and testament"—nothing can be added to it or taken away from it. The third verse of Jude's letter makes it clear that this aspect of revelation has ceased: "I was very eager to write to you about the salvation we share, I felt I had to write and urge you to contend for the faith that was once for all entrusted to the saints." Observe that "the faith"—the body of truth known as God's revelation—has been deposited "once for all" into the hands of God's people.

A final thought about revelation. Whereas in the past God used the prophets and the writers of Scripture as His foremost instruments of revelation, now He has spoken or revealed Himself to us by His Son, Jesus Christ, who is supreme over all things. God's Word through His Son is final; it fulfills all previous words by God. Look at what the author of the letter to the Hebrews wrote: "In the past God spoke to our forefathers through the prophets at many times and in various ways, but in these last days he has spoken to us by his Son, whom he appointed heir of all things, and through whom he made the universe" (Hebrews 1:1–2).

The Doctrine of Inspiration

The doctrine of inspiration can be defined as follows: the supernatural act of God whereby He so directed human authors of Scripture that without destroying their own individuality, literary style or personality, His complete and connected thought toward humanity was recorded without error or contradiction—each and every word being supernaturally recorded and preserved so as to result in an infallible document in the original writings. Inspiration is God's method of communicating His truth in such a way that humans receive it and record it accurately.

There are four important factors in this definition: First, there was a source, a cause: The Holy Spirit was the One who was engaged in this process of guarding the truth that was transferred from heaven to earth, from God's mind to the writing instruments of humans. In his second letter to Timothy, Paul puts it this way: "All Scripture is God-breathed and is useful for teaching, rebuking, correcting and training in righteousness, so that the man of God may be thoroughly equipped for every good work" (2 Timothy 3:16–17).

Second, the agent was a human writer as directed by God. Look at Peter's words in his second letter: "For prophecy never had its origin in the will of man, but men spoke from God as they were carried along by the Holy Spirit" (2 Peter 1:21).

Third, the result was an inerrant, completely trustworthy, once-for-all record given by God and thoroughly accredited. Human writers, without losing their personality, their individual style, were led by the Spirit of God to write these words from God, and they were in the process "inspired" to do so.

Fourth, the process was one in which God "carried along" the human writers (see 2 Peter 1:21) to the end that they, apart from anything unique in themselves, recorded His Word. Just as a boat without sail or motor is carried along by the wind and the waves, so these writers were carried along outside of their own power and ingenuity (without sacrificing their own personality or individual style) to record the words that have come down to us as Holy Scripture.

Because God's written revelation has ceased, it stands to reason that inspiration has also ceased. The process of revelation and inspiration occurred over a period of about 1,600 years, during which time God chose to use about forty human writers to record His revelation. God is no longer inspiring people to record without error His Word. It is an established fact that we have within our possession a copy of God's breathed-out revelation.

The Doctrine of Illumination

The doctrine of illumination can be defined as follows: the supernatural influence of the Holy Spirit on those who are in right relation with God so that our lives are transformed by God's power as He enables us to understand and apply God's truth, His inspired Word, to our lives. Illumination is God's method of communicating His truth in such a way that it opens our eyes and our hearts to know Him and to know His will for our lives.

One of the basic functions of the Holy Spirit is to move among people in the family of God and show us the living truth right before our very eyes, so that it will make a difference in the way we think and act. John describes it this way in his Gospel: "But when he, the Spirit of truth, comes, he will guide you into all truth. He will not speak on his own; he will speak only what he hears, and he will tell you what is yet to come" (John 16:13).

The apostle Paul gives us further insight into the work of the Holy Spirit in illuminating our hearts and minds so that we could grasp God's inspired truth:

> *For who among men knows the thoughts of a man except the man's spirit within him? In the same way no one knows the thoughts of God except the Spirit of God. We have not received the spirit of the world but the Spirit who is from God, that we may understand what God has freely given us. This is what we speak, not in words taught us by human wisdom but in words taught by the Spirit, expressing spiritual truths in spiritual words. The man without the Spirit does not accept the things that come from the Spirit of God, for they are foolishness to him, and he cannot understand them, because they are spiritually discerned. The spiritual man makes judgments about all things, but he himself is not subject to any man's judgment: "For who has known the mind of the Lord that he may instruct him?" But we have the mind of Christ (1 Corinthians 2:11–16).*

Observe that Paul distinguishes between the inability of the man without the Spirit (verse 14) and the spiritual man's ability (verses 11–13,15–16). Reading carefully you will note first that the man without the Spirit "does not accept" (*dechomai*—"welcome," or "receive" in the Greek) God's truths and second, he "cannot understand" (*ginosko*—"know, come to know by experience" in the Greek). Seeing this truth helps to explain why the unsaved get no pleasure out of Bible exposition and fail to enter into the joyful reality of Bible application. If it weren't for the Spirit of God using the Word of God, we could not know the thoughts of God. The Spirit takes God's written truth and makes known the depths of God's mind to His people.

You will discover, if you haven't already, that illumination still goes on. Every time you turn to God's enduring, infinitely powerful Word, He will provide new measures of light for your path and a clearer direction for your life. Every time you grasp spiritual truth and are able to store it in your reservoir of knowledge and apply it to your personal life, you are the recipient of the illumination of the Holy Spirit. Illumination certainly has not ceased! Thank God that He gave us His truth to change our lives, so that we can lift His truth from the pages of His inspired revelation and by the power of the Spirit live another kind of life on this earth.

Entering the Gates

I encourage you to walk with boldness through the gates that stand open before you—gates that will help you appreciate and become more confident in the Book that God has so graciously preserved for you. Those who would gain all God has in mind for them are those who understand the truths of revelation, inspiration and illumination. Learn well these three lessons I briefly share in conclusion.

First, *if God had not given us His revelation, we would still be living our lives in spiritual ignorance and in unmitigated despair*. God has revealed His truth in order to open our minds, to give us a standard, to give us assurance, to give us direction, to give us hope. No other book will do that in a reliable manner.

Second, *if God had not protected His revelation from error, the Bible would be an unreliable book*. We would never know exactly where to turn, where we could count on it to say the truth. But God has protected and preserved it. There isn't one single thing in His Book that would make us think it is unreliable. We have, thank God, a standard we can trust!

Third, *if God does not open our eyes and our hearts, we will never know His will*. And that is, in the final analysis, what we want to know. I would challenge us to let our minds be open to the Word of God, that we might see comfort, find relief and be given direction with respect to His will for us and His purposes for us. May God bless us as we grow in understanding, as we appropriate His Word into our daily lives, and as we experience the thrilling and life-changing reality of His *illumination*!

Psalm 120

A song of ascents.

1 I call on the LORD in my distress, Jnh 2:2
and he answers me.
2 Save me, O LORD, from lying lips Pr 12:22
and from deceitful tongues. Ps 52:4

3 What will he do to you,
and what more besides, O deceitful tongue?
4 He will punish you with a warrior's sharp arrows, Ps 45:5
with burning coals of the broom tree.

5 Woe to me that I dwell in Meshech,
that I live among the tents of Kedar! Ge 25:13
6 Too long have I lived
among those who hate peace.
7 I am a man of peace;
but when I speak, they are for war.

Psalm 121

A song of ascents.

1 I lift up my eyes to the hills—
where does my help come from?
2 My help comes from the LORD,
the Maker of heaven and earth. Ps 124:8

3 He will not let your foot slip—
he who watches over you will not slumber;
4 indeed, he who watches over Israel Ps 127:1
will neither slumber nor sleep.

5 The LORD watches over you— Isa 25:4
the LORD is your shade at your right hand;
6 the sun will not harm you by day, Ps 91:5
nor the moon by night.

7 The LORD will keep you from all harm—
he will watch over your life;
8 the LORD will watch over your coming and going
both now and forevermore. Dt 28:6

Psalm 122

A song of ascents. Of David.

1 I rejoiced with those who said to me,
"Let us go to the house of the LORD."
2 Our feet are standing
in your gates, O Jerusalem.

3 Jerusalem is built like a city
that is closely compacted together.
4 That is where the tribes go up,
the tribes of the LORD,
to praise the name of the LORD
according to the statute given to Israel.
5 There the thrones for judgment stand,
the thrones of the house of David.

6 Pray for the peace of Jerusalem:
"May those who love you be secure. Ps 51:18
7 May there be peace within your walls 1Sa 25:6
and security within your citadels." Ps 48:3
8 For the sake of my brothers and friends,
I will say, "Peace be within you."
9 For the sake of the house of the LORD our God,
I will seek your prosperity. Ne 2:10

Psalm 123

A song of ascents.

1 I lift up my eyes to you,
to you whose throne is in heaven. Ps 11:4
2 As the eyes of slaves look to the hand of their master,
as the eyes of a maid look to the hand of her mistress,
so our eyes look to the LORD our God, Ps 25:15
till he shows us his mercy.

3 Have mercy on us, O LORD, have mercy on us,
for we have endured much contempt.
4 We have endured much ridicule from the proud,
much contempt from the arrogant.

Psalm 124

A song of ascents. Of David.

1 If the LORD had not been on our side—
let Israel say— Ps 129:1
2 if the LORD had not been on our side
when men attacked us,
3 when their anger flared against us,
they would have swallowed us alive;
4 the flood would have engulfed us,
the torrent would have swept over us,
5 the raging waters
would have swept us away.

6 Praise be to the LORD,
who has not let us be torn by their teeth.
7 We have escaped like a bird
out of the fowler's snare; Ps 91:3; Pr 6:5
the snare has been broken,
and we have escaped.
8 Our help is in the name of the LORD,
the Maker of heaven and earth. Ge 1:1; Ps 121:2

Psalm 125

A song of ascents.

[1]Those who trust in the LORD are like Mount
Zion, Ps 46:5
which cannot be shaken but endures
forever.
[2]As the mountains surround Jerusalem,
so the LORD surrounds his people Ps 121:8
both now and forevermore.
[3]The scepter of the wicked will not remain
over the land allotted to the righteous,
for then the righteous might use
their hands to do evil. 1Sa 24:10
[4]Do good, O LORD, to those who are good,
to those who are upright in heart. Ps 7:10
[5]But those who turn to crooked ways Pr 2:15
the LORD will banish with the evildoers.

Peace be upon Israel. Ps 128:6

Psalm 126

A song of ascents.

[1]When the LORD brought back the captives to[a]
Zion, Ps 85:1
we were like men who dreamed.[b]
[2]Our mouths were filled with laughter,
our tongues with songs of joy. Ps 51:14
Then it was said among the nations,
"The LORD has done great things for
them."
[3]The LORD has done great things for us,
and we are filled with joy. Isa 25:9

[4]Restore our fortunes,[c] O LORD,
like streams in the Negev. Isa 43:19
[5]Those who sow in tears
will reap with songs of joy. Isa 35:10
[6]He who goes out weeping,
carrying seed to sow,
will return with songs of joy,
carrying sheaves with him.

Psalm 127

A song of ascents. Of Solomon.

[1]Unless the LORD builds the house, Ps 78:69
its builders labor in vain.
Unless the LORD watches over the city, Ps 121:4
the watchmen stand guard in vain.
[2]In vain you rise early
and stay up late,
toiling for food to eat— Ge 3:17
for he grants sleep to[d] those he loves.

[3]Sons are a heritage from the LORD,
children a reward from him. Ge 33:5
[4]Like arrows in the hands of a warrior Ps 112:2
are sons born in one's youth.

LIVING  **INSIGHT**

Is the Lord really building your home? Stop and think. The Lord alone can give you the skills and abilities to be there for your family. You can't do it on your own. Working independently of Him will accomplish zero. Remember, it is the Lord who gives these gifts.

(See Psalm 127:1.)

[5]Blessed is the man
whose quiver is full of them. Ps 128:2-3
They will not be put to shame
when they contend with their enemies in
the gate. Pr 27:11

Psalm 128

A song of ascents.

[1]Blessed are all who fear the LORD, Ps 112:1
who walk in his ways. Ps 119:1-3
[2]You will eat the fruit of your labor; Isa 3:10
blessings and prosperity will be yours.
[3]Your wife will be like a fruitful vine
within your house; Eze 19:10
your sons will be like olive shoots
around your table. Ps 52:8; 144:12
[4]Thus is the man blessed
who fears the LORD.

[5]May the LORD bless you from Zion Ps 134:3
all the days of your life;
may you see the prosperity of Jerusalem,
[6] and may you live to see your children's
children. Job 42:16

Peace be upon Israel. Ps 125:5

Psalm 129

A song of ascents.

[1]They have greatly oppressed me from my
youth— Ps 88:15
let Israel say— Ps 124:1
[2]they have greatly oppressed me from my
youth,

[a]1 Or *LORD restored the fortunes of* [b]1 Or *men restored to health* [c]4 Or *Bring back our captives* [d]2 Or *eat— / for while they sleep he provides for*

but they have not gained the victory over
me. Mt 16:18
3Plowmen have plowed my back
and made their furrows long.
4But the LORD is righteous; Ps 119:137
he has cut me free from the cords of the
wicked.

5May all who hate Zion Mic 4:11
be turned back in shame. Ps 71:13
6May they be like grass on the roof,
which withers before it can grow; Ps 37:2
7with it the reaper cannot fill his hands, Dt 28:38
nor the one who gathers fill his arms.
8May those who pass by not say,
"The blessing of the LORD be upon you;
we bless you in the name of the LORD."

Psalm 130

A song of ascents.

1Out of the depths I cry to you, O LORD; Ps 42:7
2 O Lord, hear my voice. Ps 28:2
Let your ears be attentive Ps 64:1
to my cry for mercy.

3If you, O LORD, kept a record of sins,
O Lord, who could stand? Ps 143:2
4But with you there is forgiveness; Ex 34:7; Jer 33:8
therefore you are feared. 1Ki 8:40
5I wait for the LORD, my soul waits, Ps 27:14; 33:20
and in his word I put my hope. Ps 119:81
6My soul waits for the Lord
more than watchmen wait for the morning,
more than watchmen wait for the morning.

7O Israel, put your hope in the LORD, Ps 131:3
for with the LORD is unfailing love
and with him is full redemption.
8He himself will redeem Israel Lk 1:68
from all their sins.

Psalm 131

A song of ascents. Of David.

1My heart is not proud, O LORD, Ro 12:16
my eyes are not haughty;
I do not concern myself with great matters
or things too wonderful for me.
2But I have stilled and quieted my soul; Ps 116:7
like a weaned child with its mother,
like a weaned child is my soul within me.

3O Israel, put your hope in the LORD Ps 130:7
both now and forevermore.

Psalm 132

A song of ascents.

1O LORD, remember David
and all the hardships he endured. 1Sa 18:11
2He swore an oath to the LORD
and made a vow to the Mighty One of
Jacob: Ge 49:24
3"I will not enter my house
or go to my bed—
4I will allow no sleep to my eyes,
no slumber to my eyelids,
5till I find a place for the LORD, Ac 7:46
a dwelling for the Mighty One of Jacob."
6We heard it in Ephrathah, 1Sa 17:12
we came upon it in the fields of Jaar:[a,b]
7"Let us go to his dwelling place; Ps 5:7
let us worship at his footstool— Ps 99:5
8arise, O LORD, and come to your resting
place,
you and the ark of your might.
9May your priests be clothed with
righteousness; Job 29:14; Isa 61:3,10
may your saints sing for joy."

10For the sake of David your servant,
do not reject your anointed one.

11The LORD swore an oath to David, Ps 89:3-4,35
a sure oath that he will not revoke:
"One of your own descendants 2Sa 7:12
I will place on your throne—
12if your sons keep my covenant
and the statutes I teach them,
then their sons will sit
on your throne for ever and ever."

13For the LORD has chosen Zion, Ps 48:1-2
he has desired it for his dwelling:
14"This is my resting place for ever and ever;
here I will sit enthroned, for I have desired
it—
15I will bless her with abundant provisions;
her poor will I satisfy with food. Ps 147:14
16I will clothe her priests with salvation,
and her saints will ever sing for joy.

17"Here I will make a horn[c] grow for David
and set up a lamp for my anointed one.
18I will clothe his enemies with shame, Ps 35:26
but the crown on his head will be
resplendent."

[a]6 That is, Kiriath Jearim [b]6 Or *heard of it in Ephrathah, / we found it in the fields of Jaar.* (And no quotes around verses 7-9) [c]17 *Horn* here symbolizes strong one, that is, king.

Psalm 133

A song of ascents. Of David.

1 How good and pleasant it is
when brothers live together in unity! Ge 13:8
2 It is like precious oil poured on the head,
running down on the beard,
running down on Aaron's beard,
down upon the collar of his robes.
3 It is as if the dew of Hermon Dt 4:48
were falling on Mount Zion.
For there the LORD bestows his blessing,
even life forevermore. Ps 42:8

Psalm 134

A song of ascents.

1 Praise the LORD, all you servants of the LORD
who minister by night in the house of the
LORD. 1Ch 9:33
2 Lift up your hands in the sanctuary 1Ti 2:8
and praise the LORD.

3 May the LORD, the Maker of heaven and earth,
bless you from Zion. Ps 128:5

Psalm 135

1 Praise the LORD.[a]

Praise the name of the LORD;
praise him, you servants of the LORD,
2 you who minister in the house of the LORD,
in the courts of the house of our God.

3 Praise the LORD, for the LORD is good; Ps 119:68
sing praise to his name, for that is pleasant.
4 For the LORD has chosen Jacob to be his own,
Israel to be his treasured possession. Ex 19:5

5 I know that the LORD is great, Ps 48:1
that our Lord is greater than all gods.
6 The LORD does whatever pleases him, Ps 115:3
in the heavens and on the earth,
in the seas and all their depths.

LIVING  **INSIGHT**

What we think about God enhances our worship and prompts our praise. What we think about God stimulates hope to go on, regardless. What we think about God is the foundation upon which everything rests!
(See Psalm 135:3–7.)

[a] 1 Hebrew *Hallelu Yah;* also in verses 3 and 21

7 He makes clouds rise from the ends of the
earth;
he sends lightning with the rain Jer 10:13
and brings out the wind from his
storehouses.

8 He struck down the firstborn of Egypt, Ex 12:12
the firstborn of men and animals.
9 He sent his signs and wonders into your
midst, O Egypt,
against Pharaoh and all his servants.
10 He struck down many nations Nu 21:21-25
and killed mighty kings—
11 Sihon king of the Amorites, Nu 21:21
Og king of Bashan
and all the kings of Canaan— Jos 12:7-24
12 and he gave their land as an inheritance,
an inheritance to his people Israel.

13 Your name, O LORD, endures forever, Ex 3:15
your renown, O LORD, through all
generations. Ps 102:12
14 For the LORD will vindicate his people Heb 10:30
and have compassion on his servants.

15 The idols of the nations are silver and gold,
made by the hands of men.
16 They have mouths, but cannot speak, 1Ki 18:26
eyes, but they cannot see;
17 they have ears, but cannot hear,
nor is there breath in their mouths. Jer 10:14
18 Those who make them will be like them,
and so will all who trust in them.

19 O house of Israel, praise the LORD; Ps 22:23
O house of Aaron, praise the LORD;
20 O house of Levi, praise the LORD;
you who fear him, praise the LORD.
21 Praise be to the LORD from Zion, Ps 134:3
to him who dwells in Jerusalem.

Praise the LORD.

Psalm 136

1 Give thanks to the LORD, for he is good.
His love endures forever.
2 Give thanks to the God of gods. Dt 10:17
His love endures forever.
3 Give thanks to the Lord of lords:
His love endures forever.

4 to him who alone does great wonders, Ps 72:18
His love endures forever.
5 who by his understanding made the heavens,
His love endures forever.
6 who spread out the earth upon the waters,
His love endures forever.
7 who made the great lights— Ge 1:14,16
His love endures forever.

8 the sun to govern the day,
His love endures forever.
9 the moon and stars to govern the night;
His love endures forever.

10 to him who struck down the firstborn of
Egypt Ex 12:29; Ps 135:8
His love endures forever.
11 and brought Israel out from among them
His love endures forever.
12 with a mighty hand and outstretched arm;
His love endures forever.

13 to him who divided the Red Sea[a] asunder
His love endures forever.
14 and brought Israel through the midst of it,
His love endures forever.
15 but swept Pharaoh and his army into the Red
Sea; Ex 14:27
His love endures forever.

16 to him who led his people through the desert,
His love endures forever.
17 who struck down great kings, Ps 135:9-12
His love endures forever.
18 and killed mighty kings— Dt 29:7
His love endures forever.
19 Sihon king of the Amorites
His love endures forever.
20 and Og king of Bashan—
His love endures forever.
21 and gave their land as an inheritance, Jos 12:1
His love endures forever.
22 an inheritance to his servant Israel;
His love endures forever.

23 to the One who remembered us in our low
estate Ps 113:7
His love endures forever.
24 and freed us from our enemies, Ps 107:2
His love endures forever.
25 and who gives food to every creature. Ps 104:27
His love endures forever.

26 Give thanks to the God of heaven. Ps 115:3
His love endures forever.

Psalm 137

1 By the rivers of Babylon we sat and wept
when we remembered Zion.
2 There on the poplars
we hung our harps, Job 30:31
3 for there our captors asked us for songs,
our tormentors demanded songs of joy;
they said, "Sing us one of the songs of
Zion!"

4 How can we sing the songs of the LORD
while in a foreign land?
5 If I forget you, O Jerusalem,
may my right hand forget ⌊its skill⌋.
6 May my tongue cling to the roof of my mouth
if I do not remember you,
if I do not consider Jerusalem
my highest joy.

7 Remember, O LORD, what the Edomites did
on the day Jerusalem fell. Ob 1:11
"Tear it down," they cried,
"tear it down to its foundations!"

8 O Daughter of Babylon, doomed to
destruction, Isa 13:1,19; Jer 25:12,26; Rev 18:6
happy is he who repays you
for what you have done to us—
9 he who seizes your infants
and dashes them against the rocks. 2Ki 8:12

Psalm 138

Of David.

1 I will praise you, O LORD, with all my heart;
before the "gods" I will sing your praise.
2 I will bow down toward your holy temple
and will praise your name
for your love and your faithfulness,
for you have exalted above all things
your name and your word. Isa 42:21
3 When I called, you answered me;
you made me bold and stouthearted. Ps 28:7

4 May all the kings of the earth praise you,
O LORD, Ps 102:15
when they hear the words of your mouth.
5 May they sing of the ways of the LORD,
for the glory of the LORD is great.

6 Though the LORD is on high, he looks upon
the lowly, Ps 113:6; Isa 57:15
but the proud he knows from afar. Pr 3:34
7 Though I walk in the midst of trouble, Ps 23:4
you preserve my life;
you stretch out your hand against the anger of
my foes, Jer 51:25
with your right hand you save me. Ps 71:20
8 The LORD will fulfill ⌊his purpose⌋ for me;
your love, O LORD, endures forever—
do not abandon the works of your hands.

Psalm 139

For the director of music. Of David. A psalm.

1 O LORD, you have searched me Ps 17:3
and you know me. Jer 12:3
2 You know when I sit and when I rise; 2Ki 19:27
you perceive my thoughts from afar. Mt 9:4
3 You discern my going out and my lying
down;

[a] 13 Hebrew *Yam Suph*; that is, Sea of Reeds; also in verse 15

you are familiar with all my ways. Job 31:4
4Before a word is on my tongue
you know it completely, O LORD. Heb 4:13

LIVING  **INSIGHT**

Before I ever know the thought myself, God already knows it and has analyzed it. Before I am thinking a thought, God has intercepted those promptings, those mental, unseen images, and He has analyzed them perfectly.
(See Psalm 139:1–4.)

5You hem me in—behind and before; Ps 34:7
you have laid your hand upon me.
6Such knowledge is too wonderful for me,
too lofty for me to attain. Job 42:3

7Where can I go from your Spirit?
Where can I flee from your presence?
8If I go up to the heavens, you are there;
if I make my bed in the depths,[a] you are
there. Pr 15:11
9If I rise on the wings of the dawn,
if I settle on the far side of the sea,
10even there your hand will guide me, Ps 23:3
your right hand will hold me fast.

11If I say, "Surely the darkness will hide me
and the light become night around me,"
12even the darkness will not be dark to you;
the night will shine like the day,
for darkness is as light to you.
13For you created my inmost being; Ps 119:73
you knit me together in my mother's
womb. Job 10:11; Isa 44:2,24

LIVING  **INSIGHT**

God reached into my life when I was merely a tiny embryo and began to shape me within. He originated me. He began to put me together while I was still in the soft silence of my mother's womb. It was there my inward parts were originated by God.
(See Psalm 139:13–16.)

14I praise you because I am fearfully and
wonderfully made;
your works are wonderful, Ps 40:5
I know that full well.
15My frame was not hidden from you
when I was made in the secret place.
When I was woven together in the depths of
the earth, Job 10:11
16 your eyes saw my unformed body.
All the days ordained for me
were written in your book
before one of them came to be.

17How precious to[b] me are your thoughts,
O God! Ps 40:5
How vast is the sum of them!
18Were I to count them,
they would outnumber the grains of sand.
When I awake,
I am still with you. Ps 3:5

19If only you would slay the wicked, O God!
Away from me, you bloodthirsty men!
20They speak of you with evil intent;
your adversaries misuse your name. Jude 15
21Do I not hate those who hate you, O LORD,
and abhor those who rise up against you?
22I have nothing but hatred for them;
I count them my enemies.

23Search me, O God, and know my heart;
test me and know my anxious thoughts.

LIVING  **INSIGHT**

Appraise your life. Occasions set aside for evaluation and regrouping are needed. Here are a few questions worth your consideration: First, am I really happy, genuinely challenged and fulfilled in life? Second, in light of eternity, am I making a consistent investment for God's glory and His cause? Third, is the direction my life is taking leading me toward a satisfying and meaningful future? Fourth, can I honestly say that I am in the nucleus of God's will for me?
(See Psalm 139:23–24.)

24See if there is any offensive way in me,
and lead me in the way everlasting. Ps 5:8

Psalm 140

For the director of music. A psalm of David.

1Rescue me, O LORD, from evil men; Ps 17:13
protect me from men of violence, Ps 18:48
2who devise evil plans in their hearts Ps 56:6
and stir up war every day.

[a] 8 Hebrew *Sheol* [b] 17 Or *concerning*

[3]They make their tongues as sharp as a
serpent's; Ps 57:4
the poison of vipers is on their lips. *Selah*

[4]Keep me, O LORD, from the hands of the
wicked; Ps 71:4
protect me from men of violence
who plan to trip my feet.
[5]Proud men have hidden a snare for me;
they have spread out the cords of their net
and have set traps for me along my path.
Selah

[6]O LORD, I say to you, "You are my God."
Hear, O LORD, my cry for mercy. Ps 116:1
[7]O Sovereign LORD, my strong deliverer, Ps 28:8
who shields my head in the day of battle—
[8]do not grant the wicked their desires, O LORD;
do not let their plans succeed,
or they will become proud. *Selah*

[9]Let the heads of those who surround me
be covered with the trouble their lips have
caused. Ps 7:16
[10]Let burning coals fall upon them;
may they be thrown into the fire, Ps 11:6; 21:9
into miry pits, never to rise.
[11]Let slanderers not be established in the land;
may disaster hunt down men of violence.

[12]I know that the LORD secures justice for the
poor
and upholds the cause of the needy. Ps 9:4
[13]Surely the righteous will praise your name
and the upright will live before you. Ps 11:7

Psalm 141

A psalm of David.

[1]O LORD, I call to you; come quickly to me.
Hear my voice when I call to you. Ps 143:1
[2]May my prayer be set before you like incense;
may the lifting up of my hands be like the
evening sacrifice. Ex 29:39,41; 1Ti 2:8

[3]Set a guard over my mouth, O LORD; Ps 34:13
keep watch over the door of my lips. Ps 12:2
[4]Let not my heart be drawn to what is evil,
to take part in wicked deeds
with men who are evildoers;
let me not eat of their delicacies. Pr 23:6

[5]Let a righteous man[a] strike me—it is a
kindness;
let him rebuke me—it is oil on my head.
My head will not refuse it.

Yet my prayer is ever against the deeds of
evildoers;
[6]their rulers will be thrown down from the
cliffs, 2Ch 25:12
and the wicked will learn that my words
were well spoken.
[7]⌊They will say,⌋ "As one plows and breaks up
the earth, Ps 129:3
so our bones have been scattered at the
mouth of the grave.[b]" Ps 53:5

[8]But my eyes are fixed on you, O Sovereign
LORD; Ps 25:15
in you I take refuge—do not give me over
to death. Ps 2:12
[9]Keep me from the snares they have laid for
me, Ps 140:4
from the traps set by evildoers. Ps 38:12
[10]Let the wicked fall into their own nets, Ps 35:8
while I pass by in safety.

Psalm 142

A *maskil*[c] of David. When he was in the cave.
A prayer.

[1]I cry aloud to the LORD;
I lift up my voice to the LORD for mercy.
[2]I pour out my complaint before him; Isa 26:16
before him I tell my trouble.

[3]When my spirit grows faint within me, Ps 140:5
it is you who know my way.
In the path where I walk
men have hidden a snare for me.
[4]Look to my right and see;
no one is concerned for me.
I have no refuge;
no one cares for my life. Ps 31:11

[5]I cry to you, O LORD;
I say, "You are my refuge,
my portion in the land of the living."
[6]Listen to my cry, Ps 17:1
for I am in desperate need; Ps 116:6
rescue me from those who pursue me, Ps 25:20
for they are too strong for me.
[7]Set me free from my prison, Ps 146:7
that I may praise your name.

Then the righteous will gather about me
because of your goodness to me. Ps 13:6

Psalm 143

A psalm of David.

[1]O LORD, hear my prayer,
listen to my cry for mercy; Ps 140:6
in your faithfulness and righteousness Ps 71:2
come to my relief.

[a]5 Or *Let the Righteous One* [b]7 Hebrew *Sheol* [c]Title: Probably a literary or musical term

2 Do not bring your servant into judgment,
for no one living is righteous before you.

3 The enemy pursues me,
he crushes me to the ground;
he makes me dwell in darkness Ps 107:10
like those long dead.
4 So my spirit grows faint within me;
my heart within me is dismayed. Ps 142:3

5 I remember the days of long ago; Ps 77:6
I meditate on all your works
and consider what your hands have
done.
6 I spread out my hands to you; Ps 63:1; 88:9
my soul thirsts for you like a parched
land. *Selah*

7 Answer me quickly, O LORD; Ps 69:17
my spirit fails.
Do not hide your face from me Ps 28:1
or I will be like those who go down to the
pit.
8 Let the morning bring me word of your
unfailing love, Ps 46:5
for I have put my trust in you.
Show me the way I should go, Ps 27:11
for to you I lift up my soul. Ps 25:1-2
9 Rescue me from my enemies, O LORD, Ps 31:15
for I hide myself in you.
10 Teach me to do your will,
for you are my God;
may your good Spirit
lead me on level ground. Ne 9:20; 25:4-5

LIVING  **INSIGHT**

To be used by God to serve Him! Is there anything more encouraging, more fulfilling? Perhaps not, but there is something more basic: to meet with God! To linger in His presence, to shut out the noise of the city and, in quietness, give Him the praise He deserves. Before we immerse ourselves in His work, let's meet Him in His Word . . . in prayer . . . in worship.

(See Psalm 143:5–10.)

11 For your name's sake, O LORD, preserve my
life; Ps 119:25
in your righteousness, bring me out of
trouble. Ps 31:1
12 In your unfailing love, silence my enemies;
destroy all my foes, Ps 54:5
for I am your servant. Ps 116:16

Psalm 144

Of David.

1 Praise be to the LORD my Rock, Ps 18:2,34
who trains my hands for war,
my fingers for battle.
2 He is my loving God and my fortress, Ps 59:9
my stronghold and my deliverer,
my shield, in whom I take refuge, Ps 84:9
who subdues peoples[a] under me.

3 O LORD, what is man that you care for him,
the son of man that you think of him?
4 Man is like a breath;
his days are like a fleeting shadow. Ps 102:11

5 Part your heavens, O LORD, and come down;
touch the mountains, so that they smoke.
6 Send forth lightning and scatter ⌞the enemies⌟;
shoot your arrows and rout them. Ps 18:14
7 Reach down your hand from on high;
deliver me and rescue me
from the mighty waters,
from the hands of foreigners Ps 18:44
8 whose mouths are full of lies,
whose right hands are deceitful. Ps 12:2; 41:6

9 I will sing a new song to you, O God;
on the ten-stringed lyre I will make music
to you, Ps 33:2-3
10 to the One who gives victory to kings,
who delivers his servant David from the
deadly sword. Ps 18:50

11 Deliver me and rescue me
from the hands of foreigners
whose mouths are full of lies,
whose right hands are deceitful. Ps 12:2

12 Then our sons in their youth
will be like well-nurtured plants, Ps 128:3
and our daughters will be like pillars SS 4:4
carved to adorn a palace.
13 Our barns will be filled Pr 3:10
with every kind of provision.
Our sheep will increase by thousands,
by tens of thousands in our fields;
14 our oxen will draw heavy loads.[b] Pr 14:4
There will be no breaching of walls, 2Ki 25:11
no going into captivity,
no cry of distress in our streets. Isa 24:11

15 Blessed are the people of whom this is true;
blessed are the people whose God is the
LORD.

[a]2 Many manuscripts of the Masoretic Text, Dead Sea Scrolls, Aquila, Jerome and Syriac; most manuscripts of the Masoretic Text *subdues my people* [b]14 Or *our chieftains will be firmly established*

Psalm 145[a]

A psalm of praise. Of David.

1 I will exalt you, my God the King; Ps 30:1; 34:1
I will praise your name for ever and ever.
2 Every day I will praise you Ps 71:6
and extol your name for ever and ever.

3 Great is the LORD and most worthy of praise;
his greatness no one can fathom. Job 5:9
4 One generation will commend your works to another; Isa 38:19
they will tell of your mighty acts.
5 They will speak of the glorious splendor of your majesty,
and I will meditate on your wonderful works.[b] Ps 119:27
6 They will tell of the power of your awesome works, Ps 66:3
and I will proclaim your great deeds. Dt 32:3
7 They will celebrate your abundant goodness
and joyfully sing of your righteousness.

8 The LORD is gracious and compassionate,
slow to anger and rich in love.
9 The LORD is good to all; Ps 100:5
he has compassion on all he has made.
10 All you have made will praise you, O LORD;
your saints will extol you. Ps 68:26
11 They will tell of the glory of your kingdom
and speak of your might,
12 so that all men may know of your mighty acts
and the glorious splendor of your kingdom.
13 Your kingdom is an everlasting kingdom,
and your dominion endures through all generations.

The LORD is faithful to all his promises Dt 7:9
and loving toward all he has made.[c]
14 The LORD upholds all those who fall Ps 37:24
and lifts up all who are bowed down.
15 The eyes of all look to you,
and you give them their food at the proper time. Ps 104:27
16 You open your hand
and satisfy the desires of every living thing.

17 The LORD is righteous in all his ways
and loving toward all he has made.
18 The LORD is near to all who call on him, Dt 4:7
to all who call on him in truth.
19 He fulfills the desires of those who fear him;
he hears their cry and saves them. Pr 15:29
20 The LORD watches over all who love him,
but all the wicked he will destroy. Ps 9:5

21 My mouth will speak in praise of the LORD.
Let every creature praise his holy name
for ever and ever.

Psalm 146

1 Praise the LORD.[d]

Praise the LORD, O my soul. Ps 103:1
2 I will praise the LORD all my life; Ps 104:33
I will sing praise to my God as long as I live.

3 Do not put your trust in princes, Ps 118:9
in mortal men, who cannot save. Isa 2:22
4 When their spirit departs, they return to the ground; Ecc 12:7
on that very day their plans come to nothing. Ps 33:10; 1Co 2:6

5 Blessed is he whose help is the God of Jacob,
whose hope is in the LORD his God,
6 the Maker of heaven and earth, Rev 14:7
the sea, and everything in them—
the LORD, who remains faithful forever.
7 He upholds the cause of the oppressed Ps 103:6
and gives food to the hungry. Ps 107:9
The LORD sets prisoners free, Ps 68:6
8 the LORD gives sight to the blind, Mt 9:30
the LORD lifts up those who are bowed down,
the LORD loves the righteous.
9 The LORD watches over the alien
and sustains the fatherless and the widow,
but he frustrates the ways of the wicked.

10 The LORD reigns forever, Ex 15:18; Ps 10:16
your God, O Zion, for all generations.

Praise the LORD.

Psalm 147

1 Praise the LORD.[e]

How good it is to sing praises to our God,
how pleasant and fitting to praise him!

2 The LORD builds up Jerusalem; Ps 102:16
he gathers the exiles of Israel. Dt 30:3
3 He heals the brokenhearted
and binds up their wounds.

4 He determines the number of the stars Isa 40:26
and calls them each by name.
5 Great is our Lord and mighty in power; Ps 48:1
his understanding has no limit. Isa 40:28
6 The LORD sustains the humble Ps 146:8-9
but casts the wicked to the ground.

[a] This psalm is an acrostic poem, the verses of which (including verse 13b) begin with the successive letters of the Hebrew alphabet. [b] 5 Dead Sea Scrolls and Syriac (see also Septuagint); Masoretic Text *On the glorious splendor of your majesty / and on your wonderful works I will meditate* [c] 13 One manuscript of the Masoretic Text, Dead Sea Scrolls and Syriac (see also Septuagint); most manuscripts of the Masoretic Text do not have the last two lines of verse 13. [d] 1 Hebrew *Hallelu Yah*; also in verse 10 [e] 1 Hebrew *Hallelu Yah*; also in verse 20

7Sing to the LORD with thanksgiving; Ps 33:3
make music to our God on the harp.
8He covers the sky with clouds;
he supplies the earth with rain Job 38:26
and makes grass grow on the hills. Ps 104:14
9He provides food for the cattle Ps 104:27-28
and for the young ravens when they call.

10His pleasure is not in the strength of the horse, 1Sa 16:7; Ps 33:16-17
nor his delight in the legs of a man;
11the LORD delights in those who fear him,
who put their hope in his unfailing love.

12Extol the LORD, O Jerusalem; Ps 48:1
praise your God, O Zion,
13for he strengthens the bars of your gates
and blesses your people within you. Lev 25:21
14He grants peace to your borders Isa 60:17-18
and satisfies you with the finest of wheat.

15He sends his command to the earth;
his word runs swiftly.
16He spreads the snow like wool Job 37:6
and scatters the frost like ashes.
17He hurls down his hail like pebbles.
Who can withstand his icy blast?
18He sends his word and melts them; Ps 33:9
he stirs up his breezes, and the waters flow.

19He has revealed his word to Jacob,
his laws and decrees to Israel. Mal 4:4
20He has done this for no other nation;
they do not know his laws.

Praise the LORD.

Psalm 148

1Praise the LORD.[a] Ps 33:2; 103:1

Praise the LORD from the heavens,
praise him in the heights above.
2Praise him, all his angels, Ps 103:20
praise him, all his heavenly hosts.
3Praise him, sun and moon, Ps 19:1
praise him, all you shining stars.
4Praise him, you highest heavens
and you waters above the skies. Ge 1:7
5Let them praise the name of the LORD,
for he commanded and they were created.
6He set them in place for ever and ever;
he gave a decree that will never pass away.

7Praise the LORD from the earth,
you great sea creatures and all ocean depths, Ps 74:13-14
8lightning and hail, snow and clouds,
stormy winds that do his bidding, Ps 147:15-18
9you mountains and all hills, Isa 44:23; 49:13; 55:12
fruit trees and all cedars,
10wild animals and all cattle,
small creatures and flying birds,
11kings of the earth and all nations,
you princes and all rulers on earth,
12young men and maidens,
old men and children.

13Let them praise the name of the LORD, Isa 12:4
for his name alone is exalted;
his splendor is above the earth and the heavens. Ps 113:4
14He has raised up for his people a horn,[b]
the praise of all his saints,
of Israel, the people close to his heart.

Praise the LORD.

Psalm 149

1Praise the LORD.[c] Ps 33:2

Sing to the LORD a new song,
his praise in the assembly of the saints.

2Let Israel rejoice in their Maker; Ps 95:6
let the people of Zion be glad in their King.
3Let them praise his name with dancing
and make music to him with tambourine and harp. Ps 81:2; 150:4
4For the LORD takes delight in his people;
he crowns the humble with salvation.
5Let the saints rejoice in this honor
and sing for joy on their beds. Job 35:10

6May the praise of God be in their mouths
and a double-edged sword in their hands,
7to inflict vengeance on the nations Nu 31:3
and punishment on the peoples, Ps 81:15
8to bind their kings with fetters, 2Sa 3:34
their nobles with shackles of iron, 2Ch 33:11
9to carry out the sentence written against them.
This is the glory of all his saints. Ps 148:14

Praise the LORD.

Psalm 150

1Praise the LORD.[d]

Praise God in his sanctuary; Ps 102:19
praise him in his mighty heavens.
2Praise him for his acts of power; Dt 3:24

[a] *1* Hebrew *Hallelu Yah*; also in verse 14 [b] *14* *Horn* here symbolizes strong one, that is, king. [c] *1* Hebrew *Hallelu Yah*; also in verse 9 [d] *1* Hebrew *Hallelu Yah*; also in verse 6

praise him for his surpassing greatness.
[3]Praise him with the sounding of the trumpet,
praise him with the harp and lyre, Ps 149:3
[4]praise him with tambourine and dancing,
praise him with the strings and flute,
[5]praise him with the clash of cymbals, 1Ch 15:16
praise him with resounding cymbals.

[6]Let everything that has breath praise the LORD.

Praise the LORD.

INTRODUCTION

PROVERBS

Up to this point in the Bible we have found history and biography, prophecy and poetry . . . but not much philosophy—except perhaps in the book of Job. The book of Proverbs offers a wealth of information to aid us in wise living. What the psalms are to our devotional life, the proverbs are to our practical life. In terse and striking ways, the profound genius of these maxims lies in their shrewd concentration of truth. They remain to this very day a marvelous source of insightful and penetrating wisdom. Look no further for no-nonsense advice on just about any topic that affects daily life. When you do, you will soon discover that the wisdom that comes from God is the only sure guide—it is reliable counsel for right living!

WRITERS: *Solomon and others*

DATE: *c.970–930 B.C.*

PURPOSE: *To capture all sources of knowledge and give wisdom for living*

KEY VERSE: *1:7 "The fear of the LORD is the beginning of knowledge."*

SOLOMON'S SHORT STORY: *The Rich Life of Wisdom*

TIME LINE 1400BC 1300 1200 1100 1000 900 800 700 600 500 400

David's reign (1010-970 B.C.)
Solomon's reign (970-930 B.C.)
Many proverbs written (c.970-930 B.C.)
Division of the kingdom (930 B.C.)
Exile of Israel (722 B.C.)
Hezekiah's reign (715-686 B.C.)
Proverbs compiled and edited (715-686 B.C.)
Fall of Jerusalem (586 B.C.)

Reliable Counsel for Right Living

	THE WAY OF WISDOM *"The fear of the Lord is the beginning of knowledge" (1:7).* ***CHAPTERS 1–9***	**WISDOM FOR THE TRENCHES** *"The fear of the Lord teaches a man wisdom, and humility comes before honor" (15:33).* ***CHAPTERS 10:1–22:16***	**THE REST OF THE BEST** *"Charm is deceptive, and beauty is fleeting; but a woman who fears the Lord is to be praised" (31:30).* ***CHAPTERS 22:17–31:31***
EMPHASIS	**Wisdom especially for youth**	**Wisdom especially for families**	**Wisdom for all**
TOPICS	**Subjects and statements . . .**	**People and problems . . .**	**Counseling and correction**
STYLE	**A book filled with short statements that declare a profound truth providing wisdom for life**		

One of the qualities that has always attracted me to the Bible is its intense practicality. There is no question that the sweeping themes of prophecy are impressive and that the deep, swelling tide of doctrine is invaluable to the Christian. But in my opinion there is nothing to compare with the straightforward, helpful, day-to-day counsel of Scripture that is practical and ready to be applied.

I have a theory that God will hold accountable those who teach the Word and somehow fail to make it practical. Some of us spent years in churches where the Bible lost its significance and relevance because it seemed to lack practicality. To the contrary! The Bible is startlingly fresh and ingeniously practical. I find, even in the prophetic passages, a strong dose of practicality. As a matter of fact, the great doctrinal sections of Scripture that some would dismiss as "boring" will also help us in our everyday lives when we read them and the Holy Spirit speaks to our hearts.

When we come to the book of Proverbs, we have arrived at the most practical book in the Old Testament and, in many ways, the most practical book in all the Bible.

Proverbs and Psalms . . . Knowing the Difference

As we study Proverbs, it is helpful to understand the differences between the books of Proverbs and Psalms. The psalms tell us how to get along with God. The proverbs tells us how to get along with our family, friends and neighbors. The psalms talk about spending time on our knees in prayer. The proverbs talk about spending time on our feet in the streets of our cities, in the jungle of competition, in the midst of the heavy demands of work, the pressures of life and the relentless challenges at home. The book of Psalms teaches us how to praise our Lord. The book of Proverbs teaches us how to appraise our lives. The psalms are vertical, turning our hearts toward heavenly realms. The proverbs are horizontal, directing our thoughts toward earthly responsibilities.

Proverbs for a Month

It's interesting that Proverbs has 31 chapters—the same number of days in many of the months of a year. I can't promise you that a chapter a day will keep the devil away, but I can surely tell you it'll help keep him at arm's length! I have a close friend who reads the book of Proverbs through every month. It's been my observation that the man increases in wisdom year by year. In my opinion, it's not by mistake that God has given us 31 chapters of such practical wisdom—all in one powerful book. I would suggest you try this "Proverbs for a Month" exercise for yourself.

The Wisdom of Solomon

In the very first verse of the book we read that these are "the proverbs of Solomon son of David, king of Israel." These are Solomon's proverbs, and, for the most part, the entire book is his. There are a few other authors whose proverbs have been included in the collection; their writings are found toward the end of the book. However, the vast majority of the proverbs come from Solomon's pen.

Solomon was well known for his great wisdom. The author of 1 Kings spoke glowingly of his renown in these words: "God gave Solomon wisdom and very great insight, and a breadth of understanding as measureless as the sand on the seashore" (1 Kings 4:29).

I believe wisdom is among the greatest of gifts God can give. He can give us money, but if we don't have the wisdom to handle the money, we won't have it long. He can give us fame, but if we do not have the wisdom to handle the fame and all that goes with it, we will eventually deteriorate and pride will take its toll. He can give us earthly power, but without wisdom, power reaps a harvest of destruction. He can even give us length of life, but who wants to live long without the wisdom to handle life?

When God gives a person wisdom and a breadth of understanding, He has equipped that person for meaningful, fulfilling life. Wisdom for daily living is one treasure that keeps us digging into the Bible. Keen discernment is a gracious gift of God that helps us handle the challenges of life.

The person who is wise has the ability to recognize truth, to apply it directly and to rivet it into the mind like a well-driven nail. Solomon was like that. He is credited as the creator of three thousand proverbs and more than one thousand songs (1 Kings 4:32). What a gifted man! He had more than four thousand pieces of writing attributed to his name. That's quite a record.

Understanding a Proverb

When you write a proverb, you don't simply splash a pile of words on paper. You think through what you want to say and you condense it into capsule form. A proverb is a concentrated kernel of truth. It takes time to think through a proverb—both when you write one and when you read one!

Frequently in this book of the Bible you will see the writer take something that is familiar and ordinary and teach a deep truth that is extraordinary. Now that's someone who's been blessed with penetrating wisdom! What an example of the art of illustration! You illustrate something when you take the known and you use it, based on the principle of analogy, to teach the unknown. Solomon was a master of this technique.

The Latin word *proverbia* means "in place of words," or "for words." If you could give the book of Proverbs a definition it may look like this: "It is a book filled with short statements that declare a profound truth providing wisdom for life." The book of Proverbs is a veritable treasure chest of such truth. Brevity is part of the secret of the book's appeal. Solomon could have written book after book, but he stopped with enough material to fill 31 chapters. He is brief and concise, and he provides truth you can take in daily doses. This wealth of wisdom brings about tremendous results when we let it sink into our hearts and influence our lives.

Getting the Picture

Proverbs is filled with word pictures such as the one found in 1:20: "Wisdom calls aloud in the street, she raises her voice in the public squares." Solomon personifies wisdom as a woman of grace standing in busy, noisy traffic, saying as it were, "Learn from me. Be different than those around you. Be distinctive." The book of Proverbs offers this kind of peerless wisdom. I guarantee you, you won't find this much practical discernment in any other literature. The kind of profound wisdom contained in God's divine truth is just not to be found anywhere else.

The contents of Proverbs, of course, are broad and varied, filled with incredible truth for living. In many ways the book defies outlining, but if I had to divide it broadly, I would note three topics in particular: First, *subjects and statements*. The book of Proverbs touches on numerous subjects and weaves certain threads into a tapestry of true and reliable thoughts. Second, *people and problems*. Every conceivable kind of person is mentioned in Proverbs, with a vast array of life problems. Third, *counseling and correction*. The book of Proverbs contains advice for any number of life situations, advice that is, as the apostle Paul once wrote about all Scripture, "useful for teaching, rebuking, correcting and training in righteousness" (2 Timothy 3:16).

Five Keys to the Wisdom of Proverbs

What does the book of Proverbs seek to achieve? I would suggest five purposes. First, *God gave the book of Proverbs to create a desire in our hearts "for attaining wisdom and discipline"* (1:2). God inspired the writing of these proverbs to help us in heeding His warnings—so that our hearts would revere our great and glorious God. Most folks in our day don't take God seriously; generally speaking, the generations that have gone before us did. They lived in fear of God's judgment. Not so today! There is an all-too-casual look of pompous arrogance on the faces of many of us as we come into God's presence. Reading the proverbs will strip off our facade of familiarity and will replace it with a holy reverence. We'll start taking God more seriously the more we meditate on this book.

Second, *the book of Proverbs is designed to provide us with "words of insight"* (1:2). A person who has insight is able to differentiate between good and evil, the authentic and the phony. That individual is also able to see in advance the consequences of his or her decisions. In other words, a person with insight has a better "internal filtering system"—the ability to "see" consequences that are neither obvious nor visible. Reading the proverbs will help you use discernment in your actions. It will fill you with the insight of prudence and common sense; it will help you become a person of good judgment and high integrity.

Third, *the book of Proverbs helps us develop alertness as we walk through life*. Proverbs assists us when we're on the move. As we walk through our day, we want to model wisdom. The writers of the proverbs say, "This will help make it happen." Proverbs keeps us alert, sensitive, aware.

Fourth, *the book of Proverbs will help give direction and meaning to life*. The one thing I notice in the youth of today that is different from the youth of yesteryear is an aimlessness—almost a hollow despair that there can be any sense of successful, joyful, meaningful living. You ask one of any number of college students today, "Where are you going?" and you'll often hear, "I just don't know." Reading the proverbs assists us with needed direction for living.

Fifth and finally, *the book of Proverbs cultivates keenness of mind*. Reading the proverbs cultivates the ability to think deeply and to capture the significance of subjects and issues. How we need this gift—to be able to reflect on and think through important issues that affect not only us but our children and our cities and our nation! Isn't it amazing how mentally lazy we have become? How dull? How lacking in keenness of mind? The writers of the proverbs say, "As you begin to dig into these kernels of truth, you will learn the secret to many of the riddles of life." And remember, we're not talking here about truth for truth's sake. Developing this keenness of mind is not just another intellectual exercise. The proverbs are not just formidable puzzles to be solved to prove how bright we are. No, these are truths God intended to drive home to the heart, where they will shape our behavior and our attitudes to God, to our fellow humans and to ourselves.

Wisdom for Life

The ultimate goal of the book of Proverbs is to take captive all of the sources of knowledge and give us wisdom for living in accordance with them. According to Proverbs, we can grow in wisdom through cultivating a close relationship with the Lord and getting to know Him better, through listening to the advice and observing the actions of our parents, and through our experiences as we go about our daily activities and as we cultivate our relationships with others. As you take the time to read the book of Proverbs, I greatly suspect that your experience will be the same as that of my "Proverbs for a Month" friend: You will grow in wisdom as you choose to live by Proverbs. You will gain a practical understanding of life that will stand you in good stead throughout the rest of your days on earth.

The Way of Wisdom Chapters 1–9

The book of Proverbs begins with a straightforward statement of its purpose—to provide wisdom and understanding for right living. Wisdom is directly related to "the fear of the LORD," as verse 7 of chapter 1 makes clear. Any other wisdom is really a false wisdom; these chapters take great pains to substantiate that claim. Chapters 1–9 contain a series of 13 discourses such as a father would give to his son who is entering his teen years. Solomon contrasts the way and benefits of wisdom with the way of the fool. In this section, Lady Wisdom is pitted against Lady Folly, each trying to entice "simple" youths to follow her ways. The contest is really no contest at all: *The one who finds wisdom will be greatly blessed.* The heart of the message of chapters 1–9 is summed up in Wisdom's final words in this section: "If you are wise, your wisdom will reward you; if you are a mocker, you alone will suffer" (9:12).

Prologue: Purpose and Theme

1 The proverbs of Solomon son of David, king of Israel: 1Ki 4:29-34; Pr 10:1; 25:1

[2]for attaining wisdom and discipline;
for understanding words of insight;
[3]for acquiring a disciplined and prudent life,
doing what is right and just and fair;
[4]for giving prudence to the simple, Pr 8:5
knowledge and discretion to the young—
[5]let the wise listen and add to their learning,
and let the discerning get guidance—
[6]for understanding proverbs and parables,
the sayings and riddles of the wise.

LIVING  **INSIGHT**

In a loud, volatile world marked by surface issues and shallow thoughts, let's commit not to add to it. As we spend time alone with God, we will gain a new respect for His wisdom and a new resolve to live by it.
(See Proverbs 1:1–7.)

[7]The fear of the LORD is the beginning of
knowledge, Job 28:28; Ps 111:10; Ecc 12:13
but fools[a] despise wisdom and discipline.

Exhortations to Embrace Wisdom

Warning Against Enticement

[8]Listen, my son, to your father's instruction
and do not forsake your mother's teaching.
[9]They will be a garland to grace your head
and a chain to adorn your neck. Pr 4:1-9

[10]My son, if sinners entice you, Ge 39:7
do not give in to them. Dt 13:8
[11]If they say, "Come along with us;
let's lie in wait for someone's blood,
let's waylay some harmless soul;
[12]let's swallow them alive, like the grave,[b]
and whole, like those who go down to the
pit; Ps 28:1
[13]we will get all sorts of valuable things
and fill our houses with plunder;
[14]throw in your lot with us,
and we will share a common purse"—
[15]my son, do not go along with them,
do not set foot on their paths; Ps 1:1; 119:101
[16]for their feet rush into sin,
they are swift to shed blood. Isa 59:7
[17]How useless to spread a net
in full view of all the birds!
[18]These men lie in wait for their own blood;
they waylay only themselves!
[19]Such is the end of all who go after ill-gotten
gain;
it takes away the lives of those who get it.

Warning Against Rejecting Wisdom

[20]Wisdom calls aloud in the street, Pr 8:1
she raises her voice in the public squares;
[21]at the head of the noisy streets[c] she cries out,
in the gateways of the city she makes her
speech:

[22]"How long will you simple ones[d] love your
simple ways? Pr 8:5
How long will mockers delight in mockery
and fools hate knowledge?
[23]If you had responded to my rebuke,
I would have poured out my heart to you
and made my thoughts known to you.
[24]But since you rejected me when I called
and no one gave heed when I stretched out
my hand, 1Sa 8:19
[25]since you ignored all my advice
and would not accept my rebuke,
[26]I in turn will laugh at your disaster; Ps 2:4
I will mock when calamity overtakes you—
[27]when calamity overtakes you like a storm,
when disaster sweeps over you like a
whirlwind,
when distress and trouble overwhelm you.

[28]"Then they will call to me but I will not
answer; Isa 1:15; Mic 3:4
they will look for me but will not find me.
[29]Since they hated knowledge
and did not choose to fear the LORD,
[30]since they would not accept my advice
and spurned my rebuke, Ps 81:11

[a]7 The Hebrew words rendered *fool* in Proverbs, and often elsewhere in the Old Testament, denote one who is morally deficient. [b]12 Hebrew *Sheol* [c]21 Hebrew; Septuagint / *on the tops of the walls* [d]22 The Hebrew word rendered *simple* in Proverbs generally denotes one without moral direction and inclined to evil.

[31]they will eat the fruit of their ways
and be filled with the fruit of their schemes.
[32]For the waywardness of the simple will kill them,
and the complacency of fools will destroy them;
[33]but whoever listens to me will live in safety
and be at ease, without fear of harm."

Moral Benefits of Wisdom

2 My son, if you accept my words
and store up my commands within you,
[2]turning your ear to wisdom
and applying your heart to understanding,
[3]and if you call out for insight
and cry aloud for understanding,
[4]and if you look for it as for silver
and search for it as for hidden treasure,
[5]then you will understand the fear of the LORD
and find the knowledge of God. Pr 1:7
[6]For the LORD gives wisdom, 1Ki 3:9,12; Jas 1:5
and from his mouth come knowledge and understanding.
[7]He holds victory in store for the upright,
he is a shield to those whose walk is blameless, Ps 84:11; Pr 30:5-6
[8]for he guards the course of the just
and protects the way of his faithful ones.

[9]Then you will understand what is right and just Dt 1:16
and fair—every good path.
[10]For wisdom will enter your heart, Pr 14:33
and knowledge will be pleasant to your soul.
[11]Discretion will protect you,
and understanding will guard you. Pr 6:22

[12]Wisdom will save you from the ways of wicked men,
from men whose words are perverse,
[13]who leave the straight paths
to walk in dark ways, Jn 3:19
[14]who delight in doing wrong
and rejoice in the perverseness of evil,
[15]whose paths are crooked Ps 125:5
and who are devious in their ways. Pr 21:8

[16]It will save you also from the adulteress,
from the wayward wife with her seductive words,
[17]who has left the partner of her youth
and ignored the covenant she made before God.[a] Mal 2:14
[18]For her house leads down to death
and her paths to the spirits of the dead.
[19]None who go to her return
or attain the paths of life. Ecc 7:26
[20]Thus you will walk in the ways of good men
and keep to the paths of the righteous.
[21]For the upright will live in the land, Ps 37:29
and the blameless will remain in it;
[22]but the wicked will be cut off from the land,
and the unfaithful will be torn from it.

Further Benefits of Wisdom

3 My son, do not forget my teaching, Pr 4:5
but keep my commands in your heart,
[2]for they will prolong your life many years
and bring you prosperity.

[3]Let love and faithfulness never leave you;
bind them around your neck,
write them on the tablet of your heart.
[4]Then you will win favor and a good name
in the sight of God and man. 1Sa 2:26; Lk 2:52

LIVING 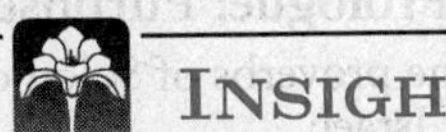 **INSIGHT**

Over and over, we need to underscore God's reliability as we talk to our children. "The Lord is our God, children. We must trust Him without reservation. There is no one more reliable. His will is perfect. All that is happening fits beautifully into His wise plan for us."

(See Proverbs 3:1–6.)

[5]Trust in the LORD with all your heart Ps 37:3,5
and lean not on your own understanding;
[6]in all your ways acknowledge him,
and he will make your paths straight.[b]

[7]Do not be wise in your own eyes; Ro 12:16
fear the LORD and shun evil. Pr 16:6
[8]This will bring health to your body Pr 4:22
and nourishment to your bones. Job 21:24

[9]Honor the LORD with your wealth,
with the firstfruits of all your crops; Ex 22:29
[10]then your barns will be filled to overflowing,
and your vats will brim over with new wine. Joel 2:24

[11]My son, do not despise the LORD's discipline
and do not resent his rebuke,
[12]because the LORD disciplines those he loves,
as a father[c] the son he delights in. Dt 8:5

[13]Blessed is the man who finds wisdom,
the man who gains understanding,
[14]for she is more profitable than silver
and yields better returns than gold. Job 28:15
[15]She is more precious than rubies; Job 28:18
nothing you desire can compare with her.
[16]Long life is in her right hand;

[a] 17 Or *covenant of her God* [b] 6 Or *will direct your paths* [c] 12 Hebrew; Septuagint / *and he punishes*

in her left hand are riches and honor.
17Her ways are pleasant ways,
and all her paths are peace. Pr 16:7; Mt 11:28-30
18She is a tree of life to those who embrace her;
those who lay hold of her will be blessed.

19By wisdom the LORD laid the earth's
foundations, Ps 104:24
by understanding he set the heavens in
place; Pr 8:27-29
20by his knowledge the deeps were divided,
and the clouds let drop the dew.

21My son, preserve sound judgment and
discernment,
do not let them out of your sight; Pr 4:20-22
22they will be life for you,
an ornament to grace your neck. Pr 1:8-9
23Then you will go on your way in safety,
and your foot will not stumble; Pr 4:12
24when you lie down, you will not be afraid;
when you lie down, your sleep will be
sweet. Job 11:18
25Have no fear of sudden disaster
or of the ruin that overtakes the wicked,
26for the LORD will be your confidence
and will keep your foot from being snared.

27Do not withhold good from those who
deserve it,
when it is in your power to act.
28Do not say to your neighbor,
"Come back later; I'll give it tomorrow"—
when you now have it with you. Lev 19:13

LIVING  **INSIGHT**

Procrastination. No liar is better respected. No bandit better rewarded. No giant better treated. He can outthink any executive when it comes to correspondence. He can outlast any parent when it comes to discipline. He has one basic product, and he centers all his energy toward that single goal: defeat.

(See Proverbs 3:27–28.)

29Do not plot harm against your neighbor,
who lives trustfully near you.
30Do not accuse a man for no reason—
when he has done you no harm.

31Do not envy a violent man Ps 37:1; Pr 24:1-2
or choose any of his ways,
32for the LORD detests a perverse man Pr 11:20
but takes the upright into his confidence.
33The LORD's curse is on the house of the
wicked, Zec 5:4; Mal 2:2
but he blesses the home of the righteous.
34He mocks proud mockers
but gives grace to the humble. Jas 4:6*; 1Pe 5:5*
35The wise inherit honor,
but fools he holds up to shame.

Wisdom Is Supreme

4 Listen, my sons, to a father's instruction;
pay attention and gain understanding.
2I give you sound learning,
so do not forsake my teaching.
3When I was a boy in my father's house,
still tender, and an only child of my
mother,
4he taught me and said,
"Lay hold of my words with all your heart;
keep my commands and you will live. Pr 7:2
5Get wisdom, get understanding; Pr 16:16
do not forget my words or swerve from
them.
6Do not forsake wisdom, and she will protect
you; 2Th 2:10
love her, and she will watch over you.
7Wisdom is supreme; therefore get wisdom.
Though it cost all you have,[a] get
understanding. Pr 23:23; Mt 13:44-46
8Esteem her, and she will exalt you;
embrace her, and she will honor you.
9She will set a garland of grace on your head
and present you with a crown of splendor."

10Listen, my son, accept what I say,
and the years of your life will be many.
11I guide you in the way of wisdom 1Sa 12:23
and lead you along straight paths.
12When you walk, your steps will not be
hampered;
when you run, you will not stumble. Job 18:7
13Hold on to instruction, do not let it go;
guard it well, for it is your life. Pr 3:22
14Do not set foot on the path of the wicked
or walk in the way of evil men. Ps 1:1; Pr 1:15
15Avoid it, do not travel on it;
turn from it and go on your way.
16For they cannot sleep till they do evil; Ps 36:4
they are robbed of slumber till they make
someone fall.
17They eat the bread of wickedness
and drink the wine of violence. Pr 1:10-19

18The path of the righteous is like the first
gleam of dawn, Isa 26:7
shining ever brighter till the full light of
day. 2Sa 23:4; Php 2:15
19But the way of the wicked is like deep
darkness; Job 18:5; Isa 59:9-10; Jn 12:35

[a]7 Or *Whatever else you get*

they do not know what makes them
stumble.

20My son, pay attention to what I say;
listen closely to my words. Pr 5:1
21Do not let them out of your sight, Pr 3:21
keep them within your heart;
22for they are life to those who find them
and health to a man's whole body. Pr 3:8
23Above all else, guard your heart,
for it is the wellspring of life. Mt 12:34; Lk 6:45

LIVING  INSIGHT

The Bible says little about success, but a lot about heart, the place where true success originates. How important is the heart! It is there that character is formed. It alone holds the secrets of true success. Its treasures are priceless—but they can be stolen. Are you guarding it?
(See Proverbs 4:23.)

24Put away perversity from your mouth;
keep corrupt talk far from your lips.
25Let your eyes look straight ahead,
fix your gaze directly before you.
26Make level[a] paths for your feet Heb 12:13*
and take only ways that are firm.
27Do not swerve to the right or the left; Dt 5:32
keep your foot from evil.

Warning Against Adultery

5 My son, pay attention to my wisdom,
listen well to my words of insight, Pr 4:20
2that you may maintain discretion
and your lips may preserve knowledge.
3For the lips of an adulteress drip honey,
and her speech is smoother than oil; Ps 55:21
4but in the end she is bitter as gall, Ecc 7:26
sharp as a double-edged sword.
5Her feet go down to death;
her steps lead straight to the grave.[b]
6She gives no thought to the way of life;
her paths are crooked, but she knows it
not. Pr 30:20

7Now then, my sons, listen to me; Pr 7:24
do not turn aside from what I say.
8Keep to a path far from her, Pr 7:1-27
do not go near the door of her house,
9lest you give your best strength to others
and your years to one who is cruel,
10lest strangers feast on your wealth
and your toil enrich another man's house.
11At the end of your life you will groan,
when your flesh and body are spent.
12You will say, "How I hated discipline!
How my heart spurned correction! Pr 1:29
13I would not obey my teachers
or listen to my instructors.
14I have come to the brink of utter ruin Pr 1:24-27
in the midst of the whole assembly."

15Drink water from your own cistern,
running water from your own well.
16Should your springs overflow in the streets,
your streams of water in the public squares?
17Let them be yours alone,
never to be shared with strangers.
18May your fountain be blessed, SS 4:12-15
and may you rejoice in the wife of your
youth. Ecc 9:9; Mal 2:14
19A loving doe, a graceful deer— SS 2:9; 4:5
may her breasts satisfy you always,
may you ever be captivated by her love.
20Why be captivated, my son, by an adulteress?
Why embrace the bosom of another man's
wife?

21For a man's ways are in full view of the LORD,
and he examines all his paths. Job 31:4; 34:21
22The evil deeds of a wicked man ensnare him;
the cords of his sin hold him fast. Nu 32:23
23He will die for lack of discipline, Job 4:21; 36:12
led astray by his own great folly.

Warnings Against Folly

6 My son, if you have put up security for
your neighbor, Pr 17:18
if you have struck hands in pledge for
another, Pr 11:15; 22:26-27
2if you have been trapped by what you said,
ensnared by the words of your mouth,
3then do this, my son, to free yourself,
since you have fallen into your neighbor's
hands:
Go and humble yourself;
press your plea with your neighbor!
4Allow no sleep to your eyes,
no slumber to your eyelids. Ps 132:4
5Free yourself, like a gazelle from the hand of
the hunter,
like a bird from the snare of the fowler.

6Go to the ant, you sluggard; Pr 20:4
consider its ways and be wise!
7It has no commander,
no overseer or ruler,
8yet it stores its provisions in summer
and gathers its food at harvest. Pr 10:4

9How long will you lie there, you sluggard?
When will you get up from your sleep?
10A little sleep, a little slumber,

[a]26 Or *Consider the* [b]5 Hebrew *Sheol*

a little folding of the hands to rest—
[11]and poverty will come on you like a bandit
and scarcity like an armed man.[a]

[12]A scoundrel and villain,
who goes about with a corrupt mouth,
[13] who winks with his eye, Ps 35:19
signals with his feet
and motions with his fingers,
[14] who plots evil with deceit in his heart—
he always stirs up dissension. ver 16-19
[15]Therefore disaster will overtake him in an
instant;
he will suddenly be destroyed—without
remedy. 2Ch 36:16

[16]There are six things the LORD hates,
seven that are detestable to him:
[17] haughty eyes,
a lying tongue, Ps 120:2; Pr 12:22
hands that shed innocent blood, Isa 1:15
[18] a heart that devises wicked schemes,
feet that are quick to rush into evil, Ge 6:5
[19] a false witness who pours out lies Ps 27:12
and a man who stirs up dissension
among brothers. ver 12-15

Warning Against Adultery

[20]My son, keep your father's commands
and do not forsake your mother's teaching.
[21]Bind them upon your heart forever;
fasten them around your neck. Pr 3:3; 7:1-3
[22]When you walk, they will guide you;
when you sleep, they will watch over you;
when you awake, they will speak to you.

LIVING  INSIGHT

God promises that our growing children will later be able to use what they learn. They will be guided when they walk . . . protected when they sleep . . . encouraged when they awaken. Such are the dividends of parental investment.
(See Proverbs 6:20–23.)

[23]For these commands are a lamp,
this teaching is a light, Ps 19:8; 119:105
and the corrections of discipline
are the way to life,
[24]keeping you from the immoral woman,
from the smooth tongue of the wayward
wife. Pr 2:16; 7:5
[25]Do not lust in your heart after her beauty
or let her captivate you with her eyes,
[26]for the prostitute reduces you to a loaf of
bread,
and the adulteress preys upon your very
life. Pr 7:22-23; 29:3
[27]Can a man scoop fire into his lap
without his clothes being burned?
[28]Can a man walk on hot coals
without his feet being scorched?
[29]So is he who sleeps with another man's wife;
no one who touches her will go
unpunished.

[30]Men do not despise a thief if he steals
to satisfy his hunger when he is starving.
[31]Yet if he is caught, he must pay sevenfold,
though it costs him all the wealth of his
house.
[32]But a man who commits adultery lacks
judgment; Pr 7:7
whoever does so destroys himself.
[33]Blows and disgrace are his lot,
and his shame will never be wiped away;
[34]for jealousy arouses a husband's fury, Ge 34:7
and he will show no mercy when he takes
revenge.
[35]He will not accept any compensation;
he will refuse the bribe, however great it is.

Warning Against the Adulteress

7 My son, keep my words Pr 2:1
and store up my commands within you.
[2]Keep my commands and you will live; Pr 4:4
guard my teachings as the apple of your
eye.
[3]Bind them on your fingers;
write them on the tablet of your heart.
[4]Say to wisdom, "You are my sister,"
and call understanding your kinsman;

LIVING  INSIGHT

Those who sustain a close companionship with wisdom tend to be more tender, compassionate, sympathetic and tolerant than those whose world revolves simply around themselves.
(See Proverbs 7:4.)

[5]they will keep you from the adulteress,
from the wayward wife with her seductive
words. Pr 2:16; 6:24

[6]At the window of my house
I looked out through the lattice.
[7]I saw among the simple,
I noticed among the young men,

[a]11 *Or like a vagrant / and scarcity like a beggar*

a youth who lacked judgment. Pr 6:32
8He was going down the street near her corner,
walking along in the direction of her house
9at twilight, as the day was fading, Job 24:15
as the dark of night set in.

10Then out came a woman to meet him,
dressed like a prostitute and with crafty intent.
11(She is loud and defiant, Pr 9:13; 1Ti 5:13
her feet never stay at home;
12now in the street, now in the squares,
at every corner she lurks.) Pr 8:1-36
13She took hold of him and kissed him Ge 39:12
and with a brazen face she said:

14"I have fellowship offerings[a] at home;
today I fulfilled my vows.
15So I came out to meet you;
I looked for you and have found you!
16I have covered my bed
with colored linens from Egypt.
17I have perfumed my bed Est 1:6
with myrrh, aloes and cinnamon. Ge 37:25
18Come, let's drink deep of love till morning;
let's enjoy ourselves with love! Ge 39:7
19My husband is not at home;
he has gone on a long journey.
20He took his purse filled with money
and will not be home till full moon."
21With persuasive words she led him astray;
she seduced him with her smooth talk.
22All at once he followed her
like an ox going to the slaughter,
like a deer[b] stepping into a noose[c] Job 18:10
23 till an arrow pierces his liver, Job 15:22
like a bird darting into a snare,
little knowing it will cost him his life.

24Now then, my sons, listen to me; Pr 1:8-9
pay attention to what I say.
25Do not let your heart turn to her ways
or stray into her paths. Pr 5:7-8
26Many are the victims she has brought down;
her slain are a mighty throng.
27Her house is a highway to the grave,[d]
leading down to the chambers of death.

Wisdom's Call

8 Does not wisdom call out? Pr 1:20; 9:3
Does not understanding raise her voice?
2On the heights along the way,
where the paths meet, she takes her stand;
3beside the gates leading into the city,
at the entrances, she cries aloud: Job 29:7
4"To you, O men, I call out;
I raise my voice to all mankind.
5You who are simple, gain prudence; Pr 1:4,22
you who are foolish, gain understanding.
6Listen, for I have worthy things to say;
I open my lips to speak what is right.
7My mouth speaks what is true, Ps 37:30; Jn 8:14
for my lips detest wickedness.
8All the words of my mouth are just;
none of them is crooked or perverse.
9To the discerning all of them are right;
they are faultless to those who have knowledge.
10Choose my instruction instead of silver,
knowledge rather than choice gold, Pr 3:14-15
11for wisdom is more precious than rubies,
and nothing you desire can compare with her. Pr 3:13-15

12"I, wisdom, dwell together with prudence;
I possess knowledge and discretion. Pr 1:4
13To fear the LORD is to hate evil; Pr 16:6
I hate pride and arrogance, Jer 44:4
evil behavior and perverse speech.
14Counsel and sound judgment are mine;
I have understanding and power. Ecc 7:19
15By me kings reign
and rulers make laws that are just; Da 2:21
16by me princes govern,
and all nobles who rule on earth.[e]
17I love those who love me, 1Sa 2:30; Jn 14:21-24
and those who seek me find me. Pr 1:28; Jas 1:5
18With me are riches and honor, Pr 3:16
enduring wealth and prosperity. Mt 6:33
19My fruit is better than fine gold;
what I yield surpasses choice silver. Pr 3:13-14
20I walk in the way of righteousness,
along the paths of justice,
21bestowing wealth on those who love me
and making their treasuries full. Pr 15:6; 24:4

22"The LORD brought me forth as the first of his works,[f,g]
before his deeds of old;
23I was appointed[h] from eternity,
from the beginning, before the world began.
24When there were no oceans, I was given birth,
when there were no springs abounding with water; Ge 7:11
25before the mountains were settled in place,
before the hills, I was given birth, Job 15:7
26before he made the earth or its fields
or any of the dust of the world. Ps 90:2
27I was there when he set the heavens in place,
when he marked out the horizon on the face of the deep,
28when he established the clouds above

[a] 14 Traditionally *peace offerings* [b] 22 Syriac (see also Septuagint); Hebrew *fool* [c] 22 The meaning of the Hebrew for this line is uncertain. [d] 27 Hebrew *Sheol* [e] 16 Many Hebrew manuscripts and Septuagint; most Hebrew manuscripts *and nobles—all righteous rulers* [f] 22 Or *way*; or *dominion* [g] 22 Or *The LORD possessed me at the beginning of his work*; or *The LORD brought me forth at the beginning of his work* [h] 23 Or *fashioned*

and fixed securely the fountains of the deep,
[29]when he gave the sea its boundary Ge 1:9
so the waters would not overstep his command, Ps 104:9
and when he marked out the foundations of the earth. Job 38:5
30 Then I was the craftsman at his side. Jn 1:1-3
I was filled with delight day after day,
rejoicing always in his presence,
[31]rejoicing in his whole world
and delighting in mankind. Ps 16:3; 104:1-30

[32]"Now then, my sons, listen to me;
blessed are those who keep my ways.
[33]Listen to my instruction and be wise;
do not ignore it.
[34]Blessed is the man who listens to me, Pr 3:13,18
watching daily at my doors,
waiting at my doorway.
[35]For whoever finds me finds life Pr 3:13-18
and receives favor from the LORD. Pr 12:2
[36]But whoever fails to find me harms himself;
all who hate me love death."

Invitations of Wisdom and of Folly

9 Wisdom has built her house; Eph 2:20-22; 1Pe 2:5
she has hewn out its seven pillars.
[2]She has prepared her meat and mixed her wine;
she has also set her table. Lk 14:16-23
[3]She has sent out her maids, and she calls
from the highest point of the city.
[4]"Let all who are simple come in here!"
she says to those who lack judgment. Pr 6:32
[5]"Come, eat my food
and drink the wine I have mixed. Isa 55:1
[6]Leave your simple ways and you will live;
walk in the way of understanding.

[7]"Whoever corrects a mocker invites insult;
whoever rebukes a wicked man incurs abuse. Pr 23:9
[8]Do not rebuke a mocker or he will hate you;
rebuke a wise man and he will love you.
[9]Instruct a wise man and he will be wiser still;
teach a righteous man and he will add to his learning. Pr 1:5,7

[10]"The fear of the LORD is the beginning of wisdom, Job 28:28; Pr 1:7
and knowledge of the Holy One is understanding. Dt 4:6
[11]For through me your days will be many,
and years will be added to your life. Pr 3:16
[12]If you are wise, your wisdom will reward you;
if you are a mocker, you alone will suffer."

[13]The woman Folly is loud; Pr 7:11
she is undisciplined and without knowledge.
[14]She sits at the door of her house,
on a seat at the highest point of the city,
[15]calling out to those who pass by,
who go straight on their way.
[16]"Let all who are simple come in here!"
she says to those who lack judgment. Pr 1:22
[17]"Stolen water is sweet;
food eaten in secret is delicious!" Pr 20:17
[18]But little do they know that the dead are there,
that her guests are in the depths of the grave.[a] Pr 2:18; 7:26-27

Wisdom for the Trenches **Chapters 10:1–22:16**

This next section in Proverbs represents the main collection of Solomon's proverbs. These proverbs cover a wide range of topics. On the surface, there doesn't seem to be any discernible arrangement, but many of these proverbs contain important advice about family relationships. Most of the proverbs in this section are two lines long (called a "couplet"), and many of them express a contrast. At times Solomon will simply make a general observation, but it is typical that he will evaluate and give advice about behavior. A number of these proverbs also describe the consequences of a particular action or character trait. We have here good, solid wisdom aimed at giving us a subtle and practical understanding of life. Its education prepares us for the street and for the marketplace, not simply for the classroom. It is "wisdom for the trenches!"

Proverbs of Solomon

10 The proverbs of Solomon: Pr 1:1

A wise son brings joy to his father, Pr 15:20
but a foolish son grief to his mother.

[2]Ill-gotten treasures are of no value, Pr 21:6
but righteousness delivers from death.

[3]The LORD does not let the righteous go hungry Mt 6:25-34
but he thwarts the craving of the wicked.

[4]Lazy hands make a man poor, Pr 19:15
but diligent hands bring wealth. Pr 13:4
[5]He who gathers crops in summer is a wise son,
but he who sleeps during harvest is a disgraceful son.

[6]Blessings crown the head of the righteous,
but violence overwhelms the mouth of the wicked.[b]

[7]The memory of the righteous will be a blessing, Ps 112:6
but the name of the wicked will rot. Ps 109:13

[a]18 Hebrew *Sheol* [b]6 Or *but the mouth of the wicked conceals violence*; also in verse 11

[8]The wise in heart accept commands,
but a chattering fool comes to ruin.

[9]The man of integrity walks securely, Ps 23:4
but he who takes crooked paths will be found out. Pr 28:18

[10]He who winks maliciously causes grief,
and a chattering fool comes to ruin.

[11]The mouth of the righteous is a fountain of life, Ps 37:30
but violence overwhelms the mouth of the wicked.

[12]Hatred stirs up dissension,
but love covers over all wrongs. 1Pe 4:8

[13]Wisdom is found on the lips of the discerning,
but a rod is for the back of him who lacks judgment. Pr 26:3

[14]Wise men store up knowledge,
but the mouth of a fool invites ruin. Pr 18:6-7

[15]The wealth of the rich is their fortified city,
but poverty is the ruin of the poor. Pr 19:7

[16]The wages of the righteous bring them life,
but the income of the wicked brings them punishment. Pr 11:18-19

[17]He who heeds discipline shows the way to life,
but whoever ignores correction leads others astray.

[18]He who conceals his hatred has lying lips,
and whoever spreads slander is a fool.

[19]When words are many, sin is not absent,
but he who holds his tongue is wise. Pr 17:28

[20]The tongue of the righteous is choice silver,
but the heart of the wicked is of little value.

[21]The lips of the righteous nourish many,
but fools die for lack of judgment.

[22]The blessing of the LORD brings wealth, Ge 24:35
and he adds no trouble to it.

[23]A fool finds pleasure in evil conduct, Pr 15:21

LIVING  **INSIGHT**

Think first before you speak. Before your lips start moving, pause ten seconds and mentally preview your words. Are they accurate or exaggerated? Kind or cutting? Necessary or needless? Wholesome or vile? Grateful or complaining?
(See Proverbs 10:18–21.)

but a man of understanding delights in wisdom.

[24]What the wicked dreads will overtake him;
what the righteous desire will be granted.

[25]When the storm has swept by, the wicked are gone,
but the righteous stand firm forever. Ps 15:5

[26]As vinegar to the teeth and smoke to the eyes,
so is a sluggard to those who send him.

[27]The fear of the LORD adds length to life,
but the years of the wicked are cut short.

[28]The prospect of the righteous is joy,
but the hopes of the wicked come to nothing. Job 8:13; Pr 11:7

[29]The way of the LORD is a refuge for the righteous,
but it is the ruin of those who do evil.

[30]The righteous will never be uprooted,
but the wicked will not remain in the land.

[31]The mouth of the righteous brings forth wisdom, Ps 37:30
but a perverse tongue will be cut out.

[32]The lips of the righteous know what is fitting,
but the mouth of the wicked only what is perverse.

11 The LORD abhors dishonest scales,
but accurate weights are his delight.

[2]When pride comes, then comes disgrace,
but with humility comes wisdom. Pr 18:12

LIVING  **INSIGHT**

False humility stinks worse than raw conceit. The answer is not in trying to appear worthless and "wormy" but in consistently taking notice of others' achievements, recognizing others' skills and contributions . . . and saying so. Indeed, the way of true humility is the truly wise way.
(See Proverbs 11:2.)

[3]The integrity of the upright guides them,
but the unfaithful are destroyed by their duplicity. Pr 13:6

[4]Wealth is worthless in the day of wrath,
but righteousness delivers from death. Ge 7:1

[5]The righteousness of the blameless makes a straight way for them,
but the wicked are brought down by their own wickedness. Pr 5:21-23

[6]The righteousness of the upright delivers them,
but the unfaithful are trapped by evil desires. Est 7:9

[7]When a wicked man dies, his hope perishes;
all he expected from his power comes to nothing. Pr 10:28

[8]The righteous man is rescued from trouble,
and it comes on the wicked instead. Pr 21:18

[9]With his mouth the godless destroys his neighbor,
but through knowledge the righteous escape. Jer 45:5

[10]When the righteous prosper, the city rejoices;
when the wicked perish, there are shouts of joy.

[11]Through the blessing of the upright a city is exalted,
but by the mouth of the wicked it is destroyed. Pr 29:8

[12]A man who lacks judgment derides his neighbor, Pr 14:21
but a man of understanding holds his tongue.

[13]A gossip betrays a confidence, Lev 19:16; Pr 20:19
but a trustworthy man keeps a secret.

[14]For lack of guidance a nation falls,
but many advisers make victory sure.

[15]He who puts up security for another will surely suffer, Pr 6:1
but whoever refuses to strike hands in pledge is safe.

[16]A kindhearted woman gains respect, Pr 31:31
but ruthless men gain only wealth.

[17]A kind man benefits himself,
but a cruel man brings trouble on himself.

[18]The wicked man earns deceptive wages,
but he who sows righteousness reaps a sure reward. Hos 10:12-13

[19]The truly righteous man attains life, Dt 30:15
but he who pursues evil goes to his death.

[20]The LORD detests men of perverse heart
but he delights in those whose ways are blameless. Ps 119:1; Pr 12:2,22

[21]Be sure of this: The wicked will not go unpunished,
but those who are righteous will go free.

[22]Like a gold ring in a pig's snout
is a beautiful woman who shows no discretion.

[23]The desire of the righteous ends only in good,
but the hope of the wicked only in wrath.

[24]One man gives freely, yet gains even more;
another withholds unduly, but comes to poverty.

[25]A generous man will prosper;
he who refreshes others will himself be refreshed. Mt 5:7; 2Co 9:6-9

[26]People curse the man who hoards grain,
but blessing crowns him who is willing to sell.

[27]He who seeks good finds goodwill,
but evil comes to him who searches for it.

[28]Whoever trusts in his riches will fall, Mk 10:25
but the righteous will thrive like a green leaf. Ps 1:3; Jer 17:8

[29]He who brings trouble on his family will inherit only wind,
and the fool will be servant to the wise.

[30]The fruit of the righteous is a tree of life,
and he who wins souls is wise.

[31]If the righteous receive their due on earth,
how much more the ungodly and the sinner!

12 Whoever loves discipline loves knowledge,
but he who hates correction is stupid.

[2]A good man obtains favor from the LORD,
but the LORD condemns a crafty man.

[3]A man cannot be established through wickedness,
but the righteous cannot be uprooted.

[4]A wife of noble character is her husband's crown,
but a disgraceful wife is like decay in his bones. Pr 14:30

[5]The plans of the righteous are just,
but the advice of the wicked is deceitful.

[6]The words of the wicked lie in wait for blood,
but the speech of the upright rescues them.

[7]Wicked men are overthrown and are no more,
but the house of the righteous stands firm.

[8]A man is praised according to his wisdom,
but men with warped minds are despised.

[9]Better to be a nobody and yet have a servant
than pretend to be somebody and have no food.

[10]A righteous man cares for the needs of his animal, Nu 22:29
but the kindest acts of the wicked are cruel.

[11]He who works his land will have abundant
food,
but he who chases fantasies lacks judgment.

[12]The wicked desire the plunder of evil men,
but the root of the righteous flourishes.

[13]An evil man is trapped by his sinful talk,
but a righteous man escapes trouble. 2Pe 2:9

[14]From the fruit of his lips a man is filled with
good things Pr 13:2
as surely as the work of his hands rewards
him. Isa 3:10-11

[15]The way of a fool seems right to him, Pr 14:12
but a wise man listens to advice.

[16]A fool shows his annoyance at once,
but a prudent man overlooks an insult.

[17]A truthful witness gives honest testimony,
but a false witness tells lies. Pr 14:5,25

[18]Reckless words pierce like a sword, Ps 57:4
but the tongue of the wise brings healing.

[19]Truthful lips endure forever,
but a lying tongue lasts only a moment.

[20]There is deceit in the hearts of those who plot
evil,
but joy for those who promote peace.

[21]No harm befalls the righteous, Ps 91:10
but the wicked have their fill of trouble.

[22]The LORD detests lying lips, Pr 6:17; Rev 22:15
but he delights in men who are truthful.

[23]A prudent man keeps his knowledge to
himself, Pr 13:16
but the heart of fools blurts out folly.

[24]Diligent hands will rule,
but laziness ends in slave labor. Pr 10:4

[25]An anxious heart weighs a man down, Pr 15:13
but a kind word cheers him up.

[26]A righteous man is cautious in friendship,[a]
but the way of the wicked leads them
astray.

[27]The lazy man does not roast[b] his game,
but the diligent man prizes his possessions.

[28]In the way of righteousness there is life;
along that path is immortality.

13

A wise son heeds his father's instruction,
but a mocker does not listen to rebuke.

[2]From the fruit of his lips a man enjoys good
things, Pr 12:14
but the unfaithful have a craving for
violence.

[3]He who guards his lips guards his life, Pr 21:23
but he who speaks rashly will come to ruin.

[4]The sluggard craves and gets nothing,
but the desires of the diligent are fully
satisfied.

[5]The righteous hate what is false, Ps 119:128
but the wicked bring shame and disgrace.

[6]Righteousness guards the man of integrity,
but wickedness overthrows the sinner.

[7]One man pretends to be rich, yet has nothing;
another pretends to be poor, yet has great
wealth. 2Co 6:10

[8]A man's riches may ransom his life,
but a poor man hears no threat.

[9]The light of the righteous shines brightly,
but the lamp of the wicked is snuffed out.

[10]Pride only breeds quarrels,
but wisdom is found in those who take
advice.

[11]Dishonest money dwindles away, Pr 10:2
but he who gathers money little by little
makes it grow.

[12]Hope deferred makes the heart sick,
but a longing fulfilled is a tree of life.

[13]He who scorns instruction will pay for it,
but he who respects a command is
rewarded.

[14]The teaching of the wise is a fountain of life,
turning a man from the snares of death.

[15]Good understanding wins favor,
but the way of the unfaithful is hard.[c]

[16]Every prudent man acts out of knowledge,
but a fool exposes his folly. Pr 12:23

[17]A wicked messenger falls into trouble,
but a trustworthy envoy brings healing.

[18]He who ignores discipline comes to poverty
and shame,
but whoever heeds correction is honored.

[19]A longing fulfilled is sweet to the soul,
but fools detest turning from evil.

[20]He who walks with the wise grows wise,
but a companion of fools suffers harm.

[21]Misfortune pursues the sinner,
but prosperity is the reward of the
righteous. Ps 32:10

[a]26 Or *man is a guide to his neighbor* [b]27 The meaning of the Hebrew for this word is uncertain. [c]15 Or *unfaithful does not endure*

[22]A good man leaves an inheritance for his
children's children,
but a sinner's wealth is stored up for the
righteous. Job 27:17; Ecc 2:26

[23]A poor man's field may produce abundant
food,
but injustice sweeps it away.

[24]He who spares the rod hates his son,
but he who loves him is careful to
discipline him. Pr 19:18; 22:15; 29:15,17

LIVING  **INSIGHT**

It was insightful of Solomon to link love with discipline. Those who truly love their children realize the importance of consistent discipline. A child senses that parents who stand their ground and maintain established parameters deeply care about him or her. That kind of love provides an emotional undergirding essential for mature adulthood.

(See Proverbs 13:24.)

[25]The righteous eat to their hearts' content,
but the stomach of the wicked goes hungry.

14 The wise woman builds her house, Pr 24:3
but with her own hands the foolish one
tears hers down.

[2]He whose walk is upright fears the LORD,
but he whose ways are devious despises
him.

[3]A fool's talk brings a rod to his back, Pr 10:14
but the lips of the wise protect them. Pr 12:6

[4]Where there are no oxen, the manger is
empty,
but from the strength of an ox comes an
abundant harvest.

[5]A truthful witness does not deceive,
but a false witness pours out lies. Pr 6:19; 12:17

[6]The mocker seeks wisdom and finds none,
but knowledge comes easily to the
discerning. Pr 9:9

[7]Stay away from a foolish man,
for you will not find knowledge on his lips.

[8]The wisdom of the prudent is to give thought
to their ways, Pr 15:28
but the folly of fools is deception. ver 24

[9]Fools mock at making amends for sin,
but goodwill is found among the upright.

[10]Each heart knows its own bitterness,
and no one else can share its joy.

[11]The house of the wicked will be destroyed,
but the tent of the upright will flourish.

LIVING  **INSIGHT**

Our thoughts form the thermostat that regulates what we accomplish in life . . . You and I become what we think about.

(See Proverbs 14:8.)

[12]There is a way that seems right to a man,
but in the end it leads to death. Pr 16:25

[13]Even in laughter the heart may ache, Ecc 2:2
and joy may end in grief.

[14]The faithless will be fully repaid for their
ways, Pr 1:31
and the good man rewarded for his. Pr 12:14

[15]A simple man believes anything,
but a prudent man gives thought to his
steps.

[16]A wise man fears the LORD and shuns evil,
but a fool is hotheaded and reckless.

[17]A quick-tempered man does foolish things,
and a crafty man is hated.

[18]The simple inherit folly,
but the prudent are crowned with
knowledge.

[19]Evil men will bow down in the presence of the
good,
and the wicked at the gates of the
righteous. Pr 11:29

[20]The poor are shunned even by their
neighbors,
but the rich have many friends. Pr 19:4,7

[21]He who despises his neighbor sins, Pr 11:12
but blessed is he who is kind to the needy.

[22]Do not those who plot evil go astray? Pr 4:16-17
But those who plan what is good find[a]
love and faithfulness.

[23]All hard work brings a profit,
but mere talk leads only to poverty.

[24]The wealth of the wise is their crown,
but the folly of fools yields folly. ver 8

[25]A truthful witness saves lives,
but a false witness is deceitful. ver 5

[a]22 Or *show*

26He who fears the LORD has a secure fortress,
and for his children it will be a refuge.

27The fear of the LORD is a fountain of life,
turning a man from the snares of death.

28A large population is a king's glory,
but without subjects a prince is ruined.

29A patient man has great understanding, Pr 17:27
but a quick-tempered man displays folly.

30A heart at peace gives life to the body,
but envy rots the bones. Pr 12:4

31He who oppresses the poor shows contempt for their Maker, Pr 17:5
but whoever is kind to the needy honors God. Dt 24:14

32When calamity comes, the wicked are brought down, Pr 6:15
but even in death the righteous have a refuge. Job 13:15; 2Ti 4:18

33Wisdom reposes in the heart of the discerning
and even among fools she lets herself be known.[a]

34Righteousness exalts a nation, Pr 11:11
but sin is a disgrace to any people.

35A king delights in a wise servant,
but a shameful servant incurs his wrath.

15 A gentle answer turns away wrath,
but a harsh word stirs up anger.

2The tongue of the wise commends knowledge,
but the mouth of the fool gushes folly.

3The eyes of the LORD are everywhere, 2Ch 16:9
keeping watch on the wicked and the good.

4The tongue that brings healing is a tree of life,
but a deceitful tongue crushes the spirit.

5A fool spurns his father's discipline,
but whoever heeds correction shows prudence. Pr 13:1

6The house of the righteous contains great treasure, Pr 8:21
but the income of the wicked brings them trouble. Pr 10:16

7The lips of the wise spread knowledge; Pr 10:13
not so the hearts of fools.

8The LORD detests the sacrifice of the wicked,
but the prayer of the upright pleases him.

9The LORD detests the way of the wicked Pr 6:16
but he loves those who pursue righteousness. Pr 21:21; 1Ti 6:11

10Stern discipline awaits him who leaves the path;
he who hates correction will die. Pr 1:31-32

11Death and Destruction[b] lie open before the LORD— Job 26:6; Ps 139:8
how much more the hearts of men! 2Ch 6:30

12A mocker resents correction; Am 5:10
he will not consult the wise.

13A happy heart makes the face cheerful,
but heartache crushes the spirit. Pr 12:25; 17:22

LIVING  **INSIGHT**

Smile often. Develop a cheerful countenance. A frowning face repels. A smile reaches and attracts. God gave you this wonderful gift that radiates encouragement. Don't fence it in . . . loosen up, break that concrete mask—smile!

(See Proverbs 15:13.)

14The discerning heart seeks knowledge, Pr 18:15
but the mouth of a fool feeds on folly.

15All the days of the oppressed are wretched,
but the cheerful heart has a continual feast.

16Better a little with the fear of the LORD
than great wealth with turmoil. Ps 37:16-17

17Better a meal of vegetables where there is love
than a fattened calf with hatred. Pr 17:1

18A hot-tempered man stirs up dissension,
but a patient man calms a quarrel. Ge 13:8

19The way of the sluggard is blocked with thorns, Pr 22:5
but the path of the upright is a highway.

20A wise son brings joy to his father, Pr 10:1
but a foolish man despises his mother.

21Folly delights a man who lacks judgment,
but a man of understanding keeps a straight course.

22Plans fail for lack of counsel,
but with many advisers they succeed.

23A man finds joy in giving an apt reply—
and how good is a timely word! Pr 25:11

24The path of life leads upward for the wise
to keep him from going down to the grave.[c]

[a] 33 Hebrew; Septuagint and Syriac / *but in the heart of fools she is not known*
[b] 11 Hebrew *Sheol and Abaddon*
[c] 24 Hebrew *Sheol*

[25]The LORD tears down the proud man's house
but he keeps the widow's boundaries intact.

[26]The LORD detests the thoughts of the wicked,
but those of the pure are pleasing to him.

[27]A greedy man brings trouble to his family,
but he who hates bribes will live. Ex 23:8

[28]The heart of the righteous weighs its answers,
but the mouth of the wicked gushes evil.

[29]The LORD is far from the wicked
but he hears the prayer of the righteous.

[30]A cheerful look brings joy to the heart,
and good news gives health to the bones.

[31]He who listens to a life-giving rebuke
will be at home among the wise. ver 5

[32]He who ignores discipline despises himself,
but whoever heeds correction gains
understanding. Pr 9:7-9

[33]The fear of the LORD teaches a man wisdom,[a]
and humility comes before honor. Pr 18:12

16 To man belong the plans of the heart,
but from the LORD comes the reply of
the tongue. Pr 19:21

[2]All a man's ways seem innocent to him,
but motives are weighed by the LORD. Pr 21:2

[3]Commit to the LORD whatever you do,
and your plans will succeed. Ps 37:5-6; Pr 3:5-6

LIVING  **INSIGHT**

God has a perfect will for our lives. He has the ability to "pull things off" in our lives. We must depend and count on Him!

(See Proverbs 16:3.)

[4]The LORD works out everything for his own
ends— Isa 43:7
even the wicked for a day of disaster. Ro 9:22

[5]The LORD detests all the proud of heart.
Be sure of this: They will not go
unpunished. Pr 11:20-21

[6]Through love and faithfulness sin is atoned
for;
through the fear of the LORD a man avoids
evil. Pr 14:16

[7]When a man's ways are pleasing to the LORD,
he makes even his enemies live at peace
with him. Ps 105:15

[8]Better a little with righteousness
than much gain with injustice. Ps 37:16

[9]In his heart a man plans his course,
but the LORD determines his steps. Jer 10:23

[10]The lips of a king speak as an oracle,
and his mouth should not betray justice.

[11]Honest scales and balances are from the LORD;
all the weights in the bag are of his making.

[12]Kings detest wrongdoing,
for a throne is established through
righteousness. Pr 25:5

[13]Kings take pleasure in honest lips;
they value a man who speaks the truth.

[14]A king's wrath is a messenger of death, Pr 19:12
but a wise man will appease it. Ecc 10:4

[15]When a king's face brightens, it means life;
his favor is like a rain cloud in spring.

[16]How much better to get wisdom than gold,
to choose understanding rather than silver!

[17]The highway of the upright avoids evil;
he who guards his way guards his life.

[18]Pride goes before destruction, 1Sa 17:42
a haughty spirit before a fall. Pr 11:2; 18:12

[19]Better to be lowly in spirit and among the
oppressed
than to share plunder with the proud.

[20]Whoever gives heed to instruction prospers,
and blessed is he who trusts in the LORD.

[21]The wise in heart are called discerning,
and pleasant words promote instruction.[b]

[22]Understanding is a fountain of life to those
who have it, Pr 13:14
but folly brings punishment to fools.

[23]A wise man's heart guides his mouth, Job 15:5
and his lips promote instruction.[c] ver 21

[24]Pleasant words are a honeycomb, 1Sa 14:27
sweet to the soul and healing to the bones.

[25]There is a way that seems right to a man,
but in the end it leads to death. Pr 14:12

[26]The laborer's appetite works for him;
his hunger drives him on.

[27]A scoundrel plots evil, Ps 140:2
and his speech is like a scorching fire. Jas 3:6

[28]A perverse man stirs up dissension, Pr 15:18
and a gossip separates close friends. Pr 17:9

[29]A violent man entices his neighbor

[a]33 Or *Wisdom teaches the fear of the LORD* [b]21 Or *words make a man persuasive* [c]23 Or *mouth / and makes his lips persuasive*

and leads him down a path that is not
good. Pr 1:10; 12:26

30 He who winks with his eye is plotting
perversity; Pr 6:13
he who purses his lips is bent on evil.

31 Gray hair is a crown of splendor; Pr 20:29
it is attained by a righteous life.

32 Better a patient man than a warrior,
a man who controls his temper than one
who takes a city.

33 The lot is cast into the lap, 1Sa 10:21; Eze 21:21
but its every decision is from the LORD.

17 Better a dry crust with peace and quiet
than a house full of feasting,[a] with
strife. Pr 15:16-17

2 A wise servant will rule over a disgraceful son,
and will share the inheritance as one of the
brothers.

3 The crucible for silver and the furnace for
gold, Pr 27:21
but the LORD tests the heart. Ps 26:2; Jer 17:10

4 A wicked man listens to evil lips;
a liar pays attention to a malicious tongue.

5 He who mocks the poor shows contempt for
their Maker; Pr 14:31
whoever gloats over disaster will not go
unpunished. Ob 1:12

6 Children's children are a crown to the aged,
and parents are the pride of their children.

7 Arrogant[b] lips are unsuited to a fool—
how much worse lying lips to a ruler!

8 A bribe is a charm to the one who gives it;
wherever he turns, he succeeds. Ex 23:8

9 He who covers over an offense promotes love,
but whoever repeats the matter separates
close friends. Pr 16:28

10 A rebuke impresses a man of discernment
more than a hundred lashes a fool.

11 An evil man is bent only on rebellion;
a merciless official will be sent against him.

12 Better to meet a bear robbed of her cubs
than a fool in his folly. 1Sa 25:25

13 If a man pays back evil for good, Ps 109:4-5
evil will never leave his house.

14 Starting a quarrel is like breaching a dam;
so drop the matter before a dispute breaks
out. Pr 20:3

15 Acquitting the guilty and condemning the
innocent— Pr 18:5
the LORD detests them both. Ex 23:6-7; Isa 5:23

16 Of what use is money in the hand of a fool,
since he has no desire to get wisdom?

17 A friend loves at all times,
and a brother is born for adversity. Pr 27:10

18 A man lacking in judgment strikes hands in
pledge
and puts up security for his neighbor.

19 He who loves a quarrel loves sin;
he who builds a high gate invites
destruction.

20 A man of perverse heart does not prosper;
he whose tongue is deceitful falls into
trouble.

21 To have a fool for a son brings grief;
there is no joy for the father of a fool.

22 A cheerful heart is good medicine,
but a crushed spirit dries up the bones.

23 A wicked man accepts a bribe in secret Ex 23:8
to pervert the course of justice. Job 34:33

24 A discerning man keeps wisdom in view,
but a fool's eyes wander to the ends of the
earth. Ecc 2:14

25 A foolish son brings grief to his father
and bitterness to the one who bore him.

26 It is not good to punish an innocent man,
or to flog officials for their integrity.

27 A man of knowledge uses words with
restraint, Job 6:24
and a man of understanding is
even-tempered. Pr 14:29; Jas 1:19

LIVING  **INSIGHT**

When we are prompted to talk too much, God says, "Hold it! Better keep that to yourself!" Restraint of the tongue is a mark of wisdom. It is a slippery eel in need of being in check between our cheeks.
(See Proverbs 17:27–28.)

28 Even a fool is thought wise if he keeps silent,
and discerning if he holds his tongue.

18 An unfriendly man pursues selfish ends;
he defies all sound judgment.

[a] 1 Hebrew *sacrifices* [b] 7 Or *Eloquent*

[2]A fool finds no pleasure in understanding
but delights in airing his own opinions.

[3]When wickedness comes, so does contempt,
and with shame comes disgrace.

[4]The words of a man's mouth are deep waters,
but the fountain of wisdom is a bubbling brook.

[5]It is not good to be partial to the wicked
or to deprive the innocent of justice. Pr 17:15

[6]A fool's lips bring him strife,
and his mouth invites a beating.

[7]A fool's mouth is his undoing,
and his lips are a snare to his soul. Ps 140:9

[8]The words of a gossip are like choice morsels;
they go down to a man's inmost parts.

[9]One who is slack in his work
is brother to one who destroys. Pr 28:24

[10]The name of the LORD is a strong tower;
the righteous run to it and are safe. Pr 14:26

[11]The wealth of the rich is their fortified city;
they imagine it an unscalable wall.

[12]Before his downfall a man's heart is proud,
but humility comes before honor. Pr 11:2

[13]He who answers before listening—
that is his folly and his shame. Pr 20:25; Jn 7:51

[14]A man's spirit sustains him in sickness,
but a crushed spirit who can bear? Pr 15:13

[15]The heart of the discerning acquires knowledge;
the ears of the wise seek it out. Pr 15:14

[16]A gift opens the way for the giver Ge 32:20
and ushers him into the presence of the great.

[17]The first to present his case seems right,
till another comes forward and questions him.

[18]Casting the lot settles disputes Pr 16:33
and keeps strong opponents apart.

[19]An offended brother is more unyielding than a fortified city, 1Sa 17:28
and disputes are like the barred gates of a citadel.

[20]From the fruit of his mouth a man's stomach is filled;
with the harvest from his lips he is satisfied.

[21]The tongue has the power of life and death,
and those who love it will eat its fruit.

[22]He who finds a wife finds what is good Pr 12:4
and receives favor from the LORD. Pr 19:14

[23]A poor man pleads for mercy,
but a rich man answers harshly.

[24]A man of many companions may come to ruin,
but there is a friend who sticks closer than a brother. Pr 17:17; Jn 15:13-15

LIVING  **INSIGHT**

Moms and dads, pastors and teachers, counselors and coaches, your tongue possesses the power of life and death. Let us never think our words will be overlooked and easily erased. **Death words** ***destroy, hurt, create humiliating feelings.*** **Life words** ***build and increase strength of character. They center on the truth, and therefore they set the other person free.***

(See Proverbs 18:21.)

19

[1]Better a poor man whose walk is blameless
than a fool whose lips are perverse. Pr 28:6

[2]It is not good to have zeal without knowledge,
nor to be hasty and miss the way. Pr 29:20

[3]A man's own folly ruins his life, Ps 14:1
yet his heart rages against the LORD.

[4]Wealth brings many friends,
but a poor man's friend deserts him. Pr 14:20

[5]A false witness will not go unpunished, Ex 23:1
and he who pours out lies will not go free.

[6]Many curry favor with a ruler, Pr 29:26
and everyone is the friend of a man who gives gifts. Pr 17:8

[7]A poor man is shunned by all his relatives—
how much more do his friends avoid him!
Though he pursues them with pleading,
they are nowhere to be found.[a] Ps 38:11

[8]He who gets wisdom loves his own soul;
he who cherishes understanding prospers.

[9]A false witness will not go unpunished,
and he who pours out lies will perish. ver 5

[10]It is not fitting for a fool to live in luxury—
how much worse for a slave to rule over princes! Pr 30:21-23

[a]7 The meaning of the Hebrew for this sentence is uncertain.

[11]A man's wisdom gives him patience; Pr 16:32
it is to his glory to overlook an offense.

[12]A king's rage is like the roar of a lion, Pr 20:2
but his favor is like dew on the grass.

[13]A foolish son is his father's ruin, Pr 10:1
and a quarrelsome wife is like a constant
dripping. Pr 21:9

[14]Houses and wealth are inherited from parents,
but a prudent wife is from the LORD. Pr 18:22

[15]Laziness brings on deep sleep,
and the shiftless man goes hungry. Pr 6:9; 10:4

[16]He who obeys instructions guards his life,
but he who is contemptuous of his ways
will die. Lk 10:28

[17]He who is kind to the poor lends to the LORD,
and he will reward him for what he has
done. Mt 10:42; 2Co 9:6-8

[18]Discipline your son, for in that there is hope;
do not be a willing party to his death.

LIVING  INSIGHT

Discipline your children while they are young enough to learn. If you don't, you may very well be helping them to destroy themselves.
(See Proverbs 19:18.)

[19]A hot-tempered man must pay the penalty;
if you rescue him, you will have to do it
again.

[20]Listen to advice and accept instruction, Pr 4:1
and in the end you will be wise. Pr 12:15

[21]Many are the plans in a man's heart,
but it is the LORD's purpose that prevails.

[22]What a man desires is unfailing love[a];
better to be poor than a liar.

[23]The fear of the LORD leads to life:
Then one rests content, untouched by
trouble. Pr 12:21; 1Ti 4:8

[24]The sluggard buries his hand in the dish;
he will not even bring it back to his mouth!

[25]Flog a mocker, and the simple will learn
prudence;
rebuke a discerning man, and he will gain
knowledge. Pr 9:9

[26]He who robs his father and drives out his
mother Pr 28:24
is a son who brings shame and disgrace.

[27]Stop listening to instruction, my son, Pr 1:8
and you will stray from the words of
knowledge.

[28]A corrupt witness mocks at justice,
and the mouth of the wicked gulps down
evil. Job 15:16

[29]Penalties are prepared for mockers,
and beatings for the backs of fools. Pr 26:3

20

Wine is a mocker and beer a brawler;
whoever is led astray by them is not
wise. Pr 31:4

[2]A king's wrath is like the roar of a lion;
he who angers him forfeits his life. Pr 8:36

[3]It is to a man's honor to avoid strife,
but every fool is quick to quarrel. Pr 17:14

[4]A sluggard does not plow in season; Pr 6:6
so at harvest time he looks but finds
nothing. Ecc 10:18

[5]The purposes of a man's heart are deep
waters, Ps 18:16
but a man of understanding draws them
out.

[6]Many a man claims to have unfailing love,
but a faithful man who can find? Ps 12:1

[7]The righteous man leads a blameless life;
blessed are his children after him. Ps 37:25-26

[8]When a king sits on his throne to judge,
he winnows out all evil with his eyes. ver 26

[9]Who can say, "I have kept my heart pure;
I am clean and without sin"? 1Ki 8:46

[10]Differing weights and differing measures—
the LORD detests them both. ver 23; Pr 11:1

[11]Even a child is known by his actions,
by whether his conduct is pure and right.

[12]Ears that hear and eyes that see—
the LORD has made them both. Ps 94:9

[13]Do not love sleep or you will grow poor;
stay awake and you will have food to spare.

[14]"It's no good, it's no good!" says the buyer;
then off he goes and boasts about his
purchase.

[15]Gold there is, and rubies in abundance,
but lips that speak knowledge are a rare
jewel.

[16]Take the garment of one who puts up security
for a stranger;
hold it in pledge if he does it for a
wayward woman. Ex 22:26; Pr 27:13

[a]22 Or *A man's greed is his shame*

[17]Food gained by fraud tastes sweet to a man,
but he ends up with a mouth full of gravel.

[18]Make plans by seeking advice;
if you wage war, obtain guidance. Pr 24:6

[19]A gossip betrays a confidence; Pr 11:13
so avoid a man who talks too much.

[20]If a man curses his father or mother, Pr 30:11
his lamp will be snuffed out in pitch darkness. Job 18:5

[21]An inheritance quickly gained at the beginning
will not be blessed at the end.

[22]Do not say, "I'll pay you back for this wrong!"
Wait for the LORD, and he will deliver you.

[23]The LORD detests differing weights,
and dishonest scales do not please him.

[24]A man's steps are directed by the LORD.
How then can anyone understand his own way? Jer 10:23

[25]It is a trap for a man to dedicate something rashly
and only later to consider his vows.

[26]A wise king winnows out the wicked;
he drives the threshing wheel over them.

[27]The lamp of the LORD searches the spirit of a man[a]; Ps 119:105
it searches out his inmost being. Pr 16:2

[28]Love and faithfulness keep a king safe;
through love his throne is made secure.

[29]The glory of young men is their strength,
gray hair the splendor of the old. Pr 16:31

[30]Blows and wounds cleanse away evil, Pr 22:15
and beatings purge the inmost being. Isa 1:5

21 The king's heart is in the hand of the LORD;
he directs it like a watercourse wherever he pleases. Est 5:1

[2]All a man's ways seem right to him,
but the LORD weighs the heart. Pr 16:2; 24:12

[3]To do what is right and just
is more acceptable to the LORD than sacrifice. 1Sa 15:22; Isa 1:11; Mic 6:6-8

[4]Haughty eyes and a proud heart, Pr 6:17
the lamp of the wicked, are sin!

[5]The plans of the diligent lead to profit Pr 10:4
as surely as haste leads to poverty.

[6]A fortune made by a lying tongue
is a fleeting vapor and a deadly snare.[b]

[7]The violence of the wicked will drag them away, Pr 11:5
for they refuse to do what is right.

[8]The way of the guilty is devious, Pr 2:15
but the conduct of the innocent is upright.

[9]Better to live on a corner of the roof
than share a house with a quarrelsome wife.

[10]The wicked man craves evil;
his neighbor gets no mercy from him.

[11]When a mocker is punished, the simple gain wisdom;
when a wise man is instructed, he gets knowledge. Pr 19:25

[12]The Righteous One[c] takes note of the house of the wicked
and brings the wicked to ruin. Pr 14:11

[13]If a man shuts his ears to the cry of the poor,
he too will cry out and not be answered.

[14]A gift given in secret soothes anger,
and a bribe concealed in the cloak pacifies great wrath. Pr 18:16; 19:6

[15]When justice is done, it brings joy to the righteous
but terror to evildoers. Pr 10:29

[16]A man who strays from the path of understanding
comes to rest in the company of the dead.

[17]He who loves pleasure will become poor;
whoever loves wine and oil will never be rich. Pr 23:20-21,29-35

[18]The wicked become a ransom for the righteous, Pr 11:8
and the unfaithful for the upright.

[19]Better to live in a desert
than with a quarrelsome and ill-tempered wife. ver 9

[20]In the house of the wise are stores of choice food and oil,
but a foolish man devours all he has.

[21]He who pursues righteousness and love
finds life, prosperity[d] and honor. Mt 5:6

[22]A wise man attacks the city of the mighty
and pulls down the stronghold in which they trust.

[23]He who guards his mouth and his tongue
keeps himself from calamity. Pr 12:13

[a]27 Or *The spirit of man is the LORD's lamp*
[b]6 Some Hebrew manuscripts, Septuagint and Vulgate; most Hebrew manuscripts *vapor for those who seek death*
[c]12 Or *The righteous man*
[d]21 Or *righteousness*

24The proud and arrogant man—"Mocker" is his name; Ps 1:1
he behaves with overweening pride.

25The sluggard's craving will be the death of him, Pr 13:4
because his hands refuse to work.
26All day long he craves for more,
but the righteous give without sparing.

27The sacrifice of the wicked is detestable—
how much more so when brought with evil intent! Pr 15:8

28A false witness will perish, Pr 19:5
and whoever listens to him will be destroyed forever.[a]

29A wicked man puts up a bold front,
but an upright man gives thought to his ways. Pr 14:8

30There is no wisdom, no insight, no plan
that can succeed against the LORD. Isa 8:10

31The horse is made ready for the day of battle,
but victory rests with the LORD. Ps 3:8

22 A good name is more desirable than great riches;
to be esteemed is better than silver or gold.
2Rich and poor have this in common:
The LORD is the Maker of them all. Job 31:15

3A prudent man sees danger and takes refuge,
but the simple keep going and suffer for it.

4Humility and the fear of the LORD
bring wealth and honor and life. Pr 10:27; 15:33

5In the paths of the wicked lie thorns and snares, Pr 15:19
but he who guards his soul stays far from them.

6Train[b] a child in the way he should go,
and when he is old he will not turn from it.

7The rich rule over the poor,
and the borrower is servant to the lender.

LIVING  **INSIGHT**

Watch your child in action. Get involved. Open your eyes. Perk up your ears. Learn the bents, the abilities, the characteristics, the good, the bad, and then adapt your training accordingly.

(See Proverbs 22:6.)

8He who sows wickedness reaps trouble, Job 4:8
and the rod of his fury will be destroyed.

9A generous man will himself be blessed, 2Co 9:6
for he shares his food with the poor. Pr 19:17

10Drive out the mocker, and out goes strife;
quarrels and insults are ended. Pr 26:20

11He who loves a pure heart and whose speech is gracious
will have the king for his friend. Mt 5:8

12The eyes of the LORD keep watch over knowledge,
but he frustrates the words of the unfaithful.
13The sluggard says, "There is a lion outside!"
or, "I will be murdered in the streets!"
14The mouth of an adulteress is a deep pit;
he who is under the LORD's wrath will fall into it. Ecc 7:26
15Folly is bound up in the heart of a child,
but the rod of discipline will drive it far from him. Pr 13:24; 23:14

16He who oppresses the poor to increase his wealth
and he who gives gifts to the rich—both come to poverty.

The Rest of the Best **Chapters 22:17–31:31**

These chapters contain sections within sections moving toward the book's striking conclusion. Chapters 22:17–24:22 highlight thirty "sayings of the wise"; most of them are two or three verses long. Many are in the form of admonitions that point us to trust in the Lord (22:19). A few additional wise sayings are recorded in 24:23–34, followed by another collection of Solomon's proverbs (25:1–29:27). The book ends with an appendix featuring the words of Agur (chapter 30) and the words of King Lemuel (31:1–9) and an epilogue honoring the "wife of noble character" (31:10–31). What a fitting way to end such a powerfully practical book! Proverbs began by *telling* us that wisdom begins when we acknowledge who God is and offer Him the worship He deserves (1:7). And Proverbs ends by *showing* us wisdom at work in a woman who truly fears the Lord (31:30).

Sayings of the Wise

17Pay attention and listen to the sayings of the wise; Pr 5:1
apply your heart to what I teach, Pr 2:2
18for it is pleasing when you keep them in your heart
and have all of them ready on your lips.
19So that your trust may be in the LORD,

[a]28 Or / *but the words of an obedient man will live on* [b]6 Or *Start*

I teach you today, even you.
20Have I not written thirty[a] sayings for you,
sayings of counsel and knowledge,
21teaching you true and reliable words, Lk 1:3-4
so that you can give sound answers
to him who sent you?

22Do not exploit the poor because they are poor
and do not crush the needy in court, Ex 23:6
23for the LORD will take up their case Ps 12:5
and will plunder those who plunder them.

24Do not make friends with a hot-tempered
man,
do not associate with one easily angered,
25or you may learn his ways
and get yourself ensnared. 1Co 15:33

26Do not be a man who strikes hands in pledge
or puts up security for debts;
27if you lack the means to pay,
your very bed will be snatched from under
you. Pr 17:18

28Do not move an ancient boundary stone
set up by your forefathers.

29Do you see a man skilled in his work?
He will serve before kings; Ge 41:46
he will not serve before obscure men.

23 When you sit to dine with a ruler,
note well what[b] is before you,
2and put a knife to your throat
if you are given to gluttony.
3Do not crave his delicacies, ver 6-8
for that food is deceptive.

4Do not wear yourself out to get rich;
have the wisdom to show restraint.
5Cast but a glance at riches, and they are gone,
for they will surely sprout wings
and fly off to the sky like an eagle. Pr 27:24

6Do not eat the food of a stingy man,
do not crave his delicacies; Ps 141:4
7for he is the kind of man
who is always thinking about the cost.[c]
"Eat and drink," he says to you,
but his heart is not with you.
8You will vomit up the little you have eaten
and will have wasted your compliments.

9Do not speak to a fool,
for he will scorn the wisdom of your words.

10Do not move an ancient boundary stone
or encroach on the fields of the fatherless,
11for their Defender is strong; Job 19:25
he will take up their case against you.

12Apply your heart to instruction Pr 2:2
and your ears to words of knowledge.

13Do not withhold discipline from a child;
if you punish him with the rod, he will not
die.
14Punish him with the rod
and save his soul from death.[d] Pr 13:24

15My son, if your heart is wise,
then my heart will be glad;
16my inmost being will rejoice
when your lips speak what is right. ver 24

17Do not let your heart envy sinners, Ps 37:1
but always be zealous for the fear of the
LORD.
18There is surely a future hope for you,
and your hope will not be cut off.

19Listen, my son, and be wise, Dt 4:9
and keep your heart on the right path.

LIVING INSIGHT

The quest for character requires that certain things be kept in the heart as well as kept from the heart. An unguarded heart spells disaster. A well-guarded heart means survival. If you hope to survive the jungle, overcoming each treacherous attack, you will have to guard your heart as you seek to keep it on the right path.

(See Proverbs 23:19.)

20Do not join those who drink too much wine
or gorge themselves on meat,
21for drunkards and gluttons become poor,
and drowsiness clothes them in rags.

22Listen to your father, who gave you life,
and do not despise your mother when she
is old. Pr 1:8; Eph 6:1-2
23Buy the truth and do not sell it;
get wisdom, discipline and understanding.
24The father of a righteous man has great joy;
he who has a wise son delights in him.
25May your father and mother be glad;
may she who gave you birth rejoice! Pr 10:1

26My son, give me your heart Pr 5:1-6
and let your eyes keep to my ways, Ps 18:21
27for a prostitute is a deep pit Pr 22:14
and a wayward wife is a narrow well.
28Like a bandit she lies in wait, Pr 7:11-12; Ecc 7:26
and multiplies the unfaithful among men.

29Who has woe? Who has sorrow?
Who has strife? Who has complaints?

[a] 20 Or *not formerly written*; or *not written excellent* [b] 1 Or *who* [c] 7 Or *for as he thinks within himself, / so he is*; or *for as he puts on a feast, / so he is* [d] 14 Hebrew *Sheol*

Who has needless bruises? Who has
bloodshot eyes?
30Those who linger over wine, Ps 75:8; Isa 5:11
who go to sample bowls of mixed wine.
31Do not gaze at wine when it is red,
when it sparkles in the cup,
when it goes down smoothly!
32In the end it bites like a snake
and poisons like a viper.
33Your eyes will see strange sights
and your mind imagine confusing things.
34You will be like one sleeping on the high seas,
lying on top of the rigging.
35"They hit me," you will say, "but I'm not
hurt!
They beat me, but I don't feel it!
When will I wake up
so I can find another drink?" Pr 20:1

24 Do not envy wicked men, Ps 37:1; Pr 3:31-32
do not desire their company;
2for their hearts plot violence, Ps 2:1; Isa 32:6
and their lips talk about making trouble.

3By wisdom a house is built, Pr 14:1
and through understanding it is established;
4through knowledge its rooms are filled
with rare and beautiful treasures. Pr 8:21

LIVING  **INSIGHT**

Families become strong, not because they have gone to school and learned the rules, but because parents pay the price to be different . . . because they inculcate Biblical truth in everyday life, conducting their relationships in the realm of wisdom, understanding and knowledge.

(See Proverbs 24:3–4.)

5A wise man has great power,
and a man of knowledge increases strength;
6for waging war you need guidance,
and for victory many advisers. Pr 11:14

7Wisdom is too high for a fool;
in the assembly at the gate he has nothing
to say.

8He who plots evil
will be known as a schemer.
9The schemes of folly are sin,
and men detest a mocker.

10If you falter in times of trouble,
how small is your strength! Jer 51:46; Heb 12:3

11Rescue those being led away to death;
hold back those staggering toward
slaughter. Ps 82:4; Isa 58:6-7

12If you say, "But we knew nothing about this,"
does not he who weighs the heart perceive
it? Pr 21:2
Does not he who guards your life know it?
Will he not repay each person according to
what he has done? Ro 2:6

13Eat honey, my son, for it is good;
honey from the comb is sweet to your taste.
14Know also that wisdom is sweet to your soul;
if you find it, there is a future hope for
you,
and your hope will not be cut off. Ps 119:103

15Do not lie in wait like an outlaw against a
righteous man's house,
do not raid his dwelling place;
16for though a righteous man falls seven times,
he rises again,
but the wicked are brought down by
calamity. Mic 7:8

17Do not gloat when your enemy falls; Ob 1:12
when he stumbles, do not let your heart
rejoice, Job 31:29
18or the LORD will see and disapprove
and turn his wrath away from him. Job 31:29

19Do not fret because of evil men Ps 37:1
or be envious of the wicked,
20for the evil man has no future hope,
and the lamp of the wicked will be snuffed
out. Pr 23:17-18

21Fear the LORD and the king, my son, Ro 13:1-5
and do not join with the rebellious,
22for those two will send sudden destruction
upon them, Ps 73:19
and who knows what calamities they can
bring?

Further Sayings of the Wise

23These also are sayings of the wise: Pr 1:6

To show partiality in judging is not good:
24Whoever says to the guilty, "You are
innocent"— Pr 17:15
peoples will curse him and nations
denounce him.
25But it will go well with those who convict the
guilty,
and rich blessing will come upon them.

26An honest answer
is like a kiss on the lips.

27Finish your outdoor work
and get your fields ready;
after that, build your house.

28Do not testify against your neighbor without
cause, Eph 4:25
or use your lips to deceive.

[29]Do not say, "I'll do to him as he has done to me;
I'll pay that man back for what he did."

[30]I went past the field of the sluggard, Pr 6:6-11
past the vineyard of the man who lacks judgment;
[31]thorns had come up everywhere,
the ground was covered with weeds,
and the stone wall was in ruins.
[32]I applied my heart to what I observed
and learned a lesson from what I saw:
[33]A little sleep, a little slumber,
a little folding of the hands to rest— Pr 6:10
[34]and poverty will come on you like a bandit
and scarcity like an armed man.[a] Pr 10:4

More Proverbs of Solomon

25 These are more proverbs of Solomon, copied by the men of Hezekiah king of Judah:

[2]It is the glory of God to conceal a matter;
to search out a matter is the glory of kings.
[3]As the heavens are high and the earth is deep,
so the hearts of kings are unsearchable.

[4]Remove the dross from the silver,
and out comes material for[b] the silversmith;
[5]remove the wicked from the king's presence,
and his throne will be established through righteousness. Pr 16:12

[6]Do not exalt yourself in the king's presence,
and do not claim a place among great men;
[7]it is better for him to say to you, "Come up here," Lk 14:7-10
than for him to humiliate you before a nobleman.

What you have seen with your eyes
[8] do not bring[c] hastily to court,
for what will you do in the end
if your neighbor puts you to shame?

[9]If you argue your case with a neighbor,
do not betray another man's confidence,
[10]or he who hears it may shame you
and you will never lose your bad reputation.

[11]A word aptly spoken
is like apples of gold in settings of silver.
[12]Like an earring of gold or an ornament of fine gold
is a wise man's rebuke to a listening ear.

[13]Like the coolness of snow at harvest time
is a trustworthy messenger to those who send him;
he refreshes the spirit of his masters. Pr 13:17

[14]Like clouds and wind without rain
is a man who boasts of gifts he does not give.

[15]Through patience a ruler can be persuaded,
and a gentle tongue can break a bone.

[16]If you find honey, eat just enough—
too much of it, and you will vomit. ver 27
[17]Seldom set foot in your neighbor's house—
too much of you, and he will hate you.

[18]Like a club or a sword or a sharp arrow
is the man who gives false testimony against his neighbor. Pr 12:18

[19]Like a bad tooth or a lame foot
is reliance on the unfaithful in times of trouble.

[20]Like one who takes away a garment on a cold day,
or like vinegar poured on soda,
is one who sings songs to a heavy heart.

[21]If your enemy is hungry, give him food to eat;
if he is thirsty, give him water to drink.
[22]In doing this, you will heap burning coals on his head, Ps 18:8
and the LORD will reward you. 2Sa 16:12

LIVING  **INSIGHT**

The most effective form of retaliation is an absence of retaliation . . . leaving all vengeance to God. In doing so, we "will heap burning coals" on the head of an adversary, which is nothing more than overcoming evil with good (read Romans 12:20–21).

(See Proverbs 25:21–22.)

[23]As a north wind brings rain,
so a sly tongue brings angry looks.

[24]Better to live on a corner of the roof
than share a house with a quarrelsome wife.

[25]Like cold water to a weary soul
is good news from a distant land. Pr 15:30

[26]Like a muddied spring or a polluted well
is a righteous man who gives way to the wicked.

[27]It is not good to eat too much honey, ver 16

[a]34 Or *like a vagrant / and scarcity like a beggar* [b]4 Or *comes a vessel from* [c]7,8 Or *nobleman / on whom you had set your eyes. / [8]Do not go*

nor is it honorable to seek one's own
honor. Pr 27:2

28Like a city whose walls are broken down
is a man who lacks self-control.

26 Like snow in summer or rain in harvest,
honor is not fitting for a fool. Pr 19:10

2Like a fluttering sparrow or a darting swallow,
an undeserved curse does not come to rest.

3A whip for the horse, a halter for the donkey,
and a rod for the backs of fools! Pr 10:13

4Do not answer a fool according to his folly,
or you will be like him yourself. ver 5; Isa 36:21

5Answer a fool according to his folly,
or he will be wise in his own eyes. ver 4; Pr 3:7

6Like cutting off one's feet or drinking violence
is the sending of a message by the hand of
a fool. Pr 10:26

7Like a lame man's legs that hang limp
is a proverb in the mouth of a fool. ver 9

8Like tying a stone in a sling
is the giving of honor to a fool. ver 1

9Like a thornbush in a drunkard's hand
is a proverb in the mouth of a fool. ver 7

10Like an archer who wounds at random
is he who hires a fool or any passer-by.

11As a dog returns to its vomit, 2Pe 2:22*
so a fool repeats his folly. Ex 8:15

12Do you see a man wise in his own eyes? Pr 3:7
There is more hope for a fool than for him.

13The sluggard says, "There is a lion in the
road, Pr 6:6-11
a fierce lion roaming the streets!" Pr 22:13

14As a door turns on its hinges,
so a sluggard turns on his bed. Pr 6:9

15The sluggard buries his hand in the dish;
he is too lazy to bring it back to his mouth.

16The sluggard is wiser in his own eyes
than seven men who answer discreetly.

17Like one who seizes a dog by the ears
is a passer-by who meddles in a quarrel not
his own.

18Like a madman shooting
firebrands or deadly arrows
19is a man who deceives his neighbor
and says, "I was only joking!"

20Without wood a fire goes out;
without gossip a quarrel dies down. Pr 22:10

21As charcoal to embers and as wood to fire,
so is a quarrelsome man for kindling strife.

22The words of a gossip are like choice morsels;
they go down to a man's inmost parts.

LIVING  **INSIGHT**

Garbled messages provide the perfect fuel for gossip sessions and just the right ingredient for slanderous slams. Exaggerate this detail or rearrange that fact, and you've got a recipe that'll make more mouths water than hot fudge on a rainy night.

(See Proverbs 26:20–22.)

23Like a coating of glaze[a] over earthenware
are fervent lips with an evil heart.

24A malicious man disguises himself with his
lips, Ps 31:18
but in his heart he harbors deceit. Ps 41:6

25Though his speech is charming, do not believe
him, Ps 28:3
for seven abominations fill his heart. Jer 9:4-8

26His malice may be concealed by deception,
but his wickedness will be exposed in the
assembly.

27If a man digs a pit, he will fall into it; Ps 7:15
if a man rolls a stone, it will roll back on
him. Pr 28:10; 29:6

28A lying tongue hates those it hurts,
and a flattering mouth works ruin. Pr 29:5

27 Do not boast about tomorrow, 1Ki 20:11
for you do not know what a day may
bring forth. Lk 12:19-20; Jas 4:13-16

2Let another praise you, and not your own
mouth;
someone else, and not your own lips.

3Stone is heavy and sand a burden, Job 6:3
but provocation by a fool is heavier than
both.

LIVING  **INSIGHT**

"Self-praise," says an ancient adage, "smells bad." In other words, it stinks up the works. How much better to "let another praise you"!

(See Proverbs 27:2.)

[a]23 With a different word division of the Hebrew; Masoretic Text *of silver dross*

[4]Anger is cruel and fury overwhelming,
but who can stand before jealousy? Nu 5:14

[5]Better is open rebuke
than hidden love.

[6]Wounds from a friend can be trusted,
but an enemy multiplies kisses. Ps 141:5

[7]He who is full loathes honey,
but to the hungry even what is bitter tastes sweet.

[8]Like a bird that strays from its nest Isa 16:2
is a man who strays from his home.

[9]Perfume and incense bring joy to the heart,
and the pleasantness of one's friend springs from his earnest counsel.

[10]Do not forsake your friend and the friend of your father,
and do not go to your brother's house when disaster strikes you— Pr 17:17
better a neighbor nearby than a brother far away.

[11]Be wise, my son, and bring joy to my heart;
then I can answer anyone who treats me with contempt. Ge 24:60

[12]The prudent see danger and take refuge,
but the simple keep going and suffer for it.

[13]Take the garment of one who puts up security for a stranger;
hold it in pledge if he does it for a wayward woman. Pr 20:16

[14]If a man loudly blesses his neighbor early in the morning,
it will be taken as a curse.

[15]A quarrelsome wife is like
a constant dripping on a rainy day; Pr 19:13
[16]restraining her is like restraining the wind
or grasping oil with the hand.

[17]As iron sharpens iron,
so one man sharpens another.

[18]He who tends a fig tree will eat its fruit, 1Co 9:7
and he who looks after his master will be honored. Lk 19:12-27

[19]As water reflects a face,
so a man's heart reflects the man.

[20]Death and Destruction[a] are never satisfied,
and neither are the eyes of man. Ecc 1:8

[21]The crucible for silver and the furnace for gold, Pr 17:3
but man is tested by the praise he receives.

[22]Though you grind a fool in a mortar,
grinding him like grain with a pestle,
you will not remove his folly from him.

[23]Be sure you know the condition of your flocks, Pr 12:10
give careful attention to your herds;
[24]for riches do not endure forever, Pr 23:5
and a crown is not secure for all generations.
[25]When the hay is removed and new growth appears
and the grass from the hills is gathered in,
[26]the lambs will provide you with clothing,
and the goats with the price of a field.
[27]You will have plenty of goats' milk
to feed you and your family
and to nourish your servant girls.

28

The wicked man flees though no one pursues, Lev 26:17; Ps 53:5
but the righteous are as bold as a lion.

[2]When a country is rebellious, it has many rulers,
but a man of understanding and knowledge maintains order.

[3]A ruler[b] who oppresses the poor
is like a driving rain that leaves no crops.

[4]Those who forsake the law praise the wicked,
but those who keep the law resist them.

[5]Evil men do not understand justice,
but those who seek the LORD understand it fully.

[6]Better a poor man whose walk is blameless
than a rich man whose ways are perverse.

[7]He who keeps the law is a discerning son,
but a companion of gluttons disgraces his father. Pr 23:19-21

[8]He who increases his wealth by exorbitant interest Ex 18:21
amasses it for another, who will be kind to the poor. Pr 13:22; Lk 14:12-14

[9]If anyone turns a deaf ear to the law,
even his prayers are detestable. Ps 66:18; 109:7

[10]He who leads the upright along an evil path
will fall into his own trap, Pr 26:27
but the blameless will receive a good inheritance.

[11]A rich man may be wise in his own eyes,
but a poor man who has discernment sees through him.

[12]When the righteous triumph, there is great elation; 2Ki 11:20

[a]20 Hebrew *Sheol and Abaddon* [b]3 Or *A poor man*

but when the wicked rise to power, men go
into hiding. Pr 11:10

13He who conceals his sins does not prosper,
but whoever confesses and renounces them
finds mercy. Ps 32:1-5; 1Jn 1:9

LIVING  INSIGHT

Discernment is the ability to detect, to recognize, to perceive beyond what is said. It is the ability to "sense" by means of intuition. It is insight apart from the obvious, outside the realm of facts. People with discernment have the ability to read between the lines.

(See Proverbs 28:11.)

14Blessed is the man who always fears the LORD,
but he who hardens his heart falls into
trouble.

15Like a roaring lion or a charging bear
is a wicked man ruling over a helpless
people.

16A tyrannical ruler lacks judgment,
but he who hates ill-gotten gain will enjoy
a long life.

17A man tormented by the guilt of murder
will be a fugitive till death; Ge 9:6
let no one support him.

18He whose walk is blameless is kept safe,
but he whose ways are perverse will
suddenly fall. Pr 10:9

19He who works his land will have abundant
food,
but the one who chases fantasies will have
his fill of poverty. Pr 12:11

20A faithful man will be richly blessed,
but one eager to get rich will not go
unpunished. ver 22; 1Ti 6:9

21To show partiality is not good— Pr 18:5
yet a man will do wrong for a piece of
bread. Eze 13:19

22A stingy man is eager to get rich
and is unaware that poverty awaits him.

23He who rebukes a man will in the end gain
more favor
than he who has a flattering tongue. Pr 27:5-6

24He who robs his father or mother Pr 19:26
and says, "It's not wrong"—
he is partner to him who destroys. Pr 18:9

25A greedy man stirs up dissension, Pr 14:17
but he who trusts in the LORD will prosper.

26He who trusts in himself is a fool, Ps 4:5
but he who walks in wisdom is kept safe.

27He who gives to the poor will lack nothing,
but he who closes his eyes to them receives
many curses. Ps 109:17

28When the wicked rise to power, people go
into hiding; ver 12
but when the wicked perish, the righteous
thrive.

29 A man who remains stiff-necked after
many rebukes Ex 32:9
will suddenly be destroyed—without
remedy. 2Ch 36:16; Pr 6:15

2When the righteous thrive, the people rejoice;
when the wicked rule, the people groan.

3A man who loves wisdom brings joy to his
father, Pr 10:1
but a companion of prostitutes squanders
his wealth. Pr 5:8-10; Lk 15:11-32

4By justice a king gives a country stability,
but one who is greedy for bribes tears it
down.

5Whoever flatters his neighbor
is spreading a net for his feet. Pr 26:28

6An evil man is snared by his own sin, Ecc 9:12
but a righteous one can sing and be glad.

7The righteous care about justice for the poor,
but the wicked have no such concern.

8Mockers stir up a city,
but wise men turn away anger. Pr 11:11; 16:14

9If a wise man goes to court with a fool,
the fool rages and scoffs, and there is no
peace.

10Bloodthirsty men hate a man of integrity
and seek to kill the upright. 1Jn 3:12

11A fool gives full vent to his anger, Job 15:13
but a wise man keeps himself under
control. Pr 12:16

12If a ruler listens to lies, 2Ki 21:9
all his officials become wicked. Job 34:30

LIVING  INSIGHT

We are foolish if we respond angrily to every criticism or offense. Who knows—God may be using those words to teach us some essential lessons, painful though they may be.

(See Proverbs 29:11.)

13The poor man and the oppressor have this in common:
The LORD gives sight to the eyes of both.

14If a king judges the poor with fairness,
his throne will always be secure. Ps 72:1-5

15The rod of correction imparts wisdom,
but a child left to himself disgraces his mother. Pr 13:24

16When the wicked thrive, so does sin,
but the righteous will see their downfall.

17Discipline your son, and he will give you peace;
he will bring delight to your soul. Pr 10:1

18Where there is no revelation, the people cast off restraint;
but blessed is he who keeps the law. Ps 1:1-2

19A servant cannot be corrected by mere words;
though he understands, he will not respond.

20Do you see a man who speaks in haste?
There is more hope for a fool than for him.

21If a man pampers his servant from youth,
he will bring grief[a] in the end.

22An angry man stirs up dissension,
and a hot-tempered one commits many sins. Pr 14:17

23A man's pride brings him low, Est 5:12
but a man of lowly spirit gains honor.

24The accomplice of a thief is his own enemy;
he is put under oath and dare not testify.

25Fear of man will prove to be a snare, 1Sa 15:24
but whoever trusts in the LORD is kept safe.

26Many seek an audience with a ruler, Pr 19:6
but it is from the LORD that man gets justice. Pr 16:33

27The righteous detest the dishonest;
the wicked detest the upright. ver 10

Sayings of Agur

30 The sayings of Agur son of Jakeh—an oracle[b]: Pr 22:17

This man declared to Ithiel,
to Ithiel and to Ucal:[c]

2"I am the most ignorant of men;
I do not have a man's understanding.
3I have not learned wisdom,
nor have I knowledge of the Holy One.
4Who has gone up to heaven and come down?
Who has gathered up the wind in the hollow of his hands? Isa 40:12
Who has wrapped up the waters in his cloak?
Who has established all the ends of the earth?
What is his name, and the name of his son?
Tell me if you know!

5"Every word of God is flawless; Ps 12:6; 18:30
he is a shield to those who take refuge in him. Ps 84:11
6Do not add to his words, Dt 4:2; Rev 22:18
or he will rebuke you and prove you a liar.

7"Two things I ask of you, O LORD;
do not refuse me before I die:
8Keep falsehood and lies far from me;
give me neither poverty nor riches,
but give me only my daily bread. Mt 6:11
9Otherwise, I may have too much and disown you Jos 24:27
and say, 'Who is the LORD?' Dt 8:10-14; Hos 13:6
Or I may become poor and steal,
and so dishonor the name of my God.

10"Do not slander a servant to his master,
or he will curse you, and you will pay for it.

11"There are those who curse their fathers
and do not bless their mothers; Pr 20:20
12those who are pure in their own eyes Lk 18:11
and yet are not cleansed of their filth;
13those whose eyes are ever so haughty, Pr 6:17
whose glances are so disdainful;
14those whose teeth are swords Job 29:17
and whose jaws are set with knives Ps 57:4
to devour the poor from the earth, Ps 14:4; Am 8:4
the needy from among mankind. Job 19:22

15"The leech has two daughters.
'Give! Give!' they cry.

"There are three things that are never satisfied,
four that never say, 'Enough!':
16the grave,[d] the barren womb, Pr 27:20; Hab 2:5
land, which is never satisfied with water,
and fire, which never says, 'Enough!'

17"The eye that mocks a father, Dt 21:18-21
that scorns obedience to a mother,
will be pecked out by the ravens of the valley,
will be eaten by the vultures. Job 15:23

18"There are three things that are too amazing for me,
four that I do not understand:

[a]21 The meaning of the Hebrew for this word is uncertain. [b]1 Or *Jakeh of Massa* [c]1 Masoretic Text; with a different word division of the Hebrew *declared, "I am weary, O God; / I am weary, O God, and faint.* [d]16 Hebrew *Sheol*

19the way of an eagle in the sky,
the way of a snake on a rock,
the way of a ship on the high seas,
and the way of a man with a maiden.

20"This is the way of an adulteress:
She eats and wipes her mouth
and says, 'I've done nothing wrong.' Pr 5:6

21"Under three things the earth trembles,
under four it cannot bear up:
22a servant who becomes king, Pr 19:10
a fool who is full of food,
23an unloved woman who is married,
and a maidservant who displaces her mistress.

24"Four things on earth are small,
yet they are extremely wise:
25Ants are creatures of little strength,
yet they store up their food in the summer;
26coneys[a] are creatures of little power, Ps 104:18
yet they make their home in the crags;
27locusts have no king, Ex 10:4
yet they advance together in ranks;
28a lizard can be caught with the hand,
yet it is found in kings' palaces.

29"There are three things that are stately in their stride,
four that move with stately bearing:
30a lion, mighty among beasts,
who retreats before nothing;
31a strutting rooster, a he-goat,
and a king with his army around him.[b]

32"If you have played the fool and exalted yourself,
or if you have planned evil,
clap your hand over your mouth! Job 21:5
33For as churning the milk produces butter,
and as twisting the nose produces blood,
so stirring up anger produces strife."

Sayings of King Lemuel

31 The sayings of King Lemuel—an oracle[c] his mother taught him: Pr 22:17

2"O my son, O son of my womb,
O son of my vows,[d] Isa 49:15
3do not spend your strength on women,
your vigor on those who ruin kings. Dt 17:17

4"It is not for kings, O Lemuel—
not for kings to drink wine, Pr 20:1; Ecc 10:16-17
not for rulers to crave beer,
5lest they drink and forget what the law decrees, 1Ki 16:9; Pr 16:12
and deprive all the oppressed of their rights.
6Give beer to those who are perishing,
wine to those who are in anguish; Ge 14:18
7let them drink and forget their poverty Est 1:10
and remember their misery no more.

8"Speak up for those who cannot speak for themselves, Job 29:12-17
for the rights of all who are destitute.
9Speak up and judge fairly;
defend the rights of the poor and needy."

Epilogue: The Wife of Noble Character

10[e]A wife of noble character who can find?
She is worth far more than rubies.
11Her husband has full confidence in her Ge 2:18
and lacks nothing of value. Pr 12:4
12She brings him good, not harm,
all the days of her life.
13She selects wool and flax
and works with eager hands. 1Ti 2:9-10
14She is like the merchant ships,
bringing her food from afar.
15She gets up while it is still dark;
she provides food for her family
and portions for her servant girls.
16She considers a field and buys it;
out of her earnings she plants a vineyard.
17She sets about her work vigorously;
her arms are strong for her tasks.
18She sees that her trading is profitable,
and her lamp does not go out at night.
19In her hand she holds the distaff
and grasps the spindle with her fingers.
20She opens her arms to the poor
and extends her hands to the needy. Dt 15:11
21When it snows, she has no fear for her household;
for all of them are clothed in scarlet.
22She makes coverings for her bed;
she is clothed in fine linen and purple.
23Her husband is respected at the city gate,
where he takes his seat among the elders of the land. Ru 4:1,11; Pr 12:4
24She makes linen garments and sells them,
and supplies the merchants with sashes.
25She is clothed with strength and dignity;
she can laugh at the days to come.
26She speaks with wisdom,
and faithful instruction is on her tongue.
27She watches over the affairs of her household
and does not eat the bread of idleness.

[a]26 That is, the hyrax or rock badger [b]31 Or *king secure against revolt* [c]1 Or *of Lemuel king of Massa, which* [d]2 Or */ the answer to my prayers* [e]10 Verses 10-31 are an acrostic, each verse beginning with a successive letter of the Hebrew alphabet.

28Her children arise and call her blessed;
her husband also, and he praises her:
29"Many women do noble things,
but you surpass them all."
30Charm is deceptive, and beauty is fleeting;
but a woman who fears the LORD is to be
praised.
31Give her the reward she has earned,
and let her works bring her praise at the
city gate. Pr 11:16

INTRODUCTION

ECCLESIASTES

This book, short though it may be, is one of the most mysterious works in the whole Bible . . . something like Winston Churchill's description of another nation's actions during his lifetime: ". . . a riddle wrapped in a mystery inside an enigma." Ecclesiastes looms before us as the sphinx of Hebrew literature, with its unanswered arguments and cynical observations about life. All this is compounded by the fact that the writer refers to himself as "the Teacher" throughout the book. Its content marks a decided departure from the orthodox, a bold and even impudent alienation from the Lord . . . and yet a few verses later we read strong words in defense of a life devoted to the living Lord. Come along as we try to unravel the riddle and understand the confessions of a cynic.

WRITER: *Solomon*

DATE: *c.970–930 B.C.*

PURPOSE: *To examine the world as one man had experienced it*

KEY MESSAGE: *Life not centered on God is meaningless and purposeless*

KEY VERSE: *2:11*

KEY TERMS: *"Meaningless"; "labor"; "do not know"*

SOLOMON'S SHORT STORY: *The Empty Life of Folly*

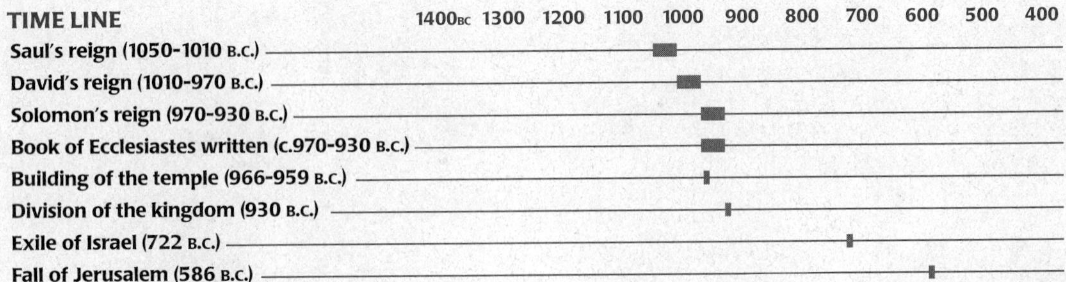

Confessions of a Cynic

	INTRODUCTION	INVESTIGATION AND DISCOVERIES			ADMONITION	CONCLUSION
		"I devoted myself to study and to explore by wisdom..."				
	Writer Theme Questions and illustrations	PURSUITS Knowledge Amusements Possessions Madness and Folly Labor Philosophy Riches	VANITY	CONCLUSIONS **Without God's help:** Humans cannot discover what is good for them to do... **Without God's revelation:** Humans do not know what will come after them...	A warning to the young A picture of old age A final admission	THE END OF THE SEARCH Fear God! Obey Him! Someday you will face Him!
	CHAPTER 1:1–11	*CHAPTERS 1:12–6:9*		*CHAPTERS 6:10–11:6*	*CHAPTERS 11:7–12:8*	*CHAPTER 12:9–14*
SEARCH	**Scientific**	**Philosophic Materialistic**		**Fatalistic Socialistic**	**Theological**	
STYLE	**Narrative**	**Proverbs Poems**		**Maxims**	**Narrative**	

There are at least two different types of people who might best understand the book of Ecclesiastes. First, those who are very bright (or who have raised children who are bright). That may sound strange, but I think Solomon, who was indeed the brightest of the bright, illustrates the intellectual struggles of a person who is extremely intelligent.

It has been my experience that the more brilliant a person is intellectually, the greater their struggles. Those who are highly intelligent often find that the simple answers to life's questions do not satisfy. As a result, many individuals with outstanding mental abilities grow to view the world with a cynical attitude. This cynicism can often be directed toward spiritual things. That very thing, I believe, is what happened to Solomon.

The second group of people who resonate with the themes of Ecclesiastes are those who are going through, or are living with someone who is going through, a time in their life often labeled a "mid-life crisis." This is an interesting phenomenon that has taken on a new tone in our time. Going through mid-life struggles has always been a challenge, but it seems to have intensified in these days. When some people reach middle age, they hit a plateau where they begin to question those things they have embraced all their lives.

I have observed a great number of people struggling through a mid-life crisis. It isn't uncommon to find that many have pushed God out of their lives. As far as they are concerned, God can wait for awhile. They'll answer to Him later. So they cast off all restraint and off they go, in a sort of quasi-psychological, spiritual tailspin until they crash and burn . . . or until the opposite occurs—they get control of their life.

Two Strikes Against Him

Solomon may very well have been in a mid-life crisis when he recorded the book of Ecclesiastes. I believe he wrote down these honest feelings when he reached that time where nothing seemed to satisfy.

In that sense, Ecclesiastes is more like a journal than a book. It is intensely personal, much of it recorded in the first person. Furthermore, Solomon was a man of great intellectual ability who seemed to have grown cynical. You might say he had two strikes against him at the time the Holy Spirit inspired his writing of the book of Ecclesiastes.

Meeting the Author

Before we go any further, let's ask and then answer some questions I think are essential to an appreciation for and understanding of this book of Scripture. First: "Who wrote Ecclesiastes?" Verses 1 and 12 of chapter 1 answer this question: "The words of the Teacher, son of David, king in Jerusalem . . . I, the Teacher, was king over Israel in Jerusalem."

This is the same person who was called Solomon in other parts of the Bible. At the time of his writing, he was an adult. He had reached the pinnacle of success. He had ascended to the highest position in the land. Suddenly, as he occupied that high-ranking position some chinks began to appear in his thinking. We don't know exactly what occurred to bring Solomon to this point at this particular time; we only know that his thinking and his attitudes changed dramatically. At this time of his life, Solomon apparently began to question some of the foundational beliefs that had been passed down from his father David. Whatever the case, Solomon was in a time of great emotional turmoil when he wrote this book.

It's sad in a way, isn't it? Solomon had brains, money, power and fame. We would say today that he had the world by the tail. He was eminently successful, but that didn't prevent him from having to go through a deep time of crisis, the experience of which he recorded in Ecclesiastes. We must understand that every public figure is unmistakably human, and each has struggles that are just as deep and painful as anyone else's. It should never shock us when the pains and struggles and failures of humanity invade the lives of public figures. At times, immorality will emerge from the life of a politician, pastor, counselor or teacher we have greatly admired. It is shockingly tragic . . . but we have little reason to be disillusioned. His or her humanity is the same humanity that resides in all of us.

Solomon is honest enough to say, in effect, "I had struggles like you can't believe! And in the midst of those struggles, when things began to fracture and my mind became jaded, I kept a journal." For some divinely ordained reason God has preserved the journal of this teacher of wisdom named Solomon. His anguished questions, struggles, depression and ponderings are openly recorded for us in Holy Scripture.

About the Title

The second question to ask about the book is this: "What is the meaning of the title—Ecclesiastes?" It's a long title that seems to have a religious ring to it. Our English title "Ecclesiates" comes from the Greek word *ekklesiastes*, which is used in the *Septuagint* (the Greek translation of the Old Testament) to translate the Hebrew *qoheleth* ("Teacher" in verse 1 of chapter 1). The term means "master of assemblies; one who holds and addresses an assembly." It's the idea of one who communicates as the official speaker. Perhaps "Teacher", or "Preacher" (as some translations render it), says it best—someone who gathers thoughts and ideas and shares them with others.

A Divinely Inspired Secular Message

Ecclesiastes is the most "secular" of all Bible books. If I were to speak to audiences made up of those who have not made a commitment to Jesus Christ, and I were asked to select a book in the Bible on which to speak, Ecclesiastes would be my preference. It hits people right where they live; it speaks to a world trying to find its way without God. It speaks to people looking for meaning—but looking in all the wrong places. You'll see the graphic portrayal of life lived apart from God as you read through Ecclesiastes. Here's just one example:

> *For the wise man, like the fool, will not be long remembered; in days to come both will be forgotten. Like the fool, the wise man too must die! So I hated life, because the work that is done under the sun was grievous to me. All of it is meaningless, a chasing after the wind (2:16–17).*

"It's emptiness. It's futility. It's useless striving. It's meaninglessness. It has no purpose. There is no satisfaction." These words of hopelessness, or words similar to it, appear 35–40 times in this book. Ecclesiastes is a book that includes lots and lots of questions—but not many answers. This is a book filled with pessimism and even certain attitudes and statements that might shock some Christian readers today.

Inspiration Does Not Equal a Good Example

The words you are about to read in Ecclesiastes may shock some of you who have not thought through your view of inspiration. Please realize that inspiration does *not* guarantee that everything recorded in this book of Scripture is meant to be a guideline for living. What inspiration does guarantee is this: what was written is accurate and has been miraculously preserved and *all of it* is "God-breathed and is useful for teaching, rebuking, correcting and training in righteousness" (2 Timothy 3:16).

God breathed out His message through the pen of human beings. However, not everything in this book is intended to be a rule to live by. Many of the arguments in Ecclesiastes are not God's arguments; they are God's accurate record of human arguments. Remember that! Secular writers often attack inspiration and take the book of Ecclesiastes as their illustration: "How can you believe that's inspired? Listen to what it says!" I've seen it done in college classrooms and in bully pulpits in many locations—perhaps you have as well. This is my confession: God's Word is a completely accurate and reliable record. But inspiration doesn't mean that everything written is truth to live by. At times the Bible includes instruction on how we should *not* live or think.

No God . . . No Hope

There is no more convincing literary work that declares that satisfaction cannot be found apart from a relationship with the triune God—Father, Son and Holy Spirit—than the book of Ecclesiastes. If you're beginning to teeter on the tightrope of life, wondering if maybe your life would be a lot better off if you turned your back on God, let me make a suggestion: Get a good dose of Ecclesiastes. Chew on this book for a few days and digest it well. You can choose to grab for all the garish gusto life has to offer; you can choose to spend your life "getting and spending," running after the world and away from God. But in the end, you *will* experience the same emptiness, the same meaninglessness Solomon discovered. May I offer a morsel of gentle advice: Learn *now* from Solomon's example and experiences—and you will avoid the bleak despair and tragic emptiness that permeated Solomon's life. Solomon learned the hard way; let him be your teacher today. Avoid at all costs the search for satisfaction that draws you away from the One who *alone* can provide purpose and meaning for your life. But if you been on Solomon's road, if you've tried it all, if you've come to the end of your rainbow and you don't know where else to turn, I urge you: Run to God—the One who loves you and will never let you go.

Make Room for God

If there is *a key verse to live by* in Ecclesiastes, I believe it is found in verse 11 of chapter 2:

> *Yet when I surveyed all that my hands had done and what I had toiled to achieve, everything was meaningless, a chasing after the wind; nothing was gained under the sun.*

Solomon was saying in effect, "I've tried it all. Yet I cannot find any satisfaction in life." The reason for this was simple: Solomon had "X"ed out God. He possessed everything a person could ever want—but he had put God, as it were, on the shelf in the storage closet. He had rejected his heritage, the ideals of his nation and even his God, the One whose name was Yahweh. Solomon decided he would pursue happiness apart from God. And when it was all said and done, his response was predictable—but heartbreaking: "You know, I didn't get what I needed. What I wound up with was a mouth full of sickeningly sweet cotton candy, an open hand full of air, a cup full of froth." By the end of all his pursuits, he was a "hollow" man! He was empty through and through! Ecclesiastes is the diary of his aimless wanderings, his fruitless searching for satisfaction apart from God.

What is the bottom line of all this? What can we learn from this book of restless wanderings? Two simple but incredibly important lessons, I believe: Number one: *Fear God*. That means take Him seriously; give Him the respect and the reverence He deserves. Make room for Him in your life. Number two: *Obey God*. That means do what He says. If you do these two things, you will find meaning in your life—I guarantee it. Anything less will leave you empty and unsatisfied. Just ask Solomon!

One Ultimate Question **Chapters 1–4**

Behind everything Solomon wrote in this journal was one key question: *Is life really worth living*? As Solomon looked at his life and at the world around him, he saw a never-ending cycle of monotonous boredom. Generations come and generations go . . . death is inevitable. The sun rises and then it sets again. The wind blows across the face of the earth with no apparent direction. The rivers and streams flow to the sea in a never-ending pattern. As Solomon looked around, he was overcome by feelings of hopelessness, despair, emptiness and purposelessness.

With the seeds of cynicism and despair firmly planted in his heart, Solomon embarked on a search for meaning. Chapter 1 records his search for wisdom. Chapter 2 chronicles his pursuit of worldly pleasures and his attempt to find satisfaction in toilsome labor. All of it left him empty, unfulfilled, unhappy. In chapter 3 he reflected on time and the things of time—which cannot fully and permanently satisfy. Solomon had tried it all: a laugh a day, a bottle a day, a woman a day, a book a day, a project a day, a big financial deal a day—and the search went on. Nothing could fill the void in his heart. He felt just as empty as when he had started his search . . . maybe even emptier! By chapter 4, Solomon stepped back to reflect on what he had experienced. In the end he had not found answers in his journey for self-satisfaction . . . only anguished questions and penetrating emptiness.

Everything Is Meaningless

1 The words of the Teacher,[a] son of David,
king in Jerusalem: Pr 1:1; Ecc 7:27

2 "Meaningless! Meaningless!"
says the Teacher.
"Utterly meaningless!
Everything is meaningless." Ps 39:5-6; 62:9

3 What does man gain from all his labor
at which he toils under the sun? Ecc 2:11,22
4 Generations come and generations go,
but the earth remains forever. Ps 104:5; 119:90
5 The sun rises and the sun sets,
and hurries back to where it rises. Ps 19:5-6
6 The wind blows to the south
and turns to the north;
round and round it goes,
ever returning on its course.
7 All streams flow into the sea,
yet the sea is never full.
To the place the streams come from,
there they return again. Job 36:28
8 All things are wearisome,
more than one can say.
The eye never has enough of seeing,
nor the ear its fill of hearing. Pr 27:20
9 What has been will be again,
what has been done will be done again;
there is nothing new under the sun.
10 Is there anything of which one can say,
"Look! This is something new"?
It was here already, long ago;
it was here before our time.
11 There is no remembrance of men of old,
and even those who are yet to come
will not be remembered
by those who follow. Ecc 2:16

Wisdom Is Meaningless

12 I, the Teacher, was king over Israel in Jerusalem. 13 I devoted myself to study and to explore by
wisdom all that is done under heaven. What a
heavy burden God has laid on men! 14 I have seen
all the things that are done under the sun; all of
them are meaningless, a chasing after the wind.

15 What is twisted cannot be straightened; Ecc 7:13
what is lacking cannot be counted.

16 I thought to myself, "Look, I have grown and
increased in wisdom more than anyone who has
ruled over Jerusalem before me; I have experienced much of wisdom and knowledge." 17 Then I
applied myself to the understanding of wisdom,
and also of madness and folly, but I learned that
this, too, is a chasing after the wind. 1Ki 3:12

18 For with much wisdom comes much sorrow;
the more knowledge, the more grief.

Pleasures Are Meaningless

2 I thought in my heart, "Come now, I will test
you with pleasure to find out what is good."
But that also proved to be meaningless. 2 "Laughter," I said, "is foolish. And what does pleasure
accomplish?" 3 I tried cheering myself with wine,
and embracing folly—my mind still guiding me
with wisdom. I wanted to see what was worthwhile
for men to do under heaven during the few days
of their lives. Ecc 1:17; 7:6; Lk 12:19
4 I undertook great projects: I built houses for
myself and planted vineyards. 5 I made gardens
and parks and planted all kinds of fruit trees in
them. 6 I made reservoirs to water groves of flourishing trees. 7 I bought male and female slaves and
had other slaves who were born in my house. I also
owned more herds and flocks than anyone in Jerusalem before me. 8 I amassed silver and gold for
myself, and the treasure of kings and provinces. I
acquired men and women singers, and a harem[b]
as well—the delights of the heart of man. 9 I became greater by far than anyone in Jerusalem before me. In all this my wisdom stayed with me.

10 I denied myself nothing my eyes desired;
I refused my heart no pleasure.
My heart took delight in all my work,
and this was the reward for all my labor.

[a] *1* Or *leader of the assembly*; also in verses 2 and 12 [b] *8* The meaning of the Hebrew for this phrase is uncertain.

[11]Yet when I surveyed all that my hands had done
and what I had toiled to achieve,
everything was meaningless, a chasing after the wind; Ecc 1:14
nothing was gained under the sun. Ecc 1:3

Wisdom and Folly Are Meaningless

[12]Then I turned my thoughts to consider wisdom,
and also madness and folly. Ecc 1:17
What more can the king's successor do
than what has already been done? Ecc 1:9
[13]I saw that wisdom is better than folly,
just as light is better than darkness.
[14]The wise man has eyes in his head,
while the fool walks in the darkness;
but I came to realize
that the same fate overtakes them both.

[15]Then I thought in my heart,

"The fate of the fool will overtake me also.
What then do I gain by being wise?" Ecc 6:8
I said in my heart,
"This too is meaningless."
[16]For the wise man, like the fool, will not be long remembered;
in days to come both will be forgotten.
Like the fool, the wise man too must die!

Toil Is Meaningless

[17]So I hated life, because the work that is done
under the sun was grievous to me. All of it is
meaningless, a chasing after the wind. [18]I hated all
the things I had toiled for under the sun, because
I must leave them to the one who comes after me.
[19]And who knows whether he will be a wise man
or a fool? Yet he will have control over all the work
into which I have poured my effort and skill under
the sun. This too is meaningless. [20]So my heart
began to despair over all my toilsome labor under

LIVING  **INSIGHT**

Self-pity is the smog that pollutes and obscures the light of the Son.
(See Ecclesiastes 2:17–20.)

the sun. [21]For a man may do his work with wisdom, knowledge and skill, and then he must leave
all he owns to someone who has not worked for it.
This too is meaningless and a great misfortune.
[22]What does a man get for all the toil and anxious
striving with which he labors under the sun? [23]All
his days his work is pain and grief; even at night
his mind does not rest. This too is meaningless.
[24]A man can do nothing better than to eat and
drink and find satisfaction in his work. This too, I
see, is from the hand of God, [25]for without him,
who can eat or find enjoyment? [26]To the man who
pleases him, God gives wisdom, knowledge and
happiness, but to the sinner he gives the task of
gathering and storing up wealth to hand it over to
the one who pleases God. This too is meaningless,
a chasing after the wind. Job 27:17; Pr 13:22; Ecc 3:12-13

A Time for Everything

3 There is a time for everything,
and a season for every activity under heaven:

2 a time to be born and a time to die,
a time to plant and a time to uproot,
3 a time to kill and a time to heal,
a time to tear down and a time to build,
4 a time to weep and a time to laugh,
a time to mourn and a time to dance,
5 a time to scatter stones and a time to gather them,
a time to embrace and a time to refrain,
6 a time to search and a time to give up,
a time to keep and a time to throw away,
7 a time to tear and a time to mend,
a time to be silent and a time to speak,
8 a time to love and a time to hate,
a time for war and a time for peace.

LIVING  **INSIGHT**

The Master is neither mute nor careless as He alters our times and changes our seasons. Take time today to delight in His presence as you acknowledge His right and His power to bring change into your life. Are you sensitive to His working? Are you listening? Are you available and open to change?
(See Ecclesiastes 3:1–8.)

[9]What does the worker gain from his toil? [10]I
have seen the burden God has laid on men. [11]He
has made everything beautiful in its time. He has
also set eternity in the hearts of men; yet they
cannot fathom what God has done from beginning
to end. [12]I know that there is nothing better for
men than to be happy and do good while they live.
[13]That everyone may eat and drink, and find satisfaction in all his toil—this is the gift of God. [14]I
know that everything God does will endure forever; nothing can be added to it and nothing taken
from it. God does it so that men will revere him.

[15]Whatever is has already been, Ecc 6:10

and what will be has been before; Ecc 1:9
and God will call the past to account.[a]

16 And I saw something else under the sun:
In the place of judgment—wickedness was
there,
in the place of justice—wickedness was
there.

17 I thought in my heart,

"God will bring to judgment Ro 2:6-8; 2Th 1:6-7
both the righteous and the wicked,
for there will be a time for every activity,
a time for every deed." ver 1

18 I also thought, "As for men, God tests them so
that they may see that they are like the animals.
19 Man's fate is like that of the animals; the same
fate awaits them both: As one dies, so dies the
other. All have the same breath[b]; man has no
advantage over the animal. Everything is meaningless. 20 All go to the same place; all come from dust,
and to dust all return. 21 Who knows if the spirit of
man rises upward and if the spirit of the animal[c]
goes down into the earth?" Ps 73:22; Ge 3:19; Ecc 12:7
22 So I saw that there is nothing better for a man
than to enjoy his work, because that is his lot. For
who can bring him to see what will happen after
him? Job 31:2; Ecc 2:24; 5:18

Oppression, Toil, Friendlessness

4 Again I looked and saw all the oppression
that was taking place under the sun: Ps 12:5

I saw the tears of the oppressed—
and they have no comforter;
power was on the side of their oppressors—
and they have no comforter. La 1:16
2 And I declared that the dead, Jer 20:17-18; 22:10
who had already died,
are happier than the living,
who are still alive. Job 3:17; 10:18
3 But better than both
is he who has not yet been, Job 3:16; Ecc 6:3
who has not seen the evil
that is done under the sun. Job 3:22

4 And I saw that all labor and all achievement
spring from man's envy of his neighbor. This too
is meaningless, a chasing after the wind. Ecc 1:14

5 The fool folds his hands Pr 6:10
and ruins himself.
6 Better one handful with tranquillity
than two handfuls with toil Pr 15:16-17; 16:8
and chasing after the wind.

7 Again I saw something meaningless under the sun:

8 There was a man all alone;
he had neither son nor brother.
There was no end to his toil,
yet his eyes were not content with his
wealth. Pr 27:20
"For whom am I toiling," he asked,
"and why am I depriving myself of
enjoyment?"
This too is meaningless—
a miserable business!

9 Two are better than one,
because they have a good return for their
work:
10 If one falls down,
his friend can help him up.
But pity the man who falls
and has no one to help him up!
11 Also, if two lie down together, they will keep
warm.
But how can one keep warm alone?
12 Though one may be overpowered,
two can defend themselves.
A cord of three strands is not quickly broken.

Advancement Is Meaningless

13 Better a poor but wise youth than an old but
foolish king who no longer knows how to take
warning. 14 The youth may have come from prison
to the kingship, or he may have been born in
poverty within his kingdom. 15 I saw that all who
lived and walked under the sun followed the
youth, the king's successor. 16 There was no end to
all the people who were before them. But those
who came later were not pleased with the successor. This too is meaningless, a chasing after the
wind.

A Momentary Breakthrough **Chapter 5**

In these verses a glimmer of hope breaks through the unrelenting darkness. The first seven verses show Solomon turning his attention back to God, but only briefly. He acknowledged the importance of keeping commitments made to God and fulfilling vows. However, in the next stroke of the pen Solomon brought back to mind the pitfalls of seeking the material goods of this world. They only multiply troubles, and ultimately they bring no satisfaction either.

Stand in Awe of God

5 Guard your steps when you go to the house of God. Go near to listen rather than to offer the sacrifice of fools, who do not know that they do wrong.

2 Do not be quick with your mouth,

[a] 15 *Or God calls back the past* [b] 19 *Or spirit* [c] 21 *Or Who knows the spirit of man, which rises upward, or the spirit of the animal, which*

do not be hasty in your heart
to utter anything before God. Jdg 11:35
God is in heaven
and you are on earth,
so let your words be few. Pr 10:19; 20:25
3As a dream comes when there are many cares,
so the speech of a fool when there are
many words. Ecc 10:14

4When you make a vow to God, do not delay in
fulfilling it. He has no pleasure in fools; fulfill your
vow. 5It is better not to vow than to make a vow

LIVING 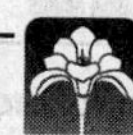 **INSIGHT**

Judging yourself on the matter of keeping your word, are you encouraging or discouraging others? Here are a few familiar situations to help you answer this question: When you tell someone they can depend on you to help them out—can they? When you say you'll be there at such-and-such a time—are you? When someone makes a request for prayer and you reply, "Yes, I'll pray for you"—do you?
(See Ecclesiastes 5:4–5.)

and not fulfill it. 6Do not let your mouth lead you
into sin. And do not protest to the ⌊temple⌋ messenger, "My vow was a mistake." Why should God
be angry at what you say and destroy the work of
your hands? 7Much dreaming and many words are
meaningless. Therefore stand in awe of God.

Riches Are Meaningless

8If you see the poor oppressed in a district, and
justice and rights denied, do not be surprised at
such things; for one official is eyed by a higher one,
and over them both are others higher still. 9The
increase from the land is taken by all; the king
himself profits from the fields. Ps 12:5; Ecc 4:1

10Whoever loves money never has money
enough;
whoever loves wealth is never satisfied with
his income.
This too is meaningless.

11As goods increase,
so do those who consume them.
And what benefit are they to the owner
except to feast his eyes on them?

12The sleep of a laborer is sweet,
whether he eats little or much,
but the abundance of a rich man
permits him no sleep. Job 20:20

13I have seen a grievous evil under the sun:

wealth hoarded to the harm of its owner,
14 or wealth lost through some misfortune,
so that when he has a son
there is nothing left for him.
15Naked a man comes from his mother's womb,
and as he comes, so he departs. Job 1:21
He takes nothing from his labor Ps 49:17; 1Ti 6:7
that he can carry in his hand. Ecc 1:3

16This too is a grievous evil:

As a man comes, so he departs,
and what does he gain,
since he toils for the wind? Pr 11:29; Ecc 1:3
17All his days he eats in darkness,
with great frustration, affliction and anger.

18Then I realized that it is good and proper for
a man to eat and drink, and to find satisfaction in
his toilsome labor under the sun during the few
days of life God has given him—for this is his lot.
19Moreover, when God gives any man wealth and
possessions, and enables him to enjoy them, to
accept his lot and be happy in his work—this is a
gift of God. 20He seldom reflects on the days of his
life, because God keeps him occupied with gladness of heart. Dt 12:7,18; Ecc 2:24; 3:13

Continued Wanderings **Chapters 6–10**

Chapters 6–10 are a smorgasbord of reflections and comments. Solomon's search for meaning continued. His tone became caustic. Yet some of his best practical advice in this section is recorded in chapter 7. Here's what Solomon had learned the hard way: Honor is better than luxury (7:1); sobriety is better than levity (7:2–7); caution is better than risk (7:8–10); wisdom is better than wealth (7:11–12); and balance is better than extremes (7:13–18).

6 I have seen another evil under the sun, and it
weighs heavily on men: 2God gives a man
wealth, possessions and honor, so that he lacks
nothing his heart desires, but God does not enable
him to enjoy them, and a stranger enjoys them
instead. This is meaningless, a grievous evil.
3A man may have a hundred children and live
many years; yet no matter how long he lives, if he
cannot enjoy his prosperity and does not receive
proper burial, I say that a stillborn child is better
off than he. 4It comes without meaning, it departs
in darkness, and in darkness its name is shrouded.
5Though it never saw the sun or knew anything, it
has more rest than does that man— 6even if he
lives a thousand years twice over but fails to enjoy
his prosperity. Do not all go to the same place?

7All man's efforts are for his mouth,
yet his appetite is never satisfied. Pr 16:26; 27:20
8What advantage has a wise man
over a fool? Ecc 2:15
What does a poor man gain

by knowing how to conduct himself before
others?
9Better what the eye sees
than the roving of the appetite.
This too is meaningless,
a chasing after the wind. Ecc 1:14

10Whatever exists has already been named,
and what man is has been known;
no man can contend
with one who is stronger than he.
11The more the words,
the less the meaning,
and how does that profit anyone?

12For who knows what is good for a man in life,
during the few and meaningless days he passes
through like a shadow? Who can tell him what will
happen under the sun after he is gone? Ps 39:6

Wisdom

7 A good name is better than fine perfume,
and the day of death better than the day of
birth. Job 10:18
2It is better to go to a house of mourning
than to go to a house of feasting,
for death is the destiny of every man; Ps 90:12
the living should take this to heart.
3Sorrow is better than laughter, Pr 14:13
because a sad face is good for the heart.
4The heart of the wise is in the house of
mourning,
but the heart of fools is in the house of
pleasure. Ecc 2:1; Jer 16:8
5It is better to heed a wise man's rebuke Ps 141:5
than to listen to the song of fools.
6Like the crackling of thorns under the pot,
so is the laughter of fools. Ecc 2:2
This too is meaningless.

7Extortion turns a wise man into a fool,
and a bribe corrupts the heart. Ex 23:8; Dt 16:19
8The end of a matter is better than its
beginning,
and patience is better than pride. Pr 14:29
9Do not be quickly provoked in your spirit,
for anger resides in the lap of fools. Pr 14:29
10Do not say, "Why were the old days better
than these?" Ps 77:5
For it is not wise to ask such questions.
11Wisdom, like an inheritance, is a good thing
and benefits those who see the sun. Ecc 11:7
12Wisdom is a shelter
as money is a shelter,
but the advantage of knowledge is this:
that wisdom preserves the life of its
possessor.

13Consider what God has done: Ecc 2:24
Who can straighten
what he has made crooked? Ecc 1:15
14When times are good, be happy;
but when times are bad, consider:
God has made the one
as well as the other. Job 1:21; Ecc 2:24
Therefore, a man cannot discover
anything about his future.

LIVING  **INSIGHT**

Suffering is essential, not only because it softens our spirits and makes us sensitive to the voice of God, but also because it reveals our true nature. It shows us the truth about ourselves.

(See Ecclesiastes 7:14.)

15In this meaningless life of mine I have seen
both of these:

a righteous man perishing in his
righteousness,
and a wicked man living long in his
wickedness. Ecc 8:12-14; Jer 12:1
16Do not be overrighteous,
neither be overwise—
why destroy yourself?
17Do not be overwicked,
and do not be a fool—
why die before your time? Job 15:32; Ps 55:23
18It is good to grasp the one
and not let go of the other.
The man who fears God will avoid all
⌞extremes⌟.[a] Ecc 3:14
19Wisdom makes one wise man more powerful
than ten rulers in a city.

20There is not a righteous man on earth Ps 14:3
who does what is right and never sins.

21Do not pay attention to every word people
say,
or you may hear your servant cursing
you— Pr 30:10
22for you know in your heart
that many times you yourself have cursed
others.

23All this I tested by wisdom and I said,

"I am determined to be wise"— Ecc 1:17; Ro 1:22
but this was beyond me.
24Whatever wisdom may be,
it is far off and most profound—

[a]18 Or *will follow them both*

who can discover it? Job 28:12
[25]So I turned my mind to understand,
to investigate and to search out wisdom
and the scheme of things Job 28:3
and to understand the stupidity of wickedness
and the madness of folly. Ecc 1:17

[26]I find more bitter than death
the woman who is a snare, Ex 10:7; Jdg 14:15
whose heart is a trap
and whose hands are chains.
The man who pleases God will escape her,
but the sinner she will ensnare. Pr 5:3-5; 7:23

[27]"Look," says the Teacher,[a] "this is what I
have discovered: Ecc 1:1

"Adding one thing to another to discover the
scheme of things—
28 while I was still searching
but not finding—
I found one ⌊upright⌋ man among a thousand,
but not one ⌊upright⌋ woman among them
all. 1Ki 11:3
[29]This only have I found:
God made mankind upright,
but men have gone in search of many
schemes."

8 Who is like the wise man?
Who knows the explanation of things?
Wisdom brightens a man's face
and changes its hard appearance.

Obey the King

[2]Obey the king's command, I say, because you
took an oath before God. [3]Do not be in a hurry to
leave the king's presence. Do not stand up for a
bad cause, for he will do whatever he pleases.
[4]Since a king's word is supreme, who can say to
him, "What are you doing?" Job 9:12; Est 1:19; Da 4:35

[5]Whoever obeys his command will come to no
harm,
and the wise heart will know the proper
time and procedure.
[6]For there is a proper time and procedure for
every matter, Ecc 3:1
though a man's misery weighs heavily upon
him.

[7]Since no man knows the future,
who can tell him what is to come?
[8]No man has power over the wind to contain
it[b];
so no one has power over the day of his
death.
As no one is discharged in time of war,
so wickedness will not release those who
practice it.

[9]All this I saw, as I applied my mind to everything done under the sun. There is a time when a
man lords it over others to his own[c] hurt. [10]Then
too, I saw the wicked buried—those who used
to come and go from the holy place and receive
praise[d] in the city where they did this. This too is
meaningless. Ecc 1:11
[11]When the sentence for a crime is not quickly
carried out, the hearts of the people are filled with
schemes to do wrong. [12]Although a wicked man
commits a hundred crimes and still lives a long
time, I know that it will go better with God-fearing
men, who are reverent before God. [13]Yet because
the wicked do not fear God, it will not go well with
them, and their days will not lengthen like a
shadow. Dt 4:40; Isa 3:11
[14]There is something else meaningless that occurs on earth: righteous men who get what the
wicked deserve, and wicked men who get what the
righteous deserve. This too, I say, is meaningless.
[15]So I commend the enjoyment of life, because
nothing is better for a man under the sun than to
eat and drink and be glad. Then joy will accompany him in his work all the days of the life God has
given him under the sun. Ecc 2:24; 3:12-13; 5:18

LIVING  **INSIGHT**

There is an old Greek motto that says, "You will break the bow if you keep it always bent"—which, being translated loosely from the original, means, "There's more to life than hard work." Loosening the strings on our bow means when we have some leisure, we live it up.

(See Ecclesiastes 8:15.)

[16]When I applied my mind to know wisdom
and to observe man's labor on earth—his eyes not
seeing sleep day or night— [17]then I saw all that
God has done. No one can comprehend what goes
on under the sun. Despite all his efforts to search
it out, man cannot discover its meaning. Even if a
wise man claims he knows, he cannot really comprehend it. Ecc 3:11; Ro 11:33

A Common Destiny for All

9 So I reflected on all this and concluded that
the righteous and the wise and what they do
are in God's hands, but no man knows whether
love or hate awaits him. [2]All share a common destiny—the righteous and the wicked, the good and

[a]27 Or *leader of the assembly* [b]8 Or *over his spirit to retain it* [c]9 Or *to their* [d]10 Some Hebrew manuscripts and Septuagint (Aquila); most Hebrew manuscripts *and are forgotten*

the bad,[a] the clean and the unclean, those who
offer sacrifices and those who do not. Dt 33:3

As it is with the good man,
so with the sinner;
as it is with those who take oaths,
so with those who are afraid to take them.

3This is the evil in everything that happens under the sun: The same destiny overtakes all. The
hearts of men, moreover, are full of evil and there
is madness in their hearts while they live, and afterward they join the dead. 4Anyone who is among
the living has hope[b]—even a live dog is better off
than a dead lion! Job 21:26; Ecc 2:14

5For the living know that they will die,
but the dead know nothing; Job 14:21
they have no further reward,
and even the memory of them is forgotten.
6Their love, their hate
and their jealousy have long since vanished;
never again will they have a part
in anything that happens under the sun.

7Go, eat your food with gladness, and drink
your wine with a joyful heart, for it is now that
God favors what you do. 8Always be clothed in
white, and always anoint your head with oil. 9En-
joy life with your wife, whom you love, all the days
of this meaningless life that God has given you
under the sun— all your meaningless days. For
this is your lot in life and in your toilsome labor
under the sun. 10Whatever your hand finds to do,
do it with all your might, for in the grave,[c] where
you are going, there is neither working nor planning nor knowledge nor wisdom. 1Sa 10:7; Ecc 2:24

11I have seen something else under the sun:

The race is not to the swift
or the battle to the strong, Am 2:14-15
nor does food come to the wise Job 32:13; Jer 9:23
or wealth to the brilliant
or favor to the learned;
but time and chance happen to them all.

12Moreover, no man knows when his hour will
come:

As fish are caught in a cruel net,
or birds are taken in a snare,
so men are trapped by evil times Pr 29:6
that fall unexpectedly upon them. Ps 73:22

Wisdom Better Than Folly

13I also saw under the sun this example of wisdom that greatly impressed me: 14There was once
a small city with only a few people in it. And a
powerful king came against it, surrounded it and
built huge siegeworks against it. 15Now there lived
in that city a man poor but wise, and he saved the
city by his wisdom. But nobody remembered that
poor man. 16So I said, "Wisdom is better than
strength." But the poor man's wisdom is despised,
and his words are no longer heeded. Pr 21:22

17The quiet words of the wise are more to be
heeded
than the shouts of a ruler of fools.
18Wisdom is better than weapons of war, ver 16
but one sinner destroys much good.

10 As dead flies give perfume a bad smell,
so a little folly outweighs wisdom and
honor. Pr 13:16; 18:2
2The heart of the wise inclines to the right,
but the heart of the fool to the left.
3Even as he walks along the road,
the fool lacks sense
and shows everyone how stupid he is.
4If a ruler's anger rises against you,
do not leave your post; Ecc 8:3
calmness can lay great errors to rest. Pr 25:15

5There is an evil I have seen under the sun,
the sort of error that arises from a ruler:
6Fools are put in many high positions, Pr 29:2
while the rich occupy the low ones.
7I have seen slaves on horseback,
while princes go on foot like slaves. Pr 19:10

8Whoever digs a pit may fall into it; Ps 7:15
whoever breaks through a wall may be
bitten by a snake. Est 2:23; Ps 9:16; Am 5:19
9Whoever quarries stones may be injured by
them;
whoever splits logs may be endangered by
them. Pr 26:27
10If the ax is dull
and its edge unsharpened,
more strength is needed
but skill will bring success.

11If a snake bites before it is charmed,
there is no profit for the charmer. Ps 58:5

12Words from a wise man's mouth are gracious,
but a fool is consumed by his own lips.
13At the beginning his words are folly;
at the end they are wicked madness—
14 and the fool multiplies words. Pr 15:2; Ecc 5:3

No one knows what is coming—
who can tell him what will happen after
him? Ecc 9:1

15A fool's work wearies him;
he does not know the way to town.

[a]2 Septuagint (Aquila), Vulgate and Syriac; Hebrew does not have *and the bad.* [b]4 Or *What then is to be chosen? With all who live, there is hope* [c]10 Hebrew *Sheol*

[16]Woe to you, O land whose king was a servant[a] Isa 3:4-5,12
and whose princes feast in the morning.
[17]Blessed are you, O land whose king is of noble birth
and whose princes eat at a proper time—
for strength and not for drunkenness.

[18]If a man is lazy, the rafters sag;
if his hands are idle, the house leaks. Pr 20:4

LIVING  **INSIGHT**

The overindulgence and underachievement of our age have created a monster whose brain is lazy, vision is blurred, hands are greedy, skin is thin, middle is round and seat is wide. This does not need to be our reality. Under the operation of the Spirit of God, we have the inner strength to resist and refrain, the strength not to indulge, not to act on impulse.
(See Ecclesiastes 10:18.)

[19]A feast is made for laughter,
and wine makes life merry, Ge 14:18; Jdg 9:13
but money is the answer for everything.

[20]Do not revile the king even in your thoughts,
or curse the rich in your bedroom,
because a bird of the air may carry your words,
and a bird on the wing may report what you say.

Advice About Life **Chapter 11**

By the time we come to chapter 11 Solomon had grown in wisdom. (It seems there is nothing like a big dose of reality to draw our attention to the counsel of wisdom.) In these verses we find a brief record of Solomon's advice on how to live. First, he wrote of the importance of investing in this life. A mother's investment in the life of her child, a worker's investment in his or her labors and a farmer's investment in his field are all to be praised. Next, Solomon praised the enjoyment of life. Finally, he acknowledged the fleeting pleasures of youth. He seemed eager to pass on the lessons he had learned, perhaps wanting to spare his readers from learning the hard way. Solomon's conclusion is important to us today: *True satisfaction cannot be found outside of a relationship with your Maker and your Sustainer.*

Bread Upon the Waters

11 Cast your bread upon the waters, ver 6
for after many days you will find it again.
[2]Give portions to seven, yes to eight,
for you do not know what disaster may come upon the land.

[3]If clouds are full of water,
they pour rain upon the earth.
Whether a tree falls to the south or to the north,
in the place where it falls, there will it lie.
[4]Whoever watches the wind will not plant;
whoever looks at the clouds will not reap.

[5]As you do not know the path of the wind,
or how the body is formed[b] in a mother's womb, Ps 139:14-16
so you cannot understand the work of God,
the Maker of all things.
[6]Sow your seed in the morning,
and at evening let not your hands be idle,
for you do not know which will succeed,
whether this or that,
or whether both will do equally well.

LIVING  **INSIGHT**

It's when we pull back, close our doors, turn off our internal lights and sit in selfish silence that we begin to shrivel. Give of yourself. Stay in touch with the mainstream of life. Let the benchmark of your life be generosity. Let it flow. Let it go.
(See Ecclesiastes 11:5–6.)

Remember Your Creator While Young

[7]Light is sweet,
and it pleases the eyes to see the sun.
[8]However many years a man may live,
let him enjoy them all.
But let him remember the days of darkness,
for they will be many.
Everything to come is meaningless.

[9]Be happy, young man, while you are young,
and let your heart give you joy in the days of your youth.
Follow the ways of your heart
and whatever your eyes see,
but know that for all these things
God will bring you to judgment. Ecc 12:14
[10]So then, banish anxiety from your heart
and cast off the troubles of your body,
for youth and vigor are meaningless. Ecc 2:24

[a]16 Or *king is a child* [b]5 Or *know how life* (or *the spirit*) / *enters the body being formed*

Putting It in Perspective **Chapter 12**

At the end of the search, there was only one thing left to say. Solomon exhorted his readers to revere God and allow Him to take the central place in their lives. God must be part of every area of our lives, from the small to the large. And he issued a strong challenge to obey God. We must not yield to our inner instincts and drives; we must not bow to the majority opinion of the day when it contradicts God's will; we must not heed the advice of counselors who promote the godless philosophies of the day. First and foremost, we must obey the Word of the Lord and revere only Him. In the end, that is the only path to meaning in life.

12 Remember your Creator Ecc 11:8
in the days of your youth,
before the days of trouble come 2Sa 19:35
and the years approach when you will say,
"I find no pleasure in them"—
2before the sun and the light
and the moon and the stars grow dark,
and the clouds return after the rain;
3when the keepers of the house tremble,
and the strong men stoop,
when the grinders cease because they are few,
and those looking through the windows
grow dim;
4when the doors to the street are closed
and the sound of grinding fades;
when men rise up at the sound of birds,
but all their songs grow faint; Jer 25:10
5when men are afraid of heights
and of dangers in the streets;
when the almond tree blossoms
and the grasshopper drags himself along
and desire no longer is stirred.
Then man goes to his eternal home Job 17:13
and mourners go about the streets. Jer 9:17
6Remember him—before the silver cord is
severed,
or the golden bowl is broken;
before the pitcher is shattered at the spring,
or the wheel broken at the well,
7and the dust returns to the ground it came
from, Ge 3:19; Job 34:15; Ps 146:4
and the spirit returns to God who gave it.

8"Meaningless! Meaningless!" says the
Teacher.[a]
"Everything is meaningless!" Ecc 1:2

The Conclusion of the Matter

9Not only was the Teacher wise, but also he
imparted knowledge to the people. He pondered
and searched out and set in order many proverbs.
10The Teacher searched to find just the right
words, and what he wrote was upright and true.
11The words of the wise are like goads, their
collected sayings like firmly embedded nails—giv-
en by one Shepherd. 12Be warned, my son, of anything in addition to them. Ezr 9:8
Of making many books there is no end, and
much study wearies the body. Ecc 1:18

13Now all has been heard;
here is the conclusion of the matter:
Fear God and keep his commandments, Dt 4:2
for this is the whole ⌞duty⌟ of man. Mic 6:8
14For God will bring every deed into judgment,
including every hidden thing, Mt 10:26; 1Co 4:5
whether it is good or evil.

[a] 8 Or *the leader of the assembly*; also in verses 9 and 10

SONG OF SONGS

This lyric poem in dialogue form has been the target of some of the most ingenious interpretations imaginable. It is quite likely that Solomon himself would be stunned to hear some of them! It seems best that we allow Solomon's song to simply say what it says rather than attempting to force on these eight chapters an allegorical interpretation of the love relationship between God and Israel. Song of Songs is an intimate, tender, romantic depiction of physical love between a man and a woman. This love is a gift of God that is to be received with gratitude and celebration. At the same time, when we see a love so rich and so unashamed, it is quite natural to think about and give thanks for Jesus Christ and His devoted love for His bride, the church.

WRITER: *Solomon*

DATE: *c.970–930 B.C.*

PURPOSE: *To disclose love's exquisite charm and beauty as one of God's great gifts*

KEY THEME: *The joy and intimacy of love within the committed marriage relationship*

SOLOMON'S SHORT STORY: *The Full Life of Love*

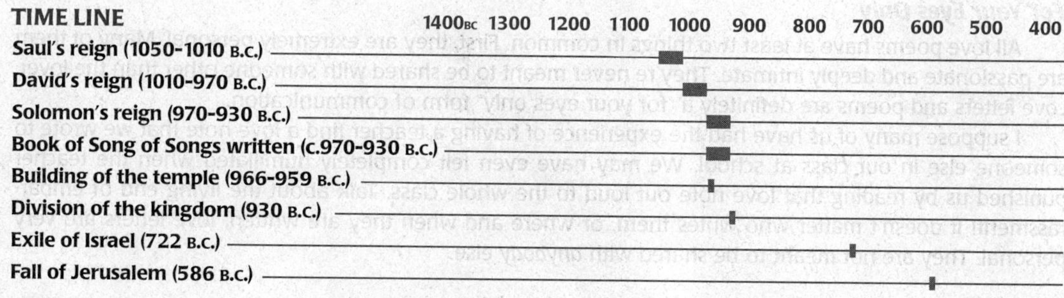

A Poem of Faithful Love

	DAYS OF ROMANTIC COURTSHIP	THE WEDDING DAY	THE JOYS OF MARRIED LIFE		
	CHAPTERS 1:2–3:5	*CHAPTERS 3:6–5:1*	*CHAPTERS 5:2–8:14*		
EMPHASIS	**Bride muses about courtship days**	**Groom speaks tenderly of the day of the wedding**	**Wife affectionately describes her loving husband**	**Husband speaks of his wife in intimate terms**	**Both partners declare a permanent seal on their love**
CHIEF SPEAKER	**The Bride *("Beloved")***	**Solomon *("Lover")***	**Wife *("Beloved")***	**Husband *("Lover")***	**Duet**

Down through the centuries men and women have employed various means of expressing their love to one another. I suppose if you're gifted at writing songs, you have, like many others, written a song to the one you love. If you're able to go one step beyond and put your lyrics to music, all the better! But then—if you are *particularly* gifted, or courageous, and dare to *sing* this song to your beloved, that's the best! There is something very special about singing your own words of love to your sweetheart.

Throughout history, some have had the time, the money and the creativity to build monuments to their beloved. Statues, buildings, and even cities have been built as monuments of love. But of all the ways men and women have picked to try to describe and/or demonstrate their love for one another, the most common is the writing of poetic verse. A love letter or poem has been a favorite for thousands of years.

For Your Eyes Only

All love poems have at least two things in common. First, they are extremely personal. Many of them are passionate and deeply intimate. They're never meant to be shared with someone other than the lover. Love letters and poems are definitely a "for your eyes only" form of communication.

I suppose many of us have had the experience of having a teacher find a love note that we wrote to someone else in our class at school. We may have even felt completely humiliated when the teacher punished us by reading that love note out loud to the whole class. Talk about the living end of embarrassment! It doesn't matter who writes them, or where and when they are written, love letters are very personal. They are not meant to be shared with *anybody* else.

Confessions of a Weekend Poet

Many years ago I used to write poetry to my wife. Once, when our children were teenagers, I decided to express my affection for Cynthia through poetry. Just before I left for a trip, I wrote her a poem expressing my heartfelt love. To my amazement, when I arrived home, she had taken that little love note and had posted it on the window in front of the kitchen sink. There it was, a note expressing my deepest feelings for my wife right out where everyone could read it. To my dismay, our teenagers had been reading that love note the whole time I was gone, and you can imagine what fun they were having with my poetry!

Needless to say, it brought a lot of laughter to my home during my absence and even a few chuckles after I was home. My love note was meant for one person, and one person only . . . certainly not a family full of teenagers.

Solomon's Love Letter

Song of Songs is among the greatest love letters ever written. There is only one love poem celebrating the intimacy of human love that has been completely inspired by the Holy Spirit—and this is it. Solomon and his lover, who became his bride, never dreamed that centuries of people would be reading their love notes over and over again. Although the Holy Spirit knew what He was doing when He inspired this wonderful poem of love, I am convinced that Solomon and his bride-to-be had no idea we would be looking over their shoulders and reading their very intimate remarks to one another. After all, living in another place and another time, how could we understand fully what they meant?

Song of Songs is a lengthy love letter of eight chapters. It's really not meant to be overanalyzed or interpreted to the point of potentially ruining its poetic and romantic beauty. Nevertheless, through the centuries many people have tried to interpret this book of Scripture in some mighty fanciful ways. When it comes right down to it, this book is simply a small vignette of a love relationship between a man and a woman in the days of Solomon. Inspired . . . yes! But let's read Song of Songs for what it is—a wonderful and passionate love letter—rather than feeling the need to spiritualize it and force it to say something different from what it was intended to say.

Setting the Scene

Let's ask a couple of introductory questions that will help as we study this book. First, *who wrote Song of Songs*? The first verse assures us that this is Solomon's work: "Solomon's Song of Songs." It is the most exquisite of all of his 1,005 songs. Verse 32 of 1 Kings 4 tells us that he wrote over a thousand songs—and this is the best of the best. Second, *when was the book written*? There is no date referred to in the book, and there is no general agreement among scholars as to the exact time of its writing. Solomon wrote three books that ultimately found their way into the Bible: Song of Songs, Ecclesiastes and Proverbs. In our English Bibles they appear in the opposite order—first comes Proverbs and then Ecclesiates and then the love letter, Song of Songs.

I believe that Solomon wrote this song relatively early in life, when his love was warm and innocent, beautiful and unmarred. Next in order, I believe he wrote Ecclesiastes—while in the throes of a mid-life crisis. Finally, I conclude that Proverbs was penned in his later years, when he had grown in wisdom and had learned, the hard way, some of the lessons that wisdom teaches.

How Should We Read This Letter?

I suggest that Solomon wrote Song of Songs when newly on the throne in the land of Israel. I believe this love letter was preserved to accent the humanity of a king like Solomon. It's easy sometimes to forget that greatly talented men and women are altogether human—very much like you and me. Song of Songs will help us see Solomon in the context of the human experience of intimate love. It is a song that extols human love. It shines the spotlight on romance and on intimate affection between married partners.

As you read Song of Songs, why not take it at face value. As I wrote earlier, in my opinion it is a mistake to force any other interpretation on it. It is a song that celebrates love between a newly married couple—a love letter between a man and a woman. At the same time, Song of Songs presents a love so rich and so full that it seems natural to think about the love of Christ for His church, as many have done. But I would urge that we stay true to what I believe is its primary intent. Let's read Song of Songs with its plain meaning in full focus . . . a poetic work praising romantic love as a gift of God, to be received with gratitude and celebration.

My Darling, My Beloved

Throughout the book you will read of "my darling" (also called "beloved" in the sectional headings in the book), which is a reference to the woman, and "my lover," which is a reference to the man. These two dialogue back and forth in this love song. The language of the book is exceedingly intimate—among the most intimate expressions found in all the Bible. As you read through Song of Songs, you are reading over the shoulders of two people who were madly in love with one another.

There is a dialogue that progresses through Song of Songs. The bride (the "beloved") is the chief speaker in chapters 1:2–3:5, and then Solomon (the "lover") becomes the chief speaker in chapters 4:1–5:1. His beloved answers him in chapters 5:2–6:3. And he responds again, as her husband, in 6:4–9. Finally both of them "sing a duet" together in the last part of the song. It's quite a creative expression of love. (Look too for the interludes provided by the "friends" throughout the book—see the sectional headings.)

Love Lessons

We can learn much from reading this book. The pace of our lives has in many cases so altered our steps that reading a love song like this, rather than softening our hearts, may humor us. Rather than motivating us to passionate expressions of love with our life partner, we're tempted to take it as some kind of a strange joke. The simple fact is, there are some who read these words with a longing that their mate would respond to them in ways similar to what is recorded here. But the best many of us can manage is a candlelight meal maybe twice a year—and even then it takes two months of planning to make it happen!

We need to know that physical love is an art comprised of sensitive techniques that cannot grow without being nurtured. If left alone, marital affection can and does decay. No amount of Bible study can replace it. No amount of church attendance, good intentions or religious activities can negate the need to cultivate physical love in our relationship with our marriage partner. If we are married, we *must* nurture an intimate and romantic relationship with our spouse. It takes time and creativity, but it is absolutely essential.

If you are excusing your lack of creative love because you're so involved in a plethora of spiritual things, you're choosing a poor excuse. Our heavenly Father, who gave us bodies as well as souls and spirits, meant for the body to be nurtured through the beauty of marital love. If there is anyone who ought to have a romantic life, it is the couple whose relationship is based on the will and the Word of God! We should joyfully participate in the intimacy God has provided in and through our spouse. Such romance and intimacy involves care, conversation, respect and physical satisfaction in the arms of your beloved. All of our interplay and intimacy helps to build a strong marriage. When you discover this beautiful romance in a marriage relationship, you will enjoy a rare gift indeed!

Days of Romantic Courtship Chapters 1:1–3:5

In these opening chapters we find a record of Solomon's courtship with his bride-to-be. The "beloved" was the first to speak, and her words were full of affection and passion for her husband-to-be. This section of the song is filled with symbolic pictures and images of beauty, grace, loveliness, charm and elegance. As we read these words, why not let ourselves be swept into the current of the romance and love that is expressed. These are not words to be analyzed so much as they are to be appreciated. Allow yourself to imagine the love and romance shared between a newly married man and woman who look forward to a life of intimacy with each other.

1 Solomon's Song of Songs. 1Ki 4:32

Beloved[a]

2Let him kiss me with the kisses of his
mouth—
for your love is more delightful than wine.
3Pleasing is the fragrance of your perfumes;
your name is like perfume poured out.
No wonder the maidens love you! Ps 45:14
4Take me away with you—let us hurry!
Let the king bring me into his chambers.

Friends

We rejoice and delight in you[b]; SS 2:3
we will praise your love more than wine.

Beloved

How right they are to adore you!

5Dark am I, yet lovely, SS 2:14; 4:3
O daughters of Jerusalem, SS 2:7; 5:8
dark like the tents of Kedar, Ge 25:13
like the tent curtains of Solomon.[c]
6Do not stare at me because I am dark,
because I am darkened by the sun.
My mother's sons were angry with me
and made me take care of the vineyards;
my own vineyard I have neglected.
7Tell me, you whom I love, where you graze
your flock
and where you rest your sheep at midday.
Why should I be like a veiled woman Ge 24:65
beside the flocks of your friends?

Friends

8If you do not know, most beautiful of women,
follow the tracks of the sheep
and graze your young goats
by the tents of the shepherds.

Lover

9I liken you, my darling, to a mare
harnessed to one of the chariots of
Pharaoh. 2Ch 1:17
10Your cheeks are beautiful with earrings, SS 5:13
your neck with strings of jewels. Isa 61:10
11We will make you earrings of gold,
studded with silver.

Beloved

12While the king was at his table,
my perfume spread its fragrance. SS 4:11-14
13My lover is to me a sachet of myrrh Ge 37:25
resting between my breasts.
14My lover is to me a cluster of henna blossoms
from the vineyards of En Gedi. 1Sa 23:29

Lover

15How beautiful you are, my darling! SS 4:7; 7:6
Oh, how beautiful!
Your eyes are doves. SS 14:1; 5:2,12

Beloved

16How handsome you are, my lover!
Oh, how charming!
And our bed is verdant.

Lover

17The beams of our house are cedars; 1Ki 6:9
our rafters are firs.

Beloved[d]

2 I am a rose[e] of Sharon, Isa 35:1
a lily of the valleys. SS 5:13; Hos 14:5

Lover

2Like a lily among thorns
is my darling among the maidens.

Beloved

3Like an apple tree among the trees of the
forest
is my lover among the young men. SS 1:14
I delight to sit in his shade, SS 1:4
and his fruit is sweet to my taste. SS 4:16
4He has taken me to the banquet hall, Est 1:11
and his banner over me is love. Nu 1:52
5Strengthen me with raisins,
refresh me with apples, SS 7:8
for I am faint with love. SS 5:8
6His left arm is under my head,
and his right arm embraces me. SS 8:3
7Daughters of Jerusalem, I charge you SS 5:8
by the gazelles and by the does of the field:

[a]Primarily on the basis of the gender of the Hebrew pronouns used, male and female speakers are indicated in the margins by the captions *Lover* and *Beloved* respectively. The words of others are marked *Friends*. In some instances the divisions and their captions are debatable. [b]4 The Hebrew is masculine singular. [c]5 Or *Salma* [d]1 Or *Lover* [e]1 Possibly a member of the crocus family

Do not arouse or awaken love
until it so desires. SS 3:5; 8:4

8Listen! My lover!
Look! Here he comes,
leaping across the mountains,
bounding over the hills. ver 17; SS 8:14
9My lover is like a gazelle or a young stag.
Look! There he stands behind our wall,
gazing through the windows,
peering through the lattice.
10My lover spoke and said to me,
"Arise, my darling,
my beautiful one, and come with me.
11See! The winter is past;
the rains are over and gone.
12Flowers appear on the earth;
the season of singing has come,
the cooing of doves
is heard in our land.
13The fig tree forms its early fruit; Isa 28:4; Jer 24:2
the blossoming vines spread their fragrance.
Arise, come, my darling;
my beautiful one, come with me."

Lover

14My dove in the clefts of the rock, Ge 8:8; SS 1:15
in the hiding places on the mountainside,
show me your face,
let me hear your voice;
for your voice is sweet,
and your face is lovely. SS 1:5; 8:13
15Catch for us the foxes, Jdg 15:4
the little foxes
that ruin the vineyards, SS 1:6
our vineyards that are in bloom. SS 7:12

LIVING  INSIGHT

Often it's the little things that weaken a marriage. The slow leaks, not the blowouts. The insidious "pests" we seldom even consider that cut away at the heart of a home until finally it crumbles. Watch out for those "foxes"—always present, always ready to devour the blossoms of your relationship.

(See Song of Songs 2:14–15.)

Beloved

16My lover is mine and I am his; SS 7:10
he browses among the lilies. SS 6:3
17Until the day breaks
and the shadows flee, SS 4:6
turn, my lover, SS 1:14
and be like a gazelle
or like a young stag ver 9
on the rugged hills.[a] ver 8

3 All night long on my bed
I looked for the one my heart loves; SS 5:6
I looked for him but did not find him.
2I will get up now and go about the city,
through its streets and squares;
I will search for the one my heart loves.
So I looked for him but did not find him.
3The watchmen found me
as they made their rounds in the city. SS 5:7
"Have you seen the one my heart loves?"
4Scarcely had I passed them
when I found the one my heart loves.
I held him and would not let him go
till I had brought him to my mother's
house, SS 8:2
to the room of the one who conceived me.
5Daughters of Jerusalem, I charge you SS 2:7
by the gazelles and by the does of the field:
Do not arouse or awaken love
until it so desires. SS 8:4

The Wedding Day — Chapters 3:6–5:1

Fantasy and longing become reality in these chapters. As the groom gazed at his bride, he painted a picture of her charm and beauty in his eyes. With adoration he praised every part of her face and body. Although the images he used do not make as much sense to us as they did thousands of years ago, they are still vivid pictures of beauty and an expression of the groom's passionate affection for his new bride.

6Who is this coming up from the desert SS 8:5
like a column of smoke,
perfumed with myrrh and incense SS 1:13; 4:6,14
made from all the spices of the merchant?
7Look! It is Solomon's carriage,
escorted by sixty warriors, 1Sa 8:11
the noblest of Israel,
8all of them wearing the sword,
all experienced in battle,
each with his sword at his side,
prepared for the terrors of the night.
9King Solomon made for himself the carriage;
he made it of wood from Lebanon.
10Its posts he made of silver,
its base of gold.
Its seat was upholstered with purple,
its interior lovingly inlaid
by[b] the daughters of Jerusalem.
11Come out, you daughters of Zion, Isa 4:4
and look at King Solomon wearing the
crown,

[a] 17 Or *the hills of Bether* [b] 10 Or *its inlaid interior a gift of love / from*

the crown with which his mother crowned
him
on the day of his wedding,
the day his heart rejoiced. Isa 62:5

Lover

4 How beautiful you are, my darling!
Oh, how beautiful!
Your eyes behind your veil are doves.
Your hair is like a flock of goats
descending from Mount Gilead. Mic 7:14
2Your teeth are like a flock of sheep just shorn,
coming up from the washing.
Each has its twin;
not one of them is alone. SS 6:6
3Your lips are like a scarlet ribbon;
your mouth is lovely. SS 5:16
Your temples behind your veil
are like the halves of a pomegranate. SS 6:7
4Your neck is like the tower of David, SS 7:4
built with elegance[a];
on it hang a thousand shields, Eze 27:10
all of them shields of warriors.
5Your two breasts are like two fawns, SS 7:3
like twin fawns of a gazelle Pr 5:19
that browse among the lilies. SS 2:16
6Until the day breaks
and the shadows flee, SS 2:17
I will go to the mountain of myrrh
and to the hill of incense.
7All beautiful you are, my darling; SS 1:15
there is no flaw in you.
8Come with me from Lebanon, my bride, SS 5:1
come with me from Lebanon.
Descend from the crest of Amana,
from the top of Senir, the summit of
Hermon, Dt 3:9; 1Ch 5:23
from the lions' dens
and the mountain haunts of the leopards.
9You have stolen my heart, my sister, my
bride;
you have stolen my heart
with one glance of your eyes,
with one jewel of your necklace. Ge 41:42
10How delightful is your love, my sister, my
bride! SS 1:2; 7:6
How much more pleasing is your love than
wine,
and the fragrance of your perfume than any
spice! Ps 45:8
11Your lips drop sweetness as the honeycomb,
my bride;
milk and honey are under your tongue.
The fragrance of your garments is like that
of Lebanon. Hos 14:6
12You are a garden locked up, my sister, my
bride;
you are a spring enclosed, a sealed
fountain. Pr 5:15-18
13Your plants are an orchard of pomegranates
with choice fruits,
with henna and nard, SS 1:14
14nard and saffron,
calamus and cinnamon, Ex 30:23
with every kind of incense tree,
with myrrh and aloes SS 3:6
and all the finest spices. SS 1:12
15You are[b] a garden fountain,
a well of flowing water
streaming down from Lebanon.

LIVING  INSIGHT

If you ever had the notion that God was some sort of puritanical prude, put the idea out of your head. He desires that our marriages provide us with ecstatic sexual delights, exhilarating and pleasurable to the maximum.

(See Song of Songs 4:12–16.)

Beloved

16Awake, north wind,
and come, south wind!
Blow on my garden,
that its fragrance may spread abroad.
Let my lover come into his garden
and taste its choice fruits. SS 2:3; 5:1

Lover

5 I have come into my garden, my sister, my
bride; SS 4:8
I have gathered my myrrh with my spice.
I have eaten my honeycomb and my honey;
I have drunk my wine and my milk. SS 4:11

Friends

Eat, O friends, and drink;
drink your fill, O lovers.

The Joys of Married Life **Chapters 5:2–8:14**

In this section a vivid portrait of married life is painted. I suggest four examples of intimacy and care that are often lacking in our relationships today. First, *we often fail to give intimate attention to our spouse.* Solomon and his bride were wild about each other, and they made a point of showing each other unrestrained attention and affection. Second, *we often lack time simply to enjoy being together.* These two married lovers *made time* to be with each

[a]4 The meaning of the Hebrew for this word is uncertain. [b]15 Or *I am* (spoken by the *Beloved*)

other to enjoy the intimate pleasures of marital bliss. Third, *we often fail to plan times just to get away with each other.* When our schedules get so full, often we allow that need to go unfulfilled. Solomon and his bride made a regular habit of getting away for romantic times of escape. Fourth, *we often lack deep, unguarded and meaningful intimacy in our relationships with our spouse.* These partners openly praised each other and spoke intimately about their love. As we read these chapters with a teachable heart, we will learn to better express our love and our care for our spouse.

Beloved

[2]I slept but my heart was awake.
Listen! My lover is knocking:
"Open to me, my sister, my darling,
my dove, my flawless one. SS 4:7; 6:9
My head is drenched with dew,
my hair with the dampness of the night."
[3]I have taken off my robe—
must I put it on again?
I have washed my feet—
must I soil them again?
[4]My lover thrust his hand through the
latch-opening;
my heart began to pound for him.
[5]I arose to open for my lover,
and my hands dripped with myrrh,
my fingers with flowing myrrh,
on the handles of the lock.
[6]I opened for my lover, SS 6:1
but my lover had left; he was gone. SS 6:2
My heart sank at his departure.[a]
I looked for him but did not find him. SS 3:1
I called him but he did not answer.
[7]The watchmen found me
as they made their rounds in the city. SS 3:3
They beat me, they bruised me;
they took away my cloak,
those watchmen of the walls!
[8]O daughters of Jerusalem, I charge you—
if you find my lover,
what will you tell him?
Tell him I am faint with love. SS 2:5

Friends

[9]How is your beloved better than others,
most beautiful of women? SS 1:8; 6:1
How is your beloved better than others,
that you charge us so?

Beloved

[10]My lover is radiant and ruddy,
outstanding among ten thousand. Ps 45:2
[11]His head is purest gold;
his hair is wavy
and black as a raven.
[12]His eyes are like doves SS 1:15; 4:1
by the water streams,
washed in milk, Ge 49:12
mounted like jewels.
[13]His cheeks are like beds of spice SS 1:10; 6:2
yielding perfume.
His lips are like lilies SS 2:1
dripping with myrrh.
[14]His arms are rods of gold
set with chrysolite.
His body is like polished ivory
decorated with sapphires.[b] Job 28:6
[15]His legs are pillars of marble
set on bases of pure gold.
His appearance is like Lebanon, 1Ki 4:33; SS 7:4
choice as its cedars.
[16]His mouth is sweetness itself; SS 4:3
he is altogether lovely.
This is my lover, this my friend, SS 7:9
O daughters of Jerusalem. SS 1:5

Friends

6 Where has your lover gone, SS 5:6
most beautiful of women? SS 1:8
Which way did your lover turn,
that we may look for him with you?

Beloved

[2]My lover has gone down to his garden, SS 4:12
to the beds of spices, SS 5:13
to browse in the gardens
and to gather lilies.
[3]I am my lover's and my lover is mine; SS 7:10
he browses among the lilies. SS 2:16

Lover

[4]You are beautiful, my darling, as Tirzah,
lovely as Jerusalem, Ps 48:2; 50:2
majestic as troops with banners. ver 10
[5]Turn your eyes from me;
they overwhelm me.
Your hair is like a flock of goats
descending from Gilead. SS 4:1
[6]Your teeth are like a flock of sheep
coming up from the washing.
Each has its twin,
not one of them is alone. SS 4:2
[7]Your temples behind your veil Ge 24:65
are like the halves of a pomegranate. SS 4:3
[8]Sixty queens there may be, Ps 45:9
and eighty concubines, Ge 22:24
and virgins beyond number;
[9]but my dove, my perfect one, is unique, SS 1:15
the only daughter of her mother,
the favorite of the one who bore her. SS 3:4
The maidens saw her and called her blessed;
the queens and concubines praised her.

[a]6 Or *heart had gone out to him when he spoke* [b]14 Or *lapis lazuli*

Friends

[10]Who is this that appears like the dawn,
fair as the moon, bright as the sun,
majestic as the stars in procession?

Lover

[11]I went down to the grove of nut trees
to look at the new growth in the valley,
to see if the vines had budded
or the pomegranates were in bloom. SS 7:12
[12]Before I realized it,
my desire set me among the royal chariots
of my people.[a]

Friends

[13]Come back, come back, O Shulammite;
come back, come back, that we may gaze
on you!

Lover

Why would you gaze on the Shulammite
as on the dance of Mahanaim? Ex 15:20

7 How beautiful your sandaled feet,
O prince's daughter! Ps 45:13
Your graceful legs are like jewels,
the work of a craftsman's hands.
[2]Your navel is a rounded goblet
that never lacks blended wine.
Your waist is a mound of wheat
encircled by lilies.
[3]Your breasts are like two fawns, SS 4:5
twins of a gazelle.
[4]Your neck is like an ivory tower. Ps 144:12; SS 4:4
Your eyes are the pools of Heshbon Nu 21:26
by the gate of Bath Rabbim.
Your nose is like the tower of Lebanon SS 5:15
looking toward Damascus.
[5]Your head crowns you like Mount Carmel.
Your hair is like royal tapestry;
the king is held captive by its tresses.
[6]How beautiful you are and how pleasing,
O love, with your delights! SS 4:10
[7]Your stature is like that of the palm,
and your breasts like clusters of fruit. SS 4:5
[8]I said, "I will climb the palm tree;
I will take hold of its fruit."
May your breasts be like the clusters of the
vine,
the fragrance of your breath like apples,
9 and your mouth like the best wine.

Beloved

May the wine go straight to my lover, SS 5:16
flowing gently over lips and teeth.[b]
[10]I belong to my lover,
and his desire is for me. Ps 45:11; SS 2:16; 6:3
[11]Come, my lover, let us go to the countryside,
let us spend the night in the villages.[c]
[12]Let us go early to the vineyards SS 1:6
to see if the vines have budded, SS 2:15
if their blossoms have opened, SS 2:13
and if the pomegranates are in bloom—
there I will give you my love.
[13]The mandrakes send out their fragrance,
and at our door is every delicacy,
both new and old,
that I have stored up for you, my lover.

8 If only you were to me like a brother,
who was nursed at my mother's breasts!
Then, if I found you outside,
I would kiss you,
and no one would despise me.
[2]I would lead you
and bring you to my mother's house—
she who has taught me.
I would give you spiced wine to drink,
the nectar of my pomegranates.
[3]His left arm is under my head
and his right arm embraces me.
[4]Daughters of Jerusalem, I charge you:
Do not arouse or awaken love
until it so desires. SS 2:7; 3:5

Friends

[5]Who is this coming up from the desert SS 3:6
leaning on her lover?

Beloved

Under the apple tree I roused you;
there your mother conceived you, SS 3:4
there she who was in labor gave you birth.
[6]Place me like a seal over your heart,
like a seal on your arm;
for love is as strong as death, SS 1:2
its jealousy[d] unyielding as the grave.[e]
It burns like blazing fire,
like a mighty flame.[f] Nu 5:14
[7]Many waters cannot quench love;
rivers cannot wash it away.
If one were to give
all the wealth of his house for love,
it[g] would be utterly scorned. Pr 6:35

Friends

[8]We have a young sister,
and her breasts are not yet grown.
What shall we do for our sister
for the day she is spoken for?

[a]12 Or *among the chariots of Amminadab*; or *among the chariots of the people of the prince* [b]9 Septuagint, Aquila, Vulgate and Syriac; Hebrew *lips of sleepers* [c]11 Or *henna bushes* [d]6 Or *ardor* [e]6 Hebrew *Sheol* [f]6 Or / *like the very flame of the LORD* [g]7 Or *he*

[9]If she is a wall,
we will build towers of silver on her.
If she is a door,
we will enclose her with panels of cedar.

Beloved

[10]I am a wall,
and my breasts are like towers.
Thus I have become in his eyes
like one bringing contentment.
[11]Solomon had a vineyard in Baal Hamon;
he let out his vineyard to tenants.
Each was to bring for its fruit
a thousand shekels[a] of silver. Isa 7:23
[12]But my own vineyard is mine to give; SS 1:6
the thousand shekels are for you,
O Solomon,
and two hundred[b] are for those who tend
its fruit.

Lover

[13]You who dwell in the gardens
with friends in attendance,
let me hear your voice!

Beloved

[14]Come away, my lover,
and be like a gazelle Pr 5:19
or like a young stag SS 2:9
on the spice-laden mountains. SS 2:8,17

[a]*11* That is, about 25 pounds (about 11.5 kilograms); also in verse 12
[b]*12* That is, about 5 pounds (about 2.3 kilograms)

PROFILE OF A PROPHET

"Before I formed you in the womb I knew you,
before you were born I set you apart;
I appointed you as a prophet to the nations."
—JEREMIAH 1:5

The Old Testament prophets were dynamic figures who continue to speak to our age with an undeniable relevance. It is doubtful that any other group of people in all literature present a more impressive or colorful picture. They were men who knew God and trusted Him in the face of seemingly insurmountable odds. Sometimes ignored and sometimes hated, mocked and attacked, they stood firm (usually all alone) against the most imposing and influential people of their day. Through them, however, God warned and rebuked and announced inescapable judgment, most of which was simply shrugged off as extreme fanaticism. But to this day, the prophets' messages throb with biting realism. Their voices may be silent to our ears, but their words live on.

Characteristics of a Prophet

We can identify eight traits that characterized the lives of those whom the Lord raised up as prophets to His people down through the history of Bible times. First, *the prophets were uncompromising individualists.* Look at the way Isaiah began his prophecy:

Hear, O heavens, listen, O earth!
For the LORD has spoken:
"I reared children and brought them up,
but they have rebelled against me.
The ox knows his master,
the donkey his owner's manger,
but Israel does not know,
my people do not understand."
Ah, sinful nation,
a people loaded with guilt,
a brood of evildoers,
children given to corruption! (Isaiah 1:2–4a).

Isaiah minced no words as he began his prophecy with a direct condemnation of those who rebelled against God. He was speaking as an uncompromising individualist. He sounded very much like a prophet of doom, and so he was—uncompromising to the core. So were all the prophets.

Second, *the prophets stood alone in times of great moral decay and social and political chaos.* The prophets often had to pay a steep price for following the call of God on their lives. Never was this more apparent than in the case of Jeremiah, whose struggles are known to us in greater detail than those of any other Old Testament prophet. Jeremiah truly did "stand alone" among his fellow citizens as He proclaimed God's message of judgment on the nation of Judah. Jeremiah testified to the depth of loneliness in chapter 15 of the book that bears his name: "I never sat in the company of revelers, never made merry with them; I sat alone because your hand was on me" (Jeremiah 15:17). Jeremiah stood alone, and he also stood firm, because the Lord came alongside to encourage him and to strengthen him to do the work to which He had called him. Even when no one else would stand, even when public opinion swayed against him, the prophet would declare, "This is what the LORD says" (Jeremiah 2:5).

Third, *the prophets were God's mouthpiece.* In the first chapter of his prophecy, Jeremiah made it abundantly clear that he was not speaking his own message; in fact, he made it clear that he had no message in and of himself that he could speak: " 'Ah, Sovereign LORD,' I said. 'I do not know how to speak; I am only a child' " (Jeremiah 1:6). But look at the Lord's response to Jeremiah: "Do not say, 'I am only a child.' You must go to everyone I send you to and say whatever I command you" (Jeremiah 1:7). Then see this dramatic act: "Then the LORD reached out his hand and touched my mouth and said to me, 'Now, I have put my words in your mouth' " (Jeremiah 1:9). There was no question: God spoke through His prophets.

Fourth, *the prophets were men of rugged determination.* The call of Ezekiel stands as an eloquent and eye-popping illustration of this truth. This is how Ezekiel recorded it in verses 3–6 of chapter 2:

> *I am sending you to the Israelites, to a rebellious nation that has rebelled against me; they and their fathers have been in revolt against me to this very day. The people to whom I am sending you are obstinate and stubborn. Say to them, "This is what the Sovereign LORD says." And whether they listen or fail to listen—for they are a rebellious house—they will know that a prophet has been among them. And you, son of man, do not be afraid of them or their words. Do not be afraid, though briers and thorns are all around you and you live among scorpions. Do not be afraid of what they say or terrified by them, though they are a rebellious house.*

The prophets had to be rugged people to go through that kind of prickly, scorpion-like experience. They stood. They spoke. They declared God's truth in the street, in the synagogue, in the temple and they were turned off and tuned out by the people. But they kept declaring it. They were told to shut up. They were told to get on the "feel-good" bandwagon. They were told if they didn't tow the party line they would be killed. But they stood firm, because they were rugged men of determination. May their tribe increase! How we need in this day of shaky values and shady ethics those who will bring a genuine message from God that will call for turning from sin and finding purpose for living according to the will and the Word of the Lord. All too often people are being told what they want to hear. There's nothing wrong with common courtesy, but a servant of God who will not speak the Word of God loses the respect of the people of God. We can learn much from the Old Testament prophets about being people of rugged determination.

Fifth, *the prophets were men of prayer and communion with God.* In Daniel 6 there's a remarkable verse that I think stands out as an amazing tribute to the character of one of God's faithful prophets. Daniel was an exiled Jew who occupied a rather high office in the Babylonian and later in the Persian governments. Daniel had a group of colleagues around him who were jealous of him and who began to search his life in an attempt to find any trace of corruption they could use against him. They set out on a pursuit to find fault and to pinpoint a breakdown in his integrity:

> *The administrators and the satraps tried to find grounds for charges against Daniel in his conduct of government affairs, but they were unable to do so. They could find no corruption in him, because he was trustworthy and neither corrupt nor negligent (Daniel 6:4).*

These men could find no shred of evidence of corruption in Daniel's life, and that blew them away. They watched him when he was alone. They watched him when he was with other people. They scoured his books, they dug into his financial affairs. They looked at his efficiency. They checked his charts—the way he dealt with people. They could not find one flaw in Daniel's life. They finally decided that the only way they could incriminate Daniel was by using his faith against him.

These jealous leaders then manipulated King Darius to pass a law that required all citizens to pray to no one except Darius. If they prayed to their own God, they would receive the death penalty. In Daniel 6:10, we read of Daniel's response to the king's edict:

> *Now when Daniel learned that the decree had been published, he went home to his upstairs room where the windows opened toward Jerusalem. Three times a day he got down on his knees and prayed, giving thanks to his God, just as he had done before.*

Even under the threat of death, Daniel prayed consistently and sought fellowship with his God. That's the power of a prophet's prayer life whose commitment to God was unbending!

Sixth, *the prophets were men of absolute obedience and dedication.* Nowhere is this better illustrated than in the experience of that prophet Hosea, who received a most unusual order from the Lord, and who obeyed without questioning:

> *When the LORD began to speak through Hosea, the LORD said to him, "Go, take to yourself an adulterous wife and children of unfaithfulness, because the land is guilty of the vilest adultery in departing from the LORD." So he married Gomer daughter of Diblaim, and she conceived and bore him a son (Hosea 1:2–3).*

No one ever said the prophets lived on easy street. These were serious times in the life of the nations of Israel and Judah, and serious times called for serious measures from the Lord. Hosea was asked to submit himself to great emotional trauma in order to convey a powerful and dramatic lesson that the Lord had for His people. This scene of an unfaithful wife and a faithful husband mirrors the scene of an unfaithful nation and a faithful God, whose love and faithfulness could not—finally—let Israel go. Certainly Hosea, like all the prophets of God, was a man who responded to God's call with absolute obedience and dedication, even through those times when he surely must have wondered why.

Seventh, *the prophets were outspoken critics of evil.* The prophecy of Amos contains a striking illustration of a prophet who was an outspoken critic of the moral degradation of his times.

In chapter 7 Amos was at the sanctuary at Bethel—the center of religious and political pretension, the place where the upper echelons of the northern kingdom worshiped. Amos was standing out on the street shouting his prophecies against the king and the nation. Amaziah the priest heard Amos and reported back to the king the words of the prophecy. Amaziah confronted Amos with these words: "Get out, you seer! Go back to the land of Judah. Earn your bread there and do your prophesying there. Don't prophesy anymore at Bethel, because this is the king's sanctuary and the temple of the kingdom." Note Amos's reply: "I was neither a prophet nor a prophet's son, but I was a shepherd, and I also took care of sycamore-fig trees. But the LORD took me from tending the flock and said to me, 'Go, prophesy to my people Israel' " (7:12–15).

You know what Amos was? He was a fig picker from Tekoa. Here he was, the prophetic country boy, in overalls, barefooted, standing there in front of the palace of the king declaring God's judgment against the king. And Amaziah said, in effect, "Get him out of here." And Amos responded with words to this effect: "I'm not leaving." And the very next prophetic word Amos spoke went something like this: "Listen up, Amaziah, your wife will become a prostitute, and your sons and daughters will lose their lives and you will too, and your nation will go into exile." How's that for winning friends and influencing people? You can be sure, if prophets lived today as they lived in those days, they would make us uncomfortable. God's prophets could be expected to stand up and speak out against evil—whenever and wherever they found it.

Eighth, *the prophets revealed future events.* Although much of what the prophets spoke about pertained to their day and to the people who heard their words, they also proclaimed what God was going to do in the future. Inspired by the Holy Spirit, they were given eyes to see beyond the natural course of human history to the supernatural work of God in the future. With clarity and boldness they proclaimed what God was going to do. In Malachi 3:1 we read of the coming of both John the Baptist and the Messiah hundreds of years before either was born:

> *"See, I will send my messenger, who will prepare the way before me. Then suddenly the Lord you are seeking will come to his temple; the messenger of the covenant, whom you desire, will come," says the LORD Almighty.*

There is no question: These messengers of God pointed ahead to what God would do in the future.

Getting the Message Out Today

In the technical sense of the word, prophets passed off the scene after the canon of Scripture was completed. In a broader sense God is still raising up those who are willing to stand alone and speak His message, boldly confronting the evils of our times. There is a sense in which He still calls us today to stand in the prophetic tradition and to carry out the prophetic tasks of preaching the gospel, getting the message out, announcing and doing the will of God, and serving our God in a word and deed ministry that honors and obeys Jesus Christ, the supreme Prophet who came to unite and reconcile all things to Himself.

INTRODUCTION

ISAIAH

The final forty years of the eighth century B.C. produced several great servants of God, but perhaps the most significant of these was a well-educated, blue-blooded prophet named Isaiah. That's quite a statement when you consider that his contemporaries were Amos, Hosea and Micah. As Isaiah received his call to ministry, world forces were gearing up for a battle for supremacy. The nation of Judah had experienced a time of peace and prosperity during King Uzziah's reign, but all was not well in the land. Abuses of power, land-grabbing, extortion, idleness, indifference, corrupt government and excessive drinking marked those times. The people of Judah had lost their religious distinctive and had fallen under the sway of idolatry and pagan customs and pathetically low moral standards. The religious leaders of the day had no stirring message to bring, no compelling exhortation to proclaim. For the whole of Isaiah's ministry this "prince among the prophets" stood virtually alone as a voice crying out a message of judgment and of comfort.

WRITER: *Isaiah*

DATE: *c.700–680 B.C.*

PURPOSE: *To warn God's people of judgment and to offer hope and the promise of restoration*

KEY VERSES: *6:1-13; 9:1-7; 40:1-11,18-31; 52:13–53:12; 55:1-13*

KEY DISTINCTIVE: *No other Old Testament book has such vivid portrayals of the Messiah*

TIME LINE 1300BC 1200 1100 1000 900 800 700 600 500 400

Division of the kingdom (930 B.C.)

Ministries of Elijah and Elisha in Israel (c.875-797 B.C.)

Ministries of Amos and Hosea in Israel (c.760-715 B.C.)

Micah's ministry in Judah (c.742-687 B.C.)

Isaiah's ministry in Judah (c.740-681 B.C.)

Exile of Israel (722 B.C.)

Book of Isaiah written (c.700-680 B.C.)

Fall of Jerusalem (586 B.C.)

Prince Among the Prophets

	THE JUDGMENT OF GOD	THE DELIVERANCE OF GOD		
		THE SUPREMACY OF THE LORD	THE SERVANT OF THE LORD **Servant Songs:** *42:1-9* *49:1-13* *50:4-11* *52:13–53:12*	THE FUTURE PLAN OF THE LORD
	CHAPTERS 1–39	*CHAPTERS 40–48*	*CHAPTERS 49–53*	*CHAPTERS 54–66*
EMPHASIS	**The law and judgment for disobedience**	**God's grace and deliverance** Comfort . . .	promise . . .	hope . . .
"BIBLE WITHIN BIBLE"	**Old Testament**	**New Testament**		

Isaiah is the first among the 17 prophetic books in the Old Testament. What a great man Isaiah was! What Michelangelo was among the artists; what Beethoven was among the musical composers; what Abraham Lincoln was among the presidents; what Charles Spurgeon was among the preachers—in my opinion Isaiah was among the prophets. He was, in many ways, outstanding in his field—one might even say, without equal. Perhaps that claim needs to be explained, lest you think I'm playing unfair favorites.

Isaiah was the most highly educated of all the prophets. He was both intelligent and articulate in all that he wrote. And, with the possible exception of Daniel, he occupied the most influential position of all the prophets. Some men and women are called to minister in obscure, low-profile positions. Many still labor behind the scenes in forgotten spots across the world today. That was *not* the case for Isaiah.

High-profile Prophet

Isaiah was called to minister in a place of high visibility and influential dignity. He was a "blue blood" among the prophets. We might even call him an aristocrat. His Hebrew was the finest of classic, ancient Hebrew. Anyone who studies this book in depth realizes quickly that the man had a style that was altogether unique . . . eloquent, it is safe to say. But, as is true of most of the prophets, he lived a sadly misunderstood life. Greatness often is accompanied by misunderstanding, and Isaiah was no exception.

We must be introduced to his time in order to appreciate what he wrote. Isaiah 1:1 contains this title: "The vision concerning Judah and Jerusalem that Isaiah son of Amoz saw during the reigns of Uzziah, Jotham, Ahaz and Hezekiah, kings of Judah." Here was a prophet who ministered in the city of Jerusalem, which was the capital of Judah. Judah was in the southern part of the finger of land we know today as Israel. Quite a place to minister! It reminds me of the days of the late Peter Marshall in Washington, D.C., when he had such a significant impact on the politicians of the land as he served as the Chaplain of the Senate. Isaiah was in that type of position, only higher. He had *direct access* to the kings of the land.

About the Prophet

God called Isaiah to bring a prophecy of judgment upon the nation of Judah. The news he would bring was not good news for the people: "See now, the Lord, the LORD Almighty, is about to take from Jerusalem and Judah both supply and support: all supplies of food and all supplies of water" (3:1). The message was certainly not a popular one. In many ways, though the situation was bleak for their neighbors to the north (the kingdom of Israel, which was to fall to the Assyrians in 722 B.C.), the people of Judah were enjoying a time of some relative prosperity and security.

Socially, the times in which Isaiah prophesied were unusual. It may surprise you to hear this, because we often think of the prophets as wearing the latest in "ragbag" fashion and down to their last pair of sandals with holes in the soles. Not Isaiah. He was affluent, educated and very influential. His times were affluent times, not times of poverty. God does not call all of His servants to places of poverty and obscurity. Some are to minister among the rich and famous. Both kinds of ministries have their opportunities and their challenges; both have their joys and their sorrows, their privileges and their pressures.

Isaiah's ministry lasted a total of forty years, from 740–700 B.C. During these years he served God as a prophet during the reign of four kings. (By the way, there were twenty monarchs in the days of Judah—19 kings and one queen. Eight of them were righteous monarchs who did good; others were wicked rulers who did evil in the eyes of the Lord.) Isaiah lived and ministered among the good rulers (like Uzziah, Jotham and Hezekiah) as well as the evil (like Ahaz). That was his calling—and he was faithful to carry it out.

Standing Alone

Isaiah's was an eloquent pen from a well-trained man who had the guts to stand alone in some pretty tough times. In some ways, it's easier to minister in an economic depression than in a time of affluence. Interestingly, if you check the dates on the cornerstones of some of the great churches of our land, you will find that many were placed there in the days of the Great Depression. Many churches grew and flourished in depression times. But when times of affluence and ease come, you reap the backwash of *self-sufficiency*: "Who needs God? Don't call me; I'll call You." This kind of an attitude toward God can prevail when earthly riches abound. You see, we forget God not when we are in need; we forget God when we think we have no needs. So Isaiah was called to remind the people that their need was *great*, even though they had everything they thought they needed; he was to remind them that they were poor, even though they had everything money could buy.

Another all-too-familiar characteristic of an affluent, indulgent people is a *lack of compassion*. People who have accumulated much tend to forget about those who have little. The cry of the orphan is ignored in the courts of the powerful; the plea of the hungry is not acknowledged by those who eat at banquet tables. Isaiah struck at the heart of their apathy and indulgence. Isaiah indicted the people . . . not for having so much, but for caring so little. Look at what he said in verse 16 of chapter 3: "The LORD says, 'The women of Zion are haughty, walking along with outstretched necks, flirting with their eyes, tripping along with mincing steps, with ornaments jingling on their ankles.' "

Now that's pretty descriptive language, isn't it? The man had been right there in the city. He had observed it firsthand. He saw their behavior; he knew the condition of their hearts and how their actions exposed their hardhearted attitudes. And he wasn't about to back down! Thankfully, he talked straight and delivered a hard message. But such is the prophet's job. It's not for the weak of heart or the faint of spirit. No, it's a tough calling—sometimes brutal, sometimes bitter, but, in the end, always blessed. I'm reminded of Jesus' words: "Blessed are those who are persecuted because of righteousness, for theirs is the kingdom of heaven" (Matthew 5:10).

Standing for the Truth

It's relatively easy for us to sit in our comfortable chairs and applaud people like Isaiah. We say, "Right on, prophet! Do that! Tell it to 'em. Say the tough thing!" But will *we* stand up and be counted among the prophets? Will *we* take this role among God's people? How difficult it is to find someone who is willing to stand alone and declare what may very well be an unpopular word from God.

Socially, Isaiah was living in a time when people were indulged—and loving it! They certainly did not want anybody laying a guilt trip on them. And yet God was urging Isaiah, "Tell 'em the truth, man! Tell 'em the truth." So he did! When you take a stand for the truth, you may never win the majority votes, you may never win a popularity contest, but you will influence the lives of others more by standing firm for your convictions than you will by going along with the crowd. Stand strong, people of God. If you don't pay close attention in your study of the prophets, you will fail to learn a crucial lesson from these strong, gritty servants of God who spoke the truth in love—even when it made people uncomfortable.

The Danger of Idolatry

Judah was a nation given over to idolatry in the days of Isaiah. The people had forsaken their commitment to the one true God—Yahweh God of the Hebrews—and had become infatuated with the polytheistic concepts of the pagan religions. It was almost as if the thinking went something like this: "If one God is good, well then certainly two or three or four or fifty would be better—you know, a God for every occasion, every need. You can never have enough—just in case." It was in response to that kind of thinking that Isaiah sounded the clarion trumpet call to the people to return to the Lord and forsake the worthless idols the people craved (41:22–24). Isaiah spoke the truth: "Those who trust in idols, who say to images, 'you are our gods,' will be turned back in utter shame" (42:17).

Woe!

In chapter 5 we find a section of "woes." In fact, the last half of chapter 5 is full of woes. "Woe" to this. "Woe" to that. Look at verses 11 and 12 and you'll get the picture:

> *Woe to those who rise early in the morning to run after their drinks, who stay up late at night till they are inflamed with wine. They have harps and lyres at their banquets, tambourines and flutes and wine, but they have no regard for the deeds of the LORD, no respect for the work of his hands.*

Notice that the banquets were filled with all of the fine things of the court, but when the things of God were mentioned, they didn't pay any attention. They took care of the tiniest details—right down to the most exquisite taste of the finest wine, but when it came to the things of God they turned a blind eye and a deaf ear and a hard heart. Look at the consequences of this wandering condition of the heart: "Therefore my people will go into exile for lack of understanding; their men of rank will die of hunger and their masses will be parched with thirst" (5:13).

The time would come when they were going to have to "pay the piper" for their arrogant disobedience. The entertainment would cease, the music would die, the food would disappear, the wine barrels would run dry. The "woes" would be realized. The word of God that came through the pen of the prophet Isaiah would be fulfilled. The people of Judah would go into exile—in 586 B.C.

A Bible Within the Bible

The Bible is one library of 66 books, divided into two main parts: the Old Testament, made up of 39 books, and the New Testament, comprised of 27 books. Interestingly, the book of Isaiah is divided into two sections, the first one containing 39 chapters and the second having 27 chapters. The first 39 chapters of Isaiah highlight the theme of God's judgment on humanity because of disobedience, much like the central theme of the Old Testament. The final 27 chapters of Isaiah contain words of comfort and hope that emphasize God's grace and mercy, much like the 27 books of the New Testament. By keeping in mind this general division of the book of Isaiah, you may find it easier to identify the general division of the whole Bible.

In analyzing the structure of the book of Isaiah, some scholars explain the division into two sections by claiming that the prophet Isaiah wrote the first 39 chapters and someone else wrote the last 27 chapters (40–66). I strongly disagree. I believe that the traditional opinion that Isaiah wrote the entire book is the correct one—one Isaiah, writing with two different styles; one Isaiah, writing with a whole different emphasis in mind in the second section. In chapters 1–39, Isaiah brought a message of judgment; in chapters 40–66, he brought a message of comfort—the promise of God to His people, not the threat of judgment against the nation, as proclaimed in the first section.

As you read through the second section of Isaiah, be especially alert to the call and mission of "the servant." Isaiah contains four "servant songs" in which the servant is the Messiah (42:1–9; 49:1–13; 50:4–11; and 52:13–53:12). Some of the most glorious and vivid pictures of the Messiah are found in this section in the book of Isaiah—in some ways, more picturesque than even the Gospels themselves. Isaiah wrote of the Messiah, Jesus Christ, as though he literally saw Him on a cross, suffering as the Servant sent by the Father. You cannot undertake a thorough study of Christology (the doctrine of Jesus Christ) if you skip over Isaiah, because there are hints of His coming found nowhere else quite like here in the book of Isaiah.

Lessons From Isaiah

There are many lessons to be learned from the book of Isaiah. Four come to mind. First, *true greatness often resides deep within a misunderstood person.* Second, *loneliness is the price we may very well have to pay for standing on our convictions.* Third, *when everything else fades and fails, God's Word still stands and will stand forever.* Fourth, *our concept of sin is formed by our idea of God.* If we take God lightly, we will take sin lightly; if our image of God is one of an impotent, weak "deity-in-training," we will sin without restraint. Conversely, if we take God seriously, if we have a deep sense of His holiness and His power and His majesty, we will take sin seriously; we will be quick to bow in humility, confessing our inadequacy, our inability to measure up, our need to have the rags of sinfulness replaced by robes of righteousness. If we have no relationship, or a superficial relationship, with Almighty God, then we will care not a whit about how our sin hurts God and harms our relationship with Him. On the other hand, if we have an intimate relationship, a love relationship, with Almighty God, then we will be grieved by our sins and failings, and we will rush to God to confess them and to find His forgiveness. Our idea of God determines our concept of sin.

Dare to Be an Isaiah

Let me ask you some direct questions: Are you an Isaiah of today . . . in your home, in your neighborhood, in your place of employment, in your church, in your school? Are you being called to stand alone and not aloof in your own sphere of influence? You're the only you around in that particular place of service—that place where your "no" is the only "no" in the room, or your "yes" is the only "yes" to be heard. You are, in today's terms, an Isaiah. If so, stand firm. Please! Hold your ground and dare to be an Isaiah!

And when the time comes for you to stand up and be counted, try not to be afraid. Ask God to give you the zeal of a prophet who will not be intimidated by the number of those who stand in opposition. Just remember, others are watching you; someday, somewhere, somebody just may come up to you and say, "Hey, I'd like to talk to you about how you're able to stand alone." What a witness you'll be privileged to have as you tell others about the God who gives you the strength to stand for the truth!

Have the courage to be a lone voice crying in the desert, if need be. Consider it *an honor* to proclaim the truth of God—not a dreadful cross to bear. It is the highest privilege on earth to take a stand for Jesus Christ. But keep in mind, if there is to be anything that proves to be a stumbling block, it is to be the cross of Jesus Christ, not the Christian (see 1 Corinthians 1:23).

The Judgment of God **Chapters 1–39**

The first 39 chapters describe the coming judgment on the nation of Judah, God's people. These chapters also predict divine judgment on Babylon, Philistia, Moab, Damascus, Egypt, Edom, Arabia and Tyre. These oracles of coming doom are focused on cities in the Gentile world that surrounded God's promised land. The phrase "the day of the LORD" is mentioned again and again as a reference to coming judgment and divine wrath.

1 The vision concerning Judah and Jerusalem
that Isaiah son of Amoz saw during the reigns
of Uzziah, Jotham, Ahaz and Hezekiah, kings of
Judah. Isa 2:1; 2Ki 16:1

A Rebellious Nation

2Hear, O heavens! Listen, O earth!
For the LORD has spoken: Mic 1:2
"I reared children and brought them up,
but they have rebelled against me. Isa 30:1,9
3The ox knows his master,
the donkey his owner's manger,
but Israel does not know, Jer 9:3,6; Hos 2:8
my people do not understand." Dt 32:28

4Ah, sinful nation,
a people loaded with guilt, Isa 5:18
a brood of evildoers, Isa 14:20; Jer 23:14
children given to corruption! Ps 14:3
They have forsaken the LORD; Ps 119:87
they have spurned the Holy One of Israel
and turned their backs on him. Pr 30:9

5Why should you be beaten anymore? Pr 20:30
Why do you persist in rebellion? Isa 31:6
Your whole head is injured,
your whole heart afflicted. Isa 33:6,24
6From the sole of your foot to the top of your head
there is no soundness— Ps 38:3
only wounds and welts
and open sores,
not cleansed or bandaged Isa 30:26; Jer 8:22
or soothed with oil. Lk 10:34

7Your country is desolate, Lev 26:34
your cities burned with fire; Lev 26:31
your fields are being stripped by foreigners
right before you,
laid waste as when overthrown by strangers.
8The Daughter of Zion is left Ps 9:14
like a shelter in a vineyard,
like a hut in a field of melons, Job 27:18
like a city under siege.
9Unless the LORD Almighty
had left us some survivors, Isa 10:20-22; 37:4,31-32
we would have become like Sodom,
we would have been like Gomorrah. Ge 19:24

10Hear the word of the LORD, Isa 28:14
you rulers of Sodom; Eze 16:49; Rev 11:8
listen to the law of our God, Isa 8:20
you people of Gomorrah! Isa 13:19
11"The multitude of your sacrifices—
what are they to me?" says the LORD.
"I have more than enough of burnt offerings,
of rams and the fat of fattened animals;
I have no pleasure
in the blood of bulls and lambs and goats.
12When you come to appear before me,
who has asked this of you, Ex 23:17; Dt 31:11
this trampling of my courts?
13Stop bringing meaningless offerings! Isa 66:3
Your incense is detestable to me. Jer 7:9
New Moons, Sabbaths and convocations—
I cannot bear your evil assemblies.
14Your New Moon festivals and your appointed feasts Nu 28:11-29:39; Isa 29:1
my soul hates. Ps 11:5
They have become a burden to me;
I am weary of bearing them. Isa 43:22,24
15When you spread out your hands in prayer,
I will hide my eyes from you; Isa 8:17; 59:2
even if you offer many prayers,
I will not listen. Isa 59:3; Jer 2:34
Your hands are full of blood;
16 wash and make yourselves clean. Mt 27:24
Take your evil deeds
out of my sight! Isa 52:11
Stop doing wrong, Isa 55:7; Jer 25:5
17 learn to do right! Ps 34:14
Seek justice, Zep 2:3
encourage the oppressed.[a] Dt 14:29
Defend the cause of the fatherless, Ps 82:3; 94:6
plead the case of the widow. Ex 22:22; Jas 1:27

18"Come now, let us reason together," Isa 41:1
says the LORD.
"Though your sins are like scarlet,
they shall be as white as snow; Ps 51:7; Rev 7:14
though they are red as crimson,
they shall be like wool. Isa 55:7
19If you are willing and obedient, Job 36:11; Isa 50:10
you will eat the best from the land;
20but if you resist and rebel, 1Sa 12:15
you will be devoured by the sword." Isa 3:25
For the mouth of the LORD has spoken.

21See how the faithful city
has become a harlot! Jer 2:20
She once was full of justice;
righteousness used to dwell in her— Isa 5:7
but now murderers! Pr 6:17
22Your silver has become dross, Ps 119:119
your choice wine is diluted with water.
23Your rulers are rebels,
companions of thieves; Dt 19:14; Mic 2:1-2

[a] 17 Or / *rebuke the oppressor*

they all love bribes Ex 23:8; Am 5:12
and chase after gifts.
They do not defend the cause of the fatherless;
the widow's case does not come before
them. Jer 5:28; Eze 22:6-7; Zec 7:10
24Therefore the Lord, the LORD Almighty,
the Mighty One of Israel, declares: Ge 49:24
"Ah, I will get relief from my foes
and avenge myself on my enemies. Isa 35:4
25I will turn my hand against you; Dt 28:63
I will thoroughly purge away your dross
and remove all your impurities. Eze 22:22
26I will restore your judges as in days of old,
your counselors as at the beginning.
Afterward you will be called
the City of Righteousness, Isa 33:5; Zec 8:3
the Faithful City." Isa 60:14; 62:2

27Zion will be redeemed with justice,
her penitent ones with righteousness.
28But rebels and sinners will both be broken,
and those who forsake the LORD will perish.

29"You will be ashamed because of the sacred
oaks Isa 57:5
in which you have delighted;
you will be disgraced because of the gardens
that you have chosen.
30You will be like an oak with fading leaves,
like a garden without water.
31The mighty man will become tinder
and his work a spark;
both will burn together,
with no one to quench the fire." Isa 5:24

The Mountain of the LORD

2 This is what Isaiah son of Amoz saw concerning Judah and Jerusalem: Isa 1:1

2In the last days
the mountain of the LORD's temple will be
established Mic 4:7
as chief among the mountains;
it will be raised above the hills, Zec 14:10
and all nations will stream to it. Ps 102:15

3Many peoples will come and say,
"Come, let us go up to the mountain of the
LORD, Ps 137:5; Isa 45:14
to the house of the God of Jacob.
He will teach us his ways,
so that we may walk in his paths."
The law will go out from Zion, Isa 51:4,7
the word of the LORD from Jerusalem.
4He will judge between the nations Isa 1:27
and will settle disputes for many peoples.
They will beat their swords into plowshares
and their spears into pruning hooks. Joel 3:10
Nation will not take up sword against nation,
nor will they train for war anymore. Mic 4:1-3
5Come, O house of Jacob, Isa 58:1
let us walk in the light of the LORD.

LIVING INSIGHT

There is nothing like light, however small and distant, to put us on tiptoes in the darkness.
(See Isaiah 2:2–5.)

The Day of the LORD

6You have abandoned your people, Dt 31:17
the house of Jacob.
They are full of superstitions from the East;
they practice divination like the Philistines
and clasp hands with pagans. 2Ki 16:7; Pr 6:1
7Their land is full of silver and gold; Dt 17:17
there is no end to their treasures. Ps 17:14
Their land is full of horses; Dt 17:16
there is no end to their chariots. Isa 31:1
8Their land is full of idols; Isa 10:9-11
they bow down to the work of their hands,
to what their fingers have made. Isa 17:8
9So man will be brought low Ps 62:9
and mankind humbled— Isa 5:15
do not forgive them.[a] Ne 4:5

10Go into the rocks,
hide in the ground
from dread of the LORD
and the splendor of his majesty! 2Th 1:9
11The eyes of the arrogant man will be humbled
and the pride of men brought low; Isa 5:15
the LORD alone will be exalted in that day.

12The LORD Almighty has a day in store Am 5:18
for all the proud and lofty, 2Sa 22:28
for all that is exalted Isa 24:4,21; Mal 4:1
(and they will be humbled), Job 40:11
13for all the cedars of Lebanon, tall and lofty,
and all the oaks of Bashan, Zec 11:2
14for all the towering mountains
and all the high hills, Isa 30:25; 40:4
15for every lofty tower Isa 30:25
and every fortified wall, Isa 25:2,12
16for every trading ship[b] 1Ki 10:22
and every stately vessel.
17The arrogance of man will be brought low
and the pride of men humbled; ver 9
the LORD alone will be exalted in that day,
18 and the idols will totally disappear. Isa 21:9
19Men will flee to caves in the rocks Isa 7:19
and to holes in the ground

[a] 9 Or *not raise them up* [b] 16 Hebrew *every ship of Tarshish*

from dread of the LORD Dt 2:25
and the splendor of his majesty, Ps 145:12
when he rises to shake the earth. Heb 12:26
20In that day men will throw away
to the rodents and bats Lev 11:19
their idols of silver and idols of gold, Rev 9:20
which they made to worship. Eze 7:19-20
21They will flee to caverns in the rocks
and to the overhanging crags
from dread of the LORD
and the splendor of his majesty, Ps 145:12
when he rises to shake the earth. ver 19
22Stop trusting in man, Ps 146:3
who has but a breath in his nostrils.
Of what account is he? Ps 8:4; Jas 4:14

Judgment on Jerusalem and Judah

3 See now, the Lord,
the LORD Almighty,
is about to take from Jerusalem and Judah
both supply and support: Ps 18:18
all supplies of food and all supplies of water,
2 the hero and warrior, Eze 17:13
the judge and prophet,
the soothsayer and elder, 2Ki 24:14; Isa 9:14-15
3the captain of fifty and man of rank,
the counselor, skilled craftsman and clever
enchanter. 2Ki 24:14 Ecc 10:11

4I will make boys their officials;
mere children will govern them. Ecc 10:16 [fn]
5People will oppress each other—
man against man, neighbor against
neighbor. Mic 7:2,6; Isa 9:19; Jer 9:8
The young will rise up against the old,
the base against the honorable.

6A man will seize one of his brothers
at his father's home, and say,
"You have a cloak, you be our leader;
take charge of this heap of ruins!"
7But in that day he will cry out,
"I have no remedy. Eze 34:4; Hos 5:13
I have no food or clothing in my house;
do not make me the leader of the people."

8Jerusalem staggers,
Judah is falling; Isa 1:7
their words and deeds are against the LORD,
defying his glorious presence. Ps 73:9,11
9The look on their faces testifies against them;
they parade their sin like Sodom; Ge 13:13
they do not hide it.
Woe to them!
They have brought disaster upon
themselves. Pr 8:36; Ro 6:23

10Tell the righteous it will be well with them,
for they will enjoy the fruit of their deeds.
11Woe to the wicked! Disaster is upon them!
They will be paid back for what their hands
have done. 2Ch 6:23

12Youths oppress my people, ver 4
women rule over them.
O my people, your guides lead you astray;
they turn you from the path.

13The LORD takes his place in court;
he rises to judge the people. Mic 6:2
14The LORD enters into judgment Job 22:4
against the elders and leaders of his people:
"It is you who have ruined my vineyard;
the plunder from the poor is in your
houses. Jas 2:6
15What do you mean by crushing my people
and grinding the faces of the poor?" Isa 10:6
declares the Lord, the LORD Almighty.

16The LORD says,
"The women of Zion are haughty, SS 3:11
walking along with outstretched necks,
flirting with their eyes,
tripping along with mincing steps,
with ornaments jingling on their ankles.
17Therefore the Lord will bring sores on the
heads of the women of Zion;
the LORD will make their scalps bald."

18In that day the Lord will snatch away their
finery: the bangles and headbands and crescent
necklaces, 19the earrings and bracelets and veils,
20the headdresses and ankle chains and sashes, the
perfume bottles and charms, 21the signet rings and
nose rings, 22the fine robes and the capes and
cloaks, the purses 23and mirrors, and the linen
garments and tiaras and shawls. Isa 2:11; Eze 16:10

24Instead of fragrance there will be a stench;
instead of a sash, a rope; Pr 31:24
instead of well-dressed hair, baldness; Isa 22:12
instead of fine clothing, sackcloth; La 2:10
instead of beauty, branding. 1Pe 3:3
25Your men will fall by the sword, Isa 1:20
your warriors in battle.
26The gates of Zion will lament and mourn;
destitute, she will sit on the ground. La 2:10

4 In that day seven women
will take hold of one man Isa 13:12
and say, "We will eat our own food 2Th 3:12
and provide our own clothes;
only let us be called by your name.
Take away our disgrace!" Ge 30:23

The Branch of the LORD

2In that day the Branch of the LORD will be
beautiful and glorious, and the fruit of the land will
be the pride and glory of the survivors in Israel.
3Those who are left in Zion, who remain in Jerusalem, will be called holy, all who are recorded
among the living in Jerusalem. 4The Lord will

wash away the filth of the women of Zion; he will cleanse the bloodstains from Jerusalem by a spirit[a] of judgment and a spirit[a] of fire.
5Then the LORD will create over all of Mount Zion and over those who assemble there a cloud of smoke by day and a glow of flaming fire by night; over all the glory will be a canopy.
6It will be a shelter and shade from the heat of the day, and a refuge and hiding place from the storm and rain. Jer 23:5-6

The Song of the Vineyard

5 I will sing for the one I love
a song about his vineyard: Ps 80:8-9
My loved one had a vineyard
on a fertile hillside.
2He dug it up and cleared it of stones
and planted it with the choicest vines.
He built a watchtower in it
and cut out a winepress as well.
Then he looked for a crop of good grapes,
but it yielded only bad fruit. Lk 13:6

3"Now you dwellers in Jerusalem and men of Judah,
judge between me and my vineyard. Mt 21:40
4What more could have been done for my vineyard
than I have done for it? Mt 23:37
When I looked for good grapes,
why did it yield only bad?
5Now I will tell you
what I am going to do to my vineyard:
I will take away its hedge,
and it will be destroyed;
I will break down its wall, Ps 80:12
and it will be trampled. Lk 21:24
6I will make it a wasteland,
neither pruned nor cultivated,
and briers and thorns will grow there.
I will command the clouds
not to rain on it."

7The vineyard of the LORD Almighty
is the house of Israel, Ps 80:8
and the men of Judah
are the garden of his delight.
And he looked for justice, but saw bloodshed;
for righteousness, but heard cries of distress.

Woes and Judgments

8Woe to you who add house to house Jer 22:13
and join field to field Mic 2:2; Hab 2:9-12
till no space is left
and you live alone in the land.

9The LORD Almighty has declared in my hearing: Isa 22:14

"Surely the great houses will become desolate,
the fine mansions left without occupants.
10A ten-acre[b] vineyard will produce only a bath[c] of wine,
a homer[d] of seed only an ephah[e] of grain." Lev 26:26

11Woe to those who rise early in the morning
to run after their drinks,
who stay up late at night
till they are inflamed with wine. Pr 23:29-30
12They have harps and lyres at their banquets,
tambourines and flutes and wine,
but they have no regard for the deeds of the LORD, Job 34:27
no respect for the work of his hands. Ps 28:5
13Therefore my people will go into exile
for lack of understanding; Isa 1:3; Hos 4:6
their men of rank will die of hunger
and their masses will be parched with thirst.
14Therefore the grave[f] enlarges its appetite
and opens its mouth without limit; Nu 16:30
into it will descend their nobles and masses
with all their brawlers and revelers.
15So man will be brought low Isa 10:33
and mankind humbled, Isa 2:9
the eyes of the arrogant humbled. Isa 2:11
16But the LORD Almighty will be exalted by his justice, Isa 28:17; 30:18; 33:5
and the holy God will show himself holy by his righteousness. Isa 29:23
17Then sheep will graze as in their own pasture;
lambs will feed[g] among the ruins of the rich.

18Woe to those who draw sin along with cords of deceit,
and wickedness as with cart ropes, Isa 59:4-8
19to those who say, "Let God hurry,
let him hasten his work
so we may see it.
Let it approach,
let the plan of the Holy One of Israel come,
so we may know it." Jer 17:15; Eze 12:22; 2Pe 3:4

20Woe to those who call evil good
and good evil,
who put darkness for light
and light for darkness, Mt 6:22-23; Lk 11:34-35
who put bitter for sweet
and sweet for bitter. Am 5:7

21Woe to those who are wise in their own eyes
and clever in their own sight.

22Woe to those who are heroes at drinking wine

[a]4 Or *the Spirit* [b]10 Hebrew *ten-yoke,* that is, the land plowed by 10 yoke of oxen in one day [c]10 That is, probably about 6 gallons (about 22 liters) [d]10 That is, probably about 6 bushels (about 220 liters) [e]10 That is, probably about 3/5 bushel (about 22 liters) [f]14 Hebrew *Sheol* [g]17 Septuagint; Hebrew / *strangers will eat*

and champions at mixing drinks,
23who acquit the guilty for a bribe, Ex 23:8
but deny justice to the innocent. Ps 94:21
24Therefore, as tongues of fire lick up straw
and as dry grass sinks down in the flames,
so their roots will decay Job 18:16
and their flowers blow away like dust;
for they have rejected the law of the LORD Almighty
and spurned the word of the Holy One of Israel. Isa 8:6; 30:9,12
25Therefore the LORD's anger burns against his people; 2Ki 22:13
his hand is raised and he strikes them down.
The mountains shake,
and the dead bodies are like refuse in the streets. 2Ki 9:37

Yet for all this, his anger is not turned away,
his hand is still upraised. Isa 9:12,17,21; 10:4

26He lifts up a banner for the distant nations,
he whistles for those at the ends of the earth.
Here they come,
swiftly and speedily!
27Not one of them grows tired or stumbles,
not one slumbers or sleeps;
not a belt is loosened at the waist, Job 12:18
not a sandal thong is broken. Joel 2:7-8
28Their arrows are sharp, Ps 45:5
all their bows are strung; Ps 7:12
their horses' hoofs seem like flint,
their chariot wheels like a whirlwind.
29Their roar is like that of the lion, Jer 51:38; Zep 3:3
they roar like young lions;
they growl as they seize their prey Isa 10:6
and carry it off with no one to rescue.
30In that day they will roar over it
like the roaring of the sea. Lk 21:25
And if one looks at the land,
he will see darkness and distress; Isa 8:22
even the light will be darkened by the clouds. Joel 2:10

The Call of Isaiah **Chapter 6**

To understand this chapter we must recognize Isaiah's state of mind. His friend Uzziah, the king, had died, and Isaiah was mourning his passing. Isaiah sought the Lord in the midst of his agony of heart and received a life-changing vision. This chapter presents the glory, grandeur and majesty of the Holy God of heaven and earth. It also reveals the need for humans to be cleansed. Isaiah's first response to the glory of the Lord was a deep realization of his own need for cleansing. Not only did the Lord offer clean lips to Isaiah, but He also called him to use his newly consecrated lips to be His messenger to the nation of Judah.

Isaiah's Commission

6 In the year that King Uzziah died, I saw the
Lord seated on a throne, high and exalted,
and the train of his robe filled the temple. 2Above
him were seraphs, each with six wings: With two
wings they covered their faces, with two they covered their feet, and with two they were flying. 3And
they were calling to one another: 2Ch 6:22-23; Rev 4:8

"Holy, holy, holy is the LORD Almighty;
the whole earth is full of his glory." Ps 72:19

4At the sound of their voices the doorposts and
thresholds shook and the temple was filled with
smoke.
5"Woe to me!" I cried. "I am ruined! For I am
a man of unclean lips, and I live among a people
of unclean lips, and my eyes have seen the King,
the LORD Almighty." Jer 9:3-8; 51:57
6Then one of the seraphs flew to me with a live
coal in his hand, which he had taken with tongs
from the altar. 7With it he touched my mouth and
said, "See, this has touched your lips; your guilt is
taken away and your sin atoned for." Jer 1:9; 1Jn 1:7

LIVING  **INSIGHT**

Knowing God reveals the truth about ourselves. God always tells us the truth. And it is the truth that sets us free! When we see ourselves as we really are, we are prompted to lean on Him and to trust Him to make us like He is.

(See Isaiah 6:1–7.)

8Then I heard the voice of the Lord saying,
"Whom shall I send? And who will go for us?"
And I said, "Here am I. Send me!" Ge 22:1
9He said, "Go and tell this people: Eze 3:11

"'Be ever hearing, but never understanding;
be ever seeing, but never perceiving.'
10Make the heart of this people calloused;
make their ears dull
and close their eyes.[a]
Otherwise they might see with their eyes,
hear with their ears, Jer 5:21
understand with their hearts,
and turn and be healed." Mk 4:12*; Ac 28:26-27*

11Then I said, "For how long, O Lord?" Ps 79:5
And he answered:

"Until the cities lie ruined Lev 26:31

[a] 9,10 Hebrew; Septuagint *'You will be ever hearing, but never understanding; / you will be ever seeing, but never perceiving.' / 10This people's heart has become calloused; / they hardly hear with their ears, / and they have closed their eyes*

ISAIAH

"Here Am I. Send Me!"

"Then I heard the voice of the Lord saying, 'Whom shall I send? And who will go for us?' And I said, 'Here am I. Send me!'"

—ISAIAH 6:8

The year was approximately 740 B.C. when Isaiah was given a vision that would serve as his commission to be God's messenger to His people. At this point in history the Assyrians had not yet invaded Israel; the Babylonians had not yet invaded Judah. To the casual observer all was well with the people of God. The nation of Judah, where Isaiah lived, seemed strong. There was an outer veneer of prosperity and peace. And yet off in the distance there was the ominous rumble of an approaching thunderstorm signaling imminent disaster. Moral and spiritual decay was doing its devastating work on the hearts and minds of the people; the growing empires of Egypt and Assyria were on the outside looking in menacingly. It was only a matter of time before the storm would hit, leaving death and destruction in its wake.

Can you imagine what it must have been like for Isaiah, a sophisticated young man not yet thirty years old, to walk into the temple and see something that was to turn his life so completely around? "In the year that King Uzziah died, I saw the Lord seated on a throne, high and exalted, and the train of his robe filled the temple" (Isaiah 6:1). Isaiah saw the Lord—God Himself, sitting on a throne. He witnessed the power and glory of the Lord, a sight that changed his life forever and prepared him to accept his calling. Adding to the glory of this vision were the seraphs, those mysterious angelic creatures who thundered out God's attributes, "Holy, holy, holy is the LORD Almighty," so loud that Isaiah must have had to cover his ears.

As Isaiah watched and listened, he caught a glimpse of where he stood in all this. Look at the response this vision evoked: "Woe to me!" It's fascinating, isn't it? In the previous chapter, we see Isaiah pronouncing woes on everybody else. Now as he came face to face with the Lord, heard the angels, felt the earth shake under his feet and smelled the smoke, he was compelled to point the finger at himself. Suddenly he was humbled before a God who is utterly pure, holy and righteous—majestic beyond comprehension.

For whatever it's worth, I think Isaiah had struggled for quite some time with a tendency toward profanity. Notice what part of Isaiah's body the angel touched when he approached the shaken prophet—his lips, his mouth. That was the area that was at the center of Isaiah's conviction about himself. Look at the grace of God! Immediately Isaiah's barrier to freedom was demolished as the angel hastened to bring a message that went something like this: "You're free, Isaiah! Your sin is gone! You're clean and ready to be used by God!" We all have our own faults—and we may have become convinced those faults must disqualify us for God's service. But let me tell you this: He can use any one of us, broken vessels that we are, for His service.

The cleansing had taken place, and at last God's call came. Isaiah heard the Lord speak: "Who will go?" And Isaiah responded excitedly, "Here am I. Send me." Isaiah had entered the temple broken and discouraged. His friend Uzziah had just died. It must have seemed to Isaiah that he was carrying the weight of the world on his shoulders. Then he "saw the Lord," and he walked out as God's fully devoted prophet. For Isaiah, and for us today, God is ready to say "Go" only when we're really ready to say "Send me!"

Now look at the rest of the chapter. God told Isaiah it was going to be tough. In fact, he was told right from the outset that people would listen but not learn from his message. But he was to be faithful to God's call, regardless! When we're called to obey, we're also called to rely on God to produce the results that *He* wants.

In our lives, as in Isaiah's life, God uses our circumstances to make us aware of His presence. He reveals His character to bring us face to face with our need. He gives us hope to help us see that He can make us useful, then He expands our vision to help us evaluate our ability and step out in faith. Finally, He tells us the truth to make us focus on reality. That's what it means to be truly open to His calling in our lives.

and without inhabitant,
until the houses are left deserted
and the fields ruined and ravaged, Ps 79:1
12until the LORD has sent everyone far away
and the land is utterly forsaken. Jer 4:29; 30:17
13And though a tenth remains in the land, Isa 1:9
it will again be laid waste.
But as the terebinth and oak
leave stumps when they are cut down,
so the holy seed will be the stump in the
land." Dt 14:2; Job 14:7

The Sign of Immanuel

7 When Ahaz son of Jotham, the son of Uzziah,
was king of Judah, King Rezin of Aram and
Pekah son of Remaliah king of Israel marched up
to fight against Jerusalem, but they could not overpower it. 2Ki 15:25,37; 2Ch 28:5
2Now the house of David was told, "Aram has
allied itself with[a] Ephraim"; so the hearts of Ahaz
and his people were shaken, as the trees of the
forest are shaken by the wind. ver 13; Isa 9:9; 22:22
3Then the LORD said to Isaiah, "Go out, you and
your son Shear-Jashub,[b] to meet Ahaz at the end
of the aqueduct of the Upper Pool, on the road to
the Washerman's Field. 4Say to him, 'Be careful,
keep calm and don't be afraid. Do not lose heart
because of these two smoldering stubs of firewood—because of the fierce anger of Rezin and
Aram and of the son of Remaliah. 5Aram, Ephraim
and Remaliah's son have plotted your ruin, saying,
6"Let us invade Judah; let us tear it apart and divide it among ourselves, and make the son of Tabeel king over it." 7Yet this is what the Sovereign
LORD says: Isa 10:24; 30:15

" 'It will not take place,
it will not happen, Isa 8:10; Ac 4:25
8for the head of Aram is Damascus, Ge 14:15
and the head of Damascus is only Rezin.
Within sixty-five years
Ephraim will be too shattered to be a
people. Isa 17:1-3
9The head of Ephraim is Samaria,
and the head of Samaria is only Remaliah's
son.
If you do not stand firm in your faith, 2Ch 20:20
you will not stand at all.' " Isa 8:6-8; 30:12-14

10Again the LORD spoke to Ahaz, 11"Ask the
LORD your God for a sign, whether in the deepest
depths or in the highest heights." Ex 7:9; Dt 13:2
12But Ahaz said, "I will not ask; I will not put
the LORD to the test." Dt 6:16; Mt 4:7
13Then Isaiah said, "Hear now, you house of
David! Is it not enough to try the patience of men?
Will you try the patience of my God also? 14There-
fore the Lord himself will give you[c] a sign: The
virgin will be with child and will give birth to a
son, and[d] will call him Immanuel.[e] 15He will eat
curds and honey when he knows enough to reject
the wrong and choose the right. 16But before the
boy knows enough to reject the wrong and choose
the right, the land of the two kings you dread will
be laid waste. 17The LORD will bring on you and on
your people and on the house of your father a time
unlike any since Ephraim broke away from Judah—he will bring the king of Assyria." Isa 8:8,10
18In that day the LORD will whistle for flies from
the distant streams of Egypt and for bees from the
land of Assyria. 19They will all come and settle in
the steep ravines and in the crevices in the rocks,
on all the thornbushes and at all the water holes.
20In that day the Lord will use a razor hired from
beyond the River[f]—the king of Assyria—to
shave your head and the hair of your legs, and to
take off your beards also. 21In that day, a man will
keep alive a young cow and two goats. 22And because of the abundance of the milk they give, he
will have curds to eat. All who remain in the land
will eat curds and honey. 23In that day, in every
place where there were a thousand vines worth a
thousand silver shekels,[g] there will be only briers
and thorns. 24Men will go there with bow and
arrow, for the land will be covered with briers and
thorns. 25As for all the hills once cultivated by the
hoe, you will no longer go there for fear of the
briers and thorns; they will become places where
cattle are turned loose and where sheep run.

Assyria, the LORD's Instrument

8 The LORD said to me, "Take a large scroll and
write on it with an ordinary pen: Maher-
Shalal-Hash-Baz.[h] 2And I will call in Uriah the
priest and Zechariah son of Jeberekiah as reliable
witnesses for me." Isa 30:8; Hab 2:2
3Then I went to the prophetess, and she conceived and gave birth to a son. And the LORD said
to me, "Name him Maher-Shalal-Hash-Baz. 4Be-
fore the boy knows how to say 'My father' or 'My
mother,' the wealth of Damascus and the plunder
of Samaria will be carried off by the king of Assyria." Isa 7:8,16
5The LORD spoke to me again:

6"Because this people has rejected Isa 5:24
the gently flowing waters of Shiloah Jn 9:7
and rejoices over Rezin
and the son of Remaliah, Isa 7:1
7therefore the Lord is about to bring against
them

[a]2 Or *has set up camp in* [b]3 *Shear-Jashub* means *a remnant will return.* [c]14 The Hebrew is plural. [d]14 Masoretic Text; Dead Sea Scrolls *and he* or *and they* [e]14 *Immanuel* means *God with us.* [f]20 That is, the Euphrates [g]23 That is, about 25 pounds (about 11.5 kilograms) [h]1 *Maher-Shalal-Hash-Baz* means *quick to the plunder, swift to the spoil*; also in verse 3.

the mighty floodwaters of the River[a]—
the king of Assyria with all his pomp.
It will overflow all its channels,
run over all its banks
8and sweep on into Judah, swirling over it,
passing through it and reaching up to the neck.
Its outspread wings will cover the breadth of your land,
O Immanuel[b]!" Isa 7:14

9Raise the war cry,[c] you nations, and be shattered! Isa 17:12-13
Listen, all you distant lands.
Prepare for battle, and be shattered! Joel 3:9
Prepare for battle, and be shattered!
10Devise your strategy, but it will be thwarted;
propose your plan, but it will not stand,
for God is with us.[d] Ro 8:31

Fear God

11The LORD spoke to me with his strong hand
upon me, warning me not to follow the way of this
people. He said: Eze 2:8; 3:14

12"Do not call conspiracy Isa 7:2
everything that these people call conspiracy[e];
do not fear what they fear, Isa 7:4; Mt 10:28
and do not dread it. 1Pe 3:14*
13The LORD Almighty is the one you are to regard as holy, Nu 20:12
he is the one you are to fear,
he is the one you are to dread, Isa 29:23
14and he will be a sanctuary; Isa 4:6; Eze 11:16
but for both houses of Israel he will be
a stone that causes men to stumble Lk 2:34
and a rock that makes them fall. Isa 24:17-18
And for the people of Jerusalem he will be
a trap and a snare.
15Many of them will stumble; Lk 20:18; Ro 9:32
they will fall and be broken,
they will be snared and captured."
16Bind up the testimony
and seal up the law among my disciples.
17I will wait for the LORD, Hab 2:3
who is hiding his face from the house of Jacob. Dt 31:17; Isa 54:8
I will put my trust in him. Heb 2:13*

18Here am I, and the children the LORD has
given me. We are signs and symbols in Israel from
the LORD Almighty, who dwells on Mount Zion.
19When men tell you to consult mediums and
spiritists, who whisper and mutter, should not a
people inquire of their God? Why consult the dead
on behalf of the living? 20To the law and to the
testimony! If they do not speak according to this
word, they have no light of dawn. 21Distressed and
hungry, they will roam through the land; when
they are famished, they will become enraged and,
looking upward, will curse their king and their
God. 22Then they will look toward the earth and
see only distress and darkness and fearful gloom,
and they will be thrust into utter darkness.

To Us a Child Is Born

9 Nevertheless, there will be no more gloom for
those who were in distress. In the past he
humbled the land of Zebulun and the land of
Naphtali, but in the future he will honor Galilee of
the Gentiles, by the way of the sea, along the Jordan— 2Ki 15:29

2The people walking in darkness Isa 8:20
have seen a great light; Eph 5:8
on those living in the land of the shadow of death[f] Lk 1:79
a light has dawned. Mt 4:15-16*
3You have enlarged the nation Job 12:23
and increased their joy; Isa 25:9
they rejoice before you
as people rejoice at the harvest,
as men rejoice
when dividing the plunder. Ps 119:162
4For as in the day of Midian's defeat, Jdg 7:25
you have shattered Job 34:24
the yoke that burdens them, Isa 14:25
the bar across their shoulders, Isa 10:27
the rod of their oppressor. Isa 14:4; 49:26
5Every warrior's boot used in battle
and every garment rolled in blood
will be destined for burning, Isa 2:4
will be fuel for the fire.
6For to us a child is born, Lk 2:11
to us a son is given, Jn 3:16
and the government will be on his shoulders. Mt 28:18

LIVING  **INSIGHT**

Immanuel has come—in a feeding trough in lowly Bethlehem—and the cry from the Infant's throat broke the centuries of silence. For the first time in all of time, God's voice could literally be heard coming from human vocal cords. Everybody should have believed, but they didn't. Many still don't. But we do. Immanuel has come!

(See Isaiah 9:6.)

[a] 7 That is, the Euphrates [b] 8 *Immanuel* means *God with us.* [c] 9 Or *Do your worst* [d] 10 Hebrew *Immanuel*
[e] 12 Or *Do not call for a treaty / every time these people call for a treaty* [f] 2 Or *land of darkness*

And he will be called
Wonderful Counselor,[a] Mighty God,
Everlasting Father, Prince of Peace. Lk 2:14
7Of the increase of his government and peace
there will be no end. Da 2:44; Lk 1:33
He will reign on David's throne
and over his kingdom,
establishing and upholding it
with justice and righteousness Isa 11:4; 16:5
from that time on and forever.
The zeal of the LORD Almighty
will accomplish this. Isa 37:32; 59:17

The LORD's Anger Against Israel

8The Lord has sent a message against Jacob;
it will fall on Israel.
9All the people will know it—
Ephraim and the inhabitants of Samaria—
who say with pride
and arrogance of heart, Isa 46:12
10"The bricks have fallen down,
but we will rebuild with dressed stone;
the fig trees have been felled, Lk 19:4
but we will replace them with cedars."
11But the LORD has strengthened Rezin's foes
against them Isa 7:8
and has spurred their enemies on.
12Arameans from the east and Philistines from
the west 2Ch 28:18
have devoured Israel with open mouth.

Yet for all this, his anger is not turned away,
his hand is still upraised. Isa 5:25

13But the people have not returned to him who
struck them, Jer 5:3
nor have they sought the LORD Almighty.
14So the LORD will cut off from Israel both head
and tail,
both palm branch and reed in a single day;
15the elders and prominent men are the head,
the prophets who teach lies are the tail.
16Those who guide this people mislead them,
and those who are guided are led astray.
17Therefore the Lord will take no pleasure in
the young men, Jer 18:21
nor will he pity the fatherless and widows,
for everyone is ungodly and wicked, Isa 1:4; 10:6
every mouth speaks vileness. Mt 12:34

Yet for all this, his anger is not turned away,
his hand is still upraised. Isa 5:25

18Surely wickedness burns like a fire; Mal 4:1
it consumes briers and thorns,
it sets the forest thickets ablaze, Ps 83:14
so that it rolls upward in a column of
smoke.
19By the wrath of the LORD Almighty Isa 13:9,13
the land will be scorched
and the people will be fuel for the fire; Isa 1:31
no one will spare his brother. Mic 7:2,6
20On the right they will devour,
but still be hungry; Lev 26:26
on the left they will eat, Isa 49:26
but not be satisfied.
Each will feed on the flesh of his own
offspring[b]:
21 Manasseh will feed on Ephraim, and
Ephraim on Manasseh;
together they will turn against Judah.

Yet for all this, his anger is not turned away,
his hand is still upraised. Isa 5:25

10 Woe to those who make unjust laws,
to those who issue oppressive decrees,
2to deprive the poor of their rights
and withhold justice from the oppressed of
my people, Isa 5:23
making widows their prey
and robbing the fatherless. Dt 10:18; Isa 1:17
3What will you do on the day of reckoning,
when disaster comes from afar? Lk 19:44
To whom will you run for help? Isa 20:6
Where will you leave your riches?
4Nothing will remain but to cringe among the
captives Isa 24:22
or fall among the slain. Isa 22:2; 66:16

Yet for all this, his anger is not turned away,
his hand is still upraised.

God's Judgment on Assyria

5"Woe to the Assyrian, the rod of my anger,
in whose hand is the club of my wrath!
6I send him against a godless nation, Isa 9:17
I dispatch him against a people who anger
me, Isa 9:19
to seize loot and snatch plunder, Isa 5:29
and to trample them down like mud in the
streets.
7But this is not what he intends, Ge 50:20; Ac 4:23-28
this is not what he has in mind;
his purpose is to destroy,
to put an end to many nations.
8'Are not my commanders all kings?' he says.
9 'Has not Calno fared like Carchemish?
Is not Hamath like Arpad,
and Samaria like Damascus? 2Ki 16:9; 17:6
10As my hand seized the kingdoms of the idols,
kingdoms whose images excelled those of
Jerusalem and Samaria—
11shall I not deal with Jerusalem and her images
as I dealt with Samaria and her idols?' "

12When the Lord has finished all his work
against Mount Zion and Jerusalem, he will say, "I

[a]6 Or *Wonderful, Counselor* [b]20 Or *arm*

will punish the king of Assyria for the willful pride of his heart and the haughty look in his eyes. [13]For he says: 2Ki 19:31; Jer 50:18

"'By the strength of my hand I have done
this, Isa 37:24; Da 4:30
and by my wisdom, because I have
understanding.
I removed the boundaries of nations,
I plundered their treasures; Eze 28:4
like a mighty one I subdued[a] their kings.
[14]As one reaches into a nest, Jer 49:16; Ob 1:4
so my hand reached for the wealth of the
nations; Job 31:25
as men gather abandoned eggs,
so I gathered all the countries;
not one flapped a wing,
or opened its mouth to chirp.'"

[15]Does the ax raise itself above him who swings
it,
or the saw boast against him who uses it?
As if a rod were to wield him who lifts it up,
or a club brandish him who is not wood!
[16]Therefore, the Lord, the LORD Almighty,
will send a wasting disease upon his sturdy
warriors; ver 18; Isa 17:4
under his pomp a fire will be kindled Isa 8:7
like a blazing flame.
[17]The Light of Israel will become a fire, Isa 31:9
their Holy One a flame; Isa 37:23
in a single day it will burn and consume
his thorns and his briers. Nu 11:1-3; Isa 9:18
[18]The splendor of his forests and fertile fields
it will completely destroy,
as when a sick man wastes away.
[19]And the remaining trees of his forests will be
so few Isa 21:17
that a child could write them down.

The Remnant of Israel

[20]In that day the remnant of Israel, Isa 11:10-11
the survivors of the house of Jacob,
will no longer rely on him 2Ki 16:7
who struck them down 2Ch 28:20
but will truly rely on the LORD, Isa 17:7
the Holy One of Israel.
[21]A remnant will return,[b] a remnant of Jacob
will return to the Mighty God. Isa 9:6
[22]Though your people, O Israel, be like the sand
by the sea, Ge 12:2; Isa 48:19
only a remnant will return. Ro 9:27-28
Destruction has been decreed, Isa 28:22; Da 9:27
overwhelming and righteous.
[23]The Lord, the LORD Almighty, will carry out
the destruction decreed upon the whole
land. Isa 28:22; Ro 9:27-28*

[24]Therefore, this is what the Lord, the LORD Almighty, says:

"O my people who live in Zion, Ps 87:5-6
do not be afraid of the Assyrians,
who beat you with a rod Ex 5:14
and lift up a club against you, as Egypt did.
[25]Very soon my anger against you will end
and my wrath will be directed to their
destruction." Da 11:36

[26]The LORD Almighty will lash them with a
whip, Isa 37:36-38
as when he struck down Midian at the rock
of Oreb; Isa 9:4
and he will raise his staff over the waters,
as he did in Egypt.
[27]In that day their burden will be lifted from
your shoulders,
their yoke from your neck; Isa 9:4; 14:25
the yoke will be broken
because you have grown so fat.[c]

[28]They enter Aiath;
they pass through Migron; 1Sa 14:2
they store supplies at Micmash. 1Sa 13:2
[29]They go over the pass, and say,
"We will camp overnight at Geba."
Ramah trembles; Jos 18:25
Gibeah of Saul flees. Jdg 19:14
[30]Cry out, O Daughter of Gallim! 1Sa 25:44
Listen, O Laishah!
Poor Anathoth! Ne 11:32
[31]Madmenah is in flight;
the people of Gebim take cover.
[32]This day they will halt at Nob; 1Sa 21:1
they will shake their fist
at the mount of the Daughter of Zion, Jer 6:23
at the hill of Jerusalem.

[33]See, the Lord, the LORD Almighty,
will lop off the boughs with great power.
The lofty trees will be felled,
the tall ones will be brought low. Am 2:9
[34]He will cut down the forest thickets with an
ax;
Lebanon will fall before the Mighty One.

The Branch From Jesse

11 A shoot will come up from the stump of
Jesse; Rev 5:5
from his roots a Branch will bear fruit.
[2]The Spirit of the LORD will rest on him—
the Spirit of wisdom and of understanding,
the Spirit of counsel and of power, 2Ti 1:7
the Spirit of knowledge and of the fear of
the LORD—
[3]and he will delight in the fear of the LORD.

[a]13 Or / *I subdued the mighty,* [b]21 Hebrew *shear-jashub*; also in verse 22 [c]27 Hebrew; Septuagint *broken / from your shoulders*

He will not judge by what he sees with his
 eyes, Jn 7:24
 or decide by what he hears with his ears;
[4]but with righteousness he will judge the needy,
 with justice he will give decisions for the
 poor of the earth. Isa 3:14; 9:7
He will strike the earth with the rod of his
 mouth; Mal 4:6
 with the breath of his lips he will slay the
 wicked. Job 4:9; 2Th 2:8
[5]Righteousness will be his belt
 and faithfulness the sash around his waist.

[6]The wolf will live with the lamb, Isa 65:25
 the leopard will lie down with the goat,
the calf and the lion and the yearling[a]
 together;
 and a little child will lead them.
[7]The cow will feed with the bear,
 their young will lie down together,
 and the lion will eat straw like the ox.
[8]The infant will play near the hole of the cobra,
 and the young child put his hand into the
 viper's nest. Isa 14:29
[9]They will neither harm nor destroy Job 5:23
 on all my holy mountain,
for the earth will be full of the knowledge of
 the LORD Hab 2:14; Ps 98:2-3
 as the waters cover the sea.

[10]In that day the Root of Jesse will stand as a
banner for the peoples; the nations will rally to
him, and his place of rest will be glorious. [11]In that
day the Lord will reach out his hand a second time
to reclaim the remnant that is left of his people
from Assyria, from Lower Egypt, from Upper
Egypt,[b] from Cush,[c] from Elam, from Babylonia,[d] from Hamath and from the islands of the
sea. Ro 15:12*; Mic 7:12; Zec 10:10
[12]He will raise a banner for the nations Ps 20:5
 and gather the exiles of Israel; Ps 106:47; Isa 14:1
he will assemble the scattered people of Judah
 from the four quarters of the earth. Ps 48:10
[13]Ephraim's jealousy will vanish,
 and Judah's enemies[e] will be cut off;
Ephraim will not be jealous of Judah,
 nor Judah hostile toward Ephraim. Jer 3:18
[14]They will swoop down on the slopes of
 Philistia to the west;
 together they will plunder the people to the
 east.
They will lay hands on Edom and Moab,
 and the Ammonites will be subject to them.
[15]The LORD will dry up
 the gulf of the Egyptian sea;
with a scorching wind he will sweep his hand
 over the Euphrates River.[f] Isa 7:20
He will break it up into seven streams
 so that men can cross over in sandals.
[16]There will be a highway for the remnant of
 his people Isa 19:23; 62:10
 that is left from Assyria,
as there was for Israel
 when they came up from Egypt. Ex 14:26-31

Songs of Praise

12 In that day you will say:

"I will praise you, O LORD. Isa 25:1
 Although you were angry with me,
your anger has turned away Job 13:16
 and you have comforted me. Ps 71:21
[2]Surely God is my salvation; Isa 17:10
 I will trust and not be afraid. Isa 26:3
The LORD, the LORD, is my strength and my
 song; Ps 18:1
 he has become my salvation." Ex 15:2; Ps 118:14
[3]With joy you will draw water Jn 4:10,14
 from the wells of salvation. Ex 15:25

[4]In that day you will say:

"Give thanks to the LORD, call on his name;
 make known among the nations what he
 has done, Isa 54:5; 60:3
 and proclaim that his name is exalted.

LIVING  **INSIGHT**

Thanksgiving speaks in clear, crisp tones of often-forgotten terms like integrity, bravery, respect, faith, vigilance, dignity, honor, freedom, discipline, sacrifice, godliness.

(See Isaiah 12:4–6.)

[5]Sing to the LORD, for he has done glorious
 things; Ex 15:1; Ps 98:1
 let this be known to all the world.
[6]Shout aloud and sing for joy, people of Zion,
 for great is the Holy One of Israel among
 you." Isa 49:26; Zep 3:14-17

A Prophecy Against Babylon

13 An oracle concerning Babylon that Isaiah son of Amoz saw: Ge 10:10; Isa 14:4; 20:2; Rev 14:8

[2]Raise a banner on a bare hilltop, Jer 50:2; 51:27
 shout to them;
beckon to them
 to enter the gates of the nobles.
[3]I have commanded my holy ones;

[a]6 Hebrew; Septuagint *lion will feed* [b]11 Hebrew *from Pathros* [c]11 That is, the upper Nile region [d]11 Hebrew *Shinar* [e]13 Or *hostility* [f]15 Hebrew *the River*

I have summoned my warriors to carry out
my wrath— Joel 3:11
those who rejoice in my triumph. Ps 149:2

4 Listen, a noise on the mountains,
like that of a great multitude! Joel 3:14
Listen, an uproar among the kingdoms, Ps 46:6
like nations massing together!
The LORD Almighty is mustering
an army for war. Isa 47:4; Jer 50:41
5 They come from faraway lands,
from the ends of the heavens— Isa 5:26
the LORD and the weapons of his wrath—
to destroy the whole country. Isa 24:1

6 Wail, for the day of the LORD is near; Eze 30:2
it will come like destruction from the
Almighty.[a] Ge 17:1
7 Because of this, all hands will go limp, 2Ki 19:26
every man's heart will melt. Eze 21:7
8 Terror will seize them, Isa 21:4
pain and anguish will grip them; Ex 15:14
they will writhe like a woman in labor.
They will look aghast at each other,
their faces aflame. Na 2:10

9 See, the day of the LORD is coming Isa 2:12
—a cruel day, with wrath and fierce anger—
to make the land desolate
and destroy the sinners within it.
10 The stars of heaven and their constellations
will not show their light.
The rising sun will be darkened Isa 5:30; Rev 8:12
and the moon will not give its light. Eze 32:7
11 I will punish the world for its evil, Isa 3:11
the wicked for their sins.
I will put an end to the arrogance of the
haughty Ps 10:5; Pr 16:18
and will humble the pride of the ruthless.
12 I will make man scarcer than pure gold, Isa 4:1
more rare than the gold of Ophir. Ge 10:29
13 Therefore I will make the heavens tremble;
and the earth will shake from its place
at the wrath of the LORD Almighty, Isa 9:19
in the day of his burning anger. Job 9:5

LIVING  **INSIGHT**

We hear regularly about the love of God, and surely we should. But to the exclusion of God's anger? I think not. How easy it is to forget that He is holy. How seldom we are taught about the anger of God, about how zealous He is for the purity of His people.

(See Isaiah 13:9–13.)

14 Like a hunted gazelle,
like sheep without a shepherd, 1Ki 22:17
each will return to his own people,
each will flee to his native land. Jer 50:16
15 Whoever is captured will be thrust through;
all who are caught will fall by the sword.
16 Their infants will be dashed to pieces before
their eyes; Ps 137:9
their houses will be looted and their wives
ravished. Ge 34:29; Hos 13:16

17 See, I will stir up against them the Medes,
who do not care for silver
and have no delight in gold. Pr 6:34-35
18 Their bows will strike down the young men;
they will have no mercy on infants Isa 47:6
nor will they look with compassion on
children. Isa 14:22
19 Babylon, the jewel of kingdoms,
the glory of the Babylonians'[b] pride, Da 4:30
will be overthrown by God Rev 14:8
like Sodom and Gomorrah. Ge 19:24
20 She will never be inhabited Isa 14:23; 34:10-15
or lived in through all generations;
no Arab will pitch his tent there, 2Ch 17:11
no shepherd will rest his flocks there.
21 But desert creatures will lie there, Rev 18:2
jackals will fill her houses;
there the owls will dwell, Dt 14:15-17
and there the wild goats will leap about.
22 Hyenas will howl in her strongholds, Isa 25:2
jackals in her luxurious palaces. Isa 34:13
Her time is at hand, Jer 51:33
and her days will not be prolonged.

14 The LORD will have compassion on
Jacob; Ps 102:13; Isa 49:10,13
once again he will choose Israel Zec 1:17; 2:12
and will settle them in their own land.
Aliens will join them Eph 2:12-19
and unite with the house of Jacob.
2 Nations will take them
and bring them to their own place. Isa 60:9
And the house of Israel will possess the
nations Isa 49:7,23
as menservants and maidservants in the
LORD's land.
They will make captives of their captors
and rule over their oppressors. Isa 60:14

3 On the day the LORD gives you relief from suffering and turmoil and cruel bondage, 4 you will
take up this taunt against the king of Babylon:

How the oppressor has come to an end! Isa 9:4
How his fury[c] has ended!

[a] 6 Hebrew *Shaddai* [b] 19 Or *Chaldeans'* [c] 4 Dead Sea Scrolls, Septuagint and Syriac; the meaning of the word in the Masoretic Text is uncertain.

[5]The LORD has broken the rod of the wicked,
the scepter of the rulers,
[6]which in anger struck down peoples Isa 10:14
with unceasing blows,
and in fury subdued nations
with relentless aggression. Isa 47:6
[7]All the lands are at rest and at peace; Ps 98:1
they break into singing.
[8]Even the pine trees and the cedars of Lebanon
exult over you and say,
"Now that you have been laid low,
no woodsman comes to cut us down."

[9]The grave[a] below is all astir Eze 32:21
to meet you at your coming;
it rouses the spirits of the departed to greet
you—
all those who were leaders in the world;
it makes them rise from their thrones—
all those who were kings over the nations.
[10]They will all respond,
they will say to you,
"You also have become weak, as we are;
you have become like us." Eze 32:21
[11]All your pomp has been brought down to the
grave,
along with the noise of your harps;
maggots are spread out beneath you
and worms cover you. Isa 51:8

[12]How you have fallen from heaven, Isa 34:4
O morning star, son of the dawn! 2Pe 1:19
You have been cast down to the earth,
you who once laid low the nations!
[13]You said in your heart,
"I will ascend to heaven; Da 8:10; Mt 11:23
I will raise my throne Eze 28:2; 2Th 2:4
above the stars of God;
I will sit enthroned on the mount of assembly,
on the utmost heights of the sacred
mountain.[b]
[14]I will ascend above the tops of the clouds;
I will make myself like the Most High."
[15]But you are brought down to the grave,
to the depths of the pit. Mt 11:23; Lk 10:15

[16]Those who see you stare at you,
they ponder your fate: Jer 50:23
"Is this the man who shook the earth
and made kingdoms tremble,
[17]the man who made the world a desert, Joel 2:3
who overthrew its cities Ps 52:7
and would not let his captives go home?"
[18]All the kings of the nations lie in state,
each in his own tomb.
[19]But you are cast out of your tomb Isa 22:16-18
like a rejected branch;
you are covered with the slain,
with those pierced by the sword,
those who descend to the stones of the pit.
Like a corpse trampled underfoot,
[20]you will not join them in burial,
for you have destroyed your land
and killed your people.

The offspring of the wicked Job 18:19; Isa 1:4
will never be mentioned again. Ps 21:10
[21]Prepare a place to slaughter his sons
for the sins of their forefathers; Ex 20:5
they are not to rise to inherit the land
and cover the earth with their cities.

[22]"I will rise up against them,"
declares the LORD Almighty.
"I will cut off from Babylon her name and
survivors,
her offspring and descendants," 1Ki 14:10
declares the LORD.
[23]"I will turn her into a place for owls Isa 34:11-15
and into swampland;
I will sweep her with the broom of
destruction,"
declares the LORD Almighty.

A Prophecy Against Assyria

[24]The LORD Almighty has sworn, Isa 45:23

"Surely, as I have planned, so it will be,
and as I have purposed, so it will stand.
[25]I will crush the Assyrian in my land; Isa 10:5,12
on my mountains I will trample him down.
His yoke will be taken from my people, Isa 9:4
and his burden removed from their
shoulders." Isa 10:27

[26]This is the plan determined for the whole
world; Isa 23:9
this is the hand stretched out over all
nations. Ex 15:12
[27]For the LORD Almighty has purposed, and
who can thwart him?
His hand is stretched out, and who can
turn it back? 2Ch 20:6; Isa 43:13; Da 4:35

A Prophecy Against the Philistines

[28]This oracle came in the year King Ahaz died:

[29]Do not rejoice, all you Philistines, 2Ch 26:6
that the rod that struck you is broken;
from the root of that snake will spring up a
viper, Isa 11:8
its fruit will be a darting, venomous
serpent. Dt 8:15
[30]The poorest of the poor will find pasture,
and the needy will lie down in safety.
But your root I will destroy by famine; Isa 8:21
it will slay your survivors. Jer 25:16

[a]9 Hebrew *Sheol*; also in verses 11 and 15 [b]13 Or *the north*; Hebrew *Zaphon*

31 Wail, O gate! Howl, O city! Isa 3:26
Melt away, all you Philistines!
A cloud of smoke comes from the north,
and there is not a straggler in its ranks.
32 What answer shall be given
to the envoys of that nation? Isa 37:9
"The LORD has established Zion, Ps 87:2,5; Isa 44:28
and in her his afflicted people will find
refuge." Isa 4:6; Jas 2:5

A Prophecy Against Moab

15 An oracle concerning Moab: Isa 11:14

Ar in Moab is ruined, Jer 48:24,41
destroyed in a night!
Kir in Moab is ruined, 2Ki 3:25
destroyed in a night!
2 Dibon goes up to its temple,
to its high places to weep; Jer 48:35
Moab wails over Nebo and Medeba.
Every head is shaved Lev 21:5
and every beard cut off. 2Sa 10:4
3 In the streets they wear sackcloth;
on the roofs and in the public squares
they all wail,
prostrate with weeping. Isa 22:4
4 Heshbon and Elealeh cry out, Nu 32:3
their voices are heard all the way to Jahaz.
Therefore the armed men of Moab cry out,
and their hearts are faint.

5 My heart cries out over Moab; Jer 48:31
her fugitives flee as far as Zoar,
as far as Eglath Shelishiyah.
They go up the way to Luhith,
weeping as they go;
on the road to Horonaim Jer 48:3,34
they lament their destruction. Jer 48:5
6 The waters of Nimrim are dried up Isa 19:5-7
and the grass is withered; Joel 1:12
the vegetation is gone
and nothing green is left. Jer 14:5
7 So the wealth they have acquired and stored
up Isa 30:6; Jer 48:36
they carry away over the Ravine of the
Poplars.
8 Their outcry echoes along the border of
Moab;
their wailing reaches as far as Eglaim,
their lamentation as far as Beer Elim.
9 Dimon's[a] waters are full of blood,
but I will bring still more upon Dimon[a]—
a lion upon the fugitives of Moab 2Ki 17:25
and upon those who remain in the land.

16 Send lambs as tribute 2Ki 3:4
to the ruler of the land,
from Sela, across the desert, 2Ki 14:7
to the mount of the Daughter of Zion.
2 Like fluttering birds
pushed from the nest, Pr 27:8
so are the women of Moab
at the fords of the Arnon. Nu 21:13-14; Jer 48:20

3 "Give us counsel,
render a decision.
Make your shadow like night—
at high noon.
Hide the fugitives, 1Ki 18:4
do not betray the refugees.
4 Let the Moabite fugitives stay with you;
be their shelter from the destroyer."

The oppressor will come to an end, Isa 9:4
and destruction will cease; Isa 2:2-4
the aggressor will vanish from the land.
5 In love a throne will be established; Da 7:14
in faithfulness a man will sit on it—
one from the house[b] of David— Lk 1:32
one who in judging seeks justice Isa 9:7
and speeds the cause of righteousness.

6 We have heard of Moab's pride— Am 2:1; Ob 1:3
her overweening pride and conceit,
her pride and her insolence—
but her boasts are empty.
7 Therefore the Moabites wail, Jer 48:20
they wail together for Moab.
Lament and grieve
for the men[c] of Kir Hareseth. 2Ki 3:25
8 The fields of Heshbon wither, Isa 15:6
the vines of Sibmah also.
The rulers of the nations
have trampled down the choicest vines,
which once reached Jazer
and spread toward the desert.
Their shoots spread out Job 8:16
and went as far as the sea. Ps 80:11
9 So I weep, as Jazer weeps, Isa 15:3
for the vines of Sibmah.
O Heshbon, O Elealeh,
I drench you with tears! Job 7:3
The shouts of joy over your ripened fruit
and over your harvests have been stilled.
10 Joy and gladness are taken away from the
orchards; Isa 24:7-8
no one sings or shouts in the vineyards;
no one treads out wine at the presses, Jdg 9:27
for I have put an end to the shouting.
11 My heart laments for Moab like a harp, Isa 15:5
my inmost being for Kir Hareseth. Isa 63:15
12 When Moab appears at her high place,
she only wears herself out;
when she goes to her shrine to pray, Isa 15:2
it is to no avail. Jer 48:29-36; 1Ki 18:29

[a] 9 Masoretic Text; Dead Sea Scrolls, some Septuagint manuscripts and Vulgate *Dibon* [b] 5 Hebrew *tent* [c] 7 Or "*raisin cakes*," a wordplay

[13]This is the word the LORD has already spoken
concerning Moab. [14]But now the LORD says:
"Within three years, as a servant bound by contract would count them, Moab's splendor and all her many people will be despised, and her survivors will be very few and feeble." Isa 21:17; 25:10

An Oracle Against Damascus

17 An oracle concerning Damascus: Jer 49:23

"See, Damascus will no longer be a city
but will become a heap of ruins. Am 1:3
[2]The cities of Aroer will be deserted
and left to flocks, which will lie down,
with no one to make them afraid. Jer 7:33
[3]The fortified city will disappear from Ephraim,
and royal power from Damascus;
the remnant of Aram will be
like the glory of the Israelites," ver 4; Isa 7:8,16
declares the LORD Almighty.

[4]"In that day the glory of Jacob will fade;
the fat of his body will waste away. Isa 10:16
[5]It will be as when a reaper gathers the
standing grain
and harvests the grain with his arm—
as when a man gleans heads of grain
in the Valley of Rephaim. 1Ch 11:15
[6]Yet some gleanings will remain, Isa 24:13
as when an olive tree is beaten, Isa 27:12
leaving two or three olives on the topmost
branches,
four or five on the fruitful boughs,"
declares the LORD, the God of Israel.
[7]In that day men will look to their Maker
and turn their eyes to the Holy One of
Israel. Mic 7:7
[8]They will not look to the altars,
the work of their hands, Isa 2:18,20; 30:22
and they will have no regard for the Asherah
poles[a] Jdg 3:7; 2Ki 17:10
and the incense altars their fingers have
made. Isa 2:8

[9]In that day their strong cities, which they left
because of the Israelites, will be like places abandoned to thickets and undergrowth. And all will be desolation. Isa 7:19
[10]You have forgotten God your Savior; Ps 68:19
you have not remembered the Rock, your
fortress. Ps 18:2
Therefore, though you set out the finest plants
and plant imported vines,
[11]though on the day you set them out, you
make them grow,
and on the morning when you plant them,
you bring them to bud, Ps 90:6
yet the harvest will be as nothing Hos 8:7
in the day of disease and incurable pain.

[12]Oh, the raging of many nations—
they rage like the raging sea! Ps 18:4; Jer 6:23
Oh, the uproar of the peoples—
they roar like the roaring of great waters!
[13]Although the peoples roar like the roar of
surging waters,
when he rebukes them they flee far away,
driven before the wind like chaff on the hills,
like tumbleweed before a gale. Job 21:18
[14]In the evening, sudden terror!
Before the morning, they are gone! 2Ki 19:35
This is the portion of those who loot us,
the lot of those who plunder us.

A Prophecy Against Cush

18 Woe to the land of whirring wings[b]
along the rivers of Cush,[c] Isa 20:3-5
[2]which sends envoys by sea
in papyrus boats over the water. Ex 2:3

Go, swift messengers,
to a people tall and smooth-skinned,
to a people feared far and wide,
an aggressive nation of strange speech, Ge 10:8-9
whose land is divided by rivers. ver 7

[3]All you people of the world,
you who live on the earth,
when a banner is raised on the mountains,
you will see it,
and when a trumpet sounds,
you will hear it.
[4]This is what the LORD says to me:
"I will remain quiet and will look on from
my dwelling place, Isa 26:21; Hos 5:15
like shimmering heat in the sunshine,
like a cloud of dew in the heat of harvest."
[5]For, before the harvest, when the blossom is
gone
and the flower becomes a ripening grape,
he will cut off the shoots with pruning knives,
and cut down and take away the spreading
branches. Isa 17:10-11; Eze 17:6
[6]They will all be left to the mountain birds of
prey
and to the wild animals; Isa 56:9; Jer 7:33; Eze 32:4
the birds will feed on them all summer,
the wild animals all winter.

[7]At that time gifts will be brought to the LORD
Almighty 2Ch 9:24

from a people tall and smooth-skinned,
from a people feared far and wide, Hab 1:7
an aggressive nation of strange speech,
whose land is divided by rivers—

[a]8 That is, symbols of the goddess Asherah [b]1 Or *of locusts* [c]1 That is, the upper Nile region

the gifts will be brought to Mount Zion, the place of the Name of the LORD Almighty. Ps 68:31

A Prophecy About Egypt

19 An oracle concerning Egypt: Ex 12:12

See, the LORD rides on a swift cloud Ps 18:10
and is coming to Egypt.
The idols of Egypt tremble before him,
and the hearts of the Egyptians melt within them. Jos 2:11

[2]"I will stir up Egyptian against Egyptian—
brother will fight against brother, Jdg 7:22
neighbor against neighbor,
city against city,
kingdom against kingdom. 2Ch 20:23
[3]The Egyptians will lose heart, Ps 18:45
and I will bring their plans to nothing;
they will consult the idols and the spirits of the dead,
the mediums and the spiritists. Isa 8:19; 47:13
[4]I will hand the Egyptians over
to the power of a cruel master,
and a fierce king will rule over them," Isa 20:4
declares the Lord, the LORD Almighty.

[5]The waters of the river will dry up, Jer 51:36
and the riverbed will be parched and dry.
[6]The canals will stink; Ex 7:18
the streams of Egypt will dwindle and dry up. Isa 37:25; Eze 30:12
The reeds and rushes will wither, Isa 15:6
7 also the plants along the Nile, Isa 23:3
at the mouth of the river.
Every sown field along the Nile
will become parched, will blow away and be no more.
[8]The fishermen will groan and lament, Eze 47:10
all who cast hooks into the Nile; Hab 1:15
those who throw nets on the water
will pine away.
[9]Those who work with combed flax will despair,
the weavers of fine linen will lose hope.
[10]The workers in cloth will be dejected,
and all the wage earners will be sick at heart.

[11]The officials of Zoan are nothing but fools;
the wise counselors of Pharaoh give senseless advice. Ge 41:37
How can you say to Pharaoh,
"I am one of the wise men, 1Ki 4:30; Ac 7:22
a disciple of the ancient kings"?

[12]Where are your wise men now? 1Co 1:20
Let them show you and make known
what the LORD Almighty
has planned against Egypt. Isa 14:24; Ro 9:17
[13]The officials of Zoan have become fools,
the leaders of Memphis[a] are deceived;
the cornerstones of her peoples
have led Egypt astray.
[14]The LORD has poured into them
a spirit of dizziness; Mt 17:17
they make Egypt stagger in all that she does,
as a drunkard staggers around in his vomit.
[15]There is nothing Egypt can do—
head or tail, palm branch or reed. Isa 9:14

[16]In that day the Egyptians will be like women.
They will shudder with fear at the uplifted hand
that the LORD Almighty raises against them. [17]And
the land of Judah will bring terror to the Egyptians; everyone to whom Judah is mentioned will
be terrified, because of what the LORD Almighty is
planning against them. Isa 11:15; 14:24
[18]In that day five cities in Egypt will speak the
language of Canaan and swear allegiance to the
LORD Almighty. One of them will be called the City
of Destruction.[b] Zep 3:9
[19]In that day there will be an altar to the LORD
in the heart of Egypt, and a monument to the LORD
at its border. [20]It will be a sign and witness to the
LORD Almighty in the land of Egypt. When they
cry out to the LORD because of their oppressors, he
will send them a savior and defender, and he will
rescue them. [21]So the LORD will make himself
known to the Egyptians, and in that day they will
acknowledge the LORD. They will worship with
sacrifices and grain offerings; they will make vows
to the LORD and keep them. [22]The LORD will strike
Egypt with a plague; he will strike them and heal
them. They will turn to the LORD, and he will respond to their pleas and heal them. Isa 45:14
[23]In that day there will be a highway from Egypt
to Assyria. The Assyrians will go to Egypt and the
Egyptians to Assyria. The Egyptians and Assyrians
will worship together. [24]In that day Israel will be
the third, along with Egypt and Assyria, a blessing
on the earth. [25]The LORD Almighty will bless them,
saying, "Blessed be Egypt my people, Assyria my
handiwork, and Israel my inheritance." Hos 2:23

A Prophecy Against Egypt and Cush

20 In the year that the supreme commander,
sent by Sargon king of Assyria, came to
Ashdod and attacked and captured it— [2]at that
time the LORD spoke through Isaiah son of Amoz.
He said to him, "Take off the sackcloth from your
body and the sandals from your feet." And he did
so, going around stripped and barefoot. 1Sa 19:24
[3]Then the LORD said, "Just as my servant Isaiah
has gone stripped and barefoot for three years, as

[a]13 Hebrew *Noph* [b]18 Most manuscripts of the Masoretic Text; some manuscripts of the Masoretic Text, Dead Sea Scrolls and Vulgate *City of the Sun* (that is, Heliopolis)

a sign and portent against Egypt and Cush,[a] [4]so
the king of Assyria will lead away stripped and
barefoot the Egyptian captives and Cushite exiles,
young and old, with buttocks bared—to Egypt's
shame. [5]Those who trusted in Cush and boasted in
Egypt will be afraid and put to shame. [6]In that day
the people who live on this coast will say, 'See what
has happened to those we relied on, those we fled
to for help and deliverance from the king of Assyria! How then can we escape?' " 2Ki 18:21; Jer 30:15-17

A Prophecy Against Babylon

21 An oracle concerning the Desert by the Sea: Isa 13:21; Jer 51:43

Like whirlwinds sweeping through the
southland, Zec 9:14
an invader comes from the desert,
from a land of terror.

[2]A dire vision has been shown to me: Ps 60:3
The traitor betrays, the looter takes loot.
Elam, attack! Media, lay siege! Jer 49:34
I will bring to an end all the groaning she
caused.

[3]At this my body is racked with pain,
pangs seize me, like those of a woman in
labor; Ps 48:6; Isa 26:17
I am staggered by what I hear,
I am bewildered by what I see.
[4]My heart falters,
fear makes me tremble; Isa 13:8
the twilight I longed for
has become a horror to me. Ps 55:5

[5]They set the tables,
they spread the rugs,
they eat, they drink! Jer 51:39,57; Da 5:2
Get up, you officers,
oil the shields! 2Sa 1:21; 1Ki 10:16-17

[6]This is what the Lord says to me:

"Go, post a lookout 2Ki 9:17
and have him report what he sees.
[7]When he sees chariots ver 9
with teams of horses,
riders on donkeys
or riders on camels,
let him be alert,
fully alert."

[8]And the lookout[b] shouted, Hab 2:1

"Day after day, my lord, I stand on the
watchtower;
every night I stay at my post.
[9]Look, here comes a man in a chariot
with a team of horses.
And he gives back the answer:
'Babylon has fallen, has fallen! Jer 51:8; Rev 14:8
All the images of its gods Isa 46:1; Jer 50:2; 51:44
lie shattered on the ground!' "
[10]O my people, crushed on the threshing floor,
I tell you what I have heard
from the LORD Almighty,
from the God of Israel.

A Prophecy Against Edom

[11]An oracle concerning Dumah[c]: Ge 25:14

Someone calls to me from Seir, Ge 32:3
"Watchman, what is left of the night?
Watchman, what is left of the night?"
[12]The watchman replies,
"Morning is coming, but also the night.
If you would ask, then ask;
and come back yet again."

A Prophecy Against Arabia

[13]An oracle concerning Arabia: Isa 13:1

You caravans of Dedanites,
who camp in the thickets of Arabia,
[14] bring water for the thirsty;
you who live in Tema, Ge 25:15
bring food for the fugitives.
[15]They flee from the sword, Isa 13:14
from the drawn sword,
from the bent bow
and from the heat of battle.

[16]This is what the Lord says to me: "Within one
year, as a servant bound by contract would count
it, all the pomp of Kedar will come to an end.
[17]The survivors of the bowmen, the warriors of
Kedar, will be few." The LORD, the God of Israel,
has spoken. Ps 120:5; Isa 16:14; 60:7

A Prophecy About Jerusalem

22 An oracle concerning the Valley of Vision:

What troubles you now,
that you have all gone up on the roofs,
[2]O town full of commotion,
O city of tumult and revelry? Isa 32:13
Your slain were not killed by the sword,
nor did they die in battle.
[3]All your leaders have fled together;
they have been captured without using the
bow. 2Ki 25:6
All you who were caught were taken prisoner
together,
having fled while the enemy was still far
away.
[4]Therefore I said, "Turn away from me;
let me weep bitterly. Isa 15:3; Lk 19:41

[a] 3 That is, the upper Nile region; also in verse 5 [b] 8 Dead Sea Scrolls and Syriac; Masoretic Text *A lion* [c] 11 *Dumah* means *silence* or *stillness*, a wordplay on *Edom*.

Do not try to console me
over the destruction of my people." Jer 9:1

5The Lord, the LORD Almighty, has a day
of tumult and trampling and terror La 1:5
in the Valley of Vision,
a day of battering down walls Jer 39:8; Eze 13:14
and of crying out to the mountains.
6Elam takes up the quiver, Isa 21:2; Jer 49:35
with her charioteers and horses;
Kir uncovers the shield. 2Ki 16:9
7Your choicest valleys are full of chariots,
and horsemen are posted at the city gates;
8 the defenses of Judah are stripped away.

And you looked in that day
to the weapons in the Palace of the Forest;
9you saw that the City of David
had many breaches in its defenses;
you stored up water
in the Lower Pool. 2Ch 32:4
10You counted the buildings in Jerusalem
and tore down houses to strengthen the
wall. 2Ch 32:5
11You built a reservoir between the two walls
for the water of the Old Pool, 2Ch 32:4
but you did not look to the One who made it,
or have regard for the One who planned it
long ago. 2Ki 19:25

12The Lord, the LORD Almighty,
called you on that day
to weep and to wail, Joel 2:17
to tear out your hair and put on sackcloth.
13But see, there is joy and revelry,
slaughtering of cattle and killing of sheep,
eating of meat and drinking of wine!
"Let us eat and drink," you say,
"for tomorrow we die!" 1Co 15:32*

14The LORD Almighty has revealed this in my
hearing: "Till your dying day this sin will not be
atoned for," says the Lord, the LORD Almighty.

15This is what the Lord, the LORD Almighty,
says:

"Go, say to this steward,
to Shebna, who is in charge of the palace:
16What are you doing here and who gave you
permission
to cut out a grave for yourself here, Mt 27:60
hewing your grave on the height
and chiseling your resting place in the rock?
17"Beware, the LORD is about to take firm hold
of you
and hurl you away, O you mighty man.
18He will roll you up tightly like a ball
and throw you into a large country. Isa 17:13
There you will die
and there your splendid chariots will
remain—
you disgrace to your master's house!
19I will depose you from your office,
and you will be ousted from your position.

20"In that day I will summon my servant, Eliakim son of Hilkiah. 21I will clothe him with your
robe and fasten your sash around him and hand
your authority over to him. He will be a father to
those who live in Jerusalem and to the house of
Judah. 22I will place on his shoulder the key to the
house of David; what he opens no one can shut,
and what he shuts no one can open. 23I will drive
him like a peg into a firm place; he will be a seat[a]
of honor for the house of his father. 24All the glory
of his family will hang on him: its offspring and
offshoots—all its lesser vessels, from the bowls to
all the jars. Job 36:7; Ezr 9:8; Rev 3:7

25"In that day," declares the LORD Almighty,
"the peg driven into the firm place will give way;
it will be sheared off and will fall, and the load
hanging on it will be cut down." The LORD has
spoken. ver 23; Isa 46:11; Mic 4:4

A Prophecy About Tyre

23 An oracle concerning Tyre: Jer 47:4; Zec 9:2-4

Wail, O ships of Tarshish! Ge 10:4; 1Ki 10:22
For Tyre is destroyed
and left without house or harbor.
From the land of Cyprus[b]
word has come to them.

2Be silent, you people of the island
and you merchants of Sidon, Jdg 1:31; Eze 27:5-24
whom the seafarers have enriched.
3On the great waters
came the grain of the Shihor;
the harvest of the Nile[c] was the revenue of
Tyre, Isa 19:7; Eze 27:3
and she became the marketplace of the
nations.

4Be ashamed, O Sidon, and you, O fortress of
the sea, Ge 10:15,19
for the sea has spoken:
"I have neither been in labor nor given birth;
I have neither reared sons nor brought up
daughters."
5When word comes to Egypt,
they will be in anguish at the report from
Tyre. Eze 26:17-18

6Cross over to Tarshish;
wail, you people of the island.
7Is this your city of revelry, Isa 22:2; 32:13

[a] 23 Or *throne* [b] 1 Hebrew *Kittim* [c] 2,3 Masoretic Text; one Dead Sea Scroll *Sidon, / who cross over the sea; / your envoys* 3*are on the great waters. / The grain of the Shihor, / the harvest of the Nile,*

the old, old city,
whose feet have taken her
to settle in far-off lands?
8Who planned this against Tyre,
the bestower of crowns,
whose merchants are princes,
whose traders are renowned in the earth?
9The LORD Almighty planned it,
to bring low the pride of all glory Job 40:11
and to humble all who are renowned on the earth. Isa 5:13; 13:11

10Till[a] your land as along the Nile,
O Daughter of Tarshish,
for you no longer have a harbor.
11The LORD has stretched out his hand over the sea Ex 14:21
and made its kingdoms tremble. Ps 46:6
He has given an order concerning Phoenicia[b]
that her fortresses be destroyed. Isa 25:2
12He said, "No more of your reveling, Rev 18:22
O Virgin Daughter of Sidon, now crushed!

"Up, cross over to Cyprus[c];
even there you will find no rest."
13Look at the land of the Babylonians,[d]
this people that is now of no account!
The Assyrians have made it Isa 10:5
a place for desert creatures;
they raised up their siege towers,
they stripped its fortresses bare
and turned it into a ruin. Isa 10:7

14Wail, you ships of Tarshish; Isa 2:16 [fn]
your fortress is destroyed!

15At that time Tyre will be forgotten for seventy
years, the span of a king's life. But at the end of
these seventy years, it will happen to Tyre as in the
song of the prostitute: Jer 25:22

16"Take up a harp, walk through the city,
O prostitute forgotten;
play the harp well, sing many a song,
so that you will be remembered."

17At the end of seventy years, the LORD will deal
with Tyre. She will return to her hire as a prostitute
and will ply her trade with all the kingdoms on the
face of the earth. 18Yet her profit and her earnings
will be set apart for the LORD; they will not be
stored up or hoarded. Her profits will go to those
who live before the LORD, for abundant food and
fine clothes. Isa 60:5-9; Eze 16:26; Rev 17:1

The LORD's Devastation of the Earth

24 See, the LORD is going to lay waste the earth Isa 2:19-21; 33:9
and devastate it;
he will ruin its face
and scatter its inhabitants—
2it will be the same
for priest as for people, Hos 4:9
for master as for servant,
for mistress as for maid,
for seller as for buyer, Eze 7:12
for borrower as for lender,
for debtor as for creditor. Lev 25:35-37; Dt 23:19-20
3The earth will be completely laid waste
and totally plundered. Isa 6:11-12
The LORD has spoken this word.

4The earth dries up and withers,
the world languishes and withers,
the exalted of the earth languish. Isa 2:12
5The earth is defiled by its people; Ge 3:17; Nu 35:33
they have disobeyed the laws, Isa 10:6; 59:12
violated the statutes
and broken the everlasting covenant.
6Therefore a curse consumes the earth;
its people must bear their guilt.
Therefore earth's inhabitants are burned up,
and very few are left.
7The new wine dries up and the vine withers;
all the merrymakers groan. Isa 16:8-10
8The gaiety of the tambourines is stilled, Isa 5:12
the noise of the revelers has stopped,
the joyful harp is silent. Eze 26:13; Rev 18:22
9No longer do they drink wine with a song;
the beer is bitter to its drinkers. Isa 5:20
10The ruined city lies desolate; Isa 6:11
the entrance to every house is barred.
11In the streets they cry out for wine;
all joy turns to gloom, Isa 16:10; 32:13; Jer 14:3
all gaiety is banished from the earth.
12The city is left in ruins, Isa 19:18
its gate is battered to pieces. Isa 3:26
13So will it be on the earth
and among the nations,
as when an olive tree is beaten, Isa 17:6
or as when gleanings are left after the grape harvest.

14They raise their voices, they shout for joy;
from the west they acclaim the LORD's majesty.
15Therefore in the east give glory to the LORD;
exalt the name of the LORD, the God of Israel, Mal 1:11
in the islands of the sea.
16From the ends of the earth we hear singing:
"Glory to the Righteous One." Isa 28:5

But I said, "I waste away, I waste away!
Woe to me!
The treacherous betray!
With treachery the treacherous betray!"

[a]10 Dead Sea Scrolls and some Septuagint manuscripts; Masoretic Text *Go through* [b]11 Hebrew *Canaan* [c]12 Hebrew *Kittim* [d]13 Or *Chaldeans*

17Terror and pit and snare await you, Jer 48:43
O people of the earth. Lk 21:35
18Whoever flees at the sound of terror Job 20:24
will fall into a pit;
whoever climbs out of the pit
will be caught in a snare.

The floodgates of the heavens are opened,
the foundations of the earth shake. Ps 18:7
19The earth is broken up,
the earth is split asunder, Dt 11:6
the earth is thoroughly shaken.
20The earth reels like a drunkard, Isa 19:14
it sways like a hut in the wind;
so heavy upon it is the guilt of its rebellion
that it falls—never to rise again. Ps 46:2

21In that day the LORD will punish Isa 10:12
the powers in the heavens above
and the kings on the earth below. Isa 2:12
22They will be herded together
like prisoners bound in a dungeon; Isa 10:4
they will be shut up in prison
and be punished[a] after many days. Eze 38:8
23The moon will be abashed, the sun ashamed;
for the LORD Almighty will reign Rev 22:5
on Mount Zion and in Jerusalem, Heb 12:22
and before its elders, gloriously. Isa 60:19

Praise to the LORD

25 O LORD, you are my God; Isa 7:13
I will exalt you and praise your name,
for in perfect faithfulness Isa 11:5
you have done marvelous things, Ps 98:1
things planned long ago. Nu 23:19; Eph 1:11
2You have made the city a heap of rubble,
the fortified town a ruin, Isa 17:3
the foreigners' stronghold a city no more;
it will never be rebuilt.
3Therefore strong peoples will honor you; Ex 6:2
cities of ruthless nations will revere you.
4You have been a refuge for the poor, Isa 4:6
a refuge for the needy in his distress,
a shelter from the storm Ps 55:8
and a shade from the heat.
For the breath of the ruthless Isa 29:5; 49:25
is like a storm driving against a wall
5 and like the heat of the desert.
You silence the uproar of foreigners; Jer 51:55
as heat is reduced by the shadow of a
cloud,
so the song of the ruthless is stilled.

6On this mountain the LORD Almighty will
prepare Isa 2:2
a feast of rich food for all peoples, Mt 8:11
a banquet of aged wine—
the best of meats and the finest of wines.
7On this mountain he will destroy
the shroud that enfolds all peoples,
the sheet that covers all nations;
8 he will swallow up death forever. Hos 13:14
The Sovereign LORD will wipe away the tears
from all faces;
he will remove the disgrace of his people
from all the earth.
The LORD has spoken.

9In that day they will say,

"Surely this is our God; Isa 40:9
we trusted in him, and he saved us. Ps 20:5
This is the LORD, we trusted in him;
let us rejoice and be glad in his salvation."
10The hand of the LORD will rest on this
mountain; Isa 2:2
but Moab will be trampled under him
as straw is trampled down in the manure.
11They will spread out their hands in it,
as a swimmer spreads out his hands to
swim.
God will bring down their pride Job 40:12; Isa 5:25
despite the cleverness[b] of their hands.
12He will bring down your high fortified walls
and lay them low; Isa 15:1
he will bring them down to the ground,
to the very dust.

A Song of Praise

26 In that day this song will be sung in the land of Judah:

We have a strong city; Isa 14:32
God makes salvation
its walls and ramparts. Isa 60:18; Zec 2:5
2Open the gates
that the righteous nation may enter, Isa 54:14
the nation that keeps faith.
3You will keep in perfect peace Php 4:7
him whose mind is steadfast,
because he trusts in you. Ps 22:5; Isa 12:2

LIVING  **INSIGHT**

God wants our total trust. Nothing held back. No games. No empty, pious-sounding words. No, He commands our absolute confidence. There is no area that He is unable to handle. God is a specialist in every circumstance—including yours. Today.

(See Isaiah 26:3–4.)

4Trust in the LORD forever, Isa 12:2; 50:10
for the LORD, the LORD, is the Rock eternal.
5He humbles those who dwell on high,

[a] 22 Or *released* [b] 11 The meaning of the Hebrew for this word is uncertain.

he lays the lofty city low;
he levels it to the ground Isa 25:12
and casts it down to the dust.
6Feet trample it down—
the feet of the oppressed,
the footsteps of the poor. Isa 3:15

7The path of the righteous is level;
O upright One, you make the way of the righteous smooth. Isa 42:16
8Yes, LORD, walking in the way of your laws,[a]
we wait for you; Ps 37:9
your name and renown Isa 12:4
are the desire of our hearts.
9My soul yearns for you in the night;
in the morning my spirit longs for you.
When your judgments come upon the earth,
the people of the world learn righteousness.
10Though grace is shown to the wicked,
they do not learn righteousness;
even in a land of uprightness they go on doing evil Isa 32:6
and regard not the majesty of the LORD.
11O LORD, your hand is lifted high,
but they do not see it. Isa 44:9,18
Let them see your zeal for your people and be put to shame;
let the fire reserved for your enemies
consume them. Heb 10:27

12LORD, you establish peace for us; Ps 119:165; Isa 9:6
all that we have accomplished you have done for us. Ps 68:28
13O LORD, our God, other lords besides you
have ruled over us, Isa 2:8; 10:5,11
but your name alone do we honor. Isa 63:7
14They are now dead, they live no more; Dt 4:28
those departed spirits do not rise.
You punished them and brought them to ruin; Isa 10:3
you wiped out all memory of them.
15You have enlarged the nation, O LORD;
you have enlarged the nation. Isa 14:2
You have gained glory for yourself;
you have extended all the borders of the land. Isa 33:17

16LORD, they came to you in their distress;
when you disciplined them,
they could barely whisper a prayer.[b]
17As a woman with child and about to give birth Jn 16:21
writhes and cries out in her pain,
so were we in your presence, O LORD.
18We were with child, we writhed in pain,
but we gave birth to wind. Isa 33:11; 59:4
We have not brought salvation to the earth;
we have not given birth to people of the world. Isa 42:6
19But your dead will live; Isa 25:8; Eph 5:14
their bodies will rise.
You who dwell in the dust, Ps 22:29
wake up and shout for joy.
Your dew is like the dew of the morning;
the earth will give birth to her dead.

20Go, my people, enter your rooms
and shut the doors behind you; Ex 12:23
hide yourselves for a little while Ps 91:1,4
until his wrath has passed by. Ps 30:5; Isa 54:7-8
21See, the LORD is coming out of his dwelling
to punish the people of the earth for their sins. Isa 13:9,11; 30:12-14
The earth will disclose the blood shed upon her; Job 16:18; Lk 11:50-51
she will conceal her slain no longer.

Deliverance of Israel

27 In that day,

the LORD will punish with his sword, Isa 34:6
his fierce, great and powerful sword,
Leviathan the gliding serpent, Job 3:8
Leviathan the coiling serpent;
he will slay the monster of the sea. Ps 74:13

2In that day—

"Sing about a fruitful vineyard: Jer 2:21
3 I, the LORD, watch over it;
I water it continually. Isa 58:11
I guard it day and night Ps 91:4
so that no one may harm it. Jn 6:39
4 I am not angry.
If only there were briers and thorns
confronting me!
I would march against them in battle;
I would set them all on fire. Isa 10:17; Mt 3:12
5Or else let them come to me for refuge; Isa 25:4
let them make peace with me, Job 22:21; Ro 5:1
yes, let them make peace with me."

6In days to come Jacob will take root, Isa 11:10
Israel will bud and blossom Hos 14:5-6
and fill all the world with fruit. Isa 37:31

7Has ⌞the LORD⌟ struck her
as he struck down those who struck her?
Has she been killed
as those were killed who killed her?
8By warfare[c] and exile you contend with her— Isa 50:1; 54:7
with his fierce blast he drives her out,
as on a day the east wind blows.
9By this, then, will Jacob's guilt be atoned for,

[a] 8 Or *judgments* [b] 16 The meaning of the Hebrew for this clause is uncertain. [c] 8 See Septuagint; the meaning of the Hebrew for this word is uncertain.

and this will be the full fruitage of the
removal of his sin: Ro 11:27*
When he makes all the altar stones
to be like chalk stones crushed to pieces,
no Asherah poles[a] or incense altars Ex 34:13
will be left standing.
10 The fortified city stands desolate, Isa 32:14; Jer 26:6
an abandoned settlement, forsaken like the
desert; Isa 5:5
there the calves graze,
there they lie down; Isa 17:2
they strip its branches bare.
11 When its twigs are dry, they are broken off
and women come and make fires with
them.
For this is a people without understanding;
so their Maker has no compassion on
them,
and their Creator shows them no favor.

12 In that day the LORD will thresh from the flowing Euphrates[b] to the Wadi of Egypt, and you,
O Israelites, will be gathered up one by one. 13 And
in that day a great trumpet will sound. Those who
were perishing in Assyria and those who were exiled in Egypt will come and worship the LORD on
the holy mountain in Jerusalem. Isa 2:2; Lev 25:9

Woe to Ephraim

28 Woe to that wreath, the pride of
Ephraim's drunkards, ver 3; Isa 9:9
to the fading flower, his glorious beauty,
set on the head of a fertile valley— ver 4
to that city, the pride of those laid low by
wine! Hos 7:5
2 See, the Lord has one who is powerful and
strong. Isa 40:10
Like a hailstorm and a destructive wind,
like a driving rain and a flooding downpour,
he will throw it forcefully to the ground.
3 That wreath, the pride of Ephraim's
drunkards,
will be trampled underfoot. Job 40:12; Isa 5:5
4 That fading flower, his glorious beauty,
set on the head of a fertile valley,
will be like a fig ripe before harvest— Hos 9:10
as soon as someone sees it and takes it in
his hand,
he swallows it.

5 In that day the LORD Almighty
will be a glorious crown, Isa 62:3
a beautiful wreath
for the remnant of his people. Isa 1:9
6 He will be a spirit of justice Isa 11:2-4
to him who sits in judgment, Jn 5:30
a source of strength
to those who turn back the battle at the
gate. 2Ch 32:8

7 And these also stagger from wine Isa 22:13
and reel from beer: Isa 56:10-12
Priests and prophets stagger from beer Isa 9:15
and are befuddled with wine;
they reel from beer,
they stagger when seeing visions, Isa 29:11
they stumble when rendering decisions.
8 All the tables are covered with vomit Jer 48:26
and there is not a spot without filth.

9 "Who is it he is trying to teach? ver 26; Isa 30:20
To whom is he explaining his message?
To children weaned from their milk, Ps 131:2
to those just taken from the breast?
10 For it is:
Do and do, do and do,
rule on rule, rule on rule[c];
a little here, a little there."

11 Very well then, with foreign lips and strange
tongues Isa 33:19
God will speak to this people, 1Co 14:21*
12 to whom he said,
"This is the resting place, let the weary
rest"; Mt 11:28-29; Isa 11:10
and, "This is the place of repose"—
but they would not listen.
13 So then, the word of the LORD to them will
become:
Do and do, do and do,
rule on rule, rule on rule;
a little here, a little there—
so that they will go and fall backward,
be injured and snared and captured. Mt 21:44

14 Therefore hear the word of the LORD, you
scoffers Isa 1:10
who rule this people in Jerusalem.
15 You boast, "We have entered into a covenant
with death,
with the grave[d] we have made an
agreement.
When an overwhelming scourge sweeps by,
it cannot touch us,
for we have made a lie our refuge Isa 9:15
and falsehood[e] our hiding place." Isa 29:15

16 So this is what the Sovereign LORD says:

"See, I lay a stone in Zion,
a tested stone, Ps 118:22; Ac 4:11; Eph 2:20
a precious cornerstone for a sure foundation;
the one who trusts will never be dismayed.

[a] 9 That is, symbols of the goddess Asherah [b] 12 Hebrew *River* [c] 10 Hebrew / *sav lasav sav lasav* / *kav lakav kav lakav* (possibly meaningless sounds; perhaps a mimicking of the prophet's words); also in verse 13 [d] 15 Hebrew *Sheol*; also in verse 18 [e] 15 Or *false gods*

17 I will make justice the measuring line Isa 5:16
and righteousness the plumb line; 2Ki 21:13
hail will sweep away your refuge, the lie,
and water will overflow your hiding place.
18 Your covenant with death will be annulled;
your agreement with the grave will not stand. Isa 7:7
When the overwhelming scourge sweeps by,
you will be beaten down by it. Da 8:13
19 As often as it comes it will carry you away;
morning after morning, by day and by night,
it will sweep through."

The understanding of this message
will bring sheer terror. Job 18:11
20 The bed is too short to stretch out on,
the blanket too narrow to wrap around you. Isa 59:6
21 The LORD will rise up as he did at Mount Perazim, 1Ch 14:11
he will rouse himself as in the Valley of Gibeon— Jos 10:10,12; 1Ch 14:16
to do his work, his strange work, Isa 10:12
and perform his task, his alien task.
22 Now stop your mocking,
or your chains will become heavier;
the Lord, the LORD Almighty, has told me
of the destruction decreed against the whole land. Isa 10:22-23

23 Listen and hear my voice; Isa 32:9
pay attention and hear what I say.
24 When a farmer plows for planting, does he plow continually? Ecc 3:2
Does he keep on breaking up and harrowing the soil?
25 When he has leveled the surface,
does he not sow caraway and scatter cummin? Mt 23:23
Does he not plant wheat in its place,[a]
barley in its plot,[a]
and spelt in its field? Ex 9:32
26 His God instructs him
and teaches him the right way. Ps 94:10

27 Caraway is not threshed with a sledge, Job 41:30
nor is a cartwheel rolled over cummin;
caraway is beaten out with a rod, Isa 10:5
and cummin with a stick.
28 Grain must be ground to make bread;
so one does not go on threshing it forever.
Though he drives the wheels of his threshing cart over it, Isa 21:10
his horses do not grind it.
29 All this also comes from the LORD Almighty,
wonderful in counsel and magnificent in wisdom. Isa 9:6; Ro 11:33

Woe to David's City

29 Woe to you, Ariel, Ariel, 2Sa 5:9; Isa 22:12-13
the city where David settled! 2Sa 5:7
Add year to year
and let your cycle of festivals go on. Isa 1:14
2 Yet I will besiege Ariel;
she will mourn and lament, Isa 3:26; La 2:5
she will be to me like an altar hearth.[b]
3 I will encamp against you all around;
I will encircle you with towers Lk 19:43-44
and set up my siege works against you.
4 Brought low, you will speak from the ground;
your speech will mumble out of the dust.
Your voice will come ghostlike from the earth;
out of the dust your speech will whisper.

5 But your many enemies will become like fine dust,
the ruthless hordes like blown chaff. Isa 17:13
Suddenly, in an instant, Isa 17:14 1Th 5:3
6 the LORD Almighty will come Zec 14:1-5
with thunder and earthquake and great noise,
with windstorm and tempest and flames of a devouring fire. Ps 83:13-15
7 Then the hordes of all the nations that fight against Ariel, Mic 4:11-12; Zec 12:9
that attack her and her fortress and besiege her,
will be as it is with a dream, Job 20:8
with a vision in the night—
8 as when a hungry man dreams that he is eating,
but he awakens, and his hunger remains;
as when a thirsty man dreams that he is drinking,
but he awakens faint, with his thirst unquenched.
So will it be with the hordes of all the nations
that fight against Mount Zion. Isa 17:12-14; 54:17

9 Be stunned and amazed, Jer 4:9; Hab 1:5
blind yourselves and be sightless; Isa 6:10
be drunk, but not from wine, Isa 51:21-22
stagger, but not from beer. Isa 3:12
10 The LORD has brought over you a deep sleep:
He has sealed your eyes (the prophets);
he has covered your heads (the seers).

11 For you this whole vision is nothing but words
sealed in a scroll. And if you give the scroll to
someone who can read, and say to him, "Read
this, please," he will answer, "I can't; it is sealed."
12 Or if you give the scroll to someone who cannot
read, and say, "Read this, please," he will answer,
"I don't know how to read." Isa 8:16; Mt 13:11; Rev 5:1-2

13 The Lord says:

[a] 25 The meaning of the Hebrew for this word is uncertain. [b] 2 The Hebrew for *altar hearth* sounds like the Hebrew for *Ariel*.

"These people come near to me with their
mouth Jer 14:11; Hag 1:2
and honor me with their lips, Ps 50:16
but their hearts are far from me. Eze 33:31
Their worship of me
is made up only of rules taught by
men.[a]
14Therefore once more I will astound these
people
with wonder upon wonder; Hab 1:5
the wisdom of the wise will perish, Jer 49:7
the intelligence of the intelligent will
vanish." 1Co 1:19*
15Woe to those who go to great depths
to hide their plans from the LORD, Isa 28:15
who do their work in darkness and think,
"Who sees us? Who will know?" Job 22:13
16You turn things upside down,
as if the potter were thought to be like the
clay! Job 10:9
Shall what is formed say to him who formed
it, Ge 2:7
"He did not make me"?
Can the pot say of the potter, Isa 45:9; Ro 9:20-21*
"He knows nothing"? Job 9:12

17In a very short time, will not Lebanon be
turned into a fertile field Ps 84:6
and the fertile field seem like a forest?
18In that day the deaf will hear the words of the
scroll, Mk 7:37
and out of gloom and darkness
the eyes of the blind will see. Isa 35:5; Mt 11:5
19Once more the humble will rejoice in the
LORD; Isa 61:1; Mt 5:5; 11:29
the needy will rejoice in the Holy One of
Israel. Jas 2:5; Isa 14:30
20The ruthless will vanish,
the mockers will disappear, Isa 28:22
and all who have an eye for evil will be cut
down— Isa 59:4; Mic 2:1
21those who with a word make a man out to be
guilty,
who ensnare the defender in court Am 5:10,15
and with false testimony deprive the
innocent of justice. Isa 32:7

22Therefore this is what the LORD, who redeemed Abraham, says to the house of Jacob:

"No longer will Jacob be ashamed; Isa 49:23
no longer will their faces grow pale.
23When they see among them their children,
the work of my hands, Isa 19:25
they will keep my name holy; Mt 6:9
they will acknowledge the holiness of the
Holy One of Jacob, Isa 5:19
and will stand in awe of the God of Israel.
24Those who are wayward in spirit will gain
understanding; Isa 28:7; Heb 5:2; Isa 41:20
those who complain will accept
instruction." Isa 30:21

LIVING  **INSIGHT**

When we take the time to reflect on and get to know our Almighty God, we discover He's holy and we're unholy. We discover that He's perfect and we're imperfect; He's strong and we're weak. Something occurs in the contrast that causes His character to overshadow our need. The result is marvelous—the knowledge of the Holy One equips us to see the truth and to begin to change.

(See Isaiah 29:22–24.)

Woe to the Obstinate Nation

30 "Woe to the obstinate children," Isa 29:15
declares the LORD,
"to those who carry out plans that are not
mine,
forming an alliance, but not by my Spirit,
heaping sin upon sin;
2who go down to Egypt Isa 31:1
without consulting me; Nu 27:21
who look for help to Pharaoh's protection,
to Egypt's shade for refuge.
3But Pharaoh's protection will be to your shame,
Egypt's shade will bring you disgrace.
4Though they have officials in Zoan Isa 19:11
and their envoys have arrived in Hanes,
5everyone will be put to shame
because of a people useless to them, ver 7
who bring neither help nor advantage, Jer 37:3-5
but only shame and disgrace." 2Ki 18:21

6An oracle concerning the animals of the Negev:

Through a land of hardship and distress,
of lions and lionesses,
of adders and darting snakes, Dt 8:15
the envoys carry their riches on donkeys' backs,
their treasures on the humps of camels,
to that unprofitable nation,
7 to Egypt, whose help is utterly useless.
Therefore I call her
Rahab the Do-Nothing. Job 9:13

8Go now, write it on a tablet for them, Dt 27:8
inscribe it on a scroll, Isa 8:1; Hab 2:2
that for the days to come
it may be an everlasting witness. Jos 24:26-27
9These are rebellious people, deceitful children,

[a]13 Hebrew; Septuagint *They worship me in vain; / their teachings are but rules taught by men*

children unwilling to listen to the LORD's
instruction. Isa 1:10
10They say to the seers,
"See no more visions!" Jer 11:21; Am 7:13
and to the prophets,
"Give us no more visions of what is right!
Tell us pleasant things, 1Ki 22:8
prophesy illusions. Eze 13:7; Ro 16:18
11Leave this way, ver 21; Pr 3:6
get off this path,
and stop confronting us Job 21:14
with the Holy One of Israel!" Isa 29:19

12Therefore, this is what the Holy One of Israel
says: Isa 5:19

"Because you have rejected this message,
relied on oppression Isa 5:7
and depended on deceit,
13this sin will become for you
like a high wall, cracked and bulging, Ps 62:3
that collapses suddenly, in an instant.
14It will break in pieces like pottery, Ps 2:9
shattered so mercilessly
that among its pieces not a fragment will be
found
for taking coals from a hearth
or scooping water out of a cistern."

15This is what the Sovereign LORD, the Holy One
of Israel, says:

"In repentance and rest is your salvation,
in quietness and trust is your strength,
but you would have none of it. Isa 8:6; 42:24

LIVING  **INSIGHT**

What's something you feel pressured about? Are you trusting God with it? How about talking to Him right now about the pressure you're feeling. Trust God with it today, tomorrow and however long it takes for you to sense His—not your—control of it.

(See Isaiah 30:15.)

16You said, 'No, we will flee on horses.' Isa 31:1,3
Therefore you will flee!
You said, 'We will ride off on swift horses.'
Therefore your pursuers will be swift!
17A thousand will flee
at the threat of one;
at the threat of five Lev 26:8; Jos 23:10
you will all flee away, Dt 28:25
till you are left Isa 1:8
like a flagstaff on a mountaintop,
like a banner on a hill." Ps 20:5
18Yet the LORD longs to be gracious to you;
he rises to show you compassion. Ps 78:38
For the LORD is a God of justice. Isa 5:16
Blessed are all who wait for him! Isa 25:9

19O people of Zion, who live in Jerusalem, you
will weep no more. How gracious he will be when
you cry for help! As soon as he hears, he will
answer you. 20Although the Lord gives you the
bread of adversity and the water of affliction, your
teachers will be hidden no more; with your own
eyes you will see them. 21Whether you turn to the
right or to the left, your ears will hear a voice
behind you, saying, "This is the way; walk in it."
22Then you will defile your idols overlaid with silver and your images covered with gold; you will
throw them away like a menstrual cloth and say to
them, "Away with you!" Ps 74:9; Isa 29:24; Am 8:11

23He will also send you rain for the seed you
sow in the ground, and the food that comes from
the land will be rich and plentiful. In that day your
cattle will graze in broad meadows. 24The oxen
and donkeys that work the soil will eat fodder and
mash, spread out with fork and shovel. 25In the
day of great slaughter, when the towers fall,
streams of water will flow on every high mountain
and every lofty hill. 26The moon will shine like the
sun, and the sunlight will be seven times brighter,
like the light of seven full days, when the LORD
binds up the bruises of his people and heals the
wounds he inflicted. Isa 1:5; 60:19-20; Rev 21:23

27See, the Name of the LORD comes from afar,
with burning anger and dense clouds of
smoke; Isa 66:14
his lips are full of wrath, Isa 10:5
and his tongue is a consuming fire. Job 41:21
28His breath is like a rushing torrent, Isa 11:4
rising up to the neck. Isa 8:8
He shakes the nations in the sieve of
destruction; Am 9:9
he places in the jaws of the peoples
a bit that leads them astray. 2Ki 19:28; Isa 37:29
29And you will sing
as on the night you celebrate a holy festival;
your hearts will rejoice Isa 12:1
as when people go up with flutes
to the mountain of the LORD, Ps 42:4
to the Rock of Israel. Ge 49:24
30The LORD will cause men to hear his majestic
voice Ps 68:33
and will make them see his arm coming
down Isa 9:12; 40:10
with raging anger and consuming fire, Isa 10:25
with cloudburst, thunderstorm and hail.
31The voice of the LORD will shatter Assyria;
with his scepter he will strike them down.
32Every stroke the LORD lays on them
with his punishing rod

will be to the music of tambourines and harps,
as he fights them in battle with the blows of his arm. Isa 11:15; Eze 32:10
33Topheth has long been prepared;
it has been made ready for the king.
Its fire pit has been made deep and wide,
with an abundance of fire and wood;
the breath of the LORD,
like a stream of burning sulfur, Ge 19:24
sets it ablaze. Isa 1:31

Woe to Those Who Rely on Egypt

31 Woe to those who go down to Egypt for help, Isa 30:2,5
who rely on horses,
who trust in the multitude of their chariots
and in the great strength of their horsemen,
but do not look to the Holy One of Israel,
or seek help from the LORD. Ps 20:7; Da 9:13
2Yet he too is wise and can bring disaster;
he does not take back his words. Nu 23:19
He will rise up against the house of the wicked, Isa 32:6
against those who help evildoers.
3But the Egyptians are men and not God;
their horses are flesh and not spirit. Isa 30:16
When the LORD stretches out his hand,
he who helps will stumble,
he who is helped will fall; Isa 30:5-7
both will perish together. Isa 20:6; Jer 17:5

4This is what the LORD says to me:

"As a lion growls, Am 3:8
a great lion over his prey—
and though a whole band of shepherds
is called together against him,
he is not frightened by their shouts
or disturbed by their clamor—
so the LORD Almighty will come down Isa 42:13
to do battle on Mount Zion and on its heights.
5Like birds hovering overhead,
the LORD Almighty will shield Jerusalem;
he will shield it and deliver it, Isa 37:35; 38:6
he will 'pass over' it and will rescue it."

6Return to him you have so greatly revolted
against, O Israelites. 7For in that day every one of
you will reject the idols of silver and gold your
sinful hands have made. Isa 2:20; 30:22

8"Assyria will fall by a sword that is not of man; Isa 10:12
a sword, not of mortals, will devour them.
They will flee before the sword
and their young men will be put to forced labor. Ge 49:15
9Their stronghold will fall because of terror;
at sight of the battle standard their
commanders will panic," Isa 18:3; Jer 51:9
declares the LORD,
whose fire is in Zion, Isa 10:17
whose furnace is in Jerusalem. Mal 4:1

The Kingdom of Righteousness

32 See, a king will reign in righteousness
and rulers will rule with justice. Isa 9:7
2Each man will be like a shelter from the wind
and a refuge from the storm, Ps 55:8
like streams of water in the desert Ps 23:2; 107:35
and the shadow of a great rock in a thirsty land.

3Then the eyes of those who see will no longer be closed, Isa 29:18
and the ears of those who hear will listen.
4The mind of the rash will know and understand, Isa 29:24
and the stammering tongue will be fluent and clear. Isa 35:6
5No longer will the fool be called noble 1Sa 25:25
nor the scoundrel be highly respected.
6For the fool speaks folly, Pr 19:3
his mind is busy with evil: Pr 24:2; Isa 26:10
He practices ungodliness Isa 9:17
and spreads error concerning the LORD;
the hungry he leaves empty Isa 3:15
and from the thirsty he withholds water.
7The scoundrel's methods are wicked, Jer 5:26-28
he makes up evil schemes Mic 7:3
to destroy the poor with lies,
even when the plea of the needy is just.
8But the noble man makes noble plans,
and by noble deeds he stands. Pr 11:25

The Women of Jerusalem

9You women who are so complacent,
rise up and listen to me; Isa 28:23
you daughters who feel secure, Isa 47:8; Am 6:1
hear what I have to say!
10In little more than a year
you who feel secure will tremble;
the grape harvest will fail, Isa 5:5-6; 24:7
and the harvest of fruit will not come.
11Tremble, you complacent women;
shudder, you daughters who feel secure!
Strip off your clothes, Isa 47:2
put sackcloth around your waists. Isa 3:24
12Beat your breasts for the pleasant fields, Na 2:7
for the fruitful vines Isa 16:9
13and for the land of my people,
a land overgrown with thorns and briers—
yes, mourn for all houses of merriment
and for this city of revelry. Isa 22:2
14The fortress will be abandoned, Isa 13:22
the noisy city deserted; Isa 6:11

citadel and watchtower will become a
wasteland forever, Isa 34:13
the delight of donkeys, a pasture for flocks,
15till the Spirit is poured upon us from on high,
and the desert becomes a fertile field,
and the fertile field seems like a forest.
16Justice will dwell in the desert Isa 9:7; 35:1,6; 42:11
and righteousness live in the fertile field.
17The fruit of righteousness will be peace;
the effect of righteousness will be quietness
and confidence forever. Isa 30:15
18My people will live in peaceful dwelling places,
in secure homes, Isa 26:1; Am 9:14
in undisturbed places of rest. Hos 2:18-23
19Though hail flattens the forest Isa 30:30; Zec 11:2
and the city is leveled completely, Isa 24:10
20how blessed you will be,
sowing your seed by every stream, Ecc 11:1
and letting your cattle and donkeys range
free. Isa 30:24

Distress and Help

33 Woe to you, O destroyer,
you who have not been destroyed!
Woe to you, O traitor,
you who have not been betrayed!
When you stop destroying,
you will be destroyed; Hab 2:8; Mt 7:2
when you stop betraying,
you will be betrayed. Isa 21:2

2O LORD, be gracious to us;
we long for you.
Be our strength every morning, Isa 40:10; 51:9
our salvation in time of distress. Isa 5:30; 25:9
3At the thunder of your voice, the peoples flee;
when you rise up, the nations scatter.
4Your plunder, O nations, is harvested as by
young locusts; Joel 1:4
like a swarm of locusts men pounce on it.

5The LORD is exalted, for he dwells on high;
he will fill Zion with justice and
righteousness. Isa 1:26; 28:6
6He will be the sure foundation for your times,
a rich store of salvation and wisdom and
knowledge; Isa 51:6
the fear of the LORD is the key to this
treasure.[a] Isa 11:2-3; Mt 6:33

7Look, their brave men cry aloud in the streets;
the envoys of peace weep bitterly. 2Ki 18:37
8The highways are deserted,
no travelers are on the roads. Jdg 5:6; Isa 35:8
The treaty is broken,
its witnesses[b] are despised,
no one is respected.
9The land mourns[c] and wastes away, Isa 3:26
Lebanon is ashamed and withers; Isa 2:13; 24:4
Sharon is like the Arabah, 1Ch 27:29
and Bashan and Carmel drop their leaves.

10"Now will I arise," says the LORD. Ps 12:5; Isa 2:21
"Now will I be exalted; Isa 5:16
now will I be lifted up.
11You conceive chaff, Ps 7:14; Isa 59:4
you give birth to straw; Isa 26:18
your breath is a fire that consumes you.
12The peoples will be burned as if to lime;
like cut thornbushes they will be set
ablaze." Isa 10:17

13You who are far away, hear what I have done;
you who are near, acknowledge my power!
14The sinners in Zion are terrified;
trembling grips the godless: Isa 32:11
"Who of us can dwell with the consuming
fire? Isa 30:30; Heb 12:29
Who of us can dwell with everlasting
burning?"
15He who walks righteously Isa 58:8
and speaks what is right, Ps 15:2; 24:4
who rejects gain from extortion
and keeps his hand from accepting bribes,
who stops his ears against plots of murder
and shuts his eyes against contemplating
evil— Ps 119:37
16this is the man who will dwell on the heights,
whose refuge will be the mountain fortress.
His bread will be supplied,
and water will not fail him. Isa 49:10

17Your eyes will see the king in his beauty Isa 6:5
and view a land that stretches afar. Isa 26:15
18In your thoughts you will ponder the former
terror: Isa 17:14
"Where is that chief officer?
Where is the one who took the revenue?
Where is the officer in charge of the
towers?" Isa 2:15
19You will see those arrogant people no more,
those people of an obscure speech,
with their strange, incomprehensible
tongue. Isa 28:11; Jer 5:15

20Look upon Zion, the city of our festivals;
your eyes will see Jerusalem,
a peaceful abode, a tent that will not be
moved; Ps 46:5; 125:1-2; Isa 32:18
its stakes will never be pulled up,
nor any of its ropes broken.
21There the LORD will be our Mighty One.
It will be like a place of broad rivers and
streams. Isa 41:18; 48:18
No galley with oars will ride them,
no mighty ship will sail them.
22For the LORD is our judge, Isa 11:4
the LORD is our lawgiver, Isa 2:3; Jas 4:12

[a]6 Or *is a treasure from him* [b]8 Dead Sea Scrolls; Masoretic Text / *the cities* [c]9 Or *dries up*

the LORD is our king; Ps 89:18
it is he who will save us. Isa 25:9

23Your rigging hangs loose:
The mast is not held secure,
the sail is not spread.
Then an abundance of spoils will be divided
and even the lame will carry off plunder.
24No one living in Zion will say, "I am ill";
and the sins of those who dwell there will
be forgiven. Jer 50:20; 1Jn 1:7-9

Judgment Against the Nations

34 Come near, you nations, and listen;
pay attention, you peoples! Isa 41:1; 43:9
Let the earth hear, and all that is in it, Ps 49:1
the world, and all that comes out of it!
2The LORD is angry with all nations;
his wrath is upon all their armies.
He will totally destroy[a] them, Isa 13:5
he will give them over to slaughter. Isa 30:25
3Their slain will be thrown out,
their dead bodies will send up a stench;
the mountains will be soaked with their
blood. Eze 14:19; 35:6; 38:22
4All the stars of the heavens will be dissolved
and the sky rolled up like a scroll; Eze 32:7-8
all the starry host will fall Joel 2:31; Mt 24:29*; Rev 6:13
like withered leaves from the vine, Isa 15:6
like shriveled figs from the fig tree.

5My sword has drunk its fill in the heavens;
see, it descends in judgment on Edom,
the people I have totally destroyed. Mal 1:4
6The sword of the LORD is bathed in blood,
it is covered with fat—
the blood of lambs and goats,
fat from the kidneys of rams.
For the LORD has a sacrifice in Bozrah Ge 36:33
and a great slaughter in Edom. Isa 30:25
7And the wild oxen will fall with them,
the bull calves and the great bulls. Ps 68:30
Their land will be drenched with blood,
and the dust will be soaked with fat.

8For the LORD has a day of vengeance, Isa 63:4
a year of retribution, to uphold Zion's
cause. Isa 59:18; Joel 3:4
9Edom's streams will be turned into pitch,
her dust into burning sulfur; Ge 19:24
her land will become blazing pitch!
10It will not be quenched night and day;
its smoke will rise forever. Rev 14:10-11; 19:3
From generation to generation it will lie
desolate; Isa 13:20; Eze 29:12; Mal 1:3
no one will ever pass through it again.
11The desert owl[b] and screech owl[b] will
possess it; Zep 2:14
the great owl[b] and the raven will nest
there.
God will stretch out over Edom Isa 21:11; Eze 35:15
the measuring line of chaos
and the plumb line of desolation. 2Ki 21:13
12Her nobles will have nothing there to be
called a kingdom,
all her princes will vanish away. Isa 41:11-12
13Thorns will overrun her citadels,
nettles and brambles her strongholds.
She will become a haunt for jackals, Ps 44:19
a home for owls.
14Desert creatures will meet with hyenas, Isa 13:22
and wild goats will bleat to each other;
there the night creatures will also repose
and find for themselves places of rest.
15The owl will nest there and lay eggs,
she will hatch them, and care for her young
under the shadow of her wings;
there also the falcons will gather, Dt 14:13
each with its mate.

16Look in the scroll of the LORD and read:

None of these will be missing, Isa 40:26
not one will lack her mate.
For it is his mouth that has given the order,
and his Spirit will gather them together.
17He allots their portions; Isa 17:14; Jer 13:25
his hand distributes them by measure.
They will possess it forever
and dwell there from generation to
generation. ver 10

Joy of the Redeemed

35 The desert and the parched land will be
glad; Isa 27:10; 41:18-19
the wilderness will rejoice and blossom.
Like the crocus, 2it will burst into bloom;
it will rejoice greatly and shout for joy.
The glory of Lebanon will be given to it,
the splendor of Carmel and Sharon; SS 7:5
they will see the glory of the LORD, Ex 16:7; Isa 4:5
the splendor of our God. Isa 25:9

3Strengthen the feeble hands,
steady the knees that give way; Job 4:4
4say to those with fearful hearts, Isa 40:2; Zec 1:13
"Be strong, do not fear; Isa 7:4; Da 10:19
your God will come, Isa 62:11
he will come with vengeance; Isa 1:24
with divine retribution
he will come to save you." Isa 25:9

5Then will the eyes of the blind be opened
and the ears of the deaf unstopped. Isa 29:18
6Then will the lame leap like a deer, Mt 15:30
and the mute tongue shout for joy. Mt 9:32-33

[a]2 The Hebrew term refers to the irrevocable giving over of things or persons to the LORD, often by totally destroying them; also in verse 5. [b]11 The precise identification of these birds is uncertain.

Water will gush forth in the wilderness
and streams in the desert. Isa 41:18; Jn 7:38
7The burning sand will become a pool,
the thirsty ground bubbling springs. Isa 49:10
In the haunts where jackals once lay, Isa 13:22
grass and reeds and papyrus will grow.

8And a highway will be there; Isa 11:16; Mt 7:13-14
it will be called the Way of Holiness. Isa 4:3
The unclean will not journey on it; Isa 52:1
it will be for those who walk in that Way;
wicked fools will not go about on it.[a]
9No lion will be there, Isa 30:6
nor will any ferocious beast get up on it;
they will not be found there.
But only the redeemed will walk there, Isa 51:11
10 and the ransomed of the LORD will return.
They will enter Zion with singing;
everlasting joy will crown their heads.
Gladness and joy will overtake them, Ps 51:8
and sorrow and sighing will flee away.

LIVING  **INSIGHT**

When God's joy invades our lives, it spills over into everything we do and onto everyone we touch.

(See Isaiah 35:10.)

Sennacherib Threatens Jerusalem

36 In the fourteenth year of King Hezekiah's
reign, Sennacherib king of Assyria attacked
all the fortified cities of Judah and captured them.
2Then the king of Assyria sent his field commander with a large army from Lachish to King Hezekiah at Jerusalem. When the commander stopped at
the aqueduct of the Upper Pool, on the road to the
Washerman's Field, 3Eliakim son of Hilkiah the
palace administrator, Shebna the secretary, and
Joah son of Asaph the recorder went out to him.
4The field commander said to them, "Tell Hezekiah,

" 'This is what the great king, the king of
Assyria, says: On what are you basing this
confidence of yours? 5You say you have
strategy and military strength—but you
speak only empty words. On whom are you
depending, that you rebel against me? 6Look
now, you are depending on Egypt, that
splintered reed of a staff, which pierces a
man's hand and wounds him if he leans on
it! Such is Pharaoh king of Egypt to all who
depend on him. 7And if you say to me, "We
are depending on the LORD our God"—isn't
he the one whose high places and altars
Hezekiah removed, saying to Judah and
Jerusalem, "You must worship before this
altar"?

8" 'Come now, make a bargain with my
master, the king of Assyria: I will give you
two thousand horses—if you can put riders
on them! 9How then can you repulse one
officer of the least of my master's officials,
even though you are depending on Egypt for
chariots and horsemen? 10Furthermore, have
I come to attack and destroy this land without the LORD? The LORD himself told me to
march against this country and destroy it.' "

11Then Eliakim, Shebna and Joah said to the
field commander, "Please speak to your servants
in Aramaic, since we understand it. Don't speak to
us in Hebrew in the hearing of the people on the
wall." Ezr 4:7
12But the commander replied, "Was it only to
your master and you that my master sent me to
say these things, and not to the men sitting on the
wall—who, like you, will have to eat their own
filth and drink their own urine?"
13Then the commander stood and called out in
Hebrew, "Hear the words of the great king, the
king of Assyria! 14This is what the king says: Do
not let Hezekiah deceive you. He cannot deliver
you! 15Do not let Hezekiah persuade you to trust
in the LORD when he says, 'The LORD will surely
deliver us; this city will not be given into the hand
of the king of Assyria.' 2Ch 32:18; Isa 37:10
16"Do not listen to Hezekiah. This is what the
king of Assyria says: Make peace with me and
come out to me. Then every one of you will eat
from his own vine and fig tree and drink water
from his own cistern, 17until I come and take you
to a land like your own—a land of grain and new
wine, a land of bread and vineyards. Pr 5:15
18"Do not let Hezekiah mislead you when he
says, 'The LORD will deliver us.' Has the god of any
nation ever delivered his land from the hand of the
king of Assyria? 19Where are the gods of Hamath
and Arpad? Where are the gods of Sepharvaim?
Have they rescued Samaria from my hand? 20Who
of all the gods of these countries has been able to
save his land from me? How then can the LORD
deliver Jerusalem from my hand?" 1Ki 20:23
21But the people remained silent and said nothing in reply, because the king had commanded,
"Do not answer him." Pr 9:7-8
22Then Eliakim son of Hilkiah the palace administrator, Shebna the secretary, and Joah son of
Asaph the recorder went to Hezekiah, with their
clothes torn, and told him what the field commander had said. 2Ki 18:17-37; 2Ch 32:9-19

[a]8 Or / *the simple will not stray from it*

Jerusalem's Deliverance Foretold

37 When King Hezekiah heard this, he tore his clothes and put on sackcloth and went into the temple of the LORD. 2He sent Eliakim the palace administrator, Shebna the secretary, and the leading priests, all wearing sackcloth, to the prophet Isaiah son of Amoz. 3They told him, "This is what Hezekiah says: This day is a day of distress and rebuke and disgrace, as when children come to the point of birth and there is no strength to deliver them. 4It may be that the LORD your God will hear the words of the field commander, whom his master, the king of Assyria, has sent to ridicule the living God, and that he will rebuke him for the words the LORD your God has heard. Therefore pray for the remnant that still survives." 1Sa 7:8

5When King Hezekiah's officials came to Isaiah, 6Isaiah said to them, "Tell your master, 'This is what the LORD says: Do not be afraid of what you have heard—those words with which the underlings of the king of Assyria have blasphemed me. 7Listen! I am going to put a spirit in him so that when he hears a certain report, he will return to his own country, and there I will have him cut down with the sword.' " Isa 7:4

8When the field commander heard that the king of Assyria had left Lachish, he withdrew and found the king fighting against Libnah. Nu 33:20

9Now Sennacherib received a report that Tirhakah, the Cushite[a] king ⌞of Egypt⌟, was marching out to fight against him. When he heard it, he sent messengers to Hezekiah with this word: 10"Say to Hezekiah king of Judah: Do not let the god you depend on deceive you when he says, 'Jerusalem will not be handed over to the king of Assyria.' 11Surely you have heard what the kings of Assyria have done to all the countries, destroying them completely. And will you be delivered? 12Did the gods of the nations that were destroyed by my forefathers deliver them—the gods of Gozan, Haran, Rezeph and the people of Eden who were in Tel Assar? 13Where is the king of Hamath, the king of Arpad, the king of the city of Sepharvaim, or of Hena or Ivvah?" 2Ki 19:1-13

Hezekiah's Prayer

14Hezekiah received the letter from the messengers and read it. Then he went up to the temple of the LORD and spread it out before the LORD. 15And Hezekiah prayed to the LORD: 16"O LORD Almighty, God of Israel, enthroned between the cherubim, you alone are God over all the kingdoms of the earth. You have made heaven and earth. 17Give ear, O LORD, and hear; open your eyes, O LORD, and see; listen to all the words Sennacherib has sent to insult the living God.

18"It is true, O LORD, that the Assyrian kings have laid waste all these peoples and their lands. 19They have thrown their gods into the fire and destroyed them, for they were not gods but only wood and stone, fashioned by human hands. 20Now, O LORD our God, deliver us from his hand, so that all kingdoms on earth may know that you alone, O LORD, are God.[b]" 2Ki 19:14-19; Ps 46:10

Sennacherib's Fall

21Then Isaiah son of Amoz sent a message to Hezekiah: "This is what the LORD, the God of Israel, says: Because you have prayed to me concerning Sennacherib king of Assyria, 22this is the word the LORD has spoken against him:

"The Virgin Daughter of Zion
despises and mocks you.
The Daughter of Jerusalem
tosses her head as you flee. Job 16:4
23Who is it you have insulted and blasphemed?
Against whom have you raised your voice
and lifted your eyes in pride? Isa 2:11
Against the Holy One of Israel! Isa 1:4; 12:6
24By your messengers
you have heaped insults on the Lord.
And you have said,
'With my many chariots
I have ascended the heights of the mountains,
the utmost heights of Lebanon. Isa 14:8
I have cut down its tallest cedars,
the choicest of its pines. 1Ki 5:8-10; Isa 41:19
I have reached its remotest heights,
the finest of its forests.
25I have dug wells in foreign lands[c]
and drunk the water there.
With the soles of my feet
I have dried up all the streams of Egypt.'

26"Have you not heard?
Long ago I ordained it. Ac 2:23; 4:27-28; 1Pe 2:8
In days of old I planned it; Isa 10:6; 25:1
now I have brought it to pass,
that you have turned fortified cities
into piles of stone. Isa 25:2
27Their people, drained of power,
are dismayed and put to shame.
They are like plants in the field,
like tender green shoots,
like grass sprouting on the roof, Ps 129:6
scorched[d] before it grows up.

28"But I know where you stay
and when you come and go Ps 139:1-3

[a] 9 That is, from the upper Nile region [b] 20 Dead Sea Scrolls (see also 2 Kings 19:19); Masoretic Text *alone are the LORD* [c] 25 Dead Sea Scrolls (see also 2 Kings 19:24); Masoretic Text does not have *in foreign lands.* [d] 27 Some manuscripts of the Masoretic Text, Dead Sea Scrolls and some Septuagint manuscripts (see also 2 Kings 19:26); most manuscripts of the Masoretic Text *roof / and terraced fields*

and how you rage against me. Ps 2:1
29Because you rage against me
and because your insolence has reached my ears, Isa 10:12
I will put my hook in your nose Isa 30:28; Eze 38:4
and my bit in your mouth,
and I will make you return
by the way you came. ver 34

30"This will be the sign for you, O Hezekiah:

"This year you will eat what grows by itself,
and the second year what springs from that.
But in the third year sow and reap, Isa 16:14
plant vineyards and eat their fruit. Ps 107:37
31Once more a remnant of the house of Judah
will take root below and bear fruit above.
32For out of Jerusalem will come a remnant,
and out of Mount Zion a band of survivors.
The zeal of the LORD Almighty
will accomplish this. Isa 9:7

33"Therefore this is what the LORD says concerning the king of Assyria:

"He will not enter this city
or shoot an arrow here.
He will not come before it with shield
or build a siege ramp against it.
34By the way that he came he will return; ver 29
he will not enter this city,"
declares the LORD.
35"I will defend this city and save it, Isa 38:6
for my sake and for the sake of David my servant!" 2Ki 20:6; Isa 43:25

36Then the angel of the LORD went out and put
to death a hundred and eighty-five thousand men
in the Assyrian camp. When the people got up the
next morning—there were all the dead bodies!
37So Sennacherib king of Assyria broke camp and
withdrew. He returned to Nineveh and stayed
there. Ge 10:11; Isa 10:12
38One day, while he was worshiping in the temple of his god Nisroch, his sons Adrammelech and
Sharezer cut him down with the sword, and they
escaped to the land of Ararat. And Esarhaddon his
son succeeded him as king. 2Ki 19:20-37; 2Ch 32:20-21

Hezekiah's Illness

38 In those days Hezekiah became ill and was
at the point of death. The prophet Isaiah
son of Amoz went to him and said, "This is what
the LORD says: Put your house in order, because
you are going to die; you will not recover."
2Hezekiah turned his face to the wall and
prayed to the LORD, 3"Remember, O LORD, how I
have walked before you faithfully and with wholehearted devotion and have done what is good in
your eyes." And Hezekiah wept bitterly. Ne 13:14
4Then the word of the LORD came to Isaiah:
5"Go and tell Hezekiah, 'This is what the LORD, the
God of your father David, says: I have heard your
prayer and seen your tears; I will add fifteen years
to your life. 6And I will deliver you and this city
from the hand of the king of Assyria. I will defend
this city. 2Ki 18:2; Isa 37:35
7" 'This is the LORD's sign to you that the LORD
will do what he has promised: 8I will make the
shadow cast by the sun go back the ten steps it has
gone down on the stairway of Ahaz.' " So the sunlight went back the ten steps it had gone down.

9A writing of Hezekiah king of Judah after his
illness and recovery:

10I said, "In the prime of my life Ps 102:24
must I go through the gates of death[a]
and be robbed of the rest of my years?"
11I said, "I will not again see the LORD,
the LORD, in the land of the living; Ps 27:13
no longer will I look on mankind,
or be with those who now dwell in this world.[b]
12Like a shepherd's tent my house 2Co 5:1,4
has been pulled down and taken from me.
Like a weaver I have rolled up my life, Heb 1:12
and he has cut me off from the loom;
day and night you made an end of me.
13I waited patiently till dawn,
but like a lion he broke all my bones;
day and night you made an end of me.
14I cried like a swift or thrush,
I moaned like a mourning dove. Isa 59:11
My eyes grew weak as I looked to the heavens. Ps 6:7
I am troubled; O Lord, come to my aid!"
15But what can I say?
He has spoken to me, and he himself has done this. Ps 39:9
I will walk humbly all my years 1Ki 21:27
because of this anguish of my soul. Job 7:11
16Lord, by such things men live;
and my spirit finds life in them too.
You restored me to health
and let me live. Ps 119:25
17Surely it was for my benefit Heb 12:11
that I suffered such anguish.
In your love you kept me
from the pit of destruction; Ps 30:3
you have put all my sins Jer 31:34
behind your back. Isa 43:25; Mic 7:19
18For the grave[a] cannot praise you, Ecc 9:10
death cannot sing your praise; Ps 6:5; 88:10-11
those who go down to the pit Ps 30:9
cannot hope for your faithfulness.

[a] 10,18 Hebrew *Sheol* [b] 11 A few Hebrew manuscripts; most Hebrew manuscripts *in the place of cessation*

[19]The living, the living—they praise you, Dt 6:7
as I am doing today;
fathers tell their children Dt 11:19
about your faithfulness.

[20]The LORD will save me,
and we will sing with stringed instruments
all the days of our lives Ps 116:2
in the temple of the LORD. Ps 116:17-19

[21]Isaiah had said, "Prepare a poultice of figs and
apply it to the boil, and he will recover."
[22]Hezekiah had asked, "What will be the sign
that I will go up to the temple of the LORD?"

Envoys From Babylon

39 At that time Merodach-Baladan son of
Baladan king of Babylon sent Hezekiah letters and a gift, because he had heard of his illness
and recovery. [2]Hezekiah received the envoys gladly and showed them what was in his storehouses—
the silver, the gold, the spices, the fine oil, his
entire armory and everything found among his
treasures. There was nothing in his palace or in all
his kingdom that Hezekiah did not show them.
[3]Then Isaiah the prophet went to King Hezekiah and asked, "What did those men say, and
where did they come from?"
"From a distant land," Hezekiah replied. "They
came to me from Babylon." Dt 28:49
[4]The prophet asked, "What did they see in your
palace?"
"They saw everything in my palace," Hezekiah
said. "There is nothing among my treasures that I
did not show them."
[5]Then Isaiah said to Hezekiah, "Hear the word
of the LORD Almighty: [6]The time will surely come
when everything in your palace, and all that your
fathers have stored up until this day, will be carried
off to Babylon. Nothing will be left, says the LORD.
[7]And some of your descendants, your own flesh
and blood who will be born to you, will be taken
away, and they will become eunuchs in the palace
of the king of Babylon." Jer 20:5; Da 1:1-7
[8]"The word of the LORD you have spoken is
good," Hezekiah replied. For he thought, "There
will be peace and security in my lifetime."

The Supremacy of the Lord Chapters 40–48

The final section of Isaiah (40–66) divides into three parts. The first nine chapters (40–48) extol the supremacy of *Yahweh*, the Lord God of Judah. The theme here changes from judgment to comfort. God was no longer speaking of wrath but promised deliverance for His people. Some scholars have suggested that a different author penned these final chapters because the tone and themes shift so dramatically and even the vocabulary of the prophet is somewhat different. This dramatic change can be explained by simply understanding that the language and tone of divine judgment are completely different than the tender language of God's comfort and love. These chapters are laden with praise for the Lord, who reigns supreme over all!

Comfort for God's People

40 Comfort, comfort my people, Isa 12:1; 49:13
says your God.
[2]Speak tenderly to Jerusalem, Isa 35:4
and proclaim to her
that her hard service has been completed,
that her sin has been paid for,
that she has received from the LORD's hand
double for all her sins. Isa 61:7; Jer 16:18

[3]A voice of one calling:
"In the desert prepare
the way for the LORD[a]; Mal 3:1
make straight in the wilderness Pr 3:5-6
a highway for our God.[b] Mt 3:3*; Mk 1:3*
[4]Every valley shall be raised up,
every mountain and hill made low;
the rough ground shall become level, Isa 45:2,13
the rugged places a plain.
[5]And the glory of the LORD will be revealed,
and all mankind together will see it.
For the mouth of the LORD
has spoken."

[6]A voice says, "Cry out."
And I said, "What shall I cry?"

"All men are like grass, Job 14:2
and all their glory is like the flowers of the
field.
[7]The grass withers and the flowers fall, Isa 15:6
because the breath of the LORD blows on
them. Job 41:21; Ps 103:16
Surely the people are grass.
[8]The grass withers and the flowers fall,
but the word of our God stands forever."

[9]You who bring good tidings to Zion, Isa 52:7-10
go up on a high mountain.
You who bring good tidings to Jerusalem,[c]
lift up your voice with a shout,
lift it up, do not be afraid;
say to the towns of Judah,
"Here is your God!" Isa 25:9
[10]See, the Sovereign LORD comes with power,
and his arm rules for him. Isa 9:6-7; 59:16
See, his reward is with him, Isa 62:11; Rev 22:12
and his recompense accompanies him.
[11]He tends his flock like a shepherd: Eze 34:23
He gathers the lambs in his arms Nu 11:12
and carries them close to his heart; Dt 26:19
he gently leads those that have young.

[a]3 Or *A voice of one calling in the desert: / "Prepare the way for the LORD* [b]3 Hebrew; Septuagint *make straight the paths of our God* [c]9 Or *O Zion, bringer of good tidings, / go up on a high mountain. / O Jerusalem, bringer of good tidings*

[12]Who has measured the waters in the hollow of
his hand, Job 38:10; Pr 30:4
or with the breadth of his hand marked off
the heavens? Heb 1:10-12
Who has held the dust of the earth in a
basket,
or weighed the mountains on the scales
and the hills in a balance? Pr 16:11
[13]Who has understood the mind[a] of the LORD,
or instructed him as his counselor? Ro 11:34*
[14]Whom did the LORD consult to enlighten him,
and who taught him the right way?
Who was it that taught him knowledge
or showed him the path of understanding?

[15]Surely the nations are like a drop in a bucket;
they are regarded as dust on the scales;
he weighs the islands as though they were
fine dust. Dt 9:21
[16]Lebanon is not sufficient for altar fires,
nor its animals enough for burnt offerings.
[17]Before him all the nations are as nothing;
they are regarded by him as worthless
and less than nothing. Da 4:35

[18]To whom, then, will you compare God? Ex 8:10
What image will you compare him to?
[19]As for an idol, a craftsman casts it, Ps 115:4
and a goldsmith overlays it with gold Isa 2:20
and fashions silver chains for it.
[20]A man too poor to present such an offering
selects wood that will not rot.
He looks for a skilled craftsman
to set up an idol that will not topple. 1Sa 5:3

[21]Do you not know?
Have you not heard?
Has it not been told you from the beginning?
Have you not understood since the earth
was founded? Ro 1:19; Isa 48:13; 51:13
[22]He sits enthroned above the circle of the
earth,
and its people are like grasshoppers. Ps 104:2
He stretches out the heavens like a canopy,
and spreads them out like a tent to live in.
[23]He brings princes to naught Isa 34:12
and reduces the rulers of this world to
nothing. Job 12:21; Ps 107:40
[24]No sooner are they planted,
no sooner are they sown,
no sooner do they take root in the ground,
than he blows on them and they wither,
and a whirlwind sweeps them away like
chaff. Job 24:24; Isa 41:2

[25]"To whom will you compare me? ver 18; 1Ch 16:25
Or who is my equal?" says the Holy One.
[26]Lift your eyes and look to the heavens: Isa 51:6
Who created all these? Ps 89:11-13; Isa 42:5
He who brings out the starry host one by one,
and calls them each by name.
Because of his great power and mighty
strength, Isa 45:24; Eph 1:19
not one of them is missing. Isa 34:16

[27]Why do you say, O Jacob,
and complain, O Israel,
"My way is hidden from the LORD;
my cause is disregarded by my God"?
[28]Do you not know?
Have you not heard?
The LORD is the everlasting God, Ps 90:2
the Creator of the ends of the earth. Isa 37:16
He will not grow tired or weary, Isa 44:12
and his understanding no one can fathom.

LIVING  **INSIGHT**

One of the marks of spiritual maturity is the quiet confidence that God is in control . . . without the need to understand why He does what He does. When we hope in the Lord—seeking Him, waiting on Him—we experience a strengthening we never knew before. As we release our panic, we turn over to God all the things He has designed and can do so much better than we ever could.

(See Isaiah 40:28–31.)

[29]He gives strength to the weary Isa 50:4; Jer 31:25
and increases the power of the weak.
[30]Even youths grow tired and weary,
and young men stumble and fall; Isa 9:17
[31]but those who hope in the LORD Lk 18:1
will renew their strength. 2Co 4:16
They will soar on wings like eagles; Ps 103:5
they will run and not grow weary,
they will walk and not be faint. 2Co 4:1

The Helper of Israel

41 "Be silent before me, you islands! Zec 2:13
Let the nations renew their strength!
Let them come forward and speak; Isa 48:16
let us meet together at the place of
judgment. Isa 34:1; 50:8

[2]"Who has stirred up one from the east, Ezr 1:2
calling him in righteousness to his
service[b]?
He hands nations over to him
and subdues kings before him.
He turns them to dust with his sword, 2Sa 22:43
to windblown chaff with his bow. Isa 40:24
[3]He pursues them and moves on unscathed,
by a path his feet have not traveled before.

[a]13 Or *Spirit*; or *spirit* [b]2 Or / *whom victory meets at every step*

4Who has done this and carried it through,
calling forth the generations from the beginning? Isa 46:10
I, the LORD—with the first of them
and with the last—I am he." Isa 44:6; Rev 1:8,17

5The islands have seen it and fear; Eze 26:17-18
the ends of the earth tremble. Isa 11:12
They approach and come forward;
6 each helps the other
and says to his brother, "Be strong!" Jos 1:6
7The craftsman encourages the goldsmith,
and he who smooths with the hammer
spurs on him who strikes the anvil.
He says of the welding, "It is good."
He nails down the idol so it will not topple.

8"But you, O Israel, my servant, Ps 136:22; Isa 27:11
Jacob, whom I have chosen, Isa 14:1
you descendants of Abraham my friend,
9I took you from the ends of the earth, Isa 11:12
from its farthest corners I called you.
I said, 'You are my servant';
I have chosen you and have not rejected you. Dt 7:6
10So do not fear, for I am with you; Isa 43:2,5
do not be dismayed, for I am your God.
I will strengthen you and help you; ver 13-14
I will uphold you with my righteous right hand. Ps 18:35; 119:117

11"All who rage against you Isa 17:12
will surely be ashamed and disgraced;
those who oppose you Ex 23:22
will be as nothing and perish. Isa 29:8
12Though you search for your enemies,
you will not find them. Ps 37:35-36
Those who wage war against you
will be as nothing at all. Isa 17:14
13For I am the LORD, your God,
who takes hold of your right hand Isa 42:6
and says to you, Do not fear;
I will help you. ver 10
14Do not be afraid, O worm Jacob, Ge 15:1; Job 4:19
O little Israel,
for I myself will help you," declares the LORD,
your Redeemer, the Holy One of Israel.
15"See, I will make you into a threshing sledge,
new and sharp, with many teeth.
You will thresh the mountains and crush them, Ex 19:18; Ps 107:33
and reduce the hills to chaff.
16You will winnow them, the wind will pick them up, Jer 51:2
and a gale will blow them away. Isa 40:24
But you will rejoice in the LORD Isa 25:9
and glory in the Holy One of Israel. Isa 45:25

17"The poor and needy search for water, Isa 43:20
but there is none;
their tongues are parched with thirst.
But I the LORD will answer them; Isa 30:19
I, the God of Israel, will not forsake them.
18I will make rivers flow on barren heights,
and springs within the valleys.
I will turn the desert into pools of water,
and the parched ground into springs. Isa 35:7
19I will put in the desert Isa 35:1
the cedar and the acacia, the myrtle and the olive. Ex 25:5,10,13
I will set pines in the wasteland,
the fir and the cypress together, Isa 60:13
20so that people may see and know, Ex 6:7
may consider and understand, Isa 29:24
that the hand of the LORD has done this, Ezr 7:6
that the Holy One of Israel has created it.

21"Present your case," says the LORD.
"Set forth your arguments," says Jacob's King. Isa 43:15; 44:6
22"Bring in ⌞your idols⌟ to tell us
what is going to happen. Isa 45:21
Tell us what the former things were,
so that we may consider them
and know their final outcome.
Or declare to us the things to come, Isa 46:10
23 tell us what the future holds,
so we may know that you are gods. Isa 42:9
Do something, whether good or bad, Jer 10:5
so that we will be dismayed and filled with fear.
24But you are less than nothing Isa 44:9; 1Co 8:4
and your works are utterly worthless;
he who chooses you is detestable. Ps 115:8

25"I have stirred up one from the north, and he comes— ver 2; Jer 50:9,41
one from the rising sun who calls on my name.
He treads on rulers as if they were mortar,
as if he were a potter treading the clay.
26Who told of this from the beginning, so we could know,
or beforehand, so we could say, 'He was right'?
No one told of this,
no one foretold it,
no one heard any words from you.
27I was the first to tell Zion, 'Look, here they are!' Isa 48:3,16
I gave to Jerusalem a messenger of good tidings. Isa 40:9
28I look but there is no one— Isa 63:5
no one among them to give counsel,
no one to give answer when I ask them.
29See, they are all false!
Their deeds amount to nothing; ver 24
their images are but wind and confusion.

The Servant of the LORD

42 "Here is my servant, whom I uphold,
my chosen one in whom I delight;
I will put my Spirit on him Mt 3:16-17; Jn 3:34
and he will bring justice to the nations.
2He will not shout or cry out,
or raise his voice in the streets.
3A bruised reed he will not break, Isa 36:6
and a smoldering wick he will not snuff out.
In faithfulness he will bring forth justice;
4 he will not falter or be discouraged
till he establishes justice on earth. Isa 2:4
In his law the islands will put their hope."

5This is what God the LORD says—
he who created the heavens and stretched them out, Ge 1:6; Ps 102:25
who spread out the earth and all that comes out of it, Ps 24:2
who gives breath to its people, Ac 17:25
and life to those who walk on it:
6"I, the LORD, have called you in righteousness;
I will take hold of your hand.
I will keep you and will make you Isa 26:3
to be a covenant for the people Isa 49:8
and a light for the Gentiles, Lk 2:32; Ac 13:47
7to open eyes that are blind, Isa 35:5
to free captives from prison Isa 61:1; Lk 4:19
and to release from the dungeon those who sit in darkness. Ps 107:10,14

8"I am the LORD; that is my name! Ex 3:15
I will not give my glory to another Isa 48:11
or my praise to idols. Ex 8:10
9See, the former things have taken place,
and new things I declare;
before they spring into being
I announce them to you." Isa 40:21

Song of Praise to the LORD

10Sing to the LORD a new song, Ps 33:3; 40:3; 98:1
his praise from the ends of the earth, Isa 49:6
you who go down to the sea, and all that is in it, 1Ch 16:32; Ps 96:11
you islands, and all who live in them.
11Let the desert and its towns raise their voices;
let the settlements where Kedar lives rejoice.
Let the people of Sela sing for joy;
let them shout from the mountaintops.
12Let them give glory to the LORD Isa 24:15
and proclaim his praise in the islands.
13The LORD will march out like a mighty man,
like a warrior he will stir up his zeal;
with a shout he will raise the battle cry
and will triumph over his enemies. Isa 66:14

14"For a long time I have kept silent, Ps 50:21
I have been quiet and held myself back.
But now, like a woman in childbirth,
I cry out, I gasp and pant. Jer 4:31
15I will lay waste the mountains and hills
and dry up all their vegetation;
I will turn rivers into islands
and dry up the pools. Isa 50:2; Na 1:4-6
16I will lead the blind by ways they have not known, Lk 1:78-79; Isa 32:3
along unfamiliar paths I will guide them;
I will turn the darkness into light before them
and make the rough places smooth. Lk 3:5
These are the things I will do;
I will not forsake them. Heb 13:5
17But those who trust in idols,
who say to images, 'You are our gods,'
will be turned back in utter shame. Ps 97:7

Israel Blind and Deaf

18"Hear, you deaf; Isa 35:5
look, you blind, and see!
19Who is blind but my servant, Isa 43:8; Eze 12:2
and deaf like the messenger I send? Isa 44:26
Who is blind like the one committed to me,
blind like the servant of the LORD?
20You have seen many things, but have paid no attention;
your ears are open, but you hear nothing."
21It pleased the LORD
for the sake of his righteousness
to make his law great and glorious. ver 4
22But this is a people plundered and looted,
all of them trapped in pits Isa 24:18
or hidden away in prisons. Isa 24:22
They have become plunder,
with no one to rescue them; Isa 5:29
they have been made loot,
with no one to say, "Send them back."

23Which of you will listen to this
or pay close attention in time to come?
24Who handed Jacob over to become loot,
and Israel to the plunderers? 2Ki 17:6
Was it not the LORD,
against whom we have sinned?
For they would not follow his ways; Isa 30:15
they did not obey his law. Ps 119:136
25So he poured out on them his burning anger,
the violence of war.
It enveloped them in flames, yet they did not understand; 2Ki 25:9
it consumed them, but they did not take it to heart. Isa 29:13; Hos 7:9

Israel's Only Savior

43 But now, this is what the LORD says—
he who created you, O Jacob,
he who formed you, O Israel: Isa 44:21
"Fear not, for I have redeemed you; Isa 44:2,6
I have summoned you by name; you are mine. Isa 45:3-4

[2]When you pass through the waters, Isa 8:7
I will be with you; Dt 31:6,8
and when you pass through the rivers,
they will not sweep over you.
When you walk through the fire, Isa 29:6; 30:27
you will not be burned;
the flames will not set you ablaze. Ps 66:12
[3]For I am the LORD, your God, Ex 20:2
the Holy One of Israel, your Savior; Ps 3:8
I give Egypt for your ransom, Ps 68:31
Cush[a] and Seba in your stead. Pr 21:18
[4]Since you are precious and honored in my sight, Isa 49:5
and because I love you, Isa 63:9
I will give men in exchange for you,
and people in exchange for your life.
[5]Do not be afraid, for I am with you; Isa 44:2
I will bring your children from the east
and gather you from the west. Isa 24:14; Zec 8:7
[6]I will say to the north, 'Give them up!'
and to the south, 'Do not hold them back.'
Bring my sons from afar
and my daughters from the ends of the earth— 2Co 6:18
[7]everyone who is called by my name, Isa 56:5
whom I created for my glory,
whom I formed and made." Ps 100:3; Eph 2:10

[8]Lead out those who have eyes but are blind,
who have ears but are deaf. Isa 42:20; Eze 12:2
[9]All the nations gather together Isa 41:1
and the peoples assemble.
Which of them foretold this
and proclaimed to us the former things?
Let them bring in their witnesses to prove they were right,
so that others may hear and say, "It is true."
[10]"You are my witnesses," declares the LORD,
"and my servant whom I have chosen,
so that you may know and believe me Ex 6:7
and understand that I am he.
Before me no god was formed, Isa 44:6,8
nor will there be one after me. Dt 4:35; Jer 14:22
[11]I, even I, am the LORD,
and apart from me there is no savior.
[12]I have revealed and saved and proclaimed—
I, and not some foreign god among you.
You are my witnesses," declares the LORD,
"that I am God. Isa 44:8
[13] Yes, and from ancient days I am he. Ps 90:2
No one can deliver out of my hand.
When I act, who can reverse it?" Isa 14:27

God's Mercy and Israel's Unfaithfulness

[14]This is what the LORD says—
your Redeemer, the Holy One of Israel:
"For your sake I will send to Babylon
and bring down as fugitives all the Babylonians,[b] Isa 23:13
in the ships in which they took pride.
[15]I am the LORD, your Holy One, Isa 42:8
Israel's Creator, your King." Isa 27:11; 41:21

[16]This is what the LORD says—
he who made a way through the sea,
a path through the mighty waters, Isa 51:10
[17]who drew out the chariots and horses, Ps 118:12
the army and reinforcements together,
and they lay there, never to rise again,
extinguished, snuffed out like a wick:
[18]"Forget the former things; Isa 41:22
do not dwell on the past.
[19]See, I am doing a new thing! 2Co 5:17; Rev 21:5
Now it springs up; do you not perceive it?
I am making a way in the desert Ex 17:6; Nu 20:11
and streams in the wasteland. Ps 126:4
[20]The wild animals honor me,
the jackals and the owls, Isa 13:22
because I provide water in the desert Isa 48:21
and streams in the wasteland,
to give drink to my people, my chosen,
[21] the people I formed for myself Mal 3:17
that they may proclaim my praise. Ps 102:18

[22]"Yet you have not called upon me, O Jacob,
you have not wearied yourselves for me, O Israel. Isa 30:11
[23]You have not brought me sheep for burnt offerings,
nor honored me with your sacrifices.
I have not burdened you with grain offerings
nor wearied you with demands for incense.
[24]You have not bought any fragrant calamus for me, Ex 30:23
or lavished on me the fat of your sacrifices.
But you have burdened me with your sins
and wearied me with your offenses. Isa 1:14

[25]"I, even I, am he who blots out
your transgressions, for my own sake,
and remembers your sins no more. Jer 31:34

LIVING  **INSIGHT**

When God forgives, He forgets. He is not only willing but pleased to use any vessel—just as long as it is clean today.

(See Isaiah 43:25.)

[26]Review the past for me,
let us argue the matter together; Isa 1:18
state the case for your innocence. Isa 41:1; 50:8
[27]Your first father sinned;
your spokesmen rebelled against me. Isa 9:15

[a]3 That is, the upper Nile region [b]14 Or *Chaldeans*

28So I will disgrace the dignitaries of your
temple,
and I will consign Jacob to destruction[a]
and Israel to scorn. Jer 24:9; Eze 5:15

Israel the Chosen

44 "But now listen, O Jacob, my servant,
Israel, whom I have chosen.
2This is what the LORD says—
he who made you, who formed you in the
womb, Ps 139:13; 149:2
and who will help you: Isa 41:10
Do not be afraid, O Jacob, my servant,
Jeshurun, whom I have chosen. Dt 32:15
3For I will pour water on the thirsty land,
and streams on the dry ground; Isa 32:2
I will pour out my Spirit on your offspring,
and my blessing on your descendants.
4They will spring up like grass in a meadow,
like poplar trees by flowing streams. Lev 23:40
5One will say, 'I belong to the LORD'; Ps 116:16
another will call himself by the name of
Jacob;
still another will write on his hand, 'The
LORD's,' Ex 13:9; Zec 8:20-22
and will take the name Israel.

The LORD, Not Idols

6"This is what the LORD says—
Israel's King and Redeemer, the LORD
Almighty: Isa 43:1
I am the first and I am the last; Isa 41:4; Rev 1:8,17
apart from me there is no God. Dt 6:4
7Who then is like me? Let him proclaim it.
Let him declare and lay out before me
what has happened since I established my
ancient people,
and what is yet to come—
yes, let him foretell what will come.
8Do not tremble, do not be afraid.
Did I not proclaim this and foretell it long
ago?
You are my witnesses. Is there any God
besides me? Isa 43:10
No, there is no other Rock; I know not
one." Dt 4:35; 1Sa 2:2
9All who make idols are nothing,
and the things they treasure are worthless.
Those who would speak up for them are
blind;
they are ignorant, to their own shame.
10Who shapes a god and casts an idol,
which can profit him nothing? Isa 41:29; Jer 10:5
11He and his kind will be put to shame; Isa 1:29
craftsmen are nothing but men.
Let them all come together and take their
stand;
they will be brought down to terror and
infamy. Isa 42:17
12The blacksmith takes a tool Isa 40:19; 41:6-7
and works with it in the coals;
he shapes an idol with hammers,
he forges it with the might of his arm.
He gets hungry and loses his strength;
he drinks no water and grows faint. Isa 40:28
13The carpenter measures with a line Isa 41:7
and makes an outline with a marker;
he roughs it out with chisels
and marks it with compasses.
He shapes it in the form of man, Ps 115:4-7
of man in all his glory,
that it may dwell in a shrine. Jdg 17:4-5
14He cut down cedars,
or perhaps took a cypress or oak.
He let it grow among the trees of the forest,
or planted a pine, and the rain made it
grow.
15It is man's fuel for burning;
some of it he takes and warms himself,
he kindles a fire and bakes bread.
But he also fashions a god and worships it;
he makes an idol and bows down to it.
16Half of the wood he burns in the fire;
over it he prepares his meal,
he roasts his meat and eats his fill.
He also warms himself and says,
"Ah! I am warm; I see the fire."
17From the rest he makes a god, his idol;
he bows down to it and worships.
He prays to it and says, 1Ki 18:26
"Save me; you are my god." Isa 45:20
18They know nothing, they understand nothing;
their eyes are plastered over so they cannot
see, Isa 6:9-10
and their minds closed so they cannot
understand.
19No one stops to think,
no one has the knowledge or understanding
to say, Isa 45:20
"Half of it I used for fuel;
I even baked bread over its coals,
I roasted meat and I ate.
Shall I make a detestable thing from what is
left? Dt 27:15
Shall I bow down to a block of wood?"
20He feeds on ashes, a deluded heart misleads
him; Ps 102:9; Job 15:31; Ro 1:21-23,28
he cannot save himself, or say,
"Is not this thing in my right hand a lie?"
21"Remember these things, O Jacob, Isa 46:8
for you are my servant, O Israel.
I have made you, you are my servant; ver 1-2
O Israel, I will not forget you. Isa 49:15

[a]28 The Hebrew term refers to the irrevocable giving over of things or persons to the LORD, often by totally destroying them.

22I have swept away your offenses like a cloud,
your sins like the morning mist.
Return to me, Isa 55:7
for I have redeemed you." 1Co 6:20
23Sing for joy, O heavens, for the LORD has
done this; Isa 42:10
shout aloud, O earth beneath. Ps 148:7
Burst into song, you mountains, Ps 98:8
you forests and all your trees,
for the LORD has redeemed Jacob,
he displays his glory in Israel. Isa 61:3

Jerusalem to Be Inhabited

24"This is what the LORD says—
your Redeemer, who formed you in the
womb: Ps 139:13; Isa 43:14

I am the LORD,
who has made all things,
who alone stretched out the heavens, Isa 42:5
who spread out the earth by myself,

25who foils the signs of false prophets Ps 33:10
and makes fools of diviners, Isa 47:13
who overthrows the learning of the wise
and turns it into nonsense, 2Sa 15:31; 1Co 1:19-20
26who carries out the words of his servants
and fulfills the predictions of his
messengers, Isa 55:11; Mt 5:18

who says of Jerusalem, 'It shall be inhabited,'
of the towns of Judah, 'They shall be built,'
and of their ruins, 'I will restore them,'
27who says to the watery deep, 'Be dry,
and I will dry up your streams,' Isa 11:15
28who says of Cyrus, 'He is my shepherd
and will accomplish all that I please;
he will say of Jerusalem, "Let it be rebuilt,"
and of the temple, "Let its foundations be
laid." ' Ezr 1:2-4

45 "This is what the LORD says to his
anointed,
to Cyrus, whose right hand I take hold of
to subdue nations before him Jer 50:35
and to strip kings of their armor,
to open doors before him
so that gates will not be shut:
2I will go before you Ex 23:20
and will level the mountains[a]; Isa 40:4
I will break down gates of bronze
and cut through bars of iron. Ps 107:16; Jer 51:30
3I will give you the treasures of darkness,
riches stored in secret places, Jer 41:8
so that you may know that I am the LORD,
the God of Israel, who summons you by
name. Ex 33:12; Isa 43:1
4For the sake of Jacob my servant, Isa 41:8-9
of Israel my chosen,
I summon you by name
and bestow on you a title of honor,
though you do not acknowledge me. Ac 17:23
5I am the LORD, and there is no other; Isa 44:8
apart from me there is no God. Ps 18:31
I will strengthen you, Ps 18:39
though you have not acknowledged me,
6so that from the rising of the sun
to the place of its setting Isa 43:5; Mal 1:11
men may know there is none besides me.
I am the LORD, and there is no other.
7I form the light and create darkness,
I bring prosperity and create disaster;
I, the LORD, do all these things.

8"You heavens above, rain down righteousness;
let the clouds shower it down.
Let the earth open wide,
let salvation spring up, Isa 12:3
let righteousness grow with it;
I, the LORD, have created it.

9"Woe to him who quarrels with his Maker,
to him who is but a potsherd among the
potsherds on the ground.
Does the clay say to the potter, Isa 29:16
'What are you making?'
Does your work say,
'He has no hands'?
10Woe to him who says to his father,
'What have you begotten?'
or to his mother,
'What have you brought to birth?'

11"This is what the LORD says—
the Holy One of Israel, and its Maker:
Concerning things to come,
do you question me about my children,
or give me orders about the work of my
hands? Isa 19:25
12It is I who made the earth
and created mankind upon it.
My own hands stretched out the heavens;
I marshaled their starry hosts. Ne 9:6
13I will raise up Cyrus[b] in my righteousness:
I will make all his ways straight. Ps 26:12
He will rebuild my city
and set my exiles free,
but not for a price or reward, Isa 52:3
says the LORD Almighty."

14This is what the LORD says:

"The products of Egypt and the merchandise
of Cush,[c] 2Sa 8:2
and those tall Sabeans— Isa 2:3
they will come over to you

[a] 2 Dead Sea Scrolls and Septuagint; the meaning of the word in the Masoretic Text is uncertain. [b] 13 Hebrew *him*
[c] 14 That is, the upper Nile region

and will be yours;
they will trudge behind you,
coming over to you in chains. Isa 14:1-2
They will bow down before you
and plead with you, saying, Jer 16:19; Zec 8:20-23
'Surely God is with you, and there is no other;
there is no other god.'" Ps 18:31

[15]Truly you are a God who hides himself,
O God and Savior of Israel.
[16]All the makers of idols will be put to shame
and disgraced; Isa 44:9,11
they will go off into disgrace together.
[17]But Israel will be saved by the LORD Ro 11:26
with an everlasting salvation; Isa 26:4
you will never be put to shame or disgraced,
to ages everlasting.

[18]For this is what the LORD says—
he who created the heavens,
he is God;
he who fashioned and made the earth,
he founded it;
he did not create it to be empty, Ge 1:2
but formed it to be inhabited— Ge 1:26
he says:
"I am the LORD,
and there is no other. ver 5; Dt 4:35
[19]I have not spoken in secret, Isa 48:16
from somewhere in a land of darkness;
I have not said to Jacob's descendants, Isa 41:8
'Seek me in vain.' 2Ch 15:2
I, the LORD, speak the truth;
I declare what is right. Dt 30:11

[20]"Gather together and come; Isa 43:9
assemble, you fugitives from the nations.
Ignorant are those who carry about idols of
wood, Isa 44:19; Jer 10:5
who pray to gods that cannot save. Isa 46:6-7
[21]Declare what is to be, present it—
let them take counsel together.
Who foretold this long ago, Isa 41:22
who declared it from the distant past?
Was it not I, the LORD?
And there is no God apart from me, ver 5
a righteous God and a Savior; Ps 11:7; Isa 25:9
there is none but me.

[22]"Turn to me and be saved, Nu 21:8-9; Zec 12:10
all you ends of the earth; Isa 49:6,12
for I am God, and there is no other. Hos 13:4
[23]By myself I have sworn, Ge 22:16
my mouth has uttered in all integrity
a word that will not be revoked: Isa 55:11
Before me every knee will bow;
by me every tongue will swear. Ro 14:11*
[24]They will say of me, 'In the LORD alone
are righteousness and strength.'" Jer 33:16
All who have raged against him
will come to him and be put to shame.
[25]But in the LORD all the descendants of Israel
will be found righteous and will exult.

Gods of Babylon

46 Bel bows down, Nebo stoops low; Isa 21:9
their idols are borne by beasts of
burden.[a] 1Sa 5:2
The images that are carried about are
burdensome, Isa 45:20
a burden for the weary.
[2]They stoop and bow down together;
unable to rescue the burden,
they themselves go off into captivity.

[3]"Listen to me, O house of Jacob, ver 12; Isa 48:12
all you who remain of the house of Israel,
you whom I have upheld since you were
conceived, Ps 139:13
and have carried since your birth. Ps 22:10
[4]Even to your old age and gray hairs Ps 71:18
I am he, I am he who will sustain you.
I have made you and I will carry you;
I will sustain you and I will rescue you.

[5]"To whom will you compare me or count me
equal?
To whom will you liken me that we may be
compared? Isa 40:18,25
[6]Some pour out gold from their bags
and weigh out silver on the scales;
they hire a goldsmith to make it into a god,
and they bow down and worship it. Isa 44:17
[7]They lift it to their shoulders and carry it;
they set it up in its place, and there it
stands.
From that spot it cannot move.
Though one cries out to it, it does not answer;
it cannot save him from his troubles.

[8]"Remember this, fix it in mind, Isa 44:21
take it to heart, you rebels.
[9]Remember the former things, those of long
ago; Dt 32:7
I am God, and there is no other;
I am God, and there is none like me.
[10]I make known the end from the beginning,
from ancient times, what is still to come.
I say: My purpose will stand, Pr 19:21; Ac 5:39
and I will do all that I please.
[11]From the east I summon a bird of prey;
from a far-off land, a man to fulfill my
purpose.
What I have said, that will I bring about;
what I have planned, that will I do. Isa 25:1
[12]Listen to me, you stubborn-hearted, ver 3; Isa 9:9
you who are far from righteousness. Jer 2:5
[13]I am bringing my righteousness near, Isa 1:26

[a]1 Or *are but beasts and cattle*

it is not far away;
and my salvation will not be delayed. Ps 85:9
I will grant salvation to Zion, Ps 74:2
my splendor to Israel. Isa 44:23

The Fall of Babylon

47 "Go down, sit in the dust,
Virgin Daughter of Babylon; Isa 23:12
sit on the ground without a throne,
Daughter of the Babylonians.[a] Jer 51:33; Zec 2:7
No more will you be called
tender or delicate. Dt 28:56
2Take millstones and grind flour; Ex 11:5; Mt 24:41
take off your veil. Ge 24:65
Lift up your skirts, bare your legs, Isa 32:11
and wade through the streams.
3Your nakedness will be exposed Eze 16:37; Na 3:5
and your shame uncovered. Isa 20:4
I will take vengeance; Isa 34:8
I will spare no one."

4Our Redeemer—the LORD Almighty is his
name— Jer 50:34; Am 4:13
is the Holy One of Israel. Isa 1:4

5"Sit in silence, go into darkness, Isa 13:10
Daughter of the Babylonians; Isa 21:9
no more will you be called
queen of kingdoms. Isa 13:19; Rev 17:18
6I was angry with my people 2Ch 28:9
and desecrated my inheritance; Dt 13:15
I gave them into your hand, Isa 10:13
and you showed them no mercy. Isa 14:6
Even on the aged
you laid a very heavy yoke.
7You said, 'I will continue forever—
the eternal queen!' ver 5; Rev 18:7
But you did not consider these things
or reflect on what might happen. Dt 32:29

8"Now then, listen, you wanton creature,
lounging in your security Isa 32:9
and saying to yourself,
'I am, and there is none besides me. Isa 45:6
I will never be a widow Rev 18:7
or suffer the loss of children.'
9Both of these will overtake you
in a moment, on a single day: 1Th 5:3
loss of children and widowhood. Isa 13:18
They will come upon you in full measure,
in spite of your many sorceries Na 3:4
and all your potent spells. Rev 18:23
10You have trusted in your wickedness Ps 52:7
and have said, 'No one sees me.' Isa 29:15
Your wisdom and knowledge mislead you
when you say to yourself,
'I am, and there is none besides me.'
11Disaster will come upon you, Isa 10:3; 14:15
and you will not know how to conjure it
away.
A calamity will fall upon you
that you cannot ward off with a ransom;
a catastrophe you cannot foresee
will suddenly come upon you. 1Th 5:3

12"Keep on, then, with your magic spells
and with your many sorceries, ver 9; Ex 7:11
which you have labored at since childhood.
Perhaps you will succeed,
perhaps you will cause terror.
13All the counsel you have received has only
worn you out! Isa 57:10; Jer 51:58
Let your astrologers come forward, Isa 44:25
those stargazers who make predictions month
by month,
let them save you from what is coming
upon you. Isa 5:29
14Surely they are like stubble; Isa 5:24; Na 1:10
the fire will burn them up.
They cannot even save themselves
from the power of the flame. Isa 10:17
Here are no coals to warm anyone;
here is no fire to sit by.
15That is all they can do for you—
these you have labored with
and trafficked with since childhood. Rev 18:11
Each of them goes on in his error;
there is not one that can save you. ver 13

Stubborn Israel

48 "Listen to this, O house of Jacob,
you who are called by the name of Israel
and come from the line of Judah,
you who take oaths in the name of the LORD
and invoke the God of Israel— Isa 58:2
but not in truth or righteousness— Jer 4:2
2you who call yourselves citizens of the holy
city Isa 52:1
and rely on the God of Israel— Mic 3:11
the LORD Almighty is his name: Isa 47:4
3I foretold the former things long ago, Isa 41:22
my mouth announced them and I made
them known; Isa 45:21
then suddenly I acted, and they came to
pass.
4For I knew how stubborn you were; Dt 31:27
the sinews of your neck were iron, Ex 32:9
your forehead was bronze. Eze 3:9
5Therefore I told you these things long ago;
before they happened I announced them to
you Isa 40:21
so that you could not say,
'My idols did them; Jer 44:15-18
my wooden image and metal god ordained
them.'

[a] 1 Or *Chaldeans*; also in verse 5

[6]You have heard these things; look at them all.
Will you not admit them?

"From now on I will tell you of new things,
of hidden things unknown to you.
[7]They are created now, and not long ago;
you have not heard of them before today.
So you cannot say,
'Yes, I knew of them.' Ex 6:7
[8]You have neither heard nor understood; Isa 1:3
from of old your ear has not been open.
Well do I know how treacherous you are;
you were called a rebel from birth. Dt 9:7,24
[9]For my own name's sake I delay my wrath;
for the sake of my praise I hold it back
from you,
so as not to cut you off. Ne 9:31
[10]See, I have refined you, though not as silver;
I have tested you in the furnace of
affliction. 1Ki 8:51
[11]For my own sake, for my own sake, I do this.
How can I let myself be defamed? Dt 32:27
I will not yield my glory to another. Isa 42:8

Israel Freed

[12]"Listen to me, O Jacob, Isa 46:3
Israel, whom I have called:
I am he; Isa 43:13
I am the first and I am the last. Isa 41:4
[13]My own hand laid the foundations of the
earth, Heb 1:10-12
and my right hand spread out the heavens;
when I summon them,
they all stand up together. Isa 40:26

[14]"Come together, all of you, and listen: Isa 43:9
Which of ⌊the idols⌋ has foretold these
things? Isa 41:22
The LORD's chosen ally
will carry out his purpose against Babylon;
his arm will be against the Babylonians.[a]
[15]I, even I, have spoken;
yes, I have called him. Isa 45:1
I will bring him,
and he will succeed in his mission.

[16]"Come near me and listen to this: Isa 41:1

"From the first announcement I have not
spoken in secret; Isa 45:19
at the time it happens, I am there."

And now the Sovereign LORD has sent me,
with his Spirit. Isa 11:2

[17]This is what the LORD says—
your Redeemer, the Holy One of Israel:
"I am the LORD your God,
who teaches you what is best for you,
who directs you in the way you should go.
[18]If only you had paid attention to my
commands, Dt 32:29
your peace would have been like a river,
your righteousness like the waves of the sea.
[19]Your descendants would have been like the
sand, Ge 12:2
your children like its numberless grains;
their name would never be cut off Isa 56:5; 66:22
nor destroyed from before me."

[20]Leave Babylon,
flee from the Babylonians! Jer 50:8; 51:6,45
Announce this with shouts of joy Isa 49:13
and proclaim it.
Send it out to the ends of the earth;
say, "The LORD has redeemed his servant
Jacob." Isa 52:9; 63:9
[21]They did not thirst when he led them through
the deserts; Isa 41:17
he made water flow for them from the
rock; Isa 30:25
he split the rock
and water gushed out. Ex 17:6; Nu 20:11; Ps 105:41

[22]"There is no peace," says the LORD, "for the
wicked." Isa 57:21

The Servant of the Lord **Chapters 49–53**

These chapters are filled with references to the "servant" of the Lord. Many scholars refer to this person as the "Suffering Servant." This section of Isaiah is dominated by poetic expressions or songs extolling the servant who suffered selflessly for others. Looking back from our New Testament perspective, we can see that this Servant is none other than our Lord Jesus Christ. Certainly the most familiar portion of this section is found in chapter 53, where we read of the One who was "pierced for our transgressions" and "crushed for our iniquities" (verse 5). As you read this moving section of Isaiah, you will encounter the "Lamb of God, who takes away the sin of the world!" (John 1:29).

The Servant of the LORD

49 Listen to me, you islands;
hear this, you distant nations:
Before I was born the LORD called me; Isa 44:24
from my birth he has made mention of my
name. Isa 43:1
[2]He made my mouth like a sharpened sword,
in the shadow of his hand he hid me; Ps 91:1
he made me into a polished arrow Dt 32:23
and concealed me in his quiver.
[3]He said to me, "You are my servant, Zec 3:8
Israel, in whom I will display my splendor."
[4]But I said, "I have labored to no purpose;
I have spent my strength in vain and for
nothing. Isa 65:23

[a]14 Or *Chaldeans*; also in verse 20

Yet what is due me is in the LORD's hand,
and my reward is with my God." Isa 35:4

5 And now the LORD says—
he who formed me in the womb to be his
servant Ps 139:13
to bring Jacob back to him
and gather Israel to himself, Isa 11:12
for I am honored in the eyes of the LORD
and my God has been my strength— Ps 18:1
6 he says:
"It is too small a thing for you to be my
servant
to restore the tribes of Jacob
and bring back those of Israel I have kept.
I will also make you a light for the Gentiles,
that you may bring my salvation to the
ends of the earth." Jn 11:52; Ac 13:47*

7 This is what the LORD says—
the Redeemer and Holy One of Israel—
to him who was despised and abhorred by the
nation, Ps 22:6; 69:7-9
to the servant of rulers:
"Kings will see you and rise up, Isa 52:15
princes will see and bow down,
because of the LORD, who is faithful, 1Co 1:9
the Holy One of Israel, who has chosen
you." Isa 14:1

Restoration of Israel

8 This is what the LORD says:

"In the time of my favor I will answer you,
and in the day of salvation I will help you;
I will keep you and will make you Isa 26:3
to be a covenant for the people, Isa 42:6
to restore the land Isa 44:26
and to reassign its desolate inheritances,
9 to say to the captives, 'Come out,' Isa 42:7; Lk 4:19
and to those in darkness, 'Be free!'

"They will feed beside the roads
and find pasture on every barren hill.
10 They will neither hunger nor thirst, Isa 33:16
nor will the desert heat or the sun beat
upon them. Ps 121:6; Rev 7:16
He who has compassion on them will guide
them Isa 14:1
and lead them beside springs of water.
11 I will turn all my mountains into roads,
and my highways will be raised up. Isa 11:16
12 See, they will come from afar— Isa 43:5-6
some from the north, some from the west,
some from the region of Aswan.[a]"

13 Shout for joy, O heavens; Isa 48:20
rejoice, O earth;
burst into song, O mountains! Isa 44:23
For the LORD comforts his people Isa 40:1; 2Co 1:4
and will have compassion on his afflicted
ones. Ps 9:12; Isa 14:1
14 But Zion said, "The LORD has forsaken me,
the Lord has forgotten me."

15 "Can a mother forget the baby at her breast
and have no compassion on the child she
has borne? 1Ki 3:26
Though she may forget,
I will not forget you! Isa 44:21
16 See, I have engraved you on the palms of my
hands; SS 8:6
your walls are ever before me. Ps 48:12-13
17 Your sons hasten back,
and those who laid you waste depart from
you. Isa 10:6
18 Lift up your eyes and look around;
all your sons gather and come to you.
As surely as I live," declares the LORD, Ro 14:11*
"you will wear them all as ornaments;
you will put them on, like a bride.

19 "Though you were ruined and made desolate
and your land laid waste, Isa 5:6
now you will be too small for your people,
and those who devoured you will be far
away. Isa 1:20
20 The children born during your bereavement
will yet say in your hearing,
'This place is too small for us;
give us more space to live in.' Isa 54:1-3
21 Then you will say in your heart,
'Who bore me these?
I was bereaved and barren;
I was exiled and rejected. Isa 5:13
Who brought these up?
I was left all alone, Isa 1:8
but these—where have they come from?'"

22 This is what the Sovereign LORD says: Ge 15:2

"See, I will beckon to the Gentiles,
I will lift up my banner to the peoples;
they will bring your sons in their arms Isa 11:12
and carry your daughters on their
shoulders. Isa 60:4
23 Kings will be your foster fathers, Isa 60:3,10-11
and their queens your nursing mothers.
They will bow down before you with their
faces to the ground;
they will lick the dust at your feet. Ps 72:9
Then you will know that I am the LORD;
those who hope in me will not be
disappointed." Ps 37:9; Isa 41:11

24 Can plunder be taken from warriors, Mt 12:29
or captives rescued from the fierce[b]?

[a] *12* Dead Sea Scrolls; Masoretic Text *Sinim*
[b] *24* Dead Sea Scrolls, Vulgate and Syriac (see also Septuagint and verse 25); Masoretic Text *righteous*

[25]But this is what the LORD says:

"Yes, captives will be taken from warriors,
and plunder retrieved from the fierce;
I will contend with those who contend with
you, Jer 50:34
and your children I will save. Isa 25:9; 35:4
[26]I will make your oppressors eat their own
flesh; Isa 9:4,20
they will be drunk on their own blood, as
with wine. Rev 16:6
Then all mankind will know Eze 39:7
that I, the LORD, am your Savior, Isa 25:9
your Redeemer, the Mighty One of Jacob."

Israel's Sin and the Servant's Obedience

50 This is what the LORD says:

"Where is your mother's certificate of divorce
with which I sent her away?
Or to which of my creditors
did I sell you? Ne 5:5; Mt 18:25
Because of your sins you were sold; Dt 32:30
because of your transgressions your mother
was sent away.
[2]When I came, why was there no one?
When I called, why was there no one to
answer? Isa 41:28
Was my arm too short to ransom you? Nu 11:23
Do I lack the strength to rescue you?
By a mere rebuke I dry up the sea, Ex 14:22
I turn rivers into a desert; Ps 107:33
their fish rot for lack of water
and die of thirst.
[3]I clothe the sky with darkness
and make sackcloth its covering." Rev 6:12

[4]The Sovereign LORD has given me an
instructed tongue, Ex 4:12
to know the word that sustains the weary.
He wakens me morning by morning, Ps 5:3
wakens my ear to listen like one being
taught. Isa 28:9
[5]The Sovereign LORD has opened my ears,
and I have not been rebellious; Mt 26:39
I have not drawn back.
[6]I offered my back to those who beat me,
my cheeks to those who pulled out my
beard; 2Sa 10:4
I did not hide my face
from mocking and spitting. La 3:30; Mt 26:67
[7]Because the Sovereign LORD helps me, Isa 42:1
I will not be disgraced.
Therefore have I set my face like flint, Eze 3:8-9
and I know I will not be put to shame.
[8]He who vindicates me is near. Isa 26:2; 49:4
Who then will bring charges against me?
Let us face each other! Isa 41:1
Who is my accuser?
Let him confront me!
[9]It is the Sovereign LORD who helps me. Isa 41:10
Who is he that will condemn me? Ro 8:1,34
They will all wear out like a garment;
the moths will eat them up. Job 13:28; Isa 51:8

[10]Who among you fears the LORD
and obeys the word of his servant? Isa 49:3
Let him who walks in the dark,
who has no light, Ps 107:14
trust in the name of the LORD Isa 26:4
and rely on his God.
[11]But now, all you who light fires
and provide yourselves with flaming torches,
go, walk in the light of your fires Jas 3:6
and of the torches you have set ablaze.
This is what you shall receive from my hand:
You will lie down in torment. Isa 65:13-15

Everlasting Salvation for Zion

51 "Listen to me, you who pursue
righteousness Ps 94:15; Isa 46:3; Ro 9:30-31
and who seek the LORD: Isa 55:6
Look to the rock from which you were cut
and to the quarry from which you were
hewn;
[2]look to Abraham, your father, Heb 11:11; Isa 29:22
and to Sarah, who gave you birth.

LIVING  **INSIGHT**

Looking to the quarry, the pit from which we were hewn, has a way of keeping us all on the same level—recipients of God's amazing grace.

(See Isaiah 51:1.)

When I called him he was but one,
and I blessed him and made him many.
[3]The LORD will surely comfort Zion Isa 40:1
and will look with compassion on all her
ruins; Isa 52:9
he will make her deserts like Eden, Ge 2:8
her wastelands like the garden of the LORD.
Joy and gladness will be found in her, Isa 25:9
thanksgiving and the sound of singing.

[4]"Listen to me, my people; Ps 50:7
hear me, my nation:
The law will go out from me; Dt 18:18
my justice will become a light to the
nations. Isa 2:4; 42:4,6
[5]My righteousness draws near speedily,
my salvation is on the way, Isa 46:13
and my arm will bring justice to the
nations. Isa 40:10; 63:1,5
The islands will look to me Isa 11:11
and wait in hope for my arm. Ge 49:10; Ps 37:9

6 Lift up your eyes to the heavens,
look at the earth beneath;
the heavens will vanish like smoke, Mt 24:35
the earth will wear out like a garment
and its inhabitants die like flies.
But my salvation will last forever, Ps 119:89
my righteousness will never fail. Ps 89:33

7 "Hear me, you who know what is right,
you people who have my law in your
hearts: Ps 37:31
Do not fear the reproach of men
or be terrified by their insults. Mt 5:11; Ac 5:41
8 For the moth will eat them up like a garment;
the worm will devour them like wool.
But my righteousness will last forever, ver 6
my salvation through all generations."

9 Awake, awake! Clothe yourself with strength,
O arm of the LORD;
awake, as in days gone by,
as in generations of old. Dt 4:34
Was it not you who cut Rahab to pieces,
who pierced that monster through? Ps 74:13
10 Was it not you who dried up the sea, Ex 14:22
the waters of the great deep,
who made a road in the depths of the sea
so that the redeemed might cross over?
11 The ransomed of the LORD will return. Isa 35:9
They will enter Zion with singing; Ps 109:28
everlasting joy will crown their heads.
Gladness and joy will overtake them, Jer 33:11
and sorrow and sighing will flee away.

12 "I, even I, am he who comforts you. 2Co 1:4
Who are you that you fear mortal men,
the sons of men, who are but grass, 1Pe 1:24
13 that you forget the LORD your Maker, Isa 17:10
who stretched out the heavens Ps 104:2; Isa 48:13
and laid the foundations of the earth,
that you live in constant terror every day
because of the wrath of the oppressor,
who is bent on destruction?
For where is the wrath of the oppressor? Isa 9:4
14 The cowering prisoners will soon be set
free;
they will not die in their dungeon,
nor will they lack bread. Isa 49:10
15 For I am the LORD your God,
who churns up the sea so that its waves
roar— Jer 31:35
the LORD Almighty is his name. Isa 13:4
16 I have put my words in your mouth Dt 18:18
and covered you with the shadow of my
hand— Ex 33:22
I who set the heavens in place,
who laid the foundations of the earth,
and who say to Zion, 'You are my
people.'" Jer 7:23

The Cup of the LORD's Wrath

17 Awake, awake! Isa 52:1
Rise up, O Jerusalem,
you who have drunk from the hand of the
LORD
the cup of his wrath, Job 21:20; Rev 14:10
you who have drained to its dregs Ps 75:8
the goblet that makes men stagger. Ps 60:3
18 Of all the sons she bore Ps 88:18
there was none to guide her; Isa 49:21
of all the sons she reared
there was none to take her by the hand.
19 These double calamities have come upon
you— Isa 47:9
who can comfort you?— Isa 49:13; Jer 15:5
ruin and destruction, famine and sword—
who can[a] console you?
20 Your sons have fainted;
they lie at the head of every street, Isa 5:25
like antelope caught in a net.
They are filled with the wrath of the LORD
and the rebuke of your God. Dt 28:20

21 Therefore hear this, you afflicted one, Isa 14:32
made drunk, but not with wine. Isa 29:9
22 This is what your Sovereign LORD says,
your God, who defends his people: Isa 49:25
"See, I have taken out of your hand
the cup that made you stagger; ver 17; Jer 25:15
from that cup, the goblet of my wrath,
you will never drink again.
23 I will put it into the hands of your
tormentors, Jer 25:15-17,26,28; 49:12
who said to you,
'Fall prostrate that we may walk over you.'
And you made your back like the ground,
like a street to be walked over." Ps 66:12

52 Awake, awake, O Zion, Isa 51:17
clothe yourself with strength. Isa 51:9
Put on your garments of splendor, Ps 110:3
O Jerusalem, the holy city. Ne 11:1; Mt 4:5
The uncircumcised and defiled
will not enter you again. Rev 21:27
2 Shake off your dust; Isa 29:4
rise up, sit enthroned, O Jerusalem.
Free yourself from the chains on your neck,
O captive Daughter of Zion. Ps 9:14

3 For this is what the LORD says:

"You were sold for nothing, Ps 44:12
and without money you will be redeemed."

4 For this is what the Sovereign LORD says:

"At first my people went down to Egypt to
live; Ge 46:6
lately, Assyria has oppressed them.

[a]19 Dead Sea Scrolls, Septuagint, Vulgate and Syriac; Masoretic Text / *how can I*

5“And now what do I have here?” declares the
LORD.
“For my people have been taken away for
nothing,
and those who rule them mock,[a]”
declares the LORD.
“And all day long
my name is constantly blasphemed. Eze 36:20
6Therefore my people will know my name;
therefore in that day they will know Isa 10:20
that it is I who foretold it. Isa 41:26
Yes, it is I.”

7How beautiful on the mountains
are the feet of those who bring good news,
who proclaim peace, Eph 6:15
who bring good tidings,
who proclaim salvation,
who say to Zion,
“Your God reigns!” Ps 93:1
8Listen! Your watchmen lift up their voices;
together they shout for joy. Isa 12:6
When the LORD returns to Zion, Isa 59:20
they will see it with their own eyes.
9Burst into songs of joy together, Ps 98:4
you ruins of Jerusalem, Isa 51:3
for the LORD has comforted his people, Lk 2:25
he has redeemed Jerusalem. Isa 48:20
10The LORD will lay bare his holy arm Ps 44:3
in the sight of all the nations, Isa 66:18
and all the ends of the earth will see Isa 11:9
the salvation of our God. Ps 98:2-3; Lk 3:6

11Depart, depart, go out from there! Isa 48:20
Touch no unclean thing! 2Co 6:17*
Come out from it and be pure, 2Ti 2:19
you who carry the vessels of the LORD.
12But you will not leave in haste Ex 12:11
or go in flight;
for the LORD will go before you, Mic 2:13
the God of Israel will be your rear guard.

The Suffering and Glory of the Servant

13See, my servant will act wisely[b]; Isa 42:1
he will be raised and lifted up and highly
exalted. Php 2:9
14Just as there were many who were appalled at
him[c]— Job 18:20
his appearance was so disfigured beyond
that of any man 2Sa 10:4
and his form marred beyond human
likeness— Job 2:12
15so will he sprinkle many nations,[d] Lev 14:7
and kings will shut their mouths because of
him. Isa 49:7
For what they were not told, they will see,
and what they have not heard, they will
understand. Ro 15:21*; Eph 3:4-5

53 Who has believed our message Ro 10:16*
and to whom has the arm of the LORD
been revealed? Jn 12:38*
2He grew up before him like a tender shoot,
and like a root out of dry ground. Isa 11:10
He had no beauty or majesty to attract us to
him,
nothing in his appearance that we should
desire him. Isa 52:14
3He was despised and rejected by men,
a man of sorrows, and familiar with
suffering. Lk 18:31-33
Like one from whom men hide their faces
he was despised, and we esteemed him not.
4Surely he took up our infirmities
and carried our sorrows, Mt 8:17*
yet we considered him stricken by God, Jn 19:7
smitten by him, and afflicted. Ge 12:17; Ru 1:21
5But he was pierced for our transgressions,
he was crushed for our iniquities; Ps 34:18
the punishment that brought us peace was
upon him, Isa 9:6; 50:6
and by his wounds we are healed. 1Pe 2:24-25
6We all, like sheep, have gone astray, Ps 95:10
each of us has turned to his own way;
and the LORD has laid on him
the iniquity of us all. Ex 28:38; Ro 4:25

7He was oppressed and afflicted, Isa 49:26
yet he did not open his mouth; Mk 14:61
he was led like a lamb to the slaughter, Ps 44:22
and as a sheep before her shearers is silent,
so he did not open his mouth.
8By oppression[e] and judgment he was taken
away. Mk 14:49
And who can speak of his descendants?
For he was cut off from the land of the living;
for the transgression of my people he was
stricken.[f] Ps 39:8
9He was assigned a grave with the wicked,
and with the rich in his death, Mt 27:57-60
though he had done no violence, Isa 42:1-3
nor was any deceit in his mouth. 1Pe 2:22*

10Yet it was the LORD's will to crush him and
cause him to suffer, Isa 46:10; Ge 12:17
and though the LORD makes[g] his life a
guilt offering, Lev 5:15; Jn 3:17
he will see his offspring and prolong his days,
and the will of the LORD will prosper in his
hand. Isa 49:4
11After the suffering of his soul, Jn 10:14-18

[a]5 Dead Sea Scrolls and Vulgate; Masoretic Text *wail* [b]13 Or *will prosper* [c]14 Hebrew *you* [d]15 Hebrew; Septuagint *so will many nations marvel at him* [e]8 Or *From arrest* [f]8 Or *away. / Yet who of his generation considered / that he was cut off from the land of the living / for the transgression of my people, / to whom the blow was due?* [g]10 Hebrew *though you make*

he will see the light ⌞of life⌟[a] and be
satisfied[b]; Job 33:30
by his knowledge[c] my righteous servant will
justify many, Ro 5:18-19
and he will bear their iniquities. Ex 28:38
12 Therefore I will give him a portion among the
great,[d] Php 2:9
and he will divide the spoils with the
strong,[e] Lk 11:22
because he poured out his life unto death,
and was numbered with the transgressors.
For he bore the sin of many, 1Pe 2:24
and made intercession for the transgressors.

The Future Plan of the Lord **Chapters 54–66**

Isaiah closed his book with words of hope and a bright anticipation of the millennial promises yet to be fulfilled. Not every one of the prophets ended their writings with this kind of stirring crescendo, but Isaiah promised the realization of a great and glorious hope that can only come by the hand of *Yahweh*, the Lord God, the Holy One of Israel.

The Future Glory of Zion

54 "Sing, O barren woman, Ge 30:1
you who never bore a child;
burst into song, shout for joy, Ge 21:6
you who were never in labor; Isa 66:7
because more are the children of the desolate
woman Isa 49:20
than of her who has a husband," Gal 4:27*
says the LORD.
2 "Enlarge the place of your tent, Isa 49:19-20
stretch your tent curtains wide,
do not hold back;
lengthen your cords,
strengthen your stakes. Ex 35:18; 39:40
3 For you will spread out to the right and to the
left;
your descendants will dispossess nations
and settle in their desolate cities. Isa 49:19

4 "Do not be afraid; you will not suffer shame.
Do not fear disgrace; you will not be
humiliated. Ge 30:23
You will forget the shame of your youth Jer 2:2
and remember no more the reproach of
your widowhood. Isa 51:7
5 For your Maker is your husband— Jer 3:14
the LORD Almighty is his name—
the Holy One of Israel is your Redeemer;
he is called the God of all the earth. Isa 6:3
6 The LORD will call you back Isa 49:14-21
as if you were a wife deserted and
distressed in spirit— Isa 62:4,12
a wife who married young, Ex 20:14; Mal 2:15
only to be rejected," says your God.
7 "For a brief moment I abandoned you, Isa 26:20
but with deep compassion I will bring you
back. Isa 49:18
8 In a surge of anger Isa 60:10
I hid my face from you for a moment,
but with everlasting kindness Ps 25:6; Isa 55:3
I will have compassion on you," Ps 102:13
says the LORD your Redeemer. Isa 48:17

9 "To me this is like the days of Noah,
when I swore that the waters of Noah
would never again cover the earth.
So now I have sworn not to be angry with
you, Isa 12:1; 57:16
never to rebuke you again. Dt 28:20
10 Though the mountains be shaken Ps 46:2; Rev 6:14
and the hills be removed,
yet my unfailing love for you will not be
shaken Isa 51:6; Ps 6:4
nor my covenant of peace be removed,"
says the LORD, who has compassion on you.

11 "O afflicted city, lashed by storms and not
comforted, Isa 14:32; 28:2; 51:19
I will build you with stones of turquoise,[f]
your foundations with sapphires.[g] Isa 28:16
12 I will make your battlements of rubies,
your gates of sparkling jewels,
and all your walls of precious stones.
13 All your sons will be taught by the LORD,
and great will be your children's peace.
14 In righteousness you will be established: Isa 26:2
Tyranny will be far from you; Isa 9:4
you will have nothing to fear. Zep 3:15
Terror will be far removed; Isa 17:14
it will not come near you.
15 If anyone does attack you, it will not be my
doing;
whoever attacks you will surrender to you.
16 "See, it is I who created the blacksmith Isa 44:12
who fans the coals into flame
and forges a weapon fit for its work. Isa 10:5
And it is I who have created the destroyer to
work havoc; Isa 13:5
17 no weapon forged against you will prevail,
and you will refute every tongue that
accuses you. Isa 45:24-25
This is the heritage of the servants of the
LORD, Isa 56:6-8
and this is their vindication from me,"
declares the LORD.

Invitation to the Thirsty

55 "Come, all you who are thirsty, Jn 4:14; 7:37
come to the waters; Jer 2:13

[a] *11* Dead Sea Scrolls (see also Septuagint); Masoretic Text does not have *the light ⌞of life⌟*. [b] *11* Or (with Masoretic Text) *11He will see the result of the suffering of his soul / and be satisfied* [c] *11* Or *by knowledge of him* [d] *12* Or *many* [e] *12* Or *numerous* [f] *11* The meaning of the Hebrew for this word is uncertain. [g] *11* Or *lapis lazuli*

and you who have no money,
come, buy and eat! Rev 3:18
Come, buy wine and milk SS 5:1
without money and without cost. Hos 14:4
2 Why spend money on what is not bread,
and your labor on what does not satisfy?
Listen, listen to me, and eat what is good,
and your soul will delight in the richest of
fare. Isa 30:23
3 Give ear and come to me;
hear me, that your soul may live. Lev 18:5
I will make an everlasting covenant with you,
my faithful love promised to David. Ac 13:34*
4 See, I have made him a witness to the peoples,
a leader and commander of the peoples.
5 Surely you will summon nations you know
not, Isa 49:6
and nations that do not know you will
hasten to you, Isa 2:3
because of the LORD your God,
the Holy One of Israel, Isa 12:6
for he has endowed you with splendor."

6 Seek the LORD while he may be found; Ps 32:6
call on him while he is near. Isa 65:24
7 Let the wicked forsake his way 2Ch 7:14
and the evil man his thoughts. Isa 32:7; 59:7
Let him turn to the LORD, and he will have
mercy on him, Isa 44:22; 54:10
and to our God, for he will freely pardon.

8 "For my thoughts are not your thoughts,
neither are your ways my ways," Isa 53:6
declares the LORD.

LIVING  **INSIGHT**

The Creator needs no creature to interpret His way, His reasons, His style. His vantage point is infinity. It is too high. We cannot attain it. And so we accept rather than explain. We trust rather than try to make it all fit together so perfectly it squeaks.

(See Isaiah 55:8–9.)

9 "As the heavens are higher than the earth,
so are my ways higher than your ways
and my thoughts than your thoughts.
10 As the rain and the snow Isa 30:23
come down from heaven,
and do not return to it
without watering the earth
and making it bud and flourish, Ps 67:6
so that it yields seed for the sower and
bread for the eater, 2Co 9:10
11 so is my word that goes out from my mouth:
It will not return to me empty, Isa 45:23
but will accomplish what I desire
and achieve the purpose for which I sent it.
12 You will go out in joy Ps 98:4
and be led forth in peace; Isa 54:10,13
the mountains and hills
will burst into song before you, Ps 65:12-13
and all the trees of the field 1Ch 16:33
will clap their hands. Ps 98:8
13 Instead of the thornbush will grow the pine
tree,
and instead of briers the myrtle will grow.
This will be for the LORD's renown, Isa 63:12
for an everlasting sign,
which will not be destroyed."

Salvation for Others

56 This is what the LORD says:

"Maintain justice Isa 1:17
and do what is right, Isa 26:8
for my salvation is close at hand Ps 85:9
and my righteousness will soon be revealed.
2 Blessed is the man who does this, Ps 119:2
the man who holds it fast,
who keeps the Sabbath without desecrating it,
and keeps his hand from doing any evil."

3 Let no foreigner who has bound himself to
the LORD say, Ex 12:43
"The LORD will surely exclude me from his
people." Dt 23:3
And let not any eunuch complain, Ac 8:27
"I am only a dry tree."

4 For this is what the LORD says:

"To the eunuchs who keep my Sabbaths,
who choose what pleases me
and hold fast to my covenant— Ex 31:13
5 to them I will give within my temple and its
walls Isa 26:1; 60:18
a memorial and a name
better than sons and daughters;
I will give them an everlasting name
that will not be cut off. Isa 48:19; 55:13
6 And foreigners who bind themselves to the
LORD
to serve him, Isa 60:7,10; 61:5
to love the name of the LORD, Mal 1:11
and to worship him,
all who keep the Sabbath without desecrating
it ver 2,4
and who hold fast to my covenant—
7 these I will bring to my holy mountain Isa 2:2
and give them joy in my house of prayer.
Their burnt offerings and sacrifices Ro 12:1
will be accepted on my altar;
for my house will be called
a house of prayer for all nations." Mt 21:13*
8 The Sovereign LORD declares—
he who gathers the exiles of Israel:

"I will gather still others to them Isa 11:12; Jn 10:16
besides those already gathered."

God's Accusation Against the Wicked

9Come, all you beasts of the field, Jer 12:9
come and devour, all you beasts of the forest!
10Israel's watchmen are blind, Eze 3:17
they all lack knowledge; Jer 2:8
they are all mute dogs,
they cannot bark;
they lie around and dream,
they love to sleep. Na 3:18
11They are dogs with mighty appetites;
they never have enough.
They are shepherds who lack understanding;
they all turn to their own way, Isa 53:6
each seeks his own gain. Mic 3:11
12"Come," each one cries, "let me get wine!
Let us drink our fill of beer!
And tomorrow will be like today,
or even far better." Lk 12:18-19

57 The righteous perish, Ps 12:1
and no one ponders it in his heart;
devout men are taken away,
and no one understands
that the righteous are taken away
to be spared from evil. 2Ki 22:20
2Those who walk uprightly Isa 26:7
enter into peace;
they find rest as they lie in death. Da 12:13

3"But you—come here, you sons of a sorceress, Ex 22:18
you offspring of adulterers and prostitutes!
4Whom are you mocking?
At whom do you sneer
and stick out your tongue?
Are you not a brood of rebels, Isa 1:2
the offspring of liars?
5You burn with lust among the oaks
and under every spreading tree; 2Ki 16:4
you sacrifice your children in the ravines
and under the overhanging crags.
6⌞The idols⌟ among the smooth stones of the ravines are your portion; Jer 3:9
they, they are your lot.
Yes, to them you have poured out drink offerings Jer 7:18
and offered grain offerings.
In the light of these things, should I relent?
7You have made your bed on a high and lofty hill; Jer 3:6; Eze 16:16
there you went up to offer your sacrifices.
8Behind your doors and your doorposts
you have put your pagan symbols.
Forsaking me, you uncovered your bed,
you climbed into it and opened it wide;
you made a pact with those whose beds you love, Eze 16:26; 23:7
and you looked on their nakedness. Eze 23:18
9You went to Molech[a] with olive oil 1Ki 11:5
and increased your perfumes.
You sent your ambassadors[b] far away;
you descended to the grave[c] itself! Isa 8:19
10You were wearied by all your ways,
but you would not say, 'It is hopeless.'
You found renewal of your strength,
and so you did not faint.

11"Whom have you so dreaded and feared
that you have been false to me,
and have neither remembered me Jer 2:32; 3:21
nor pondered this in your hearts? Isa 42:23
Is it not because I have long been silent
that you do not fear me?
12I will expose your righteousness and your works, Isa 29:15; Mic 3:2-4,8
and they will not benefit you.
13When you cry out for help, Jer 22:20; 30:15
let your collection ⌞of idols⌟ save you!
The wind will carry all of them off,
a mere breath will blow them away. Is 40:7,24
But the man who makes me his refuge Ps 118:8
will inherit the land Ps 37:9
and possess my holy mountain." Isa 65:9-11

Comfort for the Contrite

14And it will be said:

"Build up, build up, prepare the road!
Remove the obstacles out of the way of my people." Isa 62:10; Jer 18:15
15For this is what the high and lofty One says—
he who lives forever, whose name is holy:
"I live in a high and holy place, Job 16:19
but also with him who is contrite and lowly in spirit, Ps 34:18; 51:17; 147:3
to revive the spirit of the lowly
and to revive the heart of the contrite.
16I will not accuse forever,
nor will I always be angry, Ps 85:5; 103:9; Mic 7:18
for then the spirit of man would grow faint before me—
the breath of man that I have created. Ge 2:7
17I was enraged by his sinful greed; Isa 56:11
I punished him, and hid my face in anger,
yet he kept on in his willful ways. Isa 1:4
18I have seen his ways, but I will heal him;
I will guide him and restore comfort to him, Isa 61:1-3
19 creating praise on the lips of the mourners in Israel. Heb 13:15
Peace, peace, to those far and near," Ac 2:39
says the LORD. "And I will heal them."

[a]9 Or *to the king* [b]9 Or *idols* [c]9 Hebrew *Sheol*

20 But the wicked are like the tossing sea,
which cannot rest,
whose waves cast up mire and mud. Ps 69:14
21 "There is no peace," says my God, "for the
wicked." Isa 48:22; 59:8

True Fasting

58 "Shout it aloud, do not hold back. Isa 40:6
Raise your voice like a trumpet. Ex 20:18
Declare to my people their rebellion Isa 48:8
and to the house of Jacob their sins. Isa 57:12
2 For day after day they seek me out; Isa 48:1
they seem eager to know my ways,
as if they were a nation that does what is right
and has not forsaken the commands of its
God. Ps 119:87
They ask me for just decisions
and seem eager for God to come near
them. Isa 29:13
3 'Why have we fasted,' they say, Lev 16:29
'and you have not seen it?
Why have we humbled ourselves, Ex 10:3
and you have not noticed?' Mal 3:14

"Yet on the day of your fasting, you do as
you please Isa 22:13; Zec 7:5-6
and exploit all your workers.
4 Your fasting ends in quarreling and strife,
and in striking each other with wicked fists.
You cannot fast as you do today
and expect your voice to be heard on high.
5 Is this the kind of fast I have chosen, Zec 7:5
only a day for a man to humble himself?
Is it only for bowing one's head like a reed
and for lying on sackcloth and ashes? Job 2:8
Is that what you call a fast,
a day acceptable to the LORD?

6 "Is not this the kind of fasting I have chosen:
to loose the chains of injustice Ne 5:10-11
and untie the cords of the yoke,
to set the oppressed free Jer 34:9
and break every yoke? Isa 9:4
7 Is it not to share your food with the hungry
and to provide the poor wanderer with
shelter— Isa 16:4; Heb 13:2
when you see the naked, to clothe him,
and not to turn away from your own flesh
and blood? Ge 29:14; Lk 10:31-32
8 Then your light will break forth like the dawn,
and your healing will quickly appear;
then your righteousness[a] will go before you,
and the glory of the LORD will be your rear
guard. Ex 14:19
9 Then you will call, and the LORD will answer;
you will cry for help, and he will say: Here
am I.

"If you do away with the yoke of oppression,
with the pointing finger and malicious talk,
10 and if you spend yourselves in behalf of the
hungry
and satisfy the needs of the oppressed,
then your light will rise in the darkness,
and your night will become like the
noonday. Job 11:17
11 The LORD will guide you always; Ps 48:14
he will satisfy your needs in a sun-scorched
land Ps 107:9
and will strengthen your frame. Ps 72:16
You will be like a well-watered garden, SS 4:15
like a spring whose waters never fail. Jn 4:14
12 Your people will rebuild the ancient ruins
and will raise up the age-old foundations;
you will be called Repairer of Broken Walls,
Restorer of Streets with Dwellings.

LIVING  **INSIGHT**

Need a fresh and challenging goal? Consider the possibility of filling these three roles: a rebuilder, a repairer, a restorer. All three are yours for the taking. Ask God for a sensitive heart to those around you. Thank Him for rebuilding, repairing and restoring you. Tell Him you are all His—no conditions, no reservations.

(See Isaiah 58:11–12.)

13 "If you keep your feet from breaking the
Sabbath Isa 56:2
and from doing as you please on my holy
day,
if you call the Sabbath a delight Ps 84:2,10
and the LORD's holy day honorable,
and if you honor it by not going your own
way
and not doing as you please or speaking
idle words,
14 then you will find your joy in the LORD,
and I will cause you to ride on the heights
of the land Dt 32:13
and to feast on the inheritance of your
father Jacob." Ps 105:10-11
The mouth of the LORD has spoken.

Sin, Confession and Redemption

59 Surely the arm of the LORD is not too
short to save, Nu 11:23; Isa 50:2
nor his ear too dull to hear. Isa 58:9; 65:24
2 But your iniquities have separated
you from your God;
your sins have hidden his face from you,
so that he will not hear. Isa 1:15; 58:4
3 For your hands are stained with blood, Isa 1:15

[a] 8 Or *your righteous One*

your fingers with guilt. Ps 7:3
Your lips have spoken lies, Isa 3:8
and your tongue mutters wicked things.
4No one calls for justice; Isa 5:23
no one pleads his case with integrity.
They rely on empty arguments and speak lies;
they conceive trouble and give birth to evil.
5They hatch the eggs of vipers Isa 11:8
and spin a spider's web. Job 8:14
Whoever eats their eggs will die,
and when one is broken, an adder is hatched.
6Their cobwebs are useless for clothing;
they cannot cover themselves with what they make. Isa 28:20
Their deeds are evil deeds,
and acts of violence are in their hands.
7Their feet rush into sin;
they are swift to shed innocent blood.
Their thoughts are evil thoughts; Mk 7:21-22
ruin and destruction mark their ways.
8The way of peace they do not know; Ro 3:15-17*
there is no justice in their paths.
They have turned them into crooked roads;
no one who walks in them will know peace.

9So justice is far from us,
and righteousness does not reach us.
We look for light, but all is darkness; Isa 5:30
for brightness, but we walk in deep shadows.
10Like the blind we grope along the wall, Dt 28:29
feeling our way like men without eyes.
At midday we stumble as if it were twilight;
among the strong, we are like the dead.
11We all growl like bears;
we moan mournfully like doves. Isa 38:14
We look for justice, but find none;
for deliverance, but it is far away.

12For our offenses are many in your sight, Ezr 9:6
and our sins testify against us. Isa 3:9
Our offenses are ever with us,
and we acknowledge our iniquities: Ps 51:3
13rebellion and treachery against the LORD,
turning our backs on our God, Tit 1:16
fomenting oppression and revolt, Isa 5:7
uttering lies our hearts have conceived.
14So justice is driven back, Isa 29:21
and righteousness stands at a distance;
truth has stumbled in the streets, Isa 48:1
honesty cannot enter.
15Truth is nowhere to be found, Jer 7:28
and whoever shuns evil becomes a prey.

The LORD looked and was displeased
that there was no justice. Isa 5:7
16He saw that there was no one, Isa 41:28
he was appalled that there was no one to intervene; Isa 53:12
so his own arm worked salvation for him,
and his own righteousness sustained him.
17He put on righteousness as his breastplate,
and the helmet of salvation on his head;
he put on the garments of vengeance Isa 63:3
and wrapped himself in zeal as in a cloak.
18According to what they have done,
so will he repay Mt 16:27
wrath to his enemies
and retribution to his foes;
he will repay the islands their due.
19From the west, men will fear the name of the LORD, Isa 49:12
and from the rising of the sun, they will revere his glory. Ps 113:3
For he will come like a pent-up flood
that the breath of the LORD drives along.[a]

20"The Redeemer will come to Zion, Job 19:25
to those in Jacob who repent of their sins,"
declares the LORD.

LIVING  INSIGHT

Be open. Stay that way. Don't manufacture conclusions. Don't even think in terms of "this is the way things will turn out." God has a beautiful way of bringing good vibrations out of broken chords. When the Lord is in it, anything is possible.
(See Isaiah 59:1, 20.)

21"As for me, this is my covenant with them,"
says the LORD. "My Spirit, who is on you, and my
words that I have put in your mouth will not depart from your mouth, or from the mouths of your
children, or from the mouths of their descendants
from this time on and forever," says the LORD.

The Glory of Zion

60 "Arise, shine, for your light has come,
and the glory of the LORD rises upon you. Isa 4:5; Rev 21:11
2See, darkness covers the earth
and thick darkness is over the peoples,
but the LORD rises upon you
and his glory appears over you.
3Nations will come to your light, Isa 45:14; Rev 21:24
and kings to the brightness of your dawn.

4"Lift up your eyes and look about you:
All assemble and come to you; Isa 11:12
your sons come from afar, Jer 30:10
and your daughters are carried on the arm.

[a] 19 Or *When the enemy comes in like a flood, / the Spirit of the LORD will put him to flight*

[5]Then you will look and be radiant, Ex 34:29
your heart will throb and swell with joy;
the wealth on the seas will be brought to you,
to you the riches of the nations will come.
[6]Herds of camels will cover your land,
young camels of Midian and Ephah. Ge 25:2,4
And all from Sheba will come, Ps 72:10
bearing gold and incense Isa 43:23; Mt 2:11
and proclaiming the praise of the LORD.
[7]All Kedar's flocks will be gathered to you,
the rams of Nebaioth will serve you;
they will be accepted as offerings on my altar,
and I will adorn my glorious temple.

[8]"Who are these that fly along like clouds,
like doves to their nests?
[9]Surely the islands look to me; Isa 11:11
in the lead are the ships of Tarshish,[a]
bringing your sons from afar, Isa 14:2; 43:6
with their silver and gold,
to the honor of the LORD your God, Ps 22:23
the Holy One of Israel,
for he has endowed you with splendor.

[10]"Foreigners will rebuild your walls, Isa 14:1-2
and their kings will serve you. Isa 49:23
Though in anger I struck you,
in favor I will show you compassion. Isa 54:8
[11]Your gates will always stand open, Isa 62:10
they will never be shut, day or night,
so that men may bring you the wealth of the nations— Rev 21:26
their kings led in triumphal procession.
[12]For the nation or kingdom that will not serve you will perish; Isa 14:2
it will be utterly ruined. Ps 110:5; Da 2:34

[13]"The glory of Lebanon will come to you,
the pine, the fir and the cypress together,
to adorn the place of my sanctuary;
and I will glorify the place of my feet.
[14]The sons of your oppressors will come bowing before you; Isa 14:2
all who despise you will bow down at your feet Isa 49:23; Rev 3:9
and will call you the City of the LORD, Isa 1:26
Zion of the Holy One of Israel. Heb 12:22

[15]"Although you have been forsaken and hated,
with no one traveling through, Isa 33:8
I will make you the everlasting pride Isa 4:2
and the joy of all generations. Isa 65:18
[16]You will drink the milk of nations
and be nursed at royal breasts. Isa 49:23
Then you will know that I, the LORD, am your Savior, Ex 14:30
your Redeemer, the Mighty One of Jacob.
[17]Instead of bronze I will bring you gold,
and silver in place of iron.
Instead of wood I will bring you bronze,
and iron in place of stones.
I will make peace your governor Ps 85:8; Isa 66:12
and righteousness your ruler. Isa 9:7
[18]No longer will violence be heard in your land,
nor ruin or destruction within your borders,
but you will call your walls Salvation Isa 26:1
and your gates Praise. Isa 61:11; Zep 3:20
[19]The sun will no more be your light by day,
nor will the brightness of the moon shine on you,
for the LORD will be your everlasting light,
and your God will be your glory. Zec 2:5
[20]Your sun will never set again, Isa 30:26
and your moon will wane no more;
the LORD will be your everlasting light,
and your days of sorrow will end. Isa 35:10
[21]Then will all your people be righteous Rev 21:27
and they will possess the land forever.
They are the shoot I have planted, Mt 15:13
the work of my hands, Isa 29:23; Eph 2:10
for the display of my splendor. Isa 52:1
[22]The least of you will become a thousand,
the smallest a mighty nation. Ge 12:2
I am the LORD;
in its time I will do this swiftly." Isa 5:19

The Year of the LORD's Favor

61 The Spirit of the Sovereign LORD is on me, Isa 11:2
because the LORD has anointed me Ps 45:7
to preach good news to the poor. Mt 11:5
He has sent me to bind up the brokenhearted,
to proclaim freedom for the captives Isa 42:7
and release from darkness for the prisoners,[b]
[2]to proclaim the year of the LORD's favor
and the day of vengeance of our God,
to comfort all who mourn, Isa 57:18; Mt 5:4
[3] and provide for those who grieve in Zion—
to bestow on them a crown of beauty Isa 3:23
instead of ashes,
the oil of gladness Isa 1:6
instead of mourning,
and a garment of praise
instead of a spirit of despair.
They will be called oaks of righteousness,
a planting of the LORD Ps 1:3; 92:12-13
for the display of his splendor. Isa 60:20-21
[4]They will rebuild the ancient ruins Isa 49:8
and restore the places long devastated;
they will renew the ruined cities
that have been devastated for generations.
[5]Aliens will shepherd your flocks; Isa 14:1-2
foreigners will work your fields and vineyards.

[a]9 Or *the trading ships* [b]1 Hebrew; Septuagint *the blind*

6And you will be called priests of the LORD,
you will be named ministers of our God.
You will feed on the wealth of nations, Isa 60:11
and in their riches you will boast.

7Instead of their shame
my people will receive a double portion,
and instead of disgrace
they will rejoice in their inheritance;
and so they will inherit a double portion in
their land, Isa 60:21
and everlasting joy will be theirs. Isa 25:9

8"For I, the LORD, love justice; Ps 11:7; Isa 5:16
I hate robbery and iniquity.
In my faithfulness I will reward them
and make an everlasting covenant with
them. Isa 55:3
9Their descendants will be known among the
nations Isa 43:5
and their offspring among the peoples.
All who see them will acknowledge
that they are a people the LORD has
blessed." Dt 28:3-12

10I delight greatly in the LORD;
my soul rejoices in my God. Isa 25:9; Hab 3:18
For he has clothed me with garments of
salvation
and arrayed me in a robe of righteousness,
as a bridegroom adorns his head like a priest,
and as a bride adorns herself with her
jewels. Isa 49:18; Rev 21:2
11For as the soil makes the sprout come up
and a garden causes seeds to grow,
so the Sovereign LORD will make righteousness
and praise Ps 85:11
spring up before all nations.

Zion's New Name

62 For Zion's sake I will not keep silent,
for Jerusalem's sake I will not remain
quiet,
till her righteousness shines out like the dawn,
her salvation like a blazing torch. Ps 67:2
2The nations will see your righteousness,
and all kings your glory;
you will be called by a new name ver 4,12; Isa 1:26
that the mouth of the LORD will bestow.
3You will be a crown of splendor in the LORD's
hand, Zec 9:16; 1Th 2:19
a royal diadem in the hand of your God.
4No longer will they call you Deserted, Isa 54:6
or name your land Desolate. Isa 49:19
But you will be called Hephzibah,[a]
and your land Beulah[b];
for the LORD will take delight in you, Jer 32:41
and your land will be married. Jer 3:14; Hos 2:19
5As a young man marries a maiden,
so will your sons[c] marry you;
as a bridegroom rejoices over his bride,
so will your God rejoice over you. Isa 65:19

6I have posted watchmen on your walls,
O Jerusalem; Isa 52:8; Eze 3:17
they will never be silent day or night.
You who call on the LORD,
give yourselves no rest,
7and give him no rest till he establishes
Jerusalem Mt 15:21-28; Lk 18:1-8
and makes her the praise of the earth.

8The LORD has sworn by his right hand
and by his mighty arm:
"Never again will I give your grain
as food for your enemies, Dt 28:30-33; Isa 1:7
and never again will foreigners drink the new
wine
for which you have toiled;
9but those who harvest it will eat it Isa 1:19
and praise the LORD, Dt 12:7; Joel 2:26
and those who gather the grapes will drink it
in the courts of my sanctuary." Lev 23:39

10Pass through, pass through the gates! Isa 60:11
Prepare the way for the people.
Build up, build up the highway! Isa 11:16; 57:14
Remove the stones.
Raise a banner for the nations. Isa 11:10

11The LORD has made proclamation
to the ends of the earth: Dt 30:4
"Say to the Daughter of Zion, Zec 9:9; Mt 21:5
'See, your Savior comes! Rev 22:12
See, his reward is with him,
and his recompense accompanies him.' "
12They will be called the Holy People, ver 4
the Redeemed of the LORD; Isa 35:9
and you will be called Sought After,
the City No Longer Deserted. Isa 42:16

God's Day of Vengeance and Redemption

63 Who is this coming from Edom, 2Ch 28:17
from Bozrah, with his garments stained
crimson? Am 1:12
Who is this, robed in splendor,
striding forward in the greatness of his
strength? Isa 45:24
"It is I, speaking in righteousness,
mighty to save." Isa 46:13; Zep 3:17

2Why are your garments red,
like those of one treading the winepress?

3"I have trodden the winepress alone; Rev 14:20
from the nations no one was with me.
I trampled them in my anger
and trod them down in my wrath; Isa 22:5
their blood spattered my garments, Rev 19:13

[a]4 *Hephzibah* means *my delight is in her.* [b]4 *Beulah* means *married.* [c]5 Or *Builder*

and I stained all my clothing.
[4]For the day of vengeance was in my heart,
and the year of my redemption has come.
[5]I looked, but there was no one to help, Isa 41:28
I was appalled that no one gave support;
so my own arm worked salvation for me,
and my own wrath sustained me. Isa 59:16
[6]I trampled the nations in my anger; Ps 108:13
in my wrath I made them drunk Isa 29:9
and poured their blood on the ground."

Praise and Prayer

[7]I will tell of the kindnesses of the LORD, Isa 54:8
the deeds for which he is to be praised,
according to all the LORD has done for us—
yes, the many good things he has done Ex 18:9
for the house of Israel,
according to his compassion and many kindnesses. Ps 51:1; Eph 2:4
[8]He said, "Surely they are my people, Isa 51:4
sons who will not be false to me";
and so he became their Savior. Isa 25:9
[9]In all their distress he too was distressed,
and the angel of his presence saved them.
In his love and mercy he redeemed them;
he lifted them up and carried them Dt 1:31
all the days of old. Dt 32:7; Job 37:23
[10]Yet they rebelled Ps 78:40
and grieved his Holy Spirit. Ps 51:11; Ac 7:51
So he turned and became their enemy Ps 106:40
and he himself fought against them. Jos 10:14

[11]Then his people recalled[a] the days of old,
the days of Moses and his people—
where is he who brought them through the sea, Ex 14:22,30
with the shepherd of his flock?
Where is he who set
his Holy Spirit among them, Nu 11:17
[12]who sent his glorious arm of power
to be at Moses' right hand,
who divided the waters before them, Ex 14:21-22
to gain for himself everlasting renown,
[13]who led them through the depths? Dt 32:12
Like a horse in open country,
they did not stumble; Jer 31:9
[14]like cattle that go down to the plain,
they were given rest by the Spirit of the LORD. Dt 12:9
This is how you guided your people
to make for yourself a glorious name.

[15]Look down from heaven and see Dt 26:15; Ps 80:14
from your lofty throne, holy and glorious.
Where are your zeal and your might? Isa 9:7
Your tenderness and compassion are withheld from us. Jer 31:20; Hos 11:8
[16]But you are our Father, Ex 4:22
though Abraham does not know us
or Israel acknowledge us; Job 14:21
you, O LORD, are our Father,
our Redeemer from of old is your name.
[17]Why, O LORD, do you make us wander from your ways
and harden our hearts so we do not revere you? Isa 29:13
Return for the sake of your servants, Nu 10:36
the tribes that are your inheritance. Ex 34:9
[18]For a little while your people possessed your holy place, Dt 4:26; 11:17
but now our enemies have trampled down your sanctuary. Ps 74:3-8
[19]We are yours from of old;
but you have not ruled over them,
they have not been called by your name.[b]

64 Oh, that you would rend the heavens
and come down, Ps 144:5; Mic 1:3
that the mountains would tremble before you! Ex 19:18
[2]As when fire sets twigs ablaze
and causes water to boil,
come down to make your name known to your enemies
and cause the nations to quake before you!
[3]For when you did awesome things that we did not expect, Ps 65:5
you came down, and the mountains
trembled before you.
[4]Since ancient times no one has heard,
no ear has perceived,
no eye has seen any God besides you,
who acts on behalf of those who wait for him. Isa 30:18; 1Co 2:9*
[5]You come to the help of those who gladly do right, Isa 26:8
who remember your ways.
But when we continued to sin against them,
you were angry. Isa 10:4
How then can we be saved?
[6]All of us have become like one who is unclean, Lev 5:2
and all our righteous acts are like filthy rags; Isa 46:12; 48:1
we all shrivel up like a leaf, Ps 90:5-6
and like the wind our sins sweep us away.
[7]No one calls on your name Isa 59:4
or strives to lay hold of you;
for you have hidden your face from us Dt 31:18
and made us waste away because of our sins. Isa 9:18
[8]Yet, O LORD, you are our Father. Isa 63:16
We are the clay, you are the potter; Isa 29:16
we are all the work of your hand. Isa 19:25

[a]11 Or *But may he recall* [b]19 Or *We are like those you have never ruled, / like those never called by your name*

9Do not be angry beyond measure, O LORD;
do not remember our sins forever. Isa 43:25
Oh, look upon us, we pray,
for we are all your people. Isa 51:4
10Your sacred cities have become a desert;
even Zion is a desert, Jerusalem a desolation. Dt 29:23
11Our holy and glorious temple, where our fathers praised you, Ps 74:3-7
has been burned with fire,
and all that we treasured lies in ruins.
12After all this, O LORD, will you hold yourself back? Ps 74:10-11; Isa 42:14
Will you keep silent and punish us beyond measure? Ps 83:1

Judgment and Salvation

65 "I revealed myself to those who did not ask for me;
I was found by those who did not seek me.
To a nation that did not call on my name,
I said, 'Here am I, here am I.'
2All day long I have held out my hands
to an obstinate people, Ro 10:21*; Isa 1:2,23
who walk in ways not good,
pursuing their own imaginations—
3a people who continually provoke me
to my very face, Job 1:11
offering sacrifices in gardens Isa 1:29
and burning incense on altars of brick;
4who sit among the graves Lev 19:31
and spend their nights keeping secret vigil;
who eat the flesh of pigs, Lev 11:7
and whose pots hold broth of unclean meat;
5who say, 'Keep away; don't come near me,
for I am too sacred for you!' Mt 9:11; Lk 18:9-12
Such people are smoke in my nostrils,
a fire that keeps burning all day.

6"See, it stands written before me:
I will not keep silent but will pay back in full; Ps 50:3; Jer 16:18
I will pay it back into their laps— Ps 79:12
7both your sins and the sins of your fathers,"
says the LORD.
"Because they burned sacrifices on the mountains
and defied me on the hills, Isa 57:7
I will measure into their laps
the full payment for their former deeds."

8This is what the LORD says:

"As when juice is still found in a cluster of grapes
and men say, 'Don't destroy it,
there is yet some good in it,'
so will I do in behalf of my servants; Isa 54:17
I will not destroy them all.
9I will bring forth descendants from Jacob,
and from Judah those who will possess my mountains; Am 9:11-15
my chosen people will inherit them, Isa 14:1
and there will my servants live. Isa 32:18
10Sharon will become a pasture for flocks,
and the Valley of Achor a resting place for herds, Jos 7:26
for my people who seek me. Isa 51:1

11"But as for you who forsake the LORD
and forget my holy mountain, Ps 137:5
who spread a table for Fortune
and fill bowls of mixed wine for Destiny,
12I will destine you for the sword, Isa 27:1
and you will all bend down for the slaughter;
for I called but you did not answer, Pr 1:24-25
I spoke but you did not listen. 2Ch 36:15-16
You did evil in my sight
and chose what displeases me." Isa 1:24; 66:4

13Therefore this is what the Sovereign LORD says:

"My servants will eat, Isa 1:19
but you will go hungry; Job 18:12
my servants will drink, Isa 33:16
but you will go thirsty; Isa 41:17
my servants will rejoice, Isa 60:5
but you will be put to shame. Isa 44:9
14My servants will sing
out of the joy of their hearts,
but you will cry out Mt 8:12; Lk 13:28
from anguish of heart
and wail in brokenness of spirit.
15You will leave your name
to my chosen ones as a curse; Zec 8:13
the Sovereign LORD will put you to death,
but to his servants he will give another name. Rev 2:17
16Whoever invokes a blessing in the land Dt 29:19
will do so by the God of truth; Ps 31:5
he who takes an oath in the land
will swear by the God of truth. Isa 19:18
For the past troubles will be forgotten Job 11:16
and hidden from my eyes.

New Heavens and a New Earth

17"Behold, I will create
new heavens and a new earth. Isa 66:22; 2Pe 3:13
The former things will not be remembered,
nor will they come to mind.
18But be glad and rejoice forever Ps 98:1-9; Isa 25:9
in what I will create,
for I will create Jerusalem to be a delight
and its people a joy.
19I will rejoice over Jerusalem Isa 35:10; 62:5
and take delight in my people;

the sound of weeping and of crying Isa 25:8
will be heard in it no more.

20"Never again will there be in it
an infant who lives but a few days,
or an old man who does not live out his
years; Ecc 8:13
he who dies at a hundred
will be thought a mere youth;
he who fails to reach[a] a hundred
will be considered accursed.
21They will build houses and dwell in them;
they will plant vineyards and eat their fruit.
22No longer will they build houses and others
live in them, Dt 28:30
or plant and others eat.
For as the days of a tree, Ps 92:12-14
so will be the days of my people; Ps 21:4; 91:16
my chosen ones will long enjoy Isa 14:1
the works of their hands.
23They will not toil in vain Isa 49:4
or bear children doomed to misfortune;
for they will be a people blessed by the LORD,
they and their descendants with them.
24Before they call I will answer; Isa 55:6
while they are still speaking I will hear.
25The wolf and the lamb will feed together,
and the lion will eat straw like the ox,
but dust will be the serpent's food. Ge 3:14
They will neither harm nor destroy
on all my holy mountain,"
says the LORD.

Judgment and Hope

66 This is what the LORD says:

"Heaven is my throne, Mt 23:22
and the earth is my footstool. 1Ki 8:27
Where is the house you will build for me?
Where will my resting place be?
2Has not my hand made all these things,
and so they came into being?"
declares the LORD.

"This is the one I esteem:
he who is humble and contrite in spirit,
and trembles at my word. Ezr 9:4
3But whoever sacrifices a bull Isa 1:11
is like one who kills a man,
and whoever offers a lamb,
like one who breaks a dog's neck;
whoever makes a grain offering
is like one who presents pig's blood,
and whoever burns memorial incense, Lev 2:2
like one who worships an idol.
They have chosen their own ways, Isa 57:17
and their souls delight in their
abominations; Dt 27:15
4so I also will choose harsh treatment for them
and will bring upon them what they dread.
For when I called, no one answered, Pr 1:24
when I spoke, no one listened.
They did evil in my sight 2Ki 21:2,4,6
and chose what displeases me." Isa 65:12
5Hear the word of the LORD,
you who tremble at his word:
"Your brothers who hate you, Ps 38:20
and exclude you because of my name, have
said,
'Let the LORD be glorified,
that we may see your joy!'
Yet they will be put to shame. Lk 13:17
6Hear that uproar from the city,
hear that noise from the temple!
It is the sound of the LORD Ps 68:33
repaying his enemies all they deserve.

7"Before she goes into labor, Isa 54:1
she gives birth;
before the pains come upon her,
she delivers a son. Rev 12:5
8Who has ever heard of such a thing?
Who has ever seen such things? Isa 64:4
Can a country be born in a day
or a nation be brought forth in a moment?
Yet no sooner is Zion in labor
than she gives birth to her children. Isa 49:21
9Do I bring to the moment of birth Isa 37:3
and not give delivery?" says the LORD.
"Do I close up the womb
when I bring to delivery?" says your God.
10"Rejoice with Jerusalem and be glad for her,
all you who love her; Ps 26:8
rejoice greatly with her,
all you who mourn over her. Isa 57:19
11For you will nurse and be satisfied Isa 60:16
at her comforting breasts;
you will drink deeply
and delight in her overflowing abundance."

12For this is what the LORD says:

"I will extend peace to her like a river, Isa 48:18

LIVING INSIGHT

When we spend time in the quiet, comforting presence of the living Lord, we are more ready to get on with life with a lighter heart, better sight and a calmer spirit. Watch for Him to pour out His peace "like a river"—abundant and overflowing.

(See Isaiah 66:12–13.)

[a]20 Or / *the sinner who reaches*

and the wealth of nations like a flooding
stream; Isa 60:5; 61:6
you will nurse and be carried on her arm
and dandled on her knees.
13As a mother comforts her child,
so will I comfort you; Isa 40:1; 2Co 1:4
and you will be comforted over Jerusalem."

14When you see this, your heart will rejoice
and you will flourish like grass;
the hand of the LORD will be made known to
his servants, Isa 54:17
but his fury will be shown to his foes.
15See, the LORD is coming with fire, Isa 1:31
and his chariots are like a whirlwind;
he will bring down his anger with fury,
and his rebuke with flames of fire. Ps 9:5
16For with fire and with his sword Isa 27:1; 30:30
the LORD will execute judgment upon all
men, Eze 36:5
and many will be those slain by the LORD.

17"Those who consecrate and purify themselves
to go into the gardens, following the one in the
midst of[a] those who eat the flesh of pigs and rats
and other abominable things—they will meet
their end together," declares the LORD. Ps 37:20
18"And I, because of their actions and their
imaginations, am about to come[b] and gather all
nations and tongues, and they will come and see
my glory. Isa 59:19
19"I will set a sign among them, and I will send
some of those who survive to the nations—to Tarshish, to the Libyans[c] and Lydians (famous as
archers), to Tubal and Greece, and to the distant
islands that have not heard of my fame or seen my
glory. They will proclaim my glory among the nations. 20And they will bring all your brothers, from
all the nations, to my holy mountain in Jerusalem
as an offering to the LORD—on horses, in chariots
and wagons, and on mules and camels," says the
LORD. "They will bring them, as the Israelites bring
their grain offerings, to the temple of the LORD in
ceremonially clean vessels. 21And I will select some
of them also to be priests and Levites," says the
LORD. Ex 19:6; Isa 61:6; 1Pe 2:5,9

22"As the new heavens and the new earth that I
make will endure before me," declares the LORD,
"so will your name and descendants endure.
23From one New Moon to another and from one
Sabbath to another, all mankind will come and
bow down before me," says the LORD. 24"And they
will go out and look upon the dead bodies of those
who rebelled against me; their worm will not die,
nor will their fire be quenched, and they will be
loathsome to all mankind." Isa 1:31; Mk 9:48*

[a] 17 Or *gardens behind one of your temples, and* [b] 18 The meaning of the Hebrew for this clause is uncertain.
[c] 19 Some Septuagint manuscripts *Put* (Libyans); Hebrew *Pul*

INTRODUCTION

JEREMIAH

Jeremiah would not have been considered to be the brightest among the prophets of God. Isaiah would have been awarded that distinction. Nor was he the most difficult to understand. Very likely that label would have fit Ezekiel best. Not even the most influential (probably Daniel), or the most notorious (probably Jonah), or the most to be pitied (probably Hosea). But of all the prophets, Jeremiah was certainly the most heroic. Consider this: For 42 years he stood virtually alone in the nation of Judah—preaching, warning, pleading, trying to wake up the nation to the reality that judgment would surely come if they didn't turn around and seek the Lord's forgiveness and compassion. At times he must have been convinced that he was talking to a brick wall. No one seemed to listen. And when doom finally fell, Jeremiah saw the very thing he hoped he would never live to see: the destruction of the holy city, the city of Jerusalem. He lived to see his prediction come true.

WRITER: *Jeremiah*

DATE: *c.585–580 B.C.*

PURPOSE: *To warn God's people of judgment and to urge them to repent, before it was too late*

KEY MESSAGE: *Those who will not turn from evil will face severe consequences*

TIME LINE 1300BC 1200 1100 1000 900 800 700 600 500 400

Division of the kingdom (930 B.C.)

Ministries of Elijah and Elisha in Israel (c.875-797 B.C.)

Ministries of Amos and Hosea in Israel (c.760-715 B.C.)

Ministries of Micah and Isaiah in Judah (c.742-681 B.C.)

Exile of Israel (722 B.C.)

Jeremiah's ministry in Judah (c.626-585 B.C.)

Fall of Jerusalem (586 B.C.)

Book of Jeremiah written (c.585-580 B.C.)

Weeping, Warning and Waiting

A CESSPOOL OF SIN	WARNINGS AND JUDGMENT	WORDS TO THE NATIONS	A SOBERING ENDING
Weak leadership Moral compromise	Exhortations to Judah Promises of restoration *(30–33)* Fall of Jerusalem *(39)*	Egypt, Damascus Philistia, Arabia Moab, Elam Ammon, Babylon Edom	Jerusalem in ruins
CHAPTERS 1–17	***CHAPTERS 18–45***	***CHAPTERS 46–51***	***CHAPTER 52***

I would like to blow the dust off an ancient proverb you may recall having read but may not have brought to mind for a while. I'm thinking of the first line of Proverbs 13:20: "He who walks with the wise grows wise."

We may be tempted to think of that profound and practical truth only in the context of those who are still living. If we want to be wise like someone we admire and respect, then we need to rub shoulders with that person. We need to spend time with him or her. Certainly that is true.

Yet there is another way we can walk with the wise: through reading biographies. Carl Sandburg wrote eloquently about Abraham Lincoln in a four-volume set titled, *Lincoln in the War Years*. Sandburg titled one of the chapters, "A tree is best measured when it's down." Sometimes a biographer can capture the secret of a life and measure it best when that life is done.

That was true with respect to the life of the martyred missionary Jim Elliot. It was through the reading of his biography, titled *Through Gates of Splendor*, and a later book called *Shadow of the Almighty*, that God really got hold of my own life. Biography has a way of capturing the essence of someone's life and feeding us the truth about that life in such a way that wisdom penetrates our own lives. Phillips Brooks wrote back in 1886, "A biography is, indeed, a book. But far more than a book, it is a man. Never lay a biography down until the man is a living, breathing, acting person to you."

It is the reality of this concept that makes the study of the prophets of the Bible so profitable. These were not simply grumpy naysayers who declared doom to the people of their day; they were intense, passionate men of wisdom. I want these men to come out of the pages of the Bible and become for us living, breathing, acting persons from whom we can gain wisdom.

The book of Jeremiah is, in many ways, the autobiography of a great man whom God raised up in a particular place at a particular time to do a particular work. No prophet exposed his feelings more than Jeremiah. No prophet lived his wisdom more passionately; one might even say no prophet lived his wisdom more reluctantly. To study his life is to grow wise ourselves, as we learn what it means to follow God in spite of everything that threatens to undo us.

Getting to Know This Tough and Tender Prophet

We find in the prophet Jeremiah an endearing balance of tenderness and toughness. He possessed a warmth of spirit that was very sensitive to people's needs; his relationship to God was marked by a willingness to lay himself bare in total honesty before Him and to fearlessly serve Him. Yet at the same time, he had a hard, bronze-like determination to stand firm against the turbulent tidal flow of his times. That's why J. Oswald Sanders, in his book, *Robust in Faith*, defined Jeremiah as "a figure of bronze dissolving into tears."

We need to understand this man, I think, before we can begin to understand the book that bears his name. We need to see this man as he was, and from his life learn how to become wise. There is a brief and seemingly insignificant preface that appears in the first three verses of the book. It sets the stage for his life—and as such these few verses take on great importance:

> *The words of Jeremiah son of Hilkiah [Jeremiah is the son of a priest. He's an ancient P.K.], one of the priests at Anathoth in the territory of Benjamin (1:1).*

Anathoth was a quiet little village north of Jerusalem—a place where a man would love to spend all of his years, if he's the quiet type. I take it that Jeremiah might very well have been content to stay there for the rest of his life. But that was not God's plan for him.

> *The word of the Lord came to him in the thirteenth year of the reign of Josiah son of Amon king of Judah, and through the reign of Jehoiakim son of Josiah king of Judah, down to the fifth month of the eleventh year of Zedekiah son of Josiah king of Judah, when the people of Jerusalem went into exile (1:2–3).*

There were two other kings in Jeremiah's day beside the three mentioned here, but their reigns were so brief God doesn't even bother to record their names here. What I find significant is that Jeremiah lived and prophesied during the generations of five kings. That's quite a segment of time—almost five decades of ministry!

There's some question as to whether Jeremiah ministered 42 years or 47 years but most students of the Bible agree that it was less than 50 years. We have no record of any positive response to his ministry during this span of time. I want you to think about this. For almost five decades there was no measurable change in the lives of the people of Judah—but God continued to use Jeremiah to speak His message with boldness.

Jeremiah watched the slow deterioration of a nation. He watched the people to whom he ministered harden their hearts and walk away from his prophecies and warnings. But he kept on prophesying, kept on warning the people, right up to the exile of the people of Jerusalem in the days of Zedekiah. Jeremiah stayed faithful to his calling—even though his was a gloomy message in a gloomy time. He stayed faithful, even as he watched his nation destroyed by war and his people carried into captivity.

The Call of Jeremiah

After the brief preface (1:1–3), Jeremiah let us in on how it was he came to be in the position he occupied (1:4–5):

> *The word of the Lord came to me [notice it's an autobiography that Jeremiah is writing], saying,*
>
> *"Before I formed you in the womb I knew you,*
> *before you were born I set you apart;*
> *I appointed you as a prophet to the nations."*

God had a life plan for Jeremiah. He had a purpose for him, decided before Jeremiah's birth, and He communicated that in a striking way in verse 5. In the face of such an awesome responsibility and task, Jeremiah did what many other servants of God have done. He hesitated. He protested. He recognized his weaknesses and his lack of qualification, as he shrunk back and said, "Ah, Sovereign Lord . . . I do not know how to speak; I am only a child" (1:6). In effect, Jeremiah was saying, "I don't have the proper skills. I'm not experienced in speaking as a prophet."

By the way, if you're only 19 or 20 years old, don't think you have to wait until you get older before God's voice can be heard through you. God spoke to Jeremiah *before* he was what we might consider the age of adulthood—let's just say, 21 years of age. Jeremiah was probably in his late teens at the time of his call. God often captures the heart of a person in the young years of life and says to him or her, "This is the calling I have for you. Now get at it. Do it." For some, it may happen in the mid-life years, for others, even later in life. Here, Jeremiah is told early on, "You're to be a prophet for Me . . . My messenger to the nations."

God said in effect, "Jeremiah, before you were ever in the womb I knew you. I chose you. I had plans for you. I set you apart. I endowed you with prophetic gifts and I determined that you would be My man for the nation of Judah during these years of their history." And Jeremiah's response went something like this: "Thanks, but no thanks, Lord. I am not experienced. I don't have what it takes . . . all the glitz, the seasoned experience, those superior skills required to be Your spokesman."

A Hard Road

The Lord sensed what was going through Jeremiah's mind. Can't you just imagine? "A prophet to the nations." Jeremiah must have been terrified of those to whom he would speak. He was young. He was inexperienced. He was intimidated. And so the Lord hastened to reassure the young man: "Do not be afraid of them, for I am with you and will rescue you" (1:8).

In effect, God said, "When you're with Me, Jeremiah, we're a majority! We can handle whatever comes. We can handle anybody who will oppose you. I'll give you the words to say. I'll be your voice. Jeremiah, it's not *your* prophecy, it's *Mine*. You just be My mouthpiece. Don't be intimidated."

Then the Lord went on to give him this mysterious assignment: "See, today I appoint you over nations and kingdoms to uproot and tear down, to destroy and overthrow, to build and to plant" (1:10). If I count the verbs in Jeremiah's divine calling correctly, there were six of them. Interestingly, the first two pairs are negative; the last is positive. If this meant anything, it meant Jeremiah would have more of a negative than a positive ministry. He would be doing more uprooting, tearing down, destroying and overthrowing than he would building and planting. His would not be, on the whole, a happy, positive kind of ministry.

I think it's fair to say that most people want to have a positive ministry. They want to make people happy and have people like them and say good things about them. But that's normally not the calling of a prophet. God's view of things went something like this: "Jeremiah, here's the reality: You're not going to be liked. You're going to stand alone in a nation that is going south and you're going to be saying, 'north.' They're on the way to hell and you're going to be saying, 'Heaven.' They're going to say, 'But the majority says,' and you're going to reply, 'But God says.' They will be laughing and having a great time, but, Jeremiah, I'm taking away your mirth and joy and you're going to cry your way through more than forty years of ministry. It's going to be hard, Jeremiah." Now look at verses 17 and 18 of chapter 1 to see how the Lord expressed in the actual Bible text what was ahead for Jeremiah:

> *"Get yourself ready! Stand up and say to them whatever I command you. Do not be terrified by them, or I will terrify you before them . . . They will fight against you but will not overcome you, for I am with you and will rescue you," declares the* LORD.

If Jeremiah's writings were a musical score, it would be written in a minor key. Some of God's prophets, God's servants, write their scores in a major key. God made us—each of us—unique, one-of-a-kind, gifted, special. And to each of us He's given a very special task to undertake for Him and for the building up of His people. He's given us what we need to carry that out. Some He's called to be those who bring positive words of encouragement and comfort and hope. Some He's called to be those who exhort and rebuke and correct. Some have a sunny disposition. Some, like Jeremiah, are melancholy and sad. Let's give the people of God room to be who they are, just the way God made them! Let's be very careful that we don't place God's messengers in a box of our own making. Each has a place in the community of believers. Each has a special gift to contribute. Whatever our gift, with whatever personality God's given us, let's learn from Jeremiah's willingness to follow his Lord, in spite of hardship, pain and depression, in spite of everything!

Lessons From Jeremiah

Four lessons linger as we read Jeremiah. First, *God chooses and uses unlikely people for unbelievable tasks.* Who would have ever thought a man like Jeremiah would qualify for this great a task? But he did. It may be that you're one of those called to undertake a great work for the Lord. It may very well be that in your own mind you are feeling like you would be the last person on earth to do this; you may be feeling totally inept. Consider this: You may be the very one God is telling, "That's your task. I'm calling you to fill this role!"

Second, *when God's Word is ignored, you will pay the price.* If you ignore God's Word, I can virtually guarantee you severe consequences. I don't care if you are incredibly intelligent, astoundingly clever or dripping with charisma; you will reap what you sow. No matter how old you are or how much money you have, if you ignore God's Word, you will pay a price.

Third, *no amount of carnal pleasure can erase the lonely and tragic misery of a disobedient life.* At the time you give in, you may think, "Oh, this is so much fun no amount of consequences could make me forget the pleasure. This is worth it!" I can assure you, it is not.

Fourth and finally, *sometimes the most deserving people are the least rewarded.* Jeremiah deserved to have all the applause and the credit that could possibly cascade down on the best of God's people. But you know what he lived to see? The fall and destruction of his nation, and his people, captured and depressed, trudging off to Babylon.

Remember Psalm 137. How vividly it portrays what the people of Judah experienced. By the rivers of Babylon there they sat down. They hung their hearts on the weeping willow trees. And then those Babylonian mockers came and said, "Sing one of the Lord's songs here in this land." And they replied, "How can we sing the Lord's song in a foreign land?" Can't you just imagine? "Come on. Break out with 'Amazing Grace' or 'The God of Abraham Praise.' " And those broken Jerusalemites hung their heads and said, "We have no song." They were broken. They had ignored God's message to them through the prophet Jeremiah—and now they were paying the price. They had sought the temporary pleasures of sin at the expense of the permanent blessings of obedience—and they lost their ability, and their will, to sing.

Yet, before we close the book on Jeremiah, I want to bring into view one last picture of the prophet Jeremiah. He knew that God would bring judgment on the people of Judah—after all, that was the focus of his message. But think back: There was one more element to Jeremiah's call. In the midst of all the uprooting and tearing down and destroying and overthrowing, Jeremiah had been called *to build and to plant* (1:10). To a people who were going to lose their song, Jeremiah offered hope beyond judgment, through the Lord's promise to His people: "I will restore the fortunes of Jacob's tents . . . From them will come songs of thanksgiving and the sound of rejoicing" (30:19). The people would one day have a new song to sing.

Thank God for Jeremiah—wise man of long ago! We have walked with him through a summary of his life; may we have grown in wisdom and may we apply that wisdom as we fulfill the calling that the Lord has issued to us. Remember: *Those who walk with the wise grow wise!*

Living in a Cesspool **Chapters 1–17**

The book of Jeremiah was directed toward a time in the history of the nation of Judah when the people were living in a cesspool of sin and rebellion. Any semblance of morality that remained from previous years was quickly eroding. There was weak leadership on a national level and also within the religious hierarchy. Moral integrity and commitment to the God of Judah had been exchanged for compromise and idolatry. In this climate, there was room for only one of two outcomes—radical repentance on a national level, or divine judgment executed on a rebellious, disobedient nation. The book of Jeremiah unveils which of these two paths the nation chose to take.

1 The words of Jeremiah son of Hilkiah, one of
the priests at Anathoth in the territory of
Benjamin. 2The word of the LORD came to him in
the thirteenth year of the reign of Josiah son of
Amon king of Judah, 3and through the reign of
Jehoiakim son of Josiah king of Judah, down to the
fifth month of the eleventh year of Zedekiah son of
Josiah king of Judah, when the people of Jerusalem
went into exile. Jos 21:18; 1Ch 6:60; Jer 52:15

The Call of Jeremiah

4The word of the LORD came to me, saying,

5"Before I formed you in the womb I knew[a]
you, Ps 139:16
before you were born I set you apart;
I appointed you as a prophet to the
nations." ver 10; Jer 25:15-26

6"Ah, Sovereign LORD," I said, "I do not know
how to speak; I am only a child." Ex 4:10; 1Ki 3:7
7But the LORD said to me, "Do not say, 'I am
only a child.' You must go to everyone I send you
to and say whatever I command you. 8Do not be
afraid of them, for I am with you and will rescue
you," declares the LORD. Jer 15:20; Eze 2:6
9Then the LORD reached out his hand and
touched my mouth and said to me, "Now, I have
put my words in your mouth. 10See, today I appoint you over nations and kingdoms to uproot
and tear down, to destroy and overthrow, to build
and to plant." Jer 18:7-10; Isa 6:7
11The word of the LORD came to me: "What do
you see, Jeremiah?" Jer 24:3; Am 7:8
"I see the branch of an almond tree," I replied.
12The LORD said to me, "You have seen correctly, for I am watching[b] to see that my word is
fulfilled." Jer 44:27
13The word of the LORD came to me again:
"What do you see?" Zec 4:2
"I see a boiling pot, tilting away from the
north," I answered.
14The LORD said to me, "From the north disaster
will be poured out on all who live in the land. 15I
am about to summon all the peoples of the northern kingdoms," declares the LORD. Isa 14:31

"Their kings will come and set up their
thrones
in the entrance of the gates of Jerusalem;
they will come against all her surrounding
walls
and against all the towns of Judah. Jer 4:16
16I will pronounce my judgments on my people
because of their wickedness in forsaking
me, Dt 28:20; Jer 17:13
in burning incense to other gods Jer 7:9
and in worshiping what their hands have
made. Ps 115:4-8

17"Get yourself ready! Stand up and say to them
whatever I command you. Do not be terrified by
them, or I will terrify you before them. 18Today I
have made you a fortified city, an iron pillar and
a bronze wall to stand against the whole land—
against the kings of Judah, its officials, its priests
and the people of the land. 19They will fight against
you but will not overcome you, for I am with you
and will rescue you," declares the LORD. Isa 50:7

Israel Forsakes God

2 The word of the LORD came to me: 2"Go and
proclaim in the hearing of Jerusalem:

" 'I remember the devotion of your youth,
how as a bride you loved me
and followed me through the desert, Dt 2:7
through a land not sown.
3Israel was holy to the LORD, Ex 19:6
the firstfruits of his harvest; Jas 1:18; Rev 14:4
all who devoured her were held guilty, Isa 41:11
and disaster overtook them,' "
declares the LORD.

4Hear the word of the LORD, O house of Jacob,
all you clans of the house of Israel.

5This is what the LORD says:

"What fault did your fathers find in me,
that they strayed so far from me?
They followed worthless idols Dt 32:21
and became worthless themselves. 2Ki 17:15
6They did not ask, 'Where is the LORD,
who brought us up out of Egypt Hos 13:4
and led us through the barren wilderness,
through a land of deserts and rifts, Dt 8:15
a land of drought and darkness,[c]
a land where no one travels and no one
lives?' Jer 51:43
7I brought you into a fertile land
to eat its fruit and rich produce. Nu 13:27
But you came and defiled my land
and made my inheritance detestable.

[a]5 Or *chose* [b]12 The Hebrew for *watching* sounds like the Hebrew for *almond tree.* [c]6 Or *and the shadow of death*

JEREMIAH

The Prophet Who Cried a Lot

"The words of Jeremiah son of Hilkiah, one of the priests at Anathoth in the territory of Benjamin."

—JEREMIAH 1:1

In our culture, we tend to think that tears are not appropriate, that somehow they're a sign of weakness and the inability to cope. I don't think that's true at all. Some of life's deepest feelings are expressed through tears. And Jeremiah is an outstanding example to us of complete vulnerability and honesty before God.

Jeremiah was a prophet who just did not fit his times. His very name, which means, "The LORD throws," conveys this message. He was, as it were, hurled into his times. This weeping prophet came from a small town in the suburbs of Jerusalem—a small village called Anathoth. I imagine it was a nice, quiet, clean place to raise a family, far from the corruption and pollution of Jerusalem. But God didn't want Jeremiah to stay there. He called his prophet to a forty-year ministry to people who had turned a deaf ear to Him and who would oppose Jeremiah at every turn. Yet Jeremiah had the assurance of God's blessing to hold him securely in place—like an anchor to keep him steady when the storms raged all around him. Listen to the word of the Lord that came to Jeremiah so many years ago: "Before I formed you in the womb I knew you, before you were born I set you apart; I appointed you as a prophet to the nations" (Jeremiah 1:5). Not bad when it comes to discovering one's purpose in life, right?

God threw this man into hostile times, saying, in effect, "You're not going to have a delightful, prosperous ministry, Jeremiah. You'd better prepare yourself, Jeremiah, because when the people hear what you have to tell them, they're going to reject it. And they're going to reject you—despising you and your words the whole way through. But I'll be with you, Jeremiah."

That was Jeremiah's situation. Now let's take a look at his personality. First, *Jeremiah was sad and lonely*. When push came to shove, when he felt he was really up against a wall, Jeremiah cried. He was almost inconsolably sad: "Oh, that my head were a spring of water and my eyes a fountain of tears! I would weep day and night for the slain of my people" (9:1). And look at verses 1 and 2 of chapter 16, where God told Jeremiah he would spend his entire life without a wife or children. He must have felt so rejected, so alone, so consumed by the weight of his burden.

Second, *Jeremiah was introspective and underappreciated*. Chapter 20 records the story of the priest who had Jeremiah beaten and thrown into prison simply because he was doing what he had been called to do. It was at this point that Jeremiah reached rock-bottom, and he cried out to God, "Cursed be the day I was born!" (20:14). But even though Jeremiah despaired, he could not abandon his calling.

Third, and finally, *Jeremiah was faithful and determined*. Look carefully at verse 9 of chapter 20: "But if I say, 'I will not mention him or speak any more in his name,' his word is in my heart like a fire, a fire shut up in my bones. I am weary of holding it in; indeed, I cannot." Wow! This man who often complained bitterly about the role God had given him couldn't help but proclaim God's message. In effect, Jeremiah said, "Just when I think I've been burned for the last time, His word is like a fire in my bones. When I hold it in it starts to boil within me, until all of a sudden it explodes into a world that desperately needs to hear it." Do you see the depth of Jeremiah's true character and calling?

Into a corrupt culture God threw this fragile and fallible man. Jeremiah was a sensitive man given to tears and even disillusionment at times. But God wanted him to know that he was His man. Jeremiah was just what God created him to be. Please don't fail to notice how God looked after His weeping prophet and encouraged him. Jeremiah may have been the "weeping prophet," but observe this: Whenever Jeremiah cried, he cried out to God in prayer. And God never, ever, turned a deaf ear.

8The priests did not ask,
'Where is the LORD?'
Those who deal with the law did not know me; Jer 4:22
the leaders rebelled against me.
The prophets prophesied by Baal, Jer 23:13
following worthless idols. Jer 16:19

9"Therefore I bring charges against you again,"
declares the LORD.
"And I will bring charges against your children's children.
10Cross over to the coasts of Kittim[a] and look,
send to Kedar[b] and observe closely; Ge 25:13
see if there has ever been anything like this:
11Has a nation ever changed its gods?
(Yet they are not gods at all.) Isa 37:19; Jer 16:20
But my people have exchanged their[c] Glory
for worthless idols.
12Be appalled at this, O heavens,
and shudder with great horror,"
declares the LORD.
13"My people have committed two sins:
They have forsaken me,
the spring of living water, Ps 36:9; Jn 4:14
and have dug their own cisterns,
broken cisterns that cannot hold water.
14Is Israel a servant, a slave by birth? Ex 4:22
Why then has he become plunder?
15Lions have roared; Jer 4:7; 50:17
they have growled at him.
They have laid waste his land; Isa 1:7
his towns are burned and deserted. 2Ki 25:9
16Also, the men of Memphis[d] and Tahpanhes
have shaved the crown of your head.[e]
17Have you not brought this on yourselves
by forsaking the LORD your God Isa 1:28
when he led you in the way?
18Now why go to Egypt Isa 30:2
to drink water from the Shihor[f]? Jos 13:3
And why go to Assyria Hos 5:13
to drink water from the River[g]? Isa 7:20
19Your wickedness will punish you;
your backsliding will rebuke you. Jer 3:11,22
Consider then and realize
how evil and bitter it is for you Job 20:14
when you forsake the LORD your God Jer 19:4
and have no awe of me," Ps 36:1
declares the Lord, the LORD Almighty.

20"Long ago you broke off your yoke Lev 26:13
and tore off your bonds;
you said, 'I will not serve you!'
Indeed, on every high hill Isa 57:7; Jer 17:2
and under every spreading tree Dt 12:2
you lay down as a prostitute. Isa 1:21
21I had planted you like a choice vine Ex 15:17
of sound and reliable stock.
How then did you turn against me
into a corrupt, wild vine? Isa 5:4
22Although you wash yourself with soda Ps 51:2
and use an abundance of soap,
the stain of your guilt is still before me,"
declares the Sovereign LORD.
23"How can you say, 'I am not defiled; Pr 30:12
I have not run after the Baals'? Jer 9:14
See how you behaved in the valley; Jer 7:31
consider what you have done.
You are a swift she-camel
running here and there, Jer 31:22
24a wild donkey accustomed to the desert,
sniffing the wind in her craving—
in her heat who can restrain her?
Any males that pursue her need not tire themselves;
at mating time they will find her.
25Do not run until your feet are bare
and your throat is dry.
But you said, 'It's no use!
I love foreign gods, Dt 32:16; Jer 3:13; 14:10
and I must go after them.'

26"As a thief is disgraced when he is caught,
so the house of Israel is disgraced—
they, their kings and their officials,
their priests and their prophets. Jer 32:32
27They say to wood, 'You are my father,'
and to stone, 'You gave me birth.' Jer 3:9
They have turned their backs to me Ps 14:3
and not their faces; Jer 18:17; 32:33
yet when they are in trouble, they say, Isa 26:16
'Come and save us!' Hos 5:15
28Where then are the gods you made for yourselves? Isa 45:20
Let them come if they can save you
when you are in trouble! Dt 32:37
For you have as many gods
as you have towns, O Judah. Jer 11:13

29"Why do you bring charges against me?
You have all rebelled against me," Jer 5:1; 6:13
declares the LORD.
30"In vain I punished your people;
they did not respond to correction.
Your sword has devoured your prophets
like a ravening lion.

31"You of this generation, consider the word of the LORD:

"Have I been a desert to Israel
or a land of great darkness? Isa 45:19
Why do my people say, 'We are free to roam;
we will come to you no more'?
32Does a maiden forget her jewelry,

[a] *10* That is, Cyprus and western coastlands
[b] *10* The home of Bedouin tribes in the Syro-Arabian desert
[c] *11* Masoretic Text; an ancient Hebrew scribal tradition *my*
[d] *16* Hebrew *Noph*
[e] *16* Or *have cracked your skull*
[f] *18* That is, a branch of the Nile
[g] *18* That is, the Euphrates

a bride her wedding ornaments?
Yet my people have forgotten me, Isa 57:11
days without number.
33 How skilled you are at pursuing love!
Even the worst of women can learn from
your ways.
34 On your clothes men find
the lifeblood of the innocent poor, 2Ki 21:16
though you did not catch them breaking in.
Yet in spite of all this
35 you say, ‘I am innocent; Pr 30:12
he is not angry with me.’
But I will pass judgment on you Jer 25:31
because you say, ‘I have not sinned.’
36 Why do you go about so much,
changing your ways? Jer 31:22
You will be disappointed by Egypt Isa 30:2-3,7
as you were by Assyria.
37 You will also leave that place
with your hands on your head, 2Sa 13:19
for the LORD has rejected those you trust;
you will not be helped by them. Jer 37:7

3 “If a man divorces his wife Dt 24:1-4
and she leaves him and marries another
man,
should he return to her again?
Would not the land be completely defiled?
But you have lived as a prostitute with many
lovers— Jer 2:20,25; Eze 16:26,29
would you now return to me?” Hos 2:7
declares the LORD.
2 “Look up to the barren heights and see.
Is there any place where you have not been
ravished?
By the roadside you sat waiting for lovers,
sat like a nomad[a] in the desert.
You have defiled the land Jer 2:7
with your prostitution and wickedness.
3 Therefore the showers have been withheld,
and no spring rains have fallen. Jer 14:4
Yet you have the brazen look of a prostitute;
you refuse to blush with shame. Jer 6:15; 8:12
4 Have you not just called to me:
‘My Father, my friend from my youth,
5 will you always be angry? Isa 57:16
Will your wrath continue forever?’
This is how you talk,
but you do all the evil you can.”

Unfaithful Israel

6 During the reign of King Josiah, the LORD said
to me, “Have you seen what faithless Israel has
done? She has gone up on every high hill and
under every spreading tree and has committed
adultery there. 7 I thought that after she had done
all this she would return to me but she did not, and
her unfaithful sister Judah saw it. 8 I gave faithless
Israel her certificate of divorce and sent her away
because of all her adulteries. Yet I saw that her
unfaithful sister Judah had no fear; she also went
out and committed adultery. 9 Because Israel's immorality mattered so little to her, she defiled the
land and committed adultery with stone and
wood. 10 In spite of all this, her unfaithful sister
Judah did not return to me with all her heart, but
only in pretense,” declares the LORD. Jer 12:2
11 The LORD said to me, “Faithless Israel is more
righteous than unfaithful Judah. 12 Go, proclaim
this message toward the north: Eze 16:52; 23:11

“ ‘Return, faithless Israel,’ declares the LORD,
‘I will frown on you no longer,
for I am merciful,’ declares the LORD, Ps 6:2
‘I will not be angry forever. Ps 86:15
13 Only acknowledge your guilt— Dt 30:1-3
you have rebelled against the LORD your
God,
you have scattered your favors to foreign gods
under every spreading tree, Dt 12:2
and have not obeyed me,’ ” ver 25
declares the LORD.

14 “Return, faithless people,” declares the LORD,
“for I am your husband. I will choose you—one
from a town and two from a clan—and bring you
to Zion. 15 Then I will give you shepherds after my
own heart, who will lead you with knowledge and
understanding. 16 In those days, when your numbers have increased greatly in the land,” declares
the LORD, “men will no longer say, ‘The ark of the
covenant of the LORD.’ It will never enter their
minds or be remembered; it will not be missed,
nor will another one be made. 17 At that time they
will call Jerusalem The Throne of the LORD, and all
nations will gather in Jerusalem to honor the name
of the LORD. No longer will they follow the stubbornness of their evil hearts. 18 In those days the
house of Judah will join the house of Israel, and
together they will come from a northern land to
the land I gave your forefathers as an inheritance.
19 “I myself said,

“ ‘How gladly would I treat you like sons
and give you a desirable land,
the most beautiful inheritance of any
nation.’
I thought you would call me ‘Father’ Isa 63:16
and not turn away from following me.
20 But like a woman unfaithful to her husband,
so you have been unfaithful to me, O house
of Israel,”
declares the LORD.
21 A cry is heard on the barren heights,

[a] 2 Or *an Arab*

the weeping and pleading of the people of
Israel,
because they have perverted their ways
and have forgotten the LORD their God.

22 "Return, faithless people; Hos 14:4
I will cure you of backsliding." Hos 6:1

"Yes, we will come to you,
for you are the LORD our God.
23 Surely the ⌞idolatrous⌟ commotion on the hills
and mountains is a deception;
surely in the LORD our God
is the salvation of Israel. Ps 3:8; Jer 17:14
24 From our youth shameful gods have
consumed Hos 9:10
the fruits of our fathers' labor—
their flocks and herds,
their sons and daughters.
25 Let us lie down in our shame, Ezr 9:6
and let our disgrace cover us.
We have sinned against the LORD our God,
both we and our fathers; Jer 14:20
from our youth till this day Jer 22:21
we have not obeyed the LORD our God."

4 "If you will return, O Israel, Jer 3:1,22; Joel 2:12
return to me,"
declares the LORD.
"If you put your detestable idols out of my
sight Jer 35:15
and no longer go astray,
2 and if in a truthful, just and righteous way
you swear, 'As surely as the LORD lives,'
then the nations will be blessed by him Ge 22:18
and in him they will glory."

3 This is what the LORD says to the men of Judah
and to Jerusalem:

"Break up your unplowed ground Hos 10:12
and do not sow among thorns. Mk 4:18
4 Circumcise yourselves to the LORD,
circumcise your hearts, Dt 10:16; Jer 9:26; Ro 2:28-29
you men of Judah and people of Jerusalem,
or my wrath will break out and burn like fire
because of the evil you have done— Ex 32:22
burn with no one to quench it. Am 5:6

Disaster From the North

5 "Announce in Judah and proclaim in
Jerusalem and say: Jer 5:20
'Sound the trumpet throughout the land!'
Cry aloud and say:
'Gather together!
Let us flee to the fortified cities!' Jos 10:20
6 Raise the signal to go to Zion! Ps 74:4; Isa 11:10
Flee for safety without delay!
For I am bringing disaster from the north,
even terrible destruction."

7 A lion has come out of his lair; 2Ki 24:1; Jer 2:15
a destroyer of nations has set out. Jer 6:26
He has left his place
to lay waste your land. Isa 1:7
Your towns will lie in ruins Jer 25:9
without inhabitant.
8 So put on sackcloth, Isa 22:12; Jer 6:26
lament and wail, Jer 7:29
for the fierce anger of the LORD
has not turned away from us. Jer 30:24

9 "In that day," declares the LORD,
"the king and the officials will lose heart,
the priests will be horrified,
and the prophets will be appalled." Isa 29:9

10 Then I said, "Ah, Sovereign LORD, how completely you have deceived this people and Jerusalem by saying, 'You will have peace,' when the
sword is at our throats." 2Th 2:11; Jer 14:13
11 At that time this people and Jerusalem will be
told, "A scorching wind from the barren heights in
the desert blows toward my people, but not to
winnow or cleanse; 12 a wind too strong for that
comes from me.[a] Now I pronounce my judgments against them." Jer 1:16; Eze 17:10; Hos 13:15

13 Look! He advances like the clouds, Isa 19:1
his chariots come like a whirlwind, Isa 5:28
his horses are swifter than eagles. Dt 28:49; Hab 1:8
Woe to us! We are ruined! Isa 6:11; 24:3
14 O Jerusalem, wash the evil from your heart
and be saved. Jas 4:8
How long will you harbor wicked thoughts?
15 A voice is announcing from Dan, Jer 8:16
proclaiming disaster from the hills of
Ephraim. Jer 31:6
16 "Tell this to the nations,
proclaim it to Jerusalem:
'A besieging army is coming from a distant
land,
raising a war cry against the cities of Judah.
17 They surround her like men guarding a field,
because she has rebelled against me,'"
declares the LORD.
18 "Your own conduct and actions Ps 107:17; Isa 50:1
have brought this upon you. Jer 2:17
This is your punishment.
How bitter it is! Jer 2:19
How it pierces to the heart!"

19 Oh, my anguish, my anguish! Isa 22:4; Jer 9:10
I writhe in pain.
Oh, the agony of my heart!
My heart pounds within me, Jer 23:9
I cannot keep silent. Jer 20:9
For I have heard the sound of the trumpet;

[a] 12 Or *comes at my command*

I have heard the battle cry. Nu 10:9; Jer 49:2
20Disaster follows disaster; Ps 42:7; Eze 7:26
the whole land lies in ruins.
In an instant my tents are destroyed, Jer 10:20
my shelter in a moment.
21How long must I see the battle standard Nu 2:2
and hear the sound of the trumpet? Jos 6:20

22"My people are fools; Jer 10:8
they do not know me. Jer 2:8
They are senseless children;
they have no understanding.
They are skilled in doing evil; Jer 13:23; 1Co 14:20
they know not how to do good." Ro 16:19

23I looked at the earth,
and it was formless and empty; Ge 1:2
and at the heavens,
and their light was gone. Job 9:7; 30:26
24I looked at the mountains,
and they were quaking; Isa 5:25; Eze 38:20
all the hills were swaying.
25I looked, and there were no people;
every bird in the sky had flown away.
26I looked, and the fruitful land was a desert;
all its towns lay in ruins Isa 6:11
before the LORD, before his fierce anger.

27This is what the LORD says:

"The whole land will be ruined,
though I will not destroy it completely.
28Therefore the earth will mourn Hos 4:3
and the heavens above grow dark, Isa 5:30
because I have spoken and will not relent,
I have decided and will not turn back."

29At the sound of horsemen and archers Jer 6:23
every town takes to flight. 2Ki 25:4
Some go into the thickets;
some climb up among the rocks. 1Sa 26:20
All the towns are deserted; Isa 6:12
no one lives in them.

30What are you doing, O devastated one?
Why dress yourself in scarlet
and put on jewels of gold? Eze 23:40
Why shade your eyes with paint? 2Ki 9:30
You adorn yourself in vain.
Your lovers despise you; La 1:2; Eze 23:9,22
they seek your life. Ps 35:4

31I hear a cry as of a woman in labor, Jer 13:21
a groan as of one bearing her first child—
the cry of the Daughter of Zion gasping for
breath,
stretching out her hands and saying, Isa 42:14; Isa 1:15
"Alas! I am fainting;
my life is given over to murderers." La 2:21

Not One Is Upright

5 "Go up and down the streets of Jerusalem,
look around and consider, Ps 45:10
search through her squares.
If you can find but one person Ge 18:32
who deals honestly and seeks the truth,
I will forgive this city. Ge 18:24
2Although they say, 'As surely as the LORD
lives,' Jer 4:2
still they are swearing falsely." Lev 19:12
3O LORD, do not your eyes look for truth?
You struck them, but they felt no pain;
you crushed them, but they refused
correction. Jer 2:30; Zep 3:2
They made their faces harder than stone
and refused to repent. 2Ch 28:22; Isa 1:5
4I thought, "These are only the poor;
they are foolish, Jer 4:22
for they do not know the way of the LORD,
the requirements of their God.
5So I will go to the leaders Mic 3:1,9
and speak to them;
surely they know the way of the LORD,
the requirements of their God."
But with one accord they too had broken off
the yoke
and torn off the bonds. Ps 2:3; Jer 2:20
6Therefore a lion from the forest will attack
them, Ps 17:12
a wolf from the desert will ravage them,
a leopard will lie in wait near their towns
to tear to pieces any who venture out,
for their rebellion is great
and their backslidings many. Jer 30:14
7"Why should I forgive you?
Your children have forsaken me
and sworn by gods that are not gods.
I supplied all their needs,
yet they committed adultery Nu 25:1
and thronged to the houses of prostitutes.
8They are well-fed, lusty stallions,
each neighing for another man's wife.
9Should I not punish them for this?" Jer 9:9
declares the LORD.
"Should I not avenge myself Isa 57:6
on such a nation as this?

10"Go through her vineyards and ravage them,
but do not destroy them completely. Jer 4:27
Strip off her branches,
for these people do not belong to the LORD.
11The house of Israel and the house of Judah
have been utterly unfaithful to me," Jer 3:20
declares the LORD.
12They have lied about the LORD;
they said, "He will do nothing!
No harm will come to us; Jer 23:17
we will never see sword or famine. Jer 14:13

13 The prophets are but wind Jer 14:15
and the word is not in them;
so let what they say be done to them."

14 Therefore this is what the LORD God Almighty says:

"Because the people have spoken these words,
I will make my words in your mouth a fire
and these people the wood it consumes.
15 O house of Israel," declares the LORD,
"I am bringing a distant nation against
you— Dt 28:49; Isa 5:26; Jer 4:16
an ancient and enduring nation,
a people whose language you do not know,
whose speech you do not understand.
16 Their quivers are like an open grave;
all of them are mighty warriors.
17 They will devour your harvests and food,
devour your sons and daughters; Dt 28:32
they will devour your flocks and herds, Dt 28:31
devour your vines and fig trees. Nu 16:14
With the sword they will destroy Lev 26:25
the fortified cities in which you trust.

18 "Yet even in those days," declares the LORD, "I
will not destroy you completely. 19 And when the
people ask, 'Why has the LORD our God done all
this to us?' you will tell them, 'As you have forsak-
en me and served foreign gods in your own land,
so now you will serve foreigners in a land not your
own.' Dt 28:48; Jer 4:27

20 "Announce this to the house of Jacob
and proclaim it in Judah:
21 Hear this, you foolish and senseless people,
who have eyes but do not see, Isa 6:10; Eze 12:2
who have ears but do not hear: Mt 13:15
22 Should you not fear me?" declares the LORD.
"Should you not tremble in my presence?
I made the sand a boundary for the sea, Ge 1:9
an everlasting barrier it cannot cross.
The waves may roll, but they cannot prevail;
they may roar, but they cannot cross it.
23 But these people have stubborn and rebellious
hearts; Dt 21:18
they have turned aside and gone away.
24 They do not say to themselves,
'Let us fear the LORD our God,
who gives autumn and spring rains in season,
who assures us of the regular weeks of
harvest.' Ge 8:22; Ac 14:17
25 Your wrongdoings have kept these away;
your sins have deprived you of good.

26 "Among my people are wicked men
who lie in wait like men who snare birds
and like those who set traps to catch men.
27 Like cages full of birds,
their houses are full of deceit; Jer 9:6
they have become rich and powerful Jer 12:1
28 and have grown fat and sleek. Dt 32:15
Their evil deeds have no limit;
they do not plead the case of the fatherless
to win it, Zec 7:10
they do not defend the rights of the poor.
29 Should I not punish them for this?"
declares the LORD.
"Should I not avenge myself
on such a nation as this?

30 "A horrible and shocking thing Hos 6:10
has happened in the land:
31 The prophets prophesy lies, Eze 13:6; Mic 2:11
the priests rule by their own authority,
and my people love it this way.
But what will you do in the end?

Jerusalem Under Siege

6 "Flee for safety, people of Benjamin!
Flee from Jerusalem!
Sound the trumpet in Tekoa! 2Ch 11:6
Raise the signal over Beth Hakkerem!
For disaster looms out of the north, Jer 4:6
even terrible destruction.
2 I will destroy the Daughter of Zion, Ps 9:14
so beautiful and delicate. La 4:5
3 Shepherds with their flocks will come against
her; Jer 12:10
they will pitch their tents around her,
each tending his own portion."

4 "Prepare for battle against her!
Arise, let us attack at noon! Jer 15:8
But, alas, the daylight is fading,
and the shadows of evening grow long.
5 So arise, let us attack at night
and destroy her fortresses!"

6 This is what the LORD Almighty says:

"Cut down the trees Dt 20:19-20
and build siege ramps against Jerusalem.
This city must be punished;
it is filled with oppression. Jer 25:38
7 As a well pours out its water,
so she pours out her wickedness.
Violence and destruction resound in her;
her sickness and wounds are ever before
me.
8 Take warning, O Jerusalem,
or I will turn away from you Eze 23:18; Hos 9:12
and make your land desolate
so no one can live in it."

9 This is what the LORD Almighty says:

"Let them glean the remnant of Israel
as thoroughly as a vine;
pass your hand over the branches again,
like one gathering grapes."

10 To whom can I speak and give warning?

Who will listen to me?
Their ears are closed[a] Ac 7:51
so they cannot hear. Isa 42:20
The word of the LORD is offensive to them;
they find no pleasure in it.
11But I am full of the wrath of the LORD, Jer 7:20
and I cannot hold it in. Job 32:20

"Pour it out on the children in the street
and on the young men gathered together;
both husband and wife will be caught in it,
and the old, those weighed down with
years. La 2:21
12Their houses will be turned over to others,
together with their fields and their wives,
when I stretch out my hand Isa 5:25
against those who live in the land,"
declares the LORD.
13"From the least to the greatest,
all are greedy for gain; Isa 56:11
prophets and priests alike,
all practice deceit. Jer 8:10
14They dress the wound of my people
as though it were not serious.
'Peace, peace,' they say,
when there is no peace. Jer 4:10; 8:11; Eze 13:10
15Are they ashamed of their loathsome conduct?
No, they have no shame at all;
they do not even know how to blush. Jer 3:3
So they will fall among the fallen;
they will be brought down when I punish
them," 2Ch 25:16; Jer 27:15
says the LORD.

16This is what the LORD says:

"Stand at the crossroads and look;
ask for the ancient paths, Jer 18:15
ask where the good way is, and walk in it,
and you will find rest for your souls.
But you said, 'We will not walk in it.'
17I appointed watchmen over you and said,
'Listen to the sound of the trumpet!'
But you said, 'We will not listen.' Jer 11:7-8
18Therefore hear, O nations;
observe, O witnesses,
what will happen to them.
19Hear, O earth: Isa 1:2; Jer 22:29
I am bringing disaster on this people, Jos 23:15
the fruit of their schemes, Pr 1:31
because they have not listened to my words
and have rejected my law. Jer 8:9
20What do I care about incense from Sheba
or sweet calamus from a distant land?
Your burnt offerings are not acceptable;
your sacrifices do not please me." Isa 1:11

21Therefore this is what the LORD says:

"I will put obstacles before this people.
Fathers and sons alike will stumble over
them; Isa 8:14
neighbors and friends will perish."

22This is what the LORD says:

"Look, an army is coming
from the land of the north; Jer 1:15; 10:22
a great nation is being stirred up
from the ends of the earth.
23They are armed with bow and spear;
they are cruel and show no mercy. Isa 13:18
They sound like the roaring sea
as they ride on their horses; Jer 4:29
they come like men in battle formation
to attack you, O Daughter of Zion."

24We have heard reports about them,
and our hands hang limp.
Anguish has gripped us, Jer 4:19
pain like that of a woman in labor. Jer 4:31
25Do not go out to the fields
or walk on the roads,
for the enemy has a sword,
and there is terror on every side. Jer 49:29
26O my people, put on sackcloth Jer 4:8
and roll in ashes; Jer 25:34; Mic 1:10
mourn with bitter wailing
as for an only son, Zec 12:10
for suddenly the destroyer Ex 12:23
will come upon us.

27"I have made you a tester of metals Jer 9:7
and my people the ore,
that you may observe
and test their ways.
28They are all hardened rebels, Jer 5:23
going about to slander. Jer 9:4
They are bronze and iron; Eze 22:18
they all act corruptly.
29The bellows blow fiercely
to burn away the lead with fire,
but the refining goes on in vain;
the wicked are not purged out.
30They are called rejected silver,
because the LORD has rejected them."

False Religion Worthless

7 This is the word that came to Jeremiah from
the LORD: 2"Stand at the gate of the LORD's
house and there proclaim this message: Jer 17:19
" 'Hear the word of the LORD, all you people of
Judah who come through these gates to worship
the LORD. 3This is what the LORD Almighty, the
God of Israel, says: Reform your ways and your
actions, and I will let you live in this place. 4Do not
trust in deceptive words and say, "This is the temple of the LORD, the temple of the LORD, the temple
of the LORD!" 5If you really change your ways and

[a] 10 Hebrew *uncircumcised*

your actions and deal with each other justly, 6if
you do not oppress the alien, the fatherless or the
widow and do not shed innocent blood in this
place, and if you do not follow other gods to your
own harm, 7then I will let you live in this place, in
the land I gave your forefathers for ever and ever.
8But look, you are trusting in deceptive words that
are worthless. Jer 18:11; 26:13; Mic 3:11

9" 'Will you steal and murder, commit adultery
and perjury,[a] burn incense to Baal and follow
other gods you have not known, 10and then come
and stand before me in this house, which bears my
Name, and say, "We are safe"—safe to do all these
detestable things? 11Has this house, which bears
my Name, become a den of robbers to you? But I
have been watching! declares the LORD. Mk 11:17*

12" 'Go now to the place in Shiloh where I first
made a dwelling for my Name, and see what I did
to it because of the wickedness of my people Israel.
13While you were doing all these things, declares
the LORD, I spoke to you again and again, but you
did not listen; I called you, but you did not answer.
14Therefore, what I did to Shiloh I will now do to
the house that bears my Name, the temple you
trust in, the place I gave to you and your fathers.
15I will thrust you from my presence, just as I did
all your brothers, the people of Ephraim.' Ps 78:67

16"So do not pray for this people nor offer any
plea or petition for them; do not plead with me,
for I will not listen to you. 17Do you not see what
they are doing in the towns of Judah and in the
streets of Jerusalem? 18The children gather wood,
the fathers light the fire, and the women knead the
dough and make cakes of bread for the Queen of
Heaven. They pour out drink offerings to other
gods to provoke me to anger. 19But am I the one
they are provoking? declares the LORD. Are they
not rather harming themselves, to their own
shame? Ex 32:10; Jer 9:19

20" 'Therefore this is what the Sovereign LORD
says: My anger and my wrath will be poured out
on this place, on man and beast, on the trees of the
field and on the fruit of the ground, and it will
burn and not be quenched. Jer 42:18; La 2:3-5

21" 'This is what the LORD Almighty, the God of
Israel, says: Go ahead, add your burnt offerings to
your other sacrifices and eat the meat yourselves!
22For when I brought your forefathers out of Egypt
and spoke to them, I did not just give them commands about burnt offerings and sacrifices, 23but
I gave them this command: Obey me, and I will be
your God and you will be my people. Walk in all
the ways I command you, that it may go well with
you. 24But they did not listen or pay attention;
instead, they followed the stubborn inclinations of
their evil hearts. They went backward and not forward. 25From the time your forefathers left Egypt
until now, day after day, again and again I sent you
my servants the prophets. 26But they did not listen
to me or pay attention. They were stiff-necked and
did more evil than their forefathers.' Ex 19:5

27"When you tell them all this, they will not
listen to you; when you call to them, they will not
answer. 28Therefore say to them, 'This is the nation
that has not obeyed the LORD its God or responded
to correction. Truth has perished; it has vanished
from their lips. 29Cut off your hair and throw it
away; take up a lament on the barren heights, for
the LORD has rejected and abandoned this generation that is under his wrath. Jer 6:30; Eze 3:7

The Valley of Slaughter

30" 'The people of Judah have done evil in my
eyes, declares the LORD. They have set up their
detestable idols in the house that bears my Name
and have defiled it. 31They have built the high
places of Topheth in the Valley of Ben Hinnom to
burn their sons and daughters in the fire—something I did not command, nor did it enter my
mind. 32So beware, the days are coming, declares
the LORD, when people will no longer call it Topheth or the Valley of Ben Hinnom, but the Valley
of Slaughter, for they will bury the dead in Topheth until there is no more room. 33Then the
carcasses of this people will become food for the
birds of the air and the beasts of the earth, and
there will be no one to frighten them away. 34I will
bring an end to the sounds of joy and gladness and
to the voices of bride and bridegroom in the towns
of Judah and the streets of Jerusalem, for the land
will become desolate. Isa 24:8; Rev 18:23

8 " 'At that time, declares the LORD, the bones
of the kings and officials of Judah, the bones
of the priests and prophets, and the bones of the
people of Jerusalem will be removed from their
graves. 2They will be exposed to the sun and the
moon and all the stars of the heavens, which they
have loved and served and which they have followed and consulted and worshiped. They will not
be gathered up or buried, but will be like refuse
lying on the ground. 3Wherever I banish them, all
the survivors of this evil nation will prefer death to
life, declares the LORD Almighty.' Job 3:22; Rev 9:6

Sin and Punishment

4"Say to them, 'This is what the LORD says:

" 'When men fall down, do they not get up?
When a man turns away, does he not
return?
5Why then have these people turned away?
Why does Jerusalem always turn away?
They cling to deceit; Jer 5:27
they refuse to return. Jer 7:24; 9:6
6I have listened attentively,

[a]9 Or *and swear by false gods*

but they do not say what is right.
No one repents of his wickedness, Rev 9:20
saying, "What have I done?"
Each pursues his own course Ps 14:1-3
like a horse charging into battle.
7Even the stork in the sky
knows her appointed seasons,
and the dove, the swift and the thrush
observe the time of their migration.
But my people do not know Isa 1:3; Jer 5:4-5
the requirements of the LORD.

8" 'How can you say, "We are wise,
for we have the law of the LORD," Ro 2:17
when actually the lying pen of the scribes
has handled it falsely?
9The wise will be put to shame; Jer 6:15
they will be dismayed and trapped. Job 5:13
Since they have rejected the word of the LORD,
what kind of wisdom do they have? Pr 1:7
10Therefore I will give their wives to other men
and their fields to new owners. Jer 6:12
From the least to the greatest,
all are greedy for gain; Isa 56:11
prophets and priests alike, La 2:14
all practice deceit. Jer 23:11,15
11They dress the wound of my people
as though it were not serious.
"Peace, peace," they say,
when there is no peace. Jer 6:14
12Are they ashamed of their loathsome conduct?
No, they have no shame at all; Jer 3:3
they do not even know how to blush.
So they will fall among the fallen;
they will be brought down when they are
punished, Ps 52:5-7; Isa 3:9
says the LORD.

13" 'I will take away their harvest,
declares the LORD.
There will be no grapes on the vine. Joel 1:7
There will be no figs on the tree, Lk 13:6
and their leaves will wither. Mt 21:19
What I have given them
will be taken from them.[a] ' " Jer 5:17

14"Why are we sitting here?
Gather together!
Let us flee to the fortified cities Jer 4:5; 35:11
and perish there!
For the LORD our God has doomed us to
perish
and given us poisoned water to drink,
because we have sinned against him.
15We hoped for peace ver 11
but no good has come,
for a time of healing
but there was only terror. Jer 14:19
16The snorting of the enemy's horses
is heard from Dan; Jer 4:15
at the neighing of their stallions
the whole land trembles.
They have come to devour Jer 5:17
the land and everything in it,
the city and all who live there."

17"See, I will send venomous snakes among you,
vipers that cannot be charmed, Ps 58:5
and they will bite you,"
declares the LORD.

18O my Comforter[b] in sorrow,
my heart is faint within me. La 5:17
19Listen to the cry of my people
from a land far away: Jer 9:16
"Is the LORD not in Zion?
Is her King no longer there?" Mic 4:9

"Why have they provoked me to anger with
their images, Jer 44:3
with their worthless foreign idols?" Dt 32:21

20"The harvest is past,
the summer has ended,
and we are not saved."

21Since my people are crushed, I am crushed;
I mourn, and horror grips me. Jer 14:17
22Is there no balm in Gilead? Ge 37:25
Is there no physician there?
Why then is there no healing Jer 30:12
for the wound of my people?

9 1Oh, that my head were a spring of water
and my eyes a fountain of tears! Ps 119:136
I would weep day and night Jer 13:17; La 2:11,18
for the slain of my people. Isa 22:4
2Oh, that I had in the desert Ps 55:7
a lodging place for travelers,
so that I might leave my people
and go away from them;
for they are all adulterers, Jer 5:7-8; 23:10; Hos 4:2
a crowd of unfaithful people. 1Ki 19:10

3"They make ready their tongue
like a bow, to shoot lies; Ps 64:3
it is not by truth
that they triumph[c] in the land.
They go from one sin to another;
they do not acknowledge me," Isa 1:3
declares the LORD.

4"Beware of your friends; 2Sa 15:12
do not trust your brothers. Mic 7:5-6
For every brother is a deceiver,[d] Ge 27:35
and every friend a slanderer. Ex 20:16
5Friend deceives friend, Lev 6:2
and no one speaks the truth. Ps 15:2
They have taught their tongues to lie; Ps 52:3

[a] 13 The meaning of the Hebrew for this sentence is uncertain.
[c] 3 Or *lies; / they are not valiant for truth*
[d] 4 Or *a deceiving Jacob*
[b] 18 The meaning of the Hebrew for this word is uncertain.

they weary themselves with sinning.
6You[a] live in the midst of deception; Jer 5:27
in their deceit they refuse to acknowledge
me,"
declares the LORD.

7Therefore this is what the LORD Almighty says:

"See, I will refine and test them, Isa 1:25; Jer 6:27
for what else can I do
because of the sin of my people?
8Their tongue is a deadly arrow; ver 3; Ps 35:20
it speaks with deceit.
With his mouth each speaks cordially to his
neighbor, Isa 3:5
but in his heart he sets a trap for him.
9Should I not punish them for this?"
declares the LORD.
"Should I not avenge myself Jer 5:9,29
on such a nation as this?"

10I will weep and wail for the mountains
and take up a lament concerning the desert
pastures.
They are desolate and untraveled,
and the lowing of cattle is not heard.
The birds of the air have fled
and the animals are gone. Jer 4:25; 12:4; Hos 4:3

11"I will make Jerusalem a heap of ruins,
a haunt of jackals; Isa 34:13
and I will lay waste the towns of Judah Jer 1:15
so no one can live there." Isa 25:2; Jer 26:9

12What man is wise enough to understand this?
Who has been instructed by the LORD and can
explain it? Why has the land been ruined and laid
waste like a desert that no one can cross?
13The LORD said, "It is because they have forsak-
en my law, which I set before them; they have not
obeyed me or followed my law. 14Instead, they
have followed the stubbornness of their hearts;
they have followed the Baals, as their fathers taught
them." 15Therefore, this is what the LORD Almighty, the God of Israel, says: "See, I will make
this people eat bitter food and drink poisoned water. 16I will scatter them among nations that neither they nor their fathers have known, and I will
pursue them with the sword until I have destroyed
them." Lev 26:33; Dt 28:64; Jer 44:27

17This is what the LORD Almighty says:

"Consider now! Call for the wailing women to
come; Ecc 12:5; Am 5:16
send for the most skillful of them.
18Let them come quickly
and wail over us
till our eyes overflow with tears
and water streams from our eyelids. Jer 14:17
19The sound of wailing is heard from Zion:
'How ruined we are! Jer 4:13
How great is our shame!
We must leave our land
because our houses are in ruins.'"
20Now, O women, hear the word of the LORD;
open your ears to the words of his mouth.
Teach your daughters how to wail;
teach one another a lament. Isa 32:9-13
21Death has climbed in through our windows
and has entered our fortresses;
it has cut off the children from the streets
and the young men from the public
squares. 2Ch 36:17

22Say, "This is what the LORD declares:

"'The dead bodies of men will lie
like refuse on the open field, Jer 8:2
like cut grain behind the reaper,
with no one to gather them.'"

23This is what the LORD says:

"Let not the wise man boast of his wisdom
or the strong man boast of his strength
or the rich man boast of his riches, Eze 28:4-5

LIVING  **INSIGHT**

I am more convinced than ever that life's major pursuit is not knowing self . . . but knowing God. Today make it your aim. Consciously think, "Lord, use these few quiet moments to enhance my knowledge of You. Take first place in my heart. Reveal Yourself to me."

(See Jeremiah 9:23–24.)

24but let him who boasts boast about this:
that he understands and knows me, Ps 36:10
that I am the LORD, who exercises kindness,
justice and righteousness on earth, Ps 36:6
for in these I delight,"
declares the LORD.

25"The days are coming," declares the LORD,
"when I will punish all who are circumcised only
in the flesh— 26Egypt, Judah, Edom, Ammon,
Moab and all who live in the desert in distant
places.[b] For all these nations are really uncircumcised, and even the whole house of Israel is uncircumcised in heart." Lev 26:41; Ro 2:8-9,28

God and Idols

10 Hear what the LORD says to you, O house
of Israel. 2This is what the LORD says:

"Do not learn the ways of the nations Lev 20:23

[a]6 That is, Jeremiah (the Hebrew is singular) [b]26 Or *desert and who clip the hair by their foreheads*

KNOWING GOD — LIFE'S MAJOR PURSUIT

" 'Let not the wise man boast of his wisdom
or the strong man boast of his strength
or the rich man boast of his riches,
but let him who boasts boast about this:
that he understands and knows me,
that I am the LORD, who exercises kindness,
justice and righteousness on earth,
for in these I delight,' declares the LORD."

—JEREMIAH 9:23–24

I am convinced that there is nothing more important for us than what we think about God. Here are just a few of the reasons I believe our view of God is so important. It:

Enhances our worship and prompts our praise.
Shapes our moral and ethical standards.
Directly affects our response to pain and hardship.
Motivates our response toward fortune, fame, power and pleasure.
Gives us strength when we are tempted.
Keeps us faithful and courageous when we are outnumbered.
Determines our lifestyle and dictates our behavior.
Gives meaning and significance to relationships.
Sensitizes our conscience and creates the desire to be obedient.
Stimulates hope to go on, regardless of what lies ahead of us.
Enables us to know what to reject and what to respect while riveted to planet Earth.
Is the foundation upon which EVERYTHING rests!

Never think that what you think about God doesn't make much difference. The reality is this: *It determines everything*!

The Heavens Declare God's Glory

God has given us a general revelation of Himself through creation and the testimony of the heavens—so much so that the apostle Paul tells us the whole created world reveals God in such a way that no one has an excuse for not honoring God: "For since the creation of the world God's invisible qualities—his eternal power and his divine nature—have been clearly seen, being understood from what has been made, so that men are without excuse" (Romans 1:20). The psalmist also testifies that God has written His handiwork in the heavens: "The heavens declare the glory of God; the skies proclaim the work of his hands" (Psalm 19:1).

You look up into the starry skies and you realize, if you conduct any kind of serious study of those stars, they didn't just tumble into space. The rising and the lowering of the tide; the dropping of seed into the ground and the growing of plants; the climates, the wind, the weather, the seasons, the temperature, the humidity, the torrential wind currents that sweep across this earth—those things don't "just happen." They are so obviously from the hand of the living God that you have to train yourself not to think that God is alive and actively involved in His world. In fact, I personally believe you have to teach a child *not* to believe in God. The most natural thing in the world in the heart of a child is to believe that someone outside himself or herself organized and arranged things and is keeping them in motion. If you question that statement, you haven't listened to children lately.

The Transforming Power of Knowing God

But there's more. There is also special revelation in history as well as in Scripture. God specifically reveals Himself in both. Because God graciously provides the way to know Him, I'd like to elaborate on five reasons why it's important for us to know God and seek to know Him increasingly better.

First, *knowing God gives us the desire to be like Him*. Listen carefully once again to Jeremiah's words in verse 24 of chapter 9:

> *"but let him who boasts boast about this:*
> *that he understands and knows me,*
> *that I am the LORD, who exercises kindness,*
> *justice and righteousness on earth,*
> *for in these I delight," declares the LORD.*

Interesting, isn't it? When the Lord talks about Himself, He reveals His attributes, His character traits like kindness, justice and righteousness. He wants us to know what He's like—because He wants us to be like Him. In 1 Peter we read that the Lord is holy; in fact, we even read the command, "Be holy, because I am holy" (1:16). And Paul in his letter to the Ephesians reminds us that we were called to a new way of life: "You were taught, with regard to your former way of life, to put off your old self, which is being corrupted by its deceitful desires; to be made new in the attitude of your minds; and to put on the new self, created to be like God in true righteousness and holiness" (Ephesians 4:22–24).

The most natural thing in the world is to become like our parents, even when we don't want to! Isn't that amazing? I've heard people say, "When I grow up, I'm not going to be like my father!" Or, "I'm never going to be like my mother." Yet when they grow up, they are just like their father or mother. Why? Because they know their parents; they've been around them. Their mother's or father's thumbprint is indelibly imprinted on their lives. That's the way it is with God our Father. The better I get to know my God, the more I become like Him. I discover He's holy; I want to be holy. I discover He's good; I want to exhibit His goodness. I discover He's strong; I want to be more confident. I discover He's in control; I don't want to panic my way through life. I want to move through life calmly and consistently. I want to be like my Father. And in order to be like Him, I need to know what He is like.

Second, *knowing God reveals the truth about ourselves*. Spending some time gazing at the awesome, wonder-filled scene in Isaiah 6 will help support this fact. What a great section of Scripture!

> *In the year that King Uzziah died, I saw the Lord seated on a throne, high and exalted, and the train of his robe filled the temple. Above him were seraphs, each with six wings: With two wings they covered their faces, with two they covered their feet, and with two they were flying (Isaiah 6:1–2).*

Here are six-winged angelic creatures, hovering about the throne of heaven, giving praise to God. They are saying, "Holy, holy, holy, is the LORD Almighty" (Isaiah 6:3). One group stands to declare it, and another answers in antiphonal voice. Still another praises, and another responds. This group praises, and that group responds. The whole throne is so filled with God's glory and the sound of their voices that the place begins to shake. Having seen the Lord high and exalted, Isaiah suddenly got a startling glimpse of himself:

> *"Woe to me!" I cried, "I am ruined! For I am a man of unclean lips, and I live among a people of unclean lips, and my eyes have seen the King, the LORD Almighty" (Isaiah 6:5).*

When we encounter, examine and experience the Lord God, we discover that He is holy and we're unholy. It doesn't hurt us to know that; it helps us. We discover that He's perfect and we're imperfect . . . He's strong and we're weak . . . He's patient and we're impatient . . . He's impartial and we're prejudiced. He's in control, yet our lives are often fractured by worry and full of fear. And something occurs in the awareness of that immense contrast that causes His character to overshadow our need. The result is marvelous—

the knowledge of the Holy One equips us to see the truth and to change. I cannot explain how it works; I just know it does.

God will help you see yourself just as you are—with all your strengths and certainly with all your weaknesses. And every time you turn to His Word or to a time of abiding in His presence in prayer, you'll see another flaw, another need, another weakness in your life that needs to be addressed. God always tells us the truth. And it is truth that sets us free! When we see ourselves as we really are, we are prompted to lean on Him and to trust Him to make us like He is.

Third, *knowing God enables us to interpret our world*. Toward the end of Daniel 4, we meet a rather remarkable individual by the name of Nebuchadnezzar. He was the king of Babylon. In great arrogance the king lived as though he needed no one else. Full of conceit, he strutted around the kingdom with his thumbs under his suspenders, saying, "How great I am. How wonderful I am. Look at this kingdom I've built. What a magnificent person I have become. Everybody, together, say it with me again and again: Nebuchadnezzar . . ." Then, very suddenly, he lost his mind. This once-powerful and arrogant king was reduced to a wild beast, living out in the field day and night. What a terrible, insane existence! I can't fully explain my next statement. I can only tell you it's often been proven true: *For some people it takes a temporary period of insanity to come to the end of themselves and to find God*. That's the way it was with Nebuchadnezzar. Not all breakdowns are the end of a person's life. Sometimes they are the beginning, which means we should perhaps call them break-*ups*. One day the Nebuchadnezzar-beast paused in the middle of his grazing and looked up toward heaven. A shaft of light broke through the darkened mind; his sanity was restored, and he proceeded to praise, exalt, honor and glorify Almighty God. He discovered God, and he found a new way to interpret his world. Not unlike the lost son who at last came to his senses (Luke 15:17), Nebuchadnezzar saw *everything* with new eyes . . . including his own need for the Lord God.

When you take hold of the knowledge of God and begin to see that He is in charge, you won't panic every time you read the newspaper. You won't give up hope because an earthquake somewhere sent buildings toppling. You won't live in fear of terrorism or possible disease. In fact, you'll be able to sing your way through the front page, the business section, the editorial page . . . even the sports page! Why? Because you know the God who is in control of all things.

People have this weird idea that God is gingerly sitting on the edge of heaven going, "Ooh! Oh, no! How am I going to handle all this? HELLLPPPP!" My friend, that's *not* the God of the Scriptures. That isn't the living God who holds everything in His hands. He may be invisible, but He is most assuredly in touch. You may not be able to see Him or hear Him, but He is in control of everything. Yes, *everything*! And that includes you—and your circumstances. That includes all of life . . . past, present, future.

Fourth, *knowing God makes us stronger and more secure*. Goodness knows, we all need to experience this! Daniel 11:32a says: "With flattery he [the king of the North, historically identified as Antiochus IV Epiphanes] will corrupt those who have violated the covenant . . ." This verse is placed in a tough setting—a scene of conflict and warfare. There's a battle going on between good and evil. And right in the middle of that horrid prophecy of corruption, Daniel finishes his thought this way: ". . . but the people who know their God will firmly resist him [Antiochus]" (Daniel 11:32*b*). What was true way back in the centuries before Jesus Christ came to earth is equally true today. The people who know their God will firmly resist the forces of evil—in the strength of an all-powerful God who has promised us the victory!

So take heart: Things aren't out of hand! Our God is in control. He can handle it. And what's more, He can handle you. He knows you thoroughly . . . He even knows the number of the hairs on your head (see Matthew 10:30). He's got everything wired! He's got it all together! He is the sovereign God of the universe and He's never once lost control. He strengthens and He sustains His people. Those who know their God operate in such a context of confidence that they can face *whatever* may come their way.

See the value of knowing God? See what it does to your perspective? See how much calmer you become? Lift up your eyes. Behold His incredible glory, see Him high and exalted. Worthy is the Lamb, who was slain, to give power and authority over this place (see Revelation 5:12). His kingdom will not fail. His will cannot be restrained.

Fifth, and finally, *knowing God introduces us to the eternal dimension of existence*. Ponder carefully the words of Jesus as He prays to the Father: "Now this is eternal life: that they may know you, the only true God, and Jesus Christ, whom you have sent" (John 17:3). Knowing God introduces me to the world of God's kingdom. I see through eyes that aren't given to everyone. We read elsewhere, "No eye has seen, no ear has heard, no mind has conceived what God has prepared for those who love him" (1 Corinthians 2:9).

The natural person isn't born with this kind of insight. It's given at the new birth. That's why I talk so often about coming to know Jesus Christ, believing in the Lord Jesus, turning one's life over to Christ, coming to the door of one's heart and opening it by faith and saying, "Jesus Christ, come into my life. Take charge"—because when He comes in, He introduces us to a whole new way of thinking, a whole new way of living, a whole new perspective—an eternal dimension for living. And that perspective lifts the mind above the present, irksome details of life to be able to see a greater vision of a greater purpose for living. What we gain is an eternal dimension of life. And may we never forget, there's no better way to live!

There are two crucial ways to help us gain this eternal perspective: through reading and meditating on Scripture and through praying. As we read and reflect on God's Word, it informs us and transforms us. His Word is dynamic and powerful, and it accomplishes great things. It releases grace and power by which we can grow in our faith and in our commitment to Jesus Christ. The more we focus on God's Word, the better we come to know God and ourselves. The same can be said about prayer. God desires our intimate fellowship; by prayer we nurture our relationship with Him. Prayer is really a relationship in which God's Spirit speaks to our spirit (see Romans 8:16,26–27). All too often we think of prayer as a one-way relationship in which we do all the talking. True prayer is more like a healthy dialogue in which each person speaks and listens. Often it's during the period of silent listening that we discover the most about ourselves and about God.

Incomprehensible Subjects

There will be times in your life when you will simply have to admit that you just don't get it. You will not have enough intelligence to figure it all out. Remember those words when you travel down the road in hopes of understanding and knowing your God. Realize in advance that you will come to some streets that are mysterious and shrouded in fog—and to some extent impassable. Don't let the mystery surprise you or disturb you. God planned it that way. He is, after all, the One who is recorded as having said, "For my thoughts are not your thoughts, neither are your ways my ways, declares the LORD" (Isaiah 55:8). This is known among theologians as "the incomprehensibility of God."

It occurs to me that there are at least three theological thoughts that are incomprehensible. First, *the Trinity* . . . There is one God, yet three distinct *persons*. The Godhead is coequal, coeternal, coexistent: God the Father, God the Son, God the Holy Spirit. And at the same time, God is one . . . one in essence, one in nature. So much of that remains a profound mystery. Don't lose sleep if you cannot unravel the truth of the Trinity; no one else fully grasps it either. Even when we try to illustrate it, something falls short.

Second, *God's glory* . . . The Trinity has to do with the *person* of God. Glory has to do with the *presence* of God. "Glory" has something to do with light—with blinding brilliance. It was called the *shekinah* glory of God (a Hebrew word, meaning "dwelling"). The people of Bible times sensed God's presence in the tabernacle and the temple because the light of His glory was there. That same glory of God was later lifted from the place of worship and removed because of the unbelief of the people (see Ezekiel 10:4,18–19). There is something terribly mysterious about the glory of God, revealed in and through Scripture. Don't weary yourself trying to unscrew the inscrutable.

Third, *God's sovereignty* . . . This has to do with the *plan* of God. Certainly God is in control of all things; yet, even though He is perfectly holy, sin is alive and thriving in this world. God permits it; He allows it. Without being contaminated by sin, our holy God is working out His plan. If you want to engage in a futile study, try to reconcile those inescapable realities. Seriously, quit trying to reconcile them! Accept the reality of His sovereignty, His power and authority over all things; take that reality by faith!

Some Essential Facts

Yes, there are mysteries when it comes to our quest to know God; yet there are some things we *can* understand that are very practical and absolutely essential. These truths are not mysterious. They can be grasped and applied by all believers. First, *God is pleased when we walk by faith*. From cover to cover the Bible testifies to that fact. Nothing pleases the Lord more than when we walk by faith.

Second, *God is glorified when we worship in spirit and truth.* When I come across something that I can't handle or explain, God is pleased when I trust Him to get me through it. And when I am all alone in His presence or when I gather with other believers and I worship my God, He's glorified in it.

Third, *God is our Father when we believe in His Son . . . and not until.* Scripture never teaches that God is the Father of everyone, even though He graciously "causes his sun to rise on the evil and the good, and sends rain on the righteous and the unrighteous" (Matthew 5:45). By grace through faith, He becomes the Father of only those who believe in His Son.

Fourth, *God rejoices when we love him with our whole hearts.* Those who truly love the Lord have experienced His power to deliver, so their fears are gone. Perfect love casts out fear. They have received His peace and forgiveness, so their guilt has been relieved. And what a relief it is! We don't have to spend our days wallowing in how wrong we are or how ashamed we are of ourselves or how badly we feel. We have claimed His mercy. Thanks to His grace we are free from guilt. Shame is gone. Those who truly love God have felt His strong and sure presence through affliction, and their faith has been strengthened. Isn't that astounding? Through weakness you've become stronger. You know what's happened in the process? You and your Lord have become close friends . . . so close that the relationship can't really be explained in human terms. You have linked yourself with the Almighty and you and He are in league together. Nothing breaks that fellowship. That's the way it is with God. He relates on that basis with His children.

You need to know that God rejoices when we show our love to Him. God wants our hearts embracing Him. God wants to hear us say, "I love You, Father. I trust You. Whatever You want to give me I accept. I need You. I cling to You. In obedience I walk with You. I adore You." The better you get to know your God, the more comfortable you will be in making that kind of response. And as you gain comfort in your relationship with your loving Father, come to Him—just as you are. Sing your songs to Him. Talk to Him in prayer. Lay your burdens on Him. Trust Him with all your heart and strength. Give Him your utmost praise. He will be honored as you participate in such significant activities.

or be terrified by signs in the sky,
though the nations are terrified by them.
3 For the customs of the peoples are worthless;
they cut a tree out of the forest,
and a craftsman shapes it with his chisel.
4 They adorn it with silver and gold; Hos 13:2
they fasten it with hammer and nails
so it will not totter. Isa 41:7
5 Like a scarecrow in a melon patch,
their idols cannot speak; 1Co 12:2
they must be carried
because they cannot walk. Ps 115:5,7
Do not fear them;
they can do no harm
nor can they do any good." Isa 41:24; 46:7

6 No one is like you, O LORD;
you are great, Ps 48:1
and your name is mighty in power.
7 Who should not revere you,
O King of the nations? Ps 22:28; Rev 15:4
This is your due.
Among all the wise men of the nations
and in all their kingdoms,
there is no one like you.
8 They are all senseless and foolish; Isa 40:19; Jer 4:22
they are taught by worthless wooden idols.
9 Hammered silver is brought from Tarshish
and gold from Uphaz.
What the craftsman and goldsmith have made
is then dressed in blue and purple—
all made by skilled workers.
10 But the LORD is the true God;
he is the living God, the eternal King.
When he is angry, the earth trembles; Ps 29:8
the nations cannot endure his wrath. Ps 76:7

11 "Tell them this: 'These gods, who did not
make the heavens and the earth, will perish from
the earth and from under the heavens.' "[a]

12 But God made the earth by his power;
he founded the world by his wisdom
and stretched out the heavens by his
understanding. Ge 1:1,8; Isa 40:22
13 When he thunders, the waters in the heavens
roar; Job 36:29
he makes clouds rise from the ends of the
earth.
He sends lightning with the rain Ps 135:7
and brings out the wind from his
storehouses. Dt 28:12

14 Everyone is senseless and without knowledge;
every goldsmith is shamed by his idols.
His images are a fraud; Isa 44:20
they have no breath in them.
15 They are worthless, the objects of mockery;
when their judgment comes, they will
perish.
16 He who is the Portion of Jacob is not like
these, Dt 32:9; Ps 119:57
for he is the Maker of all things, ver 12
including Israel, the tribe of his inheritance—
the LORD Almighty is his name. Jer 51:15-19

Coming Destruction

17 Gather up your belongings to leave the land,
you who live under siege.
18 For this is what the LORD says:
"At this time I will hurl out 1Sa 25:29
those who live in this land;
I will bring distress on them Dt 28:52
so that they may be captured."

19 Woe to me because of my injury!
My wound is incurable! Jer 14:17
Yet I said to myself,
"This is my sickness, and I must endure it."
20 My tent is destroyed; Jer 4:20
all its ropes are snapped.
My sons are gone from me and are no more;
no one is left now to pitch my tent
or to set up my shelter.
21 The shepherds are senseless Jer 22:22
and do not inquire of the LORD; Isa 56:10
so they do not prosper
and all their flock is scattered. Jer 23:2
22 Listen! The report is coming—
a great commotion from the land of the
north!
It will make the towns of Judah desolate,
a haunt of jackals. Jer 9:11

Jeremiah's Prayer

23 I know, O LORD, that a man's life is not his
own;
it is not for man to direct his steps. Pr 20:24
24 Correct me, LORD, but only with justice—
not in your anger, Ps 6:1; 38:1
lest you reduce me to nothing. Jer 30:11
25 Pour out your wrath on the nations Zep 3:8
that do not acknowledge you,
on the peoples who do not call on your
name. Job 18:21; Ps 14:4
For they have devoured Jacob; Ps 79:7; Jer 8:16
they have devoured him completely
and destroyed his homeland. Ps 79:6-7

The Covenant Is Broken

11 This is the word that came to Jeremiah
from the LORD: 2 "Listen to the terms of this
covenant and tell them to the people of Judah and
to those who live in Jerusalem. 3 Tell them that this
is what the LORD, the God of Israel, says: 'Cursed
is the man who does not obey the terms of this

[a] *11* The text of this verse is in Aramaic.

covenant— 4the terms I commanded your forefathers when I brought them out of Egypt, out of the iron-smelting furnace.' I said, 'Obey me and do everything I command you, and you will be my people, and I will be your God. 5Then I will fulfill the oath I swore to your forefathers, to give them a land flowing with milk and honey'—the land you possess today." Ex 24:8; Jer 7:23

I answered, "Amen, LORD." Dt 27:26

6The LORD said to me, "Proclaim all these words in the towns of Judah and in the streets of Jerusalem: 'Listen to the terms of this covenant and follow them. 7From the time I brought your forefathers up from Egypt until today, I warned them again and again, saying, "Obey me." 8But they did not listen or pay attention; instead, they followed the stubbornness of their evil hearts. So I brought on them all the curses of the covenant I had commanded them to follow but that they did not keep.'" Dt 15:5; Ro 2:13; Jas 1:22

9Then the LORD said to me, "There is a conspiracy among the people of Judah and those who live in Jerusalem. 10They have returned to the sins of their forefathers, who refused to listen to my words. They have followed other gods to serve them. Both the house of Israel and the house of Judah have broken the covenant I made with their forefathers. 11Therefore this is what the LORD says: 'I will bring on them a disaster they cannot escape. Although they cry out to me, I will not listen to them. 12The towns of Judah and the people of Jerusalem will go and cry out to the gods to whom they burn incense, but they will not help them at all when disaster strikes. 13You have as many gods as you have towns, O Judah; and the altars you have set up to burn incense to that shameful god Baal are as many as the streets of Jerusalem.'

14"Do not pray for this people nor offer any plea or petition for them, because I will not listen when they call to me in the time of their distress.

15"What is my beloved doing in my temple
as she works out her evil schemes with
many?
Can consecrated meat avert ⌞your
punishment⌟?
When you engage in your wickedness,
then you rejoice.[a]" Jer 7:9-10

16The LORD called you a thriving olive tree Ps 1:3
with fruit beautiful in form.
But with the roar of a mighty storm
he will set it on fire, Jer 21:14
and its branches will be broken. Isa 27:11

17The LORD Almighty, who planted you, has decreed disaster for you, because the house of Israel and the house of Judah have done evil and provoked me to anger by burning incense to Baal.

Plot Against Jeremiah

18Because the LORD revealed their plot to me, I knew it, for at that time he showed me what they were doing. 19I had been like a gentle lamb led to the slaughter; I did not realize that they had plotted against me, saying, Jer 18:18; 20:10

"Let us destroy the tree and its fruit;
let us cut him off from the land of the
living, Isa 53:8
that his name be remembered no more."
20But, O LORD Almighty, you who judge
righteously Ps 7:11
and test the heart and mind, Ps 7:9
let me see your vengeance upon them, Ps 58:10
for to you I have committed my cause.

21"Therefore this is what the LORD says about the men of Anathoth who are seeking your life and saying, 'Do not prophesy in the name of the LORD or you will die by our hands'— 22therefore this is what the LORD Almighty says: 'I will punish them. Their young men will die by the sword, their sons and daughters by famine. 23Not even a remnant will be left to them, because I will bring disaster on the men of Anathoth in the year of their punishment.'" Jer 6:9; 23:12

Jeremiah's Complaint

12 You are always righteous, O LORD,
when I bring a case before you.
Yet I would speak with you about your
justice: Eze 18:25
Why does the way of the wicked prosper?
Why do all the faithless live at ease?
2You have planted them, and they have taken
root; Jer 11:17
they grow and bear fruit.
You are always on their lips
but far from their hearts. Mt 15:8; Tit 1:16
3Yet you know me, O LORD;
you see me and test my thoughts about
you. Ps 139:1-4; Jer 11:20
Drag them off like sheep to be butchered!
Set them apart for the day of slaughter!
4How long will the land lie parched[b] Jer 4:28
and the grass in every field be withered?
Because those who live in it are wicked,
the animals and birds have perished. Jer 4:25
Moreover, the people are saying,
"He will not see what happens to us."

God's Answer

5"If you have raced with men on foot
and they have worn you out,
how can you compete with horses?

[a]15 Or *Could consecrated meat avert your punishment? / Then you would rejoice*
[b]4 Or *land mourn*

If you stumble in safe country,[a]
how will you manage in the thickets by[b]
the Jordan? Jer 49:19; 50:44
6Your brothers, your own family—
even they have betrayed you;
they have raised a loud cry against
you.
Do not trust them,
though they speak well of you. Ps 12:2

7"I will forsake my house, 2Ki 21:14
abandon my inheritance; Jer 7:29
I will give the one I love Isa 5:1
into the hands of her enemies. Jer 17:4
8My inheritance has become to me
like a lion in the forest.
She roars at me;
therefore I hate her. Hos 9:15; Am 6:8
9Has not my inheritance become to me
like a speckled bird of prey
that other birds of prey surround and
attack?
Go and gather all the wild beasts;
bring them to devour. Isa 56:9; Jer 15:3; Eze 23:25
10Many shepherds will ruin my vineyard Jer 23:1
and trample down my field;
they will turn my pleasant field
into a desolate wasteland. Isa 5:1-7
11It will be made a wasteland,
parched and desolate before me; Isa 42:25
the whole land will be laid waste
because there is no one who cares.
12Over all the barren heights in the desert
destroyers will swarm,
for the sword of the LORD will devour Jer 47:6
from one end of the land to the other;
no one will be safe. Jer 7:10
13They will sow wheat but reap thorns;
they will wear themselves out but gain
nothing. Lev 26:20; Dt 28:38; Mic 6:15
So bear the shame of your harvest
because of the LORD's fierce anger." Jer 4:26

14This is what the LORD says: "As for all my
wicked neighbors who seize the inheritance I gave
my people Israel, I will uproot them from their
lands and I will uproot the house of Judah from
among them. 15But after I uproot them, I will again
have compassion and will bring each of them back
to his own inheritance and his own country. 16And
if they learn well the ways of my people and swear
by my name, saying, 'As surely as the LORD
lives'—even as they once taught my people to
swear by Baal—then they will be established
among my people. 17But if any nation does not
listen, I will completely uproot and destroy it,"
declares the LORD. Isa 60:12; Jer 4:2; Zec 2:7-9

A Linen Belt

13 This is what the LORD said to me: "Go and
buy a linen belt and put it around your
waist, but do not let it touch water." 2So I bought
a belt, as the LORD directed, and put it around my
waist.

3Then the word of the LORD came to me a second time: 4"Take the belt you bought and are
wearing around your waist, and go now to Perath[c] and hide it there in a crevice in the rocks."
5So I went and hid it at Perath, as the LORD
told me. Ex 40:16

6Many days later the LORD said to me, "Go now
to Perath and get the belt I told you to hide there."
7So I went to Perath and dug up the belt and took
it from the place where I had hidden it, but now
it was ruined and completely useless.

8Then the word of the LORD came to me: 9"This
is what the LORD says: 'In the same way I will ruin
the pride of Judah and the great pride of Jerusalem. 10These wicked people, who refuse to listen to
my words, who follow the stubbornness of their
hearts and go after other gods to serve and worship them, will be like this belt—completely useless! 11For as a belt is bound around a man's waist,
so I bound the whole house of Israel and the whole
house of Judah to me,' declares the LORD, 'to be my
people for my renown and praise and honor. But
they have not listened.' Lev 26:19; Jer 7:26; 32:20

Wineskins

12"Say to them: 'This is what the LORD, the God
of Israel, says: Every wineskin should be filled with
wine.' And if they say to you, 'Don't we know that
every wineskin should be filled with wine?' 13then
tell them, 'This is what the LORD says: I am going
to fill with drunkenness all who live in this land,
including the kings who sit on David's throne, the
priests, the prophets and all those living in Jerusalem. 14I will smash them one against the other,
fathers and sons alike, declares the LORD. I will
allow no pity or mercy or compassion to keep me
from destroying them.' " Isa 51:17; Jer 16:5; Eze 5:10

Threat of Captivity

15Hear and pay attention,
do not be arrogant,
for the LORD has spoken. Ps 95:7-8
16Give glory to the LORD your God Jos 7:19
before he brings the darkness,
before your feet stumble Jer 23:12
on the darkening hills.
You hope for light,
but he will turn it to thick darkness
and change it to deep gloom. Isa 59:9
17But if you do not listen, Mal 2:2
I will weep in secret

[a]5 Or *If you put your trust in a land of safety* [b]5 Or *the flooding of* [c]4 Or possibly *the Euphrates*; also in verses 5-7

because of your pride;
my eyes will weep bitterly,
overflowing with tears, Jer 9:1
because the LORD's flock will be taken
captive. Jer 14:18

LIVING INSIGHT

Glorifying God means being occupied with and committed to His ways rather than preoccupied with and determined to go my own way. It is being so thrilled with Him, so devoted to Him, so committed to Him that we cannot get enough of Him!

(See Jeremiah 13:16.)

[18]Say to the king and to the queen mother,
"Come down from your thrones,
for your glorious crowns 2Sa 12:30; La 5:16
will fall from your heads."
[19]The cities in the Negev will be shut up,
and there will be no one to open them.
All Judah will be carried into exile, Jer 20:4; 52:30
carried completely away.

[20]Lift up your eyes and see
those who are coming from the north.
Where is the flock that was entrusted to you,
the sheep of which you boasted?
[21]What will you say when ⌞the LORD⌟ sets over
you
those you cultivated as your special allies?
Will not pain grip you
like that of a woman in labor? Jer 4:31
[22]And if you ask yourself,
"Why has this happened to me?"—
it is because of your many sins Jer 16:10-12
that your skirts have been torn off Isa 20:4
and your body mistreated. Eze 16:37; Na 3:5-6
[23]Can the Ethiopian[a] change his skin
or the leopard its spots?
Neither can you do good
who are accustomed to doing evil. 2Ch 6:36

[24]"I will scatter you like chaff Ps 1:4
driven by the desert wind. Lev 26:33
[25]This is your lot,
the portion I have decreed for you," Job 20:29
declares the LORD,
"because you have forgotten me Isa 17:10
and trusted in false gods. Ps 4:2
[26]I will pull up your skirts over your face
that your shame may be seen— La 1:8
[27]your adulteries and lustful neighings,
your shameless prostitution! Jer 2:20
I have seen your detestable acts
on the hills and in the fields. Eze 6:13
Woe to you, O Jerusalem!
How long will you be unclean?" Hos 8:5

Drought, Famine, Sword

14 This is the word of the LORD to Jeremiah
concerning the drought: Isa 5:6

[2]"Judah mourns, Isa 3:26; Jer 8:21
her cities languish;
they wail for the land,
and a cry goes up from Jerusalem.
[3]The nobles send their servants for water;
they go to the cisterns
but find no water. 2Ki 18:31; Job 6:19-20
They return with their jars unfilled;
dismayed and despairing,
they cover their heads. 2Sa 15:30
[4]The ground is cracked
because there is no rain in the land; Jer 3:3
the farmers are dismayed
and cover their heads.
[5]Even the doe in the field
deserts her newborn fawn
because there is no grass. Isa 15:6
[6]Wild donkeys stand on the barren heights
and pant like jackals;
their eyesight fails
for lack of pasture."
[7]Although our sins testify against us, Hos 5:5
O LORD, do something for the sake of your
name. Ps 79:9
For our backsliding is great; Jer 5:6
we have sinned against you. Jer 8:14
[8]O Hope of Israel, Jer 17:13
its Savior in times of distress, Ps 46:1
why are you like a stranger in the land,
like a traveler who stays only a night?
[9]Why are you like a man taken by surprise,
like a warrior powerless to save? Isa 50:2
You are among us, O LORD, Jer 8:19
and we bear your name; Isa 63:19; Jer 15:16
do not forsake us! Ps 27:9

[10]This is what the LORD says about this people:

"They greatly love to wander;
they do not restrain their feet. Ps 119:101
So the LORD does not accept them; Jer 6:20
he will now remember their wickedness
and punish them for their sins." Hos 8:13

[11]Then the LORD said to me, "Do not pray for
the well-being of this people. [12]Although they fast,
I will not listen to their cry; though they offer
burnt offerings and grain offerings, I will not accept them. Instead, I will destroy them with the
sword, famine and plague." Ex 32:10; Isa 1:15; Jer 7:21
[13]But I said, "Ah, Sovereign LORD, the prophets

[a]23 Hebrew *Cushite* (probably a person from the upper Nile region)

keep telling them, 'You will not see the sword or
suffer famine. Indeed, I will give you lasting peace
in this place.'" Jer 5:12
14Then the LORD said to me, "The prophets are
prophesying lies in my name. I have not sent them
or appointed them or spoken to them. They are
prophesying to you false visions, divinations, idol-
atries[a] and the delusions of their own minds.
15Therefore, this is what the LORD says about the
prophets who are prophesying in my name: I did
not send them, yet they are saying, 'No sword or
famine will touch this land.' Those same prophets
will perish by sword and famine. 16And the people
they are prophesying to will be thrown out into the
streets of Jerusalem because of the famine and
sword. There will be no one to bury them or their
wives, their sons or their daughters. I will pour out
on them the calamity they deserve. Jer 5:12-13; 27:14

17"Speak this word to them:

"'Let my eyes overflow with tears Jer 9:1
night and day without ceasing;
for my virgin daughter—my people— 2Ki 19:21
has suffered a grievous wound,
a crushing blow. Jer 8:21
18If I go into the country,
I see those slain by the sword;
if I go into the city,
I see the ravages of famine. Eze 7:15
Both prophet and priest
have gone to a land they know not.'"
19Have you rejected Judah completely? Jer 7:29
Do you despise Zion?
Why have you afflicted us
so that we cannot be healed? Jer 30:12-13
We hoped for peace
but no good has come,
for a time of healing
but there is only terror. Jer 8:15
20O LORD, we acknowledge our wickedness
and the guilt of our fathers; 1Ki 8:47
we have indeed sinned against you. Da 9:7-8
21For the sake of your name do not despise us;
do not dishonor your glorious throne.
Remember your covenant with us
and do not break it. Ex 2:24
22Do any of the worthless idols of the nations
bring rain? Ps 135:7
Do the skies themselves send down
showers?
No, it is you, O LORD our God.
Therefore our hope is in you,
for you are the one who does all this.

15 Then the LORD said to me: "Even if Moses
and Samuel were to stand before me, my
heart would not go out to this people. Send them
away from my presence! Let them go! 2And if they
ask you, 'Where shall we go?' tell them, 'This is
what the LORD says: Jer 7:16; Eze 14:14,20

"'Those destined for death, to death;
those for the sword, to the sword; Jer 43:11
those for starvation, to starvation; Jer 14:12
those for captivity, to captivity.' Rev 13:10

3"I will send four kinds of destroyers against
them," declares the LORD, "the sword to kill and
the dogs to drag away and the birds of the air and
the beasts of the earth to devour and destroy. 4I
will make them abhorrent to all the kingdoms of
the earth because of what Manasseh son of Hezekiah king of Judah did in Jerusalem. Dt 28:25

5"Who will have pity on you, O Jerusalem?
Who will mourn for you?
Who will stop to ask how you are?
6You have rejected me," declares the LORD.
"You keep on backsliding.
So I will lay hands on you and destroy you;
I can no longer show compassion. Jer 7:20
7I will winnow them with a winnowing fork
at the city gates of the land.
I will bring bereavement and destruction on
my people, Jer 18:21
for they have not changed their ways.
8I will make their widows more numerous
than the sand of the sea.
At midday I will bring a destroyer Jer 6:4
against the mothers of their young men;
suddenly I will bring down on them
anguish and terror. Job 18:11
9The mother of seven will grow faint 1Sa 2:5
and breathe her last.
Her sun will set while it is still day;
she will be disgraced and humiliated. Jer 7:19
I will put the survivors to the sword Jer 21:7
before their enemies," 2Ki 25:7
declares the LORD.
10Alas, my mother, that you gave me birth,
a man with whom the whole land strives
and contends! Jer 1:19
I have neither lent nor borrowed, Lev 25:36
yet everyone curses me. Jer 6:10

11The LORD said,

"Surely I will deliver you for a good purpose;
surely I will make your enemies plead with
you Jer 21:1-2; 37:3; 42:1-3
in times of disaster and times of distress.

12"Can a man break iron—
iron from the north—or bronze? Jer 28:14
13Your wealth and your treasures 2Ki 25:15
I will give as plunder, without charge,
because of all your sins

[a]14 Or *visions, worthless divinations*

throughout your country. Jer 17:3
14I will enslave you to your enemies
in[a] a land you do not know, Jer 16:13
for my anger will kindle a fire Dt 32:22; Ps 21:9
that will burn against you."

15You understand, O LORD;
remember me and care for me.
Avenge me on my persecutors. Jer 12:3
You are long-suffering—do not take me
away; Ex 34:6
think of how I suffer reproach for your
sake. Ps 69:7-9
16When your words came, I ate them; Eze 3:3
they were my joy and my heart's delight,
for I bear your name, Jer 14:9
O LORD God Almighty.
17I never sat in the company of revelers, Ps 1:1
never made merry with them;
I sat alone because your hand was on me
and you had filled me with indignation.
18Why is my pain unending
and my wound grievous and incurable?
Will you be to me like a deceptive brook,
like a spring that fails? Job 6:15

19Therefore this is what the LORD says:

"If you repent, I will restore you
that you may serve me; Zec 3:7
if you utter worthy, not worthless, words,
you will be my spokesman. Ex 4:16
Let this people turn to you,
but you must not turn to them.
20I will make you a wall to this people,
a fortified wall of bronze;
they will fight against you
but will not overcome you,
for I am with you
to rescue and save you," Jer 20:11; Eze 3:8
declares the LORD.
21"I will save you from the hands of the wicked
and redeem you from the grasp of the
cruel." Ge 48:16; Jer 50:34

Day of Disaster

16 Then the word of the LORD came to me:
2"You must not marry and have sons or
daughters in this place." 3For this is what the LORD
says about the sons and daughters born in this
land and about the women who are their mothers
and the men who are their fathers: 4"They will die
of deadly diseases. They will not be mourned or
buried but will be like refuse lying on the ground.
They will perish by sword and famine, and their
dead bodies will become food for the birds of the
air and the beasts of the earth." Ps 83:10; 1Co 7:26-27
5For this is what the LORD says: "Do not enter
a house where there is a funeral meal; do not go to
mourn or show sympathy, because I have withdrawn my blessing, my love and my pity from this
people," declares the LORD. 6"Both high and low
will die in this land. They will not be buried or
mourned, and no one will cut himself or shave his
head for them. 7No one will offer food to comfort
those who mourn for the dead—not even for a
father or a mother—nor will anyone give them a
drink to console them. Jer 15:5; Eze 9:5-6
8"And do not enter a house where there is feasting and sit down to eat and drink. 9For this is what
the LORD Almighty, the God of Israel, says: Before
your eyes and in your days I will bring an end to
the sounds of joy and gladness and to the voices of
bride and bridegroom in this place. Rev 18:23
10"When you tell these people all this and they
ask you, 'Why has the LORD decreed such a great
disaster against us? What wrong have we done?
What sin have we committed against the LORD our
God?' 11then say to them, 'It is because your fathers forsook me,' declares the LORD, 'and followed
other gods and served and worshiped them. They
forsook me and did not keep my law. 12But you
have behaved more wickedly than your fathers.
See how each of you is following the stubbornness
of his evil heart instead of obeying me. 13So I will
throw you out of this land into a land neither you
nor your fathers have known, and there you will
serve other gods day and night, for I will show you
no favor.' Dt 29:24; Jer 5:19; 13:10
14"However, the days are coming," declares the
LORD, "when men will no longer say, 'As surely as
the LORD lives, who brought the Israelites up out of
Egypt,' 15but they will say, 'As surely as the LORD
lives, who brought the Israelites up out of the land
of the north and out of all the countries where he
had banished them.' For I will restore them to the
land I gave their forefathers. Jer 23:7-8; 24:6
16"But now I will send for many fishermen,"
declares the LORD, "and they will catch them. After
that I will send for many hunters, and they will
hunt them down on every mountain and hill and
from the crevices of the rocks. 17My eyes are on all
their ways; they are not hidden from me, nor is
their sin concealed from my eyes. 18I will repay
them double for their wickedness and their sin,
because they have defiled my land with the lifeless
forms of their vile images and have filled my inheritance with their detestable idols." Pr 15:3

19O LORD, my strength and my fortress,
my refuge in time of distress, Ps 46:1
to you the nations will come Isa 2:2; Jer 3:17
from the ends of the earth and say,
"Our fathers possessed nothing but false gods,
worthless idols that did them no good.

[a] 14 Some Hebrew manuscripts, Septuagint and Syriac (see also Jer. 17:4); most Hebrew manuscripts *I will cause your enemies to bring you / into*

[20]Do men make their own gods?
Yes, but they are not gods!" Isa 37:19; Jer 2:11

[21]"Therefore I will teach them—
this time I will teach them
my power and might.
Then they will know
that my name is the LORD. Ex 3:15

17 "Judah's sin is engraved with an iron
tool, Job 19:24
inscribed with a flint point,
on the tablets of their hearts Pr 3:3; 2Co 3:3
and on the horns of their altars. Ex 27:2
[2]Even their children remember
their altars and Asherah poles[a] 2Ch 24:18
beside the spreading trees
and on the high hills. Jer 2:20
[3]My mountain in the land
and your[b] wealth and all your treasures
I will give away as plunder, 2Ki 24:13
together with your high places, Jer 26:18
because of sin throughout your country.
[4]Through your own fault you will lose
the inheritance I gave you. La 5:2
I will enslave you to your enemies Dt 28:48
in a land you do not know, Jer 16:13
for you have kindled my anger,
and it will burn forever." Jer 15:14

[5]This is what the LORD says:

"Cursed is the one who trusts in man, Isa 2:22
who depends on flesh for his strength
and whose heart turns away from the LORD.
[6]He will be like a bush in the wastelands;
he will not see prosperity when it comes.
He will dwell in the parched places of the
desert,
in a salt land where no one lives. Dt 29:23

[7]"But blessed is the man who trusts in the
LORD, Ps 34:8; Pr 16:20
whose confidence is in him.
[8]He will be like a tree planted by the water
that sends out its roots by the stream.
It does not fear when heat comes;
its leaves are always green.
It has no worries in a year of drought Jer 14:1-6
and never fails to bear fruit." Ps 1:3; 92:12-14

[9]The heart is deceitful above all things Ecc 9:3
and beyond cure.
Who can understand it?

[10]"I the LORD search the heart 1Sa 16:7; Rev 2:23
and examine the mind, Jer 20:12; Ro 8:27
to reward a man according to his conduct,
according to what his deeds deserve." Ro 2:6

[11]Like a partridge that hatches eggs it did not
lay
is the man who gains riches by unjust
means.
When his life is half gone, they will desert
him,
and in the end he will prove to be a fool.

[12]A glorious throne, exalted from the beginning,
is the place of our sanctuary.
[13]O LORD, the hope of Israel, Jer 14:8
all who forsake you will be put to shame.
Those who turn away from you will be written
in the dust Ps 69:28
because they have forsaken the LORD,
the spring of living water. Jn 4:10

[14]Heal me, O LORD, and I will be healed; Isa 30:26
save me and I will be saved, Ps 119:94
for you are the one I praise. Ps 109:1
[15]They keep saying to me,
"Where is the word of the LORD?
Let it now be fulfilled!" Isa 5:19; 2Pe 3:4
[16]I have not run away from being your
shepherd;
you know I have not desired the day of
despair.
What passes my lips is open before you.
[17]Do not be a terror to me; Ps 88:15-16
you are my refuge in the day of disaster.
[18]Let my persecutors be put to shame,
but keep me from shame;
let them be terrified,
but keep me from terror.
Bring on them the day of disaster;
destroy them with double destruction.

Keeping the Sabbath Holy

[19]This is what the LORD said to me: "Go and
stand at the gate of the people, through which the
kings of Judah go in and out; stand also at all the
other gates of Jerusalem. [20]Say to them, 'Hear
the word of the LORD, O kings of Judah and all
people of Judah and everyone living in Jerusalem
who come through these gates. [21]This is what the
LORD says: Be careful not to carry a load on the
Sabbath day or bring it through the gates of Jeru-

LIVING INSIGHT

Beautiful branches and lacy leaves, no matter how attractive, fail to fortify us as the velocity increases. It takes roots, stubborn, deep powerful roots, to keep us standing.

(See Jeremiah 17:8.)

[a]2 That is, symbols of the goddess Asherah [b]2,3 Or *hills* / [3]*and the mountains of the land. / Your*

salem. 22Do not bring a load out of your houses or
do any work on the Sabbath, but keep the Sabbath
day holy, as I commanded your forefathers. 23Yet
they did not listen or pay attention; they were
stiff-necked and would not listen or respond to
discipline. 24But if you are careful to obey me,
declares the LORD, and bring no load through the
gates of this city on the Sabbath, but keep the
Sabbath day holy by not doing any work on it,
25then kings who sit on David's throne will come
through the gates of this city with their officials.
They and their officials will come riding in chariots
and on horses, accompanied by the men of Judah
and those living in Jerusalem, and this city will be
inhabited forever. 26People will come from the
towns of Judah and the villages around Jerusalem,
from the territory of Benjamin and the western
foothills, from the hill country and the Negev,
bringing burnt offerings and sacrifices, grain offerings, incense and thank offerings to the house of
the LORD. 27But if you do not obey me to keep the
Sabbath day holy by not carrying any load as you
come through the gates of Jerusalem on the Sabbath day, then I will kindle an unquenchable fire
in the gates of Jerusalem that will consume her
fortresses.'" 2Ki 25:9; Jer 22:5; Am 2:5

Warnings and Judgment **Chapters 18–45**

Jeremiah was called to be God's messenger in one of the toughest times in Hebrew history. Equipped with the word of God as his only implement of "warfare," Jeremiah stood as God's mouthpiece in a time when the people wanted him to simply keep quiet. Through his tears he proclaimed the judgment of God, and with a broken heart he leveled warning after warning against a deaf and hardhearted nation. (Yet, beyond judgment would come restoration and renewal. Look in particular at chapters 30–33 for magnificent promises of restoration.)

Jeremiah told the people that the sound of wedding bells in the land would cease (7:34). Delight, fun and romance would be nothing but a distant memory when God's judgment came on the nation. That was the sobering message Jeremiah was called to bring to Judah. If you have ever wondered if God's servants struggle with broken hearts and feelings of depression, look no further than Jeremiah. He lived life in a state of sadness—lonely and utterly disappointed. However, even in his bitterness of soul, he remained faithful to proclaim the message God called him to preach.

At the Potter's House

18 This is the word that came to Jeremiah
from the LORD: 2"Go down to the potter's
house, and there I will give you my message." 3So
I went down to the potter's house, and I saw him
working at the wheel. 4But the pot he was shaping
from the clay was marred in his hands; so the
potter formed it into another pot, shaping it as
seemed best to him.
5Then the word of the LORD came to me: 6"O
house of Israel, can I not do with you as this potter
does?" declares the LORD. "Like clay in the hand of
the potter, so are you in my hand, O house of

LIVING  **INSIGHT**

God is committed to our being changed, no matter how long or how painful the process. While being changed, we may feel like a shapeless mass. But trust the Father. He's changing you. He knows what He's about.

(See Jeremiah 18:6.)

Israel. 7If at any time I announce that a nation or
kingdom is to be uprooted, torn down and destroyed, 8and if that nation I warned repents of its
evil, then I will relent and not inflict on it the
disaster I had planned. 9And if at another time I
announce that a nation or kingdom is to be built
up and planted, 10and if it does evil in my sight and
does not obey me, then I will reconsider the good
I had intended to do for it. Isa 45:9; Ro 9:20-21; Jer 1:10
11"Now therefore say to the people of Judah and
those living in Jerusalem, 'This is what the LORD
says: Look! I am preparing a disaster for you and
devising a plan against you. So turn from your evil
ways, each one of you, and reform your ways and
your actions.' 12But they will reply, 'It's no use. We
will continue with our own plans; each of us will
follow the stubbornness of his evil heart.'"

13Therefore this is what the LORD says:

"Inquire among the nations:
  Who has ever heard anything like this?
A most horrible thing has been done Jer 5:30
  by Virgin Israel. 2Ki 19:21
14Does the snow of Lebanon
  ever vanish from its rocky slopes?
Do its cool waters from distant sources
  ever cease to flow?[a]
15Yet my people have forgotten me; Isa 17:10
  they burn incense to worthless idols, Jer 10:15
which made them stumble in their ways
  and in the ancient paths. Jer 6:16
They made them walk in bypaths
  and on roads not built up. Isa 57:14; 62:10
16Their land will be laid waste, Jer 25:9
  an object of lasting scorn; Jer 19:8
all who pass by will be appalled
  and will shake their heads. Ps 22:7
17Like a wind from the east, Jer 13:24
  I will scatter them before their enemies;

[a]14 The meaning of the Hebrew for this sentence is uncertain.

I will show them my back and not my face
in the day of their disaster."

18They said, "Come, let's make plans against Jeremiah; for the teaching of the law by the priest will not be lost, nor will counsel from the wise, nor the word from the prophets. So come, let's attack him with our tongues and pay no attention to anything he says." Jer 11:19; Mal 2:7

19Listen to me, O LORD;
hear what my accusers are saying! Ps 71:13
20Should good be repaid with evil? Ge 44:4
Yet they have dug a pit for me. Ps 35:7; 57:6
Remember that I stood before you Jer 15:1
and spoke in their behalf Ps 106:23
to turn your wrath away from them.
21So give their children over to famine; Jer 11:22
hand them over to the power of the sword.
Let their wives be made childless and widows;
let their men be put to death,
their young men slain by the sword in
battle. Isa 9:17
22Let a cry be heard from their houses Jer 6:26
when you suddenly bring invaders against
them,
for they have dug a pit to capture me
and have hidden snares for my feet. Ps 140:5
23But you know, O LORD,
all their plots to kill me. Jer 11:21
Do not forgive their crimes Ps 109:14
or blot out their sins from your sight.
Let them be overthrown before you;
deal with them in the time of your anger.

19 This is what the LORD says: "Go and buy a clay jar from a potter. Take along some of the elders of the people and of the priests 2and go out to the Valley of Ben Hinnom, near the entrance of the Potsherd Gate. There proclaim the words I tell you, 3and say, 'Hear the word of the LORD, O kings of Judah and people of Jerusalem. This is what the LORD Almighty, the God of Israel, says: Listen! I am going to bring a disaster on this place that will make the ears of everyone who hears of it tingle. 4For they have forsaken me and made this a place of foreign gods; they have burned sacrifices in it to gods that neither they nor their fathers nor the kings of Judah ever knew, and they have filled this place with the blood of the innocent. 5They have built the high places of Baal to burn their sons in the fire as offerings to Baal—something I did not command or mention, nor did it enter my mind. 6So beware, the days are coming, declares the LORD, when people will no longer call this place Topheth or the Valley of Ben Hinnom, but the Valley of Slaughter. 1Sa 3:11

7"'In this place I will ruin[a] the plans of Judah and Jerusalem. I will make them fall by the sword before their enemies, at the hands of those who seek their lives, and I will give their carcasses as food to the birds of the air and the beasts of the earth. 8I will devastate this city and make it an object of scorn; all who pass by will be appalled and will scoff because of all its wounds. 9I will make them eat the flesh of their sons and daughters, and they will eat one another's flesh during the stress of the siege imposed on them by the enemies who seek their lives.' Dt 28:49-57; Jer 18:16

10"Then break the jar while those who go with you are watching, 11and say to them, 'This is what the LORD Almighty says: I will smash this nation and this city just as this potter's jar is smashed and cannot be repaired. They will bury the dead in Topheth until there is no more room. 12This is what I will do to this place and to those who live here, declares the LORD. I will make this city like Topheth. 13The houses in Jerusalem and those of the kings of Judah will be defiled like this place, Topheth—all the houses where they burned incense on the roofs to all the starry hosts and poured out drink offerings to other gods.'"

14Jeremiah then returned from Topheth, where the LORD had sent him to prophesy, and stood in the court of the LORD's temple and said to all the people, 15"This is what the LORD Almighty, the God of Israel, says: 'Listen! I am going to bring on this city and the villages around it every disaster I pronounced against them, because they were stiff-necked and would not listen to my words.'"

Jeremiah and Pashhur

20 When the priest Pashhur son of Immer, the chief officer in the temple of the LORD, heard Jeremiah prophesying these things, 2he had Jeremiah the prophet beaten and put in the stocks at the Upper Gate of Benjamin at the LORD's temple. 3The next day, when Pashhur released him from the stocks, Jeremiah said to him, "The LORD's name for you is not Pashhur, but Magor-Missabib.[b] 4For this is what the LORD says: 'I will make you a terror to yourself and to all your friends; with your own eyes you will see them fall by the sword of their enemies. I will hand all Judah over to the king of Babylon, who will carry them away to Babylon or put them to the sword. 5I will hand over to their enemies all the wealth of this city—all its products, all its valuables and all the treasures of the kings of Judah. They will take it away as plunder and carry it off to Babylon. 6And you, Pashhur, and all who live in your house will go into exile to Babylon. There you will die and be

[a]7 The Hebrew for *ruin* sounds like the Hebrew for *jar* (see verses 1 and 10). [b]3 *Magor-Missabib* means *terror on every side.*

buried, you and all your friends to whom you have prophesied lies.' " 2Ki 20:17; Jer 52:27

Jeremiah's Complaint

7O LORD, you deceived[a] me, and I was
deceived[a]; Ex 5:23
you overpowered me and prevailed. Isa 8:11
I am ridiculed all day long; Job 12:4
everyone mocks me. Job 17:2; Ps 119:21
8Whenever I speak, I cry out
proclaiming violence and destruction. Jer 6:7
So the word of the LORD has brought me
insult and reproach all day long. 2Ch 36:16
9But if I say, "I will not mention him
or speak any more in his name,"
his word is in my heart like a fire, Ps 39:3
a fire shut up in my bones.
I am weary of holding it in; Job 32:18-20; Ac 4:20
indeed, I cannot.
10I hear many whispering,
"Terror on every side! Jer 6:25
Report him! Let's report him!" Isa 29:21
All my friends Ps 41:9
are waiting for me to slip, saying, Lk 11:53-54
"Perhaps he will be deceived;
then we will prevail over him 1Ki 19:2
and take our revenge on him." Jer 11:19

11But the LORD is with me like a mighty warrior;
so my persecutors will stumble and not
prevail. Jer 15:20; 17:18
They will fail and be thoroughly disgraced;
their dishonor will never be forgotten.
12O LORD Almighty, you who examine the
righteous
and probe the heart and mind, Jer 17:10
let me see your vengeance upon them, Ps 54:7
for to you I have committed my cause.

13Sing to the LORD! Isa 12:6
Give praise to the LORD!
He rescues the life of the needy Ps 35:10
from the hands of the wicked. Ps 97:10

14Cursed be the day I was born! Job 3:3; Jer 15:10
May the day my mother bore me not be
blessed!
15Cursed be the man who brought my father
the news,
who made him very glad, saying,
"A child is born to you—a son!"
16May that man be like the towns Ge 19:25
the LORD overthrew without pity.
May he hear wailing in the morning,
a battle cry at noon.
17For he did not kill me in the womb, Job 10:18-19
with my mother as my grave,
her womb enlarged forever.
18Why did I ever come out of the womb
to see trouble and sorrow Ge 3:17
and to end my days in shame? Ps 90:9

God Rejects Zedekiah's Request

21 The word came to Jeremiah from the LORD
when King Zedekiah sent to him Pashhur
son of Malkijah and the priest Zephaniah son of
Maaseiah. They said: 2"Inquire now of the LORD
for us because Nebuchadnezzar[b] king of Babylon
is attacking us. Perhaps the LORD will perform
wonders for us as in times past so that he will
withdraw from us." 2Ki 24:18; 25:18
3But Jeremiah answered them, "Tell Zedekiah,
4'This is what the LORD, the God of Israel, says: I
am about to turn against you the weapons of war
that are in your hands, which you are using to fight
the king of Babylon and the Babylonians[c] who
are outside the wall besieging you. And I will gather them inside this city. 5I myself will fight against
you with an outstretched hand and a mighty arm
in anger and fury and great wrath. 6I will strike
down those who live in this city—both men and
animals—and they will die of a terrible plague.
7After that, declares the LORD, I will hand over
Zedekiah king of Judah, his officials and the people in this city who survive the plague, sword and
famine, to Nebuchadnezzar king of Babylon and
to their enemies who seek their lives. He will put
them to the sword; he will show them no mercy or
pity or compassion.' 2Ch 36:17; Jer 37:17; 39:5
8"Furthermore, tell the people, 'This is what the
LORD says: See, I am setting before you the way of
life and the way of death. 9Whoever stays in this
city will die by the sword, famine or plague. But
whoever goes out and surrenders to the Babylonians who are besieging you will live; he will escape
with his life. 10I have determined to do this city
harm and not good, declares the LORD. It will be
given into the hands of the king of Babylon, and
he will destroy it with fire.' Jer 44:11,27; 52:13
11"Moreover, say to the royal house of Judah,
'Hear the word of the LORD; 12O house of David,
this is what the LORD says: Jer 13:18

" 'Administer justice every morning; Jer 22:3
rescue from the hand of his oppressor
the one who has been robbed,
or my wrath will break out and burn like fire
because of the evil you have done— Jer 23:2
burn with no one to quench it. Isa 1:31
13I am against you, ⌊Jerusalem,⌋ Eze 13:8
you who live above this valley Ps 125:2
on the rocky plateau,
declares the LORD—
you who say, "Who can come against us?
Who can enter our refuge?" Jer 49:4; Ob 1:3-4

[a] 7 Or *persuaded* [b] 2 Hebrew *Nebuchadrezzar,* of which *Nebuchadnezzar* is a variant; here and often in Jeremiah and Ezekiel
[c] 4 Or *Chaldeans*; also in verse 9

14 I will punish you as your deeds deserve,
declares the LORD.
I will kindle a fire in your forests 2Ch 36:19
that will consume everything around you.' "

Judgment Against Evil Kings

22 This is what the LORD says: "Go down to
the palace of the king of Judah and proclaim this message there: 2 'Hear the word of the
LORD, O king of Judah, you who sit on David's
throne—you, your officials and your people who
come through these gates. 3 This is what the LORD
says: Do what is just and right. Rescue from the
hand of his oppressor the one who has been
robbed. Do no wrong or violence to the alien, the
fatherless or the widow, and do not shed innocent
blood in this place. 4 For if you are careful to carry
out these commands, then kings who sit on David's throne will come through the gates of this
palace, riding in chariots and on horses, accompanied by their officials and their people. 5 But if you
do not obey these commands, declares the LORD, I
swear by myself that this palace will become a
ruin.' " Jer 17:27; Mic 6:8; Heb 6:13
6 For this is what the LORD says about the palace
of the king of Judah:

"Though you are like Gilead to me, Ge 31:21
like the summit of Lebanon,
I will surely make you like a desert, Mic 3:12
like towns not inhabited.
7 I will send destroyers against you, Jer 4:7
each man with his weapons,
and they will cut up your fine cedar beams
and throw them into the fire. 2Ch 36:19

8 "People from many nations will pass by this
city and will ask one another, 'Why has the LORD
done such a thing to this great city?' 9 And the
answer will be: 'Because they have forsaken the
covenant of the LORD their God and have worshiped and served other gods.' " 2Ki 22:17; 2Ch 34:25

10 Do not weep for the dead ⌊king⌋ or mourn
his loss; Ecc 4:2
rather, weep bitterly for him who is exiled,
because he will never return Jer 24:9
nor see his native land again.

11 For this is what the LORD says about Shallum[a]
son of Josiah, who succeeded his father as king of
Judah but has gone from this place: "He will never
return. 12 He will die in the place where they have
led him captive; he will not see this land again."

13 "Woe to him who builds his palace by
unrighteousness, Mic 3:10; Hab 2:9
his upper rooms by injustice,
making his countrymen work for nothing,
not paying them for their labor. Jas 5:4
14 He says, 'I will build myself a great palace
with spacious upper rooms.'
So he makes large windows in it,
panels it with cedar 2Sa 7:2
and decorates it in red. Eze 23:14

15 "Does it make you a king
to have more and more cedar?
Did not your father have food and drink?
He did what was right and just, 2Ki 23:25
so all went well with him. Ps 128:2; Isa 3:10
16 He defended the cause of the poor and needy,
and so all went well.
Is that not what it means to know me?"
declares the LORD.
17 "But your eyes and your heart
are set only on dishonest gain, Isa 56:11
on shedding innocent blood 2Ki 24:4
and on oppression and extortion." Dt 28:33

18 Therefore this is what the LORD says about Jehoiakim son of Josiah king of Judah:

"They will not mourn for him: 2Sa 1:26
'Alas, my brother! Alas, my sister!'
They will not mourn for him:
'Alas, my master! Alas, his splendor!'
19 He will have the burial of a donkey—
dragged away and thrown Jer 36:30
outside the gates of Jerusalem."

20 "Go up to Lebanon and cry out,
let your voice be heard in Bashan, Ps 68:15
cry out from Abarim, Nu 27:12
for all your allies are crushed. Jer 30:14
21 I warned you when you felt secure,
but you said, 'I will not listen!'
This has been your way from your youth;
you have not obeyed me. Jer 7:23-28
22 The wind will drive all your shepherds away,
and your allies will go into exile. ver 20
Then you will be ashamed and disgraced
because of all your wickedness.
23 You who live in 'Lebanon,'[b] 1Ki 7:2
who are nestled in cedar buildings,
how you will groan when pangs come upon
you,
pain like that of a woman in labor! Jer 4:31

24 "As surely as I live," declares the LORD, "even
if you, Jehoiachin[c] son of Jehoiakim king of Judah, were a signet ring on my right hand, I would
still pull you off. 25 I will hand you over to those
who seek your life, those you fear—to Nebuchadnezzar king of Babylon and to the Babylonians.[d]
26 I will hurl you and the mother who gave you
birth into another country, where neither of you
was born, and there you both will die. 27 You will

[a] 11 Also called *Jehoahaz*
[b] 23 That is, the palace in Jerusalem (see 1 Kings 7:2)
[c] 24 Hebrew *Coniah*, a variant of *Jehoiachin*; also in verse 28
[d] 25 Or *Chaldeans*

never come back to the land you long to return to." 2Ki 24:8; 2Ch 36:10

28Is this man Jehoiachin a despised, broken pot,
an object no one wants?
Why will he and his children be hurled out,
cast into a land they do not know? Jer 17:4
29O land, land, land, Jer 6:19; Mic 1:2
hear the word of the LORD!
30This is what the LORD says:
"Record this man as if childless, 1Ch 3:18; Mt 1:12
a man who will not prosper in his lifetime,
for none of his offspring will prosper, Job 18:19
none will sit on the throne of David Ps 94:20
or rule anymore in Judah."

The Righteous Branch

23 "Woe to the shepherds who are destroying
and scattering the sheep of my pasture!"
declares the LORD. 2Therefore this is what the
LORD, the God of Israel, says to the shepherds who
tend my people: "Because you have scattered my
flock and driven them away and have not bestowed care on them, I will bestow punishment on
you for the evil you have done," declares the LORD.
3"I myself will gather the remnant of my flock out
of all the countries where I have driven them and
will bring them back to their pasture, where they
will be fruitful and increase in number. 4I will
place shepherds over them who will tend them,
and they will no longer be afraid or terrified, nor
will any be missing," declares the LORD. Jer 3:15

5"The days are coming," declares the LORD,
"when I will raise up to David[a] a
righteous Branch, Isa 4:2
a King who will reign wisely Isa 9:7
and do what is just and right in the land.
6In his days Judah will be saved
and Israel will live in safety.
This is the name by which he will be called:
The LORD Our Righteousness. Ro 3:21-22

7"So then, the days are coming," declares the
LORD, "when people will no longer say, 'As surely
as the LORD lives, who brought the Israelites up out
of Egypt,' 8but they will say, 'As surely as the LORD
lives, who brought the descendants of Israel up out
of the land of the north and out of all the countries
where he had banished them.' Then they will live
in their own land." Isa 43:5-6; Am 9:14-15

Lying Prophets

9Concerning the prophets:

My heart is broken within me;
all my bones tremble.
I am like a drunken man,
like a man overcome by wine,
because of the LORD
and his holy words. Jer 20:8-9
10The land is full of adulterers; Jer 9:2
because of the curse[b] the land lies
parched[c] Dt 28:23-24
and the pastures in the desert are withered.
The ⌞prophets⌟ follow an evil course
and use their power unjustly.

11"Both prophet and priest are godless; Jer 6:13
even in my temple I find their wickedness,"
declares the LORD.
12"Therefore their path will become slippery;
they will be banished to darkness
and there they will fall.
I will bring disaster on them
in the year they are punished," Jer 11:23
declares the LORD.

13"Among the prophets of Samaria
I saw this repulsive thing:
They prophesied by Baal Jer 2:8
and led my people Israel astray. Eze 13:10
14And among the prophets of Jerusalem
I have seen something horrible: Jer 5:30
They commit adultery and live a lie. Jer 29:23
They strengthen the hands of evildoers,
so that no one turns from his wickedness.
They are all like Sodom to me; Ge 18:20
the people of Jerusalem are like
Gomorrah." Jer 20:16

15Therefore, this is what the LORD Almighty says
concerning the prophets:

"I will make them eat bitter food
and drink poisoned water, Jer 8:14; 9:15
because from the prophets of Jerusalem
ungodliness has spread throughout the
land." Jer 8:10

16This is what the LORD Almighty says:
"Do not listen to what the prophets are
prophesying to you; Jer 27:9-10,14; Mt 7:15
they fill you with false hopes.
They speak visions from their own minds,
not from the mouth of the LORD. Jer 9:20
17They keep saying to those who despise me,
'The LORD says: You will have peace.' Jer 8:11
And to all who follow the stubbornness of
their hearts Jer 13:10
they say, 'No harm will come to you.'
18But which of them has stood in the council of
the LORD Ro 11:34
to see or to hear his word?
Who has listened and heard his word?
19See, the storm of the LORD Jer 25:32; 30:23
will burst out in wrath,
a whirlwind swirling down Zec 7:14

[a]5 Or *up from David's line* [b]10 Or *because of these things* [c]10 Or *land mourns*

on the heads of the wicked.
20 The anger of the LORD will not turn back
until he fully accomplishes
the purposes of his heart.
In days to come
you will understand it clearly.
21 I did not send these prophets, Jer 14:14; 27:15
yet they have run with their message;
I did not speak to them,
yet they have prophesied.
22 But if they had stood in my council, 1Ki 22:19
they would have proclaimed my words to
my people
and would have turned them from their evil
ways Jer 25:5; Zec 1:4
and from their evil deeds.

23 "Am I only a God nearby," Ps 139:1-10
declares the LORD,
"and not a God far away?
24 Can anyone hide in secret places Job 22:12-14
so that I cannot see him?"
declares the LORD.
"Do not I fill heaven and earth?" 1Ki 8:27
declares the LORD.

25 "I have heard what the prophets say who prophesy lies in my name. They say, 'I had a dream! I had a dream!' 26 How long will this continue in the hearts of these lying prophets, who prophesy the delusions of their own minds? 27 They think the dreams they tell one another will make my people forget my name, just as their fathers forgot my name through Baal worship. 28 Let the prophet who has a dream tell his dream, but let the one who has my word speak it faithfully. For what has straw to do with grain?" declares the LORD. 29 "Is not my word like fire," declares the LORD, "and like a hammer that breaks a rock in pieces?

30 "Therefore," declares the LORD, "I am against the prophets who steal from one another words supposedly from me. 31 Yes," declares the LORD, "I am against the prophets who wag their own tongues and yet declare, 'The LORD declares.' 32 Indeed, I am against those who prophesy false dreams," declares the LORD. "They tell them and lead my people astray with their reckless lies, yet I did not send or appoint them. They do not benefit these people in the least," declares the LORD.

False Oracles and False Prophets

33 "When these people, or a prophet or a priest, ask you, 'What is the oracle[a] of the LORD?' say to them, 'What oracle?[b] I will forsake you, declares the LORD.' 34 If a prophet or a priest or anyone else claims, 'This is the oracle of the LORD,' I will punish that man and his household. 35 This is what each of you keeps on saying to his friend or relative: 'What is the LORD's answer?' or 'What has the LORD spoken?' 36 But you must not mention 'the oracle of the LORD' again, because every man's own word becomes his oracle and so you distort the words of the living God, the LORD Almighty, our God. 37 This is what you keep saying to a prophet: 'What is the LORD's answer to you?' or 'What has the LORD spoken?' 38 Although you claim, 'This is the oracle of the LORD,' this is what the LORD says: You used the words, 'This is the oracle of the LORD,' even though I told you that you must not claim, 'This is the oracle of the LORD.' 39 Therefore, I will surely forget you and cast you out of my presence along with the city I gave to you and your fathers. 40 I will bring upon you everlasting disgrace—everlasting shame that will not be forgotten." Jer 20:11; Eze 5:14-15

Two Baskets of Figs

24 After Jehoiachin[c] son of Jehoiakim king of Judah and the officials, the craftsmen and the artisans of Judah were carried into exile from Jerusalem to Babylon by Nebuchadnezzar king of Babylon, the LORD showed me two baskets of figs placed in front of the temple of the LORD. 2 One basket had very good figs, like those that ripen early; the other basket had very poor figs, so bad they could not be eaten. Isa 5:4; Am 8:1-2

3 Then the LORD asked me, "What do you see, Jeremiah?" Jer 1:11; Am 8:2

"Figs," I answered. "The good ones are very good, but the poor ones are so bad they cannot be eaten."

4 Then the word of the LORD came to me: 5 "This is what the LORD, the God of Israel, says: 'Like these good figs, I regard as good the exiles from Judah, whom I sent away from this place to the land of the Babylonians.[d] 6 My eyes will watch over them for their good, and I will bring them back to this land. I will build them up and not tear them down; I will plant them and not uproot them. 7 I will give them a heart to know me, that I

LIVING  **INSIGHT**

What is it that will make an unfaithful person faithful? What is it that will cause an individual who has turned to treachery to become gentle and gracious and giving, demonstrating a heart for God? It is understanding and knowing the living God.
(See Jeremiah 24:7.)

[a] 33 Or *burden* (see Septuagint and Vulgate) [b] 33 Hebrew; Septuagint and Vulgate *'You are the burden.* (The Hebrew for *oracle* and *burden* is the same.) [c] 1 Hebrew *Jeconiah,* a variant of *Jehoiachin* [d] 5 Or *Chaldeans*

am the LORD. They will be my people, and I will be
their God, for they will return to me with all their
heart. Jer 31:33; 32:40
8“‘But like the poor figs, which are so bad they
cannot be eaten,’ says the LORD, ‘so will I deal with
Zedekiah king of Judah, his officials and the survivors from Jerusalem, whether they remain in this
land or live in Egypt. 9I will make them abhorrent
and an offense to all the kingdoms of the earth, a
reproach and a byword, an object of ridicule and
cursing, wherever I banish them. 10I will send the
sword, famine and plague against them until they
are destroyed from the land I gave to them and
their fathers.’” Jer 15:4; 32:4-5

Seventy Years of Captivity

25 The word came to Jeremiah concerning all
the people of Judah in the fourth year of
Jehoiakim son of Josiah king of Judah, which was
the first year of Nebuchadnezzar king of Babylon.
2So Jeremiah the prophet said to all the people of
Judah and to all those living in Jerusalem: 3For
twenty-three years—from the thirteenth year of
Josiah son of Amon king of Judah until this very
day—the word of the LORD has come to me and I
have spoken to you again and again, but you have
not listened. Jer 1:2; 7:26; 36:1
4And though the LORD has sent all his servants
the prophets to you again and again, you have not
listened or paid any attention. 5They said, “Turn
now, each of you, from your evil ways and your
evil practices, and you can stay in the land the
LORD gave to you and your fathers for ever and
ever. 6Do not follow other gods to serve and worship them; do not provoke me to anger with what
your hands have made. Then I will not harm you.”
7“But you did not listen to me,” declares the
LORD, “and you have provoked me with what your
hands have made, and you have brought harm to
yourselves.” Dt 32:21; 2Ki 21:15
8Therefore the LORD Almighty says this: “Because you have not listened to my words, 9I will
summon all the peoples of the north and my servant Nebuchadnezzar king of Babylon,” declares
the LORD, “and I will bring them against this land
and its inhabitants and against all the surrounding
nations. I will completely destroy[a] them and
make them an object of horror and scorn, and an
everlasting ruin. 10I will banish from them the
sounds of joy and gladness, the voices of bride and
bridegroom, the sound of millstones and the light
of the lamp. 11This whole country will become a
desolate wasteland, and these nations will serve the
king of Babylon seventy years. Jer 18:16; 27:6
12“But when the seventy years are fulfilled, I will
punish the king of Babylon and his nation, the
land of the Babylonians,[b] for their guilt,” declares
the LORD, “and will make it desolate forever. 13I
will bring upon that land all the things I have
spoken against it, all that are written in this book
and prophesied by Jeremiah against all the nations. 14They themselves will be enslaved by many
nations and great kings; I will repay them according to their deeds and the work of their hands.”

The Cup of God’s Wrath

15This is what the LORD, the God of Israel, said
to me: “Take from my hand this cup filled with the
wine of my wrath and make all the nations to
whom I send you drink it. 16When they drink it,
they will stagger and go mad because of the sword
I will send among them.” Isa 51:17; Na 3:11
17So I took the cup from the LORD’s hand and
made all the nations to whom he sent me drink it:
18Jerusalem and the towns of Judah, its kings and
officials, to make them a ruin and an object of
horror and scorn and cursing, as they are today;
19Pharaoh king of Egypt, his attendants, his officials and all his people, 20and all the foreign people
there; all the kings of Uz; all the kings of the Philistines (those of Ashkelon, Gaza, Ekron, and the
people left at Ashdod); 21Edom, Moab and Ammon; 22all the kings of Tyre and Sidon; the kings
of the coastlands across the sea; 23Dedan, Tema,
Buz and all who are in distant places[c]; 24all the
kings of Arabia and all the kings of the foreign
people who live in the desert; 25all the kings of
Zimri, Elam and Media; 26and all the kings of the
north, near and far, one after the other—all the
kingdoms on the face of the earth. And after all of
them, the king of Sheshach[d] will drink it too.
27“Then tell them, ‘This is what the LORD Almighty, the God of Israel, says: Drink, get drunk
and vomit, and fall to rise no more because of the
sword I will send among you.’ 28But if they refuse
to take the cup from your hand and drink, tell
them, ‘This is what the LORD Almighty says: You
must drink it! 29See, I am beginning to bring disaster on the city that bears my Name, and will you
indeed go unpunished? You will not go unpunished, for I am calling down a sword upon all who
live on the earth, declares the LORD Almighty.’
30“Now prophesy all these words against them
and say to them:

“ ‘The LORD will roar from on high; Isa 16:10
he will thunder from his holy dwelling
and roar mightily against his land.
He will shout like those who tread the grapes,
shout against all who live on the earth.
31The tumult will resound to the ends of the
earth,

[a]9 The Hebrew term refers to the irrevocable giving over of things or persons to the LORD, often by totally destroying them.
[b]12 Or *Chaldeans*
[c]23 Or *who clip the hair by their foreheads*
[d]26 *Sheshach* is a cryptogram for Babylon.

for the LORD will bring charges against the
nations; Hos 4:1; Joel 3:2; Mic 6:2
he will bring judgment on all mankind Jer 2:35
and put the wicked to the sword,'" Jer 15:9
declares the LORD.

32This is what the LORD Almighty says:

"Look! Disaster is spreading
from nation to nation; Isa 34:2
a mighty storm is rising Jer 23:19
from the ends of the earth." Dt 28:49

33At that time those slain by the LORD will be everywhere—from one end of the earth to the other.
They will not be mourned or gathered up or buried, but will be like refuse lying on the ground.

34Weep and wail, you shepherds;
roll in the dust, you leaders of the flock.
For your time to be slaughtered has come;
you will fall and be shattered like fine
pottery. Jer 22:28
35The shepherds will have nowhere to flee,
the leaders of the flock no place to escape.
36Hear the cry of the shepherds, Jer 23:1; Zec 11:3
the wailing of the leaders of the flock,
for the LORD is destroying their pasture.
37The peaceful meadows will be laid waste
because of the fierce anger of the LORD.
38Like a lion he will leave his lair, Jer 4:7
and their land will become desolate Jer 44:22
because of the sword[a] of the oppressor
and because of the LORD's fierce anger.

Jeremiah Threatened With Death

26 Early in the reign of Jehoiakim son of Josiah king of Judah, this word came from the
LORD: 2"This is what the LORD says: Stand in the
courtyard of the LORD's house and speak to all
the people of the towns of Judah who come to
worship in the house of the LORD. Tell them everything I command you; do not omit a word. 3Per-
haps they will listen and each will turn from his
evil way. Then I will relent and not bring on them
the disaster I was planning because of the evil they
have done. 4Say to them, 'This is what the LORD
says: If you do not listen to me and follow my law,
which I have set before you, 5and if you do not
listen to the words of my servants the prophets,
whom I have sent to you again and again (though
you have not listened), 6then I will make this house
like Shiloh and this city an object of cursing
among all the nations of the earth.'" Lev 26:14

7The priests, the prophets and all the people
heard Jeremiah speak these words in the house of
the LORD. 8But as soon as Jeremiah finished telling
all the people everything the LORD had commanded him to say, the priests, the prophets and all the
people seized him and said, "You must die! 9Why
do you prophesy in the LORD's name that this
house will be like Shiloh and this city will be desolate and deserted?" And all the people crowded
around Jeremiah in the house of the LORD.

10When the officials of Judah heard about these
things, they went up from the royal palace to the
house of the LORD and took their places at the
entrance of the New Gate of the LORD's house.
11Then the priests and the prophets said to the
officials and all the people, "This man should be
sentenced to death because he has prophesied
against this city. You have heard it with your own
ears!" Jer 38:4; Mt 26:66; Ac 6:11

12Then Jeremiah said to all the officials and all
the people: "The LORD sent me to prophesy against
this house and this city all the things you have
heard. 13Now reform your ways and your actions
and obey the LORD your God. Then the LORD will
relent and not bring the disaster he has pronounced against you. 14As for me, I am in your
hands; do with me whatever you think is good and
right. 15Be assured, however, that if you put me to
death, you will bring the guilt of innocent blood
on yourselves and on this city and on those who
live in it, for in truth the LORD has sent me to you
to speak all these words in your hearing." Jer 7:5
16Then the officials and all the people said to the
priests and the prophets, "This man should not be
sentenced to death! He has spoken to us in the
name of the LORD our God." Ac 5:34-39; 23:9,29
17Some of the elders of the land stepped forward and said to the entire assembly of people,
18"Micah of Moresheth prophesied in the days of
Hezekiah king of Judah. He told all the people of
Judah, 'This is what the LORD Almighty says:

"'Zion will be plowed like a field, Isa 2:3
Jerusalem will become a heap of rubble,
the temple hill a mound overgrown with
thickets.'[b] Jer 17:3; Zec 8:3

19"Did Hezekiah king of Judah or anyone else in
Judah put him to death? Did not Hezekiah fear the
LORD and seek his favor? And did not the LORD
relent, so that he did not bring the disaster he
pronounced against them? We are about to bring
a terrible disaster on ourselves!" 2Sa 24:16
20(Now Uriah son of Shemaiah from Kiriath
Jearim was another man who prophesied in the
name of the LORD; he prophesied the same things
against this city and this land as Jeremiah did.
21When King Jehoiakim and all his officers and
officials heard his words, the king sought to put
him to death. But Uriah heard of it and fled in fear
to Egypt. 22King Jehoiakim, however, sent Elna-

[a] *38* Some Hebrew manuscripts and Septuagint (see also Jer. 46:16 and 50:16); most Hebrew manuscripts *anger*
[b] *18* Micah 3:12

than son of Acbor to Egypt, along with some other men. 23They brought Uriah out of Egypt and took him to King Jehoiakim, who had him struck down with a sword and his body thrown into the burial place of the common people.) Jer 36:12,25; Mt 10:23

24Furthermore, Ahikam son of Shaphan supported Jeremiah, and so he was not handed over to the people to be put to death. 2Ki 22:12

Judah to Serve Nebuchadnezzar

27 Early in the reign of Zedekiah[a] son of Josiah king of Judah, this word came to Jeremiah from the LORD: 2This is what the LORD said to me: "Make a yoke out of straps and crossbars and put it on your neck. 3Then send word to the kings of Edom, Moab, Ammon, Tyre and Sidon through the envoys who have come to Jerusalem to Zedekiah king of Judah. 4Give them a message for their masters and say, 'This is what the LORD Almighty, the God of Israel, says: "Tell this to your masters: 5With my great power and outstretched arm I made the earth and its people and the animals that are on it, and I give it to anyone I please. 6Now I will hand all your countries over to my servant Nebuchadnezzar king of Babylon; I will make even the wild animals subject to him. 7All nations will serve him and his son and his grandson until the time for his land comes; then many nations and great kings will subjugate him.

8" ' "If, however, any nation or kingdom will not serve Nebuchadnezzar king of Babylon or bow its neck under his yoke, I will punish that nation with the sword, famine and plague, declares the LORD, until I destroy it by his hand. 9So do not listen to your prophets, your diviners, your interpreters of dreams, your mediums or your sorcerers who tell you, 'You will not serve the king of Babylon.' 10They prophesy lies to you that will only serve to remove you far from your lands; I will banish you and you will perish. 11But if any nation will bow its neck under the yoke of the king of Babylon and serve him, I will let that nation remain in its own land to till it and to live there, declares the LORD." ' " Jer 21:9; 23:25

12I gave the same message to Zedekiah king of Judah. I said, "Bow your neck under the yoke of the king of Babylon; serve him and his people, and you will live. 13Why will you and your people die by the sword, famine and plague with which the LORD has threatened any nation that will not serve the king of Babylon? 14Do not listen to the words of the prophets who say to you, 'You will not serve the king of Babylon,' for they are prophesying lies to you. 15'I have not sent them,' declares the LORD. 'They are prophesying lies in my name. Therefore, I will banish you and you will perish, both you and the prophets who prophesy to you.' " Jer 6:15; 14:14

16Then I said to the priests and all these people, "This is what the LORD says: Do not listen to the prophets who say, 'Very soon now the articles from the LORD's house will be brought back from Babylon.' They are prophesying lies to you. 17Do not listen to them. Serve the king of Babylon, and you will live. Why should this city become a ruin? 18If they are prophets and have the word of the LORD, let them plead with the LORD Almighty that the furnishings remaining in the house of the LORD and in the palace of the king of Judah and in Jerusalem not be taken to Babylon. 19For this is what the LORD Almighty says about the pillars, the Sea, the movable stands and the other furnishings that are left in this city, 20which Nebuchadnezzar king of Babylon did not take away when he carried Jehoiachin[b] son of Jehoiakim king of Judah into exile from Jerusalem to Babylon, along with all the nobles of Judah and Jerusalem— 21yes, this is what the LORD Almighty, the God of Israel, says about the things that are left in the house of the LORD and in the palace of the king of Judah and in Jerusalem: 22'They will be taken to Babylon and there they will remain until the day I come for them,' declares the LORD. 'Then I will bring them back and restore them to this place.' " Ezr 1:7; 7:19

The False Prophet Hananiah

28 In the fifth month of that same year, the fourth year, early in the reign of Zedekiah king of Judah, the prophet Hananiah son of Azzur, who was from Gibeon, said to me in the house of the LORD in the presence of the priests and all the people: 2"This is what the LORD Almighty, the God of Israel, says: 'I will break the yoke of the king of Babylon. 3Within two years I will bring back to this place all the articles of the LORD's house that Nebuchadnezzar king of Babylon removed from here and took to Babylon. 4I will also bring back to this place Jehoiachin[b] son of Jehoiakim king of Judah and all the other exiles from Judah who went to Babylon,' declares the LORD, 'for I will break the yoke of the king of Babylon.' " 2Ki 24:13

5Then the prophet Jeremiah replied to the prophet Hananiah before the priests and all the people who were standing in the house of the LORD. 6He said, "Amen! May the LORD do so! May the LORD fulfill the words you have prophesied by bringing the articles of the LORD's house and all the exiles back to this place from Babylon. 7Nevertheless, listen to what I have to say in your hearing and in the hearing of all the people: 8From early times the prophets who preceded you and me have prophesied war, disaster and plague

[a] *1* A few Hebrew manuscripts and Syriac (see also Jer. 27:3, 12 and 28:1); most Hebrew manuscripts *Jehoiakim* (Most Septuagint manuscripts do not have this verse.) [b] *20,4* Hebrew *Jeconiah*, a variant of *Jehoiachin*

against many countries and great kingdoms. 9But
the prophet who prophesies peace will be recognized as one truly sent by the LORD only if his
prediction comes true." Lev 26:14-17; Dt 18:22
10Then the prophet Hananiah took the yoke off
the neck of the prophet Jeremiah and broke it,
11and he said before all the people, "This is what
the LORD says: 'In the same way will I break the
yoke of Nebuchadnezzar king of Babylon off the
neck of all the nations within two years.'" At this,
the prophet Jeremiah went on his way. Jer 14:14
12Shortly after the prophet Hananiah had broken the yoke off the neck of the prophet Jeremiah,
the word of the LORD came to Jeremiah: 13"Go and
tell Hananiah, 'This is what the LORD says: You
have broken a wooden yoke, but in its place you
will get a yoke of iron. 14This is what the LORD
Almighty, the God of Israel, says: I will put an iron
yoke on the necks of all these nations to make
them serve Nebuchadnezzar king of Babylon, and
they will serve him. I will even give him control
over the wild animals.'" Dt 28:48; Jer 27:6
15Then the prophet Jeremiah said to Hananiah
the prophet, "Listen, Hananiah! The LORD has not
sent you, yet you have persuaded this nation to
trust in lies. 16Therefore, this is what the LORD says:
'I am about to remove you from the face of the
earth. This very year you are going to die, because
you have preached rebellion against the LORD.'"
17In the seventh month of that same year, Hananiah the prophet died. 2Ki 1:17

A Letter to the Exiles

29 This is the text of the letter that the prophet
Jeremiah sent from Jerusalem to the surviving elders among the exiles and to the priests,
the prophets and all the other people Nebuchadnezzar had carried into exile from Jerusalem to
Babylon. 2(This was after King Jehoiachin[a] and
the queen mother, the court officials and the leaders of Judah and Jerusalem, the craftsmen and the
artisans had gone into exile from Jerusalem.) 3He
entrusted the letter to Elasah son of Shaphan and
to Gemariah son of Hilkiah, whom Zedekiah king
of Judah sent to King Nebuchadnezzar in Babylon.
It said: 2Ki 24:12; Jer 22:24-28

4This is what the LORD Almighty, the God
of Israel, says to all those I carried into exile
from Jerusalem to Babylon: 5"Build houses
and settle down; plant gardens and eat what
they produce. 6Marry and have sons and
daughters; find wives for your sons and give
your daughters in marriage, so that they too
may have sons and daughters. Increase in
number there; do not decrease. 7Also, seek
the peace and prosperity of the city to which
I have carried you into exile. Pray to the
LORD for it, because if it prospers, you too
will prosper." 8Yes, this is what the LORD Almighty, the God of Israel, says: "Do not let
the prophets and diviners among you deceive you. Do not listen to the dreams you
encourage them to have. 9They are prophesying lies to you in my name. I have not sent
them," declares the LORD. Jer 14:14; 1Ti 2:1-2
10This is what the LORD says: "When seventy years are completed for Babylon, I will
come to you and fulfill my gracious promise

LIVING  **INSIGHT**

Hope doesn't require a massive chain where heavy links of logic hold it together. A thin wire will do . . . just strong enough to get us through the night until the winds die down.

(See Jeremiah 29:10–14.)

to bring you back to this place. 11For I know
the plans I have for you," declares the LORD,
"plans to prosper you and not to harm you,
plans to give you hope and a future. 12Then
you will call upon me and come and pray to
me, and I will listen to you. 13You will seek
me and find me when you seek me with all
your heart. 14I will be found by you," declares the LORD, "and will bring you back
from captivity.[b] I will gather you from all
the nations and places where I have banished
you," declares the LORD, "and will bring you
back to the place from which I carried you
into exile." Jer 24:7; 25:12; Da 9:2
15You may say, "The LORD has raised up
prophets for us in Babylon," 16but this is
what the LORD says about the king who sits
on David's throne and all the people who
remain in this city, your countrymen who
did not go with you into exile— 17yes, this is
what the LORD Almighty says: "I will send the
sword, famine and plague against them and
I will make them like poor figs that are so
bad they cannot be eaten. 18I will pursue
them with the sword, famine and plague and
will make them abhorrent to all the kingdoms of the earth and an object of cursing
and horror, of scorn and reproach, among all
the nations where I drive them. 19For they
have not listened to my words," declares the
LORD, "words that I sent to them again and
again by my servants the prophets. And you
exiles have not listened either," declares the
LORD. Jer 6:19; 25:4
20Therefore, hear the word of the LORD, all

[a]2 Hebrew *Jeconiah*, a variant of *Jehoiachin* [b]14 Or *will restore your fortunes*

you exiles whom I have sent away from Jerusalem to Babylon. 21This is what the LORD
Almighty, the God of Israel, says about Ahab
son of Kolaiah and Zedekiah son of Maaseiah, who are prophesying lies to you in my
name: "I will hand them over to Nebuchadnezzar king of Babylon, and he will put them
to death before your very eyes. 22Because of
them, all the exiles from Judah who are in
Babylon will use this curse: 'The LORD treat
you like Zedekiah and Ahab, whom the king
of Babylon burned in the fire.' 23For they
have done outrageous things in Israel; they
have committed adultery with their neighbors' wives and in my name have spoken lies,
which I did not tell them to do. I know it and
am a witness to it," declares the LORD.

Message to Shemaiah

24Tell Shemaiah the Nehelamite, 25"This is what
the LORD Almighty, the God of Israel, says: You
sent letters in your own name to all the people
in Jerusalem, to Zephaniah son of Maaseiah the
priest, and to all the other priests. You said to
Zephaniah, 26'The LORD has appointed you priest
in place of Jehoiada to be in charge of the house of
the LORD; you should put any madman who acts
like a prophet into the stocks and neck-irons. 27So
why have you not reprimanded Jeremiah from
Anathoth, who poses as a prophet among you?
28He has sent this message to us in Babylon: It will
be a long time. Therefore build houses and settle
down; plant gardens and eat what they produce.' "

29Zephaniah the priest, however, read the letter
to Jeremiah the prophet. 30Then the word of the
LORD came to Jeremiah: 31"Send this message to all
the exiles: 'This is what the LORD says about Shemaiah the Nehelamite: Because Shemaiah has
prophesied to you, even though I did not send
him, and has led you to believe a lie, 32this is what
the LORD says: I will surely punish Shemaiah the
Nehelamite and his descendants. He will have no
one left among this people, nor will he see the
good things I will do for my people, declares the
LORD, because he has preached rebellion
against me.' " Jer 14:14; 28:15-16

Restoration of Israel

30 This is the word that came to Jeremiah
from the LORD: 2"This is what the LORD, the
God of Israel, says: 'Write in a book all the words
I have spoken to you. 3The days are coming,' declares the LORD, 'when I will bring my people Israel
and Judah back from captivity[a] and restore them
to the land I gave their forefathers to possess,' says
the LORD." Isa 30:8; Jer 16:15; 29:14

4These are the words the LORD spoke concerning Israel and Judah: 5"This is what the LORD says:

" 'Cries of fear are heard— Jer 6:25
terror, not peace.
6Ask and see:
Can a man bear children?
Then why do I see every strong man
with his hands on his stomach like a
woman in labor, Jer 4:31
every face turned deathly pale? Isa 29:22
7How awful that day will be! Isa 2:12; Joel 2:11
None will be like it.
It will be a time of trouble for Jacob, Zep 1:15
but he will be saved out of it. Jer 23:3
8" 'In that day,' declares the LORD Almighty,
'I will break the yoke off their necks Isa 9:4
and will tear off their bonds; Ps 107:14
no longer will foreigners enslave them.
9Instead, they will serve the LORD their God
and David their king, Eze 34:23-24; 37:24; Hos 3:5
whom I will raise up for them.

10" 'So do not fear, O Jacob my servant; Isa 43:5
do not be dismayed, O Israel,'
declares the LORD.
'I will surely save you out of a distant place,
your descendants from the land of their exile.
Jacob will again have peace and security,
and no one will make him afraid.
11I am with you and will save you,'
declares the LORD.
'Though I completely destroy all the nations
among which I scatter you,
I will not completely destroy you. Jer 4:27
I will discipline you but only with justice;
I will not let you go entirely unpunished.'

12"This is what the LORD says:

" 'Your wound is incurable, Jer 10:19
your injury beyond healing. Jer 15:18
13There is no one to plead your cause,
no remedy for your sore,
no healing for you. Jer 8:22; 14:19; 46:11
14All your allies have forgotten you; La 1:2
they care nothing for you.
I have struck you as an enemy would Job 13:24
and punished you as would the cruel,
because your guilt is so great
and your sins so many. Jer 5:6
15Why do you cry out over your wound,
your pain that has no cure? Jer 10:19
Because of your great guilt and many sins
I have done these things to you. Pr 1:31

16" 'But all who devour you will be devoured;
all your enemies will go into exile. Isa 14:2
Those who plunder you will be plundered;

[a]3 Or *will restore the fortunes of my people Israel and Judah*

all who make spoil of you I will despoil.
17 But I will restore you to health
and heal your wounds,' Isa 1:5
declares the LORD,
'because you are called an outcast, Jer 33:24
Zion for whom no one cares.' Ps 142:4

18 "This is what the LORD says:

" 'I will restore the fortunes of Jacob's tents
and have compassion on his dwellings;
the city will be rebuilt on her ruins, Jer 31:4,24,38
and the palace will stand in its proper
place.
19 From them will come songs of thanksgiving
and the sound of rejoicing. Ps 126:1-2; Jer 31:4
I will add to their numbers, Jer 33:22
and they will not be decreased;
I will bring them honor, Isa 60:9
and they will not be disdained.
20 Their children will be as in days of old,
and their community will be established
before me; Isa 54:14
I will punish all who oppress them. Ex 23:22
21 Their leader will be one of their own; Jer 23:5-6
their ruler will arise from among them.
I will bring him near and he will come close
to me, Nu 16:5
for who is he who will devote himself
to be close to me?'
declares the LORD.
22 " 'So you will be my people, Isa 19:25; Hos 2:23
and I will be your God.' " Lev 26:12
23 See, the storm of the LORD Jer 23:19
will burst out in wrath,
a driving wind swirling down
on the heads of the wicked.
24 The fierce anger of the LORD will not turn
back Jer 4:8,28
until he fully accomplishes
the purposes of his heart.
In days to come
you will understand this. Jer 23:19-20

31 "At that time," declares the LORD, "I will be
the God of all the clans of Israel, and they
will be my people." Jer 30:22
2 This is what the LORD says:

"The people who survive the sword
will find favor in the desert; Nu 14:20
I will come to give rest to Israel." Ex 33:14

3 The LORD appeared to us in the past,[a] saying:

"I have loved you with an everlasting love;
I have drawn you with loving-kindness.
4 I will build you up again
and you will be rebuilt, O Virgin Israel.
Again you will take up your tambourines
and go out to dance with the joyful. Jer 30:19
5 Again you will plant vineyards
on the hills of Samaria; Jer 50:19
the farmers will plant them
and enjoy their fruit. Isa 65:21; Am 9:14
6 There will be a day when watchmen cry out
on the hills of Ephraim,
'Come, let us go up to Zion,
to the LORD our God.' " Isa 2:3; Jer 50:4-5; Mic 4:2

7 This is what the LORD says:

"Sing with joy for Jacob;
shout for the foremost of the nations.
Make your praises heard, and say,
'O LORD, save your people, Ps 14:7; 28:9
the remnant of Israel.' Isa 37:31
8 See, I will bring them from the land of the
north Jer 3:18; 23:8
and gather them from the ends of the
earth. Dt 30:4; Eze 34:12-14
Among them will be the blind and the lame,
expectant mothers and women in labor;
a great throng will return.
9 They will come with weeping; Ps 126:5
they will pray as I bring them back.
I will lead them beside streams of water
on a level path where they will not stumble,
because I am Israel's father, Ex 4:22; Jer 3:4
and Ephraim is my firstborn son.

10 "Hear the word of the LORD, O nations;
proclaim it in distant coastlands: Isa 66:19
'He who scattered Israel will gather them
and will watch over his flock like a
shepherd.' Isa 40:11; Eze 34:12
11 For the LORD will ransom Jacob
and redeem them from the hand of those
stronger than they. Ps 142:6; Isa 44:23; 48:20
12 They will come and shout for joy on the
heights of Zion; Eze 17:23; Mic 4:1
they will rejoice in the bounty of the
LORD— Joel 3:18
the grain, the new wine and the oil, Hos 2:21-22
the young of the flocks and herds.
They will be like a well-watered garden,
and they will sorrow no more. Isa 65:19; Jn 16:22
13 Then maidens will dance and be glad,
young men and old as well.
I will turn their mourning into gladness;
I will give them comfort and joy instead of
sorrow. Ps 30:11; Isa 51:11
14 I will satisfy the priests with abundance,
and my people will be filled with my
bounty," Isa 30:23
declares the LORD.

15 This is what the LORD says:

[a] 3 Or *LORD has appeared to us from afar*

"A voice is heard in Ramah, Jos 18:25
mourning and great weeping,
Rachel weeping for her children
and refusing to be comforted, Ge 37:35
because her children are no more."

16 This is what the LORD says:

"Restrain your voice from weeping
and your eyes from tears, Isa 25:8; 30:19
for your work will be rewarded," Ru 2:12
declares the LORD.
"They will return from the land of the
enemy. Eze 11:17
17 So there is hope for your future," Job 8:7; La 3:29
declares the LORD.
"Your children will return to their own
land. Jer 30:20

18 "I have surely heard Ephraim's moaning:
'You disciplined me like an unruly calf,
and I have been disciplined.
Restore me, and I will return, Ps 80:3
because you are the LORD my God.
19 After I strayed, Eze 36:31
I repented;
after I came to understand,
I beat my breast. Eze 21:12; Lk 18:13
I was ashamed and humiliated Ezr 9:6
because I bore the disgrace of my youth.'
20 Is not Ephraim my dear son,
the child in whom I delight?
Though I often speak against him,
I still remember him. Hos 4:4; 11:8
Therefore my heart yearns for him;
I have great compassion for him," Isa 63:15
declares the LORD.

LIVING  **INSIGHT**

The word delight means "to take great satisfaction in; to approve of someone." It even means "to admire, or to affirm." Does your spouse, your child, your mother or father, your sister or brother, your friend, know you admire him or her? Your admiration helps them admire themselves. Affirmation works wonders!

(See Jeremiah 31:20.)

21 "Set up road signs;
put up guideposts.
Take note of the highway, Jer 50:5
the road that you take.
Return, O Virgin Israel, Isa 52:11
return to your towns.
22 How long will you wander, Jer 2:23
O unfaithful daughter? Jer 3:6
The LORD will create a new thing on earth—
a woman will surround[a] a man." Dt 32:10

23 This is what the LORD Almighty, the God of
Israel, says: "When I bring them back from captivity,[b] the people in the land of Judah and in its
towns will once again use these words: 'The LORD
bless you, O righteous dwelling, O sacred mountain.' 24 People will live together in Judah and all its
towns—farmers and those who move about with
their flocks. 25 I will refresh the weary and satisfy
the faint." Jn 4:14; Isa 1:26; Zec 8:4-8

26 At this I awoke and looked around. My sleep
had been pleasant to me. Zec 4:1

27 "The days are coming," declares the LORD,
"when I will plant the house of Israel and the
house of Judah with the offspring of men and of
animals. 28 Just as I watched over them to uproot
and tear down, and to overthrow, destroy and
bring disaster, so I will watch over them to build
and to plant," declares the LORD. 29 "In those days
people will no longer say, Jer 1:10; 18:8; 44:27

'The fathers have eaten sour grapes, La 5:7
and the children's teeth are set on edge.'

30 Instead, everyone will die for his own sin; whoever eats sour grapes—his own teeth will be set on
edge. Isa 3:11; Gal 6:7

31 "The time is coming," declares the LORD,
"when I will make a new covenant
with the house of Israel
and with the house of Judah.
32 It will not be like the covenant Ex 24:8
I made with their forefathers Dt 5:3
when I took them by the hand
to lead them out of Egypt, Jer 11:4
because they broke my covenant,
though I was a husband to[c] them,[d]"
declares the LORD.
33 "This is the covenant I will make with the
house of Israel
after that time," declares the LORD.
"I will put my law in their minds
and write it on their hearts. 2Co 3:3
I will be their God,
and they will be my people. Jer 24:7; Heb 10:16
34 No longer will a man teach his neighbor,
or a man his brother, saying, 'Know the
LORD,'
because they will all know me, Jn 6:45
from the least of them to the greatest,"
declares the LORD.
"For I will forgive their wickedness Isa 54:13
and will remember their sins no more."

35 This is what the LORD says,

[a] 22 Or *will go about* ⌊*seeking*⌋; or *will protect* [b] 23 Or *I restore their fortunes* [c] 32 Hebrew; Septuagint and Syriac / *and I turned away from* [d] 32 Or *was their master*

he who appoints the sun Ps 136:7-9
to shine by day,
who decrees the moon and stars
to shine by night, Ge 1:16
who stirs up the sea Ex 14:21
so that its waves roar— Ps 93:3
the LORD Almighty is his name: Jer 10:16
36“Only if these decrees vanish from my sight,”
declares the LORD,
“will the descendants of Israel ever cease
to be a nation before me.”

37This is what the LORD says:

“Only if the heavens above can be measured
and the foundations of the earth below be
searched out
will I reject all the descendants of Israel
because of all they have done,”
declares the LORD.

38“The days are coming,” declares the LORD,
“when this city will be rebuilt for me from the
Tower of Hananel to the Corner Gate. 39The measuring line will stretch from there straight to the
hill of Gareb and then turn to Goah. 40The whole
valley where dead bodies and ashes are thrown,
and all the terraces out to the Kidron Valley on the
east as far as the corner of the Horse Gate, will be
holy to the LORD. The city will never again be
uprooted or demolished.” Joel 3:17; Zec 14:21

Jeremiah Buys a Field

32 This is the word that came to Jeremiah
from the LORD in the tenth year of Zedekiah king of Judah, which was the eighteenth year of
Nebuchadnezzar. 2The army of the king of Babylon was then besieging Jerusalem, and Jeremiah
the prophet was confined in the courtyard of the
guard in the royal palace of Judah. 2Ki 25:1; Ne 3:25
3Now Zedekiah king of Judah had imprisoned
him there, saying, “Why do you prophesy as you
do? You say, ‘This is what the LORD says: I am
about to hand this city over to the king of Babylon,
and he will capture it. 4Zedekiah king of Judah will
not escape out of the hands of the Babylonians[a]
but will certainly be handed over to the king of
Babylon, and will speak with him face to face and
see him with his own eyes. 5He will take Zedekiah
to Babylon, where he will remain until I deal with
him, declares the LORD. If you fight against the
Babylonians, you will not succeed.’ ” Jer 34:2-3
6Jeremiah said, “The word of the LORD came to
me: 7Hanamel son of Shallum your uncle is going
to come to you and say, ‘Buy my field at Anathoth,
because as nearest relative it is your right and duty
to buy it.’ Lev 25:24-25; Ru 4:3-4; Mt 27:10*
8“Then, just as the LORD had said, my cousin
Hanamel came to me in the courtyard of the guard
and said, ‘Buy my field at Anathoth in the territory
of Benjamin. Since it is your right to redeem it and
possess it, buy it for yourself.’
“I knew that this was the word of the LORD; 9so
I bought the field at Anathoth from my cousin
Hanamel and weighed out for him seventeen shekels[b] of silver. 10I signed and sealed the deed, had
it witnessed, and weighed out the silver on the
scales. 11I took the deed of purchase—the sealed
copy containing the terms and conditions, as well
as the unsealed copy— 12and I gave this deed to
Baruch son of Neriah, the son of Mahseiah, in the
presence of my cousin Hanamel and of the witnesses who had signed the deed and of all the Jews
sitting in the courtyard of the guard. Jer 36:4; 51:59
13“In their presence I gave Baruch these instructions: 14‘This is what the LORD Almighty, the God
of Israel, says: Take these documents, both the
sealed and unsealed copies of the deed of purchase, and put them in a clay jar so they will last
a long time. 15For this is what the LORD Almighty,
the God of Israel, says: Houses, fields and vineyards will again be bought in this land.’ Jer 30:18
16“After I had given the deed of purchase to
Baruch son of Neriah, I prayed to the LORD:

17“Ah, Sovereign LORD, you have made the
heavens and the earth by your great power
and outstretched arm. Nothing is too hard

LIVING  **INSIGHT**

***Do you realize that whatever thing or things you're calling "impossibilities" could be superimposed over what God says is "nothing" to Him?* Nothing! *I don't have to know your situation. All I need to know—and all you need to know—is God and His promises. He is Lord, the bottom line of life, and nothing is too hard for* Him.**

(See Jeremiah 32:17.)

for you. 18You show love to thousands but
bring the punishment for the fathers' sins
into the laps of their children after them.
O great and powerful God, whose name is
the LORD Almighty, 19great are your purposes
and mighty are your deeds. Your eyes are
open to all the ways of men; you reward
everyone according to his conduct and as his
deeds deserve. 20You performed miraculous
signs and wonders in Egypt and have continued them to this day, both in Israel and
among all mankind, and have gained the renown that is still yours. 21You brought your

[a]4 Or *Chaldeans*; also in verses 5, 24, 25, 28, 29 and 43
[b]9 That is, about 7 ounces (about 200 grams)

people Israel out of Egypt with signs and
wonders, by a mighty hand and an outstretched arm and with great terror. 22You
gave them this land you had sworn to give
their forefathers, a land flowing with milk
and honey. 23They came in and took possession of it, but they did not obey you or follow
your law; they did not do what you commanded them to do. So you brought all this
disaster upon them. Ps 44:2; Jer 11:8; Da 9:14

24"See how the siege ramps are built up to
take the city. Because of the sword, famine
and plague, the city will be handed over to
the Babylonians who are attacking it. What
you said has happened, as you now see.
25And though the city will be handed over to
the Babylonians, you, O Sovereign LORD, say
to me, 'Buy the field with silver and have the
transaction witnessed.'" Dt 4:25-26; Jer 14:12

26Then the word of the LORD came to Jeremiah:
27"I am the LORD, the God of all mankind. Is anything too hard for me? 28Therefore, this is what the
LORD says: I am about to hand this city over to the
Babylonians and to Nebuchadnezzar king of Babylon, who will capture it. 29The Babylonians who
are attacking this city will come in and set it on
fire; they will burn it down, along with the houses
where the people provoked me to anger by burning incense on the roofs to Baal and by pouring
out drink offerings to other gods. Ge 18:14; Jer 21:10
30"The people of Israel and Judah have done
nothing but evil in my sight from their youth;
indeed, the people of Israel have done nothing but
provoke me with what their hands have made,
declares the LORD. 31From the day it was built until
now, this city has so aroused my anger and wrath
that I must remove it from my sight. 32The people
of Israel and Judah have provoked me by all the
evil they have done—they, their kings and officials, their priests and prophets, the men of Judah
and the people of Jerusalem. 33They turned their
backs to me and not their faces; though I taught
them again and again, they would not listen or
respond to discipline. 34They set up their abominable idols in the house that bears my Name and
defiled it. 35They built high places for Baal in the
Valley of Ben Hinnom to sacrifice their sons and
daughters[a] to Molech, though I never commanded, nor did it enter my mind, that they should do
such a detestable thing and so make Judah sin.
36"You are saying about this city, 'By the sword,
famine and plague it will be handed over to the
king of Babylon'; but this is what the LORD, the
God of Israel, says: 37I will surely gather them from
all the lands where I banish them in my furious
anger and great wrath; I will bring them back to
this place and let them live in safety. 38They will be
my people, and I will be their God. 39I will give
them singleness of heart and action, so that they
will always fear me for their own good and the
good of their children after them. 40I will make an

LIVING  **INSIGHT**

The church can seldom resurrect what the home puts to death. The very best proof of the genuineness of your Christianity occurs within the framework of your home. If you must become overinvolved—become overinvolved in your role as character builder in the home.
(See Jeremiah 32:39.)

everlasting covenant with them: I will never stop
doing good to them, and I will inspire them to fear
me, so that they will never turn away from me. 41I
will rejoice in doing them good and will assuredly
plant them in this land with all my heart and soul.
42"This is what the LORD says: As I have brought
all this great calamity on this people, so I will give
them all the prosperity I have promised them.
43Once more fields will be bought in this land of
which you say, 'It is a desolate waste, without men
or animals, for it has been handed over to the
Babylonians.' 44Fields will be bought for silver, and
deeds will be signed, sealed and witnessed in the
territory of Benjamin, in the villages around Jerusalem, in the towns of Judah and in the towns of
the hill country, of the western foothills and of the
Negev, because I will restore their fortunes,[b] declares the LORD." Jer 17:26; 33:7,11,26

Promise of Restoration

33 While Jeremiah was still confined in the
courtyard of the guard, the word of the
LORD came to him a second time: 2"This is what
the LORD says, he who made the earth, the LORD
who formed it and established it—the LORD is his
name: 3'Call to me and I will answer you and tell
you great and unsearchable things you do not
know.' 4For this is what the LORD, the God of
Israel, says about the houses in this city and the
royal palaces of Judah that have been torn down to
be used against the siege ramps and the sword 5in
the fight with the Babylonians[c]: 'They will be
filled with the dead bodies of the men I will slay in
my anger and wrath. I will hide my face from this
city because of all its wickedness. Isa 55:6; Jer 29:12
6" 'Nevertheless, I will bring health and healing
to it; I will heal my people and will let them enjoy
abundant peace and security. 7I will bring Judah

[a]35 Or *to make their sons and daughters pass through ⌞the fire⌟*
[c]5 Or *Chaldeans*
[b]44 Or *will bring them back from captivity*

and Israel back from captivity[a] and will rebuild
them as they were before. 8I will cleanse them from
all the sin they have committed against me and will
forgive all their sins of rebellion against me. 9Then
this city will bring me renown, joy, praise and
honor before all nations on earth that hear of all
the good things I do for it; and they will be in awe
and will tremble at the abundant prosperity and
peace I provide for it.' Heb 9:13-14; Jer 3:17

10"This is what the LORD says: 'You say about
this place, "It is a desolate waste, without men or
animals." Yet in the towns of Judah and the streets
of Jerusalem that are deserted, inhabited by neither men nor animals, there will be heard once
more 11the sounds of joy and gladness, the voices
of bride and bridegroom, and the voices of those
who bring thank offerings to the house of the
LORD, saying, Lev 7:12; Jer 32:43

"Give thanks to the LORD Almighty,
for the LORD is good; Ps 136:1
his love endures forever." 2Ch 5:13

For I will restore the fortunes of the land as they
were before,' says the LORD. Ps 14:7; Isa 1:26

12"This is what the LORD Almighty says: 'In this
place, desolate and without men or animals—in
all its towns there will again be pastures for shepherds to rest their flocks. 13In the towns of the hill
country, of the western foothills and of the Negev,
in the territory of Benjamin, in the villages around
Jerusalem and in the towns of Judah, flocks will
again pass under the hand of the one who counts
them,' says the LORD. Lev 27:32; Isa 65:10; Jer 17:26

14" 'The days are coming,' declares the LORD,
'when I will fulfill the gracious promise I made to
the house of Israel and to the house of Judah.

15" 'In those days and at that time
I will make a righteous Branch sprout from
David's line; Ps 72:2; Isa 4:2; 11:1; Jer 23:5
he will do what is just and right in the
land.
16In those days Judah will be saved Isa 45:17
and Jerusalem will live in safety.
This is the name by which it[b] will be called:
The LORD Our Righteousness.' 1Co 1:30

17For this is what the LORD says: 'David will never
fail to have a man to sit on the throne of the house
of Israel, 18nor will the priests, who are Levites,
ever fail to have a man to stand before me continually to offer burnt offerings, to burn grain offerings
and to present sacrifices.' " 2Sa 7:13; 1Ki 2:4; Lk 1:33

19The word of the LORD came to Jeremiah:
20"This is what the LORD says: 'If you can break my
covenant with the day and my covenant with the
night, so that day and night no longer come at
their appointed time, 21then my covenant with David my servant—and my covenant with the Levites who are priests ministering before me—can
be broken and David will no longer have a descendant to reign on his throne. 22I will make the
descendants of David my servant and the Levites
who minister before me as countless as the stars of
the sky and as measureless as the sand on the
seashore.' " Ge 15:5; Ps 89:34

23The word of the LORD came to Jeremiah:
24"Have you not noticed that these people are saying, 'The LORD has rejected the two kingdoms[c] he
chose'? So they despise my people and no longer
regard them as a nation. 25This is what the LORD
says: 'If I have not established my covenant with
day and night and the fixed laws of heaven and
earth, 26then I will reject the descendants of Jacob
and David my servant and will not choose one of
his sons to rule over the descendants of Abraham,
Isaac and Jacob. For I will restore their fortunes[d]
and have compassion on them.' " Ps 74:16-17

Warning to Zedekiah

34 While Nebuchadnezzar king of Babylon
and all his army and all the kingdoms and
peoples in the empire he ruled were fighting
against Jerusalem and all its surrounding towns,
this word came to Jeremiah from the LORD: 2"This
is what the LORD, the God of Israel, says: Go to
Zedekiah king of Judah and tell him, 'This is what
the LORD says: I am about to hand this city over to
the king of Babylon, and he will burn it down.
3You will not escape from his grasp but will surely
be captured and handed over to him. You will see
the king of Babylon with your own eyes, and he
will speak with you face to face. And you will go
to Babylon. 2Ki 25:1; Jer 32:4,29

4" 'Yet hear the promise of the LORD,
O Zedekiah king of Judah. This is what the LORD
says concerning you: You will not die by the
sword; 5you will die peacefully. As people made a
funeral fire in honor of your fathers, the former
kings who preceded you, so they will make a fire
in your honor and lament, "Alas, O master!" I
myself make this promise, declares the LORD.' "

6Then Jeremiah the prophet told all this to Zedekiah king of Judah, in Jerusalem, 7while the army
of the king of Babylon was fighting against Jerusalem and the other cities of Judah that were still
holding out—Lachish and Azekah. These were the
only fortified cities left in Judah. Jos 10:3; 2Ch 11:9

Freedom for Slaves

8The word came to Jeremiah from the LORD
after King Zedekiah had made a covenant with all
the people in Jerusalem to proclaim freedom for

[a]7 Or *will restore the fortunes of Judah and Israel from captivity* [b]16 Or *he* [c]24 Or *families* [d]26 Or *will bring them back*

the slaves. 9Everyone was to free his Hebrew
slaves, both male and female; no one was to hold
a fellow Jew in bondage. 10So all the officials and
people who entered into this covenant agreed that
they would free their male and female slaves and
no longer hold them in bondage. They agreed, and
set them free. 11But afterward they changed their
minds and took back the slaves they had freed and
enslaved them again. Ex 21:2; Lev 25:39-46

12Then the word of the LORD came to Jeremiah:
13"This is what the LORD, the God of Israel, says:
I made a covenant with your forefathers when I
brought them out of Egypt, out of the land of
slavery. I said, 14'Every seventh year each of you
must free any fellow Hebrew who has sold himself
to you. After he has served you six years, you must
let him go free.'[a] Your fathers, however, did not
listen to me or pay attention to me. 15Recently you
repented and did what is right in my sight: Each of
you proclaimed freedom to his countrymen. You
even made a covenant before me in the house that
bears my Name. 16But now you have turned
around and profaned my name; each of you has
taken back the male and female slaves you had set
free to go where they wished. You have forced
them to become your slaves again. Ex 20:7; Lev 19:12

17"Therefore, this is what the LORD says: You
have not obeyed me; you have not proclaimed
freedom for your fellow countrymen. So I now
proclaim 'freedom' for you, declares the LORD—
'freedom' to fall by the sword, plague and famine.
I will make you abhorrent to all the kingdoms of
the earth. 18The men who have violated my covenant and have not fulfilled the terms of the covenant they made before me, I will treat like the calf
they cut in two and then walked between its pieces.
19The leaders of Judah and Jerusalem, the court
officials, the priests and all the people of the land
who walked between the pieces of the calf, 20I will
hand over to their enemies who seek their lives.
Their dead bodies will become food for the birds
of the air and the beasts of the earth. Dt 28:26

21"I will hand Zedekiah king of Judah and his
officials over to their enemies who seek their lives,
to the army of the king of Babylon, which has
withdrawn from you. 22I am going to give the order, declares the LORD, and I will bring them back
to this city. They will fight against it, take it and
burn it down. And I will lay waste the towns of
Judah so no one can live there." Jer 37:5; 39:1-2

The Recabites

35 This is the word that came to Jeremiah
from the LORD during the reign of Jehoiakim son of Josiah king of Judah: 2"Go to the Recabite family and invite them to come to one of the
side rooms of the house of the LORD and give them
wine to drink." 1Ki 6:5; 2Ki 10:15; 1Ch 2:55

3So I went to get Jaazaniah son of Jeremiah, the
son of Habazziniah, and his brothers and all his
sons—the whole family of the Recabites. 4I
brought them into the house of the LORD, into the
room of the sons of Hanan son of Igdaliah the
man of God. It was next to the room of the officials, which was over that of Maaseiah son of Shallum the doorkeeper. 5Then I set bowls full of wine
and some cups before the men of the Recabite
family and said to them, "Drink some wine."

6But they replied, "We do not drink wine, because our forefather Jonadab son of Recab gave us
this command: 'Neither you nor your descendants
must ever drink wine. 7Also you must never build
houses, sow seed or plant vineyards; you must
never have any of these things, but must always
live in tents. Then you will live a long time in the
land where you are nomads.' 8We have obeyed
everything our forefather Jonadab son of Recab
commanded us. Neither we nor our wives nor our
sons and daughters have ever drunk wine 9or built
houses to live in or had vineyards, fields or crops.
10We have lived in tents and have fully obeyed
everything our forefather Jonadab commanded us.
11But when Nebuchadnezzar king of Babylon invaded this land, we said, 'Come, we must go to
Jerusalem to escape the Babylonian[b] and Aramean armies.' So we have remained in Jerusalem."

12Then the word of the LORD came to Jeremiah,
saying: 13"This is what the LORD Almighty, the God
of Israel, says: Go and tell the men of Judah and
the people of Jerusalem, 'Will you not learn a
lesson and obey my words?' declares the LORD.
14'Jonadab son of Recab ordered his sons not to
drink wine and this command has been kept. To
this day they do not drink wine, because they obey
their forefather's command. But I have spoken to
you again and again, yet you have not obeyed me.
15Again and again I sent all my servants the prophets to you. They said, "Each of you must turn from
your wicked ways and reform your actions; do not
follow other gods to serve them. Then you will live
in the land I have given to you and your fathers."
But you have not paid attention or listened to me.
16The descendants of Jonadab son of Recab have
carried out the command their forefather gave
them, but these people have not obeyed me.'

17"Therefore, this is what the LORD God Almighty, the God of Israel, says: 'Listen! I am going
to bring on Judah and on everyone living in Jerusalem every disaster I pronounced against them. I
spoke to them, but they did not listen; I called to
them, but they did not answer.'" Isa 65:12; Jer 7:13

18Then Jeremiah said to the family of the Recabites, "This is what the LORD Almighty, the God of

[a] *14* Deut. 15:12 [b] *11* Or *Chaldean*

Israel, says: 'You have obeyed the command of your forefather Jonadab and have followed all his instructions and have done everything he ordered.' 19Therefore, this is what the LORD Almighty, the God of Israel, says: 'Jonadab son of Recab will never fail to have a man to serve me.' "

Jehoiakim Burns Jeremiah's Scroll

36 In the fourth year of Jehoiakim son of Josiah king of Judah, this word came to Jeremiah from the LORD: 2"Take a scroll and write on it all the words I have spoken to you concerning Israel, Judah and all the other nations from the time I began speaking to you in the reign of Josiah till now. 3Perhaps when the people of Judah hear about every disaster I plan to inflict on them, each of them will turn from his wicked way; then I will forgive their wickedness and their sin." Jer 18:8

4So Jeremiah called Baruch son of Neriah, and while Jeremiah dictated all the words the LORD had spoken to him, Baruch wrote them on the scroll. 5Then Jeremiah told Baruch, "I am restricted; I cannot go to the LORD's temple. 6So you go to the house of the LORD on a day of fasting and read to the people from the scroll the words of the LORD that you wrote as I dictated. Read them to all the people of Judah who come in from their towns. 7Perhaps they will bring their petition before the LORD, and each will turn from his wicked ways, for the anger and wrath pronounced against this people by the LORD are great." Jer 32:12; Eze 2:9

8Baruch son of Neriah did everything Jeremiah the prophet told him to do; at the LORD's temple he read the words of the LORD from the scroll. 9In the ninth month of the fifth year of Jehoiakim son of Josiah king of Judah, a time of fasting before the LORD was proclaimed for all the people in Jerusalem and those who had come from the towns of Judah. 10From the room of Gemariah son of Shaphan the secretary, which was in the upper courtyard at the entrance of the New Gate of the temple, Baruch read to all the people at the LORD's temple the words of Jeremiah from the scroll. 2Ch 20:3

11When Micaiah son of Gemariah, the son of Shaphan, heard all the words of the LORD from the scroll, 12he went down to the secretary's room in the royal palace, where all the officials were sitting: Elishama the secretary, Delaiah son of Shemaiah, Elnathan son of Acbor, Gemariah son of Shaphan, Zedekiah son of Hananiah, and all the other officials. 13After Micaiah told them everything he had heard Baruch read to the people from the scroll, 14all the officials sent Jehudi son of Nethaniah, the son of Shelemiah, the son of Cushi, to say to Baruch, "Bring the scroll from which you have read to the people and come." So Baruch son of Neriah went to them with the scroll in his hand. 15They said to him, "Sit down, please, and read it to us."

So Baruch read it to them. 16When they heard all these words, they looked at each other in fear and said to Baruch, "We must report all these words to the king." 17Then they asked Baruch, "Tell us, how did you come to write all this? Did Jeremiah dictate it?" Jer 30:2

18"Yes," Baruch replied, "he dictated all these words to me, and I wrote them in ink on the scroll." ver 4

19Then the officials said to Baruch, "You and Jeremiah, go and hide. Don't let anyone know where you are." 1Ki 17:3

20After they put the scroll in the room of Elishama the secretary, they went to the king in the courtyard and reported everything to him. 21The king sent Jehudi to get the scroll, and Jehudi brought it from the room of Elishama the secretary and read it to the king and all the officials standing beside him. 22It was the ninth month and the king was sitting in the winter apartment, with a fire burning in the firepot in front of him. 23Whenever Jehudi had read three or four columns of the scroll, the king cut them off with a scribe's knife and threw them into the firepot, until the entire scroll was burned in the fire. 24The king and all his attendants who heard all these words showed no fear, nor did they tear their clothes. 25Even though Elnathan, Delaiah and Gemariah urged the king not to burn the scroll, he would not listen to them. 26Instead, the king commanded Jerahmeel, a son of the king, Seraiah son of Azriel and Shelemiah son of Abdeel to arrest Baruch the scribe and Jeremiah the prophet. But the LORD had hidden them. 1Ki 22:8; Jer 15:21

27After the king burned the scroll containing the words that Baruch had written at Jeremiah's dictation, the word of the LORD came to Jeremiah: 28"Take another scroll and write on it all the words that were on the first scroll, which Jehoiakim king of Judah burned up. 29Also tell Jehoiakim king of Judah, 'This is what the LORD says: You burned that scroll and said, "Why did you write on it that the king of Babylon would certainly come and destroy this land and cut off both men and animals from it?" 30Therefore, this is what the LORD says about Jehoiakim king of Judah: He will have no one to sit on the throne of David; his body will be thrown out and exposed to the heat by day and the frost by night. 31I will punish him and his children and his attendants for their wickedness; I will bring on them and those living in Jerusalem and the people of Judah every disaster I pronounced against them, because they have not listened.' " Isa 30:10; Jer 22:19

32So Jeremiah took another scroll and gave it to the scribe Baruch son of Neriah, and as Jeremiah dictated, Baruch wrote on it all the words of the scroll that Jehoiakim king of Judah had burned in the fire. And many similar words were added to them. ver 4; Ex 34:1

Jeremiah in Prison

37 Zedekiah son of Josiah was made king of Judah by Nebuchadnezzar king of Babylon; he reigned in place of Jehoiachin[a] son of Jehoiakim. 2Neither he nor his attendants nor the people of the land paid any attention to the words the LORD had spoken through Jeremiah the prophet. 2Ch 36:12,14; Jer 22:24

3King Zedekiah, however, sent Jehucal son of Shelemiah with the priest Zephaniah son of Maaseiah to Jeremiah the prophet with this message: "Please pray to the LORD our God for us."

4Now Jeremiah was free to come and go among the people, for he had not yet been put in prison. 5Pharaoh's army had marched out of Egypt, and when the Babylonians[b] who were besieging Jerusalem heard the report about them, they withdrew from Jerusalem. 2Ki 24:7; Eze 17:15

6Then the word of the LORD came to Jeremiah the prophet: 7"This is what the LORD, the God of Israel, says: Tell the king of Judah, who sent you to inquire of me, 'Pharaoh's army, which has marched out to support you, will go back to its own land, to Egypt. 8Then the Babylonians will return and attack this city; they will capture it and burn it down.'

9"This is what the LORD says: Do not deceive yourselves, thinking, 'The Babylonians will surely leave us.' They will not! 10Even if you were to defeat the entire Babylonian[c] army that is attacking you and only wounded men were left in their tents, they would come out and burn this city down." Jer 34:22

11After the Babylonian army had withdrawn from Jerusalem because of Pharaoh's army, 12Jeremiah started to leave the city to go to the territory of Benjamin to get his share of the property among the people there. 13But when he reached the Benjamin Gate, the captain of the guard, whose name was Irijah son of Shelemiah, the son of Hananiah, arrested him and said, "You are deserting to the Babylonians!" Jer 32:9

14"That's not true!" Jeremiah said. "I am not deserting to the Babylonians." But Irijah would not listen to him; instead, he arrested Jeremiah and brought him to the officials. 15They were angry with Jeremiah and had him beaten and imprisoned in the house of Jonathan the secretary, which they had made into a prison. Jer 38:26; 40:4

16Jeremiah was put into a vaulted cell in a dungeon, where he remained a long time. 17Then King Zedekiah sent for him and had him brought to the palace, where he asked him privately, "Is there any word from the LORD?" Jer 15:11; 38:16

"Yes," Jeremiah replied, "you will be handed over to the king of Babylon." Jer 21:7

18Then Jeremiah said to King Zedekiah, "What crime have I committed against you or your officials or this people, that you have put me in prison? 19Where are your prophets who prophesied to you, 'The king of Babylon will not attack you or this land'? 20But now, my lord the king, please listen. Let me bring my petition before you: Do not send me back to the house of Jonathan the secretary, or I will die there." 1Sa 26:18; Jn 10:32

21King Zedekiah then gave orders for Jeremiah to be placed in the courtyard of the guard and given bread from the street of the bakers each day until all the bread in the city was gone. So Jeremiah remained in the courtyard of the guard. Jer 32:2

Jeremiah Thrown Into a Cistern

38 Shephatiah son of Mattan, Gedaliah son of Pashhur, Jehucal[d] son of Shelemiah, and Pashhur son of Malkijah heard what Jeremiah was telling all the people when he said, 2"This is what the LORD says: 'Whoever stays in this city will die by the sword, famine or plague, but whoever goes over to the Babylonians[e] will live. He will escape with his life; he will live.' 3And this is what the LORD says: 'This city will certainly be handed over to the army of the king of Babylon, who will capture it.'" Jer 21:4,10; 32:3; 37:3

4Then the officials said to the king, "This man should be put to death. He is discouraging the soldiers who are left in this city, as well as all the people, by the things he is saying to them. This man is not seeking the good of these people but their ruin." Jer 26:11; 36:12

5"He is in your hands," King Zedekiah answered. "The king can do nothing to oppose you."

6So they took Jeremiah and put him into the cistern of Malkijah, the king's son, which was in the courtyard of the guard. They lowered Jeremiah by ropes into the cistern; it had no water in it, only mud, and Jeremiah sank down into the mud.

7But Ebed-Melech, a Cushite,[f] an official[g] in the royal palace, heard that they had put Jeremiah into the cistern. While the king was sitting in the Benjamin Gate, 8Ebed-Melech went out of the palace and said to him, 9"My lord the king, these men have acted wickedly in all they have done to Jeremiah the prophet. They have thrown him into a cistern, where he will starve to death when there is no longer any bread in the city." Jer 37:21; Ac 8:27

10Then the king commanded Ebed-Melech the Cushite, "Take thirty men from here with you and lift Jeremiah the prophet out of the cistern before he dies."

11So Ebed-Melech took the men with him and

[a] 1 Hebrew *Coniah,* a variant of *Jehoiachin* [b] 5 Or *Chaldeans*; also in verses 8, 9, 13 and 14 [c] 10 Or *Chaldean*; also in verse 11 [d] 1 Hebrew *Jucal,* a variant of *Jehucal* [e] 2 Or *Chaldeans*; also in verses 18, 19 and 23 [f] 7 Probably from the upper Nile region [g] 7 Or *a eunuch*

went to a room under the treasury in the palace.
He took some old rags and worn-out clothes from
there and let them down with ropes to Jeremiah in
the cistern. 12Ebed-Melech the Cushite said to Jeremiah, "Put these old rags and worn-out clothes
under your arms to pad the ropes." Jeremiah did
so, 13and they pulled him up with the ropes and
lifted him out of the cistern. And Jeremiah remained in the courtyard of the guard. Jer 37:21

Zedekiah Questions Jeremiah Again

14Then King Zedekiah sent for Jeremiah the
prophet and had him brought to the third entrance to the temple of the LORD. "I am going to
ask you something," the king said to Jeremiah.
"Do not hide anything from me." 1Sa 3:17; Jer 37:3
15Jeremiah said to Zedekiah, "If I give you an
answer, will you not kill me? Even if I did give you
counsel, you would not listen to me."
16But King Zedekiah swore this oath secretly to
Jeremiah: "As surely as the LORD lives, who has
given us breath, I will neither kill you nor hand
you over to those who are seeking your life."
17Then Jeremiah said to Zedekiah, "This is what
the LORD God Almighty, the God of Israel, says: 'If
you surrender to the officers of the king of Babylon, your life will be spared and this city will not
be burned down; you and your family will live.
18But if you will not surrender to the officers of the
king of Babylon, this city will be handed over to
the Babylonians and they will burn it down; you
yourself will not escape from their hands.' "
19King Zedekiah said to Jeremiah, "I am afraid
of the Jews who have gone over to the Babylonians, for the Babylonians may hand me over to
them and they will mistreat me." Isa 51:12; Jn 12:42
20"They will not hand you over," Jeremiah replied. "Obey the LORD by doing what I tell you.
Then it will go well with you, and your life will be
spared. 21But if you refuse to surrender, this is
what the LORD has revealed to me: 22All the women
left in the palace of the king of Judah will be
brought out to the officials of the king of Babylon.
Those women will say to you: Jer 6:12; 11:4

" 'They misled you and overcame you—
those trusted friends of yours. Jer 13:21
Your feet are sunk in the mud; Ps 69:14
your friends have deserted you.'

23"All your wives and children will be brought
out to the Babylonians. You yourself will not escape from their hands but will be captured by the
king of Babylon; and this city will[a] be burned
down." 2Ki 25:6; Jer 41:10
24Then Zedekiah said to Jeremiah, "Do not let
anyone know about this conversation, or you may
die. 25If the officials hear that I talked with you,
and they come to you and say, 'Tell us what you
said to the king and what the king said to you; do
not hide it from us or we will kill you,' 26then tell
them, 'I was pleading with the king not to send me
back to Jonathan's house to die there.' " Jer 37:15
27All the officials did come to Jeremiah and
question him, and he told them everything the
king had ordered him to say. So they said no more
to him, for no one had heard his conversation with
the king.
28And Jeremiah remained in the courtyard of
the guard until the day Jerusalem was captured.

The Fall of Jerusalem

39 This is how Jerusalem was taken: 1In the
ninth year of Zedekiah king of Judah, in
the tenth month, Nebuchadnezzar king of Babylon
marched against Jerusalem with his whole army
and laid siege to it. 2And on the ninth day of the
fourth month of Zedekiah's eleventh year, the city
wall was broken through. 3Then all the officials of
the king of Babylon came and took seats in the
Middle Gate: Nergal-Sharezer of Samgar, Nebo-
Sarsekim[b] a chief officer, Nergal-Sharezer a high
official and all the other officials of the king of
Babylon. 4When Zedekiah king of Judah and all
the soldiers saw them, they fled; they left the city
at night by way of the king's garden, through the
gate between the two walls, and headed toward the
Arabah.[c] Jer 25:29; 2Ch 36:11
5But the Babylonian[d] army pursued them and
overtook Zedekiah in the plains of Jericho. They
captured him and took him to Nebuchadnezzar
king of Babylon at Riblah in the land of Hamath,
where he pronounced sentence on him. 6There at
Riblah the king of Babylon slaughtered the sons of
Zedekiah before his eyes and also killed all the
nobles of Judah. 7Then he put out Zedekiah's eyes
and bound him with bronze shackles to take him
to Babylon. 2Ki 23:33; Jer 32:5; Eze 12:13
8The Babylonians[e] set fire to the royal palace
and the houses of the people and broke down the
walls of Jerusalem. 9Nebuzaradan commander of
the imperial guard carried into exile to Babylon
the people who remained in the city, along with
those who had gone over to him, and the rest of
the people. 10But Nebuzaradan the commander of
the guard left behind in the land of Judah some
of the poor people, who owned nothing; and at
that time he gave them vineyards and fields.
11Now Nebuchadnezzar king of Babylon had
given these orders about Jeremiah through Nebuzaradan commander of the imperial guard:
12"Take him and look after him; don't harm him
but do for him whatever he asks." 13So Nebuzara-

[a]23 Or *and you will cause this city to* [b]3 Or *Nergal-Sharezer, Samgar-Nebo, Sarsekim* [c]4 Or *the Jordan Valley*
[d]5 Or *Chaldean* [e]8 Or *Chaldeans*

dan the commander of the guard, Nebushazban a
chief officer, Nergal-Sharezer a high official and all
the other officers of the king of Babylon 14sent and
had Jeremiah taken out of the courtyard of the
guard. They turned him over to Gedaliah son of
Ahikam, the son of Shaphan, to take him back to
his home. So he remained among his own people.
15While Jeremiah had been confined in the
courtyard of the guard, the word of the LORD came
to him: 16"Go and tell Ebed-Melech the Cushite,
'This is what the LORD Almighty, the God of Israel,
says: I am about to fulfill my words against this
city through disaster, not prosperity. At that time
they will be fulfilled before your eyes. 17But I will
rescue you on that day, declares the LORD; you will
not be handed over to those you fear. 18I will save
you; you will not fall by the sword but will escape
with your life, because you trust in me, declares
the LORD.'" Jer 21:9; 45:5

Jeremiah Freed

40 The word came to Jeremiah from the LORD
after Nebuzaradan commander of the imperial guard had released him at Ramah. He had
found Jeremiah bound in chains among all the
captives from Jerusalem and Judah who were being carried into exile to Babylon. 2When the commander of the guard found Jeremiah, he said to
him, "The LORD your God decreed this disaster for
this place. 3And now the LORD has brought it
about; he has done just as he said he would. All
this happened because you people sinned against
the LORD and did not obey him. 4But today I am
freeing you from the chains on your wrists. Come
with me to Babylon, if you like, and I will look
after you; but if you do not want to, then don't
come. Look, the whole country lies before you; go
wherever you please." 5However, before Jeremiah
turned to go,[a] Nebuzaradan added, "Go back
to Gedaliah son of Ahikam, the son of Shaphan,
whom the king of Babylon has appointed over the
towns of Judah, and live with him among the people, or go anywhere else you please." Jer 39:11-12
Then the commander gave him provisions and
a present and let him go. 6So Jeremiah went to
Gedaliah son of Ahikam at Mizpah and stayed
with him among the people who were left behind
in the land. Jdg 20:1; 1Sa 7:5-17

Gedaliah Assassinated

7When all the army officers and their men who
were still in the open country heard that the king
of Babylon had appointed Gedaliah son of Ahikam
as governor over the land and had put him in
charge of the men, women and children who were
the poorest in the land and who had not been
carried into exile to Babylon, 8they came to Gedaliah at Mizpah—Ishmael son of Nethaniah, Johanan and Jonathan the sons of Kareah, Seraiah son
of Tanhumeth, the sons of Ephai the Netophathite,
and Jaazaniah[b] the son of the Maacathite, and
their men. 9Gedaliah son of Ahikam, the son of
Shaphan, took an oath to reassure them and their
men. "Do not be afraid to serve the Babylonians,[c]" he said. "Settle down in the land and serve
the king of Babylon, and it will go well with you.
10I myself will stay at Mizpah to represent you
before the Babylonians who come to us, but
you are to harvest the wine, summer fruit and oil,
and put them in your storage jars, and live in the
towns you have taken over." Dt 1:39; Jer 38:20
11When all the Jews in Moab, Ammon, Edom
and all the other countries heard that the king of
Babylon had left a remnant in Judah and had appointed Gedaliah son of Ahikam, the son of Shaphan, as governor over them, 12they all came back
to the land of Judah, to Gedaliah at Mizpah, from
all the countries where they had been scattered.
And they harvested an abundance of wine and
summer fruit. Jer 43:5
13Johanan son of Kareah and all the army officers still in the open country came to Gedaliah at
Mizpah 14and said to him, "Don't you know that
Baalis king of the Ammonites has sent Ishmael son
of Nethaniah to take your life?" But Gedaliah son
of Ahikam did not believe them. Jer 41:10
15Then Johanan son of Kareah said privately to
Gedaliah in Mizpah, "Let me go and kill Ishmael
son of Nethaniah, and no one will know it. Why
should he take your life and cause all the Jews who
are gathered around you to be scattered and the
remnant of Judah to perish?" 2Ki 21:14; Isa 1:9; Ro 11:5
16But Gedaliah son of Ahikam said to Johanan
son of Kareah, "Don't do such a thing! What you
are saying about Ishmael is not true."
41 In the seventh month Ishmael son of Nethaniah, the son of Elishama, who was of
royal blood and had been one of the king's officers, came with ten men to Gedaliah son of Ahikam at Mizpah. While they were eating together
there, 2Ishmael son of Nethaniah and the ten men
who were with him got up and struck down Gedaliah son of Ahikam, the son of Shaphan, with the
sword, killing the one whom the king of Babylon
had appointed as governor over the land. 3Ishmael
also killed all the Jews who were with Gedaliah at
Mizpah, as well as the Babylonian[d] soldiers who
were there. 2Ki 25:22-26; Jer 40:5,8
4The day after Gedaliah's assassination, before
anyone knew about it, 5eighty men who had
shaved off their beards, torn their clothes and cut
themselves came from Shechem, Shiloh and Sa-

[a] 5 Or *Jeremiah answered* [b] 8 Hebrew *Jezaniah*, a variant of *Jaazaniah* [c] 9 Or *Chaldeans*; also in verse 10
[d] 3 Or *Chaldean*

maria, bringing grain offerings and incense with
them to the house of the LORD. 6Ishmael son of
Nethaniah went out from Mizpah to meet them,
weeping as he went. When he met them, he said,
"Come to Gedaliah son of Ahikam." 7When they
went into the city, Ishmael son of Nethaniah and
the men who were with him slaughtered them and
threw them into a cistern. 8But ten of them said to
Ishmael, "Don't kill us! We have wheat and barley,
oil and honey, hidden in a field." So he let them
alone and did not kill them with the others. 9Now
the cistern where he threw all the bodies of the
men he had killed along with Gedaliah was the one
King Asa had made as part of his defense against
Baasha king of Israel. Ishmael son of Nethaniah
filled it with the dead. 1Ki 15:22; 2Ch 16:1,6

10Ishmael made captives of all the rest of the
people who were in Mizpah—the king's daughters
along with all the others who were left there, over
whom Nebuzaradan commander of the imperial
guard had appointed Gedaliah son of Ahikam.
Ishmael son of Nethaniah took them captive and
set out to cross over to the Ammonites. Jer 40:14

11When Johanan son of Kareah and all the army
officers who were with him heard about all the
crimes Ishmael son of Nethaniah had committed,
12they took all their men and went to fight Ishmael
son of Nethaniah. They caught up with him near
the great pool in Gibeon. 13When all the people
Ishmael had with him saw Johanan son of Kareah
and the army officers who were with him, they
were glad. 14All the people Ishmael had taken captive at Mizpah turned and went over to Johanan
son of Kareah. 15But Ishmael son of Nethaniah
and eight of his men escaped from Johanan and
fled to the Ammonites. 2Sa 2:13; Pr 28:17

Flight to Egypt

16Then Johanan son of Kareah and all the army
officers who were with him led away all the survivors from Mizpah whom he had recovered from
Ishmael son of Nethaniah after he had assassinated
Gedaliah son of Ahikam: the soldiers, women,
children and court officials he had brought from
Gibeon. 17And they went on, stopping at Geruth
Kimham near Bethlehem on their way to Egypt
18to escape the Babylonians.[a] They were afraid of
them because Ishmael son of Nethaniah had killed
Gedaliah son of Ahikam, whom the king of Babylon had appointed as governor over the land.

42 Then all the army officers, including Johanan son of Kareah and Jezaniah[b] son of
Hoshaiah, and all the people from the least to the
greatest approached 2Jeremiah the prophet and
said to him, "Please hear our petition and pray to
the LORD your God for this entire remnant. For as
you now see, though we were once many, now
only a few are left. 3Pray that the LORD your God
will tell us where we should go and what we
should do." Ps 86:11; Pr 3:6

4"I have heard you," replied Jeremiah the
prophet. "I will certainly pray to the LORD your
God as you have requested; I will tell you everything the LORD says and will keep nothing back
from you." 1Ki 22:14; 1Sa 3:17

5Then they said to Jeremiah, "May the LORD be
a true and faithful witness against us if we do not
act in accordance with everything the LORD your
God sends you to tell us. 6Whether it is favorable
or unfavorable, we will obey the LORD our God, to
whom we are sending you, so that it will go well
with us, for we will obey the LORD our God."

7Ten days later the word of the LORD came to
Jeremiah. 8So he called together Johanan son of
Kareah and all the army officers who were with
him and all the people from the least to the greatest. 9He said to them, "This is what the LORD, the
God of Israel, to whom you sent me to present
your petition, says: 10'If you stay in this land, I will
build you up and not tear you down; I will plant
you and not uproot you, for I am grieved over the
disaster I have inflicted on you. 11Do not be afraid
of the king of Babylon, whom you now fear. Do
not be afraid of him, declares the LORD, for I am
with you and will save you and deliver you from
his hands. 12I will show you compassion so that he
will have compassion on you and restore you to
your land.' Ps 106:44-46; Ro 8:31

13"However, if you say, 'We will not stay in this
land,' and so disobey the LORD your God, 14and if
you say, 'No, we will go and live in Egypt, where
we will not see war or hear the trumpet or be
hungry for bread,' 15then hear the word of the
LORD, O remnant of Judah. This is what the LORD
Almighty, the God of Israel, says: 'If you are determined to go to Egypt and you do go to settle there,
16then the sword you fear will overtake you there,
and the famine you dread will follow you into
Egypt, and there you will die. 17Indeed, all who are
determined to go to Egypt to settle there will die by
the sword, famine and plague; not one of them will
survive or escape the disaster I will bring on them.'

LIVING  **INSIGHT**

All who fly risk crashing. All who drive risk colliding. All who run risk falling. All who walk risk stumbling. All who live risk something. Effectiveness—sometimes greatness—awaits those who refuse to run scared.

(See Jeremiah 42:11.)

[a] 18 Or *Chaldeans* [b] 1 Hebrew; Septuagint (see also 43:2) *Azariah*

18This is what the LORD Almighty, the God of Israel, says: 'As my anger and wrath have been poured
out on those who lived in Jerusalem, so will my
wrath be poured out on you when you go to Egypt.
You will be an object of cursing and horror, of
condemnation and reproach; you will never see
this place again.' Jer 7:20; 29:18; 44:13
19"O remnant of Judah, the LORD has told you,
'Do not go to Egypt.' Be sure of this: I warn you
today 20that you made a fatal mistake[a] when
you sent me to the LORD your God and said, 'Pray
to the LORD our God for us; tell us everything he
says and we will do it.' 21I have told you today, but
you still have not obeyed the LORD your God in all
he sent me to tell you. 22So now, be sure of this:
You will die by the sword, famine and plague in
the place where you want to go to settle."
43 When Jeremiah finished telling the people
all the words of the LORD their God—everything the LORD had sent him to tell them—
2Azariah son of Hoshaiah and Johanan son of Kareah and all the arrogant men said to Jeremiah,
"You are lying! The LORD our God has not sent
you to say, 'You must not go to Egypt to settle
there.' 3But Baruch son of Neriah is inciting you
against us to hand us over to the Babylonians,[b] so
they may kill us or carry us into exile to Babylon."
4So Johanan son of Kareah and all the army
officers and all the people disobeyed the LORD's
command to stay in the land of Judah. 5Instead,
Johanan son of Kareah and all the army officers
led away all the remnant of Judah who had come
back to live in the land of Judah from all the nations where they had been scattered. 6They also led
away all the men, women and children and the
king's daughters whom Nebuzaradan commander
of the imperial guard had left with Gedaliah son of
Ahikam, the son of Shaphan, and Jeremiah the
prophet and Baruch son of Neriah. 7So they entered Egypt in disobedience to the LORD and went
as far as Tahpanhes. Jer 40:12; 44:1
8In Tahpanhes the word of the LORD came to
Jeremiah: 9"While the Jews are watching, take
some large stones with you and bury them in clay
in the brick pavement at the entrance to Pharaoh's
palace in Tahpanhes. 10Then say to them, 'This is
what the LORD Almighty, the God of Israel, says: I
will send for my servant Nebuchadnezzar king of
Babylon, and I will set his throne over these stones
I have buried here; he will spread his royal canopy
above them. 11He will come and attack Egypt,
bringing death to those destined for death, captivity to those destined for captivity, and the sword to
those destined for the sword. 12He[c] will set fire to
the temples of the gods of Egypt; he will burn their
temples and take their gods captive. As a shepherd
wraps his garment around him, so will he wrap
Egypt around himself and depart from there unscathed. 13There in the temple of the sun[d] in
Egypt he will demolish the sacred pillars and will
burn down the temples of the gods of Egypt.'"

Disaster Because of Idolatry

44 This word came to Jeremiah concerning all
the Jews living in Lower Egypt—in Migdol, Tahpanhes and Memphis[e]—and in Upper
Egypt[f]: 2"This is what the LORD Almighty, the
God of Israel, says: You saw the great disaster I
brought on Jerusalem and on all the towns of Judah. Today they lie deserted and in ruins 3because
of the evil they have done. They provoked me to
anger by burning incense and by worshiping other
gods that neither they nor you nor your fathers
ever knew. 4Again and again I sent my servants the
prophets, who said, 'Do not do this detestable
thing that I hate!' 5But they did not listen or pay
attention; they did not turn from their wickedness
or stop burning incense to other gods. 6Therefore,
my fierce anger was poured out; it raged against
the towns of Judah and the streets of Jerusalem
and made them the desolate ruins they are today.
7"Now this is what the LORD God Almighty, the
God of Israel, says: Why bring such great disaster
on yourselves by cutting off from Judah the men
and women, the children and infants, and so leave
yourselves without a remnant? 8Why provoke me
to anger with what your hands have made, burning incense to other gods in Egypt, where you have
come to live? You will destroy yourselves and
make yourselves an object of cursing and reproach
among all the nations on earth. 9Have you forgotten the wickedness committed by your fathers and
by the kings and queens of Judah and the wickedness committed by you and your wives in the land
of Judah and the streets of Jerusalem? 10To this day
they have not humbled themselves or shown reverence, nor have they followed my law and the
decrees I set before you and your fathers.
11"Therefore, this is what the LORD Almighty,
the God of Israel, says: I am determined to bring
disaster on you and to destroy all Judah. 12I will
take away the remnant of Judah who were determined to go to Egypt to settle there. They will all
perish in Egypt; they will fall by the sword or die
from famine. From the least to the greatest, they
will die by sword or famine. They will become an
object of cursing and horror, of condemnation
and reproach. 13I will punish those who live in
Egypt with the sword, famine and plague, as I
punished Jerusalem. 14None of the remnant of Judah who have gone to live in Egypt will escape or
survive to return to the land of Judah, to which

[a] 20 Or *you erred in your hearts* [b] 3 Or *Chaldeans* [c] 12 Or *I* [d] 13 Or *in Heliopolis* [e] 1 Hebrew *Noph*
[f] 1 Hebrew *in Pathros*

they long to return and live; none will return except a few fugitives." Jer 21:10; 22:24-27; Am 9:4

15Then all the men who knew that their wives were burning incense to other gods, along with all the women who were present—a large assembly—and all the people living in Lower and Upper Egypt,[a] said to Jeremiah, 16"We will not listen to the message you have spoken to us in the name of the LORD! 17We will certainly do everything we said we would: We will burn incense to the Queen of Heaven and will pour out drink offerings to her just as we and our fathers, our kings and our officials did in the towns of Judah and in the streets of Jerusalem. At that time we had plenty of food and were well off and suffered no harm. 18But ever since we stopped burning incense to the Queen of Heaven and pouring out drink offerings to her, we have had nothing and have been perishing by sword and famine." Dt 23:23; Jer 7:18

19The women added, "When we burned incense to the Queen of Heaven and poured out drink offerings to her, did not our husbands know that we were making cakes like her image and pouring out drink offerings to her?" Jer 7:18

20Then Jeremiah said to all the people, both men and women, who were answering him, 21"Did not the LORD remember and think about the incense burned in the towns of Judah and the streets of Jerusalem by you and your fathers, your kings and your officials and the people of the land? 22When the LORD could no longer endure your wicked actions and the detestable things you did, your land became an object of cursing and a desolate waste without inhabitants, as it is today. 23Because you have burned incense and have sinned against the LORD and have not obeyed him or followed his law or his decrees or his stipulations, this disaster has come upon you, as you now see."

24Then Jeremiah said to all the people, including the women, "Hear the word of the LORD, all you people of Judah in Egypt. 25This is what the LORD Almighty, the God of Israel, says: You and your wives have shown by your actions what you promised when you said, 'We will certainly carry out the vows we made to burn incense and pour out drink offerings to the Queen of Heaven.'

"Go ahead then, do what you promised! Keep your vows! 26But hear the word of the LORD, all Jews living in Egypt: 'I swear by my great name,' says the LORD, 'that no one from Judah living anywhere in Egypt will ever again invoke my name or swear, "As surely as the Sovereign LORD lives." 27For I am watching over them for harm, not for good; the Jews in Egypt will perish by sword and famine until they are all destroyed. 28Those who escape the sword and return to the land of Judah from Egypt will be very few. Then the whole remnant of Judah who came to live in Egypt will know whose word will stand—mine or theirs. Jer 31:28

29" 'This will be the sign to you that I will punish you in this place,' declares the LORD, 'so that you will know that my threats of harm against you will surely stand.' 30This is what the LORD says: 'I am going to hand Pharaoh Hophra king of Egypt over to his enemies who seek his life, just as I handed Zedekiah king of Judah over to Nebuchadnezzar king of Babylon, the enemy who was seeking his life.' " Jer 39:5; 46:26

A Message to Baruch

45 This is what Jeremiah the prophet told Baruch son of Neriah in the fourth year of Jehoiakim son of Josiah king of Judah, after Baruch had written on a scroll the words Jeremiah was then dictating: 2"This is what the LORD, the God of Israel, says to you, Baruch: 3You said, 'Woe to me! The LORD has added sorrow to my pain; I am worn out with groaning and find no rest.' " Jer 36:4,18,32

4⌊The LORD said,⌋ "Say this to him: 'This is what the LORD says: I will overthrow what I have built and uproot what I have planted, throughout the land. 5Should you then seek great things for yourself? Seek them not. For I will bring disaster on all people, declares the LORD, but wherever you go I will let you escape with your life.' " Jer 21:9; 38:2

Words to the Nations **Chapters 46–51**

As you might have guessed, Jeremiah was not popular with his own people. They wanted good news; he brought bad news. They wanted a word of affirmation; he brought an edict of despair. They hungered for a prophet who would tell them what they wanted to hear, but Jeremiah was committed to speak only what the Lord had told him to say. In these chapters, Jeremiah spoke out against the surrounding nations, and his words condemned them as well. Speaking the word of the Lord in truth will not always make you popular. It will, however, keep you faithful.

A Message About Egypt

46 This is the word of the LORD that came to Jeremiah the prophet concerning the nations: Jer 25:15-38

2Concerning Egypt:

This is the message against the army of Pharaoh Neco king of Egypt, which was defeated at Carchemish on the Euphrates River by Nebuchadnezzar king of Babylon in the fourth year of Jehoiakim son of Josiah king of Judah: 2Ki 23:29; 2Ch 35:20

3"Prepare your shields, both large and small,
and march out for battle!
4Harness the horses,

[a]15 Hebrew *in Egypt and Pathros*

mount the steeds!
Take your positions
with helmets on!
Polish your spears, Eze 21:9-11
put on your armor! 1Sa 17:5,38; 2Ch 26:14
5What do I see?
They are terrified,
they are retreating,
their warriors are defeated.
They flee in haste Jer 48:44
without looking back,
and there is terror on every side," Jer 49:29
declares the LORD.
6"The swift cannot flee Isa 30:16
nor the strong escape.
In the north by the River Euphrates
they stumble and fall. Da 11:19
7"Who is this that rises like the Nile,
like rivers of surging waters? Jer 47:2
8Egypt rises like the Nile, Eze 29:3,9
like rivers of surging waters.
She says, 'I will rise and cover the earth;
I will destroy cities and their people.'
9Charge, O horses!
Drive furiously, O charioteers! Jer 47:3
March on, O warriors—
men of Cush[a] and Put who carry shields,
men of Lydia who draw the bow. Isa 66:19
10But that day belongs to the Lord, the LORD
Almighty— Joel 1:15
a day of vengeance, for vengeance on his
foes. Dt 32:41
The sword will devour till it is satisfied, Dt 32:42
till it has quenched its thirst with blood.
For the Lord, the LORD Almighty, will offer
sacrifice Zep 1:7
in the land of the north by the River
Euphrates. Ge 2:14
11"Go up to Gilead and get balm, Jer 8:22
O Virgin Daughter of Egypt. Isa 47:1
But you multiply remedies in vain;
there is no healing for you. Mic 1:9
12The nations will hear of your shame;
your cries will fill the earth.
One warrior will stumble over another;
both will fall down together." Isa 19:4; Na 3:8-10

13This is the message the LORD spoke to Jeremiah the prophet about the coming of Nebuchadnezzar king of Babylon to attack Egypt: Isa 19:1

14"Announce this in Egypt, and proclaim it in
Migdol;
proclaim it also in Memphis[b] and
Tahpanhes: Jer 43:8
'Take your positions and get ready,
for the sword devours those around you.'
15Why will your warriors be laid low?
They cannot stand, for the LORD will push
them down. Isa 66:15-16
16They will stumble repeatedly; Lev 26:37
they will fall over each other.
They will say, 'Get up, let us go back
to our own people and our native lands,
away from the sword of the oppressor.'
17There they will exclaim,
'Pharaoh king of Egypt is only a loud noise;
he has missed his opportunity.' Isa 19:11-16
18"As surely as I live," declares the King, Jer 48:15
whose name is the LORD Almighty,
"one will come who is like Tabor among the
mountains, Jos 19:22
like Carmel by the sea. 1Ki 18:42
19Pack your belongings for exile, Isa 20:4
you who live in Egypt,
for Memphis will be laid waste Eze 29:10,12
and lie in ruins without inhabitant.
20"Egypt is a beautiful heifer,
but a gadfly is coming
against her from the north. Jer 47:2
21The mercenaries in her ranks 2Ki 7:6
are like fattened calves.
They too will turn and flee together,
they will not stand their ground,
for the day of disaster is coming upon them,
the time for them to be punished. Job 18:20
22Egypt will hiss like a fleeing serpent
as the enemy advances in force;
they will come against her with axes,
like men who cut down trees.
23They will chop down her forest,"
declares the LORD,
"dense though it be.
They are more numerous than locusts, Jdg 7:12
they cannot be counted.
24The Daughter of Egypt will be put to shame,
handed over to the people of the north."

25The LORD Almighty, the God of Israel, says: "I
am about to bring punishment on Amon god of
Thebes,[c] on Pharaoh, on Egypt and her gods and
her kings, and on those who rely on Pharaoh. 26I
will hand them over to those who seek their lives,
to Nebuchadnezzar king of Babylon and his officers. Later, however, Egypt will be inhabited as in
times past," declares the LORD. Eze 29:11-16; 32:11

27"Do not fear, O Jacob my servant; Isa 41:13; 43:5
do not be dismayed, O Israel.
I will surely save you out of a distant place,
your descendants from the land of their
exile. Isa 11:11; Jer 50:19
Jacob will again have peace and security,
and no one will make him afraid.

[a]9 That is, the upper Nile region [b]14 Hebrew *Noph*; also in verse 19 [c]25 Hebrew *No*

[28]Do not fear, O Jacob my servant,
for I am with you," declares the LORD.
"Though I completely destroy all the nations
among which I scatter you,
I will not completely destroy you.
I will discipline you but only with justice;
I will not let you go entirely unpunished."

A Message About the Philistines

47 This is the word of the LORD that came to
Jeremiah the prophet concerning the Philistines before Pharaoh attacked Gaza: Am 1:6

[2]This is what the LORD says:

"See how the waters are rising in the north;
they will become an overflowing torrent.
They will overflow the land and everything in it,
the towns and those who live in them.
The people will cry out;
all who dwell in the land will wail Isa 15:3
[3]at the sound of the hoofs of galloping steeds,
at the noise of enemy chariots Jer 46:9; Eze 23:24
and the rumble of their wheels.
Fathers will not turn to help their children;
their hands will hang limp. Isa 13:7
[4]For the day has come
to destroy all the Philistines
and to cut off all survivors
who could help Tyre and Sidon. Am 1:9-10
The LORD is about to destroy the Philistines,
the remnant from the coasts of Caphtor.[a]
[5]Gaza will shave her head in mourning; Jer 41:5
Ashkelon will be silenced. Jer 25:20
O remnant on the plain,
how long will you cut yourselves?

[6]"'Ah, sword of the LORD,' ⌞you cry,⌟ Jer 12:12
'how long till you rest?
Return to your scabbard;
cease and be still.' Eze 21:30
[7]But how can it rest
when the LORD has commanded it,
when he has ordered it
to attack Ashkelon and the coast?"

A Message About Moab

48 Concerning Moab: Ge 19:37

This is what the LORD Almighty, the God of Israel, says:

"Woe to Nebo, for it will be ruined. Nu 32:38
Kiriathaim will be disgraced and captured;
the stronghold[b] will be disgraced and shattered.
[2]Moab will be praised no more; Isa 16:14
in Heshbon[c] men will plot her downfall:
'Come, let us put an end to that nation.'
You too, O Madmen,[d] will be silenced;
the sword will pursue you.
[3]Listen to the cries from Horonaim, Isa 15:5
cries of great havoc and destruction.
[4]Moab will be broken;
her little ones will cry out.[e]
[5]They go up the way to Luhith, Isa 15:5
weeping bitterly as they go;
on the road down to Horonaim
anguished cries over the destruction are heard.
[6]Flee! Run for your lives;
become like a bush[f] in the desert. Jer 17:6
[7]Since you trust in your deeds and riches,
you too will be taken captive,
and Chemosh will go into exile, Nu 21:29; Isa 46:1-2
together with his priests and officials. Am 2:3
[8]The destroyer will come against every town,
and not a town will escape.
The valley will be ruined
and the plateau destroyed, Jos 13:9
because the LORD has spoken.
[9]Put salt on Moab, Jdg 9:45
for she will be laid waste[g]; Jer 51:29
her towns will become desolate,
with no one to live in them.

[10]"A curse on him who is lax in doing the LORD's work!
A curse on him who keeps his sword from bloodshed! 1Ki 20:42; 2Ki 13:15-19; Jer 47:6

[11]"Moab has been at rest from youth, Zec 1:15
like wine left on its dregs, Zep 1:12
not poured from one jar to another—
she has not gone into exile.
So she tastes as she did,
and her aroma is unchanged.
[12]But days are coming,"
declares the LORD,
"when I will send men who pour from jars,
and they will pour her out;
they will empty her jars
and smash her jugs.
[13]Then Moab will be ashamed of Chemosh,
as the house of Israel was ashamed
when they trusted in Bethel. Jos 7:2

[14]"How can you say, 'We are warriors, Ps 33:16
men valiant in battle'?
[15]Moab will be destroyed and her towns invaded;
her finest young men will go down in the slaughter," Jer 50:27

[a]4 That is, Crete [b]1 Or / *Misgab* [c]2 The Hebrew for *Heshbon* sounds like the Hebrew for *plot.* [d]2 The name of the Moabite town Madmen sounds like the Hebrew for *be silenced.* [e]4 Hebrew; Septuagint / *proclaim it to Zoar* [f]6 Or *like Aroer* [g]9 Or *Give wings to Moab, / for she will fly away*

declares the King, whose name is the LORD
Almighty. Jer 46:18; 51:57
16"The fall of Moab is at hand; Isa 13:22
her calamity will come quickly.
17Mourn for her, all who live around her,
all who know her fame; 2Ki 3:4-5
say, 'How broken is the mighty scepter, Ps 110:2
how broken the glorious staff!'

18"Come down from your glory
and sit on the parched ground, Isa 47:1
O inhabitants of the Daughter of Dibon,
for he who destroys Moab
will come up against you
and ruin your fortified cities.
19Stand by the road and watch,
you who live in Aroer. Dt 2:36
Ask the man fleeing and the woman escaping,
ask them, 'What has happened?'
20Moab is disgraced, for she is shattered.
Wail and cry out! Isa 16:7
Announce by the Arnon Nu 21:13
that Moab is destroyed.
21Judgment has come to the plateau—
to Holon, Jahzah and Mephaath, Nu 21:23
22 to Dibon, Nebo and Beth Diblathaim,
23 to Kiriathaim, Beth Gamul and Beth Meon,
24 to Kerioth and Bozrah— Am 2:2
to all the towns of Moab, far and near.
25Moab's horn[a] is cut off; Ps 75:10
her arm is broken," Ps 10:15; Eze 30:21
declares the LORD.

26"Make her drunk, Jer 25:16,27
for she has defied the LORD. 1Sa 17:26
Let Moab wallow in her vomit; Isa 28:8
let her be an object of ridicule.
27Was not Israel the object of your ridicule?
Was she caught among thieves, 2Ki 17:3-6
that you shake your head in scorn Jer 18:16
whenever you speak of her?
28Abandon your towns and dwell among the
rocks,
you who live in Moab.
Be like a dove that makes its nest Ps 55:6-7
at the mouth of a cave. Jdg 6:2

29"We have heard of Moab's pride— Isa 16:6
her overweening pride and conceit,
her pride and arrogance
and the haughtiness of her heart. Pr 16:18
30I know her insolence but it is futile,"
declares the LORD,
"and her boasts accomplish nothing. Ps 10:3
31Therefore I wail over Moab, Isa 15:5-8
for all Moab I cry out,
I moan for the men of Kir Hareseth. 2Ki 3:25
32I weep for you, as Jazer weeps, Jos 13:25
O vines of Sibmah. Isa 16:8-9
Your branches spread as far as the sea;
they reached as far as the sea of Jazer.
The destroyer has fallen
on your ripened fruit and grapes.
33Joy and gladness are gone
from the orchards and fields of Moab.
I have stopped the flow of wine from the
presses; Isa 16:10
no one treads them with shouts of joy.
Although there are shouts,
they are not shouts of joy.

34"The sound of their cry rises
from Heshbon to Elealeh and Jahaz, Isa 15:4
from Zoar as far as Horonaim and Eglath
Shelishiyah, Isa 15:5
for even the waters of Nimrim are dried up.
35In Moab I will put an end
to those who make offerings on the high
places Isa 15:2; 16:12
and burn incense to their gods," Jer 11:13
declares the LORD.
36"So my heart laments for Moab like a flute;
it laments like a flute for the men of Kir
Hareseth. 2Ki 3:25
The wealth they acquired is gone. Isa 16:6-12
37Every head is shaved Isa 15:2; Jer 41:5
and every beard cut off; 2Sa 10:4
every hand is slashed
and every waist is covered with sackcloth.
38On all the roofs in Moab
and in the public squares
there is nothing but mourning,
for I have broken Moab
like a jar that no one wants," Jer 22:28
declares the LORD.
39"How shattered she is! How they wail!
How Moab turns her back in shame!
Moab has become an object of ridicule,
an object of horror to all those around
her."

40This is what the LORD says:

"Look! An eagle is swooping down, Dt 28:49
spreading its wings over Moab. Isa 8:8
41Kerioth[b] will be captured Isa 15:1
and the strongholds taken.
In that day the hearts of Moab's warriors
will be like the heart of a woman in labor.
42Moab will be destroyed as a nation Ps 83:4
because she defied the LORD. ver 26
43Terror and pit and snare await you, Isa 24:17
O people of Moab,"
declares the LORD.
44"Whoever flees from the terror 1Ki 19:17; Isa 24:18
will fall into a pit,
whoever climbs out of the pit
will be caught in a snare;

[a] 25 *Horn* here symbolizes strength. [b] 41 Or *The cities*

for I will bring upon Moab
the year of her punishment," Jer 11:23
declares the LORD.

45"In the shadow of Heshbon
the fugitives stand helpless,
for a fire has gone out from Heshbon,
a blaze from the midst of Sihon; Nu 21:21,26-28
it burns the foreheads of Moab,
the skulls of the noisy boasters. Nu 24:17
46Woe to you, O Moab! Nu 21:29
The people of Chemosh are destroyed;
your sons are taken into exile
and your daughters into captivity.

47"Yet I will restore the fortunes of Moab
in days to come,"
declares the LORD.

Here ends the judgment on Moab.

A Message About Ammon

49 Concerning the Ammonites: Am 1:13

This is what the LORD says:

"Has Israel no sons?
Has she no heirs?
Why then has Molech[a] taken possession of
Gad? Lev 18:21
Why do his people live in its towns?
2But the days are coming,"
declares the LORD,
"when I will sound the battle cry Jer 4:19
against Rabbah of the Ammonites; Dt 3:11
it will become a mound of ruins, Dt 13:16
and its surrounding villages will be set on
fire.
Then Israel will drive out
those who drove her out," Isa 14:2; Eze 21:28-32
says the LORD.
3"Wail, O Heshbon, for Ai is destroyed! Jos 8:28
Cry out, O inhabitants of Rabbah!
Put on sackcloth and mourn;
rush here and there inside the walls,
for Molech will go into exile, Jer 48:7
together with his priests and officials.
4Why do you boast of your valleys,
boast of your valleys so fruitful?
O unfaithful daughter, Jer 3:6
you trust in your riches and say, Jer 9:23
'Who will attack me?' Jer 21:13
5I will bring terror on you
from all those around you,"
declares the Lord, the LORD Almighty.
"Every one of you will be driven away,
and no one will gather the fugitives.

6"Yet afterward, I will restore the fortunes of
the Ammonites," ver 39; Jer 48:47
declares the LORD.

A Message About Edom

7Concerning Edom: Eze 25:12

This is what the LORD Almighty says:

"Is there no longer wisdom in Teman?
Has counsel perished from the prudent?
Has their wisdom decayed?
8Turn and flee, hide in deep caves,
you who live in Dedan, Jer 25:23
for I will bring disaster on Esau
at the time I punish him.
9If grape pickers came to you,
would they not leave a few grapes?
If thieves came during the night,
would they not steal only as much as they
wanted?
10But I will strip Esau bare;
I will uncover his hiding places,
so that he cannot conceal himself.
His children, relatives and neighbors will
perish,
and he will be no more. Ob 1:5-6; Mal 1:2-5
11Leave your orphans; I will protect their lives.
Your widows too can trust in me." Dt 10:18

12This is what the LORD says: "If those who do
not deserve to drink the cup must drink it, why
should you go unpunished? You will not go unpunished, but must drink it. 13I swear by myself,"
declares the LORD, "that Bozrah will become a ruin
and an object of horror, of reproach and of cursing; and all its towns will be in ruins forever."

14I have heard a message from the LORD:
An envoy was sent to the nations to say,
"Assemble yourselves to attack it!
Rise up for battle!"

15"Now I will make you small among the
nations,
despised among men.
16The terror you inspire
and the pride of your heart have deceived
you,
you who live in the clefts of the rocks,
who occupy the heights of the hill.
Though you build your nest as high as the
eagle's, Job 39:27; Am 9:2
from there I will bring you down,"
declares the LORD.
17"Edom will become an object of horror;
all who pass by will be appalled and will
scoff
because of all its wounds. Jer 50:13; Eze 35:7
18As Sodom and Gomorrah were overthrown,

[a] 1 Or *their king*; Hebrew *malcam*; also in verse 3

along with their neighboring towns,"
says the LORD,
"so no one will live there;
no man will dwell in it." Isa 34:10

19"Like a lion coming up from Jordan's thickets
to a rich pastureland,
I will chase Edom from its land in an instant.
Who is the chosen one I will appoint for
this?
Who is like me and who can challenge me?
And what shepherd can stand against me?"
20Therefore, hear what the LORD has planned
against Edom, Isa 34:5
what he has purposed against those who
live in Teman: Isa 14:27
The young of the flock will be dragged away;
he will completely destroy their pasture
because of them. Mal 1:3-4
21At the sound of their fall the earth will
tremble; Eze 26:15
their cry will resound to the Red Sea.[a]
22Look! An eagle will soar and swoop down,
spreading its wings over Bozrah. Ge 36:33
In that day the hearts of Edom's warriors
will be like the heart of a woman in labor.

A Message About Damascus

23Concerning Damascus: Ge 14:15; 2Ch 16:2; Ac 9:2

"Hamath and Arpad are dismayed, Isa 10:9
for they have heard bad news.
They are disheartened,
troubled like[b] the restless sea. Isa 57:20
24Damascus has become feeble,
she has turned to flee
and panic has gripped her;
anguish and pain have seized her,
pain like that of a woman in labor.
25Why has the city of renown not been
abandoned,
the town in which I delight?
26Surely, her young men will fall in the streets;
all her soldiers will be silenced in that day,"
declares the LORD Almighty.
27"I will set fire to the walls of Damascus; Am 1:4
it will consume the fortresses of
Ben-Hadad." 1Ki 15:18

A Message About Kedar and Hazor

28Concerning Kedar and the kingdoms of Hazor, which Nebuchadnezzar king of Babylon attacked: Ge 25:13

This is what the LORD says:

"Arise, and attack Kedar
and destroy the people of the East. Jdg 6:3
29Their tents and their flocks will be taken;
their shelters will be carried off
with all their goods and camels.
Men will shout to them,
'Terror on every side!' Jer 6:25; 46:5

30"Flee quickly away!
Stay in deep caves, you who live in Hazor,"
declares the LORD.
"Nebuchadnezzar king of Babylon has plotted
against you; Jer 10:22
he has devised a plan against you.

31"Arise and attack a nation at ease,
which lives in confidence,"
declares the LORD,
"a nation that has neither gates nor bars;
its people live alone.
32Their camels will become plunder, Jdg 6:5
and their large herds will be booty.
I will scatter to the winds those who are in
distant places[c] Jer 9:26
and will bring disaster on them from every
side,"
declares the LORD.
33"Hazor will become a haunt of jackals, Isa 13:22
a desolate place forever. Jer 10:22
No one will live there;
no man will dwell in it." ver 18; Jer 51:37

A Message About Elam

34This is the word of the LORD that came to
Jeremiah the prophet concerning Elam, early in
the reign of Zedekiah king of Judah: Ge 10:22

35This is what the LORD Almighty says:

"See, I will break the bow of Elam, Isa 22:6
the mainstay of their might.
36I will bring against Elam the four winds ver 32
from the four quarters of the heavens;
I will scatter them to the four winds,
and there will not be a nation
where Elam's exiles do not go.
37I will shatter Elam before their foes,
before those who seek their lives;
I will bring disaster upon them,
even my fierce anger," Jer 30:24
declares the LORD.
"I will pursue them with the sword Jer 9:16
until I have made an end of them.
38I will set my throne in Elam
and destroy her king and officials,"
declares the LORD.

39"Yet I will restore the fortunes of Elam Jer 48:47
in days to come,"
declares the LORD.

[a]21 Hebrew *Yam Suph*; that is, Sea of Reeds [b]23 Hebrew *on* or *by* [c]32 *Or who clip the hair by their foreheads*

A Message About Babylon

50 This is the word the LORD spoke through Jeremiah the prophet concerning Babylon and the land of the Babylonians[a]: Ge 10:10; Isa 13:1

2"Announce and proclaim among the nations,
lift up a banner and proclaim it; Ps 20:5
keep nothing back, but say,
'Babylon will be captured; Jer 51:31
Bel will be put to shame, Isa 46:1
Marduk filled with terror. Jer 51:47
Her images will be put to shame
and her idols filled with terror.' Lev 26:30
3A nation from the north will attack her
and lay waste her land.
No one will live in it; Isa 14:22-23
both men and animals will flee away. Zep 1:3

4"In those days, at that time,"
declares the LORD,
"the people of Israel and the people of Judah
together Hos 1:11
will go in tears to seek the LORD their God.
5They will ask the way to Zion Jer 31:21
and turn their faces toward it.
They will come and bind themselves to the
LORD Jer 33:7
in an everlasting covenant Isa 55:3; Jer 32:40
that will not be forgotten.

6"My people have been lost sheep; Isa 53:6; Mt 9:36
their shepherds have led them astray Jer 23:32
and caused them to roam on the
mountains.
They wandered over mountain and hill Jer 3:6
and forgot their own resting place.
7Whoever found them devoured them;
their enemies said, 'We are not guilty, Jer 2:3
for they sinned against the LORD, their true
pasture,
the LORD, the hope of their fathers.' Jer 14:8

8"Flee out of Babylon; Isa 48:20; Jer 51:6; Rev 18:4
leave the land of the Babylonians,
and be like the goats that lead the flock.
9For I will stir up and bring against Babylon
an alliance of great nations from the land
of the north. Isa 41:25; Jer 25:26
They will take up their positions against her,
and from the north she will be captured.
Their arrows will be like skilled warriors
who do not return empty-handed.
10So Babylonia[b] will be plundered; Jer 30:16
all who plunder her will have their fill,"
declares the LORD.

11"Because you rejoice and are glad,
you who pillage my inheritance, Isa 47:6
because you frolic like a heifer threshing grain
and neigh like stallions,
12your mother will be greatly ashamed;
she who gave you birth will be disgraced.
She will be the least of the nations—
a wilderness, a dry land, a desert. Isa 21:1
13Because of the LORD's anger she will not be
inhabited
but will be completely desolate. Jer 9:11
All who pass Babylon will be horrified and
scoff Jer 18:16
because of all her wounds. Jer 49:17

14"Take up your positions around Babylon,
all you who draw the bow.
Shoot at her! Spare no arrows, Isa 13:18
for she has sinned against the LORD.
15Shout against her on every side! Jer 51:14
She surrenders, her towers fall,
her walls are torn down. Jer 51:44,58
Since this is the vengeance of the LORD, Jer 51:6
take vengeance on her;
do to her as she has done to others. Ps 137:8
16Cut off from Babylon the sower,
and the reaper with his sickle at harvest.
Because of the sword of the oppressor Jer 25:38
let everyone return to his own people,
let everyone flee to his own land. Jer 51:9

17"Israel is a scattered flock Ps 119:176
that lions have chased away. Jer 2:15
The first to devour him
was the king of Assyria; 2Ki 17:6
the last to crush his bones Nu 24:8
was Nebuchadnezzar king of Babylon."

18Therefore this is what the LORD Almighty, the God of Israel, says:

"I will punish the king of Babylon and his
land
as I punished the king of Assyria. Isa 10:12
19But I will bring Israel back to his own pasture
and he will graze on Carmel and Bashan;
his appetite will be satisfied
on the hills of Ephraim and Gilead.
20In those days, at that time,"
declares the LORD,
"search will be made for Israel's guilt,
but there will be none,
and for the sins of Judah, Mic 7:18-19
but none will be found,
for I will forgive the remnant I spare. Isa 1:9

21"Attack the land of Merathaim
and those who live in Pekod. Eze 23:23
Pursue, kill and completely destroy[c] them,"
declares the LORD.
"Do everything I have commanded you.

[a] 1 Or *Chaldeans*; also in verses 8, 25, 35 and 45 [b] 10 Or *Chaldea* [c] 21 The Hebrew term refers to the irrevocable giving over of things or persons to the LORD, often by totally destroying them; also in verse 26.

22The noise of battle is in the land, Jer 4:19-21; 51:54
the noise of great destruction!
23How broken and shattered
is the hammer of the whole earth! Isa 10:5
How desolate is Babylon Isa 14:16
among the nations!
24I set a trap for you, O Babylon, Da 5:30-31
and you were caught before you knew it;
you were found and captured Jer 51:31
because you opposed the LORD. Job 9:4
25The LORD has opened his arsenal
and brought out the weapons of his wrath,
for the Sovereign LORD Almighty has work to do
in the land of the Babylonians. Jer 51:25,55
26Come against her from afar.
Break open her granaries;
pile her up like heaps of grain.
Completely destroy her Isa 14:22-23
and leave her no remnant.
27Kill all her young bulls; Ps 68:30
let them go down to the slaughter! Isa 30:25
Woe to them! For their day has come, Job 18:20
the time for them to be punished. Jer 51:6
28Listen to the fugitives and refugees from Babylon
declaring in Zion Isa 48:20; Jer 51:10
how the LORD our God has taken vengeance,
vengeance for his temple. 2Ki 24:13; Jer 51:11

29"Summon archers against Babylon,
all those who draw the bow.
Encamp all around her;
let no one escape. Isa 13:18
Repay her for her deeds; Jer 51:56; Rev 18:6
do to her as she has done.
For she has defied the LORD, Isa 47:10
the Holy One of Israel. Ps 78:41
30Therefore, her young men will fall in the streets; Isa 13:18; Jer 49:26
all her soldiers will be silenced in that day,"
declares the LORD.
31"See, I am against you, O arrogant one,"
declares the Lord, the LORD Almighty,
"for your day has come,
the time for you to be punished.
32The arrogant one will stumble and fall Ps 119:21
and no one will help her up; Am 5:2
I will kindle a fire in her towns Jer 21:14; 49:27
that will consume all who are around her."

33This is what the LORD Almighty says:

"The people of Israel are oppressed, Isa 58:6
and the people of Judah as well.
All their captors hold them fast,
refusing to let them go. Isa 14:17
34Yet their Redeemer is strong; Job 19:25
the LORD Almighty is his name. Jer 51:19
He will vigorously defend their cause Jer 15:21
so that he may bring rest to their land,
but unrest to those who live in Babylon.

35"A sword against the Babylonians!" Jer 47:6
declares the LORD—
"against those who live in Babylon
and against her officials and wise men!
36A sword against her false prophets!
They will become fools.
A sword against her warriors! Jer 49:22
They will be filled with terror.
37A sword against her horses and chariots
and all the foreigners in her ranks!
They will become women. Jer 51:30; Na 3:13
A sword against her treasures! Isa 45:3
They will be plundered.
38A drought on[a] her waters!
They will dry up. Ps 137:1; Jer 51:13
For it is a land of idols, Jer 51:36
idols that will go mad with terror.

39"So desert creatures and hyenas will live there,
and there the owl will dwell.
It will never again be inhabited
or lived in from generation to generation.
40As God overthrew Sodom and Gomorrah
along with their neighboring towns,"
declares the LORD,
"so no one will live there;
no man will dwell in it. Jer 51:62

41"Look! An army is coming from the north;
a great nation and many kings
are being stirred up from the ends of the earth. Isa 13:4; Jer 51:22-28
42They are armed with bows and spears;
they are cruel and without mercy. Isa 13:18
They sound like the roaring sea Isa 5:30
as they ride on their horses;
they come like men in battle formation
to attack you, O Daughter of Babylon.
43The king of Babylon has heard reports about them,
and his hands hang limp. Jer 47:3
Anguish has gripped him,
pain like that of a woman in labor. Jer 6:22-24
44Like a lion coming up from Jordan's thickets
to a rich pastureland,
I will chase Babylon from its land in an instant.
Who is the chosen one I will appoint for this? Nu 16:5
Who is like me and who can challenge me?
And what shepherd can stand against me?"
45Therefore, hear what the LORD has planned against Babylon,
what he has purposed against the land of the Babylonians: Isa 14:24; Jer 51:11

[a]38 Or *A sword against*

The young of the flock will be dragged away;
he will completely destroy their pasture
because of them.
46 At the sound of Babylon's capture the earth
will tremble; Jer 49:21
its cry will resound among the nations.

51

This is what the LORD says:

"See, I will stir up the spirit of a destroyer
against Babylon and the people of Leb
Kamai.[a] Jer 25:12
2 I will send foreigners to Babylon
to winnow her and to devastate her land;
they will oppose her on every side
in the day of her disaster. Isa 13:9
3 Let not the archer string his bow, Jer 50:29
nor let him put on his armor. Jer 46:4
Do not spare her young men;
completely destroy[b] her army.
4 They will fall down slain in Babylon,[c] Isa 13:15
fatally wounded in her streets. Jer 49:26; 50:30
5 For Israel and Judah have not been forsaken
by their God, the LORD Almighty,
though their land[d] is full of guilt Hos 4:1
before the Holy One of Israel.

6 "Flee from Babylon! Jer 50:8
Run for your lives!
Do not be destroyed because of her sins.
It is time for the LORD's vengeance; Jer 50:15
he will pay her what she deserves. Jer 25:14
7 Babylon was a gold cup in the LORD's hand;
she made the whole earth drunk.
The nations drank her wine;
therefore they have now gone mad.
8 Babylon will suddenly fall and be broken.
Wail over her!
Get balm for her pain; Jer 46:11
perhaps she can be healed.

9 " 'We would have healed Babylon,
but she cannot be healed;
let us leave her and each go to his own land,
for her judgment reaches to the skies,
it rises as high as the clouds.'

10 " 'The LORD has vindicated us; Mic 7:9
come, let us tell in Zion
what the LORD our God has done.' Jer 50:28

11 "Sharpen the arrows, Jer 50:9
take up the shields! Jer 46:4
The LORD has stirred up the kings of the
Medes, Isa 41:2
because his purpose is to destroy Babylon.
The LORD will take vengeance,
vengeance for his temple. Jer 50:28

12 Lift up a banner against the walls of Babylon!
Reinforce the guard,
station the watchmen, 2Sa 18:24
prepare an ambush! Jer 50:24
The LORD will carry out his purpose, Ps 33:11
his decree against the people of Babylon.
13 You who live by many waters Rev 17:1,15
and are rich in treasures, Isa 45:3; Hab 2:9
your end has come,
the time for you to be cut off. Jer 50:3
14 The LORD Almighty has sworn by himself:
I will surely fill you with men, as with a
swarm of locusts, Na 3:15
and they will shout in triumph over you.

15 "He made the earth by his power;
he founded the world by his wisdom
and stretched out the heavens by his
understanding. Ge 1:1; Ps 104:2; 136:5
16 When he thunders, the waters in the heavens
roar; Ps 18:11-13
he makes clouds rise from the ends of the
earth.
He sends lightning with the rain
and brings out the wind from his
storehouses. Ps 13:7; Jnh 1:4

17 "Every man is senseless and without
knowledge;
every goldsmith is shamed by his idols.
His images are a fraud; Isa 44:20; Hab 2:18-19
they have no breath in them.
18 They are worthless, the objects of mockery;
when their judgment comes, they will
perish.
19 He who is the Portion of Jacob is not like
these, Ps 119:57
for he is the Maker of all things,
including the tribe of his inheritance— Ex 34:9
the LORD Almighty is his name.

20 "You are my war club, Isa 10:5
my weapon for battle—
with you I shatter nations, Mic 4:13
with you I destroy kingdoms,
21 with you I shatter horse and rider, Ex 15:1
with you I shatter chariot and driver,
22 with you I shatter man and woman,
with you I shatter old man and youth,
with you I shatter young man and maiden,
23 with you I shatter shepherd and flock,
with you I shatter farmer and oxen,
with you I shatter governors and officials.

24 "Before your eyes I will repay Babylon and all
who live in Babylonia[e] for all the wrong they have
done in Zion," declares the LORD. Jer 50:15

[a] 1 *Leb Kamai* is a cryptogram for Chaldea, that is, Babylonia. [b] 3 The Hebrew term refers to the irrevocable giving over of things or persons to the LORD, often by totally destroying them. [c] 4 Or *Chaldea* [d] 5 Or / *and the land ⌊of the Babylonians⌋* [e] 24 Or *Chaldea*; also in verse 35

25"I am against you, O destroying mountain,
you who destroy the whole earth,"
declares the LORD.
"I will stretch out my hand against you,
roll you off the cliffs,
and make you a burned-out mountain.
26No rock will be taken from you for a
cornerstone,
nor any stone for a foundation,
for you will be desolate forever,"
declares the LORD.

27"Lift up a banner in the land! Isa 13:2; Jer 50:2
Blow the trumpet among the nations!
Prepare the nations for battle against her;
summon against her these kingdoms:
Ararat, Minni and Ashkenaz. Ge 8:4; 10:3
Appoint a commander against her;
send up horses like a swarm of locusts.
28Prepare the nations for battle against her—
the kings of the Medes, ver 11
their governors and all their officials,
and all the countries they rule.
29The land trembles and writhes, Jer 49:21
for the LORD's purposes against Babylon
stand— Ps 33:11
to lay waste the land of Babylon Jer 48:9
so that no one will live there. Isa 13:20
30Babylon's warriors have stopped fighting;
they remain in their strongholds.
Their strength is exhausted;
they have become like women. Isa 19:16
Her dwellings are set on fire; Isa 47:14
the bars of her gates are broken. La 2:9; Na 3:13
31One courier follows another 2Sa 18:19-31
and messenger follows messenger
to announce to the king of Babylon
that his entire city is captured, Jer 50:2
32the river crossings seized,
the marshes set on fire, Isa 47:14
and the soldiers terrified." Jer 50:36

33This is what the LORD Almighty, the God of
Israel, says:

"The Daughter of Babylon is like a threshing
floor Isa 21:10
at the time it is trampled;
the time to harvest her will soon come."
34"Nebuchadnezzar king of Babylon has
devoured us, Jer 50:17; Hos 8:8
he has thrown us into confusion,
he has made us an empty jar.
Like a serpent he has swallowed us
and filled his stomach with our delicacies,
and then has spewed us out. Lev 18:25
35May the violence done to our flesh[a] be upon
Babylon," Hab 2:17
say the inhabitants of Zion.
"May our blood be on those who live in
Babylonia,"
says Jerusalem. Ps 137:8

36Therefore, this is what the LORD says:

"See, I will defend your cause Ps 140:12; Jer 50:34
and avenge you; Ro 12:19
I will dry up her sea Jer 50:38
and make her springs dry.
37Babylon will be a heap of ruins,
a haunt of jackals, Isa 13:22; Rev 18:2
an object of horror and scorn,
a place where no one lives. Jer 50:13,39
38Her people all roar like young lions,
they growl like lion cubs.
39But while they are aroused,
I will set out a feast for them
and make them drunk, Isa 21:5
so that they shout with laughter—
then sleep forever and not awake," Ps 13:3
declares the LORD.
40"I will bring them down
like lambs to the slaughter,
like rams and goats. Eze 39:18

41"How Sheshach[b] will be captured, Isa 13:19
the boast of the whole earth seized!
What a horror Babylon will be
among the nations!
42The sea will rise over Babylon;
its roaring waves will cover her. Isa 8:7
43Her towns will be desolate,
a dry and desert land,
a land where no one lives,
through which no man travels. Isa 13:20; Jer 2:6
44I will punish Bel in Babylon Isa 46:1
and make him spew out what he has
swallowed.
The nations will no longer stream to him.
And the wall of Babylon will fall. Jer 50:15

45"Come out of her, my people! Rev 18:4
Run for your lives! Jer 50:8
Run from the fierce anger of the LORD.
46Do not lose heart or be afraid Jer 46:27
when rumors are heard in the land; 2Ki 19:7
one rumor comes this year, another the next,
rumors of violence in the land
and of ruler against ruler.
47For the time will surely come
when I will punish the idols of Babylon;
her whole land will be disgraced Jer 50:12
and her slain will all lie fallen within her.
48Then heaven and earth and all that is in them
will shout for joy over Babylon, Isa 44:23

[a]35 Or *done to us and to our children* [b]41 *Sheshach* is a cryptogram for Babylon.

for out of the north Isa 41:25
destroyers will attack her,"
declares the LORD.

49"Babylon must fall because of Israel's slain,
just as the slain in all the earth
have fallen because of Babylon. Jer 50:29
50You who have escaped the sword,
leave and do not linger! ver 45
Remember the LORD in a distant land, Ps 137:6
and think on Jerusalem."

51"We are disgraced, Ps 44:13-16; 79:4
for we have been insulted
and shame covers our faces,
because foreigners have entered
the holy places of the LORD's house." La 1:10

52"But days are coming," declares the LORD,
"when I will punish her idols,
and throughout her land
the wounded will groan.
53Even if Babylon reaches the sky Isa 14:13-14
and fortifies her lofty stronghold,
I will send destroyers against her," Jer 49:16
declares the LORD.

54"The sound of a cry comes from Babylon,
the sound of great destruction Jer 50:22
from the land of the Babylonians.[a]
55The LORD will destroy Babylon;
he will silence her noisy din.
Waves ⌊of enemies⌋ will rage like great waters;
the roar of their voices will resound.
56A destroyer will come against Babylon;
her warriors will be captured,
and their bows will be broken. Ps 46:9
For the LORD is a God of retribution;
he will repay in full. Ps 94:1-2; Hab 2:8
57I will make her officials and wise men drunk,
her governors, officers and warriors as well;
they will sleep forever and not awake," Ps 76:5
declares the King, whose name is the LORD
Almighty. Jer 46:18; 48:15

58This is what the LORD Almighty says:

"Babylon's thick wall will be leveled Isa 15:1
and her high gates set on fire; Isa 13:2
the peoples exhaust themselves for nothing,
the nations' labor is only fuel for the flames."

59This is the message Jeremiah gave to the staff
officer Seraiah son of Neriah, the son of Mahseiah,
when he went to Babylon with Zedekiah king of
Judah in the fourth year of his reign. 60Jeremiah
had written on a scroll about all the disasters that
would come upon Babylon—all that had been recorded concerning Babylon. 61He said to Seraiah,
"When you get to Babylon, see that you read all
these words aloud. 62Then say, 'O LORD, you have
said you will destroy this place, so that neither
man nor animal will live in it; it will be desolate
forever.' 63When you finish reading this scroll, tie
a stone to it and throw it into the Euphrates.
64Then say, 'So will Babylon sink to rise no more
because of the disaster I will bring upon her. And
her people will fall.'" Rev 18:21; Jer 50:13,39

The words of Jeremiah end here.

A Sobering Ending **Chapter 52**

In this final chapter we find the city of Jerusalem in total ruins. It is a tragic, baleful, bitter scene. All around him Jeremiah saw the smoldering ruins of elegant mansions, lovely homes, splendid places of worship and once-fertile gardens. It had all been completely destroyed! The prophet had watched it with his own eyes, and now he looked on the barren city with a broken heart. The only way to truly plumb the depths of Jeremiah's despair is to read the book of Lamentations, which chronicles his response to the destruction of the holy city.

The Fall of Jerusalem

52 Zedekiah was twenty-one years old when
he became king, and he reigned in Jerusalem eleven years. His mother's name was Hamutal
daughter of Jeremiah; she was from Libnah. 2He
did evil in the eyes of the LORD, just as Jehoiakim
had done. 3It was because of the LORD's anger that
all this happened to Jerusalem and Judah, and in
the end he thrust them from his presence.
Now Zedekiah rebelled against the king of Babylon. 2Ki 24:18-20; 2Ch 36:11-16
4So in the ninth year of Zedekiah's reign, on the
tenth day of the tenth month, Nebuchadnezzar
king of Babylon marched against Jerusalem with
his whole army. They camped outside the city and
built siege works all around it. 5The city was kept
under siege until the eleventh year of King Zedekiah. 2Ki 25:1-7; Jer 39:1
6By the ninth day of the fourth month the famine in the city had become so severe that there was
no food for the people to eat. 7Then the city wall
was broken through, and the whole army fled.
They left the city at night through the gate between
the two walls near the king's garden, though the
Babylonians[b] were surrounding the city. They
fled toward the Arabah,[c] 8but the Babylonian[d]
army pursued King Zedekiah and overtook him in
the plains of Jericho. All his soldiers were separated from him and scattered, 9and he was captured.

He was taken to the king of Babylon at Riblah
in the land of Hamath, where he pronounced sentence on him. 10There at Riblah the king of Babylon slaughtered the sons of Zedekiah before his
eyes; he also killed all the officials of Judah. 11Then
he put out Zedekiah's eyes, bound him with

[a]54 Or *Chaldeans* [b]7 Or *Chaldeans*; also in verse 17 [c]7 Or *the Jordan Valley* [d]8 Or *Chaldean*; also in verse 14

bronze shackles and took him to Babylon, where he put him in prison till the day of his death.

12 On the tenth day of the fifth month, in the nineteenth year of Nebuchadnezzar king of Babylon, Nebuzaradan commander of the imperial guard, who served the king of Babylon, came to Jerusalem. 13 He set fire to the temple of the LORD, the royal palace and all the houses of Jerusalem. Every important building he burned down. 14 The whole Babylonian army under the commander of the imperial guard broke down all the walls around Jerusalem. 15 Nebuzaradan the commander of the guard carried into exile some of the poorest people and those who remained in the city, along with the rest of the craftsmen[a] and those who had gone over to the king of Babylon. 16 But Nebuzaradan left behind the rest of the poorest people of the land to work the vineyards and fields. Jer 39:1-10

17 The Babylonians broke up the bronze pillars, the movable stands and the bronze Sea that were at the temple of the LORD and they carried all the bronze to Babylon. 18 They also took away the pots, shovels, wick trimmers, sprinkling bowls, dishes and all the bronze articles used in the temple service. 19 The commander of the imperial guard took away the basins, censers, sprinkling bowls, pots, lampstands, dishes and bowls used for drink offerings—all that were made of pure gold or silver.

20 The bronze from the two pillars, the Sea and the twelve bronze bulls under it, and the movable stands, which King Solomon had made for the temple of the LORD, was more than could be weighed. 21 Each of the pillars was eighteen cubits high and twelve cubits in circumference[b]; each was four fingers thick, and hollow. 22 The bronze capital on top of the one pillar was five cubits[c] high and was decorated with a network and pomegranates of bronze all around. The other pillar, with its pomegranates, was similar. 23 There were ninety-six pomegranates on the sides; the total number of pomegranates above the surrounding network was a hundred. 2Ki 25:1-21; 2Ch 36:17-20

24 The commander of the guard took as prisoners Seraiah the chief priest, Zephaniah the priest next in rank and the three doorkeepers. 25 Of those still in the city, he took the officer in charge of the fighting men, and seven royal advisers. He also took the secretary who was chief officer in charge of conscripting the people of the land and sixty of his men who were found in the city. 26 Nebuzaradan the commander took them all and brought them to the king of Babylon at Riblah. 27 There at Riblah, in the land of Hamath, the king had them executed. 2Ki 25:18; Jer 21:1; 37:3

So Judah went into captivity, away from her land. 28 This is the number of the people Nebuchadnezzar carried into exile: 2Ki 24:14-16; 2Ch 36:20

in the seventh year, 3,023 Jews;
29 in Nebuchadnezzar's eighteenth year,
832 people from Jerusalem;
30 in his twenty-third year,
745 Jews taken into exile by Nebuzaradan
the commander of the imperial guard.
There were 4,600 people in all. Jer 13:19

Jehoiachin Released

31 In the thirty-seventh year of the exile of Jehoiachin king of Judah, in the year Evil-Merodach[d] became king of Babylon, he released Jehoiachin king of Judah and freed him from prison on the twenty-fifth day of the twelfth month. 32 He spoke kindly to him and gave him a seat of honor higher than those of the other kings who were with him in Babylon. 33 So Jehoiachin put aside his prison clothes and for the rest of his life ate regularly at the king's table. 34 Day by day the king of Babylon gave Jehoiachin a regular allowance as long as he lived, till the day of his death. 2Ki 25:27-30

[a] *15* Or *populace* [b] *21* That is, about 27 feet (about 8.1 meters) high and 18 feet (about 5.4 meters) in circumference
[c] *22* That is, about 7 1/2 feet (about 2.3 meters) [d] *31* Also called *Amel-Marduk*

INTRODUCTION

LAMENTATIONS

Most of us have never been involved in a mop-up scene after a battle or after a calamity of one kind or another. But those who have been involved testify that it is one of the most painful and pathetic experiences a human being can endure. The ravages of war and the consequences of a disaster are usually beyond belief or description. Few are those who can capture the tragic scene in words. Jeremiah was one of the few who could. His brief, powerfully moving journal of what he saw and what he felt following the fall of his beloved nation is contained in this short book that bears the name "Lamentations." It is one of the most vivid reminders in all the Bible of this inspired truth once recorded by the apostle Paul: "A man reaps what he sows" (Galatians 6:7). And so will a city. And so will a nation. There is no exception. God plays no favorites.

WRITER: *Jeremiah*

DATE: *c.586–580* B.C.

PURPOSE: *To express personal and corporate grief and to encourage repentance*

KEY MESSAGE: *High calling flaunted by low living leads to deep suffering*

KEY VERSES: *3:21-26*

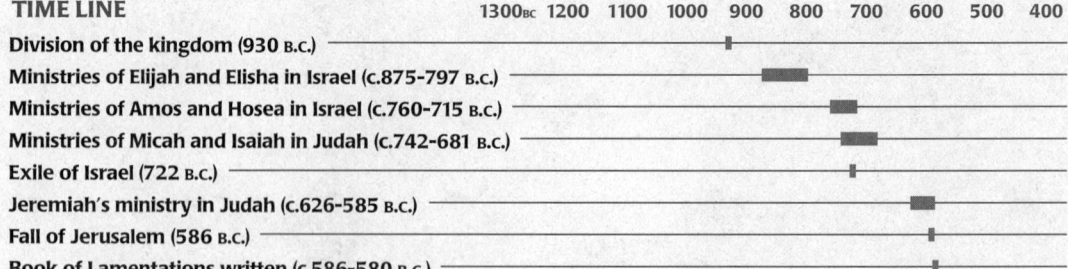

TIME LINE 1300BC 1200 1100 1000 900 800 700 600 500 400

Division of the kingdom (930 B.C.)

Ministries of Elijah and Elisha in Israel (c.875-797 B.C.)

Ministries of Amos and Hosea in Israel (c.760-715 B.C.)

Ministries of Micah and Isaiah in Judah (c.742-681 B.C.)

Exile of Israel (722 B.C.)

Jeremiah's ministry in Judah (c.626-585 B.C.)

Fall of Jerusalem (586 B.C.)

Book of Lamentations written (c.586-580 B.C.)

The Flip Side of Sin

	Voice of the CITY *CHAPTER 1*	Voice of the LORD *CHAPTER 2*	Voice of the PROPHET *CHAPTER 3*	Voice of the POSSESSIONS *CHAPTER 4*	Voice of the CAPTIVES *CHAPTER 5*
UNDERLYING EMOTION	**Lonely, groaning**	**Angry, exhorting**	**Broken, weeping**	**Empty, unsatisfying**	**Hungry, hurting**
KEY VERSES	***1:5***	***2:17***	***3:17-18***	***4:11-12***	***5:5,15***
SHORT PRAYERS	***1:20-22*** ***"See us!"***	***2:20-22*** ***"Help us!"***	***3:55-66*** ***"Judge us!"***	***4:20*** ***"Deliver us!"***	***5:21*** ***"Restore us!"***

In a city in southeast West Germany near Munich, there stands a monument. It is an unpretentious, mute reminder of a horror of inconceivable proportions; people who pass by read the words engraved there and shake their heads in silent disbelief. The monument contains three statues of gaunt, emaciated men—mere shells of humanity. The statues represent the Germans, the Jews and the Christians who died in the slave camp and in the ovens of Dachau. This small monument, erected in a place where, as tradition has it, the sun never shines, reads: "Remember the Victims." It is, however, too late for the victims.

Strangely, in the early 1940s there once stood another sign—a sign that bore a message that turned out to be a lie. But those who put the sign there hoped it would be believed as the truth. That sign read: "Work Makes You Free." Captured prisoners were brought into the concentration camp at Dachau with that large sign prominently placed before them. You and I know that this sign—though it sounded so good—could not have been further from the truth, for at Dachau those who worked the hardest died the youngest. The prisoners believed the deceitful message until it was too late to understand that it was really a lie. Those in that torturous concentration camp no doubt wondered if there was such a thing as justice. Sin was in full swing, and those many criminal acts seemed strangely victorious. Today there are 32 slabs of cement that stand as stark, naked, stunning reminders of the real truth of Dachau. Strange as it may sound, rather than a monument of honor to the value of hard work, it stands as a monument of disgrace. It is a never-to-be forgotten reminder for all the world to see.

In God's Book He has written a sign. It is a strange sign, and really quite brief; many who are in a hurry may pass by because it's wedged between the books of Jeremiah and Ezekiel. It may seem both overly emotional and insignificant. It really doesn't even represent much of a prophecy. Prophecy buffs would very likely pass it by, looking for the morsels found in the other great books of prophecy. Nevertheless, the sign hangs as a mute reminder for all who are trying to convince themselves that sin has no consequences. It is a one-word sign: *LAMENTATIONS*.

Sin Never Pays

Lamentations stands as a warning sign, a never-to-be-forgotten assessment that sin does not pay. There is a neon sign flashing brightly out of the book of Lamentations that reads: "Remember the Victims." You see, the people of Judah believed forty years earlier that another message spoke the truth: "Sin Pays

Rich Dividends." They believed that there were ecstasies connected with sinful activities—and that those pleasures would overshadow whatever consequences might ensue. Forty years later, Jeremiah, virtually alone in Jerusalem, most of his fellow citizens taken into exile, writes another epilogue that says in effect: "No! Sin does *not* pay. Remember the victims."

The name given to this book is unusual. All the other prophecies in the Bible bear the names of the primary character (the prophet), but this one is named from the action of a prophet. Jeremiah's "lamentations" were deep and anguished. To "lament" means "to wail, to cry out in grief, to regret strongly, to mourn aloud." Lamentations are what you would expect to hear at a funeral procession . . . and that is precisely what this book is! This book bears an extremely emotional title because it represents an extremely emotional message.

A Year of Infamy

The date of the event described in Lamentations, 586 B.C., may not mean much to you, but it means everything to the Jewish historian. It is the year of infamy in Hebrew history. It is the year the nation died. It is the year the truth finally won out—God's truth—and the nation fell.

On this day Jeremiah shoved aside the sophistication that prophets sometimes wrapped themselves in, and he cried with the people. But like a war correspondent walking through the cratered, corpse-ridden fields of battle, he wrote down some notes in a journal—notes of what he saw and what he felt—and they have come down to us in the book called Lamentations.

The Author of Lamentations

Although the Bible never specifically says Jeremiah wrote Lamentations, tradition says he did. This book follows the book of Jeremiah in our English Bibles for this very reason: the same person wrote both books. Lamentations is written in Jeremiah's style. It contains his characteristic Hebrew phrases. Furthermore, the *Septuagint* (the Greek version of the Old Testament) puts a unique prefix before the beginning of the book. It reads, "It came to pass after Israel was taken captive and Jerusalem made desolate, Jeremiah sat weeping and lamented this lamentation over Jerusalem." The Latin Vulgate adds, "He wrote it in bitterness of heart, sighing and crying."

The Message of Lamentations

It is crucial that we never forget the dominant message of the book of Lamentations: *Sin always has its consequences.* It is a book of consequences, and it tells the truth about the steep cost of sin. It tells it again and again and again and again—for five chapters—so we will never forget it. But alas, we will—sinful beings that we are. Whether we choose to read what is written in this book or not, it will forever stand in God's Word as a memorial. When we have eyes to see and ears to hear, this is what Lamentations shows and tells us: *Sin, like crime, never pays. Never forget it.*

The Voices of Lamentations

There are five voices that speak from the book of Lamentations—one in each chapter. In chapter 1 there's the *voice of the city,* personified by Jeremiah. He allows Jerusalem to speak through him in colorful Hebrew fashion and with great passion. The message in chapter 1 is this: *sin's pleasures are often shared, but its consequences must be endured alone.* We will never be more alone than when we suffer the consequences of a lifestyle of disobedience. Never. The loneliest people who come to visit pastors for counsel are those individuals who come in the backwash of a sinful, disobedient lifestyle. Invariably they say, "I feel so alone."

In chapter 2 there's the *voice of the Lord* that communicates His anger against His people, leaving the reader with the book's second message: *The Lord plays no favorites. All who sin suffer its consequences.* We have no corner of protection because we have walked with Him, lo, these many years. Nor will we be spared the consequences of sin just because our mother and father were godly. If you sin, you SUFFER. Remember what the apostle Paul wrote: "Do not be deceived: God cannot be mocked. A man reaps what he sows" (Galatians 6:7). It's the truth!

In chapter 3 we hear the *voice of the prophet* admitting openly that the misery the people are experiencing is the fault of the people. *We will never come fully clean with our life until we take full responsibility for how we live our life.* When consequences come, there is never any reason to blame God. Unfortunately, there is plenty of reason for God to blame us. The road to healing and restoration begins with confession.

Chapter 4 contains the *voice of the possessions*—the things people held so tightly in the days of their sinfulness. *Sin's consequences often bring the exact opposite of the very things we once held so dear and enjoyed so much*—starvation where there had been delicacies (4:5), rags where there had been robes (4:5), fear where there had once been security (4:18). This chapter is full of such illustrations. You'll be astonished, at times, how precisely God brings His judgment.

And finally, in chapter 5, there is the *voice of the captives* on their way to Babylon as they appeal for restoration and for God's forgiveness. The final lesson is unmistakable: *There is no misery greater than the misery that follows open disobedience.*

The Pain of Lamentations

Lamentations is dripping with emotion. Look at the underlying emotions that come pouring out of its five chapters: loneliness, groanings, anger, desperate pleadings, brokenness, weeping, emptiness, unfulfillment, hunger and deep hurt. Wrap all of that up in a package and tuck it away in your memory, because that is the payback of sin. No matter how fun or exciting, exhilarating or ecstatic a life of sin may seem on the surface, pain and sorrow are what you have at the end of the road.

Think of it like this—and you'll never forget it: If you wish to buy into a lifestyle of sinfulness, it's like buying one of those phonograph recordings from days gone by. You got the side that contained the songs you enjoyed, but you got the flip side as well. It always accompanied the side you enjoyed. Lamentations says to us, "This is the flip side, and you can't escape it. Play one side all you want, but there will always be the other side. And one day that side *will* play out. God plays no favorites. There are no exceptions. You will reap what you sow. It's the law of the harvest." And it's the law of Lamentations.

The Bottom Line

Let me share with you the enduring principle that can be derived from this little book: *High calling flaunted by low living leads to deep suffering.* I guarantee you the enemy knows you have learned this message; he knows that deep down *you* know it's true. And he stands ready with a whole new persuasive strategy to wink in your direction as he says, "Ah! But this time it's different." That is a lie! You have heard the truth from the pages of Lamentations . . . sin has a unbelievably expensive price tag. Lamentations gives us a never-to-be-forgotten, mournful reminder throughout the book: "Remember the Victims."

The Voice of the City — Chapter 1

In the first chapter the voice of the prophet represented the city and echoed her pain. She had fallen on hard times, and she uncovered all her wounds and screamed out in agony. There was no relief from the pain, no dignity in her shame and no companionship in her barren nakedness. All was desolation. All those who helped bring about her ruin by willingly taking part in her sin have now fled. She was alone. The lesson was clear: *Sin's pleasures are shared with others, but its consequences are endured alone.*

1[a] How deserted lies the city, Lev 26:43
once so full of people! Jer 42:2
How like a widow is she, Isa 47:8
who once was great among the nations!
She who was queen among the provinces
has now become a slave. Isa 3:26; Jer 40:9

2 Bitterly she weeps at night, Ps 6:6
tears are upon her cheeks.
Among all her lovers Jer 3:1
there is none to comfort her.
All her friends have betrayed her; Jer 4:30; Mic 7:5
they have become her enemies. Jer 30:14

3 After affliction and harsh labor,
Judah has gone into exile. Jer 13:19
She dwells among the nations;
she finds no resting place. Dt 28:65
All who pursue her have overtaken her
in the midst of her distress.

4 The roads to Zion mourn, Ps 137:1
for no one comes to her appointed feasts.
All her gateways are desolate, Jer 9:11
her priests groan,
her maidens grieve,
and she is in bitter anguish. Joel 1:8-13

5 Her foes have become her masters;
her enemies are at ease.
The LORD has brought her grief Jer 30:15
because of her many sins. Ps 5:10
Her children have gone into exile, Jer 52:28-30
captive before the foe. Ps 137:3

6 All the splendor has departed
from the Daughter of Zion. Jer 13:18
Her princes are like deer
that find no pasture;
in weakness they have fled
before the pursuer.

7 In the days of her affliction and wandering
Jerusalem remembers all the treasures
that were hers in days of old.
When her people fell into enemy hands,
there was no one to help her. Jer 37:7; La 4:17
Her enemies looked at her
and laughed at her destruction.

8 Jerusalem has sinned greatly Isa 59:2-13
and so has become unclean. Jer 2:22
All who honored her despise her,
for they have seen her nakedness; Jer 13:22,26
she herself groans Ps 6:6
and turns away.

9 Her filthiness clung to her skirts;
she did not consider her future. Dt 32:28-29
Her fall was astounding; Jer 13:18
there was none to comfort her. Ecc 4:1; Jer 16:7
"Look, O LORD, on my affliction, Ps 25:18
for the enemy has triumphed."

10 The enemy laid hands
on all her treasures; Isa 64:11
she saw pagan nations
enter her sanctuary— Ps 74:7-8; Jer 51:51
those you had forbidden Dt 23:3
to enter your assembly.

11 All her people groan Ps 38:8
as they search for bread; Jer 52:6
they barter their treasures for food
to keep themselves alive.
"Look, O LORD, and consider,
for I am despised."

12 "Is it nothing to you, all you who pass by?
Look around and see.
Is any suffering like my suffering
that was inflicted on me,
that the LORD brought on me
in the day of his fierce anger? Jer 30:24

13 "From on high he sent fire,
sent it down into my bones. Job 30:30
He spread a net for my feet
and turned me back.
He made me desolate, Jer 44:6
faint all the day long. Hab 3:16

14 "My sins have been bound into a yoke[b];
by his hands they were woven together.
They have come upon my neck
and the Lord has sapped my strength.
He has handed me over Jer 32:5
to those I cannot withstand.

15 "The Lord has rejected
all the warriors in my midst; Jer 37:10
he has summoned an army against me Isa 41:2
to[c] crush my young men. Jer 18:21
In his winepress the Lord has trampled Jdg 6:11
the Virgin Daughter of Judah. Jer 14:17

16 "This is why I weep
and my eyes overflow with tears. La 2:11,18

[a]This chapter is an acrostic poem, the verses of which begin with the successive letters of the Hebrew alphabet. [b]*14* Most Hebrew manuscripts; Septuagint *He kept watch over my sins* [c]*15* Or *has set a time for me* / *when he will*

No one is near to comfort me, Ps 69:20; Ecc 4:1
no one to restore my spirit.
My children are destitute
because the enemy has prevailed." Jer 13:17

17Zion stretches out her hands, Jer 4:31
but there is no one to comfort her.
The LORD has decreed for Jacob
that his neighbors become his foes; Ex 23:21
Jerusalem has become
an unclean thing among them. Lev 18:25-28

18"The LORD is righteous, Ex 9:27
yet I rebelled against his command. 1Sa 12:14
Listen, all you peoples;
look upon my suffering.
My young men and maidens
have gone into exile. Dt 28:32,41

19"I called to my allies
but they betrayed me.
My priests and my elders
perished in the city Jer 14:15; La 2:20
while they searched for food
to keep themselves alive.

20"See, O LORD, how distressed I am! Jer 4:19
I am in torment within, La 2:11
and in my heart I am disturbed,
for I have been most rebellious.
Outside, the sword bereaves;
inside, there is only death. Dt 32:25; Eze 7:15

21"People have heard my groaning, ver 8; Ps 6:6
but there is no one to comfort me. ver 4
All my enemies have heard of my distress;
they rejoice at what you have done. La 2:15
May you bring the day you have announced
so they may become like me.

22"Let all their wickedness come before you;
deal with them
as you have dealt with me
because of all my sins. Ne 4:5
My groans are many Ps 6:6
and my heart is faint."

The Voice of the Lord Chapter 2

The city had become silent, and the voice of Almighty God was heard. When we are hopelessly entangled in sin, as Jerusalem's people were, it may be difficult to hear the voice of the Lord. His voice may sound muffled. We may very well ignore the messages we hear or twist God's words to fit our rebellious lifestyle and make them say what we want to hear. In this chapter the voice of God broke through the noise and a clear message burst forth: *The Lord has no favorites. All who sin will suffer its consequences.*

2[a] How the Lord has covered the Daughter of Zion
with the cloud of his anger[b]! La 3:44
He has hurled down the splendor of Israel
from heaven to earth;
he has not remembered his footstool Ps 99:5
in the day of his anger. Jer 12:7

2Without pity the Lord has swallowed up
all the dwellings of Jacob;
in his wrath he has torn down
the strongholds of the Daughter of Judah.
He has brought her kingdom and its princes
down to the ground in dishonor. Isa 25:12

3In fierce anger he has cut off
every horn[c] of Israel. Ps 75:5,10
He has withdrawn his right hand Ps 74:11
at the approach of the enemy.
He has burned in Jacob like a flaming fire
that consumes everything around it. Isa 42:25

4Like an enemy he has strung his bow; La 3:12-13
his right hand is ready.
Like a foe he has slain
all who were pleasing to the eye; Eze 24:16,25
he has poured out his wrath like fire Jer 7:20
on the tent of the Daughter of Zion. Jer 4:20

5The Lord is like an enemy; Jer 30:14
he has swallowed up Israel.
He has swallowed up all her palaces
and destroyed her strongholds. ver 2
He has multiplied mourning and lamentation
for the Daughter of Judah. Jer 9:17-20

6He has laid waste his dwelling like a garden;
he has destroyed his place of meeting.
The LORD has made Zion forget
her appointed feasts and her Sabbaths;
in his fierce anger he has spurned
both king and priest. La 4:16

7The Lord has rejected his altar
and abandoned his sanctuary. Eze 7:24
He has handed over to the enemy
the walls of her palaces; Ps 74:7-8; Isa 64:11
they have raised a shout in the house of the LORD
as on the day of an appointed feast.

8The LORD determined to tear down
the wall around the Daughter of Zion.
He stretched out a measuring line 2Ki 21:13
and did not withhold his hand from destroying.
He made ramparts and walls lament; Ps 48:13
together they wasted away. Isa 3:26

9Her gates have sunk into the ground; Ne 1:3

[a]This chapter is an acrostic poem, the verses of which begin with the successive letters of the Hebrew alphabet. [b]1 Or *How the Lord in his anger / has treated the Daughter of Zion with contempt* [c]3 Or */ all the strength*; or *every king*; *horn* here symbolizes strength.

their bars he has broken and destroyed.
Her king and her princes are exiled among
the nations, Dt 28:36
the law is no more, 2Ch 15:3
and her prophets no longer find
visions from the LORD. Jer 14:14

10 The elders of the Daughter of Zion
sit on the ground in silence;
they have sprinkled dust on their heads Job 2:12
and put on sackcloth. Isa 15:3
The young women of Jerusalem
have bowed their heads to the ground.

11 My eyes fail from weeping, La 13:48-51
I am in torment within, La 1:20
my heart is poured out on the ground ver 19
because my people are destroyed,
because children and infants faint La 4:4
in the streets of the city.

LIVING  **INSIGHT**

Some of God's dearest saints and most trusted disciples are (and have been) people of pain.

(See Lamentations 2:11.)

12 They say to their mothers,
"Where is bread and wine?"
as they faint like wounded men
in the streets of the city,
as their lives ebb away
in their mothers' arms. La 4:4

13 What can I say for you?
With what can I compare you,
O Daughter of Jerusalem?
To what can I liken you,
that I may comfort you,
O Virgin Daughter of Zion? Isa 37:22
Your wound is as deep as the sea. Jer 14:17
Who can heal you?

14 The visions of your prophets
were false and worthless; Jer 28:15
they did not expose your sin
to ward off your captivity. Isa 58:1
The oracles they gave you
were false and misleading. Jer 2:8; 29:9

15 All who pass your way
clap their hands at you; Eze 25:6
they scoff and shake their heads Jer 19:8
at the Daughter of Jerusalem: La 1:21
"Is this the city that was called
the perfection of beauty, Ps 50:2
the joy of the whole earth?" Ps 48:2

16 All your enemies open their mouths
wide against you; Ps 56:2; La 3:46
they scoff and gnash their teeth Job 16:9
and say, "We have swallowed her up.
This is the day we have waited for;
we have lived to see it." Mic 4:11

17 The LORD has done what he planned;
he has fulfilled his word,
which he decreed long ago. Dt 28:15-45
He has overthrown you without pity, ver 2
he has let the enemy gloat over you, Ps 22:17
he has exalted the horn[a] of your foes.

18 The hearts of the people
cry out to the Lord. Ps 119:145
O wall of the Daughter of Zion,
let your tears flow like a river La 1:16
day and night; Jer 9:1
give yourself no relief,
your eyes no rest. La 3:49

19 Arise, cry out in the night,
as the watches of the night begin;
pour out your heart like water 1Sa 1:15; Ps 62:8
in the presence of the Lord. Isa 26:9
Lift up your hands to him
for the lives of your children,
who faint from hunger Isa 51:20
at the head of every street.

20 "Look, O LORD, and consider:
Whom have you ever treated like this?
Should women eat their offspring, Jer 19:9
the children they have cared for? La 4:10
Should priest and prophet be killed Ps 78:64
in the sanctuary of the Lord? La 1:19

21 "Young and old lie together
in the dust of the streets;
my young men and maidens
have fallen by the sword. 2 Ch 36:17; Ps 78:62-63
You have slain them in the day of your anger;
you have slaughtered them without pity.

22 "As you summon to a feast day,
so you summoned against me terrors on
every side. Ps 31:13; Jer 6:25
In the day of the LORD's anger
no one escaped or survived; Jer 11:11
those I cared for and reared, Hos 9:13
my enemy has destroyed."

The Voice of the Prophet **Chapter 3**

The prophet had waited in silence as the city poured out her agony and the Lord proclaimed His message. Then Jeremiah spoke. Peering out of his cave of despair he discovered a glimmer of hope. From the depths of judgment he looked up and saw a God who is compassionate and who brings new mercies

[a] 17 *Horn* here symbolizes strength.

with each sunrise (3:21–24). Although the Lord is just in his judgment, He is still a God of grace and love and mercy. Jeremiah had learned a profound lesson: *There is never any reason to blame God when consequences come.*

3[a] I am the man who has seen affliction
by the rod of his wrath. Job 19:21; Ps 88:7
2He has driven me away and made me walk
in darkness rather than light; Jer 4:23
3indeed, he has turned his hand against me
again and again, all day long.

4He has made my skin and my flesh grow old
and has broken my bones. Ps 51:8; Isa 38:13
5He has besieged me and surrounded me
with bitterness and hardship. ver 19; Jer 23:15
6He has made me dwell in darkness
like those long dead. Ps 88:5-6

7He has walled me in so I cannot escape;
he has weighed me down with chains.
8Even when I call out or cry for help,
he shuts out my prayer. Job 30:20; Ps 22:2
9He has barred my way with blocks of stone;
he has made my paths crooked. Isa 63:17

10Like a bear lying in wait,
like a lion in hiding, Hos 13:8; Am 5:18-19
11he dragged me from the path and mangled
me Hos 6:1
and left me without help.
12He drew his bow La 2:4
and made me the target for his arrows.

13He pierced my heart
with arrows from his quiver. Job 6:4
14I became the laughingstock of all my people;
they mock me in song all day long. Job 30:9
15He has filled me with bitter herbs
and sated me with gall. Jer 9:15

16He has broken my teeth with gravel; Pr 20:17
he has trampled me in the dust. Ps 7:5
17I have been deprived of peace;
I have forgotten what prosperity is.
18So I say, "My splendor is gone
and all that I had hoped from the LORD."

19I remember my affliction and my wandering,
the bitterness and the gall.
20I well remember them,
and my soul is downcast within me.
21Yet this I call to mind
and therefore I have hope:

22Because of the LORD's great love we are not
consumed, Ps 103:11; Hos 11:9
for his compassions never fail. Ps 78:38; Mal 3:6
23They are new every morning;
great is your faithfulness. Zep 3:5
24I say to myself, "The LORD is my portion;
therefore I will wait for him."

25The LORD is good to those whose hope is in
him,
to the one who seeks him; Isa 25:9; 30:18
26it is good to wait quietly Isa 30:15
for the salvation of the LORD. Ps 37:7; 40:1

LIVING  **INSIGHT**

Where do you go to find enough stillness to rediscover that God is God? Where do you turn when your days and nights start running together? As in days of old, Jesus is waiting in that little boat, ready to sail with you to a quieter shore. But getting in requires first some letting go.

(See Lamentations 3:26.)

27It is good for a man to bear the yoke
while he is young.

28Let him sit alone in silence, Jer 15:17
for the LORD has laid it on him.
29Let him bury his face in the dust—
there may yet be hope. Jer 31:17
30Let him offer his cheek to one who would
strike him, Job 16:10; Isa 50:6
and let him be filled with disgrace.

31For men are not cast off
by the Lord forever. Ps 94:14; Isa 54:7
32Though he brings grief, he will show
compassion,
so great is his unfailing love. Ps 78:38; Hos 11:8
33For he does not willingly bring affliction
or grief to the children of men. Eze 33:11

34To crush underfoot
all prisoners in the land,
35to deny a man his rights
before the Most High,
36to deprive a man of justice—
would not the Lord see such things? Jer 22:3

37Who can speak and have it happen
if the Lord has not decreed it? Ps 33:9-11
38Is it not from the mouth of the Most High
that both calamities and good things come?
39Why should any living man complain
when punished for his sins? Jer 30:15; Mic 7:9

40Let us examine our ways and test them,
and let us return to the LORD. Ps 119:59
41Let us lift up our hearts and our hands
to God in heaven, and say: Ps 25:1; 28:2

[a]This chapter is an acrostic poem; the verses of each stanza begin with the successive letters of the Hebrew alphabet, and the verses within each stanza begin with the same letter.

42"We have sinned and rebelled Da 9:5
and you have not forgiven. Jer 5:7-9

43"You have covered yourself with anger and
pursued us;
you have slain without pity. La 2:2,17,21
44You have covered yourself with a cloud Ps 97:2
so that no prayer can get through. Zec 7:13
45You have made us scum and refuse 1Co 4:13
among the nations.

46"All our enemies have opened their mouths
wide against us. La 2:16
47We have suffered terror and pitfalls, Jer 48:43
ruin and destruction." Isa 24:17-18
48Streams of tears flow from my eyes La 1:16
because my people are destroyed. La 2:11

49My eyes will flow unceasingly,
without relief, Jer 14:17
50until the LORD looks down
from heaven and sees. Isa 63:15
51What I see brings grief to my soul
because of all the women of my city.

52Those who were my enemies without cause
hunted me like a bird. Ps 35:7
53They tried to end my life in a pit Jer 37:16
and threw stones at me;
54the waters closed over my head, Ps 69:2; Jnh 2:3-5
and I thought I was about to be cut off.

55I called on your name, O LORD,
from the depths of the pit. Ps 130:1; Jnh 2:2
56You heard my plea: "Do not close your ears
to my cry for relief."
57You came near when I called you, Ps 46:1
and you said, "Do not fear." Isa 41:10

58O Lord, you took up my case; Jer 51:36
you redeemed my life. Ps 34:22; Jer 50:34
59You have seen, O LORD, the wrong done to
me. Jer 18:19-20
Uphold my cause!
60You have seen the depth of their vengeance,
all their plots against me. Jer 11:20; 18:18

61O LORD, you have heard their insults, Ps 89:50
all their plots against me—
62what my enemies whisper and mutter
against me all day long. Eze 36:3
63Look at them! Sitting or standing,
they mock me in their songs.

64Pay them back what they deserve, O LORD,
for what their hands have done. Ps 28:4
65Put a veil over their hearts, Isa 6:10
and may your curse be on them!
66Pursue them in anger and destroy them
from under the heavens of the LORD.

The Voice of the Possessions — Chapter 4

In this chapter the possessions of the city spoke. All those lovely things that seemed so valuable, so worth pursuing and possessing, are now seen as empty, meaningless, futile, worthless. All of the things that promised hope, fulfillment, happiness and contentment were gone, and another painful lesson was learned: *Sin's consequences often bring the very opposite of what we thought would occur.*

4[a] How the gold has lost its luster,
the fine gold become dull!
The sacred gems are scattered
at the head of every street. Eze 7:19

2How the precious sons of Zion, Isa 51:18
once worth their weight in gold,
are now considered as pots of clay,
the work of a potter's hands!

3Even jackals offer their breasts
to nurse their young,
but my people have become heartless
like ostriches in the desert. Job 39:16

4Because of thirst the infant's tongue
sticks to the roof of its mouth; Ps 22:15
the children beg for bread,
but no one gives it to them. La 2:11-12

5Those who once ate delicacies
are destitute in the streets.
Those nurtured in purple Jer 6:2
now lie on ash heaps. Am 6:3-7

6The punishment of my people
is greater than that of Sodom, Ge 19:25
which was overthrown in a moment
without a hand turned to help her.

7Their princes were brighter than snow
and whiter than milk,
their bodies more ruddy than rubies,
their appearance like sapphires.[b]

8But now they are blacker than soot; Job 30:28
they are not recognized in the streets.
Their skin has shriveled on their bones;
it has become as dry as a stick.

9Those killed by the sword are better off
than those who die of famine;
racked with hunger, they waste away
for lack of food from the field. Jer 15:2; 16:4

10With their own hands compassionate women
have cooked their own children, Dt 28:53-57
who became their food
when my people were destroyed.

[a]This chapter is an acrostic poem, the verses of which begin with the successive letters of the Hebrew alphabet.
[b]7 Or *lapis lazuli*

[11]The LORD has given full vent to his wrath;
he has poured out his fierce anger. Zep 2:2; 3:8
He kindled a fire in Zion Jer 17:27
that consumed her foundations. Dt 32:22

[12]The kings of the earth did not believe,
nor did any of the world's people,
that enemies and foes could enter
the gates of Jerusalem. 1Ki 9:9; Jer 21:13

[13]But it happened because of the sins of her prophets
and the iniquities of her priests, Jer 6:13
who shed within her
the blood of the righteous. 2Ki 21:16

[14]Now they grope through the streets
like men who are blind. Isa 59:10
They are so defiled with blood Jer 2:34; 19:4
that no one dares to touch their garments.

[15]"Go away! You are unclean!" men cry to them.
"Away! Away! Don't touch us!"
When they flee and wander about,
people among the nations say,
"They can stay here no longer." Lev 13:46

[16]The LORD himself has scattered them;
he no longer watches over them. Isa 9:14-16
The priests are shown no honor,
the elders no favor. La 5:12

[17]Moreover, our eyes failed,
looking in vain for help; Isa 20:5; La 1:7; Eze 29:16
from our towers we watched
for a nation that could not save us. Jer 37:7

[18]Men stalked us at every step,
so we could not walk in our streets.
Our end was near, our days were numbered,
for our end had come. Eze 7:2-12; Am 8:2

[19]Our pursuers were swifter
than eagles in the sky; Dt 28:49
they chased us over the mountains Isa 5:26-28
and lay in wait for us in the desert. Jer 52:7

[20]The LORD's anointed, our very life breath,
was caught in their traps. Jer 39:5; Eze 12:12-13
We thought that under his shadow
we would live among the nations.

[21]Rejoice and be glad, O Daughter of Edom,
you who live in the land of Uz.
But to you also the cup will be passed; Jer 25:15
you will be drunk and stripped naked.

[22]O Daughter of Zion, your punishment will end;
Isa 40:2; Jer 33:8
he will not prolong your exile.
But, O Daughter of Edom, he will punish your sin
and expose your wickedness. Ps 137:7; Mal 1:4

The Voice of the Captives — Chapter 5

Finally, the people of Jerusalem cried out in bitterness of soul as they looked upon their beloved city, now a heap of rubble. Their eyes were beholding what they never even dreamed could have happened. Their hearts were filled with disgrace. Their bodies were weary and worn. They were completely miserable. Their sin had caught up with them, and they were broken. They had learned one of the most painful lessons known to humanity: *There is no greater misery than the misery of living a life of disobedience.*

5 Remember, O LORD, what has happened to us;
look, and see our disgrace. Ps 44:13-16; 89:50
[2]Our inheritance has been turned over to aliens, Ps 79:1
our homes to foreigners. Zep 1:13
[3]We have become orphans and fatherless,
our mothers like widows. Jer 15:8; 18:21
[4]We must buy the water we drink;
our wood can be had only at a price. Isa 3:1
[5]Those who pursue us are at our heels;
we are weary and find no rest. Jos 1:13; Ne 9:37
[6]We submitted to Egypt and Assyria Hos 9:3
to get enough bread.
[7]Our fathers sinned and are no more,
and we bear their punishment. Jer 14:20; 16:12
[8]Slaves rule over us, Ne 5:15
and there is none to free us from their hands. Zec 11:6
[9]We get our bread at the risk of our lives
because of the sword in the desert.
[10]Our skin is hot as an oven,
feverish from hunger. La 4:8-9
[11]Women have been ravished in Zion, Zec 14:2
and virgins in the towns of Judah.
[12]Princes have been hung up by their hands;
elders are shown no respect. La 4:16
[13]Young men toil at the millstones;
boys stagger under loads of wood.
[14]The elders are gone from the city gate;
the young men have stopped their music.
[15]Joy is gone from our hearts;
our dancing has turned to mourning.
[16]The crown has fallen from our head. Ps 89:39
Woe to us, for we have sinned! Isa 3:11
[17]Because of this our hearts are faint, Isa 1:5
because of these things our eyes grow dim
[18]for Mount Zion, which lies desolate, Mic 3:12
with jackals prowling over it.

[19]You, O LORD, reign forever;
your throne endures from generation to
generation. Ps 45:6; 102:12,24-27
[20]Why do you always forget us? Ps 13:1; 44:24
Why do you forsake us so long?

[21]Restore us to yourself, O LORD, that we may
return; Ps 80:3
renew our days as of old
[22]unless you have utterly rejected us Ps 53:5; 60:1-2
and are angry with us beyond measure.

INTRODUCTION

EZEKIEL

When we open the Bible to the book of Ezekiel and begin reading, we are not into this prophet's writings three minutes before we're encountering the strange, the phenomenal, the wonderful. In his own unpredictable manner, Ezekiel tells his readers about the Lord. He genuinely desires that people understand who God is. How needed that is in our day too! Ezekiel wrote, preached, acted out powerful dramas, warned and prophesied for over two decades. With great enthusiasm and imagination, he vigorously declared God's message to an exiled generation of Jews—discouraged captives who needed a strong leader. Because modern minds often see humans as awesome and God as tiresome, a big dose of Ezekiel is long overdue. May the Lord Almighty emerge and in all His glory eclipse humanity beneath His all-embracing shadow as we hear and heed Ezekiel's message.

WRITER: *Ezekiel*

DATE: *c.571 B.C.*

PURPOSE: *To deliver a heartrending word of divine judgment and a consoling word of hope to Judah*

KEY THEMES: *God's glory; God's sovereignty; God's Spirit*

KEY MESSAGE: *There is hope when you focus on God's glory*

TIME LINE 1300BC 1200 1100 1000 900 800 700 600 500 400

- **Division of the kingdom (930 B.C.)**
- **Ministries of Micah and Isaiah in Judah (c.742-681 B.C.)**
- **Jeremiah's ministry in Judah (c.626-585 B.C.)**
- **Daniel's exile in Babylon (c.605-536 B.C.)**
- **Ezekiel's ministry (c.593-571 B.C.)**
- **Fall of Jerusalem (586 B.C.)**
- **Book of Ezekiel written (c.571 B.C.)**
- **First return of exiles to Jerusalem (538 B.C.)**

Strong Man of God

ABOUT THE PROPHET	JUDGMENT ON JUDAH	JUDGMENT ON THE NATIONS	RESTORATION OF GOD'S PEOPLE
EZEKIEL'S CALL AND COMMISSION God's hand on him God's word in him God's message through him	GOD'S GLORY DEPARTS	ALL NATIONS ANSWER TO GOD	GOD'S GLORY RETURNS
CHAPTERS 1–3	*CHAPTERS 4–24*	*CHAPTERS 25–32*	*CHAPTERS 33–48*

Did you ever want to become better acquainted with the man whose name graces the title of this book? He has, you see, somewhat of a reputation for strangeness, based on the contents of his book. To see if his reputation is deserved, it would benefit us to dig into what he has written. I want you to gather some pieces of information about the prophet Ezekiel before you look at his words and his actions. The opening words of the book (1:1) give insight into Ezekiel's geographical setting: "In the thirtieth year, in the fourth month on the fifth day, while I was among the exiles by the Kebar River . . ."

The Kebar River meandered around like a canal. (If you've ever traveled in south Florida, especially along the coastline, you may have seen the interweaving of many intercoastal canals.) One of the tributaries of the Kebar River (this one happened to run about 60 miles long) was attached to the fertile Euphrates River that flowed through Babylon. It provided the area around the Kebar with rich, fertile soil—and yet all the richness of the land could do nothing for Ezekiel's spirit. He was planted near an irrigation canal that was feeding the heart of the land but doing nothing for his soul. I'm convinced he was a discouraged man, surrounded by discouraged people.

Hold this image in your mind for just a moment and think about Psalm 137. Always remember Psalm 137 when you think of the captives in Babylon, because it was written from their perspective: "By the rivers of Babylon we sat and wept when we remembered Zion" (137:1). There is nothing like being in the midst of divine discipline and then remembering how good God was when you left Him, when you wandered away on your own, when you chose to oppose His will.

Look at how the psalm proceeds: "For there our captors asked us for songs, our tormentors demanded songs of joy; they said, 'Sing us one of the songs of Zion!' How can we sing the songs of the LORD while in a foreign land?" (137:3–4). How tragic! No song to sing! Captives don't sing. People whose freedom has been removed don't sing. It's hard to sing when your face is hugging the ground. It's hard to sing when your heart is broken and bleeding and your spirit is crushed. And certainly when you've turned your eyes from the living God, you've lost your song . . . all melodies within you are squelched.

Now that was the scene, spiritually, in Ezekiel's experience. He faced up to its reality in his first words in verse 1 of chapter 1: "I was among the exiles by the Kebar . . ." What a situation! What a desperate, discouraging scene! He and his compatriots were in captivity, far from their homeland, with no song to sing.

The Heartache of a Young Man

Note that Ezekiel was a thirty-year-old hostage in Babylon as his book begins. His ministry as prophet to the exiles began in his thirtieth year of life (the year was 593 B.C.). So Ezekiel was a man in the early portion of his middle-aged years—and he was in exile. That being the case, we can conclude that throughout Ezekiel's childhood and teenage years, he was living in the land of Judah while it was in the throes of death. He watched kings compromise and waver. He watched a foreign power invade his land. Can you imagine? He heard the news: Nebuchadnezzar had invaded. He watched as Babylon came and saw and conquered.

It is of interest to note that another prophet of God was in Babylon at the same time Ezekiel was there. The prophet Daniel was among the people of Judah carried off to Babylon in the first deportation (in 605 B.C.), while Ezekiel was taken to Babylon in the second wave of exiles in 597 B.C. Daniel and Ezekiel were contemporaries.

You might wonder, as I did, about the difference in their ages. This is what we know of the situation: Daniel was taken captive during the middle of his teenage years. He had been in Babylon 13 years at the time that Ezekiel began his ministry in Babylon in 593 B.C. So Daniel was at that time about 28 years old. Ezekiel recorded that he was 30 years old at the time of his call to ministry—five years after having been taken to Babylon. Consequently, Ezekiel would have been just a couple of years older than Daniel. They may very well have known each other.

Pain With No Tears

We know three specifics about Ezekiel. First, *Ezekiel was a married man who was going to lose his wife in Babylon*. At the time of the events of chapter 24 Ezekiel was about 34 years old. Four years had passed since the beginning of Ezekiel's ministry (chapter 1). Here in chapter 24 we read a tragic piece of information in verses 15–17:

> *The word of the LORD came to me: "Son of man, with one blow I am about to take away from you the delight of your eyes. Yet do not lament or weep or shed any tears. Groan quietly; do not mourn for the dead. Keep your turban fastened and your sandals on your feet; do not cover the lower part of your face or eat the customary food of mourners."*

Think of it! God gave Ezekiel advance warning of his wife's death. The light of his life would die suddenly—and he was to make it very obvious that he was *not* mourning. No loud cries of grief, no wailing, no weeping, no mourning. He was to keep his face uncovered and eat what he usually ate. He was to act as if nothing out of the ordinary had happened. Now this kind of command to someone who is going to experience the death of a loved one might seem almost sadistically cruel—until you realize that God was having Ezekiel model a powerful truth. The people were to see in Ezekiel's behavior a mirror of their own lives. *They* were the ones who had killed (as it were) their relationship with God—and they had not mourned or wept. They had not cared one iota about the death of that relationship. Ezekiel would act out before them the story of their very lives. The shock of it amazed them. They couldn't get over it!

Second, *Ezekiel modeled God's message to the people*. In effect, he announced, "I want you to know that there is a God in the land, and the same God who has led me to respond like this wants you to see that it is the very same way you responded to Him. It happened when the relationship was severed." And so Ezekiel performed several symbolic acts depicting God's judgment and the unfolding of His purposes in history. In chapters 4 and 5 Ezekiel portrayed the siege of Jerusalem; in chapters 8–11 he shared his vision of the corrupted temple; and in chapter 12 he portrayed Jerusalem's exile. One way or another, God was determined that His people would get the picture: He would bring them down, but the day was coming when He would lift them up again and breathe new life into them (chapter 37).

Exiled But Never Alone

Here's a third fact about Ezekiel: *He had the hand of God on his life*. Ezekiel, this thirty-year-old captive in a foreign land, this man whose wife died four years after his ministry began—this Ezekiel had the hand of God on his life: "The word of the LORD came to Ezekiel the priest, the son of Buzi, by the Kebar River in the land of the Babylonians. There the hand of the LORD was upon him" (1:3). It's doubtful that he was the only priest or prophet in the land of Babylon. As we have seen, Daniel was there at the time. And yet, even though there were other faithful servants of God, Ezekiel was a unique instrument in God's hand. There is a process God typically follows as He guides a leader. He puts His hand on a life. He speaks to that life. He then speaks through that life. The divine process follows that pattern.

Seek God's Glory . . . Discover Hope

God's passionate desire was to reveal Himself to those captives through this prophet. You may miss some subtleties in the book of Ezekiel, but please don't miss this point: *God wanted to reveal His person and His glory through His prophet Ezekiel to the exiles.* He wants to do that today through us as we have opportunity each day to reflect the light of His glory to all we meet.

Unless these captives in Babylon saw the glory of their majestic, all-powerful God, they would never regain their hope. The unmistakable message of Ezekiel's life is this: *There is hope when you focus on God's glory.* I believe that is the full message God wanted to speak through Ezekiel

The exiles gathered by the rivers of Babylon had no earthly reason to smile. They had no song to sing. As they looked around there was an absence of anything that would revive their hope . . . but when they observed Ezekiel's dramatic object lessons and heard his message, they were reminded: God is alive. God is at work. His glory is here, in spite of our circumstances. That fact alone gave them reason to go on.

Enduring Truths

There are four truths that shine brightly out of the book of Ezekiel. First, *those who significantly influence others for God have three things in common: God's hand is on them. God's Word is in them. God speaks through them.* Many who read these words have experienced that in your own lives. God's hand is on you. God's Word is in you. God is speaking through you. Do not underestimate the impact your life is having in a world that has neither salt nor light.

Second, *truth gains authenticity when it is modeled, not just declared.* Talk about God's all-sufficient hand in pain! Ezekiel experienced it, and so do we. God puts us through pain, and in doing so He has us model the willingness to bear up under it with grace and dignity and maturity. The truth gains authenticity in the eyes of other people when they see it modeled.

Third, *nothing is impossible with God, not even the restoration of corpses in a valley full of dry bones.* You may have crossed off certain people in your mind (or maybe even yourself). Perhaps you've said, "They're too far gone. God's through with them. There's no way in the world that person could ever come back . . . no way that person will ever be reached." Wrong! Be careful that you don't underestimate the power of the God of the universe. Nothing is impossible with God! If God can put muscle and flesh on dry bones and build a body out of them, surely He can renew someone you might think is all washed up and finished in God's sight.

Fourth, and finally, *there's always reason to hope when we focus on God's glory.* If you are looking for hope, look no further than the intimate presence of the living God. He wants to come close to you—He really does. He wants to shine His glory on you, and He wants you in turn to reflect that glory to all you meet. Concentrate on His glory, and you will discover fresh hope.

About the Prophet **Chapters 1–3**

The first three chapters give an introduction to the prophet and his message. Stuart Briscoe wrote an insightful book about Ezekiel, which he titled _All Things Weird and Wonderful_. Not bad! The book of Ezekiel is wonderful, but to the casual reader it may also seem quite strange, even mysterious. When you read these chapters closely and keep from being distracted by spinning wheels and strange flying creatures, you will notice three things about the prophet Ezekiel. First, the hand of the Lord was on him. Second, the Lord spoke to him and relieved his fear. Third, the Lord promised to speak through him and to reveal His glory through him to the people. Once Ezekiel was called, commissioned and given his marching orders, he was ready to move out into the rank and file of the Jewish exiles with a message from the Lord Himself.

The Living Creatures and the Glory of the LORD

1 In the[a] thirtieth year, in the fourth month
on the fifth day, while I was among the exiles
by the Kebar River, the heavens were opened and
I saw visions of God. Mt 3:16; Ac 7:56; Ex 24:10
2On the fifth of the month—it was the fifth year
of the exile of King Jehoiachin— 3the word of the
LORD came to Ezekiel the priest, the son of Buzi,[b]
by the Kebar River in the land of the Babylonians.[c] There the hand of the LORD was upon him.
4I looked, and I saw a windstorm coming out of
the north—an immense cloud with flashing lightning and surrounded by brilliant light. The center
of the fire looked like glowing metal, 5and in the
fire was what looked like four living creatures. In
appearance their form was that of a man, 6but each
of them had four faces and four wings. 7Their legs
were straight; their feet were like those of a calf and
gleamed like burnished bronze. 8Under their
wings on their four sides they had the hands of a
man. All four of them had faces and wings, 9and
their wings touched one another. Each one went
straight ahead; they did not turn as they moved.
10Their faces looked like this: Each of the four
had the face of a man, and on the right side each
had the face of a lion, and on the left the face of an
ox; each also had the face of an eagle. 11Such were
their faces. Their wings were spread out upward;
each had two wings, one touching the wing of
another creature on either side, and two wings
covering its body. 12Each one went straight ahead.
Wherever the spirit would go, they would go,
without turning as they went. 13The appearance of
the living creatures was like burning coals of fire or
like torches. Fire moved back and forth among the
creatures; it was bright, and lightning flashed out
of it. 14The creatures sped back and forth like
flashes of lightning. Isa 6:2; Rev 4:5,7
15As I looked at the living creatures, I saw a
wheel on the ground beside each creature with its
four faces. 16This was the appearance and structure
of the wheels: They sparkled like chrysolite, and all
four looked alike. Each appeared to be made like
a wheel intersecting a wheel. 17As they moved, they
would go in any one of the four directions the
creatures faced; the wheels did not turn about[d] as
the creatures went. 18Their rims were high and
awesome, and all four rims were full of eyes all
around. Eze 10:12; Rev 4:6
19When the living creatures moved, the wheels
beside them moved; and when the living creatures
rose from the ground, the wheels also rose.
20Wherever the spirit would go, they would go,
and the wheels would rise along with them, because the spirit of the living creatures was in the
wheels. 21When the creatures moved, they also
moved; when the creatures stood still, they also
stood still; and when the creatures rose from the
ground, the wheels rose along with them, because
the spirit of the living creatures was in the wheels.
22Spread out above the heads of the living creatures was what looked like an expanse, sparkling
like ice, and awesome. 23Under the expanse their
wings were stretched out one toward the other,
and each had two wings covering its body. 24When
the creatures moved, I heard the sound of their
wings, like the roar of rushing waters, like the
voice of the Almighty,[e] like the tumult of an
army. When they stood still, they lowered their
wings. Eze 10:5; Rev 1:15
25Then there came a voice from above the expanse over their heads as they stood with lowered
wings. 26Above the expanse over their heads was
what looked like a throne of sapphire,[f] and high
above on the throne was a figure like that of a man.
27I saw that from what appeared to be his waist up
he looked like glowing metal, as if full of fire, and
that from there down he looked like fire; and brilliant light surrounded him. 28Like the appearance
of a rainbow in the clouds on a rainy day, so was
the radiance around him. Rev 4:2; 10:1
This was the appearance of the likeness of the
glory of the LORD. When I saw it, I fell facedown,
and I heard the voice of one speaking. Eze 3:23; 8:4

Ezekiel's Call

2 He said to me, "Son of man, stand up on your
feet and I will speak to you." 2As he spoke,
the Spirit came into me and raised me to my feet,
and I heard him speaking to me. Eze 3:24; Da 8:18
3He said: "Son of man, I am sending you to the
Israelites, to a rebellious nation that has rebelled
against me; they and their fathers have been in
revolt against me to this very day. 4The people to

[a]1 Or ⌞my⌟ [b]3 Or *Ezekiel son of Buzi the priest* [c]3 Or *Chaldeans* [d]17 Or *aside* [e]24 Hebrew *Shaddai*
[f]26 Or *lapis lazuli*

whom I am sending you are obstinate and stubborn. Say to them, 'This is what the Sovereign LORD says.' 5And whether they listen or fail to listen—for they are a rebellious house—they will know that a prophet has been among them. 6And you, son of man, do not be afraid of them or their words. Do not be afraid, though briers and thorns are all around you and you live among scorpions. Do not be afraid of what they say or terrified by them, though they are a rebellious house. 7You must speak my words to them, whether they listen or fail to listen, for they are rebellious. 8But you, son of man, listen to what I say to you. Do not rebel like that rebellious house; open your mouth and eat what I give you." Jer 3:25; Rev 10:9

9Then I looked, and I saw a hand stretched out to me. In it was a scroll, 10which he unrolled before me. On both sides of it were written words of lament and mourning and woe. Eze 8:3; Rev 8:13

3 And he said to me, "Son of man, eat what is before you, eat this scroll; then go and speak to the house of Israel." 2So I opened my mouth, and he gave me the scroll to eat.

3Then he said to me, "Son of man, eat this scroll I am giving you and fill your stomach with it." So I ate it, and it tasted as sweet as honey in my mouth. Ps 19:10; Rev 10:9-10

4He then said to me: "Son of man, go now to the house of Israel and speak my words to them. 5You are not being sent to a people of obscure speech and difficult language, but to the house of Israel— 6not to many peoples of obscure speech and difficult language, whose words you cannot understand. Surely if I had sent you to them, they would have listened to you. 7But the house of Israel is not willing to listen to you because they are not willing to listen to me, for the whole house of Israel is hardened and obstinate. 8But I will make you as unyielding and hardened as they are. 9I will make your forehead like the hardest stone, harder than flint. Do not be afraid of them or terrified by them, though they are a rebellious house."

10And he said to me, "Son of man, listen carefully and take to heart all the words I speak to you. 11Go now to your countrymen in exile and speak to them. Say to them, 'This is what the Sovereign LORD says,' whether they listen or fail to listen."

12Then the Spirit lifted me up, and I heard behind me a loud rumbling sound—May the glory of the LORD be praised in his dwelling place!— 13the sound of the wings of the living creatures brushing against each other and the sound of the wheels beside them, a loud rumbling sound. 14The Spirit then lifted me up and took me away, and I went in bitterness and in the anger of my spirit, with the strong hand of the LORD upon me. 15I came to the exiles who lived at Tel Abib near the Kebar River. And there, where they were living, I sat among them for seven days—overwhelmed.

Warning to Israel

16At the end of seven days the word of the LORD came to me: 17"Son of man, I have made you a watchman for the house of Israel; so hear the word I speak and give them warning from me. 18When I say to a wicked man, 'You will surely die,' and you do not warn him or speak out to dissuade him from his evil ways in order to save his life, that wicked man will die for[a] his sin, and I will hold you accountable for his blood. 19But if you do warn the wicked man and he does not turn from his wickedness or from his evil ways, he will die for his sin; but you will have saved yourself. Isa 52:8

20"Again, when a righteous man turns from his righteousness and does evil, and I put a stumbling block before him, he will die. Since you did not warn him, he will die for his sin. The righteous things he did will not be remembered, and I will hold you accountable for his blood. 21But if you do warn the righteous man not to sin and he does not sin, he will surely live because he took warning, and you will have saved yourself." Eze 18:24; Ac 20:31

22The hand of the LORD was upon me there, and he said to me, "Get up and go out to the plain, and there I will speak to you." 23So I got up and went out to the plain. And the glory of the LORD was standing there, like the glory I had seen by the Kebar River, and I fell facedown. Eze 1:1; 8:4; Ac 9:6

24Then the Spirit came into me and raised me to my feet. He spoke to me and said: "Go, shut yourself inside your house. 25And you, son of man, they will tie with ropes; you will be bound so that you cannot go out among the people. 26I will make your tongue stick to the roof of your mouth so that you will be silent and unable to rebuke them, though they are a rebellious house. 27But when I speak to you, I will open your mouth and you shall say to them, 'This is what the Sovereign LORD says.' Whoever will listen let him listen, and whoever will refuse let him refuse; for they are a rebellious house. Eze 24:27; 33:22

Judgment on Judah **Chapters 4–24**

This section includes 21 chapters of clear, strong warnings of judgment on Judah. When reflecting on chapter 6, Andrew Blackwood noted, "It drips with blood, and its pages reek with the stench of war. Yet this chapter illustrates why an intelligent man, facing sure disaster, can still live and work in hope." God wanted His people to know that He was in charge. One line resounded repeatedly: "You will know that I am the LORD." In the midst of this declaration of judgment, the people could see only devastation and gloom. There was no hope and encouragement in sight. And yet that was precisely where Ezekiel came

[a] *18* Or *in*; also in verses 19 and 20

in. He was called to let the nation know that there was more than discouragement, judgment and heartache. Behind this veil of pain was the glory of God. The Lord was at work, and there was still hope. Ezekiel not only proclaimed this truth; he modeled it in many different and striking ways!

Siege of Jerusalem Symbolized

4 "Now, son of man, take a clay tablet, put it in
front of you and draw the city of Jerusalem
on it. 2Then lay siege to it: Erect siege works
against it, build a ramp up to it, set up camps
against it and put battering rams around it. 3Then
take an iron pan, place it as an iron wall between
you and the city and turn your face toward it. It
will be under siege, and you shall besiege it. This
will be a sign to the house of Israel. Eze 12:3-6
4"Then lie on your left side and put the sin of
the house of Israel upon yourself.[a] You are to
bear their sin for the number of days you lie on
your side. 5I have assigned you the same number
of days as the years of their sin. So for 390 days
you will bear the sin of the house of Israel.
6"After you have finished this, lie down again,
this time on your right side, and bear the sin of the
house of Judah. I have assigned you 40 days, a day
for each year. 7Turn your face toward the siege of
Jerusalem and with bared arm prophesy against
her. 8I will tie you up with ropes so that you cannot
turn from one side to the other until you have
finished the days of your siege. Nu 14:34; Eze 3:25
9"Take wheat and barley, beans and lentils, mil-
let and spelt; put them in a storage jar and use
them to make bread for yourself. You are to eat it
during the 390 days you lie on your side. 10Weigh
out twenty shekels[b] of food to eat each day and
eat it at set times. 11Also measure out a sixth of a
hin[c] of water and drink it at set times. 12Eat the
food as you would a barley cake; bake it in the
sight of the people, using human excrement for
fuel." 13The LORD said, "In this way the people
of Israel will eat defiled food among the nations
where I will drive them." Hos 9:3; Am 7:17
14Then I said, "Not so, Sovereign LORD! I have
never defiled myself. From my youth until now I
have never eaten anything found dead or torn by
wild animals. No unclean meat has ever entered
my mouth." Ex 22:31; Ac 10:14
15"Very well," he said, "I will let you bake your
bread over cow manure instead of human excrement."
16He then said to me: "Son of man, I will cut off
the supply of food in Jerusalem. The people will
eat rationed food in anxiety and drink rationed
water in despair, 17for food and water will be
scarce. They will be appalled at the sight of each
other and will waste away because of[d] their sin.

5 "Now, son of man, take a sharp sword and
use it as a barber's razor to shave your head
and your beard. Then take a set of scales and
divide up the hair. 2When the days of your siege
come to an end, burn a third of the hair with fire
inside the city. Take a third and strike it with the
sword all around the city. And scatter a third to the
wind. For I will pursue them with drawn sword.
3But take a few strands of hair and tuck them away
in the folds of your garment. 4Again, take a few of
these and throw them into the fire and burn them
up. A fire will spread from there to the whole
house of Israel. Lev 26:33
5"This is what the Sovereign LORD says: This is
Jerusalem, which I have set in the center of the
nations, with countries all around her. 6Yet in her
wickedness she has rebelled against my laws and
decrees more than the nations and countries
around her. She has rejected my laws and has not
followed my decrees. Jer 11:10; Zec 7:11
7"Therefore this is what the Sovereign LORD
says: You have been more unruly than the nations
around you and have not followed my decrees or
kept my laws. You have not even[e] conformed to
the standards of the nations around you. 2Ch 33:9
8"Therefore this is what the Sovereign LORD
says: I myself am against you, Jerusalem, and I will
inflict punishment on you in the sight of the nations. 9Because of all your detestable idols, I will do
to you what I have never done before and will
never do again. 10Therefore in your midst fathers
will eat their children, and children will eat their
fathers. I will inflict punishment on you and will
scatter all your survivors to the winds. 11Therefore
as surely as I live, declares the Sovereign LORD,
because you have defiled my sanctuary with all
your vile images and detestable practices, I myself
will withdraw my favor; I will not look on you with
pity or spare you. 12A third of your people will die
of the plague or perish by famine inside you; a
third will fall by the sword outside your walls; and
a third I will scatter to the winds and pursue with
drawn sword. Da 9:12; Zec 2:6
13"Then my anger will cease and my wrath
against them will subside, and I will be avenged.
And when I have spent my wrath upon them, they
will know that I the LORD have spoken in my zeal.
14"I will make you a ruin and a reproach among
the nations around you, in the sight of all who pass
by. 15You will be a reproach and a taunt, a warning
and an object of horror to the nations around you
when I inflict punishment on you in anger and in
wrath and with stinging rebuke. I the LORD have
spoken. 16When I shoot at you with my deadly and
destructive arrows of famine, I will shoot to destroy you. I will bring more and more famine

[a]4 Or *your side* [b]10 That is, about 8 ounces (about 0.2 kilogram) [c]11 That is, about 2/3 quart (about 0.6 liter)
[d]17 Or *away in* [e]7 Most Hebrew manuscripts; some Hebrew manuscripts and Syriac *You have*

upon you and cut off your supply of food. 17I will send famine and wild beasts against you, and they will leave you childless. Plague and bloodshed will sweep through you, and I will bring the sword against you. I the LORD have spoken." Ne 2:17

A Prophecy Against the Mountains of Israel

6 The word of the LORD came to me: 2"Son of man, set your face against the mountains of Israel; prophesy against them 3and say: 'O mountains of Israel, hear the word of the Sovereign LORD. This is what the Sovereign LORD says to the mountains and hills, to the ravines and valleys: I am about to bring a sword against you, and I will destroy your high places. 4Your altars will be demolished and your incense altars will be smashed; and I will slay your people in front of your idols. 5I will lay the dead bodies of the Israelites in front of their idols, and I will scatter your bones around your altars. 6Wherever you live, the towns will be laid waste and the high places demolished, so that your altars will be laid waste and devastated, your idols smashed and ruined, your incense altars broken down, and what you have made wiped out. 7Your people will fall slain among you, and you will know that I am the LORD.

LIVING  **INSIGHT**

What are our idols today? Fortune, fame, power, pleasure? Can we, will we, keep ourselves from idols, as John reminds us to do (1 John 5:21)? Quiet moments with the Lord are so valuable for us. To clear our focus. To correct our vision. To kindle our praise. To redirect our priorities. To shift our attention from this planet to eternal things.

(See Ezekiel 6:1–7.)

8" 'But I will spare some, for some of you will escape the sword when you are scattered among the lands and nations. 9Then in the nations where they have been carried captive, those who escape will remember me—how I have been grieved by their adulterous hearts, which have turned away from me, and by their eyes, which have lusted after their idols. They will loathe themselves for the evil they have done and for all their detestable practices. 10And they will know that I am the LORD; I did not threaten in vain to bring this calamity on them. Isa 7:13; Jer 44:28; Eze 14:22

11" 'This is what the Sovereign LORD says: Strike your hands together and stamp your feet and cry out "Alas!" because of all the wicked and detestable practices of the house of Israel, for they will fall by the sword, famine and plague. 12He that is far away will die of the plague, and he that is near will fall by the sword, and he that survives and is spared will die of famine. So will I spend my wrath upon them. 13And they will know that I am the LORD, when their people lie slain among their idols around their altars, on every high hill and on all the mountaintops, under every spreading tree and every leafy oak—places where they offered fragrant incense to all their idols. 14And I will stretch out my hand against them and make the land a desolate waste from the desert to Diblah[a]—wherever they live. Then they will know that I am the LORD.' " Eze 21:14,17; Jer 2:20; Hos 4:13

The End Has Come

7 The word of the LORD came to me: 2"Son of man, this is what the Sovereign LORD says to the land of Israel: The end! The end has come upon the four corners of the land. 3The end is now upon you and I will unleash my anger against you. I will judge you according to your conduct and repay you for all your detestable practices. 4I will not look on you with pity or spare you; I will surely repay you for your conduct and the detestable practices among you. Then you will know that I am the LORD. Eze 5:11; Am 8:2,10

5"This is what the Sovereign LORD says: Disaster! An unheard-of[b] disaster is coming. 6The end has come! The end has come! It has roused itself against you. It has come! 7Doom has come upon you—you who dwell in the land. The time has come, the day is near; there is panic, not joy, upon the mountains. 8I am about to pour out my wrath on you and spend my anger against you; I will judge you according to your conduct and repay you for all your detestable practices. 9I will not look on you with pity or spare you; I will repay you in accordance with your conduct and the detestable practices among you. Then you will know that it is I the LORD who strikes the blow.

10"The day is here! It has come! Doom has burst forth, the rod has budded, arrogance has blossomed! 11Violence has grown into[c] a rod to punish wickedness; none of the people will be left, none of that crowd—no wealth, nothing of value. 12The time has come, the day has arrived. Let not the buyer rejoice nor the seller grieve, for wrath is upon the whole crowd. 13The seller will not recover the land he has sold as long as both of them live, for the vision concerning the whole crowd will not be reversed. Because of their sins, not one of them will preserve his life. 14Though they blow the trumpet and get everything ready, no one will go

[a] 14 Most Hebrew manuscripts; a few Hebrew manuscripts *Riblah* [b] 5 Most Hebrew manuscripts; some Hebrew manuscripts and Syriac *Disaster after* [c] 11 Or *The violent one has become*

into battle, for my wrath is upon the whole crowd.
15“Outside is the sword, inside are plague and
famine; those in the country will die by the sword,
and those in the city will be devoured by famine
and plague. 16All who survive and escape will be in
the mountains, moaning like doves of the valleys,
each because of his sins. 17Every hand will go limp,
and every knee will become as weak as water.
18They will put on sackcloth and be clothed with
terror. Their faces will be covered with shame and
their heads will be shaved. 19They will throw their
silver into the streets, and their gold will be an
unclean thing. Their silver and gold will not be
able to save them in the day of the LORD’s wrath.
They will not satisfy their hunger or fill their stomachs with it, for it has made them stumble into sin.
20They were proud of their beautiful jewelry and
used it to make their detestable idols and vile images. Therefore I will turn these into an unclean
thing for them. 21I will hand it all over as plunder
to foreigners and as loot to the wicked of the earth,
and they will defile it. 22I will turn my face away
from them, and they will desecrate my treasured
place; robbers will enter it and desecrate it.
23“Prepare chains, because the land is full of
bloodshed and the city is full of violence. 24I will
bring the most wicked of the nations to take possession of their houses; I will put an end to the
pride of the mighty, and their sanctuaries will be
desecrated. 25When terror comes, they will seek
peace, but there will be none. 26Calamity upon
calamity will come, and rumor upon rumor. They
will try to get a vision from the prophet; the teaching of the law by the priest will be lost, as will the
counsel of the elders. 27The king will mourn, the
prince will be clothed with despair, and the hands
of the people of the land will tremble. I will deal
with them according to their conduct, and by their
own standards I will judge them. Then they will
know that I am the LORD.” Eze 24:21; 26:16

Idolatry in the Temple

8 In the sixth year, in the sixth month on the
fifth day, while I was sitting in my house and
the elders of Judah were sitting before me, the
hand of the Sovereign LORD came upon me there.
2I looked, and I saw a figure like that of a man.[a]
From what appeared to be his waist down he was
like fire, and from there up his appearance was as
bright as glowing metal. 3He stretched out what
looked like a hand and took me by the hair of my
head. The Spirit lifted me up between earth and
heaven and in visions of God he took me to Jerusalem, to the entrance to the north gate of the
inner court, where the idol that provokes to jealousy stood. 4And there before me was the glory of
the God of Israel, as in the vision I had seen in the
plain. Eze 1:28; 3:22
5Then he said to me, “Son of man, look toward
the north.” So I looked, and in the entrance north
of the gate of the altar I saw this idol of jealousy.
6And he said to me, “Son of man, do you see
what they are doing—the utterly detestable things
the house of Israel is doing here, things that will
drive me far from my sanctuary? But you will see
things that are even more detestable.” Eze 5:11
7Then he brought me to the entrance to the
court. I looked, and I saw a hole in the wall. 8He
said to me, “Son of man, now dig into the wall.”
So I dug into the wall and saw a doorway there.
9And he said to me, “Go in and see the wicked
and detestable things they are doing here.” 10So I
went in and looked, and I saw portrayed all over
the walls all kinds of crawling things and detestable
animals and all the idols of the house of Israel. 11In
front of them stood seventy elders of the house of
Israel, and Jaazaniah son of Shaphan was standing
among them. Each had a censer in his hand, and
a fragrant cloud of incense was rising. Ex 3:16; 20:4
12He said to me, “Son of man, have you seen
what the elders of the house of Israel are doing in
the darkness, each at the shrine of his own idol?
They say, ‘The LORD does not see us; the LORD has
forsaken the land.’ ” 13Again, he said, “You will see
them doing things that are even more detestable.”
14Then he brought me to the entrance to the
north gate of the house of the LORD, and I saw
women sitting there, mourning for Tammuz. 15He
said to me, “Do you see this, son of man? You will
see things that are even more detestable than this.”
16He then brought me into the inner court of
the house of the LORD, and there at the entrance to
the temple, between the portico and the altar, were
about twenty-five men. With their backs toward
the temple of the LORD and their faces toward the
east, they were bowing down to the sun in the east.
17He said to me, “Have you seen this, son of
man? Is it a trivial matter for the house of Judah to
do the detestable things they are doing here? Must
they also fill the land with violence and continually
provoke me to anger? Look at them putting the
branch to their nose! 18Therefore I will deal with
them in anger; I will not look on them with pity or
spare them. Although they shout in my ears, I will
not listen to them.” Isa 1:15; Jer 11:11; Mic 3:4

Idolaters Killed

9 Then I heard him call out in a loud voice,
“Bring the guards of the city here, each with
a weapon in his hand.” 2And I saw six men coming
from the direction of the upper gate, which faces
north, each with a deadly weapon in his hand.
With them was a man clothed in linen who had a

[a]2 Or *saw a fiery figure*

writing kit at his side. They came in and stood beside the bronze altar. Lev 16:4; Eze 10:2; Rev 15:6

3Now the glory of the God of Israel went up from above the cherubim, where it had been, and moved to the threshold of the temple. Then the LORD called to the man clothed in linen who had the writing kit at his side 4and said to him, "Go throughout the city of Jerusalem and put a mark on the foreheads of those who grieve and lament over all the detestable things that are done in it."

5As I listened, he said to the others, "Follow him through the city and kill, without showing pity or compassion. 6Slaughter old men, young men and maidens, women and children, but do not touch anyone who has the mark. Begin at my sanctuary." So they began with the elders who were in front of the temple. 2Ch 36:17; 1Pe 4:17

7Then he said to them, "Defile the temple and fill the courts with the slain. Go!" So they went out and began killing throughout the city. 8While they were killing and I was left alone, I fell facedown, crying out, "Ah, Sovereign LORD! Are you going to destroy the entire remnant of Israel in this outpouring of your wrath on Jerusalem?" Eze 11:13

9He answered me, "The sin of the house of Israel and Judah is exceedingly great; the land is full of bloodshed and the city is full of injustice. They say, 'The LORD has forsaken the land; the LORD does not see.' 10So I will not look on them with pity or spare them, but I will bring down on their own heads what they have done." Eze 8:18

11Then the man in linen with the writing kit at his side brought back word, saying, "I have done as you commanded."

The Glory Departs From the Temple

10 I looked, and I saw the likeness of a throne of sapphire[a] above the expanse that was over the heads of the cherubim. 2The LORD said to the man clothed in linen, "Go in among the wheels beneath the cherubim. Fill your hands with burning coals from among the cherubim and scatter them over the city." And as I watched, he went in.

3Now the cherubim were standing on the south side of the temple when the man went in, and a cloud filled the inner court. 4Then the glory of the LORD rose from above the cherubim and moved to the threshold of the temple. The cloud filled the temple, and the court was full of the radiance of the glory of the LORD. 5The sound of the wings of the cherubim could be heard as far away as the outer court, like the voice of God Almighty[b] when he speaks. Eze 1:24,28; 9:3

6When the LORD commanded the man in linen, "Take fire from among the wheels, from among the cherubim," the man went in and stood beside a wheel. 7Then one of the cherubim reached out his hand to the fire that was among them. He took up some of it and put it into the hands of the man in linen, who took it and went out. 8(Under the wings of the cherubim could be seen what looked like the hands of a man.) Eze 1:8

9I looked, and I saw beside the cherubim four wheels, one beside each of the cherubim; the wheels sparkled like chrysolite. 10As for their appearance, the four of them looked alike; each was like a wheel intersecting a wheel. 11As they moved, they would go in any one of the four directions the cherubim faced; the wheels did not turn about[c] as the cherubim went. The cherubim went in whatever direction the head faced, without turning as they went. 12Their entire bodies, including their backs, their hands and their wings, were completely full of eyes, as were their four wheels. 13I heard the wheels being called "the whirling wheels." 14Each of the cherubim had four faces: One face was that of a cherub, the second the face of a man, the third the face of a lion, and the fourth the face of an eagle. Eze 1:10; Rev 4:7

15Then the cherubim rose upward. These were the living creatures I had seen by the Kebar River. 16When the cherubim moved, the wheels beside them moved; and when the cherubim spread their wings to rise from the ground, the wheels did not leave their side. 17When the cherubim stood still, they also stood still; and when the cherubim rose, they rose with them, because the spirit of the living creatures was in them. Eze 1:20-21

18Then the glory of the LORD departed from over the threshold of the temple and stopped above the cherubim. 19While I watched, the cherubim spread their wings and rose from the ground, and as they went, the wheels went with them. They stopped at the entrance to the east gate of the LORD's house, and the glory of the God of Israel was above them. Ps 18:10; Eze 11:1,22

20These were the living creatures I had seen beneath the God of Israel by the Kebar River, and I realized that they were cherubim. 21Each had four faces and four wings, and under their wings was what looked like the hands of a man. 22Their faces had the same appearance as those I had seen by the Kebar River. Each one went straight ahead.

Judgment on Israel's Leaders

11 Then the Spirit lifted me up and brought me to the gate of the house of the LORD that faces east. There at the entrance to the gate were twenty-five men, and I saw among them Jaazaniah son of Azzur and Pelatiah son of Benaiah, leaders of the people. 2The LORD said to me, "Son of man, these are the men who are plotting evil and giving wicked advice in this city. 3They say, 'Will it not soon be time to build houses?[d] This city is a

[a] 1 Or *lapis lazuli* [b] 5 Hebrew *El-Shaddai* [c] 11 Or *aside* [d] 3 Or *This is not the time to build houses.*

cooking pot, and we are the meat.' 4Therefore prophesy against them; prophesy, son of man."

5Then the Spirit of the LORD came upon me, and he told me to say: "This is what the LORD says: That is what you are saying, O house of Israel, but I know what is going through your mind. 6You have killed many people in this city and filled its streets with the dead. Jer 17:10; Eze 7:23

7"Therefore this is what the Sovereign LORD says: The bodies you have thrown there are the meat and this city is the pot, but I will drive you out of it. 8You fear the sword, and the sword is what I will bring against you, declares the Sovereign LORD. 9I will drive you out of the city and hand you over to foreigners and inflict punishment on you. 10You will fall by the sword, and I will execute judgment on you at the borders of Israel. Then you will know that I am the LORD. 11This city will not be a pot for you, nor will you be the meat in it; I will execute judgment on you at the borders of Israel. 12And you will know that I am the LORD, for you have not followed my decrees or kept my laws but have conformed to the standards of the nations around you." Lev 18:4

13Now as I was prophesying, Pelatiah son of Benaiah died. Then I fell facedown and cried out in a loud voice, "Ah, Sovereign LORD! Will you completely destroy the remnant of Israel?" Eze 9:8

14The word of the LORD came to me: 15"Son of man, your brothers—your brothers who are your blood relatives[a] and the whole house of Israel—are those of whom the people of Jerusalem have said, 'They are[b] far away from the LORD; this land was given to us as our possession.' Eze 33:24

Promised Return of Israel

16"Therefore say: 'This is what the Sovereign LORD says: Although I sent them far away among the nations and scattered them among the countries, yet for a little while I have been a sanctuary for them in the countries where they have gone.'

17"Therefore say: 'This is what the Sovereign LORD says: I will gather you from the nations and bring you back from the countries where you have been scattered, and I will give you back the land of Israel again.' Jer 24:5-6; Eze 28:25

18"They will return to it and remove all its vile images and detestable idols. 19I will give them an undivided heart and put a new spirit in them; I will remove from them their heart of stone and give them a heart of flesh. 20Then they will follow my decrees and be careful to keep my laws. They will be my people, and I will be their God. 21But as for those whose hearts are devoted to their vile images and detestable idols, I will bring down on their own heads what they have done, declares the Sovereign LORD." Jer 32:39; Eze 18:31; 36:26

22Then the cherubim, with the wheels beside them, spread their wings, and the glory of the God of Israel was above them. 23The glory of the LORD went up from within the city and stopped above the mountain east of it. 24The Spirit lifted me up and brought me to the exiles in Babylonia[c] in the vision given by the Spirit of God. Zec 14:4; 2Co 12:2-4

Then the vision I had seen went up from me, 25and I told the exiles everything the LORD had shown me. Eze 3:4,11

LIVING 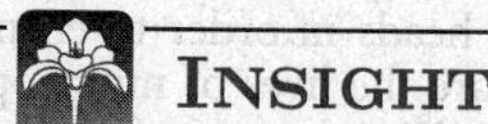 **INSIGHT**

A cold heart can be warmed only by the fire of the living God.

(See Ezekiel 11:19.)

The Exile Symbolized

12 The word of the LORD came to me: 2"Son of man, you are living among a rebellious people. They have eyes to see but do not see and ears to hear but do not hear, for they are a rebellious people.

3"Therefore, son of man, pack your belongings for exile and in the daytime, as they watch, set out and go from where you are to another place. Perhaps they will understand, though they are a rebellious house. 4During the daytime, while they watch, bring out your belongings packed for exile. Then in the evening, while they are watching, go out like those who go into exile. 5While they watch, dig through the wall and take your belongings out through it. 6Put them on your shoulder as they are watching and carry them out at dusk. Cover your face so that you cannot see the land, for I have made you a sign to the house of Israel."

7So I did as I was commanded. During the day I brought out my things packed for exile. Then in the evening I dug through the wall with my hands. I took my belongings out at dusk, carrying them on my shoulders while they watched. Eze 24:18

8In the morning the word of the LORD came to me: 9"Son of man, did not that rebellious house of Israel ask you, 'What are you doing?' Eze 17:12

10"Say to them, 'This is what the Sovereign LORD says: This oracle concerns the prince in Jerusalem and the whole house of Israel who are there.' 11Say to them, 'I am a sign to you.' Zec 3:8

"As I have done, so it will be done to them. They will go into exile as captives. Jer 15:2; 52:15

12"The prince among them will put his things

[a] 15 Or *are in exile with you* (see Septuagint and Syriac)
[b] 15 Or *those to whom the people of Jerusalem have said, 'Stay*
[c] 24 Or *Chaldea*

on his shoulder at dusk and leave, and a hole will be dug in the wall for him to go through. He will cover his face so that he cannot see the land. 13I will spread my net for him, and he will be caught in my snare; I will bring him to Babylonia, the land of the Chaldeans, but he will not see it, and there he will die. 14I will scatter to the winds all those around him—his staff and all his troops—and I will pursue them with drawn sword. 2Ki 25:5

15"They will know that I am the LORD, when I disperse them among the nations and scatter them through the countries. 16But I will spare a few of them from the sword, famine and plague, so that in the nations where they go they may acknowledge all their detestable practices. Then they will know that I am the LORD." Jer 22:8-9; Eze 6:8-10; 14:22

17The word of the LORD came to me: 18"Son of man, tremble as you eat your food, and shudder in fear as you drink your water. 19Say to the people of the land: 'This is what the Sovereign LORD says about those living in Jerusalem and in the land of Israel: They will eat their food in anxiety and drink their water in despair, for their land will be stripped of everything in it because of the violence of all who live there. 20The inhabited towns will be laid waste and the land will be desolate. Then you will know that I am the LORD.'" Isa 7:23-24; Jer 4:7

21The word of the LORD came to me: 22"Son of man, what is this proverb you have in the land of Israel: 'The days go by and every vision comes to nothing'? 23Say to them, 'This is what the Sovereign LORD says: I am going to put an end to this proverb, and they will no longer quote it in Israel.' Say to them, 'The days are near when every vision will be fulfilled. 24For there will be no more false visions or flattering divinations among the people of Israel. 25But I the LORD will speak what I will, and it shall be fulfilled without delay. For in your days, you rebellious house, I will fulfill whatever I say, declares the Sovereign LORD.'" Eze 13:23

26The word of the LORD came to me: 27"Son of man, the house of Israel is saying, 'The vision he sees is for many years from now, and he prophesies about the distant future.' Da 10:14

28"Therefore say to them, 'This is what the Sovereign LORD says: None of my words will be delayed any longer; whatever I say will be fulfilled, declares the Sovereign LORD.'"

False Prophets Condemned

13 The word of the LORD came to me: 2"Son of man, prophesy against the prophets of Israel who are now prophesying. Say to those who prophesy out of their own imagination: 'Hear the word of the LORD! 3This is what the Sovereign LORD says: Woe to the foolish[a] prophets who follow their own spirit and have seen nothing! 4Your prophets, O Israel, are like jackals among ruins. 5You have not gone up to the breaks in the wall to repair it for the house of Israel so that it will stand firm in the battle on the day of the LORD. 6Their visions are false and their divinations a lie. They say, "The LORD declares," when the LORD has not sent them; yet they expect their words to be fulfilled. 7Have you not seen false visions and uttered lying divinations when you say, "The LORD declares," though I have not spoken? Eze 22:28,30

8"'Therefore this is what the Sovereign LORD says: Because of your false words and lying visions, I am against you, declares the Sovereign LORD. 9My hand will be against the prophets who see false visions and utter lying divinations. They will not belong to the council of my people or be listed in the records of the house of Israel, nor will they enter the land of Israel. Then you will know that I am the Sovereign LORD. Jer 17:13; Eze 20:38

10"'Because they lead my people astray, saying, "Peace," when there is no peace, and because, when a flimsy wall is built, they cover it with whitewash, 11therefore tell those who cover it with whitewash that it is going to fall. Rain will come in torrents, and I will send hailstones hurtling down, and violent winds will burst forth. 12When the wall collapses, will people not ask you, "Where is the whitewash you covered it with?" Eze 22:28; 38:22

13"'Therefore this is what the Sovereign LORD says: In my wrath I will unleash a violent wind, and in my anger hailstones and torrents of rain will fall with destructive fury. 14I will tear down the wall you have covered with whitewash and will level it to the ground so that its foundation will be laid bare. When it[b] falls, you will be destroyed in it; and you will know that I am the LORD. 15So I will spend my wrath against the wall and against those who covered it with whitewash. I will say to you, "The wall is gone and so are those who whitewashed it, 16those prophets of Israel who prophesied to Jerusalem and saw visions of peace for her when there was no peace, declares the Sovereign LORD."' Isa 57:21; Jer 6:14

17"Now, son of man, set your face against the daughters of your people who prophesy out of their own imagination. Prophesy against them 18and say, 'This is what the Sovereign LORD says: Woe to the women who sew magic charms on all their wrists and make veils of various lengths for their heads in order to ensnare people. Will you ensnare the lives of my people but preserve your own? 19You have profaned me among my people for a few handfuls of barley and scraps of bread. By lying to my people, who listen to lies, you have killed those who should not have died and have spared those who should not live. Pr 28:21; Rev 2:20

20"'Therefore this is what the Sovereign LORD

[a] 3 Or *wicked* [b] 14 Or *the city*

says: I am against your magic charms with which you ensnare people like birds and I will tear them from your arms; I will set free the people that you ensnare like birds. 21I will tear off your veils and save my people from your hands, and they will no longer fall prey to your power. Then you will know that I am the LORD. 22Because you disheartened the righteous with your lies, when I had brought them no grief, and because you encouraged the wicked not to turn from their evil ways and so save their lives, 23therefore you will no longer see false visions or practice divination. I will save my people from your hands. And then you will know that I am the LORD.'" Eze 12:24; Mic 3:6

Idolaters Condemned

14 Some of the elders of Israel came to me and sat down in front of me. 2Then the word of the LORD came to me: 3"Son of man, these men have set up idols in their hearts and put wicked stumbling blocks before their faces. Should I let them inquire of me at all? 4Therefore speak to them and tell them, 'This is what the Sovereign LORD says: When any Israelite sets up idols in his heart and puts a wicked stumbling block before his face and then goes to a prophet, I the LORD will answer him myself in keeping with his great idolatry. 5I will do this to recapture the hearts of the people of Israel, who have all deserted me for their idols.' Eze 7:19; Zec 11:8

6"Therefore say to the house of Israel, 'This is what the Sovereign LORD says: Repent! Turn from your idols and renounce all your detestable practices! Isa 2:20; 30:22

7" 'When any Israelite or any alien living in Israel separates himself from me and sets up idols in his heart and puts a wicked stumbling block before his face and then goes to a prophet to inquire of me, I the LORD will answer him myself. 8I will set my face against that man and make him an example and a byword. I will cut him off from my people. Then you will know that I am the LORD.

9" 'And if the prophet is enticed to utter a prophecy, I the LORD have enticed that prophet, and I will stretch out my hand against him and destroy him from among my people Israel. 10They will bear their guilt—the prophet will be as guilty as the one who consults him. 11Then the people of Israel will no longer stray from me, nor will they defile themselves anymore with all their sins. They will be my people, and I will be their God, declares the Sovereign LORD.' " Eze 11:19-20; 48:11

Judgment Inescapable

12The word of the LORD came to me: 13"Son of man, if a country sins against me by being unfaithful and I stretch out my hand against it to cut off its food supply and send famine upon it and kill its men and their animals, 14even if these three men—Noah, Daniel[a] and Job—were in it, they could save only themselves by their righteousness, declares the Sovereign LORD. Jer 15:1; Eze 18:20

15"Or if I send wild beasts through that country and they leave it childless and it becomes desolate so that no one can pass through it because of the beasts, 16as surely as I live, declares the Sovereign LORD, even if these three men were in it, they could not save their own sons or daughters. They alone would be saved, but the land would be desolate.

17"Or if I bring a sword against that country and say, 'Let the sword pass throughout the land,' and I kill its men and their animals, 18as surely as I live, declares the Sovereign LORD, even if these three men were in it, they could not save their own sons or daughters. They alone would be saved. Eze 5:12

19"Or if I send a plague into that land and pour out my wrath upon it through bloodshed, killing its men and their animals, 20as surely as I live, declares the Sovereign LORD, even if Noah, Daniel and Job were in it, they could save neither son nor daughter. They would save only themselves by their righteousness. ver 14; Eze 38:22

21"For this is what the Sovereign LORD says: How much worse will it be when I send against Jerusalem my four dreadful judgments—sword and famine and wild beasts and plague—to kill its men and their animals! 22Yet there will be some survivors—sons and daughters who will be brought out of it. They will come to you, and when you see their conduct and their actions, you will be consoled regarding the disaster I have brought upon Jerusalem—every disaster I have brought upon it. 23You will be consoled when you see their conduct and their actions, for you will know that I have done nothing in it without cause, declares the Sovereign LORD." Jer 22:8-9

Jerusalem, A Useless Vine

15 The word of the LORD came to me: 2"Son of man, how is the wood of a vine better than that of a branch on any of the trees in the forest? 3Is wood ever taken from it to make anything useful? Do they make pegs from it to hang things on? 4And after it is thrown on the fire as fuel and the fire burns both ends and chars the middle, is it then useful for anything? 5If it was not useful for anything when it was whole, how much less can it be made into something useful when the fire has burned it and it is charred? Jn 15:6; Hos 10:1

6"Therefore this is what the Sovereign LORD says: As I have given the wood of the vine among the trees of the forest as fuel for the fire, so will I treat the people living in Jerusalem. 7I will set my face against them. Although they have come out of

[a] 14 Or *Danel*; the Hebrew spelling may suggest a person other than the prophet Daniel; also in verse 20.

the fire, the fire will yet consume them. And when I set my face against them, you will know that I am the LORD. [8]I will make the land desolate because they have been unfaithful, declares the Sovereign LORD." Isa 24:18; Am 9:1-4

An Allegory of Unfaithful Jerusalem

16 The word of the LORD came to me: [2]"Son of man, confront Jerusalem with her detestable practices [3]and say, 'This is what the Sovereign LORD says to Jerusalem: Your ancestry and birth were in the land of the Canaanites; your father was an Amorite and your mother a Hittite. [4]On the day you were born your cord was not cut, nor were you washed with water to make you clean, nor were you rubbed with salt or wrapped in cloths. [5]No one looked on you with pity or had compassion enough to do any of these things for you. Rather, you were thrown out into the open field, for on the day you were born you were despised. Eze 20:4; 22:2; Hos 2:3

[6]" 'Then I passed by and saw you kicking about in your blood, and as you lay there in your blood I said to you, "Live!"[a] [7]I made you grow like a plant of the field. You grew up and developed and became the most beautiful of jewels.[b] Your breasts were formed and your hair grew, you who were naked and bare. Ex 19:4; Dt 1:10

[8]" 'Later I passed by, and when I looked at you and saw that you were old enough for love, I spread the corner of my garment over you and covered your nakedness. I gave you my solemn oath and entered into a covenant with you, declares the Sovereign LORD, and you became mine.

[9]" 'I bathed[c] you with water and washed the blood from you and put ointments on you. [10]I clothed you with an embroidered dress and put leather sandals on you. I dressed you in fine linen and covered you with costly garments. [11]I adorned you with jewelry: I put bracelets on your arms and a necklace around your neck, [12]and I put a ring on your nose, earrings on your ears and a beautiful crown on your head. [13]So you were adorned with gold and silver; your clothes were of fine linen and costly fabric and embroidered cloth. Your food was fine flour, honey and olive oil. You became very beautiful and rose to be a queen. [14]And your fame spread among the nations on account of your beauty, because the splendor I had given you made your beauty perfect, declares the Sovereign LORD. 1Ki 10:24; La 2:15

[15]" 'But you trusted in your beauty and used your fame to become a prostitute. You lavished your favors on anyone who passed by and your beauty became his.[d] [16]You took some of your garments to make gaudy high places, where you carried on your prostitution. Such things should not happen, nor should they ever occur. [17]You also took the fine jewelry I gave you, the jewelry made of my gold and silver, and you made for yourself male idols and engaged in prostitution with them. [18]And you took your embroidered clothes to put on them, and you offered my oil and incense before them. [19]Also the food I provided for you—the fine flour, olive oil and honey I gave you to eat—you offered as fragrant incense before them. That is what happened, declares the Sovereign LORD.

[20]" 'And you took your sons and daughters whom you bore to me and sacrificed them as food to the idols. Was your prostitution not enough? [21]You slaughtered my children and sacrificed them[e] to the idols. [22]In all your detestable practices and your prostitution you did not remember the days of your youth, when you were naked and bare, kicking about in your blood. Ps 106:37-38

[23]" 'Woe! Woe to you, declares the Sovereign LORD. In addition to all your other wickedness, [24]you built a mound for yourself and made a lofty shrine in every public square. [25]At the head of every street you built your lofty shrines and degraded your beauty, offering your body with increasing promiscuity to anyone who passed by. [26]You engaged in prostitution with the Egyptians, your lustful neighbors, and provoked me to anger with your increasing promiscuity. [27]So I stretched out my hand against you and reduced your territory; I gave you over to the greed of your enemies, the daughters of the Philistines, who were shocked by your lewd conduct. [28]You engaged in prostitution with the Assyrians too, because you were insatiable; and even after that, you still were not satisfied. [29]Then you increased your promiscuity to include Babylonia,[f] a land of merchants, but even with this you were not satisfied. Isa 57:7

[30]" 'How weak-willed you are, declares the Sovereign LORD, when you do all these things, acting like a brazen prostitute! [31]When you built your mounds at the head of every street and made your lofty shrines in every public square, you were unlike a prostitute, because you scorned payment.

[32]" 'You adulterous wife! You prefer strangers to your own husband! [33]Every prostitute receives a fee, but you give gifts to all your lovers, bribing them to come to you from everywhere for your illicit favors. [34]So in your prostitution you are the opposite of others; no one runs after you for your favors. You are the very opposite, for you give payment and none is given to you. Hos 8:9-10

[35]" 'Therefore, you prostitute, hear the word of the LORD! [36]This is what the Sovereign LORD says:

[a]6 A few Hebrew manuscripts, Septuagint and Syriac; most Hebrew manuscripts *"Live!" And as you lay there in your blood I said to you, "Live!"* [b]7 Or *became mature* [c]9 Or *I had bathed* [d]15 Most Hebrew manuscripts; one Hebrew manuscript (see some Septuagint manuscripts) *by. Such a thing should not happen* [e]21 Or *and made them pass through* ⌊*the fire*⌋ [f]29 Or *Chaldea*

Because you poured out your wealth[a] and exposed your nakedness in your promiscuity with
your lovers, and because of all your detestable
idols, and because you gave them your children's
blood, 37therefore I am going to gather all your
lovers, with whom you found pleasure, those you
loved as well as those you hated. I will gather them
against you from all around and will strip you in
front of them, and they will see all your nakedness.
38I will sentence you to the punishment of women
who commit adultery and who shed blood; I will
bring upon you the blood vengeance of my wrath
and jealous anger. 39Then I will hand you over to
your lovers, and they will tear down your mounds
and destroy your lofty shrines. They will strip you
of your clothes and take your fine jewelry and
leave you naked and bare. 40They will bring a mob
against you, who will stone you and hack you to
pieces with their swords. 41They will burn down
your houses and inflict punishment on you in the
sight of many women. I will put a stop to your
prostitution, and you will no longer pay your lovers. 42Then my wrath against you will subside and
my jealous anger will turn away from you; I will be
calm and no longer angry. Eze 5:13; 39:29

43"'Because you did not remember the days of
your youth but enraged me with all these things, I
will surely bring down on your head what you
have done, declares the Sovereign LORD. Did you
not add lewdness to all your other detestable practices? Ps 78:42; Eze 11:21; 22:31

44"'Everyone who quotes proverbs will quote
this proverb about you: "Like mother, like daughter." 45You are a true daughter of your mother,
who despised her husband and her children; and
you are a true sister of your sisters, who despised
their husbands and their children. Your mother
was a Hittite and your father an Amorite. 46Your
older sister was Samaria, who lived to the north of
you with her daughters; and your younger sister,
who lived to the south of you with her daughters,
was Sodom. 47You not only walked in their ways
and copied their detestable practices, but in all
your ways you soon became more depraved than
they. 48As surely as I live, declares the Sovereign
LORD, your sister Sodom and her daughters never
did what you and your daughters have done.

49"'Now this was the sin of your sister Sodom:
She and her daughters were arrogant, overfed and
unconcerned; they did not help the poor and
needy. 50They were haughty and did detestable
things before me. Therefore I did away with them
as you have seen. 51Samaria did not commit half
the sins you did. You have done more detestable
things than they, and have made your sisters seem
righteous by all these things you have done. 52Bear
your disgrace, for you have furnished some justification for your sisters. Because your sins were
more vile than theirs, they appear more righteous
than you. So then, be ashamed and bear your disgrace, for you have made your sisters appear righteous. Ge 13:13; Lk 12:16-20

53"'However, I will restore the fortunes of Sodom and her daughters and of Samaria and her
daughters, and your fortunes along with them,
54so that you may bear your disgrace and be
ashamed of all you have done in giving them comfort. 55And your sisters, Sodom with her daughters
and Samaria with her daughters, will return to
what they were before; and you and your daughters will return to what you were before. 56You
would not even mention your sister Sodom in the
day of your pride, 57before your wickedness was
uncovered. Even so, you are now scorned by the
daughters of Edom[b] and all her neighbors and
the daughters of the Philistines—all those around
you who despise you. 58You will bear the consequences of your lewdness and your detestable
practices, declares the LORD. 2Ki 16:6; Eze 23:49

59"'This is what the Sovereign LORD says: I will
deal with you as you deserve, because you have
despised my oath by breaking the covenant. 60Yet
I will remember the covenant I made with you in
the days of your youth, and I will establish an
everlasting covenant with you. 61Then you will remember your ways and be ashamed when you
receive your sisters, both those who are older than
you and those who are younger. I will give them to
you as daughters, but not on the basis of my covenant with you. 62So I will establish my covenant
with you, and you will know that I am the LORD.
63Then, when I make atonement for you for all you
have done, you will remember and be ashamed
and never again open your mouth because of your
humiliation, declares the Sovereign LORD.'"

Two Eagles and a Vine

17 The word of the LORD came to me: 2"Son
of man, set forth an allegory and tell the
house of Israel a parable. 3Say to them, 'This is
what the Sovereign LORD says: A great eagle with
powerful wings, long feathers and full plumage of
varied colors came to Lebanon. Taking hold of the
top of a cedar, 4he broke off its topmost shoot and
carried it away to a land of merchants, where he
planted it in a city of traders. Jer 22:23; Eze 20:49

5"'He took some of the seed of your land and
put it in fertile soil. He planted it like a willow by
abundant water, 6and it sprouted and became a
low, spreading vine. Its branches turned toward
him, but its roots remained under it. So it became
a vine and produced branches and put out leafy
boughs. Dt 8:7-9; Isa 44:4

7"'But there was another great eagle with pow-

[a]36 Or *lust* [b]57 Many Hebrew manuscripts and Syriac; most Hebrew manuscripts, Septuagint and Vulgate *Aram*

erful wings and full plumage. The vine now sent
out its roots toward him from the plot where it was
planted and stretched out its branches to him for
water. [8]It had been planted in good soil by abundant water so that it would produce branches, bear
fruit and become a splendid vine.' Eze 31:4
[9]"Say to them, 'This is what the Sovereign LORD
says: Will it thrive? Will it not be uprooted and
stripped of its fruit so that it withers? All its new
growth will wither. It will not take a strong arm or
many people to pull it up by the roots. [10]Even if it
is transplanted, will it thrive? Will it not wither
completely when the east wind strikes it—wither
away in the plot where it grew?'" Hos 13:15
[11]Then the word of the LORD came to me: [12]"Say
to this rebellious house, 'Do you not know what
these things mean?' Say to them: 'The king of Babylon went to Jerusalem and carried off her king
and her nobles, bringing them back with him to
Babylon. [13]Then he took a member of the royal
family and made a treaty with him, putting him
under oath. He also carried away the leading men
of the land, [14]so that the kingdom would be
brought low, unable to rise again, surviving only
by keeping his treaty. [15]But the king rebelled
against him by sending his envoys to Egypt to get
horses and a large army. Will he succeed? Will he
who does such things escape? Will he break the
treaty and yet escape? 2Ch 36:13; Eze 12:9; 29:14
[16]"'As surely as I live, declares the Sovereign
LORD, he shall die in Babylon, in the land of the
king who put him on the throne, whose oath he
despised and whose treaty he broke. [17]Pharaoh
with his mighty army and great horde will be of no
help to him in war, when ramps are built and siege
works erected to destroy many lives. [18]He despised
the oath by breaking the covenant. Because he had
given his hand in pledge and yet did all these
things, he shall not escape. 1Ch 29:24; Eze 29:6-7
[19]"'Therefore this is what the Sovereign LORD
says: As surely as I live, I will bring down on his
head my oath that he despised and my covenant
that he broke. [20]I will spread my net for him, and
he will be caught in my snare. I will bring him to
Babylon and execute judgment upon him there
because he was unfaithful to me. [21]All his fleeing
troops will fall by the sword, and the survivors will
be scattered to the winds. Then you will know that
I the LORD have spoken. Eze 12:13-14; 20:36
[22]"'This is what the Sovereign LORD says: I myself will take a shoot from the very top of a cedar
and plant it; I will break off a tender sprig from its
topmost shoots and plant it on a high and lofty
mountain. [23]On the mountain heights of Israel I
will plant it; it will produce branches and bear fruit
and become a splendid cedar. Birds of every kind
will nest in it; they will find shelter in the shade of
its branches. [24]All the trees of the field will know
that I the LORD bring down the tall tree and make
the low tree grow tall. I dry up the green tree and
make the dry tree flourish. Ps 96:12; Jer 23:5
"'I the LORD have spoken, and I will do it.'"

The Soul Who Sins Will Die

18 The word of the LORD came to me: [2]"What
do you people mean by quoting this proverb about the land of Israel:

"'The fathers eat sour grapes,
and the children's teeth are set on edge'?

[3]"As surely as I live, declares the Sovereign
LORD, you will no longer quote this proverb in
Israel. [4]For every living soul belongs to me, the
father as well as the son—both alike belong to me.
The soul who sins is the one who will die.

[5]"Suppose there is a righteous man
who does what is just and right.
[6]He does not eat at the mountain shrines
or look to the idols of the house of Israel.
He does not defile his neighbor's wife
or lie with a woman during her period.
[7]He does not oppress anyone, Ex 22:21
but returns what he took in pledge for a
loan. Dt 24:12
He does not commit robbery Ex 20:15
but gives his food to the hungry Job 22:7
and provides clothing for the naked. Dt 15:11
[8]He does not lend at usury
or take excessive interest.[a] Ex 22:25; Lev 25:35-37
He withholds his hand from doing wrong
and judges fairly between man and man.
[9]He follows my decrees Lev 19:37
and faithfully keeps my laws.
That man is righteous; Hab 2:4
he will surely live, Lev 18:5; Am 5:4
declares the Sovereign LORD.

[10]"Suppose he has a violent son, who sheds
blood or does any of these other things[b] [11](though
the father has done none of them):

"He eats at the mountain shrines.
He defiles his neighbor's wife.
[12]He oppresses the poor and needy. Am 4:1
He commits robbery.
He does not return what he took in pledge.
He looks to the idols.
He does detestable things. Isa 59:6-7; Eze 8:6,17
[13]He lends at usury and takes excessive interest.

Will such a man live? He will not! Because he has
done all these detestable things, he will surely be
put to death and his blood will be on his own head.
[14]"But suppose this son has a son who sees all

[a] 8 Or *take interest*; similarly in verses 13 and 17 [b] 10 Or *things to a brother*

the sins his father commits, and though he sees
them, he does not do such things: 2Ch 34:21; Pr 23:24

15"He does not eat at the mountain shrines
 or look to the idols of the house of Israel.
He does not defile his neighbor's wife.
16He does not oppress anyone
 or require a pledge for a loan.
He does not commit robbery
 but gives his food to the hungry
 and provides clothing for the naked. Ps 41:1
17He withholds his hand from sin[a]
 and takes no usury or excessive interest.
He keeps my laws and follows my decrees.

He will not die for his father's sin; he will surely
live. 18But his father will die for his own sin, because he practiced extortion, robbed his brother
and did what was wrong among his people.
19"Yet you ask, 'Why does the son not share the
guilt of his father?' Since the son has done what is
just and right and has been careful to keep all my
decrees, he will surely live. 20The soul who sins is
the one who will die. The son will not share the
guilt of the father, nor will the father share the guilt
of the son. The righteousness of the righteous man
will be credited to him, and the wickedness of the
wicked will be charged against him. Dt 24:16; Isa 3:11
21"But if a wicked man turns away from all the
sins he has committed and keeps all my decrees
and does what is just and right, he will surely live;
he will not die. 22None of the offenses he has committed will be remembered against him. Because
of the righteous things he has done, he will live.
23Do I take any pleasure in the death of the wicked? declares the Sovereign LORD. Rather, am I not
pleased when they turn from their ways and live?
24"But if a righteous man turns from his righteousness and commits sin and does the same detestable things the wicked man does, will he live?
None of the righteous things he has done will be
remembered. Because of the unfaithfulness he is
guilty of and because of the sins he has committed,
he will die. Eze 3:20; 20:27; 2Pe 2:20-22
25"Yet you say, 'The way of the Lord is not just.'
Hear, O house of Israel: Is my way unjust? Is it not
your ways that are unjust? 26If a righteous man
turns from his righteousness and commits sin, he
will die for it; because of the sin he has committed
he will die. 27But if a wicked man turns away from
the wickedness he has committed and does what is
just and right, he will save his life. 28Because he
considers all the offenses he has committed and
turns away from them, he will surely live; he will
not die. 29Yet the house of Israel says, 'The way of
the Lord is not just.' Are my ways unjust, O house
of Israel? Is it not your ways that are unjust?
30"Therefore, O house of Israel, I will judge
you, each one according to his ways, declares the
Sovereign LORD. Repent! Turn away from all your
offenses; then sin will not be your downfall. 31Rid
yourselves of all the offenses you have committed,
and get a new heart and a new spirit. Why will you
die, O house of Israel? 32For I take no pleasure in
the death of anyone, declares the Sovereign LORD.
Repent and live! Eze 7:3; 11:19

A Lament for Israel's Princes

19 "Take up a lament concerning the princes
of Israel 2and say: 2Ki 24:6; Eze 26:17

" 'What a lioness was your mother
 among the lions!
She lay down among the young lions
 and reared her cubs.
3She brought up one of her cubs,
 and he became a strong lion.
He learned to tear the prey
 and he devoured men.
4The nations heard about him,
 and he was trapped in their pit.
They led him with hooks
 to the land of Egypt. 2Ki 23:33-34; 2Ch 36:4

5" 'When she saw her hope unfulfilled,
 her expectation gone,
she took another of her cubs
 and made him a strong lion. 2Ki 23:34
6He prowled among the lions,
 for he was now a strong lion.
He learned to tear the prey
 and he devoured men. 2Ki 24:9; 2Ch 36:9
7He broke down[b] their strongholds
 and devastated their towns. Eze 30:12
The land and all who were in it
 were terrified by his roaring.
8Then the nations came against him, 2Ki 24:2
 those from regions round about.
They spread their net for him,
 and he was trapped in their pit. 2Ki 24:11
9With hooks they pulled him into a cage
 and brought him to the king of Babylon.
They put him in prison,
 so his roar was heard no longer
 on the mountains of Israel. 2Ki 24:15

10" 'Your mother was like a vine in your
 vineyard[c]
 planted by the water; Ps 80:8-11
it was fruitful and full of branches
 because of abundant water.
11Its branches were strong,
 fit for a ruler's scepter.
It towered high
 above the thick foliage,

[a] 17 Septuagint (see also verse 8); Hebrew *from the poor* [b] 7 Targum (see Septuagint); Hebrew *He knew*
[c] 10 Two Hebrew manuscripts; most Hebrew manuscripts *your blood*

conspicuous for its height
and for its many branches. Eze 31:3; Da 4:11
12But it was uprooted in fury Eze 17:10
and thrown to the ground.
The east wind made it shrivel,
it was stripped of its fruit;
its strong branches withered
and fire consumed them. Eze 28:17; Hos 13:15
13Now it is planted in the desert, Eze 20:35
in a dry and thirsty land. Hos 2:3
14Fire spread from one of its main[a] branches
and consumed its fruit. Eze 20:47
No strong branch is left on it
fit for a ruler's scepter.' Eze 15:4

This is a lament and is to be used as a lament."

Rebellious Israel

20 In the seventh year, in the fifth month on
the tenth day, some of the elders of Israel
came to inquire of the LORD, and they sat down in
front of me. Eze 8:1
2Then the word of the LORD came to me: 3"Son
of man, speak to the elders of Israel and say to
them, 'This is what the Sovereign LORD says: Have
you come to inquire of me? As surely as I live, I
will not let you inquire of me, declares the Sovereign LORD.' Eze 14:3; Mic 3:7
4"Will you judge them? Will you judge them,
son of man? Then confront them with the detestable practices of their fathers 5and say to them:
'This is what the Sovereign LORD says: On the day
I chose Israel, I swore with uplifted hand to the
descendants of the house of Jacob and revealed
myself to them in Egypt. With uplifted hand I said
to them, "I am the LORD your God." 6On that day
I swore to them that I would bring them out of
Egypt into a land I had searched out for them, a
land flowing with milk and honey, the most beautiful of all lands. 7And I said to them, "Each of you,
get rid of the vile images you have set your eyes on,
and do not defile yourselves with the idols of
Egypt. I am the LORD your God." Ex 6:7; Dt 8:7
8" 'But they rebelled against me and would not
listen to me; they did not get rid of the vile images
they had set their eyes on, nor did they forsake the
idols of Egypt. So I said I would pour out my
wrath on them and spend my anger against them
in Egypt. 9But for the sake of my name I did what
would keep it from being profaned in the eyes of
the nations they lived among and in whose sight I
had revealed myself to the Israelites by bringing
them out of Egypt. 10Therefore I led them out of
Egypt and brought them into the desert. 11I gave
them my decrees and made known to them my
laws, for the man who obeys them will live by
them. 12Also I gave them my Sabbaths as a sign
between us, so they would know that I the LORD
made them holy. Lev 18:5; Dt 4:7-8; Ro 10:5
13" 'Yet the people of Israel rebelled against me
in the desert. They did not follow my decrees but
rejected my laws—although the man who obeys
them will live by them—and they utterly desecrated my Sabbaths. So I said I would pour out my
wrath on them and destroy them in the desert.
14But for the sake of my name I did what would
keep it from being profaned in the eyes of the
nations in whose sight I had brought them out.
15Also with uplifted hand I swore to them in the
desert that I would not bring them into the land I
had given them—a land flowing with milk and
honey, most beautiful of all lands— 16because
they rejected my laws and did not follow my decrees and desecrated my Sabbaths. For their hearts
were devoted to their idols. 17Yet I looked on them
with pity and did not destroy them or put an end
to them in the desert. 18I said to their children in
the desert, "Do not follow the statutes of your
fathers or keep their laws or defile yourselves with
their idols. 19I am the LORD your God; follow my
decrees and be careful to keep my laws. 20Keep my
Sabbaths holy, that they may be a sign between us.
Then you will know that I am the LORD your God."
21" 'But the children rebelled against me: They
did not follow my decrees, they were not careful to
keep my laws—although the man who obeys them
will live by them—and they desecrated my Sabbaths. So I said I would pour out my wrath on
them and spend my anger against them in the
desert. 22But I withheld my hand, and for the sake
of my name I did what would keep it from being
profaned in the eyes of the nations in whose sight
I had brought them out. 23Also with uplifted hand
I swore to them in the desert that I would disperse
them among the nations and scatter them through
the countries, 24because they had not obeyed my
laws but had rejected my decrees and desecrated
my Sabbaths, and their eyes ⌞lusted⌟ after their
fathers' idols. 25I also gave them over to statutes
that were not good and laws they could not live by;

LIVING  **INSIGHT**

I find that defiance, more than any other attitude, is the thing that kindles God's anger. Let us never forget that our defiance gives Him every right to be angry. We've broken His holy plan for us. He wants us to walk in the light, in fellowship with Him, just as He is in the light.

(See Ezekiel 20:8.)

[a] 14 Or *from under its*

26I let them become defiled through their gifts—the sacrifice of every firstborn[a]—that I might fill them with horror so they would know that I am the LORD.' Lev 26:33; Dt 28:64; Ps 81:12

27"Therefore, son of man, speak to the people of Israel and say to them, 'This is what the Sovereign LORD says: In this also your fathers blasphemed me by forsaking me: 28When I brought them into the land I had sworn to give them and they saw any high hill or any leafy tree, there they offered their sacrifices, made offerings that provoked me to anger, presented their fragrant incense and poured out their drink offerings. 29Then I said to them: What is this high place you go to?'" (It is called Bamah[b] to this day.) Eze 6:13; Ro 2:24

Judgment and Restoration

30"Therefore say to the house of Israel: 'This is what the Sovereign LORD says: Will you defile yourselves the way your fathers did and lust after their vile images? 31When you offer your gifts—the sacrifice of your sons in[c] the fire—you continue to defile yourselves with all your idols to this day. Am I to let you inquire of me, O house of Israel? As surely as I live, declares the Sovereign LORD, I will not let you inquire of me. Ps 106:37-39

32"'You say, "We want to be like the nations, like the peoples of the world, who serve wood and stone." But what you have in mind will never happen. 33As surely as I live, declares the Sovereign LORD, I will rule over you with a mighty hand and an outstretched arm and with outpoured wrath. 34I will bring you from the nations and gather you from the countries where you have been scattered—with a mighty hand and an outstretched arm and with outpoured wrath. 35I will bring you into the desert of the nations and there, face to face, I will execute judgment upon you. 36As I judged your fathers in the desert of the land of Egypt, so I will judge you, declares the Sovereign LORD. 37I will take note of you as you pass under my rod, and I will bring you into the bond of the covenant. 38I will purge you of those who revolt and rebel against me. Although I will bring them out of the land where they are living, yet they will not enter the land of Israel. Then you will know that I am the LORD. Lev 27:32; Jer 33:13; Eze 16:62

39"'As for you, O house of Israel, this is what the Sovereign LORD says: Go and serve your idols, every one of you! But afterward you will surely listen to me and no longer profane my holy name with your gifts and idols. 40For on my holy mountain, the high mountain of Israel, declares the Sovereign LORD, there in the land the entire house of Israel will serve me, and there I will accept them. There I will require your offerings and your choice gifts,[d] along with all your holy sacrifices. 41I will accept you as fragrant incense when I bring you out from the nations and gather you from the countries where you have been scattered, and I will show myself holy among you in the sight of the nations. 42Then you will know that I am the LORD, when I bring you into the land of Israel, the land I had sworn with uplifted hand to give to your fathers. 43There you will remember your conduct and all the actions by which you have defiled yourselves, and you will loathe yourselves for all the evil you have done. 44You will know that I am the LORD, when I deal with you for my name's sake and not according to your evil ways and your corrupt practices, O house of Israel, declares the Sovereign LORD.'" Eze 16:61; Hos 5:15

Prophecy Against the South

45The word of the LORD came to me: 46"Son of man, set your face toward the south; preach against the south and prophesy against the forest of the southland. 47Say to the southern forest: 'Hear the word of the LORD. This is what the Sovereign LORD says: I am about to set fire to you, and it will consume all your trees, both green and dry. The blazing flame will not be quenched, and every face from south to north will be scorched by it. 48Everyone will see that I the LORD have kindled it; it will not be quenched.'" Jer 7:20; 21:14

49Then I said, "Ah, Sovereign LORD! They are saying of me, 'Isn't he just telling parables?'"

Babylon, God's Sword of Judgment

21 The word of the LORD came to me: 2"Son of man, set your face against Jerusalem and preach against the sanctuary. Prophesy against the land of Israel 3and say to her: 'This is what the LORD says: I am against you. I will draw my sword from its scabbard and cut off from you both the righteous and the wicked. 4Because I am going to cut off the righteous and the wicked, my sword will be unsheathed against everyone from south to north. 5Then all people will know that I the LORD have drawn my sword from its scabbard; it will not return again.' Eze 20:46-47; Na 1:9

6"Therefore groan, son of man! Groan before them with broken heart and bitter grief. 7And when they ask you, 'Why are you groaning?' you shall say, 'Because of the news that is coming. Every heart will melt and every hand go limp; every spirit will become faint and every knee become as weak as water.' It is coming! It will surely take place, declares the Sovereign LORD." Isa 22:4

8The word of the LORD came to me: 9"Son of man, prophesy and say, 'This is what the Lord says:

[a]26 Or *—making every firstborn pass through* ⌞*the fire*⌟ [b]29 *Bamah* means *high place.* [c]31 Or *—making your sons pass through* [d]40 Or *and the gifts of your firstfruits*

"'A sword, a sword,
sharpened and polished—
10 sharpened for the slaughter, Ps 110:5-6; Isa 34:5-6
polished to flash like lightning!

"'Shall we rejoice in the scepter of my son ⌞Ju-
dah⌟? The sword despises every such stick.

11 "'The sword is appointed to be polished,
to be grasped with the hand;
it is sharpened and polished,
made ready for the hand of the slayer.
12 Cry out and wail, son of man,
for it is against my people;
it is against all the princes of Israel.
They are thrown to the sword
along with my people.
Therefore beat your breast. Jer 31:19

13 "'Testing will surely come. And what if the
scepter ⌞of Judah⌟, which the sword despises, does
not continue? declares the Sovereign LORD.'

14 "So then, son of man, prophesy
and strike your hands together. Nu 24:10
Let the sword strike twice,
even three times.
It is a sword for slaughter—
a sword for great slaughter,
closing in on them from every side. Eze 6:11
15 So that hearts may melt 2Sa 17:10
and the fallen be many,
I have stationed the sword for slaughter[a]
at all their gates.
Oh! It is made to flash like lightning,
it is grasped for slaughter.
16 O sword, slash to the right,
then to the left,
wherever your blade is turned.
17 I too will strike my hands together, Eze 22:13
and my wrath will subside. Eze 5:13
I the LORD have spoken." Eze 6:11

18 The word of the LORD came to me: 19 "Son of
man, mark out two roads for the sword of the king
of Babylon to take, both starting from the same
country. Make a signpost where the road branches
off to the city. 20 Mark out one road for the sword
to come against Rabbah of the Ammonites and
another against Judah and fortified Jerusalem.
21 For the king of Babylon will stop at the fork in
the road, at the junction of the two roads, to seek
an omen: He will cast lots with arrows, he will
consult his idols, he will examine the liver. 22 Into
his right hand will come the lot for Jerusalem,
where he is to set up battering rams, to give the
command to slaughter, to sound the battle cry, to
set battering rams against the gates, to build a
ramp and to erect siege works. 23 It will seem like
a false omen to those who have sworn allegiance to
him, but he will remind them of their guilt and
take them captive. Nu 23:23; Eze 4:2

24 "Therefore this is what the Sovereign LORD
says: 'Because you people have brought to mind
your guilt by your open rebellion, revealing your
sins in all that you do—because you have done
this, you will be taken captive.

25 "'O profane and wicked prince of Israel,
whose day has come, whose time of punishment
has reached its climax, 26 this is what the Sovereign
LORD says: Take off the turban, remove the crown.
It will not be as it was: The lowly will be exalted
and the exalted will be brought low. 27 A ruin! A
ruin! I will make it a ruin! It will not be restored
until he comes to whom it rightfully belongs; to
him I will give it.' Ps 2:6; Eze 37:24; Hag 2:21-22

28 "And you, son of man, prophesy and say,
'This is what the Sovereign LORD says about the
Ammonites and their insults: Zep 2:8

"'A sword, a sword, Jer 12:12
drawn for the slaughter,
polished to consume
and to flash like lightning!
29 Despite false visions concerning you
and lying divinations about you,
it will be laid on the necks
of the wicked who are to be slain,
whose day has come,
whose time of punishment has reached its
climax. Eze 22:28; 35:5
30 Return the sword to its scabbard. Jer 47:6
In the place where you were created,
in the land of your ancestry, Eze 16:3
I will judge you.
31 I will pour out my wrath upon you
and breathe out my fiery anger against you;
I will hand you over to brutal men,
men skilled in destruction. Jer 51:20-23
32 You will be fuel for the fire, Mal 4:1
your blood will be shed in your land,
you will be remembered no more; Eze 25:10
for I the LORD have spoken.'"

Jerusalem's Sins

22 The word of the LORD came to me: 2 "Son
of man, will you judge her? Will you judge
this city of bloodshed? Then confront her with all
her detestable practices 3 and say: 'This is what the
Sovereign LORD says: O city that brings on herself
doom by shedding blood in her midst and defiles
herself by making idols, 4 you have become guilty
because of the blood you have shed and have become defiled by the idols you have made. You
have brought your days to a close, and the end of
your years has come. Therefore I will make you an
object of scorn to the nations and a laughingstock
to all the countries. 5 Those who are near and those

[a] 15 Septuagint; the meaning of the Hebrew for this word is uncertain.

who are far away will mock you, O infamous city,
full of turmoil. 2Ki 21:16; Eze 5:14; Na 3:1
6“ ‘See how each of the princes of Israel who are
in you uses his power to shed blood. 7In you they
have treated father and mother with contempt; in
you they have oppressed the alien and mistreated
the fatherless and the widow. 8You have despised
my holy things and desecrated my Sabbaths. 9In
you are slanderous men bent on shedding blood;
in you are those who eat at the mountain shrines
and commit lewd acts. 10In you are those who
dishonor their fathers' bed; in you are those who
violate women during their period, when they are
ceremonially unclean. 11In you one man commits
a detestable offense with his neighbor's wife, another shamefully defiles his daughter-in-law, and
another violates his sister, his own father's daughter. 12In you men accept bribes to shed blood; you
take usury and excessive interest[a] and make unjust gain from your neighbors by extortion. And
you have forgotten me, declares the Sovereign
LORD. Lev 18:15; Dt 27:25; Mic 7:3
13“ ‘I will surely strike my hands together at the
unjust gain you have made and at the blood you
have shed in your midst. 14Will your courage endure or your hands be strong in the day I deal with
you? I the LORD have spoken, and I will do it. 15I
will disperse you among the nations and scatter
you through the countries; and I will put an end to
your uncleanness. 16When you have been defiled[b]
in the eyes of the nations, you will know that I am
the LORD.’ ” Dt 4:27; Eze 21:7; 23:27
17Then the word of the LORD came to me:
18“Son of man, the house of Israel has become
dross to me; all of them are the copper, tin, iron
and lead left inside a furnace. They are but the
dross of silver. 19Therefore this is what the Sovereign LORD says: ‘Because you have all become
dross, I will gather you into Jerusalem. 20As men
gather silver, copper, iron, lead and tin into a furnace to melt it with a fiery blast, so will I gather
you in my anger and my wrath and put you inside
the city and melt you. 21I will gather you and I will
blow on you with my fiery wrath, and you will be
melted inside her. 22As silver is melted in a furnace, so you will be melted inside her, and you will
know that I the LORD have poured out my wrath
upon you.’ ” Jer 6:28-30; Eze 20:8,33; Mal 3:2
23Again the word of the LORD came to me:
24“Son of man, say to the land, ‘You are a land that
has had no rain or showers[c] in the day of wrath.’
25There is a conspiracy of her princes[d] within her
like a roaring lion tearing its prey; they devour
people, take treasures and precious things and
make many widows within her. 26Her priests do
violence to my law and profane my holy things;
they do not distinguish between the holy and the
common; they teach that there is no difference
between the unclean and the clean; and they shut
their eyes to the keeping of my Sabbaths, so that
I am profaned among them. 27Her officials within
her are like wolves tearing their prey; they shed
blood and kill people to make unjust gain. 28Her
prophets whitewash these deeds for them by false
visions and lying divinations. They say, ‘This is
what the Sovereign LORD says’—when the LORD
has not spoken. 29The people of the land practice
extortion and commit robbery; they oppress the
poor and needy and mistreat the alien, denying
them justice. Ex 23:9; Eze 13:2,6-7
30“I looked for a man among them who would
build up the wall and stand before me in the gap
on behalf of the land so I would not have to destroy it, but I found none. 31So I will pour out my
wrath on them and consume them with my fiery
anger, bringing down on their own heads all they
have done, declares the Sovereign LORD.” Jer 5:1

Two Adulterous Sisters

23 The word of the LORD came to me: 2“Son
of man, there were two women, daughters
of the same mother. 3They became prostitutes in
Egypt, engaging in prostitution from their youth.
In that land their breasts were fondled and their
virgin bosoms caressed. 4The older was named
Oholah, and her sister was Oholibah. They were
mine and gave birth to sons and daughters. Oholah is Samaria, and Oholibah is Jerusalem. Jer 3:7
5“Oholah engaged in prostitution while she was
still mine; and she lusted after her lovers, the Assyrians—warriors 6clothed in blue, governors and
commanders, all of them handsome young men,
and mounted horsemen. 7She gave herself as a
prostitute to all the elite of the Assyrians and defiled herself with all the idols of everyone she lusted after. 8She did not give up the prostitution she
began in Egypt, when during her youth men slept
with her, caressed her virgin bosom and poured
out their lust upon her. 2Ki 16:7; Hos 8:9
9“Therefore I handed her over to her lovers, the
Assyrians, for whom she lusted. 10They stripped
her naked, took away her sons and daughters and
killed her with the sword. She became a byword
among women, and punishment was inflicted on
her. Eze 16:36; Hos 11:5
11“Her sister Oholibah saw this, yet in her lust
and prostitution she was more depraved than her
sister. 12She too lusted after the Assyrians—governors and commanders, warriors in full dress,
mounted horsemen, all handsome young men. 13I
saw that she too defiled herself; both of them went
the same way. 2Ki 16:7-15; Jer 3:8-11

[a]12 Or *usury and interest* [b]16 Or *When I have allotted you your inheritance* [c]24 Septuagint; Hebrew *has not been cleansed or rained on* [d]25 Septuagint; Hebrew *prophets*

14“But she carried her prostitution still further. She saw men portrayed on a wall, figures of Chaldeans[a] portrayed in red, 15with belts around their waists and flowing turbans on their heads; all of them looked like Babylonian chariot officers, natives of Chaldea.[b] 16As soon as she saw them, she lusted after them and sent messengers to them in Chaldea. 17Then the Babylonians came to her, to the bed of love, and in their lust they defiled her. After she had been defiled by them, she turned away from them in disgust. 18When she carried on her prostitution openly and exposed her nakedness, I turned away from her in disgust, just as I had turned away from her sister. 19Yet she became more and more promiscuous as she recalled the days of her youth, when she was a prostitute in Egypt. 20There she lusted after her lovers, whose genitals were like those of donkeys and whose emission was like that of horses. 21So you longed for the lewdness of your youth, when in Egypt your bosom was caressed and your young breasts fondled.[c] Jer 40:9; Eze 16:29

22“Therefore, Oholibah, this is what the Sovereign LORD says: I will stir up your lovers against you, those you turned away from in disgust, and I will bring them against you from every side— 23the Babylonians and all the Chaldeans, the men of Pekod and Shoa and Koa, and all the Assyrians with them, handsome young men, all of them governors and commanders, chariot officers and men of high rank, all mounted on horses. 24They will come against you with weapons,[d] chariots and wagons and with a throng of people; they will take up positions against you on every side with large and small shields and with helmets. I will turn you over to them for punishment, and they will punish you according to their standards. 25I will direct my jealous anger against you, and they will deal with you in fury. They will cut off your noses and your ears, and those of you who are left will fall by the sword. They will take away your sons and daughters, and those of you who are left will be consumed by fire. 26They will also strip you of your clothes and take your fine jewelry. 27So I will put a stop to the lewdness and prostitution you began in Egypt. You will not look on these things with longing or remember Egypt anymore.

28“For this is what the Sovereign LORD says: I am about to hand you over to those you hate, to those you turned away from in disgust. 29They will deal with you in hatred and take away everything you have worked for. They will leave you naked and bare, and the shame of your prostitution will be exposed. Your lewdness and promiscuity 30have brought this upon you, because you lusted after the nations and defiled yourself with their idols. 31You have gone the way of your sister; so I will put her cup into your hand. Jer 34:20; Eze 6:9

32“This is what the Sovereign LORD says:

“You will drink your sister’s cup,
a cup large and deep;
it will bring scorn and derision,
for it holds so much. Ps 60:3; Isa 51:17; Jer 25:15
33You will be filled with drunkenness and sorrow,
the cup of ruin and desolation,
the cup of your sister Samaria. Jer 25:15-16
34You will drink it and drain it dry; Ps 75:8
you will dash it to pieces
and tear your breasts.

I have spoken, declares the Sovereign LORD.

35“Therefore this is what the Sovereign LORD says: Since you have forgotten me and thrust me behind your back, you must bear the consequences of your lewdness and prostitution.”

36The LORD said to me: “Son of man, will you judge Oholah and Oholibah? Then confront them with their detestable practices, 37for they have committed adultery and blood is on their hands. They committed adultery with their idols; they even sacrificed their children, whom they bore to me,[e] as food for them. 38They have also done this to me: At that same time they defiled my sanctuary and desecrated my Sabbaths. 39On the very day they sacrificed their children to their idols, they entered my sanctuary and desecrated it. That is what they did in my house. 2Ki 21:4; Jer 7:10

40“They even sent messengers for men who came from far away, and when they arrived you bathed yourself for them, painted your eyes and put on your jewelry. 41You sat on an elegant couch, with a table spread before it on which you had placed the incense and oil that belonged to me. Isa 57:9; Am 6:4

42“The noise of a carefree crowd was around her; Sabeans[f] were brought from the desert along with men from the rabble, and they put bracelets on the arms of the woman and her sister and beautiful crowns on their heads. 43Then I said about the one worn out by adultery, ‘Now let them use her as a prostitute, for that is all she is.’ 44And they slept with her. As men sleep with a prostitute, so they slept with those lewd women, Oholah and Oholibah. 45But righteous men will sentence them to the punishment of women who commit adultery and shed blood, because they are adulterous and blood is on their hands. Eze 16:38; Hos 6:5

46“This is what the Sovereign LORD says: Bring a mob against them and give them over to terror and plunder. 47The mob will stone them and cut

[a] 14 Or *Babylonians* [b] 15 Or *Babylonia*; also in verse 16 [c] 21 Syriac (see also verse 3); Hebrew *caressed because of your young breasts* [d] 24 The meaning of the Hebrew for this word is uncertain. [e] 37 Or *even made the children they bore to me pass through ⌊the fire⌋* [f] 42 Or *drunkards*

them down with their swords; they will kill their
sons and daughters and burn down their houses.
48“So I will put an end to lewdness in the land,
that all women may take warning and not imitate
you. 49You will suffer the penalty for your lewdness and bear the consequences of your sins of
idolatry. Then you will know that I am the Sovereign LORD.” Eze 7:4; 2Pe 2:6

The Cooking Pot

24 In the ninth year, in the tenth month on
the tenth day, the word of the LORD came
to me: 2“Son of man, record this date, this very
date, because the king of Babylon has laid siege to
Jerusalem this very day. 3Tell this rebellious house
a parable and say to them: ‘This is what the Sovereign LORD says: Jer 39:1; Eze 17:2

“ ‘Put on the cooking pot; put it on
and pour water into it. Jer 1:13; Eze 11:3
4Put into it the pieces of meat,
all the choice pieces—the leg and the
shoulder.
Fill it with the best of these bones;
5 take the pick of the flock. Jer 52:10
Pile wood beneath it for the bones;
bring it to a boil
and cook the bones in it. Jer 52:24-27

6“ ‘For this is what the Sovereign LORD says:

“ ‘Woe to the city of bloodshed, Eze 22:2
to the pot now encrusted,
whose deposit will not go away!
Empty it piece by piece
without casting lots for them. Ob 1:11; Na 3:10
7“ ‘For the blood she shed is in her midst:
She poured it on the bare rock;
she did not pour it on the ground,
where the dust would cover it. Lev 17:13
8To stir up wrath and take revenge
I put her blood on the bare rock,
so that it would not be covered.

9“ ‘Therefore this is what the Sovereign LORD says:

“ ‘Woe to the city of bloodshed!
I, too, will pile the wood high.
10So heap on the wood
and kindle the fire.
Cook the meat well,
mixing in the spices;
and let the bones be charred.
11Then set the empty pot on the coals
till it becomes hot and its copper glows
so its impurities may be melted
and its deposit burned away. Jer 21:10; Eze 22:15
12It has frustrated all efforts;
its heavy deposit has not been removed,
not even by fire.

13“ ‘Now your impurity is lewdness. Because I
tried to cleanse you but you would not be cleansed
from your impurity, you will not be clean again
until my wrath against you has subsided.

14“ ‘I the LORD have spoken. The time has come
for me to act. I will not hold back; I will not have
pity, nor will I relent. You will be judged according
to your conduct and your actions, declares the
Sovereign LORD.’ ” Eze 18:30; 36:19

Ezekiel’s Wife Dies

15The word of the LORD came to me: 16“Son of
man, with one blow I am about to take away from
you the delight of your eyes. Yet do not lament or
weep or shed any tears. 17Groan quietly; do not
mourn for the dead. Keep your turban fastened
and your sandals on your feet; do not cover the
lower part of your face or eat the customary food
⌊of mourners⌋.” Jer 13:17; 16:7
18So I spoke to the people in the morning, and
in the evening my wife died. The next morning I
did as I had been commanded.
19Then the people asked me, “Won’t you tell us
what these things have to do with us?” Eze 12:9
20So I said to them, “The word of the LORD
came to me: 21Say to the house of Israel, ‘This is
what the Sovereign LORD says: I am about to desecrate my sanctuary—the stronghold in which you
take pride, the delight of your eyes, the object of
your affection. The sons and daughters you left
behind will fall by the sword. 22And you will do as
I have done. You will not cover the lower part of
your face or eat the customary food ⌊of mourners⌋.
23You will keep your turbans on your heads and
your sandals on your feet. You will not mourn or
weep but will waste away because of[a] your sins
and groan among yourselves. 24Ezekiel will be a
sign to you; you will do just as he has done. When
this happens, you will know that I am the Sovereign LORD.’ Eze 4:3; 12:11
25“And you, son of man, on the day I take away
their stronghold, their joy and glory, the delight of
their eyes, their heart’s desire, and their sons and
daughters as well— 26on that day a fugitive will
come to tell you the news. 27At that time your
mouth will be opened; you will speak with him
and will no longer be silent. So you will be a sign
to them, and they will know that I am the LORD.”

Destruction of the Nations **Chapters 25–32**

These chapters are historical in nature, featuring declarations of judgment against various nations—Ammon, Tyre, Sidon, Egypt and Edom. These chap-

[a]23 Or *away in*

ters remind us that there is not a nation that does not answer to God. The God of Israel, the one true God, is still in control, and He rules over all. There are no borders of national limitations on His sovereign rule. In the final analysis, all nations answer to the Maker of heaven and earth.

A Prophecy Against Ammon

25 The word of the LORD came to me: 2“Son of man, set your face against the Ammonites and prophesy against them. 3Say to them, ‘Hear the word of the Sovereign LORD. This is what the Sovereign LORD says: Because you said “Aha!” over my sanctuary when it was desecrated and over the land of Israel when it was laid waste and over the people of Judah when they went into exile, 4therefore I am going to give you to the people of the East as a possession. They will set up their camps and pitch their tents among you; they will eat your fruit and drink your milk. 5I will turn Rabbah into a pasture for camels and Ammon into a resting place for sheep. Then you will know that I am the LORD. 6For this is what the Sovereign LORD says: Because you have clapped your hands and stamped your feet, rejoicing with all the malice of your heart against the land of Israel, 7therefore I will stretch out my hand against you and give you as plunder to the nations. I will cut you off from the nations and exterminate you from the countries. I will destroy you, and you will know that I am the LORD.’” Zep 2:8-9; Eze 21:31

A Prophecy Against Moab

8“This is what the Sovereign LORD says: ‘Because Moab and Seir said, “Look, the house of Judah has become like all the other nations,” 9therefore I will expose the flank of Moab, beginning at its frontier towns—Beth Jeshimoth, Baal Meon and Kiriathaim—the glory of that land. 10I will give Moab along with the Ammonites to the people of the East as a possession, so that the Ammonites will not be remembered among the nations; 11and I will inflict punishment on Moab. Then they will know that I am the LORD.’”

A Prophecy Against Edom

12“This is what the Sovereign LORD says: ‘Because Edom took revenge on the house of Judah and became very guilty by doing so, 13therefore this is what the Sovereign LORD says: I will stretch out my hand against Edom and kill its men and their animals. I will lay it waste, and from Teman to Dedan they will fall by the sword. 14I will take vengeance on Edom by the hand of my people Israel, and they will deal with Edom in accordance with my anger and my wrath; they will know my vengeance, declares the Sovereign LORD.’”

A Prophecy Against Philistia

15“This is what the Sovereign LORD says: ‘Because the Philistines acted in vengeance and took revenge with malice in their hearts, and with ancient hostility sought to destroy Judah, 16therefore this is what the Sovereign LORD says: I am about to stretch out my hand against the Philistines, and I will cut off the Kerethites and destroy those remaining along the coast. 17I will carry out great vengeance on them and punish them in my wrath. Then they will know that I am the LORD, when I take vengeance on them.’” 2Ch 28:18; Jer 47:1-7

A Prophecy Against Tyre

26 In the eleventh year, on the first day of the month, the word of the LORD came to me: 2“Son of man, because Tyre has said of Jerusalem, ‘Aha! The gate to the nations is broken, and its doors have swung open to me; now that she lies in ruins I will prosper,’ 3therefore this is what the Sovereign LORD says: I am against you, O Tyre, and I will bring many nations against you, like the sea casting up its waves. 4They will destroy the walls of Tyre and pull down her towers; I will scrape away her rubble and make her a bare rock. 5Out in the sea she will become a place to spread fishnets, for I have spoken, declares the Sovereign LORD. She will become plunder for the nations, 6and her settlements on the mainland will be ravaged by the sword. Then they will know that I am the LORD. Isa 23; Eze 27:32

7“For this is what the Sovereign LORD says: From the north I am going to bring against Tyre Nebuchadnezzar[a] king of Babylon, king of kings, with horses and chariots, with horsemen and a great army. 8He will ravage your settlements on the mainland with the sword; he will set up siege works against you, build a ramp up to your walls and raise his shields against you. 9He will direct the blows of his battering rams against your walls and demolish your towers with his weapons. 10His horses will be so many that they will cover you with dust. Your walls will tremble at the noise of the war horses, wagons and chariots when he enters your gates as men enter a city whose walls have been broken through. 11The hoofs of his horses will trample all your streets; he will kill your people with the sword, and your strong pillars will fall to the ground. 12They will plunder your wealth and loot your merchandise; they will break down your walls and demolish your fine houses and throw your stones, timber and rubble into the sea. 13I will put an end to your noisy songs, and the music of your harps will be heard no more. 14I will make you a bare rock, and you will become a place to spread fishnets. You will never be rebuilt, for

[a]7 Hebrew *Nebuchadrezzar,* of which *Nebuchadnezzar* is a variant; here and often in Ezekiel and Jeremiah

I the LORD have spoken, declares the Sovereign
LORD. Jer 27:6; Mal 1:4
15"This is what the Sovereign LORD says to Tyre:
Will not the coastlands tremble at the sound of
your fall, when the wounded groan and the
slaughter takes place in you? 16Then all the princes
of the coast will step down from their thrones and
lay aside their robes and take off their embroidered garments. Clothed with terror, they will sit
on the ground, trembling every moment, appalled
at you. 17Then they will take up a lament concerning you and say to you: Eze 27:32

" 'How you are destroyed, O city of renown,
peopled by men of the sea!
You were a power on the seas,
you and your citizens;
you put your terror
on all who lived there. Isa 14:12
18Now the coastlands tremble
on the day of your fall;
the islands in the sea
are terrified at your collapse.' Isa 23:5; 41:5

19"This is what the Sovereign LORD says: When
I make you a desolate city, like cities no longer
inhabited, and when I bring the ocean depths over
you and its vast waters cover you, 20then I will
bring you down with those who go down to the
pit, to the people of long ago. I will make you dwell
in the earth below, as in ancient ruins, with those
who go down to the pit, and you will not return or
take your place[a] in the land of the living. 21I will
bring you to a horrible end and you will be no
more. You will be sought, but you will never again
be found, declares the Sovereign LORD." Eze 27:36

A Lament for Tyre

27 The word of the LORD came to me: 2"Son
of man, take up a lament concerning Tyre.
3Say to Tyre, situated at the gateway to the sea,
merchant of peoples on many coasts, 'This is what
the Sovereign LORD says: Eze 19:1; Hos 9:13

" 'You say, O Tyre,
"I am perfect in beauty." Eze 28:2
4Your domain was on the high seas;
your builders brought your beauty to
perfection.
5They made all your timbers
of pine trees from Senir[b]; Dt 3:9
they took a cedar from Lebanon Isa 2:13
to make a mast for you.
6Of oaks from Bashan Nu 21:33; Jer 22:20; Zec 11:2
they made your oars;
of cypress wood[c] from the coasts of
Cyprus[d] Ge 10:4; Isa 23:12
they made your deck, inlaid with ivory.
7Fine embroidered linen from Egypt was your
sail Ex 26:36
and served as your banner;
your awnings were of blue and purple Ex 25:4
from the coasts of Elishah. Ge 10:4
8Men of Sidon and Arvad were your oarsmen;
your skilled men, O Tyre, were aboard as
your seamen. 1Ki 9:27
9Veteran craftsmen of Gebal[e] were on board
as shipwrights to caulk your seams.
All the ships of the sea and their sailors
came alongside to trade for your wares.

10" 'Men of Persia, Lydia and Put Eze 30:5; 38:5
served as soldiers in your army.
They hung their shields and helmets on your
walls,
bringing you splendor.
11Men of Arvad and Helech
manned your walls on every side;
men of Gammad
were in your towers.
They hung their shields around your walls;
they brought your beauty to perfection.

12" 'Tarshish did business with you because of
your great wealth of goods; they exchanged silver,
iron, tin and lead for your merchandise. Ge 10:4
13" 'Greece, Tubal and Meshech traded with
you; they exchanged slaves and articles of bronze
for your wares. Ge 10:2 Rev 18:13
14" 'Men of Beth Togarmah exchanged work
horses, war horses and mules for your merchandise. Ge 10:3; Eze 38:6
15" 'The men of Rhodes[f] traded with you, and
many coastlands were your customers; they paid
you with ivory tusks and ebony. Ge 10:7; Rev 18:12
16" 'Aram[g] did business with you because of
your many products; they exchanged turquoise,
purple fabric, embroidered work, fine linen, coral
and rubies for your merchandise. Jdg 10:6; Eze 28:13
17" 'Judah and Israel traded with you; they exchanged wheat from Minnith and confections,[h]
honey, oil and balm for your wares. Jdg 11:33
18" 'Damascus, because of your many products
and great wealth of goods, did business with you
in wine from Helbon and wool from Zahar.
19" 'Danites and Greeks from Uzal bought your
merchandise; they exchanged wrought iron, cassia
and calamus for your wares. Ge 10:2
20" 'Dedan traded in saddle blankets with you.
21" 'Arabia and all the princes of Kedar were

[a]20 Septuagint; Hebrew *return, and I will give glory* [b]5 That is, Hermon [c]6 Targum; the Masoretic Text has a different division of the consonants. [d]6 Hebrew *Kittim* [e]9 That is, Byblos [f]15 Septuagint; Hebrew *Dedan* [g]16 Most Hebrew manuscripts; some Hebrew manuscripts and Syriac *Edom* [h]17 The meaning of the Hebrew for this word is uncertain.

your customers; they did business with you in
lambs, rams and goats. Ge 25:13; Isa 60:7
22"'The merchants of Sheba and Raamah traded with you; for your merchandise they exchanged
the finest of all kinds of spices and precious stones,
and gold. Ge 10:7,28; 1Ki 10:1-2; Isa 60:6
23"'Haran, Canneh and Eden and merchants of
Sheba, Asshur and Kilmad traded with you. 24In
your marketplace they traded with you beautiful
garments, blue fabric, embroidered work and multicolored rugs with cords twisted and tightly knot-
ted. 2Ki 19:12; Isa 37:12

25"'The ships of Tarshish serve Isa 2:16 [fn]
as carriers for your wares.
You are filled with heavy cargo
in the heart of the sea.
26Your oarsmen take you
out to the high seas.
But the east wind will break you to pieces
in the heart of the sea.
27Your wealth, merchandise and wares, Pr 11:4
your mariners, seamen and shipwrights,
your merchants and all your soldiers,
and everyone else on board
will sink into the heart of the sea Eze 28:8
on the day of your shipwreck.
28The shorelands will quake Eze 26:15
when your seamen cry out.
29All who handle the oars
will abandon their ships;
the mariners and all the seamen
will stand on the shore.
30They will raise their voice
and cry bitterly over you;
they will sprinkle dust on their heads 2Sa 1:2
and roll in ashes. Jer 6:26; Rev 18:18-19
31They will shave their heads because of you
and will put on sackcloth.
They will weep over you with anguish of soul
and with bitter mourning. Isa 22:12; Eze 7:18
32As they wail and mourn over you,
they will take up a lament concerning you:
"Who was ever silenced like Tyre,
surrounded by the sea?" Eze 26:5
33When your merchandise went out on the seas,
you satisfied many nations;
with your great wealth and your wares ver 12
you enriched the kings of the earth.
34Now you are shattered by the sea
in the depths of the waters;
your wares and all your company
have gone down with you. Zec 9:4
35All who live in the coastlands Eze 26:15
are appalled at you; Lev 26:32
their kings shudder with horror
and their faces are distorted with fear.
36The merchants among the nations hiss at you;
you have come to a horrible end
and will be no more.'" Ps 37:10,36; Eze 26:21

A Prophecy Against the King of Tyre

28 The word of the LORD came to me: 2"Son
of man, say to the ruler of Tyre, 'This is
what the Sovereign LORD says: Isa 13:11

"'In the pride of your heart
you say, "I am a god;
I sit on the throne of a god Isa 14:13
in the heart of the seas." Zep 2:15
But you are a man and not a god,
though you think you are as wise as a god.
3Are you wiser than Daniel[a]? Da 1:20; 5:11-12
Is no secret hidden from you?
4By your wisdom and understanding
you have gained wealth for yourself
and amassed gold and silver
in your treasuries. Zec 9:3
5By your great skill in trading Isa 23:8
you have increased your wealth, Eze 27:33
and because of your wealth
your heart has grown proud. Ps 52:7; 62:10

6"'Therefore this is what the Sovereign LORD
says:

"'Because you think you are wise,
as wise as a god,
7I am going to bring foreigners against you,
the most ruthless of nations; Eze 30:11; 31:12
they will draw their swords against your
beauty and wisdom Jer 9:23
and pierce your shining splendor.
8They will bring you down to the pit, Eze 32:30
and you will die a violent death
in the heart of the seas. Eze 27:27
9Will you then say, "I am a god,"
in the presence of those who kill you?
You will be but a man, not a god, Isa 31:3
in the hands of those who slay you. Eze 16:49
10You will die the death of the uncircumcised
at the hands of foreigners.

I have spoken, declares the Sovereign LORD.'"

11The word of the LORD came to me: 12"Son of
man, take up a lament concerning the king of Tyre
and say to him: 'This is what the Sovereign LORD
says: Eze 19:1

"'You were the model of perfection,
full of wisdom and perfect in beauty.
13You were in Eden, Ge 2:8
the garden of God; Eze 31:8-9
every precious stone adorned you:
ruby, topaz and emerald,
chrysolite, onyx and jasper,

[a] 3 Or *Danel*; the Hebrew spelling may suggest a person other than the prophet Daniel.

sapphire,[a] turquoise and beryl.[b] Eze 27:16
Your settings and mountings[c] were made of
gold;
on the day you were created they were
prepared. Rev 21:20
14You were anointed as a guardian cherub,
for so I ordained you.
You were on the holy mount of God;
you walked among the fiery stones.
15You were blameless in your ways
from the day you were created
till wickedness was found in you.
16Through your widespread trade
you were filled with violence, Hab 2:17
and you sinned.
So I drove you in disgrace from the mount of
God,
and I expelled you, O guardian cherub,
from among the fiery stones.
17Your heart became proud Eze 31:10
on account of your beauty,
and you corrupted your wisdom
because of your splendor.
So I threw you to the earth;
I made a spectacle of you before kings.
18By your many sins and dishonest trade
you have desecrated your sanctuaries.
So I made a fire come out from you,
and it consumed you,
and I reduced you to ashes on the ground
in the sight of all who were watching.
19All the nations who knew you
are appalled at you;
you have come to a horrible end
and will be no more.'" Eze 26:21; 27:36

A Prophecy Against Sidon

20The word of the LORD came to me: 21"Son of
man, set your face against Sidon; prophesy against
her 22and say: 'This is what the Sovereign LORD
says: Jer 25:22; Eze 6:2

"'I am against you, O Sidon,
and I will gain glory within you. Eze 39:13
They will know that I am the LORD,
when I inflict punishment on her Eze 30:19
and show myself holy within her. Lev 10:3
23I will send a plague upon her
and make blood flow in her streets.
The slain will fall within her,
with the sword against her on every side.
Then they will know that I am the LORD.

24"'No longer will the people of Israel have malicious neighbors who are painful briers and sharp
thorns. Then they will know that I am the Sovereign LORD. Nu 33:55; Jos 23:13; Eze 2:6

25"'This is what the Sovereign LORD says: When
I gather the people of Israel from the nations
where they have been scattered, I will show myself
holy among them in the sight of the nations. Then
they will live in their own land, which I gave to my
servant Jacob. 26They will live there in safety and
will build houses and plant vineyards; they will live
in safety when I inflict punishment on all their
neighbors who maligned them. Then they will
know that I am the LORD their God.'" Isa 11:12

A Prophecy Against Egypt

29 In the tenth year, in the tenth month on
the twelfth day, the word of the LORD came
to me: 2"Son of man, set your face against Pharaoh
king of Egypt and prophesy against him and
against all Egypt. 3Speak to him and say: 'This is
what the Sovereign LORD says: Isa 19:1-17; Jer 46:2

"'I am against you, Pharaoh king of Egypt,
you great monster lying among your
streams. Ps 74:13; Isa 27:1; Eze 32:2
You say, "The Nile is mine; Jer 46:8
I made it for myself."
4But I will put hooks in your jaws 2Ki 19:28
and make the fish of your streams stick to
your scales.
I will pull you out from among your streams,
with all the fish sticking to your scales.
5I will leave you in the desert,
you and all the fish of your streams.
You will fall on the open field
and not be gathered or picked up.
I will give you as food
to the beasts of the earth and the birds of
the air. Jer 7:33; 34:20; Eze 32:4-6

6Then all who live in Egypt will know that I am the
LORD.

"'You have been a staff of reed for the house of
Israel. 7When they grasped you with their hands,
you splintered and you tore open their shoulders;
when they leaned on you, you broke and their
backs were wrenched.[d] Isa 36:6; Eze 17:15-17
8"'Therefore this is what the Sovereign LORD
says: I will bring a sword against you and kill your
men and their animals. 9Egypt will become a desolate wasteland. Then they will know that I am the
LORD. Eze 14:17; 32:11-13
"'Because you said, "The Nile is mine; I made
it," 10therefore I am against you and against your
streams, and I will make the land of Egypt a ruin
and a desolate waste from Migdol to Aswan, as far
as the border of Cush.[e] 11No foot of man or
animal will pass through it; no one will live there
for forty years. 12I will make the land of Egypt

[a]*13* Or *lapis lazuli* [b]*13* The precise identification of some of these precious stones is uncertain. [c]*13* The meaning of the Hebrew for this phrase is uncertain. [d]*7* Syriac (see also Septuagint and Vulgate); Hebrew *and you caused their backs to stand* [e]*10* That is, the upper Nile region

desolate among devastated lands, and her cities
will lie desolate forty years among ruined cities.
And I will disperse the Egyptians among the nations and scatter them through the countries.
13“ ‘Yet this is what the Sovereign LORD says: At
the end of forty years I will gather the Egyptians
from the nations where they were scattered. 14I will
bring them back from captivity and return them to
Upper Egypt,[a] the land of their ancestry. There
they will be a lowly kingdom. 15It will be the lowliest of kingdoms and will never again exalt itself
above the other nations. I will make it so weak that
it will never again rule over the nations. 16Egypt
will no longer be a source of confidence for the
people of Israel but will be a reminder of their sin
in turning to her for help. Then they will know
that I am the Sovereign LORD.’ ” Isa 30:2; Hos 8:13

17In the twenty-seventh year, in the first month
on the first day, the word of the LORD came to me:
18“Son of man, Nebuchadnezzar king of Babylon
drove his army in a hard campaign against Tyre;
every head was rubbed bare and every shoulder
made raw. Yet he and his army got no reward
from the campaign he led against Tyre. 19There-
fore this is what the Sovereign LORD says: I am
going to give Egypt to Nebuchadnezzar king of
Babylon, and he will carry off its wealth. He will
loot and plunder the land as pay for his army. 20I
have given him Egypt as a reward for his efforts
because he and his army did it for me, declares the
Sovereign LORD. Isa 10:6-7; Jer 25:9
21“On that day I will make a horn[b] grow for
the house of Israel, and I will open your mouth
among them. Then they will know that I am the
LORD.” Ps 132:17; Eze 24:27

A Lament for Egypt

30 The word of the LORD came to me: 2“Son
of man, prophesy and say: ‘This is what the
Sovereign LORD says:

“ ‘Wail and say, Isa 13:6
“Alas for that day!”
3For the day is near, Joel 2:1,11; Ob 1:15
the day of the LORD is near— Eze 7:12,19
a day of clouds,
a time of doom for the nations.
4A sword will come against Egypt, Da 11:43
and anguish will come upon Cush.[c]
When the slain fall in Egypt,
her wealth will be carried away
and her foundations torn down. Eze 29:19
5Cush and Put, Lydia and all Arabia, Libya[d] and
the people of the covenant land will fall by the
sword along with Egypt. Jer 25:20

6“ ‘This is what the LORD says:

“ ‘The allies of Egypt will fall
and her proud strength will fail.
From Migdol to Aswan Eze 29:10
they will fall by the sword within her,
declares the Sovereign LORD.
7“ ‘They will be desolate
among desolate lands,
and their cities will lie
among ruined cities. Eze 29:12
8Then they will know that I am the LORD,
when I set fire to Egypt Jer 49:27
and all her helpers are crushed. Eze 29:9

9“ ‘On that day messengers will go out from me
in ships to frighten Cush out of her complacency.
Anguish will take hold of them on the day of
Egypt’s doom, for it is sure to come. Isa 18:1-2

10“ ‘This is what the Sovereign LORD says:

“ ‘I will put an end to the hordes of Egypt
by the hand of Nebuchadnezzar king of
Babylon. Eze 29:19
11He and his army—the most ruthless of
nations— Eze 28:7
will be brought in to destroy the land.
They will draw their swords against Egypt
and fill the land with the slain.
12I will dry up the streams of the Nile Isa 19:6
and sell the land to evil men;
by the hand of foreigners
I will lay waste the land and everything in
it. Eze 19:7

I the LORD have spoken.

13“ ‘This is what the Sovereign LORD says:

“ ‘I will destroy the idols Jer 43:12
and put an end to the images in
Memphis.[e] Isa 19:13
No longer will there be a prince in Egypt,
and I will spread fear throughout the land.
14I will lay waste Upper Egypt,[f] Eze 29:14
set fire to Zoan Ps 78:12,43
and inflict punishment on Thebes.[g] Jer 46:25
15I will pour out my wrath on Pelusium,[h]
the stronghold of Egypt,
and cut off the hordes of Thebes.
16I will set fire to Egypt; Jos 7:15
Pelusium will writhe in agony.
Thebes will be taken by storm;
Memphis will be in constant distress.
17The young men of Heliopolis[i] and
Bubastis[j] Ge 41:45
will fall by the sword,

[a] 14 Hebrew *to Pathros* [b] 21 *Horn* here symbolizes strength. [c] 4 That is, the upper Nile region; also in verses 5 and 9
[d] 5 Hebrew *Cub* [e] 13 Hebrew *Noph*; also in verse 16 [f] 14 Hebrew *waste Pathros* [g] 14 Hebrew *No*; also in verses 15 and 16 [h] 15 Hebrew *Sin*; also in verse 16 [i] 17 Hebrew *Awen* (or *On*) [j] 17 Hebrew *Pi Beseth*

and the cities themselves will go into
captivity.
[18]Dark will be the day at Tahpanhes
when I break the yoke of Egypt; Lev 26:13
there her proud strength will come to an
end.
She will be covered with clouds,
and her villages will go into captivity.
[19]So I will inflict punishment on Egypt, Eze 28:22
and they will know that I am the LORD.' "

[20]In the eleventh year, in the first month on the
seventh day, the word of the LORD came to me:
[21]"Son of man, I have broken the arm of Pharaoh
king of Egypt. It has not been bound up for healing or put in a splint so as to become strong
enough to hold a sword. [22]Therefore this is what
the Sovereign LORD says: I am against Pharaoh
king of Egypt. I will break both his arms, the good
arm as well as the broken one, and make the sword
fall from his hand. [23]I will disperse the Egyptians
among the nations and scatter them through the
countries. [24]I will strengthen the arms of the king
of Babylon and put my sword in his hand, but I
will break the arms of Pharaoh, and he will groan
before him like a mortally wounded man. [25]I will
strengthen the arms of the king of Babylon, but the
arms of Pharaoh will fall limp. Then they will
know that I am the LORD, when I put my sword
into the hand of the king of Babylon and he bran-
dishes it against Egypt. [26]I will disperse the Egyptians among the nations and scatter them through
the countries. Then they will know that I am the
LORD." Zep 2:12; Zec 10:6,12

A Cedar in Lebanon

31 In the eleventh year, in the third month on
the first day, the word of the LORD came to
me: [2]"Son of man, say to Pharaoh king of Egypt
and to his hordes: Jer 52:5; Eze 30:20

" 'Who can be compared with you in majesty?
[3]Consider Assyria, once a cedar in Lebanon,
with beautiful branches overshadowing the
forest;
it towered on high,
its top above the thick foliage. Isa 10:34
[4]The waters nourished it, Eze 17:7
deep springs made it grow tall;
their streams flowed
all around its base
and sent their channels
to all the trees of the field. Da 4:10
[5]So it towered higher
than all the trees of the field;
its boughs increased
and its branches grew long,
spreading because of abundant waters.
[6]All the birds of the air
nested in its boughs,
all the beasts of the field
gave birth under its branches;
all the great nations
lived in its shade. Eze 17:23; Mt 13:32
[7]It was majestic in beauty,
with its spreading boughs,
for its roots went down
to abundant waters.
[8]The cedars in the garden of God Ps 80:10
could not rival it,
nor could the pine trees
equal its boughs,
nor could the plane trees Ge 30:37
compare with its branches—
no tree in the garden of God
could match its beauty. Ge 2:8-9
[9]I made it beautiful
with abundant branches,
the envy of all the trees of Eden Ge 2:8
in the garden of God. Ge 13:10; Eze 28:13

[10]" 'Therefore this is what the Sovereign LORD
says: Because it towered on high, lifting its top
above the thick foliage, and because it was proud
of its height, [11]I handed it over to the ruler of the
nations, for him to deal with according to its wickedness. I cast it aside, [12]and the most ruthless of
foreign nations cut it down and left it. Its boughs
fell on the mountains and in all the valleys; its
branches lay broken in all the ravines of the land.
All the nations of the earth came out from under
its shade and left it. [13]All the birds of the air settled
on the fallen tree, and all the beasts of the field
were among its branches. [14]Therefore no other
trees by the waters are ever to tower proudly on
high, lifting their tops above the thick foliage. No
other trees so well-watered are ever to reach such
a height; they are all destined for death, for the
earth below, among mortal men, with those who
go down to the pit. Eze 28:7; Da 5:20
[15]" 'This is what the Sovereign LORD says: On
the day it was brought down to the grave[a] I covered the deep springs with mourning for it; I held
back its streams, and its abundant waters were
restrained. Because of it I clothed Lebanon with
gloom, and all the trees of the field withered away.
[16]I made the nations tremble at the sound of its fall
when I brought it down to the grave with those
who go down to the pit. Then all the trees of Eden,
the choicest and best of Lebanon, all the trees that
were well-watered, were consoled in the earth below. [17]Those who lived in its shade, its allies
among the nations, had also gone down to the
grave with it, joining those killed by the sword.
[18]" 'Which of the trees of Eden can be compared
with you in splendor and majesty? Yet you, too,

[a]15 Hebrew *Sheol*; also in verses 16 and 17

will be brought down with the trees of Eden to the earth below; you will lie among the uncircumcised, with those killed by the sword. Eze 32:19,21

"'This is Pharaoh and all his hordes, declares the Sovereign LORD.'"

A Lament for Pharaoh

32 In the twelfth year, in the twelfth month on the first day, the word of the LORD came to
me: 2"Son of man, take up a lament concerning Pharaoh king of Egypt and say to him: Eze 27:2

"'You are like a lion among the nations;
you are like a monster in the seas
thrashing about in your streams,
churning the water with your feet
and muddying the streams. Eze 29:3; 34:18

3"'This is what the Sovereign LORD says:

"'With a great throng of people
I will cast my net over you,
and they will haul you up in my net.
4I will throw you on the land
and hurl you on the open field.
I will let all the birds of the air settle on you
and all the beasts of the earth gorge
themselves on you. Isa 18:6; Eze 31:12-13
5I will spread your flesh on the mountains
and fill the valleys with your remains.
6I will drench the land with your flowing blood
all the way to the mountains,
and the ravines will be filled with your
flesh.
7When I snuff you out, I will cover the heavens
and darken their stars;
I will cover the sun with a cloud,
and the moon will not give its light.
8All the shining lights in the heavens
I will darken over you; Ps 102:26
I will bring darkness over your land, Joel 2:10
declares the Sovereign LORD.
9I will trouble the hearts of many peoples
when I bring about your destruction among
the nations,
among[a] lands you have not known.
10I will cause many peoples to be appalled at
you,
and their kings will shudder with horror
because of you
when I brandish my sword before them.
On the day of your downfall Jer 46:10
each of them will tremble
every moment for his life. Eze 26:16; 27:35

11"'For this is what the Sovereign LORD says:

"'The sword of the king of Babylon Jer 46:26
will come against you. Eze 29:19
12I will cause your hordes to fall
by the swords of mighty men—
the most ruthless of all nations. Eze 28:7
They will shatter the pride of Egypt,
and all her hordes will be overthrown.
13I will destroy all her cattle
from beside abundant waters
no longer to be stirred by the foot of man
or muddied by the hoofs of cattle. Eze 29:8,11
14Then I will let her waters settle
and make her streams flow like oil,
declares the Sovereign LORD.
15When I make Egypt desolate
and strip the land of everything in it,
when I strike down all who live there,
then they will know that I am the LORD.'

16"This is the lament they will chant for her. The
daughters of the nations will chant it; for Egypt
and all her hordes they will chant it, declares the
Sovereign LORD." 2Ch 35:25; Eze 26:17

17In the twelfth year, on the fifteenth day of the
month, the word of the LORD came to me: 18"Son
of man, wail for the hordes of Egypt and consign
to the earth below both her and the daughters of
mighty nations, with those who go down to the pit.
19Say to them, 'Are you more favored than others?
Go down and be laid among the uncircumcised.'
20They will fall among those killed by the sword.
The sword is drawn; let her be dragged off with all
her hordes. 21From within the grave[b] the mighty
leaders will say of Egypt and her allies, 'They have
come down and they lie with the uncircumcised,
with those killed by the sword.' Isa 14:9; Eze 28:10

22"Assyria is there with her whole army; she is
surrounded by the graves of all her slain, all who
have fallen by the sword. 23Their graves are in the
depths of the pit and her army lies around her
grave. All who had spread terror in the land of the
living are slain, fallen by the sword. Isa 14:15

24"Elam is there, with all her hordes around her
grave. All of them are slain, fallen by the sword. All
who had spread terror in the land of the living
went down uncircumcised to the earth below.
They bear their shame with those who go down to
the pit. 25A bed is made for her among the slain,
with all her hordes around her grave. All of them
are uncircumcised, killed by the sword. Because
their terror had spread in the land of the living,
they bear their shame with those who go down to
the pit; they are laid among the slain. Jer 49:37

26"Meshech and Tubal are there, with all their
hordes around their graves. All of them are uncircumcised, killed by the sword because they spread
their terror in the land of the living. 27Do they not
lie with the other uncircumcised warriors who
have fallen, who went down to the grave with their
weapons of war, whose swords were placed under

[a] 9 Hebrew; Septuagint *bring you into captivity among the nations, / to*
[b] 21 Hebrew *Sheol*; also in verse 27

their heads? The punishment for their sins rested
on their bones, though the terror of these warriors
had stalked through the land of the living.
28“You too, O Pharaoh, will be broken and will
lie among the uncircumcised, with those killed by
the sword.
29“Edom is there, her kings and all her princes;
despite their power, they are laid with those killed
by the sword. They lie with the uncircumcised,
with those who go down to the pit. Isa 34:5-15
30“All the princes of the north and all the Sidonians are there; they went down with the slain in
disgrace despite the terror caused by their power.
They lie uncircumcised with those killed by the
sword and bear their shame with those who go
down to the pit. Eze 38:6; 39:2
31“Pharaoh—he and all his army—will see
them and he will be consoled for all his hordes that
were killed by the sword, declares the Sovereign
LORD. 32Although I had him spread terror in the
land of the living, Pharaoh and all his hordes will
be laid among the uncircumcised, with those killed
by the sword, declares the Sovereign LORD.”

Restoration of God's People **Chapters 33–48**

The last section is the most positive and reassuring section in the whole book. As we read these chapters we get the sense that God's glory was returning and His promises would be kept. Chapter 34 is one of the most memorable portrayals of a shepherd in all the Old Testament (except for perhaps Psalm 23). Here Ezekiel described the dramatic contrast between false shepherds who look out for their own selfish gain and true shepherds who care for the flock. This section also contains hope for future restoration and healing in the land. Who can forget the promise of the new heart in chapter 36 or the new life given to dry bones in chapter 37? As Ezekiel concludes his vivid and dramatic prophecy with his description of the restoration of the temple, we learn that the glory of the Lord will one day return and that everyone will know that the Lord is God!

Ezekiel a Watchman

33 The word of the LORD came to me: 2“Son
of man, speak to your countrymen and say
to them: ‘When I bring the sword against a land,
and the people of the land choose one of their men
and make him their watchman, 3and he sees the
sword coming against the land and blows the
trumpet to warn the people, 4then if anyone hears
the trumpet but does not take warning and the
sword comes and takes his life, his blood will be on
his own head. 5Since he heard the sound of the
trumpet but did not take warning, his blood will
be on his own head. If he had taken warning, he
would have saved himself. 6But if the watchman
sees the sword coming and does not blow the
trumpet to warn the people and the sword comes
and takes the life of one of them, that man will be
taken away because of his sin, but I will hold the
watchman accountable for his blood.’ Eze 3:11,18
7“Son of man, I have made you a watchman for
the house of Israel; so hear the word I speak and
give them warning from me. 8When I say to the
wicked, ‘O wicked man, you will surely die,’ and
you do not speak out to dissuade him from his
ways, that wicked man will die for[a] his sin, and I
will hold you accountable for his blood. 9But if you
do warn the wicked man to turn from his ways and
he does not do so, he will die for his sin, but you
will have saved yourself. Eze 3:17-19
10“Son of man, say to the house of Israel, ‘This
is what you are saying: “Our offenses and sins
weigh us down, and we are wasting away because
of[b] them. How then can we live?” ’ 11Say to them,
‘As surely as I live, declares the Sovereign LORD, I
take no pleasure in the death of the wicked, but
rather that they turn from their ways and live.
Turn! Turn from your evil ways! Why will you die,
O house of Israel?’ Eze 18:32; 2Pe 3:9
12“Therefore, son of man, say to your countrymen, ‘The righteousness of the righteous man will
not save him when he disobeys, and the wickedness of the wicked man will not cause him to fall
when he turns from it. The righteous man, if he
sins, will not be allowed to live because of his
former righteousness.’ 13If I tell the righteous man
that he will surely live, but then he trusts in his
righteousness and does evil, none of the righteous
things he has done will be remembered; he will die
for the evil he has done. 14And if I say to the
wicked man, ‘You will surely die,’ but he then
turns away from his sin and does what is just and
right— 15if he gives back what he took in pledge
for a loan, returns what he has stolen, follows the
decrees that give life, and does no evil, he will
surely live; he will not die. 16None of the sins he
has committed will be remembered against him.
He has done what is just and right; he will surely
live. Eze 18:22; 20:11
17“Yet your countrymen say, ‘The way of the
Lord is not just.’ But it is their way that is not just.
18If a righteous man turns from his righteousness
and does evil, he will die for it. 19And if a wicked
man turns away from his wickedness and does
what is just and right, he will live by doing so.
20Yet, O house of Israel, you say, ‘The way of the
Lord is not just.’ But I will judge each of you
according to his own ways.” Eze 3:20; 18:26

Jerusalem's Fall Explained

21In the twelfth year of our exile, in the tenth
month on the fifth day, a man who had escaped

[a] 8 Or *in*; also in verse 9 [b] 10 Or *away in*

from Jerusalem came to me and said, "The city has
fallen!" 22Now the evening before the man arrived,
the hand of the LORD was upon me, and he opened
my mouth before the man came to me in the
morning. So my mouth was opened and I was no
longer silent. Eze 24:27
23Then the word of the LORD came to me:
24"Son of man, the people living in those ruins in
the land of Israel are saying, 'Abraham was only
one man, yet he possessed the land. But we are
many; surely the land has been given to us as our
possession.' 25Therefore say to them, 'This is what
the Sovereign LORD says: Since you eat meat with
the blood still in it and look to your idols and shed
blood, should you then possess the land? 26You
rely on your sword, you do detestable things, and
each of you defiles his neighbor's wife. Should you
then possess the land?' Eze 22:6,11,27
27"Say this to them: 'This is what the Sovereign
LORD says: As surely as I live, those who are left in
the ruins will fall by the sword, those out in the
country I will give to the wild animals to be devoured, and those in strongholds and caves will
die of a plague. 28I will make the land a desolate
waste, and her proud strength will come to an end,
and the mountains of Israel will become desolate
so that no one will cross them. 29Then they will
know that I am the LORD, when I have made the
land a desolate waste because of all the detestable
things they have done.' 1Sa 13:6; Isa 2:19
30"As for you, son of man, your countrymen are
talking together about you by the walls and at the
doors of the houses, saying to each other, 'Come
and hear the message that has come from the
LORD.' 31My people come to you, as they usually
do, and sit before you to listen to your words, but
they do not put them into practice. With their
mouths they express devotion, but their hearts are

> **LIVING**  **INSIGHT**
>
> ***Beware of the temptation to alter your theology instead of adjusting your life. By accommodating one's theology, it is remarkable what the mind can do to remove even the slightest trace of guilt!***
>
> **(See Ezekiel 33:30–32.)**

greedy for unjust gain. 32Indeed, to them you are
nothing more than one who sings love songs with
a beautiful voice and plays an instrument well, for
they hear your words but do not put them into
practice. Mk 6:20; Ps 78:36-37
33"When all this comes true—and it surely
will—then they will know that a prophet has been
among them." 1Sa 3:20; Eze 2:5

Shepherds and Sheep

34 The word of the LORD came to me: 2"Son
of man, prophesy against the shepherds of
Israel; prophesy and say to them: 'This is what the
Sovereign LORD says: Woe to the shepherds of Israel who only take care of themselves! Should not
shepherds take care of the flock? 3You eat the
curds, clothe yourselves with the wool and slaughter the choice animals, but you do not take care of
the flock. 4You have not strengthened the weak or
healed the sick or bound up the injured. You have
not brought back the strays or searched for the
lost. You have ruled them harshly and brutally. 5So
they were scattered because there was no shepherd, and when they were scattered they became
food for all the wild animals. 6My sheep wandered
over all the mountains and on every high hill. They
were scattered over the whole earth, and no one
searched or looked for them. Jer 23:1; Jn 10:11
7" 'Therefore, you shepherds, hear the word of
the LORD: 8As surely as I live, declares the Sovereign LORD, because my flock lacks a shepherd and
so has been plundered and has become food for all
the wild animals, and because my shepherds did
not search for my flock but cared for themselves
rather than for my flock, 9therefore, O shepherds,
hear the word of the LORD: 10This is what the Sovereign LORD says: I am against the shepherds and
will hold them accountable for my flock. I will
remove them from tending the flock so that the
shepherds can no longer feed themselves. I will
rescue my flock from their mouths, and it will no
longer be food for them. Jer 21:13; Zec 10:3
11" 'For this is what the Sovereign LORD says: I
myself will search for my sheep and look after
them. 12As a shepherd looks after his scattered
flock when he is with them, so will I look after my
sheep. I will rescue them from all the places where
they were scattered on a day of clouds and darkness. 13I will bring them out from the nations and
gather them from the countries, and I will bring
them into their own land. I will pasture them on
the mountains of Israel, in the ravines and in all
the settlements in the land. 14I will tend them in a
good pasture, and the mountain heights of Israel
will be their grazing land. There they will lie down
in good grazing land, and there they will feed in a
rich pasture on the mountains of Israel. 15I myself
will tend my sheep and have them lie down, declares the Sovereign LORD. 16I will search for the
lost and bring back the strays. I will bind up the
injured and strengthen the weak, but the sleek and
the strong I will destroy. I will shepherd the flock
with justice. Isa 10:16; Lk 5:32
17" 'As for you, my flock, this is what the Sovereign LORD says: I will judge between one sheep and
another, and between rams and goats. 18Is it not
enough for you to feed on the good pasture? Must
you also trample the rest of your pasture with your

feet? Is it not enough for you to drink clear water?
Must you also muddy the rest with your feet?
19Must my flock feed on what you have trampled
and drink what you have muddied with your feet?

LIVING  **INSIGHT**

If you're in a position of authority, no matter how small or how large, the temptation to manipulate will never go away. You may have the authority to claim certain honors, to call attention to your right to be listened to. Don't yield. Resist at all cost!

(See Ezekiel 34:16.)

20“ ‘Therefore this is what the Sovereign LORD
says to them: See, I myself will judge between the
fat sheep and the lean sheep. 21Because you shove
with flank and shoulder, butting all the weak sheep
with your horns until you have driven them away,
22I will save my flock, and they will no longer be
plundered. I will judge between one sheep and
another. 23I will place over them one shepherd, my
servant David, and he will tend them; he will tend
them and be their shepherd. 24I the LORD will be
their God, and my servant David will be prince
among them. I the LORD have spoken. Isa 40:11
25“ ‘I will make a covenant of peace with them
and rid the land of wild beasts so that they may live
in the desert and sleep in the forests in safety.
26I will bless them and the places surrounding
my hill.[a] I will send down showers in season; there
will be showers of blessing. 27The trees of the field
will yield their fruit and the ground will yield its
crops; the people will be secure in their land. They
will know that I am the LORD, when I break the
bars of their yoke and rescue them from the hands
of those who enslaved them. 28They will no longer
be plundered by the nations, nor will wild animals
devour them. They will live in safety, and no one
will make them afraid. 29I will provide for them a
land renowned for its crops, and they will no longer be victims of famine in the land or bear the
scorn of the nations. 30Then they will know that I,
the LORD their God, am with them and that they,
the house of Israel, are my people, declares the
Sovereign LORD. 31You my sheep, the sheep of my
pasture, are people, and I am your God, declares
the Sovereign LORD.’ ” Ps 100:3; Jer 23:1

A Prophecy Against Edom

35 The word of the LORD came to me: 2“Son
of man, set your face against Mount Seir;
prophesy against it 3and say: ‘This is what the
Sovereign LORD says: I am against you, Mount
Seir, and I will stretch out my hand against you
and make you a desolate waste. 4I will turn your
towns into ruins and you will be desolate. Then
you will know that I am the LORD. Jer 6:12
5“ ‘Because you harbored an ancient hostility
and delivered the Israelites over to the sword at the
time of their calamity, the time their punishment
reached its climax, 6therefore as surely as I live,
declares the Sovereign LORD, I will give you over to
bloodshed and it will pursue you. Since you did
not hate bloodshed, bloodshed will pursue you. 7I
will make Mount Seir a desolate waste and cut
off from it all who come and go. 8I will fill your
mountains with the slain; those killed by the sword
will fall on your hills and in your valleys and in all
your ravines. 9I will make you desolate forever;
your towns will not be inhabited. Then you will
know that I am the LORD. Ps 137:7; Eze 21:29
10“ ‘Because you have said, “These two nations
and countries will be ours and we will take possession of them,” even though I the LORD was there,
11therefore as surely as I live, declares the Sovereign LORD, I will treat you in accordance with the
anger and jealousy you showed in your hatred of
them and I will make myself known among them
when I judge you. 12Then you will know that I the
LORD have heard all the contemptible things you
have said against the mountains of Israel. You
said, “They have been laid waste and have been
given over to us to devour.” 13You boasted against
me and spoke against me without restraint, and I
heard it. 14This is what the Sovereign LORD says:
While the whole earth rejoices, I will make you
desolate. 15Because you rejoiced when the inheritance of the house of Israel became desolate, that
is how I will treat you. You will be desolate,
O Mount Seir, you and all of Edom. Then they will
know that I am the LORD.’ ” Jer 50:11-13; La 4:21; Ob 1:12

A Prophecy to the Mountains of Israel

36 “Son of man, prophesy to the mountains
of Israel and say, ‘O mountains of Israel,
hear the word of the LORD. 2This is what the Sovereign LORD says: The enemy said of you, “Aha! The
ancient heights have become our possession.” ’
3Therefore prophesy and say, ‘This is what the
Sovereign LORD says: Because they ravaged and
hounded you from every side so that you became
the possession of the rest of the nations and the
object of people's malicious talk and slander,
4therefore, O mountains of Israel, hear the word
of the Sovereign LORD: This is what the Sovereign
LORD says to the mountains and hills, to the ravines and valleys, to the desolate ruins and the
deserted towns that have been plundered and ridiculed by the rest of the nations around you— 5this
is what the Sovereign LORD says: In my burning

[a]26 Or *I will make them and the places surrounding my hill a blessing*

zeal I have spoken against the rest of the nations,
and against all Edom, for with glee and with malice
in their hearts they made my land their own possession so that they might plunder its pastureland.'
6Therefore prophesy concerning the land of Israel
and say to the mountains and hills, to the ravines
and valleys: 'This is what the Sovereign LORD says:
I speak in my jealous wrath because you have suffered the scorn of the nations. 7Therefore this is
what the Sovereign LORD says: I swear with uplifted
hand that the nations around you will also suffer
scorn. Ps 123:3-4; Eze 34:29; 35:10,15
8" 'But you, O mountains of Israel, will produce
branches and fruit for my people Israel, for they
will soon come home. 9I am concerned for you
and will look on you with favor; you will be
plowed and sown, 10and I will multiply the number of people upon you, even the whole house of
Israel. The towns will be inhabited and the ruins
rebuilt. 11I will increase the number of men and
animals upon you, and they will be fruitful and
become numerous. I will settle people on you as in
the past and will make you prosper more than
before. Then you will know that I am the LORD. 12I
will cause people, my people Israel, to walk upon
you. They will possess you, and you will be their
inheritance; you will never again deprive them of
their children. Eze 47:14,22
13" 'This is what the Sovereign LORD says: Because people say to you, "You devour men and
deprive your nation of its children," 14therefore
you will no longer devour men or make your nation childless, declares the Sovereign LORD. 15No
longer will I make you hear the taunts of the nations, and no longer will you suffer the scorn of the
peoples or cause your nation to fall, declares the
Sovereign LORD.' " Nu 13:32; Eze 34:29
16Again the word of the LORD came to me:
17"Son of man, when the people of Israel were
living in their own land, they defiled it by their
conduct and their actions. Their conduct was like
a woman's monthly uncleanness in my sight. 18So
I poured out my wrath on them because they had
shed blood in the land and because they had defiled it with their idols. 19I dispersed them among
the nations, and they were scattered through the
countries; I judged them according to their conduct and their actions. 20And wherever they went
among the nations they profaned my holy name,
for it was said of them, 'These are the LORD's people, and yet they had to leave his land.' 21I had
concern for my holy name, which the house of
Israel profaned among the nations where they had
gone. Ps 74:18; Isa 48:9
22"Therefore say to the house of Israel, 'This is
what the Sovereign LORD says: It is not for your
sake, O house of Israel, that I am going to do these
things, but for the sake of my holy name, which
you have profaned among the nations where you
have gone. 23I will show the holiness of my great
name, which has been profaned among the nations, the name you have profaned among them.
Then the nations will know that I am the LORD,
declares the Sovereign LORD, when I show myself
holy through you before their eyes. Ps 126:2; Isa 5:16
24" 'For I will take you out of the nations; I will
gather you from all the countries and bring you
back into your own land. 25I will sprinkle clean
water on you, and you will be clean; I will cleanse
you from all your impurities and from all your

LIVING  INSIGHT

Because the Holy Spirit is real and relevant, we are able to feel Him giving us power and perseverance. When He does that, He fills us. Ask the Spirit of God to fill you.

(See Ezekiel 36:25–27.)

idols. 26I will give you a new heart and put a new
spirit in you; I will remove from you your heart of
stone and give you a heart of flesh. 27And I will put
my Spirit in you and move you to follow my decrees and be careful to keep my laws. 28You will
live in the land I gave your forefathers; you will be
my people, and I will be your God. 29I will save you
from all your uncleanness. I will call for the grain
and make it plentiful and will not bring famine
upon you. 30I will increase the fruit of the trees and
the crops of the field, so that you will no longer
suffer disgrace among the nations because of famine. 31Then you will remember your evil ways and
wicked deeds, and you will loathe yourselves for
your sins and detestable practices. 32I want you to
know that I am not doing this for your sake, declares the Sovereign LORD. Be ashamed and disgraced for your conduct, O house of Israel!
33" 'This is what the Sovereign LORD says: On
the day I cleanse you from all your sins, I will
resettle your towns, and the ruins will be rebuilt.
34The desolate land will be cultivated instead of
lying desolate in the sight of all who pass through
it. 35They will say, "This land that was laid waste
has become like the garden of Eden; the cities that
were lying in ruins, desolate and destroyed, are
now fortified and inhabited." 36Then the nations
around you that remain will know that I the LORD
have rebuilt what was destroyed and have replant-
ed what was desolate. I the LORD have spoken, and
I will do it.' Eze 22:14; 37:14; 39:27-28
37"This is what the Sovereign LORD says: Once
again I will yield to the plea of the house of Israel
and do this for them: I will make their people as
numerous as sheep, 38as numerous as the flocks
for offerings at Jerusalem during her appointed
feasts. So will the ruined cities be filled with flocks

of people. Then they will know that I am the LORD." 1Ki 8:63; 2Ch 35:7-9

The Valley of Dry Bones

37 The hand of the LORD was upon me, and he brought me out by the Spirit of the LORD and set me in the middle of a valley; it was full of bones. 2He led me back and forth among them, and I saw a great many bones on the floor of the valley, bones that were very dry. 3He asked me, "Son of man, can these bones live?" Eze 1:3; 8:3

I said, "O Sovereign LORD, you alone know."

4Then he said to me, "Prophesy to these bones and say to them, 'Dry bones, hear the word of the LORD! 5This is what the Sovereign LORD says to these bones: I will make breath[a] enter you, and you will come to life. 6I will attach tendons to you and make flesh come upon you and cover you with skin; I will put breath in you, and you will come to life. Then you will know that I am the LORD.'" Ps 104:29-30; Joel 2:27; 3:17

7So I prophesied as I was commanded. And as I was prophesying, there was a noise, a rattling sound, and the bones came together, bone to bone. 8I looked, and tendons and flesh appeared on them and skin covered them, but there was no breath in them.

9Then he said to me, "Prophesy to the breath; prophesy, son of man, and say to it, 'This is what the Sovereign LORD says: Come from the four winds, O breath, and breathe into these slain, that they may live.'" 10So I prophesied as he commanded me, and breath entered them; they came to life and stood up on their feet—a vast army.

11Then he said to me: "Son of man, these bones are the whole house of Israel. They say, 'Our bones are dried up and our hope is gone; we are cut off.' 12Therefore prophesy and say to them: 'This is what the Sovereign LORD says: O my people, I am going to open your graves and bring you up from them; I will bring you back to the land of Israel. 13Then you, my people, will know that I am the LORD, when I open your graves and bring you up from them. 14I will put my Spirit in you and you will live, and I will settle you in your own land. Then you will know that I the LORD have spoken, and I have done it, declares the LORD.'" Hos 13:14

One Nation Under One King

15The word of the LORD came to me: 16"Son of man, take a stick of wood and write on it, 'Belonging to Judah and the Israelites associated with him.' Then take another stick of wood, and write on it, 'Ephraim's stick, belonging to Joseph and all the house of Israel associated with him.' 17Join them together into one stick so that they will become one in your hand. Nu 17:2-3; 2Ch 15:9

18"When your countrymen ask you, 'Won't you tell us what you mean by this?' 19say to them, 'This is what the Sovereign LORD says: I am going to take the stick of Joseph—which is in Ephraim's hand—and of the Israelite tribes associated with him, and join it to Judah's stick, making them a single stick of wood, and they will become one in my hand.' 20Hold before their eyes the sticks you have written on 21and say to them, 'This is what the Sovereign LORD says: I will take the Israelites out of the nations where they have gone. I will gather them from all around and bring them back into their own land. 22I will make them one nation in the land, on the mountains of Israel. There will be one king over all of them and they will never again be two nations or be divided into two kingdoms. 23They will no longer defile themselves with their idols and vile images or with any of their offenses, for I will save them from all their sinful backsliding,[b] and I will cleanse them. They will be my people, and I will be their God. Eze 36:25,28

24"'My servant David will be king over them, and they will all have one shepherd. They will follow my laws and be careful to keep my decrees. 25They will live in the land I gave to my servant Jacob, the land where your fathers lived. They and their children and their children's children will live there forever, and David my servant will be their prince forever. 26I will make a covenant of peace with them; it will be an everlasting covenant. I will establish them and increase their numbers, and I will put my sanctuary among them forever. 27My dwelling place will be with them; I will be their God, and they will be my people. 28Then the nations will know that I the LORD make Israel holy, when my sanctuary is among them forever.'"

A Prophecy Against Gog

38 The word of the LORD came to me: 2"Son of man, set your face against Gog, of the land of Magog, the chief prince of[c] Meshech and Tubal; prophesy against him 3and say: 'This is what the Sovereign LORD says: I am against you, O Gog, chief prince of[d] Meshech and Tubal. 4I will turn you around, put hooks in your jaws and bring you out with your whole army—your horses, your horsemen fully armed, and a great horde with large and small shields, all of them brandishing their swords. 5Persia, Cush[e] and Put will be with them, all with shields and helmets, 6also Gomer with all its troops, and Beth Togarmah from the far north with all its troops—the many nations with you. Ge 10:2; Eze 39:11

7"'Get ready; be prepared, you and all the

[a]5 The Hebrew for this word can also mean *wind* or *spirit* (see verses 6-14). [b]23 Many Hebrew manuscripts (see also Septuagint); most Hebrew manuscripts *all their dwelling places where they sinned* [c]2 Or *the prince of Rosh,* [d]3 Or *Gog, prince of Rosh,* [e]5 That is, the upper Nile region

hordes gathered about you, and take command of
them. 8After many days you will be called to arms.
In future years you will invade a land that has
recovered from war, whose people were gathered
from many nations to the mountains of Israel,
which had long been desolate. They had been
brought out from the nations, and now all of them
live in safety. 9You and all your troops and the
many nations with you will go up, advancing like
a storm; you will be like a cloud covering the land.
10" 'This is what the Sovereign LORD says: On
that day thoughts will come into your mind and
you will devise an evil scheme. 11You will say, "I
will invade a land of unwalled villages; I will attack
a peaceful and unsuspecting people—all of them
living without walls and without gates and bars. 12I
will plunder and loot and turn my hand against
the resettled ruins and the people gathered from
the nations, rich in livestock and goods, living at
the center of the land." 13Sheba and Dedan and the
merchants of Tarshish and all her villages[a] will
say to you, "Have you come to plunder? Have you
gathered your hordes to loot, to carry off silver
and gold, to take away livestock and goods and to
seize much plunder?" ' Eze 27:22; Jer 15:13
14"Therefore, son of man, prophesy and say to
Gog: 'This is what the Sovereign LORD says: In that
day, when my people Israel are living in safety, will
you not take notice of it? 15You will come from
your place in the far north, you and many nations
with you, all of them riding on horses, a great
horde, a mighty army. 16You will advance against
my people Israel like a cloud that covers the land.
In days to come, O Gog, I will bring you against
my land, so that the nations may know me when
I show myself holy through you before their eyes.
17" 'This is what the Sovereign LORD says: Are
you not the one I spoke of in former days by my
servants the prophets of Israel? At that time they
prophesied for years that I would bring you
against them. 18This is what will happen in that
day: When Gog attacks the land of Israel, my hot
anger will be aroused, declares the Sovereign LORD.
19In my zeal and fiery wrath I declare that at that
time there shall be a great earthquake in the land
of Israel. 20The fish of the sea, the birds of the air,
the beasts of the field, every creature that moves
along the ground, and all the people on the face of
the earth will tremble at my presence. The mountains will be overturned, the cliffs will crumble and
every wall will fall to the ground. 21I will summon
a sword against Gog on all my mountains, declares
the Sovereign LORD. Every man's sword will be
against his brother. 22I will execute judgment upon
him with plague and bloodshed; I will pour down
torrents of rain, hailstones and burning sulfur on
him and on his troops and on the many nations
with him. 23And so I will show my greatness and
my holiness, and I will make myself known in the
sight of many nations. Then they will know that I
am the LORD.' 1Sa 14:20; Hag 2:6,21

39 "Son of man, prophesy against Gog and
say: 'This is what the Sovereign LORD says:
I am against you, O Gog, chief prince of[b] Meshech and Tubal. 2I will turn you around and drag
you along. I will bring you from the far north and
send you against the mountains of Israel. 3Then I
will strike your bow from your left hand and make
your arrows drop from your right hand. 4On the
mountains of Israel you will fall, you and all your
troops and the nations with you. I will give you as
food to all kinds of carrion birds and to the wild
animals. 5You will fall in the open field, for I have
spoken, declares the Sovereign LORD. 6I will send
fire on Magog and on those who live in safety in
the coastlands, and they will know that I am the
LORD. Jer 25:22; Am 1:4
7" 'I will make known my holy name among my
people Israel. I will no longer let my holy name be
profaned, and the nations will know that I the
LORD am the Holy One in Israel. 8It is coming! It
will surely take place, declares the Sovereign LORD.
This is the day I have spoken of. Ex 20:7; Eze 36:16,23
9" 'Then those who live in the towns of Israel
will go out and use the weapons for fuel and burn
them up—the small and large shields, the bows
and arrows, the war clubs and spears. For seven
years they will use them for fuel. 10They will not
need to gather wood from the fields or cut it from
the forests, because they will use the weapons for
fuel. And they will plunder those who plundered
them and loot those who looted them, declares the
Sovereign LORD. Isa 14:2; 33:1; Hab 2:8
11" 'On that day I will give Gog a burial place in
Israel, in the valley of those who travel east toward[c] the Sea.[d] It will block the way of travelers,
because Gog and all his hordes will be buried
there. So it will be called the Valley of Hamon
Gog.[e] Eze 38:2
12" 'For seven months the house of Israel will be
burying them in order to cleanse the land. 13All the
people of the land will bury them, and the day I am
glorified will be a memorable day for them, declares the Sovereign LORD. Dt 21:23; Eze 28:22
14" 'Men will be regularly employed to cleanse
the land. Some will go throughout the land and, in
addition to them, others will bury those that remain on the ground. At the end of the seven
months they will begin their search. 15As they go
through the land and one of them sees a human
bone, he will set up a marker beside it until the
gravediggers have buried it in the Valley of Ha-

[a] 13 Or *her strong lions*
[b] 1 Or *Gog, prince of Rosh,*
[c] 11 Or *of*
[d] 11 That is, the Dead Sea
[e] 11 *Hamon Gog* means *hordes of Gog.*

mon Gog. 16(Also a town called Hamonah[a] will
be there.) And so they will cleanse the land.'
17"Son of man, this is what the Sovereign LORD
says: Call out to every kind of bird and all the wild
animals: 'Assemble and come together from all
around to the sacrifice I am preparing for you, the
great sacrifice on the mountains of Israel. There
you will eat flesh and drink blood. 18You will eat
the flesh of mighty men and drink the blood of
the princes of the earth as if they were rams and
lambs, goats and bulls—all of them fattened animals from Bashan. 19At the sacrifice I am preparing for you, you will eat fat till you are glutted and
drink blood till you are drunk. 20At my table you
will eat your fill of horses and riders, mighty men
and soldiers of every kind,' declares the Sovereign
LORD. Ps 22:12; Rev 19:17-18
21"I will display my glory among the nations,
and all the nations will see the punishment I inflict
and the hand I lay upon them. 22From that day
forward the house of Israel will know that I am the
LORD their God. 23And the nations will know that
the people of Israel went into exile for their sin,
because they were unfaithful to me. So I hid my
face from them and handed them over to their
enemies, and they all fell by the sword. 24I dealt
with them according to their uncleanness and their
offenses, and I hid my face from them. Eze 36:19
25"Therefore this is what the Sovereign LORD
says: I will now bring Jacob back from captivity[b]
and will have compassion on all the people of
Israel, and I will be zealous for my holy name.
26They will forget their shame and all the unfaithfulness they showed toward me when they lived in
safety in their land with no one to make them
afraid. 27When I have brought them back from the
nations and have gathered them from the countries of their enemies, I will show myself holy
through them in the sight of many nations. 28Then
they will know that I am the LORD their God, for
though I sent them into exile among the nations,
I will gather them to their own land, not leaving
any behind. 29I will no longer hide my face from
them, for I will pour out my Spirit on the house of
Israel, declares the Sovereign LORD." Joel 2:28

The New Temple Area

40 In the twenty-fifth year of our exile, at the
beginning of the year, on the tenth of the
month, in the fourteenth year after the fall of
the city—on that very day the hand of the LORD
was upon me and he took me there. 2In visions of
God he took me to the land of Israel and set me
on a very high mountain, on whose south side
were some buildings that looked like a city. 3He
took me there, and I saw a man whose appearance
was like bronze; he was standing in the gateway
with a linen cord and a measuring rod in his hand.
4The man said to me, "Son of man, look with your
eyes and hear with your ears and pay attention to
everything I am going to show you, for that is why
you have been brought here. Tell the house of
Israel everything you see." Jer 26:2; Eze 44:5

The East Gate to the Outer Court

5I saw a wall completely surrounding the temple
area. The length of the measuring rod in the man's
hand was six long cubits, each of which was a
cubit[c] and a handbreadth.[d] He measured the
wall; it was one measuring rod thick and one rod
high. Eze 42:20
6Then he went to the gate facing east. He
climbed its steps and measured the threshold of
the gate; it was one rod deep.[e] 7The alcoves for
the guards were one rod long and one rod wide,
and the projecting walls between the alcoves were
five cubits thick. And the threshold of the gate next
to the portico facing the temple was one rod deep.
8Then he measured the portico of the gateway;
9it[f] was eight cubits deep and its jambs were two
cubits thick. The portico of the gateway faced the
temple.
10Inside the east gate were three alcoves on each
side; the three had the same measurements, and
the faces of the projecting walls on each side had
the same measurements. 11Then he measured the
width of the entrance to the gateway; it was ten
cubits and its length was thirteen cubits. 12In front
of each alcove was a wall one cubit high, and the
alcoves were six cubits square. 13Then he measured the gateway from the top of the rear wall of
one alcove to the top of the opposite one; the
distance was twenty-five cubits from one parapet
opening to the opposite one. 14He measured along
the faces of the projecting walls all around the
inside of the gateway—sixty cubits. The measurement was up to the portico[g] facing the courtyard.[h] 15The distance from the entrance of the
gateway to the far end of its portico was fifty cubits. 16The alcoves and the projecting walls inside
the gateway were surmounted by narrow parapet
openings all around, as was the portico; the openings all around faced inward. The faces of the projecting walls were decorated with palm trees.

The Outer Court

17Then he brought me into the outer court.
There I saw some rooms and a pavement that had

[a]16 *Hamonah* means *horde.* [b]25 Or *now restore the fortunes of Jacob* [c]5 The common cubit was about 1 1/2 feet (about 0.5 meter). [d]5 That is, about 3 inches (about 8 centimeters) [e]6 Septuagint; Hebrew *deep, the first threshold, one rod deep* [f]8,9 Many Hebrew manuscripts, Septuagint, Vulgate and Syriac; most Hebrew manuscripts *gateway facing the temple; it was one rod deep. 9Then he measured the portico of the gateway; it* [g]14 Septuagint; Hebrew *projecting wall* [h]14 The meaning of the Hebrew for this verse is uncertain.

been constructed all around the court; there were thirty rooms along the pavement. 18It abutted the sides of the gateways and was as wide as they were long; this was the lower pavement. 19Then he measured the distance from the inside of the lower gateway to the outside of the inner court; it was a hundred cubits on the east side as well as on the north. Eze 41:6; 46:1

The North Gate

20Then he measured the length and width of the gate facing north, leading into the outer court. 21Its alcoves—three on each side—its projecting walls and its portico had the same measurements as those of the first gateway. It was fifty cubits long and twenty-five cubits wide. 22Its openings, its portico and its palm tree decorations had the same measurements as those of the gate facing east. Seven steps led up to it, with its portico opposite them. 23There was a gate to the inner court facing the north gate, just as there was on the east. He measured from one gate to the opposite one; it was a hundred cubits. ver 49

The South Gate

24Then he led me to the south side and I saw a gate facing south. He measured its jambs and its portico, and they had the same measurements as the others. 25The gateway and its portico had narrow openings all around, like the openings of the others. It was fifty cubits long and twenty-five cubits wide. 26Seven steps led up to it, with its portico opposite them; it had palm tree decorations on the faces of the projecting walls on each side. 27The inner court also had a gate facing south, and he measured from this gate to the outer gate on the south side; it was a hundred cubits. ver 22,32

Gates to the Inner Court

28Then he brought me into the inner court through the south gate, and he measured the south gate; it had the same measurements as the others. 29Its alcoves, its projecting walls and its portico had the same measurements as the others. The gateway and its portico had openings all around. It was fifty cubits long and twenty-five cubits wide. 30(The porticoes of the gateways around the inner court were twenty-five cubits wide and five cubits deep.) 31Its portico faced the outer court; palm trees decorated its jambs, and eight steps led up to it. ver 21-22

32Then he brought me to the inner court on the east side, and he measured the gateway; it had the same measurements as the others. 33Its alcoves, its projecting walls and its portico had the same measurements as the others. The gateway and its portico had openings all around. It was fifty cubits long and twenty-five cubits wide. 34Its portico faced the outer court; palm trees decorated the jambs on either side, and eight steps led up to it. ver 22

35Then he brought me to the north gate and measured it. It had the same measurements as the others, 36as did its alcoves, its projecting walls and its portico, and it had openings all around. It was fifty cubits long and twenty-five cubits wide. 37Its portico[a] faced the outer court; palm trees decorated the jambs on either side, and eight steps led up to it. Eze 44:4; 47:2

The Rooms for Preparing Sacrifices

38A room with a doorway was by the portico in each of the inner gateways, where the burnt offerings were washed. 39In the portico of the gateway were two tables on each side, on which the burnt offerings, sin offerings and guilt offerings were slaughtered. 40By the outside wall of the portico of the gateway, near the steps at the entrance to the north gateway were two tables, and on the other side of the steps were two tables. 41So there were four tables on one side of the gateway and four on the other—eight tables in all—on which the sacrifices were slaughtered. 42There were also four tables of dressed stone for the burnt offerings, each a cubit and a half long, a cubit and a half wide and a cubit high. On them were placed the utensils for slaughtering the burnt offerings and the other sacrifices. 43And double-pronged hooks, each a handbreadth long, were attached to the wall all around. The tables were for the flesh of the offerings. Lev 4:3,28; 7:1

Rooms for the Priests

44Outside the inner gate, within the inner court, were two rooms, one[b] at the side of the north gate and facing south, and another at the side of the south[c] gate and facing north. 45He said to me, "The room facing south is for the priests who have charge of the temple, 46and the room facing north is for the priests who have charge of the altar. These are the sons of Zadok, who are the only Levites who may draw near to the LORD to minister before him." 1Ki 2:35; Eze 43:19; 44:15

47Then he measured the court: It was square—a hundred cubits long and a hundred cubits wide. And the altar was in front of the temple.

The Temple

48He brought me to the portico of the temple and measured the jambs of the portico; they were five cubits wide on either side. The width of the entrance was fourteen cubits and its projecting walls were[d] three cubits wide on either side. 49The

[a]37 Septuagint (see also verses 31 and 34); Hebrew *jambs*
[b]44 Septuagint; Hebrew *were rooms for singers, which were*
[c]44 Septuagint; Hebrew *east*
[d]48 Septuagint; Hebrew *entrance was*

portico was twenty cubits wide, and twelve[a] cubits from front to back. It was reached by a flight of stairs,[b] and there were pillars on each side of the jambs. 1Ki 6:3; 7:15

41 Then the man brought me to the outer sanctuary and measured the jambs; the width of the jambs was six cubits[c] on each side.[d] 2The entrance was ten cubits wide, and the projecting walls on each side of it were five cubits wide. He also measured the outer sanctuary; it was forty cubits long and twenty cubits wide. ver 23

3Then he went into the inner sanctuary and measured the jambs of the entrance; each was two cubits wide. The entrance was six cubits wide, and the projecting walls on each side of it were seven cubits wide. 4And he measured the length of the inner sanctuary; it was twenty cubits, and its width was twenty cubits across the end of the outer sanctuary. He said to me, "This is the Most Holy Place." 1Ki 6:20; Heb 9:3-8

5Then he measured the wall of the temple; it was six cubits thick, and each side room around the temple was four cubits wide. 6The side rooms were on three levels, one above another, thirty on each level. There were ledges all around the wall of the temple to serve as supports for the side rooms, so that the supports were not inserted into the wall of the temple. 7The side rooms all around the temple were wider at each successive level. The structure surrounding the temple was built in ascending stages, so that the rooms widened as one went upward. A stairway went up from the lowest floor to the top floor through the middle floor.

8I saw that the temple had a raised base all around it, forming the foundation of the side rooms. It was the length of the rod, six long cubits. 9The outer wall of the side rooms was five cubits thick. The open area between the side rooms of the temple 10and the ⌞priests'⌟ rooms was twenty cubits wide all around the temple. 11There were entrances to the side rooms from the open area, one on the north and another on the south; and the base adjoining the open area was five cubits wide all around.

12The building facing the temple courtyard on the west side was seventy cubits wide. The wall of the building was five cubits thick all around, and its length was ninety cubits.

13Then he measured the temple; it was a hundred cubits long, and the temple courtyard and the building with its walls were also a hundred cubits long. 14The width of the temple courtyard on the east, including the front of the temple, was a hundred cubits. Eze 40:47

15Then he measured the length of the building facing the courtyard at the rear of the temple, including its galleries on each side; it was a hundred cubits. Eze 42:3

The outer sanctuary, the inner sanctuary and the portico facing the court, 16as well as the thresholds and the narrow windows and galleries around the three of them—everything beyond and including the threshold was covered with wood. The floor, the wall up to the windows, and the windows were covered. 17In the space above the outside of the entrance to the inner sanctuary and on the walls at regular intervals all around the inner and outer sanctuary 18were carved cherubim and palm trees. Palm trees alternated with cherubim. Each cherub had two faces: 19the face of a man toward the palm tree on one side and the face of a lion toward the palm tree on the other. They were carved all around the whole temple. 20From the floor to the area above the entrance, cherubim and palm trees were carved on the wall of the outer sanctuary. 1Ki 6:29; 7:36; Eze 10:14

21The outer sanctuary had a rectangular doorframe, and the one at the front of the Most Holy Place was similar. 22There was a wooden altar three cubits high and two cubits square[e]; its corners, its base[f] and its sides were of wood. The man said to me, "This is the table that is before the LORD." 23Both the outer sanctuary and the Most Holy Place had double doors. 24Each door had two leaves—two hinged leaves for each door. 25And on the doors of the outer sanctuary were carved cherubim and palm trees like those carved on the walls, and there was a wooden overhang on the front of the portico. 26On the sidewalls of the portico were narrow windows with palm trees carved on each side. The side rooms of the temple also had overhangs. Eze 44:16; Mal 1:7,12

Rooms for the Priests

42 Then the man led me northward into the outer court and brought me to the rooms opposite the temple courtyard and opposite the outer wall on the north side. 2The building whose door faced north was a hundred cubits[c] long and fifty cubits wide. 3Both in the section twenty cubits from the inner court and in the section opposite the pavement of the outer court, gallery faced gallery at the three levels. 4In front of the rooms was an inner passageway ten cubits wide and a hundred cubits[g] long. Their doors were on the north. 5Now the upper rooms were narrower, for the galleries took more space from them than from the rooms on the lower and middle floors of the building. 6The rooms on the third floor had no pillars, as the courts had; so they were smaller in floor

[a] *49* Septuagint; Hebrew *eleven* [b] *49* Hebrew; Septuagint *Ten steps led up to it* [c] *1,2* The common cubit was about 1 1/2 feet (about 0.5 meter). [d] *1* One Hebrew manuscript and Septuagint; most Hebrew manuscripts *side, the width of the tent* [e] *22* Septuagint; Hebrew *long* [f] *22* Septuagint; Hebrew *length* [g] *4* Septuagint and Syriac; Hebrew *and one cubit*

space than those on the lower and middle floors.
7There was an outer wall parallel to the rooms and
the outer court; it extended in front of the rooms
for fifty cubits. 8While the row of rooms on the
side next to the outer court was fifty cubits long,
the row on the side nearest the sanctuary was a
hundred cubits long. 9The lower rooms had an
entrance on the east side as one enters them from
the outer court. Eze 41:12-14; 44:5

10On the south side[a] along the length of the
wall of the outer court, adjoining the temple courtyard and opposite the outer wall, were rooms
11with a passageway in front of them. These were
like the rooms on the north; they had the same
length and width, with similar exits and dimensions. Similar to the doorways on the north 12were
the doorways of the rooms on the south. There
was a doorway at the beginning of the passageway
that was parallel to the corresponding wall extending eastward, by which one enters the rooms.

13Then he said to me, "The north and south
rooms facing the temple courtyard are the priests'
rooms, where the priests who approach the LORD
will eat the most holy offerings. There they will put
the most holy offerings—the grain offerings, the
sin offerings and the guilt offerings—for the place
is holy. 14Once the priests enter the holy precincts,
they are not to go into the outer court until they
leave behind the garments in which they minister,
for these are holy. They are to put on other clothes
before they go near the places that are for the
people." Ex 29:9; Lev 8:7-9

15When he had finished measuring what was
inside the temple area, he led me out by the east
gate and measured the area all around: 16He measured the east side with the measuring rod; it was
five hundred cubits.[b] 17He measured the north
side; it was five hundred cubits[c] by the measuring
rod. 18He measured the south side; it was five hundred cubits by the measuring rod. 19Then he
turned to the west side and measured; it was five
hundred cubits by the measuring rod. 20So he
measured the area on all four sides. It had a wall
around it, five hundred cubits long and five hundred cubits wide, to separate the holy from the
common. Eze 45:2; Rev 21:16

The Glory Returns to the Temple

43 Then the man brought me to the gate facing east, 2and I saw the glory of the God of
Israel coming from the east. His voice was like the
roar of rushing waters, and the land was radiant
with his glory. 3The vision I saw was like the vision
I had seen when he[d] came to destroy the city and
like the visions I had seen by the Kebar River, and
I fell facedown. 4The glory of the LORD entered the
temple through the gate facing east. 5Then the
Spirit lifted me up and brought me into the inner
court, and the glory of the LORD filled the temple.

6While the man was standing beside me, I heard
someone speaking to me from inside the temple.
7He said: "Son of man, this is the place of my
throne and the place for the soles of my feet. This
is where I will live among the Israelites forever.
The house of Israel will never again defile my holy
name—neither they nor their kings—by their
prostitution[e] and the lifeless idols[f] of their kings
at their high places. 8When they placed their
threshold next to my threshold and their doorposts beside my doorposts, with only a wall between me and them, they defiled my holy name by
their detestable practices. So I destroyed them in
my anger. 9Now let them put away from me their
prostitution and the lifeless idols of their kings,
and I will live among them forever. Eze 37:26-28

10"Son of man, describe the temple to the people of Israel, that they may be ashamed of their
sins. Let them consider the plan, 11and if they are
ashamed of all they have done, make known to
them the design of the temple—its arrangement,
its exits and entrances—its whole design and all its
regulations[g] and laws. Write these down before
them so that they may be faithful to its design and
follow all its regulations. Eze 16:61; 44:5

12"This is the law of the temple: All the surrounding area on top of the mountain will be most
holy. Such is the law of the temple. Eze 40:2

The Altar

13"These are the measurements of the altar in
long cubits, that cubit being a cubit[h] and a handbreadth[i]: Its gutter is a cubit deep and a cubit
wide, with a rim of one span[j] around the edge.
And this is the height of the altar: 14From the
gutter on the ground up to the lower ledge it is two
cubits high and a cubit wide, and from the smaller
ledge up to the larger ledge it is four cubits high
and a cubit wide. 15The altar hearth is four cubits
high, and four horns project upward from the
hearth. 16The altar hearth is square, twelve cubits
long and twelve cubits wide. 17The upper ledge
also is square, fourteen cubits long and fourteen
cubits wide, with a rim of half a cubit and a gutter
of a cubit all around. The steps of the altar face
east." Ex 20:26; 2Ch 4:1

18Then he said to me, "Son of man, this is what
the Sovereign LORD says: These will be the regulations for sacrificing burnt offerings and sprinkling

[a] *10* Septuagint; Hebrew *Eastward* [b] *16* See Septuagint of verse 17; Hebrew *rods*; also in verses 18 and 19. [c] *17* Septuagint; Hebrew *rods* [d] *3* Some Hebrew manuscripts and Vulgate; most Hebrew manuscripts *I* [e] *7* Or *their spiritual adultery*; also in verse 9 [f] *7* Or *the corpses*; also in verse 9 [g] *11* Some Hebrew manuscripts and Septuagint; most Hebrew manuscripts *regulations and its whole design* [h] *13* The common cubit was about 1 1/2 feet (about 0.5 meter). [i] *13* That is, about 3 inches (about 8 centimeters) [j] *13* That is, about 9 inches (about 22 centimeters)

blood upon the altar when it is built: 19You are to give a young bull as a sin offering to the priests, who are Levites, of the family of Zadok, who come near to minister before me, declares the Sovereign LORD. 20You are to take some of its blood and put it on the four horns of the altar and on the four corners of the upper ledge and all around the rim, and so purify the altar and make atonement for it. 21You are to take the bull for the sin offering and burn it in the designated part of the temple area outside the sanctuary. Ex 29:14; Heb 13:11

22"On the second day you are to offer a male goat without defect for a sin offering, and the altar is to be purified as it was purified with the bull. 23When you have finished purifying it, you are to offer a young bull and a ram from the flock, both without defect. 24You are to offer them before the LORD, and the priests are to sprinkle salt on them and sacrifice them as a burnt offering to the LORD.

25"For seven days you are to provide a male goat daily for a sin offering; you are also to provide a young bull and a ram from the flock, both without defect. 26For seven days they are to make atonement for the altar and cleanse it; thus they will dedicate it. 27At the end of these days, from the eighth day on, the priests are to present your burnt offerings and fellowship offerings[a] on the altar. Then I will accept you, declares the Sovereign LORD." Lev 8:33; 17:5

The Prince, the Levites, the Priests

44 Then the man brought me back to the outer gate of the sanctuary, the one facing east, and it was shut. 2The LORD said to me, "This gate is to remain shut. It must not be opened; no one may enter through it. It is to remain shut because the LORD, the God of Israel, has entered through it. 3The prince himself is the only one who may sit inside the gateway to eat in the presence of the LORD. He is to enter by way of the portico of the gateway and go out the same way." Eze 46:2,8

4Then the man brought me by way of the north gate to the front of the temple. I looked and saw the glory of the LORD filling the temple of the LORD, and I fell facedown. Eze 1:28; 3:23

5The LORD said to me, "Son of man, look carefully, listen closely and give attention to everything I tell you concerning all the regulations regarding the temple of the LORD. Give attention to the entrance of the temple and all the exits of the sanctuary. 6Say to the rebellious house of Israel, 'This is what the Sovereign LORD says: Enough of your detestable practices, O house of Israel! 7In addition to all your other detestable practices, you brought foreigners uncircumcised in heart and flesh into my sanctuary, desecrating my temple while you offered me food, fat and blood, and you broke my covenant. 8Instead of carrying out your duty in regard to my holy things, you put others in charge of my sanctuary. 9This is what the Sovereign LORD says: No foreigner uncircumcised in heart and flesh is to enter my sanctuary, not even the foreigners who live among the Israelites.

10" 'The Levites who went far from me when Israel went astray and who wandered from me after their idols must bear the consequences of their sin. 11They may serve in my sanctuary, having charge of the gates of the temple and serving in it; they may slaughter the burnt offerings and sacrifices for the people and stand before the people and serve them. 12But because they served them in the presence of their idols and made the house of Israel fall into sin, therefore I have sworn with uplifted hand that they must bear the consequences of their sin, declares the Sovereign LORD. 13They are not to come near to serve me as priests or come near any of my holy things or my most holy offerings; they must bear the shame of their detestable practices. 14Yet I will put them in charge of the duties of the temple and all the work that is to be done in it. 2Ki 23:8; Nu 18:23

15" 'But the priests, who are Levites and descendants of Zadok and who faithfully carried out the duties of my sanctuary when the Israelites went astray from me, are to come near to minister before me; they are to stand before me to offer sacrifices of fat and blood, declares the Sovereign LORD. 16They alone are to enter my sanctuary; they alone are to come near my table to minister before me and perform my service. Nu 18:5; Eze 40:46

17" 'When they enter the gates of the inner court, they are to wear linen clothes; they must not wear any woolen garment while ministering at the gates of the inner court or inside the temple. 18They are to wear linen turbans on their heads and linen undergarments around their waists. They must not wear anything that makes them perspire. 19When they go out into the outer court where the people are, they are to take off the clothes they have been ministering in and are to leave them in the sacred rooms, and put on other clothes, so that they do not consecrate the people by means of their garments. Eze 42:14; 46:20

20" 'They must not shave their heads or let their hair grow long, but they are to keep the hair of their heads trimmed. 21No priest is to drink wine when he enters the inner court. 22They must not marry widows or divorced women; they may marry only virgins of Israelite descent or widows of priests. 23They are to teach my people the difference between the holy and the common and show them how to distinguish between the unclean and the clean. Eze 22:26; Mal 2:7

24" 'In any dispute, the priests are to serve as

[a]27 Traditionally *peace offerings*

judges and decide it according to my ordinances.
They are to keep my laws and my decrees for all
my appointed feasts, and they are to keep my Sabbaths holy. Dt 17:8-9; 2Ch 19:8

25 "'A priest must not defile himself by going
near a dead person; however, if the dead person
was his father or mother, son or daughter, brother
or unmarried sister, then he may defile himself.
26 After he is cleansed, he must wait seven days.
27 On the day he goes into the inner court of the
sanctuary to minister in the sanctuary, he is to
offer a sin offering for himself, declares the Sovereign LORD. Lev 21:1-4; Nu 19:14

28 "'I am to be the only inheritance the priests
have. You are to give them no possession in Israel;
I will be their possession. 29 They will eat the grain
offerings, the sin offerings and the guilt offerings;
and everything in Israel devoted[a] to the LORD will
belong to them. 30 The best of all the firstfruits and
of all your special gifts will belong to the priests.
You are to give them the first portion of your
ground meal so that a blessing may rest on your
household. 31 The priests must not eat anything,
bird or animal, found dead or torn by wild animals. Nu 18:20; Dt 10:9; 18:1-2

Division of the Land

45 "'When you allot the land as an inheritance, you are to present to the LORD a
portion of the land as a sacred district, 25,000
cubits long and 20,000[b] cubits wide; the entire
area will be holy. 2 Of this, a section 500 cubits
square is to be for the sanctuary, with 50 cubits
around it for open land. 3 In the sacred district,
measure off a section 25,000 cubits[c] long and
10,000 cubits[d] wide. In it will be the sanctuary,
the Most Holy Place. 4 It will be the sacred portion
of the land for the priests, who minister in the
sanctuary and who draw near to minister before
the LORD. It will be a place for their houses as well
as a holy place for the sanctuary. 5 An area 25,000
cubits long and 10,000 cubits wide will belong to
the Levites, who serve in the temple, as their possession for towns to live in.[e] Eze 47:21-22; 48:13

6 "'You are to give the city as its property an
area 5,000 cubits wide and 25,000 cubits long, adjoining the sacred portion; it will belong to the
whole house of Israel. Eze 48:15-18

7 "'The prince will have the land bordering each
side of the area formed by the sacred district and
the property of the city. It will extend westward
from the west side and eastward from the east side,
running lengthwise from the western to the eastern border parallel to one of the tribal portions.
8 This land will be his possession in Israel. And my
princes will no longer oppress my people but will
allow the house of Israel to possess the land according to their tribes. Eze 46:18; 48:21

9 "'This is what the Sovereign LORD says: You
have gone far enough, O princes of Israel! Give up
your violence and oppression and do what is just
and right. Stop dispossessing my people, declares
the Sovereign LORD. 10 You are to use accurate
scales, an accurate ephah[f] and an accurate
bath.[g] 11 The ephah and the bath are to be the
same size, the bath containing a tenth of a homer[h] and the ephah a tenth of a homer; the homer is to be the standard measure for both. 12 The
shekel[i] is to consist of twenty gerahs. Twenty
shekels plus twenty-five shekels plus fifteen shekels equal one mina.[j] Jer 22:3; Zec 7:9-10; 8:16

Offerings and Holy Days

13 "'This is the special gift you are to offer: a
sixth of an ephah from each homer of wheat and
a sixth of an ephah from each homer of barley.
14 The prescribed portion of oil, measured by the
bath, is a tenth of a bath from each cor (which
consists of ten baths or one homer, for ten baths
are equivalent to a homer). 15 Also one sheep is to
be taken from every flock of two hundred from the
well-watered pastures of Israel. These will be used
for the grain offerings, burnt offerings and fellowship offerings[k] to make atonement for the people,
declares the Sovereign LORD. 16 All the people of the
land will participate in this special gift for the use
of the prince in Israel. 17 It will be the duty of the
prince to provide the burnt offerings, grain offerings and drink offerings at the festivals, the New
Moons and the Sabbaths—at all the appointed
feasts of the house of Israel. He will provide the sin
offerings, grain offerings, burnt offerings and fellowship offerings to make atonement for the
house of Israel. 1Ki 8:62; 2Ch 31:3

18 "'This is what the Sovereign LORD says: In the
first month on the first day you are to take a young
bull without defect and purify the sanctuary. 19 The
priest is to take some of the blood of the sin offering and put it on the doorposts of the temple, on
the four corners of the upper ledge of the altar and
on the gateposts of the inner court. 20 You are to do
the same on the seventh day of the month for
anyone who sins unintentionally or through ignorance; so you are to make atonement for the temple. Lev 4:27; Eze 43:20

21 "'In the first month on the fourteenth day you

[a] *29* The Hebrew term refers to the irrevocable giving over of things or persons to the LORD. [b] *1* Septuagint (see also verses 3 and 5 and 48:9); Hebrew *10,000* [c] *3* That is, about 7 miles (about 12 kilometers) [d] *3* That is, about 3 miles (about 5 kilometers) [e] *5* Septuagint; Hebrew *temple; they will have as their possession 20 rooms* [f] *10* An ephah was a dry measure. [g] *10* A bath was a liquid measure. [h] *11* A homer was a dry measure. [i] *12* A shekel weighed about 2/5 ounce (about 11.5 grams). [j] *12* That is, 60 shekels; the common mina was 50 shekels. [k] *15* Traditionally *peace offerings*; also in verse 17

are to observe the Passover, a feast lasting seven days, during which you shall eat bread made without yeast. 22On that day the prince is to provide a bull as a sin offering for himself and for all the people of the land. 23Every day during the seven days of the Feast he is to provide seven bulls and seven rams without defect as a burnt offering to the LORD, and a male goat for a sin offering. 24He is to provide as a grain offering an ephah for each bull and an ephah for each ram, along with a hin[a] of oil for each ephah. Ex 12:11; Lev 23:5-6

25" 'During the seven days of the Feast, which begins in the seventh month on the fifteenth day, he is to make the same provision for sin offerings, burnt offerings, grain offerings and oil.

46 " 'This is what the Sovereign LORD says: The gate of the inner court facing east is to be shut on the six working days, but on the Sabbath day and on the day of the New Moon it is to be opened. 2The prince is to enter from the outside through the portico of the gateway and stand by the gatepost. The priests are to sacrifice his burnt offering and his fellowship offerings.[b] He is to worship at the threshold of the gateway and then go out, but the gate will not be shut until evening. 3On the Sabbaths and New Moons the people of the land are to worship in the presence of the LORD at the entrance to that gateway. 4The burnt offering the prince brings to the LORD on the Sabbath day is to be six male lambs and a ram, all without defect. 5The grain offering given with the ram is to be an ephah,[c] and the grain offering with the lambs is to be as much as he pleases, along with a hin[a] of oil for each ephah. 6On the day of the New Moon he is to offer a young bull, six lambs and a ram, all without defect. 7He is to provide as a grain offering one ephah with the bull, one ephah with the ram, and with the lambs as much as he wants to give, along with a hin of oil with each ephah. 8When the prince enters, he is to go in through the portico of the gateway, and he is to come out the same way. Eze 40:19; 44:3

9" 'When the people of the land come before the LORD at the appointed feasts, whoever enters by the north gate to worship is to go out the south gate; and whoever enters by the south gate is to go out the north gate. No one is to return through the gate by which he entered, but each is to go out the opposite gate. 10The prince is to be among them, going in when they go in and going out when they go out. Ex 23:14; Ps 42:4

11" 'At the festivals and the appointed feasts, the grain offering is to be an ephah with a bull, an ephah with a ram, and with the lambs as much as one pleases, along with a hin of oil for each ephah. 12When the prince provides a freewill offering to the LORD—whether a burnt offering or fellowship offerings—the gate facing east is to be opened for him. He shall offer his burnt offering or his fellowship offerings as he does on the Sabbath day. Then he shall go out, and after he has gone out, the gate will be shut. Eze 45:17

13" 'Every day you are to provide a year-old lamb without defect for a burnt offering to the LORD; morning by morning you shall provide it. 14You are also to provide with it morning by morning a grain offering, consisting of a sixth of an ephah with a third of a hin of oil to moisten the flour. The presenting of this grain offering to the LORD is a lasting ordinance. 15So the lamb and the grain offering and the oil shall be provided morning by morning for a regular burnt offering.

16" 'This is what the Sovereign LORD says: If the prince makes a gift from his inheritance to one of his sons, it will also belong to his descendants; it is to be their property by inheritance. 17If, however, he makes a gift from his inheritance to one of his servants, the servant may keep it until the year of freedom; then it will revert to the prince. His inheritance belongs to his sons only; it is theirs. 18The prince must not take any of the inheritance of the people, driving them off their property. He is to give his sons their inheritance out of his own property, so that none of my people will be separated from his property.' " Eze 45:8; Mic 2:1-2

19Then the man brought me through the entrance at the side of the gate to the sacred rooms facing north, which belonged to the priests, and showed me a place at the western end. 20He said to me, "This is the place where the priests will cook the guilt offering and the sin offering and bake the grain offering, to avoid bringing them into the outer court and consecrating the people."

21He then brought me to the outer court and led me around to its four corners, and I saw in each corner another court. 22In the four corners of the outer court were enclosed[d] courts, forty cubits long and thirty cubits wide; each of the courts in the four corners was the same size. 23Around the inside of each of the four courts was a ledge of stone, with places for fire built all around under the ledge. 24He said to me, "These are the kitchens where those who minister at the temple will cook the sacrifices of the people."

The River From the Temple

47 The man brought me back to the entrance of the temple, and I saw water coming out from under the threshold of the temple toward the east (for the temple faced east). The water was coming down from under the south side of the temple, south of the altar. 2He then brought me

[a] 24,5 That is, probably about 4 quarts (about 4 liters) [b] 2 Traditionally *peace offerings*; also in verse 12 [c] 5 That is, probably about 3/5 bushel (about 22 liters) [d] 22 The meaning of the Hebrew for this word is uncertain.

out through the north gate and led me around the
outside to the outer gate facing east, and the water
was flowing from the south side. Joel 3:18; Rev 22:1
3As the man went eastward with a measuring
line in his hand, he measured off a thousand cubits[a] and then led me through water that was
ankle-deep. 4He measured off another thousand
cubits and led me through water that was knee-
deep. He measured off another thousand and led
me through water that was up to the waist. 5He
measured off another thousand, but now it was a
river that I could not cross, because the water had
risen and was deep enough to swim in—a river
that no one could cross. 6He asked me, "Son of
man, do you see this?" Isa 11:9; Eze 40:3
Then he led me back to the bank of the river.
7When I arrived there, I saw a great number of
trees on each side of the river. 8He said to me,
"This water flows toward the eastern region and
goes down into the Arabah,[b] where it enters the
Sea.[c] When it empties into the Sea,[c] the water
there becomes fresh. 9Swarms of living creatures
will live wherever the river flows. There will be
large numbers of fish, because this water flows
there and makes the salt water fresh; so where the
river flows everything will live. 10Fishermen will
stand along the shore; from En Gedi to En Eglaim
there will be places for spreading nets. The fish will
be of many kinds—like the fish of the Great Sea.[d]
11But the swamps and marshes will not become
fresh; they will be left for salt. 12Fruit trees of all
kinds will grow on both banks of the river. Their
leaves will not wither, nor will their fruit fail. Every
month they will bear, because the water from the
sanctuary flows to them. Their fruit will serve for
food and their leaves for healing." Ps 1:3; Jer 17:8

The Boundaries of the Land

13This is what the Sovereign LORD says: "These
are the boundaries by which you are to divide the
land for an inheritance among the twelve tribes of
Israel, with two portions for Joseph. 14You are to
divide it equally among them. Because I swore
with uplifted hand to give it to your forefathers,
this land will become your inheritance. Dt 1:8

15"This is to be the boundary of the land:

"On the north side it will run from the Great Sea
by the Hethlon road past Lebo[e] Hamath to
Zedad, 16Berothah[f] and Sibraim (which lies
on the border between Damascus and Hamath), as far as Hazer Hatticon, which is on
the border of Hauran. 17The boundary will extend from the sea to Hazar Enan,[g] along the
northern border of Damascus, with the border
of Hamath to the north. This will be the north
boundary. Eze 48:1
18"On the east side the boundary will run between
Hauran and Damascus, along the Jordan between Gilead and the land of Israel, to the
eastern sea and as far as Tamar.[h] This will be
the east boundary. Eze 27:18
19"On the south side it will run from Tamar as far
as the waters of Meribah Kadesh, then along
the Wadi ⌞of Egypt⌟ to the Great Sea. This will
be the south boundary. Eze 48:28
20"On the west side, the Great Sea will be the
boundary to a point opposite Lebo[i] Hamath.
This will be the west boundary. Nu 34:6; Eze 48:1

21"You are to distribute this land among yourselves according to the tribes of Israel. 22You are to
allot it as an inheritance for yourselves and for the
aliens who have settled among you and who have
children. You are to consider them as native-born
Israelites; along with you they are to be allotted an
inheritance among the tribes of Israel. 23In whatever tribe the alien settles, there you are to give
him his inheritance," declares the Sovereign LORD.

The Division of the Land

48 "These are the tribes, listed by name: At
the northern frontier, Dan will have one
portion; it will follow the Hethlon road to Lebo[j]
Hamath; Hazar Enan and the northern border of
Damascus next to Hamath will be part of its border from the east side to the west side. Ge 30:6
2"Asher will have one portion; it will border the
territory of Dan from east to west. Jos 19:24-31
3"Naphtali will have one portion; it will border
the territory of Asher from east to west.
4"Manasseh will have one portion; it will border
the territory of Naphtali from east to west.
5"Ephraim will have one portion; it will border
the territory of Manasseh from east to west.
6"Reuben will have one portion; it will border
the territory of Ephraim from east to west.
7"Judah will have one portion; it will border the
territory of Reuben from east to west. Jos 15:1-63
8"Bordering the territory of Judah from east to
west will be the portion you are to present as a
special gift. It will be 25,000 cubits[k] wide, and its
length from east to west will equal one of the tribal
portions; the sanctuary will be in the center of it.
9"The special portion you are to offer to the
LORD will be 25,000 cubits long and 10,000 cubits[l]
wide. 10This will be the sacred portion for the
priests. It will be 25,000 cubits long on the north

[a] 3 That is, about 1,500 feet (about 450 meters) [b] 8 Or *the Jordan Valley* [c] 8 That is, the Dead Sea [d] 10 That is, the Mediterranean; also in verses 15, 19 and 20 [e] 15 Or *past the entrance to* [f] 15,16 See Septuagint and Ezekiel 48:1; Hebrew *road to go into Zedad, 16Hamath, Berothah* [g] 17 Hebrew *Enon,* a variant of *Enan* [h] 18 Septuagint and Syriac; Hebrew *Israel. You will measure to the eastern sea* [i] 20 Or *opposite the entrance to* [j] 1 Or *to the entrance to* [k] 8 That is, about 7 miles (about 12 kilometers) [l] 9 That is, about 3 miles (about 5 kilometers)

side, 10,000 cubits wide on the west side, 10,000
cubits wide on the east side and 25,000 cubits long
on the south side. In the center of it will be the
sanctuary of the LORD. [11]This will be for the consecrated priests, the Zadokites, who were faithful in
serving me and did not go astray as the Levites did
when the Israelites went astray. [12]It will be a special
gift to them from the sacred portion of the land, a
most holy portion, bordering the territory of the
Levites. Eze 44:15
[13]"Alongside the territory of the priests, the Levites will have an allotment 25,000 cubits long and
10,000 cubits wide. Its total length will be 25,000
cubits and its width 10,000 cubits. [14]They must not
sell or exchange any of it. This is the best of the
land and must not pass into other hands, because
it is holy to the LORD. Lev 25:34; 27:10,28
[15]"The remaining area, 5,000 cubits wide and
25,000 cubits long, will be for the common use of
the city, for houses and for pastureland. The city
will be in the center of it [16]and will have these
measurements: the north side 4,500 cubits, the
south side 4,500 cubits, the east side 4,500 cubits,
and the west side 4,500 cubits. [17]The pastureland
for the city will be 250 cubits on the north, 250
cubits on the south, 250 cubits on the east, and 250
cubits on the west. [18]What remains of the area,
bordering on the sacred portion and running the
length of it, will be 10,000 cubits on the east side
and 10,000 cubits on the west side. Its produce will
supply food for the workers of the city. [19]The
workers from the city who farm it will come from
all the tribes of Israel. [20]The entire portion will be
a square, 25,000 cubits on each side. As a special
gift you will set aside the sacred portion, along
with the property of the city. Rev 21:16
[21]"What remains on both sides of the area
formed by the sacred portion and the city property
will belong to the prince. It will extend eastward
from the 25,000 cubits of the sacred portion to the
eastern border, and westward from the 25,000 cubits to the western border. Both these areas running the length of the tribal portions will belong to
the prince, and the sacred portion with the temple
sanctuary will be in the center of them. [22]So the
property of the Levites and the property of the city
will lie in the center of the area that belongs to the
prince. The area belonging to the prince will lie
between the border of Judah and the border of
Benjamin. Eze 45:7
[23]"As for the rest of the tribes: Benjamin will
have one portion; it will extend from the east side
to the west side. Jos 18:11-28
[24]"Simeon will have one portion; it will border
the territory of Benjamin from east to west.
[25]"Issachar will have one portion; it will border
the territory of Simeon from east to west.
[26]"Zebulun will have one portion; it will border
the territory of Issachar from east to west.
[27]"Gad will have one portion; it will border the
territory of Zebulun from east to west. Jos 13:24-28
[28]"The southern boundary of Gad will run
south from Tamar to the waters of Meribah Kadesh, then along the Wadi ⌞of Egypt⌟ to the Great
Sea.[a] Eze 47:19
[29]"This is the land you are to allot as an inheritance to the tribes of Israel, and these will be their
portions," declares the Sovereign LORD. Eze 45:1

The Gates of the City

[30]"These will be the exits of the city: Beginning
on the north side, which is 4,500 cubits long, [31]the
gates of the city will be named after the tribes of
Israel. The three gates on the north side will be the
gate of Reuben, the gate of Judah and the gate of
Levi.
[32]"On the east side, which is 4,500 cubits long,
will be three gates: the gate of Joseph, the gate of
Benjamin and the gate of Dan.
[33]"On the south side, which measures 4,500 cubits, will be three gates: the gate of Simeon, the
gate of Issachar and the gate of Zebulun.
[34]"On the west side, which is 4,500 cubits long,
will be three gates: the gate of Gad, the gate of
Asher and the gate of Naphtali. Rev 21:12-13
[35]"The distance all around will be 18,000 cubits.
"And the name of the city from that time on
will be:

THE LORD IS THERE."

[a]*28* That is, the Mediterranean

INTRODUCTION

DANIEL

It is doubtful that any Old Testament prophet played a more significant role in the history of Israel than Daniel. Taken from his homeland while still a teenager (probably no older than 15 years of age) and pushed through a highly competitive crash course in a foreign culture, Daniel emerged as the premier prophet during the reigns of several kings during the captivity era. In his *person* we find a model of integrity, flawless to the core. And in his *prophecies* we discover a panorama of truth regarding God's plan for the Gentile nations outlined nowhere else in such clear detail. With its New Testament counterpart, the book of Revelation, we can fit together a fairly complete account of future events set forth in the pages of Scripture.

WRITER: *Daniel*

DATE: *c.536–530 B.C.*

PURPOSE: *To encourage the exiles in Babylon by reminding them of God's ultimate control*

KEY THEME: *God's sovereignty*

KEY VERSES: *2:22; 4:34-35; 5:21*

TIME LINE 1400BC 1300 1200 1100 1000 900 800 700 600 500 400

Jeremiah's ministry in Judah (c.626-585 B.C.)

Daniel's exile in Babylon (c.605-536 B.C.)

Fall of Jerusalem (586 B.C.)

Persia's conquest of Babylon (539 B.C.)

Daniel in the lions' den (c.539 B.C.)

First return of exiles to Jerusalem (538 B.C.)

Book of Daniel written (c.536-530 B.C.)

End of Daniel's ministry (c.536 B.C.)

Integrity and Faith Personified

BIOGRAPHICAL SECTION	PROPHETICAL SECTION
Daniel Interprets Others' Dreams	**Angel Interprets Daniel's Dreams**
MAIN EMPHASIS: **DANIEL THE PROPHET**	MAIN EMPHASIS: **THE PROPHECIES OF DANIEL**
Introduction and setting *(1)*	Daniel's major vision *(7)*
Nebuchadnezzar's major dream *(2)*	Prophetic visions (near and far) *(8–12)*
Historical narratives (political and personal) *(3–6)*	
CHAPTERS 1–6	***CHAPTERS 7–12***

POLITICAL POWERS	. . . IN DANIEL'S DAY		. . . AND AFTERWARD
BABYLONIAN RULE	**MEDO-PERSIAN RULE**	**GRECIAN RULE**	**ROMAN RULE**
Nebuchadnezzar	**Darius (Media)**	**Alexander the Great**	**Last of the**
Belshazzar	**Cyrus (Persia)**	**Four Generals**	**Gentile powers**

As I was growing up, there were several Bible characters who were my favorites. They became my heroes. All of them had physical strength—I suppose that's the way it is with young boys. My number-one hero was Samson. A body-builder named Charles Atlas was "hot stuff" in my younger years. I can still remember reading about and being impressed by "dynamic tension" (I'm not sure I knew what it was, but it sounded impressive!), as his little ads came out in magazines and newspapers. I was convinced that if anybody ever possessed it, Samson did. He was tough. He was rugged. Anybody who could whip a thousand people with the jawbone of a donkey had to have "dynamic tension." He was my hero.

Second on my list of heoes was David. David was also a man of great physical strength. He killed a bear, a lion and even a giant—all while he was still a teenager. I admired David greatly because of his physical strength. There was, I suppose, a tie for third place between Joshua and Gideon. Both were men of great courage. I often identified with what it must have been like to lead an army against incalculable odds and to come out on the victorious side. These men were my childhood heroes.

Frankly, I didn't think a great deal about Daniel. The only picture of Daniel I had was that time when he was in a lions' den (chapter 6). But as I conjured up the picture in my mind, he wasn't fighting the lions; he was just sleeping by them. I always thought if a man really possessed courage, he would fight lions—he wouldn't sleep with them, like Daniel did. He obviously didn't have "dynamic tension." So he never made it on to my list of heroes.

Having grown older, I've come to realize that physical strength is not really the best example of true strength. Some of the most physically strong persons on earth are terribly weak. They are putty in the hands of whatever whim or temptation comes along. Later in life I learned a hymn that Philip Bliss wrote. It goes like this:

> *Standing by a purpose true, heeding God's command.*
> *Honor them, the faithful few! All hail to Daniel's band.*

Dare to be a Daniel, dare to stand alone!
Dare to have a purpose firm! Dare to make it known.

The longer I live, the more I have seen Daniel rise in the standings until he is now number one on my hero list. (Samson is now last!) Daniel was a man of the finest kind of strength. He was a man of absolute integrity—a character trait that when found in a person's life invariably makes that life a sterling example of God's indwelling presence.

The Setting of Daniel

If you take the time to read the introduction to the book of Ezekiel (see page 824), you will know the background to the book of Daniel; each of these men lived during the same era. They were only a very few years apart in age (Ezekiel being about two years older). The nation of Judah had been invaded and conquered by Babylon. As a young man, Daniel watched that invasion take place. Daniel was of noble blood. He was certainly a prime candidate to be selected for captivity—a bright, gifted young man. He would be very qualified to help in the captor's government—the government of Babylon. As the Babylonian troops invaded, King Nebuchadnezzar, according to verse 1 of chapter 1, "came to Jerusalem and besieged it." He took control of the city; he took his pick of the spoil of the city and the precious articles of the temple. Over the course of about twenty years he took captive the whole nation. Daniel was included in the first deportation, which took place in 605 B.C. The second deportation occurred in 597 B.C. and included Ezekiel, while the third took place in 586 B.C. when the Babylonians destroyed Jerusalem and the temple. Some have suggested that anywhere from 8,000 to 15,000 people were taken to Babylon during the span of time from 605 to 586 B.C.

From this number, the king would have selected a small number of exiles who were unusually gifted and who could be of value to him in his government. Daniel was one of those men. Many students of the Bible believe he was not more than 15 years old at the time, which makes his integrity and his solid devotion to God so striking. As the Bible records it,

Then the king ordered Ashpenaz, chief of his court officials, to bring in some of the Israelites from the royal family and the nobility—young men . . . (1:3).

"Young men." We would say "teenagers"—those beyond the ages of 11 or 12 but not yet having reached the age of 20. It is reasonable to assume that these were men in young manhood.

Now these were not supposed to be just any young men. Notice the qualifications that are required for the job:

. . . young men without any physical defect, handsome, showing aptitude for every kind of learning, well informed, quick to understand, and qualified to serve in the king's palace. He was to teach them the language and literature of the Babylonians (1:4).

Look at the clever plan of the Babylonians. A crash course to teach Daniel and his colleagues the literature, the philosophy and the language of Babylon. Remember that from his infancy Daniel had been taught, probably by his parents, about the God of the Jews—that this God was the one true God, the God of heaven and earth, the Creator of all things, that this God was to be served in such a way that would bring Him glory among the nations. Suddenly a young man who had grown up in a protected environment was to be plunged into a setting designed to rip out his traditional, well-defined roots and make him a broadminded, Babylonian-thinking young man. Daniel and his friends would be taught an entirely different set of standards. They would be exposed to a different lifestyle in a city viewed by many as one of the "wonders of the world"—a beautiful city containing all the latest in luxuries and sensual pleasures.

The king hoped to train these men for unique positions in his own government, for they were physically strong, attractive, highly intelligent and young. For three years these teens would be enrolled in this curriculum. Rubbing shoulders with one another, they would go through a series of classes and field education for three years—brainwashing experiences, if you will—in the hope of being equipped to serve the king and his purposes.

Bringing It Home . . . to You and Me

Take a moment to think about how would you feel—you're suddenly removed from your home, your roots, your religion. Your Bible is taken away and replaced with a new "religious book" that speaks another language and promotes another philosophy and lifestyle that run contrary to most of what you have known, loved and believed all your life. In essence that's what happened to four Jewish young men named Daniel, Hananiah, Mishael and Azariah. They were dislodged from their roots and given new names with new meanings. And the process of melding into Babylonian culture went on for three uninterrupted years.

It's one thing to sit and merely think about it, to intellectually enter into the experience of being asked to assume a new identity, as it were. It's something else entirely to *be* there and to experience the pressure that pounds incessantly against your character. There's no escape from it. There's no vacation. It's every day. It's boot camp for three years, away from everything that's familiar—and its purpose is to turn you away from the things of God. I wonder how many of us would be drawn into that new philosophy of life?

Taking a Stand

Look at the temptation that faced these young exiles from the very first day: "The king assigned them a daily amount of food and wine from the king's table" (1:5). Now this wasn't just any food or wine; this was "royal"—from the kitchens of the king! They were ordered to eat the same food the king ate—and you better believe it was tasty food! Yet it was contaminated food in the eyes of the young Jews, for the first portion of the food would have been offered to idols; furthermore, ceremonially unclean animals were used and therefore unsuitable for Jews to eat.

The pressure was there, believe me! With the court officials hovering nearby, Daniel and his friends were undoubtedly tempted to just pick up the fork and start eating. "Just one little exception. Shouldn't hurt anything, right?" they might have thought. Verse 8 of chapter 1 tells us how Daniel responded to the temptation: "But Daniel resolved not to defile himself with the royal food and wine."

Look at that! Plain and simple, Daniel made up his mind. He knew what he had to do—and he did it. Integrity takes root as a mental attitude that says, "Nothing will move me from my faith! I am determined to stand firm. If no one else stands with me, that's okay. I have made up my mind! No amount of pressure will change my decision."

Daniel requested that he and his friends be given an alternative menu—nothing but vegetables and water. And he offered a ten-day testing time. That alone would be a test for teenagers, wouldn't it? Just vegetables! Daniel was very gracious when he made his request. He didn't demand a change. He wasn't obnoxious. He didn't lead a march against the establishment or preach some dramatic, loud sermon. Very simply and tactfully, he asked for the plan to be rearranged. And, wonder of wonders, the guard agreed to the new plan. Permission granted! And in God's good providence, this was the result: "At the end of the ten days they looked healthier and better nourished than any of the young men who ate the royal food" (1:15).

Are you maybe wondering whether those four young men stood up under the pressure for the balance of the three-year course? If you read on in chapter 1 of Daniel, you'll get the answer. They graduated at the top of their class: "In every matter of wisdom and understanding about which the king questioned them, he found them ten times better than all the magicians and enchanters in his whole kingdom" (1:20).

There's a verse in the book of Proverbs that promises, "When a man's ways are pleasing to the LORD, he makes even his enemies live at peace with him" (16:7). Daniel's ways pleased the Lord, and the promise of the proverb was fulfilled—those who were enemies of God had peace with Daniel. Daniel was privileged to lead a life of influence as counselor to Nebuchadnezzar and later as supervisor of all the wise men of Babylon (2:48).

You can't sufficiently appreciate the impact of this Bible hero's walk with the Lord without knowing the flow of history. His ways were pleasing to the Lord *his whole life through*. Throughout the reigns of several monarchs, throughout numerous decades, Daniel served in that responsible position in the Babylonian and then the Persian governments. (Remember that the Persians and the Medes conquered Babylon in 539 B.C.) For how long? Until he was almost 90 years old! Throughout all those years he maintained his integrity. He stayed the course. He pleased the Lord.

God Is Sovereign!

God used Daniel in such tremendous ways. As we read through this book we find some of the best-loved stories in the Old Testament. The accounts of Shadrach, Meshach and Abednego in the fiery furnace and Daniel in the lions' den are sandwiched between other awe-inspiring illustrations of God's power. In chapters 2, 4, 5 and 7 Daniel and his friends demonstrated God's power to provide the revelation necessary to interpret dreams and other extraordinary experiences. (Remember the mysterious hand that appeared out of nowhere to write a message on a wall!) The destinies of the nations of the world are clearly in view in chapters 2–7, while the destiny of the nation of Israel is in view in chapters 8–12. Throughout the entire book the theme of God's sovereignty comes shining through: "The Most High God is sovereign over the kingdoms of men" (5:21). Daniel's visions always show God as triumphant. *He has won the victory*! The day of climax is coming, and that truth is described in the book of Revelation: "The kingdom of the world has become the kingdom of our Lord and of his Christ, and he will reign for ever and ever" (Revelation 11:15).

Lessons From Daniel

I find many lasting truths emerging from this grand prophetic book. Two stand out as paramount. First, *a promise with authority is a calm assurance in the hearts of men and women*. When God speaks a promise, He keeps it. When He promises to care about us and to care for us, He keeps that promise. When He promises to reward those who stay true, who live in ways that are pleasing to Him, He is faithful to carry out what He has promised. Second, *a person of integrity is a powerful instrument in the hand of God*. When you do what is right, you may be viewed as weird, you may be maligned, you may have people think and say things about you that are not true. For reasons known only to God, your integrity will incite the anger and resentment of some. But this one truth remains: You *will* become a powerful instrument in the hand of God.

When you do what is right, when you take a stand for integrity, some will misunderstand. It's the price you pay. But as you live consciously clean before God, He will give you a freedom and a power that is beyond anything you could imagine. He will free you from the chains of human opinion. He will free you to live for Him. So continue to live with integrity. Dare to be a Daniel. Dare to do the right thing, for God has honored that kind of conviction in the past, He honors it today and He will continue to honor it in the future.

Getting the Setting **Chapter 1**

It is hard to enter fully into the situation that Daniel and his three young friends faced. Their homeland had been invaded. Their holy city had been plundered. Many of their people had been killed and many others had been taken captive. They became strangers in a strange land. Nebuchadnezzar, the king of Babylon, desired to train a few of the most gifted young Hebrew men to be leaders in his government; Daniel and his friends were among this chosen group. They were given new clothes and new names and introduced to a new language and a completely new culture. They were also offered rich food and wine from the king's table during their time of training. Their commitment to obey God and remain pure and faithful to Him in the midst of incredible adversity stands as an enduring example to all believers, both young and old.

Daniel's Training in Babylon

1 In the third year of the reign of Jehoiakim
king of Judah, Nebuchadnezzar king of Babylon came to Jerusalem and besieged it. 2And the
Lord delivered Jehoiakim king of Judah into his
hand, along with some of the articles from the
temple of God. These he carried off to the temple
of his god in Babylonia[a] and put in the treasure
house of his god. 2Ch 36:6; Jer 27:19-20; Zec 5:5-11
3Then the king ordered Ashpenaz, chief of his
court officials, to bring in some of the Israelites
from the royal family and the nobility— 4young
men without any physical defect, handsome,
showing aptitude for every kind of learning, well
informed, quick to understand, and qualified to
serve in the king's palace. He was to teach them
the language and literature of the Babylonians.[b]
5The king assigned them a daily amount of food
and wine from the king's table. They were to be
trained for three years, and after that they were to
enter the king's service. Isa 39:7
6Among these were some from Judah: Daniel,
Hananiah, Mishael and Azariah. 7The chief official
gave them new names: to Daniel, the name Belteshazzar; to Hananiah, Shadrach; to Mishael, Meshach; and to Azariah, Abednego. Da 4:8; 5:12
8But Daniel resolved not to defile himself with
the royal food and wine, and he asked the chief
official for permission not to defile himself this
way. 9Now God had caused the official to show
favor and sympathy to Daniel, 10but the official
told Daniel, "I am afraid of my lord the king, who
has assigned your[c] food and drink. Why should
he see you looking worse than the other young
men your age? The king would then have my head
because of you." Ge 39:21; 1Ki 8:50
11Daniel then said to the guard whom the chief
official had appointed over Daniel, Hananiah,
Mishael and Azariah, 12"Please test your servants
for ten days: Give us nothing but vegetables to eat
and water to drink. 13Then compare our appearance with that of the young men who eat the royal
food, and treat your servants in accordance with
what you see." 14So he agreed to this and tested
them for ten days. Rev 2:10
15At the end of the ten days they looked healthier and better nourished than any of the young
men who ate the royal food. 16So the guard took
away their choice food and the wine they were to
drink and gave them vegetables instead. Ex 23:25
17To these four young men God gave knowledge and understanding of all kinds of literature
and learning. And Daniel could understand visions and dreams of all kinds. Da 2:19,30; 7:1; 8:1

LIVING  **INSIGHT**

Wisdom comes privately from God as a by-product of right decisions, godly reactions and the application of Scriptural principles to daily circumstances.

(See Daniel 1:17–20.)

18At the end of the time set by the king to bring
them in, the chief official presented them to Nebuchadnezzar. 19The king talked with them, and he
found none equal to Daniel, Hananiah, Mishael
and Azariah; so they entered the king's service.
20In every matter of wisdom and understanding
about which the king questioned them, he found
them ten times better than all the magicians and
enchanters in his whole kingdom. 1Ki 4:30; Da 2:13,28
21And Daniel remained there until the first year
of King Cyrus. Da 6:28; 10:1

Stories of Faith **Chapters 2–6**

These five chapters contain some of the most familiar and beloved stories of faith in all the Old Testament. Nebuchadnezzar's dream and Daniel's interpretation (chapter 2) teach us that *only the Lord knows and reveals the mysteries and visions of the human mind.* The three Hebrew men who were thrown into the fiery furnace because they wouldn't bow down to the golden idol teach us that *standing firm in our faith is often hard, but it is always right.* Daniel's experience of surviving the lions' den teaches us that *the commitment to follow the Lord, whatever the cost, is the path of the faithful.* Sometimes this path will take us through dungeon and danger, but during those times of trial we must remember that we are never alone. All of these stories call us to remain faithful, even when the cost is greater than we might ever imagine paying. These chapters also remind us that God is in control of the destinies of the nations, for He is sovereign over all.

[a]2 Hebrew *Shinar* [b]4 Or *Chaldeans* [c]10 The Hebrew for *your* and *you* in this verse is plural.

The God we serve is faithful to care for us in all the circumstances of life, for He reigns over our lives and over all the kingdoms of this world!

Nebuchadnezzar's Dream

2 In the second year of his reign, Nebuchadnezzar had dreams; his mind was troubled and he could not sleep. 2So the king summoned the magicians, enchanters, sorcerers and astrologers[a] to tell him what he had dreamed. When they came in and stood before the king, 3he said to them, "I have had a dream that troubles me and I want to know what it means.[b]" Da 4:5-6

4Then the astrologers answered the king in Aramaic,[c] "O king, live forever! Tell your servants the dream, and we will interpret it." Ezr 4:7; Da 3:9

5The king replied to the astrologers, "This is what I have firmly decided: If you do not tell me what my dream was and interpret it, I will have you cut into pieces and your houses turned into piles of rubble. 6But if you tell me the dream and explain it, you will receive from me gifts and rewards and great honor. So tell me the dream and interpret it for me." Da 5:7,16

7Once more they replied, "Let the king tell his servants the dream, and we will interpret it."

8Then the king answered, "I am certain that you are trying to gain time, because you realize that this is what I have firmly decided: 9If you do not tell me the dream, there is just one penalty for you. You have conspired to tell me misleading and wicked things, hoping the situation will change. So then, tell me the dream, and I will know that you can interpret it for me." Est 4:11; Isa 41:22-24

10The astrologers answered the king, "There is not a man on earth who can do what the king asks! No king, however great and mighty, has ever asked such a thing of any magician or enchanter or astrologer. 11What the king asks is too difficult. No one can reveal it to the king except the gods, and they do not live among men." Da 5:8,11

12This made the king so angry and furious that he ordered the execution of all the wise men of Babylon. 13So the decree was issued to put the wise men to death, and men were sent to look for Daniel and his friends to put them to death. Da 1:20

14When Arioch, the commander of the king's guard, had gone out to put to death the wise men of Babylon, Daniel spoke to him with wisdom and tact. 15He asked the king's officer, "Why did the king issue such a harsh decree?" Arioch then explained the matter to Daniel. 16At this, Daniel went in to the king and asked for time, so that he might interpret the dream for him.

17Then Daniel returned to his house and explained the matter to his friends Hananiah, Mishael and Azariah. 18He urged them to plead for mercy from the God of heaven concerning this mystery, so that he and his friends might not be executed with the rest of the wise men of Babylon. 19During the night the mystery was revealed to Daniel in a vision. Then Daniel praised the God of heaven 20and said: Job 33:15; Da 1:17

"Praise be to the name of God for ever and ever;
wisdom and power are his. Jer 32:19
21He changes times and seasons; Da 7:25
he sets up kings and deposes them. Ps 75:6-7
He gives wisdom to the wise Jas 1:5
and knowledge to the discerning. 2Sa 14:17
22He reveals deep and hidden things; Da 5:11
he knows what lies in darkness, Ps 139:11-12
and light dwells with him. Isa 45:7; Jas 1:17
23I thank and praise you, O God of my fathers:
You have given me wisdom and power,
you have made known to me what we asked of you,
you have made known to us the dream of the king." Eze 28:3

Daniel Interprets the Dream

24Then Daniel went to Arioch, whom the king had appointed to execute the wise men of Babylon, and said to him, "Do not execute the wise men of Babylon. Take me to the king, and I will interpret his dream for him." ver 14

25Arioch took Daniel to the king at once and said, "I have found a man among the exiles from Judah who can tell the king what his dream means." Da 1:6; 5:13; 6:13

26The king asked Daniel (also called Belteshazzar), "Are you able to tell me what I saw in my dream and interpret it?" Da 1:7

27Daniel replied, "No wise man, enchanter, magician or diviner can explain to the king the mystery he has asked about, 28but there is a God in heaven who reveals mysteries. He has shown King Nebuchadnezzar what will happen in days to come. Your dream and the visions that passed through your mind as you lay on your bed are these: Da 4:5; Am 4:13

29"As you were lying there, O king, your mind turned to things to come, and the revealer of mysteries showed you what is going to happen. 30As for me, this mystery has been revealed to me, not because I have greater wisdom than other living men, but so that you, O king, may know the interpretation and that you may understand what went through your mind. Isa 45:3; Da 1:17; Am 4:13

31"You looked, O king, and there before you stood a large statue—an enormous, dazzling statue, awesome in appearance. 32The head of the statue was made of pure gold, its chest and arms of silver, its belly and thighs of bronze, 33its legs of iron, its feet partly of iron and partly of baked clay.

[a] 2 Or *Chaldeans*; also in verses 4, 5 and 10 [b] 3 Or *was* [c] 4 The text from here through chapter 7 is in Aramaic.

34While you were watching, a rock was cut out, but not by human hands. It struck the statue on its feet of iron and clay and smashed them. 35Then the iron, the clay, the bronze, the silver and the gold were broken to pieces at the same time and became like chaff on a threshing floor in the summer. The wind swept them away without leaving a trace. But the rock that struck the statue became a huge mountain and filled the whole earth.

36"This was the dream, and now we will interpret it to the king. 37You, O king, are the king of kings. The God of heaven has given you dominion and power and might and glory; 38in your hands he has placed mankind and the beasts of the field and the birds of the air. Wherever they live, he has made you ruler over them all. You are that head of gold. Da 4:21-22

39"After you, another kingdom will rise, inferior to yours. Next, a third kingdom, one of bronze, will rule over the whole earth. 40Finally, there will be a fourth kingdom, strong as iron—for iron breaks and smashes everything—and as iron breaks things to pieces, so it will crush and break all the others. 41Just as you saw that the feet and toes were partly of baked clay and partly of iron, so this will be a divided kingdom; yet it will have some of the strength of iron in it, even as you saw iron mixed with clay. 42As the toes were partly iron and partly clay, so this kingdom will be partly strong and partly brittle. 43And just as you saw the iron mixed with baked clay, so the people will be a mixture and will not remain united, any more than iron mixes with clay. Da 7:7,23

44"In the time of those kings, the God of heaven will set up a kingdom that will never be destroyed, nor will it be left to another people. It will crush all those kingdoms and bring them to an end, but it will itself endure forever. 45This is the meaning of the vision of the rock cut out of a mountain, but not by human hands—a rock that broke the iron, the bronze, the clay, the silver and the gold to pieces. Isa 9:7; Lk 1:33

"The great God has shown the king what will take place in the future. The dream is true and the interpretation is trustworthy." Ge 41:25

46Then King Nebuchadnezzar fell prostrate before Daniel and paid him honor and ordered that an offering and incense be presented to him. 47The king said to Daniel, "Surely your God is the God of gods and the Lord of kings and a revealer of mysteries, for you were able to reveal this mystery." Da 11:36; Ac 10:25

48Then the king placed Daniel in a high position and lavished many gifts on him. He made him ruler over the entire province of Babylon and placed him in charge of all its wise men. 49Moreover, at Daniel's request the king appointed Shadrach, Meshach and Abednego administrators over the province of Babylon, while Daniel himself remained at the royal court. Da 4:9; 5:11

The Image of Gold and the Fiery Furnace

3 King Nebuchadnezzar made an image of gold, ninety feet high and nine feet[a] wide, and set it up on the plain of Dura in the province of Babylon. 2He then summoned the satraps, prefects, governors, advisers, treasurers, judges, magistrates and all the other provincial officials to come to the dedication of the image he had set up. 3So the satraps, prefects, governors, advisers, treasurers, judges, magistrates and all the other provincial officials assembled for the dedication of the image that King Nebuchadnezzar had set up, and they stood before it. Isa 46:6; Hab 2:19

4Then the herald loudly proclaimed, "This is what you are commanded to do, O peoples, nations and men of every language: 5As soon as you hear the sound of the horn, flute, zither, lyre, harp, pipes and all kinds of music, you must fall down and worship the image of gold that King Nebuchadnezzar has set up. 6Whoever does not fall down and worship will immediately be thrown into a blazing furnace." Jer 29:22; Da 6:7

7Therefore, as soon as they heard the sound of the horn, flute, zither, lyre, harp and all kinds of music, all the peoples, nations and men of every language fell down and worshiped the image of gold that King Nebuchadnezzar had set up.

8At this time some astrologers[b] came forward and denounced the Jews. 9They said to King Nebuchadnezzar, "O king, live forever! 10You have issued a decree, O king, that everyone who hears the sound of the horn, flute, zither, lyre, harp, pipes and all kinds of music must fall down and worship the image of gold, 11and that whoever does not fall down and worship will be thrown into a blazing furnace. 12But there are some Jews whom you have set over the affairs of the province of Babylon—Shadrach, Meshach and Abednego—who pay no attention to you, O king. They neither serve your gods nor worship the image of gold you have set up." Da 2:49; 6:13

13Furious with rage, Nebuchadnezzar summoned Shadrach, Meshach and Abednego. So these men were brought before the king, 14and Nebuchadnezzar said to them, "Is it true, Shadrach, Meshach and Abednego, that you do not serve my gods or worship the image of gold I have set up? 15Now when you hear the sound of the horn, flute, zither, lyre, harp, pipes and all kinds of music, if you are ready to fall down and worship the image I made, very good. But if you do not worship it, you will be thrown immediately into a

[a] 1 Aramaic *sixty cubits high and six cubits wide* (about 27 meters high and 2.7 meters wide) [b] 8 Or *Chaldeans*

blazing furnace. Then what god will be able to rescue you from my hand?" Isa 36:18-20

[16]Shadrach, Meshach and Abednego replied to the king, "O Nebuchadnezzar, we do not need to defend ourselves before you in this matter. [17]If we are thrown into the blazing furnace, the God we serve is able to save us from it, and he will rescue us from your hand, O king. [18]But even if he does not, we want you to know, O king, that we will not serve your gods or worship the image of gold you have set up." Ps 27:1-2

LIVING  **INSIGHT**

Those whom God uses most effectively have been hammered, filed and tempered in the furnace of trials and heartache.

(See Daniel 3:16–18.)

[19]Then Nebuchadnezzar was furious with Shadrach, Meshach and Abednego, and his attitude toward them changed. He ordered the furnace heated seven times hotter than usual [20]and commanded some of the strongest soldiers in his army to tie up Shadrach, Meshach and Abednego and throw them into the blazing furnace. [21]So these men, wearing their robes, trousers, turbans and other clothes, were bound and thrown into the blazing furnace. [22]The king's command was so urgent and the furnace so hot that the flames of the fire killed the soldiers who took up Shadrach, Meshach and Abednego, [23]and these three men, firmly tied, fell into the blazing furnace. Lev 26:18-28

[24]Then King Nebuchadnezzar leaped to his feet in amazement and asked his advisers, "Weren't there three men that we tied up and threw into the fire?"

They replied, "Certainly, O king."

[25]He said, "Look! I see four men walking around in the fire, unbound and unharmed, and the fourth looks like a son of the gods."

[26]Nebuchadnezzar then approached the opening of the blazing furnace and shouted, "Shadrach, Meshach and Abednego, servants of the Most High God, come out! Come here!" Da 4:2,34

So Shadrach, Meshach and Abednego came out of the fire, [27]and the satraps, prefects, governors and royal advisers crowded around them. They saw that the fire had not harmed their bodies, nor was a hair of their heads singed; their robes were not scorched, and there was no smell of fire on them. Heb 11:32-34

[28]Then Nebuchadnezzar said, "Praise be to the God of Shadrach, Meshach and Abednego, who has sent his angel and rescued his servants! They trusted in him and defied the king's command and were willing to give up their lives rather than serve or worship any god except their own God. [29]Therefore I decree that the people of any nation or language who say anything against the God of Shadrach, Meshach and Abednego be cut into pieces and their houses be turned into piles of rubble, for no other god can save in this way."

[30]Then the king promoted Shadrach, Meshach and Abednego in the province of Babylon.

Nebuchadnezzar's Dream of a Tree

4 King Nebuchadnezzar,

To the peoples, nations and men of every language, who live in all the world: Da 3:4

May you prosper greatly! Da 6:25

[2]It is my pleasure to tell you about the miraculous signs and wonders that the Most High God has performed for me. Ps 74:9

[3]How great are his signs,
how mighty his wonders! Da 6:27
His kingdom is an eternal kingdom;
his dominion endures from generation
to generation. Da 2:44

[4]I, Nebuchadnezzar, was at home in my palace, contented and prosperous. [5]I had a dream that made me afraid. As I was lying in my bed, the images and visions that passed through my mind terrified me. [6]So I commanded that all the wise men of Babylon be brought before me to interpret the dream for me. [7]When the magicians, enchanters, astrologers[a] and diviners came, I told them the dream, but they could not interpret it for me. [8]Finally, Daniel came into my presence and I told him the dream. (He is called Belteshazzar, after the name of my god, and the spirit of the holy gods is in him.) Da 2:1

[9]I said, "Belteshazzar, chief of the magicians, I know that the spirit of the holy gods is in you, and no mystery is too difficult for you. Here is my dream; interpret it for me. [10]These are the visions I saw while lying in my bed: I looked, and there before me stood a tree in the middle of the land. Its height was enormous. [11]The tree grew large and strong and its top touched the sky; it was visible to the ends of the earth. [12]Its leaves were beautiful, its fruit abundant, and on it was food for all. Under it the beasts of the field found shelter, and the birds of the air lived in its branches; from it every creature was fed.

[13]"In the visions I saw while lying in my bed, I looked, and there before me was a

[a]7 Or *Chaldeans*

messenger,[a] a holy one, coming down from
heaven. 14He called in a loud voice: 'Cut
down the tree and trim off its branches; strip
off its leaves and scatter its fruit. Let the animals flee from under it and the birds from its
branches. 15But let the stump and its roots,
bound with iron and bronze, remain in the
ground, in the grass of the field. Eze 31:12
"'Let him be drenched with the dew of
heaven, and let him live with the animals
among the plants of the earth. 16Let his mind
be changed from that of a man and let him
be given the mind of an animal, till seven
times[b] pass by for him. ver 23,32
17"'The decision is announced by messengers, the holy ones declare the verdict, so that
the living may know that the Most High is
sovereign over the kingdoms of men and
gives them to anyone he wishes and sets over
them the lowliest of men.' Da 5:18-21; Mt 23:12
18"This is the dream that I, King Nebuchadnezzar, had. Now, Belteshazzar, tell me
what it means, for none of the wise men in
my kingdom can interpret it for me. But you
can, because the spirit of the holy gods is in
you." Ge 41:8; Da 1:20

Daniel Interprets the Dream

19Then Daniel (also called Belteshazzar)
was greatly perplexed for a time, and his
thoughts terrified him. So the king said, "Belteshazzar, do not let the dream or its meaning alarm you." Da 7:15,28
Belteshazzar answered, "My lord, if only
the dream applied to your enemies and its
meaning to your adversaries! 20The tree you
saw, which grew large and strong, with its
top touching the sky, visible to the whole
earth, 21with beautiful leaves and abundant
fruit, providing food for all, giving shelter to
the beasts of the field, and having nesting
places in its branches for the birds of the
air— 22you, O king, are that tree! You have
become great and strong; your greatness has
grown until it reaches the sky, and your dominion extends to distant parts of the earth.
23"You, O king, saw a messenger, a holy
one, coming down from heaven and saying,
'Cut down the tree and destroy it, but leave
the stump, bound with iron and bronze, in
the grass of the field, while its roots remain in
the ground. Let him be drenched with the
dew of heaven; let him live like the wild animals, until seven times pass by for him.'
24"This is the interpretation, O king, and
this is the decree the Most High has issued
against my lord the king: 25You will be driven
away from people and will live with the wild
animals; you will eat grass like cattle and
be drenched with the dew of heaven. Seven
times will pass by for you until you acknowledge that the Most High is sovereign over the
kingdoms of men and gives them to anyone
he wishes. 26The command to leave the
stump of the tree with its roots means that
your kingdom will be restored to you when
you acknowledge that Heaven rules. 27There-
fore, O king, be pleased to accept my advice:
Renounce your sins by doing what is right,
and your wickedness by being kind to the
oppressed. It may be that then your prosperity will continue." Isa 55:6-7; Eze 18:22

The Dream Is Fulfilled

28All this happened to King Nebuchadnezzar. 29Twelve months later, as the king
was walking on the roof of the royal palace of
Babylon, 30he said, "Is not this the great Babylon I have built as the royal residence, by
my mighty power and for the glory of my
majesty?" Da 5:20; Hab 2:4
31The words were still on his lips when a
voice came from heaven, "This is what is
decreed for you, King Nebuchadnezzar:
Your royal authority has been taken from
you. 32You will be driven away from people
and will live with the wild animals; you will
eat grass like cattle. Seven times will pass by
for you until you acknowledge that the Most
High is sovereign over the kingdoms of men
and gives them to anyone he wishes."
33Immediately what had been said about
Nebuchadnezzar was fulfilled. He was driven
away from people and ate grass like cattle.
His body was drenched with the dew of
heaven until his hair grew like the feathers of
an eagle and his nails like the claws of a bird.
34At the end of that time, I, Nebuchadnezzar, raised my eyes toward heaven, and my
sanity was restored. Then I praised the Most
High; I honored and glorified him who lives
forever. Da 12:7; Rev 4:10

His dominion is an eternal dominion;
  his kingdom endures from generation to
    generation. Lk 1:33
35All the peoples of the earth
  are regarded as nothing. Isa 40:17
He does as he pleases Ps 115:3; 135:6
  with the powers of heaven
  and the peoples of the earth.
No one can hold back his hand
  or say to him: "What have you done?"

36At the same time that my sanity was

[a] 13 Or *watchman*; also in verses 17 and 23 [b] 16 Or *years*; also in verses 23, 25 and 32

restored, my honor and splendor were returned to me for the glory of my kingdom.
My advisers and nobles sought me out, and
I was restored to my throne and became even
greater than before. 37Now I, Nebuchadnezzar, praise and exalt and glorify the King of
heaven, because everything he does is right
and all his ways are just. And those who walk
in pride he is able to humble. Da 5:20,23

LIVING  **INSIGHT**

Before we get all enamored with our high-and-mighty importance, it's a good idea to take a backward glance at the pit from which Jesus Christ lifted us. And let's not just think about it; let's admit it. It has a way of keeping us all on the same level—undeserving recipients of His amazing grace.

(See Daniel 4:37.)

The Writing on the Wall

5 King Belshazzar gave a great banquet for a
thousand of his nobles and drank wine with
them. 2While Belshazzar was drinking his wine, he
gave orders to bring in the gold and silver goblets
that Nebuchadnezzar his father[a] had taken from
the temple in Jerusalem, so that the king and his
nobles, his wives and his concubines might drink
from them. 3So they brought in the gold goblets
that had been taken from the temple of God in
Jerusalem, and the king and his nobles, his wives
and his concubines drank from them. 4As they
drank the wine, they praised the gods of gold and
silver, of bronze, iron, wood and stone. Da 1:2

5Suddenly the fingers of a human hand appeared and wrote on the plaster of the wall, near
the lampstand in the royal palace. The king
watched the hand as it wrote. 6His face turned pale
and he was so frightened that his knees knocked
together and his legs gave way. Eze 7:17; Da 4:5

7The king called out for the enchanters, astrologers[b] and diviners to be brought and said to these
wise men of Babylon, "Whoever reads this writing
and tells me what it means will be clothed in purple and have a gold chain placed around his neck,
and he will be made the third highest ruler in the
kingdom." Da 2:5-6,48

8Then all the king's wise men came in, but they
could not read the writing or tell the king what it
meant. 9So King Belshazzar became even more
terrified and his face grew more pale. His nobles
were baffled. Isa 21:4

10The queen,[c] hearing the voices of the king
and his nobles, came into the banquet hall.
"O king, live forever!" she said. "Don't be
alarmed! Don't look so pale! 11There is a man in
your kingdom who has the spirit of the holy gods
in him. In the time of your father he was found to
have insight and intelligence and wisdom like that
of the gods. King Nebuchadnezzar your father—
your father the king, I say—appointed him chief
of the magicians, enchanters, astrologers and diviners. 12This man Daniel, whom the king called
Belteshazzar, was found to have a keen mind and
knowledge and understanding, and also the ability
to interpret dreams, explain riddles and solve difficult problems. Call for Daniel, and he will tell you
what the writing means." Da 1:7; 6:3

13So Daniel was brought before the king, and
the king said to him, "Are you Daniel, one of the
exiles my father the king brought from Judah? 14I
have heard that the spirit of the gods is in you and
that you have insight, intelligence and outstanding
wisdom. 15The wise men and enchanters were
brought before me to read this writing and tell me
what it means, but they could not explain it. 16Now
I have heard that you are able to give interpretations and to solve difficult problems. If you can
read this writing and tell me what it means, you
will be clothed in purple and have a gold chain
placed around your neck, and you will be made
the third highest ruler in the kingdom." Da 6:13

17Then Daniel answered the king, "You may
keep your gifts for yourself and give your rewards
to someone else. Nevertheless, I will read the writing for the king and tell him what it means.

18"O king, the Most High God gave your father
Nebuchadnezzar sovereignty and greatness and
glory and splendor. 19Because of the high position
he gave him, all the peoples and nations and men
of every language dreaded and feared him. Those
the king wanted to put to death, he put to death;
those he wanted to spare, he spared; those he
wanted to promote, he promoted; and those he
wanted to humble, he humbled. 20But when his
heart became arrogant and hardened with pride,
he was deposed from his royal throne and stripped
of his glory. 21He was driven away from people
and given the mind of an animal; he lived with the
wild donkeys and ate grass like cattle; and his body
was drenched with the dew of heaven, until he
acknowledged that the Most High God is sovereign over the kingdoms of men and sets over them
anyone he wishes. Da 4:16-17,35; Eze 17:24

22"But you his son,[d] O Belshazzar, have not
humbled yourself, though you knew all this. 23In-
stead, you have set yourself up against the Lord
of heaven. You had the goblets from his temple
brought to you, and you and your nobles, your

[a] 2 Or *ancestor*; or *predecessor*; also in verses 11, 13 and 18 [b] 7 Or *Chaldeans*; also in verse 11 [c] 10 Or *queen mother*
[d] 22 Or *descendant*; or *successor*

wives and your concubines drank wine from them.
You praised the gods of silver and gold, of bronze,
iron, wood and stone, which cannot see or hear or
understand. But you did not honor the God who
holds in his hand your life and all your ways.
24Therefore he sent the hand that wrote the inscription. Ps 115:4-8; Jer 10:23
25"This is the inscription that was written:

MENE, MENE, TEKEL, PARSIN[a]

26"This is what these words mean:

Mene[b]: God has numbered the days of
your reign and brought it to an
end. Isa 13:6; Jer 27:7
27*Tekel*[c]: You have been weighed on the
scales and found wanting. Ps 62:9
28*Peres*[d]: Your kingdom is divided and
given to the Medes and Persians."

29Then at Belshazzar's command, Daniel was
clothed in purple, a gold chain was placed around
his neck, and he was proclaimed the third highest
ruler in the kingdom. Da 2:6
30That very night Belshazzar, king of the Babylonians,[e] was slain, 31and Darius the Mede took
over the kingdom, at the age of sixty-two. Da 6:1

Daniel in the Den of Lions

6 It pleased Darius to appoint 120 satraps to
rule throughout the kingdom, 2with three administrators over them, one of whom was Daniel.
The satraps were made accountable to them so
that the king might not suffer loss. 3Now Daniel so
distinguished himself among the administrators
and the satraps by his exceptional qualities that the
king planned to set him over the whole kingdom.
4At this, the administrators and the satraps tried to
find grounds for charges against Daniel in his conduct of government affairs, but they were unable
to do so. They could find no corruption in him,
because he was trustworthy and neither corrupt
nor negligent. 5Finally these men said, "We will
never find any basis for charges against this man
Daniel unless it has something to do with the law
of his God." Est 10:3; Da 5:12-14
6So the administrators and the satraps went as
a group to the king and said: "O King Darius, live
forever! 7The royal administrators, prefects, satraps, advisers and governors have all agreed that
the king should issue an edict and enforce the
decree that anyone who prays to any god or man
during the next thirty days, except to you, O king,
shall be thrown into the lions' den. 8Now, O king,
issue the decree and put it in writing so that it
cannot be altered—in accordance with the laws
of the Medes and Persians, which cannot be repealed." 9So King Darius put the decree in writing.
10Now when Daniel learned that the decree had
been published, he went home to his upstairs
room where the windows opened toward Jerusalem. Three times a day he got down on his knees
and prayed, giving thanks to his God, just as he
had done before. 11Then these men went as a
group and found Daniel praying and asking God
for help. 12So they went to the king and spoke to
him about his royal decree: "Did you not publish
a decree that during the next thirty days anyone
who prays to any god or man except to you,
O king, would be thrown into the lions' den?"
The king answered, "The decree stands—in accordance with the laws of the Medes and Persians,
which cannot be repealed." Da 3:8-12
13Then they said to the king, "Daniel, who is
one of the exiles from Judah, pays no attention to
you, O king, or to the decree you put in writing.
He still prays three times a day." 14When the king
heard this, he was greatly distressed; he was determined to rescue Daniel and made every effort until
sundown to save him. Est 3:8; Mk 6:26
15Then the men went as a group to the king and
said to him, "Remember, O king, that according
to the law of the Medes and Persians no decree or
edict that the king issues can be changed." Est 8:8
16So the king gave the order, and they brought
Daniel and threw him into the lions' den. The king
said to Daniel, "May your God, whom you serve
continually, rescue you!" Ps 37:39-40
17A stone was brought and placed over the
mouth of the den, and the king sealed it with his
own signet ring and with the rings of his nobles,
so that Daniel's situation might not be changed.
18Then the king returned to his palace and spent
the night without eating and without any enter-

LIVING  INSIGHT

Generally speaking, there are two kinds of tests in life: adversity and prosperity. Of the two, the latter is the more difficult. When adversity strikes, things get simple; survival is the goal. It is a test on maintaining the basics of food, clothing and shelter. But when prosperity comes, watch out! Things get complicated. All kinds of subtle temptations arrive, pleading for satisfaction. It is then that one's integrity is put to the test.

(See Daniel 6:4.)

[a]*25* Aramaic *UPARSIN* (that is, *AND PARSIN*) [b]*26* *Mene* can mean *numbered* or *mina* (a unit of money). [c]*27* *Tekel* can mean *weighed* or *shekel.* [d]*28* *Peres* (the singular of *Parsin*) can mean *divided* or *Persia* or *a half mina* or *a half shekel.*
[e]*30* Or *Chaldeans*

DANIEL

A Man of Integrity

"They could find no corruption in him, because he was trustworthy and neither corrupt nor negligent."
—DANIEL 6:4b

Daniel was a man of the finest kind of strength. He was a man of absolute integrity. When integrity marks a person's life, it makes that life a striking illustration of God's power and presence on display.

Chapter 6 of the book of Daniel gives us insight into the depths of Daniel's faith and helps us see what integrity is all about. First, *Daniel had an excellent attitude.* When King Nebuchadnezzar appointed Daniel as one of the three rulers to look after his financial affairs, Daniel wasn't paranoid or intimidated because he was surrounded by people who marched to a different beat. His attitude and his "exceptional qualities" (6:3) distinguished him above all of his peers.

Second, *Daniel was trustworthy in his responsibilities.* The men who plotted against Daniel tried to find *a single ground* in order to bring charges against him, just *one* flaw they could exploit. Imagine! They investigated Daniel's life so closely that they would have settled for *one* piece of evidence showing that he didn't have integrity. They looked for an area of compromise, a blotch on his record, some place where he was unfaithful, some time when he had messed up. But they couldn't find it. Daniel was a man who could be trusted to do the right thing, no matter what, no matter where, no matter when.

Third, *Daniel was privately pure.* When Daniel's peers found themselves rebuffed because of his character, they intensified their search and expanded into all areas of Daniel's life. They pulled his files and scrutinized them. They looked when nobody else was looking. They asked around. They probed his private life and found him spotless. Look at the frustration expressed in the conclusion they reached: "We will never find any basis for charges against this man Daniel unless it has something to do with the law of his God" (6:5). That's when they hatched their best-laid plan. They would set Daniel up. They would catch him in the practice of his religion, the single, most significant point on which he differed from Darius. They would attack him in the only area in which he seemed vulnerable. On the surface, it was a brilliant plan that seemed guaranteed to succeed (6:7–9). But no one took into account the awesome power of Daniel's God, the great King above all gods, or the unwavering faithfulness of God's devoted servant, Daniel.

Fourth, *Daniel had a consistent walk with God.* When Darius took the advice of his officials and proclaimed himself the god of the month, who alone must be prayed to and worshiped, Daniel refused to comply with the decree. Now remember, this decree was in effect for only thirty days. Daniel could have simply shut himself up in his closet and prayed to God and not made a big deal out of it. But he was not ashamed of his relationship with his God, and the consistency of his walk with Him demanded that he live as he always lived. Imagine this scene: "When Daniel learned that the decree had been published, he went home to his upstairs room where the windows opened toward Jerusalem. Three times a day he got down on his knees and prayed, giving thanks to his God, just as he had done before" (6:10).

Oh, how Daniel's peers must have rejoiced! What glee they must have felt as they rushed to the king with their report of what they had observed! As a result, Daniel was convicted and thrown into the den of lions. But as long as Daniel was in that den, those lions experienced the greatest case of lockjaw in history. Not one cat nibbled on him. Not one even came near. When King Darius found Daniel alive the next day, he was overjoyed. Then, "at the king's command, the men who had falsely accused Daniel were brought in and thrown into the lions' den . . . And before they reached the floor of the den, the lions overpowered them and crushed all their bones" (6:24).

Remember, to be a man or a woman of integrity is not easy; in fact, that's the last thing it is. People who live lives of integrity are often misunderstood, falsely accused and maligned in many different ways. It goes against the grain of the way most people choose to live. But Daniel's life proves that a person of integrity is a powerful instrument in the hand of God.

tainment being brought to him. And he could not
sleep. Mt 27:66
19At the first light of dawn, the king got up and
hurried to the lions' den. 20When he came near the
den, he called to Daniel in an anguished voice,
"Daniel, servant of the living God, has your God,
whom you serve continually, been able to rescue
you from the lions?" Da 3:17
21Daniel answered, "O king, live forever! 22My
God sent his angel, and he shut the mouths of the
lions. They have not hurt me, because I was found
innocent in his sight. Nor have I ever done any
wrong before you, O king." Heb 11:33; 2Ti 4:17
23The king was overjoyed and gave orders to lift
Daniel out of the den. And when Daniel was lifted
from the den, no wound was found on him, because he had trusted in his God. 1Ch 5:20; Da 3:27
24At the king's command, the men who had
falsely accused Daniel were brought in and thrown
into the lions' den, along with their wives and
children. And before they reached the floor of the
den, the lions overpowered them and crushed all
their bones. Dt 24:16; 2Ki 14:6
25Then King Darius wrote to all the peoples,
nations and men of every language throughout the
land: Da 3:4

"May you prosper greatly! Da 4:1

26"I issue a decree that in every part of my
kingdom people must fear and reverence the
God of Daniel. Da 3:29

"For he is the living God Jos 2:11
and he endures forever; Rev 1:18
his kingdom will not be destroyed,
his dominion will never end. Da 2:44
27He rescues and he saves;
he performs signs and wonders Da 4:3
in the heavens and on the earth.
He has rescued Daniel
from the power of the lions."

28So Daniel prospered during the reign of Darius and the reign of Cyrus[a] the Persian. Da 1:21

Dreams and Visions Chapters 7–12

The main focus in these chapters is on the prophecies of Daniel. These chapters are set in an apocalyptic language common in those days but foreign to us in this century. Daniel's dreams and visions point to what the Lord is doing in the present and to what he will do in the future. His visions predict the rise and fall of nations and ultimately the rise of a kingdom that will last eternally. This kingdom will replace all other nations and will be ruled by the Maker of heaven and earth. Earthly rulers may think they govern the affairs on the earth, and their nations may endure for a time—but the sovereign Lord, alone, rules over all!

[a]28 Or *Darius, that is, the reign of Cyrus*

Daniel's Dream of Four Beasts

7 In the first year of Belshazzar king of Babylon, Daniel had a dream, and visions passed
through his mind as he was lying on his bed. He
wrote down the substance of his dream. Da 1:17
2Daniel said: "In my vision at night I looked,
and there before me were the four winds of heaven
churning up the great sea. 3Four great beasts, each
different from the others, came up out of the sea.
4"The first was like a lion, and it had the wings
of an eagle. I watched until its wings were torn off
and it was lifted from the ground so that it stood
on two feet like a man, and the heart of a man was
given to it. Jer 4:7; Eze 17:3
5"And there before me was a second beast,
which looked like a bear. It was raised up on one
of its sides, and it had three ribs in its mouth
between its teeth. It was told, 'Get up and eat your
fill of flesh!' Da 2:39
6"After that, I looked, and there before me was
another beast, one that looked like a leopard. And
on its back it had four wings like those of a bird.
This beast had four heads, and it was given authority to rule. Rev 13:2
7"After that, in my vision at night I looked, and
there before me was a fourth beast—terrifying and
frightening and very powerful. It had large iron
teeth; it crushed and devoured its victims and
trampled underfoot whatever was left. It was different from all the former beasts, and it had ten
horns. Da 2:40; Rev 12:3
8"While I was thinking about the horns, there
before me was another horn, a little one, which
came up among them; and three of the first horns
were uprooted before it. This horn had eyes like
the eyes of a man and a mouth that spoke boast-
fully. Rev 13:5-6
9"As I looked,

"thrones were set in place,
and the Ancient of Days took his seat.
His clothing was as white as snow; Mt 28:3
the hair of his head was white like wool.
His throne was flaming with fire,
and its wheels were all ablaze. Eze 1:15
10A river of fire was flowing, Ps 50:3
coming out from before him. Rev 5:11
Thousands upon thousands attended him;
ten thousand times ten thousand stood
before him.
The court was seated,
and the books were opened. Rev 20:11-15

11"Then I continued to watch because of the
boastful words the horn was speaking. I kept looking until the beast was slain and its body destroyed
and thrown into the blazing fire. 12(The other

beasts had been stripped of their authority, but
were allowed to live for a period of time.)
13"In my vision at night I looked, and there
before me was one like a son of man, coming with
the clouds of heaven. He approached the Ancient
of Days and was led into his presence. 14He was
given authority, glory and sovereign power; all
peoples, nations and men of every language worshiped him. His dominion is an everlasting dominion that will not pass away, and his kingdom
is one that will never be destroyed. Heb 12:28

The Interpretation of the Dream

15"I, Daniel, was troubled in spirit, and the visions that passed through my mind disturbed me.
16I approached one of those standing there and
asked him the true meaning of all this. Da 4:19
"So he told me and gave me the interpretation
of these things: 17'The four great beasts are four
kingdoms that will rise from the earth. 18But the
saints of the Most High will receive the kingdom
and will possess it forever—yes, for ever and ever.'
19"Then I wanted to know the true meaning of
the fourth beast, which was different from all the
others and most terrifying, with its iron teeth and
bronze claws—the beast that crushed and devoured its victims and trampled underfoot whatever was left. 20I also wanted to know about the ten
horns on its head and about the other horn that
came up, before which three of them fell—the
horn that looked more imposing than the others
and that had eyes and a mouth that spoke boast-
fully. 21As I watched, this horn was waging war
against the saints and defeating them, 22until
the Ancient of Days came and pronounced
judgment in favor of the saints of the Most High,
and the time came when they possessed the
kingdom.
23"He gave me this explanation: 'The fourth
beast is a fourth kingdom that will appear on
earth. It will be different from all the other kingdoms and will devour the whole earth, trampling
it down and crushing it. 24The ten horns are ten
kings who will come from this kingdom. After
them another king will arise, different from the
earlier ones; he will subdue three kings. 25He will
speak against the Most High and oppress his saints
and try to change the set times and the laws. The

VISIONS IN DANIEL

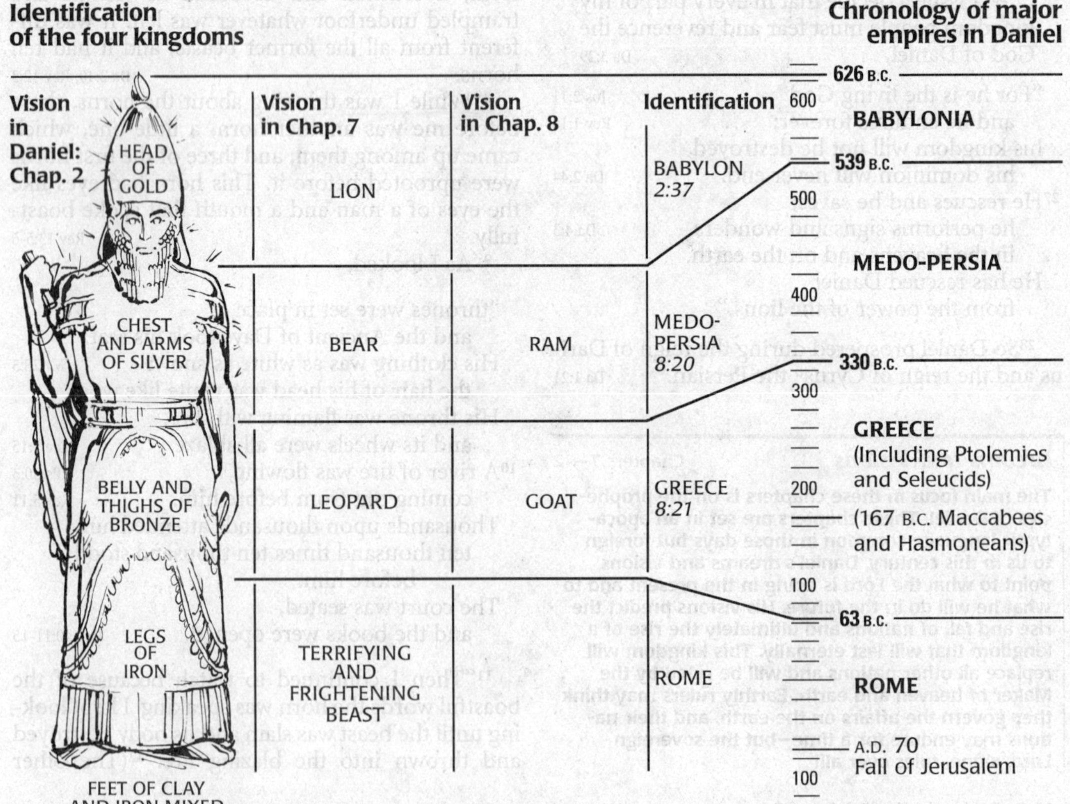

saints will be handed over to him for a time, times and half a time.[a] Da 2:21; Rev 17:12

26"'But the court will sit, and his power will be taken away and completely destroyed forever. 27Then the sovereignty, power and greatness of the kingdoms under the whole heaven will be handed over to the saints, the people of the Most High. His kingdom will be an everlasting kingdom, and all rulers will worship and obey him.' Ps 22:27; 72:11

28"This is the end of the matter. I, Daniel, was deeply troubled by my thoughts, and my face turned pale, but I kept the matter to myself."

Daniel's Vision of a Ram and a Goat

8 In the third year of King Belshazzar's reign, I, Daniel, had a vision, after the one that had already appeared to me. 2In my vision I saw myself in the citadel of Susa in the province of Elam; in the vision I was beside the Ulai Canal. 3I looked up, and there before me was a ram with two horns, standing beside the canal, and the horns were long. One of the horns was longer than the other but grew up later. 4I watched the ram as he charged toward the west and the north and the south. No animal could stand against him, and none could rescue from his power. He did as he pleased and became great. Da 11:3,16

5As I was thinking about this, suddenly a goat with a prominent horn between his eyes came from the west, crossing the whole earth without touching the ground. 6He came toward the two-horned ram I had seen standing beside the canal and charged at him in great rage. 7I saw him attack the ram furiously, striking the ram and shattering his two horns. The ram was powerless to stand against him; the goat knocked him to the ground and trampled on him, and none could rescue the ram from his power. 8The goat became very great, but at the height of his power his large horn was broken off, and in its place four prominent horns grew up toward the four winds of heaven.

9Out of one of them came another horn, which started small but grew in power to the south and to the east and toward the Beautiful Land. 10It grew until it reached the host of the heavens, and it threw some of the starry host down to the earth and trampled on them. 11It set itself up to be as great as the Prince of the host; it took away the daily sacrifice from him, and the place of his sanctuary was brought low. 12Because of rebellion, the host ⌞of the saints⌟[b] and the daily sacrifice were given over to it. It prospered in everything it did, and truth was thrown to the ground. Da 11:16,31

13Then I heard a holy one speaking, and another holy one said to him, "How long will it take for the vision to be fulfilled—the vision concerning the daily sacrifice, the rebellion that causes desolation, and the surrender of the sanctuary and of the host that will be trampled underfoot?" Da 4:23; 12:6

14He said to me, "It will take 2,300 evenings and mornings; then the sanctuary will be reconsecrated." Da 12:11-12

The Interpretation of the Vision

15While I, Daniel, was watching the vision and trying to understand it, there before me stood one who looked like a man. 16And I heard a man's voice from the Ulai calling, "Gabriel, tell this man the meaning of the vision." Da 10:16-18; Lk 1:19

17As he came near the place where I was standing, I was terrified and fell prostrate. "Son of man," he said to me, "understand that the vision concerns the time of the end." Eze 1:28; Rev 1:17

18While he was speaking to me, I was in a deep sleep, with my face to the ground. Then he touched me and raised me to my feet. Eze 2:2

19He said: "I am going to tell you what will happen later in the time of wrath, because the vision concerns the appointed time of the end.[c] 20The two-horned ram that you saw represents the kings of Media and Persia. 21The shaggy goat is the king of Greece, and the large horn between his eyes is the first king. 22The four horns that replaced the one that was broken off represent four kingdoms that will emerge from his nation but will not have the same power. Hab 2:3

23"In the latter part of their reign, when rebels have become completely wicked, a stern-faced king, a master of intrigue, will arise. 24He will become very strong, but not by his own power. He will cause astounding devastation and will succeed in whatever he does. He will destroy the mighty men and the holy people. 25He will cause deceit to prosper, and he will consider himself superior. When they feel secure, he will destroy many and take his stand against the Prince of princes. Yet he will be destroyed, but not by human power.

26"The vision of the evenings and mornings that has been given you is true, but seal up the vision, for it concerns the distant future." Da 10:1,14

27I, Daniel, was exhausted and lay ill for several days. Then I got up and went about the king's business. I was appalled by the vision; it was beyond understanding. Da 7:28

Daniel's Prayer

9 In the first year of Darius son of Xerxes[d] (a Mede by descent), who was made ruler over the Babylonian[e] kingdom— 2in the first year of his reign, I, Daniel, understood from the Scriptures, according to the word of the LORD given to Jeremiah the prophet, that the desolation of Jeru-

[a]25 Or *for a year, two years and half a year* [b]12 Or *rebellion, the armies* [c]19 Or *because the end will be at the appointed time* [d]1 Hebrew *Ahasuerus* [e]1 Or *Chaldean*

salem would last seventy years. 3So I turned to the Lord God and pleaded with him in prayer and petition, in fasting, and in sackcloth and ashes. 4I prayed to the LORD my God and confessed:

"O Lord, the great and awesome God, who keeps his covenant of love with all who love him and obey his commands, 5we have sinned and done wrong. We have been wicked and have rebelled; we have turned away from your commands and laws. 6We have not listened to your servants the prophets, who spoke in your name to our kings, our princes and our fathers, and to all the people of the land. 2Ch 36:16; Ps 106:6

7"Lord, you are righteous, but this day we are covered with shame—the men of Judah and people of Jerusalem and all Israel, both near and far, in all the countries where you have scattered us because of our unfaithfulness to you. 8O LORD, we and our kings, our princes and our fathers are covered with shame because we have sinned against you. 9The Lord our God is merciful and forgiving, even though we have rebelled against him; 10we have not obeyed the LORD our God or kept the laws he gave us through his servants the prophets. 11All Israel has transgressed your law and turned away, refusing to obey you. 2Ki 17:13-15; Ne 9:17

"Therefore the curses and sworn judgments written in the Law of Moses, the servant of God, have been poured out on us, because we have sinned against you. 12You have fulfilled the words spoken against us and against our rulers by bringing upon us great disaster. Under the whole heaven nothing has ever been done like what has been done to Jerusalem. 13Just as it is written in the Law of Moses, all this disaster has come upon us, yet we have not sought the favor of the LORD our God by turning from our sins and giving attention to your truth. 14The LORD did not hesitate to bring the disaster upon us, for the LORD our God is righteous in everything he does; yet we have not obeyed him. Isa 1:4-6; Eze 5:9

15"Now, O Lord our God, who brought your people out of Egypt with a mighty hand and who made for yourself a name that endures to this day, we have sinned, we have done wrong. 16O Lord, in keeping with all your righteous acts, turn away your anger and your wrath from Jerusalem, your city, your holy hill. Our sins and the iniquities of our fathers have made Jerusalem and your people an object of scorn to all those around us. Ps 31:1; Zec 8:3

17"Now, our God, hear the prayers and petitions of your servant. For your sake, O Lord, look with favor on your desolate sanctuary. 18Give ear, O God, and hear; open your eyes and see the desolation of the city that bears your Name. We do not make requests of you because we are righteous, but because of your great mercy. 19O Lord, listen! O Lord, forgive! O Lord, hear and act! For your sake, O my God, do not delay, because your city and your people bear your Name." Isa 37:17; Jer 7:10-12; 25:29

The Seventy "Sevens"

20While I was speaking and praying, confessing my sin and the sin of my people Israel and making my request to the LORD my God for his holy hill—21while I was still in prayer, Gabriel, the man I had seen in the earlier vision, came to me in swift flight about the time of the evening sacrifice. 22He instructed me and said to me, "Daniel, I have now come to give you insight and understanding. 23As soon as you began to pray, an answer was given, which I have come to tell you, for you are highly esteemed. Therefore, consider the message and understand the vision: Mt 24:15

24"Seventy 'sevens'[a] are decreed for your people and your holy city to finish[b] transgression, to put an end to sin, to atone for wickedness, to bring in everlasting righteousness, to seal up vision and prophecy and to anoint the most holy.[c] Isa 53:10

25"Know and understand this: From the issuing of the decree[d] to restore and rebuild Jerusalem until the Anointed One,[e] the ruler, comes, there will be seven 'sevens,' and sixty-two 'sevens.' It will be rebuilt with streets and a trench, but in times of trouble. 26After the sixty-two 'sevens,' the Anointed One will be cut off and will have nothing.[f] The people of the ruler who will come will destroy the city and the sanctuary. The end will come like a flood: War will continue until the end, and desolations have been decreed. 27He will confirm a covenant with many for one 'seven.'[g] In the middle of the 'seven'[g] he will put an end to sacrifice and offering. And on a wing ⌞of the temple⌟ he will set up an abomination that causes desolation, until the end that is decreed is poured out on him.[h]"[i]

Daniel's Vision of a Man

10 In the third year of Cyrus king of Persia, a revelation was given to Daniel (who was called Belteshazzar). Its message was true and it

[a]24 Or *'weeks'*; also in verses 25 and 26 [b]24 Or *restrain* [c]24 Or *Most Holy Place*; or *most holy One* [d]25 Or *word* [e]25 Or *an anointed one*; also in verse 26 [f]26 Or *off and will have no one*; or *off, but not for himself* [g]27 Or *'week'* [h]27 Or *it* [i]27 Or *And one who causes desolation will come upon the pinnacle of the abominable ⌞temple⌟, until the end that is decreed is poured out on the desolated ⌞city⌟*

concerned a great war.[a] The understanding of the
message came to him in a vision. Da 8:26
2At that time I, Daniel, mourned for three
weeks. 3I ate no choice food; no meat or wine
touched my lips; and I used no lotions at all until
the three weeks were over. Ezr 9:4
4On the twenty-fourth day of the first month, as
I was standing on the bank of the great river, the
Tigris, 5I looked up and there before me was a man
dressed in linen, with a belt of the finest gold
around his waist. 6His body was like chrysolite, his
face like lightning, his eyes like flaming torches, his
arms and legs like the gleam of burnished bronze,
and his voice like the sound of a multitude.
7I, Daniel, was the only one who saw the vision;
the men with me did not see it, but such terror
overwhelmed them that they fled and hid themselves. 8So I was left alone, gazing at this great
vision; I had no strength left, my face turned
deathly pale and I was helpless. 9Then I heard him
speaking, and as I listened to him, I fell into a deep
sleep, my face to the ground. 2Ki 6:17-20; Da 8:18,27
10A hand touched me and set me trembling on
my hands and knees. 11He said, "Daniel, you who
are highly esteemed, consider carefully the words
I am about to speak to you, and stand up, for I
have now been sent to you." And when he said this
to me, I stood up trembling. Da 9:23; Eze 2:1
12Then he continued, "Do not be afraid, Daniel.
Since the first day that you set your mind to gain
understanding and to humble yourself before your
God, your words were heard, and I have come in
response to them. 13But the prince of the Persian
kingdom resisted me twenty-one days. Then Michael, one of the chief princes, came to help me,
because I was detained there with the king of Persia. 14Now I have come to explain to you what will
happen to your people in the future, for the vision
concerns a time yet to come." Da 2:28; 8:26; Hab 2:3
15While he was saying this to me, I bowed with
my face toward the ground and was speechless.
16Then one who looked like a man[b] touched my
lips, and I opened my mouth and began to speak.
I said to the one standing before me, "I am overcome with anguish because of the vision, my lord,
and I am helpless. 17How can I, your servant, talk
with you, my lord? My strength is gone and I can
hardly breathe." Jer 1:9; Da 4:19
18Again the one who looked like a man touched
me and gave me strength. 19"Do not be afraid,
O man highly esteemed," he said. "Peace! Be
strong now; be strong." Jdg 6:23; Isa 35:4
When he spoke to me, I was strengthened and
said, "Speak, my lord, since you have given me
strength." Isa 6:1-8
20So he said, "Do you know why I have come to
you? Soon I will return to fight against the prince
of Persia, and when I go, the prince of Greece will
come; 21but first I will tell you what is written in
the Book of Truth. (No one supports me against
11 them except Michael, your prince. 1And in
the first year of Darius the Mede, I took my
stand to support and protect him.) Da 11:2; Jude 1:9

The Kings of the South and the North

2"Now then, I tell you the truth: Three more
kings will appear in Persia, and then a fourth, who
will be far richer than all the others. When he has
gained power by his wealth, he will stir up everyone against the kingdom of Greece. 3Then a
mighty king will appear, who will rule with great
power and do as he pleases. 4After he has appeared, his empire will be broken up and parceled
out toward the four winds of heaven. It will not go
to his descendants, nor will it have the power he
exercised, because his empire will be uprooted and
given to others. Da 8:4,21-22
5"The king of the South will become strong, but
one of his commanders will become even stronger
than he and will rule his own kingdom with great
power. 6After some years, they will become allies.
The daughter of the king of the South will go to the
king of the North to make an alliance, but she will
not retain her power, and he and his power[c] will
not last. In those days she will be handed over,
together with her royal escort and her father[d] and
the one who supported her.
7"One from her family line will arise to take her
place. He will attack the forces of the king of the
North and enter his fortress; he will fight against
them and be victorious. 8He will also seize their
gods, their metal images and their valuable articles
of silver and gold and carry them off to Egypt. For
some years he will leave the king of the North
alone. 9Then the king of the North will invade the
realm of the king of the South but will retreat to his
own country. 10His sons will prepare for war and
assemble a great army, which will sweep on like an
irresistible flood and carry the battle as far as his
fortress. Isa 8:8; Da 9:26
11"Then the king of the South will march out in
a rage and fight against the king of the North, who
will raise a large army, but it will be defeated.
12When the army is carried off, the king of the
South will be filled with pride and will slaughter
many thousands, yet he will not remain triumphant. 13For the king of the North will muster
another army, larger than the first; and after several years, he will advance with a huge army fully
equipped. Da 8:7-8
14"In those times many will rise against the king
of the South. The violent men among your own

[a] 1 Or *true and burdensome* [b] 16 Most manuscripts of the Masoretic Text; one manuscript of the Masoretic Text, Dead Sea Scrolls and Septuagint *Then something that looked like a man's hand* [c] 6 Or *offspring* [d] 6 Or *child* (see Vulgate and Syriac)

people will rebel in fulfillment of the vision, but without success. 15Then the king of the North will come and build up siege ramps and will capture a fortified city. The forces of the South will be powerless to resist; even their best troops will not have the strength to stand. 16The invader will do as he pleases; no one will be able to stand against him. He will establish himself in the Beautiful Land and will have the power to destroy it. 17He will determine to come with the might of his entire kingdom and will make an alliance with the king of the South. And he will give him a daughter in marriage in order to overthrow the kingdom, but his plans[a] will not succeed or help him. 18Then he will turn his attention to the coastlands and will take many of them, but a commander will put an end to his insolence and will turn his insolence back upon him. 19After this, he will turn back toward the fortresses of his own country but will stumble and fall, to be seen no more. Ps 27:2

20"His successor will send out a tax collector to maintain the royal splendor. In a few years, however, he will be destroyed, yet not in anger or in battle. Isa 60:17

21"He will be succeeded by a contemptible person who has not been given the honor of royalty. He will invade the kingdom when its people feel secure, and he will seize it through intrigue. 22Then an overwhelming army will be swept away before him; both it and a prince of the covenant will be destroyed. 23After coming to an agreement with him, he will act deceitfully, and with only a few people he will rise to power. 24When the richest provinces feel secure, he will invade them and will achieve what neither his fathers nor his forefathers did. He will distribute plunder, loot and wealth among his followers. He will plot the overthrow of fortresses—but only for a time. Ne 9:25; Da 8:25

25"With a large army he will stir up his strength and courage against the king of the South. The king of the South will wage war with a large and very powerful army, but he will not be able to stand because of the plots devised against him. 26Those who eat from the king's provisions will try to destroy him; his army will be swept away, and many will fall in battle. 27The two kings, with their hearts bent on evil, will sit at the same table and lie to each other, but to no avail, because an end will still come at the appointed time. 28The king of the North will return to his own country with great wealth, but his heart will be set against the holy covenant. He will take action against it and then return to his own country. Ps 64:6; Hab 2:3

29"At the appointed time he will invade the South again, but this time the outcome will be different from what it was before. 30Ships of the western coastlands[b] will oppose him, and he will lose heart. Then he will turn back and vent his fury against the holy covenant. He will return and show favor to those who forsake the holy covenant.

31"His armed forces will rise up to desecrate the temple fortress and will abolish the daily sacrifice. Then they will set up the abomination that causes desolation. 32With flattery he will corrupt those who have violated the covenant, but the people who know their God will firmly resist him.

33"Those who are wise will instruct many, though for a time they will fall by the sword or be burned or captured or plundered. 34When they fall, they will receive a little help, and many who are not sincere will join them. 35Some of the wise will stumble, so that they may be refined, purified and made spotless until the time of the end, for it will still come at the appointed time. Da 12:10

The King Who Exalts Himself

36"The king will do as he pleases. He will exalt and magnify himself above every god and will say unheard-of things against the God of gods. He will be successful until the time of wrath is completed, for what has been determined must take place. 37He will show no regard for the gods of his fathers or for the one desired by women, nor will he regard any god, but will exalt himself above them all. 38Instead of them, he will honor a god of fortresses; a god unknown to his fathers he will honor with gold and silver, with precious stones and costly gifts. 39He will attack the mightiest fortresses with the help of a foreign god and will greatly honor those who acknowledge him. He will make them rulers over many people and will distribute the land at a price.[c] Da 7:25; Rev 13:5-6

40"At the time of the end the king of the South will engage him in battle, and the king of the North will storm out against him with chariots and cavalry and a great fleet of ships. He will invade many countries and sweep through them like a flood. 41He will also invade the Beautiful Land. Many countries will fall, but Edom, Moab and the leaders of Ammon will be delivered from his hand. 42He will extend his power over many countries; Egypt will not escape. 43He will gain control of the treasures of gold and silver and all the riches of Egypt, with the Libyans and Nubians in submission. 44But reports from the east and the north will alarm him, and he will set out in a great rage to destroy and annihilate many. 45He will pitch his royal tents between the seas at[d] the beautiful holy mountain. Yet he will come to his end, and no one will help him. Isa 5:28; 21:1; Eze 38:4

The End Times

12 "At that time Michael, the great prince who protects your people, will arise. There

[a]17 Or *but she* [b]30 Hebrew *of Kittim* [c]39 Or *land for a reward* [d]45 Or *the sea and*

The Promise of Eternal Life

"Multitudes who sleep in the dust of the earth will awake:
some to everlasting life, others to shame and everlasting contempt."
—DANIEL 12:2

When it comes to the topic of life after death, I am grateful that we aren't limited to the opinions of observers and the feelings of people on deathbeds. Scripture addresses the subject of life after death often and freely. These passages provide us with great peace when the chilling winds of death blow around us. Each one gives the Christian hope and comfort. Look, for example, at the stirring words of John that have, ever since they were first written, encouraged and strengthened Christians:

> *I heard a loud voice from the throne saying, "Now the dwelling of God is with men, and he will live with them. They will be his people, and God himself will be with them and be their God. He will wipe every tear from their eyes. There will be no more death or mourning or crying or pain, for the old order of things has passed away"* (Revelation 21:3–4).

Remember this: Every time you attend the funeral or memorial service of a believer, you are merely viewing the physical remains of the deceased individual. You are not viewing the person. You are seeing only the body. Regardless of how we refer to the remains—slumbering, at rest, at peace—or how "natural" he or she may look, we are looking at that which is going to be changed and glorified. The soul, that invisible part of the Christian, has already been taken to be in the presence of the Lord. That happened immediately at death. What you are seeing before you is the external "suit of clothes," or as 2 Corinthians 5:1 calls it, "the earthly tent" that is now destroyed. The funeral service provides us a time to thank God for the memory of the person and as a time to be reminded that his or her body will be raised some day in the future.

One of my favorite comments as the funeral party gathers at the grave site pertains to that future day when the dead will be raised. As we're standing there together I will usually say, "Whether you realize it or not, at this very moment you are standing on resurrection ground." (I've actually seen people look down, then step aside two or three feet!)

There will be a time when the graves will be opened and the bodies will be removed in a glorified state to be forever with the Lord Jesus. Plain and simple, the Christian has no reason to fear death, because the future is so full of hope and happiness. This hope builds our joy as we realize with great thankfulness the amazing gift that Jesus has given to us. As Paul states, "But thanks be to God! He gives us the victory through our Lord Jesus Christ (1 Corinthians 15:57). Does your life reflect that gratitude as you look ahead to the future and anticipate your own resurrection in Christ?

Ultimate Realities for Unbelievers

In the Gospel of Luke (16:19–31) there is a vivid account of an interview with a deceased *unbeliever.* Don't misunderstand, this is not the story of another fascinating "out-of-the-body" experience, but a startling narrative of the afterlife told by the ultimate Authority on the subject—the Son of God Himself. While a number of commentators interpret this passage as a parable, I'm not so sure. By naming two of the key characters, I believe that Jesus gives us ample reason to see these verses as recording an actual historical event—a true story of two men . . . and their contrasting eternal destinies. There is a rich man who, as we will see, is eternally lost. There is a poor man who is eternally saved. They lived in two completely different worlds during their earthly lives, but there was a remarkable change of circumstances at death. Death, the greatest of all levelers, reduces everything to the lowest common denominator.

When Lazarus, the beggar, died, his body was probably tossed in the local dump, the refuse pile. Chances are good that he didn't even receive a decent burial. But his soul was taken immediately into the presence of the Lord, a presence called here "Abraham's side" (Luke 16:22).

When we read, "The rich man also died and was buried" (Luke 16:22), we can be sure his burial was one of great pomp and elaborate ceremony. So much for his body. It is his eternal soul that interests us. We find him in hell as we continue to read Jesus' words: "In hell, where he was in torment, he looked up and saw Abraham far away, with Lazarus by his side" (Luke 16:23). The verse that follows does not contain a record of some paranormal experience reported by a man who saw lights and heard buzzing. It is, I believe, an event, not a vision. It becomes an interview, as it were. Notice first that there is *agony*. There is literal pain. The rich man is tormented. And somehow he catches a glimpse of those who are at peace. Second, he is *fully conscious*. Third, he not only has his *senses*, he also has his *memory*. Neither is obliterated by death.

The scene becomes increasingly bleak. Scripture pulls no punches: "So he called to him, 'Father Abraham, have pity on me and send Lazarus to dip the tip of his finger in water and cool my tongue, because I am in agony in this fire' " (Luke 16:24). Earlier Luke mentioned "torment." Now it's "agony." Note that the man could still reason and visualize his surroundings. He still possessed the ability to feel, hear and taste. It was as if he still had a tongue and all five senses.

Abraham (who seems to speak for the Lord) answers the man's request in verse 25: "Son, remember that in your lifetime you received your good things, while Lazarus received bad things, but now he is comforted here and you are in agony." For those who joke about hell and say, "Well, we'll be there for a while and somebody will just pray us out," take a good look at the next verse: "And besides all this, between us and you a great chasm has been fixed, so that those who want to go from here to you cannot, nor can anyone cross over from there to us" (Luke 16:26). The "great chasm" that "has been fixed" suggests a permanent situation. In other words, it is impossible to change destinies or escape one's location after death. Even if others wish for you to be released, they cannot come to your rescue. Realizing this, the man begins to bargain. This is where the account becomes extremely moving. The man in torment remembers his family at home. His concern for them is enormous—and understandably so.

Let me interrupt the story long enough to ask a question: Is it your feeling that the lost who are dead care about the lost who are alive? If you're uncertain about your answer, read verse 28: "I have five brothers. Let him warn them, so that they will not also come to this place of torment." Because the rich man was unable to escape, his number-one concern was that someone would go to his brothers and communicate the truth about hell to those who are still living. Talk about a missionary message! Talk about evangelistic zeal! If it exists nowhere else, an evangelistic passion exists in hell. This scene certainly silences the superficial comments we hear from some who joke, "Aw . . . I'll just be in hell with all my buddies." All it takes is a few verses from this account to realize there's no companionship there. On the contrary, there is an awful, gnawing, inescapable loneliness.

In response to the rich man's request, Abraham says to him, "They have Moses and the Prophets" (Luke 16:29). Meaning what? They have the Scriptures, the very Word of God. They have God's voice in God's Book. In other words, "Let those who are alive hear the truth of Scripture. They have ample opportunity to hear the truth. Let them pick up the Bible and read it for themselves. Let them hear the preachers. Let them hear the gospel as it is contained in God's Word."

And then listen to Father Abraham's remarkable response to the rich man's insistence that an appearance from beyond would make the difference: "He said to him, 'If they do not listen to Moses and the Prophets, they will not be convinced even if someone rises from the dead' " (Luke 16:31). You talk about the power of Scripture! If you could bring someone back from beyond—someone who has been in hell—to tell people what the future holds, it would not be as effective as Holy Scripture! The most invincible, convincing power on earth is the Word of God as the Holy Spirit uses the truth to convict the lost.

We have sufficient truth available to us in the Bible to do the job of bringing the lost to Jesus. It is all that is needed to convince people who have not yet bowed the knee to Jesus Christ that they are missing out on what life is all about. Even if we could do something miraculous, like bring someone back from beyond, it would not have as great an impact as simply presenting the Scriptures. Be careful to grasp the message of this powerful portion of Scripture from Luke's Gospel: *Those who ignore the Word of God in life will not be ignored by the God of the Word in eternity.*

Major Questions Worth Answering

If I were sitting where you're sitting, having read what you have just read, I believe I would have some significant questions buzzing around in my head. Let me try these out: First, *how can a loving God send people to hell*? My initial reaction to that question is this: I'm bothered by the way it's worded. Even though it is commonly asked that way, I don't like what it implies. So if you'll allow me to analyze the question before I answer it, I think it will help.

The question seems to imply that God is indulgent and even a bit impotent . . . and that humanity is being taken advantage of, handled cruelly and treated unfairly—with very little feeling on God's part. Almost like God is taking great delight in watching people squirm, as He says, "Get out of My sight," and pushes people into hell against their will. So if that is what is meant by the question, then let's face that right up front. Suffice it to say, that is *not* what Scripture teaches. But if it's an honest question in which you are wrestling with God's loving character and hell's awful consequences, then I would begin by saying that God has established the ground rules. That's His sovereign right. As the Creator of life, His divine rule states that those who believe in His Son will have eternal life with Him. Those who do not believe in His Son will not have eternal life with Him. Believers will enjoy the blessedness of heaven. Unbelievers who reject the message must face the punishment for that rejection. And lest you think God is calloused and unconcerned over that scene, turn to the words of Peter in his second letter (2 Peter 3:8–9):

> *But do not forget this one thing, dear friends: With the Lord a day is like a thousand years, and a thousand years are like a day. The Lord is not slow in keeping his promise, as some understand slowness. He is patient with you, not wanting anyone to perish, but everyone to come to repentance.*

Never forget these verses! When people present to you the idea that God cruelly and gleefully dances about heaven as every last unbeliever is dumped against his or her will into hell, remind them of Peter's words. With incredible patience and astounding grace God offers the gift of eternal life to all who will accept it. Those who refuse the gift He offers must suffer the consequences, having made their own decision about eternity.

Second, *what about those who have never heard*? Or, *what about those who sincerely follow their own beliefs and their own religion*? We must always be careful about stepping into the role of God. Only He knows the destiny of people. People you and I may think are in the family may not be . . . and vice versa. God alone knows the heart. He alone is the One who makes the final determination. Not all who call Him Lord will enter the kingdom (see Matthew 7:21). And conversely, not all who fear that they are lost are actually lost. Some have genuinely come to know Christ and live under the misguided assumption that they've lost their salvation.

The only way to have eternal life with God is through faith in the Lord Jesus Christ. God has wonderful ways of getting our attention. He uses natural phenomena. He uses general revelation through His glory revealed in nature. He uses circumstances of all kinds, outpourings of blessing and the refining fires of suffering. He uses people. He uses written material. He uses human beings who make the message known. He will use tragedies and calamities, the loss of a loved one, a crippling disease, bankruptcy, the threat of death, divorce and a hundred other situations. The marvel of His plan is that He has an endless number of ways to reach the lost. As the Holy Spirit uses the truth of Scripture to convince them, they will believe.

Let's understand that no one without a saving relationship with Jesus spends eternity in heaven. The *specifics* of how God handles those who do not know Jesus because they have heard so little might be answered by the idea of degrees of punishment. But we do know this: Heaven will not be their home.

Third, *what about deathbed repentance*? This is another gnawing issue. I hear about people who turn to the Lord their last day on earth . . . maybe even their last hour. They have spent their entire life without faith in the Lord Jesus and now, as they lie dying, they express strong and confident faith in the Lord. Is that valid?

Once again, remember that no one on earth can determine with absolute certainty the eternal destiny of any other individual, for God alone knows the heart. But who is to say it is not possible for someone to become a Christian at the end of his or her life? Remember the criminal on the cross (see Luke 23:42–43)? He had lived the life of a criminal and had lived his entire life without Christ. But in his final breath he made a statement regarding eternity, and Christ acknowledged it. There is no doubt in my mind that this criminal will spend eternity in heaven. The Lord read the language of his heart. Only He can do that. Yes, deathbed repentance can be sincere and effective.

Fourth, *what about the death of babies*? This question is extremely important to those who have lost an infant at birth or a little child who never reached an age of spiritual comprehension. It's my understanding that small children who die before reaching a primary level of maturity (when they are able to reason with the basic issues of salvation and faith in the Lord Jesus) go immediately into the presence of the Lord. No passage of Scripture is clearer on this subject than 2 Samuel 12:23, where David said of his infant who had just died, "I will go to him, but he will not return to me." Somehow, in God's wonderful plan, He has reserved in heaven a place for the precious infants and little people whose lives ended prematurely on this earth. David stated the truth as he testified to the inability of his baby to return to earth. But when David himself died, he would see his child as he entered the presence of the Lord. (By the way, the erroneous teaching of reincarnation is nullified by David's remark, "he will not return to me"—which brings me to my final question.)

Where Are You Going to Spend Eternity?

Only you can answer this all-important question. Read the question once again: *Where are you going to spend eternity*? I plead with you, grapple with it until you have come to terms with it. Our country has been a death-denying culture for generations. What concerns me a great deal more than that is that the majority are still a Christ-rejecting people. But since when do thinking people like you take your cues from the majority? I ask you directly, *do you know Jesus Christ as your personal Savior*? Do you know the joy and do you have the undeniable hope that when you die you will live eternally in the presence of God?

To be a death-denying individual is not nearly as tragic as being a Christ-rejecting individual. One simply means you'd rather not talk about it, which is fine. The other means you refuse to *believe* in the One who is the way, the truth and the life (see John 14:6), the One in whom there is eternal life (see John 5:24)—and that refusal is in the end final, and it is fatal. Before you decide to die like that, it is good to remember a certain "rich man" Jesus talked about. While he was alive, he didn't believe either. He does now.

will be a time of distress such as has not happened
from the beginning of nations until then. But at
that time your people—everyone whose name is
found written in the book—will be delivered.
2Multitudes who sleep in the dust of the earth will
awake: some to everlasting life, others to shame
and everlasting contempt. 3Those who are wise[a]
will shine like the brightness of the heavens, and
those who lead many to righteousness, like the
stars for ever and ever. 4But you, Daniel, close up
and seal the words of the scroll until the time of
the end. Many will go here and there to increase
knowledge." Isa 8:16; Rev 22:10

5Then I, Daniel, looked, and there before me
stood two others, one on this bank of the river and
one on the opposite bank. 6One of them said to the
man clothed in linen, who was above the waters of
the river, "How long will it be before these astonishing things are fulfilled?" Da 8:13; 10:4

7The man clothed in linen, who was above the
waters of the river, lifted his right hand and his left
hand toward heaven, and I heard him swear by
him who lives forever, saying, "It will be for a time,
times and half a time.[b] When the power of the
holy people has been finally broken, all these
things will be completed." Lk 21:24; Rev 10:7

8I heard, but I did not understand. So I
asked, "My lord, what will the outcome of all
this be?"

9He replied, "Go your way, Daniel, because the
words are closed up and sealed until the time of
the end. 10Many will be purified, made spotless
and refined, but the wicked will continue to be
wicked. None of the wicked will understand, but
those who are wise will understand. Isa 32:7

11"From the time that the daily sacrifice is abolished and the abomination that causes desolation
is set up, there will be 1,290 days. 12Blessed is the
one who waits for and reaches the end of the 1,335
days. Isa 30:18; Da 8:14

13"As for you, go your way till the end. You will
rest, and then at the end of the days you will rise
to receive your allotted inheritance." Rev 14:13

[a] 3 Or *who impart wisdom* [b] 7 Or *a year, two years and half a year*

INTRODUCTION

HOSEA

The prophet Hosea was sent to the northern kingdom, called Israel. His contemporaries were Amos, Isaiah, Jonah and Micah. Once we begin to understand his role, we'll know why he has often been called "the other Jeremiah of the Old Testament." His was in many respects a pathetic life, a life characterized by tragedy. Few people in Scripture will arouse our sense of sympathy more than Hosea. The first section of Hosea's prophecy is *personal*—a narrative that records Hosea's life with an adulterous wife (which parallels God's life with an unfaithful nation). The second section is *national* in scope—a series of sermons declaring God's holiness and justice and His love for an adulterous people.

WRITER: *Hosea*

DATE: *c.715 B.C.*

PURPOSE: *To proclaim God's compassion and love that cannot let go of His people*

KEY THEME: *God's love relationship with Israel*

KEY VERSES: *3:1; 11:1-4*

TIME LINE 1300BC 1200 1100 1000 900 800 700 600 500 400

Division of the kingdom (930 B.C.)

Ministries of Elijah and Elisha in Israel (c.875-797 B.C.)

Amos's ministry in Israel (c.760-750 B.C.)

Hosea's ministry in Israel (c.753-715 B.C.)

Ministries of Micah and Isaiah in Judah (c.742-681 B.C.)

Exile of Israel (722 B.C.)

Book of Hosea written (c.715 B.C.)

Fall of Jerusalem (586 B.C.)

Scandal in the Parsonage

PERSONAL: The Private Agony of an Unfaithful Mate . . .		NATIONAL: The Public Tragedy of an Unfaithful People . . .		
760 B.C. — Marriage, Children, Separation, Reunion — *CHAPTERS 1–3*		Series of sermons declaring the sin of the people and the character of God; Model of the message as Hosea remains true to his wife in spite of her infidelity — *CHAPTERS 4–14* — 715 B.C.		
Adulterous wife yet faithful husband		**Adulterous nation yet faithful God**		
God: *"Go, take to yourself an adulterous wife and children . . ."*	**God: *"Go, show your love to your wife again, though she is . . . an adulteress."***	**Nation is guilty** **God is holy**	**Nation needs judgment** **God is just**	**Nation has hope** **God is love**

There are many virtues we value in a marriage, but there is one that ranks at the top in importance. That virtue is faithfulness. Marital fidelity is of the highest importance in a home that plans to build from year to year on a love relationship. If faithfulness marks our relationship, there is nothing we cannot work through, because we know that our partner is there and will not leave. If faithfulness is absent, we stand on terribly shaky ground. We never know if our partner will stick it out, "for better or for worse."

Most would agree that we can forgive our spouse of anything if we know that he or she is faithful to us. But when there isn't that absolute commitment in the intimate areas of life, everything else fades and diminishes in importance. Faithfulness is a nonnegotiable issue between partners.

In every marriage ceremony conducted in a place of worship, words of serious commitment are agreed to and stated by the bride and groom. They are called "vows," and they sound something like this: "I promise to be faithful, no matter what the sacrifice or cost required. I will love you for better or for worse, so long as we both shall live, till death do us part, for the rest of my life." Those are words of commitment, a term rarely mentioned today in the media's messages about marriage and in some secular books on marriage.

Fidelity, unfortunately, is neither automatic nor guaranteed. Married couples make a decision every day to say "yes" to their spouse and "no" to every other person. The Bible speaks very boldly as it warns against extramarital relations. It deals severely with those who break their vows with their spouse, either secretly or publicly.

The Theme of Hosea

The book of Hosea is the one book in the Bible that has infidelity as its underlying theme—and not just infidelity, but the faithfulness of a husband in spite of the infidelity of his wife. Yes, you read that correctly! This is a most unusual book about a most unusual marriage.

If you have a tender heart, you'll feel deeply as you read. You'll find yourself heartbroken along with this prophet. Hosea was a man of God who, in spite of his unfaithful wife, stood true to her as an illustration of God's standing true to the nation Israel, who was His adulterous wife (spiritually speaking).

The Days of Hosea

As we seek to understand this book, we need to answer this question: "What was the nation of Israel like in Hosea's day?" Bible commentator J. Sidlow Baxter wrote, "Hosea is the prophet of Israel's zero hour. The nation had sunk to a point of such corruption that a major stroke of divine judgment could no longer be staved off."

Let me point out three specific areas so we won't be vague about the times in which Hosea lived. Not only was his home life in pathetic condition, his nation's life was as well.

In Hosea's opening words, he described the era of time in which he lived. Look carefully: "The word of the LORD that came to Hosea son of Beeri during the reigns of Uzziah, Jotham, Ahaz and Hezekiah, kings of Judah, and during the reign of Jeroboam son of Jehoash king of Israel" (1:1).

You'll recall, the united kingdom had been split by civil war (1 Kings 12). There were tribes up in the north (Israel) and there were tribes that remained in the south (Judah). The prophets of God ministered to either one nation or the other during this civil conflict that lasted better than 300 years.

Hosea was a prophet to the *northern kingdom of Israel.* In the entire history of that land, there was not one godly king. Politically, it was a world of anarchy, bloodshed and revolt. Kyle Yates wrote, "Jeroboam's son, Zechariah, was murdered within six months after he had mounted the throne. His assassin, after a month as king, was dethroned and killed by a vigorous band of men. Anarchy was having its inning. No king was safe except as he was able to maintain a strong guard to keep the assassins from him."

Socially, it was a world of compromise and corruption. Look at verses 1 and 2 of chapter 4:

There is no faithfulness, no love,
no acknowledgment of God in the land.
There is only cursing, lying and murder,
stealing and adultery;
they break all bounds,
and bloodshed follows bloodshed.

That's the world in which this prophet lived. Justice was nowhere to be found. The courtroom was a joke in the day of Hosea, filled with judges who accepted excessive bribes from the people. Family life was equally corrupt and was rapidly disintegrating. The teaching and nurturing roles of parents were eroding at a drastic pace, leaving the children to figure out life on their own. Politically, the rulers were evil through and through, thinking nothing of leading others into a lascivious lifestyle: "Even when their drinks are gone, they continue their prostitution; their rulers dearly love shameful ways" (4:18). Loose living was the accepted standard. Religiously, Hosea's world was one of idolatry and immorality. The priests, if you read Hosea, accepted, even encouraged, the whole thing. It was a sick scene.

To cast it in today's terms, Hosea's nation was a nation "in the pits." This prophet was chosen to stand for God in that kind of a cesspool. Like a beautiful blooming flower growing over a garbage dump, he stood alone for purity and righteousness, yielding a rare fragrance of godliness.

The Home Life of Hosea

We must understand what Hosea's home life was like in order to glean the meaning for us as it relates to faithfulness. To grasp this picture is what makes the story so poignant and inspiring to us. First of all, he was told to get married: "When the LORD began to speak through Hosea, the LORD said to him, 'Go, take to yourself an adulterous wife . . .' "(1:2).

Hosea, whose name means "salvation, deliverance," was a tender, godly young man. And yet God told him to marry a woman named Gomer who, at first glance, seemed to be a prostitute. Some interpret this command literally, insisting that Gomer was, in fact, unfaithful even before she married Hosea. Others say the command is to be interpreted as merely an allegory—that Hosea was writing an imaginary story in the first person and using it as an allegory of the unfaithfulness of Israel in relationship to God.

I believe Hosea was instructed to take a woman who was not *currently* engaged in prostitution . . . but perhaps had that bent. Why do I say this? Because it seems wholly unlike the character of God to introduce a man to a known prostitute and have them marry. In my mind Gomer was faithful at first and became a prostitute later on. She acted on that bent or tendency toward a lifestyle of unfaithfulness and sensuality.

If I read chapter 2 correctly, it wasn't long into the marriage before Gomer walked away. She left her family and lived in the street. She left the care of the children to Hosea. She had no compassion for the family and lost all interest in her husband. She lived as she pleased as she ran wild after other lovers.

Surely there must have been times when Hosea threw up his arms and said, "Why, God? Why me? Why this woman? I contend with immorality all day long. I face sin constantly in the street, and now I have to come home to it! It's totally unfair." He may have been a prophet, but he was still a man with human feelings that occasionally erupted.

A Lesson of Love

Hosea heard from God a second time (3:1), and this message was the hardest of all:

> *The LORD said to me, "Go, show your love to your wife again, though she is loved by another and is an adulteress. Love her as the LORD loves the Israelites, though they turn to other gods and love the sacred raisin cakes."*

The cost of restitution for a slave gored by a bull was thirty shekels of silver (Exodus 21:32), thought to be the standard price for a slave. (Interestingly, Judas betrayed Jesus for the price of thirty silver coins—Matthew 26:15.) Hosea bought Gomer in the street for half the price of a slave. She was hanging around the back streets and dark alleys of Israel, persistently; she had pursued numerous lovers, regularly. Yet God said to Hosea, in effect, "Go and find that woman and buy her back. Love her again." Incredible!

Why would God have him do that? As I mentioned earlier, this is a most unusual book. Hosea was now asked to model God's message to Israel. Do you see the grand analogy in this book that highlights the faithfulness of God? God showed infinite, long-suffering love for a people who despised Him and shook their fists in His face, built their gold-plated statues and carved their wooden idols, and openly worshiped at false temples of worship. In that sense, they "played the harlot." But look at God's response. He faithfully stayed with His people. He did not leave them. They remained the apple of His eye. He loved them to the very end, in spite of their adulterous unfaithfulness.

Maybe some of you are like the people of Israel. God found you and pledged Himself to you in love and faithfulness. You may have walked with Him for a time, but then, in the anguish of despair and cynicism, you've run from the Lord. And now, like Gomer, perhaps you're living a life of unfaithfulness. I'd like you to see what Hosea saw. I'd like you to get a picture of a God who keeps loving you and who longs to take you back, as Hosea took back Gomer. I'd like you to see that our disloyalty to God is really spiritual adultery. We can confess that to our God, and then we can return to Him, who has never left us. His love—finally—cannot, and will not, let us go!

Enduring Lessons From Hosea

Let me share two things I observe while ministering to those who attempt to escape from God. First, *sin destroys the sensitive nerves of the conscience and takes away the tenderness of the heart.* It makes the conscience calloused. It makes the heart stony. There's a hardness that sin breeds—a hardness that curls its lip into a sneer and says, "What do I care about that?" When the sensitive nerves of your conscience are hardened and calloused, sin is paying its wages.

Second, *running from God is an absolute impossibility*. Where do you think you're going to hide? How do you think you're going to get away with it? You can't run from omnipresence. Who are you kidding? You know, King David, the great Old Testament shepherd king, knew the truth. Remember what he said in Psalm 139: "Where can I go from your Spirit? Where can I flee from your presence? If I go up to the heavens, you are there; if I make my bed in the depths, you are there" (Psalm 139:7–9). No, we can't run from God, but we can run to Him. There really is only one solution to our unfaithfulness . . . and that solution is repentance. Stopping right where we are and turning around by the grace and power of God—turning around and running in the opposite direction—into His faithful arms of love. He longs to welcome us home!

Unfaithful Wife, Private Agony **Chapters 1–3**

Hosea's life and faith stand out as an example of spiritual integrity and authenticity among a rebellious people. He was called by God to marry a woman who eventually left him to live a life of prostitution. In his pain and anguish, Hosea heard his Lord's voice calling him to seek his wayward wife and extend love and forgiveness to her. It is hard for us to imagine the hurt, humiliation and public embarrassment Hosea must have felt as he bought back his own wife from the street . . . taking her from a life of prostitution. Through his example we begin to see the depth of God's love for his wayward bride, the children of Israel.

1 The word of the LORD that came to Hosea son
of Beeri during the reigns of Uzziah, Jotham,
Ahaz and Hezekiah, kings of Judah, and during
the reign of Jeroboam son of Jehoash[a] king of
Israel: Jer 1:2; 2Ki 13:13

Hosea's Wife and Children

2When the LORD began to speak through Hosea,
the LORD said to him, "Go, take to yourself an
adulterous wife and children of unfaithfulness, because the land is guilty of the vilest adultery in
departing from the LORD." 3So he married Gomer
daughter of Diblaim, and she conceived and bore
him a son. Dt 31:16; Hos 5:3
4Then the LORD said to Hosea, "Call him Jezreel,
because I will soon punish the house of Jehu for
the massacre at Jezreel, and I will put an end to the
kingdom of Israel. 5In that day I will break Israel's
bow in the Valley of Jezreel." 2Ki 10:1-14; 15:29
6Gomer conceived again and gave birth to a
daughter. Then the LORD said to Hosea, "Call her
Lo-Ruhamah,[b] for I will no longer show love to
the house of Israel, that I should at all forgive
them. 7Yet I will show love to the house of Judah;
and I will save them—not by bow, sword or battle,
or by horses and horsemen, but by the LORD their
God." Ps 44:6; Zec 4:6
8After she had weaned Lo-Ruhamah, Gomer
had another son. 9Then the LORD said, "Call him
Lo-Ammi,[c] for you are not my people, and I am
not your God. Eze 11:19-20; 1Pe 2:10
10"Yet the Israelites will be like the sand on the
seashore, which cannot be measured or counted.
In the place where it was said to them, 'You are not
my people,' they will be called 'sons of the living
God.' 11The people of Judah and the people of
Israel will be reunited, and they will appoint one
leader and will come up out of the land, for great
will be the day of Jezreel. Ro 9:26*; Jos 3:10

2 "Say of your brothers, 'My people,' and of
your sisters, 'My loved one.' 1Pe 2:10

Israel Punished and Restored

2"Rebuke your mother, rebuke her, Isa 50:1; Hos 1:2
for she is not my wife,
and I am not her husband.
Let her remove the adulterous look from her
face Eze 23:45
and the unfaithfulness from between her
breasts.
3Otherwise I will strip her naked
and make her as bare as on the day she
was born; Eze 16:4,22
I will make her like a desert, Isa 32:13-14
turn her into a parched land,
and slay her with thirst.
4I will not show my love to her children,
because they are the children of adultery.
5Their mother has been unfaithful
and has conceived them in disgrace.
She said, 'I will go after my lovers, Jer 3:6
who give me my food and my water,
my wool and my linen, my oil and my
drink.' Jer 44:17-18
6Therefore I will block her path with
thornbushes;
I will wall her in so that she cannot find
her way. La 3:9
7She will chase after her lovers but not catch
them;
she will look for them but not find them.
Then she will say,
'I will go back to my husband as at first,
for then I was better off than now.' Eze 16:8
8She has not acknowledged that I was the one
who gave her the grain, the new wine and
oil,
who lavished on her the silver and gold—
which they used for Baal. Eze 16:15-19; Hos 8:4
9"Therefore I will take away my grain when it
ripens, Hos 8:7
and my new wine when it is ready. Hos 9:2
I will take back my wool and my linen,
intended to cover her nakedness.
10So now I will expose her lewdness
before the eyes of her lovers;
no one will take her out of my hands.
11I will stop all her celebrations: Jer 7:34
her yearly festivals, her New Moons,
her Sabbath days—all her appointed feasts.
12I will ruin her vines and her fig trees, Isa 7:23
which she said were her pay from her
lovers;
I will make them a thicket, Isa 5:6
and wild animals will devour them. Hos 13:8
13I will punish her for the days
she burned incense to the Baals; Hos 11:2
she decked herself with rings and jewelry,
and went after her lovers, Hos 4:13
but me she forgot," Hos 4:6; 8:14
declares the LORD.

[a]1 Hebrew *Joash,* a variant of *Jehoash* [b]6 *Lo-Ruhamah* means *not loved.* [c]9 *Lo-Ammi* means *not my people.*

[14]"Therefore I am now going to allure her;
I will lead her into the desert
and speak tenderly to her.
[15]There I will give her back her vineyards,
and will make the Valley of Achor[a] a door of hope. Jos 7:24,26
There she will sing[b] as in the days of her youth, Jer 2:2
as in the day she came up out of Egypt.

LIVING  INSIGHT

We shouldn't deny the pain of what happens in our lives. We should just refuse to focus only on the valleys.
(See Hosea 2:15.)

[16]"In that day," declares the LORD,
"you will call me 'my husband'; Isa 54:5
you will no longer call me 'my master.[c]'
[17]I will remove the names of the Baals from her lips; Ex 23:13; Ps 16:4
no longer will their names be invoked.
[18]In that day I will make a covenant for them
with the beasts of the field and the birds of the air
and the creatures that move along the ground. Job 5:22
Bow and sword and battle
I will abolish from the land, Isa 2:4
so that all may lie down in safety. Eze 34:25
[19]I will betroth you to me forever; Isa 62:4
I will betroth you in[d] righteousness and justice, Isa 1:27
in[e] love and compassion. Isa 54:8
[20]I will betroth you in faithfulness,
and you will acknowledge the LORD. Jer 31:34

[21]"In that day I will respond,"
declares the LORD—
"I will respond to the skies, Isa 55:10; Zec 8:12
and they will respond to the earth;
[22]and the earth will respond to the grain,
the new wine and oil, Jer 31:12; Joel 2:19
and they will respond to Jezreel.[f] Hos 1:4
[23]I will plant her for myself in the land; Jer 31:27
I will show my love to the one I called 'Not my loved one.[g]' Hos 1:6
I will say to those called 'Not my people,[h]'
'You are my people'; Hos 1:10
and they will say, 'You are my God.'"

Hosea's Reconciliation With His Wife

3 The LORD said to me, "Go, show your love to
your wife again, though she is loved by another and is an adulteress. Love her as the LORD
loves the Israelites, though they turn to other gods
and love the sacred raisin cakes." 2Sa 6:19; Hos 1:2
[2]So I bought her for fifteen shekels[i] of silver
and about a homer and a lethek[j] of barley. [3]Then
I told her, "You are to live with[k] me many days;
you must not be a prostitute or be intimate with
any man, and I will live with[k] you."
[4]For the Israelites will live many days without
king or prince, without sacrifice or sacred stones,
without ephod or idol. [5]Afterward the Israelites
will return and seek the LORD their God and David
their king. They will come trembling to the LORD
and to his blessings in the last days. Jer 50:4-5

Sinful People, Public Tragedy **Chapters 4–14**

One writer has called the book of Hosea "a succession of sobs." Indeed it is! I find three messages Hosea proclaimed to the people of Israel in these 11 chapters. First, *the people were sinful; God is holy.* The nation was corrupt through and through; a holy God could not tolerate the people's sinfulness. Second, *judgment was sure because God is just.* The God of righteousness and justice would surely judge the people if they continued on their path of rebellion. Third, *although the people strayed from God's ways, He still loved them.* There was a longing in God's heart for His bride to repent, to turn from her sinful ways and return to Him. God wanted His people to know that if they would just repent, return and remain at His side, they would find forgiveness and healing in the embrace of His loving arms. Although the Israelites had been unfaithful, prostituting themselves in their idolatry, the Lord remained faithful in all things!

The Charge Against Israel

4 Hear the word of the LORD, you Israelites,
because the LORD has a charge to bring
against you who live in the land: Joel 1:2,14
"There is no faithfulness, no love, Pr 24:2
no acknowledgment of God in the land.
[2]There is only cursing,[l] lying and murder,
stealing and adultery; Hos 7:1
they break all bounds,
and bloodshed follows bloodshed. 2Ki 21:16
[3]Because of this the land mourns,[m] Jer 4:28
and all who live in it waste away; Isa 33:9
the beasts of the field and the birds of the air
and the fish of the sea are dying. Jer 4:25

[4]"But let no man bring a charge,
let no man accuse another,

[a]15 *Achor* means *trouble.* [b]15 Or *respond* [c]16 Hebrew *baal* [d]19 Or *with;* also in verse 20 [e]19 Or *with* [f]22 *Jezreel* means *God plants.* [g]23 Hebrew *Lo-Ruhamah* [h]23 Hebrew *Lo-Ammi* [i]2 That is, about 6 ounces (about 170 grams) [j]2 That is, probably about 10 bushels (about 330 liters) [k]3 Or *wait for* [l]2 That is, to pronounce a curse upon [m]3 Or *dries up*

for your people are like those
who bring charges against a priest. Dt 17:12
5 You stumble day and night, Eze 14:7
and the prophets stumble with you.
So I will destroy your mother— Hos 2:2
6 my people are destroyed from lack of
knowledge. Hos 2:13; Mal 2:7-8

"Because you have rejected knowledge,
I also reject you as my priests;
because you have ignored the law of your
God, Hos 8:1,12
I also will ignore your children.
7 The more the priests increased,
the more they sinned against me;
they exchanged[a] their[b] Glory for
something disgraceful. Hos 10:1,6; 13:6
8 They feed on the sins of my people
and relish their wickedness. Isa 56:11; Mic 3:11
9 And it will be: Like people, like priests. Isa 24:2
I will punish both of them for their ways
and repay them for their deeds. Jer 5:31

10 "They will eat but not have enough; Lev 26:26
they will engage in prostitution but not
increase,
because they have deserted the LORD Hos 7:14
to give themselves 11 to prostitution, Hos 5:4
to old wine and new,
which take away the understanding 12 of my
people. Pr 20:1
They consult a wooden idol Jer 2:27
and are answered by a stick of wood.
A spirit of prostitution leads them astray;
they are unfaithful to their God. Ps 73:27
13 They sacrifice on the mountaintops
and burn offerings on the hills,
under oak, poplar and terebinth, Isa 1:29
where the shade is pleasant. Jer 3:6; Hos 11:2
Therefore your daughters turn to prostitution
and your daughters-in-law to adultery.

14 "I will not punish your daughters
when they turn to prostitution,
nor your daughters-in-law
when they commit adultery,
because the men themselves consort with
harlots ver 11
and sacrifice with shrine prostitutes—
a people without understanding will come
to ruin! Pr 10:21

15 "Though you commit adultery, O Israel,
let not Judah become guilty.

"Do not go to Gilgal; Hos 9:15; 12:11; Am 4:4
do not go up to Beth Aven.[c] Hos 5:8
And do not swear, 'As surely as the LORD
lives!' Jer 4:2
16 The Israelites are stubborn, Ex 32:9
like a stubborn heifer. Jer 31:18
How then can the LORD pasture them
like lambs in a meadow? Isa 5:17; 7:25
17 Ephraim is joined to idols;
leave him alone!
18 Even when their drinks are gone,
they continue their prostitution;
their rulers dearly love shameful ways.
19 A whirlwind will sweep them away, Hos 12:1
and their sacrifices will bring them shame.

Judgment Against Israel

5 "Hear this, you priests!
Pay attention, you Israelites!
Listen, O royal house!
This judgment is against you: Job 10:2
You have been a snare at Mizpah, Hos 6:9; 9:8
a net spread out on Tabor. Jer 5:26
2 The rebels are deep in slaughter. Hos 4:2
I will discipline all of them. Hos 9:15
3 I know all about Ephraim;
Israel is not hidden from me.
Ephraim, you have now turned to
prostitution;
Israel is corrupt. Hos 6:10

4 "Their deeds do not permit them
to return to their God.
A spirit of prostitution is in their heart;
they do not acknowledge the LORD. Hos 4:6
5 Israel's arrogance testifies against them; Hos 7:10
the Israelites, even Ephraim, stumble in
their sin; Eze 14:7
Judah also stumbles with them. Hos 14:1
6 When they go with their flocks and herds
to seek the LORD, Mic 6:6-7
they will not find him;
he has withdrawn himself from them. Pr 1:28
7 They are unfaithful to the LORD; Hos 6:7
they give birth to illegitimate children.
Now their New Moon festivals Isa 1:14
will devour them and their fields. Hos 2:11-12

8 "Sound the trumpet in Gibeah, Hos 9:9; 10:9
the horn in Ramah. Isa 10:29
Raise the battle cry in Beth Aven[c]; Hos 4:15
lead on, O Benjamin.
9 Ephraim will be laid waste
on the day of reckoning. Isa 37:3; Hos 9:11-17
Among the tribes of Israel
I proclaim what is certain. Isa 46:10; Zec 1:6
10 Judah's leaders are like those
who move boundary stones. Dt 19:14
I will pour out my wrath on them
like a flood of water. Eze 7:8
11 Ephraim is oppressed,

[a] 7 Syriac and an ancient Hebrew scribal tradition; Masoretic Text *I will exchange* [b] 7 Masoretic Text; an ancient Hebrew scribal tradition *my* [c] 15,8 *Beth Aven* means *house of wickedness* (a name for Bethel, which means *house of God*).

trampled in judgment,
intent on pursuing idols.[a] Hos 9:16; Mic 6:16
12I am like a moth to Ephraim, Isa 51:8
like rot to the people of Judah.

13"When Ephraim saw his sickness, Isa 7:16
and Judah his sores,
then Ephraim turned to Assyria, Hos 7:11; 8:9
and sent to the great king for help. Hos 10:6
But he is not able to cure you, Hos 14:3
not able to heal your sores. Jer 30:12
14For I will be like a lion to Ephraim, Am 3:4
like a great lion to Judah.
I will tear them to pieces and go away; Hos 6:1
I will carry them off, with no one to rescue them. Mic 5:8
15Then I will go back to my place
until they admit their guilt.
And they will seek my face; Hos 3:5
in their misery they will earnestly seek me."

Israel Unrepentant

6 "Come, let us return to the LORD. Isa 10:20
He has torn us to pieces Hos 5:14
but he will heal us; Jer 3:22
he has injured us
but he will bind up our wounds. Dt 32:39

LIVING  **INSIGHT**

You who truly love the Lord have experienced His power to deliver, so your fears are gone. You could sing your own song of praise. Your fears have been taken away. Perfect love casts out fear, doesn't it?

(See Hosea 6:1–3.)

2After two days he will revive us; Ps 30:5
on the third day he will restore us, Ps 71:20
that we may live in his presence.
3Let us acknowledge the LORD;
let us press on to acknowledge him.
As surely as the sun rises,
he will appear;
he will come to us like the winter rains,
like the spring rains that water the earth."

4"What can I do with you, Ephraim? Hos 11:8
What can I do with you, Judah?
Your love is like the morning mist,
like the early dew that disappears. Hos 7:1; 13:3
5Therefore I cut you in pieces with my prophets,
I killed you with the words of my mouth;
my judgments flashed like lightning upon you. Heb 4:12
6For I desire mercy, not sacrifice, Isa 1:11; Mt 9:13*
and acknowledgment of God rather than burnt offerings. Hos 2:20
7Like Adam,[b] they have broken the covenant— Hos 8:1
they were unfaithful to me there. Hos 5:7
8Gilead is a city of wicked men, Hos 12:11
stained with footprints of blood.
9As marauders lie in ambush for a man, Ps 10:8
so do bands of priests;
they murder on the road to Shechem,
committing shameful crimes. Jer 7:9-10; Eze 22:9
10I have seen a horrible thing Jer 5:30
in the house of Israel.
There Ephraim is given to prostitution
and Israel is defiled. Hos 5:3

11"Also for you, Judah,
a harvest is appointed. Joel 3:13

"Whenever I would restore the fortunes of my people, Ps 126:1; Zep 2:7
7 1whenever I would heal Israel,
the sins of Ephraim are exposed
and the crimes of Samaria revealed. Hos 6:4
They practice deceit,
thieves break into houses, Hos 4:2
bandits rob in the streets; Hos 6:9
2but they do not realize
that I remember all their evil deeds. Jer 14:10
Their sins engulf them; Jer 2:19
they are always before me.

3"They delight the king with their wickedness,
the princes with their lies. Mic 7:3
4They are all adulterers, Jer 9:2
burning like an oven
whose fire the baker need not stir
from the kneading of the dough till it rises.
5On the day of the festival of our king
the princes become inflamed with wine,
and he joins hands with the mockers. Ps 1:1
6Their hearts are like an oven; Ps 21:9
they approach him with intrigue.
Their passion smolders all night;
in the morning it blazes like a flaming fire.
7All of them are hot as an oven;
they devour their rulers.
All their kings fall, Hos 13:10
and none of them calls on me. Ps 14:4

8"Ephraim mixes with the nations; Ps 106:35
Ephraim is a flat cake not turned over.
9Foreigners sap his strength, Isa 1:7; Hos 8:7
but he does not realize it.
His hair is sprinkled with gray,
but he does not notice.
10Israel's arrogance testifies against him, Hos 5:5
but despite all this

[a] *11* The meaning of the Hebrew for this word is uncertain. [b] *7* Or *As at Adam*; or *Like men*

he does not return to the LORD his God
or search for him. Isa 9:13
11"Ephraim is like a dove, Hos 11:11
easily deceived and senseless—
now calling to Egypt, Hos 9:6
now turning to Assyria. Hos 5:13; 12:1
12When they go, I will throw my net over them;
I will pull them down like birds of the air.
When I hear them flocking together,
I will catch them.
13Woe to them, Hos 9:12
because they have strayed from me! Jer 14:10
Destruction to them,
because they have rebelled against me!
I long to redeem them
but they speak lies against me. Mt 23:37
14They do not cry out to me from their hearts
but wail upon their beds.
They gather together[a] for grain and new
wine Am 2:8
but turn away from me. Hos 13:16
15I trained them and strengthened them,
but they plot evil against me. Na 1:9,11
16They do not turn to the Most High;
they are like a faulty bow. Ps 78:9,57
Their leaders will fall by the sword
because of their insolent words.
For this they will be ridiculed Eze 23:32
in the land of Egypt. Hos 9:3

Israel to Reap the Whirlwind

8 "Put the trumpet to your lips!
An eagle is over the house of the LORD
because the people have broken my covenant
and rebelled against my law. Hos 4:6; 6:7
2Israel cries out to me,
'O our God, we acknowledge you!'
3But Israel has rejected what is good;
an enemy will pursue him. Tit 1:16
4They set up kings without my consent;
they choose princes without my approval.
With their silver and gold
they make idols for themselves Hos 2:8
to their own destruction.
5Throw out your calf-idol, O Samaria! Hos 10:5
My anger burns against them.
How long will they be incapable of purity?
6 They are from Israel!
This calf—a craftsman has made it;
it is not God. Hos 14:3
It will be broken in pieces,
that calf of Samaria. Ex 32:4

7"They sow the wind
and reap the whirlwind. Pr 22:8; Isa 66:15
The stalk has no head;
it will produce no flour. Hos 9:16
Were it to yield grain,
foreigners would swallow it up. Hos 2:9
8Israel is swallowed up; Jer 51:34
now she is among the nations
like a worthless thing. Jer 22:28
9For they have gone up to Assyria
like a wild donkey wandering alone.
Ephraim has sold herself to lovers. Eze 23:5
10Although they have sold themselves among
the nations,
I will now gather them together. Eze 16:37
They will begin to waste away Jer 42:2
under the oppression of the mighty king.
11"Though Ephraim built many altars for sin
offerings,
these have become altars for sinning.
12I wrote for them the many things of my law,
but they regarded them as something alien.
13They offer sacrifices given to me
and they eat the meat, Jer 7:21
but the LORD is not pleased with them.
Now he will remember their wickedness Hos 7:2
and punish their sins: Hos 4:9
They will return to Egypt. Hos 9:3,6
14Israel has forgotten his Maker Dt 32:18; Hos 2:13
and built palaces;
Judah has fortified many towns.
But I will send fire upon their cities
that will consume their fortresses." Jer 17:27

Punishment for Israel

9 Do not rejoice, O Israel;
do not be jubilant like the other nations.
For you have been unfaithful to your God;
you love the wages of a prostitute Ge 30:15
at every threshing floor.
2Threshing floors and winepresses will not feed
the people;
the new wine will fail them. Hos 2:9
3They will not remain in the LORD's land;
Ephraim will return to Egypt Hos 8:13
and eat unclean[b] food in Assyria. Eze 4:13
4They will not pour out wine offerings to the
LORD,
nor will their sacrifices please him. Hos 8:13
Such sacrifices will be to them like the bread
of mourners; Jer 16:7
all who eat them will be unclean. Hag 2:13-14
This food will be for themselves;
it will not come into the temple of the
LORD. Eze 4:13-14

5What will you do on the day of your
appointed feasts, Isa 10:3; Jer 5:31; Hos 2:11
on the festival days of the LORD?

[a] *14* Most Hebrew manuscripts; some Hebrew manuscripts and Septuagint *They slash themselves* [b] *3* That is, ceremonially unclean

6 Even if they escape from destruction,
Egypt will gather them, Hos 7:11
and Memphis will bury them. Isa 19:13
Their treasures of silver will be taken over by briers,
and thorns will overrun their tents. Isa 5:6
7 The days of punishment are coming, Isa 34:8
the days of reckoning are at hand.
Let Israel know this.
Because your sins are so many Jer 16:18
and your hostility so great,
the prophet is considered a fool, Isa 44:25; La 2:14
the inspired man a maniac. Hos 14:1
8 The prophet, along with my God,
is the watchman over Ephraim,[a]
yet snares await him on all his paths, Hos 5:1
and hostility in the house of his God.
9 They have sunk deep into corruption,
as in the days of Gibeah. Jdg 19:16-30; Hos 5:8
God will remember their wickedness Hos 8:13
and punish them for their sins. Hos 4:9

10 "When I found Israel,
it was like finding grapes in the desert;
when I saw your fathers,
it was like seeing the early fruit on the fig tree.
But when they came to Baal Peor, Nu 25:1-5
they consecrated themselves to that shameful idol Jer 11:13; Hos 4:14
and became as vile as the thing they loved.
11 Ephraim's glory will fly away like a bird—
no birth, no pregnancy, no conception.
12 Even if they rear children,
I will bereave them of every one. Eze 24:21
Woe to them Hos 7:13
when I turn away from them! Dt 31:17
13 I have seen Ephraim, like Tyre,
planted in a pleasant place. Eze 27:3
But Ephraim will bring out
their children to the slayer."

14 Give them, O LORD—
what will you give them?
Give them wombs that miscarry
and breasts that are dry. Lk 23:29

15 "Because of all their wickedness in Gilgal,
I hated them there.
Because of their sinful deeds, Hos 7:2
I will drive them out of my house.
I will no longer love them;
all their leaders are rebellious. Isa 1:23; Hos 4:9
16 Ephraim is blighted, Hos 5:11
their root is withered,
they yield no fruit. Hos 8:7
Even if they bear children,
I will slay their cherished offspring." ver 12

17 My God will reject them
because they have not obeyed him; Hos 4:10
they will be wanderers among the nations.

10 Israel was a spreading vine; Eze 15:2
he brought forth fruit for himself.
As his fruit increased,
he built more altars; 1Ki 14:23
as his land prospered,
he adorned his sacred stones. Hos 8:11; 12:11
2 Their heart is deceitful, 1Ki 18:21
and now they must bear their guilt. Hos 13:16
The LORD will demolish their altars ver 8
and destroy their sacred stones. Mic 5:13

3 Then they will say, "We have no king
because we did not revere the LORD.
But even if we had a king,
what could he do for us?"
4 They make many promises,
take false oaths Hos 4:2
and make agreements; Eze 17:19; Am 5:7
therefore lawsuits spring up
like poisonous weeds in a plowed field.
5 The people who live in Samaria fear
for the calf-idol of Beth Aven.[b] Hos 5:8
Its people will mourn over it,
and so will its idolatrous priests, 2Ki 23:5
those who had rejoiced over its splendor,
because it is taken from them into exile.
6 It will be carried to Assyria Hos 11:5
as tribute for the great king. Hos 5:13
Ephraim will be disgraced; Hos 4:7
Israel will be ashamed of its wooden idols.[c] Jer 48:13
7 Samaria and its king will float away Hos 13:11
like a twig on the surface of the waters.
8 The high places of wickedness[d] will be destroyed— 1Ki 12:28-30; Hos 4:13
it is the sin of Israel.
Thorns and thistles will grow up
and cover their altars. Isa 32:13; Hos 9:6
Then they will say to the mountains, "Cover us!"
and to the hills, "Fall on us!" Lk 23:30*; Rev 6:16

9 "Since the days of Gibeah, you have sinned,
O Israel, Hos 5:8
and there you have remained.[e]
Did not war overtake
the evildoers in Gibeah?
10 When I please, I will punish them; Eze 5:13
nations will be gathered against them
to put them in bonds for their double sin.
11 Ephraim is a trained heifer

[a] 8 Or *The prophet is the watchman over Ephraim, / the people of my God* [b] 5 *Beth Aven* means *house of wickedness* (a name for Bethel, which means *house of God*). [c] 6 Or *its counsel* [d] 8 Hebrew *aven,* a reference to Beth Aven (a derogatory name for Bethel) [e] 9 Or *there a stand was taken*

that loves to thresh;
so I will put a yoke
on her fair neck.
I will drive Ephraim,
Judah must plow,
and Jacob must break up the ground.
12Sow for yourselves righteousness, Pr 11:18
reap the fruit of unfailing love,
and break up your unplowed ground; Jer 4:3
for it is time to seek the LORD, Hos 12:6
until he comes
and showers righteousness on you. Isa 45:8
13But you have planted wickedness,
you have reaped evil, Job 4:8; Gal 6:7-8
you have eaten the fruit of deception.
Because you have depended on your own strength
and on your many warriors, Ps 33:16
14the roar of battle will rise against your people,
so that all your fortresses will be devastated— Isa 17:3
as Shalman devastated Beth Arbel on the day of battle, 2Ki 17:3
when mothers were dashed to the ground with their children. Hos 13:16
15Thus will it happen to you, O Bethel,
because your wickedness is great.
When that day dawns,
the king of Israel will be completely destroyed.

God's Love for Israel

11 "When Israel was a child, I loved him,
and out of Egypt I called my son.
2But the more I[a] called Israel,
the further they went from me.[b]
They sacrificed to the Baals Hos 2:13
and they burned incense to images. 2Ki 17:15
3It was I who taught Ephraim to walk,
taking them by the arms; Dt 1:31; Hos 7:15
but they did not realize
it was I who healed them. Jer 30:17
4I led them with cords of human kindness,
with ties of love; Jer 31:2-3
I lifted the yoke from their neck Lev 26:13
and bent down to feed them. Ps 78:25

5"Will they not return to Egypt Hos 7:16
and will not Assyria rule over them Hos 10:6
because they refuse to repent?
6Swords will flash in their cities, Hos 13:16
will destroy the bars of their gates
and put an end to their plans.
7My people are determined to turn from me.
Even if they call to the Most High,
he will by no means exalt them.

8"How can I give you up, Ephraim? Hos 6:4
How can I hand you over, Israel?
How can I treat you like Admah?
How can I make you like Zeboiim? Ge 14:8
My heart is changed within me;
all my compassion is aroused. 1Ki 3:26; Ps 25:6
9I will not carry out my fierce anger, Dt 13:17
nor will I turn and devastate Ephraim.
For I am God, and not man— Nu 23:19
the Holy One among you. Isa 31:1
I will not come in wrath.[c]
10They will follow the LORD;
he will roar like a lion.
When he roars,
his children will come trembling from the west. Hos 6:1-3
11They will come trembling
like birds from Egypt,
like doves from Assyria. Isa 11:11
I will settle them in their homes," Eze 28:26
declares the LORD.

Israel's Sin

12Ephraim has surrounded me with lies, Hos 4:2
the house of Israel with deceit.
And Judah is unruly against God,
even against the faithful Holy One. Hos 10:13
12 1Ephraim feeds on the wind; Eze 17:10
he pursues the east wind all day
and multiplies lies and violence. Hos 4:19
He makes a treaty with Assyria Hos 5:13
and sends olive oil to Egypt. 2Ki 17:4
2The LORD has a charge to bring against Judah;
he will punish Jacob[d] according to his ways
and repay him according to his deeds.
3In the womb he grasped his brother's heel;
as a man he struggled with God. Ge 32:24-29
4He struggled with the angel and overcame him;
he wept and begged for his favor.
He found him at Bethel Ge 28:12-15; 35:15
and talked with him there—
5the LORD God Almighty,
the LORD is his name of renown! Ex 3:15
6But you must return to your God; Isa 19:22
maintain love and justice, Mic 6:8
and wait for your God always. Hos 6:1-3; 10:12

7The merchant uses dishonest scales; Am 8:5
he loves to defraud.
8Ephraim boasts,
"I am very rich; I have become wealthy.
With all my wealth they will not find in me
any iniquity or sin."

9"I am the LORD your God,

[a]2 Some Septuagint manuscripts; Hebrew *they* [b]2 Septuagint; Hebrew *them* [c]9 Or *come against any city*
[d]2 *Jacob* means *he grasps the heel* (figuratively, *he deceives*).

⌊who brought you⌋ out of[a] Egypt; Lev 23:43
I will make you live in tents again, Ne 8:17
as in the days of your appointed feasts.
10I spoke to the prophets,
gave them many visions
and told parables through them." 2Ki 17:13

11Is Gilead wicked? Hos 6:8
Its people are worthless!
Do they sacrifice bulls in Gilgal? Hos 4:15
Their altars will be like piles of stones
on a plowed field. Hos 8:11
12Jacob fled to the country of Aram[b]; Ge 28:5
Israel served to get a wife,
and to pay for her he tended sheep. Ge 29:18
13The LORD used a prophet to bring Israel up
from Egypt, Hos 11:1
by a prophet he cared for him. Isa 63:11-14
14But Ephraim has bitterly provoked him to
anger;
his Lord will leave upon him the guilt of
his bloodshed Eze 18:13
and will repay him for his contempt.

The LORD's Anger Against Israel

13 When Ephraim spoke, men trembled;
he was exalted in Israel. Jdg 8:1
But he became guilty of Baal worship and
died. Hos 11:2
2Now they sin more and more;
they make idols for themselves from their
silver, Isa 46:6; Jer 10:4
cleverly fashioned images,
all of them the work of craftsmen.
It is said of these people,
"They offer human sacrifice
and kiss[c] the calf-idols." Isa 44:17-20
3Therefore they will be like the morning mist,
like the early dew that disappears, Hos 6:4
like chaff swirling from a threshing floor,
like smoke escaping through a window.

4"But I am the LORD your God,
⌊who brought you⌋ out of[a] Egypt. Hos 12:9
You shall acknowledge no God but me, Ex 20:3
no Savior except me. Isa 43:11; 45:21-22
5I cared for you in the desert, Dt 1:19
in the land of burning heat.
6When I fed them, they were satisfied;
when they were satisfied, they became
proud;
then they forgot me. Dt 32:12-15; Hos 2:13
7So I will come upon them like a lion,
like a leopard I will lurk by the path.
8Like a bear robbed of her cubs, 2Sa 17:8
I will attack them and rip them open.
Like a lion I will devour them; Ps 17:12
a wild animal will tear them apart. Ps 50:22

9"You are destroyed, O Israel,
because you are against me, against your
helper. Dt 33:29; Jer 2:17-19
10Where is your king, that he may save you?
Where are your rulers in all your towns,
of whom you said,
'Give me a king and princes'? Hos 8:4
11So in my anger I gave you a king,
and in my wrath I took him away. 1Ki 14:10
12The guilt of Ephraim is stored up,
his sins are kept on record. Dt 32:34
13Pains as of a woman in childbirth come to
him, Mic 4:9-10
but he is a child without wisdom;
when the time arrives, 2Ki 19:3
he does not come to the opening of the
womb. Isa 66:9

14"I will ransom them from the power of the
grave[d]; Eze 37:12-13
I will redeem them from death. Isa 25:8
Where, O death, are your plagues?
Where, O grave,[d] is your destruction?

"I will have no compassion,
15 even though he thrives among his brothers.
An east wind from the LORD will come,
blowing in from the desert;
his spring will fail
and his well dry up. Jer 51:36
His storehouse will be plundered Jer 20:5
of all its treasures.
16The people of Samaria must bear their guilt,
because they have rebelled against their
God. Hos 7:14
They will fall by the sword; Hos 11:6
their little ones will be dashed to the
ground, Hos 10:14
their pregnant women ripped open."

Repentance to Bring Blessing

14 Return, O Israel, to the LORD your God.
Your sins have been your downfall!
2Take words with you
and return to the LORD.
Say to him:
"Forgive all our sins
and receive us graciously, Mic 7:18-19
that we may offer the fruit of our lips.[e]
3Assyria cannot save us;
we will not mount war-horses. Isa 31:1
We will never again say 'Our gods' Hos 8:6
to what our own hands have made,
for in you the fatherless find compassion."

[a]9,4 Or *God / ever since you were in* [b]12 That is, Northwest Mesopotamia [c]2 Or *"Men who sacrifice / kiss*
[d]14 Hebrew *Sheol* [e]2 Or *offer our lips as sacrifices of bulls*

4"I will heal their waywardness Hos 6:1
and love them freely, Zep 3:17
for my anger has turned away from
them.
5I will be like the dew to Israel;
he will blossom like a lily. SS 2:1
Like a cedar of Lebanon Isa 35:2
he will send down his roots; Job 29:19
6 his young shoots will grow.
His splendor will be like an olive tree, Ps 52:8
his fragrance like a cedar of Lebanon. SS 4:11
7Men will dwell again in his shade. Ps 91:1-4
He will flourish like the grain.
He will blossom like a vine,
and his fame will be like the wine from
Lebanon. Eze 17:23; Hos 2:22
8O Ephraim, what more have I[a] to do with
idols?
I will answer him and care for him.
I am like a green pine tree; Isa 37:24
your fruitfulness comes from me."

9Who is wise? He will realize these things.
Who is discerning? He will understand
them. Pr 10:29; Isa 1:28
The ways of the LORD are right; Ps 111:7-8; Zep 3:5
the righteous walk in them, Isa 26:7
but the rebellious stumble in them.

[a]8 Or *What more has Ephraim*

INTRODUCTION

JOEL

The name Joel is a combination of two divine names in the Hebrew language: *Yahweh* and *Elohim*, meaning "The LORD is God." The prophet who bears this name believed that definition, without reservation! He was called by God to interpret the contemporary events of the nation of Judah as well as to predict some of the cataclysmic events of the future. Having very likely known Elijah, Joel must have remembered the powerful ministry of this outstanding role model. He knew that *repentance must precede revival*, so he made that issue a cornerstone of his message. In Judah a plague of locusts had devoured every green thing, leaving only desolation in its trail. Joel announced his conviction that the plague had been sent by God because of the sin of His people. But he also proclaimed hope beyond their present circumstances. His message is sorely needed today as well.

WRITER: *Joel*

DATE: *c.835 B.C.*

PURPOSE: *To urge the people of Judah to turn again to God*

KEY THEME: *God's desire for intimacy with His beloved people*

KEY MESSAGE: *Repentance must precede revival*

KEY VERSES: *2:18-27*

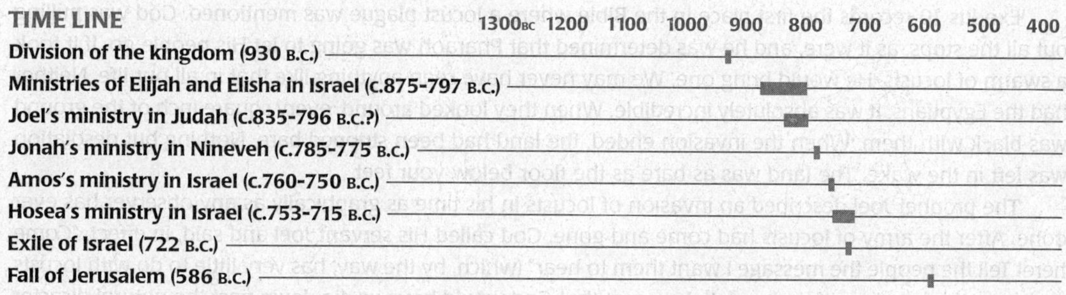

The Eleventh-Hour Alarm

	830 B.C				825 B.C
	THE PLAGUE OF LOCUSTS	**THE CALL TO REPENTANCE**		**THE MESSAGE FOR ISRAEL**	
	The historical event The prophet's warning	The actual call The character of God KEY: *2:13* The universal appeal	**The greatest promise of hope in all the Old Testament**	Concerning the Spirit of God Concerning the judgment of God Concerning the kingdom of God	
	CHAPTERS 1:1–2:11	***CHAPTER 2:12-17***	***CHAPTER 2:18-27***	***CHAPTERS 2:28–3:21***	
EMPHASIS	**Desolation**	**Exhortation**	**Restoration**		
EMOTION	**Mourning now** → **Rejoicing later**				
PARALLEL VERSE	***"His anger lasts only a moment, but his favor lasts a lifetime; weeping may remain for a night, but rejoicing comes in the morning" (Psalm 30:5).***				

For most of my life as a Christian I have known of the book of Joel. But it was not until a few years ago that I came to realize that the background of Joel was *a locust plague*. The closest I have ever come to seeing a locust plague was watching an episode of "Little House on the Prairie." From what was pictured on the tube, such an event must be devastating. I also recall articles I had read and a documentary I had seen about locust plagues. It was incredible. I saw barren objects sticking out of the ground like a naked microphone rod—big stalks that had once been trees. There was not a leaf in sight, not a sign of vegetation on the ground. Everything had turned a bland, brown-gray color. In fact, recordings had been made of the plague as the locusts were flying in their swarm, and you couldn't see through the thick darkness. The light of the sun was blocked out.

Exodus 10 records the first place in the Bible where a locust plague was mentioned. God was pulling out all the stops, as it were, and he was determined that Pharaoh was going to let His people go. If it took a swarm of locusts, He would bring one. We may never have seen anything like that in all our life. Neither had the Egyptians. It was absolutely incredible. When they looked around, every square inch of the ground was black with them. When the invasion ended, the land had been stripped bare. Nothing but desolation was left in the wake. The land was as bare as the floor below your feet.

The prophet Joel described an invasion of locusts in his time as graphically as any observer has ever done. After the army of locusts had come and gone, God called His servant Joel and said, in effect, "Come here! Tell the people the message I want them to hear" (which, by the way, has very little to do with locusts and everything to do with judgment). I suggest that God would have us dig down past the natural disaster of a locust invasion and uncover deep insights into God's universal plan. To do so will help us appreciate the alarm Joel sounds in this book.

The Anonymous Prophet

What was Joel's purpose? Where was he coming from? What message was he communicating? Before we look at his message, we should find out something about the man. His name means "The LORD is God." There are 12 other men in the Old Testament who have the name Joel. We know very little about the prophet Joel, for whom this book is named. He is simply called the "son of Pethuel" (1:1). From the way he wrote and the things he said, some have suggested he might have been a priest as well as a prophet. He has been called by some "the anonymous prophet." He is certainly an obscure one. Like John the Baptist, he spoke as the voice of God, and then, almost as soon as he had come, he was gone. He had delivered the message. He had done what he was called to do. And he left us with an unforgettable glimpse of God's desire that His people would come close to Him as He poured out on them His blessings.

Joel's brief message contains a pungent, penetrating announcement of coming judgment. However, it is balanced beautifully with hope. (In my opinion, one of the greatest promises of hope in all the Old Testament is found in the second chapter of Joel.) All the way through Joel's message we can't help but get the point: *The Lord is God*. This plague of locusts was no accident: God sent them. "See the Lord in this experience" is a pivotal part of Joel's message.

The Message of Joel

Joel prophesied in the southern kingdom; many students of the Bible believe his ministry took place around 835 B.C. during the early days of King Joash (2 Kings 11:21). The people of that day were apathetic and sluggish. They worshiped false gods. They were nonchalant toward the Lord God, and Joel was commissioned to tell them repentance was essential before there could be revival. And there *must* be revival if they hoped to stave off God's judgment. That truth is at the heart of Joel's message. Repentance must precede revival. If we do not repent, God will not hold back his judgment. God used Joel, His man, to bring His message to His people.

By the way, I want to suggest an interesting sidelight to think about. There is something unique about calamity when it strikes a nation. So often it has a way of softening people and making them more teachable. It can bring about a time of intense soul-searching, of perhaps asking, "Could God be in this?" When the citizens of a nation undergo a calamity of catastrophic proportion, often that nation is then humbled and turns to God in repentance and revival.

The Structure of Joel

The book of Joel divides neatly into two parts (1:1–2:17 and 2:18–3:21), by subject matter. First, *Joel brought a word of devastation and warning.* He not only told the people what had happened, he told them why. So often when tragedy strikes, we want to know why. Joel, as God's man for the hour, did just that for the people of his day.

> *Hear this, you elders;*
> *listen, all who live in the land.*
> *Has anything like this ever happened in your days*
> *or in the days of your forefathers? [Implied "no"] (1:2).*

Remember, he was standing before the people—a gaunt servant of God, surrounded by barren stalks that once were large, leafy trees and by bushes that were now nothing but splinters sticking out of the ground. The desolation of the scene was mind-boggling. Joel wanted the people to know that God controlled the locusts. There was a reason for what had happened. It was the first barrel of God's double-barreled plan for His wayward people—punishment for sin. Later, Joel was to unload the second barrel—a promise of restoration and transformation.

Joel sounded an alarm as he responded to God's order to him, which said, in effect, "Stand before the people and point your finger in their direction and say, 'Wake up! The end is near. In fact, it is judgment like you've never seen before. The locusts may have been devastating, but they're just a harbinger of the day of divine judgment yet to come.' "

Joel picked up on the picture of the locusts and said, in essence, "As the locusts have done this to our crops, there will be an invading army that will swarm across our land and invade our houses. People, wake up!" Read these words from verse 11 of chapter 2:

The LORD thunders
at the head of his army;
his forces are beyond number,
and mighty are those who obey his command.
The day of the LORD is great;
it is dreadful.
Who can endure it?

Second, *Joel brought a message of hope.* Joel discharged the second barrel of God's double-barreled plan for His people, as he turned his thoughts from destruction to the blessings God would pour out on His repentant people. The time was coming when God would roll back the destruction and His people would emerge with a new and strong confidence in God's love. God's Spirit would one day transform God's people (2:28–29), and there would be renewal in the land. Restoration and blessing would come after judgment and repentance. Notice how Joel ended his book: "The LORD dwells in Zion!" He is with His people, and everything will be all right in the end! What an encouraging note on which to end the prophecy of this man of God.

Excuses, Excuses, Excuses!

Why do people resist coming back to God? The prophet Joel reminded us of the need to return to the One who is gracious and compassionate (2:13), but so many refuse. Why? I suggest three reasons. First, *some think it's too late to return.* They've wandered too far. It's been too many years now since they've walked with God. It's just too late to stop and turn back. And God whispers, "Yet even now, do it now. It's never too late. I'm ready to welcome you back."

Second, *some think it's futile to return because they've tried it before and they've failed.* And God comes with penetrating honesty and says, "Rend your heart and not your garments" (2:13b). God has the power to see right through His people, and He knows when we've been genuine and when we've gone through the motions. There are times when we must hear from Him, in effect, "What you did before was a garment-rending. You just adjusted your clothes. Now go right to the core . . . the very heart, and deal deeply with it, as for the very first time."

Third, *some think it's no use to come back because God is through with them.* He's done all He can and now He's written them off as beyond hope. Hear this again and again: "Return to the LORD your God, for he is gracious and compassionate, slow to anger and abounding in love" (2:13). Please don't ever think God is through with you. In grace He speaks this message to your heart: "If you come back, I'll take you back! I'm waiting for you."

Lingering Lessons

God desperately wants to get our attention. He wants our heart. He wants our love. He wants our lives. In the days of Joel, He used an army of locusts. Today He may meet us on the home front. He may meet us at work. He may meet us at school. He'll meet us at those points where we struggle to give up whatever keeps us from giving ourselves totally to Him. And He may say, "Wake up. Listen to Me! The young locusts have come to take the place of the great locusts. I'm sending them to stop you, because I'm serious about your walk with Me."

When God restores the afflicted, He does so abundantly. Some of the tenderest people I know were the hardest a few months ago. What's the difference? God did a great work in their lives. He renewed them. He poured out His Spirit on them. He repaid them "for the years the locusts had eaten" (2:25). Isn't that awesome how God does that? He says, "You turn and come back to Me, and I will make up for the years that brought shame and heartache." There is no shame-based probationary period with our heavenly Father. As with the father of the lost son (Luke 15:11–32), when we return, He forgives and the angels in heaven rejoice! It's called grace—amazing grace!

The Plague of Locusts Chapters 1:1–2:11

These chapters record the unthinkable devastation the people of Israel experienced due to a locust plague that descended on their land. A lonely, shrill cry rang out in the deathly silence that followed the plague. In the midst of utter destruction the prophet Joel spoke and recorded the warning of the Lord. Joel's exhortation to the people was simple: "Tell it . . ." (1:3).

As devastating as the locust plague was for the nation, the coming judgment of God would be even more severe. Joel challenged the people to realize the almost unthinkable consequences they would experience if they continued to rebel and disobey.

1 The word of the LORD that came to Joel son of Pethuel. Jer 1:2; Ac 2:16

An Invasion of Locusts

2Hear this, you elders; Hos 5:1
listen, all who live in the land. Hos 4:1
Has anything like this ever happened in your days
or in the days of your forefathers? Joel 2:2
3Tell it to your children, Ex 10:2 Ps 78:4
and let your children tell it to their children,
and their children to the next generation.
4What the locust swarm has left Ex 10:14
the great locusts have eaten;
what the great locusts have left
the young locusts have eaten;
what the young locusts have left Ex 10:5
other locusts[a] have eaten. Dt 28:39; Na 3:15

5Wake up, you drunkards, and weep!
Wail, all you drinkers of wine; Joel 3:3
wail because of the new wine,
for it has been snatched from your lips.
6A nation has invaded my land,
powerful and without number; Joel 2:2,11,25
it has the teeth of a lion, Rev 9:8
the fangs of a lioness.
7It has laid waste my vines Isa 5:6
and ruined my fig trees. Am 4:9
It has stripped off their bark
and thrown it away,
leaving their branches white.

8Mourn like a virgin[b] in sackcloth Isa 22:12
grieving for the husband[c] of her youth.
9Grain offerings and drink offerings Hos 9:4
are cut off from the house of the LORD.
The priests are in mourning, Isa 22:12
those who minister before the LORD.
10The fields are ruined,
the ground is dried up[d]; Isa 24:4
the grain is destroyed,
the new wine is dried up, Hos 9:2
the oil fails.
11Despair, you farmers, Jer 14:3-4; Am 5:16
wail, you vine growers;
grieve for the wheat and the barley,
because the harvest of the field is destroyed.
12The vine is dried up
and the fig tree is withered;
the pomegranate, the palm and the apple tree—
all the trees of the field—are dried up.
Surely the joy of mankind
is withered away.

A Call to Repentance

13Put on sackcloth, O priests, and mourn; Jer 4:8
wail, you who minister before the altar.
Come, spend the night in sackcloth,
you who minister before my God;
for the grain offerings and drink offerings
are withheld from the house of your God.
14Declare a holy fast; 2Ch 20:3
call a sacred assembly.
Summon the elders
and all who live in the land
to the house of the LORD your God,
and cry out to the LORD. Jnh 3:8

15Alas for that day! Jer 30:7
For the day of the LORD is near; Joel 2:1,11,31
it will come like destruction from the Almighty.[e] Ge 17:1

16Has not the food been cut off Isa 3:7
before our very eyes—
joy and gladness
from the house of our God? Dt 12:7
17The seeds are shriveled
beneath the clods.[f] Isa 17:10-11
The storehouses are in ruins,
the granaries have been broken down,
for the grain has dried up.
18How the cattle moan!
The herds mill about
because they have no pasture;
even the flocks of sheep are suffering.

19To you, O LORD, I call, Ps 50:15
for fire has devoured the open pastures
and flames have burned up all the trees of the field.
20Even the wild animals pant for you; Ps 104:21
the streams of water have dried up 1Ki 17:7
and fire has devoured the open pastures.

[a]4 The precise meaning of the four Hebrew words used here for locusts is uncertain. [b]8 Or *young woman* [c]8 Or *betrothed* [d]10 Or *ground mourns* [e]15 Hebrew *Shaddai* [f]17 The meaning of the Hebrew for this word is uncertain.

An Army of Locusts

2 Blow the trumpet in Zion; Jer 4:5
sound the alarm on my holy hill. Ex 15:17
Let all who live in the land tremble,
for the day of the LORD is coming. Zep 1:14-16
It is close at hand— Ob 1:15
2 a day of darkness and gloom, Da 9:12; Am 5:18
a day of clouds and blackness. Rev 9:2
Like dawn spreading across the mountains
a large and mighty army comes, Joel 1:6
such as never was of old Joel 1:2
nor ever will be in ages to come.

3 Before them fire devours,
behind them a flame blazes.
Before them the land is like the garden of
Eden, Ge 2:8
behind them, a desert waste— Ps 105:34-35
nothing escapes them.
4 They have the appearance of horses; Rev 9:7
they gallop along like cavalry.
5 With a noise like that of chariots Rev 9:9
they leap over the mountaintops,
like a crackling fire consuming stubble, Isa 5:24
like a mighty army drawn up for battle.

6 At the sight of them, nations are in anguish;
every face turns pale. Na 2:10
7 They charge like warriors;
they scale walls like soldiers.
They all march in line,
not swerving from their course. Isa 5:27
8 They do not jostle each other;
each marches straight ahead.
They plunge through defenses
without breaking ranks.
9 They rush upon the city;
they run along the wall.
They climb into the houses;
like thieves they enter through the windows.

10 Before them the earth shakes, Ps 18:7
the sky trembles,
the sun and moon are darkened, Mt 24:29
and the stars no longer shine. Isa 13:10; Eze 32:8
11 The LORD thunders Joel 1:15
at the head of his army;
his forces are beyond number,
and mighty are those who obey his
command.
The day of the LORD is great; Zep 1:14; Rev 18:8
it is dreadful.
Who can endure it? Eze 22:14

A Promise of Hope **Chapter 2:12–27**

The beauty of the book of Joel is that it does not simply point a finger in the face of the guilty; it also holds out hope. These sinful people needed a message of hope even on the morning after doomsday. They got that message—but it was offered on God's terms. Joel reminded them of three truths: First, *it is never too late to turn around*; second, *true repentance is an internal transformation, not a superficial external change*; and third, *restoration is possible only because of the gracious character of God.* Joel urged the people to use the teachable moment that resided in this calamity and bow in repentance and receive the gracious offer of restoration.

Rend Your Heart

12 "Even now," declares the LORD,
"return to me with all your heart, Jer 4:1
with fasting and weeping and mourning."
13 Rend your heart Isa 57:15
and not your garments. Job 1:20
Return to the LORD your God, Isa 19:22
for he is gracious and compassionate, Dt 4:31
slow to anger and abounding in love, Ex 34:6
and he relents from sending calamity.
14 Who knows? He may turn and have pity
and leave behind a blessing— Hag 2:19
grain offerings and drink offerings Joel 1:13
for the LORD your God.

15 Blow the trumpet in Zion, Nu 10:2
declare a holy fast, Jer 36:9
call a sacred assembly. Joel 1:14
16 Gather the people,
consecrate the assembly; Ex 19:10,22
bring together the elders, Joel 1:2
gather the children,
those nursing at the breast.
Let the bridegroom leave his room Ps 19:5
and the bride her chamber.
17 Let the priests, who minister before the LORD,
weep between the temple porch and the
altar. Eze 8:16; Mt 23:35
Let them say, "Spare your people, O LORD.
Do not make your inheritance an object of
scorn, Ps 44:13
a byword among the nations. 1Ki 9:7
Why should they say among the peoples,
'Where is their God?'" Ps 42:3

The LORD's Answer

18 Then the LORD will be jealous for his land
and take pity on his people. Ps 72:13

19 The LORD will reply[a] to them:

"I am sending you grain, new wine and oil,
enough to satisfy you fully; Lev 26:5
never again will I make you
an object of scorn to the nations. Eze 34:29

20 "I will drive the northern army far from you,

[a] 18,19 Or *LORD was jealous . . . / and took pity . . . / 19The LORD replied*

pushing it into a parched and barren land,
with its front columns going into the eastern
sea[a] Zec 14:8
and those in the rear into the western
sea.[b]
And its stench will go up; Isa 34:3
its smell will rise."

Surely he has done great things.[c]
21 Be not afraid, O land; Isa 54:4; Zep 3:16-17
be glad and rejoice. Ps 9:2
Surely the LORD has done great things. Ps 126:3
22 Be not afraid, O wild animals,
for the open pastures are becoming green.
The trees are bearing their fruit;
the fig tree and the vine yield their riches.
23 Be glad, O people of Zion,
rejoice in the LORD your God, Isa 41:16; Hab 3:18
for he has given you
the autumn rains in righteousness.[d]
He sends you abundant showers, Eze 34:26
both autumn and spring rains, as before.
24 The threshing floors will be filled with grain;
the vats will overflow with new wine and
oil. Am 9:13; Mal 3:10

25 "I will repay you for the years the locusts have
eaten— Dt 28:39
the great locust and the young locust,
the other locusts and the locust swarm[e]—
my great army that I sent among you. Joel 1:6
26 You will have plenty to eat, until you are full,
and you will praise the name of the LORD
your God, Isa 62:9
who has worked wonders for you; Isa 25:1
never again will my people be shamed. Isa 29:22
27 Then you will know that I am in Israel, Ex 6:7
that I am the LORD your God, Joel 3:17
and that there is no other;
never again will my people be shamed. Zep 3:11

A Word to God's People **Chapters 2:28–3:21**

Through Joel the Lord extended an offer of hope and restoration. God promised national healing if the people would repent and follow Him, and He assured them of an outpouring of His Spirit on them. Joel pointed to a time when God's ultimate judgment would be poured out and when His glorious kingdom would finally come in its fullness. The prophetic promise of the Lord's future reign is clearly set forth in the book of Joel.

The Day of the LORD

28 "And afterward,
I will pour out my Spirit on all people.
Your sons and daughters will prophesy,
your old men will dream dreams, Jer 23:25
your young men will see visions.
29 Even on my servants, both men and women,
I will pour out my Spirit in those days.
30 I will show wonders in the heavens Lk 21:11

LIVING  **INSIGHT**

The Spirit of God is the dynamic of life. Like air, the Spirit may be invisible—but let us never be misled by equating invisible with impotent. This Spirit is vital to life.

(See Joel 2:28.)

and on the earth, Mk 13:24-25
blood and fire and billows of smoke.
31 The sun will be turned to darkness Mt 24:29
and the moon to blood
before the coming of the great and dreadful
day of the LORD. Isa 13:9-10; Mal 4:1,5
32 And everyone who calls
on the name of the LORD will be saved;
for on Mount Zion and in Jerusalem Isa 46:13
there will be deliverance, Ob 1:17
as the LORD has said,
among the survivors Mic 4:7; Ro 9:27
whom the LORD calls. Ac 2:39

The Nations Judged

3 "In those days and at that time,
when I restore the fortunes of Judah and
Jerusalem, Jer 16:15
2 I will gather all nations Zep 3:8
and bring them down to the Valley of
Jehoshaphat.[f] Isa 22:1
There I will enter into judgment against them
concerning my inheritance, my people
Israel,
for they scattered my people among the
nations Lev 26:33
and divided up my land.
3 They cast lots for my people Eze 24:6
and traded boys for prostitutes;
they sold girls for wine Am 2:6
that they might drink.

4 "Now what have you against me, O Tyre and
Sidon and all you regions of Philistia? Are you
repaying me for something I have done? If you are
paying me back, I will swiftly and speedily return
on your own heads what you have done. 5 For you
took my silver and my gold and carried off my
finest treasures to your temples. 6 You sold the

[a] 20 That is, the Dead Sea [b] 20 That is, the Mediterranean [c] 20 *Or rise. / Surely it has done great things."* [d] 23 Or / *the teacher for righteousness:* [e] 25 The precise meaning of the four Hebrew words used here for locusts is uncertain. [f] 2 *Jehoshaphat* means *the LORD judges*; also in verse 12.

GOD'S INDWELLING PRESENCE

"And afterward,
I will pour out my Spirit on all people.
Your sons and daughters will prophesy,
your old men will dream dreams,
your young men will see visions.
Even on my servants, both men and women,
I will pour out my Spirit in those days."

—JOEL 2:28–29

Have you ever really thought about air? You can't feel it. You can't see it or smell it. You can't, except in the most technical sense, measure it or weigh it. But it keeps you alive every minute. If I were to take air away from you for less than five minutes, you would become brain damaged. We cannot live without it. Yet when a businessman flies in an airplane, when a trucker puts on the brakes, or when a mechanic removes a lug nut with an air wrench, we think nothing of it. Amazing stuff, air. It may be invisible, but it is still powerful.

The Wind of the Spirit

Never think that just because something is invisible it is unimportant or weak. You may be surprised to know that the Bible talks a lot about *air*. The Old Testament Hebrew term for it is *ruach*. The New Testament Greek term is *pneuma*. (We get our English word *pneumatic* from it.) The English Bible, however, doesn't translate either of these words as air. No, our Bibles typically choose one of three words to convey the nuances of the Hebrew and the Greek—first, *breath*: God "breathed into his nostrils the breath of life" (Genesis 2:7); second, *wind*: "Like the blowing of a violent wind" (Acts 2:2); or, third, and most commonly, *spirit*: "my spirit rejoices in God my Savior" (Luke 1:47) or *the Holy Spirit*, as in "But the Counselor, the Holy Spirit, whom the Father will send in my name, will teach you all things and will remind you of everything I have said to you" (John 14:26).

A number of synonyms have been used for the Holy Spirit—words like helper, advocate, counselor, convicter, restrainer, exhorter and reprover. The Spirit is portrayed by symbols as well, such as a dove, fire, wind, and even water. In the Gospel of John Jesus calls this power "living water." Listen to what Jesus said: "If anyone is thirsty, let him come to me and drink. Whoever believes in me, as the Scripture has said, streams of living water will flow from within him" (John 7:37–38).

Let me paraphrase verse 38: "From the believer's inner life there will be a reservoir of enormous, immeasurable power. It will gush forth. It will pour out like a torrential river that causes rapids, waterfalls and endless movement to the ocean." That's the idea. It's not a picture of some blasé, passive force. The Spirit of God is the dynamic of life. In fact, the Greek word for power often associated with the Spirit is *dunamis*, from which we get our English word "dynamite." Like air, the Spirit may be invisible—but let us never be misled by equating "invisible" with "impotent." The Spirit is vital to life.

Who Is the Holy Spirit?

Many people hold some pretty strange ideas about the Holy Spirit, most of them erroneous. In fact, when people attempt to explain their beliefs, they are often most confused about the doctrine of the Holy Spirit. Let's examine four important truths. First, *the Holy Spirit is a distinct person*. He is a "Him," or a "He." In Jesus' powerful discourse about the Holy Spirit in John 14, He spoke these words:

> *You may ask me for anything in my name, and I will do it. If you love me, you will obey what I command. And I will ask the Father, and he will give you another Counselor to be with you forever—the Spirit of truth. The world cannot accept him, because it neither sees him nor knows him. But you know him, for he lives with you and will be in you (John 14:14–17).*

What a helpful revelation! While Jesus was on earth, the Spirit of God was with the people of God. But when Jesus left the earth, He sent another Counselor (another of the same kind, literally), like Himself. The Counselor came and became a part of their lives deep within. No longer merely *with* them, but *in* them. That's a mind-staggering truth. And notice that He is called "He" or "Him"—never "It." Nowhere in any version of Scripture is the Spirit of God referred to as "It."

Second, *the Holy Spirit is active and involved.* What will the Holy Spirit do in our lives? Lie around, take it easy, relax, casually exist within us? No. Listen again to what Jesus said just a little later on in His conversation with His disciples:

> *But I tell you the truth: It is for your good that I am going away. Unless I go away, the Counselor will not come to you; but if I go, I will send him to you. When he comes, he will convict the world of guilt in regard to sin and righteousness and judgment . . . But when he, the Spirit of truth, comes, he will guide you into all truth. He will not speak on his own; he will speak only what he hears, and he will tell you what is yet to come. He will bring glory to me by taking from what is mine and making it known to you (John 16:7–8,13–14).*

Oftentimes we can sense the Spirit's presence. On some occasions His presence is so real, so obvious, it's almost as though we can touch Him. When He moves among a body of people, He mobilizes and empowers. He brings an understanding of spiritual truth from the Scriptures as well as a conviction of sin within our inner being. We become sensitive, motivated, spiritually alive. We are cleansed. We are purged, enthusiastic, actively excited about the right things. In that setting we can become spontaneously responsive. Who hasn't been in worship services or in meetings where the Spirit's presence made the place electric? But when He is absent, the atmosphere is dreadfully dead, desperately, horribly lifeless. I have witnessed both. The contrast is undeniable.

Never doubt that the Spirit of God is incessantly on the move. As with air, we cannot see Him; nevertheless, He is hard at work convicting, guiding, instructing, disclosing and glorifying. And that's just a few of His activities! He's involved. He's always working.

Third, *the Holy Spirit is real and relevant.* Just before Jesus' ascension into heaven, He met with a group of His followers. They had questions; He had answers. He also had some crucial news regarding the Spirit who would soon take His place: "But you will receive power when the Holy Spirit comes on you; and you will be my witnesses in Jerusalem, and in all Judea and Samaria, and to the ends of the earth" (Acts 1:8).

Familiar words . . . packed with incredible significance. Note especially that the Spirit is no imaginary, vague hope, but a promise from our Savior. It is as if He were saying, "You will have His presence, and wherever you go He will be in you. He will be your 'dynamic' . . . a real and relevant force for your future."

Fourth, and finally, *the Holy Spirit is deity.* He is God! That truth will heighten your respect for the Holy Spirit's work, if nothing else will. Christians have been known to stand in strong defense of the deity of Jesus Christ . . . and we certainly should. But what about the deity of the Spirit? Pause and ponder this: The third member of the Godhead, the invisible, yet all-powerful representation of deity, is actually living inside your being. Therefore, the limitless capabilities of God Himself are resident within you, because He indwells you (see 1 Corinthians 3:16) . . . at all times.

You think you can't handle what life throws at you? You think you can't withstand the lure of life's temptations? Well, you certainly could not if you were all alone. You—*alone*—can't do that any more than you can sprout wings and fly alone. But with the right kind of power put into operation, the very power and presence of God, you can handle it. As a matter of fact, all the pressure will be shifted and the weight transferred from you to Him. It's a radically different way to live. And because He is God, He can handle it through you and for you. What relief this brings!

The Holy Spirit exists in an invisible realm. You will never see His presence or power, though you are convinced of His reality. You will only see His working—the results of His enabling, His filling, His guiding. But when He, the Spirit of God, is in control, the results are nothing short of phenomenal!

The Spirit Is Working Among Non-Christians

You may be surprised to know that the Spirit is also involved among the unsaved at all times. As a matter of fact, in Paul's second letter to the Thessalonians we read that the Spirit is actively involved in holding back sin (2 Thessalonians 2:7). Do you have any idea how much evil would be present and active on this earth if the Spirit of God were suddenly removed? His omnipresence is like a worldwide envelope of righteousness, an all-inclusive bubble of invisible restraint. He constantly holds evil in check. But when He is removed, literally all hell will break loose on this globe! Thankfully, He currently holds back sin.

We know that the Holy Spirit "convicts the world of guilt in regard to sin and righteousness and judgment" (John 16:8). I am comforted when I read that. It frees me from the need to moralize when I'm with a group of unsaved people. I don't have to try to convince lost people about how unrighteous they are. Most already know they're unrighteous. How? The Spirit is already convincing them. My ministry is not to convince someone else that he or she is sinful. That's the Spirit's ministry. His convicting work is much more effective than mine ever could be. My job is to present Jesus Christ.

The Holy Spirit makes it clear that all have sinned and fall short of God's glory and perfection (see Romans 3:23). Every person who comes into the family of God has been pursued ahead of time by the Spirit, who is like the prosecuting attorney saying, "These are the facts. Here is the evidence. All these things demonstrate guilt beyond the shadow of a doubt." And sinful people's mouths are shut. They are left speechless and without excuse in light of the facts and evidence. Many without Jesus Christ today struggle with guilt and unbelief and a sense of purposelessness. They try every way in the world to run away from it—through a bottle, drugs, gambling, athletics, busyness, education, philosophy of one kind or another, or countless other means of escape. Inescapable guilt haunts them, thanks to the work of the Holy Spirit.

The Spirit not only convicts the world of sin but also of righteousness. There is simply no way sin-ridden people can measure up to God's righteous demands. They may try (and often do), but the Spirit of God will convince them of their need for a relationship with Jesus Christ in order to measure up to the standard of perfection God requires. No one but the Holy Spirit can reveal to us that to be right with God does not depend on doing the right number of good deeds but on Jesus Christ's sacrificial death on the cross.

When human sin is confronted by the righteousness of Christ, inevitable judgment is brought into ever-sharper focus. And the reason this time of judgment is so significant is because the ruler of this world (Satan himself) stands judged. Satan was judged at the cross, and every moment that Satan exists since that great watershed in history, he stands judged. Each tick of the clock moves him closer to his doom. He's a defeated foe, and he knows it.

The Spirit Is Working Among Christians

The Spirit of truth is actively at work in the lives of believers as well. Remember Jesus' words: "But when he, the Spirit of truth, comes, he will guide you into all truth. He will not speak on his own; he will speak only what he hears, and he will tell you what is yet to come. He will bring glory to me by taking from what is mine and making it known to you" (John 16:13–14).

The Holy Spirit not only takes the Scriptures and makes them clear and understandable to us, but He takes circumstances in which we find ourselves and gives us insight into them. He takes pressure-filled predicaments and uses them to mature us. He guides us into all realms of the truth. He nurtures us. He comforts us when we are frightened by some fear. He tells us there's hope even when we can't see the light at the end of the tunnel. He gives us reasons to go on, even as we advance in years and death is near. All of that is included in the thought, "He will guide you into all truth."

Let me pass along something I hope you *never* forget. If you get involved in a ministry that glorifies itself instead of Jesus Christ, the Spirit of God is not in that ministry. If you follow a leader who is redirecting the glory to himself or to that ministry instead of to Jesus, the Spirit of God isn't empowering his leadership. If you're a part of a church, a Christian school, a mission organization or a Christian camping ministry in which someone other than Jesus is being glorified, it is not being empowered by the Spirit of God. Mark it down: THE SPIRIT GLORIFIES JESUS CHRIST. I'll take it even one step further: If the Holy Spirit Himself is being emphasized and magnified, He isn't in it! *Jesus Christ* is the One who is glorified when the Spirit is at work. The Spirit does His work behind the scenes, never in the limelight. I admire that as much as anything about His work.

There is an additional significant way in which the Holy Spirit works in Christians. Listen to Paul as he lays the foundation for this aspect of the Spirit's work in his designation of spiritual gifts: "There are different kinds of gifts, but the same Spirit. There are different kinds of service, but the same Lord. There are different kinds of working, but the same God works all of them in all men" (1 Corinthians 12:4–6).

Notice what he says. There are many different spiritual gifts (see Romans 12:6–8; 1 Corinthians 12:7–11; Ephesians 4:11; 1 Peter 4:9–11), but they all come from the same Spirit. These gifts inspire different forms of ministry, but they all spring from the same Lord. Each Christian receives at least one spiritual gift. The purpose is not to draw attention to oneself, to brag, boast or impress others. Rather, these spiritual gifts are intended to be used for the good of the church and for the glorification of God in the world.

God endows each Christian with certain gifts to send us forth in service. We are meant to continue the work and ministry of Jesus Christ today. Remember, Jesus has no representatives if we aren't living out our life for Him. The gifts of the Spirit make this possible so we can reflect and reveal Jesus Christ.

Signs of the Spirit

How do we experience the Holy Spirit? I suggest four ways. First, *because the Spirit is a person, we feel Him as He heals relationships.* When He does that, He *melts* us. I realize that you may never have entered into the work of the Spirit in this realm. Perhaps you have erected big thick walls around your life, barriers of resistance, heavy fortifications that keep you coolly distant and safely separated. To break through those walls, a melting process is needed. The Holy Spirit can do that, because He wants to heal strained relationships. It may be with your child who is now grown. Or with a parent. Or with a person who was once a very close, trusted friend. Somehow, some way, there has to be the melting work of the Spirit before such healing can happen and forgiveness can occur. Right now, ask the Spirit of God to begin melting you so you may be relieved of resentment, blame and bitterness as the walls of separation come tumbling down!

Second, *because the Holy Spirit is active and involved, we feel Him comforting us In our sorrows and guiding us in our pursuits.* When He does that, He *molds* us. By the way, these works of the Spirit go in order: first there's melting (as relationships are healed), and not until then can He begin to mold us. It's nothing short of amazing how such healing in our lives clears up our sight, freeing us to pursue new directions. The Spirit's presence is there to mold us and reshape us. Let me add that it can get pretty painful when He begins to poke and prod. Yet the Spirit who shapes us is also "the Counselor" . . . He will be with you to help you. Right now, right where you are, ask the Spirit to mold you into what He would have you be.

Third, *because the Holy Spirit is real and relevant, we feel Him giving us power and an attitude of perseverance.* When He does that, He *fills* us. I often begin my day by praying something like this: "Lord God, I don't know what my day holds. I don't know what's in it for You and me, but I'm Yours. Today belongs to You, not me. You are the Potter, I am the clay. I want You to guide me one step at a time. And I want Your power to mark my every step. Stop me if I'm moving in a wrong direction. Push me if I'm sluggish. Shake me back to my senses if I get out of line, but don't let me go my own way. Fill me today with Your peace and Your power." Because the Spirit is real and relevant, it is remarkable how He turns that day you may have dreaded into opportunities to experience His power and feel His peace, as we "run with perseverance the race marked out for us" (Hebrews 12:1).

Fourth, *because the Holy Spirit is God, we feel Him as He controls our circumstances and transforms our lives.* When He does that, He *uses* us. He melts us in relationships. He molds us in the pursuit and the direction of His will. He fills us with power and the perseverance to keep at it. He uses us as He controls our circumstances and transforms our lives. Ask the Spirit of God to use you, just as you are, with the gifts and abilities that He's given you. Secure in the confidence that God is in control of your life, you will be free to serve Him with joy and effectiveness.

Our God loves to hear us use these eight words: "Melt me. Mold me. Fill me. Use me." If you are sincerely willing to be restored, reshaped, refreshed and renewed by the Spirit of God, you will begin to discover a dimension of living you've never known before. A whole new process will start in your life. And the best part is this: Jesus Christ alone will be glorified!

people of Judah and Jerusalem to the Greeks, that
you might send them far from their homeland.
7"See, I am going to rouse them out of the
places to which you sold them, and I will return on
your own heads what you have done. 8I will sell
your sons and daughters to the people of Judah,
and they will sell them to the Sabeans, a nation far
away." The LORD has spoken. Isa 43:5-6; Jer 23:8

9Proclaim this among the nations:
Prepare for war! Isa 8:9
Rouse the warriors! Jer 46:4
Let all the fighting men draw near and
attack.
10Beat your plowshares into swords
and your pruning hooks into spears. Isa 2:4
Let the weakling say, Zec 12:8
"I am strong!" Jos 1:6
11Come quickly, all you nations from every side,
and assemble there. Eze 38:15-16; Zep 3:8

Bring down your warriors, O LORD! Isa 13:3
12"Let the nations be roused;
let them advance into the Valley of
Jehoshaphat,
for there I will sit
to judge all the nations on every side. Isa 2:4
13Swing the sickle, Mk 4:29
for the harvest is ripe. Hos 6:11; Mt 13:39
Come, trample the grapes, Jer 25:30
for the winepress is full Rev 14:20
and the vats overflow—
so great is their wickedness!"
14Multitudes, multitudes
in the valley of decision!
For the day of the LORD is near Isa 34:2-8; Joel 1:15
in the valley of decision. Eze 36:5
15The sun and moon will be darkened,
and the stars no longer shine. Eze 32:7
16The LORD will roar from Zion
and thunder from Jerusalem; Am 1:2
the earth and the sky will tremble. Eze 38:19
But the LORD will be a refuge for his people,
a stronghold for the people of Israel.

Blessings for God's People

17"Then you will know that I, the LORD your
God,
Joel 2:27
dwell in Zion, my holy hill. Isa 4:3
Jerusalem will be holy; Jer 31:40
never again will foreigners invade her.

18"In that day the mountains will drip new
wine,
and the hills will flow with milk; Ex 3:8
all the ravines of Judah will run with water.
A fountain will flow out of the LORD's house
and will water the valley of acacias.[a]
19But Egypt will be desolate, Isa 19:1
Edom a desert waste, Isa 11:14
because of violence done to the people of
Judah, Ob 1:10
in whose land they shed innocent blood.
20Judah will be inhabited forever Am 9:15
and Jerusalem through all generations.
21Their bloodguilt, which I have not pardoned,
I will pardon." Eze 36:25

The LORD dwells in Zion!

[a] 18 Or *Valley of Shittim*

INTRODUCTION

AMOS

The prophet Amos was called to proclaim God's message to the northern kingdom, also known as Israel. A strong voice was needed in this nation that was steeped in religiosity, immorality, compromise and complacency. Amos was just the determined, disciplined, courageous man of God needed to proclaim the truth and to denounce the sins that separated people from God. Born of humble means, brought up to work with his hands, rugged and unflappable, Amos became one of the most colorful personalities among the prophets. God's severe predictions of judgment had to be delivered by a man who modeled that message. Like Elijah before him, and John the Baptist after him, Amos fearlessly stormed the king's palace. With relentless zeal he stuck to the task, refusing to be intimidated by insults and threats. *Sin always brings judgment.* There was no way that Amos was going to allow that message to be muffled or changed.

WRITER: *Amos*

DATE: *c.760–750 B.C.*

PURPOSE: *To challenge the materialism and immorality of the people of Israel*

KEY THEMES: *God's justice; God's righteousness*

KEY MESSAGE: *"Prepare to meet your God, O Israel" (4:12)*

COMMUNICATION METHODS: *Oracles, sermons, visions, promises*

TIME LINE

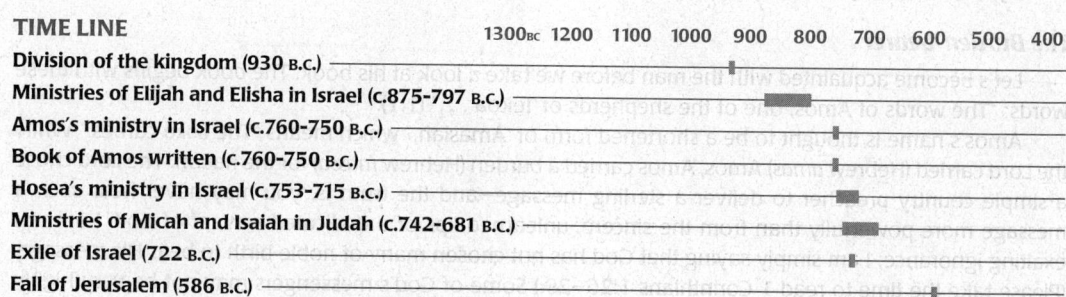

1300BC 1200 1100 1000 900 800 700 600 500 400

Division of the kingdom (930 B.C.)
Ministries of Elijah and Elisha in Israel (c.875-797 B.C.)
Amos's ministry in Israel (c.760-750 B.C.)
Book of Amos written (c.760-750 B.C.)
Hosea's ministry in Israel (c.753-715 B.C.)
Ministries of Micah and Isaiah in Judah (c.742-681 B.C.)
Exile of Israel (722 B.C.)
Fall of Jerusalem (586 B.C.)

Fig-Picker and Prophet-Preacher

760 B.C.

INTRODUCTION	ORACLES AGAINST GENTILE NATIONS	SERMONS AGAINST NATION OF ISRAEL	VISIONS OF JUDGMENT	PROMISES OF HOPE
	Aram Philistia Phoenicia Edom Ammon Moab	*"Hear this word the LORD has spoken against you, O people of Israel . . . cows of Bashan . . . O house of Israel . . . who are complacent in Zion" (3:1; 4:1; 5:1; 6:1).*	Locusts Fire Plumb line Ripe fruit The Lord by the altar	*"I will restore David's fallen tent . . . I will bring back my exiled people Israel" (9:11,14).*
CHAPTER 1:1-2	***CHAPTERS 1:3–2:16***	***CHAPTERS 3–6***	***CHAPTERS 7:1–9:10***	***CHAPTER 9:11-15***

750 B.C.

When you stop long enough to consider it, God has chosen and used some very unusual instruments as His messengers. Dotted across the landscape of our vast continent, the majority of spokespersons for God are not of noble birth. They are not men and women whom people would travel hundreds and hundreds of miles to hear. They're just plain folks. If Amos were alive today, he would be one of those instruments. If you're looking in your Bible for a "good ol' boy," you found him.

Amos was from the country, but he didn't stay in the country. He was called, probably against his preference, to the city. He went to the northern kingdom (Israel) and laid down the law as the people had never heard it before. Certainly the king of Israel, Jeroboam II (793–753 B.C.), had never heard this kind of preaching. And all those sophisticated, unbelieving advisers surrounding the king were equally appalled by Amos's message.

I think the old adage applies here: "You can take the boy out of the country, but you can't take the country out of the boy." This common preacher just blew 'em away. I love it!

The Burden-bearer

Let's become acquainted with the man before we take a look at his book. The book begins with these words: "The words of Amos, one of the shepherds of Tekoa . . ." (1:1).

Amos's name is thought to be a shortened form of "Amasiah," which means "The LORD carries." While the Lord carried (Hebrew *amas*) Amos, Amos carried a burden (Hebrew *massa*) for the nation. The Lord chose a simple country preacher to deliver a sterling message—and the truth is, you may never hear such a message more powerfully than from the sincere, unlearned lips of a dedicated servant of God. I am not exalting ignorance; I am simply saying that God has not chosen many of noble birth to bear His message. (Please take the time to read 1 Corinthians 1:26–29.) Some of God's messengers may not be very highly trained, but they have a message we need to hear, and they are faithful to the end.

Amos was one of those persons . . . a simple and committed burden-bearer. You will never read a word about his family, not even a reference to a distant relative. In fact, he is never mentioned by name elsewhere in all the Bible. He simply and humbly lived his life, delivered the message and then dropped off the scene, having done what the Lord had called him to do.

Amos's Roots

Amos was a native of Tekoa, a country village about six miles south of Bethlehem. As a matter of fact, Tekoa was so far off the beaten path that it wasn't even along the caravan route running from Jerusalem down into Beersheba. It was just a small, out-of-the-way town, a little-known, rugged place.

When questioned about his prophetic ministry, Amos said, "I was neither a prophet nor a prophet's son, but I was a shepherd, and I also took care of sycamore-fig trees" (7:14). Don't miss this. Amos wasn't saying that he didn't have a prophet's message. No, what it means is that, unlike Isaiah, for example, he was not officially recognized and respected as a skilled prophet. His father was not a prophet. He did not go to the schools of the prophets. In a sense, he didn't have the normal background or training of a prophet. He was just a country boy taking care of business—keeping sheep and tending fruit trees.

The fruit of the sycamore-fig tree was a fruit normally eaten by the poor. A unique thing about this fruit was that it needed to be pierced and mashed to make it edible. It was Amos's job not only to pick the fruit but also to pierce it with a knife, mash it, then sell it in the marketplace. It was a process that would leave him with stained hands. Try to get the picture in your mind . . . Amos, a rawboned, unsophisticated country boy with stained hands from his days in the sycamore figs, with the audacity to look kings and nobles in the eye and vigorously declare the message of God.

A Reluctant Prophet

By now you can see that Amos's background was nothing to brag about. He was an ordinary, God-fearing man. He was a hardworking shepherd and farmer. *And he was called to be a prophet*: "But the LORD took me from tending the flock and said to me, 'Go, prophesy to my people Israel' " (7:15). Amos didn't wake up one day and decide to volunteer to be a prophet . . . he was drafted! And I strongly suspect there were more than a few times during his ministry when he felt terribly unqualified for the job.

I like what A.W. Tozer wrote about leadership: "I believe it might be accepted as a fairly reliable rule of thumb that the man who is ambitious to lead is disqualified as a leader. The true leader will have no desire to lord it over God's heritage." That's a good description of Amos. He may not have been impressive to look at, but he stood tall before his Lord—because he was ready to answer the call and humbly serve. Hudson Taylor was right when he said that all God's giants have been weak persons.

Amos simply obeyed the voice of God. Obedience takes all the strain out of the call, by the way. That's why Amos wasn't intimidated by the king's presence or the king's priest. He hadn't asked for the job. The Lord appointed him, and he willingly moved out to be God's man for that crucial time in Israel's history.

The World in Amos's Day

What was the world like in the days of Amos? Irving Jensen described the times this way: "A spirit of self-sufficiency and smug complacency thrived on material prosperity. The rich were getting richer and the poor were getting poorer. Idolatry, hypocrisy, moral corruption and social injustices were everywhere. The nation was truly on the brink of disaster." Into this scene Amos was dispatched as a layman to get out of the fig-picking business and leave the sheep, at least for a while. He would go to Bethel, Israel's main religious sanctuary (7:13), and announce God's message. He was to tell the people, from the king on down, that they were walking down the wrong road. If they didn't repent, judgment was coming. That was his job—and he did it very well.

Prepare to Meet Your God

The theme of Amos is clear and simple: "Prepare to meet your God" (4:12). In effect, Amos was called to say, "Now, Israel, I stand before you as God's spokesman. Get ready. Judgment is coming if you don't return to Him." You already know the story. The Israelites didn't return, and, just as Amos prophesied, judgment came. The northern kingdom of Israel fell to the Assyrians in 722 B.C., just 25 years or so after Amos's ministry came to an end.

Life Lessons From Amos

There are some specific principles from this book that remain timeless and true. Each is worthy of serious thought. The tendency on the part of some who read the minor prophets is to stop with the teaching and say, "Now may the Lord apply it to *your* life." I think if the Lord would have us *interpret* it, He would also have us *apply* it to ourselves.

Let me give you four principles that we can apply to our lives. First, *there is always a place for a dedicated messenger of God*. Amos is a great illustration of that. You don't have to be well-schooled or have a lot of initials behind your name. You don't have to go to seminary. You don't have to know Hebrew and Greek. You don't have to preach in a big church. You don't have to bear the name "Reverend." You don't have to be clever or skilled or impressive or brilliant. You don't have to be a man. You can be a spokesperson for God as a woman, as a teenager, as a hardworking laborer who has never sensed a "call" to ministry or, for that matter, even finished high school. But you *do* need to be dedicated and you do need to be faithful.

Second, *some of God's choicest instruments emerge from obscure places*. Some of the finest evangelists and pastors and messengers of God of any age have come from small country towns. It's a surprise to many people to read about the background of people like Charles Spurgeon and Dwight Moody and Billy Graham and Dawson Troutman and Corrie ten Boom . . . the list goes on and on.

Third, *God always warns before He judges*. God is not cruel. I would be so bold as to say some who read these words have heard warnings over and over again and yet have not repented. You have not yet changed your mind about a relationship with Jesus Christ. Or you have not yet changed your heart about your walk with Him. He may be warning you this very moment. And let me gently remind you, His warning always precedes His judgment. There is an end to His long-suffering. There are cases in the Book of God where He reached the end of His patience and said, in effect, "That's enough!" If He's issuing a warning, take heed.

Fourth, *one of the greatest privileges on earth is to be fed the good Word of God*. Chapter 8 speaks about a coming famine—a famine of hearing the words of the Lord. It's hard for us to imagine the horror of famine. Thank God most of us don't know of famine personally. One of the greatest privileges we have is to be exposed to a solid Scriptural diet, to be able to read from it and learn from it, to have it laid before us consistently.

Speak Up, Listen Up

If I were asked to apply the book of Amos as a whole, my answer would be very simple. First of all, I would say, "If you are an Amos, speak! *Speak up*! In a dedicated and consistent and sensitive manner, speak the truth. Do not be intimidated! Refuse to be silenced because of a few challenges that may come your way. God has placed you where you are to be one of His messengers. So speak, on His behalf." It is so encouraging to see a modern-day Amos in action, consistently making Jesus Christ known in word and in deed.

The second part of my answer is this: If you are an "Israel," listen. *Listen up*! If you are represented in this book as one who is being told, "Prepare to meet your God. Return to the Lord," then I urge you to listen to that warning. Repent. Turn around. Come running. God will be there to meet you.

Oracles Against Gentile Nations Chapters 1–2

These opening chapters contain a series of oracles (divinely ordained messages) against the Gentile nations surrounding Israel. Each oracle listed their sins and clearly let them know that the wrath of God would not be held back. After focusing on the Gentile nations, Amos turned his attention to an indictment against the nation of Judah. At this time in history, Judah and Israel were estranged. The Israelites may well have taken perverse pleasure in hearing the convicting words spoken against her backslidden neighbor in verses 4 and 5 of chapter 2. But just when they were settling back in self-satisfaction, Amos turned his attention to them (2:6). The message was clear: God's judgment would rain down on all who were rebellious and faithless.

1 The words of Amos, one of the shepherds of
Tekoa—what he saw concerning Israel two
years before the earthquake, when Uzziah was
king of Judah and Jeroboam son of Jehoash[a] was
king of Israel. 2Sa 14:2; 2Ki 14:23; Zec 14:5

2He said:

"The LORD roars from Zion Isa 42:13
and thunders from Jerusalem; Joel 3:16
the pastures of the shepherds dry up,[b]
and the top of Carmel withers." Jer 12:4; Am 9:3

Judgment on Israel's Neighbors

3This is what the LORD says:

"For three sins of Damascus, Isa 8:4; 17:1-3
even for four, I will not turn back ⌞my
wrath⌟. Am 2:6
Because she threshed Gilead
with sledges having iron teeth,
4I will send fire upon the house of Hazael
that will consume the fortresses of
Ben-Hadad. 2Ki 6:24; Jer 17:27
5I will break down the gate of Damascus;
I will destroy the king who is in[c] the
Valley of Aven[d]
and the one who holds the scepter in Beth
Eden.
The people of Aram will go into exile to
Kir," 2Ki 16:9
says the LORD.

6This is what the LORD says:

"For three sins of Gaza, 1Sa 6:17; Zep 2:4
even for four, I will not turn back ⌞my
wrath⌟.
Because she took captive whole communities
and sold them to Edom, Ob 1:11
7I will send fire upon the walls of Gaza
that will consume her fortresses.
8I will destroy the king[e] of Ashdod 2Ch 26:6
and the one who holds the scepter in
Ashkelon.
I will turn my hand against Ekron, Ps 81:14
till the last of the Philistines is dead,"
says the Sovereign LORD.

9This is what the LORD says:

"For three sins of Tyre, Isa 23:1-18; Mt 11:21
even for four, I will not turn back ⌞my
wrath⌟.
Because she sold whole communities of
captives to Edom,
disregarding a treaty of brotherhood, 1Ki 5:12
10I will send fire upon the walls of Tyre
that will consume her fortresses." Zec 9:1-4

11This is what the LORD says:

"For three sins of Edom, Nu 20:14-21; Jer 49:7-22
even for four, I will not turn back ⌞my
wrath⌟.
Because he pursued his brother with a sword,
stifling all compassion,[f]
because his anger raged continually
and his fury flamed unchecked, Eze 25:12-14
12I will send fire upon Teman Ob 1:9-10
that will consume the fortresses of Bozrah."

13This is what the LORD says:

"For three sins of Ammon, Jer 49:1-6; Eze 21:28; 25:2-7
even for four, I will not turn back ⌞my
wrath⌟.
Because he ripped open the pregnant women
of Gilead Hos 13:16
in order to extend his borders,
14I will set fire to the walls of Rabbah Dt 3:11
that will consume her fortresses
amid war cries on the day of battle, Am 2:2
amid violent winds on a stormy day.
15Her king[g] will go into exile,
he and his officials together," Jer 25:21
says the LORD.

2 This is what the LORD says:

"For three sins of Moab, Isa 16:6
even for four, I will not turn back ⌞my
wrath⌟.
Because he burned, as if to lime,
the bones of Edom's king,
2I will send fire upon Moab
that will consume the fortresses of
Kerioth.[h] Jer 48:24
Moab will go down in great tumult
amid war cries and the blast of the
trumpet. Jos 6:20
3I will destroy her ruler Ps 2:10

[a] *1* Hebrew *Joash,* a variant of *Jehoash* [b] *2* Or *shepherds mourn* [c] *5* Or *the inhabitants of* [d] *5* *Aven* means *wickedness.* [e] *8* Or *inhabitants* [f] *11* Or *sword / and destroyed his allies* [g] *15* Or / *Molech;* Hebrew *malcam* [h] *2* Or *of her cities*

and kill all her officials with him," Isa 40:23
says the LORD.

4This is what the LORD says:

"For three sins of Judah, 2Ki 17:19
even for four, I will not turn back ⌊my
wrath⌋.
Because they have rejected the law of the LORD
and have not kept his decrees, Eze 20:24
because they have been led astray by false
gods,[a] Isa 9:16; 28:15
the gods[b] their ancestors followed, 2Ki 22:13
5I will send fire upon Judah
that will consume the fortresses of
Jerusalem." Jer 17:27; Hos 8:14

Judgment on Israel

6This is what the LORD says:

"For three sins of Israel,
even for four, I will not turn back ⌊my
wrath⌋.
They sell the righteous for silver,
and the needy for a pair of sandals. Joel 3:3
7They trample on the heads of the poor
as upon the dust of the ground
and deny justice to the oppressed.
Father and son use the same girl
and so profane my holy name. Am 5:11-12; 8:4
8They lie down beside every altar
on garments taken in pledge. Ex 22:26
In the house of their god
they drink wine taken as fines. Am 4:1; 6:6

9"I destroyed the Amorite before them,
though he was tall as the cedars
and strong as the oaks. Ps 29:9
I destroyed his fruit above
and his roots below. Eze 17:9; Mal 4:1

10"I brought you up out of Egypt, Ex 20:2; Am 3:1
and I led you forty years in the desert Dt 2:7
to give you the land of the Amorites. Ex 3:8
11I also raised up prophets from among your
sons Dt 18:18; Jer 7:25
and Nazirites from among your young
men. Nu 6:2-3; Jdg 13:5
Is this not true, people of Israel?"
declares the LORD.
12"But you made the Nazirites drink wine
and commanded the prophets not to
prophesy. Isa 30:10; Jer 11:21; Mic 2:6

13"Now then, I will crush you
as a cart crushes when loaded with grain.
14The swift will not escape,
the strong will not muster their strength,
and the warrior will not save his life. Ps 33:16
15The archer will not stand his ground, Eze 39:3
the fleet-footed soldier will not get away,
and the horseman will not save his life.
16Even the bravest warriors Jer 48:41
will flee naked on that day,"
declares the LORD.

Sermons Against Israel — Chapters 3–6

The Israelites must have taken some delight when they heard the strong words of judgment against all of their neighbors (1:3–2:5). There had been no love lost between Israel and any of the nations Amos spoke against. But suddenly the focus shifted to Israel and her sins, and with the same powerful conviction, Amos spoke of God's coming wrath on the nation of Israel. No nation is exempt from judgment when its citizens willfully disobey the King of kings. These chapters contain a shocking catalogue of Israel's sins and underscore the certainty of God's judgment. Some of the more familiar words of Amos are recorded in this section, as the prophet called the people to "seek good, not evil, that you may live" (5:14) and "let justice roll on like a river, righteousness like a never-failing stream" (5:24). Amos passionately confronted injustice and proclaimed God's unwavering concern for the poor.

Witnesses Summoned Against Israel

3 Hear this word the LORD has spoken against
you, O people of Israel—against the whole
family I brought up out of Egypt: Am 2:10

2"You only have I chosen Dt 7:6; Lk 12:47
of all the families of the earth;
therefore I will punish you
for all your sins." Jer 14:10

3Do two walk together
unless they have agreed to do so?
4Does a lion roar in the thicket
when he has no prey? Ps 104:21; Hos 5:14
Does he growl in his den
when he has caught nothing?
5Does a bird fall into a trap on the ground
where no snare has been set?
Does a trap spring up from the earth
when there is nothing to catch?
6When a trumpet sounds in a city,
do not the people tremble?
When disaster comes to a city,
has not the LORD caused it? Isa 14:24-27; 45:7

7Surely the Sovereign LORD does nothing
without revealing his plan Ge 18:17; Jn 15:15
to his servants the prophets. Jer 23:22

8The lion has roared—
who will not fear?
The Sovereign LORD has spoken—
who can but prophesy? Jer 20:9; Ac 4:20

9Proclaim to the fortresses of Ashdod

[a]4 Or *by lies* [b]4 Or *lies*

and to the fortresses of Egypt:
"Assemble yourselves on the mountains of
Samaria; Am 4:1; 6:1
see the great unrest within her
and the oppression among her people."

10"They do not know how to do right," declares
the LORD, Jer 4:22; Am 5:7; 6:12
"who hoard plunder and loot in their
fortresses." Hab 2:8; Zep 1:9

11Therefore this is what the Sovereign LORD
says:

"An enemy will overrun the land;
he will pull down your strongholds
and plunder your fortresses." Am 2:5; 6:14

12This is what the LORD says:

"As a shepherd saves from the lion's mouth
only two leg bones or a piece of an ear,
so will the Israelites be saved,
those who sit in Samaria
on the edge of their beds
and in Damascus on their couches.[a]"

13"Hear this and testify against the house of
Jacob," declares the Lord, the LORD God Almighty.

14"On the day I punish Israel for her sins,
I will destroy the altars of Bethel; Am 5:5-6
the horns of the altar will be cut off
and fall to the ground.
15I will tear down the winter house Jer 36:22
along with the summer house; Jdg 3:20
the houses adorned with ivory will be
destroyed 1Ki 22:39
and the mansions will be demolished,"
declares the LORD.

Israel Has Not Returned to God

4 Hear this word, you cows of Bashan on
Mount Samaria, Ps 22:12; Am 3:9
you women who oppress the poor and
crush the needy Dt 24:14
and say to your husbands, "Bring us some
drinks!" Am 2:8; 5:11; 8:6
2The Sovereign LORD has sworn by his holiness:
"The time will surely come Jer 31:31
when you will be taken away with hooks,
the last of you with fishhooks.
3You will each go straight out
through breaks in the wall, Eze 12:5
and you will be cast out toward
Harmon,[b]"
declares the LORD.
4"Go to Bethel and sin;
go to Gilgal and sin yet more. Hos 4:15
Bring your sacrifices every morning, Nu 28:3
your tithes every three years.[c] Dt 14:28
5Burn leavened bread as a thank offering
and brag about your freewill offerings—
boast about them, you Israelites,
for this is what you love to do,"
declares the Sovereign LORD.

6"I gave you empty stomachs[d] in every city
and lack of bread in every town,
yet you have not returned to me,"
declares the LORD.

7"I also withheld rain from you
when the harvest was still three months
away.
I sent rain on one town,
but withheld it from another. Dt 11:17; 2Ch 7:13
One field had rain;
another had none and dried up.
8People staggered from town to town for water
but did not get enough to drink,
yet you have not returned to me," Jer 3:7
declares the LORD.

9"Many times I struck your gardens and
vineyards,
I struck them with blight and mildew.
Locusts devoured your fig and olive trees,
yet you have not returned to me," Jer 3:10
declares the LORD.

10"I sent plagues among you Ex 9:3; Dt 28:27
as I did to Egypt. Ex 11:5
I killed your young men with the sword,
along with your captured horses.
I filled your nostrils with the stench of your
camps, Isa 34:3
yet you have not returned to me," Dt 28:21
declares the LORD.

11"I overthrew some of you
as I[e] overthrew Sodom and Gomorrah.
You were like a burning stick snatched from
the fire, Isa 7:4
yet you have not returned to me,"
declares the LORD.

12"Therefore this is what I will do to you, Israel,
and because I will do this to you,
prepare to meet your God, O Israel."

13He who forms the mountains, Ps 65:6
creates the wind,
and reveals his thoughts to man, Da 2:28
he who turns dawn to darkness,
and treads the high places of the earth—
the LORD God Almighty is his name. Isa 47:4

[a] 12 The meaning of the Hebrew for this line is uncertain.
[b] 3 Masoretic Text; with a different word division of the Hebrew (see Septuagint) *out, O mountain of oppression*
[c] 4 Or *tithes on the third day*
[d] 6 Hebrew *you cleanness of teeth*
[e] 11 Hebrew *God*

A Lament and Call to Repentance

5 Hear this word, O house of Israel, this lament
I take up concerning you: Eze 19:1

2 “Fallen is Virgin Israel, Jer 14:17
never to rise again,
deserted in her own land,
with no one to lift her up.” Jer 50:32; Am 8:14

3 This is what the Sovereign LORD says:

“The city that marches out a thousand strong
for Israel
will have only a hundred left;
the town that marches out a hundred strong
will have only ten left.” Isa 6:13; Am 6:9

4 This is what the LORD says to the house of
Israel:

“Seek me and live; Isa 55:3; Jer 29:13
5 do not seek Bethel,
do not go to Gilgal, Am 4:4
do not journey to Beersheba. Am 8:14
For Gilgal will surely go into exile,
and Bethel will be reduced to nothing.[a]”
6 Seek the LORD and live, Isa 55:6
or he will sweep through the house of
Joseph like a fire; Dt 4:24
it will devour,
and Bethel will have no one to quench it.

LIVING  INSIGHT

Walk away from evil. You can say, “Lord, right now, at this moment, I am weak. You are strong. By Your strength I'm stepping away from this evil, and Your power is going to give me the grace to get through it victoriously. Take charge in my life right now.”

(See Amos 5:1–6.)

7 You who turn justice into bitterness Am 6:12
and cast righteousness to the ground
8 (he who made the Pleiades and Orion, Job 9:9
who turns blackness into dawn Isa 42:16
and darkens day into night, Ps 104:20; Am 8:9
who calls for the waters of the sea
and pours them out over the face of the
land—
the LORD is his name— Ps 104:6-9; Am 4:13
9 he flashes destruction on the stronghold
and brings the fortified city to ruin), Mic 5:11
10 you hate the one who reproves in court
and despise him who tells the truth. 1Ki 22:8

11 You trample on the poor Am 8:6
and force him to give you grain.
Therefore, though you have built stone
mansions, Am 3:15
you will not live in them; Mic 1:6
though you have planted lush vineyards,
you will not drink their wine. Mic 6:15
12 For I know how many are your offenses
and how great your sins. Hos 5:3

You oppress the righteous and take bribes
and you deprive the poor of justice in the
courts. Isa 5:23; Am 2:6-7
13 Therefore the prudent man keeps quiet in
such times,
for the times are evil. Mic 2:3

14 Seek good, not evil,
that you may live. ver 6
Then the LORD God Almighty will be with
you,
just as you say he is.
15 Hate evil, love good; Ro 12:9
maintain justice in the courts. Isa 1:17
Perhaps the LORD God Almighty will have
mercy Joel 2:14
on the remnant of Joseph. Mic 5:7-8

16 Therefore this is what the Lord, the LORD God
Almighty, says:

“There will be wailing in all the streets Jer 9:17
and cries of anguish in every public square.
The farmers will be summoned to weep
and the mourners to wail.
17 There will be wailing in all the vineyards,
for I will pass through your midst,” Ex 12:12
says the LORD.

The Day of the LORD

18 Woe to you who long
for the day of the LORD! Joel 1:15
Why do you long for the day of the LORD?
That day will be darkness, not light.
19 It will be as though a man fled from a lion
only to meet a bear,
as though he entered his house
and rested his hand on the wall
only to have a snake bite him. Job 20:24
20 Will not the day of the LORD be darkness, not
light—
pitch-dark, without a ray of brightness?

21 “I hate, I despise your religious feasts; Lev 26:31
I cannot stand your assemblies. Isa 1:11-16
22 Even though you bring me burnt offerings
and grain offerings,
I will not accept them. Ps 40:6

[a]5 Or *grief*; or *wickedness*; Hebrew *aven*, a reference to Beth Aven (a derogatory name for Bethel)

Though you bring choice fellowship
offerings,[a]
I will have no regard for them. Isa 66:3
23Away with the noise of your songs!
I will not listen to the music of your harps.
24But let justice roll on like a river, Jer 22:3
righteousness like a never-failing stream!

25"Did you bring me sacrifices and offerings
forty years in the desert, O house of Israel?
26You have lifted up the shrine of your king,
the pedestal of your idols,
the star of your god[b]—
which you made for yourselves.
27Therefore I will send you into exile beyond
Damascus,"
says the LORD, whose name is God
Almighty. Am 4:13; Ac 7:42-43*

Woe to the Complacent

6 Woe to you who are complacent in Zion,
and to you who feel secure on Mount
Samaria, Am 3:9
you notable men of the foremost nation,
to whom the people of Israel come!
2Go to Calneh and look at it; Ge 10:10
go from there to great Hamath, 2Ki 18:34
and then go down to Gath in Philistia.
Are they better off than your two kingdoms?
Is their land larger than yours?
3You put off the evil day
and bring near a reign of terror. Isa 56:12
4You lie on beds inlaid with ivory
and lounge on your couches.
You dine on choice lambs
and fattened calves. Eze 34:2-3; Am 3:12
5You strum away on your harps like David
and improvise on musical instruments.
6You drink wine by the bowlful Am 2:8
and use the finest lotions,
but you do not grieve over the ruin of
Joseph. Eze 9:4
7Therefore you will be among the first to go
into exile; Am 5:27
your feasting and lounging will end. Jer 16:9

The LORD Abhors the Pride of Israel

8The Sovereign LORD has sworn by himself—
the LORD God Almighty declares: Ge 22:16; Heb 6:13

"I abhor the pride of Jacob Ps 47:4
and detest his fortresses;
I will deliver up the city Am 4:2
and everything in it." Dt 32:19

9If ten men are left in one house, they too will
die. 10And if a relative who is to burn the bodies
comes to carry them out of the house and asks
anyone still hiding there, "Is anyone with you?"
and he says, "No," then he will say, "Hush! We
must not mention the name of the LORD." Am 5:3

11For the LORD has given the command,
and he will smash the great house into
pieces Am 3:15
and the small house into bits. Isa 55:11
12Do horses run on the rocky crags?
Does one plow there with oxen?
But you have turned justice into poison
and the fruit of righteousness into
bitterness— Am 5:7
13you who rejoice in the conquest of Lo
Debar[c]
and say, "Did we not take Karnaim[d] by
our own strength?" Job 8:15; Isa 28:14-15
14For the LORD God Almighty declares,
"I will stir up a nation against you,
O house of Israel, Jer 5:15
that will oppress you all the way
from Lebo[e] Hamath to the valley of the
Arabah." 1Ki 8:65; Am 3:11

Visions of Judgment **Chapters 7:1–9:10**

In chapter 7 we move from oracles and sermons to visions. Notice how the language of Amos shifted. No longer did he say, "Hear this word the LORD has spoken," but he said, "This is what the Sovereign LORD showed me." These words clearly record the visions the Lord had given Amos: locusts, fire, a plumb line, a basket of ripe fruit, and the Lord standing by an altar. Each vision had a message for Israel. I might add that each also has a message for God's people today.

Locusts, Fire and a Plumb Line

7 This is what the Sovereign LORD showed me:
He was preparing swarms of locusts after the
king's share had been harvested and just as the
second crop was coming up. 2When they had
stripped the land clean, I cried out, "Sovereign
LORD, forgive! How can Jacob survive? He is so
small!" Isa 37:4; Eze 11:13
3So the LORD relented. Dt 32:36; Jnh 3:10
"This will not happen," the LORD said. Hos 11:8
4This is what the Sovereign LORD showed me:
The Sovereign LORD was calling for judgment by
fire; it dried up the great deep and devoured the
land. 5Then I cried out, "Sovereign LORD, I beg
you, stop! How can Jacob survive? He is so small!"
6So the LORD relented. Jnh 3:10
"This will not happen either," the Sovereign
LORD said. Eze 9:8

[a]22 Traditionally *peace offerings* [b]26 Or *lifted up Sakkuth your king / and Kaiwan your idols, / your star-gods*; Septuagint *lifted up the shrine of Molech / and the star of your god Rephan, / their idols* [c]13 *Lo Debar* means *nothing.* [d]13 *Karnaim* means *horns*; *horn* here symbolizes strength. [e]14 Or *from the entrance to*

[7]This is what he showed me: The Lord was
standing by a wall that had been built true to
plumb, with a plumb line in his hand. [8]And the
LORD asked me, "What do you see, Amos?"

"A plumb line," I replied. 2Ki 21:13

Then the Lord said, "Look, I am setting a
plumb line among my people Israel; I will spare
them no longer. Jer 15:6; Eze 7:2-9

[9]"The high places of Isaac will be destroyed
and the sanctuaries of Israel will be ruined;
with my sword I will rise against the house
of Jeroboam." 2Ki 15:9; Hos 10:8

Amos and Amaziah

[10]Then Amaziah the priest of Bethel sent a message to Jeroboam king of Israel: "Amos is raising
a conspiracy against you in the very heart of Israel.
The land cannot bear all his words. [11]For this is
what Amos is saying: 1Ki 12:32; 2Ki 14:23

" 'Jeroboam will die by the sword,
and Israel will surely go into exile, Am 5:27
away from their native land.' " Jer 36:16

[12]Then Amaziah said to Amos, "Get out, you
seer! Go back to the land of Judah. Earn your
bread there and do your prophesying there.
[13]Don't prophesy anymore at Bethel, because this
is the king's sanctuary and the temple of the kingdom." Am 2:12; Ac 4:18

[14]Amos answered Amaziah, "I was neither a
prophet nor a prophet's son, but I was a shepherd,
and I also took care of sycamore-fig trees. [15]But
the LORD took me from tending the flock and said
to me, 'Go, prophesy to my people Israel.' [16]Now
then, hear the word of the LORD. You say, 2Ki 2:5

" 'Do not prophesy against Israel, Eze 20:46; Mic 2:6
and stop preaching against the house of
Isaac.'

[17]"Therefore this is what the LORD says:

" 'Your wife will become a prostitute in the
city, Hos 4:13
and your sons and daughters will fall by the
sword.
Your land will be measured and divided up,
and you yourself will die in a pagan[a]
country.
And Israel will certainly go into exile,
away from their native land.' " Eze 4:13; Hos 9:3

A Basket of Ripe Fruit

8 This is what the Sovereign LORD showed me:
a basket of ripe fruit. [2]"What do you see,
Amos?" he asked. Am 7:8

"A basket of ripe fruit," I answered. Ge 40:16

Then the LORD said to me, "The time is ripe for
my people Israel; I will spare them no longer.

[3]"In that day," declares the Sovereign LORD,
"the songs in the temple will turn to wailing.[b]
Many, many bodies—flung everywhere! Silence!"

[4]Hear this, you who trample the needy
and do away with the poor of the land,

[5]saying,

"When will the New Moon be over
that we may sell grain,
and the Sabbath be ended
that we may market wheat?"—
skimping the measure,
boosting the price
and cheating with dishonest scales,
[6]buying the poor with silver
and the needy for a pair of sandals,
selling even the sweepings with the wheat.

[7]The LORD has sworn by the Pride of Jacob: "I
will never forget anything they have done.

[8]"Will not the land tremble for this, Hos 4:3
and all who live in it mourn?
The whole land will rise like the Nile;
it will be stirred up and then sink
like the river of Egypt. Jer 46:8; Am 9:5

[9]"In that day," declares the Sovereign LORD,

"I will make the sun go down at noon
and darken the earth in broad daylight.
[10]I will turn your religious feasts into mourning
and all your singing into weeping.
I will make all of you wear sackcloth Jer 48:37
and shave your heads.
I will make that time like mourning for an
only son Jer 6:26; Zec 12:10
and the end of it like a bitter day. Eze 7:18

[11]"The days are coming," declares the Sovereign
LORD, 1Sa 3:1; 2Ch 15:3
"when I will send a famine through the
land—

LIVING  **INSIGHT**

There is a famine in the land—but not the kind of famine sweeping across India or sections of Africa. This famine is virtually everywhere. Not a famine of food or water . . . not a famine of churches or religious ministries. This is a famine like the one the ancient prophets mentioned—a famine of hearing the truth of the Word of God.

(See Amos 8:11.)

[a]17 Hebrew *an unclean* [b]3 Or *"the temple singers will wail*

not a famine of food or a thirst for water,
but a famine of hearing the words of the LORD.
12Men will stagger from sea to sea
and wander from north to east,
searching for the word of the LORD,
but they will not find it. Eze 20:3,31

13"In that day

"the lovely young women and strong young men
will faint because of thirst. Isa 41:17; Hos 2:3
14They who swear by the shame[a] of Samaria,
or say, 'As surely as your god lives, O Dan,'
or, 'As surely as the god[b] of Beersheba lives'—
they will fall,
never to rise again." Am 5:2

Israel to Be Destroyed

9 I saw the Lord standing by the altar, and he said:

"Strike the tops of the pillars
so that the thresholds shake.
Bring them down on the heads of all the people; Ps 68:21
those who are left I will kill with the sword.
Not one will get away,
none will escape.
2Though they dig down to the depths of the grave,[c] Ps 139:8
from there my hand will take them.
Though they climb up to the heavens, Jer 51:53
from there I will bring them down. Ob 1:4
3Though they hide themselves on the top of Carmel, Am 1:2
there I will hunt them down and seize them. Ps 139:8-10
Though they hide from me at the bottom of the sea,
there I will command the serpent to bite them. Jer 16:16-17
4Though they are driven into exile by their enemies,
there I will command the sword to slay them. Lev 26:33; Eze 5:12
I will fix my eyes upon them
for evil and not for good." Jer 21:10; 39:16

5The Lord, the LORD Almighty,
he who touches the earth and it melts,
and all who live in it mourn—
the whole land rises like the Nile,
then sinks like the river of Egypt— Am 8:8
6he who builds his lofty palace[d] in the heavens
and sets its foundation[e] on the earth,
who calls for the waters of the sea
and pours them out over the face of the land—
the LORD is his name. Ps 104:1-3,5-6,13; Am 5:8
7"Are not you Israelites
the same to me as the Cushites[f]?" Isa 20:4
declares the LORD.
"Did I not bring Israel up from Egypt,
the Philistines from Caphtor[g] Dt 2:23
and the Arameans from Kir? Isa 22:6; Am 1:5

8"Surely the eyes of the Sovereign LORD
are on the sinful kingdom.
I will destroy it
from the face of the earth—
yet I will not totally destroy
the house of Jacob,"
declares the LORD.
9"For I will give the command,
and I will shake the house of Israel
among all the nations
as grain is shaken in a sieve, Isa 30:28; Lk 22:31
and not a pebble will reach the ground.
10All the sinners among my people
will die by the sword,
all those who say,
'Disaster will not overtake or meet us.'

Promises of Hope **Chapter 9:11–15**

This closing section is brief, but its message must be heard. Up to this point everything Amos said had been focused on wrath and judgment. As he ended his book he brought a word of hope. The Lord told the people of Israel that He would not bring total destruction on the nation and that one day He would raise up, restore and rebuild. As with so many of the prophets, Amos's message was one of judgment accompanied by the promise of restoration in the future.

Israel's Restoration

11"In that day I will restore
David's fallen tent. Isa 7:2
I will repair its broken places,
restore its ruins, Ps 53:6
and build it as it used to be, Ps 80:12
12so that they may possess the remnant of Edom Nu 24:18
and all the nations that bear my name,[h]"
declares the LORD, who will do these things.

13"The days are coming," declares the LORD,

[a] 14 Or *by Ashima*; or *by the idol* [b] 14 Or *power* [c] 2 Hebrew *to Sheol* [d] 6 The meaning of the Hebrew for this phrase is uncertain. [e] 6 The meaning of the Hebrew for this word is uncertain. [f] 7 That is, people from the upper Nile region [g] 7 That is, Crete [h] 12 Hebrew; Septuagint *so that the remnant of men / and all the nations that bear my name may seek* ⌞*the Lord*⌟

"when the reaper will be overtaken by the
plowman Lev 26:5
and the planter by the one treading grapes.
New wine will drip from the mountains
and flow from all the hills. Joel 3:18
14I will bring back my exiled[a] people Israel;
they will rebuild the ruined cities and live
in them. Isa 61:4
They will plant vineyards and drink their
wine;
they will make gardens and eat their fruit.
15I will plant Israel in their own land, Isa 60:21
never again to be uprooted
from the land I have given them," Isa 65:9
says the LORD your God.

[a] 14 Or *will restore the fortunes of my*

Introduction

OBADIAH

Obadiah, the shortest book in the Old Testament, is addressed, not to God's chosen people, the Israelites, but to long-standing enemies of Israel, the Edomites, who also happened to be a nation of distant blood relatives. We know virtually nothing about the bearer of this word of judgment, except for his name, which means "servant (or worshiper) of the LORD." His book is a prophetic cameo of doom without a hint of restoration. The Lord promised to humble this proud and self-confident people of the nation of Edom, and that He did. Their rock fortress still stands, but their name and their nation have perished.

WRITER: *Obadiah*

DATE: *c.853–841 B.C.*

PURPOSE: *To condemn the arrogance of the Edomites and to pronounce judgment on them*

KEY THEMES: *God's justice; human pride*

KEY MESSAGE: *Pride and revenge will ultimately lead to total destruction*

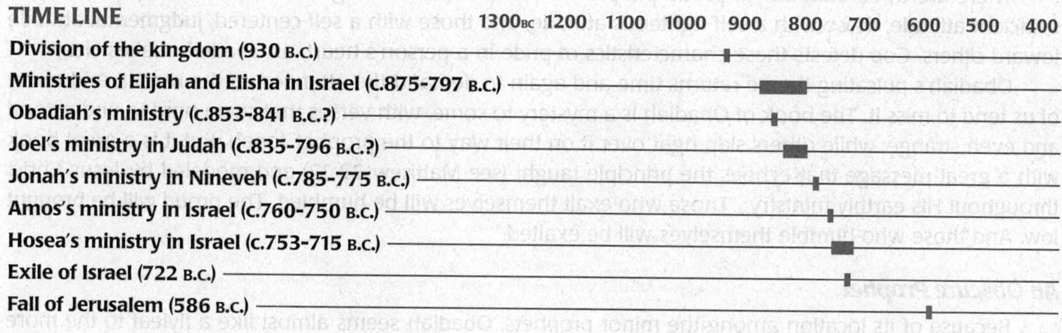

Strong Warnings to the Proud

	EDOM'S HUMILIATION AND DESTRUCTION *VERSES 1–9*	EDOM'S CRUELTY AND CRIMES *VERSES 10–14*	EDOM'S JUDGMENT AND DOOM *VERSES 15–21*
PORTENT	**Prediction**	**Denunciation**	**Annihilation**
EVENT	**What will happen**	**Why it will happen**	**How it will happen**
CONTENT	***"The pride of your heart has deceived you . . . I will bring you down" (verses 3-4).***	***. . . you stood aloof . . . rejoiced . . . boasted . . . seized their wealth . . . handed them over . . . (verses 11-14).***	***"As you have done, it will be done to you" (verse 15).***

The most severe words in all the Bible are not necessarily addressed to sinners who are broken and ashamed of their wrongdoing. They are addressed to the proud, to the self-righteous, to those who are smug in their own self-reliance and indifference. Remember the list in Proverbs of the seven things God detests (Proverbs 6:16–19)? Remember the first thing on the list? "Haughty eyes" (Proverbs 6:17). Of all the things God detests, if that list is in the order of importance, "haughty eyes," or possessing a proud heart, would be the thing He hates the most.

There are three attitudes of proud people described in the message of Obadiah: those with a self-sufficient attitude, those with a self-righteous attitude, and those with a self-centered, judgmental attitude toward others. God detests these characteristics of pride in a person's heart, as Obadiah makes clear.

Obadiah's pulsating theme returns time and again to demand the attention of the reader, and many of us tend to miss it. The book of Obadiah is a mystery to some, with verses that seem hard to understand and even strange, while others skip right over it on their way to the prophet Jonah. But it is a great book with a great message that echoes the principle taught (see Matthew 23:12) and modeled by Jesus Christ throughout His earthly ministry: "Those who exalt themselves will be humbled. The proud will be brought low. And those who humble themselves will be exalted."

An Obscure Prophet

Because of its location among the minor prophets, Obadiah seems almost like a flyleaf to the more popular and better known book of Jonah. Jonah gets all the attention in this section, not Obadiah. However, if it's true that the smallest packages hold the best gifts, then Obadiah certainly will not let us down. It is a book of only 21 verses. We know nothing about the writer—nothing except his name, which means "servant (or worshiper) of the LORD." We know Obadiah had a vision and wrote it down—but that's about all we know.

It would be safe to say that Obadiah is the most obscure of all the Old Testament prophets. He wrote strange things like: "The pride of your heart has deceived you, you who live in the clefts of the rocks" (verse 3). And, " 'Though you soar like the eagle and make your nest among the stars, from there I will bring you down,' declares the LORD" (verse 4). And, "You should not look down on your brother in the day of his misfortune" (verse 12).

What is Obadiah talking about? What does all this mean? Where are "the clefts of the rocks"? Why mention soaring like an eagle? Who is the brother? What is the misfortune? In our hurry to deal with Obadiah and be done, we may very well rush into the book without taking the time to examine the background. We may shrug our shoulders and say, "It's another one of those strange prophets—no wonder they're called *minor*." And so we may move quickly on to Jonah. But trust me on this one: There is nothing minor about Obadiah's message. As a matter of fact, it is potent! It is even severe! It's delivered to people who are proud. And if we're honest with ourselves, we might even confess that we know more than a little bit about that subject.

A Family Feud

Let's get a little background information, because without a context we can't fully appreciate what Obadiah had to say. Historically, you may be surprised to know that the context of the message was a family feud, one that was far, far worse than the Hatfields and the McCoys in America, far worse than the prejudice between two different ethnic groups, far worse than the rivalry between any athletic teams.

This family feud went back centuries ago to a set of twins born into an ancient Hebrew family . . . and those twins were named Jacob and Esau. (Isn't it interesting we almost always put Jacob first even though the older brother was Esau? We really should say Esau and Jacob!) You see, Jacob ripped off his brother's birthright (Genesis 25:19–34). He took unfair advantage of him (the little sneak!), and as a result, father Isaac's blessings fell on Jacob, the younger, rather than on Esau, the older (Genesis 27:41–45). Esau never forgot it. But he had his own set of problems: Because he was a man of passion and fleshly appetite, he went for the food. He cared little for the document that declared his rights as the older brother. He gave it all up. And Jacob, chiseler that he was, got it from him and cashed in on the benefits. It was way back then that the conflict began.

Time passed. Esau lived like a Bedouin in the desert until finally he settled in the land of Edom, a little finger of land south of the Dead Sea about 100 miles long and 40 to 50 miles wide. There he and his descendants after him lived and made life miserable for the Israelites. Why? Because of the family feud! Because of lingering hatred toward the people of Israel, Jacob's descendants. Because Jacob had at one time taken advantage of their forefather Esau.

The Edomites lived in a rugged landscape that provided a formidable, impregnable fortress, or so they thought. They would go down from their mountain stronghold, buzz the community of Israel and make life downright miserable. After the skirmishes they would quickly return to their rocky residence high on the hillside, look down and enjoy a round of hearty laughter.

As a matter of fact, when Jerusalem was invaded by foreign troops on several occasions, the Edomites rejoiced over her calamity. Can't you picture it? Gloating over Israel's misfortune. Sitting high atop their perch, saying to themselves, "How great it is to see our brothers hurt." Centuries passed . . . and those feelings of prejudice just intensified. It looked like Edom would be secure forever and Israel would be vulnerable forever. With cruel delight they took pleasure in Israel's pain.

That's the background of the book of Obadiah, and unless we know it, this little book will remain what seems to be hopelessly irrelevant. But armed with that information, the book takes on a whole new meaning for us.

The Message of Obadiah

How is the message of Obadiah relevant for us today? Let's understand it on the front end, at face value. Obadiah wrote his vision as an ongoing warning to those who would take delight in their enemies' failure. To Christians today who occasionally find themselves vengeful, who deep within, when they hear of the calamity of a brother or a sister, applaud and say, "It's about time. He had it coming; she deserved it," the book of Obadiah stands as a permanent warning. Those who possess an attitude of pride and a desire for vengeance will be reduced to nothing. It's very, very easy for the proud to feel secure when those who have done wrong get it in the neck. But let me just gently remind us: In a brief moment of time we can be cut down to size. You know the wisdom of Proverbs: "Pride goes before destruction, a haughty spirit before a fall" (Proverbs 16:18).

Whenever you take refuge in your own might, you take refuge in a very temporary and limited source of strength. It doesn't matter whether it's your own personal physical strength or your intellectual power or your emotional fortitude or the power you've gained in your position in the workplace. If you walk in pride or if you carry around a grudge, you are preparing for a fall.

Charles Spurgeon, at the height of his ministry, once wrote, "Success can go to my head, and it will, unless I remember that it is God who accomplishes the work. That He can continue to do so without my help, and that He will be able to make out with other means whenever He chooses, cuts me down to size." At any time God sovereignly chooses, He can jerk the rug out from under us and put us on our faces. Present-day Edomites, whoever you may be, hear the warning from the Book. Though you feel secure and are living high and mighty, He can bring you down . . . fast.

Life Lessons From Obadiah

There are three primary lessons to be learned from the book of Obadiah. First, *if we hold grudges or attempt to take revenge, our own failure is certain*. What is it that God states in Romans 12:19? "It is mine to avenge; I will repay." God says, in effect, "Leave it to Me. I know the wrong done against you. I know all about the unfair treatment. Let Me deal with those who have hurt you. You forgive. Remember My sovereign power; don't you attempt to take vengeance. I'll do it." If we step in and try to do what God says *He* will do for us (in His time!), we're certain to fail.

Second, *if we are proud and take pleasure in another's calamity, our own success will be diminished.* I am often convicted by the words of the New Testament that we must "rejoice with those who rejoice" (Romans 12:15). How difficult that seems to be at times! Furthermore, the genuine, Spirit-filled Christian weeps with those who weep, and there are no exceptions given in God's Word. When those around us weep, we must set aside any grudge and weep with our brothers and sisters who are hurting.

Third, *if we think we are secure in what we have earned and erected, our situation is sure to change.* A heart of pride can so very easily backfire on us. We can become so arrogant, so convinced of our own invincibility, that we may not realize that we are setting ourselves up for destruction. Remember the law of the harvest? Whatever we sow we will reap. Obadiah reminded us of this truth in these words: "As you have done, it will be done to you; your deeds will return upon your own head" (verse 15).

Beware of the attitudes of a prideful heart. Keep in mind these attitudes of self-sufficiency, self-righteousness, and self-centered judgmentalism. These are deadly attitudes in the end. They'll lead to a hard heart, a heart of stone, a heart that cannot and will not get along with God, a heart that will not get along with others. Let Obadiah remind you of the consequences of the prideful heart that dwells on vengeance.

Judgment on Edom

The theme of this book hit the mark in Obadiah's day, as it does in our day as well. Obadiah taught that an attitude of pride and a desire for revenge would ultimately lead to destruction. The nation of Edom had stood idly by and watched its brother Israel suffer at the hands of enemies. The Edomites had viewed the attacks on the Israelites with fiendish delight, laughed with joy and even willingly participated in harming the nation of Israel. Obadiah announced judgment on the Edomites for their pride and hardness of heart, and blessings on the house of Jacob.

1 The vision of Obadiah.

This is what the Sovereign LORD says about Edom— Jer 49:7-22; Eze 25:12-14

We have heard a message from the LORD:
An envoy was sent to the nations to say,
"Rise, and let us go against her for battle"—

2 "See, I will make you small among the nations;
you will be utterly despised.
3 The pride of your heart has deceived you,
you who live in the clefts of the rocks[a]
and make your home on the heights,
you who say to yourself,
'Who can bring me down to the ground?'
4 Though you soar like the eagle
and make your nest among the stars, Hab 2:9
from there I will bring you down,"
declares the LORD.
5 "If thieves came to you,
if robbers in the night—
Oh, what a disaster awaits you—
would they not steal only as much as they wanted?
If grape pickers came to you,
would they not leave a few grapes? Jer 49:9-10
6 But how Esau will be ransacked,
his hidden treasures pillaged!
7 All your allies will force you to the border;
your friends will deceive and overpower you;
those who eat your bread will set a trap for you,[b] Ps 41:9
but you will not detect it.

8 "In that day," declares the LORD,
"will I not destroy the wise men of Edom,
men of understanding in the mountains of Esau?
9 Your warriors, O Teman, will be terrified,
and everyone in Esau's mountains
will be cut down in the slaughter.
10 Because of the violence against your brother Jacob, Joel 3:19; Am 1:11-12
you will be covered with shame;
you will be destroyed forever. Eze 35:9
11 On the day you stood aloof
while strangers carried off his wealth
and foreigners entered his gates
and cast lots for Jerusalem, Na 3:10
you were like one of them.
12 You should not look down on your brother
in the day of his misfortune, Job 31:29
nor rejoice over the people of Judah Eze 35:15
in the day of their destruction, Pr 17:5
nor boast so much Ps 137:7
in the day of their trouble. Mic 4:11
13 You should not march through the gates of my people
in the day of their disaster,
nor look down on them in their calamity
in the day of their disaster,
nor seize their wealth
in the day of their disaster.
14 You should not wait at the crossroads
to cut down their fugitives,
nor hand over their survivors
in the day of their trouble.

15 "The day of the LORD is near Eze 30:3
for all nations.
As you have done, it will be done to you;
your deeds will return upon your own head. Jer 50:29; Hab 2:8

LIVING  **INSIGHT**

It's helpful to remember that the deadliest killer of humanity is not heart disease or cancer . . . it is depravity. Every one of us has it. Every one of us suffers from its consequences. And to make matters even worse, we pass it on to each new generation. This is why we all need God's grace.

(See Obadiah 15–17.)

16 Just as you drank on my holy hill,
so all the nations will drink continually;
they will drink and drink
and be as if they had never been.
17 But on Mount Zion will be deliverance;
it will be holy, Isa 4:3
and the house of Jacob
will possess its inheritance. Zec 8:12

[a] 3 Or *of Sela* [b] 7 The meaning of the Hebrew for this clause is uncertain.

[18]The house of Jacob will be a fire
and the house of Joseph a flame;
the house of Esau will be stubble,
and they will set it on fire and consume it.
There will be no survivors Jer 49:10
from the house of Esau."
The LORD has spoken.

[19]People from the Negev will occupy
the mountains of Esau,
and people from the foothills will possess
the land of the Philistines. Isa 11:14
They will occupy the fields of Ephraim and
Samaria, Jer 31:5
and Benjamin will possess Gilead.
[20]This company of Israelite exiles who are in
Canaan
will possess ⌞the land⌟ as far as Zarephath;
the exiles from Jerusalem who are in Sepharad
will possess the towns of the Negev. Jer 33:13
[21]Deliverers will go up on[a] Mount Zion
to govern the mountains of Esau.
And the kingdom will be the LORD's.

[a]21 Or *from*

INTRODUCTION

JONAH

Who hasn't heard of Jonah? The brunt of numerous jokes, the classic example of a disobedient rebel, Jonah stands in many ways as the best-known of all the prophets. His story—familiar to young and old alike—has been proclaimed, analyzed, criticized and assaulted for centuries. To many scholars, the book of Jonah is merely a *myth,* little more than a humorous legend that originated in the mind of a creative soul in antiquity. Nevertheless, it remains to this day, preserved and inspired by God. It serves up practical "food for thought" for each generation. And, to the surprise of many, it is the clearest revelation of the missionary heart of our God in all the Old Testament. Jonah is *not* the story of a great fish, but rather of a nation in desperate need of deliverance . . . and a messenger who was reluctant to go and announce the truth.

WRITER: *Jonah*

DATE: *c.785–750 B.C.*

PURPOSE: *To show God's concern even for the enemies of His people*

KEY THEME: *The great and unmeasurable mercy of the Lord*

KEY VERSE: *2:9 "Salvation comes from the LORD."*

KEY TERMS: *"Go"; "Jonah prayed"; "God provided"*

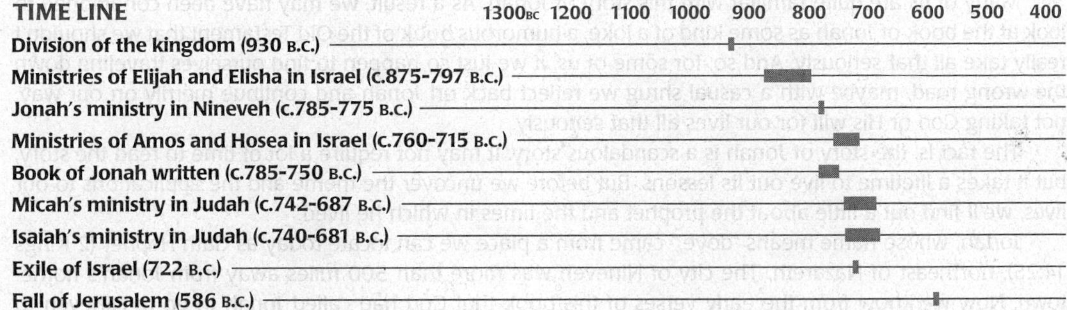

The Prodigal Prophet

RUNNING FROM GOD	RUNNING TO GOD	RUNNING WITH GOD	RUNNING AGAINST GOD
Commission of Jonah	Prayer of Jonah	Second commission of Jonah	Prejudice of Jonah
Results of disobedience	Communication from the Lord	Results of obedience	Preparations of the Lord
CHAPTER 1	*CHAPTER 2*	*CHAPTER 3*	*CHAPTER 4*

Many years ago the noted English agnostic Thomas Huxley was in Dublin, Ireland, fulfilling a number of speaking engagements. He had to leave early one morning to go from one assignment to another. He decided to take one of those famous horse-drawn taxis from the hotel to the train station. He assumed the doorman had told the driver of the carriage his destination. And so as he got in, he shouted to the driver, "Drive fast!" So off they went. Because he was somewhat familiar with the landscape of Dublin, he realized as they were speeding on their way that they were actually going in the opposite direction of the train station. He yelled to the driver, "Do you know where you are going?" And without looking back, the driver yelled back, "No, your honor, but I am driving very fast."

Many of us can hear this story and say, "I've been there!" Psychologist Rollo May was right: "Man is the strangest creature who ever lived. He is the only one who runs faster when he loses his way." John Ray, the eighteenth-century naturalist, wrote, "What is the use of running if you are on the wrong road?" But of all the quotes we could cite to illustrate a life headed in the wrong direction, none would be better than simply reading this brief, yet never-to-be-forgotten book of Jonah . . . the story of the prodigal prophet.

A New Look at an Old Story

Many of us are quite familiar with this story of Jonah. As a result, we may have been conditioned to look at the book of Jonah as some kind of a joke, a humorous book of the Old Testament that we shouldn't really take all that seriously. And so, for some of us, if we just so happen to find ourselves traveling down the wrong road, maybe with a casual shrug we reflect back on Jonah and continue merrily on our way, not taking God or His will for our lives all that seriously.

The fact is, the story of Jonah is a scandalous story. It may not require a lot of time to read the story, but it takes a lifetime to live out its lessons. But before we uncover the theme and the applications to our lives, we'll find out a little about the prophet and the times in which he lived.

Jonah, whose name means "dove," came from a place we can locate today as Gath Hepher (2 Kings 14:25), northeast of Nazareth. The city of Nineveh was more than 500 miles away from Jonah's hometown. Now we know from the early verses of this book that God had called Jonah to go to Nineveh to preach but he was determined to avoid that task. He set out for the city of Tarshish, thought to be a city in southwest Spain. Tarshish was located in the opposite direction from Nineveh. Nineveh and Tarshish represented opposite ends of the geographical boundaries in ancient times—Nineveh in the east and

Tarshish in the west. In some ways, by heading to Tarshish Jonah had his sights set on what seemed to be the far end of the world in his time. What lengths he was willing to go to escape his divinely appointed task!

Nineveh was a place of imposing military might. It was the place where the enemy resided. It was the heart and center of the nation of Assyria, a sleeping giant that would eventually sweep down on Israel and annihilate her. Jonah's clear call from God was to travel 500 miles east and bring God's message of repentance to the people of Nineveh. And Jonah wanted no part of it.

The theme of the book is really not that difficult to understand. If you look at it from God's perspective, it's the story of His marvelous and measureless mercy. If you look at it from Jonah's life, it's the story of stubborn rebellion, prompted by a mixture of pride and prejudice. If you see it through the Ninevites' eyes, it's an incredible opportunity to turn to the Lord and stave off His judgment. If you view it from the standpoint of God's world program, it is God's heart of compassion expressed to a nation that has not heard His name, has not heard His message and is facing certain doom unless repentance occurs.

A Proper Focus

There's a distinction we need to make in order to grasp and appreciate the full meaning of the book of Jonah. It is not a book about a great fish. It is not a book about a vine. It is not a book about a storm at sea or a near shipwreck. It is a book of God's dealing with a wayward man, so that he would obey Him and carry His message to others in need.

In light of the whole sweep of these four chapters, the giant fish is somewhat insignificant. The important thing is Jonah and his God, and bringing them back together so that God's life-giving message could be proclaimed. That's what the book is about—a man who is on the run and through an incredible turn of events runs back and does what God wanted done.

A Wicked Nation

Nineveh, even by our standards, was a huge city. The capital city of the Assyrians, it numbered from 600,000 to 750,000 people. The people of Assyria were brutal, vicious, godless people. It is a known fact that after they would plunder an area, they would behead the victims and stack the heads in mounds resembling a huge pyramid to serve as a visual reminder to all nations of the power of Assyria. They were a cruel people, wicked to the core. And God saw who they were and what they were doing, and this was what He said: "Its wickedness has come up before me" (1:2).

God knew the condition of the Ninevites just as He knew all the people of Assyria. He knew they were so wicked because they did not know and love Him. God didn't turn His back on them; His desire was to dispatch one of His messengers to them. The goal of God's great mission to the nations is that the message of salvation will be proclaimed to people who don't know Him—and that mission is often undertaken at great cost and with great difficulty.

A Compassionate God and a Hardhearted Prophet

God instructed Jonah to go to a place that was totally foreign to him and to his lifestyle. He told a zealous Jewish prophet to go to a group of Gentiles. In my opinion, the book of Jonah is the most mission-oriented book in the Old Testament. It is a book that reveals the merciful and compassionate heart of God that was committed first to His chosen people, the Israelites, and then to people from every nation.

God spoke plainly to Jonah and told him to get to Nineveh and declare God's message. You know the outcome, don't you? "But Jonah ran away from the LORD and headed for Tarshish" (1:3). Jonah headed in the opposite direction. That is like God saying to you, "Go to Honolulu," and you take the next plane out to Berlin. Jonah had no plans whatsoever to go to Nineveh. Plain and simple, he wasn't going. He fully intended to ignore God's call. He told us why in verse 2 of chapter 4: He knew God would take that message he proclaimed and would change the Ninevites, and *he didn't want them changed—he wanted them judged.* They were Israel's enemies. They were Gentiles. They had done horrible things. They needed to be judged, but Jonah knew God's heart. He knew the power of God's word. He knew that if God's message came to them, they would change, and that was the last thing he wanted to happen.

This book of Jonah is a very realistic book. It exposes the ulterior motives many of us have but aren't willing to admit. Jonah said, with the utmost honesty, in effect, "No, I won't go. I don't want them to hear. I don't want You to love those who are different from us. I don't want them to repent. I want You to judge them."

Lessons From Jonah

Two memorable lessons remain as we read Jonah. First, *it is utterly impossible to escape from God.* Quit trying. I am sure that some right now who read these words are running from Him. What a futile, wasteful effort! David knew it. Remember what he said? "Where can I go from your Spirit? Where can I flee from your presence? If I go up to the heavens, you are there; if I make my bed in the depths, you are there" (Psalm 139:7–8). Jeremiah knew it. Look at the truth the Lord communicated through him: " 'Am I only a God nearby,' declares the LORD, 'and not a God far away? Can anyone hide in secret places so that I cannot see him?' declares the LORD. 'Do I not fill heaven and earth?' declares the LORD" (Jeremiah 23:23–24). Jonah knew it. And you and I, if we're honest with ourselves, know that it is utterly impossible to escape from God . . . so stop trying.

Second, and showing the other side of the coin, *it is absolutely essential to submit to God* . . . so quit resisting. The book of Jonah is in the Bible for a reason. Jonah serves as a lasting reminder of the compassionate heart of God for the lost and His determination to use us regardless of our will. He will bend our will and, if necessary, break it in order to get His message declared.

Running From God — Chapter 1

This chapter records the commissioning of a very reluctant prophet. The call was clear. The source of the call was a distinct word of the Lord. The destination was Nineveh. The message was "Repent." How much more clearly could the Lord have spoken? Jonah's response was anything but positive. He got on the first ship going in the opposite direction as he attempted to run from God. Jonah learned a lesson many of us learn the hard way . . . you can't run from a God who is everywhere present. He sees exactly where you are, and He'll catch you every time.

Jonah Flees From the LORD

1 The word of the LORD came to Jonah son of
Amittai: 2"Go to the great city of Nineveh and
preach against it, because its wickedness has come
up before me." Ge 10:11; Mt 12:39-41
3But Jonah ran away from the LORD and headed
for Tarshish. He went down to Joppa, where he
found a ship bound for that port. After paying the
fare, he went aboard and sailed for Tarshish to flee
from the LORD. Jos 19:46; Ps 139:7; Ac 9:36,43
4Then the LORD sent a great wind on the sea,
and such a violent storm arose that the ship threatened to break up. 5All the sailors were afraid and
each cried out to his own god. And they threw the
cargo into the sea to lighten the ship. Ps 107:23-26
But Jonah had gone below deck, where he lay
down and fell into a deep sleep. 6The captain went
to him and said, "How can you sleep? Get up and
call on your god! Maybe he will take notice of us,
and we will not perish." Jnh 3:8; Ps 107:28
7Then the sailors said to each other, "Come, let
us cast lots to find out who is responsible for this
calamity." They cast lots and the lot fell on Jonah.
8So they asked him, "Tell us, who is responsible
for making all this trouble for us? What do you do?
Where do you come from? What is your country?
From what people are you?"
9He answered, "I am a Hebrew and I worship
the LORD, the God of heaven, who made the sea
and the land." Ps 146:6; Ac 17:24
10This terrified them and they asked, "What
have you done?" (They knew he was running away
from the LORD, because he had already told
them so.)
11The sea was getting rougher and rougher. So
they asked him, "What should we do to you to
make the sea calm down for us?"
12"Pick me up and throw me into the sea," he
replied, "and it will become calm. I know that it is
my fault that this great storm has come upon you."
13Instead, the men did their best to row back to
land. But they could not, for the sea grew even
wilder than before. 14Then they cried to the LORD,
"O LORD, please do not let us die for taking this
man's life. Do not hold us accountable for killing
an innocent man, for you, O LORD, have done as
you pleased." 15Then they took Jonah and threw
him overboard, and the raging sea grew calm. 16At
this the men greatly feared the LORD, and they
offered a sacrifice to the LORD and made vows to
him. Lk 8:24; Dt 21:8
17But the LORD provided a great fish to swallow
Jonah, and Jonah was inside the fish three days
and three nights. Mt 12:40; 16:4; Lk 11:30

Running to God — Chapter 2

This chapter contains the prayer of Jonah from the belly of a great fish. The first six verses record Jonah's near-death experience and the salvation God extended to him. God sent a great fish to swallow the wayward prophet and deliver him onto dry land three days later. Jonah acknowledged that his deliverance came wholly from the Lord. The closing verses of his prayer document the prophet's promise to respond to the Lord with thanksgiving and obedience.

Jonah's Prayer

2 From inside the fish Jonah prayed to the
LORD his God. 2He said:

"In my distress I called to the LORD, Ps 18:6; 120:1
and he answered me.
From the depths of the grave[a] I called for
help,
and you listened to my cry.

LIVING  INSIGHT

One of the most encouraging things about new years, new weeks and new days is the word* new*. It's a place to start over. Refresh yourself. Change directions. Begin anew. But that requires knowing where you are—taking time to honestly admit your present condition. Openly and freely declare your need to the One who cares deeply.

(See Jonah 2:2–7.)

3You hurled me into the deep, Ps 88:6
into the very heart of the seas,
and the currents swirled about me;
all your waves and breakers
swept over me. Ps 42:7
4I said, 'I have been banished
from your sight; Ps 31:22
yet I will look again
toward your holy temple.'
5The engulfing waters threatened me,[b]
the deep surrounded me;

[a]2 Hebrew *Sheol* [b]5 Or *waters were at my throat*

JONAH

The Running Prophet

"The word of the LORD came to Jonah son of Amittai: 'Go to the great city of Nineveh and preach against it.'"

–JONAH 1:1–2a

Contrary to what many think, the book of Jonah is not mainly about a fish. Rather, it is about the greatest missionary campaign in all the Old Testament; in all the Bible it is second only to the book of Acts as a famous missionary book. It's the story of Jonah whom God selected to take His message of repentance and reconciliation to a pagan land. It won't take you long to discover that this man Jonah was reluctant to do as God said. Based on his actions, I would call Jonah "the running prophet." Notice how the direction he ran changed during the course of the book.

In chapter 1, Jonah was running *away from* God. You see, Jonah was a zealot, a Jewish nationalist. Nineveh was the capital of the nation of Assyria, one of the superpowers of the day, and a major threat to Israel's peace and prosperity. Therefore Jonah wanted to see Nineveh destroyed, not saved. He wanted more than anything else for Israel to escape the brutality of Assyria. So when God called Jonah to go, Jonah went all right—in the opposite direction: "But Jonah ran away from the LORD and headed for Tarshish" (1:3).

Being a prophet, Jonah should have known how difficult it is to run away from God's presence—in fact, it's impossible. God followed Jonah on his way to Tarshish. "Then the LORD sent a great wind on the sea, and such a violent storm arose that the ship threatened to break up" (1:4). Please notice, it does not simply say that a storm arose. It says that *the Lord* made it happen. That's "step one" in God's divinely persuasive plan. Step two had to do with the great fish God appointed to bring Jonah to his senses.

Chapter 2 shows Jonah running *to* God. Here we see the strangest prayer meeting ever held. This was one callous prophet, believe me! After slogging around inside the fish for days, he said to himself, "You know, maybe I should pray about this situation." And the Lord heard him. Look at Jonah's testimony: "You hurled me into the deep, into the very heart of the seas" (2:3). Jonah must have had opportunity to cultivate wisdom during those long hours inside that fish—the kind of wisdom that comes from looking at life from God's point of view. Who threw him overboard? God did! It wasn't the sailors who did it.

In chapter 3 we see Jonah running *with* God. After the amphibious landing described in verse 10 of chapter 2, Jonah never stopped running until he got to Nineveh. He bore the scars of three days and nights in the belly of that fish. (There are several modern accounts describing the appearance of those who experienced what happened to Jonah in that fish's belly: patchy, bleached hair and skin that varied in color from yellow to white, almost like parchment.) When Jonah reached the city, the people sat up and paid attention! And he never stopped preaching until he had spoken his message on every street corner: "Forty more days and Nineveh will be overturned" (3:4). Then the greatest revival in Biblical history broke out. About 600,000 people repented and turned to the Lord in worship. Not bad for an evangelistic crusade that lasted three or four days! That's the *real* miracle of this book!

Now notice what takes place in verse 1 of chapter 4: Jonah was running *up against* God. Jonah had spoken a message of doom and destruction to the Ninevites, which was exactly the kind of treatment he hoped the city would receive (3:4). But the promised destruction didn't happen, sending Jonah into a tailspin of depression and anger. He explained it to God this way: "I knew that you are a gracious and compassionate God, slow to anger and abounding in love, a God who relents from sending calamity" (4:2). Through the object lesson of the vine, God captured Jonah's attention. Then God addressed Jonah with a question and a declaration that went something like this: "You're telling me, Jonah, that I shouldn't have compassion on this great city of people? Should *you* not have had compassion toward a people who could have died without having experienced God's love and mercy—more compassion than you had toward a vine that sprang up in a day and withered in a day?" Jonah's vision was so limited that he fell in love with a dumb plant and missed the ministry he could have had—had he *run with God* throughout his life.

seaweed was wrapped around my head.
[6]To the roots of the mountains I sank down;
the earth beneath barred me in forever.
But you brought my life up from the pit,
O LORD my God.

[7]"When my life was ebbing away,
I remembered you, LORD, Ps 77:11-12
and my prayer rose to you, 2Ch 30:27
to your holy temple. Ps 18:6

[8]"Those who cling to worthless idols 2Ki 17:15
forfeit the grace that could be theirs.
[9]But I, with a song of thanksgiving,
will sacrifice to you. Ps 50:14,23
What I have vowed I will make good. Ecc 5:4-5
Salvation comes from the LORD." Ps 3:8

[10]And the LORD commanded the fish, and it vomited Jonah onto dry land.

Running With God **Chapter 3**

In this third chapter Jonah received a second commission to go to Nineveh. The mission was the same: He was to call this pagan nation to repentance. When the fish delivered him onto dry land, Jonah hit the ground running. Jonah preached the coming judgment of God wherever he went (a simple message of only eight words [3:4]: "Forty more days and Nineveh will be overturned"), and the people heard the message and repented—not just a few people but "from the greatest to the least" (3:5), throughout the entire city. Jonah brought God's message, and the Lord moved powerfully in the hearts of the people. Revival broke out in Nineveh!

Jonah Goes to Nineveh

3 Then the word of the LORD came to Jonah a second time: [2]"Go to the great city of Nineveh and proclaim to it the message I give you."

LIVING  INSIGHT

God wants to use you—stumbling, falling and all—but He won't do so if you refuse to get up.
(See Jonah 3:1–3.)

[3]Jonah obeyed the word of the LORD and went to Nineveh. Now Nineveh was a very important city—a visit required three days. [4]On the first day, Jonah started into the city. He proclaimed: "Forty more days and Nineveh will be overturned." [5]The Ninevites believed God. They declared a fast, and all of them, from the greatest to the least, put on sackcloth. Da 9:3; Lk 11:32

[6]When the news reached the king of Nineveh, he rose from his throne, took off his royal robes, covered himself with sackcloth and sat down in the dust. [7]Then he issued a proclamation in Nineveh:

"By the decree of the king and his nobles:

Do not let any man or beast, herd or flock, taste anything; do not let them eat or drink. [8]But let man and beast be covered with sackcloth. Let everyone call urgently on God. Let them give up their evil ways and their violence. [9]Who knows? God may yet relent and with compassion turn from his fierce anger so that we will not perish." Joel 2:14; Jnh 1:6

[10]When God saw what they did and how they turned from their evil ways, he had compassion and did not bring upon them the destruction he had threatened. Jer 18:8; Am 7:6

Running Against God **Chapter 4**

In the final chapter we see Jonah's prejudice as he responded with anger to the Lord's graciousness toward a pagan nation. Doesn't it seem a bit strange? Wouldn't you think Jonah would have gotten some joy out of the incredible response to his preaching?—but just the opposite happened. Jonah was furious and deeply disappointed that his preaching had such a great impact. (How peculiar!) He had grown comfortable in his hatred of the Ninevites, the vicious enemy of his people, but now they had experienced the grace of God. Usually after a revival it is the converts who need to be discipled and nurtured. In this case, of all things, it was the evangelist!

Jonah's Anger at the LORD's Compassion

4 But Jonah was greatly displeased and became angry. [2]He prayed to the LORD, "O LORD, is this not what I said when I was still at home? That is why I was so quick to flee to Tarshish. I knew that you are a gracious and compassionate God, slow to anger and abounding in love, a God who relents from sending calamity. [3]Now, O LORD, take away my life, for it is better for me to die than to live." 1Ki 19:4; Ps 86:5,15

[4]But the LORD replied, "Have you any right to be angry?" Mt 20:11-15

[5]Jonah went out and sat down at a place east of the city. There he made himself a shelter, sat in its shade and waited to see what would happen to the city. [6]Then the LORD God provided a vine and made it grow up over Jonah to give shade for his head to ease his discomfort, and Jonah was very happy about the vine. [7]But at dawn the next day God provided a worm, which chewed the vine so that it withered. [8]When the sun rose, God provided a scorching east wind, and the sun blazed on Jonah's head so that he grew faint. He wanted to die, and said, "It would be better for me to die than to live." Joel 1:12

[9]But God said to Jonah, "Do you have a right to be angry about the vine?"

"I do," he said. "I am angry enough to die."

[10]But the LORD said, "You have been concerned
about this vine, though you did not tend it or
make it grow. It sprang up overnight and died
overnight. [11]But Nineveh has more than a hundred
and twenty thousand people who cannot tell their
right hand from their left, and many cattle as well.
Should I not be concerned about that great
city?"

INTRODUCTION

MICAH

It is doubtful that the poor peasants of Judah ever had a stronger champion than Micah, this young, powerful preacher from the country. Micah defended the downtrodden with passion and zeal. He cared deeply ... and so he warned of certain judgment and punishment if no repentance were shown. For this reason we should not minimize Micah's importance or regard him as somehow inferior to his fellow prophets. No way! With a simple yet courageous style, Micah proclaimed God's strong reproofs to the rich, offered sympathy and support to the poor, predicted judgment on all the ungodly and, with an open, honest and compassionate spirit, proclaimed the message of God's truth to all who would listen.

WRITER: *Micah*

DATE: *c.740–710 B.C.*

PURPOSE: *To warn God's people of approaching judgment and to offer hope for the faithful*

KEY THEME: *Judgment and deliverance by God*

KEY PREDICTIONS: *Fall of Israel; fall of Judah; captivity; return from captivity; Messiah's birth in Bethlehem; restoration and peace*

KEY VERSES: *1:2; 6:2; 6:8; 7:18*

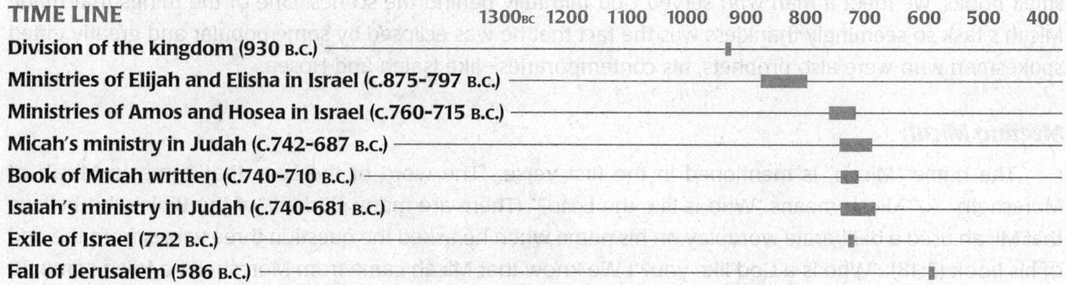

Prophet to the Poor

DOOM DECLARED	SIN EXPOSED	HOPE PREDICTED
"Hear, O peoples . . . listen, O earth . . ." (1:2)	*"Listen, you leaders . . . you rulers . . ." (3:1)*	*"Hear, O mountains . . ." (6:2)*
The capitals will be destroyed	Human corruption	Great controversy
Reasons for judgment	Divine restoration	Authentic spirituality
		Domestic scene
		Messianic mercy
CHAPTERS 1–2	*CHAPTERS 3–5*	*CHAPTERS 6–7*

735 B.C. — *710 B.C.*

So many of God's servants are never known by the public, except in that small arena in which they faithfully serve year after year. I think it is time for us to say, "Hats off to those who serve God faithfully in the less visible places." I believe if the truth could be discovered, most of us have had our lives significantly affected by someone who faithfully filled a pulpit in a small church or served us in a quiet way, behind the scenes.

I am personally convinced that one of the reasons God has preserved the messages of the minor prophets is to encourage the good people who serve God in obscure and unnoticed places. As we turn our attention to the little-known seven-chapter book of Micah tucked away in the midst of a section of many small books, we meet a man who served God faithfully behind the scenes. One of the things that made Micah's task so seemingly thankless was the fact that he was eclipsed by some popular and greatly gifted spokesmen who were also prophets, his contemporaries—like Isaiah and Hosea.

Meeting Micah

The name "Micah" is mentioned in the first verse: "The word of the LORD that came to Micah of Moresheth . . ." Micah means "Who is like the LORD?" (There are many students of the Bible who believe that Micah used a deliberate wordplay on his name when he asked the question three verses from the end of his book (7:18): "Who is a God like you?") We know that Micah came from Moresheth, a town some 20 miles southeast of Jerusalem. (We would say today that it was "off the beaten path.") It was a relatively unknown spot out in the country—located 17 miles away from another little village, Tekoa, the hometown of the prophet Amos.

Micah, like Amos, may have been a "country boy," but don't think for a moment he was unaware of his world. It's been my observation that many of the country preachers of our times have a strong and discerning message to bring to the sophisticated cities around them. So it was with Micah. He was, in every sense of the word, a genuine prophet of God who saw the world through God's eyes.

A Country Boy in the King's Court

The first verse of Micah tells us that he prophesied in the days of Kings Jotham, Ahaz and Hezekiah—all of them were kings of Judah. While Micah may have been a country preacher from a country town, he wasn't intimidated by powerful and wealthy people. As a matter of fact, his message echoed in the halls of the "Oval Office" of the eighth century B.C. time after time. His message was remembered at the birth of our Savior, for he was quoted to people in the sophisticated circles of King Herod as they searched the Scriptures to discover where the Messiah was to be born. Centuries after the man had passed from the earth's scene, religious leaders were quoting Micah, an unpretentious, clearheaded prophet in the days of Jotham, Ahaz and Hezekiah.

Micah's date of ministry was from about 735–700 B.C. He was a man who served during the same era as other great prophets of God. Consider his contemporaries. There was the highly intelligent and gifted prince of the prophets, by the name of Isaiah, who wrote a 66-chapter book. The most intelligent and sophisticated vocabulary in the Hebrew language was found in Isaiah's prophecy. There was the popular Hosea, whose compassionate heart and actions deeply influenced the nation of Israel. And just preceding Micah had been Amos from Tekoa, who was led by God to minister at Bethel, the sanctuary of the king (Amos 7:13). The greater lights overshadowed Micah . . . but in no way did they eclipse his message.

Prophet to the Poor

Micah had a burden for the poor people of the land, those who were oppressed by the land barons . . . the monopolizers and the embezzlers. The rich had used their wealth to make life miserable for the poor. Micah came down hard on those who took advantage of the poor. Micah wanted all of them to know that every cruel act against one's neighbor was an insult to God, who is deeply offended by the conduct of people who exploit others and misuse their own privileged position.

Pleading the cause of the poor, Micah's message went something like this: "Wake up, Jerusalem! Wake up, Judah! Pay attention, Israel! You're doing what is wrong, and our people are suffering. I warn you, there is doom ahead if you persist." Micah demanded their attention, and he got it. His message was characterized by vigorous language, alternating between frank predictions of doom and destruction and glorious oracles of hope and deliverance.

Sin Does Not Go Unnoticed

I want you to observe with special attention the false prophets Micah addressed in chapter 2, beginning at verse 6. Micah boldly confronted these prophets with their moral and spiritual poverty and lack of a standard to live by. The prophets were offended by Micah's rebuke and insisted that he stop predicting bad news. The way to get a receptive audience in Micah's day was to promise unending prosperity and pleasure—but Micah wasn't in it for the affirmation. He was committed to speaking the truth that Almighty God had told him to speak.

All the way through his prophecy, Micah reminded his fellow citizens, "God is alive. God is not blind. He sees and He knows the condition of our times. Doom is certain if there isn't repentance." He forcefully repeated that warning in oracle after oracle.

In chapter 3, Micah exposed the sins of the leaders of Israel with one ringing indictment after another, concentrating first on the rulers, then on the prophets and priests. For the commitment to injustice and decadence they exhibited, a price would have to be paid. Hear Micah's prophecy of the future destruction of Jerusalem (which took place in 586 B.C.): "Therefore because of you, Zion will be plowed like a field, Jerusalem will become a heap of rubble, the temple hill a mound overgrown with thickets" (3:12).

Bold Messengers

In verse 1 of chapter 6, Micah pleaded his case before the mountains as his witnesses—the case of the Lord versus Judah. He took on the role of an attorney, as it were, essentially saying to the people, "The Lord has an indictment against you. There's a case against you, and I'll tell you just exactly where you stand. Unless you repent, there will be no hope for you as a nation."

I am grateful for the men and women in my past who have been bold enough to look me in the eye and say on occasion, "That is wrong. That has no business in your life." I am grateful for a faithful mother who did that at times when I needed to hear it. I am thankful for a few mentors who loved me enough to put their arms around me at critical moments in my life and say, "Straighten up. Stop that. You need to deal with this." Straight talk from those who cared. I give thanks to this day that they cared enough to confront.

Chapter 2 records Micah's simple counsel on the key to a genuine walk with God. What is required to be godly? What is the right thing to do? According to Micah, it's not all that complicated—at least to hear it. Putting it into practice can prove to be quite another matter:

> *He has showed you, O man, what is good.*
> *And what does the LORD require of you?*
> *To act justly and to love mercy*
> *and to walk humbly with your God (6:8).*

There you have it . . . an easy-to-remember guideline for godliness:

> *Act justly.*
> *Love mercy.*
> *Walk humbly.*

Looking for a verse to memorize? Need a verse to guide you when things get complicated in your walk and you're looking for a simple summary of what the Lord wants your relationship with Him to look like? You can do no better than Micah 6:8.

Lessons From Micah

What can we learn from the book of Micah? I suggest at least these three lessons. First, *a messenger may be from an obscure place, but God's power gives him or her all the clout needed.* I want to bring a word of encouragement to those of you who serve in what some might call insignificant places. You may be in a place far removed from all the glamour and glitter, you may feel woefully unimportant, but the presence and power of God gives you all the clout you need. Be encouraged by Micah's model and message. We *need* every person who ministers in the obscure spots of our nation and our world. Just keep serving God faithfully, wherever He's placed you, for however long He's placed you there.

Second, *in times of need, God gives His faithful messengers a word in due season.* Be encouraged, you who speak for God in a decadent era like ours. It is the horror of our times that gives us a basis for our potent message. If it weren't for the needs of our land, we really wouldn't have a message that strikes a needed blow for God's truth. In times of greatest need, a nation is given God's strongest messages.

Third, *the key to living a godly life can be stated very simply.* It isn't complicated. It isn't a whole lot of fancy formulas or a whole bunch of multi-step programs. It doesn't require years of schooling or a brilliant intellect. What does the Lord require of us? To act justly, to love mercy, to walk humbly with Him—that's the heart of it. To be committed to caring that the right and fair thing be done. To respond with a heart of mercy to those around us. To be humble in all things.

I remember when a lot of very complicated things suddenly became simple for me. I was in the Marine Corps. I will never forget being stationed on an island for well over a year. While I was there I took the time to intensively study God's Word. By the end of that time it became clear to me how relatively easy it was to understand what God expected. He didn't require that I jump through a lot of religious hoops. He didn't expect me to give a hundred percent of my time to Him in formal service projects. But He made it clear to me that *I was to take Him seriously.* I was to believe *His* truth as opposed to every other kind of counsel—and when any other counsel contradicted His Word, I was not to believe that other counsel. I realized I was simply to serve Him and to take Him at His word. He showed me that I would glorify His name if I just walked with Him. And kept short accounts with Him. And spent time with Him. And trusted Him with my future. And loved others, dealing with them in grace. Simple things: to do what was right, to show compassion and kindness, and to walk humbly with my God. May God give me, and you, the desire and the strength to do it.

Doom Declared Chapters 1–2

Throughout these chapters Micah denounced the sins of the nations. More specifically, he prophesied the destruction of the two capital cities of God's chosen people. Micah predicted the certain fall of Samaria, the chief city of the northern kingdom of Israel. He also foretold the ruin of Jerusalem, the major city of the southern kingdom of Judah. Micah forcefully announced his message for all the people of the land to hear. The cloud of doom was hovering overhead. Beware, judgment was coming!

1 The word of the LORD that came to Micah of
Moresheth during the reigns of Jotham, Ahaz
and Hezekiah, kings of Judah—the vision he saw
concerning Samaria and Jerusalem. Jer 26:18; Hos 1:1

2 Hear, O peoples, all of you, Ps 50:7
listen, O earth and all who are in it, Jer 6:19
that the Sovereign LORD may witness against
you, Dt 4:26
the Lord from his holy temple. Ps 11:4

Judgment Against Samaria and Jerusalem

3 Look! The LORD is coming from his dwelling
place; Isa 18:4
he comes down and treads the high places
of the earth. Am 4:13
4 The mountains melt beneath him Ps 46:2,6
and the valleys split apart, Nu 16:31; Na 1:5
like wax before the fire,
like water rushing down a slope.
5 All this is because of Jacob's transgression,
because of the sins of the house of Israel.
What is Jacob's transgression?
Is it not Samaria? Am 8:14
What is Judah's high place?
Is it not Jerusalem?

6 "Therefore I will make Samaria a heap of
rubble,
a place for planting vineyards.
I will pour her stones into the valley Am 5:11
and lay bare her foundations. Eze 13:14
7 All her idols will be broken to pieces; Eze 6:6
all her temple gifts will be burned with fire;
I will destroy all her images. Dt 9:21
Since she gathered her gifts from the wages of
prostitutes, Dt 23:17-18
as the wages of prostitutes they will again
be used."

Weeping and Mourning

8 Because of this I will weep and wail; Isa 15:3
I will go about barefoot and naked.
I will howl like a jackal
and moan like an owl.
9 For her wound is incurable; Jer 46:11
it has come to Judah. 2Ki 18:13
It[a] has reached the very gate of my people,
even to Jerusalem itself.
10 Tell it not in Gath[b];
weep not at all.[c]
In Beth Ophrah[d]
roll in the dust.
11 Pass on in nakedness and shame, Eze 23:29
you who live in Shaphir.[e]
Those who live in Zaanan[f]
will not come out.
Beth Ezel is in mourning;
its protection is taken from you.
12 Those who live in Maroth[g] writhe in pain,
waiting for relief, Jer 14:19
because disaster has come from the LORD,
even to the gate of Jerusalem.
13 You who live in Lachish,[h] Jos 10:3
harness the team to the chariot.
You were the beginning of sin
to the Daughter of Zion, Ps 9:14
for the transgressions of Israel
were found in you.
14 Therefore you will give parting gifts 2Ki 16:8
to Moresheth Gath.
The town of Aczib[i] will prove deceptive
to the kings of Israel.
15 I will bring a conqueror against you
who live in Mareshah.[j] Jos 15:44
He who is the glory of Israel
will come to Adullam. Jos 12:15
16 Shave your heads in mourning Job 1:20
for the children in whom you delight;
make yourselves as bald as the vulture,
for they will go from you into exile. Am 5:27

Man's Plans and God's

2 Woe to those who plan iniquity,
to those who plot evil on their beds! Ps 36:4
At morning's light they carry it out
because it is in their power to do it.
2 They covet fields and seize them, Isa 5:8
and houses, and take them.
They defraud a man of his home, Jer 22:17
a fellowman of his inheritance. Eze 46:18
3 Therefore, the LORD says:

"I am planning disaster against this people,
from which you cannot save yourselves.
You will no longer walk proudly, Isa 2:12
for it will be a time of calamity.
4 In that day men will ridicule you;
they will taunt you with this mournful
song:

[a] 9 Or *He* [b] 10 *Gath* sounds like the Hebrew for *tell.* [c] 10 Hebrew; Septuagint may suggest *not in Acco.* The Hebrew for *in Acco* sounds like the Hebrew for *weep.* [d] 10 *Beth Ophrah* means *house of dust.* [e] 11 *Shaphir* means *pleasant.* [f] 11 *Zaanan* sounds like the Hebrew for *come out.* [g] 12 *Maroth* sounds like the Hebrew for *bitter.* [h] 13 *Lachish* sounds like the Hebrew for *team.* [i] 14 *Aczib* means *deception.* [j] 15 *Mareshah* sounds like the Hebrew for *conqueror.*

'We are utterly ruined; Jer 4:13
my people's possession is divided up.
He takes it from me!
He assigns our fields to traitors.'"

5Therefore you will have no one in the assembly of the LORD
to divide the land by lot. Jos 18:4

False Prophets

6"Do not prophesy," their prophets say.
"Do not prophesy about these things;
disgrace will not overtake us." Am 2:12; Mic 6:16
7Should it be said, O house of Jacob:
"Is the Spirit of the LORD angry?
Does he do such things?"

"Do not my words do good Ps 119:65
to him whose ways are upright? Ps 15:2; 84:11
8Lately my people have risen up
like an enemy.
You strip off the rich robe
from those who pass by without a care,
like men returning from battle.
9You drive the women of my people
from their pleasant homes. Jer 10:20
You take away my blessing
from their children forever.
10Get up, go away!
For this is not your resting place, Dt 12:9
because it is defiled, Lev 18:25-29; Ps 106:38-39
it is ruined, beyond all remedy.
11If a liar and deceiver comes and says, Jer 5:31
'I will prophesy for you plenty of wine and beer,'
he would be just the prophet for this people! Isa 30:10

Deliverance Promised

12"I will surely gather all of you, O Jacob;
I will surely bring together the remnant of Israel. Mic 4:7; 5:7; 7:18
I will bring them together like sheep in a pen,
like a flock in its pasture;
the place will throng with people.
13One who breaks open the way will go up before them; Isa 52:12
they will break through the gate and go out.
Their king will pass through before them,
the LORD at their head."

Sin Exposed **Chapters 3–6**

Micah openly exposed the people's sin for all to see. The doom that was coming was not arbitrary or unfair. It was the result of rebellion, idolatry and injustice. Micah stripped away all of the excuses and showed the ugly reality of the people's sinful hearts. Interestingly, in the midst of this dark picture of the sins of the people Micah interjected an interlude of hope for Israel and Judah. In chapter 4 Micah recorded a picture of the coming Millennial Age when the Messiah would reign and personally administer justice. Chapter 5 pointed to the small city of Bethlehem as the place where this Messiah would be born as He arrived for His first advent. Even in our darkest hours the unquenchable light that shines is Jesus Christ, the Lord!

Leaders and Prophets Rebuked

3 Then I said,

"Listen, you leaders of Jacob, Jer 5:5
you rulers of the house of Israel.
Should you not know justice,
2 you who hate good and love evil;
who tear the skin from my people
and the flesh from their bones; Ps 53:4
3who eat my people's flesh, Ps 14:4
strip off their skin
and break their bones in pieces; Zep 3:3
who chop them up like meat for the pan,
like flesh for the pot?" Eze 11:7

4Then they will cry out to the LORD,
but he will not answer them. Ps 18:41; Isa 1:15
At that time he will hide his face from them
because of the evil they have done. Eze 8:18

5This is what the LORD says:

"As for the prophets
who lead my people astray, Isa 3:12; 9:16
if one feeds them,
they proclaim 'peace'; Jer 4:10
if he does not,
they prepare to wage war against him.
6Therefore night will come over you, without visions,
and darkness, without divination. Isa 8:19-22
The sun will set for the prophets, Isa 29:10
and the day will go dark for them. Eze 7:26
7The seers will be ashamed Mic 7:16
and the diviners disgraced. Isa 44:25
They will all cover their faces Lev 13:45
because there is no answer from God."

8But as for me, I am filled with power,
with the Spirit of the LORD,
and with justice and might,
to declare to Jacob his transgression,
to Israel his sin. Isa 58:1
9Hear this, you leaders of the house of Jacob,
you rulers of the house of Israel,
who despise justice
and distort all that is right; Ps 58:1-2; Isa 1:23
10who build Zion with bloodshed, Jer 22:13; Hab 2:12
and Jerusalem with wickedness. Eze 22:27
11Her leaders judge for a bribe, Mal 2:9
her priests teach for a price, Eze 13:19
and her prophets tell fortunes for money.

Yet they lean upon the LORD and say,
"Is not the LORD among us?
No disaster will come upon us." Jer 7:4
12 Therefore because of you,
Zion will be plowed like a field,
Jerusalem will become a heap of rubble,
the temple hill a mound overgrown with thickets. Jer 17:3

The Mountain of the LORD

4 In the last days
the mountain of the LORD's temple will be established Zec 8:3
as chief among the mountains;
it will be raised above the hills, Eze 17:22
and peoples will stream to it. Ps 22:27; Jer 3:17

2 Many nations will come and say,

"Come, let us go up to the mountain of the LORD, Jer 31:6
to the house of the God of Jacob. Zec 2:11
He will teach us his ways, Ps 25:8-9; Isa 54:13
so that we may walk in his paths."
The law will go out from Zion,
the word of the LORD from Jerusalem.
3 He will judge between many peoples
and will settle disputes for strong nations far and wide. Isa 11:4
They will beat their swords into plowshares
and their spears into pruning hooks. Joel 3:10
Nation will not take up sword against nation,
nor will they train for war anymore. Isa 2:1-4
4 Every man will sit under his own vine
and under his own fig tree, 1Ki 4:25
and no one will make them afraid, Lev 26:6
for the LORD Almighty has spoken. Isa 1:20
5 All the nations may walk
in the name of their gods; 2Ki 17:29
we will walk in the name of the LORD
our God for ever and ever. Zec 10:12

The LORD's Plan

6 "In that day," declares the LORD,

"I will gather the lame;
I will assemble the exiles Ps 147:2
and those I have brought to grief. Eze 34:13,16
7 I will make the lame a remnant, Mic 2:12
those driven away a strong nation.
The LORD will rule over them in Mount Zion
from that day and forever. Lk 1:33; Rev 11:15
8 As for you, O watchtower of the flock,
O stronghold[a] of the Daughter of Zion,
the former dominion will be restored to you;
kingship will come to the Daughter of Jerusalem."

9 Why do you now cry aloud—
have you no king? Jer 8:19
Has your counselor perished,
that pain seizes you like that of a woman in labor? Jer 30:6
10 Writhe in agony, O Daughter of Zion,
like a woman in labor,
for now you must leave the city
to camp in the open field.
You will go to Babylon; 2Ki 20:18; Isa 43:14
there you will be rescued.
There the LORD will redeem you Isa 48:20
out of the hand of your enemies.

11 But now many nations
are gathered against you.
They say, "Let her be defiled,
let our eyes gloat over Zion!" La 2:16; Ob 1:12
12 But they do not know
the thoughts of the LORD;
they do not understand his plan, Isa 55:8
he who gathers them like sheaves to the threshing floor.

13 "Rise and thresh, O Daughter of Zion,
for I will give you horns of iron;
I will give you hoofs of bronze
and you will break to pieces many nations."

You will devote their ill-gotten gains to the LORD,
their wealth to the Lord of all the earth.

A Promised Ruler From Bethlehem

5 Marshal your troops, O city of troops,[b]
for a siege is laid against us.
They will strike Israel's ruler
on the cheek with a rod. La 3:30

2 "But you, Bethlehem Ephrathah, Jn 7:42; Ge 48:7
though you are small among the clans[c] of Judah,
out of you will come for me
one who will be ruler over Israel, 1Sa 13:14
whose origins[d] are from of old, Ps 102:25
from ancient times.[e]" Mt 2:6*

3 Therefore Israel will be abandoned
until the time when she who is in labor gives birth
and the rest of his brothers return
to join the Israelites.

4 He will stand and shepherd his flock Isa 40:11
in the strength of the LORD,
in the majesty of the name of the LORD his God.
And they will live securely, for then his
greatness Isa 52:13; Lk 1:32

[a] 8 Or *hill of eternity* [b] 1 Or *Strengthen your walls, O walled city* [c] 2 Or *rulers* [d] 2 Hebrew *goings out* [e] 2 Or *from days*

will reach to the ends of the earth.
5 And he will be their peace. Isa 9:6; Lk 2:14

Deliverance and Destruction

When the Assyrian invades our land Isa 8:7
and marches through our fortresses,
we will raise against him seven shepherds,
even eight leaders of men. Isa 10:24-27
6They will rule[a] the land of Assyria with the sword,
the land of Nimrod with drawn sword.[b]
He will deliver us from the Assyrian
when he invades our land
and marches into our borders. Na 2:11-13

7The remnant of Jacob will be
in the midst of many peoples Mic 2:12
like dew from the LORD, Ps 133:3
like showers on the grass, Isa 44:4
which do not wait for man
or linger for mankind.
8The remnant of Jacob will be among the nations,
in the midst of many peoples,
like a lion among the beasts of the forest,
like a young lion among flocks of sheep,
which mauls and mangles as it goes, Mic 4:13
and no one can rescue. Ps 50:22; Hos 5:14
9Your hand will be lifted up in triumph over your enemies, Ps 10:12
and all your foes will be destroyed.

10"In that day," declares the LORD,

"I will destroy your horses from among you
and demolish your chariots. Hos 14:3; Zec 9:10
11I will destroy the cities of your land Isa 6:11
and tear down all your strongholds. Hos 10:14
12I will destroy your witchcraft
and you will no longer cast spells. Dt 18:10-12
13I will destroy your carved images
and your sacred stones from among you;
you will no longer bow down
to the work of your hands. Eze 6:9; Zec 13:2
14I will uproot from among you your Asherah poles[c] Ex 34:13
and demolish your cities.
15I will take vengeance in anger and wrath
upon the nations that have not obeyed me."

The LORD's Case Against Israel

6 Listen to what the LORD says:

"Stand up, plead your case before the mountains; Ps 50:1; Eze 6:2
let the hills hear what you have to say.
2Hear, O mountains, the LORD's accusation;
listen, you everlasting foundations of the earth.
For the LORD has a case against his people;
he is lodging a charge against Israel. Ps 50:7

3"My people, what have I done to you?
How have I burdened you? Answer me.
4I brought you up out of Egypt Ex 3:10
and redeemed you from the land of slavery.
I sent Moses to lead you, Ex 4:16
also Aaron and Miriam. Ex 15:20; Ps 77:20
5My people, remember
what Balak king of Moab counseled Nu 22:5-6
and what Balaam son of Beor answered.
Remember ⌞your journey⌟ from Shittim to Gilgal, Nu 25:1; Jos 5:9-10
that you may know the righteous acts of the LORD." Jdg 5:11; 1Sa 12:7

6With what shall I come before the LORD
and bow down before the exalted God?
Shall I come before him with burnt offerings,
with calves a year old? Ps 40:6-8; 51:16-17
7Will the LORD be pleased with thousands of rams, Isa 40:16
with ten thousand rivers of oil? Ps 50:8-10
Shall I offer my firstborn for my transgression,
the fruit of my body for the sin of my soul?
8He has showed you, O man, what is good.
And what does the LORD require of you?
To act justly and to love mercy Isa 1:17; Jer 22:3
and to walk humbly with your God.

LIVING  INSIGHT

What we think about God shapes our moral and ethical standards. What we think about God motivates our response toward fortune, fame, power and pleasure. What we think about God directly affects our response to pain and pleasure.

(See Micah 6:8.)

Israel's Guilt and Punishment

9Listen! The LORD is calling to the city—
and to fear your name is wisdom—
"Heed the rod and the One who appointed it.[d] Isa 11:4
10Am I still to forget, O wicked house,
your ill-gotten treasures
and the short ephah,[e] which is accursed?
11Shall I acquit a man with dishonest scales,
with a bag of false weights?
12Her rich men are violent; Isa 1:23
her people are liars Isa 3:8

[a]6 Or *crush* [b]6 Or *Nimrod in its gates* [c]14 That is, symbols of the goddess Asherah [d]9 The meaning of the Hebrew for this line is uncertain. [e]10 An ephah was a dry measure.

and their tongues speak deceitfully. Jer 9:3
13Therefore, I have begun to destroy you, Isa 1:7
to ruin you because of your sins.
14You will eat but not be satisfied; Isa 9:20
your stomach will still be empty.[a]
You will store up but save nothing, Isa 30:6
because what you save I will give to the sword.
15You will plant but not harvest; Dt 28:38; Jer 12:13
you will press olives but not use the oil on yourselves,
you will crush grapes but not drink the wine. Am 5:11; Zep 1:13
16You have observed the statutes of Omri
and all the practices of Ahab's house,
and you have followed their traditions.
Therefore I will give you over to ruin Jer 25:9
and your people to derision;
you will bear the scorn of the nations.[b]"

Hope Predicted **Chapter 7**

In the closing chapter gloom turned to triumph, as Micah proclaimed the assurance of hope and the prediction of a bright future for God's people. Micah had looked straight on at the darkness of his time, but God had also allowed him to see beyond darkness. Israel would rise once again: "Do not gloat over me, my enemy! Though I have fallen, I will rise. Though I sit in darkness, the LORD will be my light" (7:8). Victory belongs to God and to His kingdom!

Israel's Misery

7 What misery is mine!
I am like one who gathers summer fruit
at the gleaning of the vineyard;
there is no cluster of grapes to eat,
none of the early figs that I crave.
2The godly have been swept from the land;
not one upright man remains. Jer 2:29
All men lie in wait to shed blood; Mic 3:10
each hunts his brother with a net. Jer 5:26
3Both hands are skilled in doing evil; Pr 4:16
the ruler demands gifts,
the judge accepts bribes, Eze 22:12
the powerful dictate what they desire—
they all conspire together.
4The best of them is like a brier, Eze 2:6
the most upright worse than a thorn hedge.
The day of your watchmen has come,
the day God visits you.
Now is the time of their confusion. Isa 22:5
5Do not trust a neighbor;
put no confidence in a friend. Jer 9:4
Even with her who lies in your embrace
be careful of your words.
6For a son dishonors his father,
a daughter rises up against her mother,
a daughter-in-law against her mother-in-law—
a man's enemies are the members of his own household. Mt 10:35-36*

7But as for me, I watch in hope for the LORD,
I wait for God my Savior;
my God will hear me. Ps 4:3

Israel Will Rise

8Do not gloat over me, my enemy! Pr 24:17
Though I have fallen, I will rise. Ps 37:24
Though I sit in darkness,
the LORD will be my light. Isa 9:2
9Because I have sinned against him,
I will bear the LORD's wrath, La 3:39-40
until he pleads my case
and establishes my right.
He will bring me out into the light;
I will see his righteousness. Isa 46:13
10Then my enemy will see it
and will be covered with shame, Ps 35:26
she who said to me,
"Where is the LORD your God?"
My eyes will see her downfall; Isa 51:23
even now she will be trampled underfoot
like mire in the streets.

11The day for building your walls will come,
the day for extending your boundaries.
12In that day people will come to you
from Assyria and the cities of Egypt,
even from Egypt to the Euphrates
and from sea to sea
and from mountain to mountain. Isa 19:23-25
13The earth will become desolate because of its inhabitants,
as the result of their deeds. Isa 3:10-11

Prayer and Praise

14Shepherd your people with your staff, Ps 23:4
the flock of your inheritance,
which lives by itself in a forest,
in fertile pasturelands.[c]
Let them feed in Bashan and Gilead Jer 50:19
as in days long ago.

15"As in the days when you came out of Egypt,
I will show them my wonders." Ex 3:20; Ps 78:12

16Nations will see and be ashamed, Isa 26:11
deprived of all their power.
They will lay their hands on their mouths
and their ears will become deaf.
17They will lick dust like a snake,
like creatures that crawl on the ground.

[a]14 The meaning of the Hebrew for this word is uncertain. [b]16 Septuagint; Hebrew *scorn due my people* [c]14 Or *in the middle of Carmel*

They will come trembling out of their dens;
they will turn in fear to the LORD our God
and will be afraid of you.
18 Who is a God like you, Ex 8:10; 1Sa 2:2
who pardons sin and forgives the
transgression Isa 43:25; Jer 50:20
of the remnant of his inheritance? Ex 34:9
You do not stay angry forever Ps 103:9
but delight to show mercy. Jer 32:41
19 You will again have compassion on us;
you will tread our sins underfoot
and hurl all our iniquities into the depths
of the sea. Isa 43:25; Jer 31:34
20 You will be true to Jacob,
and show mercy to Abraham, Gal 3:16
as you pledged on oath to our fathers Dt 7:8
in days long ago. Ps 108:4

LIVING  INSIGHT

If our perfect Lord is gracious enough to take our worst, our ugliest, our most boring, our least successful, and forgive them, burying them in the depths of the sea, then it's high time we give each other a break.

(See Micah 7:18–19.)

INTRODUCTION

NAHUM

Next to nothing is known about Nahum. Like his three-chapter book, the man is rather obscure. And that is most unfortunate... especially because his message is so directly linked to one of the most popular of the minor prophets—Jonah. Nahum's prophecy was addressed to the descendants of the same people who had been evangelized as a result of Jonah's ministry—the people of Nineveh, the capital of the nation of Assyria. One hundred years later Nahum wrote his prophecy in which he announced judgment on the Ninevites because those who had been converted neglected to pass on the knowledge and fear of the true God to their children and grandchildren (the people of Nahum's day). Negligence led to terrible consequences. The result: Nineveh fell, never to rise again.

WRITER: *Nahum*

DATE: *c.663–609 B.C.*

PURPOSE: *To assure God's people that evil does not endure forever*

KEY THEME: *The impending doom of Nineveh, the Assyrian capital*

KEY STATEMENT: *"Woe to the city of blood... Nineveh is in ruins" (3:1,7)*

CONTEMPORARIES: *Zephaniah; Jeremiah; Habakkuk*

TIME LINE 1300BC 1200 1100 1000 900 800 700 600 500 400

Ministries of Micah and Isaiah in Judah (c.742-681 B.C.)

Exile of Israel (722 B.C.)

Nahum's ministry (c.663-612 B.C.)

Zephaniah's ministry in Judah (c.640-621 B.C.)

Book of Nahum written (c.663-609 B.C.)

Jeremiah's ministry in Judah (c.626-585 B.C.)

Habakkuk's ministry in Judah (c.612-588 B.C.)

Fall of Jerusalem (586 B.C.)

Ministries of Haggai and Zechariah (c.520-480 B.C.)

Consequences of Negligence

	THE PROPHET OF GOD	THE CHARACTER OF GOD	THE JUDGMENT OF GOD
		His majestic attributes in contrast to humanity's puny abilities	Predicted and described Justified and defended Inevitable and inescapable
	CHAPTER 1:1	*CHAPTER 1:2-15*	*CHAPTERS 2–3*
CONTENT	**Biographical**	**Theological**	**Prophetical**
EMPHASIS	**God's majestic character qualifies Him to be the Judge, the Sovereign over all.**		**Nineveh's willful and pathetic decline justifies the judgment of Almighty God.**

Anything, if it happens slowly enough, if tolerated long enough, can lead to our ruin. It happened to King Solomon. It happened to King Saul. It happened to Judas—one of Jesus' disciples. And it happens to men and women today. The severity of such an erosion is often not realized until death has come knocking on the door . . . and by then it may very well be too late to do anything.

In the book of Nahum (just three chapters long—47 verses in the English text), we witness the death of a city. Strange as it may sound, the city had sinned itself to death. But the tragedy is that it was living so well about a hundred years earlier. Just a century before Nahum, a reluctant prophet named Jonah led the greatest revival of Biblical times. The entire city of Nineveh, possibly over three-quarters of a million people in total, repented. They believed the message of Jonah, a warning from God that took Jonah eight words to speak (Jonah 3:4), and turned their hearts to the Lord.

But one hundred years later, the city of Nineveh had for all intents and purposes died. Spiritually it was doomed. Its fall was imminent and certain. When Nahum brought his message of judgment, the city didn't even kick or scream. It didn't resist or repent. It didn't attempt to argue with God or His spokesperson. It just rolled over and died.

Here's the reason: Back when Jonah witnessed to the Ninevites and they repented, that particular generation failed to pass it on. Those who had discovered the living God and had embraced and experienced His grace failed to share the story with the generations that followed. Although they had the responsibility to tell their children, grandchildren and great-grandchildren about the grace of God, they neglected to do so. We shouldn't be surprised, therefore, that the city died.

A Messenger of Doom

Nahum had the awful responsibility of announcing God's judgment on Nineveh. It would take someone with boldness and integrity of character to predict the downfall of such a powerful nation and proclaim that severe a judgment. Nahum introduces himself very briefly in the opening verse—he calls himself by name, a name that means "comfort."

We don't know much about Nahum, except for his hometown (Elkosh), but we're not even sure where it's located. His simple message was, "Nineveh will be destroyed." That's all he had to say, but like a good preacher, he took three chapters to say it! He got it said—and he said it well. Nahum, writing in passionate and vivid poetic style, blazed a trail through Nineveh with words that were sure to come back to haunt them when the Babylonians, the Medes and the Scythians came to conquer Nineveh in 612 B.C.

An Introduction to the Almighty

Nahum introduced the Almighty God by describing four attributes or character traits. First, *God is infinitely holy and just.*

The LORD is a jealous and avenging God;
the LORD takes vengeance and is filled with wrath.
The LORD takes vengeance on his foes
and maintains his wrath against his enemies (1:2).

Notice that God is jealous for the people's faithfulness. He takes sin personally, and He reveals Himself in vengeance and wrath, because He is holy and just. God sees sin as a direct attack against Himself, as opposition deliberately undertaken by those He calls "his foes."

Second, *God is awesomely all-powerful.* One of my favorite verses in all the writings of the minor prophets is Nahum 1:3. I absolutely love this verse:

The LORD is slow to anger and great in power;
the LORD will not leave the guilty unpunished.
His way is in the whirlwind and the storm,
and clouds are the dust of his feet.

Isn't that beautiful? Written as only a poet could describe it. But it isn't just good poetry—it's truth! God is unparalleled in power and undeniably revealed in the phenomena of the natural world.

I remember hearing a story years ago about Dr. Donald Barnhouse. At his church in Philadelphia, he would regularly hold an open forum, where he would stand before a microphone with his Bible in his hands and answer questions from the congregation. The house of worship would be filled. On one occasion a young student spoke from the balcony and asked, "Dr. Barnhouse, how could it be that the children of Israel could walk through the desert 40 years and never wear out their shoes and never wear out their garments?" Barnhouse responded, profoundly, with one word, "God." The student in the balcony immediately smiled and said, "Oh, now I understand." With great wisdom Barnhouse responded, "No, you don't, son. Nobody understands."

We need that reminder today. Don't think you can fully understand Almighty God. Don't think you can put Him in a box. No way. He is the living God. He is "the great King above all gods" (Psalm 95:3). And when He speaks, everybody stays quiet. When He acts, everybody gets out of His way.

Third, *God is not only great, He is also good.* Praise His name! He is omnipotent. He is so far above us. And yet He relates to us in a personal way. He loves us. Nahum testifies that "the LORD is good" (1:7). In fact, He is a refuge to those who are in trouble. He knows everyone who will take refuge in Him. God opens His arms to those running for refuge. He stands ready to take in those who are afraid of life and don't know quite how to make sense of it. As the chorus of worship states it so simply and so profoundly, "God is so good, He's so good to me."

Fourth, *God is truth.* His word can be trusted. What He says He'll do, He will do. Therefore, He must be taken seriously. What He promises He fulfills. The Ninevites certainly found it out. Through Nahum, this was God's judgment on them: "You will have no descendants to bear your name. I will destroy the carved images and cast idols that are in the temple of your gods. I will prepare your grave, for you are vile" (1:14). That's what we would call a direct confrontation! Because God is truth, He always tells the truth—even though others may not want to hear it. In effect, He told the wicked nation of Nineveh, "Nineveh, you are contemptible. You are wrong. You follow images that were made by humans, and I will take action against you. Your doom is sure. You cannot escape My judgment." God is truth, and He will not hold back declaring the truth, even when it hurts.

Prophets like Nahum teach us about the awesome character of God. You don't read the prophets, then casually walk away unaffected. You walk away in silent awe. You take God seriously. Each prophet, in his own way and in his own time, broadcast the message loud and clear: Don't mess around with God!

So complete and effective was the judgment of God on Nineveh that the existence of the city disappeared for ages. In fact, some critics have even argued there may never have been a Nineveh. I tell you, when God did His work, it was thorough and conclusive. And the judgment was severe!

Lessons From Nahum

We can glean at least one powerful and lasting lesson from Nahum. *We must take God seriously because of His awesome character.* Nineveh didn't do that. At one time Nineveh's citizens listened to God speak through Jonah and responded in repentance and reverence. But time passed, and the people forgot. They reverted to their evil, vicious patterns of living and got back to business as usual—with not one solitary thought about the God who is King above all other gods. And they would pay the ultimate price. God's patience would run out, and destruction would come.

An awareness of God's almighty power demands that we respond with the highest respect and reverence. He is King of kings and Lord of lords (Revelation 17:14; 19:16). There is no other like our God—infinitely great beyond our ability to comprehend, and yet One who comes near in love to care for those who trust in Him (1:7)! Will we hear Nahum's call to us to take God seriously in our day, and will we respond with the commitment of our lives?

The Character of God **Chapter 1**

The message proclaimed by Nahum had to be tough enough to grab the attention of those living in a fast-moving urban environment. Nineveh, the capital of the Assyrian nation, was as sophisticated and secular as any city in the Old Testament era. The only way this message had a chance of turning the heads and touching the hearts of these resistant people would be if it were spoken directly from the throne room of heaven . . . and it was!

Nahum was careful to tell the people that this message came from the Lord of heaven. In the entire first chapter Nahum described the Lord God and established His perfect right to judge. As the Lord's majestic attributes were extolled, the puny abilities of humanity grew pale in comparison. Nahum taught that the Lord is holy, just, omnipotent, good and trustworthy, and therefore He holds the course of human history in His hands. God is majestic beyond description and has every right to rule over and judge the earth.

1 An oracle concerning Nineveh. The book of the vision of Nahum the Elkoshite. Jnh 1:2

The LORD's Anger Against Nineveh

2The LORD is a jealous and avenging God;
the LORD takes vengeance and is filled with wrath. Dt 32:41; Ps 94:1
The LORD takes vengeance on his foes
and maintains his wrath against his enemies.
3The LORD is slow to anger and great in power;
the LORD will not leave the guilty unpunished. Ex 34:7
His way is in the whirlwind and the storm,
and clouds are the dust of his feet. Ps 104:3

LIVING  **INSIGHT**

Life is literally filled with God-appointed storms. We all experience them; we all need them. The massive blows and shattering blasts (not to mention the little, constant irritations) smooth us and humble us and force us to submit to the script God has written and the role He has chosen for us.

(See Nahum 1:2–3.)

4He rebukes the sea and dries it up; Ex 14:22
he makes all the rivers run dry.
Bashan and Carmel wither Isa 33:9
and the blossoms of Lebanon fade.
5The mountains quake before him Ex 19:18
and the hills melt away. Mic 1:4
The earth trembles at his presence,
the world and all who live in it. Eze 38:20

6Who can withstand his indignation? Ps 130:3
Who can endure his fierce anger? Mal 3:2
His wrath is poured out like fire; Jer 10:10
the rocks are shattered before him. 1Ki 19:11

7The LORD is good, Jer 33:11
a refuge in times of trouble. Jer 17:17
He cares for those who trust in him, Ps 1:6
8 but with an overwhelming flood
he will make an end of ⌊Nineveh⌋;
he will pursue his foes into darkness.

9Whatever they plot against the LORD
he[a] will bring to an end;
trouble will not come a second time.
10They will be entangled among thorns 2Sa 23:6
and drunk from their wine;
they will be consumed like dry stubble.[b]
11From you, ⌊O Nineveh,⌋ has one come forth
who plots evil against the LORD
and counsels wickedness.

12This is what the LORD says:

"Although they have allies and are numerous,
they will be cut off and pass away. Isa 10:34
Although I have afflicted you, ⌊O Judah,⌋
I will afflict you no more. Isa 54:6-8; La 3:31-32
13Now I will break their yoke from your neck
and tear your shackles away." Ps 107:14

14The LORD has given a command concerning you, ⌊Nineveh⌋:
"You will have no descendants to bear your name. Isa 14:22
I will destroy the carved images and cast idols
that are in the temple of your gods.
I will prepare your grave, Eze 32:22-23
for you are vile."

15Look, there on the mountains,
the feet of one who brings good news,
who proclaims peace! Isa 52:7
Celebrate your festivals, O Judah, Lev 23:2-4
and fulfill your vows.
No more will the wicked invade you; Isa 52:1
they will be completely destroyed.

The Judgment of God **Chapters 2–3**

In these chapters the judgment of God is clearly declared. As you read the opening verses you notice that God did not call the people to repentance. The time for a change of heart was past. Judgment was rapidly advancing. The alarm was sounded, with words to this effect: "Nineveh, your sins have caught up with you and judgment is inevitable and inescapable." Nahum defended the righteousness of God's decision to judge. Nineveh was saturated with sin, for her people were corrupt. They thought the 100-foot walls around the city could protect them from any invasion or other consequences for their

[a]9 Or *What do you foes plot against the LORD? / He*

[b]10 The meaning of the Hebrew for this verse is uncertain.

evil acts. But the Maker of heaven and earth is not stopped by human walls of stone or by the best-laid plans of deceitful human hearts. The Ninevites' pride and sinfulness condemned them, and the judgment of God came down.

Nineveh to Fall

2 An attacker advances against you,
⌊Nineveh⌋. Jer 51:20
Guard the fortress,
watch the road,
brace yourselves,
marshal all your strength!

2The LORD will restore the splendor of Jacob
like the splendor of Israel,
though destroyers have laid them waste
and have ruined their vines.

3The shields of his soldiers are red;
the warriors are clad in scarlet. Eze 23:14-15
The metal on the chariots flashes
on the day they are made ready;
the spears of pine are brandished.[a]
4The chariots storm through the streets, Jer 4:13
rushing back and forth through the squares.
They look like flaming torches;
they dart about like lightning.

5He summons his picked troops,
yet they stumble on their way. Jer 46:12
They dash to the city wall;
the protective shield is put in place.
6The river gates are thrown open Na 3:13
and the palace collapses.
7It is decreed[b] that ⌊the city⌋
be exiled and carried away.
Its slave girls moan like doves Isa 59:11
and beat upon their breasts. Isa 32:12
8Nineveh is like a pool,
and its water is draining away.
"Stop! Stop!" they cry,
but no one turns back.
9Plunder the silver!
Plunder the gold!
The supply is endless,
the wealth from all its treasures!
10She is pillaged, plundered, stripped!
Hearts melt, knees give way,
bodies tremble, every face grows pale.

11Where now is the lions' den, Isa 5:29
the place where they fed their young,
where the lion and lioness went,
and the cubs, with nothing to fear?
12The lion killed enough for his cubs Jer 51:34
and strangled the prey for his mate,
filling his lairs with the kill Jer 4:7
and his dens with the prey. Isa 37:18

13"I am against you," Jer 21:13; Na 3:5
declares the LORD Almighty.
"I will burn up your chariots in smoke, Ps 46:9
and the sword will devour your young lions.
I will leave you no prey on the earth.
The voices of your messengers
will no longer be heard." Mic 5:6

Woe to Nineveh

3 Woe to the city of blood, Eze 22:2; Mic 3:10
full of lies, Ps 12:2
full of plunder,
never without victims!
2The crack of whips,
the clatter of wheels,
galloping horses
and jolting chariots!
3Charging cavalry,
flashing swords
and glittering spears!
Many casualties,
piles of dead,
bodies without number,
people stumbling over the corpses—
4all because of the wanton lust of a harlot,
alluring, the mistress of sorceries, Isa 47:9
who enslaved nations by her prostitution
and peoples by her witchcraft.

5"I am against you," declares the LORD
Almighty. Na 2:13
"I will lift your skirts over your face. Jer 13:22
I will show the nations your nakedness Isa 47:3
and the kingdoms your shame.
6I will pelt you with filth, Job 9:31
I will treat you with contempt Jer 51:37
and make you a spectacle. Isa 14:16
7All who see you will flee from you and say,
'Nineveh is in ruins—who will mourn for her?' Jer 15:5
Where can I find anyone to comfort you?"

8Are you better than Thebes,[c] Jer 46:25; Am 6:2
situated on the Nile, Isa 19:6-9
with water around her?
The river was her defense,
the waters her wall.
9Cush[d] and Egypt were her boundless
strength; 2Ch 12:3
Put and Libya were among her allies.
10Yet she was taken captive Isa 20:4
and went into exile.
Her infants were dashed to pieces Isa 13:16
at the head of every street.
Lots were cast for her nobles, Job 6:27
and all her great men were put in chains.

[a]3 Hebrew; Septuagint and Syriac / *the horsemen rush to and fro*
[b]7 The meaning of the Hebrew for this word is uncertain.
[c]8 Hebrew *No Amon*
[d]9 That is, the upper Nile region

[11]You too will become drunk; Isa 49:26
you will go into hiding Isa 2:10
and seek refuge from the enemy.

[12]All your fortresses are like fig trees
with their first ripe fruit;
when they are shaken,
the figs fall into the mouth of the eater.
[13]Look at your troops—
they are all women! Isa 19:16; Jer 50:37
The gates of your land Na 2:6
are wide open to your enemies;
fire has consumed their bars. Isa 45:2

[14]Draw water for the siege, 2Ch 32:4
strengthen your defenses! Na 2:1
Work the clay,
tread the mortar,
repair the brickwork!
[15]There the fire will devour you;
the sword will cut you down
and, like grasshoppers, consume you.
Multiply like grasshoppers,
multiply like locusts! Joel 1:4
[16]You have increased the number of your merchants
till they are more than the stars of the sky,
but like locusts they strip the land Ex 10:13
and then fly away.
[17]Your guards are like locusts, Jer 51:27
your officials like swarms of locusts
that settle in the walls on a cold day—
but when the sun appears they fly away,
and no one knows where.

[18]O king of Assyria, your shepherds[a] slumber;
your nobles lie down to rest. Isa 56:10
Your people are scattered on the mountains
with no one to gather them.
[19]Nothing can heal your wound; Mic 1:9
your injury is fatal.
Everyone who hears the news about you
claps his hands at your fall, La 2:15; Zep 2:15
for who has not felt
your endless cruelty? Isa 37:18

[a]18 Or *rulers*

INTRODUCTION

HABAKKUK

The Book called the Bible may date from ancient times, but it is so relevant to us today. There is no doubt that it is living and active, sharper than a double-edged sword (see Hebrews 4:12). The book of Habakkuk is a perfect example of that enduring Biblical relevance. Time and again we find that we see ourselves and our times in the verses of Habakkuk! The ancient prophet, witnessing the evils around him, wrestled with God's seemingly indifferent attitude. It seemed to be a contradiction to His holy nature. But when the Lord revealed His plan, an even greater problem arose. So Habakkuk decided to get alone and wait for his mind to clear. God gave him a fresh vision . . . hope beyond his despair, which resulted in a time of meaningful prayer as Habakkuk praised the awesome Lord of heaven and earth.

WRITER: *Habakkuk*

DATE: *c.610–605 B.C.*

PURPOSE: *To assure God's people that evil does not endure forever*

KEY THEME: *Wrestling with God over His unfathomable ways*

KEY VERSES: *2:1-4*

STYLE: *Literary dialogue between the prophet and the Lord*

TIME LINE 1300BC 1200 1100 1000 900 800 700 600 500 400

Ministries of Micah and Isaiah in Judah (c.742-681 B.C.)

Exile of Israel (722 B.C.)

Nahum's ministry (c.663-612 B.C.)

Zephaniah's ministry in Judah (c.640-621 B.C.)

Jeremiah's ministry in Judah (c.626-585 B.C.)

Habakkuk's ministry in Judah (c.612-588 B.C.)

Book of Habakkuk written (c.610-605 B.C.)

Fall of Jerusalem (586 B.C.)

Wrestling, Waiting, Praying and Praising

	THE BURDEN	THE WATCH	THE VISION	THE PRAYER
	WRESTLINGS: God's silence Human evil God's character The Lord: How long? Why?		THE LORD REPLIED Record the vision! Wait for it! Woe to the Babylonians!	THE PROPHET KNEELS: Lord, I've heard ...I stand in awe ...I wait ...I praise ...I rejoice
	CHAPTER 1	*CHAPTER 2:1*	*CHAPTER 2:2-20*	*CHAPTER 3*
CONFESSION	*"Lord... You confuse me."*	*"Lord... I wait for You."*		*"Lord... I praise You."*
REACTION	**Horizontal**	**Vertical**		
DIRECTION	**Looking around and worrying**	**Looking in and listening**		**Looking up and believing**

The first time I taught the book of Habakkuk was back in 1969. To illustrate how unknown this book really is, I decided I would carry out an unusual experiment. (I'd always wanted to conduct a street interview about the Bible.) I asked a simple question to various people I met in my normal routine of a week: at the dry cleaners, restaurants, service stations, hospitals. I asked everyone the same question: "What does Habakkuk mean to you?"

I got some amazing answers. A man at a service station frowned and thought for a few moments and said, "I think it's a word spelled backwards." A secretary told me she thought it sounded like a Jewish holiday. A waitress said it was probably a village in Vietnam. A teenager told me it was a new horror movie that had just come out. One merchant thought I must be a salesman selling a product, an abacus—he also told me he didn't want one. Another person was convinced it referred to a game, though he had never played it. The classic answer came from an older gentleman who grimaced, stared at me, then answered very seriously, "I think it is a disease of the lower back."

Those remarkable responses hint to us that not very many people know what Habakkuk is all about. It's a challenge just to know how to pronounce the name, to say nothing of understanding what's in the book. I'm going to tip my hand and tell you that when it comes to the 12 minor prophets, Habakkuk is my man! I identify with the struggles he experienced. I also appreciate how the book seems to teach itself. I would say to all who decide to study and teach this book, we simply need to get out of God's way and let Him communicate how meaningful it really is.

The Setting of Habakkuk

Just as every song is born in a certain context, every book of the Bible is born out of a certain historical womb. The prophecy of Habakkuk is no exception. Times were hard in the days of Habakkuk. Judah, his nation, was a nation that boldly and unashamedly rebelled against the Lord God. The prophet's peers lived as though there were no God.

Right around this time there was a sleeping giant arousing—Babylon, by name. Babylon was a godless nation just coming into its own. We think we see evil nations and ruthless military might today. We have seen nothing like the ancient Babylonians! They were a wicked people with an insensitive spirit. When they came into villages, they literally raped their way through. They had no conscience, and they showed no compassion on their enemies.

As Habakkuk, a sensitive man with a tender heart for God, looked on and saw all of Judah's wickedness and the increasing strength of Babylon, he wondered, "Where in the world could God be? How could God stand back and let His people become more and more wicked without stepping in and bringing the nation to its knees as in days past?"

The Burden of the Prophet

The book begins with the carrying of a burden, which is a possible meaning for the word "oracle" (Hebrew *massa*) in verse 1. A heavy weight rested on Habakkuk's shoulders. He had a number of unanswered questions, a number of complaints to register. (By the way, I should point out that he is the only minor prophet who never addressed the people directly. In other words, his prophecy is a written dialogue, an interchange, between the prophet and his Lord. It's like a journal in which he asked his questions and wrote his complaints, then recorded God's answers. It's a book that began with a sob but ended with a song.)

Habakkuk's burden was this:

How long, O LORD, must I call for help,
but you do not listen?
Or cry out to you, "Violence!"
but you do not save?
Why do you make me look at injustice?
Why do you tolerate wrong?
Destruction and violence are before me;
there is strife, and conflict abounds (1:2–3).

Habakkuk had come to some sad conclusions about his time—four of them altogether: First, "the law is paralyzed"; second, "justice never prevails"; third, "the wicked hem in the righteous"; and fourth, "justice is perverted" (1:4). And all Habakkuk could think was, "Why does the evil in Judah go unpunished?"

It is interesting to note that God never told Habakkuk why He tolerated wrong or how long before He would give an answer. Habakkuk looked at his world and said, in effect, "This nation reeks, Lord! And if You are the Holy God of heaven, how can You stand back and let this condition continue? Lord, step in. Give me some help. I'm seeing my country go down the tubes, and I cannot tell where You are. Do You care even a little bit?" Oh, Habakkuk's burden was heavy!

To put it simply, Habakkuk said, "God, what are You going to do?" God answered, "You wouldn't believe it if I told you." Habakkuk said, "Tell me. I'll believe it." God said, "No, you wouldn't." The prophet said, "Yes, I would!" So the Lord informed Habakkuk, "I'm going to use the Babylonians to judge My people." The prophet said, "I can't believe it." Look at Habakkuk's second complaint:

O LORD, are you not from everlasting?
My God, my Holy One, we will not die.
O LORD, you have appointed them to execute judgment;
O Rock, you have ordained them to punish (1:12).

I love this dialogue. It reminds us so much of us, doesn't it? "Lord, aren't You going to come to my rescue? Aren't You going to deal with this situation? Look how bad it is! Now come on, prove Your character." And then when He begins to solve our problem in a way we didn't expect, we reply, "Oh, I can't believe You're going to do *that*."

Habakkuk said, in effect, "God, You're my Holy One. We're Judah. We're Your chosen people, remember? We're promised an eternal destiny. You're planning to use the Babylonians? Lord, Lord, You've established *them* to correct *us*? They're more godless than *we* are! Your eyes are too pure to approve of such evil."

Watch and Wait

So by now totally confused, Habakkuk made the most significant decision of his entire ministry. He decided to stand back and to wait and to watch. This is the pivot upon which the book is hinged: "I will stand at my watch and station myself on the ramparts" (2:1)

Habakkuk was confused. He was uncertain. He didn't know what to say to the people any more. He didn't know how to pray. He was concerned about giving an unreliable answer or being vague, because, as the saying goes, "a mist in the pulpit puts a fog in the pew." If he were not confident and secure, the people to whom he ministered would definitely be uncertain.

We are perhaps most effective when we deliberately decide to stop and wait as we rest in our God. When we commit to stop the complaining. When we agree to stop the wrestling, stop the fighting. When we cease the inner churning. That's what Habakkuk did. He made that climactic decision: "I'm going to wait and see what God says to me."

I can testify that before every significant decision in my adult life, there has been a time when I have had no other alternative but to wait on God . . . because His answer did not come according to my schedule. He forced me to step aside—sometimes to take a trip to be alone, to pull away for a day or two or even more. Sometimes I needed to wait for Him to gently blow away the fog, to quiet my spirit. I can recall a two-and-a-half-year period of waiting. It was occasionally excruciating . . . and at other times, ecstatic. When the Lord finally answered, how sweet it was!

It is terribly important when you read verse 2 of chapter 2 that you do not miss the significance of the first word—*Then*. "Then the LORD replied" . . . When? After Habakkuk waited. After he determined to stand still and let God's timing run its course. *Then* God answered.

God answered him and said a number of things that Habakkuk needed to hear. (Isn't it amazing that in our frustration we so often feel the need to inform God of what's going on and let Him know about the situation?) God knew all about the Babylonians and He knew exactly what He was going to do. He spelled out for Habakkuk a vision that described not only the pride and power of the Babylonians but their sure doom. He knew the Babylonian situation, and He knew that their kingdom would crumble before Him.

He knows your enemies too. He knows the frustration you're experiencing. He knows why. He knows how long. He knows what impact your troubling situation has and will have in your life. And He knows the depths to which you may have to go spiritually before He will lift you up. You don't have to inform Him of it. Just keep standing still before His sovereign will. And hear His word of comfort to you through Habakkuk—that you may trust in God's loving providence regardless of circumstances (3:17–19).

Lessons From Habakkuk

Three lasting lessons come to mind when I review the wonderful little book of Habakkuk. First, *God can handle all of our questions, but He may answer only a few.* You can ask Him all the questions you wish. You can bring Him all the complaints you have. But please know this: He may not, in fact, very likely will not, give you answers to all your questions—but He will give you Himself.

Second, *the bottom line of faith is not to silence all of our doubts so that we never struggle again, but it's to make us sure of God and confident of His care.* Peace-producing confidence and an unwavering faith in Him are more important than our own ability to fully understand all that happens in and around us.

Third, *waiting strengthens our patience and lengthens our perspective.* I have discovered in my years on earth that the short view is usually the false view of life. First impressions are sometimes wrong impressions. Initial impressions of the way God is working and why He does what He does can be incorrect ones. So in waiting, we have our perspective lengthened as we have our patience deepened.

And so? May God teach us anew the value of waiting on Him and trusting in Him, no matter what!

The Burden **Chapter 1**

In the first chapter Habakkuk spoke with great intensity and emotion. He carried a heavy burden in his heart, and he lifted it to God honestly and without apology. His prophetic complaint was focused on two questions, both asked in the opening verses of this chapter: "How long?" and "Why?" Habakkuk wanted to know when God was going to do something about the rebellion and sinfulness of the nation of Judah . . . and why He was allowing sin to intensify and go unchecked.

The Lord did not give a specific date when He would act or an answer to Habakkuk's "why," but He did tell the prophet that judgment on Judah would come at the hands of the Babylonians—news that was almost unbelievable because that dreaded pagan nation was fierce, violent and godless. The prophet was confused, knowing that his people would have a hard time comprehending why God would use a nation more wicked than they as His instrument of judgment. However, whether they understood or not, judgment was coming, and Habakkuk's heart was heavy.

1 The oracle that Habakkuk the prophet received. Na 1:1

Habakkuk's Complaint

2How long, O LORD, must I call for help,
but you do not listen? Ps 13:1-2; 22:1-2
Or cry out to you, "Violence!"
but you do not save? Jer 14:9
3Why do you make me look at injustice?
Why do you tolerate wrong? Job 9:23
Destruction and violence are before me; Jer 20:8
there is strife, and conflict abounds. Ps 55:9
4Therefore the law is paralyzed, Ps 119:126
and justice never prevails.
The wicked hem in the righteous,
so that justice is perverted. Isa 5:20; Eze 9:9

The LORD's Answer

5"Look at the nations and watch—
and be utterly amazed. Isa 29:9
For I am going to do something in your days
that you would not believe,
even if you were told. Ac 13:41*
6I am raising up the Babylonians,[a] 2Ki 24:2
that ruthless and impetuous people,
who sweep across the whole earth
to seize dwelling places not their own.
7They are a feared and dreaded people; Isa 18:7
they are a law to themselves
and promote their own honor.
8Their horses are swifter than leopards, Jer 4:13
fiercer than wolves at dusk.
Their cavalry gallops headlong;
their horsemen come from afar.
They fly like a vulture swooping to devour;
9 they all come bent on violence.
Their hordes[b] advance like a desert wind
and gather prisoners like sand. Hab 2:5
10They deride kings
and scoff at rulers. 2Ch 36:6
They laugh at all fortified cities;
they build earthen ramps and capture them.
11Then they sweep past like the wind and go
on— Jer 4:11-12
guilty men, whose own strength is their
god." Da 4:30

Habakkuk's Second Complaint

12O LORD, are you not from everlasting? Ge 21:33
My God, my Holy One, we will not die.
O LORD, you have appointed them to execute
judgment; Isa 10:6
O Rock, you have ordained them to
punish. Ex 33:22
13Your eyes are too pure to look on evil; Ps 18:26
you cannot tolerate wrong. La 3:34-36
Why then do you tolerate the treacherous?
Why are you silent while the wicked
swallow up those more righteous than
themselves? Job 21:7
14You have made men like fish in the sea,
like sea creatures that have no ruler.
15The wicked foe pulls all of them up with
hooks, Isa 19:8
he catches them in his net, Jer 16:16
he gathers them up in his dragnet;
and so he rejoices and is glad.
16Therefore he sacrifices to his net
and burns incense to his dragnet, Jer 44:8
for by his net he lives in luxury
and enjoys the choicest food.
17Is he to keep on emptying his net,
destroying nations without mercy? Isa 14:6

The Vision **Chapter 2**

Habakkuk decided to do the hardest thing a prophet could do: Wait. When he did, God revealed His plan. In that vision to the prophet, God called him to do three things. First, he was told to write down clearly what the Lord had to say to the people, so that everyone could read the words and recognize what would happen. Second, God told him to wait for His perfect (though strange) plan to unfold. God's word would be fulfilled, even though it would take time. Finally, God told His prophet to tell it straight. Judgment *would* come at the hands of the Babylonians, even if Habakkuk and his people didn't understand why. God let Habakkuk know that He was perfectly aware of how sinful the Babylonians were. Yet they were His chosen instrument of destruction. I can imagine Habakkuk's confusion as he thought, "Go figure! The Babylonians? And You say You're holy, Lord?" There are times we simply *cannot* understand God's master plan!

[a]6 Or *Chaldeans* [b]9 The meaning of the Hebrew for this word is uncertain.

2 I will stand at my watch Isa 21:8
and station myself on the ramparts; Ps 48:13
I will look to see what he will say to me,
and what answer I am to give to this
complaint.[a] Ps 5:3

The LORD's Answer

[2]Then the LORD replied:

"Write down the revelation Rev 1:19
and make it plain on tablets
so that a herald[b] may run with it.
[3]For the revelation awaits an appointed time;
it speaks of the end Da 8:17; 10:14
and will not prove false.
Though it linger, wait for it; Ps 27:14
it[c] will certainly come and will not delay.

[4]"See, he is puffed up;
his desires are not upright—
but the righteous will live by his faith[d]—

LIVING  **INSIGHT**

There is a very delicate line between faith and presumption. On the surface both appear daring, courageous and impressive. Underneath, however, one is met with God's approval while the other incites His wrath and prompts His judgment. Are you waiting for God's leading today? Good for you! If the light is red or even yellow, you're wise to let Him hold you back. When it turns green, you'll know it.

(See Habakkuk 2:4.)

[5]indeed, wine betrays him; Pr 20:1
he is arrogant and never at rest. Isa 2:11
Because he is as greedy as the grave[e]
and like death is never satisfied, Pr 27:20
he gathers to himself all the nations
and takes captive all the peoples. Hab 1:9

[6]"Will not all of them taunt him with ridicule
and scorn, saying, Isa 14:4

" 'Woe to him who piles up stolen goods
and makes himself wealthy by extortion!
How long must this go on?'
[7]Will not your debtors[f] suddenly arise?
Will they not wake up and make you
tremble?
Then you will become their victim. Pr 29:1
[8]Because you have plundered many nations,
the peoples who are left will plunder you.
For you have shed man's blood;
you have destroyed lands and cities and
everyone in them. Eze 39:10

[9]"Woe to him who builds his realm by unjust
gain Jer 22:13
to set his nest on high,
to escape the clutches of ruin!
[10]You have plotted the ruin of many peoples,
shaming your own house and forfeiting
your life. Na 3:6
[11]The stones of the wall will cry out, Jos 24:27
and the beams of the woodwork will echo
it.

[12]"Woe to him who builds a city with
bloodshed Mic 3:10
and establishes a town by crime!
[13]Has not the LORD Almighty determined
that the people's labor is only fuel for the
fire, Isa 50:11
that the nations exhaust themselves for
nothing? Isa 47:13
[14]For the earth will be filled with the knowledge
of the glory of the LORD, Nu 14:21
as the waters cover the sea. Isa 11:9

[15]"Woe to him who gives drink to his
neighbors,
pouring it from the wineskin till they are
drunk,
so that he can gaze on their naked bodies.
[16]You will be filled with shame instead of glory.
Now it is your turn! Drink and be
exposed[g]! La 4:21
The cup from the LORD's right hand is coming
around to you, Isa 51:22
and disgrace will cover your glory.
[17]The violence you have done to Lebanon will
overwhelm you, Jer 51:35
and your destruction of animals will terrify
you. Jer 50:15
For you have shed man's blood;
you have destroyed lands and cities and
everyone in them.

[18]"Of what value is an idol, since a man has
carved it? Jer 5:21
Or an image that teaches lies?
For he who makes it trusts in his own
creation;
he makes idols that cannot speak. Ps 115:4-5
[19]Woe to him who says to wood, 'Come to life!'
Or to lifeless stone, 'Wake up!' 1Ki 18:27
Can it give guidance?
It is covered with gold and silver; Jer 10:4
there is no breath in it. Hos 4:12
[20]But the LORD is in his holy temple; Ps 11:4
let all the earth be silent before him."

[a]1 Or *and what to answer when I am rebuked* [b]2 Or *so that whoever reads it* [c]3 Or *Though he linger, wait for him; / he* [d]4 Or *faithfulness* [e]5 Hebrew *Sheol* [f]7 Or *creditors* [g]16 Masoretic Text; Dead Sea Scrolls, Aquila, Vulgate and Syriac (see also Septuagint) *and stagger*

The Prayer Chapter 3

This closing chapter could be called a song as easily as a prayer. It is a wonderful anthem of "glory, laud and honor!" It begins with an acknowledgment of God's greatness and moves to a request for God to renew His deeds among the nation, to make known His glory, and to remember mercy and grace. Finally, this glorious hymn recalls God's mighty saving acts of old and concludes with a powerful expression of confidence and trust (3:16–19). By the end of the song Habakkuk's whole outlook had changed. Although his circumstances were the same, his attitude had been transformed because he had met the God who never changes. There is no question that prayer changes things, especially us!

Habakkuk's Prayer

3 A prayer of Habakkuk the prophet. On *shigionoth.*[a]

2LORD, I have heard of your fame; Ps 44:1
I stand in awe of your deeds, O LORD.
Renew them in our day, Ps 85:6
in our time make them known;
in wrath remember mercy. Isa 54:8

3God came from Teman,
the Holy One from Mount Paran. *Selah*[b]
His glory covered the heavens Ps 8:1
and his praise filled the earth. Ps 48:10
4His splendor was like the sunrise; Isa 18:4
rays flashed from his hand,
where his power was hidden. Job 9:6
5Plague went before him;
pestilence followed his steps.
6He stood, and shook the earth;
he looked, and made the nations tremble.
The ancient mountains crumbled Ps 46:2
and the age-old hills collapsed. Ps 114:1-6
His ways are eternal. Ge 21:33
7I saw the tents of Cushan in distress,
the dwellings of Midian in anguish. Ex 15:14

8Were you angry with the rivers, O LORD?
Was your wrath against the streams?
Did you rage against the sea
when you rode with your horses
and your victorious chariots? Ps 68:17
9You uncovered your bow,
you called for many arrows. *Selah*
You split the earth with rivers;
10 the mountains saw you and writhed.
Torrents of water swept by;
the deep roared Ps 98:7
and lifted its waves on high. Ps 93:3

11Sun and moon stood still in the heavens
at the glint of your flying arrows, Ps 18:14
at the lightning of your flashing spear.
12In wrath you strode through the earth
and in anger you threshed the nations.
13You came out to deliver your people, Ps 20:6
to save your anointed one. 2Sa 23:1
You crushed the leader of the land of
wickedness, Ps 110:6
you stripped him from head to foot. *Selah*
14With his own spear you pierced his head
when his warriors stormed out to scatter
us, Jdg 7:22
gloating as though about to devour
the wretched who were in hiding. Ps 64:2-5
15You trampled the sea with your horses,
churning the great waters. Ex 15:8; Ps 77:19

16I heard and my heart pounded,
my lips quivered at the sound;
decay crept into my bones,
and my legs trembled.
Yet I will wait patiently for the day of calamity
to come on the nation invading us.
17Though the fig tree does not bud
and there are no grapes on the vines,
though the olive crop fails
and the fields produce no food, Joel 1:10-12,18
though there are no sheep in the pen
and no cattle in the stalls, Jer 5:17
18yet I will rejoice in the LORD, Isa 61:10; Php 4:4
I will be joyful in God my Savior. Lk 1:47

19The Sovereign LORD is my strength; Dt 33:29
he makes my feet like the feet of a deer,
he enables me to go on the heights. 2Sa 22:34

For the director of music. On my stringed instruments.

[a]1 Probably a literary or musical term [b]3 A word of uncertain meaning; possibly a musical term; also in verses 9 and 13

Introduction

ZEPHANIAH

The men who spoke for God during the ninth, eighth, seventh and sixth centuries before Christ were remarkable mixtures of severity and compassion. These tough-and-tender prophets were among the most respected and yet *hated* people of all times. Such was Zephaniah, a prophet who was a descendant of the royal line and probably a man who had greater influence on King Josiah than either Nahum or Jeremiah. It is impressive that this man did not compromise his convictions even though he had access to the king—much like the prophet Isaiah—and was a familiar figure in the royal courts of his day. With a simple yet forceful style, Zephaniah announced certain judgment during the first major section of his book, then he tenderly predicted relief and God's best blessings on His people. Through it all, he emerged as another choice prophet in a long line of tough and tender men.

WRITER: *Zephaniah*

DATE: *c.635–630 B.C.*

PURPOSE: *To stir the people of Judah to repentance*

KEY THEME: *Judgment before joy*

KEY VERSES: *1:14; 3:15-17*

CONTEMPORARIES: *Nahum, Jeremiah, Habakkuk*

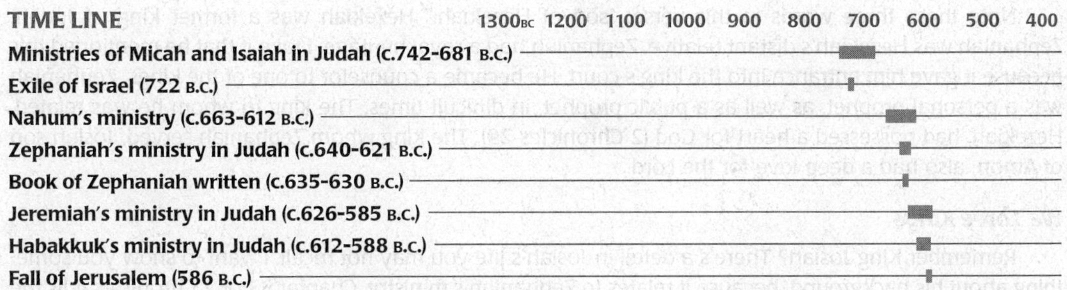

Bright Light in a Dark Day

	JUDGMENT AND DOOM			JOY AND DELIVERANCE
	"I will sweep away everything from the face of the earth," declares the Lord (1:2).			
INTRODUCTION (1:1)	DIVINE JUDGMENT ON JUDAH	INVITATION	SURE DOOM OF NATIONS	KINGDOM PROMISES TO REMNANT
	CHAPTER 1:2-18	*CHAPTER 2:1-3*	*CHAPTERS 2:4–3:7*	*CHAPTER 3:8-20*
SCOPE	**Judah**		**Nations**	**Remnant**
SUBJECT	**Sin**	**Hope**	**Desolation**	**Restoration**
KEY WORDS	***"The day of the Lord"***	***"Seek"***	***"Woe"***	***"The Lord is with you"***
RELEVANCE	**Judgment and doom are certain unless there is repentance before God. Only then can there be hope and restoration.**			

We often know more about the times in which the Old Testament prophets lived than we do about the prophets themselves. Most of the prophets give very little information about themselves beyond a statement of their name and perhaps their hometown. Some give a very brief family history. Some we know came from country towns and ordinary backgrounds. All served their God faithfully and passionately.

The prophet named Zephaniah gives us an interesting autobiographical glimpse into his identity. While education or family background didn't qualify prophets for the job—God's call did—Zephaniah came from an impressive family, and his prophecy began with a statement of his ancestry. He was from a royal line. There's a reason he revealed this information. Look at his opening statement:

> *The word of the Lord that came to Zephaniah son of Cushi, the son of Gedaliah, the son of Amariah, the son of Hezekiah, during the reign of Josiah son of Amon king of Judah (1:1).*

Note these three words in this verse: "son of Hezekiah." Hezekiah was a former king of Judah; Zephaniah was Hezekiah's distant relative. Zephaniah had a royal heritage. I take it that he mentioned this because it gave him entrance into the king's court. He became a counselor to one of the kings. Zephaniah was a personal prophet, as well as a public prophet, in difficult times. The king to whom he was related, Hezekiah, had possessed a heart for God (2 Chronicles 29). The king whom Zephaniah served, Josiah son of Amon, also had a deep love for the Lord.

We Three Kings

Remember King Josiah? There's a detail in Josiah's life you may not recall. I want to show you something about his background, because it relates to Zephaniah's ministry. Chapter 33 of 2 Chronicles tells the story of King Manasseh, who began his wicked reign when he was only 12 years old and ruled for 55 years. Manasseh brought godlessness to a new level. He did all the evil you could possibly imagine. He practiced child sacrifice and encouraged blatant idolatry and was involved in the occult like no other king before him. He built numerous high places where the people burnt incense to pagan gods. Whatever he planned or carried out was of a wicked nature. When Manasseh died, his son Amon ruled in his place.

Amon's son was Josiah, the king in the days of Zephaniah. The author of 2 Chronicles recorded these words: "Amon was twenty-two years old when he became king, and he reigned in Jerusalem two years" (33:21). Why a reign of only two years? Because he was assassinated. In fact, Amon was assassinated in his own house, the very place where Josiah was being raised. The Chronicler summarized the sad story:

> *He did evil in the eyes of the LORD, as his father Manasseh had done. Amon worshiped and offered sacrifices to all the idols Manasseh had made. But unlike his father, Manasseh, he did not humble himself before the LORD; Amon increased his guilt. Amon's officials conspired against him and assassinated him in his palace (2 Chronicles 33:22–24).*

Chapter 34 of 2 Chronicles begins with the account of the reign of Josiah, who was only eight when his father was killed. By the time Josiah was 16 he began to seek Almighty God, and when he was 20 he began to tear down the altars and smash the idols. How come? Why did young Josiah have a heart for God? If you study his life you'll see that he had a deep commitment to the Word of God, the Book of the Law, which had been found in the temple during the period of Josiah's reforms.

I also want to suggest that Josiah was a friend of Zephaniah. The prophet Zephaniah was a contemporary of King Josiah. Look again at the first verse of Zephaniah's book: "During the reign of Josiah son of Amon king of Judah" (1:1). He said, in effect, "I'm familiar with the king's court. I'm familiar, in fact, with the king and with his household." Perhaps, and I want to suggest it only as a possibility, it was partly because of Zephaniah's influence that Josiah's heart had turned to God and pulsated for God throughout his life, so much so that there was a continued emphasis on reform and revival during Josiah's reign.

The Value of Good Friends

Don't friends make a huge difference in our lives? Doesn't it even make a difference in the quality of our walk with God? Think back to your growing-up years, your years of young adulthood (or maybe you're in the stage right now). Think about the influence of friends who cared enough to come alongside you as you sensed that God was confronting you with a need to deal with His call on your life. Was it true for you that your commitment to walk with the Lord was supported by your friends who shared that commitment? Did you find yourself giving up some friends who perhaps condemned your decision and making new friends who encouraged you in your walk. Josiah had some spiritually minded individuals who undoubtedly influenced his life and encouraged his commitment to bring reform and to make a difference for the Lord in his nation.

We all need friends—and we all need to be a friend. One person in a particular place who is walking with God can affect his or her surroundings more than a hundred who are spiritually indifferent or hostile to God. We have tremendous opportunities each day to make a difference in the lives of those we encounter. Each of us, according to our own gifts and interests, can be a consistent influence. We can be there to provide what is needed for the particular moment—whether it be caring, correcting, modeling, mentoring, confronting, warning or encouraging.

The Bad News and the Good News

Note how the book of Zephaniah can be divided into two parts—a section on judgment and destruction (1:1–3:7) and another section on joy and deliverance (3:8–20). Consequently, Zephaniah's style is a study in contrasts between cutting and compassionate. He was severe at the beginning, but gracious in the end. He was not a poet like Micah. He was not a diplomat. At times he was not even very polite. In chapter 1 he represented God Himself: " 'I will sweep away everything from the face of the earth,' declares the LORD" (1:2). Yet Zephaniah ended his book on a note of triumph and hope—with stirring expressions of kingdom promises and a beautiful picture of the millennium yet to come for the nation of Israel.

The World Beyond Us

It is tempting as we study the Bible to limit our application to our own little world of our own relationships and to forget that there is a world beyond us that needs to hear the life-transforming message of Jesus Christ and His love. There are so many who struggle with emptiness and loneliness, who wonder if there's anything worth living for and dying for.

You and I possess the truth that those without Jesus need in order to fulfill their deepest longings. We have a message to bring to all we encounter, and Zephaniah reminds us that it's a message of hope for those who repent and turn to the Lord for forgiveness and healing.

Carry the Light

Zephaniah provides dazzling insight into how to carry the light of the Lord into a dark world. First, *God wants us to stay in touch with the lost world.* He does! He does not want us to build our whole frame of reference around one another. He does not want us to build walls of protection around ourselves. He wants us to break down the walls! He wants us to stay in touch in a creative way, to hear what others are saying and feeling, and to know where our fellow brothers and sisters are going so that we know how to relate when we are together.

Our great need is not to *impose* our faith; it's to *expose* our faith. *We* can't convert anybody. Converting souls and changing lives is the job of the *Spirit of God*. But you and I are the ammunition the Spirit of God uses. So whatever we do during our lives here on earth, we must stay in touch with those who are out of touch spiritually.

Second, *God wants us to hold out hope.* That's what Zephaniah did. There is a place for the warning of judgment. There is a time to speak up against the sin that is in us and around us. We must issue the call to repentance and reform. But please remember: We must also offer hope! Time is short, and those without Jesus Christ need to know of the hope that can be found only in Him.

I recall reading an apocryphal story of the day when the devil got his host of demons together to strategize a plan for this earth. Satan invited any of the demons to suggest a message that would work so that earthlings would not believe. One angel of the abyss stood up and said, "I think we should tell the people of earth that there is no heaven." Lucifer, upon hearing the suggestion, replied, "No. The heart of man knows there is such a place. The Bible proclaims the truth, and we can't deny it." Shortly thereafter another stood and said, "Then let's tell them there is no hell." And again Lucifer dismissed the suggestion with the words, "The conscience of all humanity knows there is a hell. Even in the depths of depravity and darkness people know there is ultimately a place for those who reject the Giver of eternal life. People know there is a hell." Finally a third demon stood and stated his suggestion: "Let's tell people there is no hurry." Lucifer's eyes lit up with delight. And that became the adopted strategy—to convince the world that there is no hurry.

If the prophets did nothing else, even though we may view it at times annoyingly repetitious, they kept poking their finger into the faces of people and saying, "There is an urgency. There is a reason to hurry. There is a hell. There is a heaven. And there is an invincible hope that can be fulfilled only in the Lord. Seek Him and live. Do it now!"

Judgment and Gloom **Chapters 1:1–3:8**

Zephaniah was a prophet who brought both good news and bad news. Under the inspiration of the Holy Spirit, he reported the bad news first and then the good news. The opening chapters are filled with judgment and deep gloom. Zephaniah prophesied judgment first against the nation of Judah and then the surrounding nations. The words of rebuke to Judah were severe, bold, extreme and unrelenting. Zephaniah predicted horrible judgment on those who had turned back, on the princes and priests, on the stagnant in spirit and also on those who were spiritually complacent. There was hope for those faithful individuals who repented and sought the Lord, but judgment would come on a national level.

1 The word of the LORD that came to Zephaniah son of Cushi, the son of Gedaliah, the son
of Amariah, the son of Hezekiah, during the reign
of Josiah son of Amon king of Judah: 2Ki 22:1

Warning of Coming Destruction

2"I will sweep away everything
from the face of the earth," Ge 6:7
declares the LORD.
3"I will sweep away both men and animals;
I will sweep away the birds of the air Jer 4:25
and the fish of the sea.
The wicked will have only heaps of rubble[a]
when I cut off man from the face of the
earth," Hos 4:3
declares the LORD.

Against Judah

4"I will stretch out my hand against Judah
and against all who live in Jerusalem.
I will cut off from this place every remnant of
Baal, Mic 5:13
the names of the pagan and the idolatrous
priests— Hos 10:5
5those who bow down on the roofs
to worship the starry host,
those who bow down and swear by the LORD
and who also swear by Molech,[b] Jer 5:7
6those who turn back from following the LORD
and neither seek the LORD nor inquire of
him. Isa 9:13; Hos 7:7
7Be silent before the Sovereign LORD, Hab 2:20
for the day of the LORD is near. Isa 13:6
The LORD has prepared a sacrifice; Jer 46:10
he has consecrated those he has invited.
8On the day of the LORD's sacrifice
I will punish the princes Isa 24:21
and the king's sons Jer 39:6
and all those clad
in foreign clothes.
9On that day I will punish
all who avoid stepping on the threshold,[c]
who fill the temple of their gods
with violence and deceit. Am 3:10
10"On that day," declares the LORD, Isa 22:5
"a cry will go up from the Fish Gate,
wailing from the New Quarter,
and a loud crash from the hills.
11Wail, you who live in the market district[d];
all your merchants will be wiped out,
all who trade with[e] silver will be ruined.
12At that time I will search Jerusalem with
lamps
and punish those who are complacent,
who are like wine left on its dregs, Jer 48:11
who think, 'The LORD will do nothing, Eze 8:12
either good or bad.'
13Their wealth will be plundered, Jer 15:13
their houses demolished.
They will build houses
but not live in them;
they will plant vineyards
but not drink the wine. Am 5:11; Mic 6:15

The Great Day of the LORD

14"The great day of the LORD is near— Eze 7:7
near and coming quickly.
Listen! The cry on the day of the LORD will be
bitter,
the shouting of the warrior there.
15That day will be a day of wrath,
a day of distress and anguish,
a day of trouble and ruin,
a day of darkness and gloom,
a day of clouds and blackness, Isa 22:5; Joel 2:2
16a day of trumpet and battle cry Jer 4:19
against the fortified cities
and against the corner towers. Isa 2:15
17I will bring distress on the people Dt 28:52
and they will walk like blind men, Isa 59:10
because they have sinned against the LORD.
Their blood will be poured out like dust Ps 79:3
and their entrails like filth. Jer 9:22
18Neither their silver nor their gold
will be able to save them
on the day of the LORD's wrath. Eze 7:19
In the fire of his jealousy Dt 29:20
the whole world will be consumed, Zep 3:8
for he will make a sudden end
of all who live in the earth." Ge 6:7

2 Gather together, gather together, Joel 1:14
O shameful nation, Jer 3:3; 6:15
2before the appointed time arrives
and that day sweeps on like chaff, Isa 17:13
before the fierce anger of the LORD comes
upon you, La 4:11

[a] 3 The meaning of the Hebrew for this line is uncertain. [b] 5 Hebrew *Malcam,* that is, Milcom [c] 9 See 1 Samuel 5:5.
[d] 11 Or *the Mortar* [e] 11 Or *in*

before the day of the LORD's wrath comes
upon you. Eze 7:19
3 Seek the LORD, all you humble of the land,
you who do what he commands.
Seek righteousness, seek humility; Ps 45:4
perhaps you will be sheltered Ps 57:1
on the day of the LORD's anger.

LIVING  INSIGHT

Reach the maximum of your potential—but don't talk about it. Keep uppermost in your mind the plain truth about yourself . . . you have to put your pants on one leg at a time, just like everybody else.
(See Zephaniah 2:3.)

Against Philistia

4 Gaza will be abandoned Am 1:6-8; Zec 9:5-7
and Ashkelon left in ruins.
At midday Ashdod will be emptied
and Ekron uprooted.
5 Woe to you who live by the sea,
O Kerethite people; Eze 25:16
the word of the LORD is against you, Am 3:1
O Canaan, land of the Philistines.

"I will destroy you,
and none will be left." Isa 14:30
6 The land by the sea, where the Kerethites[a]
dwell,
will be a place for shepherds and sheep
pens. Isa 5:17
7 It will belong to the remnant of the house of
Judah; Ge 45:7
there they will find pasture.
In the evening they will lie down
in the houses of Ashkelon.
The LORD their God will care for them;
he will restore their fortunes.[b] Ps 126:4

Against Moab and Ammon

8 "I have heard the insults of Moab Jer 48:27
and the taunts of the Ammonites, Eze 21:28
who insulted my people Eze 25:3
and made threats against their land. La 3:61
9 Therefore, as surely as I live,"
declares the LORD Almighty, the God of
Israel,
"surely Moab will become like Sodom, Dt 29:23
the Ammonites like Gomorrah— Jer 49:1-6
a place of weeds and salt pits,
a wasteland forever.
The remnant of my people will plunder them;
the survivors of my nation will inherit their
land." Am 2:1-3
10 This is what they will get in return for their
pride, Isa 16:6
for insulting and mocking the people of the
LORD Almighty. Jer 48:27
11 The LORD will be awesome to them Joel 2:11
when he destroys all the gods of the land.
The nations on every shore will worship him,
every one in its own land.

Against Cush

12 "You too, O Cushites,[c] Isa 18:1; 20:4
will be slain by my sword." Jer 46:10

Against Assyria

13 He will stretch out his hand against the north
and destroy Assyria,
leaving Nineveh utterly desolate
and dry as the desert. Na 1:1; Mic 5:6
14 Flocks and herds will lie down there, Isa 5:17
creatures of every kind.
The desert owl and the screech owl Ps 102:6
will roost on her columns.
Their calls will echo through the windows,
rubble will be in the doorways,
the beams of cedar will be exposed.
15 This is the carefree city Isa 32:9
that lived in safety. Isa 47:8
She said to herself,
"I am, and there is none besides me."
What a ruin she has become,
a lair for wild beasts!
All who pass by her scoff Na 3:19
and shake their fists.

The Future of Jerusalem

3 Woe to the city of oppressors,
rebellious and defiled! Jer 6:6; Eze 23:30
2 She obeys no one, Jer 22:21
she accepts no correction. Jer 7:28
She does not trust in the LORD, Dt 1:32
she does not draw near to her God. Ps 73:28
3 Her officials are roaring lions,
her rulers are evening wolves, Eze 22:27
who leave nothing for the morning.
4 Her prophets are arrogant;
they are treacherous men. Jer 9:4
Her priests profane the sanctuary
and do violence to the law. Eze 22:26
5 The LORD within her is righteous; Ezr 9:15
he does no wrong. Dt 32:4
Morning by morning he dispenses his justice,
and every new day he does not fail, La 3:23
yet the unrighteous know no shame.

[a] 6 The meaning of the Hebrew for this word is uncertain. [b] 7 Or *will bring back their captives* [c] 12 That is, people from the upper Nile region

6"I have cut off nations;
their strongholds are demolished.
I have left their streets deserted,
with no one passing through.
Their cities are destroyed; Lev 26:31
no one will be left—no one at all.
7I said to the city,
'Surely you will fear me
and accept correction!' Jer 7:28
Then her dwelling would not be cut off,
nor all my punishments come upon her.
But they were still eager
to act corruptly in all they did. Hos 9:9
8Therefore wait for me," declares the LORD,
"for the day I will stand up to testify.[a]
I have decided to assemble the nations, Joel 3:2
to gather the kingdoms
and to pour out my wrath on them—
all my fierce anger. Jer 10:25
The whole world will be consumed Zep 1:18
by the fire of my jealous anger.

Joy and Deliverance **Chapter 3:9–20**

In the final section Zephaniah wrote of the kingdom era when Messiah would reign over the people of God and deliverance would come. These verses sing to a glorious crescendo of joy and hope. There is every evidence of true praise—shouting, singing, rejoicing and pure worship. The land will be purged of evil, and Messiah will reign. By the end of this short book, our tough prophet of darkness and doom was singing the sweet melody of hope and celebration.

9"Then will I purify the lips of the peoples,
that all of them may call on the name of
the LORD Zep 2:11
and serve him shoulder to shoulder. Isa 19:18
10From beyond the rivers of Cush[b] Ps 68:31
my worshipers, my scattered people,
will bring me offerings. Isa 60:7
11On that day you will not be put to shame
for all the wrongs you have done to me,
because I will remove from this city
those who rejoice in their pride. Ps 59:12
Never again will you be haughty
on my holy hill. Ex 15:17
12But I will leave within you
the meek and humble, Isa 14:32
who trust in the name of the LORD. Na 1:7
13The remnant of Israel will do no wrong;
they will speak no lies, Rev 14:5
nor will deceit be found in their mouths.
They will eat and lie down Eze 34:15; Zep 2:7
and no one will make them afraid."

14Sing, O Daughter of Zion; Zec 2:10
shout aloud, O Israel! Isa 12:6
Be glad and rejoice with all your heart, Isa 51:11
O Daughter of Jerusalem!
15The LORD has taken away your punishment,
he has turned back your enemy.

LIVING  **INSIGHT**

The heart that loves God is a heart that bursts forth in songs of praise. It is marvelously spontaneous. It is wonderful to have your heart so in love with your Lord that the only way to express it is to sing it.
(See Zephaniah 3:14–17.)

The LORD, the King of Israel, is with you;
never again will you fear any harm. Isa 54:14
16On that day they will say to Jerusalem,
"Do not fear, O Zion;
do not let your hands hang limp. Isa 35:3-4
17The LORD your God is with you,
he is mighty to save. Isa 63:1
He will take great delight in you, Isa 62:4
he will quiet you with his love, Hos 14:4
he will rejoice over you with singing."

18"The sorrows for the appointed feasts
I will remove from you;
they are a burden and a reproach to you.[c]
19At that time I will deal
with all who oppressed you;
I will rescue the lame
and gather those who have been scattered.
I will give them praise and honor Isa 60:18
in every land where they were put to
shame.
20At that time I will gather you;
at that time I will bring you home. Jer 29:14
I will give you honor and praise Isa 56:5
among all the peoples of the earth
when I restore your fortunes[d] Joel 3:1
before your very eyes,"
says the LORD.

[a]8 Septuagint and Syriac; Hebrew *will rise up to plunder* [b]10 That is, the upper Nile region [c]18 Or *"I will gather you who mourn for the appointed feasts; / your reproach is a burden to you* [d]20 Or *I bring back your captives*

INTRODUCTION

HAGGAI

The prophet Haggai is unique for two reasons. First, he is the only person in all the Old Testament with the name *Haggai,* and second, his is the only book in all the Bible containing two chapters. But much more important than those two interesting facts is this: Haggai was God's spokesman sent to awaken and arouse the post-captivity Jews from their lethargy. With a single eye on his objective, he pursued one major goal: to complete the project of rebuilding the temple in Jerusalem. He was a "get-it-done!" type of leader, a highly motivated man who attacked indifference as the enemy it was. Haggai, and later Zechariah, were used by the Lord to afflict the comfortable, convincing them that there was no excuse for delay. His message is greatly needed in our "me-first" day of self-centeredness and apathy.

WRITER: *Haggai*

DATE: *c.520 B.C.*

PURPOSE: *To spur the people of Judah to complete the rebuilding project by showing the consequences of disobedience and of obedience*

KEY THEME: *Completing the temple*

KEY TERMS: *"Give careful thought"; the word of the LORD came"*

TIME OF PROPHECY: *Almost four months*

ERA: *Postexilic*

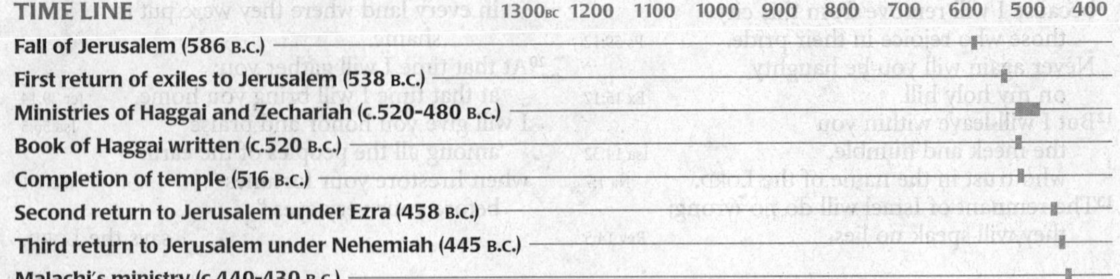

Persuasive Prophet of Priorities

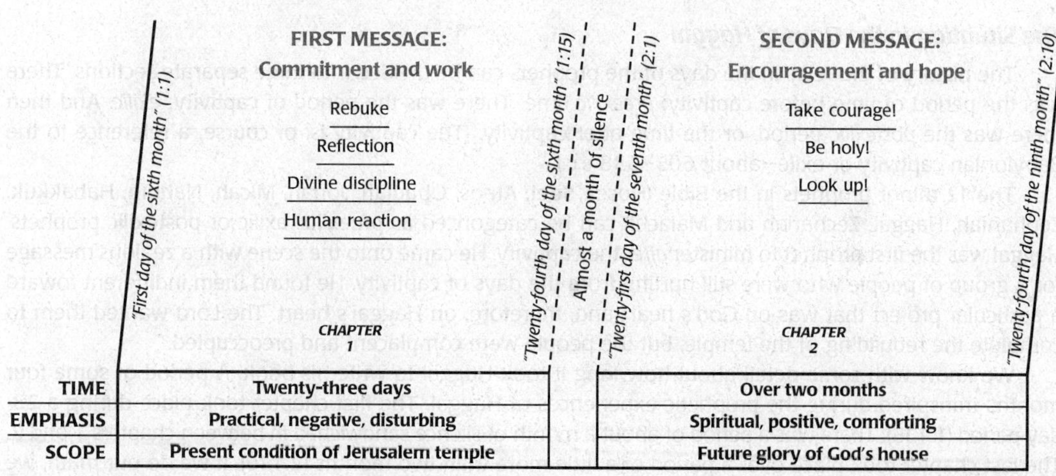

FIRST MESSAGE:
Commitment and work
Rebuke
Reflection
Divine discipline
Human reaction
SECOND MESSAGE:
Encouragement and hope
Take courage!
Be holy!
Look up!
"First day of the sixth month" (1:1)
"Twenty-fourth day of the sixth month" (1:15)
Almost a month of silence
"Twenty-first day of the seventh month" (2:1)
"Twenty-fourth day of the ninth month" (2:10)
CHAPTER 1
CHAPTER 2
TIME
Twenty-three days
Over two months
EMPHASIS
Practical, negative, disturbing
Spiritual, positive, comforting
SCOPE
Present condition of Jerusalem temple
Future glory of God's house

Even though not everyone is familiar with the book of Haggai, no one would have difficulty identifying with its message. The message of Haggai can be described in a simple five-word sentence: *Finish what has been started*. We don't have trouble understanding that message, because all of us, at one time or another, have trouble finishing what has been started.

Examples abound, like finishing the book you started weeks ago, the garage you began cleaning two months ago, the letter you started last Christmas, or the diet you adopted last year and the year before that . . . You see what I mean? The message is very, very practical. We are all pretty good at getting things started, but so often we lack the discipline to see the project through to the end.

Meeting Haggai

Before dealing with Haggai's message let's first get acquainted with the man. His name appears in verse 3 of chapter 1. Haggai means "festive," or "festal." He was the only man in all the Bible by the name of Haggai. A rather interesting name, isn't it? Why would a man who served as a prophet be named "Festive"? Stop and think about it. Obviously his parents named him. He was born during the time of captivity in Babylon. He would be something like a baby born while someone was a prisoner in the concentration camps of Auschwitz or Dachau. Perhaps the birth of that little boy was the only light in the dark tunnel of captivity for his parents—a reminder of the joy he brought them in spite of their tragic circumstances. I know of children with names like "Joy" and "Charity." I even know a young woman named "Delight"—a description of the feeling of her parents at the time of her birth. So it may very well have been with Haggai—a man who brought his parents happiness in a day in which the exiles were not singing the songs of Zion in Babylon.

Leaders in the Day of Haggai

The people of significance who surrounded Haggai were all mentioned in the first verse of his book:

> *In the second year of King Darius, on the first day of the sixth month, the word of the LORD came through the prophet Haggai to Zerubbabel son of Shealtiel, governor of Judah, and to Joshua son of Jehozadak, the high priest.*

This prophecy came in the second year of the reign of a Persian king named Darius. We can pinpoint that date as 520 B.C. And then there was a governor of Judah named Zerubbabel. There was also a priest named Joshua, not to be confused with our Old Testament friend who has a book named after him. Haggai the prophet addressed himself to the governor Zerubbabel, the priest Joshua and the remnant of the house of Israel because he was determined to get something finished that had been started.

The Situation in the Days of Haggai

The history of the Jews in the days of the prophets can be divided into three separate sections. There was the period of time before captivity: *preexilic* time. There was the period of captivity: *exilic*. And then there was the *postexilic* period, or the time after captivity. (The captivity is, of course, a reference to the Babylonian captivity or exile—about 605–538 B.C.)

The 12 minor prophets in the Bible (Hosea, Joel, Amos, Obadiah, Jonah, Micah, Nahum, Habakkuk, Zephaniah, Haggai, Zechariah and Malachi) can be categorized as preexilic, exilic or postexilic prophets. Haggai was the first prophet to minister *after* the captivity. He came onto the scene with a zealous message for a group of people who were still hurting from the days of captivity. He found them indifferent toward a particular project that was on God's heart and, therefore, on Haggai's heart. The Lord wanted them to complete the rebuilding of the temple, but the people were complacent and preoccupied.

We know with some detail about how long it took Haggai to write his book. A period of some four months transpired during the prophetic experiences of Haggai. The first chapter took place during a 23-day period (1:1,15). There was a period of about a month of silence sandwiched in between chapters 1 and 2. The last chapter took place over a period of a little more than two months (2:1,10). If we do our math, we see that the book was written in almost a four-month span of time.

Haggai's Burden

Haggai had a burden on his heart, as was true of all the prophets. Haggai's burden was God's burden. People with a prophetic heart, like the Old Testament prophets, live with burdens. They may be people in our day whom God has raised up to call people back to Him. I'm sure you know people like that. You know men and women of God who have prophetic hearts and who bring God's message for this time in history. Invariably they are the ones who say, "The Lord is calling us to an open examination of our hearts and lives. We must deal with the evil within us and around us." They're carrying the burden of a particular issue on their heart.

Haggai was just that kind of servant of God. God had a burden on His heart, and Haggai picked up on it: " 'Go up into the mountains and bring down timber and build the house, so that I may take pleasure in it and be honored,' says the LORD" (1:8).

You see, the exiles who had returned to Jerusalem had started building the temple 16 years before, but they never finished it. It's like that Model A in the garage. It's like that painting project. It's like that book. It's like the Christmas tree lights still strung around the house in mid-March. It's an unfinished project, except it was so much more significant than all the things we procrastinate about. This was the temple . . . the house of worship among the Jews in Jerusalem!

In those days, unless the temple could be rebuilt, the sign of God's visible presence (a shining light) would not reside among His people. The Spirit of God did not reside in the believers permanently then as He does now. The place where God manifested His presence was a place of worship—which was at first the tabernacle, and later the temple. And as long as there was no temple, there was no tangible presence of God. And so for 16 years, even though the people had returned to their blessed city of Zion, they had neglected God and dishonored Him by allowing the house He called home to lay in ruins. They had failed to meet with God because they had failed to rebuild the place that symbolized His presence.

Let's Get to Work

If Haggai lived today, he'd likely be saying, "Roll up your sleeves and get at it! C'mon, everybody, it's time to get the project finished!" The people were saying, "Oh, it's not time yet for the house of God to be built. We've got a lot of other things that are really, really important." It took 23 days for them to get the message. Haggai refused to lighten up. He told them, in effect, "God has spoken. His house cannot remain unfinished."

In the final analysis, it is not a building that is of greatest significance to God; it is the people. And God, through the message of Haggai, bore right down to the heart of the issue—it was their relationship with Him that was at stake. As the old saying goes, "When the heart is right, the feet are swift." The problem was ultimately one of heart, not feet! When the heart leads, the feet will follow.

The Message of Haggai

The overriding, guiding principle of this book is: *Obey God*. The same thing we learn about the priority the people of Haggai's day had to place on the temple, we can apply to our lives. If we have neglected to put God first, it's time to get back on track.

What methods does God use to renew an interest in Him? Stop and think about that. As Haggai's prophecy began, the exiles had no interest in the temple whatsoever, and suddenly, by the end of the book, they had rolled up their sleeves and were filling the air with the sounds of construction. What had happened? How did they get their spirits renewed?

I want to suggest four answers. First, *God used a messenger*. God uses human beings as His instruments. Here He tapped a man named Haggai. In your life God may very well use a parent, a teacher, a mentor or a friend. God will use an insightful person in your life to tap you on the shoulder, spiritually speaking, and say, "You seem to have gotten off the track. I love you too much to let you neglect your commitment. I want nothing more than to see you walk closely with God. I challenge you to trust Him. I challenge you to meet with Him and begin to get your life straightened out. Rebuild that temple He's called you to build." It takes a person . . . just the right individual who will come alongside and with great sensitivity and caring, hold you accountable—and keep on loving you through it all.

Second, *God used a call to personal evaluation*. Several times in this book we read the phrase, "Give careful thought to your ways"—a direct appeal to set your heart on something and to address it so deeply that you won't let that situation stay the way it's always been. Sometimes it takes a word from God through a book you are reading, or a radio or television broadcast you may be listening to, or a word fitly spoken from just the right person at just the right time. It could be that word of exhortation that says, "It's time to make some changes in the direction you're going." And you do.

Third, *God used adversity to turn the people around*. Look closely at what Haggai said about holes in their purses, about being cold even though they had a lot of clothes on, about being hungry even though they ate, about planting a lot and harvesting little (1:6). Adversity is a motivation with teeth in it. It gives an opportunity to respond with obedience and renewed commitment, to develop a spirit of faithfulness and patient endurance, to grow closer to the Lord and to the Lord's people.

Fourth, *God used encouragement to renew the spirit of the people in Haggai's day*. God raised up Haggai, and Zechariah as well, to encourage His people in the tough times of starting their life over again after years of captivity. He wanted to instill a sense of hope and a sense of purpose in them, and He wants to do that for us today as well. It may surprise you to know that we're not the only ones who have unfinished tasks. Did you know that God does too? But the only thing that's unfinished in God's work is His people. You represent the Model A in God's garage. You represent the string of lights. You and I represent the neglected painting project, the unfinished book. He's still working on us. I have a distinct feeling that some of you understand right away when I talk about how God will not quit until He brings you to a place of putting Him first.

Call to Commitment **Chapter 1**

This is a chapter of strong reproof! Those who had returned to Jerusalem from exile claimed they were living in economically hard times and therefore could not finish the rebuilding of the Lord's temple. The excuse failed to silence Haggai. Through this prophet the Lord called the people to a fresh commitment and to hard work. What would this work entail? Rebuilding the temple that was still lying in ruins while their homes had been well built and comfortably decorated. Haggai called the people to carefully evaluate their priorities and to put their commitments back in the proper order.

A Call to Build the House of the LORD

1 In the second year of King Darius, on the first day of the sixth month, the word of the LORD came through the prophet Haggai to Zerubbabel son of Shealtiel, governor of Judah, and to Joshua[a] son of Jehozadak, the high priest: Ezr 4:24; 5:3

2This is what the LORD Almighty says: "These people say, 'The time has not yet come for the LORD's house to be built.'" Ezr 1:2

3Then the word of the LORD came through the prophet Haggai: 4"Is it a time for you yourselves to be living in your paneled houses, while this house remains a ruin?" 2Sa 7:2; Ezr 5:1; Jer 33:12

5Now this is what the LORD Almighty says: "Give careful thought to your ways. 6You have planted much, but have harvested little. You eat, but never have enough. You drink, but never have your fill. You put on clothes, but are not warm. You earn wages, only to put them in a purse with holes in it." La 3:40; Hag 2:15,18

7This is what the LORD Almighty says: "Give careful thought to your ways. 8Go up into the mountains and bring down timber and build the house, so that I may take pleasure in it and be honored," says the LORD. 9"You expected much, but see, it turned out to be little. What you brought home, I blew away. Why?" declares the LORD Almighty. "Because of my house, which remains a ruin, while each of you is busy with his

LIVING  INSIGHT

Busyness feeds the ego but starves the inner person. It fills a calendar but fractures a family. It cultivates a program but plows under priorities.

(See Haggai 1:9.)

own house. 10Therefore, because of you the heavens have withheld their dew and the earth its crops. 11I called for a drought on the fields and the mountains, on the grain, the new wine, the oil and whatever the ground produces, on men and cattle, and on the labor of your hands." Ps 132:13-14

12Then Zerubbabel son of Shealtiel, Joshua son of Jehozadak, the high priest, and the whole remnant of the people obeyed the voice of the LORD their God and the message of the prophet Haggai, because the LORD their God had sent him. And the people feared the LORD. Dt 31:12; Isa 50:10

13Then Haggai, the LORD's messenger, gave this message of the LORD to the people: "I am with you," declares the LORD. 14So the LORD stirred up the spirit of Zerubbabel son of Shealtiel, governor of Judah, and the spirit of Joshua son of Jehozadak, the high priest, and the spirit of the whole remnant of the people. They came and began to work on the house of the LORD Almighty, their God, 15on the twenty-fourth day of the sixth month in the second year of King Darius. Ezr 5:2

Word of Encouragement **Chapter 2**

By the second chapter, one month had passed and the people had gotten the message. Haggai's tone had changed. His message was now filled with encouragement and hope. The construction of the temple had resumed, and the Lord wanted to affirm and motivate the people to continued obedience. Rebuke was no longer needed because repentance had taken place. The time had come for reassurance and words of blessing. Haggai's message resounds clearly to this day. We must obey the Lord, even if we have neglected our obligation for a long time. As we repent and follow the Lord, His encouragement will fill us and His hope will be our strength.

The Promised Glory of the New House

2 On the twenty-first day of the seventh month, the word of the LORD came through the prophet Haggai: 2"Speak to Zerubbabel son of Shealtiel, governor of Judah, to Joshua son of Jehozadak, the high priest, and to the remnant of the people. Ask them, 3'Who of you is left who saw this house in its former glory? How does it look to you now? Does it not seem to you like nothing? 4But now be strong, O Zerubbabel,' declares the LORD. 'Be strong, O Joshua son of Jehozadak, the high priest. Be strong, all you people of the land,' declares the LORD, 'and work. For I am with you,' declares the LORD Almighty. 5'This is what I covenanted with you when you came out of Egypt. And my Spirit remains among you. Do not fear.'

6"This is what the LORD Almighty says: 'In a little while I will once more shake the heavens and the earth, the sea and the dry land. 7I will shake all nations, and the desired of all nations will come, and I will fill this house with glory,' says the LORD Almighty. 8'The silver is mine and the gold is mine,' declares the LORD Almighty. 9'The glory of

[a]1 A variant of *Jeshua*; here and elsewhere in Haggai

this present house will be greater than the glory of
the former house,' says the LORD Almighty. 'And
in this place I will grant peace,' declares the LORD
Almighty." Heb 12:26*

Blessings for a Defiled People

10On the twenty-fourth day of the ninth month,
in the second year of Darius, the word of the LORD
came to the prophet Haggai: 11"This is what the
LORD Almighty says: 'Ask the priests what the law
says: 12If a person carries consecrated meat in the
fold of his garment, and that fold touches some
bread or stew, some wine, oil or other food, does
it become consecrated?'" Lev 10:10-11; Mt 23:19
The priests answered, "No."
13Then Haggai said, "If a person defiled by contact with a dead body touches one of these things,
does it become defiled?"
"Yes," the priests replied, "it becomes defiled."
14Then Haggai said, "'So it is with this people
and this nation in my sight,' declares the LORD.
'Whatever they do and whatever they offer there is
defiled. Isa 1:13
15"'Now give careful thought to this from this
day on[a]—consider how things were before one
stone was laid on another in the LORD's temple.
16When anyone came to a heap of twenty measures, there were only ten. When anyone went to
a wine vat to draw fifty measures, there were only
twenty. 17I struck all the work of your hands with
blight, mildew and hail, yet you did not turn to
me,' declares the LORD. 18'From this day on, from
this twenty-fourth day of the ninth month, give
careful thought to the day when the foundation of
the LORD's temple was laid. Give careful thought:
19Is there yet any seed left in the barn? Until now,
the vine and the fig tree, the pomegranate and the
olive tree have not borne fruit. Hag 1:5-6; Zec 8:9
"'From this day on I will bless you.'" Joel 2:14

Zerubbabel the LORD's Signet Ring

20The word of the LORD came to Haggai a second time on the twenty-fourth day of the month:
21"Tell Zerubbabel governor of Judah that I will
shake the heavens and the earth. 22I will overturn
royal thrones and shatter the power of the foreign
kingdoms. I will overthrow chariots and their drivers; horses and their riders will fall, each by the
sword of his brother. Jdg 7:22; Da 2:44; Mic 5:10
23"'On that day,' declares the LORD Almighty, 'I
will take you, my servant Zerubbabel son of Shealtiel,' declares the LORD, 'and I will make you like
my signet ring, for I have chosen you,' declares the
LORD Almighty." Isa 43:10

[a] 15 Or *to the days past*

INTRODUCTION

ZECHARIAH

The book of Zechariah is one of the biggest in the collection of the writings of the minor prophets. In this book Zechariah proclaimed an encouraging word of assurance to a demoralized people. The prophet Haggai had led the way in the project of rebuilding the temple . . . but the people had grown weary. Crop failures caused financial distress and the work grew tedious at the construction site. Zechariah rolled up his sleeves and plunged in with a reckless abandon as he threw himself into the work of helping his friend and fellow prophet Haggai. Zechariah relied on words of inspiration and positive encouragement to motivate the people. He was a man of vision and faith who spoke just the right word at just the right time in the history of God's people.

WRITER: *Zechariah*

DATE: *c.520* B.C.

PURPOSE: *To encourage the fainthearted to take their eyes off their distress and turn them to their sovereign Lord*

KEY THEMES: *God's sovereignty; the coming of the Messiah*

CONTEMPORARY: *Haggai*

ERA: *Postexilic*

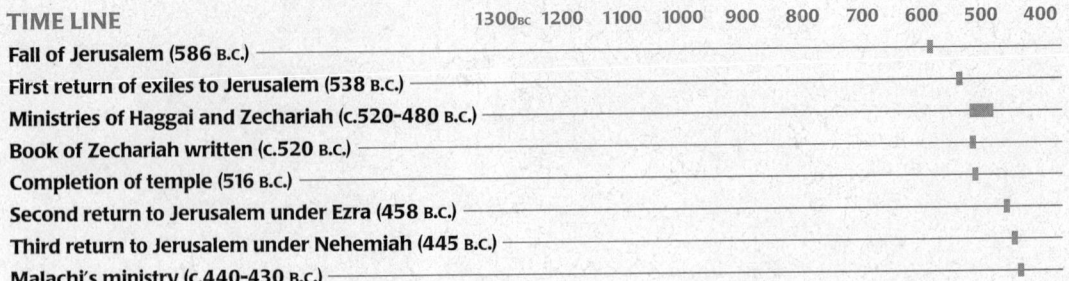

TIME LINE

1300 BC 1200 1100 1000 900 800 700 600 500 400

- Fall of Jerusalem (586 B.C.)
- First return of exiles to Jerusalem (538 B.C.)
- Ministries of Haggai and Zechariah (c.520-480 B.C.)
- Book of Zechariah written (c.520 B.C.)
- Completion of temple (516 B.C.)
- Second return to Jerusalem under Ezra (458 B.C.)
- Third return to Jerusalem under Nehemiah (445 B.C.)
- Malachi's ministry (c.440-430 B.C.)

Man of Vision and Faith

	CALL TO REPENTANCE	ENCOURAGEMENT AND MOTIVATION		ENCOURAGEMENT AND HOPE
		VISIONS	QUESTIONS	PREDICTIONS
		Horses and riders Horns and craftsmen Surveyor and measuring line Joshua (the priest) and Satan Lampstand and seven lights Flying scroll and warning Woman and a basket Chariots and judgment	Fasting Failure Future of Zion	**First "Oracle":** Historical events Messianic prophets **Second "Oracle":** Israel's final victory Messiah's final victory
	CHAPTER 1:1-6	*CHAPTERS 1:7–6:15*	*CHAPTERS 7–8*	*CHAPTERS 9–14*
TIME	**Written during the building of the temple**			**Written after completion of the temple**
PURPOSE	**To motivate those working on the temple to continue in spite of their own crop failures and financial distress. Rather than rebuking or condemning, Zechariah inspired the people to work.**			**To give the workers hope that there was a better day, a far more glorious day yet to come. Vivid scenes of Messiah are included. He is revealed as coming, rejected, returning and conquering.**

There are two distinct styles of motivation. One is the aggressive, highly charged emotional style that appeals to the will. It relies on fear and, if necessary, public demand to motivate us to get a job done. This is what we might call "extrinsic motivation." It offers tangible rewards. It provides us with visible stimuli to get a big job done.

There is a second type of motivation, which is called "intrinsic." It is quiet. It digs deep. It is at least outwardly less emotional but much more inspiring. It does not dangle the carrot and offer us a lot of external reward. It doesn't use guilt or fear to motivate us, but it appeals to our sense of purpose and/or inner feelings of deep-seated passion and concern.

Frankly, it often takes both types of motivation to get a big job done. When we think of a Biblical prophet, we probably think of an Elijah, Jonah or Ezekiel—blazing like a lightning bolt across the sky, rebuking and speaking of doom and judgment, awakening the guilt of the people. But there is another style of prophet—like Jeremiah, who could have written his book with a pen dipped in tears. Or Zechariah, who dug deep to motivate his listeners with maximum inspiration and encouragement. He believed in the intrinsic approach to motivation.

There is an appeal to the conscience, not merely to the emotions, in the book of Zechariah. And it comes on the heels of Haggai, who had rebuked the people for living in their fine homes in the suburbs, yet neglecting to finish rebuilding the temple of God. Haggai's message said, in effect, "How could you live in such beautiful places and yet allow the house of worship, God's house, to remain in rubble? Why would you start and not finish that important job? Get at the task!" And they did. Yet it's easy to see how the people might have begun to wear out and their patience wear thin.

You can motivate extrinsically only so long, and then there must be inspiration. That's when Zechariah stepped in. One writer put it this way: "He does not rebuke or condemn or berate the people. With striking colors and vivid imagination he paints glowing pictures of the presence of God to strengthen and to help the people. Words of inspiration flow from his lips. His hope for a new kingdom rests upon the faith he has in his own people." Do you sense the difference in styles between Haggai and Zechariah. I repeat, both of them helped get the job done, but there was something about Zechariah that was especially helpful in applying balm for the healing of the wounds that had remained opened since the captivity.

Haggai's message was the one side of the coin, as he said, in effect, "Shame on you for living in your houses!" Zechariah turned the coin over, saying, in effect, "Look at the way God will be lifted up when we finish this task! Look at the place where God will be glorified. Think of the benefit to Zion! Why, Israel will never be forgotten. The Messiah will inhabit this nation!" What a wonderful warmth in his leadership style.

Meeting Zechariah

The prophet has an interesting name that means "The LORD remembers," or "He whom the LORD remembers." Zechariah is the grandson of a priest named Iddo, mentioned in the first verse of the book. He apparently succeeded Iddo as head of that priestly family (Nehemiah 12:16). His ministry as a prophet began at the time of the ministry of an emotional, motivating kind of leader named Haggai.

As Zechariah began his preaching, the temple-building project was still in progress. The temple was not finished. The people were working at it, but they were getting tired. Financial worries and a poor harvest had left the people demoralized. Zechariah must have seen the strain on their faces, so he stepped in and communicated a message that went something like this: "The job can still be finished. I believe in you. More important than that, *God* believes in you. As a matter of fact, He's at work in you and through you. He plans to live with you in Jerusalem. He's making a new beginning for you."

Sometimes a compassionate style is not only inspiring—it's downright invigorating! Notice how Zechariah quickly zeroed in on the heart of the matter. Yes, the rebuilding of the temple was important. Vitally important. But more important than the building was what the building symbolized: a relationship with God. That's why it was important to get on with the work. A new beginning required a change in heart. And so at the outset of his prophecy, with a spirit of concern and care, Zechariah called the people to repentance:

> *The LORD was very angry with your forefathers. Therefore tell the people: This is what the LORD Almighty says: "Return to me," declares the LORD Almighty, "and I will return to you," says the LORD Almighty (1:2–3).*

That's intrinsic motivation at its best. Through Zechariah, God said, in effect, "You turn back to Me and when you do, believe Me, I will be there. I will return to you and you'll have power like you once had." Zechariah began with this appeal to their conscience and told them to walk with God—even though their fathers and grandfathers hadn't. Some of you grew up in homes where your parents taught you about the Lord; others of you have or had parents who had no faith in Jesus at all—but that does not need to turn you against God. God's eternal Word is directed to you and to me. It is to each of us that God speaks this message: "Come to Me. Whatever your situation, whether your parents rebelled against Me or whether they clung to Me, you return to Me, and I'll bless you beyond your wildest dreams."

A Call to Build . . . in the Power of the Spirit

The beginning of Zechariah's book dealt with the here and now: getting the temple finished. The last part of the book introduced the kind of intrinsic motivation that said, "Someday the Messiah will come back to Zion, literally, and He will reign over His people. And this temple will be a testimony to His grace for all to see."

Zechariah's prophecy was addressed to a group of people who saw an enormous obstacle in front of them. The project of finishing the temple was huge. They had very little resources. They had lost most of their crops. Their energy was draining away. And along came Zechariah the prophet with a series of eight night visions meant to encourage the builders of the temple (1:7–6:8). In the middle of the series of visions (in the fifth vision, as a matter of fact), he gave this profound message to the people that was to stand as lasting encouragement to them and to us who follow them: " 'Not by might nor by power, but by my Spirit,' says the LORD Almighty" (4:6). What a message! This obstacle that faced them would not be handled by human might or by royal power. No, it would be overcome by the Spirit of God! That's the way God works. Not in shouts and screams and cheers. Not in the tangible processes and plans we often associate with projects. Not with great, impressive powerful people or vast amounts of money. No. God's most important projects will be completed by the Spirit of God.

You and I do not overcome obstacles in the power of the flesh, but in the power of the Spirit. We don't solve the battles of life through our own effort and power. We solve them through the Spirit of God. There must come a time when we abandon ourselves to God and lean hard on Him, and Him alone. Zechariah communicated the Lord's message: " 'Not by might nor by power, but by my Spirit,' says the LORD Almighty" (4:6).

Lessons From Zechariah

There are at least two enduring lessons that minister to us through Zechariah. First, *truly effective motivation comes ultimately from being inspired*. That's the kind of motivation we need to spring into action, the kind that will bring about lasting change. You know the temptation that lies behind other forms of motivation? To use people. To manipulate them into doing something we want them to do. To shame them so they'll achieve our objectives for them. Please understand. There are times when we all need a very clearly measurable and extrinsic motivation in order to get a job done. But what could be more satisfying than to find our motivation deep within, from a deep conviction that we are doing what the Lord would have us do, that we are together relying on the all-powerful Spirit of God to carry out the task to which He has called us!

Second, *God's Spirit must be in control to accomplish something God's way and for God's glory*. That message reverberates all the way through Zechariah. "Not by might nor by power." To accomplish something for God's glory, His Spirit must be in control. You have a tough project before you? Let His Spirit direct you. Let His Spirit prompt those people who are to be part of it. Let His Spirit lead you. God's plan will not be frustrated! He is working out His purposes for His people. There is a glorious future that awaits the people of God!

Words of Motivation — Chapters 1–8

This section of Zechariah draws on visions and events to motivate the people and encourage them to get the temple rebuilt. These eight chapters focus specifically on those people who had returned to Jerusalem from captivity during the time of temple construction. There are eight "night visions" addressing various themes that would be meaningful to the workers as they continued the work on the Lord's temple. The workers were reminded that human strength would not be sufficient for the task, but only the power of God's Spirit could see them through.

A Call to Return to the LORD

1 In the eighth month of the second year of Darius, the word of the LORD came to the prophet Zechariah son of Berekiah, the son of Iddo: Ezr 4:24; Ne 12:4

2"The LORD was very angry with your forefathers. 3Therefore tell the people: This is what the LORD Almighty says: 'Return to me,' declares the LORD Almighty, 'and I will return to you,' says the LORD Almighty. 4Do not be like your forefathers, to whom the earlier prophets proclaimed: This is what the LORD Almighty says: 'Turn from your evil ways and your evil practices.' But they would not listen or pay attention to me, declares the LORD. 5Where are your forefathers now? And the prophets, do they live forever? 6But did not my words and my decrees, which I commanded my servants the prophets, overtake your forefathers?

"Then they repented and said, 'The LORD Almighty has done to us what our ways and practices deserve, just as he determined to do.'" Jer 12:14-17

The Man Among the Myrtle Trees

7On the twenty-fourth day of the eleventh month, the month of Shebat, in the second year of Darius, the word of the LORD came to the prophet Zechariah son of Berekiah, the son of Iddo.

8During the night I had a vision—and there before me was a man riding a red horse! He was standing among the myrtle trees in a ravine. Behind him were red, brown and white horses.

9I asked, "What are these, my lord?"

The angel who was talking with me answered, "I will show you what they are." Zec 4:1,4-5

10Then the man standing among the myrtle trees explained, "They are the ones the LORD has sent to go throughout the earth." Zec 6:5-8

11And they reported to the angel of the LORD, who was standing among the myrtle trees, "We have gone throughout the earth and found the whole world at rest and in peace." Isa 14:7

12Then the angel of the LORD said, "LORD Almighty, how long will you withhold mercy from Jerusalem and from the towns of Judah, which you have been angry with these seventy years?" 13So the LORD spoke kind and comforting words to the angel who talked with me. Da 9:2; Zec 4:1

14Then the angel who was speaking to me said, "Proclaim this word: This is what the LORD Almighty says: 'I am very jealous for Jerusalem and Zion, 15but I am very angry with the nations that feel secure. I was only a little angry, but they added to the calamity.' Am 1:11; Zec 8:2

16"Therefore, this is what the LORD says: 'I will return to Jerusalem with mercy, and there my house will be rebuilt. And the measuring line will be stretched out over Jerusalem,' declares the LORD Almighty. Zec 2:1-2

17"Proclaim further: This is what the LORD Almighty says: 'My towns will again overflow with prosperity, and the LORD will again comfort Zion and choose Jerusalem.'" Isa 51:3; Zec 2:12

Four Horns and Four Craftsmen

18Then I looked up—and there before me were four horns! 19I asked the angel who was speaking to me, "What are these?"

He answered me, "These are the horns that scattered Judah, Israel and Jerusalem." Am 6:13

20Then the LORD showed me four craftsmen. 21I asked, "What are these coming to do?"

He answered, "These are the horns that scattered Judah so that no one could raise his head, but the craftsmen have come to terrify them and throw down these horns of the nations who lifted up their horns against the land of Judah to scatter its people." Ps 75:4,10

A Man With a Measuring Line

2 Then I looked up—and there before me was a man with a measuring line in his hand! 2I asked, "Where are you going?"

He answered me, "To measure Jerusalem, to find out how wide and how long it is." Rev 21:15

3Then the angel who was speaking to me left, and another angel came to meet him 4and said to him: "Run, tell that young man, 'Jerusalem will be a city without walls because of the great number of men and livestock in it. 5And I myself will be a wall of fire around it,' declares the LORD, 'and I will be its glory within.' Ps 46:5; Rev 21:23

6"Come! Come! Flee from the land of the north," declares the LORD, "for I have scattered you to the four winds of heaven," declares the LORD. Eze 17:21

7"Come, O Zion! Escape, you who live in the Daughter of Babylon!" 8For this is what the LORD Almighty says: "After he has honored me and has sent me against the nations that have plundered you—for whoever touches you touches the apple of his eye— 9I will surely raise my hand against them so that their slaves will plunder them.[a] Then you will know that the LORD Almighty has sent me. Dt 32:10; Zec 4:9

10"Shout and be glad, O Daughter of Zion. For I am coming, and I will live among you," declares the LORD. 11"Many nations will be joined with the LORD in that day and will become my people. I will live among you and you will know that the LORD Almighty has sent me to you. 12The LORD will inherit Judah as his portion in the holy land and will again choose Jerusalem. 13Be still before the LORD, all mankind, because he has roused himself from his holy dwelling." Hab 2:20; Zec 1:17

Clean Garments for the High Priest

3 Then he showed me Joshua[b] the high priest standing before the angel of the LORD, and Satan[c] standing at his right side to accuse him. 2The LORD said to Satan, "The LORD rebuke you, Satan! The LORD, who has chosen Jerusalem, rebuke you! Is not this man a burning stick snatched from the fire?" Ps 109:6; Jude 1:9,23

3Now Joshua was dressed in filthy clothes as he stood before the angel. 4The angel said to those who were standing before him, "Take off his filthy clothes."

Then he said to Joshua, "See, I have taken away your sin, and I will put rich garments on you."

5Then I said, "Put a clean turban on his head." So they put a clean turban on his head and clothed him, while the angel of the LORD stood by.

6The angel of the LORD gave this charge to Joshua: 7"This is what the LORD Almighty says: 'If you will walk in my ways and keep my requirements, then you will govern my house and have charge of my courts, and I will give you a place among these standing here. Dt 17:8-11; Eze 44:15-16

8" 'Listen, O high priest Joshua and your associates seated before you, who are men symbolic of things to come: I am going to bring my servant, the Branch. 9See, the stone I have set in front of Joshua! There are seven eyes[d] on that one stone, and I will engrave an inscription on it,' says the LORD Almighty, 'and I will remove the sin of this land in a single day. Isa 28:16; Eze 12:11

10" 'In that day each of you will invite his neighbor to sit under his vine and fig tree,' declares the LORD Almighty." 1Ki 4:25; Mic 4:4

The Gold Lampstand and the Two Olive Trees

4 Then the angel who talked with me returned and wakened me, as a man is wakened from his sleep. 2He asked me, "What do you see?"

I answered, "I see a solid gold lampstand with a bowl at the top and seven lights on it, with seven channels to the lights. 3Also there are two olive trees by it, one on the right of the bowl and the other on its left." Rev 4:5; 11:4

4I asked the angel who talked with me, "What are these, my lord?"

5He answered, "Do you not know what these are?"

"No, my lord," I replied. Zec 1:9

6So he said to me, "This is the word of the LORD to Zerubbabel: 'Not by might nor by power, but by my Spirit,' says the LORD Almighty. Isa 11:2-4

7"What[e] are you, O mighty mountain? Before Zerubbabel you will become level ground. Then he will bring out the capstone to shouts of 'God bless it! God bless it!' " Ps 118:22; Jer 51:25

8Then the word of the LORD came to me: 9"The hands of Zerubbabel have laid the foundation of this temple; his hands will also complete it. Then you will know that the LORD Almighty has sent me to you. Zec 2:9; 6:12

10"Who despises the day of small things? Men will rejoice when they see the plumb line in the hand of Zerubbabel. Hag 2:3

"(These seven are the eyes of the LORD, which range throughout the earth.)" Zec 3:9; Rev 5:6

LIVING  **INSIGHT**

Those who view life through perspective's lenses have the capacity to see things in their true relation and their relative importance. They see the big picture. Perspective adds a breath of fresh air to the otherwise suffocating demands of life.

(See Zechariah 4:10.)

11Then I asked the angel, "What are these two olive trees on the right and the left of the lampstand?" Rev 11:4

12Again I asked him, "What are these two olive branches beside the two gold pipes that pour out golden oil?"

13He replied, "Do you not know what these are?"

"No, my lord," I said.

14So he said, "These are the two who are anointed to[f] serve the Lord of all the earth." Ex 29:7

The Flying Scroll

5 I looked again—and there before me was a flying scroll! Eze 2:9; Rev 5:1

2He asked me, "What do you see?"

[a] 8,9 Or *says after . . . eye:* 9"*I . . . plunder them.*" [b] 1 A variant of *Jeshua;* here and elsewhere in Zechariah [c] 1 *Satan* means *accuser.* [d] 9 Or *facets* [e] 7 Or *Who* [f] 14 Or *two who bring oil and*

I answered, "I see a flying scroll, thirty feet long and fifteen feet wide.[a]"

3And he said to me, "This is the curse that is going out over the whole land; for according to what it says on one side, every thief will be banished, and according to what it says on the other, everyone who swears falsely will be banished. 4The LORD Almighty declares, 'I will send it out, and it will enter the house of the thief and the house of him who swears falsely by my name. It will remain in his house and destroy it, both its timbers and its stones.' " Lev 14:34-45; Mal 3:5

The Woman in a Basket

5Then the angel who was speaking to me came forward and said to me, "Look up and see what this is that is appearing."

6I asked, "What is it?"

He replied, "It is a measuring basket.[b]" And he added, "This is the iniquity[c] of the people throughout the land."

7Then the cover of lead was raised, and there in the basket sat a woman! 8He said, "This is wickedness," and he pushed her back into the basket and pushed the lead cover down over its mouth.

9Then I looked up—and there before me were two women, with the wind in their wings! They had wings like those of a stork, and they lifted up the basket between heaven and earth. Lev 11:19

10"Where are they taking the basket?" I asked the angel who was speaking to me.

11He replied, "To the country of Babylonia[d] to build a house for it. When it is ready, the basket will be set there in its place." Ge 10:10; Jer 29:5,28; Da 1:2

Four Chariots

6 I looked up again—and there before me were four chariots coming out from between two mountains—mountains of bronze! 2The first chariot had red horses, the second black, 3the third white, and the fourth dappled—all of them powerful. 4I asked the angel who was speaking to me, "What are these, my lord?" Rev 6:2,5

5The angel answered me, "These are the four spirits[e] of heaven, going out from standing in the presence of the Lord of the whole world. 6The one with the black horses is going toward the north country, the one with the white horses toward the west,[f] and the one with the dappled horses toward the south." Eze 37:9; Mt 24:31; Rev 7:1

7When the powerful horses went out, they were straining to go throughout the earth. And he said, "Go throughout the earth!" So they went throughout the earth. Zec 1:10

8Then he called to me, "Look, those going toward the north country have given my Spirit[g] rest in the land of the north." Eze 5:13; 24:13

A Crown for Joshua

9The word of the LORD came to me: 10"Take ⌊silver and gold⌋ from the exiles Heldai, Tobijah and Jedaiah, who have arrived from Babylon. Go the same day to the house of Josiah son of Zephaniah. 11Take the silver and gold and make a crown, and set it on the head of the high priest, Joshua son of Jehozadak. 12Tell him this is what the LORD Almighty says: 'Here is the man whose name is the Branch, and he will branch out from his place and build the temple of the LORD. 13It is he who will build the temple of the LORD, and he will be clothed with majesty and will sit and rule on his throne. And he will be a priest on his throne. And there will be harmony between the two.' 14The crown will be given to Heldai,[h] Tobijah, Jedaiah and Hen[i] son of Zephaniah as a memorial in the temple of the LORD. 15Those who are far away will come and help to build the temple of the LORD, and you will know that the LORD Almighty has sent me to you. This will happen if you diligently obey the LORD your God." Isa 60:10; Zec 2:9-11; 3:7

Justice and Mercy, Not Fasting

7 In the fourth year of King Darius, the word of the LORD came to Zechariah on the fourth day of the ninth month, the month of Kislev. 2The people of Bethel had sent Sharezer and Regem-Melech, together with their men, to entreat the LORD 3by asking the priests of the house of the LORD Almighty and the prophets, "Should I mourn and fast in the fifth month, as I have done for so many years?" Jer 52:12-14; Zec 8:19

4Then the word of the LORD Almighty came to me: 5"Ask all the people of the land and the priests, 'When you fasted and mourned in the fifth and seventh months for the past seventy years, was it really for me that you fasted? 6And when you were eating and drinking, were you not just feasting for yourselves? 7Are these not the words the LORD proclaimed through the earlier prophets when Jerusalem and its surrounding towns were at rest and prosperous, and the Negev and the western foothills were settled?' " Jer 22:21; Zec 1:4

8And the word of the LORD came again to Zechariah: 9"This is what the LORD Almighty says: 'Administer true justice; show mercy and compassion to one another. 10Do not oppress the widow or the fatherless, the alien or the poor. In your hearts do not think evil of each other.' Isa 1:17; Zec 8:16

11"But they refused to pay attention; stubbornly they turned their backs and stopped up their ears. 12They made their hearts as hard as flint and

[a]2 Hebrew *twenty cubits long and ten cubits wide* (about 9 meters long and 4.5 meters wide) [b]6 Hebrew *an ephah*; also in verses 7-11 [c]6 Or *appearance* [d]11 Hebrew *Shinar* [e]5 Or *winds* [f]6 Or *horses after them* [g]8 Or *spirit* [h]14 Syriac; Hebrew *Helem* [i]14 Or *and the gracious one, the*

would not listen to the law or to the words that the
LORD Almighty had sent by his Spirit through the
earlier prophets. So the LORD Almighty was very
angry. Ne 9:29; Eze 11:19; Da 9:12
13"'When I called, they did not listen; so when
they called, I would not listen,' says the LORD Almighty. 14'I scattered them with a whirlwind
among all the nations, where they were strangers.
The land was left so desolate behind them that no
one could come or go. This is how they made the
pleasant land desolate.'" Isa 1:15; Jer 44:6

The LORD Promises to Bless Jerusalem

8 Again the word of the LORD Almighty came to
me. 2This is what the LORD Almighty says: "I
am very jealous for Zion; I am burning with jealousy for her." Joel 2:18

LIVING  **INSIGHT**

Our God is a jealous God. He shares His glory with no one else. From this day forward, do not allow yourself to forget the importance of glorifying His great name, regardless of your age, your status or your sphere of influence.

(See Zechariah 8:2.)

3This is what the LORD says: "I will return to
Zion and dwell in Jerusalem. Then Jerusalem will
be called the City of Truth, and the mountain of
the LORD Almighty will be called the Holy Mountain." Zec 1:16; 2:10
4This is what the LORD Almighty says: "Once
again men and women of ripe old age will sit in the
streets of Jerusalem, each with cane in hand because of his age. 5The city streets will be filled with
boys and girls playing there." Isa 65:20; Jer 30:20
6This is what the LORD Almighty says: "It may
seem marvelous to the remnant of this people at
that time, but will it seem marvelous to me?" declares the LORD Almighty. Ps 118:23; 126:1-3
7This is what the LORD Almighty says: "I will
save my people from the countries of the east and
the west. 8I will bring them back to live in Jerusalem; they will be my people, and I will be faithful
and righteous to them as their God." Zec 2:11; 10:6
9This is what the LORD Almighty says: "You
who now hear these words spoken by the prophets
who were there when the foundation was laid for
the house of the LORD Almighty, let your hands be
strong so that the temple may be built. 10Before
that time there were no wages for man or beast.
No one could go about his business safely because
of his enemy, for I had turned every man against
his neighbor. 11But now I will not deal with the
remnant of this people as I did in the past," declares the LORD Almighty. Isa 12:1; Hag 2:4
12"The seed will grow well, the vine will yield its
fruit, the ground will produce its crops, and the
heavens will drop their dew. I will give all these
things as an inheritance to the remnant of this
people. 13As you have been an object of cursing
among the nations, O Judah and Israel, so will I
save you, and you will be a blessing. Do not be
afraid, but let your hands be strong." Ge 12:2
14This is what the LORD Almighty says: "Just as
I had determined to bring disaster upon you and
showed no pity when your fathers angered me,"
says the LORD Almighty, 15"so now I have determined to do good again to Jerusalem and Judah.
Do not be afraid. 16These are the things you are to
do: Speak the truth to each other, and render true
and sound judgment in your courts; 17do not plot
evil against your neighbor, and do not love to
swear falsely. I hate all this," declares the LORD.
18Again the word of the LORD Almighty came to
me. 19This is what the LORD Almighty says: "The
fasts of the fourth, fifth, seventh and tenth months
will become joyful and glad occasions and happy
festivals for Judah. Therefore love truth and
peace." Ps 30:11
20This is what the LORD Almighty says: "Many
peoples and the inhabitants of many cities will yet
come, 21and the inhabitants of one city will go to
another and say, 'Let us go at once to entreat the
LORD and seek the LORD Almighty. I myself am
going.' 22And many peoples and powerful nations
will come to Jerusalem to seek the LORD Almighty
and to entreat him." Ps 117:1; Zec 2:11
23This is what the LORD Almighty says: "In those
days ten men from all languages and nations will
take firm hold of one Jew by the hem of his robe
and say, 'Let us go with you, because we have
heard that God is with you.'" Isa 45:14; 1Co 14:25

Words of Hope **Chapters 9–14**

In these chapters the Lord brought encouragement to the people through glorious words of hope. Zechariah looked far into the future and revealed the ultimate and climactic prophetic scenes of the nation and its Messiah as they enjoyed blessings together. These far-reaching words point to the hope of the entire nation in relationship to the future work of Messiah. Although human powers rise and fall, the kingdom of Jesus Christ will endure forever!

Judgment on Israel's Enemies

An Oracle

9 The word of the LORD is against the land of
Hadrach
and will rest upon Damascus— Isa 17:1
for the eyes of men and all the tribes of Israel

are on the LORD—[a]
2and upon Hamath too, which borders on it,
and upon Tyre and Sidon, though they are
very skillful. Eze 28:1-19
3Tyre has built herself a stronghold;
she has heaped up silver like dust,
and gold like the dirt of the streets. Job 27:16
4But the Lord will take away her possessions
and destroy her power on the sea,
and she will be consumed by fire. Isa 23:1
5Ashkelon will see it and fear; Jer 47:5
Gaza will writhe in agony,
and Ekron too, for her hope will wither.
Gaza will lose her king
and Ashkelon will be deserted.
6Foreigners will occupy Ashdod,
and I will cut off the pride of the
Philistines. Isa 14:30
7I will take the blood from their mouths,
the forbidden food from between their
teeth.
Those who are left will belong to our God
and become leaders in Judah,
and Ekron will be like the Jebusites. Jer 47:1
8But I will defend my house
against marauding forces.
Never again will an oppressor overrun my
people,
for now I am keeping watch. Isa 52:1; 54:14

The Coming of Zion's King

9Rejoice greatly, O Daughter of Zion! Isa 62:11
Shout, Daughter of Jerusalem!
See, your king[b] comes to you,
righteous and having salvation, Isa 9:6-7
gentle and riding on a donkey,
on a colt, the foal of a donkey. Mt 21:5*
10I will take away the chariots from Ephraim
and the war-horses from Jerusalem,
and the battle bow will be broken. Hos 1:7
He will proclaim peace to the nations. Isa 2:4
His rule will extend from sea to sea
and from the River[c] to the ends of the
earth.[d] Ps 72:8
11As for you, because of the blood of my
covenant with you, Ex 24:8
I will free your prisoners from the waterless
pit. Isa 42:7
12Return to your fortress, O prisoners of hope;
even now I announce that I will restore
twice as much to you. Isa 40:2
13I will bend Judah as I bend my bow
and fill it with Ephraim. Isa 49:2
I will rouse your sons, O Zion,
against your sons, O Greece, Joel 3:6
and make you like a warrior's sword.

The LORD Will Appear

14Then the LORD will appear over them; Isa 31:5
his arrow will flash like lightning. Ps 18:14
The Sovereign LORD will sound the trumpet;
he will march in the storms of the south,
15 and the LORD Almighty will shield them.
They will destroy
and overcome with slingstones.
They will drink and roar as with wine;
they will be full like a bowl
used for sprinkling[e] the corners of the
altar. Ex 27:2
16The LORD their God will save them on that
day
as the flock of his people.
They will sparkle in his land
like jewels in a crown. Isa 62:3; Jer 31:11
17How attractive and beautiful they will be!
Grain will make the young men thrive,
and new wine the young women.

The LORD Will Care for Judah

10 Ask the LORD for rain in the springtime;
it is the LORD who makes the storm
clouds.
He gives showers of rain to men, Lev 26:4
and plants of the field to everyone. Job 14:9
2The idols speak deceit, Eze 21:21
diviners see visions that lie; Isa 44:25
they tell dreams that are false,
they give comfort in vain. Isa 40:19
Therefore the people wander like sheep
oppressed for lack of a shepherd. Eze 34:5
3"My anger burns against the shepherds,
and I will punish the leaders; Jer 25:34
for the LORD Almighty will care
for his flock, the house of Judah,
and make them like a proud horse in
battle. Eze 34:8-10
4From Judah will come the cornerstone,
from him the tent peg, Isa 22:23
from him the battle bow, Zec 9:10
from him every ruler.
5Together they[f] will be like mighty men
trampling the muddy streets in battle.
Because the LORD is with them,
they will fight and overthrow the horsemen.
6"I will strengthen the house of Judah
and save the house of Joseph.
I will restore them
because I have compassion on them.
They will be as though
I had not rejected them,
for I am the LORD their God
and I will answer them. Zec 13:9

[a] *1* Or *Damascus. / For the eye of the LORD is on all mankind, / as well as on the tribes of Israel,* [b] *9* Or *King* [c] *10* That is, the Euphrates [d] *10* Or *the end of the land* [e] *15* Or *bowl, / like* [f] *4,5* Or *ruler, all of them together. / 5They*

[7]The Ephraimites will become like mighty men,
and their hearts will be glad as with wine.
Their children will see it and be joyful;
their hearts will rejoice in the LORD.
[8]I will signal for them Isa 5:26
and gather them in.
Surely I will redeem them;
they will be as numerous as before. Eze 36:11
[9]Though I scatter them among the peoples,
yet in distant lands they will remember me.
They and their children will survive,
and they will return.
[10]I will bring them back from Egypt
and gather them from Assyria. Isa 11:11
I will bring them to Gilead and Lebanon,
and there will not be room enough for
them. Isa 49:19
[11]They will pass through the sea of trouble;
the surging sea will be subdued
and all the depths of the Nile will dry up.
Assyria's pride will be brought down Zep 2:13
and Egypt's scepter will pass away. Eze 30:13
[12]I will strengthen them in the LORD
and in his name they will walk," Mic 4:5
declares the LORD.

11 Open your doors, O Lebanon, Eze 31:3
so that fire may devour your cedars!
[2]Wail, O pine tree, for the cedar has fallen;
the stately trees are ruined!
Wail, oaks of Bashan; Isa 2:13
the dense forest has been cut down! Isa 32:19
[3]Listen to the wail of the shepherds;
their rich pastures are destroyed!
Listen to the roar of the lions;
the lush thicket of the Jordan is ruined!

Two Shepherds

[4]This is what the LORD my God says: "Pasture
the flock marked for slaughter. [5]Their buyers
slaughter them and go unpunished. Those who sell
them say, 'Praise the LORD, I am rich!' Their own
shepherds do not spare them. [6]For I will no longer
have pity on the people of the land," declares the
LORD. "I will hand everyone over to his neighbor
and his king. They will oppress the land, and I will
not rescue them from their hands." Mic 5:8; 7:2-6
[7]So I pastured the flock marked for slaughter,
particularly the oppressed of the flock. Then I took
two staffs and called one Favor and the other
Union, and I pastured the flock. [8]In one month I
got rid of the three shepherds. Jer 25:34
The flock detested me, and I grew weary of
them [9]and said, "I will not be your shepherd. Let
the dying die, and the perishing perish. Let those
who are left eat one another's flesh." Jer 15:2; 43:11
[10]Then I took my staff called Favor and broke
it, revoking the covenant I had made with all the
nations. [11]It was revoked on that day, and so the
afflicted of the flock who were watching me knew
it was the word of the LORD. Jer 14:21
[12]I told them, "If you think it best, give me my
pay; but if not, keep it." So they paid me thirty
pieces of silver. Ex 21:32; Mt 26:15
[13]And the LORD said to me, "Throw it to the
potter"—the handsome price at which they priced
me! So I took the thirty pieces of silver and threw
them into the house of the LORD to the potter.
[14]Then I broke my second staff called Union,
breaking the brotherhood between Judah and Israel.
[15]Then the LORD said to me, "Take again the
equipment of a foolish shepherd. [16]For I am going
to raise up a shepherd over the land who will not
care for the lost, or seek the young, or heal the
injured, or feed the healthy, but will eat the meat
of the choice sheep, tearing off their hoofs.

[17]"Woe to the worthless shepherd, Jer 23:1
who deserts the flock!
May the sword strike his arm and his right
eye! Eze 30:21-22
May his arm be completely withered,
his right eye totally blinded!" Isa 13:1; Jer 23:1

Jerusalem's Enemies to Be Destroyed

An Oracle

12 This is the word of the LORD concerning
Israel. The LORD, who stretches out the
heavens, who lays the foundation of the earth, and
who forms the spirit of man within him, declares:
[2]"I am going to make Jerusalem a cup that sends
all the surrounding peoples reeling. Judah will be
besieged as well as Jerusalem. [3]On that day, when
all the nations of the earth are gathered against
her, I will make Jerusalem an immovable rock for
all the nations. All who try to move it will injure
themselves. [4]On that day I will strike every horse
with panic and its rider with madness," declares
the LORD. "I will keep a watchful eye over the
house of Judah, but I will blind all the horses of the
nations. [5]Then the leaders of Judah will say in their
hearts, 'The people of Jerusalem are strong, because the LORD Almighty is their God.' Ps 75:8
[6]"On that day I will make the leaders of Judah
like a firepot in a woodpile, like a flaming torch
among sheaves. They will consume right and left
all the surrounding peoples, but Jerusalem will remain intact in her place. Isa 10:17-18; Ob 1:18
[7]"The LORD will save the dwellings of Judah
first, so that the honor of the house of David and
of Jerusalem's inhabitants may not be greater than
that of Judah. [8]On that day the LORD will shield
those who live in Jerusalem, so that the feeblest
among them will be like David, and the house of
David will be like God, like the Angel of the LORD
going before them. [9]On that day I will set out to
destroy all the nations that attack Jerusalem.

Mourning for the One They Pierced

10“And I will pour out on the house of David
and the inhabitants of Jerusalem a spirit[a] of grace
and supplication. They will look on[b] me, the one
they have pierced, and they will mourn for him as
one mourns for an only child, and grieve bitterly
for him as one grieves for a firstborn son. 11On
that day the weeping in Jerusalem will be great,
like the weeping of Hadad Rimmon in the plain of
Megiddo. 12The land will mourn, each clan by itself, with their wives by themselves: the clan of the
house of David and their wives, the clan of the
house of Nathan and their wives, 13the clan of
the house of Levi and their wives, the clan of Shimei and their wives, 14and all the rest of the clans
and their wives. Jn 19:34,37*; Rev 1:7

Cleansing From Sin

13 “On that day a fountain will be opened to
the house of David and the inhabitants of
Jerusalem, to cleanse them from sin and impurity.
2“On that day, I will banish the names of the
idols from the land, and they will be remembered
no more,” declares the LORD Almighty. “I will remove both the prophets and the spirit of impurity
from the land. 3And if anyone still prophesies, his
father and mother, to whom he was born, will say
to him, ‘You must die, because you have told lies
in the LORD's name.’ When he prophesies, his own
parents will stab him. Dt 18:20; Jer 23:14-15,34
4“On that day every prophet will be ashamed of
his prophetic vision. He will not put on a prophet's
garment of hair in order to deceive. 5He will say,
‘I am not a prophet. I am a farmer; the land has
been my livelihood since my youth.[c]’ 6If someone asks him, ‘What are these wounds on your
body[d]?’ he will answer, ‘The wounds I was given
at the house of my friends.’ Mic 3:6-7; Mt 3:4

The Shepherd Struck, the Sheep Scattered

7“Awake, O sword, against my shepherd,
against the man who is close to me!”
declares the LORD Almighty.
“Strike the shepherd,
and the sheep will be scattered, Mt 26:31*
and I will turn my hand against the little
ones.
8In the whole land,” declares the LORD,
“two-thirds will be struck down and perish;
yet one-third will be left in it. Eze 5:2-4,12
9This third I will bring into the fire; Mal 3:2
I will refine them like silver 1Pe 1:6-7
and test them like gold.
They will call on my name Ps 50:15
and I will answer them; Zec 10:6
I will say, ‘They are my people,’ Jer 30:22
and they will say, ‘The LORD is our God.’ ”

The LORD Comes and Reigns

14 A day of the LORD is coming when your
plunder will be divided among you.
2I will gather all the nations to Jerusalem to fight
against it; the city will be captured, the houses
ransacked, and the women raped. Half of the city
will go into exile, but the rest of the people will not
be taken from the city. Isa 13:6; Zec 13:8
3Then the LORD will go out and fight against
those nations, as he fights in the day of battle. 4On
that day his feet will stand on the Mount of Olives,
east of Jerusalem, and the Mount of Olives will be
split in two from east to west, forming a great
valley, with half of the mountain moving north
and half moving south. 5You will flee by my
mountain valley, for it will extend to Azel. You will
flee as you fled from the earthquake[e] in the days
of Uzziah king of Judah. Then the LORD my God
will come, and all the holy ones with him.
6On that day there will be no light, no cold or
frost. 7It will be a unique day, without daytime or
nighttime—a day known to the LORD. When evening comes, there will be light. Rev 21:23-25; 22:5
8On that day living water will flow out from
Jerusalem, half to the eastern sea[f] and half to the
western sea,[g] in summer and in winter.
9The LORD will be king over the whole earth. On
that day there will be one LORD, and his name the
only name. Eph 4:5-6; Rev 11:15
10The whole land, from Geba to Rimmon, south
of Jerusalem, will become like the Arabah. But
Jerusalem will be raised up and remain in its place,
from the Benjamin Gate to the site of the First
Gate, to the Corner Gate, and from the Tower of
Hananel to the royal winepresses. 11It will be inhabited; never again will it be destroyed. Jerusalem
will be secure. Am 9:11; Zec 12:6
12This is the plague with which the LORD will
strike all the nations that fought against Jerusalem:
Their flesh will rot while they are still standing on
their feet, their eyes will rot in their sockets, and
their tongues will rot in their mouths. 13On that
day men will be stricken by the LORD with great
panic. Each man will seize the hand of another,
and they will attack each other. 14Judah too will
fight at Jerusalem. The wealth of all the surrounding nations will be collected—great quantities of
gold and silver and clothing. 15A similar plague
will strike the horses and mules, the camels and
donkeys, and all the animals in those camps.
16Then the survivors from all the nations that
have attacked Jerusalem will go up year after year

[a] 10 Or *the Spirit* [b] 10 Or *to* [c] 5 Or *farmer; a man sold me in my youth* [d] 6 Or *wounds between your hands*
[e] 5 Or 5*My mountain valley will be blocked and will extend to Azel. It will be blocked as it was blocked because of the earthquake*
[f] 8 That is, the Dead Sea [g] 8 That is, the Mediterranean

to worship the King, the LORD Almighty, and to
celebrate the Feast of Tabernacles. 17 If any of the
peoples of the earth do not go up to Jerusalem to
worship the King, the LORD Almighty, they will
have no rain. 18 If the Egyptian people do not go up
and take part, they will have no rain. The LORD[a]
will bring on them the plague he inflicts on the
nations that do not go up to celebrate the Feast
of Tabernacles. 19 This will be the punishment of
Egypt and the punishment of all the nations that
do not go up to celebrate the Feast of Tabernacles.
20 On that day HOLY TO THE LORD will be inscribed on the bells of the horses, and the cooking
pots in the LORD's house will be like the sacred
bowls in front of the altar. 21 Every pot in Jerusalem
and Judah will be holy to the LORD Almighty, and
all who come to sacrifice will take some of the pots
and cook in them. And on that day there will no
longer be a Canaanite[b] in the house of the LORD
Almighty.

1Co 10:31; Eze 44:9

[a] 18 Or *part, then the LORD* [b] 21 Or *merchant*

INTRODUCTION

MALACHI

The Jews didn't know it, but they stood on the brink of silence. God's silence. For four hundred years. J. Sidlow Baxter put it this way: "Malachi calling! . . . the last spokesman utters his soul and retires behind the misty curtains of the past. A peculiar solemnity clings about him." Prophesying after the days of Nehemiah, Malachi witnessed the settled, stagnant, corrupt indifference of his people, and he deplored what he saw. The intermarriage with foreigners, the neglect of the tithe, the compromise in offering blemished sacrifices—all these things caused this devoted and sensitive prophet to confront the people and warn them of the consequence of disobedience. Silence was soon to come, but as long as Malachi was on the scene, the nation heard plenty!

WRITER: *Malachi*

DATE: *c.430 B.C.*

PURPOSE: *To confront the spirit of complacency and indifference that had developed*

KEY THEMES: *God's passionate love; God's call for justice*

KEY SINS OF THE DAY: *Indifference; intermarriage; cynicism; blemished offerings; failure to tithe*

CONTEMPORARY: *Nehemiah*

ERA: *Postexilic*

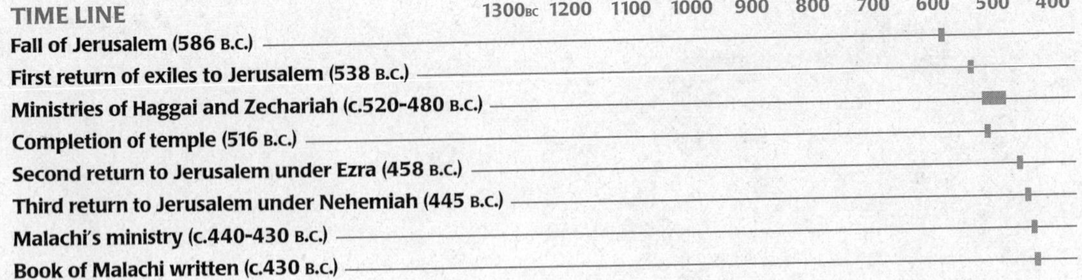

Last Call Before the Silent Years

	LOVE	REBUKE: Against the Priests	REBUKE: Against the People	HOPE
	Unconditional	Irreverence (God)	Intermarriage with pagans	Fire
	Almighty	Disobedience (work)	Indifference	Healing
	Sovereign	Cynicism (calling)	Robbing God/no tithes	"Elijah"
		Hypocrisy (self)	Blasphemy	Family
		Offense (others)		
	CHAPTER 1:1-5	*CHAPTERS 1:6–2:9*	*CHAPTERS 2:10–3:18*	*CHAPTER 4*
CONTENT	**Theological**	**Historical**		**Prophetical**
DIRECTION	**Looking up**	**Looking in**		**Looking ahead**

Sandwiched between the 39 books of the Old Testament and the 27 books of the New Testament was an almost eerie period of silence. It was as though a thick veil had been drawn between the Testaments. This was a period of time that lasted about four hundred years and was a time in which God was completely silent as far as His writing prophets were concerned. That doesn't mean that nothing happened; it simply means that God did not, during those four centuries, lead any writer to record material that would be later compiled and included in the canon of Scripture.

During that four hundred-year period of silence God worked through some very special human agents whom He personally chose. God put these persons into special roles of leadership to compile and to arrange the Old Testament books in order. He then guided the scholars of that era to translate God's Word from the Hebrew language into the common language of the day, the "vernacular" (which in that period in history was the Greek language). This translation became the most significant translation in the history of time—with the possible exception of the translation of the Bible into English. For when the Hebrew was translated into Greek, the people possessed a Bible they could use and understand. The Bible truly became an "open book" to the people who spoke that language. The Greek translation of the Old Testament is known today as the *Septuagint*.

The Final Prophet

God chose a man about whom very little is known to be His final messenger before the time between the Testaments. Just before coming into the station marking the end of the Old Testament, God raised up one man to serve as His spokesman who would be the caboose on the end of those 39 cars that have come to be known as the Scripture of the Old Testament. His name was Malachi.

Some students of the Bible believe this messenger was so significant that "Malachi" really wasn't his name. His name in Greek means "my messenger." He might very well have been a spokesman who chose not to use his own name but used a pseudonym to hide his identity—at least in part because of his select role as the last prophet before the curtain fell and brought silence across the Scriptural scene. Malachi was an exceedingly significant man!

Malachi and Nehemiah

To understand Malachi's burden and message it would help to recall the message of Nehemiah (see the introduction to Nehemiah, page 483). Remember, our English Bible is not arranged in chronological order. It can be confusing when we read the book of Nehemiah and have to remember that what was described there actually took place toward the end of the history recorded in the Old Testament (even though Nehemiah falls somewhere in the middle of our English version of the Old Testament). The fact is, Nehemiah was a contemporary of Malachi, the last prophet.

In the days of Malachi and Nehemiah, many Jews had returned to Jerusalem from captivity. A revival-like atmosphere filled the streets of that holy city. Great times! Nehemiah came on the scene in that season of revival and heard the people make great promises about what was going to happen in the days and years ahead. Remember, they had just been released from captivity, from Persian rule, where they had not been free to worship the way they could in Jerusalem.

I'm sure they joyfully sang once again the songs of Zion, and how their praise must have filled the temple when that fine structure was completed. They participated in their worship. They offered their offerings. Back in their land for the first time in decades, they announced their devotion to God and their commitment to walk with Him, regardless of what obstacles they might face! It must have been incredibly exciting for those prophets to once again see the movement of God among the people.

I think you get the picture. The people were standing tall in their faith. That's often what happens when freedom follows captivity, isn't it? Sad to say, however, this devotion didn't last. What a heartache awaits us when we turn to Nehemiah 13 and read the account of what had taken place only a few years later. The revival fires had died down to barely glowing embers. Reminds us of our New Year's resolutions, doesn't it? We make those great, vast, wonderful promises—only to break them by the end of January, if we even make it that long! Malachi was sent by God to pick up the torch that Nehemiah had lit in his time of leadership among the exiles who had returned.

A Messenger of Rebuke

Malachi's message was definitely not complicated. He began by telling the people of God's love. He established that fact, just in case any of the people would be tempted to respond after his stinging rebuke, "That proves God doesn't really love us." Malachi reminded the people right up front that God had set His love on His people Israel, and no amount of sin or compromise on their part could alter that fact!

Malachi openly rebuked God's people with a message that divided into two sections: first, a rebuke directed to the priests, and second, a rebuke directed to the people.

Malachi listed five specific evils the priests had committed: First, in their irreverence they failed to give God the respect that was due Him. Second, they were blatently disobedient. Third, they lacked devotion to their calling, having grown cynical and sarcastic. Fourth, they displayed a lack of credibility and integrity in their personal and professional lives. Fifth, they lost any sense of being godly role models that others could imitate.

The priests weren't the only ones against whom Malachi leveled his prophetic barrage. He also rebuked the people because of the sins they had been committing. They were marrying foreigners, who were to be regarded as daughters "of a foreign god" (2:11). You see, the practice of marrying those of other religions carried with it the constant danger of seduction into idolatry. The people also had begun to twist the truth of God's Word, calling into question the specifics of the standards God had set. They needed the trustworthy and honest words of a prophet . . . and Malachi was the man to deliver the goods.

Lessons From Malachi

I suggest we can learn three lessons from Malachi. First, *promises cool off when we begin to compromise*. These men and women made vast promises and, I'm sure, made them in sincerity. When they stood before Nehemiah and pledged their commitment to their covenant God, I'm confident they meant it. But after a while they began to compromise their commitment, ever so subtly. The priests began to walk another way;

ultimately they lost their sense of moral compass. And once again they were headed down the road of rebellion.

There is nothing that replaces genuine obedience. Nothing. Forgive me if this hurts too much . . . if you are really hurting right now, but no-holds-barred obedience at times is the only way you can handle God's way in your life. Trust Him when you cannot see tomorrow. When everything you have attempted to do to relieve your pain, to address your need, has blown up in your face, may I gently urge you, continue to trust Him.

Second, *all who are involved in Christian service must be alert to three especially alluring temptations: carelessness, cynicism and corruption.* It is not easy to be a godly role model. But when we fail to model Christlike attitudes and behaviors, the people among whom we serve will have greater difficulty in seeing the joy of following God. Particularly for those who have been called by God to serve Him as "shepherd" of the sheep—let me remind you how crucial it is that we stay close to our Lord, the "great Shepherd of the sheep" (Hebrews 13:20), as together we learn from Him and live according to His example. May we be the kind of role models that God would have us be!

A Messenger of Hope

Malachi ends with a message of hope. Ultimately, our great and awesome God will make all things right. He will, indeed, come. He will bring healing. He will give power. He will bring restoration. When we walk with the Lord, we walk in hope!

God's Unconditional Love Chapter 1:1–5

This prophetic book opens with a clear and resounding affirmation of God's love for His people. God assured His people that no amount of gross sin or shameful compromise would alter His love for them. As God's children, what joy and comfort there are in the knowledge that God loves us—and that nothing in all of creation can separate us from that love! (See Romans 8:38–39.) Our God is loving and filled with tender care for His own.

1 An oracle: The word of the LORD to Israel
through Malachi.[a] Na 1:1; 1Pe 4:11

Jacob Loved, Esau Hated

2“I have loved you,” says the LORD. Dt 4:37
“But you ask, ‘How have you loved us?’
“Was not Esau Jacob's brother?” the LORD says.
“Yet I have loved Jacob, 3but Esau I have hated,
and I have turned his mountains into a wasteland
and left his inheritance to the desert jackals.”
4Edom may say, “Though we have been
crushed, we will rebuild the ruins.” Isa 9:10
But this is what the LORD Almighty says: “They
may build, but I will demolish. They will be called
the Wicked Land, a people always under the wrath
of the LORD. 5You will see it with your own eyes
and say, ‘Great is the LORD—even beyond the
borders of Israel!’

Rebuking the Priests Chapters 1:6–2:9

Malachi appeared on the heels of the revival birthed through the ministries of Ezra and Nehemiah to the exiles who had returned to Jerusalem. Malachi was sent by God to speak His word to the nation in a time of indifference. We might have expected a receptive audience because of God's dazzling faithfulness, which the people had experienced in dramatic ways. But the nation was in a post-revival period, and the people and their leaders had become complacent and apathetic. In this section, Malachi rebuked the priests and religious leaders for irreverence, disobedience, cynicism, hypocrisy and offensive behavior. The leaders were taking God's call lightly, and they were castigated for their poor attitudes and compromising behavior.

Blemished Sacrifices

6“A son honors his father, and a servant his
master. If I am a father, where is the honor due
me? If I am a master, where is the respect due me?”
says the LORD Almighty. “It is you, O priests, who
show contempt for my name. Isa 1:2; Mt 15:4
“But you ask, ‘How have we shown contempt
for your name?’
7“You place defiled food on my altar. Lev 21:6
“But you ask, ‘How have we defiled you?’
“By saying that the LORD's table is contemptible.
8When you bring blind animals for sacrifice, is that
not wrong? When you sacrifice crippled or diseased animals, is that not wrong? Try offering
them to your governor! Would he be pleased with
you? Would he accept you?” says the LORD Almighty. Lev 22:22; Dt 15:21; Isa 43:23

LIVING  **INSIGHT**

God is looking out for His own. He's got our good at heart. After giving, giving, giving so many things, He warns us about forgetting Him. How easy, when blessed, to adopt a presumptuous, arrogant spirit.
(See Malachi 1:6.)

9“Now implore God to be gracious to us. With
such offerings from your hands, will he accept
you?”—says the LORD Almighty. Lev 23:33-44
10“Oh, that one of you would shut the temple
doors, so that you would not light useless fires on
my altar! I am not pleased with you,” says the
LORD Almighty, “and I will accept no offering from
your hands. 11My name will be great among the
nations, from the rising to the setting of the sun.
In every place incense and pure offerings will be
brought to my name, because my name will be
great among the nations,” says the LORD Almighty.
12“But you profane it by saying of the Lord's
table, ‘It is defiled,’ and of its food, ‘It is contemptible.’ 13And you say, ‘What a burden!’ and you
sniff at it contemptuously,” says the LORD Almighty. Isa 43:22-24
“When you bring injured, crippled or diseased
animals and offer them as sacrifices, should I accept them from your hands?” says the LORD.
14“Cursed is the cheat who has an acceptable male
in his flock and vows to give it, but then sacrifices
a blemished animal to the Lord. For I am a great
king,” says the LORD Almighty, “and my name is to
be feared among the nations. Lev 22:18-21; 1Ti 6:15

Admonition for the Priests

2 “And now this admonition is for you,
O priests. 2If you do not listen, and if you do
not set your heart to honor my name,” says the
LORD Almighty, “I will send a curse upon you, and
I will curse your blessings. Yes, I have already
cursed them, because you have not set your heart
to honor me. Dt 28:20
3“Because of you I will rebuke[b] your descendants[c]; I will spread on your faces the offal from
your festival sacrifices, and you will be carried off
with it. 4And you will know that I have sent you
this admonition so that my covenant with Levi
may continue,” says the LORD Almighty. 5“My

[a] 1 *Malachi* means *my messenger.* [b] 3 Or *cut off* (see Septuagint) [c] 3 Or *will blight your grain*

covenant was with him, a covenant of life and
peace, and I gave them to him; this called for
reverence and he revered me and stood in awe of
my name. 6“True instruction was in his mouth and
nothing false was found on his lips. He walked
with me in peace and uprightness, and turned
many from sin. Nu 25:12; Jer 23:22
7“For the lips of a priest ought to preserve
knowledge, and from his mouth men should seek
instruction—because he is the messenger of the
LORD Almighty. 8But you have turned from the
way and by your teaching have caused many to
stumble; you have violated the covenant with
Levi,” says the LORD Almighty. 9“So I have caused
you to be despised and humiliated before all
the people, because you have not followed my
ways but have shown partiality in matters of the
law.” 1Sa 2:30; Jer 18:15

Rebuking the People **Chapters 2:10–3:18**

After a clear rebuke of the priests, the Lord turned His attention to His people. They had intermarried with people from the pagan nations surrounding them, thereby compromising their faith. Their hearts had grown cold and indifferent to the things of the Lord. They were robbing God by failing to bring their tithes and the firstfruits of their labors into the treasury rooms of the Lord. In short, they had wandered from the path God had clearly set before them, and it was time for God to call them back to the straight and narrow way of faith. Malachi wrote strong but necessary words of reprimand.

Judah Unfaithful

10Have we not all one Father[a]? Did not one
God create us? Why do we profane the covenant of
our fathers by breaking faith with one another?
11Judah has broken faith. A detestable thing has
been committed in Israel and in Jerusalem: Judah
has desecrated the sanctuary the LORD loves, by
marrying the daughter of a foreign god. 12As for
the man who does this, whoever he may be, may
the LORD cut him off from the tents of Jacob[b]—
even though he brings offerings to the LORD Almighty. Mal 1:10
13Another thing you do: You flood the LORD's
altar with tears. You weep and wail because he no
longer pays attention to your offerings or accepts
them with pleasure from your hands. 14You ask,
“Why?” It is because the LORD is acting as the
witness between you and the wife of your youth,
because you have broken faith with her, though
she is your partner, the wife of your marriage covenant. Pr 5:18; Heb 13:4
15Has not ⌞the LORD⌟ made them one? In flesh
and spirit they are his. And why one? Because he
was seeking godly offspring.[c] So guard yourself in
your spirit, and do not break faith with the wife of
your youth. Mt 19:4-6; 1Co 7:14
16“I hate divorce,” says the LORD God of Israel,
“and I hate a man's covering himself[d] with violence as well as with his garment,” says the LORD
Almighty. Dt 24:1; Mt 5:31-32; 19:4-9
So guard yourself in your spirit, and do not
break faith. Ps 51:10

The Day of Judgment

17You have wearied the LORD with your words.
“How have we wearied him?” you ask. Mal 1:2
By saying, “All who do evil are good in the eyes
of the LORD, and he is pleased with them” or
“Where is the God of justice?” Ps 5:4
3 “See, I will send my messenger, who will prepare the way before me. Then suddenly the
Lord you are seeking will come to his temple; the
messenger of the covenant, whom you desire, will
come,” says the LORD Almighty. Mt 11:10*
2But who can endure the day of his coming?
Who can stand when he appears? For he will be
like a refiner's fire or a launderer's soap. 3He will
sit as a refiner and purifier of silver; he will purify
the Levites and refine them like gold and silver.
Then the LORD will have men who will bring offerings in righteousness, 4and the offerings of Judah
and Jerusalem will be acceptable to the LORD, as in
days gone by, as in former years. Rev 6:17; Isa 1:25
5“So I will come near to you for judgment. I will
be quick to testify against sorcerers, adulterers and
perjurers, against those who defraud laborers of
their wages, who oppress the widows and the fatherless, and deprive aliens of justice, but do not
fear me,” says the LORD Almighty. Lev 19:13; Jer 7:9

Robbing God

6“I the LORD do not change. So you, O descendants of Jacob, are not destroyed. 7Ever since the
time of your forefathers you have turned away
from my decrees and have not kept them.
Return to me, and I will return to you,” says the
LORD Almighty. Ac 7:51; Jas 1:17
“But you ask, ‘How are we to return?’
8“Will a man rob God? Yet you rob me.
“But you ask, ‘How do we rob you?’
“In tithes and offerings. 9You are under a
curse—the whole nation of you—because you are
robbing me. 10Bring the whole tithe into the storehouse, that there may be food in my house. Test
me in this,” says the LORD Almighty, “and see if I

[a] 10 Or *father* [b] 12 Or 12*May the LORD cut off from the tents of Jacob anyone who gives testimony in behalf of the man who does this* [c] 15 Or 15*But the one ⌞who is our father⌟ did not do this, not as long as life remained in him. And what was he seeking? An offspring from God* [d] 16 Or *his wife*

will not throw open the floodgates of heaven and pour out so much blessing that you will not have room enough for it. [11]I will prevent pests from devouring your crops, and the vines in your fields will not cast their fruit," says the LORD Almighty. [12]"Then all the nations will call you blessed, for yours will be a delightful land," says the LORD Almighty. Ne 13:10-12; Isa 62:4

[13]"You have said harsh things against me," says the LORD. Mal 2:17

"Yet you ask, 'What have we said against you?'

[14]"You have said, 'It is futile to serve God. What did we gain by carrying out his requirements and going about like mourners before the LORD Almighty? [15]But now we call the arrogant blessed. Certainly the evildoers prosper, and even those who challenge God escape.'" Isa 58:3; Jer 7:10

[16]Then those who feared the LORD talked with each other, and the LORD listened and heard. A scroll of remembrance was written in his presence concerning those who feared the LORD and honored his name. Ps 34:15; 56:8

[17]"They will be mine," says the LORD Almighty, "in the day when I make up my treasured possession.[a] I will spare them, just as in compassion a man spares his son who serves him. [18]And you will again see the distinction between the righteous and the wicked, between those who serve God and those who do not. Ps 103:13; Mt 25:32-33,41

Hope for the Future **Chapter 4**

In the closing verses of this prophecy God offered a bright word of hope and encouragement. Ultimately, God would make all things right through the promised Messiah, who would come among His people. In the Old Testament's closing words, we are told that God would bring healing and give power to His people and accomplish restoration in the land. Though we may be, and so often are, unfaithful to Him, our Lord's faithfulness endures forever!

The Day of the LORD

4 "Surely the day is coming; it will burn like a furnace. All the arrogant and every evildoer will be stubble, and that day that is coming will set them on fire," says the LORD Almighty. "Not a root or a branch will be left to them. [2]But for you who revere my name, the sun of righteousness will rise with healing in its wings. And you will go out and leap like calves released from the stall. [3]Then you will trample down the wicked; they will be ashes under the soles of your feet on the day when I do these things," says the LORD Almighty. Lk 1:78

[4]"Remember the law of my servant Moses, the decrees and laws I gave him at Horeb for all Israel.

[5]"See, I will send you the prophet Elijah before that great and dreadful day of the LORD comes. [6]He will turn the hearts of the fathers to their children, and the hearts of the children to their fathers; or else I will come and strike the land with a curse."

[a]17 Or *Almighty, "my treasured possession, in the day when I act*

FROM MALACHI TO CHRIST

The Persian Period
450-330 B.C.

For about 100 years after Nehemiah's time the Persians controlled Judah, but the Jews were allowed to carry on their religious observances and were not interfered with. During this time Judah was ruled by high priests who were responsible for Jewish government.

The Hellenistic Period
330-166 B.C.

In 333 B.C. the Persian armies stationed in Macedonia were defeated by Alexander the Great. He was convinced that Greek culture was the one force that could unify the world. Alexander permitted the Jews to observe their laws and even granted them exemption from tribute or tax during their sabbath years. The Greek conquest prepared the way for the translation of the Old Testament into Greek (Septuagint version) c.250 B.C.

The Hasmonean Period
166-63 B.C.

When this historical period began, the Jews were being greatly oppressed. The Ptolemies had been tolerant of the Jews and their religious practices, but the Seleucid rulers were determined to force Hellenism on them. Copies of the Scriptures were ordered destroyed and laws were enforced with extreme cruelty. The oppressed Jews revolted, led by Judas the Maccabee.

The Roman Period
63 B.C. . . .

In the year 63 B.C. Pompey, the Roman general, captured Jerusalem, and the provinces of Palestine became subject to Rome. The local government was entrusted part of the time to princes and the rest of the time to procurators who were appointed by the emperors. Herod the Great was ruler of all Palestine at the time of Christ's birth.

	450 B.C.
	440
	430
	420
	410
	400
	390
	380
	370
	360
	350
	340
	330
Rule of Alexander the Great	320
	310
	300
	290
	280
	270
Rule of the Ptolemies of Egypt	260
	250
	240
	230
	220
	210
	200
	190
Rule of the Seleucids of Syria	180
	170
	160
	150
	140
	130
	120
Hasmonean Dynasty	110
	100
	90
	80
	70
	60
	50
	40
	30
Herod the Great rules as king; subject to Rome	20
	10
	1
	10
	20
	A.D. 30

NEW TESTAMENT

INTRODUCTION

MATTHEW

As the flame of Christianity began spreading rapidly in the first century after Christ, the spoken testimony of the apostles was no longer adequate... therefore, the need for the truth about Jesus Christ to be recorded in written form, Matthew, a tax collector by trade, wrote his Gospel from the perspective of *Jesus Christ, the King*. It is quite clear that he had first-century Jews in mind as he arranged his material. The book, therefore, includes numerous facts and expressions that would appeal to the Jewish reader. The fulfillment of Old Testament prophecies and the presentation of Jesus as the Messiah are clearly emphasized by Matthew. When we rightly understand the Gospel of Matthew, we bow before King Jesus, the promised Messiah of Israel.

WRITER: *Matthew*

DATE: *C.A.D. 70–80*

PURPOSE: *To offer proof that Jesus is the Messiah, the One who fulfilled the Old Testament Scriptures*

KEY THEME: *Jesus is the King of Glory*

KEY MESSAGE: *Messiah has come!*

KEY TERMS: *"the kingdom of heaven" (31 times); "to fulfill what was spoken through the prophet" (or variation 10 times)*

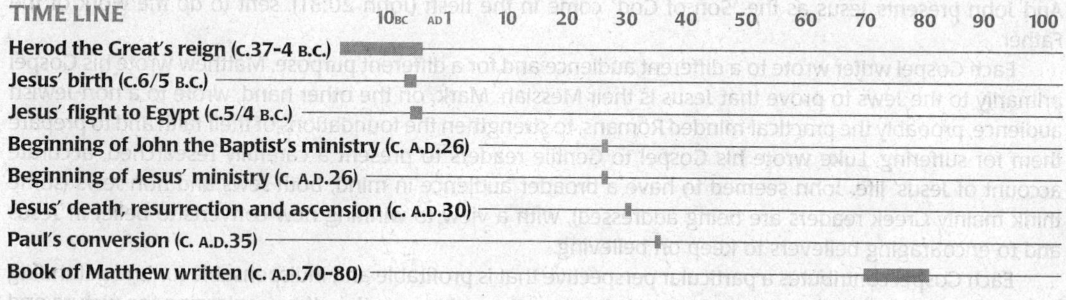

Let's Meet the King

	ARRIVAL AND ANNOUNCEMENT OF THE KING	PROCLAMATION AND RECEPTION OF THE KING	OPPOSITION AND REJECTION OF THE KING	RESURRECTION AND TRIUMPH OF THE KING
	MAIN EMPHASIS: **HIS CREDENTIALS**	MAIN EMPHASIS: **HIS MESSAGE**	MAIN EMPHASIS: **SUFFERING AND DEATH**	MAIN EMPHASIS: **HIS CONQUEST**
	Birth Baptism Temptation	Sermon on the Mount Miracles Discourses	Spread of opposition Final predictions Crucifixion	Power Commission
	CHAPTERS 1–4	*CHAPTERS 5–15*	*CHAPTERS 16–27*	*CHAPTER 28*
THE KING	**His identity: Israel's promised King**		**His destiny: *"Crucify Him!"***	
THE SCOPE	**Teaching the vast multitudes**		**Teaching the Twelve**	
LOCATION	**Bethlehem and Nazareth**	**Ministry in Galilee**	**Ministry in Judea**	
PUBLIC REACTION	**Increased popularity**		**Increased hostility**	

Each of the four Gospel accounts presents a slightly different picture of Jesus Christ that, taken together, gives us a well-rounded view of His life and teachings. Matthew, for example, shows that Jesus is the King—the son of David (Matthew 1:1), the very Messiah promised in the Old Testament. Mark presents Jesus as the Servant (Mark 10:45) who came to suffer and die for our redemption. Luke paints a compellingly beautiful picture of Jesus as fully human, the "Son of Man" who came to seek and to save the lost (Luke 19:10). And John presents Jesus as the "Son of God" come in the flesh (John 20:31), sent to do the work of the Father.

Each Gospel writer wrote to a different audience and for a different purpose. Matthew wrote his Gospel primarily to the Jews to prove that Jesus is their Messiah. Mark, on the other hand, wrote to a non-Jewish audience, probably the practical-minded Romans, to strengthen the foundations of their faith and to prepare them for suffering. Luke wrote his Gospel to Gentile readers to present a carefully researched, accurate account of Jesus' life. John seemed to have a broader audience in mind, both Jews and non-Jews (some think mainly Greek readers are being addressed), with a view to winning new converts to belief in Jesus and to encouraging believers to keep on believing.

Each Gospel contributes a particular perspective that is profitable and indispensable for understanding the earthly ministry of our Lord. Each complements and supplements the others, enlarging the picture and helping us to see Jesus more clearly and to follow Him more obediently.

The Focus of Matthew

In Matthew's Gospel, the writer was concerned with presenting the credentials of Jesus. It was very important to Matthew that his Jewish readers see the testimonials that clearly show Jesus to be the promised Messiah. When I talk with Jewish friends who have not accepted Jesus as the Messiah, I encourage them to read the Gospel of Matthew, because Matthew presents considerable Old Testament evidence that supports the claims that Jesus was the fulfillment of all that the prophets pointed to, that He was, in fact, the long-awaited deliverer of God's people.

Why did Matthew write this Gospel? Why did this tax gatherer write a book about Jesus? The answer is clear: He was interested in providing information about Jesus for the Jewish reader. He offered facts that would prove that Jesus was the promised King, the Messiah. There may very well be times when we contemporary readers scratch our heads over certain sections of Matthew, at least in part because Matthew was originally written to a Jewish audience in the first century.

Getting Things in Order

Forty-two percent of Matthew's Gospel is unique—meaning that 42 percent of the material contained within its pages is found in no other Gospel account. In Mark, only 7 percent of what he included is unique; in Luke's Gospel the percentage climbs to 59 percent. The Gospel of John is 92 percent unique to his telling of the Gospel story. Another engaging fact is that 60 percent of Matthew's Gospel contains quotations from the mouth of Jesus.

Many students of the Bible consider Mark's Gospel to be the first of the four written accounts of our Lord's earthly life. The fact that Mark is only 7 percent unique may indicate that the other Gospel writers received some of their information from Mark. (A mathematical comparison shows that 91 percent of Mark's Gospel is contained in Matthew and 53 percent of Mark is found in Luke.) I believe Matthew's account was written second and Luke's third; most scholars place John's Gospel as the fourth and final record of the life of Jesus. The Gospels comprise 46 percent of the content of the New Testament. To the surprise of many who are just becoming acquainted with the Bible, the Gospels along with the book of Acts make up 60 percent of the New Testament.

A Look at the Good News

The word "gospel" means "good news." It comes from the old Anglo-Saxon word "godspel," which means "good story"; from that term is derived the English "good news." These four books, called Gospels, give us the good news concerning Jesus.

The first three Gospels are called "synoptic Gospels." *Synoptic* comes from a blending of two Greek words, *syn*, meaning "together with," and *optic*, meaning "seeing"—combining the terms they convey the idea of "seeing together." The first three Gospels see many things together. They're quite similar. The Gospel of John, however, looks at things from a whole different point of view. As you read the fourth Gospel, you'll understand why it is unique.

Meeting the Author

Matthew was an eyewitness to the life and ministry of Jesus Christ, the Messiah. Matthew personally came into contact with the Savior, and his life would never again be the same. In chapter 9 he recorded the story of his call from the Lord. Wouldn't it have been incredible to have lived in the first century and to have been chosen by the Lord to write a book that would present Jesus Christ as the Messiah? Read the following and note Matthew's autobiographical recollection:

> *As Jesus went on from there, he saw a man named Matthew sitting at the tax collector's booth. "Follow me," he told him, and Matthew got up and followed him (9:9).*

I can't help but smile when I read the incredible response of Matthew. Surely he had examined the claims of Jesus. Surely his heart had been drawn like a magnet to the Son of God. He was ready to follow. He gave up his career at a moment's invitation. Two words were issued in his direction, and on the basis of that simple but incredibly profound invitation, "Follow Me," he dropped everything and walked with Jesus from that point on. Look closely at the very next scene:

> *While Jesus was having dinner at Matthew's house, many tax collectors and "sinners" came and ate with him and his disciples (9:10).*

When the Pharisees saw Jesus surrounded by this motley crew of ragamuffins, they could hardly contain themselves. Can't you imagine what they must have muttered among themselves: "How could it be that this one who claims to be holy sits at a table with notorious sinners and tax gatherers?" This was the real scum of society in the eyes of the religious establishment. By Jewish law, a tax collector was debarred from the synagogue and forbidden to be a witness in any legal case. Robbers, murderers and tax collectors were all lumped together as outcasts and evildoers. When Jesus called Matthew, He called a man who was hated and considered a traitor by the public.

Modern-day Matthews

Isn't it remarkable that a man with a reputation like Matthew's would be chosen to write the Gospel that would become the first book of the New Testament? But isn't that just like God? It may be that your background is filled with guilt and shame. You may be the target of hatred and rejection. You may think your poor reputation and sordid history have excluded you from God's kingdom and placed you beyond His reach. If that's what you think, let me respectfully say, you are wrong!

If Jesus could pick a man like Matthew to walk with Him and live as one of His disciples, certainly He can choose the likes of you and me to be part of His family of followers. Whatever your background, whatever your lifestyle in years gone by, God hasn't finished writing the story of your life. He still calls you, like He did Matthew, to follow Him. In the final analysis, all of us whom God has called to Himself are undeserving recipients of His mercy. It is nothing we bring that commends us to Him. No, it is all *grace—amazing grace*!

A Style All His Own

The literary style and the phrases Matthew used show us that he was a man given to systematic, orderly thinking. I've often said that he had the mind of a Certified Public Accountant! He was concerned about tracing the lineage of Jesus back to Abraham (1:1). Keep in mind that he was appealing to Jewish readers. A Jew would sit up and take notice much more readily if Jesus' roots could be traced back to Abraham, the father of the Jewish race.

Jesus was a Jew—the son of Abraham, and He was also a King—the son of David (1:1). Matthew set out to prove that this Jesus was the long-expected King, the Messiah, and so his account highlights the King and His kingdom. The phrase "the kingdom of heaven" is used 31 times in Matthew's Gospel. Guess how many other times this phrase is used in the rest of the New Testament? *Not once*! Matthew had the King on his heart, and that King has a kingdom. The kingdom is real, and it's promised to His people. The theme is this: *Jesus Christ is Israel's Messiah-King*. The King of glory has come. Jesus is Messiah!

There's a phrase (or its variation) used no less than ten times in Matthew: "To fulfill what was spoken through the prophet." Matthew was saying, in effect, to the Jewish reader, "You see, what has happened is exactly what our prophets told us would happen. This Messiah came precisely when the prophets said He would. He was born exactly as Micah said. They named Him Jesus, just as Isaiah predicted. He was called a Nazarene just as the prophets foretold." Throughout his Gospel, Matthew showed how the coming of Jesus fulfilled the Old Testament prophecies.

In other words, the purpose of Matthew's Gospel is that the Jewish reader would conclude, "Well . . . I can no longer deny it! Everything our prophets have predicted has come true. Jesus obviously is the Messiah!"

Messages From Matthew

I find Matthew divides nicely into four sections, or stages, that may reflect seasons in our own spiritual growth. The first section teaches us about the *beginning steps of faith*. We learn that when we are born again, the King arrives with all His credentials verifying that He is in fact who He says He is: Immanuel—God with us. When we give our hearts to Jesus, we receive the King. He takes up residence in our lives. That is the message of chapters 1–4 of Matthew—a beautiful section of Scripture that points us to the arrival of the King who calls us to be His disciples!

Chapters 5–15 of Matthew reflect the time in our lives when we *begin to grow*. Jesus works powerfully in us and teaches us to walk with Him. We grow closer to Him and to each other, as the King demonstrates

His power in our lives. Through a skillful blending of words and actions, Matthew tells and shows us how to live as children of the King.

The third section of Matthew introduces a new phase of spiritual life. Chapters 16–27 present what we might call the "mid-life crisis"—*a time of struggle* when the opposition seems to be winning more than it's losing. During this season, we may begin to listen to the negative voices around us. In those times when discord mounts and we feel pressure all around, we must remember that Jesus is the King. We are wise to hold on to His hand, even when, especially when, the nights are dark and long.

For some people this time of testing happens in young adulthood. Perhaps they've known Jesus since they were four or five years old; then one day they begin to question everything they've been taught, wondering if Jesus really is who He said He is. For others, maybe their marriage begins to fall apart or their career collapses around them; their faith in Jesus' power is shaken, and they find themselves asking, "Is all of this stuff about Jesus really true?" That's when the enemy swoops in, saying, "Do you think if He were God, He would let this happen? Smarten up! Crucify Him! Get rid of Him! How can a just and good God let this happen to you?" During the times of struggle we need to stand strong and listen to the voice of Jesus calling us to come to Him and to stand with Him in the times of suffering and testing.

A final phase of our spiritual growth is depicted in the last chapter of Matthew. Here the King has won out. He has emerged triumphant. He resurrects in our minds the truth of and about Himself. *The King is triumphant, and we share in the fruits of His victory.* In the joy of His resurrection power, we go out to "make disciples of all nations" (28:19), knowing that King Jesus is with us always.

All of us are at a particular place along our faith pilgrimage. We must remember that wherever we are along the way, this truth remains: Jesus is King. He has reigned supreme in the past, He reigns supreme now, and He will reign supreme forever and ever!

Arrival of the King **Chapters 1–4**

The first four chapters record the genealogy, birth, baptism and temptation of Jesus. We come to understand that Jesus is the King and that He has the credentials to get the job done. He has every right to rule over the kingdom of heaven. His birth was kingly . . . His lineage went all the way back to Abraham, the father of the Jewish nation, and to David, Israel's greatest king. At His baptism Jesus received the approval of His Father in heaven. Although tempted by the devil three times, Jesus resisted and withstood the attacks of the enemy. We are left with no doubts: The King of Israel has come. His name is Jesus.

The Genealogy of Jesus

▶ *See Ruth 4:18–22; 1 Chronicles 3:10–17; Luke 3:23–38*

1 A record of the genealogy of Jesus Christ the son of David, the son of Abraham: Ge 22:18

2 Abraham was the father of Isaac, Ge 21:3,12
Isaac the father of Jacob, Ge 25:26
Jacob the father of Judah and his brothers,
3 Judah the father of Perez and Zerah, whose mother was Tamar, Ge 38:27-30
Perez the father of Hezron,
Hezron the father of Ram,
4 Ram the father of Amminadab,
Amminadab the father of Nahshon,
Nahshon the father of Salmon,
5 Salmon the father of Boaz, whose mother was Rahab,
Boaz the father of Obed, whose mother was Ruth,
Obed the father of Jesse,
6 and Jesse the father of King David.

David was the father of Solomon, whose mother had been Uriah's wife,
7 Solomon the father of Rehoboam,
Rehoboam the father of Abijah,
Abijah the father of Asa,
8 Asa the father of Jehoshaphat,
Jehoshaphat the father of Jehoram,
Jehoram the father of Uzziah,
9 Uzziah the father of Jotham,
Jotham the father of Ahaz,
Ahaz the father of Hezekiah,
10 Hezekiah the father of Manasseh,
Manasseh the father of Amon,
Amon the father of Josiah,
11 and Josiah the father of Jeconiah[a] and his brothers at the time of the exile to Babylon. 1Ch 3:10-17

12 After the exile to Babylon:
Jeconiah was the father of Shealtiel,
Shealtiel the father of Zerubbabel,
13 Zerubbabel the father of Abiud,
Abiud the father of Eliakim,
Eliakim the father of Azor,
14 Azor the father of Zadok,
Zadok the father of Akim,
Akim the father of Eliud,
15 Eliud the father of Eleazar,
Eleazar the father of Matthan,
Matthan the father of Jacob,
16 and Jacob the father of Joseph, the husband of Mary, of whom was born Jesus, who is called Christ. Mt 27:17; Lk 1:27

17 Thus there were fourteen generations in all
from Abraham to David, fourteen from David to
the exile to Babylon, and fourteen from the exile to
the Christ.[b] Lk 3:23-38

The Birth of Jesus Christ

18 This is how the birth of Jesus Christ came
about: His mother Mary was pledged to be married to Joseph, but before they came together, she
was found to be with child through the Holy Spirit.
19 Because Joseph her husband was a righteous
man and did not want to expose her to public
disgrace, he had in mind to divorce her quietly.
20 But after he had considered this, an angel of
the Lord appeared to him in a dream and said,
"Joseph son of David, do not be afraid to take
Mary home as your wife, because what is conceived in her is from the Holy Spirit.
21 She will give
birth to a son, and you are to give him the name
Jesus,[c] because he will save his people from their
sins." Lk 2:11; Ac 13:23,28
22 All this took place to fulfill what the Lord had
said through the prophet:
23 "The virgin will be
with child and will give birth to a son, and they
will call him Immanuel"[d]—which means, "God
with us." Isa 8:8,10
24 When Joseph woke up, he did what the angel
of the Lord had commanded him and took Mary
home as his wife.
25 But he had no union with her
until she gave birth to a son. And he gave him the
name Jesus. Lk 1:31

The Visit of the Magi

2 After Jesus was born in Bethlehem in Judea,
during the time of King Herod, Magi[e] from
the east came to Jerusalem
2 and asked, "Where is
the one who has been born king of the Jews? We
saw his star in the east[f] and have come to worship him." Nu 24:17; Jer 23:5
3 When King Herod heard this he was disturbed,
and all Jerusalem with him.
4 When he had called

[a] *11* That is, Jehoiachin; also in verse 12 [b] *17* Or *Messiah*. "The Christ" (Greek) and "the Messiah" (Hebrew) both mean "the Anointed One." [c] *21* *Jesus* is the Greek form of *Joshua*, which means *the LORD saves.* [d] *23* Isaiah 7:14 [e] Traditionally *Wise Men* [f] *2* Or *star when it rose*

together all the people's chief priests and teachers of the law, he asked them where the Christ[a] was to be born. 5"In Bethlehem in Judea," they replied, "for this is what the prophet has written:

6" 'But you, Bethlehem, in the land of Judah,
are by no means least among the rulers of Judah;
for out of you will come a ruler
who will be the shepherd of my people Israel.'[b]" Jn 7:42

7Then Herod called the Magi secretly and found out from them the exact time the star had appeared. 8He sent them to Bethlehem and said, "Go and make a careful search for the child. As soon as you find him, report to me, so that I too may go and worship him."

9After they had heard the king, they went on their way, and the star they had seen in the east[c] went ahead of them until it stopped over the place where the child was. 10When they saw the star, they were overjoyed. 11On coming to the house, they saw the child with his mother Mary, and they bowed down and worshiped him. Then they opened their treasures and presented him with gifts of gold and of incense and of myrrh. 12And having been warned in a dream not to go back to Herod, they returned to their country by another route. Ps 72:10; Isa 60:3

The Escape to Egypt

13When they had gone, an angel of the Lord appeared to Joseph in a dream. "Get up," he said, "take the child and his mother and escape to Egypt. Stay there until I tell you, for Herod is going to search for the child to kill him." Rev 12:4

14So he got up, took the child and his mother during the night and left for Egypt, 15where he stayed until the death of Herod. And so was fulfilled what the Lord had said through the prophet: "Out of Egypt I called my son."[d] Ex 4:22-23

16When Herod realized that he had been outwitted by the Magi, he was furious, and he gave orders to kill all the boys in Bethlehem and its vicinity who were two years old and under, in accordance with the time he had learned from the Magi. 17Then what was said through the prophet Jeremiah was fulfilled: Mt 1:22

18"A voice is heard in Ramah,
weeping and great mourning,
Rachel weeping for her children
and refusing to be comforted,
because they are no more."[e]

The Return to Nazareth

19After Herod died, an angel of the Lord appeared in a dream to Joseph in Egypt 20and said, "Get up, take the child and his mother and go to the land of Israel, for those who were trying to take the child's life are dead." Ex 4:19

21So he got up, took the child and his mother and went to the land of Israel. 22But when he heard that Archelaus was reigning in Judea in place of his father Herod, he was afraid to go there. Having been warned in a dream, he withdrew to the district of Galilee, 23and he went and lived in a town called Nazareth. So was fulfilled what was said through the prophets: "He will be called a Nazarene." Lk 1:26; Jn 1:45-46

John the Baptist Prepares the Way

▶ *See Mark 1:3–8; Luke 3:2–17*

3 In those days John the Baptist came, preaching in the Desert of Judea 2and saying, "Repent, for the kingdom of heaven is near." 3This is he who was spoken of through the prophet Isaiah:

"A voice of one calling in the desert,
'Prepare the way for the Lord,
make straight paths for him.' "[f] Lk 1:76

4John's clothes were made of camel's hair, and he had a leather belt around his waist. His food was locusts and wild honey. 5People went out to him from Jerusalem and all Judea and the whole region of the Jordan. 6Confessing their sins, they were baptized by him in the Jordan River.

7But when he saw many of the Pharisees and Sadducees coming to where he was baptizing, he said to them: "You brood of vipers! Who warned you to flee from the coming wrath? 8Produce fruit in keeping with repentance. 9And do not think you can say to yourselves, 'We have Abraham as our father.' I tell you that out of these stones God can raise up children for Abraham. 10The ax is already at the root of the trees, and every tree that does not produce good fruit will be cut down and thrown into the fire. Mt 7:19; Ac 26:20

11"I baptize you with[g] water for repentance. But after me will come one who is more powerful than I, whose sandals I am not fit to carry. He will baptize you with the Holy Spirit and with fire. 12His winnowing fork is in his hand, and he will clear his threshing floor, gathering his wheat into the barn and burning up the chaff with unquenchable fire." Mk 1:3-8; Lk 3:2-17

The Baptism of Jesus

▶ *See Mark 1:9–11; Luke 3:21–22; John 1:31–34*

13Then Jesus came from Galilee to the Jordan to be baptized by John. 14But John tried to deter him, saying, "I need to be baptized by you, and do you come to me?" Mk 1:4

[a]4 Or *Messiah* [b]6 Micah 5:2 [c]9 Or *seen when it rose* [d]15 Hosea 11:1 [e]18 Jer. 31:15 [f]3 Isaiah 40:3
[g]11 Or *in*

[15]Jesus replied, "Let it be so now; it is proper for
us to do this to fulfill all righteousness." Then John
consented.
[16]As soon as Jesus was baptized, he went up out
of the water. At that moment heaven was opened,
and he saw the Spirit of God descending like a
dove and lighting on him. [17]And a voice from
heaven said, "This is my Son, whom I love; with
him I am well pleased." Mk 1:9-11; Lk 3:21-22; Jn 1:31-34

The Temptation of Jesus

▶ *See Mark 1:12–13; Luke 4:1–13*

4 Then Jesus was led by the Spirit into the
desert to be tempted by the devil. [2]After fasting forty days and forty nights, he was hungry.
[3]The tempter came to him and said, "If you are the
Son of God, tell these stones to become bread."

LIVING  **INSIGHT**

To be like Jesus. That is our goal, plain and simple. It sounds like a peaceful, relaxing, easy objective. But stop and think. He learned obedience by the things He suffered. So do we. He endured all kinds of temptations. So must we. To be like Jesus is our goal. But it is neither easy nor quick nor natural. It's impossible in the flesh, slow in coming and supernatural in scope. Only Jesus can accomplish it within us.

(See Matthew 4:1.)

[4]Jesus answered, "It is written: 'Man does not
live on bread alone, but on every word that comes
from the mouth of God.'[a]" Jn 4:34
[5]Then the devil took him to the holy city and
had him stand on the highest point of the temple.
[6]"If you are the Son of God," he said, "throw
yourself down. For it is written: Mt 27:53

"'He will command his angels concerning you,
and they will lift you up in their hands,
so that you will not strike your foot against a
stone.'[b]"

[7]Jesus answered him, "It is also written: 'Do not
put the Lord your God to the test.'[c]"
[8]Again, the devil took him to a very high mountain and showed him all the kingdoms of the world
and their splendor. [9]"All this I will give you," he
said, "if you will bow down and worship me."
[10]Jesus said to him, "Away from me, Satan! For
it is written: 'Worship the Lord your God, and
serve him only.'[d]"
[11]Then the devil left him, and angels came and
attended him. Mk 1:12-13; Lk 4:1-13

Jesus Begins to Preach

[12]When Jesus heard that John had been put in
prison, he returned to Galilee. [13]Leaving Nazareth,
he went and lived in Capernaum, which was by the
lake in the area of Zebulun and Naphtali— [14]to
fulfill what was said through the prophet Isaiah:

[15]"Land of Zebulun and land of Naphtali,
the way to the sea, along the Jordan,
Galilee of the Gentiles—
[16]the people living in darkness
have seen a great light;
on those living in the land of the shadow of
death
a light has dawned."[e] Lk 2:32; Jn 1:4-5,9

[17]From that time on Jesus began to preach, "Repent, for the kingdom of heaven is near." Mt 3:2

The Calling of the First Disciples

▶ *See Mark 1:16–20; Luke 5:2–11; John 1:35–42*

[18]As Jesus was walking beside the Sea of Galilee,
he saw two brothers, Simon called Peter and his
brother Andrew. They were casting a net into the
lake, for they were fishermen. [19]"Come, follow
me," Jesus said, "and I will make you fishers of
men." [20]At once they left their nets and followed him.
[21]Going on from there, he saw two other brothers, James son of Zebedee and his brother John.
They were in a boat with their father Zebedee,
preparing their nets. Jesus called them, [22]and immediately they left the boat and their father and
followed him. Mk 1:16-20; Lk 5:2-11; Jn 1:35-42

Jesus Heals the Sick

[23]Jesus went throughout Galilee, teaching in
their synagogues, preaching the good news of the
kingdom, and healing every disease and sickness
among the people. [24]News about him spread all
over Syria, and people brought to him all who
were ill with various diseases, those suffering severe pain, the demon-possessed, those having seizures, and the paralyzed, and he healed them.
[25]Large crowds from Galilee, the Decapolis,[f] Jerusalem, Judea and the region across the Jordan
followed him. Mk 1:14; Ac 10:38

Message of the King **Chapters 5–15**

The emphasis in this section is on the message of the King, which was communicated in two distinct forms—words and action. First, Jesus communicated

[a]4 Deut. 8:3 [b]6 Psalm 91:11,12 [c]7 Deut. 6:16 [d]10 Deut. 6:13 [e]16 Isaiah 9:1,2 [f]25 That is, the Ten Cities

through powerful and impressive teachings (His longest recorded speech is the Sermon on the Mount, a three-chapter discourse that contained some of the King's core teachings). Second, He declared His message through miraculous acts. The people had asked for signs (12:38), and they got what they asked for! Having witnessed the miraculous signs, more and more people believed in Jesus. These two methods of communication helped to announce the good news of Matthew's Gospel: Jesus is the King.

The Beatitudes

▶ *See Luke 6:20–23*

5 Now when he saw the crowds, he went up on
a mountainside and sat down. His disciples
came to him, 2and he began to teach them, saying:

3"Blessed are the poor in spirit,
for theirs is the kingdom of heaven. Mt 25:34
4Blessed are those who mourn,
for they will be comforted. Isa 61:2-3; Rev 7:17
5Blessed are the meek,
for they will inherit the earth. Ps 37:11; Ro 4:13
6Blessed are those who hunger and thirst for
righteousness,
for they will be filled. Isa 55:1-2
7Blessed are the merciful,
for they will be shown mercy. Jas 2:13
8Blessed are the pure in heart, Ps 24:3-4
for they will see God. Heb 12:14; Rev 22:4
9Blessed are the peacemakers, Ro 14:19; Jas 3:18
for they will be called sons of God. Ro 8:14
10Blessed are those who are persecuted because
of righteousness, 1Pe 3:14
for theirs is the kingdom of heaven. Mt 25:34

11"Blessed are you when people insult you, persecute you and falsely say all kinds of evil against
you because of me. 12Rejoice and be glad, because
great is your reward in heaven, for in the same way
they persecuted the prophets who were before you.

Salt and Light

13"You are the salt of the earth. But if the salt
loses its saltiness, how can it be made salty again?
It is no longer good for anything, except to be
thrown out and trampled by men. Mk 9:50
14"You are the light of the world. A city on a hill
cannot be hidden. 15Neither do people light a lamp
and put it under a bowl. Instead they put it on its
stand, and it gives light to everyone in the house.
16In the same way, let your light shine before men,
that they may see your good deeds and praise your
Father in heaven. Jn 8:12; 1Co 10:31

LIVING INSIGHT

When we glorify God, it has a powerful impact on others. They will learn from our example and want to glorify Him as well. Our basic reason for existence, after all, is to bring maximum glory to our God.

(See Matthew 5:14–16.)

The Fulfillment of the Law

17"Do not think that I have come to abolish the
Law or the Prophets; I have not come to abolish
them but to fulfill them. 18I tell you the truth, until
heaven and earth disappear, not the smallest letter,
not the least stroke of a pen, will by any means
disappear from the Law until everything is accomplished. 19Anyone who breaks one of the least of
these commandments and teaches others to do the
same will be called least in the kingdom of heaven,
but whoever practices and teaches these commands will be called great in the kingdom of heav-
en. 20For I tell you that unless your righteousness
surpasses that of the Pharisees and the teachers of
the law, you will certainly not enter the kingdom
of heaven. Lk 16:17; Jas 2:10

Murder

21"You have heard that it was said to the people
long ago, 'Do not murder,[a] and anyone who
murders will be subject to judgment.' 22But I tell
you that anyone who is angry with his brother[b]
will be subject to judgment. Again, anyone who
says to his brother, 'Raca,[c]' is answerable to the
Sanhedrin. But anyone who says, 'You fool!' will
be in danger of the fire of hell. 1Jn 3:15
23"Therefore, if you are offering your gift at the
altar and there remember that your brother has
something against you, 24leave your gift there in
front of the altar. First go and be reconciled to
your brother; then come and offer your gift.
25"Settle matters quickly with your adversary
who is taking you to court. Do it while you are still
with him on the way, or he may hand you over to
the judge, and the judge may hand you over to the
officer, and you may be thrown into prison. 26I tell
you the truth, you will not get out until you have
paid the last penny.[d] Lk 12:58-59

Adultery

27"You have heard that it was said, 'Do not
commit adultery.'[e] 28But I tell you that anyone
who looks at a woman lustfully has already committed adultery with her in his heart. 29If your

[a]21 Exodus 20:13 [b]22 Some manuscripts *brother without cause* [c]22 An Aramaic term of contempt [d]26 Greek *kodrantes* [e]27 Exodus 20:14

right eye causes you to sin, gouge it out and throw
it away. It is better for you to lose one part of your
body than for your whole body to be thrown into
hell. 30And if your right hand causes you to sin, cut
it off and throw it away. It is better for you to lose
one part of your body than for your whole body to
go into hell. Mk 9:42-47; Pr 6:25

Divorce

31"It has been said, 'Anyone who divorces his
wife must give her a certificate of divorce.'[a] 32But
I tell you that anyone who divorces his wife, except
for marital unfaithfulness, causes her to become an
adulteress, and anyone who marries the divorced
woman commits adultery. Lk 16:18

Oaths

33"Again, you have heard that it was said to the
people long ago, 'Do not break your oath, but
keep the oaths you have made to the Lord.' 34But
I tell you, Do not swear at all: either by heaven, for
it is God's throne; 35or by the earth, for it is his
footstool; or by Jerusalem, for it is the city of the
Great King. 36And do not swear by your head, for
you cannot make even one hair white or black.
37Simply let your 'Yes' be 'Yes,' and your 'No,'
'No'; anything beyond this comes from the evil
one. Nu 30:2; Jas 5:12

An Eye for an Eye

38"You have heard that it was said, 'Eye for eye,
and tooth for tooth.'[b] 39But I tell you, Do not
resist an evil person. If someone strikes you on the
right cheek, turn to him the other also. 40And if
someone wants to sue you and take your tunic, let
him have your cloak as well. 41If someone forces
you to go one mile, go with him two miles. 42Give
to the one who asks you, and do not turn away
from the one who wants to borrow from you.

Love for Enemies

43"You have heard that it was said, 'Love your
neighbor[c] and hate your enemy.' 44But I tell you:
Love your enemies[d] and pray for those who persecute you, 45that you may be sons of your Father
in heaven. He causes his sun to rise on the evil and
the good, and sends rain on the righteous and the
unrighteous. 46If you love those who love you,
what reward will you get? Are not even the tax
collectors doing that? 47And if you greet only your
brothers, what are you doing more than others?
Do not even pagans do that? 48Be perfect, therefore, as your heavenly Father is perfect. Lev 19:2

Giving to the Needy

6 "Be careful not to do your 'acts of righteousness' before men, to be seen by them. If you
do, you will have no reward from your Father in
heaven. Mt 23:5

LIVING  **INSIGHT**

If there was one thing Jesus despised, it was the very thing every Pharisee seemed to have majored in at seminary: showing off, or, to cushion it a bit in more formal language, being afflicted with self-righteousness.

(See Matthew 6:1.)

2"So when you give to the needy, do not announce it with trumpets, as the hypocrites do in
the synagogues and on the streets, to be honored
by men. I tell you the truth, they have received
their reward in full. 3But when you give to the
needy, do not let your left hand know what your
right hand is doing, 4so that your giving may be in
secret. Then your Father, who sees what is done in
secret, will reward you. Col 3:23-24

Prayer

▶ *See Luke 11:2–4*

5"And when you pray, do not be like the hypocrites, for they love to pray standing in the synagogues and on the street corners to be seen by
men. I tell you the truth, they have received their
reward in full. 6But when you pray, go into your
room, close the door and pray to your Father, who
is unseen. Then your Father, who sees what is
done in secret, will reward you. 7And when you
pray, do not keep on babbling like pagans, for they
think they will be heard because of their many
words. 8Do not be like them, for your Father
knows what you need before you ask him.
9"This, then, is how you should pray:

"'Our Father in heaven, Mal 2:10
hallowed be your name,
10your kingdom come, Mt 3:2
your will be done Mt 26:39
on earth as it is in heaven.
11Give us today our daily bread. Pr 30:8
12Forgive us our debts,
as we also have forgiven our debtors.
13And lead us not into temptation, Jas 1:13
but deliver us from the evil one.'[e]

14For if you forgive men when they sin against you,
your heavenly Father will also forgive you. 15But if

[a]31 Deut. 24:1 [b]38 Exodus 21:24; Lev. 24:20; Deut. 19:21 [c]43 Lev. 19:18 [d]44 Some late manuscripts *enemies, bless those who curse you, do good to those who hate you* [e]13 Or *from evil*; some late manuscripts *one, / for yours is the kingdom and the power and the glory forever. Amen.*

you do not forgive men their sins, your Father will
not forgive your sins. Mt 18:21-35; Mk 11:25,26; Luke 11:2-4

Fasting

16“When you fast, do not look somber as the
hypocrites do, for they disfigure their faces to
show men they are fasting. I tell you the truth, they
have received their reward in full. 17But when you
fast, put oil on your head and wash your face, 18so
that it will not be obvious to men that you are
fasting, but only to your Father, who is unseen;
and your Father, who sees what is done in secret,
will reward you. ver 4,6; Isa 58:5

Treasures in Heaven

19“Do not store up for yourselves treasures on
earth, where moth and rust destroy, and where
thieves break in and steal. 20But store up for yourselves treasures in heaven, where moth and rust do
not destroy, and where thieves do not break in and
steal. 21For where your treasure is, there your heart
will be also. Lk 12:33-34; Heb 13:5

LIVING  **INSIGHT**

What are you doing with the rest of your life? I'm talking about cultivating relationships, building memories that will help lift the load of future trials, and deliberately pursuing activities that will yield eternal dividends.

(See Matthew 6:19–21.)

22“The eye is the lamp of the body. If your eyes
are good, your whole body will be full of light.
23But if your eyes are bad, your whole body will be
full of darkness. If then the light within you is
darkness, how great is that darkness! Lk 11:34-36
24“No one can serve two masters. Either he will
hate the one and love the other, or he will be
devoted to the one and despise the other. You
cannot serve both God and Money. Lk 16:13

Do Not Worry

▶ *See Luke 12:22–31*

25“Therefore I tell you, do not worry about your
life, what you will eat or drink; or about your
body, what you will wear. Is not life more important than food, and the body more important than
clothes? 26Look at the birds of the air; they do not
sow or reap or store away in barns, and yet your
heavenly Father feeds them. Are you not much
more valuable than they? 27Who of you by worrying can add a single hour to his life[a]? Mt 10:29-31
28“And why do you worry about clothes? See
how the lilies of the field grow. They do not labor
or spin. 29Yet I tell you that not even Solomon in
all his splendor was dressed like one of these. 30If
that is how God clothes the grass of the field,
which is here today and tomorrow is thrown into
the fire, will he not much more clothe you, O you
of little faith? 31So do not worry, saying, ‘What
shall we eat?’ or ‘What shall we drink?’ or ‘What
shall we wear?’ 32For the pagans run after all these
things, and your heavenly Father knows that you
need them. 33But seek first his kingdom and his
righteousness, and all these things will be given to

LIVING  **INSIGHT**

Unless God is the major pursuit of our lives, all other pursuits are dead-end streets, including trying to know ourselves. They won't work. They won't satisfy. They won't result in fulfillment. They won't do for us what we think they're going to do.

(See Matthew 6:33.)

you as well. 34Therefore do not worry about tomorrow, for tomorrow will worry about itself.
Each day has enough trouble of its own.

Judging Others

▶ *See Luke 6:41–42*

7 “Do not judge, or you too will be judged. 2For
in the same way you judge others, you will be
judged, and with the measure you use, it will be
measured to you. Mk 4:24; Lk 6:38
3“Why do you look at the speck of sawdust in
your brother's eye and pay no attention to the
plank in your own eye? 4How can you say to your
brother, ‘Let me take the speck out of your eye,’
when all the time there is a plank in your own eye?
5You hypocrite, first take the plank out of your
own eye, and then you will see clearly to remove
the speck from your brother's eye. Lk 6:41-42
6“Do not give dogs what is sacred; do not throw
your pearls to pigs. If you do, they may trample
them under their feet, and then turn and tear you
to pieces.

Ask, Seek, Knock

▶ *See Luke 11:9–13*

7“Ask and it will be given to you; seek and you
will find; knock and the door will be opened to
you. 8For everyone who asks receives; he who
seeks finds; and to him who knocks, the door will
be opened. Jer 29:12-13; Jn 15:7,16

[a] 27 Or *single cubit to his height*

9“Which of you, if his son asks for bread, will
give him a stone? 10Or if he asks for a fish, will give
him a snake? 11If you, then, though you are evil,
know how to give good gifts to your children, how
much more will your Father in heaven give good
gifts to those who ask him! 12So in everything, do
to others what you would have them do to you, for
this sums up the Law and the Prophets. Lk 11:9-13

The Narrow and Wide Gates

13“Enter through the narrow gate. For wide is
the gate and broad is the road that leads to destruction, and many enter through it. 14But small
is the gate and narrow the road that leads to life,
and only a few find it. Lk 13:24; Jn 10:7,9

A Tree and Its Fruit

15“Watch out for false prophets. They come to
you in sheep’s clothing, but inwardly they are ferocious wolves. 16By their fruit you will recognize
them. Do people pick grapes from thornbushes, or
figs from thistles? 17Likewise every good tree bears
good fruit, but a bad tree bears bad fruit. 18A good
tree cannot bear bad fruit, and a bad tree cannot
bear good fruit. 19Every tree that does not bear
good fruit is cut down and thrown into the fire.
20Thus, by their fruit you will recognize them.

21“Not everyone who says to me, ‘Lord, Lord,’
will enter the kingdom of heaven, but only he who
does the will of my Father who is in heaven.
22Many will say to me on that day, ‘Lord, Lord, did
we not prophesy in your name, and in your name
drive out demons and perform many miracles?’
23Then I will tell them plainly, ‘I never knew you.
Away from me, you evildoers!’ Mt 25:12,41; Lk 13:25-27

The Wise and Foolish Builders

▶ *See Luke 6:47–49*

24“Therefore everyone who hears these words of
mine and puts them into practice is like a wise
man who built his house on the rock. 25The rain
came down, the streams rose, and the winds blew
and beat against that house; yet it did not fall,
because it had its foundation on the rock. 26But
everyone who hears these words of mine and does
not put them into practice is like a foolish man
who built his house on sand. 27The rain came
down, the streams rose, and the winds blew and
beat against that house, and it fell with a great
crash.” Lk 6:47-49

28When Jesus had finished saying these things,
the crowds were amazed at his teaching, 29because
he taught as one who had authority, and not as
their teachers of the law. Lk 4:32; Jn 7:46

The Man With Leprosy

▶ *See Mark 1:40–44; Luke 5:12–14*

8 When he came down from the mountainside,
large crowds followed him. 2A man with leprosy[a] came and knelt before him and said, “Lord,
if you are willing, you can make me clean.”

3Jesus reached out his hand and touched the
man. “I am willing,” he said. “Be clean!” Immediately he was cured[b] of his leprosy. 4Then Jesus
said to him, “See that you don’t tell anyone. But
go, show yourself to the priest and offer the gift
Moses commanded, as a testimony to them.”

The Faith of the Centurion

▶ *See Luke 7:1–10*

5When Jesus had entered Capernaum, a centurion came to him, asking for help. 6“Lord,” he
said, “my servant lies at home paralyzed and in
terrible suffering.” Mt 4:24

7Jesus said to him, “I will go and heal him.”

8The centurion replied, “Lord, I do not deserve
to have you come under my roof. But just say the
word, and my servant will be healed. 9For I myself
am a man under authority, with soldiers under
me. I tell this one, ‘Go,’ and he goes; and that one,
‘Come,’ and he comes. I say to my servant, ‘Do
this,’ and he does it.” Ps 107:20

10When Jesus heard this, he was astonished and
said to those following him, “I tell you the truth,
I have not found anyone in Israel with such great
faith. 11I say to you that many will come from the
east and the west, and will take their places at the
feast with Abraham, Isaac and Jacob in the kingdom of heaven. 12But the subjects of the kingdom
will be thrown outside, into the darkness, where
there will be weeping and gnashing of teeth.”

13Then Jesus said to the centurion, “Go! It will
be done just as you believed it would.” And his
servant was healed at that very hour. Lk 7:1-10

Jesus Heals Many

▶ *See Mark 1:29–34; Luke 4:38–41*

14When Jesus came into Peter’s house, he saw
Peter’s mother-in-law lying in bed with a fever.
15He touched her hand and the fever left her, and
she got up and began to wait on him. Mk 1:29-34

16When evening came, many who were demon-
possessed were brought to him, and he drove out
the spirits with a word and healed all the sick.
17This was to fulfill what was spoken through the
prophet Isaiah: Mt 1:22

“He took up our infirmities
  and carried our diseases.”[c]

[a]2 The Greek word was used for various diseases affecting the skin—not necessarily leprosy. [b]3 Greek *made clean*
[c]17 Isaiah 53:4

MIRACLES OF JESUS

Healing Miracles	**Matthew**	**Mark**	**Luke**	**John**
Man with leprosy	*8:2-4*	*1:40-42*	*5:12-13*	
Roman centurion's servant	*8:5-13*		*7:1-10*	
Peter's mother-in-law	*8:14-15*	*1:30-31*	*4:38-39*	
Two men from Gadara	*8:28-34*	*5:1-15*	*8:27-35*	
Paralyzed man	*9:2-7*	*2:3-12*	*5:18-25*	
Woman with bleeding	*9:20-22*	*5:25-29*	*8:43-48*	
Two blind men	*9:27-31*			
Mute, demon-possessed man	*9:32-33*			
Man with a shriveled hand	*12:10-13*	*3:1-5*	*6:6-10*	
Blind, mute, demon-possessed man	*12:22*		*11:14*	
Canaanite woman's daughter	*15:21-28*	*7:24-30*		
Boy with a demon	*17:14-18*	*9:17-29*	*9:38-43*	
Two blind men (including Bartimaeus)	*20:29-34*	*10:46-52*	*18:35-43*	
Deaf mute		*7:31-37*		
Possessed man in synagogue		*1:23-26*	*4:33-35*	
Blind man at Bethsaida		*8:22-26*		
Crippled woman			*13:11-13*	
Man with dropsy			*14:1-4*	
Ten men with leprosy			*17:11-19*	
The high priest's servant			*22:50-51*	
Official's son at Capernaum				*4:46-54*
Sick man at pool of Bethesda				*5:1-9*
Man born blind				*9:1-7*

Miracles Showing Power over Nature	**Matthew**	**Mark**	**Luke**	**John**
Calming the storm	*8:23-27*	*4:37-41*	*8:22-25*	
Walking on water	*14:25*	*6:48-51*		*6:19-21*
Feeding of the 5,000	*14:15-21*	*6:35-44*	*9:12-17*	*6:6-13*
Feeding of the 4,000	*15:32-38*	*8:1-9*		
Coin in fish	*17:24-27*			
Fig tree withered	*21:18-22*	*11:12-14,20-25*		
Large catch of fish			*5:4-11*	
Water turned into wine				*2:1-11*
Another large catch of fish				*21:1-11*

Miracles of Raising the Dead	**Matthew**	**Mark**	**Luke**	**John**
Jairus's daughter	*9:18-19,23-25*	*5:22-24,38-42*	*8:41-42,49-56*	
Widow's son at Nain			*7:11-15*	
Lazarus				*11:1-44*

The Cost of Following Jesus

▶ *See Luke 9:57–60*

18 When Jesus saw the crowd around him, he
gave orders to cross to the other side of the lake.
19 Then a teacher of the law came to him and said,
"Teacher, I will follow you wherever you go."
20 Jesus replied, "Foxes have holes and birds of
the air have nests, but the Son of Man has no place
to lay his head." Mk 8:31
21 Another disciple said to him, "Lord, first let
me go and bury my father."
22 But Jesus told him, "Follow me, and let the
dead bury their own dead." Lk 9:57-60

Jesus Calms the Storm

▶ *See Mark 4:36–41; Luke 8:22–25*

23 Then he got into the boat and his disciples
followed him. 24 Without warning, a furious storm
came up on the lake, so that the waves swept over
the boat. But Jesus was sleeping. 25 The disciples
went and woke him, saying, "Lord, save us! We're
going to drown!" Mk 4:36-41; Lk 8:22-25
26 He replied, "You of little faith, why are you so
afraid?" Then he got up and rebuked the winds
and the waves, and it was completely calm.
27 The men were amazed and asked, "What kind
of man is this? Even the winds and the waves obey
him!" Mt 14:22-33

The Healing of Two Demon-possessed Men

▶ *See Mark 5:1–17; Luke 8:26–37*

28 When he arrived at the other side in the region of the Gadarenes,[a] two demon-possessed
men coming from the tombs met him. They were
so violent that no one could pass that way.
29 "What do you want with us, Son of God?" they
shouted. "Have you come here to torture us before
the appointed time?" Mk 1:24; Jn 2:4
30 Some distance from them a large herd of pigs
was feeding. 31 The demons begged Jesus, "If you
drive us out, send us into the herd of pigs."
32 He said to them, "Go!" So they came out and
went into the pigs, and the whole herd rushed
down the steep bank into the lake and died in the
water. 33 Those tending the pigs ran off, went into
the town and reported all this, including what had
happened to the demon-possessed men. 34 Then
the whole town went out to meet Jesus. And when
they saw him, they pleaded with him to leave their
region. Mk 5:1-17; Lk 8:26-37

Jesus Heals a Paralytic

▶ *See Mark 2:3–12; Luke 5:18–26*

9 Jesus stepped into a boat, crossed over and
came to his own town. 2 Some men brought to
him a paralytic, lying on a mat. When Jesus saw
their faith, he said to the paralytic, "Take heart,
son; your sins are forgiven." Lk 7:48; Jn 16:33
3 At this, some of the teachers of the law said to
themselves, "This fellow is blaspheming!" Mt 26:65
4 Knowing their thoughts, Jesus said, "Why do
you entertain evil thoughts in your hearts? 5 Which
is easier: to say, 'Your sins are forgiven,' or to say,
'Get up and walk'? 6 But so that you may know that
the Son of Man has authority on earth to forgive
sins . . ." Then he said to the paralytic, "Get up,
take your mat and go home." 7 And the man got up
and went home. 8 When the crowd saw this, they
were filled with awe; and they praised God, who
had given such authority to men. Mk 2:3-12

The Calling of Matthew

▶ *See Mark 2:14–17; Luke 5:27–32*

9 As Jesus went on from there, he saw a man
named Matthew sitting at the tax collector's booth.
"Follow me," he told him, and Matthew got up
and followed him. Mt 4:19
10 While Jesus was having dinner at Matthew's
house, many tax collectors and "sinners" came
and ate with him and his disciples. 11 When the
Pharisees saw this, they asked his disciples, "Why
does your teacher eat with tax collectors and 'sinners'?" Mt 11:19; Gal 2:15

LIVING  **INSIGHT**

God is the One who builds trophies from the scrap pile, who draws His clay from under the bridge, who makes clean instruments of beauty from the filthy failures of yesteryear.
(See Matthew 9:10–13.)

12 On hearing this, Jesus said, "It is not the
healthy who need a doctor, but the sick. 13 But go
and learn what this means: 'I desire mercy, not
sacrifice.'[b] For I have not come to call the righteous, but sinners." Mk 2:14-17; Lk 5:27-32

Jesus Questioned About Fasting

▶ *See Mark 2:18–22; Luke 5:33–39*

14 Then John's disciples came and asked him,
"How is it that we and the Pharisees fast, but your
disciples do not fast?" Lk 18:12
15 Jesus answered, "How can the guests of the
bridegroom mourn while he is with them? The
time will come when the bridegroom will be taken
from them; then they will fast. Jn 3:29; Ac 13:2-3
16 "No one sews a patch of unshrunk cloth on an
old garment, for the patch will pull away from the
garment, making the tear worse. 17 Neither do men
pour new wine into old wineskins. If they do, the

[a] *28* Some manuscripts *Gergesenes*; others *Gerasenes* [b] *13* Hosea 6:6

skins will burst, the wine will run out and the wineskins will be ruined. No, they pour new wine into new wineskins, and both are preserved."

A Dead Girl and a Sick Woman

▶ *See Mark 5:22–43; Luke 8:41–56*

18While he was saying this, a ruler came and knelt before him and said, "My daughter has just died. But come and put your hand on her, and she will live." 19Jesus got up and went with him, and so did his disciples. Mt 8:2

20Just then a woman who had been subject to bleeding for twelve years came up behind him and touched the edge of his cloak. 21She said to herself, "If I only touch his cloak, I will be healed."

22Jesus turned and saw her. "Take heart, daughter," he said, "your faith has healed you." And the woman was healed from that moment. Lk 7:50

23When Jesus entered the ruler's house and saw the flute players and the noisy crowd, 24he said, "Go away. The girl is not dead but asleep." But they laughed at him. 25After the crowd had been put outside, he went in and took the girl by the hand, and she got up. 26News of this spread through all that region. Mk 5:22-43; Lk 8:41-56

Jesus Heals the Blind and Mute

27As Jesus went on from there, two blind men followed him, calling out, "Have mercy on us, Son of David!" Mt 15:22; Mk 10:47

28When he had gone indoors, the blind men came to him, and he asked them, "Do you believe that I am able to do this?"

"Yes, Lord," they replied. Ac 14:9

29Then he touched their eyes and said, "According to your faith will it be done to you"; 30and their sight was restored. Jesus warned them sternly, "See that no one knows about this." 31But they went out and spread the news about him all over that region. Mt 8:4; Mk 7:36

32While they were going out, a man who was demon-possessed and could not talk was brought to Jesus. 33And when the demon was driven out, the man who had been mute spoke. The crowd was amazed and said, "Nothing like this has ever been seen in Israel." Mk 2:12

34But the Pharisees said, "It is by the prince of demons that he drives out demons." Mt 12:24

The Workers Are Few

35Jesus went through all the towns and villages, teaching in their synagogues, preaching the good news of the kingdom and healing every disease and sickness. 36When he saw the crowds, he had compassion on them, because they were harassed and helpless, like sheep without a shepherd. 37Then he said to his disciples, "The harvest is plentiful but the workers are few. 38Ask the Lord of the harvest, therefore, to send out workers into his harvest field." Lk 10:2; Jn 4:35

Jesus Sends Out the Twelve

▶ *See Mark 6:8–11; Luke 9:3–5; 10:4–12*

10 He called his twelve disciples to him and gave them authority to drive out evil[a] spirits and to heal every disease and sickness.

2These are the names of the twelve apostles: first, Simon (who is called Peter) and his brother Andrew; James son of Zebedee, and his brother John; 3Philip and Bartholomew; Thomas and Matthew the tax collector; James son of Alphaeus, and Thaddaeus; 4Simon the Zealot and Judas Iscariot, who betrayed him. Mk 3:16-19; Lk 6:14-16; Ac 1:13

5These twelve Jesus sent out with the following instructions: "Do not go among the Gentiles or enter any town of the Samaritans. 6Go rather to the lost sheep of Israel. 7As you go, preach this message: 'The kingdom of heaven is near.' 8Heal the sick, raise the dead, cleanse those who have leprosy,[b] drive out demons. Freely you have received, freely give. 9Do not take along any gold or silver or copper in your belts; 10take no bag for the journey, or extra tunic, or sandals or a staff; for the worker is worth his keep. Mt 3:2; 15:24; 1Ti 5:18

11"Whatever town or village you enter, search for some worthy person there and stay at his house until you leave. 12As you enter the home, give it your greeting. 13If the home is deserving, let your peace rest on it; if it is not, let your peace return to you. 14If anyone will not welcome you or listen to your words, shake the dust off your feet when you leave that home or town. 15I tell you the truth, it will be more bearable for Sodom and Gomorrah on the day of judgment than for that town. 16I am sending you out like sheep among wolves. Therefore be as shrewd as snakes and as innocent as doves. Mk 6:8-11; Lk 9:3-5; 10:4-12

LIVING  **INSIGHT**

There's a fine line between discernment and suspicion. It's one thing to be suspicious people who question everything we hear . . . and another thing entirely to be discerning, alert, perceptive.

(See Matthew 10:16.)

17"Be on your guard against men; they will hand you over to the local councils and flog you in their synagogues. 18On my account you will be brought before governors and kings as witnesses to them and to the Gentiles. 19But when they arrest you, do

[a] *1* Greek *unclean* [b] *8* The Greek word was used for various diseases affecting the skin—not necessarily leprosy.

not worry about what to say or how to say it. At
that time you will be given what to say, 20for it will
not be you speaking, but the Spirit of your Father
speaking through you. Mk 13:9; Ac 5:40

21"Brother will betray brother to death, and a
father his child; children will rebel against their
parents and have them put to death. 22All men will
hate you because of me, but he who stands firm to
the end will be saved. 23When you are persecuted
in one place, flee to another. I tell you the truth,
you will not finish going through the cities of Israel
before the Son of Man comes. Mk 13:11-13; Lk 21:12-17

24"A student is not above his teacher, nor a
servant above his master. 25It is enough for the
student to be like his teacher, and the servant like
his master. If the head of the house has been called
Beelzebub,[a] how much more the members of his
household! Mk 3:22; Lk 6:40

26"So do not be afraid of them. There is nothing
concealed that will not be disclosed, or hidden that
will not be made known. 27What I tell you in the
dark, speak in the daylight; what is whispered in
your ear, proclaim from the roofs. 28Do not be
afraid of those who kill the body but cannot kill
the soul. Rather, be afraid of the One who can
destroy both soul and body in hell. 29Are not two
sparrows sold for a penny[b]? Yet not one of them
will fall to the ground apart from the will of your
Father. 30And even the very hairs of your head are
all numbered. 31So don't be afraid; you are worth
more than many sparrows. Mk 4:22; Heb 10:31

32"Whoever acknowledges me before men, I
will also acknowledge him before my Father in
heaven. 33But whoever disowns me before men, I
will disown him before my Father in heaven.

34"Do not suppose that I have come to bring
peace to the earth. I did not come to bring peace,
but a sword. 35For I have come to turn

" 'a man against his father,
 a daughter against her mother,
a daughter-in-law against her
 mother-in-law—
36 a man's enemies will be the members of his
 own household.'[c] Mic 7:6

37"Anyone who loves his father or mother more
than me is not worthy of me; anyone who loves his
son or daughter more than me is not worthy of
me; 38and anyone who does not take his cross and
follow me is not worthy of me. 39Whoever finds
his life will lose it, and whoever loses his life for my
sake will find it. Lk 14:26; Jn 12:25

40"He who receives you receives me, and he
who receives me receives the one who sent me.
41Anyone who receives a prophet because he is a
prophet will receive a prophet's reward, and anyone who receives a righteous man because he is a
righteous man will receive a righteous man's reward. 42And if anyone gives even a cup of cold
water to one of these little ones because he is my
disciple, I tell you the truth, he will certainly not
lose his reward." Lk 9:48; Jn 12:44; Gal 4:14

Jesus and John the Baptist

▶ *See Luke 7:18–35*

11 After Jesus had finished instructing his
twelve disciples, he went on from there to
teach and preach in the towns of Galilee.[d]

2When John heard in prison what Christ was
doing, he sent his disciples 3to ask him, "Are you
the one who was to come, or should we expect
someone else?" Mt 14:3; Jn 11:27

4Jesus replied, "Go back and report to John
what you hear and see: 5The blind receive sight,
the lame walk, those who have leprosy[e] are cured,
the deaf hear, the dead are raised, and the good
news is preached to the poor. 6Blessed is the man
who does not fall away on account of me."

7As John's disciples were leaving, Jesus began to
speak to the crowd about John: "What did you go
out into the desert to see? A reed swayed by the
wind? 8If not, what did you go out to see? A man
dressed in fine clothes? No, those who wear fine
clothes are in kings' palaces. 9Then what did you
go out to see? A prophet? Yes, I tell you, and more
than a prophet. 10This is the one about whom it is
written: Lk 1:76

" 'I will send my messenger ahead of you,
 who will prepare your way before you.'[f]

11I tell you the truth: Among those born of women
there has not risen anyone greater than John the
Baptist; yet he who is least in the kingdom of
heaven is greater than he. 12From the days of John
the Baptist until now, the kingdom of heaven has
been forcefully advancing, and forceful men lay
hold of it. 13For all the Prophets and the Law
prophesied until John. 14And if you are willing to
accept it, he is the Elijah who was to come. 15He
who has ears, let him hear. Mal 4:5; Lk 1:17

16"To what can I compare this generation? They
are like children sitting in the marketplaces and
calling out to others:

17" 'We played the flute for you,
 and you did not dance;
we sang a dirge,
 and you did not mourn.'

18For John came neither eating nor drinking, and
they say, 'He has a demon.' 19The Son of Man
came eating and drinking, and they say, 'Here is a
glutton and a drunkard, a friend of tax collectors

[a] 25 Greek *Beezeboul* or *Beelzeboul* [b] 29 Greek *an assarion* [c] 36 Micah 7:6 [d] 1 Greek *in their towns*
[e] 5 The Greek word was used for various diseases affecting the skin—not necessarily leprosy. [f] 10 Mal. 3:1

and "sinners." ' But wisdom is proved right by her
actions." Lk 7:18-35

Woe on Unrepentant Cities

▶ *See Luke 10:13–15*

20Then Jesus began to denounce the cities in
which most of his miracles had been performed,
because they did not repent. 21"Woe to you, Korazin! Woe to you, Bethsaida! If the miracles that
were performed in you had been performed in
Tyre and Sidon, they would have repented long
ago in sackcloth and ashes. 22But I tell you, it will
be more bearable for Tyre and Sidon on the day of
judgment than for you. 23And you, Capernaum,
will you be lifted up to the skies? No, you will go
down to the depths.[a] If the miracles that were
performed in you had been performed in Sodom,
it would have remained to this day. 24But I tell you
that it will be more bearable for Sodom on the day
of judgment than for you." Lk 10:13-15

Rest for the Weary

▶ *See Luke 10:21–22*

25At that time Jesus said, "I praise you, Father,
Lord of heaven and earth, because you have hidden these things from the wise and learned, and
revealed them to little children. 26Yes, Father, for
this was your good pleasure. 1Co 1:26-29

27"All things have been committed to me by my
Father. No one knows the Son except the Father,
and no one knows the Father except the Son and
those to whom the Son chooses to reveal him.

28"Come to me, all you who are weary and burdened, and I will give you rest. 29Take my yoke
upon you and learn from me, for I am gentle and
humble in heart, and you will find rest for your
souls. 30For my yoke is easy and my burden is
light." Jer 6:16; Jn 13:15

LIVING  **INSIGHT**

While so many others are demanding, Jesus is gentle. While competition is rugged and being in partnership with hard-charging, bullish leaders is tough, being yoked with Jesus is easy. Yes, easy. And instead of increasing our load of anxiety, He promises to make it lighter.

(See Matthew 11:28–30.)

Lord of the Sabbath

▶ *See Mark 2:23—3:6; Luke 6:1–11*

12 At that time Jesus went through the grainfields on the Sabbath. His disciples were
hungry and began to pick some heads of grain and
eat them. 2When the Pharisees saw this, they said
to him, "Look! Your disciples are doing what is
unlawful on the Sabbath." Ex 20:10; Lk 13:14

3He answered, "Haven't you read what David
did when he and his companions were hungry?
4He entered the house of God, and he and his
companions ate the consecrated bread—which
was not lawful for them to do, but only for the
priests. 5Or haven't you read in the Law that on the
Sabbath the priests in the temple desecrate the day
and yet are innocent? 6I tell you that one[b] greater
than the temple is here. 7If you had known what
these words mean, 'I desire mercy, not sacrifice,'[c]
you would not have condemned the innocent.
8For the Son of Man is Lord of the Sabbath."

9Going on from that place, he went into their
synagogue, 10and a man with a shriveled hand was
there. Looking for a reason to accuse Jesus, they
asked him, "Is it lawful to heal on the Sabbath?"

11He said to them, "If any of you has a sheep
and it falls into a pit on the Sabbath, will you not
take hold of it and lift it out? 12How much more
valuable is a man than a sheep! Therefore it is
lawful to do good on the Sabbath."

13Then he said to the man, "Stretch out your
hand." So he stretched it out and it was completely
restored, just as sound as the other. 14But the Pharisees went out and plotted how they might kill
Jesus. Mk 3:1-6; Lk 6:6-11

God's Chosen Servant

15Aware of this, Jesus withdrew from that place.
Many followed him, and he healed all their sick,
16warning them not to tell who he was. 17This was
to fulfill what was spoken through the prophet
Isaiah: Mt 4:23; 8:4

18"Here is my servant whom I have chosen,
the one I love, in whom I delight; Mt 3:17
I will put my Spirit on him, Jn 3:34
and he will proclaim justice to the nations.
19He will not quarrel or cry out;
no one will hear his voice in the streets.
20A bruised reed he will not break,
and a smoldering wick he will not snuff
out,
till he leads justice to victory.
21 In his name the nations will put their
hope."[d] Isa 42:1-4

Jesus and Beelzebub

▶ *See Mark 3:23–27; Luke 11:17–22*

22Then they brought him a demon-possessed
man who was blind and mute, and Jesus healed
him, so that he could both talk and see. 23All the

[a] 23 Greek *Hades* [b] 6 Or *something*; also in verses 41 and 42 [c] 7 Hosea 6:6 [d] 21 Isaiah 42:1-4

people were astonished and said, "Could this be the Son of David?" Mt 4:24; 9:32-33

24But when the Pharisees heard this, they said, "It is only by Beelzebub,[a] the prince of demons, that this fellow drives out demons." Mt 9:34; Mk 3:22

25Jesus knew their thoughts and said to them, "Every kingdom divided against itself will be ruined, and every city or household divided against itself will not stand. 26If Satan drives out Satan, he is divided against himself. How then can his kingdom stand? 27And if I drive out demons by Beelzebub, by whom do your people drive them out? So then, they will be your judges. 28But if I drive out demons by the Spirit of God, then the kingdom of God has come upon you. Mt 9:4; Ac 19:13

29"Or again, how can anyone enter a strong man's house and carry off his possessions unless he first ties up the strong man? Then he can rob his house. Mk 3:23-27; Lk 11:17-22

30"He who is not with me is against me, and he who does not gather with me scatters. 31And so I tell you, every sin and blasphemy will be forgiven men, but the blasphemy against the Spirit will not be forgiven. 32Anyone who speaks a word against the Son of Man will be forgiven, but anyone who speaks against the Holy Spirit will not be forgiven, either in this age or in the age to come. Mk 9:40

33"Make a tree good and its fruit will be good, or make a tree bad and its fruit will be bad, for a tree is recognized by its fruit. 34You brood of vipers, how can you who are evil say anything good? For out of the overflow of the heart the mouth speaks. 35The good man brings good things out of the good stored up in him, and the evil man brings evil things out of the evil stored up in him. 36But I tell you that men will have to give account on the day of judgment for every careless word they have spoken. 37For by your words you will be acquitted, and by your words you will be condemned."

The Sign of Jonah

▶ *See Luke 11:29–32*

38Then some of the Pharisees and teachers of the law said to him, "Teacher, we want to see a miraculous sign from you." Mt 16:1; Jn 2:18; 1Co 1:22

39He answered, "A wicked and adulterous generation asks for a miraculous sign! But none will be given it except the sign of the prophet Jonah. 40For as Jonah was three days and three nights in the belly of a huge fish, so the Son of Man will be three days and three nights in the heart of the earth. 41The men of Nineveh will stand up at the judgment with this generation and condemn it; for they repented at the preaching of Jonah, and now one[b] greater than Jonah is here. 42The Queen of the South will rise at the judgment with this generation and condemn it; for she came from the ends of the earth to listen to Solomon's wisdom, and now one greater than Solomon is here. Lk 11:29-32

43"When an evil[c] spirit comes out of a man, it goes through arid places seeking rest and does not find it. 44Then it says, 'I will return to the house I left.' When it arrives, it finds the house unoccupied, swept clean and put in order. 45Then it goes and takes with it seven other spirits more wicked than itself, and they go in and live there. And the final condition of that man is worse than the first. That is how it will be with this wicked generation."

Jesus' Mother and Brothers

▶ *See Mark 3:31–35; Luke 8:19–21*

46While Jesus was still talking to the crowd, his mother and brothers stood outside, wanting to speak to him. 47Someone told him, "Your mother and brothers are standing outside, wanting to speak to you."[d] Mt 13:55; Jn 2:12

48He replied to him, "Who is my mother, and who are my brothers?" 49Pointing to his disciples, he said, "Here are my mother and my brothers. 50For whoever does the will of my Father in heaven is my brother and sister and mother." Mk 3:31-35

The Parable of the Sower

▶ *See Mark 4:1–20; Luke 8:4–15*

13 That same day Jesus went out of the house and sat by the lake. 2Such large crowds gathered around him that he got into a boat and sat in it, while all the people stood on the shore. 3Then he told them many things in parables, saying: "A farmer went out to sow his seed. 4As he was scattering the seed, some fell along the path, and the birds came and ate it up. 5Some fell on rocky places, where it did not have much soil. It sprang up quickly, because the soil was shallow. 6But when the sun came up, the plants were scorched, and they withered because they had no root. 7Other seed fell among thorns, which grew up and choked the plants. 8Still other seed fell on good soil, where it produced a crop—a hundred,

LIVING  **INSIGHT**

As you study Jesus' method of communicating you will find this advice underlying it: Make it clear. Make it simple. Emphasize the essentials. Forget about impressing others. Be content to leave some things unsaid.

(See Matthew 13:3.)

[a] 24 Greek *Beezeboul* or *Beelzeboul*; also in verse 27 [b] 41 Or *something*; also in verse 42 [c] 43 Greek *unclean*
[d] 47 Some manuscripts do not have verse 47.

sixty or thirty times what was sown. 9He who has
ears, let him hear." Ge 26:12; Mt 11:15
10The disciples came to him and asked, "Why
do you speak to the people in parables?"
11He replied, "The knowledge of the secrets of
the kingdom of heaven has been given to you, but
not to them. 12Whoever has will be given more,
and he will have an abundance. Whoever does not
have, even what he has will be taken from him.
13This is why I speak to them in parables:

"Though seeing, they do not see;
though hearing, they do not hear or
understand. Dt 29:4; Jer 5:21; Eze 12:2

14In them is fulfilled the prophecy of Isaiah:

"'You will be ever hearing but never
understanding;
you will be ever seeing but never
perceiving.
15For this people's heart has become calloused;
they hardly hear with their ears,
and they have closed their eyes.
Otherwise they might see with their eyes,
hear with their ears,
understand with their hearts
and turn, and I would heal them.'[a]

16But blessed are your eyes because they see, and
your ears because they hear. 17For I tell you the
truth, many prophets and righteous men longed to
see what you see but did not see it, and to hear
what you hear but did not hear it. Lk 10:23-24
18"Listen then to what the parable of the sower
means: 19When anyone hears the message about
the kingdom and does not understand it, the evil
one comes and snatches away what was sown in
his heart. This is the seed sown along the path.
20The one who received the seed that fell on rocky
places is the man who hears the word and at once
receives it with joy. 21But since he has no root, he
lasts only a short time. When trouble or persecution comes because of the word, he quickly falls
away. 22The one who received the seed that fell
among the thorns is the man who hears the word,
but the worries of this life and the deceitfulness of
wealth choke it, making it unfruitful. 23But the one
who received the seed that fell on good soil is the
man who hears the word and understands it. He
produces a crop, yielding a hundred, sixty or thirty
times what was sown." Mk 4:13-20; Lk 8:11-15

The Parable of the Weeds

24Jesus told them another parable: "The kingdom of heaven is like a man who sowed good seed
in his field. 25But while everyone was sleeping, his
enemy came and sowed weeds among the wheat,
and went away. 26When the wheat sprouted and
formed heads, then the weeds also appeared.
27"The owner's servants came to him and said,
'Sir, didn't you sow good seed in your field? Where
then did the weeds come from?'
28"'An enemy did this,' he replied.
"The servants asked him, 'Do you want us to go
and pull them up?'
29"'No,' he answered, 'because while you are
pulling the weeds, you may root up the wheat with
them. 30Let both grow together until the harvest.
At that time I will tell the harvesters: First collect
the weeds and tie them in bundles to be burned;
then gather the wheat and bring it into my barn.'"

The Parables of the Mustard Seed and the Yeast

► *See Mark 4:30–32; Luke 13:18–21*

31He told them another parable: "The kingdom
of heaven is like a mustard seed, which a man took
and planted in his field. 32Though it is the smallest
of all your seeds, yet when it grows, it is the largest
of garden plants and becomes a tree, so that the
birds of the air come and perch in its branches."
33He told them still another parable: "The kingdom of heaven is like yeast that a woman took and
mixed into a large amount[b] of flour until it
worked all through the dough." Lk 13:18-21
34Jesus spoke all these things to the crowd in
parables; he did not say anything to them without
using a parable. 35So was fulfilled what was spoken
through the prophet: Mk 4:33; Jn 16:25

"I will open my mouth in parables,
I will utter things hidden since the creation
of the world."[c] Ps 78:2; 1Co 2:7

The Parable of the Weeds Explained

36Then he left the crowd and went into the
house. His disciples came to him and said, "Explain to us the parable of the weeds in the field."
37He answered, "The one who sowed the good
seed is the Son of Man. 38The field is the world,
and the good seed stands for the sons of the kingdom. The weeds are the sons of the evil one, 39and
the enemy who sows them is the devil. The harvest
is the end of the age, and the harvesters are angels.
40"As the weeds are pulled up and burned in the
fire, so it will be at the end of the age. 41The Son
of Man will send out his angels, and they will weed
out of his kingdom everything that causes sin and
all who do evil. 42They will throw them into the
fiery furnace, where there will be weeping and
gnashing of teeth. 43Then the righteous will shine
like the sun in the kingdom of their Father. He
who has ears, let him hear. Da 12:3; Mt 8:12; 11:15

[a] *15* Isaiah 6:9,10 [b] *33* Greek *three satas* (probably about 1/2 bushel or 22 liters) [c] *35* Psalm 78:2

The Parables of the Hidden Treasure and the Pearl

44“The kingdom of heaven is like treasure hidden in a field. When a man found it, he hid it again, and then in his joy went and sold all he had and bought that field. Isa 55:1; Php 3:7-8

45“Again, the kingdom of heaven is like a merchant looking for fine pearls. 46When he found one of great value, he went away and sold everything he had and bought it. ver 24

The Parable of the Net

47“Once again, the kingdom of heaven is like a net that was let down into the lake and caught all kinds of fish. 48When it was full, the fishermen pulled it up on the shore. Then they sat down and collected the good fish in baskets, but threw the bad away. 49This is how it will be at the end of the age. The angels will come and separate the wicked from the righteous 50and throw them into the fiery furnace, where there will be weeping and gnashing of teeth. Mt 25:32

51“Have you understood all these things?” Jesus asked.

“Yes,” they replied.

52He said to them, “Therefore every teacher of the law who has been instructed about the kingdom of heaven is like the owner of a house who brings out of his storeroom new treasures as well as old.”

A Prophet Without Honor

▶ *See Mark 6:1–6*

53When Jesus had finished these parables, he moved on from there. 54Coming to his hometown, he began teaching the people in their synagogue, and they were amazed. “Where did this man get this wisdom and these miraculous powers?” they asked. 55“Isn’t this the carpenter’s son? Isn’t his mother’s name Mary, and aren’t his brothers James, Joseph, Simon and Judas? 56Aren’t all his sisters with us? Where then did this man get all these things?” 57And they took offense at him.

But Jesus said to them, “Only in his hometown and in his own house is a prophet without honor.”

58And he did not do many miracles there because of their lack of faith. Mk 6:1-6

John the Baptist Beheaded

▶ *See Mark 6:14–29*

14 At that time Herod the tetrarch heard the reports about Jesus, 2and he said to his attendants, “This is John the Baptist; he has risen from the dead! That is why miraculous powers are at work in him.” Lk 9:7-9

3Now Herod had arrested John and bound him and put him in prison because of Herodias, his brother Philip’s wife, 4for John had been saying to him: “It is not lawful for you to have her.” 5Herod wanted to kill John, but he was afraid of the people, because they considered him a prophet.

6On Herod’s birthday the daughter of Herodias danced for them and pleased Herod so much 7that he promised with an oath to give her whatever she asked. 8Prompted by her mother, she said, “Give me here on a platter the head of John the Baptist.” 9The king was distressed, but because of his oaths and his dinner guests, he ordered that her request be granted 10and had John beheaded in the prison. 11His head was brought in on a platter and given to the girl, who carried it to her mother. 12John’s disciples came and took his body and buried it. Then they went and told Jesus. Mk 6:14-29

Jesus Feeds the Five Thousand

▶ *See Mark 6:32–44; Luke 9:10–17; John 6:1–13*

13When Jesus heard what had happened, he withdrew by boat privately to a solitary place. Hearing of this, the crowds followed him on foot from the towns. 14When Jesus landed and saw a large crowd, he had compassion on them and healed their sick. Mt 15:32-38

15As evening approached, the disciples came to him and said, “This is a remote place, and it’s already getting late. Send the crowds away, so they can go to the villages and buy themselves some food.”

16Jesus replied, “They do not need to go away. You give them something to eat.”

17“We have here only five loaves of bread and two fish,” they answered.

18“Bring them here to me,” he said. 19And he directed the people to sit down on the grass. Taking the five loaves and the two fish and looking up to heaven, he gave thanks and broke the loaves. Then he gave them to the disciples, and the disciples gave them to the people. 20They all ate and were satisfied, and the disciples picked up twelve basketfuls of broken pieces that were left over. 21The number of those who ate was about five thousand men, besides women and children.

Jesus Walks on the Water

▶ *See Mark 6:45–51; John 6:15–21*

22Immediately Jesus made the disciples get into the boat and go on ahead of him to the other side, while he dismissed the crowd. 23After he had dismissed them, he went up on a mountainside by himself to pray. When evening came, he was there alone, 24but the boat was already a considerable distance[a] from land, buffeted by the waves because the wind was against it. Lk 3:21

25During the fourth watch of the night Jesus

[a] 24 Greek *many stadia*

went out to them, walking on the lake. 26When the
disciples saw him walking on the lake, they were
terrified. "It's a ghost," they said, and cried out in
fear. Lk 24:37
27But Jesus immediately said to them: "Take
courage! It is I. Don't be afraid." Mt 17:7; Rev 1:17
28"Lord, if it's you," Peter replied, "tell me to
come to you on the water."
29"Come," he said.
Then Peter got down out of the boat, walked on
the water and came toward Jesus. 30But when he
saw the wind, he was afraid and, beginning to sink,
cried out, "Lord, save me!"
31Immediately Jesus reached out his hand and
caught him. "You of little faith," he said, "why did
you doubt?" Mt 6:30
32And when they climbed into the boat, the
wind died down. 33Then those who were in the
boat worshiped him, saying, "Truly you are
the Son of God." Mk 6:45-51; Jn 6:15-21

LIVING  **INSIGHT**

In the tragic storms of life Jesus specializes in calming waves and silencing winds. It'll just shock you sometimes. How can Jesus Christ do such a thing? How, indeed. He is God! Never doubt it, my friend.

(See Matthew 14:22–33.)

34When they had crossed over, they landed at
Gennesaret. 35And when the men of that place
recognized Jesus, they sent word to all the surrounding country. People brought all their sick to
him 36and begged him to let the sick just touch the
edge of his cloak, and all who touched him were
healed. Mk 6:53-56

Clean and Unclean

▶ *See Mark 7:1–23*

15 Then some Pharisees and teachers of the
law came to Jesus from Jerusalem and
asked, 2"Why do your disciples break the tradition
of the elders? They don't wash their hands before
they eat!" Lk 11:38
3Jesus replied, "And why do you break the command of God for the sake of your tradition? 4For
God said, 'Honor your father and mother'[a] and
'Anyone who curses his father or mother must be
put to death.'[b] 5But you say that if a man says to
his father or mother, 'Whatever help you might
otherwise have received from me is a gift devoted
to God,' 6he is not to 'honor his father[c]' with it.
Thus you nullify the word of God for the sake of
your tradition. 7You hypocrites! Isaiah was right
when he prophesied about you:

8" 'These people honor me with their lips,
but their hearts are far from me.

LIVING  **INSIGHT**

We are masters at rationalizing our inflexible behavior. We imply that change always represents a departure from the truth of Scripture. Now some changes do pull us away from Scripture. They must definitely be avoided. But let's be absolutely certain that we are standing on Scriptural rock, not the sand of tradition.

(See Matthew 15:6.)

9They worship me in vain;
their teachings are but rules taught by
men.'[d]" Col 2:20-22; Mal 2:2

10Jesus called the crowd to him and said, "Listen
and understand. 11What goes into a man's mouth
does not make him 'unclean,' but what comes out
of his mouth, that is what makes him 'unclean.' "
12Then the disciples came to him and asked,
"Do you know that the Pharisees were offended
when they heard this?"
13He replied, "Every plant that my heavenly Father has not planted will be pulled up by the roots.
14Leave them; they are blind guides.[e] If a blind
man leads a blind man, both will fall into a pit."
15Peter said, "Explain the parable to us."
16"Are you still so dull?" Jesus asked them.
17"Don't you see that whatever enters the mouth
goes into the stomach and then out of the body?
18But the things that come out of the mouth come
from the heart, and these make a man 'unclean.'
19For out of the heart come evil thoughts, murder,
adultery, sexual immorality, theft, false testimony,
slander. 20These are what make a man 'unclean';
but eating with unwashed hands does not make
him 'unclean.' " Mk 7:1-23; Gal 5:19-21

The Faith of the Canaanite Woman

▶ *See Mark 7:24–30*

21Leaving that place, Jesus withdrew to the region of Tyre and Sidon. 22A Canaanite woman
from that vicinity came to him, crying out, "Lord,
Son of David, have mercy on me! My daughter is
suffering terribly from demon-possession."
23Jesus did not answer a word. So his disciples
came to him and urged him, "Send her away, for
she keeps crying out after us."

[a] 4 Exodus 20:12; Deut. 5:16 [b] 4 Exodus 21:17; Lev. 20:9 [c] 6 Some manuscripts *father or his mother* [d] 9 Isaiah 29:13
[e] 14 Some manuscripts *guides of the blind*

24He answered, "I was sent only to the lost sheep of Israel." Mt 10:6,23; Ro 15:8

25The woman came and knelt before him. "Lord, help me!" she said. Mt 8:2

26He replied, "It is not right to take the children's bread and toss it to their dogs."

27"Yes, Lord," she said, "but even the dogs eat the crumbs that fall from their masters' table."

28Then Jesus answered, "Woman, you have great faith! Your request is granted." And her daughter was healed from that very hour.

Jesus Feeds the Four Thousand

▶ *See Mark 8:1–10*

29Jesus left there and went along the Sea of Galilee. Then he went up on a mountainside and sat down. 30Great crowds came to him, bringing the lame, the blind, the crippled, the mute and many others, and laid them at his feet; and he healed them. 31The people were amazed when they saw the mute speaking, the crippled made well, the lame walking and the blind seeing. And they praised the God of Israel. Mk 7:31-37

32Jesus called his disciples to him and said, "I have compassion for these people; they have already been with me three days and have nothing to eat. I do not want to send them away hungry, or they may collapse on the way." Mt 9:36

33His disciples answered, "Where could we get enough bread in this remote place to feed such a crowd?"

34"How many loaves do you have?" Jesus asked. "Seven," they replied, "and a few small fish."

35He told the crowd to sit down on the ground. 36Then he took the seven loaves and the fish, and when he had given thanks, he broke them and gave them to the disciples, and they in turn to the people. 37They all ate and were satisfied. Afterward the disciples picked up seven basketfuls of broken pieces that were left over. 38The number of those who ate was four thousand, besides women and children. 39After Jesus had sent the crowd away, he got into the boat and went to the vicinity of Magadan. Mt 14:13-21; Mk 8:1-10

Rejection of the King **Chapters 16–27**

In these chapters the tide began to turn. The antagonism of Jesus' opponents was no longer hidden. Because of growing opposition, Jesus began to withdraw and spend less time in public settings. He spoke more and more about His coming death and the promise of His resurrection. Before this time His teaching had been clear and pointed; now His words were veiled in parables and the core of His message known only to His closest disciples.

Chapters 23–25 record Jesus' passionate thoughts about religious hypocrisy and His predictions of the future. Soon after this discourse ended, events were set into motion that would culminate in Jesus' death on a cross. Chapters 26 and 27 tell of the plot against Jesus, the Last Supper, Jesus' arrest and trials, and finally His crucifixion. The events of these chapters break our hearts as we hear the echo of the public's opinion: "The King is dead!"

The Demand for a Sign

▶ *See Mark 8:11–21*

16 The Pharisees and Sadducees came to Jesus and tested him by asking him to show them a sign from heaven. Mt 12:38; Ac 4:1

2He replied,[a] "When evening comes, you say, 'It will be fair weather, for the sky is red,' 3and in the morning, 'Today it will be stormy, for the sky is red and overcast.' You know how to interpret the appearance of the sky, but you cannot interpret the signs of the times. 4A wicked and adulterous generation looks for a miraculous sign, but none will be given it except the sign of Jonah." Jesus then left them and went away. Mt 12:39

The Yeast of the Pharisees and Sadducees

5When they went across the lake, the disciples forgot to take bread. 6"Be careful," Jesus said to them. "Be on your guard against the yeast of the Pharisees and Sadducees." Lk 12:1

7They discussed this among themselves and said, "It is because we didn't bring any bread."

8Aware of their discussion, Jesus asked, "You of little faith, why are you talking among yourselves about having no bread? 9Do you still not understand? Don't you remember the five loaves for the five thousand, and how many basketfuls you gathered? 10Or the seven loaves for the four thousand, and how many basketfuls you gathered? 11How is it you don't understand that I was not talking to you about bread? But be on your guard against the yeast of the Pharisees and Sadducees." 12Then they understood that he was not telling them to guard against the yeast used in bread, but against the teaching of the Pharisees and Sadducees.

Peter's Confession of Christ

▶ *See Mark 8:27–29; Luke 9:18–20*

13When Jesus came to the region of Caesarea Philippi, he asked his disciples, "Who do people say the Son of Man is?" Mk 8:27-29; Lk 9:18-20

14They replied, "Some say John the Baptist; others say Elijah; and still others, Jeremiah or one of the prophets." Mt 14:2; Mk 6:15

15"But what about you?" he asked. "Who do you say I am?"

16Simon Peter answered, "You are the Christ,[b] the Son of the living God." Jn 11:27

17Jesus replied, "Blessed are you, Simon son of Jonah, for this was not revealed to you by man, but

[a]2 Some early manuscripts do not have the rest of verse 2 and all of verse 3. [b]16 Or *Messiah*; also in verse 20

PETER

A Crack in the Rock

"And I tell you that you are Peter, and on this rock I will build my church, and the gates of Hades will not overcome it."

—MATTHEW 16:18

The first-century historian Josephus was at one time a governor of Galilee, so he knew something about the Galileans. He described them as quick-tempered, impulsive, emotional, easily roused by an appeal to adventure, and intensely loyal to the end. These words perfectly describe Simon Peter, the fisherman who would become the leader of Jesus' disciples and the "rock" on which Christ would build His church.

In order to get to know this man better, we must examine four significant events in his life. First, *Jesus gave Peter a nickname*, a fact that may seem insignificant to us, but I believe it meant a lot to Peter. According to the Gospel writer John, the nicknaming took place the first time Jesus and Peter faced each other eyeball-to-eyeball. Listen to Jesus' words as He looked into the eyes of this man who was to accompany Him for the few years of His ministry: " 'You are Simon son of John. You will be called Cephas' (which, when translated, is Peter)" (1:42). Peter very likely had never had anyone point out his rock-like characteristics, possibly because he didn't have many—on the surface. Jesus, however, saw into his heart.

Second, *Peter boldly declared his faith in Jesus*. Early in His ministry, Jesus had developed a following that went well beyond the original Twelve. Some came out of a genuine, albeit self-centered, interest. Some came simply to have their stomachs filled. Others came out of curiosity. But when Jesus began to tell them what being His disciples would demand, many began to sneak away. As Jesus saw them "turning back" (6:66) He raised the question to the Twelve, "You do not want to leave too, do you?" Peter took the position of spokesman: "We believe and know that you are the Holy One of God" (6:69). Suddenly Simon was showing signs of being "the rock"—Peter! (See Matthew 16:16 for another awesome declaration of faith from the lips of Peter.)

Third, *Peter boldly boasted about his own faithfulness*. In John's account of Jesus' last night with His disciples, Jesus told it to them straight: "My children, I will be with you only a little longer. You will look for me, and just as I told the Jews, so I tell you now: Where I am going, you cannot come" (13:33). Peter's response showed a reliance on his own flesh and his own will—"Lord, why can't I follow you now? I will lay down my life for you" (13:37). Notice that the "we" had changed to an "I." Peter's reaction brings to mind the words of Solomon: "Pride goes before destruction, a haughty spirit before a fall" (Proverbs 16:18).

Fourth, *Jesus predicted Peter's denial*: "I tell you the truth, before the rooster crows, you will disown me three times!" (John 13:38). These haunting words were a direct rebuke to Peter's pride. Look at the tragic series of events that led to Peter's denial. *Peter relied on himself instead of on God when faced with opposition.* When Jesus was arrested in Gethsemane, Peter reacted impulsively, striking off a man's ear (18:10). *Peter was reluctant to stand alone when in dangerous company.* He reverted to his old habits of self-protection in the midst of the crowd (18:17). *Peter resisted being identified with Jesus when confronted with the choice.* He denied having even the faintest knowledge of this man to whom he had pledged his life just a few hours before (18:25). Finally, *Peter rejected the truth regardless of the consequences.* He knowingly and emphatically denied any association with Jesus (18:27). Matthew tells us that Peter cursed as he disowned Jesus for the third time (Matthew 26:74). That's when the rooster crowed—and the rock cracked.

Yet as you ponder Peter's life, I would urge you to look beyond the failure and read the rest of the story. I suspect William Shakespeare had it right when he wrote in his play *Julius Caesar* (Act III), "The evil that men do lives after them; the good is often interred with their bones." The story of Peter provides a remarkable example of a man who was given a second chance. You can read about it in the final chapter of John's Gospel. Aren't you relieved—and thankful—that Jesus restored him? And in the same way He did that for Peter, He'll do it for you and for me!

by my Father in heaven. 18And I tell you that you
are Peter,[a] and on this rock I will build my
church, and the gates of Hades[b] will not overcome it.[c] 19I will give you the keys of the kingdom
of heaven; whatever you bind on earth will be[d]
bound in heaven, and whatever you loose on earth
will be[d] loosed in heaven." 20Then he warned his
disciples not to tell anyone that he was the Christ.

Jesus Predicts His Death

▶ *See Mark 8:31—9:1; Luke 9:22–27*

21From that time on Jesus began to explain to
his disciples that he must go to Jerusalem and
suffer many things at the hands of the elders, chief
priests and teachers of the law, and that he must be
killed and on the third day be raised to life.

22Peter took him aside and began to rebuke
him. "Never, Lord!" he said. "This shall never happen to you!"

23Jesus turned and said to Peter, "Get behind
me, Satan! You are a stumbling block to me; you
do not have in mind the things of God, but the
things of men." Mt 4:10

24Then Jesus said to his disciples, "If anyone
would come after me, he must deny himself and
take up his cross and follow me. 25For whoever
wants to save his life[e] will lose it, but whoever
loses his life for me will find it. 26What good will
it be for a man if he gains the whole world, yet
forfeits his soul? Or what can a man give in exchange for his soul? 27For the Son of Man is going
to come in his Father's glory with his angels, and
then he will reward each person according to what
he has done. 28I tell you the truth, some who are
standing here will not taste death before they see
the Son of Man coming in his kingdom."

The Transfiguration

▶ *See Mark 9:2–13; Luke 9:28–36*

17 After six days Jesus took with him Peter,
James and John the brother of James, and
led them up a high mountain by themselves.
2There he was transfigured before them. His face
shone like the sun, and his clothes became as white
as the light. 3Just then there appeared before them
Moses and Elijah, talking with Jesus. Mt 4:21

4Peter said to Jesus, "Lord, it is good for us to
be here. If you wish, I will put up three shelters—
one for you, one for Moses and one for Elijah."

5While he was still speaking, a bright cloud enveloped them, and a voice from the cloud said,
"This is my Son, whom I love; with him I am well
pleased. Listen to him!" Mt 3:17; 2Pe 1:17

6When the disciples heard this, they fell facedown to the ground, terrified. 7But Jesus came
and touched them. "Get up," he said. "Don't be
afraid." 8When they looked up, they saw no one
except Jesus. Lk 9:28-36

9As they were coming down the mountain,
Jesus instructed them, "Don't tell anyone what you
have seen, until the Son of Man has been raised
from the dead." Mt 16:21; Mk 8:30

10The disciples asked him, "Why then do the
teachers of the law say that Elijah must come
first?"

11Jesus replied, "To be sure, Elijah comes and
will restore all things. 12But I tell you, Elijah has
already come, and they did not recognize him, but
have done to him everything they wished. In the
same way the Son of Man is going to suffer at their
hands." 13Then the disciples understood that he
was talking to them about John the Baptist.

The Healing of a Boy With a Demon

▶ *See Mark 9:14–28; Luke 9:37–42*

14When they came to the crowd, a man approached Jesus and knelt before him. 15"Lord,
have mercy on my son," he said. "He has seizures
and is suffering greatly. He often falls into the fire
or into the water. 16I brought him to your disciples, but they could not heal him." Mt 4:24

17"O unbelieving and perverse generation,"
Jesus replied, "how long shall I stay with you? How
long shall I put up with you? Bring the boy here to
me." 18Jesus rebuked the demon, and it came out
of the boy, and he was healed from that moment.

19Then the disciples came to Jesus in private
and asked, "Why couldn't we drive it out?"

20He replied, "Because you have so little faith. I
tell you the truth, if you have faith as small as a
mustard seed, you can say to this mountain, 'Move
from here to there' and it will move. Nothing will
be impossible for you.[f]" Mk 11:23; Lk 17:6

22When they came together in Galilee, he said to
them, "The Son of Man is going to be betrayed
into the hands of men. 23They will kill him, and on
the third day he will be raised to life." And the
disciples were filled with grief. Mt 16:21; Ac 2:23; 3:13

The Temple Tax

24After Jesus and his disciples arrived in Capernaum, the collectors of the two-drachma tax came
to Peter and asked, "Doesn't your teacher pay the
temple tax[g]?" Ex 30:13

25"Yes, he does," he replied.

When Peter came into the house, Jesus was the
first to speak. "What do you think, Simon?" he
asked. "From whom do the kings of the earth
collect duty and taxes—from their own sons or
from others?" Mt 22:17-21; Ro 13:7

[a]18 Peter means *rock.* [b]18 Or *hell* [c]18 Or *not prove stronger than it* [d]19 Or *have been* [e]25 The Greek word means either *life* or *soul*; also in verse 26. [f]20 Some manuscripts *you.* [21]*But this kind does not go out except by prayer and fasting.* [g]24 Greek *the two drachmas*

26"From others," Peter answered.

"Then the sons are exempt," Jesus said to him. 27"But so that we may not offend them, go to the lake and throw out your line. Take the first fish you catch; open its mouth and you will find a four-drachma coin. Take it and give it to them for my tax and yours." Jn 6:61

The Greatest in the Kingdom of Heaven

▶ *See Mark 9:33–37; Luke 9:46–48*

18 At that time the disciples came to Jesus and asked, "Who is the greatest in the kingdom of heaven?"

2He called a little child and had him stand among them. 3And he said: "I tell you the truth, unless you change and become like little children, you will never enter the kingdom of heaven. 4Therefore, whoever humbles himself like this child is the greatest in the kingdom of heaven.

5"And whoever welcomes a little child like this in my name welcomes me. 6But if anyone causes one of these little ones who believe in me to sin, it would be better for him to have a large millstone hung around his neck and to be drowned in the depths of the sea. Mk 9:33-37; Lk 9:46-48; 17:2

7"Woe to the world because of the things that cause people to sin! Such things must come, but woe to the man through whom they come! 8If your hand or your foot causes you to sin, cut it off and throw it away. It is better for you to enter life maimed or crippled than to have two hands or two feet and be thrown into eternal fire. 9And if your eye causes you to sin, gouge it out and throw it away. It is better for you to enter life with one eye than to have two eyes and be thrown into the fire of hell. Mt 5:29; Mk 9:43,45; Lk 17:1

The Parable of the Lost Sheep

▶ *See Luke 15:4–7*

10"See that you do not look down on one of these little ones. For I tell you that their angels in heaven always see the face of my Father in heaven.[a] Ge 48:16; Ps 34:7; Heb 1:14

12"What do you think? If a man owns a hundred sheep, and one of them wanders away, will he not leave the ninety-nine on the hills and go to look for the one that wandered off? 13And if he finds it, I tell you the truth, he is happier about that one sheep than about the ninety-nine that did not wander off. 14In the same way your Father in heaven is not willing that any of these little ones should be lost. Lk 15:4-7

A Brother Who Sins Against You

15"If your brother sins against you,[b] go and show him his fault, just between the two of you. If he listens to you, you have won your brother over. 16But if he will not listen, take one or two others along, so that 'every matter may be established by the testimony of two or three witnesses.'[c] 17If he refuses to listen to them, tell it to the church; and if he refuses to listen even to the church, treat him as you would a pagan or a tax collector. 1Co 6:1-6

18"I tell you the truth, whatever you bind on earth will be[d] bound in heaven, and whatever you loose on earth will be[d] loosed in heaven.

19"Again, I tell you that if two of you on earth agree about anything you ask for, it will be done for you by my Father in heaven. 20For where two or three come together in my name, there am I with them." Mt 7:7

The Parable of the Unmerciful Servant

21Then Peter came to Jesus and asked, "Lord, how many times shall I forgive my brother when he sins against me? Up to seven times?" Lk 17:4

LIVING  INSIGHT

In celebration of God's forgiveness toward you, be the first to forget and forgive an action your spouse or friend or neighbor did to you.

(See Matthew 18:21–35.)

22Jesus answered, "I tell you, not seven times, but seventy-seven times.[e] Ge 4:24

23"Therefore, the kingdom of heaven is like a king who wanted to settle accounts with his servants. 24As he began the settlement, a man who owed him ten thousand talents[f] was brought to him. 25Since he was not able to pay, the master ordered that he and his wife and his children and all that he had be sold to repay the debt. 2Ki 4:1

26"The servant fell on his knees before him. 'Be patient with me,' he begged, 'and I will pay back everything.' 27The servant's master took pity on him, canceled the debt and let him go. Mt 8:2

28"But when that servant went out, he found one of his fellow servants who owed him a hundred denarii.[g] He grabbed him and began to choke him. 'Pay back what you owe me!' he demanded.

29"His fellow servant fell to his knees and begged him, 'Be patient with me, and I will pay you back.'

30"But he refused. Instead, he went off and had the man thrown into prison until he could pay the

[a] 10 Some manuscripts *heaven.* 11*The Son of Man came to save what was lost.* [b] 15 Some manuscripts do not have *against you.* [c] 16 Deut. 19:15 [d] 18 Or *have been* [e] 22 Or *seventy times seven* [f] 24 That is, millions of dollars [g] 28 That is, a few dollars

debt. 31 When the other servants saw what had happened, they were greatly distressed and went and told their master everything that had happened.

32 "Then the master called the servant in. 'You wicked servant,' he said, 'I canceled all that debt of yours because you begged me to. 33 Shouldn't you have had mercy on your fellow servant just as I had on you?' 34 In anger his master turned him over to the jailers to be tortured, until he should pay back all he owed.

35 "This is how my heavenly Father will treat each of you unless you forgive your brother from your heart." Mt 6:14; Jas 2:13

Divorce

▶ *See Mark 10:1–12*

19 When Jesus had finished saying these things, he left Galilee and went into the region of Judea to the other side of the Jordan. 2 Large crowds followed him, and he healed them there. Mt 4:23; 7:28

3 Some Pharisees came to him to test him. They asked, "Is it lawful for a man to divorce his wife for any and every reason?" Mt 5:31

4 "Haven't you read," he replied, "that at the beginning the Creator 'made them male and female,'[a] 5 and said, 'For this reason a man will leave his father and mother and be united to his wife, and the two will become one flesh'[b]? 6 So they are no longer two, but one. Therefore what God has joined together, let man not separate."

7 "Why then," they asked, "did Moses command that a man give his wife a certificate of divorce and send her away?" Dt 24:1-4; Mt 5:31

8 Jesus replied, "Moses permitted you to divorce your wives because your hearts were hard. But it was not this way from the beginning. 9 I tell you that anyone who divorces his wife, except for marital unfaithfulness, and marries another woman commits adultery." Mk 10:1-12; Lk 16:18

10 The disciples said to him, "If this is the situation between a husband and wife, it is better not to marry."

11 Jesus replied, "Not everyone can accept this word, but only those to whom it has been given. 12 For some are eunuchs because they were born that way; others were made that way by men; and others have renounced marriage[c] because of the kingdom of heaven. The one who can accept this should accept it." Mt 13:11; 1Co 7:7-9,17

The Little Children and Jesus

▶ *See Mark 10:13–16; Luke 18:15–17*

13 Then little children were brought to Jesus for him to place his hands on them and pray for them. But the disciples rebuked those who brought them. Mk 5:23

14 Jesus said, "Let the little children come to me, and do not hinder them, for the kingdom of heaven belongs to such as these." 15 When he had placed his hands on them, he went on from there.

The Rich Young Man

▶ *See Mark 10:17–30; Luke 18:18–30*

16 Now a man came up to Jesus and asked, "Teacher, what good thing must I do to get eternal life?" Mt 25:46; Lk 10:25

17 "Why do you ask me about what is good?" Jesus replied. "There is only One who is good. If you want to enter life, obey the commandments."

18 "Which ones?" the man inquired.

Jesus replied, " 'Do not murder, do not commit adultery, do not steal, do not give false testimony, 19 honor your father and mother,'[d] and 'love your neighbor as yourself.'[e]" Lev 19:18; Jas 2:11

20 "All these I have kept," the young man said. "What do I still lack?"

21 Jesus answered, "If you want to be perfect, go, sell your possessions and give to the poor, and you will have treasure in heaven. Then come, follow me." Mt 6:20; Lk 12:33; Ac 4:34-35

22 When the young man heard this, he went away sad, because he had great wealth.

23 Then Jesus said to his disciples, "I tell you the truth, it is hard for a rich man to enter the kingdom of heaven. 24 Again I tell you, it is easier for a camel to go through the eye of a needle than for a rich man to enter the kingdom of God." Mt 13:22

25 When the disciples heard this, they were greatly astonished and asked, "Who then can be saved?"

26 Jesus looked at them and said, "With man this is impossible, but with God all things are possible." Ge 18:14; Lk 1:37; Ro 4:21

27 Peter answered him, "We have left everything to follow you! What then will there be for us?"

28 Jesus said to them, "I tell you the truth, at the renewal of all things, when the Son of Man sits on his glorious throne, you who have followed me will also sit on twelve thrones, judging the twelve tribes of Israel. 29 And everyone who has left houses or brothers or sisters or father or mother[f] or children or fields for my sake will receive a hundred times as much and will inherit eternal life. 30 But many who are first will be last, and many who are last will be first. Mk 10:17-30; Lk 18:18-30

The Parable of the Workers in the Vineyard

20 "For the kingdom of heaven is like a landowner who went out early in the morning

[a] 4 Gen. 1:27 [b] 5 Gen. 2:24 [c] 12 Or *have made themselves eunuchs* [d] 19 Exodus 20:12-16; Deut. 5:16-20
[e] 19 Lev. 19:18 [f] 29 Some manuscripts *mother or wife*

to hire men to work in his vineyard. 2He agreed to pay them a denarius for the day and sent them into his vineyard. Mt 21:28,33

3"About the third hour he went out and saw others standing in the marketplace doing nothing. 4He told them, 'You also go and work in my vineyard, and I will pay you whatever is right.' 5So they went.

"He went out again about the sixth hour and the ninth hour and did the same thing. 6About the eleventh hour he went out and found still others standing around. He asked them, 'Why have you been standing here all day long doing nothing?'

7" 'Because no one has hired us,' they answered.

"He said to them, 'You also go and work in my vineyard.'

8"When evening came, the owner of the vineyard said to his foreman, 'Call the workers and pay them their wages, beginning with the last ones hired and going on to the first.' Lev 19:13; Dt 24:15

9"The workers who were hired about the eleventh hour came and each received a denarius. 10So when those came who were hired first, they expected to receive more. But each one of them also received a denarius. 11When they received it, they began to grumble against the landowner. 12'These men who were hired last worked only one hour,' they said, 'and you have made them equal to us who have borne the burden of the work and the heat of the day.' Jnh 4:8; Jas 1:11

13"But he answered one of them, 'Friend, I am not being unfair to you. Didn't you agree to work for a denarius? 14Take your pay and go. I want to give the man who was hired last the same as I gave you. 15Don't I have the right to do what I want with my own money? Or are you envious because I am generous?' Dt 15:9; Mk 7:22

16"So the last will be first, and the first will be last." Mt 19:30

Jesus Again Predicts His Death

▶ *See Mark 10:32–34; Luke 18:31–33*

17Now as Jesus was going up to Jerusalem, he took the twelve disciples aside and said to them, 18"We are going up to Jerusalem, and the Son of Man will be betrayed to the chief priests and the teachers of the law. They will condemn him to death 19and will turn him over to the Gentiles to be mocked and flogged and crucified. On the third day he will be raised to life!" Mk 10:32-34; Lk 18:31-33

A Mother's Request

▶ *See Mark 10:35–45*

20Then the mother of Zebedee's sons came to Jesus with her sons and, kneeling down, asked a favor of him. Mt 4:21; 8:2

21"What is it you want?" he asked.

She said, "Grant that one of these two sons of mine may sit at your right and the other at your left in your kingdom." Mt 19:28

22"You don't know what you are asking," Jesus said to them. "Can you drink the cup I am going to drink?" Mt 26:39,42; Lk 22:42; Jn 18:11

"We can," they answered.

23Jesus said to them, "You will indeed drink from my cup, but to sit at my right or left is not for me to grant. These places belong to those for whom they have been prepared by my Father."

24When the ten heard about this, they were indignant with the two brothers. 25Jesus called them together and said, "You know that the rulers of the Gentiles lord it over them, and their high officials exercise authority over them. 26Not so with you. Instead, whoever wants to become great among you must be your servant, 27and whoever wants to be first must be your slave— 28just as the Son of Man did not come to be served, but to serve, and to give his life as a ransom for many." Mk 10:35-45

Two Blind Men Receive Sight

▶ *See Mark 10:46–52; Luke 18:35–43*

29As Jesus and his disciples were leaving Jericho, a large crowd followed him. 30Two blind men were sitting by the roadside, and when they heard that Jesus was going by, they shouted, "Lord, Son of David, have mercy on us!" Mt 9:27

31The crowd rebuked them and told them to be quiet, but they shouted all the louder, "Lord, Son of David, have mercy on us!"

32Jesus stopped and called them. "What do you want me to do for you?" he asked.

33"Lord," they answered, "we want our sight."

34Jesus had compassion on them and touched their eyes. Immediately they received their sight and followed him. Mk 10:46-52; Lk 18:35-43

The Triumphal Entry

▶ *See Mark 11:1–10; Luke 19:29–38; John 12:12–15*

21 As they approached Jerusalem and came to Bethphage on the Mount of Olives, Jesus sent two disciples, 2saying to them, "Go to the village ahead of you, and at once you will find a donkey tied there, with her colt by her. Untie them and bring them to me. 3If anyone says anything to you, tell him that the Lord needs them, and he will send them right away." Mk 11:1-10

4This took place to fulfill what was spoken through the prophet:

5"Say to the Daughter of Zion,
'See, your king comes to you,
gentle and riding on a donkey,
on a colt, the foal of a donkey.' "[a] Isa 62:11

6The disciples went and did as Jesus had in-

[a]5 Zech. 9:9

structed them. 7They brought the donkey and the colt, placed their cloaks on them, and Jesus sat on them. 8A very large crowd spread their cloaks on the road, while others cut branches from the trees and spread them on the road. 9The crowds that went ahead of him and those that followed shouted, 2Ki 9:13

"Hosanna[a] to the Son of David!" Mt 9:27

"Blessed is he who comes in the name of the
Lord!"[b] Lk 19:29-38

"Hosanna[a] in the highest!" Jn 12:12-15

10When Jesus entered Jerusalem, the whole city was stirred and asked, "Who is this?"

11The crowds answered, "This is Jesus, the prophet from Nazareth in Galilee." Jn 6:14; 7:40

Jesus at the Temple

▶ *See Mark 11:15–18; Luke 19:45–47*

12Jesus entered the temple area and drove out all who were buying and selling there. He overturned the tables of the money changers and the benches of those selling doves. 13"It is written," he said to them, "'My house will be called a house of prayer,'[c] but you are making it a 'den of robbers.'[d]" Ex 30:13; Dt 14:26

14The blind and the lame came to him at the temple, and he healed them. 15But when the chief priests and the teachers of the law saw the wonderful things he did and the children shouting in the temple area, "Hosanna to the Son of David," they were indignant. Mt 9:27; Lk 19:39

16"Do you hear what these children are saying?" they asked him.

"Yes," replied Jesus, "have you never read,

"'From the lips of children and infants
you have ordained praise'[e]?" Mk 11:15-18

17And he left them and went out of the city to Bethany, where he spent the night. Mt 26:6; Mk 11:1

The Fig Tree Withers

▶ *See Mark 11:12–14,20–24*

18Early in the morning, as he was on his way back to the city, he was hungry. 19Seeing a fig tree by the road, he went up to it but found nothing on it except leaves. Then he said to it, "May you never bear fruit again!" Immediately the tree withered.

20When the disciples saw this, they were amazed. "How did the fig tree wither so quickly?" they asked.

21Jesus replied, "I tell you the truth, if you have faith and do not doubt, not only can you do what was done to the fig tree, but also you can say to this mountain, 'Go, throw yourself into the sea,' and it will be done. 22If you believe, you will receive whatever you ask for in prayer."

The Authority of Jesus Questioned

▶ *See Mark 11:27–33; Luke 20:1–8*

23Jesus entered the temple courts, and, while he was teaching, the chief priests and the elders of the people came to him. "By what authority are you doing these things?" they asked. "And who gave you this authority?" Ac 4:7; 7:27

24Jesus replied, "I will also ask you one question. If you answer me, I will tell you by what authority I am doing these things. 25John's baptism—where did it come from? Was it from heaven, or from men?"

They discussed it among themselves and said, "If we say, 'From heaven,' he will ask, 'Then why didn't you believe him?' 26But if we say, 'From men'—we are afraid of the people, for they all hold that John was a prophet." Mk 6:20

27So they answered Jesus, "We don't know."

Then he said, "Neither will I tell you by what authority I am doing these things. Mk 11:27-33

The Parable of the Two Sons

28"What do you think? There was a man who had two sons. He went to the first and said, 'Son, go and work today in the vineyard.' Mt 20:1

29"'I will not,' he answered, but later he changed his mind and went.

30"Then the father went to the other son and said the same thing. He answered, 'I will, sir,' but he did not go.

31"Which of the two did what his father wanted?"

"The first," they answered.

Jesus said to them, "I tell you the truth, the tax collectors and the prostitutes are entering the kingdom of God ahead of you. 32For John came to you to show you the way of righteousness, and you did not believe him, but the tax collectors and the prostitutes did. And even after you saw this, you did not repent and believe him. Lk 7:29-30,36-50

The Parable of the Tenants

▶ *See Mark 12:1–12; Luke 20:9–19*

33"Listen to another parable: There was a landowner who planted a vineyard. He put a wall around it, dug a winepress in it and built a watchtower. Then he rented the vineyard to some farmers and went away on a journey. 34When the harvest time approached, he sent his servants to the tenants to collect his fruit. Ps 80:8; Isa 5:1-7

35"The tenants seized his servants; they beat one, killed another, and stoned a third. 36Then he sent other servants to them, more than the first

[a] *9* A Hebrew expression meaning "Save!" which became an exclamation of praise; also in verse 15 [b] *9* Psalm 118:26
[c] *13* Isaiah 56:7 [d] *13* Jer. 7:11 [e] *16* Psalm 8:2

time, and the tenants treated them the same way.
37Last of all, he sent his son to them. 'They will
respect my son,' he said. 2Ch 24:21; Mt 23:34,37
38"But when the tenants saw the son, they said
to each other, 'This is the heir. Come, let's kill him
and take his inheritance.' 39So they took him and
threw him out of the vineyard and killed him.
40"Therefore, when the owner of the vineyard
comes, what will he do to those tenants?"
41"He will bring those wretches to a wretched
end," they replied, "and he will rent the vineyard
to other tenants, who will give him his share of the
crop at harvest time." Ac 13:46; 18:6; 28:28
42Jesus said to them, "Have you never read in
the Scriptures:

"'The stone the builders rejected
has become the capstone[a];
the Lord has done this,
and it is marvelous in our eyes'[b]? Ac 4:11

43"Therefore I tell you that the kingdom of God
will be taken away from you and given to a people
who will produce its fruit. 44He who falls on this
stone will be broken to pieces, but he on whom it
falls will be crushed."[c] Mt 8:12; Lk 2:34
45When the chief priests and the Pharisees
heard Jesus' parables, they knew he was talking
about them. 46They looked for a way to arrest him,
but they were afraid of the crowd because the people held that he was a prophet. Mk 12:1-12; Lk 20:9-19

The Parable of the Wedding Banquet

22 Jesus spoke to them again in parables, saying: 2"The kingdom of heaven is like a king
who prepared a wedding banquet for his son. 3He
sent his servants to those who had been invited to
the banquet to tell them to come, but they refused
to come. Mt 21:34
4"Then he sent some more servants and said,
'Tell those who have been invited that I have prepared my dinner: My oxen and fattened cattle
have been butchered, and everything is ready.
Come to the wedding banquet.' Mt 21:36
5"But they paid no attention and went off—one
to his field, another to his business. 6The rest
seized his servants, mistreated them and killed
them. 7The king was enraged. He sent his army
and destroyed those murderers and burned their
city. Lk 19:27
8"Then he said to his servants, 'The wedding
banquet is ready, but those I invited did not deserve to come. 9Go to the street corners and invite
to the banquet anyone you find.' 10So the servants
went out into the streets and gathered all the people they could find, both good and bad, and the
wedding hall was filled with guests. Eze 21:21
11"But when the king came in to see the guests,
he noticed a man there who was not wearing wedding clothes. 12'Friend,' he asked, 'how did you get
in here without wedding clothes?' The man was
speechless. Mt 20:13; 26:50
13"Then the king told the attendants, 'Tie him
hand and foot, and throw him outside, into the
darkness, where there will be weeping and gnashing of teeth.' Mt 8:12
14"For many are invited, but few are chosen."

Paying Taxes to Caesar

▶ *See Mark 12:13–17; Luke 20:20–26*

15Then the Pharisees went out and laid plans to
trap him in his words. 16They sent their disciples
to him along with the Herodians. "Teacher," they
said, "we know you are a man of integrity and that
you teach the way of God in accordance with the
truth. You aren't swayed by men, because you pay
no attention to who they are. 17Tell us then, what
is your opinion? Is it right to pay taxes to Caesar
or not?" Mt 17:25; Mk 3:6
18But Jesus, knowing their evil intent, said,
"You hypocrites, why are you trying to trap me?
19Show me the coin used for paying the tax." They
brought him a denarius, 20and he asked them,
"Whose portrait is this? And whose inscription?"
21"Caesar's," they replied.
Then he said to them, "Give to Caesar what is
Caesar's, and to God what is God's." Ro 13:7
22When they heard this, they were amazed. So
they left him and went away. Mk 12:13-17; Lk 20:20-26

Marriage at the Resurrection

▶ *See Mark 12:18–27; Luke 20:27–40*

23That same day the Sadducees, who say there
is no resurrection, came to him with a question.
24"Teacher," they said, "Moses told us that if a
man dies without having children, his brother
must marry the widow and have children for him.
25Now there were seven brothers among us. The
first one married and died, and since he had no
children, he left his wife to his brother. 26The same
thing happened to the second and third brother,
right on down to the seventh. 27Finally, the woman
died. 28Now then, at the resurrection, whose wife
will she be of the seven, since all of them were
married to her?" Dt 25:5-6; Ac 23:8
29Jesus replied, "You are in error because you
do not know the Scriptures or the power of God.
30At the resurrection people will neither marry nor
be given in marriage; they will be like the angels in
heaven. 31But about the resurrection of the dead—
have you not read what God said to you, 32'I am
the God of Abraham, the God of Isaac, and the
God of Jacob'[d]? He is not the God of the dead but
of the living." Ex 3:6; Jn 20:9; Ac 7:32

[a]42 Or *cornerstone* [b]42 Psalm 118:22,23 [c]44 Some manuscripts do not have verse 44. [d]32 Exodus 3:6

33When the crowds heard this, they were astonished at his teaching. Mk 12:18-27; Lk 20:27-40

The Greatest Commandment

▶ *See Mark 12:28–31*

34Hearing that Jesus had silenced the Sadducees, the Pharisees got together. 35One of them, an
expert in the law, tested him with this question:
36"Teacher, which is the greatest commandment in
the Law?" Lk 7:30; 10:25; 11:45

37Jesus replied: " 'Love the Lord your God with
all your heart and with all your soul and with all
your mind.'[a] 38This is the first and greatest commandment. 39And the second is like it: 'Love your
neighbor as yourself.'[b] 40All the Law and the
Prophets hang on these two commandments."

Whose Son Is the Christ?

▶ *See Mark 12:35–37; Luke 20:41–44*

41While the Pharisees were gathered together,
Jesus asked them, 42"What do you think about the
Christ[c]? Whose son is he?"

"The son of David," they replied. Mt 9:27

43He said to them, "How is it then that David,
speaking by the Spirit, calls him 'Lord'? For he
says,

44" 'The Lord said to my Lord:
"Sit at my right hand
until I put your enemies
under your feet." '[d]

45If then David calls him 'Lord,' how can he be his
son?" 46No one could say a word in reply, and
from that day on no one dared to ask him any
more questions. Mk 12:35-37; Lk 20:41-44; Heb 1:13; 10:13

Seven Woes

▶ *See Mark 12:38–39; Luke 20:45–46*

23 Then Jesus said to the crowds and to his
disciples: 2"The teachers of the law and the
Pharisees sit in Moses' seat. 3So you must obey
them and do everything they tell you. But do not
do what they do, for they do not practice what they
preach. 4They tie up heavy loads and put them on
men's shoulders, but they themselves are not willing to lift a finger to move them. Lk 11:46; Ac 15:10

5"Everything they do is done for men to see:
They make their phylacteries[e] wide and the tassels on their garments long; 6they love the place of
honor at banquets and the most important seats in
the synagogues; 7they love to be greeted in the
marketplaces and to have men call them 'Rabbi.'

8"But you are not to be called 'Rabbi,' for you
have only one Master and you are all brothers.
9And do not call anyone on earth 'father,' for you
have one Father, and he is in heaven. 10Nor are
you to be called 'teacher,' for you have one Teacher, the Christ.[c] 11The greatest among you will be
your servant. 12For whoever exalts himself will be
humbled, and whoever humbles himself will
be exalted. Mt 20:26; Lk 14:11

13"Woe to you, teachers of the law and Pharisees, you hypocrites! You shut the kingdom of
heaven in men's faces. You yourselves do not enter, nor will you let those enter who are trying to.[f]

LIVING  **INSIGHT**

Our Lord reserved His strongest and longest sermon not for struggling sinners, discouraged disciples or prosperous people, but for hypocrites, glory hogs, legalists.

(See Matthew 23:13.)

15"Woe to you, teachers of the law and Pharisees, you hypocrites! You travel over land and sea
to win a single convert, and when he becomes one,
you make him twice as much a son of hell as you
are. Mt 5:22; Ac 2:11

16"Woe to you, blind guides! You say, 'If anyone swears by the temple, it means nothing; but if
anyone swears by the gold of the temple, he is
bound by his oath.' 17You blind fools! Which is
greater: the gold, or the temple that makes the gold
sacred? 18You also say, 'If anyone swears by the
altar, it means nothing; but if anyone swears by the
gift on it, he is bound by his oath.' 19You blind
men! Which is greater: the gift, or the altar that
makes the gift sacred? 20Therefore, he who swears
by the altar swears by it and by everything on it.
21And he who swears by the temple swears by it
and by the one who dwells in it. 22And he who
swears by heaven swears by God's throne and by
the one who sits on it. Ex 29:37; Mt 5:34

23"Woe to you, teachers of the law and Pharisees, you hypocrites! You give a tenth of your
spices—mint, dill and cummin. But you have neglected the more important matters of the law—
justice, mercy and faithfulness. You should have
practiced the latter, without neglecting the former.
24You blind guides! You strain out a gnat but swallow a camel. Lev 27:30; Lk 11:42

25"Woe to you, teachers of the law and Pharisees, you hypocrites! You clean the outside of the
cup and dish, but inside they are full of greed and
self-indulgence. 26Blind Pharisee! First clean the
inside of the cup and dish, and then the outside
also will be clean. Mk 7:4; Lk 11:39

[a] *37* Deut. 6:5 [b] *39* Lev. 19:18 [c] *42,10* Or *Messiah* [d] *44* Psalm 110:1 [e] *5* That is, boxes containing Scripture verses, worn on forehead and arm [f] *13* Some manuscripts *to.* [14] *Woe to you, teachers of the law and Pharisees, you hypocrites! You devour widows' houses and for a show make lengthy prayers. Therefore you will be punished more severely.*

[27]"Woe to you, teachers of the law and Pharisees, you hypocrites! You are like whitewashed tombs, which look beautiful on the outside but on the inside are full of dead men's bones and everything unclean. [28]In the same way, on the outside you appear to people as righteous but on the inside you are full of hypocrisy and wickedness.

[29]"Woe to you, teachers of the law and Pharisees, you hypocrites! You build tombs for the prophets and decorate the graves of the righteous. [30]And you say, 'If we had lived in the days of our forefathers, we would not have taken part with them in shedding the blood of the prophets.' [31]So you testify against yourselves that you are the descendants of those who murdered the prophets. [32]Fill up, then, the measure of the sin of your forefathers! Lk 11:47-48; Ac 7:51-52

[33]"You snakes! You brood of vipers! How will you escape being condemned to hell? [34]Therefore I am sending you prophets and wise men and teachers. Some of them you will kill and crucify; others you will flog in your synagogues and pursue from town to town. [35]And so upon you will come all the righteous blood that has been shed on earth, from the blood of righteous Abel to the blood of Zechariah son of Berekiah, whom you murdered between the temple and the altar. [36]I tell you the truth, all this will come upon this generation.

[37]"O Jerusalem, Jerusalem, you who kill the prophets and stone those sent to you, how often I have longed to gather your children together, as a hen gathers her chicks under her wings, but you were not willing. [38]Look, your house is left to you desolate. [39]For I tell you, you will not see me again until you say, 'Blessed is he who comes in the name of the Lord.'[a]" Lk 13:34-35; 2Ch 24:21

Signs of the End of the Age

▶ *See Mark 13:1-37; Luke 21:5-36*

24 Jesus left the temple and was walking away when his disciples came up to him to call his attention to its buildings. [2]"Do you see all these things?" he asked. "I tell you the truth, not one stone here will be left on another; every one will be thrown down." Mk 13:1-37; Lk 21:5-36

[3]As Jesus was sitting on the Mount of Olives, the disciples came to him privately. "Tell us," they said, "when will this happen, and what will be the sign of your coming and of the end of the age?"

[4]Jesus answered: "Watch out that no one deceives you. [5]For many will come in my name, claiming, 'I am the Christ,[b]' and will deceive many. [6]You will hear of wars and rumors of wars, but see to it that you are not alarmed. Such things must happen, but the end is still to come. [7]Nation will rise against nation, and kingdom against kingdom. There will be famines and earthquakes in various places. [8]All these are the beginning of birth pains. Isa 19:2; Ac 11:28

[9]"Then you will be handed over to be persecuted and put to death, and you will be hated by all nations because of me. [10]At that time many will turn away from the faith and will betray and hate each other, [11]and many false prophets will appear and deceive many people. [12]Because of the increase of wickedness, the love of most will grow cold, [13]but he who stands firm to the end will be saved. [14]And this gospel of the kingdom will be preached in the whole world as a testimony to all nations, and then the end will come. Ro 10:18

[15]"So when you see standing in the holy place 'the abomination that causes desolation,'[c] spoken of through the prophet Daniel—let the reader understand— [16]then let those who are in Judea flee to the mountains. [17]Let no one on the roof of his house go down to take anything out of the house. [18]Let no one in the field go back to get his cloak. [19]How dreadful it will be in those days for pregnant women and nursing mothers! [20]Pray that your flight will not take place in winter or on the Sabbath. [21]For then there will be great distress, unequaled from the beginning of the world until now—and never to be equaled again. [22]If those days had not been cut short, no one would survive, but for the sake of the elect those days will be shortened. [23]At that time if anyone says to you, 'Look, here is the Christ!' or, 'There he is!' do not believe it. [24]For false Christs and false prophets will appear and perform great signs and miracles to deceive even the elect—if that were possible. [25]See, I have told you ahead of time. Lk 17:23; 2Th 2:9-11

[26]"So if anyone tells you, 'There he is, out in the desert,' do not go out; or, 'Here he is, in the inner rooms,' do not believe it. [27]For as lightning that comes from the east is visible even in the west, so will be the coming of the Son of Man. [28]Wherever there is a carcass, there the vultures will gather.

[29]"Immediately after the distress of those days

"'the sun will be darkened,
  and the moon will not give its light;
the stars will fall from the sky,
  and the heavenly bodies will be shaken.'[d]

[30]"At that time the sign of the Son of Man will appear in the sky, and all the nations of the earth will mourn. They will see the Son of Man coming on the clouds of the sky, with power and great glory. [31]And he will send his angels with a loud trumpet call, and they will gather his elect from the four winds, from one end of the heavens to the other. Da 7:13; Isa 27:13; 1Co 15:52

[32]"Now learn this lesson from the fig tree: As soon as its twigs get tender and its leaves come out, you know that summer is near. [33]Even so, when

[a] *39* Psalm 118:26 [b] *5* Or *Messiah*; also in verse 23 [c] *15* Daniel 9:27; 11:31; 12:11 [d] *29* Isaiah 13:10; 34:4

you see all these things, you know that it[a] is near, right at the door. 34I tell you the truth, this generation[b] will certainly not pass away until all these things have happened. 35Heaven and earth will pass away, but my words will never pass away.

The Day and Hour Unknown

▶ *See Luke 12:42–46; 17:26–27*

36"No one knows about that day or hour, not even the angels in heaven, nor the Son,[c] but only the Father. 37As it was in the days of Noah, so it will be at the coming of the Son of Man. 38For in the days before the flood, people were eating and drinking, marrying and giving in marriage, up to the day Noah entered the ark; 39and they knew nothing about what would happen until the flood came and took them all away. That is how it will be at the coming of the Son of Man. 40Two men will be in the field; one will be taken and the other left. 41Two women will be grinding with a hand mill; one will be taken and the other left.

42"Therefore keep watch, because you do not know on what day your Lord will come. 43But understand this: If the owner of the house had known at what time of night the thief was coming, he would have kept watch and would not have let his house be broken into. 44So you also must be ready, because the Son of Man will come at an hour when you do not expect him. Mt 25:13

45"Who then is the faithful and wise servant, whom the master has put in charge of the servants in his household to give them their food at the proper time? 46It will be good for that servant whose master finds him doing so when he returns. 47I tell you the truth, he will put him in charge of all his possessions. 48But suppose that servant is wicked and says to himself, 'My master is staying away a long time,' 49and he then begins to beat his fellow servants and to eat and drink with drunkards. 50The master of that servant will come on a day when he does not expect him and at an hour he is not aware of. 51He will cut him to pieces and assign him a place with the hypocrites, where there will be weeping and gnashing of teeth. Lk 12:42-46

The Parable of the Ten Virgins

25 "At that time the kingdom of heaven will be like ten virgins who took their lamps and went out to meet the bridegroom. 2Five of them were foolish and five were wise. 3The foolish ones took their lamps but did not take any oil with them. 4The wise, however, took oil in jars along with their lamps. 5The bridegroom was a long time in coming, and they all became drowsy and fell asleep. 1Th 5:6; Rev 19:7

6"At midnight the cry rang out: 'Here's the bridegroom! Come out to meet him!'

7"Then all the virgins woke up and trimmed their lamps. 8The foolish ones said to the wise, 'Give us some of your oil; our lamps are going out.' Lk 12:35

9"'No,' they replied, 'there may not be enough for both us and you. Instead, go to those who sell oil and buy some for yourselves.'

10"But while they were on their way to buy the oil, the bridegroom arrived. The virgins who were ready went in with him to the wedding banquet. And the door was shut. Rev 19:9

11"Later the others also came. 'Sir! Sir!' they said. 'Open the door for us!'

12"But he replied, 'I tell you the truth, I don't know you.' Mt 7:23

13"Therefore keep watch, because you do not know the day or the hour. Mt 24:42,44; Mk 13:35

The Parable of the Talents

14"Again, it will be like a man going on a journey, who called his servants and entrusted his property to them. 15To one he gave five talents[d] of money, to another two talents, and to another one talent, each according to his ability. Then he went on his journey. 16The man who had received the five talents went at once and put his money to work and gained five more. 17So also, the one with the two talents gained two more. 18But the man who had received the one talent went off, dug a hole in the ground and hid his master's money.

19"After a long time the master of those servants returned and settled accounts with them. 20The man who had received the five talents brought the other five. 'Master,' he said, 'you entrusted me with five talents. See, I have gained five more.'

21"His master replied, 'Well done, good and faithful servant! You have been faithful with a few things; I will put you in charge of many things. Come and share your master's happiness!'

22"The man with the two talents also came. 'Master,' he said, 'you entrusted me with two talents; see, I have gained two more.'

23"His master replied, 'Well done, good and faithful servant! You have been faithful with a few things; I will put you in charge of many things. Come and share your master's happiness!' ver 21

24"Then the man who had received the one talent came. 'Master,' he said, 'I knew that you are a hard man, harvesting where you have not sown and gathering where you have not scattered seed. 25So I was afraid and went out and hid your talent in the ground. See, here is what belongs to you.'

[a] 33 Or *he* [b] 34 Or *race* [c] 36 Some manuscripts do not have *nor the Son.* [d] 15 A talent was worth more than a thousand dollars.

26“His master replied, ‘You wicked, lazy servant! So you knew that I harvest where I have not
sown and gather where I have not scattered seed?
27Well then, you should have put my money on
deposit with the bankers, so that when I returned
I would have received it back with interest.

28“ ‘Take the talent from him and give it to the
one who has the ten talents. 29For everyone who
has will be given more, and he will have an abundance. Whoever does not have, even what he has
will be taken from him. 30And throw that worthless servant outside, into the darkness, where there
will be weeping and gnashing of teeth.’ Lk 19:12-27

The Sheep and the Goats

31“When the Son of Man comes in his glory,
and all the angels with him, he will sit on his
throne in heavenly glory. 32All the nations will be
gathered before him, and he will separate the people one from another as a shepherd separates the
sheep from the goats. 33He will put the sheep on
his right and the goats on his left. Eze 34:17,20

34“Then the King will say to those on his right,
‘Come, you who are blessed by my Father; take
your inheritance, the kingdom prepared for you
since the creation of the world. 35For I was hungry
and you gave me something to eat, I was thirsty
and you gave me something to drink, I was a
stranger and you invited me in, 36I needed clothes
and you clothed me, I was sick and you looked
after me, I was in prison and you came to visit me.’ 1Co 15:50; Jas 2:15-16; Rev 13:8

37“Then the righteous will answer him, ‘Lord,
when did we see you hungry and feed you, or
thirsty and give you something to drink? 38When
did we see you a stranger and invite you in, or
needing clothes and clothe you? 39When did we
see you sick or in prison and go to visit you?’

40“The King will reply, ‘I tell you the truth,
whatever you did for one of the least of these
brothers of mine, you did for me.’ Pr 19:17

41“Then he will say to those on his left, ‘Depart
from me, you who are cursed, into the eternal
fire prepared for the devil and his angels. 42For
I was hungry and you gave me nothing to eat, I
was thirsty and you gave me nothing to drink,
43I was a stranger and you did not invite me
in, I needed clothes and you did not clothe me,
I was sick and in prison and you did not look
after me.’

44“They also will answer, ‘Lord, when did we see
you hungry or thirsty or a stranger or needing
clothes or sick or in prison, and did not help you?’

45“He will reply, ‘I tell you the truth, whatever
you did not do for one of the least of these, you did
not do for me.’ Pr 14:31; 17:5

46“Then they will go away to eternal punishment, but the righteous to eternal life.” Da 12:2

The Plot Against Jesus

▶ *See Mark 14:1–2; Luke 22:1–2*

26 When Jesus had finished saying all these
things, he said to his disciples, 2“As you
know, the Passover is two days away—and the
Son of Man will be handed over to be crucified.”

3Then the chief priests and the elders of the
people assembled in the palace of the high priest,
whose name was Caiaphas, 4and they plotted to
arrest Jesus in some sly way and kill him. 5“But not
during the Feast,” they said, “or there may be a
riot among the people.” Mk 14:1-2; Lk 22:1-2

Jesus Anointed at Bethany

▶ *See Mark 14:3–9*

6While Jesus was in Bethany in the home of a
man known as Simon the Leper, 7a woman came
to him with an alabaster jar of very expensive perfume, which she poured on his head as he was
reclining at the table. Mt 21:17

8When the disciples saw this, they were indignant. “Why this waste?” they asked. 9“This perfume could have been sold at a high price and the
money given to the poor.”

10Aware of this, Jesus said to them, “Why are
you bothering this woman? She has done a beautiful thing to me. 11The poor you will always have
with you, but you will not always have me. 12When
she poured this perfume on my body, she did it to
prepare me for burial. 13I tell you the truth, wherever this gospel is preached throughout the world,
what she has done will also be told, in memory of
her.” Mk 14:3-9; Lk 7:37-38; Jn 12:1-8

Judas Agrees to Betray Jesus

▶ *See Mark 14:10–11; Luke 22:3–6*

14Then one of the Twelve—the one called Judas
Iscariot—went to the chief priests 15and asked,
“What are you willing to give me if I hand him
over to you?” So they counted out for him thirty
silver coins. 16From then on Judas watched for an
opportunity to hand him over. Mk 14:10-11; Lk 22:3-6

The Lord’s Supper

▶ *See Mark 14:12–25; Luke 22:7–13*

17On the first day of the Feast of Unleavened
Bread, the disciples came to Jesus and asked,
“Where do you want us to make preparations for
you to eat the Passover?” Ex 12:18-20

18He replied, “Go into the city to a certain man
and tell him, ‘The Teacher says: My appointed
time is near. I am going to celebrate the Passover
with my disciples at your house.’ ” 19So the disciples did as Jesus had directed them and prepared
the Passover. Mk 14:12-16; Lk 22:7-13

20When evening came, Jesus was reclining at the
table with the Twelve. 21And while they were eat-

ing, he said, "I tell you the truth, one of you will betray me." Lk 22:21-23; Jn 13:21

22They were very sad and began to say to him one after the other, "Surely not I, Lord?"

23Jesus replied, "The one who has dipped his hand into the bowl with me will betray me. 24The Son of Man will go just as it is written about him. But woe to that man who betrays the Son of Man! It would be better for him if he had not been born." Mk 14:17-21; Jn 13:18

25Then Judas, the one who would betray him, said, "Surely not I, Rabbi?" Mt 23:7

Jesus answered, "Yes, it is you."[a]

26While they were eating, Jesus took bread, gave thanks and broke it, and gave it to his disciples, saying, "Take and eat; this is my body." 1Co 10:16

27Then he took the cup, gave thanks and offered it to them, saying, "Drink from it, all of you. 28This is my blood of the[b] covenant, which is poured out for many for the forgiveness of sins. 29I tell you, I will not drink of this fruit of the vine from now on until that day when I drink it anew with you in my Father's kingdom." Lk 22:17-20; 1Co 11:23-25

30When they had sung a hymn, they went out to the Mount of Olives. Mk 14:22-26

Jesus Predicts Peter's Denial

▶ *See Mark 14:27–31; Luke 22:31–34*

31Then Jesus told them, "This very night you will all fall away on account of me, for it is written:

"'I will strike the shepherd,
and the sheep of the flock will be
scattered.'[c]

32But after I have risen, I will go ahead of you into Galilee." Mt 28:7,10,16

33Peter replied, "Even if all fall away on account of you, I never will."

34"I tell you the truth," Jesus answered, "this very night, before the rooster crows, you will disown me three times." Jn 13:37-38

35But Peter declared, "Even if I have to die with you, I will never disown you." And all the other disciples said the same. Mk 14:27-31; Lk 22:31-34

Gethsemane

▶ *See Mark 14:32–42; Luke 22:40–46*

36Then Jesus went with his disciples to a place called Gethsemane, and he said to them, "Sit here while I go over there and pray." 37He took Peter and the two sons of Zebedee along with him, and he began to be sorrowful and troubled. 38Then he said to them, "My soul is overwhelmed with sorrow to the point of death. Stay here and keep watch with me." Mt 4:21; Jn 12:27

39Going a little farther, he fell with his face to the ground and prayed, "My Father, if it is possible, may this cup be taken from me. Yet not as I will, but as you will." Mt 20:22; Jn 6:38

40Then he returned to his disciples and found them sleeping. "Could you men not keep watch with me for one hour?" he asked Peter. 41"Watch and pray so that you will not fall into temptation. The spirit is willing, but the body is weak."

42He went away a second time and prayed, "My Father, if it is not possible for this cup to be taken away unless I drink it, may your will be done."

43When he came back, he again found them sleeping, because their eyes were heavy. 44So he left them and went away once more and prayed the third time, saying the same thing.

45Then he returned to the disciples and said to them, "Are you still sleeping and resting? Look, the hour is near, and the Son of Man is betrayed into the hands of sinners. 46Rise, let us go! Here comes my betrayer!" Mk 14:32-42; Lk 22:40-46

Jesus Arrested

▶ *See Mark 14:43–50; Luke 22:47–53*

47While he was still speaking, Judas, one of the Twelve, arrived. With him was a large crowd armed with swords and clubs, sent from the chief priests and the elders of the people. 48Now the betrayer had arranged a signal with them: "The one I kiss is the man; arrest him." 49Going at once to Jesus, Judas said, "Greetings, Rabbi!" and kissed him. Mt 23:7

50Jesus replied, "Friend, do what you came for."[d] Mt 20:13; 22:12

Then the men stepped forward, seized Jesus and arrested him. 51With that, one of Jesus' companions reached for his sword, drew it out and struck the servant of the high priest, cutting off his ear.

52"Put your sword back in its place," Jesus said to him, "for all who draw the sword will die by the sword. 53Do you think I cannot call on my Father, and he will at once put at my disposal more than twelve legions of angels? 54But how then would the Scriptures be fulfilled that say it must happen in this way?" Ge 9:6; Rev 13:10

55At that time Jesus said to the crowd, "Am I leading a rebellion, that you have come out with swords and clubs to capture me? Every day I sat in the temple courts teaching, and you did not arrest me. 56But this has all taken place that the writings of the prophets might be fulfilled." Then all the disciples deserted him and fled. Mk 14:43-50

Before the Sanhedrin

▶ *See Mark 14:53–65; John 18:12–13,19–24*

57Those who had arrested Jesus took him to

[a] 25 Or *"You yourself have said it"* [b] 28 Some manuscripts *the new* [c] 31 Zech. 13:7 [d] 50 Or *"Friend, why have you come?"*

Caiaphas, the high priest, where the teachers of the law and the elders had assembled. 58But Peter followed him at a distance, right up to the courtyard of the high priest. He entered and sat down with the guards to see the outcome. Jn 18:15

59The chief priests and the whole Sanhedrin were looking for false evidence against Jesus so that they could put him to death. 60But they did not find any, though many false witnesses came forward. Ps 27:12; 35:11; Ac 6:13

Finally two came forward 61and declared, "This fellow said, 'I am able to destroy the temple of God and rebuild it in three days.'" Dt 19:15; Jn 2:19

62Then the high priest stood up and said to Jesus, "Are you not going to answer? What is this testimony that these men are bringing against you?" 63But Jesus remained silent. Mt 27:12,14

The high priest said to him, "I charge you under oath by the living God: Tell us if you are the Christ,[a] the Son of God." Lk 22:67

64"Yes, it is as you say," Jesus replied. "But I say to all of you: In the future you will see the Son of Man sitting at the right hand of the Mighty One and coming on the clouds of heaven." Ps 110:1

65Then the high priest tore his clothes and said, "He has spoken blasphemy! Why do we need any more witnesses? Look, now you have heard the blasphemy. 66What do you think?" Mk 14:63

"He is worthy of death," they answered.

67Then they spit in his face and struck him with their fists. Others slapped him 68and said, "Prophesy to us, Christ. Who hit you?" Mk 14:53-65

Peter Disowns Jesus

▶ *See Mark 14:66–72; Luke 22:52–62; John 18:16–18,25–27*

69Now Peter was sitting out in the courtyard, and a servant girl came to him. "You also were with Jesus of Galilee," she said.

70But he denied it before them all. "I don't know what you're talking about," he said.

71Then he went out to the gateway, where another girl saw him and said to the people there, "This fellow was with Jesus of Nazareth."

72He denied it again, with an oath: "I don't know the man!"

73After a little while, those standing there went up to Peter and said, "Surely you are one of them, for your accent gives you away."

74Then he began to call down curses on himself and he swore to them, "I don't know the man!"

Immediately a rooster crowed. 75Then Peter remembered the word Jesus had spoken: "Before the rooster crows, you will disown me three times." And he went outside and wept bitterly. ver 34

Judas Hangs Himself

27 Early in the morning, all the chief priests and the elders of the people came to the decision to put Jesus to death. 2They bound him, led him away and handed him over to Pilate, the governor. Mt 20:19; Mk 15:1; Ac 3:13

3When Judas, who had betrayed him, saw that Jesus was condemned, he was seized with remorse and returned the thirty silver coins to the chief priests and the elders. 4"I have sinned," he said, "for I have betrayed innocent blood." Mt 26:14-15

"What is that to us?" they replied. "That's your responsibility." ver 24

5So Judas threw the money into the temple and left. Then he went away and hanged himself.

6The chief priests picked up the coins and said, "It is against the law to put this into the treasury, since it is blood money." 7So they decided to use the money to buy the potter's field as a burial place for foreigners. 8That is why it has been called the Field of Blood to this day. 9Then what was spoken by Jeremiah the prophet was fulfilled: "They took the thirty silver coins, the price set on him by the people of Israel, 10and they used them to buy the potter's field, as the Lord commanded me."[b]

Jesus Before Pilate

▶ *See Mark 15:2–15; Luke 23:2–3,18–25; John 18:29—19:16*

11Meanwhile Jesus stood before the governor, and the governor asked him, "Are you the king of the Jews?" Mt 2:2

"Yes, it is as you say," Jesus replied.

12When he was accused by the chief priests and the elders, he gave no answer. 13Then Pilate asked him, "Don't you hear the testimony they are bringing against you?" 14But Jesus made no reply, not even to a single charge—to the great amazement of the governor. Mt 26:62-63; Jn 19:9

15Now it was the governor's custom at the Feast to release a prisoner chosen by the crowd. 16At that time they had a notorious prisoner, called Barabbas. 17So when the crowd had gathered, Pilate asked them, "Which one do you want me to release to you: Barabbas, or Jesus who is called Christ?" 18For he knew it was out of envy that they had handed Jesus over to him. Jn 18:39

19While Pilate was sitting on the judge's seat, his wife sent him this message: "Don't have anything to do with that innocent man, for I have suffered a great deal today in a dream because of him."

20But the chief priests and the elders persuaded the crowd to ask for Barabbas and to have Jesus executed. Ac 3:14

21"Which of the two do you want me to release to you?" asked the governor.

"Barabbas," they answered.

[a]63 Or *Messiah*; also in verse 68 [b]10 See Zech. 11:12,13; Jer. 19:1-13; 32:6-9.

22“What shall I do, then, with Jesus who is
called Christ?” Pilate asked. Mt 1:16
They all answered, “Crucify him!”
23“Why? What crime has he committed?” asked
Pilate.
But they shouted all the louder, “Crucify him!”
24When Pilate saw that he was getting nowhere,
but that instead an uproar was starting, he took
water and washed his hands in front of the crowd.
“I am innocent of this man’s blood,” he said. “It is
your responsibility!” Dt 21:6-8; Mt 26:5
25All the people answered, “Let his blood be on
us and on our children!” Jos 2:19; Ac 5:28
26Then he released Barabbas to them. But he
had Jesus flogged, and handed him over to be
crucified. Mk 15:2-15; Lk 23:2-3,18-25; Jn 18:29-19:16

The Soldiers Mock Jesus

▶ *See Mark 15:16–20*

27Then the governor’s soldiers took Jesus into
the Praetorium and gathered the whole company
of soldiers around him. 28They stripped him and
put a scarlet robe on him, 29and then twisted together a crown of thorns and set it on his head.
They put a staff in his right hand and knelt in front
of him and mocked him. “Hail, king of the Jews!”
they said. 30They spit on him, and took the staff
and struck him on the head again and again. 31Af-
ter they had mocked him, they took off the robe
and put his own clothes on him. Then they led him
away to crucify him. Mk 15:16-20; Isa 53:3,7

The Crucifixion

▶ *See Mark 15:22–32; Luke 23:33–43; John 19:17–24*

32As they were going out, they met a man from
Cyrene, named Simon, and they forced him to
carry the cross. 33They came to a place called Golgotha (which means The Place of the Skull).
34There they offered Jesus wine to drink, mixed
with gall; but after tasting it, he refused to drink it.
35When they had crucified him, they divided up
his clothes by casting lots.[a] 36And sitting down,
they kept watch over him there. 37Above his head
they placed the written charge against him: THIS IS
JESUS, THE KING OF THE JEWS. 38Two robbers were
crucified with him, one on his right and one on his
left. 39Those who passed by hurled insults at him,
shaking their heads 40and saying, “You who are
going to destroy the temple and build it in three
days, save yourself! Come down from the cross, if
you are the Son of God!” Mt 26:61; Jn 2:19
41In the same way the chief priests, the teachers
of the law and the elders mocked him. 42“He saved
others,” they said, “but he can’t save himself! He’s
the King of Israel! Let him come down now from
the cross, and we will believe in him. 43He trusts in
God. Let God rescue him now if he wants him, for
he said, ‘I am the Son of God.’ ” 44In the same way
the robbers who were crucified with him also
heaped insults on him. Mk 15:22-32; Lk 23:33-43

The Death of Jesus

▶ *See Mark 15:33–41; Luke 23:44–49*

45From the sixth hour until the ninth hour
darkness came over all the land. 46About the ninth
hour Jesus cried out in a loud voice, *“Eloi, Eloi,*[b]
lama sabachthani?”—which means, “My God, my
God, why have you forsaken me?”[c] Am 8:9
47When some of those standing there heard
this, they said, “He’s calling Elijah.”
48Immediately one of them ran and got a
sponge. He filled it with wine vinegar, put it on a
stick, and offered it to Jesus to drink. 49The rest
said, “Now leave him alone. Let’s see if Elijah
comes to save him.” Ps 69:21
50And when Jesus had cried out again in a loud
voice, he gave up his spirit. Jn 19:30
51At that moment the curtain of the temple was
torn in two from top to bottom. The earth shook
and the rocks split. 52The tombs broke open and
the bodies of many holy people who had died were
raised to life. 53They came out of the tombs, and
after Jesus’ resurrection they went into the holy
city and appeared to many people. Ex 26:31-33
54When the centurion and those with him who
were guarding Jesus saw the earthquake and all
that had happened, they were terrified, and exclaimed, “Surely he was the Son[d] of God!”
55Many women were there, watching from a
distance. They had followed Jesus from Galilee to
care for his needs. 56Among them were Mary Magdalene, Mary the mother of James and Joses, and
the mother of Zebedee’s sons. Mk 15:33-41; Lk 23:44-49

The Burial of Jesus

▶ *See Mark 15:42–47; Luke 23:50–56; John 19:38–42*

57As evening approached, there came a rich
man from Arimathea, named Joseph, who had
himself become a disciple of Jesus. 58Going to Pilate, he asked for Jesus’ body, and Pilate ordered
that it be given to him. 59Joseph took the body,
wrapped it in a clean linen cloth, 60and placed it in
his own new tomb that he had cut out of the rock.
He rolled a big stone in front of the entrance to the
tomb and went away. 61Mary Magdalene and the
other Mary were sitting there opposite the tomb.

The Guard at the Tomb

62The next day, the one after Preparation Day,
the chief priests and the Pharisees went to Pilate.

[a] 35 A few late manuscripts *lots that the word spoken by the prophet might be fulfilled: “They divided my garments among themselves and cast lots for my clothing”* (Psalm 22:18) [b] 46 Some manuscripts *Eli, Eli* [c] 46 Psalm 22:1
[d] 54 Or *a son*

63“Sir,” they said, “we remember that while he was
still alive that deceiver said, ‘After three days I will
rise again.’ 64So give the order for the tomb to be
made secure until the third day. Otherwise, his
disciples may come and steal the body and tell the
people that he has been raised from the dead. This
last deception will be worse than the first.”
65“Take a guard,” Pilate answered. “Go, make
the tomb as secure as you know how.” 66So they
went and made the tomb secure by putting a seal
on the stone and posting the guard. Da 6:17

Triumph of the King **Chapter 28**

The fourth and climactic section of this Gospel declares the victory of the King. Jesus was alive! He had risen from the dead, just as He said. The King made His departure from earth as this Gospel ended, but not without giving a promise to His followers: "I am with you always" (28:20). With these words reverberating in our ears, the victory of the King over sin and death assures us that we will never be alone. The King will be with us always!

The Resurrection

▶ *See Mark 16:1–8; Luke 24:1–10*

28 After the Sabbath, at dawn on the first day
of the week, Mary Magdalene and the other Mary went to look at the tomb. Mt 27:56
2There was a violent earthquake, for an angel of
the Lord came down from heaven and, going to
the tomb, rolled back the stone and sat on it. 3His
appearance was like lightning, and his clothes were
white as snow. 4The guards were so afraid of him
that they shook and became like dead men.
5The angel said to the women, “Do not be
afraid, for I know that you are looking for Jesus,
who was crucified. 6He is not here; he has risen,
just as he said. Come and see the place where he
lay. 7Then go quickly and tell his disciples: ‘He has
risen from the dead and is going ahead of you into
Galilee. There you will see him.’ Now I have told
you.” Mk 16:1-8; Lk 24:1-10
8So the women hurried away from the tomb,
afraid yet filled with joy, and ran to tell his disciples. 9Suddenly Jesus met them. “Greetings,” he
said. They came to him, clasped his feet and worshiped him. 10Then Jesus said to them, “Do not be
afraid. Go and tell my brothers to go to Galilee;
there they will see me.” Ro 8:29; Heb 2:11-13,17

The Guards’ Report

11While the women were on their way, some of
the guards went into the city and reported to the
chief priests everything that had happened.
12When the chief priests had met with the elders
and devised a plan, they gave the soldiers a large
sum of money, 13telling them, “You are to say, ‘His
disciples came during the night and stole him
away while we were asleep.’ 14If this report gets to
the governor, we will satisfy him and keep you out
of trouble.” 15So the soldiers took the money and
did as they were instructed. And this story has
been widely circulated among the Jews to this very
day. Mt 27:2,65-66

The Great Commission

16Then the eleven disciples went to Galilee, to
the mountain where Jesus had told them to go.
17When they saw him, they worshiped him; but
some doubted. 18Then Jesus came to them and
said, “All authority in heaven and on earth has
been given to me. 19Therefore go and make disciples of all nations, baptizing them in[a] the name of
the Father and of the Son and of the Holy Spirit,

LIVING  **INSIGHT**

Trinity. There is one God, yet three distinct persons. The Godhead is coequal, coeternal, coexistent: God the Father, God the Son, God the Holy Spirit. Much of that remains a profound mystery. Don't lose sleep if your mind cannot grasp fully the truth of the Trinity.
(See Matthew 28:19.)

20and teaching them to obey everything I have
commanded you. And surely I am with you always, to the very end of the age.” Mk 16:15-16

[a] *19* Or *into*; see Acts 8:16; 19:5; Romans 6:3; 1 Cor. 1:13; 10:2 and Gal. 3:27.

INTRODUCTION

MARK

Action. Movement. Involvement. Service. *Euthus* is the Greek word repeated throughout the Gospel of Mark, appearing no less than 47 times. It is variously translated "immediately," "at once," "quickly," "just then." Although Mark has written the briefest of the four Gospels, he wastes no words as he paints a compelling portrait of the Savior serving others. The tone of this Gospel is practical, written in such a way that the material would appeal to the Roman mind. As we read the Gospel of Mark, we will want to observe the Servant at work in this account of Jesus' life, paying careful attention to Jesus' words in verse 45 of chapter 10: "For even the Son of Man did not come to be served, but to serve, and to give his life as a ransom for many."

WRITER: *John Mark (with Peter as a source)*

DATE: *C.A.D. 50–70*

PURPOSE: *To encourage suffering believers by placing before them Jesus' life*

KEY THEMES: *The cross; discipleship; Jesus as servant; Jesus as teacher*

KEY MESSAGE: *Jesus is the suffering Servant who came to die!*

KEY VERSES: *8:34-36; 10:45*

KEY TERM: *"Immediately" (or some variation)*

TIME LINE — 10BC AD1 10 20 30 40 50 60 70 80 90 100

- **Herod the Great's reign (c.37-4 B.C.)**
- **Jesus' birth (c.6/5 B.C.)**
- **Jesus' flight to Egypt (c.5/4 B.C.)**
- **Beginning of John the Baptist's ministry (C. A.D.26)**
- **Beginning of Jesus' ministry (C. A.D.26)**
- **Jesus' death, resurrection and ascension (C. A.D.30)**
- **Paul's conversion (C. A.D.35)**
- **Book of Mark written (C. A.D.50-70)**

The Servant at Work

	INTRODUCTION AND PREPARATION	THE SERVANT AT WORK . . .	THE SERVANT REJECTED . . . THEN EXALTED
		A continuous, unbroken chain of events as Jesus helped people in need:	**A growing discontent among the authorities led to Jesus' suffering and death:**
		Because people were in darkness, He enlightened.	He pressed the claim, "Messiah."
		Because people were sick/afflicted, He healed.	He spent more time alone with His disciples.
		Because people were without hope, He encouraged.	He came into open conflict with His enemies.
		Because people were in bondage to satanic control, He liberated.	He was hated, deserted, tortured, crucified and buried
		Because people were sinful, He forgave.	He was bodily raised from the dead!
	CHAPTER 1:1-13	*CHAPTERS 1:14–8:30*	*CHAPTERS 8:31–16:20*
KEY		***"For even the Son of Man did not come to be served, but to serve . . .***	***. . . and to give his life as a ransom for many" (10:45).***
EMPHASIS		**Service to others**	**Sacrifice for others**
SCOPE		**Ministry to the multitudes**	**Ministry to the Twelve**
SECTIONS		**Action . . . reaction . . . confrontation**	**Revelation . . . crucifixion . . . exaltation!**

All of the Gospel writers had at their disposal essentially the same basic information about Jesus of Nazareth. Yet we find one multicolored splash of beauty and emphasis in one of the Gospel writer's work and an altogether different one in another. Each of the Gospel accounts is different because each writer is different. That's really not all that hard to understand, is it? If each of us witnessed an automobile accident on the road, and the investigating officer were to interview four different people, he or she would very likely get four dramatically different perspectives. Same accident—but four different perspectives. So it is with the Gospels. We don't have conflicting reports. We simply have 35-millimeter snapshots taken by four different men with four different audiences and four different purposes in mind.

While Matthew viewed Jesus Christ with the eyes of a Jewish tax collector intent on carefully proving that Jesus was the Messiah, Mark approached his task with an almost breathless passion and sense of urgency dictated, it is thought, by an audience of Roman believers undergoing persecution. Mark was intent on leaving them a simple, succinct account of the life of Jesus that would remind them of Jesus' mighty works. Unlike Matthew, he was not interested in establishing the fact that Jesus is Messiah. He was interested in establishing a picture of a suffering Servant with the power to heal and, through His death, to bring life.

The Action in Mark

Mark is a fast-paced Gospel of drama and high-energy action that emphasizes events rather than words. Mark doesn't include a lot of parables; he records far fewer actual teachings of Jesus than the other Gospel writers. His emphasis is on the miracles of Jesus. His goal is to present Jesus as the Servant who came to die. And all throughout Mark's account this suffering Servant was engaged in helping, encouraging and serving other people.

As we read Mark's Gospel, we quickly notice how he packs sequences together. His favorite word (used 47 times) is threaded throughout the tapestry of his account—a Greek word variously translated "immediately," "at once," "quickly," "just then." The word resurfaces all the way through the book. Events come back to back—almost like standing dominoes that begin to fall after being nudged, one touching the other, almost without a break throughout the 16 chapters of this book.

Mark is believed to be the earliest of the four Gospels—the one from which the other Gospel writers received some of their information. In that sense it is a trailblazing Gospel covering virgin territory. At the time Mark wrote, there very likely was no Gospel of Luke. There was no Gospel of John or Gospel of Matthew either. Mark sat down and decided he would write what he remembered of the life of Jesus, and, under the inspiration of the Holy Spirit, he recorded an action-packed survey of the things that seemed important to him. He called it "the beginning of the gospel about Jesus Christ, the Son of God" (1:1)—the great Good News that God has provided salvation through the life, death and resurrection of Jesus Christ.

Mark's Source

Where did Mark get his information? Many New Testament scholars believe that his information came mainly from the one who was a common fisherman and a close friend of Jesus, namely, Peter. In fact, that belief was so firmly fixed in the minds of the early church fathers that Justin Martyr referred to Mark's Gospel as "the memoirs of Peter." Justin Martyr actually gave the Gospel of Mark the subheading: "The Gospel of Saint Peter."

A Colorful Past

To find out more about the writer, we must look at the book of Acts. The account in Acts 12 is intriguing—the story of the wonderful release of Peter from prison. Note what Peter said to himself right after his miraculous escape through the help of an angel:

> *"Now I know without a doubt that the Lord sent his angel and rescued me from Herod's clutches and from everything the Jewish people were anticipating." When this had dawned on him, he went to the house of Mary the mother of John, also called Mark (Acts 12:11–12).*

There's our man . . . the one who wrote the Gospel of Mark. One commentator has referred to Mary's home as the rallying point of the early church. It was a place where prayer meetings were held—a place in Jerusalem where many prayers were offered up to God for the sustenance, the strength and the protection of God's people. Mark was raised in that setting—perhaps a bit protected from the blows of the world around him.

Read a little further in Acts 12 and you'll see the beginning of the outreach of the gospel to "the ends of the earth" (Acts 1:8):

> *But the word of God continued to increase and spread. When Barnabas and Saul had finished their mission, they returned from Jerusalem, taking with them John, also called Mark (12:24–25).*

Saul and Barnabas had gone to Antioch and ministered there. Ultimately those men, Saul (later known as Paul—see Acts 13:9) and Barnabas, set out on the first-ever missionary journey, taking John Mark as their companion. But things got tough, and something happened that Mark would live to regret. John Mark left the group and returned to Jerusalem (13:13). Paul viewed Mark's premature departure as defecting . . . as being a quitter. Mark's name surfaced again later among Paul and Barnabas, but now the mood was decidedly different. No longer was he viewed as a warm, loving companion; he was now seen by Paul as one who shouldn't go with them on a second journey. Barnabas disagreed, which spelled the end of Barnabas and Paul's travels together (15:37–38). Mark was Barnabas's cousin (Colossians 4:10), which might help us better understand Barnabas's willingness to forgive Mark when he had . . . well, as Paul put it, "deserted them" (Acts 15:38). Mark was a family member, a relative of Barnabas. Can't you imagine that Barnabas would argue that Mark deserved another chance? But Paul would have nothing to do with it.

But there was a reunion coming. Read 2 Timothy 4:9–11 and smile with relief on Mark's behalf. Paul was in prison at the time, very close to dying and lonely for companionship. Notice what he wrote:

> *Do your best to come to me quickly, for Demas, because he loved this world, has deserted me and has gone to Thessalonica. Crescens has gone to Galatia, and Titus to Dalmatia. Only Luke is with me. Get Mark and bring him with you, because he is helpful to me in my ministry.*

Wow! Mark had been restored to partnership with Paul in the spreading of the gospel. He was acknowledged as a fellow worker in the kingdom of God (see also Colossians 4:10 and Philemon 24), as Paul said, in effect, "This man is useful to me in the service of the King." Isn't that wonderful? Forgiveness had won the day, and Mark had reason to rejoice.

Feeling Like a Mark?

Ever blown it bad? Ever quit? Ever decided you would walk away from your responsibilities and let the world go by; you just didn't want to be bothered? Ever made a stupid decision that would affect you and your reputation for years to come? Who hasn't? Take heart. One young man who did this was later given the assignment of writing an account of the life of the Lord Jesus Christ.

Have you had someone quit on you? Have you had a deserter upset your business, your home, your life? Sure you have. Have you forgiven him or her? Be greathearted enough to see that person as a potential Mark. Try to understand that the book hasn't been finished in his or her life. A chapter of it might be over, but certainly not all of it. Give your sister or brother the greatest gift that can come from one human heart to another—the gift of forgiveness. Let God's grace help you lift that person to a place of restoration and acceptance.

The Life of the Servant

The Gospel of Mark can be neatly divided into two sections: First, *the Servant at work*, performing mighty miracles and demonstrating His authority over sickness and demons (1:14–8:26), and second, *the suffering Servant* who would be rejected and crucified and ultimately vindicated at His resurrection (8:27–16:20). In the first section Jesus served others; in the last section He sacrificed Himself for others. In the first section He offered a ministry to the multitudes; in the last section His ministry was limited to a few. In the first section there was action, reaction and confrontation; in the last section there was insightful revelation, a bloody crucifixion and finally glorious exaltation. Jesus' early ministry met with credibility and belief, while His later ministry brought growing suspicion and opposition.

When you get to verse 27 of chapter 8 you've come to the turning point of Mark's Gospel. No longer would Jesus concentrate on serving the multitudes. It was time for Him to focus on the twelve disciples. Here, just before His transfiguration, Jesus disclosed both His identity and His mission to His disciples:

> *Jesus and his disciples went on to the villages around Caesarea Philippi. On the way he asked them, "Who do people say I am?" They replied, "Some say John the Baptist; others say Elijah; and still others, one of the prophets." "But what about you?" he asked. "Who do you say I am?" Peter answered, "You are the Christ." Jesus warned them not to tell anyone about him. He then began to teach them that the Son of Man must suffer . . . (8:27–31a).*

From this point on, Mark's Gospel moved quickly toward his account of the events of Jesus' last week on earth (chapters 11–15) and Jesus' resurrection (chapter 16). It is interesting to note that more than forty percent of this Gospel focuses on the suffering and sacrifice of Jesus.

Lessons From Mark

Mark teaches us some profound lessons. First, *if Jesus is our model, then servanthood is our method.* Our Lord was a Servant, in fact, the supreme Servant, encouraging us to follow His example. We must commit to a ministry of servanthood. Second, *if servanthood is the method, then people are our ministry*. You and I are not servants to activities or to administrative details or to things. We serve people. We are the Lord's servants who must direct our efforts to serving others. Third, *if people are our ministry, then involvement is the means.* Touching lives. Coming alongside. Listening. Taking time. Looking. Caring. Encouraging. Confronting when necessary. Loving always. Realizing that in every crowd there are individual people in need who crave our loving touch and caring embrace.

People are highly significant to the Savior. During His time on earth, He never considered other people to be "interruptions." People did not get in His way. To Jesus, a ministry of involvement required being drawn to people in need, not staying away from them. I hope, as you satisfy your hunger for spiritual things through reading and re-reading this Gospel, you'll realize that people are our greatest natural resource. They always have been and always will be. Let's serve them in Jesus' name and through His power.

The Servant at Work **Chapters 1:1–9:1**

In this section, the Servant rolled up His sleeves, as it were, and went to work. He called people to follow Him and to share in His work and ministry. Here Jesus met a man possessed by an evil spirit and relieved him by driving out the demon (chapter 5). He healed a woman who had been subject to bleeding and raised a young girl from the dead (chapter 5). As He traveled He was always quick to stop and care for various people in need. He took on the ministry of a servant and responded to opportunities to help those who were struggling.

Mark presented a continuous chain of events as Jesus helped those who were hurting. Because people lived in a condition of darkness, Jesus opened their eyes to the truth and brought them into the light. When He met those who were sick, He offered healing. When He encountered people without hope, He comforted and encouraged them. When He found those who were captive to evil spirits, this supreme Servant liberated them. Ultimately, as Jesus walked among those who were lost in sin, He extended the forgiveness that only He could offer. Jesus was a Servant, and these chapters chronicle His mighty work on behalf of those in need.

John the Baptist Prepares the Way

▶ *See Matthew 3:1–11; Luke 3:2–16*

1 The beginning of the gospel about Jesus
Christ, the Son of God.[a] Mt 4:3

2It is written in Isaiah the prophet:

"I will send my messenger ahead of you,
who will prepare your way"[b]— Mal 3:1
3"a voice of one calling in the desert,
'Prepare the way for the Lord,
make straight paths for him.' "[c]

4And so John came, baptizing in the desert region
and preaching a baptism of repentance for the
forgiveness of sins. 5The whole Judean countryside
and all the people of Jerusalem went out to him.
Confessing their sins, they were baptized by him in
the Jordan River. 6John wore clothing made of
camel's hair, with a leather belt around his waist,
and he ate locusts and wild honey. 7And this was
his message: "After me will come one more powerful than I, the thongs of whose sandals I am not
worthy to stoop down and untie. 8I baptize you
with[d] water, but he will baptize you with the Holy
Spirit." Mt 3:1-11; Lk 3:2-16

The Baptism and Temptation of Jesus

▶ *See Matthew 3:13–17; 4:1–11; Luke 3:21–22; 4:1–13*

9At that time Jesus came from Nazareth in Galilee and was baptized by John in the Jordan. 10As
Jesus was coming up out of the water, he saw
heaven being torn open and the Spirit descending
on him like a dove. 11And a voice came from heaven: "You are my Son, whom I love; with you I am
well pleased." Mt 3:13-17; Lk 3:21-22
12At once the Spirit sent him out into the desert,
13and he was in the desert forty days, being tempted by Satan. He was with the wild animals, and
angels attended him. Mt 4:1-11; Lk 4:1-13

The Calling of the First Disciples

▶ *See Matthew 4:18–22; Luke 5:2–11; John 1:35–42*

14After John was put in prison, Jesus went into
Galilee, proclaiming the good news of God. 15"The
time has come," he said. "The kingdom of God is
near. Repent and believe the good news!"
16As Jesus walked beside the Sea of Galilee, he
saw Simon and his brother Andrew casting a net
into the lake, for they were fishermen. 17"Come,
follow me," Jesus said, "and I will make you fishers
of men." 18At once they left their nets and followed
him. Mt 4:19
19When he had gone a little farther, he saw
James son of Zebedee and his brother John in a
boat, preparing their nets. 20Without delay he
called them, and they left their father Zebedee in
the boat with the hired men and followed him.

Jesus Drives Out an Evil Spirit

▶ *See Luke 4:31–37*

21They went to Capernaum, and when the Sabbath came, Jesus went into the synagogue and began to teach. 22The people were amazed at his
teaching, because he taught them as one who had
authority, not as the teachers of the law. 23Just then
a man in their synagogue who was possessed by an
evil[e] spirit cried out, 24"What do you want with
us, Jesus of Nazareth? Have you come to destroy
us? I know who you are—the Holy One of God!"
25"Be quiet!" said Jesus sternly. "Come out of
him!" 26The evil spirit shook the man violently and
came out of him with a shriek. Mk 9:20
27The people were all so amazed that they asked
each other, "What is this? A new teaching—and
with authority! He even gives orders to evil spirits
and they obey him." 28News about him spread
quickly over the whole region of Galilee.

Jesus Heals Many

▶ *See Matthew 8:14–17; Luke 4:38–41*

29As soon as they left the synagogue, they went
with James and John to the home of Simon and
Andrew. 30Simon's mother-in-law was in bed with
a fever, and they told Jesus about her. 31So he went
to her, took her hand and helped her up. The fever
left her and she began to wait on them. Mt 8:14-15
32That evening after sunset the people brought
to Jesus all the sick and demon-possessed. 33The

[a] *1* Some manuscripts do not have *the Son of God.* [b] *2* Mal. 3:1 [c] *3* Isaiah 40:3 [d] *8* Or *in* [e] *23* Greek *unclean;* also in verses 26 and 27

JOHN THE BAPTIST

Make Way for the Lord

"And so John came, baptizing in the desert region and preaching a baptism of repentance for the forgiveness of sins."
—MARK 1:4

What mental image pops into your mind when you think of an evangelist? If you are like most of us, you think of a person who holds high-level crusades in places all over the world—someone with lots of charisma, someone who is well respected, even admired, by people around the globe. Surrounding this person would be a well-oiled organization that helps in the day-to-day operations of the ministry. Both the evangelist and the organization would be characterized by integrity and godliness; and, if God so chose to bless this ministry, He would use the evangelist's message to draw many people to commitment to Him.

Most of us find ourselves pretty comfortable with the image of the evangelist that I've just described. We support that kind of work; we welcome the words of challenge to unbelievers to find new life in Jesus and to believers to renew their faith and their commitment. But what I find interesting is that the first evangelist who came on the scene in the New Testament, a man mentioned by all four of the Gospel writers, didn't fit this mold at all. This fellow makes us feel uncomfortable—even just reading about him. He was weird, strange—almost unbelievably unusual. In a world of dry, dusty, formal religion, in a world complacent about God and the coming of the Messiah, this man came stumbling out of the desert with a long, bony index finger stabbing the air, screaming, "Guilty! You all are guilty! Repent! Mend your ways! The kingdom of heaven is at hand! The Messiah has come!" And the people of Jesus' day were no more ready to receive a person like that than we would be ready to tolerate him today.

I view John the Baptist as a cross between Rip Van Winkle and Robinson Crusoe. He hadn't studied at any of the formal schools; he hadn't sat at the feet of the local rabbis. He wasn't even familiar to the townspeople, having left his parental home twenty or so years before in order to live in the howling waste of the desert. He appeared seemingly out of nowhere, as if having awakened from a long sleep, as if returning from a deserted island. His clothing and diet were . . . interesting, to put it mildly. Take a good long look at this man. This was *God's choice* to be an evangelist, a proclaimer of good news, the man who would prepare the way for the arrival of God's Son, the Messiah, the Savior of the world. He modeled what he preached—an austere, rugged, here's-the-truth now take-it-or-leave-it message.

John came to a community of devout Jews who had long anticipated the coming of the Messiah. This passionate preacher desperately wanted people to turn from their sins and open their hearts to the life-changing power of the one true God who was to visit them in the person of His Son, Jesus Christ.

Mark began his Gospel by outlining the prophetic credentials of this man called John the Baptist. In this quiet, reserved way, Mark described the beginning of a revolution the likes of which had never happened before and has never happened since. This man was in fact the one of whom the prophets spoke (Isaiah 40:3; Malachi 3:1); he was the one who would announce the coming of the Savior. And that he did, in a most compelling and challenging way that pointed always away from himself and toward Jesus: "He must become greater; I must become less" (John 3:30).

John came to clear the way, to prepare the way, and then to get out of the way. That was at the heart of his mission statement as recorded by Mark in verses 7 and 8 of chapter 1. After only one controversial but powerfully effective year of ministry, John was beheaded (Matthew 14:10). He didn't even live to see the age of 35. He didn't live to see the crucifixion or the resurrection of the Messiah whose way he had prepared. As a man of faith, fully committed to doing God's will, he accomplished the task for which God had called him, then stepped aside to make way for the Lord to carry out His plan of salvation—through the "Lamb of God, who takes away the sin of the world" (John 1:29).

whole town gathered at the door, [34]and Jesus
healed many who had various diseases. He also
drove out many demons, but he would not let the
demons speak because they knew who he was.

Jesus Prays in a Solitary Place

▶ *See Luke 4:42–43*

[35]Very early in the morning, while it was still
dark, Jesus got up, left the house and went off to
a solitary place, where he prayed. [36]Simon and his
companions went to look for him, [37]and when
they found him, they exclaimed: "Everyone is
looking for you!" Lk 3:21

[38]Jesus replied, "Let us go somewhere else—to
the nearby villages—so I can preach there also.
That is why I have come." [39]So he traveled
throughout Galilee, preaching in their synagogues
and driving out demons. Lk 4:42-43

LIVING  INSIGHT

To help cultivate the habit of including the Lord God in every segment of your life, meet often and alone with Him.

(See Mark 1:35.)

A Man With Leprosy

▶ *See Matthew 8:2–4; Luke 5:12–14*

[40]A man with leprosy[a] came to him and
begged him on his knees, "If you are willing, you
can make me clean." Mk 10:17

[41]Filled with compassion, Jesus reached out his
hand and touched the man. "I am willing," he said.
"Be clean!" [42]Immediately the leprosy left him and
he was cured.

[43]Jesus sent him away at once with a strong
warning: [44]"See that you don't tell this to anyone.
But go, show yourself to the priest and offer the
sacrifices that Moses commanded for your cleansing, as a testimony to them." [45]Instead he went out
and began to talk freely, spreading the news. As a
result, Jesus could no longer enter a town openly
but stayed outside in lonely places. Yet the people
still came to him from everywhere. Mt 8:2-4

Jesus Heals a Paralytic

▶ *See Matthew 9:2–8; Luke 5:18–26*

2 A few days later, when Jesus again entered
Capernaum, the people heard that he had
come home. [2]So many gathered that there was
no room left, not even outside the door, and he
preached the word to them. [3]Some men came,
bringing to him a paralytic, carried by four of
them. [4]Since they could not get him to Jesus because of the crowd, they made an opening in the
roof above Jesus and, after digging through it, lowered the mat the paralyzed man was lying on.
[5]When Jesus saw their faith, he said to the paralytic, "Son, your sins are forgiven." Mt 4:24; Lk 7:48

[6]Now some teachers of the law were sitting
there, thinking to themselves, [7]"Why does this fellow talk like that? He's blaspheming! Who can
forgive sins but God alone?" Isa 43:25

[8]Immediately Jesus knew in his spirit that this
was what they were thinking in their hearts, and he
said to them, "Why are you thinking these things?
[9]Which is easier: to say to the paralytic, 'Your sins
are forgiven,' or to say, 'Get up, take your mat and
walk'? [10]But that you may know that the Son of
Man has authority on earth to forgive sins . . ." He
said to the paralytic, [11]"I tell you, get up, take your
mat and go home." [12]He got up, took his mat and
walked out in full view of them all. This amazed
everyone and they praised God, saying, "We have
never seen anything like this!" Mt 9:2-8; Lk 5:18-26

The Calling of Levi

▶ *See Matthew 9:9–13; Luke 5:27–32*

[13]Once again Jesus went out beside the lake. A
large crowd came to him, and he began to teach
them. [14]As he walked along, he saw Levi son of
Alphaeus sitting at the tax collector's booth. "Follow me," Jesus told him, and Levi got up and
followed him. Mt 4:19; Mk 1:45

[15]While Jesus was having dinner at Levi's house,
many tax collectors and "sinners" were eating with
him and his disciples, for there were many who
followed him. [16]When the teachers of the law who
were Pharisees saw him eating with the "sinners"
and tax collectors, they asked his disciples: "Why
does he eat with tax collectors and 'sinners'?"

[17]On hearing this, Jesus said to them, "It is not
the healthy who need a doctor, but the sick. I have
not come to call the righteous, but sinners."

Jesus Questioned About Fasting

▶ *See Matthew 9:14–17; Luke 5:33–38*

[18]Now John's disciples and the Pharisees were
fasting. Some people came and asked Jesus, "How
is it that John's disciples and the disciples of the
Pharisees are fasting, but yours are not?"

[19]Jesus answered, "How can the guests of the
bridegroom fast while he is with them? They cannot, so long as they have him with them. [20]But the
time will come when the bridegroom will be taken
from them, and on that day they will fast.

[21]"No one sews a patch of unshrunk cloth on an
old garment. If he does, the new piece will pull
away from the old, making the tear worse. [22]And

[a]*40* The Greek word was used for various diseases affecting the skin—not necessarily leprosy.

no one pours new wine into old wineskins. If he does, the wine will burst the skins, and both the wine and the wineskins will be ruined. No, he pours new wine into new wineskins." Mt 9:14-17

Lord of the Sabbath

▶ *See Matthew 12:1–14; Luke 6:1–11*

[23]One Sabbath Jesus was going through the grainfields, and as his disciples walked along, they began to pick some heads of grain. [24]The Pharisees said to him, "Look, why are they doing what is unlawful on the Sabbath?" Dt 23:25; Mt 12:2

[25]He answered, "Have you never read what David did when he and his companions were hungry and in need? [26]In the days of Abiathar the high priest, he entered the house of God and ate the consecrated bread, which is lawful only for priests to eat. And he also gave some to his companions."

[27]Then he said to them, "The Sabbath was made for man, not man for the Sabbath. [28]So the Son of Man is Lord even of the Sabbath." Mt 12:1-8; Lk 6:1-5

3 Another time he went into the synagogue, and a man with a shriveled hand was there. [2]Some of them were looking for a reason to accuse Jesus, so they watched him closely to see if he would heal him on the Sabbath. [3]Jesus said to the man with the shriveled hand, "Stand up in front of everyone." Mk 1:21; Lk 14:1

[4]Then Jesus asked them, "Which is lawful on the Sabbath: to do good or to do evil, to save life or to kill?" But they remained silent.

[5]He looked around at them in anger and, deeply distressed at their stubborn hearts, said to the man, "Stretch out your hand." He stretched it out, and his hand was completely restored. [6]Then the Pharisees went out and began to plot with the Herodians how they might kill Jesus. Mt 12:9-14

Crowds Follow Jesus

▶ *See Matthew 12:15–16; Luke 6:17–19*

[7]Jesus withdrew with his disciples to the lake, and a large crowd from Galilee followed. [8]When they heard all he was doing, many people came to him from Judea, Jerusalem, Idumea, and the regions across the Jordan and around Tyre and Sidon. [9]Because of the crowd he told his disciples to have a small boat ready for him, to keep the people from crowding him. [10]For he had healed many, so that those with diseases were pushing forward to touch him. [11]Whenever the evil[a] spirits saw him, they fell down before him and cried out, "You are the Son of God." [12]But he gave them strict orders not to tell who he was. Mt 12:15-16; Lk 6:17-19

The Appointing of the Twelve Apostles

[13]Jesus went up on a mountainside and called to him those he wanted, and they came to him. [14]He appointed twelve—designating them apostles[b]—that they might be with him and that he might send them out to preach [15]and to have authority to drive out demons. [16]These are the twelve he appointed: Simon (to whom he gave the name Peter); [17]James son of Zebedee and his brother John (to them he gave the name Boanerges, which means Sons of Thunder); [18]Andrew, Philip, Bartholomew, Matthew, Thomas, James son of Alphaeus, Thaddaeus, Simon the Zealot [19]and Judas Iscariot, who betrayed him. Mt 10:2-4; Lk 6:14-16; Ac 1:13

Jesus and Beelzebub

▶ *See Matthew 12:25–29; Luke 11:17–22*

[20]Then Jesus entered a house, and again a crowd gathered, so that he and his disciples were not even able to eat. [21]When his family heard about this, they went to take charge of him, for they said, "He is out of his mind." Jn 10:20; Ac 26:24

[22]And the teachers of the law who came down from Jerusalem said, "He is possessed by Beelzebub[c]! By the prince of demons he is driving out demons." Mt 9:34; 10:25; Jn 7:20

[23]So Jesus called them and spoke to them in parables: "How can Satan drive out Satan? [24]If a kingdom is divided against itself, that kingdom cannot stand. [25]If a house is divided against itself, that house cannot stand. [26]And if Satan opposes himself and is divided, he cannot stand; his end has come. [27]In fact, no one can enter a strong man's house and carry off his possessions unless he first ties up the strong man. Then he can rob his house. [28]I tell you the truth, all the sins and blasphemies of men will be forgiven them. [29]But whoever blasphemes against the Holy Spirit will never be forgiven; he is guilty of an eternal sin."

[30]He said this because they were saying, "He has an evil spirit."

Jesus' Mother and Brothers

▶ *See Matthew 12:46–50; Luke 8:19–21*

[31]Then Jesus' mother and brothers arrived. Standing outside, they sent someone in to call him. [32]A crowd was sitting around him, and they told him, "Your mother and brothers are outside looking for you." ver 21

[33]"Who are my mother and my brothers?" he asked.

[34]Then he looked at those seated in a circle around him and said, "Here are my mother and my brothers! [35]Whoever does God's will is my brother and sister and mother." Mt 12:46-50

[a] *11* Greek *unclean*; also in verse 30 [b] *14* Some manuscripts do not have *designating them apostles.* [c] *22* Greek *Beezeboul* or *Beelzeboul*

The Parable of the Sower

▶ *See Matthew 13:1–15,18–23; Luke 8:4–15*

4 Again Jesus began to teach by the lake. The crowd that gathered around him was so large that he got into a boat and sat in it out on the lake, while all the people were along the shore at the water's edge. [2]He taught them many things by parables, and in his teaching said: [3]"Listen! A farmer went out to sow his seed. [4]As he was scattering the seed, some fell along the path, and the birds came and ate it up. [5]Some fell on rocky places, where it did not have much soil. It sprang up quickly, because the soil was shallow. [6]But when the sun came up, the plants were scorched, and they withered because they had no root. [7]Other seed fell among thorns, which grew up and choked the plants, so that they did not bear grain. [8]Still other seed fell on good soil. It came up, grew and produced a crop, multiplying thirty, sixty, or even a hundred times." Mk 3:23; Jn 15:5; Col 1:6

[9]Then Jesus said, "He who has ears to hear, let him hear." Mt 11:15

[10]When he was alone, the Twelve and the others around him asked him about the parables. [11]He told them, "The secret of the kingdom of God has been given to you. But to those on the outside everything is said in parables [12]so that, 1Co 5:12-13

"'they may be ever seeing but never
 perceiving,
 and ever hearing but never understanding;
otherwise they might turn and be
 forgiven!'[a]" Mt 13:1-15; Lk 8:4-10

[13]Then Jesus said to them, "Don't you understand this parable? How then will you understand any parable? [14]The farmer sows the word. [15]Some people are like seed along the path, where the word is sown. As soon as they hear it, Satan comes and takes away the word that was sown in them. [16]Others, like seed sown on rocky places, hear the word and at once receive it with joy. [17]But since they have no root, they last only a short time. When trouble or persecution comes because of the word, they quickly fall away. [18]Still others, like seed sown among thorns, hear the word; [19]but the worries of this life, the deceitfulness of wealth and the desires for other things come in and choke the word, making it unfruitful. [20]Others, like seed sown on good soil, hear the word, accept it, and produce a crop—thirty, sixty or even a hundred times what was sown." Mt 13:18-23; Lk 8:11-15

A Lamp on a Stand

[21]He said to them, "Do you bring in a lamp to put it under a bowl or a bed? Instead, don't you put it on its stand? [22]For whatever is hidden is meant to be disclosed, and whatever is concealed is meant to be brought out into the open. [23]If anyone has ears to hear, let him hear." Mt 5:15

[24]"Consider carefully what you hear," he continued. "With the measure you use, it will be measured to you—and even more. [25]Whoever has will be given more; whoever does not have, even what he has will be taken from him." Mt 25:29; Lk 6:38

The Parable of the Growing Seed

[26]He also said, "This is what the kingdom of God is like. A man scatters seed on the ground. [27]Night and day, whether he sleeps or gets up, the seed sprouts and grows, though he does not know how. [28]All by itself the soil produces grain—first the stalk, then the head, then the full kernel in the head. [29]As soon as the grain is ripe, he puts the sickle to it, because the harvest has come."

The Parable of the Mustard Seed

▶ *See Matthew 13:31–32; Luke 13:18–19*

[30]Again he said, "What shall we say the kingdom of God is like, or what parable shall we use to describe it? [31]It is like a mustard seed, which is the smallest seed you plant in the ground. [32]Yet when planted, it grows and becomes the largest of all garden plants, with such big branches that the birds of the air can perch in its shade."

[33]With many similar parables Jesus spoke the word to them, as much as they could understand. [34]He did not say anything to them without using a parable. But when he was alone with his own disciples, he explained everything. Jn 16:12,25

Jesus Calms the Storm

▶ *See Matthew 8:18,23–27; Luke 8:22–25*

[35]That day when evening came, he said to his disciples, "Let us go over to the other side." [36]Leaving the crowd behind, they took him along, just as he was, in the boat. There were also other boats with him. [37]A furious squall came up, and the waves broke over the boat, so that it was nearly swamped. [38]Jesus was in the stern, sleeping on a

---

LIVING  **INSIGHT**

Our Lord God specializes in roots. He plans to deepen you and strengthen you. But He won't overdo it. He is sovereignly and compassionately at work. We are more impressed with the fruit. Not God—He's watching over the roots. We like the product; He emphasizes the process.

(See Mark 4:17.)

---

[a]*12* Isaiah 6:9,10

cushion. The disciples woke him and said to him, "Teacher, don't you care if we drown?" Mk 3:9

39He got up, rebuked the wind and said to the waves, "Quiet! Be still!" Then the wind died down and it was completely calm.

40He said to his disciples, "Why are you so afraid? Do you still have no faith?" Mt 14:31

41They were terrified and asked each other, "Who is this? Even the wind and the waves obey him!" Mt 8:18,23-27; Lk 8:22-25

The Healing of a Demon-possessed Man

▶ *See Matthew 8:28–34; Luke 8:26–39*

5 They went across the lake to the region of the Gerasenes.[a] 2When Jesus got out of the boat, a man with an evil[b] spirit came from the tombs to meet him. 3This man lived in the tombs, and no one could bind him any more, not even with a chain. 4For he had often been chained hand and foot, but he tore the chains apart and broke the irons on his feet. No one was strong enough to subdue him. 5Night and day among the tombs and in the hills he would cry out and cut himself with stones. Mk 1:23; 4:1

6When he saw Jesus from a distance, he ran and fell on his knees in front of him. 7He shouted at the top of his voice, "What do you want with me, Jesus, Son of the Most High God? Swear to God that you won't torture me!" 8For Jesus had said to him, "Come out of this man, you evil spirit!"

9Then Jesus asked him, "What is your name?"

"My name is Legion," he replied, "for we are many." 10And he begged Jesus again and again not to send them out of the area.

11A large herd of pigs was feeding on the nearby hillside. 12The demons begged Jesus, "Send us among the pigs; allow us to go into them." 13He gave them permission, and the evil spirits came out and went into the pigs. The herd, about two thousand in number, rushed down the steep bank into the lake and were drowned.

14Those tending the pigs ran off and reported this in the town and countryside, and the people went out to see what had happened. 15When they came to Jesus, they saw the man who had been possessed by the legion of demons, sitting there, dressed and in his right mind; and they were afraid. 16Those who had seen it told the people what had happened to the demon-possessed man—and told about the pigs as well. 17Then the people began to plead with Jesus to leave their region. Mt 8:28-34; Lk 8:26-37

18As Jesus was getting into the boat, the man who had been demon-possessed begged to go with him. 19Jesus did not let him, but said, "Go home to your family and tell them how much the Lord has done for you, and how he has had mercy on you." 20So the man went away and began to tell in the Decapolis[c] how much Jesus had done for him. And all the people were amazed. Lk 8:38-39

A Dead Girl and a Sick Woman

▶ *See Matthew 9:18–26; Luke 8:41–56*

21When Jesus had again crossed over by boat to the other side of the lake, a large crowd gathered around him while he was by the lake. 22Then one of the synagogue rulers, named Jairus, came there. Seeing Jesus, he fell at his feet 23and pleaded earnestly with him, "My little daughter is dying. Please come and put your hands on her so that she will be healed and live." 24So Jesus went with him.

A large crowd followed and pressed around him. 25And a woman was there who had been subject to bleeding for twelve years. 26She had suffered a great deal under the care of many doctors and had spent all she had, yet instead of getting better she grew worse. 27When she heard about Jesus, she came up behind him in the crowd and touched his cloak, 28because she thought, "If I just touch his clothes, I will be healed." 29Immediately her bleeding stopped and she felt in her body that she was freed from her suffering. Lev 15:25-30; Mt 9:20

30At once Jesus realized that power had gone out from him. He turned around in the crowd and asked, "Who touched my clothes?" Lk 5:17; 6:19

31"You see the people crowding against you," his disciples answered, "and yet you can ask, 'Who touched me?' "

32But Jesus kept looking around to see who had done it. 33Then the woman, knowing what had happened to her, came and fell at his feet and, trembling with fear, told him the whole truth. 34He said to her, "Daughter, your faith has healed you. Go in peace and be freed from your suffering."

35While Jesus was still speaking, some men came from the house of Jairus, the synagogue ruler. "Your daughter is dead," they said. "Why bother the teacher any more?"

36Ignoring what they said, Jesus told the synagogue ruler, "Don't be afraid; just believe."

37He did not let anyone follow him except Peter, James and John the brother of James. 38When they came to the home of the synagogue ruler, Jesus saw a commotion, with people crying and wailing loudly. 39He went in and said to them, "Why all this commotion and wailing? The child is not dead but asleep." 40But they laughed at him. Mt 4:21

After he put them all out, he took the child's father and mother and the disciples who were with him, and went in where the child was. 41He took her by the hand and said to her, *"Talitha koum!"* (which means, "Little girl, I say to you, get up!").

[a] *1* Some manuscripts *Gadarenes*; other manuscripts *Gergesenes* [b] *2* Greek *unclean*; also in verses 8 and 13 [c] *20* That is, the Ten Cities

42Immediately the girl stood up and walked around (she was twelve years old). At this they were completely astonished. 43He gave strict orders not to let anyone know about this, and told them to give her something to eat. Mt 9:18-26

A Prophet Without Honor

▶ *See Matthew 13:54–58*

6 Jesus left there and went to his hometown, accompanied by his disciples. 2When the Sabbath came, he began to teach in the synagogue, and many who heard him were amazed. Mt 4:23

"Where did this man get these things?" they asked. "What's this wisdom that has been given him, that he even does miracles! 3Isn't this the carpenter? Isn't this Mary's son and the brother of James, Joseph,[a] Judas and Simon? Aren't his sisters here with us?" And they took offense at him.

4Jesus said to them, "Only in his hometown, among his relatives and in his own house is a prophet without honor." 5He could not do any miracles there, except lay his hands on a few sick people and heal them. 6And he was amazed at their lack of faith. Mt 13:54-58

Jesus Sends Out the Twelve

▶ *See Matthew 10:1,9–14; Luke 9:1,3–5*

Then Jesus went around teaching from village to village. 7Calling the Twelve to him, he sent them out two by two and gave them authority over evil[b] spirits. Mt 10:1; Mk 3:13; Lk 13:22

8These were his instructions: "Take nothing for the journey except a staff—no bread, no bag, no money in your belts. 9Wear sandals but not an extra tunic. 10Whenever you enter a house, stay there until you leave that town. 11And if any place will not welcome you or listen to you, shake the dust off your feet when you leave, as a testimony against them." Mt 10:1,9-14; Lk 9:1,3-5

12They went out and preached that people should repent. 13They drove out many demons and anointed many sick people with oil and healed them. Lk 9:6; Jas 5:14

John the Baptist Beheaded

▶ *See Matthew 14:1–12*

14King Herod heard about this, for Jesus' name had become well known. Some were saying,[c] "John the Baptist has been raised from the dead, and that is why miraculous powers are at work in him." Mt 3:1

15Others said, "He is Elijah." Mal 4:5

And still others claimed, "He is a prophet, like one of the prophets of long ago." Mt 16:14; Mk 8:28

16But when Herod heard this, he said, "John, the man I beheaded, has been raised from the dead!" Lk 9:7-9

17For Herod himself had given orders to have John arrested, and he had him bound and put in prison. He did this because of Herodias, his brother Philip's wife, whom he had married. 18For John had been saying to Herod, "It is not lawful for you to have your brother's wife." 19So Herodias nursed a grudge against John and wanted to kill him. But she was not able to, 20because Herod feared John and protected him, knowing him to be a righteous and holy man. When Herod heard John, he was greatly puzzled[d]; yet he liked to listen to him.

21Finally the opportune time came. On his birthday Herod gave a banquet for his high officials and military commanders and the leading men of Galilee. 22When the daughter of Herodias came in and danced, she pleased Herod and his dinner guests. Est 1:3; Lk 3:1

The king said to the girl, "Ask me for anything you want, and I'll give it to you." 23And he promised her with an oath, "Whatever you ask I will give you, up to half my kingdom." Est 5:3,6; 7:2

24She went out and said to her mother, "What shall I ask for?"

"The head of John the Baptist," she answered.

25At once the girl hurried in to the king with the request: "I want you to give me right now the head of John the Baptist on a platter."

26The king was greatly distressed, but because of his oaths and his dinner guests, he did not want to refuse her. 27So he immediately sent an executioner with orders to bring John's head. The man went, beheaded John in the prison, 28and brought back his head on a platter. He presented it to the girl, and she gave it to her mother. 29On hearing of this, John's disciples came and took his body and laid it in a tomb. Mt 14:1-12

Jesus Feeds the Five Thousand

▶ *See Matthew 14:13–21; Luke 9:10–17; John 6:5–13*

30The apostles gathered around Jesus and reported to him all they had done and taught. 31Then, because so many people were coming and

LIVING  **INSIGHT**

Renewal and restoration are not luxuries; they are essentials. Being alone and resting for a while is not selfish; it is Christlike. Taking your day off each week or rewarding yourself with a relaxing, refreshing vacation is not carnal; it's spiritual.

(See Mark 6:31.)

---

[a] 3 Greek *Joses,* a variant of *Joseph* [b] 7 Greek *unclean* [c] 14 Some early manuscripts *He was saying* [d] 20 Some early manuscripts *he did many things*

going that they did not even have a chance to eat,
he said to them, "Come with me by yourselves to
a quiet place and get some rest." Lk 9:10; Ac 1:2,26
32So they went away by themselves in a boat to
a solitary place. 33But many who saw them leaving
recognized them and ran on foot from all the
towns and got there ahead of them. 34When Jesus
landed and saw a large crowd, he had compassion
on them, because they were like sheep without a
shepherd. So he began teaching them many things.
35By this time it was late in the day, so his
disciples came to him. "This is a remote place,"
they said, "and it's already very late. 36Send the
people away so they can go to the surrounding
countryside and villages and buy themselves
something to eat." Mk 8:2-9
37But he answered, "You give them something
to eat."

They said to him, "That would take eight
months of a man's wages[a]! Are we to go and
spend that much on bread and give it to them to
eat?" 2Ki 4:42-44
38"How many loaves do you have?" he asked.
"Go and see."

When they found out, they said, "Five—and
two fish." Lk 9:10-17
39Then Jesus directed them to have all the people sit down in groups on the green grass. 40So
they sat down in groups of hundreds and fifties.
41Taking the five loaves and the two fish and looking up to heaven, he gave thanks and broke the
loaves. Then he gave them to his disciples to set
before the people. He also divided the two fish
among them all. 42They all ate and were satisfied,
43and the disciples picked up twelve basketfuls of
broken pieces of bread and fish. 44The number of
the men who had eaten was five thousand.

Jesus Walks on the Water

▶ *See Matthew 14:22–32; John 6:15–21*

45Immediately Jesus made his disciples get into
the boat and go on ahead of him to Bethsaida,
while he dismissed the crowd. 46After leaving
them, he went up on a mountainside to pray.
47When evening came, the boat was in the middle of the lake, and he was alone on land. 48He saw
the disciples straining at the oars, because the wind
was against them. About the fourth watch of the
night he went out to them, walking on the lake. He
was about to pass by them, 49but when they saw
him walking on the lake, they thought he was a
ghost. They cried out, 50because they all saw him
and were terrified. Lk 24:37

Immediately he spoke to them and said, "Take
courage! It is I. Don't be afraid." 51Then he
climbed into the boat with them, and the wind
died down. They were completely amazed, 52for
they had not understood about the loaves; their
hearts were hardened. Mt 14:22-32; Jn 6:15-21
53When they had crossed over, they landed at
Gennesaret and anchored there. 54As soon as they
got out of the boat, people recognized Jesus.
55They ran throughout that whole region and carried the sick on mats to wherever they heard he
was. 56And wherever he went—into villages,
towns or countryside—they placed the sick in the
marketplaces. They begged him to let them touch
even the edge of his cloak, and all who touched
him were healed. Mt 14:34-36

Clean and Unclean

▶ *See Matthew 15:1–20*

7 The Pharisees and some of the teachers of the
law who had come from Jerusalem gathered
around Jesus and 2saw some of his disciples eating
food with hands that were "unclean," that is, unwashed. 3(The Pharisees and all the Jews do not eat
unless they give their hands a ceremonial washing,
holding to the tradition of the elders. 4When they
come from the marketplace they do not eat unless
they wash. And they observe many other traditions, such as the washing of cups, pitchers and
kettles.[b]) Mt 23:25; Ac 10:14,28
5So the Pharisees and teachers of the law asked
Jesus, "Why don't your disciples live according to
the tradition of the elders instead of eating their
food with 'unclean' hands?" Gal 1:14; Col 2:8
6He replied, "Isaiah was right when he prophesied about you hypocrites; as it is written:

" 'These people honor me with their lips,
but their hearts are far from me.
7They worship me in vain;
their teachings are but rules taught by
men.'[c]

8You have let go of the commands of God and are
holding on to the traditions of men."
9And he said to them: "You have a fine way of
setting aside the commands of God in order to
observe[d] your own traditions! 10For Moses said,
'Honor your father and your mother,'[e] and,
'Anyone who curses his father or mother must be
put to death.'[f] 11But you say that if a man says to
his father or mother: 'Whatever help you might
otherwise have received from me is Corban' (that
is, a gift devoted to God), 12then you no longer let
him do anything for his father or mother. 13Thus
you nullify the word of God by your tradition that
you have handed down. And you do many things
like that." Mt 23:16,18; Heb 4:12
14Again Jesus called the crowd to him and said,

[a] 37 Greek *take two hundred denarii* [b] 4 Some early manuscripts *pitchers, kettles and dining couches* [c] 6,7 Isaiah 29:13
[d] 9 Some manuscripts *set up* [e] 10 Exodus 20:12; Deut. 5:16 [f] 10 Exodus 21:17; Lev. 20:9

"Listen to me, everyone, and understand this. 15Nothing outside a man can make him 'unclean' by going into him. Rather, it is what comes out of a man that makes him 'unclean.'[a]"

17After he had left the crowd and entered the house, his disciples asked him about this parable. 18"Are you so dull?" he asked. "Don't you see that nothing that enters a man from the outside can make him 'unclean'? 19For it doesn't go into his heart but into his stomach, and then out of his body." (In saying this, Jesus declared all foods "clean.") Ac 10:15; 1Ti 4:3-5

20He went on: "What comes out of a man is what makes him 'unclean.' 21For from within, out of men's hearts, come evil thoughts, sexual immorality, theft, murder, adultery, 22greed, malice, deceit, lewdness, envy, slander, arrogance and folly. 23All these evils come from inside and make a man 'unclean.' " Mt 15:1-20

The Faith of a Syrophoenician Woman

▶ *See Matthew 15:21–28*

24Jesus left that place and went to the vicinity of Tyre.[b] He entered a house and did not want anyone to know it; yet he could not keep his presence secret. 25In fact, as soon as she heard about him, a woman whose little daughter was possessed by an evil[c] spirit came and fell at his feet. 26The woman was a Greek, born in Syrian Phoenicia. She begged Jesus to drive the demon out of her daughter.

27"First let the children eat all they want," he told her, "for it is not right to take the children's bread and toss it to their dogs."

28"Yes, Lord," she replied, "but even the dogs under the table eat the children's crumbs."

29Then he told her, "For such a reply, you may go; the demon has left your daughter."

30She went home and found her child lying on the bed, and the demon gone. Mt 15:21-28

The Healing of a Deaf and Mute Man

▶ *See Matthew 15:29–31*

31Then Jesus left the vicinity of Tyre and went through Sidon, down to the Sea of Galilee and into the region of the Decapolis.[d] 32There some people brought to him a man who was deaf and could hardly talk, and they begged him to place his hand on the man. Mk 5:23; Lk 11:14

33After he took him aside, away from the crowd, Jesus put his fingers into the man's ears. Then he spit and touched the man's tongue. 34He looked up to heaven and with a deep sigh said to him, "*Ephphatha!*" (which means, "Be opened!"). 35At this, the man's ears were opened, his tongue was loosened and he began to speak plainly. Isa 35:5-6

36Jesus commanded them not to tell anyone. But the more he did so, the more they kept talking about it. 37People were overwhelmed with amazement. "He has done everything well," they said. "He even makes the deaf hear and the mute speak." Mt 15:29-31

Jesus Feeds the Four Thousand

▶ *See Matthew 15:32–39*

8 During those days another large crowd gathered. Since they had nothing to eat, Jesus called his disciples to him and said, 2"I have compassion for these people; they have already been with me three days and have nothing to eat. 3If I send them home hungry, they will collapse on the way, because some of them have come a long distance." Mt 9:36

4His disciples answered, "But where in this remote place can anyone get enough bread to feed them?"

5"How many loaves do you have?" Jesus asked.

"Seven," they replied.

6He told the crowd to sit down on the ground. When he had taken the seven loaves and given thanks, he broke them and gave them to his disciples to set before the people, and they did so. 7They had a few small fish as well; he gave thanks for them also and told the disciples to distribute them. 8The people ate and were satisfied. Afterward the disciples picked up seven basketfuls of broken pieces that were left over. 9About four thousand men were present. And having sent them away, 10he got into the boat with his disciples and went to the region of Dalmanutha. Mt 15:32-39

11The Pharisees came and began to question Jesus. To test him, they asked him for a sign from heaven. 12He sighed deeply and said, "Why does this generation ask for a miraculous sign? I tell you the truth, no sign will be given to it." 13Then he left them, got back into the boat and crossed to the other side. Mt 12:38; Mk 7:34

The Yeast of the Pharisees and Herod

14The disciples had forgotten to bring bread, except for one loaf they had with them in the boat. 15"Be careful," Jesus warned them. "Watch out for the yeast of the Pharisees and that of Herod."

16They discussed this with one another and said, "It is because we have no bread."

17Aware of their discussion, Jesus asked them: "Why are you talking about having no bread? Do you still not see or understand? Are your hearts hardened? 18Do you have eyes but fail to see, and ears but fail to hear? And don't you remember? 19When I broke the five loaves for the five thousand, how many basketfuls of pieces did you pick up?" Isa 6:9-10; Mk 6:52

[a] *15* Some early manuscripts *'unclean.' 16If anyone has ears to hear, let him hear.* [b] *24* Many early manuscripts *Tyre and Sidon* [c] *25* Greek *unclean* [d] *31* That is, the Ten Cities

"Twelve," they replied. Mt 14:20; Mk 6:41-44
20"And when I broke the seven loaves for the
four thousand, how many basketfuls of pieces did
you pick up?"
They answered, "Seven." Mt 15:37
21He said to them, "Do you still not understand?" Mk 6:52

The Healing of a Blind Man at Bethsaida

22They came to Bethsaida, and some people
brought a blind man and begged Jesus to touch
him. 23He took the blind man by the hand and led
him outside the village. When he had spit on the
man's eyes and put his hands on him, Jesus asked,
"Do you see anything?" Mk 5:23; 7:33
24He looked up and said, "I see people; they
look like trees walking around."
25Once more Jesus put his hands on the man's
eyes. Then his eyes were opened, his sight was
restored, and he saw everything clearly. 26Jesus
sent him home, saying, "Don't go into the village.[a]"

Peter's Confession of Christ

▶ *See Matthew 16:13–16; Luke 9:18–20*

27Jesus and his disciples went on to the villages
around Caesarea Philippi. On the way he asked
them, "Who do people say I am?"
28They replied, "Some say John the Baptist; others say Elijah; and still others, one of the prophets." Mt 3:1; Mal 4:5
29"But what about you?" he asked. "Who do
you say I am?"
Peter answered, "You are the Christ.[b]"
30Jesus warned them not to tell anyone about
him. Mt 8:4; 16:20; 17:9

Jesus Predicts His Death

▶ *See Matthew 16:21–28; Luke 9:22–27*

31He then began to teach them that the Son of
Man must suffer many things and be rejected by
the elders, chief priests and teachers of the law, and
that he must be killed and after three days rise
again. 32He spoke plainly about this, and Peter
took him aside and began to rebuke him.

LIVING  INSIGHT

God desires that we hold things loosely so that He might reign without a rival. With no threat to His throne. With just enough splinters in our pride to keep our hands empty and our heart warm.

(See Mark 8:34–36.)

33But when Jesus turned and looked at his disciples, he rebuked Peter. "Get behind me, Satan!" he
said. "You do not have in mind the things of God,
but the things of men." Mt 4:10
34Then he called the crowd to him along with
his disciples and said: "If anyone would come after
me, he must deny himself and take up his cross
and follow me. 35For whoever wants to save his
life[c] will lose it, but whoever loses his life for me
and for the gospel will save it. 36What good is it for
a man to gain the whole world, yet forfeit his soul?
37Or what can a man give in exchange for his soul?
38If anyone is ashamed of me and my words in this
adulterous and sinful generation, the Son of Man
will be ashamed of him when he comes in his
Father's glory with the holy angels." Mt 10:33
9 And he said to them, "I tell you the truth,
some who are standing here will not taste
death before they see the kingdom of God come
with power." Mt 16:21-28; Lk 9:22-27

The Servant Rejected — Chapters 9:2–16:20

In the second half of Mark's Gospel we typically find Jesus in smaller gatherings—with the twelve disciples or other small groups of followers. Hostility and opposition were on the rise, and Jesus became a wanted man . . . much like a fugitive on the run. Following the Last Supper with the disciples, Jesus was arrested and taken prisoner. The Servant was put on trial, falsely accused, rejected, beaten unmercifully and finally crucified. He gave the final and ultimate gift—the gift of His life in love for the world. No greater act of sacrificial service could have been given. Having served to the fullest, He gave His all.

This Gospel ends with the record of Jesus' bodily resurrection from the grave. The Servant who had died for sinful humanity had now risen to break the power of sin and death. Before Jesus ascended He called His followers and commissioned them to take up the torch of service and continue in His footsteps. We have no greater life to live than the one He modeled—the life of service.

The Transfiguration

▶ *See Matthew 17:1–13; Luke 9:28–36*

2After six days Jesus took Peter, James and John
with him and led them up a high mountain, where
they were all alone. There he was transfigured before them. 3His clothes became dazzling white,
whiter than anyone in the world could bleach
them. 4And there appeared before them Elijah and
Moses, who were talking with Jesus. Mt 28:3
5Peter said to Jesus, "Rabbi, it is good for us to
be here. Let us put up three shelters—one for you,
one for Moses and one for Elijah." 6(He did not
know what to say, they were so frightened.)
7Then a cloud appeared and enveloped them,

[a]26 Some manuscripts *Don't go and tell anyone in the village*
[b]29 Or *Messiah.* "The Christ" (Greek) and "the Messiah" (Hebrew) both mean "the Anointed One."
[c]35 The Greek word means either *life* or *soul*; also in verse 36.

and a voice came from the cloud: "This is my Son,
whom I love. Listen to him!" Ex 24:16; Mt 3:17
8Suddenly, when they looked around, they no
longer saw anyone with them except Jesus.
9As they were coming down the mountain,
Jesus gave them orders not to tell anyone what
they had seen until the Son of Man had risen from
the dead. 10They kept the matter to themselves,
discussing what "rising from the dead" meant.
11And they asked him, "Why do the teachers of
the law say that Elijah must come first?"
12Jesus replied, "To be sure, Elijah does come
first, and restores all things. Why then is it written
that the Son of Man must suffer much and be
rejected? 13But I tell you, Elijah has come, and they
have done to him everything they wished, just as
it is written about him." Mt 17:1-13

The Healing of a Boy With an Evil Spirit

▶ *See Matthew 17:14–19,22–23; Luke 9:37–45*

14When they came to the other disciples, they
saw a large crowd around them and the teachers of
the law arguing with them. 15As soon as all the
people saw Jesus, they were overwhelmed with
wonder and ran to greet him.
16"What are you arguing with them about?" he
asked.
17A man in the crowd answered, "Teacher, I
brought you my son, who is possessed by a spirit
that has robbed him of speech. 18Whenever it
seizes him, it throws him to the ground. He foams
at the mouth, gnashes his teeth and becomes rigid.
I asked your disciples to drive out the spirit, but
they could not."
19"O unbelieving generation," Jesus replied,
"how long shall I stay with you? How long shall I
put up with you? Bring the boy to me."
20So they brought him. When the spirit saw
Jesus, it immediately threw the boy into a convulsion. He fell to the ground and rolled around,
foaming at the mouth. Mk 1:26
21Jesus asked the boy's father, "How long has he
been like this?"
"From childhood," he answered. 22"It has often
thrown him into fire or water to kill him. But if
you can do anything, take pity on us and help us."
23"'If you can'?" said Jesus. "Everything is possible for him who believes." Mk 11:23; Jn 11:40
24Immediately the boy's father exclaimed, "I do
believe; help me overcome my unbelief!"
25When Jesus saw that a crowd was running to
the scene, he rebuked the evil[a] spirit. "You deaf
and mute spirit," he said, "I command you, come
out of him and never enter him again."
26The spirit shrieked, convulsed him violently
and came out. The boy looked so much like a
corpse that many said, "He's dead." 27But Jesus
took him by the hand and lifted him to his feet,
and he stood up.
28After Jesus had gone indoors, his disciples
asked him privately, "Why couldn't we drive it
out?" Mt 17:14-19; Mk 7:17
29He replied, "This kind can come out only by
prayer.[b]"
30They left that place and passed through Galilee. Jesus did not want anyone to know where they
were, 31because he was teaching his disciples. He
said to them, "The Son of Man is going to be
betrayed into the hands of men. They will kill him,
and after three days he will rise." 32But they did
not understand what he meant and were afraid to
ask him about it. Lk 9:37-45

Who Is the Greatest?

▶ *See Matthew 18:1–5; Luke 9:46–48*

33They came to Capernaum. When he was in
the house, he asked them, "What were you arguing
about on the road?" 34But they kept quiet because
on the way they had argued about who was the
greatest. Mt 4:13; Lk 22:24
35Sitting down, Jesus called the Twelve and said,
"If anyone wants to be first, he must be the very
last, and the servant of all." Mt 20:26; Mk 10:43
36He took a little child and had him stand
among them. Taking him in his arms, he said to
them, 37"Whoever welcomes one of these little
children in my name welcomes me; and whoever
welcomes me does not welcome me but the one
who sent me." Mt 18:1-5; Lk 9:46-48

Whoever Is Not Against Us Is for Us

▶ *See Luke 9:49–50*

38"Teacher," said John, "we saw a man driving
out demons in your name and we told him to stop,
because he was not one of us." Nu 11:27-29
39"Do not stop him," Jesus said. "No one who
does a miracle in my name can in the next moment say anything bad about me, 40for whoever is
not against us is for us. 41I tell you the truth, anyone who gives you a cup of water in my name
because you belong to Christ will certainly not lose
his reward. Mt 10:42; Mt 12:30; Lk 11:23

Causing to Sin

42"And if anyone causes one of these little ones
who believe in me to sin, it would be better for him
to be thrown into the sea with a large millstone
tied around his neck. 43If your hand causes you to
sin, cut it off. It is better for you to enter life
maimed than with two hands to go into hell, where
the fire never goes out.[c] 45And if your foot causes
you to sin, cut it off. It is better for you to enter life

[a]25 Greek *unclean* [b]29 Some manuscripts *prayer and fasting* [c]43 Some manuscripts *out,* [44]*where / "'their worm does not die, / and the fire is not quenched.'*

crippled than to have two feet and be thrown into hell.[a] 47And if your eye causes you to sin, pluck it out. It is better for you to enter the kingdom of God with one eye than to have two eyes and be thrown into hell, 48where

> "'their worm does not die,
> and the fire is not quenched.'[b]

49Everyone will be salted with fire. Mt 5:29; 18:9

50"Salt is good, but if it loses its saltiness, how can you make it salty again? Have salt in yourselves, and be at peace with each other." Mt 5:13

LIVING  **INSIGHT**

Extreme dilemmas are usually solved by radical adjustments. It used to be called "fighting fire with fire." Minor alterations won't do. If the situation is getting completely out of hand, a slight modification won't cut it. It's get-with-it time.

(See Mark 9:42–49.)

Divorce

▶ *See Matthew 19:1–9*

10 Jesus then left that place and went into the region of Judea and across the Jordan. Again crowds of people came to him, and as was his custom, he taught them. Jn 10:40; 11:7

2Some Pharisees came and tested him by asking, "Is it lawful for a man to divorce his wife?"

3"What did Moses command you?" he replied.

4They said, "Moses permitted a man to write a certificate of divorce and send her away."

5"It was because your hearts were hard that Moses wrote you this law," Jesus replied. 6"But at the beginning of creation God 'made them male and female.'[c] 7'For this reason a man will leave his father and mother and be united to his wife,[d] 8and the two will become one flesh.'[e] So they are no longer two, but one. 9Therefore what God has joined together, let man not separate." Ge 5:2

10When they were in the house again, the disciples asked Jesus about this. 11He answered, "Anyone who divorces his wife and marries another woman commits adultery against her. 12And if she divorces her husband and marries another man, she commits adultery." Mt 19:1-9; Lk 16:18; Ro 7:3

The Little Children and Jesus

▶ *See Matthew 19:13–15; Luke 18:15–17*

13People were bringing little children to Jesus to have him touch them, but the disciples rebuked them. 14When Jesus saw this, he was indignant. He said to them, "Let the little children come to me, and do not hinder them, for the kingdom of God belongs to such as these. 15I tell you the truth, anyone who will not receive the kingdom of God like a little child will never enter it." 16And he took the children in his arms, put his hands on them and blessed them. Mt 19:13-15; Lk 18:15-17

The Rich Young Man

▶ *See Matthew 19:16–30; Luke 18:18–30*

17As Jesus started on his way, a man ran up to him and fell on his knees before him. "Good teacher," he asked, "what must I do to inherit eternal life?" Lk 10:25; Ac 20:32

18"Why do you call me good?" Jesus answered. "No one is good—except God alone. 19You know the commandments: 'Do not murder, do not commit adultery, do not steal, do not give false testimony, do not defraud, honor your father and mother.'[f]" Ex 20:12-16; Dt 5:16-20

20"Teacher," he declared, "all these I have kept since I was a boy."

21Jesus looked at him and loved him. "One thing you lack," he said. "Go, sell everything you have and give to the poor, and you will have treasure in heaven. Then come, follow me." Mt 6:20

22At this the man's face fell. He went away sad, because he had great wealth.

23Jesus looked around and said to his disciples, "How hard it is for the rich to enter the kingdom of God!" Ps 52:7; 1Ti 6:9-10,17

24The disciples were amazed at his words. But Jesus said again, "Children, how hard it is[g] to enter the kingdom of God! 25It is easier for a camel to go through the eye of a needle than for a rich man to enter the kingdom of God." Mt 7:13-14

26The disciples were even more amazed, and said to each other, "Who then can be saved?"

27Jesus looked at them and said, "With man this is impossible, but not with God; all things are possible with God." Mt 19:26

28Peter said to him, "We have left everything to follow you!" Mt 4:19

29"I tell you the truth," Jesus replied, "no one who has left home or brothers or sisters or mother or father or children or fields for me and the gospel 30will fail to receive a hundred times as much in this present age (homes, brothers, sisters, mothers, children and fields—and with them, persecutions) and in the age to come, eternal life. 31But many who are first will be last, and the last first."

[a] 45 Some manuscripts *hell,* 46*where / "'their worm does not die, / and the fire is not quenched.'* [b] 48 Isaiah 66:24 [c] 6 Gen. 1:27 [d] 7 Some early manuscripts do not have *and be united to his wife.* [e] 8 Gen. 2:24 [f] 19 Exodus 20:12-16; Deut. 5:16-20 [g] 24 Some manuscripts *is for those who trust in riches*

Jesus Again Predicts His Death

▶ *See Matthew 20:17–19; Luke 18:31–33*

32They were on their way up to Jerusalem, with Jesus leading the way, and the disciples were astonished, while those who followed were afraid. Again he took the Twelve aside and told them what was going to happen to him. 33"We are going up to Jerusalem," he said, "and the Son of Man will be betrayed to the chief priests and teachers of the law. They will condemn him to death and will hand him over to the Gentiles, 34who will mock him and spit on him, flog him and kill him. Three days later he will rise." Mt 20:17-19; Lk 18:31-33

The Request of James and John

▶ *See Matthew 20:20–28*

35Then James and John, the sons of Zebedee, came to him. "Teacher," they said, "we want you to do for us whatever we ask."

36"What do you want me to do for you?" he asked.

37They replied, "Let one of us sit at your right and the other at your left in your glory." Mt 19:28

38"You don't know what you are asking," Jesus said. "Can you drink the cup I drink or be baptized with the baptism I am baptized with?"

39"We can," they answered.

Jesus said to them, "You will drink the cup I drink and be baptized with the baptism I am baptized with, 40but to sit at my right or left is not for me to grant. These places belong to those for whom they have been prepared." Ac 12:2; Rev 1:9

41When the ten heard about this, they became indignant with James and John. 42Jesus called them together and said, "You know that those who are regarded as rulers of the Gentiles lord it over them, and their high officials exercise authority over them. 43Not so with you. Instead, whoever wants to become great among you must be your servant, 44and whoever wants to be first must be slave of all. 45For even the Son of Man did not come to be served, but to serve, and to give his life as a ransom for many." Mt 20:20-28; Mk 9:35

Blind Bartimaeus Receives His Sight

▶ *See Matthew 20:29–34; Luke 18:35–43*

46Then they came to Jericho. As Jesus and his disciples, together with a large crowd, were leaving the city, a blind man, Bartimaeus (that is, the Son of Timaeus), was sitting by the roadside begging. 47When he heard that it was Jesus of Nazareth, he began to shout, "Jesus, Son of David, have mercy on me!" Mt 9:27; Mk 1:24

48Many rebuked him and told him to be quiet, but he shouted all the more, "Son of David, have mercy on me!"

49Jesus stopped and said, "Call him."

So they called to the blind man, "Cheer up! On your feet! He's calling you." 50Throwing his cloak aside, he jumped to his feet and came to Jesus.

51"What do you want me to do for you?" Jesus asked him.

The blind man said, "Rabbi, I want to see."

52"Go," said Jesus, "your faith has healed you." Immediately he received his sight and followed Jesus along the road. Mt 20:29-34; Lk 18:35-43

The Triumphal Entry

▶ *See Matthew 21:1–9; Luke 19:29–38; John 12:12–15*

11 As they approached Jerusalem and came to Bethphage and Bethany at the Mount of Olives, Jesus sent two of his disciples, 2saying to them, "Go to the village ahead of you, and just as you enter it, you will find a colt tied there, which no one has ever ridden. Untie it and bring it here. 3If anyone asks you, 'Why are you doing this?' tell him, 'The Lord needs it and will send it back here shortly.'" Nu 19:2; Dt 21:3; Mt 21:1

4They went and found a colt outside in the street, tied at a doorway. As they untied it, 5some people standing there asked, "What are you doing, untying that colt?" 6They answered as Jesus had told them to, and the people let them go. 7When they brought the colt to Jesus and threw their cloaks over it, he sat on it. 8Many people spread their cloaks on the road, while others spread branches they had cut in the fields. 9Those who went ahead and those who followed shouted,

"Hosanna![a]"

"Blessed is he who comes in the name of the
Lord!"[b]

10"Blessed is the coming kingdom of our father
David!"

"Hosanna in the highest!" Mt 21:1-9; Lk 19:29-38

11Jesus entered Jerusalem and went to the temple. He looked around at everything, but since it was already late, he went out to Bethany with the Twelve. Mt 21:12,17

Jesus Clears the Temple

▶ *See Matthew 21:12–16; Luke 19:45–47; John 2:13–16*

12The next day as they were leaving Bethany, Jesus was hungry. 13Seeing in the distance a fig tree in leaf, he went to find out if it had any fruit. When he reached it, he found nothing but leaves, because it was not the season for figs. 14Then he said to the tree, "May no one ever eat fruit from you again." And his disciples heard him say it. Mt 21:18-22

15On reaching Jerusalem, Jesus entered the temple area and began driving out those who were

[a]9 A Hebrew expression meaning "Save!" which became an exclamation of praise; also in verse 10 [b]9 Psalm 118:25,26

buying and selling there. He overturned the tables
of the money changers and the benches of those
selling doves, 16and would not allow anyone to
carry merchandise through the temple courts.
17And as he taught them, he said, "Is it not written:

"'My house will be called
a house of prayer for all nations'[a]?

But you have made it 'a den of robbers.'[b]"

18The chief priests and the teachers of the law
heard this and began looking for a way to kill him,
for they feared him, because the whole crowd was
amazed at his teaching. Jn 2:13-16

19When evening came, they[c] went out of the
city. Lk 21:37

The Withered Fig Tree

▶ *See Matthew 21:19–22*

20In the morning, as they went along, they saw
the fig tree withered from the roots. 21Peter remembered and said to Jesus, "Rabbi, look! The fig
tree you cursed has withered!" Mt 23:7

22"Have[d] faith in God," Jesus answered. 23"I
tell you the truth, if anyone says to this mountain,
'Go, throw yourself into the sea,' and does not
doubt in his heart but believes that what he says
will happen, it will be done for him. 24Therefore I
tell you, whatever you ask for in prayer, believe
that you have received it, and it will be yours.
25And when you stand praying, if you hold anything against anyone, forgive him, so that your
Father in heaven may forgive you your sins.[e]"

The Authority of Jesus Questioned

▶ *See Matthew 21:23–27; Luke 20:1–8*

27They arrived again in Jerusalem, and while
Jesus was walking in the temple courts, the chief
priests, the teachers of the law and the elders came
to him. 28"By what authority are you doing these
things?" they asked. "And who gave you authority
to do this?"

29Jesus replied, "I will ask you one question.
Answer me, and I will tell you by what authority
I am doing these things. 30John's baptism—was it
from heaven, or from men? Tell me!"

31They discussed it among themselves and said,
"If we say, 'From heaven,' he will ask, 'Then why
didn't you believe him?' 32But if we say, 'From
men' . . . ." (They feared the people, for everyone
held that John really was a prophet.) Mt 11:9

33So they answered Jesus, "We don't know."

Jesus said, "Neither will I tell you by what authority I am doing these things." Mt 21:23-27

The Parable of the Tenants

▶ *See Matthew 21:33–46; Luke 20:9–19*

12 He then began to speak to them in parables: "A man planted a vineyard. He put a
wall around it, dug a pit for the winepress and
built a watchtower. Then he rented the vineyard to
some farmers and went away on a journey. 2At
harvest time he sent a servant to the tenants to
collect from them some of the fruit of the vineyard. 3But they seized him, beat him and sent him
away empty-handed. 4Then he sent another servant to them; they struck this man on the head and
treated him shamefully. 5He sent still another, and
that one they killed. He sent many others; some of
them they beat, others they killed. Isa 5:1-7

6"He had one left to send, a son, whom he
loved. He sent him last of all, saying, 'They will
respect my son.' Heb 1:1-3

7"But the tenants said to one another, 'This is
the heir. Come, let's kill him, and the inheritance
will be ours.' 8So they took him and killed him,
and threw him out of the vineyard.

9"What then will the owner of the vineyard do?
He will come and kill those tenants and give the
vineyard to others. 10Haven't you read this scripture:

"'The stone the builders rejected
has become the capstone[f];
11the Lord has done this,
and it is marvelous in our eyes'[g]?" Ac 4:11

12Then they looked for a way to arrest him because they knew he had spoken the parable against
them. But they were afraid of the crowd; so they
left him and went away. Mt 21:33-46; Lk 20:9-19

Paying Taxes to Caesar

▶ *See Matthew 22:15–22; Luke 20:20–26*

13Later they sent some of the Pharisees and Herodians to Jesus to catch him in his words. 14They
came to him and said, "Teacher, we know you are
a man of integrity. You aren't swayed by men,
because you pay no attention to who they are; but
you teach the way of God in accordance with the
truth. Is it right to pay taxes to Caesar or not?
15Should we pay or shouldn't we?" Mt 12:10; 22:16

But Jesus knew their hypocrisy. "Why are you
trying to trap me?" he asked. "Bring me a denarius
and let me look at it." 16They brought the coin,
and he asked them, "Whose portrait is this? And
whose inscription?"

"Caesar's," they replied.

17Then Jesus said to them, "Give to Caesar what
is Caesar's and to God what is God's." Ro 13:7

And they were amazed at him. Mt 22:15-22

[a]17 Isaiah 56:7 [b]17 Jer. 7:11 [c]19 Some early manuscripts *he* [d]22 Some early manuscripts *If you have*
[e]25 Some manuscripts *sins.* 26*But if you do not forgive, neither will your Father who is in heaven forgive your sins.*
[f]10 Or *cornerstone* [g]11 Psalm 118:22,23

Marriage at the Resurrection

▶ *See Matthew 22:23–33; Luke 20:27–38*

18Then the Sadducees, who say there is no resurrection, came to him with a question. 19"Teacher," they said, "Moses wrote for us that if a man's
brother dies and leaves a wife but no children, the
man must marry the widow and have children for
his brother. 20Now there were seven brothers. The
first one married and died without leaving any
children. 21The second one married the widow,
but he also died, leaving no child. It was the same
with the third. 22In fact, none of the seven left any
children. Last of all, the woman died too. 23At the
resurrection[a] whose wife will be she, since the
seven were married to her?" Dt 25:5; Ac 23:8
24Jesus replied, "Are you not in error because
you do not know the Scriptures or the power of
God? 25When the dead rise, they will neither marry
nor be given in marriage; they will be like the
angels in heaven. 26Now about the dead rising—
have you not read in the book of Moses, in the
account of the bush, how God said to him, 'I am
the God of Abraham, the God of Isaac, and the
God of Jacob'[b]? 27He is not the God of the dead,
but of the living. You are badly mistaken!"

The Greatest Commandment

▶ *See Matthew 22:34–40*

28One of the teachers of the law came and heard
them debating. Noticing that Jesus had given them
a good answer, he asked him, "Of all the commandments, which is the most important?"
29"The most important one," answered Jesus,
"is this: 'Hear, O Israel, the Lord our God, the

LIVING  **INSIGHT**

Knowing God is life's major pursuit, but that's only half the story. Loving God is our ultimate response.
(See Mark 12:29–30.)

Lord is one.[c] 30Love the Lord your God with all
your heart and with all your soul and with all your
mind and with all your strength.'[d] 31The second
is this: 'Love your neighbor as yourself.'[e] There is
no commandment greater than these." Mt 5:43
32"Well said, teacher," the man replied. "You
are right in saying that God is one and there is no
other but him. 33To love him with all your heart,
with all your understanding and with all your
strength, and to love your neighbor as yourself is
more important than all burnt offerings and sacrifices." 1Sa 15:22; Mic 6:6-8
34When Jesus saw that he had answered wisely,
he said to him, "You are not far from the kingdom
of God." And from then on no one dared ask him
any more questions. Mt 22:34-40; Lk 20:40

Whose Son Is the Christ?

▶ *See Matthew 22:41–46; Luke 20:41–47*

35While Jesus was teaching in the temple courts,
he asked, "How is it that the teachers of the law say
that the Christ[f] is the son of David? 36David himself, speaking by the Holy Spirit, declared:

"'The Lord said to my Lord:
"Sit at my right hand
until I put your enemies
under your feet."'[g]

37David himself calls him 'Lord.' How then can he
be his son?" Mt 22:41-46; Lk 20:41-44
The large crowd listened to him with delight.
38As he taught, Jesus said, "Watch out for the
teachers of the law. They like to walk around in
flowing robes and be greeted in the marketplaces,
39and have the most important seats in the synagogues and the places of honor at banquets.
40They devour widows' houses and for a show
make lengthy prayers. Such men will be punished
most severely." Mt 23:1-7; Lk 20:45-47

The Widow's Offering

▶ *See Luke 21:1–4*

41Jesus sat down opposite the place where the
offerings were put and watched the crowd putting
their money into the temple treasury. Many rich
people threw in large amounts. 42But a poor widow came and put in two very small copper coins,[h]
worth only a fraction of a penny.[i] 2Ki 12:9; Jn 8:20
43Calling his disciples to him, Jesus said, "I tell
you the truth, this poor widow has put more into
the treasury than all the others. 44They all gave out
of their wealth; but she, out of her poverty, put in
everything—all she had to live on." 2Co 8:12

Signs of the End of the Age

▶ *See Matthew 24:1–51; Luke 21:5–36*

13 As he was leaving the temple, one of his
disciples said to him, "Look, Teacher!
What massive stones! What magnificent buildings!"
2"Do you see all these great buildings?" replied
Jesus. "Not one stone here will be left on another;
every one will be thrown down." Lk 19:44
3As Jesus was sitting on the Mount of Olives
opposite the temple, Peter, James, John and An-

[a]23 Some manuscripts *resurrection, when men rise from the dead,* [b]26 Exodus 3:6 [c]29 Or *the Lord our God is one Lord* [d]30 Deut. 6:4,5 [e]31 Lev. 19:18 [f]35 Or *Messiah* [g]36 Psalm 110:1 [h]42 Greek *two lepta* [i]42 Greek *kodrantes*

drew asked him privately, 4"Tell us, when will these things happen? And what will be the sign that they are all about to be fulfilled?" Mt 4:21; 21:1

5Jesus said to them: "Watch out that no one deceives you. 6Many will come in my name, claiming, 'I am he,' and will deceive many. 7When you hear of wars and rumors of wars, do not be alarmed. Such things must happen, but the end is still to come. 8Nation will rise against nation, and kingdom against kingdom. There will be earthquakes in various places, and famines. These are the beginning of birth pains. Eph 5:6; 2Th 2:3,10-12

9"You must be on your guard. You will be handed over to the local councils and flogged in the synagogues. On account of me you will stand before governors and kings as witnesses to them. 10And the gospel must first be preached to all nations. 11Whenever you are arrested and brought to trial, do not worry beforehand about what to say. Just say whatever is given you at the time, for it is not you speaking, but the Holy Spirit. Mt 10:19-20

12"Brother will betray brother to death, and a father his child. Children will rebel against their parents and have them put to death. 13All men will hate you because of me, but he who stands firm to the end will be saved. Mic 7:6; Mt 10:21-22

14"When you see 'the abomination that causes desolation'[a] standing where it[b] does not belong—let the reader understand—then let those who are in Judea flee to the mountains. 15Let no one on the roof of his house go down or enter the house to take anything out. 16Let no one in the field go back to get his cloak. 17How dreadful it will be in those days for pregnant women and nursing mothers! 18Pray that this will not take place in winter, 19because those will be days of distress unequaled from the beginning, when God created the world, until now—and never to be equaled again. 20If the Lord had not cut short those days, no one would survive. But for the sake of the elect, whom he has chosen, he has shortened them. 21At that time if anyone says to you, 'Look, here is the Christ[c]!' or, 'Look, there he is!' do not believe it. 22For false Christs and false prophets will appear and perform signs and miracles to deceive the elect—if that were possible. 23So be on your guard; I have told you everything ahead of time. Jn 4:48

24"But in those days, following that distress,

"'the sun will be darkened,
and the moon will not give its light;
25the stars will fall from the sky,
and the heavenly bodies will be shaken.'[d]

26"At that time men will see the Son of Man coming in clouds with great power and glory. 27And he will send his angels and gather his elect from the four winds, from the ends of the earth to the ends of the heavens. Da 7:13; Zec 2:6; Rev 1:7

28"Now learn this lesson from the fig tree: As soon as its twigs get tender and its leaves come out, you know that summer is near. 29Even so, when you see these things happening, you know that it is near, right at the door. 30I tell you the truth, this generation[e] will certainly not pass away until all these things have happened. 31Heaven and earth will pass away, but my words will never pass away.

The Day and Hour Unknown

32"No one knows about that day or hour, not even the angels in heaven, nor the Son, but only the Father. 33Be on guard! Be alert[f]! You do not know when that time will come. 34It's like a man going away: He leaves his house and puts his servants in charge, each with his assigned task, and tells the one at the door to keep watch. Mt 25:14

35"Therefore keep watch because you do not know when the owner of the house will come back—whether in the evening, or at midnight, or when the rooster crows, or at dawn. 36If he comes suddenly, do not let him find you sleeping. 37What I say to you, I say to everyone: 'Watch!'"

Jesus Anointed at Bethany

▶ *See Matthew 26:2–16; Luke 22:1–6*

14 Now the Passover and the Feast of Unleavened Bread were only two days away, and the chief priests and the teachers of the law were looking for some sly way to arrest Jesus and kill him. 2"But not during the Feast," they said, "or the people may riot." Mt 12:14; Jn 11:55; 13:1

3While he was in Bethany, reclining at the table in the home of a man known as Simon the Leper, a woman came with an alabaster jar of very expensive perfume, made of pure nard. She broke the jar and poured the perfume on his head. Mt 21:17

4Some of those present were saying indignantly to one another, "Why this waste of perfume? 5It could have been sold for more than a year's wages[g] and the money given to the poor." And they rebuked her harshly.

6"Leave her alone," said Jesus. "Why are you bothering her? She has done a beautiful thing to me. 7The poor you will always have with you, and you can help them any time you want. But you will not always have me. 8She did what she could. She poured perfume on my body beforehand to prepare for my burial. 9I tell you the truth, wherever the gospel is preached throughout the world, what she has done will also be told, in memory of her."

10Then Judas Iscariot, one of the Twelve, went to the chief priests to betray Jesus to them. 11They were delighted to hear this and promised to give

[a] 14 Daniel 9:27; 11:31; 12:11 [b] 14 Or *he*; also in verse 29 [c] 21 Or *Messiah* [d] 25 Isaiah 13:10; 34:4 [e] 30 Or *race*
[f] 33 Some manuscripts *alert and pray* [g] 5 Greek *than three hundred denarii*

him money. So he watched for an opportunity to
hand him over. Mt 26:2-16; Lk 22:1-6

The Lord's Supper

▶ *See Matthew 26:17–30; Luke 22:7–23*

[12]On the first day of the Feast of Unleavened
Bread, when it was customary to sacrifice the Passover lamb, Jesus' disciples asked him, "Where do
you want us to go and make preparations for you
to eat the Passover?" Ex 12:1-11; Dt 16:1-4; 1Co 5:7
[13]So he sent two of his disciples, telling them,
"Go into the city, and a man carrying a jar of water
will meet you. Follow him. [14]Say to the owner of
the house he enters, 'The Teacher asks: Where is
my guest room, where I may eat the Passover with
my disciples?' [15]He will show you a large upper
room, furnished and ready. Make preparations for
us there." Ac 1:13
[16]The disciples left, went into the city and found
things just as Jesus had told them. So they prepared the Passover.
[17]When evening came, Jesus arrived with the
Twelve. [18]While they were reclining at the table
eating, he said, "I tell you the truth, one of you will
betray me—one who is eating with me."
[19]They were saddened, and one by one they said
to him, "Surely not I?"
[20]"It is one of the Twelve," he replied, "one who
dips bread into the bowl with me. [21]The Son of
Man will go just as it is written about him. But woe
to that man who betrays the Son of Man! It would
be better for him if he had not been born."
[22]While they were eating, Jesus took bread, gave
thanks and broke it, and gave it to his disciples,
saying, "Take it; this is my body." Mt 14:19
[23]Then he took the cup, gave thanks and offered
it to them, and they all drank from it. 1Co 10:16
[24]"This is my blood of the[a] covenant, which is
poured out for many," he said to them. [25]"I tell
you the truth, I will not drink again of the fruit of
the vine until that day when I drink it anew in the
kingdom of God." 1Co 11:23-25
[26]When they had sung a hymn, they went out to
the Mount of Olives. Mt 26:17-30; Lk 22:7-23

Jesus Predicts Peter's Denial

▶ *See Matthew 26:31–35*

[27]"You will all fall away," Jesus told them, "for
it is written:

[a]24 Some manuscripts *the new*

THE LAST WEEK OF JESUS

Event	Place	Day of the Week	Matthew	Mark	Luke	John
The triumphal entry	Jerusalem	Sunday	*21:1-11*	*11:1-11*	*19:29-44*	*12:12-19*
Jesus curses the fig tree	Jerusalem	Monday	*21:18-22*	*11:12-14*		
Jesus clears the temple	Jerusalem	Monday	*21:12-13*	*11:15-18*	*19:45-48*	
The authority of Jesus questioned	Jerusalem	Tuesday	*21:23-27*	*11:27-33*	*20:1-8*	
Jesus teaches in the temple	Jerusalem	Tuesday	*21:28–23:39*	*12:1-44*	*20:9–21:4*	
Jesus' feet anointed	Bethany	Tuesday	*26:6-13*	*14:3-9*		*12:2-11*
The plot against Jesus	Jerusalem	Wednesday	*26:14-16*	*14:10-11*	*22:3-6*	
The Last Supper	Jerusalem	Thursday	*26:17-29*	*14:12-25*	*22:7-38*	*13:1-38*
Jesus comforts His disciples	Jerusalem	Thursday				*14:1–16:33*
Jesus' high priestly prayer	Jerusalem	Thursday				*17:1-26*
Gethsemane	Jerusalem	Thursday	*26:36-46*	*14:32-42*	*22:40-46*	
Jesus' arrest and trial	Jerusalem	Friday	*26:47–27:26*	*14:43–15:15*	*22:47–23:25*	*18:2–19:16*
Jesus' crucifixion and death	Golgotha	Friday	*27:27-56*	*15:16-41*	*23:26-49*	*19:17-37*
Jesus' burial	Garden tomb	Friday	*27:57-66*	*15:42-47*	*23:50-56*	*19:38-42*

"'I will strike the shepherd,
and the sheep will be scattered.'[a]

28But after I have risen, I will go ahead of you into Galilee." Mk 16:7

29Peter declared, "Even if all fall away, I will not."

30"I tell you the truth," Jesus answered, "today—yes, tonight—before the rooster crows twice[b] you yourself will disown me three times."

31But Peter insisted emphatically, "Even if I have to die with you, I will never disown you." And all the others said the same. Mt 26:31-35

Gethsemane

▶ *See Matthew 26:36–46; Luke 22:40–46*

32They went to a place called Gethsemane, and Jesus said to his disciples, "Sit here while I pray." 33He took Peter, James and John along with him, and he began to be deeply distressed and troubled. 34"My soul is overwhelmed with sorrow to the point of death," he said to them. "Stay here and keep watch." Jn 12:27

35Going a little farther, he fell to the ground and prayed that if possible the hour might pass from him. 36"*Abba*,[c] Father," he said, "everything is possible for you. Take this cup from me. Yet not what I will, but what you will." Mt 26:39; Ro 8:15

LIVING  INSIGHT

Real prayer—the kind of prayer Jesus mentioned and modeled—is realistic, spontaneous, down-to-earth communication with the living Lord that results in a relief of personal anxiety and a calm assurance that our God is in full control of our circumstances.

(See Mark 14:32–36.)

37Then he returned to his disciples and found them sleeping. "Simon," he said to Peter, "are you asleep? Could you not keep watch for one hour? 38Watch and pray so that you will not fall into temptation. The spirit is willing, but the body is weak." Mt 6:13; Ro 7:22-23

39Once more he went away and prayed the same thing. 40When he came back, he again found them sleeping, because their eyes were heavy. They did not know what to say to him.

41Returning the third time, he said to them, "Are you still sleeping and resting? Enough! The hour has come. Look, the Son of Man is betrayed into the hands of sinners. 42Rise! Let us go! Here comes my betrayer!" Mt 26:36-46; Lk 22:40-46

Jesus Arrested

▶ *See Matthew 26:47–56; Luke 22:47–50; John 18:3–11*

43Just as he was speaking, Judas, one of the Twelve, appeared. With him was a crowd armed with swords and clubs, sent from the chief priests, the teachers of the law, and the elders. Mt 10:4

44Now the betrayer had arranged a signal with them: "The one I kiss is the man; arrest him and lead him away under guard." 45Going at once to Jesus, Judas said, "Rabbi!" and kissed him. 46The men seized Jesus and arrested him. 47Then one of those standing near drew his sword and struck the servant of the high priest, cutting off his ear.

48"Am I leading a rebellion," said Jesus, "that you have come out with swords and clubs to capture me? 49Every day I was with you, teaching in the temple courts, and you did not arrest me. But the Scriptures must be fulfilled." 50Then everyone deserted him and fled. Mt 26:47-56; Lk 22:47-50; Jn 18:3-11

51A young man, wearing nothing but a linen garment, was following Jesus. When they seized him, 52he fled naked, leaving his garment behind.

Before the Sanhedrin

▶ *See Matthew 26:57–68; John 18:12–13,19–24*

53They took Jesus to the high priest, and all the chief priests, elders and teachers of the law came together. 54Peter followed him at a distance, right into the courtyard of the high priest. There he sat with the guards and warmed himself at the fire.

55The chief priests and the whole Sanhedrin were looking for evidence against Jesus so that they could put him to death, but they did not find any. 56Many testified falsely against him, but their statements did not agree. Mt 5:22

57Then some stood up and gave this false testimony against him: 58"We heard him say, 'I will destroy this man-made temple and in three days will build another, not made by man.'" 59Yet even then their testimony did not agree. Mk 15:29; Jn 2:19

60Then the high priest stood up before them and asked Jesus, "Are you not going to answer? What is this testimony that these men are bringing against you?" 61But Jesus remained silent and gave no answer. Isa 53:7; Mt 27:12,14

Again the high priest asked him, "Are you the Christ,[d] the Son of the Blessed One?" Mt 16:16

62"I am," said Jesus. "And you will see the Son of Man sitting at the right hand of the Mighty One and coming on the clouds of heaven." Rev 1:7

63The high priest tore his clothes. "Why do we need any more witnesses?" he asked. 64"You have heard the blasphemy. What do you think?"

They all condemned him as worthy of death. 65Then some began to spit at him; they blindfolded

[a] *27* Zech. 13:7 [b] *30* Some early manuscripts do not have *twice.* [c] *36* Aramaic for *Father* [d] *61* Or *Messiah*

him, struck him with their fists, and said, "Prophesy!" And the guards took him and beat him.

Peter Disowns Jesus

▶ *See Matthew 26:69–75; Luke 22:56–62; John 18:16–18,25–27*

66While Peter was below in the courtyard, one of the servant girls of the high priest came by. 67When she saw Peter warming himself, she looked closely at him. ver 54

"You also were with that Nazarene, Jesus," she said. Mk 1:24

68But he denied it. "I don't know or understand what you're talking about," he said, and went out into the entryway.[a]

69When the servant girl saw him there, she said again to those standing around, "This fellow is one of them." 70Again he denied it.

After a little while, those standing near said to Peter, "Surely you are one of them, for you are a Galilean." Ac 2:7

71He began to call down curses on himself, and he swore to them, "I don't know this man you're talking about."

72Immediately the rooster crowed the second time.[b] Then Peter remembered the word Jesus had spoken to him: "Before the rooster crows twice[c] you will disown me three times." And he broke down and wept. Mt 26:69-75; Lk 22:56-62

Jesus Before Pilate

▶ *See Matthew 27:11–26; Luke 23:2–3,18–25; John 18:29—19:16*

15 Very early in the morning, the chief priests, with the elders, the teachers of the law and the whole Sanhedrin, reached a decision. They bound Jesus, led him away and handed him over to Pilate. Mt 27:1-2

2"Are you the king of the Jews?" asked Pilate.

"Yes, it is as you say," Jesus replied.

3The chief priests accused him of many things. 4So again Pilate asked him, "Aren't you going to answer? See how many things they are accusing you of."

5But Jesus still made no reply, and Pilate was amazed. Mk 14:61

6Now it was the custom at the Feast to release a prisoner whom the people requested. 7A man called Barabbas was in prison with the insurrectionists who had committed murder in the uprising. 8The crowd came up and asked Pilate to do for them what he usually did.

9"Do you want me to release to you the king of the Jews?" asked Pilate, 10knowing it was out of envy that the chief priests had handed Jesus over to him. 11But the chief priests stirred up the crowd to have Pilate release Barabbas instead. Ac 3:14

12"What shall I do, then, with the one you call the king of the Jews?" Pilate asked them.

13"Crucify him!" they shouted.

14"Why? What crime has he committed?" asked Pilate.

But they shouted all the louder, "Crucify him!"

15Wanting to satisfy the crowd, Pilate released Barabbas to them. He had Jesus flogged, and handed him over to be crucified. Mt 27:11-26

The Soldiers Mock Jesus

▶ *See Matthew 27:27–31*

16The soldiers led Jesus away into the palace (that is, the Praetorium) and called together the whole company of soldiers. 17They put a purple robe on him, then twisted together a crown of thorns and set it on him. 18And they began to call out to him, "Hail, king of the Jews!" 19Again and again they struck him on the head with a staff and spit on him. Falling on their knees, they paid homage to him. 20And when they had mocked him, they took off the purple robe and put his own clothes on him. Then they led him out to crucify him. Mt 27:27-31; Heb 13:12

The Crucifixion

▶ *See Matthew 27:33–44; Luke 23:33–43; John 19:17–24*

21A certain man from Cyrene, Simon, the father of Alexander and Rufus, was passing by on his way in from the country, and they forced him to carry the cross. 22They brought Jesus to the place called Golgotha (which means The Place of the Skull). 23Then they offered him wine mixed with myrrh, but he did not take it. 24And they crucified him. Dividing up his clothes, they cast lots to see what each would get. Ps 22:18; Lk 23:26

25It was the third hour when they crucified him. 26The written notice of the charge against him read: THE KING OF THE JEWS. 27They crucified two robbers with him, one on his right and one on his left.[d] 29Those who passed by hurled insults at him, shaking their heads and saying, "So! You who are going to destroy the temple and build it in three days, 30come down from the cross and save yourself!" Mk 14:58; Jn 2:19

31In the same way the chief priests and the teachers of the law mocked him among themselves. "He saved others," they said, "but he can't save himself! 32Let this Christ,[e] this King of Israel, come down now from the cross, that we may see and believe." Those crucified with him also heaped insults on him. Mt 27:33-44; Lk 23:33-43; Jn 19:17-24

[a] 68 Some early manuscripts *entryway and the rooster crowed*
[b] 72 Some early manuscripts do not have *the second time.*
[c] 72 Some early manuscripts do not have *twice.*
[d] 27 Some manuscripts *left, 28and the scripture was fulfilled which says, "He was counted with the lawless ones"* (Isaiah 53:12)
[e] 32 Or *Messiah*

The Death of Jesus

▶ *See Matthew 27:45–56; Luke 23:44–49*

33At the sixth hour darkness came over the whole land until the ninth hour. 34And at the ninth hour Jesus cried out in a loud voice, *"Eloi, Eloi, lama sabachthani?"*—which means, "My God, my God, why have you forsaken me?"[a] Am 8:9

35When some of those standing near heard this, they said, "Listen, he's calling Elijah."

36One man ran, filled a sponge with wine vinegar, put it on a stick, and offered it to Jesus to drink. "Now leave him alone. Let's see if Elijah comes to take him down," he said. Ps 69:21

37With a loud cry, Jesus breathed his last.

LIVING  **INSIGHT**

It was on the cross, at one awful moment, Jesus Christ bore our sins, thus satisfying the righteous demands of the Father, completely and instantaneously clearing up our debt. Our sin is forgiven. Our enslavement is broken. We are set free from sin's penalty and sin's power once and for all.

(See Mark 15:37.)

38The curtain of the temple was torn in two from top to bottom. 39And when the centurion, who stood there in front of Jesus, heard his cry and[b] saw how he died, he said, "Surely this man was the Son[c] of God!" Mt 4:3; Heb 10:19-20

40Some women were watching from a distance. Among them were Mary Magdalene, Mary the mother of James the younger and of Joses, and Salome. 41In Galilee these women had followed him and cared for his needs. Many other women who had come up with him to Jerusalem were also there. Mt 27:45-46; Lk 23:44-49

The Burial of Jesus

▶ *See Matthew 27:57–61; Luke 23:50–56; John 19:38–42*

42It was Preparation Day (that is, the day before the Sabbath). So as evening approached, 43Joseph of Arimathea, a prominent member of the Council, who was himself waiting for the kingdom of God, went boldly to Pilate and asked for Jesus' body. 44Pilate was surprised to hear that he was already dead. Summoning the centurion, he asked him if Jesus had already died. 45When he learned from the centurion that it was so, he gave the body to Joseph. 46So Joseph bought some linen cloth, took down the body, wrapped it in the linen, and placed it in a tomb cut out of rock. Then he rolled a stone against the entrance of the tomb. 47Mary Magdalene and Mary the mother of Joses saw where he was laid. Mt 27:57-61; Lk 23:50-56; Jn 19:38-42

The Resurrection

▶ *See Matthew 28:1–8; Luke 24:1–10*

16 When the Sabbath was over, Mary Magdalene, Mary the mother of James, and Salome bought spices so that they might go to anoint Jesus' body. 2Very early on the first day of the week, just after sunrise, they were on their way to the tomb 3and they asked each other, "Who will roll the stone away from the entrance of the tomb?" Mk 15:46; Lk 23:56; Jn 19:39-40

4But when they looked up, they saw that the stone, which was very large, had been rolled away. 5As they entered the tomb, they saw a young man dressed in a white robe sitting on the right side, and they were alarmed. Jn 20:12

LIVING  **INSIGHT**

When God is involved, anything can happen. The One who directed that stone in between Goliath's eyes and split the Red Sea down the middle and leveled that wall around Jericho and brought His Son out of the tomb takes a delight in mixing up the odds as He alters the obvious and bypasses the inevitable.

(See Mark 16:4.)

6"Don't be alarmed," he said. "You are looking for Jesus the Nazarene, who was crucified. He has risen! He is not here. See the place where they laid him. 7But go, tell his disciples and Peter, 'He is going ahead of you into Galilee. There you will see him, just as he told you.'" Mk 1:24; 14:28

8Trembling and bewildered, the women went out and fled from the tomb. They said nothing to anyone, because they were afraid.

[The earliest manuscripts and some other ancient witnesses do not have Mark 16:9–20.]

9When Jesus rose early on the first day of the week, he appeared first to Mary Magdalene, out of whom he had driven seven demons. 10She went and told those who had been with him and who were mourning and weeping. 11When they heard that Jesus was alive and that she had seen him, they did not believe it. Lk 24:11; Jn 20:11-18

[a] 34 Psalm 22:1 [b] 39 Some manuscripts do not have *heard his cry and* [c] 39 Or *a son*

12Afterward Jesus appeared in a different form
to two of them while they were walking in the
country. 13These returned and reported it to the
rest; but they did not believe them either.
14Later Jesus appeared to the Eleven as they
were eating; he rebuked them for their lack of faith
and their stubborn refusal to believe those who
had seen him after he had risen. Lk 24:36-43
15He said to them, "Go into all the world and
preach the good news to all creation. 16Whoever
believes and is baptized will be saved, but whoever
does not believe will be condemned. 17And these
signs will accompany those who believe: In my
name they will drive out demons; they will speak
in new tongues; 18they will pick up snakes with
their hands; and when they drink deadly poison, it
will not hurt them at all; they will place their hands
on sick people, and they will get well." Mt 28:18-20
19After the Lord Jesus had spoken to them, he
was taken up into heaven and he sat at the right
hand of God. 20Then the disciples went out and
preached everywhere, and the Lord worked with
them and confirmed his word by the signs that
accompanied it. Lk 24:50-51; Ps 110:1

INTRODUCTION

LUKE

Doctor Luke, the apostle Paul's companion on his missionary journeys (see Colossians 4:14), was probably the only Gentile writer of any portion of the New Testament. According to Merrill Tenney, Luke's Gospel is "the most complete account of the life of Jesus that has survived from the apostolic age." Certainly none of the other three Gospel writers give us a more detailed or descriptive analysis of the Savior's birth, childhood and manhood. Writing to a Greek audience, the physician reveals his own distinctive concerns by showing an uncommon interest in various individuals, displaying an unusual emphasis on medical matters, giving a prominent place to women in his account and emphasizing the humanity of Jesus. As we might expect, Luke is extremely careful in both his research and the documentation of his facts. Luke's Gospel is the most scholarly of the four. His keen interest in Jesus' teachings provides us with a wealth of insight into the scenes and settings of Jesus' many parables.

WRITER: *Luke*

DATE: *c.A.D. 59–63*

KEY MESSAGE: *Jesus is truly human*

KEY VERSE: *19:10*

KEY TERM: *"The Son of Man"*

STYLE: *Scholarly, detailed, people-oriented*

APPEAL: *Directly to Greeks, but universal*

DISTINCTIVES: *Only Gospel addressed to an individual; over thirty sayings, parables and events mentioned nowhere else*

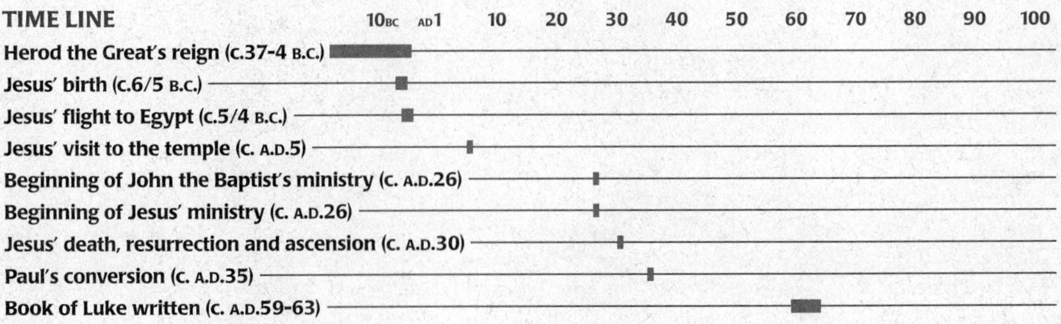

The Physician's Opinion

THE SON OF MAN . . .

Unique Introduction	. . . Announced and appearing	. . . Ministering and serving	. . . Instructing and submitting	. . . Resurrected and commissioning
	About 90 percent unique to Luke		About 60 percent unique to Luke	
	"Jesus of Nazareth . . . a prophet,	*"powerful in . . . deed . . .*	*"powerful in word . . . before God and all the people" (24:19).*	
CHAPTER 1:1-4	***CHAPTERS 1:5–4:13***	***CHAPTERS 4:14–9:50***	***CHAPTERS 9:51–23:56***	***CHAPTER 24***

KEY VERSE	***"For the Son of Man came to seek and to save what was lost" (19:10).***				
ACTIVITY	**Coming**	**Seeking**		**Saving**	
LOCATION	**Bethlehem, Nazareth and Judea**	**Galilee**	**Judea and Perea**	**Jerusalem**	
TIME	**30 years**	**1½ years**	**6 months**	**8 days**	**50 days**

Many students of the Bible call the Gospel of Luke the most scholarly work in all the New Testament. The man who wrote it had the mind of a scientist (he was a physician) and the heart of an artist. He is the only known Gentile writer of Scripture, and therefore his words appeal to those of us who are of Gentile origin, and especially to those who love details.

Our world is filled with perfectionists. It's always interesting to meet up with them and to observe how they respond to life. It is equally interesting to come across a book written by such a person. These books are typically characterized by great attention to details. It is obvious that Luke really cared about the nuts and bolts, the shadings, the fine-line issues of his subject. One might safely suspect that Luke was a perfectionist.

Bible commentator William Barclay wrote, "First and foremost, Luke's Gospel is an exceedingly careful bit of work. His Greek is notably good. The first four verses are well-nigh the best Greek in the New Testament." Look at how Luke introduced his Gospel:

> *Many have undertaken to draw up an account of the things that have been fulfilled among us, just as they were handed down to us by those who from the first were eyewitnesses and servants of the word. Therefore, since I myself have carefully investigated everything from the beginning, it seemed good also to me to write an orderly account for you, most excellent Theophilus, so that you may know the certainty of the things you have been taught.*

The words certainly sound like the writing of a perfectionist, don't they? Did you catch Luke's turn of phrase on several occasions? He stated clearly how he had "carefully investigated everything from the beginning," and he planned to write "an orderly account." He wanted to present the information so that everyone who read his words would know the "certainty of the things you have been taught."

Nothing New Under the Sun

Luke never claimed he was the first person to present information about the life of Jesus, the Messiah. He clearly stated that others had written before him; in his research he studied some of their material in preparation for the writing of this book that now bears his name. Luke illustrates the truth that a scholarly work is rarely a completely original work. In fact, some of the best works of scholarship have drawn from many different sources and put it all together in fresh and helpful ways. One of my seminary professors used to say, "I doubt you or I will ever read again a totally original piece of work." I have found it to be the case that many other writers and teachers have so affected us that it's virtually impossible not to bring what we have learned from others into what we ourselves are presenting.

Meeting Luke

Luke may have been a perfectionist, but he was certainly not dull or predictable or emotionless. Some have concluded that he was the most interesting of the four Gospel writers. Luke was a well-educated Greek. He probably studied in the schools of Tarsus, as did Paul (see Acts 22:3) and quite likely Apollos. (One commentator has suggested that these three men could have been fellow students at the same school. Isn't that an interesting thought?)

Luke and Paul were very likely good friends. In Colossians 4:14 Paul called him "our dear friend Luke, the doctor," so we know that Luke was more than a passing acquaintance of Paul. In Paul's letter to Philemon, he called Luke "a fellow worker" (Philemon 24). And Paul, writing to Timothy from prison in Rome, stated that "only Luke is with me" (2 Timothy 4:11). Luke was a brilliant and faithful man known intimately by Paul and believed by many to be Paul's personal physician and his companion at various times on the missionary journeys.

Luke was first mentioned in the Bible in Acts 16, and it is at that point in the narrative of Acts (16:10) that we find periodic sections marked by the words "we" or "our." At these points the author included himself as Paul's companion, as he signaled that he was present with Paul at the particular events described in the "we" sections.

A Warm and Sensitive Style

Luke's style is extremely appealing and interesting. He was a gifted writer who recorded such memorable stories as the Good Samaritan, the Prodigal (Lost) Son, and the Rich Man and Lazarus. It is clear that he was a master of character descriptions. His writing exuded a warm and sensitive understanding of Jesus and those around Him. And as I observed earlier, he paid exceptionally careful attention to detail. From reading the four verses that open his book, we understand that this man had done his homework, and therefore his account could be trusted.

Luke did not include much in the way of Hebrew prophecies. As I read Luke I can't find even ten Old Testament prophecies cited. In contrast, Matthew's Gospel was filled with them—over 50 in total. But as a Gentile writing to a predominantly Greek audience, most of whom had limited interest in and knowledge of the Old Testament, Luke didn't need to refer to a lot of Old Testament predictions.

Neither did Luke use many Hebrew or Aramaic words. In fact, unlike the other three Gospel writers, in his telling of the crucifixion story (23:33), Luke didn't use the word *Golgotha*, an Aramaic term. Instead he used the Greek term *kranion*, from which we get our English word "cranium," or "skull." The Bible calls Golgotha "the Place of the Skull"—and it is translated as such in Luke's Gospel. Typically Luke used language familiar to the Greek mind.

Luke's Story

I would suggest that Luke 19:10 is the key verse of this Gospel. Here the entire message of the book is capsulized: "For the Son of Man came to seek and to save what was lost." Note Luke's favorite title for Jesus: "Son of Man." Jesus, fully divine—by all means! And fully human—absolutely! He is the One sent by the Father into this world to take on human flesh. Why? For what purpose? "To seek and to save what was lost."

The early chapters of Luke (1–3) record the *coming* of Jesus into the world. Chapters 4–19 give the account of Jesus' ministry in Galilee, Judea and Perea—a word-and-deed ministry of *seeking* the lost and the hurting. And chapters 20–24 tell of the events leading up to and including Jesus' death, resurrection and ascension, as He fulfilled His great mission of *saving* sinful people through His sacrificial death on the cross.

The Stories of Luke

What I have found especially interesting in my study of Luke is that there are over thirty sayings, parables, stories and scenes found between chapters 9 and 19 that are recorded nowhere else in the Bible. When you have a storehouse like this, you have a treasured document! And because Luke was a man of great warmth and sensitivity and unbending commitment to accurate detail, he painted these scenes in such a way that brings them to life so vividly for us today.

In chapter 2, for example, Luke gave us information found nowhere else regarding the details of the Lord's birth. Most of the events in this Gospel relating to the birth and childhood of the Savior are unique to Luke. What Christmas season would be complete without the reading of Luke 2:1–15? What church school class has not taken the nativity scene right out of Luke and lived it out in bathrobes and thongs again and again, year after year? All the way through this account we come face to face with the humanity of our Lord. In Luke we get an unforgettable glimpse of our Savior, the Lord Jesus Christ, as a human being.

Think too of what emotion, sympathy and compassion flow through parables like the Good Samaritan (chapter 10), the Lost Coin (chapter 15), the Lost Son (chapter 15), the Rich Man and Lazarus (chapter 16), the Persistent Widow (chapter 18) and the Pharisee and the Tax Collector (chapter 18). Think of the power evoked as Jesus read Isaiah's prophecy of the Messiah's ministry of preaching and healing (chapter 4). Think of Jesus' response to a worried and upset Martha (chapter 10) and His stinging rebuke that silenced a small-minded synagogue ruler who protested when Jesus healed a crippled woman on the Sabbath (chapter 13). And it is only in this Gospel that we read the beautiful story of Jesus' grace extended to a man named Zacchaeus (chapter 19)—and witness Jesus looking out over Jerusalem and bursting into tears (19:41–44). What a wealth of knowledge we would be missing if we did not have this precious Gospel of Luke!

Lessons From Luke

Luke provides us with so much to ponder and to apply to our lives. Let me note two crucial areas. First, I see significance in Luke's emphasis on Jesus' prayer life, as he reminded us that Jesus took prayer with utmost seriousness. From Luke we learn that Jesus needed to spend time with His Father and pour out His heart in prayer (see, for example, 5:16; 6:12; 11:1). Has your prayer life diminished in recent days? Finding yourself just too busy? I know—involved in good things, important things, high-priority things, valuable things. Maybe the Lord is calling you back right now to a new sense of communing with Him—to gaining a new purpose and power as you come into His presence in prayer. *Let's learn from Jesus' example and become, first and foremost, people of prayer.*

Second, on numerous occasions *Jesus cared about and struggled with the hurts of people.* In chapter 4 Jesus stated directly that God had sent Him to bring healing (4:18). Later Jesus rebuked the "high fever" of Simon Peter's mother-in-law (4:38). In chapter 5 Jesus reached out to heal a man who was "covered with leprosy" (5:12). A man who was paralyzed found forgiveness and healing from Jesus (5:20,24). In chapter 7 a centurion's servant who was "sick and about to die" (7:2) had his life restored at Jesus' command. (Only a physician could tell it with such detail.) In chapter 13 Jesus healed a woman crippled for 18 years who was so affected that she was bent over . . . unable to straighten up because of a demonic attack (13:10–13). In chapter 22 a lopped-off ear suddenly, miraculously, became reattached through Jesus' healing power (22:51). Why do I take time for this kind of detail? Because it is so important to see that Jesus, in all of the momentous activity of what the Father had sent Him into the world to do, saw specific needs in people. In each case, Jesus reached out and touched those who were in need. As our "Great Physician," He is moved over the things with which we struggle. He feels the pain. He cares.

Thanks to Luke

We should be eternally grateful to Luke for four reasons. First of all, *Luke provides a trustworthy account of the life of Jesus.* Luke clearly demonstrated a commitment to thoroughness and detail, through his careful presentation of the facts. That makes me feel secure, and it can make you feel secure too.

Second, *Luke provides a realistic portrait of Jesus' humanity.* In Luke we see a beautiful picture of the Son of God who took on our human flesh, who experienced all that we experience as human beings (with the exception of sin—see Hebrews 4:15). We see that Jesus cares about our needs and hurts. We realize that we can draw near to Him, because He knows how we feel. Luke shows us that our need for identity can finally be met only in a relationship with the One who came to us to bring us back to Him. What joy there is to know that He understands us completely!

Third, *Luke provides a comforting record of mercy and compassion for the unloved and unaccepted.* He shows us that just as our need for identity is met in a relationship with Jesus, so it is with our need for acceptance. Time and again you'll find Jesus extending compassion to people, and as they experienced Jesus' acceptance, so you'll find yourself feeling accepted. Luke reminds us that our Savior cares for us tenderly like a parent whose heart breaks for a suffering child. What delight there is to know that He accepts us completely and loves us tenderly!

Fourth and finally, *Luke provides an orderly and complete account of Jesus' earthly mission to save the lost that culminates in His death, resurrection and ascension.* He points us to the sacrifice of Jesus that covers all our sins through His death on the cross. Luke shows that our need for forgiveness was met by Jesus, who was delivered to death for our sins, so that we might be declared righteous in Him. What bliss there is to know that our sins have been nailed to the cross, and we bear them no more—all praise and thanks to our Savior, Jesus Christ, in whom there is forgiveness of sins!

Thank God for the Gospel of Luke. In this account of the life of Jesus we find security, identity, acceptance and forgiveness. Luke offers us an intimate look at a Savior we can approach with confidence, knowing that He will embrace us with love and shower us with grace.

Arrival of Jesus — Chapters 1:1–4:13

In this opening section we read of the coming of the Son of Man—Jesus, the Messiah. Luke has more information about the events leading up to Jesus Christ's birth and the actual birth than any other Gospel writer. As a matter of fact, almost ninety percent of the material covered in this section is unique to the Gospel of Luke. This portion of the narrative takes place in Bethlehem, Nazareth and Judea, and it spans about thirty years—from before Jesus' birth to the temptation in the desert. As this section ends, Jesus was thirty years old and ready to enter His public ministry (3:23).

Introduction

1 Many have undertaken to draw up an account of the things that have been fulfilled[a] among us, 2just as they were handed down to us by those who from the first were eyewitnesses and servants of the word. 3Therefore, since I myself have carefully investigated everything from the beginning, it seemed good also to me to write an orderly account for you, most excellent Theophilus, 4so that you may know the certainty of the things you have been taught. Ac 1:1; 11:4; Heb 2:3

The Birth of John the Baptist Foretold

5In the time of Herod king of Judea there was a priest named Zechariah, who belonged to the priestly division of Abijah; his wife Elizabeth was also a descendant of Aaron. 6Both of them were upright in the sight of God, observing all the Lord's commandments and regulations blamelessly. 7But they had no children, because Elizabeth was barren; and they were both well along in years.

8Once when Zechariah's division was on duty and he was serving as priest before God, 9he was chosen by lot, according to the custom of the priesthood, to go into the temple of the Lord and burn incense. 10And when the time for the burning of incense came, all the assembled worshipers were praying outside. Ex 30:7-8; Lev 16:17; 1Ch 24:19

11Then an angel of the Lord appeared to him, standing at the right side of the altar of incense. 12When Zechariah saw him, he was startled and was gripped with fear. 13But the angel said to him: "Do not be afraid, Zechariah; your prayer has been heard. Your wife Elizabeth will bear you a son, and you are to give him the name John. 14He will be a joy and delight to you, and many will rejoice because of his birth, 15for he will be great in the sight of the Lord. He is never to take wine or other fermented drink, and he will be filled with the Holy Spirit even from birth.[b] 16Many of the people of Israel will he bring back to the Lord their God. 17And he will go on before the Lord, in the spirit and power of Elijah, to turn the hearts of the fathers to their children and the disobedient to the wisdom of the righteous—to make ready a people prepared for the Lord." Jer 1:5; Mt 11:14

18Zechariah asked the angel, "How can I be sure of this? I am an old man and my wife is well along in years." Ge 17:17

19The angel answered, "I am Gabriel. I stand in the presence of God, and I have been sent to speak to you and to tell you this good news. 20And now you will be silent and not able to speak until the day this happens, because you did not believe my words, which will come true at their proper time."

21Meanwhile, the people were waiting for Zechariah and wondering why he stayed so long in the temple. 22When he came out, he could not speak to them. They realized he had seen a vision in the temple, for he kept making signs to them but remained unable to speak.

23When his time of service was completed, he returned home. 24After this his wife Elizabeth became pregnant and for five months remained in seclusion. 25"The Lord has done this for me," she said. "In these days he has shown his favor and taken away my disgrace among the people."

The Birth of Jesus Foretold

26In the sixth month, God sent the angel Gabriel to Nazareth, a town in Galilee, 27to a virgin pledged to be married to a man named Joseph, a descendant of David. The virgin's name was Mary. 28The angel went to her and said, "Greetings, you who are highly favored! The Lord is with you."

29Mary was greatly troubled at his words and wondered what kind of greeting this might be. 30But the angel said to her, "Do not be afraid, Mary, you have found favor with God. 31You will be with child and give birth to a son, and you are to give him the name Jesus. 32He will be great and will be called the Son of the Most High. The Lord God will give him the throne of his father David, 33and he will reign over the house of Jacob forever; his kingdom will never end." Da 2:44; 7:14,27; Mic 4:7

34"How will this be," Mary asked the angel, "since I am a virgin?"

35The angel answered, "The Holy Spirit will come upon you, and the power of the Most High will overshadow you. So the holy one to be born will be called[c] the Son of God. 36Even Elizabeth your relative is going to have a child in her old age, and she who was said to be barren is in her sixth month. 37For nothing is impossible with God."

38"I am the Lord's servant," Mary answered. "May it be to me as you have said." Then the angel left her.

Mary Visits Elizabeth

39At that time Mary got ready and hurried to a town in the hill country of Judea, 40where she en-

[a] 1 Or *been surely believed* [b] 15 Or *from his mother's womb* [c] 35 Or *So the child to be born will be called holy,*

MARY

God's Chosen Instrument

" 'I am the Lord's servant,' Mary answered. 'May it be to me as you have said.' "

—LUKE 1:38

What must it have been like for Mary that day long ago when an angel suddenly showed up? "Greetings, you who are highly favored! The Lord is with you" (Luke 1:28). A rather simple approach, on the one hand. "Greetings. Hello, Mary. This is your special day." And yet not unlike a bolt of lightning out of a clear blue sky! "Have I got news for you, Mary! Your life is about to forever change. But don't worry, Mary. The Lord is with you. He'll never leave you." Can you imagine?

As Luke's account begins in verse 26 of chapter 1, Mary was betrothed to a man named Joseph. She was a young teenager at the time; he was very likely a few years older. Their marriage had been arranged by the parents of this young couple. Even though the marriage ceremony had not taken place, Mary and Joseph were legally bound together and could not be separated except by divorce. For Mary to become pregnant during this phase in the relationship would be scandalous. But it was at this point in her life that the angel appeared with his startling message.

The angel's first words to Mary troubled her (1:29), but not because she didn't believe. All kinds of thoughts must have been racing through her mind. What could he possibly mean: "The Lord is with you." As a devout Jew, Mary knew that God was with her and her people, even in the midst of Roman rule. We might think of Mary as saying, in today's language, "I know the Lord is with me, but exactly what are you getting at?" Notice here that *God* was the One who was active in this passage and *Mary* was the one who was passive. She was the recipient of God's grace, the one selected by God to help carry out His purposes and execute His plan through the promised Messiah, God's one and only Son.

After dispelling Mary's fear and assuring her of the Lord's favor, the angel next directly addressed the coming of the Messiah, the One for whom Mary and her people had been waiting for ages. Mary's questioning response wasn't one of disbelief, but rather one of wonder: " 'How will this be,' Mary asked the angel, 'since I am a virgin?' " (1:34). The words that follow contain the greatest statement about the virgin birth that we find in all of Scripture: "The Holy Spirit will come upon you, and the power of the Most High will overshadow you. So the holy one to be born will be called the Son of God" (1:35).

In carrying out His great redemptive plan, God could have chosen one of four options. First, He could have sent a mighty angel and given him the form of a man, but that individual would not have been truly human. Second, He could have provided a remarkably gifted individual with a wonderful set of parents who would raise their young boy in the ways of self-sacrifice, but that boy would not then have been truly divine. Third, He could have inhabited the form of a godly individual on this earth and called that person the Son of God, but this confusing mixture of human and divine would not then have been genuine. The only thing that would have worked—a stroke of divine genius—was the virgin birth. Because Jesus was born of a woman, He was fully human; because He was conceived by the Holy Spirit, He had no sin; He was at the same time fully God. Don't ever let anyone tell you that the virgin birth isn't important!

At the angel's message, Mary was stunned, surprised and puzzled, but never once did she say, "There's no way I'm going to stand before my husband and the people of my community and listen to them call my son an illegitimate child!" As she came to realize that what the angel had told her was true, that she was in fact going to give birth to the Son of God—conceived in her by the Holy Spirit—she humbly and rightly acknowledged her position in relation to God and praised Him for honoring her: "My soul glorifies the Lord and my spirit rejoices in God my Savior, for he has been mindful of the humble state of his servant. From now on all generations will call me blessed, for the Mighty One has done great things for me—holy is his name" (1:46–49). How can we as Christians do anything less than shower our God with praise and thanksgiving for the gift He gave us: His one and only Son, born of the virgin Mary—our Lord Jesus Christ?

tered Zechariah's home and greeted Elizabeth. 41 When Elizabeth heard Mary's greeting, the baby leaped in her womb, and Elizabeth was filled with the Holy Spirit. 42 In a loud voice she exclaimed: "Blessed are you among women, and blessed is the child you will bear! 43 But why am I so favored, that the mother of my Lord should come to me? 44 As soon as the sound of your greeting reached my ears, the baby in my womb leaped for joy. 45 Blessed is she who has believed that what the Lord has said to her will be accomplished!"

Mary's Song

▶ *See 1 Samuel 2:1–10*

46 And Mary said:

"My soul glorifies the Lord Ps 34:2-3
47 and my spirit rejoices in God my Savior,
48 for he has been mindful
of the humble state of his servant. Ps 138:6
From now on all generations will call me
blessed, Lk 11:27
49 for the Mighty One has done great things
for me— Ps 71:19
holy is his name. Ps 111:9
50 His mercy extends to those who fear him,
from generation to generation. Ex 20:6; Ps 103:17
51 He has performed mighty deeds with his arm;
he has scattered those who are proud in
their inmost thoughts. Ge 11:8; Jer 13:9
52 He has brought down rulers from their
thrones
but has lifted up the humble. Mt 23:12
53 He has filled the hungry with good things
but has sent the rich away empty. 1Sa 2:1-10
54 He has helped his servant Israel,
remembering to be merciful Ps 98:3
55 to Abraham and his descendants forever,
even as he said to our fathers."

56 Mary stayed with Elizabeth for about three months and then returned home.

The Birth of John the Baptist

57 When it was time for Elizabeth to have her baby, she gave birth to a son. 58 Her neighbors and relatives heard that the Lord had shown her great mercy, and they shared her joy.

59 On the eighth day they came to circumcise the child, and they were going to name him after his father Zechariah, 60 but his mother spoke up and said, "No! He is to be called John." Ge 17:12; Lk 2:21

61 They said to her, "There is no one among your relatives who has that name."

62 Then they made signs to his father, to find out what he would like to name the child. 63 He asked for a writing tablet, and to everyone's astonishment he wrote, "His name is John." 64 Immediately his mouth was opened and his tongue was loosed, and he began to speak, praising God. 65 The neighbors were all filled with awe, and throughout the hill country of Judea people were talking about all these things. 66 Everyone who heard this wondered about it, asking, "What then is this child going to be?" For the Lord's hand was with him. Ge 39:2

Zechariah's Song

67 His father Zechariah was filled with the Holy Spirit and prophesied: Joel 2:28

68 "Praise be to the Lord, the God of Israel,
because he has come and has redeemed his
people. Ps 111:9; Lk 7:16
69 He has raised up a horn[a] of salvation for us
in the house of his servant David Mt 1:1
70 (as he said through his holy prophets of long
ago), Jer 23:5
71 salvation from our enemies
and from the hand of all who hate us—
72 to show mercy to our fathers Mic 7:20
and to remember his holy covenant,
73 the oath he swore to our father Abraham:
74 to rescue us from the hand of our enemies,
and to enable us to serve him without fear
75 in holiness and righteousness before him all
our days. Eph 4:24
76 And you, my child, will be called a prophet of
the Most High; Mt 11:9
for you will go on before the Lord to
prepare the way for him, Mal 3:1
77 to give his people the knowledge of salvation
through the forgiveness of their sins, Jer 31:34
78 because of the tender mercy of our God,
by which the rising sun will come to us
from heaven Mal 4:2
79 to shine on those living in darkness
and in the shadow of death, Isa 9:2; Mt 4:16
to guide our feet into the path of peace."

80 And the child grew and became strong in spirit; and he lived in the desert until he appeared publicly to Israel. Lk 2:40,52

The Birth of Jesus

2 In those days Caesar Augustus issued a decree that a census should be taken of the entire Roman world. 2 (This was the first census that took place while Quirinius was governor of Syria.) 3 And everyone went to his own town to register.

4 So Joseph also went up from the town of Nazareth in Galilee to Judea, to Bethlehem the town of David, because he belonged to the house and line of David. 5 He went there to register with Mary, who was pledged to be married to him and was expecting a child. 6 While they were there, the time

[a] 69 *Horn* here symbolizes strength.

came for the baby to be born, [7]and she gave birth to her firstborn, a son. She wrapped him in cloths and placed him in a manger, because there was no room for them in the inn. Jn 7:42

LIVING  **INSIGHT**

Luke 2 may comprise "the greatest story ever told." Don't limit this magnificent account to Christmas Eve! It's too important, too encouraging, to be put on the shelf as a "yearly tradition." Read this passage out loud. Reflect on what it meant for God to become a baby . . . to take upon Himself our flesh and to make His dwelling among us. Come, let us adore Him—today!

(See Luke 2:1–20.)

The Shepherds and the Angels

[8]And there were shepherds living out in the fields nearby, keeping watch over their flocks at night. [9]An angel of the Lord appeared to them, and the glory of the Lord shone around them, and they were terrified. [10]But the angel said to them, "Do not be afraid. I bring you good news of great joy that will be for all the people. [11]Today in the town of David a Savior has been born to you; he is Christ[a] the Lord. [12]This will be a sign to you: You will find a baby wrapped in cloths and lying in a manger." Isa 7:14; Mt 1:21

[13]Suddenly a great company of the heavenly host appeared with the angel, praising God and saying,

[14]"Glory to God in the highest,
and on earth peace to men on whom his favor rests." Ro 5:1; Eph 2:14,17

[15]When the angels had left them and gone into heaven, the shepherds said to one another, "Let's go to Bethlehem and see this thing that has happened, which the Lord has told us about."

[16]So they hurried off and found Mary and Joseph, and the baby, who was lying in the manger.
[17]When they had seen him, they spread the word concerning what had been told them about this child, [18]and all who heard it were amazed at what the shepherds said to them. [19]But Mary treasured up all these things and pondered them in her heart. [20]The shepherds returned, glorifying and praising God for all the things they had heard and seen, which were just as they had been told.

Jesus Presented in the Temple

[21]On the eighth day, when it was time to circumcise him, he was named Jesus, the name the angel had given him before he had been conceived.

[22]When the time of their purification according to the Law of Moses had been completed, Joseph and Mary took him to Jerusalem to present him to the Lord [23](as it is written in the Law of the Lord, "Every firstborn male is to be consecrated to the Lord"[b]), [24]and to offer a sacrifice in keeping with what is said in the Law of the Lord: "a pair of doves or two young pigeons."[c] Ex 13:2,12,15; Lev 12:8

[25]Now there was a man in Jerusalem called Simeon, who was righteous and devout. He was waiting for the consolation of Israel, and the Holy Spirit was upon him. [26]It had been revealed to him by the Holy Spirit that he would not die before he had seen the Lord's Christ. [27]Moved by the Spirit, he went into the temple courts. When the parents brought in the child Jesus to do for him what the custom of the Law required, [28]Simeon took him in his arms and praised God, saying: Lk 1:6; 23:51

[29]"Sovereign Lord, as you have promised, ver 26
you now dismiss[d] your servant in peace.
[30]For my eyes have seen your salvation, Isa 52:10
[31] which you have prepared in the sight of all people,
[32]a light for revelation to the Gentiles
and for glory to your people Israel." Isa 42:6

[33]The child's father and mother marveled at what was said about him. [34]Then Simeon blessed them and said to Mary, his mother: "This child is destined to cause the falling and rising of many in Israel, and to be a sign that will be spoken against, [35]so that the thoughts of many hearts will be revealed. And a sword will pierce your own soul too." Mt 21:44; 1Co 1:23; 1Pe 2:7-8

[36]There was also a prophetess, Anna, the daughter of Phanuel, of the tribe of Asher. She was very old; she had lived with her husband seven years after her marriage, [37]and then was a widow until she was eighty-four.[e] She never left the temple but worshiped night and day, fasting and praying. [38]Coming up to them at that very moment, she gave thanks to God and spoke about the child to all who were looking forward to the redemption of Jerusalem. Lk 1:68; 1Ti 5:5

[39]When Joseph and Mary had done everything required by the Law of the Lord, they returned to Galilee to their own town of Nazareth. [40]And the child grew and became strong; he was filled with wisdom, and the grace of God was upon him.

The Boy Jesus at the Temple

[41]Every year his parents went to Jerusalem for the Feast of the Passover. [42]When he was twelve years old, they went up to the Feast, according to

[a]*11* Or *Messiah.* "The Christ" (Greek) and "the Messiah" (Hebrew) both mean "the Anointed One"; also in verse 26.
[b]*23* Exodus 13:2,12 [c]*24* Lev. 12:8 [d]*29* Or *promised, / now dismiss* [e]*37* Or *widow for eighty-four years*

the custom. [43]After the Feast was over, while his parents were returning home, the boy Jesus stayed behind in Jerusalem, but they were unaware of it. [44]Thinking he was in their company, they traveled on for a day. Then they began looking for him among their relatives and friends. [45]When they did not find him, they went back to Jerusalem to look for him. [46]After three days they found him in the temple courts, sitting among the teachers, listening to them and asking them questions. [47]Everyone who heard him was amazed at his understanding and his answers. [48]When his parents saw him, they were astonished. His mother said to him, "Son, why have you treated us like this? Your father and I have been anxiously searching for you." Ex 23:15

[49]"Why were you searching for me?" he asked. "Didn't you know I had to be in my Father's house?" [50]But they did not understand what he was saying to them. Mk 9:32; Jn 2:16

[51]Then he went down to Nazareth with them and was obedient to them. But his mother treasured all these things in her heart. [52]And Jesus grew in wisdom and stature, and in favor with God and men. Mt 2:23; Lk 1:80

John the Baptist Prepares the Way

▶ *See Matthew 3:1–10; Mark 1:3–5*

3 In the fifteenth year of the reign of Tiberius Caesar—when Pontius Pilate was governor of Judea, Herod tetrarch of Galilee, his brother Philip tetrarch of Iturea and Traconitis, and Lysanias tetrarch of Abilene— [2]during the high priesthood of Annas and Caiaphas, the word of God came to John son of Zechariah in the desert. [3]He went into all the country around the Jordan, preaching a baptism of repentance for the forgiveness of sins. [4]As is written in the book of the words of Isaiah the prophet: Mk 1:4; Jn 18:13; Ac 4:6

"A voice of one calling in the desert,
'Prepare the way for the Lord,
make straight paths for him.
[5]Every valley shall be filled in,
every mountain and hill made low.
The crooked roads shall become straight,
the rough ways smooth.
[6]And all mankind will see God's salvation.'"[a]

[7]John said to the crowds coming out to be baptized by him, "You brood of vipers! Who warned you to flee from the coming wrath? [8]Produce fruit in keeping with repentance. And do not begin to say to yourselves, 'We have Abraham as our father.' For I tell you that out of these stones God can raise up children for Abraham. [9]The ax is already at the root of the trees, and every tree that does not produce good fruit will be cut down and thrown into the fire." Jn 8:33,39; Gal 3:7

[10]"What should we do then?" the crowd asked.

[11]John answered, "The man with two tunics should share with him who has none, and the one who has food should do the same." Isa 58:7

[12]Tax collectors also came to be baptized. "Teacher," they asked, "what should we do?"

[13]"Don't collect any more than you are required to," he told them. Lk 19:8

[14]Then some soldiers asked him, "And what should we do?"

He replied, "Don't extort money and don't accuse people falsely—be content with your pay."

[15]The people were waiting expectantly and were all wondering in their hearts if John might possibly be the Christ.[b] [16]John answered them all, "I baptize you with[c] water. But one more powerful than I will come, the thongs of whose sandals I am not worthy to untie. He will baptize you with the Holy Spirit and with fire. [17]His winnowing fork is in his hand to clear his threshing floor and to gather the wheat into his barn, but he will burn up the chaff with unquenchable fire." [18]And with many other words John exhorted the people and preached the good news to them. Mt 3:11-12; Mk 1:7-8

[19]But when John rebuked Herod the tetrarch because of Herodias, his brother's wife, and all the other evil things he had done, [20]Herod added this to them all: He locked John up in prison.

The Baptism and Genealogy of Jesus

▶ *See Matthew 1:1–17; 3:13–17; Mark 1:9–11*

[21]When all the people were being baptized, Jesus was baptized too. And as he was praying, heaven was opened [22]and the Holy Spirit descended on him in bodily form like a dove. And a voice came from heaven: "You are my Son, whom I love; with you I am well pleased." Mt 3:13-17; Mk 1:9-11

[23]Now Jesus himself was about thirty years old when he began his ministry. He was the son, so it was thought, of Joseph, Mt 4:17; Lk 1:27; Ac 1:1

the son of Heli, [24]the son of Matthat,
the son of Levi, the son of Melki,
the son of Jannai, the son of Joseph,
[25]the son of Mattathias, the son of Amos,
the son of Nahum, the son of Esli,
the son of Naggai, [26]the son of Maath,
the son of Mattathias, the son of Semein,
the son of Josech, the son of Joda,
[27]the son of Joanan, the son of Rhesa,
the son of Zerubbabel, the son of Shealtiel,
the son of Neri, [28]the son of Melki,
the son of Addi, the son of Cosam,
the son of Elmadam, the son of Er,
[29]the son of Joshua, the son of Eliezer,
the son of Jorim, the son of Matthat,
the son of Levi, [30]the son of Simeon,

[a]6 Isaiah 40:3-5 [b]15 Or *Messiah* [c]16 Or *in*

the son of Judah, the son of Joseph,
the son of Jonam, the son of Eliakim,
31 the son of Melea, the son of Menna,
the son of Mattatha, the son of Nathan,
the son of David, 32 the son of Jesse,
the son of Obed, the son of Boaz,
the son of Salmon,[a] the son of Nahshon,
33 the son of Amminadab, the son of Ram,[b]
the son of Hezron, the son of Perez,
the son of Judah, 34 the son of Jacob,
the son of Isaac, the son of Abraham,
the son of Terah, the son of Nahor,
35 the son of Serug, the son of Reu,
the son of Peleg, the son of Eber,
the son of Shelah, 36 the son of Cainan,
the son of Arphaxad, the son of Shem,
the son of Noah, the son of Lamech,
37 the son of Methuselah, the son of Enoch,
the son of Jared, the son of Mahalalel,
the son of Kenan, 38 the son of Enosh,
the son of Seth, the son of Adam,
the son of God. Mt 1:1-17

The Temptation of Jesus

▶ *See Matthew 4:1–11; Mark 1:12–13*

4 Jesus, full of the Holy Spirit, returned from the Jordan and was led by the Spirit in the desert, 2 where for forty days he was tempted by the devil. He ate nothing during those days, and at the end of them he was hungry. Ex 34:28; Lk 2:27

3 The devil said to him, "If you are the Son of God, tell this stone to become bread." Mt 4:3

4 Jesus answered, "It is written: 'Man does not live on bread alone.'[c]" Dt 8:3

5 The devil led him up to a high place and showed him in an instant all the kingdoms of the world. 6 And he said to him, "I will give you all their authority and splendor, for it has been given to me, and I can give it to anyone I want to. 7 So if you worship me, it will all be yours." Jn 12:31

8 Jesus answered, "It is written: 'Worship the Lord your God and serve him only.'[d]" Dt 6:13

9 The devil led him to Jerusalem and had him stand on the highest point of the temple. "If you are the Son of God," he said, "throw yourself down from here. 10 For it is written:

" 'He will command his angels concerning you
to guard you carefully;
11 they will lift you up in their hands,
so that you will not strike your foot against
a stone.'[e]" Ps 91:11-12

12 Jesus answered, "It says: 'Do not put the Lord your God to the test.'[f]" Dt 6:16

13 When the devil had finished all this tempting, he left him until an opportune time. Mt 4:1-11; Mk 1

Ministry of Jesus Chapters 4:14–9:50

In these chapters, the Son of Man is seeking those who are lost. Luke records the ministry and service of Jesus as he reached out with compassion to those who were in need. The action in this section took place in Galilee as well as regions around Galilee. Almost two years transpire as we follow the mighty ministry of the Son of Man.

Jesus Rejected at Nazareth

14 Jesus returned to Galilee in the power of the Spirit, and news about him spread through the whole countryside. 15 He taught in their synagogues, and everyone praised him. Mt 4:12; 9:26

16 He went to Nazareth, where he had been brought up, and on the Sabbath day he went into the synagogue, as was his custom. And he stood up to read. 17 The scroll of the prophet Isaiah was handed to him. Unrolling it, he found the place where it is written: Mt 13:54

18 "The Spirit of the Lord is on me, Jn 3:34
because he has anointed me
to preach good news to the poor. Mk 16:15
He has sent me to proclaim freedom for the
prisoners
and recovery of sight for the blind,
to release the oppressed,
19 to proclaim the year of the Lord's favor."[g]

20 Then he rolled up the scroll, gave it back to the attendant and sat down. The eyes of everyone in the synagogue were fastened on him, 21 and he began by saying to them, "Today this scripture is fulfilled in your hearing." Mt 26:55

22 All spoke well of him and were amazed at the gracious words that came from his lips. "Isn't this Joseph's son?" they asked. Mt 13:54-55; Jn 6:42; 7:15

23 Jesus said to them, "Surely you will quote this proverb to me: 'Physician, heal yourself! Do here in your hometown what we have heard that you did in Capernaum.'" Mk 1:21-28; 2:1-12

24 "I tell you the truth," he continued, "no prophet is accepted in his hometown. 25 I assure you that there were many widows in Israel in Elijah's time, when the sky was shut for three and a half years and there was a severe famine throughout the land. 26 Yet Elijah was not sent to any of them, but to a widow in Zarephath in the region of Sidon. 27 And there were many in Israel with leprosy[h] in the time of Elisha the prophet, yet not one of them was cleansed—only Naaman the Syrian."

28 All the people in the synagogue were furious

[a] *32* Some early manuscripts *Sala* [b] *33* Some manuscripts *Amminadab, the son of Admin, the son of Arni*; other manuscripts vary widely. [c] *4* Deut. 8:3 [d] *8* Deut. 6:13 [e] *11* Psalm 91:11,12 [f] *12* Deut. 6:16 [g] *19* Isaiah 61:1,2
[h] *27* The Greek word was used for various diseases affecting the skin—not necessarily leprosy.

MINISTRY OF JESUS

Event	Place	Matthew	Mark	Luke	John
Jesus baptized	Jordan River	*3:13-17*	*1:9-11*	*3:21-22*	*1:29-34*
Jesus tempted by Satan	Desert	*4:1-11*	*1:12-13*	*4:1-13*	
Jesus' first miracle	Cana				*2:1-11*
Jesus and Nicodemus	Judea				*3:1-21*
Jesus talks to a Samaritan woman	Samaria				*4:5-42*
Jesus heals an official's son	Cana				*4:46-54*
The people of Nazareth try to kill Jesus	Nazareth			*4:16-30*	
Jesus calls four fishermen	Sea of Galilee	*4:18-22*	*1:16-20*	*5:1-11*	
Jesus heals Peter's mother-in-law	Capernaum	*8:14-15*	*1:29-31*	*4:38-39*	
Jesus begins preaching in Galilee	Galilee	*4:23-25*	*1:35-39*	*4:42-44*	
Matthew decides to follow Jesus	Capernaum	*9:9-13*	*2:13-17*	*5:27-32*	
Jesus chooses twelve disciples	Galilee	*10:2-4*	*3:13-19*	*6:12-15*	
Jesus preaches the Sermon on the Mount	Galilee	*5:1–7:29*		*6:20-49*	
A sinful woman anoints Jesus	Capernaum			*7:36-50*	
Jesus travels again through Galilee	Galilee			*8:1-3*	
Jesus tells kingdom parables	Galilee	*13:1-52*	*4:1-34*	*8:4-18*	
Jesus quiets the storm	Sea of Galilee	*8:23-27*	*4:35-41*	*8:22-25*	
Jairus's daughter raised to life	Capernaum	*9:18-26*	*5:21-43*	*8:40-56*	
Jesus sends out the Twelve	Galilee	*9:35–11:1*	*6:6-13*	*9:1-6*	
John the Baptist killed by Herod	Machaerus in Judea	*14:1-12*	*6:14-29*	*9:7-9*	
Jesus feeds the 5,000	Bethsaida	*14:13-21*	*6:30-44*	*9:10-17*	*6:1-14*
Jesus walks on water	Sea of Galilee	*14:22-32*	*6:47-52*		*6:16-21*
Jesus feeds the 4,000	Sea of Galilee	*15:32-39*	*8:1-10*		
Peter confesses Jesus as the Son of God	Caesarea Philippi	*16:13-20*	*8:27-30*	*9:18-21*	
Jesus predicts His death	Caesarea Philippi	*16:21-26*	*8:31-37*	*9:22-25*	
Jesus is transfigured	Mount Hermon	*17:1-13*	*9:2-13*	*9:28-36*	
Jesus pays His temple taxes	Capernaum	*17:24-27*			
Jesus attends the Feast of Tabernacles	Jerusalem				*7:10-52*
Jesus heals a man born blind	Jerusalem				*9:1-41*
Jesus visits Mary and Martha	Bethany			*10:38-42*	
Jesus raises Lazarus from the dead	Bethany				*11:1-44*
Jesus begins His last trip to Jerusalem	Border road			*17:11*	
Jesus blesses the little children	Transjordan	*19:13-15*	*10:13-16*	*18:15-17*	
Jesus talks to the rich young man	Transjordan	*19:16-30*	*10:17-31*	*18:18-30*	
Jesus again predicts His death	Near the Jordan	*20:17-19*	*10:32-34*	*18:31-34*	
Jesus heals blind Bartimaeus	Jericho	*20:29-34*	*10:46-52*	*18:35-43*	
Jesus talks to Zacchaeus	Jericho			*19:1-10*	
Jesus visits Mary and Martha again	Bethany				*12:1-11*

when they heard this. 29They got up, drove him
out of the town, and took him to the brow of the
hill on which the town was built, in order to throw
him down the cliff. 30But he walked right through
the crowd and went on his way. Jn 8:59; 10:39

Jesus Drives Out an Evil Spirit

31Then he went down to Capernaum, a town in
Galilee, and on the Sabbath began to teach the
people. 32They were amazed at his teaching, because his message had authority. Mt 7:28-29
33In the synagogue there was a man possessed
by a demon, an evil[a] spirit. He cried out at the
top of his voice, 34"Ha! What do you want with us,
Jesus of Nazareth? Have you come to destroy us?
I know who you are—the Holy One of God!"
35"Be quiet!" Jesus said sternly. "Come out of
him!" Then the demon threw the man down before them all and came out without injuring him.
36All the people were amazed and said to each
other, "What is this teaching? With authority and
power he gives orders to evil spirits and they come
out!" 37And the news about him spread throughout the surrounding area. Mk 1:21-28

Jesus Heals Many

▶ *See Matthew 8:14–17; Mark 1:29–38*

38Jesus left the synagogue and went to the home
of Simon. Now Simon's mother-in-law was suffering from a high fever, and they asked Jesus to help
her. 39So he bent over her and rebuked the fever,
and it left her. She got up at once and began to
wait on them.
40When the sun was setting, the people brought
to Jesus all who had various kinds of sickness, and
laying his hands on each one, he healed them.
41Moreover, demons came out of many people,
shouting, "You are the Son of God!" But he rebuked them and would not allow them to speak,
because they knew he was the Christ.[b] Mt 8:14-17
42At daybreak Jesus went out to a solitary place.
The people were looking for him and when they
came to where he was, they tried to keep him from
leaving them. 43But he said, "I must preach the
good news of the kingdom of God to the other
towns also, because that is why I was sent." 44And
he kept on preaching in the synagogues of Judea.[c]

The Calling of the First Disciples

▶ *See Matthew 4:18–22; Mark 1:16–20; John 1:40–42*

5 One day as Jesus was standing by the Lake
of Gennesaret,[d] with the people crowding
around him and listening to the word of God, 2he
saw at the water's edge two boats, left there by the
fishermen, who were washing their nets. 3He got
into one of the boats, the one belonging to Simon,
and asked him to put out a little from shore. Then
he sat down and taught the people from the boat.
4When he had finished speaking, he said to Simon, "Put out into deep water, and let down[e] the
nets for a catch." Jn 21:6
5Simon answered, "Master, we've worked hard
all night and haven't caught anything. But because
you say so, I will let down the nets." Lk 8:24,45
6When they had done so, they caught such a
large number of fish that their nets began to break.
7So they signaled their partners in the other boat
to come and help them, and they came and filled
both boats so full that they began to sink.
8When Simon Peter saw this, he fell at Jesus'
knees and said, "Go away from me, Lord; I am a
sinful man!" 9For he and all his companions were
astonished at the catch of fish they had taken,
10and so were James and John, the sons of Zebedee, Simon's partners. Ge 18:27; Job 42:6; Isa 6:5
Then Jesus said to Simon, "Don't be afraid;
from now on you will catch men." 11So they pulled
their boats up on shore, left everything and followed him. Mt 4:18-22; Mk 1:16-20; Jn 1:40-42

The Man With Leprosy

▶ *See Matthew 8:2–4; Mark 1:40–44*

12While Jesus was in one of the towns, a man
came along who was covered with leprosy.[f]
When he saw Jesus, he fell with his face to the
ground and begged him, "Lord, if you are willing,
you can make me clean." Mt 8:2
13Jesus reached out his hand and touched the
man. "I am willing," he said. "Be clean!" And immediately the leprosy left him.
14Then Jesus ordered him, "Don't tell anyone,
but go, show yourself to the priest and offer the
sacrifices that Moses commanded for your cleansing, as a testimony to them." Mt 8:2-4; Mk 1:40-44
15Yet the news about him spread all the more,
so that crowds of people came to hear him and to
be healed of their sicknesses. 16But Jesus often
withdrew to lonely places and prayed. Mt 14:23

LIVING  **INSIGHT**

Feeling crushed by the crowds these days? Pushed into a corner from which there seems to be no escape? Anxiety reaching a fever pitch? Stop. Pray. Turn it over to the One who can handle your load.

(See Luke 5:15–16.)

[a]33 Greek *unclean*; also in verse 36 [b]41 Or *Messiah* [c]44 Or *the land of the Jews*; some manuscripts *Galilee*
[d]1 That is, Sea of Galilee [e]4 The Greek verb is plural. [f]12 The Greek word was used for various diseases affecting the skin—not necessarily leprosy.

Jesus Heals a Paralytic

▶ *See Matthew 9:2–8; Mark 2:3–12*

[17]One day as he was teaching, Pharisees and teachers of the law, who had come from every village of Galilee and from Judea and Jerusalem, were sitting there. And the power of the Lord was present for him to heal the sick. [18]Some men came carrying a paralytic on a mat and tried to take him into the house to lay him before Jesus. [19]When they could not find a way to do this because of the crowd, they went up on the roof and lowered him on his mat through the tiles into the middle of the crowd, right in front of Jesus. Mk 5:30; Lk 6:19

[20]When Jesus saw their faith, he said, "Friend, your sins are forgiven." Lk 7:48-49

[21]The Pharisees and the teachers of the law began thinking to themselves, "Who is this fellow who speaks blasphemy? Who can forgive sins but God alone?" Isa 43:25

[22]Jesus knew what they were thinking and asked, "Why are you thinking these things in your hearts? [23]Which is easier: to say, 'Your sins are forgiven,' or to say, 'Get up and walk'? [24]But that you may know that the Son of Man has authority on earth to forgive sins . . ." He said to the paralyzed man, "I tell you, get up, take your mat and go home." [25]Immediately he stood up in front of them, took what he had been lying on and went home praising God. [26]Everyone was amazed and gave praise to God. They were filled with awe and said, "We have seen remarkable things today."

The Calling of Levi

▶ *See Matthew 9:9–13; Mark 2:14–17*

[27]After this, Jesus went out and saw a tax collector by the name of Levi sitting at his tax booth. "Follow me," Jesus said to him, [28]and Levi got up, left everything and followed him. Mt 4:19

[29]Then Levi held a great banquet for Jesus at his house, and a large crowd of tax collectors and others were eating with them. [30]But the Pharisees and the teachers of the law who belonged to their sect complained to his disciples, "Why do you eat and drink with tax collectors and 'sinners'?"

[31]Jesus answered them, "It is not the healthy who need a doctor, but the sick. [32]I have not come to call the righteous, but sinners to repentance."

Jesus Questioned About Fasting

▶ *See Matthew 9:14–17; Mark 2:18–22*

[33]They said to him, "John's disciples often fast and pray, and so do the disciples of the Pharisees, but yours go on eating and drinking." Lk 7:18

[34]Jesus answered, "Can you make the guests of the bridegroom fast while he is with them? [35]But the time will come when the bridegroom will be taken from them; in those days they will fast."

[36]He told them this parable: "No one tears a patch from a new garment and sews it on an old one. If he does, he will have torn the new garment, and the patch from the new will not match the old. [37]And no one pours new wine into old wineskins. If he does, the new wine will burst the skins, the wine will run out and the wineskins will be ruined.

LIVING  **INSIGHT**

Our Lord is distinguishing between things that are essential (the wine: that which is primary . . . the timeless and changeless gospel) and things that are useful but not primary (the skins: that which is secondary . . . like structure, traditions and fixed patterns of doing things).

(See Luke 5:37.)

[38]No, new wine must be poured into new wineskins. [39]And no one after drinking old wine wants the new, for he says, 'The old is better.' "

Lord of the Sabbath

▶ *See Matthew 12:1–14; Mark 2:23—3:6*

6 One Sabbath Jesus was going through the grainfields, and his disciples began to pick some heads of grain, rub them in their hands and eat the kernels. [2]Some of the Pharisees asked, "Why are you doing what is unlawful on the Sabbath?" Dt 23:25

[3]Jesus answered them, "Have you never read what David did when he and his companions were hungry? [4]He entered the house of God, and taking the consecrated bread, he ate what is lawful only for priests to eat. And he also gave some to his companions." [5]Then Jesus said to them, "The Son of Man is Lord of the Sabbath." Lev 24:5,9; 1Sa 21:6

[6]On another Sabbath he went into the synagogue and was teaching, and a man was there whose right hand was shriveled. [7]The Pharisees and the teachers of the law were looking for a reason to accuse Jesus, so they watched him closely to see if he would heal on the Sabbath. [8]But Jesus knew what they were thinking and said to the man with the shriveled hand, "Get up and stand in front of everyone." So he got up and stood there.

[9]Then Jesus said to them, "I ask you, which is lawful on the Sabbath: to do good or to do evil, to save life or to destroy it?"

[10]He looked around at them all, and then said to the man, "Stretch out your hand." He did so, and his hand was completely restored. [11]But they were furious and began to discuss with one another what they might do to Jesus. Mt 12:1-14; Mk 2:23-3:6

The Twelve Apostles

▶ *See Matthew 10:2–4; Mark 3:16–19; Acts 1:13*

12One of those days Jesus went out to a mountainside to pray, and spent the night praying to
God. 13When morning came, he called his disciples to him and chose twelve of them, whom he
also designated apostles: 14Simon (whom he
named Peter), his brother Andrew, James, John,
Philip, Bartholomew, 15Matthew, Thomas, James
son of Alphaeus, Simon who was called the Zealot,
16Judas son of James, and Judas Iscariot, who became a traitor. Mt 10:2-4; Mk 3:16-19; Ac 1:13

Blessings and Woes

▶ *See Matthew 5:3–12*

17He went down with them and stood on a level
place. A large crowd of his disciples was there and
a great number of people from all over Judea, from
Jerusalem, and from the coast of Tyre and Sidon,
18who had come to hear him and to be healed of
their diseases. Those troubled by evil[a] spirits were
cured, 19and the people all tried to touch him,
because power was coming from him and healing
them all. Mt 14:36; Lk 5:17

20Looking at his disciples, he said:

"Blessed are you who are poor,
 for yours is the kingdom of God. Mt 25:34
21Blessed are you who hunger now,
 for you will be satisfied. Isa 55:1-2; Mt 5:6
Blessed are you who weep now,
 for you will laugh. Isa 61:2-3; Mt 5:4; Rev 7:17
22Blessed are you when men hate you,
 when they exclude you and insult you
 and reject your name as evil,
 because of the Son of Man. Jn 15:21

23"Rejoice in that day and leap for joy, because
great is your reward in heaven. For that is how
their fathers treated the prophets. Mt 5:12

24"But woe to you who are rich, Jas 5:1
 for you have already received your
 comfort.
25Woe to you who are well fed now,
 for you will go hungry. Isa 65:13
Woe to you who laugh now,
 for you will mourn and weep. Pr 14:13
26Woe to you when all men speak well
 of you,
 for that is how their fathers treated
 the false prophets. Mt 7:15

Love for Enemies

27"But I tell you who hear me: Love your enemies, do good to those who hate you, 28bless those
who curse you, pray for those who mistreat you.
29If someone strikes you on one cheek, turn to him
the other also. If someone takes your cloak, do not
stop him from taking your tunic. 30Give to everyone who asks you, and if anyone takes what belongs to you, do not demand it back. 31Do to
others as you would have them do to you.

32"If you love those who love you, what credit is
that to you? Even 'sinners' love those who love
them. 33And if you do good to those who are good
to you, what credit is that to you? Even 'sinners' do
that. 34And if you lend to those from whom you
expect repayment, what credit is that to you? Even
'sinners' lend to 'sinners,' expecting to be repaid in
full. 35But love your enemies, do good to them,
and lend to them without expecting to get anything back. Then your reward will be great, and
you will be sons of the Most High, because he is
kind to the ungrateful and wicked. 36Be merciful,
just as your Father is merciful. Jas 2:13; Mt 5:48

Judging Others

▶ *See Matthew 7:1–5*

37"Do not judge, and you will not be judged. Do
not condemn, and you will not be condemned.

LIVING  INSIGHT

Did you blow it this week? Satan smiles smugly when we get discouraged and throw in the towel. Let's not give him that satisfaction. Knowing how our enemy hates love and forgiveness, let's give those very things to ourselves and to others . . . starting today.

(See Luke 6:37.)

Forgive, and you will be forgiven. 38Give, and it
will be given to you. A good measure, pressed
down, shaken together and running over, will be
poured into your lap. For with the measure you
use, it will be measured to you." Mt 7:1; Mk 4:24

39He also told them this parable: "Can a blind
man lead a blind man? Will they not both fall into
a pit? 40A student is not above his teacher, but
everyone who is fully trained will be like his
teacher. Mt 10:24; Jn 13:16

41"Why do you look at the speck of sawdust in
your brother's eye and pay no attention to the
plank in your own eye? 42How can you say to your
brother, 'Brother, let me take the speck out of your
eye,' when you yourself fail to see the plank in
your own eye? You hypocrite, first take the plank
out of your eye, and then you will see clearly to
remove the speck from your brother's eye.

[a] 18 Greek *unclean*

A Tree and Its Fruit

▶ *See Matthew 7:16,18,20*

43“No good tree bears bad fruit, nor does a bad
tree bear good fruit. 44Each tree is recognized by its
own fruit. People do not pick figs from thornbushes, or grapes from briers. 45The good man
brings good things out of the good stored up in his
heart, and the evil man brings evil things out of the
evil stored up in his heart. For out of the overflow
of his heart his mouth speaks. Mt 12:33-35

The Wise and Foolish Builders

▶ *See Matthew 7:24–27*

46“Why do you call me, ‘Lord, Lord,’ and do
not do what I say? 47I will show you what he is like
who comes to me and hears my words and puts
them into practice. 48He is like a man building a
house, who dug down deep and laid the foundation on rock. When a flood came, the torrent
struck that house but could not shake it, because
it was well built. 49But the one who hears my
words and does not put them into practice is like
a man who built a house on the ground without
a foundation. The moment the torrent struck
that house, it collapsed and its destruction was
complete.”

The Faith of the Centurion

▶ *See Matthew 8:5–13*

7 When Jesus had finished saying all this in the
hearing of the people, he entered Capernaum. 2There a centurion’s servant, whom his master valued highly, was sick and about to die. 3The
centurion heard of Jesus and sent some elders of
the Jews to him, asking him to come and heal his
servant. 4When they came to Jesus, they pleaded
earnestly with him, “This man deserves to have
you do this, 5because he loves our nation and has
built our synagogue.” 6So Jesus went with them.

He was not far from the house when the centurion sent friends to say to him: “Lord, don’t trouble yourself, for I do not deserve to have you come
under my roof. 7That is why I did not even consider myself worthy to come to you. But say the word,
and my servant will be healed. 8For I myself am a
man under authority, with soldiers under me. I tell
this one, ‘Go,’ and he goes; and that one, ‘Come,’
and he comes. I say to my servant, ‘Do this,’ and
he does it.” Ps 107:20

9When Jesus heard this, he was amazed at
him, and turning to the crowd following him, he
said, “I tell you, I have not found such great faith
even in Israel.” 10Then the men who had been
sent returned to the house and found the servant well.

Jesus Raises a Widow’s Son

11Soon afterward, Jesus went to a town called
Nain, and his disciples and a large crowd went
along with him. 12As he approached the town gate,
a dead person was being carried out—the only
son of his mother, and she was a widow. And a
large crowd from the town was with her. 13When
the Lord saw her, his heart went out to her and he
said, “Don’t cry.” Jn 11:1-44

14Then he went up and touched the coffin, and
those carrying it stood still. He said, “Young man,
I say to you, get up!” 15The dead man sat up and
began to talk, and Jesus gave him back to his
mother. 1Ki 17:17-24; 2Ki 4:32-37

16They were all filled with awe and praised God.
“A great prophet has appeared among us,” they
said. “God has come to help his people.” 17This
news about Jesus spread throughout Judea[a] and
the surrounding country. Mk 5:21-24,35-43

Jesus and John the Baptist

▶ *See Matthew 11:2–19*

18John’s disciples told him about all these
things. Calling two of them, 19he sent them to the
Lord to ask, “Are you the one who was to come,
or should we expect someone else?” Mt 3:1; Lk 5:33

20When the men came to Jesus, they said, “John
the Baptist sent us to you to ask, ‘Are you the one
who was to come, or should we expect someone
else?’ ”

21At that very time Jesus cured many who had
diseases, sicknesses and evil spirits, and gave sight
to many who were blind. 22So he replied to the
messengers, “Go back and report to John what
you have seen and heard: The blind receive sight,
the lame walk, those who have leprosy[b] are cured,
the deaf hear, the dead are raised, and the good
news is preached to the poor. 23Blessed is the man
who does not fall away on account of me.”

24After John’s messengers left, Jesus began to
speak to the crowd about John: “What did you go
out into the desert to see? A reed swayed by the
wind? 25If not, what did you go out to see? A man
dressed in fine clothes? No, those who wear expensive clothes and indulge in luxury are in palaces.
26But what did you go out to see? A prophet? Yes,
I tell you, and more than a prophet. 27This is the
one about whom it is written: Mt 11:9

> “ ‘I will send my messenger ahead of you,
> who will prepare your way before you.’[c]

28I tell you, among those born of women there is
no one greater than John; yet the one who is least
in the kingdom of God is greater than he.”

29(All the people, even the tax collectors, when
they heard Jesus’ words, acknowledged that God’s

[a] 17 Or *the land of the Jews*
[b] 22 The Greek word was used for various diseases affecting the skin—not necessarily leprosy.
[c] 27 Mal. 3:1

way was right, because they had been baptized by John. [30]But the Pharisees and experts in the law rejected God's purpose for themselves, because they had not been baptized by John.) Mt 22:35

[31]"To what, then, can I compare the people of this generation? What are they like? [32]They are like children sitting in the marketplace and calling out to each other:

"'We played the flute for you,
  and you did not dance;
we sang a dirge,
  and you did not cry.'

[33]For John the Baptist came neither eating bread nor drinking wine, and you say, 'He has a demon.' [34]The Son of Man came eating and drinking, and you say, 'Here is a glutton and a drunkard, a friend of tax collectors and "sinners." ' [35]But wisdom is proved right by all her children." Mt 11:2-19; Lk 1:15

Jesus Anointed by a Sinful Woman

[36]Now one of the Pharisees invited Jesus to have dinner with him, so he went to the Pharisee's house and reclined at the table. [37]When a woman who had lived a sinful life in that town learned that Jesus was eating at the Pharisee's house, she brought an alabaster jar of perfume, [38]and as she stood behind him at his feet weeping, she began to wet his feet with her tears. Then she wiped them with her hair, kissed them and poured perfume on them.

[39]When the Pharisee who had invited him saw this, he said to himself, "If this man were a prophet, he would know who is touching him and what kind of woman she is—that she is a sinner."

[40]Jesus answered him, "Simon, I have something to tell you."

"Tell me, teacher," he said.

[41]"Two men owed money to a certain moneylender. One owed him five hundred denarii,[a] and the other fifty. [42]Neither of them had the money to pay him back, so he canceled the debts of both. Now which of them will love him more?"

[43]Simon replied, "I suppose the one who had the bigger debt canceled."

"You have judged correctly," Jesus said.

[44]Then he turned toward the woman and said to Simon, "Do you see this woman? I came into your house. You did not give me any water for my feet, but she wet my feet with her tears and wiped them with her hair. [45]You did not give me a kiss, but this woman, from the time I entered, has not stopped kissing my feet. [46]You did not put oil on my head, but she has poured perfume on my feet. [47]Therefore, I tell you, her many sins have been forgiven—for she loved much. But he who has been forgiven little loves little." Ge 18:4; Ps 23:5

[48]Then Jesus said to her, "Your sins are forgiven." Mt 9:2

[49]The other guests began to say among themselves, "Who is this who even forgives sins?"

[50]Jesus said to the woman, "Your faith has saved you; go in peace." Mk 5:34; Lk 8:48; Ac 15:33

The Parable of the Sower

▶ *See Matthew 13:2–23; Mark 4:1–20*

8 After this, Jesus traveled about from one town and village to another, proclaiming the good news of the kingdom of God. The Twelve were with him, [2]and also some women who had been cured of evil spirits and diseases: Mary (called Magdalene) from whom seven demons had come out; [3]Joanna the wife of Cuza, the manager of Herod's household; Susanna; and many others. These women were helping to support them out of their own means. Mt 4:23; 14:1; 27:55-56

[4]While a large crowd was gathering and people were coming to Jesus from town after town, he told this parable: [5]"A farmer went out to sow his seed. As he was scattering the seed, some fell along the path; it was trampled on, and the birds of the air ate it up. [6]Some fell on rock, and when it came up, the plants withered because they had no moisture. [7]Other seed fell among thorns, which grew up with it and choked the plants. [8]Still other seed fell on good soil. It came up and yielded a crop, a hundred times more than was sown."

When he said this, he called out, "He who has ears to hear, let him hear." Mt 11:15

[9]His disciples asked him what this parable meant. [10]He said, "The knowledge of the secrets of the kingdom of God has been given to you, but to others I speak in parables, so that, Mt 13:11

"'though seeing, they may not see;
  though hearing, they may not
    understand.'[b] Isa 6:9; Mt 13:13-14

[11]"This is the meaning of the parable: The seed is the word of God. [12]Those along the path are the ones who hear, and then the devil comes and takes away the word from their hearts, so that they may not believe and be saved. [13]Those on the rock are the ones who receive the word with joy when they hear it, but they have no root. They believe for a while, but in the time of testing they fall away. [14]The seed that fell among thorns stands for those who hear, but as they go on their way they are choked by life's worries, riches and pleasures, and they do not mature. [15]But the seed on good soil stands for those with a noble and good heart, who hear the word, retain it, and by persevering produce a crop. Mt 13:2-23; Mk 4:1-20

[a] *41* A denarius was a coin worth about a day's wages. [b] *10* Isaiah 6:9

A Lamp on a Stand

16“No one lights a lamp and hides it in a jar or puts it under a bed. Instead, he puts it on a stand, so that those who come in can see the light. 17For there is nothing hidden that will not be disclosed, and nothing concealed that will not be known or brought out into the open. 18Therefore consider carefully how you listen. Whoever has will be given more; whoever does not have, even what he thinks he has will be taken from him.” Mt 5:15

Jesus’ Mother and Brothers

▶ *See Matthew 12:46–50; Mark 3:31–35*

19Now Jesus’ mother and brothers came to see him, but they were not able to get near him because of the crowd. 20Someone told him, “Your mother and brothers are standing outside, wanting to see you.” Jn 7:5

21He replied, “My mother and brothers are those who hear God’s word and put it into practice.” Mt 12:46-50; Mk 3:31-35

Jesus Calms the Storm

▶ *See Matthew 8:23–27; Mark 4:36–41*

22One day Jesus said to his disciples, “Let’s go over to the other side of the lake.” So they got into a boat and set out. 23As they sailed, he fell asleep. A squall came down on the lake, so that the boat was being swamped, and they were in great danger.

24The disciples went and woke him, saying, “Master, Master, we’re going to drown!”

He got up and rebuked the wind and the raging waters; the storm subsided, and all was calm. 25“Where is your faith?” he asked his disciples.

LIVING  **INSIGHT**

If finding God’s way in the suddenness of storms makes our faith grow broad, then trusting God’s wisdom in the “dailyness” of living makes it grow deep. And strong.

(See Luke 8:24.)

In fear and amazement they asked one another, “Who is this? He commands even the winds and the water, and they obey him.” Mk 4:36-41

The Healing of a Demon-possessed Man

▶ *See Matthew 8:28–34; Mark 5:1–20*

26They sailed to the region of the Gerasenes,[a] which is across the lake from Galilee. 27When Jesus stepped ashore, he was met by a demon-possessed man from the town. For a long time this man had not worn clothes or lived in a house, but had lived in the tombs. 28When he saw Jesus, he cried out and fell at his feet, shouting at the top of his voice, “What do you want with me, Jesus, Son of the Most High God? I beg you, don’t torture me!” 29For Jesus had commanded the evil[b] spirit to come out of the man. Many times it had seized him, and though he was chained hand and foot and kept under guard, he had broken his chains and had been driven by the demon into solitary places. Mt 8:29; Mk 5:7

30Jesus asked him, “What is your name?”

“Legion,” he replied, because many demons had gone into him. 31And they begged him repeatedly not to order them to go into the Abyss.

32A large herd of pigs was feeding there on the hillside. The demons begged Jesus to let them go into them, and he gave them permission. 33When the demons came out of the man, they went into the pigs, and the herd rushed down the steep bank into the lake and was drowned. ver 22-23

34When those tending the pigs saw what had happened, they ran off and reported this in the town and countryside, 35and the people went out to see what had happened. When they came to Jesus, they found the man from whom the demons had gone out, sitting at Jesus’ feet, dressed and in his right mind; and they were afraid. 36Those who had seen it told the people how the demon-possessed man had been cured. 37Then all the people of the region of the Gerasenes asked Jesus to leave them, because they were overcome with fear. So he got into the boat and left. Mt 8:28-34

38The man from whom the demons had gone out begged to go with him, but Jesus sent him away, saying, 39“Return home and tell how much God has done for you.” So the man went away and told all over town how much Jesus had done for him. Mk 5:1-20

A Dead Girl and a Sick Woman

▶ *See Matthew 9:18–26; Mark 5:22–43*

40Now when Jesus returned, a crowd welcomed him, for they were all expecting him. 41Then a man named Jairus, a ruler of the synagogue, came and fell at Jesus’ feet, pleading with him to come to his house 42because his only daughter, a girl of about twelve, was dying. Mk 5:22

As Jesus was on his way, the crowds almost crushed him. 43And a woman was there who had been subject to bleeding for twelve years,[c] but no one could heal her. 44She came up behind him and touched the edge of his cloak, and immediately her bleeding stopped. Lev 15:25-30; Mt 9:20

[a] *26* Some manuscripts *Gadarenes*; other manuscripts *Gergesenes*; also in verse 37 [b] *29* Greek *unclean* [c] *43* Many manuscripts *years, and she had spent all she had on doctors*

45“Who touched me?” Jesus asked.

When they all denied it, Peter said, “Master, the people are crowding and pressing against you.”

46But Jesus said, “Someone touched me; I know that power has gone out from me.” Lk 5:17; 6:19

47Then the woman, seeing that she could not go unnoticed, came trembling and fell at his feet. In the presence of all the people, she told why she had touched him and how she had been instantly healed. 48Then he said to her, “Daughter, your faith has healed you. Go in peace.” Mt 9:22; Ac 15:33

49While Jesus was still speaking, someone came from the house of Jairus, the synagogue ruler. “Your daughter is dead,” he said. “Don’t bother the teacher any more.” ver 41

50Hearing this, Jesus said to Jairus, “Don’t be afraid; just believe, and she will be healed.”

51When he arrived at the house of Jairus, he did not let anyone go in with him except Peter, John and James, and the child’s father and mother. 52Meanwhile, all the people were wailing and mourning for her. “Stop wailing,” Jesus said. “She is not dead but asleep.” Jn 11:11,13

53They laughed at him, knowing that she was dead. 54But he took her by the hand and said, “My child, get up!” 55Her spirit returned, and at once she stood up. Then Jesus told them to give her something to eat. 56Her parents were astonished, but he ordered them not to tell anyone what had happened. Mt 9:18-26; Mk 5:22-43

Jesus Sends Out the Twelve

▶ *See Matthew 10:9–15; Mark 6:8–11*

9 When Jesus had called the Twelve together, he gave them power and authority to drive out all demons and to cure diseases, 2and he sent them out to preach the kingdom of God and to heal the sick. 3He told them: “Take nothing for the journey—no staff, no bag, no bread, no money, no extra tunic. 4Whatever house you enter, stay there until you leave that town. 5If people do not welcome you, shake the dust off your feet when you leave their town, as a testimony against them.” 6So they set out and went from village to village, preaching the gospel and healing people everywhere. Mt 10:9-15; Mk 6:8-11

7Now Herod the tetrarch heard about all that was going on. And he was perplexed, because some were saying that John had been raised from the dead, 8others that Elijah had appeared, and still others that one of the prophets of long ago had come back to life. 9But Herod said, “I beheaded John. Who, then, is this I hear such things about?” And he tried to see him. Mt 14:1-2; Mk 6:14-16

Jesus Feeds the Five Thousand

▶ *See Matthew 14:13–21; Mark 6:32–44; John 6:5–13*

10When the apostles returned, they reported to Jesus what they had done. Then he took them with him and they withdrew by themselves to a town called Bethsaida, 11but the crowds learned about it and followed him. He welcomed them and spoke to them about the kingdom of God, and healed those who needed healing. Mt 11:21; Mk 6:30

12Late in the afternoon the Twelve came to him and said, “Send the crowd away so they can go to the surrounding villages and countryside and find food and lodging, because we are in a remote place here.”

13He replied, “You give them something to eat.”

They answered, “We have only five loaves of bread and two fish—unless we go and buy food for all this crowd.” 14(About five thousand men were there.) Jn 6:5-13

But he said to his disciples, “Have them sit down in groups of about fifty each.” 15The disciples did so, and everybody sat down. 16Taking the five loaves and the two fish and looking up to heaven, he gave thanks and broke them. Then he gave them to the disciples to set before the people. 17They all ate and were satisfied, and the disciples picked up twelve basketfuls of broken pieces that were left over. 2Ki 4:42-44

Peter’s Confession of Christ

▶ *See Matthew 16:13–16; Mark 8:27–29*

18Once when Jesus was praying in private and his disciples were with him, he asked them, “Who do the crowds say I am?” Lk 3:21

19They replied, “Some say John the Baptist; others say Elijah; and still others, that one of the prophets of long ago has come back to life.”

20“But what about you?” he asked. “Who do you say I am?” Mt 16:13-16

Peter answered, “The Christ[a] of God.”

21Jesus strictly warned them not to tell this to anyone. 22And he said, “The Son of Man must suffer many things and be rejected by the elders, chief priests and teachers of the law, and he must be killed and on the third day be raised to life.”

23Then he said to them all: “If anyone would come after me, he must deny himself and take up his cross daily and follow me. 24For whoever wants to save his life will lose it, but whoever loses his life for me will save it. 25What good is it for a man to gain the whole world, and yet lose or forfeit his very self? 26If anyone is ashamed of me and my words, the Son of Man will be ashamed of him when he comes in his glory and in the glory of the Father and of the holy angels. 27I tell you the truth,

[a]20 Or *Messiah*

some who are standing here will not taste death before they see the kingdom of God." Mt 16:21-28

The Transfiguration

▶ *See Matthew 17:1–8; Mark 9:2–8*

[28]About eight days after Jesus said this, he took Peter, John and James with him and went up onto a mountain to pray. [29]As he was praying, the appearance of his face changed, and his clothes became as bright as a flash of lightning. [30]Two men, Moses and Elijah, [31]appeared in glorious splendor, talking with Jesus. They spoke about his departure, which he was about to bring to fulfillment at Jerusalem. [32]Peter and his companions were very sleepy, but when they became fully awake, they saw his glory and the two men standing with him. [33]As the men were leaving Jesus, Peter said to him, "Master, it is good for us to be here. Let us put up three shelters—one for you, one for Moses and one for Elijah." (He did not know what he was saying.) Lk 3:21; 2Pe 1:15

[34]While he was speaking, a cloud appeared and enveloped them, and they were afraid as they entered the cloud. [35]A voice came from the cloud, saying, "This is my Son, whom I have chosen; listen to him." [36]When the voice had spoken, they found that Jesus was alone. The disciples kept this to themselves, and told no one at that time what they had seen. Mt 17:1-8; Mk 9:2-8

The Healing of a Boy With an Evil Spirit

▶ *See Matthew 17:14–18,22–23; Mark 9:14–27,30–32*

[37]The next day, when they came down from the mountain, a large crowd met him. [38]A man in the crowd called out, "Teacher, I beg you to look at my son, for he is my only child. [39]A spirit seizes him and he suddenly screams; it throws him into convulsions so that he foams at the mouth. It scarcely ever leaves him and is destroying him. [40]I begged your disciples to drive it out, but they could not." Mt 17:14-18,22-23

[41]"O unbelieving and perverse generation," Jesus replied, "how long shall I stay with you and put up with you? Bring your son here." Dt 32:5

[42]Even while the boy was coming, the demon threw him to the ground in a convulsion. But Jesus rebuked the evil[a] spirit, healed the boy and gave him back to his father. [43]And they were all amazed at the greatness of God.

While everyone was marveling at all that Jesus did, he said to his disciples, [44]"Listen carefully to what I am about to tell you: The Son of Man is going to be betrayed into the hands of men." [45]But they did not understand what this meant. It was hidden from them, so that they did not grasp it, and they were afraid to ask him about it.

Who Will Be the Greatest?

▶ *See Matthew 18:1–5; Mark 9:33–40*

[46]An argument started among the disciples as to which of them would be the greatest. [47]Jesus, knowing their thoughts, took a little child and had him stand beside him. [48]Then he said to them, "Whoever welcomes this little child in my name welcomes me; and whoever welcomes me welcomes the one who sent me. For he who is least among you all—he is the greatest." Mt 18:1-5

[49]"Master," said John, "we saw a man driving out demons in your name and we tried to stop him, because he is not one of us." Lk 5:5

[50]"Do not stop him," Jesus said, "for whoever is not against you is for you." Mt 12:30; Lk 11:23

Teachings of Jesus **Chapters 9:51–19:27**

In this section of Luke we find the Son of Man teaching his followers. These chapters are filled with parables, exhortations, warnings and teachings. About sixty percent of the instruction recorded here is unique to the Gospel of Luke. This same Jesus who had come to earth and sought the lost was continuing His ministry of saving the lost by teaching them how to find the way to eternal life.

Samaritan Opposition

[51]As the time approached for him to be taken up to heaven, Jesus resolutely set out for Jerusalem. [52]And he sent messengers on ahead, who went into a Samaritan village to get things ready for him; [53]but the people there did not welcome him, because he was heading for Jerusalem. [54]When the disciples James and John saw this, they asked, "Lord, do you want us to call fire down from heaven to destroy them[b]?" [55]But Jesus turned and rebuked them, [56]and[c] they went to another village. 2Ki 1:10,12; Mk 16:19; Lk 13:22

The Cost of Following Jesus

▶ *See Matthew 8:19–22*

[57]As they were walking along the road, a man said to him, "I will follow you wherever you go."

[58]Jesus replied, "Foxes have holes and birds of the air have nests, but the Son of Man has no place to lay his head."

[59]He said to another man, "Follow me."

But the man replied, "Lord, first let me go and bury my father."

[60]Jesus said to him, "Let the dead bury their own dead, but you go and proclaim the kingdom of God." Mt 8:19-22

[61]Still another said, "I will follow you, Lord; but first let me go back and say good-by to my family." 1Ki 19:20

[a]42 Greek *unclean* [b]54 Some manuscripts *them, even as Elijah did* [c]55,56 Some manuscripts *them. And he said, "You do not know what kind of spirit you are of, for the Son of Man did not come to destroy men's lives, but to save them."* [56]*And*

62Jesus replied, "No one who puts his hand to
the plow and looks back is fit for service in the
kingdom of God."

Jesus Sends Out the Seventy-two

▶ *See Luke 9:3–5*

10 After this the Lord appointed seventy-
two[a] others and sent them two by two
ahead of him to every town and place where he
was about to go. 2He told them, "The harvest is
plentiful, but the workers are few. Ask the Lord
of the harvest, therefore, to send out workers
into his harvest field. 3Go! I am sending you out
like lambs among wolves. 4Do not take a purse or
bag or sandals; and do not greet anyone on the
road.

5"When you enter a house, first say, 'Peace to
this house.' 6If a man of peace is there, your peace
will rest on him; if not, it will return to you. 7Stay
in that house, eating and drinking whatever they
give you, for the worker deserves his wages. Do
not move around from house to house. Mt 10:10

8"When you enter a town and are welcomed,
eat what is set before you. 9Heal the sick who are
there and tell them, 'The kingdom of God is near
you.' 10But when you enter a town and are not
welcomed, go into its streets and say, 11'Even the
dust of your town that sticks to our feet we wipe
off against you. Yet be sure of this: The kingdom
of God is near.' 12I tell you, it will be more bearable
on that day for Sodom than for that town.

13"Woe to you, Korazin! Woe to you, Bethsaida! For if the miracles that were performed in you
had been performed in Tyre and Sidon, they
would have repented long ago, sitting in sackcloth
and ashes. 14But it will be more bearable for Tyre
and Sidon at the judgment than for you. 15And
you, Capernaum, will you be lifted up to the skies?
No, you will go down to the depths.[b] Mt 4:13

16"He who listens to you listens to me; he who
rejects you rejects me; but he who rejects me rejects him who sent me." Mt 10:40; Jn 13:20

17The seventy-two returned with joy and said,
"Lord, even the demons submit to us in your
name." Mk 16:17

18He replied, "I saw Satan fall like lightning
from heaven. 19I have given you authority to trample on snakes and scorpions and to overcome all
the power of the enemy; nothing will harm you.
20However, do not rejoice that the spirits submit to
you, but rejoice that your names are written in
heaven." Ex 32:32; Heb 12:23; Rev 13:8

21At that time Jesus, full of joy through the Holy
Spirit, said, "I praise you, Father, Lord of heaven
and earth, because you have hidden these things
from the wise and learned, and revealed them to
little children. Yes, Father, for this was your good
pleasure. 1Co 1:26-29

22"All things have been committed to me by my
Father. No one knows who the Son is except the
Father, and no one knows who the Father is except
the Son and those to whom the Son chooses to
reveal him." Mt 11:21-23,25-27

23Then he turned to his disciples and said privately, "Blessed are the eyes that see what you see.
24For I tell you that many prophets and kings
wanted to see what you see but did not see it, and
to hear what you hear but did not hear it."

The Parable of the Good Samaritan

▶ *See Matthew 22:34–40; Mark 12:28–31*

25On one occasion an expert in the law stood up
to test Jesus. "Teacher," he asked, "what must I do
to inherit eternal life?" Mt 19:16; Lk 18:18

LIVING  **INSIGHT**

"Go and do likewise." Supporting, comforting, helping . . . your arm around the hunched shoulder of another . . . your smile saying "try again" to someone who's convinced it's curtains . . . your cup of cool water held up to a brother's cracked lips, reassuring and reaffirming that he is loved.

(See Luke 10:25–37.)

26"What is written in the Law?" he replied.
"How do you read it?"

27He answered: " 'Love the Lord your God with
all your heart and with all your soul and with
all your strength and with all your mind'[c]; and,
'Love your neighbor as yourself.'[d]" Lev 19:18; Dt 6:5

28"You have answered correctly," Jesus replied.
"Do this and you will live." Mt 22:34-40; Mk 12:28-31

29But he wanted to justify himself, so he asked
Jesus, "And who is my neighbor?" Lk 16:15

30In reply Jesus said: "A man was going down
from Jerusalem to Jericho, when he fell into the
hands of robbers. They stripped him of his clothes,
beat him and went away, leaving him half dead.
31A priest happened to be going down the same
road, and when he saw the man, he passed by on
the other side. 32So too, a Levite, when he came to
the place and saw him, passed by on the other side.
33But a Samaritan, as he traveled, came where the
man was; and when he saw him, he took pity on
him. 34He went to him and bandaged his wounds,
pouring on oil and wine. Then he put the man on
his own donkey, took him to an inn and took care
of him. 35The next day he took out two silver

[a] *1* Some manuscripts *seventy*; also in verse 17 [b] *15* Greek *Hades* [c] *27* Deut. 6:5 [d] *27* Lev. 19:18

coins[a] and gave them to the innkeeper. ‘Look
after him,’ he said, ‘and when I return, I will reim-
burse you for any extra expense you may have.’
36“Which of these three do you think was a
neighbor to the man who fell into the hands of
robbers?”
37The expert in the law replied, “The one who
had mercy on him.”
Jesus told him, “Go and do likewise.”

At the Home of Martha and Mary

38As Jesus and his disciples were on their way,
he came to a village where a woman named Martha opened her home to him. 39She had a sister
called Mary, who sat at the Lord’s feet listening to
what he said. 40But Martha was distracted by all
the preparations that had to be made. She came to
him and asked, “Lord, don’t you care that my
sister has left me to do the work by myself? Tell
her to help me!” Lk 8:35; Jn 11:1
41“Martha, Martha,” the Lord answered, “you
are worried and upset about many things, 42but
only one thing is needed.[b] Mary has chosen what
is better, and it will not be taken away from her.”

Jesus’ Teaching on Prayer

▶ *See Matthew 6:9–13; 7:7–11*

11 One day Jesus was praying in a certain
place. When he finished, one of his disciples said to him, “Lord, teach us to pray, just as
John taught his disciples.” Lk 3:21; Jn 13:13
2He said to them, “When you pray, say:

“ ‘Father,[c]
hallowed be your name,
your kingdom come.[d] Mt 3:2
3Give us each day our daily bread.
4Forgive us our sins,
for we also forgive everyone who sins
against us.[e] Mt 18:35; Mk 11:25
And lead us not into temptation.[f]’ ” Mt 6:9-13

5Then he said to them, “Suppose one of you has

LIVING  **INSIGHT**

At the heart of forgiveness is the very person of Jesus Christ, who forgave you. The greatest exhibition of forgiveness took place at the cross, where Jesus died for the sins of the world. Fully forgive, just as He forgave you.

(See Luke 11:4.)

a friend, and he goes to him at midnight and says,
‘Friend, lend me three loaves of bread, 6because a
friend of mine on a journey has come to me, and
I have nothing to set before him.’
7“Then the one inside answers, ‘Don’t bother
me. The door is already locked, and my children
are with me in bed. I can’t get up and give you
anything.’ 8I tell you, though he will not get up and
give him the bread because he is his friend, yet
because of the man’s boldness[g] he will get up and
give him as much as he needs. Lk 18:1-6
9“So I say to you: Ask and it will be given to
you; seek and you will find; knock and the door
will be opened to you. 10For everyone who asks
receives; he who seeks finds; and to him who
knocks, the door will be opened. Mt 7:7
11“Which of you fathers, if your son asks for[h]
a fish, will give him a snake instead? 12Or if he asks
for an egg, will give him a scorpion? 13If you then,
though you are evil, know how to give good gifts
to your children, how much more will your Father
in heaven give the Holy Spirit to those who ask
him!”

Jesus and Beelzebub

▶ *See Matthew 12:22,24–29,43–45; Mark 3:23–27*

14Jesus was driving out a demon that was mute.
When the demon left, the man who had been mute
spoke, and the crowd was amazed. 15But some of
them said, “By Beelzebub,[i] the prince of demons,
he is driving out demons.” 16Others tested him by
asking for a sign from heaven. Mt 12:22,24
17Jesus knew their thoughts and said to them:
“Any kingdom divided against itself will be ruined,
and a house divided against itself will fall. 18If Satan is divided against himself, how can his kingdom stand? I say this because you claim that I
drive out demons by Beelzebub. 19Now if I drive
out demons by Beelzebub, by whom do your followers drive them out? So then, they will be your
judges. 20But if I drive out demons by the finger of
God, then the kingdom of God has come to you.
21“When a strong man, fully armed, guards his
own house, his possessions are safe. 22But when
someone stronger attacks and overpowers him, he
takes away the armor in which the man trusted
and divides up the spoils. Mk 3:23-27
23“He who is not with me is against me, and he
who does not gather with me, scatters. Mt 12:30
24“When an evil[j] spirit comes out of a man, it
goes through arid places seeking rest and does not
find it. Then it says, ‘I will return to the house I
left.’ 25When it arrives, it finds the house swept
clean and put in order. 26Then it goes and takes

[a]35 Greek *two denarii* [b]42 Some manuscripts *but few things are needed—or only one* [c]2 Some manuscripts *Our Father in heaven* [d]2 Some manuscripts *come. May your will be done on earth as it is in heaven.* [e]4 Greek *everyone who is indebted to us* [f]4 Some manuscripts *temptation but deliver us from the evil one* [g]8 Or *persistence* [h]11 Some manuscripts *for bread, will give him a stone; or if he asks for* [i]15 Greek *Beezeboul* or *Beelzeboul*; also in verses 18 and 19 [j]24 Greek *unclean*

MARY AND MARTHA

"Only One Thing Is Needed"

"[Jesus] came to a village where a woman named Martha opened her home to him. She had a sister called Mary, who sat at the Lord's feet . . ."

—LUKE 10:38–39

Tucked away in Luke's scroll is one of the most intimate vignettes in the life of Jesus. The scene is a house in a hamlet two miles from the busy city of Jerusalem. The house was owned by Martha, the oldest of three unmarried siblings who lived together. For some reason Jesus chose this home as His place of refuge.

Moving inexorably toward the cross and the horrible dread of the iron spikes in His hands and feet, Jesus apparently cherished these moments of intimacy with close friends. On many occasions, He purposefully moved away from the crowds to be by Himself or to be with His disciples and friends. Luke records here one such occasion. In this home in Bethany, Jesus would find a safe harbor with people who didn't ask leading questions, who accepted Him for who He was, who were not overtly critical, who didn't have a hidden agenda or feel the need to pump Him for answers. It was a place to kick back and find rest.

Luke paints a scene in which Jesus was relaxing in the sitting room of Mary and Martha's home. And there was Mary, sitting at His feet. I mean, how often does the Savior stop by? How often does one get a chance to sit at the feet of the most sacred life ever to cast a shadow across the earth? Mary sat at His feet relaxed, content to sit quietly and listen. Listening to Him took priority over commonplace household tasks. But as soon as we read *Martha's* name, we find that she was "distracted." Martha, the oldest of the family's three siblings, was the take-charge person. She seemed to be the classic "type-A" personality—high-strung, intense, focused, task-oriented, even a bit driven, one might say. She was someone who took responsibility seriously. Birth-order experts tell us that's often the way it is for the oldest child in a family.

This story has nothing to do with Martha's name, or her gender, or her birth order. In Martha we see a clear picture of ourselves. How often don't we miss the moment because the incidentals take too much of our attention? Here was Martha, working away in the kitchen, trying to pull together enough food for the hungry folks talking about heavenly things out in the living room. As she worked, she reached the point of total exasperation. Finally she could stand it no longer. The lid blew off her boiling pot, and she stormed into the living room to accuse Mary and to plead for Jesus' understanding. We've all been there.

Anyone who reads her words (10:40) can't help but note the focus of Martha's thoughts. They were not on Jesus. They were not on Mary. They were not on the meal. They were on Martha. Why, of course! She had worked hard to set just the right tone for Jesus' visit. She had put it all together so well. And we applaud her motive. It's right and good! There was nothing wrong with the hospitality she was providing. It was her priorities that were out of order. She had become so concerned with the task of serving that she missed one of greater importance—taking the time to sit at the feet of Jesus.

All of us need to take time to look in the mirror that Martha provides. The frustration and anxiety that we see in Martha is the kind that can, and often does, choke us. When we become consumed by worry and buried by busyness, we can so quickly strangle our ability to distinguish the incidentals from the essentials. We can build up so many worries in our minds that we can't relax, and it siphons our joy away to the point that we can all too quickly become bitter and judgmental toward others.

Jesus responds to our anxiety in the same gentle, reassuring tones with which He spoke to Martha. He encourages all of us to enter into the spirit of the moment, to recognize the utmost importance of taking the time to be in intimate relationship with Him. For Martha, the heat of the kitchen and the busyness of the preparations and the anxiety of wanting everything to be just right caused her to take her eyes off Jesus. Would you be willing to ask yourself an honest question: Is there anything in your life that's causing *you* to take your eyes off Jesus?

seven other spirits more wicked than itself, and they go in and live there. And the final condition of that man is worse than the first." Mt 12:43-45

27 As Jesus was saying these things, a woman in the crowd called out, "Blessed is the mother who gave you birth and nursed you." Lk 23:29

28 He replied, "Blessed rather are those who hear the word of God and obey it." Lk 8:21; Jn 14:21

The Sign of Jonah

▶ *See Matthew 12:39–42*

29 As the crowds increased, Jesus said, "This is a wicked generation. It asks for a miraculous sign, but none will be given it except the sign of Jonah. 30 For as Jonah was a sign to the Ninevites, so also will the Son of Man be to this generation. 31 The Queen of the South will rise at the judgment with the men of this generation and condemn them; for she came from the ends of the earth to listen to Solomon's wisdom, and now one[a] greater than Solomon is here. 32 The men of Nineveh will stand up at the judgment with this generation and condemn it; for they repented at the preaching of Jonah, and now one greater than Jonah is here.

The Lamp of the Body

▶ *See Matthew 6:22–23*

33 "No one lights a lamp and puts it in a place where it will be hidden, or under a bowl. Instead he puts it on its stand, so that those who come in may see the light. 34 Your eye is the lamp of your body. When your eyes are good, your whole body also is full of light. But when they are bad, your body also is full of darkness. 35 See to it, then, that the light within you is not darkness. 36 Therefore, if your whole body is full of light, and no part of it dark, it will be completely lighted, as when the light of a lamp shines on you." Mt 6:22-23; Mk 4:21

Six Woes

37 When Jesus had finished speaking, a Pharisee invited him to eat with him; so he went in and reclined at the table. 38 But the Pharisee, noticing that Jesus did not first wash before the meal, was surprised. Mk 7:3-4

39 Then the Lord said to him, "Now then, you Pharisees clean the outside of the cup and dish, but inside you are full of greed and wickedness. 40 You foolish people! Did not the one who made the outside make the inside also? 41 But give what is inside ⌞the dish⌟[b] to the poor, and everything will be clean for you. Mt 23:25-26; Lk 12:33

42 "Woe to you Pharisees, because you give God a tenth of your mint, rue and all other kinds of garden herbs, but you neglect justice and the love of God. You should have practiced the latter without leaving the former undone. Mic 6:8; Mt 23:23

43 "Woe to you Pharisees, because you love the most important seats in the synagogues and greetings in the marketplaces. Mt 23:6-7; Mk 12:38-39

44 "Woe to you, because you are like unmarked graves, which men walk over without knowing it."

45 One of the experts in the law answered him, "Teacher, when you say these things, you insult us also." Mt 22:35

46 Jesus replied, "And you experts in the law, woe to you, because you load people down with burdens they can hardly carry, and you yourselves will not lift one finger to help them. Mt 23:4

47 "Woe to you, because you build tombs for the prophets, and it was your forefathers who killed them. 48 So you testify that you approve of what your forefathers did; they killed the prophets, and you build their tombs. 49 Because of this, God in his wisdom said, 'I will send them prophets and apostles, some of whom they will kill and others they will persecute.' 50 Therefore this generation will be held responsible for the blood of all the prophets that has been shed since the beginning of the world, 51 from the blood of Abel to the blood of Zechariah, who was killed between the altar and the sanctuary. Yes, I tell you, this generation will be held responsible for it all. Mt 23:29-32,34-36

52 "Woe to you experts in the law, because you have taken away the key to knowledge. You yourselves have not entered, and you have hindered those who were entering." Mt 23:13

53 When Jesus left there, the Pharisees and the teachers of the law began to oppose him fiercely and to besiege him with questions, 54 waiting to catch him in something he might say. Mk 12:13

Warnings and Encouragements

▶ *See Matthew 10:26–33*

12 Meanwhile, when a crowd of many thousands had gathered, so that they were trampling on one another, Jesus began to speak first to his disciples, saying: "Be on your guard against the yeast of the Pharisees, which is hypocrisy. 2 There is nothing concealed that will not be disclosed, or hidden that will not be made known. 3 What you have said in the dark will be heard in the daylight, and what you have whispered in the ear in the inner rooms will be proclaimed from the roofs. Mk 4:22; Lk 8:17

4 "I tell you, my friends, do not be afraid of those who kill the body and after that can do no more. 5 But I will show you whom you should fear: Fear him who, after the killing of the body, has power to throw you into hell. Yes, I tell you, fear him. 6 Are not five sparrows sold for two pennies[c]? Yet not one of them is forgotten by God. 7 Indeed, the very hairs of your head are all numbered. Don't be afraid; you are worth more than many sparrows.

[a] 31 Or *something*; also in verse 32 [b] 41 Or *what you have* [c] 6 Greek *two assaria*

8"I tell you, whoever acknowledges me before men, the Son of Man will also acknowledge him before the angels of God. 9But he who disowns me before men will be disowned before the angels of God. 10And everyone who speaks a word against the Son of Man will be forgiven, but anyone who blasphemes against the Holy Spirit will not be forgiven. Mt 10:26-33; 1Jn 5:16

LIVING  **INSIGHT**

God is in control. He can handle it. He can handle you. He knows you thoroughly . . . He even knows the number of the hairs on your head. He's got everything wired! He's got it all together!

(See Luke 12:4–7.)

11"When you are brought before synagogues, rulers and authorities, do not worry about how you will defend yourselves or what you will say, 12for the Holy Spirit will teach you at that time what you should say." Mt 10:20; Mk 13:11

The Parable of the Rich Fool

13Someone in the crowd said to him, "Teacher, tell my brother to divide the inheritance with me."

14Jesus replied, "Man, who appointed me a judge or an arbiter between you?" 15Then he said to them, "Watch out! Be on your guard against all kinds of greed; a man's life does not consist in the abundance of his possessions." Job 20:20; Ps 62:10

16And he told them this parable: "The ground of a certain rich man produced a good crop. 17He thought to himself, 'What shall I do? I have no place to store my crops.'

18"Then he said, 'This is what I'll do. I will tear down my barns and build bigger ones, and there I will store all my grain and my goods. 19And I'll say to myself, "You have plenty of good things laid up for many years. Take life easy; eat, drink and be merry." '

20"But God said to him, 'You fool! This very night your life will be demanded from you. Then who will get what you have prepared for yourself?'

21"This is how it will be with anyone who stores up things for himself but is not rich toward God."

LIVING  **INSIGHT**

The soul possesses this God-shaped vacuum. And not until God invades and fills it can we be at peace within—which is another way of saying, "If God isn't in first place, you can't handle success."

(See Luke 12:16–21.)

Do Not Worry

▶ *See Matthew 6:25–33*

22Then Jesus said to his disciples: "Therefore I tell you, do not worry about your life, what you will eat; or about your body, what you will wear. 23Life is more than food, and the body more than clothes. 24Consider the ravens: They do not sow or reap, they have no storeroom or barn; yet God feeds them. And how much more valuable you are than birds! 25Who of you by worrying can add a single hour to his life[a]? 26Since you cannot do this very little thing, why do you worry about the rest?

27"Consider how the lilies grow. They do not labor or spin. Yet I tell you, not even Solomon in all his splendor was dressed like one of these. 28If that is how God clothes the grass of the field, which is here today, and tomorrow is thrown into the fire, how much more will he clothe you, O you of little faith! 29And do not set your heart on what you will eat or drink; do not worry about it. 30For the pagan world runs after all such things, and your Father knows that you need them. 31But seek his kingdom, and these things will be given to you as well. Mt 6:25-33

32"Do not be afraid, little flock, for your Father has been pleased to give you the kingdom. 33Sell your possessions and give to the poor. Provide purses for yourselves that will not wear out, a treasure in heaven that will not be exhausted, where no thief comes near and no moth destroys. 34For where your treasure is, there your heart will be also. Mt 6:20-21; 14:27

Watchfulness

▶ *See Matthew 24:43–51; Mark 13:33–37*

35"Be dressed ready for service and keep your lamps burning, 36like men waiting for their master to return from a wedding banquet, so that when he comes and knocks they can immediately open the door for him. 37It will be good for those servants whose master finds them watching when he comes. I tell you the truth, he will dress himself to serve, will have them recline at the table and will come and wait on them. 38It will be good for those servants whose master finds them ready, even if he comes in the second or third watch of the night. 39But understand this: If the owner of the house had known at what hour the thief was coming, he would not have let his house be broken into. 40You also must be ready, because the Son of Man will come at an hour when you do not expect him."

[a]25 Or *single cubit to his height*

41Peter asked, "Lord, are you telling this parable to us, or to everyone?"

42The Lord answered, "Who then is the faithful and wise manager, whom the master puts in charge of his servants to give them their food allowance at the proper time? 43It will be good for that servant whom the master finds doing so when he returns. 44I tell you the truth, he will put him in charge of all his possessions. 45But suppose the servant says to himself, 'My master is taking a long time in coming,' and he then begins to beat the menservants and maidservants and to eat and drink and get drunk. 46The master of that servant will come on a day when he does not expect him and at an hour he is not aware of. He will cut him to pieces and assign him a place with the unbelievers. Mt 24:43-51

47"That servant who knows his master's will and does not get ready or does not do what his master wants will be beaten with many blows. 48But the one who does not know and does things deserving punishment will be beaten with few blows. From everyone who has been given much, much will be demanded; and from the one who has been entrusted with much, much more will be asked.

Not Peace but Division

▶ *See Matthew 10:34–36*

49"I have come to bring fire on the earth, and how I wish it were already kindled! 50But I have a baptism to undergo, and how distressed I am until it is completed! 51Do you think I came to bring peace on earth? No, I tell you, but division. 52From now on there will be five in one family divided against each other, three against two and two against three. 53They will be divided, father against son and son against father, mother against daughter and daughter against mother, mother-in-law against daughter-in-law and daughter-in-law against mother-in-law." Mt 10:34-36

Interpreting the Times

54He said to the crowd: "When you see a cloud rising in the west, immediately you say, 'It's going to rain,' and it does. 55And when the south wind blows, you say, 'It's going to be hot,' and it is. 56Hypocrites! You know how to interpret the appearance of the earth and the sky. How is it that you don't know how to interpret this present time?

57"Why don't you judge for yourselves what is right? 58As you are going with your adversary to the magistrate, try hard to be reconciled to him on the way, or he may drag you off to the judge, and the judge turn you over to the officer, and the officer throw you into prison. 59I tell you, you will not get out until you have paid the last penny.[a]"

Repent or Perish

13 Now there were some present at that time who told Jesus about the Galileans whose blood Pilate had mixed with their sacrifices. 2Jesus answered, "Do you think that these Galileans were worse sinners than all the other Galileans because they suffered this way? 3I tell you, no! But unless you repent, you too will all perish. 4Or those eighteen who died when the tower in Siloam fell on them—do you think they were more guilty than all the others living in Jerusalem? 5I tell you, no! But unless you repent, you too will all perish."

6Then he told this parable: "A man had a fig tree, planted in his vineyard, and he went to look for fruit on it, but did not find any. 7So he said to the man who took care of the vineyard, 'For three years now I've been coming to look for fruit on this fig tree and haven't found any. Cut it down! Why should it use up the soil?' Mt 3:10; 21:19

8" 'Sir,' the man replied, 'leave it alone for one more year, and I'll dig around it and fertilize it. 9If it bears fruit next year, fine! If not, then cut it down.' "

A Crippled Woman Healed on the Sabbath

10On a Sabbath Jesus was teaching in one of the synagogues, 11and a woman was there who had been crippled by a spirit for eighteen years. She was bent over and could not straighten up at all. 12When Jesus saw her, he called her forward and said to her, "Woman, you are set free from your infirmity." 13Then he put his hands on her, and immediately she straightened up and praised God.

14Indignant because Jesus had healed on the Sabbath, the synagogue ruler said to the people, "There are six days for work. So come and be healed on those days, not on the Sabbath."

15The Lord answered him, "You hypocrites! Doesn't each of you on the Sabbath untie his ox or donkey from the stall and lead it out to give it water? 16Then should not this woman, a daughter of Abraham, whom Satan has kept bound for eighteen long years, be set free on the Sabbath day from what bound her?" Lk 14:5; 19:9

17When he said this, all his opponents were humiliated, but the people were delighted with all the wonderful things he was doing. Isa 66:5

The Parables of the Mustard Seed and the Yeast

▶ *See Matthew 13:31–33; Mark 4:30–32*

18Then Jesus asked, "What is the kingdom of God like? What shall I compare it to? 19It is like a mustard seed, which a man took and planted in his garden. It grew and became a tree, and the birds of the air perched in its branches."

[a]59 Greek *lepton*

20Again he asked, "What shall I compare the
kingdom of God to? 21It is like yeast that a woman
took and mixed into a large amount[a] of flour
until it worked all through the dough." Mt 13:31-33

The Narrow Door

22Then Jesus went through the towns and villages, teaching as he made his way to Jerusalem.
23Someone asked him, "Lord, are only a few people going to be saved?" Lk 9:51

He said to them, 24"Make every effort to enter
through the narrow door, because many, I tell you,
will try to enter and will not be able to. 25Once the
owner of the house gets up and closes the door,
you will stand outside knocking and pleading, 'Sir,
open the door for us.' Mt 7:13

"But he will answer, 'I don't know you or where
you come from.' Mt 7:23; 25:10-12

26"Then you will say, 'We ate and drank with
you, and you taught in our streets.'

27"But he will reply, 'I don't know you or where
you come from. Away from me, all you evildoers!'

28"There will be weeping there, and gnashing of
teeth, when you see Abraham, Isaac and Jacob and
all the prophets in the kingdom of God, but you
yourselves thrown out. 29People will come from
east and west and north and south, and will take
their places at the feast in the kingdom of God.
30Indeed there are those who are last who will be
first, and first who will be last." Mt 19:30

Jesus' Sorrow for Jerusalem

▶ *See Matthew 23:37–39*

31At that time some Pharisees came to Jesus and
said to him, "Leave this place and go somewhere
else. Herod wants to kill you." Mt 14:1

32He replied, "Go tell that fox, 'I will drive out
demons and heal people today and tomorrow, and
on the third day I will reach my goal.' 33In any
case, I must keep going today and tomorrow and
the next day—for surely no prophet can die outside Jerusalem! Mt 21:11; Heb 2:10

34"O Jerusalem, Jerusalem, you who kill the
prophets and stone those sent to you, how often I
have longed to gather your children together, as a
hen gathers her chicks under her wings, but you
were not willing! 35Look, your house is left to you
desolate. I tell you, you will not see me again until
you say, 'Blessed is he who comes in the name of
the Lord.'[b]" Mt 23:37-39; Lk 19:41

Jesus at a Pharisee's House

14 One Sabbath, when Jesus went to eat in the
house of a prominent Pharisee, he was being carefully watched. 2There in front of him was
a man suffering from dropsy. 3Jesus asked the
Pharisees and experts in the law, "Is it lawful to
heal on the Sabbath or not?" 4But they remained
silent. So taking hold of the man, he healed him
and sent him away. Mt 12:2; 22:35

5Then he asked them, "If one of you has a son[c]
or an ox that falls into a well on the Sabbath day,
will you not immediately pull him out?" 6And they
had nothing to say. Lk 13:15

7When he noticed how the guests picked the
places of honor at the table, he told them this
parable: 8"When someone invites you to a wedding feast, do not take the place of honor, for a
person more distinguished than you may have
been invited. 9If so, the host who invited both of
you will come and say to you, 'Give this man your
seat.' Then, humiliated, you will have to take the
least important place. 10But when you are invited,
take the lowest place, so that when your host
comes, he will say to you, 'Friend, move up to a
better place.' Then you will be honored in the
presence of all your fellow guests. 11For everyone
who exalts himself will be humbled, and he who
humbles himself will be exalted." Pr 25:6-7

LIVING  **INSIGHT**

Regardless of your elevated position or high pile of honors or row of degrees or endless list of achievements, just stay real. Junk any idea that you deserve some kind of pat on the back or a nice gold wristwatch for a job well done. If you did it for God, He has an infinite number of unseen ways to reward you. If you did it to impress others, no wonder you're clawing for glory!

(See Luke 14:11.)

12Then Jesus said to his host, "When you give a
luncheon or dinner, do not invite your friends,
your brothers or relatives, or your rich neighbors;
if you do, they may invite you back and so you will
be repaid. 13But when you give a banquet, invite
the poor, the crippled, the lame, the blind, 14and
you will be blessed. Although they cannot repay
you, you will be repaid at the resurrection of the
righteous." Ac 24:15

The Parable of the Great Banquet

15When one of those at the table with him heard
this, he said to Jesus, "Blessed is the man who will
eat at the feast in the kingdom of God." Rev 19:9

16Jesus replied: "A certain man was preparing a
great banquet and invited many guests. 17At the
time of the banquet he sent his servant to tell those
who had been invited, 'Come, for everything is
now ready.'

[a]21 Greek *three satas* (probably about 1/2 bushel or 22 liters) [b]35 Psalm 118:26 [c]5 Some manuscripts *donkey*

18“But they all alike began to make excuses. The
first said, ‘I have just bought a field, and I must go
and see it. Please excuse me.’
19“Another said, ‘I have just bought five yoke of
oxen, and I'm on my way to try them out. Please
excuse me.’
20“Still another said, ‘I just got married, so I
can't come.’
21“The servant came back and reported this to
his master. Then the owner of the house became
angry and ordered his servant, ‘Go out quickly
into the streets and alleys of the town and bring in
the poor, the crippled, the blind and the lame.’
22“ ‘Sir,’ the servant said, ‘what you ordered has
been done, but there is still room.’
23“Then the master told his servant, ‘Go out to
the roads and country lanes and make them come
in, so that my house will be full. 24I tell you, not
one of those men who were invited will get a taste
of my banquet.’ ” Mt 22:2-14; Ac 13:46

The Cost of Being a Disciple

25Large crowds were traveling with Jesus, and
turning to them he said: 26“If anyone comes to me
and does not hate his father and mother, his wife
and children, his brothers and sisters—yes, even
his own life—he cannot be my disciple. 27And
anyone who does not carry his cross and follow
me cannot be my disciple. Mt 10:37-38; Lk 9:23
28“Suppose one of you wants to build a tower.
Will he not first sit down and estimate the cost to
see if he has enough money to complete it? 29For
if he lays the foundation and is not able to finish
it, everyone who sees it will ridicule him, 30saying,
‘This fellow began to build and was not able to
finish.’
31“Or suppose a king is about to go to war
against another king. Will he not first sit down and
consider whether he is able with ten thousand men
to oppose the one coming against him with twenty
thousand? 32If he is not able, he will send a delegation while the other is still a long way off and will
ask for terms of peace. 33In the same way, any of
you who does not give up everything he has cannot be my disciple. Php 3:7-8
34“Salt is good, but if it loses its saltiness, how
can it be made salty again? 35It is fit neither for the
soil nor for the manure pile; it is thrown out.
“He who has ears to hear, let him hear.”

The Parable of the Lost Sheep

▶ *See Matthew 18:12–14*

15 Now the tax collectors and “sinners” were
all gathering around to hear him. 2But the
Pharisees and the teachers of the law muttered,
“This man welcomes sinners and eats with them.”
3Then Jesus told them this parable: 4“Suppose
one of you has a hundred sheep and loses one of
them. Does he not leave the ninety-nine in the
open country and go after the lost sheep until he
finds it? 5And when he finds it, he joyfully puts it
on his shoulders 6and goes home. Then he calls his
friends and neighbors together and says, ‘Rejoice
with me; I have found my lost sheep.’ 7I tell you
that in the same way there will be more rejoicing
in heaven over one sinner who repents than over
ninety-nine righteous persons who do not need to
repent. Mt 18:12-14

The Parable of the Lost Coin

8“Or suppose a woman has ten silver coins[a]
and loses one. Does she not light a lamp, sweep the
house and search carefully until she finds it? 9And
when she finds it, she calls her friends and neighbors together and says, ‘Rejoice with me; I have
found my lost coin.’ 10In the same way, I tell you,
there is rejoicing in the presence of the angels of
God over one sinner who repents.” ver 6-7

The Parable of the Lost Son

11Jesus continued: “There was a man who had
two sons. 12The younger one said to his father,
‘Father, give me my share of the estate.’ So he
divided his property between them. Dt 21:17
13“Not long after that, the younger son got together all he had, set off for a distant country and
there squandered his wealth in wild living. 14After
he had spent everything, there was a severe famine
in that whole country, and he began to be in need.
15So he went and hired himself out to a citizen of
that country, who sent him to his fields to feed
pigs. 16He longed to fill his stomach with the pods
that the pigs were eating, but no one gave him
anything. Lev 11:7; Lk 16:1
17“When he came to his senses, he said, ‘How
many of my father's hired men have food to spare,
and here I am starving to death! 18I will set out and
go back to my father and say to him: Father, I have
sinned against heaven and against you. 19I am no
longer worthy to be called your son; make me like
one of your hired men.’ 20So he got up and went
to his father. Lev 26:40; Mt 3:2
“But while he was still a long way off, his father
saw him and was filled with compassion for him;
he ran to his son, threw his arms around him and
kissed him. Ge 45:14-15; Ac 20:37
21“The son said to him, ‘Father, I have sinned
against heaven and against you. I am no longer
worthy to be called your son.[b]’ Ps 51:4
22“But the father said to his servants, ‘Quick!
Bring the best robe and put it on him. Put a ring
on his finger and sandals on his feet. 23Bring the

[a] 8 Greek *ten drachmas,* each worth about a day's wages

[b] 21 Some early manuscripts *son. Make me like one of your hired men.*

PARABLES OF JESUS

Parable	Matthew	Mark	Luke
Lamp under a bowl	*5:14-15*	*4:21-22*	*8:16; 11:33*
Wise and foolish builders	*7:24-27*		*6:47-49*
New cloth on an old coat	*9:16*	*2:21*	*5:36*
New wine in old wineskins	*9:17*	*2:22*	*5:37-38*
Sower and the soils	*13:3-8,18-23*	*4:3-8,14-20*	*8:5-8,11-15*
Weeds	*13:24-30,36-43*		
Mustard seed	*13:31-32*	*4:30-32*	*13:18-19*
Yeast	*13:33*		*13:20-21*
Hidden treasure	*13:44*		
Valuable pearl	*13:45-46*		
Net	*13:47-50*		
Owner of a house	*13:52*		
Lost sheep	*18:12-14*		*15:4-7*
Unmerciful servant	*18:23-34*		
Workers in the vineyard	*20:1-16*		
Two sons	*21:28-32*		
Tenants	*21:33-44*	*12:1-11*	*20:9-18*
Wedding banquet	*22:2-14*		
Fig tree	*24:32-35*	*13:28-29*	*21:29-31*
Faithful and wise servant	*24:45-51*		*12:42-48*
Ten virgins	*25:1-13*		
Talents (minas)	*25:14-30*		*19:12-27*
Sheep and goats	*25:31-46*		
Growing seed		*4:26-29*	
Watchful servants		*13:35-37*	*12:35-40*
Moneylender			*7:41-43*
Good Samaritan			*10:30-37*
Friend in need			*11:5-8*
Rich fool			*12:16-21*
Unfruitful fig tree			*13:6-9*
Lowest seat at the feast			*14:7-14*
Great banquet			*14:16-24*
Cost of discipleship			*14:28-33*
Lost coin			*15:8-10*
Lost (prodigal) son			*15:11-32*
Shrewd manager			*16:1-8*
Rich man and Lazarus			*16:19-31*
Master and his servant			*17:7-10*
Persistent widow			*18:2-8*
Pharisee and tax collector			*18:10-14*

fattened calf and kill it. Let's have a feast and celebrate. [24]For this son of mine was dead and is alive again; he was lost and is found.' So they began to celebrate. Eph 2:1,5; 5:14; 1Ti 5:6

[25]"Meanwhile, the older son was in the field. When he came near the house, he heard music and dancing. [26]So he called one of the servants and asked him what was going on. [27]'Your brother has come,' he replied, 'and your father has killed the fattened calf because he has him back safe and sound.'

[28]"The older brother became angry and refused to go in. So his father went out and pleaded with him. [29]But he answered his father, 'Look! All these years I've been slaving for you and never disobeyed your orders. Yet you never gave me even a young goat so I could celebrate with my friends. [30]But when this son of yours who has squandered your property with prostitutes comes home, you kill the fattened calf for him!' Pr 29:3; Jnh 4:1

[31]" 'My son,' the father said, 'you are always with me, and everything I have is yours. [32]But we had to celebrate and be glad, because this brother of yours was dead and is alive again; he was lost and is found.' " Mal 3:17

The Parable of the Shrewd Manager

16 Jesus told his disciples: "There was a rich man whose manager was accused of wasting his possessions. [2]So he called him in and asked him, 'What is this I hear about you? Give an account of your management, because you cannot be manager any longer.' Lk 15:13,30

[3]"The manager said to himself, 'What shall I do now? My master is taking away my job. I'm not strong enough to dig, and I'm ashamed to beg— [4]I know what I'll do so that, when I lose my job here, people will welcome me into their houses.'

[5]"So he called in each one of his master's debtors. He asked the first, 'How much do you owe my master?'

[6]" 'Eight hundred gallons[a] of olive oil,' he replied.

"The manager told him, 'Take your bill, sit down quickly, and make it four hundred.'

[7]"Then he asked the second, 'And how much do you owe?'

" 'A thousand bushels[b] of wheat,' he replied.

"He told him, 'Take your bill and make it eight hundred.'

[8]"The master commended the dishonest manager because he had acted shrewdly. For the people of this world are more shrewd in dealing with their own kind than are the people of the light. [9]I tell you, use worldly wealth to gain friends for yourselves, so that when it is gone, you will be welcomed into eternal dwellings. Mt 19:21; Jn 12:36

[10]"Whoever can be trusted with very little can also be trusted with much, and whoever is dishonest with very little will also be dishonest with much. [11]So if you have not been trustworthy in handling worldly wealth, who will trust you with true riches? [12]And if you have not been trustworthy with someone else's property, who will give you property of your own? Mt 25:21,23; Lk 19:17

[13]"No servant can serve two masters. Either he will hate the one and love the other, or he will be devoted to the one and despise the other. You cannot serve both God and Money." Mt 6:24

[14]The Pharisees, who loved money, heard all this and were sneering at Jesus. [15]He said to them, "You are the ones who justify yourselves in the eyes of men, but God knows your hearts. What is highly valued among men is detestable in God's sight. 1Sa 16:7; Lk 23:35; 1Ti 3:3

Additional Teachings

[16]"The Law and the Prophets were proclaimed until John. Since that time, the good news of the kingdom of God is being preached, and everyone is forcing his way into it. [17]It is easier for heaven and earth to disappear than for the least stroke of a pen to drop out of the Law. Mt 5:18; 11:12-13

[18]"Anyone who divorces his wife and marries another woman commits adultery, and the man who marries a divorced woman commits adultery.

The Rich Man and Lazarus

[19]"There was a rich man who was dressed in purple and fine linen and lived in luxury every day. [20]At his gate was laid a beggar named Lazarus, covered with sores [21]and longing to eat what fell from the rich man's table. Even the dogs came and licked his sores. Eze 16:49; Ac 3:2

[22]"The time came when the beggar died and the angels carried him to Abraham's side. The rich man also died and was buried. [23]In hell,[c] where he was in torment, he looked up and saw Abraham far away, with Lazarus by his side. [24]So he called to him, 'Father Abraham, have pity on me and send Lazarus to dip the tip of his finger in water and cool my tongue, because I am in agony in this fire.'

[25]"But Abraham replied, 'Son, remember that in your lifetime you received your good things, while Lazarus received bad things, but now he is comforted here and you are in agony. [26]And besides all this, between us and you a great chasm has been fixed, so that those who want to go from here to you cannot, nor can anyone cross over from there to us.' Ps 17:14; Lk 6:21,24-25

[27]"He answered, 'Then I beg you, father, send

[a]6 Greek *one hundred batous* (probably about 3 kiloliters) [b]7 Greek *one hundred korous* (probably about 35 kiloliters)
[c]23 Greek *Hades*

Lazarus to my father's house, 28for I have five brothers. Let him warn them, so that they will not also come to this place of torment.' Ac 2:40; 1Th 4:6

29"Abraham replied, 'They have Moses and the Prophets; let them listen to them.' Lk 4:17; Jn 5:45-47

LIVING  **INSIGHT**

The most invincible, convincing power on earth is the Word of God as the Holy Spirit uses the truth to convince the lost. It is all that is needed to convince those without Christ that they are missing what life is all about.

(See Luke 16:29–31.)

30" 'No, father Abraham,' he said, 'but if someone from the dead goes to them, they will repent.'

31"He said to him, 'If they do not listen to Moses and the Prophets, they will not be convinced even if someone rises from the dead.' "

Sin, Faith, Duty

17 Jesus said to his disciples: "Things that cause people to sin are bound to come, but woe to that person through whom they come. 2It would be better for him to be thrown into the sea with a millstone tied around his neck than for him to cause one of these little ones to sin. 3So watch yourselves. Mt 18:7; Mk 10:24; Lk 10:21

"If your brother sins, rebuke him, and if he repents, forgive him. 4If he sins against you seven times in a day, and seven times comes back to you and says, 'I repent,' forgive him." Mt 18:15,21-22

5The apostles said to the Lord, "Increase our faith!" Mk 6:30; Lk 7:13

6He replied, "If you have faith as small as a mustard seed, you can say to this mulberry tree, 'Be uprooted and planted in the sea,' and it will obey you. Mt 17:20; 21:21

7"Suppose one of you had a servant plowing or looking after the sheep. Would he say to the servant when he comes in from the field, 'Come along now and sit down to eat'? 8Would he not rather say, 'Prepare my supper, get yourself ready and wait on me while I eat and drink; after that you may eat and drink'? 9Would he thank the servant because he did what he was told to do? 10So you also, when you have done everything you were told to do, should say, 'We are unworthy servants; we have only done our duty.' " Lk 12:37; 1Co 9:16

Ten Healed of Leprosy

11Now on his way to Jerusalem, Jesus traveled along the border between Samaria and Galilee. 12As he was going into a village, ten men who had leprosy[a] met him. They stood at a distance 13and called out in a loud voice, "Jesus, Master, have pity on us!" Lk 5:5; 9:51; Jn 4:3-4

14When he saw them, he said, "Go, show yourselves to the priests." And as they went, they were cleansed. Lev 14:2; Mt 8:4

15One of them, when he saw he was healed, came back, praising God in a loud voice. 16He threw himself at Jesus' feet and thanked him—and he was a Samaritan. Mt 9:8; 10:5

17Jesus asked, "Were not all ten cleansed? Where are the other nine? 18Was no one found to return and give praise to God except this foreigner?" 19Then he said to him, "Rise and go; your faith has made you well." Mt 9:22

The Coming of the Kingdom of God

20Once, having been asked by the Pharisees when the kingdom of God would come, Jesus replied, "The kingdom of God does not come with your careful observation, 21nor will people say, 'Here it is,' or 'There it is,' because the kingdom of God is within[b] you." ver 23; Mt 3:2

22Then he said to his disciples, "The time is coming when you will long to see one of the days of the Son of Man, but you will not see it. 23Men will tell you, 'There he is!' or 'Here he is!' Do not go running off after them. 24For the Son of Man in his day[c] will be like the lightning, which flashes and lights up the sky from one end to the other. 25But first he must suffer many things and be rejected by this generation. Mt 9:15; Lk 9:22; 21:8

26"Just as it was in the days of Noah, so also will it be in the days of the Son of Man. 27People were eating, drinking, marrying and being given in marriage up to the day Noah entered the ark. Then the flood came and destroyed them all. Ge 7:6-24

28"It was the same in the days of Lot. People were eating and drinking, buying and selling, planting and building. 29But the day Lot left Sodom, fire and sulfur rained down from heaven and destroyed them all. Ge 19:1-28

30"It will be just like this on the day the Son of Man is revealed. 31On that day no one who is on the roof of his house, with his goods inside, should go down to get them. Likewise, no one in the field should go back for anything. 32Remember Lot's wife! 33Whoever tries to keep his life will lose it, and whoever loses his life will preserve it. 34I tell you, on that night two people will be in one bed; one will be taken and the other left. 35Two women will be grinding grain together; one will be taken and the other left.[d]" Mt 24:41; Mk 13:15-16

[a] 12 The Greek word was used for various diseases affecting the skin—not necessarily leprosy. [b] 21 Or *among*
[c] 24 Some manuscripts do not have *in his day.* [d] 35 Some manuscripts *left.* 36*Two men will be in the field; one will be taken and the other left.*

37“Where, Lord?” they asked.

He replied, “Where there is a dead body, there the vultures will gather.” Mt 24:28

The Parable of the Persistent Widow

18 Then Jesus told his disciples a parable to show them that they should always pray and not give up. 2He said: “In a certain town there was a judge who neither feared God nor cared about men. 3And there was a widow in that town who kept coming to him with the plea, ‘Grant me justice against my adversary.’ Isa 40:31; Lk 11:5-8

4“For some time he refused. But finally he said to himself, ‘Even though I don’t fear God or care about men, 5yet because this widow keeps bothering me, I will see that she gets justice, so that she won’t eventually wear me out with her coming!’ ”

6And the Lord said, “Listen to what the unjust judge says. 7And will not God bring about justice for his chosen ones, who cry out to him day and night? Will he keep putting them off? 8I tell you, he will see that they get justice, and quickly. However, when the Son of Man comes, will he find faith on the earth?” Mt 8:20; Rev 6:10

The Parable of the Pharisee and the Tax Collector

9To some who were confident of their own righteousness and looked down on everybody else, Jesus told this parable: 10“Two men went up to the temple to pray, one a Pharisee and the other a tax collector. 11The Pharisee stood up and prayed about[a] himself: ‘God, I thank you that I am not like other men—robbers, evildoers, adulterers—or even like this tax collector. 12I fast twice a week and give a tenth of all I get.’ Isa 65:5; Lk 16:15

13“But the tax collector stood at a distance. He would not even look up to heaven, but beat his breast and said, ‘God, have mercy on me, a sinner.’

14“I tell you that this man, rather than the other, went home justified before God. For everyone who exalts himself will be humbled, and he who humbles himself will be exalted.” Mt 23:12; Lk 14:11

The Little Children and Jesus

▶ *See Matthew 19:13–15; Mark 10:13–16*

15People were also bringing babies to Jesus to have him touch them. When the disciples saw this, they rebuked them. 16But Jesus called the children to him and said, “Let the little children come to me, and do not hinder them, for the kingdom of God belongs to such as these. 17I tell you the truth, anyone who will not receive the kingdom of God like a little child will never enter it.” Mt 18:3

The Rich Ruler

▶ *See Matthew 19:16–29; Mark 10:17–30*

18A certain ruler asked him, “Good teacher, what must I do to inherit eternal life?” Lk 10:25

19“Why do you call me good?” Jesus answered. “No one is good—except God alone. 20You know the commandments: ‘Do not commit adultery, do not murder, do not steal, do not give false testimony, honor your father and mother.’[b]” Ex 20:12-16

21“All these I have kept since I was a boy,” he said.

22When Jesus heard this, he said to him, “You still lack one thing. Sell everything you have and give to the poor, and you will have treasure in heaven. Then come, follow me.” Mt 6:20; Ac 2:45

LIVING  **INSIGHT**

We are often hindered from giving up our treasures out of fear for their safety. But wait. Everything committed to our God is safe. In fact, nothing is really safe that is not so committed. No child. No job. No romance. No friend. No future. No dream.

(See Luke 18:22.)

23When he heard this, he became very sad, because he was a man of great wealth. 24Jesus looked at him and said, “How hard it is for the rich to enter the kingdom of God! 25Indeed, it is easier for a camel to go through the eye of a needle than for a rich man to enter the kingdom of God.”

26Those who heard this asked, “Who then can be saved?”

27Jesus replied, “What is impossible with men is possible with God.” Mt 19:26

28Peter said to him, “We have left all we had to follow you!” Mt 4:19

29“I tell you the truth,” Jesus said to them, “no one who has left home or wife or brothers or parents or children for the sake of the kingdom of God 30will fail to receive many times as much in this age and, in the age to come, eternal life.”

Jesus Again Predicts His Death

▶ *See Matthew 20:17–19; Mark 10:32–34*

31Jesus took the Twelve aside and told them, “We are going up to Jerusalem, and everything that is written by the prophets about the Son of Man will be fulfilled. 32He will be handed over to the Gentiles. They will mock him, insult him, spit on him, flog him and kill him. 33On the third day he will rise again.” Mt 20:17-19; Mk 10:32-34

34The disciples did not understand any of this.

[a] *11* Or *to* [b] *20* Exodus 20:12-16; Deut. 5:16-20

Its meaning was hidden from them, and they did
not know what he was talking about. Mk 9:32

A Blind Beggar Receives His Sight

▶ *See Matthew 20:29–34; Mark 10:46–52*

35As Jesus approached Jericho, a blind man was
sitting by the roadside begging. 36When he heard
the crowd going by, he asked what was happening.
37They told him, "Jesus of Nazareth is passing by."
38He called out, "Jesus, Son of David, have mercy on me!" Mt 9:27; 17:15; Lk 18:13
39Those who led the way rebuked him and told
him to be quiet, but he shouted all the more, "Son
of David, have mercy on me!"
40Jesus stopped and ordered the man to be
brought to him. When he came near, Jesus asked
him, 41"What do you want me to do for you?"
"Lord, I want to see," he replied.
42Jesus said to him, "Receive your sight; your
faith has healed you." 43Immediately he received
his sight and followed Jesus, praising God. When
all the people saw it, they also praised God.

Zacchaeus the Tax Collector

19 Jesus entered Jericho and was passing
through. 2A man was there by the name of
Zacchaeus; he was a chief tax collector and was
wealthy. 3He wanted to see who Jesus was, but
being a short man he could not, because of the
crowd. 4So he ran ahead and climbed a sycamore-
fig tree to see him, since Jesus was coming that
way. 1Ki 10:27; 1Ch 27:28
5When Jesus reached the spot, he looked up
and said to him, "Zacchaeus, come down immediately. I must stay at your house today." 6So he
came down at once and welcomed him gladly.
7All the people saw this and began to mutter,
"He has gone to be the guest of a 'sinner.'"
8But Zacchaeus stood up and said to the Lord,
"Look, Lord! Here and now I give half of my possessions to the poor, and if I have cheated anybody
out of anything, I will pay back four times the
amount." Ex 22:1; Lk 7:13
9Jesus said to him, "Today salvation has come
to this house, because this man, too, is a son of
Abraham. 10For the Son of Man came to seek and
to save what was lost." Lk 3:8; Jn 3:17

The Parable of the Ten Minas

11While they were listening to this, he went on
to tell them a parable, because he was near Jerusalem and the people thought that the kingdom of
God was going to appear at once. 12He said: "A
man of noble birth went to a distant country to
have himself appointed king and then to return.
13So he called ten of his servants and gave them ten
minas.[a] 'Put this money to work,' he said, 'until
I come back.' Mk 13:34; Lk 17:20
14"But his subjects hated him and sent a delegation after him to say, 'We don't want this man to
be our king.'
15"He was made king, however, and returned
home. Then he sent for the servants to whom he
had given the money, in order to find out what
they had gained with it.
16"The first one came and said, 'Sir, your mina
has earned ten more.'
17"'Well done, my good servant!' his master
replied. 'Because you have been trustworthy in a
very small matter, take charge of ten cities.'
18"The second came and said, 'Sir, your mina
has earned five more.'
19"His master answered, 'You take charge of
five cities.'
20"Then another servant came and said, 'Sir,
here is your mina; I have kept it laid away in a
piece of cloth. 21I was afraid of you, because you
are a hard man. You take out what you did not put
in and reap what you did not sow.' Mt 25:24
22"His master replied, 'I will judge you by your
own words, you wicked servant! You knew, did
you, that I am a hard man, taking out what I did
not put in, and reaping what I did not sow? 23Why
then didn't you put my money on deposit, so that
when I came back, I could have collected it with
interest?' 2Sa 1:16; Mt 25:26
24"Then he said to those standing by, 'Take his
mina away from him and give it to the one who
has ten minas.'
25"'Sir,' they said, 'he already has ten!'
26"He replied, 'I tell you that to everyone who
has, more will be given, but as for the one who
has nothing, even what he has will be taken away.
27But those enemies of mine who did not want me
to be king over them—bring them here and kill
them in front of me.'" Mt 25:14-30

Sacrifice of Jesus **Chapters 19:28–23:56**

This section of Luke centers in Jerusalem, where Jesus entered the city on a donkey to the cheers of the crowd, cleansed the temple, kept the Passover with His disciples at the Last Supper, prayed in Gethsemane, and experienced arrest, trial and death on the cross. The One who came to seek and to save the lost gave His life in the ultimate act of sacrifice, thereby bringing salvation for all who believe in Him.

The Triumphal Entry

▶ *See Matthew 21:1–9; Mark 11:1–10; John 12:12–15*

28After Jesus had said this, he went on ahead,
going up to Jerusalem. 29As he approached Bethphage and Bethany at the hill called the Mount of
Olives, he sent two of his disciples, saying to them,

[a] *13* A mina was about three months' wages.

ZACCHAEUS

Seeking the Sinner, Saving the Lost

"Today salvation has come to this house, because this man, too, is a son of Abraham. For the Son of Man came to seek and to save what was lost."

–LUKE 19:9–10

The ancient city of Jericho was a little paradise on earth. It was a very wealthy and important town. It had great palm forests and world-famous balsam trees. Its gardens of roses were famous the world over. Its climate was delightful. The ancient historian Josephus called this area "a divine region, the fattest in Palestine." This city was also at the heart of a vast trade route, with connections as far away as Egypt.

Where there's that kind of beauty and that kind of climate, there will be many people. Where there's trade, there will be wealth. Where there's wealth, there will be taxation, and the Roman government exacted an enormous amount of money from the people of Jericho. That means that some of the most hated people in the city were Rome's representatives—the tax collectors. They were known as rogues and as traitors. They were corrupt, known for skimming off for themselves up to half of the money they collected.

Enter Zacchaeus, whom Luke called a "chief tax collector" (Luke 19:2). Not only did this man pad his own pockets by ripping people off; he supervised other tax collectors who did the same. This man, the Bible tells us, was wealthy, probably enormously wealthy—and enormously hated. But that doesn't mean he had lost all capacity to feel the wide range of human emotions we all feel. I am sure there was something within Zacchaeus's life that felt empty and meaningless; there were human needs that weren't being met as he lived under the critical eye of the citizens of Jericho day after day. Apparently Zacchaeus heard through the grapevine that this man named Jesus and many of His followers were on their way through the garden spot of Jericho. Zacchaeus decided to go take a look—perhaps, at least in part, because the years of being an object of hatred had taken its toll on him.

The seeking aspect of this story doesn't begin with Zacchaeus, however; it begins with Jesus (19:5). What strikes me first is that Jesus knew his name. Here was Zacchaeus, probably hoping that no one would notice him, standing in a tree to get a glimpse of Jesus. And Jesus approached him and called him by name. What's more, there was an urgency in Jesus' message. He didn't ask to be wedged into Zacchaeus's busy schedule; He didn't ask if it was convenient for Him to come over. He said, in effect, "Hurry up, Zacchaeus. Get on down here. Today's the day you and I need to take care of some things." His words weren't meant to be embarrassing or tactless, but they do convey a sense of gracious urgency.

A conversation took place that day between Jesus and Zacchaeus about the condition of his soul. We don't know what went on, and Luke, ever the stickler for detail, doesn't speculate. But we can see the results of this conversation in this tax collector's life. There was a moment when this little man stood taller that he'd ever stood in his life, and he pledged to change his ways: "Look, Lord! Here and now I give half of my possessions to the poor, and if I have cheated anybody out of anything, I will pay back four times the amount" (19:8). Jesus Christ came in and transformed this man's life. Why else would a man who had spent his entire life *taking* money suddenly start talking about *giving* it to others?

Do you know a modern-day Zacchaeus, someone who's looking at Jesus Christ with curiosity, from a safe distance, hoping he or she won't be noticed? Can you think of someone who may be living with a profound emptiness at the center of his or her life? Are you willing to meet with that person on his or her own turf and share the good news of the fullness of life that can be found in Jesus Christ? When He walked the earth, Jesus went out of His way to spend time with people like Zacchaeus. Still today He seeks people far more intensely than people ever seek Him. He saves people who acknowledge their sinfulness and look to Him for mercy. And, like Zacchaeus, any person who has experienced the power and the saving grace of Jesus Christ can have the assurance of eternal life—right now, yes *today*!

30"Go to the village ahead of you, and as you enter
it, you will find a colt tied there, which no one has
ever ridden. Untie it and bring it here. 31If anyone
asks you, 'Why are you untying it?' tell him, 'The
Lord needs it.'" Mt 21:1-9; Mk 10:32
32Those who were sent ahead went and found it
just as he had told them. 33As they were untying
the colt, its owners asked them, "Why are you
untying the colt?" Lk 22:13
34They replied, "The Lord needs it."
35They brought it to Jesus, threw their cloaks on
the colt and put Jesus on it. 36As he went along,
people spread their cloaks on the road. Mk 11:1-10
37When he came near the place where the road
goes down the Mount of Olives, the whole crowd
of disciples began joyfully to praise God in loud
voices for all the miracles they had seen: Mt 21:1

38"Blessed is the king who comes in the name
of the Lord!"[a] Ps 118:26; Lk 13:35

"Peace in heaven and glory in the highest!"

39Some of the Pharisees in the crowd said to
Jesus, "Teacher, rebuke your disciples!"
40"I tell you," he replied, "if they keep quiet, the
stones will cry out." Hab 2:11
41As he approached Jerusalem and saw the city,
he wept over it 42and said, "If you, even you, had
only known on this day what would bring you
peace—but now it is hidden from your eyes. 43The
days will come upon you when your enemies will
build an embankment against you and encircle
you and hem you in on every side. 44They will dash
you to the ground, you and the children within
your walls. They will not leave one stone on another, because you did not recognize the time of
God's coming to you." Lk 21:6; 1Pe 2:12

Jesus at the Temple

▶ *See Matthew 21:12–16; Mark 11:15–18; John 2:13–16*

45Then he entered the temple area and began
driving out those who were selling. 46"It is written," he said to them, "'My house will be a house
of prayer'[b]; but you have made it 'a den of robbers.'[c]" Mt 21:12-16; Isa 56:7; Jer 7:11
47Every day he was teaching at the temple. But
the chief priests, the teachers of the law and the
leaders among the people were trying to kill him.
48Yet they could not find any way to do it, because
all the people hung on his words. Mt 26:55; Mk 11:18

The Authority of Jesus Questioned

▶ *See Matthew 21:23–27; Mark 11:27–33*

20 One day as he was teaching the people in
the temple courts and preaching the gospel, the chief priests and the teachers of the law,
together with the elders, came up to him. 2"Tell us
by what authority you are doing these things,"
they said. "Who gave you this authority?" Lk 8:1
3He replied, "I will also ask you a question. Tell
me, 4John's baptism—was it from heaven, or from
men?" Mk 1:4
5They discussed it among themselves and said,
"If we say, 'From heaven,' he will ask, 'Why didn't
you believe him?' 6But if we say, 'From men,' all
the people will stone us, because they are persuaded that John was a prophet." Mt 11:9; Lk 7:29
7So they answered, "We don't know where it
was from."
8Jesus said, "Neither will I tell you by what authority I am doing these things." Mt 21:23-27

The Parable of the Tenants

▶ *See Matthew 21:33–46; Mark 12:1–12*

9He went on to tell the people this parable: "A
man planted a vineyard, rented it to some farmers
and went away for a long time. 10At harvest time
he sent a servant to the tenants so they would give
him some of the fruit of the vineyard. But the
tenants beat him and sent him away empty-handed. 11He sent another servant, but that one also
they beat and treated shamefully and sent away
empty-handed. 12He sent still a third, and they
wounded him and threw him out. Isa 5:1-7; Mt 25:14
13"Then the owner of the vineyard said, 'What
shall I do? I will send my son, whom I love; perhaps they will respect him.' Mt 3:17
14"But when the tenants saw him, they talked
the matter over. 'This is the heir,' they said. 'Let's
kill him, and the inheritance will be ours.' 15So
they threw him out of the vineyard and killed him.
"What then will the owner of the vineyard do to
them? 16He will come and kill those tenants and
give the vineyard to others." Lk 19:27
When the people heard this, they said, "May
this never be!"
17Jesus looked directly at them and asked,
"Then what is the meaning of that which is written:

"'The stone the builders rejected
has become the capstone[d]'[e]?

18Everyone who falls on that stone will be broken
to pieces, but he on whom it falls will be crushed."
19The teachers of the law and the chief priests
looked for a way to arrest him immediately, because they knew he had spoken this parable
against them. But they were afraid of the people.

Paying Taxes to Caesar

▶ *See Matthew 22:15–22; Mark 12:13–17*

20Keeping a close watch on him, they sent spies,
who pretended to be honest. They hoped to catch
Jesus in something he said so that they might hand

[a]38 Psalm 118:26 [b]46 Isaiah 56:7 [c]46 Jer. 7:11 [d]17 Or *cornerstone* [e]17 Psalm 118:22

him over to the power and authority of the governor. 21So the spies questioned him: "Teacher, we know that you speak and teach what is right, and that you do not show partiality but teach the way of God in accordance with the truth. 22Is it right for us to pay taxes to Caesar or not?" Mt 12:10

23He saw through their duplicity and said to them, 24"Show me a denarius. Whose portrait and inscription are on it?"

25"Caesar's," they replied.

He said to them, "Then give to Caesar what is Caesar's, and to God what is God's." Lk 23:2

26They were unable to trap him in what he had said there in public. And astonished by his answer, they became silent. Mt 22:15-22; Mk 12:13-17

The Resurrection and Marriage

▶ *See Matthew 22:23–33; Mark 12:18–27*

27Some of the Sadducees, who say there is no resurrection, came to Jesus with a question. 28"Teacher," they said, "Moses wrote for us that if a man's brother dies and leaves a wife but no children, the man must marry the widow and have children for his brother. 29Now there were seven brothers. The first one married a woman and died childless. 30The second 31and then the third married her, and in the same way the seven died, leaving no children. 32Finally, the woman died too. 33Now then, at the resurrection whose wife will she be, since the seven were married to her?" Dt 25:5

34Jesus replied, "The people of this age marry and are given in marriage. 35But those who are considered worthy of taking part in that age and in the resurrection from the dead will neither marry nor be given in marriage, 36and they can no longer die; for they are like the angels. They are God's children, since they are children of the resurrection. 37But in the account of the bush, even Moses showed that the dead rise, for he calls the Lord 'the God of Abraham, and the God of Isaac, and the God of Jacob.'[a] 38He is not the God of the dead, but of the living, for to him all are alive." Ex 3:6

39Some of the teachers of the law responded, "Well said, teacher!" 40And no one dared to ask him any more questions. Mt 22:23-33; Mk 12:18-27

Whose Son Is the Christ?

▶ *See Matthew 22:41—23:7; Mark 12:35–40*

41Then Jesus said to them, "How is it that they say the Christ[b] is the Son of David? 42David himself declares in the Book of Psalms: Mt 1:1

"'The Lord said to my Lord:
"Sit at my right hand
43until I make your enemies
a footstool for your feet."'[c] Ps 110:1; Mt 22:44

44David calls him 'Lord.' How then can he be his son?"

45While all the people were listening, Jesus said to his disciples, 46"Beware of the teachers of the law. They like to walk around in flowing robes and love to be greeted in the marketplaces and have the most important seats in the synagogues and the places of honor at banquets. 47They devour widows' houses and for a show make lengthy prayers. Such men will be punished most severely."

The Widow's Offering

▶ *See Mark 12:41–44*

21 As he looked up, Jesus saw the rich putting their gifts into the temple treasury. 2He also saw a poor widow put in two very small copper coins.[d] 3"I tell you the truth," he said, "this poor widow has put in more than all the others. 4All these people gave their gifts out of their wealth; but she out of her poverty put in all she had to live on." Mk 12:41-44

Signs of the End of the Age

▶ *See Matthew 24; Mark 13*

5Some of his disciples were remarking about how the temple was adorned with beautiful stones and with gifts dedicated to God. But Jesus said, 6"As for what you see here, the time will come when not one stone will be left on another; every one of them will be thrown down." Lk 19:44

7"Teacher," they asked, "when will these things happen? And what will be the sign that they are about to take place?"

8He replied: "Watch out that you are not deceived. For many will come in my name, claiming, 'I am he,' and, 'The time is near.' Do not follow them. 9When you hear of wars and revolutions, do not be frightened. These things must happen first, but the end will not come right away." Lk 17:23

10Then he said to them: "Nation will rise against nation, and kingdom against kingdom. 11There will be great earthquakes, famines and pestilences in various places, and fearful events and great signs from heaven. 2Ch 15:6; Isa 29:6

12"But before all this, they will lay hands on you and persecute you. They will deliver you to synagogues and prisons, and you will be brought before kings and governors, and all on account of my name. 13This will result in your being witnesses to them. 14But make up your mind not to worry beforehand how you will defend yourselves. 15For I will give you words and wisdom that none of your adversaries will be able to resist or contradict. 16You will be betrayed even by parents, brothers, relatives and friends, and they will put some of you to death. 17All men will hate you because of me.

[a] 37 Exodus 3:6 [b] 41 Or *Messiah* [c] 43 Psalm 110:1 [d] 2 Greek *two lepta*

18But not a hair of your head will perish. 19By standing firm you will gain life. Mt 10:17-22

20"When you see Jerusalem being surrounded by armies, you will know that its desolation is near. 21Then let those who are in Judea flee to the mountains, let those in the city get out, and let those in the country not enter the city. 22For this is the time of punishment in fulfillment of all that has been written. 23How dreadful it will be in those days for pregnant women and nursing mothers! There will be great distress in the land and wrath against this people. 24They will fall by the sword and will be taken as prisoners to all the nations. Jerusalem will be trampled on by the Gentiles until the times of the Gentiles are fulfilled. Isa 63:18

25"There will be signs in the sun, moon and stars. On the earth, nations will be in anguish and perplexity at the roaring and tossing of the sea. 26Men will faint from terror, apprehensive of what is coming on the world, for the heavenly bodies will be shaken. 27At that time they will see the Son of Man coming in a cloud with power and great glory. 28When these things begin to take place, stand up and lift up your heads, because your redemption is drawing near." Lk 18:7; Rev 1:7

29He told them this parable: "Look at the fig tree and all the trees. 30When they sprout leaves, you can see for yourselves and know that summer is near. 31Even so, when you see these things happening, you know that the kingdom of God is near. Mt 3:2

32"I tell you the truth, this generation[a] will certainly not pass away until all these things have happened. 33Heaven and earth will pass away, but my words will never pass away. Mt 5:18; Lk 11:50

34"Be careful, or your hearts will be weighed down with dissipation, drunkenness and the anxieties of life, and that day will close on you unexpectedly like a trap. 35For it will come upon all those who live on the face of the whole earth. 36Be always on the watch, and pray that you may be able to escape all that is about to happen, and that you may be able to stand before the Son of Man."

37Each day Jesus was teaching at the temple, and each evening he went out to spend the night on the hill called the Mount of Olives, 38and all the people came early in the morning to hear him at the temple. Mk 11:19; Jn 8:2

Judas Agrees to Betray Jesus

▶ *See Matthew 26:2–5; Mark 14:1–2,10–11*

22 Now the Feast of Unleavened Bread, called the Passover, was approaching, 2and the chief priests and the teachers of the law were looking for some way to get rid of Jesus, for they were afraid of the people. 3Then Satan entered Judas, called Iscariot, one of the Twelve. 4And Judas went to the chief priests and the officers of the temple guard and discussed with them how he might betray Jesus. 5They were delighted and agreed to give him money. 6He consented, and watched for an opportunity to hand Jesus over to them when no crowd was present. Mt 26:2-5; Mk 14:1-2,10-11

The Last Supper

▶ *See Matthew 26:17–19,26–29; Mark 14:12–16,22–25*

7Then came the day of Unleavened Bread on which the Passover lamb had to be sacrificed. 8Jesus sent Peter and John, saying, "Go and make preparations for us to eat the Passover." Dt 16:5-8

9"Where do you want us to prepare for it?" they asked.

10He replied, "As you enter the city, a man carrying a jar of water will meet you. Follow him to the house that he enters, 11and say to the owner of the house, 'The Teacher asks: Where is the guest room, where I may eat the Passover with my disciples?' 12He will show you a large upper room, all furnished. Make preparations there."

13They left and found things just as Jesus had told them. So they prepared the Passover.

14When the hour came, Jesus and his apostles reclined at the table. 15And he said to them, "I have eagerly desired to eat this Passover with you before I suffer. 16For I tell you, I will not eat it again until it finds fulfillment in the kingdom of God."

17After taking the cup, he gave thanks and said, "Take this and divide it among you. 18For I tell you I will not drink again of the fruit of the vine until the kingdom of God comes."

19And he took bread, gave thanks and broke it, and gave it to them, saying, "This is my body given for you; do this in remembrance of me."

20In the same way, after the supper he took the cup, saying, "This cup is the new covenant in my blood, which is poured out for you. 21But the hand of him who is going to betray me is with mine on the table. 22The Son of Man will go as it has been decreed, but woe to that man who betrays him." 23They began to question among themselves which of them it might be who would do this.

24Also a dispute arose among them as to which of them was considered to be greatest. 25Jesus said to them, "The kings of the Gentiles lord it over them; and those who exercise authority over them call themselves Benefactors. 26But you are not to be like that. Instead, the greatest among you should be like the youngest, and the one who rules like the one who serves. 27For who is greater, the one who is at the table or the one who serves? Is it not the one who is at the table? But I am among you as one who serves. 28You are those who have

[a]32 Or *race*

A Gift to the Church

"He took bread, gave thanks and broke it, and gave it to them, saying, 'This is my body given for you; do this in remembrance of me.' In the same way, after the supper he took the cup, saying, 'This cup is the new covenant in my blood, which is poured out for you.' "

—LUKE 22:19–20

"Repent and be baptized, every one of you, in the name of Jesus Christ for the forgiveness of your sins. And you will receive the gift of the Holy Spirit. The promise is for you and your children and for all who are far off—for all whom the Lord our God will call."

—ACTS 2:38–39

To the wonderful body called the church, God has given two unique sacraments or celebrations. In no other institution will you find such things. One is called the Lord's Supper (your church might call it Communion, the Eucharist, or simply "the Table"). The other is water baptism. The Lord's Supper is a memorial of remembrance, and baptism is a celebration of initiation and belonging. With no desire to offend anyone, I sometimes think of them as sacred pantomimes. They are sermons without words . . . full of symbolic significance. The Lord's Supper is saying, "He died for me." The baptismal celebration is saying, "He lives in me."

Both require only a few words of explanation. Both are rich in symbolism, yet beautiful in simplicity. And both make bold statements to the world regarding the Christian faith. Both sacraments exist *because* of salvation; neither, however, is essential for salvation. Neither is to be treated lightly or viewed as if they are of little importance.

The Lord's Supper . . . He Died for Me

Have you ever stopped to think about the Lord's Supper? What a simple ceremony—and so strange in the eyes of the world! A little bit of bread and a swallow of liquid—how very odd. In places all around the world there are little pieces of bread and there are little cups of wine or juice used among those who worship the Lord Jesus Christ. Regardless of the exact substance, the style in which these elements are served, or the amount, it is what each represents that is so important—the bread representing our Savior's body and the cup representing His blood, both given for us at the cross. Both cause us to recall that He died for us and that He rose again in triumph over sin and death.

I've often stated publicly that one of my most memorable communion times takes me back to the early 1960s when I was with a large group of Christian collegians up on the northern California coastline. It was a church-sponsored outing. We were sitting around a fire on a windswept, chilly beach. We had sung a few songs before sunset. All we had to serve were chips and cola. Yet it was marvelous! I had never before (or have ever since) served chips and cola at the Lord's Supper, but the elements were insignificant. Our Lord's presence was there in the sunset over the Pacific, in the pounding of the surf, in the faces of those young believers, in the tears that fell, in the testimonies that were spoken. And we worshiped our God at that open place, sand between our toes, swimming suits on, towels wrapped around us as we shivered around the fire and passed the chips and cola among us. In quiet worship we did this all in remembrance of Jesus.

The Biblical basis for the Lord's Supper takes us back to the last meal Jesus had with His disciples the night before He was crucified. Matthew records the event in the simplest of terms:

While they were eating, Jesus took bread, gave thanks and broke it, and gave it to his disciples, saying, "Take and eat; this is my body." Then he took the cup, gave thanks and offered it to

> *them, saying, "Drink from it, all of you. This is my blood of the covenant, which is poured out for many for the forgiveness of sins. I tell you, I will not drink of this fruit of the vine from now on until that day when I drink it anew with you in my Father's kingdom." When they had sung a hymn, they went out to the Mount of Olives (Matthew 26:26–30).*

The apostle Paul recalled that scene when years later he wrote these words in his first letter to the Corinthians:

> *For I received from the Lord what I also passed on to you: The Lord Jesus, on the night he was betrayed, took bread, and when he had given thanks, he broke it and said, "This is my body, which is for you; do this in remembrance of me"(1 Corinthians 11:23–24).*

Obviously, participation in the Lord's Supper is not optional; it is a command: "Do this . . . !" Don't look at the Lord's Supper simply as a secondary, optional part of your worship. We are commanded by God to do it—and to do it regularly. In fact, the command is a present imperative: "Keep on doing this in remembrance of Me!" Some observe the Lord's Supper every time they meet for worship. Some observe it every other week. Some "keep on doing this" once a month. Some do it once every three or four months. However often we celebrate together at the Lord's table, we do well to remember our Lord's command to "keep on doing this" in remembrance of Him.

One of the basic reasons for celebrating the Lord's Supper frequently is that it both celebrates and reinforces the spiritual union that exists between Jesus Christ and other Christians. It is interesting to note that John is the only Gospel that does not specifically record the act, or institution, of the Lord's Supper. In its place John chronicles Jesus' words about the vine and the branches (see John 15:1–17). Jesus is the true vine, God is the gardener and we are the branches. To be alive and vital in our faith, bearing fruit and giving glory to God, requires that we "remain" in Christ. As we come to the Lord's table, we are reminded that Jesus Christ lives in us and seeks to daily lead us in our Christian living.

Think of it this way. Each time we come to the Lord's Supper we are receiving food and drink to nourish and strengthen us for our Christian walk. Our souls are fed not so much physically by the bread and juice but spiritually by remembering and reliving His sacrifice for us, His abiding presence with us and His wondrous promises to us.

Paul continued his reflection on the institution of the Lord's Supper by giving us insight into how long we are to keep on eating the bread and drinking from the cup:

> *In the same way, after supper he took the cup, saying, "This cup is the new covenant in my blood; do this, whenever you drink it, in remembrance of me." For whenever you eat this bread and drink this cup, you proclaim the Lord's death until he comes (1 Corinthians 11:25–26).*

We will be eating this symbolic, simple meal together in our churches until our Savior returns. It will be regularly observed by believers in rugged churches with thatched roofs as well as in beautiful cathedrals with high ceilings and ornate walls lined with stained-glass windows. In brand-new places of worship only a week or two old, as well as in places centuries old, we will still be observing the Lord's Supper—"until he comes."

The place we celebrate the Lord's Supper may not be significant, but the condition of the heart is. Before we ever eat the bread or drink from that cup, each Christian asks within himself or herself, "Is there anything that comes between my Father and me? Is my heart clean?" A strong warning is attached to the instruction:

> *Therefore, whoever eats the bread or drinks the cup of the Lord in an unworthy manner will be guilty of sinning against the body and blood of the Lord. A man ought to examine himself before he eats of the bread and drinks of the cup. For anyone who eats and drinks without recognizing the body of the Lord eats and drinks judgment on himself (1 Corinthians 11:27–29).*

The Corinthians had turned the Lord's Supper into a profane event. Instead of promoting an atmosphere of worship and humble confession, they had made light of the event by eating too much, drinking too much and showing favoritism to various cliques in the church. A circus atmosphere had ruined what was designed to be the most memorable moments of worship a church family could enter into together. Paul drew his warning from their carnal display of disobedience. Each believer must examine his or her own heart before participating in the eating and drinking of the elements at the communion table. Otherwise it is nothing more than empty religious ritual.

How then should we approach the table? What should our attitude be? Let's be honest: For too long, in too many churches, the atmosphere surrounding the Lord's Supper resembled more the somberness of a funeral than the exuberant joy of remembering Christ's sacrificial death and triumphant resurrection and His victory over sin and death. Consider your own experience. In your participation in the Lord's Supper has there been a profound sense of thanksgiving and expectant joy in Jesus Christ for all He has done for you?

As we come to the Lord's Supper, it is good for us to examine what Christ has done. Even a quick review of God's mercy to us and care for us will send our spirits soaring. Remember, this is the feast of joy that we will one day celebrate with Jesus Christ in heaven. Until then let's get ready by coming in the proper spirit and recognizing that we are eating and drinking not only with our fellow family members in our own church but also with Christians from every part of God's vast kingdom.

Water Baptism . . . He Lives in Me

Through the centuries, Christians have also declared their commitment to Jesus Christ by submitting themselves to water baptism, a public act of deep significance. Christians practice two variations of baptism. Some churches practice a child-dedication ceremony, others infant baptism, whereby the parents pledge to bring their children up in a Christian environment and encourage them to make their own profession of faith as they grow to the age of understanding. This approach emphasizes the richness of God's grace in calling children and adults to believe in Jesus Christ. Other churches believe it is necessary for a person to wait until he or she is old enough to make his or her own profession of faith and receive baptism as a believer. This approach emphasizes the importance of repentance, or turning around, and making a decision to accept Christ as Savior and Lord. But notice that both approaches share a common theme that it is *God* who calls and invites us to pledge our faith and follow Jesus Christ. The basis of God's call is the previous love that God has for each of us.

Baptism is carried out in the name of Jesus Christ. The Biblical imagery of Romans 6 is helpful in understanding this: "Don't you know that all of us who were baptized into Christ Jesus were baptized into his death?" (Romans 6:3). In the first century the term baptism often conveyed the concept of "identification." In fact, it was a fuller's term—used by the dry cleaner of ancient days. When he took a white garment and dipped it into a scarlet dye, he was said to have "baptized" the garment. The white garment's identity was changed to scarlet. *Baptizo* was the term used when he "changed its identity." That's the word used here, transliterated "baptized."

Paul goes on to say more about baptism in the next verse: "We were therefore buried with him through baptism into death in order that, just as Christ was raised from the dead through the glory of the Father, we too may live a new life" (Romans 6:4). Did you know that in the sacrament of baptism the water represents death? Have you ever been told that when a person goes under the water (immersion), or has the water sprinkled or poured over him or her, that the water is a picture of their identification with the death of Jesus Christ? If not, this is a good time to learn that important lesson. And as the water runs off, or as the person is brought up out of the water, it is symbolic of the resurrection of Jesus Christ out of death into new life. The person being baptized is "acting out" his or her death to sin and the subsequent newness of their walk in Jesus Christ.

Remember this, however: This act of obedience isn't simply a take-it-or-leave-it issue. Not at all. While the act itself isn't essential for salvation, it is a powerful expression of our union with Christ. That is why all believers are expected to participate in the sacrament of baptism. It is a public declaration of our absolute faith in the Lord Jesus Christ as well as a "sermon without words," portraying our having been united with Christ Jesus in His death and His resurrection.

And one thing more. As we think together about our union with Jesus Christ, remember that He wants us to live for Him daily. Some people actually talk about baptism as God's calling in our life. That means as we seek to live out our baptism, dying to sin and living in newness of life in Christ, we will seek to be

His representatives in our daily walk. Regardless of what we do, whether we are a teacher, electrician, homemaker, computer technician, construction worker, student, restaurant server, trucker—whatever we do and wherever we are, we are expected to connect our faith with our week-day world. Paul reminds us of the great importance of this. Listen to his call for consistent living: "So whether you eat or drink or whatever you do, do it all for the glory of God" (1 Corinthians 10:31). Keep this in mind the next time you observe the sacrament of baptism. Unlike the Lord's Supper, which is celebrated regularly, this sacrament is received only once. But that should not limit its power, but it should remind us that we are called to follow Jesus because He loves us and first called us out of darkness into His wonderful light (1 Peter 2:9) in order that we would follow Him closely every step of the way, to the praise of His glorious grace!

stood by me in my trials. 29And I confer on you a
kingdom, just as my Father conferred one on me,
30so that you may eat and drink at my table in my
kingdom and sit on thrones, judging the twelve
tribes of Israel. Mt 20:25-28; Mk 10:42-45
31"Simon, Simon, Satan has asked to sift you[a]
as wheat. 32But I have prayed for you, Simon, that
your faith may not fail. And when you have turned
back, strengthen your brothers." Jn 21:15-17

LIVING  INSIGHT

Failures are only temporary tests to prepare us for permanent triumphs.

(See Luke 22:31–32.)

33But he replied, "Lord, I am ready to go with
you to prison and to death." Jn 11:16
34Jesus answered, "I tell you, Peter, before the
rooster crows today, you will deny three times that
you know me." Mt 26:33-35; Mk 14:29-31; Jn 13:37-38
35Then Jesus asked them, "When I sent you
without purse, bag or sandals, did you lack anything?" Mt 10:9-10; Lk 9:3; 10:4
"Nothing," they answered.
36He said to them, "But now if you have a purse,
take it, and also a bag; and if you don't have a
sword, sell your cloak and buy one. 37It is written:
'And he was numbered with the transgressors'[b];
and I tell you that this must be fulfilled in me. Yes,
what is written about me is reaching its fulfillment." Isa 53:12
38The disciples said, "See, Lord, here are two
swords."
"That is enough," he replied.

Jesus Prays on the Mount of Olives

▶ *See Matthew 26:36–46; Mark 14:32–42*

39Jesus went out as usual to the Mount of Olives, and his disciples followed him. 40On reaching
the place, he said to them, "Pray that you will
not fall into temptation." 41He withdrew about a
stone's throw beyond them, knelt down and
prayed, 42"Father, if you are willing, take this cup
from me; yet not my will, but yours be done." 43An
angel from heaven appeared to him and strengthened him. 44And being in anguish, he prayed more
earnestly, and his sweat was like drops of blood
falling to the ground.[c] Mt 4:11; 6:13; Lk 21:37
45When he rose from prayer and went back to
the disciples, he found them asleep, exhausted
from sorrow. 46"Why are you sleeping?" he asked
them. "Get up and pray so that you will not fall
into temptation." Mt 26:36-46; Mk 14:32-42

LIVING  INSIGHT

Does Jesus understand what trauma is all about? Remember, He's the One whose sweat became like drops of blood in the agony of Gethsemane. If anybody understands trauma, He does—completely. Come to Him, and He will give you rest.

(See Luke 22:39–46.)

Jesus Arrested

▶ *See Matthew 26:47–56; Mark 14:43–50; John 18:3–11*

47While he was still speaking a crowd came up,
and the man who was called Judas, one of the
Twelve, was leading them. He approached Jesus to
kiss him, 48but Jesus asked him, "Judas, are you
betraying the Son of Man with a kiss?"
49When Jesus' followers saw what was going to
happen, they said, "Lord, should we strike with
our swords?" 50And one of them struck the servant
of the high priest, cutting off his right ear.
51But Jesus answered, "No more of this!" And
he touched the man's ear and healed him.
52Then Jesus said to the chief priests, the officers
of the temple guard, and the elders, who had come
for him, "Am I leading a rebellion, that you have
come with swords and clubs? 53Every day I was
with you in the temple courts, and you did not lay
a hand on me. But this is your hour—when darkness reigns." Mt 26:47-56; Mk 14:43-50; Jn 18:3-11

Peter Disowns Jesus

▶ *See Matthew 26:69–75; Mark 14:66–72; John 18:16–18,25–27*

54Then seizing him, they led him away and took
him into the house of the high priest. Peter followed at a distance. 55But when they had kindled
a fire in the middle of the courtyard and had sat
down together, Peter sat down with them. 56A servant girl saw him seated there in the firelight. She
looked closely at him and said, "This man was
with him." Mt 26:57-58; Mk 14:53-54
57But he denied it. "Woman, I don't know
him," he said.
58A little later someone else saw him and said,
"You also are one of them."
"Man, I am not!" Peter replied.
59About an hour later another asserted, "Certainly this fellow was with him, for he is a Galilean." Lk 23:6
60Peter replied, "Man, I don't know what you're
talking about!" Just as he was speaking, the rooster
crowed. 61The Lord turned and looked straight at

[a] *31* The Greek is plural. [b] *37* Isaiah 53:12 [c] *44* Some early manuscripts do not have verses 43 and 44.

Peter. Then Peter remembered the word the Lord had spoken to him: "Before the rooster crows today, you will disown me three times." [62]And he went outside and wept bitterly. Mt 26:69-75

The Guards Mock Jesus

▶ *See Matthew 26:67–68; Mark 14:65; John 18:22–23*

[63]The men who were guarding Jesus began mocking and beating him. [64]They blindfolded him and demanded, "Prophesy! Who hit you?" [65]And they said many other insulting things to him.

Jesus Before Pilate and Herod

▶ *See Matthew 26:63–66; Mark 14:61–63; John 18:19–21*

[66]At daybreak the council of the elders of the people, both the chief priests and teachers of the law, met together, and Jesus was led before them. [67]"If you are the Christ,[a]" they said, "tell us."

Jesus answered, "If I tell you, you will not believe me, [68]and if I asked you, you would not answer. [69]But from now on, the Son of Man will be seated at the right hand of the mighty God."

[70]They all asked, "Are you then the Son of God?" Mt 4:3

He replied, "You are right in saying I am."

[71]Then they said, "Why do we need any more testimony? We have heard it from his own lips."

23 Then the whole assembly rose and led him off to Pilate. [2]And they began to accuse him, saying, "We have found this man subverting our nation. He opposes payment of taxes to Caesar and claims to be Christ,[b] a king." Lk 20:22

[3]So Pilate asked Jesus, "Are you the king of the Jews?"

"Yes, it is as you say," Jesus replied. Mt 27:11-14

[4]Then Pilate announced to the chief priests and the crowd, "I find no basis for a charge against this man." Mt 27:23; 2Co 5:21

[5]But they insisted, "He stirs up the people all over Judea[c] by his teaching. He started in Galilee and has come all the way here." Mk 1:14

[6]On hearing this, Pilate asked if the man was a Galilean. [7]When he learned that Jesus was under Herod's jurisdiction, he sent him to Herod, who was also in Jerusalem at that time. Mt 14:1; Lk 3:1

[8]When Herod saw Jesus, he was greatly pleased, because for a long time he had been wanting to see him. From what he had heard about him, he hoped to see him perform some miracle. [9]He plied him with many questions, but Jesus gave him no answer. [10]The chief priests and the teachers of the law were standing there, vehemently accusing him. [11]Then Herod and his soldiers ridiculed and mocked him. Dressing him in an elegant robe, they sent him back to Pilate. [12]That day Herod and Pilate became friends—before this they had been enemies. Mk 15:17-19; Lk 9:9; Ac 4:27

[13]Pilate called together the chief priests, the rulers and the people, [14]and said to them, "You brought me this man as one who was inciting the people to rebellion. I have examined him in your presence and have found no basis for your charges against him. [15]Neither has Herod, for he sent him back to us; as you can see, he has done nothing to deserve death. [16]Therefore, I will punish him and then release him.[d]" Mt 27:26; Jn 19:1

[18]With one voice they cried out, "Away with this man! Release Barabbas to us!" [19](Barabbas had been thrown into prison for an insurrection in the city, and for murder.) Ac 3:13-14

[20]Wanting to release Jesus, Pilate appealed to them again. [21]But they kept shouting, "Crucify him! Crucify him!"

[22]For the third time he spoke to them: "Why? What crime has this man committed? I have found in him no grounds for the death penalty. Therefore I will have him punished and then release him." ver 16

[23]But with loud shouts they insistently demanded that he be crucified, and their shouts prevailed. [24]So Pilate decided to grant their demand. [25]He released the man who had been thrown into prison for insurrection and murder, the one they asked for, and surrendered Jesus to their will.

The Crucifixion

▶ *See Matthew 27:33–44; Mark 15:22–32; John 19:17–24*

[26]As they led him away, they seized Simon from Cyrene, who was on his way in from the country, and put the cross on him and made him carry it behind Jesus. [27]A large number of people followed him, including women who mourned and wailed for him. [28]Jesus turned and said to them, "Daughters of Jerusalem, do not weep for me; weep for yourselves and for your children. [29]For the time will come when you will say, 'Blessed are the barren women, the wombs that never bore and the breasts that never nursed!' [30]Then Mt 24:19

"'they will say to the mountains, "Fall on us!"
and to the hills, "Cover us!"'[e]

[31]For if men do these things when the tree is green, what will happen when it is dry?" Eze 20:47; Hos 10:8

[32]Two other men, both criminals, were also led out with him to be executed. [33]When they came to the place called the Skull, there they crucified him, along with the criminals—one on his right, the other on his left. [34]Jesus said, "Father, forgive them, for they do not know what they are do-

[a]67 Or *Messiah* [b]2 Or *Messiah*; also in verses 35 and 39 [c]5 Or *over the land of the Jews* [d]16 Some manuscripts *him."* [17]*Now he was obliged to release one man to them at the Feast.* [e]30 Hosea 10:8

ing."[a] And they divided up his clothes by casting lots. Ps 22:18; Mt 27:38

35The people stood watching, and the rulers even sneered at him. They said, "He saved others; let him save himself if he is the Christ of God, the Chosen One." Ps 22:17; Isa 42:1

36The soldiers also came up and mocked him. They offered him wine vinegar 37and said, "If you are the king of the Jews, save yourself." Mt 27:48

38There was a written notice above him, which read: THIS IS THE KING OF THE JEWS. Mt 2:2

39One of the criminals who hung there hurled insults at him: "Aren't you the Christ? Save yourself and us!" ver 35,37

40But the other criminal rebuked him. "Don't you fear God," he said, "since you are under the same sentence? 41We are punished justly, for we are getting what our deeds deserve. But this man has done nothing wrong."

42Then he said, "Jesus, remember me when you come into your kingdom.[b]" Mt 16:27

43Jesus answered him, "I tell you the truth, today you will be with me in paradise." Mt 27:33-44

Jesus' Death

▶ *See Matthew 27:45–56; Mark 15:33–41*

44It was now about the sixth hour, and darkness came over the whole land until the ninth hour, 45for the sun stopped shining. And the curtain of the temple was torn in two. 46Jesus called out with a loud voice, "Father, into your hands I commit my spirit." When he had said this, he breathed his last. Ps 31:5; Jn 19:30

47The centurion, seeing what had happened, praised God and said, "Surely this was a righteous man." 48When all the people who had gathered to witness this sight saw what took place, they beat their breasts and went away. 49But all those who knew him, including the women who had followed him from Galilee, stood at a distance, watching these things. Mt 27:45-56; Mk 15:33-41

Jesus' Burial

▶ *See Matthew 27:57–61; Mark 15:42–47; John 19:38–42*

50Now there was a man named Joseph, a member of the Council, a good and upright man, 51who had not consented to their decision and action. He came from the Judean town of Arimathea and he was waiting for the kingdom of God. 52Going to Pilate, he asked for Jesus' body. 53Then he took it down, wrapped it in linen cloth and placed it in a tomb cut in the rock, one in which no one had yet been laid. 54It was Preparation Day, and the Sabbath was about to begin. Mt 27:62; Lk 2:25,38

55The women who had come with Jesus from Galilee followed Joseph and saw the tomb and how his body was laid in it. 56Then they went home and prepared spices and perfumes. But they rested on the Sabbath in obedience to the commandment.

Resurrection of Jesus **Chapter 24**

The Son of Man is alive! In the final chapter Luke told of the victorious resurrection of the Lord Jesus, the walk to Emmaus, Jesus' appearance to the disciples, the commissioning of the disciples and Jesus' ascension into heaven. Although the Son of Man was returning to glory, He still had a mission on earth. His messengers would preach in His name to every nation of the world. He promised them that they would be "clothed with power from on high" (24:49). This promise was fulfilled in Luke's second book, the Acts of the Apostles, when the Holy Spirit descended on the believers (Acts 2:4).

The Resurrection

▶ *See Matthew 28:1–8; Mark 16:1–8; John 20:1–8*

24 On the first day of the week, very early in the morning, the women took the spices they had prepared and went to the tomb. 2They found the stone rolled away from the tomb, 3but when they entered, they did not find the body of the Lord Jesus. 4While they were wondering about this, suddenly two men in clothes that gleamed like lightning stood beside them. 5In their fright the women bowed down with their faces to the ground, but the men said to them, "Why do you look for the living among the dead? 6He is not here; he has risen! Remember how he told you, while he was still with you in Galilee: 7'The Son of Man must be delivered into the hands of sinful men, be crucified and on the third day be raised again.'" 8Then they remembered his words.

9When they came back from the tomb, they told all these things to the Eleven and to all the others. 10It was Mary Magdalene, Joanna, Mary the mother of James, and the others with them who told this to the apostles. 11But they did not believe the women, because their words seemed to them like nonsense. 12Peter, however, got up and ran to the tomb. Bending over, he saw the strips of linen lying by themselves, and he went away, wondering to himself what had happened. Mk 16:1-8; Jn 20:1-8

On the Road to Emmaus

13Now that same day two of them were going to a village called Emmaus, about seven miles[c] from Jerusalem. 14They were talking with each other about everything that had happened. 15As they talked and discussed these things with each other, Jesus himself came up and walked along with them; 16but they were kept from recognizing him.

[a] 34 Some early manuscripts do not have this sentence. [b] 42 Some manuscripts *come with your kingly power* [c] 13 Greek *sixty stadia* (about 11 kilometers)

17 He asked them, "What are you discussing together as you walk along?"

They stood still, their faces downcast. 18 One of them, named Cleopas, asked him, "Are you only a visitor to Jerusalem and do not know the things that have happened there in these days?" Jn 19:25

19 "What things?" he asked.

"About Jesus of Nazareth," they replied. "He was a prophet, powerful in word and deed before God and all the people. 20 The chief priests and our rulers handed him over to be sentenced to death, and they crucified him; 21 but we had hoped that he was the one who was going to redeem Israel. And what is more, it is the third day since all this took place. 22 In addition, some of our women amazed us. They went to the tomb early this morning 23 but didn't find his body. They came and told us that they had seen a vision of angels, who said he was alive. 24 Then some of our companions went to the tomb and found it just as the women had said, but him they did not see." Mt 21:11; Mk 1:24

25 He said to them, "How foolish you are, and how slow of heart to believe all that the prophets have spoken! 26 Did not the Christ[a] have to suffer these things and then enter his glory?" 27 And beginning with Moses and all the Prophets, he explained to them what was said in all the Scriptures concerning himself. Jn 1:45

28 As they approached the village to which they were going, Jesus acted as if he were going farther. 29 But they urged him strongly, "Stay with us, for it is nearly evening; the day is almost over." So he went in to stay with them.

30 When he was at the table with them, he took bread, gave thanks, broke it and began to give it to them. 31 Then their eyes were opened and they recognized him, and he disappeared from their sight. 32 They asked each other, "Were not our hearts burning within us while he talked with us on the road and opened the Scriptures to us?" Ps 39:3

33 They got up and returned at once to Jerusalem. There they found the Eleven and those with them, assembled together 34 and saying, "It is true! The Lord has risen and has appeared to Simon." 35 Then the two told what had happened on the way, and how Jesus was recognized by them when he broke the bread. 1Co 15:5

Jesus Appears to the Disciples

36 While they were still talking about this, Jesus himself stood among them and said to them, "Peace be with you." Jn 20:19,21,26

37 They were startled and frightened, thinking they saw a ghost. 38 He said to them, "Why are you troubled, and why do doubts rise in your minds? 39 Look at my hands and my feet. It is I myself! Touch me and see; a ghost does not have flesh and bones, as you see I have." Mk 6:49; Jn 20:27

40 When he had said this, he showed them his hands and feet. 41 And while they still did not believe it because of joy and amazement, he asked them, "Do you have anything here to eat?" 42 They gave him a piece of broiled fish, 43 and he took it and ate it in their presence. Ac 10:41

44 He said to them, "This is what I told you while I was still with you: Everything must be fulfilled that is written about me in the Law of Moses, the Prophets and the Psalms." Mt 18:31-33

45 Then he opened their minds so they could understand the Scriptures. 46 He told them, "This is what is written: The Christ will suffer and rise from the dead on the third day, 47 and repentance and forgiveness of sins will be preached in his name to all nations, beginning at Jerusalem. 48 You are witnesses of these things. 49 I am going to send you what my Father has promised; but stay in the city until you have been clothed with power from on high." Ac 1:4,8

The Ascension

50 When he had led them out to the vicinity of Bethany, he lifted up his hands and blessed them. 51 While he was blessing them, he left them and was taken up into heaven. 52 Then they worshiped him and returned to Jerusalem with great joy. 53 And they stayed continually at the temple, praising God. 2Ki 2:11; Ac 2:46

[a] 26 Or *Messiah*; also in verse 46

INTRODUCTION

JOHN

New Christians frequently ask, "Which book of the Bible should I study first?" Bible translating teams often ask a similar question: "Which book should we translate first?" Believers occasionally wonder, "Which section of the Scriptures would be especially helpful for my "seeking" friends to read?" All three questions can be answered in the same way: the Gospel of John. The fourth Gospel is considered a *primer,* a book containing the basics of Christianity. Jesus Christ, God's one and only Son, is clearly and preeminently exalted as deity. In simple yet profound terms, Jesus is set forth so that all may believe that He is indeed the Son of God. In the end, as we read this Gospel we are brought to see that life eternal, for time and eternity, begins with Jesus Christ.

WRITER: *John*

DATE: *c.A.D. 80–95*

PURPOSE: *To bring about a response of faith from the reader*

KEY MESSAGE: *Jesus is the divine Son of God*

KEY VERSE: *20:31 "that you may believe that Jesus is the Christ, the Son of God"*

KEY TERMS: *"Life"; "witness"; "believe"; "world"; "know"; "glorify"*

DISTINCTIVES: *Seven self-descriptions of Jesus that begin with "I am"; upper room discourse; "signs" confirming that Jesus is the Son of God*

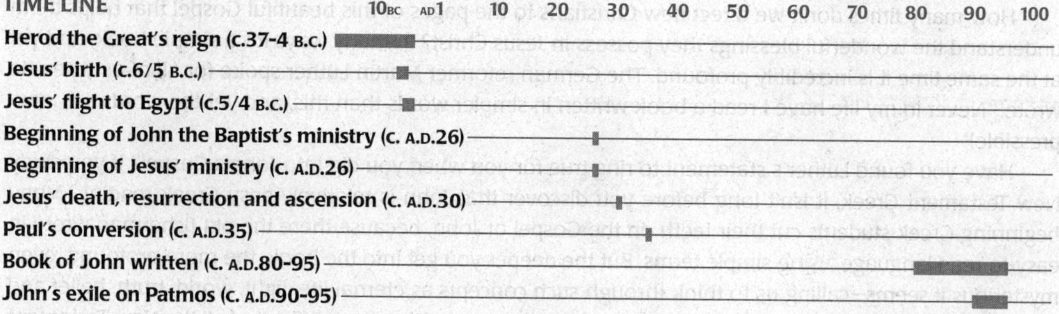

The Book That Helps Us Believe

	"THE WORD WAS GOD" (1:1)	*"THE LAMB OF GOD" (1:29)*					
	DEITY	GOD-MAN	MINISTRY	DISCOURSE		EMPTY TOMB	ASSURANCE
		Great Miracles	**Great Miracles**	**Quiet Talks**		**Quiet Talks**	**Quiet Talks**
		Water-wine *(2)* Heals son *(4)*	Heals man *(5)* Feeds 5,000 *(6)* Walks on water *(6)* Heals blind *(9)* Raises dead *(11)*	Heaven *(14)* Fruit *(15)* Promises (16) Prayer *(17)*		Appear-ances *(20)*	Future *(21)*
	CHAPTER 1:1-18	*CHAPTERS 1:19–4:54*	*CHAPTERS 5–12*	*CHAPTERS 13–17*	*CHAPTERS 18–19*	*CHAPTER 20*	*CHAPTER 21*
	PROLOGUE						**EPILOGUE**
STAGE	**Acceptance**		**Conflict**	**Preparation**	**Crucifixion**	**Triumph**	
AUDIENCE	**Public message**			**CHANGE**	**Private message**		
TIME	**Three years**				**Several days**		

How frequently do we turn to the book of Psalms to find comfort? Even people who don't know the contents of the Bible all that well can usually quote a part of Psalm 23 or Psalm 100. In many ways Psalms is the central book of the Old Testament. What the book of Psalms is to the Old Testament I believe the Gospel of John is to the New Testament. It is a refuge, a harbor. I am confident that many of us turn to it spontaneously to find comfort and rest for our anxious and weary souls. The Gospel of John is a marvelous haven of hope, bringing a word of encouragement to people who are depressed and disillusioned. There's nothing like the book of John to inspire, comfort and encourage.

How many times don't we direct new Christians to the pages of this beautiful Gospel that helps them understand the wonderful blessings they possess in Jesus Christ? In many ways it's a simple book, and yet at the same time it is incredibly profound. The German reformer Martin Luther spoke for all of us when he wrote: "Never in my life have I read a book written in simpler words than this, and yet the words are inexpressible!"

Have you found Luther's statement to ring true for you when you dig into John's Gospel? If you study New Testament Greek, it isn't long before you discover that John is relatively easy Greek reading. Many beginning Greek students cut their teeth on the Gospel of John, because there the old fisherman wrote in easy-to-read language, using simple terms. But the deeper you get into the book, the more profound, even mysterious it seems—calling us to think through such concepts as eternal life, light, world, truth, belief and love. There are times when this Gospel seems to contain some of the most difficult of all the New Testament writings.

Meeting John

This Gospel was written by the apostle John—one of the closest friends of Jesus during His life on earth. You may very well be familiar with Peter, James and John—three of Jesus' closest disciples. John was the one who seemed to have stayed closest to the Lord. Even at the Last Supper he reclined at Jesus' side (13:23). And it was at the foot of the cross on which Jesus hung that John received this charge to care for Jesus' mother, Mary: "Here is your mother" (19:27).

John was a man of warm affection who was obviously gripped by the power of love. He pointed out the love of the Father for His Son, Jesus Christ, as well as the love of the Son for the Father. He recorded Jesus' words of love for His disciples, for all believers and for the world, as well as Jesus' command that His disciples love Him and one another. Even in the midst of a growing darkness of opposition and awareness of Jesus' imminent death, John found in Jesus acceptance and security and hope. Nothing could shake his faith in the Son of God!

Jesus Is God

The question that may arise in our minds is this: "Why did God direct four different men to write the story of the life of Jesus?" Just a quick review: four different writers with four different audiences with four different purposes. Matthew portrayed Jesus as the King—the Messiah promised in the Old Testament—and wrote to a primarily Jewish audience. Mark presented Jesus as the suffering Servant and wrote to practical-minded Romans. Writing to a Greek audience, Luke showed Jesus to be the Son of Man and presented a striking picture of Jesus' humanity. John highlighted the deity of Jesus as the Son of God sent to earth to do the work of the Father. From John's grand declaration "The Word was God . . . The Word became flesh and made his dwelling among us" (1:1,14) to Thomas's confession "My Lord and my God!" (20:28), Jesus is God the Son come in the flesh.

John very clearly stated his purpose for writing his Gospel in verses 30 and 31 of chapter 20:

> *Jesus did many other miraculous signs in the presence of his disciples, which are not recorded in this book. But these are written that you may believe that Jesus is the Christ, the Son of God, and that by believing you may have life in his name.*

John said, in effect, "I have written this Gospel, this account, so that you may realize that Jesus is the Son of God; He is very God of very God; He is not only true humanity, He is undiminished deity!" And you will see this theme permeating the book. When John comes to his purpose statement late in his Gospel, we're not surprised. All he has written has led up to this conclusion: "I've written this so that you will realize that Jesus is God."

John told us that Jesus also performed many other miraculous signs (20:30). The Greek term translated "signs" was John's way of conveying the idea of "miracles." John was saying, in effect, 'Jesus did a number of miracles that are not even included in my account. He performed many of them, in fact, which I purposely did not record; they're not written in this book. I have selected a few, however. The ones I have included I have done so for one purpose: that you may believe that Jesus is the Christ."

An Invitation to Believe

As John stated his motive for writing, he used his favorite word to describe the response he desired from his readers. The term "believe" (or a related term) is used 98 times in these 21 chapters. It's amazing that one book of the Bible would use the same word almost a hundred times—there's no mistaking John's longing for us to believe in Jesus!

What does it mean to believe in Jesus? It includes at least two elements. First, *I acknowledge the facts are what they are—true, beyond dispute.* Before I can respond in belief, I need facts—facts that I can trust, facts that are accurate, reliable and spelled out in terms I can understand. I need to examine the facts as they are presented, and I need to agree that Jesus is who He said He is and that the words He spoke are true. I am then able to say, "I acknowledge that what the Bible says about Jesus is true. I see Him as more than just a good man, more than just an outstanding teacher, more than just an extraordinary servant. I acknowledge Him as the Son of God, who died so that I might live."

Second, *I personally abandon myself to the truth of those facts.* I rely on those facts to come true in my life and to make a difference in the way I live. There are various synonyms for it: receiving Christ; accepting Jesus as my Savior; becoming born again; surrendering my life to Him. As I abandon myself, I respond with my heart, "More than just agreeing that Jesus' words are true, more than just an intellectual assent to a body of facts, I trust in Jesus Christ alone for my salvation and my strength for living. I commit my life to Him; I abandon myself to Him; I place my hope, my trust, my confidence in Him; I will live for Him—and thereby I believe."

That's why John wrote his Gospel—to communicate the truth that Jesus is God, so that in seeing the facts his readers might respond positively with the commitment of their lives.

Seeing and Believing

John's method was this: to show signs that would help his readers believe. Look at the signs. In chapter 2 Jesus turned water into wine. That's the kind of sign that will help you believe—and the disciples did. Jesus healed a royal official's son in chapter 4 and healed a man by a pool in chapter 5. He fed a crowd of 5,000 in chapter 6, and shortly thereafter He walked on water. Later He healed a man born blind (chapter 9) and tossed aside the question of who was guilty—the man or his parents. In effect, He told His disciples, "The real issue here is this: I want you to believe that My power will be displayed in this situation." He used the experience of physical disability to urge people to believe. One last example: When Jesus raised Lazarus from the dead (chapter 11), many who were there with Mary and Martha believed (11:45). They had been mourning Lazarus's ill-timed, seemingly meaningless death, but immediately after he came out of the tomb, many of them believed. They saw the signs Jesus performed, and they believed in Jesus.

John always referred to Jesus' miracles as "signs." In Scripture, a "sign" as it related to a miraculous event was "an act of supernatural origin with deep meaning behind it." But get this: The *act* was of secondary importance. What was important when a miracle was performed was not so much the act itself, though it was marvelous, but the *significance* of the act—to glean the meaning behind it.

That's why Jesus, after performing a miracle, would deliver a discourse. Sometimes His teaching lasted only a few statements; sometimes it went on for a chapter or more. You see, the purpose of the miracle was to help people realize, "This Man is from God! This individual is, in fact, supernatural in origin!" Behind the doing of the miracle was a desire to show the observers some deep, profound truth—usually about Himself personally.

It's time to bring it all home—to you and to me. Let me make this suggestion, if I could: *Spend some time in the Gospel of John.* Honestly examine the claims. Examine your own reaction to those claims and your response to the One who is the foundation for those claims. Encourage your family, friends and acquaintances to do the same thing, particularly if they have resisted a relationship with Jesus Christ. Within the Gospel of John there lies a strong challenge to make a decision either for and against the Son of God. Remaining neutral is not an option. Everything John wrote he carefully crafted with a view to showing us that Jesus is the Son of God, that He is worthy of our love and our worship and our trust. How will we respond? May it be a response of belief and an experience of life in the name of Jesus!

Public Ministry of Jesus **Chapters 1–12**

In this first section we meet Jesus, the One who is fully divine and fully human. John wanted everyone to understand exactly who Jesus is . . . God in human flesh. To help us believe in Jesus, John recorded seven miraculous signs: Jesus turned water to wine, healed a young boy, healed a paralyzed man, fed a crowd of 5,000, walked on water, healed a man born blind and raised a dead man. In these chapters, Jesus, the Word of God, taught and performed His work in open and public settings. Personal encounters with Jesus were featured throughout these chapters, and, almost without exception, these individuals were challenged to believe in Him. Jesus met Nicodemus (chapter 3), the woman at the well (chapter 4), a paralyzed man (chapter 5), a woman caught in adultery (chapter 8), and many others; they were all invited to believe in the Son of God. These 12 chapters span three years of Jesus' public ministry.

The Word Became Flesh

1 In the beginning was the Word, and the
Word was with God, and the Word was God.
2He was with God in the beginning. Php 2:6; 1Jn 1:2
3Through him all things were made; without
him nothing was made that has been made. 4In
him was life, and that life was the light of men.
5The light shines in the darkness, but the darkness
has not understood[a] it. Jn 3:19; 5:26; Col 1:16
6There came a man who was sent from God; his
name was John. 7He came as a witness to testify
concerning that light, so that through him all men
might believe. 8He himself was not the light; he
came only as a witness to the light. 9The true light
that gives light to every man was coming into the
world.[b] Isa 49:6; 1Jn 2:8
10He was in the world, and though the world
was made through him, the world did not recognize him. 11He came to that which was his own,
but his own did not receive him. 12Yet to all who
received him, to those who believed in his name,
he gave the right to become children of God—
13children born not of natural descent,[c] nor of
human decision or a husband's will, but born of
God. Jn 3:6; 1Pe 1:23
14The Word became flesh and made his dwelling among us. We have seen his glory, the glory of
the One and Only,[d] who came from the Father,
full of grace and truth. Gal 4:4; 1Ti 3:16
15John testifies concerning him. He cries out,
saying, "This was he of whom I said, 'He who
comes after me has surpassed me because he was
before me.'" 16From the fullness of his grace we
have all received one blessing after another. 17For
the law was given through Moses; grace and truth
came through Jesus Christ. 18No one has ever seen
God, but God the One and Only,[d,e] who is at the
Father's side, has made him known. Ex 33:20; 1Jn 4:9

LIVING  **INSIGHT**

How magnificent is grace! How malignant is guilt! How sweet are the promises! How sour is the past! How precious and broad is God's love! How petty and narrow are humanity's limitations! How refreshing is the Lord! How rigid is the legalist!

(See John 1:14.)

John the Baptist Denies Being the Christ

19Now this was John's testimony when the Jews
of Jerusalem sent priests and Levites to ask him
who he was. 20He did not fail to confess, but confessed freely, "I am not the Christ.[f]" Lk 3:15-16
21They asked him, "Then who are you? Are you
Elijah?" Mt 11:14
He said, "I am not."
"Are you the Prophet?" Dt 18:15
He answered, "No."
22Finally they said, "Who are you? Give us an
answer to take back to those who sent us. What do
you say about yourself?"
23John replied in the words of Isaiah the prophet, "I am the voice of one calling in the desert,
'Make straight the way for the Lord.'"[g] Isa 40:3
24Now some Pharisees who had been sent
25questioned him, "Why then do you baptize if
you are not the Christ, nor Elijah, nor the
Prophet?"
26"I baptize with[h] water," John replied, "but
among you stands one you do not know. 27He is
the one who comes after me, the thongs of whose
sandals I am not worthy to untie." Mk 1:4,7
28This all happened at Bethany on the other side
of the Jordan, where John was baptizing. Jn 3:26

Jesus the Lamb of God

29The next day John saw Jesus coming toward
him and said, "Look, the Lamb of God, who takes
away the sin of the world! 30This is the one I meant
when I said, 'A man who comes after me has surpassed me because he was before me.' 31I myself
did not know him, but the reason I came baptizing
with water was that he might be revealed to Israel."
32Then John gave this testimony: "I saw the
Spirit come down from heaven as a dove and remain on him. 33I would not have known him,
except that the one who sent me to baptize with

[a]5 Or *darkness, and the darkness has not overcome into the world* [b]9 Or *This was the true light that gives light to every man who comes* [c]13 Greek *of bloods* [d]14,18 Or *the Only Begotten* [e]18 Some manuscripts *but the only* (or *only begotten) Son* [f]20 Or *Messiah.* "The Christ" (Greek) and "the Messiah" (Hebrew) both mean "the Anointed One"; also in verse 25. [g]23 Isaiah 40:3 [h]26 Or *in*; also in verses 31 and 33

GOD IN HUMAN FLESH

"In the beginning was the Word, and the Word was with God, and the Word was God . . . The Word became flesh and made his dwelling among us. We have seen his glory, the glory of the One and Only, who came from the Father, full of grace and truth."

—JOHN 1:1,14

The most significant event of all the centuries took place not in a glitzy palace, not in a convention center ballroom, but in a stable in an insignificant little city named Bethlehem. In a lowly manger, in a feeding trough. It wasn't the announcement of a stunning breakthrough in disease control or the signing of a new peace accord. It was the birth nearly two thousand years ago of a baby boy to a humble Jewish virgin named Mary, who was married to a carpenter named Joseph.

Don't you wonder what Mary must have thought as she held that precious little baby close to her chest? I wonder if the words of the prophet Isaiah came flooding into her mind. Surely she knew those words well: "Therefore the Lord himself will give you a sign: The virgin will be with child and will give birth to a son, and will call him Immanuel" (Isaiah 7:14).

There Mary was, holding in her arms "Immanuel . . . God with us." Can you imagine? The Word become flesh. Deity in a mother's arms!

Perhaps Mary remembered the angel Gabriel who had visited her nine months earlier and said, "Do not be afraid" (Luke 1:30). Just like the Lord, isn't it? You see, God doesn't issue edicts like humans do. Caesar makes a decree; it is announced, and the world jumps to attention. But God's concern is for the one who will hear the message, so He sent this word to Mary through His angel: "Don't be afraid, Mary. Something amazing is going to happen. Behold, having never intimately known a man, you will conceive in your womb. You will bear a Son, and you will call His name Jesus" (Luke 1:30–31, paraphrased). A never-to-be-repeated event! A virgin will have a baby . . . even though most people then would never believe it—and still have trouble believing it to this day.

The Supreme Question

Just who is this person called Jesus Christ? Would it surprise you to know that this question has been asked ever since the first century when He walked the paths of ancient Palestine? His identity has never failed to cause a stir. Who exactly is Jesus? The answer has ranged from demon to deity. It is imperative that we know the right answer to this question. If we don't, we will not know how to interpret what He has done. And if we are unable to interpret what He has done, we will never be able to give ourselves to Him, as He invites us to do.

Who is Jesus Christ? The divine-human Savior—the most unique Person who ever lived. The awesome Son of God. Here are three stories from the Gospels that point us to the awesome wonder of who Jesus is. Each story helps us see both the human and the divine natures in the same Person, as we answer the supreme question, WHO IS JESUS?

Humans Have Compassion . . . Only God Heals the Sick

Mark records a compelling glimpse at Jesus as fully divine and fully human when he records the healing of a man who had leprosy, who came to Jesus. Down on his knees, the man with leprosy begged Jesus, "If you are willing, you can make me clean" (Mark 1:40).

I don't know if you've ever seen what leprosy looks like. I have. While in Southeast Asia during my days in the Marine Corps, it was customary for my military outfit to visit a leprosarium once or twice a year. We went to entertain and encourage the residents. I have never seen such helpless, tragic sights. The hands and feet of those poor folks are often just bleeding stumps. No shoes can be worn, and it's obvious some of them don't even have toes.

I can imagine this suffering man, with his bleeding stumps, saying to Jesus, "If you're willing, cleanse me." Do you see it? The man with leprosy said to Jesus, in effect, "You can do it. Ah, I know You can cleanse me if You're willing. You can make me clean, Jesus! I've heard about you. You are the gentle Healer. You have power, Jesus, a power that is not of this world."

Now watch carefully. Watch what happens next. As a man, the Lord Jesus expressed the powerful feelings of compassion as He saw a fellow human being in need. You know how it is when you walk by a scene that just breaks your heart, or when you watch a tragic story on television or read one in a magazine or a newspaper; you are moved with compassion for those who hurt. Your heart goes out to them. You literally ache for those people who are in trouble, for those who suffer pain and heartache or who grieve the death of a loved one. That's the powerful feelings of human tenderness in the presence of great human misery. That's how Jesus ached. That's how Jesus in His human nature expressed His compassionate heart. But He did more than feel compassion. "Filled with compassion, Jesus reached out his hand and touched the man" (Mark 1:41). He *reached out and touched him*. What an incredible picture! Jesus, the One who was fully human and yet fully divine, bringing a physical touch of gentle care to a desperately hurting man.

Note well what happened next: "Filled with compassion, Jesus reached out his hand and touched the man. 'I am willing,' he said. 'Be clean!' Immediately the leprosy left him and he was cured" (Mark 1:41–42).

Only God can do that. Only One who is fully divine can bring instant healing for our diseases. Can you imagine it? The pain that had plagued that man disappeared, the hemorrhaging stopped. Healing had taken place—immediately. The gentle Healer had done His work, revealing beyond the shadow of a doubt that He was, in fact, the Word become flesh.

Humans Sleep . . . Only God Calms Storms

In his Gospel, Luke reports another wonderful story that took place on the Sea of Galilee. In the middle of Jesus' heavy schedule of traveling from town to town in Galilee, He and His disciples got into a boat one day and started out for the other side. Note these words of Luke as he tells what Jesus did in the boat: "As they sailed, he fell asleep" (Luke 8:23a).

I've not done a great deal of sailing, but the little I have done, I've usually fallen asleep while on board. It's the most natural response to the rhythm of the sea as it gently massages the weariness of my bones. Most people I know would agree—easygoing sailing and restful sleeping are meant for each other! But Scripture never says that God sleeps. In fact, it specifically says, "He who watches over Israel will neither slumber nor sleep" (Psalm 121:4). Yet humans sleep. Men and women, boys and girls—all must sleep.

As a man weary from the press of the day's activities, Jesus fell sound asleep in the boat. Now watch carefully. Here's when things start to happen:

> *A squall came down on the lake, so that the boat was being swamped, and they were in great danger. The disciples went and woke him, saying, "Master, Master, we're going to drown!" (Luke 8:23b–24a).*

Do you sense the panic in their actions and in their voices as they shook Jesus awake, with words to this effect, "Master, wake up, wake up! We're going to die!" Now isn't that something? The disciples had already witnessed water turned into wine at a wedding feast (John 2:1–11), but they hadn't yet grasped the reality of Jesus' power.

They'd seen Him cleanse a man who had leprosy, raise a widow's son from the dead (Luke 7:11–15), and perform many other miracles—but they hadn't put one miracle together with another miracle and come up with "deity." So here they were in a boat with God in human flesh, and all they could say was, "We're going to sink." (You can't sink with God in the same boat!) And suddenly with a few gentle words, everything turned calm. Only God could do such a thing! Here's how Luke describes it: "He got up and rebuked the wind and the raging waters; the storm subsided, and all was calm" (Luke 8:24b).

I may not have done much sailing, but I have certainly done a lot of fishing in my day, and I can tell you that I've occasionally seen the sea become what we fishermen like to call "a slick." It's an eerie sight—especially in the ocean. The water is so smooth that if you flipped a penny into it you could count the ripples. But never in my life have I seen a slick occur suddenly. Yet in this case a storming, raging sea—stirred up by incredible wind velocity—instantly became a slick. You could hear the sound of your own breathing. The boat may have taken a moment to stop rocking . . . but the sea was as calm as glass. Talk about *eerie*!

Take a close look at the disciples' response. It's great. They don't know what to think: "In fear and amazement they asked one another, 'Who is this? He commands even the winds and the water, and they obey him' " (Luke 8:25). Does that sound like strong, believing followers? "Who is this?" Can't you see Peter, that veteran fisherman, mumbling under his breath, "Even the winds and the water obey Him. This is GOD." Yes, Peter, the One you woke up a moment ago is indeed God. HE IS GOD.

Never doubt it, my friend. In the tragic storms of life Almighty God specializes in calming waves and silencing winds. It'll shock you at times. How can Jesus Christ do such a thing? How, indeed! He is God!

Humans Weep . . . Only God Raises the Dead

In his Gospel John paints a memorable scene that involved Jesus' friend, Lazarus, who became ill and suddenly died. Four days after Lazarus's death Jesus arrived at this dark, depressing scene of mourning in Bethany. There He was greeted with words of confusion and admonition for not having dropped everything and come alongside the grieving family. It's bad enough to be blamed: "Lord, if you had been here, my brother would not have died" (John 11:32)—but to have to face the unmitigated, raw grief of His friends, oh, that's another matter:

> *When Jesus saw her weeping, and the Jews who had come along with her also weeping, he was deeply moved in spirit and troubled. "Where have you laid him?" he asked. "Come and see, Lord," they replied. Jesus wept (John 11:33–35).*

Take some time to reflect on the depth of Jesus' emotions. In His humanity He experienced all we experience as human beings. The Gospels paint a full picture of Jesus' humanity as He faced the heartbreak and suffering caused by all the evil in the world. They record his expressions of being "moved . . . and troubled." They document the deep sympathy He feels for the sorrow of His people. He wept as He grieved, not only because of the waning faith of those around Him, but because of the loss of His friend and the sorrow of His companions. It was a scene that would make any of us cry. Watch what happens next:

> *Jesus, once more deeply moved, came to the tomb. It was a cave with a stone laid across the entrance. "Take away the stone," he said. "But Lord," said Martha, the sister of the dead man, "by this time there is a bad odor, for he has been there four days." Then Jesus said, "Did I not tell you that if you believed, you would see the glory of God?" So they took away the stone . . . (John 11:38–41).*

People don't argue much with Jesus, you'll notice. Maybe all you can stammer out is one measly little line. And then you wait to hear Jesus' response: "Take away the stone." So they took it away. Jesus was going to bring Lazarus back to life. A person, dead for four days, wrapped in grave clothes, yet now by the mighty command of Jesus restored to the fullness of life. Little wonder that Jesus declared that He was "the resurrection and the life" (John 11:25). Not only does He give life, He *is* life! With Him and through Him final death is impossible. And so He gave the command, "Take away the stone." What happened next?

> *So they took away the stone. Then Jesus looked up and said, "Father, I thank you that you have heard me. I knew that you always hear me, but I said this for the benefit of the people standing here, that they may believe that you sent me." When he had said this, Jesus called in a loud voice, "Lazarus, come out!" (John 11:41–43).*

I love one country preacher's comment, "If He hadn't limited that command to Lazarus, every corpse in the graveyard would have come forth!" It was as if He said, "Just Lazarus, this time, just Lazarus." Someday He'll bring them all back!

The final scene of this amazing miracle reveals Lazarus emerging from the tomb. Jesus, who is God in human flesh, has the power to triumph over death!

The dead man came out, his hands and feet wrapped with strips of linen, and a cloth around his face. Jesus said to them, "Take off the grave clothes and let him go" (John 11:44).

Isn't that an electric moment? Wouldn't you love to have had supper with Lazarus that night? "How was it, Lazarus? What was it like, Lazarus, to walk out of that tomb and watch the grave clothes tumble to the ground?"

Humanity weeps in grief and distress. Jesus experienced those powerful emotions in the presence of misery and suffering and loss. Remember, He was fully human. He experienced all we experience as human beings. And He was fully divine. Only God can raise the dead. And Jesus did. He is, after all, who He claimed to be—very God of very God, deity come in human form to serve, to suffer, to die, to be raised to life, that we might see how magnificent He really is!

Is There Room in Your Heart?

It all began in a manger, but it ends in your heart. Has there been a time in your personal life when you have asked Jesus to occupy your heart, as surely as He once occupied the manger? Honestly now, does He have first place? Does He reign there without a rival? The Lord Jesus Christ is available in the same form He has been for centuries—the Son of God who died for you, who paid the price to redeem you from your sin, who was miraculously and bodily raised from the dead, who is alive and seated at the right hand of the Father in glory, and who will one day come again. If you will, by personal invitation, ask Jesus to become your Savior from sin, your personal Redeemer, He *will* come in. In the solitude of this quiet moment, make room in your heart for the Lord Jesus. Pause now and tell Him that you are ready to give Him the place of honor and authority in your life.

water told me, 'The man on whom you see the Spirit come down and remain is he who will baptize with the Holy Spirit.' 34I have seen and I testify that this is the Son of God." Mt 3:11,16; Mk 1:10

Jesus' First Disciples

35The next day John was there again with two of his disciples. 36When he saw Jesus passing by, he said, "Look, the Lamb of God!" ver 29

37When the two disciples heard him say this, they followed Jesus. 38Turning around, Jesus saw them following and asked, "What do you want?"

They said, "Rabbi" (which means Teacher), "where are you staying?" Mt 23:7

39"Come," he replied, "and you will see."

So they went and saw where he was staying, and spent that day with him. It was about the tenth hour.

40Andrew, Simon Peter's brother, was one of the two who heard what John had said and who

LIVING INSIGHT

Don't read people a long list of rules of spirituality en route to salvation. You present to them the Savior. You press the issue of their relationship to the Lord Jesus. Your job isn't to clean up the fish bowl, certainly not initially. It's to fish—just to fish.

(See John 1:40–42.)

had followed Jesus. 41The first thing Andrew did was to find his brother Simon and tell him, "We have found the Messiah" (that is, the Christ). 42And he brought him to Jesus. Jn 4:25

Jesus looked at him and said, "You are Simon son of John. You will be called Cephas" (which, when translated, is Peter[a]). Mt 4:18-22; Mk 1:16-20

Jesus Calls Philip and Nathanael

43The next day Jesus decided to leave for Galilee. Finding Philip, he said to him, "Follow me."

44Philip, like Andrew and Peter, was from the town of Bethsaida. 45Philip found Nathanael and told him, "We have found the one Moses wrote about in the Law, and about whom the prophets also wrote—Jesus of Nazareth, the son of Joseph."

46"Nazareth! Can anything good come from there?" Nathanael asked. Jn 7:41-42,52

"Come and see," said Philip.

47When Jesus saw Nathanael approaching, he said of him, "Here is a true Israelite, in whom there is nothing false." Ps 32:2; Ro 9:4,6

48"How do you know me?" Nathanael asked.

Jesus answered, "I saw you while you were still under the fig tree before Philip called you."

49Then Nathanael declared, "Rabbi, you are the Son of God; you are the King of Israel." Mt 4:3

50Jesus said, "You believe[b] because I told you I saw you under the fig tree. You shall see greater things than that." 51He then added, "I tell you[c] the truth, you[c] shall see heaven open, and the angels of God ascending and descending on the Son of Man." Ge 28:12; Mt 3:16; 8:20

Jesus Changes Water to Wine

2 On the third day a wedding took place at Cana in Galilee. Jesus' mother was there, 2and Jesus and his disciples had also been invited to the wedding. 3When the wine was gone, Jesus' mother said to him, "They have no more wine." Mt 12:46

4"Dear woman, why do you involve me?" Jesus replied. "My time has not yet come." Jn 7:6; 19:26

5His mother said to the servants, "Do whatever he tells you." Ge 41:55

6Nearby stood six stone water jars, the kind used by the Jews for ceremonial washing, each holding from twenty to thirty gallons.[d] Mk 7:3-4

7Jesus said to the servants, "Fill the jars with water"; so they filled them to the brim.

8Then he told them, "Now draw some out and take it to the master of the banquet."

They did so, 9and the master of the banquet tasted the water that had been turned into wine. He did not realize where it had come from, though the servants who had drawn the water knew. Then he called the bridegroom aside 10and said, "Everyone brings out the choice wine first and then the cheaper wine after the guests have had too much to drink; but you have saved the best till now."

11This, the first of his miraculous signs, Jesus performed at Cana in Galilee. He thus revealed his glory, and his disciples put their faith in him.

Jesus Clears the Temple

▶ *See Matthew 21:12–13; Mark 11:15–17; Luke 19:45–46*

12After this he went down to Capernaum with his mother and brothers and his disciples. There they stayed for a few days. Mt 12:46

13When it was almost time for the Jewish Passover, Jesus went up to Jerusalem. 14In the temple courts he found men selling cattle, sheep and doves, and others sitting at tables exchanging money. 15So he made a whip out of cords, and drove all from the temple area, both sheep and cattle; he scattered the coins of the money changers and overturned their tables. 16To those who sold doves he said, "Get these out of here! How dare you turn my Father's house into a market!"

[a]42 Both *Cephas* (Aramaic) and *Peter* (Greek) mean *rock.* [b]50 Or *Do you believe . . . ?* [c]51 The Greek is plural.
[d]6 Greek *two to three metretes* (probably about 75 to 115 liters)

17His disciples remembered that it is written: "Zeal for your house will consume me."[a] Ps 69:9

18Then the Jews demanded of him, "What miraculous sign can you show us to prove your authority to do all this?" Mt 12:38

19Jesus answered them, "Destroy this temple, and I will raise it again in three days." Mt 26:61

20The Jews replied, "It has taken forty-six years to build this temple, and you are going to raise it in three days?" 21But the temple he had spoken of was his body. 22After he was raised from the dead, his disciples recalled what he had said. Then they believed the Scripture and the words that Jesus had spoken. Lk 24:5-8; 1Co 6:19

23Now while he was in Jerusalem at the Passover Feast, many people saw the miraculous signs he was doing and believed in his name.[b] 24But Jesus would not entrust himself to them, for he knew all men. 25He did not need man's testimony about man, for he knew what was in a man. Jn 6:61,64

Jesus Teaches Nicodemus

3 Now there was a man of the Pharisees named Nicodemus, a member of the Jewish ruling council. 2He came to Jesus at night and said, "Rabbi, we know you are a teacher who has come from God. For no one could perform the miraculous signs you are doing if God were not with him."

3In reply Jesus declared, "I tell you the truth, no one can see the kingdom of God unless he is born again.[c]" Jn 1:13; 1Pe 1:23

4"How can a man be born when he is old?" Nicodemus asked. "Surely he cannot enter a second time into his mother's womb to be born!"

5Jesus answered, "I tell you the truth, no one can enter the kingdom of God unless he is born of water and the Spirit. 6Flesh gives birth to flesh, but the Spirit[d] gives birth to spirit. 7You should not be surprised at my saying, 'You[e] must be born again.' 8The wind blows wherever it pleases. You hear its sound, but you cannot tell where it comes from or where it is going. So it is with everyone born of the Spirit." Jn 1:13; Tit 3:5

9"How can this be?" Nicodemus asked.

10"You are Israel's teacher," said Jesus, "and do you not understand these things? 11I tell you the truth, we speak of what we know, and we testify to what we have seen, but still you people do not accept our testimony. 12I have spoken to you of earthly things and you do not believe; how then will you believe if I speak of heavenly things? 13No one has ever gone into heaven except the one who came from heaven—the Son of Man.[f] 14Just as Moses lifted up the snake in the desert, so the Son of Man must be lifted up, 15that everyone who believes in him may have eternal life.[g] Nu 21:8-9

16"For God so loved the world that he gave his one and only Son,[h] that whoever believes in him shall not perish but have eternal life. 17For God did not send his Son into the world to condemn the world, but to save the world through him. 18Whoever believes in him is not condemned, but whoever does not believe stands condemned already because he has not believed in the name of God's one and only Son.[i] 19This is the verdict: Light has come into the world, but men loved darkness instead of light because their deeds were evil. 20Everyone who does evil hates the light, and will not come into the light for fear that his deeds will be exposed. 21But whoever lives by the truth comes into the light, so that it may be seen plainly that what he has done has been done through God."[j]

John the Baptist's Testimony About Jesus

22After this, Jesus and his disciples went out into the Judean countryside, where he spent some time with them, and baptized. 23Now John also was baptizing at Aenon near Salim, because there was plenty of water, and people were constantly coming to be baptized. 24(This was before John was put in prison.) 25An argument developed between some of John's disciples and a certain Jew[k] over the matter of ceremonial washing. 26They came to John and said to him, "Rabbi, that man who was with you on the other side of the Jordan—the one you testified about—well, he is baptizing, and everyone is going to him." Jn 1:7; 4:2

27To this John replied, "A man can receive only what is given him from heaven. 28You yourselves can testify that I said, 'I am not the Christ[l] but am sent ahead of him.' 29The bride belongs to the bridegroom. The friend who attends the bridegroom waits and listens for him, and is full of joy when he hears the bridegroom's voice. That joy is mine, and it is now complete. 30He must become greater; I must become less. Jn 1:20,23; 16:24

31"The one who comes from above is above all; the one who is from the earth belongs to the earth, and speaks as one from the earth. The one who comes from heaven is above all. 32He testifies to what he has seen and heard, but no one accepts his testimony. 33The man who has accepted it has certified that God is truthful. 34For the one whom God has sent speaks the words of God, for God[m] gives the Spirit without limit. 35The Father loves the Son and has placed everything in his hands. 36Whoever believes in the Son has eternal life, but

[a] 17 Psalm 69:9 [b] 23 Or *and believed in him* [c] 3 Or *born from above*; also in verse 7 [d] 6 Or *but spirit*
[e] 7 The Greek is plural. [f] 13 Some manuscripts *Man, who is in heaven* [g] 15 Or *believes may have eternal life in him*
[h] 16 Or *his only begotten Son* [i] 18 Or *God's only begotten Son* [j] 21 Some interpreters end the quotation after verse 15.
[k] 25 Some manuscripts *and certain Jews* [l] 28 Or *Messiah* [m] 34 Greek *he*

NICODEMUS

Religion Meets Regeneration

"Now there was a man of the Pharisees named Nicodemus, a member of the Jewish ruling council. He came to Jesus at night . . ."

—JOHN 3:1–2a

There's a world of difference between religion and regeneration. Correction: There's an eternity's difference. Religion says this: "By an external system of deeds, you can gain God's favor." Regeneration says, "No; by an internal gift of grace, God gives you His life through Jesus Christ." Religion says, "I can achieve God's favor by what I do. And when the judgment day comes, God will see that my good outweighs my evil." Regeneration says, "All my righteous actions are as filthy rags. I have no good in myself. I can only rely on Christ's death on my behalf." It's in this context that we need to look at Nicodemus.

Nicodemus was part of the religious ruling class in Jesus' day. He was a Pharisee, a member of a brotherhood known for splitting religious hairs. He was a prominent member of the Sanhedrin, the ruling body that had religious jurisdiction over every Jew in the world. In fact, Jesus called him "Israel's teacher" (John 3:10). Nicodemus was, without question, the "voice" of the Jews. He was the spokesman when it came to rabbinical teachings. We know that this man carried a lot of influence.

It's no wonder, then, that he would approach Jesus "at night" (3:2). Nicodemus knew he would be seen by people around the city if he came during the day. Furthermore, the night hours afforded him a chance for conversation about this crucial issue with which he was wrestling. I believe he came to Jesus in all sincerity, not knowing the conversation would take a dramatic turn from religion to regeneration.

Note that Nicodemus acknowledged right up front that Jesus was a teacher sent from God, one who seemed uniquely gifted (see 3:2). As a Pharisee, he was very likely enamored with Jesus' human achievement. He may well have been impressed with His growing popularity—so he laid a bit of flattery on Jesus to break the ice. What did Jesus think of that approach? He went right for the jugular: "I tell you the truth, no one can see the kingdom of God unless he is born again" (3:3). Now we may wonder what Jesus' response had to do with what Nicodemus had just said! Zero. But Jesus knew exactly what he needed.

As Jesus amplified His response we see that regeneration is something that *God* prompts, not humans. Religion is something that *humans* prompt, not God. With his spiritually blind eyes, Nicodemus couldn't get his arms around the concept of spiritual rebirth. Jesus knew that only a work of grace through the power of the Holy Spirit could open his spiritual eyes. In essence, Jesus said to Nicodemus in verses 5–7 of chapter 3, "This new birth is not that complicated. There must be an inward cleansing that God will make possible through His Spirit. When you accept Me as your personal Savior, a marvelous inward change will take over. No longer will you be driven by the ladders that you've propped up to try to climb to heaven. In your own power, you'll never make it. When you accept Me, you will immediately have a God-given bridge that will take you to Me and bring Me to you."

To nail His point home, Jesus used a story that was near to Nicodemus's heart. The ancient account of the snake in the desert (Numbers 21:4–9) perfectly illustrates the diametric opposition of religion and regeneration. These ancient Israelites who had been bitten by venomous snakes found themselves completely helpless, dependent on God's mercy. They thought the best strategy would be to implore God to take away the snakes, to come up with some extermination process that would eliminate the problem. Yet notice what God told Moses to do: "Make a snake and put it up on a pole; anyone who is bitten can look at it and live" (Numbers 21:8). Having reminded Nicodemus of that awesome scene, He outlined for him the same basic plan for eternal salvation from the snakebite of sin and death: "The Son of Man must be lifted up, that everyone who believes in him may have eternal life" (John 3:14b–15).

How can a simple belief from the heart create such new birth and incredible transformation? It's the same basic plan today as it was when Jesus spoke these words to Nicodemus. We are urged to believe it—and live!

whoever rejects the Son will not see life, for God's wrath remains on him."[a] Mt 28:18; Jn 5:20,22; 17:2

Jesus Talks With a Samaritan Woman

4 The Pharisees heard that Jesus was gaining and baptizing more disciples than John, 2although in fact it was not Jesus who baptized, but his disciples. 3When the Lord learned of this, he left Judea and went back once more to Galilee.

4Now he had to go through Samaria. 5So he came to a town in Samaria called Sychar, near the plot of ground Jacob had given to his son Joseph. 6Jacob's well was there, and Jesus, tired as he was from the journey, sat down by the well. It was about the sixth hour. Ge 33:19; 48:22; Jos 24:32

7When a Samaritan woman came to draw water, Jesus said to her, "Will you give me a drink?" 8(His disciples had gone into the town to buy food.) Ge 24:17; 1Ki 17:10

9The Samaritan woman said to him, "You are a Jew and I am a Samaritan woman. How can you ask me for a drink?" (For Jews do not associate with Samaritans.[b]) Lk 9:52-53

10Jesus answered her, "If you knew the gift of God and who it is that asks you for a drink, you would have asked him and he would have given you living water." Isa 44:3; Rev 21:6; 22:1,17

11"Sir," the woman said, "you have nothing to draw with and the well is deep. Where can you get this living water? 12Are you greater than our father Jacob, who gave us the well and drank from it himself, as did also his sons and his flocks and herds?" ver 6

13Jesus answered, "Everyone who drinks this water will be thirsty again, 14but whoever drinks the water I give him will never thirst. Indeed, the water I give him will become in him a spring of water welling up to eternal life." Jn 6:35; 7:38

15The woman said to him, "Sir, give me this water so that I won't get thirsty and have to keep coming here to draw water." Jn 6:34

16He told her, "Go, call your husband and come back."

17"I have no husband," she replied.

Jesus said to her, "You are right when you say you have no husband. 18The fact is, you have had five husbands, and the man you now have is not your husband. What you have just said is quite true."

19"Sir," the woman said, "I can see that you are a prophet. 20Our fathers worshiped on this mountain, but you Jews claim that the place where we must worship is in Jerusalem." Dt 11:29; Lk 9:53

21Jesus declared, "Believe me, woman, a time is coming when you will worship the Father neither on this mountain nor in Jerusalem. 22You Samaritans worship what you do not know; we worship what we do know, for salvation is from the Jews. 23Yet a time is coming and has now come when the true worshipers will worship the Father in spirit and truth, for they are the kind of worshipers the Father seeks. 24God is spirit, and his worshipers must worship in spirit and in truth." Mal 1:11

LIVING  **INSIGHT**

The Lord our God seeks our worship. He still awaits the praise of His people . . . the wondrous worship of His children. He still longs to inhabit our hearts and our houses of worship. Beware, lest worship become a lost art, the missing jewel of this hurried and efficient generation.

(See John 4:21–24.)

25The woman said, "I know that Messiah" (called Christ) "is coming. When he comes, he will explain everything to us." Mt 1:16; Jn 1:41

26Then Jesus declared, "I who speak to you am he." Jn 8:24; 9:35-37

The Disciples Rejoin Jesus

27Just then his disciples returned and were surprised to find him talking with a woman. But no one asked, "What do you want?" or "Why are you talking with her?" ver 8

28Then, leaving her water jar, the woman went back to the town and said to the people, 29"Come, see a man who told me everything I ever did. Could this be the Christ[c]?" 30They came out of the town and made their way toward him.

31Meanwhile his disciples urged him, "Rabbi, eat something." Mt 23:7

32But he said to them, "I have food to eat that you know nothing about." Job 23:12; Mt 4:4; Jn 6:27

33Then his disciples said to each other, "Could someone have brought him food?"

34"My food," said Jesus, "is to do the will of him who sent me and to finish his work. 35Do you not say, 'Four months more and then the harvest'? I tell you, open your eyes and look at the fields! They are ripe for harvest. 36Even now the reaper draws his wages, even now he harvests the crop for eternal life, so that the sower and the reaper may be glad together. 37Thus the saying 'One sows and another reaps' is true. 38I sent you to reap what you have not worked for. Others have done the hard work, and you have reaped the benefits of their labor." Mt 9:37; Jn 6:38; Ro 1:13

Many Samaritans Believe

39Many of the Samaritans from that town be-

[a] 36 Some interpreters end the quotation after verse 30. [b] 9 Or *do not use dishes Samaritans have used* [c] 29 Or *Messiah*

lieved in him because of the woman's testimony,
"He told me everything I ever did." 40So when the
Samaritans came to him, they urged him to stay
with them, and he stayed two days. 41And because
of his words many more became believers.
42They said to the woman, "We no longer believe just because of what you said; now we have
heard for ourselves, and we know that this man
really is the Savior of the world." Lk 2:11; 1Jn 4:14

Jesus Heals the Official's Son

43After the two days he left for Galilee. 44(Now
Jesus himself had pointed out that a prophet has
no honor in his own country.) 45When he arrived
in Galilee, the Galileans welcomed him. They had
seen all that he had done in Jerusalem at the Passover Feast, for they also had been there. Mt 13:57
46Once more he visited Cana in Galilee, where
he had turned the water into wine. And there was
a certain royal official whose son lay sick at Capernaum. 47When this man heard that Jesus had arrived in Galilee from Judea, he went to him and
begged him to come and heal his son, who was
close to death. Jn 2:1-11
48"Unless you people see miraculous signs and
wonders," Jesus told him, "you will never believe."
49The royal official said, "Sir, come down before
my child dies."
50Jesus replied, "You may go. Your son will
live."
The man took Jesus at his word and departed.
51While he was still on the way, his servants met
him with the news that his boy was living. 52When
he inquired as to the time when his son got better,
they said to him, "The fever left him yesterday at
the seventh hour."
53Then the father realized that this was the exact
time at which Jesus had said to him, "Your son will
live." So he and all his household believed.
54This was the second miraculous sign that
Jesus performed, having come from Judea to Galilee. Jn 2:11

The Healing at the Pool

5 Some time later, Jesus went up to Jerusalem
for a feast of the Jews. 2Now there is in Jerusalem near the Sheep Gate a pool, which in Aramaic
is called Bethesda[a] and which is surrounded by
five covered colonnades. 3Here a great number of
disabled people used to lie—the blind, the lame,
the paralyzed.[b] 5One who was there had been an
invalid for thirty-eight years. 6When Jesus saw
him lying there and learned that he had been in
this condition for a long time, he asked him, "Do
you want to get well?" Ne 3:1; 12:39; Jn 19:13,17,20
7"Sir," the invalid replied, "I have no one to
help me into the pool when the water is stirred.
While I am trying to get in, someone else goes
down ahead of me."
8Then Jesus said to him, "Get up! Pick up your
mat and walk." 9At once the man was cured; he
picked up his mat and walked. Mt 9:5-6; Mk 2:11
The day on which this took place was a Sabbath,
10and so the Jews said to the man who had been
healed, "It is the Sabbath; the law forbids you to
carry your mat." Ne 13:15-22; Mt 12:2; Jn 9:14
11But he replied, "The man who made me well
said to me, 'Pick up your mat and walk.' "
12So they asked him, "Who is this fellow who
told you to pick it up and walk?"
13The man who was healed had no idea who it
was, for Jesus had slipped away into the crowd that
was there.
14Later Jesus found him at the temple and said
to him, "See, you are well again. Stop sinning or
something worse may happen to you." 15The man
went away and told the Jews that it was Jesus who
had made him well. Jn 1:19; 8:11

Life Through the Son

16So, because Jesus was doing these things on
the Sabbath, the Jews persecuted him. 17Jesus said
to them, "My Father is always at his work to this
very day, and I, too, am working." 18For this reason the Jews tried all the harder to kill him; not
only was he breaking the Sabbath, but he was even
calling God his own Father, making himself equal
with God. Jn 7:1; 10:30,33
19Jesus gave them this answer: "I tell you the
truth, the Son can do nothing by himself; he can
do only what he sees his Father doing, because
whatever the Father does the Son also does. 20For
the Father loves the Son and shows him all he
does. Yes, to your amazement he will show him
even greater things than these. 21For just as the
Father raises the dead and gives them life, even so
the Son gives life to whom he is pleased to give it.
22Moreover, the Father judges no one, but has entrusted all judgment to the Son, 23that all may
honor the Son just as they honor the Father. He
who does not honor the Son does not honor the
Father, who sent him. Ac 10:42; 1Jn 2:23
24"I tell you the truth, whoever hears my word
and believes him who sent me has eternal life and
will not be condemned; he has crossed over from
death to life. 25I tell you the truth, a time is coming
and has now come when the dead will hear the
voice of the Son of God and those who hear will
live. 26For as the Father has life in himself, so he
has granted the Son to have life in himself. 27And
he has given him authority to judge because he is
the Son of Man. Jn 3:18; 1Jn 3:14

[a]2 Some manuscripts *Bethzatha*; other manuscripts *Bethsaida* [b]3 Some less important manuscripts *paralyzed—and they waited for the moving of the waters. 4From time to time an angel of the Lord would come down and stir up the waters. The first one into the pool after each such disturbance would be cured of whatever disease he had.*

[28]"Do not be amazed at this, for a time is coming when all who are in their graves will hear his voice [29]and come out—those who have done good will rise to live, and those who have done evil will rise to be condemned. [30]By myself I can do nothing; I judge only as I hear, and my judgment is just, for I seek not to please myself but him who sent me. Da 12:2; Mt 25:46; 26:39

Testimonies About Jesus

[31]"If I testify about myself, my testimony is not valid. [32]There is another who testifies in my favor, and I know that his testimony about me is valid.

[33]"You have sent to John and he has testified to the truth. [34]Not that I accept human testimony; but I mention it that you may be saved. [35]John was a lamp that burned and gave light, and you chose for a time to enjoy his light. Jn 1:7; 2Pe 1:19

[36]"I have testimony weightier than that of John. For the very work that the Father has given me to finish, and which I am doing, testifies that the Father has sent me. [37]And the Father who sent me has himself testified concerning me. You have never heard his voice nor seen his form, [38]nor does his word dwell in you, for you do not believe the one he sent. [39]You diligently study[a] the Scriptures because you think that by them you possess eternal life. These are the Scriptures that testify about me, [40]yet you refuse to come to me to have life.

[41]"I do not accept praise from men, [42]but I know you. I know that you do not have the love of God in your hearts. [43]I have come in my Father's name, and you do not accept me; but if someone else comes in his own name, you will accept him. [44]How can you believe if you accept praise from one another, yet make no effort to obtain the praise that comes from the only God[b]?

[45]"But do not think I will accuse you before the Father. Your accuser is Moses, on whom your hopes are set. [46]If you believed Moses, you would believe me, for he wrote about me. [47]But since you do not believe what he wrote, how are you going to believe what I say?" Lk 16:29,31; Jn 9:28; Ro 2:17

Jesus Feeds the Five Thousand

▶ *See Matthew 14:13–21; Mark 6:32–44; Luke 9:10–17*

6 Some time after this, Jesus crossed to the far shore of the Sea of Galilee (that is, the Sea of Tiberias), [2]and a great crowd of people followed him because they saw the miraculous signs he had performed on the sick. [3]Then Jesus went up on a mountainside and sat down with his disciples. [4]The Jewish Passover Feast was near. Jn 2:11; 11:55

[5]When Jesus looked up and saw a great crowd coming toward him, he said to Philip, "Where shall we buy bread for these people to eat?" [6]He asked this only to test him, for he already had in mind what he was going to do. Jn 1:43

[7]Philip answered him, "Eight months' wages[c] would not buy enough bread for each one to have a bite!"

[8]Another of his disciples, Andrew, Simon Peter's brother, spoke up, [9]"Here is a boy with five small barley loaves and two small fish, but how far will they go among so many?" 2Ki 4:43; Jn 1:40

[10]Jesus said, "Have the people sit down." There was plenty of grass in that place, and the men sat down, about five thousand of them. [11]Jesus then took the loaves, gave thanks, and distributed to those who were seated as much as they wanted. He did the same with the fish. Mt 14:19

[12]When they had all had enough to eat, he said to his disciples, "Gather the pieces that are left over. Let nothing be wasted." [13]So they gathered them and filled twelve baskets with the pieces of the five barley loaves left over by those who had eaten. Mt 14:13-21; Mk 6:32-44; Lk 9:10-17

[14]After the people saw the miraculous sign that Jesus did, they began to say, "Surely this is the Prophet who is to come into the world." [15]Jesus, knowing that they intended to come and make him king by force, withdrew again to a mountain by himself. Mt 14:23; Jn 18:36; Dt 18:15,18

Jesus Walks on the Water

▶ *See Matthew 14:22–33; Mark 6:47–51*

[16]When evening came, his disciples went down to the lake, [17]where they got into a boat and set off across the lake for Capernaum. By now it was dark, and Jesus had not yet joined them. [18]A strong wind was blowing and the waters grew rough. [19]When they had rowed three or three and a half miles,[d] they saw Jesus approaching the boat, walking on the water; and they were terrified. [20]But he said to them, "It is I; don't be afraid." [21]Then they were willing to take him into the boat, and immediately the boat reached the shore where they were heading. Mt 14:22-33; Mk 6:47-51

[22]The next day the crowd that had stayed on the opposite shore of the lake realized that only one boat had been there, and that Jesus had not entered it with his disciples, but that they had gone away alone. [23]Then some boats from Tiberias landed near the place where the people had eaten the bread after the Lord had given thanks. [24]Once the crowd realized that neither Jesus nor his disciples were there, they got into the boats and went to Capernaum in search of Jesus.

Jesus the Bread of Life

[25]When they found him on the other side of the

[a]39 Or *Study diligently* (the imperative) [b]44 Some early manuscripts *the Only One* [c]7 Greek *two hundred denarii*
[d]19 Greek *rowed twenty-five or thirty stadia* (about 5 or 6 kilometers)

lake, they asked him, "Rabbi, when did you get here?" Mt 23:7

26Jesus answered, "I tell you the truth, you are looking for me, not because you saw miraculous signs but because you ate the loaves and had your fill. 27Do not work for food that spoils, but for food that endures to eternal life, which the Son of Man will give you. On him God the Father has placed his seal of approval." Isa 55:2; Jn 4:14; Ro 4:11

28Then they asked him, "What must we do to do the works God requires?"

29Jesus answered, "The work of God is this: to believe in the one he has sent." Jn 3:17; 1Jn 3:23

30So they asked him, "What miraculous sign then will you give that we may see it and believe you? What will you do? 31Our forefathers ate the manna in the desert; as it is written: 'He gave them bread from heaven to eat.'[a]" Ex 16:4,15; Nu 11:7-9

32Jesus said to them, "I tell you the truth, it is not Moses who has given you the bread from heaven, but it is my Father who gives you the true bread from heaven. 33For the bread of God is he who comes down from heaven and gives life to the world." Jn 3:13,31

34"Sir," they said, "from now on give us this bread." Jn 4:15

35Then Jesus declared, "I am the bread of life. He who comes to me will never go hungry, and he who believes in me will never be thirsty. 36But as I told you, you have seen me and still you do not believe. 37All that the Father gives me will come to me, and whoever comes to me I will never drive

LIVING  **INSIGHT**

Our salvation really rests on God's strength, not ours. Our safety is in Jesus Christ's power, not ours. Our protection depends on the Father's firm grip, not ours. No one, including the devil, can sever the vital union that connects us with the Lord Jesus Christ. Why? Because it was Christ's death and resurrection that perfected us . . . because of His finished work, not ours.

(See John 6:37–39.)

away. 38For I have come down from heaven not to do my will but to do the will of him who sent me. 39And this is the will of him who sent me, that I shall lose none of all that he has given me, but raise them up at the last day. 40For my Father's will is that everyone who looks to the Son and believes in him shall have eternal life, and I will raise him up at the last day." Jn 3:15-16; 10:28

41At this the Jews began to grumble about him because he said, "I am the bread that came down from heaven." 42They said, "Is this not Jesus, the son of Joseph, whose father and mother we know? How can he now say, 'I came down from heaven'?"

43"Stop grumbling among yourselves," Jesus answered. 44"No one can come to me unless the Father who sent me draws him, and I will raise him up at the last day. 45It is written in the Prophets: 'They will all be taught by God.'[b] Everyone who listens to the Father and learns from him comes to me. 46No one has seen the Father except the one who is from God; only he has seen the Father. 47I tell you the truth, he who believes has everlasting life. 48I am the bread of life. 49Your forefathers ate the manna in the desert, yet they died. 50But here is the bread that comes down from heaven, which a man may eat and not die. 51I am the living bread that came down from heaven. If anyone eats of this bread, he will live forever. This bread is my flesh, which I will give for the life of the world." Isa 54:13; Jn 1:18; Heb 10:10

52Then the Jews began to argue sharply among themselves, "How can this man give us his flesh to eat?" Jn 9:16; 10:19

53Jesus said to them, "I tell you the truth, unless you eat the flesh of the Son of Man and drink his blood, you have no life in you. 54Whoever eats my flesh and drinks my blood has eternal life, and I will raise him up at the last day. 55For my flesh is real food and my blood is real drink. 56Whoever eats my flesh and drinks my blood remains in me, and I in him. 57Just as the living Father sent me and I live because of the Father, so the one who feeds on me will live because of me. 58This is the bread that came down from heaven. Your forefathers ate manna and died, but he who feeds on this bread will live forever." 59He said this while teaching in the synagogue in Capernaum. 1Jn 3:24; 4:15

Many Disciples Desert Jesus

60On hearing it, many of his disciples said, "This is a hard teaching. Who can accept it?"

61Aware that his disciples were grumbling about this, Jesus said to them, "Does this offend you? 62What if you see the Son of Man ascend to where he was before! 63The Spirit gives life; the flesh counts for nothing. The words I have spoken to you are spirit[c] and they are life. 64Yet there are some of you who do not believe." For Jesus had known from the beginning which of them did not believe and who would betray him. 65He went on to say, "This is why I told you that no one can come to me unless the Father has enabled him."

66From this time many of his disciples turned back and no longer followed him. ver 60

67"You do not want to leave too, do you?" Jesus asked the Twelve. Mt 10:2

[a] *31* Exodus 16:4; Neh. 9:15; Psalm 78:24,25 [b] *45* Isaiah 54:13 [c] *63* Or *Spirit*

68Simon Peter answered him, "Lord, to whom shall we go? You have the words of eternal life. 69We believe and know that you are the Holy One of God." Mk 8:29; Lk 9:20

70Then Jesus replied, "Have I not chosen you, the Twelve? Yet one of you is a devil!" 71(He meant Judas, the son of Simon Iscariot, who, though one of the Twelve, was later to betray him.) Jn 13:27

Jesus Goes to the Feast of Tabernacles

7 After this, Jesus went around in Galilee, purposely staying away from Judea because the Jews there were waiting to take his life. 2But when the Jewish Feast of Tabernacles was near, 3Jesus' brothers said to him, "You ought to leave here and go to Judea, so that your disciples may see the miracles you do. 4No one who wants to become a public figure acts in secret. Since you are doing these things, show yourself to the world." 5For even his own brothers did not believe in him.

6Therefore Jesus told them, "The right time for me has not yet come; for you any time is right. 7The world cannot hate you, but it hates me because I testify that what it does is evil. 8You go to the Feast. I am not yet[a] going up to this Feast, because for me the right time has not yet come." 9Having said this, he stayed in Galilee. Mt 26:18

10However, after his brothers had left for the Feast, he went also, not publicly, but in secret. 11Now at the Feast the Jews were watching for him and asking, "Where is that man?" Jn 11:56

12Among the crowds there was widespread whispering about him. Some said, "He is a good man."

Others replied, "No, he deceives the people." 13But no one would say anything publicly about him for fear of the Jews. Jn 9:22; 12:42; 19:38

Jesus Teaches at the Feast

14Not until halfway through the Feast did Jesus go up to the temple courts and begin to teach. 15The Jews were amazed and asked, "How did this man get such learning without having studied?"

16Jesus answered, "My teaching is not my own. It comes from him who sent me. 17If anyone chooses to do God's will, he will find out whether my teaching comes from God or whether I speak on my own. 18He who speaks on his own does so to gain honor for himself, but he who works for the honor of the one who sent him is a man of truth; there is nothing false about him. 19Has not Moses given you the law? Yet not one of you keeps the law. Why are you trying to kill me?" Jn 5:41

20"You are demon-possessed," the crowd answered. "Who is trying to kill you?"

21Jesus said to them, "I did one miracle, and you are all astonished. 22Yet, because Moses gave you circumcision (though actually it did not come from Moses, but from the patriarchs), you circumcise a child on the Sabbath. 23Now if a child can be circumcised on the Sabbath so that the law of Moses may not be broken, why are you angry with me for healing the whole man on the Sabbath? 24Stop judging by mere appearances, and make a right judgment." Jn 8:15,48; 10:20

Is Jesus the Christ?

25At that point some of the people of Jerusalem began to ask, "Isn't this the man they are trying to kill? 26Here he is, speaking publicly, and they are not saying a word to him. Have the authorities really concluded that he is the Christ[b]? 27But we know where this man is from; when the Christ comes, no one will know where he is from."

28Then Jesus, still teaching in the temple courts, cried out, "Yes, you know me, and you know where I am from. I am not here on my own, but he who sent me is true. You do not know him, 29but I know him because I am from him and he sent me." Mt 11:27; Jn 8:14,26,42

30At this they tried to seize him, but no one laid a hand on him, because his time had not yet come. 31Still, many in the crowd put their faith in him. They said, "When the Christ comes, will he do more miraculous signs than this man?" Jn 2:11

32The Pharisees heard the crowd whispering such things about him. Then the chief priests and the Pharisees sent temple guards to arrest him.

33Jesus said, "I am with you for only a short time, and then I go to the one who sent me. 34You will look for me, but you will not find me; and where I am, you cannot come." Jn 8:21; 13:33

35The Jews said to one another, "Where does this man intend to go that we cannot find him? Will he go where our people live scattered among the Greeks, and teach the Greeks? 36What did he mean when he said, 'You will look for me, but you will not find me,' and 'Where I am, you cannot come'?" Jas 1:1; 1Pe 1:1

37On the last and greatest day of the Feast, Jesus stood and said in a loud voice, "If anyone is thirsty, let him come to me and drink. 38Whoever believes in me, as[c] the Scripture has said, streams of living water will flow from within him." 39By this he meant the Spirit, whom those who believed in him were later to receive. Up to that time the Spirit had not been given, since Jesus had not yet been glorified. Isa 55:1; Joel 2:28; Jn 12:23

40On hearing his words, some of the people said, "Surely this man is the Prophet." Mt 21:11

41Others said, "He is the Christ."

Still others asked, "How can the Christ come

[a]8 Some early manuscripts do not have *yet.* [b]26 Or *Messiah*; also in verses 27, 31, 41 and 42 [c]37,38 Or / *If anyone is thirsty, let him come to me. / And let him drink,* 38*who believes in me. / As*

from Galilee? 42Does not the Scripture say that the Christ will come from David's family[a] and from Bethlehem, the town where David lived?" 43Thus the people were divided because of Jesus. 44Some wanted to seize him, but no one laid a hand on him. Mic 5:2; Jn 9:16; 10:19

Unbelief of the Jewish Leaders

45Finally the temple guards went back to the chief priests and Pharisees, who asked them, "Why didn't you bring him in?"

46"No one ever spoke the way this man does," the guards declared. Mt 7:28

47"You mean he has deceived you also?" the Pharisees retorted. 48"Has any of the rulers or of the Pharisees believed in him? 49No! But this mob that knows nothing of the law—there is a curse on them." Jn 12:42

50Nicodemus, who had gone to Jesus earlier and who was one of their own number, asked, 51"Does our law condemn anyone without first hearing him to find out what he is doing?" Jn 3:1; 19:39

52They replied, "Are you from Galilee, too? Look into it, and you will find that a prophet[b] does not come out of Galilee."

[The earliest manuscripts and many other ancient witnesses do not have John 7:53–8:11.]

53Then each went to his own home.

8 But Jesus went to the Mount of Olives. 2At dawn he appeared again in the temple courts, where all the people gathered around him, and he sat down to teach them. 3The teachers of the law and the Pharisees brought in a woman caught in adultery. They made her stand before the group 4and said to Jesus, "Teacher, this woman was caught in the act of adultery. 5In the Law Moses commanded us to stone such women. Now what

> **LIVING**  **INSIGHT**
>
> ***Be careful about people who lift lines from Scripture and adapt them to what they want those passages to say. Pharisees and teachers of the law live on today. Their problem? They may quote the Bible correctly, but they fail to maintain the correct meaning of God's Word.***
>
> **(See John 8:5.)**

do you say?" 6They were using this question as a trap, in order to have a basis for accusing him.

But Jesus bent down and started to write on the ground with his finger. 7When they kept on questioning him, he straightened up and said to them, "If any one of you is without sin, let him be the first to throw a stone at her." 8Again he stooped down and wrote on the ground. Dt 17:7; Ro 2:1,22

9At this, those who heard began to go away one at a time, the older ones first, until only Jesus was left, with the woman still standing there. 10Jesus straightened up and asked her, "Woman, where are they? Has no one condemned you?"

11"No one, sir," she said.

"Then neither do I condemn you," Jesus declared. "Go now and leave your life of sin."

The Validity of Jesus' Testimony

12When Jesus spoke again to the people, he said, "I am the light of the world. Whoever follows me will never walk in darkness, but will have the light of life." Jn 1:4; 6:35; Pr 4:18; Mt 5:14

13The Pharisees challenged him, "Here you are, appearing as your own witness; your testimony is not valid." Jn 5:31

14Jesus answered, "Even if I testify on my own behalf, my testimony is valid, for I know where I came from and where I am going. But you have no idea where I come from or where I am going. 15You judge by human standards; I pass judgment on no one. 16But if I do judge, my decisions are right, because I am not alone. I stand with the Father, who sent me. 17In your own Law it is written that the testimony of two men is valid. 18I am one who testifies for myself; my other witness is the Father, who sent me." Mt 18:16; Jn 5:37; 7:28

19Then they asked him, "Where is your father?"

"You do not know me or my Father," Jesus replied. "If you knew me, you would know my Father also." 20He spoke these words while teaching in the temple area near the place where the offerings were put. Yet no one seized him, because his time had not yet come. Mk 12:41; Jn 16:3; 1Jn 2:23

21Once more Jesus said to them, "I am going away, and you will look for me, and you will die in your sin. Where I go, you cannot come." Jn 7:34

22This made the Jews ask, "Will he kill himself? Is that why he says, 'Where I go, you cannot come'?"

23But he continued, "You are from below; I am from above. You are of this world; I am not of this world. 24I told you that you would die in your sins; if you do not believe that I am ⌞the one I claim to be⌟,[c] you will indeed die in your sins." Jn 3:31

25"Who are you?" they asked.

"Just what I have been claiming all along," Jesus replied. 26"I have much to say in judgment of you.

[a] 42 Greek *seed* [b] 52 Two early manuscripts *the Prophet* [c] 24 Or *I am he*; also in verse 28

But he who sent me is reliable, and what I have heard from him I tell the world." Jn 3:32; 7:28; 15:15

27They did not understand that he was telling them about his Father. 28So Jesus said, "When you have lifted up the Son of Man, then you will know that I am ⌊the one I claim to be⌋ and that I do nothing on my own but speak just what the Father has taught me. 29The one who sent me is with me; he has not left me alone, for I always do what pleases him." 30Even as he spoke, many put their faith in him. Jn 4:34; 7:31; 12:32

The Children of Abraham

31To the Jews who had believed him, Jesus said, "If you hold to my teaching, you are really my disciples. 32Then you will know the truth, and the truth will set you free." Jn 15:7; Ro 8:2; Jas 2:12

33They answered him, "We are Abraham's descendants[a] and have never been slaves of anyone. How can you say that we shall be set free?"

34Jesus replied, "I tell you the truth, everyone who sins is a slave to sin. 35Now a slave has no permanent place in the family, but a son belongs to it forever. 36So if the Son sets you free, you will be free indeed. 37I know you are Abraham's descendants. Yet you are ready to kill me, because you have no room for my word. 38I am telling you what I have seen in the Father's presence, and you do what you have heard from your father.[b]"

39"Abraham is our father," they answered.

"If you were Abraham's children," said Jesus, "then you would[c] do the things Abraham did. 40As it is, you are determined to kill me, a man who has told you the truth that I heard from God. Abraham did not do such things. 41You are doing the things your own father does." Ro 9:7; Gal 3:7

"We are not illegitimate children," they protested. "The only Father we have is God himself."

The Children of the Devil

42Jesus said to them, "If God were your Father, you would love me, for I came from God and now am here. I have not come on my own; but he sent me. 43Why is my language not clear to you? Because you are unable to hear what I say. 44You belong to your father, the devil, and you want to carry out your father's desire. He was a murderer from the beginning, not holding to the truth, for there is no truth in him. When he lies, he speaks his native language, for he is a liar and the father of lies. 45Yet because I tell the truth, you do not believe me! 46Can any of you prove me guilty of sin? If I am telling the truth, why don't you believe me? 47He who belongs to God hears what God says. The reason you do not hear is that you do not belong to God." Jn 18:37; 1Jn 4:6

The Claims of Jesus About Himself

48The Jews answered him, "Aren't we right in saying that you are a Samaritan and demon-possessed?" Mt 10:5; Jn 7:20

49"I am not possessed by a demon," said Jesus, "but I honor my Father and you dishonor me. 50I am not seeking glory for myself; but there is one who seeks it, and he is the judge. 51I tell you the truth, if anyone keeps my word, he will never see death." Jn 5:41; 11:26

52At this the Jews exclaimed, "Now we know that you are demon-possessed! Abraham died and so did the prophets, yet you say that if anyone keeps your word, he will never taste death. 53Are you greater than our father Abraham? He died, and so did the prophets. Who do you think you are?" Mk 3:22; Jn 4:12

54Jesus replied, "If I glorify myself, my glory means nothing. My Father, whom you claim as your God, is the one who glorifies me. 55Though you do not know him, I know him. If I said I did not, I would be a liar like you, but I do know him and keep his word. 56Your father Abraham rejoiced at the thought of seeing my day; he saw it and was glad." Jn 7:28-29; Heb 11:13

57"You are not yet fifty years old," the Jews said to him, "and you have seen Abraham!"

58"I tell you the truth," Jesus answered, "before Abraham was born, I am!" 59At this, they picked up stones to stone him, but Jesus hid himself, slipping away from the temple grounds. Ex 3:14

Jesus Heals a Man Born Blind

9 As he went along, he saw a man blind from birth. 2His disciples asked him, "Rabbi, who sinned, this man or his parents, that he was born blind?" Ex 20:5; Mt 23:7

3"Neither this man nor his parents sinned," said Jesus, "but this happened so that the work of God might be displayed in his life. 4As long as it is day, we must do the work of him who sent me. Night is coming, when no one can work. 5While I am in the world, I am the light of the world." Jn 8:12

6Having said this, he spit on the ground, made some mud with the saliva, and put it on the man's eyes. 7"Go," he told him, "wash in the Pool of Siloam" (this word means Sent). So the man went and washed, and came home seeing. Mk 7:33; 8:23

8His neighbors and those who had formerly seen him begging asked, "Isn't this the same man who used to sit and beg?" 9Some claimed that he was. Ac 3:2,10

Others said, "No, he only looks like him."

But he himself insisted, "I am the man."

10"How then were your eyes opened?" they demanded.

[a] 33 Greek *seed*; also in verse 37 [b] 38 Or *presence. Therefore do what you have heard from the Father.* [c] 39 Some early manuscripts *"If you are Abraham's children," said Jesus, "then*

11He replied, "The man they call Jesus made some mud and put it on my eyes. He told me to go to Siloam and wash. So I went and washed, and then I could see." ver 7

12"Where is this man?" they asked him.

"I don't know," he said.

The Pharisees Investigate the Healing

13They brought to the Pharisees the man who had been blind. 14Now the day on which Jesus had made the mud and opened the man's eyes was a Sabbath. 15Therefore the Pharisees also asked him how he had received his sight. "He put mud on my eyes," the man replied, "and I washed, and now I see." Jn 5:9

16Some of the Pharisees said, "This man is not from God, for he does not keep the Sabbath."

But others asked, "How can a sinner do such miraculous signs?" So they were divided. Jn 7:43

17Finally they turned again to the blind man, "What have you to say about him? It was your eyes he opened."

The man replied, "He is a prophet." Mt 21:11

18The Jews still did not believe that he had been blind and had received his sight until they sent for the man's parents. 19"Is this your son?" they asked. "Is this the one you say was born blind? How is it that now he can see?" Jn 1:19

20"We know he is our son," the parents answered, "and we know he was born blind. 21But how he can see now, or who opened his eyes, we don't know. Ask him. He is of age; he will speak for himself." 22His parents said this because they were afraid of the Jews, for already the Jews had decided that anyone who acknowledged that Jesus was the Christ[a] would be put out of the synagogue. 23That was why his parents said, "He is of age; ask him." Jn 7:13; 12:42

24A second time they summoned the man who had been blind. "Give glory to God,[b]" they said. "We know this man is a sinner." ver 16; Jos 7:19

25He replied, "Whether he is a sinner or not, I don't know. One thing I do know. I was blind but now I see!"

26Then they asked him, "What did he do to you? How did he open your eyes?"

27He answered, "I have told you already and you did not listen. Why do you want to hear it again? Do you want to become his disciples, too?"

28Then they hurled insults at him and said, "You are this fellow's disciple! We are disciples of Moses! 29We know that God spoke to Moses, but as for this fellow, we don't even know where he comes from." Jn 5:45; 8:14

30The man answered, "Now that is remarkable! You don't know where he comes from, yet he opened my eyes. 31We know that God does not listen to sinners. He listens to the godly man who does his will. 32Nobody has ever heard of opening the eyes of a man born blind. 33If this man were not from God, he could do nothing." Ps 34:15-16

34To this they replied, "You were steeped in sin at birth; how dare you lecture us!" And they threw him out. Isa 66:5

LIVING  **INSIGHT**

When your eyes are opened, when the blindness is removed, and especially when you begin to tell the story of your pilgrimage from blindness to faith in Jesus Christ, hang on! Don't be surprised if you encounter the most resistance from religious people. Religious folks are often uncomfortable around authentic people whose lives have been changed by the living Christ.

(See John 9:24–34.)

Spiritual Blindness

35Jesus heard that they had thrown him out, and when he found him, he said, "Do you believe in the Son of Man?" Mt 8:20; Jn 3:15

36"Who is he, sir?" the man asked. "Tell me so that I may believe in him." Ro 10:14

37Jesus said, "You have now seen him; in fact, he is the one speaking with you." Jn 4:26

38Then the man said, "Lord, I believe," and he worshiped him. Mt 28:9

39Jesus said, "For judgment I have come into this world, so that the blind will see and those who see will become blind." Mt 13:13; Jn 5:22

40Some Pharisees who were with him heard him say this and asked, "What? Are we blind too?"

41Jesus said, "If you were blind, you would not be guilty of sin; but now that you claim you can see, your guilt remains. Jn 15:22,24

The Shepherd and His Flock

10 "I tell you the truth, the man who does not enter the sheep pen by the gate, but climbs in by some other way, is a thief and a robber. 2The man who enters by the gate is the shepherd of his sheep. 3The watchman opens the gate for him, and the sheep listen to his voice. He calls his own sheep by name and leads them out. 4When he has brought out all his own, he goes on ahead of them, and his sheep follow him because they know his voice. 5But they will never follow a stranger; in fact, they will run away from him because they do not recognize a stranger's voice." 6Jesus used this

[a]22 Or *Messiah* [b]24 A solemn charge to tell the truth (see Joshua 7:19)

figure of speech, but they did not understand what he was telling them. Mk 9:32; Jn 16:25

7Therefore Jesus said again, "I tell you the truth, I am the gate for the sheep. 8All who ever came before me were thieves and robbers, but the sheep did not listen to them. 9I am the gate; whoever enters through me will be saved.[a] He will come in and go out, and find pasture. 10The thief comes only to steal and kill and destroy; I have come that they may have life, and have it to the full. Jn 1:4

11"I am the good shepherd. The good shepherd lays down his life for the sheep. 12The hired hand is not the shepherd who owns the sheep. So when he sees the wolf coming, he abandons the sheep and runs away. Then the wolf attacks the flock and scatters it. 13The man runs away because he is a hired hand and cares nothing for the sheep.

14"I am the good shepherd; I know my sheep and my sheep know me— 15just as the Father knows me and I know the Father—and I lay down my life for the sheep. 16I have other sheep that are not of this sheep pen. I must bring them also. They too will listen to my voice, and there shall be one flock and one shepherd. 17The reason my Father loves me is that I lay down my life—only to take it up again. 18No one takes it from me, but I lay it down of my own accord. I have authority to lay it down and authority to take it up again. This command I received from my Father." Mt 11:27; Jn 15:10

19At these words the Jews were again divided. 20Many of them said, "He is demon-possessed and raving mad. Why listen to him?" Jn 7:20,43

21But others said, "These are not the sayings of a man possessed by a demon. Can a demon open the eyes of the blind?" Ex 4:11; Jn 9:32-33

The Unbelief of the Jews

22Then came the Feast of Dedication[b] at Jerusalem. It was winter, 23and Jesus was in the temple area walking in Solomon's Colonnade. 24The Jews gathered around him, saying, "How long will you keep us in suspense? If you are the Christ,[c] tell us plainly." Jn 16:25,29; Ac 3:11

25Jesus answered, "I did tell you, but you do not believe. The miracles I do in my Father's name speak for me, 26but you do not believe because you are not my sheep. 27My sheep listen to my voice; I know them, and they follow me. 28I give them eternal life, and they shall never perish; no one can snatch them out of my hand. 29My Father, who has given them to me, is greater than all[d]; no one can snatch them out of my Father's hand. 30I and the Father are one." Jn 17:21-23

31Again the Jews picked up stones to stone him, 32but Jesus said to them, "I have shown you many great miracles from the Father. For which of these do you stone me?" Jn 8:59

33"We are not stoning you for any of these," replied the Jews, "but for blasphemy, because you, a mere man, claim to be God." Lev 24:16; Jn 5:18

LIVING  **INSIGHT**

God's great net of security spans this globe. No matter where His children live, He has stretched out His everlasting arms beneath them. As a result, every one of us can live and work freely and fearlessly, knowing that we are protected, securely sealed and kept safe by His power.

(See John 10:28.)

34Jesus answered them, "Is it not written in your Law, 'I have said you are gods'[e]? 35If he called them 'gods,' to whom the word of God came—and the Scripture cannot be broken— 36what about the one whom the Father set apart as his very own and sent into the world? Why then do you accuse me of blasphemy because I said, 'I am God's Son'? 37Do not believe me unless I do what my Father does. 38But if I do it, even though you do not believe me, believe the miracles, that you may know and understand that the Father is in me, and I in the Father." 39Again they tried to seize him, but he escaped their grasp. Jn 14:10-11,20; 15:24

40Then Jesus went back across the Jordan to the place where John had been baptizing in the early days. Here he stayed 41and many people came to him. They said, "Though John never performed a miraculous sign, all that John said about this man was true." 42And in that place many believed in Jesus. Jn 1:28; 7:31

The Death of Lazarus

11 Now a man named Lazarus was sick. He was from Bethany, the village of Mary and her sister Martha. 2This Mary, whose brother Lazarus now lay sick, was the same one who poured perfume on the Lord and wiped his feet with her hair. 3So the sisters sent word to Jesus, "Lord, the one you love is sick." Lk 10:38; Jn 12:3

4When he heard this, Jesus said, "This sickness will not end in death. No, it is for God's glory so that God's Son may be glorified through it." 5Jesus loved Martha and her sister and Lazarus. 6Yet when he heard that Lazarus was sick, he stayed where he was two more days. Jn 9:3

7Then he said to his disciples, "Let us go back to Judea." Jn 10:40

[a]9 Or *kept safe* [b]22 That is, Hanukkah [c]24 Or *Messiah* [d]29 Many early manuscripts *What my Father has given me is greater than all* [e]34 Psalm 82:6

8"But Rabbi," they said, "a short while ago the Jews tried to stone you, and yet you are going back there?" Mt 23:7; Jn 10:31

9Jesus answered, "Are there not twelve hours of daylight? A man who walks by day will not stumble, for he sees by this world's light. 10It is when he walks by night that he stumbles, for he has no light." Jn 9:4; 12:35

11After he had said this, he went on to tell them, "Our friend Lazarus has fallen asleep; but I am going there to wake him up." Ac 7:60

12His disciples replied, "Lord, if he sleeps, he will get better." 13Jesus had been speaking of his death, but his disciples thought he meant natural sleep. Mt 9:24

14So then he told them plainly, "Lazarus is dead, 15and for your sake I am glad I was not there, so that you may believe. But let us go to him."

16Then Thomas (called Didymus) said to the rest of the disciples, "Let us also go, that we may die with him." Mt 10:3; Jn 14:5; 20:24-28

Jesus Comforts the Sisters

17On his arrival, Jesus found that Lazarus had already been in the tomb for four days. 18Bethany was less than two miles[a] from Jerusalem, 19and many Jews had come to Martha and Mary to comfort them in the loss of their brother. 20When Martha heard that Jesus was coming, she went out to meet him, but Mary stayed at home. Job 2:11

21"Lord," Martha said to Jesus, "if you had been here, my brother would not have died. 22But I know that even now God will give you whatever you ask." Jn 9:31

23Jesus said to her, "Your brother will rise again."

24Martha answered, "I know he will rise again in the resurrection at the last day." Jn 5:28-29; Ac 24:15

25Jesus said to her, "I am the resurrection and the life. He who believes in me will live, even though he dies; 26and whoever lives and believes in me will never die. Do you believe this?" Jn 1:4; 3:15

27"Yes, Lord," she told him, "I believe that you are the Christ,[b] the Son of God, who was to come into the world." Mt 16:16; Jn 6:14

28And after she had said this, she went back and called her sister Mary aside. "The Teacher is here," she said, "and is asking for you." 29When Mary heard this, she got up quickly and went to him. 30Now Jesus had not yet entered the village, but was still at the place where Martha had met him. 31When the Jews who had been with Mary in the house, comforting her, noticed how quickly she got up and went out, they followed her, supposing she was going to the tomb to mourn there.

32When Mary reached the place where Jesus was and saw him, she fell at his feet and said, "Lord, if you had been here, my brother would not have died." Mt 9:32

33When Jesus saw her weeping, and the Jews who had come along with her also weeping, he was deeply moved in spirit and troubled. 34"Where have you laid him?" he asked. Jn 12:27

"Come and see, Lord," they replied.

35Jesus wept. Lk 19:41

LIVING  **INSIGHT**

When words fail, tears flow.
Tears have a language all their own,
a tongue that needs no interpreter.
(See John 11:35.)

36Then the Jews said, "See how he loved him!"

37But some of them said, "Could not he who opened the eyes of the blind man have kept this man from dying?" Jn 9:6-7

Jesus Raises Lazarus From the Dead

38Jesus, once more deeply moved, came to the tomb. It was a cave with a stone laid across the entrance. 39"Take away the stone," he said.

"But, Lord," said Martha, the sister of the dead man, "by this time there is a bad odor, for he has been there four days."

40Then Jesus said, "Did I not tell you that if you believed, you would see the glory of God?"

41So they took away the stone. Then Jesus looked up and said, "Father, I thank you that you have heard me. 42I knew that you always hear me, but I said this for the benefit of the people standing here, that they may believe that you sent me."

43When he had said this, Jesus called in a loud voice, "Lazarus, come out!" 44The dead man came out, his hands and feet wrapped with strips of linen, and a cloth around his face. Jn 19:40; 20:7

Jesus said to them, "Take off the grave clothes and let him go."

The Plot to Kill Jesus

45Therefore many of the Jews who had come to visit Mary, and had seen what Jesus did, put their faith in him. 46But some of them went to the Pharisees and told them what Jesus had done. 47Then the chief priests and the Pharisees called a meeting of the Sanhedrin. Mt 26:3; Jn 2:23; 7:31

"What are we accomplishing?" they asked. "Here is this man performing many miraculous signs. 48If we let him go on like this, everyone will believe in him, and then the Romans will come and take away both our place[c] and our nation."

49Then one of them, named Caiaphas, who was

[a] 18 Greek *fifteen stadia* (about 3 kilometers) [b] 27 Or *Messiah* [c] 48 Or *temple*

high priest that year, spoke up, "You know nothing at all! 50You do not realize that it is better for you that one man die for the people than that the whole nation perish." Mt 26:3; Jn 18:13-14

51He did not say this on his own, but as high priest that year he prophesied that Jesus would die for the Jewish nation, 52and not only for that nation but also for the scattered children of God, to bring them together and make them one. 53So from that day on they plotted to take his life.

54Therefore Jesus no longer moved about publicly among the Jews. Instead he withdrew to a region near the desert, to a village called Ephraim, where he stayed with his disciples. Jn 7:1

55When it was almost time for the Jewish Passover, many went up from the country to Jerusalem for their ceremonial cleansing before the Passover. 56They kept looking for Jesus, and as they stood in the temple area they asked one another, "What do you think? Isn't he coming to the Feast at all?" 57But the chief priests and Pharisees had given orders that if anyone found out where Jesus was, he should report it so that they might arrest him.

Jesus Anointed at Bethany

12 Six days before the Passover, Jesus arrived at Bethany, where Lazarus lived, whom Jesus had raised from the dead. 2Here a dinner was given in Jesus' honor. Martha served, while Lazarus was among those reclining at the table with him. 3Then Mary took about a pint[a] of pure nard, an expensive perfume; she poured it on Jesus' feet and wiped his feet with her hair. And the house was filled with the fragrance of the perfume.

4But one of his disciples, Judas Iscariot, who was later to betray him, objected, 5"Why wasn't this perfume sold and the money given to the poor? It was worth a year's wages.[b]" 6He did not say this because he cared about the poor but because he was a thief; as keeper of the money bag, he used to help himself to what was put into it.

7"Leave her alone," Jesus replied. "⌊It was intended⌋ that she should save this perfume for the day of my burial. 8You will always have the poor among you, but you will not always have me."

9Meanwhile a large crowd of Jews found out that Jesus was there and came, not only because of him but also to see Lazarus, whom he had raised from the dead. 10So the chief priests made plans to kill Lazarus as well, 11for on account of him many of the Jews were going over to Jesus and putting their faith in him. Jn 7:31; 11:43-44

The Triumphal Entry

▶ *See Matthew 21:4–9; Mark 11:7–10; Luke 19:35–38*

12The next day the great crowd that had come for the Feast heard that Jesus was on his way to Jerusalem. 13They took palm branches and went out to meet him, shouting, Lev 23:40

"Hosanna![c]"

"Blessed is he who comes in the name of the Lord!"[d] Ps 118:25-26

"Blessed is the King of Israel!"

14Jesus found a young donkey and sat upon it, as it is written,

15"Do not be afraid, O Daughter of Zion;
see, your king is coming,
seated on a donkey's colt."[e] Mt 21:4-9

16At first his disciples did not understand all this. Only after Jesus was glorified did they realize that these things had been written about him and that they had done these things to him. Jn 7:39

17Now the crowd that was with him when he called Lazarus from the tomb and raised him from the dead continued to spread the word. 18Many people, because they had heard that he had given this miraculous sign, went out to meet him. 19So the Pharisees said to one another, "See, this is getting us nowhere. Look how the whole world has gone after him!" Jn 11:42,47-48

Jesus Predicts His Death

20Now there were some Greeks among those who went up to worship at the Feast. 21They came to Philip, who was from Bethsaida in Galilee, with a request. "Sir," they said, "we would like to see Jesus." 22Philip went to tell Andrew; Andrew and Philip in turn told Jesus. Mt 11:21; Jn 1:44; 7:35

23Jesus replied, "The hour has come for the Son of Man to be glorified. 24I tell you the truth, unless a kernel of wheat falls to the ground and dies, it remains only a single seed. But if it dies, it produces many seeds. 25The man who loves his life will lose it, while the man who hates his life in this world will keep it for eternal life. 26Whoever serves me must follow me; and where I am, my servant also will be. My Father will honor the one who serves me. Mt 10:39; Jn 13:32; 14:3

27"Now my heart is troubled, and what shall I say? 'Father, save me from this hour'? No, it was for this very reason I came to this hour. 28Father, glorify your name!" Mt 26:38-39; Jn 11:33,38

Then a voice came from heaven, "I have glorified it, and will glorify it again." 29The crowd that was there and heard it said it had thundered; others said an angel had spoken to him. Mt 3:17

30Jesus said, "This voice was for your benefit, not mine. 31Now is the time for judgment on this world; now the prince of this world will be driven

[a] *3* Greek *a litra* (probably about 0.5 liter) [b] *5* Greek *three hundred denarii* [c] *13* A Hebrew expression meaning "Save!" which became an exclamation of praise [d] *13* Psalm 118:25, 26 [e] *15* Zech. 9:9

out. 32But I, when I am lifted up from the earth, will draw all men to myself." 33He said this to show the kind of death he was going to die. Jn 11:42

34The crowd spoke up, "We have heard from the Law that the Christ[a] will remain forever, so how can you say, 'The Son of Man must be lifted up'? Who is this 'Son of Man'?" Ps 110:4; Eze 37:25

35Then Jesus told them, "You are going to have the light just a little while longer. Walk while you have the light, before darkness overtakes you. The man who walks in the dark does not know where he is going. 36Put your trust in the light while you have it, so that you may become sons of light." When he had finished speaking, Jesus left and hid himself from them. Jn 8:59; Eph 5:8; 1Jn 2:11

LIVING  **INSIGHT**

Only one Person can step into a life and give it happiness even when health fails . . . and give it peace even when possessions fade . . . and give it security when savings fly away. That Person is Jesus Christ.

(See John 12:36.)

The Jews Continue in Their Unbelief

37Even after Jesus had done all these miraculous signs in their presence, they still would not believe in him. 38This was to fulfill the word of Isaiah the prophet: Jn 2:11

"Lord, who has believed our message
and to whom has the arm of the Lord been revealed?"[b] Ro 10:16

39For this reason they could not believe, because, as Isaiah says elsewhere:

40"He has blinded their eyes
and deadened their hearts,
so they can neither see with their eyes,
nor understand with their hearts,
nor turn—and I would heal them."[c]

41Isaiah said this because he saw Jesus' glory and spoke about him. Isa 6:1-4; Mt 13:13,15

42Yet at the same time many even among the leaders believed in him. But because of the Pharisees they would not confess their faith for fear they would be put out of the synagogue; 43for they loved praise from men more than praise from God. Jn 5:44; 7:13; 9:22

44Then Jesus cried out, "When a man believes in me, he does not believe in me only, but in the one who sent me. 45When he looks at me, he sees the one who sent me. 46I have come into the world as a light, so that no one who believes in me should stay in darkness. Mt 10:40; Jn 3:19; 14:9

47"As for the person who hears my words but does not keep them, I do not judge him. For I did not come to judge the world, but to save it. 48There is a judge for the one who rejects me and does not accept my words; that very word which I spoke will condemn him at the last day. 49For I did not speak of my own accord, but the Father who sent me commanded me what to say and how to say it. 50I know that his command leads to eternal life. So whatever I say is just what the Father has told me to say." Jn 3:17; 14:31

Private Ministry of Jesus **Chapters 13–21**

As chapter 13 begins, John is describing the final days of Jesus' life. These last nine chapters record in detail Jesus' private ministry and teaching. Chapters 13–17 contain Jesus' final teaching and ministry to His disciples as it took place in the upper room. In these chapters we read of Jesus washing the disciples' feet, teaching about the branches and the vine, and praying with His followers. Chapters 18 and 19 record the passion and death of Jesus, the Son of God. Finally, the last two chapters tell of the resurrection of Jesus and His appearances to many different people. In this section Jesus confronted a doubting Thomas and invited the skeptical disciple to touch the nail prints in His hands. The response of Thomas confirmed the whole purpose of John's Gospel. When challenged to believe in Jesus, Thomas's response was clear and powerful: "My Lord and my God!" (20:28).

Jesus Washes His Disciples' Feet

13 It was just before the Passover Feast. Jesus knew that the time had come for him to leave this world and go to the Father. Having loved his own who were in the world, he now showed them the full extent of his love.[d] Jn 11:55; 16:28

2The evening meal was being served, and the devil had already prompted Judas Iscariot, son of Simon, to betray Jesus. 3Jesus knew that the Father had put all things under his power, and that he had come from God and was returning to God; 4so he got up from the meal, took off his outer clothing, and wrapped a towel around his waist. 5After that, he poured water into a basin and began to wash his disciples' feet, drying them with the towel that was wrapped around him. Mt 28:18; Jn 8:42

6He came to Simon Peter, who said to him, "Lord, are you going to wash my feet?"

7Jesus replied, "You do not realize now what I am doing, but later you will understand."

8"No," said Peter, "you shall never wash my feet."

Jesus answered, "Unless I wash you, you have no part with me."

[a]34 Or *Messiah* [b]38 Isaiah 53:1 [c]40 Isaiah 6:10 [d]1 Or *he loved them to the last*

9"Then, Lord," Simon Peter replied, "not just
my feet but my hands and my head as well!"
10Jesus answered, "A person who has had a bath
needs only to wash his feet; his whole body is
clean. And you are clean, though not every one of
you." 11For he knew who was going to betray him,
and that was why he said not every one was clean.
12When he had finished washing their feet, he
put on his clothes and returned to his place. "Do
you understand what I have done for you?" he
asked them. 13"You call me 'Teacher' and 'Lord,'
and rightly so, for that is what I am. 14Now that I,
your Lord and Teacher, have washed your feet,
you also should wash one another's feet. 15I have
set you an example that you should do as I have

LIVING INSIGHT

Truth is more permanently transferred from a parent's* life *than from his or her lips. Modeling the truth far outweighs preaching it to the young.

(See John 13:15.)

done for you. 16I tell you the truth, no servant is
greater than his master, nor is a messenger greater
than the one who sent him. 17Now that you know
these things, you will be blessed if you do them.

Jesus Predicts His Betrayal

18"I am not referring to all of you; I know those
I have chosen. But this is to fulfill the scripture:
'He who shares my bread has lifted up his heel
against me.'[a] Ps 41:9; Jn 6:70; 15:16,19
19"I am telling you now before it happens, so
that when it does happen you will believe that I am
He. 20I tell you the truth, whoever accepts anyone
I send accepts me; and whoever accepts me accepts the one who sent me." Lk 10:16; Jn 14:29; 16:4
21After he had said this, Jesus was troubled in
spirit and testified, "I tell you the truth, one of you
is going to betray me." Mt 26:21; Jn 12:27
22His disciples stared at one another, at a loss to
know which of them he meant. 23One of them, the
disciple whom Jesus loved, was reclining next to
him. 24Simon Peter motioned to this disciple and
said, "Ask him which one he means." Jn 19:26; 20:2
25Leaning back against Jesus, he asked him,
"Lord, who is it?" Jn 21:20
26Jesus answered, "It is the one to whom I will
give this piece of bread when I have dipped it in
the dish." Then, dipping the piece of bread, he
gave it to Judas Iscariot, son of Simon. 27As soon
as Judas took the bread, Satan entered into him.
"What you are about to do, do quickly," Jesus
told him, 28but no one at the meal understood why
Jesus said this to him. 29Since Judas had charge of
the money, some thought Jesus was telling him to
buy what was needed for the Feast, or to give
something to the poor. 30As soon as Judas had
taken the bread, he went out. And it was night.

Jesus Predicts Peter's Denial

▶ *See Matthew 26:33–35; Mark 14:29–31; Luke 22:33–34*

31When he was gone, Jesus said, "Now is the
Son of Man glorified and God is glorified in him.
32If God is glorified in him,[b] God will glorify the
Son in himself, and will glorify him at once.
33"My children, I will be with you only a little
longer. You will look for me, and just as I told the
Jews, so I tell you now: Where I am going, you
cannot come. Jn 7:33-34
34"A new command I give you: Love one another. As I have loved you, so you must love one
another. 35By this all men will know that you are
my disciples, if you love one another." Lev 19:18
36Simon Peter asked him, "Lord, where are you
going?"
Jesus replied, "Where I am going, you cannot
follow now, but you will follow later." Jn 21:18-19
37Peter asked, "Lord, why can't I follow you
now? I will lay down my life for you."
38Then Jesus answered, "Will you really lay
down your life for me? I tell you the truth, before
the rooster crows, you will disown me three times!

Jesus Comforts His Disciples

14 "Do not let your hearts be troubled. Trust
in God[c]; trust also in me. 2In my Father's
house are many rooms; if it were not so, I would
have told you. I am going there to prepare a place
for you. 3And if I go and prepare a place for you,
I will come back and take you to be with me that
you also may be where I am. 4You know the way
to the place where I am going." Jn 12:26; 13:33,36

Jesus the Way to the Father

5Thomas said to him, "Lord, we don't know
where you are going, so how can we know the way?"

LIVING INSIGHT

Apart from the Way there is no going . . . Apart from the Truth there is no knowing . . . Apart from the Life there is no living. God says, "Remain in Christ, and rest yourself. He is the way and the truth and the life."

(See John 14:6.)

[a] *18* Psalm 41:9 [b] *32* Many early manuscripts do not have *If God is glorified in him.* [c] *1* Or *You trust in God*

JUDAS ISCARIOT

The World's Best-Known Traitor

"Then, dipping the piece of bread, he gave it to Judas Iscariot, son of Simon. As soon as Judas took the bread, Satan entered into him."
—JOHN 13:26b–27

Judas Iscariot is an enigma to any serious Bible student. Here was a man who had all the advantages the eleven other disciples had. He had been chosen to be a disciple in this elite band of twelve. He had sat at the feet of the Master and listened to over three years of profound teaching. He had heard Jesus speak to the crowds. He had seen Jesus perform many miracles. He had so gained the trust of the others that he served as the group's treasurer—he was the keeper of the money bag. And in spite of all this, when it came down to the wire, when all was said and done, Judas became the world's best-known traitor.

I don't think anyone *suddenly* becomes villainous and corrupt. It's a process. It takes time. One step leads to another, which in turn leads the person deeper, which in turn leads the person still deeper, which leads to the act itself that goes down in infamy. That was true in Judas's life.

First, *Judas possessed the wrong motives for following Jesus*. Judas was a Judean, the only one of the Twelve who was not a Galilean. Biographers tell us that he was the "odd man out" in the group of disciples. As such, we can assume that Judas was defensive. But there's more. Judas was from the town of Kerioth in Judea (hence the name "Iscariot," which means "a man from Kerioth"), an area known for its conservative and zealous mind-set. He was a nationalist who probably turned to Jesus in the hope that his own dreams for the nation of Israel might be fulfilled through Him. Judas undoubtedly felt that Jesus was the answer to his nationalistic zeal, and he wanted to get in "on the ground floor" of the rebellion against Rome.

Second, *Judas became bitter*. In chapter 6 of John's Gospel he records the story of Jesus withdrawing to the hillsides after the crowd wanted Him to become their political representative. Judas must have seen this event as the perfect opportunity for Jesus to make His move politically, to begin driving the wedge between the Jewish people and the Roman empire. I'm suggesting that when Jesus said "No" to an earthly empire, the seeds of bitterness and anger were planted in Judas's heart.

Third, *Judas developed a spirit of revenge and hatred*. Just six chapters later the bitterness that had taken root in Judas exploded. Judas could no longer keep silent and voiced his contempt that Mary of Bethany would deign to anoint Jesus' feet (John 12:5). I think Judas was thinking, "Why is Mary taking this expensive ointment and pouring it on *His* feet, of all people? Why this One, who wouldn't take the kingdom when it was handed to Him on a silver platter?" John shows us the pinnacle of Judas's hypocrisy. In reality, Judas had absolutely no concern for the poor. He was, in fact, revealed to be a thief. Jesus' rebuke (12:7) exposed Judas's pious and hypocritical words, which probably led to the next major event in Judas's life—his commitment to betray the Master.

Fourth, *Judas opened himself up to satanic possession*. Luke makes it plain in these words: "Then Satan entered Judas, called Iscariot, one of the Twelve. And Judas went to the chief priests and the officers of the temple guard and discussed with them how he might betray Jesus" (Luke 22:3–4). Satan possessed this weakened man and drove him to seek out the chief priests. There he agreed to betray Jesus for the price of an insignificant slave (Exodus 21:32)—thirty pieces of silver. And when Judas went to betray Jesus, he did so with a kiss, not with a slap or with a sword. Deep down in his heart he wasn't even strong enough to openly declare himself as one who had defected to the enemy.

Judas Iscariot's actions followed a progression that led to his final act of betrayal. For thirty pieces of silver, Judas sold *himself* out as Satan's slave. This man, although he was filled with emotional remorse (see Matthew 27:1–5), never truly repented; sadly, tragically, he died in this disillusioned, terrible, suicidal manner.

6Jesus answered, "I am the way and the truth and the life. No one comes to the Father except through me. 7If you really knew me, you would know[a] my Father as well. From now on, you do know him and have seen him." Jn 1:14; 10:9; 11:25

8Philip said, "Lord, show us the Father and that will be enough for us." Jn 1:43

9Jesus answered: "Don't you know me, Philip, even after I have been among you such a long time? Anyone who has seen me has seen the Father. How can you say, 'Show us the Father'?

LIVING  **INSIGHT**

Memorize John 14:9 so that you will have an answer for those who say, "Jesus may have been a great teacher—but He wasn't God."

(See John 14:9–13.)

10Don't you believe that I am in the Father, and that the Father is in me? The words I say to you are not just my own. Rather, it is the Father, living in me, who is doing his work. 11Believe me when I say that I am in the Father and the Father is in me; or at least believe on the evidence of the miracles themselves. 12I tell you the truth, anyone who has faith in me will do what I have been doing. He will do even greater things than these, because I am going to the Father. 13And I will do whatever you ask in my name, so that the Son may bring glory to the Father. 14You may ask me for anything in my name, and I will do it. Jn 10:38; 12:45

Jesus Promises the Holy Spirit

15"If you love me, you will obey what I command. 16And I will ask the Father, and he will give you another Counselor to be with you forever— 17the Spirit of truth. The world cannot accept him, because it neither sees him nor knows him. But you know him, for he lives with you and will be[b] in you. 18I will not leave you as orphans; I will come to you. 19Before long, the world will not see me anymore, but you will see me. Because I live, you also will live. 20On that day you will realize that I am in my Father, and you are in me, and I am in you. 21Whoever has my commands and obeys them, he is the one who loves me. He who loves me will be loved by my Father, and I too will love him and show myself to him." Jn 15:10; 1Jn 5:3

22Then Judas (not Judas Iscariot) said, "But, Lord, why do you intend to show yourself to us and not to the world?" Lk 6:16; Ac 10:41

23Jesus replied, "If anyone loves me, he will obey my teaching. My Father will love him, and we will come to him and make our home with him. 24He who does not love me will not obey my teaching. These words you hear are not my own; they belong to the Father who sent me. Jn 7:16

25"All this I have spoken while still with you. 26But the Counselor, the Holy Spirit, whom the Father will send in my name, will teach you all things and will remind you of everything I have said to you. 27Peace I leave with you; my peace I give you. I do not give to you as the world gives. Do not let your hearts be troubled and do not be afraid. Jn 15:26; Php 4:7; 1Jn 2:20,27

LIVING  **INSIGHT**

Peace is the divine gift of the ability to remain faithful, calm and patient in spite of the panic of unfulfilled dreams, unpleasant circumstances and unavoidable uncertainty.

(See John 14:27.)

28"You heard me say, 'I am going away and I am coming back to you.' If you loved me, you would be glad that I am going to the Father, for the Father is greater than I. 29I have told you now before it happens, so that when it does happen you will believe. 30I will not speak with you much longer, for the prince of this world is coming. He has no hold on me, 31but the world must learn that I love the Father and that I do exactly what my Father has commanded me. Jn 10:18; 12:31; 13:19

"Come now; let us leave.

The Vine and the Branches

15 "I am the true vine, and my Father is the gardener. 2He cuts off every branch in me that bears no fruit, while every branch that does bear fruit he prunes[c] so that it will be even more fruitful. 3You are already clean because of the word I have spoken to you. 4Remain in me, and I will remain in you. No branch can bear fruit by itself; it must remain in the vine. Neither can you bear fruit unless you remain in me. Isa 5:1-7; 1Jn 2:6

5"I am the vine; you are the branches. If a man remains in me and I in him, he will bear much fruit; apart from me you can do nothing. 6If anyone does not remain in me, he is like a branch that is thrown away and withers; such branches are picked up, thrown into the fire and burned. 7If you remain in me and my words remain in you, ask whatever you wish, and it will be given you. 8This is to my Father's glory, that you bear much fruit, showing yourselves to be my disciples. Mt 7:7

[a]7 Some early manuscripts *If you really have known me, you will know* [b]17 Some early manuscripts *and is*
[c]2 The Greek for *prunes* also means *cleans.*

9“As the Father has loved me, so have I loved
you. Now remain in my love. 10If you obey my
commands, you will remain in my love, just as I
have obeyed my Father’s commands and remain
in his love. 11I have told you this so that my joy
may be in you and that your joy may be complete.
12My command is this: Love each other as I have

LIVING  **INSIGHT**

No one who actually hates himself or herself can adequately share the love of Jesus. Our Lord taught that we were to love our neighbors as we love ourselves. If we don’t properly love ourselves, where does that leave our neighbors?

(See John 15:12.)

loved you. 13Greater love has no one than this, that
he lay down his life for his friends. 14You are my
friends if you do what I command. 15I no longer
call you servants, because a servant does not know
his master’s business. Instead, I have called you
friends, for everything that I learned from my Father I have made known to you. 16You did not
choose me, but I chose you and appointed you to
go and bear fruit—fruit that will last. Then the
Father will give you whatever you ask in my name.
17This is my command: Love each other.

The World Hates the Disciples

18“If the world hates you, keep in mind that it
hated me first. 19If you belonged to the world, it
would love you as its own. As it is, you do not
belong to the world, but I have chosen you out of
the world. That is why the world hates you. 20Re-
member the words I spoke to you: ‘No servant is
greater than his master.’[a] If they persecuted me,
they will persecute you also. If they obeyed my
teaching, they will obey yours also. 21They will
treat you this way because of my name, for they do
not know the One who sent me. 22If I had not
come and spoken to them, they would not be
guilty of sin. Now, however, they have no excuse
for their sin. 23He who hates me hates my Father
as well. 24If I had not done among them what no
one else did, they would not be guilty of sin. But
now they have seen these miracles, and yet they
have hated both me and my Father. 25But this is to
fulfill what is written in their Law: ‘They hated me
without reason.’[b] Jn 9:41; 1Jn 3:13
26“When the Counselor comes, whom I will
send to you from the Father, the Spirit of truth
who goes out from the Father, he will testify about
me. 27And you also must testify, for you have been
with me from the beginning. Jn 14:17; 1Jn 5:7

16 “All this I have told you so that you will
not go astray. 2They will put you out of the
synagogue; in fact, a time is coming when anyone
who kills you will think he is offering a service to
God. 3They will do such things because they have
not known the Father or me. 4I have told you this,
so that when the time comes you will remember
that I warned you. I did not tell you this at first
because I was with you. Mt 11:6; Jn 9:22; 15:21

The Work of the Holy Spirit

5“Now I am going to him who sent me, yet
none of you asks me, ‘Where are you going?’ 6Be-
cause I have said these things, you are filled with
grief. 7But I tell you the truth: It is for your good
that I am going away. Unless I go away, the Counselor will not come to you; but if I go, I will send

LIVING  **INSIGHT**

While Jesus was on the earth, the Spirit of God was with the people of God. But when Jesus left the earth and sent another Helper like Himself, the Helper came and became a part of their lives deep within. No longer merely with them, but in them.

(See John 16:7.)

him to you. 8When he comes, he will convict the
world of guilt[c] in regard to sin and righteousness
and judgment: 9in regard to sin, because men do
not believe in me; 10in regard to righteousness,
because I am going to the Father, where you can
see me no longer; 11and in regard to judgment,
because the prince of this world now stands condemned. Jn 7:33,39; 14:16,26
12“I have much more to say to you, more than
you can now bear. 13But when he, the Spirit of
truth, comes, he will guide you into all truth. He
will not speak on his own; he will speak only what
he hears, and he will tell you what is yet to come.
14He will bring glory to me by taking from what is
mine and making it known to you. 15All that belongs to the Father is mine. That is why I said the
Spirit will take from what is mine and make it
known to you. Jn 14:17,26; 17:10
16“In a little while you will see me no more, and
then after a little while you will see me.”

The Disciples’ Grief Will Turn to Joy

17Some of his disciples said to one another,
“What does he mean by saying, ‘In a little while
you will see me no more, and then after a little

[a] *20* John 13:16 [b] *25* Psalms 35:19; 69:4 [c] *8* Or *will expose the guilt of the world*

while you will see me,' and 'Because I am going to the Father'?" 18They kept asking, "What does he mean by 'a little while'? We don't understand what he is saying."

19Jesus saw that they wanted to ask him about this, so he said to them, "Are you asking one another what I meant when I said, 'In a little while you will see me no more, and then after a little while you will see me'? 20I tell you the truth, you will weep and mourn while the world rejoices. You will grieve, but your grief will turn to joy. 21A woman giving birth to a child has pain because her time has come; but when her baby is born she forgets the anguish because of her joy that a child is born into the world. 22So with you: Now is your time of grief, but I will see you again and you will rejoice, and no one will take away your joy. 23In that day you will no longer ask me anything. I tell you the truth, my Father will give you whatever you ask in my name. 24Until now you have not asked for anything in my name. Ask and you will receive, and your joy will be complete. Mt 7:7

25"Though I have been speaking figuratively, a time is coming when I will no longer use this kind of language but will tell you plainly about my Father. 26In that day you will ask in my name. I am not saying that I will ask the Father on your behalf. 27No, the Father himself loves you because you have loved me and have believed that I came from God. 28I came from the Father and entered the world; now I am leaving the world and going back to the Father." Jn 10:6; 14:21,23

29Then Jesus' disciples said, "Now you are speaking clearly and without figures of speech. 30Now we can see that you know all things and that you do not even need to have anyone ask you questions. This makes us believe that you came from God." Jn 13:3

31"You believe at last!"[a] Jesus answered. 32"But a time is coming, and has come, when you will be scattered, each to his own home. You will leave me all alone. Yet I am not alone, for my Father is with me. Mt 26:31; Jn 8:16,29

33"I have told you these things, so that in me you may have peace. In this world you will have trouble. But take heart! I have overcome the world." Jn 14:27; Ro 8:37

Jesus Prays for Himself

17 After Jesus said this, he looked toward heaven and prayed: Jn 11:41

"Father, the time has come. Glorify your Son, that your Son may glorify you. 2For you granted him authority over all people that he might give eternal life to all those you have given him. 3Now this is eternal life: that they may know you, the only true God, and Jesus Christ, whom you have sent. 4I have brought you glory on earth by completing the work you gave me to do. 5And now, Father, glorify me in your presence with the glory I had with you before the world began. Jn 1:2; Php 2:6

Jesus Prays for His Disciples

6"I have revealed you[b] to those whom you gave me out of the world. They were yours; you gave them to me and they have obeyed your word. 7Now they know that everything you have given me comes from you. 8For I gave them the words you gave me and they accepted them. They knew with certainty that I came from you, and they believed that you sent me. 9I pray for them. I am not praying for the world, but for those you have given me, for they are yours. 10All I have is yours, and all you have is mine. And glory has come to me through them. 11I will remain in the world no longer, but they are still in the world, and I am coming to you. Holy Father, protect them by the power of your name—the name you gave me—so that they may be one as we are one. 12While I was with them, I protected them and kept them safe by that name you gave me. None has been lost except the one doomed to destruction so that Scripture would be fulfilled. Jn 6:39,70

13"I am coming to you now, but I say these things while I am still in the world, so that they may have the full measure of my joy within them. 14I have given them your word and the world has hated them, for they are not of the world any more than I am of the world. 15My prayer is not that you take them out of the world but that you protect them from the evil one. 16They are not of the world, even as I am not of it. 17Sanctify[c] them by the truth; your word is truth. 18As you sent me into the world, I have sent them into the world. 19For them I sanctify myself, that they too may be truly sanctified. Jn 8:23

Jesus Prays for All Believers

20"My prayer is not for them alone. I pray also for those who will believe in me through their message, 21that all of them may be one, Father, just as you are in me and I am in you. May they also be in us so that the world may believe that you have sent me. 22I have given them the glory that you gave me, that they may be one as we are one: 23I in them and you in me. May they be brought to complete unity to let the world know that you sent

[a] 31 Or *"Do you now believe?"* [b] 6 Greek *your name*; also in verse 26 [c] 17 Greek *hagiazo (set apart for sacred use* or *make holy)*; also in verse 19

me and have loved them even as you have loved me. Jn 10:38; 14:20

24“Father, I want those you have given me to be with me where I am, and to see my glory, the glory you have given me because you loved me before the creation of the world. Jn 12:26

25“Righteous Father, though the world does not know you, I know you, and they know that you have sent me. 26I have made you known to them, and will continue to make you known in order that the love you have for me may be in them and that I myself may be in them.” Jn 15:9,21; 16:27

Jesus Arrested

▶ *See Matthew 26:47–56; Mark 14:43–50; Luke 22:47–53*

18 When he had finished praying, Jesus left with his disciples and crossed the Kidron Valley. On the other side there was an olive grove, and he and his disciples went into it. 2Sa 15:23

2Now Judas, who betrayed him, knew the place, because Jesus had often met there with his disciples. 3So Judas came to the grove, guiding a detachment of soldiers and some officials from the chief priests and Pharisees. They were carrying torches, lanterns and weapons. Lk 21:37; 22:39; Ac 1:16

4Jesus, knowing all that was going to happen to him, went out and asked them, “Who is it you want?” Jn 6:64; 13:1,11

5“Jesus of Nazareth,” they replied. Mk 1:24

“I am he,” Jesus said. (And Judas the traitor was standing there with them.) 6When Jesus said, “I am he,” they drew back and fell to the ground.

7Again he asked them, “Who is it you want?”

And they said, “Jesus of Nazareth.”

8“I told you that I am he,” Jesus answered. “If you are looking for me, then let these men go.” 9This happened so that the words he had spoken would be fulfilled: “I have not lost one of those you gave me.”[a] Jn 17:12

10Then Simon Peter, who had a sword, drew it and struck the high priest’s servant, cutting off his right ear. (The servant’s name was Malchus.)

11Jesus commanded Peter, “Put your sword away! Shall I not drink the cup the Father has given me?” Mt 26:47-56; Mk 14:43-50; Lk 22:47-53

Jesus Taken to Annas

▶ *See Matthew 26:57*

12Then the detachment of soldiers with its commander and the Jewish officials arrested Jesus. They bound him 13and brought him first to Annas, who was the father-in-law of Caiaphas, the high priest that year. 14Caiaphas was the one who had advised the Jews that it would be good if one man died for the people. Mt 26:57; Jn 11:49-51

Peter’s First Denial

▶ *See Matthew 26:69–70; Mark 14:66–68; Luke 22:55–57*

15Simon Peter and another disciple were following Jesus. Because this disciple was known to the high priest, he went with Jesus into the high priest’s courtyard, 16but Peter had to wait outside at the door. The other disciple, who was known to the high priest, came back, spoke to the girl on duty there and brought Peter in. Mt 26:58; Mk 14:54

17“You are not one of his disciples, are you?” the girl at the door asked Peter.

He replied, “I am not.”

18It was cold, and the servants and officials stood around a fire they had made to keep warm. Peter also was standing with them, warming himself. Mt 26:69-70; Mk 14:66-68; Lk 22:55-57

The High Priest Questions Jesus

▶ *See Matthew 26:59–68; Mark 14:55–65; Luke 22:63–71*

19Meanwhile, the high priest questioned Jesus about his disciples and his teaching.

20“I have spoken openly to the world,” Jesus replied. “I always taught in synagogues or at the temple, where all the Jews come together. I said nothing in secret. 21Why question me? Ask those who heard me. Surely they know what I said.”

22When Jesus said this, one of the officials nearby struck him in the face. “Is this the way you answer the high priest?” he demanded. Jn 19:3

23“If I said something wrong,” Jesus replied, “testify as to what is wrong. But if I spoke the truth, why did you strike me?” 24Then Annas sent him, still bound, to Caiaphas the high priest.[b]

Peter’s Second and Third Denials

▶ *See Matthew 26:71–75; Mark 14:69–72; Luke 22:58–62*

25As Simon Peter stood warming himself, he was asked, “You are not one of his disciples, are you?”

He denied it, saying, “I am not.”

26One of the high priest’s servants, a relative of the man whose ear Peter had cut off, challenged him, “Didn’t I see you with him in the olive grove?” 27Again Peter denied it, and at that moment a rooster began to crow. Mt 26:71-75; Mk 14:69-72

Jesus Before Pilate

▶ *See Matthew 27:11–18,20–23; Mark 15:2–15; Luke 23:2–3,18–25*

28Then the Jews led Jesus from Caiaphas to the palace of the Roman governor. By now it was early

[a] 9 John 6:39 [b] 24 Or *(Now Annas had sent him, still bound, to Caiaphas the high priest.)*

morning, and to avoid ceremonial uncleanness the Jews did not enter the palace; they wanted to be able to eat the Passover. 29So Pilate came out to them and asked, "What charges are you bringing against this man?" Mt 27:2; Mk 15:1; Jn 11:55

30"If he were not a criminal," they replied, "we would not have handed him over to you."

31Pilate said, "Take him yourselves and judge him by your own law."

"But we have no right to execute anyone," the Jews objected. 32This happened so that the words Jesus had spoken indicating the kind of death he was going to die would be fulfilled. Mt 20:19

33Pilate then went back inside the palace, summoned Jesus and asked him, "Are you the king of the Jews?" Lk 23:3; Jn 19:9

34"Is that your own idea," Jesus asked, "or did others talk to you about me?"

35"Am I a Jew?" Pilate replied. "It was your people and your chief priests who handed you over to me. What is it you have done?"

36Jesus said, "My kingdom is not of this world. If it were, my servants would fight to prevent my arrest by the Jews. But now my kingdom is from another place." Mt 26:53; Jn 6:15

37"You are a king, then!" said Pilate.

Jesus answered, "You are right in saying I am a king. In fact, for this reason I was born, and for this I came into the world, to testify to the truth. Everyone on the side of truth listens to me."

38"What is truth?" Pilate asked. With this he went out again to the Jews and said, "I find no basis for a charge against him. 39But it is your custom for me to release to you one prisoner at the time of the Passover. Do you want me to release 'the king of the Jews'?" Lk 23:4; Jn 19:4,6

40They shouted back, "No, not him! Give us Barabbas!" Now Barabbas had taken part in a rebellion. Ac 3:14

Jesus Sentenced to Be Crucified

▶ *See Matthew 27:27–31; Mark 15:16–20*

19 Then Pilate took Jesus and had him flogged. 2The soldiers twisted together a crown of thorns and put it on his head. They clothed him in a purple robe 3and went up to him again and again, saying, "Hail, king of the Jews!" And they struck him in the face. Mt 27:26,29; Jn 18:22

4Once more Pilate came out and said to the Jews, "Look, I am bringing him out to you to let you know that I find no basis for a charge against him." 5When Jesus came out wearing the crown of thorns and the purple robe, Pilate said to them, "Here is the man!" Lk 23:4; Jn 18:38

6As soon as the chief priests and their officials saw him, they shouted, "Crucify! Crucify!"

But Pilate answered, "You take him and crucify him. As for me, I find no basis for a charge against him." Lk 23:4; Ac 3:13

7The Jews insisted, "We have a law, and according to that law he must die, because he claimed to be the Son of God." Lev 24:16; Mt 26:63-66

8When Pilate heard this, he was even more afraid, 9and he went back inside the palace. "Where do you come from?" he asked Jesus, but Jesus gave him no answer. 10"Do you refuse to speak to me?" Pilate said. "Don't you realize I have power either to free you or to crucify you?"

11Jesus answered, "You would have no power over me if it were not given to you from above. Therefore the one who handed me over to you is guilty of a greater sin." Jn 18:28-30; Ac 3:13; Ro 13:1

12From then on, Pilate tried to set Jesus free, but the Jews kept shouting, "If you let this man go, you are no friend of Caesar. Anyone who claims to be a king opposes Caesar." Lk 23:2

13When Pilate heard this, he brought Jesus out and sat down on the judge's seat at a place known as the Stone Pavement (which in Aramaic is Gabbatha). 14It was the day of Preparation of Passover Week, about the sixth hour. Mt 27:62; Mk 15:25; Jn 5:2

"Here is your king," Pilate said to the Jews.

15But they shouted, "Take him away! Take him away! Crucify him!"

"Shall I crucify your king?" Pilate asked.

"We have no king but Caesar," the chief priests answered.

16Finally Pilate handed him over to them to be crucified. Mt 27:27-31; Mk 15:16-20

The Crucifixion

▶ *See Matthew 27:33–44; Mark 15:22–32; Luke 23:33–43*

So the soldiers took charge of Jesus. 17Carrying his own cross, he went out to the place of the Skull (which in Aramaic is called Golgotha). 18Here they crucified him, and with him two others—one on each side and Jesus in the middle. Lk 23:26,32-33; Jn 5:2

19Pilate had a notice prepared and fastened to the cross. It read: JESUS OF NAZARETH, THE KING OF THE JEWS. 20Many of the Jews read this sign, for the place where Jesus was crucified was near the city, and the sign was written in Aramaic, Latin and Greek. 21The chief priests of the Jews protested to Pilate, "Do not write 'The King of the Jews,' but that this man claimed to be king of the Jews."

22Pilate answered, "What I have written, I have written."

23When the soldiers crucified Jesus, they took his clothes, dividing them into four shares, one for each of them, with the undergarment remaining. This garment was seamless, woven in one piece from top to bottom.

24"Let's not tear it," they said to one another. "Let's decide by lot who will get it."

This happened that the scripture might be fulfilled which said, Mt 1:22

"They divided my garments among them
and cast lots for my clothing."[a] Ps 22:18

So this is what the soldiers did. Mt 27:33-44
25Near the cross of Jesus stood his mother, his
mother's sister, Mary the wife of Clopas, and Mary
Magdalene. 26When Jesus saw his mother there,
and the disciple whom he loved standing nearby,
he said to his mother, "Dear woman, here is your
son," 27and to the disciple, "Here is your mother."
From that time on, this disciple took her into his
home. Mk 15:40-41; Lk 24:18; Jn 13:23

The Death of Jesus

▶ *See Matthew 27:48,50; Mark 15:36–37; Luke 23:36*

28Later, knowing that all was now completed,
and so that the Scripture would be fulfilled, Jesus
said, "I am thirsty." 29A jar of wine vinegar was
there, so they soaked a sponge in it, put the sponge
on a stalk of the hyssop plant, and lifted it to Jesus'
lips. 30When he had received the drink, Jesus said,
"It is finished." With that, he bowed his head and
gave up his spirit. Mt 27:48,50; Mk 15:36-37; Lk 23:36

LIVING  **INSIGHT**

When Jesus died on that cross and poured out His blood once for all, He cried out,* tetelestai! *IT IS FINISHED! The Greek term has as its root,* telos, *"completion, end." "It's over. It's done. It's accomplished. It's complete!" The sacrifice of the Lamb of God was once for all. We will never have to offer another sacrifice. His death on the cross finished the task.

(See John 19:30.)

31Now it was the day of Preparation, and the
next day was to be a special Sabbath. Because the
Jews did not want the bodies left on the crosses
during the Sabbath, they asked Pilate to have the
legs broken and the bodies taken down. 32The soldiers therefore came and broke the legs of the first
man who had been crucified with Jesus, and then
those of the other. 33But when they came to Jesus
and found that he was already dead, they did not
break his legs. 34Instead, one of the soldiers
pierced Jesus' side with a spear, bringing a sudden
flow of blood and water. 35The man who saw it has
given testimony, and his testimony is true. He
knows that he tells the truth, and he testifies so
that you also may believe. 36These things happened so that the scripture would be fulfilled: "Not
one of his bones will be broken,"[b] 37and, as another scripture says, "They will look on the one
they have pierced."[c] 1Jn 5:6,8; Rev 1:7

The Burial of Jesus

▶ *See Matthew 27:57–61; Mark 15:42–47; Luke 23:50–56*

38Later, Joseph of Arimathea asked Pilate for
the body of Jesus. Now Joseph was a disciple of
Jesus, but secretly because he feared the Jews. With
Pilate's permission, he came and took the body
away. 39He was accompanied by Nicodemus, the
man who earlier had visited Jesus at night. Nicodemus brought a mixture of myrrh and aloes, about
seventy-five pounds.[d] 40Taking Jesus' body, the
two of them wrapped it, with the spices, in strips
of linen. This was in accordance with Jewish burial
customs. 41At the place where Jesus was crucified,
there was a garden, and in the garden a new tomb,
in which no one had ever been laid. 42Because it
was the Jewish day of Preparation and since the
tomb was nearby, they laid Jesus there. Mt 27:57-61

The Empty Tomb

▶ *See Matthew 28:1–8; Mark 16:1–8; Luke 24:1–10*

20 Early on the first day of the week, while it
was still dark, Mary Magdalene went to the
tomb and saw that the stone had been removed
from the entrance. 2So she came running to Simon
Peter and the other disciple, the one Jesus loved,
and said, "They have taken the Lord out of the
tomb, and we don't know where they have put
him!"
3So Peter and the other disciple started for the
tomb. 4Both were running, but the other disciple
outran Peter and reached the tomb first. 5He bent
over and looked in at the strips of linen lying there
but did not go in. 6Then Simon Peter, who was
behind him, arrived and went into the tomb. He
saw the strips of linen lying there, 7as well as the
burial cloth that had been around Jesus' head. The
cloth was folded up by itself, separate from the
linen. 8Finally the other disciple, who had reached
the tomb first, also went inside. He saw and believed. 9(They still did not understand from Scripture that Jesus had to rise from the dead.)

Jesus Appears to Mary Magdalene

10Then the disciples went back to their homes,
11but Mary stood outside the tomb crying. As she
wept, she bent over to look into the tomb 12and
saw two angels in white, seated where Jesus' body
had been, one at the head and the other at the foot.
13They asked her, "Woman, why are you crying?"
"They have taken my Lord away," she said,
"and I don't know where they have put him." 14At

[a] *24* Psalm 22:18 [b] *36* Exodus 12:46; Num. 9:12; Psalm 34:20 [c] *37* Zech. 12:10 [d] *39* Greek *a hundred litrai* (about 34 kilograms)

this, she turned around and saw Jesus standing
there, but she did not realize that it was Jesus.
15“Woman,” he said, “why are you crying? Who
is it you are looking for?”
Thinking he was the gardener, she said, “Sir, if
you have carried him away, tell me where you have
put him, and I will get him.”
16Jesus said to her, “Mary.”
She turned toward him and cried out in Aramaic, “Rabboni!” (which means Teacher). Mt 23:7
17Jesus said, “Do not hold on to me, for I have
not yet returned to the Father. Go instead to my
brothers and tell them, ‘I am returning to my
Father and your Father, to my God and your
God.’ ”
18Mary Magdalene went to the disciples with the
news: “I have seen the Lord!” And she told them
that he had said these things to her. Lk 24:10,22-23

Jesus Appears to His Disciples

19On the evening of that first day of the week,
when the disciples were together, with the doors
locked for fear of the Jews, Jesus came and stood
among them and said, “Peace be with you!” 20After he said this, he showed them his hands and
side. The disciples were overjoyed when they saw
the Lord. Lk 24:36-39; Jn 16:20,22
21Again Jesus said, “Peace be with you! As the
Father has sent me, I am sending you.” 22And with
that he breathed on them and said, “Receive the
Holy Spirit. 23If you forgive anyone his sins, they
are forgiven; if you do not forgive them, they are
not forgiven.” Mt 16:19; 18:18; 28:19

Jesus Appears to Thomas

24Now Thomas (called Didymus), one of the
Twelve, was not with the disciples when Jesus

RESURRECTION APPEARANCES

Event	Place	Day of the Week	Matthew	Mark	Luke	John	Acts	1Cor
The empty tomb	Jerusalem	Resurrection Sunday	*28:1-8*	*16:1-8*	*24:1-12*	*20:1-10*		
To Mary Magdalene in the garden	Jerusalem	Resurrection Sunday		*16:9-11*		*20:11-18*		
To other women	Jerusalem	Resurrection Sunday	*28:9-10*					
To two people going to Emmaus	Road to Emmaus	Resurrection Sunday		*16:12-13*	*24:13-32*			
To Peter	Jerusalem	Resurrection Sunday			*24:34*			*15:5*
To the ten disciples in the upper room	Jerusalem	Resurrection Sunday			*24:36-43*	*20:19-25*		
To the eleven disciples in the upper room	Jerusalem	Following Sunday		*16:14*		*20:26-31*		*15:5*
To seven disciples fishing	Sea of Galilee	Some time later				*21:1-14*		
To the eleven disciples on a mountain	Galilee	Some time later	*28:16-20*	*16:15-18*				
To more than five hundred	Unknown	Some time later						*15:6*
To James	Unknown	Some time later						*15:7*
To the disciples at His ascension	Mount of Olives	Forty days after Jesus' resurrection			*24:44-49*		*1:3-9*	
To Paul	Damascus	Several years later					*9:1-19* *22:3-16* *26:9-18*	*9:1*

came. [25]So the other disciples told him, "We have seen the Lord!" Jn 11:16

But he said to them, "Unless I see the nail marks in his hands and put my finger where the nails were, and put my hand into his side, I will not believe it." Mk 16:11

[26]A week later his disciples were in the house again, and Thomas was with them. Though the doors were locked, Jesus came and stood among them and said, "Peace be with you!" [27]Then he said to Thomas, "Put your finger here; see my hands. Reach out your hand and put it into my side. Stop doubting and believe." Lk 24:40; Jn 14:27

[28]Thomas said to him, "My Lord and my God!"

[29]Then Jesus told him, "Because you have seen me, you have believed; blessed are those who have not seen and yet have believed." Jn 3:15; 1Pe 1:8

[30]Jesus did many other miraculous signs in the presence of his disciples, which are not recorded in this book. [31]But these are written that you may[a] believe that Jesus is the Christ, the Son of God, and that by believing you may have life in his name.

LIVING  **INSIGHT**

How tragic to move through the seasons without realizing their ultimate purpose! And what is that? The purpose is obvious: that we might be saved . . . that we might not trust in ourselves but in Jesus Christ, our Creator Lord, and in doing so, receive from Him the assurance of abundant life now and eternal life forever.

(See John 20:31.)

Jesus and the Miraculous Catch of Fish

21 Afterward Jesus appeared again to his disciples, by the Sea of Tiberias.[b] It happened this way: [2]Simon Peter, Thomas (called Didymus), Nathanael from Cana in Galilee, the sons of Zebedee, and two other disciples were together. [3]"I'm going out to fish," Simon Peter told them, and they said, "We'll go with you." So they went out and got into the boat, but that night they caught nothing. Mt 4:21; Lk 5:5

[4]Early in the morning, Jesus stood on the shore, but the disciples did not realize that it was Jesus.

[5]He called out to them, "Friends, haven't you any fish?"

"No," they answered.

[6]He said, "Throw your net on the right side of the boat and you will find some." When they did, they were unable to haul the net in because of the large number of fish. Lk 5:4-7

[7]Then the disciple whom Jesus loved said to Peter, "It is the Lord!" As soon as Simon Peter heard him say, "It is the Lord," he wrapped his outer garment around him (for he had taken it off) and jumped into the water. [8]The other disciples followed in the boat, towing the net full of fish, for they were not far from shore, about a hundred yards.[c] [9]When they landed, they saw a fire of burning coals there with fish on it, and some bread. Jn 13:23; 18:18

[10]Jesus said to them, "Bring some of the fish you have just caught."

[11]Simon Peter climbed aboard and dragged the net ashore. It was full of large fish, 153, but even with so many the net was not torn. [12]Jesus said to them, "Come and have breakfast." None of the disciples dared ask him, "Who are you?" They knew it was the Lord. [13]Jesus came, took the bread and gave it to them, and did the same with the fish. [14]This was now the third time Jesus appeared to his disciples after he was raised from the dead.

Jesus Reinstates Peter

[15]When they had finished eating, Jesus said to Simon Peter, "Simon son of John, do you truly love me more than these?"

"Yes, Lord," he said, "you know that I love you." Mt 26:33,35; Jn 13:37

Jesus said, "Feed my lambs." Lk 12:32

[16]Again Jesus said, "Simon son of John, do you truly love me?"

He answered, "Yes, Lord, you know that I love you."

Jesus said, "Take care of my sheep." Ac 20:28

[17]The third time he said to him, "Simon son of John, do you love me?"

Peter was hurt because Jesus asked him the third time, "Do you love me?" He said, "Lord, you know all things; you know that I love you."

Jesus said, "Feed my sheep. [18]I tell you the truth, when you were younger you dressed yourself and

LIVING  **INSIGHT**

When it comes to the matter of doing God's will, God has not said that you must answer for anyone else except yourself. Quit looking around for equality! Stop concerning yourself with your need for others to do what you are doing or endure what you have been called to endure. God chooses the roles we play, and each part is unique.

(See John 21:20–23.)

[a]*31* Some manuscripts *may continue to* [b]*1* That is, Sea of Galilee [c]*8* Greek *about two hundred cubits* (about 90 meters)

THOMAS

In Defense of a Doubter

"'Put your finger here; see my hands. Reach out your hand and put it into my side. Stop doubting and believe.' Thomas said to him, 'My Lord and my God!'"

—JOHN 20:27–28

The disciple named Thomas has been saddled with a label that has stuck for centuries; to many he has gone down in history as "the doubter." He has been called a skeptic, a rationalist, an empiricist—the one who needed incontrovertible proof before he would be satisfied. He's been seen as the prototype for all who dismiss the reality of Jesus Christ on the basis of rational arguments. Many people have been taught that Thomas was the one disciple who lived as close as you can get to disbelief. It's time we see him in a different light, more as a prototype of all of us who are, at one time or another, plagued by doubts.

This Thomas is the same man who, when Jesus told his disciples that He was ready to go back to Judea to raise Lazarus, said to his friends, "Let us also go, that we may die with him" (John 11:16). Now that's quite something, isn't it? This man was committed and courageous. He was ready to go to the cross for Jesus. Thomas was the kind of guy who, when he gave himself to someone, gave with all his heart. He had sold himself out to the Lord—lock, stock and barrel.

The problem with Thomas was that he became disillusioned after Jesus' death. When a person who has invested so much into a relationship sees that the relationship didn't meet up to expectation, that it ended on a sour note, the pendulum often swings the other way. In the end Thomas wanted to draw back to a safe distance, thinking thoughts that may have gone something like this: "I'm not going to get burned again. Next time it's going to take the Rock of Gibraltar, someone I can count on to be there for me for all my life, before I give of myself so completely." That was Thomas. He had believed once upon a time. He was convinced that Jesus was the answer to his heart's deepest longings, the fulfillment of all his dreams. But then the absolute worst thing that *could* have happened *did* happen. He saw Jesus go to the cross. He saw Jesus buried. He saw the tomb and the massive rock rolled up against it. And all of his dreams died with Jesus. So when he heard the incredible, the thoroughly unbelievable, word of the other disciples that Jesus was alive and had appeared to them, Thomas needed proof before he could recommit his life.

I think if it had happened any other way, Jesus would have been far more severe with Thomas. But He understood Thomas's doubts. He recognized Thomas's fears. He helps people like Thomas, and thank God for that, because there are a lot of us around. After giving Thomas eight days to scratch his head over this issue, Jesus appeared to the disciples once again and said, first of all, "Peace" (John 20:26). No rebuke, no censure, no attack on Thomas's character. Simply a gentle word of peace. A calming word of acceptance. And then, looking into Thomas's eyes he said, in rapid succession, "Put your finger here; see my hands. Reach out your hand and put it into my side"—oh, I'm so impressed with the way Jesus handled this doubter! He met his need. He showed Thomas just what Thomas had required in order to have the strength to go on living for God all his days on earth.

Don't tell me you haven't had doubts like Thomas's. Wondering if maybe your belief in the Lord Jesus isn't just some great exercise in futility. Facing struggles that make it seem as if God is more absent in your life than present. Dealing with disappointments that have led you to question the validity of your relationship with God. And in those doubting moments when the lights have gone out and the pit is so deep and there's nobody around and tomorrow seems bleak, you and I also are very tempted to say, "He'll have to *prove* it to me next time before I could ever trust Him again." And He does. He does! He comes in like a flood of grace and compassion, and He shows you His hands and He shows you His side. And He says, "Here, my child, here's proof. I am alive, and I live forever! And I will *never* leave you or forsake you."

went where you wanted; but when you are old you
will stretch out your hands, and someone else will
dress you and lead you where you do not want to
go." 19 Jesus said this to indicate the kind of death
by which Peter would glorify God. Then he said to
him, "Follow me!" 2Pe 1:14

20 Peter turned and saw that the disciple whom
Jesus loved was following them. (This was the one
who had leaned back against Jesus at the supper
and had said, "Lord, who is going to betray you?")
21 When Peter saw him, he asked, "Lord, what
about him?" Jn 13:23,25

22 Jesus answered, "If I want him to remain alive
until I return, what is that to you? You must follow
me." 23 Because of this, the rumor spread among
the brothers that this disciple would not die. But
Jesus did not say that he would not die; he only
said, "If I want him to remain alive until I return,
what is that to you?" Mt 16:27; Ac 1:16

24 This is the disciple who testifies to these things
and who wrote them down. We know that his
testimony is true. Jn 19:35

25 Jesus did many other things as well. If every
one of them were written down, I suppose that
even the whole world would not have room for the
books that would be written. Jn 20:30

NIV HARMONY OF THE GOSPELS

	Matthew	Mark	Luke	John
A PREVIEW OF WHO JESUS IS				
Luke's purpose in writing a Gospel			*1:1-4*	
John's prologue: Jesus Christ, the preexistent Word incarnate				*1:1-18*
Jesus' legal lineage through Joseph and natural lineage through Mary	*1:1-17*		*3:23b-38*	
THE EARLY YEARS OF JOHN THE BAPTIST				
John's birth foretold to Zechariah			*1:5-25*	
Jesus' birth foretold to Mary			*1:26-38*	
Mary's visit to Elizabeth, and Elizabeth's song			*1:39-45*	
Mary's song of joy			*1:46-56*	
John's birth			*1:57-66*	
Zechariah's prophetic song			*1:67-79*	
John's growth and early life			*1:80*	
THE EARLY YEARS OF JESUS CHRIST				
Circumstances of Jesus' birth explained to Joseph	*1:18-25*			
Birth of Jesus			*2:1-7*	
Praise of the angels and witness of the shepherds			*2:8-20*	
Circumcision of Jesus			*2:21*	
Jesus presented in the temple with the homage of Simeon and Anna			*2:22-38*	
Visit of the Magi	*2:1-12*			
Escape into Egypt and murder of boys in Bethlehem	*2:13-18*			
Return to Nazareth	*2:19-23*		*2:39*	
Growth and early life of Jesus			*2:40*	
Jesus' first Passover in Jerusalem			*2:41-50*	
Jesus' growth to adulthood			*2:51-52*	
THE PUBLIC MINISTRY OF JOHN THE BAPTIST				
His ministry launched		*1:1*	*3:1-2*	
His person, proclamation and baptism	*3:1-6*	*1:2-6*	*3:3-6*	
His messages to the Pharisees, Sadducees, crowds, tax collectors and soldiers	*3:7-10*		*3:7-14*	
His description of Jesus Christ	*3:11-12*	*1:7-8*	*3:15-18*	
THE END OF JOHN'S MINISTRY AND THE BEGINNING OF JESUS' PUBLIC MINISTRY				
Jesus' baptism by John	*3:13-17*	*1:9-11*	*3:21-23a*	
Jesus' temptation in the desert	*4:1-11*	*1:12-13*	*4:1-13*	
John's testimony about himself to the priests and Levites				*1:19-28*
John's testimony to Jesus as the Son of God				*1:29-34*
Jesus' first followers				*1:35-51*
Jesus' first miracle: water becomes wine				*2:1-11*
Jesus' first stay in Capernaum with His relatives and early disciples				*2:12*
First cleansing of the temple at the Passover				*2:13-22*
Early response to Jesus' miracles				*2:23-25*
Nicodemus's interview with Jesus				*3:1-21*
John superseded by Jesus				*3:22-36*
Jesus' departure from Judea	*4:12*	*1:14a*	*3:19-20; 4:14a*	*4:1-4*
Discussion with a Samaritan woman				*4:5-26*
Challenge of a spiritual harvest				*4:27-38*
Evangelization of Sychar				*4:39-42*
Arrival in Galilee				*4:43-45*
THE MINISTRY OF JESUS IN GALILEE				
Opposition at Home and a New Headquarters				
Nature of the Galilean ministry	*4:17*	*1:14b-15*	*4:14b-15*	
Child at Capernaum healed by Jesus while at Cana				*4:46-54*
Ministry and rejection at Nazareth			*4:16-31a*	
Move to Capernaum	*4:13-16*			

NIV HARMONY OF THE GOSPELS (CONTINUED)

	Matthew	Mark	Luke	John
Disciples Called and Ministry Throughout Galilee				
Call of the four	*4:18-22*	*1:16-20*	*5:1-11*	
Teaching in the synagogue of Capernaum authenticated by healing a demoniac		*1:21-28*	*4:31b-37*	
Peter's mother-in-law and others healed	*8:14-17*	*1:29-34*	*4:38-41*	
Tour of Galilee with Simon and others	*4:23-25*	*1:35-39*	*4:42-44*	
Cleansing of a man with leprosy, followed by much publicity	*8:2-4*	*1:40-45*	*5:12-16*	
Forgiving and healing of a paralytic	*9:1-8*	*2:1-12*	*5:17-26*	
Call of Matthew	*9:9*	*2:13-14*	*5:27-28*	
Banquet at Matthew's house	*9:10-13*	*2:15-17*	*5:29-32*	
Jesus defends His disciples for feasting instead of fasting with three parables	*9:14-17*	*2:18-22*	*5:33-39*	
Sabbath Controversies and Withdrawals				
Jesus heals an invalid on the Sabbath				*5:1-9*
Effort to kill Jesus for breaking the Sabbath and saying He was equal with God				*5:10-18*
Discourse demonstrating the Son's equality with the Father				*5:19-47*
Controversy over disciples' picking grain on the Sabbath	*12:1-8*	*2:23-28*	*6:1-5*	
Healing of a man's shriveled hand on the Sabbath	*12:9-14*	*3:1-6*	*6:6-11*	
Withdrawal to the Sea of Galilee with large crowds from many places	*12:15-21*	*3:7-12*		
Appointment of the Twelve and Sermon on the Mount				
Twelve apostles chosen		*3:13-19*	*6:12-16*	
Setting of the Sermon	*5:1-2*		*6:17-19*	
Blessings on those who inherit the kingdom and woes to those who do not	*5:3-12*		*6:20-26*	
Responsibility while awaiting the kingdom	*5:13-16*			
Law, righteousness and the kingdom	*5:17-20*			
Six contrasts in interpreting the law	*5:21-48*		*6:27-30,32-36*	
Three hypocritical "acts of righteousness" to be avoided	*6:1-18*			
Three prohibitions against avarice, harsh judgment and unwise exposure of sacred things	*6:19–7:6*		*6:37-42*	
Application and conclusion	*7:7-27*		*6:31,43-49*	
Reaction of the crowds	*7:28–8:1*			
Growing Fame and Emphasis on Repentance				
A centurion's faith and the healing of his servant	*8:5-13*		*7:1-10*	
A widow's son raised at Nain			*7:11-17*	
John the Baptist's relationship to the kingdom	*11:2-19*		*7:18-35*	
Woes to Korazin and Bethsaida for failure to repent	*11:20-30*			
Jesus' feet anointed by a sinful but contrite woman			*7:36-50*	
First Public Rejection by Jewish Leaders				
A tour with the Twelve and other followers			*8:1-3*	
Blasphemous accusation by the teachers of the law and the Pharisees	*12:22-37*	*3:20-30*		
Request for a sign refused	*12:38-45*			
Announcement of a new spiritual kinship	*12:46-50*	*3:31-35*	*8:19-21*	
Secrets About the Kingdom Given in Parables				
To the Crowds by the Sea				
The setting of the parables	*13:1-3a*	*4:1-2*	*8:4*	
The parable of the soils	*13:3b-23*	*4:3-25*	*8:5-18*	
The parable of the seed's spontaneous growth		*4:26-29*		
The parable of the weeds	*13:24-30*			
The parable of the mustard seed	*13:31-32*	*4:30-32*		
The parable of the leavened loaf	*13:33-35*	*4:33-34*		
To the Disciples in the House				
The parable of the weeds explained	*13:36-43*			
The parable of the hidden treasure	*13:44*			
The parable of the valuable pearl	*13:45-46*			

NIV HARMONY OF THE GOSPELS (CONTINUED)

	Matthew	Mark	Luke	John
The parable of the net	*13:47-50*			
The parable of the house owner	*13:51-53*			
Continuing Opposition				
Crossing the lake and calming the storm	*8:18,23-27*	*4:35-41*	*8:22-25*	
Healing the Gerasene demoniacs and resultant opposition	*8:28-34*	*5:1-20*	*8:26-39*	
Return to Galilee, healing of a woman who touched Jesus' garment and raising of Jairus's daughter	*9:18-26*	*5:21-43*	*8:40-56*	
Three miracles of healing and another blasphemous accusation		*9:27-34*		
Final visit to unbelieving Nazareth	*13:54-58*	*6:1-6a*		
Final Galilean Campaign				
Shortage of workers	*9:35-38*	*6:6b*		
Commissioning of the Twelve	*10:1-42*	*6:7-11*	*9:1-5*	
Workers sent out	*11:1*	*6:12-13*	*9:6*	
Herod Antipas's mistaken identification of Jesus	*14:1-2*	*6:14-16*	*9:7-9*	
Earlier imprisonment and beheading of John the Baptist	*14:3-12*	*6:17-29*		
THE MINISTRY OF JESUS AROUND GALILEE				
Lesson on the Bread of Life				
Return of the workers		*6:30*	*9:10a*	
Withdrawal from Galilee	*14:13-14*	*6:31-34*	*9:10b-11*	*6:1-3*
Feeding the five thousand	*14:15-21*	*6:35-44*	*9:12-17*	*6:4-13*
A premature attempt to make Jesus king blocked	*14:22-23*	*6:45-46*		*6:14-15*
Walking on the water during a storm on the lake	*14:24-33*	*6:47-52*		*6:16-21*
Healings at Gennesaret	*14:34-36*	*6:53-56*		
Discourse on the true bread of life				*6:22-59*
Defection among the disciples				*6:60-71*
Lesson on the Yeast of the Pharisees, Sadducees and Herodians				
Conflict over the tradition of ceremonial uncleanness	*15:1-3a,7-9, 3b-6,10-20*	*7:1-23*		*7:1*
Ministry to a believing Greek woman in Tyre and Sidon	*15:21-28*	*7:24-30*		
Healings in Decapolis	*15:29-31*	*7:31-37*		
Feeding the four thousand in Decapolis	*15:32-38*	*8:1-9a*		
Return to Galilee and encounter with the Pharisees and Sadducees	*15:39–16:4*	*8:9b-12*		
Warning about the error of the Pharisees, Sadducees and Herodians	*16:5-12*	*8:13-21*		
Healing a blind man at Bethsaida		*8:22-26*		
Lesson of Messiahship Learned and Confirmed				
Peter's identification of Jesus as the Christ and first prophecy of the church	*16:13-20*	*8:27-30*	*9:18-21*	
First direct prediction of the rejection, crucifixion and resurrection	*16:21-26*	*8:31-37*	*9:22-25*	
Coming of the Son of Man and judgment	*16:27-28*	*8:38-9:1*	*9:26-27*	
Transfiguration of Jesus	*17:1-8*	*9:2-8*	*9:28-36a*	
Discussion of resurrection, Elijah and John the Baptist	*17:9-13*	*9:9-13*	*9:36b*	
Lessons on Responsibility to Others				
Healing of demoniac boy and unbelief rebuked	*17:14-20*	*9:14-29*	*9:37-43a*	
Second prediction of Jesus' death and resurrection	*17:22-23*	*9:30-32*	*9:43b-45*	
Payment of temple tax	*17:24-27*			
Rivalry over greatness in the kingdom	*18:1-5*	*9:33-37*	*9:46-48*	
Warning against causing believers to sin	*18:6-14*	*9:38-50*	*9:49-50*	
Treatment and forgiveness of a sinning brother	*18:15-35*			
Journey to Jerusalem for the Feast of Tabernacles				
Complete commitment required of followers	*8:19-22*		*9:57-62*	
Ridicule by Jesus' half brothers				*7:2-9*
Journey through Samaria			*9:51-56*	*7:10*

NIV HARMONY OF THE GOSPELS (CONTINUED)

	Matthew	Mark	Luke	John
THE LATER JUDEAN MINISTRY OF JESUS				
Ministry Beginning at the Feast of Tabernacles				
Mixed reaction to Jesus' teaching and miracles				*7:11-31*
Frustrated attempt to arrest Jesus				*7:32-52*
Jesus' forgiveness of a woman caught in adultery				*[7:53–8:11]*
Conflict over Jesus' claim to be the light of the world				*8:12-20*
Jesus' relationship to God the Father				*8:21-30*
Jesus' relationship to Abraham, and attempted stoning				*8:31-59*
Healing of a man born blind				*9:1-7*
Response of the blind man's neighbors				*9:8-12*
Examination and excommunication of the blind man by the Pharisees				*9:13-34*
Jesus' identification of Himself to the blind man				*9:35-38*
Spiritual blindness of the Pharisees				*9:39-41*
Allegory of the good shepherd and the thief				*10:1-18*
Further division among the Jews				*10:19-21*
Private Lessons on Loving Service and Prayer				
Commissioning of the seventy			*10:1-16*	
Return of the seventy			*10:17-24*	
Story of the good Samaritan			*10:25-37*	
Jesus' visit with Mary and Martha			*10:38-42*	
Lesson on how to pray and parable of the bold friend			*11:1-13*	
Second Debate With the Teachers of the Law and the Pharisees				
A third blasphemous accusation and a second debate			*11:14-36*	
Woes to the Pharisees and the teachers of the law while eating with a Pharisee			*11:37-54*	
Warning the disciples about hypocrisy			*12:1-12*	
Warning about greed and trust in wealth			*12:13-34*	
Warning against being unprepared for the Son of Man's coming			*12:35-48*	
Warning about the coming division			*12:49-53*	
Warning against failing to discern the present time			*12:54-59*	
Two alternatives: repent or perish			*13:1-9*	
Opposition from a synagogue ruler for healing a woman on the Sabbath			*13:10-21*	
Another attempt to stone or arrest Jesus for blasphemy at the Feast of Dedication				*10:22-39*
THE MINISTRY OF JESUS IN AND AROUND PEREA				
Principles of Discipleship				
From Jerusalem to Perea				*10:40-42*
Question about salvation and entering the kingdom			*13:22-30*	
Anticipation of Jesus' coming death and His sorrow over Jerusalem			*13:31-35*	
Healing of a man with dropsy while eating with a prominent Pharisee on the Sabbath, and three parables suggested by the occasion			*14:1-24*	
Cost of discipleship			*14:25-35*	
Parables in defense of association with sinners			*15:1-32*	
Parable to teach the proper use of money			*16:1-13*	
Story to teach the danger of wealth			*16:14-31*	
Four lessons on discipleship			*17:1-10*	
Sickness and death of Lazarus				*11:1-16*
Lazarus raised from the dead				*11:17-44*
Decision of the Sanhedrin to put Jesus to death				*11:45-54*
Teaching While on Final Journey to Jerusalem				
Healing of ten lepers while passing through Samaria and Galilee			*17:11-21*	
Instructions regarding the Son of Man's coming			*17:22-37*	
Two parables on prayer: the persistent widow, and the Pharisee and the tax collector			*18:1-14*	

NIV HARMONY OF THE GOSPELS (CONTINUED)

	Matthew	Mark	Luke	John
Conflict with Pharisaic teaching on divorce	*19:1-12*	*10:1-12*		
Example of little children in relation to the kingdom	*19:13-15*	*10:13-16*	*18:15-17*	
Riches and the kingdom	*19:16-30*	*10:17-31*	*18:18-30*	
Parable of the landowner's sovereignty	*20:1-16*			
Third prediction of Jesus' death and resurrection	*20:17-19*	*10:32-34*	*18:31-34*	
Warning against ambitious pride	*20:20-28*	*10:35-45*		
Healing of blind Bartimaeus and his companion	*20:29-34*	*10:46-52*	*18:35-43*	
Salvation of Zacchaeus			*19:1-10*	
Parable to teach responsibility while the kingdom is delayed			*19:11-28*	
THE FORMAL PRESENTATION OF JESUS TO ISRAEL AND THE RESULTING CONFLICT				
Triumphal Entry and the Fig Tree				
Arrival at Bethany				*11:55–12:1,9-11*
Triumphal entry into Jerusalem	*21:1-3,6-7, 4-5,8-11,14-17*	*11:1-11*	*19:29-44*	*12:12-19*
Cursing of the fig tree having leaves but no figs	*21:18-19a*	*11:12-14*		
Second cleansing of the temple	*21:12-13*	*11:15-18*	*19:45-48*	
Request of some Greeks to see Jesus and necessity of the Son of Man's being lifted up				*12:20-36a*
Different responses to Jesus and Jesus' response to the crowds				*12:36b-50*
Withered fig tree and the lesson on faith	*21:19b-22*	*11:19-25*	*21:37-38*	
Official Challenge to Jesus' Authority				
Questioning of Jesus' authority by the chief priests, teachers of the law and elders	*21:23-27*	*11:27-33*	*20:1-8*	
Jesus' response with His own question and three parables	*21:28–22:14*	*12:1-12*	*20:9-19*	
Attempts by Pharisees and Herodians to trap Jesus with a question about paying taxes to Caesar	*22:15-22*	*12:13-17*	*20:20-26*	
Sadducees' puzzling question about the resurrection	*22:23-33*	*12:18-27*	*20:27-40*	
A Pharisee's legal question	*22:34-40*	*12:28-34*		
Jesus' Response to His Enemies' Challenges				
Jesus Christ's relationship to David as son and Lord	*22:41-46*	*12:35-37*	*20:41-44*	
Seven woes against the teachers of the law and Pharisees	*23:1-36*	*12:38-40*	*20:45-47*	
Jesus' sorrow over Jerusalem	*23:37-39*			
A poor widow's gift of all she had		*12:41-44*	*21:1-4*	
PROPHECIES IN PREPARATION FOR THE DEATH OF JESUS				
The Olivet Discourse: Jesus Speaks Prophetically About the Temple and His Own Second Coming				
Setting of the discourse	*24:1-3*	*13:1-4*	*21:5-7*	
Beginning of birth pains	*24:4-14*	*13:5-13*	*21:8-19*	
Abomination of desolation and subsequent distress	*24:15-28*	*13:14-23*	*21:20-24*	
Coming of the Son of Man	*24:29-31*	*13:24-27*	*21:25-27*	
Signs of nearness but unknown time	*24:32-41*	*13:28-32*	*21:28-33*	
Five parables to teach watchfulness and faithfulness	*24:42–25:30*	*13:33-37*	*21:34-36*	
Judgment at the Son of Man's coming	*25:31-46*			
Arrangements for Betrayal				
Plot by the Sanhedrin to arrest and kill Jesus	*26:1-5*	*14:1-2*	*22:1-2*	
Mary's anointing of Jesus for burial	*26:6-13*	*14:3-9*		*12:2-8*
Judas's agreement to betray Jesus	*26:14-16*	*14:10-11*	*22:3-6*	
The Last Supper				
Preparation for the Passover meal	*26:17-19*	*14:12-16*	*22:7-13*	
Beginning of the Passover meal and dissension among the disciples over greatness	*26:20*	*14:17*	*22:14-16,24-30*	
Washing the disciples' feet				*13:1-20*
Identification of the betrayer	*26:21-25*	*14:18-21*	*22:21-23*	*13:21-30*

NIV HARMONY OF THE GOSPELS (CONTINUED)

	Matthew	Mark	Luke	John
Prediction of Peter's denial	*26:31-35*	*14:27-31*	*22:31-38*	*13:31-38*
Conclusion of the meal and the Lord's Supper instituted *(1 Cor. 11:23-26)*	*26:26-29*	*14:22-25*	*22:17-20*	
Discourse and Prayers From the Upper Room to Gethsemane				
Questions about His destination, the Father and the Holy Spirit answered				*14:1-31*
The vine and the branches				*15:1-17*
Opposition from the world				*15:18–16:4*
Coming and ministry of the Spirit				*16:5-15*
Prediction of joy over His resurrection				*16:16-22*
Promise of answered prayer and peace				*16:23-33*
Jesus' prayer for His disciples and all who believe				*17:1-26*
Jesus' three agonizing prayers in Gethsemane	*26:30,36-46*	*14:26,32-42*	*22:39-46*	*18:1*
THE DEATH OF JESUS				
Betrayal and Arrest				
Jesus betrayed, arrested and forsaken	*26:47-56*	*14:43-52*	*22:47-53*	*18:2-12*
Trial				
First Jewish phase, before Annas				*18:13-14,19-23*
Second Jewish phase, before Caiaphas and the Sanhedrin	*26:57,59-68*	*14:53,55-65*	*22:54a,63-65*	*18:24*
Peter's denials	*26:58,69-75*	*14:54,66-72*	*22:54b-62*	*18:15-18,25-27*
Third Jewish phase, before the Sanhedrin	*27:1*	*15:1a*	*22:66-71*	
Remorse and suicide of Judas Iscariot *(Acts 1:18-19)*	*27:3-10*			
First Roman phase, before Pilate	*27:2,11-14*	*15:1b-5*	*23:1-5*	*18:28-38*
Second Roman phase, before Herod Antipas			*23:6-12*	
Third Roman phase, before Pilate	*27:15-26*	*15:6-15*	*23:13-25*	*18:39–19:16a*
Crucifixion				
Mockery by the Roman soldiers	*27:27-30*	*15:16-19*		
Journey to Golgotha	*27:31-34*	*15:20-23*	*23:26-33a*	*19:16b-17*
First three hours of crucifixion	*27:35-44*	*15:24-32*	*23:33b-43*	*19:18,23-24, 19-22,25-27*
Last three hours of crucifixion	*27:45-50*	*15:33-37*	*23:44-45a,46*	*19:28-30*
Witness of Jesus' death	*27:51-56*	*15:38-41*	*23:45b,47-49*	
Burial				
Certification of Jesus' death and procurement of His body	*27:57-58*	*15:42-45*	*23:50-52*	*19:31-38*
Jesus' body placed in a tomb	*27:59-60*	*15:46*	*23:53-54*	*19:39-42*
The tomb watched by the women and guarded by the soldiers	*27:61-66*	*15:47*	*23:55-56*	
THE RESURRECTION AND ASCENSION OF JESUS				
The Empty Tomb				
The tomb visited by the women	*28:1*	*16:1*		
The stone rolled away	*28:2-4*			
The tomb found to be empty by the women	*28:5-8*	*16:2-8*	*24:1-8*	*20:1*
The tomb found to be empty by Peter and John			*24:9-12*	*20:2-10*
The Post-Resurrection Appearances				
Appearance to Mary Magdalene		*[16:9-11]*		*20:11-18*
Appearance to the other women	*28:9-10*			
Report of the soldiers to the Jewish authorities	*28:11-15*			
Appearance to the two disciples traveling to Emmaus		*[16:12-13]*	*24:13-32*	
Report of the two disciples to the rest *(1 Cor. 15:5a)*			*24:33-35*	
Appearance to the ten assembled disciples		*[16:14]*	*24:36-43*	*20:19-25*
Appearance to the eleven assembled disciples *(1 Cor. 15:5b)*				*20:26-31*
Appearance to the seven disciples while fishing				*21:1-25*
Appearance to the Eleven in Galilee *(1 Cor. 15:6)*	*28:16-20*	*[16:15-18]*		
Appearance to James, Jesus' brother *(1 Cor. 15:7)*				
Appearance to the disciples in Jerusalem *(Acts 1:3-8)*			*24:44-49*	
The Ascension				
Jesus' parting blessing and departure *(Acts 1:9-12)*		*[16:19-20]*	*24:50-53*	

ACTS

All too often Christians look at their religious roots with a much-too-low esteem. Intimidated by the giant boot-stomping of secular events that occupy the attention of most history books, we entertain the false idea that the church of Jesus Christ is little more than a piece of lint on the page . . . a tiny, fragile thread woven through the centuries. Not so! The church is rather "like a mighty army" marching through time deliberately, confidently, victoriously . . . spurred on by the promise of its Founder that "the gates of Hades will not overcome it" (Matthew 16:18). No other book in the Bible underscores the richness of the history of the church better than Acts. And no other book affirms more clearly its God-given power to persevere. Although the church may be comparatively small in number, no remnant was ever more sure of its destiny.

WRITER: *Luke*

DATE: *C.A.D. 63–70*

PURPOSE: *To tell the story of what happened after Jesus' resurrection*

KEY THEME: *The growth of the early church*

KEY VERSE: *1:8 "You will receive power . . . and you will be my witnesses"*

KEY PEOPLE: *Peter and Paul*

PREDICTION FULFILLED: *"I will build my church" (Matthew 16:18)*

ORIGINS: *Coming of Holy Spirit; apostolic authority; world missions*

TIME LINE

10BC AD1 10 20 30 40 50 60 70 80 90 100

- **Jesus' life (c.6/5 B.C.–A.D.30)**
- **Paul's conversion (c. A.D.35)**
- **Paul's first missionary journey (c. A.D.46-48)**
- **Council at Jerusalem (c. A.D.50-51)**
- **Paul's second missionary journey (c. A.D.50-52)**
- **Paul's third missionary journey (c. A.D.53-57)**
- **Paul's fourth missionary journey (c. A.D.62-67)**
- **Paul's imprisonment and death in Rome (c. A.D.67-68)**
- **Book of Acts written (c. A.D.63-70)**

Like a Mighty Army

	THE CHURCH ESTABLISHED AT *"JERUSALEM"*	THE CHURCH ENLARGED TO *"JUDEA AND SAMARIA"*	THE CHURCH EXPANDED TO *"THE ENDS OF THE EARTH"*
A.D. 30	THE CHURCH IS . . . . . . born . . . tested . . . purified . . . strengthened	THE GOSPEL IS . . . . . . spreading . . . multiplying . . . changing lives . . . breaking traditions	THE WITNESS IS . . . . . . extended . . . received and rejected . . . changing lives . . . unifying Jews and Gentiles *A.D. 60*
	CHAPTERS 1–7	*CHAPTERS 8–12*	*CHAPTERS 13–28*
LEADERS	**The apostle Peter**		**The apostle Paul**
EMPHASIS	**Jewish evangelism**	**Transition**	**Gentile evangelism**
TIME	A.D. 30 *(1:1–2:47)*	A.D. 33 *(8:1)* A.D. 37 *(9:32)*	A.D. 47 *(13:1)* A.D. 56 *(21:18)*
SCOPE	**Home missions**	**World missions**	

At the risk of sounding simplistic, I suggest that everything we read in the Bible could be boiled down to three basic categories: people, events and great truths. From Genesis to Revelation—everything fits neatly into one of these three classifications.

It's stimulating to trace our way through the Scriptures using those three ingredients as a guideline. I challenge you to begin by choosing a Biblical character (Adam, for example) and trace your way from Genesis to Revelation. You can do the same with notable Biblical events. Starting with creation and the fall of humanity, you could follow God's plan of re-creation through Scripture all the way to the description of a new heaven and a new earth and humanity's complete restoration to God as pictured at the end of Revelation.

It is a little more difficult, but feasible, to begin with the great truths taught in the book of Genesis and build on those truths throughout the Bible. In some sense that's what systematic theologians do as they glean the meaning of the great doctrines and teachings of the Bible and trace their themes throughout Scripture—from Genesis to Revelation.

There are times when we read a book of the Bible and find that it focuses on the same few characters all throughout the book—chapter after chapter we read about one person or a few people. Perhaps there's just one important event in a person's life that the Biblical author zooms in on. But there are other times when there's rapid action and high drama, and we hang on to the saddle as we gallop through that book. One person after another comes on to the scene; one event after another tumbles into view. And one great truth after another vies for our attention as the words and actions unfold. The book of Acts falls into this latter category.

A High-Speed Church History

The book of Acts presents people, events and great truths at a blistering pace. There's nothing slow and relaxed in the book of Acts. We find some old friends from the Gospels who reappear in this account.

We meet some new friends. We see event after event after event, progressing so quickly that we wish we could spend more time analyzing each one because of its impact on the rest of the days of the church. And the same is true with the great truths and weighty doctrines found here . . . they fill the pages of Acts.

A Refreshing Follow-Up

Frankly, I find the book of Acts an encouraging and indispensable follow-up to the Gospels. How important it is that we see the impact of Jesus' life *after* He left this earth, as well as while He was on this earth! In Acts we possess an account of the ministry of Christians who took up the message of Jesus Christ and took leadership in establishing the early church. Many of the same roots that supported the establishment and fashioning of this powerful church are still forming the solid and secure foundation for Christ's church today. That truth makes me thankful.

Jesus lit the torch of faith with the light of His life, and as the book of Acts begins He had passed on the torch to fearful, intimidated disciples huddled together behind locked doors. But by the time you get halfway through the book, those timid followers of Jesus were courageous, ardent apostles who were setting the world on fire for Jesus Christ!

The Four W's

In tracing a path through this book, I find it is helpful to do some investigative reporting and answer four fundamental questions: "Who, why, what and where?"

Who wrote this book, and to whom was it written? The answer is given in the first verse of the book: "In my former book, Theophilus, I wrote about all that Jesus began to do and to teach" (1:1). The author addressed his words to a person named Theophilus. There is little doubt that we have the same writer addressing Theophilus for a second volume of writings—having also directed a first volume to this man (see Luke 1:3). The author of the book of Acts, therefore, was none other than Luke . . . the Gentile physician, missionary, and traveling companion and friend of the apostle Paul.

Luke's writing was originally one monumental volume that was divided into two parts in the second century. The first part of Luke's work was called "The Gospel According to Luke," while the second part was titled "The Acts of the Apostles."

Why did Luke write a second volume of his writings? The answer is twofold. First, Luke wrote the book of Acts to preserve an inspired record of and commentary on the earliest history of the church. The book of Acts is the most reliable volume on early church history we will ever read. God has given us this book to provide an accurate history of the church's birth and infant years. Second, Luke wrote to strengthen the faith of believers and to commend the preaching of the gospel of Jesus Christ to the whole world.

What do we discover as we read the book of Acts? We find thirty years of history written as only a skilled writer and careful historian such as Dr. Luke could record it. Every page of Acts abounds with sharp, precise details, dramatic description and literary excellence. Remember the three categories I mentioned earlier? All three are woven into the fabric of the Acts of the Apostles: people, events and great truths.

Let's take people, as an example. For the first 12 chapters of Acts, the main character is the apostle Peter. He preached a powerful sermon on the day of Pentecost as the Holy Spirit gave birth to the church (chapter 2). He became one of the leaders among the first converts. As the gospel began to spread throughout Palestine, Peter was learning about the power of God's grace at the same time he was struggling with the role of the Old Testament laws (chapter 10). God did a beautiful work in his life to free him from his legalistic background and to reveal the earth-shattering new message being proclaimed in this dynamic era of church history—the message that the gospel was for Gentiles as well as for Jews.

When we get to chapter 13, Peter had faded into the background and Paul had emerged onto center stage. (It's amazing how a man so dominant in the first section of a book can so quietly pass off the scene.) The rest of Acts records Paul's great missionary journeys "to the ends of the earth" (1:8). The call of Jesus to take the gospel to the whole world (Matthew 28:19–20; Luke 24:47–49) was unfolding before our very eyes in the missionary journeys of the apostle Paul.

Where will all this activity described in the book of Acts take place? Jesus Himself answered this question for the disciples before He ascended to heaven: "You will be my witnesses in Jerusalem, and in all Judea and Samaria, and to the ends of the earth" (1:8). This verse gives a prophetic unfolding of the geography of Acts. (This is where a basic knowledge of the book's geography will serve us well.) Luke's account began in Jerusalem as the Holy Spirit descended in power on the believers, who were then driven out of the holy city and dispersed across Judea and Samaria. Finally, through the missionary work of Paul and his companions, the gospel was proclaimed "to the ends of the earth."

When we understand the who, why, what and where of Acts, the whole book begins to make sense. Keep these questions and answers in mind as you read this stirring account of the early church.

A Book of Beginnings

Somewhat like in the book of Genesis, many things find their beginning in Acts. Among them: the coming of the Holy Spirit, the birth of the church, the introduction of the gifts of the Spirit and the beginning of apostolic authority. Acts also records the first martyrdom of a Christian—his name was Stephen (chapter 7). From the beginning of the Christian faith, believers have suffered intense misunderstanding, cruel persecution and even death because of their faith. In this book we find the beginning of world missions described, as well as the proclamation of God's acceptance based on grace instead of adherence to the law (chapters 10, 11 and 15). As we read Acts we find ourselves blazing new trails with the Holy Spirit as we observe His powerful work and presence among His people.

Stages of Growth

The book of Acts divides nicely into three stages that reflect the growth of the church. By application they can also teach us about the process God uses to bring growth in our lives as we walk with Jesus today.

In the first stage *God establishes us as His people and church*. He brings us into His family. He holds us close and shields us. He watches over us and protects us. He nurtures us like a mother with her newborn baby.

In the second stage *God enlarges us as His people and church*. Here we have grown out of infancy and are becoming more aware of ourselves and others around us. We begin to discover the gifts God has given us. We no longer need as much hand-holding and nurturing. We can begin to shoulder our own burdens, and when they get too heavy, we find we can carry them to the Lord on our own behalf. We're becoming more mature as we grow closer to God and to each other. We're being enlarged . . . We're becoming firmly grounded in our faith.

In the third stage *God expands us as His people and church*. The book of Acts paints a life-sized growth portrait of the Christian life. At this third stage, the action seems to fly at us hot and heavy in our Christian adventure! God may very well move us from one place to another. We have to be able to shift gears, to change hats, to handle persecution as well as great blessing. We may have to endure criticism, because we're making tough decisions. In this stage God says, "Now you're ready to be used." So He may send us in the same way He sent Paul—"to the ends of the earth." And we need to be ready to go where He directs, being willing to wait patiently as He works in and through us and to endure the afflictions He permits.

In whatever stage you find yourself, keep following the Savior. He will lead you just as He led the Christians in the early church. And keep walking in the power of the Spirit. The same Holy Spirit who came with power on the church at Pentecost is at work in your life. Follow Jesus and walk in the Spirit, and you will be thrilled at how God brings growth through all the stages of your life.

Acts is an exhilarating book about fascinating people, dramatic events and great truths. It's the only "unfinished" book of the Bible, practically speaking, because we are still "writing" the history of the church day by day. How exciting to be a part of what God continues to do in and through His church!

The Church Established Chapters 1–7

The opening chapters tell how the church was born, tested, purified and strengthened by the presence and power of the Holy Spirit. The events in this section took place in the city of Jerusalem. The Holy Spirit descended in power and gave birth to a new spiritual entity . . . the church. The apostle Peter was the central character in these chapters as he gave leadership to the young church. The focus of church growth was among the Jews. We might say this represented a "home missions" effort focused almost exclusively on Jews who would have known the Old Testament prophecies about the Messiah. These seven chapters span about the first three years of church history.

Jesus Taken Up Into Heaven

1 In my former book, Theophilus, I wrote
about all that Jesus began to do and to teach
[2]until the day he was taken up to heaven, after
giving instructions through the Holy Spirit to the
apostles he had chosen. [3]After his suffering, he
showed himself to these men and gave many convincing proofs that he was alive. He appeared to
them over a period of forty days and spoke about
the kingdom of God. [4]On one occasion, while he
was eating with them, he gave them this command: "Do not leave Jerusalem, but wait for the
gift my Father promised, which you have heard
me speak about. [5]For John baptized with[a] water,
but in a few days you will be baptized with the
Holy Spirit." Lk 1:1-4; Jn 14:16

[6]So when they met together, they asked him,
"Lord, are you at this time going to restore the
kingdom to Israel?" Mt 17:11

[7]He said to them: "It is not for you to know the
times or dates the Father has set by his own authority. [8]But you will receive power when the Holy
Spirit comes on you; and you will be my witnesses
in Jerusalem, and in all Judea and Samaria, and to
the ends of the earth." Mt 24:36; Lk 24:48

[9]After he said this, he was taken up before their
very eyes, and a cloud hid him from their sight.
[10]They were looking intently up into the sky as
he was going, when suddenly two men dressed in
white stood beside them. [11]"Men of Galilee," they
said, "why do you stand here looking into the sky?
This same Jesus, who has been taken from you
into heaven, will come back in the same way you
have seen him go into heaven." Mt 16:27; Jn 20:12

LIVING  **INSIGHT**

Jesus Christ is coming back. Looking up won't bring Him any sooner. We're never told simply to stand around gazing up to heaven. In fact, we're told not to do that. We aren't even commanded to do a lot of talking about it. There's a bigger job to be done than sitting around discussing the details of His return!

(See Acts 1:8–11.)

Matthias Chosen to Replace Judas

[12]Then they returned to Jerusalem from the hill
called the Mount of Olives, a Sabbath day's walk[b]
from the city. [13]When they arrived, they went upstairs to the room where they were staying. Those
present were Peter, John, James and Andrew; Philip and Thomas, Bartholomew and Matthew; James
son of Alphaeus and Simon the Zealot, and Judas
son of James. [14]They all joined together constantly
in prayer, along with the women and Mary the
mother of Jesus, and with his brothers. Ac 2:42

[15]In those days Peter stood up among the believers[c] (a group numbering about a hundred
and twenty) [16]and said, "Brothers, the Scripture
had to be fulfilled which the Holy Spirit spoke long
ago through the mouth of David concerning Judas, who served as guide for those who arrested
Jesus— [17]he was one of our number and shared in
this ministry." Jn 6:70-71; 13:18

[18](With the reward he got for his wickedness,
Judas bought a field; there he fell headlong, his
body burst open and all his intestines spilled out.
[19]Everyone in Jerusalem heard about this, so they
called that field in their language Akeldama, that
is, Field of Blood.) Mt 26:14-15; 27:3-10

[20]"For," said Peter, "it is written in the book of
Psalms,

" 'May his place be deserted;
let there be no one to dwell in it,'[d] Ps 69:25

and,

" 'May another take his place of leadership.'[e]

[21]Therefore it is necessary to choose one of the
men who have been with us the whole time the
Lord Jesus went in and out among us, [22]beginning
from John's baptism to the time when Jesus was
taken up from us. For one of these must become
a witness with us of his resurrection." Mk 1:4

[23]So they proposed two men: Joseph called Barsabbas (also known as Justus) and Matthias.
[24]Then they prayed, "Lord, you know everyone's
heart. Show us which of these two you have chosen
[25]to take over this apostolic ministry, which Judas
left to go where he belongs." [26]Then they cast lots,
and the lot fell to Matthias; so he was added to the
eleven apostles. 1Sa 16:7; Jer 17:10; Rev 2:23

[a]5 Or *in* [b]12 That is, about 3/4 mile (about 1,100 meters) [c]15 Greek *brothers* [d]20 Psalm 69:25
[e]20 Psalm 109:8

The Holy Spirit Comes at Pentecost

2 When the day of Pentecost came, they were
all together in one place. 2Suddenly a sound
like the blowing of a violent wind came from heav-
en and filled the whole house where they were
sitting. 3They saw what seemed to be tongues of
fire that separated and came to rest on each of
them. 4All of them were filled with the Holy Spirit
and began to speak in other tongues[a] as the Spirit
enabled them. Mk 16:17; 1Co 12:10

LIVING  INSIGHT

Never think that something is insignificant just because it's invisible. The Holy Spirit is ready to work within us and move among us in revolutionary ways, transforming our lives.
(See Acts 2:1–4.)

5Now there were staying in Jerusalem God-
fearing Jews from every nation under heaven.
6When they heard this sound, a crowd came together in bewilderment, because each one heard
them speaking in his own language. 7Utterly
amazed, they asked: "Are not all these men who
are speaking Galileans? 8Then how is it that each
of us hears them in his own native language? 9Par-
thians, Medes and Elamites; residents of Mesopotamia, Judea and Cappadocia, Pontus and Asia,
10Phrygia and Pamphylia, Egypt and the parts of
Libya near Cyrene; visitors from Rome 11(both
Jews and converts to Judaism); Cretans and
Arabs—we hear them declaring the wonders of
God in our own tongues!" 12Amazed and perplexed, they asked one another, "What does this
mean?" Ac 1:11; 16:6
13Some, however, made fun of them and said,
"They have had too much wine.[b]" 1Co 14:23

Peter Addresses the Crowd

14Then Peter stood up with the Eleven, raised
his voice and addressed the crowd: "Fellow Jews
and all of you who live in Jerusalem, let me explain
this to you; listen carefully to what I say. 15These
men are not drunk, as you suppose. It's only nine
in the morning! 16No, this is what was spoken by
the prophet Joel: 1Th 5:7

17" 'In the last days, God says,
I will pour out my Spirit on all people.
Your sons and daughters will prophesy, Ac 21:9
your young men will see visions,
your old men will dream dreams.
18Even on my servants, both men and women,
I will pour out my Spirit in those days,
and they will prophesy. Ac 21:9-12
19I will show wonders in the heaven above
and signs on the earth below,
blood and fire and billows of smoke.
20The sun will be turned to darkness
and the moon to blood Mt 24:29
before the coming of the great and glorious
day of the Lord.
21And everyone who calls
on the name of the Lord will be saved.'[c]

22"Men of Israel, listen to this: Jesus of Nazareth
was a man accredited by God to you by miracles,
wonders and signs, which God did among you
through him, as you yourselves know. 23This man
was handed over to you by God's set purpose and
foreknowledge; and you, with the help of wicked
men,[d] put him to death by nailing him to the
cross. 24But God raised him from the dead, freeing
him from the agony of death, because it was impossible for death to keep its hold on him. 25David
said about him: Jn 4:48; 2Co 4:14; Eph 1:20

" 'I saw the Lord always before me.
Because he is at my right hand,
I will not be shaken.
26Therefore my heart is glad and my tongue
rejoices;
my body also will live in hope,
27because you will not abandon me to the grave,
nor will you let your Holy One see decay.
28You have made known to me the paths of life;
you will fill me with joy in your
presence.'[e] Ps 16:8-11

29"Brothers, I can tell you confidently that the
patriarch David died and was buried, and his tomb
is here to this day. 30But he was a prophet and
knew that God had promised him on oath that he
would place one of his descendants on his throne.
31Seeing what was ahead, he spoke of the resurrection of the Christ,[f] that he was not abandoned to
the grave, nor did his body see decay. 32God has
raised this Jesus to life, and we are all witnesses of
the fact. 33Exalted to the right hand of God, he has
received from the Father the promised Holy Spirit
and has poured out what you now see and hear.
34For David did not ascend to heaven, and yet he
said, Ac 10:45; 13:36

" 'The Lord said to my Lord:
"Sit at my right hand
35until I make your enemies
a footstool for your feet." '[g] Mt 22:44

[a]4 Or *languages*; also in verse 11 [b]13 Or *sweet wine* [c]21 Joel 2:28-32 [d]23 Or *of those not having the law* (that is, Gentiles) [e]28 Psalm 16:8-11 [f]31 Or *Messiah*. "The Christ" (Greek) and "the Messiah" (Hebrew) both mean "the Anointed One"; also in verse 36. [g]35 Psalm 110:1

36“Therefore let all Israel be assured of this: God has made this Jesus, whom you crucified, both Lord and Christ.” Lk 2:11

37When the people heard this, they were cut to the heart and said to Peter and the other apostles, “Brothers, what shall we do?” Lk 3:10,12,14

38Peter replied, “Repent and be baptized, every one of you, in the name of Jesus Christ for the forgiveness of your sins. And you will receive the gift of the Holy Spirit. 39The promise is for you and your children and for all who are far off—for all whom the Lord our God will call.” Lk 24:47

40With many other words he warned them; and he pleaded with them, “Save yourselves from this corrupt generation.” 41Those who accepted his message were baptized, and about three thousand were added to their number that day. Dt 32:5

The Fellowship of the Believers

42They devoted themselves to the apostles' teaching and to the fellowship, to the breaking of bread and to prayer. 43Everyone was filled with awe, and many wonders and miraculous signs were done by the apostles. 44All the believers were together and had everything in common. 45Selling their possessions and goods, they gave to anyone as he had need. 46Every day they continued to meet together in the temple courts. They broke bread in their homes and ate together with glad and sincere hearts, 47praising God and enjoying the favor of all the people. And the Lord added to their number daily those who were being saved.

LIVING  INSIGHT

The depth of a church is determined by the quality of its worship and instruction. We must always keep that near the top of our awareness. The breadth of a church is determined by its commitment to fellowship and evangelism. We must keep reaching out to people who are in need. After all, that is what love is all about.

(See Acts 2:42–47.)

Peter Heals the Crippled Beggar

3 One day Peter and John were going up to the temple at the time of prayer—at three in the afternoon. 2Now a man crippled from birth was being carried to the temple gate called Beautiful, where he was put every day to beg from those going into the temple courts. 3When he saw Peter and John about to enter, he asked them for money. 4Peter looked straight at him, as did John. Then Peter said, “Look at us!” 5So the man gave them his attention, expecting to get something from them. Ps 55:17; Ac 14:8

6Then Peter said, “Silver or gold I do not have, but what I have I give you. In the name of Jesus Christ of Nazareth, walk.” 7Taking him by the right hand, he helped him up, and instantly the man's feet and ankles became strong. 8He jumped to his feet and began to walk. Then he went with them into the temple courts, walking and jumping, and praising God. 9When all the people saw him walking and praising God, 10they recognized him as the same man who used to sit begging at the temple gate called Beautiful, and they were filled with wonder and amazement at what had happened to him. Ac 4:10,16,21

Peter Speaks to the Onlookers

11While the beggar held on to Peter and John, all the people were astonished and came running to them in the place called Solomon's Colonnade. 12When Peter saw this, he said to them: “Men of Israel, why does this surprise you? Why do you stare at us as if by our own power or godliness we had made this man walk? 13The God of Abraham, Isaac and Jacob, the God of our fathers, has glorified his servant Jesus. You handed him over to be killed, and you disowned him before Pilate, though he had decided to let him go. 14You disowned the Holy and Righteous One and asked that a murderer be released to you. 15You killed the author of life, but God raised him from the dead. We are witnesses of this. 16By faith in the name of Jesus, this man whom you see and know was made strong. It is Jesus' name and the faith that comes through him that has given this complete healing to him, as you can all see. Mk 1:24

17“Now, brothers, I know that you acted in ignorance, as did your leaders. 18But this is how God fulfilled what he had foretold through all the prophets, saying that his Christ[a] would suffer. 19Repent, then, and turn to God, so that your sins may be wiped out, that times of refreshing may come from the Lord, 20and that he may send the Christ, who has been appointed for you—even Jesus. 21He must remain in heaven until the time comes for God to restore everything, as he promised long ago through his holy prophets. 22For Moses said, ‘The Lord your God will raise up for you a prophet like me from among your own people; you must listen to everything he tells you. 23Anyone who does not listen to him will be completely cut off from among his people.’[b]

24“Indeed, all the prophets from Samuel on, as many as have spoken, have foretold these days. 25And you are heirs of the prophets and of the covenant God made with your fathers. He said to

[a] 18 Or *Messiah*; also in verse 20 [b] 23 Deut. 18:15,18,19

Abraham, 'Through your offspring all peoples on earth will be blessed.'[a] [26]When God raised up his servant, he sent him first to you to bless you by turning each of you from your wicked ways."

Peter and John Before the Sanhedrin

4 The priests and the captain of the temple guard and the Sadducees came up to Peter and John while they were speaking to the people. [2]They were greatly disturbed because the apostles were teaching the people and proclaiming in Jesus the resurrection of the dead. [3]They seized Peter and John, and because it was evening, they put them in jail until the next day. [4]But many who heard the message believed, and the number of men grew to about five thousand. Lk 22:4; Ac 5:18

[5]The next day the rulers, elders and teachers of the law met in Jerusalem. [6]Annas the high priest was there, and so were Caiaphas, John, Alexander and the other men of the high priest's family. [7]They had Peter and John brought before them and began to question them: "By what power or what name did you do this?" Mt 26:3; Lk 3:2; 23:13

[8]Then Peter, filled with the Holy Spirit, said to them: "Rulers and elders of the people! [9]If we are being called to account today for an act of kindness shown to a cripple and are asked how he was healed, [10]then know this, you and all the people of Israel: It is by the name of Jesus Christ of Nazareth, whom you crucified but whom God raised from the dead, that this man stands before you healed. [11]He is Lk 23:13; Ac 2:24

"'the stone you builders rejected,
which has become the capstone.[b]'[c]

[12]Salvation is found in no one else, for there is no other name under heaven given to men by which we must be saved." Mt 1:21; Ac 10:43; 1Ti 2:5

[13]When they saw the courage of Peter and John and realized that they were unschooled, ordinary men, they were astonished and they took note that these men had been with Jesus. [14]But since they could see the man who had been healed standing there with them, there was nothing they could say. [15]So they ordered them to withdraw from the Sanhedrin and then conferred together. [16]"What are we going to do with these men?" they asked. "Everybody living in Jerusalem knows they have done an outstanding miracle, and we cannot deny it. [17]But to stop this thing from spreading any further among the people, we must warn these men to speak no longer to anyone in this name."

[18]Then they called them in again and commanded them not to speak or teach at all in the name of Jesus. [19]But Peter and John replied, "Judge for yourselves whether it is right in God's sight to obey you rather than God. [20]For we cannot help speaking about what we have seen and heard." Ac 5:29,40

[21]After further threats they let them go. They could not decide how to punish them, because all the people were praising God for what had happened. [22]For the man who was miraculously healed was over forty years old. Ac 5:26

The Believers' Prayer

[23]On their release, Peter and John went back to their own people and reported all that the chief priests and elders had said to them. [24]When they heard this, they raised their voices together in prayer to God. "Sovereign Lord," they said, "you made the heaven and the earth and the sea, and everything in them. [25]You spoke by the Holy Spirit through the mouth of your servant, our father David: Ac 1:16

"'Why do the nations rage
and the peoples plot in vain?
[26]The kings of the earth take their stand
and the rulers gather together
against the Lord
and against his Anointed One.[d]'[e]

[27]Indeed Herod and Pontius Pilate met together with the Gentiles and the people[f] of Israel in this city to conspire against your holy servant Jesus, whom you anointed. [28]They did what your power and will had decided beforehand should happen. [29]Now, Lord, consider their threats and enable your servants to speak your word with great boldness. [30]Stretch out your hand to heal and perform miraculous signs and wonders through the name of your holy servant Jesus." Lk 4:18; Ac 2:23; 10:38

[31]After they prayed, the place where they were meeting was shaken. And they were all filled with the Holy Spirit and spoke the word of God boldly.

The Believers Share Their Possessions

[32]All the believers were one in heart and mind. No one claimed that any of his possessions was his own, but they shared everything they had. [33]With great power the apostles continued to testify to the resurrection of the Lord Jesus, and much grace was upon them all. [34]There were no needy persons among them. For from time to time those who owned lands or houses sold them, brought the money from the sales [35]and put it at the apostles' feet, and it was distributed to anyone as he had need. Ac 2:44-45; 6:1

[36]Joseph, a Levite from Cyprus, whom the apostles called Barnabas (which means Son of Encouragement), [37]sold a field he owned and brought the money and put it at the apostles' feet. Ac 5:2; 9:27

[a]*25* Gen. 22:18; 26:4 [b]*11* Or *cornerstone* [c]*11* Psalm 118:22 [d]*26* That is, Christ or Messiah [e]*26* Psalm 2:1,2
[f]*27* The Greek is plural.

Ananias and Sapphira

5 Now a man named Ananias, together with his wife Sapphira, also sold a piece of property. [2]With his wife's full knowledge he kept back part of the money for himself, but brought the rest and put it at the apostles' feet. Ac 4:35,37

[3]Then Peter said, "Ananias, how is it that Satan has so filled your heart that you have lied to the Holy Spirit and have kept for yourself some of the money you received for the land? [4]Didn't it belong to you before it was sold? And after it was sold, wasn't the money at your disposal? What made you think of doing such a thing? You have not lied to men but to God." Lev 6:2; Dt 23:21

[5]When Ananias heard this, he fell down and died. And great fear seized all who heard what had happened. [6]Then the young men came forward, wrapped up his body, and carried him out and buried him. Jn 19:40

[7]About three hours later his wife came in, not knowing what had happened. [8]Peter asked her, "Tell me, is this the price you and Ananias got for the land?"

"Yes," she said, "that is the price."

[9]Peter said to her, "How could you agree to test the Spirit of the Lord? Look! The feet of the men who buried your husband are at the door, and they will carry you out also."

[10]At that moment she fell down at his feet and died. Then the young men came in and, finding her dead, carried her out and buried her beside her husband. [11]Great fear seized the whole church and all who heard about these events. Ac 19:17

The Apostles Heal Many

[12]The apostles performed many miraculous signs and wonders among the people. And all the believers used to meet together in Solomon's Colonnade. [13]No one else dared join them, even though they were highly regarded by the people. [14]Nevertheless, more and more men and women believed in the Lord and were added to their number. [15]As a result, people brought the sick into the streets and laid them on beds and mats so that at least Peter's shadow might fall on some of them as he passed by. [16]Crowds gathered also from the towns around Jerusalem, bringing their sick and those tormented by evil[a] spirits, and all of them were healed. Ac 2:47; 3:11; 19:12

The Apostles Persecuted

[17]Then the high priest and all his associates, who were members of the party of the Sadducees, were filled with jealousy. [18]They arrested the apostles and put them in the public jail. [19]But during the night an angel of the Lord opened the doors of the jail and brought them out. [20]"Go, stand in the temple courts," he said, "and tell the people the full message of this new life." Jn 6:63,68; Ac 4:1

[21]At daybreak they entered the temple courts, as they had been told, and began to teach the people.

When the high priest and his associates arrived, they called together the Sanhedrin—the full assembly of the elders of Israel—and sent to the jail for the apostles. [22]But on arriving at the jail, the officers did not find them there. So they went back and reported, [23]"We found the jail securely locked, with the guards standing at the doors; but when we opened them, we found no one inside." [24]On hearing this report, the captain of the temple guard and the chief priests were puzzled, wondering what would come of this. Ac 4:1,5-6

[25]Then someone came and said, "Look! The men you put in jail are standing in the temple courts teaching the people." [26]At that, the captain went with his officers and brought the apostles. They did not use force, because they feared that the people would stone them. Ac 4:21

[27]Having brought the apostles, they made them appear before the Sanhedrin to be questioned by the high priest. [28]"We gave you strict orders not to teach in this name," he said. "Yet you have filled Jerusalem with your teaching and are determined to make us guilty of this man's blood." Mt 23:35

[29]Peter and the other apostles replied: "We must obey God rather than men! [30]The God of our fathers raised Jesus from the dead—whom you had killed by hanging him on a tree. [31]God exalted him to his own right hand as Prince and Savior that he might give repentance and forgiveness of sins to Israel. [32]We are witnesses of these things, and so is the Holy Spirit, whom God has given to those who obey him." Jn 15:26; Ac 3:13; 4:19

[33]When they heard this, they were furious and wanted to put them to death. [34]But a Pharisee named Gamaliel, a teacher of the law, who was honored by all the people, stood up in the Sanhedrin and ordered that the men be put outside for a little while. [35]Then he addressed them: "Men of Israel, consider carefully what you intend to do to these men. [36]Some time ago Theudas appeared, claiming to be somebody, and about four hundred men rallied to him. He was killed, all his followers were dispersed, and it all came to nothing. [37]After him, Judas the Galilean appeared in the days of the census and led a band of people in revolt. He too was killed, and all his followers were scattered. [38]Therefore, in the present case I advise you: Leave these men alone! Let them go! For if their purpose or activity is of human origin, it will fail. [39]But if it is from God, you will not be able to stop these men; you will only find yourselves fighting against God." Ac 7:51; 11:17

[40]His speech persuaded them. They called the

[a]16 Greek *unclean*

apostles in and had them flogged. Then they ordered them not to speak in the name of Jesus, and let them go. Mt 10:17

41The apostles left the Sanhedrin, rejoicing because they had been counted worthy of suffering disgrace for the Name. 42Day after day, in the temple courts and from house to house, they never stopped teaching and proclaiming the good news that Jesus is the Christ.[a] Jn 15:21; Ac 2:46

The Choosing of the Seven

6 In those days when the number of disciples was increasing, the Grecian Jews among them complained against the Hebraic Jews because their widows were being overlooked in the daily distribution of food. 2So the Twelve gathered all the disciples together and said, "It would not be right for us to neglect the ministry of the word of God in order to wait on tables. 3Brothers, choose seven men from among you who are known to be full of the Spirit and wisdom. We will turn this responsibility over to them 4and will give our attention to prayer and the ministry of the word." Ac 4:35; 9:29

LIVING  **INSIGHT**

What often gets overlooked in the midst of our breakneck schedules? It can be summarized in just a single, simple (but oh, so important) word: helping.

(See Acts 6:3.)

5This proposal pleased the whole group. They chose Stephen, a man full of faith and of the Holy Spirit; also Philip, Procorus, Nicanor, Timon, Parmenas, and Nicolas from Antioch, a convert to Judaism. 6They presented these men to the apostles, who prayed and laid their hands on them.

7So the word of God spread. The number of disciples in Jerusalem increased rapidly, and a large number of priests became obedient to the faith. Ac 12:24; 19:20

Stephen Seized

8Now Stephen, a man full of God's grace and power, did great wonders and miraculous signs among the people. 9Opposition arose, however, from members of the Synagogue of the Freedmen (as it was called)—Jews of Cyrene and Alexandria as well as the provinces of Cilicia and Asia. These men began to argue with Stephen, 10but they could not stand up against his wisdom or the Spirit by whom he spoke. Lk 21:15; Jn 4:48

11Then they secretly persuaded some men to say, "We have heard Stephen speak words of blasphemy against Moses and against God."

12So they stirred up the people and the elders and the teachers of the law. They seized Stephen and brought him before the Sanhedrin. 13They produced false witnesses, who testified, "This fellow never stops speaking against this holy place and against the law. 14For we have heard him say that this Jesus of Nazareth will destroy this place and change the customs Moses handed down to us." Mt 5:22; Ac 15:1

15All who were sitting in the Sanhedrin looked intently at Stephen, and they saw that his face was like the face of an angel. Mt 5:22

Stephen's Speech to the Sanhedrin

7 Then the high priest asked him, "Are these charges true?"

2To this he replied: "Brothers and fathers, listen to me! The God of glory appeared to our father Abraham while he was still in Mesopotamia, before he lived in Haran. 3'Leave your country and your people,' God said, 'and go to the land I will show you.'[b] Ac 22:1; Ge 11:31; 15:7

4"So he left the land of the Chaldeans and settled in Haran. After the death of his father, God sent him to this land where you are now living. 5He gave him no inheritance here, not even a foot of ground. But God promised him that he and his descendants after him would possess the land, even though at that time Abraham had no child. 6God spoke to him in this way: 'Your descendants will be strangers in a country not their own, and they will be enslaved and mistreated four hundred years. 7But I will punish the nation they serve as slaves,' God said, 'and afterward they will come out of that country and worship me in this place.'[c] 8Then he gave Abraham the covenant of circumcision. And Abraham became the father of Isaac and circumcised him eight days after his birth. Later Isaac became the father of Jacob, and Jacob became the father of the twelve patriarchs.

9"Because the patriarchs were jealous of Joseph, they sold him as a slave into Egypt. But God was with him 10and rescued him from all his troubles. He gave Joseph wisdom and enabled him to gain the goodwill of Pharaoh king of Egypt; so he made him ruler over Egypt and all his palace.

11"Then a famine struck all Egypt and Canaan, bringing great suffering, and our fathers could not find food. 12When Jacob heard that there was grain in Egypt, he sent our fathers on their first visit. 13On their second visit, Joseph told his brothers who he was, and Pharaoh learned about Joseph's family. 14After this, Joseph sent for his father Jacob and his whole family, seventy-five in all. 15Then Jacob went down to Egypt, where he and our fa-

[a] 42 Or *Messiah* [b] 3 Gen. 12:1 [c] 7 Gen. 15:13,14

STEPHEN

Life on the Raw Edge of Faith

"Now Stephen, a man full of God's grace and power, did great wonders and miraculous signs among the people."
—ACTS 6:8

Every once in a while I see a meteor flash across the sky. And when I do, I always think of Stephen. In the book of Acts, Stephen appears in a bright flash—suddenly he's there, suddenly he's gone. Stephen was a man who lived on the raw edge of faith. He operated with a paradigm that set him free from the shackles of sight. He didn't have to *see* in order to believe; he simply faced opposition with eyes fixed on the Lord.

Stephen was "a man full of faith and of the Holy Spirit" (Acts 6:5). From this point on through chapter 7 the Bible's zoom lens focuses in on this man. Stephen's name means "crown," or "wreath," the laurels given to champion athletes at the earliest Olympic games. I like to think that in the heart of Stephen's mother there rested a great dream of success for her son. He certainly lived the life of a champion of faith.

Stephen was a layperson who was picked by the believers to help the apostles in serving the Greek-speaking members of the early church. He emerged as a leader in that gifted group of seven. But did he do anything worth remembering? The Bible says that he "did great wonders and miraculous signs among the people" (6:8). So God clearly used Stephen in that diaconal capacity in a most striking way, authenticating Stephen's actions with miraculous power. But with that power came opposition.

Stephen's speech to the Sanhedrin (Acts 7) takes no more than ten minutes to read. But consider the circumstances under which Stephen was speaking. These people weren't an adoring audience—they hated him! His opponents had done their homework—piling up false testimonies against him (6:11–12). But God's Spirit was so obviously and so powerfully at work in this man of God (6:15). Stephen's face shone with God's quiet, empowering presence, giving him uncommon confidence. In response he unveiled merely a small part of the iceberg of truth that was resident within him. These are the last words we hear from Stephen; in effect, this was his last will and testament. And his words centered around the truth about the Messiah, the One who had made such a incredibly transforming difference in his life.

Stephen responded to the false charges with a simple presentation of the facts. In verses 2–50 of chapter 7, he showed his deep respect for Moses, for God's law, for the temple and for the testimony of his Jewish forefathers. His words stand in direct contrast to the false accusations brought against him (6:13–14). Next, Stephen confronted the sin of the Sanhedrin by speaking the truth: "You stiff-necked people, with uncircumcised hearts and ears! You are just like your fathers: You always resist the Holy Spirit!" (7:51). Take a moment to observe the reaction of those who clung to a dry, dusty, lifeless religious system instead of to a living Christ. When confronted with sin, they became infuriated, not repentant. I see this respectable council of religious leaders growling at Stephen, their lips curled up like a pack of angry dogs (7:54). Upon hearing this speech, delivered with perfect theology, accurate history, and even the physical manifestation of God's blessing, they responded not by heeding the message but by killing the messenger. They dragged Stephen out of the city and stoned him.

Even as Stephen anticipated his death, he looked up to see the heavens opened and God's glory shining in incomparable majesty. He saw Jesus, waiting to receive him. As the stones battered his body, he fell to his knees in prayer. His words echoed not only Jesus' last words on the cross, but also the words of many saints down through the centuries: "Lord, do not hold this sin against them" (7:60).

The stones lie in silent testimony on the ground—giving us a sense of perspective on our own lives. Reading this passage gives me the same sort of feeling I get when I walk through a great battleground or stand next to a war memorial. The sands of time erase the noise of now. Stephen's story stands as a testament, a memorial, to all people who have died in faithful service to the living Christ—and as a challenge to all of us to consider what *we* are willing to sacrifice in order to live for God.

thers died. [16]Their bodies were brought back to Shechem and placed in the tomb that Abraham had bought from the sons of Hamor at Shechem for a certain sum of money. Ge 45:1-4; Dt 10:22; Jos 24:32

[17]"As the time drew near for God to fulfill his promise to Abraham, the number of our people in Egypt greatly increased. [18]Then another king, who knew nothing about Joseph, became ruler of Egypt. [19]He dealt treacherously with our people and oppressed our forefathers by forcing them to throw out their newborn babies so that they would die. Ex 1:10-22

[20]"At that time Moses was born, and he was no ordinary child.[a] For three months he was cared for in his father's house. [21]When he was placed outside, Pharaoh's daughter took him and brought him up as her own son. [22]Moses was educated in all the wisdom of the Egyptians and was powerful in speech and action. 1Ki 4:30; Isa 19:11

[23]"When Moses was forty years old, he decided to visit his fellow Israelites. [24]He saw one of them being mistreated by an Egyptian, so he went to his defense and avenged him by killing the Egyptian. [25]Moses thought that his own people would realize that God was using him to rescue them, but they did not. [26]The next day Moses came upon two Israelites who were fighting. He tried to reconcile them by saying, 'Men, you are brothers; why do you want to hurt each other?'

[27]"But the man who was mistreating the other pushed Moses aside and said, 'Who made you ruler and judge over us? [28]Do you want to kill me as you killed the Egyptian yesterday?'[b] [29]When Moses heard this, he fled to Midian, where he settled as a foreigner and had two sons. Ex 2:11-15

[30]"After forty years had passed, an angel appeared to Moses in the flames of a burning bush in the desert near Mount Sinai. [31]When he saw this, he was amazed at the sight. As he went over to look more closely, he heard the Lord's voice: [32]'I am the God of your fathers, the God of Abraham, Isaac and Jacob.'[c] Moses trembled with fear and did not dare to look. Ex 3:1-4,6

[33]"Then the Lord said to him, 'Take off your sandals; the place where you are standing is holy ground. [34]I have indeed seen the oppression of my people in Egypt. I have heard their groaning and have come down to set them free. Now come, I will send you back to Egypt.'[d] Ex 3:5,7-10

[35]"This is the same Moses whom they had rejected with the words, 'Who made you ruler and judge?' He was sent to be their ruler and deliverer by God himself, through the angel who appeared to him in the bush. [36]He led them out of Egypt and did wonders and miraculous signs in Egypt, at the Red Sea[e] and for forty years in the desert.

[37]"This is that Moses who told the Israelites, 'God will send you a prophet like me from your own people.'[f] [38]He was in the assembly in the desert, with the angel who spoke to him on Mount Sinai, and with our fathers; and he received living words to pass on to us. Dt 18:15,18; Ro 3:2

[39]"But our fathers refused to obey him. Instead, they rejected him and in their hearts turned back to Egypt. [40]They told Aaron, 'Make us gods who will go before us. As for this fellow Moses who led us out of Egypt—we don't know what has happened to him!'[g] [41]That was the time they made an idol in the form of a calf. They brought sacrifices to it and held a celebration in honor of what their hands had made. [42]But God turned away and gave them over to the worship of the heavenly bodies. This agrees with what is written in the book of the prophets:

"'Did you bring me sacrifices and offerings
forty years in the desert, O house of Israel?
[43]You have lifted up the shrine of Molech
and the star of your god Rephan,
the idols you made to worship.
Therefore I will send you into exile'[h] beyond
Babylon. Am 5:25-27

[44]"Our forefathers had the tabernacle of the Testimony with them in the desert. It had been made as God directed Moses, according to the pattern he had seen. [45]Having received the tabernacle, our fathers under Joshua brought it with them when they took the land from the nations God drove out before them. It remained in the land until the time of David, [46]who enjoyed God's favor and asked that he might provide a dwelling place for the God of Jacob.[i] [47]But it was Solomon who built the house for him. Jos 3:14-17; 2Sa 7:8-16

[48]"However, the Most High does not live in houses made by men. As the prophet says:

[49]"'Heaven is my throne,
and the earth is my footstool. Mt 5:34-35
What kind of house will you build for me?
says the Lord.
Or where will my resting place be?
[50]Has not my hand made all these things?'[j]

[51]"You stiff-necked people, with uncircumcised hearts and ears! You are just like your fathers: You always resist the Holy Spirit! [52]Was there ever a prophet your fathers did not persecute? They even killed those who predicted the coming of the Righteous One. And now you have betrayed and murdered him— [53]you who have received the law that was put into effect through angels but have not obeyed it." Ac 3:14; Gal 3:19

[a]20 Or *was fair in the sight of God* [b]28 Exodus 2:14 [c]32 Exodus 3:6 [d]34 Exodus 3:5,7,8,10 [e]36 That is, Sea of Reeds [f]37 Deut. 18:15 [g]40 Exodus 32:1 [h]43 Amos 5:25-27 [i]46 Some early manuscripts *the house of Jacob* [j]50 Isaiah 66:1,2

The Stoning of Stephen

[54]When they heard this, they were furious and gnashed their teeth at him. [55]But Stephen, full of the Holy Spirit, looked up to heaven and saw the glory of God, and Jesus standing at the right hand of God. [56]"Look," he said, "I see heaven open and the Son of Man standing at the right hand of God."

[57]At this they covered their ears and, yelling at the top of their voices, they all rushed at him, [58]dragged him out of the city and began to stone him. Meanwhile, the witnesses laid their clothes at the feet of a young man named Saul. Lev 24:14,16

[59]While they were stoning him, Stephen prayed, "Lord Jesus, receive my spirit." [60]Then he fell on his knees and cried out, "Lord, do not hold this sin against them." When he had said this, he fell asleep. Ps 31:5; Ac 9:40

The Church Enlarged **Chapters 8–12**

This section pictures a time of dynamic growth for the church. The gospel of Jesus Christ, the good news of salvation, was changing lives daily—and even beginning to break down some of the walls between Jews and Gentiles. Peter remained the central character as he continued to provide leadership for the growing church.

In these chapters a period of about 12 years went by as the church was enlarged. The outreach of the church stretched into Judea and even up into the region of the once-hated Samaritans. God was at work. Walls of prejudice were crumbling. The Holy Spirit empowered believers as the gospel of Jesus spread all over the land.

8 And Saul was there, giving approval to his death. Ac 7:58

The Church Persecuted and Scattered

On that day a great persecution broke out against the church at Jerusalem, and all except the apostles were scattered throughout Judea and Samaria. [2]Godly men buried Stephen and mourned deeply for him. [3]But Saul began to destroy the church. Going from house to house, he dragged off men and women and put them in prison.

Philip in Samaria

[4]Those who had been scattered preached the word wherever they went. [5]Philip went down to a city in Samaria and proclaimed the Christ[a] there. [6]When the crowds heard Philip and saw the miraculous signs he did, they all paid close attention to what he said. [7]With shrieks, evil[b] spirits came out of many, and many paralytics and cripples were healed. [8]So there was great joy in that city.

Simon the Sorcerer

[9]Now for some time a man named Simon had practiced sorcery in the city and amazed all the people of Samaria. He boasted that he was someone great, [10]and all the people, both high and low, gave him their attention and exclaimed, "This man is the divine power known as the Great Power." [11]They followed him because he had amazed them for a long time with his magic. [12]But when they believed Philip as he preached the good news of the kingdom of God and the name of Jesus Christ, they were baptized, both men and women. [13]Simon himself believed and was baptized. And he followed Philip everywhere, astonished by the great signs and miracles he saw. Ac 13:6; 19:11

[14]When the apostles in Jerusalem heard that Samaria had accepted the word of God, they sent Peter and John to them. [15]When they arrived, they prayed for them that they might receive the Holy Spirit, [16]because the Holy Spirit had not yet come upon any of them; they had simply been baptized into[c] the name of the Lord Jesus. [17]Then Peter and John placed their hands on them, and they received the Holy Spirit. Ac 6:6; 19:2

[18]When Simon saw that the Spirit was given at the laying on of the apostles' hands, he offered them money [19]and said, "Give me also this ability so that everyone on whom I lay my hands may receive the Holy Spirit."

[20]Peter answered: "May your money perish with you, because you thought you could buy the gift of God with money! [21]You have no part or share in this ministry, because your heart is not right before God. [22]Repent of this wickedness and pray to the Lord. Perhaps he will forgive you for having such a thought in your heart. [23]For I see that you are full of bitterness and captive to sin." 2Ki 5:16

[24]Then Simon answered, "Pray to the Lord for me so that nothing you have said may happen to me." Ex 8:8; Nu 21:7; 1Ki 13:6

[25]When they had testified and proclaimed the word of the Lord, Peter and John returned to Jerusalem, preaching the gospel in many Samaritan villages. Ac 13:48

Philip and the Ethiopian

[26]Now an angel of the Lord said to Philip, "Go south to the road—the desert road—that goes down from Jerusalem to Gaza." [27]So he started out, and on his way he met an Ethiopian[d] eunuch, an important official in charge of all the treasury of Candace, queen of the Ethiopians. This man had gone to Jerusalem to worship, [28]and on his way home was sitting in his chariot reading the book of Isaiah the prophet. [29]The Spirit told Philip, "Go to that chariot and stay near it." Jn 12:20

[30]Then Philip ran up to the chariot and heard the man reading Isaiah the prophet. "Do you understand what you are reading?" Philip asked.

[a]5 Or *Messiah* [b]7 Greek *unclean* [c]16 Or *in* [d]27 That is, from the upper Nile region

31“How can I,” he said, “unless someone explains it to me?” So he invited Philip to come up
and sit with him.

32The eunuch was reading this passage of Scripture:

“He was led like a sheep to the slaughter,
and as a lamb before the shearer is silent,
so he did not open his mouth.
33In his humiliation he was deprived of justice.
Who can speak of his descendants?
For his life was taken from the earth.”[a]

34The eunuch asked Philip, “Tell me, please,
who is the prophet talking about, himself or someone else?” 35Then Philip began with that very passage of Scripture and told him the good news
about Jesus. Lk 24:27; Ac 18:28

36As they traveled along the road, they came to
some water and the eunuch said, “Look, here is
water. Why shouldn’t I be baptized?”[b] 38And he
gave orders to stop the chariot. Then both Philip
and the eunuch went down into the water and
Philip baptized him. 39When they came up out of
the water, the Spirit of the Lord suddenly took
Philip away, and the eunuch did not see him again,
but went on his way rejoicing. 40Philip, however,
appeared at Azotus and traveled about, preaching
the gospel in all the towns until he reached Caesarea. 1Ki 18:12; 2Ki 2:16; Ac 10:47

Saul’s Conversion

9 Meanwhile, Saul was still breathing out murderous threats against the Lord’s disciples. He
went to the high priest 2and asked him for letters
to the synagogues in Damascus, so that if he found
any there who belonged to the Way, whether men
or women, he might take them as prisoners to
Jerusalem. 3As he neared Damascus on his journey, suddenly a light from heaven flashed around
him. 4He fell to the ground and heard a voice say
to him, “Saul, Saul, why do you persecute me?”

5“Who are you, Lord?” Saul asked.

“I am Jesus, whom you are persecuting,” he
replied. 6“Now get up and go into the city, and you
will be told what you must do.” Eze 3:22

7The men traveling with Saul stood there
speechless; they heard the sound but did not see
anyone. 8Saul got up from the ground, but when
he opened his eyes he could see nothing. So they
led him by the hand into Damascus. 9For three
days he was blind, and did not eat or drink anything. Da 10:7; Ac 22:9

10In Damascus there was a disciple named Ananias. The Lord called to him in a vision, “Ananias!” Ac 10:3,17,19

“Yes, Lord,” he answered.

11The Lord told him, “Go to the house of Judas
on Straight Street and ask for a man from Tarsus
named Saul, for he is praying. 12In a vision he has
seen a man named Ananias come and place his
hands on him to restore his sight.” Ac 21:39; 22:3

13“Lord,” Ananias answered, “I have heard
many reports about this man and all the harm he
has done to your saints in Jerusalem. 14And he has
come here with authority from the chief priests to
arrest all who call on your name.” Ro 1:7; 16:2,15

15But the Lord said to Ananias, “Go! This man
is my chosen instrument to carry my name before
the Gentiles and their kings and before the people
of Israel. 16I will show him how much he must
suffer for my name.” Ac 13:2; 20:23; Ro 11:13

17Then Ananias went to the house and entered
it. Placing his hands on Saul, he said, “Brother
Saul, the Lord—Jesus, who appeared to you on
the road as you were coming here—has sent me so
that you may see again and be filled with the Holy
Spirit.” 18Immediately, something like scales fell
from Saul’s eyes, and he could see again. He got up
and was baptized, 19and after taking some food, he
regained his strength. Ac 22:4-16; 26:9-18

Saul in Damascus and Jerusalem

Saul spent several days with the disciples in Damascus. 20At once he began to preach in the synagogues that Jesus is the Son of God. 21All those
who heard him were astonished and asked, “Isn’t
he the man who raised havoc in Jerusalem among
those who call on this name? And hasn’t he come
here to take them as prisoners to the chief priests?”
22Yet Saul grew more and more powerful and baffled the Jews living in Damascus by proving that
Jesus is the Christ.[c] Ac 8:3; 18:5,28

23After many days had gone by, the Jews conspired to kill him, 24but Saul learned of their plan.
Day and night they kept close watch on the city
gates in order to kill him. 25But his followers took
him by night and lowered him in a basket through
an opening in the wall. 1Sa 19:12; Ac 20:3,19

26When he came to Jerusalem, he tried to join
the disciples, but they were all afraid of him, not
believing that he really was a disciple. 27But Barnabas took him and brought him to the apostles. He
told them how Saul on his journey had seen the
Lord and that the Lord had spoken to him, and
how in Damascus he had preached fearlessly in the
name of Jesus. 28So Saul stayed with them and
moved about freely in Jerusalem, speaking boldly
in the name of the Lord. 29He talked and debated
with the Grecian Jews, but they tried to kill him.
30When the brothers learned of this, they took him
down to Caesarea and sent him off to Tarsus.

31Then the church throughout Judea, Galilee

[a] 33 Isaiah 53:7,8 [b] 36 Some late manuscripts *baptized?” 37Philip said, “If you believe with all your heart, you may.” The eunuch answered, “I believe that Jesus Christ is the Son of God.”* [c] 22 Or *Messiah*

PHILIP

The Evangelist

"Then Philip began with that very passage of Scripture and told him the good news about Jesus."

—ACTS 8:35

Many Christians wrestle with that little ten-letter word called "evangelism." Whether out of fear, intimidation, ignorance or indifference, many followers of Jesus choose to declare themselves "silent witnesses" of God's work in their lives. Some who carry on the work of evangelism may end up offending listeners with an in-your-face, occasionally even rude, approach. Others may squeeze the life out of a living relationship with Christ by keeping matters entirely on an intellectual level.

Philip illustrates the Biblical method of evangelism. He was, quite simply, a Christian who was on fire for the Lord. He had been summoned into Samaria, an area shunned by the Jews for racial and religious reasons, where he spread the good news about Jesus Christ. And the results were incredible! God confirmed Philip's office among the Samaritans by performing many miracles through him (Acts 8:6–7). Philip's approach to evangelism was neither vague nor rude nor mute.

First, *Philip was sensitive to God's leading*. Here he was in the midst of an exciting crusade in Samaria, witnessing all sorts of bright new beginnings and hundreds of lives being changed—excitement that could only be generated if God was in that revival. But God called him out to the middle of a desert wasteland (8:26)—and Philip had the sensitivity to go where God led. You see, effective witnesses don't just suddenly arrive at the scene; they're led there as they meet regularly with God and seek His guidance and counsel. Philip possessed this discipline, and the Spirit of God moved in him when the time was right.

Second, *Philip was available*. He left immediately. Availability is sensitivity's twin. You can't have one without the other. Where was he going? Philip didn't know for sure, but God did. He was sending his evangelist out to meet an Ethiopian official at the precise moment of that man's greatest need.

Third, *Philip was proactive*. At the Spirit's leading he took the initiative and ran up to this man's chariot, not knowing what he would find. And here was this guy reading aloud from Isaiah 53. Don't tell me God doesn't know what he's doing!

Fourth, *Philip was tactful*. When Philip greeted the Ethiopian official, he didn't hit him with 17 theological positions on and 12 hermeneutical approaches to the text of Isaiah. He undoubtedly could have run intellectual circles around that politician at that moment, but his initial question was gentle and gracious: "Do you understand what you are reading?" (8:30). Then he waited for the man to answer: "How can I . . . unless someone explains it to me?" (8:31). And Philip *didn't* say, "I thought you would never ask"; he had simply waited for an invitation, and then came up alongside and told him the good news.

Fifth, *Philip was explicit and exact in his message*. Philip told this politician about Jesus, plain and simple. He didn't talk about the work in Samaria, the financial conditions in Ethiopia, or anything else. He simply presented the story of Jesus to this man who was hungry to learn more about it.

Sixth, and finally, *Philip was decisive*. Look at what happened as the story unfolds: "As they traveled along the road, they came to some water" (8:36). The eunuch, being of a religious background, saw water and must have thought to himself, "That's what I need! I need to be baptized!" Philip saw the sincerity of the man's commitment, ordered the chariot to come to a stop and baptized him right on the spot.

The Lord is in the business of bringing people into His family by means of human mouths, human hands, human lives—imperfect though we are—in order to introduce lost people to the greatest Person they could ever meet—the Lord Jesus Christ. There is no more exciting Book in all the world than the one you hold in your hands—the Bible! It contains the most relevant, beautiful message that humanity could ever hear! It is alive with power and with truth. And its missionary vision is as vital and exciting today as it was in the days of Philip and the early church.

and Samaria enjoyed a time of peace. It was strengthened; and encouraged by the Holy Spirit, it grew in numbers, living in the fear of the Lord.

Aeneas and Dorcas

32As Peter traveled about the country, he went to visit the saints in Lydda. 33There he found a man named Aeneas, a paralytic who had been bedridden for eight years. 34"Aeneas," Peter said to him, "Jesus Christ heals you. Get up and take care of your mat." Immediately Aeneas got up. 35All those who lived in Lydda and Sharon saw him and turned to the Lord. Ac 3:6,16; 11:21

36In Joppa there was a disciple named Tabitha (which, when translated, is Dorcas[a]), who was always doing good and helping the poor. 37About that time she became sick and died, and her body was washed and placed in an upstairs room. 38Lydda was near Joppa; so when the disciples heard that Peter was in Lydda, they sent two men to him and urged him, "Please come at once!" 1Ti 2:10

39Peter went with them, and when he arrived he was taken upstairs to the room. All the widows stood around him, crying and showing him the robes and other clothing that Dorcas had made while she was still with them. Ac 6:1

40Peter sent them all out of the room; then he got down on his knees and prayed. Turning toward the dead woman, he said, "Tabitha, get up." She opened her eyes, and seeing Peter she sat up. 41He took her by the hand and helped her to her feet. Then he called the believers and the widows and presented her to them alive. 42This became known all over Joppa, and many people believed in the Lord. 43Peter stayed in Joppa for some time with a tanner named Simon. Lk 7:14; Ac 7:60; 10:6

Cornelius Calls for Peter

10 At Caesarea there was a man named Cornelius, a centurion in what was known as the Italian Regiment. 2He and all his family were devout and God-fearing; he gave generously to those in need and prayed to God regularly. 3One day at about three in the afternoon he had a vision. He distinctly saw an angel of God, who came to him and said, "Cornelius!" Ac 3:1; 5:19

4Cornelius stared at him in fear. "What is it, Lord?" he asked.

The angel answered, "Your prayers and gifts to the poor have come up as a memorial offering before God. 5Now send men to Joppa to bring back a man named Simon who is called Peter. 6He is staying with Simon the tanner, whose house is by the sea." Ac 9:43; Rev 8:4

7When the angel who spoke to him had gone, Cornelius called two of his servants and a devout soldier who was one of his attendants. 8He told them everything that had happened and sent them to Joppa. Ac 9:36

Peter's Vision

9About noon the following day as they were on their journey and approaching the city, Peter went up on the roof to pray. 10He became hungry and wanted something to eat, and while the meal was being prepared, he fell into a trance. 11He saw heaven opened and something like a large sheet being let down to earth by its four corners. 12It contained all kinds of four-footed animals, as well as reptiles of the earth and birds of the air. 13Then a voice told him, "Get up, Peter. Kill and eat."

14"Surely not, Lord!" Peter replied. "I have never eaten anything impure or unclean." Dt 14:3-20

15The voice spoke to him a second time, "Do not call anything impure that God has made clean." Ro 14:14,17,20; 1Co 10:25; 1Ti 4:3-4

16This happened three times, and immediately the sheet was taken back to heaven.

17While Peter was wondering about the meaning of the vision, the men sent by Cornelius found out where Simon's house was and stopped at the gate. 18They called out, asking if Simon who was known as Peter was staying there.

19While Peter was still thinking about the vision, the Spirit said to him, "Simon, three[b] men are looking for you. 20So get up and go downstairs. Do not hesitate to go with them, for I have sent them." Ac 8:29; 15:7-9

21Peter went down and said to the men, "I'm the one you're looking for. Why have you come?"

22The men replied, "We have come from Cornelius the centurion. He is a righteous and God-fearing man, who is respected by all the Jewish people. A holy angel told him to have you come to his house so that he could hear what you have to say." 23Then Peter invited the men into the house to be his guests. Ac 11:14

Peter at Cornelius' House

The next day Peter started out with them, and some of the brothers from Joppa went along. 24The following day he arrived in Caesarea. Cornelius was expecting them and had called together his relatives and close friends. 25As Peter entered the house, Cornelius met him and fell at his feet in reverence. 26But Peter made him get up. "Stand up," he said, "I am only a man myself." Rev 19:10

27Talking with him, Peter went inside and found a large gathering of people. 28He said to

[a]36 Both *Tabitha* (Aramaic) and *Dorcas* (Greek) mean *gazelle*.

[b]19 One early manuscript *two*; other manuscripts do not have the number.

them: "You are well aware that it is against our law for a Jew to associate with a Gentile or visit him. But God has shown me that I should not call any man impure or unclean. 29So when I was sent for, I came without raising any objection. May I ask why you sent for me?" Jn 4:9; Ac 15:8-9

30Cornelius answered: "Four days ago I was in my house praying at this hour, at three in the afternoon. Suddenly a man in shining clothes stood before me 31and said, 'Cornelius, God has heard your prayer and remembered your gifts to the poor. 32Send to Joppa for Simon who is called Peter. He is a guest in the home of Simon the tanner, who lives by the sea.' 33So I sent for you immediately, and it was good of you to come. Now we are all here in the presence of God to listen to everything the Lord has commanded you to tell us." Ac 11:5-14

34Then Peter began to speak: "I now realize how true it is that God does not show favoritism 35but accepts men from every nation who fear him and do what is right. 36You know the message God sent to the people of Israel, telling the good news of peace through Jesus Christ, who is Lord of all. 37You know what has happened throughout Judea, beginning in Galilee after the baptism that John preached— 38how God anointed Jesus of Nazareth with the Holy Spirit and power, and how he went around doing good and healing all who were under the power of the devil, because God was with him. Mt 28:18; Jn 3:2

39"We are witnesses of everything he did in the country of the Jews and in Jerusalem. They killed him by hanging him on a tree, 40but God raised him from the dead on the third day and caused him to be seen. 41He was not seen by all the people, but by witnesses whom God had already chosen—by us who ate and drank with him after he rose from the dead. 42He commanded us to preach to the people and to testify that he is the one whom God appointed as judge of the living and the dead. 43All the prophets testify about him that everyone who believes in him receives forgiveness of sins through his name." Isa 53:11; Ac 2:24; 5:30

44While Peter was still speaking these words, the Holy Spirit came on all who heard the message. 45The circumcised believers who had come with Peter were astonished that the gift of the Holy Spirit had been poured out even on the Gentiles. 46For they heard them speaking in tongues[a] and praising God. Mk 16:17; Ac 11:18

Then Peter said, 47"Can anyone keep these people from being baptized with water? They have received the Holy Spirit just as we have." 48So he ordered that they be baptized in the name of Jesus Christ. Then they asked Peter to stay with them for a few days. Ac 2:38; 8:36; 11:17

Peter Explains His Actions

11 The apostles and the brothers throughout Judea heard that the Gentiles also had received the word of God. 2So when Peter went up to Jerusalem, the circumcised believers criticized him 3and said, "You went into the house of uncircumcised men and ate with them." Ac 10:25,28

4Peter began and explained everything to them precisely as it had happened: 5"I was in the city of Joppa praying, and in a trance I saw a vision. I saw something like a large sheet being let down from heaven by its four corners, and it came down to where I was. 6I looked into it and saw four-footed animals of the earth, wild beasts, reptiles, and birds of the air. 7Then I heard a voice telling me, 'Get up, Peter. Kill and eat.' Ac 10:9-32

8"I replied, 'Surely not, Lord! Nothing impure or unclean has ever entered my mouth.'

9"The voice spoke from heaven a second time, 'Do not call anything impure that God has made clean.' 10This happened three times, and then it was all pulled up to heaven again. Ac 10:15

11"Right then three men who had been sent to me from Caesarea stopped at the house where I was staying. 12The Spirit told me to have no hesitation about going with them. These six brothers also went with me, and we entered the man's house. 13He told us how he had seen an angel appear in his house and say, 'Send to Joppa for Simon who is called Peter. 14He will bring you a message through which you and all your household will be saved.' Ac 8:29; 15:9

15"As I began to speak, the Holy Spirit came on them as he had come on us at the beginning. 16Then I remembered what the Lord had said: 'John baptized with[b] water, but you will be baptized with the Holy Spirit.' 17So if God gave them the same gift as he gave us, who believed in the Lord Jesus Christ, who was I to think that I could oppose God?" Ac 2:4; 10:45,47

18When they heard this, they had no further objections and praised God, saying, "So then, God has granted even the Gentiles repentance unto life." Ro 10:12-13; 2Co 7:10

The Church in Antioch

19Now those who had been scattered by the persecution in connection with Stephen traveled as far as Phoenicia, Cyprus and Antioch, telling the message only to Jews. 20Some of them, however, men from Cyprus and Cyrene, went to Antioch and began to speak to Greeks also, telling them the good news about the Lord Jesus. 21The Lord's hand was with them, and a great number of people believed and turned to the Lord. Lk 1:66; Ac 2:47

22News of this reached the ears of the church at Jerusalem, and they sent Barnabas to Antioch.

[a]46 Or *other languages* [b]16 Or *in*

23When he arrived and saw the evidence of the
grace of God, he was glad and encouraged them all
to remain true to the Lord with all their hearts.
24He was a good man, full of the Holy Spirit and
faith, and a great number of people were brought
to the Lord. Ac 5:14; 13:43

25Then Barnabas went to Tarsus to look for
Saul, 26and when he found him, he brought him to
Antioch. So for a whole year Barnabas and Saul
met with the church and taught great numbers of
people. The disciples were called Christians first at
Antioch. Ac 9:11; 26:28; 1Pe 4:16

27During this time some prophets came down
from Jerusalem to Antioch. 28One of them, named
Agabus, stood up and through the Spirit predicted
that a severe famine would spread over the entire
Roman world. (This happened during the reign of
Claudius.) 29The disciples, each according to his
ability, decided to provide help for the brothers
living in Judea. 30This they did, sending their gift
to the elders by Barnabas and Saul. Ac 12:25

Peter's Miraculous Escape From Prison

12 It was about this time that King Herod
arrested some who belonged to the church,
intending to persecute them. 2He had James, the
brother of John, put to death with the sword.
3When he saw that this pleased the Jews, he proceeded to seize Peter also. This happened during
the Feast of Unleavened Bread. 4After arresting
him, he put him in prison, handing him over to be
guarded by four squads of four soldiers each. Herod intended to bring him out for public trial after
the Passover. Ex 12:15; 23:15; Mt 4:21

5So Peter was kept in prison, but the church was
earnestly praying to God for him. Eph 6:18

6The night before Herod was to bring him to
trial, Peter was sleeping between two soldiers,
bound with two chains, and sentries stood guard
at the entrance. 7Suddenly an angel of the Lord
appeared and a light shone in the cell. He struck
Peter on the side and woke him up. "Quick, get
up!" he said, and the chains fell off Peter's wrists.

8Then the angel said to him, "Put on your
clothes and sandals." And Peter did so. "Wrap
your cloak around you and follow me," the angel
told him. 9Peter followed him out of the prison,
but he had no idea that what the angel was doing
was really happening; he thought he was seeing a
vision. 10They passed the first and second guards
and came to the iron gate leading to the city. It
opened for them by itself, and they went through
it. When they had walked the length of one street,
suddenly the angel left him. Ac 16:26

11Then Peter came to himself and said, "Now I
know without a doubt that the Lord sent his angel
and rescued me from Herod's clutches and from
everything the Jewish people were anticipating."

12When this had dawned on him, he went to the
house of Mary the mother of John, also called
Mark, where many people had gathered and were
praying. 13Peter knocked at the outer entrance,
and a servant girl named Rhoda came to answer
the door. 14When she recognized Peter's voice, she
was so overjoyed she ran back without opening it
and exclaimed, "Peter is at the door!" Lk 24:41

15"You're out of your mind," they told her.
When she kept insisting that it was so, they said,
"It must be his angel." Mt 18:10

16But Peter kept on knocking, and when they
opened the door and saw him, they were astonished. 17Peter motioned with his hand for them to
be quiet and described how the Lord had brought
him out of prison. "Tell James and the brothers
about this," he said, and then he left for another
place. Ac 13:16; 19:33

18In the morning, there was no small commotion among the soldiers as to what had become of
Peter. 19After Herod had a thorough search made
for him and did not find him, he cross-examined
the guards and ordered that they be executed.

Herod's Death

Then Herod went from Judea to Caesarea and
stayed there a while. 20He had been quarreling
with the people of Tyre and Sidon; they now
joined together and sought an audience with him.
Having secured the support of Blastus, a trusted
personal servant of the king, they asked for peace,
because they depended on the king's country for
their food supply. 1Ki 5:9,11; Eze 27:17; Ac 8:40

21On the appointed day Herod, wearing his royal robes, sat on his throne and delivered a public
address to the people. 22They shouted, "This is the
voice of a god, not of a man." 23Immediately, because Herod did not give praise to God, an angel
of the Lord struck him down, and he was eaten by
worms and died. 1Sa 25:38; 2Sa 24:16-17

24But the word of God continued to increase
and spread. Ac 6:7; Heb 4:12

25When Barnabas and Saul had finished their
mission, they returned from[a] Jerusalem, taking
with them John, also called Mark. Ac 11:30

The Church Expanded **Chapters 13–28**

In this final section the witness of the church was extended far beyond the neighboring communities of Jerusalem. Many accepted the gospel; some rejected it. However, the proclamation of the gospel moved further and further into uncharted territories. By now the apostle Paul had become the central character, and Peter had slipped into the shadows. By the powerful hand of the Holy Spirit and under

[a]25 Some manuscripts *to*

Paul's sensitive leadership, Jews and Gentiles were bound together into one family of faith, sharing a world mission of bringing the gospel to the ends of the earth.

Barnabas and Saul Sent Off

13 In the church at Antioch there were prophets and teachers: Barnabas, Simeon called
Niger, Lucius of Cyrene, Manaen (who had been
brought up with Herod the tetrarch) and Saul.
2While they were worshiping the Lord and fasting,
the Holy Spirit said, "Set apart for me Barnabas
and Saul for the work to which I have called
them." 3So after they had fasted and prayed, they
placed their hands on them and sent them off.

On Cyprus

4The two of them, sent on their way by the Holy
Spirit, went down to Seleucia and sailed from there
to Cyprus. 5When they arrived at Salamis, they
proclaimed the word of God in the Jewish synagogues. John was with them as their helper.
6They traveled through the whole island until
they came to Paphos. There they met a Jewish
sorcerer and false prophet named Bar-Jesus, 7who
was an attendant of the proconsul, Sergius Paulus.
The proconsul, an intelligent man, sent for Barnabas and Saul because he wanted to hear the word
of God. 8But Elymas the sorcerer (for that is what
his name means) opposed them and tried to turn
the proconsul from the faith. 9Then Saul, who was
also called Paul, filled with the Holy Spirit, looked
straight at Elymas and said, 10"You are a child of
the devil and an enemy of everything that is right!
You are full of all kinds of deceit and trickery. Will
you never stop perverting the right ways of the
Lord? 11Now the hand of the Lord is against you.
You are going to be blind, and for a time you will
be unable to see the light of the sun." 1Sa 5:6-7
Immediately mist and darkness came over him,
and he groped about, seeking someone to lead him
by the hand. 12When the proconsul saw what had
happened, he believed, for he was amazed at the
teaching about the Lord.

In Pisidian Antioch

13From Paphos, Paul and his companions sailed
to Perga in Pamphylia, where John left them to
return to Jerusalem. 14From Perga they went on to
Pisidian Antioch. On the Sabbath they entered the
synagogue and sat down. 15After the reading from
the Law and the Prophets, the synagogue rulers
sent word to them, saying, "Brothers, if you have
a message of encouragement for the people, please
speak." Ac 14:19,21; 16:13
16Standing up, Paul motioned with his hand
and said: "Men of Israel and you Gentiles who
worship God, listen to me! 17The God of the people of Israel chose our fathers; he made the people
prosper during their stay in Egypt, with mighty
power he led them out of that country, 18he endured their conduct[a] for about forty years in the
desert, 19he overthrew seven nations in Canaan
and gave their land to his people as their inheritance. 20All this took about 450 years. Dt 1:31; 7:6-8

LIVING  **INSIGHT**

God's people need to turn on the encouragement! The family of God is not a place for verbal put-downs, sarcastic jabs, critical comments or harsh judgment. We get enough of that from the world. This is the place we need where we can go to be encouraged . . . the place where we are free to be ourselves.

(See Acts 13:15.)

"After this, God gave them judges until the time
of Samuel the prophet. 21Then the people asked
for a king, and he gave them Saul son of Kish, of
the tribe of Benjamin, who ruled forty years. 22Af-
ter removing Saul, he made David their king. He
testified concerning him: 'I have found David son
of Jesse a man after my own heart; he will do
everything I want him to do.' 1Sa 13:14; 15:23,26
23"From this man's descendants God has
brought to Israel the Savior Jesus, as he promised.
24Before the coming of Jesus, John preached repentance and baptism to all the people of Israel.
25As John was completing his work, he said: 'Who
do you think I am? I am not that one. No, but he
is coming after me, whose sandals I am not worthy
to untie.' Mt 1:21; 3:11; Jn 1:27
26"Brothers, children of Abraham, and you
God-fearing Gentiles, it is to us that this message
of salvation has been sent. 27The people of Jerusalem and their rulers did not recognize Jesus, yet in
condemning him they fulfilled the words of the
prophets that are read every Sabbath. 28Though
they found no proper ground for a death sentence,
they asked Pilate to have him executed. 29When
they had carried out all that was written about
him, they took him down from the tree and laid
him in a tomb. 30But God raised him from the
dead, 31and for many days he was seen by those
who had traveled with him from Galilee to Jerusalem. They are now his witnesses to our people.
32"We tell you the good news: What God promised our fathers 33he has fulfilled for us, their children, by raising up Jesus. As it is written in the
second Psalm: Ac 5:42; Ro 4:13

[a] 18 Some manuscripts *and cared for them*

"'You are my Son;
today I have become your Father.'[a][b]

34The fact that God raised him from the dead,
never to decay, is stated in these words:

"'I will give you the holy and sure blessings
promised to David.'[c]

35So it is stated elsewhere:

"'You will not let your Holy One see decay.'[d]

36"For when David had served God's purpose in
his own generation, he fell asleep; he was buried
with his fathers and his body decayed. 37But the
one whom God raised from the dead did not see
decay. Ac 2:24,29; 1Ki 2:10
38"Therefore, my brothers, I want you to know
that through Jesus the forgiveness of sins is proclaimed to you. 39Through him everyone who believes is justified from everything you could not be
justified from by the law of Moses. 40Take care that
what the prophets have said does not happen to
you: Lk 24:47; Jn 3:15; Ro 3:28

41"'Look, you scoffers,
wonder and perish,
for I am going to do something in your days
that you would never believe,
even if someone told you.'[e]" Hab 1:5

42As Paul and Barnabas were leaving the synagogue, the people invited them to speak further
about these things on the next Sabbath. 43When
the congregation was dismissed, many of the Jews
and devout converts to Judaism followed Paul and
Barnabas, who talked with them and urged them
to continue in the grace of God. Ac 11:23; 14:22
44On the next Sabbath almost the whole city
gathered to hear the word of the Lord. 45When the
Jews saw the crowds, they were filled with jealousy
and talked abusively against what Paul was saying.
46Then Paul and Barnabas answered them boldly: "We had to speak the word of God to you first.
Since you reject it and do not consider yourselves
worthy of eternal life, we now turn to the Gentiles.
47For this is what the Lord has commanded us:

"'I have made you[f] a light for the Gentiles,
that you[f] may bring salvation to the ends
of the earth.'[g]" Lk 2:32; Isa 49:6

48When the Gentiles heard this, they were glad
and honored the word of the Lord; and all who
were appointed for eternal life believed. Ac 8:25
49The word of the Lord spread through the
whole region. 50But the Jews incited the God-fearing women of high standing and the leading men
of the city. They stirred up persecution against
Paul and Barnabas, and expelled them from their
region. 51So they shook the dust from their feet in
protest against them and went to Iconium. 52And
the disciples were filled with joy and with the Holy
Spirit. Mt 10:14; Lk 1:15

In Iconium

14 At Iconium Paul and Barnabas went as
usual into the Jewish synagogue. There
they spoke so effectively that a great number of
Jews and Gentiles believed. 2But the Jews who refused to believe stirred up the Gentiles and poisoned their minds against the brothers. 3So Paul
and Barnabas spent considerable time there,
speaking boldly for the Lord, who confirmed the
message of his grace by enabling them to do miraculous signs and wonders. 4The people of the
city were divided; some sided with the Jews, others
with the apostles. 5There was a plot afoot among
the Gentiles and Jews, together with their leaders,
to mistreat them and stone them. 6But they found
out about it and fled to the Lycaonian cities of
Lystra and Derbe and to the surrounding country,
7where they continued to preach the good news.

In Lystra and Derbe

8In Lystra there sat a man crippled in his feet,
who was lame from birth and had never walked.
9He listened to Paul as he was speaking. Paul
looked directly at him, saw that he had faith to be
healed 10and called out, "Stand up on your feet!"
At that, the man jumped up and began to walk.
11When the crowd saw what Paul had done,
they shouted in the Lycaonian language, "The
gods have come down to us in human form!"
12Barnabas they called Zeus, and Paul they called
Hermes because he was the chief speaker. 13The
priest of Zeus, whose temple was just outside the
city, brought bulls and wreaths to the city gates
because he and the crowd wanted to offer sacrifices to them. Ac 8:10; 28:6
14But when the apostles Barnabas and Paul
heard of this, they tore their clothes and rushed
out into the crowd, shouting: 15"Men, why are you

LIVING  **INSIGHT**

If you are overly impressed while in the presence of celebrities, it may be because you worship stardom and those individuals who've reached it. If you're not careful, you will erect secret idols in your mind. God, and God alone, is worthy of our worship!

(See Acts 14:15.)

[a] 33 Or *have begotten you* [b] 33 Psalm 2:7 [c] 34 Isaiah 55:3 [d] 35 Psalm 16:10 [e] 41 Hab. 1:5 [f] 47 The Greek is singular. [g] 47 Isaiah 49:6

doing this? We too are only men, human like you. We are bringing you good news, telling you to turn from these worthless things to the living God, who made heaven and earth and sea and everything in them. 16In the past, he let all nations go their own way. 17Yet he has not left himself without testimony: He has shown kindness by giving you rain from heaven and crops in their seasons; he provides you with plenty of food and fills your hearts with joy." 18Even with these words, they had difficulty keeping the crowd from sacrificing to them. Ac 10:26; Jas 5:17; Ro 1:20

19Then some Jews came from Antioch and Iconium and won the crowd over. They stoned Paul and dragged him outside the city, thinking he was dead. 20But after the disciples had gathered around him, he got up and went back into the city. The next day he and Barnabas left for Derbe. Ac 13:45

The Return to Antioch in Syria

21They preached the good news in that city and won a large number of disciples. Then they returned to Lystra, Iconium and Antioch, 22strengthening the disciples and encouraging them to remain true to the faith. "We must go through many hardships to enter the kingdom of God," they said. 23Paul and Barnabas appointed elders[a] for them in each church and, with prayer and fasting, committed them to the Lord, in whom they had put their trust. 24After going through Pisidia, they came into Pamphylia, 25and when they had preached the word in Perga, they went down to Attalia. 2Ti 3:12; Tit 1:5

26From Attalia they sailed back to Antioch, where they had been committed to the grace of God for the work they had now completed. 27On arriving there, they gathered the church together and reported all that God had done through them and how he had opened the door of faith to the Gentiles. 28And they stayed there a long time with the disciples. Ac 13:1,3; 1Co 16:9; 2Co 2:12

The Council at Jerusalem

15 Some men came down from Judea to Antioch and were teaching the brothers: "Unless you are circumcised, according to the custom taught by Moses, you cannot be saved." 2This brought Paul and Barnabas into sharp dispute and debate with them. So Paul and Barnabas were appointed, along with some other believers, to go up to Jerusalem to see the apostles and elders about this question. 3The church sent them on their way, and as they traveled through Phoenicia and Samaria, they told how the Gentiles had been converted. This news made all the brothers very glad. 4When they came to Jerusalem, they were welcomed by the church and the apostles and elders, to whom they reported everything God had done through them. Ac 14:27; Gal 5:2-3

5Then some of the believers who belonged to the party of the Pharisees stood up and said, "The Gentiles must be circumcised and required to obey the law of Moses." Ac 5:17

6The apostles and elders met to consider this question. 7After much discussion, Peter got up and addressed them: "Brothers, you know that some time ago God made a choice among you that the Gentiles might hear from my lips the message of the gospel and believe. 8God, who knows the heart, showed that he accepted them by giving the Holy Spirit to them, just as he did to us. 9He made no distinction between us and them, for he purified their hearts by faith. 10Now then, why do you try to test God by putting on the necks of the disciples a yoke that neither we nor our fathers have been able to bear? 11No! We believe it is through the grace of our Lord Jesus that we are saved, just as they are." Mt 23:4; Ac 10:44,47; Ro 3:24

12The whole assembly became silent as they listened to Barnabas and Paul telling about the miraculous signs and wonders God had done among the Gentiles through them. 13When they finished, James spoke up: "Brothers, listen to me. 14Simon[b] has described to us how God at first showed his concern by taking from the Gentiles a people for himself. 15The words of the prophets are in agreement with this, as it is written: Ac 12:17; 14:27

16" 'After this I will return
and rebuild David's fallen tent.
Its ruins I will rebuild,
and I will restore it,
17that the remnant of men may seek the Lord,
and all the Gentiles who bear my name,
says the Lord, who does these things'[c]
18 that have been known for ages.[d] Isa 45:21

19"It is my judgment, therefore, that we should not make it difficult for the Gentiles who are turning to God. 20Instead we should write to them, telling them to abstain from food polluted by idols, from sexual immorality, from the meat of strangled animals and from blood. 21For Moses has been preached in every city from the earliest times and is read in the synagogues on every Sabbath." Ac 13:15; 1Co 10:14-28

The Council's Letter to Gentile Believers

22Then the apostles and elders, with the whole church, decided to choose some of their own men and send them to Antioch with Paul and Barnabas. They chose Judas (called Barsabbas) and Silas, two men who were leaders among the brothers. 23With them they sent the following letter: Ac 16:19,25,29

[a] 23 Or *Barnabas ordained elders*; or *Barnabas had elders elected*
[b] 14 Greek *Simeon*, a variant of *Simon*; that is, Peter
[c] 17 Amos 9:11,12
[d] 17,18 Some manuscripts *things'— / 18known to the Lord for ages is his work*

The apostles and elders, your brothers,

To the Gentile believers in Antioch, Syria and Cilicia: Ac 6:9; 11:19

Greetings. Jas 1:1

24 We have heard that some went out from us without our authorization and disturbed you, troubling your minds by what they said. 25 So we all agreed to choose some men and send them to you with our dear friends Barnabas and Paul— 26 men who have risked their lives for the name of our Lord Jesus Christ. 27 Therefore we are sending Judas and Silas to confirm by word of mouth what we are writing. 28 It seemed good to the Holy Spirit and to us not to burden you with anything beyond the following requirements: 29 You are to abstain from food sacrificed to idols, from blood, from the meat of strangled animals and from sexual immorality. You will do well to avoid these things. Ac 14:19

Farewell.

30 The men were sent off and went down to Antioch, where they gathered the church together and delivered the letter. 31 The people read it and were glad for its encouraging message. 32 Judas and Silas, who themselves were prophets, said much to encourage and strengthen the brothers. 33 After spending some time there, they were sent off by the brothers with the blessing of peace to return to those who had sent them.[a] 35 But Paul and Barnabas remained in Antioch, where they and many others taught and preached the word of the Lord.

Disagreement Between Paul and Barnabas

36 Some time later Paul said to Barnabas, "Let us go back and visit the brothers in all the towns where we preached the word of the Lord and see how they are doing." 37 Barnabas wanted to take John, also called Mark, with them, 38 but Paul did not think it wise to take him, because he had deserted them in Pamphylia and had not continued with them in the work. 39 They had such a sharp disagreement that they parted company. Barnabas took Mark and sailed for Cyprus, 40 but Paul chose Silas and left, commended by the brothers to the grace of the Lord. 41 He went through Syria and Cilicia, strengthening the churches. Ac 12:12; 13:13

Timothy Joins Paul and Silas

16 He came to Derbe and then to Lystra, where a disciple named Timothy lived, whose mother was a Jewess and a believer, but whose father was a Greek. 2 The brothers at Lystra and Iconium spoke well of him. 3 Paul wanted to take him along on the journey, so he circumcised him because of the Jews who lived in that area, for they all knew that his father was a Greek. 4 As they traveled from town to town, they delivered the decisions reached by the apostles and elders in Jerusalem for the people to obey. 5 So the churches were strengthened in the faith and grew daily in numbers. Ac 9:31; 11:30; 15:28-29

Paul's Vision of the Man of Macedonia

6 Paul and his companions traveled throughout the region of Phrygia and Galatia, having been kept by the Holy Spirit from preaching the word in the province of Asia. 7 When they came to the border of Mysia, they tried to enter Bithynia, but the Spirit of Jesus would not allow them to. 8 So they passed by Mysia and went down to Troas. 9 During the night Paul had a vision of a man of Macedonia standing and begging him, "Come over to Macedonia and help us." 10 After Paul had seen the vision, we got ready at once to leave for Macedonia, concluding that God had called us to preach the gospel to them. Ac 9:10; Ro 8:9; 2Co 2:12

Lydia's Conversion in Philippi

11 From Troas we put out to sea and sailed straight for Samothrace, and the next day on to Neapolis. 12 From there we traveled to Philippi, a Roman colony and the leading city of that district of Macedonia. And we stayed there several days.

13 On the Sabbath we went outside the city gate to the river, where we expected to find a place of prayer. We sat down and began to speak to the women who had gathered there. 14 One of those listening was a woman named Lydia, a dealer in purple cloth from the city of Thyatira, who was a worshiper of God. The Lord opened her heart to respond to Paul's message. 15 When she and the members of her household were baptized, she invited us to her home. "If you consider me a believer in the Lord," she said, "come and stay at my house." And she persuaded us. Lk 24:45; Ac 13:14

Paul and Silas in Prison

16 Once when we were going to the place of prayer, we were met by a slave girl who had a spirit by which she predicted the future. She earned a great deal of money for her owners by fortune-telling. 17 This girl followed Paul and the rest of us, shouting, "These men are servants of the Most High God, who are telling you the way to be saved." 18 She kept this up for many days. Finally Paul became so troubled that he turned around and said to the spirit, "In the name of Jesus Christ I command you to come out of her!" At that moment the spirit left her. Mk 16:17; 1Sa 28:3,7

19 When the owners of the slave girl realized that

[a] 33 Some manuscripts *them,* 34 *but Silas decided to remain there*

their hope of making money was gone, they seized
Paul and Silas and dragged them into the marketplace to face the authorities. 20They brought them
before the magistrates and said, "These men are
Jews, and are throwing our city into an uproar 21by
advocating customs unlawful for us Romans to
accept or practice." Ac 17:6; 19:25-26
22The crowd joined in the attack against Paul
and Silas, and the magistrates ordered them to be
stripped and beaten. 23After they had been severely
flogged, they were thrown into prison, and the
jailer was commanded to guard them carefully.
24Upon receiving such orders, he put them in the
inner cell and fastened their feet in the stocks.
25About midnight Paul and Silas were praying
and singing hymns to God, and the other prison-

LIVING  **INSIGHT**

I believe the single most significant decision I can make on a day-to-day basis is my choice of attitude. Attitude is that one thing that keeps me going or cripples my progress. It alone fuels my fire or assaults my hope.

(See Acts 16:25.)

ers were listening to them. 26Suddenly there was
such a violent earthquake that the foundations of
the prison were shaken. At once all the prison
doors flew open, and everybody's chains came
loose. 27The jailer woke up, and when he saw the
prison doors open, he drew his sword and was
about to kill himself because he thought the prisoners had escaped. 28But Paul shouted, "Don't
harm yourself! We are all here!" Ac 4:31; 12:19
29The jailer called for lights, rushed in and fell
trembling before Paul and Silas. 30He then brought
them out and asked, "Sirs, what must I do to be
saved?" Ac 2:37
31They replied, "Believe in the Lord Jesus, and
you will be saved—you and your household."
32Then they spoke the word of the Lord to him
and to all the others in his house. 33At that hour of
the night the jailer took them and washed their
wounds; then immediately he and all his family
were baptized. 34The jailer brought them into his
house and set a meal before them; he was filled
with joy because he had come to believe in God—
he and his whole family. Jn 3:15; Ro 11:14
35When it was daylight, the magistrates sent
their officers to the jailer with the order: "Release
those men." 36The jailer told Paul, "The magistrates have ordered that you and Silas be released.
Now you can leave. Go in peace." Ac 15:33
37But Paul said to the officers: "They beat us
publicly without a trial, even though we are Roman citizens, and threw us into prison. And now
do they want to get rid of us quietly? No! Let them
come themselves and escort us out." Ac 22:25-29
38The officers reported this to the magistrates,
and when they heard that Paul and Silas were Roman citizens, they were alarmed. 39They came to
appease them and escorted them from the prison,
requesting them to leave the city. 40After Paul and
Silas came out of the prison, they went to Lydia's
house, where they met with the brothers and encouraged them. Then they left. Mt 8:34; Ac 1:16

In Thessalonica

17 When they had passed through Amphipolis and Apollonia, they came to Thessalonica, where there was a Jewish synagogue. 2As his
custom was, Paul went into the synagogue, and on
three Sabbath days he reasoned with them from
the Scriptures, 3explaining and proving that the
Christ[a] had to suffer and rise from the dead.
"This Jesus I am proclaiming to you is the
Christ,[a]" he said. 4Some of the Jews were persuaded and joined Paul and Silas, as did a large
number of God-fearing Greeks and not a few
prominent women. Ac 15:22; 18:28
5But the Jews were jealous; so they rounded
up some bad characters from the marketplace,
formed a mob and started a riot in the city. They
rushed to Jason's house in search of Paul and Silas
in order to bring them out to the crowd.[b] 6But
when they did not find them, they dragged Jason
and some other brothers before the city officials,
shouting: "These men who have caused trouble all
over the world have now come here, 7and Jason
has welcomed them into his house. They are all
defying Caesar's decrees, saying that there is another king, one called Jesus." 8When they heard
this, the crowd and the city officials were thrown
into turmoil. 9Then they made Jason and the others post bond and let them go. Lk 23:2; Ro 16:21

In Berea

10As soon as it was night, the brothers sent Paul
and Silas away to Berea. On arriving there, they
went to the Jewish synagogue. 11Now the Bereans
were of more noble character than the Thessalonians, for they received the message with great eagerness and examined the Scriptures every day to
see if what Paul said was true. 12Many of the Jews
believed, as did also a number of prominent Greek
women and many Greek men. Lk 16:29; Jn 5:39; Ac 20:4
13When the Jews in Thessalonica learned that
Paul was preaching the word of God at Berea, they
went there too, agitating the crowds and stirring
them up. 14The brothers immediately sent Paul to
the coast, but Silas and Timothy stayed at Berea.

[a]3 Or *Messiah* [b]5 Or *the assembly of the people*

15The men who escorted Paul brought him to Athens and then left with instructions for Silas and
Timothy to join him as soon as possible. Ac 16:1

LIVING  **INSIGHT**

What we want to do is not nearly as important as what we want to be. Doing is usually connected with a vocation or career, and how we make a living. Being is much deeper. It relates to character—who we are, and how we make a life.

(See Acts 17:11.)

In Athens

16While Paul was waiting for them in Athens, he
was greatly distressed to see that the city was full
of idols. 17So he reasoned in the synagogue with
the Jews and the God-fearing Greeks, as well as in
the marketplace day by day with those who happened to be there. 18A group of Epicurean and
Stoic philosophers began to dispute with him.
Some of them asked, "What is this babbler trying
to say?" Others remarked, "He seems to be advocating foreign gods." They said this because Paul
was preaching the good news about Jesus and the
resurrection. 19Then they took him and brought
him to a meeting of the Areopagus, where they
said to him, "May we know what this new teaching
is that you are presenting? 20You are bringing
some strange ideas to our ears, and we want to
know what they mean." 21(All the Athenians and
the foreigners who lived there spent their time
doing nothing but talking about and listening to
the latest ideas.) Ac 4:2; 9:20
22Paul then stood up in the meeting of the Areopagus and said: "Men of Athens! I see that in
every way you are very religious. 23For as I walked
around and looked carefully at your objects of
worship, I even found an altar with this inscription: TO AN UNKNOWN GOD. Now what you worship
as something unknown I am going to proclaim to
you. Jn 4:22
24"The God who made the world and everything in it is the Lord of heaven and earth and does
not live in temples built by hands. 25And he is not
served by human hands, as if he needed anything,
because he himself gives all men life and breath
and everything else. 26From one man he made
every nation of men, that they should inhabit the
whole earth; and he determined the times set for
them and the exact places where they should live.
27God did this so that men would seek him and
perhaps reach out for him and find him, though he
is not far from each one of us. 28'For in him we live
and move and have our being.' As some of your
own poets have said, 'We are his offspring.'
29"Therefore since we are God's offspring, we
should not think that the divine being is like gold
or silver or stone—an image made by man's design and skill. 30In the past God overlooked such
ignorance, but now he commands all people everywhere to repent. 31For he has set a day when he
will judge the world with justice by the man he has
appointed. He has given proof of this to all men by
raising him from the dead." Lk 24:47; Tit 2:11-12
32When they heard about the resurrection of
the dead, some of them sneered, but others said,
"We want to hear you again on this subject." 33At
that, Paul left the Council. 34A few men became
followers of Paul and believed. Among them was
Dionysius, a member of the Areopagus, also a
woman named Damaris, and a number of others.

In Corinth

18 After this, Paul left Athens and went to
Corinth. 2There he met a Jew named Aquila, a native of Pontus, who had recently come from
Italy with his wife Priscilla, because Claudius had
ordered all the Jews to leave Rome. Paul went to
see them, 3and because he was a tentmaker as they
were, he stayed and worked with them. 4Every
Sabbath he reasoned in the synagogue, trying to
persuade Jews and Greeks. Ro 16:3; 1Co 16:19; 2Ti 4:19
5When Silas and Timothy came from Macedo-
nia, Paul devoted himself exclusively to preaching,
testifying to the Jews that Jesus was the Christ.[a]
6But when the Jews opposed Paul and became
abusive, he shook out his clothes in protest and
said to them, "Your blood be on your own heads!
I am clear of my responsibility. From now on I will
go to the Gentiles." Ac 13:46; 20:26
7Then Paul left the synagogue and went next
door to the house of Titius Justus, a worshiper of
God. 8Crispus, the synagogue ruler, and his entire
household believed in the Lord; and many of the
Corinthians who heard him believed and were
baptized. Mk 5:22; 1Co 1:14
9One night the Lord spoke to Paul in a vision:
"Do not be afraid; keep on speaking, do not be
silent. 10For I am with you, and no one is going to
attack and harm you, because I have many people
in this city." 11So Paul stayed for a year and a half,
teaching them the word of God. Mt 28:20
12While Gallio was proconsul of Achaia, the
Jews made a united attack on Paul and brought
him into court. 13"This man," they charged, "is
persuading the people to worship God in ways
contrary to the law." Ro 15:26; 1Co 16:15
14Just as Paul was about to speak, Gallio said to
the Jews, "If you Jews were making a complaint

[a]5 Or *Messiah;* also in verse 28

about some misdemeanor or serious crime, it
would be reasonable for me to listen to you. 15But
since it involves questions about words and names
and your own law—settle the matter yourselves. I
will not be a judge of such things." 16So he had
them ejected from the court. 17Then they all
turned on Sosthenes the synagogue ruler and beat
him in front of the court. But Gallio showed no
concern whatever. Ac 23:29; 1Co 1:1

Priscilla, Aquila and Apollos

18Paul stayed on in Corinth for some time.
Then he left the brothers and sailed for Syria, accompanied by Priscilla and Aquila. Before he
sailed, he had his hair cut off at Cenchrea because
of a vow he had taken. 19They arrived at Ephesus,
where Paul left Priscilla and Aquila. He himself
went into the synagogue and reasoned with the
Jews. 20When they asked him to spend more time
with them, he declined. 21But as he left, he promised, "I will come back if it is God's will." Then he
set sail from Ephesus. 22When he landed at Caesarea, he went up and greeted the church and then
went down to Antioch. Ac 11:19; 1Co 4:19
23After spending some time in Antioch, Paul set
out from there and traveled from place to place
throughout the region of Galatia and Phrygia,
strengthening all the disciples. Ac 14:22; 16:6
24Meanwhile a Jew named Apollos, a native of
Alexandria, came to Ephesus. He was a learned
man, with a thorough knowledge of the Scriptures.
25He had been instructed in the way of the Lord,
and he spoke with great fervor[a] and taught about
Jesus accurately, though he knew only the baptism
of John. 26He began to speak boldly in the synagogue. When Priscilla and Aquila heard him, they
invited him to their home and explained to him
the way of God more adequately. Ac 19:3; 1Co 1:12
27When Apollos wanted to go to Achaia, the
brothers encouraged him and wrote to the disciples there to welcome him. On arriving, he was a
great help to those who by grace had believed.
28For he vigorously refuted the Jews in public debate, proving from the Scriptures that Jesus was
the Christ. Ac 9:22; 17:2

Paul in Ephesus

19 While Apollos was at Corinth, Paul took
the road through the interior and arrived
at Ephesus. There he found some disciples 2and
asked them, "Did you receive the Holy Spirit
when[b] you believed?" Ac 18:1,19
They answered, "No, we have not even heard
that there is a Holy Spirit."
3So Paul asked, "Then what baptism did you
receive?"
"John's baptism," they replied.
4Paul said, "John's baptism was a baptism of
repentance. He told the people to believe in the
one coming after him, that is, in Jesus." 5On hearing this, they were baptized into[c] the name of the
Lord Jesus. 6When Paul placed his hands on them,
the Holy Spirit came on them, and they spoke
in tongues[d] and prophesied. 7There were about
twelve men in all. Ac 2:4; 6:6; 10:46
8Paul entered the synagogue and spoke boldly
there for three months, arguing persuasively about
the kingdom of God. 9But some of them became
obstinate; they refused to believe and publicly maligned the Way. So Paul left them. He took the
disciples with him and had discussions daily in the
lecture hall of Tyrannus. 10This went on for two
years, so that all the Jews and Greeks who lived in
the province of Asia heard the word of the Lord.
11God did extraordinary miracles through Paul,
12so that even handkerchiefs and aprons that had
touched him were taken to the sick, and their illnesses were cured and the evil spirits left them.
13Some Jews who went around driving out evil
spirits tried to invoke the name of the Lord Jesus
over those who were demon-possessed. They
would say, "In the name of Jesus, whom Paul
preaches, I command you to come out." 14Seven
sons of Sceva, a Jewish chief priest, were doing
this. 15⌊One day⌋ the evil spirit answered them,
"Jesus I know, and I know about Paul, but who are
you?" 16Then the man who had the evil spirit
jumped on them and overpowered them all. He
gave them such a beating that they ran out of the
house naked and bleeding. Mt 12:27; Mk 9:38
17When this became known to the Jews and
Greeks living in Ephesus, they were all seized with
fear, and the name of the Lord Jesus was held in
high honor. 18Many of those who believed now
came and openly confessed their evil deeds. 19A
number who had practiced sorcery brought their
scrolls together and burned them publicly. When
they calculated the value of the scrolls, the total
came to fifty thousand drachmas.[e] 20In this way
the word of the Lord spread widely and grew in
power. Ac 5:5,11; 6:7; 12:24
21After all this had happened, Paul decided to
go to Jerusalem, passing through Macedonia and
Achaia. "After I have been there," he said, "I must
visit Rome also." 22He sent two of his helpers,
Timothy and Erastus, to Macedonia, while he
stayed in the province of Asia a little longer.

The Riot in Ephesus

23About that time there arose a great disturbance about the Way. 24A silversmith named Demetrius, who made silver shrines of Artemis,

[a]25 Or *with fervor in the Spirit* [b]2 Or *after* [c]5 Or *in* [d]6 Or *other languages* [e]19 A drachma was a silver coin worth about a day's wages.

brought in no little business for the craftsmen.
25He called them together, along with the workmen in related trades, and said: "Men, you know
we receive a good income from this business.
26And you see and hear how this fellow Paul has
convinced and led astray large numbers of people
here in Ephesus and in practically the whole province of Asia. He says that man-made gods are no
gods at all. 27There is danger not only that our
trade will lose its good name, but also that the
temple of the great goddess Artemis will be discredited, and the goddess herself, who is worshiped throughout the province of Asia and the
world, will be robbed of her divine majesty."

28When they heard this, they were furious and
began shouting: "Great is Artemis of the Ephesians!" 29Soon the whole city was in an uproar. The
people seized Gaius and Aristarchus, Paul's traveling companions from Macedonia, and rushed as
one man into the theater. 30Paul wanted to appear
before the crowd, but the disciples would not let
him. 31Even some of the officials of the province,
friends of Paul, sent him a message begging him
not to venture into the theater. Ac 20:4; 27:2; Col 4:10

32The assembly was in confusion: Some were
shouting one thing, some another. Most of the
people did not even know why they were there.
33The Jews pushed Alexander to the front, and
some of the crowd shouted instructions to him. He
motioned for silence in order to make a defense
before the people. 34But when they realized he was
a Jew, they all shouted in unison for about two
hours: "Great is Artemis of the Ephesians!"

35The city clerk quieted the crowd and said:
"Men of Ephesus, doesn't all the world know that
the city of Ephesus is the guardian of the temple of
the great Artemis and of her image, which fell
from heaven? 36Therefore, since these facts are undeniable, you ought to be quiet and not do anything rash. 37You have brought these men here,
though they have neither robbed temples nor blasphemed our goddess. 38If, then, Demetrius and his
fellow craftsmen have a grievance against anybody, the courts are open and there are procon-
suls. They can press charges. 39If there is anything
further you want to bring up, it must be settled in
a legal assembly. 40As it is, we are in danger of
being charged with rioting because of today's
events. In that case we would not be able to account for this commotion, since there is no reason
for it." 41After he had said this, he dismissed the
assembly. Ac 18:19; Ro 2:22

Through Macedonia and Greece

20 When the uproar had ended, Paul sent for
the disciples and, after encouraging them,
said good-by and set out for Macedonia. 2He traveled through that area, speaking many words of
encouragement to the people, and finally arrived
in Greece, 3where he stayed three months. Because
the Jews made a plot against him just as he was
about to sail for Syria, he decided to go back
through Macedonia. 4He was accompanied by So-
pater son of Pyrrhus from Berea, Aristarchus and
Secundus from Thessalonica, Gaius from Derbe,
Timothy also, and Tychicus and Trophimus from
the province of Asia. 5These men went on ahead
and waited for us at Troas. 6But we sailed from
Philippi after the Feast of Unleavened Bread, and
five days later joined the others at Troas, where we
stayed seven days. Ac 9:23-24; 16:9

Eutychus Raised From the Dead at Troas

7On the first day of the week we came together
to break bread. Paul spoke to the people and, because he intended to leave the next day, kept on
talking until midnight. 8There were many lamps in
the upstairs room where we were meeting. 9Seated
in a window was a young man named Eutychus,
who was sinking into a deep sleep as Paul talked
on and on. When he was sound asleep, he fell to
the ground from the third story and was picked up
dead. 10Paul went down, threw himself on the
young man and put his arms around him. "Don't
be alarmed," he said. "He's alive!" 11Then he went
upstairs again and broke bread and ate. After talking until daylight, he left. 12The people took the
young man home alive and were greatly comforted. Mt 9:23-24; Ac 1:13; 1Co 16:2

Paul's Farewell to the Ephesian Elders

13We went on ahead to the ship and sailed for
Assos, where we were going to take Paul aboard.
He had made this arrangement because he was
going there on foot. 14When he met us at Assos, we
took him aboard and went on to Mitylene. 15The
next day we set sail from there and arrived off
Kios. The day after that we crossed over to Samos,
and on the following day arrived at Miletus. 16Paul
had decided to sail past Ephesus to avoid spending
time in the province of Asia, for he was in a hurry
to reach Jerusalem, if possible, by the day of Pentecost. Ac 2:1; 19:21

17From Miletus, Paul sent to Ephesus for the
elders of the church. 18When they arrived, he said
to them: "You know how I lived the whole time I
was with you, from the first day I came into the
province of Asia. 19I served the Lord with great
humility and with tears, although I was severely
tested by the plots of the Jews. 20You know that I
have not hesitated to preach anything that would
be helpful to you but have taught you publicly and
from house to house. 21I have declared to both
Jews and Greeks that they must turn to God in
repentance and have faith in our Lord Jesus.

22"And now, compelled by the Spirit, I am going to Jerusalem, not knowing what will happen to
me there. 23I only know that in every city the Holy

Spirit warns me that prison and hardships are facing me. 24However, I consider my life worth nothing to me, if only I may finish the race and complete the task the Lord Jesus has given me—the
task of testifying to the gospel of God's grace.

LIVING  **INSIGHT**

Paul made this statement as he was saying good-bye to a group of friends. What an honest admission! "I am going . . . not knowing what will happen . . ." That's what this thing called the Christian life is all about, isn't it? Going . . . yet not knowing.

(See Acts 20:22.)

25"Now I know that none of you among whom
I have gone about preaching the kingdom will ever
see me again. 26Therefore, I declare to you today
that I am innocent of the blood of all men. 27For
I have not hesitated to proclaim to you the whole
will of God. 28Keep watch over yourselves and all
the flock of which the Holy Spirit has made you
overseers.[a] Be shepherds of the church of God,[b]
which he bought with his own blood. 29I know that
after I leave, savage wolves will come in among
you and will not spare the flock. 30Even from your
own number men will arise and distort the truth in
order to draw away disciples after them. 31So be on
your guard! Remember that for three years I never
stopped warning each of you night and day with
tears. Ac 19:10; 1Pe 5:2
32"Now I commit you to God and to the word
of his grace, which can build you up and give you
an inheritance among all those who are sanctified.
33I have not coveted anyone's silver or gold or
clothing. 34You yourselves know that these hands
of mine have supplied my own needs and the
needs of my companions. 35In everything I did, I
showed you that by this kind of hard work we
must help the weak, remembering the words the
Lord Jesus himself said: 'It is more blessed to give
than to receive.'" Ac 18:3; 1Co 9:12; Col 1:12
36When he had said this, he knelt down with all
of them and prayed. 37They all wept as they embraced him and kissed him. 38What grieved them
most was his statement that they would never see
his face again. Then they accompanied him to the
ship. Lk 15:20; Ac 21:5

On to Jerusalem

21 After we had torn ourselves away from
them, we put out to sea and sailed straight
to Cos. The next day we went to Rhodes and from
there to Patara. 2We found a ship crossing over to
Phoenicia, went on board and set sail. 3After sight-
ing Cyprus and passing to the south of it, we sailed
on to Syria. We landed at Tyre, where our ship was
to unload its cargo. 4Finding the disciples there, we
stayed with them seven days. Through the Spirit
they urged Paul not to go on to Jerusalem. 5But
when our time was up, we left and continued on
our way. All the disciples and their wives and children accompanied us out of the city, and there on
the beach we knelt to pray. 6After saying good-by
to each other, we went aboard the ship, and they
returned home. Ac 20:23,36
7We continued our voyage from Tyre and landed at Ptolemais, where we greeted the brothers and
stayed with them for a day. 8Leaving the next day,
we reached Caesarea and stayed at the house of
Philip the evangelist, one of the Seven. 9He had
four unmarried daughters who prophesied. Ac 6:5
10After we had been there a number of days, a
prophet named Agabus came down from Judea.
11Coming over to us, he took Paul's belt, tied his
own hands and feet with it and said, "The Holy
Spirit says, 'In this way the Jews of Jerusalem will
bind the owner of this belt and will hand him over
to the Gentiles.'" 1Ki 22:11; Ac 11:28
12When we heard this, we and the people there
pleaded with Paul not to go up to Jerusalem.
13Then Paul answered, "Why are you weeping and
breaking my heart? I am ready not only to be
bound, but also to die in Jerusalem for the name
of the Lord Jesus." 14When he would not be dis-
suaded, we gave up and said, "The Lord's will be
done." Ac 9:16; 20:24
15After this, we got ready and went up to Jerusalem. 16Some of the disciples from Caesarea accompanied us and brought us to the home of Mnason,
where we were to stay. He was a man from Cyprus
and one of the early disciples. Ac 8:40; 19:21

Paul's Arrival at Jerusalem

17When we arrived at Jerusalem, the brothers
received us warmly. 18The next day Paul and the
rest of us went to see James, and all the elders were
present. 19Paul greeted them and reported in detail
what God had done among the Gentiles through
his ministry. Ac 1:17; 15:4
20When they heard this, they praised God. Then
they said to Paul: "You see, brother, how many
thousands of Jews have believed, and all of them
are zealous for the law. 21They have been informed
that you teach all the Jews who live among the
Gentiles to turn away from Moses, telling them not
to circumcise their children or live according to
our customs. 22What shall we do? They will certainly hear that you have come, 23so do what we
tell you. There are four men with us who have
made a vow. 24Take these men, join in their purifi-

[a]28 Traditionally *bishops* [b]28 Many manuscripts *of the Lord*

cation rites and pay their expenses, so that they can have their heads shaved. Then everybody will know there is no truth in these reports about you, but that you yourself are living in obedience to the law. [25]As for the Gentile believers, we have written to them our decision that they should abstain from food sacrificed to idols, from blood, from the meat of strangled animals and from sexual immorality."

[26]The next day Paul took the men and purified himself along with them. Then he went to the temple to give notice of the date when the days of purification would end and the offering would be made for each of them. Nu 6:13-20; Ac 24:18

Paul Arrested

[27]When the seven days were nearly over, some Jews from the province of Asia saw Paul at the temple. They stirred up the whole crowd and seized him, [28]shouting, "Men of Israel, help us! This is the man who teaches all men everywhere against our people and our law and this place. And besides, he has brought Greeks into the temple area and defiled this holy place." [29](They had previously seen Trophimus the Ephesian in the city with Paul and assumed that Paul had brought him into the temple area.) Ac 20:4; 24:18

[30]The whole city was aroused, and the people came running from all directions. Seizing Paul, they dragged him from the temple, and immediately the gates were shut. [31]While they were trying to kill him, news reached the commander of the Roman troops that the whole city of Jerusalem was in an uproar. [32]He at once took some officers and soldiers and ran down to the crowd. When the rioters saw the commander and his soldiers, they stopped beating Paul. Ac 23:27; 26:21

[33]The commander came up and arrested him and ordered him to be bound with two chains. Then he asked who he was and what he had done. [34]Some in the crowd shouted one thing and some another, and since the commander could not get at the truth because of the uproar, he ordered that Paul be taken into the barracks. [35]When Paul reached the steps, the violence of the mob was so great he had to be carried by the soldiers. [36]The crowd that followed kept shouting, "Away with him!" Lk 23:18; Ac 22:22

Paul Speaks to the Crowd

[37]As the soldiers were about to take Paul into the barracks, he asked the commander, "May I say something to you?"

"Do you speak Greek?" he replied. [38]"Aren't you the Egyptian who started a revolt and led four thousand terrorists out into the desert some time ago?" Mt 24:26; Ac 5:36

[39]Paul answered, "I am a Jew, from Tarsus in Cilicia, a citizen of no ordinary city. Please let me speak to the people." Ac 9:11; 22:3

[40]Having received the commander's permission, Paul stood on the steps and motioned to the crowd. When they were all silent, he said to them

22 in Aramaic[a]: [1]"Brothers and fathers, listen now to my defense." Ac 7:2; 12:17

[2]When they heard him speak to them in Aramaic, they became very quiet. Jn 5:2; Ac 21:40

Then Paul said: [3]"I am a Jew, born in Tarsus of Cilicia, but brought up in this city. Under Gamaliel I was thoroughly trained in the law of our fathers and was just as zealous for God as any of you are

LIVING  INSIGHT

One time-honored and effective method of evangelism is the giving of your personal testimony. The skeptic may deny your doctrine or attack your church, but he cannot honestly ignore the fact that your life has been changed. If you have not discovered the value of telling others how God has rearranged your life, you've missed a vital link in the chain of His blessing.

(See Acts 22:3–21.)

today. [4]I persecuted the followers of this Way to their death, arresting both men and women and throwing them into prison, [5]as also the high priest and all the Council can testify. I even obtained letters from them to their brothers in Damascus, and went there to bring these people as prisoners to Jerusalem to be punished. Ac 21:20; 26:5

[6]"About noon as I came near Damascus, suddenly a bright light from heaven flashed around me. [7]I fell to the ground and heard a voice say to me, 'Saul! Saul! Why do you persecute me?'

[8]"'Who are you, Lord?' I asked.

"'I am Jesus of Nazareth, whom you are persecuting,' he replied. [9]My companions saw the light, but they did not understand the voice of him who was speaking to me. Ac 9:7; 26:13

[10]"'What shall I do, Lord?' I asked.

"'Get up,' the Lord said, 'and go into Damascus. There you will be told all that you have been assigned to do.' [11]My companions led me by the hand into Damascus, because the brilliance of the light had blinded me. Ac 9:8; 16:30

[12]"A man named Ananias came to see me. He was a devout observer of the law and highly respected by all the Jews living there. [13]He stood beside me and said, 'Brother Saul, receive your sight!' And at that very moment I was able to see him. Ac 9:17; 10:22

[a]40 Or possibly *Hebrew*; also in 22:2

14 "Then he said: 'The God of our fathers has chosen you to know his will and to see the Righteous One and to hear words from his mouth. 15 You will be his witness to all men of what you have seen and heard. 16 And now what are you waiting for? Get up, be baptized and wash your sins away, calling on his name.' Ac 9:1-22; 26:9-18

17 "When I returned to Jerusalem and was praying at the temple, I fell into a trance 18 and saw the Lord speaking. 'Quick!' he said to me. 'Leave Jerusalem immediately, because they will not accept your testimony about me.' Ac 9:26; 10:10

19 " 'Lord,' I replied, 'these men know that I went from one synagogue to another to imprison and beat those who believe in you. 20 And when the blood of your martyr[a] Stephen was shed, I stood there giving my approval and guarding the clothes of those who were killing him.' Ac 8:1,3

21 "Then the Lord said to me, 'Go; I will send you far away to the Gentiles.' " Ac 9:15; 13:46

Paul the Roman Citizen

22 The crowd listened to Paul until he said this. Then they raised their voices and shouted, "Rid the earth of him! He's not fit to live!" Ac 21:36

23 As they were shouting and throwing off their cloaks and flinging dust into the air, 24 the commander ordered Paul to be taken into the barracks. He directed that he be flogged and questioned in order to find out why the people were shouting at him like this. 25 As they stretched him out to flog him, Paul said to the centurion standing there, "Is it legal for you to flog a Roman citizen who hasn't even been found guilty?"

26 When the centurion heard this, he went to the commander and reported it. "What are you going to do?" he asked. "This man is a Roman citizen."

27 The commander went to Paul and asked, "Tell me, are you a Roman citizen?"

"Yes, I am," he answered.

28 Then the commander said, "I had to pay a big price for my citizenship."

"But I was born a citizen," Paul replied.

29 Those who were about to question him withdrew immediately. The commander himself was alarmed when he realized that he had put Paul, a Roman citizen, in chains. Ac 16:38

Before the Sanhedrin

30 The next day, since the commander wanted to find out exactly why Paul was being accused by the Jews, he released him and ordered the chief priests and all the Sanhedrin to assemble. Then he brought Paul and had him stand before them.

23 Paul looked straight at the Sanhedrin and said, "My brothers, I have fulfilled my duty to God in all good conscience to this day." 2 At this the high priest Ananias ordered those standing near Paul to strike him on the mouth. 3 Then Paul said to him, "God will strike you, you whitewashed wall! You sit there to judge me according to the law, yet you yourself violate the law by commanding that I be struck!" Dt 25:1-2; Jn 7:51

4 Those who were standing near Paul said, "You dare to insult God's high priest?"

5 Paul replied, "Brothers, I did not realize that he was the high priest; for it is written: 'Do not speak evil about the ruler of your people.'[b]" Ex 22:28

6 Then Paul, knowing that some of them were Sadducees and the others Pharisees, called out in the Sanhedrin, "My brothers, I am a Pharisee, the son of a Pharisee. I stand on trial because of my hope in the resurrection of the dead." 7 When he said this, a dispute broke out between the Pharisees and the Sadducees, and the assembly was divided. 8 (The Sadducees say that there is no resurrection, and that there are neither angels nor spirits, but the Pharisees acknowledge them all.)

9 There was a great uproar, and some of the teachers of the law who were Pharisees stood up and argued vigorously. "We find nothing wrong with this man," they said. "What if a spirit or an angel has spoken to him?" 10 The dispute became so violent that the commander was afraid Paul would be torn to pieces by them. He ordered the troops to go down and take him away from them by force and bring him into the barracks.

11 The following night the Lord stood near Paul and said, "Take courage! As you have testified about me in Jerusalem, so you must also testify in Rome." Ac 18:9; 19:21

The Plot to Kill Paul

12 The next morning the Jews formed a conspiracy and bound themselves with an oath not to eat or drink until they had killed Paul. 13 More than forty men were involved in this plot. 14 They went to the chief priests and elders and said, "We have taken a solemn oath not to eat anything until we have killed Paul. 15 Now then, you and the Sanhedrin petition the commander to bring him before you on the pretext of wanting more accurate information about his case. We are ready to kill him before he gets here." Ac 22:30

16 But when the son of Paul's sister heard of this plot, he went into the barracks and told Paul.

17 Then Paul called one of the centurions and said, "Take this young man to the commander; he has something to tell him." 18 So he took him to the commander.

The centurion said, "Paul, the prisoner, sent for me and asked me to bring this young man to you because he has something to tell you." Eph 3:1

19 The commander took the young man by the

[a] 20 Or *witness* [b] 5 Exodus 22:28

hand, drew him aside and asked, "What is it you
want to tell me?"
[20]He said: "The Jews have agreed to ask you to
bring Paul before the Sanhedrin tomorrow on the
pretext of wanting more accurate information
about him. [21]Don't give in to them, because more
than forty of them are waiting in ambush for him.
They have taken an oath not to eat or drink until
they have killed him. They are ready now, waiting
for your consent to their request." ver 14-15
[22]The commander dismissed the young man
and cautioned him, "Don't tell anyone that you
have reported this to me."

Paul Transferred to Caesarea

[23]Then he called two of his centurions and ordered them, "Get ready a detachment of two hundred soldiers, seventy horsemen and two hundred
spearmen[a] to go to Caesarea at nine tonight.
[24]Provide mounts for Paul so that he may be taken
safely to Governor Felix." Ac 24:1-3,10
[25]He wrote a letter as follows:

[26]Claudius Lysias,

To His Excellency, Governor Felix: Ac 24:3

Greetings. Ac 15:23

[27]This man was seized by the Jews and
they were about to kill him, but I came with
my troops and rescued him, for I had learned
that he is a Roman citizen. [28]I wanted to
know why they were accusing him, so I
brought him to their Sanhedrin. [29]I found
that the accusation had to do with questions
about their law, but there was no charge
against him that deserved death or imprisonment. [30]When I was informed of a plot to be
carried out against the man, I sent him to
you at once. I also ordered his accusers to
present to you their case against him.

[31]So the soldiers, carrying out their orders, took
Paul with them during the night and brought him
as far as Antipatris. [32]The next day they let the
cavalry go on with him, while they returned to the
barracks. [33]When the cavalry arrived in Caesarea,
they delivered the letter to the governor and handed Paul over to him. [34]The governor read the letter
and asked what province he was from. Learning
that he was from Cilicia, [35]he said, "I will hear your
case when your accusers get here." Then he ordered that Paul be kept under guard in Herod's
palace. Ac 21:39; 24:27; 25:16

The Trial Before Felix

24 Five days later the high priest Ananias
went down to Caesarea with some of the
elders and a lawyer named Tertullus, and they
brought their charges against Paul before the governor. [2]When Paul was called in, Tertullus presented his case before Felix: "We have enjoyed a
long period of peace under you, and your foresight
has brought about reforms in this nation. [3]Everywhere and in every way, most excellent Felix, we
acknowledge this with profound gratitude. [4]But in
order not to weary you further, I would request
that you be kind enough to hear us briefly.
[5]"We have found this man to be a troublemaker, stirring up riots among the Jews all over the
world. He is a ringleader of the Nazarene sect [6]and
even tried to desecrate the temple; so we seized
him. [8]By[b] examining him yourself you will be
able to learn the truth about all these charges we
are bringing against him." Ac 16:20; 21:28
[9]The Jews joined in the accusation, asserting
that these things were true. 1Th 2:16
[10]When the governor motioned for him to
speak, Paul replied: "I know that for a number of
years you have been a judge over this nation; so I
gladly make my defense. [11]You can easily verify
that no more than twelve days ago I went up to
Jerusalem to worship. [12]My accusers did not find
me arguing with anyone at the temple, or stirring
up a crowd in the synagogues or anywhere else
in the city. [13]And they cannot prove to you the
charges they are now making against me. [14]However, I admit that I worship the God of our fathers
as a follower of the Way, which they call a sect. I
believe everything that agrees with the Law and
that is written in the Prophets, [15]and I have the
same hope in God as these men, that there will be
a resurrection of both the righteous and the wicked. [16]So I strive always to keep my conscience clear
before God and man. Ac 9:2; 23:1; 25:8
[17]"After an absence of several years, I came to
Jerusalem to bring my people gifts for the poor
and to present offerings. [18]I was ceremonially

LIVING  **INSIGHT**

If you're wrong in what you're doing, stop. No amount of rationalization will make it right. If you're right, relax. Rationalization will only confuse the issue. The main thing is that you please the Lord with a clear conscience.

(See Acts 24:16.)

[a]23 The meaning of the Greek for this word is uncertain. [b]6-8 Some manuscripts *him and wanted to judge him according to our law. [7]But the commander, Lysias, came and with the use of much force snatched him from our hands [8]and ordered his accusers to come before you. By*

clean when they found me in the temple courts doing this. There was no crowd with me, nor was I involved in any disturbance. 19But there are some Jews from the province of Asia, who ought to be here before you and bring charges if they have anything against me. 20Or these who are here should state what crime they found in me when I stood before the Sanhedrin— 21unless it was this one thing I shouted as I stood in their presence: 'It is concerning the resurrection of the dead that I am on trial before you today.' " Ac 11:29-30; 23:6

22Then Felix, who was well acquainted with the Way, adjourned the proceedings. "When Lysias the commander comes," he said, "I will decide your case." 23He ordered the centurion to keep Paul under guard but to give him some freedom and permit his friends to take care of his needs.

24Several days later Felix came with his wife Drusilla, who was a Jewess. He sent for Paul and listened to him as he spoke about faith in Christ Jesus. 25As Paul discoursed on righteousness, self-control and the judgment to come, Felix was afraid and said, "That's enough for now! You may leave. When I find it convenient, I will send for you." 26At the same time he was hoping that Paul would offer him a bribe, so he sent for him frequently and talked with him. Ac 20:21; 2Pe 1:6

27When two years had passed, Felix was succeeded by Porcius Festus, but because Felix wanted to grant a favor to the Jews, he left Paul in prison. Ac 12:3; 25:1,4,9,14

The Trial Before Festus

25 Three days after arriving in the province, Festus went up from Caesarea to Jerusalem, 2where the chief priests and Jewish leaders appeared before him and presented the charges against Paul. 3They urgently requested Festus, as a favor to them, to have Paul transferred to Jerusalem, for they were preparing an ambush to kill him along the way. 4Festus answered, "Paul is being held at Caesarea, and I myself am going there soon. 5Let some of your leaders come with me and press charges against the man there, if he has done anything wrong." Ac 24:1,23

6After spending eight or ten days with them, he went down to Caesarea, and the next day he convened the court and ordered that Paul be brought before him. 7When Paul appeared, the Jews who had come down from Jerusalem stood around him, bringing many serious charges against him, which they could not prove. Mk 15:3; Ac 24:5-6

8Then Paul made his defense: "I have done nothing wrong against the law of the Jews or against the temple or against Caesar." Ac 6:13; 24:12

9Festus, wishing to do the Jews a favor, said to Paul, "Are you willing to go up to Jerusalem and stand trial before me there on these charges?"

10Paul answered: "I am now standing before Caesar's court, where I ought to be tried. I have not done any wrong to the Jews, as you yourself know very well. 11If, however, I am guilty of doing anything deserving death, I do not refuse to die. But if the charges brought against me by these Jews are not true, no one has the right to hand me over to them. I appeal to Caesar!" Ac 26:32; 28:19

12After Festus had conferred with his council, he declared: "You have appealed to Caesar. To Caesar you will go!"

Festus Consults King Agrippa

13A few days later King Agrippa and Bernice arrived at Caesarea to pay their respects to Festus. 14Since they were spending many days there, Festus discussed Paul's case with the king. He said: "There is a man here whom Felix left as a prisoner. 15When I went to Jerusalem, the chief priests and elders of the Jews brought charges against him and asked that he be condemned. Ac 24:1,27

16"I told them that it is not the Roman custom to hand over any man before he has faced his accusers and has had an opportunity to defend himself against their charges. 17When they came here with me, I did not delay the case, but convened the court the next day and ordered the man to be brought in. 18When his accusers got up to speak, they did not charge him with any of the crimes I had expected. 19Instead, they had some points of dispute with him about their own religion and about a dead man named Jesus who Paul claimed was alive. 20I was at a loss how to investigate such matters; so I asked if he would be willing to go to Jerusalem and stand trial there on these charges. 21When Paul made his appeal to be held over for the Emperor's decision, I ordered him held until I could send him to Caesar." Ac 18:15

22Then Agrippa said to Festus, "I would like to hear this man myself."

He replied, "Tomorrow you will hear him."

Paul Before Agrippa

23The next day Agrippa and Bernice came with great pomp and entered the audience room with the high ranking officers and the leading men of the city. At the command of Festus, Paul was brought in. 24Festus said: "King Agrippa, and all who are present with us, you see this man! The whole Jewish community has petitioned me about him in Jerusalem and here in Caesarea, shouting that he ought not to live any longer. 25I found he had done nothing deserving of death, but because he made his appeal to the Emperor I decided to send him to Rome. 26But I have nothing definite to write to His Majesty about him. Therefore I have brought him before all of you, and especially before you, King Agrippa, so that as a result of this investigation I may have something to write. 27For

I think it is unreasonable to send on a prisoner
without specifying the charges against him."

26 Then Agrippa said to Paul, "You have permission to speak for yourself." Ac 9:15; 25:22

So Paul motioned with his hand and began his
defense: 2"King Agrippa, I consider myself fortu-
nate to stand before you today as I make my defense against all the accusations of the Jews, 3and
especially so because you are well acquainted with
all the Jewish customs and controversies. Therefore, I beg you to listen to me patiently. Ac 6:14
4"The Jews all know the way I have lived ever
since I was a child, from the beginning of my life
in my own country, and also in Jerusalem. 5They
have known me for a long time and can testify, if
they are willing, that according to the strictest sect
of our religion, I lived as a Pharisee. 6And now it
is because of my hope in what God has promised
our fathers that I am on trial today. 7This is the
promise our twelve tribes are hoping to see fulfilled as they earnestly serve God day and night.
O king, it is because of this hope that the Jews are
accusing me. 8Why should any of you consider it
incredible that God raises the dead? 1Th 3:10; 1Ti 5:5
9"I too was convinced that I ought to do all that
was possible to oppose the name of Jesus of Nazareth. 10And that is just what I did in Jerusalem. On
the authority of the chief priests I put many of the
saints in prison, and when they were put to death,
I cast my vote against them. 11Many a time I went
from one synagogue to another to have them punished, and I tried to force them to blaspheme. In
my obsession against them, I even went to foreign
cities to persecute them. Ac 8:3; 1Ti 1:13
12"On one of these journeys I was going to Damascus with the authority and commission of the
chief priests. 13About noon, O king, as I was on
the road, I saw a light from heaven, brighter than
the sun, blazing around me and my companions.
14We all fell to the ground, and I heard a voice
saying to me in Aramaic,[a] 'Saul, Saul, why do you
persecute me? It is hard for you to kick against the
goads.' Ac 9:7
15"Then I asked, 'Who are you, Lord?'
" 'I am Jesus, whom you are persecuting,' the
Lord replied. 16'Now get up and stand on your
feet. I have appeared to you to appoint you as a
servant and as a witness of what you have seen of
me and what I will show you. 17I will rescue you
from your own people and from the Gentiles. I am
sending you to them 18to open their eyes and turn
them from darkness to light, and from the power
of Satan to God, so that they may receive forgiveness of sins and a place among those who are
sanctified by faith in me.' Isa 35:5; 42:7,16; 1Pe 2:9
19"So then, King Agrippa, I was not disobedient
to the vision from heaven. 20First to those in Damascus, then to those in Jerusalem and in all Judea, and to the Gentiles also, I preached that they
should repent and turn to God and prove their
repentance by their deeds. 21That is why the Jews

LIVING  **INSIGHT**

A witness simply reports what he or she has seen and experienced—it doesn't have to be a "sermon" or a dump-truck load of information. Just a word at the right time about the greatest Hope in all the world.

(See Acts 26:16.)

seized me in the temple courts and tried to kill me.
22But I have had God's help to this very day, and
so I stand here and testify to small and great alike.
I am saying nothing beyond what the prophets
and Moses said would happen— 23that the
Christ[b] would suffer and, as the first to rise from
the dead, would proclaim light to his own people
and to the Gentiles." Lk 2:32; Ac 21:27,30; 1Co 15:20,23
24At this point Festus interrupted Paul's defense. "You are out of your mind, Paul!" he shouted. "Your great learning is driving you insane."
25"I am not insane, most excellent Festus," Paul
replied. "What I am saying is true and reasonable.
26The king is familiar with these things, and I can
speak freely to him. I am convinced that none of
this has escaped his notice, because it was not done
in a corner. 27King Agrippa, do you believe the
prophets? I know you do." Ac 23:26
28Then Agrippa said to Paul, "Do you think that
in such a short time you can persuade me to be a
Christian?" Ac 11:26
29Paul replied, "Short time or long—I pray God
that not only you but all who are listening to me
today may become what I am, except for these
chains." Ac 21:33
30The king rose, and with him the governor and
Bernice and those sitting with them. 31They left the
room, and while talking with one another, they
said, "This man is not doing anything that deserves death or imprisonment." Ac 23:9; 25:23
32Agrippa said to Festus, "This man could have
been set free if he had not appealed to Caesar."

Paul Sails for Rome

27 When it was decided that we would sail for
Italy, Paul and some other prisoners were
handed over to a centurion named Julius, who
belonged to the Imperial Regiment. 2We boarded
a ship from Adramyttium about to sail for ports
along the coast of the province of Asia, and we put

[a]14 Or *Hebrew* [b]23 Or *Messiah*

out to sea. Aristarchus, a Macedonian from Thessalonica, was with us. Ac 19:29; 25:12,25
3The next day we landed at Sidon; and Julius, in
kindness to Paul, allowed him to go to his friends
so they might provide for his needs. 4From there
we put out to sea again and passed to the lee of
Cyprus because the winds were against us. 5When
we had sailed across the open sea off the coast of
Cilicia and Pamphylia, we landed at Myra in Lycia.
6There the centurion found an Alexandrian ship
sailing for Italy and put us on board. 7We made
slow headway for many days and had difficulty
arriving off Cnidus. When the wind did not allow
us to hold our course, we sailed to the lee of Crete,
opposite Salmone. 8We moved along the coast
with difficulty and came to a place called Fair
Havens, near the town of Lasea. Ac 24:23; 28:11
9Much time had been lost, and sailing had already become dangerous because by now it was
after the Fast.[a] So Paul warned them, 10"Men, I
can see that our voyage is going to be disastrous
and bring great loss to ship and cargo, and to our
own lives also." 11But the centurion, instead of
listening to what Paul said, followed the advice of
the pilot and of the owner of the ship. 12Since the
harbor was unsuitable to winter in, the majority
decided that we should sail on, hoping to reach
Phoenix and winter there. This was a harbor in
Crete, facing both southwest and northwest.

The Storm

13When a gentle south wind began to blow, they
thought they had obtained what they wanted; so
they weighed anchor and sailed along the shore
of Crete. 14Before very long, a wind of hurricane
force, called the "northeaster," swept down from
the island. 15The ship was caught by the storm and
could not head into the wind; so we gave way to
it and were driven along. 16As we passed to the lee
of a small island called Cauda, we were hardly able
to make the lifeboat secure. 17When the men had
hoisted it aboard, they passed ropes under the ship
itself to hold it together. Fearing that they would
run aground on the sandbars of Syrtis, they lowered the sea anchor and let the ship be driven
along. 18We took such a violent battering from the
storm that the next day they began to throw the
cargo overboard. 19On the third day, they threw
the ship's tackle overboard with their own hands.
20When neither sun nor stars appeared for many
days and the storm continued raging, we finally
gave up all hope of being saved. Jnh 1:5; Mk 4:37
21After the men had gone a long time without
food, Paul stood up before them and said: "Men,
you should have taken my advice not to sail from
Crete; then you would have spared yourselves this
damage and loss. 22But now I urge you to keep up
your courage, because not one of you will be lost;
only the ship will be destroyed. 23Last night an
angel of the God whose I am and whom I serve
stood beside me 24and said, 'Do not be afraid,
Paul. You must stand trial before Caesar; and God
has graciously given you the lives of all who sail
with you.' 25So keep up your courage, men, for I
have faith in God that it will happen just as he told
me. 26Nevertheless, we must run aground on some
island." Ac 23:11; 28:1

The Shipwreck

27On the fourteenth night we were still being
driven across the Adriatic[b] Sea, when about midnight the sailors sensed they were approaching
land. 28They took soundings and found that the
water was a hundred and twenty feet[c] deep. A
short time later they took soundings again and
found it was ninety feet[d] deep. 29Fearing that we
would be dashed against the rocks, they dropped
four anchors from the stern and prayed for daylight. 30In an attempt to escape from the ship, the
sailors let the lifeboat down into the sea, pretend-
ing they were going to lower some anchors from
the bow. 31Then Paul said to the centurion and the
soldiers, "Unless these men stay with the ship, you
cannot be saved." 32So the soldiers cut the ropes
that held the lifeboat and let it fall away. ver 16,24
33Just before dawn Paul urged them all to eat.
"For the last fourteen days," he said, "you have
been in constant suspense and have gone without
food—you haven't eaten anything. 34Now I urge
you to take some food. You need it to survive. Not
one of you will lose a single hair from his head."
35After he said this, he took some bread and gave
thanks to God in front of them all. Then he broke
it and began to eat. 36They were all encouraged
and ate some food themselves. 37Altogether there
were 276 of us on board. 38When they had eaten
as much as they wanted, they lightened the ship by
throwing the grain into the sea. Mt 10:30; 14:19
39When daylight came, they did not recognize
the land, but they saw a bay with a sandy beach,
where they decided to run the ship aground if they
could. 40Cutting loose the anchors, they left them
in the sea and at the same time untied the ropes
that held the rudders. Then they hoisted the fore-
sail to the wind and made for the beach. 41But the
ship struck a sandbar and ran aground. The bow
stuck fast and would not move, and the stern was
broken to pieces by the pounding of the surf.
42The soldiers planned to kill the prisoners to
prevent any of them from swimming away and
escaping. 43But the centurion wanted to spare
Paul's life and kept them from carrying out their

[a] *9* That is, the Day of Atonement (Yom Kippur) [b] *27* In ancient times the name referred to an area extending well south of Italy. [c] *28* Greek *twenty orguias* (about 37 meters) [d] *28* Greek *fifteen orguias* (about 27 meters)

plan. He ordered those who could swim to jump overboard first and get to land. 44The rest were to get there on planks or on pieces of the ship. In this way everyone reached land in safety. ver 22,31

Ashore on Malta

28 Once safely on shore, we found out that the island was called Malta. 2The islanders showed us unusual kindness. They built a fire and welcomed us all because it was raining and cold. 3Paul gathered a pile of brushwood and, as he put it on the fire, a viper, driven out by the heat, fastened itself on his hand. 4When the islanders saw the snake hanging from his hand, they said to each other, "This man must be a murderer; for though he escaped from the sea, Justice has not allowed him to live." 5But Paul shook the snake off into the fire and suffered no ill effects. 6The people expected him to swell up or suddenly fall dead, but after waiting a long time and seeing nothing unusual happen to him, they changed their minds and said he was a god. Lk 10:19; Ac 14:11

7There was an estate nearby that belonged to Publius, the chief official of the island. He welcomed us to his home and for three days entertained us hospitably. 8His father was sick in bed, suffering from fever and dysentery. Paul went in to see him and, after prayer, placed his hands on him and healed him. 9When this had happened, the rest of the sick on the island came and were cured. 10They honored us in many ways and when we were ready to sail, they furnished us with the supplies we needed. Ac 9:40; Jas 5:14-15

Arrival at Rome

11After three months we put out to sea in a ship that had wintered in the island. It was an Alexandrian ship with the figurehead of the twin gods Castor and Pollux. 12We put in at Syracuse and stayed there three days. 13From there we set sail and arrived at Rhegium. The next day the south wind came up, and on the following day we reached Puteoli. 14There we found some brothers who invited us to spend a week with them. And so we came to Rome. 15The brothers there had heard that we were coming, and they traveled as far as the Forum of Appius and the Three Taverns to meet us. At the sight of these men Paul thanked God and was encouraged. 16When we got to Rome, Paul was allowed to live by himself, with a soldier to guard him. Ac 1:16; 24:23; 27:6

Paul Preaches at Rome Under Guard

17Three days later he called together the leaders of the Jews. When they had assembled, Paul said to them: "My brothers, although I have done nothing against our people or against the customs of our ancestors, I was arrested in Jerusalem and handed over to the Romans. 18They examined me and wanted to release me, because I was not guilty of any crime deserving death. 19But when the Jews objected, I was compelled to appeal to Caesar—not that I had any charge to bring against my own people. 20For this reason I have asked to see you and talk with you. It is because of the hope of Israel that I am bound with this chain." Ac 25:11

21They replied, "We have not received any letters from Judea concerning you, and none of the brothers who have come from there has reported or said anything bad about you. 22But we want to hear what your views are, for we know that people everywhere are talking against this sect." Ac 22:5

23They arranged to meet Paul on a certain day, and came in even larger numbers to the place where he was staying. From morning till evening he explained and declared to them the kingdom of God and tried to convince them about Jesus from the Law of Moses and from the Prophets. 24Some were convinced by what he said, but others would not believe. 25They disagreed among themselves and began to leave after Paul had made this final statement: "The Holy Spirit spoke the truth to your forefathers when he said through Isaiah the prophet: Ac 14:4; 19:8

26" 'Go to this people and say,
"You will be ever hearing but never
understanding;
you will be ever seeing but never
perceiving."
27For this people's heart has become calloused;
they hardly hear with their ears,
and they have closed their eyes.
Otherwise they might see with their eyes,
hear with their ears,
understand with their hearts
and turn, and I would heal them.'[a] Mt 13:15

28"Therefore I want you to know that God's salvation has been sent to the Gentiles, and they will listen!"[b] Ac 13:46

30For two whole years Paul stayed there in his own rented house and welcomed all who came to see him. 31Boldly and without hindrance he preached the kingdom of God and taught about the Lord Jesus Christ. Ac 4:29

[a] 27 Isaiah 6:9,10 [b] 28 Some manuscripts *listen!" 29After he said this, the Jews left, arguing vigorously among themselves.*

INTRODUCTION

ROMANS

Paul's letter to the Romans has earned the title, "the most widely influential letter ever written," because it touches on every major doctrine of the Christian faith. God has used this letter in a powerful way to save souls and to shape the minds of Christianity's towering "giants." In this letter Paul reveals the universality of the problem of sin and explains the message of salvation through Jesus Christ. More than any other book in the Bible, the letter to the Romans explains the basis and the benefits of a relationship with God. As we explore the deep, rich mine of God's truth in Romans, we do so with great gratitude to God for providing these words that form the doctrinal cornerstone for a Christianity that gets lived out in practical ways every day.

WRITER: *Paul*

DATE: *C.A.D. 57*

PURPOSE: *To prepare the way for Paul's upcoming visit to Rome and to present the basic system of salvation*

KEY THEME: *Righteousness from God*

EMPHASES: *Sin; salvation; grace; faith; righteousness; justification; sanctification; redemption; death; resurrection*

KEY TERMS: *"Righteousness"; "law"; "faith"; "sin"; "Holy Spirit"; "in Christ"*

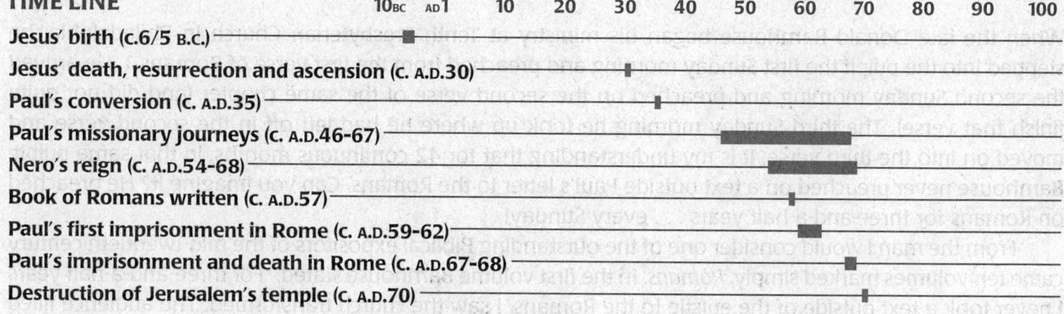

Cornerstone of Christian Faith

INTRODUCTION—Personal (1:1-17)

	THE GOSPEL: Saving the sinner	THE GOSPEL: Concerning Israel	THE GOSPEL: Concerning Christian conduct
	Depravity of humanity	Divine sovereignty and human will	Social
	Grace of God	Past, present and future of nation	Civil
	Justification by faith		Personal
	Sanctification through the Spirit		
	Security of the saint		
	CHAPTERS 1:18–8:39	*CHAPTERS 9–11*	*CHAPTERS 12:1–15:13*
EMPHASIS	**Doctrinal**	**National**	**Practical**
THEME	**Faith**	**Hope**	**Love**
DOCTRINE OF GOD	**GOD'S: Wrath . . . Righteousness . . . Glory . . . Grace**		
DOCTRINE OF HUMANITY	**HUMANITY: Fallen . . . Dead . . . Saved . . . Struggling . . . Freed . . .**		
DOCTRINE OF SIN	**SIN: Exposed . . . Conquered . . . Explained . . . Forgiven . . .**		
SCOPE	**Dead in sin . . . Dead to sin . . . Peace with God . . . Love for others . . .**		

CONCLUSION—Relational (15:14–16:27)

When the late Donald Barnhouse began his ministry at Tenth Presbyterian Church in Philadelphia, he stepped into the pulpit the first Sunday morning and preached from the first verse of Romans 1. He arrived the second Sunday morning and preached on the second verse of the same chapter (and did not quite finish that verse). The third Sunday morning he took up where he had left off in the second verse and moved on into the third verse. It is my understanding that for 42 continuous months, in that same pulpit, Barnhouse never preached on a text outside Paul's letter to the Romans. Can you imagine it? He preached on Romans for three-and-a-half years . . . every Sunday!

From the man I would consider one of the outstanding Biblical expositors of the mid-twentieth century came ten volumes marked simply, *Romans*. In the first volume Barnhouse stated, "For three-and-a-half years I never took a text outside of the epistle to the Romans. I saw the church transformed. The audience filled the pews and then the galleries, and the work went on with great blessing. But just as important as the transformation of the church was the transformation of the preacher. The disciplined necessity of treating every verse in an entire letter formed habits of study that organized the mind of this preacher for the whole of his task." This great preacher taught the book of Romans slowly as he studied it thoroughly. Every preacher and student of the Word would be wise to emulate that man's dedication and discipline.

The Grandest of the Grand

Samuel Taylor Coleridge called the letter to the Romans "the profoundest piece of writing in existence." Martin Luther said, "It's the chief book of the New Testament. It deserves to be known by heart by every Christian." John Chrysostom, never to be outdone in eloquence, called it "the cathedral of the Christian faith." J. Sidlow Baxter wrote, "This is Paul's *magnum opus*—the most important book in the Bible; more than any other it has determined the course of Christian thought."

Romans is one of the grandest books, if not the single most significant book, for the Christian to explore and apply to his or her life.

Not an Easy Read

Romans is the first book that appears in our English Bible from the mind and heart of the apostle Paul. He also wrote 12 other New Testament letters—an immense amount of correspondence covering 87 chapters in all. In his writings we have what I would call the skeleton, the spine and the bloodstream of the church. Romans contains some of the most insightful truths for the Christian life found anywhere in the Bible. None of Paul's works is light reading, and Romans may be the deepest of all.

If you want easy reading, don't choose the Pauline letters. Most of them were written to churches—so they have a direct appeal and application to the church today. Three of his letters were not only written to pastors but were about pastors (they are known as the Pastoral Letters of Paul—1 Timothy, 2 Timothy and Titus). To this day, these letters are a guide for church life and pastoral care in local congregations.

We will not discover "the how and the why" of living the Christian life until we become careful students of the New Testament letters. I believe if individuals decide to get serious about their Christian walk, it won't be long before they get into this marvelous section of God's inspired Word—Romans through Jude. It is there that we learn how to live by the Spirit on a daily basis. If you're serious about your walk with the Lord, I urge you to dig into the letters of the New Testament regularly.

A Slave of Jesus

Paul signed his name at the beginning of the letter, making it clear that he wrote it: "Paul, a servant of Christ Jesus . . ." (1:1). With regard to his relationship to the Master, he was a slave, in bondage to Jesus Christ. Paul went on to define his mission: "Called to be an apostle . . ." With regard to his calling, he was an apostle, one who was specially commissioned by Christ. Finally, the writer gave one last significant piece of information: "Set apart for the gospel of God." With regard to his work, he was marked off to undertake a specific task—to proclaim the good news that God has provided salvation through the life, death and resurrection of Jesus. The apostle Paul—once a persecutor of Christians (Acts 9:1) before his dramatic conversion on the Damascus road (Acts 9:3–6)—this Paul was the writer of the letter to the Romans.

A Letter From Corinth

Romans was most likely written from the city of Corinth, probably while Paul was on his third missionary journey. S. Lewis Johnson wrote these descriptive words about the writing of Romans: "It was winter in the city of Corinth—the vanity fair of the ancient world, the Paris of the first century. Two quiet and dignified men, guests in the house of Gaius (a Christian businessman of Corinth), sat down to engage in the work of correspondence. Paul, the older of the two, a man who appeared to be in his late 50s, prepared himself to dictate a letter to the younger, whose name was Tertius. The words on the papyrus scroll, which flowed from the hand of Tertius, would be sufficient to change the course of the history of the western world." What a monumental thought!

These two men undertook a mutual project—to write a letter in the winter of A.D. 57. It is interesting to notice this detail: Paul did not actually take stylus in hand, put ink on pages and write this letter. A man named Tertius did the actual writing. The last chapter of the letter to the Romans clues us in to the role of this humble servant who was Paul's scribe: "I, Tertius, who wrote down this letter, greet you in the Lord" (16:22).

A "Capital" Letter

The capital of the world at this time was Rome. You weren't anyone of influence until you made it to Rome. If your influence were great enough, from there you could move the world, like a puppeteer controlling the strings of a puppet. The most famous politicians, the most significant philosophers, poets and statesmen settled in Rome. From there they influenced and even manipulated the empire.

It was in that environment of impressive political power and magnificent human achievement that the church at Rome had to stand firm for the gospel of Jesus Christ. These believers in Rome needed a constitution; they needed a document that would declare a core statement of the Christian faith. Knowing that this church had not yet received the teaching of an apostle, Paul saw the need and under the Holy Spirit's influence decided, with the help of Tertius, to produce a written document that Christians in Rome could read and pass around, so that there would be no misunderstanding or ambiguity regarding the gospel. When these two men sat down to write, they were putting together a document that would become, if you will, the Christian constitution. The letter to the Romans is a bold declaration of the major doctrines of the Christian faith.

Who Needs Romans?

Who really needs to read the letter to the Romans? I think of three different groups of people. First, *sinners need the message of Romans.* There is no broader group than this one. All of us are sinful by nature. Paul stated it so clearly in this letter: "There is no one righteous, not even one . . . all have sinned and fall short of the glory of God" (3:10,23). All of us as sinners need to see how we appear before God. We all need to face the truth about our dreadful and doomed condition apart from the righteousness that comes by grace to all who believe. If you're not convinced of the need for the good news of the gospel in your own life, please read the first five chapters of Romans; if you know of someone who is living in the grip of sin, don't be afraid to ask him or her to read these chapters. Sinners need the message of Romans to honestly face up to their desperate and miserable condition before God and seek the cure through Jesus Christ.

Second, *skeptics need the message of Romans.* The letter addresses some very knotty issues and difficult questions in a rational, reasonable manner. Paul seems to anticipate the objections of the skeptics who say, "Your faith isn't logical," and ever so carefully Paul develops his arguments and unfolds his logical defense of the gospel thought by thought. If you're convinced that the Christian faith is illogical and irrational, please reserve judgment until you've read the first 11 chapters of Romans; if you have friends who are skeptical, encourage them to read the letter to the Romans. Its logic has a way of silencing the skeptic.

Third, *saints need the message of Romans.* It is here that believers get grounded in faith. It is here that we read of the essentials of the Christian faith. This letter provides a guide for understanding the content of the gospel so Christians in turn can present the gospel to those who don't know the Lord Jesus. (There's even a "Roman Road" of key verses from the letter to the Romans that summarizes the way of salvation.) In this powerful book of Scripture we receive instruction on how to think through our faith and how to live out our faith on a day-to-day basis. The last five chapters (12–16) in particular provide practical advice on how to live the Christian life.

Lessons From Rome

Let me offer several applications from this letter: *If it's a reality check we need, we need Romans 1–3.* Read these chapters slowly and drink in the truth. We human beings have gotten ourselves into a world of trouble! Sin has its hooks in us, and we need help to get out. We have no excuse before God. We are all sinners in need of salvation.

If it's a standard we need to reorder our life, we need Romans 4 and 5. When we have recognized our wretched condition and our need for a cure, when we are ready to reorganize our lives according to God's plans, we need to read these chapters and learn from them. In a standardless society, how desperately we need a principle by which to live! Paul points to the joy of trusting God for providing the cure through Jesus and the joy and peace of living by faith—the standard by which we order our lives.

If it's understanding we need to grasp the working out of the gospel in our lives, we need Romans 6–8. If we struggle with what it means to experience the Spirit-filled life, if the abundant life seems to escape us, then we'll find our struggle explained in chapters 6 and 7. In Romans 8 we'll discover the secret to overcoming our sinful nature—the indwelling presence and power of the Holy Spirit. These chapters give a hard-hitting presentation of the victory that is in Jesus Christ, as well as a realistic description of our continuing struggle with sin. When we need perspective and understanding, it is good to turn to these chapters and let the Word of God instruct us.

If it's clarification we need to see how we fit into God's sovereign plan, we need Romans 9–11. If we're wondering if God has given up on us, we'll find reassurance in these chapters that God is still at work, that His ultimate purpose in our life is to show mercy (11:25–32). If nothing more, we'll be impressively reminded in chapter 11 of the awesome power and majesty of God: "How unsearchable his judgments and his paths beyond tracing out!" (11:33). As we read these chapters we may still puzzle over difficult questions, but the picture of God's sovereign power will become clearer and our circumstances may begin to make more sense in the light of God's truth.

Finally, *if it's love and encouragement we need, we need Romans 12–16.* These chapters will lift our spirit and warm our heart. Turn to them often and let the Holy Spirit remind you of the width, length, height and depth of God's love for you—and the response that He desires from you. As we read Romans we will see that our faith must express itself in action. In this section of practical application, Paul shows us that Jesus Christ is to be Lord of every area of our lives. Let the love that God longs to share with you and the encouragement you need to live for Him leap off the pages of this letter and into your heart and life.

Saving Sinners Chapters 1–8

The first eight chapters focus on the essentials of Christian doctrine. In this section, sinners are exposed in all of their ugliness. Here Paul poignantly describes depravity and the deep need for a Savior. Although all who have sinned are condemned, God does not leave us to die in our brokenness. Jesus Christ is introduced as the Redeemer who satisfied God's just demand against sin. God offers justification for the sinner through Christ. Although we are lost in our sin, we can be made right through the finished work of Jesus, our Savior and Liberator.

Paul also addressed the struggle between living according to the Spirit and living according to our flesh. We are set free from sin, yet we still struggle daily with the weakness of our flesh. In chapter 8 we read some of the most uplifting and encouraging words in all of Scripture. Through the power and presence of the Holy Spirit in our lives we can walk in victory and live with joy and confidence!

1 Paul, a servant of Christ Jesus, called to be an apostle and set apart for the gospel of God— 2the gospel he promised beforehand through his prophets in the Holy Scriptures 3regarding his Son, who as to his human nature was a descendant of David, 4and who through the Spirit[a] of holiness was declared with power to be the Son of God[b] by his resurrection from the dead: Jesus Christ our Lord. 5Through him and for his name's sake, we received grace and apostleship to call people from among all the Gentiles to the obedience that comes from faith. 6And you also are among those who are called to belong to Jesus Christ.

7To all in Rome who are loved by God and called to be saints: Ro 8:39

Grace and peace to you from God our Father and from the Lord Jesus Christ. 1Co 1:3; 1Pe 1:2

Paul's Longing to Visit Rome

8First, I thank my God through Jesus Christ for all of you, because your faith is being reported all over the world. 9God, whom I serve with my whole heart in preaching the gospel of his Son, is my witness how constantly I remember you 10in my prayers at all times; and I pray that now at last by God's will the way may be opened for me to come to you. Ro 15:32; 2Ti 1:3

11I long to see you so that I may impart to you some spiritual gift to make you strong— 12that is, that you and I may be mutually encouraged by each other's faith. 13I do not want you to be unaware, brothers, that I planned many times to come to you (but have been prevented from doing so until now) in order that I might have a harvest among you, just as I have had among the other Gentiles. Ro 15:22-23

14I am obligated both to Greeks and non-Greeks, both to the wise and the foolish. 15That is why I am so eager to preach the gospel also to you who are at Rome. Ro 15:20; 1Co 9:16

16I am not ashamed of the gospel, because it is the power of God for the salvation of everyone who believes: first for the Jew, then for the Gentile. 17For in the gospel a righteousness from God is revealed, a righteousness that is by faith from first to last,[c] just as it is written: "The righteous will live by faith."[d] Ro 3:21; 1Co 1:18; Gal 3:11

God's Wrath Against Mankind

18The wrath of God is being revealed from heaven against all the godlessness and wickedness of men who suppress the truth by their wickedness, 19since what may be known about God is plain to them, because God has made it plain to them. 20For since the creation of the world God's invisible qualities—his eternal power and divine nature—have been clearly seen, being understood from what has been made, so that men are without excuse. Ps 19:1-6; Ac 14:17

21For although they knew God, they neither glorified him as God nor gave thanks to him, but their thinking became futile and their foolish hearts were darkened. 22Although they claimed to be wise, they became fools 23and exchanged the glory of the immortal God for images made to look like mortal man and birds and animals and reptiles.

24Therefore God gave them over in the sinful desires of their hearts to sexual impurity for the degrading of their bodies with one another. 25They exchanged the truth of God for a lie, and worshiped and served created things rather than the Creator—who is forever praised. Amen. Jer 10:14

26Because of this, God gave them over to shameful lusts. Even their women exchanged natural relations for unnatural ones. 27In the same way the men also abandoned natural relations with women and were inflamed with lust for one another. Men committed indecent acts with other men, and received in themselves the due penalty for their perversion. Lev 18:22; 1Th 4:5

28Furthermore, since they did not think it worthwhile to retain the knowledge of God, he gave them over to a depraved mind, to do what ought not to be done. 29They have become filled with every kind of wickedness, evil, greed and depravity. They are full of envy, murder, strife, deceit and malice. They are gossips, 30slanderers, God-haters, insolent, arrogant and boastful; they invent ways of doing evil; they disobey their parents; 31they are senseless, faithless, heartless, ruthless. 32Although they know God's righteous decree that those who do such things deserve death, they not

[a]4 Or *who as to his spirit* [b]4 Or *was appointed to be the Son of God with power* [c]17 Or *is from faith to faith*
[d]17 Hab. 2:4

PAUL
The Hunted

"Paul, a servant of Christ Jesus, called to be an apostle and set apart for the gospel of God."
—ROMANS 1:1

There is no one more persistent than God. When He goes seeking someone, He finds that person. As proof of God's persistent and loving heart, simply note the lengths to which God goes in His search for sinners. These are the words of His Son, who declared His purpose for coming to earth: "For the Son of Man came to seek and to save what was lost" (Luke 19:10).

Many years ago in England there lived a man named Francis Thompson. After failing in successive careers in the priesthood, medicine and the military, he wandered the streets of London. Within weeks he was addicted to opium and was living out of garbage cans. But beneath the skin of this vagabond beat a heart that God was searching after. God aroused in this man a tremendous ability to create poetry. Many literary critics have called his ode, "The Hound of Heaven," the greatest English poem ever written.

Seventeen centuries before Thompson lived, God hunted down another man. This man was not a vagrant; he was a scholar. He was, in fact, one of the keenest minds in all the Middle East—intelligent, persuasive, dogmatic. He was a Jewish zealot who despised the very name of Jesus of Nazareth. He was a man who, according to Acts 8 and the first part of chapter 9, was a one-man army against Christianity. He was mean. He was merciless. He burst into people's houses, dragging off both men and women and throwing them into prison (Acts 8:3). He hated Christians! The very mention of the name turned his stomach.

Now watch very carefully what was about to happen in this man's life. Paul (he was still called Saul at that time; see 13:9 for the first mention of the name Paul) was traveling down the road to Damascus with every intention of wreaking maximum havoc on Christians there. Damascus was about 140 miles from Jerusalem, but Paul didn't care—he would have traveled for a month to stop those deluded people who had become followers of the One who had claimed to be the Messiah. About five or six days into the journey, as Paul was walking along the road, the "Hound of Heaven" caught up to him.

Notice the divine phenomena. First there was light, brighter by far than even the noonday sun (9:3). Then there was a voice: "Saul, Saul, why do you persecute me?" (9:4). Now, Saul (let's just refer to him as Paul) had never read this story—it hadn't yet been written. He may not have known for sure whose voice this was, but I dare say he must have had a sneaking suspicion he was in the presence of deity. Look at his response: "Who are you, Lord?" (9:5). Then Jesus made His name known to Paul: "I am Jesus, whom you are persecuting." Catch the net effect as Jesus revealed Himself: "I'm not dead, Paul. You're dead! And I've come to give you life." Paul, the aggressor, was on his knees, blinded, helpless.

The "Hound of Heaven" found His man. He sank his teeth into the man who was "my chosen instrument to carry my name before the Gentiles and their kings and before the people of Israel" (9:15). This was the man who would turn the Roman world on to Jesus. He would reach the emperor Caesar before he died. He would establish churches and write inspired letters of instruction to them that would enliven and encourage the church of Christ down through the centuries.

What a story! The Lord saw Paul not for who he was, but for who he would become—"a servant of Christ Jesus, called to be an apostle and set apart for the gospel of God" (Romans 1:1). And what a servant he proved to be!

How about it, my friends? Do you remember when the "Hound of Heaven" caught up with you? Remember when you heard that voice that said, "I'm Jesus, and you can put me off no longer. Do you believe I am the Son of God who died to redeem you from your sins and give you joyful and abundant life?" I simply urge you to live in the joy of that faith, in the excitement you felt as you came to experience the Lord's unfailing love for you. And then share that excitement with someone who needs to see the light of Jesus' power and love in his or her own life.

only continue to do these very things but also approve of those who practice them. Ro 6:23; 2Ti 3:2

God's Righteous Judgment

2 You, therefore, have no excuse, you who pass judgment on someone else, for at whatever point you judge the other, you are condemning yourself, because you who pass judgment do the same things. 2 Now we know that God's judgment against those who do such things is based on truth. 3 So when you, a mere man, pass judgment on them and yet do the same things, do you think you will escape God's judgment? 4 Or do you show contempt for the riches of his kindness, tolerance and patience, not realizing that God's kindness leads you toward repentance? Ex 34:6; Ro 3:25; 2Pe 3:9

LIVING  **INSIGHT**

One of the worst forms of pride among Christians is a militant, harsh, abrasive attitude that expresses itself in judging others. The most accepting people on earth should be Christians. And the most winsome, magnetic place in the world should be the church. Both can be true if we will stop judging others and start opening doors of Christ-centered giving.

(See Romans 2:1–4.)

5 But because of your stubbornness and your unrepentant heart, you are storing up wrath against yourself for the day of God's wrath, when his righteous judgment will be revealed. 6 God "will give to each person according to what he has done."[a] 7 To those who by persistence in doing good seek glory, honor and immortality, he will give eternal life. 8 But for those who are self-seeking and who reject the truth and follow evil, there will be wrath and anger. 9 There will be trouble and distress for every human being who does evil: first for the Jew, then for the Gentile; 10 but glory, honor and peace for everyone who does good: first for the Jew, then for the Gentile. 11 For God does not show favoritism. Ac 10:34; 2Th 2:12

12 All who sin apart from the law will also perish apart from the law, and all who sin under the law will be judged by the law. 13 For it is not those who hear the law who are righteous in God's sight, but it is those who obey the law who will be declared righteous. 14 (Indeed, when Gentiles, who do not have the law, do by nature things required by the law, they are a law for themselves, even though they do not have the law, 15 since they show that the requirements of the law are written on their hearts, their consciences also bearing witness, and their thoughts now accusing, now even defending them.) 16 This will take place on the day when God will judge men's secrets through Jesus Christ, as my gospel declares. Ac 10:42; Jas 1:22-23,25

The Jews and the Law

17 Now you, if you call yourself a Jew; if you rely on the law and brag about your relationship to God; 18 if you know his will and approve of what is superior because you are instructed by the law; 19 if you are convinced that you are a guide for the blind, a light for those who are in the dark, 20 an instructor of the foolish, a teacher of infants, because you have in the law the embodiment of knowledge and truth— 21 you, then, who teach others, do you not teach yourself? You who preach against stealing, do you steal? 22 You who say that people should not commit adultery, do you commit adultery? You who abhor idols, do you rob temples? 23 You who brag about the law, do you dishonor God by breaking the law? 24 As it is written: "God's name is blasphemed among the Gentiles because of you."[b] Isa 52:5; Mic 3:11

25 Circumcision has value if you observe the law, but if you break the law, you have become as though you had not been circumcised. 26 If those who are not circumcised keep the law's requirements, will they not be regarded as though they were circumcised? 27 The one who is not circumcised physically and yet obeys the law will condemn you who, even though you have the[c] written code and circumcision, are a lawbreaker.

28 A man is not a Jew if he is only one outwardly, nor is circumcision merely outward and physical. 29 No, a man is a Jew if he is one inwardly; and circumcision is circumcision of the heart, by the Spirit, not by the written code. Such a man's praise is not from men, but from God. 2Co 10:18; Gal 6:15

God's Faithfulness

3 What advantage, then, is there in being a Jew, or what value is there in circumcision? 2 Much in every way! First of all, they have been entrusted with the very words of God. Dt 4:8; Ps 147:19

3 What if some did not have faith? Will their lack of faith nullify God's faithfulness? 4 Not at all! Let God be true, and every man a liar. As it is written:

"So that you may be proved right when you
speak
and prevail when you judge."[d] Ps 51:4

5 But if our unrighteousness brings out God's righteousness more clearly, what shall we say? That God is unjust in bringing his wrath on us? (I am using a human argument.) 6 Certainly not! If that were so, how could God judge the world? 7 Someone might argue, "If my falsehood enhances

[a] 6 Psalm 62:12; Prov. 24:12 [b] 24 Isaiah 52:5; Ezek. 36:22 [c] 27 Or *who, by means of a* [d] 4 Psalm 51:4

God's truthfulness and so increases his glory, why
am I still condemned as a sinner?" 8Why not say—
as we are being slanderously reported as saying
and as some claim that we say—"Let us do evil
that good may result"? Their condemnation is deserved. Ge 18:25; Gal 3:15

No One Is Righteous

9What shall we conclude then? Are we any better[a]? Not at all! We have already made the charge
that Jews and Gentiles alike are all under sin. 10As
it is written: Gal 3:22

"There is no one righteous, not even one;
11 there is no one who understands,
no one who seeks God.
12All have turned away,
they have together become worthless;
there is no one who does good,
not even one."[b] Ps 14:1-3
13"Their throats are open graves;
their tongues practice deceit."[c] Ps 5:9
"The poison of vipers is on their lips."[d]
14 "Their mouths are full of cursing and
bitterness."[e] Ps 10:7
15"Their feet are swift to shed blood;
16 ruin and misery mark their ways,
17and the way of peace they do not know."[f]
18 "There is no fear of God before their
eyes."[g] Ps 36:1

19Now we know that whatever the law says, it
says to those who are under the law, so that every
mouth may be silenced and the whole world held
accountable to God. 20Therefore no one will be
declared righteous in his sight by observing the
law; rather, through the law we become conscious
of sin. Ac 13:39; Ro 7:7

Righteousness Through Faith

21But now a righteousness from God, apart
from law, has been made known, to which the Law
and the Prophets testify. 22This righteousness from
God comes through faith in Jesus Christ to all who
believe. There is no difference, 23for all have sinned
and fall short of the glory of God, 24and are justified freely by his grace through the redemption
that came by Christ Jesus. 25God presented him as
a sacrifice of atonement,[h] through faith in his
blood. He did this to demonstrate his justice, because in his forbearance he had left the sins committed beforehand unpunished— 26he did it to
demonstrate his justice at the present time, so as to
be just and the one who justifies those who have
faith in Jesus. Ro 1:17; 4:16; 10:12
27Where, then, is boasting? It is excluded. On
what principle? On that of observing the law? No,
but on that of faith. 28For we maintain that a man
is justified by faith apart from observing the law.
29Is God the God of Jews only? Is he not the God
of Gentiles too? Yes, of Gentiles too, 30since there

LIVING  **INSIGHT**

We all "fall short." We can't get out of the dungeon, not even if we try. Our own sin holds us in bondage. We need someone to rescue us from the hole. We need an advocate in the courtroom of justice. We need someone who will present our case. We need someone to be our substitute. So God provided the Savior.

(See Romans 3:23.)

is only one God, who will justify the circumcised
by faith and the uncircumcised through that same
faith. 31Do we, then, nullify the law by this faith?
Not at all! Rather, we uphold the law. 1Co 1:29-31

Abraham Justified by Faith

4 What then shall we say that Abraham, our
forefather, discovered in this matter? 2If, in
fact, Abraham was justified by works, he had
something to boast about—but not before God.
3What does the Scripture say? "Abraham believed
God, and it was credited to him as righteousness."[i] Ge 15:6; 1Co 1:31; Gal 3:6
4Now when a man works, his wages are not
credited to him as a gift, but as an obligation.
5However, to the man who does not work but
trusts God who justifies the wicked, his faith is
credited as righteousness. 6David says the same
thing when he speaks of the blessedness of the
man to whom God credits righteousness apart
from works: Ro 11:6

7"Blessed are they
whose transgressions are forgiven,
whose sins are covered.
8Blessed is the man
whose sin the Lord will never count against
him."[j] Ps 32:1-2; 2Co 5:19

9Is this blessedness only for the circumcised, or
also for the uncircumcised? We have been saying
that Abraham's faith was credited to him as righteousness. 10Under what circumstances was it
credited? Was it after he was circumcised, or before? It was not after, but before! 11And he received
the sign of circumcision, a seal of the righteousness that he had by faith while he was still uncircumcised. So then, he is the father of all who

[a]9 Or *worse* [b]12 Psalms 14:1-3; 53:1-3; Eccles. 7:20 [c]13 Psalm 5:9 [d]13 Psalm 140:3 [e]14 Psalm 10:7
[f]17 Isaiah 59:7,8 [g]18 Psalm 36:1 [h]25 Or *as the one who would turn aside his wrath, taking away sin* [i]3 Gen. 15:6;
also in verse 22 [j]8 Psalm 32:1,2

THE REMEDY FOR OUR DISEASE

"For all have sinned and fall short of the glory of God, and are justified freely by his grace through the redemption that came by Christ Jesus."

—ROMANS 3:23–24

God is righteous, perfect and infinitely holy. That's His standard. It is sometimes called "glory" in the New Testament. Look closely at Romans 3:23. Let me paraphrase it: "For all have sinned [our condition] and fall short of the perfection, holiness, righteousness and glory [His standard] of God."

Unlike all humanity, God operates from a different level of expectation. His existence is in the realm of absolute perfection. He requires the same from others. The apostle Peter cites God's words first uttered through Moses: "Be holy, because I am holy" (1 Peter 1:16). Whoever hopes to relate to God must be as righteous as He is righteous. How different from us! To relate to me you don't have to be perfect. In fact, if you act like you are perfect, I get very uncomfortable. "Just be who and what you are," we say. But God isn't like that. God doesn't shrug, wink and say, "Ah, that's okay."

Let me put it another way. Perfection requires matching perfection. Ah, there's the rub! We all have sinned and fall short of the perfection of God. No one qualifies as perfect. Don't misunderstand; there are times when our goodness is rather astounding. We may take great strides, we may produce great achievements. We may even surprise ourselves with moments of goodness, gentleness and compassion. But "perfect"? Never. Or "infinitely holy"? Hardly. How about "pure"? No. Only God is those things. Romans 3:21 attributes to God perfection, holiness and purity: "But now a righteousness from God, apart from law, has been made known, to which the Law and the Prophets testify." Compared to *that* standard, all humans come up short.

J.B. Phillips paraphrased Romans 3:21 this way: ". . . indeed it is the straight edge of the Law that shows us how crooked we are." How true! God is perfect and spotless. Not a drop of gray. Not a hint of the blue that describes our depravity (see "The Bad News and the Good News," page 12). There is no way we can work up enough goodness to match His righteousness. Think about this illustration: Catalina Island is located 26 miles off the Southern California coastline. You cannot *jump* to Catalina. No one can, not even a gold medal-winning Olympian long jumper! Some can jump 27 feet. Some, 28 feet. Maybe someday one will jump 30 feet. But nobody can jump 26 miles. To get to Catalina, you have to take a boat. In the same way, no one can match God by human effort.

Our Need: A Substitute

We are sinners by birth, sinners by nature, sinners by choice, trying to reach and attain a relationship with the holy God who made us. And we "fall short." We can't make it, because we're spiritually crippled. In fact, the New Testament teaches that we're "dead in . . . transgressions and sins" (Ephesians 2:1).

What do we need? Let me put it plain and simple: We need help from outside ourselves. Just as we need a boat to get to Catalina, we need help from another source to become clean within so that we can relate to a God who is perfect. Scripture says, "God is light; in him there is no darkness at all" (1 John 1:5). If we hope to know God and walk with God and relate to God in an intimate manner, we must be able to stand the scrutiny of that kind of light. But without Christ our light does not shine; it's out. We're all dark, and He is all light.

In his immortal hymn, Charles Wesley envisioned our sin placing us in a dark dungeon, chained and helpless: "Long my imprisoned spirit lay fast bound in sin and nature's night." We can't get out of the dungeon, not even if we spent every last ounce of energy trying. Our own sin holds us in bondage. We need someone to rescue us from the deep, permanent pit of sin. We need someone to be our Redeemer, our substitute. So God provided Jesus Christ as our Savior. His death on the cross was the sufficient payment for our sin. It wiped out the debt that had been held against us and set us free to be restored to a right relationship with God.

A Prophecy: A Suffering Savior Will Come

In the Old Testament there were two great, lengthy predictions of Jesus' death on the cross. One is in Psalm 22 and the other one is in Isaiah 53. Psalm 22 emphasizes Jesus' person; Isaiah 53 emphasizes His work. Psalm 22 helps us hear and feel Christ's agony on the cross. Isaiah 53 causes us to appreciate the completed work of Christ, which was predicted by the prophet. Isaiah's words describe our condition, as well as the solution to our dilemma:

Who has believed our message
and to whom has the arm of the LORD been revealed?
He grew up before him like a tender shoot,
and like a root out of dry ground.
He had no beauty or majesty to attract us to him,
nothing in his appearance that we should desire him (Isaiah 53:1–2).

What does all this mean? Consider this: There was nothing in Jesus' physique that was attractive. There was nothing in His person, as far as appearance was concerned, that caused Him to stand out from anyone else in His day. He looked like any other Jewish man in the first century. You probably would not have been attracted to Him had you lived in His day. There was no visible aura around Him or halo above His head. When He walked across the sandy path, He got dirty like everyone else. When He slept, He slept like everyone else. When He awoke in the morning, I would imagine His hair was mussed just like everyone else's. He had all of the marks of humanity just as we have. The difference was that He was perfect within. In nature, He was not only human, He was divine. But you couldn't tell it from the outside. With the next stroke of his pen, the prophet Isaiah went deeper and addressed the sacrifice Jesus paid:

He was despised and rejected by men,
a man of sorrows, and familiar with suffering.
Like one from whom men hide their faces
he was despised, and we esteemed him not.
Surely he took up our infirmities
and carried our sorrows,
yet we considered him stricken by God,
smitten by him and afflicted.
But he was pierced for our transgressions,
he was crushed for our iniquities;
the punishment that brought us peace was upon him,
and by his wounds we are healed (Isaiah 53:3–5).

Notice that it was *our* griefs and it was *our* sorrows that He bore on *our* behalf. Not His. The burden of the cross was that He took the weight of that which was not His and carried it to the full. That explains our need for the Substitute. And people's response to Him? Look again at the words of Isaiah: "He was despised and we esteemed him not" (verse 3). An unwillingness to value His worth as the Bearer of our sins. Let us honestly examine our own hearts today as we ask ourselves the question of how we will respond to Jesus, the One who took on Himself our punishment, the One by whose wounds we are healed. Will we despise and reject Him? Will we hide our faces from Him and fail to hold Him in the highest honor? Or will we accept Him for who He is: the sinless Son of God who took on human flesh, who lived on this earth, who suffered and died and rose again, who won the victory over sin and death?

God's Provision: A Savior

What about this Jesus—the One the prophets said would come to set His people free? What is the New Testament's testimony? Now hear this:

> *[We] are justified freely by his grace through the redemption that came by Christ Jesus. God presented him as a sacrifice of atonement, through faith in his blood. He did this to demonstrate his justice, because in his forbearance he had left the sins committed beforehand unpunished—he did it to demonstrate his justice at the present time, so as to be just and the one who justifies those who have faith in Jesus (Romans 3:24–26).*

Isn't that great news? You have just been introduced to your substitute. He is Christ, the sinless and perfect Son of God. He is the One who accomplished your rescue. It occurred on a cross. It was effective because He was the only One who could qualify as our substitute before God. Sin requires a penalty—death—in order for God's righteous demands to be satisfied. The ransom must be paid. And Christ filled that role to perfection. You and I need to be washed. We need to be made sparkling clean. And God can't give up on His plan, for He hates sin. Being perfect, He cannot relate to sinful things. He couldn't even if He tried, because His nature is repelled by sin. Sin calls for judgment—and that is why the cross is so significant. It became the place of judgment. It was there the price for our redemption was paid in full.

In verse 24 of Romans 3, please take note of the term "justified." It does *not* simply mean "just as if I'd never sinned," as some have suggested. That doesn't go far enough! Neither does it mean that God makes me righteous so that I never sin again. It means to be "declared righteous." Justification is the sovereign act of God whereby He declares righteous the believing sinner while he or she is still in his or her sinning state. He sees us in our need, hopelessly lost and unable to escape from the swamp of our sin. He sees us looking to Jesus Christ and trusting Him completely, by faith, to cleanse us from our sin. And though we come to Him with all of our needs and in all of our darkness, God says to us, "Declared righteous! Forgiven! Pardoned!" Because of us? No way! Because of what Christ accomplished on our behalf when He paid for our sins.

All of that is included in what it means to be "justified." I come to God in all my need. I am hopelessly lost, spiritually dead. And I present myself to Him, just as I am. I have nothing to give that would earn my way into restoration with Him. If I could I would, but I can't. So the only way I can present myself to Him in my lost condition is by faith. Coming in recognition of my need, expressing faith in His Son who died for me, I understand that God sees me coming by faith and admitting my sinfulness. At that epochal moment, He declares me righteous.

On occasion I think of the cross as a sponge . . . a "spiritual sponge" that has taken the sins of humanity—past, present and future—and absorbed them all. At that one awful moment on Good Friday, Jesus Christ bore our sins, thus satisfying the righteous demands of the Father, completely and instantaneously clearing up my debt. My sin is forgiven. My enslavement is broken. I am set free from sin's power over me once and for all. *Redemption* (ah, another significant word in verse 24!) also occurs. I am instantaneously set free from sin's hold on me, so that I will never again return to the slave market of sin—never again to be in bondage to it. And remember, the rescue occurred because of what Jesus did—not because of what I did!

I love the way Romans 3:28 reads: "For we maintain that a man is justified by faith apart from observing the law." I remember hearing a seasoned Bible teacher say with a sigh, "Man is incurably addicted to doing something for his own salvation." What wasted effort! Scripture teaches that salvation is a by-faith, not a by-works transaction. In Romans 4:4–5, Paul makes this truth ever so clear: "Now when a man works, his wages are not credited to him as a gift, but as an obligation. However, to the man who does not work but trusts God who justifies the wicked, his faith is credited as righteousness."

Just think about your paycheck. When your boss or someone from your boss's office brings you your paycheck, you take it. You take it, I might add, without a great deal of gratitude. You don't drop to your knees and say, "Oh, thank you—thank you so very much for this gift." You probably grab the check and don't give a moment's thought to saying thanks. Why? Because you earned it. You worked hard for it. Now if your boss attaches a bonus of a thousand bucks (and maybe even adds, "Although you're dropping in your efficiency, I want you to know that I love you"), wouldn't that be great? "Great?" you respond. "That would be a miracle!" There's a big difference between a wage and a gift.

God looks at us in all of our need, and He sees nothing worth commending. Not only are we dropping in our spiritual efficiency, we have no light, no purity, no holiness. We're moving in the opposite direction, despising Him, living in a dungeon of sin, habitually acting out the lifestyle of our sinful nature. Realizing our need, we accept His miraculous, eternal bonus—the gift of His Son.

Three Crucial Questions

It seems to me that there are three crucial questions we must answer. Each has a succinct, two-word answer.

Question:	*Answer:*
Is there any hope for lost sinners?	Yes, Jesus.
Is there any work a seeker can do?	No, believe.
Is there any way for the saved to lose the gift?	No, never!

Now let me spell this out in slightly greater detail. First question: *Is there any hope for lost sinners*? Yes, our only hope is Jesus Christ. Not Christ and the church. Not Christ and good deeds. Not Christ and sincerity. Not Christ and trying real hard. Not Christ and baptism, Christ and morality or Christ and a good family. No! Jesus Christ. (Period, exclamation point!) Anything else is deeds, and "deeds" spells trouble. Jesus died for our sins and was placed in the grave as proof of His death. He rose from the dead bodily, miraculously, in proof of His life beyond. If you believe that He died and rose for you, you *have* eternal life (see John 3:15,36; 5:24). It's a gift.

Second question: *Is there any work a seeker can do*? Don't I have to add to Christ's work? Answer: No (period). Believe in the Lord Jesus! Consider this illustration—one of my favorite ones about the importance of believing in the Lord Jesus and not trusting in your own deeds to save you: You and I are going to enjoy a nice meal together. You invite me over. I come to your home. We have planned this for quite some time, and you've worked hard in the kitchen. You have prepared my favorite meal. You are thrilled because you have a great recipe you're going to follow. And I'm happy because it's going to be a delightful evening with you. I knock on your door. I walk in and can smell the meal (ahh!) all the way to the front door. I'm starved. We sit down together at the table, and you serve this delicious meal. We dine and dialogue together. What a thoroughly enjoyable evening! We visit, laugh, tell a few stories and have a relaxing time together. Then, as I get up to leave, I reach into my pocket, grab my wallet and say, "Now, what do I owe you?" You're shocked! In fact, you may even feel insulted. You knew what I needed, and out of love for me, you fixed it and served it. For me to suggest that I'll pay for it is a slap in the face. You don't even want me to help with the dishes. Love motivated your providing me this great meal. It is your gift to me. To ask to pay for it repels your love.

Third question: *Is there any way for the saved to lose the gift*? No, never! Now stop and think before you disagree. Listen to Biblical logic here, not human reasoning. If you work for your salvation, then you can certainly lose it. And that would mean it is not a gift; it's what you've earned. We really confuse things when we try to turn a gift into a wage. Furthermore, just as no one can say how much work is enough to *earn* the gift of eternal life, no one can ever say how little work is enough to *lose* it. If God required His own dear Son to die for you, He will certainly see to it that you are kept and protected through the various challenges and times of turmoil. So be confident and trust in God's security, not your own faithfulness!

Salvation is simply a gift. It's simple, but it wasn't easy. It's free, but it wasn't cheap. It's yours, but it isn't automatic. You must receive it. And when you do, it is yours forever!

believe but have not been circumcised, in order
that righteousness might be credited to them.
12And he is also the father of the circumcised who
not only are circumcised but who also walk in the
footsteps of the faith that our father Abraham had
before he was circumcised. Ge 17:10-11; Lk 19:9
13It was not through law that Abraham and his
offspring received the promise that he would be
heir of the world, but through the righteousness
that comes by faith. 14For if those who live by law
are heirs, faith has no value and the promise is
worthless, 15because law brings wrath. And where
there is no law there is no transgression. Ro 3:20
16Therefore, the promise comes by faith, so that
it may be by grace and may be guaranteed to all
Abraham's offspring—not only to those who are
of the law but also to those who are of the faith of
Abraham. He is the father of us all. 17As it is written: "I have made you a father of many nations."[a]
He is our father in the sight of God, in whom he
believed—the God who gives life to the dead and
calls things that are not as though they were.
18Against all hope, Abraham in hope believed
and so became the father of many nations, just as
it had been said to him, "So shall your offspring
be."[b] 19Without weakening in his faith, he faced
the fact that his body was as good as dead—since
he was about a hundred years old—and that Sarah's womb was also dead. 20Yet he did not waver
through unbelief regarding the promise of God,
but was strengthened in his faith and gave glory to
God, 21being fully persuaded that God had power
to do what he had promised. 22This is why "it was
credited to him as righteousness." 23The words "it
was credited to him" were written not for him
alone, 24but also for us, to whom God will credit
righteousness—for us who believe in him who
raised Jesus our Lord from the dead. 25He was
delivered over to death for our sins and was raised
to life for our justification. Ac 2:24; Ro 15:4; Heb 11:19

Peace and Joy

5 Therefore, since we have been justified
through faith, we[c] have peace with God
through our Lord Jesus Christ, 2through whom we
have gained access by faith into this grace in which
we now stand. And we[c] rejoice in the hope of the
glory of God. 3Not only so, but we[c] also rejoice in
our sufferings, because we know that suffering
produces perseverance; 4perseverance, character;
and character, hope. 5And hope does not disappoint us, because God has poured out his love into
our hearts by the Holy Spirit, whom he has giv-
en us. Eph 2:18; Jas 1:2-3
6You see, at just the right time, when we were
still powerless, Christ died for the ungodly. 7Very
rarely will anyone die for a righteous man, though
for a good man someone might possibly dare to
die. 8But God demonstrates his own love for us in
this: While we were still sinners, Christ died for us.
9Since we have now been justified by his blood,

LIVING  **INSIGHT**

I've found that it helps if I remember that I am not in charge of my day . . . God is. And while I'm sure He wants me to use my time wisely, He is more concerned with the development of my character and the cultivation of the qualities that make me Christlike within.

(See Romans 5:3–5.)

how much more shall we be saved from God's
wrath through him! 10For if, when we were God's
enemies, we were reconciled to him through the
death of his Son, how much more, having been
reconciled, shall we be saved through his life!
11Not only is this so, but we also rejoice in God
through our Lord Jesus Christ, through whom we
have now received reconciliation. Ro 11:28

Death Through Adam, Life Through Christ

12Therefore, just as sin entered the world
through one man, and death through sin, and in
this way death came to all men, because all
sinned— 13for before the law was given, sin was in
the world. But sin is not taken into account when
there is no law. 14Nevertheless, death reigned from
the time of Adam to the time of Moses, even over
those who did not sin by breaking a command, as
did Adam, who was a pattern of the one to come.
15But the gift is not like the trespass. For if the
many died by the trespass of the one man, how
much more did God's grace and the gift that came
by the grace of the one man, Jesus Christ, overflow

LIVING  **INSIGHT**

Salvation is, quite simply, a gift. It's simple, but it wasn't easy. It's free, but it wasn't cheap. It's yours, but it isn't automatic. You must receive it. When you do, it is yours forever.

(See Romans 5:15–17.)

to the many! 16Again, the gift of God is not like the
result of the one man's sin: The judgment followed
one sin and brought condemnation, but the gift
followed many trespasses and brought justification. 17For if, by the trespass of the one man, death

[a]*17* Gen. 17:5 [b]*18* Gen. 15:5 [c]*1,2,3* Or *let us*

reigned through that one man, how much more will those who receive God's abundant provision of grace and of the gift of righteousness reign in life through the one man, Jesus Christ. Ac 15:11

18 Consequently, just as the result of one trespass was condemnation for all men, so also the result of one act of righteousness was justification that brings life for all men. 19 For just as through the disobedience of the one man the many were made sinners, so also through the obedience of the one man the many will be made righteous. Ro 4:25

20 The law was added so that the trespass might increase. But where sin increased, grace increased all the more, 21 so that, just as sin reigned in death, so also grace might reign through righteousness to bring eternal life through Jesus Christ our Lord.

Dead to Sin, Alive in Christ

6 What shall we say, then? Shall we go on sinning so that grace may increase? 2 By no means! We died to sin; how can we live in it any longer? 3 Or don't you know that all of us who were baptized into Christ Jesus were baptized into his death? 4 We were therefore buried with him through baptism into death in order that, just as Christ was raised from the dead through the glory of the Father, we too may live a new life. Col 2:12

LIVING  **INSIGHT**

There are limits to our freedom. Grace does not condone license. Love has its Biblical restrictions. The opposite of legalism is not "do as you please." But let me urge you to understand this: The limitations are far broader than most of us realize.

(See Romans 6:1–4.)

5 If we have been united with him like this in his death, we will certainly also be united with him in his resurrection. 6 For we know that our old self was crucified with him so that the body of sin might be done away with,[a] that we should no longer be slaves to sin— 7 because anyone who has died has been freed from sin. Ro 7:24; Gal 2:20

8 Now if we died with Christ, we believe that we will also live with him. 9 For we know that since Christ was raised from the dead, he cannot die again; death no longer has mastery over him. 10 The death he died, he died to sin once for all; but the life he lives, he lives to God. Ac 2:24; Rev 1:18

11 In the same way, count yourselves dead to sin but alive to God in Christ Jesus. 12 Therefore do not let sin reign in your mortal body so that you obey its evil desires. 13 Do not offer the parts of your body to sin, as instruments of wickedness, but rather offer yourselves to God, as those who have been brought from death to life; and offer the parts of your body to him as instruments of righteousness. 14 For sin shall not be your master, because you are not under law, but under grace. Ro 3:24

Slaves to Righteousness

15 What then? Shall we sin because we are not under law but under grace? By no means! 16 Don't you know that when you offer yourselves to someone to obey him as slaves, you are slaves to the one whom you obey—whether you are slaves to sin, which leads to death, or to obedience, which leads to righteousness? 17 But thanks be to God that, though you used to be slaves to sin, you wholeheartedly obeyed the form of teaching to which you were entrusted. 18 You have been set free from sin and have become slaves to righteousness.

19 I put this in human terms because you are weak in your natural selves. Just as you used to offer the parts of your body in slavery to impurity and to ever-increasing wickedness, so now offer them in slavery to righteousness leading to holiness. 20 When you were slaves to sin, you were free from the control of righteousness. 21 What benefit did you reap at that time from the things you are now ashamed of? Those things result in death! 22 But now that you have been set free from sin and have become slaves to God, the benefit you reap leads to holiness, and the result is eternal life. 23 For the wages of sin is death, but the gift of God is eternal life in[b] Christ Jesus our Lord. Ro 5:12

LIVING  **INSIGHT**

Sin requires a penalty—death—in order for God's righteous demands to be satisfied. The ransom must be paid. And Jesus Christ fills that role to perfection. You and I need to be washed. And God can't give up on His plan, for He hates sin. Sin calls for judgment. And that is why the cross is so significant. It became the place of judgment. It was there that the price was paid in full.

(See Romans 6:23.)

An Illustration From Marriage

7 Do you not know, brothers—for I am speaking to men who know the law—that the law has authority over a man only as long as he lives? 2 For example, by law a married woman is bound to her husband as long as he is alive, but if her husband dies, she is released from the law of mar-

[a] 6 Or *be rendered powerless* [b] 23 Or *through*

riage. 3So then, if she marries another man while her husband is still alive, she is called an adulteress. But if her husband dies, she is released from that law and is not an adulteress, even though she marries another man. Ro 1:13; 1Co 7:39

4So, my brothers, you also died to the law through the body of Christ, that you might belong to another, to him who was raised from the dead, in order that we might bear fruit to God. 5For when we were controlled by the sinful nature,[a] the sinful passions aroused by the law were at work in our bodies, so that we bore fruit for death. 6But now, by dying to what once bound us, we have been released from the law so that we serve in the new way of the Spirit, and not in the old way of the written code. Ro 2:29; 6:13

Struggling With Sin

7What shall we say, then? Is the law sin? Certainly not! Indeed I would not have known what sin was except through the law. For I would not have known what coveting really was if the law had not said, "Do not covet."[b] 8But sin, seizing the opportunity afforded by the commandment, produced in me every kind of covetous desire. For apart from law, sin is dead. 9Once I was alive apart from law; but when the commandment came, sin sprang to life and I died. 10I found that the very commandment that was intended to bring life actually brought death. 11For sin, seizing the opportunity afforded by the commandment, deceived me, and through the commandment put me to death. 12So then, the law is holy, and the commandment is holy, righteous and good. Lev 18:5

13Did that which is good, then, become death to me? By no means! But in order that sin might be recognized as sin, it produced death in me through what was good, so that through the commandment sin might become utterly sinful. Ro 6:23

14We know that the law is spiritual; but I am unspiritual, sold as a slave to sin. 15I do not understand what I do. For what I want to do I do not do, but what I hate I do. 16And if I do what I do not want to do, I agree that the law is good. 17As it is, it is no longer I myself who do it, but it is sin living in me. 18I know that nothing good lives in me, that is, in my sinful nature.[c] For I have the desire to do what is good, but I cannot carry it out. 19For what I do is not the good I want to do; no, the evil I do not want to do—this I keep on doing. 20Now if I do what I do not want to do, it is no longer I who do it, but it is sin living in me that does it.

21So I find this law at work: When I want to do good, evil is right there with me. 22For in my inner being I delight in God's law; 23but I see another law at work in the members of my body, waging war against the law of my mind and making me a prisoner of the law of sin at work within my members. 24What a wretched man I am! Who will rescue me from this body of death? 25Thanks be to God—through Jesus Christ our Lord! Ro 6:6

So then, I myself in my mind am a slave to God's law, but in the sinful nature a slave to the law of sin. Ro 6:16,22

Life Through the Spirit

8 Therefore, there is now no condemnation for those who are in Christ Jesus,[d] 2because through Christ Jesus the law of the Spirit of life set me free from the law of sin and death. 3For what the law was powerless to do in that it was weakened by the sinful nature,[e] God did by sending his own Son in the likeness of sinful man to be a sin offering.[f] And so he condemned sin in sinful man,[g] 4in order that the righteous requirements of the law might be fully met in us, who do not live according to the sinful nature but according to the Spirit. 1Co 15:45; Gal 5:16; Heb 7:18

5Those who live according to the sinful nature have their minds set on what that nature desires; but those who live in accordance with the Spirit have their minds set on what the Spirit desires. 6The mind of sinful man[h] is death, but the mind

LIVING  **INSIGHT**

Our performance in life is directly related to the thoughts we deposit in our memory bank. We can only draw on what we deposit.

(See Romans 8:6.)

controlled by the Spirit is life and peace; 7the sinful mind[i] is hostile to God. It does not submit to God's law, nor can it do so. 8Those controlled by the sinful nature cannot please God. Gal 6:8; Jas 4:4

9You, however, are controlled not by the sinful nature but by the Spirit, if the Spirit of God lives in you. And if anyone does not have the Spirit of Christ, he does not belong to Christ. 10But if Christ is in you, your body is dead because of sin, yet your spirit is alive because of righteousness. 11And if the Spirit of him who raised Jesus from the dead is living in you, he who raised Christ from the dead will also give life to your mortal bodies through his Spirit, who lives in you. Ac 2:24; Gal 4:6

12Therefore, brothers, we have an obligation—but it is not to the sinful nature, to live according to it. 13For if you live according to the sinful na-

[a]5 Or *the flesh*; also in verse 25 [b]7 Exodus 20:17; Deut. 5:21 [c]18 Or *my flesh* [d]1 Some later manuscripts *Jesus, who do not live according to the sinful nature but according to the Spirit,* [e]3 Or *the flesh*; also in verses 4, 5, 8, 9, 12 and 13 [f]3 Or *man, for sin* [g]3 Or *in the flesh* [h]6 Or *mind set on the flesh* [i]7 Or *the mind set on the flesh*

ture, you will die; but if by the Spirit you put to
death the misdeeds of the body, you will live, 14be-
cause those who are led by the Spirit of God are
sons of God. 15For you did not receive a spirit that
makes you a slave again to fear, but you received
the Spirit of sonship.[a] And by him we cry,
"*Abba*,[b] Father." 16The Spirit himself testifies
with our spirit that we are God's children. 17Now
if we are children, then we are heirs—heirs of God
and co-heirs with Christ, if indeed we share in his
sufferings in order that we may also share in his
glory. Gal 4:7; 1Pe 4:13

Future Glory

18I consider that our present sufferings are not
worth comparing with the glory that will be revealed in us. 19The creation waits in eager expectation for the sons of God to be revealed. 20For the
creation was subjected to frustration, not by its
own choice, but by the will of the one who subjected it, in hope 21that[c] the creation itself will be
liberated from its bondage to decay and brought
into the glorious freedom of the children of God.
22We know that the whole creation has been
groaning as in the pains of childbirth right up to
the present time. 23Not only so, but we ourselves,
who have the firstfruits of the Spirit, groan inwardly as we wait eagerly for our adoption as sons, the
redemption of our bodies. 24For in this hope we
were saved. But hope that is seen is no hope at all.
Who hopes for what he already has? 25But if we
hope for what we do not yet have, we wait for it
patiently. 2Co 5:2,4; Gal 5:5
26In the same way, the Spirit helps us in our
weakness. We do not know what we ought to pray
for, but the Spirit himself intercedes for us with
groans that words cannot express. 27And he who
searches our hearts knows the mind of the Spirit,
because the Spirit intercedes for the saints in accordance with God's will. Eph 6:18; Rev 2:23

More Than Conquerors

28And we know that in all things God works for
the good of those who love him,[d] who[e] have
been called according to his purpose. 29For those
God foreknew he also predestined to be conformed to the likeness of his Son, that he might be
the firstborn among many brothers. 30And those
he predestined, he also called; those he called, he
also justified; those he justified, he also glorified.
31What, then, shall we say in response to this? If
God is for us, who can be against us? 32He who did
not spare his own Son, but gave him up for us
all—how will he not also, along with him, graciously give us all things? 33Who will bring any
charge against those whom God has chosen? It is
God who justifies. 34Who is he that condemns?
Christ Jesus, who died—more than that, who was
raised to life—is at the right hand of God and is
also interceding for us. 35Who shall separate us

LIVING  **INSIGHT**

God is committed to the task of conforming you and me to the image of His Son. Not physically—He's not making us look like Jesus looked physically—but inwardly: in character, in patience, in gentleness, in goodness, in grace, in truth, in discipline. He's committed to conforming our lives to the inner character of His Son.

(See Romans 8:29.)

from the love of Christ? Shall trouble or hardship
or persecution or famine or nakedness or danger
or sword? 36As it is written: Ps 118:6; Jn 3:16; Heb 7:25

"For your sake we face death all day long;
we are considered as sheep to be
slaughtered."[f]

37No, in all these things we are more than conquerors through him who loved us. 38For I am
convinced that neither death nor life, neither angels nor demons,[g] neither the present nor the
future, nor any powers, 39neither height nor depth,
nor anything else in all creation, will be able to
separate us from the love of God that is in Christ
Jesus our Lord. Ps 44:22; 1Co 15:57; 2Co 4:11

Concerning Israel **Chapters 9–11**

Chapter 9 records the strongest defense of the sovereignty of God of any part of the New Testament. When we read chapter 10, we discover that men and women must have hearts that believe and respond when they hear the gospel of the Lord Jesus. Though our minds may not be able to comprehend fully *God's sovereign freedom* to choose whomever He wants and *human responsibility* to respond in faith to God's call, both doctrines are clearly taught in God's Word. All of it is so unfathomable that when we get into chapter 11, we're relieved to read that Paul himself says that God's ways are beyond us (11:33–36). We cannot search the unsearchable, we cannot trace out the untraceable.

It's comforting that we don't have to understand everything completely. I appreciate men and women who are honest enough after intense study to say, "I've reached the limits of my understanding." And believe me, the longer I live, the more I see

[a]15 Or *adoption* [b]15 Aramaic for *Father* [c]20,21 Or *subjected it in hope. 21For* [d]28 Some manuscripts *And we know that all things work together for good to those who love God* [e]28 Or *works together with those who love him to bring about what is good—with those who* [f]36 Psalm 44:22 [g]38 Or *nor heavenly rulers*

how unsearchable God is. It makes me grateful that I have an all-powerful, all-knowing heavenly Father who will one day unravel it all.

God's Sovereign Choice

9 I speak the truth in Christ—I am not lying,
my conscience confirms it in the Holy Spirit— 2I have great sorrow and unceasing anguish in
my heart. 3For I could wish that I myself were
cursed and cut off from Christ for the sake of my
brothers, those of my own race, 4the people of
Israel. Theirs is the adoption as sons; theirs the
divine glory, the covenants, the receiving of the
law, the temple worship and the promises. 5Theirs
are the patriarchs, and from them is traced the
human ancestry of Christ, who is God over all,
forever praised![a] Amen. Jn 1:1; Heb 9:1
6It is not as though God's word had failed. For
not all who are descended from Israel are Israel.
7Nor because they are his descendants are they
all Abraham's children. On the contrary, "It is
through Isaac that your offspring will be reckoned."[b] 8In other words, it is not the natural children who are God's children, but it is the children
of the promise who are regarded as Abraham's
offspring. 9For this was how the promise was stated: "At the appointed time I will return, and Sarah
will have a son."[c] Ge 18:10,14; Gal 6:16
10Not only that, but Rebekah's children had one
and the same father, our father Isaac. 11Yet, before
the twins were born or had done anything good
or bad—in order that God's purpose in election
might stand: 12not by works but by him who
calls—she was told, "The older will serve the
younger."[d] 13Just as it is written: "Jacob I loved,
but Esau I hated."[e] Ge 25:21,23; Ro 8:28
14What then shall we say? Is God unjust? Not at
all! 15For he says to Moses, 2Ch 19:7

"I will have mercy on whom I have mercy,
and I will have compassion on whom I
have compassion."[f]

16It does not, therefore, depend on man's desire or
effort, but on God's mercy. 17For the Scripture
says to Pharaoh: "I raised you up for this very
purpose, that I might display my power in you and
that my name might be proclaimed in all the
earth."[g] 18Therefore God has mercy on whom he
wants to have mercy, and he hardens whom he
wants to harden. Ex 4:21; 9:16; 33:19
19One of you will say to me: "Then why does
God still blame us? For who resists his will?" 20But
who are you, O man, to talk back to God? "Shall
what is formed say to him who formed it, 'Why
did you make me like this?'"[h] 21Does not the
potter have the right to make out of the same lump
of clay some pottery for noble purposes and some
for common use? 2Ti 2:20
22What if God, choosing to show his wrath and
make his power known, bore with great patience
the objects of his wrath—prepared for destruction? 23What if he did this to make the riches of his
glory known to the objects of his mercy, whom he
prepared in advance for glory— 24even us, whom
he also called, not only from the Jews but also
from the Gentiles? 25As he says in Hosea: Ro 3:29

"I will call them 'my people' who are not my
people;
and I will call her 'my loved one' who is
not my loved one,"[i]

26and,

"It will happen that in the very place where it
was said to them,
'You are not my people,'
they will be called 'sons of the living God.'"[j]

27Isaiah cries out concerning Israel:

"Though the number of the Israelites be like
the sand by the sea, Ge 22:17; Hos 1:10
only the remnant will be saved. Ro 11:5
28For the Lord will carry out
his sentence on earth with speed and
finality."[k]

29It is just as Isaiah said previously:

"Unless the Lord Almighty Jas 5:4
had left us descendants,
we would have become like Sodom,
we would have been like Gomorrah."[l]

Israel's Unbelief

30What then shall we say? That the Gentiles,
who did not pursue righteousness, have obtained
it, a righteousness that is by faith; 31but Israel, who
pursued a law of righteousness, has not attained it.
32Why not? Because they pursued it not by faith
but as if it were by works. They stumbled over the
"stumbling stone." 33As it is written:

"See, I lay in Zion a stone that causes men to
stumble
and a rock that makes them fall,
and the one who trusts in him will never be
put to shame."[m] Isa 28:16; Ro 10:11

10 Brothers, my heart's desire and prayer to
God for the Israelites is that they may be
saved. 2For I can testify about them that they are
zealous for God, but their zeal is not based on
knowledge. 3Since they did not know the righ-

[a]5 Or *Christ, who is over all. God be forever praised!* Or *Christ. God who is over all be forever praised!* [b]7 Gen. 21:12
[c]9 Gen. 18:10,14 [d]12 Gen. 25:23 [e]13 Mal. 1:2,3 [f]15 Exodus 33:19 [g]17 Exodus 9:16 [h]20 Isaiah 29:16; 45:9
[i]25 Hosea 2:23 [j]26 Hosea 1:10 [k]28 Isaiah 10:22,23 [l]29 Isaiah 1:9 [m]33 Isaiah 8:14; 28:16

teousness that comes from God and sought to establish their own, they did not submit to God's righteousness. 4Christ is the end of the law so that there may be righteousness for everyone who believes. Ac 21:20; Ro 1:17; Gal 3:24

5Moses describes in this way the righteousness that is by the law: "The man who does these things will live by them."[a] 6But the righteousness that is by faith says: "Do not say in your heart, 'Who will ascend into heaven?'[b]" (that is, to bring Christ down) 7"or 'Who will descend into the deep?'[c]" (that is, to bring Christ up from the dead). 8But what does it say? "The word is near you; it is in your mouth and in your heart,"[d] that is, the word of faith we are proclaiming: 9That if you confess with your mouth, "Jesus is Lord," and believe in your heart that God raised him from the dead, you will be saved. 10For it is with your heart that you believe and are justified, and it is with your mouth that you confess and are saved. 11As the Scripture says, "Anyone who trusts in him will never be put to shame."[e] 12For there is no difference between Jew and Gentile—the same Lord is Lord of all and richly blesses all who call on him, 13for, "Everyone who calls on the name of the Lord will be saved."[f]

14How, then, can they call on the one they have not believed in? And how can they believe in the one of whom they have not heard? And how can they hear without someone preaching to them? 15And how can they preach unless they are sent? As it is written, "How beautiful are the feet of those who bring good news!"[g] Isa 52:7; Na 1:15

16But not all the Israelites accepted the good news. For Isaiah says, "Lord, who has believed our message?"[h] 17Consequently, faith comes from hearing the message, and the message is heard through the word of Christ. 18But I ask: Did they not hear? Of course they did: Col 3:16; Gal 3:2,5

"Their voice has gone out into all the earth,
their words to the ends of the world."[i]

19Again I ask: Did Israel not understand? First, Moses says,

"I will make you envious by those who are
not a nation; Ro 11:11,14
I will make you angry by a nation that has
no understanding."[j]

20And Isaiah boldly says,

"I was found by those who did not seek me;
I revealed myself to those who did not ask
for me."[k]

21But concerning Israel he says,

"All day long I have held out my hands
to a disobedient and obstinate people."[l]

The Remnant of Israel

11 I ask then: Did God reject his people? By no means! I am an Israelite myself, a descendant of Abraham, from the tribe of Benjamin. 2God did not reject his people, whom he foreknew. Don't you know what the Scripture says in the passage about Elijah—how he appealed to God against Israel: 3"Lord, they have killed your prophets and torn down your altars; I am the only one left, and they are trying to kill me"[m]? 4And what was God's answer to him? "I have reserved for myself seven thousand who have not bowed the knee to Baal."[n] 5So too, at the present time there is a remnant chosen by grace. 6And if by grace, then it is no longer by works; if it were, grace would no longer be grace.[o] Ro 4:4; 9:27

7What then? What Israel sought so earnestly it did not obtain, but the elect did. The others were hardened, 8as it is written: Ro 9:18,31

"God gave them a spirit of stupor,
eyes so that they could not see
and ears so that they could not hear,
to this very day."[p]

9And David says:

"May their table become a snare and a trap,
a stumbling block and a retribution for
them.
10May their eyes be darkened so they cannot
see,
and their backs be bent forever."[q]

Ingrafted Branches

11Again I ask: Did they stumble so as to fall beyond recovery? Not at all! Rather, because of their transgression, salvation has come to the Gentiles to make Israel envious. 12But if their transgression means riches for the world, and their loss means riches for the Gentiles, how much greater riches will their fullness bring! Ac 13:46; Ro 10:19

13I am talking to you Gentiles. Inasmuch as I am the apostle to the Gentiles, I make much of my ministry 14in the hope that I may somehow arouse my own people to envy and save some of them. 15For if their rejection is the reconciliation of the world, what will their acceptance be but life from the dead? 16If the part of the dough offered as firstfruits is holy, then the whole batch is holy; if the root is holy, so are the branches. Lk 15:24,32

[a] *5* Lev. 18:5 [b] *6* Deut. 30:12 [c] *7* Deut. 30:13 [d] *8* Deut. 30:14 [e] *11* Isaiah 28:16 [f] *13* Joel 2:32 [g] *15* Isaiah 52:7 [h] *16* Isaiah 53:1 [i] *18* Psalm 19:4 [j] *19* Deut. 32:21 [k] *20* Isaiah 65:1 [l] *21* Isaiah 65:2 [m] *3* 1 Kings 19:10,14 [n] *4* 1 Kings 19:18 [o] *6* Some manuscripts *by grace. But if by works, then it is no longer grace; if it were, work would no longer be work.* [p] *8* Deut. 29:4; Isaiah 29:10 [q] *10* Psalm 69:22,23

17 If some of the branches have been broken off,
and you, though a wild olive shoot, have been
grafted in among the others and now share in the
nourishing sap from the olive root, 18 do not boast
over those branches. If you do, consider this: You
do not support the root, but the root supports you.
19 You will say then, "Branches were broken off so
that I could be grafted in." 20 Granted. But they
were broken off because of unbelief, and you stand
by faith. Do not be arrogant, but be afraid. 21 For
if God did not spare the natural branches, he will
not spare you either. 1Co 10:12; 1Ti 6:17; 1Pe 1:17
22 Consider therefore the kindness and sternness
of God: sternness to those who fell, but kindness to
you, provided that you continue in his kindness.
Otherwise, you also will be cut off. 23 And if they do
not persist in unbelief, they will be grafted in, for
God is able to graft them in again. 24 After all, if you
were cut out of an olive tree that is wild by nature,
and contrary to nature were grafted into a cultivated olive tree, how much more readily will these,
the natural branches, be grafted into their own
olive tree! Jn 15:2; 1Co 15:2; 2Co 3:16

All Israel Will Be Saved

25 I do not want you to be ignorant of this mystery, brothers, so that you may not be conceited:
Israel has experienced a hardening in part until the
full number of the Gentiles has come in. 26 And so
all Israel will be saved, as it is written: Lk 21:24

"The deliverer will come from Zion;
he will turn godlessness away from Jacob.
27 And this is[a] my covenant with them
when I take away their sins."[b] Heb 8:10,12

28 As far as the gospel is concerned, they are
enemies on your account; but as far as election is
concerned, they are loved on account of the patriarchs, 29 for God's gifts and his call are irrevocable.
30 Just as you who were at one time disobedient to
God have now received mercy as a result of their
disobedience, 31 so they too have now become disobedient in order that they too may now[c] receive
mercy as a result of God's mercy to you. 32 For God
has bound all men over to disobedience so that he
may have mercy on them all. Dt 7:8; Ro 3:9; Heb 7:21

LIVING  **INSIGHT**

God is too kind to do anything cruel . . .
Too wise to make a mistake . . .
Too deep to explain Himself.
(See Romans 11:33–36.)

Doxology

33 Oh, the depth of the riches of the wisdom
and[d] knowledge of God! Ps 92:5
How unsearchable his judgments,
and his paths beyond tracing out! Job 11:7
34 "Who has known the mind of the Lord?
Or who has been his counselor?"[e]
35 "Who has ever given to God,
that God should repay him?"[f] Job 35:7
36 For from him and through him and to him
are all things. 1Co 8:6; Col 1:16
To him be the glory forever! Amen. Ro 16:27

Concerning Christian Conduct **Chapters 12–16**

Chapters 12–16 will help us live in a more peaceful, loving manner. Chapters 1–8 focus on *faith*; chapters 9–11 give us *hope*; chapters 12–16 show us *love*. You'll find some of the greatest truths for living the Christian life and the most practical, down-to-earth help in all the New Testament in chapters 12–16. Paul gives us wise instruction that will help us know how to conduct ourselves in social, civil and personal settings. We don't have to stumble blindly in the dark. God sheds light through His Word as He tells us how He wants us to live.

Living Sacrifices

12 Therefore, I urge you, brothers, in view of
God's mercy, to offer your bodies as living
sacrifices, holy and pleasing to God—this is your
spiritual[g] act of worship. 2 Do not conform any
longer to the pattern of this world, but be transformed by the renewing of your mind. Then you
will be able to test and approve what God's will
is—his good, pleasing and perfect will. Eph 4:23
3 For by the grace given me I say to every one of
you: Do not think of yourself more highly than
you ought, but rather think of yourself with sober
judgment, in accordance with the measure of faith
God has given you. 4 Just as each of us has one
body with many members, and these members do
not all have the same function, 5 so in Christ we
who are many form one body, and each member
belongs to all the others. 6 We have different gifts,
according to the grace given us. If a man's gift is
prophesying, let him use it in proportion to his[h]
faith. 7 If it is serving, let him serve; if it is teaching,
let him teach; 8 if it is encouraging, let him encourage; if it is contributing to the needs of others, let
him give generously; if it is leadership, let him
govern diligently; if it is showing mercy, let him do
it cheerfully. Ac 15:32; 2Co 9:5-13; Eph 4:11

Love

9 Love must be sincere. Hate what is evil; cling

[a] 27 Or *will be the wisdom and the* [b] 27 Isaiah 59:20,21; 27:9; Jer. 31:33,34 [c] 31 Some manuscripts do not have *now.* [d] 33 Or *riches and* [e] 34 Isaiah 40:13 [f] 35 Job 41:11 [g] 1 Or *reasonable* [h] 6 Or *in agreement with the*

to what is good. 10Be devoted to one another in
brotherly love. Honor one another above yourselves. 11Never be lacking in zeal, but keep your
spiritual fervor, serving the Lord. 12Be joyful in
hope, patient in affliction, faithful in prayer.
13Share with God's people who are in need. Practice hospitality. 1Ti 3:2; Heb 10:32,36
14Bless those who persecute you; bless and do
not curse. 15Rejoice with those who rejoice; mourn
with those who mourn. 16Live in harmony with
one another. Do not be proud, but be willing to
associate with people of low position.[a] Do not be
conceited. Mt 5:44; Ro 15:5
17Do not repay anyone evil for evil. Be careful to

LIVING  **INSIGHT**

Forgiveness is the key to handling our enemies, not revenge.
(See Romans 12:17–21)

do what is right in the eyes of everybody. 18If it is
possible, as far as it depends on you, live at peace
with everyone. 19Do not take revenge, my friends,
but leave room for God's wrath, for it is written:
"It is mine to avenge; I will repay,"[b] says the
Lord. 20On the contrary: Lev 19:18; Ro 14:19; 2Co 8:21

"If your enemy is hungry, feed him;
if he is thirsty, give him something to
drink.
In doing this, you will heap burning coals on
his head."[c] Mt 5:44; Lk 6:27

21Do not be overcome by evil, but overcome evil
with good.

Submission to the Authorities

13 Everyone must submit himself to the governing authorities, for there is no authority
except that which God has established. The authorities that exist have been established by God.
2Consequently, he who rebels against the authority
is rebelling against what God has instituted, and
those who do so will bring judgment on themselves. 3For rulers hold no terror for those who do
right, but for those who do wrong. Do you want to
be free from fear of the one in authority? Then do
what is right and he will commend you. 4For he
is God's servant to do you good. But if you do
wrong, be afraid, for he does not bear the sword
for nothing. He is God's servant, an agent of wrath
to bring punishment on the wrongdoer. 5There-
fore, it is necessary to submit to the authorities,
not only because of possible punishment but also
because of conscience. 1Th 4:6; 1Pe 2:14

6This is also why you pay taxes, for the authorities are God's servants, who give their full time to
governing. 7Give everyone what you owe him: If
you owe taxes, pay taxes; if revenue, then revenue;
if respect, then respect; if honor, then honor.

Love, for the Day Is Near

8Let no debt remain outstanding, except the
continuing debt to love one another, for he who
loves his fellowman has fulfilled the law. 9The
commandments, "Do not commit adultery," "Do
not murder," "Do not steal," "Do not covet,"[d]
and whatever other commandment there may be,
are summed up in this one rule: "Love your neighbor as yourself."[e] 10Love does no harm to its
neighbor. Therefore love is the fulfillment of the
law. Mt 19:19; 22:39-40
11And do this, understanding the present time.
The hour has come for you to wake up from your
slumber, because our salvation is nearer now than
when we first believed. 12The night is nearly over;
the day is almost here. So let us put aside the deeds
of darkness and put on the armor of light. 13Let us
behave decently, as in the daytime, not in orgies
and drunkenness, not in sexual immorality and
debauchery, not in dissension and jealousy.

LIVING  **INSIGHT**

Make no mistake about it, God is pleased when married partners enjoy a healthy sex life together. He applauds it. And why shouldn't He? He invented it. But the implied warning is clear: If we remove sex from its original, God-given context, it becomes sexual immorality, lustful passion and impurity.
(See Romans 13:13–14.)

14Rather, clothe yourselves with the Lord Jesus
Christ, and do not think about how to gratify the
desires of the sinful nature.[f] Gal 3:27; 5:19-21

The Weak and the Strong

14 Accept him whose faith is weak, without
passing judgment on disputable matters.
2One man's faith allows him to eat everything, but
another man, whose faith is weak, eats only vegetables. 3The man who eats everything must not
look down on him who does not, and the man
who does not eat everything must not condemn
the man who does, for God has accepted him.
4Who are you to judge someone else's servant? To
his own master he stands or falls. And he will
stand, for the Lord is able to make him stand.

[a] 16 Or *willing to do menial work* [b] 19 Deut. 32:35 [c] 20 Prov. 25:21,22 [d] 9 Exodus 20:13-15,17; Deut. 5:17-19,21
[e] 9 Lev. 19:18 [f] 14 Or *the flesh*

5One man considers one day more sacred than
another; another man considers every day alike.
Each one should be fully convinced in his own
mind. 6He who regards one day as special, does so
to the Lord. He who eats meat, eats to the Lord, for
he gives thanks to God; and he who abstains, does
so to the Lord and gives thanks to God. 7For none
of us lives to himself alone and none of us dies to
himself alone. 8If we live, we live to the Lord; and
if we die, we die to the Lord. So, whether we live
or die, we belong to the Lord. Gal 2:20; Php 1:20

9For this very reason, Christ died and returned
to life so that he might be the Lord of both the
dead and the living. 10You, then, why do you judge
your brother? Or why do you look down on your
brother? For we will all stand before God's judgment seat. 11It is written: Mt 7:1; 2Co 5:10

"'As surely as I live,' says the Lord, Isa 49:18
'every knee will bow before me;
every tongue will confess to God.'"[a]

12So then, each of us will give an account of himself to God. Isa 45:23; Mt 12:36; Php 2:10-11; 1Pe 4:5

13Therefore let us stop passing judgment on one
another. Instead, make up your mind not to put
any stumbling block or obstacle in your brother's
way. 14As one who is in the Lord Jesus, I am fully
convinced that no food[b] is unclean in itself. But
if anyone regards something as unclean, then for
him it is unclean. 15If your brother is distressed
because of what you eat, you are no longer acting
in love. Do not by your eating destroy your brother for whom Christ died. 16Do not allow what you
consider good to be spoken of as evil. 17For the
kingdom of God is not a matter of eating and
drinking, but of righteousness, peace and joy in
the Holy Spirit, 18because anyone who serves
Christ in this way is pleasing to God and approved
by men. Ro 15:13; 1Co 8:8; 2Co 8:21

19Let us therefore make every effort to do what
leads to peace and to mutual edification. 20Do not
destroy the work of God for the sake of food. All
food is clean, but it is wrong for a man to eat
anything that causes someone else to stumble. 21It
is better not to eat meat or drink wine or to do
anything else that will cause your brother to fall.

22So whatever you believe about these things
keep between yourself and God. Blessed is the man
who does not condemn himself by what he approves. 23But the man who has doubts is condemned if he eats, because his eating is not from
faith; and everything that does not come from
faith is sin.

15 We who are strong ought to bear with the
failings of the weak and not to please ourselves. 2Each of us should please his neighbor for
his good, to build him up. 3For even Christ did not
please himself but, as it is written: "The insults of
those who insult you have fallen on me."[c] 4For
everything that was written in the past was written
to teach us, so that through endurance and the
encouragement of the Scriptures we might have
hope. Ro 14:1,19; 1Co 10:33

5May the God who gives endurance and encouragement give you a spirit of unity among
yourselves as you follow Christ Jesus, 6so that with
one heart and mouth you may glorify the God and
Father of our Lord Jesus Christ. Ps 34:3; Ro 12:16

7Accept one another, then, just as Christ accepted you, in order to bring praise to God. 8For I tell

LIVING  **INSIGHT**

As long as our knowledge is imperfect and our preferences vary and our opinions differ, let's leave a lot of room in areas that don't really matter. Diversity and variety provide the body of believers with a beautiful blend of balance . . . but a squint-eyed, severe spirit is a killer, strangling its victim in a noose of caustic criticism.

(See Romans 15:7.)

you that Christ has become a servant of the Jews[d]
on behalf of God's truth, to confirm the promises
made to the patriarchs 9so that the Gentiles may
glorify God for his mercy, as it is written:

"Therefore I will praise you among the
Gentiles;
I will sing hymns to your name."[e]

10Again, it says,

"Rejoice, O Gentiles, with his people."[f]

11And again,

"Praise the Lord, all you Gentiles,
and sing praises to him, all you peoples."[g]

12And again, Isaiah says,

"The Root of Jesse will spring up, Rev 5:5
one who will arise to rule over the nations;
the Gentiles will hope in him."[h] Dt 32:43

13May the God of hope fill you with all joy and
peace as you trust in him, so that you may overflow with hope by the power of the Holy Spirit.

Paul the Minister to the Gentiles

14I myself am convinced, my brothers, that you
yourselves are full of goodness, complete in

[a] 11 Isaiah 45:23 [b] 14 Or *that nothing* [c] 3 Psalm 69:9 [d] 8 Greek *circumcision* [e] 9 2 Samuel 22:50; Psalm 18:49
[f] 10 Deut. 32:43 [g] 11 Psalm 117:1 [h] 12 Isaiah 11:10

knowledge and competent to instruct one another. 15I have written you quite boldly on some points, as if to remind you of them again, because of the grace God gave me 16to be a minister of Christ Jesus to the Gentiles with the priestly duty of proclaiming the gospel of God, so that the Gentiles might become an offering acceptable to God, sanctified by the Holy Spirit. Ro 1:1; 12:3

17Therefore I glory in Christ Jesus in my service to God. 18I will not venture to speak of anything except what Christ has accomplished through me in leading the Gentiles to obey God by what I have said and done— 19by the power of signs and miracles, through the power of the Spirit. So from Jerusalem all the way around to Illyricum, I have fully proclaimed the gospel of Christ. 20It has always been my ambition to preach the gospel where Christ was not known, so that I would not be building on someone else's foundation. 21Rather, as it is written: Ac 21:19; 2Co 10:15-16

"Those who were not told about him will see,
and those who have not heard will
understand."[a]

22This is why I have often been hindered from coming to you. Isa 52:15; Ro 1:13

Paul's Plan to Visit Rome

23But now that there is no more place for me to work in these regions, and since I have been longing for many years to see you, 24I plan to do so when I go to Spain. I hope to visit you while passing through and to have you assist me on my journey there, after I have enjoyed your company for a while. 25Now, however, I am on my way to Jerusalem in the service of the saints there. 26For Macedonia and Achaia were pleased to make a contribution for the poor among the saints in Jerusalem. 27They were pleased to do it, and indeed they owe it to them. For if the Gentiles have shared in the Jews' spiritual blessings, they owe it to the Jews to share with them their material blessings. 28So after I have completed this task and have made sure that they have received this fruit, I will go to Spain and visit you on the way. 29I know that when I come to you, I will come in the full measure of the blessing of Christ. Ro 1:10-11; 1Co 9:11

30I urge you, brothers, by our Lord Jesus Christ and by the love of the Spirit, to join me in my struggle by praying to God for me. 31Pray that I may be rescued from the unbelievers in Judea and that my service in Jerusalem may be acceptable to the saints there, 32so that by God's will I may come to you with joy and together with you be refreshed. 33The God of peace be with you all. Amen.

Personal Greetings

16 I commend to you our sister Phoebe, a servant[b] of the church in Cenchrea. 2I ask you to receive her in the Lord in a way worthy of the saints and to give her any help she may need from you, for she has been a great help to many people, including me.

3Greet Priscilla[c] and Aquila, my fellow workers in Christ Jesus. 4They risked their lives for me. Not only I but all the churches of the Gentiles are grateful to them. Ac 18:2; Ro 8:1,39

5Greet also the church that meets at their house.

Greet my dear friend Epenetus, who was the first convert to Christ in the province of Asia.

6Greet Mary, who worked very hard for you.

7Greet Andronicus and Junias, my relatives who have been in prison with me. They are outstanding among the apostles, and they were in Christ before I was. ver 11,21

8Greet Ampliatus, whom I love in the Lord.

9Greet Urbanus, our fellow worker in Christ, and my dear friend Stachys. ver 3

10Greet Apelles, tested and approved in Christ.

Greet those who belong to the household of Aristobulus. Ac 11:14

11Greet Herodion, my relative. ver 7,21

Greet those in the household of Narcissus who are in the Lord. Ac 11:14

12Greet Tryphena and Tryphosa, those women who work hard in the Lord.

Greet my dear friend Persis, another woman who has worked very hard in the Lord.

13Greet Rufus, chosen in the Lord, and his mother, who has been a mother to me, too.

14Greet Asyncritus, Phlegon, Hermes, Patrobas, Hermas and the brothers with them.

15Greet Philologus, Julia, Nereus and his sister, and Olympas and all the saints with them.

16Greet one another with a holy kiss.

All the churches of Christ send greetings.

17I urge you, brothers, to watch out for those who cause divisions and put obstacles in your way that are contrary to the teaching you have learned. Keep away from them. 18For such people are not serving our Lord Christ, but their own appetites. By smooth talk and flattery they deceive the minds of naive people. 19Everyone has heard about your obedience, so I am full of joy over you; but I want you to be wise about what is good, and innocent about what is evil. Mt 10:16; 1Co 14:20

20The God of peace will soon crush Satan under your feet. Ge 3:15; Ro 15:33

The grace of our Lord Jesus be with you.

21Timothy, my fellow worker, sends his greetings to you, as do Lucius, Jason and Sosipater, my relatives. Ac 13:1; 16:1; 17:5

[a]*21* Isaiah 52:15 [b]*1* Or *deaconess* [c]*3* Greek *Prisca*, a variant of *Priscilla*

[22]I, Tertius, who wrote down this letter, greet you in the Lord.

[23]Gaius, whose hospitality I and the whole church here enjoy, sends you his greetings.

Erastus, who is the city's director of public works, and our brother Quartus send you their greetings.[a] Ac 19:22; 2Ti 4:20

[25]Now to him who is able to establish you by my gospel and the proclamation of Jesus Christ, according to the revelation of the mystery hidden for long ages past, [26]but now revealed and made known through the prophetic writings by the command of the eternal God, so that all nations might believe and obey him— [27]to the only wise God be glory forever through Jesus Christ! Amen.

[a] 23 Some manuscripts *their greetings.* [24]*May the grace of our Lord Jesus Christ be with all of you. Amen.*

INTRODUCTION

1 CORINTHIANS

The city of Corinth. Color her purple . . . gaudy . . . fast and vile yet rich and influential. A city of about 200,000 free citizens, plus half a million slaves, Corinth represented a lifestyle of loose living. In fact, the immorality of Corinth became so widely known that the Greek verb *korinthiazomai* (to "Corinthianize") was coined to describe a person who lived a sexually immoral life. Into the fast lane of this wicked city came Paul, who lived and worked among them, ultimately establishing a church there. No ministry ever faced a greater challenge to survive . . . and few churches ever experienced greater conflicts. This sixteen-chapter letter is comprised mainly of troubleshooting, confronting, exhorting and correcting. No other new Testament letter gives the pastor of a church in conflict a broader base of preaching material to lead the flock into new territories of purity and unity.

WRITER: *Paul*

DATE: *C.A.D. 54–55*

PURPOSE: *To instruct believers in Christian conduct and to attack strife and division in the church*

KEY THEME: *Christian conduct in the local church*

EMPHASES: *Developing a holy character; proper worship; love; resurrection*

BACKGROUND: *Acts 18:1–18a*

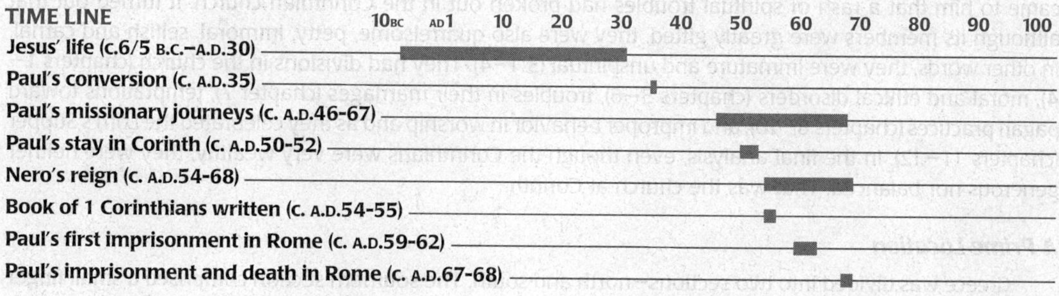

Conflicts in the Church

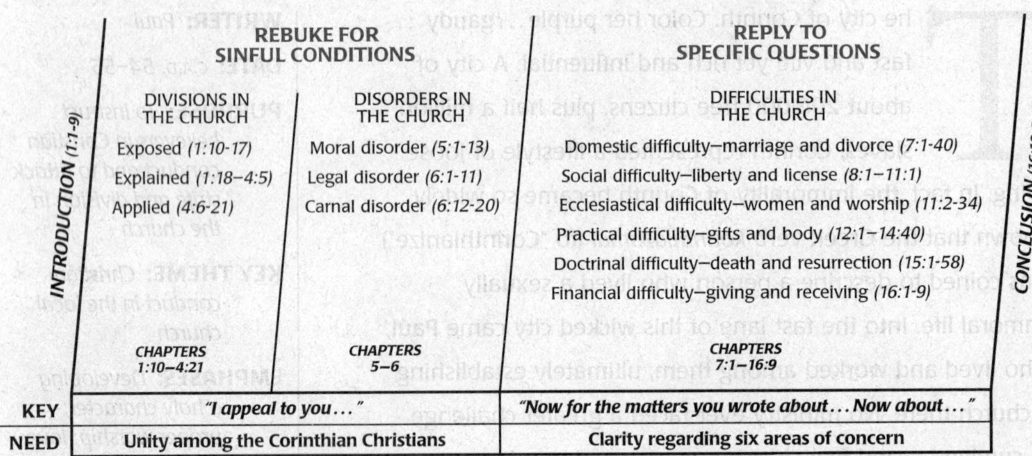

REBUKE FOR SINFUL CONDITIONS
REPLY TO SPECIFIC QUESTIONS
INTRODUCTION (1:1-9)
DIVISIONS IN THE CHURCH
Exposed (1:10-17)
Explained (1:18–4:5)
Applied (4:6-21)
CHAPTERS 1:10–4:21
DISORDERS IN THE CHURCH
Moral disorder (5:1-13)
Legal disorder (6:1-11)
Carnal disorder (6:12-20)
CHAPTERS 5–6
DIFFICULTIES IN THE CHURCH
Domestic difficulty—marriage and divorce (7:1-40)
Social difficulty—liberty and license (8:1–11:1)
Ecclesiastical difficulty—women and worship (11:2-34)
Practical difficulty—gifts and body (12:1–14:40)
Doctrinal difficulty—death and resurrection (15:1-58)
Financial difficulty—giving and receiving (16:1-9)
CHAPTERS 7:1–16:9
CONCLUSION (16:10-24)
KEY
"I appeal to you . . ."
"Now for the matters you wrote about . . . Now about . . ."
NEED
Unity among the Corinthian Christians
Clarity regarding six areas of concern

It's not unusual to find situations today of squabbles and infighting within our local churches and within our denominations. We hear reports of conflict and trouble in our churches over any number of issues, and we often experience that conflict firsthand. What church body doesn't have its share of disagreements and divisions? Those experiences lead us to conclude that the first letter to the Corinthians is a thoroughly modern letter with a powerfully pertinent message for us.

The church at Corinth was founded by the apostle Paul (Acts 18) in the spring of A.D. 52 and established as only the grand apostle could have done it. It had been well-grounded in the faith (Paul had worked there for 18 months); it appeared to be well-heeled financially and greatly gifted. It seemed to be growing by leaps and bounds under Paul's care. Yet several years after Paul left Corinth to go to Ephesus, reports came to him that a rash of spiritual troubles had broken out in the Corinthian church. It turned out that although its members were greatly gifted, they were also quarrelsome, petty, immoral, selfish and carnal. In other words, they were immature and unspiritual (3:1–4). They had divisions in the church (chapters 1–4), moral and ethical disorders (chapters 5–6), troubles in their marriages (chapter 7), temptations toward pagan practices (chapters 8–10), and improper behavior in worship and as they celebrated the Lord's Supper (chapters 11–12). In the final analysis, even though the Corinthians were very wealthy, they were neither generous nor balanced. That was the church at Corinth.

A Prime Location

Greece was divided into two sections—north and south. The southern section comprised a small finger of land not more than four miles wide and ten miles long that connected north to south—the Mediterranean Sea on the left and the Aegean Sea on the right, as you look at a map. Within that finger of land lay the city of Corinth.

It doesn't take a graduate of Harvard Business School to know that if you were an entrepreneur, the place you'd want to set up shop was in the commercial gold mine of Corinth. Any person traveling from Athens in the north to Sparta in the south needed to go through Corinth. It was a significant crossroads for travelers and traders.

Furthermore, if you were a sailor who needed to travel from east to west or vice versa, you had a problem, because you had to go around the Cape of Malea. The Greeks had two sayings about those who voyaged around Malea: "Let him who sails around Malea forget his home," and "Let him who sails around Malea first write his will." Now obviously those sayings didn't encourage sailing experiences around the cape. As a result of the difficulties in navigating the seas, many sailing vessels were literally dragged into the vicinity of this slender stretch of land in which Corinth was located. In the process, sailors poured into the city.

Because Corinth was along one of the Roman empire's most vital trade routes, merchants and traders from all directions entered the city as well. There was an endless hubbub of activity in this place of free-flowing wealth. Corinth was busy, loud, full of vice, unruly and heavily populated—a city of military personnel and mariners, entertainment and the arts. Corinth was the place to live if you wanted to "let the good times roll."

What's Missing From This Picture?

The city seemed to possess just about anything anyone could want, including all kinds of religious options—but no church of Jesus Christ. Prior to the apostle Paul's trip to the city, there was not one gospel-preaching church in the ancient, fast-moving metropolis. On a hill high above this isthmus was a temple dedicated to the worship of the goddess of sensuality—Aphrodite, whose worshipers practiced prostitution in the name of religion. The debauched lifestyle this brought into the city defied description. There was plenty of religious fervor, but no true faith; there were many temples, but not one church of Jesus Christ. Ultimately the apostle Paul came to Corinth and established a church there, but the new converts may very well have brought their bad habits with them right into the church. In the wild and crazy setting of Corinth, the hotbed of unbridled immorality, it is no wonder that it wasn't long before deep problems plagued the Corinthian church.

First Corinthians?

Paul wrote 1 Corinthians after hearing about the church members' conflicts and quarrels. While in Ephesus several things happened that caused him to become concerned about the church in Corinth, and so he wrote them this letter.

You may be surprised to know that we don't even possess the very first letter Paul wrote to the church at Corinth. The letter we call 1 Corinthians is really the *second* letter and the second letter is really the *third*. The first letter never made it into the canon of Scripture. Paul noted in 1 Corinthians that he had written to them earlier (5:9), and they appeared to have misunderstood what Paul had communicated to them. Now Paul wrote another letter based on new and troubling reports he had heard about the church.

Quarrels Among God's People

What caused Paul to take the time to write to the Corinthians? Let me point out something from the first and last chapters that will help you understand the reason. In 1 Corinthians 1:11 we read that he had received some disturbing news about them: "My brothers, some from Chloe's household have informed me that there are quarrels among you." Furthermore, Paul had been visited by three men from Corinth, whom he named in the last chapter. When these three came to him, they undoubtedly reported their concerns as well:

> *You know that the household of Stephanas were the first converts in Achaia, and they have devoted themselves to the service of the saints. I urge you, brothers, to submit to such as these and to everyone who joins in the work, and labors at it. I was glad when Stephanas, Fortunatus and Achaicus arrived, because they have supplied what was lacking from you (16:15–17).*

In effect, Paul concluded, "I was concerned about the church at Corinth after hearing from Chloe's household, and so when these men came, they supplied what I needed to know. As a result, I'm writing this letter. I know enough to realize there are problems and conflicts in the church at Corinth."

On occasion we may have to be the bearer of bad news. It isn't a pleasant role. We probably wouldn't volunteer for it. Yet part of our role as a follower of Jesus is to speak the truth in love. To hold each other accountable. To confront wrongdoing wherever we find it. To tell the truth to someone who can do something about it. That's what the members of Chloe's household did, as well as Stephanas, Fortunatus and Achaicus. They told Paul, and he not only *could* do something about it . . . he *did* do something about it.

The tone of the letter is direct, even sarcastic and angry in places. There is strong exhortation here; at times there is a firm rebuke. Some have maintained that no other letter in the New Testament showed such a wide range of Paul's emotions. Clearly the Corinthians needed a good scolding!

Six Questions and Six Answers

I would suggest that Paul raises and answers six key questions in this letter. First, *Do we solve conflicts, or do we let them fester*? (See 1:10–17.) Paul's response went something like this: "Solve conflicts! Deal with divisions! Don't just shrug your shoulders and hope they'll go away." This question spawns others: "Do we keep grudges and nurse resentments? Do we have an outstanding memory when it comes to offenses?" If we want to be conflict solvers, we've got to learn from Jesus' life and His teachings about forgiveness and unity. We must deal with conflicts and divisions quickly—because if we ignore them, they will come back to bite us.

Second, *Do we resist the temptation to boast in or even to worship other human beings, or do we yield to it*? (See chapter 3.) Paul's message to the Corinthians was this: "Resist it. Follow the leaders God gives, by all means, but don't worship them. You belong to God, not to any human leader. God alone is worthy of your worship." If we yield to this temptation, we'll remain infant Christians or, at best, adolescents, and we'll keep waiting to get our signals from that person in whom we invested all our adoration. And that person will only fail us in the end. Paul said, in effect, "Don't worship other believers, no matter how gifted or godly they may be. Grow up. Become mature in the Lord."

Third, *Are we absolutely pure in our relationship with the other sex, or are we calculating and compromising*? (See 6:12–20.) Paul was unequivocal in his response: "Flee from immorality" (6:18). Avoid even the appearance of evil. Don't even play around with it. If we're committed to purity in our relationship with the other sex, we won't tolerate immorality. We won't set ourselves up for failure or for compromise of our integrity.

Fourth, *Are we using our spiritual gifts to build up all the members of the Christian community, or are we hoarding our gifts or using them for our own selfish advantage*? (See chapters 12 and 14.) Paul gave a memorable lesson on the diversity and unity of spiritual gifts in the church, the body of Christ. In effect, Paul said, "We need the gifts of each member in order to be a healthy church; please make sure you contribute your unique spiritual gift and don't minimize the contributions of others. We need each other! We are one body, with many members." Certainly a timely issue in our day, as we seek to celebrate our unity in Jesus Christ, the Head of the church, and our diversity as members of the one body of Christ, the church that embraces people from every nation, tribe, people and language.

Fifth, *Are our actions motivated by love, or by some other inferior motivation*? (See chapter 13.) Paul didn't hesitate to give his answer: "I will show you the most excellent way. If I speak in the tongues of men and of angels, but have not love, I am only a resounding gong or a clanging cymbal" (13:1). It is love that unifies the church. It is love that must control all we are and all we do.

Sixth, and finally, *Are we givers, or takers*? Chapter 16 discusses the behaviors and attitudes of giving and receiving. And Paul's message to the Corinthians was this: "Be a giver. Release your abundance. Give of your time. Give of yourself. Give of your money. Give now—and give often. Don't wait until later. After all, you can't take one thin dime with you." God calls us to be cheerful givers who generously and freely share with others what He has so generously given to us.

These six questions are just as relevant and challenging today as they were almost 2,000 years ago. As you read 1 Corinthians, allow the Holy Spirit to ask you these questions, and then answer them for yourself with penetrating honesty. If there are areas in your life where you stand convicted, where you sense the need to make a change, pray for strength and get at it! There is immense power available to us through the convicting and life-transforming Word of God. It's time to read that Word and follow its wisdom.

Divisions in the Church **Chapters 1–4**

In these opening chapters we learn of divisions and factions in the church. Paul warned the Corinthian believers about the dangers of division in the body of Christ. The church was split by a schism based on personalities–groups had formed around different leaders in the church. Paul rebuked the church for such childish worship of human leaders like Paul and Apollos, whom church members had begun to esteem more highly than they should. Paul wanted to get their feet back on solid ground and help them realize there was no room for worship of other humans. Our unity is found when we come together in worship of our Lord Jesus alone.

1 Paul, called to be an apostle of Christ Jesus by the will of God, and our brother Sosthenes,

2To the church of God in Corinth, to those sanctified in Christ Jesus and called to be holy, together with all those everywhere who call on the name of our Lord Jesus Christ—their Lord and ours: Ac 18:1; Ro 1:7

3Grace and peace to you from God our Father and the Lord Jesus Christ. Ro 1:7

Thanksgiving

4I always thank God for you because of his grace given you in Christ Jesus. 5For in him you have been enriched in every way—in all your speaking and in all your knowledge— 6because our testimony about Christ was confirmed in you. 7Therefore you do not lack any spiritual gift as you eagerly wait for our Lord Jesus Christ to be revealed. 8He will keep you strong to the end, so that you will be blameless on the day of our Lord Jesus Christ. 9God, who has called you into fellowship with his Son Jesus Christ our Lord, is faithful.

Divisions in the Church

10I appeal to you, brothers, in the name of our Lord Jesus Christ, that all of you agree with one another so that there may be no divisions among you and that you may be perfectly united in mind and thought. 11My brothers, some from Chloe's household have informed me that there are quarrels among you. 12What I mean is this: One of you says, "I follow Paul"; another, "I follow Apollos"; another, "I follow Cephas[a]"; still another, "I follow Christ." Jn 1:42; 1Co 3:4,22

13Is Christ divided? Was Paul crucified for you? Were you baptized into[b] the name of Paul? 14I am thankful that I did not baptize any of you except Crispus and Gaius, 15so no one can say that you were baptized into my name. 16(Yes, I also baptized the household of Stephanas; beyond that, I don't remember if I baptized anyone else.) 17For Christ did not send me to baptize, but to preach the gospel—not with words of human wisdom, lest the cross of Christ be emptied of its power.

Christ the Wisdom and Power of God

18For the message of the cross is foolishness to those who are perishing, but to us who are being saved it is the power of God. 19For it is written:

"I will destroy the wisdom of the wise;
the intelligence of the intelligent I will
frustrate."[c] Isa 29:14

20Where is the wise man? Where is the scholar? Where is the philosopher of this age? Has not God made foolish the wisdom of the world? 21For since in the wisdom of God the world through its wisdom did not know him, God was pleased through the foolishness of what was preached to save those who believe. 22Jews demand miraculous signs and Greeks look for wisdom, 23but we preach Christ crucified: a stumbling block to Jews and foolishness to Gentiles, 24but to those whom God has called, both Jews and Greeks, Christ the power of God and the wisdom of God. 25For the foolishness of God is wiser than man's wisdom, and the weakness of God is stronger than man's strength.

26Brothers, think of what you were when you were called. Not many of you were wise by human standards; not many were influential; not many were of noble birth. 27But God chose the foolish things of the world to shame the wise; God chose the weak things of the world to shame the strong. 28He chose the lowly things of this world and the despised things—and the things that are not—to nullify the things that are, 29so that no one may boast before him. 30It is because of him that you are in Christ Jesus, who has become for us wisdom from God—that is, our righteousness, holiness and redemption. 31Therefore, as it is written: "Let him who boasts boast in the Lord."[d] 2Co 10:17

2 When I came to you, brothers, I did not come with eloquence or superior wisdom as I proclaimed to you the testimony about God.[e] 2For I resolved to know nothing while I was with you except Jesus Christ and him crucified. 3I came to you in weakness and fear, and with much trembling. 4My message and my preaching were not with wise and persuasive words, but with a demonstration of the Spirit's power, 5so that your faith might not rest on men's wisdom, but on God's power. Ro 15:19; 2Co 4:7; 6:7

Wisdom From the Spirit

6We do, however, speak a message of wisdom among the mature, but not the wisdom of this age or of the rulers of this age, who are coming to nothing. 7No, we speak of God's secret wisdom, a

[a] *12* That is, Peter [b] *13* Or *in;* also in verse 15 [c] *19* Isaiah 29:14 [d] *31* Jer. 9:24 [e] *1* Some manuscripts *as I proclaimed to you God's mystery*

wisdom that has been hidden and that God destined for our glory before time began. 8None of the
rulers of this age understood it, for if they had,
they would not have crucified the Lord of glory.
9However, as it is written: Ac 7:2; 1Co 1:20; Eph 4:13

"No eye has seen,
no ear has heard,
no mind has conceived
what God has prepared for those who love
him"[a]—

10but God has revealed it to us by his Spirit.
The Spirit searches all things, even the deep

LIVING  INSIGHT

Human knowledge seems impressive—even awesome. But when it comes to tomorrow, our knowledge plunges to zero. Tomorrow lies hidden in the depths of God's unfathomable, intricately interwoven plan. Is your trust in God, your attitude of dependence, sufficiently stable to sustain you regardless?
(See 1 Corinthians 2:9–10.)

things of God. 11For who among men knows the
thoughts of a man except the man's spirit within
him? In the same way no one knows the thoughts
of God except the Spirit of God. 12We have not
received the spirit of the world but the Spirit who
is from God, that we may understand what God
has freely given us. 13This is what we speak, not in
words taught us by human wisdom but in words
taught by the Spirit, expressing spiritual truths in
spiritual words.[b] 14The man without the Spirit
does not accept the things that come from the
Spirit of God, for they are foolishness to him, and
he cannot understand them, because they are spiritually discerned. 15The spiritual man makes judgments about all things, but he himself is not subject to any man's judgment: 1Co 1:17-18

16"For who has known the mind of the Lord
that he may instruct him?"[c] Isa 40:13

But we have the mind of Christ. Jn 15:15

On Divisions in the Church

3 Brothers, I could not address you as spiritual
but as worldly—mere infants in Christ. 2I
gave you milk, not solid food, for you were not yet
ready for it. Indeed, you are still not ready. 3You
are still worldly. For since there is jealousy and
quarreling among you, are you not worldly? Are
you not acting like mere men? 4For when one says,
"I follow Paul," and another, "I follow Apollos,"
are you not mere men? Gal 5:20; Heb 5:13
5What, after all, is Apollos? And what is Paul?
Only servants, through whom you came to believe—as the Lord has assigned to each his task. 6I
planted the seed, Apollos watered it, but God
made it grow. 7So neither he who plants nor he
who waters is anything, but only God, who makes
things grow. 8The man who plants and the man
who waters have one purpose, and each will be
rewarded according to his own labor. 9For we are
God's fellow workers; you are God's field, God's
building. 2Co 6:1; Eph 2:20-22
10By the grace God has given me, I laid a foundation as an expert builder, and someone else is
building on it. But each one should be careful how
he builds. 11For no one can lay any foundation
other than the one already laid, which is Jesus
Christ. 12If any man builds on this foundation using gold, silver, costly stones, wood, hay or straw,
13his work will be shown for what it is, because the
Day will bring it to light. It will be revealed with
fire, and the fire will test the quality of each man's
work. 14If what he has built survives, he will receive
his reward. 15If it is burned up, he will suffer loss;
he himself will be saved, but only as one escaping
through the flames. 2Th 1:7-10; Jude 23
16Don't you know that you yourselves are God's
temple and that God's Spirit lives in you? 17If anyone destroys God's temple, God will destroy him;
for God's temple is sacred, and you are that temple. 2Co 6:16
18Do not deceive yourselves. If any one of you
thinks he is wise by the standards of this age, he
should become a "fool" so that he may become
wise. 19For the wisdom of this world is foolishness
in God's sight. As it is written: "He catches the
wise in their craftiness"[d]; 20and again, "The Lord
knows that the thoughts of the wise are futile."[e]
21So then, no more boasting about men! All things
are yours, 22whether Paul or Apollos or Cephas[f]
or the world or life or death or the present or the
future—all are yours, 23and you are of Christ, and
Christ is of God. 2Co 10:7; Gal 3:29

Apostles of Christ

4 So then, men ought to regard us as servants
of Christ and as those entrusted with the secret things of God. 2Now it is required that those
who have been given a trust must prove faithful. 3I
care very little if I am judged by you or by any
human court; indeed, I do not even judge myself.
4My conscience is clear, but that does not make
me innocent. It is the Lord who judges me. 5There-
fore judge nothing before the appointed time; wait
till the Lord comes. He will bring to light what is

[a] *9* Isaiah 64:4 [b] *13* Or *Spirit, interpreting spiritual truths to spiritual men* [c] *16* Isaiah 40:13 [d] *19* Job 5:13
[e] *20* Psalm 94:11 [f] *22* That is, Peter

hidden in darkness and will expose the motives of
men's hearts. At that time each will receive his
praise from God. Ro 2:1,29
6Now, brothers, I have applied these things to
myself and Apollos for your benefit, so that you
may learn from us the meaning of the saying, "Do
not go beyond what is written." Then you will not
take pride in one man over against another. 7For
who makes you different from anyone else? What
do you have that you did not receive? And if you
did receive it, why do you boast as though you did
not? Jn 3:27; 1Co 1:12
8Already you have all you want! Already you
have become rich! You have become kings—and
that without us! How I wish that you really had
become kings so that we might be kings with you!
9For it seems to me that God has put us apostles
on display at the end of the procession, like men
condemned to die in the arena. We have been
made a spectacle to the whole universe, to angels
as well as to men. 10We are fools for Christ, but
you are so wise in Christ! We are weak, but you are
strong! You are honored, we are dishonored! 11To
this very hour we go hungry and thirsty, we are
in rags, we are brutally treated, we are homeless.
12We work hard with our own hands. When we
are cursed, we bless; when we are persecuted, we
endure it; 13when we are slandered, we answer
kindly. Up to this moment we have become the
scum of the earth, the refuse of the world.
14I am not writing this to shame you, but to
warn you, as my dear children. 15Even though you
have ten thousand guardians in Christ, you do not
have many fathers, for in Christ Jesus I became
your father through the gospel. 16Therefore I urge
you to imitate me. 17For this reason I am sending
to you Timothy, my son whom I love, who is
faithful in the Lord. He will remind you of my way
of life in Christ Jesus, which agrees with what I
teach everywhere in every church. 1Co 7:17; 1Th 1:6
18Some of you have become arrogant, as if I
were not coming to you. 19But I will come to you
very soon, if the Lord is willing, and then I will find
out not only how these arrogant people are talking, but what power they have. 20For the kingdom
of God is not a matter of talk but of power. 21What
do you prefer? Shall I come to you with a whip, or
in love and with a gentle spirit? Ro 15:13; 2Co 1:15-16

Disorders in the Church Chapters 5–6

In this second section we read of three distinct types of disorders in the church of Corinth. First, there was *moral disorder*. The church knew about but deliberately did not deal with an open case of incest. Paul reminded the believers that these practices were not even accepted among unbelieving pagans. He offered a sharp rebuke and a strong call to repentance. Next, Paul raised the issue of a *legal disorder* in the church. One believer was taking another to the civil courts and marring the image of Christ and the reputation of the church in the process. Paul urged believers to deal with these issues in the church and not shame the name of Jesus by dragging their disputes into court. Third and finally, Paul addressed the issue of numerous *carnal disorders* in the church. Fleshly desires had gone unrestrained in Corinth, and there was a need to call people back into line with God's desires.

Expel the Immoral Brother!

5 It is actually reported that there is sexual immorality among you, and of a kind that does
not occur even among pagans: A man has his father's wife. 2And you are proud! Shouldn't you
rather have been filled with grief and have put out
of your fellowship the man who did this? 3Even
though I am not physically present, I am with you
in spirit. And I have already passed judgment on
the one who did this, just as if I were present.
4When you are assembled in the name of our Lord
Jesus and I am with you in spirit, and the power
of our Lord Jesus is present, 5hand this man over
to Satan, so that the sinful nature[a] may be destroyed and his spirit saved on the day of the Lord.
6Your boasting is not good. Don't you know
that a little yeast works through the whole batch of
dough? 7Get rid of the old yeast that you may be
a new batch without yeast—as you really are. For
Christ, our Passover lamb, has been sacrificed.
8Therefore let us keep the Festival, not with the old
yeast, the yeast of malice and wickedness, but with
bread without yeast, the bread of sincerity and
truth. Gal 5:9; 1Pe 1:19
9I have written you in my letter not to associate
with sexually immoral people— 10not at all meaning the people of this world who are immoral, or
the greedy and swindlers, or idolaters. In that case
you would have to leave this world. 11But now I
am writing you that you must not associate with
anyone who calls himself a brother but is sexually
immoral or greedy, an idolater or a slanderer, a
drunkard or a swindler. With such a man do not
even eat. 1Co 10:27; Eph 5:11
12What business is it of mine to judge those
outside the church? Are you not to judge those
inside? 13God will judge those outside. "Expel the
wicked man from among you."[b] Mk 4:11; 1Co 6:1-4

Lawsuits Among Believers

6 If any of you has a dispute with another, dare
he take it before the ungodly for judgment
instead of before the saints? 2Do you not know
that the saints will judge the world? And if you are
to judge the world, are you not competent to judge
trivial cases? 3Do you not know that we will judge
angels? How much more the things of this life!

[a]5 Or *that his body*; or *that the flesh* [b]*13* Deut. 17:7; 19:19; 21:21; 22:21,24; 24:7

4Therefore, if you have disputes about such matters, appoint as judges even men of little account
in the church![a] 5I say this to shame you. Is it
possible that there is nobody among you wise
enough to judge a dispute between believers? 6But
instead, one brother goes to law against another—
and this in front of unbelievers! Mt 19:28; 2Co 6:14-15

7The very fact that you have lawsuits among
you means you have been completely defeated already. Why not rather be wronged? Why not rather be cheated? 8Instead, you yourselves cheat and
do wrong, and you do this to your brothers.

9Do you not know that the wicked will not inherit the kingdom of God? Do not be deceived:
Neither the sexually immoral nor idolaters nor
adulterers nor male prostitutes nor homosexual
offenders 10nor thieves nor the greedy nor drunkards nor slanderers nor swindlers will inherit the
kingdom of God. 11And that is what some of you
were. But you were washed, you were sanctified,
you were justified in the name of the Lord Jesus
Christ and by the Spirit of our God. 1Co 1:2

Sexual Immorality

12"Everything is permissible for me"—but not
everything is beneficial. "Everything is permissible
for me"—but I will not be mastered by anything.
13"Food for the stomach and the stomach for
food"—but God will destroy them both. The body
is not meant for sexual immorality, but for the
Lord, and the Lord for the body. 14By his power
God raised the Lord from the dead, and he will
raise us also. 15Do you not know that your bodies
are members of Christ himself? Shall I then take
the members of Christ and unite them with a prostitute? Never! 16Do you not know that he who
unites himself with a prostitute is one with her in
body? For it is said, "The two will become one
flesh."[b] 17But he who unites himself with the Lord
is one with him in spirit. Jn 17:21-23; Gal 2:20

18Flee from sexual immorality. All other sins a
man commits are outside his body, but he who
sins sexually sins against his own body. 19Do you
not know that your body is a temple of the Holy
Spirit, who is in you, whom you have received
from God? You are not your own; 20you were
bought at a price. Therefore honor God with your
body. Ro 6:12; Heb 13:4; Rev 5:9

Difficulties in the Church — Chapters 7–16

The final section addressed a series of difficulties in the church at Corinth. First, Paul dealt with *domestic difficulties* as he gave advice on issues relating to marriage and divorce (chapter 7). Next, he addressed *social difficulties* in the church. Certain people were doing almost anything they wanted to do—in essence, turning liberty into license. Paul called them to walk in the freedom found in Christ but also in obedience to His call to holy living (chapters 8–10). Paul also needed to clarify issues relating to the *communal life* of the church. The Corinthians were trying to understand the place of women in worship, so Paul taught them on this topic (11:2–16). They needed instruction on how spiritual gifts were to be used in a loving and edifying context, and Paul obliged with three powerful chapters on the use of gifts among God's people (chapters 12–14). Furthermore, Paul had to clarify the correct *doctrinal position* on death and the resurrection—so chapter 15 records perhaps the grandest presentation of this doctrine found anywhere in the Bible. Finally, the Corinthians needed admonishing about a *financial difficulty*—and Paul responded with instruction about giving and receiving (chapter 16). The counsel given in these ten chapters speaks as powerfully to difficulties in the church today as it did almost 2,000 years ago.

Marriage

7 Now for the matters you wrote about: It is
good for a man not to marry.[c] 2But since
there is so much immorality, each man should
have his own wife, and each woman her own husband. 3The husband should fulfill his marital duty
to his wife, and likewise the wife to her husband.
4The wife's body does not belong to her alone but
also to her husband. In the same way, the husband's body does not belong to him alone but also
to his wife. 5Do not deprive each other except by
mutual consent and for a time, so that you may
devote yourselves to prayer. Then come together
again so that Satan will not tempt you because of
your lack of self-control. 6I say this as a concession, not as a command. 7I wish that all men were
as I am. But each man has his own gift from God;
one has this gift, another has that. 1Co 9:5; 12:4,11

8Now to the unmarried and the widows I say: It
is good for them to stay unmarried, as I am. 9But
if they cannot control themselves, they should
marry, for it is better to marry than to burn with
passion. 1Ti 5:14

10To the married I give this command (not I,
but the Lord): A wife must not separate from her

LIVING  INSIGHT

Pause and ponder this, all who believe in the Lord Jesus: The third member of the Godhead, the invisible, yet all-powerful Holy Spirit, is actually living inside your being. His limitless capabilities are resident within you, for He indwells you.

(See 1 Corinthians 6:19.)

[a]4 Or *matters, do you appoint as judges men of little account in the church?* [b]16 Gen. 2:24 [c]1 Or "*It is good for a man not to have sexual relations with a woman.*"

husband. 11But if she does, she must remain unmarried or else be reconciled to her husband. And
a husband must not divorce his wife. Mal 2:14-16
12To the rest I say this (I, not the Lord): If any
brother has a wife who is not a believer and she is
willing to live with him, he must not divorce her.
13And if a woman has a husband who is not a
believer and he is willing to live with her, she must
not divorce him. 14For the unbelieving husband
has been sanctified through his wife, and the unbelieving wife has been sanctified through her believing husband. Otherwise your children would be
unclean, but as it is, they are holy. Mal 2:15
15But if the unbeliever leaves, let him do so. A
believing man or woman is not bound in such
circumstances; God has called us to live in peace.
16How do you know, wife, whether you will save
your husband? Or, how do you know, husband,
whether you will save your wife? Ro 14:19; 1Pe 3:1
17Nevertheless, each one should retain the place
in life that the Lord assigned to him and to which
God has called him. This is the rule I lay down in
all the churches. 18Was a man already circumcised
when he was called? He should not become uncircumcised. Was a man uncircumcised when he was
called? He should not be circumcised. 19Circumci-
sion is nothing and uncircumcision is nothing.
Keeping God's commands is what counts. 20Each
one should remain in the situation which he was in
when God called him. 21Were you a slave when
you were called? Don't let it trouble you—although if you can gain your freedom, do so. 22For
he who was a slave when he was called by the Lord
is the Lord's freedman; similarly, he who was a free
man when he was called is Christ's slave. 23You
were bought at a price; do not become slaves of
men. 24Brothers, each man, as responsible to God,
should remain in the situation God called him to.
25Now about virgins: I have no command from
the Lord, but I give a judgment as one who by
the Lord's mercy is trustworthy. 26Because of the
present crisis, I think that it is good for you to
remain as you are. 27Are you married? Do not seek
a divorce. Are you unmarried? Do not look for a
wife. 28But if you do marry, you have not sinned;
and if a virgin marries, she has not sinned. But
those who marry will face many troubles in this
life, and I want to spare you this. 1Ti 1:13,16
29What I mean, brothers, is that the time is
short. From now on those who have wives should
live as if they had none; 30those who mourn, as if
they did not; those who are happy, as if they were
not; those who buy something, as if it were not
theirs to keep; 31those who use the things of the
world, as if not engrossed in them. For this world
in its present form is passing away. Ro 13:11-12
32I would like you to be free from concern. An
unmarried man is concerned about the Lord's affairs—how he can please the Lord. 33But a married
man is concerned about the affairs of this world—
how he can please his wife— 34and his interests
are divided. An unmarried woman or virgin is
concerned about the Lord's affairs: Her aim is to

LIVING 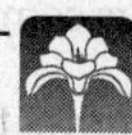 **INSIGHT**

I think we miss the mark if all we say to the many who are single is that the ultimate in God's plan for all of them is **marriage.** ***The ultimate in God's plan is that you who are unmarried seek the Lord and listen to what He is saying to you. Your singleness could become one of the highest spiritual plateaus you have ever known in your life.***

(See 1 Corinthians 7:29–31.)

be devoted to the Lord in both body and spirit.
But a married woman is concerned about the affairs of this world—how she can please her husband. 35I am saying this for your own good, not to
restrict you, but that you may live in a right way
in undivided devotion to the Lord. Ps 86:11; 1Ti 5:5
36If anyone thinks he is acting improperly toward the virgin he is engaged to, and if she is
getting along in years and he feels he ought to
marry, he should do as he wants. He is not sinning. They should get married. 37But the man who
has settled the matter in his own mind, who is
under no compulsion but has control over his own
will, and who has made up his mind not to marry
the virgin—this man also does the right thing.
38So then, he who marries the virgin does right,
but he who does not marry her does even better.[a]
39A woman is bound to her husband as long as
he lives. But if her husband dies, she is free to
marry anyone she wishes, but he must belong to
the Lord. 40In my judgment, she is happier if she
stays as she is—and I think that I too have the
Spirit of God. Ro 7:2-3; 2Co 6:14

Food Sacrificed to Idols

8 Now about food sacrificed to idols: We know
that we all possess knowledge.[b] Knowledge
puffs up, but love builds up. 2The man who thinks
he knows something does not yet know as he

[a] 36-38 Or *36If anyone thinks he is not treating his daughter properly, and if she is getting along in years, and he feels he ought to marry, he should do as he wants. He is not sinning. He should let her get married. 37But the man who has settled the matter in his own mind, who is under no compulsion but has control over his own will, and who has made up his mind to keep the virgin unmarried—this man also does the right thing. 38So then, he who gives his virgin in marriage does right, but he who does not give her in marriage does even better.* [b] 1 Or *"We all possess knowledge," as you say*

ought to know. 3But the man who loves God is known by God. Ac 15:20; 1Co 13:8-9,12; Gal 4:9

4So then, about eating food sacrificed to idols: We know that an idol is nothing at all in the world and that there is no God but one. 5For even if there are so-called gods, whether in heaven or on earth (as indeed there are many "gods" and many "lords"), 6yet for us there is but one God, the Father, from whom all things came and for whom we live; and there is but one Lord, Jesus Christ, through whom all things came and through whom we live. Ro 11:36; Mal 2:10

7But not everyone knows this. Some people are still so accustomed to idols that when they eat such food they think of it as having been sacrificed to an idol, and since their conscience is weak, it is defiled. 8But food does not bring us near to God; we are no worse if we do not eat, and no better if we do. Ro 14:14,17

9Be careful, however, that the exercise of your freedom does not become a stumbling block to the weak. 10For if anyone with a weak conscience sees you who have this knowledge eating in an idol's temple, won't he be emboldened to eat what has been sacrificed to idols? 11So this weak brother, for whom Christ died, is destroyed by your knowledge. 12When you sin against your brothers in this way and wound their weak conscience, you sin against Christ. 13Therefore, if what I eat causes my brother to fall into sin, I will never eat meat again, so that I will not cause him to fall. Mt 18:6; Ro 14:21

The Rights of an Apostle

9 Am I not free? Am I not an apostle? Have I not seen Jesus our Lord? Are you not the result of my work in the Lord? 2Even though I may not be an apostle to others, surely I am to you! For you are the seal of my apostleship in the Lord.

3This is my defense to those who sit in judgment on me. 4Don't we have the right to food and drink? 5Don't we have the right to take a believing wife along with us, as do the other apostles and the Lord's brothers and Cephas[a]? 6Or is it only I and Barnabas who must work for a living? Ac 4:36

7Who serves as a soldier at his own expense? Who plants a vineyard and does not eat of its grapes? Who tends a flock and does not drink of the milk? 8Do I say this merely from a human point of view? Doesn't the Law say the same thing? 9For it is written in the Law of Moses: "Do not muzzle an ox while it is treading out the grain."[b] Is it about oxen that God is concerned? 10Surely he says this for us, doesn't he? Yes, this was written for us, because when the plowman plows and the thresher threshes, they ought to do so in the hope of sharing in the harvest. 11If we have sown spiritual seed among you, is it too much if we reap a material harvest from you? 12If others have this right of support from you, shouldn't we have it all the more? Ro 15:27; 2Ti 2:6

But we did not use this right. On the contrary, we put up with anything rather than hinder the gospel of Christ. 13Don't you know that those who work in the temple get their food from the temple, and those who serve at the altar share in what is offered on the altar? 14In the same way, the Lord has commanded that those who preach the gospel should receive their living from the gospel.

15But I have not used any of these rights. And I am not writing this in the hope that you will do such things for me. I would rather die than have anyone deprive me of this boast. 16Yet when I preach the gospel, I cannot boast, for I am compelled to preach. Woe to me if I do not preach the gospel! 17If I preach voluntarily, I have a reward; if not voluntarily, I am simply discharging the trust committed to me. 18What then is my reward? Just this: that in preaching the gospel I may offer it free of charge, and so not make use of my rights in preaching it. 1Co 3:8,14; Gal 2:7

19Though I am free and belong to no man, I make myself a slave to everyone, to win as many as possible. 20To the Jews I became like a Jew, to win the Jews. To those under the law I became like one under the law (though I myself am not under the law), so as to win those under the law. 21To those not having the law I became like one not having the law (though I am not free from God's law but am under Christ's law), so as to win those not having the law. 22To the weak I became weak, to win the weak. I have become all things to all men so that by all possible means I might save some. 23I do all this for the sake of the gospel, that I may share in its blessings. Ro 2:12,14; 1Co 10:33

24Do you not know that in a race all the runners run, but only one gets the prize? Run in such a way as to get the prize. 25Everyone who competes in the games goes into strict training. They do it to get a crown that will not last; but we do it to get a crown that will last forever. 26Therefore I do not run like a man running aimlessly; I do not fight like a man beating the air. 27No, I beat my body and make it my slave so that after I have preached to others, I myself will not be disqualified for the prize.

Warnings From Israel's History

10 For I do not want you to be ignorant of the fact, brothers, that our forefathers were all under the cloud and that they all passed through the sea. 2They were all baptized into Moses in the cloud and in the sea. 3They all ate the same spiritual food 4and drank the same spiritual drink; for they drank from the spiritual rock that accompanied them, and that rock was Christ. 5Neverthe-

[a] 5 That is, Peter [b] 9 Deut. 25:4

less, God was not pleased with most of them; their
bodies were scattered over the desert. Nu 14:29
6Now these things occurred as examples[a] to
keep us from setting our hearts on evil things as
they did. 7Do not be idolaters, as some of them
were; as it is written: "The people sat down to eat
and drink and got up to indulge in pagan revelry."[b] 8We should not commit sexual immorality,
as some of them did—and in one day twenty-
three thousand of them died. 9We should not test
the Lord, as some of them did—and were killed by
snakes. 10And do not grumble, as some of them
did—and were killed by the destroying angel.

LIVING  **INSIGHT**

Instead of griping or complaining about that boring job or that persistent chore (for example, picking up after your kids for the nth time, or taking out the trash yet again), do it with a thankful heart. Be glad you have that job, those kids, the strength to do the task.

(See 1 Corinthians 10:10.)

11These things happened to them as examples
and were written down as warnings for us, on
whom the fulfillment of the ages has come. 12So, if
you think you are standing firm, be careful that
you don't fall! 13No temptation has seized you except what is common to man. And God is faithful;
he will not let you be tempted beyond what you
can bear. But when you are tempted, he will also
provide a way out so that you can stand up under it. Ro 11:20; 2Pe 2:9

Idol Feasts and the Lord's Supper

14Therefore, my dear friends, flee from idolatry.
15I speak to sensible people; judge for yourselves
what I say. 16Is not the cup of thanksgiving for
which we give thanks a participation in the blood
of Christ? And is not the bread that we break a
participation in the body of Christ? 17Because
there is one loaf, we, who are many, are one body,
for we all partake of the one loaf. Mt 26:26-28
18Consider the people of Israel: Do not those
who eat the sacrifices participate in the altar? 19Do
I mean then that a sacrifice offered to an idol is
anything, or that an idol is anything? 20No, but the
sacrifices of pagans are offered to demons, not to
God, and I do not want you to be participants with
demons. 21You cannot drink the cup of the Lord
and the cup of demons too; you cannot have a part
in both the Lord's table and the table of demons.
22Are we trying to arouse the Lord's jealousy? Are
we stronger than he? Dt 32:16,21; Isa 45:9

The Believer's Freedom

23"Everything is permissible"—but not everything is beneficial. "Everything is permissible"—
but not everything is constructive. 24Nobody
should seek his own good, but the good of others.
25Eat anything sold in the meat market without
raising questions of conscience, 26for, "The earth is
the Lord's, and everything in it."[c] Ps 24:1; Ac 10:15
27If some unbeliever invites you to a meal and
you want to go, eat whatever is put before you
without raising questions of conscience. 28But if
anyone says to you, "This has been offered in sacrifice," then do not eat it, both for the sake of the
man who told you and for conscience' sake[d]—
29the other man's conscience, I mean, not yours.
For why should my freedom be judged by another's conscience? 30If I take part in the meal with
thankfulness, why am I denounced because of
something I thank God for? Lk 10:7; Ro 14:6
31So whether you eat or drink or whatever you
do, do it all for the glory of God. 32Do not cause
anyone to stumble, whether Jews, Greeks or the
church of God— 33even as I try to please everybody in every way. For I am not seeking my own
good but the good of many, so that they may be
11 saved. 1Follow my example, as I follow the
example of Christ. Ro 11:14; 15:2

Propriety in Worship

2I praise you for remembering me in everything
and for holding to the teachings,[e] just as I passed
them on to you. 1Co 4:17; 15:2-3
3Now I want you to realize that the head of
every man is Christ, and the head of the woman is
man, and the head of Christ is God. 4Every man
who prays or prophesies with his head covered
dishonors his head. 5And every woman who prays
or prophesies with her head uncovered dishonors
her head—it is just as though her head were
shaved. 6If a woman does not cover her head, she
should have her hair cut off; and if it is a disgrace
for a woman to have her hair cut or shaved off, she
should cover her head. 7A man ought not to cover
his head,[f] since he is the image and glory of God;
but the woman is the glory of man. 8For man did
not come from woman, but woman from man;
9neither was man created for woman, but woman
for man. 10For this reason, and because of the

[a]6 Or *types*; also in verse 11 [b]7 Exodus 32:6 [c]26 Psalm 24:1 [d]28 Some manuscripts *conscience' sake, for "the earth is the Lord's and everything in it"* [e]2 Or *traditions* [f]4-7 Or *4Every man who prays or prophesies with long hair dishonors his head. 5And every woman who prays or prophesies with no covering* ⌞*of hair*⌟ *on her head dishonors her head—she is just like one of the "shorn women." 6If a woman has no covering, let her be for now with short hair, but since it is a disgrace for a woman to have her hair shorn or shaved, she should grow it again. 7A man ought not to have long hair*

angels, the woman ought to have a sign of authority on her head. Ge 2:21-23; Jas 3:9
11In the Lord, however, woman is not independent of man, nor is man independent of woman.
12For as woman came from man, so also man is
born of woman. But everything comes from God.
13Judge for yourselves: Is it proper for a woman to
pray to God with her head uncovered? 14Does not
the very nature of things teach you that if a man
has long hair, it is a disgrace to him, 15but that if
a woman has long hair, it is her glory? For long
hair is given to her as a covering. 16If anyone wants
to be contentious about this, we have no other
practice—nor do the churches of God. Ro 11:36

The Lord's Supper

17In the following directives I have no praise for
you, for your meetings do more harm than good.
18In the first place, I hear that when you come
together as a church, there are divisions among
you, and to some extent I believe it. 19No doubt
there have to be differences among you to show
which of you have God's approval. 20When you
come together, it is not the Lord's Supper you eat,
21for as you eat, each of you goes ahead without
waiting for anybody else. One remains hungry,
another gets drunk. 22Don't you have homes to eat
and drink in? Or do you despise the church of God
and humiliate those who have nothing? What shall
I say to you? Shall I praise you for this? Certainly
not! 1Co 1:10-12; 1Jn 2:19
23For I received from the Lord what I also
passed on to you: The Lord Jesus, on the night he
was betrayed, took bread, 24and when he had given
thanks, he broke it and said, "This is my body,
which is for you; do this in remembrance of me."
25In the same way, after supper he took the cup,
saying, "This cup is the new covenant in my blood;
do this, whenever you drink it, in remembrance of
me." 26For whenever you eat this bread and drink
this cup, you proclaim the Lord's death until he
comes. Mt 26:26-28; Mk 14:22-24; Lk 22:17-20
27Therefore, whoever eats the bread or drinks
the cup of the Lord in an unworthy manner will be
guilty of sinning against the body and blood of the
Lord. 28A man ought to examine himself before he
eats of the bread and drinks of the cup. 29For
anyone who eats and drinks without recognizing
the body of the Lord eats and drinks judgment on
himself. 30That is why many among you are weak
and sick, and a number of you have fallen asleep.
31But if we judged ourselves, we would not come
under judgment. 32When we are judged by the
Lord, we are being disciplined so that we will not
be condemned with the world. Ps 94:12; Heb 12:7-10
33So then, my brothers, when you come together to eat, wait for each other. 34If anyone is hungry,
he should eat at home, so that when you meet
together it may not result in judgment. ver 21-22
And when I come I will give further directions.

LIVING  **INSIGHT**

When participating in the Lord's Supper, the place may not be significant, but the condition of the heart is. Before we ever eat the bread or drink from the cup, each Christian asks within himself or herself, "Is there anything between my Father and me? Is my heart clean?"

(See 1 Corinthians 11:28.)

Spiritual Gifts

12 Now about spiritual gifts, brothers, I do
not want you to be ignorant. 2You know
that when you were pagans, somehow or other you
were influenced and led astray to mute idols.
3Therefore I tell you that no one who is speaking
by the Spirit of God says, "Jesus be cursed," and
no one can say, "Jesus is Lord," except by the Holy
Spirit. Ro 1:11; 1Th 1:9; 1Jn 4:2-3
4There are different kinds of gifts, but the same
Spirit. 5There are different kinds of service, but the
same Lord. 6There are different kinds of working,
but the same God works all of them in all men.

LIVING  **INSIGHT**

Relax and enjoy your spiritual species. Cultivate your own capabilities, your own style. Appreciate the members of your family or your fellowship for who they are, even though their outlook or style may be miles different from yours.

(See 1 Corinthians 12:4.)

7Now to each one the manifestation of the Spirit
is given for the common good. 8To one there is
given through the Spirit the message of wisdom, to
another the message of knowledge by means of the
same Spirit, 9to another faith by the same Spirit, to
another gifts of healing by that one Spirit, 10to
another miraculous powers, to another prophecy,
to another distinguishing between spirits, to another speaking in different kinds of tongues,[a] and
to still another the interpretation of tongues.[a]
11All these are the work of one and the same Spirit,
and he gives them to each one, just as he determines. Eph 4:12; 1Co 2:6

[a]10 Or *languages*; also in verse 28

One Body, Many Parts

12 The body is a unit, though it is made up of
many parts; and though all its parts are many, they
form one body. So it is with Christ. 13 For we were
all baptized by[a] one Spirit into one body—
whether Jews or Greeks, slave or free—and we
were all given the one Spirit to drink. Gal 3:28

14 Now the body is not made up of one part but
of many. 15 If the foot should say, "Because I am
not a hand, I do not belong to the body," it would
not for that reason cease to be part of the body.
16 And if the ear should say, "Because I am not an
eye, I do not belong to the body," it would not for
that reason cease to be part of the body. 17 If the
whole body were an eye, where would the sense of
hearing be? If the whole body were an ear, where
would the sense of smell be? 18 But in fact God has
arranged the parts in the body, every one of them,
just as he wanted them to be. 19 If they were all one
part, where would the body be? 20 As it is, there are
many parts, but one body. Ro 12:5

21 The eye cannot say to the hand, "I don't need
you!" And the head cannot say to the feet, "I don't
need you!" 22 On the contrary, those parts of the
body that seem to be weaker are indispensable,
23 and the parts that we think are less honorable we
treat with special honor. And the parts that are
unpresentable are treated with special modesty,
24 while our presentable parts need no special treatment. But God has combined the members of the
body and has given greater honor to the parts that
lacked it, 25 so that there should be no division in
the body, but that its parts should have equal concern for each other. 26 If one part suffers, every part
suffers with it; if one part is honored, every part
rejoices with it.

LIVING  **INSIGHT**

We need each other. You need someone and someone needs you. Isolated islands we are not. To make this experience called "life" work, we've got to lean and support. And relate and respond. And give and take. And confess and forgive. And reach out and embrace. And release and rely.

(See 1 Corinthians 12:26.)

27 Now you are the body of Christ, and each one
of you is a part of it. 28 And in the church God has
appointed first of all apostles, second prophets,
third teachers, then workers of miracles, also those
having gifts of healing, those able to help others,
those with gifts of administration, and those
speaking in different kinds of tongues. 29 Are all
apostles? Are all prophets? Are all teachers? Do all
work miracles? 30 Do all have gifts of healing? Do
all speak in tongues[b]? Do all interpret? 31 But eagerly desire[c] the greater gifts. 1Co 14:1,39; Eph 4:11

Love

And now I will show you the most excellent
way.

13 If I speak in the tongues[d] of men and of
angels, but have not love, I am only a resounding gong or a clanging cymbal. 2 If I have the
gift of prophecy and can fathom all mysteries and
all knowledge, and if I have a faith that can move
mountains, but have not love, I am nothing. 3 If I
give all I possess to the poor and surrender my
body to the flames,[e] but have not love, I gain
nothing. Mt 6:2; 1Co 14:2

4 Love is patient, love is kind. It does not envy,
it does not boast, it is not proud. 5 It is not rude,
it is not self-seeking, it is not easily angered, it
keeps no record of wrongs. 6 Love does not delight
in evil but rejoices with the truth. 7 It always protects, always trusts, always hopes, always perseveres. 1Co 10:24; 2Jn 4

8 Love never fails. But where there are prophecies, they will cease; where there are tongues, they
will be stilled; where there is knowledge, it will pass
away. 9 For we know in part and we prophesy in
part, 10 but when perfection comes, the imperfect
disappears. 11 When I was a child, I talked like a
child, I thought like a child, I reasoned like a child.
When I became a man, I put childish ways behind
me. 12 Now we see but a poor reflection as in a
mirror; then we shall see face to face. Now I know
in part; then I shall know fully, even as I am fully
known. 1Co 8:3; 2Co 5:7; 1Jn 3:2

13 And now these three remain: faith, hope and
love. But the greatest of these is love. 1Co 16:14

Gifts of Prophecy and Tongues

14 Follow the way of love and eagerly desire
spiritual gifts, especially the gift of prophecy. 2 For anyone who speaks in a tongue[f] does not
speak to men but to God. Indeed, no one understands him; he utters mysteries with his spirit.[g]
3 But everyone who prophesies speaks to men for
their strengthening, encouragement and comfort.
4 He who speaks in a tongue edifies himself, but he
who prophesies edifies the church. 5 I would like
every one of you to speak in tongues,[h] but I
would rather have you prophesy. He who prophesies is greater than one who speaks in tongues,[h]
unless he interprets, so that the church may be
edified. Nu 11:29; 1Co 12:31

[a] 13 Or *with*; or *in* [b] 30 Or *other languages* [c] 31 Or *But you are eagerly desiring* [d] 1 Or *languages* [e] 3 Some early manuscripts *body that I may boast* [f] 2 Or *another language*; also in verses 4, 13, 14, 19, 26 and 27 [g] 2 Or *by the Spirit* [h] 5 Or *other languages*; also in verses 6, 18, 22, 23 and 39

GOD'S "BODY-BUILDING" PROGRAM

"The body is a unit, though it is made up of many parts; and though all its parts are many, they form one body. So it is with Christ."

—1 CORINTHIANS 12:12

I think of the church as God's "body-building" program. Do you know the materials God uses for building the church? He uses all who follow Jesus. He begins by recruiting people through evangelism and outreach efforts. The lost are found as they respond positively to the Good News of Jesus Christ. Then they begin to be built up in Christ and become personally involved in God's world program of seeking those who are lost and bringing the gospel of salvation. The church's mission is a never-ending project, drawing its power and its resources from those people who have caught the vision and have become devoted to Jesus Christ.

When I speak of the church, I am not writing about some local congregation or a particular denomination. I don't have any particular geographical location in mind either . . . or color of skin or nation of origin or culture or language. I'm referring to the universal church when I speak of the body of Christ. I must admit, the more I study God's plan and program for the body, the more I believe in it, the more I admire what He has done and is doing, and the more I want to be involved.

When I meet folks who bad-mouth the church or see little significance in its existence, I pity those individuals rather than feel offended. I realize they simply don't understand. It's a little like attending a symphony with someone who has no understanding of or appreciation for classical music. The whole event seems a waste of time and energy when, in actuality, the problem lies within his or her own mind.

Defining the Church

There is nothing like a definition to clarify the meaning of terms. Let me try out this definition for "church": *The ever-enlarging body of born-again believers who comprise the universal body of Christ over whom Jesus reigns as Lord.* I believe that covers all the essential bases. The church is ever-enlarging, it is universal in scope, it is continually in process, it is exclusive in membership and it is impervious to destruction. Let me ask you: Can you think of anything more worthy of your time and energy?

The church is in the business of cultivating a passion for living with eternal dimensions. When people begin to realize this, it revolutionizes their whole frame of reference. Their world suddenly enlarges from preoccupation with this tiny speck of time and circumstances to a worldwide, invincible project over which Jesus Christ serves as Lord.

Vital Signs of a Healthy Church

Sometimes people ask, "Do I have to join a church to become a Christian?" My answer is, "No, but God always joins you to the church." No, you don't have to join some local church in order to become a Christian. God wants you to be connected with a local church—certainly—but that's a separate issue from becoming a Christian. But you automatically become a member of the universal body of Christ, His church, when you believe. No problem there. But if you do encounter problems with respect to the church, it will be when you cast your lot with a local church. It need not be an unhappy experience, but it sometimes is. Why? Because the vital signs of health and wholeness may be missing.

When we think about a healthy physical body, the vital signs are important. So it is with the body of Christ, the church. Look with me at the six vital signs of a healthy church. I find each one either mentioned or implied in 1 Corinthians 12. First, *there will be the presence of unity and harmony*: "The body is a unit, though it is made up of many parts; and though all its parts are many, they form one body. So it is with Christ" (1 Corinthians 12:12). Such unity in the body is also emphasized in John 17:20–23 and Ephesians 4:1–6.

Second, *there will be the absence of favoritism, status and prejudice*: "For we were all baptized by one Spirit into one body—whether Jews or Greeks, slave or free—and we were all given the one Spirit to drink (1 Corinthians 12:13). In the first-century Roman world, the equality found in the church was much more significant than it is today. In that day there were definite castes (still familiar to the people of India, but not as much to the people of western culture). In those days there was nobility and there was slavery. There was the slave owner and there was the slave, who was nothing more than a human "tool" in the hands of his owner. In another letter written by Paul, he recorded a thought similar to the one he communicated to the Corinthians: "You are all sons of God through faith in Christ Jesus, for all of you who were baptized into Christ have clothed yourselves with Christ. There is neither Jew nor Greek, slave nor free, male nor female, for you are all one in Christ Jesus" (Galatians 3:26–28).

In a healthy church one of the vital signs is an absence of favoritism, status and prejudice. In any other earthly organization, when you bring together a number of human beings, you're going to have prejudice, emphasis on status and a display of favoritism. It is not to be so in the body of Christ! This is one place that has no room for "preferred customers" or second-class citizens.

Third, *there is an emphasis on individual dignity and mutual variety*. We find this vital sign in 1 Corinthians 12:14–20. I love this passage. Watch for the humor in it. Think of the human body as you take a moment and read these words:

> *Now the body is not made up of one part but of many. If the foot should say, "Because I am not a hand, I do not belong to the body," it would not for that reason cease to be part of the body. And if the ear should say, "Because I am not an eye, I do not belong to the body," it would not for that reason cease to be part of the body. If the whole body were an eye, where would the sense of hearing be? If the whole body were an ear, where would the sense of smell be? But in fact God has arranged the parts in the body, every one of them, just as he wanted them to be. If they were all one part, where would the body be? As it is, there are many parts, but one body.*

It is impossible for feet to go on strike, isn't it? Because feet are part of the body, they stay connected to the body. Paul shows us how ridiculous it would be for one part of the body to try to leave. As we keep reading, he carries the analogy to the ultimate extreme! Try to picture an "eye-body"—one massive six-foot eye! (verse 17). How useless, how unattractive. You couldn't hug it or kiss it. You wouldn't have anything to kiss with, unless you "batted" each other when you got up close. You'd get dirt in your eye all the time as you rolled around the house. You couldn't move around. Think of trying to drive a car or getting into bed. Hilarious! The same could be said for an "ear-body," or any other component as well.

By now you are smiling . . . and that's what you're supposed to do! The point is so ridiculous that it's humorous. We make six-foot eyeballs out of some people. We make five-foot nine-inch ears out of others. We make them our stars, celebrities, big-time "pedestal types." But they're just eyes and ears. They're just noses. They're just lips. No one person in the body of Christ is the whole body. Let's stop making idols out of people in the body! Sure, we need heroes—people we admire and love and respect. But we don't need six-foot eyeballs. Keep this truth in mind: "But in fact God has arranged the parts in the body, every one of them, just as he wanted them to be. If they were all one part, where would the body be? As it is, there are many parts, but one body" (verses 18–20).

Fourth, *there is a de-emphasis on independence and self-sufficiency*. Listen to this, all you self-sufficient, strong and natural leaders! Pay attention, all entrepreneurs! Hear ye, hear ye, you who would be an independent-minded Lone Ranger!

> *The eye cannot say to the hand, "I don't need you!" And the head cannot say to the feet, "I don't need you!" On the contrary, those parts of the body that seem to be weaker are indispensable, and the parts that we think are less honorable we treat with special honor. And the parts that are unpresentable are treated with special modesty, while our presentable parts need no special treatment. But God has combined the members of the body and has given greater honor to the parts that lacked it (1 Corinthians 12:21–24).*

Our daughter has a chronic problem with her pancreas. The tiny duct that secretes fluid is too narrow, so that every once in a while something will get lodged in that duct—perhaps a very small stone—and her whole body will go into an incredible spasm of pain that immobilizes her. You wouldn't think the duct of a pancreas could be that big a deal. It's hard to believe something that small could affect her whole body, but that's the way God made the body. *No organ is completely independent and unrelated*.

So it is in the body of Christ. There's a little member of the body down in there somewhere. And the happiness or sadness of some part of the family of God rests on the functioning of that little, tiny part of the body. The body needs every member; every member needs the body. Interdependence is a principle that cannot be ignored among the body members.

Fifth, *there is the support of others, whether they are hurting or being honored*. Paul testifies to God's amazing wisdom in giving "greater honor to the parts that lacked it, so that there should be no division in the body, but that its parts should have equal concern for each other. If one part suffers, every part suffers with it; if one part is honored, every part rejoices with it" (1 Corinthians 12:25–26).

Isn't that great? Talk about a healthy church! Someone is hurting . . . you feel the sting of pain. You mourn with those who mourn. Someone can't keep up . . . you slow down and encourage him or her. You are promoted and honored . . . others sincerely applaud and cheer. They rejoice as you rejoice. Is that the way it works? I hope so. What one member feels, all the others feel. That's the way it is supposed to be in a healthy body.

Sixth, and finally, *there is the exaltation of Christ as Head and supreme authority*: "Now you are the body of Christ, and each one of you is a part of it" (1 Corinthians 12:27). Let us never forget our name: "the body of Christ." We are not called "the body of Chuck, or Sue, or Jennifer, or George"—but the body of Christ. Christ is the Head. Christ is the only Lord needed to make the church alive and healthy. Don't fall into the temptation of following substitutes for the real thing. The Head is Jesus Christ. He alone is Lord.

What the Church Means to the World

Why is the church significant to the world? Because it represents penetrating light and undiluted salt in a lost, confused, insipid society (see Matthew 5:13–16). Mark these words well: We come to the church not to escape the world but to be equipped to be sent out into the world with the transforming power of the gospel of Jesus Christ. Interestingly, when a church remains neutral on a moral issue that affects the community, the public will criticize that church. The public will accuse the church of letting the community down. In the public arena, the church of Jesus Christ is *expected* to stand for righteousness. Even the uncommitted, the unchurched crowd, know in their hearts that a church that is weak on sin has lost its way. Although Paul wrote the following words to reflect his own personal situation, let me broaden the application to include the church today:

> *Now I want you to know, brothers, that what has happened to me has really served to advance the gospel. As a result, it has become clear throughout the whole palace guard and to everyone else that I am in chains for Christ. Because of my chains, most of the brothers in the Lord have been encouraged to speak the word of God more courageously and fearlessly (Philippians 1:12-14).*

I remember reading the story about former United States president Calvin Coolidge, who returned home from attending church. He was asked by his wife what the minister spoke on. "Sin," Coolidge replied. Wanting to know more, she pressed him for some words of explanation. "What did he say about it?" And being a man of few words with his wife, he responded, "I think he was against it."

When the pulpit denounces sin, people are influenced to stand against it. When the pulpit speaks passionately and prophetically on moral issues, people learn to penetrate the fog of compromise and gain courage to stand alone. For many years the church gave our nation its conscience. As its pulpits stood, so its people stood.

"You are the salt of the earth," said Jesus. "You are the light of the world." Let the light shine. Let the salt bite. Let it give flavor, let it preserve from corruption. That's your role, Christian! The world expects it from us, even though in most cases it will not agree with us. In Paul's day "the whole palace guard" became aware of Jesus Christ! Even though many today will not enter the doors of a local church (though they are invited), they expect us to stand for the truth as we see it in Scripture. To do less is to diminish our distinctive and to lose our integrity.

What the Church Means to the Community

Are you ready for a surprise? What follows may make a few of my readers swallow hard. Some of you who fix a squint-eyed look at other ministries, criticizing them because they don't agree with you, may be shocked by these words from the apostle Paul:

> *It is true that some preach Christ out of envy and rivalry, but others out of goodwill. The latter do so in love, knowing that I am put here for the defense of the gospel. The former preach Christ out of selfish ambition, not sincerely, supposing that they can stir up trouble for me while I am in chains. But what does it matter? The important thing is that in every way, whether from false motives or true, Christ is preached. And because of this I rejoice (Philippians 1:15–18).*

Why is the church significant to the community? For at least two very important reasons. First, *because churches provide the availability of variety.* And second, *because churches offer a singularity of message.* In effect, Paul is affirming that there will be churches of all different kinds. Think of the windshield wipers on your car. Churches run the spectrum from one extreme to another. Churches that are worth attending and supporting have the same pivot point—the Lord Jesus Christ. Christ is exalted. Christ is declared. Christ is central. But some will approach from one direction, while others from another. A different style of worship. Another emphasis and methodology. Perhaps even a difference in motive. But one true message.

I have a strong word to any who may be prone to publicly criticize other ministries. Watch yourself! Rather than being discerning, you may have become too narrow and rigid! Learn from Paul, whose testimony went something like this: "I rejoice that at least the Lord Jesus Christ is being proclaimed." My advice? Don't waste your time criticizing other ministries. Just attend the one you prefer and give God praise that in churches throughout the world Jesus Christ is exalted. You may be thinking, "Sounds pretty liberal to me." Yet to me it sounds Biblical. If Philippians 1:15–20 isn't teaching that, then I'm at a loss to know what it means. In our zeal it is very easy to think we've got the *only* church with the *only* answers for the entire community. The simple truth is: *we don't.*

What the Church Means to the Christian

The church is significant not only to the world and to the community but to the Christian as well. Read Philippians 1:23–30 and see what the apostle Paul had to say about this topic. This passage tells us something that the city council or the school board or the bowling team will never tell us. The church alone tells Christians to "conduct yourselves in a manner worthy of the gospel of Christ" (Philippians 1:27).

You won't hear that from any other organization! No one else will confront you and urge, "Shape up your life. Get with it. You say you're a Christian? Walk like it. Your life should reflect Jesus Christ. You've done wrong? Confess it and come back to God." No one else does that. Only the church.

Furthermore, only those who continue faithfully in the attendance of church services will hear exhortation and encouragement and rebuke that will help keep their lives on track. In fact, there at least four specific benefits of church attendance: accountability, consistency, unity and stability. These wonderful benefits are beautifully interwoven through the first chapter of Paul's letter to the Philippians.

What I have observed is that Christians who lose their trust in a local church and walk away, saying, "No thanks, I don't need it," have struggles, without exception, in one or more of these four areas—sometimes all four. They lose (or wish to lose) accountability. They lack consistency in their walk. They cultivate an independent spirit rather than a spirit of interdependence that encourages mutual love and concern. And when pressure strikes, they lack stability. Why? The answer isn't that complicated: There's no family or source of support around. They're out there on their own.

My counsel is predictable: Before you decide you don't need a church, think carefully about the consequences. Especially if you have available to you a small group of caring, loving folks with whom you are free to interact, share the details of your life and enter into theirs as well. There may be challenges involved in being an active part of a local church, but let me remind you of something very important: You need them and they need you; that's the way God has designed His body, the church of Jesus Christ.

6 Now, brothers, if I come to you and speak in tongues, what good will I be to you, unless I bring you some revelation or knowledge or prophecy or word of instruction? 7 Even in the case of lifeless things that make sounds, such as the flute or harp, how will anyone know what tune is being played unless there is a distinction in the notes? 8 Again, if the trumpet does not sound a clear call, who will get ready for battle? 9 So it is with you. Unless you speak intelligible words with your tongue, how will anyone know what you are saying? You will just be speaking into the air. 10 Undoubtedly there are all sorts of languages in the world, yet none of them is without meaning. 11 If then I do not grasp the meaning of what someone is saying, I am a foreigner to the speaker, and he is a foreigner to me. 12 So it is with you. Since you are eager to have spiritual gifts, try to excel in gifts that build up the church.

13 For this reason anyone who speaks in a tongue should pray that he may interpret what he says. 14 For if I pray in a tongue, my spirit prays, but my mind is unfruitful. 15 So what shall I do? I will pray with my spirit, but I will also pray with my mind; I will sing with my spirit, but I will also sing with my mind. 16 If you are praising God with your spirit, how can one who finds himself among those who do not understand[a] say "Amen" to your thanksgiving, since he does not know what you are saying? 17 You may be giving thanks well enough, but the other man is not edified.

18 I thank God that I speak in tongues more than all of you. 19 But in the church I would rather speak five intelligible words to instruct others than ten thousand words in a tongue. ver 6

20 Brothers, stop thinking like children. In regard to evil be infants, but in your thinking be adults. 21 In the Law it is written:

"Through men of strange tongues
and through the lips of foreigners
I will speak to this people,
but even then they will not listen to me,"[b]
says the Lord.

LIVING  INSIGHT

We are the product of what we think about. Our actions and our reactions originate in our minds. What do you think about? Upon what do you spend most of your mental energy? How much independent, hard-core, no-nonsense, controlled mental input goes into your day on the average?

(See 1 Corinthians 14:20–21.)

22 Tongues, then, are a sign, not for believers but for unbelievers; prophecy, however, is for believers, not for unbelievers. 23 So if the whole church comes together and everyone speaks in tongues, and some who do not understand[c] or some unbelievers come in, will they not say that you are out of your mind? 24 But if an unbeliever or someone who does not understand[d] comes in while everybody is prophesying, he will be convinced by all that he is a sinner and will be judged by all, 25 and the secrets of his heart will be laid bare. So he will fall down and worship God, exclaiming, "God is really among you!" Isa 45:14; Zec 8:23; Ac 2:13

Orderly Worship

26 What then shall we say, brothers? When you come together, everyone has a hymn, or a word of instruction, a revelation, a tongue or an interpretation. All of these must be done for the strengthening of the church. 27 If anyone speaks in a tongue, two—or at the most three—should speak, one at a time, and someone must interpret. 28 If there is no interpreter, the speaker should keep quiet in the church and speak to himself and God.

29 Two or three prophets should speak, and the others should weigh carefully what is said. 30 And if a revelation comes to someone who is sitting down, the first speaker should stop. 31 For you can all prophesy in turn so that everyone may be instructed and encouraged. 32 The spirits of prophets are subject to the control of prophets. 33 For God is not a God of disorder but of peace. 1Co 12:10

As in all the congregations of the saints, 34 women should remain silent in the churches. They are not allowed to speak, but must be in submission, as the Law says. 35 If they want to inquire about something, they should ask their own husbands at home; for it is disgraceful for a woman to speak in the church. 1Ti 2:11-12

36 Did the word of God originate with you? Or are you the only people it has reached? 37 If anybody thinks he is a prophet or spiritually gifted, let him acknowledge that what I am writing to you is the Lord's command. 38 If he ignores this, he himself will be ignored.[e] 2Co 10:7; 1Jn 4:6

39 Therefore, my brothers, be eager to prophesy, and do not forbid speaking in tongues. 40 But everything should be done in a fitting and orderly way. 1Co 12:31

The Resurrection of Christ

15 Now, brothers, I want to remind you of the gospel I preached to you, which you received and on which you have taken your stand.

[a]16 Or *among the inquirers* [b]21 Isaiah 28:11,12 [c]23 Or *some inquirers* [d]24 Or *or some inquirer* [e]38 Some manuscripts *If he is ignorant of this, let him be ignorant*

2By this gospel you are saved, if you hold firmly to
the word I preached to you. Otherwise, you have
believed in vain. Ro 1:16; 11:22
3For what I received I passed on to you as of
first importance[a]: that Christ died for our sins
according to the Scriptures, 4that he was buried,
that he was raised on the third day according to
the Scriptures, 5and that he appeared to Peter,[b]
and then to the Twelve. 6After that, he appeared to
more than five hundred of the brothers at the
same time, most of whom are still living, though
some have fallen asleep. 7Then he appeared to
James, then to all the apostles, 8and last of all he
appeared to me also, as to one abnormally born.
9For I am the least of the apostles and do not
even deserve to be called an apostle, because I

LIVING  **INSIGHT**

I have begun to realize that secure, mature people are best described in fifteen words: They know who they are . . . they like who they are . . . they are who they are. They are real.

(See 1 Corinthians 15:9–11.)

persecuted the church of God. 10But by the grace
of God I am what I am, and his grace to me was
not without effect. No, I worked harder than all of
them—yet not I, but the grace of God that was
with me. 11Whether, then, it was I or they, this is
what we preach, and this is what you believed.

The Resurrection of the Dead

12But if it is preached that Christ has been raised
from the dead, how can some of you say that there
is no resurrection of the dead? 13If there is no
resurrection of the dead, then not even Christ has
been raised. 14And if Christ has not been raised,
our preaching is useless and so is your faith.
15More than that, we are then found to be false
witnesses about God, for we have testified about
God that he raised Christ from the dead. But he
did not raise him if in fact the dead are not raised.
16For if the dead are not raised, then Christ has not
been raised either. 17And if Christ has not been
raised, your faith is futile; you are still in your sins.
18Then those also who have fallen asleep in Christ
are lost. 19If only for this life we have hope in
Christ, we are to be pitied more than all men.
20But Christ has indeed been raised from the
dead, the firstfruits of those who have fallen asleep.
21For since death came through a man, the resurrection of the dead comes also through a man.
22For as in Adam all die, so in Christ all will be
made alive. 23But each in his own turn: Christ, the
firstfruits; then, when he comes, those who belong
to him. 24Then the end will come, when he hands
over the kingdom to God the Father after he has

LIVING  **INSIGHT**

Be sure that the one you believe in has conquered death; otherwise he or she won't get you into heaven. Hell awaits you. The only way to get beyond the grave and into the Lord's presence is to place your trust on One who has gone before you and has paved the way.

(See 1 Corinthians 15:20.)

destroyed all dominion, authority and power.
25For he must reign until he has put all his enemies
under his feet. 26The last enemy to be destroyed
is death. 27For he "has put everything under his
feet."[c] Now when it says that "everything" has
been put under him, it is clear that this does not
include God himself, who put everything under
Christ. 28When he has done this, then the Son
himself will be made subject to him who put everything under him, so that God may be all in all.
29Now if there is no resurrection, what will
those do who are baptized for the dead? If the dead
are not raised at all, why are people baptized for
them? 30And as for us, why do we endanger ourselves every hour? 31I die every day—I mean that,
brothers—just as surely as I glory over you in
Christ Jesus our Lord. 32If I fought wild beasts in
Ephesus for merely human reasons, what have I
gained? If the dead are not raised, 2Co 1:8; 11:26

"Let us eat and drink,
for tomorrow we die."[d]

33Do not be misled: "Bad company corrupts good
character." 34Come back to your senses as you
ought, and stop sinning; for there are some who
are ignorant of God—I say this to your shame.

The Resurrection Body

35But someone may ask, "How are the dead
raised? With what kind of body will they come?"
36How foolish! What you sow does not come to life
unless it dies. 37When you sow, you do not plant
the body that will be, but just a seed, perhaps of
wheat or of something else. 38But God gives it a
body as he has determined, and to each kind of
seed he gives its own body. 39All flesh is not the
same: Men have one kind of flesh, animals have
another, birds another and fish another. 40There
are also heavenly bodies and there are earthly bodies; but the splendor of the heavenly bodies is one

[a]3 Or *you at the first* [b]5 Greek *Cephas* [c]27 Psalm 8:6 [d]32 Isaiah 22:13

kind, and the splendor of the earthly bodies is
another. 41The sun has one kind of splendor, the
moon another and the stars another; and star differs from star in splendor. Eze 37:3; Jn 12:24
42So will it be with the resurrection of the dead.
The body that is sown is perishable, it is raised
imperishable; 43it is sown in dishonor, it is raised
in glory; it is sown in weakness, it is raised in
power; 44it is sown a natural body, it is raised a
spiritual body. Mt 13:43; Php 3:21

If there is a natural body, there is also a spiritual
body. 45So it is written: "The first man Adam became a living being"[a]; the last Adam, a life-giving
spirit. 46The spiritual did not come first, but the
natural, and after that the spiritual. 47The first man
was of the dust of the earth, the second man from
heaven. 48As was the earthly man, so are those who
are of the earth; and as is the man from heaven, so
also are those who are of heaven. 49And just as we
have borne the likeness of the earthly man, so shall
we[b] bear the likeness of the man from heaven.
50I declare to you, brothers, that flesh and blood
cannot inherit the kingdom of God, nor does the

LIVING  **INSIGHT**

The marvelous good news is that when our final change at Jesus' return occurs, death will never again have charge of us. At that glorious moment we shall begin a timeless, ageless existence.

(See 1 Corinthians 15:50–57.)

perishable inherit the imperishable. 51Listen, I tell
you a mystery: We will not all sleep, but we will all
be changed— 52in a flash, in the twinkling of an
eye, at the last trumpet. For the trumpet will
sound, the dead will be raised imperishable, and
we will be changed. 53For the perishable must
clothe itself with the imperishable, and the mortal
with immortality. 54When the perishable has been
clothed with the imperishable, and the mortal with
immortality, then the saying that is written will
come true: "Death has been swallowed up in victory."[c] Mt 24:31; 2Co 5:2,4

55"Where, O death, is your victory?
Where, O death, is your sting?"[d]

56The sting of death is sin, and the power of sin is
the law. 57But thanks be to God! He gives us the
victory through our Lord Jesus Christ. Hos 13:14
58Therefore, my dear brothers, stand firm. Let
nothing move you. Always give yourselves fully to
the work of the Lord, because you know that your
labor in the Lord is not in vain. 1Co 16:10

The Collection for God's People

16 Now about the collection for God's people:
Do what I told the Galatian churches to do.
2On the first day of every week, each one of you
should set aside a sum of money in keeping with
his income, saving it up, so that when I come no
collections will have to be made. 3Then, when I
arrive, I will give letters of introduction to the men
you approve and send them with your gift to Jerusalem. 4If it seems advisable for me to go also, they
will accompany me. Ac 20:7; 24:17

Personal Requests

5After I go through Macedonia, I will come
to you—for I will be going through Macedonia.
6Perhaps I will stay with you awhile, or even spend
the winter, so that you can help me on my journey,
wherever I go. 7I do not want to see you now and
make only a passing visit; I hope to spend some
time with you, if the Lord permits. 8But I will stay
on at Ephesus until Pentecost, 9because a great
door for effective work has opened to me, and
there are many who oppose me. Ac 18:21; 1Co 4:19
10If Timothy comes, see to it that he has nothing
to fear while he is with you, for he is carrying on
the work of the Lord, just as I am. 11No one, then,
should refuse to accept him. Send him on his way
in peace so that he may return to me. I am expecting him along with the brothers. 1Co 15:58; 1Ti 4:12
12Now about our brother Apollos: I strongly
urged him to go to you with the brothers. He was
quite unwilling to go now, but he will go when he
has the opportunity. Ac 18:24; 1Co 1:12
13Be on your guard; stand firm in the faith; be
men of courage; be strong. 14Do everything in
love. 1Co 14:1; Php 1:27

LIVING  **INSIGHT**

The real tests of courage are the inner tests, like remaining faithful when nobody's looking . . . like enduring pain when the room is empty . . . like standing alone when you're misunderstood.

(See 1 Corinthians 16:13.)

15You know that the household of Stephanas
were the first converts in Achaia, and they have
devoted themselves to the service of the saints. I
urge you, brothers, 16to submit to such as these
and to everyone who joins in the work, and labors
at it. 17I was glad when Stephanas, Fortunatus and
Achaicus arrived, because they have supplied what
was lacking from you. 18For they refreshed my

[a] 45 Gen. 2:7 [b] 49 Some early manuscripts *so let us* [c] 54 Isaiah 25:8 [d] 55 Hosea 13:14

spirit and yours also. Such men deserve recognition. 2Co 11:9; Php 2:29

Final Greetings

19The churches in the province of Asia send you
greetings. Aquila and Priscilla[a] greet you warmly
in the Lord, and so does the church that meets at
their house. 20All the brothers here send you greetings. Greet one another with a holy kiss.
21I, Paul, write this greeting in my own hand.
22If anyone does not love the Lord—a curse be
on him. Come, O Lord[b]! Ro 9:3; Eph 6:24
23The grace of the Lord Jesus be with you.
24My love to all of you in Christ Jesus. Amen.[c]

[a] 19 Greek *Prisca*, a variant of *Priscilla*
[b] 22 In Aramaic the expression *Come, O Lord* is *Marana tha.*
[c] 24 Some manuscripts do not have *Amen.*

INTRODUCTION

2 CORINTHIANS

There are many who would call Paul's second letter to the Corinthians the letter of a "transparent apostle." Here, as in no other letter Paul wrote, the man bears his soul. This is the most autobiographical of all of Paul's correspondence. It allows us to see the man and his ministry in genuine, unveiled terms. Because Paul's apostleship was under attack, the style is strong and forceful. In many ways it is the least systematic of Paul's writings. These are the words of a man who expresses himself without hiding the truth of his heart about both himself and his ministry. Yet behind the forceful style is a heart tender toward God and committed to ministry—a beautiful, rare blend of strength and compassion.

WRITER: *Paul*

DATE: *c.a.d. 55*

PURPOSE: *To address lingering concerns in the church and to declare the truth about himself*

KEY THEMES: *Suffering; forgiveness; ministry; reconciliation; servanthood; giving*

STYLE: *Personal and unguarded*

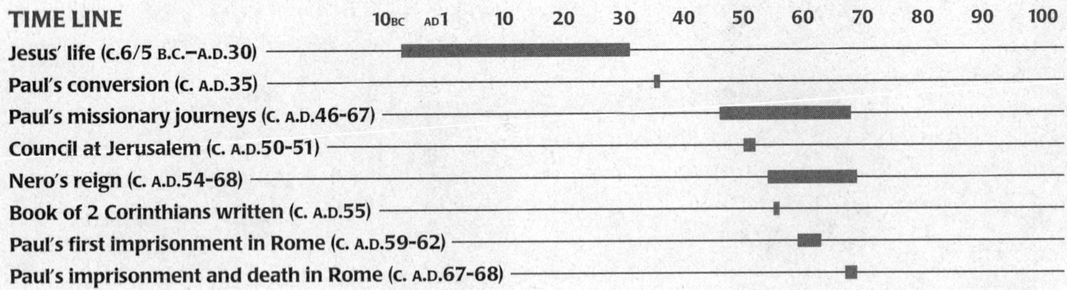

A Man and His Ministry

INTRODUCTION—Greeting (1:1-2)

	CRUCIAL CONCERNS	GRACE GIVING	APOSTOLIC AUTHORITY
	Suffering and God's sufficiency Ministry and our involvement Godliness and its impact	Example of Macedonians Command to Corinthians	Reply to critics Justification of ministry False teachers Visions, revelations, credentials, warnings
	CHAPTERS 1:3–7:16	*CHAPTERS 8–9*	*CHAPTERS 10:1–13:10*
SCOPE	**Past**	**Present**	**Future**
ISSUE	**Misunderstandings, concerns, explanations**	**Financial project**	**Vindication of Paul's ministry**
TONE	**Forgiving, grateful, bold**	**Confident**	**Defensive and strong**
KEY WORDS	***"For we do not preach ourselves, but Jesus Christ as Lord . . ." (4:5)***	***"God loves a cheerful giver" (9:7)***	***"I will not be ashamed of it" (10:8)***

CONCLUSION—Farewell (13:11-14)

In the letter called 2 Corinthians Paul opened his personal journal to us. It was unedited and unguarded. It had been published essentially without his permission. He undoubtedly had no idea it would be preserved for centuries to follow. If you want to see a man who stood up and took it on the chin or, if you prefer, fell flat on his face in weakness and humility, you'll meet him in 2 Corinthians. He groaned. He wept. He confessed. He revealed deep inner feelings. He defended himself. He boasted. He exposed the reality of his life. He revealed himself for all to see. And he did it in such a self-effacing way that we walk away shaking our heads at the honesty and vulnerability of the man.

We learn from this letter that Paul was not a highly polished silver goblet sitting on a shelf, to be admired and observed but not touched. Rather, he was a used, misused and broken piece of pottery—an ordinary "jar of clay" (4:7), if you will.

In 2 Corinthians Paul confessed to despairing of life (1:8). He admitted to being afflicted, pressured, perplexed, knocked down—but not knocked out (4:8–9). In 2 Corinthians Paul confessed he was neither invincible nor perfect, as he exposed the pain of his pilgrimage (chapters 6–11). In chapters 10–13 Paul showed that he didn't respond well to criticism, as he did his best to defend himself. But in the last analysis, he reminds us of a wandering dog that turns over and exposes his belly and says, "Kick me if you wish," or "Love me if you can."

It is also in this letter that Paul told us about a thorn so deeply embedded in him that not even a thrice-offered prayer prompted God to relieve him of the pain (12:7–10). He lived with it until he died, though he never specified exactly what it was. Frankly I'm glad he didn't, because it allows all of us who have our own "thorns" (who doesn't?) to identify with him when he cited God's response to him: "My grace is sufficient for you" (12:9). Woven through the fabric of 2 Corinthians were the colors of pain and weakness and sorrow and brokenness. Paul allowed us to see the cracks in his life. Our respect for the man only grows as we get to know him better. As a result, we want to embrace him and thank God for using him to teach us so much through his vulnerable spirit.

Why a Second Letter?

There are a number of reasons Paul wrote this letter. The first I'll call a *public* reason: Paul was still disturbed about some of the Corinthians' conduct, so he wrote to correct them—ornery lot that they were. The first letter didn't seem to do it. Reminds me of my childhood! One reminder never seemed to do it for me. Were you like that? In fact, dozens of reminders, and even several spankings, over a brief period of time, it seemed, still didn't stop me! For the Corinthians Paul couldn't seem to warn them enough to get them back in line, so he wrote them again in another effort to correct their lifestyle.

Second, there's a *personal* reason: Paul was being criticized, and he needed to defend his integrity. You'll notice that his enemies were challenging his authority as an apostle as well as his personal integrity. In memorable fashion Paul offered a spirited self-defense and boldly confronted his critics (see especially the last four chapters).

Third, there's a *practical* reason: Paul had been promoting a fund-raising effort on behalf of the needy in Jerusalem, and the Corinthians had made some commitments to the project but had seemingly lost all their momentum. So Paul encouraged the Christians in Corinth to seize the moment and respond in compassion and demonstrate in a tangible way their unity with the Jewish Christians in Jerusalem (see chapters 8–9).

Fourth, there were *doctrinal* reasons: Paul wanted to explain in greater detail some of the doctrines the Corinthians had misunderstood, possibly because of the false teachers who had infiltrated the Corinthian church. This letter clarifies some central doctrines of the Christian faith that the believers in Corinth needed to learn in greater depth—such as the adequacy of God's grace, the future life, reconciliation and the proper view of Jesus Christ. This is not only a practical letter but a doctrinal one as well.

An Emotional Letter

Paul expressed himself with a maximum of emotion and passion in this letter. R.G. Lee once wrote, "Tracing your way through 2 Corinthians is like tracing your way along a river. It is deep and profound at places—almost mysterious—and then it moves into narrow straits and the rapids become intense. And it leads, all of a sudden, to an eruption and a waterfall—only to go over and find yourself in another deep, quiet pool a little further on."

And so at times there were eruptions of emotions in this letter and at other times deep and profound thoughts and feelings. It was not only Paul's most autobiographical letter, it was one of his most passionately emotional as well. He was pensive. He was humble. He was broken. He was bruised. At other times he put on the gloves and rolled up his sleeves, willing to take the Corinthians on one at a time or, if they preferred, as a group. Paul rode the roller coaster of emotion up and down throughout this letter.

News From a Friend

Paul's friend Titus had delivered the first letter to the Corinthians. Because Paul had not heard the results of that letter from Titus's own lips, he grew uneasy about the lack of information and traveled back to Macedonia, in northern Greece. While there, he linked up with Titus and heard about the Corinthians' reaction to the first letter he had sent.

Notice Paul's state of mind and body as he entered Macedonia: "For when we came into Macedonia, this body of ours had no rest, but we were harassed at every turn—conflicts on the outside, fears within" (7:5). Does that sound like something you might be familiar with? See, not even Paul entered into peaceful rest 24 hours a day. Nor will you. Nor will I. Give yourself a break. We can't expect God to provide a struggle-free journey. But take comfort in this truth: He still loves you and still assures you of His presence and His power in your life. Paul's mind and body were certainly not at rest as he awaited news about the situation at Corinth. He was afraid . . . and then he met Titus:

But God, who comforts the downcast, comforted us by the coming of Titus, and not only by his coming but also by the comfort you had given him. He told us about your longing for me, your deep sorrow, your ardent concern for me, so that my joy was greater than ever (7:6–7).

Look at that! Look at how Paul's spirit soared as he heard Titus's news. He was encouraged that the Corinthians had repented and wanted to restore ties with him—and so Paul used the writing of 2 Corinthians to rebuild his relationship and to prepare for a visit to them. It is clear that Titus had also brought with him some information about the church that concerned Paul, as well as informed him of some criticism of Paul's integrity and authority as an apostle. It was to those charges that Paul addressed himself in the final four chapters.

Lessons From Corinth

This letter, filled as it is with passion and emotion, is a compellingly honest look at the pains and struggles of the life of faith. Within the chapters of this letter there are profound lessons that endure and speak with power to the church today—lessons you may not have expected to learn from an apostle named Paul:

First, *brokenness gives a ministry wholeness*. If you're broken, if you're bruised, if you're beaten, if you bleed, if you cry out with raw and deep emotion, if you tend to get discouraged, you're right on stream with Paul. He knew pain and struggle; in his mind, it was all part of being a "jar of clay" at the disposal of the divine Potter. Ministry involves suffering, which in turn teaches us some important lessons about God's grace and our dependence on Him.

Second, *meekness communicates strength in life*. The person who always has to be in control is in reality a very weak individual. A person who is genuinely meek is indeed genuinely strong. That's also a helpful insight on servanthood. You truly want to be a servant? Don't try to maintain such tight control over everything. Release control as you find strength in meekness.

Third, *loneliness makes us place a high value on friendships*. Paul came to this truth in chapter 11 when he described all that had happened to him—the terrible pain of having seemingly everyone turn against him and having to constantly look over his shoulder (11:23–28). It's loneliness that makes us value friendships, as we realize how agonizing it is when we have no one to hold us or no one to love us, and how wonderful it is when someone cares. Paul learned this lesson in a most painful way, and his words help us value our friendships all the more.

Fourth, *weakness puts power on display*. Sometimes we think having our act together and being self-sufficient make us powerful. We ask for all our thorns to be removed . . . but the Lord may very well have other, more profound plans for us. Listen to Paul's testimony: "Three times I pleaded with the Lord to take it away from me. But he said to me, 'My grace is sufficient for you, for my power is made perfect in weakness' " (12:8–9).

Paul desperately wanted that thorn removed. When he finally accepted God's "no," he learned that God's grace *was* sufficient. Paul teaches us that we can find strength in times of weakness when we are forced to cast ourselves on the One who grants more power than we could ever imagine. In our weakness we discover God's power, and that is power indeed! May we experience His power at work in *our* lives as we face trials, struggles and times of weakness.

Crucial Concerns **Chapters 1–7**

In this section Paul addressed three central and critical concerns—each of them as significant to the church today as they were in the first century. First, he dealt with the issue of suffering and God's sufficiency. In short, his testimony was this: While all of us will suffer, God's presence and comfort will always be sufficient for our needs. Next, he addressed the issue of our place in ministry. Paul wanted all believers to know that they have a ministry of sharing the great news of God's forgiveness and reconciliation. Finally, Paul discussed the issue of godliness and its impact on the world around us. He wanted the believers in Corinth to know that their lives and witness had a profound impact on others. This section records Paul's wise and passionate explanations of how believers must live out their faith.

1 Paul, an apostle of Christ Jesus by the will of
God, and Timothy our brother, Col 1:1; 2Ti 1:1

To the church of God in Corinth, together with
all the saints throughout Achaia: Ac 18:12; 1Co 10:32

2Grace and peace to you from God our Father
and the Lord Jesus Christ. Ro 1:7

The God of All Comfort

3Praise be to the God and Father of our Lord
Jesus Christ, the Father of compassion and the

LIVING  INSIGHT

God allows suffering so that we might have the capacity to enter into another's sorrow and affliction. God gives His children the capacity to empathize, to understand, by bringing similar sufferings into our lives.

(See 2 Corinthians 1:3–11.)

God of all comfort, 4who comforts us in all our
troubles, so that we can comfort those in any trouble with the comfort we ourselves have received
from God. 5For just as the sufferings of Christ flow
over into our lives, so also through Christ our
comfort overflows. 6If we are distressed, it is for
your comfort and salvation; if we are comforted, it
is for your comfort, which produces in you patient
endurance of the same sufferings we suffer. 7And
our hope for you is firm, because we know that
just as you share in our sufferings, so also you
share in our comfort. 2Co 4:10,15; Eph 1:3

8We do not want you to be uninformed, brothers, about the hardships we suffered in the province of Asia. We were under great pressure, far
beyond our ability to endure, so that we despaired
even of life. 9Indeed, in our hearts we felt the sentence of death. But this happened that we might
not rely on ourselves but on God, who raises the
dead. 10He has delivered us from such a deadly
peril, and he will deliver us. On him we have set
our hope that he will continue to deliver us, 11as
you help us by your prayers. Then many will give
thanks on our[a] behalf for the gracious favor
granted us in answer to the prayers of many.

Paul's Change of Plans

12Now this is our boast: Our conscience testifies
that we have conducted ourselves in the world,
and especially in our relations with you, in the
holiness and sincerity that are from God. We have
done so not according to worldly wisdom but according to God's grace. 13For we do not write you
anything you cannot read or understand. And I
hope that, 14as you have understood us in part,
you will come to understand fully that you can
boast of us just as we will boast of you in the day
of the Lord Jesus. 1Co 1:8; 2:1,4,13

15Because I was confident of this, I planned to
visit you first so that you might benefit twice. 16I
planned to visit you on my way to Macedonia and
to come back to you from Macedonia, and then to
have you send me on my way to Judea. 17When I
planned this, did I do it lightly? Or do I make my
plans in a worldly manner so that in the same
breath I say, "Yes, yes" and "No, no"? 1Co 16:5-7

18But as surely as God is faithful, our message to
you is not "Yes" and "No." 19For the Son of God,
Jesus Christ, who was preached among you by me
and Silas[b] and Timothy, was not "Yes" and "No,"
but in him it has always been "Yes." 20For no
matter how many promises God has made, they
are "Yes" in Christ. And so through him the
"Amen" is spoken by us to the glory of God.
21Now it is God who makes both us and you stand
firm in Christ. He anointed us, 22set his seal of
ownership on us, and put his Spirit in our hearts
as a deposit, guaranteeing what is to come.

23I call God as my witness that it was in order
to spare you that I did not return to Corinth. 24Not
that we lord it over your faith, but we work with
you for your joy, because it is by faith you stand
2 firm. 1So I made up my mind that I would
not make another painful visit to you. 2For if
I grieve you, who is left to make me glad but you
whom I have grieved? 3I wrote as I did so that
when I came I should not be distressed by those
who ought to make me rejoice. I had confidence in
all of you, that you would all share my joy. 4For I
wrote you out of great distress and anguish of
heart and with many tears, not to grieve you but
to let you know the depth of my love for you.

Forgiveness for the Sinner

5If anyone has caused grief, he has not so much

[a] 11 Many manuscripts *your* [b] 19 Greek *Silvanus*, a variant of *Silas*

grieved me as he has grieved all of you, to some extent—not to put it too severely. 6The punishment inflicted on him by the majority is sufficient for him. 7Now instead, you ought to forgive and comfort him, so that he will not be overwhelmed

LIVING  **INSIGHT**

Discouraged people don't need critics. They hurt enough already. They don't need someone to pile on more guilt or distress. They need encouragement. They need a refuge. A place to hide and to find healing.

(See 2 Corinthians 2:7.)

by excessive sorrow. 8I urge you, therefore, to reaffirm your love for him. 9The reason I wrote you was to see if you would stand the test and be obedient in everything. 10If you forgive anyone, I also forgive him. And what I have forgiven—if there was anything to forgive—I have forgiven in the sight of Christ for your sake, 11in order that Satan might not outwit us. For we are not unaware of his schemes. 2Co 10:6; Gal 6:1

Ministers of the New Covenant

12Now when I went to Troas to preach the gospel of Christ and found that the Lord had opened a door for me, 13I still had no peace of mind, because I did not find my brother Titus there. So I said good-by to them and went on to Macedonia. Ac 16:8; 2Co 7:5-6,13

14But thanks be to God, who always leads us in triumphal procession in Christ and through us spreads everywhere the fragrance of the knowledge of him. 15For we are to God the aroma of Christ among those who are being saved and those who are perishing. 16To the one we are the smell of death; to the other, the fragrance of life. And who is equal to such a task? 17Unlike so many, we do not peddle the word of God for profit. On the contrary, in Christ we speak before God with sincerity, like men sent from God. Lk 2:34; 2Co 1:12

3 Are we beginning to commend ourselves again? Or do we need, like some people, letters of recommendation to you or from you? 2You yourselves are our letter, written on our hearts, known and read by everybody. 3You show that you are a letter from Christ, the result of our ministry, written not with ink but with the Spirit of the living God, not on tablets of stone but on tablets of human hearts. Jer 31:33; Eze 11:19

4Such confidence as this is ours through Christ before God. 5Not that we are competent in ourselves to claim anything for ourselves, but our competence comes from God. 6He has made us competent as ministers of a new covenant—not of the letter but of the Spirit; for the letter kills, but the Spirit gives life. Jn 6:63; 1Co 15:10

The Glory of the New Covenant

7Now if the ministry that brought death, which was engraved in letters on stone, came with glory, so that the Israelites could not look steadily at the face of Moses because of its glory, fading though it was, 8will not the ministry of the Spirit be even more glorious? 9If the ministry that condemns men is glorious, how much more glorious is the ministry that brings righteousness! 10For what was glorious has no glory now in comparison with the surpassing glory. 11And if what was fading away came with glory, how much greater is the glory of that which lasts! Ex 34:29-35; Ro 1:17

12Therefore, since we have such a hope, we are very bold. 13We are not like Moses, who would put a veil over his face to keep the Israelites from gazing at it while the radiance was fading away. 14But their minds were made dull, for to this day the same veil remains when the old covenant is read. It has not been removed, because only in Christ is it taken away. 15Even to this day when Moses is read, a veil covers their hearts. 16But whenever anyone turns to the Lord, the veil is taken away. 17Now the Lord is the Spirit, and where the Spirit of the Lord is, there is freedom. 18And we, who with unveiled faces all reflect[a] the Lord's glory, are being transformed into his likeness with ever-increasing glory, which comes from the Lord, who is the Spirit. Ro 8:29; 1Co 13:12

LIVING  **INSIGHT**

God is committed to the task of working in us, developing us, rearranging, firming up and deepening us so that the character traits of His Son begin to take shape. The emerging of the Son's image in us is of primary importance to the Father.

(See 2 Corinthians 3:18.)

Treasures in Jars of Clay

4 Therefore, since through God's mercy we have this ministry, we do not lose heart. 2Rather, we have renounced secret and shameful ways; we do not use deception, nor do we distort the word of God. On the contrary, by setting forth the truth plainly we commend ourselves to every man's conscience in the sight of God. 3And even if our gospel is veiled, it is veiled to those who are perishing. 4The god of this age has blinded the

[a]18 Or *contemplate*

minds of unbelievers, so that they cannot see the light of the gospel of the glory of Christ, who is the image of God. 5For we do not preach ourselves, but Jesus Christ as Lord, and ourselves as your servants for Jesus' sake. 6For God, who said, "Let light shine out of darkness,"[a] made his light shine in our hearts to give us the light of the knowledge of the glory of God in the face of Christ. Ge 1:3; 2Pe 1:19

7But we have this treasure in jars of clay to show that this all-surpassing power is from God and not from us. 8We are hard pressed on every side, but

LIVING  INSIGHT

Surrendering to despair is humanity's favorite pastime. God offers a far better plan for joy-filled living, but it takes effort to grab it and faith to claim it.

(See 2 Corinthians 4:8.)

not crushed; perplexed, but not in despair; 9persecuted, but not abandoned; struck down, but not destroyed. 10We always carry around in our body the death of Jesus, so that the life of Jesus may also be revealed in our body. 11For we who are alive are always being given over to death for Jesus' sake, so that his life may be revealed in our mortal body. 12So then, death is at work in us, but life is at work in you. 1Co 2:5; 2Co 7:5; Heb 13:5

13It is written: "I believed; therefore I have spoken."[b] With that same spirit of faith we also believe and therefore speak, 14because we know that the one who raised the Lord Jesus from the dead will also raise us with Jesus and present us with you in his presence. 15All this is for your benefit, so that the grace that is reaching more and more people may cause thanksgiving to overflow to the glory of God. 2Co 1:11; Eph 5:27

16Therefore we do not lose heart. Though outwardly we are wasting away, yet inwardly we are being renewed day by day. 17For our light and momentary troubles are achieving for us an eternal glory that far outweighs them all. 18So we fix our eyes not on what is seen, but on what is unseen. For what is seen is temporary, but what is unseen is eternal. Ro 8:24; Heb 11:1

Our Heavenly Dwelling

5 Now we know that if the earthly tent we live in is destroyed, we have a building from God, an eternal house in heaven, not built by human hands. 2Meanwhile we groan, longing to be clothed with our heavenly dwelling, 3because when we are clothed, we will not be found naked. 4For while we are in this tent, we groan and are burdened, because we do not wish to be unclothed but to be clothed with our heavenly dwelling, so that what is mortal may be swallowed up by life. 5Now it is God who has made us for this very purpose and has given us the Spirit as a deposit, guaranteeing what is to come. Ro 8:23; 1Co 15:53-54

6Therefore we are always confident and know that as long as we are at home in the body we are away from the Lord. 7We live by faith, not by sight. 8We are confident, I say, and would prefer to be away from the body and at home with the Lord. 9So we make it our goal to please him, whether we are at home in the body or away from it. 10For we must all appear before the judgment seat of Christ, that each one may receive what is due him for the things done while in the body, whether good or bad. Ro 14:10; Eph 6:8

The Ministry of Reconciliation

11Since, then, we know what it is to fear the Lord, we try to persuade men. What we are is plain to God, and I hope it is also plain to your conscience. 12We are not trying to commend ourselves to you again, but are giving you an opportunity to take pride in us, so that you can answer those who take pride in what is seen rather than in what is in the heart. 13If we are out of our mind, it is for the sake of God; if we are in our right mind, it is for you. 14For Christ's love compels us, because we are convinced that one died for all, and therefore all died. 15And he died for all, that those who live should no longer live for themselves but for him who died for them and was raised again.

16So from now on we regard no one from a worldly point of view. Though we once regarded Christ in this way, we do so no longer. 17Therefore, if anyone is in Christ, he is a new creation; the old has gone, the new has come! 18All this is from God, who reconciled us to himself through Christ and gave us the ministry of reconciliation: 19that God was reconciling the world to himself in Christ, not counting men's sins against them. And he has committed to us the message of reconciliation. 20We are therefore Christ's ambassadors, as

LIVING  INSIGHT

The work of salvation is finished work. It is provided for me as a sinner if I will simply come to Jesus Christ. It is as if the Savior looks each one of us in the eye and says, "I've paid your debt in full at the cross. If you come to Me, I will give you perfect righteousness."

(See 2 Corinthians 5:21.)

[a]6 Gen. 1:3 [b]13 Psalm 116:10 [c]21 Or *be a sin offering*

though God were making his appeal through us.
We implore you on Christ's behalf: Be reconciled
to God. 21God made him who had no sin to be
sin[c] for us, so that in him we might become the
righteousness of God. 1Pe 2:22,24; 1Jn 3:5

6 As God's fellow workers we urge you not to
receive God's grace in vain. 2For he says,

"In the time of my favor I heard you,
and in the day of salvation I helped you."[a]

I tell you, now is the time of God's favor, now is
the day of salvation. Ps 69:13; Isa 55:6

Paul's Hardships

3We put no stumbling block in anyone's path,
so that our ministry will not be discredited. 4Rath-
er, as servants of God we commend ourselves in
every way: in great endurance; in troubles, hardships and distresses; 5in beatings, imprisonments
and riots; in hard work, sleepless nights and hunger; 6in purity, understanding, patience and kindness; in the Holy Spirit and in sincere love; 7in
truthful speech and in the power of God; with
weapons of righteousness in the right hand and in
the left; 8through glory and dishonor, bad report
and good report; genuine, yet regarded as impostors; 9known, yet regarded as unknown; dying,
and yet we live on; beaten, and yet not killed;
10sorrowful, yet always rejoicing; poor, yet making
many rich; having nothing, and yet possessing everything. Ro 8:32; 2Co 1:8-10

11We have spoken freely to you, Corinthians,
and opened wide our hearts to you. 12We are not
withholding our affection from you, but you are
withholding yours from us. 13As a fair exchange—
I speak as to my children—open wide your hearts
also. 1Co 4:14; 2Co 7:3

Do Not Be Yoked With Unbelievers

14Do not be yoked together with unbelievers.
For what do righteousness and wickedness have in
common? Or what fellowship can light have with
darkness? 15What harmony is there between Christ
and Belial[b]? What does a believer have in common with an unbeliever? 16What agreement is
there between the temple of God and idols? For we
are the temple of the living God. As God has said:
"I will live with them and walk among them, and
I will be their God, and they will be my people."[c]

17"Therefore come out from them Rev 18:4
and be separate,
says the Lord.
Touch no unclean thing,
and I will receive you."[d]
18"I will be a Father to you,
and you will be my sons and daughters,
says the Lord Almighty."[e]

7 Since we have these promises, dear friends,
let us purify ourselves from everything that
contaminates body and spirit, perfecting holiness
out of reverence for God. 2Co 6:17-18

Paul's Joy

2Make room for us in your hearts. We have
wronged no one, we have corrupted no one, we
have exploited no one. 3I do not say this to condemn you; I have said before that you have such
a place in our hearts that we would live or die with
you. 4I have great confidence in you; I take great
pride in you. I am greatly encouraged; in all our
troubles my joy knows no bounds. 2Co 6:10-13

5For when we came into Macedonia, this body
of ours had no rest, but we were harassed at every
turn—conflicts on the outside, fears within. 6But
God, who comforts the downcast, comforted us by
the coming of Titus, 7and not only by his coming
but also by the comfort you had given him. He
told us about your longing for me, your deep sorrow, your ardent concern for me, so that my joy
was greater than ever. 2Co 2:13; 4:8

8Even if I caused you sorrow by my letter, I do
not regret it. Though I did regret it—I see that my
letter hurt you, but only for a little while— 9yet
now I am happy, not because you were made sorry, but because your sorrow led you to repentance.
For you became sorrowful as God intended and so
were not harmed in any way by us. 10Godly sorrow
brings repentance that leads to salvation and
leaves no regret, but worldly sorrow brings death.
11See what this godly sorrow has produced in you:
what earnestness, what eagerness to clear yourselves, what indignation, what alarm, what longing, what concern, what readiness to see justice
done. At every point you have proved yourselves
to be innocent in this matter. 12So even though I
wrote to you, it was not on account of the one who
did the wrong or of the injured party, but rather
that before God you could see for yourselves how
devoted to us you are. 13By all this we are encouraged. 1Co 5:1-2; 2Co 2:2,4

In addition to our own encouragement, we
were especially delighted to see how happy Titus
was, because his spirit has been refreshed by all of
you. 14I had boasted to him about you, and you
have not embarrassed me. But just as everything
we said to you was true, so our boasting about you
to Titus has proved to be true as well. 15And his
affection for you is all the greater when he remembers that you were all obedient, receiving him with
fear and trembling. 16I am glad I can have complete confidence in you. 2Co 2:9; Php 2:12

[a] *2* Isaiah 49:8 [b] *15* Greek *Beliar*, a variant of *Belial* [c] *16* Lev. 26:12; Jer. 32:38; Ezek. 37:27 [d] *17* Isaiah 52:11; Ezek. 20:34,41 [e] *18* 2 Samuel 7:14; 7:8

Grace Giving — Chapters 8–9

These chapters contain some of the Bible's greatest teaching on the subject of giving. Paul lifted up an unforgettable example of giving found among the Macedonians. They had been generous and free in their giving, providing a sterling example for all the churches of the first century as well as churches today. Paul urged the Corinthians to learn from them and to share cheerfully and wholeheartedly in the ministry of giving. He did not use gimmicks or tricks to motivate; he simply gave an example and called his readers to obedience. We have much to learn from these chapters, as we encourage each other to give with generosity and joy.

Generosity Encouraged

8 And now, brothers, we want you to know about the grace that God has given the Macedonian churches. 2Out of the most severe trial, their overflowing joy and their extreme poverty welled up in rich generosity. 3For I testify that they gave as much as they were able, and even beyond their ability. Entirely on their own, 4they urgently pleaded with us for the privilege of sharing in this service to the saints. 5And they did not do as we expected, but they gave themselves first to the Lord and then to us in keeping with God's will. 6So we urged Titus, since he had earlier made a beginning, to bring also to completion this act of grace on your part. 7But just as you excel in everything—in faith, in speech, in knowledge, in complete earnestness and in your love for us[a]—see that you also excel in this grace of giving. 1Co 1:5

8I am not commanding you, but I want to test the sincerity of your love by comparing it with the earnestness of others. 9For you know the grace of our Lord Jesus Christ, that though he was rich, yet for your sakes he became poor, so that you through his poverty might become rich. 1Co 7:6

10And here is my advice about what is best for you in this matter: Last year you were the first not only to give but also to have the desire to do so. 11Now finish the work, so that your eager willingness to do it may be matched by your completion of it, according to your means. 12For if the willingness is there, the gift is acceptable according to what one has, not according to what he does not have. Mk 12:43-44; Lk 21:3; 1Co 7:25,40

13Our desire is not that others might be relieved while you are hard pressed, but that there might be equality. 14At the present time your plenty will supply what they need, so that in turn their plenty will supply what you need. Then there will be equality, 15as it is written: "He who gathered much did not have too much, and he who gathered little did not have too little."[b] Ex 16:18; 2Co 9:12

[a] 7 Some manuscripts *in our love for you* [b] 15 Exodus 16:18

Titus Sent to Corinth

16I thank God, who put into the heart of Titus the same concern I have for you. 17For Titus not only welcomed our appeal, but he is coming to you with much enthusiasm and on his own initiative. 18And we are sending along with him the

LIVING  INSIGHT

Knowledge without enthusiasm is like a bed without sheets . . . like a "thank you" without a smile. Remove enthusiasm from a worship service and you have the makings of a memorial service at a mortuary. Remove enthusiasm from the daily whirl of family activities and you've made a grinding mill out of a merry-go-round.

(See 2 Corinthians 8:17.)

brother who is praised by all the churches for his service to the gospel. 19What is more, he was chosen by the churches to accompany us as we carry the offering, which we administer in order to honor the Lord himself and to show our eagerness to help. 20We want to avoid any criticism of the way we administer this liberal gift. 21For we are taking pains to do what is right, not only in the eyes of the Lord but also in the eyes of men. Ro 12:17; 14:18

22In addition, we are sending with them our brother who has often proved to us in many ways that he is zealous, and now even more so because of his great confidence in you. 23As for Titus, he is my partner and fellow worker among you; as for our brothers, they are representatives of the churches and an honor to Christ. 24Therefore show these men the proof of your love and the reason for our pride in you, so that the churches can see it. 2Co 9:2; Php 2:25

9 There is no need for me to write to you about this service to the saints. 2For I know your eagerness to help, and I have been boasting about it to the Macedonians, telling them that since last year you in Achaia were ready to give; and your enthusiasm has stirred most of them to action. 3But I am sending the brothers in order that our boasting about you in this matter should not prove hollow, but that you may be ready, as I said you would be. 4For if any Macedonians come with me and find you unprepared, we—not to say anything about you—would be ashamed of having been so confident. 5So I thought it necessary to urge the brothers to visit you in advance and finish the arrangements for the generous gift you had

promised. Then it will be ready as a generous gift, not as one grudgingly given. Php 4:17; 2Co 12:17-18

Sowing Generously

6Remember this: Whoever sows sparingly will also reap sparingly, and whoever sows generously will also reap generously. 7Each man should give what he has decided in his heart to give, not reluctantly or under compulsion, for God loves a cheerful giver. 8And God is able to make all grace abound to you, so that in all things at all times, having all that you need, you will abound in every good work. 9As it is written: Eph 3:20; Php 4:19

> "He has scattered abroad his gifts to the poor;
> his righteousness endures forever."[a]

10Now he who supplies seed to the sower and bread for food will also supply and increase your store of seed and will enlarge the harvest of your righteousness. 11You will be made rich in every way so that you can be generous on every occasion, and through us your generosity will result in thanksgiving to God. Ps 112:9; Isa 55:10; Hos 10:12

12This service that you perform is not only supplying the needs of God's people but is also overflowing in many expressions of thanks to God. 13Because of the service by which you have proved yourselves, men will praise God for the obedience that accompanies your confession of the gospel of Christ, and for your generosity in sharing with them and with everyone else. 14And in their prayers for you their hearts will go out to you, because of the surpassing grace God has given you. 15Thanks be to God for his indescribable gift!

Apostolic Authority **Chapters 10–13**

In the closing chapters Paul defended his apostolic authority. He had fallen under severe criticism and hostile attack. This was his opportunity to respond and address issues of his identity in Christ Jesus. In this section Paul gave a clear justification for his ministry. His authority came from God and not from other humans. He also rebuked those false teachers who refuted his ministry and Christ's teachings. In contrast, he held up his own credentials. He listed his visions, revelations and sufferings as evidence of the authenticity of his ministry. By the end of the letter Paul's defense was irrefutable and his ministry was vindicated. No one could deny that He was an apostle of Jesus Christ called to preach the gospel to all who had ears to hear.

Paul's Defense of His Ministry

10 By the meekness and gentleness of Christ, I appeal to you—I, Paul, who am "timid" when face to face with you, but "bold" when away! 2I beg you that when I come I may not have to be as bold as I expect to be toward some people who think that we live by the standards of this world. 3For though we live in the world, we do not wage war as the world does. 4The weapons we fight with are not the weapons of the world. On the contrary, they have divine power to demolish strongholds. 5We demolish arguments and every pretension that sets itself up against the knowledge of God, and we take captive every thought to make it obedient to Christ. 6And we will be ready to punish every act of disobedience, once your obedience is complete. Jer 1:10; 2Co 2:9

LIVING  **INSIGHT**

We need to refocus our minds from the horizontal to the vertical. We need to rise above the nonsense of human viewpoint and tedious worries about non-eternal issues. We need to get on with thoughts that really matter.

(See 2 Corinthians 10:5.)

7You are looking only on the surface of things.[b] If anyone is confident that he belongs to Christ, he should consider again that we belong to Christ just as much as he. 8For even if I boast somewhat freely about the authority the Lord gave us for building you up rather than pulling you down, I will not be ashamed of it. 9I do not want to seem to be trying to frighten you with my letters. 10For some say, "His letters are weighty and forceful, but in person he is unimpressive and his speaking amounts to nothing." 11Such people should realize that what we are in our letters when we are absent, we will be in our actions when we are present. 1Co 1:17; 2:3

12We do not dare to classify or compare ourselves with some who commend themselves. When they measure themselves by themselves and compare themselves with themselves, they are not wise. 13We, however, will not boast beyond proper limits, but will confine our boasting to the field God has assigned to us, a field that reaches even to you. 14We are not going too far in our boasting, as would be the case if we had not come to you, for we did get as far as you with the gospel of Christ. 15Neither do we go beyond our limits by boasting of work done by others.[c] Our hope is that, as your faith continues to grow, our area of activity among you will greatly expand, 16so that we can preach the gospel in the regions beyond you. For

[a] 9 Psalm 112:9 [b] 7 Or *Look at the obvious facts* [c] 13-15 Or [13]*We, however, will not boast about things that cannot be measured, but we will boast according to the standard of measurement that the God of measure has assigned us—a measurement that relates even to you.* [14] *. . . .* [15]*Neither do we boast about things that cannot be measured in regard to the work done by others.*

we do not want to boast about work already done
in another man's territory. 17But, "Let him who
boasts boast in the Lord."[a] 18For it is not the one
who commends himself who is approved, but the
one whom the Lord commends. Ro 2:29; 1Co 4:5

Paul and the False Apostles

11 I hope you will put up with a little of my
foolishness; but you are already doing that.
2I am jealous for you with a godly jealousy. I
promised you to one husband, to Christ, so that I
might present you as a pure virgin to him. 3But
I am afraid that just as Eve was deceived by the
serpent's cunning, your minds may somehow be
led astray from your sincere and pure devotion to
Christ. 4For if someone comes to you and preaches
a Jesus other than the Jesus we preached, or if you
receive a different spirit from the one you received,
or a different gospel from the one you accepted,
you put up with it easily enough. 5But I do not
think I am in the least inferior to those "super-
apostles." 6I may not be a trained speaker, but I do
have knowledge. We have made this perfectly clear
to you in every way. 1Co 1:17; Eph 3:4

7Was it a sin for me to lower myself in order to
elevate you by preaching the gospel of God to you
free of charge? 8I robbed other churches by receiving support from them so as to serve you. 9And
when I was with you and needed something, I was
not a burden to anyone, for the brothers who
came from Macedonia supplied what I needed. I
have kept myself from being a burden to you in
any way, and will continue to do so. 10As surely as
the truth of Christ is in me, nobody in the regions
of Achaia will stop this boasting of mine. 11Why?
Because I do not love you? God knows I do! 12And
I will keep on doing what I am doing in order to
cut the ground from under those who want an
opportunity to be considered equal with us in the
things they boast about. 1Co 9:18; 2Co 12:13; Php 4:15,18

13For such men are false apostles, deceitful
workmen, masquerading as apostles of Christ.
14And no wonder, for Satan himself masquerades
as an angel of light. 15It is not surprising, then, if
his servants masquerade as servants of righteousness. Their end will be what their actions deserve.

Paul Boasts About His Sufferings

16I repeat: Let no one take me for a fool. But if
you do, then receive me just as you would a fool,
so that I may do a little boasting. 17In this self-confident boasting I am not talking as the Lord would,
but as a fool. 18Since many are boasting in the way
the world does, I too will boast. 19You gladly put
up with fools since you are so wise! 20In fact, you
even put up with anyone who enslaves you or
exploits you or takes advantage of you or pushes
himself forward or slaps you in the face. 21To my
shame I admit that we were too weak for that!

What anyone else dares to boast about—I am
speaking as a fool—I also dare to boast about.

LIVING  **INSIGHT**

There is not a single achievement worth remembering that isn't stained with the blood of diligence and etched with the scars of disappointment.

(See 2 Corinthians 11:21–29.)

22Are they Hebrews? So am I. Are they Israelites?
So am I. Are they Abraham's descendants? So am
I. 23Are they servants of Christ? (I am out of my
mind to talk like this.) I am more. I have worked
much harder, been in prison more frequently,
been flogged more severely, and been exposed to
death again and again. 24Five times I received from
the Jews the forty lashes minus one. 25Three times
I was beaten with rods, once I was stoned, three
times I was shipwrecked, I spent a night and a day
in the open sea, 26I have been constantly on the
move. I have been in danger from rivers, in danger
from bandits, in danger from my own countrymen, in danger from Gentiles; in danger in the
city, in danger in the country, in danger at sea; and
in danger from false brothers. 27I have labored and
toiled and have often gone without sleep; I have
known hunger and thirst and have often gone
without food; I have been cold and naked. 28Be-
sides everything else, I face daily the pressure of
my concern for all the churches. 29Who is weak,
and I do not feel weak? Who is led into sin, and I
do not inwardly burn? Ro 9:4; 1Co 15:10

30If I must boast, I will boast of the things that
show my weakness. 31The God and Father of the
Lord Jesus, who is to be praised forever, knows
that I am not lying. 32In Damascus the governor
under King Aretas had the city of the Damascenes
guarded in order to arrest me. 33But I was lowered
in a basket from a window in the wall and slipped
through his hands. Ac 9:24-25; 1Co 2:3

Paul's Vision and His Thorn

12 I must go on boasting. Although there is
nothing to be gained, I will go on to visions
and revelations from the Lord. 2I know a man in
Christ who fourteen years ago was caught up to
the third heaven. Whether it was in the body or
out of the body I do not know—God knows. 3And
I know that this man—whether in the body or
apart from the body I do not know, but God
knows— 4was caught up to paradise. He heard

[a] 17 Jer. 9:24

inexpressible things, things that man is not permitted to tell. [5]I will boast about a man like that, but I will not boast about myself, except about my weaknesses. [6]Even if I should choose to boast, I would not be a fool, because I would be speaking the truth. But I refrain, so no one will think more of me than is warranted by what I do or say.

[7]To keep me from becoming conceited because of these surpassingly great revelations, there was given me a thorn in my flesh, a messenger of Satan, to torment me. [8]Three times I pleaded with the Lord to take it away from me. [9]But he said to me, "My grace is sufficient for you, for my power is made perfect in weakness." Therefore I will boast all the more gladly about my weaknesses, so that Christ's power may rest on me. [10]That is why, for Christ's sake, I delight in weaknesses, in insults, in hardships, in persecutions, in difficulties. For when I am weak, then I am strong. 2Co 13:4; 2Th 1:4

Paul's Concern for the Corinthians

[11]I have made a fool of myself, but you drove me to it. I ought to have been commended by you, for I am not in the least inferior to the "super-apostles," even though I am nothing. [12]The things that mark an apostle—signs, wonders and miracles—were done among you with great perseverance. [13]How were you inferior to the other churches, except that I was never a burden to you? Forgive me this wrong! 1Co 9:12,18; 2Co 11:7

[14]Now I am ready to visit you for the third time, and I will not be a burden to you, because what I want is not your possessions but you. After all, children should not have to save up for their parents, but parents for their children. [15]So I will very gladly spend for you everything I have and expend myself as well. If I love you more, will you love me less? [16]Be that as it may, I have not been a burden to you. Yet, crafty fellow that I am, I caught you by trickery! [17]Did I exploit you through any of the men I sent you? [18]I urged Titus to go to you and I sent our brother with him. Titus did not exploit you, did he? Did we not act in the same spirit and follow the same course? 2Co 8:18; 11:9; Php 2:17

[19]Have you been thinking all along that we have been defending ourselves to you? We have been speaking in the sight of God as those in Christ; and everything we do, dear friends, is for your strengthening. [20]For I am afraid that when I come I may not find you as I want you to be, and you may not find me as you want me to be. I fear that there may be quarreling, jealousy, outbursts of anger, factions, slander, gossip, arrogance and disorder. [21]I am afraid that when I come again my God will humble me before you, and I will be grieved over many who have sinned earlier and have not repented of the impurity, sexual sin and debauchery in which they have indulged. 1Co 14:33; 2Co 13:2

Final Warnings

13 This will be my third visit to you. "Every matter must be established by the testimony of two or three witnesses."[a] [2]I already gave you a warning when I was with you the second time. I now repeat it while absent: On my return I will not spare those who sinned earlier or any of the others, [3]since you are demanding proof that Christ is speaking through me. He is not weak in dealing with you, but is powerful among you. [4]For to be sure, he was crucified in weakness, yet he lives by God's power. Likewise, we are weak in him, yet by God's power we will live with him to serve you. Ro 1:4; Php 2:7-8; 1Pe 3:18

[5]Examine yourselves to see whether you are in the faith; test yourselves. Do you not realize that Christ Jesus is in you—unless, of course, you fail the test? [6]And I trust that you will discover that we have not failed the test. [7]Now we pray to God that you will not do anything wrong. Not that people will see that we have stood the test but that you will do what is right even though we may seem to have failed. [8]For we cannot do anything against the truth, but only for the truth. [9]We are glad whenever we are weak but you are strong; and our prayer is for your perfection. [10]This is why I write these things when I am absent, that when I come I may not have to be harsh in my use of authority—the authority the Lord gave me for building you up, not for tearing you down. 1Co 11:28; 2Co 10:8

Final Greetings

[11]Finally, brothers, good-by. Aim for perfection, listen to my appeal, be of one mind, live in peace. And the God of love and peace will be with you. Ro 15:33; Eph 6:23

[12]Greet one another with a holy kiss. [13]All the saints send their greetings. Ro 16:16; Php 4:22

[14]May the grace of the Lord Jesus Christ, and the love of God, and the fellowship of the Holy Spirit be with you all. Ro 16:20; Php 2:1

[a] *1* Deut. 19:15

INTRODUCTION

GALATIANS

The German reformer Martin Luther is credited with writing these words about Paul's letter to the Galatians: "The epistle to the Galatians is my epistle. To it I am, as it were, in wedlock." Luther considered Galatians to be the best of all the books in the Bible. Some have described its contents as "the battle cry of the Protestant Reformation" and "the Magna Charta of spiritual emancipation." It is the New Testament book that affirms Christian liberty, an inspired echo chamber that continually resounds with three monosyllabic words: "You are free . . . you are free . . . you are free." No other book, with the possible exception of Romans, so forcefully and pointedly answers the question: "Are we saved by believing or by achieving?" No other book grabs legalism so firmly by the throat! The deeper we dig into this mine of theological and practical wealth, the richer we will be.

WRITER: *Paul*

DATE: *C.A.D. 48–53*

PURPOSE: *To offer a defense of the true gospel*

KEY THEME: *Justification by faith*

KEY VERSE: *2:16 ". . . by observing the law no one will be justified"*

STYLE: *Vigorous, blunt, direct and brief*

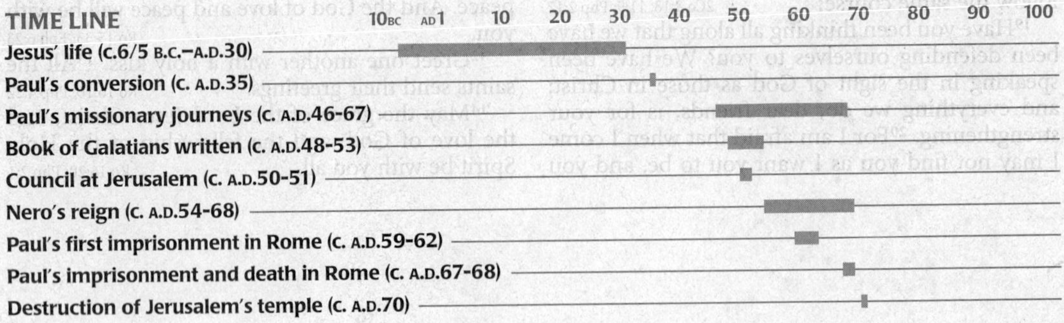

Letter of Liberation

PERSONAL WORDS FROM PAUL	DOCTRINAL TEACHING	PRACTICAL EXHORTATIONS
DEFENSE OF THE TRUE GOSPEL	FREEDOM FROM LEGALISM	FREEDOM TO LOVE AND TO SERVE
"I want you to know, brothers, that the gospel I preached is not something that man made up. I did not receive it from any man, nor was I taught it; rather, I received it by revelation from Jesus Christ" (1:11-12).	*"So the law was put in charge to lead us to Christ that we might be justified by faith. Now that faith has come, we are no longer under the supervision of the law" (3:24-25).*	*"You, my brothers, were called to be free. But do not use your freedom to indulge the sinful nature; rather, serve one another in love" (5:13).*
CHAPTERS 1–2	***CHAPTERS 3–4***	***CHAPTERS 5–6***

KEY VERSE ***"A man is not justified by observing the law, but by faith in Jesus Christ. So we too have put our faith in Christ Jesus that we may be justified by faith in Christ and not by observing the law, because by observing the law no one will be justified" (2:16).***

It happened on a Wednesday. The date was January 20, 1981. As a matter of fact, it happened at the same time an inauguration of a new President of the United States was taking place. For the first time in history an inauguration was upstaged by something happening far away. A group of American citizens sitting in an airplane on a runway in Iran (many of whom had been hostages for well over a year) were about to be released from captivity and restored to the joy of freedom in America.

While the President was delivering his inaugural address, the released hostages entered into the air space called "freedom," and then they claimed that freedom personally. We saw them restored to dignity and set free. As I watched their arrival into Algiers on the news that evening, I thought of the patriotic lyrics Samuel Smith had written over 150 years ago: "Let music swell the breeze and ring from all the trees, sweet freedom's song."

Can you imagine, in your wildest dreams, any one of those people wanting to go back into bondage and become a hostage again? I came across an article in the *Los Angeles Times* (January 24, 1981). A budget officer at the United States Embassy in Tehran who had been brought out of captivity was asked whether he might someday want to go back to Iran. He replied, "Only in a B-52." It's absurd to think that someone once in bondage and now set free would ever want to go back into captivity.

A Letter of Liberty

The apostle Paul's letter to the Galatians is a letter of liberation that declares "freedom from bondage" to all who read it. What I find amazing, and at times exasperating, is that the very thing we are willing to take up arms to defend nationally and internationally (freedom!) we are willing to give up spiritually. The letter to the Galatians declared, in no uncertain terms, "Don't give up your freedom. It is something worth fighting for. It is worth preserving. Don't give it up!"

Galatians is a forceful, potent pronouncement of freedom based on grace. It is a letter celebrating the freedom we find only in Jesus Christ—not freedom to do whatever we please, but freedom from sin and freedom to obey and serve our Savior.

Don't Give In!

This letter aims a bold frontal attack on a legalism based on the doing of good deeds. Talk about a message needed today! It is also conspicuous encouragement for those caught in the middle of a clash between two different gospels. Note what Paul wrote in verses 4 and 5 of chapter 2:

> *This matter arose because some false brothers had infiltrated our ranks to spy on the freedom we have in Christ Jesus and to make us slaves. WE DID NOT GIVE IN TO THEM FOR A MOMENT . . . (emphasis mine).*

Strong words, aren't they? Can't you picture Paul bearing down with stylus on parchment: "WE DID NOT GIVE IN TO THEM . . ." I find myself gritting my teeth as I read those words and as I imagine Paul's emotion. "Those people came in with their false message, false gospel, false hope, false freedom (which is nothing more than bondage), but we didn't yield to them." What an empowering statement for those caught in the cross fire of two ways of analyzing the Christian life and unable to defend themselves: "We're going to stand up for the truth. Whatever you do, don't give up your liberty. Stand firm in the freedom for which Christ has made you free and don't be caught in the yoke of bondage" (see 5:1).

Defend the Truth

Paul had a clear purpose in writing the letter to the Galatians: to offer a blunt declaration and vigorous defense of the true gospel in response to those who were proclaiming a false gospel.

In those days there were false teachers (in this case, Judaizers) who were preying on the church in Galatia. Paul had heard about it and decided to write a letter that would stand in defense of the true gospel. Judaizers were Jewish Christians who believed that certain Old Testament rites were still binding on the New Testament church. They taught, among other things, that the rite of circumcision was necessary for salvation. To the church in Galatia, Paul pleaded, "Don't be taken in by the false teachers. Don't be mesmerized by their outward charisma, apparent logic and smooth style. If they are saying to you, 'Believe in Jesus Christ plus circumcision, plus keeping the Sabbath, holy days and ceremonial laws,' they are not of God. That's a legalistic gospel. It's a gospel that rejects God's offer of grace and insists on works-righteousness. It's wrong! Remember the true gospel: Believe in the Lord Jesus Christ. You are justified by grace through faith."

Judaizers preached, "Sinners are saved by faith *plus* works." Paul preached, "Sinners are saved by faith *alone*." The purpose of Paul's letter was to make that declaration and to defend it.

Four Pillar Values

I see in Galatians four key values. First, *Paul issued a strong warning against abandoning the true gospel*. That warning might seem almost unnecessary for those who have heard the gospel for many years, but the temptations to forsake the truth are always present. Paul saw it happening to his friends in Galatia:

> *I am astonished that you are so quickly deserting the one who called you by the grace of Christ and are turning to a different gospel—which is really no gospel at all. Evidently some people are throwing you into confusion and are trying to pervert the gospel of Christ (1:6–7).*

There's only one true gospel of Christ. That's why Paul called it *the* gospel of Christ, using the definite article "the" on purpose. What is "the gospel of Christ"? "Christ died for our sins according to the Scriptures, that he was buried, that he was raised on the third day according to the Scriptures and that he appeared . . ." (1 Corinthians 15:3–5). This is the true gospel: Jesus Christ's death is sufficient to satisfy all of God's demands against sin. If I place my faith and trust in Christ, I am saved. Not what I have done for Christ, but what He has done for me on the cross. I believe in Him. I am saved forever because of what He has accomplished. His Holy Spirit has come into my life to revive me and to empower me to live for Him.

Second, *Paul affirmed with unwavering confidence the gospel of salvation by grace through faith*:

> *Know that a man is not justified by observing the law, but by faith in Jesus Christ. So we, too, have put our faith in Christ Jesus that we may be justified by faith in Christ and not by observing the law, because by observing the law no one will be justified (2:16).*

That old familiar hymn says it all:

Jesus paid it all, All to Him I owe.
Sin had left a crimson stain—He washed it white as snow.

Regardless of what you may have been taught or how you may feel at this moment, this is the truth of the matter: Jesus' sacrificial death wiped away the stain of sin. There is nothing you or I can do that can save our guilty souls. We cannot "earn" God's love by following the rules. The gospel of grace says, "Believe in His sufficient, 'once-for-all' death on the cross. God says that's enough. Now we must agree with heart and mind that it *is* enough." True freedom comes when we joyfully accept God's gift of grace and by faith alone live out our new life in the power of the Holy Spirit, who produces His fruit in us (5:22–23).

Third, *Paul made a powerful statement about the function of the law.* I know of no better statement on the true function of the Old Testament law than Galatians 3:23–25. Look at verse 23: "Before this faith came, we were held prisoners by the law, locked up until faith should be revealed." You can almost hear the bars as they clang shut in verse 23. We were in prison until Jesus came and perfectly obeyed the law and by His death removed the curse of the law—and now through faith in Him we are set free! Verse 24: "So the law was put in charge to lead us to Christ that we might be justified by faith." The law was like a chaperon to escort us to Christ. The law kept shouting, "You can't. You shouldn't. You must not." The law kept pushing its finger against our breastbone and warning us. "Stop that! That is sin! That is wrong!" If you ever wonder what sin is, look at the law. It'll convince you that you can't gain God's acceptance by your own human effort.

Fourth, *Paul provided the necessary balance between freedom and responsibility.* (I'm thankful for Paul's words because I strongly believe in balance.) Verses 13–16 of chapter 5 state the needed balance so that liberty isn't abused and doesn't turn into license. Every time you and I present the message of grace, every time we encourage freedom in each other, we run the risk of implying that others may just have their own way. "Oh, I'm free. Wow! I'm going to grab for all the gusto I can get." Galatians 5:13 slams the lid down on that kind of thinking: "You, my brothers, were called to be free. But do not use your freedom to indulge the sinful nature; rather, serve one another in love." Delightful touch of balance, isn't it? The wonderful thing about grace is that once it comes into our lives we are set free from a preoccupation with ourselves. Set free from the worry of whether we are doing enough to please God, we are free to serve Him in love.

Three Enduring Lessons

Let me share three thoughts about the principles found in Galatians. First, *no one is immune to the temptation to drift from the true gospel.* If these Galatian believers could drift, so can we. The first step in getting us to drift is for someone around us to question the truth and for us to tolerate that question. When we get soft on the truth about the gospel, drifting has begun.

Second, *some things are worth a vigorous defense.* Certainly, the true gospel is preeminently worthy of a vigorous defense. The message comes through loud and clear: "Quit tolerating heresy. Stand firm in the faith. Hold fast to the gospel of salvation by grace through faith."

Third, *all of us began at the same place. We all stand on the same level—sinners, every one of us, saved only by grace.* I love the words from the hymn, *Hallelujah! What a Savior!*

Guilty, vile and helpless we. Spotless Lamb of God was He.
Full atonement! can it be? Hallelujah! What a Savior!

There is no room for pride when we realize that the ground leading to the cross is level. All differences between us pale into insignificance when we stand before the cross, sinners for whom Jesus died so that all who believe in Him would have eternal life.

You may need this word of encouragement. Don't be greatly impressed or intimidated by strong believers who seem to live such a victorious life and fine teachers who handle God's Word with great skill. They are sinners saved by grace—just like the rest of us. All have sinned and have fallen short of God's standard of absolute holiness. And all find acceptance from God only by grace through faith in Jesus Christ.

The letter to the Galatians may be brief, but it is bold. It may seem innocuous, but it is of enormous importance. Those who want to understand grace, walk in grace and accurately communicate grace must become serious students of Galatians, the letter that announces our liberation.

Personal Words From Paul **Chapters 1–2**

In the first two chapters Paul's words were very personal. We read things about Paul in this section that we find nowhere else. If you like to read autobiographies, you will enjoy these chapters. Paul wanted the Galatians to know that he was an authentic apostle. As testimony to this truth, Paul listed some of his personal experiences: his history in Judaism and his conversion, his visits to Jerusalem after his conversion, and his open rebuke of Peter. Such things verified his message and ministry. Paul wanted his readers to know exactly who this man was that the Lord used to write this challenging and convicting letter.

1 Paul, an apostle—sent not from men nor by
man, but by Jesus Christ and God the Father,
who raised him from the dead— 2and all the
brothers with me, Ac 2:24; Php 4:21

To the churches in Galatia: 1Co 16:1

3Grace and peace to you from God our Father
and the Lord Jesus Christ, 4who gave himself for
our sins to rescue us from the present evil age,
according to the will of our God and Father, 5to
whom be glory for ever and ever. Amen. Mt 20:28

No Other Gospel

6I am astonished that you are so quickly deserting
the one who called you by the grace of Christ
and are turning to a different gospel— 7which is
really no gospel at all. Evidently some people are
throwing you into confusion and are trying to pervert
the gospel of Christ. 8But even if we or an
angel from heaven should preach a gospel other
than the one we preached to you, let him be eternally
condemned! 9As we have already said, so
now I say again: If anybody is preaching to you a
gospel other than what you accepted, let him be
eternally condemned! Ro 9:3; 16:17

10Am I now trying to win the approval of men,
or of God? Or am I trying to please men? If I were
still trying to please men, I would not be a servant
of Christ. Ro 2:29; 1Th 2:4

Paul Called by God

11I want you to know, brothers, that the gospel
I preached is not something that man made up. 12I
did not receive it from any man, nor was I taught
it; rather, I received it by revelation from Jesus
Christ. 1Co 11:23; 15:1

13For you have heard of my previous way of life
in Judaism, how intensely I persecuted the church
of God and tried to destroy it. 14I was advancing in
Judaism beyond many Jews of my own age and
was extremely zealous for the traditions of my fathers.
15But when God, who set me apart from
birth[a] and called me by his grace, was pleased 16to
reveal his Son in me so that I might preach him
among the Gentiles, I did not consult any man,
17nor did I go up to Jerusalem to see those who
were apostles before I was, but I went immediately
into Arabia and later returned to Damascus.

18Then after three years, I went up to Jerusalem
to get acquainted with Peter[b] and stayed with him
fifteen days. 19I saw none of the other apostles—
only James, the Lord's brother. 20I assure you before
God that what I am writing you is no lie.
21Later I went to Syria and Cilicia. 22I was personally
unknown to the churches of Judea that are in
Christ. 23They only heard the report: "The man
who formerly persecuted us is now preaching the
faith he once tried to destroy." 24And they praised
God because of me. Ro 9:1; 1Th 2:14

Paul Accepted by the Apostles

2 Fourteen years later I went up again to Jerusalem,
this time with Barnabas. I took Titus
along also. 2I went in response to a revelation and
set before them the gospel that I preach among the
Gentiles. But I did this privately to those who
seemed to be leaders, for fear that I was running or
had run my race in vain. 3Yet not even Titus, who
was with me, was compelled to be circumcised,
even though he was a Greek. 4⌊This matter arose⌋
because some false brothers had infiltrated our
ranks to spy on the freedom we have in Christ
Jesus and to make us slaves. 5We did not give in
to them for a moment, so that the truth of the
gospel might remain with you. Ac 15:1; 2Co 11:26

LIVING  **INSIGHT**

We must encourage our brothers and sisters in the family of God to become mature. Because Jesus Christ has set us free, we dare not imprison them behind the legalistic bars of our own opinions, traditions or personal preferences.

(See Galatians 2:1–5.)

6As for those who seemed to be important—
whatever they were makes no difference to me;
God does not judge by external appearance—
those men added nothing to my message. 7On the
contrary, they saw that I had been entrusted with
the task of preaching the gospel to the Gentiles,[c]
just as Peter had been to the Jews.[d] 8For God,
who was at work in the ministry of Peter as an
apostle to the Jews, was also at work in my ministry
as an apostle to the Gentiles. 9James, Peter[e]
and John, those reputed to be pillars, gave me and

[a]15 Or *from my mother's womb* [b]18 Greek *Cephas* [c]7 Greek *uncircumcised* [d]7 Greek *circumcised*; also in verses 8 and 9 [e]9 Greek *Cephas*; also in verses 11 and 14

Barnabas the right hand of fellowship when they recognized the grace given to me. They agreed that we should go to the Gentiles, and they to the Jews. 10All they asked was that we should continue to remember the poor, the very thing I was eager to do. Ac 24:17; Ro 12:3

Paul Opposes Peter

11When Peter came to Antioch, I opposed him to his face, because he was clearly in the wrong. 12Before certain men came from James, he used to eat with the Gentiles. But when they arrived, he began to draw back and separate himself from the Gentiles because he was afraid of those who belonged to the circumcision group. 13The other Jews joined him in his hypocrisy, so that by their hypocrisy even Barnabas was led astray. Ac 4:36

14When I saw that they were not acting in line with the truth of the gospel, I said to Peter in front of them all, "You are a Jew, yet you live like a Gentile and not like a Jew. How is it, then, that you force Gentiles to follow Jewish customs? Ac 10:28

15"We who are Jews by birth and not 'Gentile sinners' 16know that a man is not justified by observing the law, but by faith in Jesus Christ. So we, too, have put our faith in Christ Jesus that we may be justified by faith in Christ and not by observing the law, because by observing the law no one will be justified. Ac 13:39; Ro 9:30

17"If, while we seek to be justified in Christ, it becomes evident that we ourselves are sinners, does that mean that Christ promotes sin? Absolutely not! 18If I rebuild what I destroyed, I prove that I am a lawbreaker. 19For through the law I died to the law so that I might live for God. 20I have been crucified with Christ and I no longer live, but Christ lives in me. The life I live in the body, I live by faith in the Son of God, who loved me and gave himself for me. 21I do not set aside the grace of God, for if righteousness could be gained through the law, Christ died for nothing!"[a] 2Co 5:15; 1Pe 4:2

Doctrinal Teaching **Chapters 3–4**

This second section reads like a doctrinal treatise. (Some of it is pretty tough sledding!) The central theme is the freedom of believers. We are no longer under the curse and bondage of the law. We are God's children and are no longer slaves. In this section Paul used a number of Old Testament characters as illustrations of the spiritual realities he was teaching. If you need to be reminded of the stories of Abraham, Hagar and Sarah, turn in your Bible to chapters 12–18 of Genesis—the doctrine here is based on an understanding of those Old Testament stories. Paul teaches us about the freedom we find only in Jesus and urges us never to fall back into slavery to the law. We have been freed . . . Why would we *ever* desire to return to bondage? I love this section of Scripture!

Faith or Observance of the Law

3 You foolish Galatians! Who has bewitched you? Before your very eyes Jesus Christ was clearly portrayed as crucified. 2I would like to learn just one thing from you: Did you receive the Spirit by observing the law, or by believing what you heard? 3Are you so foolish? After beginning with the Spirit, are you now trying to attain your goal by human effort? 4Have you suffered so much for nothing—if it really was for nothing? 5Does God give you his Spirit and work miracles among you because you observe the law, or because you believe what you heard? Ro 10:17; 1Co 12:10

6Consider Abraham: "He believed God, and it was credited to him as righteousness."[b] 7Understand, then, that those who believe are children of Abraham. 8The Scripture foresaw that God would justify the Gentiles by faith, and announced the gospel in advance to Abraham: "All nations will be blessed through you."[c] 9So those who have faith are blessed along with Abraham, the man of faith.

10All who rely on observing the law are under a curse, for it is written: "Cursed is everyone who does not continue to do everything written in the Book of the Law."[d] 11Clearly no one is justified before God by the law, because, "The righteous will live by faith."[e] 12The law is not based on faith; on the contrary, "The man who does these things will live by them."[f] 13Christ redeemed us from the curse of the law by becoming a curse for us, for it is written: "Cursed is everyone who is hung on a tree."[g] 14He redeemed us in order that the blessing given to Abraham might come to the Gentiles through Christ Jesus, so that by faith we might receive the promise of the Spirit. Ac 2:33; Ro 4:9,16

The Law and the Promise

15Brothers, let me take an example from everyday life. Just as no one can set aside or add to a human covenant that has been duly established, so it is in this case. 16The promises were spoken to Abraham and to his seed. The Scripture does not say "and to seeds," meaning many people, but "and to your seed,"[h] meaning one person, who is Christ. 17What I mean is this: The law, introduced 430 years later, does not set aside the covenant previously established by God and thus do away with the promise. 18For if the inheritance depends on the law, then it no longer depends on a promise; but God in his grace gave it to Abraham through a promise. Ex 12:40; Ro 4:14

19What, then, was the purpose of the law? It was added because of transgressions until the Seed to

[a]*21* Some interpreters end the quotation after verse 14. [b]*6* Gen. 15:6 [c]*8* Gen. 12:3; 18:18; 22:18 [d]*10* Deut. 27:26 [e]*11* Hab. 2:4 [f]*12* Lev. 18:5 [g]*13* Deut. 21:23 [h]*16* Gen. 12:7; 13:15; 24:7

whom the promise referred had come. The law was put into effect through angels by a mediator. 20A mediator, however, does not represent just one party; but God is one. Ac 7:53; Heb 8:6

21Is the law, therefore, opposed to the promises of God? Absolutely not! For if a law had been given that could impart life, then righteousness would certainly have come by the law. 22But the Scripture declares that the whole world is a prisoner of sin, so that what was promised, being given through faith in Jesus Christ, might be given to those who believe. Ro 11:32; Gal 2:17

23Before this faith came, we were held prisoners by the law, locked up until faith should be revealed. 24So the law was put in charge to lead us to Christ[a] that we might be justified by faith. 25Now that faith has come, we are no longer under the supervision of the law. Ro 10:4; 11:32

Sons of God

26You are all sons of God through faith in Christ Jesus, 27for all of you who were baptized into Christ have clothed yourselves with Christ. 28There is neither Jew nor Greek, slave nor free, male nor female, for you are all one in Christ Jesus. 29If you belong to Christ, then you are Abraham's seed, and heirs according to the promise. Ro 8:14

4 What I am saying is that as long as the heir is a child, he is no different from a slave, although he owns the whole estate. 2He is subject to guardians and trustees until the time set by his father. 3So also, when we were children, we were in slavery under the basic principles of the world. 4But when the time had fully come, God sent his Son, born of a woman, born under law, 5to redeem those under law, that we might receive the full rights of sons. 6Because you are sons, God sent the Spirit of his Son into our hearts, the Spirit who calls out, "*Abba*,[b] Father." 7So you are no longer a slave, but a son; and since you are a son, God has made you also an heir. Ro 5:5; 8:15-17

Paul's Concern for the Galatians

8Formerly, when you did not know God, you were slaves to those who by nature are not gods. 9But now that you know God—or rather are known by God—how is it that you are turning back to those weak and miserable principles? Do you wish to be enslaved by them all over again? 10You are observing special days and months and seasons and years! 11I fear for you, that somehow I have wasted my efforts on you. Eph 2:12; 1Th 3:5; 4:5

12I plead with you, brothers, become like me, for I became like you. You have done me no wrong. 13As you know, it was because of an illness that I first preached the gospel to you. 14Even though my illness was a trial to you, you did not treat me with contempt or scorn. Instead, you welcomed me as if I were an angel of God, as if I were Christ Jesus himself. 15What has happened to all your joy? I can testify that, if you could have done so, you would have torn out your eyes and given them to me. 16Have I now become your enemy by telling you the truth? 1Co 2:3; Gal 6:18

17Those people are zealous to win you over, but for no good. What they want is to alienate you ⌊from us⌋, so that you may be zealous for them. 18It is fine to be zealous, provided the purpose is good, and to be so always and not just when I am with you. 19My dear children, for whom I am again in the pains of childbirth until Christ is formed in you, 20how I wish I could be with you now and change my tone, because I am perplexed about you! 1Co 4:15; Eph 4:13

Hagar and Sarah

21Tell me, you who want to be under the law, are you not aware of what the law says? 22For it is written that Abraham had two sons, one by the slave woman and the other by the free woman. 23His son by the slave woman was born in the ordinary way; but his son by the free woman was born as the result of a promise. Ro 9:7-8; Heb 11:11

24These things may be taken figuratively, for the women represent two covenants. One covenant is from Mount Sinai and bears children who are to be slaves: This is Hagar. 25Now Hagar stands for Mount Sinai in Arabia and corresponds to the present city of Jerusalem, because she is in slavery with her children. 26But the Jerusalem that is above is free, and she is our mother. 27For it is written:

"Be glad, O barren woman,
  who bears no children;
break forth and cry aloud,
  you who have no labor pains;
because more are the children of the desolate woman
  than of her who has a husband."[c] Isa 54:1

28Now you, brothers, like Isaac, are children of promise. 29At that time the son born in the ordinary way persecuted the son born by the power of the Spirit. It is the same now. 30But what does the Scripture say? "Get rid of the slave woman and her son, for the slave woman's son will never share in the inheritance with the free woman's son."[d] 31Therefore, brothers, we are not children of the slave woman, but of the free woman. Ge 21:9-10

Practical Exhortations **Chapters 5–6**

The closing chapters focus on practical teaching for the Galatian church—with words just as powerful and relevant today as they were in Paul's day. There

[a]24 Or *charge until Christ came* [b]6 Aramaic for *Father* [c]27 Isaiah 54:1 [d]30 Gen. 21:10

are three central challenges here. First, *we are called to walk in the freedom gained for us through the life, death and resurrection of Jesus.* If we still live in bondage, we have missed the good news that Jesus has set us free. Second, *we are called to live under the control of the Holy Spirit and not be ruled by the flesh.* Paul lets us know that a fierce battle still rages in the heart of every believer. We must resist the enticements of the flesh and walk in the joy, power and fruit of the Spirit. Third, *we are urged to help others.* Our faith gives us confidence and strength to reach out to others in need and extend God's love and grace to them. If we heed these words of encouragement, we will discover that true freedom comes only when we walk in the footsteps of our Savior, filled with the Holy Spirit. There is no more important message for the child of God to learn and to apply!

Freedom in Christ

5 It is for freedom that Christ has set us free.
Stand firm, then, and do not let yourselves be
burdened again by a yoke of slavery. 1Co 16:13
2Mark my words! I, Paul, tell you that if you let
yourselves be circumcised, Christ will be of no
value to you at all. 3Again I declare to every man
who lets himself be circumcised that he is obligated to obey the whole law. 4You who are trying
to be justified by law have been alienated from
Christ; you have fallen away from grace. 5But by
faith we eagerly await through the Spirit the righteousness for which we hope. 6For in Christ Jesus
neither circumcision nor uncircumcision has any
value. The only thing that counts is faith expressing itself through love. Ro 8:23-24; Heb 12:15; Jas 2:22
7You were running a good race. Who cut in on
you and kept you from obeying the truth? 8That
kind of persuasion does not come from the one
who calls you. 9"A little yeast works through the
whole batch of dough." 10I am confident in the
Lord that you will take no other view. The one
who is throwing you into confusion will pay the
penalty, whoever he may be. 11Brothers, if I am
still preaching circumcision, why am I still being
persecuted? In that case the offense of the cross has
been abolished. 12As for those agitators, I wish
they would go the whole way and emasculate
themselves! Gal 1:7; 6:12
13You, my brothers, were called to be free. But
do not use your freedom to indulge the sinful
nature[a]; rather, serve one another in love. 14The
entire law is summed up in a single command:
"Love your neighbor as yourself."[b] 15If you keep
on biting and devouring each other, watch out or
you will be destroyed by each other. Mt 22:39

Life by the Spirit

16So I say, live by the Spirit, and you will not
gratify the desires of the sinful nature. 17For the
sinful nature desires what is contrary to the Spirit,
and the Spirit what is contrary to the sinful nature.
They are in conflict with each other, so that you do
not do what you want. 18But if you are led by the
Spirit, you are not under law. Ro 7:15-23; 1Ti 1:9

LIVING  **INSIGHT**

The Spirit versus the flesh. We've all witnessed the battle. We've all experienced the difference! With the flesh in control there is comparison and struggle, agitation, irritation, force and offense. With the Spirit there is release and relief, deep satisfaction, joy that lasts, love that isn't fickle, peace that isn't fleeting.

(See Galatians 5:16.)

19The acts of the sinful nature are obvious: sexual immorality, impurity and debauchery; 20idola-
try and witchcraft; hatred, discord, jealousy, fits of
rage, selfish ambition, dissensions, factions 21and
envy; drunkenness, orgies, and the like. I warn
you, as I did before, that those who live like this
will not inherit the kingdom of God. Ro 13:13
22But the fruit of the Spirit is love, joy, peace,
patience, kindness, goodness, faithfulness, 23gen-
tleness and self-control. Against such things there
is no law. 24Those who belong to Christ Jesus have
crucified the sinful nature with its passions and
desires. 25Since we live by the Spirit, let us keep in
step with the Spirit. 26Let us not become conceited,
provoking and envying each other. Eph 5:9; Php 2:3

LIVING 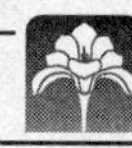 **INSIGHT**

The removal of restraint is usually neither excusable nor amusing. In fact, restraining ourselves is so important that God lists it as a fruit of the Spirit. Self-control, another word for restraint, is honored by the Lord as the "anchor virtue" on His relay team that runs life's race for His glory.

(See Galatians 5:22–23.)

Doing Good to All

6 Brothers, if someone is caught in a sin, you
who are spiritual should restore him gently.
But watch yourself, or you also may be tempted.
2Carry each other's burdens, and in this way you
will fulfill the law of Christ. 3If anyone thinks he is
something when he is nothing, he deceives himself. 4Each one should test his own actions. Then
he can take pride in himself, without comparing

[a] *13* Or *the flesh*; also in verses 16, 17, 19 and 24 [b] *14* Lev. 19:18

himself to somebody else, [5]for each one should
carry his own load. Ro 12:3; 1Co 2:15
[6]Anyone who receives instruction in the word
must share all good things with his instructor.
[7]Do not be deceived: God cannot be mocked. A
man reaps what he sows. [8]The one who sows to
please his sinful nature, from that nature[a] will
reap destruction; the one who sows to please the
Spirit, from the Spirit will reap eternal life. [9]Let us
not become weary in doing good, for at the proper
time we will reap a harvest if we do not give up.

LIVING  **INSIGHT**

Today is unique! It has never occurred before, and it will never be repeated. At midnight it will end—quietly, suddenly, totally. Forever. But the hours between now and then are opportunities with endless possibilities. With God's enablement, live this day to the full—as if it were your last day on earth.

(See Galatians 6:10.)

[10]Therefore, as we have opportunity, let us do
good to all people, especially to those who belong
to the family of believers. 1Co 15:58; Eph 2:19

Not Circumcision but a New Creation

[11]See what large letters I use as I write to you
with my own hand! 1Co 16:21
[12]Those who want to make a good impression
outwardly are trying to compel you to be circumcised. The only reason they do this is to avoid
being persecuted for the cross of Christ. [13]Not
even those who are circumcised obey the law, yet
they want you to be circumcised that they may
boast about your flesh. [14]May I never boast except
in the cross of our Lord Jesus Christ, through
which[b] the world has been crucified to me, and I
to the world. [15]Neither circumcision nor uncircumcision means anything; what counts is a new
creation. [16]Peace and mercy to all who follow this
rule, even to the Israel of God. Ro 6:2,6; Gal 5:11
[17]Finally, let no one cause me trouble, for I bear
on my body the marks of Jesus. Isa 44:5; 2Co 1:5
[18]The grace of our Lord Jesus Christ be with
your spirit, brothers. Amen. Ro 16:20; 2Ti 4:22

[a]8 Or *his flesh, from the flesh* [b]14 Or *whom*

INTRODUCTION

EPHESIANS

Although brief, the letter to the Ephesians contains a wealth of profound information about the Lord and His church. It is, in fact, foundational to the doctrine of the universal church, the body of Christ. It is in this letter that we learn about spiritual gifts and their purpose in the church, as well as receive instruction about the proper relationships among family members at home. No serious student of Scripture can afford to remain ignorant of this powerful letter. Its insights, principles and practical admonitions are essential ingredients in our growth toward maturity, as we serve our Lord together in the one body under the headship of our Savior, Jesus Christ. Read this letter carefully, for in it you will find unrestrained good news about the riches available to us in Christ.

WRITER: *Paul*

DATE: *C.A.D. 60–62*

PURPOSE: *To help Christians see the value of their position in Christ and their unity with each other*

KEY THEME: *The Christian's riches in Christ*

DOCTRINAL THEMES: *Predestination; prayer; depravity; "the mystery"; spiritual gifts; family; armor of God*

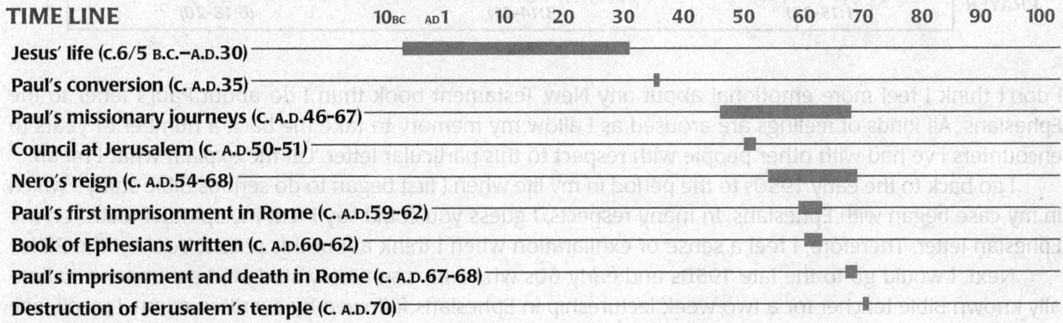

True Portrait of the Church

INTRODUCTION (1:1-2)

OUR POSITION IN CHRIST

SECTION 1: What God has done for us *(1)*
Emphasis: Sovereignty

SECTION 2: What Christ has done in us *(2)*
Emphasis: Reconciliation

SECTION 3: What the mystery means to us *(3)*
Emphasis: Grace

CHAPTERS 1–3

OUR PRACTICE ON EARTH

SECTION 1: The walk of the prisoner *(4:1-32)*
Humility
Unity
Maturity
Honesty
Harmony

SECTION 2: The life of the imitator *(5:1–6:9)*
In the world
In the home
On the job

SECTION 3: The struggle of the warrior *(6:10-20)*
Against satanic forces
Against human opposition

CHAPTERS 4–6

CONCLUSION (6:21-24)

	Chapters 1–3		Chapters 4–6
THRUST	**Theoretical . . . doctrinal**		**Practical . . . duty**
EMPHASIS	**Vertical relationship with God**		**Horizontal relationship with others**
PHRASE	***"He chose us in him . . ." (1:4)***		***"Live a life of love . . ." (5:2)***
SUBJECTS	**Declarations of heavenly truths (God's accomplishments)**		**Exhortations of earthly commands (The Christian's assignments)**
PRAYER	**Paul's prayer for Ephesians *(1:15-23)***	**Paul's prayer for the whole church *(3:14-21)***	**The Christian's prayer for power *(6:18-20)***

I don't think I feel more emotional about any New Testament book than I do about Paul's letter to the Ephesians. All kinds of feelings are aroused as I allow my memory to take me back a number of years to encounters I've had with other people with respect to this particular letter. Let me explain what I mean.

I go back to the early 1950s to the period in my life when I first began to do serious Bible study—which in my case began with Ephesians. In many respects, I guess you could say I "cut my spiritual teeth" on the Ephesian letter. Therefore, I feel a sense of exhilaration when I think about this potent book of the Bible.

Next, I would go to the late 1950s and early 60s when, as a seminary student, I sat under a nationally known Bible teacher for a two-week lectureship in Ephesians followed by a written exam. I recall feelings of great encouragement as we studied so intensely Paul's words to the Ephesian church.

However, I'd be less than honest if I didn't admit that I also have memories of boredom and disappointment associated with the letter to the Ephesians. For almost four years a certain individual preached only from Ephesians. It was a laborious, dry, theoretical, "verse-by-verse, Greek term-by-Greek term" analysis of Ephesians. At times, parts of verses would form the foundation for a 50- to 60-minute sermon. Believe me, it took years to get over the mental hang-up of those years of boredom.

I also had feelings of exasperation and irritation as I heard a particular prophet of prosperity using this letter as he promoted his claim that if you followed his own brand of teaching you would get rich. He drew on such verses as 1:7: "the riches of God's grace"; 1:18: "the riches of his glorious inheritance in the saints"; 2:7: "the incomparable riches of his grace"; 3:8: "the unsearchable riches of Christ"; and 3:16: "out of his glorious riches" (here this prophet taught that we would be strengthened with *wealth* in the inner being). I remember thinking, "What an abominable twisting of the true meaning and message of Ephesians."

And then, as is true of many of us, I have memories of delight and joy when on several occasions I have been involved in personal discipleship groups and Bible study groups where the letter to the Ephesians provided the basis for our discussion. In those small-group gatherings some of the richest cream from heaven poured into our cups.

I run the whole gamut of emotions when I open my Bible to this wonderful book that, although it has the potential to be misused, has been a source of incredible strength to so many in the church of Jesus Christ down through the ages.

The History of Ephesians

To get our foot in the door of understanding Ephesians, let me cover two sets of questions. First, *who wrote this letter and when was it written*? The letter itself reveals the author. Paul signed his name to the letter in verse 1 of chapter 1: "Paul, an apostle of Christ Jesus." Later in the letter he wrote, "For this reason I, Paul, the prisoner of Christ Jesus . . ." (3:1). Notice that twice he deliberately placed his name in the letter and it is implied on other occasions (see 3:7,13; 4:1; 6:19–20). Believe it or not, some critics still question the authorship of Ephesians.

Ephesians was written around A.D 60. Read Acts 28:30–31, and you will see the setting in which it was written. Paul had finished his major missionary journeys and had been legally detained in Rome. He was chained to a Roman soldier for a two-year period of time while under house arrest. In the last two verses of Acts, Luke wrote these words:

> *For two whole years Paul stayed there in his own rented house and welcomed all who came to see him. Boldly and without hindrance he preached the kingdom of God and taught about the Lord Jesus Christ (Acts 28:30–31).*

While he may have been chained and under arrest, Paul was still granted some limited freedom—not only to visit with those who came to visit but also to write. He wrote four letters during this two-year period, often called the "Prison Letters" (Ephesians, Philippians, Colossians and Philemon).

The second set of questions is this: *Who received this letter and where did they live*? The answers are mentioned in the first part of the letter: "Paul, an apostle of Christ Jesus by the will of God, To the saints in Ephesus, the faithful in Christ Jesus" (1:1).

Paul told us right up front who received the letter and where they were living. They were "the saints." Let me suggest that we not think of saints as some exceptionally pious, almost superhuman group of people, but as real people like you and me, thoroughly human, garden-variety, sinful people saved by the grace of God. The original Greek word translated "saint" in English means "one who is set apart for God's use." The letter was addressed to the saints, not the unsaved. It is mainly truth for the saints, truth for those set apart, for those who are faithful in Christ Jesus.

The founding of the Ephesian church is described in Acts 18. Paul had been working in Corinth for a year and a half (18:11), after which he was led by the Spirit of God to leave Corinth and to eventually make his way back to the homeland—back to Jerusalem and Antioch (18:22).

Leaders in Ephesus

When Paul left Corinth, he took Aquila and Priscilla with him (Acts 18:18). They were strong and gifted people—so strong that en route back home Paul left them in Ephesus (one of the westernmost towns in what today we call the land of Turkey). While there they did the groundwork in founding the church at Ephesus. Paul went on from Ephesus and later came back and spent two years and three months (Acts 19:8–10) helping in the work of the church there after Aquila and Priscilla had done the spadework.

The people in the church at Ephesus could boast of three very famous pastors who had lived and worked among them. They had Paul, Timothy and, toward the end of the first century, the apostle John—not to mention Aquila and Priscilla. You might think, "What a tremendous place to live. What a blessing to be under that kind of teaching for those many years." There is no question that the Ephesian church was blessed with many godly and gifted leaders . . . but keep in mind (to quote Charles Spurgeon), they were "but men, feeble, frail and apt to faint." It was the blessed and powerful Spirit of God who had empowered these leaders to establish the church at Ephesus.

True Riches

The theme of the letter is found in verse 3 of chapter 1: "Praise be to the God and Father of our Lord Jesus Christ." Not "Praise be to Artemis," not "Praise be to Diana," not "Praise be to some stone or metal image made with human hands," but "Praise be to the God and Father of our Lord Jesus Christ, who has blessed us in the heavenly realms with every spiritual blessing in Christ."

Verse 3 trumpets a clear theme: *the Christian's riches in Christ*. All the way through the letter Paul brings our spiritual wealth to our attention. These riches have nothing to do with one's bankroll or financial portfolio or earthly possessions. Our pockets don't get lined with silver coins simply by memorizing verses from Ephesians or by following its precepts. We get no automatic pay raise at work if we adhere to these principles. But we *will* be enriched in our hearts and in our relationships as we discover the gems and the riches deeply embedded in the mine of Ephesians.

Lessons From Ephesians

If I were to summarize the major truths of the letter to the Ephesians, I would suggest these four profound and priceless thoughts:

First, *God chose us in Him before creation* (1:4). We are not an afterthought when it comes to God's plan; we're a forethought. He loves us, and we remain central in His thoughts and plans.

Second, *Jesus Christ brings us to God by His blood* (2:13–16). Some today might resist the graphic nature of the language, but the truth is fundamental to the Christian faith. The blood of Jesus was the ransom He paid to redeem us from our sins.

Third, the great mystery of chapter 3: *Gentiles and Jews have been given equal status in the body of Christ, the church*. That's headline information to first-century folks—and it's so encouraging to us today too. God plays no favorites. He is color-blind and culturally neutral! Through Jesus' death He has purchased His people "from every tribe and language and people and nation" (Revelation 5:9). No matter what our nationality, we have become one in Jesus Christ!

Fourth, *the church is one body comprised of various parts, all of them important*. The church is not a team of superstars where the majority of people sit back and watch a few do the work. It is a ministering body where all of us work together (chapter 4). God expects us to live together in mutual service, peace and unity, in order that we might grow in maturity under the awesome leadership of our Head, Jesus Christ.

Our Position in Christ — Chapters 1–3

In this section Paul shares three key insights about our position in Christ. First, he declares what God has done for us. In chapter 1 we view the sovereign majesty of God as He reaches out to His people and brings them together into His church. In chapter 2 we learn of the reconciliation we have experienced through the finished work of Jesus. All the barriers between the believer and his or her Lord have been destroyed! We are now, at this very moment, reconciled to God! Finally, in chapter 3 we gain insight into the mystery of grace. God's goodness has been lavished on us, and we now stand secure before Him because of His grace. This section reminds us that ultimately we operate under the Headship of Christ, not under a pastor or a priest, not under an evangelist, not under a denominational hierarchy. The Lord Jesus Christ is the Head, the Exalted One! He is the One who makes His love known and fills us "to the measure of all the fullness of God" (3:19).

1 Paul, an apostle of Christ Jesus by the will of God, 1Co 1:1; 2Co 1:1

To the saints in Ephesus,[a] the faithful[b] in Christ Jesus: Col 1:2

2Grace and peace to you from God our Father and the Lord Jesus Christ. Ro 1:7

Spiritual Blessings in Christ

3Praise be to the God and Father of our Lord Jesus Christ, who has blessed us in the heavenly realms with every spiritual blessing in Christ. 4For he chose us in him before the creation of the world to be holy and blameless in his sight. In love 5he[c] predestined us to be adopted as his sons through Jesus Christ, in accordance with his pleasure and will— 6to the praise of his glorious grace, which he has freely given us in the One he loves. 7In him we have redemption through his blood, the forgiveness of sins, in accordance with the riches of God's grace 8that he lavished on us with all wisdom and understanding. 9And he[d] made known to us the mystery of his will according to his good pleasure, which he purposed in Christ, 10to be put into effect when the times will have reached their fulfillment—to bring all things in heaven and on earth together under one head, even Christ. Ro 8:29-30

11In him we were also chosen,[e] having been predestined according to the plan of him who works out everything in conformity with the purpose of his will, 12in order that we, who were the first to hope in Christ, might be for the praise of his glory. 13And you also were included in Christ when you heard the word of truth, the gospel of your salvation. Having believed, you were marked in him with a seal, the promised Holy Spirit, 14who is a deposit guaranteeing our inheritance until the redemption of those who are God's possession—to the praise of his glory. Eph 3:11; 4:30

Thanksgiving and Prayer

15For this reason, ever since I heard about your faith in the Lord Jesus and your love for all the saints, 16I have not stopped giving thanks for you, remembering you in my prayers. 17I keep asking that the God of our Lord Jesus Christ, the glorious Father, may give you the Spirit[f] of wisdom and revelation, so that you may know him better. 18I pray also that the eyes of your heart may be enlightened in order that you may know the hope to which he has called you, the riches of his glorious inheritance in the saints, 19and his incomparably great power for us who believe. That power is like the working of his mighty strength, 20which he exerted in Christ when he raised him from the dead and seated him at his right hand in the heavenly realms, 21far above all rule and authority, power and dominion, and every title that can be given, not only in the present age but also in the one to come. 22And God placed all things under his feet and appointed him to be head over everything for the church, 23which is his body, the fullness of him who fills everything in every way.

LIVING  **INSIGHT**

A vital sign of a healthy church is the exaltation of Christ as Head and supreme authority. Let us never forget that the body has one Head, and only one. The Head, remember, is Christ. He—alone—is Lord.

(See Ephesians 1:22–23.)

Made Alive in Christ

2 As for you, you were dead in your transgressions and sins, 2in which you used to live when you followed the ways of this world and of the ruler of the kingdom of the air, the spirit who is now at work in those who are disobedient. 3All of us also lived among them at one time, gratifying the cravings of our sinful nature[g] and following its desires and thoughts. Like the rest, we were by nature objects of wrath. 4But because of his great love for us, God, who is rich in mercy, 5made us alive with Christ even when we were dead in transgressions—it is by grace you have been saved. 6And God raised us up with Christ and seated us with him in the heavenly realms in Christ Jesus, 7in order that in the coming ages he might show the incomparable riches of his grace, expressed in his

[a]1 Some early manuscripts do not have *in Ephesus.* [b]1 Or *believers who are* [c]4,5 Or *sight in love.* [5]*He* [d]8,9 Or *us. With all wisdom and understanding,* [9]*he* [e]11 Or *were made heirs* [f]17 Or *a spirit* [g]3 Or *our flesh*

kindness to us in Christ Jesus. 8For it is by grace
you have been saved, through faith—and this not
from yourselves, it is the gift of God— 9not by
works, so that no one can boast. 10For we are
God's workmanship, created in Christ Jesus to do
good works, which God prepared in advance for
us to do. Isa 29:23; Eph 4:24; Tit 2:14

LIVING  **INSIGHT**

God watches over His workmanship. At times the tool bites in, causing the heat to increase because of the friction. We squirm and may even try to get away. But we are His workmanship, and the Father won't let us go. He holds us tightly in the lathe of His will. His goal is that we bear the image of His Son. That's the Father's task. He's committed to it. He's changing us.

(See Ephesians 2:10.)

One in Christ

11Therefore, remember that formerly you who
are Gentiles by birth and called "uncircumcised"
by those who call themselves "the circumcision"
(that done in the body by the hands of men)—
12remember that at that time you were separate
from Christ, excluded from citizenship in Israel
and foreigners to the covenants of the promise,
without hope and without God in the world. 13But
now in Christ Jesus you who once were far away
have been brought near through the blood of
Christ. Ac 2:39; Col 1:20
14For he himself is our peace, who has made the
two one and has destroyed the barrier, the dividing wall of hostility, 15by abolishing in his flesh the
law with its commandments and regulations. His
purpose was to create in himself one new man out
of the two, thus making peace, 16and in this one
body to reconcile both of them to God through the
cross, by which he put to death their hostility. 17He
came and preached peace to you who were far
away and peace to those who were near. 18For
through him we both have access to the Father by
one Spirit.
19Consequently, you are no longer foreigners
and aliens, but fellow citizens with God's people
and members of God's household, 20built on the
foundation of the apostles and prophets, with
Christ Jesus himself as the chief cornerstone. 21In
him the whole building is joined together and rises
to become a holy temple in the Lord. 22And in him
you too are being built together to become a
dwelling in which God lives by his Spirit. Mt 16:18

Paul the Preacher to the Gentiles

3 For this reason I, Paul, the prisoner of Christ
Jesus for the sake of you Gentiles— Ac 23:18
2Surely you have heard about the administration of God's grace that was given to me for you,
3that is, the mystery made known to me by revelation, as I have already written briefly. 4In reading
this, then, you will be able to understand my insight into the mystery of Christ, 5which was not
made known to men in other generations as it has
now been revealed by the Spirit to God's holy
apostles and prophets. 6This mystery is that
through the gospel the Gentiles are heirs together
with Israel, members together of one body, and
sharers together in the promise in Christ Jesus.
7I became a servant of this gospel by the gift of
God's grace given me through the working of his
power. 8Although I am less than the least of all
God's people, this grace was given me: to preach
to the Gentiles the unsearchable riches of Christ,
9and to make plain to everyone the administration
of this mystery, which for ages past was kept hidden in God, who created all things. 10His intent
was that now, through the church, the manifold
wisdom of God should be made known to the

LIVING  **INSIGHT**

It is in the church, week after week, where we learn faithfulness. It is in the church where discipleship is carried out. It is in the church where accountability is modeled. It is in the church of Jesus Christ where we find the doctrinal roots that establish us in our faith.

(See Ephesians 3:10.)

rulers and authorities in the heavenly realms, 11ac-
cording to his eternal purpose which he accomplished in Christ Jesus our Lord. 12In him and
through faith in him we may approach God with
freedom and confidence. 13I ask you, therefore,
not to be discouraged because of my sufferings for
you, which are your glory. Eph 2:18; Heb 4:16

A Prayer for the Ephesians

14For this reason I kneel before the Father,
15from whom his whole family[a] in heaven and on
earth derives its name. 16I pray that out of his
glorious riches he may strengthen you with power
through his Spirit in your inner being, 17so that
Christ may dwell in your hearts through faith. And
I pray that you, being rooted and established in
love, 18may have power, together with all the
saints, to grasp how wide and long and high and
deep is the love of Christ, 19and to know this love

[a]15 Or *whom all fatherhood*

that surpasses knowledge—that you may be filled
to the measure of all the fullness of God. Eph 1:23
20 Now to him who is able to do immeasurably
more than all we ask or imagine, according to his
power that is at work within us, 21 to him be glory
in the church and in Christ Jesus throughout all
generations, for ever and ever! Amen. Ro 11:36

Our Practice on Earth **Chapters 4–6**

Paul teaches that believers belong to a body. Not a single one of us can be a "Lone Ranger." We are a united body . . . one church under one Head. We are interdependent members of one another, not independent entities who don't need each other and aren't affected by each other. We belong to each other, like parts of a human body belong to that body. As those who serve the one Head, Jesus Christ, we are called to a new way of life—the way of maturity and purity—and to relationships that give evidence of God's power and grace at work in our lives. Finally, in verses 10–18 of chapter 6, Paul assures us that believers can stand against the enemy. We've got the armor it takes. We're not on our own. Isn't that a wonderful thought? In the battle called life we don't have to hope that if we're just clever enough we can elude the enemy. The enemy will not go away, but we are perfectly equipped to handle him. The letter to the Ephesians reminds us that we have available God's "full armor" and all we need to do is put it on and stand firm against the enemy. We can do that—and we *must* do that if we hope to walk in victory.

Unity in the Body of Christ

4 As a prisoner for the Lord, then, I urge you
to live a life worthy of the calling you have
received. 2 Be completely humble and gentle; be
patient, bearing with one another in love. 3 Make
every effort to keep the unity of the Spirit through
the bond of peace. 4 There is one body and one
Spirit— just as you were called to one hope when
you were called— 5 one Lord, one faith, one baptism; 6 one God and Father of all, who is over all
and through all and in all. Ro 11:36; Col 1:10
7 But to each one of us grace has been given as
Christ apportioned it. 8 This is why it[a] says:

"When he ascended on high,
he led captives in his train Col 2:15
and gave gifts to men."[b]

9 (What does "he ascended" mean except that he
also descended to the lower, earthly regions[c]?
10 He who descended is the very one who ascended
higher than all the heavens, in order to fill the
whole universe.) 11 It was he who gave some to be
apostles, some to be prophets, some to be evangelists, and some to be pastors and teachers, 12 to
prepare God's people for works of service, so that
the body of Christ may be built up 13 until we all
reach unity in the faith and in the knowledge of the
Son of God and become mature, attaining to the
whole measure of the fullness of Christ.
14 Then we will no longer be infants, tossed back
and forth by the waves, and blown here and there
by every wind of teaching and by the cunning and
craftiness of men in their deceitful scheming. 15 Instead, speaking the truth in love, we will in all
things grow up into him who is the Head, that is,
Christ. 16 From him the whole body, joined and
held together by every supporting ligament, grows
and builds itself up in love, as each part does its
work. 1Co 14:20; Eph 1:22

Living as Children of Light

17 So I tell you this, and insist on it in the Lord,
that you must no longer live as the Gentiles do, in
the futility of their thinking. 18 They are darkened
in their understanding and separated from the life
of God because of the ignorance that is in them
due to the hardening of their hearts. 19 Having lost
all sensitivity, they have given themselves over to
sensuality so as to indulge in every kind of impurity, with a continual lust for more. Ro 1:21; 1Ti 4:2
20 You, however, did not come to know Christ
that way. 21 Surely you heard of him and were
taught in him in accordance with the truth that is
in Jesus. 22 You were taught, with regard to your
former way of life, to put off your old self, which
is being corrupted by its deceitful desires; 23 to be
made new in the attitude of your minds; 24 and to
put on the new self, created to be like God in true
righteousness and holiness. Ro 6:4; Col 3:10
25 Therefore each of you must put off falsehood
and speak truthfully to his neighbor, for we are all
members of one body. 26 "In your anger do not
sin"[d]: Do not let the sun go down while you are

LIVING  **INSIGHT**

All of us know in our consciences when anger has become sin. Bursts of temper are sinful. Anger that slips out of control is sinful. Anger that plans to hurt another person is sinful anger.

(See Ephesians 4:26.)

still angry, 27 and do not give the devil a foothold.
28 He who has been stealing must steal no longer,
but must work, doing something useful with his
own hands, that he may have something to share
with those in need. Zec 8:16; Lk 3:11
29 Do not let any unwholesome talk come out of
your mouths, but only what is helpful for building
others up according to their needs, that it may

[a] 8 Or *God* [b] 8 Psalm 68:18 [c] 9 Or *the depths of the earth* [d] 26 Psalm 4:4

benefit those who listen. 30And do not grieve the
Holy Spirit of God, with whom you were sealed for
the day of redemption. 31Get rid of all bitterness,
rage and anger, brawling and slander, along with
every form of malice. 32Be kind and compassionate to one another, forgiving each other, just as in
Christ God forgave you. Col 3:8; 1Th 5:19

5 Be imitators of God, therefore, as dearly
loved children 2and live a life of love, just as
Christ loved us and gave himself up for us as a
fragrant offering and sacrifice to God. Lk 6:36
3But among you there must not be even a hint
of sexual immorality, or of any kind of impurity,
or of greed, because these are improper for God's
holy people. 4Nor should there be obscenity, foolish talk or coarse joking, which are out of place,
but rather thanksgiving. 5For of this you can be
sure: No immoral, impure or greedy person—
such a man is an idolater—has any inheritance in
the kingdom of Christ and of God.[a] 6Let no one
deceive you with empty words, for because of such
things God's wrath comes on those who are disobedient. 7Therefore do not be partners with
them. Ro 1:18; 1Co 6:9
8For you were once darkness, but now you are
light in the Lord. Live as children of light 9(for the
fruit of the light consists in all goodness, righteousness and truth) 10and find out what pleases
the Lord. 11Have nothing to do with the fruitless
deeds of darkness, but rather expose them. 12For it
is shameful even to mention what the disobedient
do in secret. 13But everything exposed by the light
becomes visible, 14for it is light that makes everything visible. This is why it is said: Lk 16:8; Gal 5:22

"Wake up, O sleeper, Ro 13:11
rise from the dead, Jn 5:25
and Christ will shine on you." Isa 60:1

15Be very careful, then, how you live—not as
unwise but as wise, 16making the most of every
opportunity, because the days are evil. 17Therefore
do not be foolish, but understand what the Lord's
will is. 18Do not get drunk on wine, which leads
to debauchery. Instead, be filled with the Spirit.
19Speak to one another with psalms, hymns and
spiritual songs. Sing and make music in your heart
to the Lord, 20always giving thanks to God the
Father for everything, in the name of our Lord
Jesus Christ. Ps 34:1; Col 3:16
21Submit to one another out of reverence for
Christ. Gal 5:13

LIVING  INSIGHT

Many people are caught in the trap of being too busy. Not necessarily doing bad things, just too many things. Being too busy is not a friend, it's an enemy—an evil, selfish, demanding force that requires things of us, things we have no business surrendering. Our goal is not to find more time but to use time more wisely.

(See Ephesians 5:15–16.)

Wives and Husbands

22Wives, submit to your husbands as to the
Lord. 23For the husband is the head of the wife as
Christ is the head of the church, his body, of which
he is the Savior. 24Now as the church submits to
Christ, so also wives should submit to their husbands in everything. 1Co 11:3; Eph 6:5
25Husbands, love your wives, just as Christ
loved the church and gave himself up for her 26to
make her holy, cleansing[b] her by the washing
with water through the word, 27and to present her
to himself as a radiant church, without stain or
wrinkle or any other blemish, but holy and blameless. 28In this same way, husbands ought to love
their wives as their own bodies. He who loves his
wife loves himself. 29After all, no one ever hated his
own body, but he feeds and cares for it, just as
Christ does the church— 30for we are members of
his body. 31"For this reason a man will leave his
father and mother and be united to his wife, and
the two will become one flesh."[c] 32This is a profound mystery—but I am talking about Christ
and the church. 33However, each one of you also
must love his wife as he loves himself, and the wife
must respect her husband. Mt 19:5; Col 1:22

LIVING  INSIGHT

You don't give yourself to others or consider them valuable if you don't first of all consider yourself worthy. Our own insecurities cause us to be constantly preoccupied with ourselves. Love draws on the resourcefulness of one's own esteem in order to have a sufficient supply to release it to someone else. It takes personal security to be able to do that.

(See Ephesians 5:28–29.)

Children and Parents

6 Children, obey your parents in the Lord, for
this is right. 2"Honor your father and mother"—which is the first commandment with a
promise— 3"that it may go well with you and that
you may enjoy long life on the earth."[d] Ex 20:12

[a]5 Or *kingdom of the Christ and God* [b]26 Or *having cleansed* [c]31 Gen. 2:24 [d]3 Deut. 5:16

4Fathers, do not exasperate your children; instead, bring them up in the training and instruction of the Lord. Ge 18:19; Col 3:21

Slaves and Masters

5Slaves, obey your earthly masters with respect
and fear, and with sincerity of heart, just as you
would obey Christ. 6Obey them not only to win
their favor when their eye is on you, but like slaves
of Christ, doing the will of God from your heart.
7Serve wholeheartedly, as if you were serving the
Lord, not men, 8because you know that the Lord
will reward everyone for whatever good he does,
whether he is slave or free. Col 3:22,24
9And masters, treat your slaves in the same way.
Do not threaten them, since you know that he who
is both their Master and yours is in heaven, and
there is no favoritism with him. Col 3:18-4:1

The Armor of God

10Finally, be strong in the Lord and in his
mighty power. 11Put on the full armor of God so
that you can take your stand against the devil's
schemes. 12For our struggle is not against flesh and
blood, but against the rulers, against the authorities, against the powers of this dark world and
against the spiritual forces of evil in the heavenly
realms. 13Therefore put on the full armor of God,
so that when the day of evil comes, you may be
able to stand your ground, and after you have
done everything, to stand. 14Stand firm then, with
the belt of truth buckled around your waist, with
the breastplate of righteousness in place, 15and
with your feet fitted with the readiness that comes
from the gospel of peace. 16In addition to all this,
take up the shield of faith, with which you can
extinguish all the flaming arrows of the evil one.
17Take the helmet of salvation and the sword of the
Spirit, which is the word of God. 18And pray in the
Spirit on all occasions with all kinds of prayers and
requests. With this in mind, be alert and always
keep on praying for all the saints. Lk 18:1; Heb 4:12

LIVING  **INSIGHT**

Fortune. Fame. Power. Pleasure. When it comes to temptation, these are the biggies. By resisting each, out in the open, we cultivate character down inside. So keep your eyes open and your shield handy. The battle is on right now. You can't trust Satan's cease fires.

(See Ephesians 6:18.)

19Pray also for me, that whenever I open my
mouth, words may be given me so that I will fearlessly make known the mystery of the gospel, 20for
which I am an ambassador in chains. Pray that I
may declare it fearlessly, as I should. 2Co 3:12; 5:20

Final Greetings

21Tychicus, the dear brother and faithful servant
in the Lord, will tell you everything, so that you
also may know how I am and what I am doing. 22I
am sending him to you for this very purpose, that
you may know how we are, and that he may encourage you. Ac 20:4; Col 4:7-9
23Peace to the brothers, and love with faith from
God the Father and the Lord Jesus Christ. 24Grace
to all who love our Lord Jesus Christ with an undying love. Gal 6:16; 1Pe 5:14

INTRODUCTION

PHILIPPIANS

If you need warm encouragement, a cheery boost of joy, a happy and hopeful word to lift your spirit, you have come to the right place when you open the pages of your Bible to this New Testament letter written by Paul. Philippians has it all . . . and more. Free from complicated and knotty problems, these 104 verses offer authentic reasons to be thankful, joyful and contented. And to think they were written by a man who was living under house arrest, bound by chains to a Roman guard all day long! How could he be so joyful? How could his charisma be so magnetic? Because his focus was on his Savior (whom he mentions over forty times in this brief letter) rather than on his situation. As we read Philippians, we will catch a compelling glimpse of the heart of Paul, and we will be drawn closer to the One who took first place in Paul's heart—the Lord Jesus Christ.

WRITER: *Paul*

DATE: *c.A.D. 60–62*

PURPOSE: *To thank the Philippians for their gifts, to encourage them in their suffering and to warn them about false teachers*

KEY THEME: *Joy from beginning to end*

KEY TERMS: *"Joy"; "rejoice"; "Christ"; "mind"; "all"*

STYLE: *Warm, encouraging, affirming*

DISTINCTIVES: *No major "problem passages"; no quotations from the Old Testament; written while under house arrest in Rome*

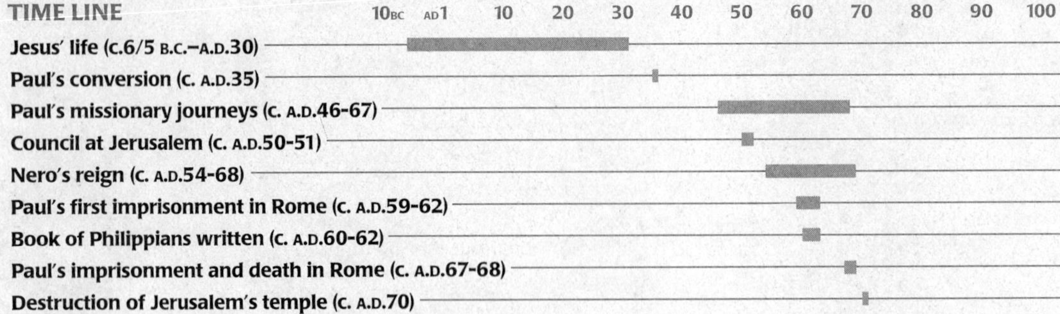

Joy in Abundance

	THERE IS... JOY IN LIVING	THERE IS... JOY IN SERVING	THERE IS... JOY IN SHARING	THERE IS... JOY IN RESTING
	Even when we don't get what we want	Starts with right attitude	A warning	Knees
	In spite of circumstances	Maintained through right theology	A testimony	Mind
	Even with conflicts	Encouraged by right models	A goal	Action
			A command	Faith
	CHAPTER 1	*CHAPTER 2*	*CHAPTER 3*	*CHAPTER 4*
CHRIST	**... my life**	**... my model**	**... my goal**	**... my contentment**
SPIRIT	**His provision *(1:19)***	**His fellowship *(2:1)***	**His worship *(3:3)***	**His peace *(4:7)***
POSITIVE REACTION	**To difficulty:** ***"Now I want you to know, brothers, that what has happened to me has really served to advance the gospel" (1:12).***	**To others:** ***"Do everything without complaining or arguing" (2:14).***	**To the past:** ***"Forgetting what is behind and straining toward what is ahead, I press on toward the goal to win the prize . . ." (3:13-14).***	**To the "unchangeables":** ***"I am not saying this because I am in need, for I have learned to be content whatever the circumstances" (4:11).***

I know of no greater need today than the need for encouragement and joy. Just look around—ours is a world of bad news and sad faces. Our stooped shoulders and deep frowns convey the heaviness of our hearts. If music and films are the pulse of a society, then little more needs to be said. Our plays and movies and television dramas depict despairing messages and themes. Watch any late-evening newscast. Read tomorrow morning's newspaper. Pick up the majority of best-selling novels. Listen to a radio talk show. Believe me, for every positive, joyful sound you hear there will be dozens of depressing and discouraging messages coming through loud and clear.

The longer I live the more convinced I become that the most magnetic quality of the Christian is not faith or mercy or courage or loyalty or even love, but joy. Those other qualities are often seen more clearly after we've gotten to know another person, but joy is the contagious magnet that draws people to one another. Joy takes the grind out of life. It is the oil in the machinery of life. Joy is the main quality that keeps the missionary on the field. The missionary without a sense of humor is the one who must come back often for furlough. There is nothing like a superlative sense of humor to get you through the day—to add joy and various dimensions of happiness to life. A joyful person is a balm of healing to hurting hearts. This is an important message for those Christians who sometimes seem to look and act more like basset hounds on the way to the pound than heaven-bound saints on their way to glory.

A Book of Joy

God has included in His Book an entire letter devoted to joy—four chapters, only 104 verses, committed to the subject of joy. If you find yourself running a little low on joy these days, I would recommend a prescription: Take one chapter of Philippians a day for several weeks, and you will see an amazing change start to take place in your life, as joy begins to flood your heart.

The message of Philippians can be summarized in one word: joy. Once you see it you cannot read the letter without smiling. You will come across the terms "joy" or "rejoice" numerous times as you read through Philippians (some 16 times in this four-chapter letter). It's a book that abounds in joy. If you find yourself feeling low and discouraged, brokenhearted, despondent, full of fear and worried about tomorrow, you need big doses of the Philippian letter. Big doses!

A Messenger of Joy

Who wrote such a pleasant and encouraging letter? The very first word in the letter provides the answer: "Paul." (I love the way they used to sign their letters back in the first century. The first thing we want to know when we get a letter is who wrote it, right? Maybe we ought to adopt that first-century custom!) Alongside Paul is a man named Timothy, a beloved brother, a disciple, a close friend. Paul refers to himself and Timothy as "servants of Christ Jesus" (1:1). Paul wrote the letter as Timothy, another servant-hearted soul, stayed near.

Now we might think, "In order to write such a joyful and delightful letter, Paul must have been sitting on the Riviera with a tall glass of lemonade, having just polished off an 18-ounce prime rib." Hardly. When we investigate what was behind Paul's current situation, we're all the more astonished at his positive attitude and cheerful disposition. In fact, he was not only joyful, he was overflowing with enthusiasm. Read the following and try to keep from smiling:

> *Now I want you to know, brothers, that what has happened to me has really served to advance the gospel. As a result, it has become clear throughout the whole palace guard and to everyone else that I am in chains for Christ (1:12–13).*

Amazing! Paul was under house arrest. He was literally chained to a Roman guard every waking moment. His situation was anything but a relaxing vacation along some seaside. Paul was in confinement. He didn't know if he would live to see another day. But he considered his plight a splendid opportunity to spread the message of Jesus Christ! In a state of deep uncertainty about the future he sat down to write a letter that went far beyond his circumstances to express a bold confidence and a living hope:

> *I know that through your prayers and the help given by the Spirit of Jesus Christ, what has happened to me will turn out for my deliverance. I eagerly expect and hope that I will in no way be ashamed, but will have sufficient courage so that now as always Christ will be exalted in my body, whether by life or by death (1:19–20).*

Paul said, in effect, "My great purpose for life is to present Jesus Christ, whether it is proclaiming Him through my voice while I'm living or through my example of facing death courageously. Whether by life or by death, it's Christ that's presented, it's Christ who is magnified and who gets the glory. For me, living is Christ, and dying, if I must, is gain." What a way to live! The man's attitude was downright infectious! To him external circumstances were incidental compared to the internal and abiding presence of Jesus Christ.

The Source of Joy

If our joy is based on daily circumstances, we might as well ship joy to the North Pole. If our joy is dependent on our circumstances, we will not have joy, because into every life comes some pain, some suffering, some displeasure, some discomfort. It will either be too hot or too cold. We'll be too confined. We'll be lonely. We will have lost something or someone very important. We will have had people disappoint us and break our heart. We will have had our business go through downturns. We will trust people only to find that they ripped us off when they promised they wouldn't, and on and on and on.

If you want your circumstances to spawn your joy, forget it! Paul said, in essence, "In spite of my imprisonment, I know people are being strengthened in the faith. I want to announce the reason I have joy: I have Christ. To me living is Christ. Dying simply means I get more of Him. The source of my joy, the secret to my joy, is Jesus Christ." Paul couldn't separate the reality of living and the reality of Jesus. If our joy is in

Jesus, our life withstands all obstacles. If our joy is in circumstances, we are setting ourselves up for one disappointment after another.

Stand Strong

One of Paul's primary reasons for writing this letter was *to encourage the Philippians in their suffering*:

> *Whatever happens, conduct yourselves in a manner worthy of the gospel of Christ. Then, whether I come and see you or only hear about you in my absence, I will know that you stand firm in one spirit, contending as one man for the faith of the gospel . . . (1:27).*

You might not have thought of the believers in Philippi as suffering people, but they were. Look at the next three verses:

> *. . . without being frightened in any way by those who oppose you. This is a sign to them that they will be destroyed, but that you will be saved—and that by God. For it has been granted to you on behalf of Christ not only to believe on him, but also to suffer for him, since you are going through the same struggle I had, and now hear that I still have (1:28–30).*

I remember going through a deep period of suffering in my own life a number of years ago, and I recall the words of a wonderful woman who empathized with me. She gave me a fine piece of information I'll never forget. She said, "Chuck, the Lord not only plans the length of a test but the depth of it as well." For some reason, that phrase made sense to me and met a need in my life. It helped me often as I brought it to mind and pondered it. I'm encouraged to know that God not only plans the length of my test but the depth of it. You may need that thought today. You may be wondering, "How long, Lord? How long is this suffering going to continue?" But an even more profound question is, "Lord, how much deeper are You going to dig in my life? How many more sensitive areas are You going to probe in order to get me to the place of total trust?" As Corrie ten Boom has taught us, "There is no pit so deep but that He is not deeper still."

Paul actually saw suffering as a privilege for the believer. Read carefully. It is not God's will that every Christian be free of pain. It is not God's will that every Christian be healthy. Put that notion out of your mind! Nor is it God's will for every Christian to be rich. That's nonsense that lacks Biblical support. It is God's will not only that we believe in Christ, but also that we "suffer for him" (1:29). He does not promise we will never suffer, but He does promise to stand with us no matter what we must endure. He will be our source of joy, no matter what awaits us.

Beware of Legalism

In chapter 3 Paul unfolded a second reason for writing this letter: *to warn the Philippian believers about those who would try to steal their joy*. Paul noted that there were "dogs" (3:2) on the prowl—vicious opponents who were preying on the believers in Philippi. "Watch out for them," urged Paul. Who were these "dogs"? Very likely they were proponents of the same false teaching Paul had to combat in the church in Galatia—namely, Judaizers. These teachers of legalism had insisted that salvation required both faith in Jesus and the keeping of such Jewish traditions as circumcision. They were taking away the joy of the gospel and turning the Christian life into a grim, merciless, harsh exercise of trying to keep religious rules in an effort to earn God's favor. In the end, all those efforts are doomed to failure, for we cannot make ourselves righteous—no matter how hard we try. The Philippians were in danger of falling into that trap and losing their joy. Paul warned the people in the church of his day, and this warning still rings true.

It's so easy for a group of believers to develop a legalistic spirit—a list of do's and don'ts. Beliefs, practices, theological dogmas, denominational loyalties, cultural customs, local church expectations and "sacred cows" are all set forth as requirements a person must fulfill before he or she could be acceptable to other believers and to God. It's impossible to hold to these teachings and at the same time truly discover the joy of knowing Christ, the joy of the gospel of grace, the joy of the "righteousness that comes from God and is by faith" (3:9). That's why I refer to such legalists as "grace killers." I don't want to be like that. I want to be an encourager. I want to be an affirmer. Don't you? I want to be a person who stays as broad as the Scriptures are broad—no broader, but no narrower. I suspect that this was one thing that blew people away when Jesus came on the scene. They didn't see or hear in Jesus all the negative, nit-picking stuff they had seen and heard so often in the religious leaders of their day. Jesus drew people to Himself, almost without a word. There was a wonderful accepting quality about Him. He wasn't a legalist; He was a lover . . . One who extended grace, accepted the undeserving and forgave the sinner.

A Grateful Heart

The third reason Paul wrote this letter was *to thank the Philippian believers for their gifts* (4:10–19). When they had learned of his detention in Rome, they had responded with a generous outpouring of love and gifts to help him as he awaited trial. Paul was determined to express his thanks, and so in joy he poured out his gratitude to the Philippians, his partners in the gospel. To this generous and caring group of believers, he said, in effect, "I want to thank you for sharing with me in your gifts. I was in the midst of affliction, and you reached out to me and you gave to me. Thank you for giving so generously."

Thankful Christians are joyful Christians, and joyful Christians are thankful Christians. There is always room for a grateful heart. Let the example of Paul speak to you today. Be a thankful person. There is so much that tempts us in the other direction—to be bitter, joyless or self-centered, to dwell on the negative. Yet Paul reminds us that nothing can stamp out the joy we have in the Lord. When we know Him, we have what we need for grateful, joyful living. When we have Him, we can be content. Then with Paul, we too can make this confession: "I can do everything through him who gives me strength" (4:13).

Joy in Living **Chapter 1**

This letter is not an ivory-tower epistle written by a scholar who never got dirt under his fingernails. The apostle Paul wrote these joy-filled words during a time of imprisonment. Through it all he experienced a joy in living that stands as an example for all of us. The message of chapter 1 is clear: Even when we don't get exactly what we want, we can still rejoice. Our joy comes not because of what we experience but because of *whom we know* . . . Jesus Christ, our Savior and Lord. Even in the midst of painful conflicts we can experience joy, because we are never alone. As a matter of fact, Paul took the harsh situation he faced and used it as an opportunity to bring the gospel to more and more people and to testify in the midst of suffering to the power and presence of his wonderful Lord. We can do the same.

1 Paul and Timothy, servants of Christ Jesus,

To all the saints in Christ Jesus at Philippi, together with the overseers[a] and deacons: 1Ti 3:1,8

2Grace and peace to you from God our Father
and the Lord Jesus Christ. Ro 1:7

Thanksgiving and Prayer

3I thank my God every time I remember you.
4In all my prayers for all of you, I always pray with
joy 5because of your partnership in the gospel
from the first day until now, 6being confident of
this, that he who began a good work in you will
carry it on to completion until the day of Christ
Jesus. Ac 16:12-40; 1Co 1:8

LIVING  **INSIGHT**

God will complete what He starts—including you. His work may seem unfair, it may be painful, it may involve changes that cause you to question His goodness. But He knows what is necessary. And He will do it.

(See Philippians 1:6.)

7It is right for me to feel this way about all of
you, since I have you in my heart; for whether I am
in chains or defending and confirming the gospel,
all of you share in God's grace with me. 8God can
testify how I long for all of you with the affection
of Christ Jesus. Ro 1:9; 2Pe 1:13

9And this is my prayer: that your love may
abound more and more in knowledge and depth
of insight, 10so that you may be able to discern
what is best and may be pure and blameless until
the day of Christ, 11filled with the fruit of righteousness that comes through Jesus Christ—to the
glory and praise of God. 1Co 1:8; 1Th 3:12

Paul's Chains Advance the Gospel

12Now I want you to know, brothers, that what
has happened to me has really served to advance
the gospel. 13As a result, it has become clear
throughout the whole palace guard[b] and to everyone else that I am in chains for Christ. 14Because
of my chains, most of the brothers in the Lord
have been encouraged to speak the word of God
more courageously and fearlessly. Ac 4:29; 21:33

15It is true that some preach Christ out of envy
and rivalry, but others out of goodwill. 16The latter
do so in love, knowing that I am put here for the
defense of the gospel. 17The former preach Christ
out of selfish ambition, not sincerely, supposing
that they can stir up trouble for me while I am in
chains.[c] 18But what does it matter? The important
thing is that in every way, whether from false motives or true, Christ is preached. And because of
this I rejoice. Php 2:3

Yes, and I will continue to rejoice, 19for I know
that through your prayers and the help given by
the Spirit of Jesus Christ, what has happened to me
will turn out for my deliverance.[d] 20I eagerly expect and hope that I will in no way be ashamed,
but will have sufficient courage so that now as
always Christ will be exalted in my body, whether
by life or by death. 21For to me, to live is Christ
and to die is gain. 22If I am to go on living in the
body, this will mean fruitful labor for me. Yet what
shall I choose? I do not know! 23I am torn between
the two: I desire to depart and be with Christ,
which is better by far; 24but it is more necessary for
you that I remain in the body. 25Convinced of this,
I know that I will remain, and I will continue with
all of you for your progress and joy in the faith,
26so that through my being with you again your
joy in Christ Jesus will overflow on account of me.
27Whatever happens, conduct yourselves in a
manner worthy of the gospel of Christ. Then,
whether I come and see you or only hear about
you in my absence, I will know that you stand firm
in one spirit, contending as one man for the faith
of the gospel 28without being frightened in any
way by those who oppose you. This is a sign to
them that they will be destroyed, but that you will
be saved—and that by God. 29For it has been
granted to you on behalf of Christ not only to
believe on him, but also to suffer for him, 30since
you are going through the same struggle you saw
I had, and now hear that I still have. Ac 16:19-40

Joy in Serving **Chapter 2**

This chapter spotlights three extraordinary examples of serving. First and foremost is that of Jesus Christ. He left the glory of heaven for a humble manger

[a] *1* Traditionally *bishops* [b] *13* Or *whole palace* [c] *16,17* Some late manuscripts have verses 16 and 17 in reverse order.
[d] *19* Or *salvation*

and finally a bloody cross. Jesus is our perfect example of servanthood. Paul also held up the examples of Timothy and Epaphroditus. What splendid models of committed service! In this chapter we learn about the joy found in serving others and following God's call to give of ourselves freely. Paul lets us know that joyous service starts with the right attitude—humility. It is maintained with the right theology—the cross. And it is encouraged by the right models—Jesus Christ above all, and other believers who have served and are serving in humility. When we commit ourselves to humble service, we will find a deep joy that can be discovered nowhere else.

Imitating Christ's Humility

2 If you have any encouragement from being
united with Christ, if any comfort from his
love, if any fellowship with the Spirit, if any tenderness and compassion, 2then make my joy complete by being like-minded, having the same love,
being one in spirit and purpose. 3Do nothing out
of selfish ambition or vain conceit, but in humility

LIVING  INSIGHT

Those who affect us the most watch out for themselves the least. They notice our needs and reach out to help, honestly concerned about our welfare. Their least-used words are "I," "me," "my" and "mine." They're unselfish.

(See Philippians 2:3–4.)

consider others better than yourselves. 4Each of
you should look not only to your own interests,
but also to the interests of others. Ro 12:10; Gal 5:26

5Your attitude should be the same as that of
Christ Jesus: Mt 11:29

6Who, being in very nature[a] God, Jn 1:1; 14:9
did not consider equality with God
something to be grasped, Jn 5:18
7but made himself nothing, 2Co 8:9
taking the very nature[b] of a servant,
being made in human likeness. Jn 1:14; Heb 2:17
8And being found in appearance as a man,
he humbled himself
and became obedient to death— Mt 26:39
even death on a cross! 1Co 1:23
9Therefore God exalted him to the highest
place Ac 2:33; Heb 2:9
and gave him the name that is above every
name, Eph 1:20-21
10that at the name of Jesus every knee should
bow, Ro 14:11
in heaven and on earth and under the
earth, Mt 28:18
11and every tongue confess that Jesus Christ is
Lord, Jn 13:13
to the glory of God the Father.

Shining as Stars

12Therefore, my dear friends, as you have always obeyed—not only in my presence, but now
much more in my absence—continue to work out
your salvation with fear and trembling, 13for it is
God who works in you to will and to act according
to his good purpose. 2Co 7:15; Ezr 1:5

14Do everything without complaining or arguing, 15so that you may become blameless and pure,
children of God without fault in a crooked and
depraved generation, in which you shine like stars
in the universe 16as you hold out[c] the word of
life—in order that I may boast on the day of
Christ that I did not run or labor for nothing.
17But even if I am being poured out like a drink
offering on the sacrifice and service coming from
your faith, I am glad and rejoice with all of you.
18So you too should be glad and rejoice with me.

Timothy and Epaphroditus

19I hope in the Lord Jesus to send Timothy to
you soon, that I also may be cheered when I receive news about you. 20I have no one else like
him, who takes a genuine interest in your welfare.
21For everyone looks out for his own interests, not
those of Jesus Christ. 22But you know that Timothy has proved himself, because as a son with his
father he has served with me in the work of the
gospel. 23I hope, therefore, to send him as soon as
I see how things go with me. 24And I am confident
in the Lord that I myself will come soon.

25But I think it is necessary to send back to you
Epaphroditus, my brother, fellow worker and fellow soldier, who is also your messenger, whom
you sent to take care of my needs. 26For he longs
for all of you and is distressed because you heard
he was ill. 27Indeed he was ill, and almost died. But
God had mercy on him, and not on him only but
also on me, to spare me sorrow upon sorrow.
28Therefore I am all the more eager to send him,
so that when you see him again you may be glad
and I may have less anxiety. 29Welcome him in the
Lord with great joy, and honor men like him, 30be-
cause he almost died for the work of Christ, risk-
ing his life to make up for the help you could not
give me. 1Co 16:17-18; 1Ti 5:17

Joy in Sharing **Chapter 3**

This chapter gives a perspective on what is of true value in this life and on into eternity. Paul teaches us that all the profit, gain and wealth of this world can't begin to compare to the surpassing worth of

[a]6 Or *in the form of* [b]7 Or *the form* [c]16 Or *hold on to*

TIMOTHY

A Man of Sincerity

"But you know that Timothy has proved himself, because as a son with his father he has served with me in the work of the gospel."

—PHILIPPIANS 2:22

Timothy—ah, Timothy. Who was this young man mentioned in Paul's writings more than any other individual?

Ponder these words, written by Paul to the church in Philippi (Philippians 2:19–22): "I hope in the Lord Jesus to send Timothy to you soon, that I also may be cheered when I receive news about you. I have no one else like him, who takes a genuine interest in your welfare. For everyone looks out for his own interests, not those of Jesus Christ. But you know that Timothy has proved himself, because as a son with his father he has served with me in the work of the gospel."

There are three characteristics Paul identified as being particularly noteworthy in the life of Timothy. First, *Timothy had a unique kindred spirit with Paul.* "I have no one else like him," wrote Paul (Philippians 2:20). Timothy and Paul were soul mates; they were like-minded, with hearts that beat virtually as one. Mathematically speaking, their triangles were congruent. When the older man (Paul) sent the younger (Timothy) on a fact-finding mission, he could rely on the report as being similar to one he himself would have brought back. Neither had to work hard at the relationship; things flowed smoothly and naturally between them. Paul took great pleasure in these relational joys he experienced with Timothy. They shared a deep spiritual bond as well—based on a common love for and commitment to the Lord Jesus Christ, whom they served and whose gospel they lived and loved to proclaimed.

Second, *Timothy had a genuine concern for others.* Paul's testimony opens a window for us into the young man's makeup. When Timothy was with others, his heart was sincerely touched over their needs. I imagine he was a man who listened empathetically and who loved deeply and who responded actively. Compassionate individuals are hard to find these days, but they were hard to find back in those days too. Remember what Paul wrote? "For everyone looks out for his own interests, not those of Jesus Christ." Well, almost everyone. Timothy seemed to be one of those rare exceptions who could look beyond himself and see others—really *see* them. Timothy modeled what Paul urged upon his readers earlier in this same letter: "Do nothing out of selfish ambition or vain conceit, but in humility consider others better than yourselves. Each of you should look not only to your own interests, but also to the interests of others" (2:3–4). That described Timothy. No wonder Paul felt so close to him. Friendships like that remind us of the importance of coming alongside one another with a genuinely caring, unselfish and open-handed attitude.

Third, *Timothy had a servant's heart.* Paul noted that Timothy had "proved himself" in the work of the gospel (2:22). He served like a child serving his father. Question: How can one grown man serve on behalf of another grown man "as a son with his father"? Answer, in one word: servanthood. In our competitive world we are so often run over by hard-charging, tough-minded, status-conscious people scrambling to make it to the top. They are willing to wield the power—and woe to those who get in the way. But it was not so with Timothy, who conformed to the Jesus model of leadership: "Whoever wants to become great among you must be your servant, and whoever wants to be first must be slave of all" (Mark 10:43–44). Timothy was a servant leader. He didn't strut his stuff; he didn't demand his due. Like his friend and mentor, the apostle Paul, he was a servant of all. By sending Timothy to the people of Philippi, or Corinth, or Ephesus, Paul knew that he was, in effect, sending *himself.* No anxiety over how the young man might handle some knotty problem he encountered. Not even a passing thought that Timothy might throw his weight around, saying, "As Paul's right-hand man, I insist that you listen to me . . ." The aging apostle could rest easy. Timothy was the man for the job! Paul must have smiled when he finally waved good-bye. Friends like Timothy relieve life's pressure and enable us to sit back and give thanks for those friends the Lord places in our lives. They bring a vast measure of joy into life's journey.

knowing Jesus. Certainly we need to be generous with our material goods, but we have a storehouse of wealth much greater than silver or gold. If we want to share something of eternal and infinite value, we need to make known the riches of Jesus Christ. If we want to discover joy, we will find it in sharing the incomparable blessings found in Jesus Christ alone.

No Confidence in the Flesh

3 Finally, my brothers, rejoice in the Lord! It is
no trouble for me to write the same things to
you again, and it is a safeguard for you. Php 2:18
2Watch out for those dogs, those men who do
evil, those mutilators of the flesh. 3For it is we who
are the circumcision, we who worship by the Spirit
of God, who glory in Christ Jesus, and who put no
confidence in the flesh— 4though I myself have
reasons for such confidence. Ps 22:16,20; Gal 6:15

If anyone else thinks he has reasons to put confidence in the flesh, I have more: 5circumcised on
the eighth day, of the people of Israel, of the tribe
of Benjamin, a Hebrew of Hebrews; in regard to
the law, a Pharisee; 6as for zeal, persecuting the
church; as for legalistic righteousness, faultless.
7But whatever was to my profit I now consider
loss for the sake of Christ. 8What is more, I consider everything a loss compared to the surpassing
greatness of knowing Christ Jesus my Lord, for
whose sake I have lost all things. I consider them
rubbish, that I may gain Christ 9and be found in
him, not having a righteousness of my own that
comes from the law, but that which is through
faith in Christ—the righteousness that comes
from God and is by faith. 10I want to know Christ
and the power of his resurrection and the fellowship of sharing in his sufferings, becoming like
him in his death, 11and so, somehow, to attain to
the resurrection from the dead. Ro 6:3-5; 8:17

Pressing on Toward the Goal

12Not that I have already obtained all this, or
have already been made perfect, but I press on to
take hold of that for which Christ Jesus took hold
of me. 13Brothers, I do not consider myself yet to
have taken hold of it. But one thing I do: Forgetting what is behind and straining toward what is
ahead, 14I press on toward the goal to win the prize
for which God has called me heavenward in Christ
Jesus. Lk 9:62; Heb 6:1
15All of us who are mature should take such a
view of things. And if on some point you think
differently, that too God will make clear to you.
16Only let us live up to what we have already attained. 1Co 2:6; Gal 5:10
17Join with others in following my example,
brothers, and take note of those who live according to the pattern we gave you. 18For, as I have
often told you before and now say again even with
tears, many live as enemies of the cross of Christ.
19Their destiny is destruction, their god is their
stomach, and their glory is in their shame. Their
mind is on earthly things. 20But our citizenship is
in heaven. And we eagerly await a Savior from
there, the Lord Jesus Christ, 21who, by the power
that enables him to bring everything under his
control, will transform our lowly bodies so that
they will be like his glorious body. 1Co 15:43-53

Joy in Resting **Chapter 4**

We live in a day when so many people clamor to climb the ladder of success. As we desperately seek things that will make us happy we often miss true joy. In this chapter Paul pointed to contentment as a secret to gaining true joy and happiness. Contentment doesn't imply a lazy, irresponsible attitude or a lack of motivation; it is simply an ability to be thankful and joyful no matter how much or how little we possess or what mountains or valleys we face. There is profound peace in thankful contentment. When we realize who has given us what we have, we can walk in contentment and experience true joy. Then the message of Philippians will not be limited to a four-chapter book in the Bible . . . It will be displayed in the everyday experiences of life.

4 Therefore, my brothers, you whom I love and
long for, my joy and crown, that is how you
should stand firm in the Lord, dear friends!

Exhortations

2I plead with Euodia and I plead with Syntyche
to agree with each other in the Lord. 3Yes, and I
ask you, loyal yokefellow,[a] help these women
who have contended at my side in the cause of the
gospel, along with Clement and the rest of my
fellow workers, whose names are in the book of
life. Php 2:2,25
4Rejoice in the Lord always. I will say it again:
Rejoice! 5Let your gentleness be evident to all. The
Lord is near. 6Do not be anxious about anything,
but in everything, by prayer and petition, with
thanksgiving, present your requests to God. 7And
the peace of God, which transcends all under-

LIVING 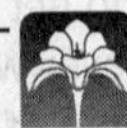 INSIGHT

God has called us to be in a spiritual growth pattern. Sometimes we're up . . . sometimes down. Sometimes we're more victorious than other times. But the progress is a movement forward and higher.

(See Philippians 3:13–14.)

[a]3 Or *loyal Syzygus*

standing, will guard your hearts and your minds in
Christ Jesus. Jn 14:27; Col 3:15
[8]Finally, brothers, whatever is true, whatever is
noble, whatever is right, whatever is pure, whatever is lovely, whatever is admirable—if anything
is excellent or praiseworthy—think about such

> **LIVING**  **INSIGHT**
>
> ***Thoughts, positive or negative, grow stronger when fertilized with constant repetition. That may explain why so many who are gloomy and gray stay in that mood, and why others who are cheery and enthusiastic continue to be so, even in the midst of difficult circumstances.***
>
> **(See Philippians 4:8.)**

things. [9]Whatever you have learned or received or
heard from me, or seen in me—put it into practice. And the God of peace will be with you.

Thanks for Their Gifts

[10]I rejoice greatly in the Lord that at last you
have renewed your concern for me. Indeed, you
have been concerned, but you had no opportunity
to show it. [11]I am not saying this because I am in
nced, for I have learned to be content whatever the
circumstances. [12]I know what it is to be in need,
and I know what it is to have plenty. I have learned
the secret of being content in any and every situation, whether well fed or hungry, whether living in
plenty or in want. [13]I can do everything through
him who gives me strength. 2Co 12:9; 1Ti 6:6,8
[14]Yet it was good of you to share in my troubles.
[15]Moreover, as you Philippians know, in the early
days of your acquaintance with the gospel, when I
set out from Macedonia, not one church shared
with me in the matter of giving and receiving,
except you only; [16]for even when I was in Thessalonica, you sent me aid again and again when I was
in need. [17]Not that I am looking for a gift, but I am
looking for what may be credited to your account.
[18]I have received full payment and even more; I
am amply supplied, now that I have received from
Epaphroditus the gifts you sent. They are a fragrant offering, an acceptable sacrifice, pleasing to
God. [19]And my God will meet all your needs according to his glorious riches in Christ Jesus.
[20]To our God and Father be glory for ever and
ever. Amen. Ro 11:36; Gal 1:4

Final Greetings

[21]Greet all the saints in Christ Jesus. The brothers who are with me send greetings. [22]All the saints
send you greetings, especially those who belong to
Caesar's household. Ac 9:13; Gal 1:2
[23]The grace of the Lord Jesus Christ be with
your spirit. Amen.[a] Ro 16:20

[a] 23 Some manuscripts do not have *Amen.*

INTRODUCTION

COLOSSIANS

One of the warriors of the faith, C.I. Scofield, once said, "Pure Christianity lives between two dangers ever present: the danger that it will evaporate into a philosophy . . . and the danger that it will freeze into a form." The letter to the Colossians is the chart and compass that will enable us to sail a straight course between those ever-present dangers. How we need this brief yet potent letter! Beset by Gnostic heresy and harassed by Greek philosophy, the saints at Colosse were caught in a cross fire. The apostle Paul wrote them a letter to help them stay on course, and in so doing he helps *all* who are tempted to take their eyes off Jesus. This letter, as much as any book in the Bible, focuses intense attention on Jesus as Lord of all and the One who is completely adequate in and for all of life's situations.

WRITER: *Paul*

DATE: *C.A.D. 60–62*

PURPOSE: *To warn the Colossians about false teachings that exalted human philosophy and depreciated Christ*

KEY THEME: *Jesus Christ is Lord*

EMPHASIS: *"In Christ" —we are united in Christ, complete in Christ, dead and risen with Christ, hidden with Christ*

STYLE: *Strong and assertive*

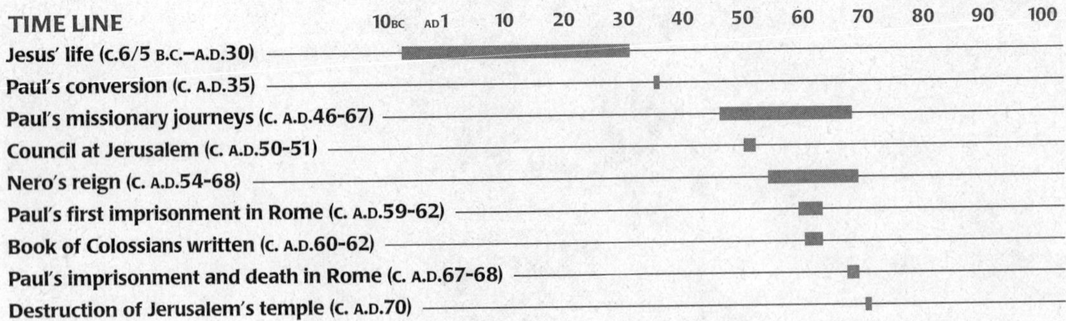

Christ, Our All in All

	CHRIST IS OUR LORD		. . . OUR LIFE	. . . OUR LOVE
	PERSONAL INTRODUCTION Lord of creation Lord of church Lord of ministry	Lord of our walk Lord of our salvation Lord of our growth	Our mind Our body Our attitude Our actions	Love for "outsiders" Love for fellow church members PERSONAL CONCLUSION
	CHAPTER 1	*CHAPTER 2*	*CHAPTER 3*	*CHAPTER 4*
SUBJECT	**Instruction**	**Warnings**	**Exhortations**	**Reminders**
CHRIST	**His person and work**		**His peace and presence**	
EMPHASIS	**Doctrinal and corrective**		**Practical and reassuring**	

In the letter to the Colossians, we encounter a very real problem that was attacking the church at Colosse. Let me first share an observation. I frequently meet Christians who have the idea that living in the first century was an enviable era in which to walk this earth. They imagine what it must have been like to have men like Peter, Paul, John, Timothy, Titus, Barnabas and Apollos to minister to them, to serve as their evangelists and their pastors. Some look back on this time in history with rose-colored glasses. You may have entertained such idealistic thoughts yourself.

Perhaps you imagined the New Testament era as a time relatively free of conflict, dissension, satanic attack and the clutches of cults. But nothing could be further from the truth. When you look in depth into the background of most of the New Testament letters, you will find that they were written to address a problem or series of problems assaulting an individual or a group of people in the church.

Read the letters to the Corinthians and those to the Thessalonians and the Galatians, for example; read about the context in which they were written and the situations they address. Someone once wrote, "The early documents could have been written in blood just as easily as ink." False teachers were everywhere. Persecution abounded. Christians had conflicts, plenty of them, even back then.

I made a list of some of the problems addressed in the New Testament, and here are just a few: schism, strife, heresy, extremism, personality conflicts, jealousy, misunderstanding and the teaching of a false gospel. On top of that there was martyrdom, defection, compromise and immorality. There was fighting. There was church discipline that had to be exercised. There was hypocrisy. There was legalism. And there was what I would call "spiritual bullying"—looking down on other people and treating them meanly.

Furthermore, the Roman government was led by rulers given to rivalry, gluttony, injustice, deceit and lust. They were men of appalling vices. Assassinations didn't even make the headlines in those days because they were so commonplace. That is the context in which the church was born and took the gospel of Jesus Christ throughout the Roman empire. The New Testament era was not nearly as attractive as some would make it out to be.

An Honest Look at Colosse

Paul's letter to the Colossians appears, on the surface, to be a relatively benign letter . . . simple and quite brief (only four chapters in length). It was written to a people living in what was called the Lycus Valley, consisting of three communities: Laodicea, Hierapolis and Colosse. Though once a leading city in Asia Minor, Colosse had paled in power by the first century to what some have called a second-rate market town. Its citizens were considered relatively insignificant, at least in comparison to residents of Rome (the hub of civilization in the empire) or Corinth or Ephesus or Philippi.

What is interesting is that false teachings had taken root there and had begun to drive a threatening wedge into the church. The impact was so severe that Paul took time to write the believers in Colosse—those virtual unknowns. Paul understood that if this heresy were given free reign, it could very well mean the demise of the three little communities in the valley and perhaps even spread like a cancer into cities like Ephesus and on across the Aegean Sea to Corinth and other important population centers. So by means of this pointed letter Paul intended to nip this false teaching in the bud before it spread out of control.

The Colossians believers had been taught well—not by Paul, but by a man named Epaphras, whose name appears in this letter (1:7; 4:12). It was very likely Epaphras who had founded the church in Colosse and had instructed the new believers in the true doctrines of the Christian faith. Now, however, the attacks of the false teachers were tempting them to forsake the truth. That temptation is experienced in every generation. It is very likely, in fact, that some who are reading this right now have been or are being tempted to drift from the true gospel of Jesus Christ. Either subtly or more overtly, you may have begun to compromise your faith. That was what was beginning to happen in Colosse.

False Teaching: Superior Knowledge

The Colossians had become the target of a mix of religious philosophies that had the potential to lead them into disaster as a church. The false teachings seemed to be a combination of Jewish legalism and a dangerous heresy called "Gnosticism." The word is derived from *gnosis*, the Greek word for "knowledge." Gnostics claimed that they had a secret knowledge that was necessary in order to gain salvation. It was secret information available only to an exclusive group of people. The net result was a message that enticed the vulnerable with this message: "There is something much deeper than Jesus Christ. Jesus is good. You need him, but you need more than that: You need this special knowledge. It'll give you a much deeper meaning to your life—and it'll give you salvation to boot!"

Notice how that arrogant message insidiously deprecated Jesus Christ and attacked His adequacy to be all we need for salvation. That's why Paul stressed the supremacy of Jesus Christ in the strongest terms:

> *He is the image of the invisible God, the firstborn over all creation . . . He is before all things, and in him all things hold together. And he is the head of the body, the church; he is the beginning and the firstborn from among the dead, so that in everything he might have the supremacy (1:15,17–18).*

You cannot point to anything beyond Jesus Christ and still possess the truth about salvation. When you go back as far as you can imagine, you come to Jesus. He is eternal. In response to the defective view that Jesus was not divine, Paul's letter to the Colossians is his greatest declaration that Jesus Christ is the eternal Son of God, the very image of God, the Creator, the preexistent sustainer of all things and the reconciler of all things (1:15–20). Look at what Paul wrote in such grand style in chapter 2:

> *For in Christ all the fullness of the Deity lives in bodily form, and you have been given fullness in Christ, who is the head over every power and authority (2:9–10).*

Gnosticism attacked the adequacy and the deity of Jesus Christ in a subtle and alluring manner. That's the way it is with most false teachings, isn't it? Most false teachers slither into a person's life in a subtle manner. They don't arrive brandishing swords. They don't burn Bibles and attack the faith, calling you "stupid" and "immature" because you have bought into the message of Scripture. They don't even necessarily reject Jesus outright; they simply include Him as one option among many. They approach with a smile. They bring a bouquet of flowers. They give you a record to listen to, a song to sing, a philosophy that seems to blend nicely into your life. But the truth is—someday their subtle tentacles will suck the joy and the power of the gospel and the hope of eternal life (and especially the awe-inspiring message of grace) right out of you. Please, please be very careful. Know what you believe and in whom you believe. If you have Jesus Christ, you have the Lord of life. Christ, and Christ alone. He is all you need for salvation, and for life.

False Teaching: Superior Behavior

The false teachers plaguing the Colossian church seemed heavily influenced by the teachings of legalists who taught that salvation required superior behavior. The Colossian believers were in danger of turning their focus from Christ alone to keeping legalistic regulations such as circumcision, dietary laws and religious ceremonies (2:6–23). Add to that the practices of various strains of asceticism (the teaching that the body is evil and thus should be treated harshly through the practice of self-denial—see 2:21–23), and you have all the ingredients for a philosophy that threatened to disconnect believers from their Head, Jesus Christ (2:19). Paul declared that Christ, and Christ alone, deserved center stage in their lives—and in ours.

Doctrine With Application

As with most of Paul's letters, this letter combines profound doctrinal teaching with practical application. The first two chapters contain some of Paul's most eloquent writing about Jesus Christ (including his majestic summary of the absolute supremacy of Christ in 1:15–20), sprinkled with practical teaching about being reconciled to God, about the way to true fullness and about the folly of following man-made rules. In these first two chapters the *person and the work* of Jesus Christ are emphasized, and the emphasis is slightly more doctrinal than practical.

In the last two chapters Paul builds on the foundation he laid as he shows us what a holy life should look like. Because we have been given salvation through Christ, and Christ alone, what should our response be? Here Paul turns very practical as he describes what the supremacy of Christ means for our everyday lives. The majestic and divine Savior comes near to offer us *His peace and His presence*, to give us the strength and the desire to follow His commands. As we remain in Him, who is our life, our relationships will be renewed and His peace will rule in all we do and say.

Lessons From Colossians

I find four rather simple lessons in this letter. First, *Jesus Christ is first—not one among many, but supreme.* Nothing can rival the place of Jesus in our lives, His lordship over all. . . nothing. If we come across anything creeping alongside, claiming to be equal to or above Jesus, it must be rejected quickly and decisively. Jesus Christ alone is Lord.

Second, *the infiltration of heresy is subtle, not bold and offensive.* I know of few teachings more outwardly appealing today than the message of the heretic. There is a powerful pull toward false teachings that add some human element to the pure gospel of Christ—whether it's the keeping of all kinds of detailed rules or whether it's the shedding of all restraint. Heresy is subtle, smooth, winsome and attractive. We must be well-grounded in the foundations of the faith in order to resist.

Third, *the way we live our lives is important.* The way we treat others is not irrelevant. The way we handle success and failure speaks volumes. Keep a careful eye on your attitude and your behavior wherever you are—at home, at church, at work, at school, in the community halls and the shopping malls. Believe it or not, the way you walk your talk is an announcement bigger than any gospel tract you put on somebody's desk. People are watching how you live. They're watching how you work. Let's face it, the eyes of the world are on those who profess to love and serve the Lord Jesus—and His eyes are on us too; ultimately, we will answer to our Maker. Our diligence underscores and reveals the substance of our doctrine.

Fourth, *people are eternal souls made in the image of God, not anonymous faces.* You never become so important that people become unimportant. Never. We are created to be in relationship, and it would be good to remind ourselves of the way God calls us to relate to each other. I urge us to be careful that we don't become so preoccupied with all the programs and all the plans and all the projects that people become unimportant to us. Our lives are a call to service—to our Lord Jesus and to our brothers and sisters whom He has placed in our lives.

A Prescription

If you're tempted to think of Colossians as nothing more than a little letter written to an insignificant church in an insignificant city, please think again. It carries an enormously significant message that speaks to believers at all times and in all places.

Reading this letter will give you a whole new perspective on the way you think about Jesus Christ. If you find that you need a fresh vision of Jesus, if you've grown too accustomed to a Christ who is too predictable, too tame, too colorless, I prescribe a month of Colossians. Read from it each day for 30 days, and the Lord Jesus will take on a new spark. Ponder its words carefully. Dwell on it. Let it penetrate your heart and soak into your spirit. Your appreciation for and reliance on the Savior will just begin to soar. Colossians is a letter committed to heightening the impact of the person and power of Jesus Christ in the minds of the reader. And believe me, it'll happen! After all, He is the One who dominates this great letter to the Colossians. He is the Lord. He is our life. He is our love. He is our everything. Christ, and Christ alone!

Jesus Is Our Lord **Chapters 1–2**

In these two chapters Paul focuses our attention on the lordship of Jesus Christ. I suspect that if we had tapped the apostle Paul on the shoulder as he was chained to the Roman guard and asked him, "What's your goal in life?" He would have responded by saying, "I want every person to know that Jesus Christ is Lord." In this brief letter, he let us know that his heart's desire was to help every person he met grow in spiritual wisdom and become mature and complete in Christ. In the first chapter Paul presents Jesus as Lord over creation, the church and all ministry. In the second chapter Jesus is exalted as the Lord of our salvation, our walk of faith and our growth. In short, He is Lord of everything! As you read these chapters you will behold the Lord of glory, Jesus Christ, who deserves first place in everything.

1 Paul, an apostle of Christ Jesus by the will of
God, and Timothy our brother, 1Co 1:1; 2Co 1:1

2To the holy and faithful[a] brothers in Christ at
Colosse:

Grace and peace to you from God our Father.[b]

Thanksgiving and Prayer

3We always thank God, the Father of our Lord
Jesus Christ, when we pray for you, 4because we
have heard of your faith in Christ Jesus and of the
love you have for all the saints— 5the faith and
love that spring from the hope that is stored up for
you in heaven and that you have already heard
about in the word of truth, the gospel 6that has
come to you. All over the world this gospel is
bearing fruit and growing, just as it has been doing
among you since the day you heard it and understood God's grace in all its truth. 7You learned it
from Epaphras, our dear fellow servant, who is a
faithful minister of Christ on our[c] behalf, 8and
who also told us of your love in the Spirit.
9For this reason, since the day we heard about
you, we have not stopped praying for you and
asking God to fill you with the knowledge of his
will through all spiritual wisdom and understanding. 10And we pray this in order that you may live
a life worthy of the Lord and may please him in
every way: bearing fruit in every good work, growing in the knowledge of God, 11being strengthened
with all power according to his glorious might so
that you may have great endurance and patience,
and joyfully 12giving thanks to the Father, who has
qualified you[d] to share in the inheritance of the
saints in the kingdom of light. 13For he has rescued
us from the dominion of darkness and brought us
into the kingdom of the Son he loves, 14in whom
we have redemption,[e] the forgiveness of sins.

The Supremacy of Christ

15He is the image of the invisible God, the firstborn over all creation. 16For by him all things were
created: things in heaven and on earth, visible and
invisible, whether thrones or powers or rulers or
authorities; all things were created by him and for
him. 17He is before all things, and in him all things
hold together. 18And he is the head of the body,
the church; he is the beginning and the firstborn
from among the dead, so that in everything he
might have the supremacy. 19For God was pleased
to have all his fullness dwell in him, 20and through
him to reconcile to himself all things, whether
things on earth or things in heaven, by making
peace through his blood, shed on the cross.
21Once you were alienated from God and were
enemies in your minds because of[f] your evil behavior. 22But now he has reconciled you by
Christ's physical body through death to present
you holy in his sight, without blemish and free
from accusation— 23if you continue in your faith,
established and firm, not moved from the hope
held out in the gospel. This is the gospel that you
heard and that has been proclaimed to every creature under heaven, and of which I, Paul, have become a servant. Ro 10:18; 1Co 3:5; Eph 3:17

Paul's Labor for the Church

24Now I rejoice in what was suffered for you,
and I fill up in my flesh what is still lacking in
regard to Christ's afflictions, for the sake of his
body, which is the church. 25I have become its
servant by the commission God gave me to
present to you the word of God in its fullness—
26the mystery that has been kept hidden for ages
and generations, but is now disclosed to the saints.
27To them God has chosen to make known among
the Gentiles the glorious riches of this mystery,
which is Christ in you, the hope of glory. Ro 8:10
28We proclaim him, admonishing and teaching
everyone with all wisdom, so that we may present

LIVING  INSIGHT

Do you imagine that your tomorrow will be just like your yesterday? Sounds like you've stopped believing in a God with the power to bring change. He can make it happen! He can shatter old habits, blast apart old attitudes, wash away old resentments and hurts, push aside old fears and limitations and stereotypes. It's His energy, His power, that's at work in our lives, making the difference.

(See Colossians 1:28–29.)

[a]2 Or *believing* [b]2 Some manuscripts *Father and the Lord Jesus Christ* [c]7 Some manuscripts *your* [d]12 Some manuscripts *us* [e]14 A few late manuscripts *redemption through his blood* [f]21 Or *minds, as shown by*

everyone perfect in Christ. 29To this end I labor, struggling with all his energy, which so powerfully works in me. 1Co 15:10; Eph 1:19; Col 2:1

2 I want you to know how much I am struggling for you and for those at Laodicea, and for all who have not met me personally. 2My purpose is that they may be encouraged in heart and united in love, so that they may have the full riches of complete understanding, in order that they may know the mystery of God, namely, Christ, 3in whom are hidden all the treasures of wisdom and knowledge. 4I tell you this so that no one may deceive you by fine-sounding arguments. 5For though I am absent from you in body, I am present with you in spirit and delight to see how orderly you are and how firm your faith in Christ is. 1Co 14:40; 1Th 2:17; 1Pe 5:9

Freedom From Human Regulations Through Life With Christ

6So then, just as you received Christ Jesus as Lord, continue to live in him, 7rooted and built up in him, strengthened in the faith as you were taught, and overflowing with thankfulness.

8See to it that no one takes you captive through hollow and deceptive philosophy, which depends on human tradition and the basic principles of this world rather than on Christ. Gal 4:3; 1Ti 6:20

9For in Christ all the fullness of the Deity lives in bodily form, 10and you have been given fullness in Christ, who is the head over every power and authority. 11In him you were also circumcised, in the putting off of the sinful nature,[a] not with a circumcision done by the hands of men but with the circumcision done by Christ, 12having been buried with him in baptism and raised with him through your faith in the power of God, who raised him from the dead. Ac 2:24; Ro 2:29; 6:5

13When you were dead in your sins and in the uncircumcision of your sinful nature,[b] God made you[c] alive with Christ. He forgave us all our sins, 14having canceled the written code, with its regulations, that was against us and that stood opposed to us; he took it away, nailing it to the cross. 15And having disarmed the powers and authorities, he made a public spectacle of them, triumphing over them by the cross.[d] Eph 2:15; 6:12

16Therefore do not let anyone judge you by what you eat or drink, or with regard to a religious festival, a New Moon celebration or a Sabbath day. 17These are a shadow of the things that were to come; the reality, however, is found in Christ. 18Do not let anyone who delights in false humility and the worship of angels disqualify you for the prize. Such a person goes into great detail about what he has seen, and his unspiritual mind puffs him up with idle notions. 19He has lost connection with the Head, from whom the whole body, supported and held together by its ligaments and sinews, grows as God causes it to grow. Eph 1:22; 4:16

20Since you died with Christ to the basic principles of this world, why, as though you still belonged to it, do you submit to its rules: 21"Do not handle! Do not taste! Do not touch!"? 22These are all destined to perish with use, because they are based on human commands and teachings. 23Such regulations indeed have an appearance of wisdom, with their self-imposed worship, their false humility and their harsh treatment of the body, but they lack any value in restraining sensual indulgence.

Jesus Is Our Life **Chapter 3**

In this chapter Paul shows that Jesus is the Lord of our way of life. He is sovereign over our mind, body, attitudes and actions. Because we belong to him, we should walk in holiness. Every area of our lives, from visible public actions to the unseen secret thoughts of our minds, should be under His lordship and control—as we see all of life through His eyes. This chapter also highlights the importance of placing our households under His rule. Jesus is Lord of our lives, and that means *all* of our lives . . . in everything!

Rules for Holy Living

3 Since, then, you have been raised with Christ, set your hearts on things above, where Christ is seated at the right hand of God. 2Set your minds on things above, not on earthly things. 3For you died, and your life is now hidden with Christ in God. 4When Christ, who is your[e] life, appears, then you also will appear with him in glory.

5Put to death, therefore, whatever belongs to your earthly nature: sexual immorality, impurity, lust, evil desires and greed, which is idolatry. 6Because of these, the wrath of God is coming.[f] 7You used to walk in these ways, in the life you once lived. 8But now you must rid yourselves of all such things as these: anger, rage, malice, slander, and filthy language from your lips. 9Do not lie to each other, since you have taken off your old self with its practices 10and have put on the new self, which is being renewed in knowledge in the image of its Creator. 11Here there is no Greek or Jew, circumcised or uncircumcised, barbarian, Scythian, slave or free, but Christ is all, and is in all. Ro 12:2

12Therefore, as God's chosen people, holy and dearly loved, clothe yourselves with compassion, kindness, humility, gentleness and patience. 13Bear with each other and forgive whatever grievances you may have against one another. Forgive as the Lord forgave you. 14And over all these virtues put

[a]11 Or *the flesh* [b]13 Or *your flesh* [c]13 Some manuscripts *us* [d]15 Or *them in him* [e]4 Some manuscripts *our*
[f]6 Some early manuscripts *coming on those who are disobedient*

on love, which binds them all together in perfect unity. Eph 4:3; Php 2:3

15 Let the peace of Christ rule in your hearts, since as members of one body you were called to peace. And be thankful. 16 Let the word of Christ dwell in you richly as you teach and admonish one another with all wisdom, and as you sing psalms, hymns and spiritual songs with gratitude in your hearts to God. 17 And whatever you do, whether in word or deed, do it all in the name of the Lord Jesus, giving thanks to God the Father through him. 1Co 10:31; Eph 5:19

LIVING  **INSIGHT**

How long will it be before we realize that others won't care how much we know until they know how much we care? If you really want to be blessed, prefer compassion to information. We need both, but in the right order.

(See Colossians 3:12–17.)

Rules for Christian Households

18 Wives, submit to your husbands, as is fitting in the Lord. Eph 5:22

19 Husbands, love your wives and do not be harsh with them.

20 Children, obey your parents in everything, for this pleases the Lord.

21 Fathers, do not embitter your children, or they will become discouraged.

22 Slaves, obey your earthly masters in everything; and do it, not only when their eye is on you and to win their favor, but with sincerity of heart and reverence for the Lord. 23 Whatever you do, work at it with all your heart, as working for the Lord, not for men, 24 since you know that you will receive an inheritance from the Lord as a reward. It is the Lord Christ you are serving. 25 Anyone who does wrong will be repaid for his wrong, and there is no favoritism. Ac 10:34; 20:32

Jesus Is Our Love **Chapter 4**

This chapter helps us see Jesus as our love. He loves us beyond measure, and we are called to respond to His love. Paul had a deep concern that the love of the Savior be extended to those both outside and inside the church. Because we have received the love of Jesus, we are called to share this overflowing love with everyone we meet. Yes, everyone!

4 Masters, provide your slaves with what is right and fair, because you know that you also have a Master in heaven. Eph 5:22-6:9

Further Instructions

2 Devote yourselves to prayer, being watchful and thankful. 3 And pray for us, too, that God may open a door for our message, so that we may proclaim the mystery of Christ, for which I am in chains. 4 Pray that I may proclaim it clearly, as I should. 5 Be wise in the way you act toward outsiders; make the most of every opportunity. 6 Let your conversation be always full of grace, seasoned with salt, so that you may know how to answer everyone. Mk 9:50; Eph 5:16; 1Pe 3:15

LIVING  **INSIGHT**

Don't let another day slip by without taking action on that issue about which you know God has been prompting you.

(See Colossians 4:5.)

Final Greetings

7 Tychicus will tell you all the news about me. He is a dear brother, a faithful minister and fellow servant in the Lord. 8 I am sending him to you for the express purpose that you may know about our[a] circumstances and that he may encourage your hearts. 9 He is coming with Onesimus, our faithful and dear brother, who is one of you. They will tell you everything that is happening here.

10 My fellow prisoner Aristarchus sends you his greetings, as does Mark, the cousin of Barnabas. (You have received instructions about him; if he comes to you, welcome him.) 11 Jesus, who is called Justus, also sends greetings. These are the only Jews among my fellow workers for the kingdom of God, and they have proved a comfort to me. 12 Epaphras, who is one of you and a servant of Christ Jesus, sends greetings. He is always wrestling in prayer for you, that you may stand firm in all the will of God, mature and fully assured. 13 I vouch for him that he is working hard for you and for those at Laodicea and Hierapolis. 14 Our dear friend Luke, the doctor, and Demas send greetings. 15 Give my greetings to the brothers at Laodicea, and to Nympha and the church in her house.

16 After this letter has been read to you, see that it is also read in the church of the Laodiceans and that you in turn read the letter from Laodicea.

17 Tell Archippus: "See to it that you complete the work you have received in the Lord." 2Ti 4:5

18 I, Paul, write this greeting in my own hand. Remember my chains. Grace be with you.

[a] 8 Some manuscripts *that he may know about your*

INTRODUCTION

1 THESSALONIANS

This letter to the Thessalonians is believed to be the first letter Paul wrote that found its way into the canon of Scripture. As such, it includes a number of very personal insights into the apostle's life. We see his heart exposed and hear it beat on several occasions, in a way similar to his second letter to the Corinthians. Although brief (less than 90 verses), Paul's first letter to the Thessalonians gives us helpful counsel on such practical matters as a church model worth emulating, a philosophy of ministry worth adopting, a commitment to purity worth remembering, a picture of Christ's return worth anticipating and a love for the body of believers worth duplicating. This letter deserves our careful attention, because it is an invaluable resource to turn to when we struggle with any one of these areas of practical living.

WRITER: *Paul*

DATE: *C.A.D. 50–51*

PURPOSE: *To encourage the Thessalonians to persevere through their trials and to excel in their walk*

KEY THEMES: *Sanctification; Jesus' return*

KEY VERSES: *1:8-10; 4:9-11*

BACKGROUND: *Acts 17:1-9*

DISTINCTIVES: *First of Paul's letters; sets forth his style of ministry; emphasizes vocational diligence*

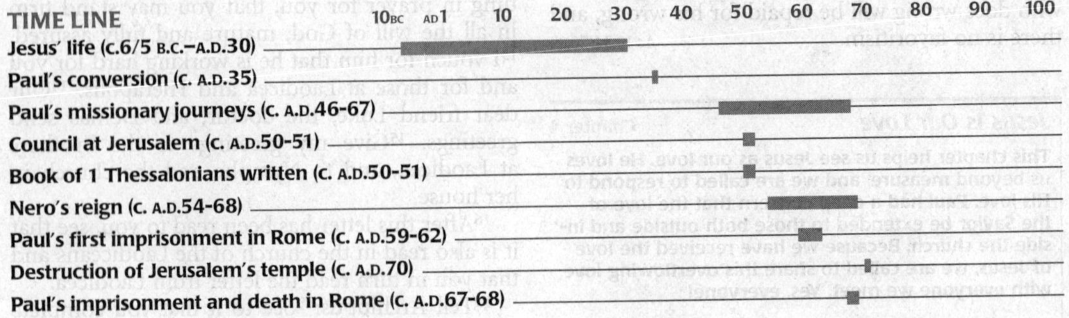

A Heart-to-Heart Talk

	CHAPTER 1	CHAPTER 2	CHAPTER 3	CHAPTER 4	CHAPTER 5
	THE PASTOR'S HEART…			THE PASTOR'S BURDEN…	
	Thanksgiving Remembering Affirming Reporting	The pastor among the flock The flock's response to him	Personal concern Comfort and relief	Sexual purity Prophetic urgency	Stay alert! Encourage one another! Live in peace!
PERSPECTIVE	Looking back			Looking ahead	
SUBJECT	The church itself	The man himself	The occasion	The concern	The balance
ESPECIALLY APPROPRIATE FOR…	…new converts	…young pastors	…suffering Christians	…tempted and uninformed Christians	…sleepy Christians

If someone were to ask me what would be a good book of the Bible for a new Christian to read, I would recommend Paul's first letter to the Thessalonians. (It is the earliest letter of Paul to have found its way into the canon of Scripture.) Paul doesn't deal with a lot of theology in this brief and essentially uncomplicated letter—and therefore new believers may find the terrain a little smoother to travel than some of the New Testament's "weightier" books and more complex teachings. What doctrine he does present gives readers enough to give them basic truths they need to know, particularly as it relates to Jesus' return to earth, and to leave them hungry for more truth to be gleaned in other portions of Scripture.

The picture painted in this letter of Paul's heart as a pastor and the life of a group of believers who are growing together in the Lord is a compelling one. As a pastor I appreciate 1 Thessalonians, because I don't know of many other Bible books that reveal the heart of a "shepherd" for the flock better than this simple yet splendid letter. Certainly Paul's teachings about holy living and a life shaped by eternity are just as relevant for us today as they were for the believers in Thessalonica more than 1,900 years ago. His letter offers an abundance of practical help in living the Christian life today, while at the same time it unveils a glimpse into the future that is both fascinating and encouraging.

Facing Opposition and Receiving Encouragement

According to Acts 17:1–9, Paul came to the city of Thessalonica and probably did not spend more than two months there. From Thessalonica he went down to Athens after a brief stay in Berea and then cut across to the city of Corinth. While in Corinth in the spring of A.D. 50 Paul wrote his first letter to the believers who lived in Thessalonica. In it he reflected on his brief ministry in their city:

> *You know, brothers, that our visit to you was not a failure. We had previously suffered and been insulted in Philippi, as you know, but with the help of our God we dared to tell you his gospel in spite of strong opposition (2:1–2).*

Some ministries are born and nurtured in a context of much opposition. That doesn't mean the person leading the ministry is being punished by God or is somehow outside of His will; it may simply mean that this period of struggle is God's choice for that particular work at a given time. Who can explain why one ministry flourishes and another ministry across town or a few counties away is in the depths of discouragement? Why are some virtually trouble-free, while others seem destined to experience struggle, conflict and hardship?

Paul's message to the Thessalonians went something like this: "When I came to Thessalonica, I faced opposition. I dealt with it in the city of Philippi, and when I came to you folks I was in the midst of it again." He simply explained, "I wanted to come back, but the enemy made it impossible for us to do that" (see 2:18). Knowing that he couldn't make a visit himself, Paul sent a messenger named Timothy:

> *But Timothy has just now come to us from you and has brought good news about your faith and love. He has told us that you always have pleasant memories of us and that you long to see us, just as we also long to see you. Therefore, brothers, in all our distress and persecution we were encouraged about you because of your faith. For now we really live, since you are standing firm in the Lord (3:6–8).*

Paul penned this letter to his friends in Thessalonica out of an encouraged and uplifted heart. He wrote them because he had heard that they were doing well, and he wanted to affirm them.

Let me share a little secret about the difference between appreciation and affirmation. We appreciate *what a person does.* We affirm *who a person is.* Most of us are fairly good at showing appreciation, but I suspect we may fall a little short when it comes to giving affirmation. Of the two, the second is far more valuable to the other person. Both responses, however, are crucial if we want to be people who offer true encouragement to another person. When we appreciate what someone does, we will want to communicate our feelings of delight and gratitude. But we also need to affirm that person for who he or she is—to affirm their growth and maturity, to affirm their character, to affirm their gifts, to affirm their walk with the Lord. I believe that Paul, first and foremost, wrote to the Thessalonians to affirm the growth that was taking place in their lives.

Power Walking

While Paul rejoiced at the good news of the Thessalonians' spiritual health, he also showed concern over the problems and trials they were facing as they lived in a culture hostile to Christian values. Paul wanted to encourage the believers in their trials (3:3–5) and give them guidelines on relationships and boundaries for living in an immoral culture (4:1–8). Listen to the encouragement and challenge from the heart of the apostle as he remembers his dear friends: "Finally, brothers, we instructed you how to live in order to please God, as in fact you are living. Now we ask you and urge you in the Lord Jesus to do this more and more" (4:1).

Paul wanted the Thessalonians to excel in their walk. He saw how well these believers were walking in the faith. As he affirmed them he urged them to continue a walk of faith that was even more powerful and more consistent and more passionate. In a society characterized by pathetically low moral standards, the Thessalonian believers were undoubtedly tempted to compromise their own beliefs and to fall into immorality. They needed Paul's reminder, and so do we, that God has another set of standards by which to live.

The Return of Jesus Christ

Paul had yet one more reason for writing this letter to the Thessalonians. Some Christians were raising questions about Jesus' return to earth. In particular, some were confused about believers who died before Jesus returned. Would these deceased believers somehow miss out on life after death? Would they be left behind when Jesus takes those "who are still alive" to be with Him forever? Paul responded to these concerns with a direct and encouraging answer:

Brothers, we do not want you to be ignorant about those who fall asleep, or to grieve like the rest of men, who have no hope. We believe that Jesus died and rose again and so we believe that God will bring with Jesus those who have fallen asleep in him (4:13–14).

Paul wrote to help clarify some of the details of Jesus' return and to offer words of encouragement. Yet he was careful not to fuel the fires of undue obsession about the future or an unhealthy speculation about how and when Jesus would return. Paul simply urged the Thessalonian believers to lead a quiet life (4:11) and live in peace with each other (5:13), secure in the strong hope of the Lord's coming again.

Four Questions for You

The message of 1 Thessalonians can be summarized with four statements and follow-up questions.

First, *we have been reached by God. Are we reaching out to others to share with them the good news of the gospel*? (See 1:4–10.) This brief letter reminds us of the truth that we have been reached with God's grace and love demonstrated in sending His Son, Jesus Christ, to die for us. When we realize the awesomeness of the gift of grace we have received, we are compelled to reach out to others with the good news. The question is this: Are we doing it?

Second, *we have been fed. Are we feeding others*? If you love to disciple people, your "theme verse" can easily be verse 8 of chapter 2: "We loved you so much that we were delighted to share with you not only the gospel of God but our lives as well, because you had become so dear to us." That's one of the grandest verses on discipleship you'll ever read. If you have been nurtured by the love of God and the love of those who have supported you, the question is this: Are you feeding others? Paul indirectly asks every believer who reads 1 Thessalonians this weighty question. How would you answer it?

Third, *we have received instruction. Are we excelling in it*? (See 4:1–12.) This letter reminds us of all the instruction we have available to us. We need to learn to feast on all of the teaching God offers us. We need to excel in learning and in growing as we walk by faith day by day.

Finally, *we have been encouraged. Are we encouraging others*? (See 5:11.) Paul wanted believers to remember that they have received encouragement and blessing from others. When we have been lifted up by the encouragement of others, we are motivated to extend this same care to others. What are we doing to bless and encourage others? I know of few needs greater than the need to give and to receive encouragement!

One of the highest of human duties is the duty of encouragement. I close with the words of a British writer: "There is a regulation of the royal Navy which says, 'No officer shall speak discouragingly to another officer in the discharge of his duties.' It is easy to laugh at people's ideals. It is easy to pour cold water on their enthusiasm. It is easy to discourage. The world is full of discouragers. We have a Christian duty to encourage one another. Many a time a word of praise or thanks or appreciation or cheer has kept a person on his feet. Blessed is the one who speaks such a word."

May I be so bold as to say that it's time for those words to be applied in your life. As you speak words of encouragement to your family, to your friends, to your neighbors, to your co-workers and even to your enemies, God ignites faint embers into flames of fresh hope.

The Pastor's Heart **Chapters 1–3**

The first three chapters look back—as if Paul were opening a photo album on his lap, thumbing through old pictures and writing down thoughts as he went through his private museum of memories. He reflected on those early weeks of ministry among the Thessalonian believers. He pondered the testimony of their lives and the way they handled the truth that came to them. In these chapters we see the tender heart of a pastor for a congregation about which he cared deeply. Paul reminded the people that he was gentle and tender with them, like a mother with her little baby (2:7). What an image of pastoral care! He also recalled how he had come with the exhortation and encouragement of a father (2:11–12). Like a caring shepherd Paul had led and fed the flock in Thessalonica, and they had responded to his pastoral leadership.

1 Paul, Silas[a] and Timothy, Ac 16:1; 2Th 1:1

To the church of the Thessalonians in God the
Father and the Lord Jesus Christ: Ac 17:1

Grace and peace to you.[b] Ro 1:7

Thanksgiving for the Thessalonians' Faith

2We always thank God for all of you, mentioning you in our prayers. 3We continually remember
before our God and Father your work produced
by faith, your labor prompted by love, and your
endurance inspired by hope in our Lord Jesus
Christ. Ro 1:8; 8:25
4For we know, brothers loved by God, that he
has chosen you, 5because our gospel came to you
not simply with words, but also with power, with
the Holy Spirit and with deep conviction. You
know how we lived among you for your sake. 6You
became imitators of us and of the Lord; in spite of
severe suffering, you welcomed the message with
the joy given by the Holy Spirit. 7And so you
became a model to all the believers in Macedonia
and Achaia. 8The Lord's message rang out from

LIVING  INSIGHT

Leadership is influence. To the extent we influence others, we lead them.

(See 1 Thessalonians 1:6–7.)

you not only in Macedonia and Achaia—your
faith in God has become known everywhere.
Therefore we do not need to say anything about it,
9for they themselves report what kind of reception
you gave us. They tell how you turned to God
from idols to serve the living and true God, 10and
to wait for his Son from heaven, whom he raised
from the dead—Jesus, who rescues us from the
coming wrath. Ac 2:24; Ro 5:9

Paul's Ministry in Thessalonica

2 You know, brothers, that our visit to you was
not a failure. 2We had previously suffered
and been insulted in Philippi, as you know, but
with the help of our God we dared to tell you his
gospel in spite of strong opposition. 3For the appeal we make does not spring from error or impure motives, nor are we trying to trick you. 4On
the contrary, we speak as men approved by God to
be entrusted with the gospel. We are not trying to
please men but God, who tests our hearts. 5You
know we never used flattery, nor did we put on a
mask to cover up greed—God is our witness. 6We
were not looking for praise from men, not from
you or anyone else. Gal 1:10; 1Th 1:5,9
As apostles of Christ we could have been a burden to you, 7but we were gentle among you, like a
mother caring for her little children. 8We loved
you so much that we were delighted to share with
you not only the gospel of God but our lives as
well, because you had become so dear to us. 9Sure-
ly you remember, brothers, our toil and hardship;
we worked night and day in order not to be a
burden to anyone while we preached the gospel of
God to you. 2Co 12:15; 2Th 3:8
10You are witnesses, and so is God, of how holy,
righteous and blameless we were among you who
believed. 11For you know that we dealt with each
of you as a father deals with his own children,
12encouraging, comforting and urging you to live
lives worthy of God, who calls you into his kingdom and glory. Eph 4:1; 1Th 1:5

LIVING  INSIGHT

To balance out your character you need to do more than guard your heart. It is the flip side that makes you authentic . . . you also need to give your heart.

(See 1 Thessalonians 2:11–12.)

13And we also thank God continually because,
when you received the word of God, which you
heard from us, you accepted it not as the word of
men, but as it actually is, the word of God, which
is at work in you who believe. 14For you, brothers,
became imitators of God's churches in Judea,
which are in Christ Jesus: You suffered from your
own countrymen the same things those churches

[a] 1 Greek *Silvanus*, a variant of *Silas* [b] 1 Some early manuscripts *you from God our Father and the Lord Jesus Christ*

suffered from the Jews, 15who killed the Lord Jesus
and the prophets and also drove us out. They displease God and are hostile to all men 16in their
effort to keep us from speaking to the Gentiles so
that they may be saved. In this way they always
heap up their sins to the limit. The wrath of God
has come upon them at last.[a] Mt 23:32; Ac 13:45,50

Paul's Longing to See the Thessalonians

17But, brothers, when we were torn away from
you for a short time (in person, not in thought),
out of our intense longing we made every effort to
see you. 18For we wanted to come to you—certainly I, Paul, did, again and again—but Satan
stopped us. 19For what is our hope, our joy, or the
crown in which we will glory in the presence of our
Lord Jesus when he comes? Is it not you? 20Indeed,
you are our glory and joy. 2Co 1:14; 1Th 3:10

3 So when we could stand it no longer, we
thought it best to be left by ourselves in Athens. 2We sent Timothy, who is our brother and
God's fellow worker[b] in spreading the gospel of
Christ, to strengthen and encourage you in your
faith, 3so that no one would be unsettled by these
trials. You know quite well that we were destined
for them. 4In fact, when we were with you, we kept
telling you that we would be persecuted. And it
turned out that way, as you well know. 5For this
reason, when I could stand it no longer, I sent to
find out about your faith. I was afraid that in some
way the tempter might have tempted you and our
efforts might have been useless. Ac 9:16; Gal 2:2

Timothy's Encouraging Report

6But Timothy has just now come to us from you
and has brought good news about your faith and
love. He has told us that you always have pleasant
memories of us and that you long to see us, just as
we also long to see you. 7Therefore, brothers, in all
our distress and persecution we were encouraged
about you because of your faith. 8For now we
really live, since you are standing firm in the Lord.
9How can we thank God enough for you in return
for all the joy we have in the presence of our God
because of you? 10Night and day we pray most
earnestly that we may see you again and supply
what is lacking in your faith. 1Th 1:2; 2Ti 1:3

11Now may our God and Father himself and
our Lord Jesus clear the way for us to come to you.
12May the Lord make your love increase and overflow for each other and for everyone else, just as
ours does for you. 13May he strengthen your hearts
so that you will be blameless and holy in the presence of our God and Father when our Lord Jesus
comes with all his holy ones. 1Co 1:8; 1Th 4:9-10

LIVING  **INSIGHT**

When our attitudes get refocused on God's power and His incredible purposes for living, hang on to your hats! Instead of running from each other in our relationships, we would be running toward one another. Before we realized it, people would become more important to us than status, fame or fortune.

(See 1 Thessalonians 3:11–13.)

The Pastor's Burden **Chapters 4–5**

From chapter 4 to the end of the book, Paul looked ahead. He closed the photo album of memories, as it were, and thought, "What are the instructions these people need?" He planned for their future with words of exhortation and encouragement. In this section Paul called the people to seek sexual purity. He knew the temptations they would face, and he challenged them to stand firm and resist impurity. He also had a burden for this congregation to understand that Jesus would return again. They needed to live with a healthy awareness of the soon-coming Savior. In the closing chapter Paul urged the believers to encourage each other. This is a timeless word to all of us: We need to be the kind of people who build up and encourage others. Finally, Paul urged believers to live in peace and joy and gratitude. As you read this section, pray that the Lord would help you sense the impact of these words on your own life.

Living to Please God

4 Finally, brothers, we instructed you how to
live in order to please God, as in fact you are
living. Now we ask you and urge you in the Lord
Jesus to do this more and more. 2For you know
what instructions we gave you by the authority of
the Lord Jesus. 2Co 5:9; 13:11

3It is God's will that you should be sanctified:
that you should avoid sexual immorality; 4that
each of you should learn to control his own
body[c] in a way that is holy and honorable, 5not
in passionate lust like the heathen, who do not
know God; 6and that in this matter no one should
wrong his brother or take advantage of him. The
Lord will punish men for all such sins, as we have
already told you and warned you. 7For God did
not call us to be impure, but to live a holy life.
8Therefore, he who rejects this instruction does
not reject man but God, who gives you his Holy
Spirit. Ro 5:5; Gal 4:6

9Now about brotherly love we do not need to
write to you, for you yourselves have been taught
by God to love each other. 10And in fact, you do

[a] 16 Or *them fully* [b] 2 Some manuscripts *brother and fellow worker*; other manuscripts *brother and God's servant*
[c] 4 Or *learn to live with his own wife*; or *learn to acquire a wife*

THE CALL TO READINESS

"For the Lord himself will come down from heaven, with a loud command, with the voice of the archangel and with the trumpet call of God, and the dead in Christ will rise first. After that, we who are still alive and are left will be caught up together with them in the clouds to meet the Lord in the air. And so we will be with the Lord forever."

–1 THESSALONIANS 4:16–17

The return of Jesus Christ never fails to create mixed emotions. For those who are ready for it, there is always a sense of comfort and anticipation. For those who are not ready for Jesus' return (or do not believe in it), there is a mixture of responses. Many are skeptical. Some are irritated. Others are intimidated. A few are afraid, maybe a little panicky. Most simply refuse to think about it. But no one can remain neutral on the subject.

Predictions That Affirm Our Assurance

Before looking at some specific verses from the Bible, let me take you on a brief safari through the Scriptures. Here are some facts about prophecy pertaining to Jesus' return that will surprise most people: One out of every thirty verses in the Bible mentions the subject of Jesus' return or the end of time. In the Old Testament, such well-known, reliable men of God as Job, Moses, David, Isaiah, Jeremiah, Daniel and most of the minor prophets spoke of the Lord's return. In the 260 chapters in the New Testament, there are well over three hundred references to Jesus' return. Only 4 of the 27 New Testament books fail to mention Jesus' return. Jesus emphasized His return often, especially after He had revealed His death. Those who followed Jesus' teachings, established churches and wrote the Scriptures frequently mentioned His return in their preaching and in their writings.

The Bible teaches that Jesus will come again. The prophets predicted it. The Lord Jesus Himself testified that He would return. The apostles declared it and wrote about it. The creeds include it and affirm it. Quite obviously, Jesus' return has not been considered an insignificant issue through the centuries. But the strange thing is that many in this generation, even a large number of believers, either ignore it or are confused by it. Too bad. It is a marvelous truth that only gains significance as each of us moves closer to death.

Look with me at several verses of Scripture that underscore Jesus' imminent coming. Pause and read Matthew 24:42–44:

> *Therefore keep watch, because you do not know on what day your Lord will come. But understand this: If the owner of the house had known at what time of night the thief was coming, he would have kept watch and would not have let his house be broken into. So you also must be ready, because the Son of Man will come at an hour when you do not expect him.*

Notice the words "when" and "will"—not "if," but "when" . . . not "may," but "will." There was no question in Jesus' mind that He would be coming back. This kind of teaching must have stunned the disciples. They had anticipated the establishment of Jesus' earthly kingdom right then and there. They expected it to be in operation before the end of their generation, when Jesus would be ruling as King of kings and Lord of lords. They envisioned themselves as charter members in His kingdom. With great delight they would witness (or so they thought) the overthrow of Rome and the conquering of Israel's numerous enemies. What a hope!

But then one dark night in a second-story flat, along some quiet street in the city of Jerusalem, Jesus ate His last meal with His disciples. There He unfolded the startling truth that His death was only hours away. They must have wanted to plug their ears to keep from hearing Him say that He was going to leave them and go back to the Father. Shortly thereafter, Jesus went to the cross. To the disciples' shock and amazement, He breathed His last while hanging suspended. After He died, He was placed in a tomb. Three days later, He came back to life and emerged in bodily form from the tomb, victorious over death. He is the only One thus far who has come back to this earth in a glorified condition. He has overcome death! In light of that, it shouldn't surprise us that He is able to bring us from the grave when He returns.

Forty days after Jesus' resurrection He stood on a mountain with His followers. While there, just before He ascended into heaven, the subject was brought up again—His return. His disciples wanted to know when He was coming back. But while these words were still on their lips they saw the Lord physically lifted to heaven.

Wow! Can you imagine that moment? We think we're pretty hot stuff because we can put people in a space capsule and send them to the moon or into an orbit around the earth a few times, then bring them back. Yet with no physical assistance, with nothing around Him or near Him, Jesus was lifted up from the earth—whoosh!—and went directly through the clouds back to heaven. His followers did just what you and I would have done—they stood with mouths open, gazing intently into the skies (Acts 1:10). I want to quote the following words to people who are preoccupied with Jesus' return, spending most of their time looking up, as if they had nothing else to do. These are the words of the angels (Acts 1:11):

> *"Men of Galilee," they said, "why do you stand here looking into the sky? This same Jesus, who has been taken from you into heaven, will come back in the same way you have seen him go into heaven."*

Jesus is coming again. Looking up won't bring Him back any sooner. We're never told simply to stand around gazing up to heaven. In fact, we're told *not* to do that. We aren't even commanded to do a lot of talking about it. There's a greater work to be done than sitting around discussing the details of His return!

While We Wait for Him to Return

Let me make four observations that will give us some guidance as we wait for Jesus to return. First, *we must be informed*. As I have said throughout my ministry, ignorance is not bliss. The Lord doesn't smile on us when we say about the future, "Well, actually, nobody can know for sure. We just hope things work out all right." He wants us to be informed and knowledgeable. We are to know what's in front of us—at least the broad brush strokes of His plan. Knowing what God has revealed to us about the future gives us confidence in the present.

Second, *we must not grieve as those without hope*. Death brings sorrow. Sorrow brings tears. Tears are a natural part of the grieving process. God never tells us, "Don't cry. Don't grieve." He says we are not to grieve like those "who have no hope" (1 Thessalonians 4:13). I am saddened when I see Christians, well-meaning though they may be, who criticize folks for crying when a loved one dies. Crying is the most natural response when we lose someone or something important to us. We have every reason to grieve, but our grief is not like those who are hopeless when they grieve. You see, those who trust in Jesus have answers beyond the grave. Unbelievers do not. It is the hope we have in Jesus Christ that ultimately brings comfort.

Third, *we must face death without fear*. The reason Jesus' own resurrection is so important is that we can anticipate rising as He did. Had He not come back from death, we couldn't expect to either. Think about the followers of the world's gurus. The guru dies. The followers later visit the grave and—there's the remains of their guru! Their great spiritual leader, their beloved guide—he's still there. If *he* didn't get out, then I ask you how is he going to get *them* out? But no one will ever see the dead body of Jesus. Why? He has been raised. His tomb is empty. Because He died and rose again He is able to provide an answer to sin, death and the grave. If we believe in Him, then we are ready to be taken with Him. He will bring us along with all those who have fallen asleep in Jesus. Because He lives, all fear is gone!

Fourth, *we must know the order of events for Jesus' return*. Paul unfolds them in 1 Thessalonians 4:14–17: First, the Lord Jesus will come down from heaven and return in glory. Next, the bodies of believers who have died will be raised. Then, all the believers who are alive will be caught up together with those who have died, been raised and changed ahead of them. Finally, we will all be caught up together in the clouds to meet the Lord and be with Him forever.

Imagine the scene! Talk about a glorious moment—"the mother of all family reunions!" Perhaps all those things will occur simultaneously . . . in one great voice, one grand sound. I smile as I write these words. They never fail to excite me! The most important thing to understand is that *He is coming again*—and *it is a comfort to you*. Why? Because you believe in Him. Be sure that the One you believe in and follow has conquered death, because if he or she hasn't, you cannot enter heaven. The only way to get beyond the grave and into the Lord's presence is to place your trust in the One who has gone before you and has paved the way (see Hebrews 4:14; 6:20).

Actions That Reveal Our Readiness

I think there are at least three ways we reveal our readiness for Jesus' return. First, *we continue to walk by faith*. Rather than walking by sight and shaping our lives on the basis of the visible, we walk by faith. Second, *we continue to live in peace*. We view the present and our future not with panic but with peace. We live ultimately hopeful, joyful, peace-filled lives— not worried, frantic, hassled lives. Third, *we continue to rely on hope*. The hope that gets me through the trials on this earth is the same hope that will get me through the grave at death, because the One in whom I have believed has gone before me. He is preparing a place for me. Because He lives, you and I shall live also . . . throughout eternity. The secret of escape from sin and pain is knowing the One who can guarantee our getting beyond the grave.

One day Jesus Christ will come for us. His coming is sure, and He will keep His promise. If you are ready, the thought of His coming is a comfort. If not, it's an awful dread. His coming is sure . . . are you?

But . . . in the Meantime

There are four words I encourage you to commit to memory—words that represent God's "marching orders" for us. They are our "in-the-meantime" standard operating procedure: *occupy, purify, watch* and *worship*. If someone were to ask you, "What are we supposed to do until Christ returns?"—these four words will provide an answer.

Luke records a parable (Luke 19:11–27) in which Jesus addressed the importance of life continuing on until He returns. As we wait for Jesus to return we are to *occupy*. Let me cite the opening words of the parable:

> *A man of noble birth went to a distant country to have himself appointed king and then to return. So he called ten of his servants and gave them ten minas. "Put this money to work," he said, "until I come back" (Luke 19:12–13).*

A "mina" was a lot of money—about a hundred day's wages (nearly twenty dollars in those days). The nobleman gave each of his ten servants one mina, instructing them to "put this money to work" while he was away. You may wish to circle the words, "Put this money to work." (Some versions of Scripture render this same command as "occupy.") The point is clear. It was not the nobleman's desire that his servants sit back and do nothing—letting the money sit on a shelf collecting dust—until he returned. Two servants put to work what they had been given and received commendation when the master returned; but at least one failed to do as he had been commanded, and he experienced judgment when the master returned (Luke 19:22–24):

> *"I will judge you by your own words, you wicked servant! You knew, did you, that I am a hard man . . . Why then didn't you put my money on deposit so that when I came back, I could have collected it with interest? Then he said to those standing by, "Take his mina away from him and give it to the one who has ten minas."*

Our Lord expects dedicated service from us, determined effort that produces results, as we put to work the gifts He's given us, as we occupy ourselves in serving Him in anticipation of His return.

Second, as we wait for Jesus' return we are to *purify*. I find Biblical support for this in Titus 2:11–14:

> *For the grace of God that brings salvation has appeared to all men. It teaches us to say "No" to ungodliness and worldly passions, and to live self-controlled, upright and godly lives in this present age, while we wait for the blessed hope—the glorious appearing of our great God and*

> *Savior, Jesus Christ, who gave himself for us to redeem us from all wickedness and to purify for himself a people that are his very own, eager to do what is good.*

Do you want to know a telltale sign of heresy? Look for a ministry that emphasizes the Lord's return but does not, with equal gusto, emphasize a godly life. Mark it down. Whoever shines the spotlight on the second coming of Jesus Christ is also responsible to teach the importance of a pure life. If indeed Jesus is coming again, there is surely one thing we want to have in order—personal purity.

I wouldn't have much confidence in a person who prides himself or herself in being a good surgeon, yet at the same time doesn't worry much about sterile instruments. I wonder how many patients would stick around if he or she said, "To tell you the truth, I've got a new plan in surgery. We do all of our surgery in the back room here at the clinic. I just push this stuff out of the way, then you crawl up on the table and I'll give you a shot. You've got nothing to worry about. It's a lot less expensive because we don't worry that much about keeping everything clean." One thing about practicing good medicine is that you must follow the rules of absolute sterilization. You can't be too careful about cleanliness. And if anyone is going to talk about the coming of the Lord Jesus, then be sure all that talk is balanced by an emphasis on purity of living.

Third, as we wait for Jesus' return we are to *watch*. Jesus' words in Mark 13:32–37 provide the context for this important activity As you read this passage, you will find that not only is the word "watch" prominently featured, it is also implied in the commands, "Be on guard! Be alert!"

> *No one knows about that day or hour, not even the angels in heaven, nor the Son, but only the Father. Be on guard! Be alert! You do not know when that time will come. It's like a man going away: He leaves his house and puts his servants in charge, each with his assigned task, and tells the one at the door to keep watch. Therefore keep watch because you do not know when the owner of the house will come back—whether in the evening, or at midnight, or when the rooster crows, or at dawn. If he comes suddenly, do not let him find you sleeping. What I say to you, I say to everyone: "Watch!"*

In light of the urgency in Jesus' words, I find it nothing short of remarkable how many days we live without a single thought of Jesus' return . . . not even a passing thought. Isn't it amazing? I've noticed that those who become sensitive to spiritual things fix more and more of their attention on His coming. And they don't need the reminder from others.

We've all had the experience of someone telling us that he's going to come see us on a particular day. He doesn't state a time, but he tells you it'll be sometime during that day. The longer the day wears on, the more often we look out the window in keen anticipation. We're watching for him. We keep waiting until night falls. We turn the front porch light on. We make sure the door is unlocked. We check it many more times to make sure! Why? Because we're anxiously anticipating our friend's coming. We watch every set of headlights that comes around the corner. We stay alert. We are thinking about that imminent arrival. That's what our Lord has in mind here.

Maintaining a balance in all this is tough. When I teach on prophetic subjects, I feel a little bit like a parent who warns a child about strangers. Hoping to guard people from fanaticism, I might go too far and talk them out of being full of anticipation. Parents who teach children to be careful about strangers have to watch out that they don't overdo it, because a child can begin to live so suspiciously that everyone comes into question and no one can be trusted. It's easy for a child to "overlearn" such warnings. So while I warn you against the extreme of foolish fanaticism, let me quickly add that God honors watching; God cherishes the heart that pumps faster with the thought of His Son's return. In fact, did you know that there's a reward promised—a crown that will be given for people who live in eager anticipation of His coming? Paul talked about it in 2 Timothy 4:8: "Now there is in store for me the crown of righteousness, which the Lord, the righteous Judge, will award to me on that day—and not only to me, but also to all who have longed for his appearing." Come, Lord Jesus, come quickly. We can't wait for Your return!

Fourth, as we wait for Jesus' return we are to *worship*. In all my years of hearing the Bible taught, I can't remember much said about the importance of this in the context of waiting for Jesus to return. Yet

Scripture clearly emphasizes it; look at 1 Corinthians 11:23–26, where Paul reflects on the institution of the Lord's Supper. Read his words as if for the first time:

> *For I received from the Lord what I also passed on to you: The Lord Jesus, on the night he was betrayed, took bread, and when he had given thanks, he broke it and said, "This is my body, which is for you; do this in remembrance of me." In the same way, after supper he took the cup, saying, "This cup is the new covenant in my blood; do this, whenever you drink it, in remembrance of me." For whenever you eat this bread and drink this cup, you proclaim the Lord's death until he comes.*

How long are Christians to participate in worship? How long are we to gather around the Lord's table and hold in our hands the elements that symbolize our Savior's body and blood? He tells us in the last three words of the passage—"until he comes." Every time we celebrate the Lord's Supper, it is another reminder that He's coming. One of these times will be our last time to observe it on earth. It's exciting to think about, isn't it? It will be our last spiritual meal on earth together. But until then we are to worship the Lord Jesus Christ. Every meal at His table is another reminder that His coming is nearer now than when we first believed. Therefore let us worship Him with great anticipation!

How to Stay Alert and Ready

There's no reason to get complicated about what we might call "in-the-meantime" living. A couple of thoughts seem worth emphasizing. First, *remember that Jesus promised His return would occur someday* (and He always tells the truth!). When you read the newspaper, think of His return. Remember His promise to return as you see events that relate to the nation of Israel or to those signs of the end of the age Jesus shared in the Gospel accounts. Each of these events—while perhaps not immediately or directly connected to Jesus' return—collectively assures us that we are certainly living in the last days. Call it to mind when you lose a loved one or when something of value is taken from you. Hope in the promises of Christ for the future takes the sting out of the present. Life won't be as hard if we learn to live in the conscious hope of His return. As the song puts it, "It will be worth it all, when we see Jesus."

Second, *realize that the promise could be fulfilled today* (and that will be the moment of truth). Let me make a suggestion: Form a new habit for getting out of bed in the morning. Just as soon as your feet hit the floor, even before you lift yourself up and head for the shower, look out the window. As you look, repeat these two lines: "Good morning, Lord. Will I see you today—face to face?"

And then . . . until He comes, what to do? Remember the watchwords: *occupy, purify, watch* and *worship.* If you're engaged in those four things, you won't have to *get ready*; you'll *be ready*! No need to try to set a date or quit your job or dress up in a white robe. Just live every day as if it were the last. You'll be surprised at the difference it'll make in how you think, how you respond . . . how you *live*!

love all the brothers throughout Macedonia. Yet we urge you, brothers, to do so more and more.

11Make it your ambition to lead a quiet life, to mind your own business and to work with your hands, just as we told you, 12so that your daily life may win the respect of outsiders and so that you will not be dependent on anybody. Eph 4:28

The Coming of the Lord

13Brothers, we do not want you to be ignorant about those who fall asleep, or to grieve like the rest of men, who have no hope. 14We believe that Jesus died and rose again and so we believe that God will bring with Jesus those who have fallen asleep in him. 15According to the Lord's own word, we tell you that we who are still alive, who are left till the coming of the Lord, will certainly not precede those who have fallen asleep. 16For the Lord himself will come down from heaven, with a loud command, with the voice of the archangel and with the trumpet call of God, and the dead in Christ will rise first. 17After that, we who are still alive and are left will be caught up together with them in the clouds to meet the Lord in the air. And so we will be with the Lord forever. 18Therefore encourage each other with these words. 1Co 15:52

LIVING  **INSIGHT**

Death brings sorrow. Sorrow brings tears. Tears are part of the grieving process. God never tells us, "Don't cry. Don't grieve." He says we are not to grieve like those "who have no hope." You see, we have an answer beyond the grave. It is this hope that ultimately brings comfort.

(See 1 Thessalonians 4:13.)

5 Now, brothers, about times and dates we do not need to write to you, 2for you know very well that the day of the Lord will come like a thief in the night. 3While people are saying, "Peace and safety," destruction will come on them suddenly, as labor pains on a pregnant woman, and they will not escape. 1Th 4:9; 2Pe 3:10

4But you, brothers, are not in darkness so that this day should surprise you like a thief. 5You are all sons of the light and sons of the day. We do not belong to the night or to the darkness. 6So then, let us not be like others, who are asleep, but let us be alert and self-controlled. 7For those who sleep, sleep at night, and those who get drunk, get drunk at night. 8But since we belong to the day, let us be self-controlled, putting on faith and love as a breastplate, and the hope of salvation as a helmet. 9For God did not appoint us to suffer wrath but to receive salvation through our Lord Jesus Christ. 10He died for us so that, whether we are awake or asleep, we may live together with him. 11Therefore encourage one another and build each other up, just as in fact you are doing. 1Th 4:18; Eph 4:29

Final Instructions

12Now we ask you, brothers, to respect those who work hard among you, who are over you in the Lord and who admonish you. 13Hold them in the highest regard in love because of their work. Live in peace with each other. 14And we urge you, brothers, warn those who are idle, encourage the timid, help the weak, be patient with everyone.

LIVING  **INSIGHT**

In neither the Old nor New Testament is laziness smiled on, especially laziness that is rationalized because one believes in the soon coming of Jesus Christ. Our Lord frowns on the lack of discipline and diligence.

(See 1 Thessalonians 5:14.)

15Make sure that nobody pays back wrong for wrong, but always try to be kind to each other and to everyone else. Eph 4:32; 2Th 3:6-7,11

16Be joyful always; 17pray continually; 18give thanks in all circumstances, for this is God's will for you in Christ Jesus. Php 4:4

19Do not put out the Spirit's fire; 20do not treat prophecies with contempt. 21Test everything. Hold on to the good. 22Avoid every kind of evil.

23May God himself, the God of peace, sanctify you through and through. May your whole spirit, soul and body be kept blameless at the coming of our Lord Jesus Christ. 24The one who calls you is faithful and he will do it. 1Co 1:9; Php 1:6

25Brothers, pray for us. 26Greet all the brothers with a holy kiss. 27I charge you before the Lord to have this letter read to all the brothers. Ro 16:16

28The grace of our Lord Jesus Christ be with you. Ro 16:20

INTRODUCTION

2 THESSALONIANS

Paul's second letter to the Thessalonians, though brief and seemingly innocuous, is both concentrated and potent. Written to correct a misunderstanding about the Lord's return, it not only clarifies issues about prophecy, it also deals with matters of great practical value. Within these 47 verses we find such helpful insights as the purpose of persecution, the importance of diligence, and the necessity of standing firm on the truth of the gospel, minding one's own business and choosing the right companions. The most pronounced contribution of this letter is the balanced perspective it brings to the subject of prophecy. We must be neither apathetic nor unduly extreme when it comes to the manner in which we wait for the return of Christ. We must be alert, aware of the deceptive forces around us, confident in God's plan, and diligently responsible in our lifestyle, our daily work and our Christian faith.

WRITER: *Paul*

DATE: *C.A.D. 51–52*

PURPOSE: *To encourage the Thessalonians to stand firm and to correct misunderstandings about Jesus' return*

KEY THEMES: *Suffering; Jesus' return*

KEY MESSAGE: *Hang tough! Be diligent!*

KEY VERSE: *2:15*

TIME LINE 10BC AD1 10 20 30 40 50 60 70 80 90 100

Jesus' life (c.6/5 B.C.–A.D.30)

Paul's conversion (c. A.D.35)

Paul's missionary journeys (c. A.D.46-67)

Book of 2 Thessalonians written (c. A.D.51-52)

Council at Jerusalem (c. A.D.50-51)

Nero's reign (c. A.D.54-68)

Paul's first imprisonment in Rome (c. A.D.59-62)

Paul's imprisonment and death in Rome (c. A.D.67-68)

Destruction of Jerusalem's temple (c. A.D.70)

Christ's Coming . . . My Response

	AFFIRMATION AMIDST AFFLICTION	EXPLANATION OF PROPHECY	CLARIFICATION REGARDING RESPONSE
	"We ought always to thank God for you" (1:3). *"We boast about your perseverance and faith" (1:4).* *"We constantly pray for you" (1:11).*	*"Don't let anyone deceive you" (2:3).* Secret power of lawlessness Restraint removed Man of lawlessness *"So then . . . stand firm" (2:15).*	*"We command you" (3:6).* *"If anyone does not obey . . . " (3:14)* *"May the Lord of peace himself give you peace" (3:16).*
	CHAPTER 1	*CHAPTER 2*	*CHAPTER 3*
QUESTION	**Why are we suffering?**	**What will occur?**	**How do I respond?**
CONTRASTS	**Peace amidst pain**	**Lawlessness versus restraint**	**Work while waiting**
STATEMENT	**The Lord knows!**	**The *"day of the Lord"* has not yet come!**	***"Never tire of doing what is right!" (3:13)***
EMPHASIS	**Commendation**	**Correction**	**Clarification**

Ever since the first century A.D., the subject of Jesus Christ's return has been a theological football. It has been kicked around, pounced on, spiked and often fumbled by people who don't know what they are talking about . . . and by those who are overly dogmatic about every last detail.

The speculation about Christ's return has also been taken to ridiculous extremes. People have set dates for His return and waited up on rooftops through the heat of the day and on into the dead of night. Then, in painful embarrassment, they slid down off those roofs after dark while the world laughed and Christians blushed at the ridiculous act of setting hard-and-fast dates.

The apostle Peter predicted the opposite extreme in his second letter—and it is a response we see today as well:

> *First of all, you must understand that in the last days scoffers will come, scoffing and following their own evil desires. They will say, "Where is this 'coming' he promised? Ever since our fathers died, everything goes on as it has since the beginning of creation"* (2 Peter 3:3–4).

Years ago there was a double-column ad in the *Los Angeles Times* (September 12, 1982). It was a letter addressed to the Reverend Billy Graham, a half-dozen other clergymen and fellow Christians all over the world. And there in bold print were the words, "Jesus Christ Will Not Come Again." At the end of the lengthy article, it was signed by an author offering his book for $8.75, detailing his reasons why Jesus Christ *will not* come again.

I confess that when I read the ad, I shrugged and thought, "So what else is new? This is absolutely predictable! Snow is white. The sun is hot. Kids are loud. The rain is wet. Scoffers scoff. No big deal, is it?"—it's just as Peter said it would be. In fact, it reminded me that we were right on stream. Peter told us that in the last days there would be scoffers who would say, "Where is this 'coming' he promised?" (2 Peter 3:4).

We see both extremes—waiting for Christ on the rooftop, and denying that He'll ever come at all. Neither reaction should disturb us or surprise us or even cause us to raise our eyebrows.

Well-informed, maturing believers aren't caught up in the silly extremes that have been associated with the second coming of Jesus Christ. They stay appropriately balanced in their attitudes and behaviors—even as they acknowledge the difficulty of maintaining balance with respect to a truth as exciting and awe-inspiring as the Lord's return. The one extreme says, "Jesus is returning. In fact, it is so sure and so soon that nothing else matters"—and so they stop working hard. They don't worry about falling more and more into debt. They leave their houses unclean and may even neglect taking care of basic personal hygiene. They exist on the raw edge of irresponsibility—because Jesus is coming.

I believe that Jesus' return is soon—at any time, in fact, but I'm praying and working like it *won't* be in my generation. I hope you are too. I do believe it is imminent, but I'm adopting a lifestyle as if it won't happen while I'm alive. I don't mean I'm living loosely or carelessly; I mean I'm living responsibly. On the other hand, I take strong issue with those on the other extreme who say, "He's not coming back. After all, look around. Everything's the same as it's always been." Why, when I look around, do I get all the more anxious for His return? I do believe it is near at hand. The key is learning to live in balance, keeping all things in their proper perspective, day in and day out.

Who, Where and Why?

Who wrote this letter of encouragement and practical advice, and to whom was it written? We simply need to turn to the first word of the letter to find the name of the writer: His name, by now so familiar to us, is Paul. The recipients are the believers in the church at Thessalonica, the largest city in the finger of land in northern Greece called Macedonia in those days. These were people who were "in God our Father and the Lord Jesus Christ" (1:1)—first-century saints, most of them friends of the apostle Paul.

Why would Paul write a second letter so soon after his first—a mere six months or so after 1 Thessalonians? A careful reading will reveal that some of the saints who had read his first letter misunderstood his teachings about the Lord's return. Apparently they had failed to listen well the first time.

To complicate matters even more, the believers were stirred up by false reports that the last days had arrived and that their completion was imminent. Note how Paul called attention to what he was hearing from the home front of the Thessalonians:

> *Concerning the coming of our Lord Jesus Christ and our being gathered to him, we ask you, brothers, not to become easily unsettled or alarmed by some prophecy, report or letter supposed to have come from us, saying that the day of the Lord has already come (2:1–2).*

Now look closely. Always apply discernment as you study the Bible, especially when confronting technical issues. You'll notice that Paul cited three sources. He didn't identify the origin of any of the three, but he said, in effect, "You people are losing your composure. You're getting all shook up over some creative prophetic utterance or by a report from some person along the way or even by some fake letter reported to be from us."

"Whatever the source," Paul explained, "I want you to know I've been misunderstood. If I was identified as the one who said that the final days have begun, we've got a major misunderstanding here. Your information is spurious." Paul hastened to write this letter we call 2 Thessalonians to correct whatever confused thinking was floating around Thessalonica.

Modern-day Thessalonians

If you hang around Christians long enough you'll find a few within the ranks who live in passionate idleness. By that I mean, you can't carry on a conversation with them without hearing them say something about the Lord's return being near. Their sometimes fanatical words are typically accompanied by irresponsible attitudes and behavior in everyday life. Look at a classic example from the days of the Thessalonians:

> *We hear that some among you are idle. They are not busy; they are busybodies. Such people we command and urge in the Lord Jesus Christ to settle down and earn the bread they eat. And*

as for you, brothers, never tire of doing what is right. If anyone does not obey our instruction in this letter, take special note of him. Do not associate with him, in order that he may feel ashamed (3:11–14).

Strong words! I think if I would have received this letter from Paul and been among the extremists, I would have been mighty uneasy. I would have felt his finger poking against my breastbone, saying, "Get back in line! You're taking this thing to a ridiculous extreme. Bring your approach to Christ's return back into balance. Yes, He's coming, and He's coming at any time. But certain things have to happen before He returns. In the meantime, stay active. Keep working. Keep living for Him. Keep doing the right thing."

Be Diligent!

Let me put your mind at ease here. You lose nothing of your commitment to the imminence of Christ's return if you live a balanced life—a life of patience and steadiness. Some folks suffer from a theological disease I call "rapture fever." Speaking with all candor, it is uncomfortable for me to be around them for very long. That preoccupation affects their commitment to their vocation, their ability to act decisively and their temptation to fall into debt . . . not to mention the way they nurture their relationships! They blame all their lack of motivation on the rapture: "So why worry about how much money you're borrowing? Why worry about how things look or how strange or insensitive some of the statements you make might sound or how you take care (or don't take care) of yourself? After all, Jesus is coming, and He's going to bail you out of all of these earthly things, so why should you concern yourself with any of it?"

We need to pay careful attention to the lesson Paul teaches us in 2 Thessalonians: Good theology creates diligent Christians, those who are faithful to the task for as long as they live here on earth. Why? Because, after all, to use the words of a popular song in years past, "The beat goes on." Unless Jesus Christ returns today, tomorrow is coming, bringing all those things with it that you have put off doing today! Be diligent, dear friends . . . always ready for His return, yet always ready to live faithfully for Him until His return.

With Perseverance in Trouble Chapter 1

The first chapter trumpets one central message: *Persevering through affliction develops maturity.* Isn't that true? Oh, how we want to be mature without having to endure the affliction! "Lord, give me patience, and give it to me right now"—you've prayed that way, and so have I. "Make me strong and bulk me up physically, but don't make me lift all those weights. Just let me wake up in the morning and be muscular." But it doesn't work like that. The reality of our journey through life is this: It is necessary to go through times of trouble. We will experience times when life seems unfair and inexplicably hard, times when the pain just won't go away. In the heat of the furnace you and I are refined and grow toward maturity, especially as we lean on our Lord.

People in the north Midwest of America say, "In the heat of the sun the corn grows." Some even say you can hear it grow. You can listen to it . . . it squeaks. Perhaps we might say that in the intense times of testing, Christians squeak. We are growing. Growing stronger. Growing deeper. This chapter is about standing strong in affliction and growing as a result of the furnace experiences of life.

1 Paul, Silas[a] and Timothy, 1Th 1:1; Ac 15:22

To the church of the Thessalonians in God our
Father and the Lord Jesus Christ: Ac 17:1

2Grace and peace to you from God the Father
and the Lord Jesus Christ. Ro 1:7

Thanksgiving and Prayer

3We ought always to thank God for you, brothers, and rightly so, because your faith is growing
more and more, and the love every one of you has
for each other is increasing. 4Therefore, among
God's churches we boast about your perseverance
and faith in all the persecutions and trials you are
enduring. 1Th 3:12; 2:14

LIVING  INSIGHT

Let us not lose heart. On tough days, you've got to have heart. Don't quit, whatever you do. Persevere. Stand firm. Be strong, resilient, determined to see it through. Ask God to build a protective shield around your heart, stabilizing you.

(See 2 Thessalonians 1:4.)

5All this is evidence that God's judgment is
right, and as a result you will be counted worthy of
the kingdom of God, for which you are suffering.
6God is just: He will pay back trouble to those who
trouble you 7and give relief to you who are troubled, and to us as well. This will happen when the
Lord Jesus is revealed from heaven in blazing fire
with his powerful angels. 8He will punish those
who do not know God and do not obey the gospel
of our Lord Jesus. 9They will be punished with
everlasting destruction and shut out from the
presence of the Lord and from the majesty of his
power 10on the day he comes to be glorified in his
holy people and to be marveled at among all those
who have believed. This includes you, because you
believed our testimony to you. 1Th 4:16; Jude 14

11With this in mind, we constantly pray for you,
that our God may count you worthy of his calling,
and that by his power he may fulfill every good
purpose of yours and every act prompted by your
faith. 12We pray this so that the name of our Lord
Jesus may be glorified in you, and you in him,
according to the grace of our God and the Lord
Jesus Christ.[b] Php 2:9-11; 1Th 1:3

With Unbending Trust Chapter 2

This chapter teaches an important lesson: *Trusting amidst confusion reveals stability.* When all you can do is simply trust in God, you demonstrate stability. You'll have folks tell you it's foolish to give up your pursuit of understanding. Some will say, "You've got to understand why you're suffering or you'll never be able to handle it." Let me tell you that half the things that happen in my life I'll never understand—and there are many things that happen to others that I'll never understand. I'll never be able to explain why God lifts up those He does and brings down others who seem more deserving than some who prosper. In the midst of the confusion I trust my God to make it all come out right. It is only when we trust in Him that we will be able to find the strength and stability to make it through the stormy struggles.

The Man of Lawlessness

2 Concerning the coming of our Lord Jesus
Christ and our being gathered to him, we ask
you, brothers, 2not to become easily unsettled or
alarmed by some prophecy, report or letter supposed to have come from us, saying that the day
of the Lord has already come. 3Don't let anyone
deceive you in any way, for ⌊that day will not
come⌋ until the rebellion occurs and the man of
lawlessness[c] is revealed, the man doomed to destruction. 4He will oppose and will exalt himself
over everything that is called God or is worshiped,
so that he sets himself up in God's temple, proclaiming himself to be God. Isa 14:13-14; 1Co 8:5

5Don't you remember that when I was with you
I used to tell you these things? 6And now you
know what is holding him back, so that he may be
revealed at the proper time. 7For the secret power
of lawlessness is already at work; but the one who
now holds it back will continue to do so till he is
taken out of the way. 8And then the lawless one

[a] *1* Greek *Silvanus,* a variant of *Silas* [b] *12* Or *God and Lord, Jesus Christ* [c] *3* Some manuscripts *sin*

will be revealed, whom the Lord Jesus will overthrow with the breath of his mouth and destroy by
the splendor of his coming. 9The coming of the
lawless one will be in accordance with the work of
Satan displayed in all kinds of counterfeit miracles,
signs and wonders, 10and in every sort of evil that
deceives those who are perishing. They perish because they refused to love the truth and so be
saved. 11For this reason God sends them a powerful delusion so that they will believe the lie 12and
so that all will be condemned who have not believed the truth but have delighted in wickedness.

Stand Firm

13But we ought always to thank God for you,
brothers loved by the Lord, because from the beginning God chose you[a] to be saved through the
sanctifying work of the Spirit and through belief in
the truth. 14He called you to this through our gospel, that you might share in the glory of our Lord
Jesus Christ. 15So then, brothers, stand firm and
hold to the teachings[b] we passed on to you,
whether by word of mouth or by letter. 1Co 11:2

16May our Lord Jesus Christ himself and God
our Father, who loved us and by his grace gave us
eternal encouragement and good hope, 17encour-
age your hearts and strengthen you in every good
deed and word. Jn 3:16; 1Th 3:2

With Patient Expectation **Chapter 3**

Paul reminds us here of a powerful truth: *Waiting with discipline cultivates responsibility.* How should we live as we await the return of our Savior? Paul urges us to lead disciplined and patient lives. We must be always ready to meet our Lord today and always prepared to live for Him tomorrow. We must work hard and not grow weary as we serve the Lord and others. We should avoid the extremes of irresponsible date setting on the one hand and skeptical scoffing on the other. The responsible believer waits for the Lord's return with patient expectation.

Maturity. Stability. Responsibility. With those qualities waiting to find their way into the lives of all who make a serious study of each chapter of 2 Thessalonians, who wouldn't want to spend time in this letter?

Request for Prayer

3 Finally, brothers, pray for us that the message
of the Lord may spread rapidly and be honored, just as it was with you. 2And pray that we
may be delivered from wicked and evil men, for
not everyone has faith. 3But the Lord is faithful,
and he will strengthen and protect you from the
evil one. 4We have confidence in the Lord that you
are doing and will continue to do the things we
command. 5May the Lord direct your hearts into
God's love and Christ's perseverance. 1Ch 29:18

Warning Against Idleness

6In the name of the Lord Jesus Christ, we command you, brothers, to keep away from every
brother who is idle and does not live according to
the teaching[c] you received from us. 7For you
yourselves know how you ought to follow our example. We were not idle when we were with you,
8nor did we eat anyone's food without paying for
it. On the contrary, we worked night and day,
laboring and toiling so that we would not be a
burden to any of you. 9We did this, not because we
do not have the right to such help, but in order to
make ourselves a model for you to follow. 10For
even when we were with you, we gave you this
rule: "If a man will not work, he shall not eat."

LIVING  **INSIGHT**

Never once in Scripture is irresponsibility excused on the basis of one's confidence in Jesus' return. Anticipation is one thing. Blind fanaticism is quite another.
(See 2 Thessalonians 3:10.)

11We hear that some among you are idle. They
are not busy; they are busybodies. 12Such people
we command and urge in the Lord Jesus Christ to
settle down and earn the bread they eat. 13And as
for you, brothers, never tire of doing what is right.
14If anyone does not obey our instruction in this
letter, take special note of him. Do not associate
with him, in order that he may feel ashamed. 15Yet
do not regard him as an enemy, but warn him as
a brother. Gal 6:1; 1Th 5:14

Final Greetings

16Now may the Lord of peace himself give you
peace at all times and in every way. The Lord be
with all of you. Ro 15:33

17I, Paul, write this greeting in my own hand,
which is the distinguishing mark in all my letters.
This is how I write. 1Co 16:21

18The grace of our Lord Jesus Christ be with
you all. Ro 16:20

[a] 13 Some manuscripts *because God chose you as his firstfruits* [b] 15 Or *traditions* [c] 6 Or *tradition*

INTRODUCTION

1 TIMOTHY

Paul's first letter to Timothy is one of three New Testament letters of special interest to churches and their pastors. These letters (1 Timothy, 2 Timothy and Titus) are commonly referred to as "the Pastoral Letters," because they give instruction concerning pastoral care. To this day these three letters remain the most accurate and very best counsel a "shepherd" and his "flock" could receive. This first letter to Timothy is the longest of the three and the most thorough treatment of Paul's pastoral advice. Look here for guidelines for life in the church. While specific problems addressed by Paul may not apply in every case to the church today, the principles that Paul teaches certainly hold true for every church in every age.

WRITER: *Paul*

DATE: *C.A.D. 63–65*

PURPOSE: *To warn Timothy about false teachers, to instruct him about ministry duties and to encourage him to educate the "flock"*

KEY THEMES: *Church leadership; church conduct; false doctrine*

KEY VERSES: *3:14-15*

STYLE: *Encouraging and exhorting*

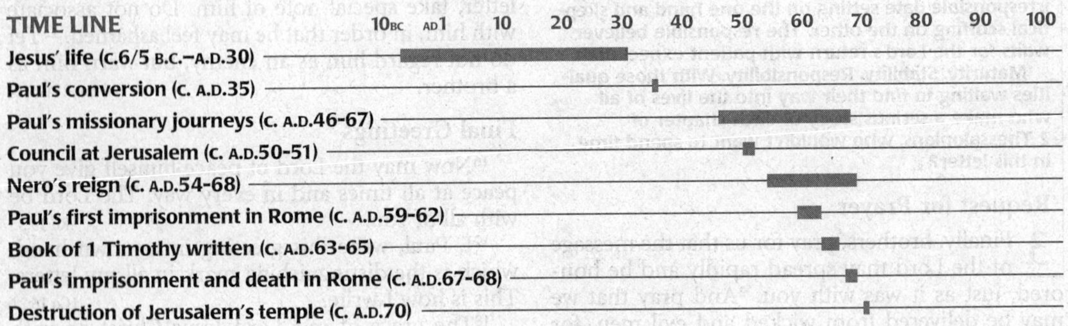

Wise Counsel for God's Servants

GREETING (1:1-2)	PERSONAL ENCOURAGEMENT AND EXHORTATION	THE MINISTRY	THE MINISTER	CONCLUSION (6:21)
	Timothy's task Paul's testimony Gospel's trust	Men and women *(2)* (Prayer and submission) Elders and deacons *(3)* (Qualifications and leadership)	Seeing the importance of *(4)*: Faithful teaching Sound doctrine True godliness Perseverance Paying attention to *(5)*: Various age groups Widows Elders Wisdom Maintaining balance with *(6)*: Masters and slaves Rich and poor Internals and externals	
	CHAPTER 1:3-20	*CHAPTERS 2–3*	*CHAPTERS 4:1–6:20*	
EMPHASIS	**The work of ministry**		**The one who ministers**	
COMMAND	**Be true!**	**Be wise!**	**Be strong and faithful!**	

I don't understand a great deal about photography. I have been told, however, that while it's difficult to photograph a single blossom or a leaf, it is much more difficult to capture a forest on film . . . or some other panoramic scene. I believe the same can be said about Scripture. Many of us may be quite skilled at understanding one verse or several verses, or we may do fairly well in explaining a paragraph of Scripture. But when it comes to an overview, to seeing a Bible book or group of books as a whole, that may well be another matter. Difficult though it may be, we need to keep the "big picture" in mind, including various "sections" of the Scriptures that fit into a thematic unit.

The letter of 1 Timothy is the first of a cluster of three letters that fit together in a single category. For several hundred years 1 Timothy, 2 Timothy and Titus have been known as the "Pastoral Letters" because they give instruction to Timothy and Titus about the pastoral care of churches.

These letters were written by a man named Paul. As he was reaching the later years of his life, this aging apostle had some concerns on his heart for two men who served churches in the city of Ephesus and on the island of Crete. These three Pastoral Letters are "must reading" for anyone who is seriously interested in filling a role of leadership in a local church. They are the divine curriculum, "Pastoring 101."

From "Father" to "Son"

The letter called 1 Timothy was written by someone with a heart for ministry and, equally important, a heart for a friend named Timothy, whom Paul called "my true son in the faith" (1:2). I find it interesting that Timothy's name appears no less than 25 times in the New Testament (six times in the book of Acts, and the rest in the letters). Paul often refers to him as "my son," which probably means that Paul led him to a relationship with Jesus Christ. He knew him well. If Paul wasn't the one responsible for his conversion, humanly speaking, then he certainly was the one who had mentored the young man and in doing so had developed a "father-son" relationship. By the time this letter was written (about A.D. 63–65), Timothy was about forty years old. Paul was past the age of sixty.

Grace, Mercy and Peace

As Paul wrote to Timothy, addressing him as a father would a son, he affirmed him with this warm salutation: "Grace, mercy and peace . . ." (1:2). In effect, Paul was saying, "May those three be yours, Timothy. May you demonstrate them throughout your life. May your ministry be characterized by grace, mercy and peace."

"Grace" is what God does for us who are so undeserving; we are not entitled to His forgiving love and His incredible kindness, nor can we earn His favor—it is unmerited, and we could never repay Him for the honor of being accepted by Him. And "mercy"? The best definition I've heard for "mercy" is this: "God's ministry to the miserable." The gift of "peace" is the experience of an inner calm, an unshakable tranquillity that settles in at the core of a person's life, even though things all around may be wild and woolly. There is a peace that only the Christian can know—because it is based on peace with God (see Romans 5:1; Philippians 4:7). And Paul's wish for his young friend was that he might know fresh measures of grace and mercy and peace rarely experienced in Timothy's day (or in our day as well).

Guard the Flock

Why did Paul write his first letter to Timothy? Paul himself revealed three reasons. First, *Paul wrote to Timothy to warn him about false teachers*:

> *As I urged you when I went into Macedonia, stay there in Ephesus so that you may command certain men not to teach false doctrines any longer nor to devote themselves to myths and endless genealogies. These promote controversies rather than God's work—which is by faith (1:3–4).*

Timothy needed that warning because there were so many heretical teachers on the loose in the church at Ephesus. False teachers have always plagued the church, from its earliest days right on down to the present day. So if you want to learn about standing firm against false teaching, become a student of 1 Timothy. You'll discover insights into discerning the differences between sound doctrine and false teachings, and you'll gain trustworthy techniques for resisting those who would distort the pure gospel of Jesus.

One of the least enjoyable tasks of "shepherding" a flock is warding off wolves who prey on the sheep. Enjoyable or not, it's an essential part of shepherding. If shepherds take their eyes off their sheep, wolves will bring destruction. Today, as in Timothy's day, pastors and church leaders need to be ready to protect their people from the cunning ways of false teachers. Note that the warning applies in all situations—to a missionary out in the bush serving a handful of people, to the pastor of a small country church, or to the staff of a large urban church. Shepherds who are faithful to the task find themselves at times needing to roll up their sleeves and deal directly with the wolves. The mark of a good shepherd is the ability to discern when the flock is in danger and to know how best to deal with the opposition.

Do the Work

Second, *Paul wrote to Timothy to instruct him on how to conduct himself as he carried out his duties.* Paul stated it clearly in chapter 3:

> *Although I hope to come to you soon, I am writing you these instructions so that if I am delayed, you will know how people ought to conduct themselves in God's household, which is the church of the living God, the pillar and foundation of the truth (3:14–15).*

The seasoned veteran took the time to give clear instruction to his friend about how he needed to go about the work of ministry (chapters 2–3). Paul covered topics important for public worship, including the prominence of prayer (2:1–7), the roles of men and women in the church (2:8–11), and guidelines for teaching Biblical submission (2:12–15). He also delineated the roles and qualifications of elders/overseers and deacons (chapter 3). Valuable information here, with important underlying principles for the life of the church.

The Place of Education

Third, *Paul wrote to Timothy to encourage him to educate the believers.* Look at Paul's statement in chapter 4:

> *If you point these things out to the brothers, you will be a good minister of Christ Jesus, brought up in the truths of the faith and of the good teaching that you have followed (4:6)*

I don't know of a better way to describe Paul's charge to Timothy than to use the words "to educate." The dictionary says "to educate" means "to develop mentally and morally . . . by instruction." A pastor's job description includes that incredibly significant role—at least part of which is fulfilled through modeling the message (4:12). Contrary to some popular opinion, the role of educator is so crucial to the work of a pastor—more important than that of motivator, cheerleader, fund-raiser or counselor.

My continuing word of counsel to those who serve as ministers is this: Educate your board. Educate your people. Help them to know what it means to be a congregation that is growing and maturing—not dependent, not independent, but *interdependent* with one another. Step down from the pedestal and get into the trenches of life. Instruct the flock of God. Serve as a role model your people can imitate. Patiently and consistently educate them.

Three Lessons From Timothy

There are at least three significant insights to be gleaned from this letter. First, *"shepherding" is much more practical than it is theoretical.* All the way through 1 Timothy Paul gave a lot of practical counsel on how to shepherd God's flock. The fact is, shepherds do not do their best work from behind a desk or even in a fancy building. Shepherding happens out in the fields—in other words, it takes place where the sheep are. Much of ministry is practical and down-to-earth involvement in the lives of people, carrying out hands-on training, practicing real-life role modeling.

Second, *church leadership is much less glamorous than it is demanding.* Being a pastor may look glamorous from the vantage point of people who occupy the pews Sunday after Sunday and may not have had the privilege of observing the ministry that's faithfully carried out day after day. Some church members look at a pastor as someone who has it made—after all, he only works one day a week! But the reality that all hard-working pastors understand is this: the work of ministry is much less glamorous than it is demanding. The work of ministry involves long hours, wide-ranging skills, deep commitment and steady sacrifice. The glamorous moments are few and far between. Paul helps us see a more realistic picture of ministry as he writes this letter to his young friend Timothy.

Third, and finally, *ministry is the maintenance of balance between commitment and contentment.* I glean that insight from Paul's parting advice to Timothy:

> *But godliness with contentment is great gain. For we brought nothing into the world, and we can take nothing out of it. But if we have food and clothing, we will be content with that (6:6–8).*

As God's workers we must be unwaveringly committed to Him and ready to work hard . . . that goes for all of us who serve the Lord Jesus! But we need to remember that God gives the growth. Our task is to be content with His timing and the way He chooses to work in and through us. Commitment and contentment . . . we need to walk in the balance of both.

Encouragement for Ministry Chapter 1

Paul began his letter by urging Timothy to stand firm against false teachers whose distorted teachings were leading people astray. He told Timothy to put a stop to all needlessly controversial and doctrinally dangerous teaching (1:3–7). Next, Paul gave a brief but powerful testimony to the grace of God (1:12–14). He wanted all people to know that if the Lord could extend grace to a sinner like Saul of Tarsus (see Acts 9), then surely the love of Jesus can reach anyone. Finally, Paul presented the basic and simple gospel of salvation in Jesus (1:15–17)—a message that was completely trustworthy then, is today and always will be.

1 Paul, an apostle of Christ Jesus by the command of God our Savior and of Christ Jesus our hope, Col 1:27; Tit 1:3

[2]To Timothy my true son in the faith: Ac 16:1

Grace, mercy and peace from God the Father and Christ Jesus our Lord. Ro 1:7

Warning Against False Teachers of the Law

[3]As I urged you when I went into Macedonia,
stay there in Ephesus so that you may command
certain men not to teach false doctrines any longer
[4]nor to devote themselves to myths and endless
genealogies. These promote controversies rather
than God's work—which is by faith. [5]The goal of
this command is love, which comes from a pure
heart and a good conscience and a sincere faith.
[6]Some have wandered away from these and turned
to meaningless talk. [7]They want to be teachers of
the law, but they do not know what they are talking about or what they so confidently affirm.

[8]We know that the law is good if one uses it
properly. [9]We also know that law[a] is made not
for the righteous but for lawbreakers and rebels,
the ungodly and sinful, the unholy and irreligious;
for those who kill their fathers or mothers, for
murderers, [10]for adulterers and perverts, for slave
traders and liars and perjurers—and for whatever
else is contrary to the sound doctrine [11]that conforms to the glorious gospel of the blessed God,
which he entrusted to me. Gal 2:7; 2Ti 4:3

The Lord's Grace to Paul

[12]I thank Christ Jesus our Lord, who has given
me strength, that he considered me faithful, appointing me to his service. [13]Even though I was
once a blasphemer and a persecutor and a violent
man, I was shown mercy because I acted in ignorance and unbelief. [14]The grace of our Lord was
poured out on me abundantly, along with the faith
and love that are in Christ Jesus. Ac 8:3; 2Ti 1:13

[15]Here is a trustworthy saying that deserves full
acceptance: Christ Jesus came into the world to
save sinners—of whom I am the worst. [16]But for
that very reason I was shown mercy so that in me,
the worst of sinners, Christ Jesus might display his
unlimited patience as an example for those who
would believe on him and receive eternal life.
[17]Now to the King eternal, immortal, invisible, the
only God, be honor and glory for ever and ever.
Amen. Ro 11:36; Col 1:15; Rev 15:3

[18]Timothy, my son, I give you this instruction
in keeping with the prophecies once made about
you, so that by following them you may fight the
good fight, [19]holding on to faith and a good conscience. Some have rejected these and so have
shipwrecked their faith. [20]Among them are Hymenaeus and Alexander, whom I have handed over to
Satan to be taught not to blaspheme. 1Ti 4:14

LIVING  INSIGHT

What roots are to a tree, the doctrines are to the Christian. From them we draw our emotional stability, our mental food for growth, as well as our spiritual energy and perspective on life itself. By returning to our roots, we determine precisely where we stand.

(See 1 Timothy 1:18–19.)

The Work of Ministry Chapters 2–3

These two chapters record instructions for church administration as Paul addressed issues of public worship and qualifications for church officers. His principal concern was ministry. Who should serve in ministry and how should they carry out their ministry? Chapter 3 clearly spelled out the qualifications for ministry leaders in the church—instructions not to be passed over lightly. As we seek those who would provide leadership in the body of believers, we should repeatedly return to this section of Scripture. As we examine our own sense of God's call to church leadership, these qualifications must always remain before us. Yet if you question whether you could ever meet those standards, take comfort in this thought: God has an incredible power to take broken vessels and make them useful in Jesus, through the experience of His healing touch and His amazing grace.

Instructions on Worship

2 I urge, then, first of all, that requests, prayers,
intercession and thanksgiving be made for
everyone— [2]for kings and all those in authority,
that we may live peaceful and quiet lives in all
godliness and holiness. [3]This is good, and pleases
God our Savior, [4]who wants all men to be saved
and to come to a knowledge of the truth. [5]For
there is one God and one mediator between God

[a]9 Or *that the law*

and men, the man Christ Jesus, 6who gave himself as a ransom for all men—the testimony given in its proper time. 7And for this purpose I was appointed a herald and an apostle—I am telling the truth, I am not lying—and a teacher of the true faith to the Gentiles. 1Co 1:6; Gal 3:20

8I want men everywhere to lift up holy hands in prayer, without anger or disputing. Ps 134:2; Lk 24:50

9I also want women to dress modestly, with decency and propriety, not with braided hair or gold or pearls or expensive clothes, 10but with good deeds, appropriate for women who profess to worship God. Pr 31:13; 1Pe 3:3

11A woman should learn in quietness and full submission. 12I do not permit a woman to teach or to have authority over a man; she must be silent. 13For Adam was formed first, then Eve. 14And Adam was not the one deceived; it was the woman who was deceived and became a sinner. 15But women[a] will be saved[b] through childbearing—if they continue in faith, love and holiness with propriety. Ge 3:1-6,13; 1Co 11:8

Overseers and Deacons

3 Here is a trustworthy saying: If anyone sets his heart on being an overseer,[c] he desires a noble task. 2Now the overseer must be above reproach, the husband of but one wife, temperate, self-controlled, respectable, hospitable, able to teach, 3not given to drunkenness, not violent but gentle, not quarrelsome, not a lover of money. 4He must manage his own family well and see that his children obey him with proper respect. 5(If anyone does not know how to manage his own family, how can he take care of God's church?) 6He must not be a recent convert, or he may become conceited and fall under the same judgment as the devil. 7He must also have a good reputation with outsiders, so that he will not fall into disgrace and into the devil's trap. 1Ti 6:4; 2Ti 2:26

8Deacons, likewise, are to be men worthy of respect, sincere, not indulging in much wine, and not pursuing dishonest gain. 9They must keep hold of the deep truths of the faith with a clear conscience. 10They must first be tested; and then if there is nothing against them, let them serve as deacons. 1Ti 1:19; Tit 2:3

11In the same way, their wives[d] are to be women worthy of respect, not malicious talkers but temperate and trustworthy in everything. Tit 2:3

12A deacon must be the husband of but one wife and must manage his children and his household well. 13Those who have served well gain an excellent standing and great assurance in their faith in Christ Jesus.

14Although I hope to come to you soon, I am writing you these instructions so that, 15if I am delayed, you will know how people ought to conduct themselves in God's household, which is the church of the living God, the pillar and foundation of the truth. 16Beyond all question, the mystery of godliness is great: Ro 16:25; Eph 2:21

He[e] appeared in a body,[f] Jn 1:14
was vindicated by the Spirit,
was seen by angels,
was preached among the nations, Col 1:23
was believed on in the world,
was taken up in glory. Mk 16:19

The Role of the Minister **Chapters 4–6**

In the closing chapters Paul instructed Timothy about various tasks of ministry. In chapter 4 he reminded Timothy of the importance of the faithful teaching of the Word, knowledge of sound doctrine, walking in true godliness and modeling perseverance in the faith. In chapter 5 Paul advised Timothy to care for various groups in the church, including widows and elders, urging him to always follow the path of wisdom. Finally, in chapter 6 Paul gave advice about slaves, the love of money, and internal and external issues in life. As a pastor, Timothy needed sound counsel in his ministry. These three chapters are rich with wisdom and direction for pastors, for church leaders and for church members. I know of no source of information more helpful to me as a pastor than this letter and the one that follows. How invaluable they prove to be, decade after decade!

Instructions to Timothy

4 The Spirit clearly says that in later times some will abandon the faith and follow deceiving spirits and things taught by demons. 2Such teachings come through hypocritical liars, whose consciences have been seared as with a hot iron. 3They forbid people to marry and order them to abstain from certain foods, which God created to be received with thanksgiving by those who believe and who know the truth. 4For everything God created is good, and nothing is to be rejected if it is received with thanksgiving, 5because it is consecrated by the word of God and prayer. Ro 14:14-18

LIVING  INSIGHT

Where are you in the learning process? Are you learning your way through God's Book? Is doctrine important to you? We must never stop learning and growing in our faith!

(See 1 Timothy 4:1–6.)

a15 Greek *she*
b15 Or *restored*
c1 Traditionally *bishop*; also in verse 2
d11 Or *way, deaconesses*
e16 Some manuscripts *God*
f16 Or *in the flesh*

6If you point these things out to the brothers, you will be a good minister of Christ Jesus, brought up in the truths of the faith and of the good teaching that you have followed. 7Have nothing to do with godless myths and old wives' tales; rather, train yourself to be godly. 8For physical training is of some value, but godliness has value for all things, holding promise for both the present life and the life to come. 1Ti 6:6; Ps 37:9,11; Mk 10:29-30

9This is a trustworthy saying that deserves full acceptance 10(and for this we labor and strive), that we have put our hope in the living God, who is the Savior of all men, and especially of those who believe. 1Ti 1:15

11Command and teach these things. 12Don't let anyone look down on you because you are young, but set an example for the believers in speech, in life, in love, in faith and in purity. 13Until I come, devote yourself to the public reading of Scripture, to preaching and to teaching. 14Do not neglect your gift, which was given you through a prophetic message when the body of elders laid their hands on you. 1Ti 1:14,18; Tit 2:7

15Be diligent in these matters; give yourself wholly to them, so that everyone may see your progress. 16Watch your life and doctrine closely. Persevere in them, because if you do, you will save both yourself and your hearers. Ro 11:14

Advice About Widows, Elders and Slaves

5 Do not rebuke an older man harshly, but exhort him as if he were your father. Treat younger men as brothers, 2older women as mothers, and younger women as sisters, with absolute purity. Lev 19:32; Tit 2:6

3Give proper recognition to those widows who are really in need. 4But if a widow has children or grandchildren, these should learn first of all to put their religion into practice by caring for their own family and so repaying their parents and grandparents, for this is pleasing to God. 5The widow who is really in need and left all alone puts her hope in God and continues night and day to pray and to ask God for help. 6But the widow who lives for pleasure is dead even while she lives. 7Give the people these instructions, too, so that no one may be open to blame. 8If anyone does not provide for his relatives, and especially for his immediate family, he has denied the faith and is worse than an unbeliever. 1Ti 4:11; Tit 1:16

9No widow may be put on the list of widows unless she is over sixty, has been faithful to her husband,[a] 10and is well known for her good deeds, such as bringing up children, showing hospitality, washing the feet of the saints, helping those in trouble and devoting herself to all kinds of good deeds. Lk 7:44; 1Pe 2:12

11As for younger widows, do not put them on such a list. For when their sensual desires overcome their dedication to Christ, they want to marry. 12Thus they bring judgment on themselves, because they have broken their first pledge. 13Besides, they get into the habit of being idle and going about from house to house. And not only do they become idlers, but also gossips and busybodies, saying things they ought not to. 14So I counsel younger widows to marry, to have children, to manage their homes and to give the enemy no opportunity for slander. 15Some have in fact already turned away to follow Satan. 1Co 7:9; 2Th 3:11

16If any woman who is a believer has widows in her family, she should help them and not let the church be burdened with them, so that the church can help those widows who are really in need.

17The elders who direct the affairs of the church well are worthy of double honor, especially those whose work is preaching and teaching. 18For the Scripture says, "Do not muzzle the ox while it is treading out the grain,"[b] and "The worker deserves his wages."[c] 19Do not entertain an accusation against an elder unless it is brought by two or three witnesses. 20Those who sin are to be rebuked publicly, so that the others may take warning.

21I charge you, in the sight of God and Christ Jesus and the elect angels, to keep these instructions without partiality, and to do nothing out of favoritism. 1Ti 6:13; 2Ti 4:1

22Do not be hasty in the laying on of hands, and do not share in the sins of others. Keep yourself pure. Ac 6:6; Eph 5:11

23Stop drinking only water, and use a little wine because of your stomach and your frequent illnesses. 1Ti 3:8

24The sins of some men are obvious, reaching the place of judgment ahead of them; the sins of others trail behind them. 25In the same way, good deeds are obvious, and even those that are not cannot be hidden.

6 All who are under the yoke of slavery should consider their masters worthy of full respect, so that God's name and our teaching may not be slandered. 2Those who have believing masters are not to show less respect for them because they are brothers. Instead, they are to serve them even better, because those who benefit from their service are believers, and dear to them. These are the things you are to teach and urge on them.

Love of Money

3If anyone teaches false doctrines and does not agree to the sound instruction of our Lord Jesus Christ and to godly teaching, 4he is conceited and understands nothing. He has an unhealthy interest in controversies and quarrels about words that re-

[a]9 Or *has had but one husband* [b]*18* Deut. 25:4 [c]*18* Luke 10:7

sult in envy, strife, malicious talk, evil suspicions 5and constant friction between men of corrupt mind, who have been robbed of the truth and who think that godliness is a means to financial gain.

6But godliness with contentment is great gain. 7For we brought nothing into the world, and we can take nothing out of it. 8But if we have food and clothing, we will be content with that. 9People who want to get rich fall into temptation and a trap and into many foolish and harmful desires that plunge men into ruin and destruction. 10For the love of money is a root of all kinds of evil. Some people, eager for money, have wandered from the faith and pierced themselves with many griefs. 1Ti 3:3

LIVING  **INSIGHT**

I love what Corrie ten Boom used to say: "Vell, I've learned to hold every ting loosely, because it hurts ven God pries my fingers apart and takes tem from me."

(See 1 Timothy 6:6–10.)

Paul's Charge to Timothy

11But you, man of God, flee from all this, and pursue righteousness, godliness, faith, love, endurance and gentleness. 12Fight the good fight of the faith. Take hold of the eternal life to which you were called when you made your good confession in the presence of many witnesses. 13In the sight of God, who gives life to everything, and of Christ Jesus, who while testifying before Pontius Pilate made the good confession, I charge you 14to keep this command without spot or blame until the appearing of our Lord Jesus Christ, 15which God will bring about in his own time—God, the blessed and only Ruler, the King of kings and Lord of lords, 16who alone is immortal and who lives in unapproachable light, whom no one has seen or can see. To him be honor and might forever. Amen. Jn 18:33-37; 1Ti 5:21

17Command those who are rich in this present world not to be arrogant nor to put their hope in wealth, which is so uncertain, but to put their hope in God, who richly provides us with everything for our enjoyment. 18Command them to do good, to be rich in good deeds, and to be generous and willing to share. 19In this way they will lay up treasure for themselves as a firm foundation for the coming age, so that they may take hold of the life that is truly life. Lk 12:20-21; Ac 14:17

20Timothy, guard what has been entrusted to your care. Turn away from godless chatter and the opposing ideas of what is falsely called knowledge, 21which some have professed and in so doing have wandered from the faith. 2Ti 1:12,14; 2:18

Grace be with you. Col 4:18

INTRODUCTION

2 TIMOTHY

It's doubtful that we could find a more nostalgic, emotional letter written by the apostle Paul. Facing death, alone in a dungeon, lonely, surrounded by memories and exposed to the elements, this grand old man writes by candlelight a letter to his dear friend, Timothy. Paul had no assurance it would ever reach the young man, but, nevertheless, he wrote it . . . and we are so grateful he did! For obvious reasons it is a letter of sharp contrasts—strong and passionate warnings laced with insightful wisdom and firm resolve, yet in other places wearisome feelings, quiet and honest reflections, even a few unguarded admissions of decisions made in years gone by. Here is a letter for the ages written by a rugged and tired warrior; it's an essential piece of Biblical literature we need in order to construct an accurate and complete mental portrait of Paul and a spiritual understanding of our times.

WRITER: *Paul*

DATE: *C.A.D. 66–67 (shortly before Nero's death)*

PURPOSE: *To encourage, warn and charge Timothy regarding God's truth*

KEY VERSES: *1:14; 2:3; 3:14; 4:2*

STYLE: *Encouraging and exhorting*

DISTINCTIVES: *Paul's final words; written from a dungeon in Rome*

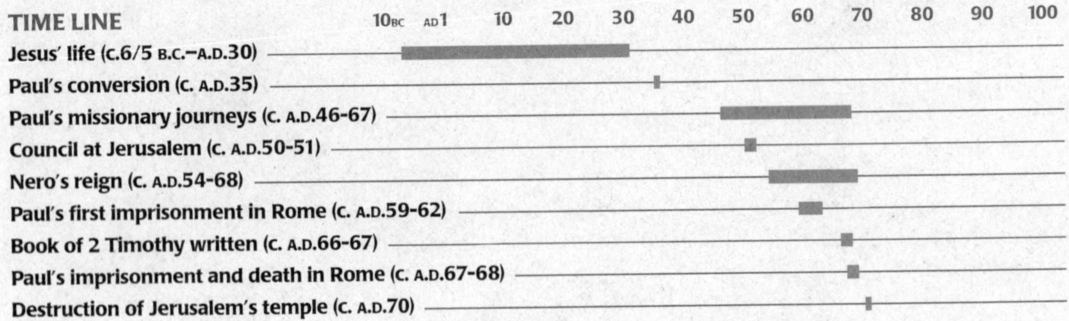

Paul's Swan Song

	GUARD THE TREASURE!	ENDURE THE HARDSHIP!	CONTINUE!	PREACH THE WORD!
	Paul's greeting Timothy's life God's treasure Our responsibility	Passing on the Truth Illustrations of the Truth (Soldier, athlete, farmer, workman, vessel, servant) Suffering for the Truth	Difficult times Evil people Standing firm Biblical basis	A solemn charge Reason for the charge Personal conclusion
	CHAPTER 1	*CHAPTER 2*	*CHAPTER 3*	*CHAPTER 4*
PERSPECTIVE	**The past**	**The present**	**The future**	
TONE	**Gratitude**	**Compassion**	**Warning**	**Command**
KEY VERSE	***"Guard the good deposit that was entrusted to you—guard it with the help of the Holy Spirit who lives in us" (1:14).***	***"Endure hardship with us like a good soldier of Christ Jesus" (2:3).***	***"But as for you, continue in what you have learned and have become convinced of, because you know those from whom you learned it" (3:14).***	***"Preach the Word; be prepared in season and out of season; correct, rebuke and encourage—with great patience and careful instruction" (4:2).***

It is often true that a person's final words are among his or her best words. By then life has been distilled into its most significant thoughts, and wisdom has tempered knowledge. As a result we seem to listen more closely when a person is about to leave this life on earth.

I never turn to 2 Timothy without trying to picture myself as a silent observer in the same dungeon as the writer of the letter—perhaps helping the old man light the candle for the evening or wrapping his cloak around his shoulders to help him stay a little warmer for the night. When I read this letter, I imagine myself, at times, hearing him cough and wheeze and sneeze as well as watching him cry and sigh as he feels the loneliness of being separated from his friends.

One of the best pieces of advice I have ever received about preaching was the suggestion that before I study a particular passage of Scripture I should try to put myself in the shoes of the person who wrote it. "If you're going to teach 1 Corinthians, join the church at Corinth!" Or "Put yourself in a dungeon if you're going to talk about 2 Timothy," was this person's advice. And so I do that, and I invite you to do the same. I think you will find that this second letter to Timothy, though brief, will take on a whole new meaning. When you know that you have received a letter written by a man only days from death, living in a dungeon, the letter carries with it a great deal of impact that perhaps it wouldn't otherwise possess.

From Paul . . . With Love

As in the first letter to Timothy, the man who wrote the letter is named in the very first verse, in the very first word. Paul called himself again simply, "an apostle of Christ Jesus" (1:1). This was Paul's swan song . . . his last will and testament. He was coming to his final end here on earth. By now a man in his mid-60s, Paul had, in his own words, "fought the good fight" and "finished the race" and "kept the faith" (4:7). And rather than simply to die in obscurity and silence, he chose to write a final note to a friend whose name appears in the second verse—"Timothy, my dear son." Timothy was a young man in the stage of life we call "mid-life" who was engaged in an active and perhaps difficult ministry in the city of Ephesus. Paul the aged wanted to pass on to Timothy the younger some words of advice about ministry and about life—ministry in particular and life in general.

Now the place from which Paul wrote is not stated anywhere, so we're left to our own judgment based on clues from the letter. Many reliable scholars believe it was the ancient Mamertine Prison in Rome—a dreadful, dismal underground dungeon. In verse 9 of chapter 2, Paul mentioned suffering hardship "even to the point of being chained like a criminal." He wrote of his need for a cloak (4:13)—undoubtedly to protect against the cold dampness of the dungeon. You and I have never been imprisoned in a dungeon as a criminal—certainly not suffering for our faith, as Paul did. But there he was, so we must vicariously enter into that dreadful and depressing hole in the bowels of ancient Rome. Read slowly verses 9–13 of chapter 4, and you can't help but feel some of his loneliness:

> *Do your best to come to me quickly, for Demas, because he loved this world, has deserted me and has gone to Thessalonica. Crescens has gone to Galatia, and Titus to Dalmatia. Only Luke is with me. Get Mark and bring him with you [Paul is lonely], because he is helpful to me in my ministry. I sent Tychicus to Ephesus. When you come, bring the cloak that I left with Carpus at Troas [he's cold], and my scrolls, especially the parchments.*

As Paul reflected on his profound sense of being abandoned, he remembered a man named Alexander who had done him much harm (4:14). Then Paul brought to mind how he had already endured his first defense—without the support of friends—though the Lord had stood with him (4:16–17). We can't miss the great surge of emotion as he expressed his longing to see Timothy: "Do your best to get here before winter" (4:21).

I really don't think we should pass hurriedly over the feelings woven through a passage like this. I want you to remember a lonely place you have been in your life. Maybe it was a time when you've felt cold and forgotten. Perhaps you saw yourself as removed from the scene, placed on a shelf, alone and useless. Maybe you're there right now. While in that place it's very easy for us to feel completely abandoned, overlooked and isolated. At times like that how desperately we need friends! We have the Lord, but we need friends. The grace of God is magnificent but it does not turn us into Superman or Wonder Woman. God's faithfulness and mercy do not deliver us from our human needs—needs like companionship and intimacy—the need to belong, to love and to be loved. Loneliness is a terrible thing with which to cope.

I can still remember Christmas of 1979 when I visited my father shortly before he died. I remember finishing the visit on Christmas Eve and going back to my car. I leaned over on the steering wheel of the car and sobbed like a baby. I remember feeling terribly alone. It wasn't that I wasn't loved or didn't feel God's presence. It was just that I was in the process of losing someone very important to me. And in the nostalgic feelings of that moment I, for some reason, thought about Paul and that place where he had been. And I admired him a great deal that he (in the horror of all he was feeling, knowing that death was imminent) . . . he would still have the wherewithal to write an urgent letter to a friend and to pass on to him so much of the wisdom of his life.

Passing the Baton

The reasons that lie behind Paul's writing are threefold. First, *Paul wrote to Timothy to equip him for a tough task.* Timothy was to pick up the baton of proclaiming the gospel of Jesus Christ—of guarding it (1:14) and preaching it (4:2). Paul was prepared to hand that baton off in the relay before he died. Timothy was to take it and run with it with all his might during the time he himself had left on earth.

Second, *Paul wrote to Timothy to stir him up, to encourage him—his dear friend and colleague in ministry.* Timothy had three things working against him. He was young. He was prone to sickness. He was passive by nature—timid may be a better word. And so Paul wrote to stir him up and to tell him not to lay back but to develop his gifts and do the job with all the strength he could muster (1:6–7).

Third, *Paul wrote to Timothy to wrap up some final personal matters before Paul's death.* Paul had some needs to communicate to Timothy, and he did so in a powerfully transparent way in his final requests and greetings (4:9–22).

The style of this letter is what I would call "urgent." Paul in effect placed a firm exclamation point after many of his statements. There's a maximum of intense emotion in the letter—expressed through many commands and contrasts that declared, "This is true now but, Timothy, you must . . ."—and then Paul would drive his point home. "And you'll find this going on, Timothy, but you must . . ." The tone is urgent. It's "if you want to survive, do this, and get at it quickly. Time's short."

The structure of the book has an inherent beauty. The key verse in chapter 1 is verse 14: "Guard the good deposit . . ." Everything Paul wrote in chapter 1 had to do with that great mandate. When you get to chapter 2, the key is verse 3: "Endure hardship . . ." Paul was telling Timothy, in effect, to roll up his sleeves and prepare for a battle: "If you think it's bad now, hang on. It will only get worse. Endure. Be tough. Be strong." In chapter 3, the key is verse 14—just one word from that verse: "Continue." Paul's counsel went something like this: "You don't need anything new or clever, quaint or cute, Timothy. You need the same old message kept constantly fresh and robust. Continue in it." In chapter 4 the key is verse 2: "Preach the Word . . ." Guard. Endure. Continue. Preach. That's 2 Timothy in four words. Excellent "marching orders" for any pastor (and for any servant of God)!

Paul's Wisdom . . . for You, for Me

The uniqueness of the letter is obvious: These are Paul's final words—special instructions for the last days, guidelines for God's "shepherds" who need encouragement for the task ahead. In light of that, let me share with you three applications.

First, *being different is not only helpful, it's essential for survival.* You want to count for Jesus Christ? You must be different from those who are willing to coast through life with seemingly no purpose, no mission, no guiding principle. Four times we read some variation of "But you . . ." in this letter. I think people who have a powerful influence on our world are courageously different. They are willing to stand up and be counted. Some of them are mild-mannered and soft-spoken; some are fiery and loud. (I've often said that the reformers of the past were some of the most intense and eccentric people you'd ever want to meet. But my did they get the job done!) Paul reminds us, "Go ahead. You be different. You hear things differently. You view things differently. You stand out from the majority." If you want to survive, you'll need to be daringly different.

Second, *godly models fill a variety of roles.* Read through this letter and you'll find many vivid word pictures—soldiers, athletes, farmers, workmen and servants. As a godly role model you will be called on to fill any number of different roles. Sometimes your involvement will be marked by excruciating loneliness and bone-chilling cold, by paralyzing fear and disabling weariness. But know this: With Christ there is never abandonment. He is with us always. He will never forsake us!

Third and finally, *younger Christians are motivated by older Christians who finish well.* It must have done something to Timothy's spirit to read the words of this grand old man, "I have fought the good fight, I have finished the race, I have kept the faith" (4:7). Most are great at starting the race, but when it comes to finding people who finish the course with great gusto and firm confidence—now that's quite another story. My! Is there anything that motivates the young more than to see those who finish well? Paul finished the race well. The question is, will we?

Guard the Treasure — Chapter 1

In this chapter Paul assured Timothy of his continuing love and prayers and encouraged him to be a faithful servant of the gospel. In response to Timothy's apparent lack of confidence, Paul reminded him of the power, love and self-discipline available in reliance on God (1:6–7) and urged him to overcome shame (1:8). As a faithful communicator of the gospel, Paul was intent on preparing Timothy to carry out his ministry of faithfully preaching and teaching the gospel of grace, and suffering for it as well (1:8). At the heart of Paul's message in chapter 1 was the command to "guard the good deposit that was entrusted to you–guard it with the help of the Holy Spirit who lives in you" (1:14). False teachers in Timothy's day were changing and adding to the message of the gospel of salvation by grace alone. That pure gospel, the great treasure entrusted to us, needed to be carefully and uncompromisingly guarded by Timothy–and by us in our day.

1 Paul, an apostle of Christ Jesus by the will of God, according to the promise of life that is in Christ Jesus, 2Co 1:1

2 To Timothy, my dear son: Ac 16:1; 1Ti 1:2

Grace, mercy and peace from God the Father and Christ Jesus our Lord. Ro 1:7

Encouragement to Be Faithful

3 I thank God, whom I serve, as my forefathers did, with a clear conscience, as night and day I constantly remember you in my prayers. 4 Recalling your tears, I long to see you, so that I may be filled with joy. 5 I have been reminded of your sincere faith, which first lived in your grandmother Lois and in your mother Eunice and, I am persuaded, now lives in you also. 6 For this reason I

LIVING  INSIGHT

If you were blessed with a good mother, you will reap the benefits the rest of your days. A mother's mark is permanent.

(See 2 Timothy 1:5.)

remind you to fan into flame the gift of God, which is in you through the laying on of my hands. 7 For God did not give us a spirit of timidity, but a spirit of power, of love and of self-discipline.

8 So do not be ashamed to testify about our Lord, or ashamed of me his prisoner. But join with me in suffering for the gospel, by the power of God, 9 who has saved us and called us to a holy life—not because of anything we have done but because of his own purpose and grace. This grace was given us in Christ Jesus before the beginning of time, 10 but it has now been revealed through the appearing of our Savior, Christ Jesus, who has destroyed death and has brought life and immortality to light through the gospel. 11 And of this gospel I was appointed a herald and an apostle and a teacher. 12 That is why I am suffering as I am. Yet I am not ashamed, because I know whom I have believed, and am convinced that he is able to guard what I have entrusted to him for that day.

13 What you heard from me, keep as the pattern of sound teaching, with faith and love in Christ Jesus. 14 Guard the good deposit that was entrusted to you—guard it with the help of the Holy Spirit who lives in us. 1Ti 1:14; Tit 1:9

15 You know that everyone in the province of Asia has deserted me, including Phygelus and Hermogenes. 2Ti 4:10-11,16

16 May the Lord show mercy to the household of Onesiphorus, because he often refreshed me and was not ashamed of my chains. 17 On the contrary, when he was in Rome, he searched hard for me until he found me. 18 May the Lord grant that he will find mercy from the Lord on that day! You know very well in how many ways he helped me in Ephesus. 2Ti 4:19; Heb 6:10

Endure Hardship — Chapter 2

In chapter 2 Paul sounded a clarion call for endurance in the face of suffering for the gospel. Paul wanted Timothy to be prepared for what might confront him as he led the church and opposed the false teachers–so he gave him three examples to follow (2:3–7). In the face of a spiritual battle for the gospel, Timothy would need to stand firm, hold to the faith and stay focused on the task to which he had been called. Through a spirit of gentleness and a commitment to "righteousness, faith, love and peace" (2:22), Timothy would be speaking a powerful message of the truth of the gospel to those who opposed him. Truly he would be a worker approved by God (2:15).

2 You then, my son, be strong in the grace that is in Christ Jesus. 2 And the things you have heard me say in the presence of many witnesses entrust to reliable men who will also be qualified to teach others. 3 Endure hardship with us like a good soldier of Christ Jesus. 4 No one serving as a soldier gets involved in civilian affairs—he wants to please his commanding officer. 5 Similarly, if anyone competes as an athlete, he does not receive the victor's crown unless he competes according to the rules. 6 The hardworking farmer should be the first to receive a share of the crops. 7 Reflect on what I am saying, for the Lord will give you insight into all this. 1Co 9:25; 1Ti 1:18

8 Remember Jesus Christ, raised from the dead, descended from David. This is my gospel, 9 for which I am suffering even to the point of being chained like a criminal. But God's word is not chained. 10 Therefore I endure everything for the sake of the elect, that they too may obtain the

salvation that is in Christ Jesus, with eternal glory.
[11]Here is a trustworthy saying: 1Ti 1:15

If we died with him,
we will also live with him; Ro 6:2-11
[12]if we endure,
we will also reign with him. Ro 8:17; 1Pe 4:13
If we disown him,
he will also disown us; Mt 10:33
[13]if we are faithless,
he will remain faithful, Nu 23:19; Ro 3:3
for he cannot disown himself.

A Workman Approved by God

[14]Keep reminding them of these things. Warn
them before God against quarreling about words;
it is of no value, and only ruins those who listen.
[15]Do your best to present yourself to God as one
approved, a workman who does not need to be
ashamed and who correctly handles the word of
truth. [16]Avoid godless chatter, because those who
indulge in it will become more and more ungodly.
[17]Their teaching will spread like gangrene. Among
them are Hymenaeus and Philetus, [18]who have
wandered away from the truth. They say that the
resurrection has already taken place, and they destroy the faith of some. [19]Nevertheless, God's solid
foundation stands firm, sealed with this inscription: "The Lord knows those who are his,"[a] and,
"Everyone who confesses the name of the Lord
must turn away from wickedness." Jn 10:14; 1Co 1:2
[20]In a large house there are articles not only of
gold and silver, but also of wood and clay; some
are for noble purposes and some for ignoble. [21]If
a man cleanses himself from the latter, he will be
an instrument for noble purposes, made holy, useful to the Master and prepared to do any good
work. Ro 9:21; 2Ti 3:17
[22]Flee the evil desires of youth, and pursue righteousness, faith, love and peace, along with those
who call on the Lord out of a pure heart. [23]Don't
have anything to do with foolish and stupid arguments, because you know they produce quarrels.
[24]And the Lord's servant must not quarrel; instead,
he must be kind to everyone, able to teach, not
resentful. [25]Those who oppose him he must gently
instruct, in the hope that God will grant them
repentance leading them to a knowledge of the
truth, [26]and that they will come to their senses and
escape from the trap of the devil, who has taken
them captive to do his will. 1Ti 1:5; 3:7

LIVING  **INSIGHT**

Our problem is not a lack of Bibles; it is a lack of people who carefully handle the Word of God, both privately and publicly. We should not simply be students of the Scriptures—sound in our theology—but we must also be careful in our interpretation of the Scriptures. And the more we teach, the greater the need for care.

(See 2 Timothy 2:15.)

Continue **Chapter 3**

Paul summarized for Timothy the times in which he lived and gave him instructions on how to combat those terrible times. How familiar the words are to us today! After a depressing litany of the depths to which people can sink (3:2–5), Paul gave Timothy good advice that pertains to us as well: "Have nothing to do with them" (3:5). Avoid them! While we might like to think that it's better to hang around with the unfaithful, the dangers are clear. All too often it isn't the godless who get better—it's we who get worse! Think of it this way. If I put on a white pair of gloves and play out in the mud on a rainy afternoon, the mud never gets "glovey." It's amazing! The gloves get muddy every time. The way to stay strong in perilous times? "Continue in what you have learned" (3:14). In reliance on the infallible and authoritative Word of God (3:14–17), Timothy was equipped—and so are we—to persevere through whatever might come in the days ahead.

Godlessness in the Last Days

3 But mark this: There will be terrible times in
the last days. [2]People will be lovers of themselves, lovers of money, boastful, proud, abusive,
disobedient to their parents, ungrateful, unholy,
[3]without love, unforgiving, slanderous, without
self-control, brutal, not lovers of the good,
[4]treacherous, rash, conceited, lovers of pleasure
rather than lovers of God— [5]having a form of
godliness but denying its power. Have nothing to
do with them. Ro 1:30; 1Ti 4:1
[6]They are the kind who worm their way into
homes and gain control over weak-willed women,
who are loaded down with sins and are swayed by
all kinds of evil desires, [7]always learning but never
able to acknowledge the truth. [8]Just as Jannes and
Jambres opposed Moses, so also these men oppose
the truth—men of depraved minds, who, as far as
the faith is concerned, are rejected. [9]But they will
not get very far because, as in the case of those
men, their folly will be clear to everyone. Ex 7:12

Paul's Charge to Timothy

[10]You, however, know all about my teaching,
my way of life, my purpose, faith, patience, love,
endurance, [11]persecutions, sufferings—what
kinds of things happened to me in Antioch, Iconium and Lystra, the persecutions I endured. Yet the

[a]*19* Num. 16:5 (see Septuagint)

GOD'S BOOK — GOD'S VOICE

"All Scripture is God-breathed and is useful for teaching, rebuking, correcting and training in righteousness, so that the man of God may be thoroughly equipped for every good work."

—2 TIMOTHY 3:16–17

What is your final authority in life? I mean, when you're cornered, when you're really up against it, when you're forced to face reality, upon what do you lean?

Before you answer too quickly, think about it for a few moments. When it comes to establishing a standard for morality, what's your guide? When you need an ethical compass to find your way out of an ethical jungle, where's north? When you're on a stormy, churning sea of emotions, which lighthouse shows you where to find the shore?

Common Crutches

It has been my observation through the years that people usually respond in one of four ways when faced with a crisis. I think of these responses as common crutches on which people lean. The first I would call, for lack of a better title, *escapism*. Most people, at least initially, escape the reality of the pain. They deny it. They run. They refuse to let reality run its course in their lives.

Second, many people turn to *cynicism*. They not only look their troubles square in the face, they become preoccupied with them. And they grow dark within. The sense of surprise at what is happening to them leads to disillusionment, which can, in turn, fester and become open wounds of resentment and finally bitterness and cynicism.

Third, there is the crutch of *humanism*. Those committed to humanism listen to the counsel of some other person rather than to God. They get their logic and their reasoning from a man or a woman or a book. They turn to self-help, other people's opinions or the panacea of self-realization. And in the end they are left empty and unfulfilled.

Fourth is the crutch of *spiritualism*. This may be mild or maddening. Some people turn to mediums. They seek information from the spirit world. A growing number of people today connect with the occult as they try to seek relief from the pain that plagues their lives.

Popular though these four crutches may be, not a one of them provides any sense of ultimate relief or genuine satisfaction. They leave the person in quicksand—more desperately confused than at the beginning of their search for satisfaction. None of the above is an acceptable "final" authority.

So I return to the question: What is your final authority in life? What holds you together when all hell breaks loose around you? There can be no more reliable authority on earth than God's Word, the Bible. This timeless, trustworthy source of truth holds the key that unlocks life's mysteries. It alone provides us with the shelter we need in times of storm.

Why the Foundation Is So Dependable

We need to understand why. Why does this Book qualify as our final authority? First, I think it will help us to know something about the *identity* of the Bible. By the way, the word *Bible* is never once found in Scripture. So what does the Bible call itself? What is its identity? Look at chapter 24 of the Gospel of Luke. Jesus is speaking with two men on the road to Emmaus. In verse 27 we read of the outcome of that historic walk together: "And beginning with Moses and all the Prophets, he explained to them what was said in all the Scriptures concerning himself."

Jesus verbally worked His way through the Old Testament, called here "the Scriptures." Notice the question the two men asked each other a few verses later: "Were not our hearts burning within us while he talked with us on the road and opened the Scriptures to us?" The reference again is to "the Scriptures."

Very interesting term, "the Scriptures." It is a translation of the Greek word *graphe*, meaning "that which is written." In other words, the Scriptures are the sacred writings. When we rely on the Bible, we rely on that which has been *written*. I linger here because I think it's significant that God didn't simply *think* His message. He didn't simply *speak* His message or reveal it in the clouds or communicate it through dreams to men and women in Biblical times. No, He saw to it that His Word was actually written down. He put it in the language of the people, so that people in all generations could read it and grasp its significance and be transformed by it. He "graphed" His Word. We're grateful we have a book that contains the very mind of our God—the Scriptures—in written form.

God's Word Is Truth

The Gospel of John contains an entire chapter that preserves for us a prayer—the longest recorded prayer of Jesus in all the Bible. While praying for His disciples Jesus said these words to the Father:

> *I have given them your word and the world has hated them, for they are not of the world any more than I am of the world. My prayer is not that you take them out of the world but that you protect them from the evil one. They are not of the world, even as I am not of it. Sanctify them by the truth; your word is truth (John 17:14–17).*

I am so grateful those verses are in the Bible. Look again at that closing comment. What an unequivocal statement from the lips of Jesus! "Your word is truth." In four monosyllabic words we find the basis for our belief in the veracity, the complete reliability, of Scripture. This is not human counsel within the pages of this Book; it is truth—it is divine counsel. It is honest. It has integrity. It is as absolute as it is timeless.

How delightful it is to make that confession before the Lord and His people: "Your Word, O God, is truth." Truth, real truth, truth you can rely on, truth that will never shrivel up or turn sour, truth that will never backfire or mislead, that's the truth in this Book. That is what this Book is about. That is why this Book provides us with *the* constant and *the* needed support.

By the way, do *you* turn to it for the truth you need? The longer I live the more I realize that most people on this earth have an amazing ability to twist truth . . . to change things so that right isn't really right; it's only partially right. And wrong isn't really wrong; it's just sort of unfortunate . . . somewhere between okay and I'm not really sure. I'm left to choose the direction I want to go. And no one is going to lay any guilt trip on me, because nobody else knows where the boundaries are. And therefore I am left not free—definitely not free—but quasi-paralyzed between bewilderment and confusion. That, my friend, is bondage!

What does it take to set us free from the aimlessness of subjectivity and the tangle of a multitude of opinions? It takes truth. Yes, *the truth*. It was Jesus Himself who once promised, "You will know the truth, and the truth will set you free" (John 8:32). In the context of human knowledge, many things are true; yet there is only one truth that will set people free: the truth of Jesus Christ found in God's Word. I've been exposed to just enough human intelligence to see the danger in it! I've gotten just enough of human wisdom not to trust in it. I don't need more of those things in my life. I need truth. I need God's "yes" and God's "no," God's light and God's mind. That explains why I appreciate the Scriptures so much. His Word provides the truth I need. It erases the doubts; it gives a sure footing even though I am surrounded by people swimming in a swamp of uncertainty.

God's Book Is God's Voice

Scripture is "God's message." It is, in fact, "God's Word." The apostle Paul testified clearly to that truth in his first letter to the Thessalonians:

> *And we also thank God continually because, when you received the word of God, which you heard from us, you accepted it not as the word of men, but as it actually is, the word of God, which is at work in you who believe (1 Thessalonians 2:13).*

Think of it this way: God's Book is, as it were, God's voice. If our Lord were to make Himself visible and return to earth and speak His message, it would be in keeping with this Book. His message of truth would tie in exactly with what you see in Scripture, in this Book you hold in your hands. His opinion, His counsel, His commands, His desires, His warnings, His very heart, His very mind. When you rely on God's voice, His very message, you have a sure foundation; you have truth that can be trusted; you have power that imparts new life and releases grace by which you can grow in faith and commitment.

God's Word Will Endure

One more thought regarding the identity of the Bible—and it leads us to consider some practical implications about how we view our lives. Referring to the same writings, the same truth, the same message of God, the apostle Peter wrote these words in his first letter (1 Peter 1:22–25):

> *Now that you have purified yourselves by obeying the truth so that you have sincere love for your brothers, love one another deeply, from the heart. For you have been born again, not of perishable seed, but of imperishable, through the living and enduring word of God. For,*
>
> *All men are like grass,*
> *and all their glory is like the flowers of the field;*
> *the grass withers and the flowers fall*
> *but the word of the Lord stands forever.*

Do you realize there are only two eternal things on earth today? Only two: people and God's Word. Everything else will ultimately be burned up—everything else. Kind of sets your priorities straight, doesn't it? The stuff we place on the shelf, the things we put frames around, the trophies and whatnots we shine and love to show off, the things we're so proud of—it's all headed for the final bonfire (see 2 Peter 3:7,10–12). But not God's Book! Peter reminds us that the truth "stands forever." Grass will grow and then it will wither; flowers will bloom and then they will die. But God's written message, the truth, will abide forever. All His promises will be fulfilled; His redemptive truth cannot be annulled or changed; His powerful Word will accomplish what He desires and achieve the purpose for which He sent it (see Isaiah 55:10–11). His Word will endure!

God's Word Is Inspired

But wait. Doesn't all this talk about the Bible lead to an important question that must be asked? The question goes like this: How can anyone get so excited about something that was written by men? We have no problem with the Giver of truth. He gave it . . . but wasn't the truth corrupted when He relayed it to earth through the hands and minds of sinful men?

This is the perfect moment for you to become acquainted with three doctrinal terms: revelation, inspiration and illumination. *Revelation* occurred when God gave His truth. *Inspiration* occurred when the writers of Scripture received and recorded His truth. Today, when we understand and apply His truth, that's *illumination.* The instrument of illumination would include discovering truth, understanding it and implementing it in our lives. Revelation has ceased. Inspiration has ceased. But illumination is going on right up to this very moment!

The critical point of your confidence in the Bible is directly related to your confidence in its inspiration. How then can we be sure that God's Word is free from error, absolutely true, and therefore deserving of our complete trust? In Paul's second letter to Timothy, he provides great help in answering this question:

> *But as for you, continue in what you have learned and have become convinced of, because you know those from whom you learned it, and how from infancy you have known the holy Scriptures, which are able to make you wise for salvation through faith in Christ Jesus. All Scripture is God-breathed and is useful for teaching, rebuking, correcting and training in righteousness, so that the man of God may be thoroughly equipped for every good work (2 Timothy 3:14–16).*

Having written these words, Paul verified his confidence in inspiration, telling Timothy, in effect, "Timothy, all *graphe*, all the writings of God, all Scripture, is God-breathed." When God revealed His truth for human writers to record, He "breathed out" His Word. Scripture is inspired because it has been miraculously "God-breathed." Not inspired like a sculpture by Michelangelo, not inspired like a great composition by Handel or Brahms, not inspired like a great sonnet by Shakespeare, but inspired as in "God-*breathed*."

Now, wait a minute. That still doesn't fully answer your question, does it? When we want to send a letter to someone, we may breathe out a message to someone, who then types what we have said—a process we call "taking dictation." Did the writers of Scripture take dictation?

If you know much about the Bible, you realize that it has been written by many different people with many different personalities. Peter doesn't sound a lot like John. And John doesn't sound like David. And Paul is altogether distinct from Peter or, for that matter, any of the other apostles. So somehow there was the preservation of each writer's personality without corrupting the text with human weakness and error. That rules out the idea of dictation. So we have a Bible full of human personality and style, and yet it is God who breathed out His message.

Then how did God produce this library of living truth that "stands forever"? How did He cause it to happen? Look at what the apostle Peter wrote in 2 Peter 1:20–21:

> *And we have the word of the prophets made more certain, and you will do well to pay attention to it, as to a light shining in a dark place, until the day dawns and the morning star rises in your hearts. Above all, you must understand that no prophecy of Scripture came about by the prophet's own interpretation. For prophecy never had its origin in the will of man, but men spoke from God as they were carried along by the Holy Spirit.*

Paul didn't sit down one day and think, "Let's see, I think I'll write 2 Corinthians." Or, "I feel like Galatians. I'll write Galatians today." No prophecy ever came to pass because of the impulse or the inner urging of the will of humans. No, in contrast to that, the key phrase in verse 21 of chapter 1 of Peter's second letter is "carried along"—"men spoke from God as they were carried along by the Holy Spirit."

This English phrase "carried along" is translated from an ancient Greek nautical term (*phero*). In extrabiblical literature it was used to describe ships at sea. When a ship was at the mercy of the winds and the waves and the currents of the sea, it was "carried along" apart from its own power. It remained a ship, but it was without its own power and energy. That's the word used here . . . not referring to ships at sea but to writers of Scripture. They raised, as it were, their sails, and the Holy Spirit filled them and carried their craft along in the direction He desired. They were "carried along" as they wrote God's abiding truth.

God's Word Will Hold You Up

So our conclusion is this: In the Bible we have the preservation of a completely dependable, authoritative, inspired text. God breathed out His message to human writers who, without losing their own style and personality, wrote His truth under His divine control. And because He superintended the process in its entirety, no error was present in the very words of the original text. What Scripture says, God says—through human agents, without error, absolutely true and utterly dependable.

The question each of us must ask ourselves is this: Can I rely on it? Is it reliable when I go through those chaotic experiences in life? My answer, and I pray it is your answer, is this: absolutely and unreservedly! And you know, the wonderful thing about relying on God's Book is that it gives you stability. It gives you that deep sense of purpose and meaning, even when you get the phone call in the middle of the night that informs you of calamity, even when your mate says, "It's over." No other counsel will get you through the long haul. No other truth will help you to stand firm in the storms of doubt and uncertainty. No other reality will give you strength for each day and deep hope for tomorrow. No other instruction has the power to give new meaning to your life.

How do I conclude an article as full as this one? Perhaps with this one thought. *The Word of God is the simple truth that holds us together in the most complex of situations.* Not simplistic, but simple. The Bible contains simple, yet incredibly profound truth that is like a warm blanket wrapped around us on a cold night. Return to this taproot of truth. Dig into it. Lean on it. Start today. It will hold you up and keep you strong. When it comes to a "final authority" in life, the Bible measures up—like nothing else!

Lord rescued me from all of them. 12In fact, everyone who wants to live a godly life in Christ Jesus will be persecuted, 13while evil men and impostors will go from bad to worse, deceiving and being deceived. 14But as for you, continue in what you have learned and have become convinced of, because you know those from whom you learned it,

LIVING  **INSIGHT**

In a world where we're encouraged to do it "if it feels good," the Bible addresses that which is holy and that which is sinful. Scripture never leaves us with a bewildered look on our faces, wondering about the issues of life. It says, "This is the way it is. That is the way it is not to be. This is the way to walk; do not walk there." It tells us straight. It provides the kind of solid foundation you and I need.

(See 2 Timothy 3:14–16.)

15and how from infancy you have known the holy Scriptures, which are able to make you wise for salvation through faith in Christ Jesus. 16All Scripture is God-breathed and is useful for teaching, rebuking, correcting and training in righteousness, 17so that the man of God may be thoroughly equipped for every good work. 2Pe 1:20-21

Preach the Word **Chapter 4**

Here it is—the final chapter of all Paul's writings, his enduring epitaph. He left Timothy a charge of the utmost importance: "Preach the Word" (4:2). In effect, Paul told Timothy, "Be ready—when you feel like it and when you don't; when it's winter and when it's summer; when it's early and when it's late; when you're tired and when you're refreshed. Be persistent. Don't give up. You'll face opposition, but stay focused on the task to which you've been called." Chapter 4 also records Paul's glorious declaration of a life well lived and a reward much anticipated (4:6–8), as well as powerfully moving personal remarks and final greetings (4:9–22).

4 In the presence of God and of Christ Jesus, who will judge the living and the dead, and in view of his appearing and his kingdom, I give you this charge: 2Preach the Word; be prepared in season and out of season; correct, rebuke and encourage—with great patience and careful instruction. 3For the time will come when men will not put up with sound doctrine. Instead, to suit their own desires, they will gather around them a great number of teachers to say what their itching ears want to hear. 4They will turn their ears away from the truth and turn aside to myths. 5But you, keep your head in all situations, endure hardship, do the work of an evangelist, discharge all the duties of your ministry. Ac 21:8; 1Ti 1:10

6For I am already being poured out like a drink offering, and the time has come for my departure. 7I have fought the good fight, I have finished the race, I have kept the faith. 8Now there is in store for me the crown of righteousness, which the Lord, the righteous Judge, will award to me on that day—and not only to me, but also to all who have longed for his appearing. 1Ti 1:18; 2Ti 1:12

Personal Remarks

9Do your best to come to me quickly, 10for Demas, because he loved this world, has deserted me and has gone to Thessalonica. Crescens has gone to Galatia, and Titus to Dalmatia. 11Only Luke is with me. Get Mark and bring him with you, because he is helpful to me in my ministry. 12I sent Tychicus to Ephesus. 13When you come, bring the cloak that I left with Carpus at Troas, and my scrolls, especially the parchments. Col 4:14; 2Ti 1:15

14Alexander the metalworker did me a great deal of harm. The Lord will repay him for what he has done. 15You too should be on your guard against him, because he strongly opposed our message. Ac 19:33; Ro 12:19

16At my first defense, no one came to my support, but everyone deserted me. May it not be held against them. 17But the Lord stood at my side and gave me strength, so that through me the message might be fully proclaimed and all the Gentiles might hear it. And I was delivered from the lion's mouth. 18The Lord will rescue me from every evil attack and will bring me safely to his heavenly kingdom. To him be glory for ever and ever. Amen. Ps 121:7; Ro 11:36

Final Greetings

19Greet Priscilla[a] and Aquila and the household of Onesiphorus. 20Erastus stayed in Corinth, and I left Trophimus sick in Miletus. 21Do your best to get here before winter. Eubulus greets you, and so do Pudens, Linus, Claudia and all the brothers. Ac 19:22; 20:4

22The Lord be with your spirit. Grace be with you. Gal 6:18; Col 4:18

[a] 19 Greek *Prisca*, a variant of *Priscilla*

Introduction

TITUS

Several books in the Bible don't get the publicity they deserve. Paul's letter to Titus is a good example. Overshadowed by the more popular letters of 1 and 2 Timothy, this "pastoral letter" seems obscure and even unimportant to some. What a shame! Equally essential and inspired by God, the letter to Titus brings needed balance to the subject of the pastoral care of churches. Paul's first letter to Timothy emphasizes doctrine; his second letter to Timothy provides a strong emotional appeal. And Paul's letter to Titus brings a word of caution, a reminder that good deeds are to accompany our proclamation of truth and our defense of the gospel. The two letters to Timothy tell God's servant to protect and to preach the gospel, while the letter to Titus tells God's servant to put into practice the gospel. While good deeds in no way earn salvation, they are the irrefutable evidence of genuine salvation. God's full-time servants in ministry need that reminder as much as anyone else does.

WRITER: *Titus*

DATE: *c.a.d. 63–65*

PURPOSE: *To give Titus guidance in facing opposition, instructions about good conduct and warnings about false teachers*

KEY THEMES: *God our Savior; soundness of doctrine and faith; "doing what is good"*

KEY VERSES: *2:10b; 3:8*

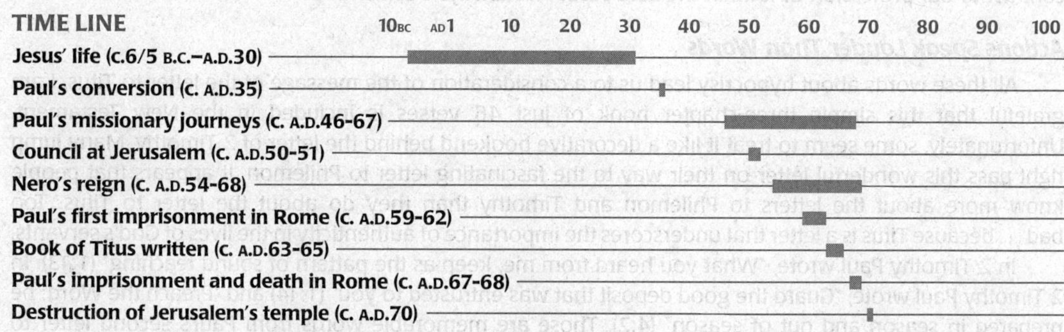

Practicing What You Preach

INTRODUCTION *(1:1-4)*

	TAKING CHARGE	GIVING ADVICE	DOING RIGHT
	Elders Rebellious people	Older men and women Young women and men Pastors Slaves and masters	The positives The negatives
	CHAPTER 1	*CHAPTER* 2	*CHAPTER* 3
PEOPLE	**Elders Enemies**	**Specific groups**	**Christians in general**
ISSUE	**Setting up the right leadership**	**Instruction for particular people**	**Attitude and conduct toward good and bad**
A CHURCH	**. . . in good order *(1:5)***	**. . . with good doctrine *(2:1)***	**. . . of good deeds *(3:1)***

CONCLUSION *(3:12-15)*

I believe it is safe to conclude that people who encounter believers in Jesus want to know if their faith is genuine. They want to know if the Christian they work next to is for real—if her commitment to Jesus keeps her from stealing from the company, if his faith keeps him from cheating on his income tax, if they conduct their business with integrity. Let's face it, people today often say they reject belief in Jesus Christ because they see so much hypocrisy in those who profess to be Christians but don't live like it. They may hear a Christian profess one thing, but practice another. Of all the things they may be interested in knowing, essentially they want to see if we are for real, if we're authentic, if the faith we profess really makes a difference in the way we live.

In the late H.A. Ironside's commentary on Paul's letter to Titus, Ironside wrote, "Never was there a time when the necessity of practical piety was so marked as in the days in which our lot is cast. Loose doctrine makes for loose living. On the other hand, it is quite possible for someone to contend earnestly for fundamental principles when his or her life is anything but consistent with the profession." Interestingly, but not surprisingly, hypocrisy is nothing new. The temptation for our attitudes and our behaviors to be in direct contrast to our profession of faith in the Lord Jesus has always been with us.

Actions Speak Louder Than Words

All these words about hypocrisy lead us to a consideration of the message of the letter to Titus. I am grateful that this simple three-chapter book of just 46 verses is included in the New Testament. Unfortunately, some seem to treat it like a decorative bookend behind the letter of 2 Timothy. Many jump right pass this wonderful letter on their way to the fascinating letter to Philemon. It appears that people know more about the letters to Philemon and Timothy than they do about the letter to Titus. Too bad . . . because Titus is a letter that underscores the importance of authenticity in the lives of God's servants.

In 2 Timothy Paul wrote, "What you heard from me, keep as the pattern of sound teaching" (1:13). In 2 Timothy Paul wrote, "Guard the good deposit that was entrusted to you" (1:14) and "Preach the Word; be prepared in season and out of season" (4:2). Those are memorable words from Paul's second letter to

Timothy, words etched in our minds and hearts. The seminary where I received my training chose its motto from 2 Timothy: "Preach the Word." Those words appear, in Greek, on Dallas Seminary's official seal.

Right on the heels of the letters to Timothy comes Titus—an often-forgotten little letter. However, all of the solid doctrine, strong exhortation and high emotion of the letters to Timothy really have nothing to offer if lives are not affected as a result, if attitudes and behaviors aren't changed. That's where the letter to Titus fits in. The net effect of Paul's message to Titus was this: "I dare you to preach powerfully and not live it out. I dare you to talk about the doctrine of godliness and not come to terms with the way it applies in your life. Your deeds will either deny or display the doctrine you preach and claim to believe." The letter to Titus taught, "Pay as much attention to your behavior as you do to your belief." I think Paul was implying that if you're not living your faith, then just be quiet and work on getting your act together—and until then, don't talk so much.

A Man of Strength and Character

This letter bears the name of the man who received it: "Titus, my true son in our common faith" (1:4). Titus was a Greek who had been converted through Paul's ministry and became his close friend. He was also one of the men with whom Paul traveled on difficult journeys. Paul took Titus with him, for example, to talk with Peter about Peter's insincerity and hypocrisy in relating to Jews and Gentiles (Galatians 2:1–16). With Titus at his side, Paul reproved Peter for playing one hand against another—living like a Jew and then when Gentiles were present, living like a Gentile. Titus got to witness that confrontation between Peter and Paul firsthand.

Titus was a gifted man who apparently had strength of character and great resourcefulness—someone with enough integrity to have served first in the church in Corinth (2 Corinthians 8:6) and then to be left on an island (Crete) to help a congregation rife with troubles become grounded in the truth of God: "The reason I left you in Crete was that you might straighten out what was left unfinished and appoint elders in every town, as I directed you" (1:5).

Paradise Island?

Titus's ministry took place on an island in the Mediterranean—but it was no "paradise island." Life on this island was rough. In fact, the behavior of its inhabitants was renowned for its coarseness and rowdiness. The dishonesty, gluttony and laziness of its people were proverbial (1:12). This was one difficult assignment given to one very gifted church leader!

The church on the island of Crete was facing the challenge of staying true to the gospel in a chaotic environment. So when Paul wrote to Titus, he offered him personal instructions to help him lead this group of believers on Crete. You can understand Titus's potential for loneliness and discouragement. And you can understand his need for advice. Paul was quick to offer both encouragement and counsel to Titus.

Putting the Pieces Back Together

Titus needed help in knowing how to deal with diverse groups in the church (chapter 2), as well as with false teachers who were sowing seeds of discord and undermining the pure gospel (chapters 1 and 3). Not surprisingly, Paul gave Titus advice on how to deal with the problems presented by each group.

Verse 5 of chapter 1 is in many ways the kernel of the whole message of the letter to Titus: "The reason I left you in Crete was that you might straighten out what was left unfinished." Pause and meditate on those words.

Titus was left on Crete to pick up the pieces of a church that was splintering and to begin to mend it, to "straighten out" some things that may have been left undone in the early stages of the church's existence—and he was going to do it in a place where not many would applaud or support his efforts. Titus had the fortitude to slug it out, alone—a rare man indeed.

The Greek term translated "straighten out" suggests "to set straight thoroughly in addition to what has already been corrected." Titus and Paul started the church on Crete, having put the foundation in place, and Titus remained there to provide the needed leadership. With extremely poor examples of moral living surrounding the believers and an environment of disunity and disharmony within the church, Titus's task was to begin bringing in the structures and the guidelines for living that the believers there so sorely needed.

This is not a complicated letter. Using a very straightforward style, Paul quickly sized up the situation on Crete and told Titus what he would prescribe. It is a letter that encouraged Titus to mix good teaching with good living. Paul advised Titus, in effect, "Blend both the words and the actions, Titus. Model the gospel in your life. You be the healing agent. If you can't find strong character qualities around you, it's your responsibility to model them before others, to show others how to walk the talk."

Lessons From Titus

I glean three significant lessons from the letter to Titus, one from each chapter. The first is found in verse 16 of chapter 1; Paul had the false teachers in mind as he leveled this charge against them:

> *They claim to know God, but by their actions they deny him. They are detestable, disobedient and unfit for doing anything good.*

The first lesson is this: *Deeds either defend or deny our doctrine*. Let someone live with you long enough, and that person will know what you *really* believe. Our lives are our doctrine on display.

The second lesson, found in verses 11 and 12 of chapter 2, applies Paul's theological teachings to real-life problems. Right behavior must be founded on right doctrine. Look at what Paul wrote:

> *For the grace of God that brings salvation has appeared to all men. It teaches us to say "No" to ungodliness and worldly passions, and to live self-controlled, upright and godly lives in this present age.*

The second lesson is this: *Grace elevates godliness; it doesn't cheapen it*. True godliness is a product of God's marvelous grace. Godliness could not be possible without grace. When we walk in grace, we grow in godliness—true godliness, authentic godliness.

The third lesson is found in what I believe to be the key verse of Paul's letter to Titus. Read the trustworthy saying that precedes this verse (3:4–7) and then ponder these words:

> *This is a trustworthy saying. And I want you to stress these things, so that those who have trusted in God may be careful to devote themselves to doing what is good. These things are excellent and profitable for everyone (3:8).*

The message is clear: *God's kindness toward us and His love for us changes the way we act*. We have been given salvation, not because of anything we have done (3:5), and out of gratitude we respond to God by "doing what is good" (3:8). The authenticity of our trust in God will come to expression in our behavior. The greatest indicator of a person's faith is to watch a person's life. How easy it is to talk big but turn soft when it's decision time. We need to do what is good, excellent and profitable for the kingdom of God, for when we live that kind of life we show that our belief is more than just theoretical theology—it is life-transforming faith!

Daily Tests of Faith

I love the story of the British pastor who had spoken powerfully to a large Sunday morning congregation about honesty. He preached his heart out, and the audience had been touched deeply by his passion. The next morning he caught the trolley to return to his study at the urban church. The driver collected his fare—and gave him too much change in return. He walked back and sat down. As he fingered the shillings in his hand, he first thought, "My, how wonderfully God provides, and in such surprising ways!" But the longer he sat, the hotter the coins became in his hand and the less he could live with himself.

When he came to his stop he walked up to the front and gave the excess change back to the driver and said, "You accidentally gave me too much change." And the driver said, "Oh no, it wasn't an accident. You see, Reverend, I was in your congregation yesterday morning when you spoke on honesty, and I thought I'd put you to the test and see if you practice what you preach."

Not all checkpoints are that overt, but they usually occur when we least expect them. How do we score on the tests we face each day? The marks we get on these tests are even more important than the ones we get on our knowledge of doctrine. Our belief and our behavior must go hand in hand. The latter gives credence to the former.

Taking Charge Chapter 1

In this chapter Paul challenged Titus to take charge of the troubled situation in the church on Crete. This exhortation had both a positive and a negative side. On the positive side, Titus was to appoint elders in every city, as directed by Paul. There was a need for leadership in the church, and Titus had the critical job of finding godly leaders who met the qualifications Paul gave in verses 6–9 of this chapter. On the negative side, Titus learned that every church needs strong, godly leaders to oppose those who teach a false gospel and contradict the truth. Paul advised Titus to deal with the rebels and not to let them gain control in the church. Taking charge in the church entailed developing strong leaders as well as dealing with those who would undermine the cause of Christ.

1 Paul, a servant of God and an apostle of Jesus
Christ for the faith of God's elect and the
knowledge of the truth that leads to godliness— 2a
faith and knowledge resting on the hope of eternal
life, which God, who does not lie, promised before
the beginning of time, 3and at his appointed season he brought his word to light through the
preaching entrusted to me by the command of
God our Savior, 2Ti 1:1,10

4To Titus, my true son in our common faith:

Grace and peace from God the Father and
Christ Jesus our Savior. Ro 1:7

Living  **Insight**

Allow the full impact of grace to flow through your thoughts, your attitudes, your responses, your words. Open the gates and let those good things stampede freely across your tough day. You stand alongside and relax.

(See Titus 1:4.)

Titus' Task on Crete

5The reason I left you in Crete was that you
might straighten out what was left unfinished and
appoint[a] elders in every town, as I directed you.
6An elder must be blameless, the husband of but
one wife, a man whose children believe and are not
open to the charge of being wild and disobedient.
7Since an overseer[b] is entrusted with God's work,
he must be blameless—not overbearing, not
quick-tempered, not given to drunkenness, not
violent, not pursuing dishonest gain. 8Rather he
must be hospitable, one who loves what is good,
who is self-controlled, upright, holy and disciplined. 9He must hold firmly to the trustworthy
message as it has been taught, so that he can encourage others by sound doctrine and refute those
who oppose it. 1Ti 3:2-4

10For there are many rebellious people, mere
talkers and deceivers, especially those of the circumcision group. 11They must be silenced, because they are ruining whole households by teaching things they ought not to teach—and that for
the sake of dishonest gain. 12Even one of their own
prophets has said, "Cretans are always liars, evil
brutes, lazy gluttons." 13This testimony is true.
Therefore, rebuke them sharply, so that they will
be sound in the faith 14and will pay no attention to
Jewish myths or to the commands of those who
reject the truth. 15To the pure, all things are pure,
but to those who are corrupted and do not believe,
nothing is pure. In fact, both their minds and consciences are corrupted. 16They claim to know God,
but by their actions they deny him. They are detestable, disobedient and unfit for doing anything
good. 1Ti 1:4; 1Jn 2:4

Giving Advice Chapter 2

Paul gave Titus good advice on specific situations and groups of people in the church on Crete—such as what to teach older men and women as well as younger men and women (2:2–6). Paul gave personal counsel and direction for Titus himself and for all pastors who read this letter today (2:7–8). Finally, Paul gave instructions on what to teach slaves and masters. If you look closely at this list of groups in chapter 2, it includes a broad spectrum of God's family members. Read carefully Paul's advice to Titus, and think about what the Lord has to say to you through it.

What Must Be Taught to Various Groups

2 You must teach what is in accord with sound
doctrine. 2Teach the older men to be temperate, worthy of respect, self-controlled, and sound
in faith, in love and in endurance. 1Ti 1:10; Tit 1:13
3Likewise, teach the older women to be reverent
in the way they live, not to be slanderers or addicted to much wine, but to teach what is good. 4Then
they can train the younger women to love their
husbands and children, 5to be self-controlled and
pure, to be busy at home, to be kind, and to be
subject to their husbands, so that no one will malign the word of God. Eph 5:22; 1Ti 6:1
6Similarly, encourage the young men to be self-
controlled. 7In everything set them an example by
doing what is good. In your teaching show integrity, seriousness 8and soundness of speech that cannot be condemned, so that those who oppose you
may be ashamed because they have nothing bad to
say about us. 1Ti 4:12; 1Pe 2:12
9Teach slaves to be subject to their masters in
everything, to try to please them, not to talk back
to them, 10and not to steal from them, but to show

[a]5 Or *ordain* [b]7 Traditionally *bishop*

that they can be fully trusted, so that in every way
they will make the teaching about God our Savior
attractive. Mt 5:16; Eph 6:5
11For the grace of God that brings salvation has
appeared to all men. 12It teaches us to say "No" to
ungodliness and worldly passions, and to live self-
controlled, upright and godly lives in this present
age, 13while we wait for the blessed hope—the
glorious appearing of our great God and Savior,
Jesus Christ, 14who gave himself for us to redeem
us from all wickedness and to purify for himself a
people that are his very own, eager to do what is
good. 2Ti 3:12; 2Pe 1:1

LIVING  INSIGHT

"Eager to do what is good." Our tendency will be anything but that. Instead of being eager to do what is good, we will feel like doing what is evil. Fume. Swear. Scream. Fight. Pout. Get irritated. Burn up all kinds of emotional BTUs. Rather than parading through that shopworn routine, stay quiet and consciously turn it all over to the Lord.

(See Titus 2:14.)

15These, then, are the things you should teach.
Encourage and rebuke with all authority. Do not
let anyone despise you.

Doing Right **Chapter 3**

This chapter contains a classic good news/bad news/good news situation. Paul first covered the good news of positive practical living, calling believers to submit humbly to those in positions of authority in all forms of human government (verses 1–2). Paul urges all of us to operate in a spirit of gentleness and humility, committing to living together in peace. In verse 3 Paul reminds us of the bad news of sin and its power to enslave us, then he hurries to a magnificent declaration of the good news of God's kindness and love (verses 4–7). Paul prompts us to remember the depths to which we had sunk in our sin, the awesomeness of the gospel of forgiveness and grace in Jesus Christ, and the necessity of doing what is good and avoiding what is evil. As one expositor wrote about Paul's letter to Titus, "This is essential reading, because ill-directed and badly formed spiritual leadership causes much damage in souls. Paul in both his life and his letters shows us how to do it right."

Doing What Is Good

3 Remind the people to be subject to rulers and
authorities, to be obedient, to be ready to do
whatever is good, 2to slander no one, to be peaceable and considerate, and to show true humility
toward all men. Eph 4:31; 2Ti 2:24
3At one time we too were foolish, disobedient,
deceived and enslaved by all kinds of passions and
pleasures. We lived in malice and envy, being hated and hating one another. 4But when the kindness and love of God our Savior appeared, 5he
saved us, not because of righteous things we had
done, but because of his mercy. He saved us

LIVING  INSIGHT

Is there any way to lose the gift of salvation? No, never! If you work for it, then you can certainly lose it. And that would mean it is not a gift; it's what you've earned. We really confuse things when we try to turn a gift into a wage. Furthermore, just as no one can say how much work is enough to earn it, no one can ever say how little work is enough to lose it.

(See Titus 3:4–8.)

through the washing of rebirth and renewal by the
Holy Spirit, 6whom he poured out on us generously through Jesus Christ our Savior, 7so that, having
been justified by his grace, we might become heirs
having the hope of eternal life. 8This is a trustworthy saying. And I want you to stress these things,
so that those who have trusted in God may be
careful to devote themselves to doing what is good.
These things are excellent and profitable for everyone. 1Ti 1:15; Tit 2:14
9But avoid foolish controversies and genealogies and arguments and quarrels about the law,
because these are unprofitable and useless. 10Warn
a divisive person once, and then warn him a second time. After that, have nothing to do with him.
11You may be sure that such a man is warped and
sinful; he is self-condemned. 1Ti 1:4; 2Ti 2:14

Final Remarks

12As soon as I send Artemas or Tychicus to you,
do your best to come to me at Nicopolis, because
I have decided to winter there. 13Do everything
you can to help Zenas the lawyer and Apollos on
their way and see that they have everything they
need. 14Our people must learn to devote themselves to doing what is good, in order that they
may provide for daily necessities and not live unproductive lives. Ac 18:24; 20:4
15Everyone with me sends you greetings. Greet
those who love us in the faith. 1Ti 1:2
Grace be with you all. Col 4:18

INTRODUCTION

PHILEMON

About six years before his execution, the apostle Paul wrote a "postcard" to his long-time friend named Philemon . . . a resident of Colosse. The briefest of all of Paul's writings, this letter is one of the grandest illustrations of grace and forgiveness in all of Scripture. It is a warm and passionate appeal to a slave owner to welcome back, forgive and reinstate his runaway slave, whose name was Onesimus. Because of the obvious analogy with sinful people being accepted by God and forgiven through His grace, this little letter has become one of the most-treasured of all the New Testament writings. May that prove to be true in your experience as you take time to read and reflect on these twenty-five powerful verses from the letter to Philemon.

WRITER: *Paul*

DATE: *C.A.D. 60–62*

PURPOSE: *To appeal to Philemon to forgive Onesimus and warmly accept him back as a Christian brother*

KEY THEMES: *Grace; the cost and joy of forgiveness*

KEY VERSES: *10-11; 18*

STYLE: *Tactful, cordial and persuasive*

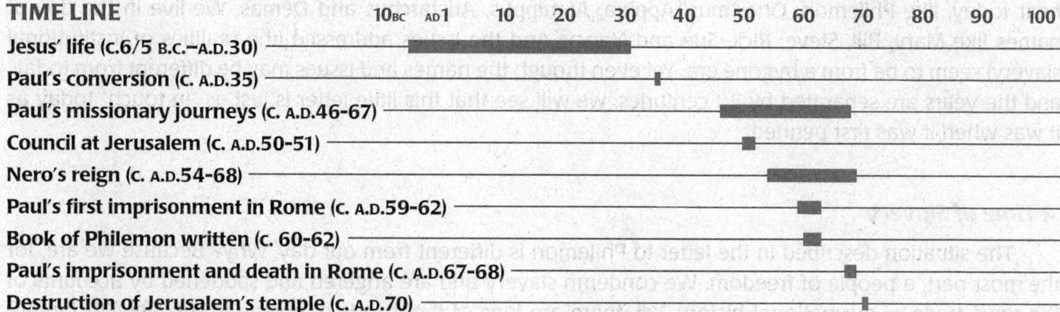

An Appeal for Grace and Forgiveness

GREETING (VERSES 1-3)	PERSONAL WORDS TO PHILEMON	STRONG APPEAL . . .	PERSONAL PROMISE FROM PAUL	CONCLUSION (VERSES 22-25)
		On the basis of the slave's conversion *(verses 8-11)*		
		On the basis of the slave owner's friendship *(verses 12-17)*		
	VERSES 4-7	***VERSES 8-17***	***VERSES 18-21***	

TONE	**Praise**	**Plea**	**Promise**
DIRECTION	**Looking back**	**Looking within**	**Looking beyond**
CENTRAL STATEMENT	***"I always thank my God . . ." (verse 4)***	***"I appeal to you . . ." (verse 10)***	***"I will pay it back . . ." (verse 19)***

Who would have ever thought that a little 468-word "postcard" from the New Testament could have anything to say to people who live in our times? Yet this little letter addressed to a man named Philemon has plenty to say to people today, especially to those who are "on the run." Philemon's story has a message for all generations and for people from every walk of life—not simply for people running from the law. It is a message of hope and grace and forgiveness—a message that needs to be heard over and over again.

To the uninformed, this letter could seem irrelevant. Strange names appear here—names you won't hear today, like Philemon, Onesimus, Apphia, Archippus, Aristarchus and Demas. We live in the day of names like Mary, Bill, Steve, Rick, Sue and Nancy. And the issues addressed (the realities of institutional slavery) seem to be from a bygone era. Yet even though the names and issues may be different from today, and the years are separated by 20 centuries, we will see that this little letter is just as "in touch" today as it was when it was first penned.

A Time of Slavery

The situation described in the letter to Philemon is different from our day. Why? Because we are, for the most part, a people of freedom. We condemn slavery and are angered and saddened by accounts of the slave trade of our national history. Yet, there are tens of thousands of people in the New Testament era who never knew freedom, for slavery was a fact of life, a position of society, in that day.

We have Edward Gibbon, the 18th-century English historian, to thank for providing insights into the realities of slavery in the Roman empire. Gibbon told us there were sixty million slaves in the Roman empire during the middle of the first century. Did you get that number? *Sixty million slaves.* Another writer summarized the typical view of a slave in that day: "A slave was not a person. He was a living tool. Any master had the right of life and death over his slaves. The master had absolute power over his slaves."

The world in which Paul wrote and in which Philemon, Onesimus, Aristarchus, Demas and Mark lived was a world as familiar with the brutalities of slavery as you and I are familiar with the athletic scenes of today. The inhuman, unmerciful treatment of slaves was a common practice in Paul's day.

Focusing the Lens

The specific setting for the writing of this little letter can best be viewed through the zoom lens of God's inspired camera. Very briefly we've glimpsed the slavery scene from a distance, but now the Spirit focuses on one particular family, directing our attention to the home of Philemon, a slave owner who had recently experienced the unspeakable—his slave had run away. The slave, Onesimus, had willfully chosen to flee Philemon's home and to blend into the blurred backdrop of the thousands of other slaves—most of them nameless faces in a crowd—who lived in the city of Rome.

A few of them bore an "F" on their forehead—Latin for *fugitivus*—"fugitive." A runaway slave who had been found and brought back (if he wasn't killed first, which the master had the legal right to order) had that sign seared on his forehead with a branding iron for all to see. The best Onesimus could expect, if he were captured and sent back to his master, Philemon, would be to receive this brand on his forehead.

The beautiful thing to observe is this: God's Spirit was at work in Onesimus's life, and he didn't even realize it. As we saw in our study of Acts, Paul was imprisoned in Rome (Acts 28:17–31). As only God could arrange it, Onesimus met Paul, who led him to a relationship with Jesus (see verse 10). The slave's conversion created a most unusual situation. We have a runaway slave who had an enormous debt to pay to his master—but now he and Philemon shared a common faith in the Lord Jesus as Savior and Lord. Onesimus recognized that he had wronged his master, Philemon, and that he needed to make things right with him. Paul became the middleman who appealed to his friend Philemon on behalf of this recently converted slave . . . and therein lies the message of this one-chapter letter.

If you read Philemon closely, you'll see how beautifully it matches what Jesus Christ has done for us. All of us who, in our bondage to sin, have been fugitives from God's perfect justice have someone who is ready to step in on our behalf to enter a plea for mercy. That "someone" is Jesus Christ, the one and only Son of God, who took on Himself our human flesh. God, in grace, accepted the Savior's sacrificial death on the cross as payment on our behalf and welcomed us back into right relationship with Him. In some sense Paul pleaded the case of Onesimus (verses 17–19) in a way that would encourage Philemon to follow the divine example, to become a living illustration of grace and welcome Onesimus back into relationship with him.

A Message for Today

We might wonder, "How does this book relate to us? I see how it related to a runaway and a slave master, and I see how it related to a day of institutional slavery, but how does it relate to me?" I find at least three analogies.

First, *every Christian was once a fugitive.* Every one of God's children was once a runaway slave. We escaped from the One who formed us and gave us life and sustains us each day, and we ran away willfully and disobediently: "All have sinned and fall short of the glory of God" (Romans 3:23).

Second, *our guilt was great and our penalty was severe.* I hope you haven't lived for so long in the family of God that you've forgotten what life was like outside of a personal relationship with Jesus Christ. Yet the reality is this: When we were wallowing in the swamp of sin, not only was our guilt great, but our consciences condemned us as well (Romans 2:15). We were worthy not of acquittal, but of conviction and the severest of sentences: "The wages of sin is death" (Romans 6:23). And through whatever means—a radio program, a verse or portion of Scripture, an evangelist, a gospel tract, a caring friend, a faithful pastor, a loving mother or a relative—something or someone, somewhere, brought to us the message of hope, just as Paul had told Onesimus about the love and acceptance to be found in the Savior.

Third, *grace opened to us the way of appeal.* There is one God and one mediator between God and human beings, Jesus Christ (see 1 Timothy 2:5). Jesus has come on our behalf to the throne of the God of justice and holiness and righteousness—pleading the blood of the cross. He has said to the Father, "This person is under My forgiveness; he has come to Me in faith, she has come to Me in faith, and on the basis of My blood they are cleansed. I come on their behalf as their advocate." As a result, our rightful Owner has bought us back. He has accepted us. We are, at this moment, clothed in God's righteousness because of the blood of our Lord Jesus Christ!

Run to Jesus

It may be that you find yourself on the run at this very moment. The message of this brief letter is to stop, right where you are, and turn around. Maybe you've come to a dramatic fork in the road, and you realize that the consequences of plunging ahead are grave and grim. If you don't stop, you're facing extremely serious charges and potentially ruinous effects on your life and the lives of others. (You see, no person is an island. The sins of our life affect others. The fact is, we never sin alone, not really, not ultimately.)

You may think that if you *stop* running you'll create greater problems than if you *keep* running. Not true! Your first need, your most urgent need, is for forgiveness from Almighty God. He freely offers grace to you through Jesus Christ. You have a loving advocate in Jesus, the righteous One, who has come to set you free. The beauty of the good news of the gospel is that He will appeal your case. No case He has presented to the Judge has ever been turned down. You can, you will, find forgiveness and grace through His advocacy.

In Jesus Christ there is cleansing available from all your sins. There's the removal of those awful, despicable, unsightly stains. It's as if Jesus walks through the art gallery of your life and takes all the pictures off the wall—pictures that represent your old way of life. He then destroys them one by one. As He forgives you, He replaces them with pictures of grace and forgiveness, purpose and power, affirmation and beauty. You may be just the one who needs to understand this truth this very moment. It is my pleasure to be the one to bring you this message of everlasting hope. My invitation to you is simple: If you are still running away . . . STOP! It is time to turn around (repent) and take the Lord Jesus by faith (believe). He alone can forgive you. He alone can clean you up. He alone can heal those scars and remove your guilt and set you free! Hallelujah! What a Savior!

A Message of Grace

This letter tells the story of a runaway slave named Onesimus and an appeal from Paul to the slave owner named Philemon to welcome this wayward slave back with grace and with love. Even a casual reading will reveal the deep concern of the apostle Paul for reconciliation between Philemon and Onesimus. As we dig deeper, however, we realize that it is more than simply the story of *one* man; it is the story of *every* man and woman who have ever walked this earth. In a real sense we are all wayward slaves who have run from our Master and who stand in need of reconciliation. Only when Jesus intercedes on our behalf, personally, can we experience true reconciliation with the Father. This little letter packs a big punch when it comes to delivering the powerful message of God's grace and forgiveness. If you need a fresh reminder of the awesomeness of grace, please read the letter to Philemon—and read it regularly.

1Paul, a prisoner of Christ Jesus, and Timothy
our brother, Eph 3:1

To Philemon our dear friend and fellow worker,
2to Apphia our sister, to Archippus our fellow soldier and to the church that meets in your home:

3Grace to you and peace from God our Father
and the Lord Jesus Christ. Ro 1:7

Thanksgiving and Prayer

4I always thank my God as I remember you in
my prayers, 5because I hear about your faith in the
Lord Jesus and your love for all the saints. 6I pray
that you may be active in sharing your faith, so
that you will have a full understanding of every
good thing we have in Christ. 7Your love has given
me great joy and encouragement, because you,
brother, have refreshed the hearts of the saints.

Paul's Plea for Onesimus

8Therefore, although in Christ I could be bold
and order you to do what you ought to do, 9yet
I appeal to you on the basis of love. I then, as
Paul—an old man and now also a prisoner of
Christ Jesus— 10I appeal to you for my son Onesimus,[a] who became my son while I was in chains.
11Formerly he was useless to you, but now he has
become useful both to you and to me. 1Co 4:15

12I am sending him—who is my very heart—
back to you. 13I would have liked to keep him with
me so that he could take your place in helping me
while I am in chains for the gospel. 14But I did not
want to do anything without your consent, so that

LIVING  **INSIGHT**

A heart kept permanently closed keeps people at a distance. A heart that risks being open invites them in, has nothing to hide, promotes generosity, prompts vulnerability, demonstrates love. If you wish to leave this earth a better place than you found it, bringing out the best in others, you'll want to give your heart.

(See Philemon 12.)

any favor you do will be spontaneous and not
forced. 15Perhaps the reason he was separated
from you for a little while was that you might have
him back for good— 16no longer as a slave, but
better than a slave, as a dear brother. He is very
dear to me but even dearer to you, both as a man
and as a brother in the Lord. 2Co 9:7; 1Ti 6:2

17So if you consider me a partner, welcome him
as you would welcome me. 18If he has done you
any wrong or owes you anything, charge it to me.
19I, Paul, am writing this with my own hand. I will
pay it back—not to mention that you owe me
your very self. 20I do wish, brother, that I may have
some benefit from you in the Lord; refresh my
heart in Christ. 21Confident of your obedience, I
write to you, knowing that you will do even more
than I ask. 2Co 2:3; 8:23

22And one thing more: Prepare a guest room for
me, because I hope to be restored to you in answer
to your prayers. 2Co 1:11; Php 1:25

23Epaphras, my fellow prisoner in Christ Jesus,
sends you greetings. 24And so do Mark, Aristarchus, Demas and Luke, my fellow workers.

25The grace of the Lord Jesus Christ be with
your spirit. 2Ti 4:22

[a]10 *Onesimus* means *useful.*

INTRODUCTION

HEBREWS

Although the letter to the Hebrews is among the longest and most significant letters in the New Testament, it remains one of the least appreciated. Profound, mysterious, deep and, admittedly, difficult to understand, it deserves our serious time and attention. Rich in Jewish history and filled with quotations from and allusions to the Old Testament, the letter to the Hebrews requires concentration and a fairly firm grasp on how God revealed Himself to His people in ancient times. Those who master this book are keen students of such subjects as the priestly system, sacrifices, traditional Jewish feasts and the tabernacle. For those who invest the time and energy in working their way through these 13 chapters, the investment yields rich and rewarding benefits.

WRITER: *Unknown*

DATE: *C.A.D. 60–70*

PURPOSE: *To warn early believers to cling to the gospel of Jesus Christ and not fall away from the faith*

KEY THEME: *The absolute superiority of Jesus Christ*

EMPHASES: *Resisting temptation; persevering in the face of hardship; growing into maturity in Christ*

KEY TERMS: *"Better", "superior"*

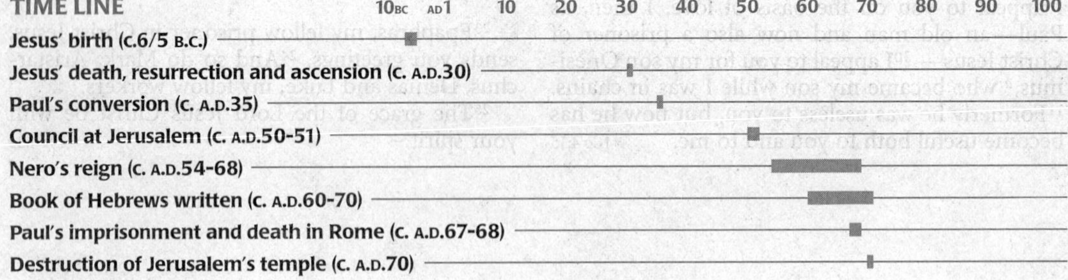

Encouragement for the Weary

	PROLOGUE (1:1-4)	JESUS CHRIST: Superior in His person	JESUS CHRIST: Superior as our Priest	JESUS CHRIST: Superior for life	EPILOGUE (13:20-25)
		Superior to: Prophets, Angels, Joshua, The Sabbath, Other priests	**Better than:** Earthly priesthood, Old covenant (Mosaic system), Animal sacrifices, Daily offerings	**Let us have:** FAITH to believe God, HOPE to endure trials, LOVE to encourage others	
		CHAPTERS 1:5–4:16	*CHAPTERS 5–10*	*CHAPTERS 11:1–13:19*	
EMPHASIS		Instruction	Instruction	Exhortation	
KEY WORDS		*"Superior to . . ." (1:4)*	*"Better . . ." (7:19)*	*"Let us . . ." (12:1)*	
KEY VERSE		*"Since we have a great high priest . . . let us hold firmly to the faith we profess" (4:14).*			
WARNINGS		*(2:1-4)* *(3:7–4:13)*	*(5:11–6:20)* *(10:19-39)*	*(12:25-29)*	

Street people. The homeless. Most of us know about them; relatively few of us know them. We see them walking the downtown streets; we see them sitting in the doorways of crumbling buildings. But we find it hard to empathize. We find it hard to walk a mile in their shoes. Our lives are so different. We have homes. Many of us have enough money to at least meet our basic needs—and many of us can sustain a pretty comfortable lifestyle.

Let's face it, most of us don't live on the street, so the issues of "just plain survival" don't grab us with much force. Perhaps that's one of the reasons this letter to the Hebrews can be so difficult for us to grasp. You see, the letter was written to first-century "street people." It was addressed to folks who had lost their homes and many of their loved ones. Many, in fact, were facing the very real fact that they could lose their own lives because they were Christians. Hebrews is full of pertinent words and profound symbols that were very meaningful to the Christians who were living in that time of intense persecution. They needed hope; they needed a bridge across swollen rivers of trouble. Hebrews is a letter of strong encouragement and exhortation for desperate times.

A Letter to the Suffering

Who wrote the letter and who received it? The second part of the question is a little more objective and certainly easier to answer.

I can't give you names of the recipients, nor can I give you the exact region where the recipients lived. What I can tell you is that they were Hebrews. They were Jewish Christians—first-century Jews who believed in Jesus. We also know they were going through terrible times of suffering and of serious temptation to forsake the faith and revert back to Judaism. The writer reminded them of all they had undergone after they had come to faith in Jesus:

> *Remember those earlier days after you had received the light, when you stood your ground in a great contest in the face of suffering. Sometimes you were publicly exposed to insult and persecution; at other times you stood side by side with those who were so treated (10:32–33).*

These were people who had "received the light." They had accepted Jesus as Savior and Lord. And then the writer divided them into categories with words to this effect: "Some of you who received this letter have been made public spectacles. You have become objects of mockery. You know firsthand what it is to be persecuted, hated and laughed at for your faith. And there are some of you who have stood beside those who were so treated. Some of you have vicariously entered into those experiences of pain as you came alongside your friends who endured them."

An Unsolved Mystery

Nobody really knows who wrote the letter to the Hebrews. But whoever did write the letter certainly understood the plight of those to whom it was written—for he was obviously well known to the original recipients. Look at what he wrote in chapter 13:

> *Pray for us. We are sure that we have a clear conscience and desire to live honorably in every way. I particularly urge you to pray so that I may be restored to you soon (13:18–19).*

Although separated from them at the time of writing, this writer knew them and looked forward to the day when they would be brought together again. Yet nowhere in the letter did he bother to give his name. We wish he had! That would have saved thousands of hours for scholars and teachers and preachers who have for years attempted to solve this mystery.

Some things are worth intense study, and other things, although they may be interesting and thought-provoking, are not worth the time. An in-depth investigation of the authorship of Hebrews is one of the things (in my opinion) not worth more of our time. The most important thing to remember is that this book has been inspired by the Holy Spirit and preserved as part of the Holy Scriptures. No matter who penned the words, God has given us this message and protected it through the centuries.

For Those Who Drift

Why was the book of Hebrews written? Some of the Jewish converts were being tempted to turn away from their faith and give up on following Jesus. In our day as well there are people who, because of suffering or because of disillusionment prompted by dashed dreams or unmet expectations, decide that following Jesus is not worth the effort . . . nothing more than an exercise in futility. Listen to the writer's passionate warning in chapter 2: "We must pay more careful attention, therefore, to what we have heard, so that we do not drift away" (2:1). Great advice! When we find ourselves drifting away from Biblical principles and a Christ-honoring lifestyle, the very best thing we can do is pay closer attention to such things. Go back to the basics; let our roots sink deeper, so that we will not drift away from the truth.

The writer shared his concern again in chapter 3, as he sensed his readers' struggle to give in to temptation and give up the fight of the faith:

> *See to it, brothers, that none of you has a sinful, unbelieving heart that turns away from the living God. But encourage one another daily, as long as it is called Today, so that none of you may be hardened by sin's deceitfulness (3:12–13).*

Verse 13 is one of those life verses to rivet into your minds: "But encourage one another daily, as long as it is called Today, so that none of you may be hardened by sin's deceitfulness." It is a great commitment for our lives as each new day dawns. The letter to the Hebrews was written to hurting believers, to those who may have been wondering if a commitment to Jesus Christ was worth the risk . . . to encourage the discouraged, to strengthen the weak, and to give relief to the burdened and rest to the weary. Bottom line—that's why we have the letter to the Hebrews.

A Fiery Time

Hebrews was written at a low-tide time for those who professed the name of Jesus Christ. Nero was on the throne of the Roman empire. In his New Testament survey book, Merrill Tenney wrote this: "In A.D. 64 a great fire broke out in Rome, which destroyed a large part of the city. Nero was suspected of having deliberately set it in order to make room for his new Golden House, a splendid palace which he built on the hill. In order to divert the blame from himself, the Christians were accused of having caused the disaster. Their attitude of aloofness from the heathen and their talk of the ultimate destruction of the world by fire lent plausibility to the charge. Many of them were brought to trial and tortured to death. Tradition says Peter and Paul perished in this persecution, the first one conducted by the state." It was during that first persecution that this letter is believed to have been written.

The longer I live, the more I'm convinced we need to identify with scenes in Scripture if we're going to glean the lessons God has for us. Can you imagine yourself in a scene of persecution where the government has decided that believers in Jesus Christ are responsible for the problems of society, where the officials who rule over us make decisions that start the pendulum swinging against us? We begin to lose our rights, personal property, church buildings and freedoms. Before we know it, we are the bull's-eye on their target. And on top of that, our family members begin to experience persecution, and we even lose some of them to martyrdom. How terrible it would be! Pause long enough to imagine how difficult such a time would have been. If you need a little help in visualizing the scene, read Hebrews 11:32–38.

I wonder how many of us would stay true to the end in the face of intense persecution because of our faith. If we no longer had homes to live in or had scarcely enough clothes to wear or food to eat, if we suddenly had our comfortable amenities taken from us, I wonder how many of us would defect. May God mercifully spare us from that experience. Or if it's His will to take us through that kind of intense testing, may the truths of these and other Scriptures hold us firm and keep us strong to the end.

The Superiority of Christ

Jesus Christ is Lord! That's the underlying theme of Hebrews. Jesus is superior over everything. As you read this letter you will encounter this theme again and again. In chapters 1–4 we learn that Jesus Christ is superior in His person. He is superior to the angels, and He is superior to Moses. In chapters 5–10 we discover He is superior as our high priest. In chapters 11–13 we are reminded that He is superior for all of life. In short, Jesus is Lord over everything.

One of the old Puritan preachers used to say, "There are two things I want to know. One: Does God speak concerning the matter? And two: What does God say?" I believe those are the two questions asked, and answered, in the letter to the Hebrews. First answer: Yes. He speaks; He speaks about subjects important for Christians of all times. Second answer: Read it, folks. Take time to read and carefully ponder each word of the letter. What God says is totally reliable, and all that He says is worth putting into practice.

This analysis may sound simple but I believe that's what this letter is about. God is speaking to hurting Christians on subjects about which we need to hear. He brings a dependable, trustworthy message. The message still rings true . . . Jesus Christ is superior! Look no further. Jesus is Lord!

Modern-day Words of Encouragement

I would like you to consider making one of your life purposes a commitment to encouragement. Encouragement is such a key thought in the letter to the Hebrews. That purpose permeated the pen of the writer, who encouraged his readers to keep going, to stay true to the faith in spite of frustrations, temptations and obstacles. He seemed to pull out all the stops in an effort to convince readers not to turn back, not to give up in the struggle—but to look to Jesus, the One who opened the way, once and for all, into the sanctuary of God's presence. We desperately need that encouragement today, and the writer of the letter to the Hebrews reminds us that others around us need that encouragement too. So on two different occasions he urges us to "encourage one another daily" (3:13) and "let us encourage one another" (10:25).

Pray that the Lord would motivate you to be one of His encouragers. The letter to the Hebrews may be directed to those who were tempted to drift, to the downcast, to the discouraged, but it doesn't leave them there. Neither should we!

Jesus: Superior in His Person Chapters 1:1–4:13

If the letter to the Hebrews were to be summarized in one brief sentence, it would be "Jesus is superior." That's it! We might ask, "Superior to what?" The answer is clear in Hebrews: "He is superior to everything!" The first section addresses the superiority of Jesus Christ's person. Note the four comparisons: Jesus is superior to the prophets, the angels, Moses and Joshua. To the Jewish mind, that was a pretty big list of central characters and issues in their faith. The writer of the letter to the Hebrews removes any doubt. There is no event or person or decision in all the Old Testament more significant than Jesus. He is God's full and final revelation, far surpassing any other. He is superior to everything.

The Son Superior to Angels

1 In the past God spoke to our forefathers
through the prophets at many times and in
various ways, 2but in these last days he has spoken
to us by his Son, whom he appointed heir of all
things, and through whom he made the universe.
3The Son is the radiance of God's glory and the
exact representation of his being, sustaining all
things by his powerful word. After he had provided purification for sins, he sat down at the right
hand of the Majesty in heaven. 4So he became as
much superior to the angels as the name he has
inherited is superior to theirs. Php 2:9-10; Heb 7:27
5For to which of the angels did God ever say,

"You are my Son;
today I have become your Father[a]"[b]?

Or again,

"I will be his Father,
and he will be my Son"[c]? 2Sa 7:14

6And again, when God brings his firstborn into the
world, he says, Heb 10:5

"Let all God's angels worship him."[d] Ps 97:7

7In speaking of the angels he says,

"He makes his angels winds,
his servants flames of fire."[e] Ps 104:4

8But about the Son he says,

"Your throne, O God, will last for ever and
ever, Lk 1:33
and righteousness will be the scepter of
your kingdom.
9You have loved righteousness and hated
wickedness;
therefore God, your God, has set you above
your companions Php 2:9
by anointing you with the oil of joy."[f]

10He also says,

"In the beginning, O Lord, you laid the
foundations of the earth,
and the heavens are the work of your
hands. Ps 8:6; Zec 12:1
11They will perish, but you remain;
they will all wear out like a garment. Isa 34:4
12You will roll them up like a robe;
like a garment they will be changed.
But you remain the same, Heb 13:8
and your years will never end."[g] Ps 102:25-27

13To which of the angels did God ever say,

"Sit at my right hand Mk 16:19
until I make your enemies
a footstool for your feet"[h]?

14Are not all angels ministering spirits sent to serve
those who will inherit salvation? Jos 10:24; Ps 103:20

Warning to Pay Attention

2 We must pay more careful attention, therefore, to what we have heard, so that we do not
drift away. 2For if the message spoken by angels
was binding, and every violation and disobedience
received its just punishment, 3how shall we escape
if we ignore such a great salvation? This salvation,
which was first announced by the Lord, was confirmed to us by those who heard him. 4God also
testified to it by signs, wonders and various miracles, and gifts of the Holy Spirit distributed according to his will. Lk 1:2; Heb 10:29

Jesus Made Like His Brothers

5It is not to angels that he has subjected the
world to come, about which we are speaking. 6But
there is a place where someone has testified:

"What is man that you are mindful of him,
the son of man that you care for him?
7You made him a little[i] lower than the angels;
you crowned him with glory and honor
8 and put everything under his feet."[j]

In putting everything under him, God left nothing

LIVING  **INSIGHT**

It isn't the literal cross we are to exalt. It is the One who hung on it whom we honor. It is what the cross represents and the rescue it provides. It was there our Substitute took our place. It was there the price for our sins was paid in full. It was the agony suffered on the cross that made the remedy for our disease effective.

(See Hebrews 2:9.)

[a]5 Or *have begotten you* [b]5 Psalm 2:7 [c]5 2 Samuel 7:14; 1 Chron. 17:13 [d]6 Deut. 32:43 (see Dead Sea Scrolls and Septuagint) [e]7 Psalm 104:4 [f]9 Psalm 45:6,7 [g]12 Psalm 102:25-27 [h]13 Psalm 110:1 [i]7 Or *him for a little while*; also in verse 9 [j]8 Psalm 8:4-6

that is not subject to him. Yet at present we do not see everything subject to him. 9But we see Jesus, who was made a little lower than the angels, now crowned with glory and honor because he suffered death, so that by the grace of God he might taste death for everyone. Jn 3:16; Ac 2:33; Php 2:7-9

10In bringing many sons to glory, it was fitting that God, for whom and through whom everything exists, should make the author of their salvation perfect through suffering. 11Both the one who makes men holy and those who are made holy are of the same family. So Jesus is not ashamed to call them brothers. 12He says, Jn 20:17; Ro 11:36

"I will declare your name to my brothers;
in the presence of the congregation I will
sing your praises."[a]

13And again,

"I will put my trust in him."[b] Isa 8:17

And again he says,

"Here am I, and the children God has given
me."[c] Isa 8:18; Jn 10:29

14Since the children have flesh and blood, he too shared in their humanity so that by his death he might destroy him who holds the power of death—that is, the devil— 15and free those who all their lives were held in slavery by their fear of death. 16For surely it is not angels he helps, but Abraham's descendants. 17For this reason he had to be made like his brothers in every way, in order that he might become a merciful and faithful high priest in service to God, and that he might make atonement for[d] the sins of the people. 18Because he himself suffered when he was tempted, he is able to help those who are being tempted.

Jesus Greater Than Moses

3 Therefore, holy brothers, who share in the heavenly calling, fix your thoughts on Jesus, the apostle and high priest whom we confess. 2He was faithful to the one who appointed him, just as Moses was faithful in all God's house. 3Jesus has been found worthy of greater honor than Moses, just as the builder of a house has greater honor than the house itself. 4For every house is built by someone, but God is the builder of everything. 5Moses was faithful as a servant in all God's house, testifying to what would be said in the future. 6But Christ is faithful as a son over God's house. And we are his house, if we hold on to our courage and the hope of which we boast. Heb 2:11,17

Warning Against Unbelief

7So, as the Holy Spirit says: Heb 9:8

"Today, if you hear his voice,
8 do not harden your hearts Heb 4:7
as you did in the rebellion,
during the time of testing in the desert,
9where your fathers tested and tried me
and for forty years saw what I did. Ac 7:36
10That is why I was angry with that generation,
and I said, 'Their hearts are always going
astray,
and they have not known my ways.'
11So I declared on oath in my anger, Dt 1:34-35
'They shall never enter my rest.' "[e] Ps 95:7-11

12See to it, brothers, that none of you has a sinful, unbelieving heart that turns away from the living God. 13But encourage one another daily, as long as it is called Today, so that none of you may

LIVING  **INSIGHT**

Families who enhance each other's esteem are families committed to understanding one another. They are learning to work at finding the good, the strength, the benefit, the hidden counsel, the "plan" in the heart of one another, then drawing it out and valuing it.
(See Hebrews 3:13.)

be hardened by sin's deceitfulness. 14We have come to share in Christ if we hold firmly till the end the confidence we had at first. 15As has just been said: Eph 4:22; Heb 10:24-25

"Today, if you hear his voice,
do not harden your hearts
as you did in the rebellion."[f] Ps 95:7-8

16Who were they who heard and rebelled? Were they not all those Moses led out of Egypt? 17And with whom was he angry for forty years? Was it not with those who sinned, whose bodies fell in the desert? 18And to whom did God swear that they would never enter his rest if not to those who disobeyed[g]? 19So we see that they were not able to enter, because of their unbelief. Jn 3:36; Nu 14:20-23

A Sabbath-Rest for the People of God

4 Therefore, since the promise of entering his rest still stands, let us be careful that none of you be found to have fallen short of it. 2For we also have had the gospel preached to us, just as they did; but the message they heard was of no value to them, because those who heard did not combine it

[a] 12 Psalm 22:22 [b] 13 Isaiah 8:17 [c] 13 Isaiah 8:18 [d] 17 Or *and that he might turn aside God's wrath, taking away*
[e] 11 Psalm 95:7-11 [f] 15 Psalm 95:7,8 [g] 18 Or *disbelieved*

with faith.[a] 3Now we who have believed enter that
rest, just as God has said, 1Th 2:13; Heb 12:15

> "So I declared on oath in my anger,
> 'They shall never enter my rest.'"[b] Ps 95:11

And yet his work has been finished since the creation of the world. 4For somewhere he has spoken
about the seventh day in these words: "And on the
seventh day God rested from all his work."[c] 5And
again in the passage above he says, "They shall
never enter my rest." Ex 20:11; Ps 95:11

6It still remains that some will enter that rest,
and those who formerly had the gospel preached
to them did not go in, because of their disobedience. 7Therefore God again set a certain day, calling it Today, when a long time later he spoke
through David, as was said before: Heb 3:18

> "Today, if you hear his voice,
> do not harden your hearts."[d]

8For if Joshua had given them rest, God would not
have spoken later about another day. 9There remains, then, a Sabbath-rest for the people of God;
10for anyone who enters God's rest also rests from
his own work, just as God did from his. 11Let us,
therefore, make every effort to enter that rest, so
that no one will fall by following their example of
disobedience. Heb 1:1; 3:18

12For the word of God is living and active.

LIVING  INSIGHT

Alive. Active. Penetrating. Powerful. That's God's Word. Unlike anything else ever written, Scripture touches hearts and changes lives. Today, as always, we need God's touch. Painful and deep though it may be, His surgery inevitably benefits us. May His Spirit prepare our hearts for the probing ministry of this double-edged sword.

(See Hebrews 4:12.)

Sharper than any double-edged sword, it penetrates even to dividing soul and spirit, joints and
marrow; it judges the thoughts and attitudes of the
heart. 13Nothing in all creation is hidden from God's
sight. Everything is uncovered and laid bare before
the eyes of him to whom we must give account.

Jesus: Superior as Priest **Chapters 4:14–10:39**

In these chapters the writer declares Jesus' priesthood. It makes sense, doesn't it? If we're going to lean with an unbending confidence on God, we have to be sure we have a qualified priest to represent us to our heavenly Father. The whole thrust of chapters 5–10 (difficult though the chapters may be to digest) is this: "Jesus is real. He's true. He qualifies. He is superior to all other priests and priesthoods. Count on Him. Lean on Him. He'll see you through." These chapters neither negate the historical value of the priesthood nor question the value of what God accomplished through the ministry of the priests in the Old Testament. Yet as awe-inspiring as those priests may have been, our high priest, Jesus Christ, is better than all of them. Once again we are reminded: Jesus is superior to everything.

Jesus the Great High Priest

14Therefore, since we have a great high priest
who has gone through the heavens,[e] Jesus the
Son of God, let us hold firmly to the faith we
profess. 15For we do not have a high priest who is
unable to sympathize with our weaknesses, but we
have one who has been tempted in every way, just
as we are—yet was without sin. 16Let us then approach the throne of grace with confidence, so that
we may receive mercy and find grace to help us in
our time of need. 2Co 5:21; Heb 3:1

5 Every high priest is selected from among men
and is appointed to represent them in matters
related to God, to offer gifts and sacrifices for sins.
2He is able to deal gently with those who are ignorant and are going astray, since he himself is subject to weakness. 3This is why he has to offer sacrifices for his own sins, as well as for the sins of the
people. Heb 7:27-28

4No one takes this honor upon himself; he must
be called by God, just as Aaron was. 5So Christ also
did not take upon himself the glory of becoming
a high priest. But God said to him, Jn 8:54; Heb 1:1

> "You are my Son;
> today I have become your Father.[f]"[g]

6And he says in another place,

> "You are a priest forever,
> in the order of Melchizedek."[h] Ps 110:4

7During the days of Jesus' life on earth, he offered up prayers and petitions with loud cries and

LIVING  INSIGHT

God's wisest saints are often people who endure pain rather than escape it. Like their Savior, they are men and women "familiar with suffering" (Isaiah 53:3). Jesus learned obedience from what He suffered, not in spite of those things.

(See Hebrews 5:8.)

[a]2 Many manuscripts *because they did not share in the faith of those who obeyed* [b]3 Psalm 95:11; also in verse 5
[c]4 Gen. 2:2 [d]7 Psalm 95:7,8 [e]14 Or *gone into heaven* [f]5 Or *have begotten you* [g]5 Psalm 2:7
[h]6 Psalm 110:4

tears to the one who could save him from death,
and he was heard because of his reverent submission. 8Although he was a son, he learned obedience from what he suffered 9and, once made perfect, he became the source of eternal salvation for
all who obey him 10and was designated by God to
be high priest in the order of Melchizedek.

Warning Against Falling Away

11We have much to say about this, but it is hard
to explain because you are slow to learn. 12In fact,
though by this time you ought to be teachers, you
need someone to teach you the elementary truths
of God's word all over again. You need milk, not
solid food! 13Anyone who lives on milk, being still
an infant, is not acquainted with the teaching
about righteousness. 14But solid food is for the
mature, who by constant use have trained themselves to distinguish good from evil. 1Co 2:6; 3:2

6 Therefore let us leave the elementary teachings about Christ and go on to maturity, not
laying again the foundation of repentance from
acts that lead to death,[a] and of faith in God,
2instruction about baptisms, the laying on of
hands, the resurrection of the dead, and eternal
judgment. 3And God permitting, we will do so.

4It is impossible for those who have once been
enlightened, who have tasted the heavenly gift,
who have shared in the Holy Spirit, 5who have
tasted the goodness of the word of God and the
powers of the coming age, 6if they fall away, to be
brought back to repentance, because[b] to their loss
they are crucifying the Son of God all over again
and subjecting him to public disgrace. Heb 10:26-31

7Land that drinks in the rain often falling on it
and that produces a crop useful to those for whom
it is farmed receives the blessing of God. 8But land
that produces thorns and thistles is worthless and
is in danger of being cursed. In the end it will be
burned. Ge 3:17-18; Isa 5:6

9Even though we speak like this, dear friends,
we are confident of better things in your case—
things that accompany salvation. 10God is not unjust; he will not forget your work and the love you
have shown him as you have helped his people and
continue to help them. 11We want each of you to
show this same diligence to the very end, in order
to make your hope sure. 12We do not want you to
become lazy, but to imitate those who through
faith and patience inherit what has been promised.

The Certainty of God's Promise

13When God made his promise to Abraham,
since there was no one greater for him to swear by,
he swore by himself, 14saying, "I will surely bless
you and give you many descendants."[c] 15And so
after waiting patiently, Abraham received what
was promised. Ge 22:16; Lk 1:73

16Men swear by someone greater than themselves, and the oath confirms what is said and puts
an end to all argument. 17Because God wanted to
make the unchanging nature of his purpose very
clear to the heirs of what was promised, he confirmed it with an oath. 18God did this so that, by
two unchangeable things in which it is impossible
for God to lie, we who have fled to take hold of the
hope offered to us may be greatly encouraged.
19We have this hope as an anchor for the soul, firm
and secure. It enters the inner sanctuary behind

LIVING  **INSIGHT**

Our Savior has gone through life, has taken all of life's beatings and buffetings, and He has gone before us. And now? Now He pulls us toward Himself! He invites His followers within the curtain. He says, "Come in. Find here the rest that you need, the relief from the burdens and the buffetings of doubt."

(See Hebrews 6:19–20.)

the curtain, 20where Jesus, who went before us, has
entered on our behalf. He has become a high priest
forever, in the order of Melchizedek. Heb 2:17; 4:14

Melchizedek the Priest

7 This Melchizedek was king of Salem and
priest of God Most High. He met Abraham
returning from the defeat of the kings and blessed
him, 2and Abraham gave him a tenth of everything. First, his name means "king of righteousness"; then also, "king of Salem" means "king of
peace." 3Without father or mother, without genealogy, without beginning of days or end of life, like
the Son of God he remains a priest forever.

4Just think how great he was: Even the patriarch
Abraham gave him a tenth of the plunder! 5Now
the law requires the descendants of Levi who become priests to collect a tenth from the people—
that is, their brothers—even though their brothers
are descended from Abraham. 6This man, however, did not trace his descent from Levi, yet he
collected a tenth from Abraham and blessed him
who had the promises. 7And without doubt the
lesser person is blessed by the greater. 8In the one
case, the tenth is collected by men who die; but in
the other case, by him who is declared to be living.
9One might even say that Levi, who collects the
tenth, paid the tenth through Abraham, 10because

[a] 1 Or *from useless rituals* [b] 6 Or *repentance while* [c] 14 Gen. 22:17

when Melchizedek met Abraham, Levi was still in
the body of his ancestor. Ro 4:13; Heb 5:6; 6:20

Jesus Like Melchizedek

11If perfection could have been attained
through the Levitical priesthood (for on the basis
of it the law was given to the people), why was
there still need for another priest to come—one in
the order of Melchizedek, not in the order of Aaron? 12For when there is a change of the priesthood,
there must also be a change of the law. 13He of
whom these things are said belonged to a different
tribe, and no one from that tribe has ever served
at the altar. 14For it is clear that our Lord descended from Judah, and in regard to that tribe Moses
said nothing about priests. 15And what we have
said is even more clear if another priest like Melchizedek appears, 16one who has become a priest
not on the basis of a regulation as to his ancestry
but on the basis of the power of an indestructible
life. 17For it is declared: Isa 11:1; Lk 3:33

"You are a priest forever,
in the order of Melchizedek."[a] Ps 110:4

18The former regulation is set aside because it
was weak and useless 19(for the law made nothing
perfect), and a better hope is introduced, by which
we draw near to God. Ro 3:20; Heb 4:16
20And it was not without an oath! Others became priests without any oath, 21but he became a
priest with an oath when God said to him:

"The Lord has sworn
and will not change his mind: 1Sa 15:29
'You are a priest forever.'"[a]

22Because of this oath, Jesus has become the guarantee of a better covenant. Heb 5:6; 8:6
23Now there have been many of those priests,
since death prevented them from continuing in
office; 24but because Jesus lives forever, he has a
permanent priesthood. 25Therefore he is able to
save completely[b] those who come to God
through him, because he always lives to intercede
for them. Ro 8:34; 11:14
26Such a high priest meets our need—one who
is holy, blameless, pure, set apart from sinners,
exalted above the heavens. 27Unlike the other high
priests, he does not need to offer sacrifices day
after day, first for his own sins, and then for the
sins of the people. He sacrificed for their sins once
for all when he offered himself. 28For the law appoints as high priests men who are weak; but the
oath, which came after the law, appointed the Son,
who has been made perfect forever. Heb 2:10; 5:2

The High Priest of a New Covenant

8 The point of what we are saying is this: We do
have such a high priest, who sat down at the
right hand of the throne of the Majesty in heaven,
2and who serves in the sanctuary, the true tabernacle set up by the Lord, not by man. Heb 9:11,24
3Every high priest is appointed to offer both
gifts and sacrifices, and so it was necessary for this
one also to have something to offer. 4If he were on
earth, he would not be a priest, for there are already men who offer the gifts prescribed by the
law. 5They serve at a sanctuary that is a copy and
shadow of what is in heaven. This is why Moses
was warned when he was about to build the tabernacle: "See to it that you make everything according to the pattern shown you on the mountain."[c]
6But the ministry Jesus has received is as superior
to theirs as the covenant of which he is mediator
is superior to the old one, and it is founded on
better promises. Ex 25:40; Lk 22:20
7For if there had been nothing wrong with that
first covenant, no place would have been sought
for another. 8But God found fault with the people
and said[d]: Heb 7:11,18

"The time is coming, declares the Lord,
when I will make a new covenant Jer 31:31
with the house of Israel
and with the house of Judah.
9It will not be like the covenant
I made with their forefathers Ex 19:5-6
when I took them by the hand
to lead them out of Egypt,
because they did not remain faithful to my
covenant,
and I turned away from them,
declares the Lord.
10This is the covenant I will make with the
house of Israel Ro 11:27
after that time, declares the Lord.
I will put my laws in their minds

LIVING  **INSIGHT**

When you need Jesus, He is there. He's there even when you don't think you need Him! You're never too early or too late. He's never in a lousy mood, nor will He ask you to call back during office hours. He's available . . . because He's immutable. He remains constant. With Him, there's no new year or old year. He is "the same" (13:8), regardless.

(See Hebrews 7:23–25.)

[a] *17,21* Psalm 110:4 [b] *25* Or *forever* [c] *5* Exodus 25:40 [d] *8* Some manuscripts may be translated *fault and said to the people.*

and write them on their hearts. Heb 10:16
I will be their God,
and they will be my people. Zec 8:8
11No longer will a man teach his neighbor,
or a man his brother, saying, 'Know the
Lord,'
because they will all know me,
from the least of them to the greatest.
12For I will forgive their wickedness
and will remember their sins no more."[a]

13By calling this covenant "new," he has made
the first one obsolete; and what is obsolete and
aging will soon disappear. 2Co 5:17

Worship in the Earthly Tabernacle

9 Now the first covenant had regulations for
worship and also an earthly sanctuary. 2A
tabernacle was set up. In its first room were the
lampstand, the table and the consecrated bread;
this was called the Holy Place. 3Behind the second
curtain was a room called the Most Holy Place,
4which had the golden altar of incense and the
gold-covered ark of the covenant. This ark contained the gold jar of manna, Aaron's staff that had
budded, and the stone tablets of the covenant.
5Above the ark were the cherubim of the Glory,
overshadowing the atonement cover.[b] But we
cannot discuss these things in detail now.
6When everything had been arranged like this,
the priests entered regularly into the outer room to
carry on their ministry. 7But only the high priest
entered the inner room, and that only once a year,
and never without blood, which he offered for
himself and for the sins the people had committed
in ignorance. 8The Holy Spirit was showing by this
that the way into the Most Holy Place had not yet
been disclosed as long as the first tabernacle was
still standing. 9This is an illustration for the
present time, indicating that the gifts and sacrifices
being offered were not able to clear the conscience
of the worshiper. 10They are only a matter of food
and drink and various ceremonial washings—external regulations applying until the time of the
new order. Col 2:16; Heb 7:16

The Blood of Christ

11When Christ came as high priest of the good
things that are already here,[c] he went through the
greater and more perfect tabernacle that is not
man-made, that is to say, not a part of this creation. 12He did not enter by means of the blood of
goats and calves; but he entered the Most Holy
Place once for all by his own blood, having obtained eternal redemption. 13The blood of goats
and bulls and the ashes of a heifer sprinkled on
those who are ceremonially unclean sanctify them
so that they are outwardly clean. 14How much
more, then, will the blood of Christ, who through
the eternal Spirit offered himself unblemished to
God, cleanse our consciences from acts that lead to
death,[d] so that we may serve the living God!
15For this reason Christ is the mediator of a new
covenant, that those who are called may receive
the promised eternal inheritance—now that he
has died as a ransom to set them free from the sins
committed under the first covenant. 1Ti 2:5; Heb 7:22
16In the case of a will,[e] it is necessary to prove
the death of the one who made it, 17because a will
is in force only when somebody has died; it never
takes effect while the one who made it is living.
18This is why even the first covenant was not put
into effect without blood. 19When Moses had proclaimed every commandment of the law to all the
people, he took the blood of calves, together with
water, scarlet wool and branches of hyssop, and
sprinkled the scroll and all the people. 20He said,
"This is the blood of the covenant, which God has
commanded you to keep."[f] 21In the same way, he
sprinkled with the blood both the tabernacle and
everything used in its ceremonies. 22In fact, the law
requires that nearly everything be cleansed with
blood, and without the shedding of blood there is
no forgiveness. Ex 24:8; Mt 26:28
23It was necessary, then, for the copies of the
heavenly things to be purified with these sacrifices,
but the heavenly things themselves with better sacrifices than these. 24For Christ did not enter a

LIVING  **INSIGHT**

Jesus Christ never again has to die! After His one-time sacrificial death, the Father said, "I am satisfied." The payment on the cross satisfied the Father's demand against sin. How do we know He's satisfied? He raised His Son from the grave. He brought Him back from death. The resurrection was God's "Amen" to Christ's, "It is finished."

(See Hebrews 9:23–28.)

man-made sanctuary that was only a copy of the
true one; he entered heaven itself, now to appear
for us in God's presence. 25Nor did he enter heav-
en to offer himself again and again, the way the
high priest enters the Most Holy Place every year
with blood that is not his own. 26Then Christ
would have had to suffer many times since the
creation of the world. But now he has appeared
once for all at the end of the ages to do away with
sin by the sacrifice of himself. 27Just as man is

[a] 12 Jer. 31:31-34 [b] 5 Traditionally *the mercy seat* [c] 11 Some early manuscripts *are to come* [d] 14 Or *from useless rituals* [e] 16 Same Greek word as *covenant*; also in verse 17 [f] 20 Exodus 24:8

destined to die once, and after that to face judgment, [28]so Christ was sacrificed once to take away the sins of many people; and he will appear a second time, not to bear sin, but to bring salvation to those who are waiting for him. 2Co 5:10; 1Pe 2:24

Christ's Sacrifice Once for All

10 The law is only a shadow of the good things that are coming—not the realities themselves. For this reason it can never, by the same sacrifices repeated endlessly year after year, make perfect those who draw near to worship. [2]If it could, would they not have stopped being offered? For the worshipers would have been cleansed once for all, and would no longer have felt guilty for their sins. [3]But those sacrifices are an annual reminder of sins, [4]because it is impossible for the blood of bulls and goats to take away sins.

[5]Therefore, when Christ came into the world, he said: Heb 1:6

"Sacrifice and offering you did not desire,
but a body you prepared for me; 1Pe 2:24
[6]with burnt offerings and sin offerings
you were not pleased.
[7]Then I said, 'Here I am—it is written about
me in the scroll— Jer 36:2
I have come to do your will, O God.'"[a]

[8]First he said, "Sacrifices and offerings, burnt offerings and sin offerings you did not desire, nor were you pleased with them" (although the law required them to be made). [9]Then he said, "Here I am, I have come to do your will." He sets aside the first to establish the second. [10]And by that will, we have been made holy through the sacrifice of the body of Jesus Christ once for all. Jn 17:19

[11]Day after day every priest stands and performs his religious duties; again and again he offers the same sacrifices, which can never take away sins. [12]But when this priest had offered for all time one sacrifice for sins, he sat down at the right hand of God. [13]Since that time he waits for his enemies to be made his footstool, [14]because by one sacrifice he has made perfect forever those who are being made holy. Eph 5:26; Heb 1:13

[15]The Holy Spirit also testifies to us about this. First he says: Heb 3:7

[16]"This is the covenant I will make with them
after that time, says the Lord.
I will put my laws in their hearts,
and I will write them on their minds."[b]

[17]Then he adds:

"Their sins and lawless acts
I will remember no more."[c]

[18]And where these have been forgiven, there is no longer any sacrifice for sin. Jer 31:33; Heb 8:10,12

A Call to Persevere

[19]Therefore, brothers, since we have confidence to enter the Most Holy Place by the blood of Jesus, [20]by a new and living way opened for us through the curtain, that is, his body, [21]and since we have a great priest over the house of God, [22]let us draw near to God with a sincere heart in full assurance of faith, having our hearts sprinkled to cleanse us from a guilty conscience and having our bodies washed with pure water. [23]Let us hold unswervingly to the hope we profess, for he who promised is faithful. [24]And let us consider how we may spur one another on toward love and good deeds. [25]Let us not give up meeting together, as some are in the habit of doing, but let us encourage one another—and all the more as you see the Day approaching.

[26]If we deliberately keep on sinning after we have received the knowledge of the truth, no sacrifice for sins is left, [27]but only a fearful expectation of judgment and of raging fire that will consume the enemies of God. [28]Anyone who rejected the law of Moses died without mercy on the testimony of two or three witnesses. [29]How much more severely do you think a man deserves to be punished who has trampled the Son of God under foot, who has treated as an unholy thing the blood of the covenant that sanctified him, and who has insulted the Spirit of grace? [30]For we know him who said, "It is mine to avenge; I will repay,"[d] and again, "The Lord will judge his people."[e] [31]It is a dreadful thing to fall into the hands of the living God.

[32]Remember those earlier days after you had received the light, when you stood your ground in a great contest in the face of suffering. [33]Sometimes you were publicly exposed to insult and persecution; at other times you stood side by side with those who were so treated. [34]You sympathized with those in prison and joyfully accepted the confiscation of your property, because you knew that you yourselves had better and lasting possessions.

[35]So do not throw away your confidence; it will be richly rewarded. [36]You need to persevere so that when you have done the will of God, you will receive what he has promised. [37]For in just a very little while, Lk 21:19; Heb 12:1

"He who is coming will come and will not
delay. Mt 11:3; Rev 22:20
[38] But my righteous one[f] will live by faith.
And if he shrinks back,
I will not be pleased with him."[g]

[39]But we are not of those who shrink back and are destroyed, but of those who believe and are saved.

[a] *7* Psalm 40:6-8 (see Septuagint) [b] *16* Jer. 31:33 [c] *17* Jer. 31:34 [d] *30* Deut. 32:35 [e] *30* Deut. 32:36; Psalm 135:14
[f] *38* One early manuscript *But the righteous* [g] *38* Hab. 2:3,4

Jesus: Superior for Life — Chapters 11–13

A good friend once said to me, "I think chapters 11–13 of Hebrews are the reward God gives us for wading through chapters 1–10." I think he's on to something! Chapter 11 records the names of men and women who lived great lives of faith. God carried them through sleepless nights and agonizing days, through times of loss and brokenness and failure and pain. These people of faith show us that Jesus is the One who gives us a superior life of faith. In Him we have the victory. But please remember, we're signed up for the long haul. A life of faith is a life of being carried, but not necessarily on a bed of ease. Chapter 12 reminds us that in the long-distance race of faith, we must be prepared to submit to discipline that will correct us and instruct us in our spiritual growth. Chapter 13 shares a number of practical rules for Christian living, urging us to love others and show compassion to the hurting. As we focus on Jesus, we will be able to accomplish many things for His glory.

By Faith

11 Now faith is being sure of what we hope for
and certain of what we do not see. 2This is
what the ancients were commended for. Ro 8:24
3By faith we understand that the universe was
formed at God's command, so that what is seen
was not made out of what was visible. Ge 1; 2Pe 3:5
4By faith Abel offered God a better sacrifice
than Cain did. By faith he was commended as a
righteous man, when God spoke well of his offerings. And by faith he still speaks, even though he
is dead. Ge 4:4; Heb 12:24
5By faith Enoch was taken from this life, so that
he did not experience death; he could not be
found, because God had taken him away. For before he was taken, he was commended as one who
pleased God. 6And without faith it is impossible to
please God, because anyone who comes to him
must believe that he exists and that he rewards
those who earnestly seek him. Ge 5:21-24; Heb 7:19
7By faith Noah, when warned about things not
yet seen, in holy fear built an ark to save his family.
By his faith he condemned the world and became
heir of the righteousness that comes by faith.
8By faith Abraham, when called to go to a place
he would later receive as his inheritance, obeyed
and went, even though he did not know where he
was going. 9By faith he made his home in the
promised land like a stranger in a foreign country;
he lived in tents, as did Isaac and Jacob, who were
heirs with him of the same promise. 10For he was
looking forward to the city with foundations,
whose architect and builder is God. Heb 6:17; 12:22
11By faith Abraham, even though he was past
age—and Sarah herself was barren—was enabled
to become a father because he[a] considered him
faithful who had made the promise. 12And so from
this one man, and he as good as dead, came
descendants as numerous as the stars in the sky
and as countless as the sand on the seashore.
13All these people were still living by faith when
they died. They did not receive the things promised; they only saw them and welcomed them from
a distance. And they admitted that they were aliens

LIVING 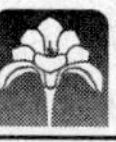 INSIGHT

God calls us "aliens and strangers" during our short stint on planet earth. People on the move, living in tents, free and unencumbered, loose and available, ready to roll, willing to break the mold—whenever and wherever He leads. No matter what!

(See Hebrews 11:13.)

and strangers on earth. 14People who say such
things show that they are looking for a country of
their own. 15If they had been thinking of the country they had left, they would have had opportunity
to return. 16Instead, they were longing for a better
country—a heavenly one. Therefore God is not
ashamed to be called their God, for he has prepared a city for them. Ex 3:6,15; Heb 13:14
17By faith Abraham, when God tested him, offered Isaac as a sacrifice. He who had received the
promises was about to sacrifice his one and only
son, 18even though God had said to him, "It is
through Isaac that your offspring[b] will be reckoned."[c] 19Abraham reasoned that God could
raise the dead, and figuratively speaking, he did
receive Isaac back from death. Ge 22:1-10; Ro 4:21
20By faith Isaac blessed Jacob and Esau in regard to their future. Ge 27:27-29,39-40
21By faith Jacob, when he was dying, blessed
each of Joseph's sons, and worshiped as he leaned
on the top of his staff. Ge 48:1,8-22
22By faith Joseph, when his end was near, spoke
about the exodus of the Israelites from Egypt and
gave instructions about his bones. Ge 50:24-25
23By faith Moses' parents hid him for three
months after he was born, because they saw he was
no ordinary child, and they were not afraid of the
king's edict. Ex 1:16,22; 2:2
24By faith Moses, when he had grown up, refused to be known as the son of Pharaoh's daughter. 25He chose to be mistreated along with the
people of God rather than to enjoy the pleasures of
sin for a short time. 26He regarded disgrace for the
sake of Christ as of greater value than the treasures
of Egypt, because he was looking ahead to his
reward. 27By faith he left Egypt, not fearing the
king's anger; he persevered because he saw him
who is invisible. 28By faith he kept the Passover

[a] *11* Or *By faith even Sarah, who was past age, was enabled to bear children because she* [b] *18* Greek *seed* [c] *18* Gen. 21:12

NOAH

The Shipbuilding Preacher

"By faith Noah, when warned about things not yet seen, in holy fear built an ark to save his family. By his faith he condemned the world and became heir of the righteousness that comes by faith."

—HEBREWS 11:7

The story of Noah is familiar to many of us, and yet I suspect there are some facts that are not very familiar to us. Consider this:

When Noah started building the ark, his sons weren't even born yet.

Noah lived five hundred miles away from the nearest large body of water.

The ark's holding capacity was equal to eight modern-day freight trains of 66 cars each.

God still remembers His promise to Noah every time He sees a rainbow.

Noah lived in a world that had degenerated into complete rebellion against God. "The LORD saw how great man's wickedness on the earth had become, and that every inclination of the thoughts of his heart was only evil all the time" (Genesis 6:5). Dreadful days. Days of moral contamination and compromise. But right smack in the middle of that flow of sewage was Noah, a godly man who would rear a godly family.

Finally God had seen enough: "The LORD was grieved that he had made man on the earth, and his heart was filled with pain. So the LORD said, 'I will wipe mankind, whom I have created, from the face of the earth' " (Genesis 6:6–7). Now that's what I would call a frightening prophecy! Never had such a word been spoken on the earth. But while God's plan of judgment was to grind completely, it would also grind slowly. For 120 years (6:3)—from the time God first spoke with Noah to the time of the flood—humanity had the opportunity to respond to God (see 1 Peter 3:20). And Noah was the model that humanity was to follow. He "walked with God" (Genesis 6:9).

The entire time that Noah was ordering wood and pounding nails he was making a dramatic announcement to a wicked generation. We've all seen huge barges and large seagoing vessels. But the people of the Noah's world had never seen the likes of Noah's ark! Here he was building this huge ship in his back yard, hundreds of miles away from any navigable body of water. So during those 120 years, this shipbuilding preacher must have been a powerful witness to God's incredible patience and power.

After this mammoth construction project was completed, God closed the door of the ark. Inside were His only followers, along with a collection of animals the likes of which hadn't been seen since the Garden of Eden. It's an amazing story. And then God's terrible judgment fell on the rest of the outside world.

Now read on just a bit and notice the first thing Noah did when he left the ark: He "built an altar to the LORD" (Genesis 8:20). Why? I think it was because he was afraid. The world was completely different from the way he had remembered it. He saw strange new mountains and valleys; the climate was alien to him. And over all the world hung an eerie silence. So Noah knelt down before God and prayed, and God responded to him with an enduring and beautiful promise: "Never again will all life be cut off by the waters of a flood . . . I have set my rainbow in the clouds, and it will be a sign of the covenant between me and the earth" (9:11,13).

You know what you need when the storms start raging around you? You need what this story offers: a good solid dose of Biblical truth to sink your anchors into. At times you may think you're at your end, that you're going to be wiped off the face of the earth. Let me offer you this gentle advice: At those times, relax. God's plan is full of rainbows, and people who trust in Him are especially honored and protected.

and the sprinkling of blood, so that the destroyer
of the firstborn would not touch the firstborn of
Israel. Ex 12:21-23; Heb 13:13
29By faith the people passed through the Red
Sea[a] as on dry land; but when the Egyptians tried
to do so, they were drowned. Ex 14:21-31
30By faith the walls of Jericho fell, after the people had marched around them for seven days.
31By faith the prostitute Rahab, because she welcomed the spies, was not killed with those who
were disobedient.[b] Jos 6:22-25; Jas 2:25
32And what more shall I say? I do not have time
to tell about Gideon, Barak, Samson, Jephthah,
David, Samuel and the prophets, 33who through
faith conquered kingdoms, administered justice,
and gained what was promised; who shut the
mouths of lions, 34quenched the fury of the flames,
and escaped the edge of the sword; whose weakness was turned to strength; and who became
powerful in battle and routed foreign armies.
35Women received back their dead, raised to life
again. Others were tortured and refused to be released, so that they might gain a better resurrection. 36Some faced jeers and flogging, while still
others were chained and put in prison. 37They
were stoned[c]; they were sawed in two; they were
put to death by the sword. They went about in
sheepskins and goatskins, destitute, persecuted
and mistreated— 38the world was not worthy of
them. They wandered in deserts and mountains,
and in caves and holes in the ground. 1Ki 18:4
39These were all commended for their faith, yet
none of them received what had been promised.
40God had planned something better for us so that
only together with us would they be made perfect.

God Disciplines His Sons

12 Therefore, since we are surrounded by
such a great cloud of witnesses, let us
throw off everything that hinders and the sin that
so easily entangles, and let us run with perseverance the race marked out for us. 2Let us fix our
eyes on Jesus, the author and perfecter of our faith,
who for the joy set before him endured the cross,
scorning its shame, and sat down at the right hand
of the throne of God. 3Consider him who endured
such opposition from sinful men, so that you will
not grow weary and lose heart. Gal 6:9; Php 2:8-9
4In your struggle against sin, you have not yet
resisted to the point of shedding your blood. 5And
you have forgotten that word of encouragement
that addresses you as sons: Heb 10:32-34

"My son, do not make light of the Lord's
discipline,
and do not lose heart when he rebukes you,
6because the Lord disciplines those he loves,
and he punishes everyone he accepts as a
son."[d] Pr 3:11-12

7Endure hardship as discipline; God is treating
you as sons. For what son is not disciplined by his
father? 8If you are not disciplined (and everyone
undergoes discipline), then you are illegitimate
children and not true sons. 9Moreover, we have all
had human fathers who disciplined us and we respected them for it. How much more should we
submit to the Father of our spirits and live! 10Our
fathers disciplined us for a little while as they
thought best; but God disciplines us for our good,
that we may share in his holiness. 11No discipline
seems pleasant at the time, but painful. Later on,
however, it produces a harvest of righteousness
and peace for those who have been trained by it.
12Therefore, strengthen your feeble arms and
weak knees. 13"Make level paths for your feet,"[e]
so that the lame may not be disabled, but rather
healed. Pr 4:26; Gal 6:1

Warning Against Refusing God

14Make every effort to live in peace with all men
and to be holy; without holiness no one will see the
Lord. 15See to it that no one misses the grace of
God and that no bitter root grows up to cause
trouble and defile many. 16See that no one is sexually immoral, or is godless like Esau, who for a
single meal sold his inheritance rights as the oldest
son. 17Afterward, as you know, when he wanted to
inherit this blessing, he was rejected. He could
bring about no change of mind, though he sought
the blessing with tears. Ge 25:29-34; 27:30-40
18You have not come to a mountain that can be
touched and that is burning with fire; to darkness,
gloom and storm; 19to a trumpet blast or to such
a voice speaking words that those who heard it
begged that no further word be spoken to them,
20because they could not bear what was commanded: "If even an animal touches the mountain, it
must be stoned."[f] 21The sight was so terrifying
that Moses said, "I am trembling with fear."[g]
22But you have come to Mount Zion, to the
heavenly Jerusalem, the city of the living God. You

LIVING  INSIGHT

About the time we are ready to give up, Jesus comes alongside and whispers, "Don't quit, keep going, keep your eyes on Me," as He provides His gentle touch of grace, joy and love at just the right moment.

(See Hebrews 12:1–3.)

[a]29 That is, Sea of Reeds [b]31 Or *unbelieving* [c]37 Some early manuscripts *stoned; they were put to the test;*
[d]6 Prov. 3:11,12 [e]13 Prov. 4:26 [f]20 Exodus 19:12,13 [g]21 Deut. 9:19

have come to thousands upon thousands of angels in joyful assembly, 23 to the church of the firstborn, whose names are written in heaven. You have come to God, the judge of all men, to the spirits of righteous men made perfect, 24 to Jesus the mediator of a new covenant, and to the sprinkled blood that speaks a better word than the blood of Abel.

25 See to it that you do not refuse him who speaks. If they did not escape when they refused him who warned them on earth, how much less will we, if we turn away from him who warns us from heaven? 26 At that time his voice shook the earth, but now he has promised, "Once more I will shake not only the earth but also the heavens."[a] 27 The words "once more" indicate the removing of what can be shaken—that is, created things—so that what cannot be shaken may remain. 1Co 7:31

28 Therefore, since we are receiving a kingdom that cannot be shaken, let us be thankful, and so worship God acceptably with reverence and awe, 29 for our "God is a consuming fire."[b] Dt 4:24

Concluding Exhortations

13 Keep on loving each other as brothers. 2 Do not forget to entertain strangers, for by so doing some people have entertained angels without knowing it. 3 Remember those in prison as if you were their fellow prisoners, and those who are mistreated as if you yourselves were suffering.

4 Marriage should be honored by all, and the marriage bed kept pure, for God will judge the

LIVING  **INSIGHT**

It is terribly important that we keep a safe distance when there is the temptation to be involved in illicit activity. We are living in a day when moral purity and marital infidelity are being rationalized and compromised. More and more people are convincing themselves it's okay to fudge a little.

(See Hebrews 13:4.)

adulterer and all the sexually immoral. 5 Keep your lives free from the love of money and be content with what you have, because God has said,

"Never will I leave you;
never will I forsake you."[c]

6 So we say with confidence,

"The Lord is my helper; I will not be afraid.
What can man do to me?"[d] Dt 31:6,8; Jos 1:5

7 Remember your leaders, who spoke the word of God to you. Consider the outcome of their way of life and imitate their faith. 8 Jesus Christ is the same yesterday and today and forever. Heb 1:12

9 Do not be carried away by all kinds of strange teachings. It is good for our hearts to be strengthened by grace, not by ceremonial foods, which are of no value to those who eat them. 10 We have an altar from which those who minister at the tabernacle have no right to eat. 1Co 9:13; Eph 4:14

11 The high priest carries the blood of animals into the Most Holy Place as a sin offering, but the bodies are burned outside the camp. 12 And so Jesus also suffered outside the city gate to make the people holy through his own blood. 13 Let us, then, go to him outside the camp, bearing the disgrace he bore. 14 For here we do not have an enduring city, but we are looking for the city that is to come.

15 Through Jesus, therefore, let us continually offer to God a sacrifice of praise—the fruit of lips that confess his name. 16 And do not forget to do good and to share with others, for with such sacrifices God is pleased. Php 4:18; Hos 14:2

17 Obey your leaders and submit to their authority. They keep watch over you as men who must give an account. Obey them so that their work will be a joy, not a burden, for that would be of no advantage to you. Isa 62:6; Ac 20:28

18 Pray for us. We are sure that we have a clear conscience and desire to live honorably in every way. 19 I particularly urge you to pray so that I may be restored to you soon. 1Th 5:25; Phm 22

20 May the God of peace, who through the blood of the eternal covenant brought back from the dead our Lord Jesus, that great Shepherd of the sheep, 21 equip you with everything good for doing his will, and may he work in us what is pleasing to him, through Jesus Christ, to whom be glory for ever and ever. Amen. Php 2:13; Jn 3:22

22 Brothers, I urge you to bear with my word of exhortation, for I have written you only a short letter. 1Pe 5:12

23 I want you to know that our brother Timothy has been released. If he arrives soon, I will come with him to see you. Ac 16:1

24 Greet all your leaders and all God's people. Those from Italy send you their greetings. Ac 18:2

25 Grace be with you all. Col 4:18

[a] 26 Haggai 2:6 [b] 29 Deut. 4:24 [c] 5 Deut. 31:6 [d] 6 Psalm 118:6,7

INTRODUCTION

JAMES

Although the German reformer Martin Luther saw the letter of James as merely "an epistle of straw," this New Testament letter stands to this day as one of the most practical and penetrating books in all the Bible. Don't be fooled by its size! It may be brief, but it's strong. It refuses to let the reader hide behind a mask of theoretical thought or within the walls of an intellectual faith. True faith produces authenticity. "No authenticity . . . no faith"—that's James's analysis of the matter. That kind of teaching may make us squirm, but it surely will force us to get out of the stands and into the playing field of living out our faith day after day after day. As James put it so plainly and so forthrightly, "Do not merely listen to the word, and so deceive yourselves. Do what it says" (1:22).

WRITER: *James*

DATE: *C.A.D. 40–50*

PURPOSE: *To instruct and encourage dispersed believers in the face of trials and oppression*

KEY THEME: *Real faith produces authentic deeds*

EMPHASES: *Vital Christianity; good deeds; faith that works*

KEY VERSES: *2:14-20*

KEY TERMS: *"Faith"; "deeds"*

ANALOGIES: *Jesus' Sermon on the Mount; wisdom writings, such as the book of Proverbs*

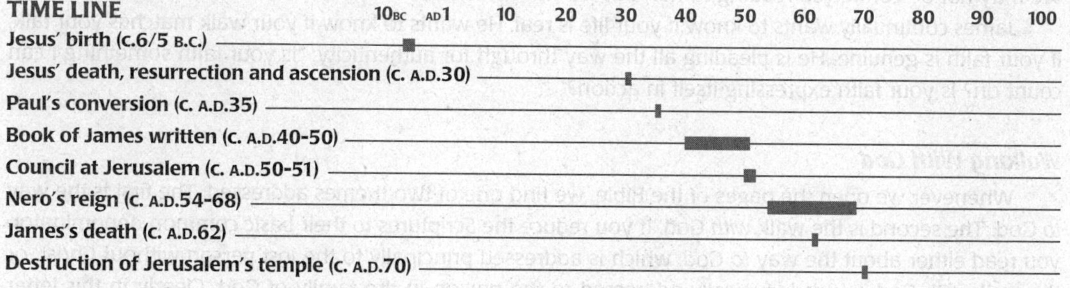

A Plea for Authenticity

FAITH . . .	**When stretched it doesn't break**	**When pressed it doesn't fail**	**When expressed it doesn't explode**	**When distressed it doesn't panic**
DEEDS . . .	**Authentic stability**	**Authentic love**	**Authentic control and humility**	**Authentic patience**
	Greeting Trials Temptation Response to Scripture	Partiality and prejudice Indifference and intellectualism Obedience and action	The tongue The heart The will	Money matters Sickness Carnality and correction
	CHAPTER 1	*CHAPTER 2*	*CHAPTERS 3–4*	*CHAPTER 5*
BACKGROUND	**The difficulties of life caused the scattered saints to drift spiritually, leading to all forms of problems—unbridled speech, wrong attitudes, doubt, strife, carnality, shallow faith.**			
CHARACTERISTICS	**"The Proverbs of the New Testament," James contains many practical, straightforward exhortations. Emphasis is on importance of balancing right belief with right behavior. Many Old Testament word pictures and references.**			

When I see complacency in my own life or in the life of any Christian, for that matter, I am tempted to offer a simple suggestion: Read the letter of James. This forthright author really grabs us by the shoulders and shakes us awake.

James is a rather brief letter—just over a hundred verses in length. Yet I don't know of a more penetrating letter we could ever read—with five no-nonsense chapters that get "down and dirty" inside our lives. We may not be comforted reading James, but we will be convicted.

James continually wants to know if your life is real. He wants to know if your walk matches your talk, if your faith is genuine. He is pleading all the way through for authenticity: "Is your faith something I can count on? Is your faith expressing itself in action?"

Walking With God

Whenever we open the pages of the Bible, we find one of two themes addressed. The first is the way *to* God. The second is the walk *with* God. If you reduce the Scriptures to their basic common denominator, you read either about the way *to* God, which is addressed principally to the lost person without Christ, or the walk *with* God, which is typically addressed to the person in the family of God. Clearly in this letter James was writing to believers. The problem was, many of these believers weren't living like believers. Sound familiar?

Over and over James drove home the point with words that went something like this: "If your faith is genuine, then your walk will be authentic." Or to put it another way, *If you say you believe like you should, then why do you behave like you shouldn't*? That's really James's question. "If you keep telling me you have the right theory, and you have placed your faith in the right message, why is it you're living a wrong life?"

James really digs deeply, like a burr under your saddle. He will work on you in areas you were convinced no one knew about. That's why this letter is as powerful today as it was centuries ago.

A Note From Jesus' Little Brother

What kind of man was this who would write such a hard-hitting letter? Notice what he called himself in the first verse: "James, a servant of God and of the Lord Jesus Christ." There were five men named James mentioned in the New Testament. Most students of the Bible believe that the writer of this letter was the brother of our Lord Jesus (see Matthew 13:55; Galatians 1:19)—to be technical about it, *His half brother*. James was raised in the family of Mary and Joseph. He was a blood son of Mary and Joseph, so James and Jesus had the same mother. (Jesus, being virgin-born, had God as his Father.)

What do we know about this man before he came to know Jesus as his Savior and Lord? We don't hear much about the family of Jesus in the Bible—we hear something about Mary, a little about Mary's husband, Joseph, not much at all about Jesus' brothers and sisters. In fact, sometimes people don't even realize that Jesus had brothers and sisters. Yet He certainly did. Read verses 54–56 of Matthew 13, and you'll find that His brothers and sisters were well-known by the people of Nazareth. In incredulous amazement at what Jesus was teaching and doing, the people said, "Isn't this the carpenter's son? Isn't his mother's name Mary, and aren't his brothers James, Joseph, Simon and Judas. Aren't all his sisters with us?" (Matthew 13:55–56a). The important thing not to overlook here is the naming of Jesus' brothers and the mentioning of "all his sisters." Jesus was the oldest in a large family.

For whatever reason, whether because of jealousy or resentment or pride, James resisted putting his faith in Jesus (see John 7:5) until the resurrection. It took this powerful miracle to convince him that this man, his brother, was indeed the Messiah (see 1 Corinthians 15:7). Later James joined the prayer group of believers awaiting the outpouring of the Holy Spirit (Acts 1:14) and was to become a leader in the Jerusalem church (Acts 15:13). This once-skeptical man came to believe that Jesus was, in fact, the promised Messiah, the One who came to bring redemption to His people. James lived, ultimately, to declare the good news of the gospel of Jesus Christ through his faithful service to the church and through the writing of this letter.

I think it's commendable that James didn't drop names and write, "I'm Jesus' brother." No, he made a very simple, direct statement of the essence of his own identity and mission: "James, a servant of God and of the Lord Jesus Christ" (1:1). Notice that he doesn't even add, in apposition, "Jesus Christ . . . my brother." James is content to acknowledge Jesus as his Lord and God. This younger-brother, once-reluctant, hard-hearted, former cynic turned believer had come a long way.

Through the Eyes of a Skeptic

This long-standing skeptic may very well have brought the practiced eye of a penetrating critic to the writing of this letter. I can just see James watching the lives of some of the followers of Jesus and seeing attitudes and behavior inconsistent with their profession of faith in Jesus. With that trained eye aimed at the hearts of his readers, James leveled his blasts at the hypocrisy that continued to plague those who claimed to believe in Jesus. Be assured that there are a lot of "James-types" who are watching you in your place of work and in your neighborhood and in other places where you spend your time. Could it be that they're saying this about you? "You listen to all of that high-powered stuff about Jesus worship service after worship service and you claim to believe it. But I watch you during the rest of the week—and I'm not convinced that it's real."

To the Believers Scattered Abroad

The letter was addressed to Jews who were scattered abroad: "To the twelve tribes scattered among the nations: Greetings" (1:1). The word "scattered" carries the idea of being spread out widely, broadly, as you would throw seed out across the field.

James directed these words to converted Jews who had been spread out across the land. Many scholars believe that these Jewish Christians had been dispersed because of persecution. The date of the writing of this letter is thought to be about A.D. 45, or maybe as late as A.D. 48—at a time when believers from the early Jerusalem church were scattered after Stephen's death (Acts 8:1; 11:19). That would place James as the earliest New Testament document written—no Gospels yet written, no inspired letters in existence and circulating among churches. Therefore, these Jewish Christians had no Scriptures available to them except the Old Testament. They had been cast out of the comfort of their homes and spread abroad. They were in great need of encouragement, as well as straight talk from someone they admired and respected.

How do we know they were Christians? On no less than 11 occasions James called his readers "brothers" (1:2,16,19; 2:1,14; 3:1; 4:11; 5:7,10,12,19). So these were believers in Jesus, who, for whatever reason, had been thrown to the wind to make it on their own. James wrote to them because he was concerned about their walk with God, worried that they were even beginning to wonder if they had been deceived by the claims of Christianity. Can't you just hear this converted skeptic bellow his response: "Wait just a minute! You say you believe the truth? You tell me you professed belief in Messiah and your life has been revolutionized? I want to probe deeper; I want to look beneath what you say. I want to address your negative attitudes, mention your lack of compassion, talk about your uncontrolled tongue, your envy, your pride, your quarrels . . . all the attitudes and behaviors that belie your faith. If you say you believe like you should, then why do you behave like you shouldn't?"

The Root and the Fruit

So disturbing has been the letter of James down the ages that the German reformer Martin Luther protested its inclusion in the New Testament canon (he called it an "an epistle of straw") and struggled to reconcile its message with that of the apostle Paul. Luther believed portions of James were downright heresy. With all due respect for a great man with a great mind, I am convinced that Luther missed the point of this letter. Rather than being a strawy epistle, it is simply a penetrating letter, urging the believer to show by his or her deeds that Jesus Christ is at work within.

While Paul left us an eloquent legacy of teaching about grace and faith (often in response to those who were slavishly legalistic), James's contribution to the balanced Christian life would be an emphasis on deeds. James always wanted to know, "How does your theology work itself out in practice? You say you have the root? I'm looking at the fruit." James's concern was, simply stated, practical Christianity. You won't find an ounce of theory in this great little letter. There was little mistaking the message: *Real faith produces authentic deeds.* Faith and deeds go together.

Many of James's commands have clear parallels with Jesus' "Sermon on the Mount" (see Matthew 5–7). Any who would accuse James of bordering on heresy in his call for a faith that expresses itself in deeds must remember Jesus' high call to moral and ethical living and His insistence that by their fruit we would recognize true believers and false believers (Matthew 7:15–23). The truth expressed by Jesus is the same truth that permeates the letter of James: "In the same way, let your light shine before men, that they may see your good deeds and praise your Father in heaven" (Matthew 5:16). James in the totality of his message agrees with the Savior's sermon, leaving us with this unmistakable exhortation stated in words to this effect: "Let's be the instruments that lead others to glorify God. Live in such a way that the world may see our good deeds and give glory to our great God." Live your faith. Show your fruit. Get real! That's what James would have us do. An authentic salvation from God results in an authentic demonstration before others.

Authentic Stability **Chapter 1**

In this chapter James teaches that if we really possess genuine faith, it will not snap when it is stretched to a breaking point. Our faith has elasticity because it is rooted in an unchanging, completely trustworthy God. Stability will emerge. If our faith is true, we will have the strength we need to abide under a trial, to stand firm under temptation. *Authentic believers are people of authentic stability.*

1 James, a servant of God and of the Lord Jesus
Christ,

To the twelve tribes scattered among the nations:

Greetings. Ac 15:23

Trials and Temptations

[2]Consider it pure joy, my brothers, whenever
you face trials of many kinds, [3]because you know
that the testing of your faith develops perseverance.
[4]Perseverance must finish its work so that
you may be mature and complete, not lacking
anything. [5]If any of you lacks wisdom, he should
ask God, who gives generously to all without finding
fault, and it will be given to him. [6]But when
he asks, he must believe and not doubt, because
he who doubts is like a wave of the sea, blown
and tossed by the wind. [7]That man should not

LIVING  **INSIGHT**

Double-mindedness is a common disease that leaves its victims paralyzed by doubt. How much better to be single-minded! No "say-one-thing-but-mean-something-else" jive. The single-minded are short on creeds and long on deeds. They care . . . really care. They are humble . . . truly humble. They love . . . genuinely love. They have character . . . authentic character.

(See James 1:5–8.)

think he will receive anything from the Lord;
[8]he is a double-minded man, unstable in all he
does.

[9]The brother in humble circumstances ought to
take pride in his high position. [10]But the one who
is rich should take pride in his low position, because
he will pass away like a wild flower. [11]For the
sun rises with scorching heat and withers the
plant; its blossom falls and its beauty is destroyed.
In the same way, the rich man will fade away even
while he goes about his business. Ps 102:4,11

[12]Blessed is the man who perseveres under trial,
because when he has stood the test, he will receive
the crown of life that God has promised to those
who love him. 1Co 9:25; Jas 2:5

[13]When tempted, no one should say, "God is
tempting me." For God cannot be tempted by evil,
nor does he tempt anyone; [14]but each one is
tempted when, by his own evil desire, he is
dragged away and enticed. [15]Then, after desire has
conceived, it gives birth to sin; and sin, when it is
full-grown, gives birth to death. Job 15:35; Ps 7:14

LIVING  **INSIGHT**

Our enemy, crafty and clever and experienced as he is, knows which lure best attracts each one of us. Our unique inner "itch" longs to be satisfied by that particular outer "scratch." And unless we draw on the all-conquering power of Jesus Christ, we'll yield. We'll bite the bait, and we'll suffer the horrible consequences.

(See James 1:13–15.)

[16]Don't be deceived, my dear brothers. [17]Every
good and perfect gift is from above, coming down
from the Father of the heavenly lights, who does
not change like shifting shadows. [18]He chose to
give us birth through the word of truth, that we
might be a kind of firstfruits of all he created.

Listening and Doing

[19]My dear brothers, take note of this: Everyone
should be quick to listen, slow to speak and slow
to become angry, [20]for man's anger does not bring
about the righteous life that God desires. [21]Therefore,
get rid of all moral filth and the evil that is so
prevalent and humbly accept the word planted in
you, which can save you. Eph 1:13; 4:22

[22]Do not merely listen to the word, and so deceive
yourselves. Do what it says. [23]Anyone who
listens to the word but does not do what it says is
like a man who looks at his face in a mirror [24]and,
after looking at himself, goes away and immediately
forgets what he looks like. [25]But the man who
looks intently into the perfect law that gives freedom,
and continues to do this, not forgetting what
he has heard, but doing it—he will be blessed in
what he does. Jn 13:17; Jas 2:12

[26]If anyone considers himself religious and yet
does not keep a tight rein on his tongue, he deceives
himself and his religion is worthless. [27]Religion
that God our Father accepts as pure and
faultless is this: to look after orphans and widows
in their distress and to keep oneself from being
polluted by the world. Isa 1:17,23; 1Pe 3:10

Authentic Love **Chapter 2**

James teaches us that when our faith is challenged, when we are forced into a corner with seemingly no way out, our love still endures. When people ask, "Where are your deeds? Can we see a demonstration of your faith?"—this is the time authentic love is produced. Authentic Christian love plays no favorites; it is not characterized by prejudice or by racist attitudes. The love that comes from God is not tainted by indifference; it is marked by true obedience. James paints a picture of a love that moves us beyond our comfort zones and personal preferences. It is an authentic love that reaches out to those who are different than we are—even to those we might consider our enemies. The love proclaimed by James sounds so much like the love Jesus extended to everyone He met as he walked this earth—and the love He extends to you and me. Our response? _Authentic believers demonstrate authentic love._

Favoritism Forbidden

2 My brothers, as believers in our glorious Lord Jesus Christ, don't show favoritism. 2Suppose a man comes into your meeting wearing a gold ring and fine clothes, and a poor man in shabby clothes also comes in. 3If you show special attention to the man wearing fine clothes and say, "Here's a good seat for you," but say to the poor man, "You stand there" or "Sit on the floor by my feet," 4have you not discriminated among yourselves and become judges with evil thoughts?

5Listen, my dear brothers: Has not God chosen those who are poor in the eyes of the world to be rich in faith and to inherit the kingdom he promised those who love him? 6But you have insulted the poor. Is it not the rich who are exploiting you? Are they not the ones who are dragging you into court? 7Are they not the ones who are slandering the noble name of him to whom you belong?

8If you really keep the royal law found in Scripture, "Love your neighbor as yourself,"[a] you are doing right. 9But if you show favoritism, you sin and are convicted by the law as lawbreakers. 10For whoever keeps the whole law and yet stumbles at just one point is guilty of breaking all of it. 11For he who said, "Do not commit adultery,"[b] also said, "Do not murder."[c] If you do not commit adultery but do commit murder, you have become a lawbreaker. Mt 5:19; Gal 3:10

12Speak and act as those who are going to be judged by the law that gives freedom, 13because judgment without mercy will be shown to anyone who has not been merciful. Mercy triumphs over judgment! Mt 5:7; Jas 1:25

Faith and Deeds

14What good is it, my brothers, if a man claims to have faith but has no deeds? Can such faith save him? 15Suppose a brother or sister is without clothes and daily food. 16If one of you says to him, "Go, I wish you well; keep warm and well fed," but does nothing about his physical needs, what good is it? 17In the same way, faith by itself, if it is not accompanied by action, is dead. Mt 7:26; 1Jn 3:17-18

LIVING  **INSIGHT**

Knowledge can be dangerous when it becomes an end in itself. God gave us His truth so that we might put it into practice, not simply store it up.

(See James 2:14–17.)

18But someone will say, "You have faith; I have deeds."

Show me your faith without deeds, and I will show you my faith by what I do. 19You believe that there is one God. Good! Even the demons believe that—and shudder. Mt 8:29; Jas 3:13

20You foolish man, do you want evidence that faith without deeds is useless[d]? 21Was not our ancestor Abraham considered righteous for what he did when he offered his son Isaac on the altar? 22You see that his faith and his actions were working together, and his faith was made complete by what he did. 23And the scripture was fulfilled that says, "Abraham believed God, and it was credited to him as righteousness,"[e] and he was called God's friend. 24You see that a person is justified by what he does and not by faith alone. 2Ch 20:7

25In the same way, was not even Rahab the prostitute considered righteous for what she did when she gave lodging to the spies and sent them off in a different direction? 26As the body without the spirit is dead, so faith without deeds is dead.

Authentic Humility **Chapters 3–4**

In these two chapters James lets us know that a genuine faith is not shared in an explosive manner. Some people communicate their faith with all the subtlety of a box of TNT. James wants us to know that we must be led by a humble, gentle and controlled spirit. We must be quick to listen to others and sensitively discern when quietness is appropriate. We must learn to control our tongues. When our faith is genuine and governed by humility and self-control, the message will come through clearly and people will hear. The words of our mouth, the longings of our heart and the expressions of our will . . . all of these things will express genuine faith. _Authentic believers are known for authentic humility._

[a] 8 Lev. 19:18 [b] 11 Exodus 20:14; Deut. 5:18 [c] 11 Exodus 20:13; Deut. 5:17 [d] 20 Some early manuscripts *dead*
[e] 23 Gen. 15:6

Taming the Tongue

3 Not many of you should presume to be teachers, my brothers, because you know that we who teach will be judged more strictly. 2We all stumble in many ways. If anyone is never at fault in what he says, he is a perfect man, able to keep his whole body in check. Mt 12:37; Jas 1:26

3When we put bits into the mouths of horses to make them obey us, we can turn the whole animal. 4Or take ships as an example. Although they are so large and are driven by strong winds, they are steered by a very small rudder wherever the pilot wants to go. 5Likewise the tongue is a small part of the body, but it makes great boasts. Consider what a great forest is set on fire by a small spark. 6The tongue also is a fire, a world of evil among the parts of the body. It corrupts the whole person, sets the whole course of his life on fire, and is itself set on fire by hell. Pr 16:27; Mt 15:11,18-19

7All kinds of animals, birds, reptiles and creatures of the sea are being tamed and have been tamed by man, 8but no man can tame the tongue. It is a restless evil, full of deadly poison. Ps 140:3

9With the tongue we praise our Lord and Father, and with it we curse men, who have been made in God's likeness. 10Out of the same mouth come praise and cursing. My brothers, this should not be. 11Can both fresh water and salt[a] water flow from the same spring? 12My brothers, can a fig tree bear olives, or a grapevine bear figs? Neither can a salt spring produce fresh water.

Two Kinds of Wisdom

13Who is wise and understanding among you? Let him show it by his good life, by deeds done in the humility that comes from wisdom. 14But if you harbor bitter envy and selfish ambition in your hearts, do not boast about it or deny the truth. 15Such "wisdom" does not come down from heaven but is earthly, unspiritual, of the devil. 16For where you have envy and selfish ambition, there you find disorder and every evil practice. 1Ti 4:1

17But the wisdom that comes from heaven is first of all pure; then peace-loving, considerate, submissive, full of mercy and good fruit, impartial and sincere. 18Peacemakers who sow in peace raise a harvest of righteousness. Pr 11:18; Ro 12:9

Submit Yourselves to God

4 What causes fights and quarrels among you? Don't they come from your desires that battle within you? 2You want something but don't get it. You kill and covet, but you cannot have what you want. You quarrel and fight. You do not have, because you do not ask God. 3When you ask, you do not receive, because you ask with wrong motives, that you may spend what you get on your pleasures. Ro 7:23; 1Jn 3:22

4You adulterous people, don't you know that friendship with the world is hatred toward God? Anyone who chooses to be a friend of the world becomes an enemy of God. 5Or do you think Scripture says without reason that the spirit he caused to live in us envies intensely?[b] 6But he gives us more grace. That is why Scripture says:

> "God opposes the proud
> but gives grace to the humble."[c] Pr 3:34

7Submit yourselves, then, to God. Resist the devil, and he will flee from you. 8Come near to God and he will come near to you. Wash your hands, you sinners, and purify your hearts, you double-minded. 9Grieve, mourn and wail. Change your laughter to mourning and your joy to gloom. 10Humble yourselves before the Lord, and he will lift you up. Isa 1:16; 1Pe 5:6-9

11Brothers, do not slander one another. Anyone who speaks against his brother or judges him speaks against the law and judges it. When you judge the law, you are not keeping it, but sitting in judgment on it. 12There is only one Lawgiver and Judge, the one who is able to save and destroy. But you—who are you to judge your neighbor?

Boasting About Tomorrow

13Now listen, you who say, "Today or tomorrow we will go to this or that city, spend a year there, carry on business and make money." 14Why, you do not even know what will happen tomorrow. What is your life? You are a mist that appears for a little while and then vanishes. 15Instead, you ought to say, "If it is the Lord's will, we will live and do this or that." 16As it is, you boast

LIVING  **INSIGHT**

Life? "A mist," answers James. Although we give the appearance of security, our lives are marked by uncertainty, adversity, brevity. All the more reason to gain perspective on how to live it. Walking with God gives us perspective. It doesn't guarantee we'll live longer, but it does help us live better. And deeper. And broader. Because you know nothing about the day, week, month or year before you, commit yourself anew to Him who knows the times and the seasons.

(See James 4:14.)

[a]11 Greek *bitter* (see also verse 14)
[b]5 Or *that God jealously longs for the spirit that he made to live in us*; or *that the Spirit he caused to live in us longs jealously*
[c]6 Prov. 3:34

and brag. All such boasting is evil. 17Anyone, then,
who knows the good he ought to do and doesn't
do it, sins. Lk 12:47; 1Co 5:6

Authentic Patience **Chapter 5**

When our faith is tested in a time of great distress, we need not panic. There is a spirit of patience that emerges in the midst of earth's struggles and storms. In this final chapter James addresses money matters, lingering sickness and carnality. All of these can bring stress and conflict to life and can remove a spirit of peace and create a spirit of panic. Genuine faith brings patience to the table when life serves up trouble. It is relatively easy to be patient when we have no struggles, when everything seems to fall into place. James asks us to gauge whether our patience shines through even in, especially in, the tough times of life. *Authentic believers exhibit authentic patience.*

Warning to Rich Oppressors

5 Now listen, you rich people, weep and wail
because of the misery that is coming upon
you. 2Your wealth has rotted, and moths have eat-
en your clothes. 3Your gold and silver are corrod-
ed. Their corrosion will testify against you and eat
your flesh like fire. You have hoarded wealth in the
last days. 4Look! The wages you failed to pay the
workmen who mowed your fields are crying out
against you. The cries of the harvesters have
reached the ears of the Lord Almighty. 5You have
lived on earth in luxury and self-indulgence. You
have fattened yourselves in the day of slaughter.[a]
6You have condemned and murdered innocent
men, who were not opposing you. Heb 10:38; Jas 4:2

Patience in Suffering

7Be patient, then, brothers, until the Lord's
coming. See how the farmer waits for the land to
yield its valuable crop and how patient he is for the
autumn and spring rains. 8You too, be patient and
stand firm, because the Lord's coming is near.
9Don't grumble against each other, brothers, or
you will be judged. The Judge is standing at the
door! Mt 24:33; Jas 4:11
10Brothers, as an example of patience in the face
of suffering, take the prophets who spoke in the
name of the Lord. 11As you know, we consider
blessed those who have persevered. You have
heard of Job's perseverance and have seen what
the Lord finally brought about. The Lord is full of
compassion and mercy. Job 42:10,12-17; Mt 5:12

LIVING  INSIGHT

Relatively few indeed are the people who finish what they start—and do a complete job of it. I'm talking about the rare but beautiful experience of carrying out a responsibility to its completion.

(See James 5:11.)

12Above all, my brothers, do not swear—not by
heaven or by earth or by anything else. Let your
"Yes" be yes, and your "No," no, or you will be
condemned. Mt 5:34-37

The Prayer of Faith

13Is any one of you in trouble? He should pray.
Is anyone happy? Let him sing songs of praise. 14Is
any one of you sick? He should call the elders of
the church to pray over him and anoint him with
oil in the name of the Lord. 15And the prayer
offered in faith will make the sick person well; the
Lord will raise him up. If he has sinned, he will be
forgiven. 16Therefore confess your sins to each
other and pray for each other so that you may be
healed. The prayer of a righteous man is powerful
and effective. Jn 9:31; 1Pe 2:24
17Elijah was a man just like us. He prayed earnestly that it would not rain, and it did not rain on
the land for three and a half years. 18Again he
prayed, and the heavens gave rain, and the earth
produced its crops. 1Ki 18:41-45; Ac 14:15
19My brothers, if one of you should wander
from the truth and someone should bring him
back, 20remember this: Whoever turns a sinner
from the error of his way will save him from death
and cover over a multitude of sins. Mt 18:15

[a]5 Or *yourselves as in a day of feasting*

1 PETER

When we take a quick glance at the first verse of Peter's first letter, we are immediately clued in to why Peter chose the major theme for his letter: "hope for the hurting." According to verse 1, the recipients were "God's elect strangers in the world, scattered . . ." These Christians were objects of social ostracism, slander, mistreatment and threats on their lives. They needed encouragement. Sitting on a powder keg of actual and potential persecution, these believers "have had to suffer grief in all kinds of trials" (1:6), as though they were "refined by fire" (1:7) day after day. Tough, tiring situations! No group of people ever needed more grace and hope to counteract feelings of panic and fear. Peter wrote them a letter to help them endure suffering . . . and, instead of facing it with grim, sober determination, to rejoice in spite of their circumstances.

WRITER: *Peter*

DATE: *C.A.D. 60–64*

PURPOSE: *To give hope and encouragement to hurting believers*

KEY THEME: *Hope for the hurting*

KEY MESSAGE: *Stand fast in the true grace of God*

EMPHASES: *Suffering and persecution; hope; pilgrimage; courage; God's grace*

IDENTITY OF CHRISTIANS: *Obedient children; newborn babies; living stones; holy priesthood; aliens and strangers; sheep; family of God; in Christ*

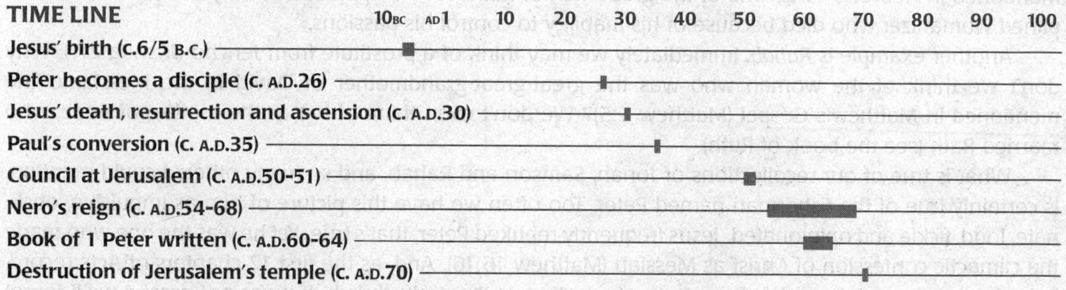

Hope for the Hurting

INTRODUCTION *(1:1)*

	OUR LIVING HOPE	**OUR "STRANGE" LIFE**	**OUR FIERY ORDEAL**
	"Grace and peace be yours . . ." (1:2) . . . as we claim our hope *(1:3-12)* . . . as we walk in holiness *(1:13-25)* . . . as we grow in Christ *(2:1-10)*	*"Dear friends, I urge you . . ." (2:11)* . . . abstain! *(2:11-12)* . . . submit! *(2:13–3:7)* . . . be humble! *(3:8-22)* . . . arm yourselves! *(4:1-6)* . . . glorify God! *(4:7-11)*	*"Dear friends, do not be surprised . . ." (4:12)* Don't be surprised *(4:12)* Keep on rejoicing *(4:13)* Commit yourselves to God *(4:19)* Cast your anxiety on God *(5:7)*
	CHAPTERS 1:2–2:10	***CHAPTERS 2:11–4:11***	***CHAPTERS 4:12–5:13***
EMPHASIS	**Informing**	**Exhorting**	**Comforting**
GRACE	**. . . to go on**	**. . . to stand firm**	**. . . to rejoice**
HOPE	**A *living* hope through Christ's resurrection *(1:3)***	**A *calm* hope through personal submission *(3:6)***	**A *firm* hope through faith *(4:19)***

CONCLUSION *(5:14)*

Even though each of us is different in personality, most of us are alike in one area when it comes to other people: We usually remember their wrongs and quickly forget the good things they've done. Take our impressions of Bible characters, for example. If I were to mention some names, the first thing that would come to your mind, and to mine too, would probably be their shortcomings. Let's try it . . . *Jonah*. I doubt very much that anyone, at the moment of hearing his name, would remember him as the evangelist who led the most extensive evangelistic campaign in Old Testament times. Through his personal message given to him by God, an entire city turned around. Remarkable! Yet when we hear the name Jonah, we usually think of a rebellious prophet who ran from God and did not want to do God's will (Jonah 1:3).

And then there's *Samson*. You and I may not recall the fact that he led Israel for twenty years (Judges 15:20), apparently with a flawless record. It was because of his faithful leadership of Israel that he was mentioned in Hebrews 11 as one of the great men of faith. Yet we think of him only as a lustful, undisciplined womanizer who died because of his inability to control his passions.

Another example is *Rahab*. Immediately we may think of a prostitute from Jericho (Joshua 2:1). Why don't we think of the woman who was the great-great-grandmother of David in the Messianic line mentioned in Matthew's Gospel (Matthew 1:5)? We don't even think of her as the mother of Boaz, who married Ruth (see the book of Ruth).

What is true of our recollections of Jonah, Samson and Rahab, and so many others I could mention, is certainly true of the fisherman named Peter. Too often we have this picture of him as impulsive, obstinate, loud, fickle and opinionated. Jesus frequently rebuked Peter, that's true. Yet he was the one who made the climactic confession of Christ as Messiah (Matthew 16:16). And, as the first 12 chapters of Acts record, Peter became a major moving force in the formation of the early church. If we're not careful we'll forget how powerfully God worked through Peter. As one man stated so well, "He was easily the most powerful figure in the Christian community. And his energetic preaching, ardent prayer, bold healing and wise direction confirmed the trust placed in him."

A Priceless Legacy

We also must never forget that it was Peter who left in his legacy two of the most wonderful letters of compassion and courage in all the New Testament—the letters of 1 and 2 Peter. Yes, this man stumbled, as we all do, but he also did so much good in the name of Jesus and in the service of His kingdom.

We all have chapters in our lives we wish we could erase. We may wish we could have changed people's opinions about us during those times in our lives. But two truths remain: First, if it hadn't been for those chapters in our lives, we would most likely be very proud people, believing that we were so good and so talented and living only in the memory of our accomplishments. Those times of testing and trial keep us humble and dependent on our merciful God. Second, we really wouldn't have grown in maturity or gained depth of character. I find in my own life that it's in the crucible, in the valley, in the times of failure, pain, misery and heartache, that I grow strong and deep. Those times of suffering build us and mold us more and more into conformity to Jesus Christ.

I'm so glad that Peter wasn't written off by our Lord! After Jesus' resurrection, the angel said to the women who had gathered at the empty tomb, "Go, tell his disciples and Peter, 'He is going ahead of you into Galilee. There you will see him, just as he told you' " (Mark 16:7). The painful chapter of failure was finished in that part of Peter's life. There was a new section of the book yet to be written. And only the Lord Himself knew what a thrill it must have been for Peter when he was singled out for special treatment and shown special concern—the very one who had disowned Jesus only days earlier (Mark 14:66–72).

Starting Where We Are

Peter signed his letter at the beginning, as was common in that day. He wrote, "Peter, an apostle of Jesus Christ" (1:1). I love the way he starts. He doesn't ridicule his past. Undoubtedly his readers knew his past. It was as if he were thinking, "I'll start right where I am." The experience of grace lets a person respond with that kind of confidence. All this may have gone through Peter's mind as he put pen to paper, "I'm an apostle—one specially commissioned, sent out to represent someone else. I am a man amazed at the grace of God in forgiving and covering my sin with the blood of Jesus. And I am able, therefore, by His grace, to write you a letter of encouragement."

Ever ask yourself something like, "Who am I to be where I am today?" Sure you have. "Who am I to help these people mature in their Christian life? Who am I to teach a church school class? Who am I to be a mother or a father of these children?" Sometimes all too clearly and painfully we see our own inadequacies, but we must also, with equal clarity, call to mind Jesus Christ's sufficiency to touch us with His grace. He wants us to start where we are: forgiven by His grace and empowered to serve others in His name.

A Word of Encouragement

The purpose of 1 Peter is to encourage and strengthen believers during times of painful and acute trial. Let me give a practical word here. Don't think of a letter like this as just being interesting material for Bible study but somehow not appropriate to apply to your life today. Don't think of this letter as providing the "stuff" for listening to great sermons but not relevant for the issues you face Monday through Friday. When you go through trials and testings, present and future, go to 1 Peter and consciously, intentionally, read the letter to yourself. Receive it as a personal missile sent from God's arsenal of encouragement targeted for your heart. Read it personally. It's a letter for people who are undergoing trials, and it speaks with power and relevance to any and every generation, most certainly to *ours*.

When Facing a Trial

What does Peter say to someone facing a trial? I find in his writings four great messages of encouragement. First, *trials may vary, but you are valuable*. Read slowly, carefully, Peter's words in verses 6 and 7 of chapter 1:

> *In this you greatly rejoice, though now for a little while you may have had to suffer grief in all kinds of trials. These have come so that your faith—of greater worth than gold, which perishes*

> *even though refined by fire—may be proved genuine and may result in praise, glory and honor when Jesus Christ is revealed.*

Peter reminds us that trials come in various shapes and sizes. According to verses 6 and 7 they all produce grief. They may vary in intensity, but they come because God sees you as gold that is incredibly valuable. He is refining your life. He is strengthening your faith. He is teaching you to depend more and more on Him. Trials fuel the furnace that God uses to reshape you from the inside out.

In the trial you will see Christ reveal Himself in your inner person. You will see the Lord Jesus come to your assistance in that very moment when you find yourself helpless—whether your trial is an illness, an emotional upheaval, a bitter disappointment or a painful loss. Whatever the trial, you will see the Lord Jesus make Himself real in the midst of the furnace.

Second, *the tests God brings may seem unreasonable and inexplicable, but they have their reason.* Look at verses 18–20 of chapter 2, and read these wise words with care:

> *Slaves, submit yourselves to your masters with all respect, not only to those who are good and considerate, but also to those who are harsh. For it is commendable if a man bears up under the pain of unjust suffering because he is conscious of God. But how is it to your credit if you receive a beating for doing wrong and endure it? But if you suffer for doing good and you endure it, this is commendable before God.*

As you walk with God, I urge you to leave yourself open to Him and to the working out of His purposes in and through your life. I cannot tell you exactly what God is saying to you in your trial; He will reveal it to you in His time. But know this: God always has a lesson to teach you. Be attentive, be teachable, be alert to His presence in your life. Remember the words of Jesus in Matthew 11:28: "Take my yoke upon you and learn from me." As the lesson emerges, the trial will be seen as a divine messenger rather than as merely an earthly misery.

Third, *trials are inevitable.* Peter made that point very clearly in verses 12 and 13 of chapter 4 of his letter:

> *Dear friends, do not be surprised at the painful trial you are suffering, as though something strange were happening to you. But rejoice that you participate in the sufferings of Christ, so that you may be overjoyed when his glory is revealed.*

We must not be surprised when we face trials. Suffering is part and parcel of the human experience of living in a broken world that groans under sin's effects. Beyond this truth of the suffering that is common to us all, we can expect to suffer as part of living a life of faith. Those who are committed to Jesus Christ with a devoted faith will face the attacks of the devil and his followers (see 5:8). Peter acknowledges the reality of suffering and even presents it as a privilege and as a way of participating in Christ's glory.

Fourth, *trials are temporal, not eternal.* Peter taught this truth in the context of a command he gave to be self-controlled and alert to the mission and motives of our enemy the devil:

> *Resist him, standing firm in the faith, because you know that your brothers throughout the world are undergoing the same kind of sufferings. And the God of all grace, who called you to his eternal glory in Christ, after you have suffered a little while, will himself restore you and make you strong, firm and steadfast (5:9–10).*

It is essential that we clearly understand and apply the truth of this final message: Yes, suffering is painful to bear, yes, trials are torturously difficult to endure, but the day of restoration is coming! We have reason to hope, whatever our circumstances—even when facing suffering or death. Those who suffer with Christ will also glory with Him in a life forever free from pain. Jesus Himself will give us our eternal reward. We need not get incurably discouraged or grow hopelessly weary! Our trials will come to an end, and one day we will experience eternal rest. There is hope for those who trust in Jesus, no matter what comes our way.

Facing Pain

I find 1 Peter to be a profoundly relevant letter, first of all, because pain is universal and inescapable. To talk about pain is to speak a universal message for all generations. You cannot slice through history and find one single day free from pain. This letter unveils the attitudes we often take toward pain and goes to great lengths to correct our often inadequate thinking.

Let me share these four negative attitudes that are familiar to most of us at least some of the time, and Peter's advice as taken from his first letter:

Our Attitude:	*Peter's Advice:*
I'm all alone in this. What's wrong with me?	You are not alone, and there's nothing wrong with you.
This isn't fair. What have I done to deserve this?	It may not seem fair, but if you and I got what we really deserved, we wouldn't be alive right now.
It seems like the pain and suffering will never end. Why doesn't it stop?	It will end. It seems unrelenting and unbearable right now, but there is hope on the horizon.
I thought God loved me. What a strange way to show it!	God does love you. He doesn't promise to keep you from the trials of life, but He does promise His grace to help you through.

To each of our negative attitudes Peter applies a new perspective and a fresh word of hope. He helps us face the pain that reaches deeply into our lives and to begin to see how God never lets go of us through it all.

An Attitude Adjustment

Peter prescribes some highly unusual, even revolutionary, treatment for those who suffer. First, *he urges us to rejoice that we suffer for Christ (4:13) and to avoid attitudes of resentment*. In order to leave yourself open to what God might be teaching you in this trial, plead with Him to give you the power to keep from becoming resentful and bitter. Find a way, in the midst of the pain and the hurt, to rejoice. That kind of attitude adjustment may take a while, but it can happen. Second, *Peter implores us to submit and not to fight*. Let what is happening happen. Don't fume. Don't fret. Submit to the Lord Jesus (2:21; 5:6). Third, *Peter counsels us to glorify God, not the pain*. Some people go through a time of suffering, and for the rest of their lives they talk about the difficulty of what they endured. Don't highlight the pain. Highlight the Lord (4:11). Fourth, and finally, *Peter commands us to humble ourselves and give up our natural tendency to defend ourselves*. As we humble ourselves, God has His ways of exalting us "in due time" (5:6). And the great promise on the heels of that firm command is this: Instead of living anxiety-ridden lives, we can rest in the realization that the Father cares for us (5:7).

Do you have trials in your life? Who doesn't? Avoid bitterness and resentment. Submit to God's method of working in and through your life. Glorify Him through it all. And humble yourself. Accept this testing. Allow the Lord to bring you through. His strength is adequate, His grace is sufficient, His plan is perfect—even when we don't fully comprehend it.

Our Living Hope **Chapters 1:1–2:10**

Peter is absolutely clear about where we find our hope. There is only one answer: Jesus. This section presents Jesus as the source of our inheritance and our hope. There is no other place to turn to find true hope to carry us through this life. We must also look to the Savior as we learn to walk in holiness. Peter reminds us of God's command to "be holy, because I am holy" (1:16), which can be carried out only by looking to Jesus. We also find in the person of Jesus the strength we need to grow in faith. Peter asks three questions in this opening section: Where do we find our hope? How can we walk in holiness? What will help us grow in faith? The answer to all three questions is the same: Jesus!

1 Peter, an apostle of Jesus Christ, 2Pe 1:1

To God's elect, strangers in the world, scattered throughout Pontus, Galatia, Cappadocia, Asia and Bithynia, 2who have been chosen according to the foreknowledge of God the Father, through the sanctifying work of the Spirit, for obedience to Jesus Christ and sprinkling by his blood: 2Th 2:13

Grace and peace be yours in abundance.

Praise to God for a Living Hope

3Praise be to the God and Father of our Lord Jesus Christ! In his great mercy he has given us new birth into a living hope through the resurrection of Jesus Christ from the dead, 4and into an inheritance that can never perish, spoil or fade—kept in heaven for you, 5who through faith are shielded by God's power until the coming of the salvation that is ready to be revealed in the last time. 6In this you greatly rejoice, though now for a little while you may have had to suffer grief in all kinds of trials. 7These have come so that your faith—of greater worth than gold, which perishes even though refined by fire—may be proved genuine and may result in praise, glory and honor when Jesus Christ is revealed. 8Though you have not seen him, you love him; and even though you do not see him now, you believe in him and are filled with an inexpressible and glorious joy, 9for you are receiving the goal of your faith, the salvation of your souls. Jn 20:29; Ro 6:22

10Concerning this salvation, the prophets, who spoke of the grace that was to come to you, searched intently and with the greatest care, 11trying to find out the time and circumstances to which the Spirit of Christ in them was pointing when he predicted the sufferings of Christ and the glories that would follow. 12It was revealed to them that they were not serving themselves but you, when they spoke of the things that have now been told you by those who have preached the gospel to you by the Holy Spirit sent from heaven. Even angels long to look into these things. Lk 24:49

LIVING  INSIGHT

Are you at the brink of despair, thinking that you cannot bear another day of heartache? As difficult as it may be for you to believe this today, the Master knows what He's doing. Your Savior knows your breaking point. The bruising and crushing and melting process is designed to reshape you, not ruin you. Your value is increasing the longer He lingers over you.

(See 1 Peter 1:6–9.)

Be Holy

13Therefore, prepare your minds for action; be self-controlled; set your hope fully on the grace to be given you when Jesus Christ is revealed. 14As obedient children, do not conform to the evil desires you had when you lived in ignorance. 15But just as he who called you is holy, so be holy in all you do; 16for it is written: "Be holy, because I am holy."[a] Ro 12:2; Eph 4:18

17Since you call on a Father who judges each man's work impartially, live your lives as strangers here in reverent fear. 18For you know that it was not with perishable things such as silver or gold that you were redeemed from the empty way of life handed down to you from your forefathers, 19but with the precious blood of Christ, a lamb without blemish or defect. 20He was chosen before the creation of the world, but was revealed in these last times for your sake. 21Through him you believe in God, who raised him from the dead and glorified him, and so your faith and hope are in God.

22Now that you have purified yourselves by obeying the truth so that you have sincere love for your brothers, love one another deeply, from the heart.[b] 23For you have been born again, not of perishable seed, but of imperishable, through the living and enduring word of God. 24For, Jn 1:13

"All men are like grass,
and all their glory is like the flowers of the field;
the grass withers and the flowers fall,
25 but the word of the Lord stands forever."[c]

And this is the word that was preached to you.

2 Therefore, rid yourselves of all malice and all deceit, hypocrisy, envy, and slander of every kind. 2Like newborn babies, crave pure spiritual milk, so that by it you may grow up in your salva-

[a] 16 Lev. 11:44,45; 19:2; 20:7 [b] 22 Some early manuscripts *from a pure heart* [c] 25 Isaiah 40:6-8

tion, 3now that you have tasted that the Lord is
good. 1Co 3:2; Heb 6:5

The Living Stone and a Chosen People

4As you come to him, the living Stone—rejected by men but chosen by God and precious to
him— 5you also, like living stones, are being built
into a spiritual house to be a holy priesthood, offering spiritual sacrifices acceptable to God
through Jesus Christ. 6For in Scripture it says:

> "See, I lay a stone in Zion,
> a chosen and precious cornerstone, Eph 2:20
> and the one who trusts in him
> will never be put to shame."[a]

7Now to you who believe, this stone is precious.
But to those who do not believe, 2Co 2:16

> "The stone the builders rejected
> has become the capstone,[b]"[c]

8and,

> "A stone that causes men to stumble
> and a rock that makes them fall."[d]

They stumble because they disobey the message—
which is also what they were destined for.

9But you are a chosen people, a royal priesthood, a holy nation, a people belonging to God,
that you may declare the praises of him who called
you out of darkness into his wonderful light.
10Once you were not a people, but now you are the
people of God; once you had not received mercy,
but now you have received mercy. Hos 1:9-10; Ac 26:18

Our "Strange" Life **Chapters 2:11–4:11**

Peter urged believers to adopt a very specific lifestyle that those who reject Jesus will label as strange. The words of Peter cut against the grain of so much of what our culture teaches about life and relationships. Look at the kind of life he describes: First, *we must abstain from any sinful desires* (2:11). Second, *we must be submissive in society, in our relationships and in our homes* (2:13–3:7). Third, *we must be humble in all of our relationships* (3:8). Finally, *in the midst of everything we face, we must glorify God in all things* (4:11). When we faithfully follow Peter's teachings, the world may look on in stunned amazement. Yet, no matter how odd we might appear to the world, we must follow the Lord's leading. His word is sure and His way is best. Peter himself answered Jesus' question, "You do not want to leave too, do you?" with these words: "Lord, to whom shall we go? You have the words of eternal life" (John 6:67–68).

11Dear friends, I urge you, as aliens and strangers in the world, to abstain from sinful desires,
which war against your soul. 12Live such good lives
among the pagans that, though they accuse you of
doing wrong, they may see your good deeds and
glorify God on the day he visits us. Mt 5:16; Php 2:15

LIVING  **INSIGHT**

If your life is an example of glorifying God, others won't see your good deeds and glorify you, because they'll know that what you are doing is for God's glory. When there is glory given to God and the action is done solely for His glory, somehow people can tell—and they will direct their gratitude and praise back to God.

(See 1 Peter 2:11–12.)

Submission to Rulers and Masters

13Submit yourselves for the Lord's sake to every
authority instituted among men: whether to the
king, as the supreme authority, 14or to governors,
who are sent by him to punish those who do
wrong and to commend those who do right. 15For
it is God's will that by doing good you should
silence the ignorant talk of foolish men. 16Live as
free men, but do not use your freedom as a cover-
up for evil; live as servants of God. 17Show proper
respect to everyone: Love the brotherhood of believers, fear God, honor the king. Ro 12:10; 13:7

18Slaves, submit yourselves to your masters with
all respect, not only to those who are good and
considerate, but also to those who are harsh. 19For
it is commendable if a man bears up under the
pain of unjust suffering because he is conscious of
God. 20But how is it to your credit if you receive
a beating for doing wrong and endure it? But if
you suffer for doing good and you endure it, this
is commendable before God. 21To this you were
called, because Christ suffered for you, leaving you
an example, that you should follow in his steps.

> 22"He committed no sin,
> and no deceit was found in his mouth."[e]

23When they hurled their insults at him, he did not
retaliate; when he suffered, he made no threats.
Instead, he entrusted himself to him who judges
justly. 24He himself bore our sins in his body on
the tree, so that we might die to sins and live
for righteousness; by his wounds you have been
healed. 25For you were like sheep going astray, but
now you have returned to the Shepherd and Overseer of your souls. Isa 53:6; Jn 10:11

Wives and Husbands

3 Wives, in the same way be submissive to your
husbands so that, if any of them do not be-

[a]6 Isaiah 28:16 [b]7 Or *cornerstone* [c]7 Psalm 118:22 [d]8 Isaiah 8:14 [e]22 Isaiah 53:9

lieve the word, they may be won over without words by the behavior of their wives, 2when they see the purity and reverence of your lives. 3Your beauty should not come from outward adornment, such as braided hair and the wearing of gold jewelry and fine clothes. 4Instead, it should be that of your inner self, the unfading beauty of a gentle and quiet spirit, which is of great worth in God's sight. 5For this is the way the holy women of the past who put their hope in God used to make themselves beautiful. They were submissive to their own husbands, 6like Sarah, who obeyed Abraham and called him her master. You are her daughters if you do what is right and do not give way to fear. Ge 18:12; 1Ti 5:5

7Husbands, in the same way be considerate as you live with your wives, and treat them with respect as the weaker partner and as heirs with you of the gracious gift of life, so that nothing will hinder your prayers. Eph 5:25-33

Suffering for Doing Good

8Finally, all of you, live in harmony with one another; be sympathetic, love as brothers, be compassionate and humble. 9Do not repay evil with evil or insult with insult, but with blessing, because to this you were called so that you may inherit a blessing. 10For, Heb 6:14; 1Pe 2:21

"Whoever would love life
    and see good days
must keep his tongue from evil
    and his lips from deceitful speech.
11He must turn from evil and do good;
    he must seek peace and pursue it.
12For the eyes of the Lord are on the righteous
    and his ears are attentive to their prayer,
but the face of the Lord is against those who
        do evil."[a] Ps 34:12-16

13Who is going to harm you if you are eager to do good? 14But even if you should suffer for what is right, you are blessed. "Do not fear what they fear[b]; do not be frightened."[c] 15But in your hearts set apart Christ as Lord. Always be prepared to give an answer to everyone who asks you to give the reason for the hope that you have. But do this with gentleness and respect, 16keeping a clear conscience, so that those who speak maliciously against your good behavior in Christ may be ashamed of their slander. 17It is better, if it is God's will, to suffer for doing good than for doing evil. 18For Christ died for sins once for all, the righteous for the unrighteous, to bring you to God. He was put to death in the body but made alive by the Spirit, 19through whom[d] also he went and preached to the spirits in prison 20who disobeyed long ago when God waited patiently in the days of Noah while the ark was being built. In it only a few people, eight in all, were saved through water, 21and this water symbolizes baptism that now saves you also—not the removal of dirt from the body but the pledge[e] of a good conscience toward God. It saves you by the resurrection of Jesus Christ, 22who has gone into heaven and is at God's right hand—with angels, authorities and powers in submission to him. Ro 8:38; 1Pe 1:3

Living for God

4 Therefore, since Christ suffered in his body, arm yourselves also with the same attitude, because he who has suffered in his body is done with sin. 2As a result, he does not live the rest of his earthly life for evil human desires, but rather for the will of God. 3For you have spent enough time in the past doing what pagans choose to do—living in debauchery, lust, drunkenness, orgies, carousing and detestable idolatry. 4They think it strange that you do not plunge with them into the same flood of dissipation, and they heap abuse on you. 5But they will have to give account to him who is ready to judge the living and the dead. 6For this is the reason the gospel was preached even to those who are now dead, so that they might be judged according to men in regard to the body, but live according to God in regard to the spirit.

7The end of all things is near. Therefore be clear minded and self-controlled so that you can pray. 8Above all, love each other deeply, because love covers over a multitude of sins. 9Offer hospitality to one another without grumbling. 10Each one should use whatever gift he has received to serve others, faithfully administering God's grace in its various forms. 11If anyone speaks, he should do it as one speaking the very words of God. If anyone serves, he should do it with the strength God provides, so that in all things God may be praised through Jesus Christ. To him be the glory and the power for ever and ever. Amen. Pr 10:12; Ro 12:6-7

Our Fiery Ordeal **Chapters 4:12–5:14**

In the closing section, Peter acknowledged that believers may encounter struggles as they follow the Lord. We should not be surprised when we face fiery ordeals, for that is part of what it means to live as a Christian. In the midst of the furnace of suffering we can rejoice that we are worthy to suffer for our faith in Jesus. We also need to entrust ourselves to our Lord, who is faithful. We are never alone, no matter how severely the battle rages. The Lord loves us and cares for us, in good times and in hard times. We can cast our burdens and anxieties on Him and

a 12 Psalm 34:12-16 *b 14* Or *not fear their threats* *c 14* Isaiah 8:12 *d 18,19* Or *alive in the spirit, 19through which*
e 21 Or *response*

know that He will *never* forsake us. Trials will come, but we must not lose hope. The Lord loves us; He is always with us—even when we cannot explain our lot or sense His presence.

Suffering for Being a Christian

12Dear friends, do not be surprised at the painful trial you are suffering, as though something
strange were happening to you. 13But rejoice that
you participate in the sufferings of Christ, so that
you may be overjoyed when his glory is revealed.

LIVING  INSIGHT

When we have responded as we should to life's blows, enduring them rather than escaping them, we are given more maturity that stays with us and new measures of wisdom that we can draw on for the balance of our lives.

(See 1 Peter 4:12–13.)

14If you are insulted because of the name of Christ,
you are blessed, for the Spirit of glory and of God
rests on you. 15If you suffer, it should not be as a
murderer or thief or any other kind of criminal, or
even as a meddler. 16However, if you suffer as a
Christian, do not be ashamed, but praise God that
you bear that name. 17For it is time for judgment
to begin with the family of God; and if it begins
with us, what will the outcome be for those who do
not obey the gospel of God? 18And, Ac 5:41; Ro 8:17

"If it is hard for the righteous to be saved,
what will become of the ungodly and the
sinner?"[a] Pr 11:31; Lk 23:31

19So then, those who suffer according to God's
will should commit themselves to their faithful
Creator and continue to do good. 1Pe 2:15; 3:17

To Elders and Young Men

5 To the elders among you, I appeal as a fellow
elder, a witness of Christ's sufferings and one
who also will share in the glory to be revealed: 2Be
shepherds of God's flock that is under your care,
serving as overseers—not because you must, but
because you are willing, as God wants you to be;
not greedy for money, but eager to serve; 3not
lording it over those entrusted to you, but being
examples to the flock. 4And when the Chief Shepherd appears, you will receive the crown of glory
that will never fade away. 1Co 9:25; 1Ti 3:3; Rev 1:9

5Young men, in the same way be submissive to
those who are older. All of you, clothe yourselves
with humility toward one another, because,

"God opposes the proud
but gives grace to the humble."[b]

6Humble yourselves, therefore, under God's
mighty hand, that he may lift you up in due time.
7Cast all your anxiety on him because he cares for
you. Heb 13:5; Jas 4:6,10

8Be self-controlled and alert. Your enemy the
devil prowls around like a roaring lion looking for
someone to devour. 9Resist him, standing firm in
the faith, because you know that your brothers
throughout the world are undergoing the same
kind of sufferings. Ac 14:22; Col 2:5

LIVING  INSIGHT

The adversary will tempt you to doubt, to hold back, to kick a few tires, to think, "We're not going to make it." Relax. Always remember that God's unusual plan ends with a rainbow of new hope.

(See 1 Peter 5:8–11.)

10And the God of all grace, who called you to
his eternal glory in Christ, after you have suffered
a little while, will himself restore you and make
you strong, firm and steadfast. 11To him be the
power for ever and ever. Amen. Ro 11:36; 2Co 4:17

Final Greetings

12With the help of Silas,[c] whom I regard as a
faithful brother, I have written to you briefly, encouraging you and testifying that this is the true
grace of God. Stand fast in it. 2Co 1:19; Heb 13:22

13She who is in Babylon, chosen together with
you, sends you her greetings, and so does my son
Mark. 14Greet one another with a kiss of love.

Peace to all of you who are in Christ. Eph 6:23

[a] *18* Prov. 11:31 [b] *5* Prov. 3:34 [c] *12* Greek *Silvanus,* a variant of *Silas*

INTRODUCTION

2 PETER

While Peter's first letter shows his concern for Christians who were undergoing suffering from external enemies, his second letter teaches Christians how to deal with internal enemies such as false teachers and other evildoers who infiltrated the church. Of special interest to Peter is the return of the Lord Jesus and our watchfulness in view of His return. Peter encourages a life of service and purity as we await that epochal event. The tone of 2 Peter is that of an urgent warning, unlike 1 Peter, which is a letter of encouragement and consolation. While this second letter may not be quite as easy to read, it is equally important. It urges all readers to beware . . . to be ready . . . to be alert, so that we don't fall into the trap of indifference and aimlessness at a time when we desperately need to be salt and light in this world.

WRITER: *Peter*

DATE: *C.A.D. 64–68*

PURPOSE: *To warn against false teaching, moral compromise and doctrinal error in the last days*

KEY THEMES: *Christian character; true knowledge*

KEY MESSAGE: *True knowledge produces holy living*

KEY TERMS: *"Knowledge/know"; "perseverance"; "corruption"*

STYLE: *Urgent and intense*

TIME LINE 10BC AD1 10 20 30 40 50 60 70 80 90 100

Jesus' birth (c.6/5 B.C.)

Jesus' death, resurrection and ascension (C. A.D.30)

Paul's conversion (C. A.D.35)

Council at Jerusalem (C. A.D.50-51)

Nero's reign (C. A.D.54-68)

Book of 2 Peter written (C. A.D.64-68)

Peter's death (C. A.D.67-68)

Destruction of Jerusalem's temple (C. A.D.70)

Beware . . . Be Ready!

INTRODUCTION (1:1-3)

	MORAL CORRUPTION	DOCTRINAL COMPROMISE	PROPHETIC CONCERN
	Answers question: How can I escape defilement?	**Answers question:** What should I expect from "prophets"?	**Answers question:** Where will all this end?
	CHAPTER 1	*CHAPTER 2*	*CHAPTER 3*
WARNING	**Be pure! *(1:4)***	**Be aware! *(2:1-3)***	**Be diligent! *(3:14)***
REMINDER	***Verses 12-13***	***Verses 21-22***	***Verses 1-2***
PROMISE	***"You will never fall" (verse 10)***	***"The Lord knows how to rescue" (verse 9)***	***"We are looking forward" (verse 13)***
PERSPECTIVE	**Looking within**	**Looking back**	**Looking ahead**

CONCLUSION (3:18)

Contrary to some popular belief, things are not always better the second time around. I can think of a number of sequels that have been inferior to the original. Perhaps you can too. If you have ever tried your hand at writing music, the first piece you wrote may have been a wonderful success. A young, budding writer of music might decide that from now on whatever he or she writes will be a success, only to discover that nothing sells like the first one. He or she is terribly disappointed. Publishers tell writers that if you have once written a best seller, there is no guarantee you will ever write another one.

Even in the sports world there is what has come to be known as "the sophomore jinx." An athlete may have a wonderful rookie season; everybody looks to that person to have a terrific second year, only to discover that his production falls way off and he doesn't even make the starting lineup by the third year of his career. To his dismay, all the bright lights and the applause of the fans the first time around are forgotten dreams.

What is true of music, books or sports is not true of the Bible. I'm pleased that when we come to 2 Peter, we come to the second in sequence of Peter's two letters, but not the second in importance. Though much shorter than the first letter—only a little over sixty verses in length—Peter's second letter is of remarkable significance for the Christian.

Three Facts About the Letter

Let me give you three facts about the letter itself. First, *this letter is more difficult to understand than Peter's first letter*. If you have been a student of Scripture for some time, you have probably read both letters more than once, perhaps many times. You may very well testify that 1 Peter reads more easily. As we saw in our study of 1 Peter (see page 1351), there is a simple theme woven through the fabric of the letter: "Hope for the Hurting." There is authoritative advice. There are encouraging words. It is a letter intended for suffering saints. When you come to 2 Peter, the message isn't as clearly discerned and is harder to grasp. It is, quite honestly, even a little tedious here and there. It carries a different style and approach from 1 Peter—which can be explained by the different circumstances to which Peter addressed himself.

While Peter's first letter carried an encouraging tone directed to those who were undergoing suffering and persecution from outside, Peter's second letter addressed the sometimes more subtle dangers of immoral behavior and false teaching inside the fellowship of believers. In response to these dangers, Peter called for a return to the true gospel:

> *So I will always remind you of these things, even though you know them and are firmly established in the truth you now have. I think it is right to refresh your memory as long as I live in the tent of this body (1:12–13).*

Second, *this letter is surprising by virtue of what it leaves out.* I made a list of some of those things. There is not a word about Jesus' resurrection in 2 Peter. Nor is there any mention of His ascension. There is no teaching about the Holy Spirit (aside from the Spirit's role in the production of Scripture—1:21), prayer, baptism, or the passionate call of men and women to follow Jesus Christ more closely. If you took all those elements out of Peter's first letter, you wouldn't have much left. But they are conspicuous by their absence from his second letter.

Third, *this letter hides its theme rather than highlights it.* While 1 Peter repeatedly and boldly underscored the theme of suffering, most of us would probably have trouble identifying a single theme uniting the letter of 2 Peter.

A Tapestry of Themes

Actually there are a number of themes that weave their way through 2 Peter. I see them in the form of an arrow with three feathers on the end of it. Let's give the arrow a stem and let's give it a point. I believe we will be going in the right direction if we see these themes working together instead of in tension.

First, the three feathers on the end are those components that keep the arrow on a straight course. Peter employed three methods of getting his message across all the way through 2 Peter: warnings, reminders and promises. Next we add diligence as the stem. Diligence, or devoted perseverance, provides the motivation to propel us toward true knowledge and right living. Warnings, reminders and promises don't automatically kick us into action, but when we apply the warnings, remember the reminders and claim the promises with great diligence, we begin to move in a purposeful direction. Finally, the point of the arrow is hope. Hope is the key to where we're going. It points the way to true meaning, true purpose. We must have hope in order to live. Without hope, we are unsharpened, useless arrows that will not penetrate the target of full life in Jesus Christ.

I would suggest, therefore, a theme revolving around five thoughts: *warnings, reminders and promises* applied with *diligence* to give us *hope.* This letter is saying, "If you want to know how and where to go, you must apply the warnings of God, remember the reminders of God, claim the promises of God, and with diligence live them out. Only then can you expect to have hope. You'll have it, and you'll never run out of it."

As you read 2 Peter, be alert to the way Peter weaves these thoughts through each chapter. Watch for the warnings, reminders and promises in chapter 1 as he seeks to stimulate Christian growth, in chapter 2 as he combats false teaching and in chapter 3 as he encourages watchfulness for the Lord's return. In each case, we are urged to respond with diligence so that we might live with hope.

How to Stay Aware and Ready

In times like these, how do we remain alert, aware and discerning in light of Jesus' promise to return? Let me give you a way to remember four important steps we can take to keep us alert. Take the word "hope" and write it vertically in a column. Using each of the four letters of *HOPE* as a starting point, we can come up with the following as a useful acrostic:

Heed
Open
Pursue
Expect

What must we do to stay alert in the last days? First, ***Heed** what you already know.* Peter provided the basis for this principle when he wrote, "So I will always remind you of these things, even though you know them and are firmly established in the truth you now have" (1:12). Isn't that great? Sometimes there are people who will say, "Well, you said that before, Chuck." Or, "You're repeating yourself. You are getting older. You may have forgotten you said that already." May I remind you? The greatest way to learn, and learn well, is repetition . . . saying it again, reviewing it over and over and over. Heed what you already know. Pay attention to it, have regard for it, take notice of it, concern yourself with it.

Many of us know what the Bible teaches. Perhaps we wade neck-deep in the truths of God. Our problem often comes in heeding what He has written. If we simply drew from the reservoir of the deposit of knowledge growing in us all these years, we would have plenty left over when the day is done. It is time to heed what we already know. That'll keep us alert in the days before Jesus returns.

Second, ***Open*** *your eyes and your ears.* Simply look and listen. If you want to be alert and stay ready, you've got to have discernment. The world will exploit you with false words and tempt you with false promises. Open your eyes. Open your ears. Peter expressed the warning this way: "Therefore, dear friends, be on your guard so that you may not be carried away by the error of lawless men and fall from your secure position" (3:17).

There are false teachers all around us who would like nothing better than to deceive us and lead us away from the truth of the gospel of Jesus. You would never believe the conversations I have had in airports and on street corners with some of the cultists. Obviously in those instances our need for discernment is essential! Don't buy their flowers. They are predators on the prowl! Don't buy their books. Don't let yourself be tempted by the sweet-sounding philosophies. Tell them what you believe and why. Open your eyes. Open your ears. Say it straight. And remember, not all false teachers will be so easily and quickly identifiable. Many come as wolves in sheep's clothing. They'll tempt you in sly and subtle ways. Let Peter's warning resound in your ears: "Be on your guard." Stay true to the pure gospel of Jesus Christ.

Third, ***Pursue*** *a godly lifestyle.* Peter laid it out in plain, unadorned language: "You ought to live holy and godly lives as you look forward to the day of God and speed its coming" (3:11–12). We simply cannot be enamored by the godless lifestyle of unbelievers and at the same time stay awake and ready for the day of Jesus' return. Distraction dulls the edge. Diligence keeps it sharp. Pursue a godly lifestyle—even if you live all alone, even if you don't have many companions around to hold you accountable. Character and godliness are something we must pursue and develop. The reality that Jesus Christ is coming again ought to make a difference in the values we hold, the attitudes we own and the behaviors we practice. Keep growing in this area of your life.

Fourth, and finally, ***Expect*** *Jesus Christ's return*. Peter said it straight: "But in keeping with his promise we are looking forward to a new heaven and a new earth, the home of righteousness" (3:13). We must live with an eager expectation that Jesus can return at any time. That sense of expectation is always held in balance with a commitment to be ready to live for Jesus in the present and in the future, should He not return immediately. Living with a genuine expectation of His return will give us a strong and a living hope that keeps us ready to meet our Lord.

Hope. We cannot go on without it. But we cannot expect to maintain it without diligently participating in those things that help keep us alert to its power and its presence in our lives. Never forget:

Heed
Open
Pursue
Expect

Moral Corruption **Chapter 1**

In chapter 1 Peter prescribes the antidote to moral corruption. I must remind you that the Christian life is not automatically victorious. You are not protected from the blast of winter in January or February simply by walking out in the weather just as you are. You have to put on the right garments. You have to prepare yourself for being outdoors, or you'll freeze to death. In this letter Peter offered just the right "clothing" to resist moral corruption, just the right advice to take to help us use the tools God has given us. This chapter gives us blunt and clear direction; our part is to follow God's teaching and resist the temptation to compromise morally.

1 Simon Peter, a servant and apostle of Jesus
Christ, Ro 1:1; 1Pe 1:1

To those who through the righteousness of our
God and Savior Jesus Christ have received a faith
as precious as ours: Ro 3:21-26; Tit 2:13

2Grace and peace be yours in abundance
through the knowledge of God and of Jesus our
Lord. Php 3:8

Making One's Calling and Election Sure

3His divine power has given us everything we
need for life and godliness through our knowledge
of him who called us by his own glory and goodness. 4Through these he has given us his very great
and precious promises, so that through them you
may participate in the divine nature and escape the
corruption in the world caused by evil desires.
5For this very reason, make every effort to add

LIVING  **INSIGHT**

Extraordinary times will require of us extraordinary wisdom, vision, boldness, flexibility, dedication, willingness to adapt and a renewed commitment to Biblical principles that never change. The secret, of course, is adapting to our times without altering God's truth.

(See 2 Peter 1:5–8.)

to your faith goodness; and to goodness, knowledge; 6and to knowledge, self-control; and to self-
control, perseverance; and to perseverance, godliness; 7and to godliness, brotherly kindness; and to
brotherly kindness, love. 8For if you possess these
qualities in increasing measure, they will keep you
from being ineffective and unproductive in your
knowledge of our Lord Jesus Christ. 9But if anyone
does not have them, he is nearsighted and blind,
and has forgotten that he has been cleansed from
his past sins. 1Jn 2:11; Eph 5:26
10Therefore, my brothers, be all the more eager
to make your calling and election sure. For if you
do these things, you will never fall, 11and you will
receive a rich welcome into the eternal kingdom of
our Lord and Savior Jesus Christ. 2Pe 3:17

Prophecy of Scripture

12So I will always remind you of these things,
even though you know them and are firmly established in the truth you now have. 13I think it is
right to refresh your memory as long as I live in
the tent of this body, 14because I know that I will
soon put it aside, as our Lord Jesus Christ has
made clear to me. 15And I will make every effort to
see that after my departure you will always be able
to remember these things. 2Co 5:1,4; 1Jn 2:21
16We did not follow cleverly invented stories
when we told you about the power and coming of
our Lord Jesus Christ, but we were eyewitnesses of
his majesty. 17For he received honor and glory
from God the Father when the voice came to him
from the Majestic Glory, saying, "This is my Son,
whom I love; with him I am well pleased."[a] 18We
ourselves heard this voice that came from heaven
when we were with him on the sacred mountain.
19And we have the word of the prophets made
more certain, and you will do well to pay attention
to it, as to a light shining in a dark place, until the
day dawns and the morning star rises in your
hearts. 20Above all, you must understand that no
prophecy of Scripture came about by the prophet's
own interpretation. 21For prophecy never had its
origin in the will of man, but men spoke from God
as they were carried along by the Holy Spirit.

Doctrinal Compromise **Chapter 2**

It is of utmost importance that believers think with razor-sharp minds about the truth of the gospel. Apply this simple test: If what someone is teaching *can be supported by Scripture*, count on it. If that teaching lacks Biblical support, question it. Anyone who claims to be a teacher of the truth will count it a privilege if you ask for Biblical support for his or her position. False prophets will often abuse their authority, exploit their hearers, rationalize their positions and try to make anyone who questions them feel embarrassed for raising a concern. When teachers cannot or will not give Biblical support for what they teach, we have every right to question them—as a matter of fact, it is our obligation. We must, in this day of doctrinal compromise, place the highest value on standing on the power and the authority of the Word of God. It is our only hope for survival.

[a] *17* Matt. 17:5; Mark 9:7; Luke 9:35

False Teachers and Their Destruction

2 But there were also false prophets among the people, just as there will be false teachers among you. They will secretly introduce destructive heresies, even denying the sovereign Lord who bought them—bringing swift destruction on themselves. [2]Many will follow their shameful ways and will bring the way of truth into disrepute. [3]In their greed these teachers will exploit you with stories they have made up. Their condemnation has long been hanging over them, and their destruction has not been sleeping. 2Co 2:17; Jude 4

[4]For if God did not spare angels when they sinned, but sent them to hell,[a] putting them into gloomy dungeons[b] to be held for judgment; [5]if he did not spare the ancient world when he brought the flood on its ungodly people, but protected Noah, a preacher of righteousness, and seven others; [6]if he condemned the cities of Sodom and Gomorrah by burning them to ashes, and made them an example of what is going to happen to the ungodly; [7]and if he rescued Lot, a righteous man, who was distressed by the filthy lives of lawless men [8](for that righteous man, living among them day after day, was tormented in his righteous soul by the lawless deeds he saw and heard)— [9]if this is so, then the Lord knows how to rescue godly men from trials and to hold the unrighteous for the day of judgment, while continuing their punishment.[c] [10]This is especially true of those who follow the corrupt desire of the sinful nature[d] and despise authority. 1Co 10:13; 2Pe 3:3

Bold and arrogant, these men are not afraid to slander celestial beings; [11]yet even angels, although they are stronger and more powerful, do not bring slanderous accusations against such beings in the presence of the Lord. [12]But these men blaspheme in matters they do not understand. They are like brute beasts, creatures of instinct, born only to be caught and destroyed, and like beasts they too will perish. Jude 8-10

[13]They will be paid back with harm for the harm they have done. Their idea of pleasure is to carouse in broad daylight. They are blots and blemishes, reveling in their pleasures while they feast with you.[e] [14]With eyes full of adultery, they never stop sinning; they seduce the unstable; they are experts in greed—an accursed brood! [15]They have left the straight way and wandered off to follow the way of Balaam son of Beor, who loved the wages of wickedness. [16]But he was rebuked for his wrongdoing by a donkey—a beast without speech—who spoke with a man's voice and restrained the prophet's madness. Nu 22:21-30

[17]These men are springs without water and mists driven by a storm. Blackest darkness is reserved for them. [18]For they mouth empty, boastful words and, by appealing to the lustful desires of sinful human nature, they entice people who are just escaping from those who live in error. [19]They promise them freedom, while they themselves are slaves of depravity—for a man is a slave to whatever has mastered him. [20]If they have escaped the corruption of the world by knowing our Lord and Savior Jesus Christ and are again entangled in it and overcome, they are worse off at the end than they were at the beginning. [21]It would have been better for them not to have known the way of righteousness, than to have known it and then to turn their backs on the sacred command that was passed on to them. [22]Of them the proverbs are true: "A dog returns to its vomit,"[f] and, "A sow that is washed goes back to her wallowing in the mud." Mt 12:45; Heb 6:4-6

Prophetic Concern **Chapter 3**

Peter ended the letter the same way he began—with a strong plea for diligence. He wanted his readers to be committed to the truth—truth that not only relates to what we have learned from the past but also to what we hope for in the future. Peter directs our attention back to the Old Testament and the flood in the days of Noah to show that God does not deal lightly with disobedience and rebellion; Peter points us forward to the future to help us realize that the return of Jesus Christ is certain. Though time may pass and people may scoff, the truth of God's Word stands firm. Count on It!

The Day of the Lord

3 Dear friends, this is now my second letter to you. I have written both of them as reminders to stimulate you to wholesome thinking. [2]I want you to recall the words spoken in the past by the holy prophets and the command given by our Lord and Savior through your apostles. 2Pe 1:13

[3]First of all, you must understand that in the last days scoffers will come, scoffing and following their own evil desires. [4]They will say, "Where is this 'coming' he promised? Ever since our fathers died, everything goes on as it has since the beginning of creation." [5]But they deliberately forget that long ago by God's word the heavens existed and the earth was formed out of water and by water. [6]By these waters also the world of that time was deluged and destroyed. [7]By the same word the present heavens and earth are reserved for fire, being kept for the day of judgment and destruction of ungodly men. Eze 12:22; 2Pe 2:10

[8]But do not forget this one thing, dear friends: With the Lord a day is like a thousand years, and

[a]4 Greek *Tartarus* [b]4 Some manuscripts *into chains of darkness* [c]9 Or *unrighteous for punishment until the day of judgment* [d]10 Or *the flesh* [e]13 Some manuscripts *in their love feasts* [f]22 Prov. 26:11

a thousand years are like a day. 9The Lord is not
slow in keeping his promise, as some understand
slowness. He is patient with you, not wanting anyone to perish, but everyone to come to repentance.

LIVING  INSIGHT

The Lord is going to return. He doesn't want anyone to perish. I call that clear, specific and reliable information. Let's not mistake our Lord's current patience for permanent absence. He is coming back.

(See 2 Peter 3:8–9.)

10But the day of the Lord will come like a thief.
The heavens will disappear with a roar; the elements will be destroyed by fire, and the earth and
everything in it will be laid bare.[a] Mt 24:35; Rev 21:1
11Since everything will be destroyed in this way,
what kind of people ought you to be? You ought
to live holy and godly lives 12as you look forward
to the day of God and speed its coming.[b] That
day will bring about the destruction of the heavens
by fire, and the elements will melt in the heat.
13But in keeping with his promise we are looking
forward to a new heaven and a new earth, the
home of righteousness. Isa 65:17; 1Co 1:7
14So then, dear friends, since you are looking
forward to this, make every effort to be found
spotless, blameless and at peace with him. 15Bear
in mind that our Lord's patience means salvation,
just as our dear brother Paul also wrote you with
the wisdom that God gave him. 16He writes the
same way in all his letters, speaking in them of
these matters. His letters contain some things that
are hard to understand, which ignorant and unstable people distort, as they do the other Scriptures,
to their own destruction. Eph 3:3; 2Pe 2:14
17Therefore, dear friends, since you already
know this, be on your guard so that you may not
be carried away by the error of lawless men and
fall from your secure position. 18But grow in the
grace and knowledge of our Lord and Savior Jesus
Christ. To him be glory both now and forever!
Amen. 2Pe 1:11; Rev 2:5

[a] 10 Some manuscripts *be burned up* [b] 12 Or *as you wait eagerly for the day of God to come*

1 JOHN

Sometimes it's easy to forget that John, one of Jesus' original twelve disciples, was responsible for five books that made their way into the canon of the New Testament. Probably the best-known of these books is the Gospel that bears his name. The next best-known may very well be the lengthy and intriguing book of prophecy called Revelation. Sandwiched between the two are three letters that reveal the heart and soul of this tender man of God. The first of these letters appears on the surface to be simple and uncomplicated, but it is in reality profound and complex. And how important! It is very likely, as some have called it, "the last apostolic message to the whole church." In John's Gospel, he declares the *way* of life through faith in God's Son, Jesus Christ. In his first letter his emphasis is on the *nature* of that life as possessed by God's children.

WRITER: *John*

DATE: *C.A.D. 85–95*

PURPOSE: *To expose false teachers and to give believers assurance of salvation*

KEY VERSES: *1:4; 2:1,26; 5:13*

KEY TERMS: *"Know"; "love"; "fellowship"*

KEY CONTRASTS: *Light and darkness; truth and error; life and death; love and hate; righteousness and lawlessness; children of God and children of the devil; Christ and antichrist*

TIME LINE 10BC AD1 10 20 30 40 50 60 70 80 90 100

Jesus' birth (c.6/5 B.C.)

John becomes a disciple (c. A.D.26)

Jesus' death, resurrection and ascension (c. A.D.30)

Nero's reign (c. A.D.54-68)

Destruction of Jerusalem's temple (c. A.D.70)

Domitian's reign (c. A.D.81-96)

Book of 1 John written (c. A.D.85-95)

John's exile on Patmos (c. A.D.90-95)

God's Life on Display

	FELLOWSHIP WITH GOD PRODUCES . . .			
	A joyful life	**A clean life**	**A discerning life**	**A confident life**
	"We write this to make our joy complete" (1:4).	*"I write this to you so that you will not sin. But if anybody does sin, we have one who speaks to the Father in our defense—Jesus Christ, the Righteous One" (2:1).*	*"I am writing these things to you about those who are trying to lead you astray" (2:26).*	*"I write these things to you who believe in the name of the Son of God so that you may know that you have eternal life" (5:13).*
	CHAPTER 1	*CHAPTER 2:1-17*	*CHAPTERS 2:18–4:6*	*CHAPTERS 4:7–5:21*
EMPHASIS	Light	Love	Truth	Knowledge
MEANS	Walking *(1:7)*	Obeying *(2:4-5)*	Testing *(4:1)*	Believing *(5:10)*
CHRIST	Son of God *(1:3,7)*	Advocate *(2:1)*	Holy One *(2:20)*	Atoning Sacrifice *(4:10)*

The very first time I had the opportunity to teach an adult church school class I chose 1 John as the topic for study. I want you to know it was *not* a good decision. I'm convinced I did it out of ignorance. This letter looked so little, sweet and innocent tucked away in the back of the New Testament, sandwiched between 2 Peter and 2 John. It seemed so simple. As I began to wade through 1 John, I realized what a bad mistake I had made. That was back in the 1950s. If I were able to gather together those four dear saints who faithfully stuck with me through the whole series of classes, I would say three words to them: "I am sorry." This book may have the appearance of a primer, but it is anything but. It may look like "bedside reading," but such a look is deceiving.

In case you missed my point, I strongly suggest, unless you are fairly well versed in Old and New Testament truth, that you undertake an in-depth study of 1 John with great care. I don't mean to leave the wrong impression. It is certainly inspired by God. It is a grand letter to learn. It simply has problems many teachers much brighter than I am have yet to unravel and maybe will never grasp completely. To put it mildly, 1 John is a *challenge*!

When the Newness Wears Off

John actually wrote five New Testament documents. Very likely his most popular is the Gospel we love and appreciate. Close behind in popularity is the book called Revelation, the last book in the New Testament. Located between these two very popular works within the canon of the New Testament are the three letters called 1 John, 2 John and 3 John.

John's writings were all undertaken toward the end of the first century; by that time the freshness of the faith had begun to wear off. You see, these three letters of John were written during an ever-widening storm of heresy called "Gnosticism" (from the Greek word *gnosis* meaning "knowledge"). Gnosticism combined such teachings as "salvation could be gained through possessing a special knowledge" and "all matter is evil; only the spirit is pure." This heresy, which thrived among the intellectual elite, had interesting side effects like "asceticism" (the practice of strict self-denial) and "antinomianism," meaning "against law" (an indifference toward personal ethics, leading to grossly immoral, licentious behavior). And, as a logical conclusion of the teaching that the physical body was evil, the Gnostics denied that God could have taken on a body in the person of Jesus Christ. Some claimed Jesus only seemed to have a body (called "Docetism," from the Greek *dokeo*, which means "to seem"), while others said God descended on Jesus at His baptism and then left Him before His death. This potentially disastrous false teaching had begun to invade the early church and take a serious toll on new believers. John wrote his first letter in the middle of that stormy setting.

As the newness of early, pristine faith had worn off, second- and in some cases third-generation Christians on the scene created a situation that left God's truth particularly open to attack. Think about this. If we're around many new Christians, we may very well have a wonderful experience in sharing the Scriptures. If we're dealing with second- and third-generation Christians, enthusiasm has sometimes waned and been replaced by complacency. Any teacher or mentor in that setting faces a difficult task.

Reflecting on the state of Christianity toward the end of the first century one historian wrote, "In the very first days of Christianity there was a glory and a splendor, a magnificence and a radiance in life. But now Christianity had become a thing of habit; it had become traditional, halfhearted, nominal. Men had grown used to it and something of the wonder had gotten lost. The first thrill was gone. The flame of devotion had died to a flicker." In a situation like that, heresy has all the opportunity it needs to grow wild. All a cult needs is an indifferent church to feed on, and it will gain numerous disciples. Though they may not look like it, complacency and indifference are some of the worst enemies authentic Christianity must confront and counteract.

Four Reasons for Writing

Why was this letter written? I find in the letter of 1 John four reasons (each marked by similar words: "I [or we] write this . . ."). First, *John wrote in order to bring back the joy that was by now missing from the church*: "We write this to make our joy complete" (1:4). He wanted to rekindle the genuine joy these believers were quickly forgetting and in danger of losing altogether. Many of us today could also use a big dose of joy in our walk with the Lord. John will help us recapture it.

Second, *John wrote to help his readers live victorious lives rather than defeated lives*: "My dear children, I write this to you so that you will not sin" (2:1). John gave these believers a reminder we need as much today as they did in John's day. There is victory in Jesus over the disastrous penalty and the oppressive power of sin. There is no reason for believers to live defeated lives; a walk in victory is not only possible, it's the norm!

Third, *John wrote to inform his readers of the deceivers among them as well as to remind them of the truth they needed to embrace*: "I am writing these things to you about those who are trying to lead you astray" (2:26). John wrote to equip believers to stand against the deception of heresy. We must know what we believe and what we don't believe (John uses two Greek verbs translated "know" some 41 times in his brief letter). While there will always be deceivers, our task is to be sure that they do not deceive us. A thoroughgoing knowledge of our faith is an excellent defense against those who are out to destroy it.

Fourth, *John wrote to reassure believers of the absolute certainty of their salvation*: "I write these things to you who believe in the name of the Son of God so that you may know that you have eternal life" (5:13). Hand in hand with John's desire that his readers regain their joy, walk in victory and resist deception was his desire to instill in them an unwavering confidence of their eternal security in Jesus Christ.

A Final Word to the Church

John's first letter was written in the later years of his life, near the end of the first century. It was a time in which loss of power and vitality had infected many believers. Potentially ruinous heresy was on the move. Because John gave no indication to whom he was writing this letter, some Bible scholars believe it was a circular letter sent to Christians in a number of places in the province of Asia. It's impossible, however, to determine the precise people to whom it was sent.

In my opinion Bible teacher G. Campbell Morgan had it right when he wrote, "Probably this is the last apostolic message to the whole church." As we suggested in our study of 2 Timothy (see page 1307), there is something significant about final words. This "last apostolic message," therefore, remains crucial for us today. While it is complex, due at least in part to the enigmatic heretical teachings of that day, we must not avoid digging into John's words in this letter as he exposes false teachers and instructs us on how our faith must affect our lives as we "walk in the light" (1:7).

A Message for Today

John provides a practical application of the gospel. He applies the truth and implies a morality in this letter that is for all generations. He writes to tell people how to have eternal life and what that eternal life includes. Look carefully at 1 John, and you will find the life of God displayed in all its glory and splendor.

The *Gospel* of John will help bring a person to a belief in Jesus Christ as Savior and Lord and to fellowship in the family of God. The first *letter* of John will help that person understand what a life in relationship with God includes. Fellowship with God involves joy, purity, assurance, discernment and confidence. All five components are directly addressed in this letter.

Because this is a letter full of contrasting figures (love and hate, light and darkness, life and death, truth and lies, Christ and antichrist, God's children and children of the devil), the lessons we can learn might best be stated in terms of contrasts.

First, *in an angry, dark world the joyful Christian is a bright light* (1:4–7). If you live a joyful life, believe me, you'll attract attention like a watermelon attracts flies. People will want to know what's happening with you. When you're joyful, you're a bright light in an angry, dark world. As Jesus taught in his immortal Sermon on the Mount, "You are the light of the world . . . Let your light shine" (Matthew 5:14,16).

Second, *in a sinful, lawless society the clean Christian is a strong witness to God's power to overcome sin* (1:8–2:2). The call from Scripture is to stay clean. Deal with sin when it arises, and don't toy with it, because you're likely to get burned. I love something I heard about John Chrysostom (347–407), called by some "the greatest of all Christian preachers." In his sermon "How to Bring Up Children," he advised parents to give their boys some great Scriptural name, teach them the story of the original bearer of that name, and thus give them a standard to live up to when they grow to manhood. Isn't that great advice? Do you know what *your* name means? Child of God. Child of light. John reminds us of the reality of forgiveness of sins through Jesus and urges us to live as Jesus did. In a society that has lost its way, a clean Christian is a beacon of hope announcing that freedom and fullness are possible in Jesus alone.

Third, *in a turbulent environment of deception the discerning Christian is a calm refuge.* What's the application? Think straight. Be discerning. Cut through the fog of lies and misrepresentation. Listen for truth. If what you're hearing conflicts with the truth of God, reject it! Listen for underlying implications that may undermine the truth. Put on your thinking cap. Those Christians in the first century, just like Christians today, had to recognize, and reject, deception.

Fourth, and finally, *in an insecure and confused age the confident Christian is a stabilizing force.* Stand firm. Let the Lord use you to bring stability in the church and in an unsteady world. You and I as Christians have a message that brings quiet confidence to a world reeling from the gale-force winds of change and the unsettling feelings of rootlessness.

Showing God's Love

There is a wonderful old story from the days of World War II about a hungry little boy and a soldier in the badly damaged city of London. The boy was peering through the fogged-up glass of a bakery shop as the bakers pulled donuts out of the oven. He wanted one so bad, but he didn't have a dime in his ragged pockets. A soldier came around the corner in his jeep and jammed on the brakes. He saw the boy and knew immediately what was happening. He walked over to the boy and asked, "You want one of those donuts?" "Yeah!" the boy said with enthusiasm. The soldier walked inside and bought a dozen hot donuts and gave them to the little boy. The boy stared at the soldier and asked, "Mister, are you God?"

If we consistently walk in the truth of God, we'll have little difficulty showing others the face of the Son of God—both in what we say and in what we do. Our lives should reflect the love and presence of God wherever we go. We are His life on display (see, for example, 2 Corinthians 2:14–3:3). John wrote his letter with the hope that his readers would be eager to have fellowship with God so sincerely, so intimately, that they would *experience* what it means to "walk in the light, as he is in the light" (1:7).

A Joyful Life **Chapter 1**

In chapter 1 John expressed his desire that believers live a *joyful* life. He had lived many years and had discovered so much about the true source of joy. John wants us to know the depth of joy that comes from Christian unity, knowing Christ, keeping short accounts with sin, and maintaining intimate fellowship with the Lord and His people. He would have us reflect on the joy we have experienced in the past, persist in a state of full joy in the present and confidently anticipate future joy. To walk in this joyous condition of heart we need to rid our lives of the anchor of sin that weighs us down and walk closely with the Savior as well as in fellowship with God's people. These things will lead to deep and abiding joy.

The Word of Life

1 That which was from the beginning, which
we have heard, which we have seen with our
eyes, which we have looked at and our hands have
touched—this we proclaim concerning the Word
of life. 2The life appeared; we have seen it and
testify to it, and we proclaim to you the eternal life,
which was with the Father and has appeared to
us. 3We proclaim to you what we have seen and
heard, so that you also may have fellowship with
us. And our fellowship is with the Father and with
his Son, Jesus Christ. 4We write this to make our[a]
joy complete. Jn 3:29; 1Jn 2:1

Walking in the Light

5This is the message we have heard from him
and declare to you: God is light; in him there is no
darkness at all. 6If we claim to have fellowship with
him yet walk in the darkness, we lie and do not live
by the truth. 7But if we walk in the light, as he is
in the light, we have fellowship with one another,
and the blood of Jesus, his Son, purifies us from
all[b] sin. Heb 9:14; Rev 1:5
8If we claim to be without sin, we deceive ourselves and the truth is not in us. 9If we confess our

LIVING  **INSIGHT**

If you have not done so already, I urge you to memorize this verse. It has become one of the most frequently quoted and beloved promises in all the Bible.

(See 1 John 1:9.)

sins, he is faithful and just and will forgive us our
sins and purify us from all unrighteousness. 10If we
claim we have not sinned, we make him out to be
a liar and his word has no place in our lives.

A Clean Life **Chapter 2:1–17**

In these verses John reminded his readers about the need for believers to live a *clean* life. He longed for God's people to lead an exemplary life, which comes as a result of knowing Jesus and His forgiveness as well as through resisting sin and walking in holiness. The key to a clean life is walking in love, a theme John came back to again and again. If we have no love in our hearts, how can we say we truly know God and love Him? John points to the atoning death of Jesus that brings us cleansing through His blood (2:2) and reminds us that we must obey His commands and walk as Jesus did (2:3,6).

2 My dear children, I write this to you so that
you will not sin. But if anybody does sin, we
have one who speaks to the Father in our defense—Jesus Christ, the Righteous One. 2He is the
atoning sacrifice for our sins, and not only for ours
but also for[c] the sins of the whole world.
3We know that we have come to know him if we
obey his commands. 4The man who says, "I know
him," but does not do what he commands is a liar,
and the truth is not in him. 5But if anyone obeys
his word, God's love[d] is truly made complete in
him. This is how we know we are in him: 6Who-
ever claims to live in him must walk as Jesus did.
7Dear friends, I am not writing you a new command but an old one, which you have had since
the beginning. This old command is the message
you have heard. 8Yet I am writing you a new command; its truth is seen in him and you, because the
darkness is passing and the true light is already
shining. Jn 1:9; 13:34
9Anyone who claims to be in the light but hates
his brother is still in the darkness. 10Whoever loves
his brother lives in the light, and there is nothing
in him[e] to make him stumble. 11But whoever
hates his brother is in the darkness and walks
around in the darkness; he does not know where
he is going, because the darkness has blinded him.

12I write to you, dear children,
because your sins have been forgiven on
account of his name. 1Jn 3:23

LIVING  **INSIGHT**

You can count on this—the past ended one second ago. From this point onward, you can be clean, filled with His Spirit and used in many different ways for His honor and to His glory.

(See 1 John 2:12.)

[a]4 Some manuscripts *your* *not only ours but also* [b]7 Or *every* [c]2 Or *He is the one who turns aside God's wrath, taking away our sins, and* [d]5 Or *word, love for God* [e]10 Or *it*

13I write to you, fathers,
because you have known him who is from
the beginning. Jn 1:1
I write to you, young men,
because you have overcome the evil one.
I write to you, dear children,
because you have known the Father.
14I write to you, fathers,
because you have known him who is from
the beginning. Jn 1:1
I write to you, young men,
because you are strong, Eph 6:10
and the word of God lives in you, Jn 5:38
and you have overcome the evil one. ver 13

Do Not Love the World

15Do not love the world or anything in the world.
If anyone loves the world, the love of the Father is
not in him. 16For everything in the world—the
cravings of sinful man, the lust of his eyes and the
boasting of what he has and does—comes not
from the Father but from the world. 17The world
and its desires pass away, but the man who does
the will of God lives forever. Pr 27:20

A Discerning Life **Chapters 2:18–4:6**

In this section John warns us against being deceived by false teachers. We need to live a *discerning* life that keeps us alert to the presence of those who teach a false gospel and who by their doctrines and lives oppose Christ. John takes pains to reassure us of God's love for His children. He is concerned that we never be led astray. At the end of this portion of the letter John gives words of hope and confidence to the reader. We must never forget that we are children of God who rely on the incomparable power of God to see us through to the very end.

Warning Against Antichrists

18Dear children, this is the last hour; and as you
have heard that the antichrist is coming, even now
many antichrists have come. This is how we know
it is the last hour. 19They went out from us, but
they did not really belong to us. For if they had
belonged to us, they would have remained with us;
but their going showed that none of them belonged to us. 1Co 11:19; 1Jn 4:1
20But you have an anointing from the Holy
One, and all of you know the truth.[a] 21I do not
write to you because you do not know the truth,
but because you do know it and because no lie
comes from the truth. 22Who is the liar? It is the
man who denies that Jesus is the Christ. Such a
man is the antichrist—he denies the Father and
the Son. 23No one who denies the Son has the
Father; whoever acknowledges the Son has the Father also. 2Pe 1:12; 1Jn 4:15
24See that what you have heard from the beginning remains in you. If it does, you also will remain in the Son and in the Father. 25And this is
what he promised us—even eternal life. Jn 14:23
26I am writing these things to you about those
who are trying to lead you astray. 27As for you, the
anointing you received from him remains in you,
and you do not need anyone to teach you. But as
his anointing teaches you about all things and as
that anointing is real, not counterfeit—just as it
has taught you, remain in him. 2Jn 7

Children of God

28And now, dear children, continue in him, so
that when he appears we may be confident and
unashamed before him at his coming. 1Jn 3:2; 4:17
29If you know that he is righteous, you know
that everyone who does what is right has been
born of him.

3 How great is the love the Father has lavished
on us, that we should be called children of
God! And that is what we are! The reason the
world does not know us is that it did not know
him. 2Dear friends, now we are children of God,
and what we will be has not yet been made known.
But we know that when he appears,[b] we shall be
like him, for we shall see him as he is. 3Everyone
who has this hope in him purifies himself, just as
he is pure. Jn 1:12; 16:3
4Everyone who sins breaks the law; in fact, sin
is lawlessness. 5But you know that he appeared so
that he might take away our sins. And in him is no
sin. 6No one who lives in him keeps on sinning.
No one who continues to sin has either seen him
or known him. 2Co 5:21; 1Jn 5:17
7Dear children, do not let anyone lead you
astray. He who does what is right is righteous, just
as he is righteous. 8He who does what is sinful is
of the devil, because the devil has been sinning
from the beginning. The reason the Son of God
appeared was to destroy the devil's work. 9No one
who is born of God will continue to sin, because
God's seed remains in him; he cannot go on sinning, because he has been born of God. 10This is
how we know who the children of God are and
who the children of the devil are: Anyone who
does not do what is right is not a child of God; nor
is anyone who does not love his brother. 1Jn 4:8

Love One Another

11This is the message you heard from the beginning: We should love one another. 12Do not be like
Cain, who belonged to the evil one and murdered
his brother. And why did he murder him? Because

[a]20 Some manuscripts *and you know all things* [b]2 Or *when it is made known*

his own actions were evil and his brother's were
righteous. 13 Do not be surprised, my brothers, if
the world hates you. 14 We know that we have
passed from death to life, because we love our
brothers. Anyone who does not love remains in
death. 15 Anyone who hates his brother is a murderer, and you know that no murderer has eternal
life in him. Mt 5:21-22; Gal 5:20-21

LIVING  **INSIGHT**

Love. No greater theme can be emphasized. No stronger message can be proclaimed. No finer song can be sung. No better truth can be imagined.

(See 1 John 3:11–18.)

16 This is how we know what love is: Jesus Christ
laid down his life for us. And we ought to lay down
our lives for our brothers. 17 If anyone has material
possessions and sees his brother in need but has
no pity on him, how can the love of God be in
him? 18 Dear children, let us not love with words or
tongue but with actions and in truth. 19 This then
is how we know that we belong to the truth, and
how we set our hearts at rest in his presence
20 whenever our hearts condemn us. For God is
greater than our hearts, and he knows everything.
21 Dear friends, if our hearts do not condemn us,
we have confidence before God 22 and receive from
him anything we ask, because we obey his commands and do what pleases him. 23 And this is his
command: to believe in the name of his Son, Jesus
Christ, and to love one another as he commanded
us. 24 Those who obey his commands live in him,
and he in them. And this is how we know that he
lives in us: We know it by the Spirit he gave us.

Test the Spirits

4 Dear friends, do not believe every spirit, but
test the spirits to see whether they are from
God, because many false prophets have gone out
into the world. 2 This is how you can recognize the
Spirit of God: Every spirit that acknowledges that
Jesus Christ has come in the flesh is from God,
3 but every spirit that does not acknowledge Jesus
is not from God. This is the spirit of the antichrist,
which you have heard is coming and even now is
already in the world. 1Co 12:3; 2Jn 7
4 You, dear children, are from God and have
overcome them, because the one who is in you is
greater than the one who is in the world. 5 They are
from the world and therefore speak from the viewpoint of the world, and the world listens to them.
6 We are from God, and whoever knows God listens to us; but whoever is not from God does not
listen to us. This is how we recognize the Spirit[a]
of truth and the spirit of falsehood. Jn 8:47; 14:17

A Confident Life — Chapters 4:7–5:21

John reminded his readers yet again of the need to live in love and in faith in Jesus as the Son of God who came to save us. In his concluding remarks, he penned words of assurance for all believers. What confidence these words bring to our hearts: "I write these things to you who believe in the name of the Son of God so that you may know that you have eternal life" (5:13). Note that John didn't write "so that you may hope that you have eternal life"; he didn't write "so that you may think that you have eternal life." No, John told us he wrote these things that we may "know," with complete confidence, that we have eternal life. In other words, we may have absolute assurance of our salvation and eternal destiny. This certainty brings a *confident* life to the believer like nothing else. As a child of God, never, ever forget this: Our eternity is secure!

God's Love and Ours

7 Dear friends, let us love one another, for love
comes from God. Everyone who loves has been
born of God and knows God. 8 Whoever does not
love does not know God, because God is love.
9 This is how God showed his love among us: He
sent his one and only Son[b] into the world that we
might live through him. 10 This is love: not that we
loved God, but that he loved us and sent his Son
as an atoning sacrifice for[c] our sins. 11 Dear
friends, since God so loved us, we also ought to
love one another. 12 No one has ever seen God; but
if we love one another, God lives in us and his love
is made complete in us. 1Jn 2:2,5
13 We know that we live in him and he in us,
because he has given us of his Spirit. 14 And we
have seen and testify that the Father has sent his
Son to be the Savior of the world. 15 If anyone
acknowledges that Jesus is the Son of God, God
lives in him and he in God. 16 And so we know and
rely on the love God has for us. Ro 10:9
God is love. Whoever lives in love lives in God,
and God in him. 17 In this way, love is made complete among us so that we will have confidence on
the day of judgment, because in this world we are
like him. 18 There is no fear in love. But perfect love
drives out fear, because fear has to do with punishment. The one who fears is not made perfect in
love. Ro 8:15; 1Jn 2:5
19 We love because he first loved us. 20 If anyone
says, "I love God," yet hates his brother, he is a
liar. For anyone who does not love his brother,
whom he has seen, cannot love God, whom he has
not seen. 21 And he has given us this command:
Whoever loves God must also love his brother.

[a] 6 Or *spirit* [b] 9 Or *his only begotten Son* [c] 10 Or *as the one who would turn aside his wrath, taking away*

Faith in the Son of God

5 Everyone who believes that Jesus is the Christ is born of God, and everyone who loves the father loves his child as well. 2This is how we know that we love the children of God: by loving God and carrying out his commands. 3This is love for God: to obey his commands. And his commands are not burdensome, 4for everyone born of God overcomes the world. This is the victory that has overcome the world, even our faith. 5Who is it that overcomes the world? Only he who believes that Jesus is the Son of God. Jn 14:15; 16:33

6This is the one who came by water and blood—Jesus Christ. He did not come by water only, but by water and blood. And it is the Spirit who testifies, because the Spirit is the truth. 7For there are three that testify: 8the[a] Spirit, the water and the blood; and the three are in agreement. 9We accept man's testimony, but God's testimony is greater because it is the testimony of God, which he has given about his Son. 10Anyone who believes in the Son of God has this testimony in his heart. Anyone who does not believe God has made him out to be a liar, because he has not believed the testimony God has given about his Son. 11And this is the testimony: God has given us eternal life, and this life is in his Son. 12He who has the Son has life; he who does not have the Son of God does not have life. Jn 3:15-16,36; 1Jn 2:25

Concluding Remarks

13I write these things to you who believe in the name of the Son of God so that you may know that you have eternal life. 14This is the confidence we have in approaching God: that if we ask anything according to his will, he hears us. 15And if we know that he hears us—whatever we ask—we know that we have what we asked of him. Jn 20:31

LIVING  **INSIGHT**

Being absolutely confident and comforted in the fact that my salvation is secure, based on God's "keeping" power, not mine, all cause for anxiety is removed. I may tremble on the Rock, but the Rock never trembles under me!

(See 1 John 5:13.)

16If anyone sees his brother commit a sin that does not lead to death, he should pray and God will give him life. I refer to those whose sin does not lead to death. There is a sin that leads to death. I am not saying that he should pray about that. 17All wrongdoing is sin, and there is sin that does not lead to death. Jas 5:15; 1Jn 3:4

18We know that anyone born of God does not continue to sin; the one who was born of God keeps him safe, and the evil one cannot harm him. 19We know that we are children of God, and that the whole world is under the control of the evil one. 20We know also that the Son of God has come and has given us understanding, so that we may know him who is true. And we are in him who is true—even in his Son Jesus Christ. He is the true God and eternal life. Lk 24:45; Jn 17:3

21Dear children, keep yourselves from idols.

[a]7,8 Late manuscripts of the Vulgate *testify in heaven: the Father, the Word and the Holy Spirit, and these three are one.* 8*And there are three that testify on earth: the* (not found in any Greek manuscript before the sixteenth century)

INTRODUCTION

2 JOHN

John's second letter is much less lengthy and certainly less complicated than his first letter. It is important to remember that this letter is a private piece of correspondence to a person rather than to a local church. It is a letter that has great application to our age of undiscerning tolerance. A much-needed balance between truth and love is set forth for all to read and heed. The word "truth" is mentioned five times, as is the word "love," in a piece of correspondence only 13 verses in length. As John writes to this Christian mother, his desire is that she continue in the truth, walking in love and standing against error. He offers a balanced perspective on life: love and truth; practice and doctrine; walking and standing; accepting and rejecting. As you read the letter, you'll quickly sense the abiding principles that apply to our day as well.

WRITER: *John*

DATE: *C.A.D. 85–95*

PURPOSE: *To warn against entertaining visitors who do not teach the truth about Jesus*

KEY THEME: *The truth of the gospel*

KEY TERMS: *"Truth"; "love"*

KEY CONCERNS: *Misplaced hospitality… undiscerning love*

DISTINCTIVES: *Only New Testament letter addressed to a lady; shortest letter (only 13 verses)*

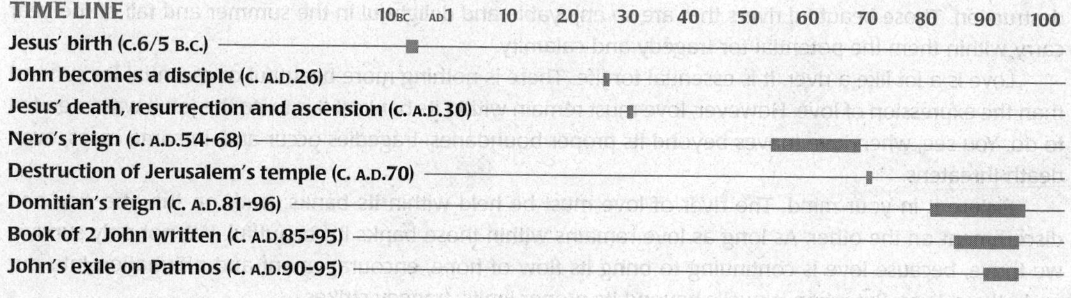

A Letter to a Lady

	INTRODUCTION	WALK IN THE TRUTH!	STAND AGAINST ERROR!	CONCLUSION
	Greeting Affirmation Encouragement	The lady's children The lady herself Love one another; walk in obedience	The circumstance (many deceivers) The warning ("Watch out!") The instruction (strong but necessary)	Personal Farewell
	VERSES 1-3	*VERSES 4-6*	*VERSES 7-11*	*VERSES 12-13*
EMPHASIS	Encouragement to love and affirm		Exhortation to be discerning	
TONE	Gracious	Concerned	Strong	Warm
PERSONAL TOUCH	*"I love you" (verse 1)*	*"I ask you" (verse 5)*	*"I warn you" (implied, verse 8)*	*"I hope to visit you" (verse 12)*

Every spring something beautiful turns into something tragic for people who live near mountainous areas. The tragedy begins when deep mounds of snow begin to thaw and torrential spring rains begin to fall. The beautiful, colorful rivers that are often the source of commerce and beauty for a city swell and overflow their banks.

Beautiful hamlets and villages that once housed and harbored life are now threatened by death thanks to the flooding river. By and by the old river begins to rage as it leaves its banks and moves into places it was never meant to be. Some residents flee their homes—if possible. When it isn't possible to flee, they hope to survive the flood. Almost without exception, year after year, springtime becomes a time of mass destruction. Those beautiful rivers that are so enjoyable and delightful in the summer and fall of the year carry within them the potential for tragedy and calamity.

Love is a lot like a river. It is essential for life. There is nothing more beautiful or essential for survival than the expression of love. However, love must remain within its banks if it is to do the job it was intended to do. You see, when love moves beyond its proper boundaries, tragedies occur and, in some cases, even death threatens.

Picture it in your mind. The river of love must be held within its banks: truth on the one side and discernment on the other. As long as love remains within those banks it's beautiful. We not only survive, we thrive, because love is continuing to bring its flow of hope, encouragement and affirmation into our and others' lives. But when it swells beyond its proper limits, tragedy strikes.

Periodically the Bible illustrates the importance of love being guarded by truth and discernment. But only on a few occasions is this particular subject addressed in concentrated form. One such place where the limits of love are emphasized is in the second letter of John.

Great Surprises in Small Packages

Each of John's last two letters (2 John and 3 John) can be read in less than two minutes. They are tiny letters, more like oversized postcards. If you had the original documents you would most likely discover that the entire letters were written on single sheets of papyrus, because neither one is more than three hundred words in the Greek language. And yet God has chosen to preserve for us these two letters—the Bible's briefest books.

If ever small packages held great surprises and delights, these letters certainly are a case in point. They are marvelous messages of instruction for God's church. I suspect that if more careful attention had been paid to 2 and 3 John throughout the years of church history, the river of love would not have left its banks quite as often as we have observed it to do. And truth mixed with discernment would have been demonstrated more often.

John's Persecution

The writer of this letter identified himself in the very first verse: "The elder." More than likely this was a reference to the writer's age rather than to his official position (though some Bible scholars believe that John functioned as an elder in his later years, perhaps in the Ephesian church). "The elder" has long been accepted as the apostle John, the same man who wrote the Gospel of John, as well as 1 John, 3 John and the book of Revelation.

At the time of the writing of this letter (about A.D. 90), the apostle John was one of the last living witnesses who had literally walked with Jesus. By now most of the other disciples had been martyred. John had been banished to Patmos to die on an island (see Revelation 1:9). Little did those who put him there realize that his writings would survive and continue to feed and bless the church through the centuries.

Christians aren't silenced simply because they have been imprisoned. Sometimes, as a result of adversity, their message is set loose and widely affirmed, even though the persecutors think they are effectively squelching it. Persecution has never succeeded in overcoming the church, just as Jesus promised it wouldn't (see Matthew 16:18). On the contrary, persecution has purified the church and helped to strengthen it. And, as in the case of John, persecution simply resulted in the message being spread even further.

A Lady or a Church?

"The chosen lady" of verse 1 has provoked a lot of interest on the part of New Testament scholars and students. There are many fine people who teach and write books about the Scriptures who believe John is using symbolic language to refer to a specific church in his day. On the other hand, there are those (I am among them) who believe that the "chosen lady" was a woman who lived in the first century. It's interesting to note that the children of the "chosen lady" are mentioned in verse 1 and her sister is referred to in verse 13—and in my judgment it would be highly unusual to address a letter to a church and refer to her children and to her sister. While some maintain that the "chosen sister" of verse 13 is a figurative description of another local church (a sister congregation), it makes more sense to me when we simply take it literally as a reference to another Christian woman. As the saying goes, "When common sense makes good sense, seek no other sense." That's helpful advice to all who wish to interpret God's Word with accuracy.

I believe this "chosen lady" was someone who opened her home to the church as a place to meet because there were no official church buildings at that time. Neither were there complete copies of the Scriptures available. By and large, believers didn't have access to much teaching. There were few long-standing pastorates either. During those times the gospel was taken from place to place by traveling evangelists and teachers who visited from house to house and from city to city as they taught God's Word to God's people.

Hospitality Tempered by Discernment

The church was in a state of flux by the end of the first century. It was a stormy time, with heresies on the rise and persecution commonplace. Not having a place of identity, the church lacked roots and therefore required the service of certain gifted men who traveled to bring the truth to God's people.

In a time when there were no comfortable hotels or inns, travelers were often accommodated in homes. John R.W. Stott described the situation for Christians as they traveled from place to place: "It was natural that Christian people on their travels should be given hospitality by members of local churches. There are many traces in the New Testament of this custom. Such hospitality was often open to abuse. There was the false teacher on the one hand who posed as a Christian. Should hospitality be extended to him? And how would you know? There was also the more obvious false prophet with false credentials who was dominated less by the creed he had to offer than by the material profit and free board and lodging he hoped to gain. It is against this background that we must read the second and the third epistles of John."

So John wrote to a woman who very likely opened her home somewhat indiscriminately to teachers who stopped on their way through the town where she lived. We don't know the woman's name or where she lived. We therefore don't know the church or the specific situation, except for the few things John says about the false teachers who were traveling through. This woman demonstrated sincere Christian hospitality. She gave herself to the ministry of entertaining these itinerant evangelists. Her intentions were pure; she wished to demonstrate the love of Christ by being hospitable to "strangers" (Hebrews 13:2). Her Christian love, however, wasn't always accompanied by clear thinking, for she carelessly received *anyone* into her home. She expressed compassion without balancing it with a commitment to maintaining solid truth. She had the problem of "misplaced hospitality." John challenged her to add a "heaping helping" of discernment to her plate of hospitality.

Lessons From John

I suggest that John shares three abiding principles in this letter, along with a corresponding command. First, *loving others is a fundamental expression of authentic Christianity. Its corresponding command is this: Let's continue walking in love.* One of the greatest messages needed in our generation is to walk in love. Christians, let's walk in love. The better you know the truth the greater your love ought to be. Let your love flow. You'll win over so many more by simply being gracious and loving to all you meet.

Second, *embracing the truth is equally essential. The command is this: Continue to take an uncompromising stand against error.* We are always to be prepared to give the reason for the hope that we have, with gentleness and yet with certainty (1 Peter 3:15). We must know the truth and be able to defend it with a mixture of boldness and grace.

Third, *when error is detected, love must be kept within its boundaries. The corresponding command is this: Let's maintain a balance, or we won't survive.* The challenge for the Christian today is to know the truth and take a stand for it without compromise. At the same time, we must extend love and walk in grace. We must keep love within the banks of truth and discernment and learn how to live in the dynamic tension between grace and truth. This is the lasting lesson of 2 John.

Walk in the Truth

This letter issues a call for a much-needed balance between truth and love in an age of undiscriminating love and undiscerning tolerance. John urged the letter's recipient, most likely a woman in the early church, to know the truth of God and to walk in this truth without wavering. She and her children were challenged to hold on to God's truth without compromise and to stand firm against error and false teaching. There were many deceivers in those days seeking to infiltrate the church with a false gospel. John urged Christians to use discretion in testing a visitor's message and to "watch out" for those who would lead believers astray. These words also resonate with us who must seek to balance love with truth and discernment. We must walk with confidence in God's truth and be ready to stand firm against falsehood.

1 The elder, 3Jn 1

To the chosen lady and her children, whom I
love in the truth—and not I only, but also all who
know the truth— 2 because of the truth, which
lives in us and will be with us forever: Jn 8:32

LIVING  INSIGHT

The essential link between God's grace and our peace is His mercy . . . not just pity. Not simply sorrow or an understanding of our plight, but divine relief that results in deep peace within.

(See 2 John 3.)

3 Grace, mercy and peace from God the Father
and from Jesus Christ, the Father's Son, will be
with us in truth and love. Ro 1:7

4 It has given me great joy to find some of your
children walking in the truth, just as the Father
commanded us. 5 And now, dear lady, I am not
writing you a new command but one we have
had from the beginning. I ask that we love one another. 6 And this is love: that we walk in obedience
to his commands. As you have heard from the
beginning, his command is that you walk in
love.
7 Many deceivers, who do not acknowledge
Jesus Christ as coming in the flesh, have gone out
into the world. Any such person is the deceiver
and the antichrist. 8 Watch out that you do not lose
what you have worked for, but that you may be
rewarded fully. 9 Anyone who runs ahead and does
not continue in the teaching of Christ does not
have God; whoever continues in the teaching has
both the Father and the Son. 10 If anyone comes
to you and does not bring this teaching, do not
take him into your house or welcome him. 11 Anyone who welcomes him shares in his wicked
work.
12 I have much to write to you, but I do not want
to use paper and ink. Instead, I hope to visit you
and talk with you face to face, so that our joy may
be complete. 3Jn 13-14

13 The children of your chosen sister send their
greetings. ver 1

INTRODUCTION

3 JOHN

There are only a few rare occasions where the New Testament lifts the veil and allows us entrance into the inner and intimate workings of a particular local church. John's third letter is one of those choice moments… and we find the scene most interesting. John names three men (verses 1,9,12) in this brief letter and singles them out for our observation and instruction. While these three men were actual personalities in the early church, Gaius, Diotrephes and Demetrius represent three different types of people in the church today. As we pay close attention, we will learn from John important lessons for our lives. We will be reminded again of the need for balance—not the practice of love to the exclusion of truth and discernment, not the holding of doctrine apart from grace and hospitality… but a proper and necessary mixture so that Jesus Christ is exalted and God's Word is obeyed.

WRITER: *John*

DATE: *C.A.D. 85–95*

PURPOSE: *To urge love and discernment in showing Christian hospitality*

KEY THEME: *The truth of the gospel*

KEY MESSAGE: *Correct doctrine and a gracious life were never meant to be separated*

KEY TERMS: *"Truth"; "love"; "hospitality"*

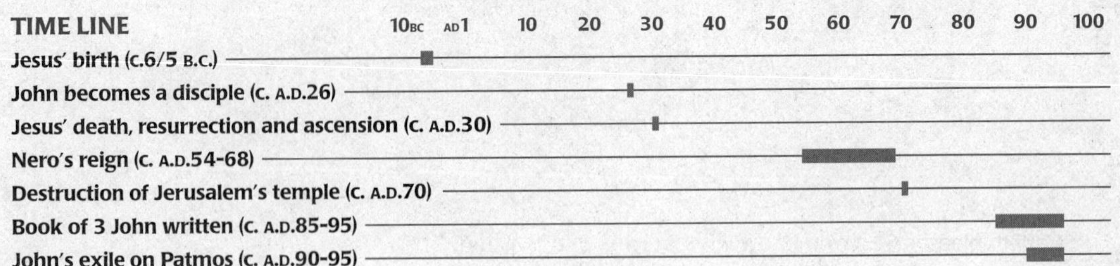

Three Men in a Church

CONFIRMATION OF GAIUS	DENUNCIATION OF DIOTREPHES	TESTIMONY OF DEMETRIUS	CONCLUSION
Sickly (?)	Proud	Good testimony	Letter is abbreviated
Obedient	Rigid and negative	Community	John hopes to visit
Hospitable	Accusing	Scriptures	Shalom!
Loving	"Church boss" complex	John	
Supportive			
VERSES 1-8	*VERSES 9-11*	*VERSE 12*	*VERSES 13-14*

TONE	**Encouraging**	**Confronting**	**Affirming**
RELATIONSHIPS	**To the truth of God**	**With other Christians**	**In the world**
EMPHASIS	**Keep it up!**	**Stop it!**	**Good for you!**
PARAPHRASE	***"I love you, and I pray for you" (verses 1-2).***	***"I call attention to your deeds" (verse 10).***	***"I hear good things about him" (verse 12).***

Whenever I hear someone dogmatically say things like, "Well, that's wrong," or "That's not good," or "I don't know how God can honor that," simply because the thing they are opposed to may be different from what they're used to, I suspect that person does not understand what the Bible has to say about the body of Christ, His church. People with such attitudes seem to be unable to accept the wonderful diversity we find among God's people.

When I read 1 Corinthians 12, I learn that the church has many members, not just one. God has placed each one of them in the body, just as it pleased Him. We're not to develop an exclusive spirit when it comes to style or taste. To be sure, we must embrace Scripture as the inspired, authoritative Word of God. Indeed we must take a stand for the things of God, but in no way is our personal "preference" to be considered the standard for the whole world. I'm convinced we must fight against this exclusive spirit that often pervades churches. We need to resist this narrow "my way or the highway" mentality that can subtly or not so subtly poison a congregation.

Variety and Disunity

Variety pleases God. You know what grieves Him? Disunity. It's the absence of unity (not the absence of *uniformity*!) that breaks the heart of God. God is saddened not when churches do things differently, but when churches are at war—either within their own body or with other parts of the body. The truth is, God rejoices in our diversity and variety, and well He should, for He is the One who created the beautiful variety we see among believers and in different churches and cultures.

The body is not diseased by variety; the body is diseased by disunity. Whenever there was disunity in the church of the first century, somebody sat down and wrote a letter—not because there was variety, because you and I know that all the churches from Ephesus to Corinth expressed themselves in different ways and had different models of leadership as well as modes of worship. Variety was accepted and encouraged. But it was when there was disunity that the apostles sat down and wrote a letter as if to say, "Straighten up. Come together."

A classic example of this is the letter of 3 John. As I said it in our study of 2 John, I say it again: It is one of the smallest letters in the New Testament. This is another postcard in the New Testament, but one that carries quite a wallop when it comes to telling God's people to "straighten up" and seek unity.

A Look at Two Postcards

I'd like to say a few words about the letters of 2 and 3 John—simply comparing and contrasting them for you. First of all, these two letters were written by the same person, but they have different purposes. Note the way 2 John begins: "The elder, to the chosen lady . . ." Now look at the opening to 3 John: "The elder, to my dear friend Gaius . . ." So we have the same writer—"the elder," who is John, one of the men in the inner circle of the twelve apostles who walked with the Savior. (Remember Peter, James and John? This "elder" is not John the Baptizer, but John the Beloved—one of Jesus' soulmates, one of those heart-to-heart disciples Jesus spent so much time with in his brief ministry on earth.) As John sat down to write this letter of concern to believers, he was more than sixty years removed from his days with Jesus.

The Balance of Love and Truth

Notice the differences in John's purpose for writing his second and third letters. In 2 John we learned about love as a river that must flow between the banks of truth and discernment. When that river of love overflows the banks in the service of falsehood, it does damage. Love has its limits. It must be controlled. The purpose of 2 John was to emphasize the value of *truth* when *love* is being expressed. To put it another way, truth and discernment give love its control.

If you reverse those two words, we make out the purpose of 3 John: to emphasize the value of *love* when *truth* is being expressed. In other words, the law of love wraps truth in a cloak of compassion and grace. In his second letter, John addressed a situation where there was an overflowing of love to the point of a lack of discernment. In 3 John he addressed a situation where there was an overflowing of truth to the point of a lack of love, grace and compassion.

By the way, there may be different varieties of ministries that serve Jesus Christ, but there must be a harmony, grace and love that pervades all of them. When you take away grace, love and a spirit of acceptance, you move dangerously close to disunity. Churches are not usually corrupted by expressions of love. Neither are they corrupted by declarations of truth. But when one of these two is emphasized *to the exclusion of the other,* trouble isn't far behind. Churches may very well go through bitter battles when they lose their balance. Seek to know the truth, by all means, but be sure that your pursuit of truth is carried out in a spirit of genuine love.

We will never grow out of the need to be filled with a spirit of compassion, grace and love. Never. I don't care if you can quote the Bible from cover to cover, you and I need love and grace. Sadly, I've met some gifted, intelligent, Bible-quoting Christians who quite plainly lack love for and especially acceptance of those who don't teach or handle the Bible the way they do. Please hear this: There is little that holds more challenge in the Christian life than the call to give up our power for the sake of love. Show yourself strong in love, willing to listen and to learn, and you'll be amazed what a ministry you can have both inside and outside the body of Christ, His church.

Two Extremes

John's second letter was written to a lady and her family (as I've noted in our study of 2 John; see page 1377). His third letter was written to a man named Gaius and, as we find out later, two acquaintances of Gaius (see 3 John 9 and 12).

The problem as described in 2 John centered around a believer receiving false teachers into her home; she was not exercising discernment as she practiced her hospitality. The problem as described in 3 John centered around a man named Diotrephes, who rejected true missionaries when he should have been extending hospitality. In 2 John a believer opened her doors to whomever knocked, seemingly without discernment. And John warned her, in effect, "Now look! You've got to understand there comes a time when we draw the line and hold back our offer of hospitality. You surely don't want to leave any impression that you're approving of the wicked work of the false teachers." And on the other end of the spectrum, 3 John was written, at least in part, to warn a man who would not accept legitimate travelers.

Words to Three Men

John's third letter revolved around three men in a church: *Gaius*, whom John encouraged and affirmed; *Diotrephes*, whom he criticized and confronted; and *Demetrius*, whom he praised and commended.

Recently I discovered that the name Gaius was the most common name in the first century. We are not sure which Gaius John wrote to, but one thing is sure: Gaius was close to John. Four times John addressed him as "dear friend." Gaius was a faithful man. John affirmed him for his faithfulness in providing hospitality and support for the brothers who shared the task of proclaiming the gospel.

Diotrephes was mentioned in verse 9. Now while Gaius was commended for his hospitality, his open heart, his generosity and his support for godly traveling ministers, Diotrephes was criticized. He evidently had a problem accepting the authority of others and consequently had conflicts with the God-given leaders of the church. I am impressed with how John handled him. John let Gaius know that should he pay a visit to Gaius's church, he was going to call Diotrephes on the carpet. He wasn't simply going to ignore the problem. He was going to deal with it swiftly and directly. He had no intentions of being diplomatic and allowing a self-appointed "church boss" to continue in his dictatorial and divisive ways.

The third gentleman was named Demetrius (verse 12). John commended him for his excellent reputation. John personally testified that Demetrius's life could be evaluated positively by the standards of Scripture. It's beautiful to read John's praise for this man who was a shining example of someone whose deeds were evidence that his life was right with God.

Words to the Wise

Let me share three practical thoughts. First, *variety will always be present in the universal church*. Please don't oppose it; please don't insist that all ministries be like the one you prefer. There is often a difference between personal preference (or taste) and what the Bible tells us is acceptable. Variety will always be present in the universal church—because that's the way God intended it. Let's value diversity in the local church; let's celebrate our differences and learn from each other as we unite in service under our Head, Jesus Christ.

Second, *disunity must never be tolerated in the local church*. We are called to live in unity with one another. It's our Lord's desire that we be united in love and grace, just as the Father and the Son are one (see John 17:21). John would not allow disunity in the church, and neither should we. We can affirm and celebrate variety and still seek unity among God's people. As Paul stated so clearly, "Make every effort to keep the unity of the Spirit through the bond of peace" (Ephesians 4:3).

The third thought is the clincher: *As long as Jesus Christ is given first place, the church can face any challenge*—and that includes exposing a "Diotrephes," as difficult as that may be. No one person, no group of persons, can rule the church. Jesus, and Jesus alone, is Lord of the church. No person may take first place in the church, for that is the place reserved for Jesus alone.

Seeking Balance

In this brief letter John teaches us the need for balance in the way we relate to others. As in John's second letter, here too we see the importance of balancing love and truth. The issue John addressed is this: Truth was being emphasized to the exclusion of love. John wanted us to understand that doctrine cannot be understood in isolation from grace and hospitality. We must seek a proper balance, a right mixture of love and truth, so that Christ will be exalted, His Word obeyed and His Spirit given the freedom to lead.

1 The elder, 2Jn 1

To my dear friend Gaius, whom I love in the
truth.

2 Dear friend, I pray that you may enjoy good
health and that all may go well with you, even as
your soul is getting along well. 3 It gave me great
joy to have some brothers come and tell about
your faithfulness to the truth and how you continue to walk in the truth. 4 I have no greater joy than
to hear that my children are walking in the truth.
5 Dear friend, you are faithful in what you are
doing for the brothers, even though they are
strangers to you. 6 They have told the church about
your love. You will do well to send them on their
way in a manner worthy of God. 7 It was for the
sake of the Name that they went out, receiving no
help from the pagans. 8 We ought therefore to
show hospitality to such men so that we may work
together for the truth. Ac 20:33,35; Ro 12:13
9 I wrote to the church, but Diotrephes, who
loves to be first, will have nothing to do with us.
10 So if I come, I will call attention to what he is
doing, gossiping maliciously about us. Not satisfied with that, he refuses to welcome the brothers.
He also stops those who want to do so and puts
them out of the church. Jn 9:22,34; 2Jn 12

Living  Insight

A lack of discernment is something like blindness. In the process of growing up in God's forever family, I plead with you to remain gracious and tolerant toward others in the same family! Gain knowledge, certainly. But as you do, guard against becoming blinded by your own importance.

(See 3 John 9–10.)

11 Dear friend, do not imitate what is evil but
what is good. Anyone who does what is good is
from God. Anyone who does what is evil has not
seen God. 12 Demetrius is well spoken of by everyone—and even by the truth itself. We also speak
well of him, and you know that our testimony is
true. Jn 21:24; 1Ti 3:7
13 I have much to write you, but I do not want
to do so with pen and ink. 14 I hope to see you
soon, and we will talk face to face. 2Jn 12

Peace to you. The friends here send their greetings. Greet the friends there by name. Jn 10:3

INTRODUCTION

JUDE

Someone has tagged this little letter with an appropriate title, "The Acts of the Apostates." The apostates at the time when this letter was written were the Gnostics—those who embraced the incipient philosophy that distinguished between matter as being inherently evil and spirit as being good. Such heresy produced and cultivated the idea that the flesh could do anything it wanted to do, because no one is under moral obligation. In that day it was called "antinomianism"; in our day it is often referred to as "hedonism." No matter what it is called, it leads to rebellion against authority, irreverence, presumptuous speech and a lifestyle marked by unbridled license. Jude wrote this letter to defend the apostolic faith and to stir up his readers to do the same. The tone of the letter is polemic, and its message is for our day as well.

WRITER: *Jude*

DATE: *C.A.D. 60–65*

PURPOSE: *To defend the orthodox faith against false teachings*

KEY THEME: *"Contend for the faith" (verse 3)*

KEY VERSES: *3; 21-23*

KEY TERMS: *"Remember"; "keep"; "ungodly"; "judge/judgment"*

STYLE: *Compassionate, intense and compelling*

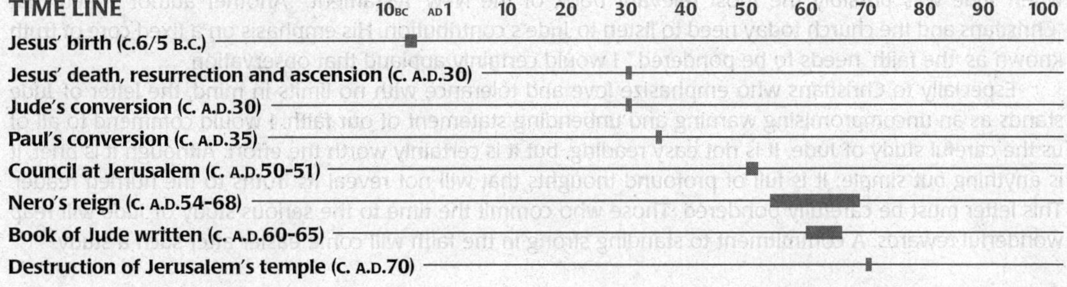

A Manual for Survival

	GREETING AND PURPOSE	EXPOSURE OF FALSE TEACHERS	WARNINGS AND COMMANDS TO CHRISTIANS	BENEDICTION
	Mercy, peace and love **What to do:** Contend for the faith! **Why:** Certain persons have secretly slipped in . . .	Doom is certain Guilt is sure Lives are godless	*"Remember!" (verse 17)* *"Keep yourselves!" (verse 21)* *"Be merciful!" (verse 22)* *"Save!" (verse 23)*	Our ultimate hope Our infinite God
	VERSES 1-4	***VERSES 5-16***	***VERSES 17-23***	***VERSES 24-25***
EMPHASIS	**Appealing**	**Revealing**	**Reminding**	**Praising**
TONE	**Personal concern**	**Bold exposure**	**Strong exhortation**	**Great hope**
DIRECTED TO	**Those *"who are loved by God the Father" (verse 1)***	**Those who *"gave them-selves up to sexual immorality" (verse 7)***	***"But, dear friends . . . But you, dear friends . . ." (verses 17,20)***	***"The only God" (verse 25)***

Although Jude is located just before the often-mentioned and more-popular book of Revelation, it is by and large an unknown piece of literature to many believers. In fact, some regard it as the most-neglected book of the New Testament; I tend to agree. It may be one of the least-known books in all the Bible—except perhaps for a few of the minor prophets.

This brief letter may be complicated and hard to understand, but it is still an impassioned cross for the church to lift high during times of confrontation and decision. Scottish Bible commentator William Barclay once wrote, "There have been times in the history of the church, and especially during the revivals, when Jude was possibly the most relevant book of the New Testament." Another author stated that "Christians and the church today need to listen to Jude's contribution. His emphasis on a fixed core of truth known as 'the faith' needs to be pondered." I would certainly applaud that observation.

Especially to Christians who emphasize love and tolerance with no limits in mind, the letter of Jude stands as an uncompromising warning and unbending statement of our faith. I would commend to all of us the careful study of Jude. It is not easy reading, but it is certainly worth the effort. Although it is brief, it is anything but simple; it is full of profound thoughts that will not reveal its truths to the hurried reader. This letter must be carefully pondered. Those who commit the time to the serious study of Jude will reap wonderful rewards. A commitment to standing strong in the faith will come easier after such a study.

My Brother's Servant

Jude identified himself as the writer and called himself "a servant of Jesus Christ" (verse 1)—which is a statement of humility. Jude was, in fact, a half brother of the Savior—he was the son of Joseph and Mary in their union, while Jesus was the son of Mary and the Son of God . . . virgin-born. Jude also described himself as "the brother of James" (verse 1)—the James who wrote the letter that bears his name.

Not until Jude became an adult did he become a believer in Jesus; in fact, it was not until the resurrection of Jesus that Jude crossed over into the ranks of Christianity (see John 7:5; Acts 1:14). Like his brother James, Jude stayed a skeptic for all his young years. This long-standing cynic may very well have brought to his writing his own ingrained desire to carefully investigate and probe deeply and profoundly into the issues of life. In many ways he seemed to approach his writing with the mind of a man who had come to faith later in life.

To God's Beloved

The letter's recipients are identified as those who are "loved by God the Father and kept by Jesus Christ" (verse 1). Because the date of Jude's writing is thought to be about A.D. 60 to 65, these were first-century believers who were slugging it out in the trenches. Persecution was abounding. Being a Christian involved paying a great price. These were believers, nevertheless, who were kept, called and declared to be "loved by God."

After a brief salutation, "Mercy, peace and love be yours in abundance" (verse 2), Jude beautifully summarized the theme of the letter:

> *Dear friends, although I was very eager to write to you about the salvation we share, I felt I had to write and urge you to contend for the faith that was once for all entrusted to the saints.*

I can never read verse 3 without calling to mind a small book authored by Frank Morison and titled *Who Moved The Stone?* Morison was an unbeliever. With the mind of an attorney, he set out to write a book that would prove that the resurrection of Jesus never happened. Convinced that belief in the resurrection was the touchstone of Christianity, which indeed it is, he believed that if he could disprove the resurrection, he would sound the death knell of Christianity.

The simple fact was that *Morison could not achieve his desire.* He admitted, "This is essentially a confession . . . the inner story of a man who originally set out to write one kind of book and found himself compelled by the sheer force of circumstances to write quite another. Somehow my perspective shifted; not suddenly, as in a flash of insight or inspiration, but slowly—almost imperceptibly by the very stubbornness of the facts themselves. The book, as it was originally planned, was left high and dry like those Thames barges when the great river goes out to meet the incoming sea. The writer discovered one day that not only could he no longer write the book as he had once conceived it, but that he would not even if he could." Morison declared that when he set his mind toward discrediting the resurrection and began to probe the facts, the facts proved quite the contrary from what he expected. He wrote an entirely different book that stood in defense of the resurrection.

Referring to his own letter, Jude, in essence, said, "I set out to write one kind of letter." And what was that? "I wanted to write about our common salvation. I wanted to write a letter about soteriology—the doctrine of salvation. But the fact is, having faced the truth of where we were in our walk with the Lord, I decided I really needed to write a letter about eschatology—the doctrine concerning the last days. I finally decided that the Spirit of God was leading me to contend earnestly for the faith that was once for all entrusted to the saints." So the theme of the letter bearing the name of Jude became: "I urge you to contend for the faith" (verse 3).

"The Faith"

"The faith" is something that is consciously and intentionally given to the saints to be vigorously defended in the face of opposition. The word "faith" is preceded by the definite article—*the* faith, which implies "the body of revealed truth as it pertains to God, sin, humanity, Christ and eternal things." We are living in a day where there is an emphasis on continued revelation—a so-called "continued body of truth" still being written. Jude reminds us of just the opposite: "The faith" was "*once for all* entrusted to the saints" (verse 3, emphasis mine). In other words, it is a nonnegotiable, completed body of information. We know it today as Biblical truth, the Word of God. It has been set forth, preserved, delivered, entrusted to the saints. It is not still in the process of being revealed. Let me quickly add that God's *will* continues to be revealed, but His *Word* has been written. His truth has been declared . . . delivered and entrusted to us.

Jude tells us we are to "contend for the faith." In other words, we are commanded to boldly guard and defend it. You'd be interested to know that the Greek word translated "contend" (*epagonizomai*) has in its root the word transliterated "agony." The sense of the Greek is "to struggle for, to exercise great effort and exertion for something." There is, on occasion, pain, even agony, connected with our contending for the truth. If you have ever had to stand your ground while surrounded by people who didn't believe the truth of God's Word, you don't need any further proof of the agony connected with this commitment. And, if truth be told, you may even have experienced the pain of having to "contend for the faith" in the fellowship of "religious" people who confess to be believers but deny or alter certain truths of God and His Word. Again, such a defense can be an "agonizing" experience.

By now you can tell that Jude has written a passionate letter. It is intense and compelling, hard-hitting and firm. It says to you, "This body of truth comes straight from God. Believe it and defend it." Jude certainly isn't light, casual reading. These are words that demand a decision—for or against the truth. Those who make a study of Jude cannot straddle a religious fence any longer.

An Important Question

What caused Jude to change his mind about his letter? What made him decide to write not about salvation but about the defense of the faith. Look at verse 4:

> *For certain men whose condemnation was written about long ago have secretly slipped in among you. They are godless men, who change the grace of our God into a license for immorality and deny Jesus Christ our only Sovereign and Lord.*

Here Jude disclosed the reason for his change of plans. The Spirit of God showed Jude that there was enough erosion occurring in the church that a clarion call to "contend for the faith" needed to be sounded.

Jude was saying, in effect, "A number of deceivers with ungodly motives have slipped into the church. They need to be exposed!" They were the hedonistic folks of that day. They were the people who said, "Pleasure at any price." They took the amazing grace of God and twisted it to meet their own selfish desires in their mad scramble to do whatever they felt like doing, whatever made them feel good. And what they felt like doing was to practice immorality. On top of that, if you look closely they "deny Jesus Christ our only Sovereign and Lord" (verse 4). Jude screamed out, in effect, "We must fight against these lies!" Strong, passionate words still needed in *our* day!

Time to Stand Strong

The insightful words of Eugene Peterson in his introduction to the book of Jude (*The Message*, page 604) deserve our undivided attention: "Our spiritual communities are as susceptible to disease as our physical bodies. But it is easier to detect whatever is wrong in our stomachs and lungs than in our worship and witness. When our physical bodies are sick or damaged, the pain calls our attention to it, and we do something quick. But a dangerous, even deadly, virus in our spiritual communities can go undetected for a long time."

Drawing on that word picture, just as we need accurate and honest physicians to diagnose our physical condition when we're sick, we need diagnosticians to examine us spiritually. Jude's letter is precisely that—an accurate and forthright diagnosis we dare not ignore.

In light of that, the time has come for you and for me to look deep within and ask ourselves some penetrating questions. As we evaluate our willingness to stand with Jude in contending for the faith, I wonder if his words cut into our hearts. I wonder if, in the process of these last number of years (or maybe even months), there has begun to be an erosion in your faith, maybe a slow, almost imperceptible hardening of your heart, a weakening of your commitment, a loosening of your lifestyle. How's the quantity and quality of your time with God in prayer and fellowship and in the Word? How teachable is your spirit, how contrite is your heart? How are you doing in showing mercy and caring for the hurting? Is your thought pattern a wholesome one? Do you still cultivate a heart for God? I say those things to myself, as well. As we honestly appraise our lives, may the words of Jude burn within us with a renewed intensity: "I . . . urge you to contend for the faith" (verse 3). Are we doing that?

No More Erosion

The message of Jude speaks directly to the threat of attack on the purity of our faith—not necessarily a bold, frontal assault, but a slow, subtle erosion of our faith. How easily it can creep in unawares. By and by the whole direction of our life's mission changes. Please hear this: The ministry of the church of Jesus Christ is a saving ministry—not only the saving of the lost, the deliverance of unbelievers from the dominion of sin to the realm of eternal life through faith in Jesus Christ, but also the deliverance of *believers* to a fresh awareness of the power of the Holy Spirit and the reality of Christ's reign in their lives. It is so easy to lose our direction as individual believers; it is so easy as a group of believers who are part of Christ's body, the church, simply to become an exclusive club where we gather as the initiated who talk only to ourselves, applaud ourselves, look at ourselves in the mirror and admire everything we see. We need to keep our calling and our mission clear. We must be ever diligent to keep our faith from eroding. The message of Jude is this: Stand firm. Contend for the faith!

1Jude, a servant of Jesus Christ and a brother of
James, Ac 1:13

To those who have been called, who are loved by God the Father and kept by[a] Jesus Christ:

2Mercy, peace and love be yours in abundance.

The Sin and Doom of Godless Men

3Dear friends, although I was very eager to write
to you about the salvation we share, I felt I had
to write and urge you to contend for the faith
that was once for all entrusted to the saints. 4For
certain men whose condemnation was written
about[b] long ago have secretly slipped in among
you. They are godless men, who change the grace
of our God into a license for immorality and deny
Jesus Christ our only Sovereign and Lord. Gal 2:4
5Though you already know all this, I want to
remind you that the Lord[c] delivered his people
out of Egypt, but later destroyed those who did not
believe. 6And the angels who did not keep their
positions of authority but abandoned their own
home—these he has kept in darkness, bound with
everlasting chains for judgment on the great Day.
7In a similar way, Sodom and Gomorrah and the
surrounding towns gave themselves up to sexual
immorality and perversion. They serve as an example of those who suffer the punishment of eternal fire. Dt 29:23; 2Pe 2:6
8In the very same way, these dreamers pollute
their own bodies, reject authority and slander celestial beings. 9But even the archangel Michael,
when he was disputing with the devil about the
body of Moses, did not dare to bring a slanderous
accusation against him, but said, "The Lord rebuke you!" 10Yet these men speak abusively
against whatever they do not understand; and
what things they do understand by instinct, like
unreasoning animals—these are the very things
that destroy them. 2Pe 2:10,12
11Woe to them! They have taken the way of
Cain; they have rushed for profit into Balaam's
error; they have been destroyed in Korah's rebellion. Nu 16:1-3,31-35; 1Jn 3:12
12These men are blemishes at your love feasts,
eating with you without the slightest qualm—
shepherds who feed only themselves. They are
clouds without rain, blown along by the wind; autumn trees, without fruit and uprooted—twice
dead. 13They are wild waves of the sea, foaming up
their shame; wandering stars, for whom blackest
darkness has been reserved forever. Isa 57:20
14Enoch, the seventh from Adam, prophesied
about these men: "See, the Lord is coming with
thousands upon thousands of his holy ones 15to
judge everyone, and to convict all the ungodly of
all the ungodly acts they have done in the ungodly
way, and of all the harsh words ungodly sinners
have spoken against him." 16These men are grumblers and faultfinders; they follow their own evil
desires; they boast about themselves and flatter
others for their own advantage. Dt 33:2; 2Pe 2:18

A Call to Persevere

17But, dear friends, remember what the apostles
of our Lord Jesus Christ foretold. 18They said to
you, "In the last times there will be scoffers who
will follow their own ungodly desires." 19These are
the men who divide you, who follow mere natural
instincts and do not have the Spirit. 1Ti 4:1; 2Pe 2:1
20But you, dear friends, build yourselves up in
your most holy faith and pray in the Holy Spirit.

LIVING  INSIGHT

Deterioration is never sudden. *No garden "suddenly" overgrows with thorns. No church "suddenly" breaks down. Slowly, almost imperceptibly, certain things are accepted that once were rejected. At the outset they may appear harmless, but the wedge they bring leaves a gap that grows wider as moral erosion joins hands with spiritual decay.* (See Jude 17–19.)

[a]1 Or *for;* or *in* [b]4 Or *men who were marked out for condemnation* [c]5 Some early manuscripts *Jesus*

[21]Keep yourselves in God's love as you wait for the mercy of our Lord Jesus Christ to bring you to eternal life. Tit 2:13; 2Pe 3:12

[22]Be merciful to those who doubt; [23]snatch others from the fire and save them; to others show mercy, mixed with fear—hating even the clothing stained by corrupted flesh. Am 4:11; Zec 3:2-5

Doxology

[24]To him who is able to keep you from falling and to present you before his glorious presence without fault and with great joy— [25]to the only God our Savior be glory, majesty, power and authority, through Jesus Christ our Lord, before all ages, now and forevermore! Amen. Ro 11:36; Col 1:22

INTRODUCTION

REVELATION

Somewhere between frightening and mysterious—that's the book of Revelation. It is notoriously considered the most difficult of all the Bible books. Unfortunately, Revelation has occasionally become the playground of religious eccentrics and has provided the fodder of the speculations of prophecy enthusiasts who seem compelled to find therein a detailed map of God's celestial timetable right on down to the very day of the Lord's return. While the book certainly provides a powerful declaration about God's plan for the future, in no way was it designed to give us a timepiece for predicting each event of tomorrow. The book of Revelation calls us to examine thoughtfully what it does say, being careful not to make it say what it does not say. At the same time, even when we have to confess that we don't understand all that is going to happen, we can take great comfort in knowing that God has the future firmly in hand.

WRITER: *John*

DATE: *C.A.D. 90–96*

PURPOSE: *To warn against falling away from the faith and to offer assurance of victory for believers*

KEY MESSAGE: *Victory belongs to Jesus Christ*

KEY VERSE: *1:19*

KEY TERMS: *"Throne"; "Lamb"*

"SEVENS": *Seven churches; seven seals; seven trumpets; seven signs; seven plagues; seven dooms*

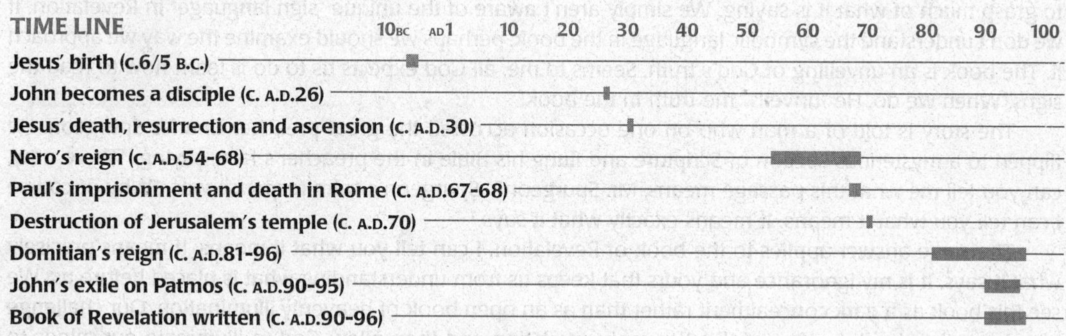

God's Final Words

"I AM THE ALPHA . . ." (1:8)	"WHAT YOU HAVE SEEN . . ."	"WHAT IS NOW . . ."	"WHAT WILL TAKE PLACE LATER . . ."	". . . AND THE OMEGA" (22:13)
	Personal and biographical	Christ's letters to the seven churches	Earthly judgments . . . Final battles . . . Ultimate doom . . . And eternal bliss	
	CHAPTER 1	*CHAPTERS 2–3*	*CHAPTERS 4–22*	
SCOPE	**History: looking back**		**Prophecy: looking ahead**	
STYLE	**Dialogue**		**Observations and questions**	
SCENE	**On earth**		**Shifts back and forth: earth and heaven**	

The book of Revelation is unlike any other section of Scripture. No other Bible book has been more controversial, suffered more abuse or been misquoted more often, yet to this day remains the most intriguing of all. To many people, just the mention of the name "The Book of Revelation" suddenly shouts "riddle, mystery, enigma—a perplexing portion of Scripture." But the strange thing is that the Greek term *apokalupsis*, from which we get the title of this book ("Revelation"—1:1), means "unveiling," or "disclosure." The name suggests revealing, not hiding. Rather than coming to this book as if it were encased in a dark, concealed cave in which truth is hidden from people, we may turn to this book in anticipation that it is an unveiling of God's unchanging truth and perfect plan. The book invites us to greater understanding of and insight into God's truth.

Sign Language

Those who have gone to the trouble of counting the symbols in the book of Revelation report that these 22 chapters contain some three hundred distinct symbols. No wonder we are unable on the surface to grasp much of what it is saying. We simply aren't aware of the unique "sign language" in Revelation. If we don't understand the symbolic language in the book, perhaps we should examine the way we approach it. The book is an unveiling of God's truth. Seems to me, all God expects us to do is learn how to read the signs. When we do, He "unveils" the truth in the book.

The story is told of a man who on one occasion accosted the great preacher Charles Spurgeon. He flipped to a mysterious section of Scripture and flung his Bible in the preacher's face, saying, "There now, can you tell me what this passage means, Mr. Spurgeon?" Spurgeon's calm response was, "Why of course I can tell you what it means. It means exactly what it says."

The same answer applies to the book of Revelation. I can tell you what it means. It means precisely what it says. It is my ignorance and yours that keeps us from understanding what is placed before us. We see this book as a dark concealment rather than as an open book of heavenly illumination. Our challenge is to learn the sign language of this heavenly revelation and then allow God to illuminate our minds to understand its message. There is no reason to feel unsettled or intimidated. Revelation is, after all, God's final words to His people. He wants us to understand what He is saying.

Meeting John

There is no mistaking who wrote the book. John gave us his signature in four places (1:1,4,9; 22:8). Also, by implication, he disclosed who he was many other times throughout the book. John wrote Revelation while living on the island of Patmos. Tradition tells us that the Roman emperor Domitian banished John as punishment for his deep commitment to his Christian faith. He was exiled to the island to work the mines. While there, John, the intimate and devoted disciple of the Savior, was led by the Spirit of God to write this book (dated about A.D. 90–96).

A Word of Assurance

Why should we take the time to read this strange book? John hints at the reason in the very first verse: "The revelation of Jesus Christ, which God gave him to show his servants what must soon take place" (1:1). Revelation gives an unparalleled picture of Jesus Christ as the conquering Ruler who wins the ultimate victory over evil and reigns victoriously over all. The purpose of Revelation is to assure its readers that God is in complete control of all future events. God gave this message to His Son, who communicated it to John, who wrote it down for the servants of Jesus in all generations. These truths are given so that we might read and learn what was said about the future plans of God.

You see, when you boil it all down, it isn't our past that presents us with our greatest worries. Certainly our past can create some present problems for us, but at least we know what's past is past. It isn't even our present that disturbs us the most. In ways sometimes miraculous but always gracious, God provides sufficient strength for handling what we face today. What seems to bring the most potent anxiety to so many people is uncertainty about the future—the unseen, unpredictable events of tomorrow. It's in this arena that we face some of our most agonizing questions about who is in control. We can look over our shoulder at the past and discover that our hindsight is invariably 20/20. We can see it all so clearly now what we couldn't see back then. Our present worries are manageable. Somehow, someway, we make it through the day. But when we gaze into tomorrow, we can't seem to see anything. The future is veiled in mystery. That reality makes most folks uneasy.

The book of Revelation unveils the major episodes of our future. God has everything carefully planned and perfectly timed. And so, in my words, the practical implication is this: "Relax. Rest assured that God knows where He's going and what He's doing. He isn't biting His nails, looking over the edge of heaven wondering what in the world He's going to do with people like us. He is in control. He knows what is going to happen in that great drama of history involving the good and the bad . . . the plagues and people like the beast, the false prophet, and those who accept the mark of the beast and buy into his whole godless system." The book is saying, in effect, "God knows what He's about." We may not completely understand all that is going to happen, but we can be assured that God has the future firmly in hand.

Reading Revelation

There are various ways to read the book of Revelation. Most who interpret the book fall into one of four categories.

There are some who say, "The book really deals exclusively with events from the past. It speaks of that which has already happened. Essentially its prophecies have been fulfilled." They view Revelation as mainly a report of past events fulfilled in their late first-century setting in the Roman empire. The term used to describe this interpretation is *preterist* (from the Latin *praeter*, meaning "past"). In the opinion of these interpreters, Revelation is essentially a closed book. There's nothing future about it (except for chapters 19–22, which await future fulfillment). To many minds, mine included, this seems absurd. There is too much in Revelation that points to the future and the final consummation of God's work in history. Furthermore, if the book is an "unveiling," what's to unveil about the *past*?

There are others who look at Revelation as a symbolic, progressive panorama of the history of the church from John's day to the end of the age. In this view, called the *historicist* interpretation, the book unfolds events from one era to the next—all symbolized by the seven churches in Revelation as described in chapters 2 and 3. For example, the church at Ephesus represents the apostolic age. The church at Smyrna would represent the era of the church fathers and on into the next period of great persecution. While there are some clues to John's meaning found in the unfolding of eras of history, to make this whole book fit into a neat and tidy system seems artificial and forced.

Still others propose what is often called the *idealist* interpretation. This view holds that everything in Revelation is symbolic and is to be spiritualized. According to these interpreters, the book does not describe actual events and people, but conveys timeless truths and moral lessons, such as the dramatic struggle between good and evil and the ultimate triumph of good. Carried to its extreme, this view would deny that Revelation describes a real devil, but provides merely a representation of evil; there are no real angels or a real God, only a representation of good; Armageddon isn't a real event, merely a representation of vast conflicts between good and evil. This nonliteral view has the potential to get you into trouble fast, because it's like opening the proverbial can of worms. You'll never get those slimy, squirmy things back in the can. The real danger of spiritualizing Scripture is that you lose any sense of being rooted in history and reality. You become vulnerable to irresponsible conjecture or speculation. Furthermore, with a good imagination, you can make a case for just about anything your heart desires.

Finally, there are those (I am among them) who hold what is called the *futurist* view. This interpretation says, "The majority of the events described in Revelation have not yet been fulfilled." Chapters 4–22 describe events that will occur at the end of the age; these events in history will be fulfilled in the future. From my perspective the futurist position is one that has the most credibility and makes the best sense. It's not without its challenges, to be sure, but in the long run, it is the most reliable. Let's understand that *no* interpretation will answer *all* the questions or solve *all* the mysteries of the future.

An Inspired Outline

The threefold division of verse 19 of chapter 1 provides a striking clue to the structure of the whole of Revelation. I'm so glad this is a Bible book that has an inspired outline. Look at this key verse where God gives John explicit directions concerning the writing of the revelation: "Write, therefore, what you have seen, what is now and what will take place later" (1:19).

This first portion of the verse reflects the theme of chapter 1: "Write, therefore, *what you have seen* . . ." (emphasis added). It's as if Jesus was saying, "The things I've shown you, things you've already seen, write it all down, John." The first chapter of Revelation deals with what had taken place in the past—what John had already seen.

Now look at the second part of this verse: "Write therefore, what you have seen, *what is now* . . ." (emphasis added). "What is now" is what we find in chapters 2 and 3. In this section John addressed seven churches that were in existence at that time, dealing with the needs of each congregation and their leadership. These words were written to real churches filled with real people, addressing real weaknesses as well as real strengths. The second and third chapters of Revelation deal with what was currently happening in the church—the things John called "what is now."

Finally, the third part of this verse instructed John to write even more: "Write therefore, what you have seen, what is now and *what will take place later*" (emphasis added). Consistent with the futuristic interpretation, I believe that much of what is described and predicted in this book has yet to be fulfilled. Not only were these chapters pointing to future events when they were first written down some 1,900 years ago, they still point to many things that are yet to be—things that "will take place later." This third section of Revelation includes 19 chapters (4–22) that point to the future.

In summary, do you see the wonderful and divinely inspired outline in Revelation 1:19? The things you *have seen* are described in chapter 1; these are past events. The things that are *now* are presented in chapters 2 and 3; these seven letters to seven churches represent present history during John's days on earth. Third and finally, the largest section of the book deals with what will take place *later*. Chapters 4–22 point to future events in God's plan for humanity. As we read Revelation 1:19, the Lord reminds us again that He is in charge of the past, the present and the future.

Three Great Truths

There are three truths that grab hold of me as I look at this book in particular, and the entire Bible in general.

First, *God's Word is a reliable map to guide us through the storms of life.* Have you ever stopped to think about those people who will live in the day when the closing events of chapters 4–22 of Revelation will unfold? Can you imagine? History tells us when Alexander the Great heard the Word of God read to him, especially when he heard Daniel's prophecy, he fell on his knees as if awestruck that God would predict the rapid movement of the Grecian army so clearly and so long before it ever happened. The Scriptures included descriptions of him!—and the realization of that overwhelmed him. I have to believe that those who go through the experiences recorded in Revelation 4–22 will have a similar response. They will be amazed at how clearly God foretold what would happen. God's Word is a reliable map to guide us through the storms. His Word communicated with power in times past, it does so today and it will continue to achieve God's purpose in the days to come (see Isaiah 55:10–11).

Second, *God's plan is a sovereign arrangement that replaces fear with peace.* What a comfort to know that He has a handle on the events that are unfolding in the future! One of the greatest verses I ever learned was Daniel 4:35:

> *All the peoples of the earth are regarded as nothing. He does as he pleases with the powers of heaven and the peoples of the earth. No one can hold back his hand or say to him: "What have you done?"*

Isn't that great? Human beings ask, "What are You doing, God?" God has every right to say, "Be quiet. I'm doing exactly as I please and what I want." (He doesn't say that, but He could.) Graciously He just keeps doing as He pleases. But how many people are wondering, "What is God up to?" Daniel says, in effect, "You don't even have to ask. Even when you can't understand it, His plan is unfolding. Count on it. He knows what He's about. He knows what He's doing." There has never been panic in heaven. Our Lord knows we have enough of it on earth! Our God is sovereign, and in our fearful turmoil and frantic confusion He comes and offers divine peace.

Third, *God's Son is the glorious Lord and conquering Ruler who deserves our allegiance and seeks our worship.* You're looking for someone to follow? A model to emulate? I present none other than Jesus Christ. There is no finer model. In fact, there is no *other* model comparable to Him. He is the glorious Lord who is worthy of our allegiance and our worship. The question is, will you commit your life to Him and bow in humble adoration? He won't force you, but He does invite you.

"What You Have Seen" **Chapter 1**

Chapter 1 describes things that have already happened. These verses paint a awe-inspiring picture of the Son of Man, Jesus Christ. He is the One who has loved us and set us free from the power of sin through His blood (1:5). All of history is under His sovereign hand. He is the One who holds the keys of death and hell (1:18). John received a revelation of the Lamb of God who is before all things and above all things. This portion of the book presents Jesus Christ with vivid and dramatic images. He is the first, the Alpha; the last, the Omega; the One "who is, and who was, and who is to come, the Almighty" (1:8).

Prologue

1 The revelation of Jesus Christ, which God
gave him to show his servants what must
soon take place. He made it known by sending his
angel to his servant John, 2who testifies to everything he saw—that is, the word of God and the
testimony of Jesus Christ. 3Blessed is the one who
reads the words of this prophecy, and blessed are
those who hear it and take to heart what is written
in it, because the time is near. Lk 11:28; 1Co 1:6

Greetings and Doxology

4John,

To the seven churches in the province of Asia:

Grace and peace to you from him who is, and
who was, and who is to come, and from the seven

LIVING 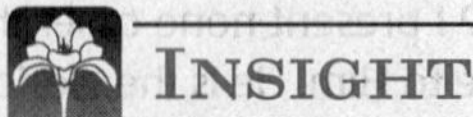 INSIGHT

Life was never meant to be two-dimensional. It's multidimensional, because our God is full of beauty, color, variety, depth and grace. Yes . . . always grace.

(See Revelation 1:4–6.)

spirits[a] before his throne, 5and from Jesus Christ,
who is the faithful witness, the firstborn from the
dead, and the ruler of the kings of the earth.

To him who loves us and has freed us from our
sins by his blood, 6and has made us to be a kingdom and priests to serve his God and Father—to
him be glory and power for ever and ever! Amen.

7Look, he is coming with the clouds, Da 7:13
and every eye will see him,
even those who pierced him; Jn 19:34,37
and all the peoples of the earth will mourn
because of him.
So shall it be! Amen.

8"I am the Alpha and the Omega," says the
Lord God, "who is, and who was, and who is to
come, the Almighty." Rev 4:8; 21:6

One Like a Son of Man

9I, John, your brother and companion in the
suffering and kingdom and patient endurance that
are ours in Jesus, was on the island of Patmos
because of the word of God and the testimony of
Jesus. 10On the Lord's Day I was in the Spirit, and
I heard behind me a loud voice like a trumpet,
11which said: "Write on a scroll what you see and
send it to the seven churches: to Ephesus, Smyrna,
Pergamum, Thyatira, Sardis, Philadelphia and Laodicea." 2Ti 2:12; Rev 4:1
12I turned around to see the voice that was
speaking to me. And when I turned I saw seven
golden lampstands, 13and among the lampstands
was someone "like a son of man,"[b] dressed in a
robe reaching down to his feet and with a golden
sash around his chest. 14His head and hair were
white like wool, as white as snow, and his eyes
were like blazing fire. 15His feet were like bronze
glowing in a furnace, and his voice was like the
sound of rushing waters. 16In his right hand he
held seven stars, and out of his mouth came a
sharp double-edged sword. His face was like the
sun shining in all its brilliance. Heb 4:12; Rev 2:12,16
17When I saw him, I fell at his feet as though
dead. Then he placed his right hand on me and
said: "Do not be afraid. I am the First and the Last.
18I am the Living One; I was dead, and behold I am
alive for ever and ever! And I hold the keys of
death and Hades. Ro 6:9; Rev 20:1
19"Write, therefore, what you have seen, what is
now and what will take place later. 20The mystery
of the seven stars that you saw in my right hand
and of the seven golden lampstands is this: The
seven stars are the angels[c] of the seven churches,
and the seven lampstands are the seven churches.

"What Is Now" **Chapters 2–3**

The second section, only two chapters long, records letters written to seven churches—centering on the things taking place at the time John recorded these words. In these seven letters, the spotlight of Christ was focused on the church. These seven churches were real churches that needed clear exhortation and affirmation, as well as confrontation and correction. Those who read this revelation in that day would have been able to identify those congregations and would have seen how its message applied to the believers in the churches of their day. These two chapters deal with the "now" portion of history as seen by the apostle John.

[a] *4* Or *the sevenfold Spirit* [b] *13* Daniel 7:13 [c] *20* Or *messengers*

To the Church in Ephesus

2 "To the angel[a] of the church in Ephesus
write: Ac 18:19

These are the words of him who holds
the seven stars in his right hand and walks
among the seven golden lampstands: 2I know
your deeds, your hard work and your perseverance. I know that you cannot tolerate
wicked men, that you have tested those who
claim to be apostles but are not, and have

LIVING INSIGHT

There is no such thing as instant endurance. The pain brought on by interruptions and disappointments, by loss and failure, by accidents and disease, is the long and arduous road to maturity. There is no other road.

(See Revelation 2:2–3.)

found them false. 3You have persevered and
have endured hardships for my name, and
have not grown weary. 1Jn 4:1; Rev 1:16
4Yet I hold this against you: You have forsaken your first love. 5Remember the height
from which you have fallen! Repent and do
the things you did at first. If you do not
repent, I will come to you and remove your
lampstand from its place. 6But you have this
in your favor: You hate the practices of the
Nicolaitans, which I also hate. Mt 24:12
7He who has an ear, let him hear what the
Spirit says to the churches. To him who overcomes, I will give the right to eat from the
tree of life, which is in the paradise of God.

To the Church in Smyrna

8"To the angel of the church in Smyrna write:

These are the words of him who is the
First and the Last, who died and came to life
again. 9I know your afflictions and your poverty—yet you are rich! I know the slander of
those who say they are Jews and are not, but
are a synagogue of Satan. 10Do not be afraid
of what you are about to suffer. I tell you, the
devil will put some of you in prison to test
you, and you will suffer persecution for ten
days. Be faithful, even to the point of death,
and I will give you the crown of life.
11He who has an ear, let him hear what the
Spirit says to the churches. He who overcomes will not be hurt at all by the second
death. Rev 21:8

To the Church in Pergamum

12"To the angel of the church in Pergamum write:

These are the words of him who has the
sharp, double-edged sword. 13I know where
you live—where Satan has his throne. Yet
you remain true to my name. You did not
renounce your faith in me, even in the days
of Antipas, my faithful witness, who was put
to death in your city—where Satan lives.
14Nevertheless, I have a few things against
you: You have people there who hold to the
teaching of Balaam, who taught Balak to entice the Israelites to sin by eating food sacrificed to idols and by committing sexual immorality. 15Likewise you also have those who
hold to the teaching of the Nicolaitans. 16Re-
pent therefore! Otherwise, I will soon come
to you and will fight against them with the
sword of my mouth. 2Th 2:8; Rev 1:16
17He who has an ear, let him hear what the
Spirit says to the churches. To him who overcomes, I will give some of the hidden manna.
I will also give him a white stone with a new
name written on it, known only to him who
receives it. Rev 19:12

To the Church in Thyatira

18"To the angel of the church in Thyatira write:

These are the words of the Son of God,
whose eyes are like blazing fire and whose
feet are like burnished bronze. 19I know your
deeds, your love and faith, your service and
perseverance, and that you are now doing
more than you did at first. Rev 1:14-15
20Nevertheless, I have this against you:
You tolerate that woman Jezebel, who calls
herself a prophetess. By her teaching she
misleads my servants into sexual immorality
and the eating of food sacrificed to idols. 21I
have given her time to repent of her immorality, but she is unwilling. 22So I will cast
her on a bed of suffering, and I will make
those who commit adultery with her suffer
intensely, unless they repent of her ways.
23I will strike her children dead. Then all
the churches will know that I am he who
searches hearts and minds, and I will repay
each of you according to your deeds. 24Now
I say to the rest of you in Thyatira, to you
who do not hold to her teaching and have
not learned Satan's so-called deep secrets (I
will not impose any other burden on you):
25Only hold on to what you have until I
come. Ac 15:28; Rev 9:20
26To him who overcomes and does my

[a] 1 Or *messenger*; also in verses 8, 12 and 18

will to the end, I will give authority over the
nations— Ps 2:8; Rev 3:21

27'He will rule them with an iron scepter;
he will dash them to pieces like
pottery'[a]— Isa 30:14; Jer 19:11

just as I have received authority from my
Father. 28I will also give him the morning
star. 29He who has an ear, let him hear what
the Spirit says to the churches. Rev 22:16

To the Church in Sardis

3 "To the angel[b] of the church in Sardis write:

These are the words of him who holds the
seven spirits[c] of God and the seven stars. I
know your deeds; you have a reputation of
being alive, but you are dead. 2Wake up!
Strengthen what remains and is about to die,
for I have not found your deeds complete in
the sight of my God. 3Remember, therefore,
what you have received and heard; obey it,
and repent. But if you do not wake up, I will
come like a thief, and you will not know at
what time I will come to you. 2Pe 3:10
4Yet you have a few people in Sardis who
have not soiled their clothes. They will walk
with me, dressed in white, for they are worthy. 5He who overcomes will, like them, be
dressed in white. I will never blot out his
name from the book of life, but will acknowledge his name before my Father and his angels. 6He who has an ear, let him hear what
the Spirit says to the churches. Mt 10:32

To the Church in Philadelphia

7"To the angel of the church in Philadelphia write:

These are the words of him who is holy
and true, who holds the key of David. What
he opens no one can shut, and what he shuts
no one can open. 8I know your deeds. See, I
have placed before you an open door that no
one can shut. I know that you have little
strength, yet you have kept my word and
have not denied my name. 9I will make those
who are of the synagogue of Satan, who
claim to be Jews though they are not, but are
liars—I will make them come and fall down
at your feet and acknowledge that I have
loved you. 10Since you have kept my command to endure patiently, I will also keep
you from the hour of trial that is going to
come upon the whole world to test those
who live on the earth. Rev 6:10; 17:8
11I am coming soon. Hold on to what you
have, so that no one will take your crown.
12Him who overcomes I will make a pillar in
the temple of my God. Never again will he
leave it. I will write on him the name of my
God and the name of the city of my God, the
new Jerusalem, which is coming down out of
heaven from my God; and I will also write on
him my new name. 13He who has an ear, let
him hear what the Spirit says to the churches.

To the Church in Laodicea

14"To the angel of the church in Laodicea write:

These are the words of the Amen, the
faithful and true witness, the ruler of God's
creation. 15I know your deeds, that you are
neither cold nor hot. I wish you were either
one or the other! 16So, because you are lukewarm—neither hot nor cold—I am about to
spit you out of my mouth. 17You say, 'I am
rich; I have acquired wealth and do not need
a thing.' But you do not realize that you are
wretched, pitiful, poor, blind and naked. 18I
counsel you to buy from me gold refined in
the fire, so you can become rich; and white
clothes to wear, so you can cover your
shameful nakedness; and salve to put on
your eyes, so you can see. Hos 12:8; 1Co 4:8
19Those whom I love I rebuke and discipline. So be earnest, and repent. 20Here I am!
I stand at the door and knock. If anyone
hears my voice and opens the door, I will
come in and eat with him, and he with me.
21To him who overcomes, I will give the
right to sit with me on my throne, just as I
overcame and sat down with my Father on
his throne. 22He who has an ear, let him hear
what the Spirit says to the churches."

"What Will Take Place Later" **Chapters 4–22**

The final section contains 19 chapters that point to the future. The focus is on what will come to pass in the history of God's work among humanity. Jesus Christ is presented as the sovereign Lord over specific future events. First, Jesus is the Lamb who controls the outcome of all history (chapters 4–5)—even as God's judgments against evil are unveiled (chapters 6–11). Jesus is the sovereign Lord in the midst of all the human turmoil during the time of the great tribulation (7:14). Next, He is sovereign Lord in the reign of His millennial kingdom, where His power and authority are displayed as He, personally, reigns on earth as King of kings and Lord of lords (17:14; 19:16). Finally, in chapters 21 and 22 we see Jesus as Lord during the judgment and final glorification of all believers. This hope-filled vision of eternal bliss in the new heaven and new earth is solidly based on the person of Jesus, who is "the Alpha and the Omega, the First and the Last, the Beginning and the End" (22:12). He is at the center throughout the entire book of Revelation—as the mighty Ruler who conquered evil and consummated hope. And be-

[a] *27* Psalm 2:9 [b] *1* Or *messenger*; also in verses 7 and 14 [c] *1* Or *the sevenfold Spirit*

cause of Him, we can face "what will take place later" with an unshakable confidence and irrepressible hope.

The Throne in Heaven

4 After this I looked, and there before me was
a door standing open in heaven. And the
voice I had first heard speaking to me like a trumpet said, "Come up here, and I will show you what
must take place after this." 2At once I was in the
Spirit, and there before me was a throne in heaven
with someone sitting on it. 3And the one who sat
there had the appearance of jasper and carnelian.
A rainbow, resembling an emerald, encircled the
throne. 4Surrounding the throne were twenty-four
other thrones, and seated on them were twenty-
four elders. They were dressed in white and had
crowns of gold on their heads. 5From the throne
came flashes of lightning, rumblings and peals of
thunder. Before the throne, seven lamps were blazing. These are the seven spirits[a] of God. 6Also
before the throne there was what looked like a sea
of glass, clear as crystal. Rev 11:16; 15:2
In the center, around the throne, were four living creatures, and they were covered with eyes, in
front and in back. 7The first living creature was
like a lion, the second was like an ox, the third had
a face like a man, the fourth was like a flying eagle.
8Each of the four living creatures had six wings
and was covered with eyes all around, even under
his wings. Day and night they never stop saying:

"Holy, holy, holy
is the Lord God Almighty,
who was, and is, and is to come."

9Whenever the living creatures give glory, honor
and thanks to him who sits on the throne and who

LIVING  INSIGHT

In worship we become preoccupied with the Lord. We don't watch something happen, we participate in it. It's coming to a place in our life, either alone, with a few or with many, where we "connect" with the living God. It is almost as though we could reach out and touch Him.
(See Revelation 4:9–11.)

lives for ever and ever, 10the twenty-four elders fall
down before him who sits on the throne, and worship him who lives for ever and ever. They lay their
crowns before the throne and say: Rev 5:8,14

11"You are worthy, our Lord and God,
to receive glory and honor and power,
for you created all things,
and by your will they were created
and have their being." Rev 10:6

The Scroll and the Lamb

5 Then I saw in the right hand of him who sat
on the throne a scroll with writing on both
sides and sealed with seven seals. 2And I saw a
mighty angel proclaiming in a loud voice, "Who is
worthy to break the seals and open the scroll?"
3But no one in heaven or on earth or under the
earth could open the scroll or even look inside it.
4I wept and wept because no one was found who
was worthy to open the scroll or look inside. 5Then
one of the elders said to me, "Do not weep! See,
the Lion of the tribe of Judah, the Root of David,
has triumphed. He is able to open the scroll and its
seven seals." Ge 49:9; Isa 11:1,10
6Then I saw a Lamb, looking as if it had been
slain, standing in the center of the throne, encircled by the four living creatures and the elders. He
had seven horns and seven eyes, which are the
seven spirits[a] of God sent out into all the earth.

LIVING  INSIGHT

Lift your eyes. Behold His glory high and lifted up. Worthy is the Lamb, who was slain to give power and authority over this place. His kingdom will not fail!
(See Revelation 5:6–10.)

7He came and took the scroll from the right hand
of him who sat on the throne. 8And when he had
taken it, the four living creatures and the twenty-
four elders fell down before the Lamb. Each one
had a harp and they were holding golden bowls
full of incense, which are the prayers of the saints.
9And they sang a new song: Ps 40:3; Rev 14:2

"You are worthy to take the scroll Rev 4:11
and to open its seals,
because you were slain,
and with your blood you purchased men
for God 1Co 6:20
from every tribe and language and people
and nation. Rev 13:7
10You have made them to be a kingdom and
priests to serve our God, 1Pe 2:5
and they will reign on the earth."

11Then I looked and heard the voice of many
angels, numbering thousands upon thousands,
and ten thousand times ten thousand. They encir-

[a] 5,6 Or *the sevenfold Spirit*

cled the throne and the living creatures and the
elders. 12In a loud voice they sang: Da 7:10; Heb 12:22

"Worthy is the Lamb, who was slain, ver 9,13
to receive power and wealth and wisdom and
strength
and honor and glory and praise!" Rev 4:11

13Then I heard every creature in heaven and on
earth and under the earth and on the sea, and all
that is in them, singing: Php 2:10

"To him who sits on the throne and to the
Lamb ver 1,7; Rev 6:16
be praise and honor and glory and power,
for ever and ever!"

14The four living creatures said, "Amen," and the
elders fell down and worshiped. 1Ch 29:11; Rev 4:10

The Seals

6 I watched as the Lamb opened the first of the
seven seals. Then I heard one of the four
living creatures say in a voice like thunder,
"Come!" 2I looked, and there before me was a
white horse! Its rider held a bow, and he was given
a crown, and he rode out as a conqueror bent on
conquest. Zec 6:11; Rev 19:11
3When the Lamb opened the second seal, I
heard the second living creature say, "Come!"
4Then another horse came out, a fiery red one. Its
rider was given power to take peace from the earth
and to make men slay each other. To him was
given a large sword. Rev 4:7
5When the Lamb opened the third seal, I heard
the third living creature say, "Come!" I looked,
and there before me was a black horse! Its rider
was holding a pair of scales in his hand. 6Then I
heard what sounded like a voice among the four
living creatures, saying, "A quart[a] of wheat for a
day's wages,[b] and three quarts of barley for a
day's wages,[b] and do not damage the oil and the
wine!" Rev 4:7; 9:4
7When the Lamb opened the fourth seal, I
heard the voice of the fourth living creature say,
"Come!" 8I looked, and there before me was a pale
horse! Its rider was named Death, and Hades was
following close behind him. They were given power over a fourth of the earth to kill by sword,
famine and plague, and by the wild beasts of the
earth. Zec 6:3; Rev 4:7
9When he opened the fifth seal, I saw under the
altar the souls of those who had been slain because
of the word of God and the testimony they had
maintained. 10They called out in a loud voice,
"How long, Sovereign Lord, holy and true, until
you judge the inhabitants of the earth and avenge
our blood?" 11Then each of them was given a white
robe, and they were told to wait a little longer,
until the number of their fellow servants and
brothers who were to be killed as they had been
was completed. Heb 11:40; Rev 20:4
12I watched as he opened the sixth seal. There
was a great earthquake. The sun turned black like
sackcloth made of goat hair, the whole moon
turned blood red, 13and the stars in the sky fell to
earth, as late figs drop from a fig tree when shaken
by a strong wind. 14The sky receded like a scroll,
rolling up, and every mountain and island was
removed from its place. Jer 4:24; Rev 8:10
15Then the kings of the earth, the princes, the
generals, the rich, the mighty, and every slave and
every free man hid in caves and among the rocks
of the mountains. 16They called to the mountains
and the rocks, "Fall on us and hide us from the
face of him who sits on the throne and from the
wrath of the Lamb! 17For the great day of their
wrath has come, and who can stand?" Ps 76:7

144,000 Sealed

7 After this I saw four angels standing at the
four corners of the earth, holding back the
four winds of the earth to prevent any wind from
blowing on the land or on the sea or on any tree.
2Then I saw another angel coming up from the
east, having the seal of the living God. He called
out in a loud voice to the four angels who had been
given power to harm the land and the sea: 3"Do
not harm the land or the sea or the trees until we
put a seal on the foreheads of the servants of our
God." 4Then I heard the number of those who
were sealed: 144,000 from all the tribes of Israel.

5From the tribe of Judah 12,000 were sealed,
from the tribe of Reuben 12,000,
from the tribe of Gad 12,000,
6from the tribe of Asher 12,000,
from the tribe of Naphtali 12,000,
from the tribe of Manasseh 12,000,
7from the tribe of Simeon 12,000,
from the tribe of Levi 12,000,
from the tribe of Issachar 12,000,
8from the tribe of Zebulun 12,000,
from the tribe of Joseph 12,000,
from the tribe of Benjamin 12,000.

The Great Multitude in White Robes

9After this I looked and there before me was a
great multitude that no one could count, from
every nation, tribe, people and language, standing
before the throne and in front of the Lamb. They
were wearing white robes and were holding palm
branches in their hands. 10And they cried out in a
loud voice: Rev 5:9

"Salvation belongs to our God, Ps 3:8; Rev 12:10

[a]6 Greek *a choinix* (probably about a liter) [b]6 Greek *a denarius*

who sits on the throne, Rev 5:1
and to the Lamb."

[11]All the angels were standing around the throne and around the elders and the four living creatures. They fell down on their faces before the throne and worshiped God, [12]saying: Rev 4:4,6,10

"Amen!
Praise and glory
and wisdom and thanks and honor
and power and strength
be to our God for ever and ever.
Amen!" Rev 5:12-14

LIVING  **INSIGHT**

Believe me, once you have tasted worship—the kind of worship that captures your heart and rivets your full attention on the living Lord—nothing less satisfies. Nothing else even comes close. Once you have tasted true worship, you will never want to "play church" again.

(See Revelation 7:9–12.)

[13]Then one of the elders asked me, "These in white robes—who are they, and where did they come from?" Rev 3:4

[14]I answered, "Sir, you know."

And he said, "These are they who have come out of the great tribulation; they have washed their robes and made them white in the blood of the Lamb. [15]Therefore, Heb 9:14; 1Jn 1:7

"they are before the throne of God ver 9
and serve him day and night in his temple;
and he who sits on the throne will spread his
tent over them. Rev 21:3
[16]Never again will they hunger;
never again will they thirst. Jn 6:35
The sun will not beat upon them,
nor any scorching heat. Isa 49:10
[17]For the Lamb at the center of the throne will
be their shepherd; Ps 23:1; Jn 10:11
he will lead them to springs of living water.
And God will wipe away every tear from their
eyes." Isa 25:8; Rev 21:4

The Seventh Seal and the Golden Censer

8 When he opened the seventh seal, there was silence in heaven for about half an hour.

[2]And I saw the seven angels who stand before God, and to them were given seven trumpets.

[3]Another angel, who had a golden censer, came and stood at the altar. He was given much incense to offer, with the prayers of all the saints, on the golden altar before the throne. [4]The smoke of the incense, together with the prayers of the saints, went up before God from the angel's hand. [5]Then the angel took the censer, filled it with fire from the altar, and hurled it on the earth; and there came peals of thunder, rumblings, flashes of lightning and an earthquake. Ex 30:1-6; Rev 5:8

The Trumpets

[6]Then the seven angels who had the seven trumpets prepared to sound them. ver 2

[7]The first angel sounded his trumpet, and there came hail and fire mixed with blood, and it was hurled down upon the earth. A third of the earth was burned up, a third of the trees were burned up, and all the green grass was burned up.

[8]The second angel sounded his trumpet, and something like a huge mountain, all ablaze, was thrown into the sea. A third of the sea turned into blood, [9]a third of the living creatures in the sea died, and a third of the ships were destroyed.

[10]The third angel sounded his trumpet, and a great star, blazing like a torch, fell from the sky on a third of the rivers and on the springs of water—[11]the name of the star is Wormwood.[a] A third of the waters turned bitter, and many people died from the waters that had become bitter. Isa 14:12

[12]The fourth angel sounded his trumpet, and a third of the sun was struck, a third of the moon, and a third of the stars, so that a third of them turned dark. A third of the day was without light, and also a third of the night. Ex 10:21-23; Rev 6:12-13

[13]As I watched, I heard an eagle that was flying in midair call out in a loud voice: "Woe! Woe! Woe to the inhabitants of the earth, because of the trumpet blasts about to be sounded by the other three angels!" Rev 9:12; 14:6

9 The fifth angel sounded his trumpet, and I saw a star that had fallen from the sky to the earth. The star was given the key to the shaft of the Abyss. [2]When he opened the Abyss, smoke rose from it like the smoke from a gigantic furnace. The sun and sky were darkened by the smoke from the Abyss. [3]And out of the smoke locusts came down upon the earth and were given power like that of scorpions of the earth. [4]They were told not to harm the grass of the earth or any plant or tree, but only those people who did not have the seal of God on their foreheads. [5]They were not given power to kill them, but only to torture them for five months. And the agony they suffered was like that of the sting of a scorpion when it strikes a man. [6]During those days men will seek death, but will not find it; they will long to die, but death will elude them. Jer 8:3; Rev 8:7

[7]The locusts looked like horses prepared for

[a] *11* That is, Bitterness

battle. On their heads they wore something like crowns of gold, and their faces resembled human faces. 8Their hair was like women's hair, and their teeth were like lions' teeth. 9They had breastplates like breastplates of iron, and the sound of their wings was like the thundering of many horses and chariots rushing into battle. 10They had tails and stings like scorpions, and in their tails they had power to torment people for five months. 11They had as king over them the angel of the Abyss, whose name in Hebrew is Abaddon, and in Greek, Apollyon.[a] Joel 1:6; 2:5

12The first woe is past; two other woes are yet to come. Rev 8:13

13The sixth angel sounded his trumpet, and I heard a voice coming from the horns[b] of the golden altar that is before God. 14It said to the sixth angel who had the trumpet, "Release the four angels who are bound at the great river Euphrates." 15And the four angels who had been kept ready for this very hour and day and month and year were released to kill a third of mankind. 16The number of the mounted troops was two hundred million. I heard their number. Rev 7:4; 16:12

17The horses and riders I saw in my vision looked like this: Their breastplates were fiery red, dark blue, and yellow as sulfur. The heads of the horses resembled the heads of lions, and out of their mouths came fire, smoke and sulfur. 18A third of mankind was killed by the three plagues of fire, smoke and sulfur that came out of their mouths. 19The power of the horses was in their mouths and in their tails; for their tails were like snakes, having heads with which they inflict injury.

20The rest of mankind that were not killed by these plagues still did not repent of the work of their hands; they did not stop worshiping demons, and idols of gold, silver, bronze, stone and wood—idols that cannot see or hear or walk. 21Nor did they repent of their murders, their magic arts, their sexual immorality or their thefts.

The Angel and the Little Scroll

10 Then I saw another mighty angel coming down from heaven. He was robed in a cloud, with a rainbow above his head; his face was like the sun, and his legs were like fiery pillars. 2He was holding a little scroll, which lay open in his hand. He planted his right foot on the sea and his left foot on the land, 3and he gave a loud shout like the roar of a lion. When he shouted, the voices of the seven thunders spoke. 4And when the seven thunders spoke, I was about to write; but I heard a voice from heaven say, "Seal up what the seven thunders have said and do not write it down."

5Then the angel I had seen standing on the sea and on the land raised his right hand to heaven. 6And he swore by him who lives for ever and ever, who created the heavens and all that is in them, the earth and all that is in it, and the sea and all that is in it, and said, "There will be no more delay! 7But in the days when the seventh angel is about to sound his trumpet, the mystery of God will be accomplished, just as he announced to his servants the prophets." Rev 4:11; 16:17

8Then the voice that I had heard from heaven spoke to me once more: "Go, take the scroll that lies open in the hand of the angel who is standing on the sea and on the land." ver 2,4

9So I went to the angel and asked him to give me the little scroll. He said to me, "Take it and eat it. It will turn your stomach sour, but in your mouth it will be as sweet as honey." 10I took the little scroll from the angel's hand and ate it. It tasted as sweet as honey in my mouth, but when I had eaten it, my stomach turned sour. 11Then I was told, "You must prophesy again about many peoples, nations, languages and kings." Jer 15:16

The Two Witnesses

11 I was given a reed like a measuring rod and was told, "Go and measure the temple of God and the altar, and count the worshipers there. 2But exclude the outer court; do not measure it, because it has been given to the Gentiles. They will trample on the holy city for 42 months. 3And I will give power to my two witnesses, and they will prophesy for 1,260 days, clothed in sackcloth." 4These are the two olive trees and the two lampstands that stand before the Lord of the earth. 5If anyone tries to harm them, fire comes from their mouths and devours their enemies. This is how anyone who wants to harm them must die. 6These men have power to shut up the sky so that it will not rain during the time they are prophesying; and they have power to turn the waters into blood and to strike the earth with every kind of plague as often as they want. Rev 13:5; Zec 4:14

7Now when they have finished their testimony, the beast that comes up from the Abyss will attack them, and overpower and kill them. 8Their bodies will lie in the street of the great city, which is figuratively called Sodom and Egypt, where also their Lord was crucified. 9For three and a half days men from every people, tribe, language and nation will gaze on their bodies and refuse them burial. 10The inhabitants of the earth will gloat over them and will celebrate by sending each other gifts, because these two prophets had tormented those who live on the earth. Est 9:19,22; Da 7:21

11But after the three and a half days a breath of life from God entered them, and they stood on their feet, and terror struck those who saw them. 12Then they heard a loud voice from heaven saying

[a] *11 Abaddon* and *Apollyon* mean *Destroyer.* [b] *13* That is, projections

to them, "Come up here." And they went up to heaven in a cloud, while their enemies looked on. 13At that very hour there was a severe earthquake and a tenth of the city collapsed. Seven thousand people were killed in the earthquake, and the survivors were terrified and gave glory to the God of heaven. Rev 6:12; 16:11

14The second woe has passed; the third woe is coming soon. Rev 8:13

The Seventh Trumpet

15The seventh angel sounded his trumpet, and there were loud voices in heaven, which said:

"The kingdom of the world has become the
kingdom of our Lord and of his
Christ, Rev 12:10
and he will reign for ever and ever."

16And the twenty-four elders, who were seated on their thrones before God, fell on their faces and worshiped God, 17saying: Rev 4:4

"We give thanks to you, Lord God Almighty,
the One who is and who was, Rev 1:4
because you have taken your great power
and have begun to reign. Rev 19:6
18The nations were angry; Ps 2:1
and your wrath has come.
The time has come for judging the dead,
and for rewarding your servants the
prophets Rev 10:7
and your saints and those who reverence your
name,
both small and great— Rev 19:5
and for destroying those who destroy the
earth."

19Then God's temple in heaven was opened, and within his temple was seen the ark of his covenant. And there came flashes of lightning, rumblings, peals of thunder, an earthquake and a great hailstorm. Rev 15:5,8; 16:21

The Woman and the Dragon

12 A great and wondrous sign appeared in heaven: a woman clothed with the sun, with the moon under her feet and a crown of twelve stars on her head. 2She was pregnant and cried out in pain as she was about to give birth. 3Then another sign appeared in heaven: an enormous red dragon with seven heads and ten horns and seven crowns on his heads. 4His tail swept a third of the stars out of the sky and flung them to the earth. The dragon stood in front of the woman who was about to give birth, so that he might devour her child the moment it was born. 5She gave birth to a son, a male child, who will rule all the nations with an iron scepter. And her child was snatched up to God and to his throne. 6The woman fled into the desert to a place prepared for her by God, where she might be taken care of for 1,260 days. Da 8:10; Rev 11:2

7And there was war in heaven. Michael and his angels fought against the dragon, and the dragon and his angels fought back. 8But he was not strong enough, and they lost their place in heaven. 9The great dragon was hurled down—that ancient serpent called the devil, or Satan, who leads the whole world astray. He was hurled to the earth, and his angels with him. Jn 12:31; Rev 20:3,8,10

10Then I heard a loud voice in heaven say:

"Now have come the salvation and the power
and the kingdom of our God, Rev 7:10
and the authority of his Christ.
For the accuser of our brothers, Job 1:9-11; Zec 3:1
who accuses them before our God day and
night,
has been hurled down.
11They overcame him Jn 16:33
by the blood of the Lamb Rev 7:14
and by the word of their testimony; Rev 6:9
they did not love their lives so much
as to shrink from death. Lk 14:26

LIVING  **INSIGHT**

In Jesus Christ we are the victors, the conquerors. There is no need to be afraid. We have "overcoming" power through Him who died that we might live. Stand firm, Christian. Through Christ we conquer.

(See Revelation 12:11–12.)

12Therefore rejoice, you heavens Ps 96:11; Rev 18:20
and you who dwell in them!
But woe to the earth and the sea, Rev 10:6
because the devil has gone down to you!
He is filled with fury,
because he knows that his time is short."

13When the dragon saw that he had been hurled to the earth, he pursued the woman who had given birth to the male child. 14The woman was given the two wings of a great eagle, so that she might fly to the place prepared for her in the desert, where she would be taken care of for a time, times and half a time, out of the serpent's reach. 15Then from his mouth the serpent spewed water like a river, to overtake the woman and sweep her away with the torrent. 16But the earth helped the woman by opening its mouth and swallowing the river that the dragon had spewed out of his mouth. 17Then the dragon was enraged at the woman and went off to make war against the rest of her offspring—those who obey God's commandments and hold

13 to the testimony of Jesus. 1And the dragon[a] stood on the shore of the sea.

The Beast out of the Sea

And I saw a beast coming out of the sea. He had ten horns and seven heads, with ten crowns on his horns, and on each head a blasphemous name. 2The beast I saw resembled a leopard, but had feet like those of a bear and a mouth like that of a lion. The dragon gave the beast his power and his throne and great authority. 3One of the heads of the beast seemed to have had a fatal wound, but the fatal wound had been healed. The whole world was astonished and followed the beast. 4Men worshiped the dragon because he had given authority to the beast, and they also worshiped the beast and asked, "Who is like the beast? Who can make war against him?" Da 7:1-6; Rev 17:8

5The beast was given a mouth to utter proud words and blasphemies and to exercise his authority for forty-two months. 6He opened his mouth to blaspheme God, and to slander his name and his dwelling place and those who live in heaven. 7He was given power to make war against the saints and to conquer them. And he was given authority over every tribe, people, language and nation. 8All inhabitants of the earth will worship the beast—all whose names have not been written in the book of life belonging to the Lamb that was slain from the creation of the world.[b] Mt 25:34

9He who has an ear, let him hear. Rev 2:7

10If anyone is to go into captivity,
  into captivity he will go.
If anyone is to be killed[c] with the sword,
  with the sword he will be killed.

This calls for patient endurance and faithfulness on the part of the saints. Heb 6:12; Rev 14:12

The Beast out of the Earth

11Then I saw another beast, coming out of the earth. He had two horns like a lamb, but he spoke like a dragon. 12He exercised all the authority of the first beast on his behalf, and made the earth and its inhabitants worship the first beast, whose fatal wound had been healed. 13And he performed great and miraculous signs, even causing fire to come down from heaven to earth in full view of men. 14Because of the signs he was given power to do on behalf of the first beast, he deceived the inhabitants of the earth. He ordered them to set up an image in honor of the beast who was wounded by the sword and yet lived. 15He was given power to give breath to the image of the first beast, so that it could speak and cause all who refused to worship the image to be killed. 16He also forced everyone, small and great, rich and poor, free and slave, to receive a mark on his right hand or on his forehead, 17so that no one could buy or sell unless he had the mark, which is the name of the beast or the number of his name. Rev 12:9; 14:11

18This calls for wisdom. If anyone has insight, let him calculate the number of the beast, for it is man's number. His number is 666. Rev 15:2; 17:9

The Lamb and the 144,000

14 Then I looked, and there before me was the Lamb, standing on Mount Zion, and with him 144,000 who had his name and his Father's name written on their foreheads. 2And I heard a sound from heaven like the roar of rushing waters and like a loud peal of thunder. The sound I heard was like that of harpists playing their harps. 3And they sang a new song before the throne and before the four living creatures and the elders. No one could learn the song except the 144,000 who had been redeemed from the earth. 4These are those who did not defile themselves with women, for they kept themselves pure. They follow the Lamb wherever he goes. They were purchased from among men and offered as firstfruits to God and the Lamb. 5No lie was found in their mouths; they are blameless. Ps 32:2; Eph 5:27

The Three Angels

6Then I saw another angel flying in midair, and he had the eternal gospel to proclaim to those who live on the earth—to every nation, tribe, language and people. 7He said in a loud voice, "Fear God and give him glory, because the hour of his judgment has come. Worship him who made the heavens, the earth, the sea and the springs of water."

8A second angel followed and said, "Fallen! Fallen is Babylon the Great, which made all the nations drink the maddening wine of her adulteries." Isa 21:9; Jer 51:8

9A third angel followed them and said in a loud voice: "If anyone worships the beast and his image and receives his mark on the forehead or on the hand, 10he, too, will drink of the wine of God's fury, which has been poured full strength into the cup of his wrath. He will be tormented with burning sulfur in the presence of the holy angels and of the Lamb. 11And the smoke of their torment rises for ever and ever. There is no rest day or night for those who worship the beast and his image, or for anyone who receives the mark of his name." 12This calls for patient endurance on the part of the saints who obey God's commandments and remain faithful to Jesus. Isa 34:10; Rev 13:10

13Then I heard a voice from heaven say, "Write:

[a] 1 Some late manuscripts *And I* [b] 8 Or *written from the creation of the world in the book of life belonging to the Lamb that was slain* [c] 10 Some manuscripts *anyone kills*

Blessed are the dead who die in the Lord from
now on." 1Co 15:18; 1Th 4:16
"Yes," says the Spirit, "they will rest from their
labor, for their deeds will follow them." Rev 2:7

LIVING INSIGHT

There's a long, demanding course to be run, most of which takes place in the trenches and without applause. I suggest we intensify our determination and head for the goal. Endurance is the secret.
(See Revelation 14:12.)

The Harvest of the Earth

14I looked, and there before me was a white
cloud, and seated on the cloud was one "like a son
of man"[a] with a crown of gold on his head and
a sharp sickle in his hand. 15Then another angel
came out of the temple and called in a loud voice
to him who was sitting on the cloud, "Take your
sickle and reap, because the time to reap has come,
for the harvest of the earth is ripe." 16So he who
was seated on the cloud swung his sickle over the
earth, and the earth was harvested. Jer 51:33; Joel 3:13
17Another angel came out of the temple in heav-
en, and he too had a sharp sickle. 18Still another
angel, who had charge of the fire, came from the
altar and called in a loud voice to him who had the
sharp sickle, "Take your sharp sickle and gather
the clusters of grapes from the earth's vine, because its grapes are ripe." 19The angel swung his
sickle on the earth, gathered its grapes and threw
them into the great winepress of God's wrath.
20They were trampled in the winepress outside the
city, and blood flowed out of the press, rising as
high as the horses' bridles for a distance of 1,600
stadia.[b] Heb 13:12; Rev 19:15

Seven Angels With Seven Plagues

15 I saw in heaven another great and marvelous sign: seven angels with the seven last
plagues—last, because with them God's wrath is
completed. 2And I saw what looked like a sea of
glass mixed with fire and, standing beside the sea,
those who had been victorious over the beast and
his image and over the number of his name. They
held harps given them by God 3and sang the song
of Moses the servant of God and the song of the
Lamb: Rev 4:6; 13:14

"Great and marvelous are your deeds, Ps 111:2
Lord God Almighty. Rev 1:8
Just and true are your ways, Ps 145:17
King of the ages.
4Who will not fear you, O Lord, Jer 10:7
and bring glory to your name? Ps 86:9
For you alone are holy.
All nations will come
and worship before you, Isa 66:23
for your righteous acts have been revealed."

5After this I looked and in heaven the temple,
that is, the tabernacle of the Testimony, was
opened. 6Out of the temple came the seven angels
with the seven plagues. They were dressed in clean,
shining linen and wore golden sashes around their
chests. 7Then one of the four living creatures gave
to the seven angels seven golden bowls filled with
the wrath of God, who lives for ever and ever.
8And the temple was filled with smoke from the
glory of God and from his power, and no one
could enter the temple until the seven plagues of
the seven angels were completed. Ex 40:34-35; Rev 4:6

The Seven Bowls of God's Wrath

16 Then I heard a loud voice from the temple
saying to the seven angels, "Go, pour out
the seven bowls of God's wrath on the earth."
2The first angel went and poured out his bowl
on the land, and ugly and painful sores broke out
on the people who had the mark of the beast and
worshiped his image. Rev 8:7; 13:15-17
3The second angel poured out his bowl on the
sea, and it turned into blood like that of a dead
man, and every living thing in the sea died.
4The third angel poured out his bowl on the
rivers and springs of water, and they became
blood. 5Then I heard the angel in charge of the
waters say: Ex 7:17-21; Rev 8:10

"You are just in these judgments, Rev 15:3
you who are and who were, the Holy One,
because you have so judged; Rev 6:10
6for they have shed the blood of your saints
and prophets, Lk 11:49-51
and you have given them blood to drink as
they deserve."

7And I heard the altar respond: Rev 6:9

"Yes, Lord God Almighty, Rev 1:8
true and just are your judgments." Isa 49:26

8The fourth angel poured out his bowl on the
sun, and the sun was given power to scorch people
with fire. 9They were seared by the intense heat
and they cursed the name of God, who had control
over these plagues, but they refused to repent and
glorify him. Rev 11:13
10The fifth angel poured out his bowl on the
throne of the beast, and his kingdom was plunged
into darkness. Men gnawed their tongues in agony
11and cursed the God of heaven because of their

[a] *14* Daniel 7:13 [b] *20* That is, about 180 miles (about 300 kilometers)

pains and their sores, but they refused to repent of
what they had done. Rev 9:2; 13:2
12The sixth angel poured out his bowl on the
great river Euphrates, and its water was dried up
to prepare the way for the kings from the East.
13Then I saw three evil[a] spirits that looked like
frogs; they came out of the mouth of the dragon,
out of the mouth of the beast and out of the mouth
of the false prophet. 14They are spirits of demons
performing miraculous signs, and they go out to
the kings of the whole world, to gather them for
the battle on the great day of God Almighty.
15"Behold, I come like a thief! Blessed is he who
stays awake and keeps his clothes with him, so that
he may not go naked and be shamefully exposed."
16Then they gathered the kings together to the
place that in Hebrew is called Armageddon.
17The seventh angel poured out his bowl into
the air, and out of the temple came a loud voice
from the throne, saying, "It is done!" 18Then there
came flashes of lightning, rumblings, peals of
thunder and a severe earthquake. No earthquake
like it has ever occurred since man has been on
earth, so tremendous was the quake. 19The great
city split into three parts, and the cities of the
nations collapsed. God remembered Babylon the
Great and gave her the cup filled with the wine of
the fury of his wrath. 20Every island fled away and
the mountains could not be found. 21From the sky
huge hailstones of about a hundred pounds each
fell upon men. And they cursed God on account of
the plague of hail, because the plague was so terrible. Ex 9:23-25; Rev 14:10

The Woman on the Beast

17 One of the seven angels who had the seven
bowls came and said to me, "Come, I will
show you the punishment of the great prostitute,
who sits on many waters. 2With her the kings of
the earth committed adultery and the inhabitants
of the earth were intoxicated with the wine of her
adulteries." Jer 51:13; Rev 16:19
3Then the angel carried me away in the Spirit
into a desert. There I saw a woman sitting on a
scarlet beast that was covered with blasphemous
names and had seven heads and ten horns. 4The
woman was dressed in purple and scarlet, and was
glittering with gold, precious stones and pearls.
She held a golden cup in her hand, filled with
abominable things and the filth of her adulteries.
5This title was written on her forehead: Jer 51:7

MYSTERY
BABYLON THE GREAT
THE MOTHER OF PROSTITUTES
AND OF THE ABOMINATIONS OF THE EARTH.

6I saw that the woman was drunk with the blood
of the saints, the blood of those who bore testimony to Jesus. Rev 18:24
When I saw her, I was greatly astonished. 7Then
the angel said to me: "Why are you astonished? I
will explain to you the mystery of the woman and
of the beast she rides, which has the seven heads
and ten horns. 8The beast, which you saw, once
was, now is not, and will come up out of the Abyss
and go to his destruction. The inhabitants of the
earth whose names have not been written in the
book of life from the creation of the world will be
astonished when they see the beast, because he
once was, now is not, and yet will come.
9"This calls for a mind with wisdom. The seven
heads are seven hills on which the woman sits.
10They are also seven kings. Five have fallen, one
is, the other has not yet come; but when he does
come, he must remain for a little while. 11The beast
who once was, and now is not, is an eighth king.
He belongs to the seven and is going to his destruction. Rev 13:18
12"The ten horns you saw are ten kings who
have not yet received a kingdom, but who for one
hour will receive authority as kings along with the
beast. 13They have one purpose and will give their
power and authority to the beast. 14They will make
war against the Lamb, but the Lamb will overcome
them because he is Lord of lords and King of
kings—and with him will be his called, chosen and
faithful followers." 1Ti 6:15; Rev 16:14
15Then the angel said to me, "The waters you
saw, where the prostitute sits, are peoples, multitudes, nations and languages. 16The beast and the
ten horns you saw will hate the prostitute. They
will bring her to ruin and leave her naked; they will
eat her flesh and burn her with fire. 17For God has
put it into their hearts to accomplish his purpose
by agreeing to give the beast their power to rule,
until God's words are fulfilled. 18The woman you
saw is the great city that rules over the kings of the
earth." Rev 10:7; 16:19

The Fall of Babylon

18 After this I saw another angel coming
down from heaven. He had great authority, and the earth was illuminated by his splendor.
2With a mighty voice he shouted: Eze 43:2; Rev 17:1

"Fallen! Fallen is Babylon the Great! Rev 14:8
She has become a home for demons
and a haunt for every evil[a] spirit, Rev 16:13
a haunt for every unclean and detestable
bird. Isa 13:21-22; Jer 50:39
3For all the nations have drunk
the maddening wine of her adulteries.
The kings of the earth committed adultery
with her, Rev 17:2

[a] 13,2 Greek *unclean*

and the merchants of the earth grew rich
from her excessive luxuries." Eze 27:9-25

[4]Then I heard another voice from heaven say:

"Come out of her, my people, Jer 50:8; 2Co 6:17
so that you will not share in her sins,
so that you will not receive any of her
plagues; Ge 19:15
[5]for her sins are piled up to heaven, Jer 51:9
and God has remembered her crimes.
[6]Give back to her as she has given;
pay her back double for what she has done.
Mix her a double portion from her own
cup. Rev 14:10; 16:19
[7]Give her as much torture and grief
as the glory and luxury she gave herself.
In her heart she boasts,
'I sit as queen; I am not a widow,
and I will never mourn.' Zep 2:15
[8]Therefore in one day her plagues will overtake
her: Isa 47:9
death, mourning and famine.
She will be consumed by fire, Rev 17:16
for mighty is the Lord God who judges her.

[9]"When the kings of the earth who committed
adultery with her and shared her luxury see the
smoke of her burning, they will weep and mourn
over her. [10]Terrified at her torment, they will stand
far off and cry: Eze 26:17-18; Rev 19:3

"'Woe! Woe, O great city,
O Babylon, city of power!
In one hour your doom has come!' Rev 17:12

[11]"The merchants of the earth will weep and
mourn over her because no one buys their cargoes
any more— [12]cargoes of gold, silver, precious
stones and pearls; fine linen, purple, silk and scarlet cloth; every sort of citron wood, and articles of
every kind made of ivory, costly wood, bronze,
iron and marble; [13]cargoes of cinnamon and spice,
of incense, myrrh and frankincense, of wine and
olive oil, of fine flour and wheat; cattle and sheep;
horses and carriages; and bodies and souls of men.
[14]"They will say, 'The fruit you longed for is
gone from you. All your riches and splendor have
vanished, never to be recovered.' [15]The merchants
who sold these things and gained their wealth
from her will stand far off, terrified at her torment.
They will weep and mourn [16]and cry out:

"'Woe! Woe, O great city,
dressed in fine linen, purple and scarlet,
and glittering with gold, precious stones
and pearls! Rev 17:4
[17]In one hour such great wealth has been
brought to ruin!' Rev 17:12,16

"Every sea captain, and all who travel by ship,
the sailors, and all who earn their living from the
sea, will stand far off. [18]When they see the smoke
of her burning, they will exclaim, 'Was there ever
a city like this great city?' [19]They will throw dust on
their heads, and with weeping and mourning cry
out: Eze 27:28-30; Rev 13:4

"'Woe! Woe, O great city, Rev 17:18
where all who had ships on the sea
became rich through her wealth!
In one hour she has been brought to ruin!
[20]Rejoice over her, O heaven! Jer 51:48
Rejoice, saints and apostles and prophets!
God has judged her for the way she treated
you.'" Rev 19:2

[21]Then a mighty angel picked up a boulder the
size of a large millstone and threw it into the sea,
and said: Jer 51:63; Rev 5:2

"With such violence
the great city of Babylon will be thrown
down, Rev 17:18
never to be found again.
[22]The music of harpists and musicians, flute
players and trumpeters,
will never be heard in you again. Eze 26:13
No workman of any trade
will ever be found in you again.
The sound of a millstone
will never be heard in you again. Jer 25:10
[23]The light of a lamp
will never shine in you again.
The voice of bridegroom and bride
will never be heard in you again. Jer 7:34
Your merchants were the world's great men.
By your magic spell all the nations were led
astray. Na 3:4
[24]In her was found the blood of prophets and
of the saints, Rev 17:6
and of all who have been killed on the
earth." Jer 51:49

Hallelujah!

19 After this I heard what sounded like the
roar of a great multitude in heaven shouting: Rev 11:15

"Hallelujah!
Salvation and glory and power belong to our
God, Rev 4:11; 7:10
[2] for true and just are his judgments. Rev 16:7
He has condemned the great prostitute Rev 17:1
who corrupted the earth by her adulteries.
He has avenged on her the blood of his
servants." Dt 32:43; Rev 6:10

[3]And again they shouted:

"Hallelujah!
The smoke from her goes up for ever and
ever." Isa 34:10; Rev 14:11

4The twenty-four elders and the four living creatures fell down and worshiped God, who was seated on the throne. And they cried: Rev 4:4,6; 5:14

"Amen, Hallelujah!"

5Then a voice came from the throne, saying:

"Praise our God,
all you his servants, Ps 134:1
you who fear him,
both small and great!" Rev 11:18

6Then I heard what sounded like a great multitude, like the roar of rushing waters and like loud peals of thunder, shouting: Rev 11:15

"Hallelujah!
For our Lord God Almighty reigns. Rev 1:8
7Let us rejoice and be glad
and give him glory! Rev 11:13
For the wedding of the Lamb has come,
and his bride has made herself ready.
8Fine linen, bright and clean, Rev 15:6
was given her to wear."

(Fine linen stands for the righteous acts of the saints.) Rev 15:4

9Then the angel said to me, "Write: 'Blessed are those who are invited to the wedding supper of the Lamb!' " And he added, "These are the true words of God." Lk 14:15; Rev 1:19

10At this I fell at his feet to worship him. But he said to me, "Do not do it! I am a fellow servant with you and with your brothers who hold to the testimony of Jesus. Worship God! For the testimony of Jesus is the spirit of prophecy." Rev 22:8-9

The Rider on the White Horse

11I saw heaven standing open and there before me was a white horse, whose rider is called Faithful and True. With justice he judges and makes war. 12His eyes are like blazing fire, and on his head are many crowns. He has a name written on him that no one knows but he himself. 13He is dressed in a robe dipped in blood, and his name is the Word of God. 14The armies of heaven were following him, riding on white horses and dressed in fine linen, white and clean. 15Out of his mouth comes a sharp sword with which to strike down the nations. "He will rule them with an iron scepter."[a] He treads the winepress of the fury of the wrath of God Almighty. 16On his robe and on his thigh he has this name written: Isa 11:4; Rev 6:2

KING OF KINGS AND LORD OF LORDS.

17And I saw an angel standing in the sun, who cried in a loud voice to all the birds flying in midair, "Come, gather together for the great supper of God, 18so that you may eat the flesh of kings, generals, and mighty men, of horses and their riders, and the flesh of all people, free and slave, small and great." Eze 39:17-20

19Then I saw the beast and the kings of the earth and their armies gathered together to make war against the rider on the horse and his army. 20But the beast was captured, and with him the false prophet who had performed the miraculous signs on his behalf. With these signs he had deluded those who had received the mark of the beast and worshiped his image. The two of them were thrown alive into the fiery lake of burning sulfur. 21The rest of them were killed with the sword that came out of the mouth of the rider on the horse, and all the birds gorged themselves on their flesh.

The Thousand Years

20 And I saw an angel coming down out of heaven, having the key to the Abyss and holding in his hand a great chain. 2He seized the dragon, that ancient serpent, who is the devil, or Satan, and bound him for a thousand years. 3He threw him into the Abyss, and locked and sealed it over him, to keep him from deceiving the nations anymore until the thousand years were ended. After that, he must be set free for a short time.

4I saw thrones on which were seated those who had been given authority to judge. And I saw the souls of those who had been beheaded because of their testimony for Jesus and because of the word of God. They had not worshiped the beast or his image and had not received his mark on their foreheads or their hands. They came to life and reigned with Christ a thousand years. 5(The rest of the dead did not come to life until the thousand years were ended.) This is the first resurrection. 6Blessed and holy are those who have part in the first resurrection. The second death has no power over them, but they will be priests of God and of Christ and will reign with him for a thousand years. Rev 1:6; 2:11

Satan's Doom

7When the thousand years are over, Satan will be released from his prison 8and will go out to deceive the nations in the four corners of the earth—Gog and Magog—to gather them for battle. In number they are like the sand on the seashore. 9They marched across the breadth of the earth and surrounded the camp of God's people, the city he loves. But fire came down from heaven and devoured them. 10And the devil, who deceived them, was thrown into the lake of burning sulfur, where the beast and the false prophet had been thrown. They will be tormented day and night for ever and ever. Eze 38:9,16; Rev 14:10-11

[a] 15 Psalm 2:9

The Dead Are Judged

[11]Then I saw a great white throne and him who was seated on it. Earth and sky fled from his presence, and there was no place for them. [12]And I saw the dead, great and small, standing before the throne, and books were opened. Another book was opened, which is the book of life. The dead were judged according to what they had done as recorded in the books. [13]The sea gave up the dead that were in it, and death and Hades gave up the dead that were in them, and each person was judged according to what he had done. [14]Then death and Hades were thrown into the lake of fire. The lake of fire is the second death. [15]If anyone's name was not found written in the book of life, he was thrown into the lake of fire. Mt 16:27; 1Co 15:26

The New Jerusalem

21 Then I saw a new heaven and a new earth, for the first heaven and the first earth had passed away, and there was no longer any sea. [2]I saw the Holy City, the new Jerusalem, coming down out of heaven from God, prepared as a bride beautifully dressed for her husband. [3]And I heard a loud voice from the throne saying, "Now the dwelling of God is with men, and he will live with them. They will be his people, and God himself will be with them and be their God. [4]He will wipe every tear from their eyes. There will be no more death or mourning or crying or pain, for the old order of things has passed away." Isa 35:10; 1Co 15:26

[5]He who was seated on the throne said, "I am making everything new!" Then he said, "Write this down, for these words are trustworthy and true."

[6]He said to me: "It is done. I am the Alpha and the Omega, the Beginning and the End. To him who is thirsty I will give to drink without cost from the spring of the water of life. [7]He who overcomes will inherit all this, and I will be his God and he will be my son. [8]But the cowardly, the unbelieving, the vile, the murderers, the sexually immoral, those who practice magic arts, the idolaters and all liars—their place will be in the fiery lake of burning sulfur. This is the second death." Rev 1:8; 16:17

[9]One of the seven angels who had the seven bowls full of the seven last plagues came and said to me, "Come, I will show you the bride, the wife of the Lamb." [10]And he carried me away in the Spirit to a mountain great and high, and showed me the Holy City, Jerusalem, coming down out of heaven from God. [11]It shone with the glory of God, and its brilliance was like that of a very precious jewel, like a jasper, clear as crystal. [12]It had a great, high wall with twelve gates, and with twelve angels at the gates. On the gates were written the names of the twelve tribes of Israel. [13]There were three gates on the east, three on the north, three on the south and three on the west. [14]The wall of the city had twelve foundations, and on them were the names of the twelve apostles of the Lamb. Eze 48:30-34; Rev 15:1,6-7

[15]The angel who talked with me had a measuring rod of gold to measure the city, its gates and its walls. [16]The city was laid out like a square, as long as it was wide. He measured the city with the rod and found it to be 12,000 stadia[a] in length, and as wide and high as it is long. [17]He measured its wall and it was 144 cubits[b] thick,[c] by man's measurement, which the angel was using. [18]The wall was made of jasper, and the city of pure gold, as pure as glass. [19]The foundations of the city walls were decorated with every kind of precious stone. The first foundation was jasper, the second sapphire, the third chalcedony, the fourth emerald, [20]the fifth sardonyx, the sixth carnelian, the seventh chrysolite, the eighth beryl, the ninth topaz, the tenth chrysoprase, the eleventh jacinth, and the twelfth amethyst.[d] [21]The twelve gates were twelve pearls, each gate made of a single pearl. The great street of the city was of pure gold, like transparent glass. Isa 54:11-12; Rev 11:1

[22]I did not see a temple in the city, because the Lord God Almighty and the Lamb are its temple. [23]The city does not need the sun or the moon to shine on it, for the glory of God gives it light, and the Lamb is its lamp. [24]The nations will walk by its light, and the kings of the earth will bring their splendor into it. [25]On no day will its gates ever be shut, for there will be no night there. [26]The glory and honor of the nations will be brought into it. [27]Nothing impure will ever enter it, nor will anyone who does what is shameful or deceitful, but only those whose names are written in the Lamb's book of life. Isa 24:23; 52:1; Rev 22:14-15

The River of Life

22 Then the angel showed me the river of the water of life, as clear as crystal, flowing from the throne of God and of the Lamb [2]down the middle of the great street of the city. On each side of the river stood the tree of life, bearing twelve crops of fruit, yielding its fruit every month. And the leaves of the tree are for the healing of the nations. [3]No longer will there be any curse. The throne of God and of the Lamb will be in the city, and his servants will serve him. [4]They will see his face, and his name will be on their foreheads. [5]There will be no more night. They will not need the light of a lamp or the light of the sun, for the Lord God will give them light. And they will reign for ever and ever. Eze 47:1; Zec 14:11; Rev 21:23

[6]The angel said to me, "These words are trust-

[a] *16* That is, about 1,400 miles (about 2,200 kilometers) [b] *17* That is, about 200 feet (about 65 meters) [c] *17* Or *high*
[d] *20* The precise identification of some of these precious stones is uncertain.

worthy and true. The Lord, the God of the spirits
of the prophets, sent his angel to show his servants
the things that must soon take place." Rev 1:1; 19:9

Jesus Is Coming

7"Behold, I am coming soon! Blessed is he who
keeps the words of the prophecy in this book."

8I, John, am the one who heard and saw these
things. And when I had heard and seen them, I fell
down to worship at the feet of the angel who had
been showing them to me. 9But he said to me, "Do
not do it! I am a fellow servant with you and with
your brothers the prophets and of all who keep the
words of this book. Worship God!" Rev 19:10

10Then he told me, "Do not seal up the words
of the prophecy of this book, because the time is
near. 11Let him who does wrong continue to do
wrong; let him who is vile continue to be vile; let
him who does right continue to do right; and let
him who is holy continue to be holy." Eze 3:27

12"Behold, I am coming soon! My reward is
with me, and I will give to everyone according to
what he has done. 13I am the Alpha and the Omega, the First and the Last, the Beginning and the
End. Isa 40:10; Rev 1:8; 21:6

14"Blessed are those who wash their robes, that
they may have the right to the tree of life and may
go through the gates into the city. 15Outside are the
dogs, those who practice magic arts, the sexually
immoral, the murderers, the idolaters and everyone who loves and practices falsehood. Gal 5:19-21

16"I, Jesus, have sent my angel to give you[a] this
testimony for the churches. I am the Root and the
Offspring of David, and the bright Morning Star."

17The Spirit and the bride say, "Come!" And let
him who hears say, "Come!" Whoever is thirsty,
let him come; and whoever wishes, let him take the
free gift of the water of life. Rev 2:7

18I warn everyone who hears the words of the
prophecy of this book: If anyone adds anything to

LIVING  **INSIGHT**

If our Lord were to make Himself visible and return to earth and speak His message, it would be in keeping with the Bible. His message of truth would tie in exactly with what we see in Scripture—His opinion, His counsel, His commands, His desires, His warnings, His very mind. When we rely on God's voice, God's very message, we have a sure foundation.

(See Revelation 22:18–19.)

them, God will add to him the plagues described
in this book. 19And if anyone takes words away
from this book of prophecy, God will take away
from him his share in the tree of life and in the
holy city, which are described in this book.

20He who testifies to these things says, "Yes, I
am coming soon." Rev 1:2

Amen. Come, Lord Jesus. 1Co 16:22

21The grace of the Lord Jesus be with God's
people. Amen. Ro 16:20

[a] *16* The Greek is plural.

Weights and Measures

	BIBLICAL UNIT		APPROXIMATE AMERICAN EQUIVALENT	APPROXIMATE METRIC EQUIVALENT
WEIGHTS	talent	(60 minas)	75 pounds	34 kilograms
	mina	(50 shekels)	1 1/4 pounds	0.6 kilogram
	shekel	(2 bekas)	2/5 ounce	11.5 grams
	pim	(2/3 shekel)	1/3 ounce	7.6 grams
	beka	(10 gerahs)	1/5 ounce	5.5 grams
	gerah		1/50 ounce	0.6 gram
LENGTH	cubit		18 inches	0.5 meter
	span		9 inches	23 centimeters
	handbreadth		3 inches	8 centimeters
CAPACITY				
Dry Measure	cor [homer]	(10 ephahs)	6 bushels	220 liters
	lethek	(5 ephahs)	3 bushels	110 liters
	ephah	(10 omers)	3/5 bushel	22 liters
	seah	(1/3 ephah)	7 quarts	7.3 liters
	omer	(1/10 ephah)	2 quarts	2 liters
	cab	(1/18 ephah)	1 quart	1 liter
Liquid Measure	bath	(1 ephah)	6 gallons	22 liters
	hin	(1/6 bath)	4 quarts	4 liters
	log	(1/72 bath)	1/3 quart	0.3 liter

The figures of the table are calculated on the basis of a shekel equaling 11.5 grams, a cubit equaling 18 inches and an ephah equaling 22 liters. The quart referred to is either a dry quart (slightly smaller than a liter) or a liquid quart (slightly larger than a liter), whichever is applicable. The ton referred to in the footnotes is the American ton of 2,000 pounds.

This table is based upon the best available information, but it is not intended to be mathematically precise; like the measurement equivalents in the footnotes, it merely gives approximate amounts and distances. Weights and measures differed somewhat at various times and places in the ancient world. There is uncertainty particularly about the ephah and the bath; further discoveries may shed more light on these units of capacity.

About the NIV

THE NEW INTERNATIONAL VERSION is a completely new translation of the Holy Bible made by over a hundred scholars working directly from the best available Hebrew, Aramaic and Greek texts. It had its beginning in 1965 when, after several years of exploratory study by committees from the Christian Reformed Church and the National Association of Evangelicals, a group of scholars met at Palos Heights, Illinois, and concurred in the need for a new translation of the Bible in contemporary English. This group, though not made up of official church representatives, was transdenominational. Its conclusion was endorsed by a large number of leaders from many denominations who met in Chicago in 1966.

Responsibility for the new version was delegated by the Palos Heights group to a self-governing body of fifteen, the Committee on Bible Translation, composed for the most part of biblical scholars from colleges, universities and seminaries. In 1967 the New York Bible Society (now the International Bible Society) generously undertook the financial sponsorship of the project—a sponsorship that made it possible to enlist the help of many distinguished scholars. The fact that participants from the United States, Great Britain, Canada, Australia and New Zealand worked together gave the project its international scope. That they were from many denominations—including Anglican, Assemblies of God, Baptist, Brethren, Christian Reformed, Church of Christ, Evangelical Free, Lutheran, Mennonite, Methodist, Nazarene, Presbyterian, Wesleyan and other churches—helped to safeguard the translation from sectarian bias.

How it was made helps to give the New International Version its distinctiveness. The translation of each book was assigned to a team of scholars. Next, one of the Intermediate Editorial Committees revised the initial translation, with constant reference to the Hebrew, Aramaic or Greek. Their work then went to one of the General Editorial Committees, which checked it in detail and made another thorough revision. This revision in turn was carefully reviewed by the Committee on Bible Translation, which made further changes and then released the final version for publication. In this way the entire Bible underwent three revisions, during each of which the translation was examined for its faithfulness to the original languages and for its English style.

All this involved many thousands of hours of research and discussion regarding the meaning of the texts and the precise way of putting them into English. It may well be that no other translation has been made by a more thorough process of review and revision from committee to committee than this one.

From the beginning of the project, the Committee on Bible Translation held to certain goals for the New International Version: that it would be an accurate translation and one that would have clarity and literary quality and so prove suitable for public and private reading, teaching, preaching, memorizing and liturgical use. The Committee also sought to preserve some measure of continuity with the long tradition of translating the Scriptures into English.

In working toward these goals, the translators were united in their commitment to the authority and infallibility of the Bible as God's Word in written form. They believe that it contains the divine answer to the deepest needs of humanity, that it sheds unique light on our path in a dark world, and that it sets forth the way to our eternal well-being.

The first concern of the translators has been the accuracy of the translation and its fidelity to the thought of the biblical writers. They have weighed the significance of the lexical and grammatical details of the Hebrew, Aramaic and Greek texts. At the same time, they have striven for more than a word-for-word translation. Because thought patterns and syntax differ from language to language, faithful communication of the meaning of the writers of the Bible demands frequent modifications in sentence structure and constant regard for the contextual meanings of words.

A sensitive feeling for style does not always accompany scholarship. Accordingly the Committee on Bible Translation submitted the developing version to a number of stylistic consultants. Two of them read every book of both Old and New Testaments twice—once before and once after the last major revision—and made invaluable suggestions. Samples of the translation were tested for clarity and ease of reading by various kinds of people—young and old, highly educated and less well educated, ministers and laymen.

Concern for clear and natural English—that the New International Version should be idiomatic but not idiosyncratic, contemporary but not dated—motivated the translators and consultants. At the same time, they tried to reflect the differing styles of the biblical writers. In view of the international use of English, the translators sought to avoid obvious Americanisms on the one hand and obvious Anglicisms on the other. A British edition reflects the comparatively few differences of significant idiom and of spelling.

As for the traditional pronouns "thou," "thee" and "thine" in reference to the Deity, the translators judged that to use these archaisms (along with the old verb forms such as "doest," "wouldest" and "hadst") would violate accuracy in translation. Neither Hebrew, Aramaic nor Greek uses special pronouns for the persons of the Godhead. A present-day translation is not enhanced by forms that in the time of the King James Version were used in everyday speech, whether referring to God or man.

For the Old Testament the standard Hebrew text, the Masoretic Text as published in the latest editions of *Biblia Hebraica,* was used throughout. The Dead Sea Scrolls contain material bearing on an earlier stage of the Hebrew text. They were consulted, as were the Samaritan Pentateuch and the ancient scribal traditions relating to textual changes. Sometimes a variant Hebrew reading in the margin of the Masoretic Text was followed instead of the text itself. Such instances, being variants within the Masoretic tradition, are not specified by footnotes. In rare cases, words in the consonantal text were divided differently from the way they appear in the Masoretic Text. Footnotes indicate this. The translators also consulted the more important early versions—the Septuagint; Aquila, Symmachus and Theodotion; the Vulgate; the Syriac Peshitta; the Targums; and for the Psalms the *Juxta Hebraica* of Jerome. Readings from these versions were occasionally followed where the Masoretic Text seemed doubtful and where accepted principles of textual criticism showed that one or more of these textual witnesses appeared to provide the correct reading. Such instances are footnoted. Sometimes vowel letters and vowel signs did not, in the judgment of the translators, represent the correct vowels for the original consonantal text. Accordingly some words were read with a different set of vowels. These instances are usually not indicated by footnotes.

The Greek text used in translating the New Testament was an eclectic one. No other piece of ancient literature has such an abundance of manuscript witnesses as does the New Testament. Where existing manuscripts differ, the translators made their choice of readings according to accepted principles of New Testament textual criticism. Footnotes call attention to places where there was uncertainty about what the original text was. The best current printed texts of the Greek New Testament were used.

There is a sense in which the work of translation is never wholly finished. This applies to all great literature and uniquely so to the Bible. In 1973 the New Testament in the New International Version was published. Since then, suggestions for corrections and revisions have been received from various sources. The Committee on Bible Translation carefully considered the suggestions and adopted a number of them. These were incorporated in the first printing of the entire Bible in 1978. Additional revisions were made by the Committee on Bible Translation in 1983 and appear in printings after that date.

As in other ancient documents, the precise meaning of the biblical texts is sometimes uncertain. This is more often the case with the Hebrew and Aramaic texts than with the Greek text. Although archaeological and linguistic discoveries in this century aid in understanding difficult passages, some uncertainties remain. The more significant of these have been called to the reader's attention in the footnotes.

In regard to the divine name *YHWH,* commonly referred to as the *Tetragrammaton,* the translators adopted the device used in most English versions of rendering that name as "LORD" in capital letters to distinguish it from *Adonai,* another Hebrew word rendered "Lord," for which small letters are used. Wherever the two names stand together in the Old Testament as a compound name of God, they are rendered "Sovereign LORD."

Because for most readers today the phrases "the LORD of hosts" and "God of hosts" have little meaning, this version renders them "the LORD Almighty" and "God Almighty." These renderings convey the sense of the Hebrew, namely, "he who is sovereign over all the 'hosts' (powers) in heaven and on earth, especially over the "hosts" (armies) of Israel." For readers unacquainted with Hebrew this does not make clear the distinction between *Sabaoth* ("hosts" or "Almighty") and *Shaddai* (which can also be translated "Almighty"), but the latter occurs infrequently and is always footnoted. When *Adonai* and *YHWH Sabaoth* occur together, they are rendered "the Lord, the LORD Almighty."

As for other proper nouns, the familiar spellings of the King James Version are generally retained. Names traditionally spelled with "ch," except where it is final, are usually spelled in this translation with "k" or "c," since the biblical languages do not have the sound that "ch" frequently indicates in English—for example, in *chant*. For well-known names such as Zechariah, however, the traditional spelling has been retained. Variation in the spelling of names in the original languages has usually not been indicated. Where a person or place has two or more different names in the Hebrew, Aramaic or Greek texts, the more familiar one has generally been used, with footnotes where needed.

To achieve clarity the translators sometimes supplied words not in the original texts but required by the context. If there was uncertainty about such material, it is enclosed in brackets. Also for the sake of clarity or style, nouns, including some proper nouns, are sometimes substituted for pronouns, and vice versa. And though the Hebrew writers often shifted back and forth between first, second and third personal pronouns without change of antecedent, this translation often makes them uniform, in accordance with English style and without the use of footnotes.

Poetical passages are printed as poetry, that is, with indentation of lines with separate stanzas. These are generally designed to reflect the structure of Hebrew poetry. This poetry is normally characterized by parallelism in balanced lines. Most of the poetry in the Bible is in the Old Testament, and scholars differ regarding the scansion of Hebrew lines. The translators determined the stanza divisions for the most part by analysis of the subject matter. The stanzas therefore serve as poetic paragraphs.

As an aid to the reader, italicized sectional headings are inserted in most of the books. They are not to be regarded as part of the NIV text, are not for oral reading, and are not intended to dictate the interpretation of the sections they head.

The footnotes in this version are of several kinds, most of which need no explanation. Those giving alternative translations begin with "Or" and generally introduce the alternative with the last word preceding it in the text, except when it is a single-word alternative; in poetry quoted in a footnote a slant mark indicates a line division. Footnotes introduced by "Or" do not have uniform significance. In some cases two possible translations were considered to have about equal validity. In other cases, though the translators were convinced that the translation in the text was correct, they judged that another interpretation was possible and of sufficient importance to be represented in a footnote.

In the New Testament, footnotes that refer to uncertainty regarding the original text are introduced by "Some manuscripts" or similar expressions. In the Old Testament, evidence for the reading chosen is given first and evidence for the alternative is added after a semicolon (for example: Septuagint; Hebrew *father*). In such notes the term "Hebrew" refers to the Masoretic Text.

It should be noted that minerals, flora and fauna, architectural details, articles of clothing and jewelry, musical instruments and other articles cannot always be identified with precision. Also measures of capacity in the biblical period are particularly uncertain (see the table of weights and measures following the text).

Like all translations of the Bible, made as they are by imperfect man, this one undoubtedly falls short of its goals. Yet we are grateful to God for the extent to which he has enabled us to realize these goals and for the strength he has given us and our colleagues to complete our task. We offer this version of the Bible to him in whose name and for whose glory it has been made. We pray that it will lead many into a better understanding of the Holy Scriptures and a fuller knowledge of Jesus Christ the incarnate Word, of whom the Scriptures so faithfully testify.

The Committee on Bible Translation

June 1978
(Revised August 1983)

Names of the translators and editors may be secured
from the International Bible Society,
translation sponsors of the New International Version,
1820 Jet Stream Drive, Colorado Springs, Colorado
80921-3696 U.S.A.

Glossary of Doctrinal Terms

One of the most helpful ways to understand the Bible is through a serious study of doctrinal terms. While such a knowledge does not guarantee spiritual success, it does give the Christian a well-grounded orientation to life and a discernment much needed in this day of confusion and error. This glossary can be especially helpful when you come across terms you've never really understood. The definitions are purposely nontechnical, designed to clarify that which can be confusing or misleading. Scripture references have been added to help identify particular terms with a Biblical setting.

Advocate One who counsels or intercedes for the cause of another. Both Jesus Christ and the Holy Spirit are recognized as those who speak on behalf of the believer (John 14:16; Romans 8:26–27; 1 John 2:1).

Agnostic One who believes that the existence of any ultimate reality (such as God) is unknown and probably unknowable. The Greek term *agnostos* appears only in Acts 17:23, where it is rendered "unknown."

Alpha and Omega The first and last letters of the Greek alphabet. This expression appears three times in the New Testament (Revelation 1:8; 21:6; 22:13) and in each case has in mind totality, infinity and/or eternity. The expression is essentially the same as God's words recorded by Isaiah: "I am the first and I am the last; apart from me there is no God" (44:6).

Amen Originally a Hebrew word (Numbers 5:22; Deuteronomy 27:15) meaning "reliable, sure, true," It now signifies one's firm belief, "I believe it," "surely," "yes, indeed!"

Amillennialism The belief that there is no sufficient ground for the expectation of a literal thousand-year reign of Christ upon the earth in the future. This view holds that there will be a general resurrection and judgment of the believers and unbelievers synchronized with the second advent of Christ. Amillennialists believe Christ is now reigning in His kingdom.

Angelology "Angel" is derived from the Greek word *angelos*, meaning "messenger" or "sent one." The angels (Daniel 6:22; Luke 1:19; Hebrews 1:14) are messengers sent from their Master. Angelology is the study of the origin, activity and personality of angels.

Anthropology *Anthropos* means "man, humanity" in Greek. This title refers to the study of humanity.

Anthropomorphism Attributing certain human forms to God; for example, "feet" of God (Exodus 24:10), "hand" of the Lord (Joshua 4:24), "arm" of the Lord (Isaiah 53:1) and "heart" of God (Hosea 11:8).

Anthropopathism Ascribing human feeling or emotion to God; for example, "grief and pain" of God (Genesis 6:6), "anger" of the Lord (Numbers 11:1) and "laughter" of God (Psalm 2:4).

Anti-Semitism Hostility in thought, word or action against the Jews.

Apostasy The act of departing from one's faith; abandonment of belief in the basic doctrines of Christianity and the renunciation of the standards of the faith (2 Thessalonians 2:3; 1 Timothy 4:1; Hebrews 3:12; 2 Peter 3:17).

Ascension The belief that Jesus Christ bodily left the earth forty days after His resurrection, thus ending His earthly ministry until His second advent (Acts 1:1–11). His acceptance into heaven by God the Father verified the Father's satisfaction with the life and death of His Son while He was on earth.

Assurance Confidence that a right relationship exists between oneself and God. Not to be confused with eternal security. See 1 John 5:10–12 for a direct statement of spiritual assurance. See ***Security***.

Atheism The denial of the existence of God. This is a Biblical term used in Ephesians 2:12, translated "without God." It is derived from the Greek: *a* (negative prefix) and *theos* (God).

Atonement An all-inclusive word that describes what Jesus Christ accomplished by His death on the cross. The term as used in the Old Testament translates the Hebrew verb *kaphar* ("to cover") and expresses the idea of covering over an offense by making a payment by blood (Leviticus 16:15–16). The New Testament describes Jesus as "a sacrifice of atonement" (Romans 3:25) and uses the word "redemption" (Romans 3:24; Ephesians 1:7) to cite our deliverance from sin through the ransom payment of Christ's death on the cross (Hebrews 9:11–15).

Atoning Sacrifice The doctrine of the satisfaction of all God's righteous demands for judgment on the sinner by the death of Jesus Christ (Romans 3:25; 1 John 2:2).

Baptism A Christian sacrament symbolizing cleansing from sin (Titus 3:5), and union with Christ and the events of Christ (Romans 6:4).

Believer A person who has received the Lord Jesus Christ as his or her personal Savior (John 1:12; 3:16; Acts 16:31). Synonymous with being a *Christian*.

Bibliology The study of the doctrines related to the Bible.

Blasphemy Taking the name of God on the lips in an empty, vulgar, idle or trifling manner; an irreverent use of God's name in oaths and curses addressed to people or things. In Matthew 12:22–37 Jesus spoke about this issue because the Pharisees attributed the work of God to the devil—a blasphemous accusation.

Canon The collection of Bible books that are recognized as genuine, inspired Holy Scripture. The canon contains the 39 Old Testament books and the 27 books of the New Testament.

Carnal See ***Worldly***.

Christian The title of one who has personally received the Lord Jesus Christ as his or her Savior. A Biblical term, appearing three times in Scripture (Acts 11:26; 26:28; 1 Peter 4:16). One who embraces the teachings of Christ as the basis of his or her faith and practice. Synonymous with *believer*.

Christology "Christ" is at the heart of this term, which refers to the study of the doctrines related to the second Person of the Trinity, the Lord Jesus Christ.

Christophany an appearance of Jesus Christ in bodily form prior to His incarnation. He is most often referred to as "the angel of the LORD" at those times (Genesis 16:7; Judges 13:3; 1 Kings 19:7).

Church Two possible meanings: (1) the *local* assembly established for the purpose of worship, prayer, fellowship, instruction and the administration of the sacraments (Acts 2:42), and (2) the *universal* body of Christ into which all believers become members at the moment of salvation. This universal church began at Pentecost (Acts 2) and will find its culmination when Jesus Christ returns in the clouds for His own (1 Thessalonians 4:13–17). A synonym for the universal church is "the bride of Christ.' (see Ephesians 5:22–27 for this analogy).

Confession (1) With reference to sin in a believer's life, this term has in mind the admission of sins for the purpose of restoring temporal fellowship with the Lord. The believer, technically, does not need to plead for forgiveness from God; rather, he or she simply and openly agrees with God that it is sin and humbly acknowledges it, then claims the forgiveness that is promised in 1 John 1:9. The term comes from a Greek word *homologeo* meaning "to say the same thing." The believer says the same thing about sin that God says, namely, that it *is* sin. (2) With reference to faith, the term describes one's belief and trust in Jesus Christ as Lord (Romans 10:9; Philippians 2:11).

Conversion Turning from evil to God (Acts 14:14; 1 Thessalonians 1:9). Such an act translates people from Satan's power to God's kingdom (Acts 26:18) and involves faith and repentance. See ***Regeneration***.

Covenant A promise or agreement between two parties binding them to undertakings on each other's behalf. God made a covenant with Abraham in Genesis 12:1–3 and with others during Bible times. God also promised a "new covenant" (Jeremiah 31:31–33) sealed by the blood of Jesus (Mark 14:24; 1 Corinthians 11:25).

Creation The doctrine of the miraculous origin of the universe through the power of the Trinity apart from previously existing matter (Genesis 1–2; note "Let us" in Genesis 1:26). The doctrine of creation is also declared in John 1:3; Colossians 1:16–17 and Hebrews 11:3.

Cross The framework of wood on which Christ was crucified (Matthew 27:32–50). At the cross salvation was achieved and the defeat of evil powers accomplished (Colossians 2:17; 1 Peter 2:24; 3:18). It is used symbolically for "denying oneself" in Luke 9:23.

Crown The believer will receive future eternal rewards as tangible evidences of God's satisfaction in his or her earthly life. These rewards are described in the New Testament as "crowns." God blesses the believer with crowns of life (1 Corinthians 9:25; 2 Timothy 2:5; James 1:12; Revelation 2:10), of righteousness (2 Timothy 4:8) and of glory (1 Peter 5:4). Ultimately, the crowns will be cast before the Lord in heavenly worship (Revelation 4:9–11).

Deacon Literally, "servant." One of the categories of leadership within the local church. Most likely, the office of deacon was instituted in Acts 6 when the rapid growth of the church reduced the apostles' ability to devote themselves to prayer and the ministry of the Word (Acts 6:1–7). The qualifications for deacons are declared in 1 Timothy 3:8–13.

Death Though there are several different kinds of deaths mentioned in the Bible (physical, spiritual, a sinful life), the idea of "separation" is prominent in each. Most commonly, the term refers to the separation of the soul/spirit from the body when *physical* death on earth occurs (Genesis 5:5,8,11; John 11:14).

Decalogue A Greek word meaning "Ten Words." Another word for the Ten Commandments (Exodus 20:1–17; Deuteronomy 5:6–21). The first four commandments summarize our devotion to God, and the last six describe our responsibility to other people.

Deity The character or essential nature of God the Father, Son and Holy Spirit.

Demons The company of fallen angels who chose to follow Satan when he was cast out of his heavenly abode in eternity past. They are his personal emissaries who carry out his evil plan on earth until their ultimate judgment and doom. They have the ability to possess animals and people, working havoc in and through the lives of their victims. They energize idolatry, immorality and every form of human wickedness (1 Corinthians 10:20; Revelation 9:20–21), inspire false teachers (1 John 4:1–3) and exercise influential power over governmental leaders in the satanic world system (Daniel 10:13; Ephesians 6:12). Demons exist today, comprising the invisible forces of darkness and wickedness that wage war against the forces of righteousness.

Depravity The effects of sin have touched every aspect of a person's life. The person without Christ is completely dead in his or her spiritual life. Apart from new life through Christ, he or she remains in this condition of spiritual death, unable to understand or experience the value of the work of Christ or the Word of God (Romans 3:22–24; 5:9–11; 1 Corinthians 2:14; Ephesians 2:1–9).

Disciple A pupil, learner or follower. A general term sometimes referring to Jesus' chosen twelve (Matthew 10:1), sometimes to many others who listened to His teachings (but not necessarily believers). All believers, however, can be called disciples in that they are taught by God through the indwelling Holy Spirit. Jesus describes the cost of genuine discipleship in Luke 14:25–33.

Dispensation A period of time on earth in which believers are given the opportunity to fellowship with God through a specified way of life in accordance with certain rules of life, and unbelievers are made aware of their inability to have fellowship with God in themselves. Each dispensation begins with a unique blessing and opportunity, contains a test of obedience and ends in judgment. Grace flows through each dispensation from beginning to end. In *every dispensation*, however, salvation is based on blood and entered into by faith.

Doctrine Derived from the Greek term *didache*, meaning

"to teach." To put it simply, doctrine means "teaching" (John 7:17; Acts 2:42; 2 Timothy 3:16).

Ecclesiology Pronounced "ee-*klee*-zee-ology," it is derived from *ekklesia,* meaning "an assembly, church" (Matthew 16:18; Ephesians 5:23). It is the study of the doctrines pertaining to the universal and the local church.

Ecumenical Worldwide in extent and influence. This term has come to signify a desire for inter-church cooperation. The ecumenical movement has tended to handle differing theological beliefs by calling together denominations for dialogue and pleading for "understanding and openmindedness" among all in attendance. The danger of this movement is Biblical compromise and the elevation of human cooperation beyond proper bounds. The term is a transliterated Greek word from *oikoumena,* meaning "the whole inhabited earth; the world" (Luke 2:1; Acts 17:31; Revelation 3:10).

Elder The title given to those called by God to be overseers in the local, visible church. Qualities expected of an elder are set forth in 1 Timothy 3:1–7 and Titus 1:6–9.

Election The sovereign act of God in choosing the individuals who comprise the select company of saints. This selection was made personally and individually by God before all ages of time (Romans 9:11–13; Ephesians 1:4).

Eschatology Pronounced "*es*-kah-tology." The Greek term *Eschatos* means "last" (2 Timothy 3:1; 1 Peter 1:5). It is the doctrinal study of the last things, future events, prophecies of Scripture.

Eternal Existence without beginning or ending—infinite time.

Evangelist In popular usage it refers to the one who has the divinely given ability to communicate the gospel with effectiveness, ease, pleasure and clarity (Acts 21:8; Ephesians 4:11).

Expiation The removal of the penalty of sin. See ***Atoning Sacrifice***.

Faith The unqualified acceptance of and dependence on the completed work of Jesus Christ to secure God's mercy toward believers. Can refer to saving faith (at the moment of salvation—Ephesians 2:8), Christian doctrines (*the* faith—Colossians 2:7; Jude 3) or to daily reliance, trust and rest in the Lord (Hebrews 11:1,6).

Fatalism The belief that events happen apart from any divine purpose or plan of a sovereign force—God or some other. Often referred to as "blind chance." This belief is opposed to the doctrine of divine providence.

Fellowship The active, intimate, Christ-controlled relationship of a believer to his or her Lord and also to other believers (1 John 1:3–7).

Flesh Our earthly human nature lived apart from divine influence and therefore prone to sin and opposed to God. Same as "the sinful nature" (Romans 7:18; 8:9; Galatians 5:17).

Foreknowledge That which God knows with certainty will come to pass because He has decreed that event (Acts 3:18; 1 Peter 1:2). It has to do not only with *what* will occur but *who* will be involved.

Forgiveness The removal or canceling of charges against a sinner because God's wrath against sin has been satisfied. Matthew 18:21–35 also applies this to relationships between one person and another. It is the solution to resentment and bitterness (Ephesians 4:32).

Fundamentalism System of beliefs in the principles that lie at the heart of Christian truth. Fundamentalists adhere to nine points of doctrine: (1) the inspiration and inerrancy of Holy Scripture, (2) the Trinity, (3) the deity and virgin birth of the Lord Jesus Christ, (4) the literal creation and fall of humanity, (5) the substitutionary atonement of Christ, (6) the bodily resurrection and ascension of Christ, (7) the regeneration of believing sinners, (8) the personal and imminent return of Christ, and (9) the bodily resurrection and assignment of all people to eternal blessedness or eternal punishment.

Gospel The "good news" of the death and resurrection of Jesus Christ on behalf of sinners (1 Corinthians 15:3–4). This "good news" brings great joy (Luke 2:10) because Jesus Christ gave Himself for us (Galatians 1:4) so that we might not die in our sins.

Grace That which God does for humanity through His Son, which we cannot earn, do not deserve and will never merit. It is God's unmerited favor in spite of what is often the rebellious response of humanity. It is summed up in the name, person and work of the Lord Jesus Christ (John 1:14,16; Ephesians 2:8–9; Titus 2:11).

Hades A transliterated Greek word that refers to the abode of the departed souls/spirits of all dead unbelievers, who are awaiting final judgment and eternal punishment in the "lake of fire" (Revelation 20:14). Translated "hell" in Luke 16:23.

Hamartiology Pronounced "*hah*-mar-tiology." *Hamartia* (meaning "sin, error, wrong") comes from the verb *hamartano,* meaning "to miss the mark"—which aptly describes sin. This is the doctrinal study of sin—its causes, categories and consequences.

Heart Biblical word to describe our entire inner being—the seat and source of motives, thoughts, passions and volition (Proverbs 4:23; Jeremiah 17:9, 1 Peter 3:4).

Heaven The future place of dwelling for all believers in Christ. Called "third heaven" and "paradise" in 2 Corinthians 12:1–4.

Hell The place of final, eternal punishment for the wicked (Matthew 18:9).

Hermeneutics The science of Biblical interpretation. See ***Interpretation***.

Holy Separate from sin, pure, sacred, clean. Applied to God, it signifies his separation from and transcendence over all His creation. Applied to humans, it signifies being set apart for God's use and for His glory.

Holy Spirit Third member of the Trinity. Possesses personality and all the attributes of deity. Has functions distinct from the Father and the Son. He came to earth at Pentecost (Acts 2:1–4; 1 Corinthians 12:13) to permanently indwell every believer (1 Corinthians 3:16). The Spirit guides, inspires, reveals and continues the work and ministry of Jesus Christ (John 16:5–15).

Hypostatic Union The unique combination of undiminished deity and true humanity that has existed in the person of Jesus Christ since His incarnation. These two natures existed without confusion or loss of separate identity, and they were inseparably united without transfer of attributes. Christ was (and still is) both God and man, no less God because of His humanity and no less human because of His deity.

Illumination The act of being enlightened with the truths of God's Word. This act is related to the work of the Holy Spirit, who takes the truths of the Bible and helps believers understand their meaning and application (John 16:13; 1 Corinthians 2:9–16).

Immutable Unchangeable. A basic description of God's nature (Malachi 3:6; James 1:17).

Impeccability The sinlessness of Jesus Christ. Because He had no sin nature or imputed sin, He never committed acts of personal sin. The New Testament reveals that He "had no sin" (2 Corinthians 5:21), "was without sin" (Hebrews 4:15) and "committed no sin" (1 Peter 2:22).

Imputation Principal meaning is "reckoning to the account of another." A legal term, it refers to the act of God whereby He credits perfect righteousness to the account of the believing sinner at the moment of salvation. The Bible also speaks of the imputation of Adam's sin to humanity (Romans 5:12–21) and the imputation of humanity's sin to Christ (Isaiah 53:4–6; 2 Corinthians 5:21; 1 Peter 2:24).

Incarnation The act of God the Son taking upon Himself the form of a person and becoming flesh and living on earth (John 1:14; Philippians 2:5–8).

Infallible Apart from error or contradiction. Sure, reliable and exact. Inerrant.

Inspiration The term is translated from a compound Greek word *theopneustos*, literally, "God-breathed" (2 Timothy 3:16). God so supernaturally directed the writers of Scripture that without affecting their literary style, vocabulary, intelligence or personal feelings, His complete message to humanity was recorded with perfect accuracy—the very words of the original manuscripts bearing the authority of divine authorship (2 Peter 1:21).

Interpretation The act of drawing from Scripture its meaning. The interpretation of Scripture is determined by a careful investigation of the context and the normal understanding of each word, taking into consideration the historical background, literary style, grammatical usage and geographical location of the writers. Also known as Biblical exegesis.

Justice The rightness of God's dealings with His creatures, either in approving and rewarding or condemning and judging. God's attitude and acts are based on His righteousness (Psalm 89:14).

Justification The judicial act of God whereby He declares righteous the believing sinner at the moment of salvation (Romans 3:24–28; 5:1).

Kenosis This term is a transliteration of a Greek word found in Philippians 2:7, translated "made himself nothing." It refers to the act of Jesus who, at the moment He became human flesh, surrendered the voluntary use of His divine attributes throughout His earthly life. At the same time, He did not empty himself of His deity. His actions were always under the direct will of the Father, empowered by the Holy Spirit (John 8:29; Hebrews 10:7–9).

Law This term may be used in three different ways: (1) the Ten Commandments God gave to Moses on Mount Sinai (Exodus 20); (2) the Old Testament Scriptures (Psalm 1:2); and (3) the period of time (or dispensation) between the reception of the Law at Mount Sinai and the death of Jesus Christ at Calvary.

Legalism Conforming to a code or system of deeds and observances by human effort, hoping to gain God's blessing and favor by such acts. Legalism invariably denies the principle of GRACE and exalts human PRIDE. The letter to the Galatians was written as a magna charta against such attitudes and practices.

Lord's Supper A sacrament or memorial that signifies the death of Christ. The two elements (bread and juice) represent the body and blood of our Lord. The local church is to observe this memorial regularly and in accordance with Scriptural instruction (1 Corinthians 11:23–34). It is to be offered to all professing believers who have confessed their sins to God (Proverbs 28:13; 1 Corinthians 11:28; 1 John 1:9).

Mediation The work of one who reconciles persons in conflict with one another. Christ is the only Mediator between God and us (1 Timothy 2:5).

Meditate The act of pondering over Scripture and God's mighty deeds, for the purpose of allowing this continued reflection to result in a deeper understanding of that portion (and related portions) of God's blessed Word or of God's powerful actions (Joshua 1:8; Psalm 1:1–3; 143:5).

Messiah Title used throughout Scripture when referring to the Lord Jesus Christ, the "Anointed One," especially with respect to His relationship to Israel (John 1:41; 4:26).

Millennium The Biblical teaching on the millennium is found in Revelation 20:1–10. This particular term is never used in Scripture. It has reference to a literal period of 1,000 years when the Lord Jesus will personally reign as King of kings and Lord of lords over this earth. This will be the time when God's promises to the nation of Israel will be completely and absolutely fulfilled.

Missions One of the primary tasks of the Christian church since its inception has been the proclamation of the gospel to the ends of the earth. This call to worldwide evangelism springs from Matthew 28:18–20 and Acts 1:8. The church's mission is the propagation of the gospel of Jesus Christ to all people across the street, across the states and across the seas.

Monotheism The belief in only one God (Deuteronomy 6:4). Many of Israel's neighbors were polytheists, believing in numerous gods.

Mystery Specific information hidden or withheld in the past but now revealed to believers. Most often has reference to God's plan for the universal church (Ephesians 3:8–10).

Natural Man Term used to refer to the unregenerate who lack the Spirit of God (1 Corinthians 2:14).

Necromancy An attempt to communicate with the spirits of the dead for the purpose of receiving comfort, gaining information or ascertaining knowledge of future events. This practice is condemned in the Bible, since it is connected with demonic influence and/or human deception. (Compare 1 Samuel 28:8–25 with 1 Chronicles 10:13–14.)

Numerology The study of the significance and meaning of numbers in Scripture.

Omnipotence The unlimited and incomparable power of God. He can do all that He wills to perform; nothing is impossible with Him (Matthew 19:26; Luke 1:37; Ephesians 3:20).

Omnipresence God's presence is universal. He is everywhere at once (Psalm 139:7–12; Jeremiah 23:23–24).

Omniscience God's knowledge is eternal and infinite. He knows everything (Psalm 139:1–4).

Ordain Commonly used to refer to appointing or setting individuals apart to a particular calling and service (Exodus 28:41; Titus 1:5).

Ordinance See ***Sacrament***

Parable A short, simple story in narrative form from which a moral or spiritual truth is drawn by comparison. The contents of the parable arise from nature; from the social, domestic or political life of the people; and from events of Biblical times. This method of instruction was used by Jesus frequently in His private ministry (Matthew 13:1–52).

Paraclete A transliterated Greek term used only by John in the New Testament and usually translated "Counselor." Literal meaning is "one called alongside." It refers to the Holy Spirit, our Comforter and Helper (John 14:16,26; 15:26; 16:7), and also to Christ, our Advocate (1 John 2:1).

Paradise Location of the soul/spirit of believers after death (Luke 23:43; 2 Corinthians 12:4). It is now located in the "third heaven" in the very presence of God. See ***Heaven***.

Pentecost A term derived from the Greek *pentecostos*, meaning "fiftieth." It applied to the fiftieth day after the Passover ceremony. On the day of Pentecost the Holy Spirit came in great power and brought into being the universal church (Acts 2). This occurred fifty days after Jesus' resurrection.

Pneumatology The Greek *pneuma* (pronounced "nooma") means "wind, breath, spirit," the most common Greek New Testament word for the Holy Spirit (Matthew 3:16; Luke 11:13; Romans 8:11). This is the study of the third Person of the Trinity, God the Holy Spirit.

Postmillennialism The belief that the world will become increasingly better as the Spirit empowers believers with spiritual strength and authority above the evil powers of the world system, until the "golden age" of the kingdom is ushered in by a great revival of spirituality. Christ's second advent will occur *after* this millennium (hence *post*-millennialism). While once popular, only rarely today do conservative, evangelical Christians hold this belief.

Predestination The belief that God has foreordained all things that come to pass, including the final salvation or reprobation of people (Acts 4:27–28; Romans 8:29–30; Ephesians 1:3–6).

Premillennialism The belief that Jesus Christ will return to earth before the establishment of His kingdom upon the earth. See ***Rapture***.

Propitiation The turning aside of God's righteous anger by Christ's sacrifice (Romans 3:21–26). See ***Atoning Sacrifice***.

Providence The belief that the events of our lives are not ruled by chance or fate but by our sovereign God and loving Lord who works out His plan and purpose in the lives of all His children (Romans 8:28; Ephesians 1:11). It also speaks of God's gracious provision and care for our daily needs (Matthew 6:25–34).

Ransom The price paid by Christ on the cross by which redemption was made possible (Mark 10:45; 1 Timothy 2:6; Hebrews 9:15).

Rapture An aspect of premillennialism. The removal of the universal church (living and dead believers) to meet Jesus in the air at the end of this present era known as the Church Age (1 Corinthians 15:51–55; 1 Thessalonians 4:13–17).

Reconciliation The removal of the barrier of sin between God and humanity by the work of the Lord Jesus Christ on the cross—with the result that no barrier to fellowship with God remains. Humanity is now reconciled to God (2 Corinthians 5:14–21).

Redemption The payment of the price of sin by the sacrifice of Christ whereby He purchased believers out of the slave market of sin and set them free, never to be under the yoke of sin's penalty again (Ephesians 1:7–8).

Regeneration The work of the Holy Spirit in salvation whereby He gives a new life and nature to the believing sinner at conversion (the moment of salvation). The new birth (John 3:1–16) is the beginning of this new nature that becomes a part of the believing sinner the instant he or she receives Christ.

Remission A sending away or passing over of sin, synonymous with forgiveness (Romans 3:25; Hebrews 9:22).

Repentance The act of changing one's inner attitude toward something or someone. From the Greek *metanoeo*, literally, "to change the mind." It encompasses all that is involved in turning *from* sin and turning *to* God (Acts 3:19; 26:20; Romans 2:4).

Resurrection The belief in a bodily rising from the dead and the joining of that body with the soul and spirit. At the time of resurrection, the body will be fashioned anew so as to endure throughout eternity. Jesus' resurrection (Matthew 28:1–10) is essential to the salvation of believers (Romans 4:25). 1 Corinthians 15 is the key chapter in the Bible on resurrection.

Revelation The supernatural act of God whereby He gave His Word to the writers of Holy Scripture (2 Peter 1:20–21). God's inspired, written revelation is now completely contained in His Word. More generally, this can refer to God's making Himself known through nature (Psalm 19:1; Romans 1:18–20).

Sacrament A ceremony instituted by the Lord for public observation and regular participation in the local church. Two sacraments remain for the church to observe: baptism and the Lord's Supper.

Sanctification "Saint," "sanctify" and "holy" all derive from the same Greek root word, *hagiazo*, "to dedicate, separate, set apart, make holy." It is the process of being set apart unto God by the Spirit to grow out of sin and more fully into Christ (2 Thessalonians 2:13; 1 Peter 1:2).

Satan The originator of evil who at first dwelt in the presence of God the Father as the "angel of light" (2 Corinthians 11:14) but who chose to rebel against God. He was cast out of heaven and made his dwelling over this earth, becoming the "god of this age" (2 Corinthians 4:4) and actively participating in leading humanity into sin against God (2 Corinthians 4:3–4). He will ultimately be judged and doomed to eternal punishment along with his myriad of demons (Revelation 20:7–10).

Second Advent The personal return of Jesus Christ to this earth in power, judgment, glory and authority (Matthew 16:27; 25:31–32; 1 Corinthians 4:5; Revelation 19:11–21). According to the premillennial view, this will occur at the end of the tribulation period, prior to the establishment of Christ's earthly kingdom.

Security The doctrine of eternal security is the teaching that once a person has received Christ as his or her Savior he or she is forever secure in God's family—never subject to being lost or rejected. This is based on the character, promises, grace and power of God (John 3:16; 6:37; 10:27–30; Romans 8:38–39; 1 Corinthians 3:15).

Session The doctrine of Christ's position of honor at the right hand of God the Father, sitting in majesty and authority as our Representative (Ephesians 1:20–23; Hebrews 10:12–13).

Soteriology Pronounced "so-*teer*-ee-ology." This comes from the Greek *soter*, meaning "savior, deliverer." After sin entered the world through Adam, there came the need for salvation. This is the study of all doctrines having to do with salvation.

Spiritual Gifts Divinely bestowed abilities given to every believer at the moment of salvation, which enable the believer to perform his or her service in the body of Christ (universal church) so that the body functions with maximum effectiveness (Romans 12:6–8; 1 Corinthians 12; Ephesians 4:11–12; 1 Peter 4:10–11).

Spirituality The lifestyle of the believer who is controlled by and walking in dependence on the Holy Spirit (1 Corinthians 2:15; Galatians 5:25; Ephesians 5:18). The Christian seeks to live all of life under the guidance of God's Spirit.

Temptation Enticement into evil prompted by the world system, the flesh or the devil. God never tempts us (James 1:13–15; 1 John 2:15–17).

Ten Commandments See ***Decalogue***.

Theology Proper *Theology* is derived from two Greek words, *theos* and *logos*, which when combined refer generally to the study of all Christian truth—all the doctrines. By adding *proper* to the title, the subject is narrowed to the study of the first Person of the Trinity, God the Father.

Tongues Reference to one of the spiritual gifts mentioned in the New Testament. Specific guidelines for tongue-speaking and interpretation were given to the Corinthians in 1 Corinthians 14.

Tribulation A period of seven literal years upon the earth (Daniel 9:24–27) following the rapture of the church and ending with the Second Advent of Christ. The events of this era are contained in Revelation 6–19. It will be a time of unprecedented evil, anguish and affliction on earth due to the unrestrained activity of Satan (2 Thessalonians 2:7–10).

Trinity The Godhead, consisting of the Father, the Son and the Holy Spirit, who are one in essence and attributes, yet three in distinct work and purpose. They are coequal, coeternal and coexistent (Matthew 28:19; 2 Corinthians 13:14; 1 Peter 1:2).

Word of God The Bible or Holy Scripture (Luke 24:27; Ephesians 6:17; Hebrews 4:12).

Worldly The term used to describe the fleshly state of a believer who is controlled by his or her sinful nature rather than by the Holy Spirit. While in this state, no eternal rewards are accrued and divine discipline frequently occurs (1 Corinthians 3:1–4).

Worship A human response to divine revelation. More specifically, the act of personal and corporate adoration, love and reverence directed toward God. Worship includes such elements as hearing God's Word, praying, singing, meditating, celebrating the sacraments and bringing gifts. The Book of Psalms directs our attention to God as the only proper focus of our worship (Psalm 95:6–7; 96:9).

Index to Subjects

The Index to Subjects will lead you to key Scripture texts on a wide variety of subjects.

A

B

G

H

S

Index to Living Insights

The Index to Living Insights will lead you to "living insight" notes on a variety of subjects.

NIV Concordance

Word or block entries marked with an asterisk (*) list every verse in the Bible in which the word appears. Words in parentheses after an entry remind the reader to check other forms of that word in locating a passage.

AARON

Genealogy of (Ex 6:16–20; Jos 21:4, 10; 1Ch 6:3–15).

Priesthood of (Ex 28:1; Nu 17; Heb 5:1–4; 7), garments (Ex 28; 39), consecration (Ex 29), ordination (Lev 8).

Spokesman for Moses (Ex 4:14–16, 27–31; 7:1–2). Supported Moses' hands in battle (Ex 17:8–13). Built golden calf (Ex 32; Dt 9:20). Talked against Moses (Nu 12). Priesthood opposed (Nu 16); staff budded (Nu 17). Forbidden to enter land (Nu 20:1–12). Death (Nu 20:22–29; 33:38–39).

ABADDON*

Rev 9:11 whose name in Hebrew is *A*,

ABANDON (ABANDONED)

Dt 4:31 he will not *a* or destroy you
1Ki 6:13 and will not *a* my people Israel."
Ne 9:19 compassion you did not *a* them
9:31 an end to them or *a* them,
Ps 16:10 you will not *a* me to the grave,
Ac 2:27 you will not *a* me to the grave,
1Ti 4:1 in later times some will *a* the faith

ABANDONED (ABANDON)

Ge 24:27 who has not *a* his kindness
2Co 4:9 persecuted, but not *a*; struck down,

ABBA*

Mk 14:36 "*A*, Father," he said, "everything is
Ro 8:15 And by him we cry, "*A*, Father."
Gal 4:6 the Spirit who calls out, "*A*, Father

ABEDNEGO

Deported to Babylon with Daniel (Da 1:1–6). Name changed from Azariah (Da 1:7). Refused defilement by food (Da 1:8–20). Refused idol worship (Da 3:1–12); saved from furnace (Da 3:13–30).

ABEL

Second son of Adam (Ge 4:2). Offered proper sacrifice (Ge 4:4; Heb 11:4). Murdered by Cain (Ge 4:8; Mt 23:35; Lk 11:51; 1Jn 3:12).

ABHOR (ABHORS)

Lev 26:30 of your idols, and I will *a* you.
Dt 7:26 Utterly *a* and detest it,
Ps 26:5 I *a* the assembly of evildoers
119:163 I hate and *a* falsehood
139:21 and *a* those who rise up against you
Am 6:8 "I *a* the pride of Jacob
Ro 2:22 You who *a* idols, do you rob

ABHORS (ABHOR)

Pr 11:1 The LORD *a* dishonest scales,

ABIATHAR

High priest in days of Saul and David (1Sa 22; 2Sa 15; 1Ki 1–2; Mk 2:26). Escaped Saul's slaughter of priests (1Sa 22:18–23). Supported David in Absalom's revolt (2Sa 15:24–29). Supported Adonijah (1Ki 1:7–42); deposed by Solomon (1Ki 2:22–35; cf. 1Sa 2:31–35).

ABIGAIL

1. Sister of David (1Ch 2:16–17).

2. Wife of Nabal (1Sa 25:30); pled for his life with David (1Sa 25:14–35). Became David's wife after Nabal's death (1Sa 25:36–42); bore him Kileab (2Sa 3:3) also known as Daniel (1Ch 3:1).

ABIHU

Son of Aaron (Ex 6:23; 24:1, 9); killed for offering unauthorized fire (Lev 10; Nu 3:2–4; 1Ch 24:1–2).

ABIJAH

1. Second son of Samuel (1Ch 6:28); a corrupt judge (1Sa 8:1–5).

2. An Aaronic priest (1Ch 24:10; Lk 1:5).

3. Son of Jeroboam I of Israel; died as prophesied by Ahijah (1Ki 14:1–18).

4. Son of Rehoboam; king of Judah who fought Jeroboam I attempting to reunite the kingdom (1Ki 14:31–15:8; 2Ch 12:16–14:1; Mt 1:7).

ABILITY (ABLE)

Ex 35:34 tribe of Dan, the *a* to teach others.
Dt 8:18 for it is he who gives you the *a*
Ezr 2:69 According to their *a* they gave
Mt 25:15 one talent, each according to his *a*.
Ac 11:29 disciples, each according to his *a*,
2Co 1:8 far beyond our *a* to endure,
8:3 were able, and even beyond their *a*.

ABIMELECH

1. King of Gerar who took Abraham's wife Sarah, believing her to be his sister (Ge 20). Later made a covenant with Abraham (Ge 21:22–33).

2. King of Gerar who took Isaac's wife Rebekah, believing her to be his sister (Ge 26:1–11). Later made a covenant with Isaac (Ge 26:12–31).

3. Son of Gideon (Jdg 8:31). Attempted to make himself king (Jdg 9).

ABISHAG*

Shunammite virgin; attendant of David in his old age (1Ki 1:1–15; 2:17–22).

ABISHAI

Son of Zeruiah, David's sister (1Sa 26:6; 1Ch 2:16). One of David's chief warriors (1Ch 11:15–21): against Edom (1Ch 18:12–13), Ammon (2Sa 10), Absalom (2Sa 18), Sheba (2Sa 20). Wanted to kill Saul (1Sa 26), killed Abner (2Sa 2:18–27; 3:22–39), wanted to kill Shimei (2Sa 16:5–13; 19:16–23).

ABLE (ABILITY ENABLE ENABLED ENABLES ENABLING)

Nu 14:16 'The LORD was not *a*
1Ch 29:14 that we should be *a* to give
2Ch 2:6 who is *a* to build a temple for him,
Eze 7:19 and gold will not be *a* to save them
Da 3:17 the God we serve is *a* to save us
4:37 walk in pride he is *a* to humble.
Mt 9:28 "Do you believe that I am *a*
Lk 13:24 will try to enter and will not be *a* to
14:30 to build and was not *a* to finish.'
21:15 none of your adversaries will be *a*
21:36 and that you may be *a* to stand
Ac 5:39 you will not be *a* to stop these men;
Ro 8:39 will be *a* to separate us
14:4 for the Lord is *a* to make him stand
16:25 to him who is *a* to establish you
2Co 9:8 God is *a* to make all grace abound
Eph 3:20 him who is *a* to do immeasurably
6:13 you may be *a* to stand your ground,
1Ti 3:2 respectable, hospitable, *a* to teach,
2Ti 1:12 and am convinced that he is *a*
2:24 kind to everyone, *a* to teach,
3:15 which are *a* to make you wise
Heb 2:18 he is *a* to help those who are being
7:25 he is *a* to save completely
Jas 3:2 *a* to keep his whole body in check.
Jude :24 To him who is *a* to keep you
Rev 5:5 He is *a* to open the scroll

ABNER

Cousin of Saul and commander of his army (1Sa 14:50; 17:55–57; 26). Made Ish-Bosheth king after Saul (2Sa 2:8–10), but later defected to David (2Sa 3:6–21). Killed Asahel (2Sa 2:18–32), for which he was killed by Joab and Abishai (2Sa 3:22–39).

ABOLISH (ABOLISHED ABOLISHING)

Hos 2:18 I will *a* from the land,
Mt 5:17 that I have come to *a* the Law

ABOLISHED (ABOLISH)

Gal 5:11 the offense of the cross has been *a*.

ABOLISHING* (ABOLISH)

Eph 2:15 by *a* in his flesh the law

ABOMINATION*

Da 11:31 set up the *a* that causes desolation.
12:11 *a* that causes desolation is set up,
Mt 24:15 the holy place 'the *a* that causes
Mk 13:14 you see 'the *a* that causes

ABOUND (ABOUNDING)

2Co 9:8 able to make all grace *a* to you,
9:8 you will *a* in every good work.
Php 1:9 that your love may *a* more

ABOUNDING (ABOUND)

Ex 34:6 slow to anger, *a* in love
Nu 14:18 *a* in love and forgiving sin
Ne 9:17 slow to anger and *a* in love.
Ps 86:5 *a* in love to all who call to you.
86:15 slow to anger, *a* in love
103:8 slow to anger, *a* in love.
Joel 2:13 slow to anger and *a* in love,
Jnh 4:2 slow to anger and *a* in love,

ABRAHAM

Abram, son of Terah (Ge 11:26–27), husband of Sarah (Ge 11:29).

Covenant relation with the LORD (Ge 12:1–3; 13:14–17; 15; 17; 22:15–18; Ex 2:24; Ne 9:8; Ps 105; Mic 7:20; Lk 1:68–75; Ro 4; Heb 6:13–15).

Called from Ur, via Haran, to Canaan (Ge 12:1; Ac 7:2–4; Heb 11:8–10). Moved to Egypt, nearly lost Sarah to Pharaoh (Ge 12:10–20). Divided the land with Lot; settled in Hebron (Ge 13). Saved Lot from four kings (Ge 14:1–16); blessed by Melchizedek (Ge 14:17–20; Heb 7:1–20). Declared righteous by faith (Ge 15:6; Ro 4:3; Gal 3:6–9). Fathered Ishmael by Hagar (Ge 16).

Name changed from Abram (Ge 17:5; Ne 9:7). Circumcised (Ge 17; Ro 4:9–12). Entertained three visitors (Ge 18); promised a son by Sarah (Ge 18:9–15; 17:16). Questioned destruction of Sodom and Gomorrah (Ge 18:16–33). Moved to Gerar; nearly lost Sarah to Abimelech (Ge 20). Fathered Isaac by Sarah (Ge 21:1–7; Ac 7:8; Heb 11:11–12); sent away Hagar and Ishmael (Ge 21:8–21; Gal 4:22–30). Covenant with Abimelech (Ge 21:22–32). Tested by offering Isaac (Ge 22; Heb 11:17–19; Jas 2:21–24). Sarah died; bought field of Ephron for burial (Ge 23). Secured wife for Isaac (Ge 24). Fathered children by Keturah (Ge 25:1–6; 1Ch 1:32–33). Death (Ge 25:7–11).

Called servant of God (Ge 26:24), friend of God (2Ch 20:7; Isa 41:8; Jas 2:23), prophet (Ge 20:7), father of Israel (Ex 3:15; Isa 51:2; Mt 3:9; Jn 8:39–58).

ABSALOM

Son of David by Maacah (2Sa 3:3; 1Ch 3:2). Killed Amnon for rape of his sister Tamar; banished by David (2Sa 13). Returned to Jerusalem; received by David (2Sa 14). Rebelled against David; seized kingdom (2Sa 15–17). Killed (2Sa 18).

ABSENT

Col 2:5 though I am *a* from you in body,

ABSOLUTE*

1Ti 5:2 women as sisters, with *a* purity.

ABSTAIN (ABSTAINS)

Ex 19:15 *A* from sexual relations."

Nu 6: 3 he must *a* from wine and other
Ac 15:20 them to *a* from food polluted
1Pe 2:11 to *a* from sinful desires,

ABSTAINS* (ABSTAIN)
Ro 14: 6 thanks to God; and he who *a*,

ABUNDANCE (ABUNDANT)
Ge 41:29 Seven years of great *a* are coming
Job 36:31 and provides food in *a*.
Ps 66:12 but you brought us to a place of *a*.
Ecc 5:12 but the *a* of a rich man
Isa 66:11 and delight in her overflowing *a*."
Jer 2:22 and use an *a* of soap,
Mt 13:12 given more, and he will have an *a*.
25:29 given more, and he will have an *a*.
Lk 12:15 consist in the *a* of his possessions."
1Pe 1: 2 Grace and peace be yours in *a*.
2Pe 1: 2 yours in *a* through the knowledge
Jude : 2 peace and love be yours in *a*.

ABUNDANT (ABUNDANCE)
Dt 28:11 will grant you *a* prosperity—
32: 2 like *a* rain on tender plants.
Job 36:28 and *a* showers fall on mankind.
Ps 68: 9 You gave *a* showers, O God;
78:15 gave them water as *a* as the seas;
132: 15 I will bless her with *a* provisions;
145: 7 will celebrate your *a* goodness
Pr 12:11 works his land will have *a* food,
28:19 works his land will have *a* food,
Jer 33: 9 and will tremble at the *a* prosperity
Ro 5:17 who receive God's *a* provision

ABUSIVE
2Ti 3: 2 *a*, disobedient to their parents,

ABYSS*
Lk 8:31 not to order them to go into the *A*.
Rev 9: 1 the key to the shaft of the *A*.
9: 2 When he opened the *A*, smoke rose
9: 2 darkened by the smoke from the *A*.
9:11 king over them the angel of the *A*,
11: 7 up from the *A* will attack them,
17: 8 and will come up out of the *A*
20: 1 having the key to the *A*
20: 3 He threw him into the *A*,

ACCEPT (ACCEPTABLE ACCEPTANCE ACCEPTED ACCEPTS)
Ex 23: 8 "Do not *a* a bribe,
Dt 16:19 Do not *a* a bribe, for a bribe blinds
Job 42: 8 and I will *a* his prayer and not deal
Pr 10: 8 The wise in heart *a* commands,
19:20 Listen to advice and *a* instruction,
Ro 15: 7 *A* one another, then, just
Jas 1:21 humbly *a* the word planted in you,

ACCEPTABLE (ACCEPT)
Pr 21: 3 is more *a* to the LORD

ACCEPTANCE* (ACCEPT)
Ro 11:15 what will their *a* be but life
1Ti 1:15 saying that deserves full *a*:
4: 9 saying that deserves full *a*

ACCEPTED (ACCEPT)
Ge 4: 7 will you not be *a*? But if you do not
Job 42: 9 and the LORD *a* Job's prayer.
Lk 4:24 "no prophet is *a* in his hometown.
Gal 1: 9 you a gospel other than what you *a*,

ACCEPTS (ACCEPT)
Ps 6: 9 the LORD *a* my prayer.
Jn 13:20 whoever *a* anyone I send *a* me;
13:20 whoever *a* me *a* the one who sent

ACCESS
Ro 5: 2 through whom we have gained *a*
Eph 2:18 For through him we both have *a*

ACCOMPANIED (ACCOMPANY)
1Co 10: 4 from the spiritual rock that *a* them,
Jas 2:17 if it is not *a* by action, is dead.

ACCOMPANIES (ACCOMPANY)
2Co 9:13 obedience that *a* your confession

ACCOMPANY (ACCOMPANIED ACCOMPANIES)
Dt 28: 2 *a* you if you obey the LORD your
Mk 16:17 these signs will *a* those who believe
Heb 6: 9 your case—things that *a* salvation.

ACCOMPLISH
Ecc 2: 2 And what does pleasure *a*?"
Isa 44:28 and will *a* all that I please;
Isa 55:11 but will *a* what I desire

ACCORD
Nu 24:13 not do anything of my own *a*,
Jn 10:18 but I lay it down of my own *a*.
12:49 For I did not speak of my own *a*,

ACCOUNT (ACCOUNTABLE)
Ge 2: 4 This is the *a* of the heavens
5: 1 This is the written *a* of Adam's line
6: 9 This is the *a* of Noah.
10: 1 This is the *a* of Shem, Ham
11:10 This is the *a* of Shem.
11:27 This is the *a* of Terah.
25:12 This is the *a* of Abraham's son
25:19 This is the *a* of Abraham's son
36: 1 This is the *a* of Esau (that is, Edom
36: 9 This is the *a* of Esau the father
37: 2 This is the *a* of Jacob.
Mt 12:36 to give *a* on the day of judgment
Lk 16: 2 Give an *a* of your management,
Ro 14:12 each of us will give an *a* of himself
Heb 4:13 of him to whom we must give *a*.

ACCOUNTABLE* (ACCOUNT)
Eze 3:18 and I will hold you *a* for his blood.
3:20 and I will hold you *a* for his blood.
33: 6 but I will hold the watchman *a*
33: 8 and I will hold you *a* for his blood.
34:10 and will hold them *a* for my flock.
Da 6: 2 The satraps were made *a* to them
Jnh 1:14 Do not hold us *a* for killing
Ro 3:19 and the whole world held *a* to God.

ACCURATE
Dt 25:15 You must have *a* and honest
Pr 11: 1 but *a* weights are his delight.

ACCURSED (CURSE)
2Pe 2:14 experts in greed—an *a* brood!

ACCUSATION (ACCUSE)
1Ti 5:19 Do not entertain an *a*

ACCUSATIONS (ACCUSE)
2Pe 2:11 do not bring slanderous *a*

ACCUSE (ACCUSATION ACCUSATIONS ACCUSER ACCUSES ACCUSING)
Pr 3:30 Do not *a* a man for no reason—
Lk 3:14 and don't *a* people falsely—

ACCUSER (ACCUSE)
Jn 5:45 Your *a* is Moses, on whom your
Rev 12:10 For the *a* of our brothers,

ACCUSES (ACCUSE)
Job 40: 2 Let him who *a* God answer him!"
Rev 12:10 who *a* them before our God day

ACCUSING (ACCUSE)
Ro 2:15 and their thoughts now *a*,

ACHAN*

Sin at Jericho caused defeat at Ai; stoned (Jos 7; 22:20; 1Ch 2:7).

ACHE*
Pr 14:13 Even in laughter the heart may *a*,

ACHIEVE
Isa 55:11 *a* the purpose for which I sent it.

ACHISH

King of Gath before whom David feigned insanity (1Sa 21:10–15). Later "ally" of David (2Sa 27–29).

ACKNOWLEDGE (ACKNOWLEDGED ACKNOWLEDGES)
Pr 3: 6 in all your ways *a* him,
Jer 3:13 Only *a* your guilt—
Hos 6: 3 let us press on to *a* him.
Mt 10:32 *a* him before my Father in heaven.
Lk 12: 8 *a* him before the angels of God.
1Jn 4: 3 spirit that does not *a* Jesus is not

ACKNOWLEDGED (ACKNOWLEDGE)
Lk 7:29 *a* that God's way was right,

ACKNOWLEDGES* (ACKNOWLEDGE)
Ps 91:14 for he *a* my name.
Mt 10:32 "Whoever *a* me before men,
Lk 12: 8 whoever *a* me before men,
1Jn 2:23 whoever *a* the Son has the Father
4: 2 Every spirit that *a* that Jesus Christ
4:15 If anyone *a* that Jesus is the Son

ACQUIRES (ACQUIRING)
Pr 18:15 of the discerning *a* knowledge;

ACQUIRING* (ACQUIRES)
Pr 1: 3 for *a* a disciplined and prudent life,

ACQUIT (ACQUITTING)
Ex 23: 7 to death, for I will not *a* the guilty.

ACQUITTING* (ACQUIT)
Dt 25: 1 *a* the innocent and condemning
Pr 17:15 *A* the guilty and condemning

ACT (ACTION ACTIONS ACTIVE ACTIVITY ACTS)
Ps 119:126 It is time for you to *a*, O LORD;

ACTION (ACT)
2Co 9: 2 has stirred most of them to *a*.
Jas 2:17 if it is not accompanied by *a*,
1Pe 1:13 minds for *a*; be self-controlled;

ACTIONS (ACT)
Mt 11:19 wisdom is proved right by her *a*."
Gal 6: 4 Each one should test his own *a*.
Tit 1:16 but by their *a* they deny him.

ACTIVE* (ACT)
Phm : 6 I pray that you may be *a*
Heb 4:12 For the word of God is living and *a*

ACTIVITY (ACT)
Ecc 3: 1 a season for every *a* under heaven:
3:17 for there will be a time for every *a*,

ACTS (ACT)
1Ch 16: 9 tell of all his wonderful *a*.
Ps 71:16 proclaim your mighty *a*,
71:24 tell of your righteous *a*
105: 2 tell of all his wonderful *a*.
106: 2 Who can proclaim the mighty *a*
145: 4 they will tell of your mighty *a*.
145: 12 all men may know of your mighty *a*
150: 2 Praise him for his *a* of power;
Isa 64: 6 all our righteous *a* are like filthy
Mt 6: 1 not to do your '*a* of righteousness'

ADAM

1. First man (Ge 1:26–2:25; Ro 5:14; 1Ti 2:13). Sin of (Ge 3; Hos 6:7; Ro 5:12–21). Children of (Ge 4:1–5:5). Death of (Ge 5:5; Ro 5:12–21; 1Co 15:22).

2. City (Jos 3:16).

ADD (ADDED)
Dt 4: 2 Do not *a* to what I command you
12:32 do not *a* to it or take away from it.
Pr 1: 5 let the wise listen and *a*
9: 9 he will *a* to his learning.
30: 6 Do not *a* to his words,
Mt 6:27 by worrying can *a* a single hour
Lk 12:25 by worrying can *a* a single hour
Rev 22:18 God will *a* to him the plagues

ADDED (ADD)
Ecc 3:14 nothing can be *a* to it and nothing
Ac 2:47 Lord *a* to their number daily those
Ro 5:20 The law was *a* so that the trespass
Gal 3:19 It was *a* because of transgressions

ADDICTED*
Tit 2: 3 to be slanderers or *a* to much wine,

ADMINISTRATION*
1Co 12:28 with gifts of *a*, and those speaking
Eph 3: 2 Surely you have heard about the *a*
3: 9 to everyone the *a* of this mystery,

ADMIRABLE*
Php 4: 8 whatever is lovely, whatever is *a*—

ADMIT
Hos 5:15 until they *a* their guilt.

ADMONISH* (ADMONISHING)
Col 3:16 and *a* one another with all wisdom,
1Th 5:12 you in the Lord and who *a* you.

ADMONISHING* (ADMONISH)
Col 1:28 *a* and teaching everyone

ADONIJAH

1. Son of David by Haggith (2Sa 3:4; 1Ch 3:2). Attempted to be king after David; killed by Solomon's order (1Ki 1–2).

2. Levite; teacher of the Law (2Ch 17:8).

ADOPTED (ADOPTION)
Eph 1: 5 In love he predestined us to be *a*

ADOPTION* (ADOPTED)
Ro 8:23 as we wait eagerly for our *a* as sons,
9:4 Theirs is the *a* as sons; theirs

ADORE*
SS 1:4 How right they are to *a* you!

ADORNMENT* (ADORNS)
1Pe 3:3 should not come from outward *a,*

ADORNS* (ADORNMENT)
Ps 93:5 holiness *a* your house
Isa 61:10 as a bride *a* herself with her jewels.
61:10 bridegroom *a* his head like a priest,

ADULTERER (ADULTERY)
Lev 20:10 both the *a* and the adulteress must
Heb 13:4 for God will judge the *a*

ADULTERERS (ADULTERY)
1Co 6:9 idolaters nor *a* nor male prostitutes
1Ti 1:10 for murderers, for *a* and perverts,

ADULTERESS (ADULTERY)
Hos 3:1 she is loved by another and is an *a.*

ADULTERIES (ADULTERY)
Jer 3:8 sent her away because of all her *a.*

ADULTEROUS (ADULTERY)
Mk 8:38 in this *a* and sinful generation,
Jas 4:4 You *a* people, don't you know that

ADULTERY (ADULTERER ADULTERERS ADULTERESS ADULTERIES ADULTEROUS)
Ex 20:14 "You shall not commit *a.*
Dt 5:18 "You shall not commit *a.*
Mt 5:27 that it was said, 'Do not commit *a.*'
5:28 lustfully has already committed *a*
5:32 the divorced woman commits *a.*
15:19 murder, *a,* sexual immorality, theft
19:9 marries another woman commits *a*
19:18 do not commit *a,* do not steal,
Mk 7:21 theft, murder, *a,* greed, malice,
10:11 marries another woman commits *a*
10:12 another man, she commits *a.*"
10:19 do not commit *a,* do not steal,
Lk 16:18 a divorced woman commits *a.*
16:18 marries another woman commits *a*
18:20 'Do not commit *a,* do not murder,
Jn 8:4 woman was caught in the act of *a.*
Rev 18:3 of the earth committed *a* with her,

ADULTS*
1Co 14:20 but in your thinking be *a.*

ADVANCE (ADVANCED)
Ps 18:29 With your help I can *a*
Php 1:12 has really served to *a* the gospel.

ADVANCED (ADVANCE)
Job 32:7 *a* years should teach wisdom.'

ADVANTAGE
Ex 22:22 "Do not take *a* of a widow
Dt 24:14 Do not take *a* of a hired man who is
Ro 3:1 What *a,* then, is there
2Co 11:20 or exploits you or takes *a* of you
1Th 4:6 should wrong his brother or take *a*

ADVERSITY*
Pr 17:17 and a brother is born for *a.*
Isa 30:20 the Lord gives you the bread of *a*

ADVICE (ADVISERS)
1Ki 12:8 rejected the *a* the elders
12:14 he followed the *a* of the young men
2Ch 10:8 rejected the *a* the elders
Pr 12:5 but the *a* of the wicked is deceitful.
12:15 but a wise man listens to *a.*
19:20 Listen to *a* and accept instruction,
20:18 Make plans by seeking *a;*

ADVISERS (ADVICE)
Pr 11:14 but many *a* make victory sure.

ADVOCATE*
Job 16:19 my *a* is on high.

AFFLICTED (AFFLICTION)
Job 2:7 and *a* Job with painful sores
36:6 but gives the *a* their rights.
Ps 9:12 he does not ignore the cry of the *a.*
9:18 nor the hope of the *a* ever perish.
119:67 Before I was *a* I went astray,
119:71 It was good for me to be *a*
119:75 and in faithfulness you have *a* me.
Isa 49:13 will have compassion on his *a* ones.
53:4 smitten by him, and *a.*
53:7 He was oppressed and *a,*
Na 1:12 Although I have *a* you, ⌞O Judah,⌟

AFFLICTION (AFFLICTED AFFLICTIONS)
Dt 16:3 bread of *a,* because you left Egypt
Ps 107:41 he lifted the needy out of their *a*
Isa 30:20 of adversity and the water of *a,*
48:10 in the furnace of *a.*
La 3:33 For he does not willingly bring *a*
Ro 12:12 patient in *a,* faithful in prayer.

AFFLICTIONS (AFFLICTION)
Col 1:24 lacking in regard to Christ's *a,*

AFRAID (FEAR)
Ge 3:10 and I was *a* because I was naked;
26:24 Do not be *a,* for I am with you;
Ex 2:14 Then Moses was *a* and thought,
3:6 because he was *a* to look at God.
Dt 1:21 Do not be *a;* do not be discouraged
1:29 "Do not be terrified; do not be *a*
20:1 do not be *a* of them,
20:3 Do not be fainthearted or *a;*
2Ki 25:24 "Do not be *a* of the Babylonian
1Ch 13:12 David was *a* of God that day
Ps 27:1 of whom shall I be *a?*
56:3 When I am *a,* / I will trust in you.
56:4 in God I trust; I will not be *a.*
Pr 3:24 lie down, you will not be *a;*
Isa 10:24 do not be *a* of the Assyrians,
12:2 I will trust and not be *a.*
44:8 Do not tremble, do not be *a.*
Jer 1:8 Do not be *a* of them, for I am
Mt 8:26 You of little faith, why are you so *a*
10:28 be *a* of the One who can destroy
10:31 So don't be *a;* you are worth more
Mk 5:36 "Don't be *a;* just believe."
Lk 9:34 and they were *a* as they entered
Jn 14:27 hearts be troubled and do not be *a.*
Ac 27:24 beside me and said, 'Do not be *a,*
Ro 11:20 Do not be arrogant, but be *a.*
Heb 13:6 Lord is my helper; I will not be *a.*

AGAG (AGAGITE)
King of Amalekites not killed by Saul (1Sa 15).

AGAGITE (AGAG)
Est 8:3 to the evil plan of Haman the *A,*

AGED (AGES)
Job 12:12 Is not wisdom found among the *a?*
Pr 17:6 children are a crown to the *a,*

AGES (AGED)
Ro 16:25 the mystery hidden for long *a* past,
Eph 2:7 that in the coming *a* he might show
3:9 which for *a* past was kept hidden
Col 1:26 that has been kept hidden for *a*
Rev 15:3 King of the *a.*

AGONY
Lk 16:24 because I am in *a* in this fire.'
Rev 16:10 Men gnawed their tongues in *a*

AGREE (AGREEMENT AGREES)
Mt 18:19 on earth *a* about anything you ask
Ro 7:16 want to do, I *a* that the law is good.
Php 4:2 with Syntyche to *a* with each other

AGREEMENT (AGREE)
2Co 6:16 What *a* is there between the temple

AGREES* (AGREE)
Ac 7:42 This *a* with what is written
24:14 I believe everything that *a*
1Co 4:17 which *a* with what I teach

AGRIPPA*
Descendant of Herod; king before whom Paul pled his case in Caesarea (Ac 25:13–26:32).

AHAB
1. Son of Omri; king of Israel (1Ki 16:28–22:40), husband of Jezebel (1Ki 16:31). Promoted Baal worship (1Ki 16:31–33); opposed by Elijah (1Ki 17:1; 18; 21), a prophet (1Ki 20:35–43), Micaiah (1Ki 22:1–28). Defeated Ben-Hadad (1Ki 20). Killed for failing to kill Ben-Hadad and for murder of Naboth (1Ki 20:35–21:40).
2. A false prophet (Jer 29:21–22).

AHAZ
1. Son of Jotham; king of Judah, (2Ki 16; 2Ch 28). Idolatry of (2Ki 16:3–4, 10–18; 2Ch 28:1–4, 22–25). Defeated by Aram and Israel (2Ki 16:5–6; 2Ch 28:5–15). Sought help from Assyria rather than the LORD (2Ki 16:7–9; 2Ch 28:16–21; Isa 7).
2. Benjamite, descendant of Saul (1Ch 8:35–36).

AHAZIAH
1. Son of Ahab; king of Israel (1Ki 22:51–2Ki 1:18; 2Ch 20:35–37). Made an unsuccessful alliance with Jehoshaphat of Judah (2Ch 20:35–37). Died for seeking Baal rather than the LORD (2Ki 1).
2. Son of Jehoram; king of Judah (2Ki 8:25–29; 9:14–29), also called Jehoahaz (2Ch 21:17–22:9; 25:23). Killed by Jehu while visiting Joram (2Ki 9:14–29; 2Ch 22:1–9).

AHIJAH
1Sa 14:18 Saul said to *A,* "Bring the ark
1Ki 14:2 *A* the prophet is there—the one

AHIMELECH
1. Priest who helped David in his flight from Saul (1Sa 21–22).
2. One of David's warriors (1Sa 26:6).

AHITHOPHEL
One of David's counselors who sided with Absalom (2Sa 15:12, 31–37; 1Ch 27:33–34); committed suicide when his advice was ignored (2Sa 16:15–17:23).

AI
Jos 7:4 they were routed by the men of *A,*
8:28 So Joshua burned *A* and made it

AID
Isa 38:14 troubled; O Lord, come to my *a!*"
Php 4:16 you sent me *a* again and again

AIM
1Co 7:34 Her *a* is to be devoted to the Lord
2Co 13:11 *A* for perfection, listen

AIR
Mt 8:20 and birds of the *a* have nests,
Lk 9:58 and birds of the *a* have nests,
1Co 9:26 not fight like a man beating the *a.*
14:9 You will just be speaking into the *a*
Eph 2:2 of the ruler of the kingdom of the *a,*
1Th 4:17 clouds to meet the Lord in the *a.*

ALABASTER*
Mt 26:7 came to him with an *a* jar
Mk 14:3 a woman came with an *a* jar
Lk 7:37 she brought an *a* jar of perfume,

ALARM (ALARMED)
2Co 7:11 indignation, what *a,* what longing,

ALARMED (ALARM)
Mk 13:7 and rumors of wars, do not be *a.*
2Th 2:2 not to become easily unsettled or *a*

ALERT*
Jos 8:4 All of you be on the *a.*
Ps 17:11 with eyes *a,* to throw me
Isa 21:7 let him be *a,* / fully *a.*"
Mk 13:33 Be *a!* You do not know
Eph 6:18 be *a* and always keep on praying
1Th 5:6 but let us be *a* and self-controlled.
1Pe 5:8 Be self-controlled and *a.*

ALIEN (ALIENATED ALIENS)
Ex 22:21 "Do not mistreat an *a*
Lev 24:22 are to have the same law for the *a*
Ps 146:9 The LORD watches over the *a*

ALIENATED (ALIEN)
Gal 5:4 by law have been *a* from Christ;
Col 1:21 Once you were *a* from God

ALIENS (ALIEN)
Ex 23:9 know how it feels to be *a,*
1Pe 2:11 as *a* and strangers in the world,

ALIVE (LIVE)
1Sa 2:6 LORD brings death and makes *a;*
Lk 24:23 vision of angels, who said he was *a.*
Ac 1:3 convincing proofs that he was *a.*
Ro 6:11 but *a* to God in Christ Jesus.
1Co 15:22 so in Christ all will be made *a.*
Eph 2:5 made us *a* with Christ

ALMIGHTY (MIGHT)
Ge 17:1 "I am God *A;* walk before me

Ex 6: 3 to Isaac and to Jacob as God *A,*
Ru 1:20 the *A* has made my life very bitter.
Job 11: 7 Can you probe the limits of the *A?*
33: 4 the breath of the *A* gives me life.
Ps 89: 8 O LORD God *A,* who is like you?
91: 1 will rest in the shadow of the *A.*
Isa 6: 3 "Holy, holy, holy is the LORD *A;*
45:13 says the LORD *A."*
47: 4 the LORD *A* is his name—
48: 2 the LORD *A* is his name:
51:15 the LORD *A* is his name.
54: 5 the LORD *A* is his name—
Am 5:14 the LORD God *A* will be with you,
5:15 the LORD God *A* will have mercy
Rev 4: 8 holy is the Lord God *A,* who was,
19: 6 For our Lord God *A* reigns.

ALPHA*
Rev 1: 8 "I am the *A* and the Omega,"
21: 6 I am the *A* and the Omega,
22:13 I am the *A* and the Omega,

ALTAR
Ge 8:20 Then Noah built an *a* to the LORD
12: 7 So he built an *a* there to the LORD
13:18 where he built an *a* to the LORD.
22: 9 Abraham built an *a* there
22: 9 his son Isaac and laid him on the *a,*
26:25 Isaac built an *a* there and called
35: 1 and build an *a* there to God,
Ex 17:15 Moses built an *a* and called it
27: 1 "Build an *a* of acacia wood,
30: 1 "Make an *a* of acacia wood
37:25 They made the *a* of incense out
Dt 27: 5 an *a* to the LORD your God, an *a*
Jos 8:30 on Mount Ebal an *a* to the LORD,
22:10 built an imposing *a* there
Jdg 6:24 So Gideon built an *a* to the LORD
21: 4 the next day the people built an *a*
1Sa 7:17 he built an *a* there to the LORD.
14:35 Then Saul built an *a* to the LORD;
2Sa 24:25 David built an *a* to the LORD
1Ki 12:33 sacrifices on the *a* he had built
13: 2 "O *a, a!* This is what the LORD
16:32 He set up an *a* for Baal
18:30 and he repaired the *a* of the LORD
2Ki 16:11 So Uriah the priest built an *a*
1Ch 21:26 David built an *a* to the LORD
2Ch 4: 1 made a bronze *a* twenty cubits
4:19 the golden *a;* the tables
15: 8 He repaired the *a* of the LORD
32:12 'You must worship before one *a*
33:16 he restored the *a* of the LORD
Ezr 3: 2 to build the *a* of the God of Israel
Isa 6: 6 taken with tongs from the *a.*
Eze 40:47 the *a* was in front of the temple.
Mt 5:23 if you are offering your gift at the *a*
Ac 17:23 found an *a* with this inscription:
Heb 13:10 We have an *a* from which those
Rev 6: 9 I saw under the *a* the souls

ALTER*
Ps 89:34 or *a* what my lips have uttered.

ALWAYS
Dt 15:11 There will *a* be poor people
Ps 16: 8 I have set the LORD *a* before me.
51: 3 and my sin is *a* before me.
Pr 23: 7 who is *a* thinking about the cost.
Mt 26:11 The poor you will *a* have with you,
28:20 And surely I am with you *a,*
Mk 14: 7 The poor you will *a* have with you,
Jn 12: 8 You will *a* have the poor
1Co 13: 7 *a* protects, *a* trusts, *a* hopes, *a*
Php 4: 4 Rejoice in the Lord *a.*
1Pe 3:15 *A* be prepared to give an answer

AMALEKITES
Ex 17: 8 *A* came and attacked the Israelites
1Sa 15: 2 'I will punish the *A*

AMASA
Nephew of David (1Ch 2:17). Commander of Absalom's forces (2Sa 17:24–27). Returned to David (2Sa 19:13). Killed by Joab (2Sa 20:4–13).

AMASSES*
Pr 28: 8 *a* it for another, who will be kind

AMAZED
Mt 7:28 the crowds were *a* at his teaching,
Mk 6: 6 And he was *a* at their lack of faith.
10:24 The disciples were *a* at his words.
Ac 2: 7 Utterly *a,* they asked: "Are not all
Ac 13:12 for he was *a* at the teaching about

AMAZIAH
1. Son of Joash; king of Judah (2Ki 14; 2Ch 25). Defeated Edom (2Ki 14:7; 2Ch 25:5–13); defeated by Israel for worshiping Edom's gods (2Ki 14:8–14; 2Ch 25:14–24).
2. Idolatrous priest who opposed Amos (Am 7:10–17).

AMBASSADOR* (AMBASSADORS)
Eph 6:20 for which I am an *a* in chains.

AMBASSADORS (AMBASSADOR)
2Co 5:20 We are therefore Christ's *a,*

AMBITION*
Ro 15:20 It has always been my *a*
Gal 5:20 fits of rage, selfish *a,* dissensions,
Php 1:17 preach Christ out of selfish *a,*
2: 3 Do nothing out of selfish *a*
1Th 4:11 Make it your *a* to lead a quiet life,
Jas 3:14 and selfish *a* in your hearts,
3:16 where you have envy and selfish *a,*

AMENDS
Pr 14: 9 Fools mock at making *a* for sin,

AMNON
Firstborn of David (2Sa 3:2; 1Ch 3:1). Killed by Absalom for raping his sister Tamar (2Sa 13).

AMON
1. Son of Manasseh; king of Judah (2Ki 21:18–26; 1Ch 3:14; 2Ch 33:21–25).
2. Ruler of Samaria under Ahab (1Ki 22:26; 2Ch 18:25).

AMOS
1. Prophet from Tekoa (Am 1:1; 7:10–17).
2. Ancestor of Jesus (Lk 3:25).

ANAK (ANAKITES)
Nu 13:28 even saw descendants of *A* there.

ANAKITES (ANAK)
Dt 1:28 We even saw the *A* there.'"
2:10 and numerous, and as tall as the *A.*
9: 2 "Who can stand up against the *A?"*

ANANIAS
1. Husband of Sapphira; died for lying to God (Ac 5:1–11).
2. Disciple who baptized Saul (Ac 9:10–19).
3. High priest at Paul's arrest (Ac 22:30–24:1).

ANCESTORS (ANCESTRY)
1Ki 19: 4 I am no better than my *a."*

ANCESTRY (ANCESTORS)
Ro 9: 5 from them is traced the human *a*

ANCHOR
Heb 6:19 We have this hope as an *a*

ANCIENT
Da 7: 9 and the *A* of Days took his seat.
7:13 He approached the *A* of Days
7:22 until the *A* of Days came

ANDREW*
Apostle; brother of Simon Peter (Mt 4:18; 10:2; Mk 1:16–18, 29; 3:18; 13:3; Lk 6:14; Jn 1:35–44; 6:8–9; 12:22; Ac 1:13).

ANGEL (ANGELS ARCHANGEL)
Ge 16: 7 The *a* of the LORD found Hagar
22:11 But the *a* of the LORD called out
Ex 23:20 I am sending an *a* ahead of you
Nu 22:23 When the donkey saw the *a*
Jdg 2: 1 The *a* of the LORD went up
6:22 Gideon realized that it was the *a*
13:15 Manoah said to the *a* of the LORD
2Sa 24:16 The *a* of the LORD was then
1Ki 19: 7 The *a* of the LORD came back
2Ki 19:35 That night the *a* of the LORD went
Ps 34: 7 The *a* of the LORD encamps
Hos 12: 4 He struggled with the *a*
Mt 2:13 an *a* of the Lord appeared
28: 2 for an *a* of the Lord came
Lk 1:26 God sent the *a* Gabriel
2: 9 An *a* of the Lord appeared to them,
22:43 An *a* from heaven appeared to him
Ac 6:15 his face was like the face of an *a.*
12: 7 Suddenly an *a* of the Lord
2Co 11:14 Satan himself masquerades as an *a*
Gal 1: 8 or an *a* from heaven should preach

ANGELS (ANGEL)
Ps 91:11 command his *a* concerning you
Mt 4: 6 command his *a* concerning you,
13:39 of the age, and the harvesters are *a.*
13:49 The *a* will come and separate
18:10 For I tell you that their *a*
25:41 prepared for the devil and his *a.*
Lk 4:10 command his *a* concerning you
20:36 for they are like the *a.*
1Co 6: 3 you not know that we will judge *a?*
13: 1 in the tongues of men and of *a,*
Col 2:18 and the worship of *a* disqualify you
Heb 1: 4 as much superior to the *a*
1: 6 "Let all God's *a* worship him."
1: 7 "He makes his *a* winds,
1:14 Are not all *a* ministering spirits
2: 7 made him a little lower than the *a;*
2: 9 was made a little lower than the *a,*
13: 2 some people have entertained *a*
1Pe 1:12 Even *a* long to look
2Pe 2: 4 For if God did not spare *a*
Jude : 6 *a* who did not keep their positions

ANGER (ANGERED ANGRY)
Ex 15: 7 You unleashed your burning *a;*
22:24 My *a* will be aroused, and I will kill
32:10 alone so that my *a* may burn
32:11 "why should your *a* burn
32:12 Turn from your fierce *a;* relent
32:19 his *a* burned and he threw
34: 6 slow to *a,* abounding in love
Lev 26:28 then in my *a* I will be hostile
Nu 14:18 slow to *a,* abounding in love
25:11 has turned my *a* away
32:10 LORD's *a* was aroused that day
32:13 The LORD's *a* burned
Dt 9:19 I feared the *a* and wrath
29:28 In furious *a* and in great wrath
Jdg 14:19 Burning with *a,* he went up
2Sa 12: 5 David burned with *a*
2Ki 22:13 Great is the LORD's *a* that burns
Ne 9:17 slow to *a* and abounding in love.
Ps 30: 5 For his *a* lasts only a moment,
78:38 Time after time he restrained his *a*
86:15 slow to *a,* abounding in love
90: 7 We are consumed by your *a*
103: 8 slow to *a,* abounding in love.
Pr 15: 1 but a harsh word stirs up *a.*
29:11 A fool gives full vent to his *a,*
30:33 so stirring up *a* produces strife."
Jnh 4: 2 slow to *a* and abounding in love,
Eph 4:26 "In your *a* do not sin": Do not let
Jas 1:20 for man's *a* does not bring about

ANGERED (ANGER)
Pr 22:24 do not associate with one easily *a,*
1Co 13: 5 it is not easily *a,* it keeps no record

ANGRY (ANGER)
Ps 2:12 Kiss the Son, lest he be *a*
95:10 For forty years I was *a*
Pr 29:22 An *a* man stirs up dissension,
Mt 5:22 But I tell you that anyone who is *a*
Jas 1:19 slow to speak and slow to become *a*

ANGUISH
Ps 118: 5 In my *a* I cried to the LORD,
Jer 4:19 Oh, my *a,* my *a!*
Zep 1:15 a day of distress and *a,*
Lk 21:25 nations will be in *a* and perplexity
22:44 in *a,* he prayed more earnestly,
Ro 9: 2 and unceasing *a* in my heart.

ANIMALS
Ge 1:24 wild *a,* each according to its kind."
7:16 The *a* going in were male
Dt 14: 4 These are the *a* you may eat: the ox
Job 12: 7 ask the *a,* and they will teach you,
Isa 43:20 The wild *a* honor me,

ANNOUNCE (ANNOUNCED)
Mt 6: 2 give to the needy, do not *a* it

ANNOUNCED (ANNOUNCE)
Isa 48: 5 before they happened I *a* them
Gal 3: 8 and *a* the gospel in advance

ANNOYANCE*
Pr 12:16 A fool shows his *a* at once,

ANNUAL*
Ex 30:10 This *a* atonement must be made
Jdg 21:19 there is the *a* festival of the LORD
1Sa 1:21 family to offer the *a* sacrifice

1Sa 2:19 husband to offer the *a* sacrifice.
20: 6 an *a* sacrifice is being made there
2Ch 8:13 New Moons and the three *a* feasts
Heb 10: 3 those sacrifices are an *a* reminder

ANOINT (ANOINTED ANOINTING)
Ex 30:26 use it to *a* the Tent of Meeting,
30:30 "*A* Aaron and his sons
1Sa 9:16 *A* him leader over my people Israel
15: 1 to *a* you king over his people Israel;
2Ki 9: 3 what the LORD says: I *a* you king
Ps 23: 5 You *a* my head with oil;
Da 9:24 prophecy and to *a* the most holy.
Jas 5:14 and *a* him with oil in the name

ANOINTED (ANOINT)
1Ch 16:22 "Do not touch my *a* ones;
Ps 105: 15 "Do not touch my *a* ones;
Isa 61: 1 because the LORD has *a* me
Da 9:26 the *A* One will be cut off
Lk 4:18 because he has *a* me
Ac 10:38 how God *a* Jesus of Nazareth

ANOINTING (ANOINT)
Lev 8:12 some of the *a* oil on Aaron's head
1Ch 29:22 *a* him before the LORD to be ruler
Ps 45: 7 by *a* you with the oil of joy.
Heb 1: 9 by *a* you with the oil of joy."
1Jn 2:20 you have an *a* from the Holy One,
2:27 about all things and as that *a* is real,

ANT* (ANTS)
Pr 6: 6 Go to the *a*, you sluggard;

ANTICHRIST* (ANTICHRISTS)
1Jn 2:18 have heard that the *a* is coming,
2:22 a man is the *a*—he denies
4: 3 of the *a*, which you have heard is
2Jn : 7 person is the deceiver and the *a*.

ANTICHRISTS* (ANTICHRIST)
1Jn 2:18 even now many *a* have come.

ANTIOCH
Ac 11:26 were called Christians first at *A*.

ANTS* (ANT)
Pr 30:25 *A* are creatures of little strength,

ANXIETIES* (ANXIOUS)
Lk 21:34 drunkenness and the *a* of life,

ANXIETY (ANXIOUS)
1Pe 5: 7 Cast all your *a* on him

ANXIOUS (ANXIETIES ANXIETY)
Pr 12:25 An *a* heart weighs a man down,
Php 4: 6 Do not be *a* about anything,

APOLLOS*
Christian from Alexandria, learned in the Scriptures; instructed by Aquila and Priscilla (Ac 18:24–28). Ministered at Corinth (Ac 19:1; 1Co 1:12; 3; Tit 3:13).

APOLLYON*
Rev 9:11 is Abaddon, and in Greek, *A*.

APOSTLE (APOSTLES APOSTLES')
Ro 11:13 as I am the *a* to the Gentiles,
1Co 9: 1 Am I not an *a*? Have I not seen
2Co 12:12 The things that mark an *a*—signs,
Gal 2: 8 of Peter as an *a* to the Jews,
1Ti 2: 7 was appointed a herald and an *a*—
2Ti 1:11 I was appointed a herald and an *a*
Heb 3: 1 *a* and high priest whom we confess.

APOSTLES (APOSTLE)
See also Andrew, Bartholomew, James, John, Judas, Matthew, Matthias, Nathanael, Paul, Peter, Philip, Simon, Thaddaeus, Thomas.
Mk 3:14 twelve—designating them *a*—
Lk 11:49 'I will send them prophets and *a*,
Ac 1:26 so he was added to the eleven *a*.
2:43 signs were done by the *a*.
1Co 12:28 God has appointed first of all *a*,
15: 9 For I am the least of the *a*
2Co 11:13 masquerading as *a* of Christ.
Eph 2:20 built on the foundation of the *a*
4:11 It was he who gave some to be *a*,
Rev 21:14 names of the twelve *a* of the Lamb.

APOSTLES' (APOSTLE)
Ac 5: 2 the rest and put it at the *a'* feet.
8:18 at the laying on of the *a'* hands,

APPEAL
Ac 25:11 I *a* to Caesar!" After Festus had
Phm : 9 yet I *a* to you on the basis of love.

APPEAR (APPEARANCE APPEARANCES APPEARED APPEARING APPEARS)
Ge 1: 9 to one place, and let dry ground *a*."
Lev 16: 2 I *a* in the cloud over the atonement
Mt 24:30 of the Son of Man will *a* in the sky,
Mk 13:22 false prophets will *a* and perform
Lk 19:11 of God was going to *a* at once.
2Co 5:10 we must all *a* before the judgment
Col 3: 4 also will *a* with him in glory.
Heb 9:24 now to *a* for us in God's presence.
9:28 and he will *a* a second time,

APPEARANCE (APPEAR)
1Sa 16: 7 Man looks at the outward *a*,
Isa 52:14 his *a* was so disfigured beyond that
53: 2 in his *a* that we should desire him.
Gal 2: 6 God does not judge by external *a*—

APPEARANCES* (APPEAR)
Jn 7:24 Stop judging by mere *a*,

APPEARED (APPEAR)
Nu 14:10 glory of the LORD *a* at the Tent
Mt 1:20 an angel of the Lord *a* to him
Lk 2: 9 An angel of the Lord *a* to them,
1Co 15: 5 and that he *a* to Peter,
Heb 9:26 now he has *a* once for all at the end

APPEARING (APPEAR)
1Ti 6:14 until the *a* of our Lord Jesus Christ,
2Ti 1:10 through the *a* of our Savior,
4: 8 to all who have longed for his *a*.
Tit 2:13 the glorious *a* of our great God

APPEARS (APPEAR)
Mal 3: 2 Who can stand when he *a*?
Col 3: 4 When Christ, who is your life, *a*,
1Pe 5: 4 And when the Chief Shepherd *a*,
1Jn 3: 2 But we know that when he *a*,

APPETITE
Pr 16:26 The laborer's *a* works for him;
Ecc 6: 7 yet his *a* is never satisfied.
Jer 50:19 his *a* will be satisfied

APPLES
Pr 25:11 is like *a* of gold in settings of silver.

APPLY (APPLYING)
Pr 22:17 *a* your heart to what I teach,
23:12 *A* your heart to instruction

APPLYING (APPLY)
Pr 2: 2 and *a* your heart to understanding,

APPOINT (APPOINTED)
Ps 61: 7 *a* your love and faithfulness
1Th 5: 9 For God did not *a* us
Tit 1: 5 and *a* elders in every town,

APPOINTED (APPOINT)
Dt 1:15 *a* them to have authority over you
Pr 8:23 I was *a* from eternity,
Da 11:27 an end will still come at the *a* time.
Hab 2: 3 For the revelation awaits an *a* time;
Jn 15:16 Chose you and *a* you to go
Ro 9: 9 "At the *a* time I will return,

APPROACH (APPROACHING)
Ex 24: 2 but Moses alone is to *a* the LORD;
Eph 3:12 in him we may *a* God with freedom
Heb 4:16 Let us then *a* the throne of grace

APPROACHING (APPROACH)
Heb 10:25 all the more as you see the Day *a*.
1Jn 5:14 is the confidence we have in *a* God:

APPROPRIATE
1Ti 2:10 *a* for women who profess

APPROVAL (APPROVE)
Jdg 18: 6 Your journey has the LORD's *a*."
Jn 6:27 the Father has placed his seal of *a*."
1Co 11:19 to show which of you have God's *a*
Gal 1:10 trying to win the *a* of men,

APPROVE (APPROVAL APPROVED APPROVES)
Ro 2:18 if you know his will and *a*
12: 2 and *a* what God's will is—

APPROVED* (APPROVE)
Ro 14:18 pleasing to God and *a* by men.
16:10 Greet Apelles, tested and *a*
2Co 10:18 who commends himself who is *a*,
1Th 2: 4 as men *a* by God to be entrusted
2Ti 2:15 to present yourself to God as one *a*,

APPROVES* (APPROVE)
Ro 14:22 not condemn himself by what he *a*.

APT*
Pr 15:23 A man finds joy in giving an *a* reply

AQUILA*
Husband of Priscilla; co-worker with Paul, instructor of Apollos (Ac 18; Ro 16:3; 1Co 16:19; 2Ti 4:19).

ARABIA
Gal 1:17 but I went immediately into *A*
4:25 Hagar stands for Mount Sinai in *A*

ARARAT
Ge 8: 4 came to rest on the mountains of *A*.

ARAUNAH
2Sa 24:16 threshing floor of *A* the Jebusite.

ARBITER* (ARBITRATE)
Lk 12:14 who appointed me a judge or an *a*

ARBITRATE* (ARBITER)
Job 9:33 If only there were someone to *a*

ARCHANGEL* (ANGEL)
1Th 4:16 with the voice of the *a*
Jude : 9 *a* Michael, when he was disputing

ARCHER
Pr 26:10 Like an *a* who wounds at random

ARCHIPPUS*
Col 4:17 Tell *A*: "See to it that you complete
Phm : 2 to *A* our fellow soldier

ARCHITECT*
Heb 11:10 whose *a* and builder is God.

AREOPAGUS*
Ac 17:19 brought him to a meeting of the *A*,
17:22 up in the meeting of the *A*
17:34 of the *A*, also a woman named

ARGUE (ARGUMENT ARGUMENTS)
Job 13: 3 and to *a* my case with God.
13: 8 Will you *a* the case for God?
Pr 25: 9 If you *a* your case with a neighbor,

ARGUMENT (ARGUE)
Heb 6:16 is said and puts an end to all *a*.

ARGUMENTS (ARGUE)
Isa 41:21 "Set forth your *a*," says Jacob's
Col 2: 4 you by fine-sounding *a*.
2Ti 2:23 to do with foolish and stupid *a*,
Tit 3: 9 and *a* and quarrels about the law,

ARK
Ge 6:14 So make yourself an *a*
Ex 25:21 and put in the *a* the Testimony,
Dt 10: 5 put the tablets in the *a* I had made,
1Sa 4:11 The *a* of God was captured,
7: 2 that the *a* remained at Kiriath
2Sa 6:17 They brought the *a* of the LORD
1Ki 8: 9 There was nothing in the *a*
1Ch 13: 9 out his hand to steady the *a*,
2Ch 35: 3 "Put the sacred *a* in the temple that
Heb 9: 4 This *a* contained the gold jar
11: 7 in holy fear built an *a*
Rev 11:19 within his temple was seen the *a*

ARM (ARMY)
Nu 11:23 "Is the LORD's *a* too short?
Dt 4:34 hand and an outstretched *a*,
7:19 mighty hand and outstretched *a*,
Ps 44: 3 it was your right hand, your *a*,
98: 1 his right hand and his holy *a*
Jer 27: 5 outstretched *a* I made the earth
1Pe 4: 1 *a* yourselves also with the same

ARMAGEDDON*
Rev 16:16 that in Hebrew is called *A*.

ARMIES (ARMY)
1Sa 17:26 Philistine that he should defy the *a*
Rev 19:14 *a* of heaven were following him,

ARMOR (ARMY)
1Ki 20:11 on his *a* should not boast like one
Jer 46: 4 put on your *a*!
Ro 13:12 deeds of darkness and put on the *a*
Eph 6:11 Put on the full *a* of God
6:13 Therefore put on the full *a* of God,

ARMS (ARMY)
Dt 33:27 underneath are the everlasting *a.*
Ps 18:32 It is God who *a* me with strength
Pr 31:17 her *a* are strong for her tasks.
31:20 She opens her *a* to the poor
Isa 40:11 He gathers the lambs in his *a*
Mk 10:16 And he took the children in his *a,*
Heb 12:12 strengthen your feeble *a*

ARMY (ARM ARMIES ARMOR ARMS)
Ps 33:16 No king is saved by the size of his *a*
Joel 2: 2 a large and mighty *a* comes,
2: 5 like a mighty *a* drawn up for battle.
2:11 thunders at the head of his *a;*
Rev 19:19 the rider on the horse and his *a.*

AROMA
Ge 8:21 The LORD smelled the pleasing *a*
Ex 29:18 a pleasing *a,* an offering made
Lev 3:16 made by fire, a pleasing *a.*
2Co 2:15 For we are to God the *a* of Christ

AROUSE (AROUSED)
Ro 11:14 I may somehow *a* my own people

AROUSED (AROUSE)
Ps 78:58 they *a* his jealousy with their idols.

ARRANGED
1Co 12:18 But in fact God has *a* the parts

ARRAYED*
Ps 110: 3 *A* in holy majesty,
Isa 61:10 and *a* me in a robe of righteousness

ARREST
Mt 10:19 But when they *a* you, do not worry

ARROGANCE (ARROGANT)
1Sa 2: 3 or let your mouth speak such *a,*
Pr 8:13 I hate pride and *a,*
Mk 7:22 lewdness, envy, slander, *a* and folly
2Co 12:20 slander, gossip, *a* and disorder.

ARROGANT (ARROGANCE)
Ps 5: 5 The *a* cannot stand
119: 78 May the *a* be put to shame
Pr 17: 7 *A* lips are unsuited to a fool—
21:24 *a* man—"Mocker" is his name;
Ro 1:30 God-haters, insolent, *a;*
11:20 Do not be *a,* but be afraid.
1Ti 6:17 in this present world not to be *a*

ARROW (ARROWS)
Ps 91: 5 nor the *a* that flies by day,
Pr 25:18 Like a club or a sword or a sharp *a*

ARROWS (ARROW)
Ps 64: 3 and aim their words like deadly *a.*
64: 7 But God will shoot them with *a;*
127: 4 Like *a* in the hands of a warrior
Pr 26:18 firebrands or deadly *a*
Eph 6:16 you can extinguish all the flaming *a*

ARTAXERXES
King of Persia; allowed rebuilding of temple under Ezra (Ezr 4; 7), and of walls of Jerusalem under his cupbearer Nehemiah (Ne 2; 5:14; 13:6).

ARTEMIS
Ac 19:28 "Great is *A* of the Ephesians!"

ASA
King of Judah (1Ki 15:8–24; 1Ch 3:10; 2Ch 14–16). Godly reformer (2Ch 15); in later years defeated Israel with help of Aram, not the LORD (1Ki 15:16–22; 2Ch 16).

ASAHEL
1. Nephew of David, one of his warriors (2Sa 23:24; 1Ch 2:16; 11:26; 27:7). Killed by Abner (2Sa 2); avenged by Joab (2Sa 3:22–39).
2. Levite; teacher (2Ch 17:8).

ASAPH
1. Recorder to Hezekiah (2Ki 18:18, 37; Isa 36:3, 22).
2. Levitical musician (1Ch 6:39; 15:17–19; 16:4–7, 37). Sons of (1Ch 25; 2Ch 5:12; 20:14; 29:13; 35:15; Ezr 2:41; 3:10; Ne 7:44; 11:17; 12:27–47). Psalms of (2Ch 29:30; Ps 50; 73–83).

ASCEND* (ASCENDED ASCENDING)
Dt 30:12 "Who will *a* into heaven to get it
Ps 24: 3 Who may *a* the hill of the LORD?
Isa 14:13 "I will *a* to heaven;
14:14 I will *a* above the tops of the clouds
Jn 6:62 of Man *a* to where he was before!
Ac 2:34 For David did not *a* to heaven,
Ro 10: 6 'Who will *a* into heaven?' " (that is,

ASCENDED (ASCEND)
Ps 68:18 When you *a* on high,
Eph 4: 8 "When he *a* on high,

ASCENDING (ASCEND)
Ge 28:12 and the angels of God were *a*
Jn 1:51 and the angels of God *a*

ASCRIBE*
1Ch 16:28 *A* to the LORD, O families
16:28 *a* to the LORD glory and strength,
16:29 *a* to the LORD the glory due his
Job 36: 3 I will *a* justice to my Maker.
Ps 29: 1 *A* to the LORD, O mighty ones,
29: 1 *a* to the LORD glory and strength.
29: 2 *A* to the LORD the glory due his
96: 7 *A* to the LORD, O families
96: 7 *a* to the LORD glory and strength.
96: 8 *A* to the LORD the glory due his

ASHAMED (SHAME)
Mk 8:38 If anyone is *a* of me and my words
Lk 9:26 If anyone is *a* of me and my words,
Ro 1:16 I am not *a* of the gospel,
2Ti 1: 8 So do not be *a* to testify about our
2:15 who does not need to be *a*

ASHER
Son of Jacob by Zilpah (Ge 30:13; 35:26; 46:17; Ex 1:4; 1Ch 2:2). Tribe of blessed (Ge 49:20; Dt 33:24–25), numbered (Nu 1:40–41; 26:44–47), allotted land (Jos 10:24–31; Eze 48:2), failed to fully possess (Jdg 1:31–32), failed to support Deborah (Jdg 5:17), supported Gideon (Jdg 6:35; 7:23) and David (1Ch 12:36), 12,000 from (Rev 7:6).

ASHERAH (ASHERAHS)
Ex 34:13 and cut down their *A* poles.
1Ki 18:19 the four hundred prophets of *A,*

ASHERAHS* (ASHERAH)
Jdg 3: 7 and served the Baals and the *A.*

ASHES
Job 42: 6 and repent in dust and *a."*
Mt 11:21 ago in sackcloth and *a.*

ASHTORETHS
Jdg 2:13 and served Baal and the *A.*
1Sa 7: 4 put away their Baals and *A,*

ASLEEP (SLEEP)
1Co 15:18 who have fallen *a* in Christ are lost.
1Th 4:13 be ignorant about those who fall *a,*

ASSEMBLY
Ps 1: 5 nor sinners in the *a* of the righteous
35:18 I will give you thanks in the great *a*
82: 1 God presides in the great *a;*
149: 1 his praise in the *a* of the saints.

ASSIGNED
1Ki 7:14 and did all the work *a* to him.
Mk 13:34 with his *a* task, and tells the one
1Co 3: 5 as the Lord has *a* to each his task.
7:17 place in life that the Lord *a* to him
2Co 10:13 to the field God has *a* to us,

ASSOCIATE
Pr 22:24 do not *a* with one easily angered,
Jn 4: 9 (For Jews do not *a* with Samaritans
Ac 10:28 law for a Jew to *a* with a Gentile
Ro 12:16 but be willing to *a* with people
1Co 5: 9 to *a* with sexually immoral people
5:11 am writing you that you must not *a*
2Th 3:14 Do not *a* with him,

ASSURANCE (ASSURED)
Heb 10:22 with a sincere heart in full *a* of faith

ASSURED (ASSURANCE)
Col 4:12 the will of God, mature and fully *a.*

ASTRAY
Ps 119: 67 Before I was afflicted I went *a,*
Pr 10:17 ignores correction leads others *a.*
20: 1 whoever is led *a* by them is not
Isa 53: 6 We all, like sheep, have gone *a,*
Jer 50: 6 their shepherds have led them *a*
Jn 16: 1 you so that you will not go *a.*
1Pe 2:25 For you were like sheep going *a,*
1Jn 3: 7 do not let anyone lead you *a.*

ASTROLOGERS
Isa 47:13 Let your *a* come forward,
Da 2: 2 *a* to tell him what he had dreamed.

ATE (EAT)
Ge 3: 6 wisdom, she took some and *a* it.
27:25 Jacob brought it to him and he *a;*
2Sa 9:11 Mephibosheth *a* at David's table
Ps 78:25 Men *a* the bread of angels;
Jer 15:16 When your words came, I *a* them;
Eze 3: 3 So I *a* it, and it tasted as sweet
Mt 14:20 They all *a* and were satisfied,
15:37 They all *a* and were satisfied.
Mk 6:42 They all *a* and were satisfied,
Lk 9:17 They all *a* and were satisfied,

ATHALIAH
Granddaughter of Omri; wife of Jehoram and mother of Ahaziah; encouraged their evil ways (2Ki 8:18, 27; 2Ch 22:2). At death of Ahaziah she made herself queen, killing all his sons but Joash (2Ki 11:1–3; 2Ch 22:10–12); killed six years later when Joash was revealed (2Ki 11:4–16; 2Ch 23:1–15).

ATHLETE*
2Ti 2: 5 if anyone competes as an *a,*

ATONE* (ATONEMENT)
Ex 30:15 to the LORD to *a* for your lives.
2Ch 29:24 for a sin offering to *a* for all Israel,
Da 9:24 an end to sin, to *a* for wickedness,

ATONED* (ATONEMENT)
Dt 21: 8 And the bloodshed will be *a* for.
1Sa 3:14 guilt of Eli's house will never be *a*
Pr 16: 6 faithfulness sin is *a* for;
Isa 6: 7 guilt is taken away and your sin *a*
22:14 your dying day this sin will not be *a*
27: 9 then, will Jacob's guilt be *a* for,

ATONEMENT (ATONE ATONED)
Ex 25:17 "Make an *a* cover of pure gold—
30:10 Once a year Aaron shall make *a*
Lev 17:11 it is the blood that makes *a*
23:27 this seventh month is the Day of *A.*
Nu 25:13 and made *a* for the Israelites."
Ro 3:25 presented him as a sacrifice of *a,*
Heb 2:17 that he might make *a* for the sins

ATTACK
Ps 109: 3 they *a* me without cause.

ATTAINED
Php 3:16 up to what we have already *a.*
Heb 7:11 If perfection could have been *a*

ATTENTION (ATTENTIVE)
Pr 4: 1 pay *a* and gain understanding.
4:20 My son, pay *a* to what I say;
5: 1 My son, pay *a* to my wisdom,
7:24 pay *a* to what I say.
22:17 Pay *a* and listen to the sayings
Ecc 7:21 Do not pay *a* to every word people
Isa 42:20 many things, but have paid no *a;*
Tit 1:14 and will pay no *a* to Jewish myths
Heb 2: 1 We must pay more careful *a,*

ATTENTIVE (ATTENTION)
Ne 1:11 let your ear be *a* to the prayer
1Pe 3:12 and his ears are *a* to their prayer,

ATTITUDE (ATTITUDES)
Eph 4:23 new in the *a* of your minds;
Php 2: 5 Your *a* should be the same
1Pe 4: 1 yourselves also with the same *a,*

ATTITUDES (ATTITUDE)
Heb 4:12 it judges the thoughts and *a*

ATTRACTIVE
Tit 2:10 teaching about God our Savior *a.*

AUDIENCE
Pr 29:26 Many seek an *a* with a ruler,

AUTHORITIES (AUTHORITY)
Ro 13: 1 *a* that exist have been established
13: 5 it is necessary to submit to the *a,*
13: 6 for the *a* are God's servants,
Eph 3:10 and *a* in the heavenly realms,
6:12 but against the rulers, against the *a,*
Col 1:16 thrones or powers or rulers or *a;*
2:15 having disarmed the powers and *a,*
Tit 3: 1 people to be subject to rulers and *a,*
1Pe 3:22 *a* and powers in submission to him.

AUTHORITY (AUTHORITIES)
Mt 7:29 because he taught as one who had *a*
9:6 the Son of Man has *a* on earth
28:18 "All *a* in heaven and on earth has
Mk 1:22 he taught them as one who had *a*,
2:10 the Son of Man has *a* on earth
Lk 4:32 because his message had *a*.
5:24 the Son of Man has *a* on earth
Jn 10:18 *a* to lay it down and *a*
Ac 1:7 the Father has set by his own *a*.
Ro 7:1 that the law has *a* over a man only
13:1 for there is no *a* except that which
13:2 rebels against the *a* is rebelling
1Co 11:10 to have a sign of *a* on her head.
15:24 he has destroyed all dominion, *a*
1Ti 2:2 for kings and all those in *a*,
2:12 to teach or to have *a* over a man;
Tit 2:15 Encourage and rebuke with all *a*.
Heb 13:17 your leaders and submit to their *a*.

AUTUMN*
Dt 11:14 both *a* and spring rains,
Ps 84:6 the *a* rains also cover it with pools.
Jer 5:24 who gives *a* and spring rains
Joel 2:23 both *a* and spring rains, as before.
Jas 5:7 and how patient he is for the *a*
Jude :12 blown along by the wind; *a* trees,

AVENGE (VENGEANCE)
Lev 26:25 sword upon you to *a* the breaking
Dt 32:35 It is mine to *a*; I will repay.
32:43 for he will *a* the blood
Ro 12:19 "It is mine to *a*; I will repay,"
Heb 10:30 "It is mine to *a*; I will repay,"
Rev 6:10 of the earth and *a* our blood?"

AVENGER (VENGEANCE)
Nu 35:27 the *a* of blood may kill the accused
Jos 20:3 find protection from the *a* of blood.
Ps 8:2 to silence the foe and the *a*.

AVENGES (VENGEANCE)
Ps 94:1 O LORD, the God who *a*,

AVENGING (VENGEANCE)
1Sa 25:26 and from *a* yourself with your own
Na 1:2 The LORD is a jealous and *a* God;

AVOID (AVOIDS)
Pr 4:15 *A* it, do not travel on it;
20:3 It is to a man's honor to *a* strife,
20:19 so *a* a man who talks too much.
Ecc 7:18 who fears God will *a* all ⌊extremes⌋.
1Th 4:3 you should *a* sexual immorality;
5:22 *A* every kind of evil.
2Ti 2:16 *A* godless chatter, because those
Tit 3:9 But *a* foolish controversies

AVOIDS* (AVOID)
Pr 16:6 of the LORD a man *a* evil.
16:17 The highway of the upright *a* evil;

AWAITS (WAIT)
Pr 15:10 Stern discipline *a* him who leaves
28:22 and is unaware that poverty *a* him.

AWAKE (WAKE)
Ps 17:15 when I *a*, I will be satisfied
Pr 6:22 when you *a*, they will speak to you.

AWARD*
2Ti 4:8 will *a* to me on that day—

AWARE
Ex 34:29 he was not *a* that his face was
Mt 24:50 and at an hour he is not *a* of.
Lk 12:46 and at an hour he is not *a* of.

AWE* (AWESOME OVERAWED)
1Sa 12:18 So all the people stood in *a*
1Ki 3:28 they held the king in *a*,
Job 25:2 "Dominion and *a* belong to God;
Ps 119:120 I stand in *a* of your laws.
Ecc 5:7 Therefore stand in *a* of God.
Isa 29:23 will stand in *a* of the God of Israel.
Jer 2:19 and have no *a* of me,"
33:9 they will be in *a* and will tremble
Hab 3:2 I stand in *a* of your deeds,
Mal 2:5 and stood in *a* of my name.
Mt 9:8 they were filled with *a*;
Lk 1:65 The neighbors were all filled with *a*
5:26 They were filled with *a* and said,
7:16 They were all filled with *a*
Ac 2:43 Everyone was filled with *a*,
Heb 12:28 acceptably with reverence and *a*,

AWESOME* (AWE)
Ge 28:17 and said, "How *a* is this place!
Ex 15:11 *a* in glory,
34:10 among will see how *a* is the work
Dt 4:34 or by great and *a* deeds,
7:21 is among you, is a great and *a* God.
10:17 the great God, mighty and *a*,
10:21 and *a* wonders you saw
28:58 revere this glorious and *a* name—
34:12 performed the *a* deeds that Moses
Jdg 13:6 like an angel of God, very *a*.
2Sa 7:23 *a* wonders by driving out nations
1Ch 17:21 *a* wonders by driving out nations
Ne 1:5 of heaven, the great and *a* God,
4:14 and *a*, and fight for your brothers,
9:32 the great, mighty and *a* God,
Job 10:16 again display your *a* power
37:22 God comes in *a* majesty.
Ps 45:4 let your right hand display *a* deeds.
47:2 How *a* is the LORD Most High,
65:5 us with *a* deeds of righteousness,
66:3 to God, "How *a* are your deeds!
66:5 how *a* his works in man's behalf!
68:35 You are *a*, O God,
89:7 he is more *a* than all who surround
99:3 praise your great and *a* name—
106:22 and *a* deeds by the Red Sea.
111:9 holy and *a* is his name.
145:6 of the power of your *a* works,
Isa 64:3 when you did *a* things that we did
Eze 1:18 Their rims were high and *a*,
1:22 expanse, sparkling like ice, and *a*.
Da 2:31 dazzling statue, *a* in appearance.
9:4 "O Lord, the great and *a* God,
Zep 2:11 The LORD will be *a* to them

AX
Mt 3:10 The *a* is already at the root
Lk 3:9 The *a* is already at the root

BAAL
Jdg 6:25 Tear down your father's altar to *B*
1Ki 16:32 *B* in the temple of *B* that he built
18:25 Elijah said to the prophets of *B*,
19:18 knees have not bowed down to *B*
2Ki 10:28 Jehu destroyed *B* worship in Israel.
Jer 19:5 places of *B* to burn their sons
Ro 11:4 have not bowed the knee to *B*."

BAASHA
King of Israel (1Ki 15:16–16:7; 2Ch 16:1–6).

BABBLER* (BABBLING)
Ac 17:18 "What is this *b* trying to say?"

BABBLING* (BABBLER)
Mt 6:7 do not keep on *b* like pagans,

BABIES* (BABY)
Ge 25:22 The *b* jostled each other within her
Ex 2:6 "This is one of the Hebrew *b*,"
Lk 18:15 also bringing *b* to Jesus
Ac 7:19 them to throw out their newborn *b*
1Pe 2:2 Like newborn *b*, crave pure

BABY* (BABIES BABY'S)
Ex 2:6 She opened it and saw the *b*.
2:7 women to nurse the *b* for you?"
2:9 So the woman took the *b*
2:9 "Take this *b* and nurse him for me,
1Ki 3:17 I had a *b* while she was there
3:18 was born, this woman also had a *b*.
3:26 give her the living *b*! Don't kill him
3:27 Give the living *b* to the first woman
Isa 49:15 "Can a mother forget the *b*
Lk 1:41 the *b* leaped in her womb,
1:44 the *b* in my womb leaped for joy.
1:57 time for Elizabeth to have her *b*,
2:6 the time came for the *b* to be born,
2:12 You will find a *b* wrapped in strips
2:16 the *b*, who was lying in the manger.
Jn 16:21 but when her *b* is born she forgets

BABY'S* (BABY)
Ex 2:8 the girl went and got the *b* mother.

BABYLON
Ps 137:1 By the rivers of *B* we sat and wept
Jer 29:10 seventy years are completed for *B*,
51:37 *B* will be a heap of ruins,
Rev 14:8 "Fallen! Fallen is *B* the Great,
17:5 MYSTERY *B* THE GREAT

BACKS
2Pe 2:21 and then to turn their *b*

BACKSLIDING* (BACKSLIDINGS)
Jer 2:19 your *b* will rebuke you.
3:22 I will cure you of *b*."
14:7 For our *b* is great;
15:6 "You keep on *b*.
Eze 37:23 them from all their sinful *b*,

BACKSLIDINGS* (BACKSLIDING)
Jer 5:6 and their *b* many.

BALAAM
Prophet who attempted to curse Israel (Nu 22–24; Dt 23:4–5; 2Pe 2:15; Jude 11). Killed in Israel's vengeance on Midianites (Nu 31:8; Jos 13:22).

BALAK
Moabite king who hired Balaam to curse Israel (Nu 22–24; Jos 24:9).

BALDHEAD
2Ki 2:23 "Go on up, you *b*!" they said.

BALM
Jer 8:22 Is there no *b* in Gilead?

BANISH (BANISHED)
Jer 25:10 I will *b* from them the sounds of joy

BANISHED (BANISH)
Dt 30:4 Even if you have been *b*

BANNER
Ex 17:15 and called it The LORD is my *B*.
SS 2:4 and his *b* over me is love.
Isa 11:10 the Root of Jesse will stand as a *b*

BANQUET
SS 2:4 He has taken me to the *b* hall,
Lk 14:13 when you give a *b*, invite the poor,

BAPTISM* (BAPTIZE)
Mt 21:25 John's *b*—where did it come from?
Mk 1:4 and preaching a *b* of repentance
10:38 baptized with the *b* I am baptized
10:39 baptized with the *b* I am baptized
11:30 John's *b*—was it from heaven,
Lk 3:3 preaching a *b* of repentance
12:50 But I have a *b* to undergo,
20:4 John's *b*—was it from heaven,
Ac 1:22 beginning from John's *b*
10:37 after the *b* that John preached—
13:24 and *b* to all the people of Israel.
18:25 though he knew only the *b* of John.
19:3 did you receive?" "John's *b*,"
19:3 "Then what *b* did you receive?"
19:4 "John's *b* was a *b* of repentance.
Ro 6:4 with him through *b* into death
Eph 4:5 one Lord, one faith, one *b*;
Col 2:12 having been buried with him in *b*
1Pe 3:21 this water symbolizes *b* that now

BAPTISMS* (BAPTIZE)
Heb 6:2 instruction about *b*, the laying

BAPTIZE* (BAPTISM BAPTISMS BAPTIZED BAPTIZING)
Mt 3:11 He will *b* you with the Holy Spirit
3:11 "I *b* you with water for repentance.
Mk 1:8 I *b* you with water, but he will
1:8 he will *b* you with the Holy Spirit."
Lk 3:16 He will *b* you with the Holy Spirit
3:16 John answered them all, "I *b* you
Jn 1:25 "Why then do you *b*
1:26 nor the Prophet?" "I *b* with water,"
1:33 and remain is he who will *b*
1:33 me to *b* with water told me,
1Co 1:14 I am thankful that I did not *b* any
1:17 For Christ did not send me to *b*,

BAPTIZED* (BAPTIZE)
Mt 3:6 they were *b* by him in the Jordan
3:13 to the Jordan to be *b* by John.
3:14 saying, "I need to be *b* by you,
3:16 as Jesus was *b*, he went up out
Mk 1:5 they were *b* by him in the Jordan
1:9 and was *b* by John in the Jordan.
10:38 or be *b* with the baptism I am
10:38 with the baptism I am *b* with?"
10:39 and be *b* with the baptism I am
10:39 with the baptism I am *b* with,
16:16 believes and is *b* will be saved,
Lk 3:7 to the crowds coming out to be *b*
3:12 Tax collectors also came to be *b*.
3:21 were being *b*, Jesus was *b* too.
7:29 because they had been *b* by John.

Lk 7:30 they had not been *b* by John.)
Jn 3:22 spent some time with them, and *b*.
3:23 were constantly coming to be *b*.
4:2 in fact it was not Jesus who *b*,
Ac 1:5 For John *b* with water,
1:5 but in a few days you will be *b*
2:38 Repent and be *b*, every one of you,
2:41 who accepted his message were *b*,
8:12 they were *b*, both men and women.
8:13 Simon himself believed and was *b*.
8:16 they had simply been *b*
8:36 Why shouldn't I be *b*?"
8:38 into the water and Philip *b* him.
9:18 was *b*, and after taking some food,
10:47 people from being *b* with water?
10:48 So he ordered that they be *b*
11:16 what the Lord had said, 'John *b*
11:16 you will be *b* with the Holy Spirit.'
16:15 members of her household were *b*,
16:33 he and all his family were *b*.
18:8 heard him believed and were *b*.
19:5 they were *b* into the name
22:16 be *b* and wash your sins away,
Ro 6:3 *b* into Christ Jesus were *b*
1Co 1:13 Were you *b* into the name of Paul?
1:15 so no one can say that you were *b*
1:16 I also *b* the household of Stephanas
1:16 I don't remember if I *b* anyone else
10:2 They were all *b* into Moses
12:13 For we were all *b* by one Spirit
15:29 what will those do who are *b*
15:29 why are people *b* for them?
Gal 3:27 all of you who were *b*

BAPTIZING* (BAPTIZE)
Mt 3:7 coming to where he was *b*,
28:19 *b* them in the name of the Father
Mk 1:4 *b* in the desert region
Jn 1:28 of the Jordan, where John was *b*.
1:31 but the reason I came *b*
3:23 also was *b* at Aenon near Salim,
3:26 he is *b*, and everyone is going
4:1 and *b* more disciples than John,
10:40 to the place where John had been *b*

BAR-JESUS*
Ac 13:6 and false prophet named *B*,

BARABBAS
Mt 27:26 Then he released *B* to them.

BARAK*
Judge who fought with Deborah against Canaanites (Jdg 4–5; 1Sa 12:11; Heb 11:32).

BARBARIAN*
Col 3:11 circumcised or uncircumcised, *b*,

BARBS*
Nu 33:55 allow to remain will become *b*

BARE
Hos 2:3 as *b* as on the day she was born;
Heb 4:13 and laid *b* before the eyes of him

BARNABAS*
Disciple, originally Joseph (Ac 4:36), prophet (Ac 13:1), apostle (Ac 14:14). Brought Paul to apostles (Ac 9:27), Antioch (Ac 11:22–29; Gal 2:1–13), on the first missionary journey (Ac 13–14). Together at Jerusalem Council, they separated over John Mark (Ac 15). Later co-workers (1Co 9:6; Col 4:10).

BARREN
Ge 11:30 Sarai was *b*; she had no children.
29:31 her womb, but Rachel was *b*.
Ps 113:9 He settles the *b* woman
Isa 54:1 "Sing, O *b* woman,
Lk 1:7 children, because Elizabeth was *b*;
Gal 4:27 "Be glad, O *b* woman,
Heb 11:11 and Sarah herself was *b*–

BARTHOLOMEW*
Apostle (Mt 10:3; Mk 3:18; Lk 6:14; Ac 1:13). Possibly also known as Nathanael (Jn 1:45–49; 21:2).

BARUCH
Jeremiah's secretary (Jer 32:12–16; 36; 43:1–6; 45:1–2).

BARZILLAI
1. Gileadite who aided David during Absalom's revolt (2Sa 17:27; 19:31–39).
2. Son-in-law of 1. (Ezr 2:61; Ne 7:63).

BASHAN
Jos 22:7 Moses had given land in *B*,
Ps 22:12 strong bulls of *B* encircle me.

BASIN
Ex 30:18 "Make a bronze *b*,

BASKET
Ex 2:3 she got a papyrus *b* for him
Ac 9:25 him in a *b* through an opening
2Co 11:33 I was lowered in a *b* from a window

BATCH*
Ro 11:16 then the whole *b* is holy;
1Co 5:6 through the whole *b* of dough?
5:7 old yeast that you may be a new *b*
Gal 5:9 through the whole *b* of dough."

BATH (BATHING)
Jn 13:10 person who has had a *b* needs only

BATHING (BATH)
2Sa 11:2 From the roof he saw a woman *b*.

BATHSHEBA*
Wife of Uriah who committed adultery with and became wife of David (2Sa 11), mother of Solomon (2Sa 12:24; 1Ki 1–2; 1Ch 3:5).

BATTLE (BATTLES)
1Sa 17:47 for the *b* is the LORD'S,
2Ch 20:15 For the *b* is not yours, but God's.
Ps 24:8 the LORD mighty in *b*.
Ecc 9:11 or the *b* to the strong,
Isa 31:4 down to do *b* on Mount Zion
Eze 13:5 in the *b* on the day of the LORD.
Rev 16:14 them for the *b* on the great day
20:8 and Magog—to gather them for *b*.

BATTLES* (BATTLE)
1Sa 8:20 to go out before us and fight our *b*."
18:17 and fight the *b* of the LORD."
25:28 because he fights the LORD'S *b*.
2Ch 32:8 God to help us and to fight our *b*."

BEAR (BEARING BEARS BIRTH BIRTHRIGHT BORE BORN CHILDBEARING CHILDBIRTH FIRSTBORN NEWBORN REBIRTH)
Ge 4:13 punishment is more than I can *b*.
Ps 38:4 like a burden too heavy to *b*.
Isa 11:7 The cow will feed with the *b*,
53:11 and he will *b* their iniquities.
Da 7:5 beast, which looked like a *b*.
Mt 7:18 A good tree cannot *b* bad fruit,
Jn 15:2 branch that does *b* fruit he prunes
15:8 glory, that you *b* much fruit,
15:16 appointed you to go and *b* fruit—
Ro 7:4 in order that we might *b* fruit
15:1 ought to *b* with the failings
1Co 10:13 tempted beyond what you can *b*.
Col 3:13 *B* with each other and forgive

BEARD
Lev 19:27 or clip off the edges of your *b*.
Isa 50:6 to those who pulled out my *b*;

BEARING (BEAR)
Eph 4:2 *b* with one another in love.
Col 1:10 *b* fruit in every good work,
Heb 13:13 outside the camp, *b* the disgrace he

BEARS (BEAR)
1Ki 8:43 house I have built *b* your Name.
Ps 68:19 who daily *b* our burdens.

BEAST (BEASTS)
Rev 13:18 him calculate the number of the *b*,
16:2 people who had the mark of the *b*
19:20 who had received the mark of the *b*

BEASTS (BEAST)
Da 7:3 Four great *b*, each different
1Co 15:32 If I fought wild *b* in Ephesus

BEAT (BEATEN BEATING BEATINGS)
Isa 2:4 They will *b* their swords
Joel 3:10 *B* your plowshares into swords
Mic 4:3 They will *b* their swords
1Co 9:27 I *b* my body and make it my slave

BEATEN (BEAT)
Lk 12:47 do what his master wants will be *b*
12:48 deserving punishment will be *b*
2Co 11:25 Three times I was *b* with rods,

BEATING (BEAT)
1Co 9:26 I do not fight like a man *b* the air.
1Pe 2:20 if you receive a *b* for doing wrong

BEATINGS (BEAT)
Pr 19:29 and *b* for the backs of fools.

BEAUTIFUL* (BEAUTY)
Ge 6:2 that the daughters of men were *b*,
12:11 "I know what a *b* woman you are.
12:14 saw that she was a very *b* woman.
24:16 The girl was very *b*, a virgin;
26:7 of Rebekah, because she is *b*."
29:17 Rachel was lovely in form, and *b*.
49:21 that bears *b* fawns.
Nu 24:5 "How *b* are your tents, O Jacob,
Dt 21:11 among the captives a *b* woman
Jos 7:21 saw in the plunder a *b* robe
1Sa 25:3 was an intelligent and *b* woman,
2Sa 11:2 The woman was very *b*,
13:1 the *b* sister of Absalom son
14:27 and she became a *b* woman.
1Ki 1:3 throughout Israel for a *b* girl
1:4 The girl was very *b*; she took care
Est 2:2 for *b* young virgins for the king.
2:3 realm to bring all these *b* girls
Job 38:31 "Can you bind the *b* Pleiades?
42:15 land were there found women as *b*
Ps 48:2 It is *b* in its loftiness,
Pr 11:22 is a *b* woman who shows no
24:4 filled with rare and *b* treasures.
Ecc 3:11 He has made everything *b*
SS 1:8 *Lover* If you do not know, most *b*
1:10 Your cheeks are *b* with earrings,
1:15 Oh, how *b*!
1:15 *Lover* How *b* you are, my darling!
2:10 my *b* one, and come with me.
2:13 my *b* one, come with me."
4:1 How *b* you are, my darling!
4:1 Oh, how *b*!
4:7 All *b* you are, my darling;
5:9 most *b* of women?
6:1 most *b* of women?
6:4 *Lover* You are *b*, my darling,
7:1 How *b* your sandaled feet,
7:6 How *b* you are and how pleasing,
Isa 4:2 of the LORD will be *b*
28:5 a *b* wreath
52:7 How *b* on the mountains
Jer 3:19 the most *b* inheritance
6:2 so *b* and delicate.
11:16 with fruit *b* in form.
46:20 "Egypt is a *b* heifer,
Eze 7:20 They were proud of their *b* jewelry
16:7 and became the most *b* of jewels.
16:12 and a *b* crown on your head.
16:13 You became very *b* and rose
20:6 and honey, the most *b* of all lands.
20:15 and honey, most *b* of all lands—
23:42 and *b* crowns on their heads.
27:24 traded with you *b* garments,
31:3 with *b* branches overshadowing
31:9 I made it *b*
33:32 who sings love songs with a *b* voice
Da 4:12 Its leaves were *b*, its fruit abundant
4:21 with *b* leaves and abundant fruit,
8:9 to the east and toward the *B* Land.
11:16 will establish himself in the *B* Land
11:41 He will also invade the *B* Land.
11:45 the seas at the *b* holy mountain.
Zec 9:17 How attractive and *b* they will be!
Mt 23:27 which look *b* on the outside
26:10 She has done a *b* thing to me.
Mk 14:6 She has done a *b* thing to me.
Lk 21:5 temple was adorned with *b* stones
Ac 3:2 carried to the temple gate called *B*,
3:10 at the temple gate called *B*,
Ro 10:15 "How *b* are the feet
1Pe 3:5 in God used to make themselves *b*.

BEAUTY* (BEAUTIFUL)
Est 1:11 order to display her *b* to the people
2:3 let *b* treatments be given to them.
2:9 her with her *b* treatments
2:12 months of *b* treatments prescribed
Ps 27:4 to gaze upon the *b* of the LORD
37:20 LORD'S enemies will be like the *b*
45:11 The king is enthralled by your *b*;
50:2 From Zion, perfect in *b*,
Pr 6:25 lust in your heart after her *b*
31:30 is deceptive, and *b* is fleeting;
Isa 3:24 instead of *b*, branding.
28:1 to the fading flower, his glorious *b*,

Isa 28: 4 That fading flower, his glorious *b*,
33:17 Your eyes will see the king in his *b*
53: 2 He had no *b* or majesty
61: 3 to bestow on them a crown of *b*
La 2:15 the perfection of *b*,
Eze 16:14 had given you made your *b* perfect,
16:14 the nations on account of your *b*,
16:15 passed by and your *b* became his.
16:15 " 'But you trusted in your *b*
16:25 lofty shrines and degraded your *b*,
27: 3 "I am perfect in *b*."
27: 4 your builders brought your *b*
27:11 they brought your *b* to perfection.
28: 7 draw their swords against your *b*
28:12 full of wisdom and perfect in *b*.
28:17 proud on account of your *b*,
31: 7 It was majestic in *b*,
31: 8 could match its *b*.
Jas 1:11 blossom falls and its *b* is destroyed.
1Pe 3: 3 Your *b* should not come
3: 4 the unfading *b* of a gentle

BED (SICKBED)
Isa 28:20 The *b* is too short to stretch out on,
Lk 11: 7 and my children are with me in *b*.
17:34 night two people will be in one *b*;
Heb 13: 4 and the marriage *b* kept pure,

BEELZEBUB*
Mt 10:25 of the house has been called *B*,
12:24 "It is only by *B*, the prince
12:27 And if I drive out demons by *B*,
Mk 3:22 possessed by *B*! By the prince
Lk 11:15 "By *B*, the prince of demons,
11:18 claim that I drive out demons by *B*.
11:19 Now if I drive out demons by *B*,

BEER
Pr 20: 1 Wine is a mocker and *b* a brawler;

BEERSHEBA
Ge 21:14 and wandered in the desert of *B*.
Jdg 20: 1 all the Israelites from Dan to *B*
1Sa 3:20 to *B* recognized that Samuel was
2Sa 3:10 and Judah from Dan to *B*."
17:11 Let all Israel, from Dan to *B*—
24: 2 the tribes of Israel from Dan to *B*
24:15 of the people from Dan to *B* died.
1Ki 4:25 from Dan to *B*, lived in safety,
1Ch 21: 2 count the Israelites from *B* to Dan.
2Ch 30: 5 throughout Israel, from *B* to Dan,

BEFALLS*
Pr 12:21 No harm *b* the righteous,

BEGGING
Ps 37:25 or their children *b* bread.
Ac 16: 9 of Macedonia standing and *b* him,

BEGINNING
Ge 1: 1 In the *b* God created the heavens
Ps 102: 25 In the *b* you laid the foundations
111: 10 of the LORD is the *b* of wisdom;
Pr 1: 7 of the LORD is the *b* of knowledge
9:10 of the LORD is the *b* of wisdom,
Ecc 3:11 fathom what God has done from *b*
Isa 40:21 Has it not been told you from the *b*
46:10 I make known the end from the *b*,
Mt 24: 8 All these are the *b* of birth pains.
Lk 1: 3 investigated everything from the *b*,
Jn 1: 1 In the *b* was the Word,
1Jn 1: 1 That which was from the *b*,
Rev 21: 6 and the Omega, the *B* and the End.
22:13 and the Last, the *B* and the End.

BEHAVE (BEHAVIOR)
Ro 13:13 Let us *b* decently, as in the daytime

BEHAVIOR (BEHAVE)
1Pe 3: 1 without words by the *b* of their wives,
3:16 maliciously against your good *b*

BEHEMOTH*
Job 40:15 "Look at the *b*,

BELIEVE (BELIEVED BELIEVER BELIEVERS BELIEVES BELIEVING)
Ex 4: 1 "What if they do not *b* me
1Ki 10: 7 I did not *b* these things until I came
2Ch 9: 6 But I did not *b* what they said
Ps 78:32 of his wonders, they did not *b*.
Hab 1: 5 that you would not *b*,
Mt 18: 6 one of these little ones who *b* in me
21:22 If you *b*, you will receive whatever
27:42 from the cross, and we will *b* in him
Mk 1:15 Repent and *b* the good news!"
5:36 ruler, "Don't be afraid; just *b*."
9:24 "I do *b*; help me overcome my
9:42 one of these little ones who *b* in me
11:24 *b* that you have received it,
15:32 the cross, that we may see and *b*."
16:16 but whoever does not *b* will be
16:17 signs will accompany those who *b*:
Lk 8:12 so that they may not *b* and be saved.
8:13 They *b* for a while, but in the time
8:50 just *b*, and she will be healed."
22:67 you will not *b* me,
24:25 to *b* all that the prophets have
Jn 1: 7 that through him all men might *b*.
3:18 does not *b* stands condemned
4:42 "We no longer *b* just
5:38 for you do not *b* the one he sent.
5:46 believed Moses, you would *b* me,
6:29 to *b* in the one he has sent."
6:69 We *b* and know that you are
7: 5 his own brothers did not *b* in him.
8:24 if you do not *b* that I am ⌞the one I
9:35 "Do you *b* in the Son of Man?"
9:36 "Tell me so that I may *b* in him."
9:38 "Lord, I *b*," and he worshiped him.
10:26 you do not *b* because you are not
10:37 Do not *b* me unless I do what my
10:38 you do not *b* me, *b* the miracles,
11:27 "I *b* that you are the Christ,
12:37 they still would not *b* in him.
12:39 For this reason they could not *b*,
12:44 in me, he does not *b* in me only,
13:19 does happen you will *b* that I am
14:10 Don't you *b* that I am in the Father
14:11 *B* me when I say that I am
14:11 or at least *b* on the evidence
16:30 This makes us *b* that you came
16:31 "You *b* at last!" Jesus answered.
17:21 that the world may *b* that you have
19:35 he testifies so that you also may *b*.
20:27 Stop doubting and *b*."
20:31 written that you may *b* that Jesus is
Ac 16:31 They replied, "*B* in the Lord Jesus,
19: 4 the people to *b* in the one coming
24:14 I *b* everything that agrees
26:27 Agrippa, do you *b* the prophets?
Ro 3:22 faith in Jesus Christ to all who *b*.
4:11 he is the father of all who *b*
10: 9 *b* in your heart that God raised him
10:10 For it is with your heart that you *b*
10:14 And how can they *b* in the one
16:26 so that all nations might *b*
1Co 1:21 preached to save those who *b*.
Gal 3:22 might be given to those who *b*.
Php 1:29 of Christ not only to *b* on him,
1Th 4:14 We *b* that Jesus died and rose again
2Th 2:11 delusion so that they will *b* the lie
1Ti 4:10 and especially of those who *b*.
Tit 1: 6 a man whose children *b*
Heb 11: 6 comes to him must *b* that he exists
Jas 1: 6 But when he asks, he must *b*
2:19 Even the demons *b* that—
2:19 You *b* that there is one God.
1Pe 2: 7 to you who *b*, this stone is precious
1Jn 3:23 to *b* in the name of his Son,
4: 1 Dear friends, do not *b* every spirit,
5:13 things to you who *b* in the name

BELIEVED (BELIEVE)
Ge 15: 6 Abram *b* the LORD, and he
Ex 4:31 signs before the people, and they *b*.
Isa 53: 1 Who has *b* our message
Jnh 3: 5 The Ninevites *b* God.
Lk 1:45 is she who has *b* that what the Lord
Jn 1:12 to those who *b* in his name,
2:22 Then they *b* the Scripture
3:18 because he has not *b* in the name
5:46 If you *b* Moses, you would believe
7:39 whom those who *b*
11:40 "Did I not tell you that if you *b*,
12:38 "Lord, who has *b* our message
20: 8 He saw and *b*.
20:29 who have not seen and yet have *b*."
Ac 13:48 were appointed for eternal life *b*.
19: 2 the Holy Spirit when you *b*?"
Ro 4: 3 Scripture say? "Abraham *b* God,
10:14 call on the one they have not *b* in?
10:16 "Lord, who has *b* our message?"
1Co 15: 2 Otherwise, you have *b* in vain.
Gal 3: 6 Consider Abraham: "He *b* God,
2Th 2:12 who have not *b* the truth
1Ti 3:16 was *b* on in the world,
2Ti 1:12 because I know whom I have *b*,
Jas 2:23 that says, "Abraham *b* God,

BELIEVER* (BELIEVE)
1Ki 18: 3 (Obadiah was a devout *b*
Ac 16: 1 whose mother was a Jewess and a *b*
16:15 "If you consider me a *b* in the Lord
1Co 7:12 brother has a wife who is not a *b*
7:13 has a husband who is not a *b*
2Co 6:15 What does a *b* have in common
1Ti 5:16 any woman who is a *b* has widows

BELIEVERS* (BELIEVE)
Jn 4:41 of his words many more became *b*.
Ac 1:15 among the *b* (a group numbering
2:44 All the *b* were together
4:32 All the *b* were one in heart
5:12 And all the *b* used to meet together
9:41 he called the *b* and the widows
10:45 The circumcised *b* who had come
11: 2 the circumcised *b* criticized him
15: 2 along with some other *b*,
15: 5 Then some of the *b* who belonged
15:23 To the Gentile *b* in Antioch,
21:25 for the Gentile *b*, we have written
1Co 6: 5 to judge a dispute between *b*?
14:22 is for *b*, not for unbelievers.
14:22 not for *b* but for unbelievers;
Gal 6:10 who belong to the family of *b*.
1Th 1: 7 a model to all the *b* in Macedonia
1Ti 4:12 set an example for the *b* in speech,
6: 2 benefit from their service are *b*,
Jas 2: 1 *b* in our glorious Lord Jesus Christ,
1Pe 2:17 Love the brotherhood of *b*,

BELIEVES* (BELIEVE)
Pr 14:15 A simple man *b* anything,
Mk 9:23 is possible for him who *b*."
11:23 *b* that what he says will happen,
16:16 Whoever *b* and is baptized will be
Jn 3:15 that everyone who *b*
3:16 that whoever *b* in him shall not
3:18 Whoever *b* in him is not
3:36 Whoever *b* in the Son has eternal
5:24 *b* him who sent me has eternal life
6:35 and he who *b* in me will never be
6:40 and *b* in him shall have eternal life,
6:47 he who *b* has everlasting life.
7:38 Whoever *b* in me, as the Scripture
11:25 He who *b* in me will live, even
11:26 and *b* in me will never die.
12:44 Jesus cried out, "When a man *b*
12:46 so that no one who *b*
Ac 10:43 about him that everyone who *b*
13:39 him everyone who *b* is justified
Ro 1:16 for the salvation of everyone who *b*
10: 4 righteousness for everyone who *b*.
1Jn 5: 1 Everyone who *b* that Jesus is
5: 5 Only he who *b* that Jesus is the Son
5:10 Anyone who *b* in the Son

BELIEVING* (BELIEVE)
Jn 20:31 and that by *b* you may have life
Ac 9:26 not *b* that he really was a disciple.
1Co 7:14 sanctified through her *b* husband.
7:15 A *b* man or woman is not bound
9: 5 right to take a *b* wife along with us,
Gal 3: 2 or by *b* what you heard? Are you
1Ti 6: 2 Those who have *b* masters are not

BELLY
Ge 3:14 You will crawl on your *b*
Da 2:32 its *b* and thighs of bronze,
Mt 12:40 three nights in the *b* of a huge fish,

BELONG (BELONGING BELONGS)
Ge 40: 8 "Do not interpretations *b* to God?
Lev 25:55 for the Israelites *b* to me
Dt 10:14 LORD your God *b* the heavens,
29:29 The secret things *b*
Job 12:13 "To God *b* wisdom and power;
12:16 To him *b* strength and victory;
25: 2 "Dominion and awe *b* to God;
Ps 47: 9 for the kings of the earth *b* to God;
95: 4 and the mountain peaks *b* to him.
115: 16 The highest heavens *b*
Jer 5:10 for these people do not *b*
Jn 8:44 You *b* to your father, the devil,
15:19 As it is, you do not *b* to the world,

Ro 1: 6 called to *b* to Jesus Christ.
7: 4 that you might *b* to another,
8: 9 of Christ, he does not *b* to Christ.
14: 8 we live or die, we *b* to the Lord.
1Co 7:39 but he must *b* to the Lord.
15:23 when he comes, those who *b*
Gal 3:29 If you *b* to Christ, then you are
5:24 Those who *b* to Christ Jesus have
1Th 5: 5 We do not *b* to the night
5: 8 But since we *b* to the day, let us be
1Jn 3:19 then is how we know that we *b*

BELONGING (BELONG)
1Pe 2: 9 a holy nation, a people *b* to God,

BELONGS (BELONG)
Lev 27:30 *b* to the LORD; it is holy
Dt 1:17 of any man, for judgment *b* to God.
Job 41:11 Everything under heaven *b* to me.
Ps 22:28 for dominion *b* to the LORD
89:18 Indeed, our shield *b* to the LORD,
111: 10 To him *b* eternal praise.
Eze 18: 4 For every living soul *b* to me,
Jn 8:47 He who *b* to God hears what God
Ro 12: 5 each member *b* to all the others.
Rev 7:10 "Salvation *b* to our God,

BELOVED* (LOVE)
Dt 33:12 "Let the *b* of the LORD rest secure
SS 5: 9 How is your *b* better than others,
5: 9 *Friends* How is your *b* better
Jer 11:15 "What is my *b* doing in my temple

BELSHAZZAR
King of Babylon in days of Daniel (Da 5).

BELT
Ex 12:11 with your cloak tucked into your *b*,
1Ki 18:46 and, tucking his cloak into his *b*,
2Ki 4:29 "Tuck your cloak into your *b*,
9: 1 "Tuck your cloak into your *b*,
Isa 11: 5 Righteousness will be his *b*
Eph 6:14 with the *b* of truth buckled

BENEFICIAL* (BENEFIT)
1Co 6:12 for me"—but not everything is *b*.
10:23 but not everything is *b*.

BENEFIT (BENEFICIAL BENEFITS)
Job 22: 2 "Can a man be of *b* to God?
Isa 38:17 Surely it was for my *b*
Ro 6:22 the *b* you reap leads to holiness,
2Co 4:15 All this is for your *b*,

BENEFITS (BENEFIT)
Ps 103: 2 and forget not all his *b*.
Jn 4:38 you have reaped the *b* of their labor

BENJAMIN
Twelfth son of Jacob by Rachel (Ge 35:16–24; 46:19–21; 1Ch 2:2). Jacob refused to send him to Egypt, but relented (Ge 42–45). Tribe of blessed (Ge 49:27; Dt 33:12), numbered (Nu 1:37; 26:41), allotted land (Jos 18:11–28; Eze 48:23), failed to fully possess (Jdg 1:21), nearly obliterated (Jdg 20–21), sided with Ish-Bosheth (2Sa 2), but turned to David (1Ch 12:2, 29). 12,000 from (Rev 7:8).

BEREANS*
Ac 17:11 the *B* were of more noble character

BESTOWING* (BESTOWS)
Pr 8:21 *b* wealth on those who love me

BESTOWS (BESTOWING)
Ps 84:11 the LORD *b* favor and honor;

BETHANY
Mk 11: 1 and *B* at the Mount of Olives,

BETHEL
Ge 28:19 He called that place *B*,

BETHLEHEM
Ru 1:19 went on until they came to *B*.
1Sa 16: 1 I am sending you to Jesse of *B*.
2Sa 23:15 from the well near the gate of *B*!"
Mic 5: 2 "But you, *B* Ephrathah,
Mt 2: 1 After Jesus was born in *B* in Judea,
2: 6 " 'But you, *B*, in the land of Judah,

BETHPHAGE
Mt 21: 1 came to *B* on the Mount of Olives,

BETHSAIDA
Jn 12:21 who was from *B* in Galilee,

BETRAY (BETRAYED BETRAYS)
Ps 89:33 nor will I ever *b* my faithfulness.
Pr 25: 9 do not *b* another man's confidence,
Mt 10:21 "Brother will *b* brother to death,
26:21 the truth, one of you will *b* me."

BETRAYED (BETRAY)
Mt 27: 4 "for I have *b* innocent blood."

BETRAYS (BETRAY)
Pr 11:13 A gossip *b* a confidence,
20:19 A gossip *b* a confidence;

BEULAH*
Isa 62: 4 and your land *B*;

BEWITCHED*
Gal 3: 1 foolish Galatians! Who has *b* you?

BEZALEL
Judahite craftsman in charge of building the tabernacle (Ex 31:1–11; 35:30–39:31).

BIDDING*
Ps 103: 20 you mighty ones who do his *b*,
148: 8 stormy winds that do his *b*,

BILDAD
One of Job's friends (Job 8; 18; 25).

BILHAH
Servant of Rachel, mother of Jacob's sons Dan and Naphtali (Ge 30:1–7; 35:25; 46:23–25).

BIND (BINDS BOUND)
Dt 6: 8 and *b* them on your foreheads.
Pr 3: 3 *b* them around your neck,
6:21 *B* them upon your heart forever;
7: 3 *B* them on your fingers;
Isa 61: 1 me to *b* up the brokenhearted,
Mt 16:19 whatever you *b* on earth will be

BINDS (BIND)
Ps 147: 3 and *b* up their wounds.
Isa 30:26 when the LORD *b* up the bruises

BIRD (BIRDS)
Pr 27: 8 Like a *b* that strays from its nest
Ecc 10:20 a *b* of the air may carry your words,

BIRDS (BIRD)
Mt 8:20 and *b* of the air have nests,
Lk 9:58 and *b* of the air have nests,

BIRTH (BEAR)
Ps 51: 5 Surely I was sinful at *b*,
58: 3 Even from *b* the wicked go astray;
Isa 26:18 but we gave *b* to wind.
Mt 1:18 This is how the *b* of Jesus Christ
24: 8 these are the beginning of *b* pains.
Jn 3: 6 Flesh gives *b* to flesh, but the Spirit
1Pe 1: 3 great mercy he has given us new *b*

BIRTHRIGHT (BEAR)
Ge 25:34 So Esau despised his *b*.

BITTEN
Nu 21: 8 anyone who is *b* can look at it

BITTER (BITTERNESS EMBITTER)
Ex 12: 8 along with *b* herbs, and bread made
Pr 27: 7 what is *b* tastes sweet.

BITTERNESS (BITTER)
Pr 14:10 Each heart knows its own *b*,
17:25 and *b* to the one who bore him.
Ro 3:14 full of cursing and *b*."
Eph 4:31 Get rid of all *b*, rage and anger,

BLACK
Zec 6: 6 The one with the *b* horses is going
Rev 6: 5 and there before me was a *b* horse!

BLAMELESS* (BLAMELESSLY)
Ge 6: 9 *b* among the people of his time,
17: 1 walk before me and be *b*.
Dt 18:13 You must be *b* before the LORD
2Sa 22:24 I have been *b* before him
22:26 to the *b* you show yourself *b*,
Job 1: 1 This man was *b* and upright;
1: 8 one on earth like him; he is *b*
2: 3 one on earth like him; he is *b*
4: 6 and your *b* ways your hope?
8:20 God does not reject a *b* man
9:20 if I were *b*, it would pronounce me
9:21 "Although I am *b*,
9:22 'He destroys both the *b*
12: 4 though righteous and *b*!
Job 22: 3 gain if your ways were *b*?
31: 6 and he will know that I am *b*—
Ps 15: 2 He whose walk is *b*
18:23 I have been *b* before him
18:25 to the *b* you show yourself *b*,
19:13 Then will I be *b*,
26: 1 for I have led a *b* life;
26:11 But I lead a *b* life;
37:18 The days of the *b* are known
37:37 Consider the *b*, observe the upright
84:11 from those whose walk is *b*.
101: 2 I will be careful to lead a *b* life—
101: 2 house with *b* heart.
101: 6 he whose walk is *b*
119: 1 Blessed are they whose ways are *b*,
119: 80 May my heart be *b*
Pr 2: 7 a shield to those whose walk is *b*,
2:21 and the *b* will remain in it;
11: 5 of the *b* makes a straight way
11:20 in those whose ways are *b*.
19: 1 Better a poor man whose walk is *b*
20: 7 The righteous man leads a *b* life;
28: 6 Better a poor man whose walk is *b*
28:10 *b* will receive a good inheritance.
28:18 He whose walk is *b* is kept safe,
Eze 28:15 You were *b* in your ways
1Co 1: 8 so that you will be *b* on the day
Eph 1: 4 world to be holy and *b* in his sight.
5:27 any other blemish, but holy and *b*.
Php 1:10 and *b* until the day of Christ,
2:15 so that you may become *b* and pure
1Th 2:10 and *b* we were among you who
3:13 hearts so that you will be *b*
5:23 and body be kept *b* at the coming
Tit 1: 6 An elder must be *b*, the husband of
1: 7 he must be *b*—not overbearing,
Heb 7:26 *b*, pure, set apart from sinners,
2Pe 3:14 effort to be found spotless, *b*
Rev 14: 5 found in their mouths; they are *b*.

BLAMELESSLY* (BLAMELESS)
Lk 1: 6 commandments and regulations *b*.

BLASPHEME* (BLASPHEMED BLASPHEMER BLASPHEMES BLASPHEMIES BLASPHEMING BLASPHEMOUS BLASPHEMY)
Ex 22:28 "Do not *b* God or curse the ruler
Ac 26:11 and I tried to force them to *b*.
1Ti 1:20 over to Satan to be taught not to *b*.
2Pe 2:12 these men *b* in matters they do not
Rev 13: 6 He opened his mouth to *b* God,

BLASPHEMED* (BLASPHEME)
Lev 24:11 of the Israelite woman *b* the Name
2Ki 19: 6 of the king of Assyria have *b* me.
19:22 Who is it you have insulted and *b*?
Isa 37: 6 of the king of Assyria have *b* me.
37:23 Who is it you have insulted and *b*?
52: 5 my name is constantly *b*.
Eze 20:27 your fathers *b* me by forsaking me:
Ac 19:37 robbed temples nor *b* our goddess.
Ro 2:24 name is *b* among the Gentiles

BLASPHEMER* (BLASPHEME)
Lev 24:14 "Take the *b* outside the camp.
24:23 they took the *b* outside the camp
1Ti 1:13 I was once a *b* and a persecutor

BLASPHEMES* (BLASPHEME)
Lev 24:16 anyone who *b* the name
24:16 native-born, when he *b* the Name,
Nu 15:30 native-born or alien, *b* the LORD,
Mk 3:29 whoever *b* against the Holy Spirit
Lk 12:10 but anyone who *b* against the Holy

BLASPHEMIES* (BLASPHEME)
Ne 9:18 or when they committed awful *b*.
9:26 to you; they committed awful *b*.
Mk 3:28 and *b* of men will be forgiven them.
Rev 13: 5 and *b* and to exercise his authority

BLASPHEMING* (BLASPHEME)
Mt 9: 3 "This fellow is *b*!" Knowing their
Mk 2: 7 He's *b*! Who can forgive sins

BLASPHEMOUS* (BLASPHEME)
Rev 13: 1 and on each head a *b* name.
17: 3 that was covered with *b* names

BLASPHEMY* (BLASPHEME)
Mt 12:31 and *b* will be forgiven men,
12:31 the *b* against the Spirit will not be
26:65 Look, now you have heard the *b*.
26:65 "He has spoken *b*! Why do we

Mk 14:64 "You have heard the *b*.
Lk 5:21 "Who is this fellow who speaks *b*?
Jn 10:33 replied the Jews, "but for *b*,
10:36 Why then do you accuse me of *b*
Ac 6:11 words of *b* against Moses

BLAST*
Ex 15: 8 By the *b* of your nostrils
19:13 horn sounds a long *b* may they go
19:16 and a very loud trumpet *b*.
Nu 10: 5 When a trumpet *b* is sounded,
10: 6 At the sounding of a second *b*,
10: 6 The *b* will be the signal
10: 9 sound a *b* on the trumpets.
Jos 6: 5 you hear them sound a long *b*
6:16 the priests sounded the trumpet *b*,
2Sa 22:16 at the *b* of breath from his nostrils.
Job 4: 9 at the *b* of his anger they perish.
39:25 At the *b* of the trumpet he snorts,
Ps 18:15 the *b* of breath from your nostrils.
98: 6 and the *b* of the ram's horn—
147: 17 Who can withstand his icy *b*?
Isa 27: 8 with his fierce *b* he drives her out,
Eze 22:20 a furnace to melt it with a fiery *b*,
Am 2: 2 tumult amid war cries and the *b*
Heb 12:19 to a trumpet *b* or to such a voice

BLEATING*
1Sa 15:14 "What then is this *b* of sheep

BLEMISH (BLEMISHES)
Lev 22:21 be without defect or *b*
Eph 5:27 or wrinkle or any other *b*,
Col 1:22 without *b* and free from accusation
1Pe 1:19 a lamb without *b* or defect.

BLEMISHES* (BLEMISH)
2Pe 2:13 and *b*, reveling in their pleasures
Jude :12 These men are *b* at your love feasts

BLESS (BLESSED BLESSES BLESSING BLESSINGS)
Ge 12: 3 I will *b* those who *b* you,
32:26 not let you go unless you *b* me."
Dt 7:13 He will love you and *b* you
33:11 *B* all his skills, O LORD,
Ps 72:15 and *b* him all day long.
Ro 12:14 Bless those who persecute you; *b*

BLESSED (BLESS)
Ge 1:22 God *b* them and said, "Be fruitful
2: 3 And God *b* the seventh day
22:18 nations on earth will be *b*,
Nu 24: 9 "May those who bless you be *b*
1Ch 17:27 have *b* it, and it will be *b* forever."
Ps 1: 1 *B* is the man
2:12 *B* are all who take refuge in him.
32: 2 *B* is the man
33:12 *B* is the nation whose God is
40: 4 *B* is the man
41: 1 *B* is he who has regard for the weak
84: 5 *B* are those whose strength is
89:15 *B* are those who have learned
94:12 *B* is the man you discipline,
106: 3 *B* are they who maintain justice,
112: 1 *B* is the man who fears the LORD,
118: 26 *B* is he who comes in the name
119: 1 *B* are they whose ways are
119: 2 *B* are they who keep his statutes
127: 5 *B* is the man
Pr 3:13 *B* is the man who finds wisdom,
8:34 *B* is the man who listens to me,
28:20 A faithful man will be richly *b*,
29:18 but *b* is he who keeps the law.
31:28 Her children arise and call her *b*;
Isa 30:18 *B* are all who wait for him!
Mal 3:12 Then all the nations will call you *b*,
3:15 But now we call the arrogant *b*.
Mt 5: 3 saying: "*B* are the poor in spirit,
5: 4 *B* are those who mourn,
5: 5 *B* are the meek,
5: 6 *B* are those who hunger
5: 7 *B* are the merciful,
5: 8 *B* are the pure in heart,
5: 9 *B* are the peacemakers,
5:10 *B* are those who are persecuted
5:11 "*B* are you when people insult you,
Lk 1:48 on all generations will call me *b*,
Jn 12:13 "*B* is he who comes in the name
Ac 20:35 'It is more *b* to give than to receive
Tit 2:13 while we wait for the *b* hope—
Jas 1:12 *B* is the man who perseveres
Rev 1: 3 *B* is the one who reads the words
Rev 22: 7 *B* is he who keeps the words
22:14 "*B* are those who wash their robes,

BLESSES (BLESS)
Ps 29:11 the LORD *b* his people with peace.
Ro 10:12 and richly *b* all who call on him,

BLESSING (BLESS)
Ge 27: 4 so that I may give you my *b*
Dt 23: 5 turned the curse into a *b* for you,
33: 1 This is the *b* that Moses the man
Pr 10:22 The *b* of the LORD brings wealth,
Eze 34:26 there will be showers of *b*.

BLESSINGS (BLESS)
Dt 11:29 proclaim on Mount Gerizim the *b*,
Jos 8:34 all the words of the law—the *b*
Pr 10: 6 *B* crown the head of the righteous,
Ro 15:27 shared in the Jews' spiritual *b*,

BLIND (BLINDED)
Mt 15:14 a *b* man leads a *b* man, both will fall
23:16 "Woe to you, *b* guides! You say,
Mk 10:46 a *b* man, Bartimaeus (that is,
Lk 6:39 "Can a *b* man lead a *b* man?
Jn 9:25 I was *b* but now I see!"

BLINDED (BLIND)
Jn 12:40 elsewhere: "He has *b* their eyes
2Co 4: 4 The god of this age has *b* the minds

BLOOD (BLOODSHED BLOODTHIRSTY)
Ge 4:10 Your brother's *b* cries out to me
9: 6 "Whoever sheds the *b* of man,
Ex 12:13 and when I see the *b*, I will pass
24: 8 "This is the *b* of the covenant that
Lev 16:15 and take its *b* behind the curtain
17:11 For the life of a creature is in the *b*,
Dt 12:23 eat the *b*, because the *b* is the life,
Ps 72:14 for precious is their *b* in his sight.
Pr 6:17 hands that shed innocent *b*,
Isa 1:11 pleasure in the *b* of bulls and lambs
Mt 26:28 This is my *b* of the covenant,
27:24 "I am innocent of this man's *b*,"
Mk 14:24 "This is my *b* of the covenant,
Lk 22:44 drops of *b* falling to the ground.
Jn 6:53 of the Son of Man and drink his *b*,
Ac 15:20 of strangled animals and from *b*.
20:26 innocent of the *b* of all men.
Ro 3:25 of atonement, through faith in his *b*
5: 9 have now been justified by his *b*,
1Co 11:25 cup is the new covenant in my *b*;
Eph 1: 7 we have redemption through his *b*,
2:13 near through the *b* of Christ.
Col 1:20 by making peace through his *b*,
Heb 9: 7 once a year, and never without *b*,
9:12 once for all by his own *b*,
9:20 "This is the *b* of the covenant,
9:22 of *b* there is no forgiveness.
12:24 word than the *b* of Abel.
1Pe 1:19 but with the precious *b* of Christ,
1Jn 1: 7 and the *b* of Jesus, his Son,
Rev 1: 5 has freed us from our sins by his *b*,
5: 9 with your *b* you purchased men
7:14 white in the *b* of the Lamb.
12:11 him by the *b* of the Lamb
19:13 He is dressed in a robe dipped in *b*,

BLOODSHED (BLOOD)
Jer 48:10 on him who keeps his sword from *b*
Eze 35: 6 did not hate *b*, *b* will pursue you.
Hab 2:12 to him who builds a city with *b*

BLOODTHIRSTY* (BLOOD)
Ps 5: 6 *b* and deceitful men
26: 9 my life with *b* men,
55:23 *b* and deceitful men
59: 2 and save me from *b* men.
139: 19 Away from me, you *b* men!
Pr 29:10 *B* men hate a man of integrity

BLOSSOM
Isa 35: 1 the wilderness will rejoice and *b*.

BLOT (BLOTS)
Ex 32:32 then *b* me out of the book you have
Ps 51: 1 *b* out my transgressions.
Rev 3: 5 I will never *b* out his name

BLOTS (BLOT)
Isa 43:25 "I, even I, am he who *b* out

BLOWN
Eph 4:14 and *b* here and there by every wind
Jas 1: 6 doubts is like a wave of the sea, *b*
Jude :12 without rain, *b* along by the wind;

BLUSH
Jer 6:15 they do not even know how to *b*.

BOAST (BOASTS)
1Ki 20:11 armor should not *b* like one who
Ps 34: 2 My soul will *b* in the LORD;
44: 8 In God we make our *b* all day long,
Pr 27: 1 Do not *b* about tomorrow,
Jer 9:23 or the rich man *b* of his riches,
1Co 1:31 Let him who boasts *b* in the Lord."
2Co 10:17 Let him who boasts *b* in the Lord."
11:30 I do not inwardly burn? If I must *b*,
Gal 6:14 May I never *b* except in the cross
Eph 2: 9 not by works, so that no one can *b*.

BOASTS (BOAST)
Jer 9:24 but let him who *b* boast about this:

BOAZ
Wealthy Bethlehemite who showed favor to Ruth (Ru 2), married her (Ru 4). Ancestor of David (Ru 4:18–22; 1Ch 2:12–15), Jesus (Mt 1:5–16; Lk 3:23–32).

BODIES (BODY)
Isa 26:19 their *b* will rise.
Ro 12: 1 to offer your *b* as living sacrifices,
1Co 6:15 not know that your *b* are members
Eph 5:28 to love their wives as their own *b*.

BODILY (BODY)
Col 2: 9 of the Deity lives in *b* form,

BODY (BODIES BODILY EMBODIMENT)
Zec 13: 6 What are these wounds on your *b*?'
Mt 10:28 afraid of those who kill the *b*
26:26 saying, "Take and eat; this is my *b*
26:41 spirit is willing, but the *b* is weak."
Mk 14:22 saying, "Take it; this is my *b*."
Lk 22:19 saying, "This is my *b* given for you;
Jn 13:10 wash his feet; his whole *b* is clean.
Ro 6:13 Do not offer the parts of your *b*
12: 4 us has one *b* with many members,
1Co 6:19 not know that your *b* is a temple
6:20 Therefore honor God with your *b*.
11:24 "This is my *b*, which is for you;
12:12 The *b* is a unit, though it is made up
12:13 baptized by one Spirit into one *b*—
15:44 a natural *b*, it is raised a spiritual *b*.
Eph 1:23 which is his *b*, the fullness
4:25 for we are all members of one *b*.
5:30 for we are members of his *b*.
Php 1:20 Christ will be exalted in my *b*,
Col 1:24 sake of his *b*, which is the church.

BOLD (BOLDNESS)
Ps 138: 3 you made me *b* and stouthearted.
Pr 21:29 A wicked man puts up a *b* front,
28: 1 but the righteous are as *b* as a lion.

BOLDNESS* (BOLD)
Lk 11: 8 of the man's *b* he will get up
Ac 4:29 to speak your word with great *b*.

BONDAGE
Ezr 9: 9 God has not deserted us in our *b*.

BONES
Ge 2:23 "This is now bone of my *b*
Ps 22:14 and all my *b* are out of joint.
22:17 I can count all my *b*;
Eze 37: 1 middle of a valley; it was full of *b*.
Jn 19:36 "Not one of his *b* will be broken,"

BOOK (BOOKS)
Ex 32:33 against me I will blot out of my *b*.
Jos 1: 8 Do not let this *B* of the Law depart
2Ki 22: 8 "I have found the *B* of the Law
2Ch 34:15 "I have found the *B* of the Law
Ne 8: 8 They read from the *B* of the Law
Ps 69:28 May they be blotted out of the *b*
Da 12: 1 name is found written in the *b*—
Jn 20:30 which are not recorded in this *b*.
Php 4: 3 whose names are in the *b* of life.
Rev 3: 5 never blot out his name from the *b*
20:12 *b* was opened, which is the *b*
20:15 was not found written in the *b*
21:27 written in the Lamb's *b* of life.
22:18 him the plagues described in this *b*.

BOOKS* (BOOK)
Ecc 12:12 Of making many *b* there is no end,
Da 7:10 and the *b* were opened.
Jn 21:25 for the *b* that would be written.

Rev 20:12 the throne, and *b* were opened.
20:12 they had done as recorded in the *b*.

BORE (BEAR)
Isa 53:12 For he *b* the sin of many,
1Pe 2:24 He himself *b* our sins in his body

BORN (BEAR)
Ecc 3: 2 a time to be *b* and a time to die,
Isa 9: 6 For to us a child is *b*,
66: 8 Can a country be *b* in a day
Lk 2:11 of David a Savior has been *b* to you
Jn 3: 3 see the kingdom of God unless he is *b* again.
3: 4 How can a man be *b* when he is old
3: 5 unless he is *b* of water
3: 7 at my saying, 'You must be *b* again
3: 8 it is with everyone *b* of the Spirit."
1Pe 1:23 For you have been *b* again,
1Jn 3: 9 because he has been *b* of God.
4: 7 Everyone who loves has been *b*
5: 1 believes that Jesus is the Christ is *b*
5: 4 for everyone *b* of God overcomes
5:18 We know that anyone *b*

BORROWER
Pr 22: 7 and the *b* is servant to the lender.

BOTHER (BOTHERING)
Lk 11: 7 one inside answers, 'Don't *b* me.

BOTHERING (BOTHER)
Lk 18: 5 yet because this widow keeps *b* me,

BOUGHT (BUY)
Ac 20:28 which he *b* with his own blood.
1Co 6:20 You are not your own; you were *b*
7:23 You were *b* at a price; do not
2Pe 2: 1 the sovereign Lord who *b* them—

BOUND (BIND)
Is 56: 3 Let no foreigner who has *b* himself
Mt 16:19 bind on earth will be *b* in heaven,
18:18 bind on earth will be *b* in heaven,
Ro 7: 2 by law a married woman is *b*
1Co 7:39 A woman is *b* to her husband
Jude : 6 *b* with everlasting chains
Rev 20: 2 and *b* him for a thousand years.

BOUNDARY (BOUNDS)
Nu 34: 3 your southern *b* will start
Pr 23:10 Do not move an ancient *b* stone
Hos 5:10 who move *b* stones.

BOUNDS (BOUNDARY)
2Co 7: 4 all our troubles my joy knows no *b*.

BOUNTY*
Ge 49:26 than the *b* of the age-old hills.
Dt 28:12 heavens, the storehouse of his *b*,
1Ki 10:13 he had given her out of his royal *b*.
Ps 65:11 You crown the year with your *b*,
68:10 from your *b*, O God, you provided
Jer 31:12 rejoice in the *b* of the LORD—
31:14 my people will be filled with my *b*

BOW (BOWED BOWS)
Dt 5: 9 You shall not *b* down to them
1Ki 22:34 But someone drew his *b* at random
Ps 5: 7 in reverence will I *b* down
44: 6 I do not trust in my *b*,
95: 6 Come, let us *b* down in worship,
138: 2 I will *b* down toward your holy
Isa 44:19 Shall I *b* down to a block of wood?"
45:23 Before me every knee will *b*;
Ro 14:11 'every knee will *b* before me;
Php 2:10 name of Jesus every knee should *b*,

BOWED (BOW)
Ps 145: 14 and lifts up all who are *b* down.
146: 8 the LORD lifts up those who are *b*

BOWS (BOW)
Isa 44:15 he makes an idol and *b* down to it.
44:17 he *b* down to it and worships.

BOY (BOY'S BOYS)
Ge 21:17 God heard the *b* crying,
22:12 not lay a hand on the *b*
Jdg 13: 5 *b* is to be a Nazirite,
1Sa 2:11 *b* ministered before the LORD.
3: 8 the LORD was calling the *b*.
Isa 7:16 before the *b* knows enough
Mt 17:18 demon, and it came out of the *b*
Lk 2:43 the *b* Jesus stayed behind

BOY'S (BOY)
1Ki 17:22 the *b* life returned to him
2Ki 4:34 the *b* body grew warm

BOYS (BOY)
Ge 25:24 twin *b* in her womb
Ex 1:18 they let the *b* live.

BRACE*
Job 38: 3 *B* yourself like a man;
40: 7 out of the storm: "*B* yourself like
Na 2: 1 *b* yourselves,

BRAG*
Am 4: 5 and *b* about your freewill offerings
Ro 2:17 *b* about your relationship to God;
2:23 temples? You who *b* about the law,
Jas 4:16 As it is, you boast and *b*.

BRAIDED
1Ti 2: 9 not with *b* hair or gold or pearls
1Pe 3: 3 as *b* hair and the wearing

BRANCH (BRANCHES)
Isa 4: 2 In that day the *B* of the LORD will
Jer 23: 5 up to David a righteous *B*,
33:15 I will make a righteous *B* sprout
Zec 3: 8 going to bring my servant, the *B*.
6:12 is the man whose name is the *B*,
Jn 15: 2 while every *b* that does bear fruit
15: 4 No *b* can bear fruit by itself;

BRANCHES (BRANCH)
Jn 15: 5 "I am the vine; you are the *b*.
Ro 11:21 if God did not spare the natural *b*,

BRAVE
2Sa 2: 7 Now then, be strong and *b*,
13:28 you this order? Be strong and *b*."

BREACH (BREAK)
Ps 106: 23 stood in the *b* before him

BREACHING (BREAK)
Pr 17:14 Starting a quarrel is like *b* a dam;

BREAD
Ex 12: 8 and *b* made without yeast.
23:15 the Feast of Unleavened *B*;
25:30 Put the *b* of the Presence
Dt 8: 3 that man does not live on *b* alone
Ps 78:25 Men ate the *b* of angels;
Pr 30: 8 but give me only my daily *b*.
Ecc 11: 1 Cast your *b* upon the waters,
Isa 55: 2 Why spend money on what is not *b*
Mt 4: 3 tell these stones to become *b*."
4: 4 'Man does not live on *b* alone,
6:11 Give us today our daily *b*.
26:26 Jesus took *b*, gave thanks
Mk 14:22 Jesus took *b*, gave thanks
Lk 4: 3 tell this stone to become *b*."
4: 4 'Man does not live on *b* alone.' "
9:13 "We have only five loaves of *b*
11: 3 Give us each day our daily *b*.
22:19 And he took *b*, gave thanks
Jn 6:33 For the *b* of God is he who comes
6:35 Jesus declared, "I am the *b* of life.
6:41 "I am the *b* that came
6:48 I am the *b* of life.
6:51 I am the living *b* that came
6:51 This *b* is my flesh, which I will give
21:13 took the *b* and gave it to them,
1Co 10:16 And is not the *b* that we break
11:23 took *b*, and when he had given
11:26 For whenever you eat this *b*

BREAK (BREACH BREACHING BREAKERS BREAKING BREAKS BROKE BROKEN BROKENNESS)
Nu 30: 2 he must not *b* his word
Jdg 2: 1 'I will never *b* my covenant
Pr 25:15 and a gentle tongue can *b* a bone.
Isa 42: 3 A bruised reed he will not *b*,
Mal 2:15 and do not *b* faith with the wife
Mt 12:20 A bruised reed he will not *b*,
Ac 20: 7 week we came together to *b* bread.
1Co 10:16 the bread that we *b* a participation
Rev 5: 2 "Who is worthy to *b* the seals

BREAKERS* (BREAK)
Ps 42: 7 all your waves and *b*
93: 4 mightier than the *b* of the sea—
Jnh 2: 3 all your waves and *b*

BREAKING (BREAK)
Jos 9:20 fall on us for *b* the oath we swore
Eze 16:59 oath by *b* the covenant.
17:18 the oath by *b* the covenant.
Ac 2:42 to the *b* of bread and to prayer.
Jas 2:10 at just one point is guilty of *b* all

BREAKS (BREAK)
Jer 23:29 "and like a hammer that *b* a rock
1Jn 3: 4 Everyone who sins *b* the law;

BREASTPIECE (BREASTPLATE)
Ex 28:15 Fashion a *b* for making decisions—

BREASTPLATE* (BREASTPIECE)
Isa 59:17 He put on righteousness as his *b*,
Eph 6:14 with the *b* of righteousness in place
1Th 5: 8 putting on faith and love as a *b*,

BREASTS
La 4: 3 Even jackals offer their *b*

BREATH (BREATHED GOD-BREATHED)
Ge 2: 7 into his nostrils the *b* of life,

BREATHED (BREATH)
Ge 2: 7 *b* into his nostrils the breath of life,
Mk 15:37 With a loud cry, Jesus *b* his last.
Jn 20:22 And with that he *b* on them

BREEDS*
Pr 13:10 Pride only *b* quarrels,

BRIBE
Ex 23: 8 "Do not accept a *b*,
Dt 16:19 for a *b* blinds the eyes of the wise
27:25 "Cursed is the man who accepts a *b*
Pr 6:35 will refuse the *b*, however great it

BRIDE
Isa 62: 5 as a bridegroom rejoices over his *b*,
Rev 19: 7 and his *b* has made herself ready.
21: 2 as a *b* beautifully dressed
21: 9 I will show you the *b*, the wife
22:17 The Spirit and the *b* say, "Come!"

BRIDEGROOM
Ps 19: 5 which is like a *b* coming forth
Mt 25: 1 and went out to meet the *b*.
25: 5 The *b* was a long time in coming,

BRIGHTENS* (BRIGHTNESS)
Pr 16:15 When a king's face *b*, it means life;
Ecc 8: 1 Wisdom *b* a man's face

BRIGHTER (BRIGHTNESS)
Pr 4:18 shining ever *b* till the full light

BRIGHTNESS* (BRIGHTENS BRIGHTER)
2Sa 22:13 Out of the *b* of his presence
23: 4 like the *b* after rain
Ps 18:12 of the *b* of his presence clouds
Isa 59: 9 for *b*, but we walk in deep shadows.
60: 3 and kings to the *b* of your dawn.
60:19 will the *b* of the moon shine on you
Da 12: 3 who are wise will shine like the *b*
Am 5:20 pitch-dark, without a ray of *b*?

BRILLIANCE* (BRILLIANT)
Ac 22:11 the *b* of the light had blinded me.
Rev 1:16 was like the sun shining in all its *b*.
21:11 its *b* was like that of a very precious

BRILLIANT* (BRILLIANCE)
Ecc 9:11 or wealth to the *b*
Eze 1: 4 and surrounded by *b* light.
1:27 and *b* light surrounded him.

BRINK*
Pr 5:14 I have come to the *b* of utter ruin

BRITTLE
Da 2:42 will be partly strong and partly *b*.

BROAD
Mt 7:13 and *b* is the road that leads

BROKE (BREAK)
Mt 26:26 took bread, gave thanks and *b* it,
Mk 14:22 took bread, gave thanks and *b* it,
Ac 2:46 They *b* bread in their homes
20:11 he went upstairs again and *b* bread
1Co 11:24 when he had given thanks, he *b* it

BROKEN (BREAK)
Ps 34:20 not one of them will be *b*.
51:17 The sacrifices of God are a *b* spirit;
Ecc 4:12 of three strands is not quickly *b*.
Lk 20:18 on that stone will be *b* to pieces,
Jn 7:23 the law of Moses may not be *b*,
10:35 and the Scripture cannot be *b*—

Jn 19:36 "Not one of his bones will be *b*,"
Ro 11:20 they were *b* off because of unbelief,

BROKENHEARTED* (HEART)
Ps 34:18 The LORD is close to the *b*
109: 16 and the needy and the *b*.
147: 3 He heals the *b*
Isa 61: 1 He has sent me to bind up the *b*,

BROKENNESS* (BREAK)
Isa 65:14 and wail in *b* of spirit.

BRONZE
Ex 27: 2 and overlay the altar with *b*.
30:18 "Make a *b* basin, with its *b* stand,
Nu 21: 9 So Moses made a *b* snake
Da 2:32 and thighs of *b*, its legs of iron,
10: 6 legs like the gleam of burnished *b*,
Rev 1:15 His feet were like *b* glowing
2:18 whose feet are like burnished *b*.

BROTHER (BROTHER'S BROTHERHOOD BROTHERLY BROTHERS)
Pr 17:17 and a *b* is born for adversity.
18:24 a friend who sticks closer than a *b*.
27:10 neighbor nearby than a *b* far away.
Mt 5:24 and be reconciled to your *b*;
18:15 "If your *b* sins against you,
Mk 3:35 Whoever does God's will is my *b*
Lk 17: 3 "If your *b* sins, rebuke him,
Ro 14:15 not by your eating destroy your *b*
14:21 anything else that will cause your *b*
1Co 8:13 if what I eat causes my *b* to fall
2Th 3: 6 away from every *b* who is idle
3:15 as an enemy, but warn him as a *b*.
Phm :16 but better than a slave, as a dear *b*.
Jas 2:15 Suppose a *b* or sister is
4:11 Anyone who speaks against his *b*
1Jn 2: 9 hates his *b* is still in the darkness.
2:10 Whoever loves his *b* lives
2:11 But whoever hates his *b* is
3:10 is anyone who does not love his *b*.
3:15 who hates his *b* is a murderer,
3:17 material possessions and sees his *b*
4:20 For anyone who does not love his *b*
4:20 yet hates his *b*, he is a liar.
4:21 loves God must also love his *b*.
5:16 If anyone sees his *b* commit a sin

BROTHER'S (BROTHER)
Ge 4: 9 "Am I my *b* keeper?" The LORD
Mt 7: 5 remove the speck from your *b* eye.
Ro 14:13 or obstacle in your *b* way.

BROTHERHOOD (BROTHER)
1Pe 2:17 Love the *b* of believers, fear God,

BROTHERLY* (BROTHER)
Ro 12:10 devoted to one another in *b* love.
1Th 4: 9 Now about *b* love we do not need
2Pe 1: 7 and to godliness, *b* kindness;
1: 7 kindness; and to *b* kindness,

BROTHERS (BROTHER)
Jos 1:14 You are to help your *b*
Ps 133: 1 is when *b* live together in unity!
Pr 6:19 who stirs up dissension among *b*.
Mt 12:49 "Here are my mother and my *b*.
19:29 everyone who has left houses or *b*
25:40 one of the least of these *b* of mine,
Mk 3:33 "Who are my mother and my *b*?"
10:29 or *b* or sisters or mother or father
Lk 21:16 will be betrayed even by parents, *b*,
22:32 turned back, strengthen your *b*."
Jn 7: 5 his own *b* did not believe in him.
Ac 15:32 to encourage and strengthen the *b*.
Ro 9: 3 off from Christ for the sake of my *b*
1Co 8:12 sin against your *b* in this way
2Co 11:26 and in danger from false *b*.
Gal 2: 4 some false *b* had infiltrated our
1Th 4:10 you do love all the *b*
5:26 Greet all the *b* with a holy kiss.
1Ti 6: 2 for them because they are *b*.
Heb 2:11 Jesus is not ashamed to call them *b*.
2:17 to be made like his *b* in every way,
13: 1 Keep on loving each other as *b*.
1Pe 1:22 you have sincere love for your *b*,
3: 8 be sympathetic, love as *b*,
1Jn 3:14 death to life, because we love our *b*.
3:16 to lay down our lives for our *b*.
3Jn :10 he refuses to welcome the *b*.
Rev 12:10 For the accuser of our *b*,

BROW
Ge 3:19 By the sweat of your *b*

BRUISED (BRUISES)
Isa 42: 3 A *b* reed he will not break,
Mt 12:20 A *b* reed he will not break,

BRUISES (BRUISED)
Isa 30:26 when the LORD binds up the *b*

BRUTAL (BRUTE)
2Ti 3: 3 slanderous, without self-control, *b*,

BRUTE* (BRUTAL)
Ps 73:22 I was a *b* beast before you.
2Pe 2:12 They are like *b* beasts, creatures

BUBBLING*
Pr 18: 4 the fountain of wisdom is a *b* brook
Isa 35: 7 the thirsty ground *b* springs.

BUCKET*
Isa 40:15 the nations are like a drop in a *b*;

BUCKLED* (BUCKLER)
Eph 6:14 belt of truth *b* around your waist,

BUCKLER* (BUCKLED)
Ps 35: 2 Take up shield and *b*;

BUD (BUDDED)
Isa 27: 6 Israel will *b* and blossom

BUDDED (BUD)
Heb 9: 4 Aaron's staff that had *b*,

BUILD (BUILDER BUILDERS BUILDING BUILDS BUILT REBUILD REBUILT)
2Sa 7: 5 Are you the one to *b* me a house
1Ki 6: 1 he began to *b* the temple
Ecc 3: 3 a time to tear down and a time to *b*,
Mt 16:18 and on this rock I will *b* my church,
Ac 20:32 which can *b* you up and give you
Ro 15: 2 neighbor for his good, to *b* him up.
1Co 14:12 excel in gifts that *b* up the church.
1Th 5:11 one another and *b* each other up,
Jude :20 *b* yourselves up in your most holy

BUILDER* (BUILD)
1Co 3:10 I laid a foundation as an expert *b*,
Heb 3: 3 the *b* of a house has greater honor
3: 4 but God is the *b* of everything.
11:10 whose architect and *b* is God.

BUILDERS (BUILD)
Ps 118: 22 The stone the *b* rejected
Mt 21:42 " 'The stone the *b* rejected
Mk 12:10 " 'The stone the *b* rejected
Lk 20:17 " 'The stone the *b* rejected
Ac 4:11 " 'the stone you *b* rejected,
1Pe 2: 7 "The stone the *b* rejected

BUILDING (BUILD)
Ezr 3: 8 to supervise the *b* of the house
Ne 4:17 of Judah who were *b* the wall.
Ro 15:20 so that I would not be *b*
1Co 3: 9 you are God's field, God's *b*.
2Co 5: 1 we have a *b* from God, an eternal
10: 8 us for *b* you up rather
13:10 the Lord gave me for *b* you up,
Eph 2:21 him the whole *b* is joined together
4:29 helpful for *b* others up according

BUILDS (BUILD)
Ps 127: 1 Unless the LORD *b* the house,
Pr 14: 1 The wise woman *b* her house,
1Co 3:10 one should be careful how he *b*.
3:12 If any man *b* on this foundation
8: 1 Knowledge puffs up, but love *b* up.
Eph 4:16 grows and *b* itself up in love,

BUILT (BUILD)
1Ki 6:14 So Solomon *b* the temple
Mt 7:24 is like a wise man who *b* his house
Lk 6:49 is like a man who *b* a house
Ac 17:24 does not live in temples *b* by hands.
1Co 3:14 If what he has *b* survives, he will
2Co 5: 1 in heaven, not *b* by human hands.
Eph 2:20 *b* on the foundation of the apostles
4:12 the body of Christ may be *b* up
Col 2: 7 live in him, rooted and *b* up in him,
1Pe 2: 5 are being *b* into a spiritual house

BULL (BULLS)
Lev 4: 3 bring to the LORD a young *b*

BULLS (BULL)
1Ki 7:25 The Sea stood on twelve *b*,
Heb 10: 4 it is impossible for the blood of *b*

BURDEN (BURDENED BURDENS BURDENSOME)
Ps 38: 4 like a *b* too heavy to bear.
Ecc 1:13 What a heavy *b* God has laid
Mt 11:30 my yoke is easy and my *b* is light."
Ac 15:28 to us not to *b* you with anything
2Co 11: 9 from being a *b* to you in any way,
12:14 and I will not be a *b* to you,
1Th 2: 9 day in order not to be a *b* to anyone
2Th 3: 8 so that we would not be a *b* to any
Heb 13:17 not a *b*, for that would be

BURDENED* (BURDEN)
Isa 43:23 have not *b* you with grain offerings
43:24 But you have *b* me with your sins
Mic 6: 3 How have I *b* you? Answer me.
Mt 11:28 all you who are weary and *b*,
2Co 5: 4 are in this tent, we groan and are *b*,
Gal 5: 1 do not let yourselves be *b* again
1Ti 5:16 not let the church be *b* with them,

BURDENS (BURDEN)
Ps 68:19 who daily bears our *b*.
Lk 11:46 down with *b* they can hardly carry,
Gal 6: 2 Carry each other's *b*,

BURDENSOME (BURDEN)
1Jn 5: 3 And his commands are not *b*,

BURIED (BURY)
Ru 1:17 die I will die, and there I will be *b*.
Ro 6: 4 *b* with him through baptism
1Co 15: 4 that he was *b*, that he was raised
Col 2:12 having been *b* with him in baptism

BURN (BURNING BURNT)
Dt 7: 5 and *b* their idols in the fire.
Ps 79: 5 long will your jealousy *b* like fire?
1Co 7: 9 to marry than to *b* with passion.

BURNING (BURN)
Ex 27:20 so that the lamps may be kept *b*.
Lev 6: 9 the fire must be kept *b* on the altar.
Ps 18:28 You, O LORD, keep my lamp *b*;
Pr 25:22 you will heap *b* coals on his head,
Ro 12:20 you will heap *b* coals on his head."
Rev 19:20 alive into the fiery lake of *b* sulfur.

BURNISHED*
1Ki 7:45 of the LORD were of *b* bronze.
Eze 1: 7 and gleamed like *b* bronze.
Da 10: 6 and legs like the gleam of *b* bronze,
Rev 2:18 and whose feet are like *b* bronze.

BURNT (BURN)
Ge 8:20 he sacrificed *b* offerings on it.
22: 2 as a *b* offering on one
Ex 10:25 and *b* offerings to present
18:12 brought a *b* offering and other
40: 6 Place the altar of *b* offering in front
Lev 1: 3 " 'If the offering is a *b* offering
Jos 8:31 offered to the LORD *b* offerings
Jdg 6:26 offer the second bull as a *b* offering
13:16 But if you prepare a *b* offering,
1Ki 3: 4 offered a thousand *b* offerings
9:25 year Solomon sacrificed *b* offerings
10: 5 and the *b* offerings he made
Ezr 3: 2 Israel to sacrifice *b* offerings on it,
Eze 43:18 for sacrificing *b* offerings

BURST
Ps 98: 4 *b* into jubilant song with music;
Isa 44:23 *B* into song, you mountains,
49:13 *b* into song, O mountains!
52: 9 *B* into songs of joy together,
54: 1 *b* into song, shout for joy,
55:12 will *b* into song before you,

BURY (BURIED)
Mt 8:22 and let the dead *b* their own dead."
Lk 9:60 "Let the dead *b* their own dead,

BUSH
Ex 3: 2 the *b* was on fire it did not burn up.
Mk 12:26 the account of the *b*, how God said
Lk 20:37 But in the account of the *b*,
Ac 7:35 who appeared to him in the *b*.

BUSINESS
Ecc 4: 8 a miserable *b*!
Da 8:27 and went about the king's *b*.
1Co 5:12 What *b* is it of mine to judge those
1Th 4:11 to mind your own *b* and to work
Jas 1:11 even while he goes about his *b*.

BUSY*
1Ki 18:27 Perhaps he is deep in thought, or *b*,
20:40 While your servant was *b* here
Isa 32: 6 his mind is *b* with evil:

Hag 1: 9 of you is *b* with his own house.
2Th 3:11 They are not *b;* they are
Tit 2: 5 to be *b* at home, to be kind,

BUSYBODIES*
2Th 3:11 They are not busy; they are *b.*
1Ti 5:13 *b,* saying things they ought not to.

BUY (BOUGHT BUYS)
Pr 23:23 *B* the truth and do not sell it;
Isa 55: 1 Come, *b* wine and milk
Rev 13:17 so that no one could *b* or sell

BUYS (BUY)
Pr 31:16 She considers a field and *b* it;

BYWORD (WORD)
1Ki 9: 7 Israel will then become a *b*
Ps 44:14 You have made us a *b*
Joel 2:17 a *b* among the nations.

CAESAR
Mt 22:21 "Give to *C* what is Caesar's,

CAIN
Firstborn of Adam (Ge 4:1), murdered brother Abel (Ge 4:1–16; 1Jn 3:12).

CAKE
Hos 7: 8 Ephraim is a flat *c* not turned over.

CALEB
Judahite who spied out Canaan (Nu 13:6); allowed to enter land because of faith (Nu 13:30–14:38; Dt 1:36). Possessed Hebron (Jos 14:6–15:19).

CALF
Ex 32: 4 into an idol cast in the shape of a *c,*
Pr 15:17 than a fattened *c* with hatred.
Lk 15:23 Bring the fattened *c* and kill it.
Ac 7:41 made an idol in the form of a *c.*

CALL (CALLED CALLING CALLS)
1Ki 18:24 I will *c* on the name of the LORD.
2Ki 5:11 *c* on the name of the LORD his
1Ch 16: 8 to the LORD, *c* on his name;
Ps 105: 1 to the LORD, *c* on his name;
116: 13 and *c* on the name of the LORD.
116: 17 and *c* on the name of the LORD.
145: 18 near to all who *c* on him,
Pr 31:28 children arise and *c* her blessed;
Isa 5:20 Woe to those who *c* evil good
12: 4 to the LORD, *c* on his name;
55: 6 *c* on him while he is near.
65:24 Before they *c* I will answer;
Jer 33: 3 '*C* to me and I will answer you
Zep 3: 9 that all of them may *c* on the name
Zec 13: 9 They will *c* on my name
Mt 9:13 come to *c* the righteous,
Mk 2:17 I have not come to *c* the righteous,
Lk 5:32 I have not come to *c* the righteous,
Ac 2:39 all whom the Lord our God will *c.*"
9:14 to arrest all who *c* on your name."
9:21 among those who *c* on this name?
Ro 10:12 and richly blesses all who *c* on him,
11:29 gifts and his *c* are irrevocable.
1Co 1: 2 with all those everywhere who *c*
1Th 4: 7 For God did not *c* us to be impure,
2Ti 2:22 along with those who *c*

CALLED (CALL)
Ge 2:23 she shall be *c* 'woman,'
5: 2 he blessed them and *c* them "man
12: 8 and *c* on the name of the LORD.
21:33 and there he *c* upon the name
26:25 and *c* on the name of the LORD.
1Sa 3: 5 and said, "Here I am; you *c* me."
2Ch 7:14 if my people, who are *c*
Ps 34: 6 This poor man *c,* and the LORD
116: 4 Then I *c* on the name of the LORD
Isa 56: 7 for my house will be *c*
La 3:55 I *c* on your name, O LORD,
Hos 11: 1 and out of Egypt I *c* my son.
Mt 1:16 was born Jesus, who is *c* Christ.
2:15 "Out of Egypt I *c* my son."
21:13 " 'My house will be *c* a house
Mk 11:17 " 'My house will be *c*
Lk 1:32 will be *c* the Son of the Most High.
1:35 to be born will be *c* the Son of God.
Ro 1: 1 *c* to be an apostle and set apart
1: 6 among those who are *c* to belong
1: 7 loved by God and *c* to be saints:
8:28 who have been *c* according
8:30 And those he predestined, he also *c*
1Co 1: 1 *c* to be an apostle of Christ Jesus
1: 2 in Christ Jesus and *c* to be holy,
1:24 but to those whom God has *c,*
1:26 of what you were when you were *c.*
7:15 God has *c* us to live in peace.
7:17 and to which God has *c* him.
Gal 1: 6 deserting the one who *c* you
1:15 from birth and *c* me by his grace,
5:13 You, my brothers, were *c* to be free
Eph 1:18 the hope to which he has *c* you,
4: 4 as you were *c* to one hope
Col 3:15 of one body you were *c* to peace.
2Th 2:14 He *c* you to this through our gospel
1Ti 6:12 life to which you were *c*
2Ti 1: 9 who has saved us and *c* us
Heb 9:15 that those who are *c* may receive
1Pe 1:15 But just as he who *c* you is holy,
2: 9 of him who *c* you out of darkness
3: 9 to this you were *c* so that you may
5:10 who *c* you to his eternal glory
2Pe 1: 3 of him who *c* us by his own glory
Jude : 1 To those who have been *c,*

CALLING (CALL)
Isa 40: 3 A voice of one *c:*
Mt 3: 3 "A voice of one *c* in the desert,
Mk 1: 3 "a voice of one *c* in the desert,
10:49 Cheer up! On your feet! He's *c* you
Lk 3: 4 "A voice of one *c* in the desert,
Jn 1:23 I am the voice of one *c* in the desert
Ac 22:16 wash your sins away, *c* on his name
Eph 4: 1 worthy of the *c* you have received.
2Th 1:11 may count you worthy of his *c,*
2Pe 1:10 all the more eager to make your *c*

CALLOUS* (CALLOUSED)
Ps 17:10 They close up their *c* hearts,
73: 7 From their *c* hearts comes iniquity;
119: 70 Their hearts are *c* and unfeeling,

CALLOUSED* (CALLOUS)
Isa 6:10 Make the heart of this people *c;*
Mt 13:15 this people's heart has become *c;*
Ac 28:27 this people's heart has become *c;*

CALLS (CALL)
Ps 147: 4 and *c* them each by name.
Isa 40:26 and *c* them each by name.
Joel 2:32 And everyone who *c*
Mt 22:43 speaking by the Spirit, *c* him 'Lord
Jn 10: 3 He *c* his own sheep by name
Ac 2:21 And everyone who *c*
Ro 10:13 "Everyone who *c* on the name
1Th 2:12 who *c* you into his kingdom
5:24 The one who *c* you is faithful

CALM (CALMS)
Ps 107: 30 They were glad when it grew *c,*
Isa 7: 4 keep *c* and don't be afraid.
Eze 16:42 I will be *c* and no longer angry.

CALMS* (CALM)
Pr 15:18 but a patient man *c* a quarrel.

CAMEL
Mt 19:24 it is easier for a *c* to go
23:24 strain out a gnat but swallow a *c.*
Mk 10:25 It is easier for a *c* to go
Lk 18:25 it is easier for a *c* to go

CAMP (ENCAMPS)
Heb 13:13 outside the *c,* bearing the disgrace

CANAAN (CANAANITE CANAANITES)
Ge 10:15 *C* was the father of Sidon his
Lev 14:34 "When you enter the land of *C,*
25:38 of Egypt to give you the land of *C*
Nu 13: 2 men to explore the land of *C,*
33:51 'When you cross the Jordan into *C,*
Jdg 4: 2 a king of *C,* who reigned in Hazor.
1Ch 16:18 "To you I will give the land of *C*
Ps 105: 11 "To you I will give the land of *C*
Ac 13:19 he overthrew seven nations in *C*

CANAANITE (CANAAN)
Ge 10:18 Later the *C* clans scattered
28: 1 "Do not marry a *C* woman.
Jos 5: 1 all the *C* kings along the seacoast
Jdg 1:32 lived among the *C* inhabitants

CANAANITES (CANAAN)
Ex 33: 2 before you and drive out the *C,*

CANCEL (CANCELED)
Dt 15: 1 seven years you must *c* debts.

CANCELED (CANCEL)
Mt 18:27 pity on him, *c* the debt
Lk 7:42 so he *c* the debts of both.
Col 2:14 having *c* the written code,

CANDLESTICKS
see LAMPSTANDS

CANOPY*
2Sa 22:12 He made darkness his *c*
2Ki 16:18 away the Sabbath *c* that had been
Ps 18:11 made darkness his covering, his *c*
Isa 4: 5 over all the glory will be a *c.*
40:22 stretches out the heavens like a *c,*
Jer 43:10 he will spread his royal *c*

CAPERNAUM
Mt 4:13 Nazareth, he went and lived in *C,*
Jn 6:59 teaching in the synagogue in *C.*

CAPITAL
Dt 21:22 guilty of a *c* offense is put to death

CAPSTONE* (STONE)
Ps 118: 22 has become the *c;*
Zec 4: 7 he will bring out the *c* to shouts
Mt 21:42 has become the *c;*
Mk 12:10 has become the *c;*
Lk 20:17 has become the *c*?
Ac 4:11 which has become the *c.*'
1Pe 2: 7 has become the *c,*"

CAPTIVATE* (CAPTIVE)
Pr 6:25 or let her *c* you with her eyes,

CAPTIVATED* (CAPTIVE)
Pr 5:19 may you ever be *c* by her love.
5:20 Why be *c,* my son, by an adulteress

CAPTIVE (CAPTIVATE CAPTIVATED CAPTIVES CAPTIVITY CAPTURED)
Ac 8:23 full of bitterness and *c* to sin."
2Co 10: 5 and we take *c* every thought
Col 2: 8 See to it that no one takes you *c*
2Ti 2:26 who has taken them *c* to do his will.

CAPTIVES (CAPTIVE)
Ps 68:18 you led *c* in your train;
Isa 61: 1 to proclaim freedom for the *c*
Eph 4: 8 he led *c* in his train

CAPTIVITY (CAPTIVE)
Dt 28:41 because they will go into *c.*
2Ki 25:21 So Judah went into *c,* away
Jer 30: 3 Israel and Judah back from *c*
52:27 So Judah went into *c,* away
Eze 29:14 I will bring them back from *c*

CAPTURED (CAPTIVE)
1Sa 4:11 The ark of God was *c,*
2Sa 5: 7 David *c* the fortress of Zion,
2Ki 17: 6 the king of Assyria *c* Samaria

CARCASS
Jdg 14: 9 taken the honey from the lion's *c.*
Mt 24:28 there is a *c,* there the vultures

CARE (CAREFUL CARES CARING)
Ps 8: 4 the son of man that you *c* for him?
65: 9 You *c* for the land and water it;
144: 3 what is man that you *c* for him,
Pr 29: 7 The righteous *c* about justice
Mk 5:26 deal under the *c* of many doctors
Lk 10:34 him to an inn and took *c* of him.
18: 4 I don't fear God or *c* about men,
Jn 21:16 Jesus said, "Take *c* of my sheep."
1Ti 3: 5 how can he take *c* of God's church
6:20 what has been entrusted to your *c.*
Heb 2: 6 the son of man that you *c* for him?
1Pe 5: 2 of God's flock that is under your *c,*

CAREFUL* (CARE)
Ge 31:24 "Be *c* not to say anything to Jacob,
31:29 'Be *c* not to say anything to Jacob,
Ex 19:12 'Be *c* that you do not go up
23:13 "Be *c* to do everything I have said
34:12 Be *c* not to make a treaty
34:15 "Be *c* not to make a treaty
Lev 18: 4 and be *c* to follow my decrees.
25:18 " 'Follow my decrees and be *c*
26: 3 and are *c* to obey my commands,
Dt 2: 4 afraid of you, but be very *c.*
4: 9 before you today? Only be *c,*
4:23 Be *c* not to forget the covenant
5:32 So be *c* to do what the LORD your
6: 3 be *c* to obey so that it may go well

Dt 6:12 be *c* that you do not forget
6:25 And if we are *c* to obey all this law
7:12 attention to these laws and are *c*
8: 1 Be *c* to follow every command I am
8:11 Be *c* that you do not forget
11:16 Be *c*, or you will be enticed
12: 1 and laws you must be *c* to follow
12:13 Be *c* not to sacrifice your burnt
12:19 Be *c* not to neglect the Levites
12:28 Be *c* to obey all these regulations I
12:30 be *c* not to be ensnared
15: 5 are *c* to follow all these commands
15: 9 Be *c* not to harbor this wicked
17:10 Be *c* to do everything they direct
24: 8 cases of leprous diseases be very *c*
Jos 1: 7 Be *c* to obey all the law my servant
1: 8 so that you may be *c*
22: 5 But be very *c* to keep
23: 6 be *c* to obey all that is written
23:11 be very *c* to love the LORD your
1Ki 8:25 if only your sons are *c* in all they do
2Ki 10:31 Yet Jehu was not *c* to keep the law
17:37 You must always be *c*
21: 8 if only they will be *c*
1Ch 22:13 if you are *c* to observe the decrees
28: 8 Be *c* to follow all the commands
2Ch 6:16 if only your sons are *c* in all they do
33: 8 if only they will be *c*
Ezr 4:22 Be *c* not to neglect this matter.
Job 36:18 Be *c* that no one entices you
Ps 101: 2 I will be *c* to lead a blameless life—
Pr 13:24 he who loves him is *c*
27:23 give *c* attention to your herds;
Isa 7: 4 Be *c*, keep calm and don't be afraid.
Jer 17:21 Be *c* not to carry a load
17:24 But if you are *c* to obey me,
22: 4 For if you are *c* to carry out these
Eze 11:20 will follow my decrees and be *c*
18:19 has been *c* to keep all my decrees,
20:19 follow my decrees and be *c*
20:21 they were not *c* to keep my laws—
36:27 you to follow my decrees and be *c*
37:24 and be *c* to keep my decrees.
Mic 7: 5 be *c* of your words.
Hag 1: 5 "Give *c* thought to your ways.
1: 7 "Give *c* thought to your ways.
2:15 give *c* thought to this from this day
2:18 Give *c* thought: Is there yet any
2:18 give *c* thought to the day
Mt 2: 8 and make a *c* search for the child.
6: 1 "Be *c* not to do your 'acts
16: 6 "Be *c*," Jesus said to them.
Mk 8:15 "Be *c*," Jesus warned them.
Lk 21:34 Be *c*, or your hearts will be weighed
Ro 12:17 Be *c* to do what is right in the eyes
1Co 3:10 each one should be *c* how he builds
8: 9 Be *c*, however, that the exercise
10:12 standing firm, be *c* that you don't
Eph 5:15 Be very *c*, then, how you live—
2Ti 4: 2 great patience and *c* instruction.
Tit 3: 8 may be *c* to devote themselves
Heb 2: 1 We must pay more *c* attention,
4: 1 let us be *c* that none

CARELESS*
Mt 12:36 for every *c* word they have spoken.

CARES* (CARE)
Dt 11:12 It is a land the LORD your God *c*
Job 39:16 she *c* not that her labor was in vain,
Ps 55:22 Cast your *c* on the LORD
142: 4 no one *c* for my life.
Pr 12:10 A righteous man *c* for the needs
Ecc 5: 3 when there are many *c*,
Jer 12:11 because there is no one who *c*.
30:17 Zion for whom no one *c*.'
Na 1: 7 He *c* for those who trust in him,
Jn 10:13 and *c* nothing for the sheep.
Eph 5:29 but he feeds and *c* for it, just
1Pe 5: 7 on him because he *c* for you.

CARING* (CARE)
1Th 2: 7 like a mother *c* for her little
1Ti 5: 4 practice by *c* for their own family

CARPENTER (CARPENTER'S)
Mk 6: 3 does miracles! Isn't this the *c*?

CARPENTER'S* (CARPENTER)
Mt 13:55 "Isn't this the *c* son? Isn't his

CARRIED (CARRY)
Ex 19: 4 and how I *c* you on eagles' wings
Dt 1:31 how the LORD your God *c* you,
Isa 53: 4 and *c* our sorrows,
63: 9 he lifted them up and *c* them
Mt 8:17 and *c* our diseases."
Heb 13: 9 Do not be *c* away by all kinds
2Pe 1:21 as they were *c* along by the Holy
3:17 so that you may not be *c* away

CARRIES (CARRY)
Dt 32:11 and *c* them on its pinions.
Isa 40:11 and *c* them close to his heart;

CARRY (CARRIED CARRIES CARRYING)
Lev 16:22 goat will *c* on itself all their sins
26:15 and fail to *c* out all my commands
Isa 46: 4 I have made you and I will *c* you;
Lk 14:27 anyone who does not *c* his cross
Gal 6: 2 *C* each other's burdens,
6: 5 for each one should *c* his own load.

CARRYING (CARRY)
Jn 19:17 *C* his own cross, he went out
1Jn 5: 2 loving God and *c* out his

CARVED (CARVES)
Nu 33:52 Destroy all their *c* images
Mic 5:13 I will destroy your *c* images

CARVES* (CARVED)
Dt 27:15 "Cursed is the man who *c* an image

CASE
Pr 18:17 to present his *c* seems right,
22:23 for the LORD will take up their *c*
23:11 he will take up their *c* against you.

CAST (CASTING)
Ex 34:17 "Do not make *c* idols.
Lev 16: 8 He is to *c* lots for the two goats—
Ps 22:18 and *c* lots for my clothing.
55:22 *C* your cares on the LORD
Pr 16:33 The lot is *c* into the lap,
Ecc 11: 1 *C* your bread upon the waters,
Jn 19:24 and *c* lots for my clothing."
1Pe 5: 7 *C* all your anxiety on him

CASTING (CAST)
Pr 18:18 *C* the lot settles disputes
Mt 27:35 divided up his clothes by *c* lots.

CATCH (CATCHES CAUGHT)
Lk 5: 4 and let down the nets for a *c*."
5:10 from now on you will *c* men."

CATCHES (CATCH)
Job 5:13 He *c* the wise in their craftiness,
1Co 3:19 "He *c* the wise in their craftiness";

CATTLE
Ps 50:10 and the *c* on a thousand hills.

CAUGHT (CATCH)
Ge 22:13 there in a thicket he saw a ram *c*
2Co 12: 2 who fourteen years ago was *c* up
1Th 4:17 and are left will be *c* up together with them

CAUSE (CAUSES)
Pr 24:28 against your neighbor without *c*,
Ecc 8: 3 Do not stand up for a bad *c*,
Mt 18: 7 of the things that *c* people to sin!
Ro 14:21 else that will *c* your brother
1Co 10:32 Do not *c* anyone to stumble,

CAUSES (CAUSE)
Ps 7:16 The trouble he *c* recoils on himself;
Isa 8:14 a stone that *c* men to stumble
Mt 5:29 If your right eye *c* you to sin,
5:30 And if your right hand *c* you to sin,
18: 6 if anyone *c* one of these little ones
18: 8 or your foot *c* you to sin,
Ro 14:20 to eat anything that *c* someone else
1Co 8:13 if what I eat *c* my brother to fall
1Pe 2: 8 "A stone that *c* men to stumble

CAUTIOUS*
Pr 12:26 A righteous man is *c* in friendship,

CEASE
Ps 46: 9 He makes wars *c* to the ends

CELEBRATE*
Ex 10: 9 we are to *c* a festival to the LORD
12:14 generations to come you shall *c* it
12:17 *C* this day as a lasting ordinance
12:17 "*C* the Feast of Unleavened Bread,
12:47 community of Israel must *c* it.
12:48 to *c* the LORD's Passover must
Ex 23:14 are to *c* a festival to me.
23:15 "*C* the Feast of Unleavened Bread;
23:16 "*C* the Feast of Harvest
23:16 "*C* the Feast of Ingathering
34:18 "*C* the Feast of Unleavened Bread.
34:22 "*C* the Feast of Weeks
Lev 23:39 *c* the festival to the LORD
23:41 *C* this as a festival to the LORD
23:41 for the generations to come; *c* it
Nu 9: 2 "Have the Israelites *c* the Passover
9: 3 *C* it at the appointed time,
9: 4 told the Israelites to *c* the Passover,
9: 6 of them could not *c* the Passover
9:10 they may still *c* the LORD's
9:11 are to *c* it on the fourteenth day
9:12 When they *c* the Passover,
9:13 on a journey fails to *c* the Passover,
9:14 to *c* the LORD's Passover must do
29:12 *C* a festival to the LORD
Dt 16: 1 *c* the Passover of the LORD your
16:10 Then *c* the Feast of Weeks
16:13 *C* the Feast of Tabernacles
16:15 For seven days *c* the Feast
Jdg 16:23 to Dagon their god and to *c*,
2Sa 6:21 the LORD's people Israel—I will *c*
2Ki 23:21 "*C* the Passover to the LORD your
2Ch 30: 1 and *c* the Passover to the LORD,
30: 2 decided to *c* the Passover
30: 3 able to *c* it at the regular time
30: 5 and *c* the Passover to the LORD,
30:13 in Jerusalem to *c* the Feast
30:23 to *c* the festival seven more days;
Ne 8:12 of food and to *c* with great joy,
12:27 to *c* joyfully the dedication
Est 9:21 to have them *c* annually
Ps 145: 7 They will *c* your abundant
Isa 30:29 as on the night you *c* a holy festival
Na 1:15 *C* your festivals, O Judah,
Zec 14:16 and to *c* the Feast of Tabernacles.
14:18 up to *c* the Feast of Tabernacles.
14:19 up to *c* the Feast of Tabernacles.
Mt 26:18 I am going to *c* the Passover
Lk 15:23 Let's have a feast and *c*.
15:24 So they began to *c*.
15:29 goat so I could *c* with my friends.
15:32 But we had to *c* and be glad,
Rev 11:10 will *c* by sending each other gifts,

CELESTIAL*
2Pe 2:10 afraid to slander *c* beings;
Jude : 8 authority and slander *c* beings.

CENSER (CENSERS)
Lev 16:12 is to take a *c* full of burning coals
Rev 8: 3 Another angel, who had a golden *c*,

CENSERS (CENSER)
Nu 16: 6 Take *c* and tomorrow put fire

CENTURION
Mt 8: 5 had entered Capernaum, a *c* came
27:54 When the *c* and those
Mk 15:39 And when the *c*, who stood there
Lk 7: 3 The *c* heard of Jesus and sent some
23:47 The *c*, seeing what had happened,
Ac 10: 1 a *c* in what was known
27: 1 handed over to a *c* named Julius,

CEPHAS* (PETER)
Jn 1:42 You will be called *C*" (which,
1Co 1:12 another, "I follow *C*"; still another,
3:22 Paul or Apollos or *C* or the world
9: 5 and the Lord's brothers and *C*?

CEREMONIAL* (CEREMONY)
Lev 14: 2 at the time of his *c* cleansing,
15:13 off seven days for his *c* cleansing;
Mk 7: 3 they give their hands a *c* washing,
Jn 2: 6 used by the Jews for *c* washing,
3:25 Jew over the matter of *c* washing.
11:55 to Jerusalem for their *c* cleansing
18:28 to avoid *c* uncleanness the Jews did
Heb 9:10 drink and various *c* washings—
13: 9 not by *c* foods, which are

CEREMONIALLY* (CEREMONY)
Lev 4:12 outside the camp to a place *c* clean,
5: 2 touches anything *c* unclean—
6:11 the camp to a place that is *c* clean.
7:19 anyone *c* clean may eat it.
7:19 touches anything *c* unclean must
10:14 Eat them in a *c* clean place;
11: 4 not have a split hoof; it is *c* unclean

Lev 12: 2 birth to a son will be *c* unclean
12: 7 and then she will be *c* clean
13: 3 he shall pronounce him *c* unclean.
14: 8 with water; then he will be *c* clean.
15:28 and after that she will be *c* clean.
15:33 lies with a woman who is *c* unclean.
17:15 he will be *c* unclean till evening.
21: 1 must not make himself *c* unclean
22: 3 of your descendants is *c* unclean
27:11 he vowed is a *c* unclean animal—
Nu 5: 2 who is *c* unclean because of a dead
6: 7 must not make himself *c* unclean
8: 6 Israelites and make them *c* clean.
9: 6 they were *c* unclean on account
9:13 But if a man who is *c* clean
18:11 household who is *c* clean may eat
18:13 household who is *c* clean may eat
19: 7 but he will be *c* unclean till evening
19: 9 and put them in a *c* clean place
19:18 Then a man who is *c* clean is
Dt 12:15 Both the *c* unclean and the clean
12:22 Both the *c* unclean and the clean
14: 7 they are *c* unclean for you.
15:22 Both the *c* unclean and the clean
1Sa 20:26 to David to make him *c* unclean—
2Ch 13:11 the bread on the *c* clean table
30:17 for all those who were not *c* clean
Ezr 6:20 themselves and were all *c* clean.
Ne 12:30 Levites had purified themselves *c*,
Isa 66:20 of the LORD in *c* clean vessels.
Eze 22:10 period, when they are *c* unclean.
Ac 24:18 I was *c* clean when they found me
Heb 9:13 those who are *c* unclean sanctify

CEREMONY* (CEREMONIAL CEREMONIALLY)
Ge 50:11 Egyptians are holding a solemn *c*
Ex 12:25 as he promised, observe this *c*.
12:26 'What does this *c* mean to you?'
13: 5 are to observe this *c* in this month:

CERTAIN (CERTAINTY)
2Pe 1:19 word of the prophets made more *c*,

CERTAINTY* (CERTAIN)
Lk 1: 4 so that you may know the *c*
Jn 17: 8 They knew with *c* that I came

CERTIFICATE* (CERTIFIED)
Dt 24: 1 and he writes her a *c* of divorce,
24: 3 and writes her a *c* of divorce,
Isa 50: 1 "Where is your mother's *c*
Jer 3: 8 I gave faithless Israel her *c*
Mt 5:31 divorces his wife must give her a *c*
19: 7 that a man give his wife a *c*
Mk 10: 4 a man to write a *c* of divorce

CERTIFIED* (CERTIFICATE)
Jn 3:33 has accepted it has *c* that God is

CHAFF
Ps 1: 4 They are like *c*
35: 5 May they be like *c* before the wind,
Da 2:35 became like *c* on a threshing floor
Mt 3:12 up the *c* with unquenchable fire."

CHAINED (CHAINS)
2Ti 2: 9 But God's word is not *c*.

CHAINS (CHAINED)
Eph 6:20 for which I am an ambassador in *c*.
Col 4:18 Remember my *c*.
2Ti 1:16 and was not ashamed of my *c*.
Jude : 6 with everlasting *c* for judgment

CHAMPION
Ps 19: 5 like a *c* rejoicing to run his course.

CHANCE
Ecc 9:11 but time and *c* happen to them all.

CHANGE (CHANGED)
1Sa 15:29 of Israel does not lie or *c* his mind;
Ps 110: 4 and will not *c* his mind:
Jer 7: 5 If you really *c* your ways
Mal 3: 6 "I the LORD do not *c*.
Mt 18: 3 unless you *c* and become like little
Heb 7:21 and will not *c* his mind:
Jas 1:17 who does not *c* like shifting

CHANGED (CHANGE)
1Sa 10: 6 you will be *c* into a different person
Hos 11: 8 My heart is *c* within me;
1Co 15:51 but we will all be *c*—in a flash,

CHARACTER*
Ru 3:11 that you are a woman of noble *c*.
Pr 12: 4 of noble *c* is her husband's crown,
31:10 A wife of noble *c* who can find?
Ac 17:11 noble *c* than the Thessalonians,
Ro 5: 4 perseverance, *c*; and *c*, hope.
1Co 15:33 "Bad company corrupts good *c*."

CHARGE (CHARGES)
Job 34:13 him in *c* of the whole world?
Ro 8:33 Who will bring any *c*
1Co 9:18 the gospel I may offer it free of *c*,
2Co 11: 7 the gospel of God to you free of *c*?
2Ti 4: 1 I give you this *c*: Preach the Word;
Phm :18 or owes you anything, *c* it to me.

CHARGES (CHARGE)
Isa 50: 8 Who then will bring *c* against me?

CHARIOT (CHARIOTS)
2Ki 2:11 suddenly a *c* of fire and horses
Ps 104: 3 He makes the clouds his *c*
Ac 8:28 sitting in his *c* reading the book

CHARIOTS (CHARIOT)
2Ki 6:17 and *c* of fire all around Elisha.
Ps 20: 7 Some trust in *c* and some in horses,
68:17 The *c* of God are tens of thousands

CHARM* (CHARMING)
Pr 17: 8 bribe is a *c* to the one who gives it;
31:30 *C* is deceptive, and beauty is

CHARMING* (CHARM)
Pr 26:25 his speech is *c*, do not believe
SS 1:16 Oh, how *c*!

CHASE (CHASES)
Lev 26: 8 Five of you will *c* a hundred,

CHASES* (CHASE)
Pr 12:11 he who *c* fantasies lacks judgment.
28:19 one who *c* fantasies will have his

CHASM*
Lk 16:26 and you a great *c* has been fixed,

CHATTER* (CHATTERING)
1Ti 6:20 Turn away from godless *c*
2Ti 2:16 Avoid godless *c*, because those

CHATTERING* (CHATTER)
Pr 10: 8 but a *c* fool comes to ruin.
10:10 and a *c* fool comes to ruin.

CHEAT* (CHEATED CHEATING CHEATS)
Mal 1:14 "Cursed is the *c* who has
1Co 6: 8 you yourselves *c* and do wrong,

CHEATED* (CHEAT)
Ge 31: 7 yet your father has *c* me
1Sa 12: 3 Whom have I *c*? Whom have I
12: 4 "You have not *c* or oppressed us,"
Lk 19: 8 if I have *c* anybody out of anything,
1Co 6: 7 Why not rather be *c*? Instead,

CHEATING* (CHEAT)
Am 8: 5 and *c* with dishonest scales,

CHEATS* (CHEAT)
Lev 6: 2 or if he *c* him, or if he finds lost

CHEEK (CHEEKS)
Mt 5:39 someone strikes you on the right *c*,
Lk 6:29 If someone strikes you on one *c*,

CHEEKS (CHEEK)
Isa 50: 6 my *c* to those who pulled out my

CHEERFUL* (CHEERS)
Pr 15:13 A happy heart makes the face *c*,
15:15 but the *c* heart has a continual feast
15:30 A *c* look brings joy to the heart,
17:22 A *c* heart is good medicine,
2Co 9: 7 for God loves a *c* giver.

CHEERS (CHEERFUL)
Pr 12:25 but a kind word *c* him up.

CHEMOSH
2Ki 23:13 for *C* the vile god of Moab,

CHERISH (CHERISHED CHERISHES)
Ps 17:14 You still the hunger of those you *c*;

CHERISHED (CHERISH)
Ps 66:18 If I had *c* sin in my heart,

CHERISHES* (CHERISH)
Pr 19: 8 he who *c* understanding prospers.

CHERUB (CHERUBIM)
Ex 25:19 Make one *c* on one end
Eze 28:14 You were anointed as a guardian *c*,

CHERUBIM (CHERUB)
Ge 3:24 side of the Garden of Eden *c*
1Sa 4: 4 who is enthroned between the *c*.
2Sa 6: 2 enthroned between the *c* that are
22:11 He mounted the *c* and flew;
1Ki 6:23 a pair of *c* of olive wood,
2Ki 19:15 of Israel, enthroned between the *c*,
1Ch 13: 6 who is enthroned between the *c*—
Ps 18:10 He mounted the *c* and flew;
80: 1 who sit enthroned between the *c*,
99: 1 he sits enthroned between the *c*,
Isa 37:16 of Israel, enthroned between the *c*,
Eze 10: 1 was over the heads of the *c*.

CHEST
Ex 25:10 "Have them make a *c*
2Ki 12: 9 Jehoiada the priest took a *c*
Da 2:32 its *c* and arms of silver, its belly
Rev 1:13 with a golden sash around his *c*.

CHEWS
Lev 11: 3 divided and that *c* the cud.

CHIEF
1Pe 5: 4 And when the *C* Shepherd appears,

CHILD (CHILDISH CHILDREN CHILDREN'S GRANDCHILDREN)
Pr 20:11 Even a *c* is known by his actions,
22: 6 Train a *c* in the way he should go,
22:15 Folly is bound up in the heart of a *c*
23:13 not withhold discipline from a *c*;
29:15 *c* left to himself disgraces his mother.
Isa 7:14 The virgin will be with *c*
9: 6 For to us a *c* is born,
11: 6 and a little *c* will lead them.
66:13 As a mother comforts her *c*,
Mt 1:23 "The virgin will be with *c*
18: 2 He called a little *c* and had him
Lk 1:42 and blessed is the *c* you will bear!
1:80 And the *c* grew and became strong
1Co 13:11 When I was a *c*, I talked like a *c*,
1Jn 5: 1 who loves the father loves his *c*

CHILDBEARING (BEAR)
Ge 3:16 greatly increase your pains in *c*;

CHILDBIRTH (BEAR)
Gal 4:19 the pains of *c* until Christ is formed

CHILDISH* (CHILD)
1Co 13:11 When I became a man, I put *c* ways

CHILDREN (CHILD)
Ex 20: 5 punishing the *c* for the sin
Dt 4: 9 Teach them to your *c*
6: 7 Impress them on your *c*.
11:19 them to your *c*, talking about them
14: 1 You are the *c* of the LORD your
24:16 nor *c* put to death for their fathers;
30:19 so that you and your *c* may live
32:46 so that you may command your *c*
Job 1: 5 "Perhaps my *c* have sinned
Ps 8: 2 From the lips of *c* and infants
78: 5 forefathers to teach their *c*,
Pr 17: 6 Children's *c* are a crown
20: 7 blessed are his *c* after him.
31:28 Her *c* arise and call her blessed;
Joel 1: 3 Tell it to your *c*,
Mal 4: 6 the hearts of the fathers to their *c*,
Mt 7:11 how to give good gifts to your *c*,
11:25 and revealed them to little *c*.
18: 3 you change and become like little *c*
19:14 "Let the little *c* come to me,
21:16 " 'From the lips of *c* and infants
Mk 9:37 one of these little *c* in my name
10:14 "Let the little *c* come to me,
10:16 And he took the *c* in his arms,
13:12 *C* will rebel against their parents
Lk 10:21 and revealed them to little *c*.
18:16 "Let the little *c* come to me,
Jn 1:12 the right to become *c* of God—
Ac 2:39 The promise is for you and your *c*
Ro 8:16 with our spirit that we are God's *c*.
1Co 14:20 Brothers, stop thinking like *c*.
2Co 12:14 parents, but parents for their *c*.
Eph 6: 1 *C*, obey your parents in the Lord,
6: 4 do not exasperate your *c*; instead,
Col 3:20 *C*, obey your parents in everything,
3:21 Fathers, do not embitter your *c*,
1Ti 3: 4 and see that his *c* obey him
3:12 and must manage his *c* and his

1Ti 5:10 bringing up *c*, showing hospitality,
Heb 2:13 and the *c* God has given me."
1Jn 3: 1 that we should be called *c* of God!

CHILDREN'S (CHILD)
Isa 54:13 and great will be your *c* peace.

CHOKE
Mk 4:19 come in and *c* the word,

CHOOSE (CHOOSES CHOSE CHOSEN)
Dt 30:19 Now *c* life, so that you
Jos 24:15 then *c* for yourselves this day
Pr 8:10 *C* my instruction instead of silver,
16:16 to *c* understanding rather
Jn 15:16 You did not *c* me, but I chose you

CHOOSES (CHOOSE)
Mt 11:27 to whom the Son *c* to reveal him.
Lk 10:22 to whom the Son *c* to reveal him."
Jn 7:17 If anyone *c* to do God's will,

CHOSE (CHOOSE)
Ge 13:11 So Lot *c* for himself the whole plain
Ps 33:12 the people he *c* for his inheritance.
Jn 15:16 but I *c* you and appointed you to go
1Co 1:27 But God *c* the foolish things
Eph 1: 4 he *c* us in him before the creation
2Th 2:13 from the beginning God *c* you

CHOSEN (CHOOSE)
Isa 41: 8 Jacob, whom I have *c*,
Mt 22:14 For many are invited, but few are *c*
Lk 10:42 Mary has *c* what is better,
23:35 the Christ of God, the *C* One."
Jn 15:19 but I have *c* you out of the world.
1Pe 1:20 He was *c* before the creation
2: 9 But you are a *c* people, a royal

CHRIST (CHRIST'S CHRISTIAN CHRISTIANS CHRISTS)
Mt 1:16 was born Jesus, who is called *C*.
16:16 Peter answered, "You are the *C*,
22:42 "What do you think about the *C*?
Mk 1: 1 of the gospel about Jesus *C*,
8:29 Peter answered, "You are the *C*."
14:61 "Are you the *C*, the Son
Lk 9:20 Peter answered, "The *C* of God."
Jn 1:41 found the Messiah" (that is, the *C*).
20:31 you may believe that Jesus is the *C*,
Ac 2:36 you crucified, both Lord and *C*."
5:42 the good news that Jesus is the *C*.
9:22 by proving that Jesus is the *C*.
9:34 said to him, "Jesus *C* heals you.
17: 3 proving that the *C* had to suffer
18:28 the Scriptures that Jesus was the *C*.
26:23 that the *C* would suffer and,
Ro 1: 4 from the dead: Jesus *C* our Lord.
3:22 comes through faith in Jesus *C*
5: 1 God through our Lord Jesus *C*,
5: 6 we were still powerless, *C* died
5: 8 While we were still sinners, *C* died
5:11 in God through our Lord Jesus *C*,
5:17 life through the one man, Jesus *C*.
6: 4 as *C* was raised from the dead
6: 9 that since *C* was raised
6:23 life in *C* Jesus our Lord.
7: 4 to the law through the body of *C*,
8: 1 for those who are in *C* Jesus,
8: 9 Spirit of *C*, he does not belong to *C*.
8:17 heirs of God and co-heirs with *C*,
8:34 Who is he that condemns? *C* Jesus,
8:35 us from the love of *C*?
9: 5 is traced the human ancestry of *C*,
10: 4 *C* is the end of the law
12: 5 so in *C* we who are many form one
13:14 yourselves with the Lord Jesus *C*,
14: 9 *C* died and returned to life
15: 3 For even *C* did not please himself
15: 5 yourselves as you follow *C* Jesus,
15: 7 then, just as *C* accepted you,
16:18 people are not serving our Lord *C*,
1Co 1: 2 to those sanctified in *C* Jesus
1: 7 for our Lord Jesus *C* to be revealed.
1:13 Is *C* divided? Was Paul crucified
1:17 For *C* did not send me to baptize,
1:23 but we preach *C* crucified:
1:30 of him that you are in *C* Jesus,
2: 2 except Jesus *C* and him crucified.
3:11 one already laid, which is Jesus *C*.
5: 7 For *C*, our Passover lamb,
6:15 bodies are members of *C* himself?
8: 6 and there is but one Lord, Jesus *C*,
8:12 conscience, you sin against *C*.
10: 4 them, and that rock was *C*.
11: 1 as I follow the example of *C*.
11: 3 the head of every man is *C*,
12:27 Now you are the body of *C*,
15: 3 that *C* died for our sins according
15:14 And if *C* has not been raised,
15:22 so in *C* all will be made alive.
15:57 victory through our Lord Jesus *C*.
2Co 1: 5 as the sufferings of *C* flow
2:14 us in triumphal procession in *C*
3: 3 show that you are a letter from *C*,
3:14 because only in *C* is it taken away.
4: 4 light of the gospel of the glory of *C*,
4: 5 not preach ourselves, but Jesus *C*
4: 6 of the glory of God in the face of *C*.
5:10 before the judgment seat of *C*,
5:17 Therefore, if anyone is in *C*,
6:15 What harmony is there between *C*
10: 1 the meekness and gentleness of *C*,
11: 2 you to one husband, to *C*,
Gal 1: 7 are trying to pervert the gospel of *C*
2: 4 on the freedom we have in *C* Jesus
2:16 but by faith in Jesus *C*.
2:17 does that mean that *C* promotes sin
2:20 I have been crucified with *C*
2:21 *C* died for nothing!" You foolish
3:13 *C* redeemed us from the curse
3:16 meaning one person, who is *C*.
3:26 of God through faith in *C* Jesus,
4:19 of childbirth until *C* is formed
5: 1 for freedom that *C* has set us free.
5: 4 by law have been alienated from *C*;
5:24 to *C* Jesus have crucified the sinful
6:14 in the cross of our Lord Jesus *C*,
Eph 1: 3 with every spiritual blessing in *C*.
1:10 together under one head, even *C*.
1:20 which he exerted in *C*
2: 5 made us alive with *C*
2:10 created in *C* Jesus
2:12 time you were separate from *C*,
2:20 with *C* Jesus himself as the chief
3: 8 the unsearchable riches of *C*,
3:17 so that *C* may dwell in your hearts
4: 7 has been given as *C* apportioned it.
4:13 measure of the fullness of *C*.
4:15 into him who is the Head, that is, *C*
4:32 just as in *C* God forgave you.
5: 2 as *C* loved us and gave himself up
5:21 out of reverence for *C*.
5:23 as *C* is the head of the church,
5:25 just as *C* loved the church
Php 1:18 motives or true, *C* is preached.
1:21 to live is *C* and to die is gain.
1:23 I desire to depart and be with *C*,
1:27 worthy of the gospel of *C*.
1:29 on behalf of *C* not only to believe
2: 5 be the same as that of *C* Jesus:
3: 7 now consider loss for the sake of *C*.
3:10 I want to know *C* and the power
3:18 as enemies of the cross of *C*.
4:19 to his glorious riches in *C* Jesus.
Col 1: 4 heard of your faith in *C* Jesus
1:27 which is *C* in you, the hope of glory
1:28 may present everyone perfect in *C*.
2: 2 the mystery of God, namely, *C*,
2: 6 as you received *C* Jesus as Lord,
2: 9 For in *C* all the fullness
2:13 God made you alive with *C*.
2:17 the reality, however, is found in *C*.
3: 1 then, you have been raised with *C*,
3: 3 and your life is now hidden with *C*
3:15 Let the peace of *C* rule
1Th 5: 9 through our Lord Jesus *C*.
2Th 2: 1 the coming of our Lord Jesus *C*
2:14 in the glory of our Lord Jesus *C*.
1Ti 1:12 I thank *C* Jesus our Lord, who has
1:15 *C* Jesus came into the world
1:16 *C* Jesus might display his unlimited
2: 5 the man *C* Jesus, who gave himself
2Ti 1: 9 us in *C* Jesus before the beginning
1:10 appearing of our Savior, *C* Jesus,
2: 1 in the grace that is in *C* Jesus.
2: 3 us like a good soldier of *C* Jesus.
2: 8 Remember Jesus *C*, raised
2:10 the salvation that is in *C* Jesus,
3:12 life in *C* Jesus will be persecuted,
3:15 salvation through faith in *C* Jesus.
4: 1 presence of God and of *C* Jesus,
Tit 2:13 our great God and Savior, Jesus *C*,
Heb 3: 6 But *C* is faithful as a son
3:14 to share in *C* if we hold firmly
5: 5 So *C* also did not take
6: 1 the elementary teachings about *C*
9:11 When *C* came as high priest
9:14 more, then, will the blood of *C*,
9:15 For this reason *C* is the mediator
9:24 For *C* did not enter a man-made
9:26 Then *C* would have had
9:28 so *C* was sacrificed once
10:10 of the body of Jesus *C* once for all.
13: 8 Jesus *C* is the same yesterday
1Pe 1: 2 for obedience to Jesus *C*
1: 3 of Jesus *C* from the dead,
1:11 he predicted the sufferings of *C*
1:19 but with the precious blood of *C*,
2:21 because *C* suffered for you,
3:15 in your hearts set apart *C* as Lord.
3:18 For *C* died for sins once for all,
3:21 you by the resurrection of Jesus *C*,
4:13 participate in the sufferings of *C*,
4:14 insulted because of the name of *C*,
2Pe 1: 1 and Savior Jesus *C* have received
1:16 and coming of our Lord Jesus *C*,
1Jn 2: 1 Jesus *C*, the Righteous One.
2:22 man who denies that Jesus is the *C*.
3:16 Jesus *C* laid down his life for us.
3:23 in the name of his Son, Jesus *C*,
4: 2 that Jesus *C* has come
5: 1 believes that Jesus is the *C* is born
5:20 even in his Son Jesus *C*.
2Jn : 9 teaching of *C* does not have God;
Jude : 4 deny Jesus *C* our only Sovereign
Rev 1: 1 The revelation of Jesus *C*,
1: 5 from Jesus *C*, who is the faithful
11:15 kingdom of our Lord and of his *C*,
20: 4 reigned with *C* a thousand years.
20: 6 they will be priests of God and of *C*

CHRIST'S (CHRIST)
1Co 9:21 from God's law but am under *C* law
2Co 5:14 For *C* love compels us,
5:20 We are therefore *C* ambassadors,
12: 9 so that *C* power may rest on me.
Col 1:22 by *C* physical body through death

CHRISTIAN* (CHRIST)
Ac 26:28 you can persuade me to be a *C*?"
1Pe 4:16 as a *C*, do not be ashamed,

CHRISTIANS* (CHRIST)
Ac 11:26 The disciples were called *C* first

CHRISTS* (CHRIST)
Mt 24:24 For false *C* and false prophets will
Mk 13:22 For false *C* and false prophets will

CHURCH
Mt 16:18 and on this rock I will build my *c*,
18:17 if he refuses to listen even to the *c*,
Ac 20:28 Be shepherds of the *c* of God,
1Co 5:12 of mine to judge those outside the *c*
14: 4 but he who prophesies edifies the *c*.
14:12 to excel in gifts that build up the *c*.
14:26 done for the strengthening of the *c*.
15: 9 because I persecuted the *c* of God.
Gal 1:13 how intensely I persecuted the *c*
Eph 5:23 as Christ is the head of the *c*,
Col 1:18 he is the head of the body, the *c*;
1:24 the sake of his body, which is the *c*.

CHURNING
Pr 30:33 For as *c* the milk produces butter,

CIRCLE
Isa 40:22 enthroned above the *c* of the earth,

CIRCUMCISE (CIRCUMCISED CIRCUMCISION)
Dt 10:16 *C* your hearts, therefore,

CIRCUMCISED (CIRCUMCISE)
Ge 17:10 Every male among you shall be *c*.
17:12 who is eight days old must be *c*,
Jos 5: 3 and *c* the Israelites at Gibeath
Gal 5: 2 that if you let yourselves be *c*,

CIRCUMCISION (CIRCUMCISE)
Ro 2:25 *C* has value if you observe the law,
2:29 and *c* is *c* of the heart, by the Spirit,
1Co 7:19 *C* is nothing and uncircumcision is

CIRCUMSTANCES
Php 4:11 to be content whatever the *c*.
1Th 5:18 continually; give thanks in all *c*,

CITIES (CITY)
Lk 19:17 small matter, take charge of ten *c*.'
19:19 'You take charge of five *c*.'

CITIZENS (CITIZENSHIP)
Eph 2:19 but fellow *c* with God's people

CITIZENSHIP* (CITIZENS)
Ac 22:28 "I had to pay a big price for my *c*."
Eph 2:12 excluded from *c* in Israel
Php 3:20 But our *c* is in heaven.

CITY (CITIES)
Mt 5:14 A *c* on a hill cannot be hidden.
Ac 18:10 I have many people in this *c*."
Heb 13:14 here we do not have an enduring *c*,
Rev 21: 2 saw the Holy *C*, the new

CIVILIAN*
2Ti 2: 4 a soldier gets involved in *c* affairs—

CLAIM (CLAIMS RECLAIM)
Pr 25: 6 do not *c* a place among great men;
1Jn 1: 6 If we *c* to have fellowship
1: 8 If we *c* to be without sin, we
1:10 If we *c* we have not sinned,

CLAIMS (CLAIM)
Jas 2:14 if a man *c* to have faith
1Jn 2: 6 Whoever *c* to live in him must walk
2: 9 Anyone who *c* to be in the light

CLANGING*
1Co 13: 1 a resounding gong or a *c* cymbal.

CLAP* (CLAPPED CLAPS)
Job 21: 5 *c* your hand over your mouth.
Ps 47: 1 *C* your hands, all you nations;
98: 8 Let the rivers *c* their hands,
Pr 30:32 *c* your hand over your mouth!
Isa 55:12 will *c* their hands.
La 2:15 *c* their hands at you;

CLAPPED* (CLAP)
2Ki 11:12 and the people *c* their hands
Eze 25: 6 Because you have *c* your hands

CLAPS* (CLAP)
Job 27:23 It *c* its hands in derision
34:37 scornfully he *c* his hands among us
Na 3:19 *c* his hands at your fall,

CLASSIFY*
2Co 10:12 dare to *c* or compare ourselves

CLAUDIUS
Ac 11:28 happened during the reign of *C*.)
18: 2 because *C* had ordered all the Jews

CLAY
Isa 45: 9 Does the *c* say to the potter,
64: 8 We are the *c*, you are the potter;
Jer 18: 6 "Like *c* in the hand of the potter,
La 4: 2 are now considered as pots of *c*,
Da 2:33 partly of iron and partly of baked *c*.
Ro 9:21 of the same lump of *c* some pottery
2Co 4: 7 we have this treasure in jars of *c*
2Ti 2:20 and *c*; some are for noble purposes

CLEAN (CLEANNESS CLEANSE CLEANSED CLEANSES CLEANSING)
Ge 7: 2 seven of every kind of *c* animal,
Lev 4:12 the camp to a place ceremonially *c*,
16:30 you will be *c* from all your sins.
Ps 24: 4 He who has *c* hands and a pure
51: 7 with hyssop, and I will be *c*;
Pr 20: 9 I am *c* and without sin"?
Eze 36:25 I will sprinkle *c* water on you,
Mt 8: 2 are willing, you can make me *c*."
12:44 the house unoccupied, swept *c*
23:25 You *c* the outside of the cup
Mk 7:19 Jesus declared all foods "*c*.")
Jn 13:10 to wash his feet; his whole body is *c*
15: 3 are already *c* because of the word
Ac 10:15 impure that God has made *c*."
Ro 14:20 All food is *c*, but it is wrong

CLEANNESS (CLEAN)
2Sa 22:25 according to my *c* in his sight.

CLEANSE (CLEAN)
Ps 51: 2 and *c* me from my sin.
51: 7 *C* me with hyssop, and I will be
Pr 20:30 Blows and wounds *c* away evil,
Heb 9:14 *c* our consciences from acts that
10:22 having our hearts sprinkled to *c* us

CLEANSED (CLEAN)
Heb 9:22 requires that nearly everything be *c*
2Pe 1: 9 has forgotten that he has been *c*

CLEANSES* (CLEAN)
2Ti 2:21 If a man *c* himself from the latter,

CLEANSING (CLEAN)
Eph 5:26 *c* her by the washing with water

CLEFT*
Ex 33:22 I will put you in a *c* in the rock

CLEVER
Isa 5:21 and *c* in their own sight.

CLING
Ro 12: 9 Hate what is evil; *c* to what is good.

CLINGS
Ps 63: 8 My soul *c* to you;

CLOAK
Ex 12:11 with your *c* tucked into your belt,
2Ki 4:29 "Tuck your *c* into your belt,
9: 1 "Tuck your *c* into your belt,
Mt 5:40 let him have your *c* as well.

CLOSE (CLOSER CLOSES)
2Ki 11: 8 Stay *c* to the king wherever he goes
2Ch 23: 7 Stay *c* to the king wherever he goes
Ps 34:18 LORD is *c* to the brokenhearted
148: 14 of Israel, the people *c* to his heart.
Isa 40:11 and carries them *c* to his heart;
Jer 30:21 himself to be *c* to me?'

CLOSER (CLOSE)
Ex 3: 5 "Do not come any *c*," God said.
Pr 18:24 there is a friend who sticks *c*

CLOSES (CLOSE)
Pr 28:27 he who *c* his eyes to them receives

CLOTHE (CLOTHED CLOTHES CLOTHING)
Ps 45: 3 *c* yourself with splendor
Isa 52: 1 *c* yourself with strength.
Ro 13:14 *c* yourselves with the Lord Jesus
Col 3:12 *c* yourselves with compassion,
1Pe 5: 5 *c* yourselves with humility

CLOTHED (CLOTHE)
Ps 30:11 removed my sackcloth and *c* me
104: 1 you are *c* with splendor
Pr 31:22 she is *c* in fine linen and purple.
31:25 She is *c* with strength and dignity;
Isa 61:10 For he has *c* me with garments
Lk 24:49 until you have been *c* with power
Gal 3:27 into Christ have *c* yourselves

CLOTHES (CLOTHE)
Dt 8: 4 Your *c* did not wear out
Mt 6:25 the body more important than *c*?
6:28 "And why do you worry about *c*?
27:35 they divided up his *c* by casting lots
Jn 11:44 Take off the grave *c* and let him go

CLOTHING (CLOTHE)
Dt 22: 5 A woman must not wear men's *c*,
Job 29:14 I put on righteousness as my *c*;
Ps 22:18 and cast lots for my *c*.
Mt 7:15 They come to you in sheep's *c*,
1Ti 6: 8 But if we have food and *c*,

CLOUD (CLOUDS)
Ex 13:21 them in a pillar of *c* to guide them
1Ki 18:44 *c* as small as a man's hand is rising
Pr 16:15 his favor is like a rain *c* in spring.
Isa 19: 1 See, the LORD rides on a swift *c*
Lk 21:27 of Man coming in a *c* with power
Heb 12: 1 by such a great *c* of witnesses,
Rev 14:14 seated on the *c* was one "like a son

CLOUDS (CLOUD)
Dt 33:26 and on the *c* in his majesty.
Ps 68: 4 extol him who rides on the *c*—
104: 3 He makes the *c* his chariot
Pr 25:14 Like *c* and wind without rain
Da 7:13 coming with the *c* of heaven.
Mt 24:30 of Man coming on the *c* of the sky,
26:64 and coming on the *c* of heaven."
Mk 13:26 coming in *c* with great power
1Th 4:17 with them in the *c* to meet the Lord
Rev 1: 7 Look, he is coming with the *c*,

CLUB
Pr 25:18 Like a *c* or a sword or a sharp arrow

CO-HEIRS* (INHERIT)
Ro 8:17 heirs of God and *c* with Christ,

COALS
Pr 25:22 you will heap burning *c* on his head
Ro 12:20 you will heap burning *c* on his head

COARSE*
Eph 5: 4 or *c* joking, which are out of place,

CODE*
Ro 2:27 even though you have the written *c*
2:29 by the Spirit, not by the written *c*.
7: 6 not in the old way of the written *c*.
Col 2:14 having canceled the written *c*,

COINS
Mt 26:15 out for him thirty silver *c*.
Lk 15: 8 suppose a woman has ten silver *c*

COLD
Pr 25:25 Like *c* water to a weary soul
Mt 10:42 if anyone gives even a cup of *c* water
24:12 the love of most will grow *c*,

COLLECTION
1Co 16: 1 Now about the *c* for God's people:

COLT
Zec 9: 9 on a *c*, the foal of a donkey.
Mt 21: 5 on a *c*, the foal of a donkey.' "

COMB
Ps 19:10 than honey from the *c*.

COMFORT* (COMFORTED COMFORTER COMFORTERS COMFORTING COMFORTS)
Ge 5:29 "He will *c* us in the labor
37:35 and daughters came to *c* him,
Ru 2:13 "You have given me *c*
1Ch 7:22 and his relatives came to *c* him.
Job 2:11 sympathize with him and *c* him.
7:13 When I think my bed will *c* me
16: 5 *c* from my lips would bring you
36:16 to the *c* of your table laden
Ps 23: 4 rod and your staff, they *c* me.
71:21 and *c* me once again.
119: 50 My *c* in my suffering is this:
119: 52 and I find *c* in them.
119: 76 May your unfailing love be my *c*,
119: 82 I say, "When will you *c* me?"
Isa 40: 1 *C*, *c* my people,
51: 3 The LORD will surely *c* Zion
51:19 who can *c* you?—
57:18 I will guide him and restore *c*
61: 2 to *c* all who mourn,
66:13 so will I *c* you;
Jer 16: 7 food to *c* those who mourn
31:13 I will give them *c* and joy instead
La 1: 2 there is none to *c* her.
1: 9 there was none to *c* her.
1:16 No one is near to *c* me,
1:17 but there is no one to *c* her.
1:21 but there is no one to *c* me.
2:13 that I may *c* you,
Eze 16:54 all you have done in giving them *c*.
Na 3: 7 Where can I find anyone to *c* you?"
Zec 1:17 and the LORD will again *c* Zion
10: 2 they give *c* in vain.
Lk 6:24 you have already received your *c*.
Jn 11:19 and Mary to *c* them in the loss
1Co 14: 3 encouragement and *c*.
2Co 1: 3 of compassion and the God of all *c*,
1: 4 so that we can *c* those
1: 4 with the *c* we ourselves have
1: 5 through Christ our *c* overflows.
1: 6 if we are comforted, it is for your *c*,
1: 6 it is for your *c* and salvation;
1: 7 so also you share in our *c*.
2: 7 you ought to forgive and *c* him,
7: 7 also by the *c* you had given him.
Php 2: 1 if any *c* from his love,
Col 4:11 and they have proved a *c* to me.

COMFORTED* (COMFORT)
Ge 24:67 Isaac was *c* after his mother's death
37:35 comfort him, but he refused to be *c*.
2Sa 12:24 Then David *c* his wife Bathsheba,
Job 42:11 They *c* and consoled him
Ps 77: 2 and my soul refused to be *c*.
86:17 have helped me and *c* me.
Isa 12: 1 and you have *c* me.
52: 9 for the LORD has *c* his people,
54:11 lashed by storms and not *c*,
66:13 and you will be *c* over Jerusalem."
Jer 31:15 and refusing to be *c*,

Mt 2:18 and refusing to be *c*,
5:4 for they will be *c*.
Lk 16:25 but now he is *c* here and you are
Ac 20:12 man home alive and were greatly *c*.
2Co 1:6 if we are *c*, it is for your comfort,
7:6 *c* us by the coming of Titus,

COMFORTER* (COMFORT)
Ecc 4:1 and they have no *c*;
4:1 and they have no *c*.
Jer 8:18 O my *C* in sorrow,

COMFORTERS* (COMFORT)
Job 16:2 miserable *c* are you all!
Ps 69:20 for *c*, but I found none.

COMFORTING* (COMFORT)
Isa 66:11 satisfied at her *c* breasts;
Zec 1:13 *c* words to the angel who talked
Jn 11:31 *c* her, noticed how quickly she got
1Th 2:12 *c* and urging you to live lives

COMFORTS* (COMFORT)
Job 29:25 I was like one who *c* mourners.
Isa 49:13 For the LORD *c* his people
51:12 "I, even I, am he who *c* you.
66:13 As a mother *c* her child,
2Co 1:4 who *c* us in all our troubles,
7:6 But God, who *c* the downcast,

COMMAND (COMMANDED COMMANDING COMMANDMENT COMMANDMENTS COMMANDS)
Ex 7:2 You are to say everything I *c* you,
Nu 14:41 are you disobeying the LORD's *c*?
24:13 to go beyond the *c* of the LORD—
Dt 4:2 Do not add to what I *c* you
8:1 to follow every *c* I am giving you
12:32 See that you do all I *c* you;
15:11 I *c* you to be openhanded
30:16 For I *c* you today to love
32:46 so that you may *c* your children
Ps 91:11 For he will *c* his angels concerning
Pr 13:13 but he who respects a *c* is rewarded
Ecc 8:2 Obey the king's *c*, I say,
Jer 1:7 you to and say whatever I *c* you.
1:17 and say to them whatever I *c* you.
7:23 Walk in all the ways I *c* you,
11:4 Obey me and do everything I *c* you
26:2 Tell them everything I *c* you;
Joel 2:11 mighty are those who obey his *c*.
Mt 4:6 He will *c* his angels concerning you
15:3 why do you break the *c* of God
Lk 4:10 " 'He will *c* his angels concerning
Jn 14:15 love me, you will obey what I *c*.
15:12 My *c* is this: Love each other
15:14 friends if you do what I *c*.
15:17 This is my *c*: Love each other.
1Co 14:37 writing to you is the Lord's *c*.
Gal 5:14 law is summed up in a single *c*:
1Ti 1:5 goal of this *c* is love, which comes
6:14 to you keep this *c* without spot
6:17 *C* those who are rich
Heb 11:3 universe was formed at God's *c*,
2Pe 2:21 on the sacred *c* that was passed
3:2 and the *c* given by our Lord
1Jn 2:7 I am not writing you a new *c*
3:23 this is his *c*: to believe in the name
4:21 And he has given us this *c*:
2Jn :6 his *c* is that you walk in love.

COMMANDED (COMMAND)
Ge 2:16 And the LORD God *c* the man,
7:5 Noah did all that the LORD *c* him.
50:12 Jacob's sons did as he had *c* them:
Ex 7:6 did just as the LORD *c* them.
19:7 all the words the LORD had *c* him
Dt 4:5 laws as the LORD my God *c* me,
6:24 The LORD *c* us to obey all these
Jos 1:9 Have I not *c* you? Be strong
1:16 Whatever you have *c* us we will do,
2Sa 5:25 So David did as the LORD *c* him,
2Ki 17:13 the entire Law that I *c* your fathers
21:8 careful to do everything I *c* them
2Ch 33:8 do everything I *c* them concerning
Ps 33:9 he *c*, and it stood firm.
78:5 which he *c* our forefathers
148:5 for he *c* and they were created.
Mt 28:20 to obey everything I have *c* you.
1Co 9:14 Lord has *c* that those who preach
1Jn 3:23 and to love one another as he *c* us.
2Jn :4 in the truth, just as the Father *c* us.

COMMANDING (COMMAND)
2Ti 2:4 he wants to please his *c* officer.

COMMANDMENT* (COMMAND)
Jos 22:5 But be very careful to keep the *c*
Mt 22:36 which is the greatest *c* in the Law?"
22:38 This is the first and greatest *c*.
Mk 12:31 There is no *c* greater than these."
Lk 23:56 the Sabbath in obedience to the *c*.
Jn 13:34 "A new *c* I give you: Love one
Ro 7:8 the opportunity afforded by the *c*,
7:9 when the *c* came, sin sprang to life
7:10 that the very *c* that was intended
7:11 and through the *c* put me to death.
7:11 the opportunity afforded by the *c*,
7:12 and the *c* is holy, righteous
7:13 through the *c* sin might become
13:9 and whatever other *c* there may be,
Eph 6:2 which is the first *c* with a promise
Heb 9:19 Moses had proclaimed every *c*

COMMANDMENTS* (COMMAND)
Ex 20:6 who love me and keep my *c*.
34:28 of the covenant—the Ten *C*.
Dt 4:13 to you his covenant, the Ten *C*,
5:10 who love me and keep my *c*.
5:22 These are the *c* the LORD
6:6 These *c* that I give you today are
9:10 were all the *c* the LORD
10:4 The Ten *C* he had proclaimed
Ecc 12:13 Fear God and keep his *c*,
Mt 5:19 one of the least of these *c*
19:17 If you want to enter life, obey the *c*
22:40 the Prophets hang on these two *c*."
Mk 10:19 You know the *c*: 'Do not murder,
12:28 "Of all the *c*, which is the most
Lk 1:6 observing all the Lord's *c*
18:20 You know the *c*: 'Do not commit
Ro 13:9 The *c*, "Do not commit adultery,"
Eph 2:15 in his flesh the law with its *c*
Rev 12:17 those who obey God's *c*
14:12 part of the saints who obey God's *c*

COMMANDS (COMMAND)
Ex 24:12 and *c* I have written for their
25:22 give you all my *c* for the Israelites.
34:32 gave them all the *c* the LORD had
Lev 22:31 "Keep my *c* and follow them.
Nu 15:39 and so you will remember all the *c*
Dt 7:9 those who love him and keep his *c*.
7:11 Therefore, take care to follow the *c*
11:1 decrees, his laws and his *c* always.
11:27 the blessing if you obey the *c*
28:1 carefully follow all his *c* I give you
30:10 LORD your God and keep his *c*
Jos 22:5 to walk in all his ways, to obey his *c*
1Ki 2:3 and keep his decrees and *c*,
8:58 in all his ways and to keep the *c*,
8:61 to live by his decrees and obey his *c*
1Ch 28:7 unswerving in carrying out my *c*
29:19 devotion to keep your *c*,
2Ch 31:21 in obedience to the law and the *c*,
Ne 1:5 those who love him and obey his *c*,
Ps 78:7 but would keep his *c*.
112:1 who finds great delight in his *c*.
119:10 do not let me stray from your *c*.
119:32 I run in the path of your *c*,
119:35 Direct me in the path of your *c*,
119:47 for I delight in your *c*
119:48 I lift up my hands to your *c*,
119:73 me understanding to learn your *c*.
119:86 All your *c* are trustworthy;
119:96 but your *c* are boundless.
119:98 Your *c* make me wiser
119:115 that I may keep the *c* of my God!
119:127 Because I love your *c*
119:131 longing for your *c*.
119:143 but your *c* are my delight.
119:151 and all your *c* are true.
119:172 for all your *c* are righteous.
119:176 for I have not forgotten your *c*.
Pr 2:1 and store up my *c* within you,
3:1 but keep my *c* in your heart,
6:23 For these *c* are a lamp,
10:8 The wise in heart accept *c*,
Isa 48:18 you had paid attention to my *c*,
Da 9:4 all who love him and obey his *c*,
Mt 5:19 teaches these *c* will be called great
Mk 7:8 You have let go of the *c* of God
7:9 way of setting aside the *c* of God
Jn 14:21 Whoever has my *c* and obeys them,
15:10 If you obey my *c*, you will remain
Ac 17:30 but now he *c* all people everywhere
1Co 7:19 Keeping God's *c* is what counts.
1Jn 2:3 come to know him if we obey his *c*.
2:4 but does not do what he *c* is a liar,
3:22 we obey his *c* and do what pleases
3:24 Those who obey his *c* live in him,
5:2 loving God and carrying out his *c*.
5:3 And his *c* are not burdensome,
5:3 This is love for God: to obey his *c*.
2Jn :6 that we walk in obedience to his *c*.

COMMEMORATE
Ex 12:14 "This is a day you are to *c*;

COMMEND* (COMMENDABLE COMMENDED COMMENDS)
Ps 145:4 One generation will *c* your works
Ecc 8:15 So I *c* the enjoyment of life,
Ro 13:3 do what is right and he will *c* you.
16:1 I *c* to you our sister Phoebe,
2Co 3:1 beginning to *c* ourselves again?
4:2 the truth plainly we *c* ourselves
5:12 trying to *c* ourselves to you again,
6:4 as servants of God we *c* ourselves
10:12 with some who *c* themselves.
1Pe 2:14 and to *c* those who do right.

COMMENDABLE* (COMMEND)
1Pe 2:19 For it is *c* if a man bears up
2:20 you endure it, this is *c* before God.

COMMENDED* (COMMEND)
Ne 11:2 The people *c* all the men who
Job 29:11 and those who saw me *c* me,
Lk 16:8 master *c* the dishonest manager
Ac 15:40 *c* by the brothers to the grace
2Co 12:11 I ought to have been *c* by you,
Heb 11:2 This is what the ancients were *c* for
11:4 By faith he was *c* as a righteous
11:5 he was *c* as one who pleased God.
11:39 These were all *c* for their faith,

COMMENDS* (COMMEND)
Pr 15:2 of the wise *c* knowledge,
2Co 10:18 but the one whom the Lord *c*.
10:18 not the one who *c* himself who is

COMMIT (COMMITS COMMITTED)
Ex 20:14 "You shall not *c* adultery.
Dt 5:18 "You shall not *c* adultery.
1Sa 7:3 and *c* yourselves to the LORD
Ps 31:5 Into your hands I *c* my spirit;
37:5 *C* your way to the LORD;
Pr 16:3 *C* to the LORD whatever you do,
Mt 5:27 that it was said, 'Do not *c* adultery.'
5:32 causes her to *c* adultery,
19:18 do not *c* adultery, do not steal,
Mk 10:19 do not *c* adultery, do not steal,
Lk 18:20 'Do not *c* adultery, do not murder,
23:46 into your hands I *c* my spirit."
Ac 20:32 I *c* you to God and to the word
Ro 2:22 do you *c* adultery? You who abhor
2:22 that people should not *c* adultery,
13:9 "Do not *c* adultery,"
1Co 10:8 We should not *c* sexual immorality,
Jas 2:11 do not *c* adultery but do *c* murder,
1Pe 4:19 to God's will should *c* themselves
Rev 2:22 I will make those who *c* adultery

COMMITS (COMMIT)
Pr 6:32 man who *c* adultery lacks
29:22 a hot-tempered one *c* many sins.
Ecc 8:12 a wicked man *c* a hundred crimes
Eze 18:12 He *c* robbery.
18:14 who sees all the sins his father *c*,
18:24 from his righteousness and *c* sin
18:26 from his righteousness and *c* sin,
22:11 you one man *c* a detestable offense
Mt 5:32 the divorced woman *c* adultery.
19:9 marries another woman *c* adultery
Mk 10:11 marries another woman *c* adultery
10:12 another man, she *c* adultery."
Lk 16:18 a divorced woman *c* adultery.
16:18 marries another woman *c* adultery,

COMMITTED (COMMIT)
Nu 5:7 and must confess the sin he has *c*.
1Ki 8:61 But your hearts must be fully *c*
15:14 Asa's heart was fully *c*
2Ch 16:9 those whose hearts are fully *c*
Mt 5:28 lustfully has already *c* adultery
11:27 "All things have been *c* to me
Lk 10:22 "All things have been *c* to me

Ac 14:23 *c* them to the Lord,
14:26 where they had been *c* to the grace
1Co 9:17 I am simply discharging the trust *c*
2Co 5:19 And he has *c* to us the message
1Pe 2:22 "He *c* no sin,
Rev 17: 2 the kings of the earth *c* adultery
18: 3 of the earth *c* adultery with her,
18: 9 kings of the earth who *c* adultery

COMMON
Ge 11: 1 had one language and a *c* speech.
Lev 10:10 between the holy and the *c*,
Pr 22: 2 Rich and poor have this in *c*:
29:13 the oppressor have this in *c*:
Ac 2:44 together and had everything in *c*.
1Co 10:13 has seized you except what is *c*
2Co 6:14 and wickedness have in *c*?

COMPANION (COMPANIONS)
Ps 55:13 my *c*, my close friend,
55:20 My *c* attacks his friends;
Pr 13:20 but a *c* of fools suffers harm.
28: 7 a *c* of gluttons disgraces his father.
29: 3 *c* of prostitutes squanders his
Rev 1: 9 your brother and *c* in the suffering

COMPANIONS (COMPANION)
Ps 45: 7 your God, has set you above your *c*
Pr 18:24 A man of many *c* may come to ruin
Heb 1: 9 your God, has set you above your *c*

COMPANY
Ps 14: 5 present in the *c* of the righteous.
Pr 21:16 comes to rest in the *c* of the dead.
24: 1 do not desire their *c*;
Jer 15:17 I never sat in the *c* of revelers,
1Co 15:33 "Bad *c* corrupts good character."

COMPARE* (COMPARED COMPARING COMPARISON)
Job 28:17 Neither gold nor crystal can *c*
28:19 The topaz of Cush cannot *c* with it;
39:13 but they cannot *c* with the pinions
Ps 86: 8 no deeds can *c* with yours.
89: 6 skies above can *c* with the LORD?
Pr 3:15 nothing you desire can *c* with her.
8:11 nothing you desire can *c* with her.
Isa 40:18 To whom, then, will you *c* God?
40:18 What image will you *c* him to?
40:25 "To whom will you *c* me?
46: 5 "To whom will you *c* me
La 2:13 With what can I *c* you,
Eze 31: 8 *c* with its branches—
Da 1:13 Then *c* our appearance with that
Mt 11:16 "To what can I *c* this generation?
Lk 7:31 I *c* the people of this generation?
13:18 What shall I *c* it to? It is like
13:20 What shall I *c* the kingdom of God
2Co 10:12 and *c* themselves with themselves,
10:12 or *c* ourselves with some who

COMPARED* (COMPARE)
Jdg 8: 2 What have I accomplished *c* to you
8: 3 What was I able to do *c* to you?"
Isa 46: 5 you liken me that we may be *c*?
Eze 31: 2 Who can be *c* with you in majesty?
31:18 the trees of Eden can be *c* with you
Php 3: 8 I consider everything a loss *c*

COMPARING* (COMPARE)
Ro 8:18 present sufferings are not worth *c*
2Co 8: 8 the sincerity of your love by *c* it
Gal 6: 4 without *c* himself to somebody else

COMPARISON* (COMPARE)
2Co 3:10 now in *c* with the surpassing glory.

COMPASSION* (COMPASSIONATE COMPASSIONS)
Ex 33:19 I will have *c* on whom I will have *c*.
Dt 13:17 he will show you mercy, have *c*
28:54 man among you will have no *c*
30: 3 restore your fortunes and have *c*
32:36 and have *c* on his servants
Jdg 2:18 for the LORD had *c* on them
1Ki 3:26 son was alive was filled with *c*
2Ki 13:23 and had *c* and showed concern
2Ch 30: 9 and your children will be shown *c*
Ne 9:19 of your great *c* you did not
9:27 and in your great *c* you gave them
9:28 in your *c* you delivered them time
Ps 51: 1 according to your great *c*
77: 9 Has he in anger withheld his *c*?"
90:13 Have *c* on your servants.
102: 13 You will arise and have *c* on Zion,
103: 4 and crowns you with love and *c*.
103: 13 As a father has *c* on his children,
103: 13 so the LORD has *c*
116: 5 our God is full of *c*.
119: 77 Let your *c* come to me that I may
119:156 Your *c* is great, O LORD;
135: 14 and have *c* on his servants.
145: 9 he has *c* on all he has made.
Isa 13:18 will they look with *c* on children.
14: 1 The LORD will have *c* on Jacob;
27:11 so their Maker has no *c* on them,
30:18 he rises to show you *c*.
49:10 He who has *c* on them will guide
49:13 and will have *c* on his afflicted ones
49:15 and have no *c* on the child she has
51: 3 and will look with *c* on all her ruins
54: 7 with deep *c* I will bring you back.
54: 8 I will have *c* on you,"
54:10 says the LORD, who has *c* on you.
60:10 in favor I will show you *c*.
63: 7 to his *c* and many kindnesses.
63:15 and *c* are withheld from us.
Jer 12:15 I will again have *c* and will bring
13:14 *c* to keep me from destroying them
15: 6 I can no longer show *c*.
21: 7 show them no mercy or pity or *c*.'
30:18 and have *c* on his dwellings;
31:20 I have great *c* for him,"
33:26 restore their fortunes and have *c*
42:12 I will show you *c* so that he will
42:12 so that he will have *c* on you
La 3:32 he brings grief, he will show *c*,
Eze 9: 5 without showing pity or *c*.
16: 5 or had *c* enough to do any
39:25 and will have *c* on all the people
Hos 2:19 in love and *c*.
11: 8 all my *c* is aroused.
13:14 "I will have no *c*,
14: 3 for in you the fatherless find *c*."
Am 1:11 stifling all *c*,
Jnh 3: 9 with *c* turn from his fierce anger
3:10 he had *c* and did not bring
Mic 7:19 You will again have *c* on us;
Zec 7: 9 show mercy and *c* to one another.
10: 6 because I have *c* on them.
Mal 3:17 as in *c* a man spares his son who
Mt 9:36 When he saw the crowds, he had *c*
14:14 he had *c* on them and healed their
15:32 "I have *c* for these people;
20:34 Jesus had *c* on them and touched
Mk 1:41 with *c*, Jesus reached out his hand
6:34 and saw a large crowd, he had *c*
8: 2 "I have *c* for these people;
Lk 15:20 and was filled with *c* for him;
Ro 9:15 and I will have *c* on whom I have *c*
2Co 1: 3 the Father of *c* and the God
Php 2: 1 and *c*, then make my joy complete
Col 3:12 clothe yourselves with *c*, kindness,
Jas 5:11 The Lord is full of *c* and mercy.

COMPASSIONATE* (COMPASSION)
Ex 22:27 out to me, I will hear, for I am *c*.
34: 6 the LORD, the *c* and gracious God
2Ch 30: 9 LORD your God is gracious and *c*.
Ne 9:17 gracious and *c*, slow to anger
Ps 86:15 O Lord, are a *c* and gracious God,
103: 8 The LORD is *c* and gracious,
111: 4 the LORD is gracious and *c*.
112: 4 the gracious and *c* and righteous
145: 8 The LORD is gracious and *c*,
La 4:10 With their own hands *c* women
Joel 2:13 for he is gracious and *c*,
Jnh 4: 2 that you are a gracious and *c* God,
Eph 4:32 Be kind and *c* to one another,
1Pe 3: 8 love as brothers, be *c* and humble.

COMPASSIONS* (COMPASSION)
La 3:22 for his *c* never fail.

COMPELLED (COMPULSION)
Ac 20:22 "And now, *c* by the Spirit,
1Co 9:16 I cannot boast, for I am *c* to preach.

COMPELS (COMPULSION)
Job 32:18 and the spirit within me *c* me;
2Co 5:14 For Christ's love *c* us, because we

COMPETENCE* (COMPETENT)
2Co 3: 5 but our *c* comes from God.

COMPETENT* (COMPETENCE)
Ro 15:14 and *c* to instruct one another.
1Co 6: 2 are you not *c* to judge trivial cases?
2Co 3: 5 Not that we are *c* in ourselves to claim
3: 6 He has made us *c* as ministers

COMPETES*
1Co 9:25 Everyone who *c* in the games goes
2Ti 2: 5 Similarly, if anyone *c* as an athlete,
2: 5 unless he *c* according to the rules.

COMPLACENCY* (COMPLACENT)
Pr 1:32 and the *c* of fools will destroy them
Eze 30: 9 ships to frighten Cush out of her *c*.

COMPLACENT* (COMPLACENCY)
Isa 32: 9 You women who are so *c*,
32:11 Tremble, you *c* women;
Am 6: 1 Woe to you who are *c* in Zion,
Zep 1:12 and punish those who are *c*,

COMPLAINING*
Php 2:14 Do everything without *c* or arguing

COMPLETE
Dt 16:15 your hands, and your joy will be *c*.
Jn 3:29 That joy is mine, and it is now *c*.
15:11 and that your joy may be *c*.
16:24 will receive, and your joy will be *c*.
17:23 May they be brought to *c* unity
Ac 20:24 *c* the task the Lord Jesus has given
Php 2: 2 then make my joy *c*
Col 4:17 to it that you *c* the work you have
Jas 1: 4 so that you may be mature and *c*,
2:22 his faith was made *c* by what he did
1Jn 1: 4 We write this to make our joy *c*.
2: 5 God's love is truly made *c* in him.
4:12 and his love is made *c* in us.
4:17 love is made *c* among us
2Jn :12 to face, so that our joy may be *c*.

COMPLIMENTS*
Pr 23: 8 and will have wasted your *c*.

COMPREHEND* (COMPREHENDED)
Job 28:13 Man does not *c* its worth;
Ecc 8:17 No one can *c* what goes
8:17 he knows, he cannot really *c* it.

COMPREHENDED* (COMPREHEND)
Job 38:18 Have you *c* the vast expanses

COMPULSION (COMPELLED COMPELS)
2Co 9: 7 not reluctantly or under *c*,

CONCEAL (CONCEALED CONCEALS)
Ps 40:10 I do not *c* your love and your truth
Pr 25: 2 It is the glory of God to *c* a matter;

CONCEALED (CONCEAL)
Jer 16:17 nor is their sin *c* from my eyes.
Mt 10:26 There is nothing *c* that will not be
Mk 4:22 and whatever is *c* is meant
Lk 8:17 nothing *c* that will not be known
12: 2 There is nothing *c* that will not be

CONCEALS* (CONCEAL)
Pr 10:18 He who *c* his hatred has lying lips,
28:13 He who *c* his sins does not prosper,

CONCEIT* (CONCEITED CONCEITS)
Isa 16: 6 her overweening pride and *c*,
Jer 48:29 her overweening pride and *c*,
Php 2: 3 out of selfish ambition or vain *c*,

CONCEITED* (CONCEIT)
1Sa 17:28 I know how *c* you are and how
Ro 11:25 brothers, so that you may not be *c*:
12:16 Do not be *c*.
2Co 12: 7 To keep me from becoming *c*
Gal 5:26 Let us not become *c*, provoking
1Ti 3: 6 or he may become *c* and fall
6: 4 he is *c* and understands nothing.
2Ti 3: 4 of the good, treacherous, rash, *c*,

CONCEITS* (CONCEIT)
Ps 73: 7 evil *c* of their minds know no

CONCEIVED (CONCEIVES)
Ps 51: 5 from the time my mother *c* me.
Mt 1:20 what is *c* in her is from the Holy
1Co 2: 9 no mind has *c*
Jas 1:15 after desire has *c*, it gives birth

CONCEIVES* (CONCEIVED)
Ps 7:14 *c* trouble gives birth

CONCERN* (CONCERNED)
Ge 39: 6 he did not *c* himself with anything

Ge 39: 8 "my master does not c himself
1Sa 23:21 "The LORD bless you for your c
2Ki 13:23 and had compassion and showed c
Job 9:21 I have no c for myself;
19: 4 my error remains my c alone.
Ps 131: 1 I do not c myself with great matters
Pr 29: 7 but the wicked have no such c.
Eze 36:21 I had c for my holy name, which
Ac 15:14 God at first showed his c by taking
18:17 But Gallio showed no c whatever.
1Co 7:32 I would like you to be free from c.
12:25 that its parts should have equal c
2Co 7: 7 your deep sorrow, your ardent c
7:11 what alarm, what longing, what c,
8:16 of Titus the same c I have for you.
11:28 of my c for all the churches.
Php 4:10 at last you have renewed your c

CONCERNED (CONCERN)
Ex 2:25 Israelites and was c about them.
Ps 142: 4 no one is c for me.
Jnh 4:10 "You have been c about this vine,
4:11 Should I not be c about that great
1Co 7:32 An unmarried man is c about
9: 9 Is it about oxen that God is c?
Php 4:10 you have been c, but you had no

CONCESSION*
1Co 7: 6 I say this as a c, not as a command.

CONDEMN* (CONDEMNATION CONDEMNED CONDEMNING CONDEMNS)
Job 9:20 innocent, my mouth would c me;
10: 2 I will say to God: Do not c me,
34:17 Will you c the just and mighty One
34:29 if he remains silent, who can c him?
40: 8 Would you c me to justify yourself?
Ps 94:21 and c the innocent to death.
109: 7 and may his prayers c him.
109: 31 from those who c him.
Isa 50: 9 Who is he that will c me?
Mt 12:41 with this generation and c it;
12:42 with this generation and c it;
20:18 They will c him to death
Mk 10:33 They will c him to death
Lk 6:37 Do not c, and you will not be
11:31 men of this generation and c them;
11:32 with this generation and c it;
Jn 3:17 Son into the world to c the world,
7:51 "Does our law c anyone
8:11 "Then neither do I c you,"
12:48 very word which I spoke will c him
Ro 2:27 yet obeys the law will c you who,
14: 3 everything must not c the man who
14:22 is the man who does not c himself
2Co 7: 3 this to c you; I have said
1Jn 3:20 presence whenever our hearts c us.
3:21 if our hearts do not c us,

CONDEMNATION* (CONDEMN)
Jer 42:18 of c and reproach; you will never
44:12 and horror, of c and reproach.
Ro 3: 8 may result"? Their c is deserved.
5:16 followed one sin and brought c,
5:18 of one trespass was c for all men,
8: 1 there is now no c for those who are
2Pe 2: 3 Their c has long been hanging
Jude : 4 certain men whose c was written

CONDEMNED* (CONDEMN)
Dt 13:17 of those c things shall be found
Job 32: 3 to refute Job, and yet had c him.
Ps 34:21 the foes of the righteous will be c.
34:22 will be c who takes refuge in him.
37:33 let them be c when brought to trial.
79:11 preserve those c to die.
102: 20 and release those c to death."
Mt 12: 7 you would not have c the innocent.
12:37 and by your words you will be c."
23:33 How will you escape being c to hell
27: 3 betrayed him, saw that Jesus was c,
Mk 14:64 They all c him as worthy of death.
16:16 whoever does not believe will be c.
Lk 6:37 condemn, and you will not be c.
Jn 3:18 Whoever believes in him is not c,
3:18 does not believe stands c already
5:24 has eternal life and will not be c;
5:29 who have done evil will rise to be c.
8:10 Has no one c you?" "No one, sir,"
16:11 prince of this world now stands c.
Ac 25:15 against him and asked that he be c.
Ro 3: 7 why am I still c as a sinner?"
8: 3 And so he c sin in sinful man,
14:23 But the man who has doubts is c
1Co 4: 9 like men c to die in the arena.
11:32 disciplined so that we will not be c
Gal 1: 8 let him be eternally c! As we have
1: 9 let him be eternally c! Am I now
2Th 2:12 that all will be c who have not
Tit 2: 8 of speech that cannot be c,
Heb 11: 7 By his faith he c the world
Jas 5: 6 You have c and murdered innocent
5:12 and your "No," no, or you will be c
2Pe 2: 6 if he c the cities of Sodom
Rev 19: 2 He has c the great prostitute

CONDEMNING* (CONDEMN)
Dt 25: 1 the innocent and c the guilty.
1Ki 8:32 c the guilty and bringing
Pr 17:15 the guilty and c the innocent—
Ac 13:27 yet in c him they fulfilled the words
Ro 2: 1 judge the other, you are c yourself,

CONDEMNS* (CONDEMN)
Job 15: 6 Your own mouth c you, not mine;
Pr 12: 2 but the LORD c a crafty man.
Ro 8:34 Who is he that c? Christ Jesus,
2Co 3: 9 the ministry that c men is glorious,

CONDITION
Pr 27:23 Be sure you know the c

CONDUCT (CONDUCTED CONDUCTS)
Pr 10:23 A fool finds pleasure in evil c,
20:11 by whether his c is pure and right.
21: 8 but the c of the innocent is upright.
Ecc 6: 8 how to c himself before others?
Jer 4:18 "Your own c and actions
17:10 to reward a man according to his c,
Eze 7: 3 I will judge you according to your c
Php 1:27 c yourselves in a manner worthy
1Ti 3:15 to c themselves in God's household

CONDUCTED* (CONDUCT)
2Co 1:12 testifies that we have c ourselves

CONDUCTS* (CONDUCT)
Ps 112: 5 who c his affairs with justice.

CONFESS* (CONFESSED CONFESSES CONFESSING CONFESSION)
Lev 5: 5 he must c in what way he has
16:21 and c over it all the wickedness
26:40 " 'But if they will c their sins
Nu 5: 7 must c the sin he has committed.
1Ki 8:33 back to you and c your name,
8:35 toward this place and c your name
2Ch 6:24 they turn back and c your name,
6:26 toward this place and c your name
Ne 1: 6 I c the sins we Israelites, including
Ps 32: 5 I said, "I will c
38:18 I c my iniquity;
Jn 1:20 fail to c, but confessed freely,
12:42 they would not c their faith
Ro 10: 9 That if you c with your mouth,
10:10 it is with your mouth that you c
14:11 every tongue will c to God.' "
Php 2:11 every tongue c that Jesus Christ is
Heb 3: 1 and high priest whom we c.
13:15 the fruit of lips that c his name.
Jas 5:16 Therefore c your sins to each other
1Jn 1: 9 If we c our sins, he is faithful

CONFESSED* (CONFESS)
1Sa 7: 6 day they fasted and there they c,
Ne 9: 2 in their places and c their sins
Da 9: 4 to the LORD my God and c:
Jn 1:20 but c freely, "I am not the Christ."
Ac 19:18 and openly c their evil deeds.

CONFESSES* (CONFESS)
Pr 28:13 whoever c and renounces them
2Ti 2:19 and, "Everyone who c the name

CONFESSING* (CONFESS)
Ezr 10: 1 While Ezra was praying and c,
Da 9:20 c my sin and the sin
Mt 3: 6 C their sins, they were baptized
Mk 1: 5 C their sins, they were baptized

CONFESSION* (CONFESS)
Ezr 10:11 Now make c to the LORD,
Ne 9: 3 and spent another quarter in c
2Co 9:13 obedience that accompanies your c
1Ti 6:12 called when you made your good c
6:13 Pontius Pilate made the good c,

CONFIDENCE* (CONFIDENT)
Jdg 9:26 and its citizens put their c in him.
2Ki 18:19 On what are you basing this c
2Ch 32: 8 And the people gained c
32:10 On what are you basing your c,
Job 4: 6 Should not your piety be your c
Ps 71: 5 my c since my youth.
Pr 3:26 for the LORD will be your c
3:32 but takes the upright into his c.
11:13 A gossip betrays a c,
20:19 A gossip betrays a c;
25: 9 do not betray another man's c,
31:11 Her husband has full c in her
Isa 32:17 will be quietness and c forever.
36: 4 On what are you basing this c
Jer 17: 7 whose c is in him.
49:31 which lives in c,"
Eze 29:16 a source of c for the people of Israel
Mic 7: 5 put no c in a friend.
2Co 2: 3 I had c in all of you, that you would
3: 4 Such c as this is ours
7: 4 I have great c in you; I take great
7:16 I am glad I can have complete c
8:22 so because of his great c in you.
Eph 3:12 God with freedom and c.
Php 3: 3 and who put no c in the flesh—
3: 4 I myself have reasons for such c.
3: 4 reasons to put c in the flesh,
2Th 3: 4 We have c in the Lord that you are
Heb 3:14 till the end the c we had at first.
4:16 the throne of grace with c,
10:19 since we have c to enter the Most
10:35 So do not throw away your c;
13: 6 So we say with c,
1Jn 3:21 we have c before God and receive
4:17 us so that we will have c on the day
5:14 This is the c we have

CONFIDENT* (CONFIDENCE)
Job 6:20 because they had been c;
Ps 27: 3 even then will I be c.
27:13 I am still c of this:
Lk 18: 9 To some who were c
2Co 1:15 Because I was c of this, I planned
5: 6 Therefore we are always c
5: 8 We are c, I say, and would prefer
9: 4 ashamed of having been so c.
10: 7 If anyone is c that he belongs
Gal 5:10 I am c in the Lord that you will
Php 1: 6 day until now, being c of this,
2:24 I am c in the Lord that I myself will
Phm :21 C of your obedience, I write to you,
Heb 6: 9 we are c of better things
1Jn 2:28 that when he appears we may be c

CONFIDES*
Ps 25:14 The LORD c in those who fear him

CONFORM* (CONFORMED CONFORMITY CONFORMS)
Ro 12: 2 Do not c any longer to the pattern
1Pe 1:14 do not c to the evil desires you had

CONFORMED* (CONFORM)
Eze 5: 7 c to the standards of the nations
11:12 but have c to the standards
Ro 8:29 predestined to be c to the likeness

CONFORMITY* (CONFORM)
Eph 1:11 in c with the purpose of his will,

CONFORMS* (CONFORM)
1Ti 1:11 to the sound doctrine that c

CONQUEROR* (CONQUERORS)
Mic 1:15 I will bring a c against you
Rev 6: 2 he rode out as a c bent on conquest.

CONQUERORS (CONQUEROR)
Ro 8:37 than c through him who loved us.

CONSCIENCE* (CONSCIENCE-STRICKEN CONSCIENCES CONSCIENTIOUS)
Ge 20: 5 I have done this with a clear c
20: 6 I know you did this with a clear c,
1Sa 25:31 have on his c the staggering burden
Job 27: 6 my c will not reproach me as long
Ac 23: 1 to God in all good c to this day."
24:16 to keep my c clear before God
Ro 9: 1 my c confirms it in the Holy Spirit
13: 5 punishment but also because of c.
1Co 4: 4 My c is clear, but that does not
8: 7 since their c is weak, it is defiled.
8:10 with a weak c sees you who have

COOLNESS*
Pr 25:13 Like the *c* of snow at harvest time

COPIES (COPY)
Heb 9:23 for the *c* of the heavenly things

COPY (COPIES)
Dt 17:18 for himself on a scroll a *c* of this law
Heb 8: 5 They serve at a sanctuary that is a *c*
9:24 sanctuary that was only a *c*

CORBAN*
Mk 7:11 received from me is *C'* (that is,

CORD (CORDS)
Jos 2:18 you have tied this scarlet *c*
Ecc 4:12 *c* of three strands is not quickly

CORDS (CORD)
Pr 5:22 the *c* of his sin hold him fast.
Isa 54: 2 lengthen your *c*,
Hos 11: 4 them with *c* of human kindness,

CORINTH
Ac 18: 1 Paul left Athens and went to *C*.
1Co 1: 2 To the church of God in *C*,
2Co 1: 1 To the church of God in *C*,

CORNELIUS*
Roman to whom Peter preached; first Gentile Christian (Ac 10).

CORNER (CORNERS)
Ru 3: 9 "Spread the *c* of your garment
Pr 21: 9 Better to live on a *c* of the roof
25:24 Better to live on a *c* of the roof
Ac 26:26 because it was not done in a *c*.

CORNERS (CORNER)
Mt 6: 5 on the street *c* to be seen by men.
22: 9 Go to the street *c* and invite

CORNERSTONE* (STONE)
Job 38: 6 or who laid its *c*—
Isa 28:16 a precious *c* for a sure foundation;
Jer 51:26 rock will be taken from you for a *c*,
Zec 10: 4 From Judah will come the *c*,
Eph 2:20 Christ Jesus himself as the chief *c*.
1Pe 2: 6 a chosen and precious *c*,

CORRECT* (CORRECTED CORRECTING CORRECTION CORRECTIONS CORRECTS)
Job 6:26 Do you mean to *c* what I say,
40: 2 contends with the Almighty *c* him?
Jer 10:24 *C* me, LORD, but only with justice
2Ti 4: 2 *c*, rebuke and encourage—

CORRECTED* (CORRECT)
Pr 29:19 A servant cannot be *c*

CORRECTING* (CORRECT)
2Ti 3:16 *c* and training in righteousness,

CORRECTION* (CORRECT)
Lev 26:23 things you do not accept my *c*
Job 36:10 He makes them listen to *c*
Pr 5:12 How my heart spurned *c*!
10:17 whoever ignores *c* leads others
12: 1 but he who hates *c* is stupid.
13:18 but whoever heeds *c* is honored.
15: 5 whoever heeds *c* shows prudence.
15:10 he who hates *c* will die.
15:12 A mocker resents *c*;
15:32 whoever heeds *c* gains
29:15 The rod of *c* imparts wisdom,
Jer 2:30 they did not respond to *c*.
5: 3 crushed them, but they refused *c*.
7:28 LORD its God or responded to *c*.
Zep 3: 2 she accepts no *c*.
3: 7 you will fear me / and accept *c*!'

CORRECTIONS* (CORRECT)
Pr 6:23 and the *c* of discipline

CORRECTS* (CORRECT)
Job 5:17 "Blessed is the man whom God *c*;
Pr 9: 7 Whoever *c* a mocker invites insult;

CORRUPT (CORRUPTED CORRUPTION CORRUPTS)
Ge 6:11 Now the earth was *c* in God's sight
Ps 14: 1 They are *c*, their deeds are vile;
14: 3 they have together become *c*;
Pr 4:24 keep *c* talk far from your lips.
6:12 who goes about with a *c* mouth,
19:28 A *c* witness mocks at justice,

CORRUPTED (CORRUPT)
2Co 7: 2 wronged no one, we have *c* no one,
Tit 1:15 but to those who are *c* and do not

CORRUPTION (CORRUPT)
2Pe 1: 4 escape the *c* in the world caused
2:20 If they have escaped the *c*

CORRUPTS* (CORRUPT)
Ecc 7: 7 and a bribe *c* the heart.
1Co 15:33 "Bad company *c* good character."
Jas 3: 6 It *c* the whole person, sets

COST (COSTS)
Nu 16:38 sinned at the *c* of their lives.
Pr 4: 7 Though it *c* all you have, get
7:23 little knowing it will *c* him his life.
Isa 55: 1 milk without money and without *c*.
Lk 14:28 and estimate the *c* to see
Rev 21: 6 to drink without *c* from the spring

COSTS (COST)
Pr 6:31 it *c* him all the wealth of his house.

COUNCIL
Ps 89: 7 In the *c* of the holy ones God is
107: 32 and praise him in the *c* of the elders

COUNSEL (COUNSELOR COUNSELS)
1Ki 22: 5 "First seek the *c* of the LORD."
2Ch 18: 4 "First seek the *c* of the LORD."
Job 38: 2 "Who is this that darkens my *c*
42: 3 'Who is this that obscures my *c*
Ps 1: 1 walk in the *c* of the wicked
73:24 You guide me with your *c*,
107: 11 despised the *c* of the Most High.
Pr 8:14 *C* and sound judgment are mine;
15:22 Plans fail for lack of *c*,
27: 9 from his earnest *c*.
Isa 28:29 wonderful in *c* and magnificent
1Ti 5:14 So I *c* younger widows to marry,
Rev 3:18 I *c* you to buy from me gold refined

COUNSELOR (COUNSEL)
Isa 9: 6 Wonderful *C*, Mighty God,
Jn 14:16 he will give you another *C* to be
14:26 But the *C*, the Holy Spirit,
15:26 "When the *C* comes, whom I will
16: 7 the *C* will not come to you;
Ro 11:34 Or who has been his *c*?"

COUNSELS (COUNSEL)
Ps 16: 7 I will praise the LORD, who *c* me;

COUNT (COUNTED COUNTING COUNTS)
Ps 22:17 I can *c* all my bones;
Ro 4: 8 whose sin the Lord will never *c*
6:11 *c* yourselves dead to sin
2Th 1:11 that our God may *c* you worthy

COUNTED (COUNT)
Ac 5:41 because they had been *c* worthy
2Th 1: 5 and as a result you will be *c* worthy

COUNTERFEIT*
2Th 2: 9 displayed in all kinds of *c* miracles,
1Jn 2:27 not *c*—just as it has taught you,

COUNTING (COUNT)
2Co 5:19 not *c* men's sins against them.

COUNTRY
Pr 28: 2 When a *c* is rebellious, it has many
29: 4 By justice a king gives a *c* stability,
Isa 66: 8 Can a *c* be born in a day
Lk 15:13 off for a distant *c* and there
Jn 4:44 prophet has no honor in his own *c*.)
2Co 11:26 in danger in the *c*, in danger at sea;
Heb 11:14 looking for a *c* of their own.

COUNTRYMEN
2Co 11:26 danger from my own *c*, in danger

COUNTS (COUNT)
Jn 6:63 The Spirit gives life; the flesh *c*
1Co 7:19 God's commands is what *c*.
Gal 5: 6 only thing that *c* is faith expressing

COURAGE* (COURAGEOUS)
Jos 2:11 everyone's *c* failed because of you,
5: 1 and they no longer had the *c*
2Sa 4: 1 he lost *c*, and all Israel became
7:27 So your servant has found *c*
1Ch 17:25 So your servant has found *c* to pray
2Ch 15: 8 son of Oded the prophet, he took *c*.
19:11 Act with *c*, and may the LORD be
Ezr 7:28 I took *c* and gathered leading men
10: 4 We will support you, so take *c*
Ps 107: 26 in their peril their *c* melted away.
Eze 22:14 Will your *c* endure or your hands
Da 11:25 and *c* against the king of the South.
Mt 14:27 said to them: "Take *c*!
Mk 6:50 spoke to them and said, "Take *c*!
Ac 4:13 When they saw the *c* of Peter
23:11 "Take *c*! As you have testified
27:22 now I urge you to keep up your *c*,
27:25 So keep up your *c*, men,
1Co 16:13 stand firm in the faith; be men of *c*;
Php 1:20 will have sufficient *c* so that now
Heb 3: 6 if we hold on to our *c* and the hope

COURAGEOUS* (COURAGE)
Dt 31: 6 Be strong and *c*.
31: 7 of all Israel, "Be strong and *c*,
31:23 son of Nun: "Be strong and *c*,
Jos 1: 6 and *c*, because you will lead these
1: 7 Be strong and very *c*.
1: 9 commanded you? Be strong and *c*.
1:18 Only be strong and *c*!"
10:25 Be strong and *c*.
1Ch 22:13 Be strong and *c*.
28:20 "Be strong and *c*, and do the work.
2Ch 26:17 priest with eighty other *c* priests
32: 7 with these words: "Be strong and *c*.

COURSE
Ps 19: 5 a champion rejoicing to run his *c*.
Pr 2: 8 for he guards the *c* of the just
15:21 of understanding keeps a straight *c*.
16: 9 In his heart a man plans his *c*,
17:23 to pervert the *c* of justice.
Jas 3: 6 sets the whole *c* of his life on fire,

COURT (COURTS)
Pr 22:22 and do not crush the needy in *c*,
25: 8 do not bring hastily to *c*,
Mt 5:25 adversary who is taking you to *c*.
1Co 4: 3 judged by you or by any human *c*;

COURTS (COURT)
Ps 84:10 Better is one day in your *c*
100: 4 and his *c* with praise;
Am 5:15 maintain justice in the *c*.
Zec 8:16 and sound judgment in your *c*;

COURTYARD
Ex 27: 9 "Make a *c* for the tabernacle.

COUSIN
Col 4:10 as does Mark, the *c* of Barnabas.

COVENANT (COVENANTS)
Ge 9: 9 "I now establish my *c* with you
17: 2 I will confirm my *c* between me
Ex 19: 5 if you obey me fully and keep my *c*,
24: 7 Then he took the Book of the *C*
Dt 4:13 declared to you his *c*, the Ten
29: 1 in addition to the *c* he had made
Jdg 2: 1 'I will never break my *c* with you,
1Sa 23:18 of them made a *c* before the LORD
1Ki 8:21 in which is the *c* of the LORD that
8:23 you who keep your *c* of love
2Ki 23: 2 the words of the Book of the *C*,
1Ch 16:15 He remembers his *c* forever,
2Ch 6:14 you who keep your *c* of love
34:30 the words of the Book of the *C*,
Ne 1: 5 who keeps his *c* of love
Job 31: 1 "I made a *c* with my eyes
Ps 105: 8 He remembers his *c* forever,
Pr 2:17 ignored the *c* she made before God
Isa 42: 6 you to be a *c* for the people
61: 8 make an everlasting *c* with them.
Jer 11: 2 "Listen to the terms of this *c*
31:31 "when I will make a new *c*
31:32 It will not be like the *c*
31:33 "This is the *c* I will make
Eze 37:26 I will make a *c* of peace with them;
Da 9:27 He will confirm a *c* with many
Hos 6: 7 Like Adam, they have broken the *c*
Mal 2:14 the wife of your marriage *c*.
3: 1 of the *c*, whom you desire,
Mt 26:28 blood of the *c*, which is poured out
Mk 14:24 "This is my blood of the *c*,
Lk 22:20 "This cup is the new *c* in my blood,
1Co 11:25 "This cup is the new *c* in my blood;
2Co 3: 6 as ministers of a new *c*—
Gal 4:24 One *c* is from Mount Sinai
Heb 8: 6 as the *c* of which he is mediator is
8: 8 when I will make a new *c*
9:15 Christ is the mediator of a new *c*,
12:24 to Jesus the mediator of a new *c*,

COVENANTS (COVENANT)
Ro 9: 4 theirs the divine glory, the *c*,

Gal 4:24 for the women represent two c.

COVER (COVER-UP COVERED COVERING COVERINGS COVERS)
Ex 25:17 "Make an atonement c of pure gold
25:21 Place the c on top of the ark
33:22 and c you with my hand
Lev 16: 2 in the cloud over the atonement c.
Ps 32: 5 and did not c up my iniquity.
91: 4 He will c you with his feathers,
Hos 10: 8 say to the mountains, "C us!"
Lk 23:30 and to the hills, "C us!"
1Co 11: 6 If a woman does not c her head,
11: 6 shaved off, she should c her head.
11: 7 A man ought not to c his head,
Jas 5:20 and c over a multitude of sins.

COVER-UP* (COVER)
1Pe 2:16 but do not use your freedom as a c

COVERED (COVER)
Ps 32: 1 whose sins are c.
85: 2 and c all their sins.
Isa 6: 2 With two wings they c their faces,
51:16 c you with the shadow of my hand
Ro 4: 7 whose sins are c.
1Co 11: 4 with his head c dishonors his head.

COVERING (COVER)
1Co 11:15 For long hair is given to her as a c.

COVERINGS (COVER)
Ge 3: 7 and made c for themselves.
Pr 31:22 She makes c for her bed;

COVERS (COVER)
Pr 10:12 but love c over all wrongs.
17: 9 He who c over an offense promotes
2Co 3:15 Moses is read, a veil c their hearts.
1Pe 4: 8 love c over a multitude of sins.

COVET* (COVETED COVETING COVETOUS)
Ex 20:17 You shall not c your neighbor's
20:17 "You shall not c your neighbor's
34:24 and no one will c your land
Dt 5:21 "You shall not c your neighbor's
7:25 Do not c the silver and gold
Mic 2: 2 They c fields and seize them,
Ro 7: 7 if the law had not said, "Do not c."
13: 9 "Do not steal," "Do not c,"
Jas 4: 2 c, but you cannot have what you

COVETED* (COVET)
Jos 7:21 weighing fifty shekels, I c them
Ac 20:33 I have not c anyone's silver or gold

COVETING
Ro 7: 7 what c really was if the law

COVETOUS* (COVET)
Ro 7: 8 in me every kind of c desire.

COWARDLY*
Rev 21: 8 But the c, the unbelieving, the vile,

COWS
Ge 41: 2 of the river there came up seven c,
Ex 25: 5 skins dyed red and hides of sea c;
Nu 4: 6 are to cover this with hides of sea c,
1Sa 6: 7 Hitch the c to the cart,

CRAFTINESS* (CRAFTY)
Job 5:13 He catches the wise in their c,
1Co 3:19 "He catches the wise in their c";
Eph 4:14 and c of men in their deceitful

CRAFTSMAN
Pr 8:30 Then I was the c at his side.

CRAFTY* (CRAFTINESS)
Ge 3: 1 the serpent was more c than any
1Sa 23:22 They tell me he is very c.
Job 5:12 He thwarts the plans of the c,
15: 5 you adopt the tongue of the c.
Pr 7:10 like a prostitute and with c intent.
12: 2 but the LORD condemns a c man.
14:17 and a c man is hated.
2Co 12:16 c fellow that I am, I caught you

CRAVE* (CRAVED CRAVES CRAVING CRAVINGS)
Nu 11: 4 with them began to c other food,
Dt 12:20 you c meat and say, "I would like
Pr 23: 3 Do not c his delicacies,
23: 6 do not c his delicacies;
31: 4 not for rulers to c beer,
Mic 7: 1 none of the early figs that I c.
1Pe 2: 2 newborn babies, c pure spiritual

CRAVED* (CRAVE)
Nu 11:34 the people who had c other food.
Ps 78:18 by demanding the food they c.
78:29 for he had given them what they c.
78:30 turned from the food they c,

CRAVES* (CRAVE)
Pr 13: 4 The sluggard c and gets nothing,
21:10 The wicked man c evil;
21:26 All day long he c for more,

CRAVING* (CRAVE)
Job 20:20 he will have no respite from his c;
Ps 106:14 In the desert they gave in to their c;
Pr 10: 3 but he thwarts the c of the wicked.
13: 2 the unfaithful have a c for violence.
21:25 The sluggard's c will be the death
Jer 2:24 sniffing the wind in her c—

CRAVINGS* (CRAVE)
Ps 10: 3 He boasts of the c of his heart;
Eph 2: 3 gratifying the c of our sinful nature
1Jn 2:16 in the world—the c of sinful man,

CRAWL
Ge 3:14 You will c on your belly

CREATE* (CREATED CREATES CREATING CREATION CREATOR)
Ps 51:10 C in me a pure heart, O God,
Isa 4: 5 Then the LORD will c over all
45: 7 I bring prosperity and c disaster;
45: 7 I form the light and c darkness,
45:18 he did not c it to be empty,
65:17 "Behold, I will c / new heavens
65:18 for I will c Jerusalem to be a delight
65:18 forever in what I will c,
Jer 31:22 The LORD will c a new thing
Mal 2:10 one Father? Did not one God c us?
Eph 2:15 His purpose was to c

CREATED* (CREATE)
Ge 1: 1 In the beginning God c the heavens
1:21 God c the great creatures of the sea
1:27 So God c man in his own image,
1:27 in the image of God he c him;
1:27 male and female he c them.
2: 4 and the earth when they were c.
5: 1 When God c man, he made him
5: 2 He c them male and female
5: 2 when they were c, he called them
6: 7 whom I have c, from the face
Dt 4:32 from the day God c man
Ps 89:12 You c the north and the south;
89:47 what futility you have c all men!
102: 18 a people not yet c may praise
104: 30 you send your Spirit, / they are c,
139: 13 For you c my inmost being;
148: 5 for he commanded and they were c
Isa 40:26 Who c all these?
41:20 that the Holy One of Israel has c it.
42: 5 he who c the heavens and stretched
43: 1 he who c you, O Jacob,
43: 7 whom I c for my glory,
45: 8 I, the LORD, have c it.
45:12 and c mankind upon it.
45:18 he who c the heavens,
48: 7 They are c now, and not long ago;
54:16 And it is I who have c the destroyer
54:16 "See, it is I who c the blacksmith
57:16 the breath of man that I have c.
Eze 21:30 In the place where you were c,
28:13 the day you were c they were
28:15 ways from the day you were c
Mk 13:19 when God c the world, until now—
Ro 1:25 and served c things rather
1Co 11: 9 neither was man c for woman,
Eph 2:10 c in Christ Jesus to do good works,
3: 9 hidden in God, who c all things.
4:24 c to be like God in true
Col 1:16 For by him all things were c:
1:16 all things were c by him
1Ti 4: 3 which God c to be received
4: 4 For everything God c is good,
Heb 12:27 c things—so that what cannot be
Jas 1:18 a kind of firstfruits of all he c.
Rev 4:11 and by your will they were c
4:11 for you c all things,
10: 6 who c the heavens and all that is

CREATES* (CREATE)
Am 4:13 c the wind,

CREATING* (CREATE)
Ge 2: 3 the work of c that he had done.
Isa 57:19 c praise on the lips of the mourners

CREATION* (CREATE)
Hab 2:18 he who makes it trusts in his own c;
Mt 13:35 hidden since the c of the world."
25:34 for you since the c of the world.
Mk 10: 6 of c God 'made them male
16:15 and preach the good news to all c.
Jn 17:24 me before the c of the world.
Ro 1:20 For since the c of the world God's
8:19 The c waits in eager expectation
8:20 For the c was subjected
8:21 in hope that the c itself will be
8:22 that the whole c has been groaning
8:39 depth, nor anything else in all c,
2Co 5:17 he is a new c; the old has gone,
Gal 6:15 anything; what counts is a new c.
Eph 1: 4 us in him before the c of the world
Col 1:15 God, the firstborn over all c.
Heb 4: 3 finished since the c of the world.
4:13 Nothing in all c is hidden
9:11 that is to say, not a part of this c.
9:26 times since the c of the world.
1Pe 1:20 chosen before the c of the world,
2Pe 3: 4 as it has since the beginning of c."
Rev 3:14 true witness, the ruler of God's c.
13: 8 slain from the c of the world.
17: 8 life from the c of the world will be

CREATOR* (CREATE)
Ge 14:19 C of heaven and earth.
14:22 God Most High, C of heaven
Dt 32: 6 Is he not your Father, your C,
Ecc 12: 1 Remember your C
Isa 27:11 and their C shows them no favor.
40:28 the C of the ends of the earth.
43:15 Israel's C, your King."
Mt 19: 4 the beginning the C 'made them
Ro 1:25 created things rather than the C—
Col 3:10 in knowledge in the image of its C.
1Pe 4:19 themselves to their faithful C

CREATURE (CREATURES)
Lev 17:11 For the life of a c is in the blood,
17:14 the life of every c is its blood.
Ps 136: 25 and who gives food to every c.
Eze 1:15 beside each c with its four faces.
Rev 4: 7 The first living c was like a lion,

CREATURES (CREATURE)
Ge 6:19 bring into the ark two of all living c,
8:21 again will I destroy all living c,
Ps 104: 24 the earth is full of your c.
Eze 1: 5 was what looked like four living c.

CREDIT (CREDITED CREDITOR CREDITS)
Lk 6:33 what c is that to you? Even
Ro 4:24 to whom God will c righteousness
1Pe 2:20 it to your c if you receive a beating

CREDITED (CREDIT)
Ge 15: 6 and he c it to him as righteousness.
Ps 106: 31 This was c to him as righteousness
Eze 18:20 of the righteous man will be c
Ro 4: 3 and it was c to him as righteousness
4: 4 his wages are not c to him as a gift,
4: 5 his faith is c as righteousness.
4: 9 saying that Abraham's faith was c
4:23 The words "it was c
Gal 3: 6 and it was c to him as righteousness
Php 4:17 for what may be c to your account.
Jas 2:23 and it was c to him as righteousness

CREDITOR (CREDIT)
Dt 15: 2 Every c shall cancel the loan he has

CREDITS (CREDIT)
Ro 4: 6 whom God c righteousness apart

CRETANS (CRETE)
Tit 1:12 "C are always liars, evil brutes,

CRETE (CRETANS)
Ac 27:12 harbor in C, facing both southwest

CRIED (CRY)
Ex 2:23 groaned in their slavery and c out,
14:10 They were terrified and c out
Nu 20:16 but when we c out to the LORD,
Jos 24: 7 But they c to the LORD for help,
Jdg 3: 9 But when they c out to the LORD,
3:15 Again the Israelites c out
4: 3 they c to the LORD for help.

Jdg 6: 6 the Israelites that they *c* out
10:12 Maonites oppressed you and you *c*
1Sa 7: 9 He *c* out to the LORD
12: 8 they *c* to the LORD for help,
12:10 They *c* out to the LORD and said,
Ps 18: 6 I *c* to my God for help.

CRIMINALS
Lk 23:32 both *c*, were also led out with him

CRIMSON
Isa 1:18 though they are red as *c*,
63: 1 with his garments stained *c*?

CRIPPLED
2Sa 9: 3 of Jonathan; he is *c* in both feet."
Mk 9:45 better for you to enter life *c*

CRISIS*
1Co 7:26 of the present *c*, I think that it is

CRITICISM*
2Co 8:20 We want to avoid any *c*

CROOKED*
Dt 32: 5 but a warped and *c* generation.
2Sa 22:27 to the *c* you show yourself shrewd.
Ps 18:26 to the *c* you show yourself shrewd.
125: 5 But those who turn to *c* ways
Pr 2:15 whose paths are *c*
5: 6 her paths are *c*, but she knows it
8: 8 none of them is *c* or perverse.
10: 9 he who takes *c* paths will be found
Ecc 7:13 what he has made *c*?
Isa 59: 8 have turned them into *c* roads;
La 3: 9 he has made my paths *c*.
Lk 3: 5 The *c* roads shall become straight,
Php 2:15 children of God without fault in a *c*

CROP (CROPS)
Mt 13: 8 where it produced a *c*—a hundred,
21:41 share of the *c* at harvest time."

CROPS (CROP)
Pr 3: 9 with the firstfruits of all your *c*;
10: 5 He who gathers *c* in summer is
28: 3 like a driving rain that leaves no *c*.
2Ti 2: 6 the first to receive a share of the *c*.

CROSS (CROSSED CROSSING)
Dt 4:21 swore that I would not *c* the Jordan
12:10 But you will *c* the Jordan
Mt 10:38 and anyone who does not take his *c*
16:24 and take up his *c* and follow me.
Mk 8:34 and take up his *c* and follow me.
Lk 9:23 take up his *c* daily and follow me.
14:27 anyone who does not carry his *c*
Jn 19:17 Carrying his own *c*, he went out
Ac 2:23 to death by nailing him to the *c*.
1Co 1:17 lest the *c* of Christ be emptied
1:18 the message of the *c* is foolishness
Gal 5:11 offense of the *c* has been abolished.
6:12 persecuted for the *c* of Christ.
6:14 in the *c* of our Lord Jesus Christ,
Eph 2:16 both of them to God through the *c*,
Php 2: 8 even death on a *c*!
3:18 as enemies of the *c* of Christ.
Col 1:20 through his blood, shed on the *c*.
2:14 he took it away, nailing it to the *c*.
2:15 triumphing over them by the *c*.
Heb 12: 2 set before him endured the *c*,

CROSSED (CROSS)
Jos 4: 7 When it *c* the Jordan, the waters
Jn 5:24 he has *c* over from death to life.

CROSSING (CROSS)
Ge 48:14 he was the younger, and *c* his arms,

CROSSROADS (ROAD)
Jer 6:16 "Stand at the *c* and look;

CROUCHING
Ge 4: 7 sin is *c* at your door; it desires

CROWD (CROWDS)
Ex 23: 2 Do not follow the *c* in doing wrong.

CROWDS (CROWD)
Mt 9:36 he saw the *c*, he had compassion

CROWED (CROWS)
Mt 26:74 the man!" Immediately a rooster *c*.

CROWN (CROWNED CROWNS)
Pr 4: 9 present you with a *c* of splendor."
10: 6 Blessings *c* the head
12: 4 noble character is her husband's *c*,
16:31 Gray hair is a *c* of splendor;
17: 6 Children's children are a *c*
Isa 35:10 everlasting joy will *c* their heads.
51:11 everlasting joy will *c* their heads.
61: 3 to bestow on them a *c* of beauty
62: 3 You will be a *c* of splendor
Eze 16:12 and a beautiful *c* on your head.
Zec 9:16 like jewels in a *c*.
Mt 27:29 and then twisted together a *c* of thorns
Mk 15:17 then twisted together a *c* of thorns
Jn 19: 2 The soldiers twisted together a *c*
19: 5 When Jesus came out wearing the *c*
1Co 9:25 it to get a *c* that will last forever.
9:25 it to get a *c* that will not last;
Php 4: 1 and long for, my joy and *c*,
1Th 2:19 or the *c* in which we will glory
2Ti 2: 5 he does not receive the victor's *c*
4: 8 store for me the *c* of righteousness,
Jas 1:12 he will receive the *c*
1Pe 5: 4 you will receive the *c*
Rev 2:10 and I will give you the *c* of life.
3:11 so that no one will take your *c*.
14:14 a son of man" with a *c* of gold

CROWNED* (CROWN)
Ps 8: 5 and *c* him with glory and honor.
Pr 14:18 the prudent are *c* with knowledge.
SS 3:11 crown with which his mother *c* him
Heb 2: 7 you *c* him with glory and honor
2: 9 now *c* with glory and honor

CROWNS (CROWN)
Ps 103: 4 and *c* me with love and compassion
149: 4 he *c* the humble with salvation.
Pr 11:26 blessing *c* him who is willing to sell.
Rev 4: 4 and had *c* of gold on their heads.
4:10 They lay their *c* before the throne
12: 3 ten horns and seven *c* on his heads.
19:12 and on his head are many *c*.

CROWS (CROWED)
Mt 26:34 this very night, before the rooster *c*

CRUCIFIED* (CRUCIFY)
Mt 20:19 to be mocked and flogged and *c*.
26: 2 of Man will be handed over to be *c*
27:26 and handed him over to be *c*.
27:35 When they had *c* him, they divided
27:38 Two robbers were *c* with him,
27:44 same way the robbers who were *c*
28: 5 looking for Jesus, who was *c*.
Mk 15:15 and handed him over to be *c*.
15:24 And they *c* him.
15:25 the third hour when they *c* him.
15:27 They *c* two robbers with him,
15:32 Those *c* with him also heaped
16: 6 for Jesus the Nazarene, who was *c*.
Lk 23:23 insistently demanded that he be *c*,
23:33 *c* him, along with the criminals—
24: 7 be *c* and on the third day be raised
24:20 sentenced to death, and they *c* him;
Jn 19:16 him over to them to be *c*.
19:18 Here they *c* him, and with him two
19:20 for the place where Jesus was *c* was
19:23 When the soldiers *c* Jesus,
19:32 of the first man who had been *c*
19:41 At the place where Jesus was *c*,
Ac 2:36 whom you *c*, both Lord and Christ
4:10 whom you *c* but whom God raised
Ro 6: 6 For we know that our old self was *c*
1Co 1:13 Is Christ divided? Was Paul *c*
1:23 but we preach Christ *c*: a stumbling
2: 2 except Jesus Christ and him *c*.
2: 8 they would not have *c* the Lord
2Co 13: 4 to be sure, he was *c* in weakness,
Gal 2:20 I have been *c* with Christ
3: 1 Christ was clearly portrayed as *c*.
5:24 Christ Jesus have *c* the sinful
6:14 which the world has been *c*
Rev 11: 8 where also their Lord was *c*.

CRUCIFY* (CRUCIFIED CRUCIFYING)
Mt 23:34 Some of them you will kill and *c*;
27:22 They all answered, "*C* him!" "Why
27:23 they shouted all the louder, "*C* him
27:31 Then they led him away to *c* him.
Mk 15:13 "*C* him!" they shouted.
15:14 they shouted all the louder, "*C* him
15:20 Then they led him out to *c* him.
Lk 23:21 they kept shouting, "*C* him! *C* him
Jn 19: 6 they shouted, "*C*! *C*!"
19: 6 "You take him and *c* him.
19:10 either to free you or to *c* you?"
19:15 Crucify him!" "Shall I *c* your king
19:15 away! Take him away! *C* him!"

CRUCIFYING* (CRUCIFY)
Heb 6: 6 to their loss they are *c* the Son

CRUSH (CRUSHED)
Ge 3:15 he will *c* your head,
Isa 53:10 it was the LORD's will to *c* him
Ro 16:20 The God of peace will soon *c* Satan

CRUSHED (CRUSH)
Ps 34:18 and saves those who are *c* in spirit.
Pr 17:22 but a *c* spirit dries up the bones.
18:14 but a *c* spirit who can bear?
Isa 53: 5 he was *c* for our iniquities;
2Co 4: 8 not *c*; perplexed, but not in despair;

CRY (CRIED)
Ex 2:23 *c* for help because of their slavery
Ps 5: 2 Listen to my *c* for help,
34:15 and his ears are attentive to their *c*;
40: 1 he turned to me and heard my *c*.
130: 1 Out of the depths I *c* to you,
Pr 21:13 to the *c* of the poor,
La 2:18 *c* out to the Lord.
Hab 2:11 The stones of the wall will *c* out,
Lk 19:40 keep quiet, the stones will *c* out."

CUNNING
2Co 11: 3 deceived by the serpent's *c*,
Eph 4:14 and by the *c* and craftiness of men

CUP
Ps 23: 5 my *c* overflows.
Isa 51:22 from that *c*, the goblet of my wrath,
51:22 the *c* that made you stagger;
Mt 10:42 if anyone gives even a *c* of cold water
20:22 "Can you drink the *c* I am going
23:25 You clean the outside of the *c*
23:26 First clean the inside of the *c*
26:27 Then he took the *c*, gave thanks
26:39 may this *c* be taken from me.
26:42 possible for this *c* to be taken away
Mk 9:41 anyone who gives you a *c* of water
10:38 "Can you drink the *c* I drink
10:39 "You will drink the *c* I drink
14:23 Then he took the *c*, gave thanks
14:36 Take this *c* from me.
Lk 11:39 Pharisees clean the outside of the *c*
22:17 After taking the *c*, he gave thanks
22:20 after the supper he took the *c*,
22:20 "This *c* is the new covenant
22:42 if you are willing, take this *c*
Jn 18:11 I not drink the *c* the Father has
1Co 10:16 Is not the *c* of thanksgiving
10:21 the *c* of the Lord and the *c*
11:25 after supper he took the *c*, saying,
11:25 "This *c* is the new covenant

CUPBEARER
Ge 40: 1 the *c* and the baker of the king
Ne 1:11 I was *c* to the king.

CURE (CURED)
Jer 17: 9 and beyond *c*.
30:15 your pain that has no *c*?
Hos 5:13 But he is not able to *c* you,
Lk 9: 1 out all demons and to *c* diseases,

CURED (CURE)
Mt 11: 5 those who have leprosy are *c*,
Lk 6:18 troubled by evil spirits were *c*,

CURSE (ACCURSED CURSED CURSES CURSING)
Ge 4:11 Now you are under a *c*
8:21 "Never again will I *c* the ground
12: 3 and whoever curses you I will *c*;
Dt 11:26 before you today a blessing and a *c*
11:28 the *c* if you disobey the commands
21:23 hung on a tree is under God's *c*.
23: 5 turned the *c* into a blessing for you,
Job 1:11 he will surely *c* you to your face."
2: 5 he will surely *c* you to your face."
2: 9 *C* God and die!" He replied,
Ps 109: 28 They may *c*, but you will bless;
Pr 3:33 The LORD's *c* is on the house
24:24 peoples will *c* him and nations
Mal 2: 2 and I will *c* your blessings.
Lk 6:28 bless those who *c* you, pray
Ro 12:14 persecute you; bless and do not *c*.

Gal 3:10 on observing the law are under a *c*,
3:13 of the law by becoming a *c* for us,
Jas 3: 9 with it we *c* men, who have been
Rev 22: 3 No longer will there be any *c*.

CURSED (CURSE)
Ge 3:17 "*C* is the ground because of you;
Dt 27:15 "*C* is the man who carves an image
27:16 "*C* is the man who dishonors his
27:17 "*C* is the man who moves his
27:18 "*C* is the man who leads the blind
27:19 *C* is the man who withholds justice
27:20 "*C* is the man who sleeps
27:21 "*C* is the man who has sexual
27:22 "*C* is the man who sleeps
27:23 "*C* is the man who sleeps
27:24 "*C* is the man who kills his
27:25 "*C* is the man who accepts a bribe
27:26 "*C* is the man who does not uphold
Jer 17: 5 "*C* is the one who trusts in man,
Mal 1:14 "*C* is the cheat who has
Ro 9: 3 I could wish that I myself were *c*
1Co 4:12 When we are *c*, we bless;
12: 3 "Jesus be *c*," and no one can say,
Gal 3:10 "*C* is everyone who does not
3:13 *C* is everyone who is hung on a tree

CURSES (CURSE)
Ex 21:17 "Anyone who *c* his father
Lev 20: 9 " 'If anyone *c* his father or mother,
Nu 5:23 is to write these *c* on a scroll
Jos 8:34 the blessings and the *c*—just
Pr 20:20 If a man *c* his father or mother,
28:27 to them receives many *c*.
Mt 15: 4 and 'Anyone who *c* his father
Mk 7:10 and, 'Anyone who *c* his father

CURSING (CURSE)
Ps 109: 18 He wore *c* as his garment;
Ro 3:14 "Their mouths are full of *c*
Jas 3:10 the same mouth come praise and *c*.

CURTAIN
Ex 26:31 "Make a *c* of blue, purple
26:33 The *c* will separate the Holy Place
Mt 27:51 At that moment the *c*
Mk 15:38 The *c* of the temple was torn in two
Lk 23:45 the *c* of the temple was torn in two.
Heb 6:19 the inner sanctuary behind the *c*,
9: 3 Behind the second *c* was a room
10:20 opened for us through the *c*,

CUSTOM
Job 1: 5 This was Job's regular *c*.
Mk 10: 1 and as was his *c*, he taught them.
Lk 4:16 into the synagogue, as was his *c*.
Ac 17: 2 As his *c* was, Paul went

CUT
Lev 19:27 " 'Do not *c* the hair at the sides
21: 5 of their beards or *c* their bodies.
1Ki 3:25 "*C* the living child in two
Isa 51: 1 to the rock from which you were *c*
53: 8 For he was *c* off from the land
Da 2:45 of the rock *c* out of a mountain,
9:26 the Anointed One will be *c* off
Mt 3:10 not produce good fruit will be *c*
24:22 If those days had not been *c* short,
1Co 11: 6 for a woman to have her hair *c*

CYMBAL* (CYMBALS)
1Co 13: 1 a resounding gong or a clanging *c*.

CYMBALS (CYMBAL)
1Ch 15:16 instruments: lyres, harps and *c*.
2Ch 5:12 dressed in fine linen and playing *c*,
Ps 150: 5 praise him with resounding *c*.

CYRUS
Persian king who allowed exiles to return (2Ch 36:22-Ezr 1:8), to rebuild temple (Ezr 5:13–6:14), as appointed by the LORD (Isa 44:28–45:13).

DAGON
Jdg 16:23 offer a great sacrifice to *D* their god
1Sa 5: 2 Dagon's temple and set it beside *D*.

DAMASCUS
Ac 9: 3 As he neared *D* on his journey,

DAN
1. Son of Jacob by Bilhah (Ge 30:4–6; 35:25; 46:23). Tribe of blessed (Ge 49:16–17; Dt 33:22), numbered (Nu 1:39; 26:43), allotted land (Jos 19:40–48; Eze 48:1), failed to fully possess (Jdg 1:34–35), failed to support Deborah (Jdg 5:17), possessed Laish/Dan (Jdg 18).
2. Northernmost city in Israel (Ge 14:14; Jdg 18; 20:1).

DANCE (DANCED DANCING)
Ecc 3: 4 a time to mourn and a time to *d*,
Mt 11:17 and you did not *d*;

DANCED (DANCE)
2Sa 6:14 *d* before the LORD
Mk 6:22 of Herodias came in and *d*,

DANCING (DANCE)
Ps 30:11 You turned my wailing into *d*;
149: 3 Let them praise his name with *d*

DANGER
Pr 22: 3 A prudent man sees *d*
27:12 The prudent see *d* and take refuge,
Mt 5:22 will be in *d* of the fire of hell.
Ro 8:35 famine or nakedness or *d* or sword?
2Co 11:26 I have been in *d* from rivers,

DANIEL
1. Hebrew exile to Babylon, name changed to Belteshazzar (Da 1:6–7). Refused to eat unclean food (Da 1:8–21). Interpreted Nebuchadnezzar's dreams (Da 2; 4), writing on the wall (Da 5). Thrown into lion's den (Da 6). Visions of (Da 7–12).
2. Son of David (1Ch 3:1).

DARIUS
1. King of Persia (Ezr 4:5), allowed rebuilding of temple (Ezr 5–6).
2. Mede who conquered Babylon (Da 5:31).

DARK (DARKENED DARKENS DARKNESS)
Job 34:22 There is no *d* place, no deep
Ps 18: 9 *d* clouds were under his feet.
Pr 31:15 She gets up while it is still *d*;
SS 1: 6 Do not stare at me because I am *d*,
Jn 12:35 in the *d* does not know where he is
Ro 2:19 a light for those who are in the *d*,
2Pe 1:19 as to a light shining in a *d* place,

DARKENED (DARK)
Joel 2:10 the sun and moon are *d*,
Mt 24:29 " 'the sun will be *d*,
Ro 1:21 and their foolish hearts were *d*.
Eph 4:18 They are *d* in their understanding

DARKENS (DARK)
Job 38: 2 "Who is this that *d* my counsel

DARKNESS (DARK)
Ge 1: 2 *d* was over the surface of the deep,
1: 4 he separated the light from the *d*.
Ex 10:22 and total *d* covered all Egypt
20:21 approached the thick *d* where God
2Sa 22:29 the LORD turns my *d* into light.
Ps 18:28 my God turns my *d* into light.
91: 6 the pestilence that stalks in the *d*,
112: 4 Even in *d* light dawns
139: 12 even the *d* will not be dark to you;
Pr 4:19 the way of the wicked is like deep *d*
Isa 5:20 and light for *d*,
42:16 I will turn the *d* into light
45: 7 I form the light and create *d*,
58:10 then your light will rise in the *d*,
61: 1 and release from *d*,
Joel 2:31 The sun will be turned to *d*
Mt 4:16 the people living in *d*
6:23 how great is that *d*! "No one can
Lk 11:34 are bad, your body also is full of *d*.
23:44 and *d* came over the whole land
Jn 1: 5 The light shines in the *d*,
3:19 but men loved *d* instead of light
Ac 2:20 The sun will be turned to *d*
2Co 4: 6 who said, "Let light shine out of *d*
6:14 fellowship can light have with *d*?
Eph 5: 8 For you were once *d*, but now you
5:11 to do with the fruitless deeds of *d*,
1Pe 2: 9 out of *d* into his wonderful light.
2Pe 2:17 Blackest *d* is reserved for them.
1Jn 1: 5 in him there is no *d* at all.
2: 9 but hates his brother is still in the *d*.
Jude : 6 in *d*, bound with everlasting chains
:13 for whom blackest *d* has been

DASH
Ps 2: 9 you will *d* them to pieces like

DAUGHTER (DAUGHTERS)
Ex 1:10 she took him to Pharaoh's *d*
Jdg 11:48 to commemorate the *d* of Jephthah
Est 2: 7 Mordecai had taken her as his own *d*
Ps 9:14 praises in the gates of the *D* of Zion
137: 8 O *D* of Babylon, doomed
Isa 62:11 "Say to the *D* of Zion,
Zec 9: 9 Shout, *D* of Jerusalem!
Mk 5:34 "*D*, your faith has healed you.
7:29 the demon has left your *d*.

DAUGHTERS (DAUGHTER)
Ge 6: 2 the *d* of men were beautiful,
19:36 Lot's *d* became pregnant
Nu 36:10 Zelophehad's *d* did as the LORD
Joel 2:28 sons and *d* will prophesy,

DAVID
Son of Jesse (Ru 4:17–22; 1Ch 2:13–15), ancestor of Jesus (Mt 1:1–17; Lk 3:31). Wives and children (1Sa 18; 25:39–44; 2Sa 3:2–5; 5:13–16; 11:27; 1Ch 3:1–9).
Anointed king by Samuel (1Sa 16:1–13). Musician to Saul (1Sa 16:14–23; 18:10). Killed Goliath (1Sa 17). Relation with Jonathan (1Sa 18:1–4; 19–20; 23:16–18; 2Sa 1). Disfavor of Saul (1Sa 18:6–23:29). Spared Saul's life (1Sa 24; 26). Among Philistines (1Sa 21:10–14; 27–30). Lament for Saul and Jonathan (2Sa 1).
Anointed king of Judah (2Sa 2:1–11). Conflict with house of Saul (2Sa 2–4). Anointed king of Israel (2Sa 5:1–4; 1Ch 11:1–3). Conquered Jerusalem (2Sa 5:6–10; 1Ch 11:4–9). Brought ark to Jerusalem (2Sa 6; 1Ch 13; 15–16). The LORD promised eternal dynasty (2Sa 7; 1Ch 17; Ps 132). Showed kindness to Mephibosheth (2Sa 9). Adultery with Bathsheba, murder of Uriah (2Sa 11–12). Son Amnon raped daughter Tamar; killed by Absalom (2Sa 13). Absalom's revolt (2Sa 14–17); death (2Sa 18). Sheba's revolt (2Sa 20). Victories: Philistines (2Sa 5:17–25; 1Ch 14:8–17; 2Sa 21:15–22; 1Ch 20:4–8), Ammonites (2Sa 10; 1Ch 19), various (2Sa 8; 1Ch 18). Mighty men (2Sa 23:8–39; 1Ch 11–12). Punished for numbering army (2Sa 24; 1Ch 21). Appointed Solomon king (1Ki 1:28–2:9). Prepared for building of temple (1Ch 22–29). Last words (2Sa 23:1–7). Death (1Ki 2:10–12; 1Ch 29:28).
Psalmist (Mt 22:43–45), musician (Am 6:5), prophet (2Sa 23:2–7; Ac 1:16; 2:30).
Psalms of: 2 (Ac 4:25), 3–32, 34–41, 51–65, 68–70, 86, 95 (Heb 4:7), 101, 103, 108–110, 122, 124, 131, 133, 138–145.

DAWN (DAWNED DAWNS)
Ps 37: 6 your righteousness shine like the *d*,
Pr 4:18 is like the first gleam of *d*,
Isa 14:12 O morning star, son of the *d*!
Am 4:13 he who turns *d* to darkness,
5: 8 who turns blackness into *d*

DAWNED (DAWN)
Isa 9: 2 a light has *d*.
Mt 4:16 a light has *d*."

DAWNS* (DAWN)
Ps 65: 8 where morning *d* and evening
112: 4 in darkness light *d* for the upright,
Hos 10:15 When that day *d*,
2Pe 1:19 until the day *d* and the morning

DAY (DAYS)
Ge 1: 5 God called the light "*d*,"
1: 5 and there was morning—the first *d*
1: 8 there was morning—the second *d*.
1:13 there was morning—the third *d*.
1:19 there was morning—the fourth *d*.
1:23 there was morning—the fifth *d*.
1:31 there was morning—the sixth *d*.
2: 2 so on the seventh *d* he rested
8:22 *d* and night
Ex 16:30 the people rested on the seventh *d*.
20: 8 "Remember the Sabbath *d*
Lev 16:30 on this *d* atonement will be made
23:28 because it is the *D* of Atonement,
Nu 14:14 before them in a pillar of cloud by *d*
Jos 1: 8 meditate on it *d* and night,
2Ki 7: 9 This is a *d* of good news
25:30 *D* by *d* the king gave Jehoiachin
1Ch 16:23 proclaim his salvation *d* after *d*.
Ne 8:18 *D* after *d*, from the first *d*
Ps 84:10 Better is one *d* in your courts
96: 2 proclaim his salvation *d* after *d*.
118: 24 This is the *d* the LORD has made;
Pr 27: 1 not know what a *d* may bring forth.
Isa 13: 9 a cruel *d*, with wrath and fierce

Jer 46:10 But that *d* belongs to the Lord,
50:31 "for your *d* has come,
Eze 30: 2 "Alas for that *d!*"
Joel 1:15 "Alas for that *d!*
2:31 and dreadful *d* of the LORD.
Am 3:14 On the *d* I punish Israel for her sins
5:20 Will not the *d* of the LORD be
Ob :15 "The *d* of the LORD is near
Zep 1:14 The great *d* of the LORD is near—
Zec 2:11 joined with the LORD in that *d*
14: 1 A *d* of the LORD is coming
14: 7 It will be a unique *d,*
Mal 4: 5 dreadful *d* of the LORD comes.
Mt 24:38 up to the *d* Noah entered the ark;
Lk 11: 3 Give us each *d* our daily bread.
17:24 in his *d* will be like the lightning,
Ac 5:42 *D* after *d,* in the temple courts
17:11 examined the Scriptures every *d*
17:17 as in the marketplace *d* by *d*
Ro 14: 5 man considers every *d* alike.
1Co 5: 5 his spirit saved on the *d* of the Lord
2Co 4:16 we are being renewed *d* by *d.*
11:25 I spent a night and a *d*
1Th 5: 2 for you know very well that the *d*
5: 4 so that this *d* should surprise you
2Th 2: 2 saying that the *d* of the Lord has
Heb 7:27 need to offer sacrifices *d* after *d,*
2Pe 3: 8 With the Lord a *d* is like
3:10 *d* of the Lord will come like a thief.
Rev 6:17 For the great *d* of their wrath has
16:14 on the great *d* of God Almighty.

DAYS (DAY)
Dt 17:19 he is to read it all the *d* of his life
32: 7 Remember the *d* of old;
Ps 23: 6 all the *d* of my life,
34:12 and desires to see many good *d,*
39: 5 have made my *d* a mere
90:10 The length of our *d* is seventy years
90:12 Teach us to number our *d* aright,
103: 15 As for man, his *d* are like grass,
128: 5 all the *d* of your life;
Pr 31:12 all the *d* of her life.
Ecc 9: 9 all the *d* of this meaningless life
12: 1 Creator in the *d* of your youth,
Isa 38:20 all the *d* of our lives
Da 7: 9 and the Ancient of *D* took his seat.
7:13 He approached the Ancient of *D*
7:22 until the Ancient of *D* came
Hos 3: 5 and to his blessings in the last *d.*
Joel 2:29 I will pour out my Spirit in those *d.*
Mic 4: 1 In the last *d*
Lk 19:43 The *d* will come upon you
Ac 2:17 by the prophet Joel: " 'In the last *d,*
2Ti 3: 1 will be terrible times in the last *d.*
Heb 1: 2 in these last *d* he has spoken to us
2Pe 3: 3 that in the last *d* scoffers will come,

DAZZLING*
Da 2:31 *d* statue, awesome in appearance.
Mk 9: 3 His clothes became *d* white,

DEACON* (DEACONS)
1Ti 3:12 A *d* must be the husband of

DEACONS* (DEACON)
Php 1: 1 together with the overseers and *d:*
1Ti 3: 8 *D,* likewise, are to be men worthy
3:10 against them, let them serve as *d.*

DEAD (DIE)
Lev 17:15 who eats anything found *d*
Dt 18:11 or spiritist or who consults the *d.*
Isa 8:19 Why consult the *d* on behalf
Mt 8:22 and let the *d* bury their own *d.*"
28: 7 'He has risen from the *d*
Lk 15:24 For this son of mine was *d*
24:46 rise from the *d* on the third day,
Ro 6:11 count yourselves *d* to sin
1Co 15:29 do who are baptized for the *d?*
Eph 2: 1 you were *d* in your transgressions
1Th 4:16 and the *d* in Christ will rise first.
Jas 2:17 is not accompanied by action, is *d.*
2:26 so faith without deeds is *d.*
Rev 14:13 Blessed are the *d* who die
20:12 And I saw the *d,* great and small,

DEADENED* (DIE)
Jn 12:40 and *d* their hearts,

DEAR* (DEARER)
2Sa 1:26 you were very *d* to me.
Ps 102: 14 For her stones are *d*
Jer 31:20 Is not Ephraim my *d* son,
Jn 2: 4 "*D* woman, why do you involve me
19:26 he said to his mother, "*D* woman,
Ac 15:25 to you with our *d* friends Barnabas
Ro 16: 5 Greet my *d* friend Epenetus,
16: 9 in Christ, and my *d* friend Stachys.
16:12 Greet my *d* friend Persis, another
1Co 4:14 but to warn you, as my *d* children.
10:14 my *d* friends, flee from idolatry.
15:58 Therefore, my *d* brothers,
2Co 7: 1 we have these promises, *d* friends,
12:19 and everything we do, *d* friends,
Gal 4:19 My *d* children, for whom I am
Eph 6:21 the *d* brother and faithful servant
Php 2:12 my *d* friends, as you have always
4: 1 firm in the Lord, *d* friends!
Col 1: 7 Epaphras, our *d* fellow servant,
4: 7 He is a *d* brother, a faithful
4: 9 our faithful and *d* brother,
4:14 Our *d* friend Luke, the doctor,
1Th 2: 8 because you had become so *d* to us.
1Ti 6: 2 their service are believers, and *d*
2Ti 1: 2 To Timothy, my *d* son: Grace,
Phm : 1 To Philemon our *d* friend
:16 He is very *d* to me but
:16 better than a slave, as a *d* brother.
Heb 6: 9 we speak like this, *d* friends,
Jas 1:16 Don't be deceived, my *d* brothers.
1:19 My *d* brothers, take note of this:
2: 5 thoughts? Listen, my *d* brothers:
1Pe 2:11 *D* friends, I urge you, as aliens
4:12 *D* friends, do not be surprised
2Pe 3: 1 *D* friends, this is now my second
3: 8 not forget this one thing, *d* friends:
3:14 *d* friends, since you are looking
3:15 just as our *d* brother Paul
3:17 *d* friends, since you already know
1Jn 2: 1 My *d* children, I write this to you
2: 7 *D* friends, I am not writing you
2:12 I write to you, *d* children,
2:13 I write to you, *d* children,
2:18 *D* children, this is the last hour;
2:28 *d* children, continue in him,
3: 2 *D* friends, now we are children
3: 7 *D* children, do not let anyone lead
3:18 love of God be in him? *D* children,
3:21 *D* friends, if our hearts do not
4: 1 *D* friends, do not believe every
4: 4 *d* children, are from God
4: 7 *D* friends, let us love one another,
4:11 *D* friends, since God so loved us,
5:21 *D* children, keep yourselves
2Jn : 5 *d* lady, I am not writing you a new
3Jn : 1 The elder, To my *d* friend Gaius,
: 2 *D* friend, I pray that you may enjoy
: 5 *D* friend, you are faithful
:11 *D* friend, do not imitate what is evil
Jude : 3 *D* friends, although I was very
:17 But, *d* friends, remember what
:20 *d* friends, build yourselves up

DEARER* (DEAR)
Phm :16 dear to me but even *d* to you,

DEATH (DIE)
Ex 21:12 kills him shall surely be put to *d.*
Nu 35:16 the murderer shall be put to *d.*
Dt 30:19 set before you life and *d,*
Ru 1:17 if anything but *d* separates you
2Ki 4:40 O man of God, there is *d* in the pot
Job 26: 6 *D* is naked before God;
Ps 23: 4 the valley of the shadow of *d,*
44:22 for your sake we face *d* all day long
89:48 What man can live and not see *d,*
116: 15 is the *d* of his saints.
Pr 8:36 all who hate me love *d.*"
11:19 he who pursues evil goes to his *d.*
14:12 but in the end it leads to *d.*
15:11 *D* and Destruction lie open
16:25 but in the end it leads to *d.*
18:21 tongue has the power of life and *d,*
19:18 do not be a willing party to his *d.*
23:14 and save his soul from *d.*
Ecc 7: 2 for *d* is the destiny of every man;
Isa 25: 8 he will swallow up *d* forever.
53:12 he poured out his life unto *d,*
Eze 18:23 pleasure in the *d* of the wicked?
18:32 pleasure in the *d* of anyone,
33:11 pleasure in the *d* of the wicked,
Hos 13:14 Where, O *d,* are your plagues?
Jn 5:24 he has crossed over from *d* to life.
Ro 4:25 delivered over to *d* for our sins
5:12 and in this way *d* came to all men,
5:14 *d* reigned from the time of Adam
6: 3 Jesus were baptized into his *d?*
6:23 For the wages of sin is *d,*
7:24 me from this body of *d?*
8:13 put to *d* the misdeeds of the body,
8:36 your sake we face *d* all day long;
1Co 15:21 For since *d* came through a man,
15:26 The last enemy to be destroyed is *d*
15:55 Where, O *d,* is your sting?"
2Ti 1:10 who has destroyed *d* and has
Heb 2:14 him who holds the power of *d*—
1Jn 5:16 There is a sin that leads to *d.*
Rev 1:18 And I hold the keys of *d* and Hades
2:11 hurt at all by the second *d.*
20: 6 The second *d* has no power
20:14 The lake of fire is the second *d.*
20:14 Then *d* and Hades were thrown
21: 4 There will be no more *d*
21: 8 This is the second *d.*"

DEBAUCHERY*
Ro 13:13 not in sexual immorality and *d,*
2Co 12:21 and *d* in which they have indulged.
Gal 5:19 impurity and *d;* idolatry
Eph 5:18 drunk on wine, which leads to *d.*
1Pe 4: 3 living in *d,* lust, drunkenness,

DEBORAH*
1. Prophetess who led Israel to victory over Canaanites (Jdg 4–5).
2. Rebekah's nurse (Ge 35:8).

DEBT* (DEBTOR DEBTORS DEBTS)
Dt 15: 3 must cancel any *d* your brother
24: 6 the upper one—as security for a *d,*
1Sa 22: 2 or in *d* or discontented gathered
Job 24: 9 of the poor is seized for a *d.*
Mt 18:25 that he had be sold to repay the *d.*
18:27 canceled the *d* and let him go.
18:30 into prison until he could pay the *d.*
18:32 'I canceled all that *d* of yours
Lk 7:43 who had the bigger *d* canceled."
Ro 13: 8 Let no *d* remain outstanding,
13: 8 continuing *d* to love one another,

DEBTOR* (DEBT)
Isa 24: 2 for *d* as for creditor.

DEBTORS* (DEBT)
Hab 2: 7 Will not your *d* suddenly arise?
Mt 6:12 as we also have forgiven our *d.*
Lk 16: 5 called in each one of his master's *d.*

DEBTS* (DEBT)
Dt 15: 1 seven years you must cancel *d.*
15: 2 time for canceling *d* has been
15: 9 the year for canceling *d,* is near,"
31:10 in the year for canceling *d,*
2Ki 4: 7 "Go, sell the oil and pay your *d.*
Ne 10:31 the land and will cancel all *d.*
Pr 22:26 or puts up security for *d;*
Mt 6:12 Forgive us our *d,*
Lk 7:42 so he canceled the *d* of both.

DECAY*
Ps 16:10 will you let your Holy One see *d.*
49: 9 and not see *d.*
49:14 their forms will *d* in the grave,
Pr 12: 4 a disgraceful wife is like *d*
Isa 5:24 so their roots will *d*
Hab 3:16 *d* crept into my bones,
Ac 2:27 will you let your Holy One see *d.*
2:31 to the grave, nor did his body see *d.*
13:34 never to *d,* is stated in these words:
13:35 will not let your Holy One see *d.*'
13:37 raised from the dead did not see *d.*
Ro 8:21 liberated from its bondage to *d*

DECEIT (DECEIVE)
Ps 5: 9 with their tongue they speak *d.*
Isa 53: 9 nor was any *d* in his mouth.
Da 8:25 He will cause *d* to prosper,
Zep 3:13 nor will *d* be found in their mouths.
Mk 7:22 greed, malice, *d,* lewdness, envy,
Ac 13:10 You are full of all kinds of *d*
Ro 1:29 murder, strife, *d* and malice.
3:13 their tongues practice *d.*"
1Pe 2: 1 yourselves of all malice and all *d,*
2:22 and no *d* was found in his mouth."

DECEITFUL (DECEIVE)
Jer 17: 9 The heart is *d* above all things

Hos 10: 2 Their heart is *d,*
2Co 11:13 men are false apostles, *d* workmen,
Eph 4:14 of men in their *d* scheming.
4:22 is being corrupted by its *d* desires;
1Pe 3:10 and his lips from *d* speech.
Rev 21:27 who does what is shameful or *d,*

DECEITFULNESS* (DECEIVE)
Ps 119:118 for their *d* is in vain.
Mt 13:22 and the *d* of wealth choke it,
Mk 4:19 the *d* of wealth and the desires
Heb 3:13 of you may be hardened by sin's *d.*

DECEIVE (DECEIT DECEITFUL DECEITFULNESS DECEIVED DECEIVER DECEIVERS DECEIVES DECEIVING DECEPTION DECEPTIVE)
Lev 19:11 " 'Do not *d* one another.
Pr 14: 5 A truthful witness does not *d,*
24:28 or use your lips to *d.*
Jer 37: 9 Do not *d* yourselves, thinking,
Zec 13: 4 garment of hair in order to *d.*
Mt 24: 5 'I am the Christ,' and will *d* many.
24:11 will appear and *d* many people.
24:24 and miracles to *d* even the elect—
Mk 13: 6 'I am he,' and will *d* many.
13:22 and miracles to *d* the elect—
Ro 16:18 and flattery they *d* the minds
1Co 3:18 Do not *d* yourselves.
Eph 5: 6 Let no one *d* you with empty words
Col 2: 4 this so that no one may *d* you
2Th 2: 3 Don't let anyone *d* you in any way,
Jas 1:22 to the word, and so *d* yourselves.
1Jn 1: 8 we *d* ourselves and the truth is not
Rev 20: 8 and will go out to *d* the nations

DECEIVED (DECEIVE)
Ge 3:13 "The serpent *d* me, and I ate."
Lk 21: 8 "Watch out that you are not *d.*
1Co 6: 9 the kingdom of God? Do not be *d:*
2Co 11: 3 Eve was *d* by the serpent's cunning
Gal 6: 7 Do not be *d:* God cannot be
1Ti 2:14 And Adam was not the one *d;*
2Ti 3:13 to worse, deceiving and being *d.*
Tit 3: 3 *d* and enslaved by all kinds
Jas 1:16 Don't be *d,* my dear brothers.
Rev 13:14 he *d* the inhabitants of the earth.
20:10 And the devil, who *d* them,

DECEIVER (DECEIVE)
Mt 27:63 while he was still alive that *d* said,
2Jn : 7 Any such person is the *d*

DECEIVERS* (DECEIVE)
Ps 49: 5 when wicked *d* surround me—
Tit 1:10 and *d,* especially those
2Jn : 7 Many *d,* who do not acknowledge

DECEIVES (DECEIVE)
Pr 26:19 is a man who *d* his neighbor
Mt 24: 4 "Watch out that no one *d* you.
Mk 13: 5 "Watch out that no one *d* you.
Gal 6: 3 when he is nothing, he *d* himself.
2Th 2:10 sort of evil that *d* those who are
Jas 1:26 he *d* himself and his religion is

DECEIVING* (DECEIVE)
Lev 6: 2 by *d* his neighbor about something
1Ti 4: 1 follow *d* spirits and things taught
2Ti 3:13 go from bad to worse, *d*
Rev 20: 3 him from *d* the nations anymore

DECENCY* (DECENTLY)
1Ti 2: 9 women to dress modestly, with *d*

DECENTLY* (DECENCY)
Ro 13:13 Let us behave *d,* as in the daytime,

DECEPTION (DECEIVE)
Pr 14: 8 but the folly of fools is *d.*
26:26 His malice may be concealed by *d,*
Mt 27:64 This last *d* will be worse
2Co 4: 2 we do not use *d,* nor do we distort

DECEPTIVE (DECEIVE)
Pr 11:18 The wicked man earns *d* wages,
31:30 Charm is *d,* and beauty is fleeting;
Jer 7: 4 Do not trust in *d* words and say,
Col 2: 8 through hollow and *d* philosophy,

DECIDED (DECISION)
2Co 9: 7 man should give what he has *d*

DECISION (DECIDED)
Ex 28:29 heart on the breastpiece of *d*
Joel 3:14 multitudes in the valley of *d!*

DECLARE (DECLARED DECLARING)
1Ch 16:24 *D* his glory among the nations,
Ps 19: 1 The heavens *d* the glory of God;
96: 3 *D* his glory among the nations,
Isa 42: 9 and new things I *d;*

DECLARED (DECLARE)
Mk 7:19 Jesus *d* all foods "clean.")
Ro 2:13 the law who will be *d* righteous.
3:20 no one will be *d* righteous

DECLARING (DECLARE)
Ps 71: 8 *d* your splendor all day long.
Ac 2:11 we hear them *d* the wonders

DECREE (DECREED DECREES)
Ex 15:25 There the LORD made a *d*
1Ch 16:17 He confirmed it to Jacob as a *d,*
Ps 2: 7 I will proclaim the *d* of the LORD:
7: 6 Awake, my God; *d* justice.
81: 4 this is a *d* for Israel,
148: 6 he gave a *d* that will never pass
Da 4:24 and this is the *d* the Most High has
Lk 2: 1 Augustus issued a *d* that a census
Ro 1:32 know God's righteous *d* that those

DECREED (DECREE)
Ps 78: 5 He *d* statutes for Jacob
Jer 40: 2 LORD your God *d* this disaster
La 3:37 happen if the Lord has not *d* it?
Da 9:24 "Seventy 'sevens' are *d*
9:26 and desolations have been *d.*
Lk 22:22 Son of Man will go as it has been *d,*

DECREES (DECREE)
Ge 26: 5 my commands, my *d* and my laws
Ex 15:26 to his commands and keep all his *d,*
18:16 inform them of God's *d* and laws."
18:20 Teach them the *d* and laws,
Lev 10:11 Israelites all the *d* the LORD has
18: 4 and be careful to follow my *d.*
18: 5 Keep my *d* and laws,
18:26 you must keep my *d* and my laws.
Ps 119: 12 teach me your *d.*
119: 16 I delight in your *d;*
119: 48 and I meditate on your *d.*
119:112 My heart is set on keeping your *d*

DEDICATE (DEDICATED DEDICATION)
Nu 6:12 He must *d* himself to the LORD
Pr 20:25 for a man to *d* something rashly

DEDICATED (DEDICATE)
Lev 21:12 he has been *d* by the anointing oil
Nu 6: 9 thus defiling the hair he has *d,*
6:18 shave off the hair that he *d.*
18: 6 *d* to the LORD to do the work
1Ki 8:63 and all the Israelites *d* the temple
2Ch 29:31 "You have now *d* yourselves
Ne 3: 1 They *d* it and set its doors in place,

DEDICATION (DEDICATE)
Nu 6:19 shaved off the hair of his *d,*
Jn 10:22 came the Feast of *D* at Jerusalem.
1Ti 5:11 sensual desires overcome their *d*

DEED (DEEDS)
Jer 32:10 and sealed the *d,* had it witnessed,
32:16 After I had given the *d* of purchase
Col 3:17 you do, whether in word or *d,*
2Th 2:17 and strengthen you in every good *d*

DEEDS (DEED)
Dt 3:24 or on earth who can do the *d*
4:34 or by great and awesome *d,*
34:12 the awesome *d* that Moses
1Sa 2: 3 and by him *d* are weighed.
1Ch 16:24 his marvelous *d* among all peoples.
Job 34:25 Because he takes note of their *d,*
Ps 26: 7 and telling of all your wonderful *d.*
45: 4 right hand display awesome *d.*
65: 5 with awesome *d* of righteousness,
66: 3 "How awesome are your *d!*
71:17 day I declare your marvelous *d.*
72:18 who alone does marvelous *d.*
73:28 I will tell of all your *d.*
75: 1 men tell of your wonderful *d.*
77:11 I will remember the *d* of the LORD
77:12 and consider all your mighty *d.*
78: 4 the praiseworthy *d* of the LORD,
78: 7 and would not forget his *d*
86: 8 no *d* can compare with yours.
86:10 you are great and do marvelous *d;*
88:12 or your righteous *d* in the land
90:16 May your *d* be shown
Ps 92: 4 For you make me glad by your *d,*
96: 3 his marvelous *d* among all peoples.
107: 8 and his wonderful *d* for men,
107: 15 and his wonderful *d* for men,
107: 21 and his wonderful *d* for men.
107: 24 his wonderful *d* in the deep.
107: 31 and his wonderful *d* for men.
111: 3 Glorious and majestic are his *d,*
145: 6 and I will proclaim your great *d.*
Jer 32:19 purposes and mighty are your *d.*
Hab 3: 2 I stand in awe of your *d,* O LORD.
Mt 5:16 that they may see your good *d*
Lk 1:51 He has performed mighty *d*
23:41 we are getting what our *d* deserve.
Ac 26:20 prove their repentance by their *d.*
1Ti 6:18 rich in good *d,* and to be generous
Heb 10:24 on toward love and good *d.*
Jas 2:14 claims to have faith but has no *d?*
2:18 Show me your faith without *d,*
2:20 faith without *d* is useless?
2:26 so faith without *d* is dead.
1Pe 2:12 they may see your good *d*
Rev 2:19 I know your *d,* your love and faith,
2:23 each of you according to your *d.*
3: 1 I know your *d;* you have
3: 2 I have not found your *d* complete
3: 8 I know your *d.*
3:15 I know your *d,* that you are neither
14:13 for their *d* will follow them."
15: 3 "Great and marvelous are your *d,*

DEEP (DEPTH DEPTHS)
Ge 1: 2 was over the surface of the *d,*
8: 2 Now the springs of the *d*
Ps 42: 7 *D* calls to *d*
Lk 5: 4 to Simon, "Put out into *d* water,
1Co 2:10 all things, even the *d* things
1Ti 3: 9 hold of the *d* truths of the faith

DEER
Ps 42: 1 As the *d* pants for streams of water,

DEFAMED*
Isa 48:11 How can I let myself be *d?*

DEFEATED
1Co 6: 7 have been completely *d* already.

DEFEND (DEFENDED DEFENDER DEFENDING DEFENDS DEFENSE)
Ps 72: 4 He will *d* the afflicted
74:22 Rise up, O God, and *d* your cause;
82: 2 "How long will you *d* the unjust
82: 3 *D* the cause of the weak
119:154 *D* my cause and redeem me;
Pr 31: 9 *d* the rights of the poor and needy
Isa 1:17 *D* the cause of the fatherless,
1:23 They do not *d* the cause
Jer 5:28 they do not *d* the rights of the poor.
50:34 He will vigorously *d* their cause

DEFENDED (DEFEND)
Jer 22:16 He *d* the cause of the poor

DEFENDER (DEFEND)
Ex 22: 2 the *d* is not guilty of bloodshed;
Ps 68: 5 to the fatherless, a *d* of widows,
Pr 23:11 for their *D* is strong;

DEFENDING (DEFEND)
Ps 10:18 *d* the fatherless and the oppressed,
Ro 2:15 now accusing, now even *d* them.)
Php 1: 7 or *d* and confirming the gospel,

DEFENDS* (DEFEND)
Dt 10:18 He *d* the cause of the fatherless
33: 7 With his own hands he *d* his cause.
Isa 51:22 your God, who *d* his people:

DEFENSE (DEFEND)
Ps 35:23 Awake, and rise to my *d!*
Php 1:16 here for the *d* of the gospel.
1Jn 2: 1 speaks to the Father in our *d*—

DEFERRED*
Pr 13:12 Hope *d* makes the heart sick,

DEFIED
1Sa 17:45 armies of Israel, whom you have *d.*
1Ki 13:26 the man of God who *d* the word

DEFILE (DEFILED)
Da 1: 8 Daniel resolved not to *d* himself
Rev 14: 4 are those who did not *d* themselves

DEFILED (DEFILE)
Isa 24: 5 The earth is *d* by its people;

DEFRAUD
Lev 19:13 Do not *d* your neighbor or rob him.
Mk 10:19 do not *d*, honor your father

DEITY*
Col 2: 9 of the *D* lives in bodily form,

DELAY
Ecc 5: 4 vow to God, do not *d* in fulfilling it.
Isa 48: 9 my own name's sake I *d* my wrath;
Heb 10:37 is coming will come and will not *d*.
Rev 10: 6 and said, "There will be no more *d*!

DELICACIES
Ps 141: 4 let me not eat of their *d*.
Pr 23: 3 Do not crave his *d*,
23: 6 do not crave his *d*;

DELICIOUS*
Pr 9:17 food eaten in secret is *d*!"

DELIGHT* (DELIGHTED DELIGHTFUL DELIGHTING DELIGHTS)
Lev 26:31 and I will take no *d* in the pleasing
Dt 30: 9 The LORD will again *d* in you
1Sa 2: 1 for I *d* in your deliverance.
15:22 "Does the LORD *d*
Ne 1:11 the prayer of your servants who *d*
Job 22:26 Surely then you will find *d*
27:10 Will he find *d* in the Almighty?
Ps 1: 2 But his *d* is in the law of the LORD
16: 3 in whom is all my *d*.
35: 9 and *d* in his salvation.
35:27 those who *d* in my vindication
37: 4 *D* yourself in the LORD
43: 4 to God, my joy and my *d*.
51:16 You do not *d* in sacrifice,
51:19 whole burnt offerings to *d* you;
62: 4 they take *d* in lies.
68:30 Scatter the nations who *d* in war.
111: 2 by all who *d* in them.
112: 1 who finds great *d* in his commands.
119: 16 I *d* in your decrees;
119: 24 Your statutes are my *d*;
119: 35 for there I find *d*.
119: 47 for I *d* in your commands
119: 70 but I *d* in your law.
119: 77 for your law is my *d*.
119: 92 If your law had not been my *d*,
119:143 but your commands are my *d*.
119:174 and your law is my *d*.
147: 10 nor his *d* in the legs of a man;
149: 4 For the LORD takes *d*
Pr 1:22 How long will mockers *d*
2:14 who *d* in doing wrong
8:30 I was filled with *d* day after day,
11: 1 but accurate weights are his *d*.
29:17 he will bring *d* to your soul.
Ecc 2:10 My heart took *d* in all my work,
SS 1: 4 We rejoice and *d* in you;
2: 3 I *d* to sit in his shade,
Isa 5: 7 are the garden of his *d*.
11: 3 he will *d* in the fear of the LORD.
13:17 and have no *d* in gold.
32:14 the *d* of donkeys, a pasture
42: 1 my chosen one in whom I *d*;
55: 2 and your soul will *d* in the richest
58:13 if you call the Sabbath a *d*
61:10 I *d* greatly in the LORD;
62: 4 for the LORD will take *d* in you,
65:18 for I will create Jerusalem to be a *d*
65:19 and take *d* in my people;
66: 3 their souls *d* in their abominations;
66:11 *d* in her overflowing abundance."
Jer 9:24 for in these I *d*,"
15:16 they were my joy and my heart's *d*,
31:20 the child in whom I *d*?
49:25 the town in which I *d*?
Eze 24:16 away from you the *d* of your eyes.
24:21 in which you take pride, the *d*
24:25 and glory, the *d* of their eyes,
Hos 7: 3 *d* the king with their wickedness,
Mic 1:16 for the children in whom you *d*;
7:18 but *d* to show mercy.
Zep 3:17 He will take great *d* in you,
Mt 12:18 the one I love, in whom I *d*;
Mk 12:37 large crowd listened to him with *d*.
Lk 1:14 He will be a joy and *d* to you,
Ro 7:22 in my inner being I *d* in God's law;
1Co 13: 6 Love does not *d* in evil
2Co 12:10 for Christ's sake, I *d* in weaknesses,
Col 2: 5 and *d* to see how orderly you are

DELIGHTED (DELIGHT)
2Sa 22:20 he rescued me because he *d* in me.
1Ki 10: 9 who has *d* in you and placed you
2Ch 9: 8 who has *d* in you and placed you
Ps 18:19 he rescued me because he *d* in me.
Lk 13:17 but the people were *d* with all

DELIGHTFUL* (DELIGHT)
Ps 16: 6 surely I have a *d* inheritance.
SS 1: 2 for your love is more *d* than wine.
4:10 How *d* is your love, my sister,
Mal 3:12 for yours will be a *d* land,"

DELIGHTING* (DELIGHT)
Pr 8:31 and *d* in mankind.

DELIGHTS (DELIGHT)
Est 6: 6 for the man the king *d* to honor?"
Ps 22: 8 since he *d* in him."
35:27 who *d* in the well-being
36: 8 from your river of *d*.
37:23 if the LORD *d* in a man's way
147: 11 the LORD *d* in those who fear him,
Pr 3:12 as a father the son he *d* in.
10:23 of understanding *d* in wisdom.
11:20 he *d* in those whose ways are
12:22 but he *d* in men who are truthful.
14:35 A king *d* in a wise servant,
18: 2 but *d* in airing his own opinions.
23:24 he who has a wise son *d* in him.
Col 2:18 Do not let anyone who *d*

DELILAH*
Woman who betrayed Samson (Jdg 16:4–22).

DELIVER (DELIVERANCE DELIVERED DELIVERER DELIVERS)
Dt 32:39 and no one can *d* out of my hand.
Ps 22: 8 Let him *d* him,
72:12 For he will *d* the needy who cry out
79: 9 *d* us and forgive our sins
109: 21 of the goodness of your love, *d* me.
119:170 *d* me according to your promise.
Mt 6:13 but *d* us from the evil one.'
2Co 1:10 hope that he will continue to *d* us,

DELIVERANCE (DELIVER)
1Sa 2: 1 for I delight in your *d*.
Ps 3: 8 From the LORD comes *d*.
32: 7 and surround me with songs of *d*.
33:17 A horse is a vain hope for *d*;
Ob :17 But on Mount Zion will be *d*;

DELIVERED (DELIVER)
Ps 34: 4 he *d* me from all my fears.
107: 6 and he *d* them from their distress.
116: 8 have *d* my soul from death,
Da 12: 1 written in the book—will be *d*.
Ro 4:25 He was *d* over to death for our sins

DELIVERER* (DELIVER)
Jdg 3: 9 for them a *d*, Othniel son of Kenaz,
3:15 and he gave them a *d*—Ehud,
2Sa 22: 2 is my rock, my fortress and my *d*;
2Ki 13: 5 The LORD provided a *d* for Israel,
Ps 18: 2 is my rock, my fortress and my *d*;
40:17 You are my help and my *d*;
70: 5 You are my help and my *d*;
140: 7 O Sovereign LORD, my strong *d*,
144: 2 my stronghold and my *d*,
Ac 7:35 sent to be their ruler and *d*
Ro 11:26 "The *d* will come from Zion;

DELIVERS (DELIVER)
Ps 34:17 he *d* them from all their troubles.
34:19 but the LORD *d* him from them all
37:40 The LORD helps them and *d* them
37:40 he *d* them from the wicked

DELUSION*
2Th 2:11 God sends them a powerful *d*

DEMAND (DEMANDED)
Lk 6:30 belongs to you, do not *d* it back.

DEMANDED (DEMAND)
Lk 12:20 This very night your life will be *d*
12:48 been given much, much will be *d*;

DEMETRIUS
Ac 19:24 A silversmith named *D*, who made

DEMON* (DEMONS)
Mt 9:33 And when the *d* was driven out,
11:18 and they say, 'He has a *d*.'
17:18 Jesus rebuked the *d*, and it came
Mk 7:26 to drive the *d* out of her daughter.
7:29 the *d* has left your daughter."
7:30 lying on the bed, and the *d* gone.
Lk 4:33 there was a man possessed by a *d*,
4:35 Then the *d* threw the man
7:33 wine, and you say, 'He has a *d*.'
8:29 driven by the *d* into solitary places.
9:42 the *d* threw him to the ground
11:14 When the *d* left, the man who had
11:14 was driving out a *d* that was mute.
Jn 8:49 "I am not possessed by a *d*,"
10:21 Can a *d* open the eyes of the blind
10:21 sayings of a man possessed by a *d*.

DEMON-POSSESSED* (DEMON-POSSESSION)
Mt 4:24 those suffering severe pain, the *d*,
8:16 many who were *d* were brought
8:28 two *d* men coming
8:33 what had happened to the *d* men.
9:32 man who was *d* and could not talk
12:22 they brought him a *d* man who was
Mk 1:32 brought to Jesus all the sick and *d*.
5:16 what had happened to the *d* man—
5:18 the man who had been *d* begged
Lk 8:27 met by a *d* man from the town.
8:36 the people how the *d* man had been
Jn 7:20 "You are *d*," the crowd answered.
8:48 that you are a Samaritan and *d*?"
8:52 "Now we know that you are *d*!
10:20 Many of them said, "He is *d*
Ac 19:13 Jesus over those who were *d*.

DEMON-POSSESSION* (DEMON-POSSESSED)
Mt 15:22 is suffering terribly from *d*."

DEMONS* (DEMON)
Dt 32:17 to *d*, which are not God—
Ps 106: 37 and their daughters to *d*.
Mt 7:22 and in your name drive out *d*
8:31 *d* begged Jesus, "If you drive us
9:34 prince of *d* that he drives out *d*."
10: 8 who have leprosy, drive out *d*.
12:24 of *d*, that this fellow drives out
12:24 that this fellow drives out *d*."
12:27 And if I drive out *d* by Beelzebub,
12:28 if I drive out *d* by the Spirit of God,
Mk 1:34 He also drove out many *d*,
1:34 but he would not let the *d* speak
1:39 their synagogues and driving out *d*.
3:15 to have authority to drive out *d*.
3:22 the prince of *d* he is driving out *d*."
5:12 The *d* begged Jesus, "Send us
5:15 possessed by the legion of *d*,
6:13 They drove out many *d*
9:38 "we saw a man driving out *d*
16: 9 out of whom he had driven seven *d*
16:17 In my name they will drive out *d*;
Lk 4:41 *d* came out of many people,
8: 2 from whom seven *d* had come out;
8:30 because many *d* had gone into him.
8:32 The *d* begged Jesus to let them go
8:33 When the *d* came out of the man,
8:35 from whom the *d* had gone out,
8:38 from whom the *d* had gone out
9: 1 and authority to drive out all *d*
9:49 "we saw a man driving out *d*
10:17 the *d* submit to us in your name."
11:15 the prince of *d*, he is driving out *d*."
11:18 you claim that I drive out *d*
11:19 Now if I drive out *d* by Beelzebub,
11:20 if I drive out *d* by the finger of God,
13:32 'I will drive out *d* and heal people
Ro 8:38 neither angels nor *d*, neither
1Co 10:20 of pagans are offered to *d*,
10:20 you to be participants with *d*.
10:21 of the Lord and the cup of *d* too;
10:21 the Lord's table and the table of *d*.
1Ti 4: 1 spirits and things taught by *d*.
Jas 2:19 Good! Even the *d* believe that—
Rev 9:20 they did not stop worshiping *d*,
16:14 of *d* performing miraculous signs,
18: 2 She has become a home for *d*

DEMONSTRATE* (DEMONSTRATES DEMONSTRATION)
Ro 3:25 He did this to *d* his justice,
3:26 he did it to *d* his justice

DEMONSTRATES* (DEMONSTRATE)
Ro 5: 8 God *d* his own love for us in this:

DEMONSTRATION* (DEMONSTRATE)
1Co 2: 4 but with a *d* of the Spirit's power,

DEN
Da 6:16 and threw him into the lions' *d.*
Mt 21:13 you are making it a '*d* of robbers.' "
Mk 11:17 you have made it 'a *d* of robbers.' "
Lk 19:46 but you have made it 'a *d* of robbers

DENARII* (DENARIUS)
Mt 18:28 who owed him a hundred *d.*
Lk 7:41 One owed him five hundred *d,*

DENARIUS (DENARII)
Mt 20: 2 agreed to pay them a *d* for the day
Mk 12:15 Bring me a *d* and let me look at it."

DENIED (DENY)
Mt 26:70 But he *d* it before them all.
Mk 14:68 But he *d* it.
Lk 22:57 But he *d* it.
Jn 18:25 He *d* it, saying, "I am not."
1Ti 5: 8 he has *d* the faith and is worse
Rev 3: 8 my word and have not *d* my name.

DENIES (DENY)
1Jn 2:22 It is the man who *d* that Jesus is
2:23 No one who *d* the Son has

DENY (DENIED DENIES DENYING)
Ex 23: 6 "Do not *d* justice to your poor
Job 27: 5 till I die, I will not *d* my integrity.
Isa 5:23 but *d* justice to the innocent.
La 3:35 to *d* a man his rights
Am 2: 7 and *d* justice to the oppressed.
Mt 16:24 he must *d* himself and take up his
Mk 8:34 he must *d* himself and take up his
Lk 9:23 he must *d* himself and take up his
22:34 you will *d* three times that you
Ac 4:16 miracle, and we cannot *d* it.
Tit 1:16 but by their actions they *d* him.
Jas 3:14 do not boast about it or *d* the truth.
Jude : 4 *d* Jesus Christ our only Sovereign

DENYING* (DENY)
Eze 22:29 mistreat the alien, *d* them justice.
2Ti 3: 5 a form of godliness but *d* its power.
2Pe 2: 1 *d* the sovereign Lord who bought

DEPART (DEPARTED DEPARTS DEPARTURE)
Ge 49:10 The scepter will not *d* from Judah,
Job 1:21 and naked I will *d.*
Mt 25:41 '*D* from me, you who are cursed,
Php 1:23 I desire to *d* and be with Christ,

DEPARTED (DEPART)
1Sa 4:21 "The glory has *d* from Israel"—
Ps 119:102 I have not *d* from your laws,

DEPARTS (DEPART)
Ecc 5:15 and as he comes, so he *d.*

DEPARTURE (DEPART)
Lk 9:31 spoke about his *d,* which he was
2Ti 4: 6 and the time has come for my *d.*
2Pe 1:15 after my *d* you will always be able

DEPEND
Ps 62: 7 My salvation and my honor *d*

DEPOSES*
Da 2:21 he sets up kings and *d* them.

DEPOSIT
Mt 25:27 money on *d* with the bankers,
Lk 19:23 didn't you put my money on *d,*
2Co 1:22 put his Spirit in our hearts as a *d,*
5: 5 and has given us the Spirit as a *d,*
Eph 1:14 who is a *d* guaranteeing our
2Ti 1:14 Guard the good *d* that was

DEPRAVED* (DEPRAVITY)
Eze 16:47 ways you soon became more *d*
23:11 and prostitution she was more *d*
Ro 1:28 he gave them over to a *d* mind,
Php 2:15 fault in a crooked and *d* generation,
2Ti 3: 8 oppose the truth—men of *d* minds,

DEPRAVITY* (DEPRAVED)
Ro 1:29 of wickedness, evil, greed and *d.*
2Pe 2:19 they themselves are slaves of *d*—

DEPRIVE
Dt 24:17 Do not *d* the alien or the fatherless
Pr 18: 5 or to *d* the innocent of justice.
31: 5 *d* all the oppressed of their rights.
Isa 10: 2 to *d* the poor of their rights
29:21 with false testimony *d* the innocent
La 3:36 to *d* a man of justice—
1Co 7: 5 Do not *d* each other
1Co 9:15 die than have anyone *d* me

DEPTH (DEEP)
Ro 8:39 any powers, neither height nor *d,*
11:33 the *d* of the riches of the wisdom

DEPTHS (DEEP)
Ps 130: 1 Out of the *d* I cry to you, O LORD;

DERIDES*
Pr 11:12 who lacks judgment *d* his neighbor,

DERIVES*
Eph 3:15 in heaven and on earth *d* its name.

DESCEND (DESCENDED DESCENDING)
Ro 10: 7 "or 'Who will *d* into the deep?' "

DESCENDED (DESCEND)
Eph 4: 9 except that he also *d* to the lower,
Heb 7:14 For it is clear that our Lord *d*

DESCENDING (DESCEND)
Ge 28:12 of God were ascending and *d* on it.
Mt 3:16 the Spirit of God *d* like a dove
Mk 1:10 and the Spirit *d* on him like a dove.
Jn 1:51 and *d* on the Son of Man."

DESECRATING*
Ne 13:17 you are doing—*d* the Sabbath day?
13:18 against Israel by *d* the Sabbath."
Isa 56: 2 who keeps the Sabbath without *d* it
56: 6 who keep the Sabbath without *d* it
Eze 44: 7 *d* my temple while you offered me

DESERT
Nu 32:13 wander in the *d* forty years,
Dt 8:16 He gave you manna to eat in the *d,*
29: 5 years that I led you through the *d,*
Ne 9:19 you did not abandon them in the *d.*
Ps 78:19 "Can God spread a table in the *d*?
78:52 led them like sheep through the *d.*
Pr 21:19 Better to live in a *d*
Isa 32: 2 like streams of water in the *d*
32:15 and the *d* becomes a fertile field,
35: 6 and streams in the *d.*
43:20 because I provide water in the *d*
Mk 1: 3 "a voice of one calling in the *d,*
1:13 and he was in the *d* forty days,
Rev 12: 6 fled into the *d* to a place prepared

DESERTED (DESERTS)
Ezr 9: 9 our God has not *d* us
Mt 26:56 all the disciples *d* him and fled.
2Ti 1:15 in the province of Asia has *d* me,

DESERTING (DESERTS)
Gal 1: 6 are so quickly *d* the one who called

DESERTS (DESERTED DESERTING)
Zec 11:17 who *d* the flock!

DESERVE* (DESERVED DESERVES)
Ge 40:15 to *d* being put in a dungeon."
Lev 26:21 times over, as your sins *d.*
Jdg 20:10 it can give them what they *d*
1Sa 26:16 you and your men *d* to die,
1Ki 2:26 You *d* to die, but I will not put you
Ps 28: 4 bring back upon them what they *d.*
94: 2 pay back to the proud what they *d.*
103: 10 he does not treat us as our sins *d*
Pr 3:27 from those who *d* it,
Ecc 8:14 men who get what the righteous *d.*
8:14 men who get what the wicked *d,*
Isa 66: 6 repaying his enemies all they *d.*
Jer 14:16 out on them the calamity they *d.*
17:10 according to what his deeds *d.*"
21:14 I will punish you as your deeds *d,*
32:19 to his conduct and as his deeds *d.*
49:12 "If those who do not *d*
La 3:64 Pay them back what they *d,*
Eze 16:59 I will deal with you as you *d,*
Zec 1: 6 to us what our ways and practices *d*
Mt 8: 8 I do not *d* to have you come
22: 8 those I invited did not *d* to come.
Lk 7: 6 for I do not *d* to have you come
23:15 he has done nothing to *d* death.
23:41 for we are getting what our deeds *d*
Ro 1:32 those who do such things *d* death,
1Co 15: 9 even *d* to be called an apostle,
16:18 Such men *d* recognition.
2Co 11:15 end will be what their actions *d.*
Rev 16: 6 blood to drink as they *d.*"

DESERVED* (DESERVE)
2Sa 19:28 descendants *d* nothing
Ezr 9:13 less than our sins have *d*
Job 33:27 but I did not get what I *d.*
Ac 23:29 charge against him that *d* death
Ro 3: 8 Their condemnation is *d.*

DESERVES* (DESERVE)
Nu 35:31 the life of a murderer, who *d* to die.
Dt 25: 2 If the guilty man *d* to be beaten,
25: 2 the number of lashes his crime *d,*
Jdg 9:16 and if you have treated him as he *d*
2Sa 12: 5 the man who did this *d* to die!
Job 34:11 upon him what his conduct *d.*
Jer 51: 6 he will pay her what she *d.*
Lk 7: 4 "This man *d* to have you do this,
10: 7 for the worker *d* his wages.
Ac 26:31 is not doing anything that *d* death
1Ti 1:15 saying that *d* full acceptance:
4: 9 saying that *d* full acceptance
5:18 and "The worker *d* his wages."
Heb 10:29 severely do you think a man *d*

DESIGNATED
Lk 6:13 also *d* apostles: Simon (whom he
Heb 5:10 and was *d* by God to be high priest

DESIRABLE* (DESIRE)
Ge 3: 6 and also *d* for gaining wisdom,
Pr 22: 1 A good name is more *d*
Jer 3:19 and give you a *d* land,

DESIRE* (DESIRABLE DESIRED DESIRES)
Ge 3:16 Your *d* will be for your husband,
Dt 5:21 You shall not set your *d*
1Sa 9:20 to whom is all the *d* of Israel turned
2Sa 19:38 anything you *d* from me I will do
23: 5 and grant me my every *d*?
1Ch 29:18 keep this *d* in the hearts
2Ch 1:11 "Since this is your heart's *d*
9: 8 and his *d* to uphold them forever,
Job 13: 3 But I *d* to speak to the Almighty
21:14 We have no *d* to know your ways.
Ps 10:17 O LORD, the *d* of the afflicted;
20: 4 May he give you the *d*
21: 2 You have granted him the *d*
27:12 me over to the *d* of my foes,
40: 6 Sacrifice and offering you did not *d*
40: 8 I *d* to do your will, O my God;
40:14 may all who *d* my ruin
41: 2 him to the *d* of his foes.
51: 6 Surely you *d* truth
70: 2 may all who *d* my ruin
73:25 earth has nothing I *d* besides you
Pr 3:15 nothing you *d* can compare
8:11 and nothing you *d* can compare
10:24 what the righteous *d* will be
11:23 The *d* of the righteous ends only
12:12 The wicked *d* the plunder
17:16 since he has no *d* to get wisdom?
24: 1 do not *d* their company;
Ecc 12: 5 and *d* no longer is stirred.
SS 6:12 my *d* set me among the royal
7:10 and his *d* is for me.
Isa 26: 8 are the *d* of our hearts.
53: 2 appearance that we should *d* him.
55:11 but will accomplish what I *d*
Eze 24:25 delight of their eyes, their heart's *d,*
Hos 6: 6 For I *d* mercy, not sacrifice,
Mic 7: 3 the powerful dictate what they *d*—
Mal 3: 1 whom you *d,* will come," says
Mt 9:13 learn what this means: 'I *d* mercy,
12: 7 what these words mean, 'I *d* mercy,
Jn 8:44 want to carry out your father's *d.*
Ro 7: 8 in me every kind of covetous *d.*
7:18 For I have the *d* to do what is good,
9:16 depend on man's *d* or effort,
10: 1 my heart's *d* and prayer to God
1Co 12:31 But eagerly *d* the greater gifts.
14: 1 and eagerly *d* spiritual gifts,
2Co 8:10 but also to have the *d* to do so.
8:13 Our *d* is not that others might be
Php 1:23 I *d* to depart and be with Christ,
Heb 10: 5 Sacrifice and offering you did not *d*
10: 8 and sin offerings you did not *d,*
13:18 *d* to live honorably in every way.
Jas 1:14 by his own evil *d,* he is dragged
1:15 Then, after *d* has conceived,
2Pe 2:10 of those who follow the corrupt *d*

DESIRED (DESIRE)
Hag 2: 7 and the *d* of all nations will come,
Lk 22:15 "I have eagerly *d* to eat this

DESIRES* (DESIRE)
Ge 4: 7 at your door; it *d* to have you,

Ge 41:16 will give Pharaoh the answer he *d.*"
2Sa 3:21 rule over all that your heart *d.*"
1Ki 11:37 rule over all that your heart *d;*
Job 17:11 and so are the *d* of my heart.
31:16 "If I have denied the *d* of the poor
Ps 34:12 and *d* to see many good days,
37:4 he will give you the *d* of your heart.
103:5 who satisfies your *d* with good things,
140:8 do not grant the wicked their *d,*
145:16 satisfy the *d* of every living thing.
145:19 He fulfills the *d* of those who fear
Pr 11:6 the unfaithful are trapped by evil *d.*
13:4 *d* of the diligent are fully satisfied.
19:22 What a man *d* is unfailing love;
Ecc 6:2 so that he lacks nothing his heart *d,*
SS 2:7 or awaken love / until it so *d.*
3:5 or awaken love / until it so *d.*
8:4 or awaken love / until it so *d.*
Hab 2:4 his *d* are not upright—
Mk 4:19 and the *d* for other things come in
Ro 1:24 over in the sinful *d* of their hearts
6:12 body so that you obey its evil *d.*
8:5 set on what that nature *d;*
8:5 set on what the Spirit *d.*
13:14 to gratify the *d* of the sinful nature.
Gal 5:16 and you will not gratify the *d*
5:17 the sinful nature *d* what is contrary
5:24 nature with its passions and *d.*
Eph 2:3 and following its *d* and thoughts.
4:22 being corrupted by its deceitful *d;*
Col 3:5 impurity, lust, evil *d* and greed,
1Ti 3:1 an overseer, he *d* a noble task.
5:11 their sensual *d* overcome their
6:9 and harmful *d* that plunge men
2Ti 2:22 Flee the evil *d* of youth,
3:6 are swayed by all kinds of evil *d,*
4:3 Instead, to suit their own *d,*
Jas 1:20 about the righteous life that God *d.*
4:1 from your *d* that battle within you?
1Pe 1:14 conform to the evil *d* you had
2:11 to abstain from sinful *d,* which war
4:2 of his earthly life for evil human *d,*
2Pe 1:4 in the world caused by evil *d.*
2:18 to the lustful *d* of sinful human
3:3 and following their own evil *d.*
1Jn 2:17 The world and its *d* pass away,
Jude :16 they follow their own evil *d;*
:18 will follow their own ungodly *d.*"

DESOLATE (DESOLATION)
Isa 54:1 are the children of the *d* woman
Gal 4:27 are the children of the *d* woman

DESOLATION (DESOLATE)
Da 11:31 up the abomination that causes *d.*
12:11 abomination that causes *d* is set up,
Mt 24:15 'the abomination that causes *d,*'

DESPAIR (DESPAIRED)
Isa 61:3 instead of a spirit of *d.*
2Co 4:8 perplexed, but not in *d;* persecuted,

DESPAIRED* (DESPAIR)
2Co 1:8 ability to endure, so that we *d*

DESPERATE*
2Sa 12:18 He may do something *d.*"
Ps 60:3 have shown your people *d* times;
79:8 for we are in *d* need.
142:6 for I am in *d* need;

DESPISE (DESPISED DESPISES)
2Sa 12:9 Why did you *d* the word
Job 5:17 so do not *d* the discipline
36:5 God is mighty, but does not *d* men;
42:6 Therefore I *d* myself
Ps 51:17 O God, you will not *d.*
102:17 he will not *d* their plea.
Pr 1:7 but fools *d* wisdom and discipline.
3:11 do not *d* the LORD's discipline
6:30 Men do not *d* a thief if he steals
23:22 do not *d* your mother
Jer 14:21 of your name do not *d* us;
Am 5:10 and *d* him who tells the truth.
5:21 "I hate, I *d* your religious feasts;
Mt 6:24 devoted to the one and *d* the other.
Lk 16:13 devoted to the one and *d* the other.
1Co 11:22 Or do you *d* the church of God
Tit 2:15 Do not let anyone *d* you.
2Pe 2:10 of the sinful nature and *d* authority.

DESPISED (DESPISE)
Ge 25:34 So Esau *d* his birthright.
Ps 22:6 by men and *d* by the people.
Pr 12:8 but men with warped minds are *d.*
Isa 53:3 He was *d* and rejected by men,
53:3 he was *d,* and we esteemed him not
1Co 1:28 of this world and the *d* things—

DESPISES (DESPISE)
Pr 14:21 He who *d* his neighbor sins,
15:20 but a foolish man *d* his mother.
15:32 who ignores discipline *d* himself,
Zec 4:10 "Who *d* the day of small things?

DESTINED (DESTINY)
Lk 2:34 "This child is *d* to cause the falling
1Co 2:7 and that God *d* for our glory
Col 2:22 These are all *d* to perish with use,
1Th 3:3 know quite well that we were *d*
Heb 9:27 Just as man is *d* to die once,
1Pe 2:8 which is also what they were *d* for.

DESTINY* (DESTINED PREDESTINED)
Job 8:13 Such is the *d* of all who forget God;
Ps 73:17 then I understood their final *d.*
Ecc 7:2 for death is the *d* of every man;
9:2 share a common *d*—the righteous
9:3 the sun: The same *d* overtakes all.
Isa 65:11 and fill bowls of mixed wine for *D,*
Php 3:19 Their *d* is destruction, their god is

DESTITUTE
Ps 102:17 to the prayer of the *d;*
Pr 31:8 for the rights of all who are *d.*
Heb 11:37 *d,* persecuted and mistreated—

DESTROY (DESTROYED DESTROYING DESTROYS DESTRUCTION DESTRUCTIVE)
Ge 6:17 floodwaters on the earth to *d* all life
9:11 will there be a flood to *d* the earth."
Pr 1:32 complacency of fools will *d* them;
Mt 10:28 of the One who can *d* both soul
Mk 14:58 'I will *d* this man-made temple
Lk 4:34 to *d* us? I know who you are—
Jn 10:10 only to steal and kill and *d;*
Ac 8:3 But Saul began to *d* the church.
Rev 11:18 destroying those who *d* the earth."

DESTROYED (DESTROY)
Dt 8:19 you today that you will surely be *d.*
Job 19:26 And after my skin has been *d,*
Pr 6:15 he will suddenly be *d*—
11:3 the unfaithful are *d*
21:28 listens to him will be *d* forever.
29:1 will suddenly be *d*—
Isa 55:13 which will not be *d.*"
Da 2:44 up a kingdom that will never be *d,*
6:26 his kingdom will not be *d,*
1Co 5:5 so that the sinful nature may be *d*
8:11 for whom Christ died, is *d*
15:24 Father after he has *d* all dominion,
15:26 The last enemy to be *d* is death.
2Co 4:9 abandoned; struck down, but not *d.*
5:1 if the earthly tent we live in is *d,*
Gal 5:15 or you will be *d* by each other.
Eph 2:14 the two one and has *d* the barrier,
2Ti 1:10 who has *d* death and has brought
Heb 10:39 of those who shrink back and are *d,*
2Pe 2:12 born only to be caught and *d,*
3:10 the elements will be *d* by fire,
3:11 Since everything will be *d*
Jude :5 later *d* those who did not believe.
:11 have been *d* in Korah's rebellion.

DESTROYING (DESTROY)
Jer 23:1 "Woe to the shepherds who are *d*

DESTROYS (DESTROY)
Pr 6:32 whoever does so *d* himself.
11:9 mouth the godless *d* his neighbor,
18:9 is brother to one who *d.*
28:24 he is partner to him who *d.*
Ecc 9:18 but one sinner *d* much good.
1Co 3:17 If anyone *d* God's temple,

DESTRUCTION (DESTROY)
Nu 32:15 and you will be the cause of their *d*
Pr 16:18 Pride goes before *d,*
17:19 he who builds a high gate invites *d.*
24:22 for those two will send sudden *d*
Hos 13:14 Where, O grave, is your *d?*
Mt 7:13 broad is the road that leads to *d,*
Lk 6:49 it collapsed and its *d* was complete
Jn 17:12 except the one doomed to *d*
Ro 9:22 of his wrath—prepared for *d?*
Gal 6:8 from that nature will reap *d;*
Php 3:19 Their destiny is *d,* their god is their
1Th 5:3 *d* will come on them suddenly,
2Th 1:9 punished with everlasting *d*
2:3 is revealed, the man doomed to *d.*
1Ti 6:9 that plunge men into ruin and *d.*
2Pe 2:1 bringing swift *d* on themselves.
2:3 and their *d* has not been sleeping.
3:7 of judgment and *d* of ungodly men.
3:12 That day will bring about the *d*
3:16 other Scriptures, to their own *d.*
Rev 17:8 out of the Abyss and go to his *d.*
17:11 to the seven and is going to his *d.*

DESTRUCTIVE (DESTROY)
2Pe 2:1 will secretly introduce *d* heresies,

DETERMINED (DETERMINES)
Job 14:5 Man's days are *d;*
Isa 14:26 This is the plan *d* for the whole
Da 11:36 for what has been *d* must take place
Ac 17:26 and he *d* the times set for them

DETERMINES* (DETERMINED)
Ps 147:4 He *d* the number of the stars
Pr 16:9 but the LORD *d* his steps.
1Co 12:11 them to each one, just as he *d.*

DETEST (DETESTABLE DETESTED DETESTS)
Lev 11:10 in the water—you are to *d.*
Pr 8:7 for my lips *d* wickedness.
13:19 but fools *d* turning from evil.
16:12 Kings *d* wrongdoing,
24:9 and men *d* a mocker.
29:27 The righteous *d* the dishonest;
29:27 the wicked *d* the upright.

DETESTABLE (DETEST)
Pr 6:16 seven that are *d* to him:
21:27 The sacrifice of the wicked is *d*—
28:9 even his prayers are *d.*
Isa 1:13 Your incense is *d* to me.
41:24 he who chooses you is *d.*
44:19 Shall I make a *d* thing
Jer 44:4 'Do not do this *d* thing that I hate!'
Eze 8:13 doing things that are even more *d.*"
Lk 16:15 among men is *d* in God's sight.
Tit 1:16 They are *d,* disobedient
1Pe 4:3 orgies, carousing and *d* idolatry.

DETESTED* (DETEST)
Zec 11:8 The flock *d* me, and I grew weary

DETESTS* (DETEST)
Dt 22:5 LORD your God *d* anyone who
23:18 the LORD your God *d* them both.
25:16 LORD your God *d* anyone who
Pr 3:32 for the LORD *d* a perverse man
11:20 The LORD *d* men
12:22 The LORD *d* lying lips,
15:8 The LORD *d* the sacrifice
15:9 The LORD *d* the way
15:26 The LORD *d* the thoughts
16:5 The LORD *d* all the proud of heart
17:15 the LORD *d* them both.
20:10 the LORD *d* them both.
20:23 The LORD *d* differing weights,

DEVIATE*
2Ch 8:15 They did not *d* from the king's

DEVICES*
Ps 81:12 to follow their own *d.*

DEVIL* (DEVIL'S)
Mt 4:1 the desert to be tempted by the *d.*
4:5 the *d* took him to the holy city
4:8 *d* took him to a very high mountain
4:11 the *d* left him, and angels came
13:39 the enemy who sows them is the *d.*
25:41 the eternal fire prepared for the *d*
Lk 4:2 forty days he was tempted by the *d.*
4:3 *d* said to him, "If you are the Son
4:5 The *d* led him up to a high place
4:9 The *d* led him to Jerusalem
4:13 When the *d* had finished all this
8:12 then the *d* comes and takes away
Jn 6:70 of you is a *d!*" (He meant Judas,
8:44 You belong to your father, the *d,*
13:2 the *d* had already prompted Judas
Ac 10:38 were under the power of the *d,*
13:10 "You are a child of the *d*
Eph 4:27 and do not give the *d* a foothold.
1Ti 3:6 under the same judgment as the *d.*
2Ti 2:26 and escape from the trap of the *d,*
Heb 2:14 the *d*—and free those who all their

Jas 3:15 but is earthly, unspiritual, of the *d.*
4: 7 Resist the *d,* and he will flee
1Pe 5: 8 Your enemy the *d* prowls
1Jn 3: 8 because the *d* has been sinning
3: 8 who does what is sinful is of the *d,*
3:10 and who the children of the *d* are:
Jude : 9 with the *d* about the body of Moses
Rev 2:10 the *d* will put some of you in prison
12: 9 that ancient serpent called the *d*
12:12 the *d* has gone down to you!
20: 2 that ancient serpent, who is the *d,*
20:10 And the *d,* who deceived them,

DEVIL'S* (DEVIL)
Eph 6:11 stand against the *d* schemes.
1Ti 3: 7 into disgrace and into the *d* trap.
1Jn 3: 8 was to destroy the *d* work.

DEVIOUS*
Pr 2:15 and who are *d* in their ways.
14: 2 he whose ways are *d* despises him.
21: 8 The way of the guilty is *d,*

DEVOTE* (DEVOTED DEVOTING DEVOTION DEVOUT)
1Ch 22:19 Now *d* your heart and soul
2Ch 31: 4 Levites so they could *d* themselves
Job 11:13 "Yet if you *d* your heart to him
Jer 30:21 for who is he who will *d* himself
Mic 4:13 You will *d* their ill-gotten gains
1Co 7: 5 so that you may *d* yourselves
Col 4: 2 *D* yourselves to prayer, being
1Ti 1: 4 nor to *d* themselves to myths
4:13 *d* yourself to the public reading
Tit 3: 8 may be careful to *d* themselves
3:14 people must learn to *d* themselves

DEVOTED (DEVOTE)
1Ki 11: 4 and his heart was not fully *d*
Ezr 7:10 For Ezra had *d* himself to the study
Ps 86: 2 Guard my life, for I am *d* to you.
Mt 6:24 or he will be *d* to the one
Mk 7:11 from me is Corban' (that is, a gift *d*
Ac 2:42 They *d* themselves
18: 5 Paul *d* himself exclusively
Ro 12:10 Be *d* to one another
1Co 7:34 Her aim is to be *d* to the Lord
16:15 and they have *d* themselves
2Co 7:12 for yourselves how *d* to us you are.

DEVOTING* (DEVOTE)
1Ti 5:10 *d* herself to all kinds of good deeds.

DEVOTION* (DEVOTE)
2Ki 20: 3 and with wholehearted *d* and have
1Ch 28: 9 and serve him with wholehearted *d*
29: 3 in my *d* to the temple
29:19 son Solomon the wholehearted *d*
2Ch 32:32 and his acts of *d* are written
35:26 of Josiah's reign and his acts of *d,*
Job 6:14 despairing man should have the *d*
15: 4 and hinder *d* to God.
Isa 38: 3 and with wholehearted *d* and have
Jer 2: 2 " 'I remember the *d* of your youth,
Eze 33:31 With their mouths they express *d,*
1Co 7:35 way in undivided *d* to the Lord.
2Co 11: 3 from your sincere and pure *d*

DEVOUR (DEVOURED DEVOURING DEVOURS)
2Sa 2:26 "Must the sword *d* forever?
Mk 12:40 They *d* widows' houses
1Pe 5: 8 lion looking for someone to *d.*

DEVOURED (DEVOUR)
Jer 30:16 But all who devour you will be *d;*

DEVOURING (DEVOUR)
Gal 5:15 keep on biting and *d* each other,

DEVOURS (DEVOUR)
2Sa 11:25 the sword *d* one as well as another.
Pr 21:20 but a foolish man *d* all he has.

DEVOUT* (DEVOTE)
1Ki 18: 3 (Obadiah was a *d* believer
Isa 57: 1 *d* men are taken away,
Lk 2:25 Simeon, who was righteous and *d.*
Ac 10: 2 his family were *d* and God-fearing;
10: 7 a *d* soldier who was one of his attendants
13:43 and *d* converts to Judaism followed
22:12 He was a *d* observer of the law

DEW
Jdg 6:37 If there is *d* only on the fleece

DICTATED
Jer 36: 4 and while Jeremiah *d* all the words

DIE (DEAD DEADENED DEATH DIED DIES DYING)
Ge 2:17 when you eat of it you will surely *d*
3: 3 you must not touch it, or you will *d*
3: 4 will not surely *d,*" the serpent said
Ex 11: 5 Every firstborn son in Egypt will *d,*
Ru 1:17 Where you *d* I will *d,* and there I
2Ki 14: 6 each is to *d* for his own sins."
Job 2: 9 Curse God and *d!*" He replied,
Pr 5:23 He will *d* for lack of discipline,
10:21 but fools *d* for lack of judgment.
15:10 he who hates correction will *d.*
23:13 with the rod, he will not *d.*
Ecc 3: 2 a time to be born and a time to *d,*
Isa 22:13 "for tomorrow we *d!*"
66:24 their worm will not *d,* nor will their
Jer 31:30 everyone will *d* for his own sin;
Eze 3:18 that wicked man will *d* for his sin,
3:19 he will *d* for his sin; but you will
3:20 block before him, he will *d.*
18: 4 soul who sins is the one who will *d.*
18:20 soul who sins is the one who will *d.*
18:31 Why will you *d,* O house of Israel?
33: 8 'O wicked man, you will surely *d,*'
Mt 26:52 "for all who draw the sword will *d*
Mk 9:48 " 'their worm does not *d,*
Jn 8:21 and you will *d* in your sin.
11:26 and believes in me will never *d.*
Ro 5: 7 Very rarely will anyone *d*
14: 8 and if we *d,* we *d* to the Lord.
1Co 15:22 in Adam all *d,* so in Christ all will
15:31 I *d* every day—I mean that,
15:32 for tomorrow we *d.*"
Php 1:21 to live is Christ and to *d* is gain.
Heb 9:27 Just as man is destined to *d* once,
1Pe 2:24 so that we might *d* to sins
Rev 14:13 Blessed are the dead who *d*

DIED (DIE)
1Ki 16:18 So he *d,* because of the sins he had
1Ch 1:51 Hadad also *d.*
10:13 Saul *d* because he was unfaithful
Lk 16:22 "The time came when the beggar *d*
Ro 5: 6 we were still powerless, Christ *d*
5: 8 we were still sinners, Christ *d*
6: 2 By no means! We *d* to sin;
6: 7 anyone who has *d* has been freed
6: 8 if we *d* with Christ, we believe that
6:10 The death he *d,* he *d* to sin once
14: 9 Christ *d* and returned to life
14:15 brother for whom Christ *d.*
1Co 8:11 for whom Christ *d,* is destroyed
15: 3 that Christ *d* for our sins according
2Co 5:14 *d* for all, and therefore all *d.*
5:15 he *d* for all, that those who live
Col 2:20 Since you *d* with Christ
3: 3 For you *d,* and your life is now
1Th 4:14 We believe that Jesus *d*
5:10 He *d* for us so that, whether we are
2Ti 2:11 If we *d* with him,
Heb 9:15 now that he has *d* as a ransom
9:17 in force only when somebody has *d*
1Pe 3:18 For Christ *d* for sins once for all,
Rev 2: 8 who *d* and came to life again.

DIES (DIE)
Job 14:14 If a man *d,* will he live again?
Pr 11: 7 a wicked man *d,* his hope perishes;
26:20 without gossip a quarrel *d* down.
Jn 11:25 in me will live, even though he *d;*
12:24 But if it *d,* it produces many seeds.
Ro 7: 2 but if her husband *d,* she is released
14: 7 and none of us *d* to himself alone.
1Co 7:39 But if her husband *d,* she is free
15:36 does not come to life unless it *d.*

DIFFERENCE* (DIFFERENT)
2Sa 19:35 Can I tell the *d* between what is
2Ch 12: 8 so that they may learn the *d*
Eze 22:26 they teach that there is no *d*
44:23 are to teach my people the *d*
Ro 3:22 There is no *d,* for all have sinned
10:12 For there is no *d* between Jew
Gal 2: 6 whatever they were makes no *d*

DIFFERENCES* (DIFFERENT)
1Co 11:19 to be *d* among you to show which

DIFFERENT* (DIFFERENCE DIFFERENCES DIFFERING DIFFERS)
Lev 19:19 " 'Do not mate *d* kinds of animals.
Nu 14:24 my servant Caleb has a *d* spirit
1Sa 10: 6 you will be changed into a *d* person
Est 1: 7 each one *d* from the other,
3: 8 whose customs are *d* from those
Da 7: 3 Four great beasts, each *d*
7: 7 It was *d* from all the former beasts,
7:19 which was *d* from all the others
7:23 It will be *d* from all the other
7:24 them another king will arise, *d*
11:29 but this time the outcome will be *d*
Mk 16:12 Jesus appeared in a *d* form
Ro 12: 6 We have *d* gifts, according
1Co 4: 7 For who makes you *d*
12: 4 There are *d* kinds of gifts,
12: 5 There are *d* kinds of service,
12: 6 There are *d* kinds of working,
12:10 speaking in *d* kinds of tongues,
12:28 and those speaking in *d* kinds
2Co 11: 4 or a *d* gospel from the one you
11: 4 or if you receive a *d* spirit
Gal 1: 6 and are turning to a *d* gospel—
4: 1 he is no *d* from a slave,
Heb 7:13 are said belonged to a *d* tribe,
Jas 2:25 and sent them off in a *d* direction?

DIFFERING* (DIFFERENT)
Dt 25:13 Do not have two *d* weights
25:14 Do not have two *d* measures
Pr 20:10 Differing weights and *d* measures
20:10 *D* weights and differing measures
20:23 The LORD detests *d* weights,

DIFFERS* (DIFFERENT)
1Co 15:41 and star *d* from star in splendor.

DIFFICULT (DIFFICULTIES)
Ex 18:22 but have them bring every *d* case
Dt 30:11 commanding you today is not too *d*
2Ki 2:10 "You have asked a *d* thing,"
Eze 3: 5 of obscure speech and *d* language,
Ac 15:19 that we should not make it *d*

DIFFICULTIES* (DIFFICULT)
Dt 31:17 and *d* will come upon them,
31:21 when many disasters and *d* come
2Co 12:10 in hardships, in persecutions, in *d.*

DIGNITY
Pr 31:25 She is clothed with strength and *d;*

DIGS
Pr 26:27 If a man *d* a pit, he will fall into it;

DILIGENCE (DILIGENT)
Ezr 5: 8 The work is being carried on with *d*
Heb 6:11 to show this same *d* to the very end

DILIGENT (DILIGENCE)
Pr 10: 4 but *d* hands bring wealth.
12:24 *D* hands will rule,
12:27 the *d* man prizes his possessions.
13: 4 of the *d* are fully satisfied.
21: 5 The plans of the *d* lead to profit
1Ti 4:15 Be *d* in these matters; give yourself

DINAH*
Only daughter of Jacob, by Leah (Ge 30:21; 46:15). Raped by Shechem; avenged by Simeon and Levi (Ge 34).

DINE
Pr 23: 1 When you sit to *d* with a ruler,

DIOTREPHES*
3Jn : 9 but *D,* who loves to be first,

DIRECT (DIRECTED DIRECTIVES DIRECTS)
Ge 18:19 so that he will *d* his children
Dt 17:10 to do everything they *d* you to do.
Ps 119: 35 *D* me in the path of your
119:133 *D* my footsteps according
Jer 10:23 it is not for man to *d* his steps.
2Th 3: 5 May the Lord *d* your hearts
1Ti 5:17 The elders who *d* the affairs

DIRECTED (DIRECT)
Ge 24:51 master's son, as the LORD has *d.*"
Nu 16:40 as the LORD *d* him through Moses
Dt 2: 1 Sea, as the LORD had *d* me.
6: 1 laws the LORD your God *d* me
Jos 11: 9 did to them as the LORD had *d:*
11:23 just as the LORD had *d* Moses,
Pr 20:24 A man's steps are *d* by the LORD.
Jer 13: 2 as the LORD *d,* and put it
Ac 7:44 It had been made as God *d* Moses,
Tit 1: 5 elders in every town, as I *d* you.

DIRECTIVES* (DIRECT)
1Co 11:17 In the following *d* I have no praise

DIRECTS (DIRECT)
Ps 42: 8 By day the LORD *d* his love,
Isa 48:17 who *d* you in the way you should

DIRGE*
Mt 11:17 we sang a *d,*
Lk 7:32 we sang a *d,*

DISABLED*
Jn 5: 3 number of *d* people used to lie—
Heb 12:13 so that the lame may not be *d,*

DISAGREEMENT*
Ac 15:39 had such a sharp *d* that they parted

DISAPPEAR (DISAPPEARED DISAPPEARS)
Mt 5:18 will by any means *d* from the Law
Lk 16:17 earth to *d* than for the least stroke
Heb 8:13 is obsolete and aging will soon *d.*
2Pe 3:10 The heavens will *d* with a roar;

DISAPPEARED (DISAPPEAR)
1Ki 20:40 busy here and there, the man *d."*

DISAPPEARS (DISAPPEAR)
1Co 13:10 perfection comes, the imperfect *d.*

DISAPPOINT* (DISAPPOINTED)
Ro 5: 5 And hope does not *d* us,

DISAPPOINTED (DISAPPOINT)
Ps 22: 5 in you they trusted and were not *d.*

DISAPPROVE*
Pr 24:18 or the LORD will see and *d*

DISARMED*
Col 2:15 And having *d* the powers

DISASTER
Ex 32:12 and do not bring *d* on your people.
Ps 57: 1 wings until the *d* has passed.
Pr 1:26 I in turn will laugh at your *d;*
3:25 Have no fear of sudden *d*
6:15 Therefore *d* will overtake him
16: 4 even the wicked for a day of *d.*
17: 5 over *d* will not go unpunished.
27:10 house when *d* strikes you—
Isa 45: 7 I bring prosperity and create *d;*
Jer 17:17 you are my refuge in the day of *d.*
Eze 7: 5 An unheard-of *d* is coming.

DISCERN (DISCERNED DISCERNING DISCERNMENT)
Ps 19:12 Who can *d* his errors?
139: 3 You *d* my going out and my lying
Php 1:10 you may be able to *d* what is best

DISCERNED (DISCERN)
1Co 2:14 because they are spiritually *d.*

DISCERNING (DISCERN)
1Ki 3: 9 So give your servant a *d* heart
3:12 I will give you a wise and *d* heart,
Pr 1: 5 and let the *d* get guidance—
8: 9 To the *d* all of them are right;
10:13 on the lips of the *d,*
14: 6 knowledge comes easily to the *d.*
14:33 in the heart of the *d*
15:14 The *d* heart seeks knowledge,
16:21 The wise in heart are called *d,*
17:24 A *d* man keeps wisdom in view,
17:28 and *d* if he holds his tongue.
18:15 heart of the *d* acquires knowledge;
19:25 rebuke a *d* man, and he will gain
28: 7 He who keeps the law is a *d* son,

DISCERNMENT (DISCERN)
Ps 119:125 I am your servant; give me *d*
Pr 3:21 preserve sound judgment and *d,*
17:10 A rebuke impresses a man of *d*
28:11 a poor man who has *d* sees

DISCHARGED* (DISCHARGING)
Ecc 8: 8 As no one is *d* in time of war,

DISCHARGING* (DISCHARGED)
1Co 9:17 I am simply *d* the trust committed

DISCIPLE (DISCIPLES DISCIPLES')
Mt 10:42 these little ones because he is my *d,*
Lk 14:26 his own life—he cannot be my *d.*
14:27 and follow me cannot be my *d.*
14:33 everything he has cannot be my *d.*
Jn 13:23 of them, the *d* whom Jesus loved,
19:26 and the *d* whom he loved standing
Jn 21: 7 Then the *d* whom Jesus loved said
21:20 saw that the *d* whom Jesus loved

DISCIPLES (DISCIPLE)
Mt 10: 1 He called his twelve *d* to him
26:56 Then all the *d* deserted him
28:19 Therefore go and make *d*
Mk 3: 7 withdrew with his *d* to the lake,
16:20 Then the *d* went out and preached
Lk 6:13 he called his *d* to him and chose
Jn 2:11 and his *d* put their faith in him.
6:66 many of his *d* turned back
8:31 to my teaching, you are really my *d*
12:16 At first his *d* did not understand all
13:35 men will know that you are my *d*
15: 8 showing yourselves to be my *d.*
20:20 The *d* were overjoyed
Ac 6: 1 the number of *d* was increasing,
11:26 The *d* were called Christians first
14:22 strengthening the *d*
18:23 Phrygia, strengthening all the *d.*

DISCIPLES' (DISCIPLE)
Jn 13: 5 and began to wash his *d* feet,

DISCIPLINE* (DISCIPLINED DISCIPLINES SELF-DISCIPLINE)
Dt 4:36 made you hear his voice to *d* you.
11: 2 and experienced the *d*
21:18 listen to them when they *d* him,
Job 5:17 so do not despise the *d*
Ps 6: 1 or *d* me in your wrath.
38: 1 or *d* me in your wrath.
39:11 You rebuke and *d* men for their sin;
94:12 Blessed is the man you *d,* O LORD
Pr 1: 2 for attaining wisdom and *d;*
1: 7 but fools despise wisdom and *d.*
3:11 do not despise the LORD's *d*
5:12 You will say, "How I hated *d!*
5:23 He will die for lack of *d,*
6:23 and the corrections of *d*
10:17 He who heeds *d* shows the way
12: 1 Whoever loves *d* loves knowledge,
13:18 He who ignores *d* comes to poverty
13:24 who loves him is careful to *d* him.
15: 5 A fool spurns his father's *d,*
15:10 Stern *d* awaits him who leaves
15:32 He who ignores *d* despises himself,
19:18 *D* your son, for in that there is hope
22:15 the rod of *d* will drive it far
23:13 Do not withhold *d* from a child;
23:23 get wisdom, *d* and understanding.
29:17 *D* your son, and he will give you
Jer 17:23 would not listen or respond to *d.*
30:11 I will *d* you but only with justice;
32:33 would not listen or respond to *d.*
46:28 I will *d* you but only with justice;
Hos 5: 2 I will *d* all of them.
Heb 12: 5 do not make light of the Lord's *d,*
12: 7 as *d;* God is treating you
12: 8 (and everyone undergoes *d),*
12:11 No *d* seems pleasant at the time,
Rev 3:19 Those whom I love I rebuke and *d.*

DISCIPLINED* (DISCIPLINE)
Pr 1: 3 for acquiring a *d* and prudent life,
Isa 26:16 when you *d* them,
Jer 31:18 and I have been *d.*
31:18 'You *d* me like an unruly calf,
1Co 11:32 we are being *d* so that we will not
Tit 1: 8 upright, holy and *d.*
Heb 12: 7 For what son is not *d* by his father?
12: 8 you are not *d* (and everyone
12: 9 all had human fathers who *d* us
12:10 Our fathers *d* us for a little while

DISCIPLINES* (DISCIPLINE)
Dt 8: 5 your heart that as a man *d* his son,
8: 5 so the LORD your God *d* you.
Ps 94:10 Does he who *d* nations not punish?
Pr 3:12 the LORD *d* those he loves,
Heb 12: 6 because the Lord *d* those he loves,
12:10 but God *d* us for our good,

DISCLOSED
Lk 8:17 is nothing hidden that will not be *d,*
Col 1:26 and generations, but is now *d*
Heb 9: 8 Holy Place had not yet been *d*

DISCORD
Gal 5:20 idolatry and witchcraft; hatred, *d,*

DISCOURAGED* (DISCOURAGEMENT)
Nu 32: 9 they *d* the Israelites
Dt 1:21 Do not be afraid; do not be *d."*
31: 8 Do not be afraid; do not be *d."*
Jos 1: 9 Do not be terrified; do not be *d,*
8: 1 "Do not be afraid; do not be *d.*
10:25 "Do not be afraid; do not be *d.*
1Ch 22:13 Do not be afraid or *d.*
28:20 or *d,* for the LORD God,
2Ch 20:15 or *d* because of this vast army.
20:17 Do not be afraid; do not be *d.*
32: 7 or *d* because of the king of Assyria
Job 4: 5 to you, and you are *d;*
Isa 42: 4 he will not falter or be *d*
Eph 3:13 to be *d* because of my sufferings
Col 3:21 children, or they will become *d.*

DISCOURAGEMENT* (DISCOURAGED)
Ex 6: 9 of their *d* and cruel bondage.

DISCOVERED
2Ki 23:24 book that Hilkiah the priest had *d*

DISCREDIT* (DISCREDITED)
Ne 6:13 would give me a bad name to *d* me.
Job 40: 8 "Would you *d* my justice?

DISCREDITED (DISCREDIT)
2Co 6: 3 so that our ministry will not be *d.*

DISCRETION*
1Ch 22:12 May the LORD give you *d*
Pr 1: 4 knowledge and *d* to the young—
2:11 *D* will protect you,
5: 2 that you may maintain *d*
8:12 I possess knowledge and *d.*
11:22 a beautiful woman who shows no *d.*

DISCRIMINATED*
Jas 2: 4 have you not *d* among yourselves

DISEASE (DISEASES)
Mt 4:23 and healing every *d* and sickness
9:35 and healing every *d* and sickness.
10: 1 and to heal every *d* and sickness.

DISEASES (DISEASE)
Ps 103: 3 and heals all my *d;*
Mt 8:17 and carried our *d."*
Mk 3:10 those with *d* were pushing forward
Lk 9: 1 drive out all demons and to cure *d,*

DISFIGURE* (DISFIGURED)
Mt 6:16 for they *d* their faces

DISFIGURED (DISFIGURE)
Isa 52:14 his appearance was so *d*

DISGRACE (DISGRACEFUL DISGRACES)
Ps 44:15 My *d* is before me all day long,
52: 1 you who are a *d* in the eyes of God?
74:21 not let the oppressed retreat in *d;*
Pr 6:33 Blows and *d* are his lot,
11: 2 When pride comes, then comes *d,*
14:34 but sin is a *d* to any people.
19:26 is a son who brings shame and *d.*
Mt 1:19 want to expose her to public *d,*
Ac 5:41 of suffering *d* for the Name.
1Co 11: 6 and if it is a *d* for a woman
11:14 it is a *d* to him, but that
1Ti 3: 7 so that he will not fall into *d*
Heb 6: 6 and subjecting him to public *d.*
11:26 He regarded *d* for the sake
13:13 the camp, bearing the *d* he bore.

DISGRACEFUL (DISGRACE)
Pr 10: 5 during harvest is a *d* son.
12: 4 a *d* wife is like decay in his bones.
17: 2 wise servant will rule over a *d* son,
1Co 14:35 for it is *d* for a woman to speak

DISGRACES (DISGRACE)
Pr 28: 7 of gluttons *d* his father.
29:15 but a child left to himself *d* his mother

DISGUISES*
Pr 26:24 A malicious man *d* himself

DISH
Pr 19:24 sluggard buries his hand in the *d;*
Mt 23:25 the outside of the cup and *d,*

DISHONEST*
Ex 18:21 trustworthy men who hate *d* gain
Lev 19:35 " 'Do not use *d* standards
1Sa 8: 3 They turned aside after *d* gain
Pr 11: 1 The LORD abhors *d* scales,
13:11 *D* money dwindles away,

Pr 20:23 and *d* scales do not please him.
29:27 The righteous detest the *d;*
Jer 22:17 are set only on *d* gain,
Eze 28:18 By your many sins and *d* trade
Hos 12: 7 The merchant uses *d* scales;
Am 8: 5 and cheating with *d* scales,
Mic 6:11 Shall I acquit a man with *d* scales,
Lk 16: 8 master commended the *d* manager
16:10 whoever is *d* with very little will
16:10 with very little will also be *d*
1Ti 3: 8 wine, and not pursuing *d* gain.
Tit 1: 7 not violent, not pursuing *d* gain.
1:11 and that for the sake of *d* gain.

DISHONOR* (DISHONORED DISHONORS)
Lev 18: 7 " 'Do not *d* your father
18: 8 wife; that would *d* your father.
18:10 daughter; that would *d* you.
18:14 " 'Do not *d* your father's brother
18:16 that would *d* your brother.
20:19 for that would *d* a close relative;
Dt 22:30 he must not *d* his father's bed.
Pr 30: 9 and so *d* the name of my God.
Jer 14:21 do not *d* your glorious throne.
20:11 their *d* will never be forgotten.
La 2: 2 princes down to the ground in *d.*
Eze 22:10 are those who *d* their fathers' bed;
Jn 8:49 I honor my Father and you *d* me.
Ro 2:23 do you *d* God by breaking the law?
1Co 15:43 it is sown in *d,* it is raised in glory;
2Co 6: 8 through glory and *d,* bad report

DISHONORED* (DISHONOR)
Lev 20:11 father's wife, he has *d* his father.
20:17 He has *d* his sister and will be held
20:20 with his aunt, he has *d* his uncle.
20:21 of impurity; he has *d* his brother.
Dt 21:14 as a slave, since you have *d* her.
Ezr 4:14 proper for us to see the king *d,*
1Co 4:10 You are honored, we are *d!*

DISHONORS* (DISHONOR)
Dt 27:16 Cursed is the man who *d* his father
27:20 for he *d* his father's bed."
Job 20: 3 I hear a rebuke that *d* me,
Mic 7: 6 For a son *d* his father,
1Co 11: 4 with his head covered *d* his head.
11: 5 her head uncovered *d* her head—

DISILLUSIONMENT*
Ps 7:14 conceives trouble gives birth to *d.*

DISMAYED
Isa 28:16 the one who trusts will never be *d.*
41:10 do not be *d,* for I am your God.

DISOBEDIENCE* (DISOBEY)
Jos 22:22 in rebellion or *d* to the LORD,
Jer 43: 7 So they entered Egypt in *d*
Ro 5:19 as through the *d* of the one man
11:30 mercy as a result of their *d,*
11:32 to *d* so that he may have mercy
2Co 10: 6 ready to punish every act of *d,*
Heb 2: 2 and *d* received its just punishment,
4: 6 go in, because of their *d.*
4:11 fall by following their example of *d.*

DISOBEDIENT* (DISOBEY)
Ne 9:26 "But they were *d* and rebelled
Lk 1:17 and the *d* to the wisdom
Ac 26:19 I was not *d* to the vision
Ro 10:21 hands to a *d* and obstinate people."
11:30 as you who were at one time *d*
11:31 so they too have now become *d*
Eph 2: 2 now at work in those who are *d.*
5: 6 comes on those who are *d.*
5:12 to mention what the *d* do in secret.
2Ti 3: 2 proud, abusive, *d* to their parents,
Tit 1: 6 to the charge of being wild and *d.*
1:16 *d* and unfit for doing anything
3: 3 At one time we too were foolish, *d,*
Heb 11:31 killed with those who were *d.*

DISOBEY* (DISOBEDIENCE DISOBEDIENT DISOBEYED DISOBEYING DISOBEYS)
Dt 11:28 the curse if you *d* the commands
2Ch 24:20 'Why do you *d* the LORD's
Est 3: 3 Why do you *d* the king's command
Jer 42:13 and so *d* the LORD your God,
Ro 1:30 they *d* their parents; they are
1Pe 2: 8 because they *d* the message—

DISOBEYED* (DISOBEY)
Nu 14:22 and in the desert but who *d* me
Nu 27:14 both of you *d* my command
Jdg 2: 2 Yet you have *d* me.
Ne 9:29 arrogant and *d* your commands.
Isa 24: 5 they have *d* the laws,
Jer 43: 4 and all the people *d* the LORD's
Lk 15:29 for you and never *d* your orders.
Heb 3:18 rest if not to those who *d?*
1Pe 3:20 the spirits in prison who *d* long ago

DISOBEYING* (DISOBEY)
Nu 14:41 "Why are you *d* the LORD's

DISOBEYS* (DISOBEY)
Eze 33:12 man will not save him when he *d,*

DISORDER
1Co 14:33 For God is not a God of *d*
2Co 12:20 slander, gossip, arrogance and *d.*
Jas 3:16 there you find *d* and every evil

DISOWN (DISOWNS)
Pr 30: 9 I may have too much and *d* you
Mt 10:33 I will *d* him before my Father
26:35 to die with you, I will never *d* you."
2Ti 2:12 If we *d* him,

DISOWNS (DISOWN)
Lk 12: 9 he who *d* me before men will be

DISPENSATION
see ADMINISTRATION, TRUST

DISPLACES
Pr 30:23 a maidservant who *d* her mistress.

DISPLAY (DISPLAYED DISPLAYS)
Ps 45: 4 your right hand *d* awesome deeds.
Eze 39:21 I will *d* my glory among the nations
Ro 9:17 that I might *d* my power in you
1Co 4: 9 on *d* at the end of the procession,
1Ti 1:16 Christ Jesus might *d* his unlimited

DISPLAYED (DISPLAY)
Jn 9: 3 work of God might be *d* in his life.
2Th 2: 9 the work of Satan *d* in all kinds

DISPLAYS (DISPLAY)
Isa 44:23 he *d* his glory in Israel.

DISPLEASE (DISPLEASED)
1Th 2:15 They *d* God and are hostile

DISPLEASED (DISPLEASE)
2Sa 11:27 David had done *d* the LORD.

DISPUTABLE* (DISPUTE)
Ro 14: 1 passing judgment on *d* matters.

DISPUTE (DISPUTABLE DISPUTES DISPUTING)
Pr 17:14 before a *d* breaks out.
1Co 6: 1 If any of you has a *d* with another,

DISPUTES (DISPUTE)
Pr 18:18 Casting the lot settles *d*

DISPUTING (DISPUTE)
1Ti 2: 8 in prayer, without anger or *d.*

DISQUALIFIED*
1Co 9:27 I myself will not be *d* for the prize.

DISREPUTE*
2Pe 2: 2 will bring the way of truth into *d.*

DISSENSION* (DISSENSIONS)
Pr 6:14 he always stirs up *d.*
6:19 and a man who stirs up *d*
10:12 Hatred stirs up *d,*
15:18 A hot-tempered man stirs up *d,*
16:28 A perverse man stirs up *d,*
28:25 A greedy man stirs up *d,*
29:22 An angry man stirs up *d,*
Ro 13:13 debauchery, not in *d* and jealousy.

DISSENSIONS* (DISSENSION)
Gal 5:20 selfish ambition, *d,* factions

DISSIPATION*
Lk 21:34 will be weighed down with *d,*
1Pe 4: 4 with them into the same flood of *d,*

DISTINCTION
Ac 15: 9 He made no *d* between us

DISTINGUISH (DISTINGUISHING)
1Ki 3: 9 and to *d* between right and wrong.
Heb 5:14 themselves to *d* good from evil.

DISTINGUISHING
1Co 12:10 the *d* between spirits,

DISTORT
Ac 20:30 and *d* the truth in order
2Co 4: 2 nor do we *d* the word of God.
2Pe 3:16 ignorant and unstable people *d,*

DISTRACTED*
Lk 10:40 But Martha was *d* by all

DISTRESS (DISTRESSED)
2Ch 15: 4 in their *d* they turned to the LORD
Ps 18: 6 In my *d* I called to the LORD;
81: 7 In your *d* you called and I rescued
120: 1 I call on the LORD in my *d,*
Jnh 2: 2 "In my *d* I called to the LORD,
Mt 24:21 For then there will be great *d,*
Jas 1:27 after orphans and widows in their *d*

DISTRESSED (DISTRESS)
Lk 12:50 how *d* I am until it is completed!
Ro 14:15 If your brother is *d*

DIVIDE (DIVIDED DIVIDING DIVISION DIVISIONS DIVISIVE)
Ps 22:18 They *d* my garments among them

DIVIDED (DIVIDE)
Mt 12:25 household *d* against itself will not
Lk 23:34 they *d* up his clothes by casting lots
1Co 1:13 Is Christ *d?* Was Paul crucified

DIVIDING (DIVIDE)
Eph 2:14 destroyed the barrier, the *d* wall
Heb 4:12 it penetrates even to *d* soul

DIVINATION
Lev 19:26 " 'Do not practice *d* or sorcery.

DIVINE
Ro 1:20 his eternal power and *d* nature—
2Co 10: 4 they have *d* power
2Pe 1: 4 you may participate in the *d* nature

DIVISION (DIVIDE)
Lk 12:51 on earth? No, I tell you, but *d.*
1Co 12:25 so that there should be no *d*

DIVISIONS (DIVIDE)
Ro 16:17 to watch out for those who cause *d*
1Co 1:10 another so that there may be no *d*
11:18 there are *d* among you,

DIVISIVE* (DIVIDE)
Tit 3:10 Warn a *d* person once,

DIVORCE* (DIVORCED DIVORCES)
Dt 22:19 he must not *d* her as long as he lives
22:29 He can never *d* her as long
24: 1 and he writes her a certificate of *d,*
24: 3 and writes her a certificate of *d,*
Isa 50: 1 is your mother's certificate of *d*
Jer 3: 8 faithless Israel her certificate of *d*
Mal 2:16 "I hate *d,*" says the LORD God
Mt 1:19 he had in mind to *d* her quietly.
5:31 must give her a certificate of *d.*'
19: 3 for a man to *d* his wife for any
19: 7 man give his wife a certificate of *d*
19: 8 permitted you to *d* your wives
Mk 10: 2 Is it lawful for a man to *d* his wife?"
10: 4 a man to write a certificate of *d*
1Co 7:11 And a husband must not *d* his wife.
7:12 to live with him, he must not *d* her.
7:13 to live with her, she must not *d* him
7:27 Are you married? Do not seek a *d.*

DIVORCED* (DIVORCE)
Lev 21: 7 or *d* from their husbands,
21:14 not marry a widow, a *d* woman,
22:13 daughter becomes a widow or is *d,*
Nu 30: 9 or *d* woman will be binding on her.
Dt 24: 4 then her first husband, who *d* her,
1Ch 8: 8 after he had *d* his wives Hushim
Eze 44:22 not marry widows or *d* women;
Mt 5:32 marries the *d* woman commits adultery.
Lk 16:18 who marries a *d* woman commits

DIVORCES* (DIVORCE)
Jer 3: 1 "If a man *d* his wife
Mt 5:31 'Anyone who *d* his wife must give
5:32 tell you that anyone who *d* his wife,
19: 9 tell you that anyone who *d* his wife,
Mk 10:11 "Anyone who *d* his wife
10:12 And if she *d* her husband
Lk 16:18 "Anyone who *d* his wife

DOCTOR
Mt 9:12 "It is not the healthy who need a *d,*

DOCTRINE* (DOCTRINES)
1Ti 1:10 to the sound of *d* that conforms
4:16 Watch your life and *d* closely.
2Ti 4: 3 men will not put up with sound *d.*
Tit 1: 9 can encourage others by sound *d*
2: 1 is in accord with sound *d.*

DOCTRINES* (DOCTRINE)
1Ti 1: 3 not to teach false *d* any longer
6: 3 If anyone teaches false *d*

DOEG*
Edomite; Saul's head shepherd; responsible for murder of priests at Nob (1Sa 21:7; 22:6–23; Ps 52).

DOG (DOGS)
Pr 26:11 As a *d* returns to its vomit,
Ecc 9: 4 a live *d* is better off than a dead lion
2Pe 2:22 "A *d* returns to its vomit," and,

DOGS (DOG)
Mt 7: 6 "Do not give *d* what is sacred;
15:26 bread and toss it to their *d.*"

DOMINION
Job 25: 2 "*D* and awe belong to God;
Ps 22:28 for *d* belongs to the LORD

DONKEY
Nu 22:30 *d* said to Balaam, "Am I not your
Zec 9: 9 gentle and riding on a *d,*
Mt 21: 5 gentle and riding on a *d,*
2Pe 2:16 for his wrongdoing by a *d*—

DOOR (DOORS)
Job 31:32 for my *d* was always open
Ps 141: 3 keep watch over the *d* of my lips.
Mt 6: 6 close the *d* and pray to your Father
7: 7 and the *d* will be opened to you.
Ac 14:27 how he had opened the *d* of faith
1Co 16: 9 a great *d* for effective work has
2Co 2:12 found that the Lord had opened a *d*
Rev 3:20 I stand at the *d* and knock.

DOORFRAMES
Dt 6: 9 Write them on the *d* of your houses

DOORKEEPER
Ps 84:10 I would rather be a *d* in the house

DOORS (DOOR)
Ps 24: 7 be lifted up, you ancient *d,*

DORCAS
Ac 9:36 is *D),* who was always doing good

DOUBLE
2Ki 2: 9 "Let me inherit a *d* portion
1Ti 5:17 church well are worthy of *d* honor,

DOUBLE-EDGED (EDGE)
Heb 4:12 Sharper than any *d* sword,
Rev 1:16 of his mouth came a sharp *d* sword.
2:12 of him who has the sharp, *d* sword.

DOUBLE-MINDED* (MIND)
Ps 119:113 I hate *d* men,
Jas 1: 8 he is a *d* man, unstable
4: 8 and purify your hearts, you *d.*

DOUBT (DOUBTING DOUBTS)
Mt 14:31 he said, "why did you *d?*"
21:21 if you have faith and do not *d,*
Mk 11:23 and does not *d* in his heart
Jas 1: 6 he must believe and not *d,*
Jude :22 Be merciful to those who *d;*

DOUBTING* (DOUBT)
Jn 20:27 Stop *d* and believe."

DOUBTS* (DOUBT)
Lk 24:38 and why do *d* rise in your minds?
Ro 14:23 the man who has *d* is condemned
Jas 1: 6 he who *d* is like a wave of the sea,

DOVE (DOVES)
Ge 8: 8 Then he sent out a *d* to see
Mt 3:16 Spirit of God descending like a *d*

DOVES (DOVE)
Lev 12: 8 is to bring two *d* or two young
Mt 10:16 as snakes and as innocent as *d.*
Lk 2:24 "a pair of *d* or two young pigeons."

DOWNCAST
Ps 42: 5 Why are you *d,* O my soul?
2Co 7: 6 But God, who comforts the *d,*

DOWNFALL
Hos 14: 1 Your sins have been your *d!*

DRAGON
Rev 12: 7 and his angels fought against the *d,*
13: 2 The *d* gave the beast his power
20: 2 He seized the *d,* that ancient

DRAW (DRAWING DRAWS)
Mt 26:52 "for all who *d* the sword will die
Jn 12:32 up from the earth, will *d* all men
Heb 10:22 let us *d* near to God

DRAWING (DRAW)
Lk 21:28 because your redemption is *d* near

DRAWS (DRAW)
Jn 6:44 the Father who sent me *d* him,

DREAD (DREADFUL)
Ps 53: 5 they were, overwhelmed with *d,*

DREADFUL (DREAD)
Mt 24:19 How *d* it will be in those days
Heb 10:31 It is a *d* thing to fall into the hands

DREAM
Joel 2:28 your old men will *d* dreams,
Ac 2:17 your old men will *d* dreams.

DRESS
1Ti 2: 9 I also want women to *d* modestly,

DRIFT*
Heb 2: 1 so that we do not *d* away.

DRINK (DRINKING DRINKS DRUNK DRUNKARD DRUNKARD'S DRUNKARDS DRUNKENNESS)
Ex 29:40 of a hin of wine as a *d* offering.
Nu 6: 3 He must not *d* grape juice
Jdg 7: 5 from those who kneel down to *d.*"
2Sa 23:15 that someone would get me a *d*
Pr 5:15 *D* water from your own cistern,
Mt 20:22 "Can you *d* the cup I am going to *d*
26:27 saying, "*D* from it, all of you.
Mk 16:18 and when they *d* deadly poison,
Lk 12:19 Take life easy; eat, *d* and be merry
Jn 7:37 let him come to me and *d.*
18:11 Shall I not *d* the cup the Father has
1Co 10: 4 and drank the same spiritual *d;*
12:13 were all given the one Spirit to *d.*
Php 2:17 being poured out like a *d* offering
2Ti 4: 6 being poured out like a *d* offering,
Rev 14:10 too, will *d* of the wine of God's fury
21: 6 to *d* without cost from the spring

DRINKING (DRINK)
Ro 14:17 God is not a matter of eating and *d,*

DRINKS (DRINK)
Isa 5:22 and champions at mixing *d,*
Jn 4:13 "Everyone who *d* this water will be
6:54 and *d* my blood has eternal life,
1Co 11:27 or *d* the cup of the Lord

DRIPPING
Pr 19:13 wife is like a constant *d.*
27:15 a constant *d* on a rainy day;

DRIVE (DRIVES)
Ex 23:30 Little by little I will *d* them out
Nu 33:52 *d* out all the inhabitants of the land
Jos 13:13 Israelites did not *d* out the people
23:13 will no longer *d* out these nations
Pr 22:10 *D* out the mocker, and out goes
Mt 10: 1 authority to *d* out evil spirits
Jn 6:37 comes to me I will never *d* away.

DRIVES (DRIVE)
Mt 12:26 If Satan *d* out Satan, he is divided
1Jn 4:18 But perfect love *d* out fear,

DROP (DROPS)
Pr 17:14 so *d* the matter before a dispute
Isa 40:15 Surely the nations are like a *d*

DROPS (DROP)
Lk 22:44 his sweat was like *d* of blood falling

DROSS
Ps 119:119 of the earth you discard like *d;*
Pr 25: 4 Remove the *d* from the silver,

DROUGHT
Jer 17: 8 It has no worries in a year of *d*

DROWNED
Ex 15: 4 are *d* in the Red Sea.
Mt 18: 6 and to be *d* in the depths of the sea.
Heb 11:29 tried to do so, they were *d.*

DROWSINESS*
Pr 23:21 and *d* clothes them in rags.

DRUNK (DRINK)
1Sa 1:13 Eli thought she was *d* and said
Ac 2:15 men are not *d,* as you suppose.
Eph 5:18 Do not get *d* on wine, which leads

DRUNKARD (DRINK)
Mt 11:19 and a *d,* a friend of tax collectors
1Co 5:11 or a slanderer, a *d* or a swindler.

DRUNKARD'S* (DRINK)
Pr 26: 9 Like a thornbush in a *d* hand

DRUNKARDS (DRINK)
Pr 23:21 for *d* and gluttons become poor,
1Co 6:10 nor the greedy nor *d* nor slanderers

DRUNKENNESS (DRINK)
Lk 21:34 weighed down with dissipation, *d*
Ro 13:13 and *d,* not in sexual immorality
Gal 5:21 factions and envy; *d,* orgies,
1Ti 3: 3 not given to *d,* not violent
1Pe 4: 3 living in debauchery, lust, *d,* orgies,

DRY
Ge 1: 9 place, and let *d* ground appear."
Ex 14:16 go through the sea on *d* ground.
Jos 3:17 the crossing on *d* ground.
Isa 53: 2 and like a root out of *d* ground.
Eze 37: 4 '*D* bones, hear the word

DULL
Isa 6:10 make their ears *d*
2Co 3:14 But their minds were made *d,*

DUST
Ge 2: 7 man from the *d* of the ground
3:19 for *d* you are
Job 42: 6 and repent in *d* and ashes."
Ps 22:15 you lay me in the *d* of death.
103: 14 he remembers that we are *d.*
Ecc 3:20 all come from *d,* and to *d* all return.
Mt 10:14 shake the *d* off your feet
1Co 15:47 was of the *d* of the earth,

DUTIES (DUTY)
2Ti 4: 5 discharge all the *d* of your ministry

DUTY (DUTIES)
Ecc 12:13 for this is the whole *d* of man.
Ac 23: 1 I have fulfilled my *d* to God
1Co 7: 3 husband should fulfill his marital *d*

DWELL (DWELLING DWELLINGS DWELLS DWELT)
Ex 25: 8 for me, and I will *d* among them.
2Sa 7: 5 the one to build me a house to *d* in?
1Ki 8:27 "But will God really *d* on earth?
Ps 23: 6 I will *d* in the house of the LORD
37: 3 *d* in the land and enjoy safe pasture
61: 4 I long to *d* in your tent forever
Pr 8:12 wisdom, *d* together with prudence;
Isa 33:14 of us can *d* with the consuming fire
43:18 do not *d* on the past.
Jn 5:38 nor does his word *d* in you,
Eph 3:17 so that Christ may *d* in your hearts
Col 1:19 to have all his fullness *d* in him,
3:16 the word of Christ *d* in you richly

DWELLING (DWELL)
Lev 26:11 I will put my *d* place among you,
Dt 26:15 from heaven, your holy *d* place,
Ps 90: 1 Lord, you have been our *d* place
2Co 5: 2 to be clothed with our heavenly *d,*
Eph 2:22 to become a *d* in which God lives

DWELLINGS (DWELL)
Lk 16: 9 will be welcomed into eternal *d.*

DWELLS (DWELL)
Ps 46: 4 holy place where the Most High *d.*
91: 1 He who *d* in the shelter

DWELT (DWELL)
Dt 33:16 of him who *d* in the burning bush.

DYING (DIE)
Ro 7: 6 by *d* to what once bound us,
2Co 6: 9 yet regarded as unknown; *d,*

EAGER
Pr 31:13 and works with *e* hands.
Ro 8:19 The creation waits in *e* expectation

1Co 14:12 Since you are *e* to have spiritual
14:39 my brothers, be *e* to prophesy,
Tit 2:14 a people that are his very own, *e*
1Pe 5:2 greedy for money, but *e* to serve;

EAGLE (EAGLE'S EAGLES)
Dt 32:11 like an *e* that stirs up its nest
Eze 1:10 each also had the face of an *e*.
Rev 4:7 the fourth was like a flying *e*.
12:14 given the two wings of a great *e*,

EAGLE'S (EAGLE)
Ps 103:5 your youth is renewed like the *e*.

EAGLES (EAGLE)
Isa 40:31 They will soar on wings like *e*;

EAR (EARS)
Ex 21:6 and pierce his *e* with an awl.
Ps 5:1 Give *e* to my words, O LORD,
Pr 2:2 turning your *e* to wisdom
1Co 2:9 no *e* has heard,
12:16 if the *e* should say, "Because I am
Rev 2:7 He who has an *e*, let him hear what

EARN (EARNED EARNINGS)
2Th 3:12 down and *e* the bread they eat.

EARNED (EARN)
Pr 31:31 Give her the reward she has *e*,

EARNESTNESS
2Co 7:11 what *e*, what eagerness
8:7 in complete *e* and in your love

EARNINGS (EARN)
Pr 31:16 out of her *e* she plants a vineyard.

EARRING (EARRINGS)
Pr 25:12 Like an *e* of gold or an ornament

EARRINGS (EARRING)
Ex 32:2 Take off the gold *e* that your wives,

EARS (EAR)
Job 42:5 My *e* had heard of you
Ps 34:15 and his *e* are attentive to their cry;
Pr 21:13 If a man shuts his *e* to the cry
26:17 Like one who seizes a dog by the *e*
Isa 6:10 hear with their *e*,
Mt 11:15 He who has *e*, let him hear.
2Ti 4:3 to say what their itching *e* want
1Pe 3:12 his *e* are attentive to their prayer,

EARTH (EARTH'S EARTHLY)
Ge 1:1 God created the heavens and the *e*.
1:2 Now the *e* was formless and empty,
7:24 The waters flooded the *e*
14:19 Creator of heaven and *e*.
1Ki 8:27 "But will God really dwell on *e*?
Job 26:7 he suspends the *e* over nothing.
Ps 24:1 *e* is the LORD's, and everything
46:6 he lifts his voice, the *e* melts.
90:2 or you brought forth the *e*
97:5 before the Lord of all the *e*.
102:25 you laid the foundations of the *e*,
108:5 and let your glory be over all the *e*.
Pr 8:26 before he made the *e* or its fields
Isa 6:3 the whole *e* is full of his glory."
24:20 The *e* reels like a drunkard,
37:16 You have made heaven and *e*.
40:22 enthroned above the circle of the *e*,
51:6 the *e* will wear out like a garment
54:5 he is called the God of all the *e*.
55:9 the heavens are higher than the *e*,
65:17 new heavens and a new *e*.
66:1 and the *e* is my footstool.
Jer 10:10 When he is angry, the *e* trembles;
23:24 "Do not I fill heaven and *e*?"
33:25 and the fixed laws of heaven and *e*,
Hab 2:20 let all the *e* be silent before him."
Mt 5:5 for they will inherit the *e*.
5:35 or by the *e*, for it is his footstool;
6:10 done on *e* as it is in heaven.
16:19 bind on *e* will be bound
24:35 Heaven and *e* will pass away,
28:18 and on *e* has been given to me.
Lk 2:14 on *e* peace to men
Jn 12:32 when I am lifted up from the *e*,
Ac 4:24 "you made the heaven and the *e*
7:49 and the *e* is my footstool.
1Co 10:26 The *e* is the Lord's, and everything
Eph 3:15 in heaven and on *e* derives its name
Php 2:10 in heaven and on *e* and under the *e*,
Heb 1:10 you laid the foundations of the *e*,
2Pe 3:13 to a new heaven and a new *e*,
Rev 8:7 A third of the *e* was burned up,
12:12 But woe to the *e* and the sea,
20:11 *E* and sky fled from his presence,
21:1 I saw a new heaven and a new *e*,
21:1 and the first *e* had passed away,

EARTH'S (EARTH)
Job 38:4 when I laid the *e* foundation?

EARTHENWARE
Pr 26:23 Like a coating of glaze over *e*

EARTHLY (EARTH)
Eph 4:9 descended to the lower, *e* regions?
Php 3:19 Their mind is on *e* things.
Col 3:2 on things above, not on *e* things.
3:5 whatever belongs to your *e* nature:

EARTHQUAKE (EARTHQUAKES)
Eze 38:19 at that time there shall be a great *e*
Mt 28:2 There was a violent *e*, for an angel
Rev 6:12 There was a great *e*.

EARTHQUAKES (EARTHQUAKE)
Mt 24:7 There will be famines and *e*

EASE
Pr 1:33 and be at *e*, without fear of harm."

EASIER (EASY)
Lk 16:17 It is *e* for heaven and earth
18:25 it is *e* for a camel to go

EAST
Ge 2:8 God had planted a garden in the *e*,
Ps 103:12 as far as the *e* is from the west,
Eze 43:2 God of Israel coming from the *e*.
Mt 2:1 Magi from the *e* came to Jerusalem
2:2 We saw his star in the *e*

EASY (EASIER)
Mt 11:30 For my yoke is *e* and my burden is

EAT (ATE EATEN EATER EATING EATS)
Ge 2:16 "You are free to *e* from any tree
2:17 but you must not *e* from the tree
3:19 you will *e* your food
Ex 12:11 *E* it in haste; it is the LORD's
Lev 11:2 these are the ones you may *e*:
17:12 "None of you may *e* blood,
Dt 8:16 He gave you manna to *e*
14:4 These are the animals you may *e*:
Jdg 14:14 "Out of the eater, something to *e*;
2Sa 9:7 and you will always *e* at my table."
Pr 31:27 and does not *e* the bread of idleness
Isa 55:1 come, buy and *e*!
65:25 and the lion will *e* straw like the ox,
Eze 3:1 *e* what is before you, *e* this scroll;
Mt 14:16 You give them something to *e*."
15:2 wash their hands before they *e*!"
26:26 "Take and *e*; this is my body."
Mk 14:14 where I may *e* the Passover
Lk 10:8 and are welcomed, *e* what is set
12:19 Take life easy; *e*, drink
12:22 what you will *e*; or about your body
Jn 4:32 to *e* that you know nothing about."
6:31 bread from heaven to *e*.'"
6:52 can this man give us his flesh to *e*?"
Ac 10:13 Kill and *e*."
Ro 14:2 faith allows him to *e* everything,
14:15 is distressed because of what you *e*,
14:20 to *e* anything that causes someone
14:21 It is better not to *e* meat
1Co 5:11 With such a man do not even *e*.
8:13 if what I *e* causes my brother to fall
10:25 *E* anything sold in the meat market
10:27 *e* whatever is put before you
10:31 So whether you *e* or drink
11:26 For whenever you *e* this bread
2Th 3:10 man will not work, he shall not *e*."
Rev 2:7 the right to *e* from the tree of life,
3:20 I will come in and *e* with him,

EATEN (EAT)
Ge 3:11 Have you *e* from the tree that I
Ac 10:14 "I have never *e* anything impure
Rev 10:10 when I had *e* it, my stomach turned

EATER (EAT)
Isa 55:10 for the sower and bread for the *e*,

EATING (EAT)
Ex 34:28 and forty nights without *e* bread
Ro 14:15 not by your *e* destroy your brother
14:17 kingdom of God is not a matter of *e*
14:23 because his *e* is not from faith;
1Co 8:4 about *e* food sacrificed to idols:
8:10 you who have this knowledge *e*
Jude :12 *e* with you without the slightest

EATS (EAT)
1Sa 14:24 "Cursed be any man who *e* food
Lk 15:2 "This man welcomes sinners and *e*
Jn 6:51 If anyone *e* of this bread, he will live
6:54 Whoever *e* my flesh and drinks my
Ro 14:2 faith is weak, *e* only vegetables.
14:3 man who *e* everything must not
14:6 He who *e* meat, *e* to the Lord,
14:23 has doubts is condemned if he *e*,
1Co 11:27 whoever *e* the bread or drinks

EBAL
Dt 11:29 and on Mount *E* the curses.
Jos 8:30 Joshua built on Mount *E* an altar

EBENEZER
1Sa 7:12 He named it *E*, saying, "Thus far

EDEN
Ge 2:8 in *E*; and there he put the man
Eze 28:13 You were in *E*,

EDGE (DOUBLE-EDGED)
Mt 9:20 and touched the *e* of his cloak.

EDICT
Heb 11:23 they were not afraid of the king's *e*.

EDIFICATION (EDIFIED EDIFIES)
Ro 14:19 leads to peace and to mutual *e*.

EDIFIED* (EDIFICATION)
1Co 14:5 so that the church may be *e*.
14:17 but the other man is not *e*.

EDIFIES* (EDIFICATION)
1Co 14:4 but he who prophesies *e* the church
14:4 speaks in a tongue *e* himself,

EDOM
Ge 36:1 the account of Esau (that is, *E*).
36:8 *E*) settled in the hill country of Seir
Isa 63:1 Who is this coming from *E*,
Ob :1 Sovereign LORD says about *E*—

EDUCATED*
Ac 7:22 Moses was *e* in all the wisdom

EFFECT* (EFFECTIVE)
Job 41:26 sword that reaches him has no *e*,
Isa 32:17 *e* of righteousness will be quietness
Ac 7:53 put into *e* through angels
1Co 15:10 his grace to me was not without *e*.
Gal 3:19 put into *e* through angels
Eph 1:10 put into *e* when the times will have
Heb 9:17 it never takes *e* while the one who
9:18 put into *e* without blood.

EFFECTIVE* (EFFECT)
1Co 16:9 a great door for *e* work has opened
Jas 5:16 a righteous man is powerful and *e*.

EFFORT*
Ecc 2:19 into which I have poured my *e*
Da 6:14 and made every *e* until sundown
Lk 13:24 "Make every *e* to enter
Jn 5:44 yet make no *e* to obtain the praise
Ro 9:16 depend on man's desire or *e*,
14:19 make every *e* to do what leads
Gal 3:3 to attain your goal by human *e*?
Eph 4:3 Make every *e* to keep the unity
1Th 2:16 to all men in their *e* to keep us
2:17 intense longing we made every *e*.
Heb 4:11 make every *e* to enter that rest,
12:14 Make every *e* to live in peace
2Pe 1:5 make every *e* to add
1:15 And I will make every *e* to see that
3:14 make every *e* to be found spotless,

EGG
Lk 11:12 for an *e*, will give him a scorpion?

EGLON
1. Fat king of Moab killed by Ehud (Jdg 3:12–30).
2. City in Canaan (Jos 10).

EGYPT (EGYPTIANS)
Ge 12:10 went down to *E* to live there
37:28 Ishmaelites, who took him to *E*.
42:3 went down to buy grain from *E*.
45:20 the best of all *E* will be yours.'
46:6 and all his offspring went to *E*.
47:27 Now the Israelites settled in *E*

Ex 3:11 and bring the Israelites out of *E?*"
12:40 lived in *E* was 430 years.
12:41 all the LORD's divisions left *E.*
32:1 Moses who brought us up out of *E,*
Nu 11:18 We were better off in *E!*"
14:4 choose a leader and go back to *E.*"
24:8 "God brought them out of *E;*
Dt 6:21 "We were slaves of Pharaoh in *E,*
1Ki 4:30 greater than all the wisdom of *E.*
10:28 horses were imported from *E*
11:40 but Jeroboam fled to *E,*
14:25 king of *E* attacked Jerusalem.
2Ch 35:20 Neco king of *E* went up to fight
36:3 The king of *E* dethroned him
Isa 19:23 a highway from *E* to Assyria.
Hos 11:1 and out of *E* I called my son.
Mt 2:15 "Out of *E* I called my son."
Heb 11:27 By faith he left *E,* not fearing
Rev 11:8 is figuratively called Sodom and *E,*

EGYPTIANS (EGYPT)
Nu 14:13 "Then the *E* will hear about it!

EHUD
Left-handed judge who delivered Israel from Moabite king, Eglon (Jdg 3:12–30).

EKRON
1Sa 5:10 So they sent the ark of God to *E.*

ELAH
Son of Baasha; king of Israel (1Ki 16:6–14).

ELATION
Pr 28:12 righteous triumph, there is great *e;*

ELDER* (ELDERLY ELDERS)
Isa 3:2 the soothsayer and *e,*
1Ti 5:19 an accusation against an *e*
Tit 1:6 *e* must be blameless, the husband
1Pe 5:1 among you, I appeal as a fellow *e,*
2Jn :1 The *e,* To the chosen lady
3Jn :1 The *e,* To my dear friend Gaius,

ELDERLY* (ELDER)
Lev 19:32 show respect for the *e*

ELDERS (ELDER)
1Ki 12:8 rejected the advice the *e* gave him
Mt 15:2 break the tradition of the *e?*
Mk 7:3 holding to the tradition of the *e.*
7:5 to the tradition of the *e* instead
Ac 11:30 gift to the *e* by Barnabas
14:23 and Barnabas appointed *e* for them
15:2 the apostles and *e* about this
15:4 the church and the apostles and *e,*
15:6 and *e* met to consider this question.
15:22 and *e,* with the whole church,
15:23 The apostles and *e,* your brothers,
16:4 and *e* in Jerusalem for the people
20:17 to Ephesus for the *e* of the church.
21:18 and all the *e* were present.
23:14 They went to the chief priests and *e*
24:1 to Caesarea with some of the *e*
1Ti 4:14 when the body of *e* laid their hands
5:17 The *e* who direct the affairs
Tit 1:5 and appoint *e* in every town,
Jas 5:14 He should call the *e* of the church
1Pe 5:1 To the *e* among you, I appeal
Rev 4:4 seated on them were twenty-four *e.*
4:10 the twenty-four *e* fall

ELEAZAR
Third son of Aaron (Ex 6:23–25). Succeeded Aaron as high priest (Nu 20:26; Dt 10:6). Allotted land to tribes (Jos 14:1). Death (Jos 24:33).

ELECT* (ELECTION)
Mt 24:22 the sake of the *e* those days will be
24:24 miracles to deceive even the *e*—
24:31 and they will gather his *e*
Mk 13:20 sake of the *e,* whom he has chosen,
13:22 and miracles to deceive the *e*—
13:27 gather his *e* from the four winds,
Ro 11:7 it did not obtain, but the *e* did.
1Ti 5:21 and Christ Jesus and the *e* angels,
2Ti 2:10 everything for the sake of the *e,*
Tit 1:1 Christ for the faith of God's *e*
1Pe 1:1 To God's *e,* strangers in the world,

ELECTION* (ELECT)
Ro 9:11 God's purpose in *e* might stand:
11:28 but as far as *e* is concerned,
2Pe 1:10 to make your calling and *e* sure.

ELEMENTARY* (ELEMENTS)
Heb 5:12 someone to teach you the *e* truths
6:1 us leave the *e* teachings about

ELEMENTS* (ELEMENTARY)
2Pe 3:10 the *e* will be destroyed by fire,
3:12 and the *e* will melt in the heat.

ELEVATE*
2Co 11:7 to *e* you by preaching the gospel

ELI
High priest in youth of Samuel (1Sa 1–4). Blessed Hannah (1Sa 1:12–18); raised Samuel (1Sa 2:11–26). Prophesied against because of wicked sons (1Sa 2:27–36). Death of Eli and sons (1Sa 4:11–22).

ELIHU
One of Job's friends (Job 32–37).

ELIJAH
Prophet; predicted famine in Israel (1Ki 17:1; Jas 5:17). Fed by ravens (1Ki 17:2–6). Raised Sidonian widow's son (1Ki 17:7–24). Defeated prophets of Baal at Carmel (1Ki 18:16–46). Ran from Jezebel (1Ki 19:1–9). Prophesied death of Azariah (2Ki 1). Succeeded by Elishah (1Ki 19:19–21; 2Ki 2:1–18). Taken to heaven in whirlwind (2Ki 2:11–12).
Return prophesied (Mal 4:5–6); equated with John the Baptist (Mt 17:9–13; Mk 9:9–13; Lk 1:17). Appeared with Moses in transfiguration of Jesus (Mt 17:1–8; Mk 9:1–8).

ELIMELECH
Ru 1:3 Now *E,* Naomi's husband, died,

ELIPHAZ
1. Firstborn of Esau (Ge 36).
2. One of Job's friends (Job 4–5; 15; 22).

ELISHA
Prophet; successor of Elijah (1Ki 19:16–21); inherited his cloak (2Ki 2:1–18). Purified bad water (2Ki 2:19–22). Cursed young men (2Ki 2:23–25). Aided Israel's defeat of Moab (2Ki 3). Provided widow with oil (2Ki 4:1–7). Raised Shunammite woman's son (2Ki 4:8–37). Purified food (2Ki 4:38–41). Fed 100 men (2Ki 4:42–44). Healed Naaman's leprosy (2Ki 5). Made axhead float (2Ki 6:1–7). Captured Arameans (2Ki 6:8–23). Political adviser to Israel (2Ki 6:24–8:6; 9:1–3; 13:14–19), Damascus (2Ki 8:7–15). Death (2Ki 13:20).

ELIZABETH*
Mother of John the Baptist, relative of Mary (Lk 1:5–58).

ELKANAH
Husband of Hannah, father of Samuel (1Sa 1–2).

ELOI*
Mt 27:46 *"E, E, lama sabachthani?"*—
Mk 15:34 *"E, E, lama sabachthani?"*—

ELOQUENCE* (ELOQUENT)
1Co 2:1 come with *e* or superior wisdom

ELOQUENT* (ELOQUENCE)
Ex 4:10 "O Lord, I have never been *e,*

ELYMAS
Ac 13:8 *E* the sorcerer (for that is what his

EMBEDDED*
Ecc 12:11 sayings like firmly *e* nails—

EMBERS
Pr 26:21 As charcoal to *e* and as wood to fire

EMBITTER* (BITTER)
Col 3:21 Fathers, do not *e* your children,

EMBODIMENT* (BODY)
Ro 2:20 have in the law the *e* of knowledge

EMPTIED (EMPTY)
1Co 1:17 the cross of Christ be *e* of its power.

EMPTY (EMPTIED)
Ge 1:2 Now the earth was formless and *e,*
Job 26:7 the northern ⌞skies⌟ over *e* space;
Isa 45:18 he did not create it to be *e,*
55:11 It will not return to me *e,*
Jer 4:23 and it was formless and *e;*
Lk 1:53 but has sent the rich away *e.*

Eph 5:6 no one deceive you with *e* words,
1Pe 1:18 from the *e* way of life handed
2Pe 2:18 For they mouth *e,* boastful words

ENABLE (ABLE)
Lk 1:74 to *e* us to serve him without fear
Ac 4:29 *e* your servants to speak your word

ENABLED* (ABLE)
Lev 26:13 *e* you to walk with heads held high.
Ru 4:13 And the LORD *e* her to conceive,
Jn 6:65 unless the Father has *e* him."
Ac 2:4 other tongues as the Spirit *e* them.
7:10 and *e* him to gain the goodwill
Heb 11:11 was *e* to become a father

ENABLES (ABLE)
Php 3:21 by the power that *e* him

ENABLING* (ABLE)
Ac 14:3 the message of his grace by *e* them

ENCAMPS* (CAMP)
Ps 34:7 The angel of the LORD *e*

ENCOURAGE* (ENCOURAGED ENCOURAGEMENT ENCOURAGES ENCOURAGING)
Dt 1:38 *E* him, because he will lead Israel
3:28 and *e* and strengthen him,
2Sa 11:25 Say this to *e* Joab."
19:7 Now go out and *e* your men.
Job 16:5 But my mouth would *e* you;
Ps 10:17 you *e* them, and you listen
64:5 They *e* each other in evil plans,
Isa 1:17 *e* the oppressed.
Jer 29:8 to the dreams you *e* them to have.
Ac 15:32 to *e* and strengthen the brothers.
Ro 12:8 if it is encouraging, let him *e;*
Eph 6:22 how we are, and that he may *e* you.
Col 4:8 and that he may *e* your hearts.
1Th 3:2 to strengthen and *e* you
4:18 Therefore *e* each other
5:11 Therefore *e* one another
5:14 those who are idle, *e* the timid,
2Th 2:17 *e* your hearts and strengthen you
2Ti 4:2 rebuke and *e*—with great patience
Tit 1:9 so that he can *e* others
2:6 *e* the young men to be
2:15 *E* and rebuke with all authority.
Heb 3:13 But *e* one another daily, as long
10:25 but let us *e* one another—

ENCOURAGED* (ENCOURAGE)
Jdg 7:11 you will be *e* to attack the camp."
20:22 But the men of Israel *e* one another
2Ch 22:3 for his mother *e* him
32:6 and *e* them with these words:
35:2 and *e* them in the service
Eze 13:22 you *e* the wicked not to turn
Ac 9:31 It was strengthened; and *e*
11:23 and *e* them all to remain true
16:40 met with the brothers and *e* them.
18:27 the brothers *e* him and wrote
27:36 They were all *e* and ate some food
28:15 men Paul thanked God and was *e.*
Ro 1:12 and I may be mutually *e*
1Co 14:31 everyone may be instructed and *e.*
2Co 7:4 I am greatly *e;* in all our troubles
7:13 By all this we are *e.*
Php 1:14 brothers in the Lord have been *e*
Col 2:2 My purpose is that they may be *e*
1Th 3:7 persecution we were *e* about you
Heb 6:18 offered to us may be greatly *e.*

ENCOURAGEMENT* (ENCOURAGE)
Ac 4:36 Barnabas (which means Son of *E),*
13:15 a message of *e* for the people,
20:2 speaking many words of *e*
Ro 15:4 *e* of the Scriptures we might have
15:5 and *e* give you a spirit of unity
1Co 14:3 to men for their strengthening, *e*
2Co 7:13 to our own *e,* we were especially
Php 2:1 If you have any *e* from being united
2Th 2:16 and by his grace gave us eternal *e*
Phm :7 love has given me great joy and *e,*
Heb 12:5 word of *e* that addresses you

ENCOURAGES* (ENCOURAGE)
Isa 41:7 The craftsman *e* the goldsmith,

ENCOURAGING* (ENCOURAGE)
Ac 14:22 *e* them to remain true to the faith.
15:31 and were glad for its *e* message.
20:1 for the disciples and, after *e* them,

Ro 12: 8 if it is *e,* let him encourage;
1Th 2:12 *e,* comforting and urging you
1Pe 5:12 *e* you and testifying that this is

ENCROACH
Pr 23:10 or *e* on the fields of the fatherless,

END (ENDS)
Ps 119: 33 then I will keep them to the *e.*
119:112 to the very *e.*
Pr 1:19 Such is the *e* of all who go
5: 4 but in the *e* she is bitter as gall,
5:11 At the *e* of your life you will groan,
14:12 but in the *e* it leads to death.
14:13 and joy may *e* in grief.
16:25 but in the *e* it leads to death.
19:20 and in the *e* you will be wise.
20:21 will not be blessed at the *e.*
23:32 In the *e* it bites like a snake
25: 8 for what will you do in the *e*
28:23 in the *e* gain more favor
29:21 he will bring grief in the *e.*
Ecc 3:11 done from beginning to *e.*
7: 8 The *e* of a matter is better
12:12 making many books there is no *e,*
Eze 7: 2 The *e!* The *e* has come
Mt 10:22 firm to the *e* will be saved.
24:13 firm to the *e* will be saved.
24:14 nations, and then the *e* will come.
Lk 21: 9 but the *e* will not come right away
Ro 10: 4 Christ is the *e* of the law
1Co 15:24 the *e* will come, when he hands
Rev 21: 6 Omega, the Beginning and the *E.*
22:13 the Last, the Beginning and the *E.*

ENDS (END)
Ps 19: 4 their words to the *e* of the world.
Pr 20:17 he *e* up with a mouth full of gravel.
Isa 49: 6 salvation to the *e* of the earth."
62:11 proclamation to the *e* of the earth:
Ac 13:47 salvation to the *e* of the earth.' "
Ro 10:18 their words to the *e* of the world."

ENDURANCE* (ENDURE)
Ro 15: 4 through *e* and the encouragement
15: 5 May the God who gives *e*
2Co 1: 6 which produces in you patient *e*
6: 4 in great *e;* in troubles, hardships
Col 1:11 might so that you may have great *e*
1Th 1: 3 and your *e* inspired by hope
1Ti 6:11 faith, love, *e* and gentleness.
2Ti 3:10 patience, love, *e,* persecutions,
Tit 2: 2 and sound in faith, in love and in *e.*
Rev 1: 9 and patient *e* that are ours in Jesus,
13:10 This calls for patient *e*
14:12 This calls for patient *e* on the part

ENDURE (ENDURANCE ENDURED ENDURES ENDURING)
Ps 72:17 May his name *e* forever;
Pr 12:19 Truthful lips *e* forever,
27:24 for riches do not *e* forever,
Ecc 3:14 everything God does will *e* forever;
Da 2:44 to an end, but it will itself *e* forever.
Mal 3: 2 who can *e* the day of his coming?
1Co 4:12 when we are persecuted, we *e* it;
2Co 1: 8 far beyond our ability to *e,*
2Ti 2: 3 *E* hardship with us like a good
2:10 Therefore I *e* everything
2:12 if we *e,* / we will also reign
4: 5 head in all situations, *e* hardship,
Heb 12: 7 *E* hardship as discipline; God is
1Pe 2:20 a beating for doing wrong and *e* it?
2:20 suffer for doing good and you *e* it,
Rev 3:10 kept my command to *e* patiently,

ENDURED* (ENDURE)
Ps 123: 3 for we have *e* much contempt.
123: 4 We have *e* much ridicule
132: 1 and all the hardships he *e.*
Ac 13:18 and *e* their conduct forty years
2Ti 3:11 and Lystra, the persecutions I *e.*
Heb 12: 2 set before him *e* the cross,
12: 3 him who *e* such opposition
Rev 2: 3 and have *e* hardships for my name,

ENDURES (ENDURE)
Ps 102: 12 renown *e* through all generations.
112: 9 his righteousness *e* forever;
136: 1 *His love e forever.*
Da 9:15 made for yourself a name that *e*
2Co 9: 9 his righteousness *e* forever."

ENDURING (ENDURE)
2Th 1: 4 persecutions and trials you are *e.*
1Pe 1:23 through the living and *e* word

ENEMIES (ENEMY)
Ps 23: 5 in the presence of my *e.*
110: 1 hand until I make your *e*
Pr 16: 7 his *e* live at peace with him.
Isa 59:18 wrath to his *e*
Mic 7: 6 a man's *e* are the members
Mt 5:44 Love your *e* and pray
10:36 a man's *e* will be the members
Lk 6:27 Love your *e,* do good
6:35 But love your *e,* do good to them,
20:43 hand until I make your *e*
Ro 5:10 For if, when we were God's *e,*
1Co 15:25 reign until he has put all his *e*
Php 3:18 many live as *e* of the cross of Christ
Heb 1:13 hand until I make your *e*
10:13 for his *e* to be made his footstool,

ENEMY (ENEMIES ENMITY)
Pr 24:17 Do not gloat when your *e* falls;
25:21 If your *e* is hungry, give him food
27: 6 but an *e* multiplies kisses.
29:24 of a thief is his own *e;*
Lk 10:19 to overcome all the power of the *e;*
Ro 12:20 "If your *e* is hungry, feed him;
1Co 15:26 The last *e* to be destroyed is death.
1Ti 5:14 and to give the *e* no opportunity
1Pe 5: 8 Your *e* the devil prowls

ENERGY*
Col 1:29 struggling with all his *e,* which

ENGRAVED
Isa 49:16 I have *e* you on the palms
2Co 3: 7 which was *e* in letters on stone,

ENHANCES*
Ro 3: 7 my falsehood *e* God's truthfulness

ENJOY (JOY)
Dt 6: 2 and so that you may *e* long life.
Ps 37: 3 dwell in the land and *e* safe pasture.
Pr 28:16 ill-gotten gain will *e* a long life.
Ecc 3:22 better for a man than to *e* his work,
Eph 6: 3 and that you may *e* long life
Heb 11:25 rather than to *e* the pleasures of sin
3Jn : 2 I pray that you may *e* good health

ENJOYMENT (JOY)
Ecc 4: 8 and why am I depriving myself of *e*
1Ti 6:17 us with everything for our *e.*

ENLARGE (ENLARGES)
2Co 9:10 *e* the harvest of your righteousness.

ENLARGES (ENLARGE)
Dt 33:20 Blessed is he who *e* Gad's domain!

ENLIGHTENED* (LIGHT)
Eph 1:18 that the eyes of your heart may be *e*
Heb 6: 4 for those who have once been *e,*

ENMITY* (ENEMY)
Ge 3:15 And I will put *e*

ENOCH
1. Son of Cain (Ge 4:17–18).
2. Descendant of Seth; walked with God and taken by him (Ge 5:18–24; Heb 11:5). Prophet (Jude 14).

ENSLAVED (SLAVE)
Gal 4: 9 Do you wish to be *e* by them all
Tit 3: 3 and *e* by all kinds of passions

ENSNARE (SNARE)
Pr 5:22 of a wicked man *e* him;
Ecc 7:26 but the sinner she will *e.*

ENSNARED* (SNARE)
Dt 7:25 for yourselves, or you will be *e* by it
12:30 be careful not to be *e*
Ps 9:16 the wicked are *e* by the work
Pr 6: 2 *e* by the words of your mouth,
22:25 and get yourself *e.*

ENTANGLED (ENTANGLES)
2Pe 2:20 and are again *e* in it and overcome,

ENTANGLES* (ENTANGLED)
Heb 12: 1 and the sin that so easily *e,*

ENTER (ENTERED ENTERING ENTERS ENTRANCE)
Ps 95:11 "They shall never *e* my rest."
100: 4 *E* his gates with thanksgiving
Pr 2:10 For wisdom will *e* your heart,
Mt 5:20 will certainly not *e* the kingdom
7:13 "*E* through the narrow gate.
7:21 Lord,' will *e* the kingdom of heaven
18: 3 you will never *e* the kingdom
18: 8 It is better for you to *e* life maimed
19:17 to *e* life, obey the commandments
19:23 man to *e* the kingdom of heaven.
Mk 9:43 It is better for you to *e* life maimed
9:45 It is better for you to *e* life crippled
9:47 for you to *e* the kingdom of God
10:15 like a little child will never *e* it."
10:23 is for the rich to *e* the kingdom
Lk 13:24 will try to *e* and will not be able to.
13:24 "Make every effort to *e*
18:17 like a little child will never *e* it."
18:24 is for the rich to *e* the kingdom
Jn 3: 5 no one can *e* the kingdom of God.
Heb 3:11 'They shall never *e* my rest.' "
4:11 make every effort to *e* that rest,

ENTERED (ENTER)
Ps 73:17 me till I *e* the sanctuary of God;
Eze 4:14 meat has ever *e* my mouth."
Ac 11: 8 or unclean has ever *e* my mouth.'
Ro 5:12 as sin *e* the world through one man,
Heb 9:12 but he *e* the Most Holy Place once

ENTERING (ENTER)
Mt 21:31 the prostitutes are *e* the kingdom
Lk 11:52 have hindered those who were *e.*"
Heb 4: 1 the promise of *e* his rest still stands,

ENTERS (ENTER)
Mk 7:18 you see that nothing that *e* a man
Jn 10: 2 The man who *e* by the gate is

ENTERTAIN* (ENTERTAINED ENTERTAINMENT)
Jdg 16:25 "Bring out Samson to *e* us."
Mt 9: 4 "Why do you *e* evil thoughts
1Ti 5:19 Do not *e* an accusation
Heb 13: 2 Do not forget to *e* strangers,

ENTERTAINED* (ENTERTAIN)
Ac 28: 7 and for three days *e* us hospitably.
Heb 13: 2 so doing some people have *e* angels

ENTERTAINMENT* (ENTERTAIN)
Da 6:18 without any *e* being brought to him

ENTHRALLED*
Ps 45:11 The king is *e* by your beauty;

ENTHRONED* (THRONE)
1Sa 4: 4 who is *e* between the cherubim.
2Sa 6: 2 who is *e* between the cherubim that
2Ki 19:15 of Israel, *e* between the cherubim,
1Ch 13: 6 who is *e* between the cherubim—
Ps 2: 4 The One *e* in heaven laughs;
9:11 to the LORD, *e* in Zion;
22: 3 Yet you are *e* as the Holy One;
29:10 The LORD sits *e* over the flood;
29:10 the LORD is *e* as King forever.
55:19 God, who is *e* forever,
61: 7 May he be *e* in God's presence
80: 1 who sit *e* between the cherubim,
99: 1 he sits *e* between the cherubim,
102: 12 But you, O LORD, sit *e* forever;
113: 5 the One who sits *e* on high,
132: 14 here I will sit *e,* for I have desired it
Isa 14:13 I will sit *e* on the mount
37:16 of Israel, *e* between the cherubim,
40:22 He sits *e* above the circle
52: 2 rise up, sit *e,* O Jerusalem.

ENTHRONES* (THRONE)
Job 36: 7 he *e* them with kings

ENTHUSIASM*
2Co 8:17 he is coming to you with much *e*
9: 2 and your *e* has stirred most of them

ENTICE* (ENTICED ENTICES)
Pr 1:10 My son, if sinners *e* you,
2Pe 2:18 they *e* people who are just escaping
Rev 2:14 who taught Balak to *e* the Israelites

ENTICED* (ENTICE)
Dt 4:19 do not be *e* into bowing
11:16 or you will be *e* to turn away
2Ki 17:21 Jeroboam *e* Israel away
Job 31: 9 If my heart has been *e* by a woman,
31:27 so that my heart was secretly *e*
Jas 1:14 desire, he is dragged away and *e.*

ENTICES* (ENTICE)
Dt 13: 6 your closest friend secretly *e* you,

Job 36:18 Be careful that no one *e* you
Pr 16:29 A violent man *e* his neighbor

ENTIRE
Gal 5:14 The *e* law is summed up

ENTRANCE (ENTER)
Mt 27:60 stone in front of the *e* to the tomb
Mk 15:46 a stone against the *e* of the tomb.
16: 3 away from the *e* of the tomb?"
Jn 11:38 cave with a stone laid across the *e*.
20: 1 had been removed from the *e*.

ENTRUST (TRUST)
Jn 2:24 Jesus would not *e* himself to them,
2Ti 2: 2 the presence of many witnesses *e*

ENTRUSTED (TRUST)
Jer 13:20 Where is the flock that was *e* to you
Jn 5:22 but has *e* all judgment to the Son,
Ro 3: 2 they have been *e* with the very
6:17 of teaching to which you were *e*.
1Co 4: 1 as those *e* with the secret things
1Th 2: 4 by God to be *e* with the gospel.
1Ti 1:11 of the blessed God, which he *e*
6:20 guard what has been *e* to your care.
2Ti 1:12 able to guard what I have *e* to him
1:14 Guard the good deposit that was *e*
Tit 1: 3 light through the preaching *e* to me
1: 7 Since an overseer is *e*
1Pe 2:23 he *e* himself to him who judges
5: 3 not lording it over those *e* to you,
Jude : 3 once for all *e* to the saints.

ENVIES
Jas 4: 5 spirit he caused to live in us *e*

ENVIOUS (ENVY)
Dt 32:21 I will make them *e*
Pr 24:19 or be *e* of the wicked,
Ro 10:19 "I will make you *e*

ENVOY
Pr 13:17 but a trustworthy *e* brings healing.

ENVY (ENVIOUS ENVYING)
Pr 3:31 Do not *e* a violent man
14:30 but *e* rots the bones.
23:17 Do not let your heart *e* sinners,
24: 1 Do not *e* wicked men,
Mk 7:22 malice, deceit, lewdness, *e*, slander
Ro 1:29 They are full of *e*, murder, strife,
11:14 arouse my own people to *e*
1Co 13: 4 It does not *e*, it does not boast,
Gal 5:21 factions and *e*; drunkenness, orgies
Php 1:15 that some preach Christ out of *e*
1Ti 6: 4 and quarrels about words that result in *e*,
Tit 3: 3 lived in malice and *e*, being hated
Jas 3:14 But if you harbor bitter *e*
3:16 where you have *e* and selfish
1Pe 2: 1 *e*, and slander of every kind.

ENVYING* (ENVY)
Gal 5:26 provoking and *e* each other.

EPHAH
Eze 45:11 The *e* and the bath are

EPHESUS
Ac 18:19 at *E*, where Paul left Priscilla
19: 1 the interior and arrived at *E*.
Eph 1: 1 To the saints in *E*, the faithful
Rev 2: 1 the angel of the church in *E* write:

EPHRAIM
1. Second son of Joseph (Ge 41:52; 46:20). Blessed as firstborn by Jacob (Ge 48). Tribe of numbered (Nu 1:33; 26:37), blessed (Dt 33:17), allotted land (Jos 16:4–9; Eze 48:5), failed to fully possess (Jos 16:10; Jdg 1:29).
2. Synonymous with Northern Kingdom (Isa 7:17; Hos 5).

EQUAL (EQUALITY EQUITY)
Dt 33:25 and your strength will *e* your days.
1Sa 9: 2 without *e* among the Israelites—
Isa 40:25 who is my *e*?" says the Holy One.
46: 5 you compare me or count me *e*?
Da 1:19 and he found none *e* to Daniel,
Jn 5:18 making himself *e* with God.
1Co 12:25 that its parts should have *e* concern
2Co 2:16 And who is *e* to such a task?

EQUALITY* (EQUAL)
2Co 8:13 pressed, but that there might be *e*.
8:14 Then there will be *e*, as it is written:
Php 2: 6 did not consider *e*

EQUIP* (EQUIPPED)
Heb 13:21 *e* you with everything good

EQUIPPED (EQUIP)
2Ti 3:17 man of God may be thoroughly *e*

EQUITY* (EQUAL)
Ps 96:10 he will judge the peoples with *e*.
98: 9 and the peoples with *e*.
99: 4 you have established *e*;

ERODES*
Job 14:18 "But as a mountain *e* and crumbles

ERROR (ERRORS)
Jas 5:20 Whoever turns a sinner from the *e*
2Pe 2:18 escaping from those who live in *e*.

ERRORS* (ERROR)
Ps 19:12 Who can discern his *e*?
Ecc 10: 4 calmness can lay great *e* to rest.

ESAU
Firstborn of Isaac, twin of Jacob (Ge 25:21–26). Also called Edom (Ge 25:30). Sold Jacob his birthright (Ge 25:29–34); lost blessing (Gen 27). Married Hittites (Ge 26:34), Ishmaelites (Ge 28:6–9). Reconciled to Jacob (Gen 33). Genealogy (Ge 36). The LORD chose Jacob over Esau (Mal 1:2–3), but gave Esau land (Dt 2:2–12). Descendants eventually obliterated (Ob 1–21; Jer 49:7–22).

ESCAPE (ESCAPED ESCAPES ESCAPING)
Ps 68:20 from the Sovereign LORD comes *e*
Pr 11: 9 through knowledge the righteous *e*.
Ro 2: 3 think you will *e* God's judgment?
1Th 5: 3 woman, and they will not *e*.
2Ti 2:26 and *e* from the trap of the devil,
Heb 2: 3 how shall we *e* if we ignore such
12:25 If they did not *e* when they refused
2Pe 1: 4 and *e* the corruption in the world

ESCAPED (ESCAPE)
2Pe 2:20 If they have *e* the corruption

ESCAPES (ESCAPE)
Pr 12:13 but a righteous man *e* trouble.

ESCAPING (ESCAPE)
1Co 3:15 only as one *e* through the flames.
2Pe 2:18 they entice people who are just *e*

ESTABLISH (ESTABLISHED ESTABLISHES)
Ge 6:18 But I will *e* my covenant with you,
17:21 But my covenant I will *e* with Isaac
2Sa 7:11 the LORD himself will *e* a house
1Ki 9: 5 I will *e* your royal throne
1Ch 28: 7 I will *e* his kingdom forever
Ps 90:17 *e* the work of our hands for us—
Isa 26:12 LORD, you *e* peace for us;
Ro 10: 3 God and sought to *e* their own,
16:25 able to *e* you by my gospel
Heb 10: 9 sets aside the first to *e* the second.

ESTABLISHED (ESTABLISH)
Ge 9:17 the sign of the covenant I have *e*
Ex 6: 4 also *e* my covenant with them
Pr 16:12 a throne is *e* through righteousness.

ESTABLISHES (ESTABLISH)
Job 25: 2 he *e* order in the heights of heaven.
Isa 42: 4 till he *e* justice on earth.

ESTATE
Ps 136: 23 who remembered us in our low *e*

ESTEEMED
Pr 22: 1 to be *e* is better than silver or gold.
Isa 53: 3 he was despised, and we *e* him not.

ESTHER
Jewess, originally named Hadassah, who lived in Persia; cousin of Mordecai (Est 2:7). Chosen queen of Xerxes (Est 2:8–18). Persuaded by Mordecai to foil Haman's plan to exterminate the Jews (Est 3–4). Revealed Haman's plans to Xerxes, resulting in Haman's death (Est 7), the Jews' preservation (Est 8–9), Mordecai's exaltation (Est 8:15; 9:4; 10). Decreed celebration of Purim (Est 9:18–32).

ETERNAL* (ETERNALLY ETERNITY)
Ge 21:33 the name of the LORD, the *E* God.
Dt 33:27 The *e* God is your refuge,
1Ki 10: 9 of the LORD's *e* love for Israel,
Ps 16:11 with *e* pleasures at your right hand.
21: 6 you have granted him *e* blessings
111: 10 To him belongs *e* praise.
119: 89 Your word, O LORD, is *e*;
119:160 all your righteous laws are *e*.
Ecc 12: 5 Then man goes to his *e* home
Isa 26: 4 LORD, the LORD, is the Rock *e*.
47: 7 the *e* queen!'
Jer 10:10 he is the living God, the *e* King.
Da 4: 3 His kingdom is an *e* kingdom;
4:34 His dominion is an *e* dominion;
Hab 3: 6 His ways are *e*.
Mt 18: 8 two feet and be thrown into *e* fire.
19:16 good thing must I do to get *e* life?"
19:29 as much and will inherit *e* life.
25:41 into the *e* fire prepared for the devil
25:46 but the righteous to *e* life."
25:46 they will go away to *e* punishment,
Mk 3:29 be forgiven; he is guilty of an *e* sin."
10:17 "what must I do to inherit *e* life?"
10:30 and in the age to come, *e* life.
Lk 10:25 "what must I do to inherit *e* life?"
16: 9 will be welcomed into *e* dwellings.
18:18 what must I do to inherit *e* life?"
18:30 and, in the age to come, *e* life."
Jn 3:15 believes in him may have *e* life.
3:16 him shall not perish but have *e* life.
3:36 believes in the Son has *e* life,
4:14 spring of water welling up to *e* life."
4:36 now he harvests the crop for *e* life,
5:24 believes him who sent me has *e* life
5:39 that by them you possess *e* life.
6:27 but for food that endures to *e* life,
6:40 believes in him shall have *e* life,
6:54 and drinks my blood has *e* life,
6:68 You have the words of *e* life.
10:28 I give them *e* life, and they shall
12:25 in this world will keep it for *e* life.
12:50 that his command leads to *e* life.
17: 2 all people that he might give *e* life
17: 3 this is *e* life: that they may know
Ac 13:46 yourselves worthy of *e* life,
13:48 were appointed for *e* life believed.
Ro 1:20 his *e* power and divine nature—
2: 7 and immortality, he will give *e* life.
5:21 righteousness to bring *e* life
6:22 to holiness, and the result is *e* life.
6:23 but the gift of God is *e* life
16:26 by the command of the *e* God,
2Co 4:17 for us an *e* glory that far outweighs
4:18 temporary, but what is unseen is *e*.
5: 1 from God, an *e* house in heaven,
Gal 6: 8 from the Spirit will reap *e* life.
Eph 3:11 to his *e* purpose which he
2Th 2:16 his grace gave us *e* encouragement
1Ti 1:16 believe on him and receive *e* life.
1:17 Now to the King *e*, immortal,
6:12 Take hold of the *e* life
2Ti 2:10 is in Christ Jesus, with *e* glory.
Tit 1: 2 resting on the hope of *e* life,
3: 7 heirs having the hope of *e* life.
Heb 5: 9 he became the source of *e* salvation
6: 2 of the dead, and *e* judgment.
9:12 having obtained *e* redemption.
9:14 through the *e* Spirit offered himself
9:15 the promised *e* inheritance—
13:20 of the *e* covenant brought back
1Pe 5:10 you to his *e* glory in Christ,
2Pe 1:11 into the *e* kingdom of our Lord
1Jn 1: 2 and we proclaim to you the *e* life,
2:25 what he promised us—even *e* life.
3:15 know that no murderer has *e* life
5:11 God has given us *e* life,
5:13 you may know that you have *e* life.
5:20 He is the true God and *e* life.
Jude : 7 who suffer the punishment of *e* fire.
:21 Christ to bring you to *e* life.
Rev 14: 6 and he had the *e* gospel to proclaim

ETERNALLY* (ETERNAL)
Gal 1: 8 let him be *e* condemned! As we
1: 9 let him be *e* condemned! Am I now

ETERNITY* (ETERNAL)
Ps 93: 2 you are from all *e*.
Pr 8:23 I was appointed from *e*,
Ecc 3:11 also set *e* in the hearts of men;

ETHIOPIAN*
Jer 13:23 Can the *E* change his skin
Ac 8:27 and on his way he met an *E* eunuch

EUNUCH (EUNUCHS)
Ac 8:27 on his way he met an Ethiopian *e,*

EUNUCHS (EUNUCH)
Isa 56: 4 "To the *e* who keep my Sabbaths,
Mt 19:12 For some are *e* because they were

EUTYCHUS*
Ac 20: 9 was a young man named *E,*

EVANGELIST* (EVANGELISTS)
Ac 21: 8 stayed at the house of Philip the *e,*
2Ti 4: 5 hardship, do the work of an *e,*

EVANGELISTS* (EVANGELIST)
Eph 4:11 some to be prophets, some to be *e,*

EVE*
Ge 3:20 Adam named his wife *E,*
4: 1 Adam lay with his wife *E,*
2Co 11: 3 as *E* was deceived by the serpent's
1Ti 2:13 For Adam was formed first, then *E*

EVEN-TEMPERED* (TEMPER)
Pr 17:27 and a man of understanding is *e.*

EVENING
Ge 1: 5 there was *e,* and there was morning

EVER (EVERLASTING FOREVER FOREVERMORE)
Ex 15:18 LORD will reign for *e* and *e."*
Dt 8:19 If you *e* forget the LORD your
1Ki 3:12 anyone like you, nor will there *e* be.
Job 4: 7 were the upright *e* destroyed?
Ps 5:11 let them *e* sing for joy.
10:16 The LORD is King for *e* and *e;*
21: 4 length of days, for *e* and *e.*
25: 3 will *e* be put to shame,
25:15 My eyes are *e* on the LORD,
26: 3 for your love is *e* before me,
45: 6 O God, will last for *e* and *e;*
45:17 nations will praise you for *e* and *e.*
48:14 For this God is our God for *e* and *e;*
52: 8 God's unfailing love for *e* and *e.*
61: 8 will I *e* sing praise to your name
71: 6 I will *e* praise you.
84: 4 they are *e* praising you.
89:33 nor will I *e* betray my faithfulness.
111: 8 They are steadfast for *e* and *e,*
119: 44 your law, for *e* and *e.*
119: 98 for they are *e* with me.
132: 12 sit on your throne for *e* and *e."*
145: 1 I will praise your name for *e* and *e.*
145: 2 and extol your name for *e* and *e.*
145: 21 his holy name for *e* and *e.*
Pr 4:18 shining *e* brighter till the full light
5:19 may you *e* be captivated
Isa 66: 8 Who has *e* heard of such a thing?
66: 8 Who has *e* seen such things?
Jer 7: 7 I gave your forefathers for *e* and *e.*
25: 5 and your fathers for *e* and *e.*
31:36 the descendants of Israel *e* cease
Da 2:20 be to the name of God for *e* and *e;*
7:18 it forever—yes, for *e* and *e.'*
12: 3 like the stars for *e* and *e.*
Mic 4: 5 our God for *e* and *e.*
Mt 13:14 you will be *e* seeing but never
13:14 "'You will be *e* hearing
Mk 4:12 *e* hearing but never understanding;
Jn 1:18 No one has *e* seen God,
Gal 1: 5 to whom be glory for *e* and *e.*
Eph 3:21 all generations, for *e* and *e!*
Php 4:20 and Father be glory for *e* and *e.*
1Ti 1:17 be honor and glory for *e* and *e.*
2Ti 4:18 To him be glory for *e* and *e.*
Heb 1: 8 O God, will last for *e* and *e,*
13:21 to whom be glory for *e* and *e.*
1Pe 4:11 the glory and the power for *e* and *e.*
5:11 To him be the power for *e* and *e.*
1Jn 4:12 No one has *e* seen God;
Rev 1: 6 him be glory and power for *e* and *e!*
1:18 and behold I am alive for *e* and *e!*
21:27 Nothing impure will *e* enter it,
22: 5 And they will reign for *e* and *e.*

EVER-INCREASING* (INCREASE)
Ro 6:19 to impurity and to *e* wickedness,
2Co 3:18 into his likeness with *e* glory,

EVERLASTING* (EVER)
Ge 9:16 and remember the *e* covenant
17: 7 an *e* covenant between me and you
17: 8 I will give as an *e* possession to you
17:13 in your flesh is to be an *e* covenant.
17:19 an *e* covenant for his descendants
48: 4 *e* possession to your descendants
Nu 18:19 It is an *e* covenant of salt
Dt 33:15 and the fruitfulness of the *e* hills;
33:27 and underneath are the *e* arms.
2Sa 23: 5 made with me an *e* covenant,
1Ch 16:17 to Israel as an *e* covenant:
16:36 from *e* to *e.*
29:10 from *e* to *e.*
Ezr 9:12 to your children as an *e* inheritance
Ne 9: 5 your God, who is from *e* to *e."*
Ps 41:13 from *e* to *e.*
52: 5 God will bring you down to *e* ruin:
74: 3 toward these *e* ruins,
78:66 he put them to *e* shame.
90: 2 from *e* to *e* you are God.
103: 17 But from *e* to *e*
105: 10 to Israel as an *e* covenant:
106: 48 from *e* to *e.*
119:142 Your righteousness is *e*
139: 24 and lead me in the way *e.*
145: 13 Your kingdom is an *e* kingdom,
Isa 9: 6 *E* Father, Prince of Peace.
24: 5 and broken the *e* covenant.
30: 8 it may be an *e* witness.
33:14 Who of us can dwell with *e* burning
35:10 *e* joy will crown their heads.
40:28 The LORD is the *e* God,
45:17 the LORD with an *e* salvation;
45:17 to ages *e.*
51:11 *e* joy will crown their heads.
54: 8 but with *e* kindness
55: 3 I will make an *e* covenant with you,
55:13 for an *e* sign,
56: 5 I will give them an *e* name
60:15 I will make you the *e* pride
60:19 for the LORD will be your *e* light,
60:20 the LORD will be your *e* light,
61: 7 and *e* joy will be theirs.
61: 8 and make an *e* covenant with them.
63:12 to gain for himself *e* renown,
Jer 5:22 an *e* barrier it cannot cross.
23:40 I will bring upon you *e* disgrace—
23:40 *e* shame that will not be forgotten."
25: 9 of horror and scorn, and an *e* ruin.
31: 3 "I have loved you with an *e* love;
32:40 I will make an *e* covenant
50: 5 the LORD in an *e* covenant
Eze 16:60 and I will establish an *e* covenant
37:26 with them; it will be an *e* covenant.
Da 7:14 dominion is an *e* dominion that will
7:27 His kingdom will be an *e* kingdom,
9:24 to bring in *e* righteousness,
12: 2 others to shame and *e* contempt.
12: 2 some to *e* life, others to shame
Mic 6: 2 you *e* foundations of the earth.
Hab 1:12 O LORD, are you not from *e?*
Jn 6:47 the truth, he who believes has *e* life.
2Th 1: 9 punished with *e* destruction
Jude 6 bound with *e* chains for judgment

EVER-PRESENT*
Ps 46: 1 an *e* help in trouble

EVIDENCE (EVIDENT)
Jn 14:11 on the *e* of the miracles themselves.
Ac 11:23 and saw the *e* of the grace of God,
2Th 1: 5 All this is *e* that God's judgment is
Jas 2:20 do you want *e* that faith

EVIDENT (EVIDENCE)
Php 4: 5 Let your gentleness be *e* to all.

EVIL (EVILDOER EVILDOERS EVILS)
Ge 2: 9 of the knowledge of good and *e.*
3: 5 be like God, knowing good and *e."*
6: 5 of his heart was only *e* all the time.
Ex 32:22 how prone these people are to *e.*
Jdg 2:11 Then the Israelites did *e* in the eyes
3: 7 The Israelites did *e* in the eyes
3:12 Once again the Israelites did *e*
4: 1 the Israelites once again did *e*
6: 1 Again the Israelites did *e*
10: 6 Again the Israelites did *e*
13: 1 Again the Israelites did *e*
1Ki 11: 6 So Solomon did *e* in the eyes
16:25 But Omri did *e* in the eyes
2Ki 15:24 Pekahiah did *e* in the eyes
Job 1: 1 he feared God and shunned *e.*
1: 8 a man who fears God and shuns *e."*
34:10 Far be it from God to do *e,*
36:21 Beware of turning to *e,*
Ps 5: 4 not a God who takes pleasure in *e;*
23: 4 I will fear no *e,*
34:13 keep your tongue from *e*
34:14 Turn from *e* and do good;
34:16 is against those who do *e,*
37: 1 Do not fret because of *e* men
37: 8 do not fret—it leads only to *e.*
37:27 Turn from *e* and do good;
49: 5 fear when *e* days come,
51: 4 and done what is *e* in your sight,
97:10 those who love the LORD hate *e,*
101: 4 I will have nothing to do with *e.*
141: 4 not my heart be drawn to what is *e,*
Pr 4:27 keep your foot from *e.*
8:13 To fear the LORD is to hate *e;*
10:23 A fool finds pleasure in *e* conduct,
11:19 he who pursues *e* goes to his death.
11:27 *e* comes to him who searches for it.
14:16 man fears the LORD and shuns *e,*
17:13 If a man pays back *e* for good,
20:30 Blows and wounds cleanse away *e,*
24:19 Do not fret because of *e* men
24:20 for the *e* man has no future hope,
26:23 are fervent lips with an *e* heart.
28: 5 *E* men do not understand justice,
29: 6 An *e* man is snared by his own sin,
Ecc 12:14 whether it is good or *e.*
Isa 5:20 Woe to those who call *e* good
13:11 I will punish the world for its *e,*
55: 7 and the *e* man his thoughts.
Jer 4:14 wash the *e* from your heart
18: 8 nation I warned repents of its *e,*
18:11 So turn from your *e* ways,
Eze 33:11 Turn! Turn from your *e* ways!
33:13 he will die for the *e* he has done.
33:15 and does no *e,* he will surely live;
Am 5:13 for the times are *e.*
Hab 1:13 Your eyes are too pure to look on *e;*
Zec 8:17 do not plot *e* against your neighbor,
Mt 5:45 He causes his sun to rise on the *e*
6:13 but deliver us from the *e* one.'
7:11 If you, then, though you are *e,*
12:34 you who are *e* say anything good?
12:35 and the *e* man brings *e* things out
12:35 out of the *e* stored up in him.
12:43 "When an *e* spirit comes out
15:19 out of the heart come *e* thoughts,
Mk 7:21 come *e* thoughts, sexual
Lk 6:45 and the *e* man brings *e* things out
11:13 If you then, though you are *e,*
Jn 3:19 of light because their deeds were *e.*
3:20 Everyone who does *e* hates
17:15 you protect them from the *e* one.
Ro 1:30 they invent ways of doing *e;*
2: 8 who reject the truth and follow *e,*
2: 9 for every human being who does *e:*
3: 8 "Let us do *e* that good may result"?
6:12 body so that you obey its *e* desires.
7:19 no, the *e* I do not want to do—
7:21 to do good, *e* is right there with me.
12: 9 Hate what is *e;* cling
12:17 Do not repay anyone *e* for *e.*
12:21 Do not be overcome by *e,*
14:16 good to be spoken of as *e.*
16:19 and innocent about what is *e.*
1Co 13: 6 Love does not delight in *e*
14:20 In regard to *e* be infants,
Eph 5:16 because the days are *e.*
6:12 forces of *e* in the heavenly realms.
6:16 all the flaming arrows of the *e* one.
Col 3: 5 impurity, lust, *e* desires and greed,
1Th 5:22 Avoid every kind of *e.*
2Th 3: 3 and protect you from the *e* one.
1Ti 6:10 of money is a root of all kinds of *e.*
2Ti 2:22 Flee the *e* desires of youth,
3: 6 are swayed by all kinds of *e* desires,
3:13 while *e* men and impostors will go
Heb 5:14 to distinguish good from *e.*
Jas 1:13 For God cannot be tempted by *e,*
1:21 and the *e* that is so prevalent,
3: 6 a world of *e* among the parts
3: 8 It is a restless *e,* full
1Pe 2:16 your freedom as a cover-up for *e;*
3: 9 Do not repay *e* with *e* or insult
3:10 must keep his tongue from *e*
3:17 for doing good than for doing *e.*
1Jn 2:13 you have overcome the *e* one.
2:14 and you have overcome the *e* one.
3:12 who belonged to the *e* one
5:18 and the *e* one cannot harm him.

1Jn 5:19 is under the control of the *e* one.
3Jn :11 do not imitate what is *e*

EVILDOER* (EVIL)
2Sa 3:39 the LORD repay the *e* according
Ps 101: 8 I will cut off every *e*
Mal 4: 1 and every *e* will be stubble,

EVILDOERS* (EVIL)
1Sa 24:13 saying goes, 'From *e* come evil
Job 8:20 or strengthen the hands of *e*.
34: 8 He keeps company with *e*;
34:22 where *e* can hide.
Ps 14: 4 Will *e* never learn—
14: 6 You *e* frustrate the plans
26: 5 I abhor the assembly of *e*
36:12 See how the *e* lie fallen—
53: 4 Will the *e* never learn—
59: 2 Deliver me from *e*
64: 2 from that noisy crowd of *e*.
92: 7 and all *e* flourish,
92: 9 all *e* will be scattered.
94: 4 all the *e* are full of boasting.
94:16 will take a stand for me against *e*?
119:115 Away from me, you *e*,
125: 5 the LORD will banish with the *e*.
141: 4 deeds with men who are *e*;
141: 5 ever against the deeds of *e*;
141: 9 from the traps set by *e*.
Pr 21:15 but terror to *e*.
Isa 1: 4 a brood of *e*,
31: 2 against those who help *e*.
Jer 23:14 They strengthen the hands of *e*,
Hos 10: 9 the *e* in Gibeah?
Mal 3:15 Certainly the *e* prosper, and
Mt 7:23 you *e*!' "Therefore everyone who
Lk 13:27 Away from me, all you *e*!'
18:11 *e*, adulterers—or even like this tax

EVILS* (EVIL)
Mk 7:23 All these *e* come from inside

EWE
2Sa 12: 3 one little *e* lamb he had bought.

EXACT*
Ge 43:21 the *e* weight—in the mouth
Est 4: 7 including the *e* amount
Mt 2: 7 from them the *e* time the star had
Jn 4:53 realized that this was the *e* time
Ac 17:26 the *e* places where they should live.
Heb 1: 3 the *e* representation of his being,

EXALT* (EXALTED EXALTS)
Ex 15: 2 my father's God, and I will *e* him.
Jos 3: 7 begin to *e* you in the eyes
1Sa 2:10 and *e* the horn of his anointed."
1Ch 25: 5 the promises of God to *e* him.
29:12 power to *e* and give strength to all.
Job 19: 5 If indeed you would *e* yourselves
Ps 30: 1 I will *e* you, O LORD,
34: 3 let us *e* his name together.
35:26 may all who *e* themselves over me
37:34 He will *e* you to inherit the land;
38:16 *e* themselves over me
75: 6 or from the desert can *e* a man.
89:17 and by your favor you *e* our horn.
99: 5 *E* the LORD our God
99: 9 *E* the LORD our God
107:32 Let them *e* him in the assembly
118:28 you are my God, and I will *e* you.
145: 1 I will *e* you, my God the King;
Pr 4: 8 Esteem her, and she will *e* you;
25: 6 Do not *e* yourself in the king's
Isa 24:15 *e* the name of the LORD, the God
25: 1 I will *e* you and praise your name,
Eze 29:15 and will never again *e* itself
Da 4:37 *e* and glorify the King of heaven,
11:36 He will *e* and magnify himself
11:37 but will *e* himself above them all.
Hos 11: 7 he will by no means *e* them.
2Th 2: 4 will *e* himself over everything that is

EXALTED* (EXALT)
Ex 15: 1 for he is highly *e*.
15:21 for he is highly *e*.
Nu 24: 7 their kingdom will be *e*.
Jos 4:14 That day the LORD *e* Joshua
2Sa 5:12 and had *e* his kingdom for the sake
22:47 *E* be God, the Rock, my Savior!
22:49 You *e* me above my foes;
23: 1 of the man *e* by the Most High,
1Ch 14: 2 that his kingdom had been highly *e*
17:17 as though I were the most *e* of men,
29:11 you are *e* as head over all.
29:25 The LORD highly *e* Solomon
Ne 9: 5 and may it be *e* above all blessing
Job 24:24 For a little while they are *e*,
36:22 "God is *e* in his power.
37:23 beyond our reach and *e* in power;
Ps 18:46 *E* be God my Savior!
18:48 You *e* me above my foes;
21:13 Be *e*, O LORD, in your strength;
27: 6 Then my head will be *e*
35:27 they always say, "The LORD be *e*,
40:16 "The LORD be *e*!"
46:10 I will be *e* among the nations,
46:10 I will be *e* in the earth."
47: 9 he is greatly *e*.
57: 5 Be *e*, O God, above the heavens;
57:11 Be *e*, O God, above the heavens;
70: 4 "Let God be *e*!"
89:13 hand is strong, your right hand *e*.
89:19 I have *e* a young man
89:24 through my name his horn will be *e*
89:27 the most *e* of the kings of the earth.
89:42 You have *e* the right hand
92: 8 But you, O LORD, are *e* forever.
92:10 You have *e* my horn like that
97: 9 you are *e* far above all gods.
99: 2 he is *e* over all the nations.
108: 5 Be *e*, O God, above the heavens,
113: 4 The LORD is *e* over all the nations
138: 2 for you have *e* above all things
148:13 for his name alone is *e*;
Pr 11:11 of the upright a city is *e*,
30:32 have played the fool and *e* yourself,
Isa 2:11 the LORD alone will be *e*
2:12 for all that is *e*
2:17 the LORD alone will be *e*
5:16 the LORD Almighty will be *e*
6: 1 *e*, and the train of his robe filled
12: 4 and proclaim that his name is *e*.
24: 4 the *e* of the earth languish.
33: 5 The LORD is *e*, for he dwells
33:10 "Now will I be *e*;
52:13 be raised and lifted up and highly *e*.
Jer 17:12 A glorious throne, *e*
La 2:17 he has *e* the horn of your foes.
Eze 21:26 The lowly will be *e* and the *e* will be
Hos 13: 1 he was *e* in Israel.
Mic 6: 6 and bow down before the *e* God?
Mt 23:12 whoever humbles himself will be *e*.
Lk 14:11 he who humbles himself will be *e*."
18:14 he who humbles himself will be *e*."
Ac 2:33 *E* to the right hand of God,
5:31 God *e* him to his own right hand
Php 1:20 always Christ will be *e* in my body,
2: 9 Therefore God *e* him
Heb 7:26 from sinners, *e* above the heavens.

EXALTS* (EXALT)
1Sa 2: 7 he humbles and he *e*.
Job 36: 7 and *e* them forever.
Ps 75: 7 He brings one down, he *e* another.
Pr 14:34 Righteousness *e* a nation,
Mt 23:12 For whoever *e* himself will be
Lk 14:11 For everyone who *e* himself will be
18:14 For everyone who *e* himself will be

EXAMINE (EXAMINED EXAMINES)
Ps 11: 4 his eyes *e* them.
17: 3 you probe my heart and *e* me
26: 2 *e* my heart and my mind;
Jer 17:10 and *e* the mind,
20:12 Almighty, you who *e* the righteous
La 3:40 Let us *e* our ways and test them,
1Co 11:28 A man ought to *e* himself
2Co 13: 5 *E* yourselves to see whether you

EXAMINED (EXAMINE)
Job 13: 9 Would it turn out well if he *e* you?
Ac 17:11 *e* the Scriptures every day to see

EXAMINES (EXAMINE)
Ps 11: 5 The LORD *e* the righteous,
Pr 5:21 and he *e* all his paths.

EXAMPLE* (EXAMPLES)
2Ki 14: 3 In everything he followed the *e*
Ecc 9:13 also saw under the sun this *e*
Eze 14: 8 and make him an *e* and a byword.
Jn 13:15 have set you an *e* that you should
Ro 7: 2 as long as he lives? For *e*,
1Co 11: 1 Follow my *e*, as I follow
11: 1 as I follow the *e* of Christ.
Gal 3:15 let me take an *e* from everyday life.
Php 3:17 Join with others in following my *e*,
2Th 3: 7 how you ought to follow our *e*.
1Ti 1:16 as an *e* for those who would believe
4:12 set an *e* for the believers in speech,
Tit 2: 7 In everything set them an *e*
Heb 4:11 fall by following their *e*
Jas 3: 4 Or take ships as an *e*.
5:10 as an *e* of patience in the face
1Pe 2:21 leaving you an *e*, that you should
2Pe 2: 6 made them an *e* of what is going
Jude : 7 as an *e* of those who suffer

EXAMPLES* (EXAMPLE)
1Co 10: 6 Now these things occurred as *e*
10:11 as *e* and were written down
1Pe 5: 3 to you, but being *e* to the flock.

EXASPERATE*
Eph 6: 4 Fathers, do not *e* your children;

EXCEL* (EXCELLENT)
Ge 49: 4 as the waters, you will no longer *e*,
1Co 14:12 to *e* in gifts that build up the church
2Co 8: 7 But just as you *e* in everything—
8: 7 also *e* in this grace of giving.

EXCELLENT (EXCEL)
1Co 12:31 now I will show you the most *e* way
Php 4: 8 if anything is *e* or praiseworthy—
1Ti 3:13 have served well gain an *e* standing
Tit 3: 8 These things are *e* and profitable

EXCESSIVE
Eze 18: 8 or take *e* interest.
2Co 2: 7 not be overwhelmed by *e* sorrow.

EXCHANGE (EXCHANGED)
Mt 16:26 Or what can a man give in *e*
Mk 8:37 Or what can a man give in *e*
2Co 6:13 As a fair *e*—I speak

EXCHANGED (EXCHANGE)
Ps 106:20 They *e* their Glory
Jer 2:11 But my people have *e* their Glory
Hos 4: 7 they *e* their Glory
Ro 1:23 *e* the glory of the immortal God
1:25 They *e* the truth of God for a lie,
1:26 their women *e* natural relations

EXCLAIM
Ps 35:10 My whole being will *e*,

EXCUSE* (EXCUSES)
Ps 25: 3 who are treacherous without *e*.
Lk 14:18 Please *e* me.'
14:19 Please *e* me.'
Jn 15:22 they have no *e* for their sin.
Ro 1:20 so that men are without *e*.
2: 1 You, therefore, have no *e*,

EXCUSES* (EXCUSE)
Lk 14:18 "But they all alike began to make *e*.

EXERTED*
Eph 1:20 which he *e* in Christ

EXHORT*
1Ti 5: 1 but *e* him as if he were your father.

EXILE
2Ki 17:23 taken from their homeland into *e*
25:11 into *e* the people who remained

EXISTED* (EXISTS)
2Pe 3: 5 ago by God's word the heavens *e*

EXISTS (EXISTED)
Heb 2:10 and through whom everything *e*,
11: 6 to him must believe that he *e*

EXPANSE
Ge 1: 7 So God made the *e* and separated
1: 8 God called the *e* "sky."

EXPECT (EXPECTATION EXPECTED EXPECTING)
Mt 24:44 at an hour when you do not *e* him.
Lk 12:40 at an hour when you do not *e* him."
Php 1:20 I eagerly *e* and hope that I will

EXPECTATION (EXPECT)
Ro 8:19 waits in eager *e* for the sons
Heb 10:27 but only a fearful *e* of judgment

EXPECTED (EXPECT)
Pr 11: 7 all he *e* from his power comes
Hag 1: 9 "You *e* much, but see, it turned out

EXPECTING (EXPECT)
Lk 6:35 and lend to them without *e*

EXPEL* (EXPELLED)
1Co 5:13 *E* the wicked man from among you

EXPELLED (EXPEL)
Eze 28:16 and I *e* you, O guardian cherub,

EXPENSE (EXPENSIVE)
1Co 9: 7 Who serves as a soldier at his own *e*

EXPENSIVE* (EXPENSE)
Mt 26: 7 jar of very *e* perfume,
Mk 14: 3 jar of very *e* perfume,
Lk 7:25 those who wear *e* clothes
Jn 12: 3 a pint of pure nard, an *e* perfume;
1Ti 2: 9 or gold or pearls or *e* clothes,

EXPERT
1Co 3:10 I laid a foundation as an *e* builder,

EXPLAINING (EXPLAINS)
Ac 17: 3 *e* and proving that the Christ had

EXPLAINS* (EXPLAINING)
Ac 8:31 he said, "unless someone *e* it to me

EXPLOIT* (EXPLOITED EXPLOITING EXPLOITS)
Pr 22:22 Do not *e* the poor because they are
Isa 58: 3 and *e* all your workers.
2Co 12:17 Did I *e* you through any
12:18 Titus did not *e* you, did he?
2Pe 2: 3 greed these teachers will *e* you

EXPLOITED* (EXPLOIT)
2Co 7: 2 no one, we have *e* no one.

EXPLOITING* (EXPLOIT)
Jas 2: 6 Is it not the rich who are *e* you?

EXPLOITS (EXPLOIT)
2Co 11:20 or *e* you or takes advantage of you

EXPLORE
Nu 13: 2 "Send some men to *e* the land

EXPOSE (EXPOSED)
1Co 4: 5 will *e* the motives of men's hearts.
Eph 5:11 of darkness, but rather *e* them.

EXPOSED (EXPOSE)
Jn 3:20 for fear that his deeds will be *e*.
Eph 5:13 everything *e* by the light becomes

EXPRESS (EXPRESSING)
Ro 8:26 us with groans that words cannot *e*.

EXPRESSING* (EXPRESS)
1Co 2:13 *e* spiritual truths in spiritual words.
Gal 5: 6 thing that counts is faith *e* itself

EXTENDS (EXTENT)
Pr 31:20 and *e* her hands to the needy.
Lk 1:50 His mercy *e* to those who fear him,

EXTENT (EXTENDS)
Jn 13: 1 he now showed them the full *e*

EXTERNAL
Gal 2: 6 judge by *e* appearance—

EXTINGUISH (EXTINGUISHED)
Eph 6:16 which you can *e* all the flaming

EXTINGUISHED (EXTINGUISH)
2Sa 21:17 the lamp of Israel will not be *e*."

EXTOL*
Job 36:24 Remember to *e* his work,
Ps 34: 1 I will *e* the LORD at all times;
68: 4 *e* him who rides on the clouds—
95: 2 and *e* him with music and song.
109: 30 mouth I will greatly *e* the LORD;
111: 1 I will *e* the LORD with all my heart
115: 18 it is we who *e* the LORD,
117: 1 *e* him, all you peoples.
145: 2 and *e* your name for ever and ever.
145: 10 your saints will *e* you.
147: 12 *E* the LORD, O Jerusalem;

EXTORT*
Lk 3:14 "Don't *e* money and don't accuse

EXTRAORDINARY*
Ac 19:11 God did *e* miracles through Paul,

EXTREME (EXTREMES)
2Co 8: 2 and their *e* poverty welled up

EXTREMES* (EXTREME)
Ecc 7:18 who fears God will avoid all *e*.

EXULT
Ps 89:16 they *e* in your righteousness.
Isa 45:25 will be found righteous and will *e*.

EYE (EYES)
Ge 3: 6 good for food and pleasing to the *e*,
Ex 21:24 you are to take life for life, *e* for *e*,
Dt 19:21 life for life, *e* for *e*, tooth for tooth,
Ps 94: 9 Does he who formed the *e* not see?
Mt 5:29 If your right *e* causes you to sin,
5:38 '*E* for *e*, and tooth for tooth.'
6:22 "The *e* is the lamp of the body.
7: 3 of sawdust in your brother's *e*
1Co 2: 9 "No *e* has seen,
12:16 I am not an *e*, I do not belong
15:52 of an *e*, at the last trumpet.
Eph 6: 6 favor when their *e* is on you,
Col 3:22 not only when their *e* is on you
Rev 1: 7 and every *e* will see him,

EYES (EYE)
Nu 15:39 the lusts of your own hearts and *e*.
33:55 remain will become barbs in your *e*
Dt 11:12 the *e* of the LORD your God are
12:25 right in the *e* of the LORD.
16:19 for a bribe blinds the *e* of the wise
Jos 23:13 on your backs and thorns in your *e*,
1Sa 15:17 you were once small in your own *e*,
1Ki 10: 7 I came and saw with my own *e*.
2Ki 9:30 heard about it, she painted her *e*,
2Ch 16: 9 For the *e* of the LORD range
Job 31: 1 "I made a covenant with my *e*
36: 7 He does not take his *e*
Ps 25:15 My *e* are ever on the LORD,
36: 1 God before his *e*.
101: 6 My *e* will be on the faithful
118: 23 and it is marvelous in our *e*.
119: 18 Open my *e* that I may see
119: 37 my *e* away from worthless things;
121: 1 I lift up my *e* to the hills—
123: 1 I lift up my *e* to you,
139: 16 your *e* saw my unformed body.
141: 8 But my *e* are fixed on you,
Pr 3: 7 Do not be wise in your own *e*;
4:25 Let your *e* look straight ahead,
15: 3 The *e* of the LORD are everywhere
17:24 a fool's *e* wander to the ends
Isa 6: 5 and my *e* have seen the King,
33:17 Your *e* will see the king
42: 7 to open *e* that are blind,
Jer 24: 6 My *e* will watch over them
Hab 1:13 Your *e* are too pure to look on evil;
Mt 6:22 If your *e* are good, your whole
21:42 and it is marvelous in our *e*'?
Lk 16:15 ones who justify yourselves in the *e*
24:31 Then their *e* were opened
Jn 4:35 open your *e* and look at the fields!
Ac 1: 9 he was taken up before their very *e*,
2Co 4:18 So we fix our *e* not on what is seen,
8:21 not only in the *e* of the Lord but
Eph 1:18 also that the *e* of your heart may be
Heb 12: 2 Let us fix our *e* on Jesus, the author
Jas 2: 5 poor in the *e* of the world to be rich
1Pe 3:12 For the *e* of the Lord are
Rev 7:17 wipe away every tear from their *e*."
21: 4 He will wipe every tear from their *e*

EYEWITNESSES* (WITNESS)
Lk 1: 2 by those who from the first were *e*
2Pe 1:16 but we were *e* of his majesty.

EZEKIEL*
Priest called to be prophet to the exiles (Eze 1–3). Symbolically acted out destruction of Jerusalem (Eze 4–5; 12; 24).

EZRA*
Priest and teacher of the Law who led a return of exiles to Israel to reestablish temple and worship (Ezr 7–8). Corrected intermarriage of priests (Ezr 9–10). Read Law at celebration of Feast of Tabernacles (Ne 8). Participated in dedication of Jerusalem's walls (Ne 12).

FACE (FACES)
Ge 32:30 "It is because I saw God *f* to *f*,
Ex 3: 6 Moses hid his *f*, because he was
33:11 would speak to Moses *f* to *f*,
33:20 But," he said, "you cannot see my *f*
34:29 was not aware that his *f* was radiant
Nu 6:25 the LORD make his *f* shine
12: 8 With him I speak *f* to *f*,
14:14 O LORD, have been seen *f* to *f*,
Dt 5: 4 The LORD spoke to you *f* to *f* out
31:17 I will hide my *f* from them,
34:10 whom the LORD knew *f* to *f*,
Jdg 6:22 the angel of the LORD *f* to *f*!"
2Ki 14: 8 challenge: "Come, meet me *f* to *f*."
1Ch 16:11 seek his *f* always.
2Ch 7:14 and seek my *f* and turn
25:17 of Israel: "Come, meet me *f* to *f*."
Ezr 9: 6 and disgraced to lift up my *f* to you,
Ps 4: 6 Let the light of your *f* shine upon us
27: 8 Your *f*, LORD, I will seek.
31:16 Let your *f* shine on your servant;
44: 3 and the light of your *f*,
44:22 Yet for your sake we *f* death all day
51: 9 Hide your *f* from my sins
67: 1 and make his *f* shine upon us; *Selah*
80: 3 make your *f* shine upon us,
105: 4 seek his *f* always.
119:135 Make your *f* shine
SS 2:14 and your *f* is lovely.
Isa 50: 7 Therefore have I set my *f* like flint,
50: 8 Let us *f* each other!
54: 8 I hid my *f* from you for a moment,
Jer 32: 4 and will speak with him *f* to *f*
34: 3 and he will speak with you *f* to *f*.
Eze 1:10 Each of the four had the *f* of a man,
20:35 *f* to *f*, I will execute judgment
Mt 17: 2 His *f* shone like the sun,
18:10 angels in heaven always see the *f*
Lk 9:29 the appearance of his *f* changed,
Ro 8:36 "For your sake we *f* death all day
1Co 13:12 mirror; then we shall see *f* to *f*.
2Co 3: 7 could not look steadily at the *f*
4: 6 the glory of God in the *f* of Christ.
10: 1 who am "timid" when *f* to *f*
1Pe 3:12 but the *f* of the Lord is
2Jn :12 to visit you and talk with you *f* to *f*,
3Jn :14 see you soon, and we will talk *f* to *f*.
Rev 1:16 His *f* was like the sun shining
22: 4 They will see his *f*, and his name

FACES (FACE)
2Co 3:18 who with unveiled *f* all reflect

FACTIONS
2Co 12:20 outbursts of anger, *f*, slander,
Gal 5:20 selfish ambition, dissensions, *f*

FADE (FADING)
Jas 1:11 the rich man will *f* away
1Pe 5: 4 of glory that will never *f* away.

FADING (FADE)
2Co 3: 7 *f* though it was, will not
3:11 if what was *f* away came with glory,
3:13 at it while the radiance was *f* away.

FAIL (FAILED FAILING FAILINGS FAILS FAILURE)
Lev 26:15 and *f* to carry out all my commands
1Ki 2: 4 you will never *f* to have a man
1Ch 28:20 He will not *f* you or forsake you
2Ch 34:33 they did not *f* to follow the LORD,
Ps 89:28 my covenant with him will never *f*.
Pr 15:22 Plans *f* for lack of counsel,
Isa 51: 6 my righteousness will never *f*.
La 3:22 for his compassions never *f*.
Lk 22:32 Simon, that your faith may not *f*.
2Co 13: 5 unless, of course, you *f* the test?

FAILED (FAIL)
Jos 23:14 has been fulfilled; not one has *f*.
1Ki 8:56 Not one word has *f*
Ps 77: 8 Has his promise *f* for all time?
Ro 9: 6 as though God's word had *f*.
2Co 13: 6 discover that we have not *f* the test.

FAILING (FAIL)
1Sa 12:23 sin against the LORD by *f* to pray

FAILINGS (FAIL)
Ro 15: 1 ought to bear with the *f* of the weak

FAILS (FAIL)
Jer 14: 6 their eyesight *f*
Joel 1:10 the oil *f*.
1Co 13: 8 Love never *f*.

FAILURE* (FAIL)
1Th 2: 1 that our visit to you was not a *f*.

FAINT
Isa 40:31 they will walk and not be *f*.

FAINTHEARTED* (HEART)
Dt 20: 3 Do not be *f* or afraid; do not be
20: 8 shall add, "Is any man afraid or *f*?

FAIR (FAIRNESS)
Pr 1: 3 doing what is right and just and *f*;
Col 4: 1 slaves with what is right and *f*,

FAIRNESS* (FAIR)
Pr 29:14 If a king judges the poor with *f*,

FAITH* (FAITHFUL FAITHFULLY FAITHFULNESS FAITHLESS)
Ex 21: 8 because he has broken *f* with her.
Dt 32:51 both of you broke *f* with me
Jos 22:16 'How could you break *f*
Jdg 9:16 and in good *f* when you made
9:19 and in good *f* toward Jerub-Baal
1Sa 14:33 "You have broken *f*," he said.
2Ch 20:20 Have *f* in the LORD your God
20:20 have *f* in his prophets and you will
Isa 7: 9 If you do not stand firm in your *f*,
26: 2 the nation that keeps *f*.
Hab 2: 4 but the righteous will live by his *f*—
Mal 2:10 by breaking *f* with one another?
2:11 one another? Judah has broken *f*.
2:14 because you have broken *f* with her
2:15 and do not break *f* with the wife
2:16 in your spirit, and do not break *f*.
Mt 6:30 O you of little *f*? So do not worry,
8:10 anyone in Israel with such great *f*.
8:26 He replied, "You of little *f*,
9: 2 When Jesus saw their *f*, he said
9:22 he said, "your *f* has healed you."
9:29 According to your *f* will it be done
13:58 there because of their lack of *f*.
14:31 of little *f*," he said, "why did you
15:28 "Woman, you have great *f*!
16: 8 Jesus asked, "You of little *f*,
17:20 if you have *f* as small as a mustard
17:20 "Because you have so little *f*.
21:21 if you have *f* and do not doubt,
24:10 many will turn away from the *f*
Mk 2: 5 When Jesus saw their *f*, he said
4:40 still have no *f*?" They were
5:34 "Daughter, your *f* has healed you.
6: 6 he was amazed at their lack of *f*.
10:52 said Jesus, "your *f* has healed you."
11:22 "Have *f* in God," Jesus answered.
16:14 he rebuked them for their lack of *f*
Lk 5:20 When Jesus saw their *f*, he said,
7: 9 I have not found such great *f*
7:50 the woman, "Your *f* has saved you;
8:25 "Where is your *f*?" he asked his
8:48 "Daughter, your *f* has healed you.
12:28 will he clothe you, O you of little *f*!
17: 5 "Increase our *f*!" He replied,
17: 6 "If you have *f* as small
17:19 your *f* has made you well."
18: 8 will he find *f* on the earth?"
18:42 your sight; your *f* has healed you."
22:32 Simon, that your *f* may not fail.
Jn 2:11 and his disciples put their *f* in him.
7:31 in the crowd put their *f* in him.
8:30 he spoke, many put their *f* in him.
11:45 had seen what Jesus did, put their *f*
12:11 to Jesus and putting their *f* in him.
12:42 they would not confess their *f*
14:12 anyone who has *f* in me will do
Ac 3:16 By *f* in the name of Jesus, this man
3:16 *f* that comes through him that has
6: 5 full of *f* and of the Holy Spirit;
6: 7 of priests became obedient to the *f*.
11:24 full of the Holy Spirit and *f*,
13: 8 to turn the proconsul from the *f*.
14: 9 saw that he had *f* to be healed
14:22 them to remain true to the *f*.
14:27 the door of *f* to the Gentiles.
15: 9 for he purified their hearts by *f*.
16: 5 were strengthened in the *f*
20:21 and have *f* in our Lord Jesus.
24:24 as he spoke about *f* in Christ Jesus.
26:18 those who are sanctified by *f*
27:25 for I have *f* in God that it will
Ro 1: 5 to the obedience that comes from *f*.
1: 8 because your *f* is being reported all
1:12 encouraged by each other's *f*.
1:17 is by *f* from first to last,
1:17 "The righteous will live by *f*."
3: 3 What if some did not have *f*?
3: 3 lack of *f* nullify God's faithfulness?
Ro 3:22 comes through *f* in Jesus Christ
3:25 a sacrifice of atonement, through *f*
3:26 one who justifies those who have *f*
3:27 the law? No, but on that of *f*.
3:28 by *f* apart from observing the law.
3:30 through that same *f*.
3:30 will justify the circumcised by *f*
3:31 nullify the law by this *f*? Not at all!
4: 5 his *f* is credited as righteousness.
4: 9 that Abraham's *f* was credited
4:11 had by *f* while he was still
4:12 of the *f* that our father Abraham
4:13 the righteousness that comes by *f*.
4:14 *f* has no value and the promise is
4:16 Therefore, the promise comes by *f*,
4:16 are of the *f* of Abraham.
4:19 Without weakening in his *f*,
4:20 but was strengthened in his *f*
5: 1 we have been justified through *f*,
5: 2 access by *f* into this grace
9:30 a righteousness that is by *f*;
9:32 Because they pursued it not by *f*
10: 6 the righteousness that is by *f* says:
10: 8 the word of *f* we are proclaiming:
10:17 *f* comes from hearing the message,
11:20 of unbelief, and you stand by *f*.
12: 3 measure of *f* God has given you.
12: 6 let him use it in proportion to his *f*.
14: 1 Accept him whose *f* is weak,
14: 2 One man's *f* allows him
14: 2 but another man, whose *f* is weak,
14:23 because his eating is not from *f*;
14:23 that does not come from *f* is sin.
1Co 2: 5 so that your *f* might not rest
12: 9 to another *f* by the same Spirit,
13: 2 and if I have a *f* that can move
13:13 And now these three remain: *f*,
15:14 is useless and so is your *f*.
15:17 has not been raised, your *f* is futile;
16:13 stand firm in the *f*; be men
2Co 1:24 Not that we lord it over your *f*,
1:24 because it is by *f* you stand firm.
4:13 With that same spirit of *f* we
5: 7 We live by *f*, not by sight.
8: 7 in *f*, in speech, in knowledge,
10:15 as your *f* continues to grow,
13: 5 to see whether you are in the *f*;
Gal 1:23 now preaching the *f* he once tried
2:16 Jesus that we may be justified by *f*
2:16 but by *f* in Jesus Christ.
2:16 have put our *f* in Christ Jesus that
2:20 I live by *f* in the Son of God,
3: 8 would justify the Gentiles by *f*,
3: 9 So those who have *f* are blessed
3: 9 along with Abraham, the man of *f*.
3:11 "The righteous will live by *f*."
3:12 based on *f*; on the contrary,
3:14 by *f* we might receive the promise
3:22 being given through *f*
3:23 Before this *f* came, we were held
3:23 up until *f* should be revealed.
3:24 that we might be justified by *f*.
3:25 that *f* has come, we are no longer
3:26 of God through *f* in Christ Jesus,
5: 5 But by *f* we eagerly await
5: 6 that counts is *f* expressing itself
Eph 1:15 ever since I heard about your *f*
2: 8 through *f*—and this not
3:12 through *f* in him we may approach
3:17 dwell in your hearts through *f*.
4: 5 one Lord, one *f*, one baptism;
4:13 up until we all reach unity in the *f*
6:16 to all this, take up the shield of *f*,
6:23 love with *f* from God the Father
Php 1:25 for your progress and joy in the *f*,
1:27 as one man for the *f* of the gospel
2:17 and service coming from your *f*,
3: 9 comes from God and is by *f*.
3: 9 that which is through *f* in Christ—
Col 1: 4 heard of your *f* in Christ Jesus
1: 5 the *f* and love that spring
1:23 continue in your *f*, established
2: 5 and how firm your *f* in Christ is.
2: 7 in the *f* as you were taught,
2:12 him through your *f* in the power
1Th 1: 3 Father your work produced by *f*,
1: 8 your *f* in God has become known
3: 2 and encourage you in your *f*,
3: 5 I sent to find out about your *f*.
3: 6 brought good news about your *f*
1Th 3: 7 about you because of your *f*.
3:10 supply what is lacking in your *f*.
5: 8 on *f* and love as a breastplate,
2Th 1: 3 because your *f* is growing more
1: 4 and *f* in all the persecutions
1:11 and every act prompted by your *f*.
3: 2 evil men, for not everyone has *f*.
1Ti 1: 2 To Timothy my true son in the *f*:
1: 4 than God's work—which is by *f*.
1: 5 a good conscience and a sincere *f*.
1:14 along with the *f* and love that are
1:19 and so have shipwrecked their *f*.
1:19 on to *f* and a good conscience.
2: 7 of the true *f* to the Gentiles.
2:15 if they continue in *f*, love
3: 9 of the *f* with a clear conscience.
3:13 assurance in their *f* in Christ Jesus.
4: 1 later times some will abandon the *f*
4: 6 brought up in the truths of the *f*
4:12 in life, in love, in *f* and in purity.
5: 8 he has denied the *f* and is worse
6:10 have wandered from the *f*
6:11 pursue righteousness, godliness, *f*,
6:12 Fight the good fight of the *f*.
6:21 so doing have wandered from the *f*.
2Ti 1: 5 been reminded of your sincere *f*,
1:13 with *f* and love in Christ Jesus.
2:18 and they destroy the *f* of some.
2:22 and pursue righteousness, *f*,
3: 8 as far as the *f* is concerned,
3:10 my purpose, *f*, patience, love,
3:15 wise for salvation through *f*
4: 7 finished the race, I have kept the *f*.
Tit 1: 1 Christ for the *f* of God's elect
1: 2 a *f* and knowledge resting
1: 4 my true son in our common *f*:
1:13 so that they will be sound in the *f*
2: 2 self-controlled, and sound in *f*,
3:15 Greet those who love us in the *f*.
Phm : 5 because I hear about your *f*
: 6 may be active in sharing your *f*,
Heb 4: 2 heard did not combine it with *f*.
4:14 firmly to the *f* we profess.
6: 1 and of *f* in God, instruction about
6:12 but to imitate those who through *f*
10:22 heart in full assurance of *f*,
10:38 But my righteous one will live by *f*.
11: 1 *f* is being sure of what we hope for
11: 3 By *f* we understand that
11: 4 And by *f* he still speaks, even
11: 4 By *f* Abel offered God a better
11: 4 By *f* he was commended
11: 5 By *f* Enoch was taken from this life
11: 6 And without *f* it is impossible
11: 7 By his *f* he condemned the world
11: 7 By *f* Noah, when warned about
11: 7 the righteousness that comes by *f*.
11: 8 By *f* Abraham, when called to go
11: 9 By *f* he made his home
11:11 By *f* Abraham, even though he was
11:13 living by *f* when they died.
11:17 By *f* Abraham, when God tested
11:20 By *f* Isaac blessed Jacob
11:21 By *f* Jacob, when he was dying,
11:22 By *f* Joseph, when his end was near
11:23 By *f* Moses' parents hid him
11:24 By *f* Moses, when he had grown up
11:27 By *f* he left Egypt, not fearing
11:28 By *f* he kept the Passover
11:29 By *f* the people passed
11:30 By *f* the walls of Jericho fell,
11:31 By *f* the prostitute Rahab,
11:33 through *f* conquered kingdoms,
11:39 were all commended for their *f*,
12: 2 the author and perfecter of our *f*,
13: 7 way of life and imitate their *f*.
Jas 1: 3 of your *f* develops perseverance.
2: 5 the eyes of the world to be rich in *f*
2:14 has no deeds? Can such *f* save him?
2:14 if a man claims to have *f*
2:17 In the same way, *f* by itself,
2:18 I will show you my *f* by what I do.
2:18 Show me your *f* without deeds,
2:18 "You have *f*; I have deeds."
2:20 do you want evidence that *f*
2:22 You see that his *f* and his actions
2:22 and his *f* was made complete
2:24 by what he does and not by *f* alone.
2:26 so *f* without deeds is dead.
5:15 in *f* will make the sick person well;

1Pe 1: 5 who through *f* are shielded
1: 7 These have come so that your *f*—
1: 9 you are receiving the goal of your *f*,
1:21 and so your *f* and hope are in God.
5: 9 Resist him, standing firm in the *f*,
2Pe 1: 1 Jesus Christ have received a *f*
1: 5 effort to add to your *f* goodness;
1Jn 5: 4 overcome the world, even our *f*.
Jude :3 to contend for the *f* that was once
:20 up in your most holy *f*
Rev 2:13 You did not renounce your *f* in me,
2:19 your love and *f*, your service

FAITHFUL* (FAITH)

Nu 12: 7 he is *f* in all my house.
Dt 7: 9 your God is God; he is the *f* God,
32: 4 A *f* God who does no wrong,
1Sa 2:35 I will raise up for myself a *f* priest,
2Sa 20:19 We are the peaceful and *f* in Israel.
22:26 "To the *f* you show yourself *f*,
1Ki 3: 6 because he was *f* to you
2Ch 31:18 were *f* in consecrating themselves.
31:20 and *f* before the LORD his God.
Ne 9: 8 You found his heart *f* to you,
Ps 12: 1 the *f* have vanished
18:25 To the *f* you show yourself *f*,
25:10 of the LORD are loving and *f*
31:23 The LORD preserves the *f*,
33: 4 he is *f* in all he does.
37:28 and will not forsake his *f* ones.
78: 8 whose spirits were not *f* to him.
78:37 they were not *f* to his covenant.
89:19 to your *f* people you said:
89:24 My *f* love will be with him,
89:37 the *f* witness in the sky."
97:10 for he guards the lives of his *f* ones
101: 6 My eyes will be on the *f* in the land,
111: 7 The works of his hands are *f*
145: 13 The LORD is *f* to all his promises
146: 6 the LORD, who remains *f* forever.
Pr 2: 8 and protects the way of his *f* ones.
20: 6 but a *f* man who can find?
28:20 A *f* man will be richly blessed,
31:26 and *f* instruction is on her tongue.
Isa 1:21 See how the *f* city has become
1:26 the *F* City."
49: 7 because of the LORD, who is *f*,
55: 3 my *f* love promised to David.
Jer 42: 5 *f* witness against us if we do not act
Eze 43:11 so that they may be *f* to its design
48:11 who were *f* in serving me
Hos 11:12 even against the *f* Holy One.
Zec 8: 8 I will be *f* and righteous to them
Mt 24:45 Who then is the *f* and wise servant,
25:21 'Well done, good and *f* servant!
25:21 You have been *f* with a few things;
25:23 You have been *f* with a few things;
25:23 'Well done, good and *f* servant!
Lk 12:42 then is the *f* and wise manager,
Ro 12:12 patient in affliction, *f* in prayer.
1Co 1: 9 his Son Jesus Christ our Lord, is *f*.
4: 2 been given a trust must prove *f*.
4:17 my son whom I love, who is *f*
10:13 And God is *f*; he will not let you be
2Co 1:18 no"? But as surely as God is *f*,
Eph 1: 1 in Ephesus, the *f* in Christ Jesus:
6:21 the dear brother and *f* servant
Col 1: 2 and *f* brothers in Christ at Colosse:
1: 7 who is a *f* minister of Christ
4: 7 a *f* minister and fellow servant
4: 9 He is coming with Onesimus, our *f*
1Th 5:24 The one who calls you is *f*
2Th 3: 3 the Lord is *f*, and he will strengthen
1Ti 1:12 he considered me *f*, appointing me
5: 9 has been *f* to her husband,
2Ti 2:13 he will remain *f*,
Heb 2:17 and *f* high priest in service to God,
3: 2 He was *f* to the one who appointed
3: 2 as Moses was *f* in all God's house.
3: 5 Moses was *f* as a servant
3: 6 But Christ is *f* as a son
8: 9 because they did not remain *f*
10:23 for he who promised is *f*.
11:11 he considered him *f* who had made
1Pe 4:19 themselves to their *f* Creator
5:12 whom I regard as a *f* brother,
1Jn 1: 9 he is *f* and just and will forgive us
3Jn :5 you are *f* in what you are doing
Rev 1: 5 who is the *f* witness, the firstborn
2:10 Be *f*, even to the point of death,
Rev 2:13 the days of Antipas, my *f* witness,
3:14 the words of the Amen, the *f*
14:12 commandments and remain *f*
17:14 his called, chosen and *f* followers."
19:11 whose rider is called *F* and True.

FAITHFULLY* (FAITH)

Dt 11:13 if you *f* obey the commands I am
Jos 2:14 *f* when the LORD gives us the land
1Sa 12:24 and serve him *f* with all your heart;
1Ki 2: 4 and if they walk *f* before me
2Ki 20: 3 how I have walked before you *f*
22: 7 because they are acting *f*."
2Ch 19: 9 must serve *f* and wholeheartedly
31:12 they *f* brought in the contributions,
31:15 and Shecaniah assisted him *f*
32: 1 all that Hezekiah had so *f* done,
34:12 The men did the work *f*.
Ne 9:33 you have acted *f*, while we did
13:14 so *f* done for the house of my God
Isa 38: 3 how I have walked before you *f*
Jer 23:28 one who has my word speak it *f*.
Eze 18: 9 and *f* keeps my laws.
44:15 and who *f* carried out the duties
1Pe 4:10 *f* administering God's grace

FAITHFULNESS* (FAITH)

Ge 24:27 not abandoned his kindness and *f*
24:49 if you will show kindness and *f*
32:10 and *f* you have shown your servant.
47:29 you will show me kindness and *f*.
Ex 34: 6 *f*, maintaining love to thousands,
Jos 24:14 the LORD and serve him with all *f*.
1Sa 26:23 man for his righteousness and *f*.
2Sa 2: 6 now show you kindness and *f*,
15:20 May kindness and *f* be with you."
Ps 30: 9 Will it proclaim your *f*?
36: 5 your *f* to the skies.
40:10 I speak of your *f* and salvation.
54: 5 in your *f* destroy them.
57: 3 God sends his love and his *f*.
57:10 your *f* reaches to the skies.
61: 7 appoint your love and *f*
71:22 the harp for your *f*, O my God;
85:10 Love and *f* meet together;
85:11 *F* springs forth from the earth,
86:15 to anger, abounding in love and *f*.
88:11 your *f* in Destruction?
89: 1 mouth I will make your *f* known
89: 2 that you established your *f*
89: 5 your *f* too, in the assembly
89: 8 and your *f* surrounds you.
89:14 love and *f* go before you.
89:33 nor will I ever betray my *f*.
89:49 which in your *f* you swore to David
91: 4 his *f* will be your shield
92: 2 and your *f* at night,
98: 3 and his *f* to the house of Israel;
100: 5 *f* continues through all
108: 4 your *f* reaches to the skies.
111: 8 done in *f* and uprightness.
115: 1 because of your love and *f*.
117: 2 the *f* of the LORD endures forever.
119: 75 and in *f* you have afflicted me.
119: 90 *f* continues through all
138: 2 name for your love and your *f*,
143: 1 in your *f* and righteousness
Pr 3: 3 Let love and *f* never leave you;
14:22 plan what is good find love and *f*.
16: 6 Through love and *f* sin is atoned for
20:28 Love and *f* keep a king safe;
Isa 11: 5 and *f* the sash around his waist.
16: 5 in *f* a man will sit on it—
25: 1 for in perfect *f*
38:18 cannot hope for your *f*.
38:19 about your *f*.
42: 3 In *f* he will bring forth justice;
61: 8 In my *f* I will reward them
La 3:23 great is your *f*.
Hos 2:20 I will betroth you in *f*,
4: 1 "There is no *f*, no love,
Mt 23:23 of the law—justice, mercy and *f*.
Ro 3: 3 lack of faith nullify God's *f*?
Gal 5:22 patience, kindness, goodness, *f*,
3Jn :3 and tell about your *f* to the truth
Rev 13:10 and *f* on the part of the saints.

FAITHLESS* (FAITH)

Ps 78:57 fathers they were disloyal and *f*,
101: 3 The deeds of *f* men I hate;
119:158 I look on the *f* with loathing,
Pr 14:14 The *f* will be fully repaid
Jer 3: 6 you seen what *f* Israel has done?
3: 8 I gave *f* Israel her certificate
3:11 "*F* Israel is more righteous
3:12 *f* Israel,' declares the LORD,
3:14 *f* people," declares the LORD,
3:22 "Return, *f* people;
12: 1 Why do all the *f* live at ease?
Ro 1:31 they are senseless, *f*, heartless,
2Ti 2:13 if we are *f*,

FALL (FALLEN FALLING FALLS)

Ps 37:24 though he stumble, he will not *f*,
55:22 he will never let the righteous *f*.
69: 9 of those who insult you *f* on me.
145: 14 The LORD upholds all those who *f*
Pr 11:28 Whoever trusts in his riches will *f*,
Isa 40: 7 The grass withers and the flowers *f*,
Mt 7:25 yet it did not *f*, because it had its
Lk 10:18 "I saw Satan *f* like lightning
11:17 a house divided against itself will *f*.
23:30 say to the mountains, "*F* on us!"
Ro 3:23 and *f* short of the glory of God,
Heb 6: 6 if they *f* away, to be brought back

FALLEN (FALL)

2Sa 1:19 How the mighty have *f*!
Isa 14:12 How you have *f* from heaven,
1Co 11:30 and a number of you have *f* asleep.
15: 6 though some have *f* asleep.
15:18 who have *f* asleep in Christ are lost.
15:20 of those who have *f* asleep.
Gal 5: 4 you have *f* away from grace.
1Th 4:15 precede those who have *f* asleep.

FALLING (FALL)

Jude :24 able to keep you from *f*

FALLS (FALL)

Pr 11:14 For lack of guidance a nation *f*,
24:17 Do not gloat when your enemy *f*;
28:14 he who hardens his heart *f*
Mt 13:21 of the word, he quickly *f* away.
21:44 He who *f* on this stone will be
Jn 12:24 a kernel of wheat *f* to the ground
Ro 14: 4 To his own master he stands or *f*.

FALSE (FALSEHOOD FALSELY)

Ex 20:16 "You shall not give *f* testimony
23: 1 "Do not spread *f* reports.
23: 7 Have nothing to do with a *f* charge
Dt 5:20 "You shall not give *f* testimony
Pr 12:17 but a *f* witness tells lies.
13: 5 The righteous hate what is *f*,
14: 5 but a *f* witness pours out lies.
14:25 but a *f* witness is deceitful.
19: 5 A *f* witness will not go unpunished,
19: 9 A *f* witness will not go unpunished,
21:28 A *f* witness will perish,
25:18 is the man who gives *f* testimony
Isa 44:25 who foils the signs of *f* prophets
Jer 23:16 they fill you with *f* hopes.
Mt 7:15 "Watch out for *f* prophets.
15:19 theft, *f* testimony, slander.
19:18 not steal, do not give *f* testimony,
24:11 and many *f* prophets will appear
24:24 For *f* Christs and *f* prophets will
Mk 10:19 do not give *f* testimony, do not
13:22 For *f* Christs and *f* prophets will
Lk 6:26 their fathers treated the *f* prophets.
18:20 not steal, do not give *f* testimony,
Jn 1:47 in whom there is nothing *f*."
1Co 15:15 found to be *f* witnesses about God,
2Co 11:13 For such men are *f* apostles,
11:26 and in danger from *f* brothers.
Gal 2: 4 some *f* brothers had infiltrated our
Php 1:18 whether from *f* motives or true,
Col 2:18 anyone who delights in *f* humility
2:23 their *f* humility and their harsh
1Ti 1: 3 not to teach *f* doctrines any longer
6: 3 If anyone teaches *f* doctrines
2Pe 2: 1 also *f* prophets among the people,
2: 1 there will be *f* teachers among you.
1Jn 4: 1 many *f* prophets have gone out
Rev 16:13 out of the mouth of the *f* prophet.
19:20 with him the *f* prophet who had
20:10 and the *f* prophet had been thrown.

FALSEHOOD* (FALSE)

Job 21:34 left of your answers but *f*!"
31: 5 "If I have walked in *f*
Ps 52: 3 *f* rather than speaking the truth.
119:163 I hate and abhor *f*

Pr 30: 8 Keep *f* and lies far from me;
Isa 28:15 and *f* our hiding place."
Ro 3: 7 "If my *f* enhances God's
Eph 4:25 each of you must put off *f*
1Jn 4: 6 Spirit of truth and the spirit of *f*.
Rev 22:15 everyone who loves and practices *f*

FALSELY (FALSE)
Lev 19:12 " 'Do not swear *f* by my name
Mt 5:11 *f* say all kinds of evil against you
Lk 3:14 and don't accuse people *f*—
1Ti 6:20 ideas of what is *f* called knowledge,

FALTER*
Pr 24:10 If you *f* in times of trouble,
Isa 42: 4 he will not *f* or be discouraged

FAME
Jos 9: 9 of the *f* of the LORD your God.
Isa 66:19 islands that have not heard of my *f*
Hab 3: 2 LORD, I have heard of your *f*;

FAMILIES (FAMILY)
Ps 68: 6 God sets the lonely in *f*,

FAMILY (FAMILIES)
Pr 15:27 greedy man brings trouble to his *f*,
31:15 she provides food for her *f*
Mk 5:19 to your *f* and tell them how much
Lk 9:61 go back and say good-by to my *f*."
12:52 in one *f* divided against each other,
Ac 10: 2 He and all his *f* were devout
16:33 and all his *f* were baptized.
16:34 he and his whole *f*.
1Ti 3: 4 He must manage his own *f* well
3: 5 how to manage his own *f*,
5: 4 practice by caring for their own *f*
5: 8 and especially for his immediate *f*,

FAMINE
Ge 12:10 Now there was a *f* in the land,
26: 1 Now there was a *f* in the land—
41:30 seven years of *f* will follow them.
Ru 1: 1 the judges ruled, there was a *f*
1Ki 18: 2 Now the *f* was severe in Samaria,
Am 8:11 but a *f* of hearing the words
Ro 8:35 or persecution or *f* or nakedness

FAN*
2Ti 1: 6 you to *f* into flame the gift of God,

FANTASIES*
Ps 73:20 you will despise them as *f*.
Pr 12:11 but he who chases *f* lacks judgment
28:19 one who chases *f* will have his fill

FAST (FASTING)
Dt 10:20 Hold *f* to him and take your oaths
11:22 in all his ways and to hold *f* to him
13: 4 serve him and hold *f* to him.
30:20 to his voice, and hold *f* to him.
Jos 22: 5 to hold *f* to him and to serve him
23: 8 to hold *f* to the LORD your God,
2Ki 18: 6 He held *f* to the LORD
Ps 119: 31 I hold *f* to your statutes, O LORD;
139: 10 your right hand will hold me *f*.
Mt 6:16 "When you *f*, do not look somber
1Pe 5:12 Stand *f* in it.

FASTING (FAST)
Ps 35:13 and humbled myself with *f*.
Ac 13: 2 were worshiping the Lord and *f*,
14:23 and *f*, committed them to the Lord

FATHER (FATHER'S FATHERED FATHERLESS FATHERS FOREFATHERS)
Ge 2:24 this reason a man will leave his *f*
17: 4 You will be the *f* of many nations.
Ex 20:12 "Honor your *f* and your mother,
21:15 "Anyone who attacks his *f*
21:17 "Anyone who curses his *f*
Lev 18: 7 " 'Do not dishonor your *f*
19: 3 you must respect his mother and *f*,
20: 9 " 'If anyone curses his *f* or mother,
Dt 1:31 carried you, as a *f* carries his son,
5:16 "Honor your *f* and your mother,
21:18 son who does not obey his *f*
32: 6 Is he not your *F*, your Creator,
2Sa 7:14 I will be his *f*, and he will be my son
1Ch 17:13 I will be his *f*, and he will be my son
22:10 will be my son, and I will be his *f*.
28: 6 to be my son, and I will be his *f*.
Job 38:28 Does the rain have a *f*?
Ps 2: 7 today I have become your *F*.
27:10 Though my *f* and mother forsake
Ps 68: 5 A *f* to the fatherless, a defender
89:26 to me, 'You are my *F*,
103: 13 As a *f* has compassion
Pr 3:12 as a *f* the son he delights in.
10: 1 A wise son brings joy to his *f*,
17:21 there is no joy for the *f* of a fool.
17:25 A foolish son brings grief to his *f*
23:22 Listen to your *f*, who gave you life,
23:24 *f* of a righteous man has great joy;
28: 7 of gluttons disgraces his *f*.
28:24 He who robs his *f* or mother
29: 3 loves wisdom brings joy to his *f*,
Isa 9: 6 Everlasting *F*, Prince of Peace.
45:10 Woe to him who says to his *f*,
63:16 But you are our *F*,
Jer 2:27 They say to wood, 'You are my *f*,'
3:19 I thought you would call me '*F*'
31: 9 because I am Israel's *f*,
Eze 18:19 the son not share the guilt of his *f*?'
Mic 7: 6 For a son dishonors his *f*,
Mal 1: 6 If I am a *f*, where is the honor due
2:10 we not all one *F*? Did not one God
Mt 3: 9 'We have Abraham as our *f*.'
5:16 and praise your *F* in heaven.
6: 9 " 'Our *F* in heaven,
6:26 yet your heavenly *F* feeds them.
10:37 "Anyone who loves his *f*
11:27 no one knows the *F* except the Son
15: 4 'Honor your *f* and mother'
18:10 the face of my *F* in heaven.
19: 5 this reason a man will leave his *f*
19:19 honor your *f* and mother,'
19:29 or brothers or sisters or *f* or mother
23: 9 And do not call anyone on earth '*f*,'
Mk 7:10 'Honor your *f* and your mother,' and,
Lk 9:59 "Lord, first let me go and bury my *f*
12:53 *f* against son and son against *f*,
14:26 and does not hate his *f* and mother,
18:20 honor your *f* and mother.' "
23:34 Jesus said, "*F*, forgive them,
Jn 3:35 The *F* loves the Son and has placed
4:21 you will worship the *F* neither
5:17 "My *F* is always at his work
5:18 he was even calling God his own *F*,
5:20 For the *F* loves the Son
6:44 the *F* who sent me draws him,
6:46 No one has seen the *F*
8:19 "You do not know me or my *F*,"
8:28 speak just what the *F* has taught me
8:41 The only *F* we have is God himself
8:42 God were your *F*, you would love
8:44 You belong to your *f*, the devil,
10:17 reason my *F* loves me is that I lay
10:30 I and the *F* are one."
10:38 and understand that the *F* is in me,
14: 6 No one comes to the *F*
14: 9 who has seen me has seen the *F*.
14:28 for the *F* is greater than I.
15: 9 "As the *F* has loved me,
15:23 He who hates me hates my *F*
20:17 'I am returning to my *F* and your *F*,
Ac 13:33 today I have become your *F*.'
Ro 4:11 he is the *f* of all who believe
4:16 He is the *f* of us all.
8:15 And by him we cry, "*Abba, F.*"
1Co 4:15 for in Christ Jesus I became your *f*
2Co 6:18 "I will be a *F* to you,
Eph 5:31 this reason a man will leave his *f*
6: 2 "Honor your *f* and mother"—
Php 2:11 to the glory of God the *F*.
Heb 1: 5 today I have become your *F*"?
12: 7 what son is not disciplined by his *f*?
1Jn 1: 3 And our fellowship is with the *F*
2:15 the love of the *F* is not in him.
2:22 he denies the *F* and the Son.

FATHER'S (FATHER)
Pr 13: 1 A wise son heeds his *f* instruction,
15: 5 A fool spurns his *f* discipline,
19:13 A foolish son is his *f* ruin,
Mt 16:27 going to come in his *F* glory
Lk 2:49 had to be in my *F* house?"
Jn 2:16 How dare you turn my *F* house
10:29 can snatch them out of my *F* hand.
14: 2 In my *F* house are many rooms;
15: 8 to my *F* glory, that you bear much

FATHERED (FATHER)
Dt 32:18 You deserted the Rock, who *f* you;

FATHERLESS (FATHER)
Dt 10:18 He defends the cause of the *f*
Dt 14:29 the *f* and the widows who live
24:17 Do not deprive the alien or the *f*
24:19 Leave it for the alien, the *f*
26:12 the alien, the *f* and the widow,
Ps 68: 5 A father to the *f*, a defender
82: 3 Defend the cause of the weak and *f*
Pr 23:10 or encroach on the fields of the *f*,

FATHERS (FATHER)
Ex 20: 5 for the sin of the *f* to the third
Jer 31:29 'The *f* have eaten sour grapes,
Mal 4: 6 the hearts of the children to their *f*;
Lk 1:17 the hearts of the *f* to their children
11:11 "Which of you *f*, if your son asks
Jn 4:20 Our *f* worshiped on this mountain,
1Co 4:15 you do not have many *f*,
Eph 6: 4 *F*, do not exasperate your children;
Col 3:21 *F*, do not embitter your children,
Heb 12: 9 all had human *f* who disciplined us

FATHOM* (FATHOMED)
Job 11: 7 "Can you *f* the mysteries of God?
Ps 145: 3 his greatness no one can *f*.
Ecc 3:11 yet they cannot *f* what God has
Isa 40:28 and his understanding no one can *f*
1Co 13: 2 and can *f* all mysteries and all

FATHOMED* (FATHOM)
Job 5: 9 performs wonders that cannot be *f*,
9:10 performs wonders that cannot be *f*,

FATTENED
Pr 15:17 than a *f* calf with hatred.
Lk 15:23 Bring the *f* calf and kill it.

FAULT (FAULTS)
1Sa 29: 3 I have found no *f* in him."
Mt 18:15 and show him his *f*, just
Php 2:15 of God without *f* in a crooked
Jas 1: 5 generously to all without finding *f*,
Jude :24 his glorious presence without *f*

FAULTFINDERS*
Jude :16 These men are grumblers and *f*;

FAULTLESS*
Pr 8: 9 they are *f* to those who have
Php 3: 6 as for legalistic righteousness, *f*.
Jas 1:27 Father accepts as pure and *f* is this:

FAULTS* (FAULT)
Job 10: 6 that you must search out my *f*
Ps 19:12 Forgive my hidden *f*.

FAVOR (FAVORITISM)
Ge 4: 4 The LORD looked with *f* on Abel
6: 8 But Noah found *f* in the eyes
Ex 33:12 and you have found *f* with me.'
34: 9 if I have found *f* in your eyes,"
Lev 26: 9 " 'I will look on you with *f*
Nu 11:15 if I have found *f* in your eyes—
Jdg 6:17 "If now I have found *f* in your eyes,
1Sa 2:26 in *f* with the LORD and with men.
2Sa 2: 6 and I too will show you the same *f*
2Ki 13: 4 Jehoahaz sought the LORD's *f*,
2Ch 33:12 In his distress he sought the *f*
Est 7: 3 "If I have found *f* with you, O king,
Ps 90:17 May the *f* of the Lord our God rest
Pr 8:35 and receives *f* from the LORD.
18:22 and receives *f* from the LORD.
19: 6 Many curry *f* with a ruler,
Isa 61: 2 proclaim the year of the LORD's *f*
Zec 11: 7 called one *F* and the other Union,
Lk 1:30 Mary, you have found *f* with God.
2:14 to men on whom his *f* rests."
2:52 and in *f* with God and men.
4:19 to proclaim the year of the Lord's *f*
2Co 6: 2 now is the time of God's *f*,

FAVORITISM* (FAVOR)
Ex 23: 3 and do not show *f* to a poor man
Lev 19:15 to the poor or *f* to the great,
Ac 10:34 true it is that God does not show *f*
Ro 2:11 For God does not show *f*.
Eph 6: 9 and there is no *f* with him.
Col 3:25 for his wrong, and there is no *f*.
1Ti 5:21 and to do nothing out of *f*.
Jas 2: 1 Lord Jesus Christ, don't show *f*.
2: 9 But if you show *f*, you sin

FEAR (AFRAID FEARED FEARS FRIGHTENED GOD-FEARING)
Dt 6:13 *F* the LORD your God, serve him
10:12 but to *f* the LORD your God,
31:12 and learn to *f* the LORD your God

Dt 31:13 and learn to *f* the LORD your God
Jos 4:24 you might always *f* the LORD
24:14 "Now *f* the LORD and serve him
1Sa 12:14 If you *f* the LORD and serve
12:24 But be sure to *f* the LORD
2Sa 23: 3 when he rules in the *f* of God,
2Ch 19: 7 let the *f* of the LORD be upon you.
26: 5 who instructed him in the *f* of God.
Job 1: 9 "Does Job *f* God for nothing?"
Ps 2:11 Serve the LORD with *f*
19: 9 The *f* of the LORD is pure,
23: 4 I will *f* no evil,
27: 1 whom shall I *f*?
33: 8 Let all the earth *f* the LORD;
34: 7 around those who *f* him,
34: 9 *F* the LORD, you his saints,
46: 2 Therefore we will not *f*,
86:11 that I may *f* your name.
90:11 great as the *f* that is due you.
91: 5 You will not *f* the terror of night,
111: 10 *f* of the LORD is the beginning
118: 4 Let those who *f* the LORD say:
128: 1 Blessed are all who *f* the LORD,
145: 19 of those who *f* him;
147: 11 delights in those who *f* him,
Pr 1: 7 *f* of the LORD is the beginning
1:33 and be at ease, without *f* of harm."
8:13 To *f* the LORD is to hate evil;
9:10 *f* of the LORD is the beginning
10:27 The *f* of the LORD adds length
14:27 The *f* of the LORD is a fountain
15:33 *f* of the LORD teaches a man
16: 6 through the *f* of the LORD a man
19:23 The *f* of the LORD leads to life:
22: 4 Humility and the *f* of the LORD
29:25 *F* of man will prove to be a snare,
31:21 she has no *f* for her household;
Ecc 12:13 *F* God and keep his
Isa 11: 3 delight in the *f* of the LORD.
33: 6 the *f* of the LORD is the key
35: 4 "Be strong, do not *f*;
41:10 So do not *f*, for I am with you;
41:13 and says to you, Do not *f*;
43: 1 "*F* not, for I have redeemed you;
51: 7 Do not *f* the reproach of men
54:14 you will have nothing to *f*.
Jer 17: 8 It does not *f* when heat comes;
Lk 12: 5 I will show you whom you should *f*:
2Co 5:11 we know what it is to *f* the Lord,
Php 2:12 to work out your salvation with *f*
1Jn 4:18 But perfect love drives out *f*,
Jude :23 to others show mercy, mixed with *f*
Rev 14: 7 "*F* God and give him glory,

FEARED (FEAR)
Job 1: 1 he *f* God and shunned evil.
Ps 76: 7 You alone are to be *f*.
Mal 3:16 those who *f* the LORD talked

FEARS (FEAR)
Job 1: 8 a man who *f* God and shuns evil."
2: 3 a man who *f* God and shuns evil.
Ps 34: 4 he delivered me from all my *f*.
112: 1 is the man who *f* the LORD,
Pr 14:16 A wise man *f* the LORD
14:26 He who *f* the LORD has a secure
31:30 a woman who *f* the LORD is
2Co 7: 5 conflicts on the outside, *f* within.
1Jn 4:18 The one who *f* is not made perfect

FEAST (FEASTING FEASTS)
Pr 15:15 the cheerful heart has a continual *f*.
2Pe 2:13 pleasures while they *f* with you.

FEASTING (FEAST)
Pr 17: 1 than a house full of *f*, with strife.

FEASTS (FEAST)
Am 5:21 "I hate, I despise your religious *f*;
Jude :12 men are blemishes at your love *f*,

FEATHERS
Ps 91: 4 He will cover you with his *f*,

FEEBLE
Job 4: 3 you have strengthened *f* hands.
Isa 35: 3 Strengthen the *f* hands,
Heb 12:12 strengthen your *f* arms

FEED (FEEDS)
Jn 21:15 Jesus said, "*F* my lambs."
21:17 Jesus said, "*F* my sheep.
Ro 12:20 "If your enemy is hungry, *f* him;
Jude :12 shepherds who *f* only themselves.

FEEDS (FEED)
Pr 15:14 but the mouth of a fool *f* on folly.
Mt 6:26 yet your heavenly Father *f* them.
Jn 6:57 so the one who *f* on me will live

FEEL
Jdg 16:26 me where I can *f* the pillars that
Ps 115: 7 they have hands, but cannot *f*,

FEET (FOOT)
Ru 3: 8 discovered a woman lying at his *f*.
Ps 8: 6 you put everything under his *f*:
22:16 have pierced my hands and my *f*.
40: 2 he set my *f* on a rock
56:13 and my *f* from stumbling,
66: 9 and kept our *f* from slipping.
73: 2 as for me, my *f* had almost slipped;
110: 1 a footstool for your *f*."
119:105 Your word is a lamp to my *f*
Pr 4:26 Make level paths for your *f*
Isa 52: 7 are the *f* of those who bring good
Da 2:33 its *f* partly of iron and partly
Na 1:15 the *f* of one who brings good news,
Mt 10:14 shake the dust off your *f*
22:44 enemies under your *f*."
Lk 1:79 to guide our *f* into the path of peace
20:43 a footstool for your *f*."
24:39 Look at my hands and my *f*.
Jn 13: 5 and began to wash his disciples' *f*,
13:14 also should wash one another's *f*.
Ro 3:15 "Their *f* are swift to shed blood;
10:15 "How beautiful are the *f*
16:20 will soon crush Satan under your *f*.
1Co 12:21 And the head cannot say to the *f*,
15:25 has put all his enemies under his *f*.
Eph 1:22 God placed all things under his *f*
1Ti 5:10 washing the *f* of the saints,
Heb 1:13 a footstool for your *f*"?
2: 8 and put everything under his *f*."
12:13 "Make level paths for your *f*,"
Rev 1:15 His *f* were like bronze glowing

FELIX
Governor before whom Paul was tried (Ac 23:23–24:27).

FELLOWSHIP
Ex 20:24 burnt offerings and *f* offerings,
Lev 3: 1 If someone's offering is a *f* offering,
1Co 1: 9 who has called you into *f*
5: 2 out of your *f* the man who did this?
2Co 6:14 what *f* can light have with darkness
13:14 and the *f* of the Holy Spirit be
Gal 2: 9 and Barnabas the right hand of *f*
Php 2: 1 if any *f* with the Spirit,
3:10 the *f* of sharing in his sufferings,
1Jn 1: 3 And our *f* is with the Father
1: 3 so that you also may have *f* with us.
1: 6 claim to have *f* with him yet walk
1: 7 we have *f* with one another,

FEMALE
Ge 1:27 male and *f* he created them.
5: 2 He created them male and *f*
Mt 19: 4 Creator 'made them male and *f*,'
Mk 10: 6 God 'made them male and *f*.'
Gal 3:28 *f*, for you are all one in Christ Jesus

FEROCIOUS
Mt 7:15 but inwardly they are *f* wolves.

FERTILE (FERTILIZE)
Isa 32:15 and the desert becomes a *f* field,
Jer 2: 7 I brought you into a *f* land

FERTILIZE* (FERTILE)
Lk 13: 8 and I'll dig around it and *f* it.

FERVOR*
Ac 18:25 and he spoke with great *f*
Ro 12:11 but keep your spiritual *f*, serving

FESTIVAL
1Co 5: 8 Therefore let us keep the *F*,
Col 2:16 or with regard to a religious *f*,

FESTUS
Successor of Felix; sent Paul to Caesar (Ac 25–26).

FEVER
Job 30:30 my body burns with *f*.
Mt 8:14 mother-in-law lying in bed with a *f*.
Lk 4:38 was suffering from a high *f*,
Jn 4:52 "The *f* left him yesterday
Ac 28: 8 suffering from *f* and dysentery.

FIELD (FIELDS)
Ge 4: 8 Abel, "Let's go out to the *f*."
Lev 19: 9 reap to the very edges of your *f*
19:19 Do not plant your *f* with two kinds
Pr 31:16 She considers a *f* and buys it;
Isa 40: 6 glory is like the flowers of the *f*.
Mt 6:28 See how the lilies of the *f* grow.
6:30 how God clothes the grass of the *f*,
13:38 *f* is the world, and the good seed
13:44 is like treasure hidden in a *f*.
Lk 14:18 I have just bought a *f*, and I must go
1Co 3: 9 you are God's *f*, God's building.
1Pe 1:24 glory is like the flowers of the *f*;

FIELDS (FIELD)
Ru 2: 2 go to the *f* and pick up the leftover
Lk 2: 8 were shepherds living out in the *f*
Jn 4:35 open your eyes and look at the *f*!

FIG (FIGS SYCAMORE-FIG)
Ge 3: 7 so they sewed *f* leaves together
Jdg 9:10 "Next, the trees said to the *f* tree,
1Ki 4:25 man under his own vine and *f* tree.
Pr 27:18 He who tends a *f* tree will eat its
Mic 4: 4 and under his own *f* tree,
Zec 3:10 to sit under his vine and *f* tree,'
Mt 21:19 Seeing a *f* tree by the road,
Lk 13: 6 "A man had a *f* tree, planted
Jas 3:12 brothers, can a *f* tree bear olives,
Rev 6:13 drop from a *f* tree when shaken

FIGHT (FIGHTING FIGHTS FOUGHT)
Ex 14:14 The LORD will *f* for you; you need
Dt 1:30 going before you, will *f* for you,
3:22 the LORD your God himself will *f*
Ne 4:20 Our God will *f* for us!"
Ps 35: 1 *f* against those who *f* against me.
Jn 18:36 my servants would *f*
1Co 9:26 I do not *f* like a man beating the air.
2Co 10: 4 The weapons we *f*
1Ti 1:18 them you may *f* the good *f*,
6:12 Fight the good *f* of the faith.
2Ti 4: 7 fought the good *f*, I have finished

FIGHTING (FIGHT)
Jos 10:14 Surely the LORD was *f* for Israel!

FIGHTS (FIGHT)
Jos 23:10 the LORD your God *f* for you,
1Sa 25:28 because he *f* the LORD's battles.
Jas 4: 1 What causes *f* and quarrels

FIGS (FIG)
Lk 6:44 People do not pick *f*
Jas 3:12 grapevine bear *f*? Neither can a salt

FILL (FILLED FILLING FILLS FULL FULLNESS FULLY)
Ge 1:28 and increase in number; *f* the earth
Ps 16:11 you will *f* me with joy
81:10 wide your mouth and I will *f* it.
Pr 28:19 who chases fantasies will have his *f*
Hag 2: 7 and I will *f* this house with glory,'
Jn 6:26 you ate the loaves and had your *f*.
Ac 2:28 you will *f* me with joy
Ro 15:13 the God of hope *f* you with all joy

FILLED (FILL)
Ex 31: 3 I have *f* him with the Spirit of God,
35:31 he has *f* him with the Spirit of God,
Dt 34: 9 son of Nun was *f* with the spirit
1Ki 8:10 the cloud *f* the temple
8:11 glory of the LORD *f* his temple.
2Ch 5:14 of the LORD *f* the temple of God.
7: 1 the glory of the LORD *f* the temple
Ps 72:19 may the whole earth be *f*
119: 64 The earth is *f* with your love,
Isa 6: 4 and the temple was *f* with smoke.
Eze 10: 3 and a cloud *f* the inner court.
10: 4 The cloud *f* the temple,
43: 5 the glory of the LORD *f* the temple
Hab 2:14 For the earth will be *f*
3: 3 and his praise *f* the earth.
Mt 5: 6 for they will be *f*.
Lk 1:15 and he will be *f* with the Holy Spirit
1:41 and Elizabeth was *f* with the Holy
1:67 His father Zechariah was *f*
2:40 and became strong; he was *f*
Jn 12: 3 the house was *f* with the fragrance
Ac 2: 2 *f* the whole house where they were
2: 4 All of them were *f*
4: 8 Then Peter, *f* with the Holy Spirit,

Ac 4:31 they were all *f* with the Holy Spirit
9:17 and be *f* with the Holy Spirit."
13: 9 called Paul, *f* with the Holy Spirit,
Eph 5:18 Instead, be *f* with the Spirit.
Php 1:11 *f* with the fruit of righteousness
Rev 15: 8 And the temple was *f* with smoke

FILLING (FILL)
Eze 44: 4 the glory of the LORD *f* the temple

FILLS (FILL)
Nu 14:21 of the LORD *f* the whole earth,
Ps 107: 9 and *f* the hungry with good things.
Eph 1:23 fullness of him who *f* everything

FILTH (FILTHY)
Isa 4: 4 The Lord will wash away the *f*
Jas 1:21 rid of all moral *f* and the evil that is

FILTHY (FILTH)
Isa 64: 6 all our righteous acts are like *f* rags;
Col 3: 8 and *f* language from your lips.
2Pe 2: 7 by the *f* lives of lawless men

FINAL (FINALITY)
Ps 73:17 then I understood their *f* destiny.

FINALITY* (FINAL)
Ro 9:28 on earth with speed and *f*."

FINANCIAL*
1Ti 6: 5 that godliness is a means to *f* gain.

FIND (FINDS FOUND)
Nu 32:23 be sure that your sin will *f* you out.
Dt 4:29 you will *f* him if you look for him
1Sa 23:16 and helped him *f* strength in God.
Job 23: 3 If only I knew where to *f* him;
Ps 36: 7 *f* refuge in the shadow
62: 5 *F* rest, O my soul, in God alone;
91: 4 under his wings you will *f* refuge;
Pr 8:17 and those who seek me *f* me.
14:22 those who plan what is good *f* love
20: 6 but a faithful man who can *f*?
24:14 if you *f* it, there is a future hope
31:10 A wife of noble character who can *f*
Jer 6:16 and you will *f* rest for your souls.
29:13 and *f* me when you seek me
Mt 7: 7 seek and you will *f*; knock
11:29 and you will *f* rest for your souls.
16:25 loses his life for me will *f* it.
22: 9 invite to the banquet anyone you *f*.'
Lk 11: 9 seek and you will *f*; knock
18: 8 will he *f* faith on the earth?"
Jn 10: 9 come in and go out, and *f* pasture.

FINDS (FIND)
Ps 62: 1 My soul *f* rest in God alone;
112: 1 who *f* great delight
119:162 like one who *f* great spoil.
Pr 3:13 Blessed is the man who *f* wisdom,
8:35 For whoever *f* me *f* life
11:27 He who seeks good *f* good will,
18:22 He who *f* a wife *f* what is good
Mt 7: 8 he who seeks *f*; and to him who
10:39 Whoever *f* his life will lose it,
Lk 11:10 he who seeks *f*; and to him who
12:37 whose master *f* them watching
12:43 servant whom the master *f* doing
15: 4 go after the lost sheep until he *f* it?
15: 8 and search carefully until she *f* it?

FINE-SOUNDING* (SOUND)
Col 2: 4 may deceive you by *f* arguments.

FINGER
Ex 8:19 to Pharaoh, "This is the *f* of God."
31:18 of stone inscribed by the *f* of God.
Dt 9:10 two stone tablets inscribed by the *f*
Lk 11:20 But if I drive out demons by the *f*
16:24 to dip the tip of his *f* in water
Jn 8: 6 to write on the ground with his *f*.
20:25 and put my *f* where the nails were,

FINISH (FINISHED)
Jn 4:34 him who sent me and to *f* his work.
5:36 that the Father has given me to *f*,
Ac 20:24 if only I may *f* the race
2Co 8:11 Now *f* the work, so that your eager
Jas 1: 4 Perseverance must *f* its work

FINISHED (FINISH)
Ge 2: 2 seventh day God had *f* the work he
Jn 19:30 the drink, Jesus said, "It is *f*."
2Ti 4: 7 I have *f* the race, I have kept

FIRE
Ex 3: 2 in flames of *f* from within a bush.
13:21 in a pillar of *f* to give them light,
Lev 6:12 *f* on the altar must be kept burning;
9:24 *F* came out from the presence
1Ki 18:38 Then the *f* of the LORD fell
2Ki 2:11 suddenly a chariot of *f*
Isa 5:24 as tongues of *f* lick up straw
30:27 and his tongue is a consuming *f*.
Jer 23:29 my word like *f*," declares
Da 3:25 four men walking around in the *f*,
Zec 3: 2 stick snatched from the *f*?"
Mal 3: 2 For he will be like a refiner's *f*
Mt 3:11 you with the Holy Spirit and with *f*.
3:12 the chaff with unquenchable *f*."
5:22 will be in danger of the *f* of hell.
18: 8 and be thrown into eternal *f*.
25:41 into the eternal *f* prepared
Mk 9:43 where the *f* never goes out.
9:48 and the *f* is not quenched.'
9:49 Everyone will be salted with *f*.
Lk 3:16 you with the Holy Spirit and with *f*.
12:49 I have come to bring *f* on the earth,
Ac 2: 3 to be tongues of *f* that separated
1Co 3:13 It will be revealed with *f*,
1Th 5:19 Do not put out the Spirit's *f*;
Heb 12:29 for our "God is a consuming *f*."
Jas 3: 5 set on *f* by a small spark.
3: 6 also is a *f*, a world of evil
2Pe 3:10 the elements will be destroyed by *f*,
Jude : 7 suffer the punishment of eternal *f*.
:23 snatch others from the *f*
Rev 1:14 and his eyes were like blazing *f*.
20:14 The lake of *f* is the second death.

FIRM*
Ex 14:13 Stand *f* and you will see
15: 8 surging waters stood *f* like a wall;
Jos 3:17 the covenant of the LORD stood *f*
2Ch 20:17 stand *f* and see the deliverance
Ezr 9: 8 giving us a *f* place in his sanctuary,
Job 11:15 you will stand *f* and without fear.
36: 5 he is mighty, and *f* in his purpose.
41:23 they are *f* and immovable.
Ps 20: 8 but we rise up and stand *f*.
30: 7 you made my mountain stand *f*;
33: 9 he commanded, and it stood *f*.
33:11 of the LORD stand *f* forever,
37:23 he makes his steps *f*;
40: 2 and gave me a *f* place to stand.
75: 3 it is I who hold its pillars *f*.
78:13 made the water stand *f* like a wall.
89: 2 that your love stands *f* forever,
89: 4 and make your throne *f*
93: 5 Your statutes stand *f*;
119: 89 it stands *f* in the heavens.
Pr 4:26 and take only ways that are *f*.
10:25 but the righteous stand *f* forever.
12: 7 the house of the righteous stands *f*.
Isa 7: 9 If you do not stand *f* in your faith,
22:17 about to take *f* hold of you
22:23 drive him like a peg into a *f* place;
22:25 into the *f* place will give way;
Eze 13: 5 so that it will stand *f* in the battle
Zec 8:23 nations will take *f* hold of one Jew
Mt 10:22 he who stands *f* to the end will be
24:13 he who stands *f* to the end will be
Mk 13:13 he who stands *f* to the end will be
Lk 21:19 By standing *f* you will gain life.
1Co 10:12 So, if you think you are standing *f*,
15:58 my dear brothers, stand *f*.
16:13 on your guard; stand *f* in the faith;
2Co 1: 7 for you is *f*, because we know that
1:21 who makes both us and you stand *f*
1:24 because it is by faith you stand *f*.
Gal 5: 1 Stand *f*, then, and do not let
Eph 6:14 Stand *f* then, with the belt
Php 1:27 I will know that you stand *f*
4: 1 that is how you should stand *f*
Col 1:23 in your faith, established and *f*,
2: 5 and how *f* your faith in Christ is.
4:12 that you may stand *f* in all the will
1Th 3: 8 since you are standing *f* in the Lord
2Th 2:15 stand *f* and hold to the teachings
1Ti 6:19 a *f* foundation for the coming age,
2Ti 2:19 God's solid foundation stands *f*,
Heb 6:19 an anchor for the soul, *f* and secure
Jas 5: 8 You too, be patient and stand *f*,
1Pe 5: 9 Resist him, standing *f* in the faith,
5:10 make you strong, *f* and steadfast.

FIRST
Ge 1: 5 and there was morning—the *f* day.
13: 4 and where he had *f* built an altar.
Ex 34:19 *f* offspring of every womb belongs
1Ki 22: 5 "*F* seek the counsel of the LORD."
Pr 18:17 *f* to present his case seems right,
Isa 44: 6 I am the *f* and I am the last;
48:12 I am the *f* and I am the last.
Mt 5:24 *F* go and be reconciled
6:33 But seek *f* his kingdom
7: 5 *f* take the plank out
19:30 But many who are *f* will be last,
20:16 last will be *f*, and the *f* will be last."
20:27 wants to be *f* must be your slave—
22:38 This is the *f* and greatest
23:26 *F* clean the inside of the cup
Mk 9:35 to be *f*, he must be the very last,
10:31 are *f* will be last, and the last *f*."
10:44 wants to be *f* must be slave
13:10 And the gospel must *f* be preached
Lk 13:30 will be *f*, and *f* who will be last."
Jn 8: 7 let him be the *f* to throw a stone
Ac 11:26 disciples were called Christians *f*
Ro 1:16 *f* for the Jew, then for the Gentile.
1:17 is by faith from *f* to last,
2: 9 *f* for the Jew, then for the Gentile;
2:10 *f* for the Jew, then for the Gentile.
1Co 12:28 in the church God has appointed *f*
15:45 "The *f* man Adam became a living
2Co 8: 5 they gave themselves *f* to the Lord
Eph 6: 2 which is the *f* commandment
1Th 4:16 and the dead in Christ will rise *f*.
1Ti 2:13 For Adam was formed *f*, then Eve.
Heb 10: 9 He sets aside the *f*
Jas 3:17 comes from heaven is *f* of all pure;
1Jn 4:19 We love because he *f* loved us.
3Jn : 9 but Diotrephes, who loves to be *f*,
Rev 1:17 I am the *F* and the Last.
2: 4 You have forsaken your *f* love.
22:13 and the Omega, the *F* and the Last,

FIRSTBORN (BEAR)
Ex 11: 5 Every *f* son in Egypt will die,
34:20 Redeem all your *f* sons.
Ps 89:27 I will also appoint him my *f*,
Lk 2: 7 and she gave birth to her *f*, a son.
Ro 8:29 that he might be the *f*
Col 1:15 image of the invisible God, the *f*
1:18 and the *f* from among the dead,
Heb 1: 6 when God brings his *f*
12:23 of the *f*, whose names are written
Rev 1: 5 who is the faithful witness, the *f*

FIRSTFRUITS
Ex 23:16 the Feast of Harvest with the *f*
23:19 "Bring the best of the *f* of your soil
Ro 8:23 who have the *f* of the Spirit,
1Co 15:23 Christ, the *f*; then, when he comes,
Rev 14: 4 offered as *f* to God and the Lamb.

FISH (FISHERS)
Ge 1:26 let them rule over the *f* of the sea
Jnh 1:17 But the LORD provided a great *f*
Mt 7:10 asks for a *f*, will give him a snake?
12:40 three nights in the belly of a huge *f*,
14:17 loaves of bread and two *f*,"
Mk 6:38 they said, "Five—and two *f*."
Lk 5: 6 of *f* that their nets began to break.
9:13 loaves of bread and two *f*—
Jn 6: 9 small barley loaves and two small *f*,
21: 5 haven't you any *f*?" "No,"
21:11 It was full of large *f*, 153, but

FISHERMEN
Mk 1:16 a net into the lake, for they were *f*.

FISHERS (FISH)
Mt 4:19 "and I will make you *f* of men."
Mk 1:17 "and I will make you *f* of men."

FISHHOOK*
Job 41: 1 pull in the leviathan with a *f*

FISTS
Mt 26:67 and struck him with their *f*.

FIT (FITTING)
Jdg 17: 6 no king; everyone did as he saw *f*.
21:25 no king; everyone did as he saw *f*.

FITTING* (FIT)
Ps 33: 1 it is *f* for the upright to praise him.
147: 1 how pleasant and *f* to praise him!
Pr 10:32 of the righteous know what is *f*,

Pr 19:10 It is not *f* for a fool to live in luxury
26: 1 honor is not *f* for a fool.
1Co 14:40 everything should be done in a *f*
Col 3:18 to your husbands, as is *f* in the Lord
Heb 2:10 sons to glory, it was *f* that God,

FIX* (FIXED)
Dt 11:18 *F* these words of mine
Job 14: 3 Do you *f* your eye on such a one?
Pr 4:25 *f* your gaze directly before you.
Isa 46: 8 "Remember this, *f* it in mind,
Am 9: 4 I will *f* my eyes upon them
2Co 4:18 we *f* our eyes not on what is seen,
Heb 3: 1 heavenly calling, *f* your thoughts
12: 2 Let us *f* our eyes on Jesus,

FIXED* (FIX)
2Ki 8:11 stared at him with a *f* gaze
Job 38:10 when I *f* limits for it
Ps 141: 8 my eyes are *f* on you, O Sovereign
Pr 8:28 *f* securely the fountains of the deep
Jer 33:25 and night and the *f* laws of heaven
Lk 16:26 and you a great chasm has been *f*,

FLAME (FLAMES FLAMING)
2Ti 1: 6 you to fan into *f* the gift of God,

FLAMES (FLAME)
1Co 3:15 only as one escaping through the *f*.
13: 3 and surrender my body to the *f*,

FLAMING (FLAME)
Eph 6:16 you can extinguish all the *f* arrows

FLANK
Eze 34:21 Because you shove with *f*

FLASH
1Co 15:52 in a *f*, in the twinkling of an eye,

FLATTER* (FLATTERING FLATTERS FLATTERY)
Job 32:21 nor will I *f* any man;
Ps 78:36 But then they would *f* him
Jude :16 *f* others for their own advantage.

FLATTERING* (FLATTER)
Ps 12: 2 their *f* lips speak with deception.
12: 3 May the LORD cut off all *f* lips
Pr 26:28 and a *f* mouth works ruin.
28:23 than he who has a *f* tongue.
Eze 12:24 or *f* divinations among the people

FLATTERS* (FLATTER)
Ps 36: 2 For in his own eyes he *f* himself
Pr 29: 5 Whoever *f* his neighbor

FLATTERY* (FLATTER)
Job 32:22 for if I were skilled in *f*,
Da 11:32 With *f* he will corrupt those who
Ro 16:18 and *f* they deceive the minds
1Th 2: 5 You know we never used *f*,

FLAWLESS*
2Sa 22:31 the word of the LORD is *f*.
Job 11: 4 You say to God, 'My beliefs are *f*
Ps 12: 6 And the words of the LORD are *f*,
18:30 the word of the LORD is *f*.
Pr 30: 5 "Every word of God is *f*;
SS 5: 2 my dove, my *f* one.

FLEE (FLEES)
Ps 139: 7 Where can I *f* from your presence?
1Co 6:18 *F* from sexual immorality.
10:14 my dear friends, *f* from idolatry.
1Ti 6:11 But you, man of God, *f* from all this
2Ti 2:22 *F* the evil desires of youth,
Jas 4: 7 Resist the devil, and he will *f*

FLEECE
Jdg 6:37 I will place a wool *f*

FLEES (FLEE)
Pr 28: 1 The wicked man *f* though no one

FLEETING*
Job 14: 2 like a *f* shadow, he does not endure
Ps 39: 4 let me know how *f* is my life.
89:47 Remember how *f* is my life.
144: 4 his days are like a *f* shadow.
Pr 21: 6 is a *f* vapor and a deadly snare.
31:30 Charm is deceptive, and beauty is *f*

FLESH
Ge 2:23 and *f* of my *f*;
2:24 and they will become one *f*.
2Ch 32: 8 With him is only the arm of *f*,
Job 19:26 yet in my *f* I will see God;
Eze 11:19 of stone and give them a heart of *f*.
36:26 of stone and give you a heart of *f*.
Mt 19: 5 and the two will become one *f*?
Mk 10: 8 and the two will become one *f*.'
Jn 1:14 The Word became *f* and made his
6:51 This bread is my *f*, which I will give
1Co 6:16 "The two will become one *f*."
15:39 All *f* is not the same: Men have one
Eph 5:31 and the two will become one *f*."
6:12 For our struggle is not against *f*
Php 3: 2 do evil, those mutilators of the *f*.
1Jn 4: 2 come in the *f* is from God,
Jude :23 the clothing stained by corrupted *f*.

FLIGHT
Dt 32:30 or two put ten thousand to *f*,

FLINT
Isa 50: 7 Therefore have I set my face like *f*,
Zec 7:12 They made their hearts as hard as *f*

FLIRTING*
Isa 3:16 *f* with their eyes,

FLOCK (FLOCKS)
Ps 77:20 You led your people like a *f*
78:52 he brought his people out like a *f*;
95: 7 the *f* under his care.
Isa 40:11 He tends his *f* like a shepherd:
Jer 10:21 and all their *f* is scattered.
23: 2 "Because you have scattered my *f*
31:10 watch over his *f* like a shepherd.'
Eze 34: 2 not shepherds take care of the *f*?
Zec 11:17 who deserts the *f*!
Mt 26:31 the sheep of the *f* will be scattered.'
Lk 12:32 little *f*, for your Father has been
Jn 10:16 shall be one *f* and one shepherd.
Ac 20:28 all the *f* of which the Holy Spirit
1Co 9: 7 Who tends a *f* and does not drink
1Pe 5: 2 Be shepherds of God's *f* that is
5: 3 but being examples to the *f*.

FLOCKS (FLOCK)
Lk 2: 8 keeping watch over their *f* at night.

FLOG (FLOGGED FLOGGING)
Pr 19:25 *F* a mocker, and the simple will
Ac 22:25 to *f* a Roman citizen who hasn't

FLOGGED (FLOG)
Jn 19: 1 Pilate took Jesus and had him *f*.
Ac 5:40 the apostles in and had them *f*.
16:23 After they had been severely *f*,
2Co 11:23 frequently, been *f* more severely,

FLOGGING (FLOG)
Heb 11:36 *f*, while still others were chained

FLOOD (FLOODGATES)
Ge 7: 7 ark to escape the waters of the *f*.
Mal 2:13 You *f* the LORD's altar with tears.
Mt 24:38 For in the days before the *f*,
2Pe 2: 5 world when he brought the *f*

FLOODGATES (FLOOD)
Ge 7:11 the *f* of the heavens were opened.
Mal 3:10 see if I will not throw open the *f*

FLOOR
Jas 2: 3 or "Sit on the *f* by my feet,"

FLOUR
Lev 2: 1 his offering is to be of fine *f*.
Nu 7:13 filled with fine *f* mixed with oil
28: 9 of an ephah of fine *f* mixed with oil.

FLOURISH (FLOURISHES FLOURISHING)
Ps 72: 7 In his days the righteous will *f*;
92: 7 and all evildoers *f*,
92:12 The righteous will *f* like a palm tree
Pr 14:11 but the tent of the upright will *f*.

FLOURISHES (FLOURISH)
Pr 12:12 but the root of the righteous *f*.

FLOURISHING (FLOURISH)
Ps 52: 8 *f* in the house of God;

FLOW (FLOWING)
Nu 13:27 and it does *f* with milk and honey!
Jn 7:38 streams of living water will *f*

FLOWER (FLOWERS)
Job 14: 2 up like a *f* and withers away;
Ps 103: 15 he flourishes like a *f* of the field;
Jas 1:10 he will pass away like a wild *f*.

FLOWERS (FLOWER)
Isa 40: 6 and all their glory is like the *f*
Isa 40: 7 The grass withers and the *f* fall,
1Pe 1:24 and all their glory is like the *f*

FLOWING (FLOW)
Ex 3: 8 a land *f* with milk and honey—
33: 3 Go up to the land *f* with milk
Nu 16:14 us into a land *f* with milk
Jos 5: 6 a land *f* with milk and honey.
Ps 107: 33 *f* springs into thirsty ground,
107: 35 the parched ground into *f* springs;
Jer 32:22 a land *f* with milk and honey.
Eze 20: 6 a land *f* with milk and honey,
Rev 22: 1 *f* from the throne of God

FLUTE
Ps 150: 4 praise him with the strings and *f*,
Mt 11:17 " 'We played the *f* for you,
1Co 14: 7 that make sounds, such as the *f*

FOAL*
Zec 9: 9 on a colt, the *f* of a donkey.
Mt 21: 5 on a colt, the *f* of a donkey.' "

FOILS*
Ps 33:10 The LORD *f* the plans
Isa 44:25 who *f* the signs of false prophets

FOLDING* (FOLDS)
Pr 6:10 a little *f* of the hands to rest—
24:33 a little *f* of the hands to rest—

FOLDS (FOLDING)
Ecc 4: 5 The fool *f* his hands

FOLLOW (FOLLOWED FOLLOWING FOLLOWS)
Ex 23: 2 Do not *f* the crowd in doing wrong.
Lev 18: 4 and be careful to *f* my decrees.
Dt 5: 1 Learn them and be sure to *f* them.
17:19 *f* carefully all the words of this law
1Ki 11: 6 he did not *f* the LORD completely,
2Ch 34:33 they did not fail to *f* the LORD,
Ps 23: 6 Surely goodness and love will *f* me
119:166 and I *f* your commands.
Mt 4:19 *f* me," Jesus said, "and I will make
8:19 I will *f* you wherever you go."
8:22 But Jesus told him, "*F* me,
16:24 and take up his cross and *f* me.
19:27 "We have left everything to *f* you!
Lk 9:23 take up his cross daily and *f* me.
9:61 Still another said, "I will *f* you,
Jn 10: 4 his sheep *f* him because they know
10: 5 But they will never *f* a stranger;
10:27 I know them, and they *f* me.
12:26 Whoever serves me must *f* me;
21:19 Then he said to him, "*F* me!"
1Co 1:12 One of you says, "I *f* Paul";
11: 1 *F* my example, as I follow
14: 1 *F* the way of love and eagerly
2Th 3: 9 ourselves a model for you to *f*.
1Pe 2:21 that you should *f* in his steps.
Rev 14: 4 They *f* the Lamb wherever he goes.

FOLLOWED (FOLLOW)
Nu 32:11 they have not *f* me wholeheartedly,
Dt 1:36 he *f* the LORD wholeheartedly."
Jos 14:14 he *f* the LORD, the God of Israel,
2Ch 10:14 he *f* the advice of the young men
Mt 4:20 once they left their nets and *f* him.
9: 9 and Matthew got up and *f* him.
26:58 But Peter *f* him at a distance,
Lk 18:43 he received his sight and *f* Jesus,

FOLLOWING (FOLLOW)
Ps 119: 14 I rejoice in *f* your statutes
Php 3:17 Join with others in *f* my example,
1Ti 1:18 by *f* them you may fight the good

FOLLOWS (FOLLOW)
Jn 8:12 Whoever *f* me will never walk

FOLLY (FOOL)
Pr 14:29 a quick-tempered man displays *f*.
19: 3 A man's own *f* ruins his life,
Ecc 10: 1 so a little *f* outweighs wisdom
Mk 7:22 envy, slander, arrogance and *f*.
2Ti 3: 9 their *f* will be clear to everyone.

FOOD (FOODS)
Ge 1:30 I give every green plant for *f*."
Pr 12: 9 to be somebody and have no *f*.
12:11 his land will have abundant *f*,
20:13 you will have *f* to spare.
20:17 *F* gained by fraud tastes sweet
21:20 of the wise are stores of choice *f*

Pr 22: 9 for he shares his *f* with the poor.
23: 3 for that *f* is deceptive.
23: 6 Do not eat the *f* of a stingy man,
25:21 If your enemy is hungry, give him *f*
31:14 bringing her *f* from afar.
31:15 she provides *f* for her family
Isa 58: 7 not to share your *f* with the hungry
Eze 18: 7 but gives his *f* to the hungry
Da 1: 8 to defile himself with the royal *f*
Mt 3: 4 His *f* was locusts and wild honey.
6:25 Is not life more important than *f*,
Jn 4:32 "I have *f* to eat that you know
4:34 have brought him *f*?" "My *f*,"
6:27 Do not work for *f* that spoils,
6:55 my flesh is real *f* and my blood is
Ac 15:20 to abstain from *f* polluted by idols,
Ro 14:14 fully convinced that no *f* is unclean
1Co 8: 1 Now about *f* sacrificed to idols:
8: 8 But *f* does not bring us near to God
2Co 11:27 and have often gone without *f*;
1Ti 6: 8 But if we have *f* and clothing,
Heb 5:14 But solid *f* is for the mature,
Jas 2:15 sister is without clothes and daily *f*.

FOODS (FOOD)
Mk 7:19 Jesus declared all *f* "clean.")

FOOL (FOLLY FOOL'S FOOLISH FOOLISHNESS FOOLS)
1Sa 25:25 his name is *F*, and folly goes
Ps 14: 1 The *f* says in his heart,
Pr 10:10 and a chattering *f* comes to ruin.
10:18 and whoever spreads slander is a *f*.
12:15 The way of a *f* seems right to him,
12:16 A *f* shows his annoyance at once,
14:16 but a *f* is hotheaded and reckless.
15: 5 A *f* spurns his father's discipline,
17:12 than a *f* in his folly.
17:16 use is money in the hand of a *f*,
17:21 To have a *f* for a son brings grief;
17:28 Even a *f* is thought wise
18: 2 A *f* finds no pleasure
20: 3 but every *f* is quick to quarrel.
23: 9 Do not speak to a *f*,
24: 7 Wisdom is too high for a *f*;
26: 4 Do not answer a *f* according
26: 5 Answer a *f* according to his folly,
26: 7 is a proverb in the mouth of a *f*.
26:11 so a *f* repeats his folly.
26:12 for a *f* than for him.
27:22 Though you grind a *f* in a mortar,
28:26 He who trusts in himself is a *f*,
29:11 A *f* gives full vent to his anger,
29:20 for a *f* than for him.
Mt 5:22 But anyone who says, 'You *f*!'
Lk 12:20 "But God said to him, 'You *f*!
1Co 3:18 he should become a "*f*"
2Co 11:21 I am speaking as a *f*—I

FOOL'S (FOOL)
Pr 14: 3 A *f* talk brings a rod to his back,
18: 7 A *f* mouth is his undoing,

FOOLISH (FOOL)
Pr 10: 1 but a *f* son grief to his mother.
14: 1 her own hands the *f* one tears hers
15:20 but a *f* man despises his mother.
17:25 A *f* son brings grief to his father
19:13 A *f* son is his father's ruin,
Mt 7:26 practice is like a *f* man who built
25: 2 of them were *f* and five were wise.
Lk 11:40 You *f* people! Did not the one who
24:25 He said to them, "How *f* you are,
1Co 1:20 Has not God made *f* the wisdom
1:27 God chose the *f* things of the world
Gal 3: 1 died for nothing!" You *f* Galatians!
Eph 5: 4 should there be obscenity, *f* talk
5:17 Therefore do not be *f*,
Tit 3: 9 But avoid *f* controversies

FOOLISHNESS (FOOL)
1Co 1:18 of the cross is *f* to those who are
1:21 through the *f* of what was preached
1:23 block to Jews and *f* to Gentiles,
1:25 For the *f* of God is wiser
2:14 for they are *f* to him, and he cannot
3:19 of this world is *f* in God's sight.

FOOLS (FOOL)
Pr 1: 7 but *f* despise wisdom and discipline
3:35 but *f* he holds up to shame.
12:23 but the heart of *f* blurts out folly.
13:19 but *f* detest turning from evil.
Pr 13:20 but a companion of *f* suffers harm.
14: 9 *F* mock at making amends for sin,
14:24 but the folly of *f* yields folly.
Ecc 7: 5 than to listen to the song of *f*.
7: 6 so is the laughter of *f*.
10: 6 *F* are put in many high positions,
Mt 23:17 You blind *f*! Which is greater:
Ro 1:22 they became *f* and exchanged
1Co 4:10 We are *f* for Christ, but you are

FOOT (FEET FOOTHOLD)
Jos 1: 3 every place where you set your *f*,
Ps 121: 3 He will not let your *f* slip—
Pr 3:23 and your *f* will not stumble;
4:27 keep your *f* from evil.
25:17 Seldom set *f* in your neighbor's
Isa 1: 6 From the sole of your *f* to the top
Mt 18: 8 or your *f* causes you to sin,
Lk 4:11 so that you will not strike your *f*
1Co 12:15 If the *f* should say, "Because I am
Rev 10: 2 He planted his right *f* on the sea

FOOTHOLD* (FOOT)
Ps 69: 2 where there is no *f*.
73: 2 I had nearly lost my *f*.
Eph 4:27 and do not give the devil a *f*.

FOOTSTEPS (STEP)
Ps 119:133 Direct my *f* according

FOOTSTOOL
Ps 99: 5 and worship at his *f*;
110: 1 a *f* for your feet."
Isa 66: 1 and the earth is my *f*.
Mt 5:35 for it is his *f*; or by Jerusalem,
Ac 7:49 and the earth is my *f*.
Heb 1:13 a *f* for your feet"?
10:13 for his enemies to be made his *f*,

FORBEARANCE*
Ro 3:25 because in his *f* he had left the sins

FORBID
1Co 14:39 and do not *f* speaking in tongues.
1Ti 4: 3 They *f* people to marry

FORCE (FORCED FORCEFUL FORCES FORCING)
Jn 6:15 to come and make him king by *f*,
Ac 26:11 and I tried to *f* them to blaspheme.
Gal 2:14 that you *f* Gentiles

FORCED (FORCE)
Mt 27:32 and they *f* him to carry the cross.
Phm :14 do will be spontaneous and not *f*.

FORCEFUL* (FORCE)
Mt 11:12 forcefully advancing, and *f* men lay
2Co 10:10 "His letters are weighty and *f*,

FORCES (FORCE)
Mt 5:41 If someone *f* you to go one mile,
Eph 6:12 and against the spiritual *f* of evil

FORCING (FORCE)
Lk 16:16 and everyone is *f* his way into it.

FOREFATHERS (FATHER)
Heb 1: 1 spoke to our *f* through the prophets
1Pe 1:18 handed down to you from your *f*,

FOREHEAD (FOREHEADS)
Ex 13: 9 a reminder on your *f* that the law
13:16 on your *f* that the LORD brought
1Sa 17:49 and struck the Philistine on the *f*.
Rev 13:16 a mark on his right hand or on his *f*,

FOREHEADS (FOREHEAD)
Dt 6: 8 hands and bind them on your *f*.
Rev 9: 4 not have the seal of God on their *f*.
14: 1 his Father's name written on their *f*

FOREIGN (FOREIGNER FOREIGNERS)
Ge 35: 2 "Get rid of the *f* gods you have
2Ch 14: 3 He removed the *f* altars
33:15 He got rid of the *f* gods
Isa 28:11 with *f* lips and strange tongues

FOREIGNER (FOREIGN)
Lk 17:18 give praise to God except this *f*?"
1Co 14:11 I am a *f* to the speaker,

FOREIGNERS (FOREIGN)
Eph 2:12 *f* to the covenants of the promise,
2:19 you are no longer *f* and aliens,

FOREKNEW* (KNOW)
Ro 8:29 For those God *f* he
Ro 11: 2 not reject his people, whom he *f*.

FOREKNOWLEDGE* (KNOW)
Ac 2:23 to you by God's set purpose and *f*;
1Pe 1: 2 to the *f* of God the Father,

FORESAW*
Gal 3: 8 Scripture *f* that God would justify

FOREST
Jas 3: 5 Consider what a great *f* is set

FOREVER (EVER)
Ge 3:22 the tree of life and eat, and live *f*."
6: 3 Spirit will not contend with man *f*,
Ex 3:15 This is my name *f*, the name
2Sa 7:26 so that your name will be great *f*.
1Ki 2:33 may there be the LORD's peace *f*."
9: 3 by putting my Name there *f*.
1Ch 16:15 He remembers his covenant *f*,
16:34 his love endures *f*.
16:41 "for his love endures *f*."
17:24 and that your name will be great *f*.
2Ch 5:13 his love endures *f*."
20:21 for his love endures *f*."
Ps 9: 7 The LORD reigns *f*;
23: 6 dwell in the house of the LORD *f*.
28: 9 be their shepherd and carry them *f*.
29:10 the LORD is enthroned as King *f*.
33:11 the plans of the LORD stand firm *f*
37:28 They will be protected *f*,
44: 8 and we will praise your name *f*.
61: 4 I long to dwell in your tent *f*
72:19 Praise be to his glorious name *f*;
73:26 and my portion *f*.
77: 8 Has his unfailing love vanished *f*?
79:13 will praise you *f*;
81:15 and their punishment would last *f*.
86:12 I will glorify your name *f*.
89: 1 of the LORD's great love *f*;
92: 8 But you, O LORD, are exalted *f*.
100: 5 is good and his love endures *f*;
102: 12 But you, O LORD, sit enthroned *f*;
104: 31 of the LORD endure *f*;
107: 1 his love endures *f*.
110: 4 "You are a priest *f*,
111: 3 and his righteousness endures *f*.
112: 6 man will be remembered *f*.
117: 2 of the LORD endures *f*.
118: 1 his love endures *f*.
119:111 Your statutes are my heritage *f*;
119:152 that you established them to last *f*.
136: 1 *His love endures* f.
146: 6 the LORD, who remains faithful *f*.
Pr 10:25 but the righteous stand firm *f*.
27:24 for riches do not endure *f*,
Isa 25: 8 he will swallow up death *f*.
26: 4 Trust in the LORD *f*,
32:17 will be quietness and confidence *f*.
40: 8 but the word of our God stands *f*."
51: 6 But my salvation will last *f*,
51: 8 But my righteousness will last *f*,
57:15 he who lives *f*, whose name is holy:
59:21 from this time on and *f*,"
Jer 33:11 his love endures *f*."
Eze 37:26 put my sanctuary among them *f*.
Da 2:44 to an end, but it will itself endure *f*.
3: 9 live *f*! You have issued a decree,
Jn 6:51 eats of this bread, he will live *f*.
14:16 Counselor to be with you *f*—
Ro 9: 5 who is God over all, *f* praised!
16:27 to the only wise God be glory *f*
1Co 9:25 it to get a crown that will last *f*.
1Th 4:17 And so we will be with the Lord *f*.
Heb 5: 6 "You are a priest *f*,
7:17 "You are a priest *f*,
7:24 Jesus lives *f*, he has a permanent
13: 8 same yesterday and today and *f*.
1Pe 1:25 but the word of the Lord stands *f*."
1Jn 2:17 who does the will of God lives *f*.
2Jn : 2 lives in us and will be with us *f*:

FOREVERMORE (EVER)
Ps 113: 2 both now and *f*.

FORFEIT
Mk 8:36 the whole world, yet *f* his soul?
Lk 9:25 and yet lose or *f* his very self?

FORGAVE (FORGIVE)
Ps 32: 5 and you *f*
65: 3 you *f* our transgressions
78:38 you *f* their iniquities

Eph 4:32 just as in Christ God *f* you.
Col 2:13 He *f* us all our sins, having
3:13 Forgive as the Lord *f* you.

FORGET (FORGETS FORGETTING FORGOT FORGOTTEN)
Dt 4:23 Be careful not to *f* the covenant
6:12 that you do not *f* the LORD,
2Ki 17:38 Do not *f* the covenant I have made
Ps 9:17 all the nations that *f* God.
10:12 Do not *f* the helpless.
50:22 "Consider this, you who *f* God,
78: 7 and would not *f* his deeds
103: 2 and *f* not all his benefits.
119: 93 I will never *f* your precepts,
137: 5 may my right hand *f* its skill.
Pr 3: 1 My son, do not *f* my teaching,
4: 5 do not *f* my words or swerve
Isa 49:15 "Can a mother *f* the baby
51:13 that you *f* the LORD your Maker,
Jer 2:32 Does a maiden *f* her jewelry,
23:39 I will surely *f* you and cast you out
Heb 6:10 he will not *f* your work
13: 2 Do not *f* to entertain strangers,
13:16 And do not *f* to do good
2Pe 3: 8 But do not *f* this one thing,

FORGETS (FORGET)
Jn 16:21 her baby is born she *f* the anguish
Jas 1:24 immediately *f* what he looks like.

FORGETTING* (FORGET)
Php 3:13 *F* what is behind and straining
Jas 1:25 to do this, not *f* what he has heard,

FORGIVE* (FORGAVE FORGIVENESS FORGIVES FORGIVING)
Ge 50:17 I ask you to *f* your brothers the sins
50:17 please *f* the sins of the servants
Ex 10:17 Now *f* my sin once more
23:21 he will not *f* your rebellion,
32:32 But now, please *f* their sin—
34: 9 *f* our wickedness and our sin,
Nu 14:19 with your great love, *f* the sin
Dt 29:20 will never be willing to *f* him;
Jos 24:19 He will not *f* your rebellion
1Sa 15:25 *f* my sin and come back with me,
25:28 Please *f* your servant's offense,
1Ki 8:30 place, and when you hear, *f*.
8:34 and *f* the sin of your people Israel
8:36 and *f* the sin of your servants,
8:39 *F* and act; deal with each man
8:50 *f* all the offenses they have
8:50 *f* your people, who have sinned
2Ki 5:18 But may the LORD *f* your servant
5:18 may the LORD *f* your servant
24: 4 and the LORD was not willing to *f*.
2Ch 6:21 place; and when you hear, *f*.
6:25 and *f* the sin of your people Israel
6:27 and *f* the sin of your servants,
6:30 *F*, and deal with each man
6:39 *f* your people, who have sinned
7:14 will *f* their sin and will heal their
Job 7:21 and *f* my sins?
Ps 19:12 *F* my hidden faults.
25:11 *f* my iniquity, though it is great.
79: 9 deliver us and *f* our sins
Isa 2: 9 do not *f* them.
Jer 5: 1 I will *f* this city.
5: 7 "Why should I *f* you?
18:23 Do not *f* their crimes
31:34 "For I will *f* their wickedness
33: 8 and will *f* all their sins of rebellion
36: 3 then I will *f* their wickedness
50:20 for I will *f* the remnant I spare.
Da 9:19 O Lord, listen! O Lord, *f*! O Lord,
Hos 1: 6 that I should at all *f* them.
14: 2 "*F* all our sins
Am 7: 2 *f*! How can Jacob survive?
Mt 6:12 *F* us our debts,
6:14 For if you *f* men when they sin
6:14 heavenly Father will also *f* you.
6:15 But if you do not *f* men their sins,
6:15 your Father will not *f* your sins.
9: 6 authority on earth to *f* sins..
18:21 many times shall I *f* my brother
18:35 you *f* your brother from your heart
Mk 2: 7 Who can *f* sins but God alone?"
2:10 authority on earth to *f* sins
11:25 anything against anyone, *f* him,
11:25 in heaven may *f* you your sins."
Lk 5:21 Who can *f* sins but God alone?"
Lk 5:24 authority on earth to *f* sins..
6:37 *F*, and you will be forgiven.
11: 4 *F* us our sins,
11: 4 *f* everyone who sins against us.
17: 3 rebuke him, and if he repents, *f* him
17: 4 and says, 'I repent,' *f* him."
23:34 Jesus said, "Father, *f* them,
Jn 20:23 If you *f* anyone his sins, they are
20:23 if you do not *f* them, they are not
Ac 8:22 Perhaps he will *f* you
2Co 2: 7 you ought to *f* and comfort him,
2:10 If you *f* anyone, I also *f* him.
2:10 if there was anything to *f*—
12:13 a burden to you? *F* me this wrong!
Col 3:13 and *f* whatever grievances you may
3:13 *F* as the Lord forgave you.
Heb 8:12 For I will *f* their wickedness
1Jn 1: 9 and just and will *f* us our sins

FORGIVENESS* (FORGIVE)
Ps 130: 4 But with you there is *f*;
Mt 26:28 out for many for the *f* of sins.
Mk 1: 4 of repentance for the *f* of sins.
Lk 1:77 salvation through the *f* of their sins,
3: 3 of repentance for the *f* of sins.
24:47 and *f* of sins will be preached
Ac 5:31 that he might give repentance and *f*
10:43 believes in him receives *f* of sins
13:38 that through Jesus the *f*
26:18 so that they may receive *f* of sins
Eph 1: 7 through his blood, the *f* of sins,
Col 1:14 in whom we have redemption, the *f*
Heb 9:22 the shedding of blood there is no *f*.

FORGIVES* (FORGIVE)
Ps 103: 3 He *f* all my sins
Mic 7:18 pardons sin and *f* the transgression
Lk 7:49 "Who is this who even *f* sins?"

FORGIVING* (FORGIVE)
Ex 34: 7 and *f* wickedness, rebellion and sin.
Nu 14:18 abounding in love and *f* sin
Ne 9:17 But you are a *f* God, gracious
Ps 86: 5 You are *f* and good, O Lord,
99: 8 you were to Israel a *f* God,
Da 9: 9 The Lord our God is merciful and *f*
Eph 4:32 to one another, *f* each other,

FORGOT (FORGET)
Dt 32:18 you *f* the God who gave you birth.
Ps 78:11 They *f* what he had done,
106: 13 But they soon *f* what he had done

FORGOTTEN (FORGET)
Job 11: 6 God has even *f* some of your sin.
Ps 44:20 If we had *f* the name of our God
Isa 17:10 You have *f* God your Savior;
Hos 8:14 Israel has *f* his Maker
Lk 12: 6 Yet not one of them is *f* by God.
2Pe 1: 9 and has *f* that he has been cleansed

FORM (FORMED)
Isa 52:14 *f* marred beyond human likeness—
2Ti 3: 5 having a *f* of godliness

FORMED (FORM)
Ge 2: 7 —the LORD God *f* the man
2:19 Now the LORD God had *f* out
Ps 103: 14 for he knows how we are *f*,
Ecc 11: 5 or how the body is *f* in a mother's
Isa 29:16 Shall what is *f* say to him who *f* it,
45:18 but *f* it to be inhabited—
49: 5 he who *f* me in the womb
Jer 1: 5 "Before I *f* you in the womb I knew
Ro 9:20 "Shall what is *f* say to him who *f* it,
Gal 4:19 of childbirth until Christ is *f* in you,
1Ti 2:13 For Adam was *f* first, then Eve.
Heb 11: 3 understand that the universe was *f*
2Pe 3: 5 and the earth was *f* out of water

FORMLESS*
Ge 1: 2 Now the earth was *f* and empty,
Jer 4:23 and it was *f* and empty;

FORSAKE (FORSAKEN)
Dt 31: 6 he will never leave you nor *f* you."
Jos 1: 5 I will never leave you nor *f* you.
24:16 "Far be it from us to *f* the LORD
2Ch 15: 2 but if you *f* him, he will *f* you.
Ps 27:10 Though my father and mother *f* me
94:14 he will never *f* his inheritance.
Isa 55: 7 Let the wicked *f* his way
Heb 13: 5 never will I *f* you."

FORSAKEN (FORSAKE)
Ps 22: 1 my God, why have you *f* me?
37:25 I have never seen the righteous *f*
Mt 27:46 my God, why have you *f* me?"
Rev 2: 4 You have *f* your first love.

FORTRESS
2Sa 22: 2 "The LORD is my rock, my *f*
Ps 18: 2 The LORD is my rock, my *f*
31: 2 a strong *f* to save me.
59:16 for you are my *f*,
71: 3 for you are my rock and my *f*.
Pr 14:26 who fears the LORD has a secure *f*,

FORTUNE-TELLING*
Ac 16:16 deal of money for her owners by *f*.

FORTY
Ge 7: 4 on the earth for *f* days and *f* nights,
18:29 "What if only *f* are found there?"
Ex 16:35 The Israelites ate manna *f* years,
24:18 on the mountain *f* days and *f* nights
Nu 14:34 For *f* years—one year for each
Jos 14: 7 I was *f* years old when Moses
1Sa 4:18 He had led Israel *f* years.
2Sa 5: 4 king, and he reigned *f* years.
1Ki 19: 8 he traveled *f* days and *f* nights
2Ki 12: 1 and he reigned in Jerusalem *f* years
2Ch 9:30 in Jerusalem over all Israel *f* years.
Eze 29:12 her cities will lie desolate *f* years
Jnh 3: 4 "*F* more days and Nineveh will be
Mt 4: 2 After fasting *f* days and *f* nights,

FOUGHT (FIGHT)
1Co 15:32 If I *f* wild beasts in Ephesus
2Ti 4: 7 I have *f* the good fight, I have

FOUND (FIND)
2Ki 22: 8 "I have *f* the Book of the Law
1Ch 28: 9 If you seek him, he will be *f* by you;
2Ch 15:15 sought God eagerly, and he was *f*
Isa 55: 6 Seek the LORD while he may be *f*;
65: 1 I was *f* by those who did not seek
Da 5:27 on the scales and *f* wanting.
Mt 1:18 she was *f* to be with child
Lk 15: 6 with me; I have *f* my lost sheep.'
15: 9 with me; I have *f* my lost coin.'
15:24 is alive again; he was lost and is *f*.'
Ac 4:12 Salvation is *f* in no one else,
Ro 10:20 "I was *f* by those who did not seek
Jas 2: 8 If you really keep the royal law *f*
Rev 5: 4 no one was *f* who was worthy

FOUNDATION (FOUNDATIONS FOUNDED)
Isa 28:16 a precious cornerstone for a sure *f*;
Mt 7:25 because it had its *f* on the rock.
Lk 14:29 For if he lays the *f* and is not able
Ro 15:20 building on someone else's *f*.
1Co 3:10 I laid a *f* as an expert builder,
3:11 For no one can lay any *f* other
Eph 2:20 built on the *f* of the apostles
1Ti 3:15 the pillar and *f* of the truth.
2Ti 2:19 God's solid *f* stands firm,
Heb 6: 1 not laying again the *f* of repentance

FOUNDATIONS (FOUNDATION)
Ps 102: 25 In the beginning you laid the *f*
Heb 1:10 O Lord, you laid the *f* of the earth,

FOUNDED (FOUNDATION)
Jer 10:12 he *f* the world by his wisdom
Heb 8: 6 and it is *f* on better promises.

FOUNTAIN
Ps 36: 9 For with you is the *f* of life;
Pr 14:27 The fear of the LORD is a *f* of life,
18: 4 the *f* of wisdom is a bubbling brook.
Zec 13: 1 "On that day a *f* will be opened

FOX (FOXES)
Lk 13:32 He replied, "Go tell that *f*,

FOXES (FOX)
SS 2:15 the little *f*
Mt 8:20 "*F* have holes and birds

FRAGRANCE (FRAGRANT)
Ex 30:38 it to enjoy its *f* must be cut
Jn 12: 3 filled with the *f* of the perfume.
2Co 2:14 us spreads everywhere the *f*
2:16 of death; to the other, the *f* of life.

FRAGRANT (FRAGRANCE)
Eph 5: 2 as a *f* offering and sacrifice to God.
Php 4:18 They are a *f* offering, an acceptable

FREE (FREED FREEDOM FREELY)
Ge 2:16 "You are *f* to eat from any tree
Ps 118: 5 and he answered by setting me *f*.
119: 32 for you have set my heart *f*.
146: 7 The LORD sets prisoners *f*,
Pr 6: 3 then do this, my son, to *f* yourself,
Jn 8:32 and the truth will set you *f*."
8:36 if the Son sets you *f*, you will be *f*
Ro 6:18 You have been set *f* from sin
8: 2 of life set me *f* from the law of sin
1Co 12:13 whether Jews or Greeks, slave or *f*
Gal 3:28 slave nor *f*, male nor female,
5: 1 for freedom that Christ has set us *f*.
1Pe 2:16 *f* men, but do not use your freedom

FREED (FREE)
Ps 116: 16 you have *f* me from my chains.
Ro 6: 7 anyone who has died has been *f*
Rev 1: 5 has *f* us from our sins by his blood,

FREEDOM (FREE)
Ps 119: 45 I will walk about in *f*,
Isa 61: 1 to proclaim *f* for the captives
Lk 4:18 me to proclaim *f* for the prisoners
Ro 8:21 into the glorious *f* of the children
1Co 7:21 although if you can gain your *f*,
2Co 3:17 the Spirit of the Lord is, there is *f*.
Gal 2: 4 ranks to spy on the *f* we have
5:13 But do not use your *f* to indulge
Jas 1:25 into the perfect law that gives *f*,
1Pe 2:16 but do not use your *f* as a cover-up

FREELY (FREE)
Isa 55: 7 and to our God, for he will *f* pardon
Mt 10: 8 Freely you have received, *f* give.
Ro 3:24 and are justified *f* by his grace
Eph 1: 6 which he has *f* given us

FRESH
Jas 3:11 Can both *f* water and salt water

FRET*
Ps 37: 1 Do not *f* because of evil men
37: 7 do not *f* when men succeed
37: 8 do not *f*—it leads only to evil.
Pr 24:19 Do not *f* because of evil men

FRICTION
1Ti 6: 5 and constant *f* between men

FRIEND (FRIENDS FRIENDSHIP)
Ex 33:11 as a man speaks with his *f*.
2Ch 20: 7 descendants of Abraham your *f*?
Pr 17:17 A *f* loves at all times,
18:24 there is a *f* who sticks closer
27: 6 Wounds from a *f* can be trusted
27:10 Do not forsake your *f* and the *f*
Isa 41: 8 you descendants of Abraham my *f*,
Mt 11:19 a *f* of tax collectors and "sinners."
Lk 11: 8 him the bread because he is his *f*,
Jn 19:12 "If you let this man go, you are no *f*
Jas 2:23 and he was called God's *f*.
4: 4 Anyone who chooses to be a *f*

FRIENDS (FRIEND)
Pr 16:28 and a gossip separates close *f*.
17: 9 the matter separates close *f*.
Zec 13: 6 given at the house of my *f*.'
Jn 15:13 that he lay down his life for his *f*.
15:14 You are my *f* if you do what I

FRIENDSHIP (FRIEND)
Jas 4: 4 don't you know that *f*

FRIGHTENED (FEAR)
Php 1:28 gospel without being *f* in any way
1Pe 3:14 fear what they fear; do not be *f*."

FROGS
Ex 8: 2 plague your whole country with *f*.
Rev 16:13 three evil spirits that looked like *f*;

FRUIT (FRUITFUL)
Jdg 9:11 'Should I give up my *f*, so good
Ps 1: 3 which yields its *f* in season
Pr 11:30 The *f* of the righteous is a tree
12:14 From the *f* of his lips a man is filled
27:18 He who tends a fig tree will eat its *f*
Isa 11: 1 from his roots a Branch will bear *f*.
27: 6 and fill all the world with *f*.
32:17 The *f* of righteousness will be peace
Jer 17: 8 and never fails to bear *f*."
Hos 10:12 reap the *f* of unfailing love,
14: 2 that we may offer the *f* of our lips.
Am 8: 1 showed me: a basket of ripe *f*.
Mt 3: 8 Produce *f* in keeping
3:10 does not produce good *f* will be cut
7:16 By their *f* you will recognize them.
7:17 good *f*, but a bad tree bears bad *f*.
7:20 by their *f* you will recognize them.
12:33 a tree good and its *f* will be good,
Lk 3: 9 does not produce good *f* will be cut
6:43 nor does a bad tree bear good *f*.
13: 6 and he went to look for *f* on it,
Jn 15: 2 branch in me that bears no *f*,
15:16 and bear *f*—*f* that will last.
Ro 7: 4 in order that we might bear *f*
Gal 5:22 But the *f* of the Spirit is love, joy,
Php 1:11 with the *f* of righteousness that
Col 1:10 bearing *f* in every good work,
Heb 13:15 the *f* of lips that confess his name.
Jas 3:17 and good *f*, impartial and sincere.
Jude :12 autumn trees, without *f*
Rev 22: 2 of *f*, yielding its *f* every month.

FRUITFUL (FRUIT)
Ge 1:22 "Be *f* and increase in number
9: 1 "Be *f* and increase in number
35:11 be *f* and increase in number.
Ex 1: 7 the Israelites were *f* and multiplied
Ps 128: 3 Your wife will be like a *f* vine
Jn 15: 2 prunes so that it will be even more *f*.
Php 1:22 this will mean *f* labor for me.

FRUITLESS*
Eph 5:11 to do with the *f* deeds of darkness,

FRUSTRATION
Ro 8:20 For the creation was subjected to *f*,

FUEL
Isa 44:19 "Half of it I used for *f*;

FULFILL (FULFILLED FULFILLMENT FULFILLS)
Nu 23:19 Does he promise and not *f*?
Ps 61: 8 and *f* my vows day after day.
116: 14 I will *f* my vows to the LORD
138: 8 The LORD will *f* ⌞his purpose⌟
Ecc 5: 5 than to make a vow and not *f* it.
Isa 46:11 far-off land, a man to *f* my purpose.
Jer 33:14 'when I will *f* the gracious promise
Mt 1:22 place to *f* what the Lord had said
3:15 us to do this to *f* all righteousness."
4:14 *f* what was said
5:17 come to abolish them but to *f* them.
8:17 This was to *f* what was spoken
12:17 This was to *f* what was spoken
21: 4 place to *f* what was spoken
Jn 12:38 This was to *f* the word
13:18 But this is to *f* the scripture:
15:25 But this is to *f* what is written
1Co 7: 3 husband should *f* his marital duty

FULFILLED (FULFILL)
Jos 21:45 of Israel failed; every one was *f*.
23:14 Every promise has been *f*;
Pr 13:12 but a longing *f* is a tree of life.
13:19 A longing *f* is sweet to the soul,
Mt 2:15 so was *f* what the Lord had said
2:17 the prophet Jeremiah was *f*:
2:23 So was *f* what was said
13:14 In them is *f* the prophecy of Isaiah:
13:35 So was *f* what was spoken
26:54 would the Scriptures be *f* that say it
26:56 of the prophets might be *f*."
27: 9 by Jeremiah the prophet was *f*:
Mk 13: 4 that they are all about to be *f*?"
14:49 But the Scriptures must be *f*."
Lk 4:21 "Today this scripture is *f*
18:31 about the Son of Man will be *f*.
24:44 Everything must be *f* that is
Jn 18: 9 words he had spoken would be *f*:
19:24 the Scripture might be *f* which said,
19:28 and so that the Scripture would be *f*
19:36 so that the Scripture would be *f*:
Ac 1:16 to be *f* which the Holy Spirit spoke
Ro 13: 8 loves his fellowman has *f* the law.
Jas 2:23 And the scripture was *f* that says,

FULFILLMENT (FULFILL)
Ro 13:10 Therefore love is the *f* of the law.

FULFILLS (FULFILL)
Ps 57: 2 to God, who *f* ⌞his purpose⌟ for me.
145: 19 He *f* the desires of those who fear

FULL (FILL)
2Ch 24:10 them into the chest until it was *f*.
Ps 127: 5 whose quiver is *f* of them.
Pr 27: 7 He who is *f* loathes honey,
31:11 Her husband has *f* confidence
Isa 6: 3 the whole earth is *f* of his glory."
11: 9 for the earth will be *f*
Lk 4: 1 Jesus, *f* of the Holy Spirit,
Jn 10:10 may have life, and have it to the *f*.
Ac 6: 3 known to be *f* of the Spirit
6: 5 a man *f* of faith and of the Holy
7:55 But Stephen, *f* of the Holy Spirit,
11:24 *f* of the Holy Spirit and faith,

FULL-GROWN* (GROW)
Jas 1:15 when it is *f*, gives birth to death.

FULLNESS* (FILL)
Dt 33:16 gifts of the earth and its *f*
Jn 1:16 From the *f* of his grace we have all
Ro 11:12 greater riches will their *f* bring!
Eph 1:23 the *f* of him who fills everything
3:19 to the measure of all the *f* of God.
4:13 to the whole measure of the *f*
Col 1:19 to have all his *f* dwell in him,
1:25 to you the word of God in its *f*—
2: 9 in Christ all the *f* of the Deity lives
2:10 and you have been given *f* in Christ

FULLY (FILL)
1Ki 8:61 your hearts must be *f* committed
2Ch 16: 9 whose hearts are *f* committed
Ps 119: 4 that are to be *f* obeyed.
119:138 they are *f* trustworthy.
Pr 13: 4 of the diligent are *f* satisfied.
Lk 6:40 everyone who is *f* trained will be
Ro 4:21 being *f* persuaded that God had
14: 5 Each one should be *f* convinced
1Co 13:12 shall know *f*, even as I am *f* known.
15:58 Always give yourselves *f*
2Ti 4:17 the message might be *f* proclaimed

FURIOUS (FURY)
Dt 29:28 In *f* anger and in great wrath
Jer 32:37 where I banish them in my *f* anger

FURNACE
Isa 48:10 in the *f* of affliction.
Da 3: 6 be thrown into a blazing *f*."
Mt 13:42 will throw them into the fiery *f*,

FURY (FURIOUS)
Isa 14: 6 and in *f* subdued nations
Jer 21: 5 and a mighty arm in anger and *f*
Rev 14:10 will drink of the wine of God's *f*,
16:19 with the wine of the *f* of his wrath.
19:15 the winepress of the *f* of the wrath

FUTILE (FUTILITY)
Mal 3:14 You have said, 'It is *f* to serve God.
1Co 3:20 that the thoughts of the wise are *f*."

FUTILITY (FUTILE)
Eph 4:17 in the *f* of their thinking.

FUTURE
Ps 37:37 there is a *f* for the man of peace.
Pr 23:18 There is surely a *f* hope for you,
Ecc 7:14 anything about his *f*.
8: 7 Since no man knows the *f*,
Jer 29:11 plans to give you hope and a *f*.
31:17 So there is hope for your *f*,"
Ro 8:38 neither the present nor the *f*,
1Co 3:22 life or death or the present or the *f*

GABRIEL*
Angel who interpreted Daniel's visions (Da 8:16–26; 9:20–27); announced births of John (Lk 1:11–20), Jesus (Lk 1:26–38).

GAD
1. Son of Jacob by Zilpah (Ge 30:9–11; 35:26; 1Ch 2:2). Tribe of blessed (Ge 49:19; Dt 33:20–21), numbered (Nu 1:25; 26:18), allotted land east of the Jordan (Nu 32; 34:14; Jos 18:7; 22), west (Eze 48:27–28), 12,000 from (Rev 7:5).
2. Prophet; seer of David (1Sa 22:5; 2Sa 24:11–19; 1Ch 29:29).

GAIN (GAINED GAINS)
Ex 14:17 And I will *g* glory through Pharaoh
Ps 60:12 With God we will *g* the victory,
Pr 4: 1 pay attention and *g* understanding.
8: 5 You who are simple, *g* prudence;
28:16 he who hates ill-gotten *g* will enjoy
28:23 in the end *g* more favor
Isa 63:12 to *g* for himself everlasting renown
Da 2: 8 that you are trying to *g* time,
Mk 8:36 it for a man to *g* the whole world,

Lk 9:25 it for a man to *g* the whole world,
21:19 standing firm you will *g* life.
1Co 13: 3 but have not love, I *g* nothing.
Php 1:21 to live is Christ and to die is *g.*
3: 8 that I may *g* Christ and be found
1Ti 3:13 have served well *g* an excellent
6: 5 godliness is a means to financial *g.*
6: 6 with contentment is great *g.*

GAINED (GAIN)
Jer 32:20 have *g* the renown that is still yours
Ro 5: 2 through whom we have *g* access

GAINS (GAIN)
Pr 3:13 the man who *g* understanding,
11:16 A kindhearted woman *g* respect,
15:32 heeds correction *g* understanding.
29:23 but a man of lowly spirit *g* honor.
Mt 16:26 for a man if he *g* the whole world,

GALILEE
Isa 9: 1 but in the future he will honor *G*
Mt 4:15 *G* of the Gentiles—
26:32 I will go ahead of you into *G.*"
28:10 Go and tell my brothers to go to *G;*

GALL
Mt 27:34 mixed with *g;* but after tasting it,

GALLIO
Ac 18:12 While *G* was proconsul of Achaia,

GALLOWS
Est 7:10 Haman on the *g* he had prepared

GAMALIEL
Ac 5:34 But a Pharisee named *G,* a teacher

GAMES
1Co 9:25 in the *g* goes into strict training.

GAP
Eze 22:30 stand before me in the *g* on behalf

GAPE*
Ps 35:21 They *g* at me and say, "Aha! Aha!

GARDEN (GARDENER)
Ge 2: 8 the LORD God had planted a *g*
2:15 put him in the *G* of Eden to work it
SS 4:12 You are a *g* locked up, my sister,
Isa 58:11 You will be like a well-watered *g,*
Jer 31:12 They will be like a well-watered *g,*
Eze 28:13 the *g* of God;
31: 9 Eden in the *g* of God.

GARDENER (GARDEN)
Jn 15: 1 true vine, and my Father is the *g.*

GARLAND*
Pr 1: 9 They will be a *g* to grace your head
4: 9 She will set a *g* of grace

GARMENT (GARMENTS)
Ps 102: 26 they will all wear out like a *g.*
Isa 50: 9 They will all wear out like a *g;*
51: 6 the earth will wear out like a *g*
61: 3 and a *g* of praise
Mt 9:16 of unshrunk cloth on an old *g,*
Jn 19:23 This *g* was seamless, woven
Heb 1:11 they will all wear out like a *g.*

GARMENTS (GARMENT)
Ge 3:21 The LORD God made *g* of skin
Ex 28: 2 Make sacred *g* for your brother
Lev 16:23 and take off the linen *g* he put
16:24 holy place and put on his regular *g.*
Isa 61:10 me with *g* of salvation
63: 1 with his *g* stained crimson?
Joel 2:13 and not your *g.*
Zec 3: 4 and I will put rich *g* on you."
Jn 19:24 "They divided my *g* among them

GATE (GATES)
Ps 118: 20 This is the *g* of the LORD
Pr 31:23 husband is respected at the city *g,*
31:31 works bring her praise at the city *g.*
Mt 7:13 For wide is the *g* and broad is
7:13 "Enter through the narrow *g.*
Jn 10: 1 not enter the sheep pen by the *g,*
10: 2 enters by the *g* is the shepherd
10: 7 "I tell you the truth, I am the *g*
10: 9 I am the *g;* whoever enters
Heb 13:12 also suffered outside the city *g*
Rev 21:21 each *g* made of a single pearl.

GATES (GATE)
Ps 24: 7 Lift up your heads, O you *g;*
24: 9 Lift up your heads, O you *g;*
100: 4 Enter his *g* with thanksgiving
118: 19 Open for me the *g* of righteousness
Isa 60:11 Your *g* will always stand open,
60:18 and your *g* Praise.
62:10 Pass through, pass through the *g!*
Mt 16:18 the *g* of Hades will not overcome it
Rev 21:12 On the *g* were written the names
21:21 The twelve *g* were twelve pearls,
21:25 On no day will its *g* ever be shut,
22:14 may go through the *g* into the city.

GATH
1Sa 17:23 the Philistine champion from *G,*
2Sa 1:20 "Tell it not in *G,*
Mic 1:10 Tell it not in *G;*

GATHER (GATHERED GATHERS)
Ps 106: 47 and *g* us from the nations,
Isa 11:12 and *g* the exiles of Israel;
Jer 3:17 and all nations will *g* in Jerusalem
23: 3 "I myself will *g* the remnant
31:10 who scattered Israel will *g* them
Zep 2: 1 *G* together, *g* together,
3:20 At that time I will *g* you;
Zec 14: 2 I will *g* all the nations to Jerusalem
Mt 12:30 he who does not *g* with me scatters
13:30 then *g* the wheat and bring it
23:37 longed to *g* your children together,
24:31 and they will *g* his elect
25:26 *g* where I have not scattered seed?
Mk 13:27 and *g* his elect from the four winds,
Lk 3:17 and to *g* the wheat into his barn,
11:23 and he who does not *g* with me,
13:34 longed to *g* your children together,

GATHERED (GATHER)
Ex 16:18 and he who *g* little did not have too
Pr 30: 4 Who has *g* up the wind
Mt 25:32 All the nations will be *g* before him
2Co 8:15 and he who *g* little did not have too
2Th 2: 1 Lord Jesus Christ and our being *g*
Rev 16:16 Then they *g* the kings together

GATHERS (GATHER)
Ps 147: 2 he *g* the exiles of Israel.
Pr 10: 5 He who *g* crops in summer is a wise
Isa 40:11 He *g* the lambs in his arms
Mt 23:37 a hen *g* her chicks under her wings,

GAVE (GIVE)
Ge 2:20 man *g* names to all the livestock,
3: 6 She also *g* some to her husband,
14:20 Abram *g* him a tenth of everything.
28: 4 the land God *g* to Abraham."
35:12 The land I *g* to Abraham
39:23 *g* him success in whatever he did.
47:11 *g* them property in the best part
Ex 4:11 to him, "Who *g* man his mouth?
31:18 he *g* him the two tablets
Dt 2:12 did in the land the LORD *g* them
2:36 The LORD our God *g* us all
3:12 I *g* the Reubenites and the Gadites
3:13 I *g* to the half tribe of Manasseh.
3:15 And I *g* Gilead to Makir.
3:16 Gadites I *g* the territory extending
8:16 He *g* you manna to eat in the desert
26: 9 us to this place and *g* us this land,
32: 8 the Most High *g* the nations their
Jos 11:23 and he *g* it as an inheritance
13:14 tribe of Levi he *g* no inheritance,
14:13 *g* him Hebron as his inheritance.
21:44 The LORD *g* them rest
24:13 I *g* you a land on which you did not
1Sa 27: 6 So on that day Achish *g* him Ziklag
2Sa 12: 8 I *g* you the house of Israel
1Ki 4:29 God *g* Solomon wisdom
5:12 The LORD *g* Solomon wisdom,
Ezr 2:69 According to their ability they *g*
Ne 9:15 In their hunger you *g* them bread
9:20 You *g* your good Spirit
9:22 You *g* them kingdoms and nations,
9:27 compassion you *g* them deliverers,
Job 1:21 LORD *g* and the LORD has taken
42:10 prosperous again and *g* him twice
Ps 69:21 and *g* me vinegar for my thirst.
135: 12 he *g* their land as an inheritance,
Ecc 12: 7 the spirit returns to God who *g* it.
Eze 3: 2 and he *g* me the scroll to eat.
Mt 1:25 And he *g* him the name Jesus.
25:35 and you *g* me something to drink,
25:42 and you *g* me nothing to drink,
26:26 Jesus took bread, *g* thanks
27:50 in a loud voice, he *g* up his spirit.
Mk 6: 7 *g* them authority over evil spirits.
Jn 1:12 he *g* the right to become children
3:16 so loved the world that he *g* his one
17: 4 by completing the work you *g* me
17: 6 you *g* them to me and they have
19:30 bowed his head and *g* up his spirit.
Ac 1: 3 *g* many convincing proofs that he
2:45 they *g* to anyone as he had need.
11:17 *g* them the same gift as he *g* us,
Ro 1:24 Therefore God *g* them
1:26 God *g* them over to shameful lusts.
1:28 he *g* them over to a depraved mind,
8:32 not spare his own Son, but *g* him up
2Co 5:18 *g* us the ministry of reconciliation:
8: 3 For I testify that they *g* as much
8: 5 they *g* themselves first to the Lord
Gal 1: 4 who *g* himself for our sins
2:20 who loved me and *g* himself for me
Eph 4: 8 and *g* gifts to men."
5: 2 as Christ loved us and *g* himself up
5:25 and *g* himself up for her
2Th 2:16 and by his grace *g* us eternal
1Ti 2: 6 who *g* himself as a ransom
Tit 2:14 who *g* himself for us to redeem us
1Jn 3:24 We know it by the Spirit he *g* us.

GAZE
Ps 27: 4 to *g* upon the beauty of the LORD
Pr 4:25 fix your *g* directly before you.

GEDALIAH
Governor of Judah appointed by Nebuchadnezzar (2Ki 25:22–26; Jer 39–41).

GEHAZI*
Servant of Elisha (2Ki 4:12–5:27; 8:4–5).

GENEALOGIES
1Ti 1: 4 themselves to myths and endless *g.*
Tit 3: 9 avoid foolish controversies and *g*

GENERATION (GENERATIONS)
Ex 3:15 am to be remembered from *g* to *g.*
Nu 32:13 until the whole of *g* of those who had
Dt 1:35 of this evil *g* shall see the good land
Jdg 2:10 After that whole *g* had been
Ps 24: 6 Such is the *g* of those who seek him
48:13 tell of them to the next *g.*
71:18 I declare your power to the next *g,*
78: 4 we will tell the next *g*
102: 18 Let this be written for a future *g,*
112: 2 the *g* of the upright will be blessed
145: 4 One *g* will commend your works
La 5:19 your throne endures from *g* to *g.*
Da 4: 3 his dominion endures from *g* to *g.*
4:34 his kingdom endures from *g* to *g.*
Joel 1: 3 and their children to the next *g.*
Mt 12:39 adulterous *g* asks for a miraculous
17:17 "O unbelieving and perverse *g,*"
23:36 all this will come upon this *g.*
24:34 this *g* will certainly not pass away
Mk 9:19 "O unbelieving *g,*" Jesus replied,
13:30 this *g* will certainly not pass away
Lk 1:50 who fear him, from *g* to *g.*
11:29 Jesus said, "This is a wicked *g.*
11:30 will the Son of Man be to this *g.*
11:50 Therefore this *g* will be held
21:32 this *g* will certainly not pass away
Ac 2:40 Save yourselves from this corrupt *g*
Php 2:15 fault in a crooked and depraved *g,*

GENERATIONS (GENERATION)
Ge 9:12 a covenant for all *g* to come:
17: 7 after you for the *g* to come,
17: 9 after you for the *g* to come.
Ex 20: 6 a thousand *g* of those
31:13 and you for the *g* to come,
Dt 7: 9 covenant of love to a thousand *g*
32: 7 consider the *g* long past.
1Ch 16:15 he commanded, for a thousand *g,*
Job 8: 8 "Ask the former *g*
Ps 22:30 future *g* will be told about the Lord
33:11 of his heart through all *g.*
45:17 your memory through all *g;*
89: 1 faithfulness known through all *g.*
90: 1 throughout all *g.*
100: 5 continues through all *g.*
102: 12 your renown endures through all *g.*
105: 8 he commanded, for a thousand *g,*
119: 90 continues through all *g;*

Ps 135: 13 renown, O LORD, through all *g*.
145: 13 dominion endures through all *g*.
146: 10 your God, O Zion, for all *g*.
Pr 27:24 and a crown is not secure for all *g*.
Isa 41: 4 forth the *g* from the beginning?
51: 8 my salvation through all *g*."
Lk 1:48 now on all *g* will call me blessed,
Eph 3: 5 not made known to men in other *g*
3:21 in Christ Jesus throughout all *g*,
Col 1:26 been kept hidden for ages and *g*,

GENEROSITY* (GENEROUS)
2Co 8: 2 poverty welled up in rich *g*.
9:11 and through us your *g* will result
9:13 and for your *g* in sharing with them

GENEROUS* (GENEROSITY)
Ps 37:26 They are always *g* and lend freely;
112: 5 Good will come to him who is *g*
Pr 11:25 A *g* man will prosper;
22: 9 A *g* man will himself be blessed,
Mt 20:15 Or are you envious because I am *g*
2Co 9: 5 Then it will be ready as a *g* gift,
9: 5 for the *g* gift you had promised.
9:11 way so that you can be *g*
1Ti 6:18 and to be *g* and willing to share.

GENTILE (GENTILES)
Ac 21:25 As for the *G* believers, we have
Ro 1:16 first for the Jew, then for the *G*.
2: 9 first for the Jew, then for the *G*;
2:10 first for the Jew, then for the *G*.
10:12 difference between Jew and *G*—

GENTILES (GENTILE)
Isa 42: 6 and a light for the *G*,
49: 6 also make you a light for the *G*,
49:22 "See, I will beckon to the *G*,
Lk 2:32 a light for revelation to the *G*
21:24 on by the *G* until the times
Ac 9:15 to carry my name before the *G*
10:45 been poured out even on the *G*.
11:18 granted even the *G* repentance unto
13:16 and you *G* who worship God,
13:46 of eternal life, we now turn to the *G*
13:47 I have made you a light for the *G*,
14:27 opened the door of faith to the *G*.
15:14 by taking from the *G* a people
18: 6 From now on I will go to the *G*."
22:21 I will send you far away to the *G*.'"
26:20 and in all Judea, and to the *G* also,
28:28 salvation has been sent to the *G*,
Ro 2:14 when *G*, who do not have the law,
3: 9 and *G* alike are all under sin.
3:29 Is he not the God of *G* too? Yes,
9:24 from the Jews but also from the *G*?
11:11 to the *G* to make Israel envious.
11:12 their loss means riches for the *G*,
11:13 as I am the apostle to the *G*,
15: 9 I will praise you among the *G*;
15: 9 so that the *G* may glorify God
1Co 1:23 block to Jews and foolishness to *G*,
Gal 1:16 I might preach him among the *G*,
2: 2 gospel that I preach among the *G*.
2: 8 my ministry as an apostle to the *G*.
2: 9 agreed that we should go to the *G*,
3: 8 that God would justify the *G*
3:14 to the *G* through Christ Jesus,
Eph 3: 6 the gospel the *G* are heirs together
3: 8 to the *G* the unsearchable riches
Col 1:27 among the *G* the glorious riches
1Ti 2: 7 a teacher of the true faith to the *G*.
2Ti 4:17 and all the *G* might hear it.

GENTLE* (GENTLENESS)
Dt 28:54 Even the most *g* and sensitive man
28:56 The most *g* and sensitive woman
28:56 and *g* that she would not venture
2Sa 18: 5 Be *g* with the young man Absalom
1Ki 19:12 And after the fire came a *g* whisper
Job 41: 3 Will he speak to you with *g* words?
Pr 15: 1 A *g* answer turns away wrath,
25:15 and a *g* tongue can break a bone.
Jer 11:19 I had been like a *g* lamb led
Zec 9: 9 *g* and riding on a donkey,
Mt 11:29 for I am *g* and humble in heart,
21: 5 *g* and riding on a donkey,
Ac 27:13 When a *g* south wind began
1Co 4:21 or in love and with a *g* spirit?
Eph 4: 2 Be completely humble and *g*;
1Th 2: 7 but we were *g* among you,
1Ti 3: 3 not violent but *g*, not quarrelsome,
1Pe 3: 4 the unfading beauty of a *g*

GENTLENESS* (GENTLE)
2Co 10: 1 By the meekness and *g* of Christ,
Gal 5:23 faithfulness, *g* and self-control.
Php 4: 5 Let your *g* be evident to all.
Col 3:12 kindness, humility, *g* and patience.
1Ti 6:11 faith, love, endurance and *g*.
1Pe 3:15 But do this with *g* and respect,

GENUINE*
2Co 6: 8 *g*, yet regarded as impostors;
Php 2:20 who takes a *g* interest
1Pe 1: 7 may be proved *g* and may result

GERIZIM
Dt 27:12 on Mount *G* to bless the people:

GERSHOM
Ex 2:22 and Moses named him *G*, saying,

GETHSEMANE*
Mt 26:36 disciples to a place called *G*,
Mk 14:32 They went to a place called *G*,

GHOST
see also SPIRIT
Lk 24:39 a *g* does not have flesh and bones,

GIBEON
Jos 10:12 "O sun, stand still over *G*,

GIDEON*
Judge, also called Jerub-Baal; freed Israel from Midianites (Jdg 6–8; Heb 11:32). Given sign of fleece (Jdg 6:36–40).

GIFT (GIFTED GIFTS)
Pr 18:16 A *g* opens the way for the giver
21:14 A *g* given in secret soothes anger,
Ecc 3:13 in all his toil—this is the *g* of God.
Mt 5:23 if you are offering your *g*
Jn 4:10 "If you knew the *g* of God
Ac 1: 4 wait for the *g* my Father promised,
2:38 And you will receive the *g*
11:17 So if God gave them the same *g*
Ro 6:23 but the *g* of God is eternal life
12: 6 If a man's *g* is prophesying,
1Co 7: 7 each man has his own *g* from God;
2Co 8:12 the *g* is acceptable according
9:15 be to God for his indescribable *g*!
Eph 2: 8 it is the *g* of God—not by works,
1Ti 4:14 not neglect your *g*, which was
2Ti 1: 6 you to fan into flame the *g* of God,
Heb 6: 4 who have tasted the heavenly *g*,
Jas 1:17 and perfect *g* is from above,
1Pe 3: 7 with you of the gracious *g* of life,
4:10 should use whatever *g* he has
Rev 22:17 let him take the free *g* of the water

GIFTED* (GIFT)
1Co 14:37 he is a prophet or spiritually *g*,

GIFTS (GIFT)
Ps 76:11 bring *g* to the One to be feared.
112: 9 He has scattered abroad his *g*
Pr 25:14 of *g* he does not give.
Mt 2:11 and presented him with *g* of gold
7:11 Father in heaven give good *g*
7:11 to give good *g* to your children,
Lk 11:13 to give good *g* to your children,
Ac 10: 4 and *g* to the poor have come up
Ro 11:29 for God's *g* and his call are
12: 6 We have different *g*, according
1Co 12: 1 Now about spiritual *g*, brothers,
12: 4 There are different kinds of *g*,
12:28 those with *g* of administration,
12:30 all work miracles? Do all have *g*
12:31 But eagerly desire the greater *g*.
14: 1 and eagerly desire spiritual *g*,
14:12 eager to have spiritual *g*,
14:12 excel in *g* that build up the church.
2Co 9: 9 "He has scattered abroad his *g*
Eph 4: 8 and gave *g* to men."
Heb 2: 4 and *g* of the Holy Spirit distributed
9: 9 indicating that the *g* and sacrifices

GILEAD
1Ch 27:21 the half-tribe of Manasseh in *G*:
Jer 8:22 Is there no balm in *G*?
46:11 "Go up to *G* and get balm,

GILGAL
Jos 5: 9 So the place has been called *G*

GIRD*
Ps 45: 3 *G* your sword upon your side,

GIRL
Ge 24:16 *g* was very beautiful, a virgin;
2Ki 5: 2 a young *g* from Israel.
Mk 5:41 Little *g*, I say to you, get up!

GIVE (GAVE GIVEN GIVER GIVES GIVING LIFE-GIVING)
Ge 28: 4 you and your descendants the blessing *g* to Abraham
28:22 that you *g* me I will *g* you a tenth."
Ex 20:16 "You shall not *g* false testimony
30:15 The rich are not to *g* more
Nu 6:26 and *g* you peace."'
Dt 5:20 "You shall not *g* false testimony
15:10 *G* generously to him and do
15:14 *G* to him as the LORD your God
1Sa 1:11 then I will *g* him to the LORD
1:28 So now I *g* him to the LORD.
2Ch 15: 7 be strong and do not *g* up,
Pr 21:26 but the righteous *g* without sparing
23:26 My son, *g* me your heart
25:21 if he is thirsty, *g* him water to drink
30: 8 but *g* me only my daily bread.
31:31 *G* her the reward she has earned,
Ecc 3: 6 a time to search and a time to *g* up,
Isa 42: 8 I will not *g* my glory to another
Eze 36:26 I will *g* you a new heart
Mt 6:11 *G* us today our daily bread.
7:11 know how to *g* good gifts
10: 8 Freely you have received, freely *g*.
16:19 I will *g* you the keys
22:21 "*G* to Caesar what is Caesar's,
Mk 8:37 Or what can a man *g* in exchange
10:19 not steal, do not *g* false testimony,
Lk 6:38 *G*, and it will be given to you.
11: 3 *G* us each day our daily bread.
11:13 Father in heaven *g* the Holy Spirit
14:33 who does not *g* up everything he
Jn 10:28 I *g* them eternal life, and they shall
13:34 "A new commandment I *g* you:
14:16 he will *g* you another Counselor
14:27 I do not *g* to you as the world gives.
14:27 leave with you; my peace I *g* you.
17: 2 people that he might *g* eternal life
Ac 20:35 blessed to *g* than to receive.'"
Ro 2: 7 immortality, he will *g* eternal life.
8:32 with him, graciously *g* us all things
12: 8 let him *g* generously;
13: 7 *G* everyone what you owe him:
14:12 each of us will *g* an account
2Co 9: 7 Each man should *g* what he has
Gal 2: 5 We did not *g* in to them
6: 9 reap a harvest if we do not *g* up.
Heb 10:25 Let us not *g* up meeting together,
Rev 14: 7 "Fear God and *g* him glory,

GIVEN (GIVE)
Nu 8:16 are to be *g* wholly to me.
Dt 26:11 things the LORD your God has *g*
Job 3:23 Why is life *g* to a man
Ps 115: 16 but the earth he has *g* to man.
Isa 9: 6 to us a son is *g*,
Mt 6:33 and all these things will be *g* to you
7: 7 "Ask and it will be *g* to you;
13:12 Whoever has will be *g* more,
22:30 people will neither marry nor be *g*
25:29 everyone who has will be *g* more,
Lk 6:38 Give, and it will be *g* to you.
8:10 kingdom of God has been *g* to you,
11: 9 Ask and it will be *g* to you;
22:19 saying, "This is my body *g* for you;
Jn 3:27 man can receive only what is *g* him
15: 7 you wish, and it will be *g* you.
17:24 I want those you have *g* me to be
17:24 the glory you have *g* me
18:11 the cup the Father has *g* me?"
Ac 5:32 whom God has *g* to those who
20:24 the task the Lord Jesus has *g* me—
Ro 5: 5 the Holy Spirit, whom he has *g* us.
1Co 4: 2 those who have been *g* a trust must
11:24 and when he had *g* thanks,
12:13 we were all *g* the one Spirit to drink
2Co 5: 5 and has *g* us the Spirit as a deposit,
Eph 1: 6 which he has freely *g* us
4: 7 to each one of us grace has been *g*
1Ti 4:14 was *g* you through a prophetic
1Jn 4:13 because he has *g* us of his Spirit.

GIVER* (GIVE)
Pr 18:16 A gift opens the way for the *g*
2Co 9: 7 for God loves a cheerful *g*.

GIVES (GIVE)
Job 35:10 who *g* songs in the night,
Ps 119:130 The unfolding of your words *g* light;
Pr 3:34 but *g* grace to the humble.
11:24 One man *g* freely, yet gains
14:30 A heart at peace *g* life to the body,
15:30 good news *g* health to the bones.
19: 6 of a man who *g* gifts.
25:26 is a righteous man who *g* way
28:27 He who *g* to the poor will lack
29: 4 justice a king *g* a country stability,
Isa 40:29 He *g* strength to the weary
Hab 2:15 "Woe to him who *g* drink
Mt 10:42 if anyone *g* even a cup of cold water
Jn 5:21 even so the Son *g* life to whom he is
6:63 The Spirit *g* life; the flesh counts
1Co 15:57 He *g* us the victory
2Co 3: 6 the letter kills, but the Spirit *g* life.
1Th 4: 8 who *g* you his Holy Spirit.
Jas 1:25 into the perfect law that *g* freedom,
4: 6 but *g* grace to the humble."
1Pe 5: 5 but *g* grace to the humble."

GIVING (GIVE)
Ne 8: 8 *g* the meaning so that the people
Est 9:19 a day for *g* presents to each other.
Ps 19: 8 *g* joy to the heart.
Pr 15:23 A man finds joy in *g* an apt reply—
Mt 6: 4 so that your *g* may be in secret.
24:38 marrying and *g* in marriage,
Ac 15: 8 them by *g* the Holy Spirit to them,
2Co 8: 7 also excel in this grace of *g*.
Php 4:15 shared with me in the matter of *g*

GLAD* (GLADDENS GLADNESS)
Ex 4:14 his heart will be *g* when he sees you
Jos 22:33 They were *g* to hear the report
Jdg 8:25 "We'll be *g* to give them."
18:20 household?" Then the priest was *g*.
1Sa 19: 5 and you saw it and were *g*.
2Sa 1:20 daughters of the Philistines be *g*,
1Ki 8:66 *g* in heart for all the good things
1Ch 16:31 heavens rejoice, let the earth be *g*;
2Ch 7:10 and *g* in heart for the good things
Ps 5:11 let all who take refuge in you be *g*;
9: 2 I will be *g* and rejoice in you;
14: 7 let Jacob rejoice and Israel be *g*!
16: 9 Therefore my heart is *g*
21: 6 made him *g* with the joy
31: 7 I will be *g* and rejoice in your love,
32:11 Rejoice in the LORD and be *g*,
40:16 rejoice and be *g* in you;
45: 8 music of the strings makes you *g*.
46: 4 whose streams make *g* the city
48:11 the villages of Judah are *g*
53: 6 let Jacob rejoice and Israel be *g*!
58:10 The righteous will be *g*
67: 4 May the nations be *g* and sing
68: 3 But may the righteous be *g*
69:32 The poor will see and be *g*—
70: 4 rejoice and be *g* in you;
90:14 for joy and be *g* all our days.
90:15 Make us *g* for as many days
92: 4 For you make me *g* by your deeds,
96:11 heavens rejoice, let the earth be *g*;
97: 1 LORD reigns, let the earth be *g*;
97: 8 and the villages of Judah are *g*
105: 38 Egypt was *g* when they left,
107: 30 They were *g* when it grew calm,
118: 24 let us rejoice and be *g* in it.
149: 2 of Zion be *g* in their King.
Pr 23:15 then my heart will be *g*;
23:25 May your father and mother be *g*;
29: 6 a righteous one can sing and be *g*.
Ecc 8:15 sun than to eat and drink and be *g*.
Isa 25: 9 let us rejoice and be *g*
35: 1 and the parched land will be *g*;
65:18 But be *g* and rejoice forever
66:10 with Jerusalem and be *g* for her,
Jer 20:15 who made him very *g*, saying,
31:13 Then maidens will dance and be *g*,
41:13 were with him, they were *g*.
50:11 "Because you rejoice and are *g*,
La 4:21 be *g*, O Daughter of Edom,
Joel 2:21 be *g* and rejoice.
2:23 Be *g*, O people of Zion,
Hab 1:15 and so he rejoices and is *g*.
Zep 3:14 Be *g* and rejoice with all your heart
Zec 2:10 and be *g*, O Daughter of Zion.
8:19 will become joyful and *g* occasions
10: 7 their hearts will be *g* as with wine.
Mt 5:12 be *g*, because great is your reward
Lk 15:32 But we had to celebrate and be *g*,
Jn 4:36 and the reaper may be *g* together.
8:56 my day; he saw it and was *g*."
11:15 for your sake I am *g* I was not there
14:28 you would be *g* that I am going
Ac 2:26 Therefore my heart is *g*
2:46 together with *g* and sincere hearts,
11:23 he was *g* and encouraged them all
13:48 they were *g* and honored the word
15: 3 news made all the brothers very *g*.
15:31 were *g* for its encouraging message.
1Co 16:17 was *g* when Stephanas, Fortunatus
2Co 2: 2 who is left to make me *g*
7:16 I am *g* I can have complete
13: 9 We are *g* whenever we are weak
Gal 4:27 "Be *g*, O barren woman,
Php 2:17 I am *g* and rejoice with all of you.
2:18 So you too should be *g* and rejoice
2:28 you see him again you may be *g*
Rev 19: 7 Let us rejoice and be *g*

GLADDENS* (GLAD)
Ps 104: 15 wine that *g* the heart of man,

GLADNESS* (GLAD)
2Ch 29:30 So they sang praises with *g*
Est 8:16 a time of happiness and joy, *g*
8:17 there was joy and *g*
Job 3:22 who are filled with *g*
Ps 35:27 shout for joy and *g*;
45:15 They are led in with joy and *g*;
51: 8 Let me hear joy and *g*;
65:12 the hills are clothed with *g*.
100: 2 Worship the LORD with *g*;
Ecc 5:20 God keeps him occupied with *g*
9: 7 Go, eat your food with *g*,
Isa 16:10 *g* are taken away from the orchards
35:10 *G* and joy will overtake them,
51: 3 Joy and *g* will be found in her,
51:11 *G* and joy will overtake them,
61: 3 the oil of *g* / instead of mourning,
Jer 7:34 and *g* and to the voices of bride
16: 9 and *g* and to the voices of bride
25:10 from them the sounds of joy and *g*,
31:13 I will turn their mourning into *g*;
33:11 once more the sounds of joy and *g*,
48:33 Joy and *g* are gone
Joel 1:16 joy and *g*

GLAZE*
Pr 26:23 of *g* over earthenware

GLEAM*
Pr 4:18 of the righteous is like the first *g*
Da 10: 6 legs like the *g* of burnished bronze,

GLOAT (GLOATS)
Pr 24:17 Do not *g* when your enemy falls;

GLOATS* (GLOAT)
Pr 17: 5 whoever *g* over disaster will not go

GLORIES* (GLORY)
1Pe 1:11 and the *g* that would follow.

GLORIFIED* (GLORY)
Isa 66: 5 'Let the LORD be *g*,
Eze 39:13 day I am *g* will be a memorable day
Da 4:34 and *g* him who lives forever.
Jn 7:39 since Jesus had not yet been *g*.
11: 4 glory so that God's Son may be *g*
12:16 after Jesus was *g* did they realize
12:23 come for the Son of Man to be *g*.
12:28 "I have *g* it, and will glorify it again
13:31 Son of Man *g* and God is *g* in him.
13:32 If God is *g* in him, God will glorify
Ac 3:13 our fathers, has *g* his servant Jesus.
Ro 1:21 they neither *g* him as God
8:30 those he justified, he also *g*.
2Th 1:10 comes to be *g* in his holy people
1:12 of our Lord Jesus may be *g* in you,
1Pe 1:21 him from the dead and *g* him,

GLORIFIES* (GLORY)
Lk 1:46 My soul *g* the Lord
Jn 8:54 as your God, is the one who *g* me.

GLORIFY* (GLORY)
Ps 34: 3 *G* the LORD with me;
63: 3 my lips will *g* you.
69:30 and *g* him with thanksgiving.
86:12 I will *g* your name forever.
Isa 60:13 and I will *g* the place of my feet.
Da 4:37 and exalt and *g* the King of heaven,
Jn 8:54 Jesus replied, "If I *g* myself,
12:28 glorified it, and will *g* it again."
12:28 *g* your name!" Then a voice came
13:32 God will *g* the Son in himself,
13:32 in himself, and will *g* him at once.
17: 1 *G* your Son, that your Son may
17: 1 your Son, that your Son may *g* you.
17: 5 *g* me in your presence
21:19 death by which Peter would *g* God.
Ro 15: 6 and mouth you may *g* the God
15: 9 so that the Gentiles may *g* God
1Pe 2:12 and *g* God on the day he visits us.
Rev 16: 9 they refused to repent and *g* him.

GLORIFYING* (GLORY)
Lk 2:20 *g* and praising God

GLORIOUS* (GLORY)
Dt 28:58 not revere this *g* and awesome
33:29 and your *g* sword.
1Ch 29:13 and praise your *g* name.
Ne 9: 5 "Blessed be your *g* name,
Ps 16: 3 they are the *g* ones
45:13 All *g* is the princess
66: 2 make his praise *g*.
72:19 Praise be to his *g* name forever;
87: 3 *G* things are said of you,
111: 3 *G* and majestic are his deeds,
145: 5 of the *g* splendor of your majesty,
145: 12 the *g* splendor of your kingdom.
Isa 3: 8 defying his *g* presence.
4: 2 the LORD will be beautiful and *g*,
11:10 and his place of rest will be *g*.
12: 5 for he has done *g* things;
28: 1 to the fading flower, his *g* beauty,
28: 4 That fading flower, his *g* beauty,
28: 5 will be a *g* crown,
42:21 to make his law great and *g*.
60: 7 and I will adorn my *g* temple.
63:12 who sent his *g* arm of power
63:14 to make for yourself a *g* name.
63:15 from your lofty throne, holy and *g*.
64:11 *g* temple, where our fathers praised
Jer 13:18 for your *g* crowns
14:21 do not dishonor your *g* throne.
17:12 A *g* throne, exalted
48:17 how broken the *g* staff!'
Mt 19:28 the Son of Man sits on his *g* throne,
Lk 9:31 appeared in *g* splendor, talking
Ac 2:20 of the great and *g* day of the Lord.
Ro 8:21 and brought into the *g* freedom
2Co 3: 8 of the Spirit be even more *g*?
3: 9 how much more *g* is the ministry
3: 9 ministry that condemns men is *g*,
3:10 For what was *g* has no glory now
Eph 1: 6 to the praise of his *g* grace,
1:17 *g* Father, may give you the Spirit
1:18 the riches of his *g* inheritance
3:16 of his *g* riches he may strengthen
Php 3:21 so that they will be like his *g* body.
4:19 to his *g* riches in Christ Jesus.
Col 1:11 all power according to his *g* might
1:27 among the Gentiles the *g* riches
1Ti 1:11 to the *g* gospel of the blessed God,
Tit 2:13 the *g* appearing of our great God
Jas 2: 1 believers in our *g* Lord Jesus Christ
1Pe 1: 8 with an inexpressible and *g* joy,
Jude :24 before his *g* presence without fault

GLORIOUSLY* (GLORY)
Isa 24:23 and before its elders, *g*.

GLORY (GLORIES GLORIFIED GLORIFIES GLORIFY GLORIFYING GLORIOUS GLORIOUSLY)
Ex 14: 4 But I will gain *g* for myself
14:17 And I will gain *g* through Pharaoh
15:11 awesome in *g*,
16:10 and there was the *g* of the LORD
24:16 and the *g* of the LORD settled
33:18 Moses said, "Now show me your *g*
40:34 and the *g* of the LORD filled
Nu 14:21 the *g* of the LORD fills the whole
Dt 5:24 LORD our God has shown us his *g*
Jos 7:19 "My son, give *g* to the LORD,
1Sa 4:21 "The *g* has departed from Israel"—
1Ch 16:10 *G* in his holy name;
16:24 Declare his *g* among the nations,
16:28 ascribe to the LORD *g*
29:11 and the *g* and the majesty
Ps 8: 1 You have set your *g*
8: 5 and crowned him with *g* and honor

Ps 19: 1 The heavens declare the *g* of God;
24: 7 that the King of *g* may come in.
26: 8 the place where your *g* dwells.
29: 1 ascribe to the LORD *g*
29: 9 And in his temple all cry, "*G*!"
57: 5 let your *g* be over all the earth.
66: 2 Sing the *g* of his name;
72:19 the whole earth be filled with his *g*.
96: 3 Declare his *g* among the nations,
102: 15 of the earth will revere your *g*.
108: 5 and let your *g* be over all the earth.
149: 9 This is the *g* of all his saints.
Pr 19:11 it is to his *g* to overlook an offense.
25: 2 It is the *g* of God to conceal
Isa 4: 5 over all the *g* will be a canopy.
6: 3 the whole earth is full of his *g*."
24:16 "*G* to the Righteous One."
26:15 You have gained *g* for yourself;
35: 2 they will see the *g* of the LORD,
40: 5 the *g* of the LORD will be revealed
42: 8 I will not give my *g* to another
42:12 Let them give *g* to the LORD
43: 7 whom I created for my *g*,
44:23 he displays his *g* in Israel.
48:11 I will not yield my *g* to another.
66:18 and they will come and see my *g*.
66:19 They will proclaim my *g*
Eze 1:28 the likeness of the *g* of the LORD.
10: 4 the radiance of the *g* of the LORD.
43: 2 and the land was radiant with his *g*.
44: 4 and saw the *g* of the LORD filling
Hab 2:14 knowledge of the *g* of the LORD,
3: 3 His *g* covered the heavens
Zec 2: 5 'and I will be its *g* within.'
Mt 16:27 in his Father's *g* with his angels,
24:30 of the sky, with power and great *g*.
25:31 sit on his throne in heavenly *g*.
25:31 the Son of Man comes in his *g*,
Mk 8:38 in his Father's *g* with the holy
13:26 in clouds with great power and *g*.
Lk 2: 9 and the *g* of the Lord shone
2:14 saying, "*G* to God in the highest,
9:26 and in the *g* of the Father
9:26 of him when he comes in his *g*
9:32 they saw his *g* and the two men
19:38 in heaven and *g* in the highest!"
21:27 in a cloud with power and great *g*.
24:26 these things and then enter his *g*?"
Jn 1:14 We have seen his *g*, the *g* of the One
2:11 He thus revealed his *g*,
8:50 I am not seeking *g* for myself;
8:54 myself, my *g* means nothing.
11: 4 for God's *g* so that God's Son may
11:40 you would see the *g* of God?"
12:41 he saw Jesus' *g* and spoke about
14:13 so that the Son may bring *g*
15: 8 is to my Father's *g*, that you bear
16:14 He will bring *g* to me by taking
17: 4 I have brought you *g* on earth
17: 5 presence with the *g* I had with you
17:10 *g* has come to me through them.
17:22 given them the *g* that you gave
17:24 to see my *g*, the *g* you have given
Ac 7: 2 The God of *g* appeared
7:55 up to heaven and saw the *g* of God,
Ro 1:23 exchanged the *g* of the immortal
2: 7 by persistence in doing good seek *g*
2:10 then for the Gentile; but *g*,
3: 7 truthfulness and so increases his *g*,
3:23 and fall short of the *g* of God,
4:20 in his faith and gave *g* to God,
8:17 that we may also share in his *g*.
8:18 with the *g* that will be revealed
9: 4 theirs the divine *g*, the covenants,
9:23 riches of his *g* known to the objects
9:23 whom he prepared in advance for *g*
11:36 To him be the *g* forever! Amen.
15:17 Therefore I *g* in Christ Jesus
16:27 to the only wise God be *g* forever
1Co 2: 7 for our *g* before time began.
10:31 whatever you do, do it all for the *g*
11: 7 but the woman is the *g* of man.
11: 7 since he is the image and *g* of God;
11:15 it is her *g*? For long hair is given
15:43 it is raised in *g*; it is sown
2Co 1:20 spoken by us to the *g* of God.
3: 7 in letters on stone, came with *g*,
3: 7 the face of Moses because of its *g*,
3:10 comparison with the surpassing *g*.
3:10 what was glorious has no *g* now
2Co 3:11 how much greater is the *g*
3:11 what was fading away came with *g*,
3:18 faces all reflect the Lord's *g*,
3:18 likeness with ever-increasing *g*,
4: 4 of the gospel of the *g* of Christ,
4: 6 of the knowledge of the *g* of God
4:15 to overflow to the *g* of God.
4:17 us an eternal *g* that far outweighs
Gal 1: 5 to whom be *g* for ever and ever.
Eph 1:12 might be for the praise of his *g*.
1:14 to the praise of his *g*.
3:13 for you, which are your *g*.
3:21 to him be *g* in the church
Php 1:11 to the *g* and praise of God.
2:11 to the *g* of God the Father.
3: 3 of God, who *g* in Christ Jesus,
4:20 and Father be *g* for ever and ever.
Col 1:27 Christ in you, the hope of *g*.
3: 4 also will appear with him in *g*.
1Th 2:12 you into his kingdom and *g*.
2:19 in which we will *g* in the presence
2:20 Indeed, you are our *g* and joy.
2Th 2:14 in the *g* of our Lord Jesus Christ.
1Ti 1:17 be honor and *g* for ever and ever.
3:16 was taken up in *g*.
2Ti 2:10 is in Christ Jesus, with eternal *g*.
4:18 To him be *g* for ever and ever.
Heb 1: 3 The Son is the radiance of God's *g*
2: 7 you crowned him with *g* and honor
2: 9 now crowned with *g* and honor
2:10 In bringing many sons to *g*,
5: 5 take upon himself the *g*
9: 5 the ark were the cherubim of the *G*,
13:21 to whom be *g* for ever and ever.
1Pe 1: 7 *g* and honor when Jesus Christ is
1:24 and all their *g* is like the flowers
4:11 To him be the *g* and the power
4:13 overjoyed when his *g* is revealed.
4:14 for the Spirit of *g* and of God rests
5: 1 will share in the *g* to be revealed:
5: 4 of *g* that will never fade away.
5:10 you to his eternal *g* in Christ,
2Pe 1: 3 of him who called us by his own *g*
1:17 and *g* from God the Father
1:17 came to him from the Majestic *G*,
3:18 To him be *g* both now and forever!
Jude :25 to the only God our Savior be *g*,
Rev 1: 6 to him be *g* and power for ever
4: 9 the living creatures give *g*,
4:11 to receive *g* and honor and power,
5:12 and honor and *g* and praise!"
5:13 and honor and *g* and power,
7:12 Praise and *g*
11:13 and gave *g* to the God of heaven.
14: 7 "Fear God and give him *g*,
15: 4 and bring *g* to your name?
15: 8 with smoke from the *g* of God
19: 1 *g* and power belong to our God,
19: 7 and give him *g*!
21:11 It shone with the *g* of God,
21:23 for the *g* of God gives it light,
21:26 *g* and honor of the nations will be

GLOWING
Eze 8: 2 was as bright as *g* metal.
Rev 1:15 His feet were like bronze *g*

GLUTTONS* (GLUTTONY)
Pr 23:21 for drunkards and *g* become poor,
28: 7 of *g* disgraces his father.
Tit 1:12 always liars, evil brutes, lazy *g*."

GLUTTONY* (GLUTTONS)
Pr 23: 2 throat if you are given to *g*.

GNASHING
Mt 8:12 where there will be weeping and *g*

GNAT* (GNATS)
Mt 23:24 You strain out a *g* but swallow

GNATS (GNAT)
Ex 8:16 of Egypt the dust will become *g*."

GOADS
Ecc 12:11 The words of the wise are like *g*,
Ac 26:14 hard for you to kick against the *g*.'

GOAL*
Lk 13:32 on the third day I will reach my *g*.'
2Co 5: 9 So we make it our *g* to please him,
Gal 3: 3 to attain your *g* by human effort?
Php 3:14 on toward the *g* to win the prize
1Ti 1: 5 The *g* of this command is love,
1Pe 1: 9 for you are receiving the *g*

GOAT (GOATS SCAPEGOAT)
Ge 15: 9 "Bring me a heifer, a *g* and a ram,
30:32 and every spotted or speckled *g*.
37:31 slaughtered a *g* and dipped
Ex 26: 7 Make curtains of *g* hair for the tent
Lev 16: 9 shall bring the *g* whose lot falls
Nu 7:16 one male *g* for a sin offering;
Isa 11: 6 the leopard will lie down with the *g*
Da 8: 5 suddenly a *g* with a prominent

GOATS (GOAT)
Nu 7:17 five male *g* and five male lambs
Mt 25:32 separates the sheep from the *g*.
Heb 10: 4 of bulls and *g* to take away sins.

GOD (GOD'S GODLINESS GODLY GODS)
Ge 1: 1 In the beginning *G* created
1: 2 and the Spirit of *G* was hovering
1: 3 And *G* said, "Let there be light,"
1: 7 So *G* made the expanse
1: 9 And *G* said, "Let the water
1:11 Then *G* said, "Let the land produce
1:20 And *G* said, "Let the water teem
1:21 So *G* created the great creatures
1:25 *G* made the wild animals according
1:26 Then *G* said, "Let us make man
1:27 So *G* created man in his own image
1:31 *G* saw all that he had made,
2: 3 And *G* blessed the seventh day
2: 7 And the LORD *G* formed the man
2: 8 the LORD *G* had planted a garden
2:18 The LORD *G* said, "It is not good
2:22 Then the LORD *G* made a woman
3: 1 to the woman, "Did *G* really say,
3: 5 you will be like *G*, knowing good
3: 8 from the LORD *G* among the trees
3: 9 But the LORD *G* called to the man
3:21 The LORD *G* made garments
3:22 LORD *G* said, "The man has now
3:23 So the LORD *G* banished him
5: 1 When *G* created man, he made him
5:22 Enoch walked with *G* 300 years
5:24 because *G* took him away.
6: 2 sons of *G* saw that the daughters
6: 9 of his time, and he walked with *G*.
6:12 *G* saw how corrupt the earth had
8: 1 But *G* remembered Noah
9: 1 Then *G* blessed Noah and his sons,
9: 6 for in the image of *G*
9:16 everlasting covenant between *G*
14:18 He was priest of *G* Most High,
14:19 Blessed be Abram by *G* Most High,
16:13 "You are the *G* who sees me,"
17: 1 "I am *G* Almighty; walk before me
17: 7 to be your *G* and the *G*
21: 4 him, as *G* commanded him.
21: 6 "*G* has brought me laughter,
21:20 *G* was with the boy as he grew up.
21:22 *G* is with you in everything you do.
21:33 name of the LORD, the Eternal *G*.
22: 1 Some time later *G* tested Abraham.
22: 8 "*G* himself will provide the lamb
22:12 Now I know that you fear *G*,
25:11 Abraham's death, *G* blessed his
28:12 and the angels of *G* were ascending
28:17 other than the house of *G*;
31:42 But *G* has seen my hardship
31:50 remember that *G* is a witness
32: 1 and the angels of *G* met him.
32:28 because you have struggled with *G*
32:30 "It is because I saw *G* face to face,
33:11 for *G* has been gracious to me
35: 1 and build an altar there to *G*,
35: 5 and the terror of *G* fell
35:10 *G* said to him, "Your name is Jacob
35:11 *G* said to him, "I am *G* Almighty;
41:51 *G* has made me forget all my
41:52 *G* has made me fruitful in the land
50:20 but *G* intended it for good
50:24 But *G* will surely come to your aid
Ex 2:24 *G* heard their groaning
3: 5 "Do not come any closer," *G* said.
3: 6 because he was afraid to look at *G*.
3:12 And *G* said, "I will be with you.
3:14 what shall I tell them?" *G* said
4:27 he met Moses at the mountain of *G*
6: 7 own people, and I will be your *G*.
8:10 is no one like the LORD our *G*.
10:16 sinned against the LORD your *G*

Ex 13:18 So *G* led the people
15: 2 He is my *G*, and I will praise him,
16:12 that I am the LORD your *G*.' "
17: 9 with the staff of *G* in my hands."
18: 5 camped near the mountain of *G*.
19: 3 Then Moses went up to *G*,
20: 1 And *G* spoke all these words:
20: 2 the LORD your *G*, who brought
20: 5 the LORD your *G*, am a jealous *G*,
20: 7 the name of the LORD your *G*,
20:10 a Sabbath to the LORD your *G*.
20:12 the LORD your *G* is giving you.
20:19 But do not have *G* speak to us
20:20 the fear of *G* will be with you
22:20 "Whoever sacrifices to any *g* other
22:28 "Do not blaspheme *G*
23:19 to the house of the LORD your *G*.
31:18 inscribed by the finger of *G*.
34: 6 the compassionate and gracious *G*,
34:14 name is Jealous, is a jealous *G*.
Lev 2:13 salt of the covenant of your *G* out
11:44 the LORD your *G*; consecrate
18:21 not profane the name of your *G*.
19: 2 the LORD your *G*, am holy.
20: 7 because I am the LORD your *G*.
21: 6 They must be holy to their *G*
22:33 out of Egypt to be your *G*.
26:12 walk among you and be your *G*,
Nu 15:40 and will be consecrated to your *G*.
22:18 the command of the LORD my *G*.
22:38 I must speak only what *G* puts
23:19 *G* is not a man, that he should lie,
25:13 zealous for the honor of his *G*
Dt 1:17 for judgment belongs to *G*.
1:21 the LORD your *G* has given you
1:30 The LORD your *G*, who is going
3:22 LORD your *G* himself will fight
3:24 For what *g* is there in heaven
4:24 is a consuming fire, a jealous *G*.
4:29 there you seek the LORD your *G*,
4:31 the LORD your *G* is a merciful *G*;
4:39 heart this day that the LORD is *G*
5: 9 the LORD your *G*, am a jealous *G*,
5:11 the name of the LORD your *G*,
5:12 the LORD your *G* has commanded
5:14 a Sabbath to the LORD your *G*.
5:15 the LORD your *G* brought you out
5:16 the LORD your *G* has commanded
5:16 the LORD your *G* is giving you.
5:24 LORD our *G* has shown us his
5:26 of the living *G* speaking out of fire,
6: 2 them may fear the LORD your *G*
6: 4 LORD our *G*, the LORD is one.
6: 5 Love the LORD your *G*
6:13 the LORD your *G*, serve him only
6:16 Do not test the LORD your *G*
7: 6 holy to the LORD your *G*.
7: 9 your *G* is *G*; he is the faithful *G*,
7:12 the LORD your *G* will keep his
7:19 LORD your *G* will do the same
7:21 is a great and awesome *G*.
8: 5 the LORD your *G* disciplines you.
8:11 do not forget the LORD your *G*,
8:18 But remember the LORD your *G*,
9:10 inscribed by the finger of *G*.
10:12 but to fear the LORD your *G*,
10:14 the LORD your *G* belong
10:17 For the LORD your *G* is *G* of gods
10:21 He is your praise; he is your *G*,
11: 1 Love the LORD your *G*
11:13 to love the LORD your *G*
12:12 rejoice before the LORD your *G*,
12:28 in the eyes of the LORD your *G*.
13: 3 The LORD your *G* is testing you
13: 4 the LORD your *G* you must
15: 6 the LORD your *G* will bless you
15:19 the LORD your *G* every firstborn
16:11 rejoice before the LORD your *G*
16:17 the LORD your *G* has blessed you.
18:13 before the LORD your *G*.
18:15 The LORD your *G* will raise up
19: 9 to love the LORD your *G*
22: 5 the LORD your *G* detests anyone
23: 5 the LORD your *G* loves you.
23:14 the LORD your *G* moves about
23:21 a vow to the LORD your *G*,
25:16 the LORD your *G* detests anyone
26: 5 declare before the LORD your *G*:
29:13 that he may be your *G*
29:29 belong to the LORD our *G*,
Dt 30: 2 return to the LORD your *G*
30: 4 the LORD your *G* will gather you
30: 6 The LORD your *G* will circumcise
30:16 today to love the LORD your *G*,
30:20 you may love the LORD your *G*,
31: 6 for the LORD your *G* goes
32: 3 Oh, praise the greatness of our *G*!
32: 4 A faithful *G* who does no wrong,
33:27 The eternal *G* is your refuge,
Jos 1: 9 for the LORD your *G* will be
14: 8 the LORD my *G* wholeheartedly.
14: 9 the LORD my *G* wholeheartedly.'
14:14 the *G* of Israel, wholeheartedly.
22: 5 to love the LORD your *G*,
22:22 The Mighty One, *G*, the LORD!
22:34 Between Us that the LORD is *G*.
23: 8 to hold fast to the LORD your *G*,
23:11 careful to love the LORD your *G*.
23:14 the LORD your *G* gave you has
23:15 of the LORD your *G* has come true
24:19 He is a holy *G*; he is a jealous *G*.
24:23 to the LORD, the *G* of Israel."
Jdg 5: 3 to the LORD, the *G* of Israel.
16:28 O *G*, please strengthen me just
Ru 1:16 be my people and your *G* my *G*.
2:12 by the LORD, the *G* of Israel,
1Sa 2: 2 there is no Rock like our *G*.
2: 3 for the LORD is a *G* who knows,
2:25 another man, *G* may mediate
10:26 men whose hearts *G* had touched.
12:12 the LORD your *G* was your king.
16:15 spirit from *G* is tormenting you.
17:26 defy the armies of the living *G*?"
17:36 defied the armies of the living *G*.
17:45 the *G* of the armies of Israel,
17:46 world will know that there is a *G*
23:16 and helped him find strength in *G*.
28:15 and *G* has turned away from me.
30: 6 strength in the LORD his *G*.
2Sa 7:22 and there is no *G* but you,
7:23 on earth that *G* went out to redeem
14:14 But *G* does not take away life;
21:14 *G* answered prayer in behalf
22: 3 my *G* is my rock, in whom I take
22:31 "As for *G*, his way is perfect;
22:32 And who is the Rock except our *G*
22:33 It is *G* who arms me with strength
22:47 Exalted be *G*, the Rock, my Savior!
1Ki 2: 3 what the LORD your *G* requires:
4:29 *G* gave Solomon wisdom
5: 5 for the Name of the LORD my *G*,
8:23 there is no *G* like you in heaven
8:27 "But will *G* really dwell on earth?
8:60 may know that the LORD is *G*
8:61 committed to the LORD our *G*,
10:24 to hear the wisdom *G* had put
15:30 he provoked the LORD, the *G*
18:21 If the LORD is *G*, follow him;
18:36 it be known today that you are *G*
18:37 are *G*, and that you are turning
20:28 a *g* of the hills and not a *g*
2Ki 5:15 "Now I know that there is no *G*
18: 5 in the LORD, the *G* of Israel.
19:15 *G* of Israel, enthroned
19:19 Now, O LORD our *G*, deliver us
1Ch 12:18 for your *G* will help you."
13: 2 if it is the will of the LORD our *G*,
16:35 Cry out, "Save us, O *G* our Savior;
17:20 and there is no *G* but you,
17:24 the *G* over Israel, is Israel's *G*!'
21: 8 said to *G*, "I have sinned greatly
22: 1 house of the LORD *G* is to be here,
22:19 soul to seeking the LORD your *G*.
28: 2 for the footstool of our *G*,
28: 9 acknowledge the *G* of your father,
28:20 for the LORD *G*, my *G*, is with you
29: 1 not for man but for the LORD *G*.
29: 2 provided for the temple of my *G*—
29: 3 of my *G* I now give my personal
29:10 *G* of our father Israel,
29:13 Now, our *G*, we give you thanks,
29:16 O LORD our *G*, as for all this
29:17 my *G*, that you test the heart
29:18 *G* of our fathers Abraham,
2Ch 2: 4 for the Name of the LORD my *G*
5:14 of the LORD filled the temple of *G*
6: 4 be to the LORD, the *G* of Israel,
6:14 there is no *G* like you in heaven
6:18 "But will *G* really dwell on earth
10:15 for this turn of events was from *G*,
2Ch 13:12 *G* is with us; he is our leader.
15: 3 was without the true *G*,
15:12 the *G* of their fathers,
15:15 They sought *G* eagerly,
18:13 I can tell him only what my *G* says
19: 3 have set your heart on seeking *G*."
19: 7 with the LORD our *G* there is no
20: 6 are you not the *G* who is in heaven?
20:20 Have faith in the LORD your *G*
25: 8 for *G* has the power to help
26: 5 sought the LORD, *G* gave him
30: 9 for the LORD your *G* is gracious
30:19 who sets his heart on seeking *G*—
31:21 he sought his *G* and worked
32:31 *G* left him to test him
33:12 the favor of the LORD his *G*
34:33 fail to follow the LORD, the *G*
Ezr 6:21 to seek the LORD, the *G* of Israel.
7:18 accordance with the will of your *G*.
7:23 Whatever the *G* of heaven has
8:22 "The gracious hand of our *G* is
8:31 The hand of our *G* was on us,
9: 6 "O my *G*, I am too ashamed
9: 9 our *G* has not deserted us
9:13 our *G*, you have punished us less
9:15 *G* of Israel, you are righteous!
Ne 1: 5 the great and awesome *G*,
5: 9 fear of our *G* to avoid the reproach
5:15 for *G* I did not act like that.
7: 2 feared *G* more than most men do.
8: 8 from the Book of the Law of *G*,
8:18 from the Book of the Law of *G*.
9: 5 and praise the LORD your *G*,
9:17 But you are a forgiving *G*,
9:31 you are a gracious and merciful *G*.
9:32 the great, mighty and awesome *G*,
10:29 oath to follow the Law of *G* given
10:39 not neglect the house of our *G*."
12:43 *G* had given them great joy.
13:11 Why is the house of *G* neglected?"
13:26 He was loved by his *G*,
13:31 Remember me with favor, O my *G*.
Job 1: 1 he feared *G* and shunned evil.
1:22 by charging *G* with wrongdoing.
2:10 Shall we accept good from *G*,
4:17 a mortal be more righteous than *G*?
5:17 is the man whom *G* corrects;
8: 3 Does *G* pervert justice?
8:20 "Surely *G* does not reject
9: 2 a mortal be righteous before *G*?
11: 7 Can you fathom the mysteries of *G*
12:13 "To *G* belong wisdom and power;
16: 7 Surely, O *G*, you have worn me out
19:26 yet in my flesh I will see *G*;
21:19 '*G* stores up a man's punishment
21:22 Can anyone teach knowledge to *G*,
22:12 "Is not *G* in the heights of heaven?
22:13 Yet you say, 'What does *G* know?
22:21 "Submit to *G* and be at peace
25: 2 "Dominion and awe belong to *G*;
25: 4 can a man be righteous before *G*?
26: 6 Death is naked before *G*;
30:20 O *G*, but you do not answer;
31: 6 let *G* weigh me in honest scales
31:14 do when *G* confronts me?
32:13 let *G* refute him, not man.'
33: 6 I am just like you before *G*;
33:14 For *G* does speak—now one way,
33:26 He prays to *G* and finds favor
34:10 Far be it from *G* to do evil,
34:12 is unthinkable that *G* would do
34:23 *G* has no need to examine men
34:33 Should *G* then reward you
36: 5 "*G* is mighty, but does not despise
36:26 is *G*—beyond our understanding!
37:22 *G* comes in awesome majesty.
Ps 5: 4 You are not a *G* who takes pleasure
7:11 *G* is a righteous judge,
10:14 O *G*, do see trouble and grief;
14: 5 for *G* is present in the company
18: 2 my *G* is my rock, in whom I take
18:28 my *G* turns my darkness into light.
18:30 As for *G*, his way is perfect;
18:31 And who is the Rock except our *G*
18:32 It is *G* who arms me with strength
18:46 Exalted be *G* my Savior!
19: 1 The heavens declare the glory of *G*;
22: 1 *G*, my *G*, why have you forsaken
22:10 womb you have been my *G*.
27: 9 O *G* my Savior.

Ps 29: 3 the *G* of glory thunders,
31: 5 redeem me, O LORD, the *G*
31:14 I say, "You are my *G*."
33:12 the nation whose *G* is the LORD,
35:24 righteousness, O LORD my *G*;
37:31 The law of his *G* is in his heart;
40: 3 a hymn of praise to our *G*.
40: 8 I desire to do your will, O my *G*;
42: 1 so my soul pants for you, O *G*.
42: 2 thirsts for *G*, for the living *G*.
42: 5 Put your hope in *G*,
42: 8 a prayer to the *G* of my life.
42:11 Put your hope in *G*,
43: 4 to *G*, my joy and my delight.
44: 8 In *G* we make our boast all day
45: 6 O *G*, will last for ever and ever;
45: 7 therefore *G*, your *G*, has set you
46: 1 *G* is our refuge and strength,
46: 5 *G* will help her at break of day.
46:10 "Be still, and know that I am *G*;
47: 1 shout to *G* with cries of joy.
47: 6 Sing praises to *G*, sing praises;
47: 7 For *G* is the King of all the earth;
48: 9 Within your temple, O *G*,
49: 7 or give to *G* a ransom for him—
50: 2 *G* shines forth.
50: 3 Our *G* comes and will not be silent;
51: 1 Have mercy on me, O *G*,
51:10 Create in me a pure heart, O *G*,
51:17 O *G*, you will not despise.
53: 2 any who seek *G*.
54: 4 Surely *G* is my help;
55:19 *G*, who is enthroned forever,
56: 4 In *G*, whose word I praise,
56:10 In *G*, whose word I praise,
56:13 that I may walk before *G*
57: 3 *G* sends his love and his
57: 7 My heart is steadfast, O *G*,
59:17 are my fortress, my loving *G*.
62: 1 My soul finds rest in *G* alone;
62: 7 my honor depend on *G*;
62: 8 for *G* is our refuge.
62:11 One thing *G* has spoken,
63: 1 O *G*, you are my *G*,
65: 5 O *G* our Savior,
66: 1 Shout with joy to *G*, all the earth!
66: 3 Say to *G*, "How awesome are your
66: 5 Come and see what *G* has done,
66:16 listen, all you who fear *G*;
66:20 Praise be to *G*,
68: 4 Sing to *G*, sing praise to his name,
68: 6 *G* sets the lonely in families,
68:20 Our *G* is a *G* who saves;
68:24 has come into view, O *G*,
68:35 You are awesome, O *G*,
69: 5 You know my folly, O *G*;
70: 1 Hasten, O *G*, to save me;
70: 4 "Let *G* be exalted!"
70: 5 come quickly to me, O *G*.
71:17 my youth, O *G*, you have taught
71:18 do not forsake me, O *G*,
71:19 reaches to the skies, O *G*,
71:22 harp for your faithfulness, O my *G*;
73:17 me till I entered the sanctuary of *G*;
73:26 but *G* is the strength of my heart
76:11 Make vows to the LORD your *G*
77:13 What *g* is so great as our God?
77:14 You are the *G* who performs
78:19 Can *G* spread a table in the desert?
79: 9 Help us, O *G* our Savior,
81: 1 Sing for joy to *G* our strength;
82: 1 *G* presides in the great assembly;
84: 2 out for the living *G*.
84:10 a doorkeeper in the house of my *G*
84:11 For the LORD *G* is a sun
86:12 O Lord my *G*, with all my heart;
86:15 a compassionate and gracious *G*,
87: 3 O city of *G*: *Selah*
89: 7 of the holy ones *G* is greatly feared;
90: 2 to everlasting you are *G*.
91: 2 my *G*, in whom I trust."
94:22 my *G* the rock in whom I take
95: 7 for he is our *G*
99: 8 you were to Israel a forgiving *G*,
99: 9 Exalt the LORD our *G*
100: 3 Know that the LORD is *G*.
108: 1 My heart is steadfast, O *G*;
113: 5 Who is like the LORD our *G*,
115: 3 Our *G* is in heaven;
116: 5 our *G* is full of compassion.

Ps 123: 2 look to the LORD our *G*,
136: 2 Give thanks to the *G* of gods.
136: 26 Give thanks to the *G* of heaven.
139: 17 to me are your thoughts, O *G*!
139: 23 Search me, O *G*, and know my
143: 10 for you are my *G*;
144: 2 He is my loving *G* and my fortress,
147: 1 is to sing praises to our *G*,
Pr 3: 4 in the sight of *G* and man.
14:31 to the needy honors *G*.
25: 2 of *G* to conceal a matter;
30: 5 "Every word of *G* is flawless;
Ecc 2:26 *G* gives wisdom, knowledge
3:11 cannot fathom what *G* has done
3:13 in all his toil—this is the gift of *G*.
3:14 *G* does it so that men will revere him.
5: 4 When you make a vow to *G*,
5:19 in his work—this is a gift of *G*.
8:12 who are reverent before *G*.
11: 5 cannot understand the work of *G*,
12: 7 the spirit returns to *G* who gave it.
12:13 Fear *G* and keep his
Isa 5:16 the holy *G* will show himself holy
9: 6 Wonderful Counselor, Mighty *G*,
12: 2 Surely *G* is my salvation;
25: 9 "Surely this is our *G*;
28:11 *G* will speak to this people,
29:23 will stand in awe of the *G* of Israel.
30:18 For the LORD is a *G* of justice.
35: 4 your *G* will come,
37:16 you alone are *G* over all
40: 1 says your *G*.
40: 3 a highway for our *G*.
40: 8 the word of our *G* stands forever."
40:18 then, will you compare *G*?
40:28 The LORD is the everlasting *G*,
41:10 not be dismayed, for I am your *G*.
41:13 For I am the LORD, your *G*,
43:10 Before me no *g* was formed,
44: 6 apart from me there is no *G*.
44:15 he also fashions a *g* and worships it;
45:18 he is *G*;
48:17 "I am the LORD your *G*,
52: 7 "Your *G* reigns!"
52:12 *G* of Israel will be your rear guard.
55: 7 to our *G*, for he will freely pardon.
57:21 says my *G*, "for the wicked."
59: 2 you from your *G*;
60:19 and your *G* will be your glory.
61: 2 and the day of vengeance of our *G*,
61:10 my soul rejoices in my *G*.
62: 5 so will your *G* rejoice over you.
Jer 7:23 I will be your *G* and you will be my
10:10 But the LORD is the true *G*;
10:12 But *G* made the earth by his power;
23:23 "Am I only a *G* nearby,"
23:36 distort the words of the living *G*,
31:33 I will be their *G*,
32:27 "I am the LORD, the *G*
42: 6 for we will obey the LORD our *G*."
51:10 what the LORD our *G* has done.'
51:56 For the LORD is a *G* of retribution
Eze 28:13 the garden of *G*;
34:31 and I am your *G*, declares
Da 2:28 there is a *G* in heaven who reveals
3:17 the *G* we serve is able to save us
3:29 for no other *g* can save in this way
6:16 "May your *G*, whom you serve
9: 4 O Lord, the great and awesome *G*,
10:12 to humble yourself before your *G*,
11:36 things against the *G* of gods.
Hos 1: 9 my people, and I am not your *G*.
1:10 will be called 'sons of the living *G*.'
4: 6 you have ignored the law of your *G*
6: 6 acknowledgment of *G* rather
9: 8 The prophet, along with my *G*,
12: 6 and wait for your *G* always.
Joel 2:13 Return to the LORD your *G*,
2:23 rejoice in the LORD your *G*,
Am 4:12 prepare to meet your *G*, O Israel."
4:13 the LORD *G* Almighty is his name
Jnh 1: 6 Get up and call on your *g*!
4: 2 a gracious and compassionate *G*,
Mic 6: 8 and to walk humbly with your *G*.
7: 7 I wait for *G* my Savior;
7:18 Who is a *G* like you,
Na 1: 2 LORD is a jealous and avenging *G*;
Hab 3:18 I will be joyful in *G* my Savior.
Zep 3:17 The LORD your *G* is with you,

Zec 14: 5 Then the LORD my *G* will come,
Mal 2:10 Father? Did not one *G* create us?
2:16 says the LORD *G* of Israel,
3: 8 Will a man rob *G*? Yet you rob me.
Mt 1:23 which means, "*G* with us."
4: 4 comes from the mouth of *G*.'"
4: 7 'Do not put the Lord your *G*
4:10 'Worship the Lord your *G*,
5: 8 for they will see *G*.
6:24 You cannot serve both *G*
19: 6 Therefore what *G* has joined
19:26 but with *G* all things are possible."
22:21 and to *G* what is God's."
22:32 He is not the *G* of the dead
22:37 "'Love the Lord your *G*
27:46 which means, "My *G*, my *G*,
Mk 2: 7 Who can forgive sins but *G* alone?"
7:13 Thus you nullify the word of *G*
10: 6 of creation *G* 'made them male
10: 9 Therefore what *G* has joined
10:18 "No one is good—except *G* alone.
10:27 all things are possible with *G*."
11:22 "Have faith in *G*," Jesus answered.
12:17 and to *G* what is God's."
12:29 the Lord our *G*, the Lord is one.
12:30 Love the Lord your *G*
15:34 which means, "My *G*, my *G*,
16:19 and he sat at the right hand of *G*.
Lk 1:30 Mary, you have found favor with *G*
1:37 For nothing is impossible with *G*."
1:47 my spirit rejoices in *G* my Savior,
2:14 "Glory to *G* in the highest,
2:52 and in favor with *G* and men.
4: 8 'Worship the Lord your *G*
5:21 Who can forgive sins but *G* alone?"
8:39 tell how much *G* has done for you."
10: 9 'The kingdom of *G* is near you.'
10:27 "'Love the Lord your *G*
13:18 "What is the kingdom of *G* like?
18:19 "No one is good—except *G* alone.
18:27 with men is possible with *G*."
20:25 and to *G* what is God's."
20:38 He is not the *G* of the dead,
22:69 at the right hand of the mighty *G*."
Jn 1: 1 was with *G*, and the Word was *G*.
1:18 ever seen *G*, but *G* the One and Only,
1:29 Lamb of *G*, who takes away the sin
3:16 "For *G* so loved the world that he
3:34 the one whom *G* has sent speaks
4:24 *G* is spirit, and his worshipers must
5:44 praise that comes from the only *G*?
6:29 answered, "The work of *G* is this:
7:17 my teaching comes from *G* or
8:42 to them, "If *G* were your Father,
8:47 belongs to *G* hears what *G* says.
11:40 you would see the glory of *G*?"
13: 3 from *G* and was returning to *G*;
13:31 of Man glorified and *G* is glorified
14: 1 Trust in *G*; trust also in me.
17: 3 the only true *G*, and Jesus Christ,
20:17 your Father, to my *G* and your *G*
20:28 "My Lord and my *G*!"
20:31 the Son of *G*, and that
Ac 2:11 wonders of *G* in our own tongues!"
2:24 But *G* raised him from the dead,
2:33 Exalted to the right hand of *G*,
2:36 *G* has made this Jesus, whom you
3:15 but *G* raised him from the dead.
3:19 Repent, then, and turn to *G*,
4:31 and spoke the word of *G* boldly.
5: 4 You have not lied to men but to *G*
5:29 "We must obey *G* rather than men!
5:31 *G* exalted him to his own right
5:32 whom *G* has given
7:55 to heaven and saw the glory of *G*,
8:21 your heart is not right before *G*.
11: 9 anything impure that *G* has made
12:24 But the word of *G* continued
13:32 What *G* promised our fathers he
15:10 to test *G* by putting on the necks
17:23 TO AN UNKNOWN *G*.
17:30 In the past *G* overlooked such
20:27 to you the whole will of *G*.
20:32 "Now I commit you to *G*
24:16 keep my conscience clear before *G*
Ro 1:16 the power of *G* for the salvation
1:17 a righteousness from *G* is revealed,
1:18 The wrath of *G* is being revealed
1:24 Therefore *G* gave them

Ro 1:26 *G* gave them over to shameful lusts
2:11 For *G* does not show favoritism.
2:16 when *G* will judge men's secrets
3: 4 Let *G* be true, and every man a liar.
3:19 world held accountable to *G.*
3:23 and fall short of the glory of *G,*
3:29 Is *G* the *G* of Jews only? Is he not
4: 3 say? "Abraham believed *G,*
4: 6 to whom *G* credits righteousness
4:17 the *G* who gives life to the dead
4:24 to whom *G* will credit
5: 1 we have peace with *G*
5: 5 because *G* has poured out his love
5: 8 *G* demonstrates his own love for us
6:22 and have become slaves to *G,*
6:23 but the gift of *G* is eternal life
8: 7 the sinful mind is hostile to *G.*
8:17 heirs of *G* and co-heirs with Christ,
8:28 in all things *G* works for the good
9:14 What then shall we say? Is *G* unjust
9:18 Therefore *G* has mercy
10: 9 in your heart that *G* raised him
11: 2 *G* did not reject his people,
11:22 the kindness and sternness of *G:*
11:32 For *G* has bound all men
13: 1 exist have been established by *G.*
14:12 give an account of himself to *G.*
16:20 *G* of peace will soon crush Satan
1Co 1:18 are being saved it is the power of *G.*
1:20 Has not *G* made foolish
1:25 For the foolishness of *G* is wiser
1:27 But *G* chose the foolish things
2: 9 what *G* has prepared
2:11 of *G* except the Spirit of *G.*
3: 6 watered it, but *G* made it grow.
3:17 God's temple, *G* will destroy
6:20 Therefore honor *G* with your body.
7: 7 each man has his own gift from *G;*
7:15 *G* has called us to live in peace.
7:20 was in when *G* called him.
7:24 each man, as responsible to *G,*
8: 3 man who loves *G* is known by *G.*
8: 8 food does not bring us near to *G;*
10:13 *G* is faithful; he will not let you be
10:31 do it all for the glory of *G.*
12:24 But *G* has combined the members
14:33 For *G* is not a *G* of disorder
15:24 over the kingdom to *G* the Father
15:28 so that *G* may be all in all.
15:34 are some who are ignorant of *G*—
15:57 be to *G!* He gives us the victory
2Co 1: 9 rely on ourselves but on *G,*
2:14 be to *G,* who always leads us
2:15 For we are to *G* the aroma of Christ
2:17 we do not peddle the word of *G*
3: 5 but our competence comes from *G.*
4: 2 nor do we distort the word of *G.*
4: 7 this all-surpassing power is from *G*
5: 5 Now it is *G* who has made us
5:19 that *G* was reconciling the world
5:20 though *G* were making his appeal
5:21 *G* made him who had no sin
6:16 we are the temple of the living *G.*
9: 7 for *G* loves a cheerful giver.
9: 8 *G* is able to make all grace abound
10:13 to the field *G* has assigned to us,
Gal 2: 6 *G* does not judge by external
3: 5 Does *G* give you his Spirit
3: 6 Abraham: "He believed *G,*
3:11 justified before *G* by the law,
3:26 You are all sons of *G* through faith
6: 7 not be deceived: *G* cannot be
Eph 1:22 *G* placed all things under his feet
2: 8 it is the gift of *G*—not by works,
2:10 which *G* prepared in advance for us
2:22 in which *G* lives by his Spirit.
4: 6 one baptism; one *G* and Father
4:24 to be like *G* in true righteousness
5: 1 Be imitators of *G,* therefore,
6: 6 doing the will of *G* from your heart.
Php 2: 6 Who, being in very nature *G,*
2: 9 Therefore *G* exalted him
2:13 for it is *G* who works in you to will
4: 7 peace of *G,* which transcends all
4:19 And my *G* will meet all your needs
Col 1:19 For *G* was pleased
2:13 *G* made you alive with Christ.
1Th 2: 4 trying to please men but *G,*
2:13 but as it actually is, the word of *G,*
3: 9 How can we thank *G* enough
1Th 4: 7 For *G* did not call us to be impure,
4: 9 taught by *G* to love each other.
5: 9 For *G* did not appoint us
1Ti 2: 5 one mediator between *G* and men,
4: 4 For everything *G* created is good,
5: 4 for this is pleasing to *G.*
2Ti 1: 6 you to fan into flame the gift of *G,*
Tit 1: 2 which *G,* who does not lie,
2:13 glorious appearing of our great *G*
Heb 1: 1 In the past *G* spoke
3: 4 but *G* is the builder of everything.
4: 4 "And on the seventh day *G* rested
4:12 For the word of *G* is living
6:10 *G* is not unjust; he will not forget
6:18 in which it is impossible for *G* to lie
7:19 by which we draw near to *G.*
7:25 come to *G* through him,
10:22 draw near to *G* with a sincere heart
10:31 to fall into the hands of the living *G*
11: 5 commended as one who pleased *G.*
11: 6 faith it is impossible to please *G,*
12: 7 as discipline; *G* is treating you
12:10 but *G* disciplines us for our good,
12:29 for our "*G* is a consuming fire."
13:15 offer to *G* a sacrifice of praise—
Jas 1:12 crown of life that *G* has promised
1:13 For *G* cannot be tempted by evil,
1:27 Religion that *G* our Father accepts
2:19 You believe that there is one *G.*
2:23 "Abraham believed *G,*
4: 4 the world becomes an enemy of *G.*
4: 6 "*G* opposes the proud
4: 8 Come near to *G* and he will come
1Pe 1:23 the living and enduring word of *G.*
2:20 this is commendable before *G.*
3:18 the unrighteous, to bring you to *G.*
4:11 it with the strength *G* provides,
5: 5 because, "*G* opposes the proud
2Pe 1:21 but men spoke from *G*
2: 4 For if *G* did not spare angels
1Jn 1: 5 *G* is light; in him there is no
2:17 the will of *G* lives forever.
3: 1 we should be called children of *G!*
3: 9 born of *G* will continue to sin,
3:10 we know who the children of *G* are
3:20 For *G* is greater than our hearts,
4: 7 for love comes from *G.*
4: 8 not know *G,* because *G* is love.
4: 9 This is how *G* showed his love
4:11 Dear friends, since *G* so loved us,
4:12 No one has ever seen *G;*
4:15 *G* lives in him and he in *G.*
4:16 *G* is love.
4:20 "I love *G,*" yet hates his brother,
4:21 Whoever loves *G* must
5: 2 that we love the children of *G:*
5: 3 love for *G:* to obey his commands.
5: 4 born of *G* overcomes the world.
5:10 does not believe *G* has made him
5:14 have in approaching *G:*
5:18 born of *G* does not continue to sin;
Rev 4: 8 holy is the Lord *G* Almighty,
7:12 be to our *G* for ever and ever.
7:17 *G* will wipe away every tear
11:16 fell on their faces and worshiped *G,*
15: 3 Lord *G* Almighty.
17:17 For *G* has put it into their hearts
19: 6 For our Lord *G* Almighty reigns.
21: 3 Now the dwelling of *G* is with men,
21:23 for the glory of *G* gives it light,

GOD-BREATHED* (BREATH)
2Ti 3:16 All Scripture is *G* and is useful

GOD-FEARING* (FEAR)
Ecc 8:12 that it will go better with *G* men,
Ac 2: 5 staying in Jerusalem *G* Jews
10: 2 all his family were devout and *G;*
10:22 He is a righteous and *G* man,
13:26 of Abraham, and you *G* Gentiles,
13:50 But the Jews incited the *G* women
17: 4 as did a large number of *G* Greeks
17:17 with the Jews and the *G* Greeks,

GOD-HATERS* (HATE)
Ro 1:30 They are gossips, slanderers, *G,*

GOD'S (GOD)
2Ch 20:15 For the battle is not yours, but *G.*
Job 37:14 stop and consider *G* wonders.
Ps 52: 8 I trust in *G* unfailing love
69:30 I will praise *G* name in song
Mk 3:35 Whoever does *G* will is my brother
Jn 7:17 If anyone chooses to do *G* will,
10:36 'I am *G* Son'? Do not believe me
Ro 2: 3 think you will escape *G* judgment?
2: 4 not realizing that *G* kindness leads
3: 3 lack of faith nullify *G* faithfulness?
7:22 in my inner being I delight in *G* law
9:16 or effort, but on *G* mercy.
11:29 for *G* gifts and his call are
12: 2 and approve what *G* will is—
12:13 Share with *G* people who are
13: 6 for the authorities are *G* servants,
1Co 7:19 Keeping *G* commands is what
2Co 6: 2 now is the time of *G* favor,
Eph 1: 7 riches of *G* grace that he lavished
1Th 4: 3 It is *G* will that you should be sanctified;
5:18 for this is *G* will for you
1Ti 6: 1 so that *G* name and our teaching
2Ti 2:19 *G* solid foundation stands firm,
Tit 1: 7 overseer is entrusted with *G* work,
Heb 1: 3 The Son is the radiance of *G* glory
9:24 now to appear for us in *G* presence.
11: 3 was formed at *G* command,
1Pe 2:15 For it is *G* will that
3: 4 which is of great worth in *G* sight.
1Jn 2: 5 *G* love is truly made complete

GODLESS
Job 20: 5 the joy of the *g* lasts but a moment.
1Ti 6:20 Turn away from *g* chatter

GODLINESS (GOD)
1Ti 2: 2 and quiet lives in all *g* and holiness.
4: 8 but *g* has value for all things,
6: 5 and who think that *g* is a means
6: 6 *g* with contentment is great gain.
6:11 and pursue righteousness, *g,* faith,
2Pe 1: 6 and to perseverance, *g;*

GODLY (GOD)
Ps 4: 3 that the LORD has set apart the *g*
2Co 7:10 *G* sorrow brings repentance that
11: 2 jealous for you with a *g* jealousy.
2Ti 3:12 everyone who wants to live a *g* life
2Pe 3:11 You ought to live holy and *g* lives

GODS (GOD)
Ex 20: 3 "You shall have no other *g*
Dt 5: 7 "You shall have no other *g*
1Ch 16:26 For all the *g* of the nations are idols
Ps 82: 6 "I said, 'You are "*g*";
Jn 10:34 have said you are *g*'? If he called
Ac 19:26 He says that man-made *g* are no *g*

GOG
Eze 38:18 When *G* attacks the land of Israel,
Rev 20: 8 *G* and Magog—to gather them

GOLD
1Ki 20: 3 'Your silver and *g* are mine,
Job 22:25 then the Almighty will be your *g,*
23:10 tested me, I will come forth as *g.*
28:15 cannot be bought with the finest *g,*
31:24 "If I have put my trust in *g*
Ps 19:10 They are more precious than *g,*
119:127 more than *g,* more than pure *g,*
Pr 3:14 and yields better returns than *g.*
22: 1 esteemed is better than silver or *g.*
Hag 2: 8 The silver is mine and the *g* is mine
Mt 2:11 and presented him with gifts of *g*
Rev 3:18 to buy from me *g* refined in the fire,

GOLGOTHA*
Mt 27:33 to a place called *G* (which means
Mk 15:22 to the place called *G* (which means
Jn 19:17 (which in Aramaic is called *G).*

GOLIATH
Philistine giant killed by David (1Sa 17; 21:9).

GOMORRAH
Ge 19:24 sulfur on Sodom and *G*—
Mt 10:15 and *G* on the day of judgment
2Pe 2: 6 and *G* by burning them to ashes,
Jude : 7 *G* and the surrounding towns gave

GOOD
Ge 1: 4 God saw that the light was *g,*
1:10 And God saw that it was *g.*
1:12 And God saw that it was *g.*
1:18 And God saw that it was *g.*
1:21 And God saw that it was *g.*
1:25 And God saw that it was *g.*

Ge 1:31 he had made, and it was very *g*.
2: 9 and the tree of the knowledge of *g*
2: 9 pleasing to the eye and *g* for food.
2:18 "It is not *g* for the man to be alone.
3:22 become like one of us, knowing *g*
50:20 but God intended it for *g*
2Ch 7: 3 "He is *g*; / his love endures
31:20 doing what was *g* and right
Job 2:10 Shall we accept *g* from God,
Ps 14: 1 there is no one who does *g*.
34: 8 Taste and see that the LORD is *g*;
34:14 Turn from evil and do *g*;
37: 3 Trust in the LORD and do *g*;
37:27 Turn from evil and do *g*;
52: 9 for your name is *g*.
53: 3 there is no one who does *g*,
84:11 no *g* thing does he withhold
86: 5 You are forgiving and *g*, O Lord
100: 5 For the LORD is *g* and his love
103: 5 satisfies your desires with *g* things,
112: 5 *G* will come to him who is
119: 68 You are *g*, and what you do is *g*;
133: 1 How *g* and pleasant it is
145: 9 The LORD is *g* to all;
147: 1 How *g* it is to sing praises
Pr 3: 4 you will win favor and a *g* name
3:27 Do not withhold *g*
11:27 He who seeks *g* finds *g* will,
13:22 A *g* man leaves an inheritance
14:22 those who plan what is *g* find love
15: 3 on the wicked and the *g*.
15:23 and how *g* is a timely word!
15:30 *g* news gives health to the bones.
17:22 A cheerful heart is *g* medicine,
18:22 He who finds a wife finds what is *g*
19: 2 It is not *g* to have zeal
22: 1 A *g* name is more desirable
31:12 She brings him *g*, not harm,
Ecc 12:14 whether it is *g* or evil.
Isa 5:20 Woe to those who call evil *g*
40: 9 You who bring *g* tidings
52: 7 the feet of those who bring *g* news,
61: 1 me to preach *g* news to the poor.
Jer 6:16 ask where the *g* way is,
13:23 Neither can you do *g*
32:39 the *g* of their children after them.
Eze 34:14 I will tend them in a *g* pasture,
Mic 6: 8 has showed you, O man, what is *g*.
Na 1:15 the feet of one who brings *g* news,
Mt 5:45 sun to rise on the evil and the *g*,
7:11 Father in heaven give *g* gifts
7:17 Likewise every *g* tree bears *g* fruit,
7:18 A *g* tree cannot bear bad fruit,
12:35 The *g* man brings *g* things out
13: 8 Still other seed fell on *g* soil,
13:24 is like a man who sowed *g* seed
13:48 and collected the *g* fish in baskets,
19:17 "There is only One who is *g*.
22:10 both *g* and bad, and the wedding
25:21 'Well done, *g* and faithful servant!
Mk 1:15 Repent and believe the *g* news!"
3: 4 lawful on the Sabbath: to do *g*
4: 8 Still other seed fell on *g* soil.
8:36 What *g* is it for a man
10:18 "No one is *g*—except God alone.
16:15 preach the *g* news to all creation.
Lk 2:10 I bring you *g* news
3: 9 does not produce *g* fruit will be
6:27 do *g* to those who hate you,
6:43 nor does a bad tree bear *g* fruit.
6:45 The *g* man brings *g* things out
8: 8 Still other seed fell on *g* soil.
9:25 What *g* is it for a man
14:34 "Salt is *g*, but if it loses its saltiness,
18:19 "No one is *g*—except God alone.
19:17 " 'Well done, my *g* servant!'
Jn 10:11 "I am the *g* shepherd.
Ro 3:12 there is no one who does *g*,
7:12 is holy, righteous and *g*.
7:16 want to do, I agree that the law is *g*.
7:18 I have the desire to do what is *g*,
8:28 for the *g* of those who love him,
10:15 feet of those who bring *g* news!"
12: 2 his *g*, pleasing and perfect will.
12: 9 Hate what is evil; cling to what is *g*.
13: 4 For he is God's servant to do you *g*
16:19 you to be wise about what is *g*,
1Co 7: 1 It is *g* for a man not to marry.
10:24 should seek his own *g*, but the *g*
15:33 Bad company corrupts *g* character
2Co 9: 8 you will abound in every *g* work.
Gal 4:18 provided the purpose is *g*,
6: 9 us not become weary in doing *g*,
6:10 as we have opportunity, let us do *g*
Eph 2:10 in Christ Jesus to do *g* works,
6: 8 everyone for whatever *g* he does,
Php 1: 6 that he who began a *g* work
Col 1:10 bearing fruit in every *g* work,
1Th 5:21 Hold on to the *g*.
1Ti 3: 7 have a *g* reputation with outsiders,
4: 4 For everything God created is *g*,
6:12 Fight the *g* fight of the faith.
6:18 them to do *g*, to be rich in *g* deeds,
2Ti 3:17 equipped for every *g* work.
4: 7 I have fought the *g* fight, I have
Tit 1: 8 loves what is *g*, who is
2: 7 an example by doing what is *g*.
2:14 his very own, eager to do what is *g*.
Heb 5:14 to distinguish *g* from evil.
10:24 on toward love and *g* deeds.
12:10 but God disciplines us for our *g*,
13:16 do not forget to do *g* and to share
Jas 4:17 who knows the *g* he ought to do
1Pe 2: 3 you have tasted that the Lord is *g*.
2:12 Live such *g* lives among the pagans
2:18 not only to those who are *g*
3:17 to suffer for doing *g*

GOODS
Ecc 5:11 As *g* increase,

GORGE
Pr 23:20 or *g* themselves on meat,

GOSHEN
Ge 45:10 You shall live in the region of *G*
Ex 8:22 differently with the land of *G*,

GOSPEL
Ro 1:16 I am not ashamed of the *g*,
15:16 duty of proclaiming the *g* of God,
15:20 to preach the *g* where Christ was
1Co 1:17 to preach the *g*—not with words
9:12 rather than hinder the *g* of Christ.
9:14 who preach the *g* should receive
9:16 Woe to me if I do not preach the *g*!
15: 1 you of the *g* I preached to you,
15: 2 By this *g* you are saved,
2Co 4: 4 light of the *g* of the glory of Christ,
9:13 your confession of the *g*
Gal 1: 7 a different *g*—which is really no *g*
Eph 6:15 comes from the *g* of peace.
Php 1:27 in a manner worthy of the *g*
Col 1:23 This is the *g* that you heard
1Th 2: 4 by God to be entrusted with the *g*.
2Th 1: 8 do not obey the *g* of our Lord Jesus
2Ti 1:10 immortality to light through the *g*.
Rev 14: 6 he had the eternal *g* to proclaim

GOSSIP*
Pr 11:13 A *g* betrays a confidence,
16:28 and a *g* separates close friends.
18: 8 of a *g* are like choice morsels;
20:19 A *g* betrays a confidence;
26:20 without *g* a quarrel dies down.
26:22 of a *g* are like choice morsels;
2Co 12:20 slander, *g*, arrogance and disorder.

GOVERN (GOVERNMENT)
Ge 1:16 the greater light to *g* the day
Job 34:17 Can he who hates justice *g*?
Ro 12: 8 it is leadership, let him *g* diligently;

GOVERNMENT (GOVERN)
Isa 9: 6 and the *g* will be on his shoulders.

GRACE* (GRACIOUS)
Ps 45: 2 lips have been anointed with *g*,
Pr 1: 9 will be a garland to *g* your head
3:22 an ornament to *g* your neck.
3:34 but gives *g* to the humble.
4: 9 She will set a garland of *g*
Isa 26:10 Though *g* is shown to the wicked,
Jnh 2: 8 forfeit the *g* that could be theirs.
Zec 12:10 of Jerusalem a spirit of *g*
Lk 2:40 and the *g* of God was upon him.
Jn 1:14 who came from the Father, full of *g*
1:16 of his *g* we have all received one
1:17 *g* and truth came through Jesus
Ac 4:33 and much *g* was upon them all.
6: 8 a man full of God's *g* and power,
11:23 saw the evidence of the *g* of God,
13:43 them to continue in the *g* of God.
14: 3 message of his *g* by enabling them
Ac 14:26 they had been committed to the *g*
15:11 We believe it is through the *g*
15:40 by the brothers to the *g* of the Lord
18:27 to those who by *g* had believed.
20:24 testifying to the gospel of God's *g*.
20:32 to God and to the word of his *g*,
Ro 1: 5 we received *g* and apostleship
1: 7 *G* and peace to you
3:24 and are justified freely by his *g*
4:16 be by *g* and may be guaranteed
5: 2 access by faith into this *g*
5:15 came by the *g* of the one man,
5:15 how much more did God's *g*
5:17 God's abundant provision of *g*
5:20 where sin increased, *g* increased all
5:21 also *g* might reign
6: 1 on sinning so that *g* may increase?
6:14 you are not under law, but under *g*.
6:15 we are not under law but under *g*?
11: 5 there is a remnant chosen by *g*.
11: 6 if by *g*, then it is no longer by works
11: 6 if it were, *g* would no longer be *g*.
12: 3 For by the *g* given me I say
12: 6 according to the *g* given us.
15:15 because of the *g* God gave me
16:20 The *g* of our Lord Jesus be
1Co 1: 3 *G* and peace to you
1: 4 of his *g* given you in Christ Jesus.
3:10 By the *g* God has given me,
15:10 But by the *g* of God I am what I am
15:10 but the *g* of God that was with me.
15:10 his *g* to me was not without effect.
16:23 The *g* of the Lord Jesus be with you
2Co 1: 2 *G* and peace to you
1:12 wisdom but according to God's *g*.
4:15 so that the *g* that is reaching more
6: 1 not to receive God's *g* in vain.
8: 1 to know about the *g* that God has
8: 6 also to completion this act of *g*
8: 7 also excel in this *g* of giving.
8: 9 For you know the *g*
9: 8 able to make all *g* abound to you,
9:14 of the surpassing *g* God has given
12: 9 "My *g* is sufficient for you,
13:14 May the *g* of the Lord Jesus Christ,
Gal 1: 3 *G* and peace to you
1: 6 the one who called you by the *g*
1:15 from birth and called me by his *g*,
2: 9 when they recognized the *g* given
2:21 I do not set aside the *g* of God,
3:18 God in his *g* gave it to Abraham
5: 4 you have fallen away from *g*.
6:18 The *g* of our Lord Jesus Christ be
Eph 1: 2 *G* and peace to you
1: 6 to the praise of his glorious *g*,
1: 7 riches of God's *g* that he lavished
2: 5 it is by *g* you have been saved.
2: 7 the incomparable riches of his *g*,
2: 8 For it is by *g* you have been saved,
3: 2 of God's *g* that was given to me
3: 7 by the gift of God's *g* given me
3: 8 God's people, this *g* was given me:
4: 7 to each one of us *g* has been given
6:24 *G* to all who love our Lord Jesus
Php 1: 2 *G* and peace to you
1: 7 all of you share in God's *g* with me.
4:23 The *g* of the Lord Jesus Christ be
Col 1: 2 *G* and peace to you
1: 6 understood God's *g* in all its truth.
4: 6 conversation be always full of *g*,
4:18 *G* be with you.
1Th 1: 1 and the Lord Jesus Christ: *G*
5:28 The *g* of our Lord Jesus Christ be
2Th 1: 2 *G* and peace to you
1:12 according to the *g* of our God
2:16 and by his *g* gave us eternal
3:18 The *g* of our Lord Jesus Christ be
1Ti 1: 2 my true son in the faith: *G*,
1:14 The *g* of our Lord was poured out
6:21 *G* be with you.
2Ti 1: 2 To Timothy, my dear son: *G*,
1: 9 This *g* was given us in Christ Jesus
1: 9 because of his own purpose and *g*.
2: 1 be strong in the *g* that is
4:22 *G* be with you.
Tit 1: 4 *G* and peace from God the Father
2:11 For the *g* of God that brings
3: 7 having been justified by his *g*,
3:15 *G* be with you all.
Phm :3 *G* to you and peace

Phm :25 The *g* of the Lord Jesus Christ be
Heb 2: 9 that by the *g* of God he might taste
4:16 find *g* to help us in our time of need
4:16 the throne of *g* with confidence,
10:29 and who has insulted the Spirit of *g*
12:15 See to it that no one misses the *g*
13: 9 hearts to be strengthened by *g*,
13:25 *G* be with you all.
Jas 4: 6 but gives *g* to the humble."
4: 6 But he gives us more *g*. That is why
1Pe 1: 2 *G* and peace be yours in abundance
1:10 who spoke of the *g* that was
1:13 fully on the *g* to be given you
4:10 faithfully administering God's *g*
5: 5 but gives *g* to the humble."
5:10 the God of all *g*, who called you
5:12 and testifying that this is the true *g*
2Pe 1: 2 *G* and peace be yours in abundance
3:18 But grow in the *g* and knowledge
2Jn : 3 and will be with us forever: *G*,
Jude : 4 who change the *g* of our God
Rev 1: 4 *G* and peace to you
22:21 The *g* of the Lord Jesus be

GRACIOUS (GRACE)
Ex 34: 6 the compassionate and *g* God,
Nu 6:25 and be *g* to you;
Ne 9:17 But you are a forgiving God, *g*
Ps 67: 1 May God be *g* to us and bless us
Pr 22:11 a pure heart and whose speech is *g*
Isa 30:18 Yet the LORD longs to be *g* to you

GRAIN
Lev 2: 1 When someone brings a *g* offering
Lk 17:35 women will be grinding *g* together;
1Co 9: 9 ox while it is treading out the *g*."

GRANDCHILDREN (CHILD)
1Ti 5: 4 But if a widow has children or *g*,

GRANDMOTHER (MOTHER)
2Ti 1: 5 which first lived in your *g* Lois

GRANT (GRANTED)
Ps 20: 5 May the LORD *g* all your requests
51:12 *g* me a willing spirit, to sustain me.

GRANTED (GRANT)
Pr 10:24 what the righteous desire will be *g*.
Mt 15:28 great faith! Your request is *g*."
Php 1:29 For it has been *g* to you on behalf

GRAPES
Nu 13:23 branch bearing a single cluster of *g*.
Jer 31:29 'The fathers have eaten sour *g*,
Eze 18: 2 " 'The fathers eat sour *g*,
Mt 7:16 Do people pick *g* from thornbushes
Rev 14:18 and gather the clusters of *g*

GRASPED
Php 2: 6 with God something to be *g*,

GRASS
Ps 103: 15 As for man, his days are like *g*,
Isa 40: 6 "All men are like *g*,
Mt 6:30 If that is how God clothes the *g*
1Pe 1:24 "All men are like *g*,

GRASSHOPPERS
Nu 13:33 We seemed like *g* in our own eyes,

GRATIFY* (GRATITUDE)
Ro 13:14 think about how to *g* the desires
Gal 5:16 and you will not *g* the desires

GRATITUDE (GRATIFY)
Col 3:16 and spiritual songs with *g*

GRAVE (GRAVES)
Nu 19:16 who touches a human bone or a *g*,
Dt 34: 6 day no one knows where his *g* is.
Ps 5: 9 Their throat is an open *g*;
49:15 will redeem my life from the *g*;
Pr 7:27 Her house is a highway to the *g*,
Hos 13:14 Where, O *g*, is your destruction?
Jn 11:44 'Take off the *g* clothes
Ac 2:27 you will not abandon me to the *g*,

GRAVES (GRAVE)
Eze 37:12 I am going to open your *g*
Jn 5:28 are in their *g* will hear his voice
Ro 3:13 "Their throats are open *g*;

GRAY
Pr 16:31 *G* hair is a crown of splendor;
20:29 *g* hair the splendor of the old.

GREAT (GREATER GREATEST GREATNESS)
Ge 12: 2 I will make your name *g*,
12: 2 "I will make you into a *g* nation
Ex 32:11 out of Egypt with *g* power
Nu 14:19 In accordance with your *g* love,
Dt 4:32 so *g* as this ever happened,
10:17 the *g* God, mighty and awesome,
29:28 in *g* wrath the LORD uprooted
Jos 7: 9 do for your own *g* name?"
Jdg 16: 5 you the secret of his *g* strength
2Sa 7:22 "How *g* you are, O Sovereign
22:36 you stoop down to make me *g*.
24:14 for his mercy is *g*; but do not let me
1Ch 17:19 made known all these *g* promises.
Ps 18:35 you stoop down to make me *g*.
19:11 in keeping them there is *g* reward.
47: 2 the *g* King over all the earth!
57:10 For *g* is your love, reaching
68:11 and *g* was the company
89: 1 of the LORD's *g* love forever;
103: 11 so *g* is his love for those who fear
107: 43 consider the *g* love of the LORD.
108: 4 For *g* is your love, higher
117: 2 For *g* is his love toward us,
119:165 *G* peace have they who love your
145: 3 *G* is the LORD and most worthy
Pr 22: 1 is more desirable than *g* riches;
23:24 of a righteous man has *g* joy;
Isa 42:21 to make his law *g* and glorious.
Jer 27: 5 With my *g* power and outstretched
32:19 *g* are your purposes and mighty are
La 3:23 *g* is your faithfulness.
Da 9: 4 "O Lord, the *g* and awesome God,
Joel 2:11 The day of the LORD is *g*;
2:20 Surely he has done *g* things.
Zep 1:14 "The *g* day of the LORD is near—
Mal 1:11 My name will be *g*
4: 5 the prophet Elijah before that *g*
Mt 20:26 whoever wants to become *g*
Mk 10:43 whoever wants to become *g*
Lk 6:23 because *g* is your reward in heaven.
6:35 Then your reward will be *g*,
21:27 in a cloud with power and *g* glory.
Eph 1:19 and his incomparably *g* power
2: 4 But because of his *g* love for us,
1Ti 6: 6 with contentment is *g* gain.
Tit 2:13 glorious appearing of our *g* God
Heb 2: 3 if we ignore such a *g* salvation?
1Jn 3: 1 How *g* is the love the Father has
Rev 6:17 For the *g* day of their wrath has
20:11 Then I saw a *g* white throne

GREATER (GREAT)
Mt 11:11 there has not risen anyone *g*
12: 6 I tell you that one *g*
12:41 and now one *g* than Jonah is here.
12:42 now one *g* than Solomon is here.
Mk 12:31 There is no commandment *g*
Jn 1:50 You shall see *g* things than that."
3:30 He must become *g*; I must become
14:12 He will do even *g* things than these
15:13 *G* love has no one than this,
1Co 12:31 But eagerly desire the *g* gifts.
2Co 3:11 how much *g* is the glory
Heb 3: 3 the builder of a house has *g* honor
3: 3 worthy of *g* honor than Moses,
7: 7 lesser person is blessed by the *g*.
11:26 as of *g* value than the treasures
1Jn 3:20 For God is *g* than our hearts,
4: 4 is in you is *g* than the one who is

GREATEST (GREAT)
Mt 22:38 is the first and *g* commandment.
23:11 *g* among you will be your servant.
Lk 9:48 least among you all—he is the *g*."
1Co 13:13 But the *g* of these is love.

GREATNESS* (GREAT)
Ex 15: 7 In the *g* of your majesty
Dt 3:24 to show to your servant your *g*
32: 3 Oh, praise the *g* of our God!
1Ch 29:11 O LORD, is the *g* and the power
2Ch 9: 6 half the *g* of your wisdom was told
Est 10: 2 account of the *g* of Mordecai
Ps 145: 3 his *g* no one can fathom.
150: 2 praise him for his surpassing *g*.
Isa 63: 1 forward in the *g* of his strength?
Eze 38:23 I will show my *g* and my holiness,
Da 4:22 your *g* has grown until it reaches
5:18 and *g* and glory and splendor.
7:27 and *g* of the kingdoms

Mic 5: 4 will live securely, for then his *g*
Lk 9:43 And they were all amazed at the *g*
Php 3: 8 compared to the surpassing *g*

GREED (GREEDY)
Lk 12:15 on your guard against all kinds of *g*
Ro 1:29 kind of wickedness, evil, *g*
Eph 5: 3 or of any kind of impurity, or of *g*,
Col 3: 5 evil desires and *g*, which is idolatry
2Pe 2:14 experts in *g*—an accursed brood!

GREEDY (GREED)
Pr 15:27 A *g* man brings trouble
1Co 6:10 nor thieves nor the *g* nor drunkards
Eph 5: 5 No immoral, impure or *g* person—
1Pe 5: 2 not *g* for money, but eager to serve;

GREEK (GREEKS)
Gal 3:28 There is neither Jew nor *G*,
Col 3:11 Here there is no *G* or Jew,

GREEKS (GREEK)
1Co 1:22 miraculous signs and *G* look

GREEN
Ps 23: 2 makes me lie down in *g* pastures,

GREW (GROW)
Lk 1:80 And the child *g* and became strong
2:52 And Jesus *g* in wisdom and stature,
Ac 9:31 by the Holy Spirit, it *g* in numbers,
16: 5 in the faith and *g* daily in numbers.

GRIEF (GRIEFS GRIEVANCES GRIEVE GRIEVED)
Ps 10:14 O God, do see trouble and *g*;
Pr 10: 1 but a foolish son *g* to his mother.
14:13 and joy may end in *g*.
17:21 To have a fool for a son brings *g*;
Ecc 1:18 the more knowledge, the more *g*.
La 3:32 Though he brings *g*, he will show
Jn 16:20 but your *g* will turn to joy.
1Pe 1: 6 had to suffer *g* in all kinds of trials.

GRIEFS* (GRIEF)
1Ti 6:10 pierced themselves with many *g*.

GRIEVANCES* (GRIEF)
Col 3:13 forgive whatever *g* you may have

GRIEVE (GRIEF)
Eph 4:30 do not *g* the Holy Spirit of God,
1Th 4:13 or to *g* like the rest of men,

GRIEVED (GRIEF)
Isa 63:10 and *g* his Holy Spirit.

GRINDING
Lk 17:35 women will be *g* grain together;

GROAN (GROANING GROANS)
Ro 8:23 *g* inwardly as we wait eagerly
2Co 5: 4 For while we are in this tent, we *g*

GROANING (GROAN)
Ex 2:24 God heard their *g* and he
Eze 21: 7 'Why are you *g*?' you shall say,
Ro 8:22 that the whole creation has been *g*

GROANS (GROAN)
Ro 8:26 with *g* that words cannot express.

GROUND
Ge 1:10 God called the dry *g* "land,"
3:17 "Cursed is the *g* because of you;
4:10 blood cries out to me from the *g*.
Ex 3: 5 where you are standing is holy *g*."
15:19 walked through the sea on dry *g*.
Isa 53: 2 and like a root out of dry *g*.
Mt 10:29 fall to the *g* apart from the will
25:25 and hid your talent in the *g*.
Jn 8: 6 to write on the *g* with his finger.
Eph 6:13 you may be able to stand your *g*,

GROW (FULL-GROWN GREW GROWING GROWS)
Pr 13:11 by little makes it *g*.
20:13 not love sleep or you will *g* poor;
Isa 40:31 they will run and not *g* weary,
Mt 6:28 See how the lilies of the field *g*.
1Co 3: 6 watered it, but God made it *g*.
2Pe 3:18 But *g* in the grace and knowledge

GROWING (GROW)
Col 1: 6 this gospel is bearing fruit and *g*,
1:10 *g* in the knowledge of God,
2Th 1: 3 your faith is *g* more and more,

GROWS (GROW)
Eph 4:16 *g* and builds itself up in love,
Col 2:19 *g* as God causes it to grow.

GRUMBLE (GRUMBLED GRUMBLERS GRUMBLING)
1Co 10:10 And do not *g*, as some of them did
Jas 5: 9 Don't *g* against each other,

GRUMBLED (GRUMBLE)
Ex 15:24 So the people *g* against Moses,
Nu 14:29 and who has *g* against me.

GRUMBLERS* (GRUMBLE)
Jude :16 These men are *g* and faultfinders;

GRUMBLING (GRUMBLE)
Jn 6:43 "Stop *g* among yourselves,"
1Pe 4: 9 to one another without *g*.

GUARANTEE (GUARANTEEING)
Heb 7:22 Jesus has become the *g*

GUARANTEEING* (GUARANTEE)
2Co 1:22 as a deposit, *g* what is to come.
5: 5 as a deposit, *g* what is to come.
Eph 1:14 who is a deposit *g* our inheritance

GUARD (GUARDS)
1Sa 2: 9 He will *g* the feet of his saints,
Ps 141: 3 Set a *g* over my mouth, O LORD;
Pr 2:11 and understanding will *g* you.
4:13 *g* it well, for it is your life.
4:23 Above all else, *g* your heart,
7: 2 *g* my teachings as the apple
Isa 52:12 the God of Israel will be your rear *g*
Mk 13:33 Be on *g*! Be alert! You do not know
Lk 12: 1 "Be on your *g* against the yeast
12:15 Be on your *g* against all kinds
Ac 20:31 So be on your *g*! Remember that
1Co 16:13 Be on your *g*; stand firm in the faith
Php 4: 7 will *g* your hearts and your minds
1Ti 6:20 *g* what has been entrusted
2Ti 1:14 *G* the good deposit that was

GUARDS (GUARD)
Pr 13: 3 He who *g* his lips *g* his life,
19:16 who obeys instructions *g* his life,
21:23 He who *g* his mouth and his tongue
22: 5 he who *g* his soul stays far

GUIDANCE (GUIDE)
Pr 1: 5 and let the discerning get *g*—
11:14 For lack of *g* a nation falls,
24: 6 for waging war you need *g*,

GUIDE (GUIDANCE GUIDED GUIDES)
Ex 13:21 of cloud to *g* them on their way
15:13 In your strength you will *g* them
Ne 9:19 cease to *g* them on their path,
Ps 25: 5 *g* me in your truth and teach me,
43: 3 let them *g* me;
48:14 he will be our *g* even to the end.
67: 4 and *g* the nations of the earth.
73:24 You *g* me with your counsel,
139: 10 even there your hand will *g* me,
Pr 4:11 I *g* you in the way of wisdom
6:22 When you walk, they will *g* you;
Isa 58:11 The LORD will *g* you always;
Jn 16:13 comes, he will *g* you into all truth.

GUIDED (GUIDE)
Ps 107: 30 he *g* them to their desired haven.

GUIDES (GUIDE)
Ps 23: 3 He *g* me in paths of righteousness
25: 9 He *g* the humble in what is right
Pr 11: 3 The integrity of the upright *g* them,
16:23 A wise man's heart *g* his mouth,
Mt 23:16 "Woe to you, blind *g*! You say,
23:24 You blind *g*! You strain out a gnat

GUILT (GUILTY)
Lev 5:15 It is a *g* offering.
Ps 32: 5 the *g* of my sin.
38: 4 My *g* has overwhelmed me
Isa 6: 7 your *g* is taken away and your sin
Jer 2:22 the stain of your *g* is still before me
Eze 18:19 'Why does the son not share the *g*

GUILTY (GUILT)
Ex 34: 7 does not leave the *g* unpunished;
Mk 3:29 Spirit will never be forgiven; he is *g*
Jn 8:46 Can any of you prove me *g* of sin?
1Co 11:27 in an unworthy manner will be *g*
Heb 10: 2 and would no longer have felt *g*
Heb 10:22 to cleanse us from a *g* conscience
Jas 2:10 at just one point is *g* of breaking all

HABAKKUK*
Prophet to Judah (Hab 1:1; 3:1).

HABIT
1Ti 5:13 they get into the *h* of being idle
Heb 10:25 as some are in the *h* of doing,

HADAD
Edomite adversary of Solomon (1Ki 11:14–25).

HADES*
Mt 16:18 the gates of *H* will not overcome it.
Rev 1:18 And I hold the keys of death and *H*
6: 8 *H* was following close behind him.
20:13 and *H* gave up the dead that were
20:14 *H* were thrown into the lake of fire.

HAGAR
Servant of Sarah, wife of Abraham, mother of Ishmael (Ge 16:1–6; 25:12). Driven away by Sarah while pregnant (Ge 16:5–16); after birth of Isaac (Ge 21:9–21; Gal 4:21–31).

HAGGAI*
Post-exilic prophet who encouraged rebuilding of the temple (Ezr 5:1; 6:14; Hag 1–2).

HAIL
Ex 9:19 the *h* will fall on every man
Rev 8: 7 and there came *h* and fire mixed

HAIR (HAIRS HAIRY)
Lev 19:27 " 'Do not cut the *h* at the sides
Nu 6: 5 he must let the *h* of his head grow
Pr 16:31 Gray *h* is a crown of splendor;
20:29 gray *h* the splendor of the old.
Lk 7:44 and wiped them with her *h*.
21:18 But not a *h* of your head will perish
Jn 11: 2 and wiped his feet with her *h*.
12: 3 and wiped his feet with her *h*.
1Co 11: 6 for a woman to have her *h* cut
11: 6 she should have her *h* cut off;
11:14 that if a man has long *h*,
11:15 For long *h* is given to her
11:15 but that if a woman has long *h*,
1Ti 2: 9 not with braided *h* or gold or pearls
1Pe 3: 3 as braided *h* and the wearing
Rev 1:14 and *h* were white like wool,

HAIRS (HAIR)
Mt 10:30 even the very *h* of your head are all
Lk 12: 7 the very *h* of your head are all

HAIRY (HAIR)
Ge 27:11 "But my brother Esau is a *h* man,

HALF
Ex 30:13 This *h* shekel is an offering
Jos 8:33 *H* of the people stood in front
1Ki 3:25 give *h* to one and *h* to the other."
10: 7 Indeed, not even *h* was told me;
Est 5: 3 Even up to *h* the kingdom,
Da 7:25 him for a time, times and *h* a time.
Mk 6:23 up to *h* my kingdom."

HALF-TRIBE (TRIBE)
Nu 32:33 and the *h* of Manasseh son

HALLELUJAH*
Rev 19: 1, 3, 4, 6.

HALLOWED* (HOLY)
Mt 6: 9 *h* be your name,
Lk 11: 2 *h* be your name,

HALT
Job 38:11 here is where your proud waves *h*'?

HALTER*
Pr 26: 3 for the horse, a *h* for the donkey,

HAM
Son of Noah (Ge 5:32; 1Ch 1:4), father of Canaan (Ge 9:18; 10:6–20; 1Ch 1:8–16). Saw Noah's nakedness (Ge 9:20–27).

HAMAN
Agagite nobleman honored by Xerxes (Est 3:1–2). Plotted to exterminate the Jews because of Mordecai (Est 3:3–15). Forced to honor Mordecai (Est 5–6). Plot exposed by Esther (Est 5:1–8; 7:1–8). Hanged (Est 7:9–10).

HAMPERED*
Pr 4:12 you walk, your steps will not be *h*;

HAND (HANDED HANDFUL HANDS OPENHANDED)
Ge 24: 2 "Put your *h* under my thigh.
47:29 put your *h* under my thigh
Ex 13: 3 out of it with a mighty *h*.
15: 6 Your right *h*, O LORD,
33:22 and cover you with my *h*
Dt 12: 7 in everything you have put your *h*
1Ki 8:42 and your mighty *h* and your
13: 4 But the *h* he stretched out
1Ch 29:14 you only what comes from your *h*.
29:16 it comes from your *h*, and all
2Ch 6:15 with your *h* you have fulfilled it—
Ne 4:17 materials did their work with one *h*
Job 40: 4 I put my *h* over my mouth.
Ps 16: 8 Because he is at my right *h*,
32: 4 your *h* was heavy upon me;
37:24 the LORD upholds him with his *h*.
44: 3 it was your right *h*, your arm,
45: 9 at your right *h* is the royal bride
63: 8 your right *h* upholds me.
75: 8 In the *h* of the LORD is a cup
91: 7 ten thousand at your right *h*,
98: 1 his right *h* and his holy arm
109: 31 at the right *h* of the needy one,
110: 1 "Sit at my right *h*
137: 5 may my right *h* forget ⌊its skill⌋.
139: 10 even there your *h* will guide me,
145: 16 You open your *h*
Pr 27:16 or grasping oil with the *h*.
Ecc 5:15 that he can carry in his *h*.
9:10 Whatever your *h* finds to do,
Isa 11: 8 the young child put his *h*
40:12 the waters in the hollow of his *h*,
41:13 who takes hold of your right *h*
44: 5 still another will write on his *h*,
48:13 My own *h* laid the foundations
64: 8 we are all the work of your *h*.
La 3: 3 he has turned his *h* against me
Da 10:10 *h* touched me and set me trembling
Jnh 4:11 people who cannot tell their right *h*
Hab 3: 4 rays flashed from his *h*,
Mt 5:30 if your right *h* causes you to sin,
6: 3 know what your right *h* is doing,
12:10 a man with a shriveled *h* was there.
18: 8 If your *h* or your foot causes you
22:44 "Sit at my right *h*
26:64 at the right *h* of the Mighty One
Mk 3: 1 a man with a shriveled *h* was there.
9:43 If your *h* causes you to sin, cut it off
12:36 "Sit at my right *h*
16:19 and he sat at the right *h* of God.
Lk 6: 6 there whose right *h* was shriveled.
20:42 "Sit at my right *h*
22:69 at the right *h* of the mighty God."
Jn 10:28 one can snatch them out of my *h*.
20:27 Reach out your *h* and put it
Ac 7:55 Jesus standing at the right *h* of God
1Co 12:15 I am not a *h*, I do not belong
Heb 1:13 "Sit at my right *h*
Rev 13:16 to receive a mark on his right *h*

HANDED (HAND)
Da 7:25 The saints will be *h* over to him
1Ti 1:20 whom I have *h* over to Satan

HANDFUL (HAND)
Ecc 4: 6 Better one *h* with tranquillity

HANDLE (HANDLES)
Col 2:21 "Do not *h*! Do not taste! Do not

HANDLES (HANDLE)
2Ti 2:15 who correctly *h* the word of truth.

HANDS (HAND)
Ge 27:22 but the *h* are the *h* of Esau."
Ex 17:11 As long as Moses held up his *h*,
29:10 his sons shall lay their *h* on its head
Dt 6: 8 Tie them as symbols on your *h*
Jdg 7: 6 lapped with their *h* to their mouths.
2Ki 11:12 and the people clapped their *h*
2Ch 6: 4 who with his *h* has fulfilled what he
Ps 22:16 they have pierced my *h*
24: 4 He who has clean *h* and a pure
31: 5 Into your *h* I commit my spirit;
31:15 My times are in your *h*;
47: 1 Clap your *h*, all you nations;
63: 4 and in your name I will lift up my *h*
Pr 10: 4 Lazy *h* make a man poor,
21:25 because his *h* refuse to work.
31:13 and works with eager *h*.

Pr 31:20 and extends her *h* to the needy.
Ecc 10:18 if his *h* are idle, the house leaks.
Isa 35: 3 Strengthen the feeble *h,*
49:16 you on the palms of my *h;*
55:12 will clap their *h.*
65: 2 All day long I have held out my *h*
La 3:41 Let us lift up our hearts and our *h*
Lk 23:46 into your *h* I commit my spirit."
Ac 6: 6 who prayed and laid their *h*
8:18 at the laying on of the apostles' *h,*
13: 3 they placed their *h* on them
19: 6 When Paul placed his *h* on them,
28: 8 placed his *h* on him and healed him
1Th 4:11 and to work with your *h,*
1Ti 2: 8 to lift up holy *h* in prayer,
4:14 body of elders laid their *h* on you.
5:22 hasty in the laying on of *h,*
2Ti 1: 6 you through the laying on of my *h.*
Heb 6: 2 the laying on of *h,* the resurrection

HANDSOME*
Ge 39: 6 Now Joseph was well-built and *h,*
1Sa 16:12 a fine appearance and *h* features.
17:42 ruddy and *h,* and he despised him.
2Sa 14:25 praised for his *h* appearance
1Ki 1: 6 also very *h* and was born next
SS 1:16 *Beloved* How *h* you are, my lover!
Eze 23: 6 all of them *h* young men,
23:12 horsemen, all *h* young men.
23:23 with them, *h* young men,
Da 1: 4 without any physical defect, *h,*
Zec 11:13 the *h* price at which they priced me

HANG (HANGED HANGING HUNG)
Mt 22:40 and the Prophets *h* on these two

HANGED (HANG)
Mt 27: 5 Then he went away and *h* himself.

HANGING (HANG)
Ac 10:39 They killed him by *h* him on a tree,

HANNAH*
Wife of Elkanah, mother of Samuel (1Sa 1). Prayer at dedication of Samuel (1Sa 2:1–10). Blessed (1Sa 2:18–21).

HAPPIER (HAPPY)
Mt 18:13 he is *h* about that one sheep
1Co 7:40 she is *h* if she stays as she is—

HAPPINESS* (HAPPY)
Dt 24: 5 bring *h* to the wife he has married.
Est 8:16 For the Jews it was a time of *h*
Job 7: 7 my eyes will never see *h* again.
Ecc 2:26 gives wisdom, knowledge and *h,*
Mt 25:21 Come and share your master's *h!'*
25:23 Come and share your master's *h!'*

HAPPY* (HAPPIER HAPPINESS)
Ge 30:13 The women will call me *h."*
30:13 Then Leah said, "How *h* I am!
1Ki 4:20 they drank and they were *h.*
10: 8 How *h* your men must be!
10: 8 men must be! How *h* your officials,
2Ch 9: 7 How *h* your men must be!
9: 7 men must be! How *h* your officials,
Est 5: 9 Haman went out that day *h*
5:14 the king to the dinner and be *h."*
Ps 10: 6 I'll always be *h* and never have
68: 3 may they be *h* and joyful.
113: 9 as a *h* mother of children.
137: 8 *h* is he who repays you
Pr 15:13 A *h* heart makes the face cheerful,
Ecc 3:12 better for men than to be *h*
5:19 to accept his lot and be *h*
7:14 When times are good, be *h;*
11: 9 Be *h,* young man, while you are
Jnh 4: 6 Jonah was very *h* about the vine.
Zec 8:19 and glad occasions and *h* festivals
1Co 7:30 those who are *h,* as if they were not
2Co 7: 9 yet now I am *h,* not because you
7:13 delighted to see how *h* Titus was,
Jas 5:13 Is anyone *h?* Let him sing songs

HARD (HARDEN HARDENED HARDENING HARDENS HARDER HARDSHIP HARDSHIPS)
Ge 18:14 Is anything too *h* for the LORD?
1Ki 10: 1 came to test him with *h* questions.
Pr 14:23 All *h* work brings a profit,
Jer 32:17 Nothing is too *h* for you.
Zec 7:12 They made their hearts as *h* as flint
Mt 19:23 it is *h* for a rich man
Mk 10: 5 your hearts were *h* that Moses
Jn 6:60 disciples said, "This is a *h* teaching.
Ac 20:35 of *h* work we must help the weak,
26:14 It is *h* for you to kick
Ro 16:12 woman who has worked very *h*
1Co 4:12 We work *h* with our own hands.
2Co 6: 5 imprisonments and riots; in *h* work
1Th 5:12 to respect those who work *h*
Rev 2: 2 your *h* work and your

HARDEN (HARD)
Ex 4:21 I will *h* his heart so that he will not
Ps 95: 8 do not *h* your hearts as you did
Ro 9:18 he hardens whom he wants to *h.*
Heb 3: 8 do not *h* your hearts

HARDENED (HARD)
Ex 10:20 But the LORD *h* Pharaoh's heart,

HARDENING* (HARD)
Ro 11:25 Israel has experienced a *h* in part
Eph 4:18 in them due to the *h* of their hearts.

HARDENS* (HARD)
Pr 28:14 he who *h* his heart falls into trouble
Ro 9:18 and he *h* whom he wants to harden.

HARDER (HARD)
1Co 15:10 No, I worked *h* than all of them—
2Co 11:23 I have worked much *h,* been

HARDHEARTED* (HEART)
Dt 15: 7 do not be *h* or tightfisted

HARDSHIP (HARD)
Ro 8:35 Shall trouble or *h* or persecution
2Ti 2: 3 Endure *h* with us like a good
4: 5 endure *h,* do the work
Heb 12: 7 Endure *h* as discipline; God is

HARDSHIPS (HARD)
Ac 14:22 go through many *h* to enter
2Co 6: 4 in troubles, *h* and distresses;
12:10 in insults, in *h,* in persecutions,
Rev 2: 3 and have endured *h* for my name,

HARM (HARMS)
1Ch 16:22 do my prophets no *h."*
Ps 105: 15 do my prophets no *h."*
121: 6 the sun will not *h* you by day,
Pr 3:29 not plot *h* against your neighbor,
12:21 No *h* befalls the righteous,
31:12 She brings him good, not *h,*
Jer 10: 5 they can do no *h*
29:11 to prosper you and not to *h* you,
Ro 13:10 Love does no *h* to its neighbor.
1Co 11:17 for your meetings do more *h*
1Jn 5:18 the evil one cannot *h* him.

HARMONY*
Zec 6:13 there will be *h* between the two.'
Ro 12:16 Live in *h* with one another.
2Co 6:15 What *h* is there between Christ
1Pe 3: 8 live in *h* with one another;

HARMS* (HARM)
Pr 8:36 whoever fails to find me *h* himself;

HARP (HARPS)
Ge 4:21 the father of all who play the *h*
1Sa 16:23 David would take his *h* and play.
Ps 33: 2 Praise the LORD with the *h;*
98: 5 with the *h* and the sound of singing
150: 3 praise him with the *h* and lyre,
Rev 5: 8 Each one had a *h* and they were

HARPS (HARP)
Ps 137: 2 we hung our *h,*

HARSH
Pr 15: 1 but a *h* word stirs up anger.
Col 2:23 and their *h* treatment of the body,
3:19 and do not be *h* with them.
1Pe 2:18 but also to those who are *h.*
Jude :15 of all the *h* words ungodly sinners

HARVEST (HARVESTERS)
Ge 8:22 seedtime and *h,*
Ex 23:16 the Feast of *H* with the firstfruits
Dt 16:15 God will bless you in all your *h*
Pr 10: 5 during *h* is a disgraceful son.
Jer 8:20 "The *h* is past,
Joel 3:13 for the *h* is ripe.
Mt 9:37 *h* is plentiful but the workers are
Lk 10: 2 He told them, "The *h* is plentiful,
Jn 4:35 at the fields! They are ripe for *h.*
1Co 9:11 if we reap a material *h* from you?
2Co 9:10 the *h* of your righteousness.
Gal 6: 9 at the proper time we will reap a *h*
Heb 12:11 it produces a *h* of righteousness
Jas 3:18 in peace raise a *h* of righteousness.
Rev 14:15 for the *h* of the earth is ripe."

HARVESTERS (HARVEST)
Ru 2: 3 to glean in the fields behind the *h.*

HASTE (HASTEN HASTY)
Ex 12:11 it in *h;* it is the LORD's Passover.
Pr 21: 5 as surely as *h* leads to poverty.
29:20 Do you see a man who speaks in *h?*

HASTEN (HASTE)
Ps 70: 1 *H,* O God, to save me;
119: 60 I will *h* and not delay

HASTY* (HASTE)
Pr 19: 2 nor to be *h* and miss the way.
Ecc 5: 2 do not be *h* in your heart
1Ti 5:22 Do not be *h* in the laying

HATE (GOD-HATERS HATED HATES HATING HATRED)
Lev 19:17 " 'Do not *h* your brother
Ps 5: 5 you *h* all who do wrong.
36: 2 too much to detect or *h* his sin.
45: 7 righteousness and *h* wickedness;
97:10 those who love the LORD *h* evil,
119:104 therefore I *h* every wrong path.
119:163 I *h* and abhor falsehood
139: 21 Do I not *h* those who *h* you,
Pr 8:13 To fear the LORD is to *h* evil;
9: 8 rebuke a mocker or he will *h* you;
13: 5 The righteous *h* what is false,
25:17 too much of you, and he will *h* you.
29:10 Bloodthirsty men *h* a man
Ecc 3: 8 a time to love and a time to *h,*
Isa 61: 8 I *h* robbery and iniquity.
Eze 35: 6 Since you did not *h* bloodshed,
Am 5:15 *H* evil, love good;
Mal 2:16 "I *h* divorce," says the LORD God
Mt 5:43 your neighbor and *h* your enemy.'
10:22 All men will *h* you because of me,
Lk 6:22 Blessed are you when men *h* you,
6:27 do good to those who *h* you,
14:26 does not *h* his father and mother,
Ro 12: 9 *H* what is evil; cling to what is good

HATED (HATE)
Mal 1: 3 loved Jacob, but Esau I have *h,*
Jn 15:18 keep in mind that it *h* me first.
Ro 9:13 "Jacob I loved, but Esau I *h."*
Eph 5:29 no one ever *h* his own body,
Heb 1: 9 righteousness and *h* wickedness;

HATES (HATE)
Pr 6:16 There are six things the LORD *h,*
13:24 He who spares the rod *h* his son,
15:27 but he who *h* bribes will live.
26:28 A lying tongue *h* those it hurts,
Jn 3:20 Everyone who does evil *h* the light,
12:25 while the man who *h* his life
1Jn 2: 9 *h* his brother is still in the darkness.
4:20 "I love God," yet *h* his brother,

HATING (HATE)
Jude :23 *h* even the clothing stained

HATRED (HATE)
Pr 10:12 *H* stirs up dissension,
15:17 than a fattened calf with *h.*
Jas 4: 4 with the world is *h* toward God?

HAUGHTY
Pr 6:17 detestable to him: / *h* eyes,
16:18 a *h* spirit before a fall.

HAVEN
Ps 107: 30 he guided them to their desired *h.*

HAY
1Co 3:12 costly stones, wood, *h* or straw,

HEAD (HEADS HOTHEADED)
Ge 3:15 he will crush your *h,*
Nu 6: 5 no razor may be used on his *h.*
Jdg 16:17 If my *h* were shaved, my strength
1Sa 9: 2 a *h* taller than any of the others.
2Sa 18: 9 Absalom's *h* got caught in the tree.
Ps 23: 5 You anoint my *h* with oil;
133: 2 is like precious oil poured on the *h,*
Pr 10: 6 Blessings crown the *h*
25:22 will heap burning coals on his *h,*
Isa 59:17 and the helmet of salvation on his *h*
Eze 33: 4 his blood will be on his own *h.*

Mt 8:20 of Man has no place to lay his *h.*"
Jn 19: 2 crown of thorns and put it on his *h.*
Ro 12:20 will heap burning coals on his *h.*"
1Co 11: 3 and the *h* of Christ is God.
11: 5 her *h* uncovered dishonors her *h*—
12:21 And the *h* cannot say to the feet,
Eph 1:22 him to be *h* over everything
5:23 For the husband is the *h* of the wife
Col 1:18 And he is the *h* of the body,
2Ti 4: 5 keep your *h* in all situations,
Rev 14:14 with a crown of gold on his *h*
19:12 and on his *h* are many crowns.

HEADS (HEAD)
Lev 26:13 you to walk with *h* held high.
Ps 22: 7 they hurl insults, shaking their *h:*
24: 7 Lift up your *h,* O you gates;
Isa 35:10 everlasting joy will crown their *h.*
51:11 everlasting joy will crown their *h.*
Mt 27:39 shaking their *h* and saying,
Lk 21:28 stand up and lift up your *h,*
Ac 18: 6 "Your blood be on your own *h!*
Rev 4: 4 and had crowns of gold on their *h.*

HEAL* (HEALED HEALING HEALS)
Nu 12:13 please *h* her!" The LORD replied
Dt 32:39 I have wounded and I will *h,*
2Ki 20: 5 and seen your tears; I will *h* you.
20: 8 the sign that the LORD will *h* me
2Ch 7:14 their sin and will *h* their land.
Job 5:18 he injures, but his hands also *h.*
Ps 6: 2 *h* me, for my bones are in agony.
41: 4 *h* me, for I have sinned against you
Ecc 3: 3 a time to kill and a time to *h,*
Isa 19:22 he will strike them and *h* them.
19:22 respond to their pleas and *h* them.
57:18 seen his ways, but I will *h* him;
57:19 "And I will *h* them."
Jer 17:14 *H* me, O LORD, and I will be
30:17 and *h* your wounds,'
33: 6 I will *h* my people and will let them
La 2:13 Who can *h* you?
Hos 5:13 not able to *h* your sores.
6: 1 but he will *h* us;
7: 1 whenever I would *h* Israel,
14: 4 "I will *h* their waywardness
Na 3:19 Nothing can *h* your wound;
Zec 11:16 or seek the young, or *h* the injured,
Mt 8: 7 said to him, "I will go and *h* him."
10: 1 to *h* every disease and sickness.
10: 8 *H* the sick, raise the dead,
12:10 "Is it lawful to *h* on the Sabbath?"
13:15 and turn, and I would *h* them.'
17:16 but they could not *h* him."
Mk 3: 2 if he would *h* him on the Sabbath.
6: 5 on a few sick people and *h* them.
Lk 4:23 to me: 'Physician, *h* yourself!
5:17 present for him to *h* the sick.
6: 7 to see if he would *h* on the Sabbath.
7: 3 him to come and *h* his servant.
8:43 years, but no one could *h* her.
9: 2 kingdom of God and to *h* the sick.
10: 9 *H* the sick who are there
13:32 and *h* people today and tomorrow,
14: 3 "Is it lawful to *h* on the Sabbath
Jn 4:47 begged him to come and *h* his son,
12:40 nor turn—and I would *h* them."
Ac 4:30 Stretch out your hand to *h*
28:27 and turn, and I would *h* them.'

HEALED* (HEAL)
Ge 20:17 to God, and God *h* Abimelech,
Ex 21:19 and see that he is completely *h.*
Lev 13:37 hair has grown in it, the itch is *h.*
14: 3 If the person has been *h*
Jos 5: 8 were in camp until they were *h.*
1Sa 6: 3 you will be *h,* and you will know
2Ki 2:21 LORD says: 'I have *h* this water.
2Ch 30:20 heard Hezekiah and *h* the people.
Ps 30: 2 and you *h* me.
107: 20 He sent forth his word and *h* them;
Isa 6:10 and turn and be *h.*"
53: 5 and by his wounds we are *h.*
Jer 14:19 us so that we cannot be *h?*
17:14 Heal me, O LORD, and I will be *h;*
51: 8 perhaps she can be *h.*
51: 9 but she cannot be *h;*
51: 9 " 'We would have *h* Babylon,
Eze 34: 4 the weak or *h* the sick
Hos 11: 3 it was I who *h* them.
Mt 4:24 and the paralyzed, and he *h* them.
Mt 8: 8 the word, and my servant will be *h.*
8:13 his servant was *h* at that very hour.
8:16 with a word and *h* all the sick.
9:21 If I only touch his cloak, I will be *h*
9:22 he said, "your faith has *h* you."
9:22 woman was *h* from that moment.
12:15 him, and he *h* all their sick,
12:22 Jesus *h* him, so that he could both
14:14 on them and *h* their sick.
14:36 and all who touched him were *h.*
15:28 And her daughter was *h*
15:30 laid them at his feet; and he *h* them
17:18 and he was *h* from that moment.
19: 2 followed him, and he *h* them there.
21:14 to him at the temple, and he *h* them
Mk 1:34 and Jesus *h* many who had various
3:10 For he had *h* many, so that those
5:23 hands on her so that she will be *h*
5:28 If I just touch his clothes, I will be *h*
5:34 "Daughter, your faith has *h* you.
6:13 people with oil and *h* them.
6:56 and all who touched him were *h.*
10:52 said Jesus, "your faith has *h* you."
Lk 4:40 hands on each one, he *h* them.
5:15 and to be *h* of their sicknesses.
6:18 and to be *h* of their diseases.
7: 7 the word, and my servant will be *h.*
8:47 and how she had been instantly *h.*
8:48 "Daughter, your faith has *h* you.
8:50 just believe, and she will be *h.*"
9:11 and *h* those who needed healing.
9:42 *h* the boy and gave him back
13:14 Jesus had *h* on the Sabbath,
13:14 So come and be *h* on those days,
14: 4 he *h* him and sent him away.
17:15 when he saw he was *h,* came back,
18:42 your sight; your faith has *h* you."
22:51 touched the man's ear and *h* him.
Jn 5:10 said to the man who had been *h,*
5:13 man who was *h* had no idea who it
Ac 4: 9 and are asked how he was *h,*
4:10 stands before you *h.*
4:14 who had been *h* standing there
4:22 man who was miraculously *h* was
5:16 evil spirits, and all of them were *h.*
8: 7 paralytics and cripples were *h.*
14: 9 saw that he had faith to be *h*
28: 8 placed his hands on him and *h* him.
Heb 12:13 may not be disabled, but rather *h.*
Jas 5:16 for each other so that you may be *h*
1Pe 2:24 by his wounds you have been *h.*
Rev 13: 3 but the fatal wound had been *h.*
13:12 whose fatal wound had been *h.*

HEALING* (HEAL)
2Ch 28:15 food and drink, and *h* balm.
Pr 12:18 but the tongue of the wise brings *h.*
13:17 but a trustworthy envoy brings *h.*
15: 4 The tongue that brings *h* is a tree
16:24 sweet to the soul and *h* to the bones
Isa 58: 8 and your *h* will quickly appear;
Jer 8:15 for a time of *h*
8:22 Why then is there no *h*
14:19 for a time of *h*
30:12 your injury beyond *h.*
30:13 no *h* for you.
33: 6 I will bring health and *h* to it;
46:11 there is no *h* for you.
Eze 30:21 It has not been bound up for *h*
47:12 for food and their leaves for *h.*"
Mal 4: 2 rise with *h* in its wings.
Mt 4:23 and *h* every disease and sickness
9:35 and *h* every disease and sickness.
Lk 6:19 coming from him and *h* them all.
9: 6 gospel and *h* people everywhere.
9:11 and healed those who needed *h.*
Jn 7:23 angry with me for *h* the whole man
Ac 3:16 him that has given this complete *h*
10:38 *h* all who were under the power
1Co 12: 9 to another gifts of *h*
12:28 also those having gifts of *h,*
12:30 Do all have gifts of *h?* Do all speak
Rev 22: 2 are for the *h* of the nations.

HEALS* (HEAL)
Ex 15:26 for I am the LORD, who *h* you."
Lev 13:18 a boil on his skin and it *h,*
Ps 103: 3 and *h* all your diseases;
147: 3 He *h* the brokenhearted
Isa 30:26 and *h* the wounds he inflicted.
Ac 9:34 said to him, "Jesus Christ *h* you.

HEALTH* (HEALTHIER HEALTHY)
1Sa 25: 6 And good *h* to all that is yours!
25: 6 Good *h* to you and your household
Ps 38: 3 of your wrath there is no *h*
38: 7 there is no *h* in my body.
Pr 3: 8 This will bring *h* to your body
4:22 and *h* to a man's whole body.
15:30 and good news gives *h* to the bones
Isa 38:16 You restored me to *h*
Jer 30:17 But I will restore you to *h*
33: 6 I will bring *h* and healing to it;
3Jn : 2 I pray that you may enjoy good *h*

HEALTHIER* (HEALTH)
Da 1:15 end of the ten days they looked *h*

HEALTHY* (HEALTH)
Ge 41: 5 Seven heads of grain, *h* and good,
41: 7 of grain swallowed up the seven *h,*
Ps 73: 4 their bodies are *h* and strong.
Zec 11:16 or heal the injured, or feed the *h,*
Mt 9:12 "It is not the *h* who need a doctor,
Mk 2:17 "It is not the *h* who need a doctor,
Lk 5:31 "It is not the *h* who need a doctor,

HEAP
Pr 25:22 you will *h* burning coals
Ro 12:20 you will *h* burning coals

HEAR (HEARD HEARING HEARS)
Ex 15:14 The nations will *h* and tremble;
22:27 I will *h,* for I am compassionate.
Nu 14:13 Then the Egyptians will *h* about it!
Dt 1:16 *H* the disputes between your
4:36 heaven he made you *h* his voice
6: 4 *H,* O Israel: The LORD our God,
19:20 The rest of the people will *h* of this
31:13 must *h* it and learn
Jos 7: 9 of the country will *h* about this
1Ki 8:30 *H* the supplication of your servant
2Ki 19:16 O LORD, and *h;* open your eyes,
2Ch 7:14 then will I *h* from heaven
Job 31:35 ("Oh, that I had someone to *h* me!
Ps 94: 9 he who implanted the ear not *h?*
95: 7 Today, if you *h* his voice,
Ecc 7:21 or you may *h* your servant cursing
Isa 21: 3 I am staggered by what I *h,*
29:18 that day the deaf will *h* the words
30:21 your ears will *h* a voice behind you,
51: 7 *H* me, you who know what is right,
59: 1 nor his ear too dull to *h.*
65:24 while they are still speaking I will *h*
Jer 5:21 who have ears but do not *h:*
Eze 33: 7 so *h* the word I speak and give
37: 4 'Dry bones, *h* the word
Mt 11: 5 the deaf *h,* the dead are raised,
11:15 He who has ears, let him *h.*
13:17 and to *h* what you *h* but did not *h* it
Mk 12:29 answered Jesus, "is this: '*H,*
Lk 7:22 the deaf *h,* the dead are raised,
Jn 8:47 reason you do not *h* is that you do
Ac 13: 7 he wanted to *h* the word of God.
13:44 gathered to *h* the word of the Lord.
17:32 "We want to *h* you again
Ro 2:13 is not those who *h* the law who are
10:14 they *h* without someone preaching
2Ti 4: 3 what their itching ears want to *h.*
Heb 3: 7 "Today, if you *h* his voice,
Rev 1: 3 and blessed are those who *h* it

HEARD (HEAR)
Ex 2:24 God *h* their groaning and he
Dt 4:32 has anything like it ever been *h* of?
2Sa 7:22 as we have *h* with our own ears.
Job 42: 5 My ears had *h* of you
Isa 40:21 Have you not *h?*
40:28 Have you not *h?*
66: 8 Who has ever *h* of such a thing?
Jer 18:13 Who has ever *h* anything like this?
Da 10:12 your words were *h,* and I have
12: 8 I *h,* but I did not understand.
Hab 3:16 I *h* and my heart pounded,
Mt 5:21 "You have *h* that it was said
5:27 "You have *h* that it was said,
5:33 you have *h* that it was said
5:38 "You have *h* that it was said,
5:43 "You have *h* that it was said,
Lk 12: 3 in the dark will be *h* in the daylight,
Jn 8:26 and what I have *h* from him I tell
Ac 2: 6 because each one *h* them speaking
1Co 2: 9 no ear has *h,*
2Co 12: 4 He *h* inexpressible things,

1Th 2:13 word of God, which you *h* from us,
2Ti 1:13 What you *h* from me, keep
Jas 1:25 not forgetting what he has *h,*
Rev 22: 8 am the one who *h* and saw these

HEARING (HEAR)
Isa 6: 9 Be ever *h,* but never understanding
Mt 13:14 will be ever *h* but never
Mk 4:12 ever *h* but never understanding;
Ac 28:26 will be ever *h* but never
Ro 10:17 faith comes from *h* the message,
1Co 12:17 where would the sense of *h* be?

HEARS (HEAR)
Jn 5:24 whoever *h* my word and believes
1Jn 5:14 according to his will, he *h* us.
Rev 3:20 If anyone *h* my voice and opens

HEART (BROKENHEARTED FAINT-HEARTED HARDHEARTED HEART'S HEARTACHE HEARTS KINDHEARTED SIMPLEHEARTED STOUTHEARTED WHOLEHEARTED WHOLEHEARTEDLY)
Ge 6: 5 of his *h* was only evil all the time.
Ex 4:21 But I will harden his *h*
25: 2 each man whose *h* prompts him
35:21 and whose *h* moved him came
Lev 19:17 Do not hate your brother in your *h.*
Dt 4: 9 or let them slip from your *h* as long
4:29 if you look for him with all your *h*
6: 5 LORD your God with all your *h*
10:12 LORD your God with all your *h*
11:13 and to serve him with all your *h*
13: 3 you love him with all your *h*
15:10 and do so without a grudging *h;*
26:16 observe them with all your *h*
29:18 you today whose *h* turns away
30: 2 and obey him with all your *h*
30: 6 you may love him with all your *h*
30:10 LORD your God with all your *h*
Jos 22: 5 and to serve him with all your *h*
23:14 You know with all your *h*
1Sa 10: 9 God changed Saul's *h,*
12:20 serve the LORD with all your *h.*
12:24 serve him faithfully with all your *h;*
13:14 sought out a man after his own *h*
14: 7 I am with you *h* and soul."
16: 7 but the LORD looks at the *h."*
17:32 "Let no one lose *h* on account
1Ki 2: 4 faithfully before me with all their *h*
3: 9 So give your servant a discerning *h*
3:12 give you a wise and discerning *h,*
8:48 back to you with all their *h*
9: 3 and my *h* will always be there.
9: 4 walk before me in integrity of *h*
10:24 the wisdom God had put in his *h.*
11: 4 and his *h* was not fully devoted
14: 8 and followed me with all his *h,*
15:14 Asa's *h* was fully committed
2Ki 22:19 Because your *h* was responsive
23: 3 with all his *h* and all his soul,
1Ch 28: 9 for the LORD searches every *h*
2Ch 6:38 back to you with all their *h*
7:16 and my *h* will always be there.
15:12 of their fathers, with all their *h*
15:17 Asa's *h* was fully committed
17: 6 His *h* was devoted to the ways
22: 9 sought the LORD with all his *h."*
34:31 with all his *h* and all his soul,
36:13 stiff-necked and hardened his *h*
Ezr 1: 5 everyone whose *h* God had moved
Ne 4: 6 the people worked with all their *h.*
Job 19:27 How my *h* yearns within me!
22:22 and lay up his words in your *h.*
37: 1 "At this my *h* pounds
Ps 9: 1 you, O LORD, with all my *h;*
14: 1 The fool says in his *h,*
16: 9 Therefore my *h* is glad
19:14 and the meditation of my *h*
20: 4 he give you the desire of your *h*
24: 4 who has clean hands and a pure *h,*
26: 2 examine my *h* and my mind;
37: 4 will give you the desires of your *h.*
37:31 The law of his God is in his *h;*
44:21 since he knows the secrets of the *h*
45: 1 My *h* is stirred by a noble theme
51:10 Create in me a pure *h,* O God,
51:17 a broken and contrite *h,*
53: 1 The fool says in his *h,*
66:18 If I had cherished sin in my *h,*
73: 1 to those who are pure in *h.*
Ps 73:26 My flesh and my *h* may fail,
86:11 give me an undivided *h,*
90:12 that we may gain a *h* of wisdom.
97:11 and joy on the upright in *h.*
108: 1 My *h* is steadfast, O God;
109: 22 and my *h* is wounded within me.
111: 1 will extol the LORD with all my *h*
112: 7 his *h* is steadfast, trusting
112: 8 His *h* is secure, he will have no fear
119: 2 and seek him with all their *h.*
119: 10 I seek you with all my *h;*
119: 11 I have hidden your word in my *h*
119: 30 I have set my *h* on your laws.
119: 32 for you have set my *h* free.
119: 34 and obey it with all my *h.*
119: 36 Turn my *h* toward your statutes
119: 58 sought your face with all my *h;*
119: 69 I keep your precepts with all my *h.*
119:111 they are the joy of my *h.*
119:112 My *h* is set on keeping your
119:145 I call with all my *h;* answer me,
125: 4 to those who are upright in *h.*
138: 1 you, O LORD, with all my *h;*
139: 23 Search me, O God, and know my *h*
Pr 2: 2 applying your *h* to understanding,
3: 1 but keep my commands in your *h,*
3: 3 write them on the tablet of your *h.*
3: 5 Trust in the LORD with all your *h*
4: 4 hold of my words with all your *h;*
4:21 keep them within your *h;*
4:23 Above all else, guard your *h,*
6:21 Bind them upon your *h* forever;
7: 3 write them on the tablet of your *h.*
10: 8 The wise in *h* accept commands,
13:12 Hope deferred makes the *h* sick,
14:13 Even in laughter the *h* may ache,
14:30 A *h* at peace gives life to the body,
15:13 A happy *h* makes the face cheerful,
15:15 the cheerful *h* has a continual feast.
15:28 *h* of the righteous weighs its
15:30 A cheerful look brings joy to the *h,*
16:23 A wise man's *h* guides his mouth,
17:22 A cheerful *h* is good medicine,
20: 9 can say, "I have kept my *h* pure;
22:11 He who loves a pure *h*
22:17 apply your *h* to what I teach,
22:18 when you keep them in your *h*
23:15 My son, if your *h* is wise,
23:19 and keep your *h* on the right path.
23:26 My son, give me your *h*
24:17 stumbles, do not let your *h* rejoice,
27:19 so a man's *h* reflects the man.
Ecc 5: 2 do not be hasty in your *h*
8: 5 wise *h* will know the proper time
11:10 banish anxiety from your *h*
SS 3: 1 I looked for the one my *h* loves;
4: 9 You have stolen my *h,* my sister,
5: 2 *Beloved* I slept but my *h* was awake
5: 4 my *h* began to pound for him.
8: 6 Place me like a seal over your *h,*
Isa 6:10 Make the *h* of this people calloused
40:11 and carries them close to his *h;*
57:15 and to revive the *h* of the contrite.
66:14 you see this, your *h* will rejoice
Jer 3:15 give you shepherds after my own *h,*
4:14 wash the evil from your *h*
9:26 of Israel is uncircumcised in *h."*
17: 9 The *h* is deceitful above all things
20: 9 is in my *h* like a fire,
24: 7 I will give them a *h* to know me,
29:13 when you seek me with all your *h.*
32:39 I will give them singleness of *h*
32:41 them in this land with all my *h*
51:46 Do not lose *h* or be afraid
Eze 11:19 I will give them an undivided *h*
18:31 and get a new *h* and a new spirit.
36:26 I will give you a new *h*
44: 7 foreigners uncircumcised in *h*
Da 7: 4 and the *h* of a man was given to it.
Joel 2:12 "return to me with all your *h,*
2:13 Rend your *h*
Zep 3:14 Be glad and rejoice with all your *h,*
Mt 5: 8 Blessed are the pure in *h,*
5:28 adultery with her in his *h.*
6:21 treasure is, there your *h* will be
11:29 for I am gentle and humble in *h,*
12:34 of the *h* the mouth speaks.
13:15 For this people's *h* has become
15:18 out of the mouth come from the *h,*
15:19 For out of the *h* come evil thoughts
Mt 18:35 forgive your brother from your *h."*
22:37 the Lord your God with all your *h*
Mk 11:23 and does not doubt in his *h*
12:30 the Lord your God with all your *h*
12:33 To love him with all your *h,*
Lk 2:19 and pondered them in her *h.*
2:51 treasured all these things in her *h.*
6:45 out of the good stored up in his *h,*
6:45 overflow of his *h* his mouth speaks.
8:15 for those with a noble and good *h,*
10:27 the Lord your God with all your *h*
12:34 treasure is, there your *h* will be
Jn 12:27 "Now my *h* is troubled,
Ac 1:24 "Lord, you know everyone's *h.*
2:37 they were cut to the *h*
4:32 All the believers were one in *h*
8:21 your *h* is not right before God.
15: 8 who knows the *h,* showed that he
16:14 The Lord opened her *h* to respond
28:27 For this people's *h* has become
Ro 1: 9 with my whole *h* in preaching
2:29 is circumcision of the *h,*
10: 9 in your *h* that God raised him
10:10 is with your *h* that you believe
15: 6 with one *h* and mouth you may
1Co 14:25 the secrets of his *h* will be laid bare.
2Co 2: 4 anguish of *h* and with many tears,
4: 1 this ministry, we do not lose *h.*
4:16 Therefore we do not lose *h.*
9: 7 give what he has decided in his *h*
Eph 1:18 eyes of your *h* may be enlightened
5:19 make music in your *h* to the Lord,
6: 5 and with sincerity of *h,* just
6: 6 doing the will of God from your *h.*
Php 1: 7 since I have you in my *h;* for
Col 2: 2 is that they may be encouraged in *h*
3:22 but with sincerity of *h*
3:23 work at it with all your *h,*
1Ti 1: 5 which comes from a pure *h*
3: 1 If anyone sets his *h*
2Ti 2:22 call on the Lord out of a pure *h.*
Phm :12 who is my very *h*—back to you.
:20 in the Lord; refresh my *h* in Christ.
Heb 4:12 the thoughts and attitudes of the *h.*
1Pe 1:22 one another deeply, from the *h.*

HEART'S* (HEART)
2Ch 1:11 "Since this is your *h* desire
Jer 15:16 they were my joy and my *h* delight,
Eze 24:25 delight of their eyes, their *h* desire,
Ro 10: 1 my *h* desire and prayer to God

HEARTACHE* (HEART)
Pr 15:13 but *h* crushes the spirit.

HEARTLESS*
La 4: 3 but my people have become *h*
Ro 1:31 they are senseless, faithless, *h,*

HEARTS (HEART)
Lev 26:41 their uncircumcised *h* are humbled
Dt 6: 6 are to be upon your *h.*
10:16 Circumcise your *h,* therefore,
11:18 Fix these words of mine in your *h*
30: 6 your God will circumcise your *h*
Jos 11:20 himself who hardened their *h*
24:23 and yield your *h* to the LORD,
1Sa 7: 3 to the LORD with all your *h,*
10:26 valiant men whose *h* God had
2Sa 15: 6 and so he stole the *h* of the men
1Ki 8:39 for you alone know the *h* of all men
8:61 your *h* must be fully committed
18:37 are turning their *h* back again."
1Ch 29:18 and keep their *h* loyal to you.
2Ch 6:30 (for you alone know the *h* of men),
11:16 tribe of Israel who set their *h*
29:31 all whose *h* were willing brought
Ps 7: 9 who searches minds and *h,*
33:21 In him our *h* rejoice,
62: 8 pour out your *h* to him,
95: 8 do not harden your *h* as you did
Ecc 3:11 also set eternity in the *h* of men;
Isa 26: 8 are the desire of our *h.*
29:13 but their *h* are far from me.
35: 4 say to those with fearful *h,*
51: 7 people who have my law in your *h:*
63:17 harden our *h* so we do not revere
65:14 out of the joy of their *h,*
Jer 4: 4 circumcise your *h,*
12: 2 but far from their *h.*
17: 1 on the tablets of their *h*
31:33 and write it on their *h.*

Mal 4: 6 He will turn the *h* of the fathers
Mt 15: 8 but their *h* are far from me.
Mk 6:52 the loaves; their *h* were hardened.
7: 6 but their *h* are far from me.
7:21 out of men's *h,* come evil thoughts,
Lk 1:17 to turn the *h* of the fathers
16:15 of men, but God knows your *h.*
24:32 "Were not our *h* burning within us
Jn 5:42 not have the love of God in your *h.*
14: 1 "Do not let your *h* be troubled.
14:27 Do not let your *h* be troubled
Ac 7:51 with uncircumcised *h* and ears!
11:23 true to the Lord with all their *h.*
15: 9 for he purified their *h* by faith.
28:27 understand with their *h*
Ro 1:21 and their foolish *h* were darkened.
2:15 of the law are written on their *h,*
5: 5 love into our *h* by the Holy Spirit,
8:27 who searches our *h* knows
1Co 4: 5 will expose the motives of men's *h.*
2Co 1:22 put his Spirit in our *h* as a deposit,
3: 2 written on our *h,* known
3: 3 but on tablets of human *h.*
4: 6 shine in our *h* to give us the light
6:11 and opened wide our *h* to you.
6:13 to my children—open wide your *h*
7: 2 Make room for us in your *h.*
Gal 4: 6 the Spirit of his Son into our *h,*
Eph 3:17 dwell in your *h* through faith.
Php 4: 7 will guard your *h* and your minds
Col 3: 1 set your *h* on things above,
3:15 the peace of Christ rule in your *h,*
3:16 with gratitude in your *h* to God.
1Th 2: 4 men but God, who tests our *h.*
3:13 May he strengthen your *h*
2Th 2:17 encourage your *h* and strengthen
Phm : 7 have refreshed the *h* of the saints.
Heb 3: 8 do not harden your *h*
8:10 and write them on their *h.*
10:16 I will put my laws in their *h,*
10:22 having our *h* sprinkled
Jas 4: 8 purify your *h,* you double-minded.
2Pe 1:19 the morning star rises in your *h.*
1Jn 3:20 For God is greater than our *h,*

HEAT
Ps 19: 6 nothing is hidden from its *h.*
2Pe 3:12 and the elements will melt in the *h.*

HEAVEN (HEAVENLY HEAVENS HEAVENWARD)
Ge 14:19 Creator of *h* and earth.
28:12 with its top reaching to *h,*
Ex 16: 4 rain down bread from *h* for you.
20:22 that I have spoken to you from *h:*
Dt 26:15 from *h,* your holy dwelling place,
30:12 "Who will ascend into *h* to get it
1Ki 8:27 the highest *h,* cannot contain you.
8:30 Hear from *h,* your dwelling place,
22:19 the host of *h* standing around him
2Ki 2: 1 up to *h* in a whirlwind,
19:15 You have made *h* and earth.
2Ch 7:14 then will I hear from *h*
Isa 14:12 How you have fallen from *h,*
66: 1 "*H* is my throne,
Da 7:13 coming with the clouds of *h.*
Mt 3: 2 for the kingdom of *h* is near."
3:16 At that moment *h* was opened,
4:17 for the kingdom of *h* is near."
5:12 because great is your reward in *h,*
5:19 great in the kingdom of *h.*
6: 9 " 'Our Father in *h,*
6:10 done on earth as it is in *h.*
6:20 up for yourselves treasures in *h,*
7:21 Lord,' will enter the kingdom of *h,*
16:19 bind on earth will be bound in *h,*
18: 3 will never enter the kingdom of *h.*
18:18 bind on earth will be bound in *h,*
19:14 the kingdom of *h* belongs to such
19:21 and you will have treasure in *h.*
19:23 man to enter the kingdom of *h.*
23:13 the kingdom of *h* in men's faces.
24:35 *H* and earth will pass away,
26:64 and coming on the clouds of *h.*"
28:18 "All authority in *h*
Mk 1:10 he saw *h* being torn open
10:21 and you will have treasure in *h.*
13:31 *H* and earth will pass away,
14:62 and coming on the clouds of *h.*"
16:19 he was taken up into *h*
Lk 3:21 *h* was opened and the Holy Spirit
Lk 10:18 saw Satan fall like lightning from *h.*
10:20 that your names are written in *h.*"
12:33 in *h* that will not be exhausted,
15: 7 in *h* over one sinner who repents
18:22 and you will have treasure in *h.*
21:33 *H* and earth will pass away,
24:51 left them and was taken up into *h.*
Jn 3:13 No one has ever gone into *h*
6:38 down from *h* not to do my will
12:28 Then a voice came from *h,*
Ac 1:11 has been taken from you into *h,*
7:49 the prophet says: " '*H* is my
7:55 looked up to *h* and saw the glory
9: 3 a light from *h* flashed around him.
26:19 disobedient to the vision from *h.*
Ro 10: 6 'Who will ascend into *h?*' " (that is,
1Co 15:47 the earth, the second man from *h.*
2Co 5: 1 an eternal house in *h,* not built
12: 2 ago was caught up to the third *h.*
Eph 1:10 to bring all things in *h*
Php 2:10 *h* and on earth and under the earth,
3:20 But our citizenship is in *h.*
Col 1:16 things in *h* and on earth, visible
4: 1 that you also have a Master in *h.*
1Th 1:10 and to wait for his Son from *h,*
4:16 himself will come down from *h,*
Heb 1: 3 hand of the Majesty in *h.*
8: 5 and shadow of what is in *h.*
9:24 he entered *h* itself, now to appear
12:23 whose names are written in *h.*
1Pe 1: 4 spoil or fade—kept in *h* for you,
3:22 who has gone into *h* and is
2Pe 3:13 we are looking forward to a new *h*
Rev 5:13 Then I heard every creature in *h*
11:19 God's temple in *h* was opened,
12: 7 And there was war in *h.*
15: 5 this I looked and in *h* the temple,
19: 1 of a great multitude in *h* shouting:
19:11 I saw *h* standing open and there
21: 1 Then I saw a new *h* and a new earth
21:10 coming down out of *h* from God.

HEAVENLY (HEAVEN)
Ps 8: 5 him a little lower than the *h* beings
2Co 5: 2 to be clothed with our *h* dwelling,
Eph 1: 3 in the *h* realms with every spiritual
1:20 at his right hand in the *h* realms,
2Ti 4:18 bring me safely to his *h* kingdom.
Heb 12:22 to the *h* Jerusalem, the city

HEAVENS (HEAVEN)
Ge 1: 1 In the beginning God created the *h*
11: 4 with a tower that reaches to the *h,*
Dt 33:26 who rides on the *h* to help you
1Ki 8:27 The *h,* even the highest heaven,
2Ch 2: 6 since the *h,* even the highest
Ezr 9: 6 and our guilt has reached to the *h.*
Ne 9: 6 You made the *h,* even the highest
Job 11: 8 They are higher than the *h*—
38:33 Do you know the laws of the *h?*
Ps 8: 3 When I consider your *h,*
19: 1 The *h* declare the glory of God;
33: 6 of the LORD were the *h* made,
57: 5 Be exalted, O God, above the *h;*
102: 25 the *h* are the work of your hands.
103: 11 as high as the *h* are above the earth,
108: 4 is your love, higher than the *h;*
115: 16 The highest *h* belong to the LORD
119: 89 it stands firm in the *h.*
135: 6 in the *h* and on the earth,
139: 8 If I go up to the *h,* you are there;
148: 1 Praise the LORD from the *h,*
Isa 40:26 Lift your eyes and look to the *h:*
45: 8 "You *h* above, rain
51: 6 Lift up your eyes to the *h,*
55: 9 "As the *h* are higher than the earth,
65:17 new *h* and a new earth.
Jer 31:37 if the *h* above can be measured
32:17 you have made the *h* and the earth
Eze 1: 1 *h* were opened and I saw visions
Da 12: 3 shine like the brightness of the *h,*
Joel 2:30 I will show wonders in the *h*
Mt 24:31 from one end of the *h* to the other.
Mk 13:27 of the earth to the ends of the *h.*
Eph 4:10 who ascended higher than all the *h,*
Heb 4:14 priest who has gone through the *h,*
7:26 from sinners, exalted above the *h.*
2Pe 3: 5 ago by God's word the *h* existed
3:10 The *h* will disappear with a roar;

HEAVENWARD (HEAVEN)
Php 3:14 for which God has called me *h*

HEAVIER (HEAVY)
Pr 27: 3 provocation by a fool is *h* than both

HEAVY (HEAVIER)
1Ki 12: 4 and the *h* yoke he put on us,
Ecc 1:13 What a *h* burden God has laid
Isa 47: 6 you laid a very *h* yoke.
Mt 23: 4 They tie up *h* loads and put them

HEBREW (HEBREWS)
Ge 14:13 and reported this to Abram the *H.*
2Ki 18:26 speak to us in *H* in the hearing
Php 3: 5 tribe of Benjamin, a *H* of Hebrews;

HEBREWS (HEBREW)
Ex 9: 1 of the *H,* says: "Let my people go,
2Co 11:22 Are they *H?* So am I.

HEBRON
Ge 13:18 near the great trees of Mamre at *H,*
23: 2 died at Kiriath Arba (that is, *H)*
Jos 14:13 and gave him *H* as his inheritance.
20: 7 *H)* in the hill country of Judah.
21:13 the priest they gave *H* (a city
2Sa 2:11 king in *H* over the house

HEDGE
Job 1:10 "Have you not put a *h* around him

HEED (HEEDS)
Ecc 7: 5 It is better to *h* a wise man's rebuke

HEEDS (HEED)
Pr 13: 1 wise son *h* his father's instruction,
13:18 whoever *h* correction is honored.
15: 5 whoever *h* correction shows
15:32 whoever *h* correction gains

HEEL
Ge 3:15 and you will strike his *h.*"

HEIR (INHERIT)
Gal 4: 7 God has made you also an *h.*
Heb 1: 2 whom he appointed *h* of all things,

HEIRS (INHERIT)
Ro 8:17 then we are *h*— *h* of God
Gal 3:29 and *h* according to the promise.
Eph 3: 6 gospel the Gentiles are *h* together
1Pe 3: 7 as *h* with you of the gracious gift

HELD (HOLD)
Ex 17:11 As long as Moses *h* up his hands,
Dt 4: 4 but all of you who *h* fast
2Ki 18: 6 He *h* fast to the LORD
SS 3: 4 I *h* him and would not let him go
Isa 65: 2 All day long I have *h* out my hands
Ro 10:21 day long I have *h* out my hands
Col 2:19 and *h* together by its ligaments

HELL*
Mt 5:22 will be in danger of the fire of *h.*
5:29 body to be thrown into *h.*
5:30 for your whole body to go into *h.*
10:28 destroy both soul and body in *h.*
18: 9 and be thrown into the fire of *h.*
23:15 as much a son of *h* as you are.
23:33 you escape being condemned to *h?*
Mk 9:43 than with two hands to go into *h,*
9:45 have two feet and be thrown into *h.*
9:47 two eyes and be thrown into *h,*
Lk 12: 5 has power to throw you into *h.*
16:23 In *h,* where he was in torment,
Jas 3: 6 and is itself set on fire by *h.*
2Pe 2: 4 but sent them to *h,* putting them

HELMET
Isa 59:17 and the *h* of salvation on his head;
Eph 6:17 Take the *h* of salvation
1Th 5: 8 and the hope of salvation as a *h.*

HELP (HELPED HELPER HELPFUL HELPING HELPLESS HELPS)
Ex 23: 5 leave it there; be sure you *h* him
Lev 25:35 *h* him as you would an alien
Dt 33:26 who rides on the heavens to *h* you
2Ch 16:12 even in his illness he did not seek *h*
Ps 18: 6 I cried to my God for *h.*
30: 2 my God, I called to you for *h*
33:20 he is our *h* and our shield.
46: 1 an ever-present *h* in trouble.
72:12 the afflicted who have no one to *h.*
79: 9 *H* us, O God our Savior,
108: 12 for the *h* of man is worthless.
115: 9 he is their *h* and shield.
121: 1 where does my *h* come from?

Ecc 4:10 his friend can *h* him up.
Isa 41:10 I will strengthen you and *h* you;
Jnh 2: 2 depths of the grave I called for *h,*
Mk 9:24 *h* me overcome my unbelief!"
Lk 11:46 will not lift one finger to *h* them.
Ac 16: 9 Come over to Macedonia and *h* us
18:27 he was a great *h* to those who
20:35 of hard work we must *h* the weak,
26:22 I have had God's *h* to this very day,
1Co 12:28 those able to *h* others, those
2Co 9: 2 For I know your eagerness to *h,*
1Ti 5:16 she should *h* them and not let

HELPED (HELP)
1Sa 7:12 "Thus far has the LORD *h* us."

HELPER (HELP)
Ge 2:18 I will make a *h* suitable for him."
Ps 10:14 you are the *h* of the fatherless.
Heb 13: 6 Lord is my *h;* I will not be afraid.

HELPFUL (HELP)
Eph 4:29 only what is *h* for building others

HELPING (HELP)
Ac 9:36 always doing good and *h* the poor.
1Ti 5:10 *h* those in trouble and devoting

HELPLESS (HELP)
Ps 10:12 Do not forget the *h.*
Mt 9:36 because they were harassed and *h,*

HELPS (HELP)
Ro 8:26 the Spirit *h* us in our weakness.

HEN
Mt 23:37 as a *h* gathers her chicks
Lk 13:34 as a *h* gathers her chicks

HERALD
1Ti 2: 7 for this purpose I was appointed a *h*
2Ti 1:11 of this gospel I was appointed a *h*

HERBS
Ex 12: 8 with bitter *h,* and bread made

HERITAGE (INHERIT)
Ps 61: 5 you have given me the *h*
119:111 Your statutes are my *h* forever;
127: 3 Sons are a *h* from the LORD,

HEROD

1. King of Judea who tried to kill Jesus (Mt 2; Lk 1:5).

2. Son of 1. Tetrarch of Galilee who arrested and beheaded John the Baptist (Mt 14:1–12; Mk 6:14–29; Lk 3:1, 19–20; 9:7–9); tried Jesus (Lk 23:6–15).

3. Grandson of 1. King of Judea who killed James (Ac 12:2); arrested Peter (Ac 12:3–19). Death (Ac 12:19–23).

HERODIAS

Wife of Herod the Tetrarch who persuaded her daughter to ask for John the Baptist's head (Mt 14:1–12; Mk 6:14–29).

HEWN
Isa 51: 1 the quarry from which you were *h;*

HEZEKIAH

King of Judah. Restored the temple and worship (2Ch 29–31). Sought the LORD for help against Assyria (2Ki 18–19; 2Ch 32:1–23; Isa 36–37). Illness healed (2Ki 20:1–11; 2Ch 32:24–26; Isa 38). Judged for showing Babylonians his treasures (2Ki 20:12–21; 2Ch 32:31; Isa 39).

HID (HIDE)
Ge 3: 8 and they *h* from the LORD God
Ex 2: 2 she *h* him for three months.
Jos 6:17 because she *h* the spies we sent.
1Ki 18:13 I *h* a hundred of the LORD's
2Ch 22:11 she *h* the child from Athaliah
Isa 54: 8 I *h* my face from you for a moment,
Mt 13:44 When a man found it, he *h* it again,
25:25 and *h* your talent in the ground.
Heb 11:23 By faith Moses' parents *h* him

HIDDEN (HIDE)
1Sa 10:22 has *h* himself among the baggage."
Job 28:11 and brings *h* things to light.
Ps 19:12 Forgive my *h* faults.
78: 2 I will utter *h* things, things from of old—
119: 11 I have *h* your word in my heart
Pr 2: 4 and search for it as for *h* treasure,
27: 5 rebuke than *h* love.
Isa 59: 2 your sins have *h* his face from you,
Da 2:22 He reveals deep and *h* things;
Mt 5:14 A city on a hill cannot be *h.*
10:26 or *h* that will not be made known.
11:25 because you have *h* these things
13:35 I will utter things *h*
13:44 of heaven is like treasure *h*
Mk 4:22 For whatever is *h* is meant
Ro 16:25 of the mystery *h* for long ages past,
1Co 2: 7 a wisdom that has been *h*
Eph 3: 9 for ages past was kept *h* in God,
Col 1:26 the mystery that has been kept *h*
2: 3 in whom are *h* all the treasures
3: 3 and your life is now *h* with Christ

HIDE (HID HIDDEN HIDING)
Dt 31:17 I will *h* my face from them,
Ps 17: 8 *h* me in the shadow of your wings
27: 5 he will *h* me in the shelter
143: 9 for I *h* myself in you.
Isa 53: 3 one from whom men *h* their faces

HIDING (HIDE)
Ps 32: 7 You are my *h* place;
Pr 28:12 to power, men go into *h.*

HIGH
Ge 14:18 He was priest of God Most *H,*
14:22 God Most *H,* Creator of heaven
Ps 21: 7 the unfailing love of the Most *H*
82: 6 you are all sons of the Most *H.'*
Isa 14:14 I will make myself like the Most *H*
Da 4:17 know that the Most *H* is sovereign
Mk 5: 7 Jesus, Son of the Most *H* God?
Heb 7: 1 and priest of God Most *H.*

HIGHWAY
Isa 40: 3 a *h* for our God.

HILL (HILLS)
Ps 24: 3 ascend the *h* of the LORD?
Isa 40: 4 every mountain and *h* made low;
Mt 5:14 A city on a *h* cannot be hidden.
Lk 3: 5 every mountain and *h* made low.

HILLS (HILL)
1Ki 20:23 "Their gods are gods of the *h.*
Ps 50:10 and the cattle on a thousand *h.*
121: 1 I lift up my eyes to the *h*—
Hos 10: 8 and to the *h,* "Fall on us!"
Lk 23:30 and to the *h,* "Cover us!"
Rev 17: 9 The seven heads are seven *h*

HINDER (HINDERED HINDERS)
1Sa 14: 6 Nothing can *h* the LORD
Mt 19:14 come to me, and do not *h* them,
1Co 9:12 anything rather than *h* the gospel
1Pe 3: 7 so that nothing will *h* your prayers.

HINDERED (HINDER)
Lk 11:52 and you have *h* those who were

HINDERS (HINDER)
Heb 12: 1 let us throw off everything that *h*

HINT*
Eph 5: 3 even a *h* of sexual immorality,

HIP
Ge 32:32 socket of Jacob's *h* was touched

HIRAM

King of Tyre; helped David build his palace (2Sa 5:11–12; 1Ch 14:1); helped Solomon build the temple (1Ki 5; 2Ch 2) and his navy (1Ki 9:10–27; 2Ch 8).

HIRED
Lk 15:15 and *h* himself out to a citizen
Jn 10:12 *h* hand is not the shepherd who

HOARDED (HOARDS)
Ecc 5:13 wealth *h* to the harm of its owner,
Jas 5: 3 You have *h* wealth in the last days.

HOARDS (HOARDED)
Pr 11:26 People curse the man who *h* grain,

HOLD (HELD HOLDS)
Ex 20: 7 LORD will not *h* anyone guiltless
Lev 19:13 " 'Do not *h* back the wages
Dt 5:11 LORD will not *h* anyone guiltless
11:22 in all his ways and to *h* fast to him
13: 4 serve him and *h* fast to him.
30:20 listen to his voice, and *h* fast to him
Jos 22: 5 to *h* fast to him and to serve him
2Ki 4:16 "you will *h* a son in your arms."
Ps 18:16 from on high and took *h* of me;
73:23 you *h* me by my right hand.
Pr 4: 4 "Lay *h* of my words
Isa 41:13 who takes *h* of your right hand
54: 2 do not *h* back;
Eze 3:18 and I will *h* you accountable
3:20 and I will *h* you accountable
33: 6 I will *h* the watchman accountable
Zec 8:23 nations will take firm *h* of one Jew
Mk 11:25 if you *h* anything against anyone,
Jn 20:17 Jesus said, "Do not *h* on to me,
Php 2:16 as you *h* out the word of life—
3:12 but I press on to take *h* of that
Col 1:17 and in him all things *h* together.
1Th 5:21 *H* on to the good.
1Ti 6:12 Take *h* of the eternal life
Heb 10:23 Let us *h* unswervingly

HOLDS (HOLD)
Pr 10:19 but he who *h* his tongue is wise.
17:28 and discerning if he *h* his tongue.

HOLES
Hag 1: 6 to put them in a purse with *h* in it."
Mt 8:20 "Foxes have *h* and birds

HOLINESS* (HOLY)
Ex 15:11 majestic in *h,*
Dt 32:51 because you did not uphold my *h*
1Ch 16:29 the LORD in the splendor of his *h.*
2Ch 20:21 him for the splendor of his *h*
Ps 29: 2 in the splendor of his *h.*
89:35 Once for all, I have sworn by my *h*
93: 5 *h* adorns your house
96: 9 in the splendor of his *h;*
Isa 29:23 they will acknowledge the *h*
35: 8 it will be called the Way of *H.*
Eze 36:23 I will show the *h* of my great name,
38:23 I will show my greatness and my *h,*
Am 4: 2 LORD has sworn by his *h:*
Lk 1:75 fear in *h* and righteousness
Ro 1: 4 the Spirit of *h* was declared
6:19 to righteousness leading to *h.*
6:22 the benefit you reap leads to *h,*
1Co 1:30 our righteousness, *h*
2Co 1:12 in the *h* and sincerity that are
7: 1 perfecting *h* out of reverence
Eph 4:24 God in true righteousness and *h.*
1Ti 2: 2 quiet lives in all godliness and *h.*
2:15 love and *h* with propriety.
Heb 12:10 that we may share in his *h.*
12:14 without *h* no one will see the Lord.

HOLY (HALLOWED HOLINESS)
Ge 2: 3 the seventh day and made it *h,*
Ex 3: 5 you are standing is *h* ground."
16:23 a *h* Sabbath to the LORD.
19: 6 kingdom of priests and a *h* nation.'
20: 8 the Sabbath day by keeping it *h.*
26:33 Place from the Most *H* Place.
26:33 curtain will separate the *H* Place
28:36 seal: *H* TO THE LORD.
29:37 Then the altar will be most *h,*
30:10 It is most *h* to the LORD."
30:29 them so they will be most *h,*
31:13 I am the LORD, who makes you *h.*
40: 9 all its furnishings, and it will be *h.*
Lev 10: 3 I will show myself *h;*
10:10 must distinguish between the *h*
10:13 in a *h* place, because it is your share
11:44 and be *h,* because I am *h.*
11:45 therefore be *h,* because I am *h.*
19: 2 'Be *h* because I, the LORD your
19: 8 he has desecrated what is *h*
19:24 the fourth year all its fruit will be *h,*
20: 3 and profaned my *h* name.
20: 7 " 'Consecrate yourselves and be *h,*
20: 8 I am the LORD, who makes you *h.*
20:26 You are to be *h* to me because I,
21: 6 They must be *h* to their God
21: 8 Consider them *h,* because I
22: 9 am the LORD, who makes them *h.*
22:32 Do not profane my *h* name.
25:12 For it is a jubilee and is to be *h*
27: 9 given to the LORD becomes *h.*
Nu 4:15 they must not touch the *h* things
6: 5 He must be *h* until the period
20:12 as *h* in the sight of the Israelites,
20:13 and where he showed himself *h*
Dt 5:12 the Sabbath day by keeping it *h,*

Dt 23:14 Your camp must be *h*,
26:15 from heaven, your *h* dwelling place
33: 2 He came with myriads of *h* ones
Jos 5:15 place where you are standing is *h*."
24:19 He is a *h* God; he is a jealous God.
1Sa 2: 2 "There is no one *h* like the LORD;
6:20 of the LORD, this *h* God?
21: 5 even on missions that are not *h*.
2Ki 4: 9 often comes our way is a *h* man
1Ch 16:10 Glory in his *h* name;
16:35 may give thanks to your *h* name,
29: 3 I have provided for this *h* temple:
2Ch 30:27 heaven, his *h* dwelling place.
Ezr 9: 2 and have mingled the *h* race
Ne 11: 1 the *h* city, while the remaining nine
Job 6:10 not denied the words of the *H* One.
Ps 2: 6 King on Zion, my *h* hill."
11: 4 The LORD is in his *h* temple;
16:10 will you let your *H* One see decay.
22: 3 you are enthroned as the *H* One;
24: 3 Who may stand in his *h* place?
30: 4 praise his *h* name.
77:13 Your ways, O God, are *h*.
78:54 to the border of his *h* land,
99: 3 he is *h*.
99: 5 he is *h*.
99: 9 for the LORD our God is *h*.
105: 3 Glory in his *h* name;
111: 9 *h* and awesome is his name.
Pr 9:10 of the *H* One is understanding.
Isa 5:16 the *h* God will show himself *h*
6: 3 *H, h, h* is the LORD Almighty;
8:13 is the one you are to regard as *h*,
29:23 they will keep my name *h*;
40:25 who is my equal?" says the *H* One.
43: 3 the *H* One of Israel, your Savior;
54: 5 *H* One of Israel is your Redeemer;
57:15 who lives forever, whose name is *h*:
58:13 and the LORD's *h* day honorable,
Jer 17:22 but keep the Sabbath day *h*,
Eze 20:41 I will show myself *h* among you
22:26 to my law and profane my *h* things;
28:22 and show myself *h* within her.
28:25 I will show myself *h* among them
36:20 nations they profaned my *h* name,
38:16 when I show myself *h* through you
44:23 the difference between the *h*
Da 9:24 prophecy and to anoint the most *h*.
Hab 2:20 But the LORD is in his *h* temple;
Zec 14: 5 and all the *h* ones with him.
14:20 On that day HOLY TO THE LORD
Mt 24:15 in the *h* place 'the abomination
Mk 1:24 the *H* One of God!" "Be quiet!"
Lk 1:35 the *h* one to be born will be called
1:49 *h* is his name.
4:34 the *H* One of God!" "Be quiet!"
Jn 6:69 and know that you are the *H* One
Ac 2:27 will you let your *H* One see decay.
13:35 will not let your *H* One see decay.'
Ro 1: 2 prophets in the *H* Scriptures
7:12 and the commandment is *h*,
11:16 if the root is *h*, so are the branches.
12: 1 as living sacrifices, *h* and pleasing
1Co 1: 2 in Christ Jesus and called to be *h*,
7:14 be unclean, but as it is, they are *h*.
Eph 1: 4 the creation of the world to be *h*
2:21 and rises to become a *h* temple
3: 5 by the Spirit to God's *h* apostles
5: 3 improper for God's *h* people.
5:26 up for her to make her *h*,
Col 1:22 death to present you *h* in his sight,
1Th 2:10 and so is God, of how *h*,
3:13 and *h* in the presence of our God
3:13 comes with all his *h* ones.
4: 7 us to be impure, but to live a *h* life.
2Th 1:10 to be glorified in his *h* people
1Ti 2: 8 to lift up *h* hands in prayer,
2Ti 1: 9 saved us and called us to a *h* life—
2:21 for noble purposes, made *h*,
3:15 you have known the *h* Scriptures,
Tit 1: 8 upright, *h* and disciplined.
Heb 2:11 Both the one who makes men *h*
7:26 one who is *h*, blameless, pure,
10:10 we have been made *h*
10:14 those who are being made *h*.
10:19 to enter the Most *H* Place
12:14 in peace with all men and to be *h*;
13:12 gate to make the people *h*
1Pe 1:15 But just as he who called you is *h*,
1:16 is written: "Be *h*, because I am *h*."
1Pe 2: 5 house to be a *h* priesthood,
2: 9 a royal priesthood, a *h* nation,
3: 5 For this is the way the *h* women
2Pe 3:11 You ought to live *h* and godly lives
Jude :14 upon thousands of his *h* ones
Rev 3: 7 are the words of him who is *h*
4: 8 "*H, h, h* is the Lord God
15: 4 For you alone are *h*.
20: 6 and *h* are those who have part
22:11 let him who is *h* continue to be *h*."

HOME (HOMES)
Dt 6: 7 Talk about them when you sit at *h*
11:19 about them when you sit at *h*
20: 5 Let him go *h*, or he may die
24: 5 is to be free to stay at *h*
Ru 1:11 "Return *h*, my daughters.
2Sa 7:10 them so that they can have a *h*
1Ch 16:43 and David returned *h* to bless his
Ps 84: 3 Even the sparrow has found a *h*,
113: 9 settles the barren woman in her *h*
Pr 3:33 but he blesses the *h* of the righteous
27: 8 is a man who strays from his *h*.
Ecc 12: 5 Then man goes to his eternal *h*
Eze 36: 8 for they will soon come *h*.
Mic 2: 2 They defraud a man of his *h*,
Mt 1:24 and took Mary *h* as his wife.
Mk 10:29 "no one who has left *h* or brothers
Lk 10:38 named Martha opened her *h*
Jn 14:23 to him and make our *h* with him.
19:27 this disciple took her into his *h*.
Ac 16:15 baptized, she invited us to her *h*.
Tit 2: 5 to be busy at *h*, to be kind,

HOMELESS*
1Co 4:11 we are brutally treated, we are *h*.

HOMES (HOME)
Ne 4:14 daughters, your wives and your *h*."
Isa 32:18 in secure *h*,
Mk 10:30 as much in this present age (*h*,
1Ti 5:14 to manage their *h* and to give

HOMETOWN
Mt 13:57 "Only in his *h*
Lk 4:24 "no prophet is accepted in his *h*.

HOMOSEXUAL*
1Co 6: 9 male prostitutes nor *h* offenders

HONEST (HONESTY)
Lev 19:36 Use *h* scales and *h* weights,
Dt 25:15 and *h* weights and measures,
Job 31: 6 let God weigh me in *h* scales
Pr 12:17 truthful witness gives *h* testimony,

HONESTY (HONEST)
2Ki 12:15 they acted with complete *h*.

HONEY (HONEYCOMB)
Ex 3: 8 a land flowing with milk and *h*—
Jdg 14: 8 a swarm of bees and some *h*,
1Sa 14:26 they saw the *h* oozing out,
Ps 19:10 than *h* from the comb.
119:103 sweeter than *h* to my mouth!
Pr 25:16 If you find *h*, eat just enough—
SS 4:11 milk and *h* are under your tongue.
Isa 7:15 and *h* when he knows enough
Eze 3: 3 it tasted as sweet as *h* in my mouth.
Mt 3: 4 His food was locusts and wild *h*.
Rev 10: 9 mouth it will be as sweet as *h*."

HONEYCOMB (HONEY)
SS 4:11 Your lips drop sweetness as the *h*,
5: 1 I have eaten my *h* and my honey;

HONOR (HONORABLE HONORABLY HONORED HONORS)
Ex 20:12 "*H* your father and your mother,
Nu 20:12 trust in me enough to *h* me
25:13 he was zealous for the *h* of his God
Dt 5:16 "*H* your father and your mother,
Jdg 4: 9 going about this, the *h* will not be
1Sa 2: 8 and has them inherit a throne of *h*.
2:30 Those who *h* me I will *h*,
1Ch 29:12 Wealth and *h* come from you;
2Ch 1:11 or *h*, nor for the death
18: 1 had great wealth and *h*,
Est 6: 6 for the man the king delights to *h*
Ps 8: 5 and crowned him with glory and *h*.
45:11 *h* him, for he is your lord.
84:11 the LORD bestows favor and *h*;
Pr 3: 9 *H* the LORD with your wealth,
3:35 The wise inherit *h*,
15:33 and humility comes before *h*.
Pr 18:12 but humility comes before *h*.
20: 3 It is to a man's *h* to avoid strife,
25:27 is it honorable to seek one's own *h*.
Isa 29:13 and *h* me with their lips,
Jer 33: 9 and *h* before all nations
Mt 13:57 own house is a prophet without *h*."
15: 4 '*H* your father and mother'
15: 8 These people *h* me with their lips,
19:19 *h* your father and mother,'
23: 6 they love the place of *h* at banquets
Mk 6: 4 own house is a prophet without *h*."
Lk 14: 8 do not take the place of *h*,
Jn 5:23 that all may *h* the Son just
7:18 does so to gain *h* for himself,
12:26 My Father will *h* the one who
Ro 12:10 *H* one another above yourselves.
1Co 6:20 Therefore *h* God with your body.
Eph 6: 2 "*H* your father and mother"—
1Ti 5:17 well are worthy of double *h*,
Heb 2: 7 you crowned him with glory and *h*
Rev 4: 9 *h* and thanks to him who sits

HONORABLE (HONOR)
1Th 4: 4 body in a way that is holy and *h*,

HONORABLY (HONOR)
Heb 13:18 and desire to live *h* in every way.

HONORED (HONOR)
Ps 12: 8 when what is vile is *h* among men.
Pr 13:18 but whoever heeds correction is *h*.
Da 4:34 I *h* and glorified him who lives
1Co 12:26 if one part is *h*, every part rejoices
Heb 13: 4 Marriage should be *h* by all,

HONORS (HONOR)
Ps 15: 4 but *h* those who fear the LORD,
Pr 14:31 to the needy *h* God.

HOOF
Ex 10:26 not a *h* is to be left behind.

HOOKS
Isa 2: 4 and their spears into pruning *h*.
Joel 3:10 and your pruning *h* into spears.
Mic 4: 3 and their spears into pruning *h*.

HOPE (HOPES)
Job 13:15 Though he slay me, yet will I *h*
Ps 25: 3 No one whose *h* is in you
33:17 A horse is a vain *h* for deliverance;
33:18 on those whose *h* is
42: 5 Put your *h* in God,
62: 5 my *h* comes from him.
119: 74 for I have put my *h* in your word.
130: 5 and in his word I put my *h*.
130: 7 O Israel, put your *h* in the LORD,
146: 5 whose *h* is in the LORD his God,
147: 11 who put their *h* in his unfailing love.
Pr 13:12 *H* deferred makes the heart sick,
23:18 There is surely a future *h* for you,
Isa 40:31 but those who *h* in the LORD
Jer 29:11 plans to give you *h* and a future.
La 3:21 and therefore I have *h*:
Zec 9:12 to your fortress, O prisoners of *h*;
Ro 5: 4 character; and character, *h*.
8:20 in *h* that the creation itself will be
8:24 But *h* that is seen is no *h* at all.
8:25 if we *h* for what we do not yet have,
12:12 Be joyful in *h*, patient in affliction,
15: 4 of the Scriptures we might have *h*.
15:13 May the God of *h* fill you
1Co 13:13 now these three remain: faith, *h*
15:19 for this life we have *h* in Christ,
Eph 2:12 without *h* and without God
Col 1:27 Christ in you, the *h* of glory.
1Th 1: 3 and your endurance inspired by *h*
5: 8 and the *h* of salvation as a helmet.
1Ti 4:10 that we have put our *h*
6:17 but to put their *h* in God,
Tit 1: 2 resting on the *h* of eternal life,
2:13 while we wait for the blessed *h*—
Heb 6:19 We have this *h* as an anchor
10:23 unswervingly to the *h* we profess,
11: 1 faith is being sure of what we *h* for
1Jn 3: 3 Everyone who has this *h*

HOPES (HOPE)
1Co 13: 7 always *h*, always perseveres.

HORN (HORNS)
Ex 19:13 when the ram's *h* sounds a long
27: 2 Make a *h* at each of the four
Da 7: 8 This *h* had eyes like the eyes

HORNS (HORN)
Da 7:24 ten *h* are ten kings who will come
Rev 5: 6 He had seven *h* and seven eyes,
12: 3 and ten *h* and seven crowns
13: 1 He had ten *h* and seven heads,
17: 3 and had seven heads and ten *h.*

HORRIBLE (HORROR)
Jer 5:30 "A *h* and shocking thing

HORROR (HORRIBLE)
Jer 2:12 and shudder with great *h,*"

HORSE
Ps 147: 10 not in the strength of the *h,*
Pr 26: 3 A whip for the *h,* a halter
Zec 1: 8 before me was a man riding a red *h*
Rev 6: 2 and there before me was a white *h!*
6: 4 Come!" Then another *h* came out,
6: 5 and there before me was a black *h!*
6: 8 and there before me was a pale *h!*
19:11 and there before me was a white *h,*

HOSANNA
Mt 21: 9 *"H* in the highest!"
Mk 11: 9 *"H!"*
Jn 12:13 *"H!"*

HOSEA
Prophet whose wife and family pictured the unfaithfulness of Israel (Hos 1–3).

HOSHEA (JOSHUA)
1. Original name of Joshua (Nu 13:16).
2. Last king of Israel (2Ki 15:30; 17:1–6).

HOSPITABLE* (HOSPITALITY)
1Ti 3: 2 self-controlled, respectable, *h,*
Tit 1: 8 Rather he must be *h,* one who loves

HOSPITABLY* (HOSPITALITY)
Ac 28: 7 and for three days entertained us *h.*

HOSPITALITY* (HOSPITABLE HOSPITABLY)
Ro 12:13 Practice *h.*
16:23 whose *h* I and the whole church
1Ti 5:10 as bringing up children, showing *h,*
1Pe 4: 9 Offer *h* to one another
3Jn : 8 therefore to show *h* to such men

HOSTILE (HOSTILITY)
Ro 8: 7 the sinful mind is *h* to God.

HOSTILITY (HOSTILE)
Eph 2:14 wall of *h,* by abolishing
2:16 by which he put to death their *h.*

HOT
1Ti 4: 2 have been seared as with a *h* iron.
Rev 3:15 that you are neither cold nor *h.*

HOT-TEMPERED (TEMPER)
Pr 15:18 A *h* man stirs up dissension,
19:19 A *h* man must pay the penalty;
22:24 Do not make friends with a *h* man,
29:22 and a *h* one commits many sins.

HOTHEADED (HEAD)
Pr 14:16 but a fool is *h* and reckless.

HOUR
Ecc 9:12 knows when his *h* will come:
Mt 6:27 you by worrying can add a single *h*
Lk 12:40 the Son of Man will come at an *h*
Jn 12:23 The *h* has come for the Son of Man
12:27 for this very reason I came to this *h*

HOUSE (HOUSEHOLD HOUSEHOLDS HOUSES STOREHOUSE)
Ex 12:22 the door of his *h* until morning.
20:17 shall not covet your neighbor's *h.*
Nu 12: 7 he is faithful in all my *h.*
Dt 5:21 desire on your neighbor's *h*
2Sa 7:11 LORD himself will establish a *h*
1Ch 17:23 and his *h* be established forever.
Ne 10:39 "We will not neglect the *h*
Ps 23: 6 I will dwell in the *h* of the LORD
27: 4 dwell in the *h* of the LORD
69: 9 for zeal for your *h* consumes me,
84:10 a doorkeeper in the *h* of my God
122: 1 "Let us go to the *h* of the LORD."
127: 1 Unless the LORD builds the *h,*
Pr 7:27 Her *h* is a highway to the grave,
21: 9 than share a *h* with a quarrelsome
Isa 56: 7 a *h* of prayer for all nations."
Jer 7:11 Has this *h,* which bears my Name,
18: 2 "Go down to the potter's *h,*
Eze 33: 7 made you a watchman for the *h*
Joel 3:18 will flow out of the LORD's *h*
Zec 13: 6 given at the *h* of my friends.'
Mt 7:24 is like a wise man who built his *h*
10:11 and stay at his *h* until you leave.
12:29 can anyone enter a strong man's *h*
21:13 My *h* will be called a *h* of prayer,'
Mk 3:25 If a *h* is divided against itself,
11:17 "'My *h* will be called
Lk 6:48 He is like a man building a *h,*
10: 7 Do not move around from *h* to *h.*
11:17 a *h* divided against itself will fall.
11:24 'I will return to the *h* I left.'
15: 8 sweep the *h* and search carefully
19: 9 Today salvation has come to this *h,*
Jn 2:16 How dare you turn my Father's *h*
2:17 "Zeal for your *h* will consume me."
12: 3 the *h* was filled with the fragrance
14: 2 In my Father's *h* are many rooms;
Ac 20:20 you publicly and from *h* to *h.*
Ro 16: 5 the church that meets at their *h.*
Heb 3: 3 the builder of a *h* has greater honor
1Pe 2: 5 built into a spiritual *h* to be a holy

HOUSEHOLD (HOUSE)
Ex 12: 3 lamb for his family, one for each *h.*
Jos 24:15 my *h,* we will serve the LORD."
Pr 31:21 it snows, she has no fear for her *h;*
31:27 over the affairs of her *h*
Mic 7: 6 are the members of his own *h.*
Mt 10:36 will be the members of his own *h.'*
12:25 or *h* divided against itself will not
Ac 16:31 you will be saved—you and your *h*
Eph 2:19 people and members of God's *h,*
1Ti 3:12 manage his children and his *h* well.
3:15 to conduct themselves in God's *h,*

HOUSEHOLDS (HOUSE)
Tit 1:11 because they are ruining whole *h*

HOUSES (HOUSE)
Ex 12:27 passed over the *h* of the Israelites
Mt 19:29 everyone who has left *h* or brothers

HOVERING* (HOVERS)
Ge 1: 2 of God was *h* over the waters.
Isa 31: 5 Like birds *h* overhead,

HOVERS* (HOVERING)
Dt 32:11 and *h* over its young,

HULDAH*
Prophetess inquired by Hilkiah for Josiah (2Ki 22; 2Ch 34:14–28).

HUMAN (HUMANITY)
Lev 24:17 If anyone takes the life of a *h* being,
Isa 52:14 his form marred beyond *h* likeness
Jn 8:15 You judge by *h* standards;
Ro 1: 3 as to his *h* nature was a descendant
9: 5 from them is traced the *h* ancestry
1Co 1:17 not with words of *h* wisdom,
1:26 of you were wise by *h* standards;
2:13 not in words taught us by *h* wisdom
2Co 3: 3 of stone but on tablets of *h* hearts.
Gal 3: 3 to attain your goal by *h* effort?
2Pe 2:18 lustful desires of sinful *h* nature,

HUMANITY* (HUMAN)
Heb 2:14 he too shared in their *h* so that

HUMBLE (HUMBLED HUMBLES HUMILIATE HUMILIATED HUMILITY)
Nu 12: 3 (Now Moses was a very *h* man,
2Ch 7:14 will *h* themselves and pray
Ps 18:27 You save the *h*
25: 9 He guides the *h* in what is right
149: 4 he crowns the *h* with salvation.
Pr 3:34 but gives grace to the *h.*
Isa 66: 2 he who is *h* and contrite in spirit,
Mt 11:29 for I am gentle and *h* in heart,
Eph 4: 2 Be completely *h* and gentle;
Jas 4: 6 but gives grace to the *h."*
4:10 *H* yourselves before the Lord,
1Pe 5: 5 but gives grace to the *h."*
5: 6 *H* yourselves,

HUMBLED (HUMBLE)
Mt 23:12 whoever exalts himself will be *h,*
Lk 14:11 who exalts himself will be *h,*
Php 2: 8 he *h* himself

HUMBLES* (HUMBLE)
1Sa 2: 7 he *h* and he exalts.
Isa 26: 5 He *h* those who dwell on high,
Mt 18: 4 whoever *h* himself like this child is
23:12 whoever *h* himself will be exalted.
Lk 14:11 he who *h* himself will be exalted."
18:14 he who *h* himself will be exalted."

HUMILIATE* (HUMBLE)
Pr 25: 7 than for him to *h* you
1Co 11:22 and *h* those who have nothing?

HUMILIATED (HUMBLE)
Jer 31:19 I was ashamed and *h*
Lk 14: 9 *h,* you will have to take the least

HUMILITY* (HUMBLE)
Ps 45: 4 of truth, *h* and righteousness;
Pr 11: 2 but with *h* comes wisdom.
15:33 and *h* comes before honor.
18:12 but *h* comes before honor.
22: 4 *H* and the fear of the LORD
Zep 2: 3 Seek righteousness, seek *h;*
Ac 20:19 I served the Lord with great *h*
Php 2: 3 but in *h* consider others better
Col 2:18 let anyone who delights in false *h*
2:23 their false *h* and their harsh
3:12 *h,* gentleness and patience.
Tit 3: 2 and to show true *h* toward all men.
Jas 3:13 in the *h* that comes from wisdom.
1Pe 5: 5 clothe yourselves with *h*

HUNG (HANG)
Dt 21:23 anyone who is *h* on a tree is
Mt 18: 6 him to have a large millstone *h*
Lk 19:48 all the people *h* on his words.
Gal 3:13 "Cursed is everyone who is *h*

HUNGER (HUNGRY)
Ne 9:15 In their *h* you gave them bread
Pr 6:30 to satisfy his *h* when he is starving.
Mt 5: 6 Blessed are those who *h*
Lk 6:21 Blessed are you who *h* now,
2Co 6: 5 sleepless nights and *h;* in purity,
11:27 I have known *h* and thirst
Rev 7:16 Never again will they *h;*

HUNGRY (HUNGER)
Job 24:10 carry the sheaves, but still go *h.*
Ps 107: 9 and fills the *h* with good things.
146: 7 and gives food to the *h.*
Pr 19:15 and the shiftless man goes *h.*
25:21 If your enemy is *h,* give him food
27: 7 to the *h* even what is bitter tastes
Isa 58: 7 not to share your food with the *h*
58:10 spend yourselves in behalf of the *h*
Eze 18: 7 but gives his food to the *h*
18:16 but gives his food to the *h*
Mt 15:32 I do not want to send them away *h,*
25:35 For I was *h* and you gave me
25:42 For I was *h* and you gave me
Lk 1:53 He has filled the *h* with good things
Jn 6:35 comes to me will never go *h,*
Ro 12:20 "If your enemy is *h,* feed him;
1Co 4:11 To this very hour we go *h*
Php 4:12 whether well fed or *h,*

HUR
Ex 17:12 Aaron and *H* held his hands up—

HURL
Mic 7:19 *h* all our iniquities into the depths

HURT (HURTS)
Ecc 8: 9 it over others to his own *h.*
Mk 16:18 deadly poison, it will not *h* them
Rev 2:11 He who overcomes will not be *h*

HURTS* (HURT)
Ps 15: 4 even when it *h,*
Pr 26:28 A lying tongue hates those it *h,*

HUSBAND (HUSBAND'S HUSBANDS)
Pr 31:11 Her *h* has full confidence in her
31:23 Her *h* is respected at the city gate,
31:28 her *h* also, and he praises her:
Isa 54: 5 For your Maker is your *h*—
Jer 3:14 the LORD, "for I am your *h.*
3:20 like a woman unfaithful to her *h,*
Jn 4:17 "I have no *h,"* she replied.
Ro 7: 2 a married woman is bound to her *h*
1Co 7: 2 and each woman her own *h.*
7: 3 The *h* should fulfill his marital duty
7:10 wife must not separate from her *h.*
7:11 And a *h* must not divorce his wife.
7:13 And if a woman has a *h* who is not
7:14 For the unbelieving *h* has been
7:39 A woman is bound to her *h* as long

1Co 7:39 But if her *h* dies, she is free
2Co 11: 2 I promised you to one *h,* to Christ,
Gal 4:27 woman than of her who has a *h."*
Eph 5:23 For the *h* is the head of the wife
5:33 and the wife must respect her *h.*
1Ti 3: 2 the *h* of but one wife, temperate,
3:12 A deacon must be the *h* of
5: 9 has been faithful to her *h,*
Tit 1: 6 An elder must be blameless, the *h*

HUSBANDMAN see GARDENER

HUSBAND'S (HUSBAND)
Dt 25: 5 Her *h* brother shall take her
Pr 12: 4 of noble character is her *h* crown,
1Co 7: 4 the *h* body does not belong

HUSBANDS (HUSBAND)
Eph 5:22 submit to your *h* as to the Lord.
5:25 *H,* love your wives, just
5:28 *h* ought to love their wives
Col 3:18 submit to your *h,* as is fitting
3:19 *H,* love your wives and do not be
Tit 2: 4 the younger women to love their *h*
2: 5 and to be subject to their *h,*
1Pe 3: 1 same way be submissive to your *h*
3: 7 *H,* in the same way be considerate

HUSHAI
Wise man of David who frustrated Ahithophel's advice and foiled Absalom's revolt (2Sa 15:32–37; 16:15–17:16; 1Ch 27:33).

HYMN* (HYMNS)
Ps 40: 3 a *h* of praise to our God.
Mt 26:30 they had sung a *h,* they went out
Mk 14:26 they had sung a *h,* they went out
1Co 14:26 everyone has a *h,* or a word

HYMNS* (HYMN)
Ac 16:25 Silas were praying and singing *h*
Ro 15: 9 I will sing *h* to your name."
Eph 5:19 to one another with psalms, *h*
Col 3:16 *h* and spiritual songs with gratitude

HYPOCRISY* (HYPOCRITE HYPOCRITES HYPOCRITICAL)
Mt 23:28 but on the inside you are full of *h*
Mk 12:15 we?" But Jesus knew their *h.*
Lk 12: 1 yeast of the Pharisees, which is *h.*
Gal 2:13 The other Jews joined him in his *h,*
2:13 by their *h* even Barnabas was led
1Pe 2: 1 *h,* envy, and slander of every kind.

HYPOCRITE* (HYPOCRISY)
Mt 7: 5 You *h,* first take the plank out
Lk 6:42 You *h,* first take the plank out

HYPOCRITES* (HYPOCRISY)
Ps 26: 4 nor do I consort with *h;*
Mt 6: 2 as the *h* do in the synagogues
6: 5 when you pray, do not be like the *h*
6:16 do not look somber as the *h* do,
15: 7 You *h!* Isaiah was right
22:18 their evil intent, said, "You *h,*
23:13 of the law and Pharisees, you *h!*
23:15 of the law and Pharisees, you *h!*
23:23 of the law and Pharisees, you *h!*
23:25 of the law and Pharisees, you *h!*
23:27 you *h!* You are like whitewashed
23:29 of the law and Pharisees, you *h!*
24:51 and assign him a place with the *h,*
Mk 7: 6 when he prophesied about you *h;*
Lk 12:56 *H!* You know how
13:15 The Lord answered him, "You *h!*

HYPOCRITICAL* (HYPOCRISY)
1Ti 4: 2 teachings come through *h* liars,

HYSSOP
Ex 12:22 Take a bunch of *h,* dip it
Ps 51: 7 with *h,* and I will be clean;
Jn 19:29 the sponge on a stalk of the *h* plant,

ICHABOD
1Sa 4:21 She named the boy *I,* saying,

IDLE* (IDLENESS IDLERS)
Dt 32:47 They are not just *i* words for you—
Job 11: 3 Will your *i* talk reduce men
Ecc 10:18 if his hands are *i,* the house leaks.
11: 6 at evening let not your hands be *i,*
Isa 58:13 as you please or speaking *i* words,
Col 2:18 mind puffs him up with *i* notions.
1Th 5:14 those who are *i,* encourage
2Th 3: 6 away from every brother who is *i*
2Th 3: 7 We were not *i* when we were
3:11 We hear that some among you are *i*
1Ti 5:13 they get into the habit of being *i*

IDLENESS* (IDLE)
Pr 31:27 and does not eat the bread of *i.*

IDLERS* (IDLE)
1Ti 5:13 And not only do they become *i,*

IDOL (IDOLATER IDOLATERS IDOLATRY IDOLS)
Ex 20: 4 make for yourself an *i* in the form
32: 4 made it into an *i* cast in the shape
Isa 40:19 As for an *i,* a craftsman casts it,
41: 7 He nails down the *i*
44:15 he makes an *i* and bows down to it.
44:17 From the rest he makes a god, his *i;*
Hab 2:18 "Of what value is an *i,*
1Co 8: 4 We know that an *i* is nothing at all

IDOLATER* (IDOL)
1Co 5:11 an *i* or a slanderer, a drunkard
Eph 5: 5 greedy person—such a man is an *i*

IDOLATERS (IDOL)
1Co 5:10 or the greedy and swindlers, or *i.*
6: 9 Neither the sexually immoral nor *i*

IDOLATRY (IDOL)
1Sa 15:23 and arrogance like the evil of *i.*
1Co 10:14 my dear friends, flee from *i.*
Gal 5:20 and debauchery; *i* and witchcraft;
Col 3: 5 evil desires and greed, which is *i.*
1Pe 4: 3 orgies, carousing and detestable *i.*

IDOLS (IDOL)
Dt 32:16 angered him with their detestable *i.*
Ps 78:58 aroused his jealousy with their *i.*
Isa 44: 9 All who make *i* are nothing,
Eze 23:39 sacrificed their children to their *i,*
Ac 15:20 to abstain from food polluted by *i,*
21:25 abstain from food sacrificed to *i,*
1Co 8: 1 Now about food sacrificed to *i:*
1Jn 5:21 children, keep yourselves from *i.*
Rev 2:14 to sin by eating food sacrificed to *i*

IGNORANT (IGNORE)
1Co 15:34 for there are some who are *i* of God
Heb 5: 2 to deal gently with those who are *i*
1Pe 2:15 good you should silence the *i* talk
2Pe 3:16 which *i* and unstable people distort

IGNORE (IGNORANT IGNORED IGNORES)
Dt 22: 1 do not *i* it but be sure
Ps 9:12 he does not *i* the cry of the afflicted
Heb 2: 3 if we *i* such a great salvation?

IGNORED (IGNORE)
Hos 4: 6 you have *i* the law of your God,
1Co 14:38 he ignores this, he himself will be *i.*

IGNORES* (IGNORE)
Pr 10:17 whoever *i* correction leads others
13:18 He who *i* discipline comes
15:32 He who *i* discipline despises
1Co 14:38 If he *i* this, he himself will be

ILL (ILLNESS)
Mt 4:24 brought to him all who were *i*

ILL-GOTTEN
Pr 1:19 the end of all who go after *i* gain;
10: 2 *I* treasures are of no value,

ILL-TEMPERED* (TEMPER)
Pr 21:19 than with a quarrelsome and *i* wife.

ILLEGITIMATE
Heb 12: 8 then you are *i* children

ILLNESS (ILL)
2Ki 8: 9 'Will I recover from this *i?'* "
2Ch 16:12 even in his *i* he did not seek help
Ps 41: 3 and restore him from his bed of *i.*
Isa 38: 9 king of Judah after his *i*

ILLUMINATED*
Rev 18: 1 and the earth was *i* by his splendor.

IMAGE (IMAGES)
Ge 1:26 "Let us make man in our *i,*
1:27 So God created man in his own *i,*
9: 6 for in the *i* of God
Dt 27:15 "Cursed is the man who carves an *i*
Isa 40:18 What *i* will you compare him to?
Da 3: 1 King Nebuchadnezzar made an *i*
1Co 11: 7 since he is the *i* and glory of God;
2Co 4: 4 glory of Christ, who is the *i* of God.
Col 1:15 He is the *i* of the invisible God,
3:10 in knowledge in the *i* of its Creator.
Rev 13:14 them to set up an *i* in honor

IMAGES (IMAGE)
Ps 97: 7 All who worship *i* are put to shame,
Jer 10:14 His *i* are a fraud;
Ro 1:23 of the immortal God for *i* made

IMAGINATION (IMAGINE)
Eze 13: 2 who prophesy out of their own *i:*

IMAGINE (IMAGINATION)
Eph 3:20 more than all we ask or *i,*

IMITATE (IMITATORS)
1Co 4:16 Therefore I urge you to *i* me.
Heb 6:12 but to *i* those who through faith
13: 7 of their way of life and *i* their faith.
3Jn :11 do not *i* what is evil but what is

IMITATORS* (IMITATE)
Eph 5: 1 Be *i* of God, therefore,
1Th 1: 6 You became *i* of us and of the Lord
2:14 became *i* of God's churches

IMMANUEL*
Isa 7:14 birth to a son, and will call him *I.*
8: 8 O *I!"*
Mt 1:23 and they will call him *I"*—

IMMORAL* (IMMORALITY)
Pr 6:24 keeping you from the *i* woman,
1Co 5: 9 to associate with sexually *i* people
5:10 the people of this world who are *i,*
5:11 but is sexually *i* or greedy,
6: 9 Neither the sexually *i* nor idolaters
Eph 5: 5 No *i,* impure or greedy person—
Heb 12:16 See that no one is sexually *i,*
13: 4 the adulterer and all the sexually *i.*
Rev 21: 8 the murderers, the sexually *i,*
22:15 the sexually *i,* the murderers,

IMMORALITY* (IMMORAL)
Nu 25: 1 in sexual *i* with Moabite women,
Jer 3: 9 Because Israel's *i* mattered so little
Mt 15:19 murder, adultery, sexual *i,* theft,
Mk 7:21 sexual *i,* theft, murder, adultery,
Ac 15:20 from sexual *i,* from the meat
15:29 animals and from sexual *i.*
21:25 animals and from sexual *i."*
Ro 13:13 not in sexual *i* and debauchery,
1Co 5: 1 reported that there is sexual *i*
6:13 The body is not meant for sexual *i,*
6:18 Flee from sexual *i.*
7: 2 But since there is so much *i,*
10: 8 We should not commit sexual *i,*
Gal 5:19 sexual *i,* impurity and debauchery;
Eph 5: 3 must not be even a hint of sexual *i,*
Col 3: 5 sexual *i,* impurity, lust, evil desires
1Th 4: 3 that you should avoid sexual *i;*
Jude : 4 grace of our God into a license for *i*
: 7 gave themselves up to sexual *i*
Rev 2:14 and by committing sexual *i.*
2:20 misleads my servants into sexual *i*
2:21 given her time to repent of her *i,*
9:21 their sexual *i* or their thefts.

IMMORTAL* (IMMORTALITY)
Ro 1:23 glory of the *i* God for images made
1Ti 1:17 Now to the King eternal, *i,*
6:16 who alone is *i* and who lives

IMMORTALITY* (IMMORTAL)
Pr 12:28 along that path is *i.*
Ro 2: 7 honor and *i,* he will give eternal life
1Co 15:53 and the mortal with *i.*
15:54 with *i,* then the saying that is
2Ti 1:10 and *i* to light through the gospel.

IMPARTIAL*
Jas 3:17 and good fruit, *i* and sincere.

IMPARTS*
Pr 29:15 The rod of correction *i* wisdom,

IMPERFECT*
1Co 13:10 perfection comes, the *i* disappears.

IMPERISHABLE
1Co 15:42 it is raised *i;* it is sown in dishonor,
15:50 nor does the perishable inherit the *i*
1Pe 1:23 not of perishable seed, but of *i,*

IMPLANTED*
Ps 94: 9 Does he who *i* the ear not hear?

IMPLORE*
Mal 1: 9 "Now *i* God to be gracious to us.
2Co 5:20 We *i* you on Christ's behalf:

IMPORTANCE* (IMPORTANT)
1Co 15: 3 passed on to you as of first *i*:

IMPORTANT (IMPORTANCE)
Mt 6:25 Is not life more *i* than food,
23:23 have neglected the more *i* matters
Mk 12:29 "The most *i* one," answered Jesus,
12:33 as yourself is more *i* than all burnt
Php 1:18 The *i* thing is that in every way,

IMPOSSIBLE
Mt 17:20 Nothing will be *i* for you."
19:26 "With man this is *i*,
Mk 10:27 "With man this is *i*, but not
Lk 1:37 For nothing is *i* with God."
18:27 "What is *i* with men is possible
Ac 2:24 it was *i* for death to keep its hold
Heb 6: 4 It is *i* for those who have once been
6:18 things in which it is *i* for God to lie,
10: 4 because it is *i* for the blood of bulls
11: 6 without faith it is *i* to please God,

IMPOSTORS
2Ti 3:13 and *i* will go from bad to worse,

IMPRESS* (IMPRESSES)
Dt 6: 7 *I* them on your children.

IMPRESSES* (IMPRESS)
Pr 17:10 A rebuke *i* a man of discernment

IMPROPER*
Eph 5: 3 these are *i* for God's holy people.

IMPURE (IMPURITY)
Ac 10:15 not call anything *i* that God has
Eph 5: 5 No immoral, *i* or greedy person—
1Th 2: 3 spring from error or *i* motives,
4: 7 For God did not call us to be *i*,
Rev 21:27 Nothing *i* will ever enter it,

IMPURITY (IMPURE)
Ro 1:24 hearts to sexual *i* for the degrading
Gal 5:19 sexual immorality, *i*
Eph 4:19 as to indulge in every kind of *i*,
5: 3 or of any kind of *i*, or of greed,
Col 3: 5 *i*, lust, evil desires and greed,

INCENSE
Ex 30: 1 altar of acacia wood for burning *i*.
40: 5 Place the gold altar of *i* in front
Ps 141: 2 my prayer be set before you like *i*;
Mt 2:11 him with gifts of gold and of *i*
Heb 9: 4 which had the golden altar of *i*
Rev 5: 8 were holding golden bowls full of *i*,
8: 4 The smoke of the *i*, together

INCLINATION (INCLINES)
Ge 6: 5 and that every *i* of the thoughts

INCLINES* (INCLINATION)
Ecc 10: 2 The heart of the wise *i* to the right,

INCOME
Ecc 5:10 wealth is never satisfied with his *i*.
1Co 16: 2 sum of money in keeping with his *i*,

INCOMPARABLE*
Eph 2: 7 ages he might show the *i* riches

INCREASE (EVER-INCREASING INCREASED INCREASES INCREASING)
Ge 1:22 "Be fruitful and *i* in number
3:16 "I will greatly *i* your pains
8:17 be fruitful and *i* in number upon it
Ps 62:10 though your riches *i*,
Pr 22:16 oppresses the poor to *i* his wealth
Isa 9: 7 Of the *i* of his government
Mt 24:12 Because of the *i* of wickedness,
Lk 17: 5 said to the Lord, "*I* our faith!"
Ac 12:24 But the word of God continued to *i*
Ro 5:20 added so that the trespass might *i*.
1Th 3:12 May the Lord make your love *i*

INCREASED (INCREASE)
Ac 6: 7 of disciples in Jerusalem *i* rapidly,
Ro 5:20 But where sin *i*, grace *i* all the more

INCREASES (INCREASE)
Pr 24: 5 and a man of knowledge *i* strength;

INCREASING (INCREASE)
Ac 6: 1 when the number of disciples was *i*,
2Th 1: 3 one of you has for each other is *i*.

2Pe 1: 8 these qualities in *i* measure,

INCREDIBLE*
Ac 26: 8 of you consider it *i* that God raises

INDECENT
Ro 1:27 Men committed *i* acts

INDEPENDENT*
1Co 11:11 however, woman is not *i* of man,
11:11 of man, nor is man *i* of woman.

INDESCRIBABLE*
2Co 9:15 Thanks be to God for his *i* gift!

INDESTRUCTIBLE*
Heb 7:16 on the basis of the power of an *i* life

INDIGNANT
Mk 10:14 When Jesus saw this, he was *i*.

INDISPENSABLE*
1Co 12:22 seem to be weaker are *i*,

INEFFECTIVE*
2Pe 1: 8 they will keep you from being *i*

INEXPRESSIBLE*
2Co 12: 4 He heard *i* things, things that man
1Pe 1: 8 are filled with an *i* and glorious joy,

INFANCY* (INFANTS)
2Ti 3:15 from *i* you have known the holy

INFANTS (INFANCY)
Ps 8: 2 From the lips of children and *i*
Mt 21:16 " 'From the lips of children and *i*
1Co 3: 1 but as worldly—mere *i* in Christ.
14:20 In regard to evil be *i*,
Eph 4:14 Then we will no longer be *i*,

INFIRMITIES*
Isa 53: 4 Surely he took up our *i*
Mt 8:17 "He took up our *i*

INFLAMED
Ro 1:27 were *i* with lust for one another.

INFLUENTIAL*
1Co 1:26 not many were *i*; not many were

INHABITANTS (INHABITED)
Nu 33:55 " 'But if you do not drive out the *i*
Rev 8:13 Woe! Woe to the *i* of the earth,

INHABITED (INHABITANTS)
Isa 45:18 but formed it to be *i*—

INHERIT (CO-HEIRS HEIR HEIRS HERITAGE INHERITANCE)
Dt 1:38 because he will lead Israel to *i* it.
Jos 1: 6 people to *i* the land I swore
Ps 37:11 But the meek will *i* the land
37:29 the righteous will *i* the land
Zec 2:12 The LORD will *i* Judah
Mt 5: 5 for they will *i* the earth.
19:29 as much and will *i* eternal life.
Mk 10:17 "what must I do to *i* eternal life?"
Lk 10:25 "what must I do to *i* eternal life?"
18:18 what must I do to *i* eternal life?"
1Co 6: 9 the wicked will not *i* the kingdom
15:50 blood cannot *i* the kingdom of God
Rev 21: 7 He who overcomes will *i* all this,

INHERITANCE (INHERIT)
Lev 20:24 I will give it to you as an *i*,
Dt 4:20 to be the people of his *i*,
10: 9 the LORD is their *i*, as the LORD
Jos 14: 3 two-and-a-half tribes their *i* east
Ps 16: 6 surely I have a delightful *i*.
33:12 the people he chose for his *i*.
136: 21 and gave their land as an *i*,
Pr 13:22 A good man leaves an *i*
Mt 25:34 blessed by my Father; take your *i*,
Eph 1:14 who is a deposit guaranteeing our *i*
5: 5 has any *i* in the kingdom of Christ
Col 1:12 you to share in the *i* of the saints
3:24 you know that you will receive an *i*
Heb 9:15 receive the promised eternal *i*—
1Pe 1: 4 and into an *i* that can never perish,

INIQUITIES (INIQUITY)
Ps 78:38 he forgave their *i*
103: 10 or repay us according to our *i*.
Isa 53: 5 he was crushed for our *i*;
53:11 and he will bear their *i*.
59: 2 But your *i* have separated
Mic 7:19 and hurl all our *i* into the depths

INIQUITY (INIQUITIES)
Ps 25:11 forgive my *i*, though it is great.
32: 5 and did not cover up my *i*.
51: 2 Wash away all my *i*
51: 9 and blot out all my *i*.
Isa 53: 6 the *i* of us all.

INJURED
Eze 34:16 will bind up the *i* and strengthen
Zec 11:16 or heal the *i*, or feed the healthy,

INJUSTICE
2Ch 19: 7 the LORD our God there is no *i*

INK
2Co 3: 3 not with *i* but with the Spirit

INN*
Lk 2: 7 there was no room for them in the *i*
10:34 took him to an *i* and took care

INNOCENT
Ex 23: 7 do not put an *i* or honest person
Dt 25: 1 acquitting the *i* and condemning
Pr 6:17 hands that shed *i* blood,
17:26 It is not good to punish an *i* man,
Mt 10:16 shrewd as snakes and as *i* as doves.
27: 4 "for I have betrayed *i* blood."
27:24 I am *i* of this man's blood," he said.
Ac 20:26 declare to you today that I am *i*
Ro 16:19 what is good, and *i* about what is
1Co 4: 4 but that does not make me *i*.

INQUIRE
Isa 8:19 should not a people *i* of their God?

INSCRIPTION
Mt 22:20 And whose *i*?" "Caesar's,"
2Ti 2:19 with this *i*: "The Lord knows those

INSIGHT
1Ki 4:29 Solomon wisdom and very great *i*,
Ps 119: 99 I have more *i* than all my teachers,
Pr 5: 1 listen well to my words of *i*,
21:30 There is no wisdom, no *i*, no plan
Php 1: 9 more in knowledge and depth of *i*,
2Ti 2: 7 for the Lord will give you *i*

INSOLENT
Ro 1:30 God-haters, *i*, arrogant

INSPIRED*
Hos 9: 7 the *i* man a maniac.
1Th 1: 3 and your endurance *i* by hope

INSTALLED
Ps 2: 6 "I have *i* my King

INSTINCT* (INSTINCTS)
2Pe 2:12 are like brute beasts, creatures of *i*,
Jude :10 things they do understand by *i*,

INSTINCTS* (INSTINCT)
Jude :19 who follow mere natural *i*

INSTITUTED
Ro 13: 2 rebelling against what God has *i*,
1Pe 2:13 to every authority *i* among men:

INSTRUCT (INSTRUCTED INSTRUCTION INSTRUCTIONS INSTRUCTOR)
Ps 32: 8 I will *i* you and teach you
105: 22 to *i* his princes as he pleased
Pr 9: 9 *I* a wise man and he will be wiser
Ro 15:14 and competent to *i* one another.
1Co 2:16 that he may *i* him?"
14:19 to *i* others than ten thousand words
2Ti 2:25 who oppose him he must gently *i*,

INSTRUCTED (INSTRUCT)
2Ch 26: 5 who *i* him in the fear of God.
Pr 21:11 a wise man is *i*, he gets knowledge.
Isa 50: 4 LORD has given me an *i* tongue,
Mt 13:52 who has been *i* about the kingdom
1Co 14:31 in turn so that everyone may be *i*

INSTRUCTION (INSTRUCT)
Pr 1: 8 Listen, my son, to your father's *i*
4: 1 Listen, my sons, to a father's *i*;
4:13 Hold on to *i*, do not let it go;
8:10 Choose my *i* instead of silver,
8:33 Listen to my *i* and be wise;
13: 1 A wise son heeds his father's *i*,
13:13 He who scorns *i* will pay for it,
16:20 Whoever gives heed to *i* prospers,
16:21 and pleasant words promote *i*.
19:20 Listen to advice and accept *i*,
23:12 Apply your heart to *i*

1Co 14: 6 or prophecy or word of *i?*
14:26 or a word of *i*, a revelation,
Eph 6: 4 up in the training and *i* of the Lord.
1Th 4: 8 he who rejects this *i* does not reject
2Th 3:14 If anyone does not obey our *i*
1Ti 1:18 I give you this *i* in keeping
6: 3 to the sound *i* of our Lord Jesus
2Ti 4: 2 with great patience and careful *i.*

INSTRUCTIONS (INSTRUCT)
1Ti 3:14 I am writing you these *i* so that,

INSTRUCTOR (INSTRUCT)
Gal 6: 6 share all good things with his *i.*

INSTRUMENT* (INSTRUMENTS)
Eze 33:32 beautiful voice and plays an *i* well,
Ac 9:15 This man is my chosen *i*
2Ti 2:21 he will be an *i* for noble purposes,

INSTRUMENTS (INSTRUMENT)
Ro 6:13 as *i* of wickedness, but rather offer

INSULT (INSULTED INSULTS)
Pr 9: 7 corrects a mocker invites *i;*
12:16 but a prudent man overlooks an *i.*
Mt 5:11 Blessed are you when people *i* you,
Lk 6:22 when they exclude you and *i* you
1Pe 3: 9 evil with evil or *i* with *i,*

INSULTED (INSULT)
Heb 10:29 and who has *i* the Spirit of grace?
Jas 2: 6 love him? But you have *i* the poor.
1Pe 4:14 If you are *i* because of the name

INSULTS (INSULT)
Ps 22: 7 they hurl *i,* shaking their heads:
69: 9 the *i* of those who insult you fall
Pr 22:10 quarrels and *i* are ended.
Mk 15:29 passed by hurled *i* at him,
Jn 9:28 Then they hurled *i* at him and said,
Ro 15: 3 "The *i* of those who insult you have
2Co 12:10 in *i,* in hardships, in persecutions,
1Pe 2:23 When they hurled their *i* at him,

INTEGRITY*
Dt 9: 5 or your *i* that you are going
1Ki 9: 4 if you walk before me in *i* of heart
1Ch 29:17 the heart and are pleased with *i.*
Ne 7: 2 because he was a man of *i*
Job 2: 3 And he still maintains his *i,*
2: 9 "Are you still holding on to your *i?*
6:29 reconsider, for my *i* is at stake.
27: 5 till I die, I will not deny my *i.*
Ps 7: 8 according to my *i,* O Most High.
25:21 May *i* and uprightness protect me,
41:12 In my *i* you uphold me
78:72 David shepherded them with *i*
Pr 10: 9 The man of *i* walks securely,
11: 3 The *i* of the upright guides them,
13: 6 Righteousness guards the man of *i,*
17:26 or to flog officials for their *i.*
29:10 Bloodthirsty men hate a man of *i*
Isa 45:23 my mouth has uttered in all *i*
59: 4 no one pleads his case with *i.*
Mt 22:16 "we know you are a man of *i*
Mk 12:14 we know you are a man of *i.*
Tit 2: 7 your teaching show *i,* seriousness

INTELLIGENCE (INTELLIGENT)
Isa 29:14 the *i* of the intelligent will vanish."
1Co 1:19 *i* of the intelligent I will frustrate."

INTELLIGENT (INTELLIGENCE)
Isa 29:14 the intelligence of the *i* will vanish

INTELLIGIBLE
1Co 14:19 I would rather speak five *i* words

INTENDED
Ge 50:20 place of God? You *i* to harm me,

INTENSE
1Th 2:17 out of our *i* longing we made every
Rev 16: 9 They were seared by the *i* heat

INTERCEDE (INTERCEDES INTERCEDING INTERCESSION INTERCESSOR)
Heb 7:25 he always lives to *i* for them.

INTERCEDES* (INTERCEDE)
Ro 8:26 but the Spirit himself *i* for us
8:27 because the Spirit *i* for the saints

INTERCEDING* (INTERCEDE)
Ro 8:34 hand of God and is also *i* for us.

INTERCESSION* (INTERCEDE)
Isa 53:12 and made *i* for the transgressors.
1Ti 2: 1 *i* and thanksgiving be made

INTERCESSOR* (INTERCEDE)
Job 16:20 My *i* is my friend

INTEREST (INTERESTS)
Lev 25:36 Do not take *i* of any kind from him,
Dt 23:20 You may charge a foreigner *i,*
Mt 25:27 would have received it back with *i.*
Php 2:20 who takes a genuine *i*

INTERESTS (INTEREST)
1Co 7:34 his wife—and his *i* are divided.
Php 2: 4 only to your own *i,* but also to the *i*
2:21 everyone looks out for his own *i,*

INTERFERE*
Ezr 6: 7 Do not *i* with the work

INTERMARRY (MARRY)
Dt 7: 3 Do not *i* with them.
Ezr 9:14 and *i* with the peoples who commit

INTERPRET (INTERPRETATION INTERPRETER INTERPRETS)
Ge 41:15 "I had a dream, and no one can *i* it.
Mt 16: 3 you cannot *i* the signs of the times.
1Co 12:30 Do all *i?* But eagerly desire
14:13 pray that he may *i* what he says.
14:27 one at a time, and someone must *i.*

INTERPRETATION (INTERPRET)
1Co 12:10 and to still another the *i* of tongues.
14:26 a revelation, a tongue or an *i.*
2Pe 1:20 about by the prophet's own *i.*

INTERPRETER (INTERPRET)
1Co 14:28 If there is no *i,* the speaker should

INTERPRETS (INTERPRET)
1Co 14: 5 he *i,* so that the church may be

INVADED
2Ki 17: 5 king of Assyria *i* the entire land,
24: 1 king of Babylon *i* the land,

INVENT* (INVENTED)
Ro 1:30 boastful; they *i* ways of doing evil;

INVENTED* (INVENT)
2Pe 1:16 We did not follow cleverly *i* stories

INVESTIGATED
Lk 1: 3 I myself have carefully *i* everything

INVISIBLE*
Ro 1:20 of the world God's *i* qualities—
Col 1:15 He is the image of the *i* God,
1:16 and on earth, visible and *i,*
1Ti 1:17 immortal, *i,* the only God,
Heb 11:27 because he saw him who is *i.*

INVITE (INVITED INVITES)
Mt 22: 9 *i* to the banquet anyone you find.'
25:38 did we see you a stranger and *i* you
Lk 14:12 do not *i* your friends, your brothers
14:13 you give a banquet, *i* the poor,

INVITED (INVITE)
Zep 1: 7 he has consecrated those he has *i.*
Mt 22:14 For many are *i,* but few are chosen
25:35 I was a stranger and you *i* me in,
Lk 14:10 But when you are *i,* take the lowest
Rev 19: 9 'Blessed are those who are *i*

INVITES (INVITE)
Pr 18: 6 and his mouth *i* a beating.
1Co 10:27 If some unbeliever *i* you to a meal

INVOLVED
2Ti 2: 4 a soldier gets *i* in civilian affairs—

IRON
2Ki 6: 6 threw it there, and made the *i* float.
Ps 2: 9 will rule them with an *i* scepter;
Pr 27:17 As *i* sharpens *i,*
Da 2:33 and thighs of bronze, its legs of *i,*
1Ti 4: 2 have been seared as with a hot *i.*
Rev 2:27 He will rule them with an *i* scepter;
12: 5 all the nations with an *i* scepter.
19:15 He will rule them with an *i* scepter

IRRELIGIOUS*
1Ti 1: 9 and sinful, the unholy and *i;*

IRREVOCABLE*
Ro 11:29 for God's gifts and his call are *i.*

ISAAC

Son of Abraham by Sarah (Ge 17:19; 21:1–7; 1Ch 1:28). Abrahamic covenant perpetuated through (Ge 17:21; 26:2–5). Offered up by Abraham (Ge 22; Heb 11:17–19). Rebekah taken as wife (Ge 24). Inherited Abraham's estate (Ge 25:5). Fathered Esau and Jacob (Ge 25:19–26; 1Ch 1:34). Nearly lost Rebekah to Abimelech (Ge 26:1–11). Covenant with Abimelech (Ge 26:12–31). Tricked into blessing Jacob (Ge 27). Death (Ge 35:27–29). Father of Israel (Ex 3:6; Dt 29:13; Ro 9:10).

ISAIAH

Prophet to Judah (Isa 1:1). Called by the LORD (Isa 6). Announced judgment to Ahaz (Isa 7), deliverance from Assyria to Hezekiah (2Ki 19; Isa 36–37), deliverance from death to Hezekiah (2Ki 20:1–11; Isa 38). Chronicler of Judah's history (2Ch 26:22; 32:32).

ISH-BOSHETH*

Son of Saul who attempted to succeed him as king (2Sa 2:8–4:12; 1Ch 8:33).

ISHMAEL

Son of Abraham by Hagar (Ge 16; 1Ch 1:28). Blessed, but not son of covenant (Ge 17:18–21; Gal 4:21–31). Sent away by Sarah (Ge 21:8–21). Children (Ge 25:12–18; 1Ch 1:29–31). Death (Ge 25:17).

ISLAND
Rev 1: 9 was on the *i* of Patmos
16:20 Every *i* fled away

ISRAEL (ISRAEL'S ISRAELITE ISRAELITES)

1. Name given to Jacob (see JACOB).

2. Corporate name of Jacob's descendants; often specifically Northern Kingdom.

Ex 28:11 Engrave the names of the sons of *I*
28:29 of the sons of *I* over his heart
Nu 24:17 a scepter will rise out of *I.*
Dt 6: 4 Hear, O *I:* The LORD our God,
10:12 O *I,* what does the LORD your
Jos 4:22 *I* crossed the Jordan on dry ground
Jdg 17: 6 In those days *I* had no king;
Ru 2:12 of *I,* under whose wings you have
1Sa 3:20 *I* from Dan to Beersheba
4:21 "The glory has departed from *I*"—
14:23 So the LORD rescued *I* that day,
15:26 has rejected you as king over *I!*"
17:46 will know that there is a God in *I.*
18:16 But all *I* and Judah loved David,
2Sa 5: 2 'You will shepherd my people *I,*
5: 3 they anointed David king over *I.*
14:25 In all *I* there was not a man
1Ki 1:35 I have appointed him ruler over *I*
10: 9 of the LORD's eternal love for *I,*
18:17 "Is that you, you troubler of *I?*"
19:18 Yet I reserve seven thousand in *I*—
2Ki 5: 8 know that there is a prophet in *I.*"
1Ch 17:22 made your people *I* your very own
21: 1 incited David to take a census of *I.*
29:25 Solomon in the sight of all *I*
2Ch 9: 8 of the love of your God for *I*
Ps 73: 1 Surely God is good to *I,*
81: 8 if you would but listen to me, O *I!*
98: 3 his faithfulness to the house of *I;*
99: 8 you were to *I* a forgiving God,
Isa 11:12 and gather the exiles of *I;*
27: 6 *I* will bud and blossom
44:21 O *I,* I will not forget you.
46:13 my splendor to *I.*
Jer 2: 3 *I* was holy to the LORD,
23: 6 and *I* will live in safety.
31: 2 I will come to give rest to *I.*"
31:10 'He who scattered *I* will gather
31:31 covenant with the house of *I*
33:17 sit on the throne of the house of *I,*
Eze 3:17 you a watchman for the house of *I;*
33: 7 you a watchman for the house of *I;*
34: 2 prophesy against the shepherds of *I*
37:28 that I the LORD make *I* holy,
39:23 of *I* went into exile for their sin,
Da 9:20 my sin and the sin of my people *I*
Hos 11: 1 "When *I* was a child, I loved him,
Am 4:12 prepare to meet your God, O *I.*"
7:11 and *I* will surely go into exile,
8: 2 "The time is ripe for my people *I;*
9:14 I will bring back my exiled people *I*
Mic 5: 2 one who will be ruler over *I,*

Zep 3:13 The remnant of *I* will do no wrong;
Zec 11:14 brotherhood between Judah and *I*.
Mal 1: 5 even beyond the borders of *I*!'
Mt 2: 6 be the shepherd of my people *I*.' "
10: 6 Go rather to the lost sheep of *I*.
15:24 only to the lost sheep of *I*."
Mk 12:29 'Hear, O *I*, the Lord our God,
Lk 22:30 judging the twelve tribes of *I*.
Ac 1: 6 going to restore the kingdom to *I*?"
9:15 and before the people of *I*.
Ro 9: 4 of my own race, the people of *I*.
9: 6 all who are descended from *I* are *I*.
9:31 but *I*, who pursued a law
11: 7 What *I* sought so earnestly it did
11:26 And so all *I* will be saved,
Gal 6:16 who follow this rule, even to the *I*
Eph 2:12 excluded from citizenship in *I*
3: 6 Gentiles are heirs together with *I*,
Heb 8: 8 covenant with the house of *I*
Rev 7: 4 144,000 from all the tribes of *I*.
21:12 the names of the twelve tribes of *I*.

ISRAEL'S (ISRAEL)
Jdg 10:16 he could bear *I* misery no longer.
2Sa 23: 1 *I* singer of songs:
Isa 44: 6 *I* King and Redeemer, the LORD
Jer 3: 9 Because *I* immorality mattered
31: 9 because I am *I* father,
Jn 3:10 "You are *I* teacher," said Jesus,

ISRAELITE (ISRAEL)
Ex 16: 1 The whole *I* community set out
35:29 All the *I* men and women who
Nu 8:16 offspring from every *I* woman.
20: 1 the whole *I* community arrived
20:22 The whole *I* community set out
Jn 1:47 "Here is a true *I*, in whom there is
Ro 11: 1 I am an *I* myself, a descendant

ISRAELITES (ISRAEL)
Ex 1: 7 the *I* were fruitful and multiplied
2:23 The *I* groaned in their slavery
3: 9 the cry of the *I* has reached me,
12:35 The *I* did as Moses instructed
12:37 The *I* journeyed from Rameses
14:22 and the *I* went through the sea
16:12 I have heard the grumbling of the *I*.
16:35 The *I* ate manna forty years,
24:17 To the *I* the glory of the LORD
28:30 decisions for the *I* over his heart
29:45 Then I will dwell among the *I*
31:16 The *I* are to observe the Sabbath,
33: 5 "Tell the *I*, 'You are a stiff-necked
39:42 The *I* had done all the work just
Lev 22:32 be acknowledged as holy by the *I*.
25:46 rule over your fellow *I* ruthlessly.
25:55 for the *I* belong to me as servants.
Nu 2:32 These are the *I*, counted according
6:23 'This is how you are to bless the *I*.
9: 2 "Have the *I* celebrate the Passover
9:17 the *I* set out; wherever the cloud
10:12 Then the *I* set out from the Desert
14: 2 All the *I* grumbled against Moses
20:12 as holy in the sight of the *I*,
21: 6 they bit the people and many *I* died
26:65 had told those *I* they would surely
27:12 and see the land I have given the *I*.
33: 3 The *I* set out from Rameses
35:10 "Speak to the *I* and say to them:
Dt 33: 1 on the *I* before his death.
Jos 1: 2 about to give to them—to the *I*.
5: 6 The *I* had moved about
7: 1 the *I* acted unfaithfully in regard
8:32 There in the presence of the *I*,
18: 1 of the *I* gathered at Shiloh
21: 3 the *I* gave the Levites the following
22: 9 of Manasseh left the *I* at Shiloh
Jdg 2:11 Then the *I* did evil in the eyes
3:12 Once again the *I* did evil
4: 1 the *I* once again did evil in the eyes
6: 1 Again the *I* did evil in the eyes
10: 6 Again the *I* did evil in the eyes
13: 1 Again the *I* did evil in the eyes
1Sa 17: 2 Saul and the *I* assembled
1Ki 8:63 and all the *I* dedicated the temple
9:22 did not make slaves of any of the *I*;
12: 1 for all the *I* had gone there
12:17 But as for the *I* who were living
2Ki 17:24 towns of Samaria to replace the *I*.
1Ch 9: 2 in their own towns were some *I*,
10: 1 fought against Israel; the *I* fled
1Ch 11: 4 and all the *I* marched to Jerusalem,
2Ch 7: 6 and all the *I* were standing.
Ne 1: 6 the sins we *I*, including myself
Jer 16:14 who brought the *I* up out of Egypt,'
Hos 1:10 "Yet the *I* will be like the sand
3: 1 Love her as the LORD loves the *I*,
Am 4: 5 boast about them, you *I*,
Mic 5: 3 return to join the *I*.
Ro 9:27 the number of the *I* be like the sand
10: 1 for the *I* is that they may be saved.
10:16 But not all the *I* accepted the good
2Co 11:22 Are they *I*? So am I.

ISSACHAR
Son of Jacob by Leah (Ge 30:18; 35:23; 1Ch 2:1). Tribe of blessed (Ge 49:14–15; Dt 33:18–19), numbered (Nu 1:29; 26:25), allotted land (Jos 19:17–23; Eze 48:25), assisted Deborah (Jdg 5:15), 12,000 from (Rev 7:7).

ISSUING*
Da 9:25 From the *i* of the decree to restore

ITALY
Ac 27: 1 decided that we would sail for *I*,
Heb 13:24 from *I* send you their greetings.

ITCHING*
2Ti 4: 3 to say what their *i* ears want to hear

ITHAMAR
Son of Aaron (Ex 6:23; 1Ch 6:3). Duties at tabernacle (Ex 38:21; Nu 4:21–33; 7:8).

ITTAI
2Sa 15:19 The king said to *I* the Gittite,

IVORY
1Ki 10:22 silver and *i*, and apes and baboons.
22:39 the palace he built and inlaid with *i*

JABBOK
Ge 32:22 and crossed the ford of the *J*.
Dt 3:16 and out to the *J* River,

JABESH
1Sa 11: 1 And all the men of *J* said to him,
31:12 wall of Beth Shan and went to *J*,
1Ch 10:12 and his sons and brought them to *J*.

JABESH GILEAD
Jdg 21: 8 that no one from *J* had come to
2Sa 2: 4 the men of *J* who had buried Saul,
1Ch 10:11 the inhabitants of *J* heard

JACOB
Second son of Isaac, twin of Esau (Ge 26:21–26; 1Ch 1:34). Bought Esau's birthright (Ge 26:29–34); tricked Isaac into blessing him (Ge 27:1–37). Fled to Haran (Ge 28:1–5). Abrahamic covenant perpetuated through (Ge 28:13–15; Mal 1:2). Vision at Bethel (Ge 28:10–22). Served Laban for Rachel and Leah (Ge 29:1–30). Children (Ge 29:31–30:24; 35:16–26; 1Ch 2–9). Flocks increased (Ge 30:25–43). Returned to Canaan (Ge 31). Wrestled with God; name changed to Israel (Ge 32:22–32). Reconciled to Esau (Ge 33). Returned to Bethel (Ge 35:1–15). Favored Joseph (Ge 37:3). Sent sons to Egypt during famine (Ge 42–43). Settled in Egypt (Ge 46). Blessed Ephraim and Manasseh (Ge 48). Blessed sons (Ge 49:1–28; Heb 11:21). Death (Ge 49:29–33). Burial (Ge 50:1–14).

JAEL*
Woman who killed Canaanite general, Sisera (Jdg 4:17–22; 5:24–27).

JAIR
Judge from Gilead (Jdg 10:3–5).

JAIRUS*
Synagogue ruler whose daughter Jesus raised (Mk 5:22–43; Lk 8:41–56).

JAMES
1. Apostle; brother of John (Mt 4:21–22; 10:2; Mk 3:17; Lk 5:1–10). At transfiguration (Mt 17:1–13; Mk 9:1–13; Lk 9:28–36). Killed by Herod (Ac 12:2).
2. Apostle; son of Alphaeus (Mt 10:3; Mk 3:18; Lk 6:15).
3. Brother of Jesus (Mt 13:55; Mk 6:3; Lk 24:10; Gal 1:19) and Judas (Jude 1). With believers before Pentecost (Ac 1:13). Leader of church at Jerusalem (Ac 12:17; 15; 21:18; Gal 2:9, 12). Author of epistle (Jas 1:1).

JAPHETH
Son of Noah (Ge 5:32; 1Ch 1:4–5). Blessed (Ge 9:18–28). Sons of (Ge 10:2–5).

JAR (JARS)
Ge 24:14 let down your *j* that I may have
1Ki 17:14 'The *j* of flour will not be used up
Jer 19: 1 "Go and buy a clay *j* from a potter.
Lk 8:16 hides it in a *j* or puts it under a bed.

JARS (JAR)
Jn 2: 6 Nearby stood six stone water *j*,
2Co 4: 7 we have this treasure in *j* of clay

JASPER
Ex 28:20 row a chrysolite, an onyx and a *j*.
Eze 28:13 chrysolite, onyx and *j*,
Rev 4: 3 sat there had the appearance of *j*
21:19 The first foundation was *j*,

JAVELIN
1Sa 17:45 me with sword and spear and *j*,

JAWBONE
Jdg 15:15 Finding a fresh *j* of a donkey,

JEALOUS (JEALOUSY)
Ex 20: 5 the LORD your God, am a *j* God,
34:14 whose name is Jealous, is a *j* God.
Dt 4:24 God is a consuming fire, a *j* God.
6:15 is a *j* God and his anger will burn
32:21 They made me *j* by what is no god
Jos 24:19 He is a holy God; he is a *j* God.
Eze 16:38 of my wrath and *j* anger.
16:42 my *j* anger will turn away from you
23:25 I will direct my *j* anger against you,
36: 6 in my *j* wrath because you have
Joel 2:18 the LORD will be *j* for his land
Na 1: 2 LORD is a *j* and avenging God;
Zep 3: 8 consumed by the fire of my *j* anger.
Zec 1:14 I am very *j* for Jerusalem and Zion,
8: 2 "I am very *j* for Zion; I am burning
2Co 11: 2 I am *j* for you with a godly jealousy

JEALOUSY (JEALOUS)
Ps 79: 5 How long will your *j* burn like fire?
Pr 6:34 for *j* arouses a husband's fury,
27: 4 but who can stand before *j*?
SS 8: 6 its *j* unyielding as the grave.
Zep 1:18 In the fire of his *j*
Zec 8: 2 I am burning with *j* for her."
Ro 13:13 debauchery, not in dissension and *j*
1Co 3: 3 For since there is *j* and quarreling
10:22 trying to arouse the Lord's *j*?
2Co 11: 2 I am jealous for you with a godly *j*.
12:20 *j*, outbursts of anger, factions,
Gal 5:20 hatred, discord, *j*, fits of rage,

JEERS*
Heb 11:36 Some faced *j* and flogging,

JEHOAHAZ
1. Son of Jehu; king of Israel (2Ki 13:1–9).
2. Son of Josiah; king of Judah (2Ki 23:31–34; 2Ch 36:1–4).

JEHOASH
1. See JOASH.
2. Son of Jehoahaz; king of Israel. Defeat of Aram prophesied by Elisha (2Ki 13:10–25). Defeated Amaziah in Jerusalem (2Ki 14:1–16; 2Ch 25:17–24).

JEHOIACHIN
Son of Jehoiakim; king of Judah exiled by Nebuchadnezzar (2Ki 24:8–17; 2Ch 36:8–10; Jer 22:24–30; 24:1). Raised from prisoner status (2Ki 25:27–30; Jer 52:31–34).

JEHOIADA
Priest who sheltered Joash from Athaliah (2Ki 11–12; 2Ch 22:11–24:16).

JEHOIAKIM
Son of Josiah; made king of Judah by Pharaoh Neco (2Ki 23:34–24:6; 2Ch 36:4–8; Jer 22:18–23). Burned scroll of Jeremiah's prophecies (Jer 36).

JEHORAM
1. Son of Jehoshaphat; king of Judah (2Ki 8:16–24). Prophesied against by Elijah; killed by the LORD (2Ch 21).
2. See JORAM.

JEHOSHAPHAT

Son of Asa; king of Judah. Strengthened his kingdom (2Ch 17). Joined with Ahab against Aram (2Ki 22; 2Ch 18). Established judges (2Ch 19). Joined with Joram against Moab (2Ki 3; 2Ch 20).

JEHU

1. Prophet against Baasha (2Ki 16:1–7).

2. King of Israel. Anointed by Elijah to obliterate house of Ahab (1Ki 19:16–17); anointed by servant of Elisha (2Ki 9:1–13). Killed Joram and Ahaziah (2Ki 9:14–29; 2Ch 22:7–9), Jezebel (2Ki 9:30–37), relatives of Ahab (2Ki 10:1–17), ministers of Baal (2Ki 10:18–29). Death (2Ki 10:30–36).

JEPHTHAH

Judge from Gilead who delivered Israel from Ammon (Jdg 10:6–12:7). Made rash vow concerning his daughter (Jdg 11:30–40).

JEREMIAH

Prophet to Judah (Jer 1:1–3). Called by the LORD (Jer 1). Put in stocks (Jer 20:1–3). Threatened for prophesying (Jer 11:18–23; 26). Opposed by Hananiah (Jer 28). Scroll burned (Jer 36). Imprisoned (Jer 37). Thrown into cistern (Jer 38). Forced to Egypt with those fleeing Babylonians (Jer 43).

JERICHO

Nu 22: 1 along the Jordan across from *J.*
Jos 3:16 the people crossed over opposite *J.*
5:10 camped at Gilgal on the plains of *J,*
Lk 10:30 going down from Jerusalem to *J,*
Heb 11:30 By faith the walls of *J* fell,

JEROBOAM

1. Official of Solomon; rebelled to become first king of Israel (1Ki 11:26–40; 12:1–20; 2Ch 10). Idolatry (1Ki 12:25–33); judgment for (1Ki 13–14; 2Ch 13).

2. Son of Jehoash; king of Israel (1Ki 14:23–29).

JERUSALEM

Jos 10: 1 of *J* heard that Joshua had taken Ai
15: 8 of the Jebusite city (that is, *J*).
Jdg 1: 8 The men of Judah attacked *J* also
1Sa 17:54 head and brought it to *J,*
2Sa 5: 5 and in *J* he reigned over all Israel
5: 6 and his men marched to *J*
9:13 And Mephibosheth lived in *J,*
11: 1 But David remained in *J.*
15:29 took the ark of God back to *J*
24:16 stretched out his hand to destroy *J,*
1Ki 3: 1 the LORD, and the wall around *J.*
9:15 the wall of *J,* and Hazor, Megiddo
9:19 whatever he desired to build in *J,*
10:26 cities and also with him in *J.*
10:27 as common in *J* as stones,
11: 7 of *J,* Solomon built a high place
11:13 my servant and for the sake of *J,*
11:36 always have a lamp before me in *J,*
11:42 Solomon reigned in *J*
12:27 at the temple of the LORD in *J,*
14:21 and he reigned seventeen years in *J*
14:25 Shishak king of Egypt attacked *J.*
15: 2 and he reigned in *J* three years.
15:10 and he reigned in *J* forty-one years.
22:42 he reigned in *J* twenty-five years.
2Ki 8:17 and he reigned in *J* eight years.
8:26 and he reigned in *J* one year.
12: 1 and he reigned in *J* forty years.
12:17 Then he turned to attack *J.*
14: 2 he reigned in *J* twenty-nine years.
14:13 Then Jehoash went to *J*
15: 2 and he reigned in *J* fifty-two years.
15:33 and he reigned in *J* sixteen years.
16: 2 and he reigned in *J* sixteen years.
16: 5 Israel marched up to fight against *J*
18: 2 he reigned in *J* twenty-nine years.
18:17 Lachish to King Hezekiah at *J.*
19:31 For out of *J* will come a remnant,
21: 1 and he reigned in *J* fifty-five years.
21:12 going to bring such disaster on *J*
21:19 and he reigned in *J* two years.
22: 1 he reigned in *J* thirty-one years.
23:27 and I will reject *J,* the city I chose,
23:31 and he reigned in *J* three months.
23:36 and he reigned in *J* eleven years.
24: 8 and he reigned in *J* three months.
24:10 king of Babylon advanced on *J*
2Ki 24:14 He carried into exile all *J:*
24:18 and he reigned in *J* eleven years.
24:20 anger that all this happened to *J*
25: 1 king of Babylon marched against *J*
25: 9 royal palace and all the houses of *J.*
1Ch 11: 4 and all the Israelites marched to *J,*
21:16 sword in his hand extended over *J.*
2Ch 1: 4 he had pitched a tent for it in *J.*
3: 1 the LORD in *J* on Mount Moriah,
6: 6 now I have chosen *J* for my Name
9: 1 she came to *J* to test him
20:15 and all who live in Judah and *J!*
20:27 and *J* returned joyfully to *J,*
29: 8 LORD has fallen on Judah and *J;*
36:19 and broke down the wall of *J;*
Ezr 1: 2 a temple for him at *J* in Judah.
2: 1 to Babylon (they returned to *J*
3: 1 people assembled as one man in *J.*
4:12 up to us from you have gone to *J*
4:24 of God in *J* came to a standstill
6:12 or to destroy this temple in *J.*
7: 8 Ezra arrived in *J* in the fifth month
9: 9 a wall of protection in Judah and *J.*
10: 7 for all the exiles to assemble in *J.*
Ne 1: 2 the exile, and also about *J.*
1: 3 The wall of *J* is broken down,
2:11 to *J,* and after staying there three
2:17 Come, let us rebuild the wall of *J,*
2:20 you have no share in *J* or any claim
3: 8 They restored *J* as far as the Broad
4: 8 fight against *J* and stir up trouble
11: 1 leaders of the people settled in *J,*
12:27 At the dedication of the wall of *J,*
12:43 in *J* could be heard far away.
Ps 51:18 build up the walls of *J.*
79: 1 they have reduced *J* to rubble.
122: 2 in your gates, O *J.*
122: 3 *J* is built like a city
122: 6 Pray for the peace of *J:*
125: 2 As the mountains surround *J,*
128: 5 may you see the prosperity of *J,*
137: 5 If I forget you, O *J,*
147: 2 The LORD builds up *J;*
147:12 Extol the LORD, O *J;*
SS 6: 4 lovely as *J,*
Isa 1: 1 and *J* that Isaiah son of Amoz saw
2: 1 saw concerning Judah and *J:*
3: 1 is about to take from *J* and Judah
3: 8 *J* staggers,
4: 3 recorded among the living in *J.*
8:14 And for the people of *J* he will be
27:13 LORD on the holy mountain in *J.*
31: 5 the LORD Almighty will shield *J;*
33:20 your eyes will see *J,*
40: 2 Speak tenderly to *J,*
40: 9 You who bring good tidings to *J,*
52: 1 O *J,* the holy city.
52: 2 rise up, sit enthroned, O *J.*
62: 6 on your walls, O *J;*
62: 7 give him no rest till he establishes *J*
65:18 for I will create *J* to be a delight
Jer 2: 2 and proclaim in the hearing of *J:*
3:17 time they will call *J* The Throne
4: 5 and proclaim in *J* and say:
4:14 O *J,* wash the evil from your heart
5: 1 "Go up and down the streets of *J,*
6: 6 and build siege ramps against *J.*
8: 5 Why does *J* always turn away?
9:11 "I will make *J* a heap of ruins,
13:27 Woe to you, O *J!*
23:14 And among the prophets of *J*
24: 1 into exile from *J* to Babylon
26:18 *J* will become a heap of rubble,
32: 2 of Babylon was then besieging *J,*
33:10 the streets of *J* that are deserted,
39: 1 This is how *J* was taken: In
51:50 and think on *J.*"
52:14 broke down all the walls around *J.*
La 1: 7 *J* remembers all the treasures
Eze 14:21 send against *J* my four dreadful
16: 2 confront *J* with her detestable
Da 6:10 the windows opened toward *J.*
9: 2 of *J* would last seventy years.
9:12 done like what has been done to *J.*
9:25 and rebuild *J* until the Anointed
Joel 3: 1 restore the fortunes of Judah and *J,*
3:16 and thunder from *J;*
3:17 *J* will be holy;
Am 2: 5 will consume the fortresses of *J.*"
Ob :11 and cast lots for *J,*
Mic 1: 5 Is it not *J?*
4: 2 the word of the LORD from *J.*
Zep 3:16 On that day they will say to *J,*
Zec 1:14 'I am very jealous for *J* and Zion,
1:17 comfort Zion and choose *J.*' "
2: 2 He answered me, "To measure *J,*
2: 4 '*J* will be a city without walls
8: 3 I will return to Zion and dwell in *J.*
8: 8 I will bring them back to live in *J;*
8:15 determined to do good again to *J*
8:22 powerful nations will come to *J*
9: 9 Shout, Daughter of *J!*
9:10 and the war-horses from *J,*
12: 3 I will make *J* an immovable rock
12:10 the inhabitants of *J* a spirit of grace
14: 2 the nations to *J* to fight against it;
14: 8 living water will flow out from *J,*
14:16 that have attacked *J* will go up
Mt 16:21 to his disciples that he must go to *J*
20:18 said to them, "We are going up to *J*
21:10 When Jesus entered *J,* the whole
23:37 "O *J, J,* you who kill the prophets
Mk 10:33 "We are going up to *J,*" he said,
Lk 2:22 Mary took him to *J* to present him
2:41 Every year his parents went to *J*
2:43 the boy Jesus stayed behind in *J,*
4: 9 The devil led him to *J*
9:31 about to bring to fulfillment at *J.*
9:51 Jesus resolutely set out for *J,*
13:34 die outside *J!* "O *J, J,*
18:31 told them, "We are going up to *J,*
19:41 As he approached *J* and saw
21:20 "When you see *J* being surrounded
21:24 *J* will be trampled
24:47 name to all nations, beginning at *J.*
Jn 4:20 where we must worship is in *J.*"
Ac 1: 4 this command: "Do not leave *J,*
1: 8 and you will be my witnesses in *J,*
6: 7 of disciples in *J* increased rapidly,
20:22 by the Spirit, I am going to *J,*
23:11 As you have testified about me in *J*
Ro 15:19 So from *J* all the way
Gal 4:25 corresponds to the present city of *J*
4:26 But the *J* that is above is free,
Heb 12:22 to the heavenly *J,* the city
Rev 3:12 the new *J,* which is coming
21: 2 I saw the Holy City, the new *J,*
21:10 and showed me the Holy City, *J,*

JESSE

Father of David (Ru 4:17–22; 1Sa 16; 1Ch 2:12–17).

JESUS

LIFE: Genealogy (Mt 1:1–17; Lk 3:21–37). Birth announced (Mt 1:18–25; Lk 1:26–45). Birth (Mt 2:1–12; Lk 2:1–40). Escape to Egypt (Mt 2:13–23). As a boy in the temple (Lk 2:41–52). Baptism (Mt 3:13–17; Mk 1:9–11; Lk 3:21–22; Jn 1:32–34). Temptation (Mt 4:1–11; Mk 1:12–13; Lk 4:1–13). Ministry in Galilee (Mt 4:12–18:35; Mk 1:14–9:50; Lk 4:14–13:9; Jn 1:35–2:11; 4; 6), Transfiguration (Mt 17:1–8; Mk 9:2–8; Lk 9:28–36), on the way to Jerusalem (Mt 19–20; Mk 10; Lk 13:10–19:27), in Jerusalem (Mt 21–25; Mk 11–13; Lk 19:28–21:38; Jn 2:12–3:36; 5; 7–12). Last supper (Mt 26:17–35; Mk 14:12–31; Lk 22:1–38; Jn 13–17). Arrest and trial (Mt 26:36–27:31; Mk 14:43–15:20; Lk 22:39–23:25; Jn 18:1–19:16). Crucifixion (Mt 27:32–66; Mk 15:21–47; Lk 23:26–55; Jn 19:28–42). Resurrection and appearances (Mt 28; Mk 16; Lk 24; Jn 20–21; Ac 1:1–11; 7:56; 9:3–6; 1Co 15:1–8; Rev 1:1–20).

MIRACLES. Healings: official's son (Jn 4:43–54), demoniac in Capernaum (Mk 1:23–26; Lk 4:33–35), Peter's mother-in-law (Mt 8:14–17; Mk 1:29–31; Lk 4:38–39), leper (Mt 8:2–4; Mk 1:40–45; Lk 5:12–16), paralytic (Mt 9:1–8; Mk 2:1–12; Lk 5:17–26), cripple (Jn 5:1–9), shriveled hand (Mt 12:10–13; Mk 3:1–5; Lk 6:6–11), centurion's servant (Mt 8:5–13; Lk 7:1–10), widow's son raised (Lk 7:11–17), demoniac (Mt 12:22–23; Lk 11:14), Gadarene demoniacs (Mt 8:28–34; Mk 5:1–20; Lk 8:26–39), woman's bleeding and Jairus' daughter (Mt 9:18–26; Mk 5:21–43; Lk 8:40–56), blind man (Mt 9:27–31), mute man (Mt 9:32–33), Canaanite woman's daughter (Mt 15:21–28; Mk 7:24–30), deaf man (Mk 7:31–37), blind man (Mk 8:22–26), demoniac boy (Mt 17:14–18; Mk 9:14–29; Lk 9:37–43), ten lepers

(Lk 17:11–19), man born blind (Jn 9:1–7), Lazarus raised (Jn 11), crippled woman (Lk 13:11–17), man with dropsy (Lk 14:1–6), two blind men (Mt 20:29–34; Mk 10:46–52; Lk 18:35–43), Malchus' ear (Lk 22:50–51). Other Miracles: water to wine (Jn 2:1–11), catch of fish (Lk 5:1–11), storm stilled (Mt 8:23–27; Mk 4:37–41; Lk 8:22–25), 5,000 fed (Mt 14:15–21; Mk 6:35–44; Lk 9:10–17; Jn 6:1–14), walking on water (Mt 14:25–33; Mk 6:48–52; Jn 6:15–21), 4,000 fed (Mt 15:32–39; Mk 8:1–9), money from fish (Mt 17:24–27), fig tree cursed (Mt 21:18–22; Mk 11:12–14), catch of fish (Jn 21:1–14).

MAJOR TEACHING: Sermon on the Mount (Mt 5–7; Lk 6:17–49), to Nicodemus (Jn 3), to Samaritan woman (Jn 4), Bread of Life (Jn 6:22–59), at Feast of Tabernacles (Jn 7–8), woes to Pharisees (Mt 23; Lk 11:37–54), Good Shepherd (Jn 10:1–18), Olivet Discourse (Mt 24–25; Mk 13; Lk 21:5–36), Upper Room Discourse (Jn 13–16).

PARABLES: Sower (Mt 13:3–23; Mk 4:3–25; Lk 8:5–18), seed's growth (Mk 4:26–29), wheat and weeds (Mt 13:24–30, 36–43), mustard seed (Mt 13:31–32; Mk 4:30–32), yeast (Mt 13:33; Lk 13:20–21), hidden treasure (Mt 13:44), valuable pearl (Mt 13:45–46), net (Mt 13:47–51), house owner (Mt 13:52), good Samaritan (Lk 10:25–37), unmerciful servant (Mt 18:15–35), lost sheep (Mt 18:10–14; Lk 15:4–7), lost coin (Lk 15:8–10), lost son (Lk 15:11–32), dishonest manager (Lk 16:1–13), rich man and Lazarus (Lk 16:19–31), persistent widow (Lk 18:1–8), Pharisee and tax collector (Lk 18:9–14), payment of workers (Mt 20:1–16), tenants and the vineyard (Mt 21:28–46; Mk 12:1–12; Lk 20:9–19), wedding banquet (Mt 22:1–14), faithful servant (Mt 24:45–51), ten virgins (Mt 25:1–13), talents (Mt 25:1–30; Lk 19:12–27).

DISCIPLES see APOSTLES. Call of (Jn 1:35–51; Mt 4:18–22; 9:9; Mk 1:16–20; 2:13–14; Lk 5:1–11, 27–28). Named Apostles (Mk 3:13–19; Lk 6:12–16). Twelve sent out (Mt 10; Mk 6:7–11; Lk 9:1–5). Seventy sent out (Lk 10:1–24). Defection of (Jn 6:60–71; Mt 26:56; Mk 14:50–52). Final commission (Mt 28:16–20; Jn 21:15–23; Ac 1:3–8).

Ac 2:32 God has raised this *J* to life,
9:5 "I am *J*, whom you are persecuting
9:34 said to him, "*J* Christ heals you.
15:11 of our Lord *J* that we are saved,
16:31 "Believe in the Lord *J*,
20:24 the task the Lord *J* has given me—
Ro 3:24 redemption that came by Christ *J*.
5:17 life through the one man, *J* Christ.
8:1 for those who are in Christ *J*,
1Co 1:7 for our Lord *J* Christ to be revealed
2:2 except *J* Christ and him crucified.
6:11 in the name of the Lord *J* Christ
8:6 and there is but one Lord, *J* Christ,
12:3 and no one can say, "*J* is Lord,"
2Co 4:5 not preach ourselves, but *J* Christ
13:5 Do you not realize that Christ *J* is
Gal 2:16 but by faith in *J* Christ.
3:28 for you are all one in Christ *J*.
5:6 in Christ *J* neither circumcision
6:17 bear on my body the marks of *J*.
Eph 1:5 as his sons through *J* Christ,
2:10 created in Christ *J*
2:20 with Christ *J* himself as the chief
Php 1:6 until the day of Christ *J*.
2:5 be the same as that of Christ *J*:
2:10 name of *J* every knee should bow,
Col 3:17 do it all in the name of the Lord *J*,
1Th 1:10 whom he raised from the dead—*J*,
4:14 We believe that *J* died
5:23 at the coming of our Lord *J* Christ.
2Th 1:7 when the Lord *J* is revealed
2:1 the coming of our Lord *J* Christ
1Ti 1:15 Christ *J* came into the world
2Ti 1:10 appearing of our Savior, Christ *J*,
2:3 us like a good soldier of Christ *J*.
3:12 life in Christ *J* will be persecuted,
Tit 2:13 our great God and Savior, *J* Christ,
Heb 2:9 But we see *J*, who was made a little
2:11 So *J* is not ashamed to call them
3:1 fix your thoughts on *J*, the apostle
3:3 *J* has been found worthy
4:14 through the heavens, *J* the Son
6:20 where *J*, who went before us,
7:22 *J* has become the guarantee
Heb 7:24 but because *J* lives forever,
8:6 But the ministry *J* has received is
12:2 Let us fix our eyes on *J*, the author
12:24 to *J* the mediator of a new
1Pe 1:3 the resurrection of *J* Christ
2Pe 1:16 and coming of our Lord *J* Christ,
1Jn 1:7 and the blood of *J*, his Son,
2:1 *J* Christ, the Righteous One.
2:6 to live in him must walk as *J* did.
4:15 anyone acknowledges that *J* is
Rev 1:1 The revelation of *J* Christ,
22:16 *J*, have sent my angel
22:20 Come, Lord *J*.

JETHRO

Father-in-law and adviser of Moses (Ex 3:1; 18). Also known as Reuel (Ex 2:18).

JEW (JEWS JEWS' JUDAISM)

Est 2:5 of Susa a *J* of the tribe of Benjamin,
Zec 8:23 of one *J* by the hem of his robe
Ac 21:39 "I am a *J*, from Tarsus in Cilicia,
Ro 1:16 first for the *J*, then for the Gentile.
2:28 A man is not a *J* if he is only one
10:12 there is no difference between *J*
1Co 9:20 To the Jews I became like a *J*,
Gal 2:14 "You are a *J*, yet you live like
3:28 There is neither *J* nor Greek,
Col 3:11 Here there is no Greek or *J*,

JEWEL (JEWELRY JEWELS)

Pr 20:15 that speak knowledge are a rare *j*.
SS 4:9 with one *j* of your necklace.
Rev 21:11 that of a very precious *j*,

JEWELRY (JEWEL)

Ex 35:22 and brought gold *j* of all kinds:
Jer 2:32 Does a maiden forget her *j*,
Eze 16:11 you with *j*: I put bracelets
1Pe 3:3 wearing of gold *j* and fine clothes.

JEWELS (JEWEL)

Isa 54:12 your gates of sparkling *j*,
61:10 as a bride adorns herself with her *j*.
Zec 9:16 like *j* in a crown.

JEWS (JEW)

Ne 4:1 He ridiculed the *J*,
Est 3:13 kill and annihilate all the *J*—
4:14 and deliverance for the *J* will arise
Mt 2:2 who has been born king of the *J*?
27:11 "Are you the king of the *J*?" "Yes,
Jn 4:9 (For *J* do not associate
4:22 for salvation is from the *J*.
19:3 saying, "Hail, king of the *J*!"
Ac 20:21 I have declared to both *J*
Ro 3:29 Is God the God of *J* only?
9:24 not only from the *J* but
15:27 they owe it to the *J* to share
1Co 1:22 *J* demand miraculous signs
9:20 To the *J* I became like a Jew,
12:13 whether *J* or Greeks, slave or free
Gal 2:8 of Peter as an apostle to the *J*,
Rev 2:9 slander of those who say they are *J*
3:9 claim to be *J* though they are not,

JEWS' (JEW)

Ro 15:27 shared in the *J* spiritual blessings,

JEZEBEL

Sidonian wife of Ahab (1Ki 16:31). Promoted Baal worship (1Ki 16:32–33). Killed prophets of the LORD (1Ki 18:4, 13). Opposed Elijah (1Ki 19:1–2). Had Naboth killed (1Ki 21). Death prophesied (1Ki 21:17–24). Killed by Jehu (2Ki 9:30–37).

JEZREEL

2Ki 9:36 at *J* dogs will devour Jezebel's flesh
10:7 and sent them to Jehu in *J*.
Hos 1:4 house of Jehu for the massacre at *J*,

JOAB

Nephew of David (1Ch 2:16). Commander of his army (2Sa 8:16). Victorious over Ammon (2Sa 10; 1Ch 19), Rabbah (2Sa 11; 1Ch 20), Jerusalem (1Ch 11:6), Absalom (2Sa 18), Sheba (2Sa 20). Killed Abner (2Sa 3:22–39), Amasa (2Sa 20:1–13). Numbered David's army (2Sa 24; 1Ch 21). Sided with Adonijah (1Ki 1:17, 19). Killed by Benaiah (1Ki 2:5–6, 28–35).

JOASH

Son of Ahaziah; king of Judah. Sheltered from Athaliah by Jehoiada (2Ki 11; 2Ch 22:10–23:21). Repaired temple (2Ki 12; 2Ch 24).

JOB

Wealthy man from Uz; feared God (Job 1:1–5). Righteousness tested by disaster (Job 1:6–22), personal affliction (Job 2). Maintained innocence in debate with three friends (Job 3–31), Elihu (Job 32–37). Rebuked by the LORD (Job 38–41). Vindicated and restored to greater stature by the LORD (Job 42). Example of righteousness (Eze 14:14, 20).

JOCHEBED*

Mother of Moses and Aaron (Ex 6:20; Nu 26:59).

JOEL

Prophet (Joel 1:1; Ac 2:16).

JOHN

1. Son of Zechariah and Elizabeth (Lk 1). Called the Baptist (Mt 3:1–12; Mk 1:2–8). Witness to Jesus (Mt 3:11–12; Mk 1:7–8; Lk 3:15–18; Jn 1:6–35; 3:27–30; 5:33–36). Doubts about Jesus (Mt 11:2–6; Lk 7:18–23). Arrest (Mt 4:12; Mk 1:14). Execution (Mt 14:1–12; Mk 6:14–29; Lk 9:7–9). Ministry compared to Elijah (Mt 11:7–19; Mk 9:11–13; Lk 7:24–35).

2. Apostle; brother of James (Mt 4:21–22; 10:2; Mk 3:17; Lk 5:1–10). At transfiguration (Mt 17:1–13; Mk 9:1–13; Lk 9:28–36). Desire to be greatest (Mk 10:35–45). Leader of church at Jerusalem (Ac 4:1–3; Gal 2:9). Elder who wrote epistles (2Jn 1; 3Jn 1). Prophet who wrote Revelation (Rev 1:1; 22:8).

3. Cousin of Barnabas, co-worker with Paul, (Ac 12:12–13:13; 15:37), see MARK.

JOIN (JOINED JOINS)

Ne 10:29 all these now *j* their brothers
Pr 23:20 Do not *j* those who drink too much
24:21 and do not *j* with the rebellious,
Jer 3:18 of Judah will *j* the house of Israel,
Eze 37:17 *J* them together into one stick
Da 11:34 who are not sincere will *j* them.
Ro 15:30 to *j* me in my struggle by praying
2Ti 1:8 *j* with me in suffering for the gospel

JOINED (JOIN)

Zec 2:11 "Many nations will be *j*
Mt 19:6 Therefore what God has *j* together,
Mk 10:9 Therefore what God has *j* together,
Ac 1:14 They all *j* together constantly
Eph 2:21 him the whole building is *j* together
4:16 *j* and held together

JOINS (JOIN)

1Co 16:16 and to everyone who *j* in the work,

JOINT (JOINTS)

Ps 22:14 and all my bones are out of *j*.

JOINTS (JOINT)

Heb 4:12 even to dividing soul and spirit, *j*

JOKING*

Ge 19:14 his sons-in-law thought he was *j*.
Pr 26:19 and says, "I was only *j*!"
Eph 5:4 or coarse *j*, which are out of place,

JONAH

Prophet in days of Jeroboam II (2Ki 14:25). Called to Nineveh; fled to Tarshish (Jnh 1:1–3). Cause of storm; thrown into sea (Jnh 1:4–16). Swallowed by fish (Jnh 1:17). Prayer (Jnh 2). Preached to Nineveh (Jnh 3). Attitude reproved by the LORD (Jnh 4). Sign of (Mt 12:39–41; Lk 11:29–32).

JONATHAN

Son of Saul (1Sa 13:16; 1Ch 8:33). Valiant warrior (1Sa 13–14). Relation to David (1Sa 18:1–4; 19–20; 23:16–18). Killed at Gilboa (1Sa 31). Mourned by David (2Sa 1).

JOPPA

Ezr 3:7 logs by sea from Lebanon to *J*,
Jnh 1:3 to *J*, where he found a ship bound
Ac 9:43 Peter stayed in *J* for some time

JORAM

1. Son of Ahab; king of Israel. Fought with Jehoshaphat against Moab (2Ki 3). Killed with Ahaziah by Jehu (2Ki 8:25–29; 9:14–26; 2Ch 22:5–9).

2. See JEHORAM.

JORDAN
Ge 13:10 plain of the *J* was well watered,
Nu 22: 1 and camped along the *J*
34:12 boundary will go down along the *J*
Dt 3:27 you are not going to cross this *J.*
Jos 1: 2 get ready to cross the *J* River
3:11 go into the *J* ahead of you.
3:17 ground in the middle of the *J,*
4:22 Israel crossed the *J* on dry ground.'
2Ki 2: 7 and Elisha had stopped at the *J.*
2:13 and stood on the bank of the *J.*
5:10 wash yourself seven times in the *J,*
6: 4 They went to the *J* and began
Ps 114: 3 the *J* turned back;
Isa 9: 1 along the *J*—The people walking
Jer 12: 5 manage in the thickets by the *J?*
Mt 3: 6 baptized by him in the *J* River.
4:15 the way to the sea, along the *J,*
Mk 1: 9 and was baptized by John in the *J.*

JOSEPH

1. Son of Jacob by Rachel (Ge 30:24; 1Ch 2:2). Favored by Jacob, hated by brothers (Ge 37:3–4). Dreams (Ge 37:5–11). Sold by brothers (Ge 37:12–36). Served Potiphar; imprisoned by false accusation (Ge 39). Interpreted dreams of Pharaoh's servants (Ge 40), of Pharaoh (Ge 41:4–40). Made greatest in Egypt (Ge 41:41–57). Sold grain to brothers (Ge 42–45). Brought Jacob and sons to Egypt (Ge 46–47). Sons Ephraim and Manasseh blessed (Ge 48). Blessed (Ge 49:22–26; Dt 33:13–17). Death (Ge 50:22–26; Ex 13:19; Heb 11:22). 12,000 from (Rev 7:8).

2. Husband of Mary, mother of Jesus (Mt 1:16–24; 2:13–19; Lk 1:27; 2; Jn 1:45).

3. Disciple from Arimathea, who gave his tomb for Jesus' burial (Mt 27:57–61; Mk 15:43–47; Lk 24:50–52).

4. Original name of Barnabas (Ac 4:36).

JOSHUA (HOSHEA)

1. Son of Nun; name changed from Hoshea (Nu 13:8, 16; 1Ch 7:27). Fought Amalekites under Moses (Ex 17:9–14). Servant of Moses on Sinai (Ex 24:13; 32:17). Spied Canaan (Nu 13). With Caleb, allowed to enter land (Nu 14:6, 30). Succeeded Moses (Dt 1:38; 31:1–8; 34:9).

Charged Israel to conquer Canaan (Jos 1). Crossed Jordan (Jos 3–4). Circumcised sons of wilderness wanderings (Jos 5). Conquered Jericho (Jos 6), Ai (Jos 7–8), five kings at Gibeon (Jos 10:1–28), southern Canaan (Jos 10:29–43), northern Canaan (Jos 11–12). Defeated at Ai (Jos 7). Deceived by Gibeonites (Jos 9). Renewed covenant (Jos 8:30–35; 24:1–27). Divided land among tribes (Jos 13–22). Last words (Jos 23). Death (Jos 24:28–31).

2. High priest during rebuilding of temple (Hag 1–2; Zec 3:1–9; 6:11).

JOSIAH

Son of Amon; king of Judah (2Ki 21:26; 1Ch 3:14). Prophesied (1Ki 13:2). Book of Law discovered during his reign (2Ki 22; 2Ch 34:14–31). Reforms (2Ki 23:1–25; 2Ch 34:1–13; 35:1–19). Killed by Pharaoh Neco (2Ki 23:29–30; 2Ch 35:20–27).

JOTHAM

1. Son of Gideon (Jdg 9).
2. Son of Azariah (Uzziah); king of Judah (2Ki 15:32–38; 2Ch 26:21–27:9).

JOURNEY
Dt 1:33 who went ahead of you on your *j,*
2: 7 over your *j* through this vast desert
Jdg 18: 6 Your *j* has the LORD's approval."
Ezr 8:21 and ask him for a safe *j* for us
Job 16:22 before I go on the *j* of no return.
Isa 35: 8 The unclean will not *j* on it;
Mt 25:14 it will be like a man going on a *j,*
Ro 15:24 to have you assist me on my *j* there

JOY* (ENJOY ENJOYMENT JOYFUL JOYOUS OVERJOYED REJOICE REJOICES REJOICING)
Ge 31:27 so I could send you away with *j*
Lev 9:24 shouted for *j* and fell facedown.
Dt 16:15 and your *j* will be complete.
Jdg 9:19 may Abimelech be your *j,*
1Ch 12:40 and sheep, for there was *j* in Israel.
16:27 strength and *j* in his dwelling place.
16:33 sing for *j* before the LORD,
1Ch 29:17 with *j* how willingly your people
29:22 drank with great *j* in the presence
2Ch 30:26 There was great *j* in Jerusalem,
Ezr 3:12 while many others shouted for *j.*
3:13 of the shouts of *j* from the sound
6:16 of the house of God with *j.*
6:22 with *j* by changing the attitude
6:22 *j* the Feast of Unleavened Bread,
Ne 8:10 for the *j* of the LORD is your
8:12 and to celebrate with great *j,*
8:17 And their *j* was very great.
12:43 God had given them great *j.*
Est 8:16 a time of happiness and *j,*
8:17 there was *j* and gladness
9:17 and made it a day of feasting and *j.*
9:18 and made it a day of feasting and *j.*
9:19 as a day of *j* and feasting,
9:22 and *j* and giving presents of food
9:22 their sorrow was turned into *j*
Job 3: 7 may no shout of *j* be heard in it.
6:10 my *j* in unrelenting pain—
8:21 and your lips with shouts of *j.*
9:25 they fly away without a glimpse of *j*
10:20 from me so I can have a moment's *j*
20: 5 the *j* of the godless lasts
33:26 he sees God's face and shouts for *j;*
38: 7 and all the angels shouted for *j?*
Ps 4: 7 have filled my heart with greater *j*
5:11 let them ever sing for *j.*
16:11 me with *j* in your presence,
19: 8 giving *j* to the heart.
20: 5 We will shout for *j*
21: 1 How great is his *j* in the victories
21: 6 with the *j* of your presence.
27: 6 will I sacrifice with shouts of *j;*
28: 7 My heart leaps for *j*
30:11 sackcloth and clothed me with *j,*
33: 3 play skillfully, and shout for *j.*
35:27 shout for *j* and gladness;
42: 4 with shouts of *j* and thanksgiving
43: 4 to God, my *j* and my delight.
45: 7 by anointing you with the oil of *j.*
45:15 They are led in with *j* and gladness;
47: 1 shout to God with cries of *j.*
47: 5 God has ascended amid shouts of *j,*
48: 2 the *j* of the whole earth.
51: 8 Let me hear *j* and gladness;
51:12 to me the *j* of your salvation
65: 8 you call forth songs of *j.*
65:13 they shout for *j* and sing.
66: 1 Shout with *j* to God, all the earth!
67: 4 the nations be glad and sing for *j,*
71:23 My lips will shout for *j*
81: 1 Sing for *j* to God our strength;
86: 4 Bring *j* to your servant,
89:12 Hermon sing for *j* at your name.
90:14 for *j* and be glad all our days.
92: 4 I sing for *j* at the works
94:19 your consolation brought *j*
95: 1 let us sing for *j* to the LORD;
96:12 the trees of the forest will sing for *j;*
97:11 and *j* on the upright in heart.
98: 4 for *j* to the LORD, all the earth,
98: 6 shout for *j* before the LORD,
98: 8 the mountains sing together for *j;*
100: 1 for *j* to the LORD, all the earth.
105: 43 his chosen ones with shouts of *j;*
106: 5 share in the *j* of your nation
107: 22 and tell of his works with songs of *j*
118: 15 Shouts of *j* and victory
119:111 they are the *j* of my heart.
126: 2 our tongues with songs of *j.*
126: 3 and we are filled with *j.*
126: 5 will reap with songs of *j.*
126: 6 will return with songs of *j,*
132: 9 may your saints sing for *j."*
132: 16 and her saints will ever sing for *j.*
137: 3 tormentors demanded songs of *j;*
137: 6 my highest *j.*
149: 5 and sing for *j* on their beds.
Pr 10: 1 A wise son brings *j* to his father,
10:28 The prospect of the righteous is *j,*
11:10 wicked perish, there are shouts of *j.*
12:20 but *j* for those who promote peace.
14:10 and no one else can share its *j.*
14:13 and *j* may end in grief.
15:20 A wise son brings *j* to his father,
15:23 A man finds *j* in giving an apt reply
15:30 A cheerful look brings *j*
17:21 there is no *j* for the father of a fool.
Pr 21:15 it brings *j* to the righteous
23:24 of a righteous man has great *j;*
27: 9 incense bring *j* to the heart,
27:11 my son, and bring *j* to my heart;
29: 3 A man who loves wisdom brings *j*
Ecc 8:15 Then *j* will accompany him
11: 9 let your heart give you *j* in the days
Isa 9: 3 and increased their *j;*
12: 3 With *j* you will draw water
12: 6 Shout aloud and sing for *j,*
16: 9 shouts of *j* over your ripened fruit
16:10 *J* and gladness are taken away
22:13 But see, there is *j* and revelry,
24:11 all *j* turns to gloom,
24:14 raise their voices, they shout for *j;*
26:19 wake up and shout for *j.*
35: 2 will rejoice greatly and shout for *j.*
35: 6 the mute tongue shout for *j.*
35:10 Gladness and *j* will overtake them,
35:10 everlasting *j* will crown their heads
42:11 Let the people of Sela sing for *j;*
44:23 Sing for *j,* O heavens,
48:20 Announce this with shouts of *j*
49:13 Shout for *j,* O heavens;
51: 3 *J* and gladness will be found in her,
51:11 Gladness and *j* will overtake them,
51:11 everlasting *j* will crown their heads
52: 8 together they shout for *j.*
52: 9 Burst into songs of *j* together,
54: 1 burst into song, shout for *j,*
55:12 You will go out in *j*
56: 7 give them *j* in my house of prayer.
58:14 then you will find your *j*
60: 5 heart will throb and swell with *j;*
60:15 and the *j* of all generations.
61: 7 and everlasting *j* will be theirs.
65:14 out of the *j* of their hearts,
65:18 and its people a *j.*
66: 5 that we may see your *j!'*
Jer 7:34 will bring an end to the sounds of *j*
15:16 they were my *j* and my heart's
16: 9 will bring an end to the sounds of *j*
25:10 banish from them the sounds of *j*
31: 7 "Sing with *j* for Jacob;
31:12 shout for *j* on the heights of Zion;
31:13 give them comfort and *j* instead
33: 9 this city will bring me renown, *j,*
33:11 be heard once more the sounds of *j*
48:33 *J* and gladness are gone
48:33 no one treads them with shouts of *j*
48:33 they are not shouts of *j.*
51:48 will shout for *j* over Babylon,
La 2:15 the *j* of the whole earth?"
5:15 *J* is gone from our hearts;
Eze 7: 7 not *j,* upon the mountains.
24:25 their *j* and glory, the delight
Joel 1:12 Surely the *j* of mankind
1:16 *j* and gladness
Mt 13:20 and at once receives it with *j.*
13:44 in his *j* went and sold all he had
28: 8 afraid yet filled with *j,*
Mk 4:16 and at once receive it with *j.*
Lk 1:14 He will be a *j* and delight to you,
1:44 the baby in my womb leaped for *j.*
1:58 great mercy, and they shared her *j.*
2:10 news of great *j* that will be
6:23 "Rejoice in that day and leap for *j,*
8:13 the word with *j* when they hear it,
10:17 The seventy-two returned with *j*
10:21 full of *j* through the Holy Spirit,
24:41 still did not believe it because of *j*
24:52 returned to Jerusalem with great *j.*
Jn 3:29 That *j* is mine, and it is now
3:29 full of *j* when he hears
15:11 and that your *j* may be complete.
15:11 this so that my *j* may be in you
16:20 but your grief will turn to *j.*
16:21 because of her *j* that a child is born
16:22 and no one will take away your *j.*
16:24 and your *j* will be complete.
17:13 measure of my *j* within them.
Ac 2:28 with *j* in your presence.'
8: 8 So there was great *j* in that city.
13:52 And the disciples were filled with *j*
14:17 and fills your hearts with *j."*
16:34 he was filled with *j* because he had come
Ro 14:17 peace and *j* in the Holy Spirit,
15:13 the God of hope fill you with all *j*
15:32 will I may come to you with *j*

Ro 16:19 so I am full of *j* over you;
2Co 1:24 but we work with you for your *j,*
2: 3 that you would all share my *j.*
7: 4 our troubles my *j* knows no
7: 7 so that my *j* was greater than ever.
8: 2 their overflowing *j* and their
Gal 4:15 What has happened to all your *j?*
5:22 *j,* peace, patience, kindness,
Php 1: 4 I always pray with *j*
1:25 for your progress and *j* in the faith,
1:26 being with you again your *j*
2: 2 then make my *j* complete
2:29 him in the Lord with great *j,*
4: 1 and long for, my *j* and crown,
1Th 1: 6 with the *j* given by the Holy Spirit.
2:19 For what is our hope, our *j,*
2:20 Indeed, you are our glory and *j.*
3: 9 you in return for all the *j* we have
2Ti 1: 4 so that I may be filled with *j.*
Phm : 7 Your love has given me great *j*
Heb 1: 9 by anointing you with the oil of *j."*
12: 2 for the *j* set before him endured
13:17 them so that their work will be a *j,*
Jas 1: 2 Consider it pure *j,* my brothers,
4: 9 to mourning and your *j* to gloom.
1Pe 1: 8 with an inexpressible and glorious *j*
1Jn 1: 4 this to make our *j* complete.
2Jn : 4 It has given me great *j* to find some
:12 so that our *j* may be complete.
3Jn : 3 It gave me great *j* to have some
: 4 I have no greater *j*
Jude :24 without fault and with great *j*—

JOYFUL* (JOY)
Dt 16:14 Be *j* at your Feast—you, your sons
1Sa 18: 6 with *j* songs and with tambourines
1Ki 8:66 *j* and glad in heart
1Ch 15:16 as singers to sing *j* songs,
2Ch 7:10 *j* and glad in heart
Ps 68: 3 may they be happy and *j.*
100: 2 come before him with *j* songs.
Ecc 9: 7 and drink your wine with a *j* heart,
Isa 24: 8 the *j* harp is silent.
Jer 31: 4 and go out to dance with the *j.*
Hab 3:18 I will be *j* in God my Savior.
Zec 8:19 and tenth months will become *j*
10: 7 Their children will see it and be *j;*
Ro 12:12 Be *j* in hope, patient in affliction,
1Th 5:16 Be *j* always; pray continually;
Heb 12:22 thousands of angels in *j* assembly,

JOYOUS* (JOY)
Est 8:15 the city of Susa held a *j* celebration.

JUBILANT
Ps 96:12 let the fields be *j,* and everything
98: 4 burst into *j* song with music;

JUBILEE
Lev 25:11 The fiftieth year shall be a *j* for you;

JUDAH (JUDEA)
1. Son of Jacob by Leah (Ge 29:35; 35:23; 1Ch 2:1). Did not want to kill Joseph (Ge 37:26–27). Among Canaanites, fathered Perez by Tamar (Ge 38). Tribe of blessed as ruling tribe (Ge 49:8–12; Dt 33:7), numbered (Nu 1:27; 26:22), allotted land (Jos 15; Eze 48:7), failed to fully possess (Jos 15:63; Jdg 1:1–20).

2. Name used for people and land of Southern Kingdom.

Ru 1: 7 take them back to the land of *J.*
2Sa 2: 4 king over the house of *J.*
Isa 1: 1 The vision concerning *J*
3: 8 *J* is falling;
Jer 13:19 All *J* will be carried into exile,
30: 3 bring my people Israel and *J* back
Hos 1: 7 I will show love to the house of *J;*
Zec 10: 4 From *J* will come the cornerstone,
Mt 2: 6 least among the rulers of *J;*
Heb 7:14 that our Lord descended from *J,*
8: 8 and with the house of *J.*
Rev 5: 5 of the tribe of *J,* the Root of David,

JUDAISM (JEW)
Ac 13:43 devout converts to *J* followed Paul
Gal 1:13 of my previous way of life in *J,*
1:14 advancing in *J* beyond many Jews

JUDAS
1. Apostle; son of James (Lk 6:16; Jn 14:22; Ac 1:13). Probably also called Thaddaeus (Mt 10:3; Mk 3:18).

2. Brother of James and Jesus (Mt 13:55; Mk 6:3), also called Jude (Jude 1).

3. Christian prophet (Ac 15:22–32).

4. Apostle, also called Iscariot, who betrayed Jesus (Mt 10:4; 26:14–56; Mk 3:19; 14:10–50; Lk 6:16; 22:3–53; Jn 6:71; 12:4; 13:2–30; 18:2–11). Suicide of (Mt 27:3–5; Ac 1:16–25).

JUDEA (JUDAH)
Mt 2: 1 born in Bethlehem in *J,*
24:16 are in *J* flee to the mountains.
Lk 3: 1 Pontius Pilate was governor of *J,*
Ac 1: 8 and in all *J* and Samaria,
9:31 Then the church throughout *J,*
1Th 2:14 imitators of God's churches in *J,*

JUDGE (JUDGED JUDGES JUDGING JUDGMENT JUDGMENTS)
Ge 16: 5 May the LORD *j* between you
18:25 Will not the *J* of all the earth do
Lev 19:15 but *j* your neighbor fairly.
Dt 1:16 between your brothers and *j* fairly,
17:12 man who shows contempt for the *j*
32:36 The LORD will *j* his people
Jdg 2:18 Whenever the LORD raised up a *j*
1Sa 2:10 the LORD will *j* the ends
3:13 that I would *j* his family forever
7:15 *j* over Israel all the days of his life.
24:12 May the LORD *j* between you
1Ki 8:32 *J* between your servants,
1Ch 16:33 for he comes to *j* the earth.
2Ch 6:23 *J* between your servants, repaying
19: 7 *J* carefully, for with the LORD our
Job 9:15 plead with my *J* for mercy.
Ps 7: 8 *J* me, O LORD, according
7: 8 let the LORD *j* the peoples.
7:11 God is a righteous *j,*
9: 8 He will *j* the world in righteousness
50: 6 for God himself is *j.*
51: 4 and justified when you *j.*
75: 2 it is I who *j* uprightly.
76: 9 when you, O God, rose up to *j,*
82: 8 Rise up, O God, *j* the earth,
94: 2 Rise up, O *J* of the earth;
96:10 he will *j* the peoples with equity.
96:13 He will *j* the world in righteousness
98: 9 He will *j* the world in righteousness
110: 6 He will *j* the nations, heaping up
Pr 31: 9 Speak up and *j* fairly;
Isa 2: 4 He will *j* between the nations
3:13 he rises to *j* the people.
11: 3 He will not *j* by what he sees
33:22 For the LORD is our *j,*
Jer 11:20 Almighty, you who *j* righteously
Eze 7: 3 I will *j* you according
7:27 by their own standards I will *j* them
18:30 O house of Israel, I will *j* you,
20:36 so I will *j* you, declares
22: 2 "Son of man, will you *j* her?
34:17 I will *j* between one sheep
Joel 3:12 sit to *j* all the nations on every side.
Mic 3:11 Her leaders *j* for a bribe,
4: 3 He will *j* between many peoples
Mt 7: 1 Do not *j,* or you too will be judged.
Lk 6:37 "Do not *j,* and you will not be
18: 2 there was a *j* who neither feared
Jn 5:27 And he has given him authority to *j*
5:30 By myself I can do nothing; I *j* only
8:16 But if I do *j,* my decisions are right,
12:47 For I did not come to *j* the world,
12:48 There is a *j* for the one who rejects
Ac 10:42 as *j* of the living and the dead.
17:31 a day when he will *j* the world
Ro 2:16 day when God will *j* men's secrets
3: 6 how could God *j* the world?
14:10 then, why do you *j* your brother?
1Co 4: 3 indeed, I do not even *j* myself.
4: 5 Therefore *j* nothing
6: 2 And if you are to *j* the world,
6: 2 that the saints will *j* the world?
Gal 2: 6 not *j* by external appearance—
Col 2:16 Therefore do not let anyone *j* you
2Ti 4: 1 who will *j* the living and the dead,
4: 8 which the Lord, the righteous *J,*
Heb 10:30 "The Lord will *j* his people."
12:23 come to God, the *j* of all men,
13: 4 for God will *j* the adulterer
Jas 4:12 There is only one Lawgiver and *J,*
4:12 who are you to *j* your neighbor?
1Pe 4: 5 to him who is ready to *j* the living
Rev 20: 4 who had been given authority to *j.*

JUDGED (JUDGE)
Mt 7: 1 "Do not judge, or you too will be *j.*
1Co 4: 3 I care very little if I am *j* by you
10:29 For why should my freedom be *j*
11:31 But if we *j* ourselves, we would not
14:24 all that he is a sinner and will be *j*
Jas 3: 1 who teach will be *j* more strictly.
Rev 20:12 The dead were *j* according

JUDGES (JUDGE)
Jdg 2:16 Then the LORD raised up *j,*
Job 9:24 he blindfolds its *j.*
Ps 58:11 there is a God who *j* the earth."
75: 7 But it is God who *j:*
Pr 29:14 If a king *j* the poor with fairness,
Jn 5:22 Moreover, the Father *j* no one,
1Co 4: 4 It is the Lord who *j* me.
Heb 4:12 it *j* the thoughts and attitudes
1Pe 1:17 on a Father who *j* each man's work
2:23 himself to him who *j* justly.
Rev 19:11 With justice he *j* and makes war.

JUDGING (JUDGE)
Ps 9: 4 on your throne, *j* righteously.
Pr 24:23 To show partiality in *j* is not good:
Isa 16: 5 one who in *j* seeks justice
Mt 19:28 *j* the twelve tribes of Israel.
Jn 7:24 Stop *j* by mere appearances,

JUDGMENT (JUDGE)
Nu 33: 4 for the LORD had brought *j*
Dt 1:17 of any man, for *j* belongs to God.
32:41 and my hand grasps it in *j,*
1Sa 25:33 May you be blessed for your good *j*
Ps 1: 5 the wicked will not stand in the *j,*
9: 7 he has established his throne for *j.*
76: 8 From heaven you pronounced *j,*
82: 1 he gives *j* among the "gods":
119: 66 Teach me knowledge and good *j,*
143: 2 Do not bring your servant into *j,*
Pr 3:21 preserve sound *j* and discernment,
6:32 man who commits adultery lacks *j;*
8:14 Counsel and sound *j* are mine;
10:21 but fools die for lack of *j.*
11:12 man who lacks *j* derides his
12:11 but he who chases fantasies lacks *j.*
17:18 A man lacking in *j* strikes hands
18: 1 he defies all sound *j.*
28:16 A tyrannical ruler lacks *j,*
Ecc 12:14 God will bring every deed into *j,*
Isa 3:14 The LORD enters into *j*
28: 6 justice to him who sits in *j,*
53: 8 By oppression and *j* he was taken
66:16 the LORD will execute *j*
Jer 2:35 But I will pass *j* on you
25:31 he will bring *j* on all mankind
51:18 when their *j* comes, they will
Eze 11:10 and I will execute *j* on you
Da 7:22 pronounced *j* in favor of the saints
Am 7: 4 Sovereign LORD was calling for *j*
Zec 8:16 and sound *j* in your courts;
Mal 3: 5 "So I will come near to you for *j.*
Mt 5:21 who murders will be subject to *j.'*
5:22 with his brother will be subject to *j.*
10:15 on the day of *j* than for that town.
11:24 on the day of *j* than for you."
12:36 have to give account on the day of *j*
12:41 up at the *j* with this generation
Jn 5:22 but has entrusted all *j* to the Son,
5:30 as I hear, and my *j* is just,
7:24 appearances, and make a right *j."*
8:26 "I have much to say in *j* of you.
9:39 "For *j* I have come into this world,
12:31 Now is the time for *j* on this world;
16: 8 to sin and righteousness and *j:*
16:11 in regard to *j,* because the prince
Ac 24:25 self-control and the *j* to come,
Ro 2: 1 you who pass *j* on someone else,
2: 2 Now we know that God's *j*
5:16 The *j* followed one sin
12: 3 rather think of yourself with sober *j*
14:10 stand before God's *j* seat.
14:13 Therefore let us stop passing *j*
1Co 7:40 In my *j,* she is happier if she stays
11:29 body of the Lord eats and drinks *j*
2Co 5:10 appear before the *j* seat of Christ,
2Th 1: 5 is evidence that God's *j* is right,
1Ti 3: 6 fall under the same *j* as the devil.
5:12 Thus they bring *j* on themselves,
Heb 6: 2 of the dead, and eternal *j.*
9:27 to die once, and after that to face *j,*

Heb 10:27 but only a fearful expectation of *j*
Jas 2:13 *j* without mercy will be shown
4:11 are not keeping it, but sitting in *j*
1Pe 4:17 For it is time for *j* to begin
2Pe 2: 9 the unrighteous for the day of *j*,
3: 7 being kept for the day of *j*
1Jn 4:17 have confidence on the day of *j*,
Jude : 6 bound with everlasting chains for *j*
Rev 14: 7 because the hour of his *j* has come.

JUDGMENTS (JUDGE)
Jer 1:16 I will pronounce my *j* on my people
Da 9:11 and sworn *j* written in the Law
Hos 6: 5 my *j* flashed like lightning
Ro 11:33 How unsearchable his *j*,
1Co 2:15 spiritual man makes *j* about all
Rev 16: 7 true and just are your *j*."

JUG
1Sa 26:12 and water *j* near Saul's head,
1Ki 17:12 of flour in a jar and a little oil in a *j*.

JUST* (JUSTICE JUSTIFICATION JUSTIFIED JUSTIFIES JUSTIFY JUSTIFYING JUSTLY)
Ge 18:19 LORD by doing what is right and *j*,
Dt 2:12 *j* as Israel did in the land
6: 3 *j* as the LORD, the God
27: 3 and honey, *j* as the LORD,
30: 9 *j* as he delighted in your fathers,
32: 4 and all his ways are *j*.
32: 4 upright and *j* is he.
32:47 They are not *j* idle words for you—
32:50 *j* as your brother Aaron died
2Sa 8:15 doing what was *j* and right
1Ch 18:14 doing what was *j* and right
2Ch 12: 6 and said, "The LORD is *j*."
Ne 9:13 and laws that are *j* and right,
9:33 you have been *j*; you have acted
Job 34:17 Will you condemn the *j*
35: 2 Elihu said: "Do you think this is *j*?
Ps 37:28 For the LORD loves the *j*
37:30 and his tongue speaks what is *j*.
99: 4 what is *j* and right.
111: 7 of his hands are faithful and *j*;
119:121 I have done what is righteous and *j*;
Pr 1: 3 doing what is right and *j* and fair;
2: 8 for he guards the course of the *j*
2: 9 will understand what is right and *j*
8: 8 All the words of my mouth are *j*;
8:15 and rulers make laws that are *j*;
12: 5 The plans of the righteous are *j*,
21: 3 To do what is right and *j*
Isa 32: 7 even when the plea of the needy is *j*
58: 2 They ask me for *j* decisions
Jer 4: 2 if in a truthful, *j* and righteous way
22: 3 what the LORD says: Do what is *j*
22:15 He did what was right and *j*,
23: 5 do what is *j* and right in the land.
33:15 he will do what is *j* and right
Eze 18: 5 who does what is *j* and right.
18:19 Since the son has done what is *j*
18:21 and does what is *j* and right,
18:25 'The way of the Lord is not *j*.'
18:27 and does what is *j* and right,
18:29 'The way of the Lord is not *j*.'
33:14 and does what is *j* and right—
33:16 He has done what is *j* and right;
33:17 But it is their way that is not *j*.
33:17 'The way of the Lord is not *j*.'
33:19 and does what is *j* and right,
33:20 'The way of the Lord is not *j*.'
45: 9 and oppression and do what is *j*
Da 4:37 does is right and all his ways are *j*.
Jn 5:30 as I hear, and my judgment is *j*,
Ro 3:26 as to be *j* and the one who justifies
2Th 1: 6 God is *j*: He will pay back trouble
Heb 2: 2 received its *j* punishment,
1Jn 1: 9 and *j* and will forgive us our sins
Rev 15: 3 *J* and true are your ways,
16: 5 "You are *j* in these judgments,
16: 7 true and *j* are your judgments."
19: 2 for true and *j* are his judgments.

JUSTICE* (JUST)
Ge 49:16 "Dan will provide *j* for his people
Ex 23: 2 do not pervert *j* by siding
23: 6 "Do not deny *j* to your poor people
Lev 19:15 " 'Do not pervert *j*; do not show
Dt 16:19 Do not pervert *j* or show partiality.
16:20 Follow *j* and *j* alone,
24:17 the alien or the fatherless of *j*,
27:19 Cursed is the man who withholds *j*
1Sa 8: 3 accepted bribes and perverted *j*.
2Sa 15: 4 and I would see that he gets *j*."
15: 6 came to the king asking for *j*,
1Ki 3:11 for discernment in administering *j*,
3:28 wisdom from God to administer *j*.
7: 7 the Hall of *J*, where he was to judge
10: 9 to maintain *j* and righteousness."
2Ch 9: 8 to maintain *j* and righteousness."
Ezr 7:25 and judges to administer *j*
Est 1:13 experts in matters of law and *j*,
Job 8: 3 Does God pervert *j*?
9:19 matter of *j*, who will summon him?
19: 7 though I call for help, there is no *j*.
27: 2 as God lives, who has denied me *j*,
29:14 *j* was my robe and my turban.
31:13 "If I have denied *j*
34: 5 but God denies me *j*.
34:12 that the Almighty would pervert *j*.
34:17 Can he who hates *j* govern?
36: 3 I will ascribe *j* to my Maker.
36:17 *j* have taken hold of you.
37:23 in his *j* and great righteousness,
40: 8 "Would you discredit my *j*?
Ps 7: 6 Awake, my God; decree *j*.
9: 8 he will govern the peoples with *j*.
9:16 The LORD is known by his *j*;
11: 7 he loves *j*;
33: 5 LORD loves righteousness and *j*;
36: 6 your *j* like the great deep.
37: 6 *j* of your cause like the noonday
45: 6 a scepter of *j* will be the scepter
72: 1 Endow the king with your *j*, O God
72: 2 your afflicted ones with *j*.
89:14 *j* are the foundation of your throne;
97: 2 *j* are the foundation of his throne.
99: 4 The King is mighty, he loves *j*—
101: 1 I will sing of your love and *j*;
103: 6 and *j* for all the oppressed.
106: 3 Blessed are they who maintain *j*,
112: 5 who conducts his affairs with *j*.
140:12 I know that the LORD secures *j*
Pr 8:20 along the paths of *j*,
16:10 and his mouth should not betray *j*.
17:23 to pervert the course of *j*.
18: 5 or to deprive the innocent of *j*.
19:28 A corrupt witness mocks at *j*,
21:15 When *j* is done, it brings joy
28: 5 Evil men do not understand *j*,
29: 4 By *j* a king gives a country stability
29: 7 The righteous care about *j*
29:26 from the LORD that man gets *j*.
Ecc 3:16 place of *j*—wickedness was there.
5: 8 poor oppressed in a district, and *j*
Isa 1:17 Seek *j*,
1:21 She once was full of *j*;
1:27 Zion will be redeemed with *j*,
5: 7 he looked for *j*, but saw bloodshed;
5:16 Almighty will be exalted by his *j*,
5:23 but deny *j* to the innocent.
9: 7 it with *j* and righteousness
10: 2 and withhold *j* from the oppressed of
11: 4 with *j* he will give decisions
16: 5 one who in judging seeks *j*
28: 6 He will be a spirit of *j*
28:17 I will make *j* the measuring line
29:21 deprive the innocent of *j*.
30:18 For the LORD is a God of *j*.
32: 1 and rulers will rule with *j*.
32:16 *J* will dwell in the desert
33: 5 with *j* and righteousness.
42: 1 and he will bring *j* to the nations.
42: 3 In faithfulness he will bring forth *j*;
42: 4 till he establishes *j* on earth.
51: 4 my *j* will become a light
51: 5 my arm will bring *j* to the nations.
56: 1 "Maintain *j*
59: 4 No one calls for *j*;
59: 8 there is no *j* in their paths.
59: 9 So *j* is far from us,
59:11 We look for *j*, but find none;
59:14 So *j* is driven back,
59:15 that there was no *j*.
61: 8 "For I, the LORD, love *j*;
Jer 9:24 *j* and righteousness on earth,
10:24 Correct me, LORD, but only with *j*
12: 1 speak with you about your *j*:
21:12 " 'Administer *j* every morning;
30:11 I will discipline you but only with *j*;
46:28 I will discipline you but only with *j*;
La 3:36 to deprive a man of *j*—
Eze 22:29 mistreat the alien, denying them *j*.
34:16 I will shepherd the flock with *j*.
Hos 2:19 you in righteousness and *j*,
12: 6 maintain love and *j*,
Am 2: 7 and deny *j* to the oppressed.
5: 7 You who turn *j* into bitterness
5:12 and you deprive the poor of *j*
5:15 maintain *j* in the courts.
5:24 But let *j* roll on like a river,
6:12 But you have turned *j* into poison
Mic 3: 1 Should you not know *j*,
3: 8 and with *j* and might,
3: 9 who despise *j*
Hab 1: 4 and *j* never prevails.
1: 4 so that *j* is perverted.
Zep 3: 5 by morning he dispenses his *j*,
Zec 7: 9 'Administer true *j*; show mercy
Mal 2:17 or "Where is the God of *j*?"
3: 5 and deprive aliens of *j*,
Mt 12:18 he will proclaim *j* to the nations.
12:20 till he leads *j* to victory.
23:23 important matters of the law—*j*,
Lk 11:42 you neglect *j* and the love of God.
18: 3 'Grant me *j* against my adversary.'
18: 5 I will see that she gets *j*,
18: 7 And will not God bring about *j*
18: 8 he will see that they get *j*,
Ac 8:33 humiliation he was deprived of *j*.
17:31 with *j* by the man he has appointed.
28: 4 *J* has not allowed him to live."
Ro 3:25 He did this to demonstrate his *j*,
3:26 it to demonstrate his *j*
2Co 7:11 what readiness to see *j* done.
Heb 11:33 administered *j*, and gained what
Rev 19:11 With *j* he judges and makes war.

JUSTIFICATION* (JUST)
Eze 16:52 for you have furnished some *j*
Ro 4:25 and was raised to life for our *j*.
5:16 many trespasses and brought *j*.
5:18 of righteousness was *j* that brings

JUSTIFIED* (JUST)
Ps 51: 4 and *j* when you judge.
Lk 18:14 rather than the other, went home *j*
Ac 13:39 from everything you could not be *j*
13:39 him everyone who believes is *j*
Ro 3:24 and are *j* freely by his grace
3:28 For we maintain that a man is *j*
4: 2 If, in fact, Abraham was *j* by works,
5: 1 since we have been *j* through faith,
5: 9 Since we have now been *j*
8:30 those he called, he also *j*; those he *j*,
10:10 heart that you believe and are *j*,
1Co 6:11 you were *j* in the name
Gal 2:16 in Christ Jesus that we may be *j*
2:16 observing the law no one will be *j*.
2:16 sinners' know that a man is not *j*
2:17 "If, while we seek to be *j* in Christ,
3:11 Clearly no one is *j* before God,
3:24 to Christ that we might be *j* by faith
5: 4 to be *j* by law have been alienated
Tit 3: 7 so that, having been *j* by his grace,
Jas 2:24 You see that a person is *j*

JUSTIFIES* (JUST)
Ro 3:26 one who *j* those who have faith
4: 5 but trusts God who *j* the wicked,
8:33 God has chosen? It is God who *j*.

JUSTIFY* (JUST)
Est 7: 4 such distress would *j* disturbing
Job 40: 8 you condemn me to *j* yourself?
Isa 53:11 my righteous servant will *j* many,
Lk 10:29 But he wanted to *j* himself,
16:15 "You are the ones who *j* yourselves
Ro 3:30 who will *j* the circumcised by faith
Gal 3: 8 that God would *j* the Gentiles

JUSTIFYING* (JUST)
Job 32: 2 angry with Job for *j* himself rather

JUSTLY* (JUST)
Ps 58: 1 Do you rulers indeed speak *j*?
67: 4 for you rule the peoples *j*
Jer 7: 5 and deal with each other *j*,
Mic 6: 8 To act *j* and to love mercy
Lk 23:41 We are punished *j*,
1Pe 2:23 himself to him who judges *j*.

KADESH
Nu 20: 1 of Zin, and they stayed at *K*.
Dt 1:46 And so you stayed in *K* many days

KADESH BARNEA
Nu 32: 8 I sent them from *K* to look over

KEBAR
Eze 1: 1 among the exiles by the *K* River,

KEDORLAOMER
Ge 14:17 Abram returned from defeating *K*

KEEP (KEEPER KEEPING KEEPS KEPT)
Ge 31:49 "May the LORD *k* watch
Ex 15:26 his commands and *k* all his
20: 6 and *k* my commandments.
Lev 15:31 You must *k* the Israelites separate
Nu 6:24 and *k* you;
Dt 4: 2 but *k* the commands of the LORD
6:17 Be sure to *k* the commands
7: 9 who love him and *k* his commands.
7:12 your God will *k* his covenant
11: 1 your God and *k* his requirements,
13: 4 *K* his commands and obey him;
30:10 your God and *k* his commands
30:16 and to *k* his commands, decrees
Jos 22: 5 careful to *k* the commandment
1Ki 8:58 and to *k* the commands,
2Ki 17:19 Judah did not *k* the commands
23: 3 the LORD and *k* his commands,
1Ch 29:18 and *k* their hearts loyal to you.
2Ch 6:14 you who *k* your covenant of love
34:31 the LORD and *k* his commands,
Job 14:16 but not *k* track of my sin.
Ps 18:28 You, O LORD, *k* my lamp burning
19:13 *K* your servant also from willful
78:10 they did not *k* God's covenant
119: 2 Blessed are they who *k* his statutes
119: 9 can a young man *k* his way pure?
121: 7 The LORD will *k* you
141: 3 *k* watch over the door of my lips.
Pr 4:21 *k* them within your heart;
4:24 *k* corrupt talk far from your lips.
30: 8 *K* falsehood and lies far from me;
Ecc 3: 6 a time to *k* and a time
12:13 and *k* his commandments,
Isa 26: 3 You will *k* in perfect peace
42: 6 I will *k* you and will make you
58:13 "If you *k* your feet
Jer 16:11 forsook me and did not *k* my law.
Eze 20:19 and be careful to *k* my laws.
Mt 10:10 for the worker is worth his *k*.
Lk 12:35 and *k* your lamps burning,
17:33 tries to *k* his life will lose it,
Jn 10:24 How long will you *k* us in suspense
12:25 in this world will *k* it for eternal life
Ac 2:24 for death to *k* its hold on him.
18: 9 "Do not be afraid; *k* on speaking,
Ro 7:19 want to do—this I *k* on doing.
12:11 but *k* your spiritual fervor,
14:22 you believe about these things *k*
16:17 *K* away from them.
1Co 1: 8 He will *k* you strong to the end,
2Co 12: 7 To *k* me from becoming conceited
Gal 5:25 let us *k* in step with the Spirit.
Eph 4: 3 Make every effort to *k* the unity
2Th 3: 6 to *k* away from every brother who
1Ti 5:22 *K* yourself pure.
2Ti 4: 5 *k* your head in all situations,
Heb 9:20 God has commanded you to *k*."
13: 5 *K* your lives free from the love
Jas 1:26 and yet does not *k* a tight rein
2: 8 If you really *k* the royal law found
3: 2 able to *k* his whole body in check.
2Pe 1: 8 will *k* you from being ineffective
Jude :21 *K* yourselves in God's love
:24 able to *k* you from falling
Rev 3:10 also *k* you from the hour
22: 9 of all who *k* the words of this book.

KEEPER (KEEP)
Ge 4: 9 I my brother's *k*?" The LORD

KEEPING (KEEP)
Ex 20: 8 the Sabbath day by *k* it holy.
Dt 5:12 the Sabbath day by *k* it holy,
13:18 *k* all his commands that I am
Ps 19:11 in *k* them there is great reward.
119:112 My heart is set on *k* your decrees
Pr 15: 3 *k* watch on the wicked
Mt 3: 8 Produce fruit in *k* with repentance.
Lk 2: 8 *k* watch over their flocks at night.
1Co 7:19 *K* God's commands is what counts.
2Co 8: 5 and then to us in *k* with God's will.
Jas 4:11 you are not *k* it, but sitting
1Pe 3:16 and respect, *k* a clear conscience,
2Pe 3: 9 Lord is not slow in *k* his promise,

KEEPS (KEEP)
Ne 1: 5 who *k* his covenant of love
Ps 15: 4 who *k* his oath
Pr 12:23 A prudent man *k* his knowledge
15:21 of understanding *k* a straight
17:28 a fool is thought wise if he *k* silent,
29:11 a wise man *k* himself under control
Isa 56: 2 who *k* the Sabbath
Da 9: 4 who *k* his covenant of love
Am 5:13 Therefore the prudent man *k* quiet
Jn 7:19 Yet not one of you *k* the law.
8:51 if anyone *k* my word, he will never
1Co 13: 5 is not easily angered, it *k* no record
Jas 2:10 For whoever *k* the whole law
Rev 22: 7 Blessed is he who *k* the words

KEILAH
1Sa 23:13 that David had escaped from *K*,

KEPT (KEEP)
Ex 12:42 Because the LORD *k* vigil that
Dt 7: 8 and *k* the oath he swore
2Ki 18: 6 he *k* the commands the LORD had
Ne 9: 8 You have *k* your promise
Ps 130: 3 If you, O LORD, *k* a record of sins,
Isa 38:17 In your love you *k* me
Mt 19:20 these I have *k*," the young man
2Co 11: 9 I have *k* myself from being
2Ti 4: 7 finished the race, I have *k* the faith.
1Pe 1: 4 spoil or fade—*k* in heaven for you,

KERNEL
Mk 4:28 then the full *k* in the head.
Jn 12:24 a *k* of wheat falls to the ground

KEY (KEYS)
Isa 33: 6 the fear of the LORD is the *k*
Rev 20: 1 having the *k* to the Abyss

KEYS* (KEY)
Mt 16:19 I will give you the *k* of the kingdom
Rev 1:18 And I hold the *k* of death

KICK*
Ac 26:14 for you to *k* against the goads.'

KILL (KILLED KILLS)
Ecc 3: 3 a time to *k* and a time to heal,
Mt 10:28 *k* the body but cannot *k* the soul.
17:23 They will *k* him, and on the third
Mk 9:31 will *k* him, and after three days
10:34 spit on him, flog him and *k* him.

KILLED (KILL)
Ge 4: 8 his brother Abel and *k* him.
Ex 2:12 he *k* the Egyptian and hid him
13:15 the LORD *k* every firstborn
Nu 35:11 who has *k* someone accidentally
1Sa 17:50 down the Philistine and *k* him.
Ne 9:26 They *k* your prophets, who had
Hos 6: 5 I *k* you with the words
Lk 11:48 they *k* the prophets, and you build
Ac 3:15 You *k* the author of life,

KILLS (KILL)
Ex 21:12 *k* him shall surely be put to death.
Lev 24:21 but whoever *k* a man must be put
2Co 3: 6 for the letter *k*, but the Spirit gives

KIND (KINDNESS KINDNESSES KINDS)
Ge 1:24 animals, each according to its *k*."
2Ch 10: 7 "If you will be *k* to these people
Pr 11:17 A *k* man benefits himself,
12:25 but a *k* word cheers him up.
14:21 blessed is he who is *k* to the needy.
14:31 whoever is *k* to the needy honors
19:17 He who is *k* to the poor lends
Da 4:27 by being *k* to the oppressed.
Lk 6:35 because he is *k* to the ungrateful
1Co 13: 4 Love is patient, love is *k*.
15:35 With what *k* of body will they
Eph 4:32 Be *k* and compassionate
1Th 5:15 but always try to be *k* to each other
2Ti 2:24 instead, he must be *k* to everyone,
Tit 2: 5 to be busy at home, to be *k*,

KINDHEARTED* (HEART)
Pr 11:16 A *k* woman gains respect,

KINDNESS (KIND)
Ge 24:12 and show *k* to my master Abraham
32:10 I am unworthy of all the *k*
39:21 he showed him *k* and granted him
Jdg 8:35 failed to show *k* to the family
Ru 2:20 has not stopped showing his *k*
2Sa 9: 3 to whom I can show God's *k*?"
22:51 he shows unfailing *k*
Ps 18:50 he shows unfailing *k*
141: 5 righteous man strike me—it is a *k*;
Isa 54: 8 but with everlasting *k*
Jer 9:24 I am the LORD, who exercises *k*,
Hos 11: 4 I led them with cords of human *k*,
Ac 14:17 He has shown *k* by giving you rain
Ro 11:22 Consider therefore the *k*
2Co 6: 6 understanding, patience and *k*;
Gal 5:22 peace, patience, *k*, goodness,
Eph 2: 7 expressed in his *k* to us
Col 3:12 yourselves with compassion, *k*,
Tit 3: 4 But when the *k* and love
2Pe 1: 7 brotherly *k*; and to brotherly *k*,

KINDNESSES* (KIND)
Ps 106: 7 did not remember your many *k*,
Isa 63: 7 I will tell of the *k* of the LORD,
63: 7 to his compassion and many *k*.

KINDS (KIND)
Ge 1:12 bearing seed according to their *k*
1Co 12: 4 There are different *k* of gifts,
1Ti 6:10 of money is a root of all *k* of evil.
1Pe 1: 6 had to suffer grief in all *k* of trials.

KING (KING'S KINGDOM KINGDOMS KINGS)
1. Kings of Judah and Israel: see Saul, David, Solomon.
2. Kings of Judah: see Rehoboam, Abijah, Asa, Jehoshaphat, Jehoram, Ahaziah, Athaliah (Queen), Joash, Amaziah, Azariah (Uzziah), Jotham, Ahaz, Hezekiah, Manasseh, Amon, Josiah, Jehoahaz, Jehoiakim, Jehoiachin, Zedekiah.
3. Kings of Israel: see Jeroboam I, Nadab, Baasha, Elah, Zimri, Tibni, Omri, Ahab, Ahaziah, Joram, Jehu, Jehoahaz, Jehoash, Jeroboam II, Zechariah, Shallum, Menahem, Pekah, Pekahiah, Hoshea.
Ex 1: 8 a new *k*, who did not know about
Dt 17:14 "Let us set a *k* over us like all
Jdg 17: 6 In those days Israel had no *k*;
1Sa 8: 5 now appoint a *k* to lead us,
11:15 as *k* in the presence of the LORD.
12:12 the LORD your God was your *k*.
2Sa 2: 4 and there they anointed David *k*
1Ki 1:30 Solomon your son shall be *k*
Ps 2: 6 "I have installed my *K*
24: 7 that the *K* of glory may come in.
44: 4 You are my *K* and my God,
47: 7 For God is the *K* of all the earth;
Isa 32: 1 See, a *k* will reign in righteousness
Jer 30: 9 and David their *k*,
Hos 3: 5 their God and David their *k*.
Mic 2:13 *k* will pass through before them,
Zec 9: 9 See, your *k* comes to you,
Mt 2: 2 is the one who has been born *k*
27:11 "Are you the *k* of the Jews?" "Yes,
Lk 19:38 "Blessed is the *k* who comes
23: 3 "Are you the *k* of the Jews?" "Yes,
23:38 THE *K* OF THE JEWS.
Jn 1:49 of God; you are the *K* of Israel."
12:13 "Blessed is the *K* of Israel!"
Ac 17: 7 saying that there is another *k*,
1Ti 1:17 Now to the *K* eternal, immortal,
6:15 the *K* of kings and Lord of lords,
Heb 7: 1 This Melchizedek was *k* of Salem
1Pe 2:13 to the *k*, as the supreme authority,
2:17 of believers, fear God, honor the *k*.
Rev 15: 3 *K* of the ages.
17:14 he is Lord of lords and *K* of kings—
19:16 *K* OF KINGS AND LORD

KING'S (KING)
Pr 21: 1 The *k* heart is in the hand
Ecc 8: 3 in a hurry to leave the *k* presence.

KINGDOM (KING)
Ex 19: 6 you will be for me a *k* of priests
Dt 17:18 When he takes the throne of his *k*,
2Sa 7:12 body, and I will establish his *k*.
1Ki 11:31 to tear the *k* out of Solomon's hand
1Ch 17:11 own sons, and I will establish his *k*.
29:11 Yours, O LORD, is the *k*;
Ps 45: 6 justice will be the scepter of your *k*.
103: 19 and his *k* rules over all.
145: 11 They will tell of the glory of your *k*
Eze 29:14 There they will be a lowly *k*.

Da 2:39 'After you, another *k* will rise,
4: 3 His *k* is an eternal *k;*
7:27 His *k* will be an everlasting *k,*
Ob :21 And the *k* will be the LORD's.
Mt 3: 2 Repent, for the *k* of heaven is near
4:17 Repent, for the *k* of heaven is near
4:23 preaching the good news of the *k,*
5: 3 for theirs is the *k* of heaven.
5:10 for theirs is the *k* of heaven.
5:19 great in the *k* of heaven.
5:19 least in the *k* of heaven,
5:20 you will certainly not enter the *k*
6:10 your *k* come,
6:33 But seek first his *k* and his
7:21 Lord,' will enter the *k* of heaven,
8:11 Isaac and Jacob in the *k* of heaven.
8:12 the subjects of the *k* will be thrown
9:35 preaching the good news of the *k*
10: 7 preach this message: 'The *k*
11:11 least in the *k* of heaven is greater
11:12 the *k* of heaven has been forcefully
12:25 "Every *k* divided against itself will
12:26 How then can his *k* stand?
12:28 then the *k* of God has come
13:11 knowledge of the secrets of the *k*
13:19 hears the message about the *k*
13:24 "The *k* of heaven is like a man who
13:31 *k* of heaven is like a mustard seed,
13:33 "The *k* of heaven is like yeast that
13:38 stands for the sons of the *k.*
13:41 of his *k* everything that causes sin
13:43 the sun in the *k* of their Father.
13:44 *k* of heaven is like treasure hidden
13:45 the *k* of heaven is like a merchant
13:47 *k* of heaven is like a net that was let
13:52 has been instructed about the *k*
16:19 the keys of the *k* of heaven;
16:28 the Son of Man coming in his *k.*"
18: 1 the greatest in the *k* of heaven?"
18: 3 you will never enter the *k*
18: 4 the greatest in the *k* of heaven.
18:23 the *k* of heaven is like a king who
19:12 because of the *k* of heaven.
19:14 for the *k* of heaven belongs to such
19:23 man to enter the *k* of heaven.
19:24 for a rich man to enter the *k* of God
20: 1 "For the *k* of heaven is like
20:21 the other at your left in your *k.*"
21:31 the prostitutes are entering the *k*
21:43 "Therefore I tell you that the *k*
22: 2 "The *k* of heaven is like a king who
23:13 You shut the *k* of heaven
24: 7 rise against nation, and *k* against *k.*
24:14 gospel of the *k* will be preached
25: 1 "At that time the *k*
25:34 the *k* prepared for you
26:29 anew with you in my Father's *k.*"
Mk 1:15 "The *k* of God is near.
3:24 If a *k* is divided against itself,
3:24 against itself, that *k* cannot stand.
4:11 "The secret of the *k*
4:26 "This is what the *k* of God is like.
4:30 "What shall we say the *k*
6:23 I will give you, up to half my *k.*"
9: 1 before they see the *k* of God come
9:47 better for you to enter the *k* of God
10:14 for the *k* of God belongs to such
10:15 anyone who will not receive the *k*
10:23 for the rich to enter the *k* of God!"
10:24 how hard it is to enter the *k* of God
10:25 for a rich man to enter the *k* of God
11:10 "Blessed is the coming *k*
12:34 "You are not far from the *k* of God
13: 8 rise against nation, and *k* against *k.*
14:25 day when I drink it anew in the *k*
15:43 who was himself waiting for the *k*
Lk 1:33 Jacob forever; his *k* will never
4:43 of the *k* of God to the other towns
6:20 for yours is the *k* of God.
7:28 in the *k* of God is greater than he."
8: 1 proclaiming the good news of the *k*
8:10 knowledge of the secrets of the *k*
9: 2 out to preach the *k* of God
9:11 spoke to them about the *k* of God,
9:27 before they see the *k* of God."
9:60 you go and proclaim the *k* of God
9:62 fit for service in the *k* of God."
10: 9 'The *k* of God is near you.'
10:11 sure of this: The *k* of God is near.'
11: 2 your *k* come.

Lk 11:17 "Any *k* divided against itself will
11:18 himself, how can his *k* stand?
11:20 then the *k* of God has come to you.
12:31 seek his *k,* and these things will be
12:32 has been pleased to give you the *k.*
13:18 "What is the *k* of God like?
13:20 What shall I compare the *k* of God
13:28 all the prophets in the *k* of God,
13:29 places at the feast in the *k* of God.
14:15 eat at the feast in the *k* of God."
16:16 the good news of the *k*
17:20 when the *k* of God would come,
17:20 *k* of God does not come with careful
17:21 because the *k* of God is within you
18:16 for the *k* of God belongs to such
18:17 anyone who will not receive the *k*
18:24 for the rich to enter the *k* of God!
18:25 for a rich man to enter the *k* of God
18:29 for the sake of the *k* of God will fail
19:11 and the people thought that the *k*
21:10 rise against nation, and *k* against *k.*
21:31 you know that the *k* of God is near.
22:16 until it finds fulfillment in the *k*
22:18 the vine until the *k* of God comes."
22:29 And I confer on you a *k,* just
22:30 and drink at my table in my *k*
23:42 me when you come into your *k.*"
23:51 he was waiting for the *k* of God.
Jn 3: 3 no one can see the *k* of God.
3: 5 no one can enter the *k* of God.
18:36 now my *k* is from another place."
18:36 "My *k* is not of this world.
Ac 1: 3 and spoke about the *k* of God.
1: 6 going to restore the *k* to Israel?"
8:12 he preached the good news of the *k*
14:22 hardships to enter the *k* of God,"
19: 8 arguing persuasively about the *k*
20:25 about preaching the *k* will ever see
28:23 and declared to them the *k* of God
28:31 hindrance he preached the *k*
Ro 14:17 For the *k* of God is not a matter
1Co 4:20 For the *k* of God is not a matter
6: 9 the wicked will not inherit the *k*
6:10 swindlers will inherit the *k* of God.
15:24 hands over the *k* to God the Father
15:50 blood cannot inherit the *k* of God,
Gal 5:21 live like this will not inherit the *k*
Eph 2: 2 and of the ruler of the *k* of the air,
5: 5 has any inheritance in the *k*
Col 1:12 of the saints in the *k* of light.
1:13 and brought us into the *k*
4:11 among my fellow workers for the *k*
1Th 2:12 who calls you into his *k* and glory.
2Th 1: 5 will be counted worthy of the *k*
2Ti 4: 1 in view of his appearing and his *k,*
4:18 bring me safely to his heavenly *k.*
Heb 1: 8 will be the scepter of your *k.*
12:28 we are receiving a *k* that cannot be
Jas 2: 5 to inherit the *k* he promised those
2Pe 1:11 into the eternal *k* of our Lord
Rev 1: 6 has made us to be a *k* and priests
1: 9 companion in the suffering and *k*
5:10 You have made them to be a *k*
11:15 of the world has become the *k*
11:15 "The *k* of the world has become
12:10 the power and the *k* of our God,
16:10 his *k* was plunged into darkness.
17:12 who have not yet received a *k,*

KINGDOMS (KING)

2Ki 19:15 God over all the *k* of the earth.
19:19 so that all *k* on earth may know
2Ch 20: 6 rule over all the *k* of the nations.
Ps 68:32 Sing to God, O *k* of the earth,
Isa 37:16 God over all the *k* of the earth.
37:20 so that all *k* on earth may know
Eze 29:15 It will be the lowliest of *k*
37:22 or be divided into two *k.*
Da 4:17 Most High is sovereign over the *k*
7:17 great beasts are four *k* that will rise
Zep 3: 8 to gather the *k*

KINGS (KING)

Ps 2: 2 The *k* of the earth take their stand
47: 9 for the *k* of the earth belong to God
68:29 *k* will bring you gifts.
72:11 All *k* will bow down to him
110: 5 he will crush *k* on the day
149: 8 to bind their *k* with fetters,
Pr 16:12 *K* detest wrongdoing,
Isa 24:21 and the *k* on the earth below.

Isa 52:15 and *k* will shut their mouths
60:11 their *k* led in triumphal procession.
Da 2:21 he sets up *k* and deposes them.
7:24 ten horns are ten *k* who will come
Lk 21:12 and you will be brought before *k*
1Co 4: 8 You have become *k*—
1Ti 2: 2 for *k* and all those in authority,
6:15 the King of *k* and Lord of lords,
Rev 1: 5 and the ruler of the *k* of the earth.
17:14 he is Lord of lords and King of *k*—
19:16 KING OF *K* AND LORD

KINSMAN-REDEEMER (REDEEM)

Ru 3: 9 over me, since you are a *k.*"
4:14 day has not left you without a *k.*

KISS (KISSED KISSES)

Ps 2:12 *K* the Son, lest he be angry
Pr 24:26 is like a *k* on the lips.
SS 1: 2 *Beloved* Let him *k* me
8: 1 I would *k* you,
Lk 22:48 the Son of Man with a *k?*"
Ro 16:16 Greet one another with a holy *k.*
1Co 16:20 Greet one another with a holy *k.*
2Co 13:12 Greet one another with a holy *k.*
1Th 5:26 Greet all the brothers with a holy *k*
1Pe 5:14 Greet one another with a *k* of love.

KISSED (KISS)

Mk 14:45 Judas said, "Rabbi!" and *k* him.
Lk 7:38 *k* them and poured perfume

KISSES* (KISS)

Pr 27: 6 but an enemy multiplies *k.*
SS 1: 2 with the *k* of his mouth—

KNEE (KNEES)

Isa 45:23 Before me every *k* will bow;
Ro 14:11 'every *k* will bow before me;
Php 2:10 name of Jesus every *k* should bow,

KNEEL (KNELT)

Est 3: 2 But Mordecai would not *k* down
Ps 95: 6 let us *k* before the LORD our
Eph 3:14 For this reason I *k*

KNEES (KNEE)

1Ki 19:18 all whose *k* have not bowed
Isa 35: 3 steady the *k* that give way;
Da 6:10 times a day he got down on his *k*
Lk 5: 8 he fell at Jesus' *k* and said,
Heb 12:12 your feeble arms and weak *k.*

KNELT* (KNEEL)

1Ki 1:16 Bathsheba bowed low and *k*
2Ch 6:13 and then *k* down before the whole
7: 3 they *k* on the pavement
29:29 everyone present with him *k* down
Est 3: 2 officials at the king's gate *k* down
Mt 8: 2 and *k* before him and said,
9:18 a ruler came and *k* before him
15:25 The woman came and *k* before him
17:14 a man approached Jesus and *k*
27:29 *k* in front of him and mocked him.
Lk 22:41 *k* down and prayed, "Father,
Ac 20:36 he *k* down with all of them
21: 5 there on the beach we *k* to pray.

KNEW (KNOW)

2Ch 33:13 Manasseh *k* that the LORD is God
Job 23: 3 If only I *k* where to find him;
Pr 24:12 "But we *k* nothing about this,"
Jer 1: 5 you in the womb I *k* you,
Jnh 4: 2 I *k* that you are a gracious
Mt 7:23 tell them plainly, 'I never *k* you.
12:25 Jesus *k* their thoughts
Jn 2:24 himself to them, for he *k* all men.
14: 7 If you really *k* me, you would know

KNIFE

Ge 22:10 and took the *k* to slay his son.
Pr 23: 2 and put a *k* to your throat

KNOCK* (KNOCKS)

Mt 7: 7 *k* and the door will be opened
Lk 11: 9 *k* and the door will be opened
Rev 3:20 I am! I stand at the door and *k.*

KNOCKS (KNOCK)

Mt 7: 8 and to him who *k,* the door will be

KNOW (FOREKNEW FOREKNOWLEDGE KNEW KNOWING KNOWLEDGE KNOWN KNOWS)

Ge 22:12 Now I *k* that you fear God,
Ex 6: 7 you will *k* that I am the LORD

Ex 14: 4 and the Egyptians will *k* that I am
33:13 teach me your ways so I may *k* you
Dt 7: 9 *K* therefore that the LORD your
18:21 "How can we *k* when a message
Jos 4:24 of the earth might *k* that the hand
23:14 You *k* with all your heart
1Sa 17:46 the whole world will *k* that there is
1Ki 8:39 heart (for you alone *k* the hearts
Job 11: 6 *K* this: God has even forgotten
19:25 I *k* that my Redeemer lives,
42: 3 things too wonderful for me to *k*.
Ps 9:10 Those who *k* your name will trust
46:10 "Be still, and *k* that I am God;
100: 3 *K* that the LORD is God.
139: 1 and you *k* me.
139: 23 Search me, O God, and *k* my heart;
145: 12 so that all men may *k*
Pr 27: 1 for you do not *k* what a day may
30: 4 Tell me if you *k*!
Ecc 8: 5 wise heart will *k* the proper time
Isa 29:15 "Who sees us? Who will *k*?"
40:21 Do you not *k*?
Jer 6:15 they do not even *k* how to blush.
22:16 Is that not what it means to *k* me?"
24: 7 I will give them a heart to *k* me,
31:34 his brother, saying, '*K* the LORD,'
33: 3 unsearchable things you do not *k*.'
Eze 2: 5 they will *k* that a prophet has been
6:10 they will *k* that I am the LORD;
Da 11:32 people who *k* their God will firmly
Mt 6: 3 let your left hand *k* what your right
7:11 *k* how to give good gifts
9: 6 But so that you may *k* that the Son
22:29 you do not *k* the Scriptures
24:42 you do not *k* on what day your
26:74 "I don't *k* the man!" Immediately
Mk 12:24 you do not *k* the Scriptures
Lk 1: 4 so that you may *k* the certainty
11:13 *k* how to give good gifts
12:48 But the one who does not *k*
13:25 'I don't *k* you or where you come
21:31 you *k* that the kingdom of God is
23:34 for they do not *k* what they are
Jn 1:26 among you stands one you do not *k*
3:11 we speak of what we *k*,
4:22 we worship what we do *k*,
4:42 and we *k* that this man really is
6:69 and *k* that you are the Holy One
7:28 You do not *k* him, but I *k* him
8:14 for I *k* where I came from
8:19 "You do not *k* me or my Father,"
8:32 Then you will *k* the truth,
8:55 Though you do not *k* him, I *k* him.
9:25 One thing I do *k*.
10: 4 him because they *k* his voice.
10:14 I *k* my sheep and my sheep *k* me—
10:27 I *k* them, and they follow me.
12:35 the dark does not *k* where he is
13:17 Now that you *k* these things,
13:35 all men will *k* that you are my
14:17 you *k* him, for he lives with you
15:21 for they do not *k* the One who sent
16:30 we can see that you *k* all things
17: 3 that they may *k* you, the only true
17:23 to let the world *k* that you sent me
21:15 he said, "you *k* that I love you."
21:24 We *k* that his testimony is true.
Ac 1: 7 "It is not for you to *k* the times
1:24 "Lord, you *k* everyone's heart.
Ro 3:17 and the way of peace they do not *k*
6: 3 Or don't you *k* that all
6: 6 For we *k* that our old self was
6:16 Don't you *k* that when you offer
7:14 We *k* that the law is spiritual;
7:18 I *k* that nothing good lives in me,
8:22 We *k* that the whole creation has
8:26 We do not *k* what we ought to pray
8:28 we *k* that in all things God works
1Co 1:21 through its wisdom did not *k* him,
2: 2 For I resolved to *k* nothing
3:16 Don't you *k* that you yourselves
5: 6 Don't you *k* that a little yeast
6: 2 Do you not *k* that the saints will
6:15 Do you not *k* that your bodies are
6:16 Do you not *k* that he who unites
6:19 Do you not *k* that your body is
7:16 How do you *k*, wife, whether you
8: 2 does not yet *k* as he ought to *k*.
9:13 Don't you *k* that those who work
9:24 Do you not *k* that

1Co 13: 9 For we *k* in part and we prophesy
13:12 Now I *k* in part; then I shall *k* fully,
15:58 because you *k* that your labor
2Co 5: 1 we *k* that if the earthly tent we live
5:11 we *k* what it is to fear the Lord,
8: 9 For you *k* the grace
Gal 1:11 you to *k*, brothers, that the gospel I
2:16 not 'Gentile sinners' *k* that a man
Eph 1:17 so that you may *k* him better.
1:18 in order that you may *k* the hope
6: 8 you *k* that the Lord will reward
6: 9 since you *k* that he who is both
Php 3:10 I want to *k* Christ and the power
4:12 I *k* what it is to be in need,
Col 2: 2 order that they may *k* the mystery
4: 1 because you *k* that you
4: 6 so that you may *k* how
1Th 3: 3 You *k* quite well that we were
5: 2 for you *k* very well that the day
2Th 1: 8 punish those who do not *k* God
1Ti 1: 7 they do not *k* what they are talking
3: 5 (If anyone does not *k* how
3:15 you will *k* how people ought
2Ti 1:12 because I *k* whom I have believed,
2:23 you *k* they produce quarrels.
3:14 you *k* those from whom you
Heb 8:11 because they will all *k* me,
11: 8 he did not *k* where he was going.
Jas 1: 3 because you *k* that the testing
3: 1 you *k* that we who teach will be
4: 4 don't you *k* that friendship
4:14 *k* what will happen tomorrow.
1Pe 1:18 For you *k* that it was not
2Pe 1:12 even though you *k* them
1Jn 2: 3 We *k* that we have come
2: 4 The man who says, "I *k* him,"
2: 5 This is how we *k* we are in him:
2:11 he does not *k* where he is going,
2:20 and all of you *k* the truth.
2:29 you *k* that everyone who does
3: 1 not *k* us is that it did not *k* him.
3: 2 But we *k* that when he appears,
3:10 This is how we *k* who the children
3:14 We *k* that we have passed
3:16 This is how we *k* what love is:
3:19 then is how we *k* that we belong
3:24 We *k* it by the Spirit he gave us.
4: 8 does not love does not *k* God,
4:13 We *k* that we live in him
4:16 so we *k* and rely on the love God
5: 2 This is how we *k* that we love
5:13 so that you may *k* that you have
5:15 And if we *k* that he hears us—
5:18 We *k* that anyone born
5:20 We *k* also that the Son
Rev 2: 2 I *k* your deeds, your hard work
2: 9 I *k* your afflictions and your
2:19 I *k* your deeds, your love and faith,
3: 3 you will not *k* at what time I will
3:15 I *k* your deeds, that you are neither

KNOWING (KNOW)

Ge 3: 5 and you will be like God, *k* good
3:22 now become like one of us, *k* good
Jn 19:28 *k* that all was now completed,
Php 3: 8 of *k* Christ Jesus my Lord,
Phm :21 *k* that you will do even more
Heb 13: 2 entertained angels without *k* it.

KNOWLEDGE (KNOW)

Ge 2: 9 the tree of the *k* of good and evil.
2:17 eat from the tree of the *k* of good
2Ch 1:10 and *k*, that I may lead this people,
Job 21:22 "Can anyone teach *k* to God,
38: 2 counsel with words without *k*?
42: 3 obscures my counsel without *k*?'
Ps 19: 2 night after night they display *k*.
73:11 Does the Most High have *k*?"
94:10 Does he who teaches man lack *k*?
119: 66 Teach me *k* and good judgment,
139: 6 Such *k* is too wonderful for me,
Pr 1: 4 *k* and discretion to the young—
1: 7 of the LORD is the beginning of *k*,
2: 5 and find the *k* of God.
2: 6 from his mouth come *k*
2:10 and *k* will be pleasant to your soul.
3:20 by his *k* the deeps were divided,
8:10 *k* rather than choice gold,
8:12 I possess *k* and discretion.
9:10 *k* of the Holy One is understanding
10:14 Wise men store up *k*,

Pr 12: 1 Whoever loves discipline loves *k*,
12:23 A prudent man keeps his *k*
13:16 Every prudent man acts out of *k*,
14: 6 *k* comes easily to the discerning.
15: 7 The lips of the wise spread *k*;
15:14 The discerning heart seeks *k*,
17:27 A man of *k* uses words
18:15 heart of the discerning acquires *k*;
19: 2 to have zeal without *k*,
19:25 discerning man, and he will gain *k*.
20:15 lips that speak *k* are a rare jewel.
23:12 and your ears to words of *k*.
24: 4 through *k* its rooms are filled
Ecc 7:12 but the advantage of *k* is this:
Isa 11: 2 the Spirit of *k* and of the fear
11: 9 full of the *k* of the LORD
40:14 Who was it that taught him *k*
Jer 3:15 who will lead you with *k*
Hos 4: 6 are destroyed from lack of *k*.
Hab 2:14 filled with the *k* of the glory
Mal 2: 7 lips of a priest ought to preserve *k*,
Mt 13:11 The *k* of the secrets of the kingdom
Lk 8:10 The *k* of the secrets of the kingdom
11:52 you have taken away the key to *k*.
Ac 18:24 with a thorough *k* of the Scriptures
Ro 1:28 worthwhile to retain the *k* of God,
10: 2 but their zeal is not based on *k*.
11:33 riches of the wisdom and *k* of God!
1Co 8: 1 *K* puffs up, but love builds up.
8:11 Christ died, is destroyed by your *k*.
12: 8 to another the message of *k*
13: 2 can fathom all mysteries and all *k*,
13: 8 where there is *k*, it will pass away.
2Co 2:14 everywhere the fragrance of the *k*
4: 6 light of the *k* of the glory of God
8: 7 in *k*, in complete earnestness
11: 6 a trained speaker, but I do have *k*.
Eph 3:19 to know this love that surpasses *k*
4:13 and in the *k* of the Son of God
Php 1: 9 and more in *k* and depth of insight,
Col 1: 9 God to fill you with the *k* of his will
1:10 every good work, growing in the *k*
2: 3 all the treasures of wisdom and *k*.
3:10 which is being renewed in *k*
1Ti 2: 4 and to come to a *k* of the truth.
6:20 ideas of what is falsely called *k*,
Tit 1: 1 and the *k* of the truth that leads
Heb 10:26 after we have received the *k*
2Pe 1: 5 and to goodness, *k*; and to *k*,
3:18 grow in the grace and *k* of our Lord

KNOWN (KNOW)

Ex 6: 3 the LORD I did not make myself *k*
Ps 16:11 You have made *k* to me the path
89: 1 I will make your faithfulness *k*
98: 2 LORD has made his salvation *k*
105: 1 make *k* among the nations what he
119:168 for all my ways are *k* to you.
Pr 20:11 Even a child is *k* by his actions,
Isa 12: 4 make *k* among the nations what he
46:10 I make *k* the end from the beginning,
61: 9 Their descendants will be *k*
Eze 38:23 I will make myself *k* in the sight
39: 7 " 'I will make *k* my holy name
Mt 10:26 or hidden that will not be made *k*.
24:43 of the house had *k* at what time
Lk 19:42 had only *k* on this day what would
Jn 15:15 from my Father I have made *k*
16:14 from what is mine and making it *k*
17:26 I have made you *k* to them,
Ac 2:28 You have made *k* to me the paths
Ro 1:19 since what may be *k* about God is
3:21 apart from law, has been made *k*,
9:22 his wrath and make his power *k*,
11:34 "Who has *k* the mind of the Lord?
15:20 the gospel where Christ was not *k*,
16:26 and made *k* through the prophetic
1Co 2:16 "For who has *k* the mind
8: 3 But the man who loves God is *k*
13:12 know fully, even as I am fully *k*.
2Co 3: 2 written on our hearts, *k*
Gal 4: 9 or rather are *k* by God—
Eph 3: 5 which was not made *k* to men
6:19 will fearlessly make *k* the mystery
2Ti 3:15 infancy you have *k* the holy
2Pe 2:21 than to have *k* it and then

KNOWS (KNOW)

1Sa 2: 3 for the LORD is a God who *k*,
Est 4:14 And who *k* but that you have come
Job 23:10 But he *k* the way that I take;

Ps 44:21 since he *k* the secrets of the heart?
94:11 The LORD *k* the thoughts of man;
103: 14 for he *k* how we are formed,
Ecc 8: 7 Since no man *k* the future,
8:17 Even if a wise man claims he *k*,
9:12 no man *k* when his hour will come:
Isa 29:16 "He *k* nothing"?
Jer 9:24 that he understands and *k* me,
Mt 6: 8 for your Father *k* what you need
11:27 No one *k* the Son
24:36 "No one *k* about that day or hour,
Lk 12:47 "That servant who *k* his master's
16:15 of men, but God *k* your hearts.
Ac 15: 8 who *k* the heart, showed that he
Ro 8:27 who searches our hearts *k* the mind
1Co 2:11 who among men *k* the thoughts
8: 2 who thinks he *k* something does
2Ti 2:19 The Lord *k* those who are his," and
Jas 4:17 who *k* the good he ought to do
1Jn 4: 6 and whoever *k* God listens to us;
4: 7 born of God and *k* God.

KOHATHITE (KOHATHITES)
Nu 3:29 The *K* clans were to camp

KOHATHITES (KOHATHITE)
Nu 3:28 The *K* were responsible
4:15 *K* are to carry those things that are

KORAH
Levite who led rebellion against Moses and Aaron (Nu 16; Jude 11).

KORAZIN
Mt 11:21 "Woe to you, *K!* Woe to you,

LABAN
Brother of Rebekah (Ge 24:29), father of Rachel and Leah (Ge 29:16). Received Abraham's servant (Ge 24:29–51). Provided daughters as wives for Jacob in exchange for Jacob's service (Ge 29:1–30). Provided flocks for Jacob's service (Ge 30:25–43). After Jacob's departure, pursued and covenanted with him (Ge 31).

LABOR (LABORING)
Ex 1:11 to oppress them with forced *l*,
20: 9 Six days you shall *l* and do all your
Dt 5:13 Six days you shall *l* and do all your
Ps 127: 1 its builders *l* in vain.
128: 2 You will eat the fruit of your *l;*
Pr 12:24 but laziness ends in slave *l*.
Isa 54: 1 you who were never in *l;*
55: 2 and your *l* on what does not satisfy
Mt 6:28 They do not *l* or spin.
Jn 4:38 have reaped the benefits of their *l*."
1Co 3: 8 rewarded according to his own *l*.
15:58 because you know that your *l*
Gal 4:27 you who have no *l* pains;
Php 2:16 day of Christ that I did not run or *l*
Rev 14:13 "they will rest from their *l*,

LABORING* (LABOR)
2Th 3: 8 *l* and toiling so that we would not

LACK (LACKED LACKING LACKS)
Ps 34: 9 for those who fear him *l* nothing.
Pr 5:23 He will die for *l* of discipline,
10:21 but fools die for *l* of judgment.
11:14 For *l* of guidance a nation falls,
15:22 Plans fail for *l* of counsel,
28:27 to the poor will *l* nothing,
Mk 6: 6 he was amazed at their *l* of faith.
16:14 he rebuked them for their *l* of faith
Ro 3: 3 Will their *l* of faith nullify God's
1Co 1: 7 you do not *l* any spiritual gift
7: 5 because of your *l* of self-control.
Col 2:23 *l* any value in restraining sensual

LACKED (LACK)
Dt 2: 7 and you have not *l* anything.
Ne 9:21 them in the desert; they *l* nothing,
1Co 12:24 honor to the parts that *l* it,

LACKING (LACK)
Pr 17:18 A man *l* in judgment strikes hands
Ro 12:11 Never be *l* in zeal, but keep your
Jas 1: 4 and complete, not *l* anything.

LACKS (LACK)
Pr 6:32 who commits adultery *l* judgment;
11:12 man who *l* judgment derides his
12:11 he who chases fantasies *l* judgment
15:21 delights a man who *l* judgment,
24:30 of the man who *l* judgment;
25:28 is a man who *l* self-control.
28:16 A tyrannical ruler *l* judgment,
31:11 and *l* nothing of value.
Eze 34: 8 because my flock *l* a shepherd
Jas 1: 5 any of you *l* wisdom, he should ask

LAID (LAY)
Isa 53: 6 and the LORD has *l* on him
Mk 6:29 took his body and *l* it in a tomb.
Lk 6:48 and *l* the foundation on rock.
Ac 6: 6 and *l* their hands on them.
1Co 3:11 other than the one already *l*,
1Ti 4:14 body of elders *l* their hands on you.
1Jn 3:16 Jesus Christ *l* down his life for us.

LAKE
Mt 8:24 a furious storm came up on the *l*,
14:25 out to them, walking on the *l*.
Mk 4: 1 into a boat and sat in it out on the *l*,
Lk 8:33 down the steep bank into the *l*
Jn 6:25 him on the other side of the *l*,
Rev 19:20 into the fiery *l* of burning sulfur.
20:14 The *l* of fire is the second death.

LAMB (LAMB'S LAMBS)
Ge 22: 8 "God himself will provide the *l*
Ex 12:21 and slaughter the Passover *l*.
Nu 9:11 are to eat the *l*, together
2Sa 12: 4 he took the ewe *l* that belonged
Isa 11: 6 The wolf will live with the *l*,
53: 7 he was led like a *l* to the slaughter,
Mk 14:12 to sacrifice the Passover *l*,
Jn 1:29 *L* of God, who takes away the sin
Ac 8:32 as a *l* before the shearer is silent,
1Co 5: 7 our Passover *l*, has been sacrificed.
1Pe 1:19 a *l* without blemish or defect.
Rev 5: 6 Then I saw a *L*, looking
5:12 "Worthy is the *L*, who was slain,
7:14 white in the blood of the *L*.
14: 4 They follow the *L* wherever he
15: 3 of God and the song of the *L:*
17:14 but the *L* will overcome them
19: 9 to the wedding supper of the *L!*' "
21:23 gives it light, and the *L* is its lamp.

LAMB'S (LAMB)
Rev 21:27 written in the *L* book of life.

LAMBS (LAMB)
Lk 10: 3 I am sending you out like *l*
Jn 21:15 Jesus said, "Feed my *l*."

LAME
Isa 33:23 even the *l* will carry off plunder.
35: 6 Then will the *l* leap like a deer,
Mt 11: 5 The blind receive sight, the *l* walk,
15:31 the *l* walking and the blind seeing.
Lk 14:21 the crippled, the blind and the *l*.'

LAMENT
2Sa 1:17 took up this *l* concerning Saul
Eze 19: 1 Take up a *l* concerning the princes

LAMP (LAMPS LAMPSTAND LAMPSTANDS)
2Sa 22:29 You are my *l*, O LORD;
Ps 18:28 You, O LORD, keep my *l* burning;
119:105 Your word is a *l* to my feet
132: 17 and set up a *l* for my anointed one.
Pr 6:23 For these commands are a *l*,
20:27 *l* of the LORD searches the spirit
31:18 and her *l* does not go out at night.
Mt 6:22 "The eye is the *l* of the body.
Lk 8:16 "No one lights a *l* and hides it
Rev 21:23 gives it light, and the Lamb is its *l*.
22: 5 They will not need the light of a *l*

LAMPS (LAMP)
Mt 25: 1 be like ten virgins who took their *l*
Lk 12:35 for service and keep your *l* burning,
Rev 4: 5 the throne, seven *l* were blazing.

LAMPSTAND (LAMP)
Ex 25:31 "Make a *l* of pure gold
Zec 4: 2 "I see a solid gold *l* with a bowl
4:11 on the right and the left of the *l?*"
Heb 9: 2 In its first room were the *l*,
Rev 2: 5 and remove your *l* from its place.

LAMPSTANDS (LAMP)
2Ch 4: 7 He made ten gold *l* according
Rev 1:12 when I turned I saw seven golden *l*,
1:20 and of the seven golden *l* is this:

LAND (LANDS)
Ge 1:10 God called the dry ground "*l*,"
1:11 "Let the *l* produce vegetation:
1:24 "Let the *l* produce living creatures
12: 1 and go to the *l* I will show you.
12: 7 To your offspring I will give this *l*."
13:15 All the *l* that you see I will give
15:18 "To your descendants I give this *l*,
50:24 out of this *l* to the *l* he promised
Ex 3: 8 a *l* flowing with milk and honey—
6: 8 to the *l* I swore with uplifted hand
33: 3 Go up to the *l* flowing with milk
Lev 25:23 *l* must not be sold permanently,
Nu 14: 8 us into that *l*, a *l* flowing with milk
35:33 Do not pollute the *l* where you are.
Dt 1: 8 See, I have given you this *l*.
8: 7 God is bringing you into a good *l*—
11:10 The *l* you are entering to take
28:21 you from the *l* you are entering
29:19 will bring disaster on the watered *l*
34: 1 LORD showed him the whole *l*—
Jos 13: 2 "This is the *l* that remains:
14: 4 Levites received no share of the *l*
14: 9 *l* on which your feet have walked
2Sa 21:14 answered prayer in behalf of the *l*.
2Ki 17: 5 of Assyria invaded the entire *l*,
24: 1 king of Babylon invaded the *l*,
25:21 into captivity, away from her *l*.
2Ch 7:14 their sin and will heal their *l*.
7:20 then I will uproot Israel from my *l*,
36:21 The *l* enjoyed its sabbath rests;
Ezr 9:11 entering to possess is a *l* polluted
Ne 9:36 in the *l* you gave our forefathers
Ps 37:11 But the meek will inherit the *l*
37:29 the righteous will inherit the *l*
136: 21 and gave their *l* as an inheritance,
142: 5 my portion in the *l* of the living."
Pr 2:21 For the upright will live in the *l*,
12:11 who works his *l* will have abundant
Isa 6:13 though a tenth remains in the *l*,
53: 8 cut off from the *l* of the living;
Jer 2: 7 But you came and defiled my *l*
Eze 36:24 and bring you back into your own *l*.

LANDS (LAND)
Ps 111: 6 giving them the *l* of other nations.
Eze 20: 6 honey, the most beautiful of all *l*.
Zec 10: 9 in distant *l* they will remember me.

LANGUAGE (LANGUAGES)
Ge 11: 1 Now the whole world had one *l*
11: 9 there the LORD confused the *l*
Ps 19: 3 There is no speech or *l*
Jn 8:44 When he lies, he speaks his native *l*
Ac 2: 6 heard them speaking in his own *l*.
Col 3: 8 slander, and filthy *l* from your lips.
Rev 5: 9 from every tribe and *l* and people
7: 9 every nation, tribe, people and *l*,
14: 6 to every nation, tribe, *l* and people.

LANGUAGES (LANGUAGE)
Zec 8:23 "In those days ten men from all *l*

LAODICEA
Rev 3:14 the angel of the church in *L* write:

LAP
Jdg 7: 5 "Separate those who *l* the water

LASHES
Pr 17:10 more than a hundred *l* a fool.
2Co 11:24 from the Jews the forty *l* minus one

LAST (LASTING LASTS LATTER)
Ex 14:24 During the *l* watch of the night
2Sa 23: 1 These are the *l* words of David:
Isa 2: 2 and Jerusalem: In the *l* days
41: 4 and with the *l*—I am he."
44: 6 I am the first and I am the *l;*
48:12 I am the first and I am the *l*.
Hos 3: 5 and to his blessings in the *l* days.
Mic 4: 1 In the *l* days
Mt 19:30 But many who are first will be *l*,
20: 8 beginning with the *l* ones hired
21:37 *L* of all, he sent his son to them.
Mk 9:35 must be the very *l*, and the servant
10:31 are first will be *l*, and the *l* first."
15:37 a loud cry, Jesus breathed his *l*.
Jn 6:40 and I will raise him up at the *l* day."
15:16 and bear fruit—fruit that will *l*.
Ac 2:17 " 'In the *l* days, God says,
Ro 1:17 is by faith from first to *l*,
1Co 15:26 *l* enemy to be destroyed is death.
15:52 of an eye, at the *l* trumpet.
2Ti 3: 1 will be terrible times in the *l* days.

2Pe 3: 3 in the *l* days scoffers will come,
Jude :18 "In the *l* times there will be
Rev 1:17 I am the First and the *L*.
22:13 the First and the *L*, the Beginning

LASTING (LAST)
Ex 12:14 to the LORD—a *l* ordinance.
Lev 24: 8 of the Israelites, as a *l* covenant.
Nu 25:13 have a covenant of a *l* priesthood,
Heb 10:34 had better and *l* possessions.

LASTS (LAST)
Ps 30: 5 For his anger *l* only a moment,
2Co 3:11 greater is the glory of that which *l*!

LATTER (LAST)
Job 42:12 The LORD blessed the *l* part
Mt 23:23 You should have practiced the *l*,
Php 1:16 *l* do so in love, knowing that I am

LAUGH (LAUGHED LAUGHS LAUGHTER)
Ps 59: 8 But you, O LORD, *l* at them;
Pr 31:25 she can *l* at the days to come.
Ecc 3: 4 a time to weep and a time to *l*,
Lk 6:21 for you will *l*.
6:25 Woe to you who *l* now,

LAUGHED (LAUGH)
Ge 17:17 Abraham fell facedown; he *l*
18:12 So Sarah *l* to herself as she thought,

LAUGHS (LAUGH)
Ps 2: 4 The One enthroned in heaven *l*;
37:13 but the Lord *l* at the wicked,

LAUGHTER (LAUGH)
Ge 21: 6 Sarah said, "God has brought me *l*,
Ps 126: 2 Our mouths were filled with *l*,
Pr 14:13 Even in *l* the heart may ache,
Jas 4: 9 Change your *l* to mourning

LAVISHED
Eph 1: 8 of God's grace that he *l* on us
1Jn 3: 1 great is the love the Father has *l*

LAW (LAWFUL LAWGIVER LAWS)
Lev 24:22 are to have the same *l* for the alien
Nu 6:13 " 'Now this is the *l* for the Nazirite
Dt 1: 5 Moses began to expound this *l*,
6:25 to obey all this *l* before the LORD
27:26 of this *l* by carrying them out."
31:11 you shall read this *l* before them
31:26 "Take this Book of the *L*
Jos 1: 7 to obey all the *l* my servant Moses
1: 8 of the *L* depart from your mouth;
22: 5 and the *l* that Moses the servant
2Ki 22: 8 of the *L* in the temple of the LORD
2Ch 6:16 walk before me according to my *l*,
17: 9 the Book of the *L* of the LORD;
34:14 of the *L* of the LORD that had
Ezr 7: 6 versed in the *L* of Moses,
Ne 8: 2 Ezra the priest brought the *L*
8: 8 from the Book of the *L* of God,
Ps 1: 2 and on his *l* he meditates day
19: 7 The *l* of the LORD is perfect,
37:31 The *l* of his God is in his heart;
40: 8 your *l* is within my heart."
119: 18 wonderful things in your *l*.
119: 70 but I delight in your *l*.
119: 72 *l* from your mouth is more precious
119: 77 for your *l* is my delight.
119: 97 Oh, how I love your *l*!
119:163 but I love your *l*.
119:165 peace have they who love your *l*,
Pr 28: 9 If anyone turns a deaf ear to the *l*,
29:18 but blessed is he who keeps the *l*.
Isa 2: 3 The *l* will go out from Zion,
8:20 To the *l* and to the testimony!
42:21 to make his *l* great and glorious.
Jer 2: 8 deal with the *l* did not know me;
8: 8 for we have the *l* of the LORD,"
31:33 "I will put my *l* in their minds
Mic 4: 2 The *l* will go out from Zion,
Hab 1: 7 they are a *l* to themselves
Zec 7:12 as flint and would not listen to the *l*
Mt 5:17 that I have come to abolish the *L*
7:12 sums up the *L* and the Prophets.
22:36 greatest commandment in the *L*?"
22:40 All the *L* and the Prophets hang
23:23 more important matters of the *l*—
Lk 11:52 "Woe to you experts in the *l*,
16:17 stroke of a pen to drop out of the *L*.
24:44 me in the *L* of Moses,
Jn 1:17 For the *l* was given through Moses;
Ac 13:39 justified from by the *l* of Moses.
Ro 2:12 All who sin apart from the *l* will
2:15 of the *l* are written on their hearts,
2:20 you have in the *l* the embodiment
2:25 value if you observe the *l*,
3:19 we know that whatever the *l* says,
3:20 in his sight by observing the *l*;
3:21 apart from *l*, has been made known
3:28 by faith apart from observing the *l*.
3:31 Not at all! Rather, we uphold the *l*.
4:13 It was not through *l* that Abraham
4:15 worthless, because *l* brings wrath.
4:16 not only to those who are of the *l*
5:13 for before the *l* was given,
5:20 *l* was added so that the trespass
6:14 because you are not under *l*,
6:15 we are not under *l* but under grace?
7: 1 that the *l* has authority
7: 4 also died to the *l* through the body
7: 5 aroused by the *l* were at work
7: 6 released from the *l* so that we serve
7: 7 then? Is the *l* sin? Certainly not!
7: 8 For apart from *l*, sin is dead.
7:12 *l* is holy, and the commandment is
7:14 We know that the *l* is spiritual;
7:22 my inner being I delight in God's *l*;
7:25 in my mind am a slave to God's *l*,
8: 2 because through Christ Jesus the *l*
8: 3 For what the *l* was powerless to do
8: 4 of the *l* might be fully met in us,
8: 7 It does not submit to God's *l*,
9: 4 covenants, the receiving of the *l*,
9:31 who pursued a *l* of righteousness,
10: 4 Christ is the end of the *l*
13: 8 his fellowman has fulfilled the *l*.
13:10 love is the fulfillment of the *l*.
1Co 6: 6 goes to *l* against another—
9: 9 For it is written in the *L* of Moses:
9:20 the *l* I became like one under the *l*
9:21 I became like one not having the *l*
15:56 and the power of sin is the *l*.
Gal 2:16 justified by observing the *l*,
2:19 For through the *l* I died to the *l*
3: 2 the Spirit by observing the *l*,
3: 5 you because you observe the *l*,
3:10 on observing the *l* are under a curse
3:11 justified before God by the *l*,
3:13 curse of the *l* by becoming a curse
3:17 The *l*, introduced 430 years later,
3:19 then, was the purpose of the *l*?
3:21 Is the *l*, therefore, opposed
3:23 we were held prisoners by the *l*,
3:24 So the *l* was put in charge to lead us
4:21 you who want to be under the *l*,
5: 3 obligated to obey the whole *l*.
5: 4 justified by *l* have been alienated
5:14 The entire *l* is summed up
5:18 by the Spirit, you are not under *l*.
6: 2 and in this way you will fulfill the *l*
Eph 2:15 flesh the *l* with its commandments
Php 3: 9 of my own that comes from the *l*,
1Ti 1: 8 We know that the *l* is good
Heb 7:12 there must also be a change of the *l*.
7:19 (for the *l* made nothing perfect),
10: 1 The *l* is only a shadow
Jas 1:25 intently into the perfect *l* that gives
2: 8 If you really keep the royal *l* found
2:10 For whoever keeps the whole *l*
4:11 or judges him speaks against the *l*
1Jn 3: 4 Everyone who sins breaks the *l*;

LAWFUL (LAW)
Mt 12:12 Therefore it is *l* to do good

LAWGIVER* (LAW)
Isa 33:22 the LORD is our *l*,
Jas 4:12 There is only one *L* and Judge,

LAWLESS (LAWLESSNESS)
2Th 2: 8 And then the *l* one will be revealed
Heb 10:17 "Their sins and *l* acts

LAWLESSNESS* (LAWLESS)
2Th 2: 3 and the man of *l* is revealed,
2: 7 power of *l* is already at work;
1Jn 3: 4 sins breaks the law; in fact, sin is *l*.

LAWS (LAW)
Ex 21: 1 "These are the *l* you are to set
Lev 25:18 and be careful to obey my *l*,
Dt 4: 1 and *l* I am about to teach you.
30:16 decrees and *l*; then you will live
Ps 119: 30 I have set my heart on your *l*.
119: 43 for I have put my hope in your *l*.
119:120 I stand in awe of your *l*.
119:164 for your righteous *l*.
119:175 and may your *l* sustain me.
Eze 36:27 and be careful to keep my *l*.
Heb 8:10 I will put my *l* in their minds
10:16 I will put my *l* in their hearts,

LAWSUITS
Hos 10: 4 therefore *l* spring up
1Co 6: 7 The very fact that you have *l*

LAY (LAID LAYING LAYS)
Ex 29:10 and his sons shall *l* their hands
Lev 1: 4 He is to *l* his hand on the head
4:15 the community are to *l* their hands
Nu 8:10 the Israelites are to *l* their hands
27:18 whom is the spirit, and *l* your hand
1Sa 26: 9 Who can *l* a hand on the LORD's
Job 1:12 on the man himself do not *l* a finger
22:22 and *l* up his words in your heart.
Ecc 10: 4 calmness can *l* great errors to rest.
Isa 28:16 "See, I *l* a stone in Zion,
Mt 8:20 of Man has no place to *l* his head."
28: 6 Come and see the place where he *l*.
Mk 6: 5 *l* his hands on a few sick people
Lk 9:58 of Man has no place to *l* his head."
Jn 10:15 and I *l* down my life for the sheep.
10:18 but I *l* it down of my own accord.
15:13 that he *l* down his life
Ac 8:19 on whom I *l* my hands may receive
Ro 9:33 I *l* in Zion a stone that causes men
1Co 3:11 no one can *l* any foundation other
1Pe 2: 6 "See, I *l* a stone in Zion,
1Jn 3:16 And we ought to *l* down our lives
Rev 4:10 They *l* their crowns

LAYING (LAY)
Lk 4:40 and *l* his hands on each one,
Ac 8:18 at the *l* on of the apostles' hands,
1Ti 5:22 Do not be hasty in the *l* on of hands
2Ti 1: 6 is in you through the *l*
Heb 6: 1 not *l* again the foundation
6: 2 instruction about baptisms, the *l*

LAYS (LAY)
Jn 10:11 The good shepherd *l* down his life

LAZARUS
1. Poor man in Jesus' parable (Lk 16:19–31).
2. Brother of Mary and Martha whom Jesus raised from the dead (Jn 11:1–12:19).

LAZINESS* (LAZY)
Pr 12:24 but *l* ends in slave labor.
19:15 *L* brings on deep sleep,

LAZY* (LAZINESS)
Ex 5: 8 They are *l*; that is why they are
5:17 Pharaoh said, "*L*, that's what you
5:17 "Lazy, that's what you are—*l*!
Pr 10: 4 *L* hands make a man poor,
12:27 The *l* man does not roast his game,
26:15 he is too *l* to bring it back
Ecc 10:18 If a man is *l*, the rafters sag;
Mt 25:26 replied, 'You wicked, *l* servant!
Tit 1:12 liars, evil brutes, *l* gluttons."
Heb 6:12 We do not want you to become *l*,

LEAD (LEADER LEADERS LEADERSHIP LEADS LED)
Ex 15:13 "In your unfailing love you will *l*
Nu 14: 8 with us, he will *l* us into that land,
Dt 31: 2 and I am no longer able to *l* you.
Jos 1: 6 because you will *l* these people
1Sa 8: 5 now appoint a king to *l* us,
2Ch 1:10 knowledge, that I may *l* this people
Ps 27:11 *l* me in a straight path
61: 2 *l* me to the rock that is higher
139: 24 and *l* me in the way everlasting.
143: 10 *l* me on level ground.
Pr 4:11 and *l* you along straight paths.
Ecc 5: 6 Do not let your mouth *l* you
Isa 11: 6 and a little child will *l* them.
49:10 and *l* them beside springs of water.
Da 12: 3 those who *l* many to righteousness,
Mt 6:13 And *l* us not into temptation,
Lk 11: 4 And *l* us not into temptation.' "
Gal 3:24 So the law was put in charge to *l* us
1Th 4:11 it your ambition to *l* a quiet life,
1Jn 3: 7 do not let anyone *l* you astray.
Rev 7:17 he will *l* them to springs

LEADER (LEAD)
1Sa 7: 6 Samuel was *l* of Israel at Mizpah.
10: 1 Has not the LORD anointed you *l*
12: 2 I have been your *l* from my youth
13:14 and appointed him *l* of his people,

LEADERS (LEAD)
Heb 13: 7 Remember your *l*, who spoke
13:17 Obey your *l* and submit

LEADERSHIP* (LEAD)
Nu 33: 1 by divisions under the *l* of Moses
Ps 109: 8 may another take his place of *l*.
Ac 1:20 " 'May another take his place of *l*.'
Ro 12: 8 if it is *l*, let him govern diligently;

LEADS (LEAD)
Dt 27:18 is the man who *l* the blind astray
Ps 23: 2 he *l* me beside quiet waters,
37: 8 do not fret—it *l* only to evil.
68: 6 he *l* forth the prisoners
Pr 2:18 For her house *l* down to death
10:17 ignores correction *l* others astray.
14:23 but mere talk *l* only to poverty.
16:25 but in the end it *l* to death.
19:23 The fear of the LORD *l* to life:
20: 7 righteous man *l* a blameless life;
21: 5 as surely as haste *l* to poverty.
Isa 40:11 he gently *l* those that have young.
Mt 7:13 and broad is the road that *l*
12:20 till he *l* justice to victory.
15:14 If a blind man *l* a blind man,
Jn 10: 3 sheep by name and *l* them out.
Ro 6:16 which *l* to death, or to obedience,
6:22 the benefit you reap *l* to holiness,
14:19 effort to do what *l* to peace
2Co 2:14 always *l* us in triumphal procession
7:10 sorrow brings repentance that *l*
Tit 1: 1 of the truth that *l* to godliness—

LEAH
Wife of Jacob (Ge 29:16–30); bore six sons and one daughter (Ge 29:31–30:21; 34:1; 35:23).

LEAN (LEANED)
Pr 3: 5 *l* not on your own understanding;

LEANED (LEAN)
Ge 47:31 as he *l* on the top of his staff.
Jn 21:20 (This was the one who had *l* back
Heb 11:21 as he *l* on the top of his staff.

LEAP (LEAPED LEAPS)
Isa 35: 6 Then will the lame *l* like a deer,
Mal 4: 2 *l* like calves released from the stall.
Lk 6:23 "Rejoice in that day and *l* for joy,

LEAPED (LEAP)
Lk 1:41 heard Mary's greeting, the baby *l*

LEAPS (LEAP)
Ps 28: 7 My heart *l* for joy

LEARN (LEARNED LEARNING LEARNS)
Dt 4:10 so that they may *l* to revere me
5: 1 *L* them and be sure to follow them.
31:12 and *l* to fear the LORD your God
Ps 119: 7 as I *l* your righteous laws.
Isa 1:17 *l* to do right!
26: 9 of the world *l* righteousness.
Mt 11:29 yoke upon you and *l* from me,
Jn 14:31 world must *l* that I love the Father
1Th 4: 4 that each of you should *l*
1Ti 2:11 A woman should *l* in quietness
5: 4 these should *l* first of all

LEARNED (LEARN)
Ps 119:152 Long ago I *l* from your statutes
Mt 11:25 things from the wise and *l*,
Php 4: 9 Whatever you have *l* or received
4:11 for I have *l* to be content whatever
2Ti 3:14 continue in what you have *l*
Heb 5: 8 he *l* obedience from what he

LEARNING (LEARN)
Pr 1: 5 let the wise listen and add to their *l*,
9: 9 man and he will add to his *l*.
Isa 44:25 who overthrows the *l* of the wise
Jn 7:15 "How did this man get such *l*
2Ti 3: 7 always *l* but never able

LEARNS (LEARN)
Jn 6:45 and *l* from him comes to me.

LEATHER
2Ki 1: 8 and with a *l* belt around his waist."
Mt 3: 4 and he had a *l* belt around his waist

LEAVES
Ge 3: 7 so they sewed fig *l* together
Eze 47:12 for food and their *l* for healing."
Rev 22: 2 the *l* of the tree are for the healing

LEBANON
Dt 11:24 from the desert to *L*,
1Ki 4:33 from the cedar of *L*

LED (LEAD)
Ex 3: 1 and he *l* the flock to the far side
Dt 8: 2 the LORD your God *l* you all
1Ki 11: 3 and his wives *l* him astray.
2Ch 26:16 his pride *l* to his downfall.
Ne 13:26 he was *l* into sin by foreign women.
Ps 68:18 you *l* captives in your train;
78:52 he *l* them like sheep
Pr 7:21 persuasive words she *l* him astray;
20: 1 whoever is *l* astray
Isa 53: 7 he was *l* like a lamb to the slaughter
Jer 11:19 I had been like a gentle lamb *l*
Am 2:10 and I *l* you forty years in the desert
Mt 4: 1 Then Jesus was *l* by the Spirit
27:31 they *l* him away to crucify him.
Lk 4: 1 was *l* by the Spirit in the desert,
Ac 8:32 "He was *l* like a sheep
Ro 8:14 those who are *l* by the Spirit
2Co 7: 9 your sorrow *l* you to repentance.
Gal 5:18 But if you are *l* by the Spirit,
Eph 4: 8 he *l* captives in his train

LEEKS*
Nu 11: 5 melons, *l*, onions and garlic.

LEFT
Dt 28:14 or to the *l*, following other gods
Jos 1: 7 turn from it to the right or to the *l*,
23: 6 aside to the right or to the *l*.
2Ki 22: 2 aside to the right or to the *l*.
Pr 4:27 Do not swerve to the right or the *l*;
Isa 30:21 turn to the right or to the *l*,
Mt 6: 3 do not let your *l* hand know what
25:33 on his right and the goats on his *l*.

LEGALISTIC*
Php 3: 6 as for *l* righteousness, faultless.

LEGION
Mk 5: 9 "My name is *L*," he replied,

LEND (LENDER LENDS MONEYLENDER)
Lev 25:37 You must not *l* him money
Dt 15: 8 freely *l* him whatever he needs.
Ps 37:26 are always generous and *l* freely;
Eze 18: 8 He does not *l* at usury
Lk 6:34 if you *l* to those from whom you

LENDER (LEND)
Pr 22: 7 and the borrower is servant to the *l*.
Isa 24: 2 for borrower as for *l*,

LENDS (LEND)
Ps 15: 5 who *l* his money without usury
112: 5 to him who is generous and *l* freely,
Pr 19:17 to the poor *l* to the LORD,

LENGTH (LONG)
Ps 90:10 The *l* of our days is seventy years—
Pr 10:27 The fear of the LORD adds *l* to life

LENGTHY* (LONG)
Mk 12:40 and for a show make *l* prayers.
Lk 20:47 and for a show make *l* prayers.

LEOPARD
Isa 11: 6 the *l* will lie down with the goat,
Da 7: 6 beast, one that looked like a *l*.
Rev 13: 2 The beast I saw resembled a *l*,

LEPROSY (LEPROUS)
Nu 12:10 toward her and saw that she had *l*;
2Ki 5: 1 was a valiant soldier, but he had *l*.
7: 3 men with *l* at the entrance
2Ch 26:21 King Uzziah had *l*
Mt 11: 5 those who have *l* are cured,
Lk 17:12 ten men who had *l* met him.

LEPROUS (LEPROSY)
Ex 4: 6 and when he took it out, it was *l*,

LETTER (LETTERS)
Mt 5:18 not the smallest *l*, not the least
2Co 3: 2 You yourselves are our *l*, written
3: 6 for the *l* kills, but the Spirit gives
2Th 3:14 not obey our instruction in this *l*,

LETTERS (LETTER)
2Co 3: 7 which was engraved in *l* on stone,
10:10 "His *l* are weighty and forceful,
2Pe 3:16 His *l* contain some things that are

LEVEL
Ps 143: 10 lead me on *l* ground.
Pr 4:26 Make *l* paths for your feet
Isa 26: 7 The path of the righteous is *l*;
40: 4 the rough ground shall become *l*,
Jer 31: 9 on a *l* path where they will not
Heb 12:13 "Make *l* paths for your feet,"

LEVI (LEVITE LEVITES LEVITICAL)
1. Son of Jacob by Leah (Ge 29:34; 46:11; 1Ch 2:1). With Simeon avenged rape of Dinah (Ge 34). Tribe of blessed (Ge 49:5–7; Dt 33:8–11), chosen as priests (Nu 3–4), numbered (Nu 3:39; 26:62), allotted cities, but not land (Nu 18; 35; Dt 10:9; Jos 13:14; 21), land (Eze 48:8–22), 12,000 from (Rev 7:7).
2. See MATTHEW.

LEVIATHAN
Job 41: 1 pull in the *l* with a fishhook
Ps 74:14 you who crushed the heads of *L*
Isa 27: 1 *L* the gliding serpent,

LEVITE (LEVI)
Dt 26:12 you shall give it to the *L*, the alien,
Jdg 19: 1 a *L* who lived in a remote area

LEVITES (LEVI)
Nu 1:53 The *L* are to be responsible
3:12 "I have taken the *L*
8: 6 "Take the *L* from among the other
18:21 I give to the *L* all the tithes in Israel
35: 7 must give the *L* forty-eight towns,
2Ch 31: 2 assigned the priests and *L*
Mal 3: 3 he will purify the *L* and refine them

LEVITICAL (LEVI)
Heb 7:11 attained through the *L* priesthood

LEWDNESS
Mk 7:22 malice, deceit, *l*, envy, slander,

LIAR* (LIE)
Dt 19:18 and if the witness proves to be a *l*,
Job 34: 6 I am considered a *l*;
Pr 17: 4 *l* pays attention to a malicious
19:22 better to be poor than a *l*.
30: 6 will rebuke you and prove you a *l*.
Mic 2:11 If a *l* and deceiver comes and says,
Jn 8:44 for he is a *l* and the father of lies.
8:55 I did not, I would be a *l* like you,
Ro 3: 4 Let God be true, and every man a *l*.
1Jn 1:10 we make him out to be a *l*
2: 4 not do what he commands is a *l*,
2:22 Who is the *l*? It is the man who
4:20 yet hates his brother, he is a *l*.
5:10 God has made him out to be a *l*,

LIARS* (LIE)
Ps 63:11 the mouths of *l* will be silenced.
116: 11 "All men are *l*."
Isa 57: 4 the offspring of *l*?
Mic 6:12 her people are *l*
1Ti 1:10 for slave traders and *l* and perjurers
4: 2 come through hypocritical *l*,
Tit 1:12 "Cretans are always *l*, evil brutes,
Rev 3: 9 though they are not, but are *l*—
21: 8 magic arts, the idolaters and all *l*—

LIBERATED*
Ro 8:21 that the creation itself will be *l*

LICENSE
Jude : 4 of our God into a *l* for immorality

LICK
Ps 72: 9 and his enemies will *l* the dust.
Isa 49:23 they will *l* the dust at your feet.
Mic 7:17 They will *l* dust like a snake,

LIE (LIAR LIARS LIED LIES LYING)
Lev 18:22 " 'Do not *l* with a man
19:11 " 'Do not *l*.
Nu 23:19 God is not a man, that he should *l*,
Dt 6: 7 when you *l* down and when you get
25: 2 the judge shall make him *l* down
1Sa 15:29 the Glory of Israel does not *l*
Ps 4: 8 I will *l* down and sleep in peace,
23: 2 me *l* down in green pastures,
89:35 and I will not *l* to David—
Pr 3:24 when you *l* down, you will not be

Isa 11: 6 leopard will *l* down with the goat,
28:15 for we have made a *l* our refuge
Jer 9: 5 They have taught their tongues to *l*
23:14 They commit adultery and live a *l*.
Eze 13: 6 are false and their divinations a *l*.
34:14 they will *l* down in good grazing
Ro 1:25 exchanged the truth of God for a *l*,
Col 3: 9 Do not *l* to each other,
2Th 2:11 so that they will believe the *l*
Tit 1: 2 which God, who does not *l*,
Heb 6:18 which it is impossible for God to *l*,
1Jn 2:21 because no *l* comes from the truth.
Rev 14: 5 No *l* was found in their mouths;

LIED (LIE)
Ac 5: 4 You have not *l* to men but to God."

LIES (LIE)
Lev 6: 3 finds lost property and *l* about it,
Ps 5: 6 You destroy those who tell *l*;
10: 7 His mouth is full of curses and *l*
12: 2 Everyone *l* to his neighbor;
34:13 and your lips from speaking *l*.
58: 3 they are wayward and speak *l*.
144: 8 whose mouths are full of *l*,
Pr 6:19 a false witness who pours out *l*
12:17 but a false witness tells *l*.
19: 5 he who pours out *l* will not go free.
19: 9 and he who pours out *l* will perish.
29:12 If a ruler listens to *l*,
30: 8 Keep falsehood and *l* far from me;
Isa 59: 3 Your lips have spoken *l*,
Jer 5:31 The prophets prophesy *l*,
9: 3 like a bow, to shoot *l*;
14:14 "The prophets are prophesying *l*
Hos 11:12 Ephraim has surrounded me with *l*,
Jn 8:44 for he is a liar and the father of *l*.

LIFE (LIVE)
Ge 1:30 everything that has the breath of *l*
2: 7 into his nostrils the breath of *l*,
2: 9 of the garden were the tree of *l*
6:17 to destroy all *l* under the heavens,
9: 5 for the *l* of his fellow man.
9:11 Never again will all *l* be cut
Ex 21: 6 Then he will be his servant for *l*.
21:23 you are to take *l* for *l*, eye for eye,
23:26 I will give you a full *l* span.
Lev 17:14 the *l* of every creature is its blood.
24:17 " 'If anyone takes the *l*
24:18 must make restitution—*l* for *l*.
Nu 35:31 a ransom for the *l* of a murderer,
Dt 4:42 one of these cities and save his *l*.
12:23 because the blood is the *l*,
19:21 Show no pity: *l* for *l*, eye for eye,
30:15 I set before you today *l*
30:19 Now choose *l*, so that you
30:20 For the LORD is your *l*,
32:39 I put to death and I bring to *l*,
32:47 words for you—they are your *l*.
1Sa 19: 5 He took his *l* in his hands
Job 2: 6 hands; but you must spare his *l*."
33: 4 of the Almighty gives me *l*.
33:30 that the light of *l* may shine on him.
Ps 16:11 known to me the path of *l*;
17:14 this world whose reward is in this *l*.
23: 6 all the days of my *l*,
27: 1 LORD is the stronghold of my *l*—
34:12 Whoever of you loves *l*
36: 9 For with you is the fountain of *l*;
39: 4 let me know how fleeting is my *l*.
41: 2 will protect him and preserve his *l*;
49: 7 No man can redeem the *l*
49: 8 the ransom for a *l* is costly,
63: 3 Because your love is better than *l*,
69:28 they be blotted out of the book of *l*
91:16 With long *l* will I satisfy him
104: 33 I will sing to the LORD all my *l*;
119: 25 preserve my *l* according to your word
Pr 1: 3 a disciplined and prudent *l*,
3: 2 will prolong your *l* many years
3:18 of *l* to those who embrace her;
4:23 for it is the wellspring of *l*.
6:23 are the way to *l*,
6:26 adulteress preys upon your very *l*.
7:23 little knowing it will cost him his *l*.
8:35 For whoever finds me finds *l*
10:11 of the righteous is a fountain of *l*,
10:27 of the LORD adds length to *l*,
11:30 of the righteous is a tree of *l*,
Pr 13: 3 He who guards his lips guards his *l*,
13:12 but a longing fulfilled is a tree of *l*.
13:14 of the wise is a fountain of *l*,
14:27 of the LORD is a fountain of *l*,
15: 4 that brings healing is a tree of *l*,
16:22 Understanding is a fountain of *l*
19: 3 A man's own folly ruins his *l*,
19:23 The fear of the LORD leads to *l*:
21:21 finds *l*, prosperity and honor.
Isa 53:10 LORD makes his *l* a guilt offering,
53:11 he will see the light ⌞of *l*⌟
53:12 he poured out his *l* unto death,
Jer 10:23 that a man's *l* is not his own;
La 3:58 you redeemed my *l*.
Eze 18:27 and right, he will save his *l*.
37: 5 enter you, and you will come to *l*.
Da 12: 2 some to everlasting *l*, others
Jnh 2: 6 you brought my *l* up from the pit,
Mal 2: 5 a covenant of *l* and peace,
Mt 6:25 Is not *l* more important than food,
7:14 and narrow the road that leads to *l*,
10:39 Whoever finds his *l* will lose it,
16:21 and on the third day be raised to *l*.
16:25 wants to save his *l* will lose it,
18: 8 better for you to enter *l* maimed
19:16 thing must I do to get eternal *l*?"
19:29 as much and will inherit eternal *l*.
20:28 to give his *l* as a ransom for many."
25:46 but the righteous to eternal *l*."
Mk 8:35 but whoever loses his *l* for me
9:43 better for you to enter *l* maimed
10:17 "what must I do to inherit eternal *l*
10:30 and in the age to come, eternal *l*.
10:45 to give his *l* as a ransom for many."
Lk 6: 9 to save *l* or to destroy it?"
9:22 and on the third day be raised to *l*."
9:24 wants to save his *l* will lose it,
12:15 a man's *l* does not consist
12:22 do not worry about your *l*,
12:25 can add a single hour to his *l*?
14:26 even his own *l*—he cannot be my
17:33 tries to keep his *l* will lose it,
21:19 standing firm you will gain *l*.
Jn 1: 4 In him was *l*, and that *l* was
3:15 believes in him may have eternal *l*.
3:36 believes in the Son has eternal *l*,
4:14 of water welling up to eternal *l*."
5:21 raises the dead and gives them *l*,
5:24 him who sent me has eternal *l*
5:26 For as the Father has *l* in himself,
5:39 that by them you possess eternal *l*.
5:40 refuse to come to me to have *l*.
6:27 for food that endures to eternal *l*,
6:33 down from heaven and gives *l*
6:35 Jesus declared, "I am the bread of *l*
6:40 believes in him shall have eternal *l*,
6:47 he who believes has everlasting *l*.
6:48 I am the bread of *l*.
6:51 give for the *l* of the world."
6:53 and drink his blood, you have no *l*
6:63 The Spirit gives *l*; the flesh counts
6:68 You have the words of eternal *l*.
8:12 but will have the light of *l*."
10:10 I have come that they may have *l*,
10:15 and I lay down my *l* for the sheep.
10:17 loves me is that I lay down my *l*—
10:28 I give them eternal *l*, and they shall
11:25 "I am the resurrection and the *l*.
12:25 The man who loves his *l* will lose it,
12:50 his command leads to eternal *l*.
13:37 I will lay down my *l* for you."
14: 6 am the way and the truth and the *l*.
15:13 lay down his *l* for his friends.
17: 2 people that he might give eternal *l*
17: 3 Now this is eternal *l*: that they may
20:31 that by believing you may have *l*
Ac 2:32 God has raised this Jesus to *l*,
3:15 You killed the author of *l*,
11:18 the Gentiles repentance unto *l*."
13:48 appointed for eternal *l* believed.
Ro 2: 7 immortality, he will give eternal *l*.
4:25 was raised to *l* for our justification.
5:10 shall we be saved through his *l*!
5:18 was justification that brings *l*
5:21 righteousness to bring eternal *l*
6: 4 the Father, we too may live a new *l*.
6:13 have been brought from death to *l*;
6:22 holiness, and the result is eternal *l*.
6:23 but the gift of God is eternal *l*
8: 6 mind controlled by the Spirit is *l*
Ro 8:11 also give *l* to your mortal bodies
8:38 convinced that neither death nor *l*,
1Co 15:19 If only for this *l* we have hope
15:36 What you sow does not come to *l*
2Co 2:16 to the other, the fragrance of *l*.
3: 6 letter kills, but the Spirit gives *l*.
4:10 so that the *l* of Jesus may
5: 4 is mortal may be swallowed up by *l*.
Gal 2:20 The *l* I live in the body, I live
3:21 had been given that could impart *l*,
6: 8 from the Spirit will reap eternal *l*.
Eph 4: 1 I urge you to live a *l* worthy
Php 2:16 as you hold out the word of *l*—
4: 3 whose names are in the book of *l*.
Col 1:10 order that you may live a *l* worthy
3: 3 your *l* is now hidden with Christ
1Th 4:12 so that your daily *l* may win
1Ti 1:16 on him and receive eternal *l*.
4: 8 for both the present *l* and the *l*
4:12 in *l*, in love, in faith and in purity.
4:16 Watch your *l* and doctrine closely.
6:12 Take hold of the eternal *l*
6:19 hold of the *l* that is truly *l*.
2Ti 1: 9 saved us and called us to a holy *l*—
1:10 destroyed death and has brought *l*
3:12 to live a godly *l* in Christ Jesus will
Tit 1: 2 resting on the hope of eternal *l*,
3: 7 heirs having the hope of eternal *l*.
Heb 7:16 of the power of an indestructible *l*.
Jas 1:12 crown of *l* that God has promised
3:13 Let him show it by his good *l*,
1Pe 3: 7 with you of the gracious gift of *l*,
3:10 "Whoever would love *l*
4: 2 rest of his earthly *l* for evil human
2Pe 1: 3 given us everything we need for *l*
1Jn 1: 1 proclaim concerning the Word of *l*.
2:25 he promised us—even eternal *l*.
3:14 we have passed from death to *l*,
3:16 Jesus Christ laid down his *l* for us.
5:11 has given us eternal *l*, and this *l* is
5:20 He is the true God and eternal *l*.
Jude :21 Christ to bring you to eternal *l*.
Rev 2: 7 the right to eat from the tree of *l*,
2: 8 who died and came to *l* again.
2:10 and I will give you the crown of *l*.
3: 5 name from the book of *l*,
13: 8 written in the book of *l* belonging
17: 8 in the book of *l* from the creation
20:12 was opened, which is the book of *l*.
20:15 not found written in the book of *l*,
21: 6 from the spring of the water of *l*.
21:27 written in the Lamb's book of *l*.
22: 1 me the river of the water of *l*,
22: 2 side of the river stood the tree of *l*,
22:14 may have the right to the tree of *l*
22:17 take the free gift of the water of *l*.
22:19 from him his share in the tree of *l*

LIFE-GIVING (GIVE)
Pr 15:31 He who listens to a *l* rebuke
1Co 15:45 being"; the last Adam, a *l* spirit.

LIFETIME (LIVE)
Ps 30: 5 but his favor lasts a *l*;
Lk 16:25 in your *l* you received your good

LIFT (LIFTED LIFTING LIFTS)
Ps 3: 3 you bestow glory on me and *l*
28: 2 as I *l* up my hands
63: 4 in your name I will *l* up my hands.
91:12 they will *l* you up in their hands,
121: 1 I *l* up my eyes to the hills—
123: 1 I *l* up my eyes to you,
134: 2 *L* up your hands in the sanctuary
143: 8 for to you I *l* up my soul.
Isa 40: 9 *l* up your voice with a shout,
La 2:19 *L* up your hands to him
3:41 Let us *l* up our hearts and our
Mt 4: 6 they will *l* you up in their hands,
Lk 21:28 stand up and *l* up your heads,
1Ti 2: 8 everywhere to *l* up holy hands
Jas 4:10 the Lord, and he will *l* you up.
1Pe 5: 6 that he may *l* you up in due time.

LIFTED (LIFT)
Ne 8: 6 and all the people *l* their hands
Ps 24: 7 be *l* up, you ancient doors,
40: 2 He *l* me out of the slimy pit,
41: 9 has *l* up his heel against me.
Isa 52:13 *l* up and highly exalted.
63: 9 he *l* them up and carried them
Jn 3:14 Moses *l* up the snake in the desert,

Jn 8:28 "When you have *l* up the Son
12:32 when I am *l* up from the earth,
12:34 'The Son of Man must be *l* up'?
13:18 shares my bread has *l* up his heel

LIFTING (LIFT)
Ps 141: 2 may the *l* up of my hands be like

LIFTS (LIFT)
Ps 113: 7 and *l* the needy from the ash heap;

LIGAMENT* (LIGAMENTS)
Eph 4:16 held together by every supporting *l*

LIGAMENTS* (LIGAMENT)
Col 2:19 held together by its *l* and sinews,

LIGHT (ENLIGHTENED LIGHTS)
Ge 1: 3 "Let there be *l*," and there was *l*.
Ex 13:21 in a pillar of fire to give them *l*,
25:37 it so that they *l* the space in front
2Sa 22:29 LORD turns my darkness into *l*.
Job 38:19 "What is the way to the abode of *l*?
Ps 4: 6 Let the *l* of your face shine upon us
18:28 my God turns my darkness into *l*.
19: 8 giving *l* to the eyes.
27: 1 LORD is my *l* and my salvation—
36: 9 in your *l* we see *l*.
56:13 God in the *l* of life.
76: 4 You are resplendent with *l*,
89:15 who walk in the *l* of your presence,
104: 2 He wraps himself in *l*
119:105 and a *l* for my path.
119:130 The unfolding of your words gives *l*;
139: 12 for darkness is as *l* to you.
Pr 4:18 till the full *l* of day.
Isa 2: 5 let us walk in the *l* of the LORD.
9: 2 have seen a great *l*;
42: 6 and a *l* for the Gentiles,
45: 7 I form the *l* and create darkness,
49: 6 also make you a *l* for the Gentiles,
53:11 he will see the *l* ⌞of life⌟
60: 1 "Arise, shine, for your *l* has come,
60:19 LORD will be your everlasting *l*,
Eze 1:27 and brilliant *l* surrounded him.
Mic 7: 8 the LORD will be my *l*.
Mt 4:16 have seen a great *l*;
5:14 "You are the *l* of the world.
5:15 it gives *l* to everyone in the house.
5:16 let your *l* shine before men,
6:22 your whole body will be full of *l*.
11:30 yoke is easy and my burden is *l*."
17: 2 his clothes became as white as the *l*
24:29 and the moon will not give its *l*;
Mk 13:24 and the moon will not give its *l*;
Lk 2:32 a *l* for revelation to the Gentiles
8:16 those who come in can see the *l*.
11:33 those who come in may see the *l*.
Jn 1: 4 and that life was the *l* of men.
1: 5 The *l* shines in the darkness,
1: 7 witness to testify concerning that *l*,
1: 9 The true *l* that gives *l*
3:19 but men loved darkness instead of *l*
3:20 Everyone who does evil hates the *l*,
8:12 he said, "I am the *l* of the world.
9: 5 in the world, I am the *l* of the world
12:35 Walk while you have the *l*,
12:46 I have come into the world as a *l*,
Ac 13:47 " 'I have made you a *l*
Ro 13:12 darkness and put on the armor of *l*.
2Co 4: 6 made his *l* shine in our hearts
6:14 Or what fellowship can *l* have
11:14 masquerades as an angel of *l*.
Eph 5: 8 but now you are *l* in the Lord.
1Th 5: 5 You are all sons of the *l*
1Ti 6:16 and who lives in unapproachable *l*,
1Pe 2: 9 of darkness into his wonderful *l*.
2Pe 1:19 as to a *l* shining in a dark place,
1Jn 1: 5 God is *l*; in him there is no
1: 7 But if we walk in the *l*,
2: 9 Anyone who claims to be in the *l*
Rev 21:23 for the glory of God gives it *l*,
22: 5 for the Lord God will give them *l*.

LIGHTNING
Ex 9:23 and *l* flashed down to the ground.
20:18 and *l* and heard the trumpet
Ps 18:12 with hailstones and bolts of *l*.
Eze 1:13 it was bright, and *l* flashed out of it.
Da 10: 6 his face like *l*, his eyes like flaming
Mt 24:27 For as the *l* that comes from the east
28: 3 His appearance was like *l*,
Lk 10:18 "I saw Satan fall like *l* from heaven.

Rev 4: 5 From the throne came flashes of *l*,

LIGHTS (LIGHT)
Ge 1:14 "Let there be *l* in the expanse
Lk 8:16 No one *l* a lamp and hides it in a jar

LIKE-MINDED* (MIND)
Php 2: 2 make my joy complete by being *l*,

LIKENESS
Ge 1:26 man in our image, in our *l*,
Ps 17:15 I will be satisfied with seeing your *l*
Isa 52:14 his form marred beyond human *l*—
Ro 8: 3 Son in the *l* of sinful man
8:29 to be conformed to the *l* of his Son,
2Co 3:18 his *l* with ever-increasing glory,
Php 2: 7 being made in human *l*.
Jas 3: 9 who have been made in God's *l*.

LILIES (LILY)
Lk 12:27 "Consider how the *l* grow.

LILY (LILIES)
SS 2: 1 a *l* of the valleys.
2: 2 Like a *l* among thorns

LIMIT
Ps 147: 5 his understanding has no *l*.
Jn 3:34 for God gives the Spirit without *l*.

LINEN
Lev 16: 4 He is to put on the sacred *l* tunic,
Pr 31:22 she is clothed in fine *l* and purple.
31:24 She makes *l* garments
Mk 15:46 So Joseph bought some *l* cloth,
Jn 20: 6 He saw the strips of *l* lying there,
Rev 15: 6 shining *l* and wore golden sashes
19: 8 Fine *l*, bright and clean,

LINGER
Hab 2: 3 Though it *l*, wait for it;

LION (LION'S LIONS')
Jdg 14: 6 power so that he tore the *l* apart
1Sa 17:34 When a *l* or a bear came
Isa 11: 7 and the *l* will eat straw like the ox.
65:25 and the *l* will eat straw like the ox,
Eze 1:10 right side each had the face of a *l*,
10:14 the third the face of a *l*,
Da 7: 4 "The first was like a *l*,
1Pe 5: 8 around like a roaring *l* looking
Rev 4: 7 The first living creature was like a *l*
5: 5 See, the *L* of the tribe of Judah,

LION'S (LION)
Ge 49: 9 You are a *l* cub, O Judah;

LIONS' (LION)
Da 6: 7 shall be thrown into the *l* den.

LIPS
Ps 8: 2 From the *l* of children and infants
34: 1 his praise will always be on my *l*.
40: 9 I do not seal my *l*,
63: 3 my *l* will glorify you.
119:171 May my *l* overflow with praise,
140: 3 the poison of vipers is on their *l*.
141: 3 keep watch over the door of my *l*.
Pr 10:13 on the *l* of the discerning,
10:18 who conceals his hatred has lying *l*,
10:32 *l* of the righteous know what is
12:22 The LORD detests lying *l*,
13: 3 He who guards his *l* guards his life,
14: 7 will not find knowledge on his *l*.
24:26 is like a kiss on the *l*.
26:23 are fervent *l* with an evil heart.
27: 2 someone else, and not your own *l*.
Isa 6: 5 For I am a man of unclean *l*,
28:11 with foreign *l* and strange tongues
29:13 and honor me with their *l*,
Mal 2: 7 "For the *l* of a priest ought
Mt 15: 8 These people honor me with their *l*
21:16 " 'From the *l* of children
Lk 4:22 words that came from his *l*.
Ro 3:13 "The poison of vipers is on their *l*."
Col 3: 8 and filthy language from your *l*.
Heb 13:15 the fruit of *l* that confess his name.
1Pe 3:10 and his *l* from deceitful speech.

LISTEN (LISTENED LISTENING LISTENS)
Dt 18:15 You must *l* to him.
30:20 *l* to his voice, and hold fast to him.
1Ki 4:34 came to *l* to Solomon's wisdom,
2Ki 21: 9 But the people did not *l*.
Pr 1: 5 let the wise *l* and add
Ecc 5: 1 Go near to *l* rather

Eze 2: 5 And whether they *l* or fail to *l*—
Mt 12:42 earth to *l* to Solomon's wisdom,
Mk 9: 7 *L* to him!" Suddenly,
Jn 10:27 My sheep *l* to my voice; I know
Ac 3:22 you must *l* to everything he tells
Jas 1:19 Everyone should be quick to *l*,
1:22 Do not merely *l* to the word,
1Jn 4: 6 not from God does not *l* to us.

LISTENED (LISTEN)
Ne 8: 3 And all the people *l* attentively
Isa 66: 4 when I spoke, no one *l*.
Da 9: 6 We have not *l* to your servants

LISTENING (LISTEN)
1Sa 3: 9 Speak, LORD, for your servant is *l*
Pr 18:13 He who answers before *l*—
Lk 10:39 at the Lord's feet *l* to what he said.

LISTENS (LISTEN)
Pr 12:15 but a wise man *l* to advice.
Lk 10:16 "He who *l* to you *l*
1Jn 4: 6 and whoever knows God *l* to us;

LIVE (ALIVE LIFE LIFETIME LIVES LIVING)
Ge 3:22 tree of life and eat, and *l* forever."
Ex 20:12 so that you may *l* long
33:20 for no one may see me and *l*."
Nu 21: 8 who is bitten can look at it and *l*."
Dt 5:24 we have seen that a man can *l*
6: 2 as you *l* by keeping all his decrees
8: 3 to teach you that man does not *l*
Job 14:14 If a man dies, will he *l* again?
Ps 15: 1 Who may *l* on your holy hill?
24: 1 the world, and all who *l* in it;
26: 8 I love the house where you *l*,
119:175 Let me *l* that I may praise you,
Pr 21: 9 Better to *l* on a corner of the roof
21:19 Better to *l* in a desert
Ecc 9: 4 a *l* dog is better off than a dead lion
Isa 26:19 But your dead will *l*;
55: 3 hear me, that your soul may *l*.
Eze 17:19 LORD says: As surely as I *l*,
20:11 for the man who obeys them will *l*
37: 3 can these bones *l*?" I said,
Am 5: 6 Seek the LORD and *l*,
Hab 2: 4 but the righteous will *l* by his faith
Zec 2:11 I will *l* among you and you will
Mt 4: 4 'Man does not *l* on bread alone,
Lk 4: 4 'Man does not *l* on bread alone.' "
Jn 14:19 Because I *l*, you also will *l*.
Ac 17:24 does not *l* in temples built by hands
17:28 'For in him we *l* and move
Ro 1:17 "The righteous will *l* by faith."
2Co 5: 7 We *l* by faith, not by sight.
6:16 "I will *l* with them and walk
Gal 2:20 The life I *l* in the body, I *l* by faith
3:11 "The righteous will *l* by faith."
5:25 Since we *l* by the Spirit, let us keep
Eph 4:17 that you must no longer *l*
Php 1:21 to *l* is Christ and to die is gain.
Col 1:10 order that you may *l* a life worthy
1Th 4: 1 we instructed you how to *l* in order
5:13 *L* in peace with each other.
1Ti 2: 2 that we may *l* peaceful
2Ti 3:12 who wants to *l* a godly life
Tit 2:12 and to *l* self-controlled, upright
Heb 10:38 But my righteous one will *l* by faith
12:14 Make every effort to *l* in peace
1Pe 1:17 *l* your lives as strangers here
3: 8 *l* in harmony with one another;

LIVES (LIVE)
Ge 45: 7 and to save your *l* by a great
Job 19:25 I know that my Redeemer *l*,
Pr 1:19 it takes away the *l*
Isa 57:15 he who *l* forever, whose name is
Da 3:28 to give up their *l* rather than serve
Jn 14:17 for he *l* with you and will be in you.
Ro 6:10 but the life he *l*, he *l* to God.
7:18 I know that nothing good *l* in me,
8: 9 if the Spirit of God *l* in you.
14: 7 For none of us *l* to himself alone
1Co 3:16 and that God's Spirit *l* in you?
Gal 2:20 I no longer live, but Christ *l* in me.
1Th 2: 8 only the gospel of God but our *l*
1Ti 2: 2 quiet *l* in all godliness and holiness.
Tit 2:12 and godly *l* in this present age,
Heb 7:24 but because Jesus *l* forever,
13: 5 Keep your *l* free from the love
1Pe 3: 2 the purity and reverence of your *l*.
2Pe 3:11 You ought to live holy and godly *l*

1Jn 3:16 to lay down our *l* for our brothers.
4:16 Whoever *l* in love *l* in God,

LIVING (LIVE)

Ge 2: 7 and the man became a *l* being.
1Sa 17:26 defy the armies of the *l* God?"
Isa 53: 8 cut off from the land of the *l*;
Jer 2:13 the spring of *l* water,
Eze 1: 5 what looked like four *l* creatures.
Zec 14: 8 On that day *l* water will flow out
Mt 22:32 the God of the dead but of the *l*."
Jn 4:10 he would have given you *l* water."
6:51 I am the *l* bread that came
7:38 streams of *l* water will flow
Ro 8:11 Jesus from the dead is *l* in you,
12: 1 to offer your bodies as *l* sacrifices,
1Co 9:14 the gospel should receive their *l*
Heb 4:12 For the word of God is *l* and active.
10:20 and *l* way opened for us
10:31 to fall into the hands of the *l* God.
1Pe 1:23 through the *l* and enduring word
Rev 1:18 I am the *L* One; I was dead,
4: 6 the throne, were four *l* creatures,
7:17 to springs of *l* water.

LOAD (LOADS)

Gal 6: 5 for each one should carry his own *l*.

LOADS (LOAD)

Mt 23: 4 They tie up heavy *l* and put them

LOAF (LOAVES)

1Co 10:17 for we all partake of the one *l*.

LOAVES (LOAF)

Mk 6:41 Taking the five *l* and the two fish
8: 6 When he had taken the seven *l*
Lk 11: 5 'Friend, lend me three *l* of bread,

LOCKED

Jn 20:26 the doors were *l*, Jesus came
Gal 3:23 *l* up until faith should be revealed.

LOCUSTS

Ex 10: 4 I will bring *l* into your country
Joel 2:25 you for the years the *l* have eaten—
Mt 3: 4 His food was *l* and wild honey.
Rev 9: 3 And out of the smoke *l* came

LOFTY

Ps 139: 6 too *l* for me to attain.
Isa 57:15 is what the high and *l* One says—

LONELY

Ps 68: 6 God sets the *l* in families,
Lk 5:16 Jesus often withdrew to *l* places

LONG (LENGTH LENGTHY LONGED LONGING LONGINGS LONGS)

Ex 17:11 As *l* as Moses held up his hands,
Nu 6: 5 the hair of his head grow *l*.
1Ki 18:21 "How *l* will you waver
Ps 119: 97 I meditate on it all day *l*.
119:174 I *l* for your salvation, O LORD,
Hos 7:13 I *l* to redeem them
Am 5:18 Why do you *l* for the day
Mt 25: 5 The bridegroom was a *l* time
Jn 9: 4 As *l* as it is day, we must do
1Co 11:14 that if a man has *l* hair,
Eph 3:18 to grasp how wide and *l* and high
Php 1: 8 God can testify how I *l* for all
1Pe 1:12 Even angels *l* to look

LONGED (LONG)

Mt 13:17 righteous men *l* to see what you see
23:37 how often I have *l*
Lk 13:34 how often I have *l*
2Ti 4: 8 to all who have *l* for his appearing.

LONGING* (LONG)

Dt 28:65 with *l*, and a despairing heart.
Job 7: 2 Like a slave *l* for the evening
Ps 119: 20 My soul is consumed with *l*
119: 81 with *l* for your salvation,
119:131 *l* for your commands.
143: 7 my spirit faints with *l*.
Pr 13:12 but a *l* fulfilled is a tree of life.
13:19 A *l* fulfilled is sweet to the soul,
Eze 23:27 look on these things with *l*
Lk 16:21 and *l* to eat what fell from the rich
Ro 15:23 since I have been *l* for many years
2Co 5: 2 *l* to be clothed with our heavenly
7: 7 He told us about your *l* for me,
7:11 what alarm, what *l*, what concern,
1Th 2:17 out of our intense *l* we made every
Heb 11:16 they were *l* for a better country—

LONGINGS* (LONG)

Ps 38: 9 All my *l* lie open before you,
112: 10 the *l* of the wicked will come

LONGS* (LONG)

Ps 63: 1 my body *l* for you,
Isa 26: 9 in the morning my spirit *l* for you.
30:18 Yet the LORD *l* to be gracious
Php 2:26 For he *l* for all of you and is

LOOK (LOOKED LOOKING LOOKS)

Ge 19:17 "Flee for your lives! Don't *l* back,
Ex 3: 6 because he was afraid to *l* at God.
Nu 21: 8 anyone who is bitten can *l* at it
32: 8 Kadesh Barnea to *l* over the land.
Dt 4:29 you will find him if you *l* for him
1Sa 16: 7 The LORD does not *l*
Job 31: 1 not to *l* lustfully at a girl.
Ps 34: 5 Those who *l* to him are radiant;
105: 4 *L* to the LORD and his strength;
113: 6 who stoops down to *l*
123: 2 As the eyes of slaves *l* to the hand
Pr 1:28 they will *l* for me but will not find
4:25 Let your eyes *l* straight ahead,
15:30 A cheerful *l* brings joy to the heart,
Isa 17: 7 In that day men will *l*
31: 1 do not *l* to the Holy One of Israel,
40:26 Lift your eyes and *l* to the heavens:
60: 5 Then you will *l* and be radiant,
Jer 3: 3 Yet you have the brazen *l*
6:16 "Stand at the crossroads and *l*;
Eze 34:11 for my sheep and *l* after them.
Hab 1:13 Your eyes are too pure to *l* on evil;
Zec 12:10 They will *l* on me, the one they
Mt 18:10 "See that you do not *l* down on one
18:12 go to *l* for the one that wandered
23:27 which *l* beautiful on the outside
Mk 13:21 '*L*, here is the Christ!' or, '*L*,
Lk 6:41 "Why do you *l* at the speck
24:39 *L* at my hands and my feet.
Jn 1:36 he said, "*L*, the Lamb of God!"
4:35 open your eyes and *l* at the fields!
19:37 "They will *l* on the one they have
Ro 14:10 why do you *l* down on your brother
Php 2: 4 Each of you should *l* not only
1Ti 4:12 Don't let anyone *l* down on you
Jas 1:27 to *l* after orphans and widows
1Pe 1:12 long to *l* into these things.
2Pe 3:12 as you *l* forward to the day of God

LOOKED (LOOK)

Ge 19:26 Lot's wife *l* back, and she became
Ex 2:25 So God *l* on the Israelites
1Sa 6:19 because they had *l* into the ark
SS 3: 1 I *l* for the one my heart loves;
Eze 22:30 "I *l* for a man among them who
34: 6 and no one searched or *l* for them.
44: 4 I *l* and saw the glory
Da 7: 9 "As I *l*,
10: 5 I *l* up and there before me was
Hab 3: 6 he *l*, and made the nations tremble.
Mt 25:36 I was sick and you *l* after me,
Lk 18: 9 and *l* down on everybody else,
22:61 The Lord turned and *l* straight
1Jn 1: 1 which we have *l* at and our hands

LOOKING (LOOK)

Ps 69: 3 *l* for my God.
119: 82 My eyes fail, *l* for your promise;
119:123 My eyes fail, *l* for your salvation,
Mk 16: 6 "You are *l* for Jesus the Nazarene,
2Co 10: 7 You are *l* only on the surface
Php 4:17 Not that I am *l* for a gift,
1Th 2: 6 We were not *l* for praise from men,
2Pe 3:13 with his promise we are *l* forward
Rev 5: 6 I saw a Lamb, *l* as if it had been

LOOKS (LOOK)

1Sa 16: 7 Man *l* at the outward appearance,
Ezr 8:22 is on everyone who *l* to him,
Ps 104: 32 who *l* at the earth, and it trembles;
138: 6 on high, he *l* upon the lowly,
Pr 27:18 he who *l* after his master will be
Eze 34:12 As a shepherd *l* after his scattered
Mt 5:28 But I tell you that anyone who *l*
16: 4 and adulterous generation *l*
Lk 9:62 and *l* back is fit for service
Jn 6:40 Father's will is that everyone who *l*
12:45 When he *l* at me, he sees the one
Php 2:21 For everyone *l* out
Jas 1:25 But the man who *l* intently

LOOSE

Isa 33:23 Your rigging hangs *l*:

Mt 16:19 and whatever you *l* on earth will be
18:18 and whatever you *l* on earth will be

LORD† (LORD'S† LORDED LORDING)

Ge 18:27 been so bold as to speak to the *L*,
Ex 15:17 O *L*, your hands established.
Nu 16:13 now you also want to *l* it over us?
Dt 10:17 God of gods and *L* of lords,
Jos 3:13 the *L* of all the earth—set foot
1Ki 3:10 *L* was pleased that Solomon had
Ne 4:14 Remember the *L*, who is great
Job 28:28 'The fear of the *L*—that is wisdom,
Ps 37:13 but the *L* laughs at the wicked,
38:22 O *L* my Savior.
54: 4 the *L* is the one who sustains me.
62:12 and that you, O *L*, are loving.
69: 6 O *L*, the LORD Almighty;
86: 5 You are forgiving and good, O *L*,
86: 8 gods there is none like you, O *L*;
89:49 O *L*, where is your former great
110: 1 The LORD says to my *L*:
110: 5 The *L* is at your right hand;
130: 3 O *L*, who could stand?
135: 5 that our *L* is greater than all gods.
136: 3 Give thanks to the *L* of lords:
147: 5 Great is our *L* and mighty in power
Isa 6: 1 I saw the *L* seated on a throne,
Da 2:47 and the *L* of kings and a revealer
9: 4 "O *L*, the great and awesome God,
9: 7 "*L*, you are righteous,
9: 9 The *L* our God is merciful
9:19 O *L*, listen! O *L*, forgive! O *L*,
Mt 3: 3 'Prepare the way for the *L*,
4: 7 'Do not put the *L* your God
4:10 'Worship the *L* your God,
7:21 "Not everyone who says to me, '*L*,
9:38 Ask the *L* of the harvest, therefore,
12: 8 Son of Man is *L* of the Sabbath."
20:25 of the Gentiles *l* it over them,
21: 9 comes in the name of the *L*!"
22:37 " 'Love the *L* your God
22:44 For he says, " 'The *L* said to my *L*:
23:39 comes in the name of the *L*.' "
Mk 1: 3 'Prepare the way for the *L*,
12:11 the *L* has done this,
12:29 the *L* our God, the *L* is one.
12:30 Love the *L* your God
Lk 2: 9 glory of the *L* shone around them,
6: 5 The Son of Man is *L* of the Sabbath
6:46 "Why do you call me, '*L*, *L*,'
10:27 " 'Love the *L* your God
11: 1 one of his disciples said to him, "*L*,
24:34 The *L* has risen and has appeared
Jn 1:23 'Make straight the way for the *L*.' "
Ac 2:21 on the name of the *L* will be saved.'
2:25 " 'I saw the *L* always before me.
2:34 " 'The *L* said to my *L*:
8:16 into the name of the *L* Jesus.
9: 5 "Who are you, *L*?" Saul asked.
10:36 through Jesus Christ, who is *L*
11:23 true to the *L* with all their hearts.
16:31 replied, "Believe in the *L* Jesus,
Ro 4:24 in him who raised Jesus our *L*
5:11 in God through our *L* Jesus Christ,
6:23 life in Christ Jesus our *L*.
8:39 of God that is in Christ Jesus our *L*.
10: 9 with your mouth, "Jesus is *L*,"
10:13 on the name of the *L* will be saved
10:16 *L*, who has believed our message?"
11:34 Who has known the mind of the *L*?
12:11 your spiritual fervor, serving the *L*.
13:14 yourselves with the *L* Jesus Christ,
14: 4 for the *L* is able to make him stand.
14: 8 we live to the *L*; and if we die,
1Co 1:31 Let him who boasts boast in the *L*."
3: 5 the *L* has assigned to each his task.
4: 5 time; wait till the *L* comes.
6:13 for the *L*, and the *L* for the body.
6:14 By his power God raised the *L*
7:32 affairs—how he can please the *L*.
7:34 to be devoted to the *L* in both body
7:35 in undivided devotion to the *L*.
7:39 but he must belong to the *L*.
8: 6 and there is but one *L*, Jesus Christ,
10: 9 We should not test the *L*,
11:23 For I received from the *L* what I
12: 3 "Jesus is *L*," except by the Holy
15:57 victory through our *L* Jesus Christ.
15:58 fully to the work of the *L*,
16:22 If anyone does not love the *L*—

2Co 1:24 Not that we *l* it over your faith,
2:12 found that the *L* had opened a door
3:17 Now the *L* is the Spirit,
4: 5 but Jesus Christ as *L,* and ourselves
5: 6 in the body we are away from the *L*
8: 5 they gave themselves first to the *L*
8:21 not only in the eyes of the *L* but
10:17 Let him who boasts boast in the *L.*"
10:18 but the one whom the *L* commends
13:10 the authority the *L* gave me
Gal 6:14 in the cross of our *L* Jesus Christ,
Eph 4: 5 one *L,* one faith, one baptism;
5: 8 but now you are light in the *L.*
5:10 and find out what pleases the *L.*
5:19 make music in your heart to the *L,*
5:22 submit to your husbands as to the *L*
6: 1 obey your parents in the *L,*
6: 7 as if you were serving the *L,*
6: 8 know that the *L* will reward
6:10 in the *L* and in his mighty power.
Php 2:11 confess that Jesus Christ is *L,*
3: 1 my brothers, rejoice in the *L!*
3: 8 of knowing Christ Jesus my *L,*
4: 1 you should stand firm in the *L,*
4: 4 Rejoice in the *L* always.
4: 5 The *L* is near.
Col 1:10 you may live a life worthy of the *L*
2: 6 as you received Christ Jesus as *L,*
3:13 Forgive as the *L* forgave you.
3:17 do it all in the name of the *L* Jesus,
3:18 your husbands, as is fitting in the *L.*
3:20 in everything, for this pleases the *L*
3:23 as working for the *L,* not for men,
3:24 It is the *L* Christ you are serving.
3:24 receive an inheritance from the *L*
4:17 work you have received in the *L.*"
1Th 3: 8 since you are standing firm in the *L*
3:12 May the *L* make your love increase
4: 1 and urge you in the *L* Jesus
4: 6 The *L* will punish men
4:15 who are left till the coming of the *L*
5: 2 day of the *L* will come like a thief
5:23 at the coming of our *L* Jesus Christ.
2Th 1: 7 when the *L* Jesus is revealed
1:12 of our *L* Jesus may be glorified
2: 1 the coming of our *L* Jesus Christ
2: 8 whom the *L* Jesus will overthrow
3: 3 *L* is faithful, and he will strengthen
3: 5 May the *L* direct your hearts
1Ti 6:15 the King of kings and *L* of lords,
2Ti 1: 8 ashamed to testify about our *L,*
2:19 "The *L* knows those who are his,"
4: 8 which the *L,* the righteous Judge,
4:17 But the *L* stood at my side
Heb 1:10 O *L,* you laid the foundations
10:30 "The *L* will judge his people."
12:14 holiness no one will see the *L.*
13: 6 *L* is my helper; I will not be afraid.
Jas 3: 9 With the tongue we praise our *L*
4:10 Humble yourselves before the *L,*
5:11 The *L* is full of compassion
1Pe 1:25 the word of the *L* stands forever."
2: 3 you have tasted that the *L* is good.
3:12 eyes of the *L* are on the righteous
3:15 in your hearts set apart Christ as *L.*
2Pe 1:11 into the eternal kingdom of our *L*
1:16 and coming of our *L* Jesus Christ,
2: 1 the sovereign *L* who bought
2: 9 then the *L* knows how
3: 9 The *L* is not slow in keeping his
3:18 and knowledge of our *L* and Savior
Jude :14 the *L* is coming with thousands
Rev 4: 8 holy, holy is the *L* God Almighty,
4:11 "You are worthy, our *L* and God,
11:15 has become the kingdom of our *L*
17:14 he is *L* of lords and King of kings—
19:16 KINGS AND *L* OF LORDS.
22: 5 for the *L* God will give them light.
22:20 Come, *L* Jesus.

LORD'S† (LORD†)
Lk 1:38 "I am the *L* servant," Mary
Ac 11:21 The *L* hand was with them,
21:14 and said, "The *L* will be done."
1Co 7:32 is concerned about the *L* affairs—
10:26 "The earth is the *L,* and everything
11:26 you proclaim the *L* death
2Co 3:18 faces all reflect the *L* glory,
Eph 5:17 but understand what the *L* will is.
2Ti 2:24 And the *L* servant must not quarrel
Heb 12: 5 light of the *L* discipline,
Jas 4:15 you ought to say, "If it is the *L* will,
5: 8 because the *L* coming is near.
1Pe 2:13 Submit yourselves for the *L* sake

LORDED* (LORD†)
Ne 5:15 Their assistants also *l* it

LORDING* (LORD†)
1Pe 5: 3 not *l* it over those entrusted to you,

LORD‡ (LORD'S‡)
Ge 2: 4 When the *L* God made the earth
2: 7 the *L* God formed the man
2:22 Then the *L* God made a woman
3:21 The *L* God made garments of skin
3:23 So the *L* God banished him
4: 4 The *L* looked with favor on Abel
4:26 began to call on the name of the *L*
6: 7 So the *L* said, "I will wipe mankind
7:16 Then the *L* shut him in.
9:26 Blessed be the *L,* the God of Shem!
11: 9 there the *L* confused the language
12: 1 *L* had said to Abram, "Leave your
15: 6 Abram believed the *L,*
15:18 On that day the *L* made a covenant
17: 1 the *L* appeared to him and said,
18: 1 The *L* appeared to Abraham
18:14 Is anything too hard for the *L?*
18:19 way of the *L* by doing what is right
21: 1 Now the *L* was gracious to Sarah
22:14 that place The *L* Will Provide.
24: 1 the *L* had blessed him in every way
26: 2 The *L* appeared to Isaac and said,
28:13 There above it stood the *L,*
31:49 "May the *L* keep watch
39: 2 The *L* was with Joseph
39:21 in the prison, the *L* was with him;
Ex 3: 2 the angel of the *L* appeared to him
4:11 Is it not I, the *L?* Now go;
4:31 heard that the *L* was concerned
6: 2 also said to Moses, "I am the *L.*
9:12 the *L* hardened Pharaoh's heart
12:27 'It is the Passover sacrifice to the *L,*
12:43 The *L* said to Moses and Aaron,
13: 9 For the *L* brought you out of Egypt
13:21 By day the *L* went ahead of them
14:13 the deliverance the *L* will bring
14:30 That day the *L* saved Israel
15: 3 The *L* is a warrior;
15:11 among the gods is like you, O *L?*
15:26 for I am the *L,* who heals you."
16:12 know that I am the *L* your God.' "
16:23 day of rest, a holy Sabbath to the *L.*
17:15 and called it The *L* is my Banner.
19: 8 will do everything the *L* has said."
19:20 The *L* descended to the top
20: 2 "I am the *L* your God, who
20: 5 the *L* your God, am a jealous God,
20: 7 for the *L* will not hold anyone
20:10 a Sabbath to the *L* your God.
20:11 in six days the *L* made the heavens
20:12 in the land the *L* your God is giving
23:25 Worship the *L* your God,
24: 3 "Everything the *L* has said we will
24:12 The *L* said to Moses, "Come up
24:16 and the glory of the *L* settled
25: 1 The *L* said to Moses, "Tell
28:36 HOLY TO THE *L.*
30:11 Then the *L* said to Moses,
31:13 so you may know that I am the *L,*
31:18 When the *L* finished speaking
33:11 The *L* would speak to Moses face
33:19 And the *L* said, "I will cause all my
34: 1 *L* said to Moses, "Chisel out two
34: 6 proclaiming, "The *L,* the *L,*
34:10 awesome is the work that I, the *L,*
34:29 because he had spoken with the *L.*
40:34 glory of the *L* filled the tabernacle.
40:38 So the cloud of the *L* was
Lev 8:36 did everything the *L* commanded
9:23 and the glory of the *L* appeared
10: 2 and they died before the *L.*
19: 2 'Be holy because I, the *L* your God,
20: 8 I am the *L,* who makes you holy.
Lev 20:26 to be holy to me because I, the *L,*
23:40 and rejoice before the *L* your God
Nu 6:24 Say to them: " 'The *L* bless you
8: 5 *L* said to Moses: "Take the Levites
11: 1 hardships in the hearing of the *L,*
14:14 O *L,* have been seen face to face,
14:18 you have declared: 'The *L* is slow
14:21 glory of the *L* fills the whole earth,
21: 6 Then the *L* sent venomous snakes
22:31 Then the *L* opened Balaam's eyes,
23:12 "Must I not speak what the *L* puts
30: 2 When a man makes a vow to the *L*
32:12 followed the *L* wholeheartedly.'
Dt 1:21 and take possession of it as the *L,*
2: 7 forty years the *L* your God has
4:29 there you seek the *L* your God,
5: 6 And he said: "I am the *L* your God,
5: 9 the *L* your God, am a jealous God,
6: 4 The *L* our God, the *L* is one.
6: 5 Love the *L* your God
Dt 6:16 Do not test the *L* your God
6:25 law before the *L* our God,
7: 1 When the *L* your God brings you
7: 6 holy to the *L* your God.
7: 8 But it was because the *L* loved you
7: 9 that the *L* your God is God;
7:12 then the *L* your God will keep his
8: 5 so the *L* your God disciplines you.
9:10 The *L* gave me two stone tablets
10:12 but to fear the *L* your God,
10:14 To the *L* your God belong
10:17 For the *L* your God is God of gods
10:20 Fear the *L* your God and serve him
10:22 now the *L* your God has made you
11: 1 Love the *L* your God and keep his
11:13 to love the *L* your God
16: 1 the Passover of the *L* your God,
17:15 the king the *L* your God chooses.
28: 1 If you fully obey the *L* your God
28:15 if you do not obey the *L* your God
29: 1 covenant the *L* commanded Moses
29:29 things belong to the *L* our God,
30: 4 from there the *L* your God will
30: 6 *L* your God will circumcise your
30:10 if you obey the *L* your God
30:16 today to love the *L* your God,
30:20 For the *L* is your life, and he will
31: 6 for the *L* your God goes with you;
34: 5 of the *L* died there in Moab,
Jos 10:14 a day when the *L* listened to a man.
22: 5 to love the *L* your God, to walk
23:11 careful to love the *L* your God.
24:15 my household, we will serve the *L*
24:18 We too will serve the *L,*
Jdg 2:12 They forsook the *L,* the God
Ru 1: 8 May the *L* show kindness to you,
4:13 And the *L* enabled her to conceive,
1Sa 1:11 him to the *L* for all the days
1:15 I was pouring out my soul to the *L.*
1:28 So now I give him to the *L.*
2: 2 "There is no one holy like the *L;*
2:25 but if a man sins against the *L,*
2:26 in favor with the *L* and with men.
3: 9 *L,* for your servant is listening.' "
3:19 The *L* was with Samuel
7:12 "Thus far has the *L* helped us."
9:17 sight of Saul, the *L* said to him,
11:15 as king in the presence of the *L.*
12:18 all the people stood in awe of the *L*
12:22 his great name the *L* will not reject
12:24 But be sure to fear the *L*
13:14 the *L* has sought out a man
14: 6 Nothing can hinder the *L*
15:22 "Does the *L* delight
16:13 Spirit of the *L* came upon David
17:45 you in the name of the *L* Almighty,
2Sa 6:14 danced before the *L*
7:22 How great you are, O Sovereign *L!*
8: 6 *L* gave David victory everywhere
12: 7 This is what the *L,* the God
22: 2 "The *L* is my rock, my fortress
22:29 You are my lamp, O *L;*
22:31 the word of the *L* is flawless.
1Ki 1:30 today what I swore to you by the *L,*
2: 3 and observe what the *L* your God
3: 7 O *L* my God, you have made your
5: 5 for the Name of the *L* my God,

‡This entry represents the translation of the Hebrew name for God. *Yahweh,* always indicated in the NIV by LORD. For Lord, see the concordance entries LORD† and LORD'S†.

1Ki 5:12 The *L* gave Solomon wisdom,
8:11 the glory of the *L* filled his temple.
8:23 toward heaven and said: "O *L*,
8:61 fully committed to the *L* our God,
9: 3 The *L* said to him: "I have heard
10: 9 Praise be to the *L* your God,
15:14 committed to the *L* all his life.
18:21 If the *L* is God, follow him;
18:36 "O *L*, God of Abraham, Isaac
18:39 "The *L*—he is God! The *L*—
21:23 also concerning Jezebel the *L* says:
2Ki 13:23 But the *L* was gracious to them
17:18 So the *L* was very angry with Israel
18: 5 Hezekiah trusted in the *L*,
19: 1 and went into the temple of the *L*.
20:11 *L* made the shadow go back the ten
21:12 Therefore this is what the *L*,
22: 2 right in the eyes of the *L*
22: 8 of the Law in the temple of the *L*."
23: 3 to follow the *L* and keep his
23:21 the Passover to the *L* your God,
23:25 a king like him who turned to the *L*
24: 2 The *L* sent Babylonian, Aramean,
24: 4 and the *L* was not willing to forgive
1Ch 10:13 because he was unfaithful to the *L*;
11: 3 with them at Hebron before the *L*,
11: 9 the *L* Almighty was with him.
13: 6 from there the ark of God the *L*, who
16: 8 Give thanks to the *L*, call
16:11 Look to the *L* and his strength;
16:14 He is the *L* our God;
16:23 Sing to the *L*, all the earth;
17: 1 covenant of the *L* is under a tent."
21:24 take for the *L* what is yours,
22: 5 to be built for the *L* should be
22:11 build the house of the *L* your God,
22:13 and laws that the *L* gave Moses
22:16 Now begin the work, and the *L* be
22:19 soul to seeking the *L* your God.
25: 7 and skilled in music for the *L*—
28: 9 for the *L* searches every heart
28:20 for the *L* God, my God, is with you
29: 1 not for man but for the *L* God.
29:11 O *L*, is the greatness and the power
29:18 O *L*, God of our fathers Abraham,
29:25 The *L* highly exalted Solomon
2Ch 1: 1 for the *L* his God was with him
5:13 to give praise and thanks to the *L*.
5:14 the glory of the *L* filled the temple
6:16 "Now *L*, God of Israel, keep
6:41 O *L* God, and come
6:42 O *L* God, do not reject your
7: 1 the glory of the *L* filled the temple.
7:12 the *L* appeared to him at night
7:21 'Why has the *L* done such a thing
9: 8 as king to rule for the *L* your God.
13:12 do not fight against the *L*,
14: 2 right in the eyes of the *L* his God.
15:14 to the *L* with loud acclamation,
16: 9 of the *L* range throughout the earth
17: 9 the Book of the Law of the *L*;
18:13 said, "As surely as the *L* lives,
19: 6 judging for man but for the *L*,
19: 9 wholeheartedly in the fear of the *L*.
20:15 This is what the *L* says to you:
20:20 Have faith in the *L* your God
20:21 appointed men to sing to the *L*
26: 5 As long as he sought the *L*,
26:16 He was unfaithful to the *L* his God,
29:30 to praise the *L* with the words
30: 9 for the *L* your God is gracious
31:20 and faithful before the *L* his God.
32: 8 with us is the *L* our God to help us
34:14 Law of the *L* that had been given
34:31 to follow the *L* and keep his
Ezr 3:10 foundation of the temple of the *L*,
7: 6 for the hand of the *L* his God was
7:10 observance of the Law of the *L*,
9: 5 hands spread out to the *L* my God
9: 8 the *L* our God has been gracious
9:15 O *L*, God of Israel, you are
Ne 1: 5 Then I said: "O *L*, God of heaven,
8: 1 which the *L* had commanded
9: 6 You alone are the *L*.
Job 1: 6 to present themselves before the *L*,
1:21 *L* gave and the *L* has taken away;
38: 1 the *L* answered Job out
42: 9 and the *L* accepted Job's prayer.
42:12 The *L* blessed the latter part
Ps 1: 2 But his delight is in the law of the *L*

Ps 1: 6 For the *L* watches over the way
4: 6 of your face shine upon us, O *L*.
4: 8 for you alone, O *L*,
5: 3 In the morning, O *L*,
6: 1 O *L*, do not rebuke me
8: 1 O *L*, our Lord,
9: 9 The *L* is a refuge for the oppressed,
9:19 Arise, O *L*, let not man triumph;
10:16 The *L* is King for ever and ever;
12: 6 And the words of the *L* are flawless
16: 5 *L*, you have assigned me my
16: 8 I have set the *L* always before me.
18: 1 I love you, O *L*, my strength.
18: 6 In my distress I called to the *L*;
18:30 the word of the *L* is flawless.
19: 7 The law of the *L* is perfect,
19:14 O *L*, my Rock and my Redeemer.
20: 5 May the *L* grant all your requests.
20: 7 in the name of the *L* our God.
22: 8 let the *L* rescue him.
23: 1 The *L* is my shepherd, I shall
23: 6 I will dwell in the house of the *L*
24: 3 Who may ascend the hill of the *L*?
24: 8 The *L* strong and mighty,
25:10 All the ways of the *L* are loving
27: 1 The *L* is my light and my salvation
27: 4 to gaze upon the beauty of the *L*
27: 6 I will sing and make music to the *L*.
29: 1 Ascribe to the *L*, O mighty ones,
29: 4 The voice of the *L* is powerful;
30: 4 Sing to the *L*, you saints of his;
31: 5 redeem me, O *L*, the God of truth.
32: 2 whose sin the *L* does not count
33: 1 joyfully to the *L*, you righteous;
33: 6 of the *L* were the heavens made,
33:12 is the nation whose God is the *L*,
33:18 But the eyes of the *L* are
34: 1 I will extol the *L* at all times;
34: 3 Glorify the *L* with me;
34: 4 I sought the *L*, and he answered me
34: 7 The angel of the *L* encamps
34: 8 Taste and see that the *L* is good;
34: 9 Fear the *L*, you his saints,
34:15 The eyes of the *L* are
34:18 The *L* is close to the brokenhearted
37: 4 Delight yourself in the *L*
37: 5 Commit your way to the *L*;
39: 4 "Show me, O *L*, my life's end
40: 1 I waited patiently for the *L*;
40: 5 Many, O *L* my God,
46: 8 Come and see the works of the *L*,
47: 2 How awesome is the *L* Most High,
48: 1 Great is the *L*, and most worthy
50: 1 The Mighty One, God, the *L*,
55:22 Cast your cares on the *L*
59: 8 But you, O *L*, laugh at them;
68: 4 his name is the *L*—
68:18 O *L* God, might dwell there.
68:20 from the Sovereign *L* comes escape
69:31 This will please the *L* more
72:18 Praise be to the *L* God, the God
75: 8 In the hand of the *L* is a cup
78: 4 the praiseworthy deeds of the *L*,
84: 8 my prayer, O *L* God Almighty;
84:11 For the *L* God is a sun and shield;
85: 7 Show us your unfailing love, O *L*,
86:11 Teach me your way, O *L*,
87: 2 the *L* loves the gates of Zion
89: 5 heavens praise your wonders, O *L*,
89: 8 O *L* God Almighty, who is like you
91: 2 I will say of the *L*, "He is my refuge
92: 1 It is good to praise the *L*
92: 4 by your deeds, O *L*;
92:13 planted in the house of the *L*,
93: 1 The *L* reigns, he is robed in majesty
93: 5 house for endless days, O *L*.
94: 1 O *L*, the God who avenges,
94:12 is the man you discipline, O *L*,
94:18 your love, O *L*, supported me.
95: 1 Come, let us sing for joy to the *L*;
95: 3 For the *L* is the great God,
95: 6 let us kneel before the *L* our Maker
96: 1 Sing to the *L* a new song;
96: 5 but the *L* made the heavens.
96: 8 to the *L* the glory due his name;
96: 9 Worship the *L* in the splendor
96:13 they will sing before the *L*,
97: 1 The *L* reigns, let the earth be glad;
97: 9 O *L*, are the Most High
98: 1 Sing to the *L* a new song,

Ps 98: 2 *L* has made his salvation known
98: 4 Shout for joy to the *L*, all the earth,
99: 1 The *L* reigns,
99: 2 Great is the *L* in Zion;
99: 5 Exalt the *L* our God
99: 9 Exalt the *L* our God
100: 1 Shout for joy to the *L*, all the earth.
100: 2 Worship the *L* with gladness;
100: 3 Know that the *L* is God.
100: 5 For the *L* is good and his love
101: 1 to you, O *L*, I will sing praise.
102: 12 But you, O *L*, sit enthroned forever
103: 1 Praise the *L*, O my soul;
103: 8 The *L* is compassionate
103: 19 The *L* has established his throne
104: 1 O *L* my God, you are very great;
104: 24 How many are your works, O *L*!
104: 33 I will sing to the *L* all my life;
105: 4 Look to the *L* and his strength;
105: 7 He is the *L* our God;
106: 2 proclaim the mighty acts of the *L*
107: 1 Give thanks to the *L*, for he is good
107: 8 to the *L* for his unfailing love
107: 21 to the *L* for his unfailing love
107: 43 and consider the great love of the *L*
108: 3 I will praise you, O *L*,
109: 26 Help me, O *L* my God;
110: 1 The *L* says to my Lord:
110: 4 The *L* has sworn
111: 2 Great are the works of the *L*;
111: 4 *L* is gracious and compassionate.
111: 10 The fear of the *L* is the beginning
112: 1 Blessed is the man who fears the *L*,
113: 1 Praise, O servants of the *L*,
113: 2 Let the name of the *L* be praised,
113: 4 *L* is exalted over all the nations,
113: 5 Who is like the *L* our God,
115: 1 Not to us, O *L*, not to us
115: 18 it is we who extol the *L*,
116: 12 How can I repay the *L*
116: 15 Precious in the sight of the *L*
117: 1 Praise the *L*, all you nations;
118: 1 Give thanks to the *L*, for he is good
118: 5 In my anguish I cried to the *L*,
118: 8 It is better to take refuge in the *L*
118: 18 The *L* has chastened me severely,
118: 23 the *L* has done this,
118: 24 This is the day the *L* has made;
118: 26 comes in the name of the *L*.
119: 1 to the law of the *L*.
119: 64 with your love, O *L*;
119: 89 Your word, O *L*, is eternal;
119:126 It is time for you to act, O *L*;
119:159 O *L*, according to your love.
120: 1 I call on the *L* in my distress,
121: 2 My help comes from the *L*,
121: 5 The *L* watches over you—
121: 8 the *L* will watch over your coming
122: 1 "Let us go to the house of the *L*."
123: 2 so our eyes look to the *L* our God,
124: 1 If the *L* had not been on our side—
124: 8 Our help is in the name of the *L*,
125: 2 so the *L* surrounds his people
126: 3 The *L* has done great things for us,
126: 4 Restore our fortunes, O *L*,
127: 1 Unless the *L* builds the house,
127: 3 Sons are a heritage from the *L*,
128: 1 Blessed are all who fear the *L*,
130: 1 O *L*; O Lord, hear my voice.
130: 3 If you, O *L*, kept a record of sins,
130: 5 I wait for the *L*, my soul waits,
131: 3 O Israel, put your hope in the *L*
132: 1 O *L*, remember David
132: 13 For the *L* has chosen Zion,
133: 3 For there the *L* bestows his
134: 3 May the *L*, the Maker of heaven
135: 4 For the *L* has chosen Jacob
135: 6 The *L* does whatever pleases him,
136: 1 Give thanks to the *L*, for he is good
137: 4 How can we sing the songs of the *L*
138: 1 I will praise you, O *L*,
138: 8 The *L* will fulfill ⸤his purpose⸥
139: 1 O *L*, you have searched me
140: 1 Rescue me, O *L*, from evil men;
141: 1 O *L*, I call to you; come quickly
141: 3 Set a guard over my mouth, O *L*;
142: 5 I cry to you, O *L*;
143: 9 Rescue me from my enemies, O *L*,
144: 3 O *L*, what is man that you care
145: 3 Great is the *L* and most worthy

Ps 145: 8 *L* is gracious and compassionate,
145: 9 The *L* is good to all;
145: 17 The *L* is righteous in all his ways
145: 18 The *L* is near to all who call on him
146: 5 whose hope is in the *L* his God,
146: 7 The *L* sets prisoners free,
147: 2 The *L* builds up Jerusalem;
147: 7 Sing to the *L* with thanksgiving;
147: 11 *L* delights in those who fear him,
147: 12 Extol the *L*, O Jerusalem;
148: 1 Praise the *L* from the heavens,
148: 7 Praise the *L* from the earth,
149: 4 For the *L* takes delight
150: 1 Praise the *L*.
150: 6 that has breath praise the *L*.
Pr 1: 7 The fear of the *L* is the beginning
1:29 and did not choose to fear the *L*,
2: 5 will understand the fear of the *L*
2: 6 For the *L* gives wisdom,
3: 5 Trust in the *L* with all your heart
3: 7 fear the *L* and shun evil.
3: 9 Honor the *L* with your wealth,
3:12 the *L* disciplines those he loves,
3:19 By wisdom the *L* laid the earth's
5:21 are in full view of the *L*,
6:16 There are six things the *L* hates,
8:13 To fear the *L* is to hate evil;
9:10 "The fear of the *L* is the beginning
10:27 The fear of the *L* adds length to life
11: 1 The *L* abhors dishonest scales,
12:22 The *L* detests lying lips,
14: 2 whose walk is upright fears the *L*,
14:26 He who fears the *L* has a secure
14:27 The fear of the *L* is a fountain
15: 3 The eyes of the *L* are everywhere,
15:16 Better a little with the fear of the *L*
15:33 of the *L* teaches a man wisdom,
16: 2 but motives are weighed by the *L*.
16: 3 Commit to the *L* whatever you do,
16: 4 The *L* works out everything
16: 5 The *L* detests all the proud of heart
16: 9 but the *L* determines his steps.
16:33 but its every decision is from the *L*.
18:10 The name of the *L* is a strong tower
18:22 and receives favor from the *L*.
19:14 but a prudent wife is from the *L*.
19:17 to the poor lends to the *L*,
19:23 The fear of the *L* leads to life:
20:10 the *L* detests them both.
21: 2 but the *L* weighs the heart.
21: 3 to the *L* than sacrifice.
21:30 that can succeed against the *L*.
21:31 but victory rests with the *L*.
22: 2 The *L* is the Maker of them all.
22:23 for the *L* will take up their case
23:17 for the fear of the *L*.
24:18 or the *L* will see and disapprove
24:21 Fear the *L* and the king, my son,
25:22 and the *L* will reward you.
28:14 is the man who always fears the *L*,
29:26 from the *L* that man gets justice.
30: 7 "Two things I ask of you, O *L*;
31:30 a woman who fears the *L* is
Isa 2: 3 up to the mountain of the *L*,
2:10 the ground from dread of the *L*
3:17 the *L* will make their scalps bald."
4: 2 of the *L* will be beautiful
5:16 the *L* Almighty will be exalted
6: 3 holy, holy is the *L* Almighty;
9: 7 The zeal of the *L* Almighty
11: 2 The Spirit of the *L* will rest on him
11: 9 full of the knowledge of the *L*
12: 2 The *L*, the *L*, is my strength
18: 7 of the Name of the *L* Almighty.
24: 1 the *L* is going to lay waste the earth
25: 1 O *L*, you are my God;
25: 6 this mountain the *L* Almighty will
25: 8 The Sovereign *L* will wipe away
26: 4 Trust in the *L* forever,
26: 8 *L*, walking in the way of your laws,
26:13 O *L*, our God, other lords
26:21 the *L* is coming out of his dwelling
27: 1 the *L* will punish with his sword,
27:12 In that day the *L* will thresh
28: 5 In that day the *L* Almighty
29: 6 the *L* Almighty will come
29:15 to hide their plans from the *L*,
30:18 For the *L* is a God of justice.
30:26 when the *L* binds up the bruises
30:27 the Name of the *L* comes from afar
Isa 30:30 The *L* will cause men
33: 2 O *L*, be gracious to us;
33: 6 the fear of the *L* is the key
33:22 For the *L* is our judge,
34: 2 The *L* is angry with all nations;
35: 2 they will see the glory of the *L*,
35:10 the ransomed of the *L* will return.
38: 7 to you that the *L* will do what he
40: 3 the way for the *L*;
40: 5 the glory of the *L* will be revealed,
40: 7 the breath of the *L* blows on them.
40:10 the Sovereign *L* comes with power,
40:14 Whom did the *L* consult
40:28 The *L* is the everlasting God,
40:31 but those who hope in the *L*
41:14 will help you," declares the *L*,
41:20 that the hand of the *L* has done this
42: 6 the *L*, have called you
42: 8 "I am the *L*; that is my name!
42:13 The *L* will march out like a mighty
42:21 It pleased the *L*
43: 3 For I am the *L*, your God,
43:11 I, even I, am the *L*,
44: 6 "This is what the *L* says—
44:24 I am the *L*,
45: 5 I am the *L*, and there is no other;
45: 7 I, the *L*, do all these things.
45:21 Was it not I, the *L*?
48:17 "I am the *L* your God,
50: 4 Sovereign *L* has given me
50:10 Who among you fears the *L*
51: 1 and who seek the *L*:
51:11 The ransomed of the *L* will return.
51:15 the *L* Almighty is his name.
53: 1 the arm of the *L* been revealed?
53: 6 and the *L* has laid on him
53:10 and the will of the *L* will prosper
54: 5 the *L* Almighty is his name—
55: 6 Seek the *L* while he may be found;
55: 7 to the *L*, and he will have mercy
56: 6 who bind themselves to the *L*
58: 8 of the *L* will be your rear guard.
58:11 The *L* will guide you always;
59: 1 the arm of the *L* is not too short
60: 1 the glory of the *L* rises upon you.
60:16 Then you will know that I, the *L*,
60:20 the *L* will be your everlasting light,
61: 1 Spirit of the Sovereign *L* is on me,
61: 3 a planting of the *L*
61:10 I delight greatly in the *L*;
61:11 so the Sovereign *L* will make
62: 4 for the *L* will take delight in you,
63: 7 I will tell of the kindnesses of the *L*,
64: 8 Yet, O *L*, you are our Father.
66:15 See, the *L* is coming with fire,
Jer 1: 9 Then the *L* reached out his hand
2:19 when you forsake the *L* your God
3:25 sinned against the *L* our God,
4: 4 Circumcise yourselves to the *L*,
8: 7 the requirements of the *L*.
9:24 I am the *L*, who exercises kindness,
10: 6 No one is like you, O *L*;
10:10 But the *L* is the true God;
12: 1 You are always righteous, O *L*,
14: 7 O *L*, do something for the sake
14:20 O *L*, we acknowledge our
16:15 will say, 'As surely as the *L* lives,
16:19 O *L*, my strength and my fortress,
17: 7 is the man who trusts in the *L*,
17:10 "I the *L* search the heart
20:11 *L* is with me like a mighty warrior;
23: 6 The *L* Our Righteousness.
24: 7 heart to know me, that I am the *L*.
28: 9 as one truly sent by the *L* only
31:11 For the *L* will ransom Jacob
31:22 The *L* will create a new thing
31:34 his brother, saying, 'Know the *L*,'
32:27 I am the *L*, the God of all mankind.
33:16 The *L* Our Righteousness.'
36: 6 the words of the *L* that you wrote
40: 3 now the *L* has brought it about;
42: 3 Pray that the *L* your God will tell
42: 4 I will tell you everything the *L* says
42: 6 we will obey the *L* our God,
50: 4 go in tears to seek the *L* their God.
51:10 " 'The *L* has vindicated us;
51:56 For the *L* is a God of retribution;
La 3:24 to myself, "The *L* is my portion;
3:25 *L* is good to those whose hope is
3:40 and let us return to the *L*.
Eze 1: 3 the word of the *L* came
1:28 of the likeness of the glory of the *L*.
4:14 Sovereign *L*! I have never defiled
10: 4 Then the glory of the *L* rose
15: 7 you will know that I am the *L*.
30: 3 the day of the *L* is near—
36:23 nations will know that I am the *L*,
37: 4 'Dry bones, hear the word of the *L*!
43: 4 glory of the *L* entered the temple
44: 4 LORD filling the temple of the *L*,
Da 9: 2 to the word of the *L* given
Hos 1: 7 horsemen, but by the *L* their God."
2:20 and you will acknowledge the *L*.
3: 1 as the *L* loves the Israelites,
3: 5 They will come trembling to the *L*
6: 1 "Come, let us return to the *L*.
6: 3 Let us acknowledge the *L*;
10:12 for it is time to seek the *L*,
12: 5 the *L* is his name of renown!
14: 1 O Israel, to the *L* your God.
Joel 1: 1 The word of the *L* that came
1:15 For the day of the *L* is near;
2: 1 for the day of the *L* is coming.
2:11 The day of the *L* is great;
2:13 Return to the *L* your God,
2:23 rejoice in the *L* your God,
2:31 the great and dreadful day of the *L*.
2:32 on the name of the *L* will be saved;
3:14 For the day of the *L* is near
3:16 the *L* will be a refuge for his people,
Am 4:13 the *L* God Almighty is his name.
5: 6 Seek the *L* and live,
5:15 Perhaps the *L* God Almighty will
5:18 long for the day of the *L*?
7:15 *L* took me from tending the flock
8:12 searching for the word of the *L*,
9: 5 The Lord, the *L* Almighty,
Ob :15 "The day of the *L* is near
Jnh 1: 3 But Jonah ran away from the *L*
1: 4 the *L* sent a great wind on the sea,
1:17 But the *L* provided a great fish
2: 9 Salvation comes from the *L*."
4: 2 He prayed to the *L*, "O *L*,
4: 6 Then the *L* God provided a vine
Mic 1: 1 The word of the *L* that came to Micah
4: 2 up to the mountain of the *L*,
5: 4 flock in the strength of the *L*,
6: 2 For the *L* has a case
6: 8 And what does the *L* require of you
7: 7 as for me, I watch in hope for the *L*,
Na 1: 2 The *L* takes vengeance on his foes
1: 3 The *L* is slow to anger
Hab 2:14 knowledge of the glory of the *L*,
2:20 But the *L* is in his holy temple;
3: 2 I stand in awe of your deeds, O *L*.
Zep 1: 1 The word of the *L* that came
1: 7 for the day of the *L* is near.
3:17 The *L* your God is with you,
Hag 1: 1 the word of the *L* came
1: 8 and be honored," says the *L*.
2:23 that day,' declares the *L* Almighty,
Zec 1: 1 the word of the *L* came
1:17 and the *L* will again comfort Zion
3: 1 standing before the angel of the *L*,
4: 6 by my Spirit,' says the *L* Almighty.
6:12 and build the temple of the *L*.
8:21 the *L* and seek the *L* Almighty.
9:16 The *L* their God will save them
14: 5 Then the *L* my God will come,
14: 9 The *L* will be king
14:16 the *L* Almighty, and to celebrate
Mal 1: 1 The word of the *L* to Israel
3: 6 "I the *L* do not change.
4: 5 and dreadful day of the *L* comes.

LORD'S‡ (LORD‡)

Ex 4:14 the *L* anger burned against Moses
12:11 Eat it in haste; it is the *L* Passover.
34:34 he entered the *L* presence
Lev 23: 4 " 'These are the *L* appointed feasts,
Nu 9:23 At the *L* command they encamped
14:41 you disobeying the *L* command?
32:13 The *L* anger burned against Israel
Dt 6:18 is right and good in the *L* sight,
10:13 and to observe the *L* commands
32: 9 For the *L* portion is his people,
Jos 21:45 Not one of all the *L* good promises
1Sa 24:10 because he is the *L* anointed.'
1Ki 10: 9 Because of the *L* eternal love

Ps 24: 1 The earth is the *L*, and everything
32:10 but the *L* unfailing love
89: 1 of the *L* great love forever;
103: 17 *L* love is with those who fear him,
118: 15 "The *L* right hand has done mighty
Pr 3:11 do not despise the *L* discipline
19:21 but it is the *L* purpose that prevails.
Isa 24:14 west they acclaim the *L* majesty.
30: 9 to listen to the *L* instruction.
49: 4 Yet what is due me is in the *L* hand
53:10 Yet it was the *L* will to crush him
55:13 This will be for the *L* renown,
61: 2 to proclaim the year of the *L* favor
62: 3 of splendor in the *L* hand,
Jer 25:17 So I took the cup from the *L* hand
48:10 lax in doing the *L* work!
51: 7 was a gold cup in the *L* hand;
La 3:22 of the *L* great love we are not
Eze 7:19 them in the day of the *L* wrath.
Joel 3:18 will flow out of the *L* house
Ob :21 And the kingdom will be the *L*.
Mic 4: 1 of the *L* temple will be established
6: 2 O mountains, the *L* accusation;
Hab 2:16 from the *L* right hand is coming
Zep 2: 3 sheltered on the day of the *L* anger.

LOSE (LOSES LOSS LOST)
Dt 1:28 Our brothers have made us *l* heart.
1Sa 17:32 "Let no one *l* heart on account
Isa 7: 4 Do not *l* heart because of these two
Mt 10:39 Whoever finds his life will *l* it,
Lk 9:25 and yet *l* or forfeit his very self?
Jn 6:39 that I shall *l* none of all that he has
2Co 4: 1 this ministry, we do not *l* heart.
4:16 Therefore we do not *l* heart.
Heb 12: 3 will not grow weary and *l* heart.
12: 5 do not *l* heart when he rebukes you
2Jn : 8 that you do not *l* what you have

LOSES (LOSE)
Mt 5:13 But if the salt *l* its saltiness,
Lk 15: 4 you has a hundred sheep and *l* one
15: 8 has ten silver coins and *l* one.

LOSS (LOSE)
Ro 11:12 and their *l* means riches
1Co 3:15 he will suffer *l*; he himself will be
Php 3: 8 I consider everything a *l* compared

LOST (LOSE)
Ps 73: 2 I had nearly *l* my foothold.
Jer 50: 6 "My people have been *l* sheep;
Eze 34: 4 the strays or searched for the *l*.
34:16 for the *l* and bring back the strays.
Mt 18:14 any of these little ones should be *l*.
Lk 15: 4 go after the *l* sheep until he finds it?
15: 6 with me; I have found my *l* sheep.'
15: 9 with me; I have found my *l* coin.'
15:24 is alive again; he was *l* and is found
19:10 to seek and to save what was *l*."
Php 3: 8 for whose sake I have *l* all things.

LOT (LOTS)
Nephew of Abraham (Ge 11:27; 12:5). Chose to live in Sodom (Ge 13). Rescued from four kings (Ge 14). Rescued from Sodom (Ge 19:1–29; 2Pe 2:7). Fathered Moab and Ammon by his daughters (Ge 19:30–38).
Est 3: 7 the *l*) in the presence of Haman
9:24 the *l*) for their ruin and destruction.
Pr 16:33 The *l* is cast into the lap,
18:18 Casting the *l* settles disputes
Ecc 3:22 his work, because that is his *l*.
Ac 1:26 Then they cast lots, and the *l* fell

LOTS (LOT)
Jos 18:10 Joshua then cast *l* for them
Ps 22:18 and cast *l* for my clothing.
Joel 3: 3 They cast *l* for my people
Ob :11 and cast *l* for Jerusalem,
Mt 27:35 divided up his clothes by casting *l*.
Ac 1:26 Then they cast *l*, and the lot fell

LOVE* (BELOVED LOVED LOVELY LOVER LOVER'S LOVERS LOVES LOVING LOVING-KINDNESS)
Ge 20:13 'This is how you can show your *l*
22: 2 your only son, Isaac, whom you *l*,
29:18 Jacob was in *l* with Rachel and said
29:20 days to him because of his *l* for her.
29:32 Surely my husband will *l* me now."
Ex 15:13 "In your unfailing *l* you will lead
20: 6 showing *l* to a thousand generations
Ex 20: 6 of those who *l* me
21: 5 'I *l* my master and my wife
34: 6 abounding in *l* and faithfulness,
34: 7 maintaining *l* to thousands,
Lev 19:18 but *l* your neighbor as yourself.
19:34 *L* him as yourself,
Nu 14:18 abounding in *l* and forgiving sin
14:19 In accordance with your great *l*,
Dt 5:10 showing *l* to a thousand generations
5:10 of those who *l* me
6: 5 *L* the LORD your God
7: 9 generations of those who *l* him
7: 9 keeping his covenant of *l*
7:12 God will keep his covenant of *l*
7:13 He will *l* you and bless you
10:12 to walk in all his ways, to *l* him,
10:19 you are to *l* those who are aliens,
11: 1 *L* the LORD your God
11:13 to *l* the LORD your God
11:22 to *l* the LORD your God,
13: 3 you *l* him with all your heart
13: 6 wife you *l*, or your closest friend
19: 9 to *l* the LORD your God
21:15 the son of the wife he does not *l*,
21:16 the son of the wife he does not *l*.
30: 6 so that you may *l* him
30:16 today to *l* the LORD your God,
30:20 and that you may *l* the LORD your
33: 3 Surely it is you who *l* the people;
Jos 22: 5 to *l* the LORD your God, to walk
23:11 careful to *l* the LORD your God.
Jdg 5:31 may they who *l* you be like the sun
14:16 You hate me! You don't really *l* me
16: 4 he fell in *l* with a woman
16:15 "How can you say, 'I *l* you,'
1Sa 18:20 Saul's daughter Michal was in *l*
20:17 had David reaffirm his oath out of *l*
2Sa 1:26 Your *l* for me was wonderful,
7:15 But my *l* will never be taken away
13: 1 son of David fell in *l* with Tamar,
13: 4 said to him, "I'm in *l* with Tamar,
16:17 "Is this the *l* you show your friend?
19: 6 You *l* those who hate you
19: 6 hate you and hate those who *l* you.
1Ki 3: 3 Solomon showed his *l*
8:23 you who keep your covenant of *l*
10: 9 of the LORD's eternal *l* for Israel,
11: 2 Solomon held fast to them in *l*.
1Ch 16:34 his *l* endures forever.
16:41 "for his *l* endures forever."
17:13 I will never take my *l* away
2Ch 5:13 his *l* endures forever."
6:14 you who keep your covenant of *l*
6:42 Remember the great *l* promised
7: 3 his *l* endures forever."
7: 6 saying, "His *l* endures forever."
9: 8 Because of the *l* of your God
19: 2 and *l* those who hate the LORD?
20:21 for his *l* endures forever."
Ezr 3:11 his *l* to Israel endures forever."
Ne 1: 5 covenant of *l* with those who *l* him
9:17 slow to anger and abounding in *l*.
9:32 who keeps his covenant of *l*,
13:22 to me according to your great *l*.
Job 15:34 of those who *l* bribes.
19:19 those I *l* have turned against me.
37:13 or to water his earth and show his *l*.
Ps 4: 2 How long will you *l* delusions
5:11 that those who *l* your name may
6: 4 save me because of your unfailing *l*.
11: 5 wicked and those who *l* violence
13: 5 But I trust in your unfailing *l*;
17: 7 Show the wonder of your great *l*,
18: 1 I *l* you, O LORD, my strength.
21: 7 through the unfailing *l*
23: 6 Surely goodness and *l* will follow
25: 6 O LORD, your great mercy and *l*,
25: 7 according to your *l* remember me,
26: 3 for your *l* is ever before me,
26: 8 I *l* the house where you live,
31: 7 I will be glad and rejoice in your *l*,
31:16 save me in your unfailing *l*.
31:21 for he showed his wonderful *l*
31:23 *L* the LORD, all his saints!
32:10 but the LORD's unfailing *l*
33: 5 the earth is full of his unfailing *l*.
33:18 whose hope is in his unfailing *l*,
33:22 May your unfailing *l* rest upon us,
36: 5 Your *l*, O LORD, reaches
36: 7 How priceless is your unfailing *l*!
Ps 36:10 Continue your *l* to those who know
40:10 I do not conceal your *l*
40:11 may your *l* and your truth always
40:16 may those who *l* your salvation
42: 8 By day the LORD directs his *l*,
44:26 of your unfailing *l*.
45: 7 You *l* righteousness and hate
48: 9 we meditate on your unfailing *l*.
51: 1 according to your unfailing *l*;
52: 3 You *l* evil rather than good,
52: 4 You *l* every harmful word,
52: 8 I trust in God's unfailing *l*
57: 3 God sends his *l* and his faithfulness
57:10 For great is your *l*, reaching
59:16 in the morning I will sing of your *l*;
60: 5 that those you *l* may be delivered.
61: 7 appoint your *l* and faithfulness
63: 3 Because your *l* is better than life,
66:20 or withheld his *l* from me!
69:13 in your great *l*, O God,
69:16 out of the goodness of your *l*;
69:36 and those who *l* his name will dwell
70: 4 may those who *l* your salvation
77: 8 Has his unfailing *l* vanished forever
85: 7 Show us your unfailing *l*, O LORD
85:10 *L* and faithfulness meet together;
86: 5 abounding in *l* to all who call
86:13 For great is your *l* toward me;
86:15 abounding in *l* and faithfulness.
88:11 Is your *l* declared in the grave,
89: 1 of the LORD's great *l* forever;
89: 2 declare that your *l* stands firm
89:14 *l* and faithfulness go before you.
89:24 My faithful *l* will be with him,
89:28 I will maintain my *l* to him forever,
89:33 but I will not take my *l* from him,
89:49 where is your former great *l*,
90:14 with your unfailing *l*,
92: 2 to proclaim your *l* in the morning
94:18 your *l*, O LORD, supported me.
97:10 Let those who *l* the LORD hate
98: 3 He has remembered his *l*
100: 5 is good and his *l* endures forever;
101: 1 I will sing of your *l* and justice;
103: 4 crowns you with *l* and compassion.
103: 8 slow to anger, abounding in *l*.
103: 11 so great is his *l* for those who fear
103: 17 LORD's *l* is with those who fear
106: 1 his *l* endures forever.
106: 45 and out of his great *l* he relented.
107: 1 his *l* endures forever.
107: 8 to the LORD for his unfailing *l*
107: 15 to the LORD for his unfailing *l*
107: 21 to the LORD for his unfailing *l*
107: 31 to the LORD for his unfailing *l*
107: 43 consider the great *l* of the LORD.
108: 4 For great is your *l*, higher
108: 6 that those you *l* may be delivered.
109: 21 out of the goodness of your *l*,
109: 26 save me in accordance with your *l*.
115: 1 because of your *l* and faithfulness.
116: 1 I *l* the LORD, for he heard my
117: 2 For great is his *l* toward us,
118: 1 his *l* endures forever.
118: 2 "His *l* endures forever."
118: 3 "His *l* endures forever."
118: 4 "His *l* endures forever."
118: 29 his *l* endures forever.
119: 41 May your unfailing *l* come to me,
119: 47 because I *l* them.
119: 48 to your commands, which I *l*,
119: 64 The earth is filled with your *l*,
119: 76 May your unfailing *l* be my
119: 88 my life according to your *l*,
119: 97 Oh, how I *l* your law!
119:113 but I *l* your law.
119:119 therefore I *l* your statutes.
119:124 your servant according to your *l*
119:127 Because I *l* your commands
119:132 to those who *l* your name.
119:149 in accordance with your *l*;
119:159 O LORD, according to your *l*.
119:159 See how I *l* your precepts;
119:163 but I *l* your law.
119:165 peace have they who *l* your law,
119:167 for I *l* them greatly.
122: 6 "May those who *l* you be secure.
130: 7 for with the LORD is unfailing *l*
136: 1-26 *His l endures forever.*
138: 2 for your *l* and your faithfulness,

Ps 138: 8 your *l,* O LORD, endures forever
143: 8 of your unfailing *l,*
143: 12 In your unfailing *l,* silence my
145: 8 slow to anger and rich in *l.*
145: 20 over all who *l* him,
147: 11 who put their hope in his unfailing *l*
Pr 1:22 you simple ones *l* your simple
3: 3 Let *l* and faithfulness never leave
4: 6 *l* her, and she will watch over you.
5:19 you ever be captivated by her *l.*
7:18 let's drink deep of *l* till morning;
7:18 let's enjoy ourselves with *l!*
8:17 I *l* those who *l* me,
8:21 wealth on those who *l* me
8:36 all who hate me *l* death."
9: 8 rebuke a wise man and he will *l* you
10:12 but *l* covers over all wrongs.
14:22 those who plan what is good find *l*
15:17 of vegetables where there is *l*
16: 6 Through *l* and faithfulness sin is
17: 9 over an offense promotes *l,*
18:21 and those who *l* it will eat its fruit.
19:22 What a man desires is unfailing *l;*
20: 6 claims to have unfailing *l,*
20:13 Do not *l* sleep or you will grow
20:28 *L* and faithfulness keep a king safe;
20:28 through *l* his throne is made secure
21:21 who pursues righteousness and *l*
27: 5 rebuke than hidden *l.*
Ecc 3: 8 a time to *l* and a time to hate,
9: 1 but no man knows whether *l*
9: 6 Their *l,* their hate
9: 9 life with your wife, whom you *l,*
SS 1: 2 for your *l* is more delightful
1: 3 No wonder the maidens *l* you!
1: 4 we will praise your *l* more
1: 7 you whom I *l,* where you graze
2: 4 and his banner over me is *l.*
2: 5 for I am faint with *l.*
2: 7 Do not arouse or awaken *l*
3: 5 Do not arouse or awaken *l*
4:10 How delightful is your *l,* my sister,
4:10 How much more pleasing is your *l*
5: 8 Tell him I am faint with *l.*
7: 6 O *l,* with your delights!
7:12 there I will give you my *l.*
8: 4 Do not arouse or awaken *l*
8: 6 for *l* is as strong as death,
8: 7 Many waters cannot quench *l;*
8: 7 all the wealth of his house for *l,*
Isa 1:23 they all *l* bribes
5: 1 I will sing for the one I *l*
16: 5 In *l* a throne will be established;
38:17 In your *l* you kept me
43: 4 and because I *l* you,
54:10 yet my unfailing *l* for you will not
55: 3 my faithful *l* promised to David.
56: 6 to *l* the name of the LORD,
56:10 they *l* to sleep.
57: 8 a pact with those whose beds you *l,*
61: 8 "For I, the LORD, *l* justice;
63: 9 In his *l* and mercy he redeemed
66:10 all you who *l* her;
Jer 2:25 I *l* foreign gods,
2:33 How skilled you are at pursuing *l!*
5:31 and my people *l* it this way.
12: 7 I will give the one I *l*
14:10 "They greatly *l* to wander;
16: 5 my *l* and my pity from this people
31: 3 you with an everlasting *l;*
32:18 You show *l* to thousands
33:11 his *l* endures forever."
La 3:22 of the LORD's great *l* we are not
3:32 so great is his unfailing *l.*
Eze 16: 8 saw that you were old enough for *l,*
23:17 of *l,* and in their lust they defiled
33:32 more than one who sings *l* songs
Da 9: 4 covenant of *l* with all who *l* him
Hos 1: 6 for I will no longer show *l*
1: 7 Yet I will show *l* to the house
2: 4 I will not show my *l* to her children
2:19 in *l* and compassion.
2:23 I will show my *l* to the one I called
3: 1 Go, show your *l* to your wife again,
3: 1 and *l* the sacred raisin cakes."
3: 1 *L* her as the LORD loves
4: 1 "There is no faithfulness, no *l,*
4:18 their rulers dearly *l* shameful ways.
6: 4 Your *l* is like the morning mist,
9: 1 you *l* the wages of a prostitute
Hos 9:15 I will no longer *l* them;
10:12 reap the fruit of unfailing *l,*
11: 4 with ties of *l;*
12: 6 maintain *l* and justice,
14: 4 and *l* them freely,
Joel 2:13 slow to anger and abounding in *l,*
Am 4: 5 for this is what you *l* to do,"
5:15 Hate evil, *l* good;
Jnh 4: 2 slow to anger and abounding in *l,*
Mic 3: 2 you who hate good and *l* evil;
6: 8 To act justly and to *l* mercy
Zep 3:17 he will quiet you with his *l,*
Zec 8:17 and do not *l* to swear falsely.
8:19 Therefore *l* truth and peace."
Mt 3:17 "This is my Son, whom I *l;*
5:43 '*L* your neighbor and hate your
5:44 *L* your enemies and pray
5:46 you *l* those who *l* you, what reward
6: 5 for they *l* to pray standing
6:24 he will hate the one and *l* the other,
12:18 the one I *l,* in whom I delight;
17: 5 "This is my Son, whom I *l;*
19:19 and '*l* your neighbor as yourself.' "
22:37 " '*L* the Lord your God
22:39 '*L* your neighbor as yourself.'
23: 6 they *l* the place of honor
23: 7 they *l* to be greeted
24:12 the *l* of most will grow cold,
Mk 1:11 "You are my Son, whom I *l;*
9: 7 "This is my Son, whom I *l.*
12:30 *L* the Lord your God
12:31 '*L* your neighbor as yourself.'
12:33 To *l* him with all your heart,
12:33 and to *l* your neighbor
Lk 3:22 "You are my Son, whom I *l;*
6:27 you who hear me: *L* your enemies,
6:32 Even 'sinners' *l* those who *l* them.
6:32 you *l* those who *l* you, what credit
6:35 *l* your enemies, do good to them,
7:42 which of them will *l* him more?"
10:27 and, '*L* your neighbor as yourself
10:27 " '*L* the Lord your God
11:42 you neglect justice and the *l* of God
11:43 you *l* the most important seats
16:13 he will hate the one and *l* the other,
20:13 whom I *l;* perhaps they will respect
20:46 *l* to be greeted in the marketplaces
Jn 5:42 I know that you do not have the *l*
8:42 were your Father, you would *l* me,
11: 3 "Lord, the one you *l* is sick."
13: 1 them the full extent of his *l.*
13:34 I give you: *L* one another.
13:34 so you must *l* one another.
13:35 disciples, if you *l* one another."
14:15 "If you *l* me, you will obey what I
14:21 I too will *l* him and show myself
14:23 My Father will *l* him, and we will
14:24 He who does not *l* me will not obey
14:31 world must learn that I *l* the Father
15: 9 Now remain in my *l.*
15:10 commands and remain in his *l.*
15:10 you will remain in my *l,*
15:12 *L* each other as I have loved you.
15:13 Greater *l* has no one than this,
15:17 This is my command: *L* each other.
15:19 to the world, it would *l* you
17:26 known in order that the *l* you have
21:15 do you truly *l* me more than these
21:15 he said, "you know that I *l* you."
21:16 Yes, Lord, you know that I *l* you."
21:16 do you truly *l* me?" He answered,
21:17 all things; you know that I *l* you."
21:17 "Do you *l* me?" He said, "Lord,
21:17 "Simon son of John, do you *l* me?"
Ro 5: 5 because God has poured out his *l*
5: 8 God demonstrates his own *l* for us
8:28 for the good of those who *l* him,
8:35 us from the *l* of Christ?
8:39 us from the *l* of God that is
12: 9 *L* must be sincere.
12:10 to one another in brotherly *l.*
13: 8 continuing debt to *l* one another,
13: 9 "*L* your neighbor as yourself."
13:10 Therefore *l* is the fulfillment
13:10 *L* does no harm to its neighbor.
14:15 you are no longer acting in *l.*
15:30 and by the *l* of the Spirit,
16: 8 Greet Ampliatus, whom I *l*
1Co 2: 9 prepared for those who *l* him"—
4:17 my son whom I *l,* who is faithful
1Co 4:21 or in *l* and with a gentle spirit?
8: 1 Knowledge puffs up, but *l* builds up
13: 1 have not *l,* I am only a resounding
13: 2 but have not *l,* I am nothing.
13: 3 but have not *l,* I gain nothing.
13: 4 Love is patient, *l* is kind.
13: 4 *L* is patient, love is kind.
13: 6 *L* does not delight in evil
13: 8 *L* never fails.
13:13 But the greatest of these is *l.*
13:13 three remain: faith, hope and *l.*
14: 1 way of *l* and eagerly desire spiritual
16:14 Do everything in *l.*
16:22 If anyone does not *l* the Lord—
16:24 My *l* to all of you in Christ Jesus.
2Co 2: 4 to let you know the depth of my *l*
2: 8 therefore, to reaffirm your *l* for him
5:14 For Christ's *l* compels us,
6: 6 in the Holy Spirit and in sincere *l;*
8: 7 complete earnestness and in your *l*
8: 8 sincerity of your *l* by comparing it
8:24 show these men the proof of your *l*
11:11 Why? Because I do not *l* you?
12:15 If I *l* you more, will you *l* me less?
13:11 And the God of *l* and peace will be
13:14 of the Lord Jesus Christ, and the *l*
Gal 5: 6 is faith expressing itself through *l.*
5:13 rather, serve one another in *l.*
5:14 "*L* your neighbor as yourself."
5:22 But the fruit of the Spirit is *l,* joy,
Eph 1: 4 In *l* he predestined us
1:15 and your *l* for all the saints,
2: 4 But because of his great *l* for us,
3:17 being rooted and established in *l,*
3:18 and high and deep is the *l* of Christ,
3:19 and to know this *l* that surpasses
4: 2 bearing with one another in *l.*
4:15 Instead, speaking the truth in *l,*
4:16 grows and builds itself up in *l,*
5: 2 loved children and live a life of *l,*
5:25 *l* your wives, just as Christ loved
5:28 husbands ought to *l* their wives
5:33 each one of you also must *l* his wife
6:23 *l* with faith from God the Father
6:24 Christ with an undying *l.*
6:24 to all who *l* our Lord Jesus Christ
Php 1: 9 that your *l* may abound more
1:16 so in *l,* knowing that I am put here
2: 1 from his *l,* if any fellowship
2: 2 having the same *l,* being one
4: 1 you whom I *l* and long for,
Col 1: 4 of the *l* you have for all the saints—
1: 5 *l* that spring from the hope that is
1: 8 also told us of your *l* in the Spirit.
2: 2 in heart and united in *l,*
3:14 And over all these virtues put on *l,*
3:19 *l* your wives and do not be harsh
1Th 1: 3 your labor prompted by *l,*
3: 6 good news about your faith and *l.*
3:12 May the Lord make your *l* increase
4: 9 about brotherly *l* we do not need
4: 9 taught by God to *l* each other.
4:10 you do *l* all the brothers
5: 8 on faith and *l* as a breastplate,
5:13 them in the highest regard in *l*
2Th 1: 3 and the *l* every one of you has
2:10 because they refused to *l* the truth
3: 5 direct your hearts into God's *l*
1Ti 1: 5 The goal of this command is *l,*
1:14 and *l* that are in Christ Jesus.
2:15 *l* and holiness with propriety.
4:12 in life, in *l,* in faith and in purity.
6:10 For the *l* of money is a root
6:11 faith, *l,* endurance and gentleness.
2Ti 1: 7 of power, of *l* and of self-discipline.
1:13 with faith and *l* in Christ Jesus.
2:22 and pursue righteousness, faith, *l*
3: 3 unholy, without *l,* unforgiving,
3:10 faith, patience, *l,* endurance,
Tit 2: 2 in faith, in *l* and in endurance.
2: 4 women to *l* their husbands
3: 4 and *l* of God our Savior appeared,
3:15 Greet those who *l* us in the faith.
Phm : 5 and your *l* for all the saints.
: 7 Your *l* has given me great joy
: 9 yet I appeal to you on the basis of *l.*
Heb 6:10 and the *l* you have shown him
10:24 may spur one another on toward *l*
13: 5 free from the *l* of money
Jas 1:12 promised to those who *l* him.

Jas 2: 5 he promised those who *l* him?
2: 8 "*L* your neighbor as yourself,"
1Pe 1: 8 you have not seen him, you *l* him;
1:22 the truth so that you have sincere *l*
1:22 *l* one another deeply,
2:17 *L* the brotherhood of believers,
3: 8 be sympathetic, *l* as brothers,
3:10 "Whoever would *l* life
4: 8 Above all, *l* each other deeply,
4: 8 *l* covers over a multitude of sins.
5:14 Greet one another with a kiss of *l.*
2Pe 1: 7 and to brotherly kindness, *l.*
1:17 "This is my Son, whom I *l;*
1Jn 2: 5 God's *l* is truly made complete
2:15 Do not *l* the world or anything
2:15 the *l* of the Father is not in him.
3: 1 How great is the *l* the Father has
3:10 anyone who does not *l* his brother.
3:11 We should *l* one another.
3:14 Anyone who does not *l* remains
3:14 because we *l* our brothers.
3:16 This is how we know what *l* is:
3:17 how can the *l* of God be in him?
3:18 let us not *l* with words or tongue
3:23 to *l* one another as he commanded
4: 7 Dear friends, let us *l* one another,
4: 7 for *l* comes from God.
4: 8 Whoever does not *l* does not know
4: 8 not know God, because God is *l.*
4: 9 This is how God showed his *l*
4:10 This is *l:* not that we loved God,
4:11 we also ought to *l* one another.
4:12 seen God; but if we *l* one another,
4:12 and his *l* is made complete in us.
4:16 God is *l.*
4:16 Whoever lives in *l* lives in God,
4:16 and rely on the *l* God has for us.
4:17 *l* is made complete among us
4:18 But perfect *l* drives out fear,
4:18 There is no fear in *l.*
4:18 who fears is not made perfect in *l.*
4:19 We *l* because he first loved us.
4:20 If anyone says, "I *l* God,"
4:20 anyone who does not *l* his brother,
4:20 whom he has seen, cannot *l* God,
4:21 loves God must also *l* his brother.
5: 2 we know that we *l* the children
5: 3 This is *l* for God: to obey his
2Jn : 1 whom I *l* in the truth—
: 3 will be with us in truth and *l.*
: 5 I ask that we *l* one another.
: 6 his command is that you walk in *l.*
: 6 this is *l:* that we walk in obedience
3Jn : 1 To my dear friend Gaius, whom I *l*
: 6 have told the church about your *l.*
Jude : 2 peace and *l* be yours in abundance.
:12 men are blemishes at your *l* feasts,
:21 Keep yourselves in God's *l*
Rev 2: 4 You have forsaken your first *l.*
2:19 I know your deeds, your *l* and faith
3:19 Those whom I *l* I rebuke
12:11 they did not *l* their lives so much

LOVED* (LOVE)
Ge 24:67 she became his wife, and he *l* her;
25:28 *l* Esau, but Rebekah *l* Jacob.
29:30 and he *l* Rachel more than Leah.
29:31 the LORD saw that Leah was not *l,*
29:33 the LORD heard that I am not *l,*
34: 3 and he *l* the girl and spoke tenderly
37: 3 Now Israel *l* Joseph more than any
37: 4 saw that their father *l* him more
Dt 4:37 Because he *l* your forefathers
7: 8 But it was because the LORD *l* you
10:15 on your forefathers and *l* them,
1Sa 1: 5 a double portion because he *l* her,
18: 1 in spirit with David, and he *l* him
18: 3 with David because he *l* him
18:16 But all Israel and Judah *l* David,
18:28 that his daughter Michal *l* David,
20:17 because he *l* him as he *l* himself.
2Sa 1:23 in life they were *l* and gracious,
12:24 The LORD *l* him; and
12:25 and because the LORD *l* him,
13:15 hated her more than he had *l* her.
1Ki 11: 1 *l* many foreign women
2Ch 11:21 Rehoboam *l* Maacah daughter
26:10 in the fertile lands, for he *l* the soil.
Ne 13:26 He was *l* by his God, and God
Ps 44: 3 light of your face, for you *l* them.
Ps 47: 4 the pride of Jacob, whom he *l.*
78:68 Mount Zion, which he *l.*
88:18 taken my companions and *l* ones
109: 17 He *l* to pronounce a curse—
Isa 5: 1 My *l* one had a vineyard
Jer 2: 2 how as a bride you *l* me
8: 2 which they have *l* and served
31: 3 "I have *l* you with an everlasting
Eze 16:37 those you *l* as well as those you
Hos 2: 1 and of your sisters, 'My *l* one.'
2:23 to the one I called 'Not my *l* one.'
3: 1 though she is *l* by another
9:10 became as vile as the thing they *l.*
11: 1 "When Israel was a child, I *l* him,
Mal 1: 2 "But you ask, 'How have you *l* us?'
1: 2 "I have *l* you," says the LORD.
1: 2 "Yet I have *l* Jacob, but Esau I
Mk 10:21 Jesus looked at him and *l* him.
12: 6 left to send, a son, whom he *l.*
Lk 7:47 been forgiven—for she *l* much.
16:14 The Pharisees, who *l* money,
Jn 3:16 so *l* the world that he gave his one
3:19 but men *l* darkness instead of light
11: 5 Jesus *l* Martha and her sister
11:36 "See how he *l* him!" But some
12:43 for they *l* praise from men more
13: 1 Having *l* his own who were
13:23 the disciple whom Jesus *l,*
13:34 As I have *l* you, so you must love
14:21 He who loves me will be *l*
14:28 If you *l* me, you would be glad that
15: 9 the Father has *l* me, so have I *l* you.
15:12 Love each other as I have *l* you.
16:27 loves you because you have *l* me
17:23 have *l* them even as you have *l* me.
17:24 you *l* me before the creation
19:26 the disciple whom he *l* standing
20: 2 one Jesus *l,* and said, "They have
21: 7 the disciple whom Jesus *l* said
21:20 whom Jesus *l* was following
Ro 1: 7 To all in Rome who are *l* by God
8:37 conquerors through him who *l* us.
9:13 "Jacob I *l,* but Esau I hated."
9:25 her 'my *l* one' who is not my *l* one,"
11:28 they are *l* on account
Gal 2:20 who *l* me and gave himself for me.
Eph 5: 1 as dearly *l* children and live a life
5: 2 as Christ *l* us and gave himself up
5:25 just as Christ *l* the church
Col 3:12 and dearly *l,* clothe yourselves
1Th 1: 4 For we know, brothers *l* by God,
2: 8 We *l* you so much that we were
2Th 2:13 for you, brothers *l* by the Lord,
2:16 who *l* us and by his grace gave us
2Ti 4:10 for Demas, because he *l* this world,
Heb 1: 9 You have *l* righteousness
2Pe 2:15 who *l* the wages of wickedness.
1Jn 4:10 This is love: not that we *l* God,
4:10 but that he *l* us and sent his Son
4:11 Dear friends, since God so *l* us,
4:19 We love because he first *l* us.
Jude : 1 who are *l* by God the Father
Rev 3: 9 and acknowledge that I have *l* you.

LOVELY* (LOVE)
Ge 29:17 but Rachel was *l* in form,
Est 1:11 and nobles, for she was *l* to look at.
2: 7 was *l* in form and features,
Ps 84: 1 How *l* is your dwelling place,
SS 1: 5 Dark am I, yet *l,*
2:14 and your face is *l.*
4: 3 your mouth is *l.*
5:16 he is altogether *l.*
6: 4 *l* as Jerusalem,
Am 8:13 *l* young women and strong young
Php 4: 8 whatever is *l,* whatever is

LOVER* (LOVE)
SS 1:13 My *l* is to me a sachet of myrrh
1:14 My *l* is to me a cluster
1:16 How handsome you are, my *l!*
2: 3 is my *l* among the young men.
2: 8 Listen! My *l!*
2: 9 My *l* is like a gazelle or a young
2:10 My *l* spoke and said to me,
2:16 *Beloved* My *l* is mine and I am his;
2:17 turn, my *l,*
4:16 Let my *l* come into his garden
5: 2 Listen! My *l* is knocking:
5: 4 My *l* thrust his hand
5: 5 I arose to open for my *l,*
SS 5: 6 I opened for my *l,*
5: 6 but my *l* had left; he was gone.
5: 8 if you find my *l,*
5:10 *Beloved* My *l* is radiant and ruddy,
5:16 This is my *l,* this my friend,
6: 1 Where has your *l* gone,
6: 1 Which way did your *l* turn,
6: 2 *Beloved* My *l* has gone
6: 3 I am my lover's and my *l* is mine;
7: 9 May the wine go straight to my *l,*
7:10 I belong to my *l,*
7:11 my *l,* let us go to the countryside,
7:13 that I have stored up for you, my *l.*
8: 5 leaning on her *l?*
8:14 *Beloved* Come away, my *l,*
1Ti 3: 3 not quarrelsome, not a *l* of money.

LOVER'S* (LOVE)
SS 6: 3 I am my *l* and my lover is mine;

LOVERS* (LOVE)
SS 5: 1 drink your fill, O *l.*
Jer 3: 1 as a prostitute with many *l*—
3: 2 the roadside you sat waiting for *l,*
4:30 Your *l* despise you;
La 1: 2 Among all her *l*
Eze 16:33 but you give gifts to all your *l,*
16:36 in your promiscuity with your *l,*
16:37 I am going to gather all your *l,*
16:39 Then I will hand you over to your *l,*
16:41 and you will no longer pay your *l.*
23: 5 she lusted after her *l,* the Assyrians
23: 9 I handed her over to her *l,*
23:20 There she lusted after her *l,*
23:22 I will stir up your *l* against you,
Hos 2: 5 She said, 'I will go after my *l,*
2: 7 She will chase after her *l*
2:10 lewdness before the eyes of her *l;*
2:12 she said were her pay from her *l;*
2:13 and went after her *l,*
8: 9 Ephraim has sold herself to *l.*
2Ti 3: 2 People will be *l* of themselves,
3: 2 *l* of money, boastful, proud,
3: 3 without self-control, brutal, not *l*
3: 4 *l* of pleasure rather than *l* of God—

LOVES* (LOVE)
Ge 44:20 sons left, and his father *l* him.'
Dt 10:18 and *l* the alien, giving him food
15:16 because he *l* you and your family
21:15 and he *l* one but not the other,
21:16 son of the wife he *l* in preference
23: 5 because the LORD your God *l* you
28:54 wife he *l* or his surviving children,
28:56 will begrudge the husband she *l*
33:12 and the one the LORD *l* rests
Ru 4:15 who *l* you and who is better to you
2Ch 2:11 "Because the LORD *l* his people,
Ps 11: 7 he *l* justice;
33: 5 The LORD *l* righteousness
34:12 Whoever of you *l* life
37:28 For the LORD *l* the just
87: 2 the LORD *l* the gates of Zion
91:14 Because he *l* me," says the LORD,
99: 4 The King is mighty, he *l* justice—
119:140 and your servant *l* them.
127: 2 for he grants sleep to those he *l.*
146: 8 the LORD *l* the righteous.
Pr 3:12 the LORD disciplines those he *l,*
12: 1 Whoever *l* discipline *l* knowledge,
13:24 he who *l* him is careful
15: 9 he *l* those who pursue
17:17 A friend *l* at all times,
17:19 He who *l* a quarrel *l* sin;
19: 8 He who gets wisdom *l* his own soul
21:17 He who *l* pleasure will become
21:17 whoever *l* wine and oil will never
22:11 He who *l* a pure heart and whose
29: 3 A man who *l* wisdom brings joy
Ecc 5:10 Whoever *l* money never has
5:10 whoever *l* wealth is never satisfied
SS 3: 1 I looked for the one my heart *l;*
3: 2 I will search for the one my heart *l.*
3: 3 "Have you seen the one my heart *l*
3: 4 when I found the one my heart *l.*
Hos 3: 1 as the LORD *l* the Israelites,
10:11 that *l* to thresh;
12: 7 he *l* to defraud.
Mal 2:11 the sanctuary the LORD *l,*
Mt 10:37 anyone who *l* his son or daughter
10:37 "Anyone who *l* his father

Lk 7: 5 because he *l* our nation
7:47 has been forgiven little *l* little."
Jn 3:35 Father *l* the Son and has placed
5:20 For the Father *l* the Son
10:17 reason my Father *l* me is that I lay
12:25 The man who *l* his life will lose it,
14:21 He who *l* me will be loved
14:21 obeys them, he is the one who *l* me.
14:23 Jesus replied, "If anyone *l* me,
16:27 the Father himself *l* you
Ro 13: 8 for he who *l* his fellowman has
1Co 8: 3 But the man who *l* God is known
2Co 9: 7 for God *l* a cheerful giver.
Eph 1: 6 has freely given us in the One he *l*.
5:28 He who *l* his wife *l* himself.
5:33 must love his wife as he *l* himself,
Col 1:13 us into the kingdom of the Son he *l*,
Tit 1: 8 one who *l* what is good, who is
Heb 12: 6 the Lord disciplines those he *l*,
1Jn 2:10 Whoever *l* his brother lives
2:15 If anyone *l* the world, the love
4: 7 Everyone who *l* has been born
4:21 Whoever *l* God must also love his
5: 1 who *l* the father *l* his child
3Jn : 9 but Diotrephes, who *l* to be first,
Rev 1: 5 To him who *l* us and has freed us
20: 9 camp of God's people, the city he *l*.
22:15 and everyone who *l* and practices

LOVING* (LOVE)
Ps 25:10 All the ways of the LORD are *l*
59:10 my *l* God.
59:17 O God, are my fortress, my *l* God.
62:12 and that you, O Lord, are *l*.
144: 2 He is my *l* God and my fortress,
145: 13 and *l* toward all he has made.
145: 17 and *l* toward all he has made.
Pr 5:19 A *l* doe, a graceful deer—
Heb 13: 1 Keep on *l* each other as brothers.
1Jn 5: 2 by *l* God and carrying out his

LOVING-KINDNESS* (LOVE)
Jer 31: 3 I have drawn you with *l*.

LOWER
Ps 8: 5 You made him a little *l*
2Co 11: 7 a sin for me to *l* myself in order
Heb 2: 7 You made him a little *l*

LOWING
1Sa 15:14 What is this *l* of cattle that I hear?"

LOWLY
Job 5:11 The *l* he sets on high,
Ps 138: 6 on high, he looks upon the *l*,
Pr 29:23 but a man of *l* spirit gains honor.
Isa 57:15 also with him who is contrite and *l*
Eze 21:26 *l* will be exalted and the exalted
1Co 1:28 He chose the *l* things of this world

LOYAL
1Ch 29:18 and keep their hearts *l* to you.
Ps 78: 8 whose hearts were not *l* to God,

LUKE*
Co-worker with Paul (Col 4:14; 2Ti 4:11; Phm 24).

LUKEWARM*
Rev 3:16 So, because you are *l*—neither hot

LUST (LUSTED LUSTS)
Pr 6:25 Do not *l* in your heart
Eze 20:30 and *l* after their vile images?
Col 3: 5 sexual immorality, impurity, *l*,
1Th 4: 5 not in passionate *l* like the heathen,
1Pe 4: 3 in debauchery, *l*, drunkenness,
1Jn 2:16 the *l* of his eyes and the boasting

LUSTED (LUST)
Eze 23: 5 she *l* after her lovers, the Assyrians

LUSTS* (LUST)
Nu 15:39 yourselves by going after the *l*
Ro 1:26 God gave them over to shameful *l*.

LUXURY
Jas 5: 5 You have lived on earth in *l*

LYDIA'S*
Ac 16:40 went to *L* house, where they met

LYING (LIE)
Pr 6:17 a *l* tongue,
12:22 The LORD detests *l* lips,
21: 6 A fortune made by a *l* tongue
26:28 A *l* tongue hates those it hurts,

MACEDONIA
Ac 16: 9 "Come over to *M* and help us."

MAD
Dt 28:34 The sights you see will drive you *m*

MADE (MAKE)
Ge 1: 7 So God *m* the expanse
1:16 God *m* two great lights—
1:16 He also *m* the stars.
1:25 God *m* the wild animals according
1:31 God saw all that he had *m*,
2:22 Then the LORD God *m* a woman
6: 6 was grieved that he had *m* man
9: 6 has God *m* man.
15:18 that day the LORD *m* a covenant
Ex 20:11 six days the LORD *m* the heavens
20:11 the Sabbath day and *m* it holy.
24: 8 the covenant that the LORD has *m*
32: 4 *m* it into an idol cast in the shape
Lev 16:34 Atonement is to be *m* once a year
Dt 32: 6 who *m* you and formed you?
Jos 24:25 On that day Joshua *m* a covenant
2Ki 19:15 You have *m* heaven and earth.
2Ch 2:12 the God of Israel, who *m* heaven
Ne 9: 6 You *m* the heavens,
9:10 You *m* a name for yourself,
Ps 33: 6 of the LORD were the heavens *m*,
95: 5 The sea is his, for he *m* it,
96: 5 but the LORD *m* the heavens.
100: 3 It is he who *m* us, and we are his;
118: 24 This is the day the LORD has *m*;
136: 7 who *m* the great lights—
139: 14 I am fearfully and wonderfully *m*;
Ecc 3:11 He has *m* everything beautiful
Isa 43: 7 whom I formed and *m*."
45:12 It is I who *m* the earth
45:18 he who fashioned and *m* the earth,
66: 2 Has not my hand *m* all these things
Jer 10:12 But God *m* the earth by his power;
27: 5 and outstretched arm I *m* the earth
32:17 you have *m* the heavens
33: 2 LORD says, he who *m* the earth,
51:15 "He *m* the earth by his power;
Eze 3:17 I have *m* you a watchman
33: 7 I have *m* you a watchman
Am 5: 8 (he who *m* the Pleiades and Orion,
Jnh 1: 9 who *m* the sea and the land."
Mk 2:27 "The Sabbath was *m* for man,
Jn 1: 3 Through him all things were *m*;
Ac 17:24 "The God who *m* the world
1Co 3: 6 watered it, but God *m* it grow.
Heb 1: 2 through whom he *m* the universe.
Jas 3: 9 who have been *m* in God's likeness
Rev 14: 7 Worship him who *m* the heavens,

MAGDALENE
Lk 8: 2 Mary (called *M*) from whom seven

MAGI
Mt 2: 1 *M* from the east came to Jerusalem

MAGIC (MAGICIANS)
Eze 13:20 I am against your *m* charms
Rev 21: 8 those who practice *m* arts,
22:15 those who practice *m* arts,

MAGICIANS (MAGIC)
Ex 7:11 the Egyptian *m* also did the same
Da 2: 2 So the king summoned the *m*,

MAGNIFICENCE* (MAGNIFICENT)
1Ch 22: 5 for the LORD should be of great *m*

MAGNIFICENT (MAGNIFICENCE)
1Ki 8:13 I have indeed built a *m* temple
Isa 28:29 in counsel and *m* in wisdom.
Mk 13: 1 stones! What *m* buildings!"

MAGOG
Eze 38: 2 of the land of *M*, the chief prince
39: 6 I will send fire on *M*
Rev 20: 8 and *M*—to gather them for battle.

MAIDEN (MAIDENS)
Pr 30:19 and the way of a man with a *m*.
Isa 62: 5 As a young man marries a *m*,
Jer 2:32 Does a *m* forget her jewelry,

MAIDENS (MAIDEN)
SS 1: 3 No wonder the *m* love you!

MAIMED
Mt 18: 8 It is better for you to enter life *m*

MAINTAIN (MAINTAINING)
Ps 82: 3 *m* the rights of the poor
106: 3 Blessed are they who *m* justice,
Hos 12: 6 *m* love and justice,
Am 5:15 *m* justice in the courts.
Ro 3:28 For we *m* that a man is justified

MAINTAINING* (MAINTAIN)
Ex 34: 7 faithfulness, *m* love to thousands,

MAJESTIC* (MAJESTY)
Ex 15: 6 was *m* in power.
15:11 *m* in holiness,
Job 37: 4 he thunders with his *m* voice.
Ps 8: 1 how *m* is your name in all the earth
8: 9 how *m* is your name in all the earth
29: 4 the voice of the LORD is *m*.
68:15 of Bashan are *m* mountains;
76: 4 more *m* than mountains rich
111: 3 Glorious and *m* are his deeds,
SS 6: 4 *m* as troops with banners.
6:10 *m* as the stars in procession?
Isa 30:30 men to hear his *m* voice
Eze 31: 7 It was *m* in beauty,
2Pe 1:17 came to him from the *M* Glory,

MAJESTY* (MAJESTIC)
Ex 15: 7 In the greatness of your *m*
Dt 5:24 has shown us his glory and his *m*,
11: 2 his *m*, his mighty hand, his
33:17 In *m* he is like a firstborn bull;
33:26 and on the clouds in his *m*.
1Ch 16:27 Splendor and *m* are before him;
29:11 and the *m* and the splendor,
Est 1: 4 the splendor and glory of his *m*.
7: 3 if it pleases your *m*, grant me my
Job 37:22 God comes in awesome *m*.
40:10 and clothe yourself in honor and *m*
Ps 21: 5 on him splendor and *m*.
45: 3 with splendor and *m*.
45: 4 In your *m* ride forth victoriously
68:34 whose *m* is over Israel,
93: 1 The LORD reigns, he is robed in *m*
93: 1 the LORD is robed in *m*
96: 6 Splendor and *m* are before him;
104: 1 clothed with splendor and *m*.
110: 3 Arrayed in holy *m*,
145: 5 of the glorious splendor of your *m*,
Isa 2:10 and the splendor of his *m*!
2:19 and the splendor of his *m*,
2:21 and the splendor of his *m*,
24:14 west they acclaim the LORD's *m*.
26:10 and regard not the *m* of the LORD.
53: 2 or *m* to attract us to him,
Eze 31: 2 can be compared with you in *m*?
31:18 with you in splendor and *m*?
Da 4:30 and for the glory of my *m*?"
Mic 5: 4 in the *m* of the name
Zec 6:13 and he will be clothed with *m*
Ac 19:27 will be robbed of her divine *m*."
25:26 to write to His *M* about him.
2Th 1: 9 and from the *m* of his power
Heb 1: 3 hand of the *M* in heaven.
8: 1 of the throne of the *M* in heaven,
2Pe 1:16 but we were eyewitnesses of his *m*.
Jude :25 only God our Savior be glory, *m*,

MAKE (MADE MAKER MAKERS MAKES MAKING MAN-MADE)
Ge 1:26 "Let us *m* man in our image,
2:18 I will *m* a helper suitable for him."
6:14 *m* yourself an ark of cypress wood;
12: 2 "I will *m* you into a great nation
Ex 22: 3 thief must certainly *m* restitution,
25: 9 *M* this tabernacle and all its
25:40 See that you *m* them according
Nu 6:25 the LORD *m* his face shine
2Sa 7: 9 Now I will *m* your name great,
Job 7:17 "What is man that you *m* so much
Ps 4: 8 *m* me dwell in safety.
20: 4 and *m* all your plans succeed.
108: 1 *m* music with all my soul.
110: 1 hand until I *m* your enemies
119:165 and nothing can *m* them stumble.
Pr 3: 6 and he will *m* your paths straight.
4:26 *M* level paths for your feet
20:18 *M* plans by seeking advice;
Isa 14:14 I will *m* myself like the Most High
29:16 "He did not *m* me"?
55: 3 I will *m* an everlasting covenant
61: 8 and *m* an everlasting covenant
Jer 31:31 "when I will *m* a new covenant

Eze 37:26 I will *m* a covenant of peace
Mt 3: 3 *m* straight paths for him.'"
28:19 and *m* disciples of all nations,
Mk 1:17 "and I will *m* you fishers of men."
Lk 13:24 "*M* every effort to enter
14:23 country lanes and *m* them come in,
Ro 14:19 *m* every effort to do what leads
2Co 5: 9 So we *m* it our goal to please him,
Eph 4: 3 *M* every effort to keep the unity
Col 4: 5 *m* the most of every opportunity.
1Th 4:11 *M* it your ambition
Heb 4:11 *m* every effort to enter that rest,
8: 5 it that you *m* everything according
12:14 *M* every effort to live in peace
2Pe 1: 5 *m* every effort to add
3:14 *m* every effort to be found spotless,

MAKER* (MAKE)
Job 4:17 Can a man be more pure than his *M*
9: 9 He is the *M* of the Bear and Orion,
32:22 my *M* would soon take me away.
35:10 no one says, 'Where is God my *M*,
36: 3 I will ascribe justice to my *M*.
40:19 yet his *M* can approach him
Ps 95: 6 kneel before the LORD our *M*;
115: 15 the *M* of heaven and earth.
121: 2 the *M* of heaven and earth.
124: 8 the *M* of heaven and earth.
134: 3 the *M* of heaven and earth,
146: 6 the *M* of heaven and earth,
149: 2 Let Israel rejoice in their *M*;
Pr 14:31 poor shows contempt for their *M*,
17: 5 poor shows contempt for their *M*;
22: 2 The LORD is the *M* of them all.
Ecc 11: 5 the *M* of all things.
Isa 17: 7 that day men will look to their *M*
27:11 so their *M* has no compassion
45: 9 to him who quarrels with his *M*,
45:11 the Holy One of Israel, and its *M*:
51:13 that you forget the LORD your *M*,
54: 5 For your *M* is your husband—
Jer 10:16 for he is the *M* of all things,
51:19 for he is the *M* of all things,
Hos 8:14 Israel has forgotten his *M*

MAKERS* (MAKE)
Isa 45:16 All the *m* of idols will be put

MAKES (MAKE)
Ps 23: 2 *m* me lie down in green pastures,
Pr 13:12 Hope deferred *m* the heart sick,
1Co 3: 7 but only God, who *m* things grow.

MAKING (MAKE)
Ps 19: 7 *m* wise the simple.
Ecc 12:12 Of *m* many books there is no end,
Jn 5:18 *m* himself equal with God.
Eph 5:16 *m* the most of every opportunity,

MALACHI*
Mal 1: 1 of the LORD to Israel through *M*.

MALE
Ge 1:27 *m* and female he created them.
Ex 13: 2 to me every firstborn *m*.
Nu 8:16 the first *m* offspring
Mt 19: 4 the Creator 'made them *m*
Gal 3:28 slave nor free, *m* nor female,

MALICE (MALICIOUS)
Mk 7:22 adultery, greed, *m*, deceit,
Ro 1:29 murder, strife, deceit and *m*.
1Co 5: 8 the yeast of *m* and wickedness,
Eph 4:31 along with every form of *m*.
Col 3: 8 *m*, slander, and filthy language
1Pe 2: 1 rid yourselves of all *m*

MALICIOUS (MALICE)
Pr 26:24 A *m* man disguises himself
1Ti 3:11 not *m* talkers but temperate
6: 4 *m* talk, evil suspicions

MALIGN
Tit 2: 5 so that no one will *m* the word

MAN (MAN'S MANKIND MEN MEN'S WOMAN WOMEN)
Ge 1:26 "Let us make *m* in our image,
2: 7 God formed the *m* from the dust
2: 8 *m* became a living being
2:15 God took the *m* and put
2:18 for the *m* to be alone
2:20 *m* gave names to all the
2:23 she was taken out of *m*.
2:25 *m* and his wife were both
3: 9 God called to the *m*,
3:22 *m* has now become like
4: 1 I have brought forth a *m*.
6: 3 not contend with *m* forever,
6: 6 grieved that he had made *m*
9: 6 Whoever sheds the blood of *m*,
Dt 8: 3 *m* does not live on bread
1Sa 13:14 a *m* after his own heart
15:29 he is not a *m* that he
16: 7 at the things *m* looks at.
Job 14: 1 *M* born of woman is of few
14:14 If a *m* dies, will he live
Ps 1: 1 Blessed is the *m* who does
8: 4 what is *m* that you are
32: 2 Blessed is the *m* whose sin
40: 4 Blessed is the *m* who makes
84:12 blessed is the *m* who trusts
103: 15 As for *m*, his days are
112: 1 Blessed is the *m* who fears
119: 9 can a young *m* keep his
127: 5 Blessed is the *m* whose quiver
144: 3 what is *m* that you care
Pr 3:13 Blessed is the *m* who finds
9: 9 Instruct a wise *m*
14:12 that seems right to a *m*,
30:19 way of a *m* with a maiden.
Isa 53: 3 a *m* of sorrows,
Jer 17: 5 the one who trusts in *m*,
17: 7 blessed is the *m* who trusts
Eze 22:30 I looked for a *m*
Mt 4: 4 *M* does not live on bread
19: 5 a *m* will leave his father
Mk 8:36 What good is it for a *m*
Lk 4: 4 '*M* does not live on bread
Ro 5:12 entered the world through one *m*
1Co 2:15 spiritual *m* makes judgments
3:12 If any *m* builds on this
7: 1 good for a *m* not to marry.
7: 2 each *m* should have his own
11: 3 head of every *m* is Christ,
11: 3 head of woman is *m*
13:11 When I became a *m*,
15:21 death came through a *m*,
15:45 first *m* Adam became a
15:47 the second *m* from heaven
2Co 12: 2 I know a *m* in Christ
Eph 2:15 create in himself one new *m*
5:31 a *m* will leave his father
Php 2: 8 found in appearance as a *m*,
1Ti 2: 5 the *m* Christ Jesus,
2:11 have authority over a *m*;
2Ti 3:17 that the *m* of God may be
Heb 2: 6 what is *m* that you are
9:27 as *m* is destined to die

MAN'S (MAN)
Pr 20:24 A *m* steps are directed by
Jer 10:23 a *m* life is not his own;
1Co 1:25 is wiser than *m* wisdom,

MAN-MADE (MAKE)
Heb 9:11 perfect tabernacle that is not *m*,
9:24 not enter a *m* sanctuary that was

MANAGE (MANAGER)
Jer 12: 5 how will you *m* in the thickets
1Ti 3: 4 He must *m* his own family well
3:12 one wife and must *m* his children
5:14 to *m* their homes and to give

MANAGER (MANAGE)
Lk 12:42 Who then is the faithful and wise *m*
16: 1 a rich man whose *m* was accused

MANASSEH
1. Firstborn of Joseph (Ge 41:51; 46:20). Blessed by Jacob but not firstborn (Ge 48). Tribe of blessed (Dt 33:17), numbered (Nu 1:35; 26:34), half allotted land east of Jordan (Nu 32; Jos 13:8–33), half west (Jos 17; Eze 48:4), failed to fully possess (Jos 17:12–13; Jdg 1:27), 12,000 from (Rev 7:6).
2. Son of Hezekiah; king of Judah (2Ki 21:1–18; 2Ch 33:1–20). Judah exiled for his detestable sins (2Ki 21:10–15). Repentance (2Ch 33:12–19).

MANDRAKES
Ge 30:14 give me some of your son's *m*."

MANGER
Lk 2:12 in strips of cloth and lying in a *m*."

MANIFESTATION*
1Co 12: 7 to each one the *m* of the Spirit is

MANKIND (MAN)
Ge 6: 7 I will wipe *m*, whom I have created
Ps 33:13 and sees all *m*;
Pr 8:31 and delighting in *m*.
Ecc 7:29 God made *m* upright,
Isa 40: 5 and all *m* together will see it.
45:12 and created *m* upon it.
Jer 32:27 "I am the LORD, the God of all *m*.
Zec 2:13 Be still before the LORD, all *m*,
Lk 3: 6 And all *m* will see God's salvation

MANNA
Ex 16:31 people of Israel called the bread *m*.
Dt 8:16 He gave you *m* to eat in the desert,
Jn 6:49 Your forefathers ate the *m*
Rev 2:17 I will give some of the hidden *m*.

MANNER
1Co 11:27 in an unworthy *m* will be guilty
Php 1:27 conduct yourselves in a *m* worthy

MANSIONS*
Ps 49:14 far from their princely *m*.
Isa 5: 9 the fine *m* left without occupants.
Am 3:15 and the *m* will be demolished,"
5:11 though you have built stone *m*,

MARCH
Jos 6: 4 *m* around the city seven times,
Isa 42:13 LORD will *m* out like a mighty

MARITAL* (MARRY)
Ex 21:10 of her food, clothing and *m* rights.
Mt 5:32 except for *m* unfaithfulness,
19: 9 except for *m* unfaithfulness,
1Co 7: 3 husband should fulfill his *m* duty

MARK (MARKS)
Cousin of Barnabas (Col 4:10; 2Ti 4:11; Phm 24; 1Pe 5:13), see JOHN.
Ge 4:15 Then the LORD put a *m* on Cain
Rev 13:16 to receive a *m* on his right hand

MARKET (MARKETPLACE MARKETPLACES)
Jn 2:16 turn my Father's house into a *m*!"

MARKETPLACE (MARKET)
Lk 7:32 are like children sitting in the *m*

MARKETPLACES (MARKET)
Mt 23: 7 they love to be greeted in the *m*

MARKS (MARK)
Jn 20:25 Unless I see the nail *m* in his hands
Gal 6:17 bear on my body the *m* of Jesus.

MARRED
Isa 52:14 his form *m* beyond human likeness

MARRIAGE (MARRY)
Mt 22:30 neither marry nor be given in *m*;
24:38 marrying and giving in *m*,
Ro 7: 2 she is released from the law of *m*.
Heb 13: 4 by all, and the *m* bed kept pure,

MARRIED (MARRY)
Dt 24: 5 happiness to the wife he has *m*.
Ezr 10:10 you have *m* foreign women,
Pr 30:23 an unloved woman who is *m*,
Mt 1:18 pledged to be *m* to Joseph,
Mk 12:23 since the seven were *m* to her?"
Ro 7: 2 by law a *m* woman is bound
1Co 7:27 Are you *m*? Do not seek a divorce.
7:33 But a *m* man is concerned about
7:36 They should get *m*.

MARRIES (MARRY)
Mt 5:32 anyone who *m* the divorced woman
19: 9 and *m* another woman commits
Lk 16:18 the man who *m* a divorced woman

MARROW
Heb 4:12 joints and *m*; it judges the thoughts

MARRY (INTERMARRY MARITAL MARRIAGE MARRIED MARRIES)
Dt 25: 5 brother shall take her and *m* her
Mt 22:30 resurrection people will neither *m*
1Co 7: 1 It is good for a man not to *m*.
7: 9 control themselves, they should *m*,
7:28 if you do *m*, you have not sinned;
1Ti 4: 3 They forbid people to *m*
5:14 So I counsel younger widows to *m*,

MARTHA*
Sister of Mary and Lazarus (Lk 10:38–42; Jn 11; 12:2).

MARVELED* (MARVELOUS)
Lk 2:33 mother *m* at what was said about
2Th 1:10 and to be *m* at among all those who

MARVELING* (MARVELOUS)
Lk 9:43 While everyone was *m*

MARVELOUS* (MARVELED MARVELING)
1Ch 16:24 his *m* deeds among all peoples.
Job 37: 5 God's voice thunders in *m* ways;
Ps 71:17 to this day I declare your *m* deeds.
72:18 who alone does *m* deeds.
86:10 For you are great and do *m* deeds;
96: 3 his *m* deeds among all peoples.
98: 1 for he has done *m* things;
118: 23 and it is *m* in our eyes.
Isa 25: 1 you have done *m* things,
Zec 8: 6 but will it seem *m* to me?"
8: 6 "It may seem *m* to the remnant
Mt 21:42 and it is *m* in our eyes'?
Mk 12:11 and it is *m* in our eyes'?"
Rev 15: 1 in heaven another great and *m* sign
15: 3 "Great and *m* are your deeds,

MARY
1. Mother of Jesus (Mt 1:16–25; Lk 1:27–56; 2:1–40). With Jesus at temple (Lk 2:41–52), at the wedding in Cana (Jn 2:1–5), questioning his sanity (Mk 3:21), at the cross (Jn 19:25–27). Among disciples after Ascension (Ac 1:14).
2. Magdalene; former demoniac (Lk 8:2). Helped support Jesus' ministry (Lk 8:1–3). At the cross (Mt 27:56; Mk 15:40; Jn 19:25), burial (Mt 27:61; Mk 15:47). Saw angel after resurrection (Mt 28:1–10; Mk 16:1–9; Lk 24:1–12); also Jesus (Jn 20:1–18).
3. Sister of Martha and Lazarus (Jn 11). Washed Jesus' feet (Jn 12:1–8).

MASQUERADES*
2Co 11:14 for Satan himself *m* as an angel

MASTER (MASTER'S MASTERED MASTERS MASTERY)
Ge 4: 7 to have you, but you must *m* it."
Hos 2:16 you will no longer call me 'my *m*.'
Mal 1: 6 If I am a *m*, where is the respect
Mt 10:24 nor a servant above his *m*.
23: 8 for you have only one *M*
24:46 that servant whose *m* finds him
25:21 "His *m* replied, 'Well done,
25:23 "His *m* replied, 'Well done,
Ro 6:14 For sin shall not be your *m*,
14: 4 To his own *m* he stands or falls.
Col 4: 1 you know that you also have a *M*
2Ti 2:21 useful to the *M* and prepared

MASTER'S (MASTER)
Mt 25:21 Come and share your *m* happiness

MASTERED* (MASTER)
1Co 6:12 but I will not be *m* by anything.
2Pe 2:19 a slave to whatever has *m* him.

MASTERS (MASTER)
Pr 25:13 he refreshes the spirit of his *m*.
Mt 6:24 "No one can serve two *m*.
Lk 16:13 "No servant can serve two *m*.
Eph 6: 5 obey your earthly *m* with respect
6: 9 And *m*, treat your slaves
Col 3:22 obey your earthly *m* in everything;
4: 1 *M*, provide your slaves
1Ti 6: 1 should consider their *m* worthy
6: 2 who have believing *m* are not
Tit 2: 9 subject to their *m* in everything,
1Pe 2:18 to your *m* with all respect,

MASTERY* (MASTER)
Ro 6: 9 death no longer has *m* over him.

MAT
Mk 2: 9 'Get up, take your *m* and walk'?
Ac 9:34 Get up and take care of your *m*."

MATCHED*
2Co 8:11 do it may be *m* by your completion

MATTHEW*
Apostle; former tax collector (Mt 9:9–13; 10:3; Mk 3:18; Lk 6:15; Ac 1:13). Also called Levi (Mk 2:14–17; Lk 5:27–32).

MATTHIAS
Ac 1:26 the lot fell to *M*; so he was added

MATURE* (MATURITY)
Lk 8:14 and pleasures, and they do not *m*.
1Co 2: 6 a message of wisdom among the *m*,
Eph 4:13 of the Son of God and become *m*,
Php 3:15 of us who are *m* should take such
Col 4:12 firm in all the will of God, *m*
Heb 5:14 But solid food is for the *m*,
Jas 1: 4 work so that you may be *m*

MATURITY* (MATURE)
Heb 6: 1 about Christ and go on to *m*,

MEAL
Pr 15:17 Better a *m* of vegetables where
1Co 10:27 some unbeliever invites you to a *m*
Heb 12:16 for a single *m* sold his inheritance

MEANING
Ne 8: 8 and giving the *m* so that the people

MEANINGLESS
Ecc 1: 2 *"M! M!"* says the Teacher.
1Ti 1: 6 from these and turned to *m* talk.

MEANS
1Co 9:22 by all possible *m* I might save some

MEASURE (MEASURED MEASURES)
Ps 71:15 though I know not its *m*.
Eze 45: 3 In the sacred district, *m*
Zec 2: 2 He answered me, "To *m* Jerusalem
Lk 6:38 A good *m*, pressed
Eph 3:19 to the *m* of all the fullness of God.
4:13 to the whole *m* of the fullness
Rev 11: 1 "Go and *m* the temple of God

MEASURED (MEASURE)
Isa 40:12 Who has *m* the waters
Jer 31:37 if the heavens above can be *m*

MEASURES (MEASURE)
Dt 25:14 Do not have two differing *m*
Pr 20:10 Differing weights and differing *m*

MEAT
Pr 23:20 or gorge themselves on *m*,
Ro 14: 6 He who eats *m*, eats to the Lord,
14:21 It is better not to eat *m*
1Co 8:13 I will never eat *m* again,
10:25 *m* market without raising questions

MEDDLER* (MEDDLES)
1Pe 4:15 kind of criminal, or even as a *m*.

MEDDLES* (MEDDLER)
Pr 26:17 is a passer-by who *m*

MEDIATOR
1Ti 2: 5 and one *m* between God and men,
Heb 8: 6 of which he is *m* is superior
9:15 For this reason Christ is the *m*
12:24 to Jesus the *m* of a new covenant,

MEDICINE*
Pr 17:22 A cheerful heart is good *m*,

MEDITATE* (MEDITATED MEDITATES MEDITATION)
Ge 24:63 out to the field one evening to *m*,
Jos 1: 8 from your mouth; *m* on it day
Ps 48: 9 we *m* on your unfailing love.
77:12 I will *m* on all your works
119: 15 I *m* on your precepts
119: 23 your servant will *m*
119: 27 then I will *m* on your wonders.
119: 48 and I *m* on your decrees.
119: 78 but I will *m* on your precepts.
119: 97 I *m* on it all day long.
119: 99 for I *m* on your statutes.
119:148 that I may *m* on your promises.
143: 5 I *m* on all your works
145: 5 I will *m* on your wonderful works.

MEDITATED* (MEDITATE)
Ps 39: 3 and as I *m*, the fire burned;

MEDITATES* (MEDITATE)
Ps 1: 2 and on his law he *m* day and night.

MEDITATION* (MEDITATE)
Ps 19:14 of my mouth and the *m* of my heart
104: 34 May my *m* be pleasing to him,

MEDIUM
Lev 20:27 " 'A man or woman who is a *m*

MEEK* (MEEKNESS)
Ps 37:11 But the *m* will inherit the land
Zep 3:12 the *m* and humble,
Mt 5: 5 Blessed are the *m*,

MEEKNESS* (MEEK)
2Co 10: 1 By the *m* and gentleness of Christ,

MEET (MEETING MEETINGS MEETS)
Ps 42: 2 When can I go and *m* with God?
85:10 Love and faithfulness *m* together;
Am 4:12 prepare to *m* your God, O Israel."
1Co 11:34 when you *m* together it may not
1Th 4:17 them in the clouds to *m* the Lord

MEETING (MEET)
Ex 40:34 the cloud covered the Tent of *M*,
Heb 10:25 Let us not give up *m* together,

MEETINGS* (MEET)
1Co 11:17 for your *m* do more harm

MEETS (MEET)
Heb 7:26 Such a high priest *m* our need—

MELCHIZEDEK
Ge 14:18 *M* king of Salem brought out bread
Ps 110: 4 in the order of *M*."
Heb 7:11 in the order of *M*, not in the order

MELT (MELTS)
2Pe 3:12 and the elements will *m* in the heat.

MELTS (MELT)
Am 9: 5 he who touches the earth and it *m*,

MEMBER (MEMBERS)
Ro 12: 5 each *m* belongs to all the others.

MEMBERS (MEMBER)
Mic 7: 6 a man's enemies are the *m*
Mt 10:36 a man's enemies will be the *m*
Ro 7:23 law at work in the *m* of my body,
12: 4 of us has one body with many *m*,
1Co 6:15 not know that your bodies are *m*
12:24 But God has combined the *m*
Eph 3: 6 *m* together of one body,
4:25 for we are all *m* of one body.
5:30 for we are *m* of his body.
Col 3:15 as *m* of one body you were called

MEMORABLE* (MEMORY)
Eze 39:13 day I am glorified will be a *m* day

MEMORIES* (MEMORY)
1Th 3: 6 us that you always have pleasant *m*

MEMORY (MEMORABLE MEMORIES)
Pr 10: 7 *m* of the righteous will be
Mt 26:13 she has done will also be told, in *m*

MEN (MAN)
Ge 6: 2 daughter of *m* were beautiful,
6: 4 heroes of old, *m* of renown
Ps 9:20 nations know they are but *m*.
11: 4 He observes the sons of *m*;
Mt 4:19 will make you fishers of *m*
5:16 your light shine before *m*
6:14 if you forgive *m* when
10:32 acknowledges me before *m*
12:31 blasphemy will be forgiven *m*,
12:36 *m* will have to give account
23: 5 is done for *m* to see:
Mk 7: 7 are but rules taught by *m*.
Lk 6:22 Blessed are you when *m*
6:26 Woe to you when all *m*
Jn 1: 4 life was the light of *m*.
2:24 for he knew all *m*.
3:19 *m* loved darkness instead
12:32 will draw all *m* to myself
13:35 all *m* will know that you
Ac 5:29 obey God rather than *m*!
Ro 1:18 wickedness of *m*
1:27 indecent acts with other *m*,
5:12 death came to all *m*,
1Co 2:11 among *m* knows the thoughts
3: 3 acting like mere *m*?
3:21 no more boasting about *m*!
9:22 all things to all *m*
13: 1 tongues of *m* and of angels
16:13 be *m* of courage;
16:18 Such *m* deserve recognition.
2Co 5:11 we try to persuade *m*.
8:21 but also in the eyes of *m*.
Gal 1: 1 sent not from *m* nor
1:10 to win approval of *m*, or
Eph 4: 8 and gave gifts to *m*.
1Th 2: 4 as *m* approved by God
2:13 not as the word of *m*,
1Ti 2: 4 wants all *m* to be saved
2: 6 as a ransom for all *m*—

1Ti 4:10 the Savior of all *m*
5: 2 younger *m* as brothers
2Ti 2: 2 entrust to reliable *m*
Tit 2:11 has appeared to all *m.*
Heb 5: 1 is selected from among *m*
7:28 high priests *m* who are weak;
2Pe 1:21 but *m* spoke from God
Rev 21: 3 dwelling of God is with *m,*

MEN'S (MAN)
2Ki 19:18 fashioned by *m* hands.
2Ch 32:19 the work of *m* hands.
1Co 2: 5 not rest on *m* wisdom,

MENAHEM*
King of Israel (2Ki 15:17–22).

MENE
Da 5:25 that was written: *M, M,*

MEPHIBOSHETH
Son of Jonathan shown kindness by David (2Sa 4:4; 9; 21:7). Accused of siding with Absalom (2Sa 16:1–4; 19:24–30).

MERCHANT
Pr 31:14 She is like the *m* ships,
Mt 13:45 of heaven is like a *m* looking

MERCIFUL (MERCY)
Dt 4:31 the LORD your God is a *m* God;
Ne 9:31 for you are a gracious and *m* God.
Ps 77: 9 Has God forgotten to be *m?*
78:38 Yet he was *m;*
Jer 3:12 for I am *m,*' declares the LORD,
Da 9: 9 The Lord our God is *m*
Mt 5: 7 Blessed are the *m,*
Lk 1:54 remembering to be *m*
6:36 Be *m,* just as your Father is *m.*
Heb 2:17 in order that he might become a *m*
Jas 2:13 to anyone who has not been *m.*
Jude :22 Be *m* to those who doubt; snatch

MERCY (MERCIFUL)
Ex 33:19 *m* on whom I will have *m,*
2Sa 24:14 of the LORD, for his *m* is great;
1Ch 21:13 for his *m* is very great;
Ne 9:31 But in your great *m* you did not put
Ps 25: 6 O LORD, your great *m* and love,
28: 6 for he has heard my cry for *m.*
57: 1 Have *m* on me, O God, have *m*
Pr 28:13 renounces them finds *m.*
Isa 63: 9 and *m* he redeemed them;
Da 9:18 but because of your great *m.*
Hos 6: 6 For I desire *m,* not sacrifice,
Am 5:15 LORD God Almighty will have *m*
Mic 6: 8 To act justly and to love *m*
7:18 but delight to show *m.*
Hab 3: 2 in wrath remember *m.*
Zec 7: 9 show *m* and compassion
Mt 5: 7 for they will be shown *m.*
9:13 learn what this means: 'I desire *m,*
12: 7 'I desire *m,* not sacrifice,' you
18:33 Shouldn't you have had *m*
23:23 justice, *m* and faithfulness.
Lk 1:50 His *m* extends to those who fear
Ro 9:15 "I will have *m* on whom I have *m,*
9:18 Therefore God has *m*
11:32 so that he may have *m* on them all.
12: 1 brothers, in view of God's *m,*
12: 8 if it is showing *m,* let him do it
Eph 2: 4 who is rich in *m,* made us alive
1Ti 1:13 I was shown *m* because I acted
1:16 for that very reason I was shown *m*
Tit 3: 5 we had done, but because of his *m.*
Heb 4:16 so that we may receive *m*
Jas 2:13 judgment without *m* will be shown
2:13 *M* triumphs over judgment!
3:17 submissive, full of *m* and good fruit
5:11 full of compassion and *m.*
1Pe 1: 3 In his great *m* he has given us new
2:10 once you had not received *m,*
Jude :23 to others show *m,* mixed with fear

MERRY
Lk 12:19 Take life easy; eat, drink and be *m*

MESHACH
Hebrew exiled to Babylon; name changed from Mishael (Da 1:6–7). Refused defilement by food (Da 1:8–20). Refused to worship idol (Da 3:1–18); saved from furnace (Da 3:19–30).

MESSAGE (MESSENGER)
Isa 53: 1 Who has believed our *m*
Jn 12:38 "Lord, who has believed our *m*
Ac 5:20 "and tell the people the full *m*
10:36 You know the *m* God sent
17:11 for they received the *m*
Ro 10:16 who has believed our *m?*"
10:17 faith comes from hearing the *m,*
1Co 1:18 For the *m* of the cross is
2: 4 My *m* and my preaching were not
2Co 5:19 to us the *m* of reconciliation.
2Th 3: 1 pray for us that the *m*
Tit 1: 9 firmly to the trustworthy *m*
Heb 4: 2 the *m* they heard was of no value
1Pe 2: 8 because they disobey the *m*—

MESSENGER (MESSAGE)
Pr 25:13 is a trustworthy *m*
Mal 3: 1 I will send my *m,* who will prepare
Mt 11:10 " 'I will send my *m* ahead of you,
2Co 12: 7 a *m* of Satan, to torment me.

MESSIAH*
Jn 1:41 "We have found the *M*" (that is,
4:25 "I know that *M*" (called Christ) "is

METHUSELAH
Ge 5:27 Altogether, *M* lived 969 years,

MICAH
1. Idolater from Ephraim (Jdg 17–18).
2. Prophet from Moresheth (Jer 26:18–19; Mic 1:1).

MICAIAH
Prophet of the LORD who spoke against Ahab (1Ki 22:1–28; 2Ch 18:1–27).

MICHAEL
Archangel (Jude 9); warrior in angelic realm, protector of Israel (Da 10:13, 21; 12:1; Rev 12:7).

MICHAL
Daughter of Saul, wife of David (1Sa 14:49; 18:20–28). Warned David of Saul's plot (1Sa 19). Saul gave her to Paltiel (1Sa 25:44); David retrieved her (2Sa 3:13–16). Criticized David for dancing before the ark (2Sa 6:16–23); 1Ch 15:29).

MIDIAN
Ex 2:15 Pharaoh and went to live in *M,*
Jdg 7: 2 me to deliver *M* into their hands.

MIDWIVES
Ex 1:17 The *m,* however, feared God

MIGHT (ALMIGHTY MIGHTIER MIGHTY)
Jdg 16:30 Then he pushed with all his *m,*
2Sa 6: 5 with all their *m* before the LORD,
6:14 before the LORD with all his *m,*
2Ch 20: 6 Power and *m* are in your hand,
Ps 21:13 we will sing and praise your *m.*
54: 1 vindicate me by your *m.*
Isa 63:15 Where are your zeal and your *m?*
Mic 3: 8 and with justice and *m,*
Zec 4: 6 'Not by *m* nor by power,
Col 1:11 power according to his glorious *m*
1Ti 6:16 To him be honor and *m* forever.

MIGHTIER (MIGHT)
Ps 93: 4 *M* than the thunder

MIGHTY (MIGHT)
Ge 49:24 of the hand of the *M* One of Jacob,
Ex 6: 1 of my *m* hand he will drive them
13: 3 out of it with a *m* hand.
Dt 5:15 out of there with a *m* hand
7: 8 he brought you out with a *m* hand
10:17 the great God, *m* and awesome,
34:12 one has ever shown the *m* power
2Sa 1:19 How the *m* have fallen!
23: 8 the names of David's *m* men:
Ne 9:32 the great, *m* and awesome God,
Job 36: 5 God is *m,* but does not despise men
Ps 24: 8 The LORD strong and *m,*
45: 3 upon your side, O *m* one;
50: 1 The *M* One, God, the LORD,
62: 7 he is my *m* rock, my refuge.
68:33 who thunders with *m* voice.
71:16 proclaim your *m* acts,
77:12 and consider all your *m* deeds.
77:15 With your *m* arm you redeemed
89: 8 You are *m,* O LORD,
93: 4 the LORD on high is *m.*
99: 4 The King is *m,* he loves justice—
110: 2 LORD will extend your *m* scepter
Ps 118:15 right hand has done *m* things!
136:12 with a *m* hand and outstretched
145: 4 they will tell of your *m* acts.
145:12 all men may know of your *m* acts
147: 5 Great is our Lord and *m* in power;
SS 8: 6 like a *m* flame.
Isa 9: 6 Wonderful Counselor, *M* God,
60:16 your Redeemer, the *M* One
63: 1 *m* to save."
Jer 10: 6 and your name is *m* in power.
20:11 with me like a *m* warrior;
32:19 your purposes and *m* are your
Eze 20:33 I will rule over you with a *m* hand
Zep 3:17 he is *m* to save.
Mt 26:64 at the right hand of the *M* One
Eph 1:19 like the working of his *m* strength,
6:10 in the Lord and in his *m* power.
1Pe 5: 6 therefore, under God's *m* hand,

MILE*
Mt 5:41 If someone forces you to go one *m,*

MILK
Ex 3: 8 a land flowing with *m* and honey—
23:19 a young goat in its mother's *m.*
Pr 30:33 as churning the *m* produces butter,
Isa 55: 1 Come, buy wine and *m*
1Co 3: 2 I gave you *m,* not solid food,
Heb 5:12 You need *m,* not solid food!
1Pe 2: 2 babies, crave pure spiritual *m,*

MILLSTONE (STONE)
Lk 17: 2 sea with a *m* tied around his neck

MIND (DOUBLE-MINDED LIKE-MINDED MINDED MINDFUL MINDS)
Nu 23:19 that he should change his *m.*
Dt 28:65 LORD will give you an anxious *m,*
1Sa 15:29 Israel does not lie or change his *m;*
1Ch 28: 9 devotion and with a willing *m,*
2Ch 30:12 the people to give them unity of *m*
Ps 26: 2 examine my heart and my *m;*
110: 4 and will not change his *m:*
Isa 26: 3 him whose *m* is steadfast,
Jer 17:10 and examine the *m,*
Mt 22:37 all your soul and with all your *m.*'
Mk 12:30 with all your *m* and with all your
Lk 10:27 your strength and with all your *m*';
Ac 4:32 believers were one in heart and *m.*
Ro 1:28 he gave them over to a depraved *m*
7:25 I myself in my *m* am a slave
8: 6 The *m* of sinful man is death,
8: 7 the sinful *m* is hostile to God.
12: 2 by the renewing of your *m.*
14:13 make up your *m* not
1Co 1:10 you may be perfectly united in *m*
2: 9 no *m* has conceived
14:14 spirit prays, but my *m* is unfruitful.
2Co 13:11 be of one *m,* live in peace.
Php 3:19 Their *m* is on earthly things.
Col 2:18 and his unspiritual *m* puffs him up
1Th 4:11 to *m* your own business
Heb 7:21 and will not change his *m:*

MINDED* (MIND)
1Pe 4: 7 be clear *m* and self-controlled

MINDFUL* (MIND)
Ps 8: 4 what is man that you are *m* of him,
Lk 1:48 God my Savior, for he has been *m*
Heb 2: 6 What is man that you are *m* of him,

MINDS (MIND)
Dt 11:18 of mine in your hearts and *m;*
Ps 7: 9 who searches *m* and hearts,
Jer 31:33 "I will put my law in their *m*
Lk 24:38 and why do doubts rise in your *m?*
24:45 Then he opened their *m*
Ro 8: 5 to the sinful nature have their *m* set
2Co 4: 4 god of this age has blinded the *m*
Eph 4:23 new in the attitude of your *m;*
Col 3: 2 Set your *m* on things above,
Heb 8:10 I will put my laws in their *m*
10:16 and I will write them on their *m.*"
1Pe 1:13 prepare your *m* for action;
Rev 2:23 I am he who searches hearts and *m,*

MINISTER (MINISTERING MINISTERS MINISTRY)
Ps 101: 6 will *m* to me.
1Ti 4: 6 you will be a good *m*

MINISTERING (MINISTER)
Heb 1:14 Are not all angels *m* spirits sent

MINISTERS (MINISTER)
2Co 3: 6 as *m* of a new covenant—

MINISTRY (MINISTER)
Ac 6: 4 to prayer and the *m* of the word."
Ro 11:13 I make much of my *m*
2Co 4: 1 God's mercy we have this *m,*
5:18 gave us the *m* of reconciliation:
6: 3 so that our *m* will not be
Gal 2: 8 who was at work in the *m* of Peter
2Ti 4: 5 discharge all the duties of your *m.*
Heb 8: 6 But the *m* Jesus has received is

MIRACLE* (MIRACLES MIRACULOUS)
Ex 7: 9 'Perform a *m,'* then say to Aaron,
Mk 9:39 "No one who does a *m*
Lk 23: 8 hoped to see him perform some *m.*
Jn 7:21 "I did one *m,* and you are all
Ac 4:16 they have done an outstanding *m,*

MIRACLES* (MIRACLE)
1Ch 16:12 his *m,* and the judgments he
Ne 9:17 to remember the *m* you performed
Job 5: 9 *m* that cannot be counted.
9:10 *m* that cannot be counted.
Ps 77:11 I will remember your *m* of long ago
77:14 You are the God who performs *m;*
78:12 He did *m* in the sight
105: 5 his *m,* and the judgments he
106: 7 they gave no thought to your *m;*
106: 22 *m* in the land of Ham
Mt 7:22 out demons and perform many *m?'*
11:20 most of his *m* had been performed,
11:21 If the *m* that were performed
11:23 If the *m* that were performed
13:58 And he did not do many *m* there
24:24 and perform great signs and *m*
Mk 6: 2 does *m!* Isn't this the carpenter?
6: 5 He could not do any *m* there,
13:22 and *m* to deceive the elect—
Lk 10:13 For if the *m* that were performed
19:37 for all the *m* they had seen:
Jn 7: 3 disciples may see the *m* you do.
10:25 *m* I do in my Father's name speak
10:32 "I have shown you many great *m*
10:38 do not believe me, believe the *m,*
14:11 the evidence of the *m* themselves.
15:24 But now they have seen these *m,*
Ac 2:22 accredited by God to you by *m,*
8:13 by the great signs and *m* he saw.
19:11 God did extraordinary *m*
Ro 15:19 by the power of signs and *m,*
1Co 12:28 third teachers, then workers of *m,*
12:29 Are all teachers? Do all work *m?*
2Co 12:12 and *m*—were done among you
Gal 3: 5 work *m* among you because you
2Th 2: 9 in all kinds of counterfeit *m,*
Heb 2: 4 it by signs, wonders and various *m,*

MIRACULOUS (MIRACLE)
Dt 13: 1 and announces to you a *m* sign
Mt 12:39 generation asks for a *m* sign!
13:54 this wisdom and these *m* powers?"
Jn 2:11 This, the first of his *m* signs,
2:23 people saw the *m* signs he was
3: 2 could perform the *m* signs you are
4:48 "Unless you people see *m* signs
7:31 will he do more *m* signs
9:16 "How can a sinner do such *m* signs
12:37 Jesus had done all these *m* signs
20:30 Jesus did many other *m* signs
Ac 2:43 *m* signs were done by the apostles.
5:12 apostles performed many *m* signs
1Co 1:22 Jews demand *m* signs and Greeks
12:10 to another *m* powers,

MIRE
Ps 40: 2 out of the mud and *m;*
Isa 57:20 whose waves cast up *m* and mud.

MIRIAM
Sister of Moses and Aaron (Nu 26:59). Led dancing at Red Sea (Ex 15:20–21). Struck with leprosy for criticizing Moses (Nu 12). Death (Nu 20:1).

MIRROR
1Co 13:12 but a poor reflection as in a *m;*
Jas 1:23 a man who looks at his face in a *m*

MISDEEDS*
Ps 99: 8 though you punished their *m.*
Ro 8:13 put to death the *m* of the body,

MISERY
Ex 3: 7 "I have indeed seen the *m*
Jdg 10:16 he could bear Israel's *m* no longer.
Hos 5:15 in their *m* they will earnestly seek
Ro 3:16 ruin and *m* mark their ways,
Jas 5: 1 of the *m* that is coming upon you.

MISFORTUNE
Ob :12 brother in the day of his *m,*

MISLEAD (MISLED)
Isa 47:10 wisdom and knowledge *m* you

MISLED (MISLEAD)
1Co 15:33 Do not be *m:* "Bad company

MISS (MISSES)
Pr 19: 2 nor to be hasty and *m* the way.

MISSES (MISS)
Heb 12:15 See to it that no one *m* the grace

MIST
Hos 6: 4 Your love is like the morning *m,*
Jas 4:14 You are a *m* that appears for a little

MISTREAT (MISTREATED)
Ex 22:21 "Do not *m* an alien or oppress him,
Eze 22:29 and needy and *m* the alien,
Lk 6:28 pray for those who *m* you.

MISTREATED (MISTREAT)
Eze 22: 7 *m* the fatherless and the widow.
Heb 11:25 to be *m* along with the people
11:37 destitute, persecuted and *m*—
13: 3 who are *m* as if you yourselves

MISUSE* (MISUSES)
Ex 20: 7 "You shall not *m* the name
Dt 5:11 "You shall not *m* the name
Ps 139: 20 your adversaries *m* your name.

MISUSES* (MISUSE)
Ex 20: 7 anyone guiltless who *m* his name.
Dt 5:11 anyone guiltless who *m* his name.

MIXED (MIXING)
Da 2:41 even as you saw iron *m* with clay.

MIXING (MIXED)
Isa 5:22 and champions at *m* drinks,

MOAB (MOABITESS)
Ge 19:37 she named him *M;* he is the father
Dt 34: 6 He buried him in *M,* in the valley
Ru 1: 1 live for a while in the country of *M.*
Isa 15: 1 An oracle concerning *M:*
Jer 48:16 "The fall of *M* is at hand;
Am 2: 1 "For three sins of *M,*

MOABITESS (MOAB)
Ru 1:22 accompanied by Ruth the *M,*

MOAN
Ps 90: 9 we finish our years with a *m.*

MOCK (MOCKED MOCKER MOCKERS MOCKING MOCKS)
Ps 22: 7 All who see me *m* me;
119: 51 The arrogant *m* me
Pr 1:26 I will *m* when calamity overtakes
14: 9 Fools *m* at making amends for sin,
Mk 10:34 who will *m* him and spit on him,

MOCKED (MOCK)
Ps 89:51 with which they have *m* every step
Mt 27:29 knelt in front of him and *m* him.
27:41 of the law and the elders *m* him.
Gal 6: 7 not be deceived: God cannot be *m.*

MOCKER (MOCK)
Pr 9: 7 corrects a *m* invites insult;
9:12 if you are a *m,* you alone will suffer
20: 1 Wine is a *m* and beer a brawler;
22:10 Drive out the *m,* and out goes strife

MOCKERS (MOCK)
Ps 1: 1 or sit in the seat of *m.*
Pr 29: 8 *M* stir up a city,

MOCKING (MOCK)
Isa 50: 6 face from *m* and spitting.

MOCKS (MOCK)
Pr 17: 5 He who *m* the poor shows
30:17 "The eye that *m* a father,

MODEL*
Eze 28:12 " 'You were the *m* of perfection,
1Th 1: 7 And so you became a *m*
2Th 3: 9 to make ourselves a *m* for you

MODESTY*
1Co 12:23 are treated with special *m,*

MOLDED*
Job 10: 9 Remember that you *m* me like clay

MOLDY
Jos 9: 5 of their food supply was dry and *m.*

MOLECH
Lev 20: 2 of his children to *M* must be put
1Ki 11:33 and *M* the god of the Ammonites,

MOMENT (MOMENTARY)
Job 20: 5 the joy of the godless lasts but a *m.*
Ps 2:12 for his wrath can flare up in a *m.*
30: 5 For his anger lasts only a *m,*
Pr 12:19 but a lying tongue lasts only a *m.*
Isa 54: 7 "For a brief *m* I abandoned you,
66: 8 or a nation be brought forth in a *m?*
Gal 2: 5 We did not give in to them for a *m,*

MOMENTARY* (MOMENT)
2Co 4:17 and *m* troubles are achieving

MONEY
Pr 13:11 Dishonest *m* dwindles away,
Ecc 5:10 Whoever loves *m* never has *m*
Isa 55: 1 and you who have no *m,*
Mt 6:24 You cannot serve both God and *M.*
27: 5 Judas threw the *m* into the temple
Lk 3:14 "Don't extort *m* and don't accuse
9: 3 no bread, no *m,* no extra tunic.
16:13 You cannot serve both God and *M*
Ac 5: 2 part of the *m* for himself,
1Co 16: 2 set aside a sum of *m* in keeping
1Ti 3: 3 not quarrelsome, not a lover of *m.*
6:10 For the love of *m* is a root
2Ti 3: 2 lovers of *m,* boastful, proud,
Heb 13: 5 free from the love of *m*
1Pe 5: 2 not greedy for *m,* but eager to serve

MONEYLENDER* (LEND)
Ex 22:25 not be like a *m;* charge him no
Lk 7:41 men owed money to a certain *m.*

MONTH (MONTHS)
Ex 12: 2 "This *m* is to be for you the first
Eze 47:12 Every *m* they will bear,
Rev 22: 2 of fruit, yielding its fruit every *m.*

MONTHS (MONTH)
Gal 4:10 and *m* and seasons and years!
Rev 11: 2 trample on the holy city for 42 *m.*
13: 5 his authority for forty-two *m.*

MOON
Jos 10:13 and the *m* stopped,
Ps 8: 3 the *m* and the stars,
74:16 you established the sun and *m.*
89:37 be established forever like the *m,*
104: 19 The *m* marks off the seasons,
121: 6 nor the *m* by night.
136: 9 the *m* and stars to govern the night;
148: 3 Praise him, sun and *m,*
SS 6:10 fair as the *m,* bright as the sun,
Joel 2:31 and the *m* to blood
Hab 3:11 and *m* stood still in the heavens
Mt 24:29 and the *m* will not give its light;
Ac 2:20 and the *m* to blood
1Co 15:41 *m* another and the stars another;
Col 2:16 a New *M* celebration or a Sabbath
Rev 6:12 the whole *m* turned blood red,
21:23 city does not need the sun or the *m*

MORAL*
Jas 1:21 rid of all *m* filth and the evil that is

MORDECAI
Benjamite exile who raised Esther (Est 2:5–15). Exposed plot to kill Xerxes (Est 2:19–23). Refused to honor Haman (Est 3:1–6; 5:9–14). Charged Esther to foil Haman's plot against the Jews (Est 4). Xerxes forced Haman to honor Mordecai (Est 6). Mordecai exalted (Est 8–10). Established Purim (Est 9:18–32).

MORIAH*
Ge 22: 2 and go to the region of *M.*
2Ch 3: 1 LORD in Jerusalem on Mount *M,*

MORNING
Ge 1: 5 and there was *m*—the first day.
Dt 28:67 In the *m* you will say, "If only it
2Sa 23: 4 he is like the light of *m* at sunrise
Ps 5: 3 In the *m,* O LORD,

Pr 27:14 blesses his neighbor early in the *m,*
Isa 14:12 O *m* star, son of the dawn!
La 3:23 They are new every *m;*
2Pe 1:19 and the *m* star rises in your hearts.
Rev 2:28 I will also give him the *m* star.
22:16 of David, and the bright *M* Star."

MORTAL
Ge 6: 3 for he is *m;* his days will be
Job 10: 4 Do you see as a *m* sees?
Ro 8:11 also give life to your *m* bodies
1Co 15:53 and the *m* with immortality.
2Co 5: 4 that what is *m* may be swallowed

MOSES
Levite; brother of Aaron (Ex 6:20; 1Ch 6:3). Put in basket into Nile; discovered and raised by Pharaoh's daughter (Ex 2:1–10). Fled to Midian after killing Egyptian (Ex 2:11–15). Married to Zipporah, fathered Gershom (Ex 2:16–22).

Called by the LORD to deliver Israel (Ex 3–4). Pharaoh's resistance (Ex 5). Ten plagues (Ex 7–11). Passover and Exodus (Ex 12–13). Led Israel through Red Sea (Ex 14). Song of deliverance (Ex 15:1–21). Brought water from rock (Ex 17:1–7). Raised hands to defeat Amalekites (Ex 17:8–16). Delegated judges (Ex 18; Dt 1:9–18).

Received Law at Sinai (Ex 19–23; 25–31; Jn 1:17). Announced Law to Israel (Ex 19:7–8; 24; 35). Broke tablets because of golden calf (Ex 32; Dt 9). Saw glory of the LORD (Ex 33–34). Supervised building of tabernacle (Ex 36–40). Set apart Aaron and priests (Lev 8–9). Numbered tribes (Nu 1–4; 26). Opposed by Aaron and Miriam (Nu 12). Sent spies into Canaan (Nu 13). Announced forty years of wandering for failure to enter land (Nu 14). Opposed by Korah (Nu 16). Forbidden to enter land for striking rock (Nu 20:1–13; Dt 1:37). Lifted bronze snake for healing (Nu 21:4–9; Jn 3:14). Final address to Israel (Dt 1–33). Succeeded by Joshua (Nu 27:12–23; Dt 34). Death (Dt 34:5–12).

"Law of Moses" (1Ki 2:3; Ezr 3:2; Mk 12:26; Lk 24:44). "Book of Moses" (2Ch 25:12; Ne 13:1). "Song of Moses" (Ex 15:1–21; Rev 15:3). "Prayer of Moses" (Ps 90).

MOTH
Mt 6:19 where *m* and rust destroy,

MOTHER (GRANDMOTHER MOTHER-IN-LAW MOTHER'S)
Ge 2:24 and *m* and be united to his wife,
3:20 because she would become the *m*
Ex 20:12 "Honor your father and your *m,*
Lev 20: 9 " 'If anyone curses his father or *m,*
Dt 5:16 "Honor your father and your *m,*
21:18 who does not obey his father and *m*
27:16 who dishonors his father or his *m."*
Jdg 5: 7 arose a *m* in Israel.
1Sa 2:19 Each year his *m* made him a little
Ps 113: 9 as a happy *m* of children.
Pr 10: 1 but a foolish son grief to his *m.*
23:22 do not despise your *m*
23:25 May your father and *m* be glad;
29:15 a child left to himself disgraces his *m.*
30:17 that scorns obedience to a *m,*
31: 1 an oracle his *m* taught him:
Isa 49:15 "Can a *m* forget the baby
66:13 As a *m* comforts her child,
Jer 20:17 with my *m* as my grave,
Mic 7: 6 a daughter rises up against her *m,*
Mt 10:35 a daughter against her *m,*
10:37 or *m* more than me is not worthy
12:48 He replied to him, "Who is my *m,*
15: 4 'Honor your father and *m'*
19: 5 and *m* and be united to his wife,
19:19 honor your father and *m,'*
Mk 7:10 'Honor your father and your *m,'* and,
10:19 honor your father and *m.' "*
Lk 11:27 "Blessed is the *m* who gave you
12:53 daughter and daughter against *m,*
18:20 honor your father and *m.' "*
Jn 19:27 to the disciple, "Here is your *m."*
Gal 4:26 is above is free, and she is our *m.*
Eph 5:31 and *m* and be united to his wife,
6: 2 "Honor your father and *m"*–
1Th 2: 7 like a *m* caring for her little
2Ti 1: 5 and in your *m* Eunice and,

MOTHER-IN-LAW (MOTHER)
Ru 2:19 Ruth told her *m* about the one
Mt 10:35 a daughter-in-law against her *m*–

MOTHER'S (MOTHER)
Job 1:21 "Naked I came from my *m* womb,
Pr 1: 8 and do not forsake your *m* teaching
Ecc 5:15 from his *m* womb,
11: 5 the body is formed in a *m* womb,
Jn 3: 4 time into his *m* womb to be born!"

MOTIVE* (MOTIVES)
1Ch 28: 9 and understands every *m*

MOTIVES* (MOTIVE)
Pr 16: 2 but *m* are weighed by the LORD.
1Co 4: 5 will expose the *m* of men's hearts.
Php 1:18 whether from false *m* or true,
1Th 2: 3 spring from error or impure *m,*
Jas 4: 3 because you ask with wrong *m,*

MOUNT (MOUNTAIN MOUNTAINS MOUNTAINTOPS)
Ps 89: 9 when its waves *m* up, you still them
Isa 14:13 enthroned on the *m* of assembly,
Eze 28:14 You were on the holy *m* of God;
Zec 14: 4 stand on the *M* of Olives,

MOUNTAIN (MOUNT)
Ge 22:14 "On the *m* of the LORD it will be
Ex 24:18 And he stayed on the *m* forty days
Dt 5: 4 face to face out of the fire on the *m.*
Job 14:18 "But as a *m* erodes and crumbles
Ps 48: 1 in the city of our God, his holy *m.*
Isa 40: 4 every *m* and hill made low;
Mic 4: 2 let us go up to the *m* of the LORD,
Mt 4: 8 the devil took him to a very high *m*
17:20 say to this *m,* 'Move from here
Mk 9: 2 with him and led them up a high *m,*
Lk 3: 5 every *m* and hill made low.
Jn 4:21 the Father neither on this *m*
2Pe 1:18 were with him on the sacred *m.*

MOUNTAINS (MOUNT)
Ps 36: 6 righteousness is like the mighty *m,*
46: 2 the *m* fall into the heart of the sea,
90: 2 Before the *m* were born
Isa 52: 7 How beautiful on the *m*
54:10 Though the *m* be shaken
55:12 the *m* and hills
Eze 34: 6 My sheep wandered over all the *m*
Mt 24:16 are in Judea flee to the *m.*
Lk 23:30 they will say to the *m,* "Fall on us!"
1Co 13: 2 if I have a faith that can move *m,*
Rev 6:16 They called to the *m* and the rocks,

MOUNTAINTOPS (MOUNT)
Isa 42:11 let them shout from the *m.*

MOURN (MOURNING MOURNS)
Ecc 3: 4 a time to *m* and a time to dance,
Isa 61: 2 to comfort all who *m,*
Mt 5: 4 Blessed are those who *m,*
Ro 12:15 *m* with those who *m.*

MOURNING (MOURN)
Isa 61: 3 instead of *m,*
Jer 31:13 I will turn their *m* into gladness;
Rev 21: 4 There will be no more death or *m*

MOURNS (MOURN)
Zec 12:10 as one *m* for an only child,

MOUTH (MOUTHS)
Nu 22:38 only what God puts in my *m."*
Dt 8: 3 comes from the *m* of the LORD.
18:18 I will put my words in his *m,*
30:14 it is in your *m* and in your heart
Jos 1: 8 of the Law depart from your *m;*
2Ki 4:34 *m* to *m,* eyes to eyes, hands
Ps 10: 7 His *m* is full of curses and lies
17: 3 resolved that my *m* will not sin.
19:14 May the words of my *m*
37:30 *m* of the righteous man utters
40: 3 He put a new song in my *m,*
71: 8 My *m* is filled with your praise,
119:103 sweeter than honey to my *m!*
141: 3 Set a guard over my *m,* O LORD;
Pr 2: 6 and from his *m* come knowledge
4:24 Put away perversity from your *m;*
10:11 The *m* of the righteous is a fountain
10:31 *m* of the righteous brings forth
16:23 A wise man's heart guides his *m,*
26:28 and a flattering *m* works ruin.
27: 2 praise you, and not your own *m;*
Ecc 5: 2 Do not be quick with your *m,*
SS 1: 2 with the kisses of his *m*–
SS 5:16 His *m* is sweetness itself;
Isa 29:13 come near to me with their *m*
40: 5 For the *m* of the LORD has spoken
45:23 my *m* has uttered in all integrity
51:16 I have put my words in your *m*
53: 7 so he did not open his *m.*
55:11 my word that goes out from my *m:*
59:21 *m* will not depart from your *m,*
Eze 3: 2 So I opened my *m,* and he gave me
Mal 2: 7 and from his *m* men should seek
Mt 4: 4 comes from the *m* of God.' "
12:34 overflow of the heart the *m* speaks.
15:11 into a man's *m* does not make him
15:18 out of the *m* come from the heart,
Lk 6:45 overflow of his heart his *m* speaks.
Ro 10: 9 That if you confess with your *m,*
15: 6 and *m* you may glorify the God
1Pe 2:22 and no deceit was found in his *m."*
Rev 1:16 and out of his *m* came a sharp
2:16 them with the sword of my *m.*
3:16 I am about to spit you out of my *m.*
19:15 Out of his *m* comes a sharp sword

MOUTHS (MOUTH)
Ps 78:36 would flatter him with their *m,*
Eze 33:31 With their *m* they express devotion
Ro 3:14 "Their *m* are full of cursing
Eph 4:29 talk come out of your *m,*
Jas 3: 3 bits into the *m* of horses

MOVE (MOVED MOVES)
Dt 19:14 Do not *m* your neighbor's
Pr 23:10 Do not *m* an ancient boundary
Ac 17:28 and *m* and have our being.'
1Co 13: 2 have a faith that can *m* mountains,
15:58 Let nothing *m* you.

MOVED (MOVE)
Ex 35:21 and whose heart *m* him came
2Ch 36:22 the LORD *m* the heart
Ezr 1: 5 everyone whose heart God had *m*
Ps 93: 1 it cannot be *m.*
Jn 11:33 he was deeply *m* in spirit
Col 1:23 not *m* from the hope held out

MOVES (MOVE)
Dt 23:14 For the LORD your God *m* about

MUD (MUDDIED)
Ps 40: 2 out of the *m* and mire;
Isa 57:20 whose waves cast up mire and *m.*
Jn 9: 6 made some *m* with the saliva,
2Pe 2:22 back to her wallowing in the *m."*

MUDDIED (MUD)
Pr 25:26 Like a *m* spring or a polluted well
Eze 32:13 or *m* by the hoofs of cattle.

MULBERRY*
Lk 17: 6 you can say to this *m* tree,

MULTITUDE (MULTITUDES)
Isa 31: 1 who trust in the *m* of their chariots
Jas 5:20 and cover over a *m* of sins.
1Pe 4: 8 love covers over a *m* of sins.
Rev 7: 9 me was a great *m* that no one could
19: 1 of a great *m* in heaven shouting:

MULTITUDES (MULTITUDE)
Ne 9: 6 and the *m* of heaven worship you.
Da 12: 2 *M* who sleep in the dust
Joel 3:14 *M, m* in the valley of decision!

MURDER (MURDERED MURDERER MURDERERS)
Ex 20:13 "You shall not *m.*
Dt 5:17 "You shall not *m.*
Pr 28:17 A man tormented by the guilt of *m*
Mt 5:21 'Do not *m,* and anyone who
15:19 *m,* adultery, sexual immorality,
Ro 1:29 *m,* strife, deceit and malice.
13: 9 "Do not *m,"* "Do not steal,"
Jas 2:11 adultery," also said, "Do not *m."*

MURDERED (MURDER)
Mt 23:31 of those who *m* the prophets.
Ac 7:52 now you have betrayed and *m* him
1Jn 3:12 to the evil one and *m* his brother.

MURDERER (MURDER)
Nu 35:16 he is a *m;* the *m* shall be put
Jn 8:44 He was a *m* from the beginning,
1Jn 3:15 who hates his brother is a *m,*

MURDERERS (MURDER)
1Ti 1: 9 for *m,* for adulterers and perverts,

Rev 21: 8 the *m*, the sexually immoral,
22:15 the sexually immoral, the *m*,

MUSIC* (MUSICAL MUSICIAN MUSICIANS)
Ge 31:27 singing to the *m* of tambourines
Jdg 5: 3 I will make *m* to the LORD,
1Ch 6:31 put in charge of the *m* in the house
6:32 They ministered with *m*
25: 6 fathers for the *m* of the temple
25: 7 and skilled in *m* for the LORD—
Ne 12:27 and with the *m* of cymbals,
Job 21:12 They sing to the *m* of tambourine
Ps 27: 6 and make *m* to the LORD.
33: 2 make *m* to him on the ten-stringed
45: 8 the *m* of the strings makes you glad
57: 7 I will sing and make *m*.
81: 2 Begin the *m*, strike the tambourine,
87: 7 As they make *m* they will sing,
92: 1 and make *m* to your name,
92: 3 to the *m* of the ten-stringed lyre
95: 2 and extol him with *m* and song.
98: 4 burst into jubilant song with *m*;
98: 5 make *m* to the LORD
108: 1 make *m* with all my soul.
144: 9 the ten-stringed lyre I will make *m*
147: 7 make *m* to our God on the harp.
149: 3 make *m* to him with tambourine
Isa 30:32 will be to the *m* of tambourines
La 5:14 young men have stopped their *m*.
Eze 26:13 *m* of your harps will be heard no
Da 3: 5 lyre, harp, pipes and all kinds of *m*,
3: 7 and all kinds of *m*, all the peoples,
3:10 and all kinds of *m* must fall down
3:15 lyre, harp, pipes and all kinds of *m*,
Am 5:23 to the *m* of your harps.
Hab 3:19 For the director of *m*.
Lk 15:25 came near the house, he heard *m*
Eph 5:19 make *m* in your heart to the Lord,
Rev 18:22 The *m* of harpists and musicians,

MUSICAL* (MUSIC)
1Ch 15:16 accompanied by *m* instruments:
23: 5 with the *m* instruments I have
2Ch 7: 6 with the LORD's *m* instruments,
23:13 with *m* instruments were leading
34:12 skilled in playing *m* instruments—
Ne 12:36 with *m* instruments prescribed
Am 6: 5 and improvise on *m* instruments.

MUSICIAN* (MUSIC)
1Ch 6:33 Heman, the *m*, the son of Joel,

MUSICIANS* (MUSIC)
1Ki 10:12 to make harps and lyres for the *m*.
1Ch 9:33 Those who were *m*, heads
15:19 The *m* Heman, Asaph
2Ch 5:12 All the Levites who were *m*—
9:11 to make harps and lyres for the *m*.
35:15 The *m*, the descendants of Asaph,
Ps 68:25 are the singers, after them the *m*;
Rev 18:22 The music of harpists and *m*,

MUSTARD
Mt 13:31 kingdom of heaven is like a *m* seed,
17:20 you have faith as small as a *m* seed,
Mk 4:31 It is like a *m* seed, which is

MUTILATORS*
Php 3: 2 those men who do evil, those *m*

MUTUAL* (MUTUALLY)
Ro 14:19 leads to peace and to *m* edification.
1Co 7: 5 by *m* consent and for a time,

MUTUALLY* (MUTUAL)
Ro 1:12 and I may be *m* encouraged

MUZZLE*
Dt 25: 4 Do not *m* an ox while it is treading
Ps 39: 1 I will put a *m* on my mouth
1Co 9: 9 "Do not *m* an ox while it is
1Ti 5:18 "Do not *m* the ox while it is

MYRRH
Ps 45: 8 All your robes are fragrant with *m*
SS 1:13 My lover is to me a sachet of *m*
Mt 2:11 of gold and of incense and of *m*.
Mk 15:23 offered him wine mixed with *m*,
Jn 19:39 Nicodemus brought a mixture of *m*
Rev 18:13 of incense, *m* and frankincense,

MYSTERIES* (MYSTERY)
Job 11: 7 "Can you fathom the *m* of God?
Da 2:28 a God in heaven who reveals *m*.
2:29 of *m* showed you what is going
2:47 Lord of kings and a revealer of *m*,
1Co 13: 2 can fathom all *m* and all knowledge
14: 2 he utters *m* with his spirit.

MYSTERY* (MYSTERIES)
Da 2:18 God of heaven concerning this *m*,
2:19 the night the *m* was revealed
2:27 to the king the *m* he has asked
2:30 this *m* has been revealed to me,
2:47 for you were able to reveal this *m*."
4: 9 and no *m* is too difficult for you.
Ro 11:25 you to be ignorant of this *m*,
16:25 to the revelation of the *m* hidden
1Co 15:51 I tell you a *m*: We will not all sleep,
Eph 1: 9 to us the *m* of his will according
3: 3 the *m* made known to me
3: 4 insight into the *m* of Christ,
3: 6 This *m* is that through the gospel
3: 9 the administration of this *m*,
5:32 This is a profound *m*—
6:19 I will fearlessly make known the *m*
Col 1:26 the *m* that has been kept hidden
1:27 the glorious riches of this *m*,
2: 2 in order that they may know the *m*
4: 3 so that we may proclaim the *m*
1Ti 3:16 the *m* of godliness is great:
Rev 1:20 *m* of the seven stars that you saw
10: 7 the *m* of God will be accomplished,
17: 5 written on her forehead: M
17: 7 explain to you the *m* of the woman

MYTHS*
1Ti 1: 4 nor to devote themselves to *m*
4: 7 Have nothing to do with godless *m*
2Ti 4: 4 from the truth and turn aside to *m*.
Tit 1:14 will pay no attention to Jewish *m*

NAAMAN
Aramean general whose leprosy was cleansed by Elisha (2Ki 5).

NABAL
Wealthy Carmelite the LORD killed for refusing to help David (1Sa 25). David married Abigail, his widow (1Sa 25:39–42).

NABOTH*
Jezreelite killed by Jezebel for his vineyard (1Ki 21). Ahab's family destroyed for this (1Ki 21:17–24; 2Ki 9:21–37).

NADAB
1. Firstborn of Aaron (Ex 6:23); killed with Abihu for offering unauthorized fire (Lev 10; Nu 3:4).
2. Son of Jeroboam I; king of Israel (1Ki 15:25–32).

NAHUM
Prophet against Nineveh (Na 1:1).

NAIL* (NAILING)
Jn 20:25 "Unless I see the *n* marks

NAILING* (NAIL)
Ac 2:23 him to death by *n* him to the cross.
Col 2:14 he took it away, *n* it to the cross.

NAIVE
Ro 16:18 they deceive the minds of *n* people.

NAKED
Ge 2:25 The man and his wife were both *n*,
Job 1:21 *N* I came from my mother's womb,
Isa 58: 7 when you see the *n*, to clothe him,
2Co 5: 3 are clothed, we will not be found *n*.

NAME (NAMES)
Ge 2:19 man to see what he would *n* them;
4:26 to call on the *n* of the LORD.
11: 4 so that we may make a *n*
12: 2 I will make your *n* great,
32:29 Jacob said, "Please tell me your *n*."
Ex 3:15 This is my *n* forever, the *n*
20: 7 "You shall not misuse the *n*
34:14 for the LORD, whose *n* is Jealous,
Lev 24:11 Israelite woman blasphemed the *N*
Dt 5:11 "You shall not misuse the *n*
12:11 choose as a dwelling for his *N*—
18: 5 minister in the LORD's *n* always.
25: 6 carry on the *n* of the dead brother
28:58 this glorious and awesome *n*—
Jos 7: 9 do for your own great *n*?"
Jdg 13:17 "What is your *n*, so that we may
1Sa 12:22 of his great *n* the LORD will not
2Sa 6: 2 which is called by the *N*, the name
7: 9 Now I will make your *n* great,
1Ki 5: 5 will build the temple for my *N*.'
8:29 you said, 'My *N* shall be there,'
1Ch 17: 8 I will make your *n* like the names
2Ch 7:14 my people, who are called by my *n*,
Ne 9:10 You made a *n* for yourself,
Ps 8: 1 how majestic is your *n*
9:10 Those who know your *n* will trust
20: 7 in the *n* of the LORD our God.
29: 2 to the LORD the glory due his *n*;
34: 3 let us exalt his *n* together.
44:20 If we had forgotten the *n*
66: 2 Sing the glory of his *n*;
68: 4 Sing to God, sing praise to his *n*,
79: 9 for the glory of your *n*;
96: 8 to the LORD the glory due his *n*;
103: 1 my inmost being, praise his holy *n*.
115: 1 but to your *n* be the glory,
138: 2 your *n* and your word.
145: 1 I will praise your *n* for ever
147: 4 and calls them each by *n*.
Pr 3: 4 you will win favor and a good *n*
18:10 *n* of the LORD is a strong tower;
22: 1 A good *n* is more desirable
30: 4 What is his *n*, and the *n* of his son?
Ecc 7: 1 A good *n* is better
SS 1: 3 your *n* is like perfume poured out.
Isa 12: 4 thanks to the LORD, call on his *n*;
26: 8 your *n* and renown
40:26 and calls them each by *n*.
42: 8 "I am the LORD; that is my *n*!
56: 5 I will give them an everlasting *n*
57:15 who lives forever, whose *n* is holy:
63:14 to make for yourself a glorious *n*.
Jer 14: 7 do something for the sake of your *n*
15:16 for I bear your *n*,
Eze 20: 9 of my *n* I did what would keep it
20:14 of my *n* I did what would keep it
20:22 of my *n* I did what would keep it
Da 12: 1 everyone whose *n* is found written
Hos 12: 5 the LORD is his *n* of renown!
Joel 2:32 on the *n* of the LORD will be saved
Mic 5: 4 in the majesty of the *n*
Zep 3: 9 call on the *n* of the LORD
Zec 6:12 is the man whose *n* is the Branch,
14: 9 one LORD, and his *n* the only *n*.
Mal 1: 6 O priests, who show contempt for my *n*.
Mt 1:21 and you are to give him the *n* Jesus,
6: 9 hallowed be your *n*,
18:20 or three come together in my *n*,
24: 5 For many will come in my *n*,
28:19 them in the *n* of the Father
Mk 9:41 gives you a cup of water in my *n*
Lk 11: 2 hallowed be your *n*,
Jn 10: 3 He calls his own sheep by *n*
14:13 I will do whatever you ask in my *n*,
16:24 asked for anything in my *n*.
Ac 2:21 on the *n* of the Lord will be saved.'
4:12 for there is no other *n*
Ro 10:13 "Everyone who calls on the *n*
Php 2: 9 him the *n* that is above every *n*,
2:10 at the *n* of Jesus every knee should
Col 3:17 do it all in the *n* of the Lord Jesus,
Heb 1: 4 as the *n* he has inherited is superior
Jas 5:14 him with oil in the *n* of the Lord.
1Jn 5:13 believe in the *n* of the Son of God
Rev 2:17 stone with a new *n* written on it,
3: 5 I will never blot out his *n*
3:12 I will also write on him my new *n*.
19:13 and his *n* is the Word of God.
20:15 If anyone's *n* was not found written

NAMES (NAME)
Ex 28: 9 engrave on them the *n* of the sons
Lk 10:20 but rejoice that your *n* are written
Php 4: 3 whose *n* are in the book of life.
Heb 12:23 whose *n* are written in heaven.
Rev 21:27 but only those whose *n* are written

NAOMI
Wife of Elimelech, mother-in-law of Ruth (Ru 1:2, 4). Left Bethlehem for Moab during famine (Ru 1:1). Returned a widow, with Ruth (Ru 1:6–22). Advised Ruth to seek marriage with Boaz (Ru 2:17–3:4). Cared for Ruth's son Obed (Ru 4:13–17).

NAPHTALI

Son of Jacob by Bilhah (Ge 30:8; 35:25; 1Ch 2:2). Tribe of blessed (Ge 49:21; Dt 33:23), numbered (Nu 1:43; 26:50), allotted land (Jos 19:32–39; Eze 48:3), failed to fully possess (Jdg 1:33), supported Deborah (Jdg 4:10; 5:18), David (1Ch 12:34), 12,000 from (Rev 7:6).

NARROW

Mt 7:13 "Enter through the *n* gate.
7:14 and *n* the road that leads to life,

NATHAN

Prophet and chronicler of Israel's history (1Ch 29:29; 2Ch 9:29). Announced the Davidic covenant (2Sa 7; 1Ch 17). Denounced David's sin with Bathsheba (2Sa 12). Supported Solomon (1Ki 1).

NATHANAEL*

Apostle (Jn 1:45–49; 21:2). Probably also called Bartholomew (Mt 10:3).

NATION (NATIONS)

Ge 12: 2 "I will make you into a great *n*
Ex 19: 6 a kingdom of priests and a holy *n*.'
Dt 4: 7 What other *n* is so great
Jos 5: 8 And after the whole *n* had been
2Sa 7:23 one *n* on earth that God went out
Ps 33:12 Blessed is the *n* whose God is
Pr 11:14 For lack of guidance a *n* falls,
14:34 Righteousness exalts a *n*,
Isa 2: 4 *N* will not take up sword
26: 2 that the righteous *n* may enter,
60:12 For the *n* or kingdom that will not
65: 1 To a *n* that did not call on my name
66: 8 a *n* be brought forth in a moment?
Mic 4: 3 *N* will not take up sword
Mt 24: 7 *N* will rise against *n*,
Mk 13: 8 *N* will rise against *n*,
1Pe 2: 9 a royal priesthood, a holy *n*,
Rev 5: 9 and language and people and *n*.
7: 9 from every *n*, tribe, people
14: 6 to every *n*, tribe, language

NATIONS (NATION)

Ge 17: 4 You will be the father of many *n*.
18:18 and all *n* on earth will be blessed
Ex 19: 5 of all *n* you will be my treasured
Lev 20:26 apart from the *n* to be my own.
Dt 7: 1 drives out before you many *n*–
15: 6 You will rule over many *n*
Jdg 3: 1 These are the *n* the LORD left
2Ch 20: 6 rule over all the kingdoms of the *n*.
Ne 1: 8 I will scatter you among the *n*,
Ps 2: 1 Why do the *n* conspire
2: 8 I will make the *n* your inheritance,
9: 5 You have rebuked the *n*
22:28 and he rules over the *n*.
46:10 I will be exalted among the *n*,
47: 8 God reigns over the *n*;
66: 7 his eyes watch the *n*–
67: 2 your salvation among all *n*.
68:30 Scatter the *n* who delight in war.
72:17 All *n* will be blessed through him,
96: 3 Declare his glory among the *n*,
99: 2 he is exalted over all the *n*.
106: 35 but they mingled with the *n*
110: 6 He will judge the *n*, heaping up
113: 4 The LORD is exalted over all the *n*
Isa 2: 2 and all *n* will stream to it.
11:10 the *n* will rally to him,
12: 4 among the *n* what he has done,
40:15 Surely the *n* are like a drop
42: 1 and he will bring justice to the *n*.
51: 4 justice will become a light to the *n*.
52:15 so will he sprinkle many *n*,
56: 7 a house of prayer for all *n*."
60: 3 *N* will come to your light,
66:18 and gather all *n* and tongues,
Jer 1: 5 you as a prophet to the *n*."
3:17 and all *n* will gather in Jerusalem
31:10 "Hear the word of the LORD, O *n*;
33: 9 and honor before all *n*
46:28 I completely destroy all the *n*
Eze 22: 4 you an object of scorn to the *n*
34:13 I will bring them out from the *n*
36:23 *n* will know that I am the LORD,
37:22 and they will never again be two *n*
39:21 I will display my glory among the *n*
Hos 7: 8 "Ephraim mixes with the *n*;
Joel 2:17 a byword among the *n*.
3: 2 I will gather all *n*
Am 9:12 and all the *n* that bear my name,"
Zep 3: 8 I have decided to assemble the *n*,
Hag 2: 7 and the desired of all *n* will come,
Zec 8:13 an object of cursing among the *n*,
8:23 *n* will take firm hold of one Jew
9:10 He will proclaim peace to the *n*.
14: 2 I will gather all the *n* to Jerusalem
Mt 12:18 he will proclaim justice to the *n*.
24: 9 and you will be hated by all *n*
24:14 whole world as a testimony to all *n*,
25:32 All the *n* will be gathered
28:19 and make disciples of all *n*,
Mk 11:17 a house of prayer for all *n*'?
Ac 4:25 " 'Why do the *n* rage
Ro 15:12 who will arise to rule over the *n*;
Gal 3: 8 All *n* will be blessed through you."
1Ti 3:16 was preached among the *n*,
Rev 15: 4 All *n* will come
21:24 The *n* will walk by its light,
22: 2 are for the healing of the *n*.

NATURAL (NATURE)

Ro 6:19 you are weak in your *n* selves.
1Co 15:44 If there is a *n* body, there is

NATURE (NATURAL)

Ro 1:20 his eternal power and divine *n*–
7:18 lives in me, that is, in my sinful *n*.
8: 4 do not live according to the sinful *n*
8: 5 to the sinful *n* have their minds set
8: 8 by the sinful *n* cannot please God.
13:14 to gratify the desires of the sinful *n*.
Gal 5:13 freedom to indulge the sinful *n*;
5:19 The acts of the sinful *n* are obvious:
5:24 Jesus have crucified the sinful *n*
Php 2: 6 Who, being in very *n* God,
Col 3: 5 whatever belongs to your earthly *n*
2Pe 1: 4 you may participate in the divine *n*

NAZARENE* (NAZARETH)

Mt 2:23 prophets: "He will be called a *N*."
Mk 14:67 "You also were with that *N*, Jesus,"
16: 6 "You are looking for Jesus the *N*,
Ac 24: 5 He is a ringleader of the *N* sect and

NAZARETH (NAZARENE)

Mt 4:13 Leaving *N*, he went and lived
Lk 4:16 to *N*, where he had been brought
Jn 1:46 "*N*! Can anything good come

NAZIRITE

Nu 6: 2 of separation to the LORD as a *N*,
Jdg 13: 7 because the boy will be a *N* of God

NEBO

Dt 34: 1 Then Moses climbed Mount *N*

NEBUCHADNEZZAR

Babylonian king. Subdued and exiled Judah (2Ki 24–25; 2Ch 36; Jer 39). Dreams interpreted by Daniel (Da 2; 4). Worshiped God (Da 3:28–29; 4:34–37).

NECESSARY*

Ac 1:21 Therefore it is *n* to choose one
Ro 13: 5 it is *n* to submit to the authorities,
2Co 9: 5 I thought it *n* to urge the brothers
Php 1:24 it is more *n* for you that I remain
2:25 But I think it is *n* to send back
Heb 8: 3 and so it was *n* for this one
9:16 it is *n* to prove the death
9:23 It was *n*, then, for the copies

NECK (STIFF-NECKED)

Pr 3:22 an ornament to grace your *n*.
6:21 fasten them around your *n*.
Mt 18: 6 a large millstone hung around his *n*

NECO

Pharaoh who killed Josiah (2Ki 23:29–30; 2Ch 35:20–22), deposed Jehoahaz (2Ki 23:33–35; 2Ch 36:3–4).

NEED (NEEDS NEEDY)

1Ki 8:59 Israel according to each day's *n*,
Ps 79: 8 for we are in desperate *n*.
116: 6 when I was in great *n*, he saved me.
142: 6 for I am in desperate *n*;
Mt 6: 8 for your Father knows what you *n*
Lk 15:14 country, and he began to be in *n*.
Ac 2:45 they gave to anyone as he had *n*.
Ro 12:13 with God's people who are in *n*.
1Co 12:21 say to the hand, "I don't *n* you!"
Eph 4:28 something to share with those in *n*.
1Ti 5: 3 to those widows who are really in *n*
Heb 4:16 grace to help us in our time of *n*.
1Jn 3:17 sees his brother in *n* but has no pity

NEEDLE

Mt 19:24 go through the eye of a *n*

NEEDS (NEED)

Isa 58:11 he will satisfy your *n*
Php 2:25 sent to take care of my *n*.
4:19 God will meet all your *n* according
Jas 2:16 does nothing about his physical *n*,

NEEDY (NEED)

Dt 15:11 toward the poor and *n* in your land.
1Sa 2: 8 and lifts the *n* from the ash heap;
Ps 35:10 and *n* from those who rob them."
69:33 The LORD hears the *n*
72:12 he will deliver the *n* who cry out,
140: 12 and upholds the cause of the *n*.
Pr 14:21 blessed is he who is kind to the *n*.
14:31 to the *n* honors God.
22:22 and do not crush the *n* in court,
31: 9 defend the rights of the poor and *n*
31:20 and extends her hands to the *n*.
Mt 6: 2 "So when you give to the *n*,

NEGLECT* (NEGLECTED)

Dt 12:19 Be careful not to *n* the Levites
14:27 And do not *n* the Levites living
Ezr 4:22 Be careful not to *n* this matter.
Ne 10:39 We will not *n* the house of our God
Est 6:10 Do not *n* anything you have
Ps 119: 16 I will not *n* your word.
Lk 11:42 you *n* justice and the love of God.
Ac 6: 2 for us to *n* the ministry of the word
1Ti 4:14 Do not *n* your gift, which was

NEGLECTED (NEGLECT)

Mt 23:23 But you have *n* the more important

NEHEMIAH

Cupbearer of Artaxerxes (Ne 2:1); governor of Israel (Ne 8:9). Returned to Jerusalem to rebuild walls (Ne 2–6). With Ezra, reestablished worship (Ne 8). Prayer confessing nation's sin (Ne 9). Dedicated wall (Ne 12).

NEIGHBOR (NEIGHBOR'S)

Ex 20:16 give false testimony against your *n*.
20:17 or anything that belongs to your *n*
Lev 19:13 Do not defraud your *n* or rob him.
19:17 Rebuke your *n* frankly
19:18 but love your *n* as yourself.
Ps 15: 3 who does his *n* no wrong
Pr 3:29 Do not plot harm against your *n*,
11:12 who lacks judgment derides his *n*,
14:21 He who despises his *n* sins,
16:29 A violent man entices his *n*
24:28 against your *n* without cause,
25:18 gives false testimony against his *n*.
27:10 better a *n* nearby than a brother far
27:14 If a man loudly blesses his *n*
29: 5 Whoever flatters his *n*
Jer 31:34 No longer will a man teach his *n*,
Zec 8:17 do not plot evil against your *n*,
Mt 5:43 Love your *n* and hate your enemy.'
19:19 and 'love your *n* as yourself.' "
Mk 12:31 The second is this: 'Love your *n*
Lk 10:27 and, 'Love your *n* as yourself.'
10:29 who is my *n*?" In reply Jesus said:
Ro 13: 9 "Love your *n* as yourself."
13:10 Love does no harm to its *n*.
15: 2 Each of us should please his *n*
Gal 5:14 "Love your *n* as yourself."
Eph 4:25 and speak truthfully to his *n*,
Heb 8:11 No longer will a man teach his *n*,
Jas 2: 8 "Love your *n* as yourself,"

NEIGHBOR'S (NEIGHBOR)

Ex 20:17 You shall not covet your *n* wife,
Dt 5:21 not set your desire on your *n* house
19:14 not move your *n* boundary stone
27:17 who moves his *n* boundary stone."
Pr 25:17 Seldom set foot in your *n* house–

NESTS

Mt 8:20 and birds of the air have *n*,

NET (NETS)

Pr 1:17 How useless to spread a *n*
Hab 1:15 he catches them in his *n*,
Mt 13:47 of heaven is like a *n* that was let
Jn 21: 6 "Throw your *n* on the right side

NETS (NET)

Ps 141: 10 Let the wicked fall into their own *n*

Mt 4:20 At once they left their *n*
Lk 5: 4 and let down the *n* for a catch."

NEVER-FAILING*
Am 5:24 righteousness like a *n* stream!

NEW
Ps 40: 3 He put a *n* song in my mouth,
98: 1 Sing to the LORD a *n* song,
Ecc 1: 9 there is nothing *n* under the sun.
Isa 42: 9 and *n* things I declare;
62: 2 you will be called by a *n* name
65:17 *n* heavens and a *n* earth.
66:22 "As the *n* heavens and the *n* earth
Jer 31:31 "when I will make a *n* covenant
La 3:23 They are *n* every morning;
Eze 11:19 undivided heart and put a *n* spirit
18:31 and get a *n* heart and a *n* spirit.
36:26 give you a *n* heart and put a *n* spirit
Zep 3: 5 and every *n* day he does not fail,
Mt 9:17 Neither do men pour *n* wine
Mk 16:17 they will speak in *n* tongues;
Lk 5:39 after drinking old wine wants the *n*
22:20 "This cup is the *n* covenant
Jn 13:34 "A *n* commandment I give you:
Ac 5:20 the full message of this *n* life."
Ro 6: 4 the Father, we too may live a *n* life.
1Co 5: 7 old yeast that you may be a *n* batch
11:25 "This cup is the *n* covenant
2Co 3: 6 as ministers of a *n* covenant—
5:17 he is a *n* creation; the old has gone,
Gal 6:15 what counts is a *n* creation.
Eph 4:23 to be made *n* in the attitude
4:24 and to put on the *n* self, created
Col 3:10 and have put on the *n* self,
Heb 8: 8 when I will make a *n* covenant
9:15 is the mediator of a *n* covenant,
10:20 by a *n* and living way opened for us
12:24 Jesus the mediator of a *n* covenant,
1Pe 1: 3 great mercy he has given us *n* birth
2Pe 3:13 to a *n* heaven and a *n* earth,
1Jn 2: 8 Yet I am writing you a *n* command;
Rev 2:17 stone with a *n* name written on it,
3:12 the *n* Jerusalem, which is coming
21: 1 I saw a *n* heaven and a *n* earth,

NEWBORN (BEAR)
1Pe 2: 2 Like *n* babies, crave pure spiritual

NEWS
2Ki 7: 9 This is a day of good *n*
Ps 112: 7 He will have no fear of bad *n;*
Pr 15:30 good *n* gives health to the bones.
25:25 is good *n* from a distant land.
Isa 52: 7 the feet of those who bring good *n,*
61: 1 me to preach good *n* to the poor.
Na 1:15 the feet of one who brings good *n,*
Mt 4:23 preaching the good *n*
9:35 preaching the good *n*
11: 5 the good *n* is preached to the poor.
Mk 1:15 Repent and believe the good *n!"*
16:15 preach the good *n* to all creation.
Lk 1:19 and to tell you this good *n.*
2:10 I bring you good *n*
3:18 and preached the good *n* to them.
4:43 "I must preach the good *n*
8: 1 proclaiming the good *n*
16:16 the good *n* of the kingdom
Ac 5:42 proclaiming the good *n* that Jesus
10:36 telling the good *n* of peace
14: 7 continued to preach the good *n.*
14:21 They preached the good *n*
17:18 preaching the good *n* about Jesus
Ro 10:15 feet of those who bring good *n!"*

NICODEMUS*
Pharisee who visted Jesus at night (Jn 3). Argued fair treatment of Jesus (Jn 7:50–52). With Joseph, prepared Jesus for burial (Jn 19:38–42).

NIGHT (NIGHTS NIGHTTIME)
Ge 1: 5 and the darkness he called *"n."*
1:16 and the lesser light to govern the *n.*
Ex 13:21 and by *n* in a pillar of fire
14:24 During the last watch of the *n.*
Dt 28:66 filled with dread both *n* and day,
Jos 1: 8 and *n,* so that you may be careful
Job 35:10 who gives songs in the *n,*
Ps 1: 2 on his law he meditates day and *n.*
19: 2 *n* after *n* they display knowledge.
42: 8 at *n* his song is with me—
63: 6 of you through the watches of the *n*
77: 6 I remembered my songs in the *n.*
Ps 90: 4 or like a watch in the *n.*
91: 5 You will not fear the terror of *n,*
119:148 through the watches of the *n,*
121: 6 nor the moon by *n.*
136: 9 the moon and stars to govern the *n;*
Pr 31:18 and her lamp does not go out at *n.*
Isa 21:11 Watchman, what is left of the *n?"*
58:10 and your *n* will become like
Jer 33:20 and my covenant with the *n,*
Lk 2: 8 watch over their flocks at *n.*
6:12 and spent the *n* praying to God.
Jn 3: 2 He came to Jesus at *n* and said,
9: 4 *N* is coming, when no one can work
1Th 5: 2 Lord will come like a thief in the *n.*
5: 5 We do not belong to the *n*
Rev 21:25 for there will be no *n* there.

NIGHTS (NIGHT)
Jnh 1:17 the fish three days and three *n.*
Mt 4: 2 After fasting forty days and forty *n*
12:40 three *n* in the belly of a huge fish,
2Co 6: 5 in hard work, sleepless *n*

NIGHTTIME* (NIGHT)
Zec 14: 7 or *n*—a day known to the LORD.

NIMROD
Ge 10: 9 "Like *N,* a mighty hunter

NINEVEH
Jnh 1: 2 "Go to the great city of *N*
Na 1: 1 An oracle concerning *N.*
Mt 12:41 The men of *N* will stand up

NOAH
Righteous man (Eze 14:14, 20) called to build ark (Ge 6–8; Heb 11:7; 1Pe 3:20; 2Pe 2:5). God's covenant with (Ge 9:1–17). Drunkenness of (Ge 9:18–23). Blessed sons, cursed Canaan (Ge 9:24–27).

NOBLE
Ru 3:11 you are a woman of *n* character.
Ps 45: 1 My heart is stirred by a *n* theme
Pr 12: 4 of *n* character is her husband's
31:10 A wife of *n* character who can find?
31:29 "Many women do *n* things,
Isa 32: 8 But the *n* man makes *n* plans,
Lk 8:15 good soil stands for those with a *n*
Ro 9:21 of clay some pottery for *n* purposes
Php 4: 8 whatever is *n,* whatever is right,
2Ti 2:20 some are for *n* purposes

NOSTRILS
Ge 2: 7 and breathed into his *n* the breath
Ex 15: 8 By the blast of your *n*
Ps 18:15 at the blast of breath from your *n.*

NOTE
Ac 4:13 and they took *n* that these men had
Php 3:17 take *n* of those who live according

NOTHING
2Sa 24:24 offerings that cost me *n."*
Ne 9:21 in the desert; they lacked *n,*
Ps 73:25 earth has *n* I desire besides you
Jer 32:17 *N* is too hard for you
Jn 15: 5 apart from me you can do *n.*

NOURISH
Pr 10:21 The lips of the righteous *n* many,

NULLIFY
Mt 15: 6 Thus you *n* the word of God
Ro 3:31 Do we, then, *n* the law by this faith

OATH
Ex 33: 1 up to the land I promised on *o*
Nu 30: 2 or takes an *o* to obligate himself
Dt 6:18 promised on *o* to your forefathers,
7: 8 and kept the *o* he swore
29:12 you this day and sealing with an *o,*
Ps 95:11 So I declared on *o* in my anger,
119:106 I have taken an *o* and confirmed it,
132: 11 The LORD swore an *o* to David,
Ecc 8: 2 because you took an *o* before God.
Mt 5:33 'Do not break your *o,* but keep
Heb 7:20 And it was not without an *o!*

OBADIAH
1. Believer who sheltered 100 prophets from Jezebel (1Ki 18:1–16).
2. Prophet against Edom (Ob 1).

OBEDIENCE* (OBEY)
Ge 49:10 and the *o* of the nations is his.
Jdg 2:17 of *o* to the LORD's commands.
1Ch 21:19 So David went up in *o*
2Ch 31:21 in *o* to the law and the commands,
Pr 30:17 that scorns *o* to a mother,
Lk 23:56 Sabbath in *o* to the commandment.
Ac 21:24 but that you yourself are living in *o*
Ro 1: 5 to the *o* that comes from faith.
5:19 also through the *o* of the one man
6:16 to *o,* which leads to righteousness?
16:19 Everyone has heard about your *o,*
2Co 9:13 for the *o* that accompanies your
10: 6 once your *o* is complete.
Phm :21 Confident of your *o,* I write to you,
Heb 5: 8 he learned *o* from what he suffered
1Pe 1: 2 for *o* to Jesus Christ and sprinkling
2Jn : 6 that we walk in *o* to his commands.

OBEDIENT* (OBEY)
Dt 30:17 heart turns away and you are not *o,*
Isa 1:19 If you are willing and *o,*
Lk 2:51 with them and was *o* to them.
Ac 6: 7 of priests became *o* to the faith.
2Co 2: 9 if you would stand the test and be *o*
7:15 he remembers that you were all *o,*
10: 5 thought to make it *o* to Christ.
Php 2: 8 and became *o* to death—
Tit 3: 1 to be *o,* to be ready
1Pe 1:14 As *o* children, do not conform

OBEY (OBEDIENCE OBEDIENT OBEYED OBEYING OBEYS)
Ex 12:24 *"O* these instructions as a lasting
19: 5 Now if you *o* me fully and keep my
24: 7 the LORD has said; we will *o."*
Lev 18: 4 You must *o* my laws and be careful
25:18 and be careful to *o* my laws,
Nu 15:40 remember to *o* all my commands
Dt 5:27 We will listen and *o."*
6: 3 careful to *o* so that it may go well
6:24 us to *o* all these decrees
11:13 if you faithfully *o* the commands I
12:28 to *o* all these regulations I am
13: 4 Keep his commands and *o* him;
21:18 son who does not *o* his father
28: 1 If you fully *o* the LORD your God
28:15 if you do not *o* the LORD your
30: 2 and *o* him with all your heart
30:10 if you *o* the LORD your God
30:14 and in your heart so you may *o* it.
32:46 children to *o* carefully all the words
Jos 1: 7 to *o* all the law my servant Moses
22: 5 in all his ways, to *o* his commands,
24:24 the LORD our God and *o* him."
1Sa 15:22 To *o* is better than sacrifice,
1Ki 8:61 by his decrees and *o* his commands
2Ki 17:13 that I commanded your fathers to *o*
2Ch 34:31 and to *o* the words of the covenant
Ne 1: 5 who love him and *o* his commands,
Ps 103: 18 and remember to *o* his precepts.
103: 20 who *o* his word.
119: 17 I will *o* your word.
119: 34 and *o* it with all my heart.
119: 57 I have promised to *o* your words.
119: 67 but now I *o* your word.
119:100 for I *o* your precepts.
119:129 therefore I *o* them.
119:167 I *o* your statutes,
Pr 5:13 I would not *o* my teachers
Jer 7:23 I gave them this command: *O* me,
11: 4 *'O* me and do everything I
11: 7 and again, saying, *"O* me."
42: 6 we will *o* the LORD our God,
Da 9: 4 who love him and *o* his commands,
Mt 8:27 the winds and the waves *o* him!"
19:17 to enter life, *o* the commandments
28:20 to *o* everything I have commanded
Lk 11:28 hear the word of God and *o* it."
Jn 14:15 you will *o* what I command.
14:23 loves me, he will *o* my teaching.
14:24 not love me will not *o* my teaching.
15:10 If you *o* my commands, you will
Ac 5:29 "We must *o* God rather than men!
5:32 given to those who *o* him."
Ro 2:13 it is those who *o* the law who will
6:12 body so that you *o* its evil desires.
6:16 slaves to the one whom you *o*—
6:16 yourselves to someone to *o* him
15:18 in leading the Gentiles to *o* God
16:26 nations might believe and *o* him—
Gal 5: 3 obligated to *o* the whole law.
Eph 6: 1 *o* your parents in the Lord,

Eph 6: 5 *o* your earthly masters with respect
Col 3:20 *o* your parents in everything,
3:22 *o* your earthly masters
2Th 3:14 anyone does not *o* our instruction
1Ti 3: 4 and see that his children *o* him
Heb 5: 9 eternal salvation for all who *o* him
13:17 *O* your leaders and submit
1Pe 4:17 for those who do not *o* the gospel
1Jn 3:24 Those who *o* his commands live
5: 3 love for God: to *o* his commands.
Rev 12:17 those who *o* God's commandments
14:12 the saints who *o* God's

OBEYED (OBEY)
Ge 22:18 blessed, because you have *o* me."
Jos 1:17 we fully *o* Moses, so we will obey
Ps 119: 4 that are to be fully *o*.
Da 9:10 we have not *o* the LORD our God
Jnh 3: 3 Jonah *o* the word of the LORD
Mic 5:15 the nations that have not *o* me."
Jn 15:10 as I have *o* my Father's commands
15:20 If they *o* my teaching, they will
17: 6 and they have *o* your word.
Ac 7:53 through angels but have not *o* it."
Ro 6:17 you wholeheartedly *o* the form
Php 2:12 as you have always *o*—not only
Heb 11: 8 *o* and went, even though he did not
1Pe 3: 6 who *o* Abraham and called him her

OBEYING (OBEY)
1Sa 15:22 as in *o* the voice of the LORD?
Ps 119: 5 steadfast in *o* your decrees!
Gal 5: 7 and kept you from *o* the truth?
1Pe 1:22 purified yourselves by *o* the truth

OBEYS (OBEY)
Lev 18: 5 for the man who *o* them will live
Pr 19:16 He who *o* instructions guards his
Eze 20:11 for the man who *o* them will live
Jn 14:21 has my commands and *o* them,
Ro 2:27 and yet *o* the law will condemn you
1Jn 2: 5 if anyone *o* his word, God's love is

OBLIGATED (OBLIGATION)
Ro 1:14 I am *o* both to Greeks
Gal 5: 3 himself be circumcised that he is *o*

OBLIGATION (OBLIGATED)
Ro 8:12 Therefore, brothers, we have an *o*

OBSCENITY*
Eph 5: 4 Nor should there be *o*, foolish talk

OBSCURES*
Job 42: 3 'Who is this that *o* my counsel

OBSERVE (OBSERVING)
Ex 31:13 'You must *o* my Sabbaths.
Lev 25: 2 the land itself must *o* a sabbath
Dt 4: 6 *O* them carefully, for this will show
5:12 "*O* the Sabbath day
8: 6 *O* the commands of the LORD
11:22 If you carefully *o* all these
26:16 carefully *o* them with all your heart
Ps 37:37 the blameless, *o* the upright;

OBSERVING (OBSERVE)
Ro 3:27 principle? On that of *o* the law?
Gal 2:16 a man is not justified by *o* the law,
3: 2 you receive the Spirit by *o* the law,
3:10 All who rely on *o* the law are

OBSOLETE
Heb 8:13 he has made the first one *o*;

OBSTACLE* (OBSTACLES)
Ro 14:13 or *o* in your brother's way.

OBSTACLES (OBSTACLE)
Ro 16:17 put *o* in your way that are contrary

OBSTINATE
Isa 65: 2 hands to an *o* people,
Ro 10:21 to a disobedient and *o* people."

OBTAIN (OBTAINED OBTAINS)
Ro 11: 7 sought so earnestly it did not *o*,
2Ti 2:10 they too may *o* the salvation that

OBTAINED (OBTAIN)
Ro 9:30 not pursue righteousness, have *o* it,
Php 3:12 Not that I have already *o* all this,
Heb 9:12 having *o* eternal redemption.

OBTAINS* (OBTAIN)
Pr 12: 2 A good man *o* favor

OBVIOUS*
Mt 6:18 so that it will not be *o*
Gal 5:19 The acts of the sinful nature are *o*:
1Ti 5:24 The sins of some men are *o*,
5:25 In the same way, good deeds are *o*,

OCCASIONS
Eph 6:18 in the Spirit on all *o* with all kinds

OFFENDED (OFFENSE)
Pr 18:19 An *o* brother is more unyielding

OFFENDERS* (OFFENSE)
1Co 6: 9 nor homosexual *o* nor thieves

OFFENSE (OFFENDED OFFENDERS OFFENSES OFFENSIVE)
Pr 17: 9 over an *o* promotes love,
19:11 it is to his glory to overlook an *o*.
Gal 5:11 In that case the *o* of the cross has

OFFENSES (OFFENSE)
Isa 44:22 swept away your *o* like a cloud,
59:12 For our *o* are many in your sight,
Eze 18:30 Repent! Turn away from all your *o*;
33:10 "Our *o* and sins weigh us down,

OFFENSIVE (OFFENSE)
Ps 139: 24 See if there is any *o* way in me,

OFFER (OFFERED OFFERING OFFERINGS OFFERS)
Ps 4: 5 *O* right sacrifices
Ro 6:13 Do not *o* the parts of your body
12: 1 to *o* your bodies as living sacrifices,
Heb 9:25 he enter heaven to *o* himself again
13:15 therefore, let us continually *o*

OFFERED (OFFER)
Isa 50: 6 I *o* my back to those who beat me,
1Co 9:13 share in what is *o* on the altar?
10:20 of pagans are *o* to demons,
Heb 7:27 once for all when he *o* himself.
9:14 the eternal Spirit *o* himself
11: 4 By faith Abel *o* God a better
11:17 when God tested him, *o* Isaac
Jas 5:15 prayer *o* in faith will make the sick

OFFERING (OFFER)
Ge 4: 3 of the soil as an *o* to the LORD.
22: 2 a burnt *o* on one of the mountains I
22: 8 provide the lamb for the burnt *o*,
Ex 29:24 before the LORD as a wave *o*.
29:40 quarter of a hin of wine as a drink *o*.
Lev 1: 3 If the *o* is a burnt *o* from the herd,
2: 4 " 'If you bring a grain *o* baked
3: 1 " 'If someone's *o* is a fellowship *o*,
4: 3 a sin *o* for the sin he has committed
5:15 It is a guilt *o*.
7:37 ordination *o* and the fellowship *o*,
9:24 and consumed the burnt *o*
22:18 to fulfill a vow or as a freewill *o*,
22:21 a special vow or as a freewill *o*,
1Sa 13: 9 And Saul offered up the burnt *o*.
1Ch 21:26 from heaven on the altar of burnt *o*.
2Ch 7: 1 and consumed the burnt *o*
Ps 40: 6 Sacrifice and *o* you did not desire,
116: 17 I will sacrifice a thank *o* to you
Isa 53:10 the LORD makes his life a guilt *o*,
Mt 5:23 if you are *o* your gift at the altar
Ro 8: 3 likeness of sinful man to be a sin *o*.
Eph 5: 2 as a fragrant *o* and sacrifice to God.
Php 2:17 I am being poured out like a drink *o*
4:18 are a fragrant *o*, an acceptable
2Ti 4: 6 being poured out like a drink *o*,
Heb 10: 5 "Sacrifice and *o* you did not desire,
1Pe 2: 5 *o* spiritual sacrifices acceptable

OFFERINGS (OFFER)
1Sa 15:22 Does the LORD delight in burnt *o*
2Ch 35: 7 and goats for the Passover *o*,
Isa 1:13 Stop bringing meaningless *o*!
Hos 6: 6 of God rather than burnt *o*.
Mal 3: 8 do we rob you?' "In tithes and *o*.
Mk 12:33 is more important than all burnt *o*
Heb 10: 8 First he said, "Sacrifices and *o*,

OFFERS (OFFER)
Heb 10:11 and again he *o* the same sacrifices,

OFFICER (OFFICIALS)
2Ti 2: 4 wants to please his commanding *o*.

OFFICIALS (OFFICER)
Ex 5:21 a stench to Pharaoh and his *o*.
Pr 17:26 or to flog *o* for their integrity.
Pr 29:12 all his *o* become wicked.

OFFSPRING
Ge 3:15 and between your *o* and hers;
12: 7 "To your *o* I will give this land."
13:16 I will make your *o* like the dust
26: 4 and through your *o* all nations
28:14 blessed through you and your *o*.
Ex 13: 2 The first *o* of every womb
Ru 4:12 Through the *o* the LORD gives
Isa 44: 3 I will pour out my Spirit on your *o*,
53:10 he will see his *o* and prolong his
Ac 3:25 'Through your *o* all peoples
17:28 own poets have said, 'We are his *o*.'
17:29 "Therefore since we are God's *o*,
Ro 4:18 said to him, "So shall your *o* be."
9: 8 who are regarded as Abraham's *o*.

OG
Nu 21:33 *O* king of Bashan and his whole
Ps 136: 20 and *O* king of Bashan—

OIL
Ex 29: 7 Take the anointing *o* and anoint
30:25 It will be the sacred anointing *o*.
Dt 14:23 tithe of your grain, new wine and *o*,
1Sa 10: 1 Then Samuel took a flask of *o*
16:13 So Samuel took the horn of *o*
1Ki 17:16 and the jug of *o* did not run dry,
2Ki 4: 6 Then the *o* stopped flowing.
Ps 23: 5 You anoint my head with *o*;
45: 7 by anointing you with the *o* of joy.
104: 15 *o* to make his face shine,
133: 2 It is like precious *o* poured
Pr 21:17 loves wine and *o* will never be
Isa 1: 6 or soothed with *o*.
61: 3 the *o* of gladness
Mt 25: 3 but did not take any *o* with them.
Heb 1: 9 by anointing you with the *o* of joy."

OLIVE (OLIVES)
Ge 8:11 beak was a freshly plucked *o* leaf!
Jdg 9: 8 said to the *o* tree, 'Be our king.'
Jer 11:16 LORD called you a thriving *o* tree
Zec 4: 3 Also there are two *o* trees by it,
Ro 11:17 and you, though a wild *o* shoot,
11:24 of an *o* tree that is wild by nature,
Rev 11: 4 These are the two *o* trees

OLIVES (OLIVE)
Zec 14: 4 stand on the Mount of *O*,
Mt 24: 3 sitting on the Mount of *O*,
Jas 3:12 a fig tree bear *o*, or a grapevine bear

OMEGA*
Rev 1: 8 "I am the Alpha and the *O*,"
21: 6 I am the Alpha and the *O*,
22:13 I am the Alpha and the *O*,

OMIT*
Jer 26: 2 I command you; do not *o* a word.

OMRI
King of Israel (1Ki 16:21–26).

ONESIMUS*
Col 4: 9 He is coming with *O*, our faithful
Phm :10 I appeal to you for my son *O*,

ONESIPHORUS*
2Ti 1:16 mercy to the household of *O*,
4:19 Aquila and the household of *O*.

ONIONS*
Nu 11: 5 melons, leeks, *o* and garlic.

ONYX
Ex 28: 9 "Take two *o* stones and engrave
28:20 in the fourth row a chrysolite, an *o*

OPENHANDED* (HAND)
Dt 15: 8 Rather be *o* and freely lend him
15:11 you to be *o* toward your brothers

OPINIONS*
1Ki 18:21 will you waver between two *o*?
Pr 18: 2 but delights in airing his own *o*.

OPPONENTS (OPPOSE)
Pr 18:18 and keeps strong *o* apart.

OPPORTUNE (OPPORTUNITY)
Lk 4:13 he left him until an *o* time.

OPPORTUNITY* (OPPORTUNE)
1Sa 18:21 "Now you have a second *o*
Jer 46:17 he has missed his *o*.'
Mt 26:16 watched for an *o* to hand him over.

Mk 14:11 So he watched for an *o* to hand him
Lk 22: 6 and watched for an *o* to hand Jesus
Ac 25:16 and has had an *o* to defend himself
Ro 7: 8 seizing the *o* afforded
7:11 seizing the *o* afforded
1Co 16:12 but he will go when he has the *o*.
2Co 5:12 are giving you an *o* to take pride
11:12 from under those who want an *o*
Gal 6:10 as we have *o*, let us do good
Eph 5:16 making the most of every *o*,
Php 4:10 but you had no *o* to show it.
Col 4: 5 make the most of every *o*.
1Ti 5:14 to give the enemy no *o* for slander.
Heb 11:15 they would have had *o* to return.

OPPOSE (OPPONENTS OPPOSED OPPOSES OPPOSING OPPOSITION)
Ex 23:22 and will *o* those who *o* you.
1Sa 2:10 those who *o* the LORD will be
Job 23:13 he stands alone, and who can *o* him
Ac 11:17 I to think that I could *o* God?"
2Ti 2:25 Those who *o* him he must gently
Tit 1: 9 doctrine and refute those who *o* it.
2: 8 so that those who *o* you may be

OPPOSED (OPPOSE)
Gal 2:11 to Antioch, I *o* him to his face,
3:21 therefore, *o* to the promises of God

OPPOSES (OPPOSE)
Jas 4: 6 "God *o* the proud
1Pe 5: 5 because, "God *o* the proud

OPPOSING (OPPOSE)
1Ti 6:20 the *o* ideas of what is falsely called

OPPOSITION (OPPOSE)
Heb 12: 3 Consider him who endured such *o*

OPPRESS (OPPRESSED OPPRESSES OPPRESSION OPPRESSOR)
Ex 1:11 masters over them to *o* them
22:21 "Do not mistreat an alien or *o* him,
Isa 3: 5 People will *o* each other—
Eze 22:29 they *o* the poor and needy
Da 7:25 the Most High and *o* his saints
Am 5:12 You *o* the righteous and take bribes
Zec 7:10 Do not *o* the widow
Mal 3: 5 who *o* the widows

OPPRESSED (OPPRESS)
Jdg 2:18 as they groaned under those who *o*
Ps 9: 9 The LORD is a refuge for the *o*,
82: 3 the rights of the poor and *o*.
146: 7 He upholds the cause of the *o*
Pr 16:19 in spirit and among the *o*
31: 5 and deprive all the *o* of their rights.
Isa 1:17 encourage the *o*.
53: 7 He was *o* and afflicted,
58:10 and satisfy the needs of the *o*,
Zec 10: 2 *o* for lack of a shepherd.
Lk 4:18 to release the *o*,

OPPRESSES (OPPRESS)
Pr 14:31 He who *o* the poor shows contempt
22:16 He who *o* the poor
Eze 18:12 He *o* the poor and needy.

OPPRESSION (OPPRESS)
Ps 12: 5 "Because of the *o* of the weak
72:14 He will rescue them from *o*
119:134 Redeem me from the *o* of men,
Isa 53: 8 By *o* and judgment he was taken
58: 9 "If you do away with the yoke of *o*,

OPPRESSOR (OPPRESS)
Ps 72: 4 he will crush the *o*.
Isa 51:13 For where is the wrath of the *o*?
Jer 22: 3 hand of his *o* the one who has been

ORDAINED
Ps 8: 2 you have *o* praise
111: 9 he *o* his covenant forever—
139: 16 All the days *o* for me
Eze 28:14 for so I *o* you.
Hab 1:12 you have *o* them to punish.
Mt 21:16 you have *o* praise'?"

ORDER (ORDERLY ORDERS)
Nu 9:23 They obeyed the LORD's *o*,
Ps 110: 4 in the *o* of Melchizedek."
Heb 5:10 priest in the *o* of Melchizedek.
9:10 until the time of the new *o*.
Rev 21: 4 for the old *o* of things has passed

ORDERLY (ORDER)
1Co 14:40 done in a fitting and *o* way.

Col 2: 5 and delight to see how *o* you are

ORDERS (ORDER)
Mk 1:27 He even gives *o* to evil spirits
3:12 But he gave them strict *o* not
9: 9 Jesus gave them *o* not

ORDINARY
Ac 4:13 that they were unschooled, *o* men,

ORGIES*
Ro 13:13 not in *o* and drunkenness,
Gal 5:21 drunkenness, *o*, and the like.
1Pe 4: 3 *o*, carousing and detestable

ORIGIN (ORIGINATE ORIGINS)
2Pe 1:21 For prophecy never had its *o*

ORIGINATE* (ORIGIN)
1Co 14:36 Did the word of God *o* with you?

ORIGINS* (ORIGIN)
Mic 5: 2 whose *o* are from of old,

ORNAMENT* (ORNAMENTED)
Pr 3:22 an *o* to grace your neck.
25:12 of gold or an *o* of fine gold

ORNAMENTED (ORNAMENT)
Ge 37: 3 and he made a richly *o* robe for him

ORPHAN* (ORPHANS)
Ex 22:22 advantage of a widow or an *o*.

ORPHANS (ORPHAN)
Jn 14:18 will not leave you as *o*; I will come
Jas 1:27 to look after *o* and widows

OTHNIEL
Nephew of Caleb (Jos 15:15–19; Jdg 1:12–15). Judge who freed Israel from Aram (Jdg 3:7–11).

OUTBURSTS*
2Co 12:20 jealousy, *o* of anger, factions,

OUTCOME
Heb 13: 7 Consider the *o* of their way of life
1Pe 4:17 what will the *o* be for those who do

OUTNUMBER
Ps 139: 18 they would *o* the grains of sand.

OUTSIDERS*
Col 4: 5 wise in the way you act toward *o*;
1Th 4:12 daily life may win the respect of *o*
1Ti 3: 7 also have a good reputation with *o*,

OUTSTANDING
SS 5:10 *o* among ten thousand.
Ro 13: 8 no debt remain *o*,

OUTSTRETCHED
Ex 6: 6 and will redeem you with an *o* arm
Dt 4:34 by a mighty hand and an *o* arm,
5:15 with a mighty hand and an *o* arm.
1Ki 8:42 your mighty hand and your *o* arm
Ps 136: 12 with a mighty hand and *o* arm;
Jer 27: 5 and *o* arm I made the earth
32:17 by your great power and *o* arm.
Eze 20:33 an *o* arm and with outpoured wrath

OUTWEIGHS (WEIGH)
2Co 4:17 an eternal glory that far *o* them all.

OUTWIT*
2Co 2:11 in order that Satan might not *o* us.

OVERAWED* (AWE)
Ps 49:16 Do not be *o* when a man grows rich

OVERBEARING*
Tit 1: 7 not *o*, not quick-tempered,

OVERCAME (OVERCOME)
Rev 3:21 as I *o* and sat down with my Father
12:11 They *o* him

OVERCOME (OVERCAME OVERCOMES)
Mt 16:18 and the gates of Hades will not *o* it.
Mk 9:24 I do believe; help me *o* my unbelief
Lk 10:19 to *o* all the power of the enemy;
Jn 16:33 But take heart! I have *o* the world."
Ro 12:21 Do not be *o* by evil, but *o* evil
2Pe 2:20 and are again entangled in it and *o*,
1Jn 2:13 because you have *o* the evil one.
4: 4 are from God and have *o* them,
5: 4 is the victory that has *o* the world,
Rev 17:14 but the Lamb will *o* them

OVERCOMES* (OVERCOME)
1Jn 5: 4 born of God *o* the world.

1Jn 5: 5 Who is it that *o* the world?
Rev 2: 7 To him who *o*, I will give the right
2:11 He who *o* will not be hurt at all
2:17 To him who *o*, I will give some
2:26 To him who *o* and does my will
3: 5 He who *o* will, like them, be
3:12 Him who *o* I will make a pillar
3:21 To him who *o*, I will give the right
21: 7 He who *o* will inherit all this,

OVERFLOW (OVERFLOWING OVERFLOWS)
Ps 65:11 and your carts *o* with abundance.
119:171 May my lips *o* with praise,
La 1:16 and my eyes *o* with tears.
Mt 12:34 out of the *o* of the heart the mouth
Lk 6:45 out of the *o* of his heart his mouth
Ro 5:15 Jesus Christ, *o* to the many! Again,
15:13 so that you may *o* with hope
2Co 4:15 to *o* to the glory of God.
1Th 3:12 *o* for each other and for everyone

OVERFLOWING (OVERFLOW)
Pr 3:10 then your barns will be filled to *o*,
2Co 8: 2 their *o* joy and their extreme
9:12 *o* in many expressions of thanks
Col 2: 7 as you were taught, and *o*

OVERFLOWS* (OVERFLOW)
Ps 23: 5 my cup *o*.
2Co 1: 5 also through Christ our comfort *o*.

OVERJOYED* (JOY)
Da 6:23 The king was *o* and gave orders
Mt 2:10 they saw the star, they were *o*.
Jn 20:20 The disciples were *o*
Ac 12:14 she was so *o* she ran back
1Pe 4:13 so that you may be *o*

OVERLOOK
Pr 19:11 it is to his glory to *o* an offense.

OVERSEER* (OVERSEERS)
Pr 6: 7 no *o* or ruler,
1Ti 3: 1 anyone sets his heart on being an *o*,
3: 2 Now the *o* must be above reproach,
Tit 1: 7 Since an *o* is entrusted
1Pe 2:25 returned to the Shepherd and *O*

OVERSEERS* (OVERSEER)
Ac 20:28 the Holy Spirit has made you *o*.
Php 1: 1 together with the *o* and deacons:
1Pe 5: 2 as *o*—not because you must,

OVERSHADOW* (OVERSHADOWING)
Lk 1:35 power of the Most High will *o* you.

OVERSHADOWING (OVERSHADOW)
Ex 25:20 wings spread upward, *o* the cover
Heb 9: 5 the glory, *o* the atonement cover.

OVERTHROW (OVERTHROWS)
2Th 2: 8 whom the Lord Jesus will *o*

OVERTHROWS (OVERTHROW)
Pr 13: 6 but wickedness *o* the sinner.
Isa 44:25 who *o* the learning of the wise

OVERWHELMED (OVERWHELMING)
2Sa 22: 5 the torrents of destruction *o* me.
1Ki 10: 5 temple of the LORD, she was *o*.
Ps 38: 4 My guilt has *o* me
65: 3 When we were *o* by sins,
Mt 26:38 "My soul is *o* with sorrow
Mk 7:37 People were *o* with amazement.
9:15 they were *o* with wonder
2Co 2: 7 so that he will not be *o*

OVERWHELMING (OVERWHELMED)
Pr 27: 4 Anger is cruel and fury *o*,
Isa 10:22 *o* and righteous.
28:15 When an *o* scourge sweeps by,

OWE
Ro 13: 7 If you *o* taxes, pay taxes; if revenue
Phm :19 to mention that you *o* me your very

OWNER'S (OWNERSHIP)
Isa 1: 3 the donkey his *o* manger,

OWNERSHIP* (OWNER'S)
2Co 1:22 He anointed us, set his seal of *o*

OX (OXEN)
Dt 25: 4 Do not muzzle an *o*
Isa 11: 7 and the lion will eat straw like the *o*
Eze 1:10 and on the left the face of an *o*;
Lk 13:15 of you on the Sabbath untie his *o*
1Co 9: 9 "Do not muzzle an *o*

1Ti 5:18 'Do not muzzle the *o*
Rev 4: 7 second was like an *o,* the third had

OXEN (OX)
1Ki 19:20 Elisha then left his *o* and ran
Lk 14:19 'I have just bought five yoke of *o,*

PAGAN (PAGANS)
Mt 18:17 as you would a *p* or a tax collector.
Lk 12:30 For the *p* world runs

PAGANS* (PAGAN)
Isa 2: 6 and clasp hands with *p.*
Mt 5:47 Do not even *p* do that? Be perfect,
6: 7 do not keep on babbling like *p,*
6:32 For the *p* run after all these things,
1Co 5: 1 that does not occur even among *p:*
10:20 but the sacrifices of *p* are offered
12: 2 You know that when you were *p,*
1Pe 2:12 such good lives among the *p* that,
4: 3 in the past doing what *p* choose
3Jn : 7 receiving no help from the *p.*

PAID (PAY)
Isa 40: 2 that her sin has been *p* for,
Zec 11:12 So they *p* me thirty pieces of silver.

PAIN (PAINFUL PAINS)
Ge 3:16 with *p* you will give birth
6: 6 and his heart was filled with *p.*
Job 6:10 my joy in unrelenting *p*–
33:19 may be chastened on a bed of *p*
Jer 4:19 I writhe in *p.*
15:18 Why is my *p* unending
Mt 4:24 suffering severe *p,*
Jn 16:21 woman giving birth to a child has *p*
1Pe 2:19 up under the *p* of unjust suffering
Rev 21: 4 or mourning or crying or *p,*

PAINFUL (PAIN)
Ge 3:17 through *p* toil you will eat of it
5:29 and *p* toil of our hands caused
Job 6:25 How *p* are honest words!
Eze 28:24 neighbors who are *p* briers
2Co 2: 1 I would not make another *p* visit
Heb 12:11 seems pleasant at the time, but *p.*
1Pe 4:12 at the *p* trial you are suffering,

PAINS (PAIN)
Ge 3:16 'I will greatly increase your *p*
Mt 24: 8 these are the beginning of birth *p.*
Ro 8:22 as in the *p* of childbirth right up
Gal 4:19 again in the *p* of childbirth
1Th 5: 3 as labor *p* on a pregnant woman,

PAIRS
Ge 7: 8 *P* of clean and unclean animals,

PALACE (PALACES)
2Sa 7: 2 'Here I am, living in a *p* of cedar,
Jer 22: 6 is what the LORD says about the *p*
22:13 'Woe to him who builds his *p*

PALACES (PALACE)
Mt 11: 8 wear fine clothes are in kings' *p.*
Lk 7:25 and indulge in luxury are in *p.*

PALE
Isa 29:22 no longer will their faces grow *p.*
Jer 30: 6 every face turned deathly *p?*
Da 10: 8 my face turned deathly *p*
Rev 6: 8 and there before me was a *p* horse!

PALM (PALMS)
Jn 12:13 They took *p* branches and went out
Rev 7: 9 and were holding *p* branches

PALMS (PALM)
Isa 49:16 you on the *p* of my hands;

PAMPERS*
Pr 29:21 If a man *p* his servant from youth,

PANIC
Dt 20: 3 or give way to *p* before them.
1Sa 14:15 It was a *p* sent by God.
Eze 7: 7 there is *p,* not joy,
Zec 14:13 by the LORD with great *p.*

PANTS
Ps 42: 1 As the deer *p* for streams of water,

PARABLES
See also JESUS: PARABLES
Ps 78: 2 I will open my mouth in *p,*
Mt 13:35 'I will open my mouth in *p,*
Lk 8:10 but to others I speak in *p,* so that,

PARADISE*
Lk 23:43 today you will be with me in *p.*"
2Co 12: 4 God knows—was caught up to *p.*
Rev 2: 7 of life, which is in the *p* of God.

PARALYTIC
Mt 9: 2 Some men brought to him a *p,*
Mk 2: 3 bringing to him a *p,* carried by four
Ac 9:33 a *p* who had been bedridden

PARCHED
Ps 143: 6 my soul thirsts for you like a *p* land.

PARCHMENTS*
2Ti 4:13 and my scrolls, especially the *p.*

PARDON* (PARDONED PARDONS)
2Ch 30:18 *p* everyone who sets his heart
Job 7:21 Why do you not *p* my offenses
Isa 55: 7 and to our God, for he will freely *p.*
Joel 3:21 I will *p.*"

PARDONED* (PARDON)
Nu 14:19 as you have *p* them from the time
Joel 3:21 bloodguilt, which I have not *p,*

PARDONS* (PARDON)
Mic 7:18 who *p* sin and forgives

PARENTS
Pr 17: 6 and *p* are the pride of their children
19:14 wealth are inherited from *p,*
Mt 10:21 children will rebel against their *p*
Lk 18:29 left home or wife or brothers or *p*
21:16 You will be betrayed even by *p,* brothers,
Jn 9: 3 Neither this man nor his *p* sinned,"
Ro 1:30 they disobey their *p;* they are
2Co 12:14 for their *p,* but *p* for their children.
Eph 6: 1 Children, obey your *p* in the Lord,
Col 3:20 obey your *p* in everything,
1Ti 5: 4 repaying their *p* and grandparents,
2Ti 3: 2 disobedient to their *p,* ungrateful,

PARTAKE*
1Co 10:17 for we all *p* of the one loaf.

PARTIAL* (PARTIALITY)
Pr 18: 5 It is not good to be *p* to the wicked

PARTIALITY (PARTIAL)
Lev 19:15 do not show *p* to the poor
Dt 1:17 Do not show *p* in judging;
10:17 who shows no *p* and accepts no
16:19 Do not pervert justice or show *p.*
2Ch 19: 7 our God there is no injustice or *p*
Job 32:21 I will show *p* to no one,
34:19 who shows no *p* to princes
Pr 24:23 To show *p* in judging is not good:
Mal 2: 9 have shown *p* in matters of the law
Lk 20:21 and that you do not show *p*
1Ti 5:21 keep these instructions without *p,*

PARTICIPANTS (PARTICIPATE)
1Co 10:20 you to be *p* with demons.

PARTICIPATE (PARTICIPANTS PARTICIPATION)
1Pe 4:13 rejoice that you *p* in the sufferings
2Pe 1: 4 that through them you may *p*

PARTICIPATION (PARTICIPATE)
1Co 10:16 is not the bread that we break a *p*

PARTNER (PARTNERS PARTNERSHIP)
Pr 2:17 who has left the *p* of her youth
Mal 2:14 though she is your *p,* the wife
1Pe 3: 7 them with respect as the weaker *p*

PARTNERS (PARTNER)
Eph 5: 7 Therefore do not be *p* with them.

PARTNERSHIP* (PARTNER)
Php 1: 5 because of your *p* in the gospel

PASS (PASSED PASSER-BY PASSING)
Ex 12:13 and when I see the blood, I will *p*
33:19 goodness to *p* in front of you,
1Ki 9: 8 all who *p* by will be appalled
19:11 for the LORD is about to *p* by."
Ps 90:10 for they quickly *p,* and we fly away.
105: 19 till what he foretold came to *p,*
Isa 31: 5 he will '*p* over' it and will rescue it
43: 2 When you *p* through the waters,
62:10 *P* through, *p* through the gates!
Jer 22: 8 'People from many nations will *p*
La 1:12 to you, all you who *p* by?
Da 7:14 dominion that will not *p* away,
Am 5:17 for I will *p* through your midst,"
Mt 24:34 will certainly not *p* away
24:35 Heaven and earth will *p* away,
Mk 13:31 Heaven and earth will *p* away,
Lk 21:33 Heaven and earth will *p* away,
1Co 13: 8 there is knowledge, it will *p* away.
Jas 1:10 he will *p* away like a wild flower.
1Jn 2:17 The world and its desires *p* away,

PASSED (PASS)
Ge 15:17 a blazing torch appeared and *p*
Ex 33:22 you with my hand until I have *p* by.
2Ch 21:20 He *p* away, to no one's regret,
Ps 57: 1 wings until the disaster has *p.*
Lk 10:32 saw him, *p* by on the other side.
1Co 15: 3 For what I received I *p* on to you
Heb 11:29 By faith the people *p*

PASSER-BY* (PASS)
Pr 26:10 is he who hires a fool or any *p.*
26:17 is a *p* who meddles

PASSING (PASS)
1Co 7:31 world in its present form is *p* away.
1Jn 2: 8 because the darkness is *p*

PASSION* (PASSIONATE PASSIONS)
Hos 7: 6 Their *p* smolders all night;
1Co 7: 9 better to marry than to burn with *p.*

PASSIONATE* (PASSION)
1Th 4: 5 not in *p* lust like the heathen,

PASSIONS* (PASSION)
Ro 7: 5 the sinful *p* aroused
Gal 5:24 crucified the sinful nature with its *p*
Tit 2:12 to ungodliness and worldly *p,*
3: 3 and enslaved by all kinds of *p*

PASSOVER
Ex 12:11 Eat it in haste; it is the LORD's *P.*
Nu 9: 2 Have the Israelites celebrate the *P*
Dt 16: 1 celebrate the *P* of the LORD your
Jos 5:10 the Israelites celebrated the *P.*
2Ki 23:21 "Celebrate the *P* to the LORD
Ezr 6:19 the exiles celebrated the *P.*
Mk 14:12 customary to sacrifice the *P* lamb,
Lk 22: 1 called the *P,* was approaching,
1Co 5: 7 our *P* lamb, has been sacrificed.
Heb 11:28 he kept the *P* and the sprinkling

PAST
Isa 43:18 do not dwell on the *p.*
65:16 For the *p* troubles will be forgotten
Ro 15: 4 in the *p* was written to teach us,
16:25 the mystery hidden for long ages *p,*
Eph 3: 9 which for ages *p* was kept hidden
Heb 1: 1 In the *p* God spoke

PASTORS*
Eph 4:11 and some to be *p* and teachers,

PASTURE (PASTURES)
Ps 37: 3 dwell in the land and enjoy safe *p.*
95: 7 and we are the people of his *p,*
100: 3 we are his people, the sheep of his *p*
Jer 50: 7 against the LORD, their true *p,*
Eze 34:13 I will *p* them on the mountains
Zec 11: 4 "*P* the flock marked for slaughter.
Jn 10: 9 come in and go out, and find *p.*

PASTURES (PASTURE)
Ps 23: 2 He makes me lie down in green *p,*

PATCH
Jer 10: 5 Like a scarecrow in a melon *p,*
Mt 9:16 No one sews a *p* of unshrunk cloth

PATH (PATHS)
Ps 16:11 known to me the *p* of life;
27:11 lead me in a straight *p*
119: 32 I run in the *p* of your commands,
119:105 and a light for my *p.*
Pr 2: 9 and fair—every good *p.*
12:28 along that *p* is immortality.
15:10 awaits him who leaves the *p;*
15:19 the *p* of the upright is a highway.
15:24 The *p* of life leads upward
21:16 from the *p* of understanding
Isa 26: 7 The *p* of the righteous is level;
Jer 31: 9 on a level *p* where they will not
Mt 13: 4 fell along the *p,* and the birds came
Lk 1:79 to guide our feet into the *p* of peace
2Co 6: 3 no stumbling block in anyone's *p,*

PATHS (PATH)
Ps 23: 3 He guides me in *p* of righteousness

Ps 25: 4 teach me your *p;*
Pr 2:13 who leave the straight *p*
3: 6 and he will make your *p* straight.
4:11 and lead you along straight *p.*
4:26 Make level *p* for your feet
5:21 and he examines all his *p.*
8:20 along the *p* of justice,
22: 5 In the *p* of the wicked lie thorns
Isa 2: 3 so that we may walk in his *p."*
Jer 6:16 ask for the ancient *p,*
Mic 4: 2 so that we may walk in his *p."*
Mt 3: 3 make straight *p* for him.' "
Ac 2:28 to me the *p* of life;
Ro 11:33 and his *p* beyond tracing out!
Heb 12:13 "Make level *p* for your feet,"

PATIENCE* (PATIENT)
Pr 19:11 A man's wisdom gives him *p;*
25:15 Through *p* a ruler can be persuaded
Ecc 7: 8 and *p* is better than pride.
Isa 7:13 Is it not enough to try the *p* of men?
7:13 Will you try the *p* of my God also?
Ro 2: 4 and *p,* not realizing that God's
9:22 bore with great *p* the objects
2Co 6: 6 understanding, *p* and kindness;
Gal 5:22 joy, peace, *p,* kindness, goodness,
Col 1:11 may have great endurance and *p,*
3:12 humility, gentleness and *p.*
1Ti 1:16 Jesus might display his unlimited *p*
2Ti 3:10 my purpose, faith, *p,* love,
4: 2 with great *p* and careful instruction
Heb 6:12 *p* inherit what has been promised.
Jas 5:10 as an example of *p* in the face
2Pe 3:15 that our Lord's *p* means salvation,

PATIENT* (PATIENCE PATIENTLY)
Ne 9:30 For many years you were *p*
Job 6:11 What prospects, that I should be *p?*
Pr 14:29 A *p* man has great understanding,
15:18 but a *p* man calms a quarrel.
16:32 Better a *p* man than a warrior,
Mt 18:26 'Be *p* with me,' he begged,
18:29 'Be *p* with me, and I will pay you
Ro 12:12 Be joyful in hope, *p* in affliction,
1Co 13: 4 Love is *p,* love is kind.
2Co 1: 6 produces in you *p* endurance
Eph 4: 2 humble and gentle; be *p,*
1Th 5:14 help the weak, be *p* with everyone.
Jas 5: 7 Be *p,* then, brothers,
5: 7 and how *p* he is for the autumn
5: 8 You too, be *p* and stand firm,
2Pe 3: 9 He is *p* with you, not wanting
Rev 1: 9 *p* endurance that are ours in Jesus,
13:10 This calls for *p* endurance
14:12 This calls for *p* endurance

PATIENTLY* (PATIENT)
Ps 37: 7 still before the LORD and wait *p*
40: 1 I waited *p* for the LORD;
Isa 38:13 I waited *p* till dawn,
Hab 3:16 Yet I will wait *p* for the day
Ac 26: 3 I beg you to listen to me *p.*
Ro 8:25 we do not yet have, we wait for it *p.*
Heb 6:15 after waiting *p,* Abraham received
1Pe 3:20 ago when God waited *p* in the days
Rev 3:10 kept my command to endure *p,*

PATTERN
Ex 25:40 according to the *p* shown you
Ro 5:14 who was a *p* of the one to come.
12: 2 longer to the *p* of this world,
2Ti 1:13 keep as the *p* of sound teaching,
Heb 8: 5 according to the *p* shown you

PAUL

Also called Saul (Ac 13:9). Pharisee from Tarsus (Ac 9:11; Php 3:5). Apostle (Gal 1). At stoning of Stephen (Ac 8:1). Persecuted Church (Ac 9:1–2; Gal 1:13). Vision of Jesus on road to Damascus (Ac 9:4–9; 26:12–18). In Arabia (Gal 1:17). Preached in Damascus; escaped death through the wall in a basket (Ac 9:19–25). In Jerusalem; sent back to Tarsus (Ac 9:26–30).

Brought to Antioch by Barnabas (Ac 11:22–26). First missionary journey to Cyprus and Galatia (Ac 13–14). Stoned at Lystra (Ac 14:19–20). At Jerusalem council (Ac 15). Split with Barnabas over Mark (Ac 15:36–41).

Second missionary journey with Silas (Ac 16–20). Called to Macedonia (Ac 16:6–10). Freed from prison in Philippi (Ac 16:16–40). In Thessalonica (Ac 17:1–9). Speech in Athens (Ac 17:16–33). In Corinth (Ac 18). In Ephesus (Ac 19). Return to Jerusalem (Ac 20). Farewell to Ephesian elders (Ac 20:13–38). Arrival in Jerusalem (Ac 21:1–26). Arrested (Ac 21:27–36). Addressed crowds (Ac 22), Sanhedrin (Ac 23:1–11). Transferred to Caesarea (Ac 23:12–35). Trial before Felix (Ac 24), Festus (Ac 25:1–12). Before Agrippa (Ac 25:13–26:32). Voyage to Rome; shipwreck (Ac 27). Arrival in Rome (Ac 28).

Epistles: Romans, 1 and 2 Corinthians, Galatians, Ephesians, Philippians, Colossians, 1 and 2 Thessalonians, 1 and 2 Timothy, Titus, Philemon.

PAVEMENT
Jn 19:13 as the Stone *P* (which

PAY (PAID PAYMENT PAYS REPAID REPAY REPAYING)
Lev 26:43 They will *p* for their sins
Dt 7:12 If you *p* attention to these laws
Pr 4: 1 *p* attention and gain understanding
4:20 My son, *p* attention to what I say;
5: 1 My son, *p* attention to my wisdom,
6:31 if he is caught, he must *p* sevenfold,
19:19 man must *p* the penalty;
22:17 *P* attention and listen
24:29 I'll *p* that man back for what he did
Eze 40: 4 and *p* attention to everything I am
Zec 11:12 give me my *p;* but if not, keep it."
Mt 20: 2 He agreed to *p* them a denarius
22:16 you *p* no attention to who they are.
22:17 Is it right to *p* taxes to Caesar
Lk 3:14 falsely—be content with your *p."*
19: 8 I will *p* back four times the amount
Ro 13: 6 This is also why you *p* taxes,
2Pe 1:19 you will do well to *p* attention to it,

PAYMENT (PAY)
Ps 49: 8 no *p* is ever enough—
Php 4:18 I have received full *p* and

PAYS (PAY)
Pr 17:13 If a man *p* back evil for good,
1Th 5:15 sure that nobody *p* back wrong

PEACE (PEACEABLE PEACEFUL PEACEMAKERS)
Lev 26: 6 " 'I will grant *p* in the land,
Nu 6:26 and give you *p."* '
25:12 him I am making my covenant of *p*
Dt 20:10 make its people an offer of *p.*
Jdg 3:11 So the land had *p* for forty years,
3:30 and the land had *p* for eighty years.
5:31 Then the land had *p* forty years.
6:24 and called it The LORD is *P.*
8:28 the land enjoyed *p* forty years.
1Sa 7:14 And there was *p* between Israel
2Sa 10:19 they made *p* with the Israelites
1Ki 2:33 may there be the LORD'S *p* forever
22:44 also at *p* with the king of Israel.
2Ki 9:17 come in *p?'* " The horseman rode
1Ch 19:19 they made *p* with David
22: 9 and I will grant Israel *p*
2Ch 14: 1 and in his days the country was at *p*
20:30 kingdom of Jehoshaphat was at *p,*
Job 3:26 I have no *p,* no quietness;
22:21 to God and be at *p* with him;
Ps 29:11 LORD blesses his people with *p.*
34:14 seek *p* and pursue it.
37:11 and enjoy great *p.*
37:37 there is a future for the man of *p.*
85:10 righteousness and *p* kiss each other
119:165 Great *p* have they who love your
120: 7 I am a man of *p;*
122: 6 Pray for the *p* of Jerusalem:
147: 14 He grants *p* to your borders
Pr 12:20 but joy for those who promote *p.*
14:30 A heart at *p* gives life to the body,
16: 7 his enemies live at *p* with him.
17: 1 Better a dry crust with *p* and quiet
Ecc 3: 8 a time for war and a time for *p.*
Isa 9: 6 Everlasting Father, Prince of *P.*
14: 7 All the lands are at rest and at *p;*
26: 3 You will keep in perfect *p*
32:17 The fruit of righteousness will be *p;*
48:18 your *p* would have been like a river,
48:22 "There is no *p,"* says the LORD,
52: 7 who proclaim *p,*
53: 5 punishment that brought us *p* was
54:10 nor my covenant of *p* be removed,"
55:12 and be led forth in *p;*
57: 2 enter into *p;*
Isa 57:19 *P, p,* to those far and near,"
57:21 "There is no *p,"* says my God,
59: 8 The way of *p* they do not know;
Jer 6:14 *'P, p,'* they say,
8:11 *"P, p,"* ... there is no *p.*
30:10 Jacob will again have *p*
46:27 Jacob will again have *p*
Eze 13:10 *"P,"* when there is no *p,*
34:25 " 'I will make a covenant of *p*
37:26 I will make a covenant of *p*
Mic 5: 5 And he will be their *p*
Zec 8:19 Therefore love truth and *p."*
9:10 He will proclaim *p* to the nations.
Mal 2: 5 a covenant of life and *p,*
2: 6 He walked with me in *p*
Mt 10:34 I did not come to bring *p,*
Mk 9:50 and be at *p* with each other."
Lk 1:79 to guide our feet into the path of *p*
2:14 on earth *p* to men on whom his
19:38 *"P* in heaven and glory
Jn 14:27 *P* I leave with you; my *p*
16:33 so that in me you may have *p.*
Ro 1: 7 and *p* to you from God our Father
2:10 and *p* for everyone who does good:
5: 1 we have *p* with God
8: 6 by the Spirit is life and *p;*
12:18 on you, live at *p* with everyone.
14:19 effort to do what leads to *p*
1Co 7:15 God has called us to live in *p.*
14:33 a God of disorder but of *p.*
2Co 13:11 be of one mind, live in *p.*
Gal 5:22 joy, *p,* patience, kindness,
Eph 2:14 he himself is our *p,* who has made
2:15 thus making *p,* and in this one body
2:17 and *p* to those who were near.
6:15 comes from the gospel of *p.*
Php 4: 7 the *p* of God, which transcends all
Col 1:20 by making *p* through his blood,
3:15 Let the *p* of Christ rule
3:15 of one body you were called to *p.*
1Th 5: 3 While people are saying, *"P*
5:13 Live in *p* with each other.
5:23 the God of *p,* sanctify you through
2Th 3:16 the Lord of *p* himself give you *p*
2Ti 2:22 righteousness, faith, love and *p,*
Heb 7: 2 "king of Salem" means "king of *p."*
12:11 *p* for those who have been trained
12:14 effort to live in *p* with all men
13:20 May the God of *p,* who
1Pe 3:11 he must seek *p* and pursue it.
2Pe 3:14 blameless and at *p* with him.
Rev 6: 4 power to take *p* from the earth

PEACEABLE* (PEACE)
Tit 3: 2 to slander no one, to be *p*

PEACEFUL (PEACE)
1Ti 2: 2 that we may live *p* and quiet lives

PEACE-LOVING
Jas 3:17 then *p,* considerate

PEACEMAKERS* (PEACE)
Mt 5: 9 Blessed are the *p,*
Jas 3:18 *P* who sow in peace raise a harvest

PEARL* (PEARLS)
Rev 21:21 each gate made of a single *p.*

PEARLS (PEARL)
Mt 7: 6 do not throw your *p* to pigs.
13:45 like a merchant looking for fine *p.*
1Ti 2: 9 or gold or *p* or expensive clothes,
Rev 21:21 The twelve gates were twelve *p,*

PEDDLE*
2Co 2:17 we do not *p* the word of God

PEG
Jdg 4:21 She drove the *p* through his temple

PEKAH

King of Israel (2Ki 15:25–31; Isa 7:1).

PEKAHIAH*

Son of Menahem; king of Israel (2Ki 15:22–26).

PEN
Ps 45: 1 my tongue is the *p*
Mt 5:18 letter, not the least stroke of a *p,*
Jn 10: 1 who does not enter the sheep *p*

PENETRATES*
Heb 4:12 it *p* even to dividing soul and spirit,

PENNIES* (PENNY)
Lk 12: 6 not five sparrows sold for two *p?*

PENNY* (PENNIES)
Mt 5:26 out until you have paid the last *p.*
10:29 Are not two sparrows sold for a *p?*
Mk 12:42 worth only a fraction of a *p.*
Lk 12:59 out until you have paid the last *p."*

PENTECOST*
Ac 2: 1 of *P* came, they were all together
20:16 if possible, by the day of *P.*
1Co 16: 8 I will stay on at Ephesus until *P,*

PEOPLE (PEOPLES)
Ge 11: 6 as one *p* speaking the same
Ex 5: 1 Let my *p* go,
6: 7 take you as my own *p,*
8:23 between my *p* and your *p.*
15:13 the *p* you have redeemed.
19: 8 The *p* all responded together,
24: 3 Moses went and told the *p*
32: 1 When the *p* saw that Moses
32: 9 they are a stiff-necked *p.*
33:13 this nation is your *p.*
Lev 9: 7 for yourself and the *p:*
16:24 the burnt offering for the *p,*
26:12 and you will be my *p.*
Nu 11:11 burden of all these *p* on
14:11 *p* treat me with contempt?
14:19 forgive the sin of these *p,*
22: 5 A *p* has come out of Egypt
Dt 4: 6 a wise and understanding *p.*
4:20 the *p* of his inheritance,
5:28 what this *p* said to you.
7: 6 a *p* holy to the LORD
26:18 that you are his *p,*
31: 7 you must go with this *p*
31:16 these *p* will soon prostitute
32: 9 the LORD's portion is his *p,*
32:43 atonement for his land and *p.*
33:29 a *p* saved by the LORD?
Jos 1: 6 you will lead this *p*
24:24 the *p* said to Joshua,
Jdg 2: 7 *p* served the LORD throughout
Ru 1:16 Your *p* will be my *p*
1Sa 8: 7 the *p* are saying to you;
12:22 LORD will not reject his *p,*
2Sa 5: 2 will shepherd my *p* Israel
7:10 provide a place for my *p*
1Ki 3: 8 among the *p* you have chosen,
8:30 your *p* Israel when they pray
8:56 has given rest to his *p*
18:39 when all the *p* saw this,
2Ki 23: 3 all the *p* pledged themselves
1Ch 17:21 to redeem *p* for himself
29:17 how willingly your *p* who are
2Ch 2:11 Because the LORD loves his *p,*
7: 5 *p* dedicated the temple
7:14 if my *p,* who are called
30: 6 *"P* of Israel, return to
36:16 was aroused against his *p*
Ezr 2: 1 These are the *p* of the
3: 1 *p* assembled as one man
Ne 1:10 your *p,* whom you redeemed
4: 6 *p* worked with all their heart
8: 1 *p* assembled as one man
Est 3: 6 to destroy all Mordecai's *p,*
Job 12: 2 Doubtless you are the *p,*
Ps 29:11 gives strength to his *p;*
33:12 *p* he chose for his inheritance
50: 4 that he may judge his *p*
53: 6 restores the fortunes of his *p,*
81:13 If my *p* would but listen
94:14 LORD will not reject his *p;*
95: 7 we are the *p* of his pasture,
95:10 a *p* whose hearts go astray,
125: 2 the LORD surrounds his *p*
135: 14 LORD will vindicate his *p*
144: 15 *p* whose God is the LORD.
Pr 14:34 sin is a disgrace to any *p.*
29: 2 righteous thrive, the *p* rejoice
29:18 the *p* cast off restraint
Isa 1: 3 my *p* do not understand.
1: 4 a *p* loaded with guilt,
5:13 my *p* will go into exile
6:10 the heart of this *p* calloused;
9: 2 the *p* walking in darkness
12:12 will assemble the scattered *p*
19:25 Blessed be Egypt my *p,*
25: 8 remove the disgrace of his *p*
Isa 29:13 These *p* come near to me
40: 1 Comfort, comfort my *p*
40: 7 Surely the *p* are grass.
42: 6 a covenant for the *p*
49:13 the LORD comforts his *p*
51: 4 "Listen to me, my *p;*
52: 6 my *p* will know my name;
53: 8 for the transgression of my *p*
60:21 will all your *p* be righteous
62:12 will be called the Holy *P,*
65:23 they will be a *p* blessed
Jer 2:11 my *p* have exchanged their
2:13 *p* have committed two sins:
2:32 my *p* have forgotten me,
4:22 My *p* are fools;
5:14 Because the *p* have spoken
5:31 my *p* love it this way
7:16 do not pray for this *p*
7:23 you will be my *p,*
18:15 my *p* have forgotten me;
30: 3 I will bring my *p* Israel
Eze 13:23 I will save my *p* from
36: 8 fruit for my *p* Israel,
36:28 you will be my *p,*
36:38 be filled with flocks of *p.*
37:13 Then you, my *p,* will know
38:14 *p* Israel are living in safety
39: 7 name among my *p* Israel.
Da 7:27 saints, the *p* of the Most High.
8:24 mighty men and the holy *p*
9:19 your *p* bear your name
9:24 are decreed for your *p*
9:26 *p* of the ruler who will come
10:14 what will happen to your *p*
11:32 *p* who know their God will
12: 1 prince who protects your *p.*
Hos 1:10 'You are not my *p,'*
2:23 'You are my *p'*;
4:14 a *p* without understanding
Joel 2:18 and take pity on his *p.*
3:16 be a refuge for his *p,*
Am 9:14 back my exiled *p* Israel;
Mic 6: 2 a case against his *p;*
7:14 Shepherd your *p* with
Hag 1:12 remnant of the *p* obeyed
Zec 2:11 and will become my *p.*
8: 7 I will save my *p*
13: 9 will say, 'They are my *p,'*
Mk 7: 6 *p* honor me with their lips
8:27 "Who do *p* say I am?"
Lk 1:17 make ready a *p* prepared
1:68 and has redeemed his *p.*
2:10 joy that will be for all the *p.*
21:23 and wrath against this *p.*
Jn 11:50 one man die for the *p*
18:14 if one man died for the *p.*
Ac 15:14 from the Gentiles a *p.*
18:10 have many *p* in this city.
Ro 9:25 will call them 'my *p.'*
11: 1 Did God reject his *p?*
15:10 O Gentiles, with his *p."*
2Co 6:16 and they will be my *p."*
Tit 2:14 a *p* that are his very own,
Heb 2:17 for the sins of the *p.*
4: 9 a Sabbath-rest for the *p*
5: 3 for the sins of the *p.*
10:30 Lord will judge his *p.*
11:25 mistreated along with the *p*
13:12 to make the *p* holy
1Pe 2: 9 you are a chosen *p,*
2:10 Once you were not a *p,*
2:10 you are the *p* of God;
2Pe 2: 1 false prophets among the *p,*
3:11 kind of *p* ought you to be ?
Rev 18: 4 "Come out of her, my *p,*
21: 3 They will be his *p,*

PEOPLES (PEOPLE)
Ge 17:16 kings of *p* will come from her
25:23 two *p* from within you will
27:29 and *p* bow down to you
28: 3 become a community of *p.*
48: 4 you a community of *p,*
Dt 14: 2 of all the *p* on the face of
28:10 Then all the *p* on earth
32: 8 set up boundaries for the *p*
Jos 4:24 all the *p* of the earth might
1Ki 8:43 all the *p* of the earth may
2Ch 7:20 of ridicule among all *p.*
Ps 9: 8 he will govern the *p*
Ps 67: 5 may all the *p* praise you.
87: 6 in the register of the *p:*
96:10 he will judge the *p*
Isa 2: 4 settle disputes for many *p.*
17:12 Oh, the uproar of the *p*–
25: 6 of rich food for all *p,*
34: 1 pay attention, you *p!*
55: 4 him a witness to the *p,*
Jer 10: 3 customs of the *p* are worthless
Da 7:14 all *p,* nations and men
Mic 4: 1 and *p* will stream to it.
4: 3 will judge between many *p*
5: 7 in the midst of many *p*
Zep 3: 9 purify the lips of the *p,*
3:20 among all the *p* of the
Zec 8:20 Many *p* and the inhabitants
12: 2 all the surrounding *p* reeling.
Rev 10:11 prophesy again about many *p,*
17:15 the prostitute sits, are *p,*

PEOR
Nu 25: 3 joined in worshiping the Baal of *P.*
Dt 4: 3 who followed the Baal of *P,*

PERCEIVE (PERCEIVING)
Ps 139: 2 you *p* my thoughts from afar.
Pr 24:12 not he who weighs the heart *p* it?

PERCEIVING* (PERCEIVE)
Isa 6: 9 be ever seeing, but never *p.'*
Mt 13:14 you will be ever seeing but never *p.*
Mk 4:12 may be ever seeing but never *p,*
Ac 28:26 you will be ever seeing but never *p*

PERFECT* (PERFECTER PERFECTING PERFECTION)
Dt 32: 4 He is the Rock, his works are *p,*
2Sa 22:31 "As for God, his way is *p;*
22:33 and makes my way *p.*
Job 36: 4 one *p* in knowledge is with you.
37:16 of him who is *p* in knowledge?
Ps 18:30 As for God, his way is *p;*
18:32 and makes my way *p.*
19: 7 The law of the LORD is *p,*
50: 2 From Zion, *p* in beauty,
64: 6 "We have devised a *p* plan!"
SS 6: 9 but my dove, my *p* one, is unique,
Isa 25: 1 for in *p* faithfulness
26: 3 You will keep in *p* peace
Eze 16:14 had given you made your beauty *p,*
27: 3 "I am *p* in beauty."
28:12 full of wisdom and *p* in beauty.
Mt 5:48 Do not even pagans do that? Be *p,*
5:48 as your heavenly Father is *p.*
19:21 answered, "If you want to be *p,*
Ro 12: 2 his good, pleasing and *p* will.
2Co 12: 9 for my power is made *p*
Php 3:12 or have already been made *p,*
Col 1:28 so that we may present everyone *p*
3:14 binds them all together in *p* unity.
Heb 2:10 the author of their salvation *p*
5: 9 what he suffered and, once made *p,*
7:19 useless (for the law made nothing *p*
7:28 who has been made *p* forever.
9:11 and more *p* tabernacle that is not
10: 1 make *p* those who draw
10:14 he has made *p* forever those who
11:40 with us would they be made *p.*
12:23 spirits of righteous men made *p,*
Jas 1:17 Every good and *p* gift is from above
1:25 into the *p* law that gives freedom,
3: 2 he is a *p* man, able
1Jn 4:18 But *p* love drives out fear,
4:18 The one who fears is not made *p*

PERFECTER* (PERFECT)
Heb 12: 2 the author and *p* of our faith,

PERFECTING* (PERFECT)
2Co 7: 1 *p* holiness out of reverence for God

PERFECTION* (PERFECT)
Ps 119: 96 To all *p* I see a limit;
La 2:15 the *p* of beauty,
Eze 27: 4 builders brought your beauty to *p.*
27:11 they brought your beauty to *p.*
28:12 " 'You were the model of *p,*
1Co 13:10 but when *p* comes, the imperfect
2Co 13: 9 and our prayer is for your *p.*
13:11 Aim for *p,* listen to my appeal,
Heb 7:11 If *p* could have been attained

PERFORM (PERFORMED PERFORMS)
Ex 3:20 with all the wonders that I will *p*

2Sa 7:23 to *p* great and awesome wonders
Jn 3: 2 no one could *p* the miraculous

PERFORMED (PERFORM)
Mt 11:21 If the miracles that were *p*
Jn 10:41 John never *p* a miraculous

PERFORMS (PERFORM)
Ps 77:14 You are the God who *p* miracles;

PERFUME
Ecc 7: 1 A good name is better than fine *p*,
SS 1: 3 your name is like *p* poured out.
Mk 14: 3 jar of very expensive *p*,

PERIL
2Co 1:10 us from such a deadly *p*,

PERISH (PERISHABLE PERISHED PERISHES PERISHING)
Ge 6:17 Everything on earth will *p*.
Est 4:16 And if I *p*, I *p*."
Ps 1: 6 but the way of the wicked will *p*.
37:20 But the wicked will *p*:
73:27 Those who are far from you will *p*;
102: 26 They will *p*, but you remain;
Pr 11:10 when the wicked *p*, there are
19: 9 and he who pours out lies will *p*.
21:28 A false witness will *p*,
28:28 when the wicked *p*, the righteous
Isa 1:28 who forsake the LORD will *p*.
29:14 the wisdom of the wise will *p*,
60:12 that will not serve you will *p*;
Zec 11: 9 the dying die, and the perishing *p*.
Lk 13: 3 unless you repent, you too will all *p*
13: 5 unless you repent, you too will all *p*
21:18 But not a hair of your head will *p*.
Jn 3:16 whoever believes in him shall not *p*
10:28 eternal life, and they shall never *p*;
Ro 2:12 apart from the law will also *p* apart
Col 2:22 These are all destined to *p* with use,
2Th 2:10 They *p* because they refused
Heb 1:11 They will *p*, but you remain;
1Pe 1: 4 into an inheritance that can never *p*
2Pe 3: 9 not wanting anyone to *p*,

PERISHABLE (PERISH)
1Co 15:42 The body that is sown is *p*,
1Pe 1:18 not with *p* things such
1:23 not of *p* seed, but of imperishable,

PERISHED (PERISH)
Ps 119: 92 I would have *p* in my affliction.

PERISHES (PERISH)
Job 8:13 so *p* the hope of the godless.
1Pe 1: 7 which *p* even though refined by fire

PERISHING (PERISH)
1Co 1:18 foolishness to those who are *p*,
2Co 2:15 being saved and those who are *p*.
4: 3 it is veiled to those who are *p*.

PERJURERS* (PERJURY)
Mal 3: 5 and *p*, against those who defraud
1Ti 1:10 for slave traders and liars and *p*—

PERJURY* (PERJURERS)
Jer 7: 9 murder, commit adultery and *p*,

PERMANENT
Heb 7:24 lives forever, he has a *p* priesthood.

PERMISSIBLE (PERMIT)
1Co 6:12 "Everything is *p* for me"—
10:23 "Everything is *p*"—but not

PERMIT (PERMISSIBLE PERMITTED)
Hos 5: 4 "Their deeds do not *p* them
1Ti 2:12 I do not *p* a woman to teach

PERMITTED (PERMIT)
Mt 19: 8 Moses *p* you to divorce your wives
2Co 12: 4 things that man is not *p* to tell.

PERSECUTE (PERSECUTED PERSECUTION PERSECUTIONS)
Ps 119: 86 for men *p* me without cause.
Mt 5:11 *p* you and falsely say all kinds
5:44 and pray for those who *p* you,
Jn 15:20 they persecuted me, they will *p* you
Ac 9: 4 why do you *p* me?" "Who are you,
Ro 12:14 Bless those who *p* you; bless

PERSECUTED (PERSECUTE)
Mt 5:10 Blessed are those who are *p*
5:12 same way they *p* the prophets who
Jn 15:20 If they *p* me, they will persecute
1Co 4:12 when we are *p*, we endure it;
15: 9 because I *p* the church of God.
2Co 4: 9 in despair; *p*, but not abandoned;
1Th 3: 4 kept telling you that we would be *p*.
2Ti 3:12 life in Christ Jesus will be *p*,
Heb 11:37 destitute, *p* and mistreated—

PERSECUTION (PERSECUTE)
Mt 13:21 When trouble or *p* comes
Ro 8:35 or hardship or *p* or famine

PERSECUTIONS (PERSECUTE)
Mk 10:30 and with them, *p*) and in the age
2Co 12:10 in hardships, in *p*, in difficulties.
2Th 1: 4 faith in all the *p* and trials you are
2Ti 3:11 love, endurance, *p*, sufferings—

PERSEVERANCE* (PERSEVERE)
Ro 5: 3 we know that suffering produces *p*;
5: 4 *p*, character; and character, hope.
2Co 12:12 were done among you with great *p*.
2Th 1: 4 churches we boast about your *p*
3: 5 into God's love and Christ's *p*.
Heb 12: 1 run with *p* the race marked out
Jas 1: 3 the testing of your faith develops *p*.
1: 4 *P* must finish its work
5:11 You have heard of Job's *p*
2Pe 1: 6 *p*; and to *p*, godliness;
Rev 2: 2 your hard work and your *p*.
2:19 and faith, your service and *p*,

PERSEVERE* (PERSEVERANCE PERSEVERED PERSEVERES PERSEVERING)
1Ti 4:16 *P* in them, because if you do,
Heb 10:36 You need to *p* so that

PERSEVERED* (PERSEVERE)
Heb 11:27 he *p* because he saw him who is
Jas 5:11 consider blessed those who have *p*.
Rev 2: 3 You have *p* and have endured

PERSEVERES* (PERSEVERE)
1Co 13: 7 trusts, always hopes, always *p*.
Jas 1:12 Blessed is the man who *p*

PERSEVERING* (PERSEVERE)
Lk 8:15 retain it, and by *p* produce a crop.

PERSIANS
Da 6:15 law of the Medes and *P* no decree

PERSISTENCE*
Ro 2: 7 To those who by *p*

PERSUADE (PERSUADED PERSUASIVE)
Ac 18: 4 trying to *p* Jews and Greeks.
2Co 5:11 is to fear the Lord, we try to *p* men.

PERSUADED (PERSUADE)
Ro 4:21 being fully *p* that God had power

PERSUASIVE (PERSUADE)
1Co 2: 4 not with wise and *p* words,

PERVERSION* (PERVERT)
Lev 18:23 sexual relations with it; that is a *p*.
20:12 What they have done is a *p*;
Ro 1:27 the due penalty for their *p*.
Jude : 7 up to sexual immorality and *p*.

PERVERT (PERVERSION PERVERTED PERVERTS)
Ex 23: 2 do not *p* justice by siding
Dt 16:19 Do not *p* justice or show partiality.
Job 34:12 that the Almighty would *p* justice.
Pr 17:23 to *p* the course of justice.
Gal 1: 7 are trying to *p* the gospel of Christ.

PERVERTED (PERVERT)
1Sa 8: 3 and accepted bribes and *p* justice.

PERVERTS* (PERVERT)
1Ti 1:10 for murderers, for adulterers and *p*,

PESTILENCE (PESTILENCES)
Ps 91: 6 nor the *p* that stalks in the darkness

PESTILENCES (PESTILENCE)
Lk 21:11 famines and *p* in various places,

PETER
Apostle, brother of Andrew, also called Simon (Mt 10:2; Mk 3:16; Lk 6:14; Ac 1:13), and Cephas (Jn 1:42). Confession of Christ (Mt 16:13–20; Mk 8:27–30; Lk 9:18–27). At transfiguration (Mt 17:1–8; Mk 9:2–8; Lk 9:28–36; 2Pe 1:16–18). Caught fish with coin (Mt 17:24–27). Denial of Jesus predicted (Mt 26:31–35; Mk 14:27–31; Lk 22:31–34; Jn 13:31–38). Denied Jesus (Mt 26:69–75; Mk 14:66–72; Lk 22:54–62; Jn 18:15–27). Commissioned by Jesus to shepherd his flock (Jn 21:15–23).

Speech at Pentecost (Ac 2). Healed beggar (Ac 3:1–10). Speech at temple (Ac 3:11–26), before Sanhedrin (Ac 4:1–22). In Samaria (Ac 8:14–25). Sent by vision to Cornelius (Ac 10). Announced salvation of Gentiles in Jerusalem (Ac 11; 15). Freed from prison (Ac 12). Inconsistency at Antioch (Gal 2:11–21). At Jerusalem Council (Ac 15).

Epistles: 1–2 Peter.

PETITION (PETITIONS)
1Ch 16: 4 to make *p*, to give thanks,
Php 4: 6 by prayer and *p*, with thanksgiving,

PETITIONS (PETITION)
Heb 5: 7 he offered up prayers and *p*

PHANTOM*
Ps 39: 6 Man is a mere *p* as he goes to

PHARAOH (PHARAOH'S)
Ge 12:15 her to *P*, and she was taken
41:14 So *P* sent for Joseph, and he was
Ex 14: 4 glory for myself through *P*
14:17 And I will gain glory through *P*

PHARAOH'S (PHARAOH)
Ex 7: 3 But I will harden *P* heart, and

PHARISEE (PHARISEES)
Ac 23: 6 brothers, I am a *P*, the son of a *P*.
Php 3: 5 in regard to the law, a *P*; as for zeal,

PHARISEES (PHARISEE)
Mt 5:20 surpasses that of the *P*
16: 6 guard against the yeast of the *P*
23:13 of the law and *P*, you hypocrites!
Jn 3: 1 a man of the *P* named Nicodemus,

PHILADELPHIA
Rev 3: 7 the angel of the church in *P* write:

PHILEMON*
Phm : 1 To *P* our dear friend and fellow

PHILIP
1. Apostle (Mt 10:3; Mk 3:18; Lk 6:14; Jn 1:43–48; 14:8; Ac 1:13).
2. Deacon (Ac 6:1–7); evangelist in Samaria (Ac 8:4–25), to Ethiopian (Ac 8:26–40).

PHILIPPI
Ac 16:12 From there we traveled to *P*,
Php 1: 1 To all the saints in Christ Jesus at *P*

PHILISTINE (PHILISTINES)
Jos 13: 3 of the five *P* rulers in Gaza,
1Sa 14: 1 let's go over to the *P* outpost
17:26 is this uncircumcised *P* that he
17:37 me from the hand of this *P*."

PHILISTINES (PHILISTINE)
Jdg 10: 7 them into the hands of the *P*
13: 1 the hands of the *P* for forty years.
16: 5 The rulers of the *P* went to her
1Sa 4: 1 at Ebenezer, and the *P* at Aphek.
5: 8 together all the rulers of the *P*
13:23 a detachment of *P* had gone out
17: 1 the *P* gathered their forces for war
23: 1 the *P* are fighting against Keilah
27: 1 is to escape to the land of the *P*.
31: 1 Now the *P* fought against Israel;
2Sa 5:17 When the *P* heard that David had
8: 1 David defeated the *P* and subdued
21:15 there was a battle between the *P*
2Ki 18: 8 he defeated the *P*, as far as Gaza
Am 1: 8 Ekron till the last of the *P* is dead,"

PHILOSOPHER* (PHILOSOPHY)
1Co 1:20 Where is the *p* of this age?

PHILOSOPHY* (PHILOSOPHER)
Col 2: 8 through hollow and deceptive *p*,

PHINEHAS
Nu 25: 7 When *P* son of Eleazar, the son
Ps 106: 30 But *P* stood up and intervened,

PHOEBE*
Ro 16: 1 I commend to you our sister *P*,

PHYLACTERIES*
Mt 23: 5 They make their *p* wide

PHYSICAL
Ro 2:28 merely outward and *p*.

Col 1:22 by Christ's *p* body through death
1Ti 4: 8 For *p* training is of some value,
Jas 2:16 but does nothing about his *p* needs,

PICK (PICKED)
Mk 16:18 they will *p* up snakes

PICKED (PICK)
Lk 14: 7 noticed how the guests *p* the places
Jn 5: 9 he *p* up his mat and walked.

PIECE (PIECES)
Jn 19:23 woven in one *p* from top to bottom.

PIECES (PIECE)
Ge 15:17 and passed between the *p.*
Jer 34:18 and then walked between its *p.*
Zec 11:12 So they paid me thirty *p* of silver.
Mt 14:20 of broken *p* that were left over.

PIERCE (PIERCED)
Ex 21: 6 and *p* his ear with an awl.
Pr 12:18 Reckless words *p* like a sword,
Lk 2:35 a sword will *p* your own soul too."

PIERCED (PIERCE)
Ps 22:16 they have *p* my hands and my feet.
40: 6 but my ears you have *p;*
Isa 53: 5 But he was *p* for our transgressions,
Zec 12:10 look on me, the one they have *p,*
Jn 19:37 look on the one they have *p."*
Rev 1: 7 even those who *p* him;

PIG'S (PIGS)
Pr 11:22 Like a gold ring in a *p* snout

PIGEONS
Lev 5:11 afford two doves or two young *p,*
Lk 2:24 "a pair of doves or two young *p."*

PIGS (PIG'S)
Mt 7: 6 do not throw your pearls to *p.*
Mk 5:11 A large herd of *p* was feeding on

PILATE
Governor of Judea. Questioned Jesus (Mt 27:1–26; Mk 15:15; Lk 22:66–23:25; Jn 18:28–19:16); sent him to Herod (Lk 23:6–12); consented to his crucifixion when crowds chose Barabbas (Mt 27:15–26; Mk 15:6–15; Lk 23:13–25; Jn 19:1–10).

PILLAR (PILLARS)
Ge 19:26 and she became a *p* of salt.
Ex 13:21 ahead of them in a *p* of cloud
1Ti 3:15 the *p* and foundation of the truth.
Rev 3:12 who overcomes I will make a *p*

PILLARS (PILLAR)
Gal 2: 9 and John, those reputed to be *p,*

PINIONS
Dt 32:11 and carries them on its *p.*

PISGAH
Dt 3:27 Go up to the top of *P* and look west

PIT
Ps 7:15 falls into the *p* he has made.
40: 2 He lifted me out of the slimy *p,*
103: 4 who redeems your life from the *p*
Pr 23:27 for a prostitute is a deep *p*
26:27 If a man digs a *p,* he will fall into it;
Isa 24:17 Terror and *p* and snare await you,
38:17 me from the *p* of destruction;
Mt 15:14 a blind man, both will fall into a *p."*

PITCH
Ge 6:14 and coat it with *p* inside and out.
Ex 2: 3 and coated it with tar and *p.*

PITIED (PITY)
1Co 15:19 we are to be *p* more than all men.

PITY (PITIED)
Ps 72:13 He will take *p* on the weak
Ecc 4:10 But *p* the man who falls
Lk 10:33 when he saw him, he took *p* on him

PLAGUE (PLAGUED PLAGUES)
2Ch 6:28 "When famine or *p* comes
Ps 91: 6 nor the *p* that destroys at midday.

PLAGUED* (PLAGUE)
Ps 73: 5 they are not *p* by human ills.
73:14 All day long I have been *p;*

PLAGUES (PLAGUE)
Hos 13:14 Where, O death, are your *p?*
Rev 21: 9 full of the seven last *p* came
22:18 to him the *p* described in this book.

PLAIN
Isa 40: 4 the rugged places a *p.*
Ro 1:19 what may be known about God is *p*

PLAN (PLANNED PLANS)
Ex 26:30 according to the *p* shown you
Job 42: 2 no *p* of yours can be thwarted.
Pr 14:22 those who *p* what is good find love
21:30 is no wisdom, no insight, no *p*
Am 3: 7 nothing without revealing his *p*
Eph 1:11 predestined according to the *p*

PLANK
Mt 7: 3 attention to the *p* in your own eye?
Lk 6:41 attention to the *p* in your own eye?

PLANNED (PLAN)
Ps 40: 5 The things you *p* for us
Isa 14:24 "Surely, as I have *p,* so it will be,
23: 9 The LORD Almighty *p* it,
46:11 what I have *p,* that will I do.
Heb 11:40 God had *p* something better for us

PLANS (PLAN)
Ps 20: 4 and make all your *p* succeed.
33:11 *p* of the LORD stand firm forever,
Pr 15:22 *P* fail for lack of counsel,
16: 3 and your *p* will succeed.
19:21 Many are the *p* in a man's heart,
20:18 Make *p* by seeking advice;
Isa 29:15 to hide their *p* from the LORD,
30: 1 those who carry out *p* that are not
32: 8 But the noble man makes noble *p,*
2Co 1:17 Or do I make my *p* in a worldly

PLANT (PLANTED PLANTING PLANTS)
Am 9:15 I will *p* Israel in their own land,
Mt 15:13 "Every *p* that my heavenly Father

PLANTED (PLANT)
Ge 2: 8 the LORD God had *p* a garden
Ps 1: 3 He is like a tree *p* by streams
Jer 17: 8 He will be like a tree *p* by the water
Mt 15:13 Father has not *p* will be pulled
21:33 was a landowner who *p* a vineyard.
Lk 13: 6 "A man had a fig tree, *p*
1Co 3: 6 I *p* the seed, Apollos watered it,
Jas 1:21 humbly accept the word *p* in you,

PLANTING (PLANT)
Isa 61: 3 a *p* of the LORD

PLANTS (PLANT)
Pr 31:16 out of her earnings she *p* a vineyard
1Co 3: 7 So neither he who *p* nor he who
9: 7 Who *p* a vineyard and does not eat

PLATTER
Mk 6:25 head of John the Baptist on a *p."*

PLAY (PLAYED)
1Sa 16:23 David would take his harp and *p.*
Isa 11: 8 The infant will *p* near the hole

PLAYED (PLAY)
Lk 7:32 " 'We *p* the flute for you,
1Co 14: 7 anyone know what tune is being *p*

PLEA (PLEAD PLEADED PLEADS)
1Ki 8:28 to your servant's prayer and his *p*
Ps 102: 17 he will not despise their *p.*
La 3:56 You heard my *p:* "Do not close

PLEAD (PLEA)
Isa 1:17 *p* the case of the widow.

PLEADED (PLEA)
2Co 12: 8 Three times I *p* with the Lord

PLEADS (PLEA)
Job 16:21 on behalf of a man he *p* with God

PLEASANT (PLEASE)
Ge 49:15 and how *p* is his land,
Ps 16: 6 for me in *p* places;
133: 1 How good and *p* it is
135: 3 sing praise to his name, for that is *p*
147: 1 how *p* and fitting to praise him!
Pr 2:10 knowledge will be *p* to your soul.
3:17 Her ways are *p* ways,
16:21 and *p* words promote instruction.
16:24 *P* words are a honeycomb,
Isa 30:10 Tell us *p* things,
1Th 3: 6 that you always have *p* memories
Heb 12:11 No discipline seems *p* at the time,

PLEASANTNESS* (PLEASE)
Pr 27: 9 the *p* of one's friend springs

PLEASE (PLEASANT PLEASANTNESS PLEASED PLEASES PLEASING PLEASURE PLEASURES)
Ps 69:31 This will *p* the LORD more
Pr 20:23 and dishonest scales do not *p* him.
Isa 46:10 and I will do all that I *p.*
Jer 6:20 your sacrifices do not *p* me."
27: 5 and I give it to anyone I *p.*
Jn 5:30 for I seek not to *p* myself
Ro 8: 8 by the sinful nature cannot *p* God.
15: 1 of the weak and not to *p* ourselves.
15: 2 Each of us should *p* his neighbor
1Co 7:32 affairs—how he can *p* the Lord.
10:33 I try to *p* everybody in every way.
2Co 5: 9 So we make it our goal to *p* him,
Gal 1:10 or of God? Or am I trying to *p* men
6: 8 the one who sows to *p* the Spirit,
Col 1:10 and may *p* him in every way:
1Th 2: 4 We are not trying to *p* men
4: 1 how to live in order to *p* God,
2Ti 2: 4 wants to *p* his commanding officer.
Tit 2: 9 to try to *p* them, not to talk back
Heb 11: 6 faith it is impossible to *p* God,

PLEASED (PLEASE)
Dt 28:63 as it *p* the LORD to make you
1Sa 12:22 LORD was *p* to make you his own.
1Ki 3:10 The Lord was *p* that Solomon had
1Ch 29:17 that you test the heart and are *p*
Mic 6: 7 Will the LORD be *p*
Mal 1:10 I am not *p* with you," says
Mt 3:17 whom I love; with him I am well *p*
17: 5 whom I love; with him I am well *p.*
Mk 1:11 whom I love; with you I am well *p*
Lk 3:22 whom I love; with you I am well *p*
1Co 1:21 God was *p* through the foolishness
Col 1:19 For God was *p* to have all his
Heb 10: 6 you were not *p.*
10: 8 nor were you *p* with them"
10:38 I will not be *p* with him."
11: 5 commended as one who *p* God.
13:16 for with such sacrifices God is *p.*
2Pe 1:17 whom I love; with him I am well *p*

PLEASES (PLEASE)
Job 23:13 He does whatever he *p.*
Ps 115: 3 he does whatever *p* him.
135: 6 The LORD does whatever *p* him,
Pr 15: 8 but the prayer of the upright *p* him.
21: 1 it like a watercourse wherever he *p.*
Ecc 2:26 To the man who *p* him, God gives
7:26 man who *p* God will escape her,
Da 4:35 He does as he *p*
Jn 3: 8 The wind blows wherever it *p.*
8:29 for I always do what *p* him."
Eph 5:10 truth) and find out what *p* the Lord
Col 3:20 in everything, for this *p* the Lord.
1Ti 2: 3 This is good, and *p* God our Savior,
1Jn 3:22 his commands and do what *p* him.

PLEASING (PLEASE)
Ge 2: 9 trees that were *p* to the eye
Lev 1: 9 an aroma *p* to the LORD.
Ps 19:14 be *p* in your sight,
104: 34 May my meditation be *p* to him,
Pr 15:26 but those of the pure are *p* to him.
16: 7 When a man's ways are *p*
SS 1: 3 *P* is the fragrance of your perfumes
4:10 How much more *p* is your love
7: 6 How beautiful you are and how *p,*
Ro 12: 1 *p* to God—this is your spiritual
14:18 Christ in this way is *p* to God
Php 4:18 an acceptable sacrifice, *p* to God.
1Ti 5: 4 grandparents, for this is *p* to God.
Heb 13:21 may he work in us what is *p* to him,

PLEASURE (PLEASE)
Ps 5: 4 You are not a God who takes *p*
51:16 you do not take *p* in burnt offerings
147: 10 His *p* is not in the strength
Pr 10:23 A fool finds *p* in evil conduct,
18: 2 A fool finds no *p* in understanding
21:17 He who loves *p* will become poor;
Isa 1:11 I have no *p*
Jer 6:10 they find no *p* in it.
Eze 18:23 Do I take any *p* in the death
18:32 For I take no *p* in the death
33:11 I take no *p* in the death
Lk 10:21 Father, for this was your good *p.*

Eph 1: 5 in accordance with his *p* and will—
1: 9 of his will according to his good *p*,
1Ti 5: 6 the widow who lives for *p* is dead
2Ti 3: 4 lovers of *p* rather than lovers
2Pe 2:13 Their idea of *p* is to carouse

PLEASURES* (PLEASE)
Ps 16:11 with eternal *p* at your right hand.
Lk 8:14 and *p*, and they do not mature.
Tit 3: 3 by all kinds of passions and *p*.
Heb 11:25 rather than to enjoy the *p* of sin
Jas 4: 3 may spend what you get on your *p*.
2Pe 2:13 reveling in their *p* while they feast

PLEDGE
Dt 24:17 take the cloak of the widow as a *p*.
1Pe 3:21 but the *p* of a good conscience

PLEIADES
Job 38:31 "Can you bind the beautiful *P*?
Am 5: 8 (he who made the *P* and Orion,

PLENTIFUL (PLENTY)
Mt 9:37 harvest is *p* but the workers are
Lk 10: 2 harvest is *p*, but the workers are

PLENTY (PLENTIFUL)
2Co 8:14 the present time your *p* will supply
Php 4:12 whether living in *p* or in want.

PLOT (PLOTS)
Est 2:22 Mordecai found out about the *p*
Ps 2: 1 and the peoples *p* in vain?
Pr 3:29 not *p* harm against your neighbor,
Zec 8:17 do not *p* evil against your neighbor,
Ac 4:25 and the peoples *p* in vain?

PLOTS (PLOT)
Pr 6:14 who *p* evil with deceit in his heart

PLOW (PLOWMAN PLOWSHARES)
Lk 9:62 "No one who puts his hand to the *p*

PLOWMAN (PLOW)
1Co 9:10 because when the *p* plows

PLOWSHARES (PLOW)
1Sa 13:20 to the Philistines to have their *p*,
Isa 2: 4 They will beat their swords into *p*
Joel 3:10 Beat your *p* into swords
Mic 4: 3 They will beat their swords into *p*

PLUCK
Mk 9:47 your eye causes you to sin, *p* it out.

PLUNDER (PLUNDERED)
Ex 3:22 And so you will *p* the Egyptians."
Est 3:13 of Adar, and to *p* their goods.
8:11 to *p* the property of their enemies.
9:10 did not lay their hands on the *p*.
Pr 22:23 and will *p* those who *p* them.
Isa 3:14 the *p* from the poor is

PLUNDERED (PLUNDER)
Eze 34: 8 lacks a shepherd and so has been *p*

PLUNGE
1Ti 6: 9 and harmful desires that *p* men
1Pe 4: 4 think it strange that you do not *p*

PODS
Lk 15:16 with the *p* that the pigs were eating,

POINT
Mt 4: 5 on the highest *p* of the temple.
26:38 with sorrow to the *p* of death.
Jas 2:10 yet stumbles at just one *p* is guilty
Rev 2:10 Be faithful, even to the *p* of death,

POISON
Ps 140: 3 the *p* of vipers is on their lips.
Mk 16:18 and when they drink deadly *p*,
Ro 3:13 "The *p* of vipers is on their lips."
Jas 3: 8 It is a restless evil, full of deadly *p*.

POLE (POLES)
Nu 21: 8 "Make a snake and put it up on a *p*;
Dt 16:21 not set up any wooden Asherah *p*

POLES (POLE)
Ex 25:13 Then make *p* of acacia wood

POLISHED
Isa 49: 2 he made me into a *p* arrow

POLLUTE* (POLLUTED POLLUTES)
Nu 35:33 "'Do not *p* the land where you are.
Jude : 8 these dreamers *p* their own bodies,

POLLUTED* (POLLUTE)
Ezr 9:11 entering to possess is a land *p*
Pr 25:26 Like a muddied spring or a *p* well
Ac 15:20 to abstain from food *p* by idols,
Jas 1:27 oneself from being *p* by the world.

POLLUTES* (POLLUTE)
Nu 35:33 Bloodshed *p* the land,

PONDER (PONDERED)
Ps 64: 9 and *p* what he has done.
119: 95 but I will *p* your statutes.

PONDERED (PONDER)
Ps 111: 2 they are *p* by all who delight
Lk 2:19 up all these things and *p* them

POOR (POVERTY)
Lev 19:10 Leave them for the *p* and the alien.
23:22 Leave them for the *p* and the alien.
27: 8 If anyone making the vow is too *p*
Dt 15: 4 there should be no *p* among you,
15: 7 is a *p* man among your brothers
15:11 There will always be *p* people
24:12 If the man is *p*, do not go to sleep
24:14 advantage of a hired man who is *p*
Job 5:16 So the *p* have hope,
24: 4 force all the *p* of the land
Ps 14: 6 frustrate the plans of the *p*,
34: 6 This *p* man called, and the LORD
35:10 You rescue the *p* from those too
40:17 Yet I am *p* and needy;
68:10 O God, you provided for the *p*.
82: 3 maintain the rights of the *p*
112: 9 scattered abroad his gifts to the *p*,
113: 7 He raises the *p* from the dust
140: 12 the LORD secures justice for the *p*
Pr 10: 4 Lazy hands make a man *p*,
13: 7 to be *p*, yet has great wealth.
14:20 The *p* are shunned
14:31 oppresses the *p* shows contempt
17: 5 who mocks the *p* shows contempt
19: 1 Better a *p* man whose walk is
19:17 to the *p* lends to the LORD,
19:22 better to be *p* than a liar.
20:13 not love sleep or you will grow *p*;
21:13 to the cry of the *p*,
21:17 who loves pleasure will become *p*;
22: 2 Rich and *p* have this in common:
22: 9 for he shares his food with the *p*.
22:22 not exploit the *p* because they are *p*
28: 6 Better a *p* man whose walk is
28:27 to the *p* will lack nothing,
29: 7 care about justice for the *p*,
31: 9 defend the rights of the *p*
31:20 She opens her arms to the *p*
Ecc 4:13 Better a *p* but wise youth
Isa 3:14 the plunder from the *p* is
10: 2 to deprive the *p* of their rights
14:30 of the *p* will find pasture,
25: 4 You have been a refuge for the *p*,
32: 7 schemes to destroy the *p* with lies,
61: 1 me to preach good news to the *p*.
Jer 22:16 He defended the cause of the *p*
Eze 18:12 He oppresses the *p* and needy.
Am 2: 7 They trample on the heads of the *p*
4: 1 you women who oppress the *p*
5:11 You trample on the *p*
Zec 7:10 or the fatherless, the alien or the *p*.
Mt 5: 3 saying: "Blessed are the *p* in spirit,
11: 5 the good news is preached to the *p*.
19:21 your possessions and give to the *p*,
26:11 The *p* you will always have
Mk 12:42 But a *p* widow came and put
14: 7 The *p* you will always have
Lk 4:18 me to preach good news to the *p*.
6:20 "Blessed are you who are *p*,
11:41 is inside ⌞the dish⌟ to the *p*,
14:13 invite the *p*, the crippled, the lame,
21: 2 also saw a *p* widow put
Jn 12: 8 You will always have the *p*
Ac 9:36 doing good and helping the *p*.
10: 4 and gifts to the *p* have come up
24:17 to bring my people gifts for the *p*
Ro 15:26 for the *p* among the saints
1Co 13: 3 If I give all I possess to the *p*
2Co 6:10 sorrowful, yet always rejoicing; *p*,
8: 9 yet for your sakes he became *p*,
Gal 2:10 continue to remember the *p*,
Jas 2: 2 and a *p* man in shabby clothes
2: 5 not God chosen those who are *p*
2: 6 But you have insulted the *p*.

POPULATION*
Pr 14:28 A large *p* is a king's glory,

PORTION
Nu 18:29 as the LORD's *p* the best
Dt 32: 9 For the LORD's *p* is his people,
1Sa 1: 5 But to Hannah he gave a double *p*
2Ki 2: 9 "Let me inherit a double *p*
Ps 73:26 and my *p* forever.
119: 57 You are my *p*, O LORD;
Isa 53:12 Therefore I will give him a *p*
Jer 10:16 He who is the *P* of Jacob is not like
La 3:24 to myself, "The LORD is my *p*;
Zec 2:12 LORD will inherit Judah as his *p*

PORTRAIT
Lk 20:24 Whose *p* and inscription are on it?"

PORTRAYED
Gal 3: 1 very eyes Jesus Christ was clearly *p*

POSITION (POSITIONS)
Ro 12:16 to associate with people of low *p*.
Jas 1: 9 ought to take pride in his high *p*.
2Pe 3:17 and fall from your secure *p*.

POSITIONS (POSITION)
2Ch 20:17 Take up your *p*; stand firm
Jude : 6 the angels who did not keep their *p*

POSSESS (POSSESSED POSSESSING POSSESSION POSSESSIONS)
Nu 33:53 for I have given you the land to *p*.
Dt 4:14 you are crossing the Jordan to *p*.
Pr 8:12 I *p* knowledge and discretion.
Jn 5:39 that by them you *p* eternal life.

POSSESSED (POSSESS)
Jn 10:21 the sayings of a man *p* by a demon.

POSSESSING* (POSSESS)
2Co 6:10 nothing, and yet *p* everything.

POSSESSION (POSSESS)
Ge 15: 7 to give you this land to take *p* of it
Ex 6: 8 I will give it to you as a *p*.
19: 5 nations you will be my treasured *p*.
Nu 13:30 "We should go up and take *p*
Dt 7: 6 to be his people, his treasured *p*.
Jos 1:11 take *p* of the land the LORD your
Ps 2: 8 the ends of the earth your *p*.
135: 4 Israel to be his treasured *p*.
Eph 1:14 of those who are God's *p*—

POSSESSIONS (POSSESS)
Mt 19:21 go, sell your *p* and give to the poor,
Lk 11:21 guards his own house, his *p* are safe
12:15 consist in the abundance of his *p*."
19: 8 now I give half of my *p* to the poor,
Ac 4:32 any of his *p* was his own,
2Co 12:14 what I want is not your *p* but you.
Heb 10:34 yourselves had better and lasting *p*.
1Jn 3:17 If anyone has material *p*

POSSIBLE
Mt 19:26 but with God all things are *p*."
26:39 if it is *p*, may this cup be taken
Mk 9:23 "Everything is *p* for him who
10:27 all things are *p* with God."
14:35 prayed that if *p* the hour might pass
Ro 12:18 If it is *p*, as far as it depends on you,
1Co 6: 5 Is it *p* that there is nobody
9:19 to everyone, to win as many as *p*.
9:22 by all *p* means I might save some.

POT (POTSHERD POTTER POTTER'S POTTERY)
2Ki 4:40 there is death in the *p*!"
Jer 18: 4 But the *p* he was shaping

POTIPHAR*
Egyptian who bought Joseph (Ge 37:36), set him over his house (Ge 39:1–6), sent him to prison (Ge 39:7–30).

POTSHERD (POT)
Isa 45: 9 a *p* among the potsherds

POTTER (POT)
Isa 29:16 Can the pot say of the *p*,
45: 9 Does the clay say to the *p*,
64: 8 We are the clay, you are the *p*;
Jer 18: 6 "Like clay in the hand of the *p*,
Zec 11:13 it to the *p*"—the handsome price
Ro 9:21 Does not the *p* have the right

POTTER'S (POT)
Mt 27: 7 to use the money to buy the *p* field

POTTERY (POT)
Ro 9:21 of clay some *p* for noble purposes

POUR (POURED POURS)
Ps 62: 8 *p* out your hearts to him,
Isa 44: 3 I will *p* out my Spirit
Eze 20: 8 So I said I would *p* out my wrath
39:29 for I will *p* out my Spirit
Joel 2:28 I will *p* out my Spirit on all people.
Zec 12:10 I will *p* out on the house of David
Mal 3:10 *p* out so much blessing that you
Ac 2:17 I will *p* out my Spirit on all people.

POURED (POUR)
Ps 22:14 I am *p* out like water,
Isa 32:15 till the Spirit is *p* upon us
Mt 26:28 which is *p* out for many
Lk 22:20 in my blood, which is *p* out for you.
Ac 2:33 and has *p* out what you now see
10:45 of the Holy Spirit had been *p* out
Ro 5: 5 because God has *p* out his love
Php 2:17 even if I am being *p* out like a drink
2Ti 4: 6 I am already being *p* out like
Tit 3: 6 whom he *p* out on us generously
Rev 16: 2 and *p* out his bowl on the land,

POURS (POUR)
Lk 5:37 And no one *p* new wine

POVERTY* (POOR)
Dt 28:48 and thirst, in nakedness and dire *p*,
1Sa 2: 7 The LORD sends *p* and wealth;
Pr 6:11 *p* will come on you like a bandit
10:15 but *p* is the ruin of the poor.
11:24 withholds unduly, but comes to *p*.
13:18 who ignores discipline comes to *p*
14:23 but mere talk leads only to *p*.
21: 5 as surely as haste leads to *p*.
22:16 to the rich—both come to *p*.
24:34 *p* will come on you like a bandit
28:19 fantasies will have his fill of *p*.
28:22 and is unaware that *p* awaits him.
30: 8 give me neither *p* nor riches,
31: 7 let them drink and forget their *p*
Ecc 4:14 born in *p* within his kingdom.
Mk 12:44 out of her *p*, put in everything—
Lk 21: 4 she out of her *p* put in all she had
2Co 8: 2 and their extreme *p* welled up
8: 9 through his *p* might become rich.
Rev 2: 9 I know your afflictions and your *p*

POWER (POWERFUL POWERS)
Ex 15: 6 was majestic in *p*.
32:11 out of Egypt with great *p*
Dt 8:17 "My *p* and the strength
34:12 one has ever shown the mighty *p*
1Sa 10: 6 LORD will come upon you in *p*,
10:10 Spirit of God came upon him in *p*,
11: 6 Spirit of God came upon him in *p*,
16:13 the LORD came upon David in *p*.
1Ch 29:11 LORD, is the greatness and the *p*
2Ch 20: 6 *P* and might are in your hand,
32: 7 for there is a greater *p* with us
Job 9: 4 wisdom is profound, his *p* is vast.
36:22 "God is exalted in his *p*.
37:23 beyond our reach and exalted in *p*;
Ps 20: 6 with the saving *p* of his right hand.
63: 2 and beheld your *p* and your glory.
66: 3 So great is your *p*
68:34 Proclaim the *p* of God,
77:14 you display your *p*
89:13 Your arm is endued with *p*;
145: 6 of the *p* of your awesome works,
147: 5 Great is our Lord and mighty in *p*;
150: 2 Praise him for his acts of *p*;
Pr 3:27 when it is in your *p* to act.
18:21 The tongue has the *p* of life
24: 5 A wise man has great *p*,
Isa 11: 2 the Spirit of counsel and of *p*,
40:10 the Sovereign LORD comes with *p*
40:26 of his great *p* and mighty strength,
63:12 who sent his glorious arm of *p*
Jer 10: 6 and your name is mighty in *p*.
10:12 But God made the earth by his *p*;
27: 5 With my great *p* and outstretched
32:17 and the earth by your great *p*
Hos 13:14 from the *p* of the grave;
Na 1: 3 to anger and great in *p*;
Zec 4: 6 nor by *p*, but by my Spirit,'
Mt 22:29 do not know the Scriptures or the *p*
24:30 on the clouds of the sky, with *p*
Lk 1:35 and the *p* of the Most High will
Lk 4:14 to Galilee in the *p* of the Spirit,
9: 1 he gave them *p* and authority
10:19 to overcome all the *p* of the enemy;
24:49 clothed with *p* from on high."
Ac 1: 8 you will receive *p* when the Holy
4:28 They did what your *p* and will had
4:33 With great *p* the apostles
10:38 with the Holy Spirit and *p*,
26:18 and from the *p* of Satan to God,
Ro 1:16 it is the *p* of God for the salvation
1:20 his eternal *p* and divine nature—
4:21 fully persuaded that God had *p*
9:17 that I might display my *p* in you
15:13 overflow with hope by the *p*
15:19 through the *p* of the Spirit.
1Co 1:17 cross of Christ be emptied of its *p*.
1:18 to us who are being saved it is the *p*
2: 4 a demonstration of the Spirit's *p*,
6:14 By his *p* God raised the Lord
15:24 all dominion, authority and *p*.
15:56 of death is sin, and the *p*
2Co 4: 7 to show that this all-surpassing *p* is
6: 7 in truthful speech and in the *p*
10: 4 they have divine *p*
12: 9 for my *p* is made perfect
13: 4 weakness, yet he lives by God's *p*.
Eph 1:19 and his incomparably great *p*
3:16 you with *p* through his Spirit
3:20 according to his *p* that is at work
6:10 in the Lord and in his mighty *p*.
Php 3:10 and the *p* of his resurrection
3:21 by the *p* that enables him
Col 1:11 strengthened with all *p* according
2:10 who is the head over every *p*
1Th 1: 5 also with *p*, with the Holy Spirit
2Ti 1: 7 but a spirit of *p*, of love
3: 5 form of godliness but denying its *p*.
Heb 2:14 might destroy him who holds the *p*
7:16 of the *p* of an indestructible life.
1Pe 1: 5 by God's *p* until the coming
2Pe 1: 3 His divine *p* has given us
Jude :25 *p* and authority, through Jesus
Rev 4:11 to receive glory and honor and *p*,
5:12 to receive *p* and wealth
11:17 you have taken your great *p*
19: 1 and glory and *p* belong to our God,
20: 6 The second death has no *p*

POWERFUL (POWER)
2Ch 27: 6 Jotham grew *p* because he walked
Est 9: 4 and he became more and more *p*.
Ps 29: 4 The voice of the LORD is *p*;
Jer 32:18 *p* God, whose name is the LORD
Zec 8:22 *p* nations will come to Jerusalem
Mk 1: 7 "After me will come one more *p*
Lk 24:19 *p* in word and deed before God
2Th 1: 7 in blazing fire with his *p* angels.
Heb 1: 3 sustaining all things by his *p* word.
Jas 5:16 The prayer of a righteous man is *p*

POWERLESS
Ro 5: 6 when we were still *p*, Christ died
8: 3 For what the law was *p* to do

POWERS (POWER)
Da 4:35 pleases with the *p* of heaven
Ro 8:38 nor any *p*, neither height nor depth
1Co 12:10 to another miraculous *p*,
Eph 6:12 against the *p* of this dark world
Col 1:16 whether thrones or *p* or rulers
2:15 And having disarmed the *p*
Heb 6: 5 and the *p* of the coming age,
1Pe 3:22 and *p* in submission to him.

PRACTICE (PRACTICED PRACTICES)
Lev 19:26 " 'Do not *p* divination or sorcery.
Ps 119: 56 This has been my *p*:
Eze 33:31 but they do not put them into *p*.
Mt 7:24 into *p* is like a wise man who built
23: 3 for they do not *p* what they preach.
Lk 8:21 hear God's word and put it into *p*."
Ro 12:13 *P* hospitality.
Php 4: 9 or seen in me—put it into *p*.
1Ti 5: 4 to put their religion into *p* by caring

PRACTICED (PRACTICE)
Mt 23:23 You should have *p* the latter,

PRACTICES (PRACTICE)
Ps 101: 7 No one who *p* deceit
Mt 5:19 but whoever *p* and teaches these
Col 3: 9 taken off your old self with its *p*

PRAISE (PRAISED PRAISES PRAISEWORTHY PRAISING)
Ex 15: 2 He is my God, and I will *p* him,
Dt 10:21 He is your *p*; he is your God,
26:19 declared that he will set you in *p*,
32: 3 Oh, *p* the greatness of our God!
Ru 4:14 said to Naomi: "*P* be to the LORD,
2Sa 22: 4 to the LORD, who is worthy of *p*,
22:47 The LORD lives! *P* be to my Rock
1Ch 16:25 is the LORD and most worthy of *p*;
16:35 that we may glory in your *p*."
23: 5 four thousand are to *p* the LORD
29:10 "*P* be to you, O LORD,
2Ch 5:13 they raised their voices in *p*
20:21 and to *p* him for the splendor
29:30 to *p* the LORD with the words
Ezr 3:10 took their places to *p* the LORD,
Ne 9: 5 and *p* the LORD your God,
Ps 8: 2 you have ordained *p*
9: 1 I will *p* you, O LORD,
16: 7 I will *p* the LORD, who counsels
26: 7 proclaiming aloud your *p*
30: 4 *p* his holy name.
33: 1 it is fitting for the upright to *p* him.
34: 1 his *p* will always be on my lips.
40: 3 a hymn of *p* to our God.
42: 5 for I will yet *p* him,
43: 5 for I will yet *p* him,
45:17 the nations will *p* you for ever
47: 7 sing to him a psalm of *p*.
48: 1 the LORD, and most worthy of *p*,
51:15 and my mouth will declare your *p*.
56: 4 In God, whose word I *p*,
57: 9 I will *p* you, O Lord,
63: 4 I will *p* you as long as I live,
65: 1 *P* awaits you, O God, in Zion;
66: 2 make his *p* glorious.
66: 8 *P* our God, O peoples,
68:19 *P* be to the Lord, to God our Savior
68:26 *p* the LORD in the assembly
69:30 I will *p* God's name in song
69:34 Let heaven and earth *p* him,
71: 8 My mouth is filled with your *p*,
71:14 I will *p* you more and more.
71:22 I will *p* you with the harp
74:21 the poor and needy *p* your name.
86:12 I will *p* you, O Lord my God,
89: 5 The heavens *p* your wonders,
92: 1 It is good to *p* the LORD
96: 2 Sing to the LORD, *p* his name;
100: 4 and his courts with *p*;
101: 1 to you, O LORD, I will sing *p*.
102: 18 not yet created may *p* the LORD:
103: 1 *P* the LORD, O my soul;
103: 20 *P* the LORD, you his angels,
104: 1 *P* the LORD, O my soul.
105: 2 Sing to him, sing *p* to him;
106: 1 *P* the LORD.
108: 3 I will *p* you, O LORD,
111: 1 *P* the LORD.
113: 1 *P* the LORD.
117: 1 *P* the LORD, all you nations;
119:175 Let me live that I may *p* you,
135: *P* the LORD.
135: 20 you who fear him, *p* the LORD.
138: 1 I will *p* you, O LORD,
139: 14 I *p* you because I am fearfully
144: 1 *P* be to the LORD my Rock,
145: 3 is the LORD and most worthy of *p*;
145: 10 All you have made will *p* you,
145: 21 Let every creature *p* his holy name
146: 1 *P* the LORD, O my soul.
147: 1 how pleasant and fitting to *p* him!
148: 1 *P* the LORD from the heavens,
148: 13 Let them *p* the name of the LORD,
149: 1 his *p* in the assembly of the saints.
149: 6 May the *p* of God be
149: 9 *P* the LORD.
150: 2 *p* him for his surpassing greatness.
150: 6 that has breath *p* the LORD.
Pr 27: 2 Let another *p* you, and not your
27:21 man is tested by the *p* he receives.
31:31 let her works bring her *p*
SS 1: 4 we will *p* your love more than wine
Isa 12: 1 "I will *p* you, O LORD.
42:10 his *p* from the ends of the earth,
61: 3 and a garment of *p*
Jer 33: 9 *p* and honor before all nations
Da 2:20 "*P* be to the name of God for ever
4:37 *p* and exalt and glorify the King

Mt 5:16 and *p* your Father in heaven.
21:16 you have ordained *p*'?"
Lk 19:37 to *p* God in loud voices
Jn 5:44 effort to obtain the *p* that comes
12:43 for they loved *p* from men more
Ro 2:29 Such a man's *p* is not from men,
15: 7 in order to bring *p* to God.
2Co 1: 3 *P* be to the God and Father
Eph 1: 3 *P* be to the God and Father
1: 6 to the *p* of his glorious grace,
1:12 might be for the *p* of his glory.
1:14 to the *p* of his glory.
1Th 2: 6 We were not looking for *p*
Heb 13:15 offer to God a sacrifice of *p*—
Jas 3: 9 With the tongue we *p* our Lord
5:13 happy? Let him sing songs of *p*.
Rev 5:13 be *p* and honor and glory
7:12 *P* and glory

PRAISED (PRAISE)
1Ch 29:10 David *p* the LORD in the presence
Ne 8: 6 Ezra *p* the LORD, the great God;
Job 1:21 may the name of the LORD be *p*."
Ps 113: 2 Let the name of the LORD be *p*,
Pr 31:30 who fears the LORD is to be *p*.
Isa 63: 7 the deeds for which he is to be *p*,
Da 2:19 Then Daniel *p* the God of heaven
4:34 Then I *p* the Most High; I honored
Lk 18:43 the people saw it, they also *p* God.
23:47 seeing what had happened, *p* God
Ro 9: 5 who is God over all, forever *p*!
Gal 1:24 And they *p* God because of me.
1Pe 4:11 that in all things God may be *p*

PRAISES (PRAISE)
2Sa 22:50 I will sing *p* to your name.
Ps 18:49 I will sing *p* to your name.
47: 6 Sing *p* to God, sing *p*;
147: 1 How good it is to sing *p* to our God,
Pr 31:28 her husband also, and he *p* her:
1Pe 2: 9 that you may declare the *p*

PRAISEWORTHY* (PRAISE)
Ps 78: 4 the *p* deeds of the LORD,
Php 4: 8 if anything is excellent or *p*—

PRAISING (PRAISE)
Lk 2:13 *p* God and saying, "Glory to God
2:20 *p* God for all the things they had
Ac 2:47 *p* God and enjoying the favor
10:46 speaking in tongues and *p* God.
1Co 14:16 If you are *p* God with your spirit,

PRAY (PRAYED PRAYER PRAYERS PRAYING PRAYS)
Dt 4: 7 is near us whenever we *p* to him?
1Sa 12:23 the LORD by failing to *p* for you.
1Ki 8:30 when they *p* toward this place.
2Ch 7:14 will humble themselves and *p*
Ezr 6:10 and *p* for the well-being of the king
Job 42: 8 My servant Job will *p* for you,
Ps 5: 2 for to you I *p*.
32: 6 let everyone who is godly *p*
122: 6 *P* for the peace of Jerusalem:
Jer 29: 7 *P* to the LORD for it,
29:12 upon me and come and *p* to me,
42: 3 *P* that the LORD your God will
Mt 5:44 and *p* for those who persecute you,
6: 5 "And when you *p*, do not be like
6: 9 "This, then, is how you should *p*:
14:23 up on a mountainside by himself to *p*.
19:13 hands on them and *p* for them.
26:36 Sit here while I go over there and *p*
Lk 6:28 *p* for those who mistreat you.
11: 1 us to *p*, just as John taught his
18: 1 them that they should always *p*
22:40 "*P* that you will not fall
Jn 17:20 I *p* also for those who will believe
Ro 8:26 do not know what we ought to *p* for,
1Co 14:13 in a tongue should *p* that he may
Eph 1:18 I *p* also that the eyes
3:16 I *p* that out of his glorious riches he
6:18 And *p* in the Spirit on all occasions
Col 1:10 we *p* this in order that you may live
4: 3 *p* for us, too, that God may open
1Th 5:17 Be joyful always; *p* continually;
2Th 1:11 in mind, we constantly *p* for you,
Jas 5:13 one of you in trouble? He should *p*.
5:16 *p* for each other so that you may be
1Pe 4: 7 self-controlled so that you can *p*.
Jude :20 up in your most holy faith and *p*

PRAYED (PRAY)
1Sa 1:27 I *p* for this child, and the LORD
1Ki 18:36 Elijah stepped forward and *p*:
19: 4 under it and *p* that he might die.
2Ki 6:17 And Elisha *p*, "O LORD,
2Ch 30:18 But Hezekiah *p* for them, saying,
Ne 4: 9 we *p* to our God and posted a guard
Job 42:10 After Job had *p* for his friends,
Da 6:10 got down on his knees and *p*,
9: 4 I *p* to the LORD my God
Jnh 2: 1 From inside the fish Jonah *p*
Mt 26:39 with his face to the ground and *p*,
Mk 1:35 off to a solitary place, where he *p*.
14:35 *p* that if possible the hour might
Lk 22:41 knelt down and *p*, "Father,
Jn 17: 1 he looked toward heaven and *p*:
Ac 4:31 After they *p*, the place where they
6: 6 who *p* and laid their hands on them
8:15 they *p* for them that they might
13: 3 So after they had fasted and *p*,

PRAYER (PRAY)
2Ch 30:27 for their *p* reached heaven,
Ezr 8:23 about this, and he answered our *p*.
Ps 4: 1 be merciful to me and hear my *p*.
6: 9 the LORD accepts my *p*.
17: 1 Give ear to my *p*—
17: 6 give ear to me and hear my *p*.
65: 2 O you who hear *p*,
66:20 who has not rejected my *p*
86: 6 Hear my *p*, O LORD;
Pr 15: 8 but the *p* of the upright pleases him
15:29 but he hears the *p* of the righteous.
Isa 56: 7 a house of *p* for all nations."
Mt 21:13 house will be called a house of *p*,'
21:22 receive whatever you ask for in *p*."
Mk 9:29 This kind can come out only by *p*."
11:24 whatever you ask for in *p*,
Jn 17:15 My *p* is not that you take them out
Ac 1:14 all joined together constantly in *p*,
2:42 to the breaking of bread and to *p*.
6: 4 and will give our attention to *p*
10:31 has heard your *p* and remembered
16:13 expected to find a place of *p*.
Ro 12:12 patient in affliction, faithful in *p*.
1Co 7: 5 you may devote yourselves to *p*.
2Co 13: 9 and our *p* is for your perfection.
Php 1: 9 this is my *p*: that your love may
4: 6 but in everything, by *p* and petition
Col 4: 2 yourselves to *p*, being watchful
1Ti 2: 8 to lift up holy hands in *p*,
4: 5 by the word of God and *p*.
Jas 5:15 *p* offered in faith will make the sick
1Pe 3:12 and his ears are attentive to their *p*,

PRAYERS (PRAY)
1Ch 5:20 He answered their *p*, because they
Isa 1:15 even if you offer many *p*,
Mk 12:40 and for a show make lengthy *p*.
2Co 1:11 as you help us by your *p*.
Eph 6:18 on all occasions with all kinds of *p*
1Ti 2: 1 then, first of all, that requests, *p*,
1Pe 3: 7 so that nothing will hinder your *p*.
Rev 5: 8 which are the *p* of the saints.
8: 3 with the *p* of all the saints,

PRAYING (PRAY)
Ge 24:45 "Before I finished *p* in my heart,
1Sa 1:12 As she kept on *p* to the LORD,
Mk 11:25 And when you stand *p*,
Lk 3:21 as he was *p*, heaven was opened
6:12 and spent the night *p* to God.
9:29 As he was *p*, the appearance
Jn 17: 9 I am not *p* for the world,
Ac 9:11 from Tarsus named Saul, for he is *p*
16:25 and Silas were *p* and singing hymns
Ro 15:30 in my struggle by *p* to God for me.
Eph 6:18 always keep on *p* for all the saints.

PRAYS (PRAY)
1Co 14:14 my spirit *p*, but my mind is

PREACH (PREACHED PREACHING)
Isa 61: 1 me to *p* good news to the poor.
Mt 10: 7 As you go, *p* this message:
23: 3 they do not practice what they *p*.
Mk 16:15 and *p* the good news to all creation.
Lk 4:18 me to *p* good news to the poor.
Ac 9:20 At once he began to *p*
16:10 us to *p* the gospel to them.
Ro 1:15 am so eager to *p* the gospel
10:15 how can they *p* unless they are sent
15:20 to *p* the gospel where Christ was
1Co 1:17 to *p* the gospel—not with words
1:23 wisdom, but we *p* Christ crucified:
9:14 that those who *p* the gospel should
9:16 Woe to me if I do not *p* the gospel!
2Co 4: 5 For we do not *p* ourselves,
10:16 so that we can *p* the gospel
Gal 1: 8 from heaven should *p* a gospel
2Ti 4: 2 I give you this charge: *P* the Word;

PREACHED (PREACH)
Mt 24:14 gospel of the kingdom will be *p*
Mk 6:12 and *p* that people should repent.
13:10 And the gospel must first be *p*
14: 9 wherever the gospel is *p*
Ac 8: 4 had been scattered *p* the word
28:31 hindrance he *p* the kingdom
1Co 9:27 so that after I have *p* to others,
15: 1 you of the gospel I *p* to you,
2Co 11: 4 other than the Jesus we *p*,
Gal 1: 8 other than the one we *p* to you,
Eph 2:17 *p* peace to you who were far away
Php 1:18 false motives or true, Christ is *p*.
1Ti 3:16 was *p* among the nations,
1Pe 1:25 this is the word that was *p* to you.
3:19 and *p* to the spirits in prison who

PREACHING (PREACH)
Lk 9: 6 *p* the gospel and healing people
Ac 18: 5 devoted himself exclusively to *p*,
Ro 10:14 hear without someone *p* to them?
1Co 2: 4 and my *p* were not with wise
9:18 in *p* the gospel I may offer it free
Gal 1: 9 If anybody is *p* to you a gospel
1Ti 4:13 the public reading of Scripture, to *p*
5:17 especially those whose work is *p*

PRECEDE*
1Th 4:15 will certainly not *p* those who have

PRECEPTS*
Dt 33:10 He teaches your *p* to Jacob
Ps 19: 8 The *p* of the LORD are right,
103: 18 and remember to obey his *p*.
105: 45 that they might keep his *p*
111: 7 all his *p* are trustworthy.
111: 10 who follow his *p* have good
119: 4 You have laid down *p*
119: 15 I meditate on your *p*
119: 27 understand the teaching of your *p*;
119: 40 How I long for your *p*!
119: 45 for I have sought out your *p*.
119: 56 I obey your *p*.
119: 63 to all who follow your *p*.
119: 69 I keep your *p* with all my heart.
119: 78 but I will meditate on your *p*.
119: 87 but I have not forsaken your *p*.
119: 93 I will never forget your *p*,
119: 94 I have sought out your *p*.
119:100 for I obey your *p*.
119:104 I gain understanding from your *p*;
119:110 but I have not strayed from your *p*.
119:128 because I consider all your *p* right,
119:134 that I may obey your *p*.
119:141 I do not forget your *p*.
119:159 See how I love your *p*;
119:168 I obey your *p* and your statutes,
119:173 for I have chosen your *p*.

PRECIOUS
Ps 19:10 They are more *p* than gold,
72:14 for *p* is their blood in his sight.
116: 15 *P* in the sight of the LORD
119: 72 from your mouth is more *p* to me
139: 17 How *p* to me are your thoughts,
Pr 8:11 for wisdom is more *p* than rubies,
Isa 28:16 a *p* cornerstone for a sure
1Pe 1:19 but with the *p* blood of Christ,
2: 4 but chosen by God and *p* to him—
2: 6 a chosen and *p* cornerstone,
2Pe 1: 1 Christ have received a faith as *p*
1: 4 us his very great and *p* promises,

PREDESTINED* (DESTINY)
Ro 8:29 *p* to be conformed to the likeness
8:30 And those he *p*, he also called;
Eph 1: 5 In love he *p* us to be adopted
1:11 having been *p* according

PREDICTED (PREDICTION)
1Sa 28:17 The LORD has done what he *p*
Ac 7:52 killed those who *p* the coming
1Pe 1:11 when he *p* the sufferings of Christ

PREDICTION* (PREDICTED PREDICTIONS)
Jer 28: 9 only if his *p* comes true."

PREDICTIONS (PREDICTION)
Isa 44:26 and fulfills the *p* of his messengers,

PREGNANT
Ex 21:22 who are fighting hit a *p* woman
Mt 24:19 be in those days for *p* women
1Th 5: 3 as labor pains on a *p* woman,

PREPARE (PREPARED)
Ps 23: 5 You *p* a table before me
Isa 25: 6 the LORD Almighty will *p*
40: 3 "In the desert *p*
Am 4:12 *p* to meet your God, O Israel."
Mal 3: 1 who will *p* the way before me.
Mt 3: 3 '*P* the way for the Lord,
Jn 14: 2 there to *p* a place for you.
Eph 4:12 to *p* God's people for works
1Pe 1:13 Therefore, *p* your minds for action;

PREPARED (PREPARE)
Ex 23:20 to bring you to the place I have *p*.
Mt 25:34 the kingdom *p* for you
Ro 9:22 of his wrath—*p* for destruction?
1Co 2: 9 what God has *p* for those who love
Eph 2:10 which God *p* in advance for us
2Ti 2:21 and *p* to do any good work.
4: 2 be *p* in season and out of season;
1Pe 3:15 Always be *p* to give an answer

PRESCRIBED
Ezr 7:23 Whatever the God of heaven has *p*,

PRESENCE (PRESENT)
Ex 25:30 Put the bread of the *P* on this table
33:14 The LORD replied, "My *P* will go
Nu 4: 7 "Over the table of the *P* they are
1Sa 6:20 in the *p* of the LORD, this
21: 6 of the *P* that had been removed
2Sa 22:13 Out of the brightness of his *p*
2Ki 17:23 LORD removed them from his *p*,
23:27 also from my *p* as I removed Israel,
Ezr 9:15 one of us can stand in your *p*."
Ps 16:11 you will fill me with joy in your *p*,
21: 6 with the joy of your *p*.
23: 5 in the *p* of my enemies.
31:20 the shelter of your *p* you hide them
41:12 and set me in your *p* forever.
51:11 Do not cast me from your *p*
52: 9 in the *p* of your saints.
89:15 who walk in the light of your *p*,
90: 8 our secret sins in the light of your *p*
114: 7 O earth, at the *p* of the Lord,
139: 7 Where can I flee from your *p*?
Isa 26:17 so were we in your *p*, O LORD.
Jer 5:22 "Should you not tremble in my *p*?
Eze 38:20 of the earth will tremble at my *p*.
Hos 6: 2 that we may live in his *p*.
Na 1: 5 The earth trembles at his *p*,
Mal 3:16 in his *p* concerning those who
Ac 2:28 you will fill me with joy in your *p*.'
1Th 3: 9 have in the *p* of our God
3:13 and holy in the *p* of our God
2Th 1: 9 and shut out from the *p* of the Lord
Heb 9:24 now to appear for us in God's *p*.
1Jn 3:19 rest in his *p* whenever our hearts
Jude :24 before his glorious *p* without fault

PRESENT (PRESENCE)
1Co 3:22 life or death or the *p* or the future—
7:26 of the *p* crisis, I think that it is good
2Co 11: 2 so that I might *p* you as a pure
Eph 5:27 and to *p* her to himself
1Ti 4: 8 holding promise for both the *p* life
2Ti 2:15 Do your best to *p* yourself to God
Jude :24 and to *p* you before his glorious

PRESERVE
Lk 17:33 and whoever loses his life will *p* it.

PRESERVES
Ps 1 19:50 Your promise *p* my life.

PRESS (PRESSED PRESSURE)
Php 3:12 but I *p* on to take hold of that
3:14 I *p* on toward the goal

PRESSED (PRESS)
Lk 6:38 *p* down, shaken together

PRESSURE (PRESS)
2Co 1: 8 We were under great *p*, far
11:28 I face daily the *p* of my concern

PRETENDED
1Sa 21:13 So he *p* to be insane

PREVAILS
1Sa 2: 9 "It is not by strength that one *p*;
Pr 19:21 but it is the LORD's purpose that *p*

PRICE (PRICELESS)
Job 28:18 the *p* of wisdom is beyond rubies.
1Co 6:20 your own; you were bought at a *p*.
7:23 bought at a *p*; do not become slaves

PRICELESS* (PRICE)
Ps 36: 7 How *p* is your unfailing love!

PRIDE (PROUD)
Pr 8:13 I hate *p* and arrogance,
11: 2 When *p* comes, then comes
13:10 *P* only breeds quarrels,
16:18 *P* goes before destruction,
29:23 A man's *p* brings him low,
Isa 25:11 God will bring down their *p*
Da 4:37 And those who walk in *p* he is able
Am 8: 7 The LORD has sworn by the *P*
2Co 5:12 giving you an opportunity to take *p*
7: 4 in you; I take great *p* in you.
8:24 and the reason for our *p* in you,
Gal 6: 4 Then he can take *p* in himself,
Jas 1: 9 ought to take *p* in his high position.

PRIEST (PRIESTHOOD PRIESTLY PRIESTS)
Ge 14:18 He was *p* of God Most High,
Nu 5:10 to the *p* will belong to the *p*.'"
2Ch 13: 9 and seven rams may become a *p*
Ps 110: 4 "You are a *p* forever,
Heb 2:17 faithful high *p* in service to God,
3: 1 and high *p* whom we confess.
4:14 have a great high *p* who has gone
4:15 do not have a high *p* who is unable
5: 6 "You are a *p* forever,
6:20 He has become a high *p* forever,
7: 3 Son of God he remains a *p* forever.
7:15 clear if another *p* like Melchizedek
7:26 Such a high *p* meets our need—
8: 1 We do have such a high *p*,
10:11 Day after day every *p* stands
13:11 The high *p* carries the blood

PRIESTHOOD (PRIEST)
Heb 7:24 lives forever, he has a permanent *p*.
1Pe 2: 5 into a spiritual house to be a holy *p*,
2: 9 you are a chosen people, a royal *p*,

PRIESTLY (PRIEST)
Ro 15:16 to the Gentiles with the *p* duty

PRIESTS (PRIEST)
Ex 19: 6 you will be for me a kingdom of *p*
Lev 21: 1 "Speak to the *p*, the sons of Aaron,
Eze 42:13 where the *p* who approach
46: 2 *p* are to sacrifice his burnt offering
Mal 1: 6 O *p*, who show contempt for my name.
Rev 5:10 to be a kingdom and *p*
20: 6 but they will be *p* of God

PRIME
Isa 38:10 recovery: I said, "In the *p* of my life

PRINCE (PRINCES PRINCESS)
Isa 9: 6 Everlasting Father, *P* of Peace.
Eze 34:24 and my servant David will be *p*
37:25 my servant will be their *p* forever.
Da 8:25 stand against the *P* of princes.
Jn 12:31 now the *p* of this world will be
Ac 5:31 as *P* and Savior that he might give

PRINCES (PRINCE)
Ps 118: 9 than to trust in *p*.
148: 11 you *p* and all rulers on earth,
Isa 40:23 He brings *p* to naught

PRINCESS* (PRINCE)
Ps 45:13 All glorious is the *p*

PRISCILLA*
Wife of Aquila; co-worker with Paul (Ac 18; Ro 16:3; 1Co 16:19; 2Ti 4:19); instructor of Apollos (Ac 18:24–28).

PRISON (PRISONER PRISONERS)
Ps 66:11 You brought us into *p*
142: 7 Set me free from my *p*,
Isa 42: 7 to free captives from *p*
Mt 25:36 I was in *p* and you came to visit me
2Co 11:23 been in *p* more frequently,
Heb 11:36 others were chained and put in *p*.
13: 3 Remember those in *p*
1Pe 3:19 spirits in *p* who disobeyed long ago
Rev 20: 7 Satan will be released from his *p*

PRISONER (PRISON)
Ro 7:23 and making me a *p* of the law of sin
Gal 3:22 declares that the whole world is a *p*
Eph 3: 1 the *p* of Christ Jesus for the sake

PRISONERS (PRISON)
Ps 68: 6 he leads forth the *p* with singing;
79:11 groans of the *p* come before you;
107: 10 *p* suffering in iron chains,
146: 7 The LORD sets *p* free,
Zec 9:12 to your fortress, O *p* of hope;
Lk 4:18 me to proclaim freedom for the *p*
Gal 3:23 we were held *p* by the law,

PRIVILEGE*
2Co 8: 4 pleaded with us for the *p* of sharing

PRIZE*
1Co 9:24 Run in such a way as to get the *p*.
9:24 but only one gets the *p*? Run
9:27 will not be disqualified for the *p*.
Php 3:14 on toward the goal to win the *p*
Col 2:18 of angels disqualify you for the *p*.

PROBE
Job 11: 7 Can you *p* the limits
Ps 17: 3 Though you *p* my heart

PROCEDURE
Ecc 8: 6 For there is a proper time and *p*

PROCESSION
Ps 68:24 Your *p* has come into view, O God,
118: 27 boughs in hand, join in the festal *p*
1Co 4: 9 on display at the end of the *p*,
2Co 2:14 us in triumphal *p* in Christ

PROCLAIM (PROCLAIMED PROCLAIMING PROCLAIMS PROCLAMATION)
Ex 33:19 and I will *p* my name, the LORD,
Lev 25:10 and *p* liberty throughout the land
Dt 30:12 and *p* it to us so we may obey it?"
2Sa 1:20 *p* it not in the streets of Ashkelon,
1Ch 16:23 *p* his salvation day after day.
Ne 8:15 and that they should *p* this word
Ps 2: 7 I will *p* the decree of the LORD:
9:11 *p* among the nations what he has
19: 1 the skies *p* the work of his hands.
22:31 They will *p* his righteousness
40: 9 I *p* righteousness in the great
50: 6 the heavens *p* his righteousness,
64: 9 they will *p* the works of God
68:34 *P* the power of God,
71:16 I will come and *p* your mighty acts,
92: 2 to *p* your love in the morning
96: 2 *p* his salvation day after day.
97: 6 The heavens *p* his righteousness,
106: 2 Who can *p* the mighty acts
118: 17 will *p* what the LORD has done.
145: 6 and I will *p* your great deeds.
Isa 12: 4 and *p* that his name is exalted.
42:12 and *p* his praise in the islands.
52: 7 who *p* salvation,
61: 1 to *p* freedom for the captives
66:19 They will *p* my glory
Jer 7: 2 house and there *p* this message:
50: 2 lift up a banner and *p* it;
Hos 5: 9 I *p* what is certain.
Zec 9:10 He will *p* peace to the nations.
Mt 10:27 in your ear, *p* from the roofs.
12:18 and he will *p* justice to the nations.
Lk 4:18 me to *p* freedom for the prisoners
9:60 you go and *p* the kingdom of God."
Ac 17:23 unknown I am going to *p*
20:27 hesitated to *p* to you the whole will
1Co 11:26 you *p* the Lord's death
Col 1:28 We *p* him, admonishing
4: 4 Pray that I may *p* it clearly,
1Jn 1: 1 this we *p* concerning the Word

PROCLAIMED (PROCLAIM)
Ex 9:16 and that my name might be *p*
34: 5 there with him and *p* his name,
Ps 68:11 was the company of those who *p* it:
Ro 15:19 I have fully *p* the gospel of Christ.
Col 1:23 that has been *p* to every creature
2Ti 4:17 me the message might be fully *p*

PROCLAIMING (PROCLAIM)
Ps 26: 7 *p* aloud your praise

Ps 92:15 *p,* "The LORD is upright;
Ac 5:42 and *p* the good news that Jesus is
Ro 10: 8 the word of faith we are *p:*

PROCLAIMS (PROCLAIM)
Dt 18:22 If what a prophet *p* in the name

PROCLAMATION (PROCLAIM)
Isa 62:11 The LORD has made *p*

PRODUCE (PRODUCES)
Mt 3: 8 *P* fruit in keeping with repentance.
3:10 tree that does not *p* good fruit will

PRODUCES (PRODUCE)
Pr 30:33 so stirring up anger *p* strife."
Ro 5: 3 that suffering *p* perseverance;
Heb 12:11 it *p* a harvest of righteousness

PROFANE (PROFANED)
Lev 19:12 and so *p* the name of your God.
22:32 Do not *p* my holy name.
Mal 2:10 Why do we *p* the covenant

PROFANED (PROFANE)
Eze 36:20 the nations they *p* my holy name,

PROFESS*
1Ti 2:10 for women who *p* to worship God.
Heb 4:14 let us hold firmly to the faith we *p.*
10:23 unswervingly to the hope we *p,*

PROFIT (PROFITABLE)
Pr 14:23 All hard work brings a *p,*
21: 5 The plans of the diligent lead to *p*
Isa 44:10 which can *p* him nothing?
2Co 2:17 not peddle the word of God for *p.*
Php 3: 7 was to my *p* I now consider loss

PROFITABLE* (PROFIT)
Pr 3:14 for she is more *p* than silver
31:18 She sees that her trading is *p,*
Tit 3: 8 These things are excellent and *p*

PROFOUND
Job 9: 4 His wisdom is *p,* his power is vast.
Ps 92: 5 how *p* your thoughts!
Eph 5:32 This is a *p* mystery—but I am

PROGRESS
Php 1:25 continue with all of you for your *p*
1Ti 4:15 so that everyone may see your *p.*

PROLONG*
Dt 5:33 *p* your days in the land that you
Ps 85: 5 Will you *p* your anger
Pr 3: 2 for they will *p* your life many years
Isa 53:10 will see his offspring and *p* his days,
La 4:22 he will not *p* your exile.

PROMISE (PROMISED PROMISES)
Nu 23:19 Does he *p* and not fulfill?
Jos 23:14 Every *p* has been fulfilled;
2Sa 7:25 keep forever the *p* you have made
1Ki 8:20 The LORD has kept the *p* he made
8:24 You have kept your *p*
Ne 5:13 man who does not keep this *p.*
9: 8 have kept your *p* because you are
Ps 77: 8 Has his *p* failed for all time?
119: 41 your salvation according to your *p;*
119: 50 Your *p* preserves my life.
119: 58 to me according to your *p.*
119:162 I rejoice in your *p*
Ac 2:39 The *p* is for you and your children
Ro 4:13 offspring received the *p* that he
4:20 unbelief regarding the *p* of God,
Gal 3:14 that by faith we might receive the *p*
Eph 2:12 foreigners to the covenants of the *p*
1Ti 4: 8 holding *p* for both the present life
Heb 6:13 When God made his *p* to Abraham
11:11 him faithful who had made the *p.*
2Pe 3: 9 Lord is not slow in keeping his *p,*
3:13 with his *p* we are looking forward

PROMISED (PROMISE)
Ge 21: 1 did for Sarah what he had *p.*
24: 7 who spoke to me and *p* me on oath,
Ex 3:17 And I have *p* to bring you up out
Nu 10:29 for the LORD has *p* good things
Dt 15: 6 your God will bless you as he has *p,*
26:18 his treasured possession as he *p,*
2Sa 7:28 and you have *p* these good things
1Ki 9: 5 I *p* David your father when I said,
2Ch 6:15 with your mouth you have *p*
Ps 119: 57 I have *p* to obey your words.
Lk 24:49 to send you what my Father has *p;*
Ac 1: 4 but wait for the gift my Father *p,*
13:32 What God *p* our fathers he has
Ro 4:21 power to do what he had *p.*
Tit 1: 2 *p* before the beginning of time,
Heb 10:23 for he who *p* is faithful.
10:36 you will receive what he has *p.*
Jas 1:12 the crown of life that God has *p*
2: 5 the kingdom he *p* those who love
2Pe 3: 4 "Where is this 'coming' he *p?*
1Jn 2:25 And this is what he *p* us—

PROMISES (PROMISE)
Jos 21:45 one of all the LORD's good *p*
23:14 of all the good *p* the LORD your
1Ki 8:56 failed of all the good *p* he gave
1Ch 17:19 and made known all these great *p.*
Ps 85: 8 he *p* peace to his people, his saints
106: 12 Then they believed his *p*
119:140 Your *p* have been thoroughly
119:148 that I may meditate on your *p.*
145: 13 The LORD is faithful to all his *p*
Ro 9: 4 the temple worship and the *p.*
2Co 1:20 matter how many *p* God has made,
7: 1 Since we have these *p,* dear friends,
Heb 8: 6 and it is founded on better *p.*
2Pe 1: 4 us his very great and precious *p,*

PROMOTE (PROMOTES)
Pr 12:20 but joy for those who *p* peace.
16:21 and pleasant words *p* instruction.
1Ti 1: 4 These *p* controversies rather

PROMOTES (PROMOTE)
Pr 17: 9 over an offense *p* love,

PROMPTED
1Th 1: 3 your labor *p* by love, and your
2Th 1:11 and every act *p* by your faith.

PRONOUNCE (PRONOUNCED)
1Ch 23:13 to *p* blessings in his name forever.

PRONOUNCED (PRONOUNCE)
1Ch 16:12 miracles, and the judgments he *p,*

PROOF (PROVE)
Ac 17:31 He has given *p* of this to all men
2Co 8:24 Therefore show these men the *p*

PROPER
Ps 104: 27 give them their food at the *p* time.
145: 15 give them their food at the *p* time.
Ecc 5:18 Then I realized that it is good and *p*
8: 5 the wise heart will know the *p* time
Mt 24:45 give them their food at the *p* time?
Lk 1:20 which will come true at their *p* time
1Co 11:13 Is it *p* for a woman to pray to God
Gal 6: 9 at the *p* time we will reap a harvest
1Ti 2: 6 the testimony given in its *p* time.
1Pe 2:17 Show *p* respect to everyone:

PROPERTY
Heb 10:34 the confiscation of your *p,*

PROPHECIES (PROPHESY)
1Co 13: 8 where there are *p,* they will cease;
1Th 5:20 do not treat *p* with contempt.

PROPHECY (PROPHESY)
Da 9:24 to seal up vision and *p*
1Co 12:10 miraculous powers, to another *p,*
13: 2 of *p* and can fathom all mysteries
14: 1 gifts, especially the gift of *p.*
14: 6 or *p* or word of instruction?
14:22 *p,* however, is for believers,
2Pe 1:20 you must understand that no *p*
Rev 22:18 the words of the *p* of this book:

PROPHESIED (PROPHESY)
Nu 11:25 the Spirit rested on them, they *p,*
1Sa 19:24 and also *p* in Samuel's presence.
Jn 11:51 that year he *p* that Jesus would
Ac 19: 6 and they spoke in tongues and *p.*
21: 9 four unmarried daughters who *p.*

PROPHESIES (PROPHESY)
Jer 28: 9 the prophet who *p* peace will be
Eze 12:27 and he *p* about the distant future.'
1Co 11: 4 *p* with his head covered dishonors
14: 3 But everyone who *p* speaks to men

PROPHESY (PROPHECIES PROPHECY PROPHESIED PROPHESIES PROPHESYING PROPHET PROPHET'S PROPHETESS PROPHETS)
1Sa 10: 6 and you will *p* with them;
Eze 13: 2 Say to those who *p* out
13:17 daughters of your people who *p* out
34: 2 *p* against the shepherds of Israel;
37: 4 "*P* to these bones and say to them,
Joel 2:28 Your sons and daughters will *p,*
Mt 7:22 Lord, did we not *p* in your name,
Ac 2:17 Your sons and daughters will *p,*
1Co 13: 9 know in part and we *p* in part,
14:39 my brothers, be eager to *p,*
Rev 11: 3 and they will *p* for 1,260 days,

PROPHESYING (PROPHESY)
1Ch 25: 1 and Jeduthun for the ministry of *p,*
Ro 12: 6 If a man's gift is *p,* let him use it

PROPHET (PROPHESY)
Ex 7: 1 your brother Aaron will be your *p.*
Nu 12: 6 "When a *p* of the LORD is
Dt 13: 1 If a *p,* or one who foretells
18:18 up for them a *p* like you
18:22 If what a *p* proclaims in the name
1Sa 3:20 that Samuel was attested as a *p*
9: 9 because the *p* of today used
1Ki 1: 8 son of Jehoiada, Nathan the *p,*
18:36 the *p* Elijah stepped forward
2Ki 5: 8 and he will know that there is a *p*
6:12 "but Elisha, the *p* who is in Israel,
20: 1 The *p* Isaiah son of Amoz went
2Ch 35:18 since the days of the *p* Samuel;
36:12 himself before Jeremiah the *p,*
Ezr 5: 1 Haggai the *p* and Zechariah the *p,*
Eze 2: 5 they will know that a *p* has been
33:33 they will know that a *p* has been
Hos 9: 7 the *p* is considered a fool,
Am 7:14 "I was neither a *p* nor a prophet's
Hab 1: 1 that Habakkuk the *p* received.
Hag 1: 1 came through the *p* Haggai
Zec 1: 1 to the *p* Zechariah son of Berekiah,
13: 4 that day every *p* will be ashamed
Mal 4: 5 I will send you the *p* Elijah
Mt 10:41 Anyone who receives a *p*
11: 9 what did you go out to see? A *p?*
12:39 except the sign of the *p* Jonah.
Lk 1:76 will be called a *p* of the Most High;
4:24 "no *p* is accepted in his hometown.
7:16 A great *p* has appeared among us,"
24:19 "He was a *p,* powerful in word
Jn 1:21 "Are you the *P?*" He answered,
Ac 7:37 'God will send you a *p* like me
21:10 a *p* named Agabus came
1Co 14:37 If anybody thinks he is a *p*
Rev 16:13 and out of the mouth of the false *p.*

PROPHET'S (PROPHESY)
2Pe 1:20 about by the *p* own interpretation.

PROPHETESS (PROPHESY)
Ex 15:20 Then Miriam the *p,* Aaron's sister,
Jdg 4: 4 a *p,* the wife of Lappidoth,
Isa 8: 3 I went to the *p,* and she conceived
Lk 2:36 a *p,* Anna, the daughter of Phanuel,

PROPHETS (PROPHESY)
Nu 11:29 that all the LORD's people were *p*
1Sa 10:11 Is Saul also among the *p?*"
28: 6 him by dreams or Urim or *p.*
1Ki 19:10 put your *p* to death with the sword.
1Ch 16:22 do my *p* no harm."
Ps 105: 15 do my *p* no harm."
Jer 23: 9 Concerning the *p:*
23:30 "I am against the *p* who steal
Eze 13: 2 prophesy against the *p*
Mt 5:17 come to abolish the Law or the *P;*
7:12 for this sums up the Law and the *P.*
7:15 "Watch out for false *p.*
22:40 and the *P* hang on these two
23:37 you who kill the *p* and stone those
24:24 false Christs and false *p* will appear
26:56 of the *p* might be fulfilled."
Lk 10:24 For I tell you that many *p*
11:49 'I will send them *p* and apostles,
24:25 believe all that the *p* have spoken!
24:44 me in the Law of Moses, the *P*
Ac 3:24 "Indeed, all the *p* from Samuel on,
10:43 All the *p* testify about him that
13: 1 the church at Antioch there were *p*
26:22 nothing beyond what the *p*
28:23 the Law of Moses and from the *P.*
Ro 1: 2 through his *p* in the Holy
3:21 to which the Law and the *P* testify.
11: 3 they have killed your *p*
1Co 12:28 second *p,* third teachers, then

1Co 12:29 Are all *p*? Are all teachers?
14:32 The spirits of *p* are subject
Eph 2:20 foundation of the apostles and *p*,
3: 5 Spirit to God's holy apostles and *p*.
4:11 some to be *p*, some
Heb 1: 1 through the *p* at many times
1Pe 1:10 Concerning this salvation, the *p*,
2Pe 1:19 word of the *p* made more certain,
3: 2 spoken in the past by the holy *p*
1Jn 4: 1 because many false *p* have gone out
Rev 11:10 these two *p* had tormented those
18:20 Rejoice, saints and apostles and *p*!

PROPORTION
Dt 16:10 by giving a freewill offering in *p*
16:17 Each of you must bring a gift in *p*

PROPRIETY*
1Ti 2: 9 with decency and *p*,
2:15 in faith, love and holiness with *p*.

PROSPECT*
Pr 10:28 The *p* of the righteous is joy,

PROSPER (PROSPERED PROSPERITY PROSPEROUS PROSPERS)
Dt 5:33 so that you may live and *p*
28:63 pleased the LORD to make you *p*
29: 9 that you may *p* in everything you
1Ki 2: 3 so that you may *p* in all you do
Ezr 6:14 and *p* under the preaching
Pr 11:10 When the righteous *p*, the city
11:25 A generous man will *p*;
17:20 A man of perverse heart does not *p*
28:13 who conceals his sins does not *p*,
28:25 he who trusts in the LORD will *p*.
Isa 53:10 of the LORD will *p* in his hand.
Jer 12: 1 Why does the way of the wicked *p*?

PROSPERED (PROSPER)
Ge 39: 2 was with Joseph and he *p*,
2Ch 14: 7 So they built and *p*.
31:21 And so he *p*.

PROSPERITY (PROSPER)
Dt 28:11 will grant you abundant *p*–
30:15 I set before you today life and *p*,
Job 36:11 will spend the rest of their days in *p*
Ps 73: 3 when I saw the *p* of the wicked.
122: 9 I will seek your *p*.
128: 2 blessings and *p* will be yours.
Pr 3: 2 and bring you *p*.
13:21 but *p* is the reward of the righteous.
21:21 finds life, *p* and honor.
Isa 45: 7 I bring *p* and create disaster;

PROSPEROUS (PROSPER)
Dt 30: 9 your God will make you most *p*
Jos 1: 8 Then you will be *p* and successful.
Job 42:10 the LORD made him *p* again

PROSPERS (PROSPER)
Ps 1: 3 Whatever he does *p*.
Pr 16:20 gives heed to instruction *p*,
19: 8 he who cherishes understanding *p*.

PROSTITUTE (PROSTITUTES PROSTITUTION)
Lev 20: 6 and spiritists to *p* himself
Nu 15:39 and not *p* yourselves by going
Jos 2: 1 the house of a *p* named Rahab
Pr 6:26 for the *p* reduces you to a loaf
7:10 like a *p* and with crafty intent.
23:27 for a *p* is a deep pit
Eze 16:15 and used your fame to become a *p*.
23: 7 a *p* to all the elite of the Assyrians
Hos 3: 3 you must not be a *p* or be intimate
1Co 6:15 of Christ and unite them with a *p*?
6:16 with a *p* is one with her in body?
Rev 17: 1 you the punishment of the great *p*,

PROSTITUTES (PROSTITUTE)
Pr 29: 3 of *p* squanders his wealth.
Mt 21:31 and the *p* are entering the kingdom
Lk 15:30 property with *p* comes home,
1Co 6: 9 male *p* nor homosexual offenders

PROSTITUTION (PROSTITUTE)
Eze 16:16 where you carried on your *p*.
23: 3 engaging in *p* from their youth.
Hos 4:10 engage in *p* but not increase,

PROSTRATE
Dt 9:18 again I fell *p* before the LORD
1Ki 18:39 they fell *p* and cried, "The LORD

PROTECT (PROTECTED PROTECTION PROTECTS)
Dt 23:14 about in your camp to *p* you
Ps 25:21 integrity and uprightness *p* me,
32: 7 you will *p* me from trouble
40:11 your truth always *p* me.
41: 2 The LORD will *p* him
91:14 I will *p* him, for he acknowledges
140: 1 *p* me from men of violence,
Pr 2:11 Discretion will *p* you,
4: 6 forsake wisdom, and she will *p* you;
Jn 17:11 *p* them by the power of your name
17:15 that you *p* them from the evil one.
2Th 3: 3 and *p* you from the evil one.

PROTECTED (PROTECT)
Jos 24:17 He *p* us on our entire journey
1Sa 30:23 He has *p* us and handed
Ps 37:28 They will be *p* forever,
Jn 17:12 I *p* them and kept them safe

PROTECTION (PROTECT)
Ezr 9: 9 he has given us a wall of *p* in Judah
Ps 5:11 Spread your *p* over them,

PROTECTS (PROTECT)
Ps 116: 6 The LORD *p* the simplehearted;
Pr 2: 8 and *p* the way of his faithful ones.
1Co 13: 7 It always *p*, always trusts,

PROUD (PRIDE)
Ps 31:23 but the *p* he pays back in full.
101: 5 has haughty eyes and a *p* heart,
138: 6 but the *p* he knows from afar.
Pr 3:34 He mocks *p* mockers
16: 5 The LORD detests all the *p*
16:19 than to share plunder with the *p*.
18:12 his downfall a man's heart is *p*,
21: 4 Haughty eyes and a *p* heart,
Isa 2:12 store for all the *p* and lofty,
Ro 12:16 Do not be *p*, but be willing
1Co 13: 4 it does not boast, it is not *p*.
2Ti 3: 2 lovers of money, boastful, *p*,
Jas 4: 6 "God opposes the *p*
1Pe 5: 5 because, "God opposes the *p*

PROVE (PROOF PROVED PROVING)
Pr 29:25 Fear of man will *p* to be a snare,
Jn 8:46 Can any of you *p* me guilty of sin?
Ac 26:20 *p* their repentance by their deeds.
1Co 4: 2 been given a trust must *p* faithful.

PROVED (PROVE)
Ps 51: 4 so that you are *p* right
Mt 11:19 wisdom is *p* right by her actions."
Ro 3: 4 "So that you may be *p* right
1Pe 1: 7 may be *p* genuine and may result

PROVIDE (PROVIDED PROVIDES PROVISION)
Ge 22: 8 "God himself will *p* the lamb
22:14 that place "The LORD will *P*."
Isa 43:20 because I *p* water in the desert
61: 3 and *p* for those who grieve in Zion
1Co 10:13 *p* a way out so that you can stand
1Ti 5: 8 If anyone does not *p*
Tit 3:14 in order that they may *p*

PROVIDED (PROVIDE)
Ps 68:10 O God, you *p* for the poor.
111: 9 He *p* redemption for his people;
Jnh 1:17 But the LORD *p* a great fish
4: 6 Then the LORD God *p* a vine
4: 7 dawn the next day God *p* a worm,
4: 8 God *p* a scorching east wind,
Gal 4:18 to be zealous, *p* the purpose is good
Heb 1: 3 After he had *p* purification for sins,

PROVIDES (PROVIDE)
Ps 111: 5 He *p* food for those who fear him;
Pr 31:15 she *p* food for her family
Eze 18: 7 and *p* clothing for the naked.
1Ti 6:17 who richly *p* us with everything
1Pe 4:11 it with the strength God *p*,

PROVING* (PROVE)
Ac 9:22 by *p* that Jesus is the Christ.
17: 3 and *p* that the Christ had to suffer
18:28 *p* from the Scriptures that Jesus

PROVISION (PROVIDE)
Ro 5:17 who receive God's abundant *p*

PROVOKED
Ecc 7: 9 Do not be quickly *p* in your spirit,
Jer 32:32 Judah have *p* me by all the evil they

PROWLS
1Pe 5: 8 Your enemy the devil *p*

PRUDENCE* (PRUDENT)
Pr 1: 4 for giving *p* to the simple,
8: 5 You who are simple, gain *p*;
8:12 "I, wisdom, dwell together with *p*;
15: 5 whoever heeds correction shows *p*.
19:25 and the simple will learn *p*;

PRUDENT* (PRUDENCE)
Pr 1: 3 acquiring a disciplined and *p* life,
12:16 but a *p* man overlooks an insult.
12:23 A *p* man keeps his knowledge
13:16 Every *p* man acts out of knowledge
14: 8 The wisdom of the *p* is
14:15 a *p* man gives thought to his steps.
14:18 the *p* are crowned with knowledge.
19:14 but a *p* wife is from the LORD.
22: 3 *p* man sees danger and takes
27:12 The *p* see danger and take refuge,
Jer 49: 7 Has counsel perished from the *p*?
Am 5:13 Therefore the *p* man keeps quiet

PRUNES (PRUNING)
Jn 15: 2 that does bear fruit he *p*

PRUNING (PRUNES)
Isa 2: 4 and their spears into *p* hooks.
Joel 3:10 and your *p* hooks into spears.

PSALMS
Eph 5:19 Speak to one another with *p*,
Col 3:16 and as you sing *p*, hymns

PUBLICLY
Ac 20:20 have taught you *p* and from house
1Ti 5:20 Those who sin are to be rebuked *p*,

PUFFS
1Co 8: 1 Knowledge *p* up, but love builds up

PULLING
2Co 10: 8 building you up rather than *p* you

PUNISH (PUNISHED PUNISHES PUNISHMENT)
Ge 15:14 But I will *p* the nation they serve
Ex 32:34 I will *p* them for their sin."
Pr 17:26 It is not good to *p* an innocent man,
23:13 if you *p* him with the rod, he will
Isa 13:11 I will *p* the world for its evil,
Jer 2:19 Your wickedness will *p* you;
21:14 I will *p* you as your deeds deserve,
Zep 1:12 and *p* those who are complacent,
Ac 7: 7 But I will *p* the nation they serve
2Th 1: 8 He will *p* those who do not know
1Pe 2:14 by him to *p* those who do wrong

PUNISHED (PUNISH)
Ezr 9:13 you have *p* us less than our sins
Ps 99: 8 though you *p* their misdeeds.
La 3:39 complain when *p* for his sins?
Mk 12:40 Such men will be *p* most severely."
Lk 23:41 the same sentence? We are *p* justly,
2Th 1: 9 be *p* with everlasting destruction
Heb 10:29 to be *p* who has trampled the Son

PUNISHES (PUNISH)
Heb 12: 6 and he *p* everyone he accepts

PUNISHMENT (PUNISH)
Isa 53: 5 the *p* that brought us peace was
Jer 4:18 This is your *p*.
Mt 25:46 Then they will go away to eternal *p*
Lk 12:48 and does things deserving *p* will be
21:22 For this is the time of *p*
Ro 13: 4 wrath to bring *p* on the wrongdoer.
Heb 2: 2 disobedience received its just *p*,
2Pe 2: 9 while continuing their *p*.

PURCHASED
Ps 74: 2 Remember the people you *p* of old,
Rev 5: 9 with your blood you *p* men for God

PURE (PURIFICATION PURIFIED PURIFIES PURIFY PURITY)
2Sa 22:27 to the *p* you show yourself *p*,
Job 14: 4 Who can bring what is *p*
Ps 19: 9 The fear of the LORD is *p*,
24: 4 who has clean hands and a *p* heart,
51:10 Create in me a *p* heart, O God,
119: 9 can a young man keep his way *p*?
Pr 15:26 those of the *p* are pleasing to him.
20: 9 can say, "I have kept my heart *p*;
Isa 52:11 Come out from it and be *p*,

Hab 1:13 Your eyes are too *p* to look on evil;
Mt 5: 8 Blessed are the *p* in heart,
2Co 11: 2 I might present you as a *p* virgin
Php 4: 8 whatever is *p*, whatever is lovely,
1Ti 1: 5 which comes from a *p* heart
5:22 Keep yourself *p*.
2Ti 2:22 call on the Lord out of a *p* heart.
Tit 1:15 To the *p*, all things are *p*,
2: 5 to be self-controlled and *p*,
Heb 7:26 blameless, *p*, set apart from sinners
13: 4 and the marriage bed kept *p*,
Jas 1:27 that God our Father accepts as *p*
3:17 comes from heaven is first of all *p*;
1Jn 3: 3 him purifies himself, just as he is *p*.

PURGE
Pr 20:30 and beatings *p* the inmost being.

PURIFICATION (PURE)
Heb 1: 3 After he had provided *p* for sins,

PURIFIED (PURE)
Ac 15: 9 for he *p* their hearts by faith.
1Pe 1:22 Now that you have *p* yourselves

PURIFIES* (PURE)
1Jn 1: 7 of Jesus, his Son, *p* us from all sin.
3: 3 who has this hope in him *p* himself,

PURIFY (PURE)
Nu 19:12 He must *p* himself with the water
2Co 7: 1 us *p* ourselves from everything that
Tit 2:14 to *p* for himself a people that are
Jas 4: 8 you sinners, and *p* your hearts,
1Jn 1: 9 and *p* us from all unrighteousness.

PURIM
Est 9:26 Therefore these days were called *P*

PURITY* (PURE)
Hos 8: 5 long will they be incapable of *p*?
2Co 6: 6 in *p*, understanding, patience
1Ti 4:12 in life, in love, in faith and in *p*.
5: 2 as sisters, with absolute *p*.
1Pe 3: 2 when they see the *p* and reverence

PURPLE
Pr 31:22 she is clothed in fine linen and *p*.
Mk 15:17 They put a *p* robe on him, then

PURPOSE (PURPOSED PURPOSES)
Ex 9:16 I have raised you up for this very *p*,
Job 36: 5 he is mighty, and firm in his *p*.
Pr 19:21 but it is the LORD's *p* that prevails
Isa 46:10 I say: My *p* will stand,
55:11 and achieve the *p* for which I sent it
Ac 2:23 handed over to you by God's set *p*
Ro 8:28 have been called according to his *p*.
9:11 in order that God's *p*
9:17 "I raised you up for this very *p*,
1Co 3: 8 the man who waters have one *p*,
2Co 5: 5 who has made us for this very *p*
Gal 4:18 be zealous, provided the *p* is good,
Eph 1:11 in conformity with the *p* of his will,
3:11 according to his eternal *p* which he
Php 2: 2 love, being one in spirit and *p*.
2:13 and to act according to his good *p*.
2Ti 1: 9 but because of his own *p* and grace.

PURPOSED (PURPOSE)
Isa 14:24 and as I have *p*, so it will stand.
14:27 For the LORD Almighty has *p*,
Eph 1: 9 which he *p* in Christ, to be put

PURPOSES (PURPOSE)
Ps 33:10 he thwarts the *p* of the peoples.
Jer 23:20 the *p* of his heart.
32:19 great are your *p* and mighty are

PURSE (PURSES)
Hag 1: 6 to put them in a *p* with holes in it."
Lk 10: 4 Do not take a *p* or bag or sandals;
22:36 "But now if you have a *p*, take it,

PURSES (PURSE)
Lk 12:33 Provide *p* for yourselves that will

PURSUE (PURSUES)
Ps 34:14 seek peace and *p* it.
Pr 15: 9 he loves those who *p* righteousness
Ro 9:30 who did not *p* righteousness,
1Ti 6:11 and *p* righteousness, godliness,
2Ti 2:22 and *p* righteousness, faith,
1Pe 3:11 he must seek peace and *p* it.

PURSUES (PURSUE)
Pr 21:21 He who *p* righteousness and love
Pr 28: 1 wicked man flees though no one *p*,

QUAIL
Ex 16:13 That evening *q* came and covered
Nu 11:31 and drove *q* in from the sea.

QUALITIES* (QUALITY)
Da 6: 3 by his exceptional *q* that the king
Ro 1:20 of the world God's invisible *q*—
2Pe 1: 8 For if you possess these *q*

QUALITY (QUALITIES)
1Co 3:13 and the fire will test the *q*

QUARREL (QUARRELING QUARRELS QUARRELSOME)
Pr 15:18 but a patient man calms a *q*.
17:14 Starting a *q* is like breaching a dam;
17:19 He who loves a *q* loves sin;
20: 3 but every fool is quick to *q*.
26:17 in a *q* not his own.
26:20 without gossip a *q* dies down.
2Ti 2:24 And the Lord's servant must not *q*;
Jas 4: 2 You *q* and fight.

QUARRELING (QUARREL)
1Co 3: 3 For since there is jealousy and *q*
2Ti 2:14 before God against *q* about words;

QUARRELS (QUARREL)
Pr 13:10 Pride only breeds *q*,
Isa 45: 9 Woe to him who *q* with his Maker,
2Ti 2:23 because you know they produce *q*.
Jas 4: 1 What causes fights and *q*

QUARRELSOME (QUARREL)
Pr 19:13 a *q* wife is like a constant dripping.
21: 9 than share a house with a *q* wife.
26:21 so is a *q* man for kindling strife.
1Ti 3: 3 not violent but gentle, not *q*,

QUEEN
1Ki 10: 1 When the *q* of Sheba heard about
2Ch 9: 1 When the *q* of Sheba heard
Mt 12:42 The *Q* of the South will rise

QUENCH (QUENCHED)
SS 8: 7 Many waters cannot *q* love;

QUENCHED (QUENCH)
Isa 66:24 nor will their fire be *q*,
Mk 9:48 and the fire is not *q*.'

QUICK-TEMPERED* (TEMPER)
Pr 14:17 A *q* man does foolish things,
14:29 but a *q* man displays folly.
Tit 1: 7 not *q*, not given to drunkenness,

QUIET (QUIETNESS)
Ps 23: 2 he leads me beside *q* waters,
Pr 17: 1 Better a dry crust with peace and *q*
Ecc 9:17 The *q* words of the wise are more
Am 5:13 Therefore the prudent man keeps *q*
Zep 3:17 he will *q* you with his love,
Lk 19:40 he replied, "if they keep *q*,
1Th 4:11 it your ambition to lead a *q* life,
1Ti 2: 2 we may live peaceful and *q* lives
1Pe 3: 4 beauty of a gentle and *q* spirit,

QUIETNESS (QUIET)
Isa 30:15 in *q* and trust is your strength,
32:17 the effect of righteousness will be *q*
1Ti 2:11 A woman should learn in *q*

QUIVER
Ps 127: 5 whose *q* is full of them.

RACE
Ecc 9:11 The *r* is not to the swift
Ac 20:24 if only I may finish the *r*
1Co 9:24 that in a *r* all the runners run,
Gal 2: 2 that I was running or had run my *r*
5: 7 You were running a good *r*.
2Ti 4: 7 I have finished the *r*, I have kept
Heb 12: 1 perseverance the *r* marked out

RACHEL

Daughter of Laban (Ge 29:16); wife of Jacob (Ge 29:28); bore two sons (Ge 30:22–24; 35:16–24; 46:19). Stole Laban's gods (Ge 31:19, 32–35). Death (Ge 35:19–20).

RADIANCE (RADIANT)
Eze 1:28 so was the *r* around him.
Heb 1: 3 The Son is the *r* of God's glory

RADIANT (RADIANCE)
Ex 34:29 he was not aware that his face was *r*
Ps 34: 5 Those who look to him are *r*;
SS 5:10 *Beloved* My lover is *r* and ruddy,
Isa 60: 5 Then you will look and be *r*,
Eph 5:27 her to himself as a *r* church,

RAGE
Ac 4:25 " 'Why do the nations *r*
Col 3: 8 *r*, malice, slander, and filthy

RAGS
Isa 64: 6 our righteous acts are like filthy *r*;

RAHAB

Prostitute of Jericho who hid Israelite spies (Jos 2; 6:22–25; Heb 11:31; Jas 2:25). Mother of Boaz (Mt 1:5).

RAIN (RAINBOW)
Ge 7: 4 from now I will send *r* on the earth
1Ki 17: 1 nor *r* in the next few years
18: 1 and I will send *r* on the land."
Mt 5:45 and sends *r* on the righteous
Jas 5:17 it did not *r* on the land for three
Jude :12 They are clouds without *r*,

RAINBOW (RAIN)
Ge 9:13 I have set my *r* in the clouds,

RAISE (RISE)
Jn 6:39 but *r* them up at the last day.
1Co 15:15 he did not *r* him if in fact the dead

RAISED (RISE)
Isa 52:13 he will be *r* and lifted up
Mt 17:23 on the third day he will be *r* to life
Lk 7:22 the deaf hear, the dead are *r*,
Ac 2:24 But God *r* him from the dead,
Ro 4:25 was *r* to life for our justification.
6: 4 as Christ was *r* from the dead
8:11 And if the Spirit of him who *r* Jesus
10: 9 in your heart that God *r* him
1Co 15: 4 that he was *r* on the third day
15:20 But Christ has indeed been *r*

RALLY*
Isa 11:10 the nations will *r* to him,

RAM (RAMS)
Ge 22:13 there in a thicket he saw a *r* caught
Da 8: 3 before me was a *r* with two horns,

RAMPART*
Ps 91: 4 will be your shield and *r*.

RAMS (RAM)
1Sa 15:22 to heed is better than the fat of *r*.
Mic 6: 7 pleased with thousands of *r*,

RAN (RUN)
Jnh 1: 3 But Jonah *r* away from the LORD

RANSOM (RANSOMED)
Isa 50: 2 Was my arm too short to *r* you?
Hos 13:14 "I will *r* them from the power
Mt 20:28 and to give his life as a *r* for many."
Mk 10:45 and to give his life as a *r* for many."
1Ti 2: 6 who gave himself as a *r* for all men
Heb 9:15 as a *r* to set them free

RANSOMED (RANSOM)
Isa 35:10 and the *r* of the LORD will return.

RARE
Pr 20:15 that speak knowledge are a *r* jewel.

RAVEN (RAVENS)
Ge 8: 7 made in the ark and sent out a *r*,
Job 38:41 Who provides food for the *r*

RAVENS (RAVEN)
1Ki 17: 6 The *r* brought him bread
Ps 147: 9 and for the young *r* when they call.
Lk 12:24 Consider the *r*: They do not sow

READ (READING READS)
Dt 17:19 he is to *r* it all the days of his life
Jos 8:34 Joshua *r* all the words of the law—
2Ki 23: 2 He *r* in their hearing all the words
Ne 8: 8 They *r* from the Book of the Law
Jer 36: 6 and *r* to the people from the scroll
2Co 3: 2 known and *r* by everybody.

READING (READ)
1Ti 4:13 to the public *r* of Scripture,

READS (READ)
Rev 1: 3 Blessed is the one who *r* the words

REAFFIRM
2Co 2: 8 therefore, to *r* your love for him.

REAL* (REALITIES REALITY)
Jn 6:55 is *r* food and my blood is *r* drink.
1Jn 2:27 all things and as that anointing is *r*,

REALITIES* (REAL)
Heb 10: 1 are coming—not the *r* themselves.

REALITY* (REAL)
Col 2:17 the *r*, however, is found in Christ.

REALM (REALMS)
Hab 2: 9 "Woe to him who builds his *r*

REALMS (REALM)
Eph 1: 3 the heavenly *r* with every spiritual
2: 6 in the heavenly *r* in Christ Jesus,

REAP (REAPER REAPS)
Job 4: 8 and those who sow trouble *r* it.
Ps 126: 5 will *r* with songs of joy.
Hos 8: 7 and *r* the whirlwind.
10:12 *r* the fruit of unfailing love,
Jn 4:38 you to *r* what you have not worked
Ro 6:22 the benefit you *r* leads to holiness,
2Co 9: 6 generously will also *r* generously.
Gal 6: 8 from that nature will *r* destruction;

REAPER (REAP)
Jn 4:36 and the *r* may be glad together.

REAPS (REAP)
Pr 11:18 who sows righteousness *r* a sure
22: 8 He who sows wickedness *r* trouble,
Gal 6: 7 A man *r* what he sows.

REASON (REASONED)
Ge 2:24 For this *r* a man will leave his
Isa 1:18 "Come now, let us *r* together,"
Mt 19: 5 'For this *r* a man will leave his
Jn 12:27 it was for this very *r* I came
15:25 'They hated me without *r*.'
1Pe 3:15 to give the *r* for the hope that you
2Pe 1: 5 For this very *r*, make every effort

REASONED (REASON)
1Co 13:11 thought like a child, I *r* like a child.

REBEKAH
Sister of Laban, secured as bride for Isaac (Ge 24). Mother of Esau and Jacob (Ge 25:19–26). Taken by Abimelech as sister of Isaac; returned (Ge 26:1–11). Encouraged Jacob to trick Isaac out of blessing (Ge 27:1–17).

REBEL (REBELLED REBELLION REBELS)
Nu 14: 9 Only do not *r* against the LORD.
1Sa 12:14 and do not *r* against his commands,
Mt 10:21 children will *r* against their parents

REBELLED (REBEL)
Ps 78:56 and *r* against the Most High;
Isa 63:10 Yet they *r*

REBELLION (REBEL)
Ex 34: 7 and forgiving wickedness, *r* and sin
Nu 14:18 in love and forgiving sin and *r*.
1Sa 15:23 For *r* is like the sin of divination,
2Th 2: 3 will not come⌋ until the *r* occurs

REBELS (REBEL)
Ro 13: 2 he who *r* against the authority is
1Ti 1: 9 but for lawbreakers and *r*,

REBIRTH* (BEAR)
Tit 3: 5 us through the washing of *r*

REBUILD (BUILD)
Ezr 5: 2 set to work to *r* the house of God
Ne 2:17 let us *r* the wall of Jerusalem,
Ps 102: 16 For the LORD will *r* Zion
Da 9:25 and *r* Jerusalem until the Anointed
Am 9:14 they will *r* the ruined cities
Ac 15:16 Its ruins I will *r*,

REBUILT (BUILD)
Zec 1:16 and there my house will be *r*.

REBUKE (REBUKED REBUKES REBUKING)
Lev 19:17 *R* your neighbor frankly
Ps 141: 5 let him *r* me—it is oil on my head.
Pr 3:11 and do not resent his *r*,
9: 8 *r* a wise man and he will love you.
15:31 He who listens to a life-giving *r*
17:10 A *r* impresses a man
19:25 *r* a discerning man, and he will gain
25:12 is a wise man's *r* to a listening ear.
27: 5 Better is open *r*
30: 6 or he will *r* you and prove you a liar
Ecc 7: 5 It is better to heed a wise man's *r*
Isa 54: 9 never to *r* you again.
Jer 2:19 your backsliding will *r* you.
Lk 17: 3 "If your brother sins, *r* him,
1Ti 5: 1 Do not *r* an older man harshly,
2Ti 4: 2 correct, *r* and encourage—
Tit 1:13 Therefore, *r* them sharply,
2:15 Encourage and *r* with all authority.
Rev 3:19 Those whom I love I *r*

REBUKED (REBUKE)
Mk 16:14 he *r* them for their lack of faith
1Ti 5:20 Those who sin are to be *r* publicly,

REBUKES (REBUKE)
Job 22: 4 "Is it for your piety that he *r* you
Pr 28:23 He who *r* a man will
29: 1 remains stiff-necked after many *r*
Heb 12: 5 do not lose heart when he *r* you,

REBUKING (REBUKE)
2Ti 3:16 *r*, correcting and training

RECEIVE (RECEIVED RECEIVES)
Mt 10:41 a righteous man will *r* a righteous
Mk 10:15 anyone who will not *r* the kingdom
Jn 20:22 and said, "*R* the Holy Spirit.
Ac 1: 8 you will *r* power when the Holy
2:38 you will *r* the gift of the Holy Spirit
19: 2 "Did you *r* the Holy Spirit
20:35 'It is more blessed to give than to *r*
1Co 9:14 the gospel should *r* their living
2Co 6:17 and I will *r* you."
1Ti 1:16 believe on him and *r* eternal life.
Jas 1: 7 should not think he will *r* anything
2Pe 1:11 and you will *r* a rich welcome
1Jn 3:22 and *r* from him anything we ask,
Rev 4:11 to *r* glory and honor and power,
5:12 to *r* power and wealth and wisdom

RECEIVED (RECEIVE)
Mt 6: 2 they have *r* their reward in full.
10: 8 Freely you have *r*, freely give.
Mk 11:24 believe that you have *r* it,
Jn 1:12 Yet to all who *r* him,
1:16 his grace we have all *r* one blessing
Ac 8:17 and they *r* the Holy Spirit.
10:47 They have *r* the Holy Spirit just
Ro 8:15 but you *r* the Spirit of sonship.
1Co 11:23 For I *r* from the Lord what I
2Co 1: 4 the comfort we ourselves have *r*
Col 2: 6 just as you *r* Christ Jesus as Lord,
1Pe 4:10 should use whatever gift he has *r*

RECEIVES (RECEIVE)
Pr 18:22 and *r* favor from the LORD.
27:21 but man is tested by the praise he *r*.
Mt 7: 8 everyone who asks *r*; he who seeks
10:40 he who *r* me *r* the one who sent me.
10:40 "He who *r* you *r* me, and he who
Ac 10:43 believes in him *r* forgiveness of sins

RECITE
Ps 45: 1 as I *r* my verses for the king;

RECKLESS
Pr 12:18 *R* words pierce like a sword,
14:16 but a fool is hotheaded and *r*.

RECKONING
Isa 10: 3 What will you do on the day of *r*,
Hos 9: 7 the days of *r* are at hand.

RECLAIM* (CLAIM)
Isa 11:11 time to *r* the remnant that is left

RECOGNITION (RECOGNIZE)
1Co 16:18 Such men deserve *r*.
1Ti 5: 3 Give proper *r* to those widows who

RECOGNIZE (RECOGNITION RECOGNIZED)
Mt 7:16 By their fruit you will *r* them.
1Jn 4: 2 This is how you can *r* the Spirit
4: 6 This is how we *r* the Spirit of truth

RECOGNIZED (RECOGNIZE)
Mt 12:33 for a tree is *r* by its fruit.
Ro 7:13 in order that sin might be *r* as sin,

RECOMPENSE*
Isa 40:10 and his *r* accompanies him.
62:11 and his *r* accompanies him.' "

RECONCILE* (RECONCILED RECONCILIATION RECONCILING)
Ac 7:26 He tried to *r* them by saying, 'Men,
Eph 2:16 in this one body to *r* both of them
Col 1:20 him to *r* to himself all things,

RECONCILED* (RECONCILE)
Mt 5:24 First go and be *r* to your brother;
Lk 12:58 try hard to be *r* to him on the way,
Ro 5:10 how much more, having been *r*,
5:10 we were *r* to him through the death
1Co 7:11 or else be *r* to her husband.
2Co 5:18 who *r* us to himself through Christ
5:20 you on Christ's behalf: Be *r* to God.
Col 1:22 he has *r* you by Christ's physical

RECONCILIATION* (RECONCILE)
Ro 5:11 whom we have now received *r*.
11:15 For if their rejection is the *r*
2Co 5:18 and gave us the ministry of *r*:
5:19 committed to us the message of *r*.

RECONCILING* (RECONCILE)
2Co 5:19 that God was *r* the world to himself

RECORD (RECORDED)
Ps 130: 3 If you, O LORD, kept a *r* of sins,
Hos 13:12 his sins are kept on *r*.
1Co 13: 5 is not easily angered, it keeps no *r*

RECORDED (RECORD)
Job 19:23 "Oh, that my words were *r*,
Jn 20:30 which are not *r* in this book.

RECOUNT*
Ps 40: 5 no one can *r* to you;
79:13 we will *r* your praise.
119: 13 With my lips I *r*

RED
Ex 15: 4 are drowned in the *R* Sea.
Ps 106: 9 He rebuked the *R* Sea,
Pr 23:31 Do not gaze at wine when it is *r*,
Isa 1:18 though they are *r* as crimson,

REDEEM (KINSMAN-REDEEMER REDEEMED REDEEMER REDEEMS REDEMPTION)
Ex 6: 6 will *r* you with an outstretched arm
2Sa 7:23 on earth that God went out to *r*
Ps 44:26 *r* us because of your unfailing love.
49: 7 No man can *r* the life of another
49:15 God will *r* my life from the grave;
130: 8 He himself will *r* Israel
Hos 13:14 I will *r* them from death.
Gal 4: 5 under law, to *r* those under law,
Tit 2:14 for us to *r* us from all wickedness

REDEEMED (REDEEM)
Job 33:28 He *r* my soul from going
Ps 71:23 I, whom you have *r*.
107: 2 Let the *r* of the LORD say this—
Isa 35: 9 But only the *r* will walk there,
63: 9 In his love and mercy he *r* them;
Gal 3:13 Christ *r* us from the curse
1Pe 1:18 or gold that you were *r*

REDEEMER (REDEEM)
Job 19:25 I know that my *R* lives,
Ps 19:14 O LORD, my Rock and my *R*.
Isa 44: 6 and *R*, the LORD Almighty:
48:17 your *R*, the Holy One of Israel:
59:20 "The *R* will come to Zion,

REDEEMS (REDEEM)
Ps 34:22 The LORD *r* his servants;
103: 4 he *r* my life from the pit

REDEMPTION (REDEEM)
Ps 130: 7 and with him is full *r*.
Lk 21:28 because your *r* is drawing near."
Ro 3:24 grace through the *r* that came
8:23 as sons, the *r* of our bodies.
1Co 1:30 our righteousness, holiness and *r*.
Eph 1: 7 In him we have *r* through his blood
1:14 until the *r* of those who are God's
4:30 you were sealed for the day of *r*.
Col 1:14 in whom we have *r*, the forgiveness
Heb 9:12 having obtained eternal *r*.

REED
Isa 42: 3 A bruised *r* he will not break,
Mt 12:20 A bruised *r* he will not break,

REFINE*
Jer 9: 7 "See, I will *r* and test them,
Zec 13: 9 I will *r* them like silver
Mal 3: 3 and *r* them like gold and silver.

REFLECT (REFLECTS)
2Co 3:18 unveiled faces all *r* the Lord's

REFLECTS (REFLECT)
Pr 27:19 As water *r* a face,

REFRESH (REFRESHED REFRESHING)
Phm :20 in the Lord; *r* my heart in Christ.

REFRESHED (REFRESH)
Pr 11:25 refreshes others will himself be *r*.

REFRESHING* (REFRESH)
Ac 3:19 that times of *r* may come

REFUGE
Nu 35:11 towns to be your cities of *r*,
Dt 33:27 The eternal God is your *r*,
Jos 20: 2 to designate the cities of *r*,
Ru 2:12 wings you have come to take *r*."
2Sa 22: 3 God is my rock, in whom I take *r*,
22:31 a shield for all who take *r* in him.
Ps 2:12 Blessed are all who take *r* in him.
5:11 But let all who take *r* in you be glad
9: 9 The LORD is a *r* for the oppressed,
16: 1 for in you I take *r*.
17: 7 those who take *r* in you
18: 2 God is my rock, in whom I take *r*.
31: 2 be my rock of *r*,
34: 8 blessed is the man who takes *r*
36: 7 find *r* in the shadow of your wings.
46: 1 God is our *r* and strength,
62: 8 for God is our *r*.
71: 1 In you, O LORD, I have taken *r*;
91: 2 "He is my *r* and my fortress,
144: 2 my shield, in whom I take *r*,
Pr 14:26 and for his children it will be a *r*.
30: 5 a shield to those who take *r* in him.
Na 1: 7 a *r* in times of trouble.

REFUSE (REFUSED)
Jn 5:40 yet you *r* to come to me to have life

REFUSED (REFUSE)
2Th 2:10 because they *r* to love the truth
Rev 16: 9 but they *r* to repent and glorify him

REGARD (REGARDS)
1Th 5:13 Hold them in the highest *r* in love

REGARDS (REGARD)
Ro 14:14 But if anyone *r* something

REGRET
2Co 7:10 leads to salvation and leaves no *r*,

REHOBOAM
Son of Solomon (1Ki 11:43; 1Ch 3:10). Harsh treatment of subjects caused divided kingdom (1Ki 12:1–24; 14:21–31; 2Ch 10–12).

REIGN (REIGNED REIGNS)
Ex 15:18 The LORD will *r*
Ps 68:16 mountain where God chooses to *r*,
Isa 9: 7 He will *r* on David's throne
24:23 for the LORD Almighty will *r*
32: 1 See, a king will *r* in righteousness
Jer 23: 5 a King who will *r* wisely
Lk 1:33 and he will *r* over the house
Ro 6:12 Therefore do not let sin *r*
1Co 15:25 For he must *r* until he has put all
2Ti 2:12 we will also *r* with him.
Rev 11:15 and he will *r* for ever and ever."
20: 6 will *r* with him for a thousand years
22: 5 And they will *r* for ever and ever.

REIGNED (REIGN)
Ro 5:21 so that, just as sin *r* in death,
Rev 20: 4 and *r* with Christ a thousand years.

REIGNS (REIGN)
Ps 9: 7 The LORD *r* forever;
47: 8 God *r* over the nations;
93: 1 The LORD *r*, he is robed
96:10 among the nations, "The LORD *r*
97: 1 The LORD *r*, let the earth be glad;
99: 1 The LORD *r*, / let the nations tremble;
146: 10 The LORD *r* forever,
Isa 52: 7 "Your God *r*!"
Rev 19: 6 For our Lord God Almighty *r*.

REIN
Jas 1:26 and yet does not keep a tight *r*

REJECT (REJECTED REJECTION REJECTS)
Ps 94:14 For the LORD will not *r* his people
Ro 11: 1 I ask then: Did God *r* his people?

REJECTED (REJECT)
1Sa 8: 7 it is not you they have *r*,
1Ki 19:10 The Israelites have *r* your covenant
2Ki 17:15 They *r* his decrees
Ps 66:20 who has not *r* my prayer
118: 22 The stone the builders *r*
Isa 5:24 for they have *r* the law
41: 9 chosen you and have not *r* you.
53: 3 He was despised and *r* by men,
Jer 8: 9 Since they have *r* the word
Mt 21:42 " 'The stone the builders *r*
1Ti 4: 4 nothing is to be *r* if it is received
1Pe 2: 4 *r* by men but chosen by God
2: 7 "The stone the builders *r*

REJECTION* (REJECT)
Ro 11:15 For if their *r* is the reconciliation

REJECTS (REJECT)
Lk 10:16 but he who *r* me *r* him who sent me
Jn 3:36 whoever *r* the Son will not see life,
1Th 4: 8 he who *r* this instruction does not

REJOICE (JOY)
Dt 12: 7 shall *r* in everything you have put
1Ch 16:10 of those who seek the LORD *r*.
16:31 Let the heavens *r*, let the earth be
Ps 2:11 and *r* with trembling.
5:11 those who love your name may *r*
9:14 and there *r* in your salvation.
34: 2 let the afflicted hear and *r*.
63:11 But the king will *r* in God;
66: 6 come, let us *r* in him.
68: 3 and *r* before God;
105: 3 of those who seek the LORD *r*.
118: 24 let us *r* and be glad in it.
119: 14 I *r* in following your statutes
119:162 I *r* in your promise
149: 2 Let Israel *r* in their Maker;
Pr 5:18 may you *r* in the wife of your youth
23:25 may she who gave you birth *r*!
24:17 stumbles, do not let your heart *r*,
Isa 9: 3 as men *r*
35: 1 the wilderness will *r* and blossom.
61: 7 they will *r* in their inheritance;
62: 5 so will your God *r* over you.
Jer 31:12 they will *r* in the bounty
Zep 3:17 he will *r* over you with singing."
Zec 9: 9 *R* greatly, O Daughter of Zion!
Lk 6:23 "*R* in that day and leap for joy,
10:20 but *r* that your names are written
15: 6 '*R* with me; I have found my lost
15: 9 '*R* with me; I have found my lost
Ro 5: 2 And we *r* in the hope of the glory
12:15 Rejoice with those who *r*; mourn
Php 2:17 I am glad and *r* with all of you.
3: 1 Finally, my brothers, *r* in the Lord!
4: 4 *R* in the Lord always.
1Pe 4:13 But *r* that you participate
Rev 19: 7 Let us *r* and be glad

REJOICES (JOY)
Ps 13: 5 my heart *r* in your salvation.
16: 9 my heart is glad and my tongue *r*;
Isa 61:10 my soul *r* in my God.
62: 5 as a bridegroom *r* over his bride,
Lk 1:47 and my spirit *r* in God my Savior,
Ac 2:26 my heart is glad and my tongue *r*;
1Co 12:26 if one part is honored, every part *r*
13: 6 delight in evil but *r* with the truth.

REJOICING (JOY)
2Sa 6:12 to the City of David with *r*.
Ne 12:43 *r* because God had given them
Ps 30: 5 but *r* comes in the morning.
Lk 15: 7 in the same way there will be more *r*
Ac 5:41 *r* because they had been counted
2Co 6:10 sorrowful, yet always *r*; poor,

RELATIVES
Pr 19: 7 A poor man is shunned by all his *r*
Mk 6: 4 among his *r* and in his own house is
Lk 21:16 betrayed even by parents, brothers, *r*
1Ti 5: 8 If anyone does not provide for his *r*

RELEASE (RELEASED)
Isa 61: 1 and *r* from darkness,
Lk 4:18 to *r* the oppressed,

RELEASED (RELEASE)
Ro 7: 6 we have been *r* from the law
Rev 20: 7 Satan will be *r* from his prison

RELENTED (RELENTS)
Ex 32:14 the LORD *r* and did not bring
Ps 106: 45 and out of his great love he *r*.

RELENTS* (RELENTED)
Joel 2:13 and he *r* from sending calamity.
Jnh 4: 2 a God who *r* from sending calamity

RELIABLE (RELY)
Pr 22:21 teaching you true and *r* words,
Jn 8:26 But he who sent me is *r*,
2Ti 2: 2 witnesses entrust to *r* men who will

RELIANCE* (RELY)
Pr 25:19 is *r* on the unfaithful in times

RELIED (RELY)
2Ch 13:18 were victorious because they *r*
16: 8 Yet when you *r* on the LORD,
Ps 71: 6 From birth I have *r* on you;

RELIEF
Job 35: 9 they plead for *r* from the arm
Ps 94:13 you grant him *r* from days
143: 1 come to my *r*.
La 3:49 without *r*,
3:56 to my cry for *r*."
2Th 1: 7 and give *r* to you who are troubled,

RELIGION* (RELIGIOUS)
Ac 25:19 dispute with him about their own *r*
26: 5 to the strictest sect of our *r*,
1Ti 5: 4 all to put their *r* into practice
Jas 1:26 himself and his *r* is worthless.
1:27 *R* that God our Father accepts

RELIGIOUS (RELIGION)
Jas 1:26 If anyone considers himself *r*

RELY (RELIABLE RELIANCE RELIED)
Isa 50:10 and *r* on his God.
Eze 33:26 you then possess the land? You *r*
2Co 1: 9 this happened that we might not *r*
Gal 3:10 All who *r* on observing the law are
1Jn 4:16 and *r* on the love God has for us.

REMAIN (REMAINS)
Nu 33:55 allow to *r* will become barbs
Ps 102: 27 But you *r* the same,
Jn 1:32 from heaven as a dove and *r* on him
15: 4 *R* in me, and I will *r* in you.
15: 7 If you *r* in me and my words
15: 9 Now *r* in my love.
Ro 13: 8 Let no debt *r* outstanding,
1Co 13:13 And now these three *r*: faith,
2Ti 2:13 he will *r* faithful,
Heb 1:11 They will perish, but you *r*;
1Jn 2:27 just as it has taught you, *r* in him.

REMAINS (REMAIN)
Ps 146: 6 the LORD, who *r* faithful forever.
Heb 7: 3 Son of God he *r* a priest forever.

REMEDY
Isa 3: 7 "I have no *r*.

REMEMBER (REMEMBERED REMEMBERS REMEMBRANCE)
Ge 9:15 I will *r* my covenant between me
Ex 20: 8 "*R* the Sabbath day
33:13 *R* that this nation is your people."
Dt 5:15 *R* that you were slaves in Egypt
1Ch 16:12 *R* the wonders he has done,
Job 36:24 *R* to extol his work,
Ps 25: 6 *R*, O LORD, your great mercy
63: 6 On my bed I *r* you;
74: 2 *R* the people you purchased of old,
77:11 I will *r* the deeds of the LORD;
Ecc 12: 1 *R* your Creator
Isa 46: 8 "*R* this, fix it in mind,
Jer 31:34 and will *r* their sins no more."
Hab 3: 2 in wrath *r* mercy.
Lk 1:72 and to *r* his holy covenant,
Gal 2:10 we should continue to *r* the poor,
Php 1: 3 I thank my God every time I *r* you.
2Ti 2: 8 *R* Jesus Christ, raised
Heb 8:12 and will *r* their sins no more."

REMEMBERED (REMEMBER)
Ex 2:24 he *r* his covenant with Abraham,
3:15 am to be *r* from generation
Ps 98: 3 He has *r* his love
106: 45 for their sake he *r* his covenant
111: 4 He has caused his wonders to be *r*;
136: 23 to the One who *r* us
Isa 65:17 The former things will not be *r*,
Eze 18:22 offenses he has committed will be *r*
33:13 things he has done will be *r*;

REMEMBERS (REMEMBER)
Ps 103: 14 he *r* that we are dust.

Ps 111: 5 he *r* his covenant forever.
Isa 43:25 and *r* your sins no more.

REMEMBRANCE (REMEMBER)
Lk 22:19 given for you; do this in *r* of me."
1Co 11:24 which is for you; do this in *r* of me
11:25 whenever you drink it, in *r* of me."

REMIND
Jn 14:26 will *r* you of everything I have said
2Pe 1:12 I will always *r* you of these things,

REMNANT
Ezr 9: 8 has been gracious in leaving us a *r*
Isa 11:11 time to reclaim the *r* that is left
Jer 23: 3 "I myself will gather the *r*
Zec 8:12 inheritance to the *r* of this people.
Ro 11: 5 the present time there is a *r* chosen

REMOVED
Ps 30:11 you *r* my sackcloth and clothed me
103: 12 so far has he *r* our transgressions
Jn 20: 1 and saw that the stone had been *r*

REND
Joel 2:13 *R* your heart

RENEW (RENEWAL RENEWED RENEWING)
Ps 51:10 and *r* a steadfast spirit within me.
Isa 40:31 will *r* their strength.

RENEWAL (RENEW)
Isa 57:10 You found *r* of your strength,
Tit 3: 5 of rebirth and *r* by the Holy Spirit,

RENEWED (RENEW)
Ps 103: 5 that your youth is *r* like the eagle's.
2Co 4:16 yet inwardly we are being *r* day

RENEWING* (RENEW)
Ro 12: 2 transformed by the *r* of your mind.

RENOUNCE (RENOUNCED RENOUNCES)
Da 4:27 *R* your sins by doing what is right,

RENOUNCED (RENOUNCE)
2Co 4: 2 we have *r* secret and shameful

RENOUNCES (RENOUNCE)
Pr 28:13 confesses and *r* them finds

RENOWN*
Ge 6: 4 were the heroes of old, men of *r*.
Ps 102: 12 *r* endures through all generations.
135: 13 *r*, O LORD, through all
Isa 26: 8 your name and *r*
55:13 This will be for the LORD's *r*,
63:12 to gain for himself everlasting *r*,
Jer 13:11 to be my people for my *r* and praise
32:20 have gained the *r* that is still yours.
33: 9 Then this city will bring me *r*, joy,
49:25 the city of *r* not been abandoned,
Eze 26:17 How you are destroyed, O city of *r*,
Hos 12: 5 the LORD is his name of *r*!

REPAID (PAY)
Lk 6:34 to 'sinners,' expecting to be *r* in full
14:14 you will be *r* at the resurrection
Col 3:25 Anyone who does wrong will be *r*

REPAY (PAY)
Dt 7:10 But those who hate him he will *r*
32:35 It is mine to avenge; I will *r*.
Ru 2:12 May the LORD *r* you
Ps 103: 10 or *r* us according to our iniquities.
116: 12 How can I *r* the LORD
Jer 25:14 I will *r* them according
Ro 12:17 Do not *r* anyone evil for evil.
12:19 "It is mine to avenge; I will *r*,"
1Pe 3: 9 Do not *r* evil with evil

REPAYING (PAY)
2Ch 6:23 *r* the guilty by bringing
1Ti 5: 4 so *r* their parents and grandparents

REPEATED
Heb 10: 1 the same sacrifices *r* endlessly year

REPENT (REPENTANCE REPENTED REPENTS)
1Ki 8:47 *r* and plead with you in the land
Job 36:10 commands them to *r* of their evil.
42: 6 and *r* in dust and ashes."
Jer 15:19 "If you *r*, I will restore you
Eze 18:30 *R*! Turn away from all your
18:32 *R* and live! "Take up a lament
Mt 3: 2 "*R*, for the kingdom of heaven is
4:17 "*R*, for the kingdom of heaven is
Mk 6:12 and preached that people should *r*.
Lk 13: 3 unless you *r*, you too will all perish.
Ac 2:38 Peter replied, "*R* and be baptized,
3:19 *R*, then, and turn to God,
17:30 all people everywhere to *r*.
26:20 also, I preached that they should *r*
Rev 2: 5 *R* and do the things you did at first.

REPENTANCE (REPENT)
Isa 30:15 "In *r* and rest is your salvation,
Mt 3: 8 Produce fruit in keeping with *r*.
Mk 1: 4 a baptism of *r* for the forgiveness
Lk 3: 8 Produce fruit in keeping with *r*.
5:32 call the righteous, but sinners to *r*."
24:47 and *r* and forgiveness of sins will be
Ac 20:21 that they must turn to God in *r*
26:20 and prove their *r* by their deeds.
Ro 2: 4 kindness leads you toward *r*?
2Co 7:10 Godly sorrow brings *r* that leads
2Pe 3: 9 but everyone to come to *r*.

REPENTED (REPENT)
Mt 11:21 they would have *r* long ago

REPENTS (REPENT)
Lk 15: 7 in heaven over one sinner who *r*
15:10 of God over one sinner who *r*."
17: 3 rebuke him, and if he *r*, forgive him

REPORTS
Ex 23: 1 "Do not spread false *r*.

REPOSES*
Pr 14:33 Wisdom *r* in the heart

REPRESENTATION*
Heb 1: 3 and the exact *r* of his being,

REPROACH
Job 27: 6 my conscience will not *r* me
Isa 51: 7 Do not fear the *r* of men
1Ti 3: 2 Now the overseer must be above *r*,

REPUTATION
1Ti 3: 7 also have a good *r* with outsiders,

REQUESTS
Ps 20: 5 May the LORD grant all your *r*.
Php 4: 6 with thanksgiving, present your *r*

REQUIRE (REQUIRED REQUIRES)
Mic 6: 8 And what does the LORD *r* of you

REQUIRED (REQUIRE)
1Co 4: 2 it is *r* that those who have been

REQUIRES (REQUIRE)
1Ki 2: 3 what the LORD your God *r*:
Heb 9:22 the law *r* that nearly everything be

RESCUE (RESCUED RESCUES)
Ps 22: 8 let the LORD *r* him.
31: 2 come quickly to my *r*;
69:14 *R* me from the mire,
91:14 says the LORD, "I will *r* him;
143: 9 *R* me from my enemies, O LORD,
Da 6:20 been able to *r* you from the lions?"
Ro 7:24 Who will *r* me from this body
Gal 1: 4 himself for our sins to *r* us
2Pe 2: 9 how to *r* godly men from trials

RESCUED (RESCUE)
Ps 18:17 He *r* me from my powerful enemy,
Pr 11: 8 The righteous man is *r*
Col 1:13 For he has *r* us from the dominion

RESCUES (RESCUE)
Da 6:27 He *r* and he saves;
1Th 1:10 who *r* us from the coming wrath.

RESENT* (RESENTFUL RESENTS)
Pr 3:11 and do not *r* his rebuke,

RESENTFUL* (RESENT)
2Ti 2:24 to everyone, able to teach, not *r*.

RESENTS* (RESENT)
Pr 15:12 A mocker *r* correction;

RESERVE (RESERVED)
1Ki 19:18 Yet I *r* seven thousand in Israel—

RESERVED (RESERVE)
Ro 11: 4 "I have *r* for myself seven

RESIST (RESISTED RESISTS)
Da 11:32 know their God will firmly *r* him.
Mt 5:39 I tell you, Do not *r* an evil person.
Lk 21:15 of your adversaries will be able to *r*
Jas 4: 7 *R* the devil, and he will flee
1Pe 5: 9 *R* him, standing firm in the faith,

RESISTED (RESIST)
Job 9: 4 Who has *r* him and come out

RESISTS* (RESIST)
Ro 9:19 For who *r* his will?" But who are

RESOLVED
Ps 17: 3 I have *r* that my mouth will not sin.
Da 1: 8 But Daniel *r* not to defile himself
1Co 2: 2 For I *r* to know nothing while I was

RESOUNDING*
Ps 150: 5 praise him with *r* cymbals.
1Co 13: 1 I am only a *r* gong or a clanging

RESPECT (RESPECTABLE RESPECTED RESPECTS)
Lev 19: 3 " 'Each of you must *r* his mother
19:32 show *r* for the elderly and revere
Pr 11:16 A kindhearted woman gains *r*,
Mal 1: 6 where is the *r* due me?" says
Eph 5:33 and the wife must *r* her husband.
6: 5 obey your earthly masters with *r*
1Th 4:12 so that your daily life may win the *r*
5:12 to *r* those who work hard
1Ti 3: 4 children obey him with proper *r*.
3: 8 are to be men worthy of *r*, sincere,
3:11 are to be women worthy of *r*,
6: 1 their masters worthy of full *r*,
Tit 2: 2 worthy of *r*, self-controlled,
1Pe 2:17 Show proper *r* to everyone:
3: 7 them with *r* as the weaker partner
3:16 But do this with gentleness and *r*,

RESPECTABLE* (RESPECT)
1Ti 3: 2 self-controlled, *r*, hospitable,

RESPECTED (RESPECT)
Pr 31:23 Her husband is *r* at the city gate,

RESPECTS (RESPECT)
Pr 13:13 he who *r* a command is rewarded.

RESPLENDENT*
Ps 76: 4 You are *r* with light,
132: 18 but the crown on his head will be *r*

RESPOND
Ps 102: 17 He will *r* to the prayer
Hos 2:21 "I will *r* to the skies,

RESPONSIBILITY (RESPONSIBLE)
Ac 18: 6 your own heads! I am clear of my *r*.

RESPONSIBLE (RESPONSIBILITY)
Nu 1:53 The Levites are to be *r* for the care
1Co 7:24 Brothers, each man, as *r* to God,

REST (RESTED RESTS SABBATH-REST)
Ex 31:15 the seventh day is a Sabbath of *r*,
33:14 go with you, and I will give you *r*."
Lev 25: 5 The land is to have a year of *r*.
Dt 31:16 going to *r* with your fathers,
Jos 14:15 Then the land had *r* from war.
21:44 The LORD gave them *r*
1Ki 5: 4 The LORD my god has given me *r*
1Ch 22: 9 who will be a man of peace and *r*,
Job 3:17 and there the weary are at *r*.
Ps 16: 9 my body also will *r* secure,
33:22 May your unfailing love *r* upon us,
62: 1 My soul finds *r* in God alone;
62: 5 Find *r*, O my soul, in God alone;
90:17 of the Lord our God *r* upon us;
91: 1 will *r* in the shadow
95:11 "They shall never enter my *r*."
Pr 6:10 a little folding of the hands to *r*—
Isa 11: 2 Spirit of the LORD will *r* on him—
11:10 and his place of *r* will be glorious.
30:15 "In repentance and *r* is your
32:18 in undisturbed places of *r*.
57:20 which cannot *r*,
Jer 6:16 and you will find *r* for your souls.
47: 6 'how long till you *r*?
Mt 11:28 and burdened, and I will give you *r*.
2Co 12: 9 so that Christ's power may *r* on me
Heb 3:11 'They shall never enter my *r*.' "
4: 3 'They shall never enter my *r*.' "
4:10 for anyone who enters God's *r*
Rev 14:13 "they will *r* from their labor,

RESTED (REST)
Ge 2: 2 so on the seventh day he *r*
Heb 4: 4 "And on the seventh day God *r*

RESTITUTION
Ex 22: 3 "A thief must certainly make *r*,
Lev 6: 5 He must make *r* in full, add a fifth
Nu 5: 8 the *r* belongs to the LORD

RESTORE (RESTORES)
Ps 51:12 *R* to me the joy of your salvation
80: 3 *R* us, O God;
126: 4 *R* our fortunes, O LORD,
Jer 31:18 *R* me, and I will return,
La 5:21 *R* us to yourself, O LORD,
Da 9:25 From the issuing of the decree to *r*
Na 2: 2 The LORD will *r* the splendor
Gal 6: 1 are spiritual should *r* him gently.
1Pe 5:10 will himself *r* you and make you

RESTORES (RESTORE)
Ps 23: 3 he *r* my soul.

RESTRAINED (RESTRAINT)
Ps 78:38 Time after time he *r* his anger

RESTRAINING (RESTRAINT)
Pr 27:16 *r* her is like *r* the wind
Col 2:23 value in *r* sensual indulgence.

RESTRAINT (RESTRAINED RESTRAINING)
Pr 17:27 of knowledge uses words with *r*,
23: 4 have the wisdom to show *r*.
29:18 no revelation, the people cast off *r*;

RESTS (REST)
Dt 33:12 and the one the LORD loves *r*
Pr 19:23 one *r* content, untouched
Lk 2:14 to men on whom his favor *r*."

RESULT
Lk 21:13 This will *r* in your being witnesses
Ro 6:22 to holiness, and the *r* is eternal life.
11:31 as a *r* of God's mercy to you.
2Co 3: 3 from Christ, the *r* of our ministry,
2Th 1: 5 as a *r* you will be counted worthy
1Pe 1: 7 may be proved genuine and may *r*

RESURRECTION*
Mt 22:23 who say there is no *r*, came to him
22:28 at the *r*, whose wife will she be
22:30 At the *r* people will neither marry
22:31 But about the *r* of the dead—
27:53 and after Jesus' *r* they went
Mk 12:18 who say there is no *r*, came to him
12:23 At the *r* whose wife will she be,
Lk 14:14 repaid at the *r* of the righteous."
20:27 who say there is no *r*, came to Jesus
20:33 at the *r* whose wife will she be,
20:35 in the *r* from the dead will neither
20:36 since they are children of the *r*.
Jn 11:24 again in the *r* at the last day."
11:25 Jesus said to her, "I am the *r*
Ac 1:22 become a witness with us of his *r*."
2:31 he spoke of the *r* of the Christ,
4: 2 in Jesus the *r* of the dead.
4:33 to testify to the *r* of the Lord Jesus,
17:18 good news about Jesus and the *r*.
17:32 When they heard about the *r*
23: 6 of my hope in the *r* of the dead."
23: 8 Sadducees say that there is no *r*,
24:15 that there will be a *r*
24:21 'It is concerning the *r*
Ro 1: 4 Son of God by his *r* from the dead:
6: 5 also be united with him in his *r*.
1Co 15:12 some of you say that there is no *r*
15:13 If there is no *r* of the dead,
15:21 the *r* of the dead comes
15:29 if there is no *r*, what will those do
15:42 So will it be with the *r* of the dead.
Php 3:10 power of his *r* and the fellowship
3:11 to attain to the *r* from the dead.
2Ti 2:18 say that the *r* has already taken
Heb 6: 2 on of hands, the *r* of the dead,
11:35 so that they might gain a better *r*.
1Pe 1: 3 hope through the *r* of Jesus Christ
3:21 It saves you by the *r* of Jesus Christ
Rev 20: 5 This is the first *r*.
20: 6 those who have part in the first *r*.

RETALIATE*
1Pe 2:23 he did not *r*; when he suffered,

RETRIBUTION
Ps 69:22 may it become *r* and a trap.
Jer 51:56 For the LORD is a God of *r*;
Ro 11: 9 a stumbling block and a *r* for them.

RETURN (RETURNED RETURNS)
Ge 3:19 and to dust you will *r*."
2Sa 12:23 go to him, but he will not *r* to me."
2Ch 30: 9 If you *r* to the LORD, then your
Ne 1: 9 but if you *r* to me and obey my
Job 10:21 joy before I go to the place of no *r*,
16:22 before I go on the journey of no *r*.
22:23 If you *r* to the Almighty, you will
Ps 80:14 *R* to us, O God Almighty!
126: 6 will *r* with songs of joy,
Isa 10:21 A remnant will *r*, a remnant
35:10 the ransomed of the LORD will *r*.
55:11 It will not *r* to me empty,
Jer 24: 7 for they will *r* to me
31: 8 a great throng will *r*.
La 3:40 and let us *r* to the LORD.
Hos 6: 1 "Come, let us *r* to the LORD.
12: 6 But you must *r* to your God;
14: 1 *R*, O Israel, to the LORD your
Joel 2:12 "*r* to me with all your heart,
Zec 1: 3 '*R* to me,' declares the LORD
10: 9 and they will *r*.

RETURNED (RETURN)
Ps 35:13 When my prayers *r*
Am 4: 6 yet you have not *r* to me,"
1Pe 2:25 now you have *r* to the Shepherd

RETURNS (RETURN)
Pr 3:14 and yields better *r* than gold.
Isa 52: 8 When the LORD *r* to Zion,
Mt 24:46 finds him doing so when he *r*.

REUBEN

Firstborn of Jacob by Leah (Ge 29:32; 46:8; 1Ch 2:1). Attempted to rescue Joseph (Ge 37:21–30). Lost birthright for sleeping with Bilhah (Ge 35:22; 49:4). Tribe of blessed (Ge 49:3–4; Dt 33:6), numbered (Nu 1:21; 26:7), allotted land east of Jordan (Nu 32; 34:14; Jos 13:15), west (Eze 48:6), failed to help Deborah (Jdg 5:15–16), supported David (1Ch 12:37), 12,000 from (Rev 7:5).

REVEAL (REVEALED REVEALS REVELATION REVELATIONS)
Mt 11:27 to whom the Son chooses to *r* him.
Gal 1:16 was pleased to *r* his Son in me

REVEALED (REVEAL)
Dt 29:29 but the things *r* belong to us
Isa 40: 5 the glory of the LORD will be *r*,
43:12 I have *r* and saved and proclaimed
53: 1 the arm of the LORD been *r*?
65: 1 I *r* myself to those who did not ask
Mt 11:25 and *r* them to little children.
Jn 12:38 the arm of the Lord been *r*?"
17: 6 "I have *r* you to those whom you
Ro 1:17 a righteousness from God is *r*,
8:18 with the glory that will be *r* in us.
10:20 I *r* myself to those who did not ask
16:26 but now *r* and made known
1Co 2:10 but God has *r* it to us by his Spirit.
2Th 1: 7 happen when the Lord Jesus is *r*
2: 3 and the man of lawlessness is *r*,
1Pe 1: 7 and honor when Jesus Christ is *r*.
1:20 but was *r* in these last times
4:13 overjoyed when his glory is *r*.

REVEALS* (REVEAL)
Nu 23: 3 Whatever he *r* to me I will tell you
Job 12:22 He *r* the deep things of darkness
Da 2:22 He *r* deep and hidden things;
2:28 a God in heaven who *r* mysteries.
Am 4:13 and *r* his thoughts to man,

REVELATION* (REVEAL)
2Sa 7:17 David all the words of this entire *r*.
1Ch 17:15 David all the words of this entire *r*.
Pr 29:18 Where there is no *r*, the people cast
Da 10: 1 a *r* was given to Daniel (who was
Hab 2: 2 "Write down the *r*
2: 3 For the *r* awaits an appointed time;
Lk 2:32 a light for *r* to the Gentiles
Ro 16:25 according to the *r*
1Co 14: 6 I bring you some *r* or knowledge
14:26 a *r*, a tongue or an interpretation.
14:30 And if a *r* comes to someone who is
Gal 1:12 I received it by *r* from Jesus Christ.
2: 2 I went in response to a *r*
Eph 1:17 you the Spirit of wisdom and *r*,
3: 3 mystery made known to me by *r*,
Rev 1: 1 *r* of Jesus Christ, which God gave

REVELATIONS* (REVEAL)
2Co 12: 1 on to visions and *r* from the Lord.
12: 7 of these surpassingly great *r*,

REVELED* (REVELRY)
Ne 9:25 they *r* in your great goodness.

REVELRY (REVELED)
Ex 32: 6 drink and got up to indulge in *r*.
1Co 10: 7 and got up to indulge in pagan *r*."

REVENGE (VENGEANCE)
Lev 19:18 " 'Do not seek *r* or bear a grudge
Ro 12:19 Do not take *r*, my friends,

REVERE* (REVERENCE REVERENT REVERING)
Lev 19:32 for the elderly and *r* your God.
Dt 4:10 so that they may learn to *r* me
13: 4 must follow, and him you must *r*.
14:23 to *r* the LORD your God always.
17:19 learn to *r* the LORD his God
28:58 and do not *r* this glorious
Job 37:24 Therefore, men *r* him,
Ps 22:23 *R* him, all you descendants
33: 8 let all the people of the world *r* him
102: 15 of the earth will *r* your glory.
Ecc 3:14 God does it so that men will *r* him.
Isa 25: 3 cities of ruthless nations will *r* you.
59:19 of the sun, they will *r* his glory.
63:17 hearts so we do not *r* you?
Jer 10: 7 Who should not *r* you,
Hos 10: 3 because we did not *r* the LORD.
Mal 4: 2 But for you who *r* my name,

REVERENCE (REVERE)
Lev 19:30 and have *r* for my sanctuary.
Ne 5:15 of *r* for God I did not act like that.
Ps 5: 7 in *r* will I bow down
Da 6:26 people must fear and *r* the God
2Co 7: 1 perfecting holiness out of *r* for God
Eph 5:21 to one another out of *r* for Christ.
Col 3:22 of heart and *r* for the Lord.
1Pe 3: 2 when they see the purity and *r*
Rev 11:18 and those who *r* your name,

REVERENT* (REVERE)
Ecc 8:12 with God-fearing men, who are *r*
Tit 2: 3 women to be *r* in the way they live,
Heb 5: 7 because of his *r* submission.
1Pe 1:17 as strangers here in *r* fear.

REVERING* (REVERE)
Dt 8: 6 walking in his ways and *r* him.
Ne 1:11 who delight in *r* your name.

REVERSE*
Isa 43:13 When I act, who can *r* it?"

REVIVE* (REVIVING)
Ps 80:18 *r* us, and we will call on your name.
85: 6 Will you not *r* us again,
Isa 57:15 and to *r* the heart of the contrite.
57:15 to *r* the spirit of the lowly
Hos 6: 2 After two days he will *r* us;

REVIVING* (REVIVE)
Ps 19: 7 *r* the soul.

REVOKED
Isa 45:23 a word that will not be *r*:

REWARD (REWARDED REWARDING REWARDS)
Ge 15: 1 your very great *r*."
1Sa 24:19 May the LORD *r* you well
Ps 19:11 in keeping them there is great *r*.
62:12 Surely you will *r* each person
127: 3 children a *r* from him.
Pr 9:12 are wise, your wisdom will *r* you;
11:18 sows righteousness reaps a sure *r*.
13:21 prosperity is the *r* of the righteous.
19:17 he will *r* him for what he has done.
25:22 and the LORD will *r* you.
31:31 Give her the *r* she has earned,
Isa 40:10 See, his *r* is with him,
49: 4 and my *r* is with my God."
61: 8 In my faithfulness I will *r* them
62:11 See, his *r* is with him,
Jer 17:10 to *r* a man according to his conduct
32:19 you *r* everyone according
Mt 5:12 because great is your *r* in heaven,
6: 1 you will have no *r*
6: 5 they have received their *r* in full.
10:41 a prophet will receive a prophet's *r*,
16:27 and then he will *r* each person
Lk 6:23 because great is your *r* in heaven.
6:35 Then your *r* will be great,
1Co 3:14 built survives, he will receive his *r*.

Eph 6: 8 know that the Lord will *r* everyone
Col 3:24 an inheritance from the Lord as a *r*.
Heb 11:26 he was looking ahead to his *r*.
Rev 22:12 I am coming soon! My *r* is with me

REWARDED (REWARD)
Ru 2:12 May you be richly *r* by the LORD,
2Sa 22:21 of my hands he has *r* me.
2Ch 15: 7 for your work will be *r*."
Ps 18:24 The LORD has *r* me according
Pr 13:13 he who respects a command is *r*.
14:14 and the good man *r* for his.
Jer 31:16 for your work will be *r*,"
1Co 3: 8 and each will be *r* according
Heb 10:35 your confidence; it will be richly *r*.
2Jn : 8 but that you may be *r* fully.

REWARDING* (REWARD)
Rev 11:18 for *r* your servants the prophets

REWARDS (REWARD)
1Sa 26:23 The LORD *r* every man
Pr 12:14 the work of his hands *r* him.
Heb 11: 6 that he *r* those who earnestly seek

RIBS
Ge 2:21 he took one of the man's *r*

RICH (RICHES RICHEST)
Job 34:19 does not favor the *r* over the poor,
Ps 49:16 overawed when a man grows *r*,
145: 8 slow to anger and *r* in love.
Pr 21:17 loves wine and oil will never be *r*.
22: 2 *R* and poor have this in common:
23: 4 Do not wear yourself out to get *r*;
28: 6 than a *r* man whose ways are
28:20 to get *r* will not go unpunished.
28:22 A stingy man is eager to get *r*
Ecc 5:12 but the abundance of a *r* man
Isa 33: 6 a *r* store of salvation and wisdom
53: 9 and with the *r* in his death,
Jer 9:23 or the *r* man boast of his riches,
Zec 3: 4 and I will put *r* garments on you."
Mt 19:23 it is hard for a *r* man
Lk 1:53 but has sent the *r* away empty.
6:24 "But woe to you who are *r*,
12:21 for himself but is not *r* toward God
16: 1 "There was a *r* man whose
21: 1 Jesus saw the *r* putting their gifts
2Co 6:10 yet making many *r*; having nothing
8: 2 poverty welled up in *r* generosity.
8: 9 he was *r*, yet for your sakes he
9:11 You will be made *r* in every way
Eph 2: 4 love for us, God, who is *r* in mercy,
1Ti 6: 9 want to get *r* fall into temptation
6:17 Command those who are *r*
6:18 to do good, to be *r* in good deeds,
Jas 1:10 the one who is *r* should take pride
2: 5 the eyes of the world to be *r* in faith
5: 1 you *r* people, weep and wail
Rev 2: 9 and your poverty—yet you are *r*!
3:18 you can become *r*; and white

RICHES (RICH)
Job 36:18 that no one entices you by *r*;
Ps 49: 6 and boast of their great *r*?
49:12 despite his *r*, does not endure;
62:10 though your *r* increase,
119: 14 as one rejoices in great *r*.
Pr 3:16 in her left hand are *r* and honor.
11:28 Whoever trusts in his *r* will fall,
22: 1 is more desirable than great *r*;
27:24 for *r* do not endure forever,
30: 8 give me neither poverty nor *r*,
Isa 10: 3 Where will you leave your *r*?
60: 5 to you the *r* of the nations will
Jer 9:23 or the rich man boast of his *r*,
Lk 8:14 *r* and pleasures, and they do not
Ro 9:23 to make the *r* of his glory known
11:33 the depth of the *r* of the wisdom
Eph 2: 7 he might show the incomparable *r*
3: 8 to the Gentiles the unsearchable *r*
Col 1:27 among the Gentiles the glorious *r*
2: 2 so that they may have the full *r*

RICHEST (RICH)
Isa 55: 2 and your soul will delight in the *r*

RID
Ge 21:10 "Get *r* of that slave woman
1Co 5: 7 Get *r* of the old yeast that you may
Gal 4:30 "Get *r* of the slave woman

RIDE (RIDER RIDING)
Ps 45: 4 In your majesty *r* forth victoriously

RIDER (RIDE)
Rev 6: 2 was a white horse! Its *r* held a bow,
19:11 whose *r* is called Faithful and True.

RIDING (RIDE)
Zec 9: 9 gentle and *r* on a donkey,
Mt 21: 5 gentle and *r* on a donkey,

RIGGING
Isa 33:23 Your *r* hangs loose:

RIGHT (RIGHTS)
Ge 4: 7 But if you do not do what is *r*,
18:19 of the LORD by doing what is *r*
18:25 the Judge of all the earth do *r*?"
48:13 on his left toward Israel's *r* hand,
Ex 15: 6 Your *r* hand, O LORD,
15:26 and do what is *r* in his eyes,
Dt 5:32 do not turn aside to the *r*
6:18 Do what is *r* and good
13:18 and doing what is *r* in his eyes.
Jos 1: 7 do not turn from it to the *r*
1Sa 12:23 you the way that is good and *r*.
1Ki 3: 9 to distinguish between *r* and wrong
15: 5 For David had done what was *r*
2Ki 7: 9 to each other, "We're not doing *r*.
Ne 9:13 and laws that are just and *r*,
Ps 16: 8 Because he is at my *r* hand,
16:11 eternal pleasures at your *r* hand.
17: 7 you who save by your *r* hand
18:35 and your *r* hand sustains me;
19: 8 The precepts of the LORD are *r*,
25: 9 He guides the humble in what is *r*
33: 4 For the word of the LORD is *r*
44: 3 it was your *r* hand, your arm,
45: 4 let your *r* hand display awesome
51: 4 so that you are proved *r*
63: 8 your *r* hand upholds me.
73:23 you hold me by my *r* hand.
91: 7 ten thousand at your *r* hand,
98: 1 his *r* hand and his holy arm
106: 3 who constantly do what is *r*.
110: 1 "Sit at my *r* hand
118: 15 LORD's *r* hand has done mighty
119:144 Your statutes are forever *r*;
137: 5 may my *r* hand forget its skill.
139: 10 your *r* hand will hold me fast.
Pr 1: 3 doing what is *r* and just and fair;
4:27 Do not swerve to the *r* or the left;
14:12 There is a way that seems *r*
18:17 The first to present his case seems *r*
Ecc 7:20 who does what is *r* and never sins.
SS 1: 4 How *r* they are to adore you!
Isa 1:17 learn to do *r*!
7:15 reject the wrong and choose the *r*.
30:10 us no more visions of what is *r*!
30:21 Whether you turn to the *r*
41:10 you with my righteous *r* hand.
41:13 who takes hold of your *r* hand
48:13 my *r* hand spread out the heavens;
64: 5 to the help of those who gladly do *r*
Jer 23: 5 and do what is just and *r* in the land
Eze 18: 5 who does what is just and *r*.
18:21 and does what is just and *r*,
33:14 and does what is just and *r*—
Hos 14: 9 The ways of the LORD are *r*;
Mt 5:29 If your *r* eye causes you to sin,
6: 3 know what your *r* hand is doing,
22:44 "Sit at my *r* hand
25:33 He will put the sheep on his *r*
Jn 1:12 he gave the *r* to become children
Ac 2:34 "Sit at my *r* hand
7:55 Jesus standing at the *r* hand of God
Ro 3: 4 "So that you may be proved *r*
8:34 is at the *r* hand of God and is
9:21 Does not the potter have the *r*
12:17 careful to do what is *r* in the eyes
1Co 9: 4 Don't we have the *r* to food
2Co 8:21 we are taking pains to do what is *r*,
Eph 1:20 and seated him at his *r* hand
6: 1 parents in the Lord, for this is *r*.
Php 4: 8 whatever is *r*, whatever is pure,
2Th 3:13 never tire of doing what is *r*.
Heb 1: 3 down at the *r* hand of the Majesty
Jas 2: 8 as yourself," you are doing *r*.
1Pe 3:14 if you should suffer for what is *r*,
1Jn 2:29 who does what is *r* has been born
Rev 2: 7 I will give the *r* to eat from the tree
3:21 I will give the *r* to sit with me
22:11 let him who does *r* continue to do *r*

RIGHTEOUS (RIGHTEOUSLY RIGHTEOUSNESS)
Ge 6: 9 Noah was a *r* man, blameless
18:23 "Will you sweep away the *r*
Nu 23:10 Let me die the death of the *r*,
Ne 9: 8 your promise because you are *r*.
Job 36: 7 He does not take his eyes off the *r*;
Ps 1: 5 nor sinners in the assembly of the *r*.
5:12 O LORD, you bless the *r*;
11: 7 For the LORD is *r*,
15: 2 and who does what is *r*,
34:15 The eyes of the LORD are on the *r*
37:16 Better the little that the *r* have
37:21 but the *r* give generously;
37:25 yet I have never seen the *r* forsaken
37:30 of the *r* man utters wisdom,
55:22 he will never let the *r* fall.
64:10 Let the *r* rejoice in the LORD
68: 3 But may the *r* be glad
112: 4 compassionate and *r* man.
118: 20 through which the *r* may enter.
119: 7 as I learn your *r* laws.
119:137 *R* are you, O LORD,
140: 13 Surely the *r* will praise your name
143: 2 for no one living is *r* before you.
145: 17 The LORD is *r* in all his ways
Pr 3:33 but he blesses the home of the *r*.
4:18 of the *r* is like the first gleam
10: 7 of the *r* will be a blessing,
10:11 The mouth of the *r* is a fountain
10:16 The wages of the *r* bring them life,
10:20 The tongue of the *r* is choice silver,
10:24 what the *r* desire will be granted.
10:28 The prospect of the *r* is joy,
10:32 of the *r* know what is fitting,
11:23 The desire of the *r* ends only
11:30 The fruit of the *r* is a tree of life,
12:10 A *r* man cares for the needs
12:21 No harm befalls the *r*,
13: 9 The light of the *r* shines brightly,
15:28 of the *r* weighs its answers,
15:29 but he hears the prayer of the *r*.
16:31 it is attained by a *r* life.
18:10 the *r* run to it and are safe.
20: 7 The *r* man leads a blameless life;
21:15 justice is done, it brings joy to the *r*
23:24 The father of a *r* man has great joy;
28: 1 but the *r* are as bold as a lion.
29: 6 but a *r* one can sing and be glad.
29: 7 The *r* care about justice
29:27 The *r* detest the dishonest;
Ecc 7:20 There is not a *r* man on earth
Isa 26: 7 The path of the *r* is level;
41:10 you with my *r* right hand.
45:21 a *r* God and a Savior;
53:11 his knowledge my *r* servant will
64: 6 and all our *r* acts are like filthy rags
Jer 23: 5 up to David a *r* Branch,
Eze 3:20 when a *r* man turns
18: 5 "Suppose there is a *r* man
18:20 of the *r* man will be credited
33:12 The *r* man, if he sins, will not be
Da 9:18 requests of you because we are *r*,
Hab 2: 4 but the *r* will live by his faith—
Zec 9: 9 *r* and having salvation,
Mal 3:18 see the distinction between the *r*
Mt 5:45 rain on the *r* and the unrighteous.
9:13 For I have not come to call the *r*,
10:41 and anyone who receives a *r* man
13:43 Then the *r* will shine like the sun
13:49 and separate the wicked from the *r*
25:37 "Then the *r* will answer him, 'Lord,
25:46 to eternal punishment, but the *r*
Ac 24:15 will be a resurrection of both the *r*
Ro 1:17 as it is written: "The *r* will live
2: 5 when his *r* judgment will be
2:13 the law who will be declared *r*.
3:10 "There is no one *r*, not even one;
3:20 Therefore no one will be declared *r*
5:19 one man the many will be made *r*.
Gal 3:11 because, "The *r* will live by faith."
1Ti 1: 9 that law is made not for the *r*
2Ti 4: 8 which the Lord, the *r* Judge,
Tit 3: 5 because of *r* things we had done,
Heb 10:38 But my *r* one will live by faith.
Jas 5:16 The prayer of a *r* man is powerful
1Pe 3:12 the eyes of the Lord are on the *r*
3:18 the *r* for the unrighteous,
4:18 "If it is hard for the *r* to be saved,
1Jn 2: 1 defense—Jesus Christ, the *R* One.

1Jn 3: 7 does what is right is *r,* just as he is *r.*
Rev 19: 8 stands for the *r* acts of the saints.)

RIGHTEOUSLY* (RIGHTEOUS)
Ps 9: 4 on your throne, judging *r.*
Isa 33:15 He who walks *r*
Jer 11:20 LORD Almighty, you who judge *r*

RIGHTEOUSNESS (RIGHTEOUS)
Ge 15: 6 and he credited it to him as *r.*
Dt 9: 4 of this land because of my *r."*
1Sa 26:23 LORD rewards every man for his *r*
1Ki 10: 9 to maintain justice and *r."*
Job 37:23 great *r,* he does not oppress.
Ps 7:17 to the LORD because of his *r*
9: 8 He will judge the world in *r;*
17:15 And I—in *r* I will see your face;
23: 3 He guides me in paths of *r*
33: 5 The LORD loves *r* and justice;
35:28 My tongue will speak of your *r*
36: 6 Your *r* is like the mighty
37: 6 He will make your *r* shine like
40: 9 I proclaim *r* in the great assembly;
45: 4 in behalf of truth, humility and *r;*
45: 7 You love *r* and hate wickedness;
48:10 your right hand is filled with *r.*
65: 5 us with awesome deeds of *r,*
71: 2 Rescue me and deliver me in your *r*
71:15 My mouth will tell of your *r,*
71:19 Your *r* reaches to the skies, O God,
85:10 *r* and peace kiss each other.
89:14 *R* and justice are the foundation
96:13 He will judge the world in *r*
98: 9 He will judge the world in *r*
103: 6 The LORD works *r*
103: 17 his *r* with their children's children
106: 31 This was credited to him as *r*
111: 3 and his *r* endures forever.
118: 19 Open for me the gates of *r;*
132: 9 May your priests be clothed with *r;*
145: 7 and joyfully sing of your *r.*
Pr 11: 5 *r* of the blameless makes a straight
11:18 he who sows *r* reaps a sure reward.
13: 6 *R* guards the man of integrity,
14:34 *R* exalts a nation,
16: 8 Better a little with *r*
16:12 a throne is established through *r.*
21:21 He who pursues *r* and love
Isa 5:16 will show himself holy by his *r.*
9: 7 it with justice and *r*
11: 4 but with *r* he will judge the needy,
16: 5 and speeds the cause of *r.*
26: 9 the people of the world learn *r.*
32:17 The fruit of *r* will be peace;
42: 6 "I, the LORD, have called you in *r;*
42:21 the LORD for the sake of his *r*
45: 8 "You heavens above, rain down *r;*
51: 1 "Listen to me, you who pursue *r*
51: 6 my *r* will never fail.
51: 8 But my *r* will last forever,
58: 8 then your *r* will go before you,
59:17 He put on *r* as his breastplate,
61:10 and arrayed me in a robe of *r,*
63: 1 "It is I, speaking in *r,*
Jer 9:24 justice and *r* on earth,
23: 6 The LORD Our *R.*
Eze 3:20 a righteous man turns from his *r*
14:20 save only themselves by their *r.*
18:20 The *r* of the righteous man will be
33:12 *r* of the righteous man will not save
Da 9:24 to bring in everlasting *r,*
12: 3 and those who lead many to *r,*
Hos 10:12 Sow for yourselves *r,*
Am 5:24 *r* like a never-failing stream!
Mic 7: 9 I will see his *r.*
Zep 2: 3 Seek *r,* seek humility;
Mal 4: 2 the sun of *r* will rise with healing
Mt 5: 6 those who hunger and thirst for *r,*
5:10 who are persecuted because of *r,*
5:20 unless your *r* surpasses that
6: 1 to do your 'acts of *r'* before men,
6:33 But seek first his kingdom and his *r*
Jn 16: 8 world of guilt in regard to sin and *r*
Ac 24:25 Paul discoursed on *r,* self-control
Ro 1:17 For in the gospel a *r* from God is
3: 5 brings out God's *r* more clearly,
3:22 This *r* from God comes
4: 3 and it was credited to him as *r."*
4: 5 wicked, his faith is credited as *r.*
4: 6 man to whom God credits *r* apart
4: 9 faith was credited to him as *r.*
Ro 4:13 through the *r* that comes by faith.
4:22 why "it was credited to him as *r."*
5:18 of *r* was justification that brings life
6:13 body to him as instruments of *r.*
6:16 or to obedience, which leads to *r?*
6:18 and have become slaves to *r.*
6:19 in slavery to *r* leading to holiness.
8:10 yet your spirit is alive because of *r.*
9:30 did not pursue *r,* have obtained it,
10: 3 they did not know the *r* that comes
14:17 but of *r,* peace and joy
1Co 1:30 our *r,* holiness and redemption.
2Co 3: 9 is the ministry that brings *r!*
5:21 that in him we might become the *r*
6: 7 with weapons of *r* in the right hand
6:14 For what do *r* and wickedness have
9: 9 his *r* endures forever."
Gal 2:21 for if *r* could be gained
3: 6 and it was credited to him as *r."*
3:21 then *r* would certainly have come
Eph 4:24 created to be like God in true *r*
5: 9 *r* and truth) and find out what
6:14 with the breastplate of *r* in place,
Php 1:11 filled with the fruit of *r* that comes
3: 6 as for legalistic *r,* faultless.
3: 9 not having a *r* of my own that
1Ti 6:11 and pursue *r,* godliness, faith, love,
2Ti 2:22 and pursue *r,* faith, love and peace,
3:16 correcting and training in *r,*
4: 8 is in store for me the crown of *r,*
Heb 1: 8 and *r* will be the scepter
5:13 with the teaching about *r.*
7: 2 his name means "king of *r";*
11: 7 became heir of the *r* that comes
12:11 it produces a harvest of *r*
Jas 2:23 and it was credited to him as *r,"*
3:18 sow in peace raise a harvest of *r.*
1Pe 2:24 die to sins and live for *r;*
2Pe 2:21 not to have known the way of *r,*
3:13 and a new earth, the home of *r.*

RIGHTS (RIGHT)
Ps 82: 3 maintain the *r* of the poor
Pr 31: 8 for the *r* of all who are destitute.
Isa 10: 2 to deprive the poor of their *r*
La 3:35 to deny a man his *r*
Gal 4: 5 that we might receive the full *r*

RING
Pr 11:22 Like a gold *r* in a pig's snout
Lk 15:22 Put a *r* on his finger and sandals

RIOTS
2Co 6: 5 imprisonments and *r;* in hard work,

RIPE
Joel 3:13 for the harvest is *r.*
Am 8: 1 showed me: a basket of *r* fruit.
Jn 4:35 at the fields! They are *r* for harvest.
Rev 14:15 for the harvest of the earth is *r."*

RISE (RAISE RAISED RISEN ROSE)
Lev 19:32 " '*R* in the presence of the aged,
Nu 24:17 a scepter will *r* out of Israel.
Isa 26:19 their bodies will *r.*
Mal 4: 2 of righteousness will *r* with healing
Mt 27:63 'After three days I will *r* again.'
Mk 8:31 and after three days *r* again.
Lk 18:33 On the third day he will *r* again."
Jn 5:29 those who have done good will *r*
20: 9 had to *r* from the dead.)
Ac 17: 3 had to suffer and *r* from the dead.
1Th 4:16 and the dead in Christ will *r* first.

RISEN (RISE)
Mt 28: 6 He is not here; he has *r,* just
Mk 16: 6 He has *r!* He is not here.
Lk 24:34 The Lord has *r* and has appeared

RIVER (RIVERS)
Ps 46: 4 There is a *r* whose streams make
Isa 66:12 "I will extend peace to her like a *r,*
Eze 47:12 grow on both banks of the *r.*
Rev 22: 1 Then the angel showed me the *r*

RIVERS (RIVER)
Ps 137: 1 By the *r* of Babylon we sat

ROAD (CROSSROADS ROADS)
Mt 7:13 and broad is the *r* that leads

ROADS (ROAD)
Lk 3: 5 crooked *r* shall become straight,

ROARING
1Pe 5: 8 prowls around like a *r* lion looking

ROB (ROBBERS ROBBERY ROBS)
Mal 3: 8 "Will a man *r* God? Yet you *r* me.

ROBBERS (ROB)
Jer 7:11 become a den of *r* to you?
Mk 15:27 They crucified two *r* with him,
Lk 19:46 but you have made it 'a den of *r.'"*
Jn 10: 8 came before me were thieves and *r,*

ROBBERY (ROB)
Isa 61: 8 I hate *r* and iniquity.

ROBE (ROBED ROBES)
Ge 37: 3 and he made a richly ornamented *r*
Isa 6: 1 the train of his *r* filled the temple.
61:10 arrayed me in a *r* of righteousness,
Rev 6:11 each of them was given a white *r,*

ROBED (ROBE)
Ps 93: 1 the LORD is *r* in majesty
Isa 63: 1 Who is this, *r* in splendor,

ROBES (ROBE)
Ps 45: 8 All your *r* are fragrant with myrrh
Rev 7:13 "These in white *r*—who are they,

ROBS* (ROB)
Pr 19:26 He who *r* his father and drives out
28:24 He who *r* his father or mother

ROCK
Ge 49:24 of the Shepherd, the *R* of Israel,
Ex 17: 6 Strike the *r,* and water will come
Nu 20: 8 Speak to that *r* before their eyes
Dt 32: 4 He is the *R,* his works are perfect,
32:13 him with honey from the *r,*
2Sa 22: 2 "The LORD is my *r,* my fortress
Ps 18: 2 The LORD is my *r,* my fortress
19:14 O LORD, my *R* and my Redeemer
40: 2 he set my feet on a *r*
61: 2 lead me to the *r* that is higher
92:15 he is my *R,* and there is no
Isa 26: 4 the LORD, is the *R* eternal.
51: 1 to the *r* from which you were cut
Da 2:34 you were watching, a *r* was cut out,
Mt 7:24 man who built his house on the *r.*
16:18 and on this *r* I will build my church
Ro 9:33 and a *r* that makes them fall,
1Co 10: 4 the spiritual *r* that accompanied
1Pe 2: 8 and a *r* that makes them fall."

ROD (RODS)
2Sa 7:14 I will punish him with the *r* of men,
Ps 23: 4 your *r* and your staff,
Pr 13:24 He who spares the *r* hates his son,
22:15 the *r* of discipline will drive it far
23:13 if you punish him with the *r,*
29:15 *r* of correction imparts wisdom,
Isa 11: 4 the earth with the *r* of his mouth;

RODS (ROD)
2Co 11:25 Three times I was beaten with *r,*

ROLL (ROLLED)
Mk 16: 3 "Who will *r* the stone away

ROLLED (ROLL)
Lk 24: 2 They found the stone *r* away

ROMAN
Ac 16:37 even though we are *R* citizens,
22:25 you to flog a *R* citizen who hasn't

ROOF (ROOFS)
Pr 21: 9 Better to live on a corner of the *r*

ROOFS
Mt 10:27 in your ear, proclaim from the *r.*

ROOM (ROOMS)
Mt 6: 6 But when you pray, go into your *r,*
Mk 14:15 He will show you a large upper *r,*
Lk 2: 7 there was no *r* for them in the inn.
Jn 8:37 because you have no *r* for my word
21:25 the whole world would not have *r*
2Co 7: 2 Make *r* for us in your hearts.

ROOMS (ROOM)
Jn 14: 2 In my Father's house are many *r;*

ROOSTER
Mt 26:34 this very night, before the *r* crows,

ROOT (ROOTED ROOTS)
Isa 11:10 In that day the *R* of Jesse will stand
53: 2 and like a *r* out of dry ground.
Mt 3:10 already at the *r* of the trees,
13:21 But since he has no *r,* he lasts only

Ro 11:16 if the *r* is holy, so are the branches.
15:12 "The *R* of Jesse will spring up,
1Ti 6:10 of money is a *r* of all kinds of evil.
Rev 5: 5 the *R* of David, has triumphed.
22:16 I am the *R* and the Offspring

ROOTED (ROOT)
Eph 3:17 being *r* and established in love,

ROOTS (ROOT)
Isa 11: 1 from his *r* a Branch will bear fruit.

ROSE (RISE)
SS 2: 1 I am a *r* of Sharon,
1Th 4:14 believe that Jesus died and *r* again

ROTS
Pr 14:30 but envy *r* the bones.

ROUGH
Isa 42:16 and make the *r* places smooth.
Lk 3: 5 the *r* ways smooth.

ROUND
Ecc 1: 6 *r* and *r* it goes,

ROYAL
Ps 45: 9 at your right hand is the *r* bride
Da 1: 8 not to defile himself with the *r* food
Jas 2: 8 If you really keep the *r* law found
1Pe 2: 9 a *r* priesthood, a holy nation,

RUBBISH*
Php 3: 8 I consider them *r*, that I may gain

RUBIES
Job 28:18 the price of wisdom is beyond *r*.
Pr 3:15 She is more precious than *r*;
8:11 for wisdom is more precious than *r*,
31:10 She is worth far more than *r*.

RUDDER*
Jas 3: 4 by a very small *r* wherever the pilot

RUDDY
1Sa 16:12 He was *r*, with a fine appearance
SS 5:10 *Beloved* My lover is radiant and *r*,

RUDE*
1Co 13: 5 It is not *r*, it is not self-seeking,

RUIN (RUINED RUINING RUINS)
Pr 10: 8 but a chattering fool comes to *r*.
10:10 and a chattering fool comes to *r*.
10:14 but the mouth of a fool invites *r*.
10:29 but it is the *r* of those who do evil.
18:24 many companions may come to *r*,
19:13 A foolish son is his father's *r*,
26:28 and a flattering mouth works *r*.
SS 2:15 that *r* the vineyards,
Eze 21:27 A *r*! A *r*! I will make it a *r*!
1Ti 6: 9 desires that plunge men into *r*

RUINED (RUIN)
Isa 6: 5 "I am *r*! For I am a man
Mt 9:17 and the wineskins will be *r*.
12:25 divided against itself will be *r*,

RUINING* (RUIN)
Tit 1:11 they are *r* whole households

RUINS (RUIN)
Pr 19: 3 A man's own folly *r* his life,
Ecc 4: 5 and *r* himself.
2Ti 2:14 and only *r* those who listen.

RULE (RULER RULERS RULES)
Ge 1:26 let them *r* over the fish of the sea
3:16 and he will *r* over you."
Jdg 8:22 said to Gideon, "*R* over us—
1Sa 12:12 'No, we want a king to *r* over us'—
Ps 2: 9 You will *r* them with an iron
67: 4 for you *r* the peoples justly
119:133 let no sin *r* over me.
Pr 17: 2 A wise servant will *r*
Isa 28:10 *r* on *r*, *r* on *r*;
Eze 20:33 I will *r* over you with a mighty
Zec 6:13 and will sit and *r* on his throne.
9:10 His *r* will extend from sea to sea
Ro 13: 9 are summed up in this one *r*:
15:12 arise to *r* over the nations;
1Co 7:17 This is the *r* I lay down in all
Gal 6:16 and mercy to all who follow this *r*,
Eph 1:21 far above all *r* and authority,
Col 3:15 the peace of Christ *r* in your hearts,
2Th 3:10 we gave you this *r*: "If a man will
Rev 2:27 He will *r* them with an iron scepter;
12: 5 who will *r* all the nations
19:15 He will *r* them with an iron scepter

RULER (RULE)
Ps 8: 6 You made him *r* over the works
Pr 19: 6 Many curry favor with a *r*,
23: 1 When you sit to dine with a *r*,
25:15 Through patience a *r* can be
29:26 Many seek an audience with a *r*,
Isa 60:17 and righteousness your *r*.
Da 9:25 the *r*, comes, there will be seven
Mic 5: 2 one who will be *r* over Israel,
Mt 2: 6 for out of you will come a *r*
Eph 2: 2 of the *r* of the kingdom of the air,
1Ti 6:15 God, the blessed and only *R*,
Rev 1: 5 and the *r* of the kings of the earth.

RULERS (RULE)
Ps 2: 2 and the *r* gather together
119:161 *R* persecute me without cause,
Isa 40:23 reduces the *r* of this world
Da 7:27 and all *r* will worship and obey him
Mt 20:25 "You know that the *r*
Ac 13:27 and their *r* did not recognize Jesus,
Ro 13: 3 For *r* hold no terror
1Co 2: 6 of this age or of the *r* of this age,
Eph 3:10 should be made known to the *r*
6:12 the *r*, against the authorities,
Col 1:16 or powers or *r* or authorities;

RULES (RULE)
Nu 15:15 is to have the same *r* for you
2Sa 23: 3 when he *r* in the fear of God,
Ps 22:28 and he *r* over the nations.
66: 7 He *r* forever by his power,
103: 19 and his kingdom *r* over all.
Isa 29:13 is made up only of *r* taught by men.
40:10 and his arm *r* for him.
Mt 15: 9 their teachings are but *r* taught
Lk 22:26 one who *r* like the one who serves.
2Ti 2: 5 he competes according to the *r*.

RUMORS
Jer 51:46 afraid when *r* are heard in the land;
Mt 24: 6 You will hear of wars and *r* of wars,

RUN (RAN RUNNERS RUNNING RUNS)
Ps 19: 5 champion rejoicing to *r* his course.
Pr 4:12 when you *r*, you will not stumble.
18:10 the righteous *r* to it and are safe.
Isa 10: 3 To whom will you *r* for help?
40:31 they will *r* and not grow weary,
Joel 3:18 ravines of Judah will *r* with water.
Hab 2: 2 so that a herald may *r* with it.
1Co 9:24 *R* in such a way as to get the prize.
Gal 2: 2 that I was running or had *r* my race
Php 2:16 on the day of Christ that I did not *r*
Heb 12: 1 let us *r* with perseverance the race

RUNNERS* (RUN)
1Co 9:24 that in a race all the *r* run,

RUNNING (RUN)
Ps 133: 2 *r* down on Aaron's beard,
Lk 17:23 Do not go *r* off after them.
1Co 9:26 I do not run like a man *r* aimlessly;
Gal 5: 7 You were *r* a good race.

RUNS (RUN)
Jn 10:12 he abandons the sheep and *r* away.

RUSH
Pr 1:16 for their feet *r* into sin,
6:18 feet that are quick to *r* into evil,
Isa 59: 7 Their feet *r* into sin;

RUST
Mt 6:19 where moth and *r* destroy,

RUTH*
Moabitess; widow who went to Bethlehem with mother-in-law Naomi (Ru 1). Gleaned in field of Boaz; shown favor (Ru 2). Proposed marriage to Boaz (Ru 3). Married (Ru 4:1–12); bore Obed, ancestor of David (Ru 4:13–22), Jesus (Mt 1:5).

RUTHLESS
Pr 11:16 but *r* men gain only wealth.
Ro 1:31 are senseless, faithless, heartless, *r*.

SABBATH (SABBATHS)
Ex 20: 8 "Remember the *S* day
31:14 " 'Observe the *S*, because it is holy
Lev 25: 2 the land itself must observe a *s*
Dt 5:12 "Observe the *S* day
Isa 56: 2 keeps the *S* without desecrating it,
56: 6 all who keep the *S*
58:13 if you call the *S* a delight
Jer 17:21 not to carry a load on the *S* day
Mt 12: 1 through the grainfields on the *S*.
Lk 13:10 On a *S* Jesus was teaching in one
Col 2:16 a New Moon celebration or a *S* day

SABBATH-REST* (REST)
Heb 4: 9 then, a *S* for the people of God;

SABBATHS (SABBATH)
2Ch 2: 4 evening and on *S* and New Moons
Eze 20:12 Also I gave them my *S*

SACKCLOTH
Ps 30:11 you removed my *s* and clothed me
Da 9: 3 in fasting, and in *s* and ashes.
Mt 11:21 would have repented long ago in *s*

SACRED
Lev 23: 2 are to proclaim as *s* assemblies.
Mt 7: 6 "Do not give dogs what is *s*;
Ro 14: 5 One man considers one day more *s*
1Co 3:17 for God's temple is *s*, and you are
2Pe 1:18 were with him on the *s* mountain.
2:21 on the *s* command that was

SACRIFICE (SACRIFICED SACRIFICES)
Ge 22: 2 *S* him there as a burnt offering
Ex 12:27 'It is the Passover *s* to the LORD,
1Sa 15:22 To obey is better than *s*,
1Ki 18:38 the LORD fell and burned up the *s*,
1Ch 21:24 or *s* a burnt offering that costs me
Ps 40: 6 *S* and offering you did not desire,
50:14 *S* thank offerings to God,
51:16 You do not delight in *s*,
54: 6 I will *s* a freewill offering to you;
107: 22 Let them *s* thank offerings
141: 2 of my hands be like the evening *s*.
Pr 15: 8 The LORD detests the *s*
21: 3 to the LORD than *s*.
Da 9:27 the 'seven' he will put an end to *s*
12:11 time that the daily *s* is abolished
Hos 6: 6 For I desire mercy, not *s*,
Mt 9:13 this means: 'I desire mercy, not *s*.'
Ro 3:25 God presented him as a *s*
Eph 5: 2 as a fragrant offering and *s* to God.
Php 4:18 an acceptable *s*, pleasing to God.
Heb 9:26 away with sin by the *s* of himself.
10: 5 "*S* and offering you did not desire,
10:10 holy through the *s* of the body
10:14 by one *s* he has made perfect
10:18 there is no longer any *s* for sin.
11: 4 faith Abel offered God a better *s*
13:15 offer to God a *s* of praise—
1Jn 2: 2 He is the atoning *s* for our sins,
4:10 as an atoning *s* for our sins.

SACRIFICED (SACRIFICE)
Ac 15:29 are to abstain from food *s* to idols,
1Co 5: 7 our Passover lamb, has been *s*.
8: 1 Now about food *s* to idols:
Heb 7:27 He *s* for their sins once for all
9:28 so Christ was *s* once

SACRIFICES (SACRIFICE)
Ps 51:17 The *s* of God are a broken spirit;
Mk 12:33 than all burnt offerings and *s*."
Ro 12: 1 to offer your bodies as living *s*,
Heb 9:23 with better *s* than these.
13:16 for with such *s* God is pleased.
1Pe 2: 5 offering spiritual *s* acceptable

SAD
Lk 18:23 he heard this, he became very *s*,

SADDUCEES
Mt 16: 6 the yeast of the Pharisees and *S*."
Mk 12:18 *S*, who say there is no resurrection,
Ac 23: 8 *S* say that there is no resurrection,

SAFE (SAVE)
Ps 27: 5 he will keep me *s* in his dwelling;
37: 3 in the land and enjoy *s* pasture.
Pr 18:10 the righteous run to it and are *s*.
28:26 he who walks in wisdom is kept *s*.
29:25 in the LORD is kept *s*.
Jer 12: 5 If you stumble in *s* country,
Jn 17:12 kept them *s* by that name you gave
1Jn 5:18 born of God keeps him *s*,

SAFETY (SAVE)
Ps 4: 8 make me dwell in *s*.
Hos 2:18 so that all may lie down in *s*.
1Th 5: 3 people are saying, "Peace and *s*,"

SAINTS
1Sa 2: 9 He will guard the feet of his *s*,
Ps 16: 3 As for the *s* who are in the land,
30: 4 Sing to the LORD, you *s* of his;
31:23 Love the LORD, all his *s*!
34: 9 Fear the LORD, you his *s*,
116: 15 is the death of his *s*.
149: 1 his praise in the assembly of the *s*.
149: 5 Let the *s* rejoice in this honor
Da 7:18 the *s* of the Most High will receive
Ro 8:27 intercedes for the *s* in accordance
1Co 6: 2 not know that the *s* will judge
Eph 1:15 Jesus and your love for all the *s*,
1:18 of his glorious inheritance in the *s*,
6:18 always keep on praying for all the *s*
Phm : 7 have refreshed the hearts of the *s*.
Rev 5: 8 which are the prayers of the *s*.
19: 8 for the righteous acts of the *s*.)

SAKE (SAKES)
1Sa 12:22 For the *s* of his great name
Ps 23: 3 righteousness for his name's *s*.
44:22 Yet for your *s* we face death all day
106: 8 Yet he saved them for his name's *s*,
Isa 42:21 for the *s* of his righteousness
43:25 your transgressions, for my own *s*,
48: 9 For my own name's *s* I delay my
48:11 For my own *s*, for my own *s*,
Jer 14: 7 for the *s* of your name.
14:21 For the *s* of your name do not
Eze 20: 9 But for the *s* of my name I did what
20:14 But for the *s* of my name I did what
20:22 and for the *s* of my name I did what
36:22 but for the *s* of my holy name,
Da 9:17 For your *s*, O Lord, look with favor
Mt 10:39 life for my *s* will find it.
19:29 for my *s* will receive a hundred
1Co 9:23 I do all this for the *s* of the gospel,
2Co 12:10 for Christ's *s*, I delight
Php 3: 7 loss for the *s* of Christ.
Heb 11:26 He regarded disgrace for the *s*
1Pe 2:13 for the Lord's *s* to every authority
3Jn : 7 was for the *s* of the Name that they

SAKES* (SAKE)
2Co 8: 9 yet for your *s* he became poor,

SALEM
Ge 14:18 king of *S* brought out bread
Heb 7: 2 "king of *S*" means "king of peace."

SALT
Ge 19:26 and she became a pillar of *s*.
Nu 18:19 covenant of *s* before the LORD
Mt 5:13 "You are the *s* of the earth.
Col 4: 6 with *s*, so that you may know how
Jas 3:11 *s* water flow from the same spring?

SALVATION* (SAVE)
Ex 15: 2 he has become my *s*.
2Sa 22: 3 my shield and the horn of my *s*.
23: 5 Will he not bring to fruition my *s*
1Ch 16:23 proclaim his *s* day after day.
2Ch 6:41 O LORD God, be clothed with *s*,
Ps 9:14 and there rejoice in your *s*.
13: 5 my heart rejoices in your *s*.
14: 7 that *s* for Israel would come out
18: 2 is my shield and the horn of my *s*,
27: 1 The LORD is my light and my *s*—
28: 8 a fortress of *s* for his anointed one.
35: 3 "I am your *s*."
35: 9 and delight in his *s*.
37:39 The *s* of the righteous comes
40:10 I speak of your faithfulness and *s*.
40:16 those who love your *s* always say,
50:23 way so that I may show him the *s*
51:12 Restore to me the joy of your *s*
53: 6 that *s* for Israel would come out
62: 1 my *s* comes from him.
62: 2 He alone is my rock and my *s*;
62: 6 He alone is my rock and my *s*;
62: 7 My *s* and my honor depend
67: 2 your *s* among all nations.
69:13 answer me with your sure *s*.
69:27 do not let them share in your *s*.
69:29 may your *s*, O God, protect me.
70: 4 those who love your *s* always say,
71:15 of your *s* all day long,
74:12 you bring *s* upon the earth.
85: 7 and grant us your *s*.
85: 9 Surely his *s* is near those who fear
91:16 and show him my *s*."
Ps 95: 1 to the Rock of our *s*.
96: 2 proclaim his *s* day after day.
98: 1 have worked *s* for him.
98: 2 The LORD has made his *s* known
98: 3 the *s* of our God.
116: 13 I will lift up the cup of *s*
118: 14 he has become my *s*.
118: 21 you have become my *s*.
119: 41 your *s* according to your promise;
119: 81 with longing for your *s*,
119:123 My eyes fail, looking for your *s*,
119:155 *S* is far from the wicked,
119:166 I wait for your *s*, O LORD,
119:174 I long for your *s*, O LORD,
132: 16 I will clothe her priests with *s*,
149: 4 he crowns the humble with *s*.
Isa 12: 2 Surely God is my *s*;
12: 2 he has become my *s*."
12: 3 from the wells of *s*.
25: 9 let us rejoice and be glad in his *s*."
26: 1 God makes *s*
26:18 We have not brought *s* to the earth;
30:15 "In repentance and rest is your *s*,
33: 2 our *s* in time of distress.
33: 6 a rich store of *s* and wisdom
45: 8 let *s* spring up,
45:17 the LORD with an everlasting *s*;
46:13 I will grant *s* to Zion,
46:13 and my *s* will not be delayed.
49: 6 that you may bring my *s*
49: 8 and in the day of *s* I will help you;
51: 5 my *s* is on the way,
51: 6 But my *s* will last forever,
51: 8 my *s* through all generations."
52: 7 who proclaim *s*,
52:10 the *s* of our God.
56: 1 for my *s* is close at hand
59:16 so his own arm worked *s* for him,
59:17 and the helmet of *s* on his head;
60:18 but you will call your walls *S*
61:10 me with garments of *s*
62: 1 her *s* like a blazing torch.
63: 5 so my own arm worked *s* for me,
Jer 3:23 is the *s* of Israel.
La 3:26 quietly for the *s* of the LORD.
Jnh 2: 9 *S* comes from the LORD."
Zec 9: 9 righteous and having *s*,
Lk 1:69 He has raised up a horn of *s* for us
1:71 of long ago), *s* from our enemies
1:77 give his people the knowledge of *s*
2:30 For my eyes have seen your *s*,
3: 6 And all mankind will see God's *s*
19: 9 "Today *s* has come to this house,
Jn 4:22 for *s* is from the Jews.
Ac 4:12 *S* is found in no one else,
13:26 message of *s* has been sent.
13:47 that you may bring *s* to the ends
28:28 to know that God's *s* has been sent
Ro 1:16 for the *s* of everyone who believes:
11:11 *s* has come to the Gentiles
13:11 because our *s* is nearer now
2Co 1: 6 it is for your comfort and *s*;
6: 2 and in the day of *s* I helped you."
6: 2 of God's favor, now is the day of *s*.
7:10 brings repentance that leads to *s*
Eph 1:13 word of truth, the gospel of your *s*.
6:17 Take the helmet of *s* and the sword
Php 2:12 to work out your *s* with fear
1Th 5: 8 and the hope of *s* as a helmet.
5: 9 to receive *s* through our Lord Jesus
2Ti 2:10 they too may obtain the *s* that is
3:15 wise for *s* through faith
Tit 2:11 of God that brings *s* has appeared
Heb 1:14 to serve those who will inherit *s*?
2: 3 This *s*, which was first announced
2: 3 escape if we ignore such a great *s*?
2:10 of their *s* perfect through suffering.
5: 9 of eternal *s* for all who obey him
6: 9 case—things that accompany *s*.
9:28 to bring *s* to those who are waiting
1Pe 1: 5 the coming of the *s* that is ready
1: 9 of your faith, the *s* of your souls.
1:10 Concerning this *s*, the prophets,
2: 2 by it you may grow up in your *s*,
2Pe 3:15 that our Lord's patience means *s*,
Jude : 3 to write to you about the *s* we share
Rev 7:10 "*S* belongs to our God,
12:10 have come the *s* and the power
19: 1 *S* and glory and power belong

SAMARIA (SAMARITAN)
1Ki 16:24 He bought the hill of *S*
2Ki 17: 6 the king of Assyria captured *S*
Jn 4: 4 Now he had to go through *S*.
4: 5 came to a town in *S* called Sychar,

SAMARITAN (SAMARIA)
Lk 10:33 But a *S*, as he traveled, came where
17:16 and thanked him—and he was a *S*.
Jn 4: 7 When a *S* woman came

SAMSON
Danite judge. Birth promised (Jdg 13). Married to Philistine, but wife given away (Jdg 14). Vengeance on Philistines (Jdg 15). Betrayed by Delilah (Jdg 16:1–22). Death (Jdg 16:23–31). Feats of strength: killed lion (Jdg 14:6), 30 Philistines (Jdg 14:19), 1,000 Philistines with jawbone (Jdg 15:13–17), carried off gates of Gaza (Jdg 16:3), pushed down temple of Dagon (Jdg 16:25–30).

SAMUEL
Ephraimite judge and prophet (Heb 11:32). Birth prayed for (1Sa 1:10–18). Dedicated to temple by Hannah (1Sa 1:21–28). Raised by Eli (1Sa 2:11, 18–26). Called as prophet (1Sa 3). Led Israel to victory over Philistines (1Sa 7). Asked by Israel for a king (1Sa 8). Anointed Saul as king (1Sa 9–10). Farewell speech (1Sa 12). Rebuked Saul for sacrifice (1Sa 13). Announced rejection of Saul (1Sa 15). Anointed David as king (1Sa 16). Protected David from Saul (1Sa 19:18–24). Death (1Sa 25:1). Returned from dead to condemn Saul (1Sa 28).

SANBALLAT
Led opposition to Nehemiah's rebuilding of Jerusalem (Ne 2:10, 19; 4; 6).

SANCTIFIED* (SANCTIFY)
Jn 17:19 that they too may be truly *s*.
Ac 20:32 among all those who are *s*.
26:18 among those who are *s* by faith
Ro 15:16 to God, *s* by the Holy Spirit.
1Co 1: 2 to those *s* in Christ Jesus
6:11 But you were washed, you were *s*,
7:14 and the unbelieving wife has been *s*
7:14 the unbelieving husband has been *s*
1Th 4: 3 It is God's will that you should be *s*
Heb 10:29 blood of the covenant that *s* him,

SANCTIFY* (SANCTIFIED SANCTIFYING)
Jn 17:17 *S* them by the truth; your word is
17:19 For them I *s* myself, that they too
1Th 5:23 *s* you through and through.
Heb 9:13 are ceremonially unclean *s* them

SANCTIFYING* (SANCTIFY)
2Th 2:13 through the *s* work of the Spirit
1Pe 1: 2 through the *s* work of the Spirit,

SANCTUARY
Ex 25: 8 "Then have them make a *s* for me,
Lev 19:30 and have reverence for my *s*,
Ps 15: 1 LORD, who may dwell in your *s*?
63: 2 I have seen you in the *s*
68:24 of my God and King into the *s*.
68:35 are awesome, O God, in your *s*;
73:17 me till I entered the *s* of God;
102: 19 looked down from his *s* on high,
134: 2 Lift up your hands in the *s*
150: 1 Praise God in his *s*;
Eze 37:26 I will put my *s* among them forever
41: 1 the man brought me to the outer *s*
Da 9:26 will destroy the city and the *s*.
Heb 6:19 It enters the inner *s*
8: 2 in the *s*, the true tabernacle set up
8: 5 They serve at a *s* that is a copy
9:24 enter a man-made *s* that was only

SAND
Ge 22:17 and as the *s* on the seashore.
Mt 7:26 man who built his house on *s*.

SANDAL (SANDALS)
Ru 4: 7 one party took off his *s*

SANDALS (SANDAL)
Ex 3: 5 off your *s*, for the place where you
Dt 25: 9 take off one of his *s*, spit in his face
Jos 5:15 off your *s*, for the place where you
Mt 3:11 whose *s* I am not fit to carry.

SANG (SING)
Ex 15: 1 and the Israelites *s* this song
15:21 Miriam *s* to them:
Nu 21:17 Then Israel *s* this song:

Jdg 5: 1 Barak son of Abinoam *s* this song:
1Sa 18: 7 As they danced, they *s:*
2Sa 22: 1 David *s* to the LORD the words
2Ch 5:13 in praise to the LORD and *s:*
29:30 So they *s* praises with gladness
Ezr 3:11 thanksgiving they *s* to the LORD:
Job 38: 7 while the morning stars *s* together
Ps 106: 12 and *s* his praise.
Rev 5: 9 And they *s* a new song:
5:12 In a loud voice they *s:*
14: 3 they *s* a new song before the throne
15: 3 and *s* the song of Moses the servant

SAP
Ro 11:17 share in the nourishing *s*

SAPPHIRA*
Ac 5: 1 together with his wife *S,*

SARAH
Wife of Abraham, originally named Sarai; barren (Ge 11:29–31; 1Pe 3:6). Taken by Pharaoh as Abraham's sister; returned (Ge 12:10–20). Gave Hagar to Abraham; sent her away in pregnancy (Ge 16). Name changed; Isaac promised (Ge 17:15–21; 18:10–15; Heb 11:11). Taken by Abimelech as Abraham's sister; returned (Ge 20). Isaac born; Hagar and Ishmael sent away (Ge 21:1–21; Gal 4:21–31). Death (Ge 23).

SARDIS
Rev 3: 1 the angel of the church in *S* write:

SASH (SASHES)
Rev 1:13 with a golden *s* around his chest.

SASHES (SASH)
Rev 15: 6 wore golden *s* around their chests.

SAT (SIT)
Ps 137: 1 By the rivers of Babylon we *s*
Mk 16:19 and he *s* at the right hand of God.
Lk 10:39 who *s* at the Lord's feet listening
Heb 1: 3 he *s* down at the right hand
8: 1 who *s* down at the right hand
10:12 he *s* down at the right hand of God.
12: 2 and *s* down at the right hand

SATAN
Job 1: 6 and *S* also came with them.
Zec 3: 2 said to *S,* "The LORD rebuke you,
Mt 12:26 If *S* drives out *S,* he is divided
16:23 *S!* You are a stumbling block to me;
Mk 4:15 *S* comes and takes away the word
Lk 10:18 "I saw *S* fall like lightning
22: 3 *S* entered Judas, called Iscariot,
Ro 16:20 The God of peace will soon crush *S*
1Co 5: 5 is present, hand this man over to *S,*
2Co 11:14 for *S* himself masquerades
12: 7 a messenger of *S,* to torment me.
1Ti 1:20 handed over to *S* to be taught not
Rev 12: 9 serpent called the devil, or *S,*
20: 2 or *S,* and bound him for a thousand
20: 7 *S* will be released from his prison

SATISFIED (SATISFY)
Ps 17:15 I will be *s* with seeing your likeness
22:26 The poor will eat and be *s;*
63: 5 My soul will be *s* as with the richest
104: 28 they are *s* with good things.
105: 40 *s* them with the bread of heaven.
Pr 13: 4 the desires of the diligent are fully *s*
30:15 are three things that are never *s,*
Ecc 5:10 whoever loves wealth is never *s*
Isa 53:11 he will see the light of life, and be *s*
Mt 14:20 They all ate and were *s,*
Lk 6:21 for you will be *s.*

SATISFIES* (SATISFY)
Ps 103: 5 who *s* your desires with good things,
107: 9 for he *s* the thirsty
147: 14 and *s* you with the finest of wheat.

SATISFY (SATISFIED SATISFIES)
Ps 90:14 *S* us in the morning
145: 16 *s* the desires of every living thing.
Pr 5:19 may her breasts *s* you always,
Isa 55: 2 and your labor on what does not *s?*
58:10 and *s* the needs of the oppressed,

SAUL
1. Benjamite; anointed by Samuel as first king of Israel (1Sa 9–10). Defeated Ammonites (1Sa 11). Rebuked for offering sacrifice (1Sa 13:1–15). Defeated Philistines (1Sa 14). Rejected as king for failing to annihilate Amalekites (1Sa 15). Soothed from evil spirit by David (1Sa 16:14–23). Sent David against Goliath (1Sa 17). Jealousy and attempted murder of David (1Sa 18:1–11). Gave David Michal as wife (1Sa 18:12–30). Second attempt to kill David (1Sa 19). Anger at Jonathan (1Sa 20:26–34). Pursued David: killed priests at Nob (1Sa 22), went to Keilah and Ziph (1Sa 23), life spared by David at En Gedi (1Sa 24) and in his tent (1Sa 26). Rebuked by Samuel's spirit for consulting witch at Endor (1Sa 28). Wounded by Philistines; took his own life (1Sa 31; 1Ch 10). Lamented by David (2Sa 1:17–27). Children (1Sa 14:49–51; 1Ch 8).
2. See PAUL

SAVAGE
Ac 20:29 *s* wolves will come in among you

SAVE (SAFE SAFETY SALVATION SAVED SAVES SAVIOR)
Ge 45: 5 to *s* lives that God sent me ahead
1Ch 16:35 Cry out, "*S* us, O God our Savior;
Job 40:14 that your own right hand can *s* you.
Ps 17: 7 you who *s* by your right hand
18:27 You *s* the humble
28: 9 *S* your people and bless your
31:16 *s* me in your unfailing love.
69:35 for God will *s* Zion
71: 2 turn your ear to me and *s* me.
72:13 and *s* the needy from death.
89:48 or *s* himself from the power
91: 3 Surely he will *s* you
109: 31 to *s* his life from those who
146: 3 in mortal men, who cannot *s.*
Pr 2:16 will *s* you also from the adulteress,
Isa 35: 4 he will come to *s* you."
38:20 The LORD will *s* me,
46: 7 it cannot *s* him from his troubles.
59: 1 of the LORD is not too short to *s,*
63: 1 mighty to *s.*"
Jer 17:14 *s* me and I will be saved,
Eze 3:18 ways in order to *s* his life,
7:19 able to *s* them in the day
14:14 they could *s* only themselves
33:12 of the righteous man will not *s* him
34:22 I will *s* my flock, and they will no
Da 3:17 the God we serve is able to *s* us
Hos 1: 7 and I will *s* them—not by bow,
Zep 1:18 will be able to *s* them
3:17 he is mighty to *s.*
Zec 8: 7 "I will *s* my people
Mt 1:21 he will *s* his people from their sins
16:25 wants to *s* his life will lose it,
Lk 19:10 to seek and to *s* what was lost."
Jn 3:17 but to *s* the world through him.
12:47 come to judge the world, but to *s* it.
Ro 11:14 people to envy and *s* some of them.
1Co 7:16 whether you will *s* your husband?
1Ti 1:15 came into the world to *s* sinners—
Heb 7:25 to *s* completely those who come
Jas 5:20 of his way will *s* him from death
Jude :23 others from the fire and *s* them;

SAVED (SAVE)
Ps 22: 5 They cried to you and were *s;*
33:16 No king is *s* by the size of his army;
34: 6 he *s* him out of all his troubles.
106: 21 They forgot the God who *s* them,
116: 6 when I was in great need, he *s* me.
Isa 25: 9 we trusted in him, and he *s* us.
45:22 "Turn to me and be *s,*
64: 5 How then can we be *s?*
Jer 4:14 from your heart and be *s.*
8:20 and we are not *s.*"
Eze 3:19 but you will have *s* yourself.
33: 5 warning, he would have *s* himself.
Joel 2:32 on the name of the LORD will be *s;*
Mt 10:22 firm to the end will be *s.*
24:13 firm to the end will be *s.*
Mk 13:13 firm to the end will be *s.*
16:16 believes and is baptized will be *s,*
Jn 10: 9 enters through me will be *s.*
Ac 2:21 on the name of the Lord will be *s.*'
2:47 daily those who were being *s.*
4:12 to men by which we must be *s.*"
15:11 of our Lord Jesus that we are *s,*
16:30 do to be *s?*" They replied,
Ro 5: 9 how much more shall we be *s*
9:27 only the remnant will be *s.*
10: 1 the Israelites is that they may be *s.*
10: 9 him from the dead, you will be *s.*
10:13 on the name of the Lord will be *s.*"
11:26 so all Israel will be *s,* as it is written:
1Co 1:18 to us who are being *s* it is the power
3:15 will suffer loss; he himself will be *s,*
5: 5 his spirit *s* on the day of the Lord.
10:33 of many, so that they may be *s.*
15: 2 By this gospel you are *s,*
Eph 2: 5 it is by grace you have been *s.*
2: 8 For it is by grace you have been *s,*
2Th 2:13 you to be *s* through the sanctifying
1Ti 2: 4 who wants all men to be *s*
2:15 But women will be *s*
2Ti 1: 9 who has *s* us and called us
Tit 3: 5 He *s* us through the washing
Heb 10:39 but of those who believe and are *s.*

SAVES (SAVE)
Ps 7:10 who *s* the upright in heart.
68:20 Our God is a God who *s;*
145: 19 he hears their cry and *s* them.
1Pe 3:21 It *s* you by the resurrection

SAVIOR* (SAVE)
Dt 32:15 and rejected the Rock his *S.*
2Sa 22: 3 stronghold, my refuge and my *s*—
22:47 Exalted be God, the Rock, my *S!*
1Ch 16:35 Cry out, "Save us, O God our *S;*
Ps 18:46 Exalted be God my *S!*
24: 5 and vindication from God his *S.*
25: 5 for you are God my *S,*
27: 9 O God my *S.*
38:22 O Lord my *S.*
42: 5 my *S* and
42:11 my *S* and my God.
43: 5 my *S* and my God.
65: 5 O God our *S,*
68:19 Praise be to the Lord, to God our *S,*
79: 9 Help us, O God our *S,*
85: 4 Restore us again, O God our *S,*
89:26 my God, the Rock my *S.*'
Isa 17:10 You have forgotten God your *S;*
19:20 he will send them a *s* and defender,
43: 3 the Holy One of Israel, your *S;*
43:11 and apart from me there is no *s.*
45:15 O God and *S* of Israel.
45:21 a righteous God and a *S;*
49:26 that I, the LORD, am your *S,*
60:16 know that I, the LORD, am your *S,*
62:11 'See, your *S* comes!
63: 8 and so he became their *S.*
Jer 14: 8 its *S* in times of distress,
Hos 13: 4 no *S* except me.
Mic 7: 7 I wait for God my *S;*
Hab 3:18 I will be joyful in God my *S.*
Lk 1:47 and my spirit rejoices in God my *S,*
2:11 of David a *S* has been born to you;
Jn 4:42 know that this man really is the *S*
Ac 5:31 *S* that he might give repentance
13:23 God has brought to Israel the *S*
Eph 5:23 his body, of which he is the *S.*
Php 3:20 we eagerly await a *S* from there,
1Ti 1: 1 by the command of God our *S*
2: 3 This is good, and pleases God our *S*
4:10 who is the *S* of all men,
2Ti 1:10 through the appearing of our *S,*
Tit 1: 3 me by the command of God our *S,*
1: 4 the Father and Christ Jesus our *S.*
2:10 about God our *S* attractive.
2:13 appearing of our great God and *S,*
3: 4 and love of God our *S* appeared,
3: 6 through Jesus Christ our *S,*
2Pe 1: 1 *S* Jesus Christ have received a faith
1:11 eternal kingdom of our Lord and *S*
2:20 and *S* Jesus Christ and are again
3: 2 and *S* through your apostles.
3:18 and knowledge of our Lord and *S*
1Jn 4:14 Son to be the *S* of the world.
Jude :25 to the only God our *S* be glory,

SCALE (SCALES)
Ps 18:29 with my God I can *s* a wall.

SCALES (SCALE)
Lev 11: 9 may eat any that have fins and *s.*
19:36 Use honest *s* and honest weights,
Pr 11: 1 The LORD abhors dishonest *s,*
Da 5:27 You have been weighed on the *s*
Rev 6: 5 Its rider was holding a pair of *s*

SCAPEGOAT (GOAT)
Lev 16:10 by sending it into the desert as a *s.*

SCARECROW*
Jer 10: 5 Like a *s* in a melon patch,

SCARLET
Jos 2:21 she tied the *s* cord in the window.
Isa 1:18 "Though your sins are like *s*,
Mt 27:28 They stripped him and put a *s* robe

SCATTER (SCATTERED SCATTERS)
Dt 4:27 The LORD will *s* you
Ne 1: 8 I will *s* you among the nations,
Jer 9:16 I will *s* them among nations that
30:11 the nations among which I *s* you,
Zec 10: 9 I *s* them among the peoples,

SCATTERED (SCATTER)
Isa 11:12 he will assemble the *s* people
Jer 31:10 'He who *s* Israel will gather them
Zec 2: 6 "for I have *s* you to the four winds
13: 7 and the sheep will be *s*,
Mt 26:31 and the sheep of the flock will be *s*.'
Jn 11:52 but also for the *s* children of God,
Ac 8: 4 who had been *s* preached the word
Jas 1: 1 To the twelve tribes *s*
1Pe 1: 1 *s* throughout Pontus, Galatia,

SCATTERS (SCATTER)
Mt 12:30 he who does not gather with me *s*.

SCEPTER
Ge 49:10 The *s* will not depart from Judah,
Nu 24:17 a *s* will rise out of Israel.
Ps 2: 9 You will rule them with an iron *s*;
45: 6 a *s* of justice will be the *s*
Heb 1: 8 and righteousness will be the *s*
Rev 2:27 'He will rule them with an iron *s*;
12: 5 rule all the nations with an iron *s*.
19:15 "He will rule them with an iron *s*."

SCHEMES
Pr 6:18 a heart that devises wicked *s*,
24: 9 The *s* of folly are sin,
2Co 2:11 For we are not unaware of his *s*.
Eph 6:11 stand against the devil's *s*.

SCHOLAR*
1Co 1:20 Where is the *s*? Where is

SCOFFERS
2Pe 3: 3 that in the last days *s* will come,

SCORN (SCORNED SCORNING SCORNS)
Ps 69: 7 For I endure *s* for your sake,
69:20 *S* has broken my heart
89:41 he has become the *s*
109: 25 I am an object of *s* to my accusers;
119: 22 Remove from me *s* and contempt,
Mic 6:16 you will bear the *s* of the nations."

SCORNED (SCORN)
Ps 22: 6 *s* by men and despised

SCORNING (SCORN)
Heb 12: 2 him endured the cross, *s* its shame,

SCORNS (SCORN)
Pr 13:13 He who *s* instruction will pay for it,
30:17 that *s* obedience to a mother,

SCORPION
Lk 11:12 will give him a *s*? If you then,
Rev 9: 5 sting of a *s* when it strikes a man.

SCOUNDREL
Pr 6:12 A *s* and villain,

SCRIPTURE (SCRIPTURES)
Jn 2:22 Then they believed the *S*
7:42 Does not the *S* say that the Christ
10:35 and the *S* cannot be broken—
Ac 8:32 was reading this passage of *S*:
1Ti 4:13 yourself to the public reading of *S*,
2Ti 3:16 All *S* is God-breathed
2Pe 1:20 that no prophecy of *S* came about

SCRIPTURES (SCRIPTURE)
Mt 22:29 because you do not know the *S*
Lk 24:27 said in all the *S* concerning himself.
24:45 so they could understand the *S*.
Jn 5:39 These are the *S* that testify about
Ac 17:11 examined the *S* every day to see
2Ti 3:15 you have known the holy *S*,
2Pe 3:16 as they do the other *S*,

SCROLL
Ps 40: 7 it is written about me in the *s*.
Isa 34: 4 and the sky rolled up like a *s*;
Eze 3: 1 eat what is before you, eat this *s*;
Heb 10: 7 it is written about me in the *s*—
Rev 6:14 The sky receded like a *s*, rolling up,
10: 8 take the *s* that lies open in the hand

SCUM
1Co 4:13 this moment we have become the *s*

SEA (SEASHORE)
Ex 14:16 go through the *s* on dry ground.
Dt 30:13 "Who will cross the *s* to get it
1Ki 7:23 He made the *S* of cast metal,
Job 11: 9 and wider than the *s*.
Ps 93: 4 mightier than the breakers of the *s*
95: 5 The *s* is his, for he made it,
Ecc 1: 7 All streams flow into the *s*,
Isa 57:20 the wicked are like the tossing *s*,
Jnh 1: 4 LORD sent a great wind on the *s*,
Mic 7:19 iniquities into the depths of the *s*.
Hab 2:14 as the waters cover the *s*.
Zec 9:10 His rule will extend from *s* to *s*
Mt 18: 6 drowned in the depths of the *s*.
1Co 10: 1 that they all passed through the *s*.
Jas 1: 6 who doubts is like a wave of the *s*,
Jude :13 They are wild waves of the *s*,
Rev 10: 2 He planted his right foot on the *s*
13: 1 I saw a beast coming out of the *s*.
20:13 The *s* gave up the dead that were
21: 1 and there was no longer any *s*.

SEAL (SEALED SEALS)
Ps 40: 9 I do not *s* my lips,
SS 8: 6 Place me like a *s* over your heart,
Da 12: 4 and *s* the words of the scroll
Jn 6:27 God the Father has placed his *s*
1Co 9: 2 For you are the *s* of my apostleship
2Co 1:22 set his *s* of ownership on us,
Eph 1:13 you were marked in him with a *s*,
Rev 6: 3 the Lamb opened the second *s*,
6: 5 When the Lamb opened the third *s*,
6: 7 the Lamb opened the fourth *s*,
6: 9 When he opened the fifth *s*,
6:12 I watched as he opened the sixth *s*.
8: 1 When he opened the seventh *s*,
9: 4 people who did not have the *s*
22:10 "Do not *s* up the words

SEALED (SEAL)
Eph 4:30 with whom you were *s* for the day
2Ti 2:19 solid foundation stands firm, *s*
Rev 5: 1 on both sides and *s* with seven seals

SEALS (SEAL)
Rev 5: 2 "Who is worthy to break the *s*
6: 1 opened the first of the seven *s*.

SEAMLESS*
Jn 19:23 This garment was *s*, woven

SEARCH (SEARCHED SEARCHES SEARCHING)
Ps 4: 4 *s* your hearts and be silent.
139: 23 *S* me, O God, and know my heart;
Pr 2: 4 and *s* for it as for hidden treasure,
25: 2 to *s* out a matter is the glory
SS 3: 2 I will *s* for the one my heart loves.
Jer 17:10 "I the LORD *s* the heart
Eze 34:11 I myself will *s* for my sheep
34:16 I will *s* for the lost and bring back
Lk 15: 8 and *s* carefully until she finds it?

SEARCHED (SEARCH)
Ps 139: 1 O LORD, you have *s* me
Ecc 12:10 The Teacher *s* to find just the right
1Pe 1:10 *s* intently and with the greatest

SEARCHES (SEARCH)
1Ch 28: 9 for the LORD *s* every heart
Ps 7: 9 who *s* minds and hearts,
Pr 11:27 but evil comes to him who *s* for it.
20:27 The lamp of the LORD *s* the spirit
Ro 8:27 And he who *s* our hearts knows
1Co 2:10 The Spirit *s* all things,
Rev 2:23 will know that I am he who *s* hearts

SEARCHING (SEARCH)
Jdg 5:15 there was much *s* of heart.
Am 8:12 *s* for the word of the LORD,

SEARED
1Ti 4: 2 whose consciences have been *s*

SEASHORE (SEA)
Jos 11: 4 as numerous as the sand on the *s*.
1Ki 4:29 as measureless as the sand on the *s*.

SEASON (SEASONED SEASONS)
Lev 26: 4 I will send you rain in its *s*,
Ps 1: 3 which yields its fruit in *s*
2Ti 4: 2 be prepared in *s* and out of *s*;

SEASONED* (SEASON)
Col 4: 6 full of grace, *s* with salt,

SEASONS (SEASON)
Ge 1:14 signs to mark *s* and days and years,
Gal 4:10 and months and *s* and years!

SEAT (SEATED SEATS)
Ps 1: 1 or sit in the *s* of mockers.
Pr 31:23 where he takes his *s*
Da 7: 9 and the Ancient of Days took his *s*.
Lk 14: 9 say to you, 'Give this man your *s*.'
2Co 5:10 before the judgment *s* of Christ,

SEATED (SEAT)
Ps 47: 8 God is *s* on his holy throne.
Isa 6: 1 I saw the Lord *s* on a throne,
Lk 22:69 of Man will be *s* at the right hand
Eph 1:20 and *s* him at his right hand
2: 6 and *s* us with him in the heavenly
Col 3: 1 where Christ is *s* at the right hand
Rev 14:14 *s* on the cloud was one "like a son
20:11 white throne and him who was *s*

SEATS (SEAT)
Lk 11:43 you love the most important *s*

SECLUSION*
Lk 1:24 and for five months remained in *s*.

SECRET (SECRETLY SECRETS)
Dt 29:29 The *s* things belong
Jdg 16: 6 Tell me the *s* of your great strength
Ps 90: 8 our *s* sins in the light
139: 15 when I was made in the *s* place.
Pr 11:13 but a trustworthy man keeps a *s*.
21:14 A gift given in *s* soothes anger,
Jer 23:24 Can anyone hide in *s* places
Mt 6: 4 so that your giving may be in *s*.
6:18 who sees what is done in *s*,
Mk 4:11 "The *s* of the kingdom
1Co 2: 7 No, we speak of God's *s* wisdom,
4: 1 entrusted with the *s* things of God.
2Co 4: 2 we have renounced *s* and shameful
Eph 5:12 what the disobedient do in *s*.
Php 4:12 I have learned the *s*

SECRETLY (SECRET)
2Pe 2: 1 They will *s* introduce destructive
Jude : 4 about long ago have *s* slipped

SECRETS (SECRET)
Ps 44:21 since he knows the *s* of the heart?
Ro 2:16 day when God will judge men's *s*
1Co 14:25 the *s* of his heart will be laid bare.
Rev 2:24 Satan's so-called deep *s* (I will not

SECURE (SECURITY)
Dt 33:12 beloved of the LORD rest *s* in him,
Ps 16: 5 you have made my lot *s*.
16: 9 my body also will rest *s*,
112: 8 His heart is *s*, he will have no fear;
Pr 14:26 fears the LORD has a *s* fortress,
Heb 6:19 an anchor for the soul, firm and *s*.
2Pe 3:17 and fall from your *s* position.

SECURITY (SECURE)
Job 31:24 or said to pure gold, 'You are my *s*,'

SEED (SEEDS SEEDTIME)
Ge 1:11 on the land that bear fruit with *s*
Isa 55:10 so that it yields *s* for the sower
Mt 13: 3 "A farmer went out to sow his *s*.
13:31 of heaven is like a mustard *s*,
17:20 have faith as small as a mustard *s*,
Lk 8:11 of the parable: The *s* is the word
1Co 3: 6 I planted the *s*, Apollos watered it,
2Co 9:10 he who supplies *s* to the sower
Gal 3:29 then you are Abraham's *s*,
1Pe 1:23 not of perishable *s*,
1Jn 3: 9 because God's *s* remains in him;

SEEDS (SEED)
Jn 12:24 But if it dies, it produces many *s*.
Gal 3:16 Scripture does not say "and to *s*,"

SEEDTIME* (SEED)
Ge 8:22 *s* and harvest,

SEEK (SEEKING SEEKS SELF-SEEKING SOUGHT)
Lev 19:18 Do not *s* revenge or bear a grudge
Dt 4:29 if from there you *s* the LORD your
1Ki 22: 5 "First *s* the counsel of the LORD."

1Ch 28: 9 If you *s* him, he will be found
2Ch 7:14 themselves and pray and *s* my face
15: 2 If you *s* him, he will be found
Ps 34:10 those who *s* the LORD lack no
105: 3 of those who *s* the LORD rejoice.
105: 4 *s* his face always.
119: 2 and *s* him with all their heart.
119: 10 I *s* you with all my heart;
119:176 *S* your servant,
Pr 8:17 and those who *s* me find me.
18:15 the ears of the wise *s* it out.
25:27 is it honorable to *s* one's own honor
28: 5 those who *s* the LORD understand
Isa 55: 6 *S* the LORD while he may be
65: 1 found by those who did not *s* me.
Jer 29:13 You will *s* me and find me
Hos 10:12 for it is time to *s* the LORD,
Am 5: 4 "*S* me and live;
Zep 2: 3 *S* the LORD, all you humble
Mt 6:33 But *s* first his kingdom
7: 7 and it will be given to you; *s*
Lk 12:31 *s* his kingdom, and these things will
19:10 For the Son of Man came to *s*
Jn 5:30 for I *s* not to please myself
Ro 10:20 found by those who did not *s* me;
1Co 7:27 you married? Do not *s* a divorce.
10:24 Nobody should *s* his own good,
Heb 11: 6 rewards those who earnestly *s* him.
1Pe 3:11 he must *s* peace and pursue it.

SEEKING (SEEK)
2Ch 30:19 who sets his heart on *s* God—
Pr 20:18 Make plans by *s* advice;
Mal 3: 1 the Lord you are *s* will come
Jn 8:50 I am not *s* glory for myself;
1Co 10:33 For I am not *s* my own good

SEEKS (SEEK)
Pr 11:27 He who *s* good finds good will,
Mt 7: 8 he who *s* finds; and to him who
Jn 4:23 the kind of worshipers the Father *s*.
Ro 3:11 no one who *s* God.

SEER
1Sa 9: 9 of today used to be called a *s*.)

SELF-CONTROL* (CONTROL)
Pr 25:28 is a man who lacks *s*.
Ac 24:25 *s* and the judgment to come,
1Co 7: 5 you because of your lack of *s*.
Gal 5:23 faithfulness, gentleness and *s*.
2Ti 3: 3 slanderous, without *s*, brutal,
2Pe 1: 6 and to knowledge, *s*; and to *s*,

SELF-CONTROLLED* (CONTROL)
1Th 5: 6 are asleep, but let us be alert and *s*.
5: 8 let us be *s*, putting on faith and love
1Ti 3: 2 *s*, respectable, hospitable,
Tit 1: 8 who is *s*, upright, holy
2: 2 worthy of respect, *s*, and sound
2: 5 to be *s* and pure, to be busy at home
2: 6 encourage the young men to be *s*.
2:12 to live *s*, upright and godly lives
1Pe 1:13 prepare your minds for action; be *s*;
4: 7 and *s* so that you can pray.
5: 8 Be *s* and alert.

SELF-DISCIPLINE* (DISCIPLINE)
2Ti 1: 7 a spirit of power, of love and of *s*.

SELF-INDULGENCE*
Mt 23:25 inside they are full of greed and *s*.
Jas 5: 5 lived on earth in luxury and *s*.

SELF-SEEKING* (SEEK)
Ro 2: 8 But for those who are *s*
1Co 13: 5 it is not *s*, it is not easily angered,

SELFISH*
Ps119: 36 and not toward *s* gain.
Pr 18: 1 An unfriendly man pursues *s* ends;
Gal 5:20 fits of rage, *s* ambition, dissensions,
Php 1:17 preach Christ out of *s* ambition,
2: 3 Do nothing out of *s* ambition
Jas 3:14 and *s* ambition in your hearts,
3:16 you have envy and *s* ambition,

SELL (SELLING SELLS SOLD)
Ge 25:31 "First *s* me your birthright."
Mk 10:21 *s* everything you have
Rev 13:17 or *s* unless he had the mark,

SELLING (SELL)
Lk 17:28 buying and *s*, planting and building

SELLS (SELL)
Pr 31:24 makes linen garments and *s* them,

SEND (SENDING SENDS SENT)
Ps 43: 3 *S* forth your light and your truth,
Isa 6: 8 *S* me!" He said, "Go and tell this
Mal 3: 1 "See, I will *s* my messenger,
Mt 9:38 to *s* out workers into his harvest
24:31 And he will *s* his angels
Mk 1: 2 I will *s* my messenger ahead of you,
Lk 20:13 I will *s* my son, whom I love;
Jn 3:17 For God did not *s* his Son
16: 7 but if I go, I will *s* him to you.
1Co 1:17 For Christ did not *s* me to baptize,

SENDING (SEND)
Mt 10:16 I am *s* you out like sheep
Jn 20:21 Father has sent me, I am *s* you."
Ro 8: 3 God did by *s* his own Son

SENDS (SEND)
Ps 57: 3 God *s* his love and his faithfulness.

SENNACHERIB
Assyrian king whose siege of Jerusalem was overthrown by the LORD following prayer of Hezekiah and Isaiah (2Ki 18:13–19:37; 2Ch 32:1–21; Isa 36–37).

SENSES*
Lk 15:17 "When he came to his *s*, he said,
1Co 15:34 Come back to your *s* as you ought,
2Ti 2:26 and that they will come to their *s*

SENSITIVITY*
Eph 4:19 Having lost all *s*, they have given

SENSUAL* (SENSUALITY)
Col 2:23 value in restraining *s* indulgence.
1Ti 5:11 For when their *s* desires overcome

SENSUALITY* (SENSUAL)
Eph 4:19 have given themselves over to *s*

SENT (SEND)
Ex 3:14 to the Israelites: 'I AM has *s* me
Isa 55:11 achieve the purpose for which I *s* it.
61: 1 He has *s* me to bind up
Jer 28: 9 as one truly *s* by the LORD only
Mt 10:40 me receives the one who *s* me.
Mk 6: 7 he *s* them out two by two
Lk 4:18 He has *s* me to proclaim freedom
9: 2 and he *s* them out to preach
10:16 rejects me rejects him who *s* me."
Jn 1: 6 There came a man who was *s*
4:34 "is to do the will of him who *s* me
5:24 believes him who *s* me has eternal
8:16 I stand with the Father, who *s* me.
9: 4 must do the work of him who *s* me.
16: 5 "Now I am going to him who *s* me,
17: 3 and Jesus Christ, whom you have *s*.
17:18 As you *s* me into the world,
20:21 As the Father has *s* me, I am
Ro 10:15 can they preach unless they are *s*?
Gal 4: 4 God *s* his Son, born of a woman,
1Jn 4:10 but that he loved us and *s* his Son

SENTENCE
2Co 1: 9 in our hearts we felt the *s* of death.

SEPARATE (SEPARATED SEPARATES SEPARATION)
Mt 19: 6 has joined together, let man not *s*."
Ro 8:35 Who shall *s* us from the love
1Co 7:10 wife must not *s* from her husband.
2Co 6:17 and be *s*, says the Lord.
Eph 2:12 at that time you were *s* from Christ,

SEPARATED (SEPARATE)
Isa 59: 2 But your iniquities have *s*
Eph 4:18 in their understanding and *s*

SEPARATES (SEPARATE)
Pr 16:28 and a gossip *s* close friends.
17: 9 repeats the matter *s* close friends.
Mt 25:32 as a shepherd *s* the sheep

SEPARATION (SEPARATE)
Nu 6: 2 a vow of *s* to the LORD

SERAPHS*
Isa 6: 2 Above him were *s*, each
6: 6 Then one of the *s* flew to me

SERIOUSNESS*
Tit 2: 7 *s* and soundness of speech that

SERPENT (SERPENT'S)
Ge 3: 1 the *s* was more crafty than any
Isa 27: 1 Leviathan the coiling *s*;
Rev 12: 9 that ancient *s* called the devil
20: 2 that ancient *s*, who is the devil,

SERPENT'S (SERPENT)
2Co 11: 3 Eve was deceived by the *s* cunning,

SERVANT (SERVANTS)
Ex 14:31 trust in him and in Moses his *s*.
21: 2 "If you buy a Hebrew *s*, he is
1Sa 3:10 "Speak, for your *s* is listening."
2Sa 7:19 the future of the house of your *s*.
1Ki 20:40 While your *s* was busy here
Job 1: 8 "Have you considered my *s* Job?
Ps 19:11 By them is your *s* warned;
19:13 Keep your *s* also from willful sins;
31:16 Let your face shine on your *s*;
89: 3 I have sworn to David my *s*,
Pr 14:35 A king delights in a wise *s*,
17: 2 wise *s* will rule over a disgraceful
22: 7 and the borrower is *s* to the lender.
31:15 and portions for her *s* girls.
Isa 41: 8 "But you, O Israel, my *s*,
49: 3 He said to me, "You are my *s*,
53:11 my righteous *s* will justify
Zec 3: 8 going to bring my *s*, the Branch.
Mal 1: 6 his father, and a *s* his master.
Mt 8:13 his *s* was healed at that very hour.
20:26 great among you must be your *s*,
24:45 Who then is the faithful and wise *s*,
25:21 'Well done, good and faithful *s*!
Lk 1:38 I am the Lord's *s*," Mary answered.
16:13 "No *s* can serve two masters.
Jn 12:26 and where I am, my *s* also will be.
Ro 1: 1 a *s* of Christ Jesus, called
13: 4 For he is God's *s* to do you good.
Php 2: 7 taking the very nature of a *s*,
Col 1:23 of which I, Paul, have become a *s*.
2Ti 2:24 And the Lord's *s* must not quarrel;

SERVANTS (SERVANT)
Lev 25:55 for the Israelites belong to me as *s*.
2Ki 17:13 to you through my *s* the prophets."
Ezr 5:11 "We are the *s* of the God of heaven
Ps 34:22 The LORD redeems his *s*;
103: 21 you his *s* who do his will.
104: 4 flames of fire his *s*.
Isa 44:26 who carries out the words of his *s*
65: 8 so will I do in behalf of my *s*;
65:13 my *s* will drink,
Lk 17:10 should say, 'We are unworthy *s*;
Jn 15:15 longer call you *s*, because a servant
Ro 13: 6 for the authorities are God's *s*,
1Co 3: 5 And what is Paul? Only *s*,
Heb 1: 7 his *s* flames of fire."

SERVE (SERVED SERVES SERVICE SERVING)
Dt 10:12 to *s* the LORD your God
11:13 and to *s* him with all your heart
13: 4 *s* him and hold fast to him.
28:47 you did not *s* the LORD your
Jos 22: 5 and to *s* him with all your heart
24:15 this day whom you will *s*,
24:18 We too will *s* the LORD,
1Sa 7: 3 to the LORD and *s* him only,
12:20 but *s* the LORD with all your heart
12:24 *s* him faithfully with all your heart;
2Ch 19: 9 "You must *s* faithfully
Job 36:11 If they obey and *s* him,
Ps 2:11 *S* the LORD with fear
Da 3:17 the God we *s* is able to save us
Mt 4:10 Lord your God, and *s* him only.'"
6:24 "No one can *s* two masters.
20:28 but to *s*, and to give his life
Ro 12: 7 If it is serving, let him *s*;
Gal 5:13 rather, *s* one another in love.
Eph 6: 7 *S* wholeheartedly,
1Ti 6: 2 they are to *s* them even better,
Heb 9:14 so that we may *s* the living God!
1Pe 4:10 gift he has received to *s* others,
5: 2 greedy for money, but eager to *s*;
Rev 5:10 kingdom and priests to *s* our God,

SERVED (SERVE)
Mt 20:28 Son of Man did not come to be *s*,
Jn 12: 2 Martha *s*, while Lazarus was
Ac 17:25 And he is not *s* by human hands,
Ro 1:25 and *s* created things rather
1Ti 3:13 Those who have *s* well gain

SERVES (SERVE)
Lk 22:26 one who rules like the one who *s*.

Lk 22:27 But I am among you as one who *s.*
Jn 12:26 Whoever *s* me must follow me;
Ro 14:18 because anyone who *s* Christ
1Pe 4:11 If anyone *s,* he should do it

SERVICE (SERVE)
Lk 9:62 fit for *s* in the kingdom
12:35 "Be dressed ready for *s*
Ro 15:17 in Christ Jesus in my *s* to God.
1Co 12:5 There are different kinds of *s,*
16:15 themselves to the *s* of the saints.
2Co 9:12 This *s* that you perform is not only
Eph 4:12 God's people for works of *s,*
Rev 2:19 and faith, your *s* and perseverance,

SERVING (SERVE)
Jos 24:15 if *s* the LORD seems undesirable
2Ch 12:8 learn the difference between *s* me
Ro 12:7 If it is *s,* let him serve;
12:11 your spiritual fervor, *s* the Lord.
16:18 people are not *s* our Lord Christ,
Eph 6:7 as if you were *s* the Lord, not men,
Col 3:24 It is the Lord Christ you are *s.*
2Ti 2:4 No one *s* as a soldier gets involved

SETH
Ge 4:25 birth to a son and named him *S,*

SETTLE
Mt 5:25 "*S* matters quickly
2Th 3:12 in the Lord Jesus Christ to *s* down

SEVEN (SEVENS SEVENTH)
Ge 7:2 Take with you *s* of every kind
Jos 6:4 march around the city *s* times,
1Ki 19:18 Yet I reserve *s* thousand in Israel—
Pr 6:16 *s* that are detestable to him:
24:16 a righteous man falls *s* times,
Isa 4:1 In that day *s* women
Da 9:25 comes, there will be *s* 'sevens,'
Mt 18:21 Up to *s* times?" Jesus answered,
Lk 11:26 takes *s* other spirits more wicked
Ro 11:4 for myself *s* thousand who have not
Rev 1:4 To the *s* churches in the province
6:1 opened the first of the *s* seals.
8:2 and to them were given *s* trumpets.
10:4 And when the *s* thunders spoke,
15:7 to the *s* angels *s* golden bowls filled

SEVENS* (SEVEN)
Da 9:24 "Seventy '*s*' are decreed
9:25 will be seven '*s*,' and sixty-two '*s*.'
9:26 the sixty-two '*s*,' the Anointed

SEVENTH (SEVEN)
Ge 2:2 By the *s* day God had finished
Ex 20:10 but the *s* day is a Sabbath
23:11 but during the *s* year let the land lie
23:12 but on the *s* day do not work,
Heb 4:4 "And on the *s* day God rested

SEVERE
2Co 8:2 Out of the most *s* trial, their
1Th 1:6 of the Lord; in spite of *s* suffering,

SEWED (SEWS)
Ge 3:7 so they *s* fig leaves together

SEWS (SEWED)
Mt 9:16 No one *s* a patch of unshrunk cloth

SEXUAL (SEXUALLY)
Ex 22:19 "Anyone who has *s* relations
Lev 18:6 relative to have *s* relations.
18:7 father by having *s* relations
18:20 Do not have *s* relations with
Mt 15:19 murder, adultery, *s* immorality,
Ac 15:20 by idols, from *s* immorality,
1Co 5:1 reported that there is *s* immorality
6:13 body is not meant for *s* immorality,
6:18 Flee from *s* immorality.
10:8 should not commit *s* immorality,
2Co 12:21 *s* sin and debauchery
Gal 5:19 *s* immorality, impurity
Eph 5:3 even a hint of *s* immorality,
Col 3:5 *s* immorality, impurity, lust,
1Th 4:3 that you should avoid *s* immorality

SEXUALLY (SEXUAL)
1Co 5:9 to associate with *s* immoral people
6:9 Neither the *s* immoral nor idolaters
6:18 he who sins *s* sins against his own
Heb 12:16 See that no one is *s* immoral,
13:4 the adulterer and all the *s* immoral.
Rev 21:8 the murderers, the *s* immoral,

SHADE
Ps 121:5 the LORD is your *s*
Isa 25:4 and a *s* from the heat.

SHADOW
Ps 17:8 hide me in the *s* of your wings
23:4 through the valley of the *s* of death,
36:7 find refuge in the *s* of your wings.
91:1 will rest in the *s* of the Almighty.
Isa 51:16 covered you with the *s* of my hand
Col 2:17 These are a *s* of the things that
Heb 8:5 and *s* of what is in heaven.
10:1 The law is only a *s*

SHADRACH
Hebrew exiled to Babylon; name changed from Hananiah (Da 1:6–7). Refused defilement by food (Da 1:8–20). Refused to worship idol (Da 3:1–18); saved from furnace (Da 3:19–30).

SHAKE (SHAKEN SHAKING)
Ps 64:8 all who see them will *s* their heads
99:1 let the earth *s.*
Hag 2:6 I will once more *s* the heavens
Heb 12:26 "Once more I will *s* not only

SHAKEN (SHAKE)
Ps 16:8 I will not be *s.*
30:6 "I will never be *s.*"
62:2 he is my fortress, I will never be *s.*
112:6 Surely he will never be *s;*
Isa 54:10 Though the mountains be *s*
Mt 24:29 and the heavenly bodies will be *s.*'
Lk 6:38 *s* together and running over,
Ac 2:25 I will not be *s.*
Heb 12:27 that what cannot be *s* may remain.

SHAKING* (SHAKE)
Ps 22:7 they hurl insults, *s* their heads:
Mt 27:39 insults at him, *s* their heads
Mk 15:29 *s* their heads and saying, "So!

SHALLUM
King of Israel (2Ki 15:10–16).

SHAME (ASHAMED SHAMED SHAMEFUL)
Ps 25:3 will ever be put to *s,*
34:5 their faces are never covered with *s*
69:6 not be put to *s* because of me,
Pr 13:18 discipline comes to poverty and *s,*
18:13 that is his folly and his *s.*
Jer 8:9 The wise will be put to *s;*
8:12 No, they have no *s* at all;
Ro 9:33 trusts in him will never be put to *s.*"
10:11 trusts in him will never be put to *s.*"
1Co 1:27 things of the world to *s* the wise;
Heb 12:2 endured the cross, scorning its *s,*

SHAMED (SHAME)
Jer 10:14 every goldsmith is *s* by his idols.
Joel 2:26 never again will my people be *s.*

SHAMEFUL (SHAME)
2Co 4:2 have renounced secret and *s* ways;
2Pe 2:2 Many will follow their *s* ways
Rev 21:27 nor will anyone who does what is *s*

SHAMGAR
Judge; killed 600 Philistines (Jdg 3:31).

SHAPE (SHAPES SHAPING)
Job 38:14 The earth takes *s* like clay

SHAPES (SHAPE)
Isa 44:10 Who *s* a god and casts an idol,

SHAPING (SHAPE)
Jer 18:4 the pot he was *s* from the clay was

SHARE (SHARED SHARERS SHARES SHARING)
Ge 21:10 that slave woman's son will never *s*
Lev 19:17 frankly so you will not *s* in his guilt.
Dt 10:9 That is why the Levites have no *s*
1Sa 30:24 All will *s* alike."
Eze 18:20 The son will not *s* the guilt
Mt 25:21 and *s* your master's happiness!'
Lk 3:11 "The man with two tunics should *s*
Ro 8:17 if indeed we *s* in his sufferings
12:13 *S* with God's people who are
2Co 1:7 as you *s* in our sufferings,
Gal 4:30 the slave woman's son will never *s*
6:6 in the word must *s* all good things
Eph 4:28 something to *s* with those in need.
Col 1:12 you to *s* in the inheritance
2Th 2:14 that you might *s* in the glory
1Ti 5:22 and do not *s* in the sins of others.
6:18 and to be generous and willing to *s.*
2Ti 2:6 the first to receive a *s* of the crops.
Heb 12:10 that we may *s* in his holiness.
13:16 to do good and to *s* with others,
Rev 22:19 from him his *s* in the tree of life

SHARED (SHARE)
Ps 41:9 he who *s* my bread,
Ac 4:32 but they *s* everything they had.
Heb 2:14 he too *s* in their humanity so that

SHARERS* (SHARE)
Eph 3:6 and *s* together in the promise

SHARES (SHARE)
Pr 22:9 for he *s* his food with the poor.
Jn 13:18 'He who *s* my bread has lifted up

SHARING (SHARE)
1Co 9:10 so in the hope of *s* in the harvest.
2Co 9:13 for your generosity in *s* with them
Php 3:10 the fellowship of *s* in his sufferings,
Phm 6 you may be active in *s* your faith,

SHARON
SS 2:1 I am a rose of *S,*

SHARP (SHARPENED SHARPENS SHARPER)
Pr 5:4 *s* as a double-edged sword.
Isa 5:28 Their arrows are *s,*
Rev 1:16 came a *s* double-edged sword.
19:15 Out of his mouth comes a *s* sword

SHARPENED (SHARP)
Eze 21:9 *s* and polished—

SHARPENS* (SHARP)
Pr 27:17 As iron *s* iron,
27:17 so one man *s* another.

SHARPER* (SHARP)
Heb 4:12 *S* than any double-edged sword,

SHATTER (SHATTERED SHATTERS)
Jer 51:20 with you I *s* nations,

SHATTERED (SHATTER)
1Sa 2:10 who oppose the LORD will be *s.*
Job 16:12 All was well with me, but he *s* me;
17:11 days have passed, my plans are *s,*
Ecc 12:6 before the pitcher is *s* at the spring,

SHATTERS (SHATTER)
Ps 46:9 he breaks the bow and *s* the spear,

SHAVED
Jdg 16:17 my head were *s,* my strength would
1Co 11:5 it is just as though her head were *s.*

SHEAF (SHEAVES)
Lev 23:11 is to wave the *s* before the LORD

SHEARER* (SHEARERS)
Ac 8:32 and as a lamb before the *s* is silent,

SHEARERS (SHEARER)
Isa 53:7 and as a sheep before her *s* is silent,

SHEAVES (SHEAF)
Ge 37:7 while your *s* gathered around mine
Ps 126:6 carrying *s* with him.

SHEBA
1. Benjamite who rebelled against David (2Sa 20).
2. See QUEEN.

SHECHEM
1. Raped Jacob's daughter Dinah; killed by Simeon and Levi (Ge 34).
2. City where Joshua renewed the covenant (Jos 24).

SHED (SHEDDING SHEDS)
Ge 9:6 by man shall his blood be *s;*
Pr 6:17 hands that *s* innocent blood,
Ro 3:15 "Their feet are swift to *s* blood;
Col 1:20 through his blood, *s* on the cross.

SHEDDING (SHED)
Heb 9:22 without the *s* of blood there is no

SHEDS (SHED)
Ge 9:6 "Whoever *s* the blood of man,

SHEEP (SHEEP'S SHEEPSKINS)
Nu 27:17 LORD's people will not be like *s*
Dt 17:1 a *s* that has any defect or flaw in it,
1Sa 15:14 "What then is this bleeding of *s*

Ps 44:22 we are considered as *s*
78:52 led them like *s* through the desert.
100: 3 we are his people, the *s*
119:176 I have strayed like a lost *s*.
SS 4: 2 teeth are like a flock of *s* just shorn,
Isa 53: 6 We all, like *s*, have gone astray,
53: 7 as a *s* before her shearers is silent,
Jer 50: 6 "My people have been lost *s*;
Eze 34:11 I myself will search for my *s*
Zec 13: 7 and the *s* will be scattered,
Mt 9:36 helpless, like *s* without a shepherd.
10:16 I am sending you out like *s*
12:11 "If any of you has a *s* and it falls
18:13 he is happier about that one *s*
25:32 as a shepherd separates the *s*
Jn 10: 1 man who does not enter the *s* pen
10: 3 He calls his own *s* by name
10: 7 the truth, I am the gate for the *s*.
10:15 and I lay down my life for the *s*.
10:27 My *s* listen to my voice; I know
21:17 Jesus said, "Feed my *s*.
1Pe 2:25 For you were like *s* going astray,

SHEEP'S* (SHEEP)
Mt 7:15 They come to you in *s* clothing,

SHEEPSKINS* (SHEEP)
Heb 11:37 They went about in *s* and goatskins

SHEKEL
Ex 30:13 This half *s* is an offering

SHELTER
Ps 27: 5 me in the *s* of his tabernacle
31:20 In the *s* of your presence you hide
55: 8 I would hurry to my place of *s*,
61: 4 take refuge in the *s* of your wings.
91: 1 in the *s* of the Most High
Ecc 7:12 Wisdom is a *s*
Isa 4: 6 It will be a *s* and shade
25: 4 a *s* from the storm
32: 2 Each man will be like a *s*
58: 7 the poor wanderer with *s*—

SHEM
Son of Noah (Ge 5:32; 6:10). Blessed (Ge 9:26). Descendants (Ge 10:21–31; 11:10–32).

SHEPHERD (SHEPHERDS)
Ge 48:15 the God who has been my *s*
49:24 because of the *S*, the Rock of Israel
Nu 27:17 will not be like sheep without a *s*."
2Sa 7: 7 commanded to *s* my people Israel,
1Ki 22:17 on the hills like sheep without a *s*,
Ps 23: 1 LORD is my *s*, I shall not be in want.
28: 9 be their *s* and carry them forever.
80: 1 Hear us, O *S* of Israel,
Isa 40:11 He tends his flock like a *s*:
Jer 31:10 will watch over his flock like a *s*.'
Eze 34: 5 scattered because there was no *s*,
34:12 As a *s* looks after his scattered
Zec 11: 9 and said, "I will not be your *s*.
11:17 "Woe to the worthless *s*,
13: 7 "Strike the *s*,
Mt 2: 6 who will be the *s* of my people
9:36 and helpless, like sheep without a *s*.
26:31 " 'I will strike the *s*,
Jn 10:11 The good *s* lays down his life
10:14 "I am the good *s*; I know my sheep
10:16 there shall be one flock and one *s*.
Heb 13:20 that great *S* of the sheep, equip you
1Pe 5: 4 And when the Chief *S* appears,
Rev 7:17 of the throne will be their *s*;

SHEPHERDS (SHEPHERD)
Jer 23: 1 "Woe to the *s* who are destroying
50: 6 their *s* have led them astray
Eze 34: 2 prophesy against the *s* of Israel;
Lk 2: 8 there were *s* living out in the fields
Ac 20:28 Be *s* of the church of God,
1Pe 5: 2 Be *s* of God's flock that is
Jude :12 *s* who feed only themselves.

SHIBBOLETH*
Jdg 12: 6 No," they said, "All right, say '*S*.' "

SHIELD (SHIELDED SHIELDS)
Ge 15: 1 I am your *s*,
2Sa 22: 3 my *s* and the horn of my salvation.
22:36 You give me your *s* of victory;
Ps 3: 3 But you are a *s* around me,
5:12 with your favor as with a *s*.
7:10 My *s* is God Most High,
18: 2 He is my *s* and the horn
Ps 28: 7 LORD is my strength and my *s*;
33:20 he is our help and our *s*.
84:11 For the LORD God is a sun and *s*;
91: 4 his faithfulness will be your *s*
115: 9 he is their help and *s*.
119:114 You are my refuge and my *s*;
144: 2 my *s*, in whom I take refuge,
Pr 2: 7 he is a *s* to those whose walk is
30: 5 he is a *s* to those who take refuge
Eph 6:16 to all this, take up the *s* of faith,

SHIELDED (SHIELD)
1Pe 1: 5 through faith are *s* by God's power

SHIELDS (SHIELD)
Dt 33:12 for he *s* him all day long,

SHIFTLESS*
Pr 19:15 and the *s* man goes hungry.

SHIMEI
Cursed David (2Sa 16:5–14); spared (2Sa 19:16–23). Killed by Solomon (1Ki 2:8–9, 36–46).

SHINE (SHINES SHINING SHONE)
Nu 6:25 the LORD make his face *s*
Job 33:30 that the light of life may *s* on him.
Ps 4: 6 Let the light of your face *s* upon us,
37: 6 make your righteousness *s* like
67: 1 and make his face *s* upon us; *Selah*
80: 1 between the cherubim, *s* forth
118:27 and he has made his light *s* upon us.
Isa 60: 1 "Arise, *s*, for your light has come,
Da 12: 3 are wise will *s* like the brightness
Mt 5:16 let your light *s* before men,
13:43 the righteous will *s* like the sun
2Co 4: 6 made his light *s* in our hearts
Eph 5:14 and Christ will *s* on you."
Php 2:15 in which you *s* like stars

SHINES (SHINE)
Ps 50: 2 God *s* forth.
Pr 13: 9 The light of the righteous *s* brightly
Jn 1: 5 The light *s* in the darkness,

SHINING (SHINE)
Pr 4:18 *s* ever brighter till the full light
2Pe 1:19 as to a light *s* in a dark place,
Rev 1:16 His face was like the sun *s*

SHIPS
Pr 31:14 She is like the merchant *s*,

SHIPWRECKED*
2Co 11:25 I was stoned, three times I was *s*,
1Ti 1:19 and so have *s* their faith.

SHISHAK
1Ki 14:25 *S* king of Egypt attacked Jerusalem
2Ch 12: 2 *S* king of Egypt attacked Jerusalem

SHOCKING*
Jer 5:30 "A horrible and *s* thing

SHONE (SHINE)
Mt 17: 2 His face *s* like the sun,
Lk 2: 9 glory of the Lord *s* around them,
Rev 21:11 It *s* with the glory of God,

SHOOT
Isa 53: 2 up before him like a tender *s*,
Ro 11:17 and you, though a wild olive *s*,

SHORE
Lk 5: 3 asked him to put out a little from *s*.

SHORT (SHORTENED)
Nu 11:23 "Is the LORD's arm too *s*?
Isa 50: 2 Was my arm too *s* to ransom you?
59: 1 of the LORD is not too *s* to save,
Mt 24:22 If those days had not been cut *s*,
Ro 3:23 and fall *s* of the glory of God,
1Co 7:29 brothers, is that the time is *s*.
Heb 4: 1 of you be found to have fallen *s* of it
Rev 20: 3 he must be set free for a *s* time.

SHORTENED (SHORT)
Mt 24:22 of the elect those days will be *s*.

SHOULDER (SHOULDERS)
Zep 3: 9 and serve him *s* to *s*.

SHOULDERS (SHOULDER)
Dt 33:12 LORD loves rests between his *s*."
Isa 9: 6 and the government will be on his *s*
Lk 15: 5 he joyfully puts it on his *s*

SHOUT (SHOUTED)
Ps 47: 1 *s* to God with cries of joy.
66: 1 *S* with joy to God, all the earth!
95: 1 let us *s* aloud to the Rock
98: 4 *S* for joy to the LORD, all the earth
100: 1 *S* for joy to the LORD, all the earth
Isa 12: 6 *S* aloud and sing for joy, people
26:19 wake up and *s* for joy.
35: 6 the mute tongue *s* for joy.
40: 9 lift up your voice with a *s*,
42: 2 He will not *s* or cry out,
44:23 *s* aloud, O earth beneath.
54: 1 burst into song, *s* for joy,
Zec 9: 9 *S*, Daughter of Jerusalem!

SHOUTED (SHOUT)
Job 38: 7 and all the angels *s* for joy?

SHOW (SHOWED)
Ex 18:20 and *s* them the way to live
33:18 Moses said, "Now *s* me your glory
2Sa 22:26 the faithful you *s* yourself faithful,
1Ki 2: 2 "So be strong, *s* yourself a man,
Ps 17: 7 *S* the wonder of your great love,
25: 4 *S* me your ways, O LORD,
39: 4 "*S* me, O LORD, my life's end
85: 7 *S* us your unfailing love, O LORD,
143: 8 *S* me the way I should go,
Pr 23: 4 have the wisdom to *s* restraint.
SS 2:14 *s* me your face,
Isa 5:16 the holy God will *s* himself holy
30:18 he rises to *s* you compassion.
Eze 28:25 I will *s* myself holy among them
Joel 2:30 I will *s* wonders in the heavens
Zec 7: 9 *s* mercy and compassion
Ac 2:19 I will *s* wonders in the heaven
10:34 it is that God does not *s* favoritism
1Co 12:31 now I will *s* you the most excellent
Eph 2: 7 ages he might *s* the incomparable
Tit 2: 7 In your teaching *s* integrity,
Jas 2:18 I will *s* you my faith by what I do.
Jude :23 to others *s* mercy, mixed with fear

SHOWED (SHOW)
1Ki 3: 3 Solomon *s* his love for the LORD
Lk 24:40 he *s* them his hands and feet.
1Jn 4: 9 This is how God *s* his love

SHOWERS
Eze 34:26 in season; there will be *s* of blessing
Hos 10:12 and *s* righteousness on you.

SHREWD
2Sa 22:27 to the crooked you show yourself *s*.
Mt 10:16 Therefore be as *s* as snakes and

SHRINK (SHRINKS)
Heb 10:39 But we are not of those who *s* back

SHRINKS* (SHRINK)
Heb 10:38 And if he *s* back,

SHRIVEL
Isa 64: 6 we all *s* up like a leaf,

SHUDDER
Eze 32:10 and their kings will *s* with horror

SHUHITE
Job 2:11 Bildad the *S* and Zophar

SHUN* (SHUNS)
Job 28:28 and to *s* evil is understanding.' "
Pr 3: 7 fear the LORD and *s* evil.

SHUNS (SHUN)
Job 1: 8 a man who fears God and *s* evil."
Pr 14:16 man fears the LORD and *s* evil,

SHUT
Ge 7:16 Then the LORD *s* him in.
Isa 22:22 what he opens no one can *s*,
60:11 they will never be *s*, day or night,
Da 6:22 and he *s* the mouths of the lions.
Heb 11:33 who *s* the mouths of lions,
Rev 3: 7 no one can *s*, and what he shuts
21:25 On no day will its gates ever be *s*,

SICK (SICKNESS)
Pr 13:12 Hope deferred makes the heart *s*,
Eze 34: 4 or healed the *s* or bound up
Mt 9:12 who need a doctor, but the *s*.
10: 8 Heal the *s*, raise the dead, cleanse
25:36 I was *s* and you looked after me,
1Co 11:30 many among you are weak and *s*,
Jas 5:14 of you *s*? He should call the elders

SICKBED* (BED)
Ps 41: 3 LORD will sustain him on his *s*

SICKLE
Joel 3:13 Swing the *s,*
Rev 14:14 gold on his head and a sharp *s*

SICKNESS (SICK)
Mt 4:23 and healing every disease and *s*

SIDE (SIDES)
Ps 91: 7 A thousand may fall at your *s,*
124: 1 If the LORD had not been on our *s*
Jn 18:37 Everyone on the *s* of truth listens
20:20 he showed them his hands and *s.*
2Ti 4:17 But the Lord stood at my *s*
Heb 10:33 at other times you stood *s* by *s*

SIDES (SIDE)
Nu 33:55 in your eyes and thorns in your *s.*

SIFT
Lk 22:31 Satan has asked to *s* you as wheat.

SIGHING
Isa 35:10 and sorrow and *s* will flee away.

SIGHT
Ps 51: 4 and done what is evil in your *s,*
90: 4 For a thousand years in your *s*
116: 15 Precious in the *s* of the LORD
Pr 3: 4 in the *s* of God and man.
Mt 11: 5 The blind receive *s,* the lame walk,
Ac 4:19 right in God's *s* to obey you rather
1Co 3:19 this world is foolishness in God's *s.*
2Co 5: 7 We live by faith, not by *s.*
1Pe 3: 4 which is of great worth in God's *s.*

SIGN (SIGNS)
Ge 9:12 "This is the *s* of the covenant I am
17:11 and it will be the *s* of the covenant
Isa 7:14 the Lord himself will give you a *s:*
55:13 for an everlasting *s,*
Eze 20:12 I gave them my Sabbaths as a *s*
Mt 12:38 to see a miraculous *s* from you."
24: 3 what will be the *s* of your coming
24:30 "At that time the *s* of the Son
Lk 2:12 This will be a *s* to you: You will
11:29 It asks for a miraculous *s,*
Ro 4:11 he received the *s* of circumcision,
1Co 11:10 to have a *s* of authority on her head
14:22 are a *s,* not for believers

SIGNS (SIGN)
Ge 1:14 let them serve as *s* to mark seasons
Ps 78:43 day he displayed his miraculous *s*
105: 27 They performed his miraculous *s*
Da 6:27 he performs *s* and wonders
Mt 24:24 and perform great *s* and miracles
Mk 16:17 these *s* will accompany those who
Jn 3: 2 perform the miraculous *s* you are
20:30 Jesus did many other miraculous *s*
Ac 2:19 and *s* on the earth below,
1Co 1:22 Jews demand miraculous *s*
2Co 12:12 *s,* wonders and miracles—
2Th 2: 9 *s* and wonders, and in every sort

SIHON
Nu 21:21 to say to *S* king of the Amorites:
Ps 136: 19 *S* king of the Amorites

SILAS*
Prophet (Ac 15:22–32); co-worker with Paul on second missionary journey (Ac 16–18; 2Co 1:19). Co-writer with Paul (1Th 1:1; 2Th 1:1); Peter (1Pe 5:12).

SILENCE (SILENCED SILENT)
1Pe 2:15 good you should *s* the ignorant talk
Rev 8: 1 there was *s* in heaven

SILENCED (SILENCE)
Ro 3:19 so that every mouth may be *s*
Tit 1:11 They must be *s,* because they are

SILENT (SILENCE)
Est 4:14 For if you remain *s* at this time,
Ps 30:12 to you and not be *s.*
32: 3 When I kept *s,*
39: 2 But when I was *s* and still,
Pr 17:28 a fool is thought wise if he keeps *s,*
Ecc 3: 7 a time to be *s* and a time to speak,
Isa 53: 7 as a sheep before her shearers is *s,*
62: 1 For Zion's sake I will not keep *s,*
Hab 2:20 let all the earth be *s* before him."
Ac 8:32 and as a lamb before the shearer is *s*
1Co 14:34 women should remain *s*
1Ti 2:12 over a man; she must be *s.*

SILVER
Ps 12: 6 like *s* refined in a furnace of clay,
66:10 you refined us like *s.*
Pr 2: 4 and if you look for it as for *s*
3:14 for she is more profitable than *s*
8:10 Choose my instruction instead of *s,*
22: 1 to be esteemed is better than *s*
25: 4 Remove the dross from the *s,*
25:11 is like apples of gold in settings of *s.*
Isa 48:10 I have refined you, though not as *s;*
Eze 22:18 They are but the dross of *s.*
Da 2:32 its chest and arms of *s,* its belly
Hag 2: 8 'The *s* is mine and the gold is mine,'
Zec 13: 9 I will refine them like *s*
Ac 3: 6 Peter said, "*S* or gold I do not have,
1Co 3:12 *s,* costly stones, wood, hay or straw
1Pe 1:18 not with perishable things such as *s*

SILVERSMITH
Ac 19:24 A *s* named Demetrius, who made

SIMEON
Son of Jacob by Leah (Ge 29:33; 35:23; 1Ch 2:1). With Levi killed Shechem for rape of Dinah (Ge 34:25–29). Held hostage by Joseph in Egypt (Ge 42:24–43:23). Tribe of blessed (Ge 49:5–7), numbered (Nu 1:23; 26:14), allotted land (Jos 19:1–9; Eze 48:24), 12,000 from (Rev 7:7).

SIMON
1. See PETER.
2. Apostle, called the Zealot (Mt 10:4; Mk 3:18; Lk 6:15; Ac 1:13).
3. Samaritan sorcerer (Ac 8:9–24).

SIMPLE
Ps 19: 7 making wise the *s.*
119:130 it gives understanding to the *s.*
Pr 8: 5 You who are *s,* gain prudence;
14:15 A *s* man believes anything,

SIMPLEHEARTED* (HEART)
Ps 116: 6 The LORD protects the *s;*

SIN (SINFUL SINNED SINNER SINNERS SINNING SINS)
Ge 4: 7 *s* is crouching at your door;
Ex 32:32 please forgive their *s*—but if not,
Nu 5: 7 and must confess the *s* he has
32:23 be sure that your *s* will find you
Dt 24:16 each is to die for his own *s.*
1Sa 12:23 it from me that I should *s*
15:23 For rebellion is like the *s*
1Ki 8:46 for there is no one who does not *s*
2Ch 7:14 and will forgive their *s* and will heal
Job 1:22 Job did not *s* by charging God
Ps 4: 4 In your anger do not *s;*
17: 3 resolved that my mouth will not *s.*
32: 2 whose *s* the LORD does not count
32: 5 Then I acknowledged my *s* to you
36: 2 too much to detect or hate his *s.*
38:18 I am troubled by my *s.*
39: 1 and keep my tongue from *s;*
51: 2 and cleanse me from my *s.*
66:18 If I had cherished *s* in my heart,
119: 11 that I might not *s* against you.
119:133 let no *s* rule over me.
Pr 5:22 the cords of his *s* hold him fast.
10:19 words are many, *s* is not absent,
14: 9 Fools mock at making amends for *s*
16: 6 faithfulness *s* is atoned for;
17:19 He who loves a quarrel loves *s;*
20: 9 I am clean and without *s*"?
Isa 3: 9 they parade their *s* like Sodom;
6: 7 is taken away and your *s* atoned
64: 5 But when we continued to *s*
Jer 31:30 everyone will die for his own *s;*
Eze 3:18 that wicked man will die for his *s,*
18:26 his righteousness and commits *s,*
33: 8 that wicked man will die for his *s,*
Am 4: 4 "Go to Bethel and *s;*
Mic 6: 7 of my body for the *s* of my soul?
7:18 who pardons *s* and forgives
Zec 3: 4 "See, I have taken away your *s,*
Mt 18: 6 little ones who believe in me to *s,*
Mk 3:29 he is guilty of an eternal *s.*"
9:43 If your hand causes you to *s,*
Lk 17: 1 people to *s* are bound to come,
Jn 1:29 who takes away the *s* of the world!
8: 7 "If any one of you is without *s,*
8:34 everyone who sins is a slave to *s.*
8:46 Can any of you prove me guilty of *s*
Ro 2:12 All who *s* apart from the law will
5:12 as *s* entered the world
5:20 where *s* increased, grace increased
6: 2 By no means! We died to *s;*
6:11 count yourselves dead to *s*
6:14 For *s* shall not be your master,
6:23 For the wages of *s* is death,
7: 7 I would not have known what *s* was
7:25 sinful nature a slave to the law of *s.*
14:23 that does not come from faith is *s.*
1Co 8:12 When you *s* against your brothers
15:56 The sting of death is *s,*
2Co 5:21 God made him who had no *s* to be *s*
Gal 6: 1 if someone is caught in a *s,*
1Ti 5:20 Those who *s* are to be rebuked
Heb 4:15 just as we are—yet was without *s.*
9:26 to do away with *s* by the sacrifice
11:25 the pleasures of *s* for a short time.
12: 1 and the *s* that so easily entangles,
Jas 1:15 it gives birth to *s;* and *s,*
1Pe 2:22 "He committed no *s,*
1Jn 1: 7 his Son, purifies us from all *s.*
1: 8 If we claim to be without *s,*
2: 1 But if anybody does *s,* we have one
3: 4 in fact, *s* is lawlessness.
3: 5 And in him is no *s.*
3: 6 No one who continues to *s* has
3: 9 born of God will continue to *s,*
5:16 There is a *s* that leads to death.
5:17 All wrongdoing is *s,* and there is *s*
5:18 born of God does not continue to *s;*

SINAI
Ex 19:20 descended to the top of Mount *S*
31:18 speaking to Moses on Mount *S,*
Ps 68:17 from *S* into his sanctuary.

SINCERE* (SINCERITY)
Da 11:34 many who are not *s* will join them.
Ac 2:46 ate together with glad and *s* hearts,
Ro 12: 9 Love must be *s.*
2Co 6: 6 in the Holy Spirit and in *s* love;
11: 3 somehow be led astray from your *s*
1Ti 1: 5 a good conscience and a *s* faith.
3: 8 *s,* not indulging in much wine,
2Ti 1: 5 have been reminded of your *s* faith,
Heb 10:22 near to God with a *s* heart
Jas 3:17 and good fruit, impartial and *s.*
1Pe 1:22 the truth so that you have *s* love

SINCERITY* (SINCERE)
1Co 5: 8 bread without yeast, the bread of *s*
2Co 1:12 in the holiness and *s* that are
2:17 speak before God with *s,*
8: 8 but I want to test the *s* of your love
Eph 6: 5 and with *s* of heart, just
Col 3:22 but with *s* of heart and reverence

SINFUL (SIN)
Ps 51: 5 Surely I was *s* at birth,
51: 5 *s* from the time my mother
Lk 5: 8 from me, Lord; I am a *s* man!"
Ro 7: 5 we were controlled by the *s* nature,
7:18 lives in me, that is, in my *s* nature.
7:25 but in the *s* nature a slave to the law
8: 3 Son in the likeness of *s* man
8: 4 not live according to the *s* nature
8: 7 the *s* mind is hostile to God.
8: 8 by the *s* nature cannot please God.
8: 9 are controlled not by the *s* nature
8:13 if you live according to the *s* nature
13:14 to gratify the desires of the *s* nature
1Co 5: 5 so that the *s* nature may be
Gal 5:13 freedom to indulge the *s* nature;
5:16 gratify the desires of the *s* nature.
5:19 The acts of the *s* nature are obvious
5:24 Jesus have crucified the *s* nature
6: 8 sows to please his *s* nature,
Col 2:11 in the putting off of the *s* nature,
Heb 3:12 brothers, that none of you has a *s,*
1Pe 2:11 abstain from *s* desires, which war
1Jn 3: 8 He who does what is *s* is

SING (SANG SINGER SINGING SINGS SONG SONGS SUNG)
Ex 15: 1 "I will *s* to the LORD,
Ps 5:11 let them ever *s* for joy.
13: 6 I will *s* to the LORD,
30: 4 *S* to the LORD, you saints of his;
33: 1 *S* joyfully to the LORD, you

Ps 47: 6 *S* praises to God, *s* praises;
57: 7 I will *s* and make music.
59:16 But I will *s* of your strength,
63: 7 I *s* in the shadow of your wings.
66: 2 *S* to the glory of his name;
89: 1 I will *s* of the LORD's great love
95: 1 Come, let us *s* for joy to the LORD
96: 1 *S* to the LORD a new song;
98: 1 *S* to the LORD a new song,
101: 1 I will *s* of your love and justice;
108: 1 I will *s* and make music
137: 3 "*S* us one of the songs of Zion!"
147: 1 is to *s* praises to our God,
149: 1 *S* to the LORD a new song,
Isa 54: 1 "*S*, O barren woman,
1Co 14:15 also pray with my mind; I will *s*
Eph 5:19 *S* and make music in your heart
Col 3:16 and as you *s* psalms, hymns
Jas 5:13 Is anyone happy? Let him *s* songs

SINGER* (SING)
2Sa 23: 1 Israel's *s* of songs:

SINGING (SING)
Ps 63: 5 with *s* lips my mouth will praise
68: 6 he leads forth the prisoners with *s;*
98: 5 with the harp and the sound of *s,*
Isa 35:10 They will enter Zion with *s;*
Zep 3:17 he will rejoice over you with *s."*
Ac 16:25 Silas were praying and *s* hymns
Rev 5:13 on the sea, and all that is in them, *s:*

SINGLE
Ex 23:29 I will not drive them out in a *s* year,
Mt 6:27 you by worrying can add a *s* hour
Gal 5:14 law is summed up in a *s* command:

SINGS (SING)
Eze 33:32 more than one who *s* love songs

SINNED (SIN)
Lev 5: 5 confess in what way he has *s*
1Sa 15:24 Then Saul said to Samuel, "I have *s*
2Sa 12:13 "I have *s* against the LORD."
24:10 I have *s* greatly in what I have done
2Ch 6:37 'We have *s*, we have done wrong
Job 1: 5 "Perhaps my children have *s*
33:27 'I *s*, and perverted what was right,
Ps 51: 4 Against you, you only, have I *s*
Jer 2:35 because you say, 'I have not *s*.'
14:20 we have indeed *s* against you.
Da 9: 5 we have *s* and done wrong.
Mic 7: 9 Because I have *s* against him,
Mt 27: 4 "I have *s*," he said,
Lk 15:18 I have *s* against heaven
Ro 3:23 for all have *s* and fall short
5:12 all *s*—for before the law was given,
2Pe 2: 4 did not spare angels when they *s*,
1Jn 1:10 claim we have not *s*, we make him

SINNER (SIN)
Ecc 9:18 but one *s* destroys much good.
Lk 15: 7 in heaven over one *s* who repents
18:13 'God, have mercy on me, a *s*.'
1Co 14:24 convinced by all that he is a *s*
Jas 5:20 Whoever turns a *s* from the error
1Pe 4:18 become of the ungodly and the *s?"*

SINNERS (SIN)
Ps 1: 1 or stand in the way of *s*
37:38 But all *s* will be destroyed;
Pr 1:10 My son, if *s* entice you,
23:17 Do not let your heart envy *s*,
Mt 9:13 come to call the righteous, but *s*."
Ro 5: 8 While we were still *s*, Christ died
Gal 2:17 evident that we ourselves are *s*,
1Ti 1:15 came into the world to save *s*—
Heb 7:26 set apart from *s*, exalted

SINNING (SIN)
Ex 20:20 be with you to keep you from *s*."
1Co 15:34 stop *s;* for there are some who are
Heb 10:26 If we deliberately keep on *s*
1Jn 3: 6 No one who lives in him keeps on *s*
3: 9 go on *s*, because he has been born

SINS (SIN)
Lev 5: 1 " 'If a person *s* because he does not
16:30 you will be clean from all your *s*.
26:40 " 'But if they will confess their *s*
Nu 15:30 " 'But anyone who *s* defiantly,
1Sa 2:25 If a man *s* against another man,
2Ki 14: 6 each is to die for his own *s*."
Ezr 9: 6 our *s* are higher than our heads
9:13 less than our *s* have deserved
Ps 19:13 your servant also from willful *s;*
32: 1 whose *s* are covered.
51: 9 Hide your face from my *s*
79: 9 deliver us and forgive our *s*
85: 2 and covered all their *s*.
103: 3 who forgives all your *s*
103: 10 does not treat us as our *s* deserve
130: 3 O LORD, kept a record of *s*,
Pr 14:21 He who despises his neighbor *s*,
28:13 who conceals his *s* does not
29:22 one commits many *s*.
Ecc 7:20 who does what is right and never *s*.
Isa 1:18 "Though your *s* are like scarlet,
38:17 you have put all my *s*
43:25 and remembers your *s* no more.
59: 2 your *s* have hidden his face
64: 6 like the wind our *s* sweep us away.
Jer 31:34 and will remember their *s* no more
La 3:39 complain when punished for his *s?*
Eze 18: 4 soul who *s* is the one who will die.
33:10 Our offenses and *s* weigh us down,
36:33 day I cleanse you from all your *s*,
Hos 14: 1 Your *s* have been your downfall!
Mt 1:21 he will save his people from their *s*
6:15 if you do not forgive men their *s*,
9: 6 authority on earth to forgive *s*...."
18:15 "If your brother *s* against you,
26:28 for many for the forgiveness of *s*.
Lk 5:24 authority on earth to forgive *s*...."
11: 4 Forgive us our *s*,
17: 3 "If your brother *s*, rebuke him,
Jn 8:24 you will indeed die in your *s*."
20:23 If you forgive anyone his *s*,
Ac 2:38 for the forgiveness of your *s*.
3:19 so that your *s* may be wiped out,
10:43 forgiveness of *s* through his name."
22:16 be baptized and wash your *s* away,
26:18 they may receive forgiveness of *s*
Ro 4: 7 whose *s* are covered.
4:25 delivered over to death for our *s*
1Co 15: 3 died for our *s* according
2Co 5:19 not counting men's *s* against them.
Gal 1: 4 himself for our *s* to rescue us
Eph 2: 1 dead in your transgressions and *s*,
Col 2:13 us all our *s*, having canceled
1Ti 5:22 and do not share in the *s* of others.
Heb 1: 3 he had provided purification for *s*,
2:17 atonement for the *s* of the people.
7:27 He sacrificed for their *s* once for all
8:12 and will remember their *s* no more
9:28 to take away the *s* of many people;
10: 4 of bulls and goats to take away *s*.
10:12 for all time one sacrifice for *s*,
10:26 of the truth, no sacrifice for *s* is left,
Jas 4:17 ought to do and doesn't do it, *s*.
5:16 Therefore confess your *s*
5:20 and cover over a multitude of *s*.
1Pe 2:24 He himself bore our *s* in his body
3:18 For Christ died for *s* once for all,
4: 8 love covers over a multitude of *s*.
1Jn 1: 9 If we confess our *s*, he is faithful
2: 2 He is the atoning sacrifice for our *s*,
3: 5 so that he might take away our *s*.
4:10 as an atoning sacrifice for our *s*.
Rev 1: 5 has freed us from our *s* by his blood

SISERA
Jdg 4: 2 The commander of his army was *S*,
5:26 She struck *S*, she crushed his head,

SISTER (SISTERS)
Lev 18: 9 have sexual relations with your *s*,
Mk 3:35 does God's will is my brother and *s*

SISTERS (SISTER)
Mt 19:29 or brothers or *s* or father or mother
1Ti 5: 2 as *s*, with absolute purity.

SIT (SAT SITS SITTING)
Dt 6: 7 them when you *s* at home
1Ki 8:25 fail to have a man to *s* before me
Ps 1: 1 or *s* in the seat of mockers.
26: 5 and refuse to *s* with the wicked.
80: 1 you who *s* enthroned
110: 1 "*S* at my right hand
139: 2 You know when I *s* and when I rise
SS 2: 3 I delight to *s* in his shade,
Isa 16: 5 in faithfulness a man will *s* on it—
Mic 4: 4 Every man will *s* under his own
Mt 20:23 to *s* at my right or left is not for me
22:44 "*S* at my right hand
Lk 22:30 in my kingdom and *s* on thrones,
Heb 1:13 "*S* at my right hand
Rev 3:21 right to *s* with me on my throne,

SITS (SIT)
Ps 99: 1 *s* enthroned between the cherubim,
Isa 40:22 He *s* enthroned above the circle
Mt 19:28 of Man *s* on his glorious throne,
Rev 4: 9 thanks to him who *s* on the throne

SITTING (SIT)
Est 2:19 Mordecai was *s* at the king's gate.
Mt 26:64 the Son of Man *s* at the right hand
Rev 4: 2 in heaven with someone *s* on it.

SITUATION (SITUATIONS)
1Co 7:24 remain in the *s* God called him
Php 4:12 of being content in any and every *s*,

SITUATIONS* (SITUATION)
2Ti 4: 5 head in all *s*, endure hardship,

SKIES (SKY)
Ps 19: 1 the *s* proclaim the work
71:19 Your righteousness reaches to the *s*
108: 4 your faithfulness reaches to the *s*.

SKILL (SKILLED SKILLFUL)
Ps 137: 5 may my right hand forget its *s*.
Ecc 10:10 but *s* will bring success.

SKILLED (SKILL)
Pr 22:29 Do you see a man *s* in his work?

SKILLFUL (SKILL)
Ps 45: 1 my tongue is the pen of a *s* writer.
78:72 with *s* hands he led them.

SKIN (SKINS)
Job 19:20 with only the *s* of my teeth.
19:26 And after my *s* has been destroyed,
Jer 13:23 Can the Ethiopian change his *s*

SKINS (SKIN)
Ex 25: 5 ram *s* dyed red and hides
Lk 5:37 the new wine will burst the *s*,

SKULL
Mt 27:33 (which means The Place of the *S*).

SKY (SKIES)
Ge 1: 8 God called the expanse "*s*."
Pr 30:19 the way of an eagle in the *s*,
Isa 34: 4 and the *s* rolled up like a scroll;
Jer 33:22 stars of the *s* and as measureless
Mt 24:29 the stars will fall from the *s*,
24:30 coming on the clouds of the *s*,
Rev 20:11 Earth and *s* fled from his presence,

SLACK*
Pr 18: 9 One who is *s* in his work

SLAIN (SLAY)
1Sa 18: 7 "Saul has *s* his thousands,
Eze 37: 9 into these *s*, that they may live.' "
Rev 5: 6 as if it had been *s*, standing
5:12 "Worthy is the Lamb, who was *s*,
6: 9 the souls of those who had been *s*

SLANDER (SLANDERED SLANDERER SLANDERERS SLANDEROUS)
Lev 19:16 " 'Do not go about spreading *s*
Ps 15: 3 and has no *s* on his tongue,
Pr 10:18 and whoever spreads *s* is a fool.
2Co 12:20 outbursts of anger, factions, *s*,
Eph 4:31 rage and anger, brawling and *s*,
1Ti 5:14 the enemy no opportunity for *s*.
Tit 3: 2 to *s* no one, to be peaceable
1Pe 3:16 in Christ may be ashamed of their *s*
2Pe 2:10 afraid to *s* celestial beings;

SLANDERED (SLANDER)
1Co 4:13 when we are *s*, we answer kindly.

SLANDERER (SLANDER)
1Co 5:11 an idolater or a *s*, a drunkard

SLANDERERS (SLANDER)
Ro 1:30 They are gossips, *s*, God-haters,
1Co 6:10 nor the greedy nor drunkards nor *s*
Tit 2: 3 not to be *s* or addicted

SLANDEROUS (SLANDER)
2Ti 3: 3 unforgiving, *s*, without self-control
2Pe 2:11 do not bring *s* accusations

SLAUGHTER (SLAUGHTERED)
Isa 53: 7 he was led like a lamb to the *s*,
Jer 11:19 been like a gentle lamb led to the *s;*

Ac 8:32 "He was led like a sheep to the *s*,

SLAUGHTERED (SLAUGHTER)
Ps 44:22 we are considered as sheep to be *s*.
Ro 8:36 we are considered as sheep to be *s*

SLAVE (ENSLAVED SLAVERY SLAVES)
Ge 21:10 "Get rid of that *s* woman
Mt 20:27 wants to be first must be your *s*—
Jn 8:34 everyone who sins is a *s* to sin.
Ro 7:14 I am unspiritual, sold as a *s* to sin.
1Co 7:21 Were you a *s* when you were called
12:13 whether Jews or Greeks, *s* or free
Gal 3:28 *s* nor free, male nor female,
4: 7 So you are no longer a *s*, but a son;
4:30 Get rid of the *s* woman and her son
Col 3:11 barbarian, Scythian, *s* or free,
1Ti 1:10 for *s* traders and liars and perjurers
Phm :16 no longer as a *s*, but better than a *s*,
2Pe 2:19 a man is a *s* to whatever has

SLAVERY (SLAVE)
Ex 2:23 The Israelites groaned in their *s*
Ro 6:19 parts of your body in *s* to impurity
Gal 4: 3 were in *s* under the basic principles
1Ti 6: 1 of *s* should consider their masters

SLAVES (SLAVE)
Ps 123: 2 As the eyes of *s* look to the hand
Ecc 10: 7 I have seen *s* on horseback,
Ro 6: 6 that we should no longer be *s* to sin
6:16 you are *s* to sin, which leads
6:22 and have become *s* to God,
Gal 2: 4 in Christ Jesus and to make us *s*.
4: 8 you were *s* to those who
Eph 6: 5 *S*, obey your earthly masters
Col 3:22 *S*, obey your earthly masters
4: 1 provide your *s* with what is right
Tit 2: 9 Teach *s* to be subject

SLAY (SLAIN)
Job 13:15 Though he *s* me, yet will I hope

SLEEP (ASLEEP SLEEPER SLEEPING SLEEPS)
Ge 2:21 the man to fall into a deep *s*;
15:12 Abram fell into a deep *s*,
28:11 it under his head and lay down to *s*.
Ps 4: 8 I will lie down and *s* in peace,
121: 4 will neither slumber nor *s*.
127: 2 for he grants *s* to those he loves.
Pr 6: 9 When will you get up from your *s*?
Ecc 5:12 The *s* of a laborer is sweet,
1Co 15:51 We will not all *s*, but we will all be
1Th 5: 7 For those who *s*, *s* at night,

SLEEPER (SLEEP)
Eph 5:14 "Wake up, O *s*,

SLEEPING (SLEEP)
Mk 13:36 suddenly, do not let him find you *s*.

SLEEPLESS*
2Co 6: 5 in hard work, *s* nights and hunger;

SLEEPS (SLEEP)
Pr 10: 5 he who *s* during harvest is

SLIMY
Ps 40: 2 He lifted me out of the *s* pit,

SLING
1Sa 17:50 over the Philistine with a *s*

SLIP (SLIPPING)
Dt 4: 9 let them *s* from your heart as long
Ps 121: 3 He will not let your foot *s*—

SLIPPING (SLIP)
Ps 66: 9 and kept our feet from *s*.

SLOW
Ex 34: 6 and gracious God, *s* to anger,
Jas 1:19 *s* to speak and *s* to become angry,
2Pe 3: 9 The Lord is not *s* in keeping his

SLUGGARD
Pr 6: 6 Go to the ant, you *s*;
13: 4 The *s* craves and gets nothing,
20: 4 A *s* does not plow in season;
26:15 The *s* buries his hand in the dish;

SLUMBER
Ps 121: 3 he who watches over you will not *s*;
Pr 6:10 A little sleep, a little *s*,
Ro 13:11 for you to wake up from your *s*,

SLUR
Ps 15: 3 and casts no *s* on his fellow man,

SMELL
Ecc 10: 1 As dead flies give perfume a bad *s*,
2Co 2:16 To the one we are the *s* of death;

SMITTEN
Isa 53: 4 *s* by him, and afflicted.

SMOKE
Ex 19:18 Mount Sinai was covered with *s*,
Ps 104: 32 touches the mountains, and they *s*.
Isa 6: 4 and the temple was filled with *s*.
Joel 2:30 blood and fire and billows of *s*.
Ac 2:19 blood and fire and billows of *s*.
Rev 15: 8 filled with *s* from the glory

SMYRNA
Rev 2: 8 the angel of the church in *S* write:

SNAKE (SNAKES)
Nu 21: 8 "Make a *s* and put it up on a pole;
Pr 23:32 In the end it bites like a *s*
Jn 3:14 Moses lifted up the *s* in the desert,

SNAKES (SNAKE)
Mt 10:16 as shrewd as *s* and as innocent
Mk 16:18 they will pick up *s* with their hands;

SNARE (ENSNARE ENSNARED SNARED)
Dt 7:16 for that will be a *s* to you.
Ps 69:22 before them become a *s*;
91: 3 from the fowler's *s*
Pr 29:25 Fear of man will prove to be a *s*,
Ro 11: 9 "May their table become a *s*

SNARED (SNARE)
Pr 3:26 will keep your foot from being *s*.

SNATCH
Jn 10:28 no one can *s* them out of my hand.
Jude :23 *s* others from the fire and save

SNOUT
Pr 11:22 Like a gold ring in a pig's *s*

SNOW
Ps 51: 7 and I will be whiter than *s*.
Isa 1:18 they shall be as white as *s*;

SNUFF (SNUFFED)
Isa 42: 3 a smoldering wick he will not *s* out.
Mt 12:20 a smoldering wick he will not *s* out,

SNUFFED (SNUFF)
Pr 13: 9 but the lamp of the wicked is *s* out.

SOAP
Mal 3: 2 a refiner's fire or a launderer's *s*.

SOAR (SOARED)
Isa 40:31 They will *s* on wings like eagles;

SOARED (SOAR)
2Sa 22:11 he *s* on the wings of the wind.

SOBER
Ro 12: 3 think of yourself with *s* judgment,

SODOM
Ge 13:12 and pitched his tents near *S*.
19:24 rained down burning sulfur on *S*
Isa 1: 9 we would have become like *S*,
Lk 10:12 on that day for *S* than for that town
Ro 9:29 we would have become like *S*,
Rev 11: 8 which is figuratively called *S*

SOIL
Ge 4: 2 kept flocks, and Cain worked the *s*.
Mt 13:23 on good *s* is the man who hears

SOLD (SELL)
1Ki 21:25 who *s* himself to do evil in the eyes
Mt 10:29 Are not two sparrows *s* for a penny
13:44 then in his joy went and *s* all he had
Ro 7:14 I am unspiritual, *s* as a slave to sin.

SOLDIER
1Co 9: 7 as a *s* at his own expense?
2Ti 2: 3 with us like a good *s* of Christ Jesus

SOLE
Dt 28:65 place for the *s* of your foot.
Isa 1: 6 From the *s* of your foot to the top

SOLID
2Ti 2:19 God's *s* foundation stands firm,
Heb 5:12 You need milk, not *s* food!

SOLOMON
Son of David by Bathsheba; king of Judah (2Sa 12:24; 1Ch 3:5, 10). Appointed king by David (1Ki 1); adversaries Adonijah, Joab, Shimei killed by Benaiah (1Ki 2). Asked for wisdom (1Ki 3; 2Ch 1). Judged between two prostitutes (1Ki 3:16–28). Built temple (1Ki 5–7; 2Ch 2–5); prayer of dedication (1Ki 8; 2Ch 6). Visited by Queen of Sheba (1Ki 10; 2Ch 9). Wives turned his heart from God (1Ki 11:1–13). Jeroboam rebelled against (1Ki 11:26–40). Death (1Ki 11:41–43; 2Ch 9:29–31).
Proverbs of (1Ki 4:32; Pr 1:1; 10:1; 25:1); psalms of (Ps 72; 127); song of (SS 1:1).

SON (SONS SONSHIP)
Ge 17:19 your wife Sarah will bear you a *s*,
21:10 rid of that slave woman and her *s*,
22: 2 "Take your *s*, your only *s*, Isaac,
Ex 11: 5 Every firstborn *s* in Egypt will die,
Dt 1:31 father carries his *s*, all the way you
6:20 In the future, when your *s* asks you,
8: 5 as a man disciplines his *s*,
21:18 rebellious *s* who does not obey his
2Sa 7:14 be his father, and he will be my *s*.
1Ki 3:20 and put her dead *s* by my breast.
Ps 2: 7 He said to me, "You are my *S*;
2:12 Kiss the *S*, lest he be angry
8: 4 the *s* of man that you care for him?
Pr 3:12 as a father the *s* he delights in.
6:20 My *s*, keep your father's
10: 1 A wise *s* brings joy to his father,
13:24 He who spares the rod hates his *s*,
29:17 Discipline your *s*, and he will give
Isa 7:14 with child and will give birth to a *s*,
Eze 18:20 The *s* will not share the guilt
Da 3:25 the fourth looks like a *s* of the gods
7:13 before me was one like a *s* of man,
Hos 11: 1 and out of Egypt I called my *s*.
Am 7:14 neither a prophet nor a prophet's *s*,
Mt 1: 1 of Jesus Christ the *s* of David,
1:21 She will give birth to a *s*,
2:15 "Out of Egypt I called my *s*."
3:17 "This is my *S*, whom I love;
4: 3 "If you are the *S* of God, tell these
8:20 but the *S* of Man has no place
11:27 one knows the *S* except the Father,
12: 8 For the *S* of Man is Lord
12:32 a word against the *S* of Man will be
12:40 so the *S* of Man will be three days
13:41 *S* of Man will send out his angels,
13:55 "Isn't this the carpenter's *s*?
14:33 "Truly you are the *S* of God."
16:16 "You are the Christ, the *S*
16:27 For the *S* of Man is going to come
17: 5 "This is my *S*, whom I love;
19:28 when the *S* of Man sits
20:18 and the *S* of Man will be betrayed
20:28 as the *S* of Man did not come
21: 9 "Hosanna to the *S* of David!"
22:42 Whose *s* is he?" "The *s* of David,"
24:27 so will be the coming of the *S*
24:30 They will see the *S* of Man coming
24:44 the *S* of Man will come at an hour
25:31 "When the *S* of Man comes
26:63 if you are the Christ, the *S* of God."
27:54 "Surely he was the *S* of God!"
28:19 and of the *S* and of the Holy Spirit,
Mk 1:11 "You are my *S*, whom I love;
2:28 So the *S* of Man is Lord
8:38 the *S* of Man will be ashamed
9: 7 "This is my *S*, whom I love.
10:45 even the *S* of Man did not come
13:32 nor the *S*, but only the Father.
14:62 you will see the *S* of Man sitting
Lk 1:32 and will be called the *S*
2: 7 she gave birth to her firstborn, a *s*.
3:22 "You are my *S*, whom I love;
9:35 This is my *S*, whom I have chosen;
9:58 but the *S* of Man has no place
12: 8 the *S* of Man will also acknowledge
15:20 he ran to his *s*, threw his arms
18: 8 when the *S* of Man comes,
18:31 written by the prophets about the *S*
19:10 For the *S* of Man came to seek
Jn 1:34 I testify that this is the *S* of God."
3:14 so the *S* of Man must be lifted up,
3:16 that he gave his one and only *S*,
3:36 believes in the *S* has eternal life,
5:19 the *S* can do nothing by himself;
6:40 is that everyone who looks to the *S*
11: 4 so that God's *S* may be glorified
17: 1 Glorify your *S*, that your *S* may
Ac 7:56 and the *S* of Man standing

Ac 13:33 " 'You are my S;
Ro 1: 4 with power to be the S of God
5:10 to him through the death of his S,
8: 3 did by sending his own S
8:29 conformed to the likeness of his S,
8:32 He who did not spare his own S,
1Co 15:28 then the S himself will be made
Gal 2:20 I live by faith in the S of God,
4: 4 God sent his S, born of a woman,
4:30 rid of the slave woman and her s,
1Th 1:10 and to wait for his S from heaven,
Heb 1: 2 days he has spoken to us by his S,
1: 5 "You are my S;
2: 6 the s of man that you care for him?
4:14 Jesus the S of God, let us hold
5: 5 "You are my S;
7:28 appointed the S, who has been
10:29 punished who has trampled the S
12: 6 everyone he accepts as a s."
2Pe 1:17 saying, "This is my S, whom I love;
1Jn 1: 3 is with the Father and with his S,
1: 7 his S, purifies us from all sin.
2:23 whoever acknowledges the S has
3: 8 reason the S of God appeared was
4: 9 only S into the world that we might
4:14 that the Father has sent his S
5: 5 he who believes that Jesus is the S
5:11 eternal life, and this life is in his S.
Rev 1:13 lampstands was someone "like a s
14:14 on the cloud was one "like a s

SONG (SING)
Ex 15: 2 LORD is my strength and my s;
Ps 40: 3 He put a new s in my mouth,
69:30 I will praise God's name in s
96: 1 Sing to the LORD a new s;
98: 4 burst into jubilant s with music;
119: 54 Your decrees are the theme of my s
149: 1 Sing to the LORD a new s,
Isa 49:13 burst into s, O mountains!
55:12 will burst into s before you,
Rev 5: 9 And they sang a new s:
15: 3 and sang the s of Moses the servant

SONGS (SING)
2Sa 23: 1 Israel's singer of s:
Job 35:10 who gives s in the night,
Ps 100: 2 come before him with joyful s.
126: 6 will return with s of joy,
137: 3 "Sing us one of the s of Zion!"
Eph 5:19 with psalms, hymns and spiritual s.
Jas 5:13 Is anyone happy? Let him sing s

SONS (SON)
Ge 6: 2 the s of God saw that the daughters
10:20 These are the s of Ham
Ru 4:15 who is better to you than seven s,
Ps 127: 3 S are a heritage from the LORD,
132: 12 if your s keep my covenant
Hos 1:10 they will be called 's
Joel 2:28 Your s and daughters will prophesy
Mt 5: 9 for they will be called s of God.
Lk 6:35 and you will be s of the Most High,
Jn 12:36 so that you may become s of light."
Ro 8:14 by the Spirit of God are s of God.
9:26 they will be called 's
2Co 6:18 and you will be my s and daughters
Gal 3:26 You are all s of God through faith
4: 5 we might receive the full rights of s.
4: 6 Because you are s, God sent
Heb 12: 7 discipline; God is treating you as s.

SONSHIP* (SON)
Ro 8:15 but you received the Spirit of s.

SORCERY
Lev 19:26 " 'Do not practice divination or s.

SORROW (SORROWS)
Ps 6: 7 My eyes grow weak with s;
116: 3 I was overcome by trouble and s.
Isa 60:20 and your days of s will end.
Jer 31:12 and they will s no more.
Ro 9: 2 I have great s and unceasing
2Co 7:10 Godly s brings repentance that

SORROWS (SORROW)
Isa 53: 3 a man of s, and familiar

SOUGHT (SEEK)
2Ch 26: 5 As long as he s the LORD,
31:21 he s his God and worked
Ps 34: 4 I s the LORD, and he answered me
119: 58 I have s your face with all my heart;

SOUL (SOULS)
Dt 6: 5 with all your s and with all your
10:12 all your heart and with all your s,
30: 6 all your heart and with all your s,
Jos 22: 5 with all your heart and all your s."
2Ki 23:25 and with all his s and with all his
Ps 23: 3 he restores my s.
34: 2 My s will boast in the LORD;
42: 1 so my s pants for you, O God.
42:11 Why are you downcast, O my s?
62: 5 Find rest, O my s, in God alone;
63: 8 My s clings to you;
94:19 consolation brought joy to my s.
103: 1 Praise the LORD, O my s;
Pr 13:19 A longing fulfilled is sweet to the s,
16:24 sweet to the s and healing
22: 5 he who guards his s stays far
Isa 55: 2 your s will delight in the richest
La 3:20 and my s is downcast within me.
Eze 18: 4 For every living s belongs to me,
Mt 10:28 kill the body but cannot kill the s.
16:26 yet forfeits his s? Or what can
22:37 with all your s and with all your
Heb 4:12 even to dividing s and spirit,
3Jn : 2 even as your s is getting along well.

SOULS (SOUL)
Pr 11:30 and he who wins s is wise.
Jer 6:16 and you will find rest for your s.
Mt 11:29 and you will find rest for your s.

SOUND (FINE-SOUNDING)
Ge 3: 8 and his wife heard the s
Pr 3:21 preserve s judgment
Eze 3:12 I heard behind me a loud rumbling s
Jn 3: 8 You hear its s, but you cannot tell
Ac 2: 2 Suddenly a s like the blowing
1Co 14: 8 if the trumpet does not s a clear call
15:52 the trumpet will s, the dead will
1Ti 1:10 to the s doctrine that conforms
2Ti 4: 3 men will not put up with s doctrine.
Tit 1: 9 can encourage others by s doctrine
2: 1 is in accord with s doctrine.

SOUR
Eze 18: 2 " 'The fathers eat s grapes,

SOURCE
Heb 5: 9 became the s of eternal salvation

SOVEREIGN (SOVEREIGNTY)
Ge 15: 2 But Abram said, "O S LORD,
2Sa 7:18 O S LORD, and what is my family,
Ps 71:16 your mighty acts, O S LORD;
Isa 25: 8 S LORD will wipe away the tears
40:10 the S LORD comes with power,
50: 4 S LORD has given me
61: 1 The Spirit of the S LORD is on me,
61:11 so the S LORD will make
Jer 32:17 to the LORD: "Ah, S LORD,
Eze 12:28 fulfilled, declares the S LORD.' "
Da 4:25 that the Most High is s
2Pe 2: 1 denying the s Lord who bought
Jude : 4 and deny Jesus Christ our only S

SOVEREIGNTY (SOVEREIGN)
Da 7:27 Then the s, power and greatness

SOW (SOWER SOWN SOWS)
Job 4: 8 and those who s trouble reap it.
Ps 126: 5 Those who s in tears
Hos 8: 7 "They s the wind
10:12 S for yourselves righteousness,
Mt 6:26 they do not s or reap or store away
13: 3 "A farmer went out to s his seed.
1Co 15:36 What you s does not come to life
Jas 3:18 Peacemakers who s
2Pe 2:22 and, "A s that is washed goes back

SOWER (SOW)
Isa 55:10 so that it yields seed for the s
Mt 13:18 to what the parable of the s means:
Jn 4:36 so that the s and the reaper may be
2Co 9:10 Now he who supplies seed to the s

SOWN (SOW)
Mt 13: 8 sixty or thirty times what was s.
Mk 4:15 along the path, where the word is s.
1Co 15:42 The body that is s is perishable,

SOWS (SOW)
Pr 11:18 he who s righteousness reaps a sure
22: 8 He who s wickedness reaps trouble
2Co 9: 6 Whoever s sparingly will
Gal 6: 7 A man reaps what he s.

SPARE (SPARES SPARING)
Est 7: 3 s my people—this is my request.
Ro 8:32 He who did not s his own Son,
11:21 natural branches, he will not s you
2Pe 2: 4 For if God did not s angels
2: 5 if he did not s the ancient world

SPARES (SPARE)
Pr 13:24 He who s the rod hates his son,

SPARING (SPARE)
Pr 21:26 but the righteous give without s.

SPARKLE
Zec 9:16 They will s in his land

SPARROW (SPARROWS)
Ps 84: 3 Even the s has found a home,

SPARROWS (SPARROW)
Mt 10:29 Are not two s sold for a penny?

SPEAR (SPEARS)
1Sa 19:10 as Saul drove the s into the wall.
Ps 46: 9 breaks the bow and shatters the s,

SPEARS (SPEAR)
Isa 2: 4 and their s into pruning hooks.
Joel 3:10 and your pruning hooks into s.
Mic 4: 3 and their s into pruning hooks.

SPECIAL
Jas 2: 3 If you show s attention

SPECK
Mt 7: 3 look at the s of sawdust

SPECTACLE
1Co 4: 9 We have been made a s
Col 2:15 he made a public s of them,

SPEECH
Ps 19: 3 There is no s or language
Pr 22:11 pure heart and whose s is gracious
2Co 8: 7 in faith, in s, in knowledge,
1Ti 4:12 set an example for the believers in s

SPEND (SPENT)
Pr 31: 3 do not s your strength on women,
Isa 55: 2 Why s money on what is not bread,
2Co 12:15 So I will very gladly s

SPENT (SPEND)
Mk 5:26 many doctors and had s all she had,
Lk 6:12 and s the night praying to God.
15:14 After he had s everything,

SPIN
Mt 6:28 They do not labor or s.

SPIRIT (SPIRIT'S SPIRITS SPIRITUAL SPIRITUALLY)
Ge 1: 2 and the S of God was hovering
6: 3 "My S will not contend
Ex 31: 3 I have filled him with the S of God,
Nu 11:25 and put the S on the seventy elders.
Dt 34: 9 filled with the s of wisdom
Jdg 6:34 Then the S of the LORD came
11:29 Then the S of the LORD came
13:25 and the S of the LORD began
1Sa 10:10 the S of God came upon him
16:13 day on the S of the LORD came
16:14 the S of the LORD had departed
2Sa 23: 2 "The S of the LORD spoke
2Ki 2: 9 inherit a double portion of your s,"
Ne 9:20 You gave your good S
9:30 By your S you admonished them
Job 33: 4 The S of God has made me;
Ps 31: 5 Into your hands I commit my s;
34:18 saves those who are crushed in s.
51:10 and renew a steadfast s within me.
51:11 or take your Holy S from me.
51:17 sacrifices of God are a broken s;
106: 33 rebelled against the S of God,
139: 7 Where can I go from your S?
143: 10 may your good S
Isa 11: 2 The S of the LORD will rest
30: 1 an alliance, but not by my S,
32:15 till the S is poured upon us
44: 3 I will pour out my S
57:15 him who is contrite and lowly in s,
61: 1 The S of the Sovereign LORD is
63:10 and grieved his Holy S.
Eze 11:19 an undivided heart and put a new s
13: 3 prophets who follow their own s
36:26 you a new heart and put a new s
Da 4: 8 and the s of the holy gods is in him

Joel 2:28 I will pour out my *S* on all people.
Zec 4: 6 but by my *S*,' says the LORD
Mt 1:18 to be with child through the Holy *S*
3:11 will baptize you with the Holy *S*
3:16 he saw the *S* of God descending
4: 1 led by the *S* into the desert
5: 3 saying: "Blessed are the poor in *s*,
10:20 but the *S* of your Father speaking
12:31 against the *S* will not be forgiven.
26:41 *s* is willing, but the body is weak."
28:19 and of the Son and of the Holy *S*,
Mk 1: 8 he will baptize you with the Holy *S*
Lk 1:35 "The Holy *S* will come upon you,
1:80 child grew and became strong in *s*;
3:16 will baptize you with the Holy *S*
4:18 "The *S* of the Lord is on me,
11:13 Father in heaven give the Holy *S*
23:46 into your hands I commit my *s*."
Jn 1:33 who will baptize with the Holy *S*.'
3: 5 a man is born of water and the *S*,
4:24 God is *s*, and his worshipers must
6:63 The *S* gives life; the flesh counts
7:39 Up to that time the *S* had not been
14:26 But the Counselor, the Holy *S*,
16:13 But when he, the *S* of truth, comes,
20:22 and said, "Receive the Holy *S*.
Ac 1: 5 will be baptized with the Holy *S*."
1: 8 when the Holy *S* comes on you;
2: 4 of them were filled with the Holy *S*
2:17 I will pour out my *S* on all people.
2:38 will receive the gift of the Holy *S*.
4:31 they were all filled with the Holy *S*
5: 3 that you have lied to the Holy *S*
6: 3 who are known to be full of the *S*
8:15 that they might receive the Holy *S*,
9:17 and be filled with the Holy *S*."
11:16 will be baptized with the Holy *S*.'
13: 2 and fasting, the Holy *S* said,
19: 2 "Did you receive the Holy *S*
Ro 8: 4 nature but according to the *S*.
8: 5 set on what the *S* desires.
8: 9 And if anyone does not have the *S*
8:13 but if by the *S* you put
8:16 The *S* himself testifies
8:23 who have the firstfruits of the *S*,
8:26 the *S* helps us in our weakness.
1Co 2:10 God has revealed it to us by his *S*.
2:14 man without the *S* does not accept
5: 3 present, I am with you in *s*.
6:19 body is a temple of the Holy *S*,
12:13 baptized by one *S* into one body—
2Co 1:22 and put his *S* in our hearts
3: 3 but with the *S* of the living God,
3: 6 the letter kills, but the *S* gives life.
3:17 Now the Lord is the *S*,
5: 5 and has given us the *S* as a deposit,
7: 1 that contaminates body and *s*,
Gal 3: 2 Did you receive the *S*
5:16 by the *S*, and you will not gratify
5:22 But the fruit of the *S* is love, joy,
5:25 let us keep in step with the *S*.
6: 8 from the *S* will reap eternal life.
Eph 1:13 with a seal, the promised Holy *S*,
2:22 in which God lives by his *S*.
4: 4 There is one body and one *S*—
4:30 do not grieve the Holy *S* of God,
5:18 Instead, be filled with the *S*.
6:17 of salvation and the sword of the *S*,
Php 2: 2 being one in *s* and purpose.
1Th 5:23 May your whole *s*, soul
2Th 2:13 the sanctifying work of the *S*
1Ti 3:16 was vindicated by the *S*,
2Ti 1: 7 For God did not give us a *s*
Heb 2: 4 of the Holy *S* distributed according
4:12 even to dividing soul and *s*,
10:29 and who has insulted the *S* of grace
1Pe 3: 4 beauty of a gentle and quiet *s*,
2Pe 1:21 carried along by the Holy *S*.
1Jn 3:24 We know it by the *S* he gave us.
4: 1 Dear friends, do not believe every *s*
4:13 because he has given us of his *S*.
Jude :20 holy faith and pray in the Holy *S*.
Rev 2: 7 let him hear what the *S* says

SPIRIT'S* (SPIRIT)
1Co 2: 4 a demonstration of the *S* power,
1Th 5:19 not put out the *S* fire; do not treat

SPIRITS (SPIRIT)
1Co 12:10 to another distinguishing between *s*,
14:32 The *s* of prophets are subject
1Jn 4: 1 test the *s* to see whether they are

SPIRITUAL (SPIRIT)
Ro 12: 1 to God—this is your *s* act of worship.
12:11 but keep your *s* fervor, serving
1Co 2:13 expressing *s* truths in *s* words.
3: 1 I could not address you as *s* but
12: 1 Now about *s* gifts, brothers,
14: 1 of love and eagerly desire *s* gifts,
15:44 a natural body, it is raised a *s* body.
Gal 6: 1 you who are *s* should restore him
Eph 1: 3 with every *s* blessing in Christ.
5:19 with psalms, hymns and *s* songs.
6:12 and against the *s* forces of evil
1Pe 2: 2 newborn babies, crave pure *s* milk,
2: 5 are being built into a *s* house

SPIRITUALLY (SPIRIT)
1Co 2:14 because they are *s* discerned.

SPIT
Mt 27:30 They *s* on him, and took the staff
Rev 3:16 I am about to *s* you out

SPLENDOR
1Ch 16:29 the LORD in the *s* of his holiness.
29:11 the glory and the majesty and the *s*,
Job 37:22 of the north he comes in golden *s*;
Ps 29: 2 in the *s* of his holiness.
45: 3 clothe yourself with *s* and majesty.
96: 6 *S* and majesty are before him;
96: 9 in the *s* of his holiness;
104: 1 you are clothed with *s* and majesty.
145: 5 of the glorious *s* of your majesty,
145: 12 and the glorious *s* of your kingdom.
148: 13 his *s* is above the earth
Pr 4: 9 and present you with a crown of *s*."
16:31 Gray hair is a crown of *s*;
20:29 gray hair the *s* of the old.
Isa 55: 5 for he has endowed you with *s*."
60:21 for the display of my *s*.
61: 3 the LORD for the display of his *s*.
63: 1 Who is this, robed in *s*,
Hab 3: 4 His *s* was like the sunrise;
Mt 6:29 in all his *s* was dressed like one
Lk 9:31 appeared in glorious *s*, talking
2Th 2: 8 and destroy by the *s* of his coming.

SPOIL (SPOILS)
Ps 119:162 like one who finds great *s*.

SPOILS (SPOIL)
Isa 53:12 he will divide the *s* with the strong,
Jn 6:27 Do not work for food that *s*,

SPONTANEOUS*
Phm :14 so that any favor you do will be *s*

SPOTLESS
2Pe 3:14 make every effort to be found *s*,

SPOTS (SPOTTED)
Jer 13:23 or the leopard its *s*?

SPOTTED (SPOTS)
Ge 30:32 and every *s* or speckled goat.

SPREAD (SPREADING SPREADS)
Ps 78:19 "Can God *s* a table in the desert?
Ac 6: 7 So the word of God *s*.
12:24 of God continued to increase and *s*.
13:49 of the Lord *s* through the whole
19:20 the word of the Lord *s* widely
2Th 3: 1 message of the Lord may *s* rapidly

SPREADING (SPREAD)
Pr 29: 5 is *s* a net for his feet.
1Th 3: 2 God's fellow worker in *s* the gospel

SPREADS (SPREAD)
Pr 10:18 and whoever *s* slander is a fool.

SPRING (SPRINGS WELLSPRING)
Jer 2:13 the *s* of living water,
Jn 4:14 in him a *s* of water welling up
Jas 3:12 can a salt *s* produce fresh water.

SPRINGS (SPRING)
2Pe 2:17 These men are *s* without water

SPRINKLE (SPRINKLED SPRINKLING)
Lev 16:14 and with his finger *s* it on the front

SPRINKLED (SPRINKLE)
Heb 10:22 having our hearts *s* to cleanse us

SPRINKLING (SPRINKLE)
1Pe 1: 2 to Jesus Christ and *s* by his blood:

SPROUT
Pr 23: 5 for they will surely *s* wings
Jer 33:15 I will make a righteous Branch *s*

SPUR*
Heb 10:24 how we may *s* one another

SPURNS*
Pr 15: 5 A fool *s* his father's discipline,

SPY
Gal 2: 4 ranks to *s* on the freedom we have

SQUANDERED (SQUANDERS)
Lk 15:13 there *s* his wealth in wild living.

SQUANDERS* (SQUANDERED)
Pr 29: 3 of prostitutes *s* his wealth.

SQUARE
Rev 21:16 The city was laid out like a *s*,

STABILITY*
Pr 29: 4 By justice a king gives a country *s*,

STAFF
Ge 49:10 the ruler's *s* from between his feet,
Ex 7:12 Aaron's *s* swallowed up their staffs.
Nu 17: 6 and Aaron's *s* was among them.
Ps 23: 4 your rod and your *s*,

STAIN (STAINED)
Eph 5:27 without *s* or wrinkle or any other

STAINED (STAIN)
Isa 63: 1 with his garments *s* crimson?

STAKES
Isa 54: 2 strengthen your *s*.

STAND (STANDING STANDS STOOD)
Ex 14:13 *S* firm and you will see
Jos 10:12 "O sun, *s* still over Gibeon,
2Ch 20:17 *s* firm and see the deliverance
Job 19:25 in the end he will *s* upon the earth.
Ps 1: 1 or *s* in the way of sinners
1: 5 Therefore the wicked will not *s*
24: 3 Who may *s* in his holy place?
33:11 of the LORD *s* firm forever,
40: 2 and gave me a firm place to *s*.
76: 7 Who can *s* before you
93: 5 Your statutes *s* firm;
119:120 I *s* in awe of your laws.
130: 3 O Lord, who could *s*?
Ecc 5: 7 Therefore *s* in awe of God.
Isa 7: 9 If you do not *s* firm in your faith,
29:23 will *s* in awe of the God of Israel.
Eze 22:30 *s* before me in the gap on behalf
Hab 3: 2 I *s* in awe of your deeds, O LORD.
Zec 14: 4 On that day his feet will *s*
Mal 3: 2 Who can *s* when he appears?
Mt 12:25 divided against itself will not *s*.
Ro 14: 4 for the Lord is able to make him *s*.
14:10 we will all *s* before God's judgment
1Co 10:13 out so that you can *s* up under it.
15:58 Therefore, my dear brothers, *s* firm
16:13 Be on your guard; *s* firm in the faith
Gal 5: 1 *S* firm, then, and do not let
Eph 6:14 *S* firm then, with the belt
2Th 2:15 *s* firm and hold to the teachings we
Jas 5: 8 You too, be patient and *s* firm,
Rev 3:20 Here I am! I *s* at the door

STANDING (STAND)
Ex 3: 5 where you are *s* is holy ground."
Jos 5:15 the place where you are *s* is holy."
Ru 2: 1 a man of *s*, whose name was Boaz.
4:11 May you have *s* in Ephrathah
Lk 21:19 By *s* firm you will gain life.
1Ti 3:13 have served well gain an excellent *s*
1Pe 5: 9 Resist him, *s* firm in the faith,

STANDS (STAND)
Ps 89: 2 that your love *s* firm forever,
119: 89 it *s* firm in the heavens.
Pr 12: 7 the house of the righteous *s* firm.
Isa 40: 8 but the word of our God *s* forever."
Mt 10:22 but he who *s* firm to the end will be
2Ti 2:19 God's solid foundation *s* firm,
1Pe 1:25 but the word of the Lord *s* forever

STAR (STARS)
Nu 24:17 A *s* will come out of Jacob;
Isa 14:12 O morning *s*, son of the dawn!
Mt 2: 2 We saw his *s* in the east
2Pe 1:19 the morning *s* rises in your hearts.
Rev 2:28 I will also give him the morning *s*.

Rev 22:16 and the bright Morning *S.*"

STARS (STAR)
Ge 1:16 He also made the *s.*
Job 38: 7 while the morning *s* sang together
Da 12: 3 like the *s* for ever and ever.
Php 2:15 in which you shine like *s*

STATURE
1Sa 2:26 boy Samuel continued to grow in *s*
Lk 2:52 And Jesus grew in wisdom and *s,*

STATUTES
Ps 19: 7 *s* of the LORD are trustworthy,
93: 5 Your *s* stand firm;
119: 2 Blessed are they who keep his *s*
119: 14 I rejoice in following your *s*
119: 24 Your *s* are my delight;
119: 36 Turn my heart toward your *s*
119: 99 for I meditate on your *s.*
119:111 Your *s* are my heritage forever;
119:125 that I may understand your *s.*
119:129 Your *s* are wonderful;
119:138 The *s* you have laid
119:152 Long ago I learned from your *s*
119:167 I obey your *s,*

STEADFAST*
Ps 51:10 and renew a *s* spirit within me.
57: 7 My heart is *s,* O God,
57: 7 my heart is *s;*
108: 1 My heart is *s,* O God;
111: 8 They are *s* for ever and ever,
112: 7 his heart is *s,* trusting in the LORD
119: 5 Oh, that my ways were *s*
Isa 26: 3 him whose mind is *s,*
1Pe 5:10 and make you strong, firm and *s.*

STEADY
Isa 35: 3 *s* the knees that give way;

STEAL (STOLEN)
Ex 20:15 "You shall not *s.*
Lev 19:11 " 'Do not *s.*
Dt 5:19 "You shall not *s.*
Mt 19:18 do not *s,* do not give false
Ro 13: 9 "Do not *s,*" "Do not covet,"
Eph 4:28 has been stealing must *s* no longer,

STEP (FOOTSTEPS STEPS)
Job 34:21 he sees their every *s.*
Gal 5:25 let us keep in *s* with the Spirit.

STEPHEN
Deacon (Ac 6:5). Arrested (Ac 6:8–15). Speech to Sanhedrin (Ac 7). Stoned (Ac 7:54–60; 22:20).

STEPS (STEP)
Ps 37:23 he makes his *s* firm;
Pr 14:15 prudent man gives thought to his *s.*
16: 9 but the LORD determines his *s.*
20:24 A man's *s* are directed
Jer 10:23 it is not for man to direct his *s.*
1Pe 2:21 that you should follow in his *s.*

STERN (STERNNESS)
Pr 15:10 *S* discipline awaits him who leaves

STERNNESS* (STERN)
Ro 11:22 and *s* of God: *s* to those who fell,

STICKS
Pr 18:24 there is a friend who *s* closer

STIFF-NECKED (NECK)
Ex 34: 9 Although this is a *s* people,
Pr 29: 1 A man who remains *s*

STILL
Jos 10:13 So the sun stood *s,*
Ps 37: 7 Be *s* before the LORD
46:10 "Be *s,* and know that I am God;
89: 9 its waves mount up, you *s* them.
Zec 2:13 Be *s* before the LORD, all mankind
Mk 4:39 said to the waves, "Quiet! Be *s!*"

STIMULATE*
2Pe 3: 1 as reminders to *s* you

STING
1Co 15:55 Where, O death, is your *s?*"

STINGY
Pr 28:22 A *s* man is eager to get rich

STIRRED (STIRS)
Ps 45: 1 My heart is *s* by a noble theme

STIRS (STIRRED)
Pr 6:19 and a man who *s* up dissension
10:12 Hatred *s* up dissension,
15: 1 but a harsh word *s* up anger.
15:18 hot-tempered man *s* up dissension,
16:28 A perverse man *s* up dissension,
28:25 A greedy man *s* up dissension,
29:22 An angry man *s* up dissension,

STOLEN (STEAL)
Lev 6: 4 he must return what he has *s*
SS 4: 9 You have *s* my heart, my sister,

STOMACH
1Co 6:13 Food for the *s* and the *s* for food"—
Php 3:19 their god is their *s,* and their glory

STONE (CAPSTONE CORNERSTONE MILLSTONE STONED STONES)
Ex 24: 4 set up twelve *s* pillars representing
28:10 on one *s* and the remaining six
34: 1 "Chisel out two *s* tablets like
Dt 4:13 then wrote them on two *s* tablets.
19:14 your neighbor's boundary *s* set up
1Sa 17:50 the Philistine with a sling and a *s;*
Ps 91:12 will not strike your foot against a *s.*
118: 22 The *s* the builders rejected
Pr 22:28 not move an ancient boundary *s*
Isa 8:14 a *s* that causes men to stumble
28:16 "See, I lay a *s* in Zion,
Eze 11:19 remove from them their heart of *s*
36:26 remove from you your heart of *s*
Mt 7: 9 will give him a *s?* Or if he asks
21:42 " 'The *s* the builders rejected
24: 2 not one *s* here will be left
Mk 16: 3 "Who will roll the *s* away
Lk 4: 3 tell this *s* to become bread."
Jn 8: 7 the first to throw a *s* at her."
Ac 4:11 " 'the *s* you builders rejected,
Ro 9:32 stumbled over the "stumbling *s.*"
2Co 3: 3 not on tablets of *s* but on tablets
1Pe 2: 6 "See, I lay a *s* in Zion,
Rev 2:17 also give him a white *s*

STONED (STONE)
2Co 11:25 once I was *s,* three times I was
Heb 11:37 They were *s;* they were sawed

STONES (STONE)
Ex 28:21 are to be twelve *s,* one for each
Jos 4: 3 to take up twelve *s* from the middle
1Sa 17:40 chose five smooth *s*
Mt 3: 9 out of these *s* God can raise up
1Co 3:12 silver, costly *s,* wood, hay or straw,
1Pe 2: 5 also, like living *s,* are being built

STOOD (STAND)
Jos 10:13 So the sun *s* still,
Lk 22:28 You are those who have *s* by me
2Ti 4:17 But the Lord *s* at my side
Jas 1:12 because when he has *s* the test,

STOOP (STOOPS)
2Sa 22:36 you *s* down to make me great.

STOOPS (STOOP)
Ps 113: 6 who *s* down to look

STOP
Job 37:14 *s* and consider God's wonders.
Isa 1:13 *S* bringing meaningless offerings!
1:16 *S* doing wrong,
2:22 *S* trusting in man,
Jer 32:40 I will never *s* doing good to them,
Mk 9:39 "Do not *s* him," Jesus said.
Jn 6:43 "*S* grumbling among yourselves,"
7:24 *S* judging by mere appearances,
20:27 *S* doubting and believe."
Ro 14:13 Therefore let us *s* passing judgment
1Co 14:20 Brothers, *s* thinking like children.

STORE (STORED)
Pr 2: 1 and *s* up my commands within you,
7: 1 and *s* up my commands within you.
10:14 Wise men *s* up knowledge,
Isa 33: 6 a rich *s* of salvation and wisdom
Mt 6:19 not *s* up for yourselves treasures
6:26 or reap or *s* away in barns,
2Ti 4: 8 Now there is in *s* for me the crown

STORED (STORE)
Lk 6:45 out of the good *s* up in his heart,
Col 1: 5 from the hope that is *s* up for you

STOREHOUSE (HOUSE)
Mal 3:10 Bring the whole tithe into the *s,*

STORIES*
2Pe 1:16 did not follow cleverly invented *s*
2: 3 you with *s* they have made up.

STORM
Job 38: 1 LORD answered Job out of the *s.*
Ps 107: 29 He stilled the *s* to a whisper;
Lk 8:24 the *s* subsided, and all was calm.

STOUTHEARTED* (HEART)
Ps 138: 3 you made me bold and *s.*

STRAIGHT
Ps 27:11 lead me in a *s* path
107: 7 He led them by a *s* way
Pr 2:13 who leave the *s* paths
3: 6 and he will make your paths *s.*
4:11 and lead you along *s* paths.
4:25 Let your eyes look *s* ahead,
11: 5 of the blameless makes a *s* way
15:21 of understanding keeps a *s* course.
Isa 40: 3 make *s* in the wilderness
Mt 3: 3 make *s* paths for him.' "
Jn 1:23 'Make *s* the way for the Lord.' "
2Pe 2:15 They have left the *s* way

STRAIN (STRAINING)
Mt 23:24 You *s* out a gnat but swallow

STRAINING (STRAIN)
Php 3:13 and *s* toward what is ahead,

STRANGE (STRANGER STRANGERS)
Isa 28:11 with foreign lips and *s* tongues
1Co 14:21 "Through men of *s* tongues
1Pe 4: 4 They think it *s* that you do not

STRANGER (STRANGE)
Ps 119: 19 I am a *s* on earth;
Mt 25:35 I was a *s* and you invited me in,
Jn 10: 5 But they will never follow a *s;*

STRANGERS (STRANGE)
Heb 13: 2 Do not forget to entertain *s,*
1Pe 2:11 as aliens and *s* in the world,

STRAW
Isa 11: 7 and the lion will eat *s* like the ox.
1Co 3:12 silver, costly stones, wood, hay or *s*

STRAYED (STRAYS)
Ps 119:176 I have *s* like a lost sheep.
Jer 31:19 After I *s,*

STRAYS (STRAYED)
Pr 21:16 A man who *s* from the path
Eze 34:16 for the lost and bring back the *s.*

STREAM (STREAMS)
Am 5:24 righteousness like a never-failing *s!*

STREAMS (STREAM)
Ps 1: 3 He is like a tree planted by *s*
46: 4 is a river whose *s* make glad
Ecc 1: 7 All *s* flow into the sea,
Jn 7:38 *s* of living water will flow

STREET
Mt 6: 5 on the *s* corners to be seen by men.
22: 9 Go to the *s* corners and invite
Rev 21:21 The great *s* of the city was of pure gold,

STRENGTH (STRONG)
Ex 15: 2 The LORD is my *s* and my song;
Dt 4:37 by his Presence and his great *s,*
6: 5 all your soul and with all your *s.*
Jdg 16:15 told me the secret of your great *s.*"
2Sa 22:33 It is God who arms me with *s*
2Ki 23:25 with all his soul and with all his *s,*
1Ch 16:11 Look to the LORD and his *s;*
16:28 ascribe to the LORD glory and *s,*
29:12 In your hands are *s* and power
Ne 8:10 for the joy of the LORD is your *s.*"
Ps 18: 1 I love you, O LORD, my *s.*
21:13 Be exalted, O LORD, in your *s;*
28: 7 The LORD is my *s* and my shield;
29:11 The LORD gives *s* to his people;
33:16 no warrior escapes by his great *s.*
46: 1 God is our refuge and *s,*
59:17 O my *S,* I sing praise to you;
65: 6 having armed yourself with *s,*
73:26 but God is the *s* of my heart
84: 5 Blessed are those whose *s* is in you,
96: 7 ascribe to the LORD glory and *s.*
105: 4 Look to the LORD and his *s;*
118: 14 The LORD is my *s* and my song;

Ps 147: 10 not in the *s* of the horse,
Pr 24: 5 a man of knowledge increases *s;*
30: 25 Ants are creatures of little *s,*
Isa 12: 2 the LORD, is my *s* and my song;
31: 1 and in the great *s* of their horsemen
40: 26 of his great power and mighty *s,*
40: 31 will renew their *s.*
63: 1 forward in the greatness of his *s?*
Jer 9: 23 or the strong man boast of his *s*
Mic 5: 4 flock in the *s* of the LORD,
Hab 3: 19 The Sovereign LORD is my *s;*
Mk 12: 30 all your mind and with all your *s.'*
1Co 1: 25 of God is stronger than man's *s.*
Eph 1: 19 is like the working of his mighty *s,*
Php 4: 13 through him who gives me *s.*
Heb 11: 34 whose weakness was turned to *s;*
1Pe 4: 11 it with the *s* God provides,

STRENGTHEN (STRONG)
2Ch 16: 9 to *s* those whose hearts are fully
Ps 119: 28 *s* me according to your word.
Isa 35: 3 *S* the feeble hands,
41: 10 I will *s* you and help you;
Lk 22: 32 have turned back, *s* your brothers."
Eph 3: 16 of his glorious riches he may *s* you
1Th 3: 13 May he *s* your hearts
2Th 2: 17 and *s* you in every good deed
Heb 12: 12 *s* your feeble arms and weak knees.

STRENGTHENED (STRONG)
Col 1: 11 being *s* with all power according
Heb 13: 9 good for our hearts to be *s* by grace,

STRENGTHENING (STRONG)
1Co 14: 26 done for the *s* of the church.

STRETCHES
Ps 104: 2 he *s* out the heavens like a tent

STRICKEN (STRIKE)
Isa 53: 8 of my people he was *s.*

STRICT
1Co 9: 25 in the games goes into *s* training.

STRIFE (STRIVE)
Pr 17: 1 than a house full of feasting, with *s.*
20: 3 It is to a man's honor to avoid *s,*
22: 10 out the mocker, and out goes *s;*
30: 33 so stirring up anger produces *s."*
1Ti 6: 4 *s,* malicious talk, evil suspicions

STRIKE (STRIKES STROKE)
Ge 3: 15 and you will *s* his heel."
Zec 13: 7 "*S* the shepherd,
Mt 4: 6 so that you will not *s* your foot
26: 31 " 'I will *s* the shepherd,

STRIKES (STRIKE)
Mt 5: 39 If someone *s* you on the right

STRIPS
Lk 2: 12 You will find a baby wrapped in *s*
Jn 20: 5 in at the *s* of linen lying there

STRIVE* (STRIFE)
Ac 24: 16 I *s* always to keep my conscience
1Ti 4: 10 (and for this we labor and *s),*

STROKE (STRIKE)
Mt 5: 18 the smallest letter, not the least *s*

STRONG (STRENGTH STRENGTHEN STRENGTHENED STRENGTHENING STRONGER)
Dt 3: 24 your greatness and your *s* hand.
31: 6 Be *s* and courageous.
Jos 1: 6 "Be *s* and courageous,
Jdg 5: 21 March on, my soul; be *s!*
2Sa 10: 12 Be *s* and let us fight bravely
1Ki 2: 2 "So be *s,* show yourself a man,
1Ch 28: 20 "Be *s* and courageous,
2Ch 32: 7 them with these words: "Be *s*
Ps 24: 8 The LORD *s* and mighty,
31: 2 a *s* fortress to save me.
62: 11 that you, O God, are *s,*
Pr 18: 10 The name of the LORD is a *s* tower
31: 17 her arms are *s* for her tasks.
Ecc 9: 11 or the battle to the *s,*
SS 8: 6 for love is as *s* as death,
Isa 35: 4 "Be *s,* do not fear;
53: 12 he will divide the spoils with the *s,*
Jer 9: 23 or the *s* man boast of his strength
50: 34 Yet their Redeemer is *s;*
Hag 2: 4 Be *s,* all you people of the land,'
Mt 12: 29 can anyone enter a *s* man's house

Lk 2: 40 And the child grew and became *s;*
Ro 15: 1 We who are *s* ought to bear
1Co 1: 8 He will keep you *s* to the end,
1: 27 things of the world to shame the *s.*
16: 13 in the faith; be men of courage; be *s*
2Co 12: 10 For when I am weak, then I am *s.*
Eph 6: 10 be *s* in the Lord and in his mighty
2Ti 2: 1 be *s* in the grace that is
1Pe 5: 10 restore you and make you *s,*

STRONGER (STRONG)
Dt 4: 38 before you nations greater and *s*
1Co 1: 25 of God is *s* than man's strength.

STRONGHOLD (STRONGHOLDS)
2Sa 22: 3 He is my *s,* my refuge and my
Ps 9: 9 a *s* in times of trouble.
18: 2 the horn of my salvation, my *s.*
27: 1 The LORD is the *s* of my life—
144: 2 my *s* and my deliverer,

STRONGHOLDS (STRONGHOLD)
Zep 3: 6 their *s* are demolished.
2Co 10: 4 have divine power to demolish *s.*

STRUGGLE (STRUGGLED STRUGGLING)
Ro 15: 30 me in my *s* by praying to God
Eph 6: 12 For our *s* is not against flesh
Heb 12: 4 In your *s* against sin, you have not

STRUGGLED (STRUGGLE)
Ge 32: 28 because you have *s* with God

STRUGGLING* (STRUGGLE)
Col 1: 29 To this end I labor, *s*
2: 1 to know how much I am *s* for you

STUDENT (STUDY)
Mt 10: 24 "A *s* is not above his teacher,

STUDY (STUDENT)
Ezr 7: 10 Ezra had devoted himself to the *s*
Ecc 12: 12 and much *s* wearies the body.
Jn 5: 39 You diligently *s* the Scriptures

STUMBLE (STUMBLES STUMBLING)
Ps 37: 24 though he *s,* he will not fall,
119: 165 and nothing can make them *s.*
Pr 3: 23 and your foot will not *s;*
Isa 8: 14 a stone that causes men to *s*
Jer 13: 16 before your feet *s*
31: 9 a level path where they will not *s,*
Eze 7: 19 for it has made them *s* into sin.
Hos 14: 9 but the rebellious *s* in them.
Mal 2: 8 teaching have caused many to *s;*
Jn 11: 9 A man who walks by day will not *s,*
Ro 9: 33 in Zion a stone that causes men to *s*
14: 20 that causes someone else to *s.*
1Co 10: 32 Do not cause anyone to *s,*
Jas 3: 2 We all *s* in many ways.
1Pe 2: 8 and, "A stone that causes men to *s*
1Jn 2: 10 nothing in him to make him *s.*

STUMBLES (STUMBLE)
Pr 24: 17 when he *s,* do not let your heart
Jn 11: 10 is when he walks by night that he *s,*
Jas 2: 10 and yet *s* at just one point is guilty

STUMBLING (STUMBLE)
Lev 19: 14 put a *s* block in front of the blind,
Ps 56: 13 and my feet from *s,*
Mt 16: 23 Satan! You are a *s* block to me;
Ro 9: 32 They stumbled over the "*s* stone."
11: 9 a *s* block and a retribution for them
14: 13 up your mind not to put any *s* block
1Co 1: 23 a *s* block to Jews and foolishness
8: 9 freedom does not become a *s* block
2Co 6: 3 We put no *s* block in anyone's path,

STUMP
Isa 6: 13 so the holy seed will be the *s*
11: 1 up from the *s* of Jesse;

STUPID
Pr 12: 1 but he who hates correction is *s.*
2Ti 2: 23 to do with foolish and *s* arguments,

STUPOR
Ro 11: 8 "God gave them a spirit of *s,*

SUBDUE (SUBDUED)
Ge 1: 28 in number; fill the earth and *s* it.

SUBDUED (SUBDUE)
Jos 10: 40 So Joshua *s* the whole region,
Ps 47: 3 He *s* nations under us,

SUBJECT (SUBJECTED)
Mt 5: 22 angry with his brother will be *s*
1Co 14: 32 of prophets are *s* to the control
15: 28 then the Son himself will be made *s*
Tit 2: 5 and to be *s* to their husbands,
2: 9 slaves to be *s* to their masters
3: 1 Remind the people to be *s* to rulers

SUBJECTED (SUBJECT)
Ro 8: 20 For the creation was *s*

SUBMISSION (SUBMIT)
1Co 14: 34 but must be in *s,* as the Law says.
1Ti 2: 11 learn in quietness and full *s.*

SUBMISSIVE (SUBMIT)
Jas 3: 17 then peace-loving, considerate, *s,*
1Pe 3: 1 in the same way be *s*
5: 5 in the same way be *s*

SUBMIT (SUBMISSION SUBMISSIVE SUBMITS)
Ro 13: 1 Everyone must *s* himself
13: 5 necessary to *s* to the authorities,
1Co 16: 16 to *s* to such as these
Eph 5: 21 *S* to one another out of reverence
Col 3: 18 Wives, *s* to your husbands,
Heb 12: 9 How much more should we *s*
13: 17 Obey your leaders and *s*
Jas 4: 7 *S* yourselves, then, to God.
1Pe 2: 18 *s* yourselves to your masters

SUBMITS* (SUBMIT)
Eph 5: 24 Now as the church *s* to Christ,

SUBTRACT*
Dt 4: 2 what I command you and do not *s*

SUCCEED (SUCCESS SUCCESSFUL)
Ps 20: 4 and make all your plans *s.*
Pr 15: 22 but with many advisers they *s.*
16: 3 and your plans will *s.*
21: 30 that can *s* against the LORD.

SUCCESS (SUCCEED)
Ge 39: 23 and gave him *s* in whatever he did.
1Sa 18: 14 In everything he did he had great *s,*
1Ch 12: 18 *S, s* to you, and *s*
22: 13 you will have *s* if you are careful
2Ch 26: 5 the LORD, God gave him *s.*
Ecc 10: 10 but skill will bring *s.*

SUCCESSFUL (SUCCEED)
Jos 1: 7 that you may be *s* wherever you go.
2Ki 18: 7 he was *s* in whatever he undertook.
2Ch 20: 20 in his prophets and you will be *s."*

SUFFER (SUFFERED SUFFERING SUFFERINGS SUFFERS)
Job 36: 15 those who *s* he delivers
Isa 53: 10 to crush him and cause him to *s,*
Mk 8: 31 the Son of Man must *s* many things
Lk 24: 26 the Christ have to *s* these things
24: 46 The Christ will *s* and rise
2Co 1: 6 of the same sufferings we *s.*
Php 1: 29 to *s* for him, since you are going
Heb 9: 26 would have had to *s* many times
1Pe 3: 17 to *s* for doing good
4: 16 However, if you *s* as a Christian,

SUFFERED (SUFFER)
Heb 2: 9 and honor because he *s* death,
2: 18 Because he himself *s*
1Pe 2: 21 Christ *s* for you, leaving you
4: 1 he who has *s* in his body is done

SUFFERING (SUFFER)
Job 36: 15 who suffer he delivers in their *s;*
Ps 22: 24 the *s* of the afflicted one;
Isa 53: 3 of sorrows, and familiar with *s.*
53: 11 After the *s* of his soul,
La 1: 12 Is any *s* like my *s*
Ac 5: 41 worthy of *s* disgrace for the Name.
Ro 5: 3 know that *s* produces
2Ti 1: 8 But join with me in *s* for the gospel,
Heb 2: 10 of their salvation perfect through *s.*
13: 3 as if you yourselves were *s.*
1Pe 4: 12 at the painful trial you are *s,*

SUFFERINGS (SUFFER)
Ro 5: 3 but we also rejoice in our *s,*
8: 17 share in his *s* in order that we may
8: 18 that our present *s* are not worth
2Co 1: 5 as the *s* of Christ flow
Php 3: 10 the fellowship of sharing in his *s,*
1Pe 4: 13 rejoice that you participate in the *s*

1Pe 5: 9 are undergoing the same kind of *s*.

SUFFERS (SUFFER)
Pr 13:20 but a companion of fools *s* harm.
1Co 12:26 If one part *s*, every part *s* with it;

SUFFICIENT
2Co 12: 9 said to me, "My grace is *s* for you,

SUITABLE
Ge 2:18 I will make a helper *s* for him."

SUMMED* (SUMS)
Ro 13: 9 there may be, are *s* up
Gal 5:14 The entire law is *s* up

SUMMONS
Ps 50: 1 speaks and *s* the earth
Isa 45: 3 God of Israel, who *s* you by name.

SUMS* (SUMMED)
Mt 7:12 for this *s* up the Law

SUN (SUNRISE)
Jos 10:13 So the *s* stood still,
Jdg 5:31 may they who love you be like the *s*
Ps 84:11 For the LORD God is a *s*
121: 6 the *s* will not harm you by day,
136: 8 the *s* to govern the day,
Ecc 1: 9 there is nothing new under the *s*.
Isa 60:19 The *s* will no more be your light
Mal 4: 2 the *s* of righteousness will rise
Mt 5:45 He causes his *s* to rise on the evil
13:43 the righteous will shine like the *s*
17: 2 His face shone like the *s*,
Lk 23:45 for the *s* stopped shining.
Eph 4:26 Do not let the *s* go
Rev 1:16 His face was like the *s* shining
21:23 The city does not need the *s*

SUNG (SING)
Mt 26:30 When they had *s* a hymn, they

SUNRISE (SUN)
2Sa 23: 4 he is like the light of morning at *s*
Hab 3: 4 His splendor was like the *s*;

SUPERIOR
Heb 1: 4 he became as much *s* to the angels
8: 6 ministry Jesus has received is as *s*

SUPERVISION
Gal 3:25 longer under the *s* of the law.

SUPPER
Lk 22:20 after the *s* he took the cup, saying,
1Co 11:25 after *s* he took the cup,
Rev 19: 9 to the wedding *s* of the Lamb!' "

SUPPLIED (SUPPLY)
Ac 20:34 of mine have *s* my own needs
Php 4:18 and even more; I am amply *s*,

SUPPLY (SUPPLIED SUPPLYING)
2Co 8:14 your plenty will *s* what they need,
1Th 3:10 and *s* what is lacking in your faith.

SUPPLYING* (SUPPLY)
2Co 9:12 you perform is not only *s* the needs

SUPPORT (SUPPORTED SUPPORTING)
Ps 18:18 but the LORD was my *s*.
Ro 11:18 consider this: You do not *s* the root
1Co 9:12 If others have this right of *s*

SUPPORTED (SUPPORT)
Ps 94:18 your love, O LORD, *s* me.
Col 2:19 *s* and held together by its ligaments

SUPPORTING (SUPPORT)
Eph 4:16 held together by every *s* ligament,

SUPPRESS*
Ro 1:18 wickedness of men who *s* the truth

SUPREMACY* (SUPREME)
Col 1:18 in everything he might have the *s*.

SUPREME (SUPREMACY)
Pr 4: 7 Wisdom is *s*; therefore get wisdom.

SURE
Nu 28:31 Be *s* the animals are without defect
32:23 you may be *s* that your sin will find
Dt 6:17 Be *s* to keep the commands
14:22 Be *s* to set aside a tenth
29:18 make *s* there is no root
Jos 23:13 then you may be *s* that the LORD
1Sa 12:24 But be *s* to fear the LORD
Ps 19: 9 The ordinances of the LORD are *s*
132:11 a *s* oath that he will not revoke:
Pr 27:23 Be *s* you know the condition
Isa 28:16 cornerstone for a *s* foundation;
Eph 5: 5 of this you can be *s*: No immoral,
Heb 11: 1 faith is being *s* of what we hope for
2Pe 1:10 to make your calling and election *s*.

SURFACE
2Co 10: 7 You are looking only on the *s*

SURPASS* (SURPASSED SURPASSES SURPASSING)
Pr 31:29 but you *s* them all."

SURPASSED* (SURPASS)
Jn 1:15 'He who comes after me has *s* me
1:30 man who comes after me has *s* me

SURPASSES* (SURPASS)
Pr 8:19 what I yield *s* choice silver.
Mt 5:20 unless your righteousness *s* that
Eph 3:19 to know this love that *s* knowledge

SURPASSING* (SURPASS)
Ps 150: 2 praise him for his *s* greatness.
2Co 3:10 in comparison with the *s* glory.
9:14 of the *s* grace God has given you.
Php 3: 8 the *s* greatness of knowing Christ

SURPRISE (SURPRISED)
1Th 5: 4 that this day should *s* you like

SURPRISED (SURPRISE)
1Pe 4:12 do not be *s* at the painful trial you
1Jn 3:13 Do not be *s*, my brothers,

SURRENDER
1Co 13: 3 and *s* my body to the flames,

SURROUND (SURROUNDED SURROUNDS)
Ps 5:12 you *s* them with your favor
32: 7 and *s* me with songs of deliverance.
89: 7 awesome than all who *s* him.
125: 2 As the mountains *s* Jerusalem,
Jer 31:22 a woman will *s* a man."

SURROUNDED (SURROUND)
Heb 12: 1 since we are *s* by such a great cloud

SURROUNDS* (SURROUND)
Ps 32:10 *s* the man who trusts in him.
89: 8 and your faithfulness *s* you.
125: 2 so the LORD *s* his people

SUSA
Ezr 4: 9 and Babylon, the Elamites of *S*,
Ne 1: 1 while I was in the citadel of *S*,

SUSPENDS*
Job 26: 7 he *s* the earth over nothing.

SUSPICIONS*
1Ti 6: 4 evil *s* and constant friction

SUSTAIN (SUSTAINING SUSTAINS)
Ps 55:22 and he will *s* you;
Isa 46: 4 I am he, I am he who will *s* you.

SUSTAINING* (SUSTAIN)
Heb 1: 3 *s* all things by his powerful word.

SUSTAINS (SUSTAIN)
Ps 18:35 and your right hand *s* me;
146: 9 and *s* the fatherless and the widow,
147: 6 The LORD *s* the humble
Isa 50: 4 to know the word that *s* the weary.

SWALLOW (SWALLOWED)
Isa 25: 8 he will *s* up death forever.
Jnh 1:17 provided a great fish to *s* Jonah,
Mt 23:24 You strain out a gnat but *s* a camel.

SWALLOWED (SWALLOW)
1Co 15:54 "Death has been *s* up in victory."
2Co 5: 4 so that what is mortal may be *s* up

SWAYED
Mt 11: 7 A reed *s* by the wind? If not,
22:16 You aren't *s* by men, because you
2Ti 3: 6 are *s* by all kinds of evil desires,

SWEAR (SWORE SWORN)
Lev 19:12 " 'Do not *s* falsely by my name
Ps 24: 4 or *s* by what is false.
Isa 45:23 by me every tongue will *s*.
Mt 5:34 Do not *s* at all: either by heaven,
Jas 5:12 Above all, my brothers, do not *s*—

SWEAT*
Ge 3:19 By the *s* of your brow
Lk 22:44 his *s* was like drops of blood falling

SWEET (SWEETER SWEETNESS)
Job 20:12 "Though evil is *s* in his mouth
Ps 119:103 How *s* are your words
Pr 9:17 "Stolen water is *s*;
13:19 A longing fulfilled is *s* to the soul,
16:24 *s* to the soul and healing
20:17 by fraud tastes *s* to a man,
24:14 also that wisdom is *s* to your soul;
Ecc 5:12 The sleep of a laborer is *s*,
Isa 5:20 and *s* for bitter.
Eze 3: 3 it tasted as *s* as honey in my mouth.
Rev 10:10 It tasted as *s* as honey in my mouth

SWEETER (SWEET)
Ps 19:10 they are *s* than honey,
119:103 *s* than honey to my mouth!

SWEETNESS* (SWEET)
SS 4:11 Your lips drop *s* as the honeycomb,
5:16 His mouth is *s* itself;

SWEPT
Mt 12:44 finds the house unoccupied, *s* clean

SWERVE*
Pr 4: 5 do not forget my words or *s*
4:27 Do not *s* to the right or the left;

SWIFT
Pr 1:16 they are *s* to shed blood.
Ecc 9:11 The race is not to the *s*
Isa 59: 7 they are *s* to shed innocent blood.
Ro 3:15 "Their feet are *s* to shed blood;
2Pe 2: 1 bringing *s* destruction

SWINDLER* (SWINDLERS)
1Co 5:11 or a slanderer, a drunkard or a *s*.

SWINDLERS* (SWINDLER)
1Co 5:10 or the greedy and *s*, or idolaters.
6:10 *s* will inherit the kingdom of God.

SWORD (SWORDS)
Ge 3:24 and a flaming *s* flashing back
Dt 32:41 when I sharpen my flashing *s*
Jos 5:13 of him with a drawn *s* in his hand.
1Sa 17:45 "You come against me with *s*
17:47 here will know that it is not by *s*
31: 4 so Saul took his own *s* and fell on it.
2Sa 12:10 therefore, the *s* will never depart
Ps 44: 6 my *s* does not bring me victory;
45: 3 Gird your *s* upon your side,
Pr 12:18 Reckless words pierce like a *s*,
Isa 2: 4 Nation will not take up *s*
Mic 4: 3 Nation will not take up *s*
Mt 10:34 come to bring peace, but a *s*.
26:52 all who draw the *s* will die by the *s*.
Lk 2:35 a *s* will pierce your own soul too."
Ro 13: 4 for he does not bear the *s*
Eph 6:17 of salvation and the *s* of the Spirit,
Heb 4:12 Sharper than any double-edged *s*,
Rev 1:16 came a sharp double-edged *s*.
19:15 Out of his mouth comes a sharp *s*

SWORDS (SWORD)
Ps 64: 3 who sharpen their tongues like *s*
Isa 2: 4 They will beat their *s*
Joel 3:10 Beat your plowshares into *s*

SWORE (SWEAR)
Heb 6:13 for him to swear by, he *s* by himself

SWORN (SWEAR)
Ps 110: 4 The LORD has *s*
Eze 20:42 the land I had *s* with uplifted hand
Heb 7:21 "The Lord has *s*

SYCAMORE-FIG (FIG)
Am 7:14 and I also took care of *s* trees.
Lk 19: 4 and climbed a *s* tree to see him,

SYMBOLIZES*
1Pe 3:21 this water *s* baptism that now saves

SYMPATHETIC* (SYMPATHY)
1Pe 3: 8 in harmony with one another; be *s*,

SYMPATHIZED* (SYMPATHY)
Heb 10:34 You *s* with those in prison

SYMPATHY (SYMPATHETIC SYMPATHIZED)
Ps 69:20 I looked for *s*, but there was none,

SYNAGOGUE
Lk 4:16 the Sabbath day he went into the *s*,
Ac 17: 2 custom was, Paul went into the *s*,

TABERNACLE (TABERNACLES)
Ex 40:34 the glory of the LORD filled the *t.*
Heb 8: 2 the true *t* set up by the Lord,
9:11 and more perfect *t* that is not
9:21 sprinkled with the blood both the *t*
Rev 15: 5 that is, the *t* of the Testimony,

TABERNACLES (TABERNACLE)
Lev 23:34 the LORD's Feast of *T* begins,
Dt 16:16 Feast of Weeks and the Feast of *T.*
Zec 14:16 and to celebrate the Feast of *T.*

TABLE (TABLES)
Ex 25:23 "Make a *t* of acacia wood—
Ps 23: 5 You prepare a *t* before me

TABLES (TABLE)
Jn 2:15 changers and overturned their *t.*
Ac 6: 2 word of God in order to wait on *t.*

TABLET (TABLETS)
Pr 3: 3 write them on the *t* of your heart.
7: 3 write them on the *t* of your heart.

TABLETS (TABLET)
Ex 31:18 he gave him the two *t*
Dt 10: 5 and put the *t* in the ark I had made,
2Co 3: 3 not on *t* of stone but on *t*

TAKE (TAKEN TAKES TAKING TOOK)
Ge 15: 7 land to *t* possession of it."
22:17 Your descendants will *t* possession
Ex 3: 5 "*T* off your sandals,
21:23 you are to *t* life for life, eye for eye,
22:22 "Do not *t* advantage of a widow
Lev 10:17 given to you to *t* away the guilt
25:14 do not *t* advantage of each other.
Nu 13:30 and *t* possession of the land,
Dt 1: 8 and *t* possession of the land that
12:32 do not add to it or *t* away from it.
31:26 "*T* this Book of the Law
1Sa 8:11 He will *t* your sons and make them
1Ch 17:13 I will never *t* my love away
Job 23:10 But he knows the way that I *t;*
Ps 2:12 Blessed are all who *t* refuge in him.
25:18 and *t* away all my sins.
27:14 be strong and *t* heart
31:24 Be strong and *t* heart,
49:17 for he will *t* nothing with him
51:11 or *t* your Holy Spirit from me.
73:24 afterward you will *t* me into glory.
118: 8 It is better to *t* refuge in the LORD
Pr 22:23 for the LORD will *t* up their case
Isa 62: 4 for the LORD will *t* delight in you,
Eze 3:10 and *t* to heart all the words I speak
33:11 I *t* no pleasure in the death
Mt 10:38 anyone who does not *t* his cross
11:29 *T* my yoke upon you and learn
16:24 deny himself and *t* up his cross
26:26 saying, "*T* and eat; this is my body
Mk 14:36 *T* this cup from me.
1Ti 6:12 *T* hold of the eternal life

TAKEN (TAKE)
Ge 2:23 for she was *t* out of man."
Lev 6: 4 must return what he has stolen or *t*
Nu 8:16 I have *t* them as my own in place
19: 3 it is to be *t* outside the camp
Ecc 3:14 added to it and nothing *t* from it.
Isa 6: 7 your guilt is *t* away and your sin
Zec 3: 4 "See, I have *t* away your sin,
Mt 13:12 even what he has will be *t* from him
24:40 one will be *t* and the other left.
26:39 may this cup be *t* from me.
Mk 16:19 he was *t* up into heaven
Ac 1: 9 he was *t* up before their very eyes,
Ro 5:13 But sin is not *t* into account
1Ti 3:16 was *t* up in glory.

TAKES (TAKE)
1Ki 20:11 should not boast like one who *t* it
Ps 5: 4 You are not a God who *t* pleasure
34: 8 blessed is the man who *t* refuge
Lk 6:30 and if anyone *t* what belongs to you
Jn 1:29 who *t* away the sin of the world!
10:18 No one *t* it from me, but I lay it
Rev 22:19 And if anyone *t* words away

TAKING (TAKE)
Ac 15:14 by *t* from the Gentiles a people
Php 2: 7 *t* the very nature of a servant,

TALENT
Mt 25:15 to another one *t,* each according

TALES*
1Ti 4: 7 with godless myths and old wives' *t*

TALL
1Sa 17: 4 He was over nine feet *t.*
1Ch 11:23 who was seven and a half feet *t.*

TAMAR

1. Wife of Judah's sons Er and Onan (Ge 38:1–10). Tricked Judah into fathering children when he refused her his third son (Ge 38:11–30).

2. Daughter of David, raped by Amnon (2Sa 13).

TAMBOURINE
Ps 150: 4 praise him with *t* and dancing,

TAME* (TAMED)
Jas 3: 8 but no man can *t* the tongue.

TAMED* (TAME)
Jas 3: 7 the sea are being *t* and have been *t*

TARSHISH
Jnh 1: 3 from the LORD and headed for *T.*

TARSUS
Ac 9:11 ask for a man from *T* named Saul,

TASK (TASKS)
1Ch 29: 1 The *t* is great, because this palatial
Mk 13:34 each with his assigned *t,*
Ac 20:24 complete the *t* the Lord Jesus has
1Co 3: 5 the Lord has assigned to each his *t.*
2Co 2:16 And who is equal to such a *t?*
1Ti 3: 1 an overseer, he desires a noble *t.*

TASKS (TASK)
Pr 31:17 her arms are strong for her *t.*

TASTE (TASTED TASTY)
Ps 34: 8 *T* and see that the LORD is good;
119:103 sweet are your words to my *t,*
Pr 24:13 from the comb is sweet to your *t.*
SS 2: 3 and his fruit is sweet to my *t.*
Col 2:21 Do not *t!* Do not touch!"?
Heb 2: 9 the grace of God he might *t* death

TASTED (TASTE)
Eze 3: 3 it *t* as sweet as honey in my mouth.
1Pe 2: 3 now that you have *t* that the Lord
Rev 10:10 It *t* as sweet as honey in my mouth,

TASTY (TASTE)
Ge 27: 4 Prepare me the kind of *t* food I like

TATTOO*
Lev 19:28 or put *t* marks on yourselves.

TAUGHT (TEACH)
1Ki 4:33 He also *t* about animals and birds,
2Ki 17:28 *t* them how to worship the LORD.
2Ch 17: 9 They *t* throughout Judah,
Ps 119:102 for you yourself have *t* me.
Pr 4: 4 he *t* me and said,
31: 1 an oracle his mother *t* him:
Isa 29:13 is made up only of rules *t* by men.
50: 4 ear to listen like one being *t.*
Mt 7:29 he *t* as one who had authority,
15: 9 their teachings are but rules *t*
Lk 4:15 He *t* in their synagogues,
Ac 20:20 have *t* you publicly and from house
1Co 2:13 but in words *t* by the Spirit,
Gal 1:12 nor was I *t* it; rather, I received it
1Ti 1:20 to Satan to be *t* not to blaspheme.
1Jn 2:27 just as it has *t* you, remain in him.

TAX (TAXES)
Mt 11:19 a friend of *t* collectors and "sinners
17:24 of the two-drachma *t* came to Peter

TAXES (TAX)
Mt 22:17 Is it right to pay *t* to Caesar or not
Ro 13: 7 If you owe *t,* pay *t;* if revenue,

TEACH (TAUGHT TEACHER TEACHERS TEACHES TEACHING TEACHINGS)
Ex 4:12 and will *t* you what to say."
18:20 *T* them the decrees and laws,
33:13 *t* me your ways so I may know you
Lev 10:11 and you must *t* the Israelites all
Dt 4: 9 *T* them to your children
6: 1 me to *t* you to observe
8: 3 to *t* you that man does not live
11:19 *T* them to your children, talking
1Sa 12:23 I will *t* you the way that is good
1Ki 8:36 *T* them the right way to live,
Job 12: 7 ask the animals, and they will *t* you
Ps 32: 8 *t* you in the way you should go;
34:11 I will *t* you the fear of the LORD.
51:13 I will *t* transgressors your ways,
78: 5 forefathers to *t* their children,
90:12 *T* us to number our days aright,
119: 33 *T* me, O LORD, to follow your
143: 10 *T* me to do your will,
Pr 9: 9 *t* a righteous man and he will add
Jer 31:34 No longer will a man *t* his neighbor
Mic 4: 2 He will *t* us his ways,
Lk 11: 1 said to him, "Lord, *t* us to pray,
12:12 for the Holy Spirit will *t* you
Jn 14:26 will *t* you all things and will remind
Ro 2:21 who *t* others, do you not *t* yourself?
15: 4 in the past was written to *t* us,
1Ti 2:12 I do not permit a woman to *t*
3: 2 respectable, hospitable, able to *t,*
2Ti 2: 2 also be qualified to *t* others.
2:24 kind to everyone, able to *t,*
Tit 2: 1 You must *t* what is in accord
2:15 then, are the things you should *t.*
Heb 8:11 No longer will a man *t* his neighbor
Jas 3: 1 know that we who *t* will be judged
1Jn 2:27 you do not need anyone to *t* you.

TEACHER (TEACH)
Ecc 1: 1 The words of the *T,* son of David,
Mt 10:24 "A student is not above his *t,*
13:52 "Therefore every *t*
23:10 Nor are you to be called '*t,*'
Lk 6:40 A student is not above his *t,*
Jn 3: 2 we know you are a *t* who has come
13:14 and *T,* have washed your feet,

TEACHERS (TEACH)
Ps 119: 99 I have more insight than all my *t,*
Pr 5:13 I would not obey my *t*
Lk 20:46 "Beware of the *t* of the law.
1Co 12:28 third *t,* then workers of miracles,
Eph 4:11 and some to be pastors and *t,*
2Ti 4: 3 around them a great number of *t*
Heb 5:12 by this time you ought to be *t,*
Jas 3: 1 of you should presume to be *t,*
2Pe 2: 1 as there will be false *t* among you.

TEACHES (TEACH)
Ps 25: 9 and *t* them his way.
94:10 Does he who *t* man lack
Pr 15:33 of the LORD *t* a man wisdom,
Isa 48:17 who *t* you what is best for you,
Mt 5:19 *t* these commands will be called
1Ti 6: 3 If anyone *t* false doctrines
Tit 2:12 It *t* us to say "No" to ungodliness
1Jn 2:27 his anointing *t* you about all things

TEACHING (TEACH)
Ezr 7:10 to *t* its decrees and laws in Israel.
Pr 1: 8 and do not forsake your mother's *t.*
3: 1 My son, do not forget my *t,*
6:23 this *t* is a light,
Mt 28:20 *t* them to obey everything I have
Jn 7:17 whether my *t* comes from God or
8:31 to my *t,* you are really my disciples.
14:23 loves me, he will obey my *t.*
Ac 2:42 themselves to the apostles' *t*
Ro 12: 7 let him serve; if it is *t,* let him teach;
Eph 4:14 and there by every wind of *t*
2Th 3: 6 to the *t* you received from us.
1Ti 4:13 of Scripture, to preaching and to *t.*
5:17 whose work is preaching and *t.*
6: 3 Lord Jesus Christ and to godly *t,*
2Ti 3:16 is God-breathed and is useful for *t,*
Tit 1:11 by *t* things they ought not
2: 7 In your *t* show integrity,
Heb 5:13 with the *t* about righteousness.
2Jn : 9 and does not continue in the *t*

TEACHINGS (TEACH)
Pr 7: 2 guard my *t* as the apple of your eye.
2Th 2:15 hold to the *t* we passed on to you,
Heb 6: 1 leave the elementary *t* about Christ

TEAR (TEARS)
Rev 7:17 God will wipe away every *t*
21: 4 He will wipe every *t*

TEARS (TEAR)
Ps 126: 5 Those who sow in *t*
Isa 25: 8 LORD will wipe away the *t*
Jer 31:16 and your eyes from *t,*
50: 4 in *t* to seek the LORD their God.
Lk 7:38 she began to wet his feet with her *t.*
2Co 2: 4 anguish of heart and with many *t,*
Php 3:18 and now say again even with *t,*

TEETH (TOOTH)
Job 19:20 with only the skin of my *t.*
Ps 35:16 they gnashed their *t* at me.
Jer 31:29 and the children's *t* are set on edge
Mt 8:12 will be weeping and gnashing of *t.*"

TEMPER (EVEN-TEMPERED HOT-TEMPERED ILL-TEMPERED QUICK-TEMPERED)
Pr 16:32 a man who controls his *t*

TEMPERANCE see SELF-CONTROL

TEMPERATE*
1Ti 3: 2 *t,* self-controlled, respectable,
3:11 not malicious talkers but *t*
Tit 2: 2 Teach the older men to be *t,*

TEMPEST
Ps 50: 3 and around him a *t* rages.
55: 8 far from the *t* and storm."

TEMPLE (TEMPLES)
1Ki 6: 1 began to build the *t* of the LORD.
6:38 the *t* was finished in all its details
8:10 the cloud filled the *t* of the LORD.
8:27 How much less this *t* I have built!
2Ch 36:19 They set fire to God's *t*
36:23 me to build a *t* for him at Jerusalem
Ezr 6:14 finished building the *t* according
Ps 27: 4 and to seek him in his *t.*
Isa 6: 1 and the train of his robe filled the *t.*
Eze 10: 4 cloud filled the *t,* and the court was
43: 4 glory of the LORD entered the *t*
Hab 2:20 But the LORD is in his holy *t;*
Mt 12: 6 that one greater than the *t* is here.
26:61 'I am able to destroy the *t* of God
27:51 of the *t* was torn in two from top
Lk 21: 5 about how the *t* was adorned
Jn 2:14 In the *t* courts he found men selling
1Co 3:16 that you yourselves are God's *t*
6:19 you not know that your body is a *t*
2Co 6:16 For we are the *t* of the living God.
Rev 21:22 I did not see a *t* in the city,

TEMPLES (TEMPLE)
Ac 17:24 does not live in *t* built by hands.

TEMPORARY
2Co 4:18 what is seen is *t,* but what is unseen

TEMPT* (TEMPTATION TEMPTED TEMPTER TEMPTING)
1Co 7: 5 again so that Satan will not *t* you
Jas 1:13 does he *t* anyone; but each one is

TEMPTATION* (TEMPT)
Mt 6:13 And lead us not into *t,*
26:41 pray so that you will not fall into *t.*
Mk 14:38 pray so that you will not fall into *t.*
Lk 11: 4 And lead us not into *t.*'"
22:40 "Pray that you will not fall into *t.*"
22:46 pray so that you will not fall into *t*
1Co 10:13 No *t* has seized you except what is
1Ti 6: 9 want to get rich fall into *t*

TEMPTED* (TEMPT)
Mt 4: 1 into the desert to be *t* by the devil.
Mk 1:13 was in the desert forty days, being *t*
Lk 4: 2 for forty days he was *t* by the devil.
1Co 10:13 But when you are *t,* he will
10:13 he will not let you be *t*
Gal 6: 1 yourself, or you also may be *t.*
1Th 3: 5 way the tempter might have *t* you
Heb 2:18 able to help those who are being *t.*
2:18 he himself suffered when he was *t,*
4:15 but we have one who has been *t*
Jas 1:13 For God cannot be *t* by evil,
1:13 When *t,* no one should say,
1:14 each one is *t* when, by his own evil

TEMPTER* (TEMPT)
Mt 4: 3 The *t* came to him and said,
1Th 3: 5 some way the *t* might have

TEMPTING* (TEMPT)
Lk 4:13 the devil had finished all this *t,*
Jas 1:13 no one should say, "God is *t* me."

TEN (TENTH TITHE TITHES)
Ex 34:28 covenant—the *T* Commandments.
Lev 26: 8 of you will chase *t* thousand,
Dt 4:13 covenant, the *T* Commandments,
10: 4 The *T* Commandments he had
Ps 91: 7 *t* thousand at your right hand,
Da 7:24 *t* horns are *t* kings who will come
Mt 25: 1 will be like *t* virgins who took
25:28 it to the one who has the *t* talents.
Lk 15: 8 suppose a woman has *t* silver coins
Rev 12: 3 and *t* horns and seven crowns

TENANTS
Mt 21:34 servants to the *t* to collect his fruit.

TEND
Jer 23: 2 to the shepherds who *t* my people:
Eze 34:14 I will *t* them in a good pasture,

TENDERNESS*
Isa 63:15 Your *t* and compassion are
Php 2: 1 fellowship with the Spirit, if any *t*

TENT (TENTMAKER TENTS)
Ex 27:21 In the *T* of Meeting,
40: 2 "Set up the tabernacle, the *T*
Isa 54: 2 "Enlarge the place of your *t,*
2Co 5: 1 that if the earthly *t* we live
2Pe 1:13 as long as I live in the *t* of this body,

TENTH (TEN)
Ge 14:20 Abram gave him a *t* of everything.
Nu 18:26 you must present a *t* of that tithe
Dt 14:22 Be sure to set aside a *t*
1Sa 8:15 He will take a *t* of your grain
Lk 11:42 you give God a *t* of your mint,
18:12 I fast twice a week and give a *t*
Heb 7: 4 patriarch Abraham gave him a *t*

TENTMAKER* (TENT)
Ac 18: 3 and because he was a *t* as they were

TENTS (TENT)
Ge 13:12 and pitched his *t* near Sodom.
Ps 84:10 than dwell in the *t* of the wicked.

TERAH
Ge 11:31 *T* took his son Abram, his

TERRIBLE (TERROR)
2Ti 3: 1 There will be *t* times

TERRIFIED (TERROR)
Dt 7:21 Do not be *t* by them,
20: 3 do not be *t* or give way to panic
Ps 90: 7 and *t* by your indignation.
Mt 14:26 walking on the lake, they were *t.*
17: 6 they fell facedown to the ground, *t.*
27:54 they were *t,* and exclaimed,
Mk 4:41 They were *t* and asked each other,

TERRIFYING (TERROR)
Heb 12:21 The sight was so *t* that Moses said,

TERRITORY
2Co 10:16 done in another man's *t.*

TERROR (TERRIBLE TERRIFIED TERRIFYING)
Dt 2:25 very day I will begin to put the *t*
28:67 of the *t* that will fill your hearts
Job 9:34 so that his *t* would frighten me no
Ps 91: 5 You will not fear the *t* of night,
Pr 21:15 but *t* to evildoers.
Isa 13: 8 *T* will seize them,
24:17 *T* and pit and snare await you,
51:13 live in constant *t* every day
54:14 *T* will be far removed;
Lk 21:26 Men will faint from *t,* apprehensive
Ro 13: 3 For rulers hold no *t*

TEST (TESTED TESTING TESTS)
Dt 6:16 Do not *t* the LORD your God
Jdg 3: 1 to *t* all those Israelites who had not
1Ki 10: 1 came to *t* him with hard questions.
1Ch 29:17 that you *t* the heart and are pleased
Ps 26: 2 *T* me, O LORD, and try me,
78:18 They willfully put God to the *t*
106: 14 wasteland they put God to the *t.*
139: 23 *t* me and know my anxious
Jer 11:20 and *t* the heart and mind,
Lk 4:12 put the Lord your God to the *t.*'"
Ac 5: 9 How could you agree to *t* the Spirit
Ro 12: 2 Then you will be able to *t*
1Co 3:13 and the fire will *t* the quality
10: 9 We should not *t* the Lord,
2Co 13: 5 unless, of course, you fail the *t?*
1Th 5:21 *T* everything.
Jas 1:12 because when he has stood the *t,*
1Jn 4: 1 *t* the spirits to see whether they are

TESTED (TEST)
Ge 22: 1 Some time later God *t* Abraham.
Job 23:10 when he has *t* me, I will come forth
34:36 that Job might be *t* to the utmost
Ps 66:10 For you, O God, *t* us;
Pr 27:21 man is *t* by the praise he receives.
Isa 28:16 a *t* stone,
48:10 I have *t* you in the furnace
1Ti 3:10 They must first be *t;* and then
Heb 11:17 By faith Abraham, when God *t* him

TESTIFIES (TESTIFY)
Jn 5:32 There is another who *t* in my favor,
Ro 8:16 The Spirit himself *t*

TESTIFY (TESTIFIES TESTIMONY)
Pr 24:28 Do not *t* against your neighbor
Jn 1: 7 a witness to *t* concerning that light,
1:34 and I *t* that this is the Son of God."
5:39 are the Scriptures that *t* about me,
7: 7 because I *t* that what it does is evil.
15:26 he will *t* about me. And you
Ac 4:33 continued to *t* to the resurrection
10:43 All the prophets *t* about him that
2Ti 1: 8 ashamed to *t* about our Lord,
1Jn 4:14 *t* that the Father has sent his Son
5: 7 For there are three that *t:* the Spirit

TESTIMONY (TESTIFY)
Ex 20:16 "You shall not give false *t*
31:18 gave him the two tablets of the *T,*
Nu 35:30 only on the *t* of witnesses.
Dt 19:18 giving false *t* against his brother,
Pr 12:17 A truthful witness gives honest *t,*
Isa 8:20 and to the *t!* If they do not speak
Mt 15:19 sexual immorality, theft, false *t,*
24:14 preached in the whole world as a *t*
Lk 18:20 not give false *t,* honor your father
Jn 2:25 He did not need man's *t* about man
21:24 We know that his *t* is true.
1Jn 5: 9 but God's *t* is greater because it is
Rev 12:11 and by the word of their *t;*

TESTING (TEST)
Lk 8:13 but in the time of *t* they fall away.
Heb 3: 8 during the time of *t* in the desert,
Jas 1: 3 because you know that the *t*

TESTS (TEST)
Pr 17: 3 but the LORD *t* the heart.
1Th 2: 4 but God, who *t* our hearts.

THADDAEUS
Apostle (Mt 10:3; Mk 3:18); probably also known as Judas son of James (Lk 6:16; Ac 1:13).

THANK (THANKFUL THANKFULNESS THANKS THANKSGIVING)
Php 1: 3 I *t* my God every time I remember
1Th 3: 9 How can we *t* God enough for you

THANKFUL (THANK)
Col 3:15 And be *t.*
Heb 12:28 let us be *t,* and so worship God

THANKFULNESS (THANK)
1Co 10:30 If I take part in the meal with *t,*
Col 2: 7 taught, and overflowing with *t.*

THANKS (THANK)
1Ch 16: 8 Give *t* to the LORD, call
Ne 12:31 assigned two large choirs to give *t.*
Ps 7:17 I will give *t* to the LORD
28: 7 and I will give *t* to him in song.
30:12 my God, I will give you *t* forever.
35:18 I will give you *t* in the great
75: 1 we give *t,* for your Name is near;
100: 4 give *t* to him and praise his name.
107: 1 Give *t* to the LORD, for he is good;
118: 28 are my God, and I will give you *t;*
136: 1 Give *t* to the LORD, for he is good.
Ro 1:21 as God nor gave *t* to him,
1Co 11:24 when he had given *t,* he broke it
15:57 *t* be to God! He gives us the victory
2Co 2:14 *t* be to God, who always leads us
9:15 *T* be to God for his indescribable
1Th 5:18 give *t* in all circumstances,
Rev 4: 9 and *t* to him who sits on the throne

THANKSGIVING (THANK)
Ps 95: 2 Let us come before him with *t*
100: 4 Enter his gates with *t*
1Co 10:16 cup of *t* for which we give thanks
Php 4: 6 by prayer and petition, with *t,*
1Ti 4: 3 created to be received with *t*

THEFT (THIEF)
Mt 15:19 sexual immorality, *t,* false

THEFTS* (THIEF)
Rev 9:21 their sexual immorality or their *t.*

THEME*
Ps 45: 1 My heart is stirred by a noble *t*
119: 54 Your decrees are the *t* of my song

THIEF (THEFT THEFTS THIEVES)
Ex 22: 3 A *t* must certainly make restitution
Pr 6:30 Men do not despise a *t* if he steals
Lk 12:39 at what hour the *t* was coming,
1Th 5: 2 day of the Lord will come like a *t*
1Pe 4:15 or *t* or any other kind of criminal,
Rev 16:15 I come like a *t*! Blessed is he who

THIEVES (THIEF)
Mt 6:19 and where *t* break in and steal.
Jn 10: 8 who ever came before me were *t*
1Co 6:10 nor homosexual offenders nor *t*

THINK (THINKING THOUGHT THOUGHTS)
Ps 63: 6 I *t* of you through the watches
Isa 44:19 No one stops to *t*,
Mt 22:42 "What do you *t* about the Christ?
Ro 12: 3 Do not *t* of yourself more highly
Php 4: 8 praiseworthy—*t* about such things

THINKING (THINK)
Pr 23: 7 who is always *t* about the cost.
1Co 14:20 Brothers, stop *t* like children.
2Pe 3: 1 to stimulate you to wholesome *t*.

THIRST (THIRSTS THIRSTY)
Ps 69:21 and gave me vinegar for my *t*.
Mt 5: 6 Blessed are those who hunger and *t*
Jn 4:14 the water I give him will never *t*.
2Co 11:27 I have known hunger and *t*
Rev 7:16 never again will they *t*.

THIRSTS (THIRST)
Ps 42: 2 My soul *t* for God,

THIRSTY (THIRST)
Ps 107: 9 for he satisfies the *t*
Pr 25:21 if he is *t*, give him water to drink.
Isa 55: 1 "Come, all you who are *t*,
Mt 25:35 I was *t* and you gave me something
Jn 7:37 "If anyone is *t*, let him come to me
Ro 12:20 if he is *t*, give him something
Rev 21: 6 To him who is *t* I will give to drink
22:17 Whoever is *t*, let him come;

THOMAS
Apostle (Mt 10:3; Mk 3:18; Lk 6:15, Jn 11:16; 14:5; 21:2; Ac 1:13). Doubted resurrection (Jn 20:24–28).

THONGS
Mk 1: 7 *t* of whose sandals I am not worthy

THORN (THORNBUSHES THORNS)
2Co 12: 7 there was given me a *t* in my flesh,

THORNBUSHES (THORN)
Lk 6:44 People do not pick figs from *t*,

THORNS (THORN)
Ge 3:18 It will produce *t* and thistles
Nu 33:55 in your eyes and *t* in your sides.
Mt 13: 7 fell among *t*, which grew up
27:29 and then twisted together a crown of *t*
Heb 6: 8 But land that produces *t*

THOUGHT (THINK)
Pr 14:15 a prudent man gives *t* to his steps.
21:29 an upright man gives *t* to his ways.
1Co 13:11 I talked like a child, I *t* like a child,

THOUGHTS (THINK)
1Ch 28: 9 every motive behind the *t*.
Ps 94:11 The LORD knows the *t* of man;
139: 23 test me and know my anxious *t*.
Isa 55: 8 "For my *t* are not your *t*,
Mt 15:19 For out of the heart come evil *t*,
1Co 2:11 among men knows the *t* of a man
Heb 4:12 it judges the *t* and attitudes

THREE
Ge 6:10 Noah had *t* sons: Shem, Ham
Ex 23:14 "*T* times a year you are
Dt 19:15 the testimony of two or *t* witnesses.
2Sa 23: 8 a Tahkemonite, was chief of the *T*;
Pr 30:15 "There are *t* things that are never
30:18 "There are *t* things that are too
30:21 "Under *t* things the earth trembles,
30:29 "There are *t* things that are stately
Ecc 4:12 of *t* strands is not quickly broken.
Da 3:24 "Weren't there *t* men that we tied up
Am 1: 3 "For *t* sins of Damascus,
Jnh 1:17 inside the fish *t* days and *t* nights.
Mt 12:40 so the Son of Man will be *t* days
12:40 *t* nights in the belly of a huge fish,
12:40 *t* nights in the heart of the earth.
17: 4 I will put up *t* shelters—one
18:20 or *t* come together in my name,
26:34 you will disown me *t* times."
26:75 you will disown me *t* times."
27:63 'After *t* days I will rise again.'
Mk 8:31 and after *t* days rise again.
9: 5 Let us put up *t* shelters—one
14:30 yourself will disown me *t* times."
Jn 2:19 and I will raise it again in *t* days."
1Co 13:13 And now these *t* remain: faith,
14:27 or at the most *t*—should speak,
2Co 13: 1 testimony of two or *t* witnesses."
1Jn 5: 7 For there are *t* that testify:

THRESHER* (THRESHING)
1Co 9:10 plowman plows and the *t* threshes,

THRESHING (THRESHER)
Ru 3: 6 So she went down to the *t* floor
2Sa 24:18 an altar to the LORD on the *t* floor
Lk 3:17 is in his hand to clear his *t* floor

THREW (THROW)
Da 6:16 and *t* him into the lions' den.
Jnh 1:15 took Jonah and *t* him overboard,

THRIVE
Pr 29: 2 When the righteous *t*, the people

THROAT (THROATS)
Ps 5: 9 Their *t* is an open grave;
Pr 23: 2 and put a knife to your *t*

THROATS (THROAT)
Ro 3:13 "Their *t* are open graves;

THROB*
Isa 60: 5 your heart will *t* and swell with joy;

THRONE (ENTHRONED ENTHRONES THRONES)
2Sa 7:16 your *t* will be established forever
1Ch 17:12 and I will establish his *t* forever.
Ps 11: 4 the LORD is on his heavenly *t*.
45: 6 Your *t*, O God, will last for ever
47: 8 God is seated on his holy *t*.
89:14 justice are the foundation of your *t*;
Isa 6: 1 I saw the Lord seated on a *t*,
66: 1 "Heaven is my *t*,
Eze 28: 2 I sit on the *t* of a god
Da 7: 9 His *t* was flaming with fire,
Mt 19:28 Son of Man sits on his glorious *t*,
Ac 7:49 prophet says: " 'Heaven is my *t*,
Heb 1: 8 "Your *t*, O God, will last for ever
4:16 Let us then approach the *t* of grace
12: 2 at the right hand of the *t* of God.
Rev 3:21 sat down with my Father on his *t*.
3:21 the right to sit with me on my *t*,
4: 2 there before me was a *t* in heaven
4:10 They lay their crowns before the *t*
20:11 Then I saw a great white *t*
22: 3 *t* of God and of the Lamb will be

THRONES (THRONE)
Mt 19:28 me will also sit on twelve *t*,
Rev 4: 4 throne were twenty-four other *t*,

THROW (THREW)
Jn 8: 7 the first to *t* a stone at her."
Heb 10:35 So do not *t* away your confidence;
12: 1 let us *t* off everything that hinders

THUNDER (THUNDERS)
Ps 93: 4 Mightier than the *t*
Mk 3:17 which means Sons of *T*); Andrew,

THUNDERS (THUNDER)
Job 37: 5 God's voice *t* in marvelous ways;
Ps 29: 3 the God of glory *t*,
Rev 10: 3 the voices of the seven *t* spoke.

THWART* (THWARTED)
Isa 14:27 has purposed, and who can *t* him?

THWARTED (THWART)
Job 42: 2 no plan of yours can be *t*.

THYATIRA
Rev 2:18 the angel of the church in *T* write:

TIBNI
King of Israel (1Ki 16:21–22).

TIDINGS
Isa 40: 9 You who bring good *t* to Jerusalem
52: 7 who bring good *t*,

TIES
Hos 11: 4 with *t* of love;
Mt 12:29 unless he first *t* up the strong man?

TIGHT*
Jas 1:26 and yet does not keep a *t* rein

TIGHTFISTED*
Dt 15: 7 or *t* toward your poor brother.

TIME (TIMES)
Est 4:14 come to royal position for such a *t*
Ecc 3: 1 There is a *t* for everything,
8: 5 wise heart will know the proper *t*
Da 7:25 to him for a *t*, times and half a *t*.
12: 7 "It will be for a *t*, times and half a *t*.
Hos 10:12 for it is *t* to seek the LORD,
Jn 2: 4 Jesus replied, "My *t* has not yet
17: 1 prayed: "Father, the *t* has come.
Ro 9: 9 "At the appointed *t* I will return,
13:11 understanding the present *t*.
1Co 7:29 brothers, is that the *t* is short.
2Co 6: 2 now is the *t* of God's favor,
2Ti 1: 9 Jesus before the beginning of *t*,
Tit 1: 2 promised before the beginning of *t*,
Heb 9:28 and he will appear a second *t*,
10:12 for all *t* one sacrifice for sins,
1Pe 4:17 For it is *t* for judgment to begin

TIMES (TIME)
Ps 9: 9 a stronghold in *t* of trouble.
31:15 My *t* are in your hands;
62: 8 Trust in him at all *t*, O people;
Pr 17:17 A friend loves at all *t*,
Isa 46:10 from ancient *t*, what is still to come
Am 5:13 for the *t* are evil.
Mt 16: 3 cannot interpret the signs of the *t*.
18:21 how many *t* shall I forgive my
Ac 1: 7 "It is not for you to know the *t*
Rev 12:14 *t* and half a time, out

TIMID (TIMIDITY)
1Th 5:14 encourage the *t*, help the weak,

TIMIDITY* (TIMID)
2Ti 1: 7 For God did not give us a spirit of *t*

TIMOTHY
Believer from Lystra (Ac 16:1). Joined Paul on second missionary journey (Ac 16–20). Sent to settle problems at Corinth (1Co 4:17; 16:10). Led church at Ephesus (1Ti 1:3). Co-writer with Paul (1Th 1:1; 2Th 1:1; Phm 1).

TIP
Job 33: 2 my words are on the *t* of my tongue

TIRE (TIRED)
2Th 3:13 never *t* of doing what is right.

TIRED (TIRE)
Ex 17:12 When Moses' hands grew *t*,
Isa 40:28 He will not grow *t* or weary,

TITHE (TEN)
Lev 27:30 " 'A *t* of everything from the land,
Dt 12:17 eat in your own towns the *t*
Mal 3:10 the whole *t* into the storehouse,

TITHES (TEN)
Nu 18:21 give to the Levites all the *t* in Israel
Mal 3: 8 'How do we rob you?' "In *t*

TITUS*
Gentile co-worker of Paul (Gal 2:1–3; 2Ti 4:10); sent to Corinth (2Co 2:13; 7–8; 12:18), Crete (Tit 1:4–5).

TODAY
Ps 2: 7 *t* I have become your Father.
95: 7 *T*, if you hear his voice,
Mt 6:11 Give us *t* our daily bread.
Lk 2:11 *T* in the town of David a Savior has
23:43 *t* you will be with me in paradise."
Ac 13:33 *t* I have become your Father.'
Heb 1: 5 *t* I have become your Father"?
3: 7 "*T*, if you hear his voice,
3:13 daily, as long as it is called *T*,
5: 5 *t* I have become your Father."
13: 8 Christ is the same yesterday and *t*

TOIL (TOILED TOILING)
Ge 3:17 through painful *t* you will eat of it

TOILED (TOIL)
2Co 11:27 and *t* and have often gone

TOILING (TOIL)
2Th 3: 8 *t* so that we would not be a burden

TOLERANCE* (TOLERATE)
Ro 2: 4 for the riches of his kindness, *t*

TOLERATE (TOLERANCE)
Hab 1:13 you cannot *t* wrong.
Rev 2: 2 that you cannot *t* wicked men,

TOMB
Mt 27:65 make the *t* as secure as you know
Lk 24: 2 the stone rolled away from the *t*,

TOMORROW
Pr 27: 1 Do not boast about *t*,
Isa 22:13 "for *t* we die!"
Mt 6:34 Therefore do not worry about *t*,
1Co 15:32 for *t* we die."
Jas 4:13 "Today or *t* we will go to this

TONGUE (TONGUES)
Ex 4:10 I am slow of speech and *t*."
Job 33: 2 my words are on the tip of my *t*.
Ps 5: 9 with their *t* they speak deceit.
34:13 keep your *t* from evil
37:30 and his *t* speaks what is just.
39: 1 and keep my *t* from sin;
51:14 my *t* will sing of your righteousness
52: 4 O you deceitful *t*!
71:24 My *t* will tell of your righteous acts
119:172 May my *t* sing of your word,
137: 6 May my *t* cling to the roof
139: 4 Before a word is on my *t*
Pr 6:17 a lying *t*,
10:19 but he who holds his *t* is wise.
12:18 but the *t* of the wise brings healing.
15: 4 The *t* that brings healing is a tree
17:20 he whose *t* is deceitful falls
21:23 He who guards his mouth and his *t*
25:15 and a gentle *t* can break a bone.
26:28 A lying *t* hates those it hurts,
28:23 than he who has a flattering *t*.
31:26 and faithful instruction is on her *t*.
SS 4:11 milk and honey are under your *t*.
Isa 32: 4 and the stammering *t* will be fluent
45:23 by me every *t* will swear.
50: 4 has given me an instructed *t*,
59: 3 and your *t* mutters wicked things.
Lk 16:24 of his finger in water and cool my *t*,
Ro 14:11 every *t* will confess to God.'"
1Co 14: 2 speaks in a *t* does not speak to men
14: 4 He who speaks in a *t* edifies himself
14: 9 intelligible words with your *t*,
14:13 in a *t* should pray that he may
14:19 than ten thousand words in a *t*.
14:26 revelation, a *t* or an interpretation.
14:27 If anyone speaks in a *t*, two—
Php 2:11 every *t* confess that Jesus Christ is
Jas 1:26 does not keep a tight rein on his *t*,
3: 5 Likewise the *t* is a small part
3: 8 but no man can tame the *t*.
1Jn 3:18 or *t* but with actions and in truth.

TONGUES (TONGUE)
Ps 12: 4 "We will triumph with our *t*;
126: 2 our *t* with songs of joy.
Isa 28:11 with foreign lips and strange *t*
66:18 and gather all nations and *t*,
Jer 23:31 the prophets who wag their own *t*
Mk 16:17 in new *t*; they will pick up snakes
Ac 2: 3 to be *t* of fire that separated
2: 4 and began to speak in other *t*
10:46 For they heard them speaking in *t*
19: 6 and they spoke in *t* and prophesied
Ro 3:13 their *t* practice deceit."
1Co 12:10 still another the interpretation of *t*.
12:28 speaking in different kinds of *t*.
12:30 Do all speak in *t*? Do all interpret?
13: 1 If I speak in the *t* of men
13: 8 where there are *t*, they will be
14: 5 greater than one who speaks in *t*,
14:18 speak in *t* more than all of you.
14:21 "Through men of strange *t*
14:39 and do not forbid speaking in *t*.

TOOK (TAKE)
Isa 53: 4 Surely he *t* up our infirmities
Mt 8:17 "He *t* up our infirmities
26:26 they were eating, Jesus *t* bread,
26:27 Then he *t* the cup, gave thanks
1Co 11:23 the night he was betrayed, *t* bread,
11:25 after supper he *t* the cup, saying,
Php 3:12 for which Christ Jesus *t* hold of me.

TOOTH (TEETH)
Ex 21:24 eye for eye, *t* for *t*, hand for hand,
Mt 5:38 'Eye for eye, and *t* for *t*.'

TOP
Dt 28:13 you will always be at the *t*,
Isa 1: 6 of your foot to the *t* of your head
Mt 27:51 torn in two from *t* to bottom.

TORMENT (TORMENTED TORMENTORS)
Lk 16:28 also come to this place of *t*.'
2Co 12: 7 a messenger of Satan, to *t* me.

TORMENTED (TORMENT)
Rev 20:10 They will be *t* day and night

TORMENTORS (TORMENT)
Ps 137: 3 our *t* demanded songs of joy;

TORN
Gal 4:15 you would have *t* out your eyes
Php 1:23 I do not know! I am *t*

TORTURED*
Mt 18:34 turned him over to the jailers to be *t*,
Heb 11:35 Others were *t* and refused

TOSSED (TOSSING)
Eph 4:14 *t* back and forth by the waves,
Jas 1: 6 of the sea, blown and *t* by the wind.

TOSSING (TOSSED)
Isa 57:20 But the wicked are like the *t* sea,

TOUCH (TOUCHED TOUCHES)
Ge 3: 3 you must not *t* it, or you will die.'"
Ex 19:12 go up the mountain or *t* the foot
Ps 105: 15 "Do not *t* my anointed ones;
Mt 9:21 If I only *t* his cloak, I will be healed
Lk 18:15 babies to Jesus to have him *t* them.
24:39 It is myself! *T* me and see;
2Co 6:17 *T* no unclean thing,
Col 2:21 Do not taste! Do not *t*!"?

TOUCHED (TOUCH)
1Sa 10:26 men whose hearts God had *t*.
Isa 6: 7 With it he *t* my mouth and said,
Mt 14:36 and all who *t* him were healed.
Lk 8:45 "Who *t* me?" Jesus asked.
1Jn 1: 1 looked at and our hands have *t*—

TOUCHES (TOUCH)
Ex 19:12 Whoever *t* the mountain shall
Zec 2: 8 for whoever *t* you *t* the apple

TOWER
Ge 11: 4 with a *t* that reaches to the heavens
Pr 18:10 of the LORD is a strong *t*;

TOWN (TOWNS)
Mt 2:23 and lived in a *t* called Nazareth.

TOWNS (TOWN)
Nu 35: 2 to give the Levites *t* to live
35:15 These six *t* will be a place of refuge
Jer 11:13 as many gods as you have *t*,
Mt 9:35 Jesus went through all the *t*

TRACING*
Ro 11:33 and his paths beyond *t* out!

TRACK
Job 14:16 but not keep *t* of my sin.

TRADERS (TRADING)
1Ti 1:10 for slave *t* and liars and perjurers—

TRADING (TRADERS)
1Ki 10:22 The king had a fleet of *t* ships at sea
Pr 31:18 She sees that her *t* is profitable,

TRADITION (TRADITIONS)
Mt 15: 2 "Why do your disciples break the *t*
15: 6 word of God for the sake of your *t*.
Mk 7:13 by your *t* that you have handed
Col 2: 8 which depends on human *t*

TRADITIONS (TRADITION)
Mk 7: 8 are holding on to the *t* of men."
Gal 1:14 zealous for the *t* of my fathers.

TRAIL
1Ti 5:24 the sins of others *t* behind them.

TRAIN* (TRAINED TRAINING)
Ps 68:18 you led captives in your *t*;
Pr 22: 6 *T* a child in the way he should go,
Isa 2: 4 nor will they *t* for war anymore.
6: 1 the *t* of his robe filled the temple.
Mic 4: 3 nor will they *t* for war anymore.
Eph 4: 8 he led captives in his *t*
1Ti 4: 7 rather, *t* yourself to be godly.
Tit 2: 4 they can *t* the younger women

TRAINED (TRAIN)
Lk 6:40 everyone who is fully *t* will be like
Ac 22: 3 Under Gamaliel I was thoroughly *t*
2Co 11: 6 I may not be a *t* speaker,
Heb 5:14 by constant use have *t* themselves
12:11 for those who have been *t* by it.

TRAINING* (TRAIN)
1Co 9:25 in the games goes into strict *t*.
Eph 6: 4 up in the *t* and instruction
1Ti 4: 8 For physical *t* is of some value,
2Ti 3:16 correcting and *t* in righteousness,

TRAITOR (TRAITORS)
Lk 6:16 and Judas Iscariot, who became a *t*.
Jn 18: 5 Judas the *t* was standing there

TRAITORS (TRAITOR)
Ps 59: 5 show no mercy to wicked *t*.

TRAMPLE (TRAMPLED)
Joel 3:13 Come, *t* the grapes,
Am 2: 7 They *t* on the heads of the poor
5:11 You *t* on the poor
8: 4 Hear this, you who *t* the needy
Mt 7: 6 they may *t* them under their feet,
Lk 10:19 I have given you authority to *t*

TRAMPLED (TRAMPLE)
Isa 63: 6 I *t* the nations in my anger;
Lk 21:24 Jerusalem will be *t*
Heb 10:29 to be punished who has *t* the Son
Rev 14:20 They were *t* in the winepress

TRANCE*
Ac 10:10 was being prepared, he fell into a *t*.
11: 5 and in a *t* I saw a vision.
22:17 into a *t* and saw the Lord speaking.

TRANQUILLITY*
Ecc 4: 6 Better one handful with *t*

TRANSACTIONS*
Ru 4: 7 method of legalizing *t* in Israel.)

TRANSCENDS*
Php 4: 7 which *t* all understanding,

TRANSFIGURED*
Mt 17: 2 There he was *t* before them.
Mk 9: 2 There he was *t* before them.

TRANSFORM* (TRANSFORMED)
Php 3:21 will *t* our lowly bodies

TRANSFORMED (TRANSFORM)
Ro 12: 2 be *t* by the renewing of your mind.
2Co 3:18 are being *t* into his likeness

TRANSGRESSED* (TRANSGRESSION)
Da 9:11 All Israel has *t* your law

TRANSGRESSION* (TRANSGRESSED TRANSGRESSIONS TRANSGRESSORS)
Ps 19:13 innocent of great *t*.
Isa 53: 8 for the *t* of my people he was
Da 9:24 and your holy city to finish *t*,
Mic 1: 5 All this is because of Jacob's *t*,
1: 5 What is Jacob's *t*?
3: 8 to declare to Jacob his *t*,
6: 7 Shall I offer my firstborn for my *t*,
7:18 who pardons sin and forgives the *t*
Ro 4:15 where there is no law there is no *t*.
11:11 Rather, because of their *t*,
11:12 if their *t* means riches for the world

TRANSGRESSIONS* (TRANSGRESSION)
Ps 32: 1 whose *t* are forgiven,
32: 5 my *t* to the LORD"—
39: 8 Save me from all my *t*;
51: 1 blot out my *t*.
51: 3 For I know my *t*,
65: 3 you forgave our *t*.
103: 12 so far has he removed our *t* from us
Isa 43:25 your *t*, for my own sake,
50: 1 of your *t* your mother was sent
53: 5 But he was pierced for our *t*,
Mic 1:13 for the *t* of Israel
Ro 4: 7 whose *t* are forgiven,
Gal 3:19 because of *t* until the Seed to whom

Eph 2: 1 you were dead in your *t* and sins,
2: 5 even when we were dead in *t*—

TRANSGRESSORS* (TRANSGRESSION)
Ps 51:13 Then I will teach *t* your ways,
Isa 53:12 and made intercession for the *t*.
53:12 and was numbered with the *t*.
Lk 22:37 'And he was numbered with the *t*';

TRAP (TRAPPED TRAPS)
Ps 69:22 may it become retribution and a *t*.
Pr 20:25 a *t* for a man to dedicate something
28:10 will fall into his own *t*,
Isa 8:14 a *t* and a snare.
Mt 22:15 and laid plans to *t* him in his words.
Lk 21:34 close on you unexpectedly like a *t*.
Ro 11: 9 their table become a snare and a *t*,
1Ti 3: 7 into disgrace and into the devil's *t*.
6: 9 and a *t* and into many foolish
2Ti 2:26 and escape from the *t* of the devil,

TRAPPED (TRAP)
Pr 6: 2 if you have been *t* by what you said
12:13 An evil man is *t* by his sinful talk,

TRAPS (TRAP)
Jos 23:13 they will become snares and *t*
La 4:20 was caught in their *t*.

TRAVEL (TRAVELER)
Pr 4:15 Avoid it, do not *t* on it;
Mt 23:15 You *t* over land and sea

TRAVELER (TRAVEL)
Job 31:32 door was always open to the *t*—
Jer 14: 8 like a *t* who stays only a night?

TREACHEROUS (TREACHERY)
Ps 25: 3 who are *t* without excuse.
2Ti 3: 4 not lovers of the good, *t*, rash,

TREACHERY (TREACHEROUS)
Isa 59:13 rebellion and *t* against the LORD,

TREAD (TREADING TREADS)
Ps 91:13 You will *t* upon the lion

TREADING (TREAD)
Dt 25: 4 an ox while it is *t* out the grain.
1Co 9: 9 an ox while it is *t* out the grain."
1Ti 5:18 the ox while it is *t* out the grain,"

TREADS (TREAD)
Rev 19:15 He *t* the winepress of the fury

TREASURE (TREASURED TREASURES TREASURY)
Pr 2: 4 and search for it as for hidden *t*,
Isa 33: 6 of the LORD is the key to this *t*.
Mt 6:21 For where your *t* is, there your
13:44 of heaven is like *t* hidden in a field.
Lk 12:33 a *t* in heaven that will not be
2Co 4: 7 But we have this *t* in jars of clay
1Ti 6:19 In this way they will lay up *t*

TREASURED (TREASURE)
Ex 19: 5 you will be my *t* possession.
Dt 7: 6 to be his people, his *t* possession.
26:18 his *t* possession as he promised,
Job 23:12 I have *t* the words
Mal 3:17 when I make up my *t* possession.
Lk 2:19 But Mary *t* up all these things
2:51 But his mother *t* all these things

TREASURES (TREASURE)
1Ch 29: 3 my God I now give my personal *t*
Pr 10: 2 Ill-gotten *t* are of no value,
Mt 6:19 up for yourselves *t* on earth,
13:52 out of his storeroom new *t*
Col 2: 3 in whom are hidden all the *t*
Heb 11:26 of greater value than the *t* of Egypt,

TREASURY (TREASURE)
Mk 12:43 more into the *t* than all the others.

TREAT (TREATED TREATING TREATMENT)
Lev 22: 2 sons to *t* with respect the sacred
Ps 103:10 he does not *t* us as our sins deserve
Mt 18:17 *t* him as you would a pagan
18:35 my heavenly Father will *t* each
Eph 6: 9 *t* your slaves in the same way.
1Th 5:20 do not *t* prophecies with contempt.
1Ti 5: 1 *T* younger men as brothers,
1Pe 3: 7 and *t* them with respect

TREATED (TREAT)
Lev 19:34 The alien living with you must be *t*
25:40 He is to be *t* as a hired worker
1Sa 24:17 "You have *t* me well, but I have
Heb 10:29 who has *t* as an unholy thing

TREATING (TREAT)
Ge 18:25 *t* the righteous and the wicked
Heb 12: 7 as discipline; God is *t* you as sons.

TREATMENT (TREAT)
Col 2:23 and their harsh *t* of the body,

TREATY
Ex 34:12 not to make a *t* with those who live
Dt 7: 2 Make no *t* with them, and show
23: 6 Do not seek a *t* of friendship with them

TREE (TREES)
Ge 2: 9 and the *t* of the knowledge of good
2: 9 of the garden were the *t* of life
Dt 21:23 hung on a *t* is under God's curse.
2Sa 18: 9 Absalom's head got caught in the *t*.
1Ki 14:23 and under every spreading *t*.
Ps 1: 3 He is like a *t* planted by streams
52: 8 But I am like an olive *t*
92:12 righteous will flourish like a palm *t*,
Pr 3:18 She is a *t* of life to those who
11:30 of the righteous is a *t* of life,
27:18 He who tends a fig *t* will eat its fruit
Isa 65:22 For as the days of a *t*,
Jer 17: 8 He will be like a *t* planted
Eze 17:24 I the LORD bring down the tall *t*
Da 4:10 before me stood a *t* in the middle
Mic 4: 4 and under his own fig *t*,
Zec 3:10 to sit under his vine and fig *t*,'
Mt 3:10 every *t* that does not produce good
12:33 for a *t* is recognized by its fruit.
Lk 19: 4 climbed a sycamore-fig *t* to see him
Ac 5:30 killed by hanging him on a *t*.
Ro 11:24 be grafted into their own olive *t*!
Gal 3:13 is everyone who is hung on a *t*."
Jas 3:12 My brothers, can a fig *t* bear olives,
1Pe 2:24 sins in his body on the *t*,
Rev 2: 7 the right to eat from the *t* of life,
22: 2 side of the river stood the *t* of life,
22:14 they may have the right to the *t*
22:19 from him his share in the *t* of life

TREES (TREE)
Jdg 9: 8 One day the *t* went out
Ps 96:12 Then all the *t* of the forest will sing
Isa 55:12 and all the *t* of the field
Mt 3:10 The ax is already at the root of the *t*
Mk 8:24 they look like *t* walking around."
Jude :12 autumn *t*, without fruit

TREMBLE (TREMBLED TREMBLES TREMBLING)
Ex 15:14 The nations will hear and *t*;
1Ch 16:30 *T* before him, all the earth!
Ps 114: 7 *T*, O earth, at the presence
Jer 5:22 'Should you not *t* in my presence?
Eze 38:20 of the earth will *t* at my presence.
Joel 2: 1 Let all who live in the land *t*,
Hab 3: 6 he looked, and made the nations *t*.

TREMBLED (TREMBLE)
Ex 19:16 Everyone in the camp *t*.
20:18 in smoke, they *t* with fear.
2Sa 22: 8 "The earth *t* and quaked,
Ac 7:32 Moses *t* with fear and did not dare

TREMBLES (TREMBLE)
Ps 97: 4 the earth sees and *t*.
104:32 he who looks at the earth, and it *t*,
Isa 66: 2 and *t* at my word.
Jer 10:10 When he is angry, the earth *t*;
Na 1: 5 The earth *t* at his presence,

TREMBLING (TREMBLE)
Ps 2:11 and rejoice with *t*.
Da 10:10 set me *t* on my hands and knees.
Php 2:12 out your salvation with fear and *t*,
Heb 12:21 terrifying that Moses said, "I am *t*

TRESPASS* (TRESPASSES)
Ro 5:15 But the gift is not like the *t*.
5:15 died by the *t* of the one man,
5:17 For if, by the *t* of the one man,
5:18 result of one *t* was condemnation
5:20 added so that the *t* might increase.

TRESPASSES* (TRESPASS)
Ro 5:16 but the gift followed many *t*

TRIAL (TRIALS)
Ps 37:33 condemned when brought to *t*.
Mk 13:11 you are arrested and brought to *t*,
2Co 8: 2 most severe *t*, their overflowing
Jas 1:12 is the man who perseveres under *t*,
1Pe 4:12 at the painful *t* you are suffering,
Rev 3:10 you from the hour of *t* that is going

TRIALS* (TRIAL)
Dt 7:19 saw with your own eyes the great *t*,
29: 3 own eyes you saw those great *t*,
Lk 22:28 who have stood by me in my *t*.
1Th 3: 3 one would be unsettled by these *t*.
2Th 1: 4 the persecutions and *t* you are
Jas 1: 2 whenever you face *t* of many kinds,
1Pe 1: 6 had to suffer grief in all kinds of *t*.
2Pe 2: 9 how to rescue godly men from *t*

TRIBE (HALF-TRIBE TRIBES)
Heb 7:13 no one from that *t* has ever served
Rev 5: 5 See, the Lion of the *t* of Judah,
5: 9 God from every *t* and language
11: 9 men from every people, *t*,
14: 6 to every nation, *t*, language

TRIBES (TRIBE)
Ge 49:28 All these are the twelve *t* of Israel,
Mt 19:28 judging the twelve *t* of Israel.

TRIBULATION*
Rev 7:14 who have come out of the great *t*;

TRICKERY*
Ac 13:10 full of all kinds of deceit and *t*.
2Co 12:16 fellow that I am, I caught you by *t*!

TRIED (TRY)
Ps 73:16 When I *t* to understand all this,
95: 9 where your fathers tested and *t* me,
Heb 3: 9 where your fathers tested and *t* me

TRIES (TRY)
Lk 17:33 Whoever *t* to keep his life will lose

TRIMMED
Mt 25: 7 virgins woke up and *t* their lamps.

TRIUMPH (TRIUMPHAL TRIUMPHED TRIUMPHING TRIUMPHS)
Ps 25: 2 nor let my enemies *t* over me.
54: 7 my eyes have looked in *t*
112: 8 in the end he will look in *t*
118: 7 I will look in *t* on my enemies.
Pr 28:12 When the righteous *t*, there is great
Isa 42:13 and will *t* over his enemies.

TRIUMPHAL* (TRIUMPH)
Isa 60:11 their kings led in *t* procession.
2Co 2:14 us in *t* procession in Christ

TRIUMPHED (TRIUMPH)
Rev 5: 5 of Judah, the Root of David, has *t*.

TRIUMPHING* (TRIUMPH)
Col 2:15 of them, *t* over them by the cross.

TRIUMPHS* (TRIUMPH)
Jas 2:13 Mercy *t* over judgment! What

TROUBLE (TROUBLED TROUBLES)
Ge 41:51 God has made me forget all my *t*
Jos 7:25 Why have you brought this *t* on us?
Job 2:10 good from God, and not *t*?"
5: 7 Yet man is born to *t*
14: 1 is of few days and full of *t*.
42:11 him over all the *t* the LORD had
Ps 7:14 conceives *t* gives birth
7:16 The *t* he causes recoils on himself;
9: 9 a stronghold in times of *t*.
10:14 But you, O God, do see *t* and grief;
22:11 for *t* is near
27: 5 For in the day of *t*
32: 7 you will protect me from *t*
37:39 he is their stronghold in time of *t*.
41: 1 LORD delivers him in times of *t*.
46: 1 an ever-present help in *t*.
50:15 and call upon me in the day of *t*;
59:16 my refuge in times of *t*.
66:14 spoke when I was in *t*.
86: 7 In the day of my *t* I will call to you,
91:15 I will be with him in *t*,
107: 6 to the LORD in their *t*,
107:13 they cried to the LORD in their *t*,
116: 3 I was overcome by *t* and sorrow.
119:143 *T* and distress have come upon me,
138: 7 Though I walk in the midst of *t*,
143:11 righteousness, bring me out of *t*.
Pr 11: 8 righteous man is rescued from *t*,

Pr 11:17 a cruel man brings *t* on himself
11:29 He who brings *t* on his family will
12:13 but a righteous man escapes *t.*
12:21 but the wicked have their fill of *t.*
15:27 A greedy man brings *t* to his family
19:23 one rests content, untouched by *t.*
22: 8 He who sows wickedness reaps *t,*
24:10 If you falter in times of *t,*
25:19 on the unfaithful in times of *t.*
28:14 he who hardens his heart falls into *t*
Jer 30: 7 It will be a time of *t* for Jacob,
Na 1: 7 a refuge in times of *t.*
Zep 1:15 a day of *t* and ruin,
Mt 6:34 Each day has enough *t* of its own.
13:21 When *t* or persecution comes
Jn 16:33 In this world you will have *t.*
Ro 8:35 Shall *t* or hardship or persecution
2Co 1: 4 those in any *t* with the comfort we
2Th 1: 6 *t* to those who *t* you
Jas 5:13 one of you in *t*? He should pray.

TROUBLED (TROUBLE)
Ps 38:18 I am *t* by my sin.
Isa 38:14 I am *t;* O Lord, come to my aid!"
Mk 14:33 began to be deeply distressed and *t.*
Jn 14: 1 "Do not let your hearts be *t.*
14:27 Do not let your hearts be *t*
2Th 1: 7 and give relief to you who are *t,*

TROUBLES (TROUBLE)
Ps 34: 6 he saved him out of all his *t.*
34:17 he delivers them from all their *t.*
34:19 A righteous man may have many *t,*
40:12 For *t* without number surround me
54: 7 he has delivered me from all my *t,*
1Co 7:28 those who marry will face many *t*
2Co 1: 4 who comforts us in all our *t,*
4:17 and momentary *t* are achieving
6: 4 in *t,* hardships and distresses;
7: 4 in all our *t* my joy knows no bounds
Php 4:14 good of you to share in my *t.*

TRUE (TRUTH)
Nu 11:23 not what I say will come *t* for you."
12: 7 this is not *t* of my servant Moses;
Dt 18:22 does not take place or come *t,*
Jos 23:15 of the LORD your God has come *t*
1Sa 9: 6 and everything he says comes *t.*
1Ki 10: 6 and your wisdom is *t.*
2Ch 6:17 your servant David come *t.*
15: 3 was without the *t* God,
Ps 33: 4 of the LORD is right and *t;*
119:142 and your law is *t.*
119:151 and all your commands are *t.*
119:160 All your words are *t;*
Pr 8: 7 My mouth speaks what is *t,*
22:21 teaching you *t* and reliable words,
Jer 10:10 But the LORD is the *t* God;
28: 9 only if his prediction comes *t.*"
Eze 33:33 "When all this comes *t*—
Lk 16:11 who will trust you with *t* riches?
Jn 1: 9 The *t* light that gives light
4:23 when the *t* worshipers will worship
6:32 Father who gives you the *t* bread
7:28 on my own, but he who sent me is *t*
15: 1 "I am the *t* vine, and my Father is
17: 3 the only *t* God, and Jesus Christ,
19:35 testimony, and his testimony is *t.*
21:24 We know that his testimony is *t.*
Ac 10:34 "I now realize how *t* it is that God
11:23 all to remain *t* to the Lord
14:22 them to remain *t* to the faith.
17:11 day to see if what Paul said was *t.*
Ro 3: 4 Let God be *t,* and every man a liar.
Php 4: 8 whatever is *t,* whatever is noble,
1Jn 2: 8 and the *t* light is already shining.
5:20 He is the *t* God and eternal life.
Rev 19: 9 "These are the *t* words of God."
22: 6 These words are trustworthy and *t.*

TRUMPET (TRUMPETS)
Isa 27:13 And in that day a great *t* will sound
Eze 33: 5 Since he heard the sound of the *t*
Zec 9:14 Sovereign LORD will sound the *t;*
Mt 24:31 send his angels with a loud *t* call,
1Co 14: 8 if the *t* does not sound a clear call,
15:52 For the *t* will sound, the dead will
1Th 4:16 and with the *t* call of God,
Rev 8: 7 The first angel sounded his *t,*

TRUMPETS (TRUMPET)
Jdg 7:19 They blew their *t* and broke the jars
Rev 8: 2 and to them were given seven *t.*

TRUST* (ENTRUST ENTRUSTED TRUSTED TRUSTFULLY TRUSTING TRUSTS TRUSTWORTHY)
Ex 14:31 put their *t* in him and in Moses his
19: 9 and will always put their *t* in you."
Nu 20:12 "Because you did not *t*
Dt 1:32 you did not *t* in the LORD your
9:23 You did not *t* him or obey him.
28:52 walls in which you *t* fall down.
Jdg 11:20 did not *t* Israel to pass
2Ki 17:14 who did not *t* in the LORD their
18:30 to *t* in the LORD when he says,
1Ch 9:22 to their positions of *t* by David
Job 4:18 If God places no *t* in his servants,
15:15 If God places no *t* in his holy ones,
31:24 "If I have put my *t* in gold
39:12 Can you *t* him to bring
Ps 4: 5 and *t* in the LORD.
9:10 Those who know your name will *t*
13: 5 But I *t* in your unfailing love;
20: 7 Some *t* in chariots and some
20: 7 we *t* in the name of the LORD our
22: 4 In you our fathers put their *t;*
22: 9 you made me *t* in you
25: 2 I lift up my soul; in you I *t,*
31: 6 I *t* in the LORD.
31:14 But I *t* in you, O LORD;
33:21 for we *t* in his holy name.
37: 3 *T* in the LORD and do good;
37: 5 *t* in him and he will do this:
40: 3 and put their *t* in the LORD.
40: 4 who makes the LORD his *t,*
44: 6 I do not *t* in my bow,
49: 6 those who *t* in their wealth
49:13 of those who *t* in themselves,
52: 8 I *t* in God's unfailing love
55:23 But as for me, I *t* in you.
56: 3 I will *t* in you.
56: 4 in God I *t;* I will not be afraid.
56:11 in God I *t;* I will not be afraid.
62: 8 *T* in him at all times, O people;
62:10 Do not *t* in extortion
78: 7 Then they would put their *t* in God
78:22 or *t* in his deliverance.
91: 2 my God, in whom I *t.*"
115: 8 and so will all who *t* in them.
115: 9 O house of Israel, *t* in the LORD—
115: 10 O house of Aaron, *t* in the LORD
115: 11 You who fear him, *t* in the LORD
118: 8 than to *t* in man.
118: 9 than to *t* in princes.
119: 42 for I *t* in your word.
125: 1 Those who *t* in the LORD are like
135: 18 and so will all who *t* in them.
143: 8 for I have put my *t* in you.
146: 3 Do not put your *t* in princes,
Pr 3: 5 *T* in the LORD with all your heart
21:22 the stronghold in which they *t.*
22:19 So that your *t* may be in the LORD
Isa 8:17 I will put my *t* in him.
12: 2 I will *t* and not be afraid.
26: 4 *T* in the LORD forever,
30:15 in quietness and *t* is your strength,
31: 1 who *t* in the multitude
36:15 to *t* in the LORD when he says,
42:17 But those who *t* in idols,
50:10 *t* in the name of the LORD
Jer 2:37 LORD has rejected those you *t;*
5:17 the fortified cities in which you *t.*
7: 4 Do not *t* in deceptive words
7:14 the temple you *t* in, the place I gave
9: 4 do not *t* your brothers.
12: 6 Do not *t* them,
28:15 you have persuaded this nation to *t*
39:18 you *t* in me, declares the LORD.'"
48: 7 Since you *t* in your deeds
49: 4 you *t* in your riches and say,
49:11 Your widows too can *t* in me."
Mic 7: 5 Do not *t* a neighbor;
Na 1: 7 He cares for those who *t* in him,
Zep 3: 2 She does not *t* in the LORD,
3:12 who *t* in the name of the LORD.
Lk 16:11 who will *t* you with true riches?
Jn 12:36 Put your *t* in the light
14: 1 *T* in God; *t* also in me.
Ac 14:23 Lord, in whom they had put their *t.*
Ro 15:13 you with all joy and peace as you *t*
1Co 4: 2 been given a *t* must prove faithful.
1Co 9:17 discharging the *t* committed
2Co 13: 6 I *t* that you will discover that we
Heb 2:13 "I will put my *t* in him."

TRUSTED* (TRUST)
1Sa 27:12 Achish *t* David and said to himself,
2Ki 18: 5 Hezekiah *t* in the LORD, the God
1Ch 5:20 their prayers, because they *t*
Job 12:20 He silences the lips of *t* advisers
Ps 5: 9 from their mouth can be *t;*
22: 4 they *t* and you delivered them.
22: 5 in you they *t* and were not
26: 1 I have *t* in the LORD
41: 9 Even my close friend, whom I *t,*
52: 7 but *t* in his great wealth
Isa 20: 5 Those who *t* in Cush and boasted
25: 9 This is the LORD, we *t* in him;
25: 9 we *t* in him, and he saved us.
47:10 You have *t* in your wickedness
Jer 13:25 and *t* in false gods.
38:22 those *t* friends of yours.
48:13 ashamed when they *t* in Bethel.
Eze 16:15 " 'But you *t* in your beauty
Da 3:28 They *t* in him and defied the king's
6:23 because he had *t* in his God.
Lk 11:22 the armor in which the man *t*
16:10 *t* with very little can also be *t*
Ac 12:20 a *t* personal servant of the king,
Tit 2:10 but to show that they can be fully *t,*
3: 8 so that those who have *t*

TRUSTFULLY* (TRUST)
Pr 3:29 who lives *t* near you.

TRUSTING* (TRUST)
Job 15:31 by *t* what is worthless,
Ps 112: 7 his heart is steadfast, *t*
Isa 2:22 Stop *t* in man,
Jer 7: 8 you are *t* in deceptive words that

TRUSTS* (TRUST)
Job 8:14 What he *t* in is fragile;
Ps 21: 7 For the king *t* in the LORD;
22: 8 "He *t* in the LORD;
28: 7 my heart *t* in him, and I am helped.
32:10 surrounds the man who *t* in him.
84:12 blessed is the man who *t* in you.
86: 2 who *t* in you.
Pr 11:28 Whoever *t* in his riches will fall,
16:20 blessed is he who *t* in the LORD.
28:25 he who *t* in the LORD will prosper.
28:26 He who *t* in himself is a fool,
29:25 whoever *t* in the LORD is kept safe
Isa 26: 3 because he *t* in you.
28:16 one who *t* will never be dismayed.
Jer 17: 5 "Cursed is the one who *t* in man,
17: 7 blessed is the man who *t*
Eze 33:13 but then he *t* in his righteousness
Hab 2:18 For he who makes it *t*
Mt 27:43 He *t* in God.
Ro 4: 5 but *t* God who justifies the wicked,
9:33 one who *t* in him will never be put
10:11 "Anyone who *t* in him will never
1Co 13: 7 always protects, always *t,*
1Pe 2: 6 and the one who *t* in him

TRUSTWORTHY* (TRUST)
Ex 18:21 *t* men who hate dishonest gain—
2Sa 7:28 you are God! Your words are *t,*
Ne 13:13 these men were considered *t.*
Ps 19: 7 The statutes of the LORD are *t,*
111: 7 all his precepts are *t.*
119: 86 All your commands are *t;*
119:138 they are fully *t.*
Pr 11:13 but a *t* man keeps a secret.
13:17 but a *t* envoy brings healing.
25:13 is a *t* messenger to those who send
Da 2:45 and the interpretation is *t.*"
6: 4 he was *t* and neither corrupt
Lk 16:11 So if you have not been *t*
16:12 And if you have not been *t*
19:17 'Because you have been *t*
1Co 7:25 one who by the Lord's mercy is *t.*
1Ti 1:15 Here is a *t* saying that deserves full
3: 1 Here is a *t* saying: If anyone sets his
3:11 but temperate and *t* in everything.
4: 9 This is a *t* saying that deserves full
2Ti 2:11 Here is a *t* saying:
Tit 1: 9 must hold firmly to the *t* message

Tit 3: 8 This is a *t* saying.
Rev 21: 5 for these words are *t* and true."
22: 6 "These words are *t* and true.

TRUTH* (TRUE TRUTHFUL TRUTHFULNESS TRUTHS)

Ge 42:16 tested to see if you are telling the *t.*
1Ki 17:24 LORD from your mouth is the *t."*
22:16 the *t* in the name of the LORD?"
2Ch 18:15 the *t* in the name of the LORD?"
Ps 15: 2 who speaks the *t* from his heart
25: 5 guide me in your *t* and teach me,
26: 3 and I walk continually in your *t.*
31: 5 redeem me, O LORD, the God of *t*
40:10 do not conceal your love and your *t*
40:11 your *t* always protect me.
43: 3 Send forth your light and your *t,*
45: 4 victoriously in behalf of *t,* humility
51: 6 Surely you desire *t*
52: 3 than speaking the *t.*
86:11 and I will walk in your *t;*
96:13 and the peoples in his *t.*
119: 30 I have chosen the way of *t;*
119: 43 of *t* from my mouth,
145: 18 to all who call on him in *t.*
Pr 16:13 they value a man who speaks the *t.*
23:23 Buy the *t* and do not sell it;
Isa 45:19 I, the LORD, speak the *t;*
48: 1 but not in *t* or righteousness—
59:14 *t* has stumbled in the streets,
59:15 *T* is nowhere to be found,
65:16 will do so by the God of *t;*
65:16 will swear by the God of *t.*
Jer 5: 1 who deals honestly and seeks the *t,*
5: 3 do not your eyes look for *t?*
7:28 *T* has perished; it has vanished
9: 3 it is not by *t*
9: 5 and no one speaks the *t.*
26:15 for in *t* the LORD has sent me
Da 8:12 and *t* was thrown to the ground.
9:13 and giving attention to your *t.*
10:21 what is written in the Book of *T.*
11: 2 "Now then, I tell you the *t:*
Am 5:10 and despise him who tells the *t.*
Zec 8: 3 will be called the City of *T,*
8:16 are to do: Speak the *t* to each other,
8:19 Therefore love *t* and peace."
Mt 5:18 I tell you the *t,* until heaven
5:26 I tell you the *t,* you will not get out
6: 2 I tell you the *t,* they have received
6: 5 I tell you the *t,* they have received
6:16 I tell you the *t,* they have received
8:10 "I tell you the *t,* I have not found
10:15 I tell you the *t,* it will be more
10:23 I tell you the *t,* you will not finish
10:42 I tell you the *t,* he will certainly not
11:11 I tell you the *t:* Among those born
13:17 For I tell you the *t,* many prophets
16:28 I tell you the *t,* some who are
17:20 I tell you the *t,* if you have faith
18: 3 And he said: "I tell you the *t,*
18:13 And if he finds it, I tell you the *t,*
18:18 "I tell you the *t,* whatever you bind
19:23 to his disciples, "I tell you the *t,*
19:28 "I tell you the *t,* at the renewal
21:21 Jesus replied, "I tell you the *t,*
21:31 Jesus said to them, "I tell you the *t,*
22:16 of God in accordance with the *t.*
23:36 I tell you the *t,* all this will come
24: 2 "I tell you the *t,* not one stone here
24:34 I tell you the *t,* this generation will
24:47 I tell you the *t,* he will put him
25:12 'I tell you the *t,* I don't know you.'
25:40 The King will reply, 'I tell you the *t*
25:45 "He will reply, 'I tell you the *t,*
26:13 tell you the *t,* wherever this gospel
26:21 "I tell you the *t,* one
26:34 "I tell you the *t,"* Jesus answered,
Mk 3:28 I tell you the *t,* all the sins
5:33 with fear, told him the whole *t.*
8:12 I tell you the *t,* no sign will be given
9: 1 he said to them, "I tell you the *t,*
9:41 I tell you the *t,* anyone who gives
10:15 I tell you the *t,* anyone who will not
10:29 "I tell you the *t,"* Jesus replied,
11:23 "I tell you the *t,* if anyone says
12:14 of God in accordance with the *t.*
12:43 Jesus said, "I tell you the *t,*
13:30 I tell you the *t,* this generation will
14: 9 I tell you the *t,* wherever the gospel
Mk 14:18 "I tell you the *t,* one
14:25 "I tell you the *t,* I will not drink
14:30 "I tell you the *t,"* Jesus answered,
Lk 4:24 "I tell you the *t,"* he continued,
9:27 I tell you the *t,* some who are
12:37 I tell you the *t,* he will dress himself
12:44 I tell you the *t,* he will put him
18:17 I tell you the *t,* anyone who will not
18:29 I tell you the *t,"* Jesus said to them,
20:21 of God in accordance with the *t.*
21: 3 "I tell you the *t,"* he said, "this
21:32 tell you the *t,* this generation will
23:43 answered him, "I tell you the *t,*
Jn 1:14 from the Father, full of grace and *t.*
1:17 and *t* came through Jesus Christ.
1:51 "I tell you the *t,* you shall see
3: 3 "I tell you the *t,* no one can see
3: 5 Jesus answered, "I tell you the *t,*
3:11 I tell you the *t,* we speak
3:21 But whoever lives by the *t* comes
4:23 worship the Father in spirit and *t,*
4:24 must worship in spirit and in *t."*
5:19 "I tell you the *t,* the Son can do
5:24 "I tell you the *t,* whoever hears my
5:25 I tell you the *t,* a time is coming
5:33 and he has testified to the *t.*
6:26 "I tell you the *t,* you are looking
6:32 Jesus said to them, "I tell you the *t,*
6:47 I tell you the *t,* he who believes has
6:53 Jesus said to them, "I tell you the *t,*
7:18 the one who sent him is a man of *t;*
8:32 Then you will know the *t,*
8:32 and the *t* will set you free."
8:34 Jesus replied, "I tell you the *t,*
8:40 who has told you the *t* that I heard
8:44 to the *t,* for there is no *t* in him.
8:45 I tell the *t,* you do not believe me!
8:46 I am telling the *t,* why don't you
8:51 I tell you the *t,* if anyone keeps my
8:58 "I tell you the *t,"* Jesus answered,
10: 1 "I tell you the *t,* the man who does
10: 7 "I tell you the *t,* I am the gate
12:24 I tell you the *t,* unless a kernel
13:16 I tell you the *t,* no servant is greater
13:20 tell you the *t,* whoever accepts
13:21 "I tell you the *t,* one of you is going
13:38 I tell you the *t,* before the rooster
14: 6 I am the way and the *t* and the life.
14:12 I tell you the *t,* anyone who has
14:17 with you forever—the Spirit of *t.*
15:26 the Spirit of *t* who goes out
16: 7 But I tell you the *t:* It is
16:13 But when he, the Spirit of *t,* comes,
16:13 comes, he will guide you into all *t.*
16:20 I tell you the *t,* you will weep
16:23 I tell you the *t,* my Father will give
17:17 them by the *t;* your word is *t.*
18:23 if I spoke the *t,* why did you strike
18:37 into the world, to testify to the *t.*
18:37 on the side of *t* listens to me."
18:38 "What is *t?"* Pilate asked.
19:35 He knows that he tells the *t,*
21:18 I tell you the *t,* when you were
Ac 20:30 and distort the *t* in order
21:24 everybody will know there is no *t*
21:34 commander could not get at the *t*
24: 8 able to learn the *t* about all these
28:25 "The Holy Spirit spoke the *t*
Ro 1:18 of men who suppress the *t*
1:25 They exchanged the *t* of God
2: 2 who do such things is based on *t.*
2: 8 who reject the *t* and follow evil,
2:20 embodiment of knowledge and *t*—
9: 1 I speak the *t* in Christ—I am not
15: 8 of the Jews on behalf of God's *t,*
1Co 5: 8 the bread of sincerity and *t.*
13: 6 in evil but rejoices with the *t.*
2Co 4: 2 setting forth the *t* plainly we
11:10 As surely as the *t* of Christ is in me,
12: 6 because I would be speaking the *t.*
13: 8 against the *t,* but only for the *t.*
Gal 2: 5 so that the *t* of the gospel might
2:14 in line with the *t* of the gospel,
4:16 enemy by telling you the *t?*
5: 7 and kept you from obeying the *t?*
Eph 1:13 when you heard the word of *t,*
4:15 Instead, speaking the *t* in love,
4:21 him in accordance with the *t* that is
5: 9 and *t*) and find out what pleases
6:14 with the belt of *t* buckled
Col 1: 5 heard about in the word of *t,*
1: 6 understood God's grace in all its *t.*
2Th 2:10 because they refused to love the *t*
2:12 who have not believed the *t*
2:13 and through belief in the *t.*
1Ti 2: 4 to come to a knowledge of the *t.*
2: 7 I am telling the *t,* I am not lying—
3:15 the pillar and foundation of the *t.*
4: 3 who believe and who know the *t.*
6: 5 who have been robbed of the *t*
2Ti 2:15 correctly handles the word of *t.*
2:18 have wandered away from the *t.*
2:25 them to a knowledge of the *t,*
3: 7 never able to acknowledge the *t.*
3: 8 so also these men oppose the *t*—
4: 4 will turn their ears away from the *t*
Tit 1: 1 the knowledge of the *t* that leads
1:14 of those who reject the *t.*
Heb 10:26 received the knowledge of the *t,*
Jas 1:18 birth through the word of *t,*
3:14 do not boast about it or deny the *t.*
5:19 of you should wander from the *t*
1Pe 1:22 by obeying the *t* so that you have
2Pe 1:12 established in the *t* you now have.
2: 2 the way of *t* into disrepute.
1Jn 1: 6 we lie and do not live by the *t.*
1: 8 deceive ourselves and the *t* is not
2: 4 commands is a liar, and the *t* is not
2: 8 its *t* is seen in him and you,
2:20 and all of you know the *t.*
2:21 because no lie comes from the *t.*
2:21 because you do not know the *t,*
3:18 or tongue but with actions and in *t.*
3:19 we know that we belong to the *t,*
4: 6 is how we recognize the Spirit of *t*
5: 6 testifies, because the Spirit is the *t.*
2Jn : 1 whom I love in the *t*—
: 2 who know the *t*—because of the *t,*
: 3 will be with us in *t* and love.
: 4 of your children walking in the *t,*
3Jn : 1 friend Gaius, whom I love in the *t.*
: 3 how you continue to walk in the *t.*
: 3 tell about your faithfulness to the *t*
: 4 my children are walking in the *t.*
: 8 we may work together for the *t.*
:12 everyone—and even by the *t* itself.

TRUTHFUL* (TRUTH)

Pr 12:17 A *t* witness gives honest testimony,
12:19 *T* lips endure forever,
12:22 but he delights in men who are *t.*
14: 5 A *t* witness does not deceive,
14:25 A *t* witness saves lives,
Jer 4: 2 and if in a *t,* just and righteous way
Jn 3:33 it has certified that God is *t.*
2Co 6: 7 in *t* speech and in the power

TRUTHFULNESS* (TRUTH)

Ro 3: 7 "If my falsehood enhances God's *t*

TRUTHS* (TRUTH)

1Co 2:13 expressing spiritual *t*
1Ti 3: 9 hold of the deep *t* of the faith
4: 6 brought up in the *t* of the faith
Heb 5:12 to teach you the elementary *t*

TRY (TRIED TRIES TRYING)

Ps 26: 2 Test me, O LORD, and *t* me,
Isa 7:13 enough to *t* the patience of men?
Lk 12:58 *t* hard to be reconciled to him
13:24 will *t* to enter and will not be able
1Co 10:33 even as I *t* to please everybody
14:12 *t* to excel in gifts that build up
2Co 5:11 is to fear the Lord, we *t*
1Th 5:15 always *t* to be kind to each other
Tit 2: 9 to *t* to please them, not to talk back

TRYING (TRY)

2Co 5:12 We are not *t* to commend ourselves
Gal 1:10 If I were still *t* to please men,
1Th 2: 4 We are not *t* to please men but God
1Pe 1:11 *t* to find out the time
1Jn 2:26 things to you about those who are *t*

TUMORS

1Sa 5: 6 them and afflicted them with *t.*

TUNE

1Co 14: 7 anyone know what *t* is being

TUNIC (TUNICS)

Lk 6:29 do not stop him from taking your *t.*

TUNICS (TUNIC)

Lk 3:11 "The man with two *t* should share

TURMOIL
Ps 65: 7 and the *t* of the nations.
Pr 15:16 than great wealth with *t*.

TURN (TURNED TURNING TURNS)
Ex 32:12 *T* from your fierce anger; relent
Nu 32:15 If you *t* away from following him,
Dt 5:32 do not *t* aside to the right
28:14 Do not *t* aside from any
30:10 and *t* to the LORD your God
Jos 1: 7 do not *t* from it to the right
1Ki 8:58 May he *t* our hearts to him,
2Ch 7:14 and *t* from their wicked ways,
30: 9 He will not *t* his face from you
Job 33:30 to *t* back his soul from the pit,
Ps 28: 1 do not *t* a deaf ear to me.
34:14 *T* from evil and do good;
51:13 and sinners will *t* back to you.
78: 6 they in *t* would tell their children.
119: 36 *T* my heart toward your statutes
119:132 *T* to me and have mercy on me,
Pr 22: 6 when he is old he will not *t* from it.
Isa 17: 7 *t* their eyes to the Holy One
28: 6 to those who *t* back the battle
29:16 You *t* things upside down,
30:21 Whether you *t* to the right
45:22 "*T* to me and be saved,
55: 7 Let him *t* to the LORD,
Jer 31:13 I will *t* their mourning
Eze 33: 9 if you do warn the wicked man to *t*
33:11 *T*! *T* from your evil ways!
Jnh 3: 9 and with compassion *t*
Mal 4: 6 He will *t* the hearts of the fathers
Mt 5:39 you on the right cheek, *t*
10:35 For I have come to *t*
Lk 1:17 to *t* the hearts of the fathers
Jn 12:40 nor *t*—and I would heal them."
16:20 but your grief will *t* to joy.
Ac 3:19 Repent, then, and *t* to God,
26:18 and *t* them from darkness to light,
1Co 14:31 For you can all prophesy in *t*
15:23 But each in his own *t*: Christ,
1Ti 6:20 *T* away from godless chatter
1Pe 3:11 He must *t* from evil and do good;

TURNED (TURN)
Dt 23: 5 *t* the curse into a blessing for you,
1Ki 11: 4 his wives *t* his heart
2Ch 15: 4 But in their distress they *t*
Est 9: 1 but now the tables were *t*
9:22 when their sorrow was *t* into joy
Ps 14: 3 All have *t* aside,
30:11 You *t* my wailing into dancing;
40: 1 he *t* to me and heard my cry.
Isa 9:12 for all this, his anger is not *t* away,
53: 6 each of us has *t* to his own way;
Hos 7: 8 Ephraim is a flat cake not *t* over.
Joel 2:31 The sun will be *t* to darkness
Lk 22:32 And when you have *t* back,
Ro 3:12 All have *t* away,

TURNING (TURN)
2Ki 21:13 wiping it and *t* it upside down.
Pr 2: 2 *t* your ear to wisdom
14:27 *t* a man from the snares of death.

TURNS (TURN)
2Sa 22:29 the LORD *t* my darkness into light
Pr 15: 1 A gentle answer *t* away wrath,
Isa 44:25 and *t* it into nonsense,
Jas 5:20 Whoever *t* a sinner from the error

TWELVE
Ge 35:22 Jacob had *t* sons: The sons of Leah:
49:28 All these are the *t* tribes of Israel,
Mt 10: 1 He called his *t* disciples to him
Lk 9:17 the disciples picked up *t* basketfuls
Rev 21:12 the names of the *t* tribes of Israel.
21:14 of the *t* apostles of the Lamb.

TWIN (TWINS)
Ge 25:24 there were *t* boys in her womb.

TWINKLING*
1Co 15:52 in a flash, in the *t* of an eye,

TWINS (TWIN)
Ro 9:11 before the *t* were born

TWISTING* (TWISTS)
Pr 30:33 and as *t* the nose produces blood,

TWISTS (TWISTING)
Ex 23: 8 and *t* the words of the righteous.

TYRANNICAL*
Pr 28:16 A *t* ruler lacks judgment,

TYRE
Eze 28:12 a lament concerning the king of *T*
Mt 11:22 it will be more bearable for *T*

UNAPPROACHABLE*
1Ti 6:16 immortal and who lives in *u* light,

UNASHAMED*
1Jn 2:28 and *u* before him at his coming.

UNBELIEF* (UNBELIEVER UNBELIEVERS UNBELIEVING)
Mk 9:24 help me overcome my *u*!"
Ro 4:20 through *u* regarding the promise
11:20 they were broken off because of *u*,
11:23 And if they do not persist in *u*,
1Ti 1:13 because I acted in ignorance and *u*.
Heb 3:19 able to enter, because of their *u*.

UNBELIEVER* (UNBELIEF)
1Co 7:15 But if the *u* leaves, let him do so.
10:27 If some *u* invites you to a meal
14:24 if an *u* or someone who does not
2Co 6:15 have in common with an *u*?
1Ti 5: 8 the faith and is worse than an *u*.

UNBELIEVERS* (UNBELIEF)
Lk 12:46 and assign him a place with the *u*.
Ro 15:31 rescued from the *u* in Judea
1Co 6: 6 another—and this in front of *u*!
14:22 however, is for believers, not for *u*.
14:22 not for believers but for *u*;
14:23 do not understand or some *u* come
2Co 4: 4 this age has blinded the minds of *u*,
6:14 Do not be yoked together with *u*.

UNBELIEVING* (UNBELIEF)
Mt 17:17 "O *u* and perverse generation,"
Mk 9:19 "O *u* generation," Jesus replied,
Lk 9:41 "O *u* and perverse generation,"
1Co 7:14 For the *u* husband has been
7:14 and the *u* wife has been sanctified
Heb 3:12 *u* heart that turns away
Rev 21: 8 But the cowardly, the *u*, the vile,

UNBLEMISHED*
Heb 9:14 the eternal Spirit offered himself *u*

UNCEASING
Ro 9: 2 and *u* anguish in my heart.

UNCERTAIN*
1Ti 6:17 which is so *u*, but to put their hope

UNCHANGEABLE* (UNCHANGING)
Heb 6:18 by two *u* things in which it is

UNCHANGING* (UNCHANGEABLE)
Heb 6:17 wanted to make the *u* nature

UNCIRCUMCISED
Lev 26:41 when their *u* hearts are humbled
1Sa 17:26 Who is this *u* Philistine that he
Jer 9:26 house of Israel is *u* in heart."
Ac 7:51 stiff-necked people, with *u* hearts
Ro 4:11 had by faith while he was still *u*.
1Co 7:18 Was a man *u* when he was called?
Col 3:11 circumcised or *u*, barbarian,

UNCIRCUMCISION
1Co 7:19 is nothing and *u* is nothing.
Gal 5: 6 neither circumcision nor *u* has any

UNCLEAN
Ge 7: 2 and two of every kind of *u* animal,
Lev 10:10 between the *u* and the clean,
11: 4 it is ceremonially *u* for you.
17:15 he will be ceremonially *u* till evening.
Isa 6: 5 ruined! For I am a man of *u* lips,
52:11 Touch no *u* thing!
Mt 15:11 mouth does not make him '*u*,'
Ac 10:14 never eaten anything impure or *u*."
Ro 14:14 fully convinced that no food is *u*
2Co 6:17 Touch no *u* thing,

UNCLOTHED*
2Co 5: 4 because we do not wish to be *u*

UNCONCERNED*
Eze 16:49 were arrogant, overfed and *u*;

UNCOVERED
Ru 3: 7 Ruth approached quietly, *u* his feet
1Co 11: 5 with her head *u* dishonors her head
11:13 to pray to God with her head *u*?

Heb 4:13 Everything is *u* and laid bare

UNDERGOES* (UNDERGOING)
Heb 12: 8 (and everyone *u* discipline),

UNDERGOING* (UNDERGOES)
1Pe 5: 9 the world are *u* the same kind

UNDERSTAND (UNDERSTANDING UNDERSTANDS UNDERSTOOD)
Ne 8: 8 the people could *u* what was being
Job 38: 4 Tell me, if you *u*.
42: 3 Surely I spoke of things I did not *u*,
Ps 14: 2 men to see if there are any who *u*,
73:16 When I tried to *u* all this,
119: 27 Let me *u* the teaching
119:125 that I may *u* your statutes.
Pr 2: 5 then you will *u* the fear
2: 9 Then you will *u* what is right
30:18 four that I do not *u*:
Ecc 7:25 to *u* the stupidity of wickedness
11: 5 so you cannot *u* the work of God,
Isa 6:10 *u* with their hearts,
44:18 know nothing, they *u* nothing;
52:15 they have not heard, they will *u*.
Jer 17: 9 Who can *u* it?
31:19 after I came to *u*,
Da 9:25 and *u* this: From the issuing
Hos 14: 9 Who is discerning? He will *u* them.
Mt 13:15 *u* with their hearts
24:15 Daniel—let the reader *u*—
Lk 24:45 so they could *u* the Scriptures.
Ac 8:30 "Do you *u* what you are reading?"
Ro 7:15 I do not *u* what I do.
15:21 those who have not heard will *u*."
1Co 2:12 that we may *u* what God has freely
2:14 and he cannot *u* them,
14:16 those who do not *u* say "Amen"
Eph 5:17 but *u* what the Lord's will is.
Heb 11: 3 By faith we *u* that the universe was
2Pe 1:20 you must *u* that no prophecy
3: 3 you must *u* that in the last days
3:16 some things that are hard to *u*,

UNDERSTANDING (UNDERSTAND)
1Ki 4:29 and a breadth of *u* as measureless
Job 12:12 Does not long life bring *u*?
28:12 Where does *u* dwell?
28:28 and to shun evil is *u*.'"
32: 8 of the Almighty, that gives him *u*.
36:26 How great is God—beyond our *u*!
37: 5 he does great things beyond our *u*.
Ps 111: 10 follow his precepts have good *u*.
119: 34 Give me *u*, and I will keep your law
119:100 I have more *u* than the elders,
119:104 I gain *u* from your precepts;
119:130 it gives *u* to the simple.
136: 5 who by his *u* made the heavens,
147: 5 his *u* has no limit.
Pr 2: 2 and applying your heart to *u*,
2: 6 his mouth come knowledge and *u*.
3: 5 and lean not on your own *u*;
3:13 the man who gains *u*,
4: 5 Get wisdom, get *u*;
4: 7 Though it cost all you have, get *u*.
7: 4 and call *u* your kinsman;
9:10 knowledge of the Holy One is *u*.
10:23 but a man of *u* delights in wisdom.
11:12 but a man of *u* holds his tongue.
14:29 A patient man has great *u*,
15:21 a man of *u* keeps a straight course.
15:32 whoever heeds correction gains *u*.
16:16 to choose *u* rather than silver!
16:22 *U* is a fountain of life
17:27 and a man of *u* is even-tempered.
18: 2 A fool finds no pleasure in *u*
19: 8 he who cherishes *u* prospers.
20: 5 but a man of *u* draws them out.
23:23 get wisdom, discipline and *u*.
Isa 11: 2 the Spirit of wisdom and of *u*,
40:28 and his *u* no one can fathom.
56:11 They are shepherds who lack *u*;
Jer 3:15 you with knowledge and *u*.
10:12 stretched out the heavens by his *u*.
Da 5:12 a keen mind and knowledge and *u*,
10:12 that you set your mind to gain *u*
Hos 4:11 which take away the *u*
Mk 4:12 and ever hearing but never *u*;
12:33 with all your *u* and with all your
Lk 2:47 who heard him was amazed at his *u*
2Co 6: 6 in purity, *u*, patience and kindness;
Eph 1: 8 on us with all wisdom and *u*.

Php 4: 7 of God, which transcends all *u*,
Col 1: 9 through all spiritual wisdom and *u*.
2: 2 have the full riches of complete *u*,
1Jn 5:20 God has come and has given us *u*,

UNDERSTANDS (UNDERSTAND)
1Ch 28: 9 and *u* every motive
Jer 9:24 that he *u* and knows me,
Mt 13:23 man who hears the word and *u* it.
Ro 3:11 there is no one who *u*,
1Ti 6: 4 he is conceited and *u* nothing.

UNDERSTOOD (UNDERSTAND)
Ne 8:12 they now *u* the words that had
Ps 73:17 then I *u* their final destiny.
Isa 40:13 Who has *u* the mind of the LORD,
40:21 Have you not *u* since the earth was
Jn 1: 5 but the darkness has not *u* it.
Ro 1:20 being *u* from what has been made,

UNDESIRABLE*
Jos 24:15 But if serving the LORD seems *u*

UNDIVIDED*
1Ch 12:33 to help David with *u* loyalty—
Ps 86:11 give me an *u* heart,
Eze 11:19 I will give them an *u* heart
1Co 7:35 way in *u* devotion to the Lord.

UNDOING
Pr 18: 7 A fool's mouth is his *u*,

UNDYING*
Eph 6:24 Lord Jesus Christ with an *u* love.

UNEQUALED*
Mt 24:21 *u* from the beginning of the world
Mk 13:19 of distress *u* from the beginning,

UNFADING*
1Pe 3: 4 the *u* beauty of a gentle

UNFAILING*
Ex 15:13 "In your *u* love you will lead
1Sa 20:14 But show me *u* kindness like that
2Sa 22:51 he shows *u* kindness
Ps 6: 4 save me because of your *u* love.
13: 5 But I trust in your *u* love;
18:50 he shows *u* kindness
21: 7 through the *u* love
31:16 save me in your *u* love.
32:10 but the LORD's *u* love
33: 5 the earth is full of his *u* love.
33:18 those whose hope is in his *u* love,
33:22 May your *u* love rest upon us,
36: 7 How priceless is your *u* love!
44:26 redeem us because of your *u* love.
48: 9 we meditate on your *u* love.
51: 1 according to your *u* love;
52: 8 I trust in God's *u* love
77: 8 Has his *u* love vanished forever?
85: 7 Show us your *u* love, O LORD,
90:14 in the morning with your *u* love,
107: 8 thanks to the LORD for his *u* love
107: 15 thanks to the LORD for his *u* love
107: 21 to the LORD for his *u* love
107: 31 to the LORD for his *u* love
119: 41 May your *u* love come to me,
119: 76 May your *u* love be my comfort,
130: 7 for with the LORD is *u* love
143: 8 bring me word of your *u* love,
143: 12 In your *u* love, silence my enemies;
147: 11 who put their hope in his *u* love.
Pr 19:22 What a man desires is *u* love;
20: 6 Many a man claims to have *u* love,
Isa 54:10 yet my *u* love for you will not be
La 3:32 so great is his *u* love.
Hos 10:12 reap the fruit of *u* love,

UNFAITHFUL (UNFAITHFULNESS)
Lev 6: 2 is *u* to the LORD by deceiving his
Nu 5: 6 and so is *u* to the LORD,
1Ch 10:13 because he was *u* to the LORD;
Pr 11: 6 the *u* are trapped by evil desires.
13: 2 the *u* have a craving for violence.
13:15 but the way of the *u* is hard.
22:12 but he frustrates the words of the *u*.
23:28 and multiplies the *u* among men.
25:19 is reliance on the *u* in times
Jer 3:20 But like a woman *u* to her husband,

UNFAITHFULNESS (UNFAITHFUL)
1Ch 9: 1 to Babylon because of their *u*.
Mt 5:32 except for marital *u*, causes her
19: 9 for marital *u*, and marries another

UNFIT*
Tit 1:16 and *u* for doing anything good.

UNFOLDING
Ps 119:130 the *u* of your words gives light;

UNFORGIVING*
2Ti 3: 3 unholy, without love, *u*, slanderous

UNFRIENDLY*
Pr 18: 1 An *u* man pursues selfish ends;

UNFRUITFUL
1Co 14:14 my spirit prays, but my mind is *u*.

UNGODLINESS (UNGODLY)
Tit 2:12 It teaches us to say "No" to *u*

UNGODLY (UNGODLINESS)
Ro 5: 6 powerless, Christ died for the *u*.
1Ti 1: 9 the *u* and sinful, the unholy
2Ti 2:16 in it will become more and more *u*.
2Pe 2: 6 of what is going to happen to the *u*;
Jude :15 and to convict all the *u*

UNGRATEFUL*
Lk 6:35 he is kind to the *u* and wicked.
2Ti 3: 2 disobedient to their parents, *u*,

UNHOLY*
1Ti 1: 9 and sinful, the *u* and irreligious;
2Ti 3: 2 ungrateful, *u*, without love,
Heb 10:29 as an *u* thing the blood

UNINTENTIONALLY
Lev 4: 2 'When anyone sins *u* and does
Nu 15:22 " 'Now if you *u* fail to keep any
Dt 4:42 flee if he had *u* killed his neighbor

UNIT
1Co 12:12 body is a *u*, though it is made up

UNITE (UNITED UNITY)
1Co 6:15 and *u* them with a prostitute?

UNITED (UNITE)
Ge 2:24 and mother and be *u* to his wife,
Mt 19: 5 and mother and be *u* to his wife,
Ro 6: 5 If we have been *u* with him like this
Eph 5:31 and mother and be *u* to his wife,
Php 2: 1 from being *u* with Christ,
Col 2: 2 encouraged in heart and *u* in love,

UNITY* (UNITE)
2Ch 30:12 the people to give them *u* of mind
Ps 133: 1 is when brothers live together in *u*!
Jn 17:23 May they be brought to complete *u*
Ro 15: 5 a spirit of *u* among yourselves
Eph 4: 3 effort to keep the *u* of the Spirit
4:13 up until we all reach *u* in the faith
Col 3:14 them all together in perfect *u*.

UNIVERSE*
1Co 4: 9 made a spectacle to the whole *u*,
Eph 4:10 in order to fill the whole *u*.)
Php 2:15 which you shine like stars in the *u*
Heb 1: 2 and through whom he made the *u*.
11: 3 understand that the *u* was formed

UNJUST
Ro 3: 5 That God is *u* in bringing his wrath
9:14 What then shall we say? Is God *u*?
1Pe 2:19 up under the pain of *u* suffering

UNKNOWN
Ac 17:23 TO AN *U* GOD.

UNLEAVENED
Ex 12:17 "Celebrate the Feast of *U* Bread,
Dt 16:16 at the Feast of *U* Bread, the Feast

UNLIMITED*
1Ti 1:16 Jesus might display his *u* patience

UNLOVED
Pr 30:23 an *u* woman who is married,

UNMARRIED
1Co 7: 8 It is good for them to stay *u*,
7:27 Are you *u*? Do not look for a wife.
7:32 An *u* man is concerned about

UNPLOWED
Ex 23:11 the seventh year let the land lie *u*
Hos 10:12 and break up your *u* ground;

UNPRODUCTIVE
Tit 3:14 necessities and not live *u* lives.
2Pe 1: 8 and *u* in your knowledge

UNPROFITABLE
Tit 3: 9 because these are *u* and useless.

UNPUNISHED
Ex 34: 7 Yet he does not leave the guilty *u*;
Pr 6:29 no one who touches her will go *u*.
11:21 of this: The wicked will not go *u*,
19: 5 A false witness will not go *u*,

UNQUENCHABLE
Lk 3:17 he will burn up the chaff with *u* fire

UNREPENTANT*
Ro 2: 5 stubbornness and your *u* heart,

UNRIGHTEOUS*
Zep 3: 5 yet the *u* know no shame.
Mt 5:45 rain on the righteous and the *u*.
1Pe 3:18 the righteous for the *u*, to bring you
2Pe 2: 9 and to hold the *u* for the day

UNSEARCHABLE
Ro 11:33 How *u* his judgments,
Eph 3: 8 preach to the Gentiles the *u* riches

UNSEEN*
Mt 6: 6 and pray to your Father, who is *u*.
6:18 who is *u*; and your Father,
2Co 4:18 on what is seen, but on what is *u*.
4:18 temporary, but what is *u* is eternal.

UNSETTLED*
1Th 3: 3 so that no one would be *u*
2Th 2: 2 not to become easily *u*

UNSHRUNK
Mt 9:16 patch of *u* cloth on an old garment,

UNSPIRITUAL*
Ro 7:14 but I am *u*, sold as a slave to sin.
Col 2:18 and his *u* mind puffs him up
Jas 3:15 down from heaven but is earthly, *u*,

UNSTABLE*
Jas 1: 8 he is a double-minded man, *u*
2Pe 2:14 they seduce the *u*; they are experts
3:16 ignorant and *u* people distort,

UNTHINKABLE*
Job 34:12 It is *u* that God would do wrong,

UNTIE
Mk 1: 7 worthy to stoop down and *u*.
Lk 13:15 each of you on the Sabbath *u* his ox

UNVEILED*
2Co 3:18 with *u* faces all reflect the Lord's

UNWHOLESOME*
Eph 4:29 Do not let any *u* talk come out

UNWISE
Eph 5:15 how you live—not as *u* but as wise,

UNWORTHY*
Ge 32:10 I am *u* of all the kindness
Job 40: 4 "I am *u*—how can I reply to you?
Lk 17:10 should say, 'We are *u* servants;
1Co 11:27 Lord in an *u* manner will be guilty

UPHOLD (UPHOLDS)
Isa 41:10 I will *u* you with my righteous right
Ro 3:31 Not at all! Rather, we *u* the law.

UPHOLDS* (UPHOLD)
Ps 37:17 but the LORD *u* the righteous.
37:24 for the LORD *u* him with his hand.
63: 8 your right hand *u* me.
140: 12 and *u* the cause of the needy.
145: 14 The LORD *u* all those who fall
146: 7 He *u* the cause of the oppressed

UPRIGHT
Dt 32: 4 *u* and just is he.
Job 1: 1 This man was blameless and *u*;
Ps 7:10 who saves the *u* in heart.
11: 7 *u* men will see his face.
25: 8 Good and *u* is the LORD;
33: 1 it is fitting for the *u* to praise him.
64:10 let all the *u* in heart praise him!
92:15 proclaiming, "The LORD is *u*;
97:11 and joy on the *u* in heart.
119: 7 I will praise you with an *u* heart
Pr 2: 7 He holds victory in store for the *u*,
3:32 but takes the *u* into his confidence.
14: 2 whose walk is *u* fears the LORD,
15: 8 but the prayer of the *u* pleases him.
21:29 an *u* man gives thought to his ways.
Isa 26: 7 O *u* One, you make the way

Tit 1: 8 who is self-controlled, *u*, holy
2:12 *u* and godly lives in this present

UPROOTED
Dt 28:63 You will be *u* from the land you are
Jer 31:40 The city will never again be *u*
Jude :12 without fruit and *u*—twice dead.

UPSET
Lk 10:41 are worried and *u* about many

URIAH
Hittite husband of Bathsheba, killed by David's order (2Sa 11).

USEFUL
Eph 4:28 doing something *u*
2Ti 2:21 *u* to the Master and prepared
3:16 Scripture is God-breathed and is *u*
Phm :11 now he has become *u* both to you

USELESS
1Co 15:14 our preaching is *u*
Tit 3: 9 these are unprofitable and *u*.
Phm :11 Formerly he was *u* to you,
Heb 7:18 *u* (for the law made nothing perfect
Jas 2:20 faith without deeds is *u*?

USURY
Ne 5:10 But let the exacting of *u* stop!
Ps 15: 5 who lends his money without *u*

UTMOST
Job 34:36 that Job might be tested to the *u*

UTTER (UTTERS)
Ps 78: 2 I will *u* hidden things, things from of old—
Mt 13:35 I will *u* things hidden

UTTERS (UTTER)
1Co 14: 2 he *u* mysteries with his spirit.

UZZIAH
Son of Amaziah; king of Judah also known as Azariah (2Ki 15:1–7; 1Ch 6:24; 2Ch 26). Struck with leprosy because of pride (2Ch 26:16–23).

VAIN
Ps 33:17 A horse is a *v* hope for deliverance;
73:13 in *v* have I kept my heart pure;
127: 1 its builders labor in *v*.
Isa 65:23 They will not toil in *v*
1Co 15: 2 Otherwise, you have believed in *v*.
15:58 labor in the Lord is not in *v*.
2Co 6: 1 not to receive God's grace in *v*.
Gal 2: 2 running or had run my race in *v*.

VALIANT
1Sa 10:26 by *v* men whose hearts God had

VALID
Jn 8:14 my own behalf, my testimony is *v*,

VALLEY (VALLEYS)
Ps 23: 4 walk through the *v* of the shadow
Isa 40: 4 Every *v* shall be raised up,
Joel 3:14 multitudes in the *v* of decision!

VALLEYS (VALLEY)
SS 2: 1 a lily of the *v*.

VALUABLE (VALUE)
Lk 12:24 And how much more *v* you are

VALUE (VALUABLE VALUED)
Lev 27: 3 set the *v* of a male between the ages
Pr 16:13 they *v* a man who speaks the truth.
31:11 and lacks nothing of *v*.
Mt 13:46 When he found one of great *v*,
1Ti 4: 8 For physical training is of some *v*,
Heb 11:26 as of greater *v* than the treasures

VALUED (VALUE)
Lk 16:15 What is highly *v* among men is

VANISHES
Jas 4:14 appears for a little while and then *v*.

VASHTI*
Queen of Persia replaced by Esther (Est 1–2).

VAST
Ge 2: 1 completed in all their *v* array.
Dt 1:19 of the Amorites through all that *v*
8:15 He led you through the *v*
Ps 139:17 How *v* is the sum of them!

VEGETABLES
Pr 15:17 of *v* where there is love

Ro 14: 2 whose faith is weak, eats only *v*.

VEIL
Ex 34:33 to them, he put a *v* over his face.
2Co 3:14 for to this day the same *v* remains

VENGEANCE (AVENGE AVENGER AVENGES AVENGING REVENGE)
Nu 31: 3 to carry out the LORD's *v* on them
Isa 34: 8 For the LORD has a day of *v*,
Na 1: 2 The LORD takes *v* on his foes

VERDICT
Jn 3:19 This is the *v*: Light has come

VICTOR'S* (VICTORY)
2Ti 2: 5 he does not receive the *v* crown

VICTORIES* (VICTORY)
2Sa 22:51 He gives his king great *v*;
Ps 18:50 He gives his king great *v*;
21: 1 great is his joy in the *v* you give!
21: 5 Through the *v* you gave, his glory is
44: 4 who decrees *v* for Jacob.

VICTORIOUS (VICTORY)
Ps 20: 5 for joy when you are *v*

VICTORIOUSLY* (VICTORY)
Ps 45: 4 In your majesty ride forth *v*

VICTORY (VICTOR'S VICTORIES VICTORIOUS VICTORIOUSLY)
2Sa 8: 6 gave David *v* wherever he
Ps 44: 6 my sword does not bring me *v*;
60:12 With God we will gain the *v*,
129: 2 they have not gained the *v* over me.
Pr 11:14 but many advisers make *v* sure.
1Co 15:54 "Death has been swallowed up in *v*
15:57 He gives us the *v* through our Lord
1Jn 5: 4 This is the *v* that has overcome

VIEW
Pr 5:21 are in full *v* of the LORD,
2Ti 4: 1 and in *v* of his appearing

VILLAGE
Mk 6: 6 went around teaching from *v* to *v*.

VINDICATED (VINDICATION)
Job 13:18 I know I will be *v*.
1Ti 3:16 was *v* by the Spirit,

VINDICATION (VINDICATED)
Ps 24: 5 and *v* from God his Savior.

VINE (VINEYARD)
Ps 128: 3 Your wife will be like a fruitful *v*
Isa 36:16 one of you will eat from his own *v*
Jnh 4: 6 Jonah was very happy about the *v*.
Jn 15: 1 "I am the true *v*, and my Father is

VINEGAR
Pr 10:26 As *v* to the teeth and smoke
Mk 15:36 filled a sponge with wine *v*,

VINEYARD (VINE)
1Ki 21: 1 an incident involving a *v* belonging
Pr 31:16 out of her earnings she plants a *v*.
SS 1: 6 my own *v* I have neglected.
Isa 5: 1 My loved one had a *v*
1Co 9: 7 Who plants a *v* and does not eat

VIOLATION
Heb 2: 2 every *v* and disobedience received

VIOLENCE (VIOLENT)
Ge 6:11 in God's sight and was full of *v*.
Isa 53: 9 though he had done no *v*,
60:18 No longer will *v* be heard
Eze 45: 9 Give up your *v* and oppression
Joel 3:19 of *v* done to the people of Judah,
Jnh 3: 8 give up their evil ways and their *v*.

VIOLENT (VIOLENCE)
Eze 18:10 "Suppose he has a *v* son, who sheds
1Ti 1:13 and a persecutor and a *v* man,
3: 3 not *v* but gentle, not quarrelsome,
Tit 1: 7 not *v*, not pursuing dishonest gain.

VIPERS
Ps 140: 3 the poison of *v* is on their lips.
Lk 3: 7 "You brood of *v*! Who warned you
Ro 3:13 "The poison of *v* is on their lips."

VIRGIN (VIRGINS)
Dt 22:15 shall bring proof that she was a *v*
Isa 7:14 The *v* will be with child
Mt 1:23 "The *v* will be with child

Lk 1:34 I am a *v*?" The angel answered,
2Co 11: 2 that I might present you as a pure *v*

VIRGINS (VIRGIN)
Mt 25: 1 will be like ten *v* who took their
1Co 7:25 Now about *v*: I have no command

VIRTUES*
Col 3:14 And over all these *v* put on love,

VISIBLE
Eph 5:13 exposed by the light becomes *v*,
Col 1:16 and on earth, *v* and invisible,

VISION (VISIONS)
Da 9:24 to seal up *v* and prophecy
Ac 26:19 disobedient to the *v* from heaven.

VISIONS (VISION)
Nu 12: 6 I reveal myself to him in *v*,
Joel 2:28 your young men will see *v*,
Ac 2:17 your young men will see *v*,

VOICE
Dt 30:20 listen to his *v*, and hold fast to him.
1Sa 15:22 as in obeying the *v* of the LORD?
Job 40: 9 and can your thunder like his?
Ps 19: 4 Their *v* goes out into all the earth,
29: 3 The *v* of the LORD is
66:19 and heard my *v* in prayer.
95: 7 Today, if you hear his *v*,
Pr 8: 1 Does not understanding raise her *v*
Isa 30:21 your ears will hear a *v* behind you,
40: 3 A *v* of one calling:
Mk 1: 3 "a *v* of one calling in the desert,
Jn 5:28 are in their graves will hear his *v*
10: 3 and the sheep listen to his *v*.
Ro 10:18 "Their *v* has gone out
Heb 3: 7 "Today, if you hear his *v*,
Rev 3:20 If anyone hears my *v* and opens

VOMIT
Lev 18:28 it will *v* you out as it vomited out
Pr 26:11 As a dog returns to its *v*,
2Pe 2:22 "A dog returns to its *v*," and,

VOW (VOWS)
Nu 6: 2 a *v* of separation to the LORD
30: 2 When a man makes a *v*
Jdg 11:30 Jephthah made a *v* to the LORD:

VOWS (VOW)
Ps 116: 14 I will fulfill my *v* to the LORD
Pr 20:25 and only later to consider his *v*.

VULTURES
Mt 24:28 is a carcass, there the *v* will gather.

WAGE (WAGES WAGING)
2Co 10: 3 we do not *w* war as the world does.

WAGES (WAGE)
Mal 3: 5 who defraud laborers of their *w*,
Lk 10: 7 for the worker deserves his *w*.
Ro 4: 4 his *w* are not credited to him
6:23 For the *w* of sin is death,
1Ti 5:18 and "The worker deserves his *w*."

WAGING (WAGE)
Ro 7:23 *w* war against the law of my mind

WAILING
Ps 30:11 You turned my *w* into dancing;

WAIST
2Ki 1: 8 and with a leather belt around his *w*."
Mt 3: 4 he had a leather belt around his *w*.

WAIT (AWAITS WAITED WAITING WAITS)
Ps 27:14 *W* for the LORD;
130: 5 I *w* for the LORD, my soul waits,
Isa 30:18 Blessed are all who *w* for him!
Ac 1: 4 *w* for the gift my Father promised,
Ro 8:23 as we *w* eagerly for our adoption
1Th 1:10 and to *w* for his Son from heaven,
Tit 2:13 while we *w* for the blessed hope—

WAITED (WAIT)
Ps 40: 1 I *w* patiently for the LORD;

WAITING (WAIT)
Heb 9:28 to those who are *w* for him.

WAITS (WAIT)
Ro 8:19 creation *w* in eager expectation

WAKE (AWAKE WAKENS)
Eph 5:14 "*W* up, O sleeper,

WAKENS* (WAKE)
Isa 50: 4 He *w* me morning by morning,
50: 4 *w* my ear to listen like one being

WALK (WALKED WALKING WALKS)
Lev 26:12 I will *w* among you and be your
Dt 5:33 *W* in all the way that the LORD
6: 7 and when you *w* along the road,
10:12 to *w* in all his ways, to love him,
11:19 and when you *w* along the road,
11:22 to *w* in all his ways and to hold fast
26:17 and that you will *w* in his ways,
Jos 22: 5 to *w* in all his ways,
Ps 1: 1 who does not *w* in the counsel
15: 2 He whose *w* is blameless
23: 4 Even though I *w*
84:11 from those whose *w* is blameless.
89:15 who *w* in the light of your presence
119: 45 I will *w* about in freedom,
Pr 4:12 When you *w*, your steps will not be
6:22 When you *w*, they will guide you;
Isa 2: 3 so that we may *w* in his paths."
2: 5 let us *w* in the light of the LORD.
30:21 saying, "This is the way; *w* in it."
40:31 they will *w* and not be faint.
57: 2 Those who *w* uprightly
Jer 6:16 ask where the good way is, and *w*
Da 4:37 And those who *w* in pride he is able
Am 3: 3 Do two *w* together
Mic 4: 5 All the nations may *w*
6: 8 and to *w* humbly with your God.
Mk 2: 9 'Get up, take your mat and *w*'?
Jn 8:12 Whoever follows me will never *w*
1Jn 1: 6 with him yet *w* in the darkness,
1: 7 But if we *w* in the light,
2Jn : 6 his command is that you *w* in love.

WALKED (WALK)
Ge 5:24 Enoch *w* with God; then he was no
Jos 14: 9 which your feet have *w* will be your
Mt 14:29 *w* on the water and came toward Jesus.

WALKING (WALK)
1Ki 3: 3 love for the LORD by *w* according
Da 3:25 I see four men *w* around in the fire,
2Jn : 4 of your children *w* in the truth,

WALKS (WALK)
Pr 10: 9 The man of integrity *w* securely,
13:20 He who *w* with the wise grows wise
Isa 33:15 He who *w* righteously
Jn 11: 9 A man who *w* by day will not

WALL (WALLS)
Jos 6:20 *w* collapsed; so every man charged
Ne 2:17 let us rebuild the *w* of Jerusalem,
Eph 2:14 the dividing *w* of hostility,
Rev 21:12 It had a great, high *w*

WALLOWING
2Pe 2:22 back to her *w* in the mud."

WALLS (WALL)
Isa 58:12 be called Repairer of Broken *W*,
60:18 but you will call your *w* Salvation
Heb 11:30 By faith the *w* of Jericho fell,

WANDER (WANDERED)
Nu 32:13 he made them *w* in the desert forty
Jas 5:19 one of you should *w* from the truth

WANDERED (WANDER)
Eze 34: 6 My sheep *w* over all the mountains
Mt 18:12 go to look for the one that *w* off?
1Ti 6:10 have *w* from the faith and pierced
2Ti 2:18 who have *w* away from the truth.

WANT (WANTED WANTING WANTS)
1Sa 8:19 "We *w* a king over us.
Mt 19:21 Jesus answered, "If you *w*
Lk 19:14 'We don't *w* this man to be our king
Ro 7:15 For what I *w* to do I do not do,
13: 3 Do you *w* to be free from fear
2Co 12:14 what I *w* is not your possessions
Php 3:10 I *w* to know Christ and the power

WANTED (WANT)
1Co 12:18 of them, just as he *w* them to be.
Heb 6:17 Because God *w* to make

WANTING (WANT)
Da 5:27 weighed on the scales and found *w*.
2Pe 3: 9 with you, not *w* anyone to perish,

WANTS (WANT)
Mt 5:42 from the one who *w* to borrow
20:26 whoever *w* to become great
Mk 8:35 For whoever *w* to save his life will
10:43 whoever *w* to become great
Ro 9:18 he hardens whom he *w* to harden.
1Ti 2: 4 who *w* all men to be saved
1Pe 5: 2 you are willing, as God *w* you to be;

WAR (WARRIOR WARS)
Jos 11:23 Then the land had rest from *w*.
1Sa 15:18 make *w* on them until you have
Ps 68:30 the nations who delight in *w*.
120: 7 but when I speak, they are for *w*.
144: 1 who trains my hands for *w*,
Isa 2: 4 nor will they train for *w* anymore.
Da 9:26 *W* will continue until the end,
Ro 7:23 waging *w* against the law
2Co 10: 3 we do not wage *w* as the world does
1Pe 2:11 which *w* against your soul.
Rev 12: 7 And there was *w* in heaven.
19:11 With justice he judges and makes *w*

WARN* (WARNED WARNING WARNINGS)
Ex 19:21 *w* the people so they do not force
Nu 24:14 let me *w* you of what this people
1Sa 8: 9 but *w* them solemnly and let them
1Ki 2:42 swear by the LORD and *w* you,
2Ch 19:10 you are to *w* them not to sin
Ps 81: 8 O my people, and I will *w* you—
Jer 42:19 I *w* you today that you made a fatal
Eze 3:18 and you do not *w* him or speak out
3:19 But if you do *w* the wicked man
3:20 Since you did not *w* him, he will die
3:21 if you do *w* the righteous man not
33: 3 blows the trumpet to *w* the people,
33: 6 blow the trumpet to *w* the people
33: 9 if you do *w* the wicked man to turn
Lk 16:28 Let him *w* them, so that they will
Ac 4:17 we must *w* these men
1Co 4:14 but to *w* you, as my dear children.
Gal 5:21 I *w* you, as I did before, that those
1Th 5:14 brothers, *w* those who are idle,
2Th 3:15 an enemy, but *w* him as a brother.
2Ti 2:14 *W* them before God
Tit 3:10 and then *w* him a second time.
3:10 *W* a divisive person once,
Rev 22:18 I *w* everyone who hears the words

WARNED (WARN)
2Ki 17:13 The LORD *w* Israel and Judah
Ps 19:11 By them is your servant *w*;
Jer 22:21 I *w* you when you felt secure,
Mt 3: 7 Who *w* you to flee
1Th 4: 6 have already told you and *w* you.
Heb 11: 7 when *w* about things not yet seen,
12:25 they refused him who *w* them

WARNING (WARN)
Jer 6: 8 Take *w*, O Jerusalem,
1Ti 5:20 so that the others may take *w*.

WARNINGS (WARN)
1Co 10:11 and were written down as *w* for us,

WARRIOR (WAR)
Ex 15: 3 The LORD is a *w*;
1Ch 28: 3 you are a *w* and have shed blood.'
Pr 16:32 Better a patient man than a *w*,

WARS (WAR)
Ps 46: 9 He makes *w* cease to the ends
Mt 24: 6 You will hear of *w* and rumors of *w*,

WASH (WASHED WASHING)
Ps 51: 7 *w* me, and I will be whiter
Jer 4:14 *w* the evil from your heart
Jn 13: 5 and began to *w* his disciples' feet,
Ac 22:16 be baptized and *w* your sins away,
Jas 4: 8 *W* your hands, you sinners,
Rev 22:14 Blessed are those who *w* their robes

WASHED (WASH)
Ps 73:13 in vain have I *w* my hands
1Co 6:11 you were *w*, you were sanctified,
Heb 10:22 and having our bodies *w*
2Pe 2:22 and, "A sow that is *w* goes back
Rev 7:14 they have *w* their robes

WASHING (WASH)
Eph 5:26 cleansing her by the *w* with water
1Ti 5:10 showing hospitality, *w* the feet
Tit 3: 5 us through the *w* of rebirth

WASTED (WASTING)
Jn 6:12 Let nothing be *w*."

WASTING (WASTED)
2Co 4:16 Though outwardly we are *w* away,

WATCH (WATCHER WATCHES WATCHING WATCHMAN)
Ge 31:49 "May the LORD keep *w*
Ps 90: 4 or like a *w* in the night.
141: 3 keep *w* over the door of my lips.
Pr 4: 6 love her, and she will *w* over you.
6:22 when you sleep, they will *w*
Jer 31:10 will *w* over his flock like a shepherd
Mic 7: 7 I *w* in hope for the LORD,
Mt 24:42 "Therefore keep *w*, because you do
26:41 *W* and pray so that you will not fall
Mk 13:35 "Therefore keep *w* because you do
Lk 2: 8 keeping *w* over their flocks at night
1Ti 4:16 *W* your life and doctrine closely.
Heb 13:17 They keep *w* over you

WATCHER* (WATCH)
Job 7:20 O *w* of men?

WATCHES* (WATCH)
Nu 19: 5 While he *w*, the heifer is
Job 24:15 The eye of the adulterer *w* for dusk;
Ps 1: 6 For the LORD *w* over the way
33:14 from his dwelling place he *w*
63: 6 of you through the *w* of the night.
119:148 through the *w* of the night,
121: 3 he who *w* over you will not slumber
121: 4 indeed, he who *w* over Israel
121: 5 The LORD *w* over you—
127: 1 Unless the LORD *w* over the city,
145: 20 LORD *w* over all who love him,
146: 9 The LORD *w* over the alien
Pr 31:27 She *w* over the affairs
Ecc 11: 4 Whoever *w* the wind will not plant;
La 2:19 as the *w* of the night begin;
4:16 he no longer *w* over them.

WATCHING (WATCH)
Lk 12:37 whose master finds them *w*

WATCHMAN (WATCH)
Eze 3:17 I have made you a *w* for the house
33: 6 but I will hold the *w* accountable

WATER (WATERED WATERING WATERS WELL-WATERED)
Ex 7:20 all the *w* was changed into blood
17: 1 but there was no *w* for the people
Nu 20: 2 there was no *w* for the community,
Ps 1: 3 like a tree planted by streams of *w*,
22:14 I am poured out like *w*,
42: 1 As the deer pants for streams of *w*,
Pr 25:21 if he is thirsty, give him *w* to drink.
Isa 12: 3 With joy you will draw *w*
30:20 of adversity and the *w* of affliction,
32: 2 like streams of *w* in the desert
49:10 and lead them beside springs of *w*.
Jer 2:13 broken cisterns that cannot hold *w*.
17: 8 will be like a tree planted by the *w*
31: 9 I will lead them beside streams of *w*
Eze 36:25 I will sprinkle clean *w* on you,
Zec 14: 8 On that day living *w* will flow out
Mt 14:29 walked on the *w* and came toward Jesus.
Mk 9:41 anyone who gives you a cup of *w*
Lk 5: 4 to Simon, "Put out into deep *w*,
Jn 3: 5 unless he is born of *w* and the Spirit.
4:10 he would have given you living *w*."
7:38 streams of living *w* will flow
Eph 5:26 washing with *w* through the word,
Heb 10:22 our bodies washed with pure *w*.
1Pe 3:21 this *w* symbolizes baptism that now
2Pe 2:17 These men are springs without *w*
1Jn 5: 6 This is the one who came by *w*
5: 6 come by *w* only, but by *w*
5: 8 the Spirit, the *w* and the blood;
Rev 7:17 to springs of living *w*.
21: 6 cost from the spring of the *w* of life.

WATERED (WATER)
1Co 3: 6 I planted the seed, Apollos *w* it,

WATERING (WATER)
Isa 55:10 it without *w* the earth

WATERS (WATER)
Ps 23: 2 he leads me beside quiet *w*,
Ecc 11: 1 Cast your bread upon the *w*,
SS 8: 7 Many *w* cannot quench love;
Isa 11: 9 as the *w* cover the sea.
43: 2 When you pass through the *w*,

Isa 55: 1 come to the *w;*
58:11 like a spring whose *w* never fail.
Hab 2:14 as the *w* cover the sea.
1Co 3: 7 plants nor he who *w* is anything,

WAVE (WAVES)
Lev 23:11 He is to *w* the sheaf
Jas 1: 6 he who doubts is like a *w* of the sea,

WAVER*
1Ki 18:21 "How long will you *w*
Ro 4:20 Yet he did not *w* through unbelief

WAVES (WAVE)
Isa 57:20 whose *w* cast up mire and mud.
Mt 8:27 Even the winds and the *w* obey him
Eph 4:14 tossed back and forth by the *w,*

WAY (WAYS)
Ex 13:21 of cloud to guide them on their *w*
18:20 and show them the *w* to live
Dt 1:33 to show you the *w* you should go.
32: 6 Is this the *w* you repay the LORD,
1Sa 12:23 I will teach you the *w* that is good
2Sa 22:31 "As for God, his *w* is perfect;
1Ki 8:23 wholeheartedly in your *w.*
8:36 Teach them the right *w* to live,
Job 23:10 But he knows the *w* that I take;
Ps 1: 1 or stand in the *w* of sinners
32: 8 teach you in the *w* you should go;
37: 5 Commit your *w* to the LORD;
86:11 Teach me your *w,* O LORD,
119: 9 can a young man keep his *w* pure?
139: 24 See if there is any offensive *w* in me
Pr 4:11 I guide you in the *w* of wisdom
12:15 The *w* of a fool seems right to him,
14:12 There is a *w* that seems right
16:17 he who guards his *w* guards his life.
19: 2 nor to be hasty and miss the *w.*
22: 6 Train a child in the *w* he should go,
30:19 and the *w* of a man with a maiden.
Isa 30:21 saying, "This is the *w;* walk in it."
35: 8 it will be called the *W* of Holiness.
40: 3 the *w* for the LORD;
48:17 you in the *w* you should go.
53: 6 each of us has turned to his own *w;*
55: 7 Let the wicked forsake his *w*
Jer 5:31 and my people love it this *w.*
Mal 3: 1 who will prepare the *w* before me.
Mt 3: 3 'Prepare the *w* for the Lord,
Lk 7:27 who will prepare your *w* before you
Jn 14: 6 "I am the *w* and the truth
Ac 1:11 in the same *w* you have seen him go
9: 2 any there who belonged to the *W,*
24:14 of the *W,* which they call a sect.
1Co 10:13 also provide a *w* out so that you can
12:31 will show you the most excellent *w.*
14: 1 Follow the *w* of love and eagerly
Col 1:10 and may please him in every *w:*
Tit 2:10 that in every *w* they will make
Heb 4:15 who has been tempted in every *w,*
9: 8 was showing by this that the *w*
10:20 and living *w* opened for us
13:18 desire to live honorably in every *w.*

WAYS (WAY)
Ex 33:13 teach me your *w* so I may know
Dt 10:12 to walk in all his *w,* to love him,
26:17 and that you will walk in his *w,*
30:16 in his *w,* and to keep his commands
32: 4 and all his *w* are just.
Jos 22: 5 in all his *w,* to obey his commands,
2Ch 11:17 walking in the *w* of David
Job 34:21 "His eyes are on the *w* of men;
Ps 25: 4 Show me your *w,* O LORD,
25:10 All the *w* of the LORD are loving
37: 7 fret when men succeed in their *w,*
51:13 I will teach transgressors your *w,*
77:13 Your *w,* O God, are holy.
119: 59 I have considered my *w*
139: 3 you are familiar with all my *w.*
145: 17 The LORD is righteous in all his *w*
Pr 3: 6 in all your *w* acknowledge him,
4:26 and take only *w* that are firm.
5:21 For a man's *w* are in full view
16: 2 All a man's *w* seem innocent
16: 7 When a man's *w* are pleasing
Isa 2: 3 He will teach us his *w,*
55: 8 neither are your *w* my *w,"*
Eze 28:15 You were blameless in your *w*
33: 8 out to dissuade him from his *w,*
Hos 14: 9 The *w* of the LORD are right;

Ro 1:30 they invent *w* of doing evil;
Jas 3: 2 We all stumble in many *w.*

WEAK (WEAKER WEAKNESS WEAKNESSES)
Ps 41: 1 is he who has regard for the *w;*
72:13 He will take pity on the *w*
82: 3 Defend the cause of the *w*
Eze 34: 4 You have not strengthened the *w*
Mt 26:41 spirit is willing, but the body is *w."*
Ac 20:35 of hard work we must help the *w,*
Ro 14: 1 Accept him whose faith is *w,*
15: 1 to bear with the failings of the *w*
1Co 1:27 God chose the *w* things
8: 9 become a stumbling block to the *w.*
9:22 To the *w* I became *w,* to win the *w.*
11:30 That is why many among you are *w*
2Co 12:10 For when I am *w,* then I am strong.
1Th 5:14 help the *w,* be patient
Heb 12:12 your feeble arms and *w* knees.

WEAK-WILLED (WILL)
2Ti 3: 6 and gain control over *w* women,

WEAKER* (WEAK)
2Sa 3: 1 the house of Saul grew *w* and *w.*
1Co 12:22 seem to be *w* are indispensable,
1Pe 3: 7 them with respect as the *w* partner

WEAKNESS* (WEAK)
La 1: 6 in *w* they have fled
Ro 8:26 the Spirit helps us in our *w.*
1Co 1:25 and the *w* of God is stronger
2: 3 I came to you in *w* and fear,
15:43 it is sown in *w,* it is raised in power;
2Co 11:30 boast of the things that show my *w.*
12: 9 for my power is made perfect in *w*
13: 4 he was crucified in *w,* yet he lives
Heb 5: 2 since he himself is subject to *w.*
11:34 whose *w* was turned to strength;

WEAKNESSES* (WEAK)
2Co 12: 5 about myself, except about my *w.*
12: 9 all the more gladly about my *w,*
12:10 I delight in *w,* in insults,
Heb 4:15 unable to sympathize with our *w,*

WEALTH
Dt 8:18 gives you the ability to produce *w,*
2Ch 1:11 and you have not asked for *w,*
Ps 39: 6 he heaps up *w,* not knowing who
Pr 3: 9 Honor the LORD with your *w,*
10: 4 but diligent hands bring *w.*
11: 4 *W* is worthless in the day of wrath,
13: 7 to be poor, yet has great *w.*
15:16 than great *w* with turmoil.
22: 4 bring *w* and honor and life.
Ecc 5:10 whoever loves *w* is never satisfied
5:13 *w* hoarded to the harm of its owner,
SS 8: 7 all the *w* of his house for love,
Mt 13:22 and the deceitfulness of *w* choke it,
Mk 10:22 away sad, because he had great *w.*
12:44 They all gave out of their *w;* but she
Lk 15:13 and there squandered his *w*
1Ti 6:17 nor to put their hope in *w,*
Jas 5: 2 Your *w* has rotted, and moths have
5: 3 You have hoarded *w*

WEAPON (WEAPONS)
Ne 4:17 work with one hand and held a *w*

WEAPONS (WEAPON)
Ecc 9:18 Wisdom is better than *w* of war,
2Co 6: 7 with *w* of righteousness
10: 4 The *w* we fight with are not

WEAR (WEARING)
Dt 8: 4 Your clothes did not *w* out
22: 5 nor a man *w* women's clothing,
Ps 102: 26 they will all *w* out like a garment.
Pr 23: 4 Do not *w* yourself out to get rich;
Isa 51: 6 the earth will *w* out like a garment
Heb 1:11 they will all *w* out like a garment.
Rev 3:18 and white clothes to *w,*

WEARIES (WEARY)
Ecc 12:12 and much study *w* the body.

WEARING (WEAR)
Jn 19: 5 When Jesus came out *w* the crown
Jas 2: 3 attention to the man *w* fine clothes
1Pe 3: 3 as braided hair and the *w*
Rev 7: 9 They were *w* white robes

WEARY (WEARIES)
Isa 40:28 He will not grow tired or *w,*
40:31 they will run and not grow *w,*

Isa 50: 4 know the word that sustains the *w.*
Mt 11:28 all you who are *w* and burdened,
Gal 6: 9 Let us not become *w* in doing good,
Heb 12: 3 so that you will not grow *w*
Rev 2: 3 my name, and have not grown *w.*

WEDDING
Mt 22:11 who was not wearing *w* clothes.
Rev 19: 7 For the *w* of the Lamb has come,

WEEDS
Mt 13:25 and sowed *w* among the wheat,

WEEK
Mt 28: 1 at dawn on the first day of the *w,*
1Co 16: 2 On the first day of every *w,*

WEEP (WEEPING WEPT)
Ecc 3: 4 a time to *w* and a time to laugh,
Lk 6:21 Blessed are you who *w* now,
23:28 *w* for yourselves and for your

WEEPING (WEEP)
Ps 30: 5 *w* may remain for a night,
126: 6 He who goes out *w,*
Jer 31:15 Rachel *w* for her children
Mt 2:18 Rachel *w* for her children
8:12 where there will be *w* and gnashing

WEIGH (OUTWEIGHS WEIGHED WEIGHS WEIGHTIER WEIGHTS)
1Co 14:29 others should *w* carefully what is

WEIGHED (WEIGH)
Job 28:15 nor can its price be *w* in silver.
Da 5:27 You have been *w* on the scales
Lk 21:34 or your hearts will be *w*

WEIGHS (WEIGH)
Pr 12:25 An anxious heart *w* a man down,
15:28 of the righteous *w* its answers,
21: 2 but the LORD *w* the heart.
24:12 not he who *w* the heart perceive

WEIGHTIER* (WEIGH)
Jn 5:36 "I have testimony *w* than that

WEIGHTS (WEIGH)
Lev 19:36 Use honest scales and honest *w,*
Dt 25:13 Do not have two differing *w*
Pr 11: 1 but accurate *w* are his delight.

WELCOME (WELCOMES)
Mk 9:37 welcomes me does not *w* me
2Pe 1:11 and you will receive a rich *w*

WELCOMES (WELCOME)
Mt 18: 5 whoever *w* a little child like this
2Jn :11 Anyone who *w* him shares

WELL (WELLED WELLING WELLS)
Mt 15:31 crippled made *w,* the lame walking
Lk 14: 5 falls into a *w* on the Sabbath day,
17:19 your faith has made you *w."*
Jas 5:15 in faith will make the sick person *w*

WELL-WATERED (WATER)
Isa 58:11 You will be like a *w* garden,

WELLED* (WELL)
2Co 8: 2 and their extreme poverty *w* up

WELLING* (WELL)
Jn 4:14 of water *w* up to eternal life."

WELLS (WELL)
Isa 12: 3 from the *w* of salvation.

WELLSPRING* (SPRING)
Pr 4:23 for it is the *w* of life.

WEPT (WEEP)
Ps 137: 1 of Babylon we sat and *w*
Lk 22:62 And he went outside and *w* bitterly
Jn 11:35 Jesus *w.*

WEST
Ps 103: 12 as far as the east is from the *w,*
107: 3 from east and *w,* from north

WHEAT
Mt 3:12 gathering his *w* into the barn
13:25 and sowed weeds among the *w,*
Lk 22:31 Satan has asked to sift you as *w.*
Jn 12:24 a kernel of *w* falls to the ground

WHEELS
Eze 1:16 appearance and structure of the *w:*

WHIRLWIND (WIND)
2Ki 2: 1 to take Elijah up to heaven in a *w,*

Hos 8: 7 and reap the *w*.
Na 1: 3 His way is in the *w* and the storm,

WHISPER (WHISPERED)
1Ki 19:12 And after the fire came a gentle *w*.
Job 26:14 how faint the *w* we hear of him!
Ps 107: 29 He stilled the storm to a *w*;

WHISPERED (WHISPER)
Mt 10:27 speak in the daylight; what is *w*

WHITE (WHITER)
Isa 1:18 they shall be as *w* as snow;
Da 7: 9 His clothing was as *w* as snow;
7: 9 the hair of his head was *w* like wool
Mt 28: 3 and his clothes were *w* as snow.
Rev 1:14 hair were *w* like wool, as *w* as snow,
3: 4 dressed in *w*, for they are worthy.
6: 2 and there before me was a *w* horse!
7:13 "These in *w* robes—who are they,
19:11 and there before me was a *w* horse,
20:11 Then I saw a great *w* throne

WHITER (WHITE)
Ps 51: 7 and I will be *w* than snow.

WHOLE
Ge 1:29 plant on the face of the *w* earth
2: 6 and watered the *w* surface
11: 1 Now the *w* world had one language
Ex 12:47 The *w* community
19: 5 Although the *w* earth is mine,
Lev 16:17 and the *w* community of Israel.
Nu 14:21 of the LORD fills the *w* earth,
32:13 until the *w* generation
Dt 13:16 *w* burnt offering to the LORD your
19: 8 gives you the *w* land he promised
Jos 2: 3 come to spy out the *w* land."
1Sa 1:28 For his *w* life he will be given
17:46 the *w* world will know that there is
1Ki 10:24 The *w* world sought audience
2Ki 21: 8 and will keep the *w* Law that my
Ps 72:19 may the *w* earth be filled
Pr 4:22 and health to a man's *w* body.
8:31 rejoicing in his *w* world
Ecc 12:13 for this is the *w* duty of man.
Isa 1: 5 Your *w* head is injured,
6: 3 the *w* earth is full of his glory."
14:26 plan determined for the *w* world;
Eze 34: 6 were scattered over the *w* earth,
37:11 these bones are the *w* house
Da 2:35 mountain and filled the *w* earth.
Zep 1:18 the *w* world will be consumed,
Zec 14: 9 will be king over the *w* earth.
Mal 3:10 the *w* tithe into the storehouse,
Mt 5:29 than for your *w* body to be thrown
6:22 your *w* body will be full of light.
16:26 for a man if he gains the *w* world,
24:14 will be preached in the *w* world
Lk 21:35 live on the face of the *w* earth.
Jn 12:19 Look how the *w* world has gone
13:10 to wash his feet; his *w* body is clean
21:25 the *w* world would not have room
Ac 17:26 they should inhabit the *w* earth;
20:27 proclaim to you the *w* will of God.
Ro 1: 9 whom I serve with my *w* heart
3:19 and the *w* world held accountable
8:22 know that the *w* creation has been
1Co 4: 9 made a spectacle to the *w* universe,
12:17 If the *w* body were an ear,
Gal 3:22 declares that the *w* world is
5: 3 obligated to obey the *w* law.
Eph 4:10 in order to fill the *w* universe.)
4:13 attaining to the *w* measure
1Th 5:23 May your *w* spirit, soul
Jas 2:10 For whoever keeps the *w* law
1Jn 2: 2 but also for the sins of the *w* world.
Rev 3:10 going to come upon the *w* world

WHOLEHEARTED* (HEART)
2Ki 20: 3 you faithfully and with *w* devotion
1Ch 28: 9 and serve him with *w* devotion
29:19 my son Solomon the *w* devotion
Isa 38: 3 you faithfully and with *w* devotion

WHOLEHEARTEDLY* (HEART)
Nu 14:24 a different spirit and follows me *w*,
32:11 they have not followed me *w*,
32:12 for they followed the LORD *w*.'
Dt 1:36 because he followed the LORD *w*
Jos 14: 8 followed the LORD my God *w*.
14: 9 followed the LORD my God *w*.'
14:14 the LORD, the God of Israel, *w*.

1Ki 8:23 with your servants who continue *w*
1Ch 29: 9 for they had given freely and *w*
2Ch 6:14 with your servants who continue *w*
15:15 oath because they had sworn it *w*.
19: 9 and *w* in the fear of the LORD.
25: 2 in the eyes of the LORD, but not *w*
31:21 he sought his God and worked *w*.
Ro 6:17 you *w* obeyed the form of teaching
Eph 6: 7 Serve *w*, as if you were serving

WHOLESOME*
2Ki 2:22 And the water has remained *w*
2Pe 3: 1 to stimulate you to *w* thinking.

WICK
Isa 42: 3 a smoldering *w* he will not snuff out
Mt 12:20 a smoldering *w* he will not snuff out

WICKED (WICKEDNESS)
Ge 13:13 Now the men of Sodom were *w*
39: 9 How then could I do such a *w* thing
Ex 23: 1 Do not help a *w* man
Nu 14:35 things to this whole *w* community,
Dt 15: 9 not to harbor this *w* thought:
Jdg 19:22 some of the *w* men
1Sa 2:12 Eli's sons were *w* men; they had no
15:18 completely destroy those *w* people,
25:17 He is such a *w* man that no one can
2Sa 13:12 in Israel! Don't do this *w* thing.
2Ki 17:11 They did *w* things that provoked
2Ch 7:14 and turn from their *w* ways,
19: 2 "Should you help the *w*
Ne 13:17 "What is this *w* thing you are doing
Ps 1: 1 walk in the counsel of the *w*
1: 5 Therefore the *w* will not stand
7: 9 to an end the violence of the *w*
10:13 Why does the *w* man revile God?
11: 5 the *w* and those who love violence
12: 8 The *w* freely strut about
26: 5 and refuse to sit with the *w*.
32:10 Many are the woes of the *w*,
36: 1 concerning the sinfulness of the *w*:
37:13 but the Lord laughs at the *w*,
49: 5 when *w* deceivers surround me—
50:16 But to the *w*, God says:
58: 3 Even from birth the *w* go astray;
73: 3 when I saw the prosperity of the *w*.
82: 2 and show partiality to the *w*? *Selah*
112: 10 the longings of the *w* will come
119: 61 Though the *w* bind me with ropes,
119:155 Salvation is far from the *w*,
140: 8 do not grant the *w* their desires,
141: 10 Let the *w* fall into their own nets,
146: 9 but he frustrates the ways of the *w*.
Pr 2:12 you from the ways of *w* men,
4:14 Do not set foot on the path of the *w*
6:18 a heart that devises *w* schemes,
9: 7 whoever rebukes a *w* man incurs
10:20 the heart of the *w* is of little value.
10:28 the hopes of the *w* come to nothing
11: 5 *w* are brought down by their own
11:10 when the *w* perish, there are shouts
11:21 The *w* will not go unpunished,
12: 5 but the advice of the *w* is deceitful.
12:10 the kindest acts of the *w* are cruel.
14:19 the *w* at the gates of the righteous.
15: 3 keeping watch on the *w*
15:26 detests the thoughts of the *w*,
21:10 The *w* man craves evil;
21:29 A *w* man puts up a bold front,
28: 1 *w* man flees though no one pursues,
28: 4 who forsake the law praise the *w*,
29: 7 but the *w* have no such concern.
29:16 When the *w* thrive, so does sin,
29:27 the *w* detest the upright.
Isa 11: 4 breath of his lips he will slay the *w*.
13:11 the *w* for their sins.
26:10 Though grace is shown to the *w*,
48:22 says the LORD, "for the *w*."
53: 9 He was assigned a grave with the *w*
55: 7 Let the *w* forsake his way
57:20 But the *w* are like the tossing sea,
Jer 35:15 of you must turn from your *w* ways
Eze 3:18 that *w* man will die for his sin,
13:22 you encouraged the *w* not to turn
14: 7 and puts a *w* stumbling block
18:21 "But if a *w* man turns away
18:23 pleasure in the death of the *w*?
21:25 "'O profane and *w* prince of Israel,
33: 8 When I say to the *w*, 'O *w* man,
33:11 pleasure in the death of the *w*,

Eze 33:14 to the *w* man, 'You will surely die,'
33:19 And if a *w* man turns away
Da 12:10 but the *w* will continue to be *w*.
Mt 12:39 *w* and adulterous generation asks
12:45 be with this *w* generation."
12:45 with it seven other spirits more *w*
Lk 6:35 he is kind to the ungrateful and *w*.
Ac 2:23 and you, with the help of *w* men,
Ro 4: 5 but trusts God who justifies the *w*,
1Co 5:13 "Expel the *w* man from among you
6: 9 not know that the *w* will not inherit
Rev 2: 2 that you cannot tolerate *w* men,

WICKEDNESS (WICKED)
Ge 6: 5 The LORD saw how great man's *w*
Ex 34: 7 and forgiving *w*, rebellion and sin.
Lev 16:21 and confess over it all the *w*
19:29 to prostitution and be filled with *w*.
Dt 9: 4 it is on account of the *w*
Ne 9: 2 and confessed their sins and the *w*
Ps 45: 7 You love righteousness and hate *w*;
92:15 he is my Rock, and there is no *w*
Pr 13: 6 but *w* overthrows the sinner.
Jer 3: 2 land with your prostitution and *w*.
8: 6 No one repents of his *w*,
14:20 O LORD, we acknowledge our *w*
Eze 18:20 the *w* of the wicked will be charged
28:15 created till *w* was found in you.
33:19 wicked man turns away from his *w*
Da 4:27 and your *w* by being kind
9:24 to atone for *w*, to bring
Jnh 1: 2 its *w* has come up before me."
Mt 24:12 Because of the increase of *w*,
Lk 11:39 inside you are full of greed and *w*.
Ac 1:18 (With the reward he got for his *w*,
Ro 1:18 who suppress the truth by their *w*,
1Co 5: 8 the yeast of malice and *w*,
2Co 6:14 what do righteousness and *w* have
2Ti 2:19 of the Lord must turn away from *w*
Tit 2:14 for us to redeem us from all *w*
Heb 1: 9 loved righteousness and hated *w*;
8:12 For I will forgive their *w*
2Pe 2:15 who loved the wages of *w*.

WIDE
Ps 81:10 Open *w* your mouth and I will fill it
Isa 54: 2 stretch your tent curtains *w*,
Mt 7:13 For *w* is the gate and broad is
2Co 6:13 my children—open *w* your hearts
Eph 3:18 to grasp how *w* and long and high

WIDOW (WIDOWS)
Ex 22:22 "Do not take advantage of a *w*
Dt 10:18 cause of the fatherless and the *w*,
Ps 146: 9 sustains the fatherless and the *w*,
Isa 1:17 plead the case of the *w*.
Lk 21: 2 saw a poor *w* put in two very small
1Ti 5: 4 But if a *w* has children

WIDOWS (WIDOW)
Ps 68: 5 to the fatherless, a defender of *w*,
Ac 6: 1 their *w* were being overlooked
1Co 7: 8 to the unmarried and the *w* I say:
1Ti 5: 3 to those *w* who are really
Jas 1:27 look after orphans and *w*

WIFE (WIVES WIVES')
Ge 2:24 and mother and be united to his *w*,
19:26 But Lot's *w* looked back,
24:67 she became his *w*, and he loved her;
Ex 20:17 shall not covet your neighbor's *w*,
Lev 20:10 adultery with another man's *w*—
Dt 5:21 shall not covet your neighbor's *w*.
24: 5 happiness to the *w* he has married.
Ru 4:13 took Ruth and she became his *w*.
Pr 5:18 in the *w* of your youth.
12: 4 *w* of noble character is her
18:22 He who finds a *w* finds what is
19:13 quarrelsome *w* is like a constant
31:10 *w* of noble character who can find?
Hos 1: 2 take to yourself an adulterous *w*
Mal 2:14 the witness between you and the *w*
Mt 1:20 to take Mary home as your *w*,
19: 3 for a man to divorce his *w* for any
Lk 17:32 Remember Lot's *w*! Whoever tries
18:29 or *w* or brothers or parents
1Co 7: 2 each man should have his own *w*,
7:33 how he can please his *w*—
Eph 5:23 the husband is the head of the *w*
5:33 must love his *w* as he loves himself,
1Ti 3: 2 husband of but one *w*, temperate,
Rev 21: 9 I will show you the bride, the *w*

WILD
Ge 1:25 God made the *w* animals according
8: 1 Noah and all the *w* animals
Lk 15:13 squandered his wealth in *w* living.
Ro 11:17 and you, though a *w* olive shoot,

WILL (WEAK-WILLED WILLFUL WILLING WILLINGNESS)
Ps 40: 8 I desire to do your *w*, O my God;
143: 10 Teach me to do your *w*,
Isa 53:10 Yet it was the LORD's *w*
Mt 6:10 your *w* be done
7:21 who does the *w* of my Father
10:29 apart from the *w* of your Father.
12:50 does the *w* of my Father
26:39 Yet not as I *w*, but as you *w*."
26:42 I drink it, may your *w* be done."
Jn 6:38 but to do the *w* of him who sent me.
7:17 If anyone chooses to do God's *w*,
Ac 20:27 to you the whole *w* of God.
Ro 12: 2 and approve what God's *w* is—
1Co 7:37 but has control over his own *w*,
Eph 5:17 understand what the Lord's *w* is.
Php 2:13 for it is God who works in you to *w*
1Th 4: 3 God's *w* that you should be sanctified:
5:18 for this is God's *w* for you
2Ti 2:26 has taken them captive to do his *w*.
Heb 2: 4 distributed according to his *w*.
9:16 In the case of a *w*, it is necessary
10: 7 I have come to do your *w*, O God
13:21 everything good for doing his *w*,
Jas 4:15 "If it is the Lord's *w*,
1Pe 3:17 It is better, if it is God's *w*,
4: 2 but rather for the *w* of God.
2Pe 1:21 never had its origin in the *w*
1Jn 5:14 we ask anything according to his *w*,
Rev 4:11 and by your *w* they were created

WILLFUL (WILL)
Ps 19:13 Keep your servant also from *w* sins;

WILLING (WILL)
1Ch 28: 9 devotion and with a *w* mind,
29: 5 who is *w* to consecrate himself
Ps 51:12 grant me a *w* spirit, to sustain me.
Da 3:28 were *w* to give up their lives rather
Mt 18:14 Father in heaven is not *w* that any
23:37 her wings, but you were not *w*.
26:41 The spirit is *w*, but the body is weak
1Ti 6:18 and to be generous and *w* to share.
1Pe 5: 2 but because you are *w*,

WILLINGNESS* (WILL)
2Co 8:11 so that your eager *w*
8:12 For if the *w* is there, the gift is

WIN (WINS WON)
1Co 9:19 myself a slave to everyone, to *w*
Php 3:14 on toward the goal to *w* the prize
1Th 4:12 your daily life may *w* the respect

WIND (WHIRLWIND WINDS)
Ps 1: 4 that the *w* blows away.
Ecc 2:11 meaningless, a chasing after the *w*;
Hos 8: 7 "They sow the *w*
Mk 4:41 Even the *w* and the waves obey
Jn 3: 8 The *w* blows wherever it pleases.
Eph 4:14 and there by every *w* of teaching
Jas 1: 6 blown and tossed by the *w*.

WINDOW
Jos 2:21 she tied the scarlet cord in the *w*.
Ac 20: 9 in a *w* was a young man named
2Co 11:33 in a basket from a *w* in the wall

WINDS (WIND)
Ps 104: 4 He makes *w* his messengers,
Mt 24:31 gather his elect from the four *w*,
Heb 1: 7 "He makes his angels *w*,

WINE
Ps 104: 15 *w* that gladdens the heart of man,
Pr 20: 1 *W* is a mocker and beer a brawler;
23:20 join those who drink too much *w*
23:31 Do not gaze at *w* when it is red,
31: 6 *w* to those who are in anguish;
SS 1: 2 your love is more delightful than *w*.
Isa 28: 7 And these also stagger from *w*
55: 1 Come, buy *w* and milk
Mt 9:17 Neither do men pour new *w*
Lk 23:36 They offered him *w* vinegar
Jn 2: 3 When the *w* was gone, Jesus'
Ro 14:21 not to eat meat or drink *w*
Eph 5:18 on *w*, which leads to debauchery.
1Ti 5:23 a little *w* because of your stomach
Rev 16:19 with the *w* of the fury of his wrath.

WINEPRESS
Isa 63: 2 like those of one treading the *w*?
Rev 19:15 He treads the *w* of the fury

WINESKINS
Mt 9:17 do men pour new wine into old *w*.

WINGS
Ex 19: 4 and how I carried you on eagles' *w*
Ru 2:12 under whose *w* you have come
Ps 17: 8 hide me in the shadow of your *w*
91: 4 under his *w* you will find refuge;
Isa 6: 2 him were seraphs, each with six *w*:
40:31 They will soar on *w* like eagles;
Eze 1: 6 of them had four faces and four *w*.
Zec 5: 9 in their *w*! They had *w* like those
Mal 4: 2 rise with healing in its *w*.
Lk 13:34 hen gathers her chicks under her *w*,
Rev 4: 8 the four living creatures had six *w*

WINS (WIN)
Pr 11:30 and he who *w* souls is wise.

WINTER
Mk 13:18 that this will not take place in *w*,

WIPE (WIPED)
Isa 25: 8 The Sovereign LORD will *w* away
Rev 7:17 God will *w* away every tear
21: 4 He will *w* every tear

WIPED (WIPE)
Lk 7:38 Then she *w* them with her hair,
Ac 3:19 so that your sins may be *w* out,

WISDOM (WISE)
Ge 3: 6 and also desirable for gaining *w*,
1Ki 4:29 God gave Solomon *w* and very
2Ch 1:10 Give me *w* and knowledge,
Ps 51: 6 you teach me *w* in the inmost place
111: 10 of the LORD is the beginning of *w*;
Pr 2: 6 For the LORD gives *w*,
3:13 Blessed is the man who finds *w*,
4: 7 *W* is supreme; therefore get
8:11 for *w* is more precious than rubies,
11: 2 but with humility comes *w*.
13:10 *w* is found in those who take advice
23:23 get *w*, discipline and understanding
29: 3 A man who loves *w* brings joy
29:15 The rod of correction imparts *w*,
31:26 She speaks with *w*,
Isa 11: 2 Spirit of *w* and of understanding,
28:29 in counsel and magnificent in *w*.
Jer 10:12 he founded the world by his *w*
Mic 6: 9 and to fear your name is *w*—
Mt 11:19 But *w* is proved right by her actions
Lk 2:52 And Jesus grew in *w* and stature,
Ac 6: 3 known to be full of the Spirit and *w*.
Ro 11:33 the depth of the riches of the *w*
1Co 1:17 not with words of human *w*,
1:30 who has become for us *w* from God
12: 8 through the Spirit the message of *w*
Eph 1:17 may give you the Spirit of *w*
Col 2: 3 are hidden all the treasures of *w*
2:23 indeed have an appearance of *w*,
Jas 1: 5 of you lacks *w*, he should ask God,
3:13 in the humility that comes from *w*.
Rev 5:12 and wealth and *w* and strength

WISE (WISDOM WISER)
1Ki 3:12 give you a *w* and discerning heart,
Job 5:13 He catches the *w* in their craftiness
Ps 19: 7 making *w* the simple.
Pr 3: 7 Do not be *w* in your own eyes;
9: 8 rebuke a *w* man and he will love
10: 1 A *w* son brings joy to his father,
11:30 and he who wins souls is *w*.
13: 1 A *w* son heeds his father's
13:20 He who walks with the *w* grows *w*,
16:23 A *w* man's heart guides his mouth,
17:28 Even a fool is thought *w*
Ecc 9:17 The quiet words of the *w* are more
Jer 9:23 "Let not the *w* man boast
Eze 28: 6 " 'Because you think you are *w*,
Da 2:21 He gives wisdom to the *w*
12: 3 Those who are *w* will shine like
Mt 11:25 hidden these things from the *w*
25: 2 them were foolish and five were *w*.
1Co 1:19 I will destroy the wisdom of the *w*;
1:27 things of the world to shame the *w*;
1Co 3:19 He catches the *w* in their craftiness
Eph 5:15 but as *w*, making the most
2Ti 3:15 able to make you *w* for salvation
Jas 3:13 Who is *w* and understanding

WISER (WISE)
Pr 9: 9 a wise man and he will be *w* still;
1Co 1:25 of God is *w* than man's wisdom,

WISH (WISHES)
Jn 15: 7 ask whatever you *w*, and it will be
Ro 9: 3 For I could *w* that I myself were
Rev 3:15 I *w* you were either one

WISHES (WISH)
Rev 22:17 let him come; and whoever *w*,

WITCHCRAFT
Dt 18:10 engages in *w*, or casts spells,
Gal 5:20 idolatry and *w*; hatred, discord,

WITHDREW
Lk 5:16 But Jesus often *w* to lonely places

WITHER (WITHERS)
Ps 1: 3 and whose leaf does not *w*.
37:19 In times of disaster they will not *w*;

WITHERS (WITHER)
Isa 40: 7 The grass *w* and the flowers fall,
1Pe 1:24 the grass *w* and the flowers fall,

WITHHELD (WITHHOLD)
Ge 22:12 you have not *w* from me your son,

WITHHOLD (WITHHELD WITHHOLDS)
Ps 84:11 no good thing does he *w*
Pr 23:13 Do not *w* discipline from a child;

WITHHOLDS (WITHHOLD)
Dt 27:19 "Cursed is the man who *w* justice

WITNESS (EYEWITNESSES WITNESSES)
Pr 12:17 truthful *w* gives honest testimony,
19: 9 A false *w* will not go unpunished,
Jn 1: 8 he came only as a *w* to the light.

WITNESSES (WITNESS)
Dt 19:15 by the testimony of two or three *w*.
Mt 18:16 by the testimony of two or three *w*.'
Ac 1: 8 and you will be my *w* in Jerusalem,

WIVES (WIFE)
Eph 5:22 *W*, submit to your husbands
5:25 love your *w*, just as Christ loved
1Pe 3: 1 words by the behavior of their *w*,

WIVES' (WIFE)
1Ti 4: 7 with godless myths and old *w* tales

WOE
Isa 6: 5 "*W* to me!" I cried.
Eze 34: 2 *W* to the shepherds
Mt 18: 7 "*W* to the world
23:13 "*W* to you, teachers of the law
Jude :11 *W* to them! They have taken

WOLF (WOLVES)
Isa 65:25 *w* and the lamb will feed together,

WOLVES (WOLF)
Mt 10:16 you out like sheep among *w*.

WOMAN (MAN)
Ge 2:22 God made a *w* from
2:23 she shall be called '*w*,'
3: 6 *w* saw that the fruit
3:12 The *w* you put here with
3:15 between you and the *w*,
3:16 To the *w* he said,
12:11 a beautiful *w* you are.
20: 3 because of the *w* you have
24: 5 if the *w* is unwilling
Ex 2: 1 married a Levite *w*
3:22 Every *w* is to ask her
21:10 If he marries another *w*
21:22 hit a pregnant *w*
Lev 12: 2 *w* who becomes pregnant
15:19 *w* has her regular flow
15:25 a *w* has a discharge
18:17 sexual relations with both a *w*
20:13 as one lies with a *w*,
Nu 5:29 when a *w* goes astray
30: 3 young *w* still living in
30: 9 by a widow or divorced *w*
30:10 *w* living with her husband
Dt 20: 7 become pledged to a *w*
21:11 the captives a beautiful *w*

Dt 22: 5 *w* must not wear men's
22:13 married this *w* but when
Jdg 4: 9 hand Sisera over to a *w.*
13: 6 the *w* went to her husband
14: 2 have seen a Philistine *w*
16: 4 he fell in love with a *w*
20: 4 husband of the murdered *w*
Ru 3:11 a *w* of noble character
1Sa 1:15 a *w* who is deeply troubled
25: 3 intelligent and beautiful *w,*
28: 7 a *w* who is a medium,
2Sa 11: 2 he saw a *w* bathing
13:17 "Get this *w* out of here
14: 2 had a wise *w* brought
20:16 a wise *w* called from
1Ki 3:18 this *w* also had a baby.
17:24 the *w* said to Elijah,
2Ki 4: 8 a well-to-do *w* was there,
8: 1 Elisha had said to the *w*
9:34 "Take care of that cursed *w,*"
Job 14: 1 Man born of *w* is of few
Pr 11:16 A kindhearted *w* gains respect,
11:22 a beautiful *w* who shows no
14: 1 a wise *w* builds her house,
30:23 unloved *w* who is married,
31:30 a *w* who fears the LORD
Isa 54: 1 O barren *w,* you who never
Mt 5:28 looks at a *w* lustfully
9:20 a *w* who had been subject
15:28 *W* you have great faith!
26: 7 a *w* came to him with
Mk 5:25 a *w* was there who had
7:25 a *w* whose little daughter
Lk 7:39 what kind of a *w* she is
10:38 a *w* named Martha opened
13:12 "*W,* you are set free
15: 8 suppose a *w* has ten silver
Jn 2: 4 *w,* why do you involve
4: 7 a Samaritan *w* came
8: 3 a *w* caught in adultery.
19:26 *w,* here is your son,"
20:15 *W,* 'he said, "Why are you crying?
Ac 9:40 Turning toward the dead *w,*
16:14 was a *w* named Lydia,
Ro 7: 2 a married *w* is bound to
1Co 7: 2 each *w* her own husband
7:15 a believing man or *w* is
7:34 an unmarried *w* or virgin
7:39 *w* is bound to her husband
11: 3 the head of the *w* is man,
11: 7 the *w* is the glory of man
11:13 a *w* to pray to God with
Gal 4: 4 his Son, born of a *w,*
4:31 not children of the slave *w,*
1Ti 2:11 A *w* should learn in
5:16 any *w* who is a believer
Rev 2:20 You tolerate that *w* Jezebel,
12: 1 a *w* clothed with the sun
12:13 he pursued the *w* who had
17: 3 a *w* sitting on a scarlet

WOMEN (MAN)
Mt 11:11 among those born of *w,*
28: 5 The angel said to the *w,*
Mk 15:41 Many other *w* who had come
Lk 1:42 Blessed are you among *w,*
8: 2 also some *w* who had been
23:27 *w* who mourned and wailed
24:11 they did not believe the *w,*
Ac 1:14 along with the *w* and Mary
16:13 speak to the *w* who had
17: 4 not a few prominent *w.*
Ro 1:26 *w* exchanged natural relations
1Co 14:34 *w* should remain silent in
Php 4: 3 help these *w* who have
1Ti 2: 9 want *w* to dress modestly
5: 2 older *w* as mothers,
Tit 2: 3 teach the older *w* to be
2: 4 train the younger *w* to love
Heb 11:35 *W* received back their dead
1Pe 3: 5 the holy *w* of the past

WOMB
Job 1:21 Naked I came from my mother's *w,*
Ps 139: 13 in my mother's *w.*
Pr 31: 2 "O my son, O son of my *w,*
Jer 1: 5 you in the *w* I knew you,
Lk 1:44 the baby in my *w* leaped for joy.
Jn 3: 4 into his mother's *w* to be born!"

WON (WIN)
1Pe 3: 1 they may be *w* over without words

WONDER (WONDERFUL WONDERS)
Ps 17: 7 Show the *w* of your great love,
SS 1: 3 No *w* the maidens love you!

WONDERFUL* (WONDER)
2Sa 1:26 Your love for me was *w,*
1:26 more *w* than that of women.
1Ch 16: 9 tell of all his *w* acts.
Job 42: 3 things too *w* for me to know.
Ps 26: 7 and telling of all your *w* deeds.
31:21 for he showed his *w* love to me
75: 1 men tell of your *w* deeds.
105: 2 tell of all his *w* acts.
107: 8 and his *w* deeds for men,
107: 15 and his *w* deeds for men,
107: 21 and his *w* deeds for men.
107: 24 his *w* deeds in the deep.
107: 31 and his *w* deeds for men.
119: 18 *w* things in your law.
119:129 Your statutes are *w;*
131: 1 or things too *w* for me.
139: 6 Such knowledge is too *w* for me,
139: 14 your works are *w,*
145: 5 I will meditate on your *w* works.
Isa 9: 6 *W* Counselor, Mighty God,
28:29 *w* in counsel and magnificent
Mt 21:15 of the law saw the *w* things he did
Lk 13:17 with all the *w* things he was doing.
1Pe 2: 9 out of darkness into his *w* light.

WONDERS (WONDER)
Ex 3:20 with all the *w* that I will perform
Dt 10:21 and awesome *w* you saw
2Sa 7:23 awesome *w* by driving out nations
Job 37:14 stop and consider God's *w.*
Ps 9: 1 I will tell of all your *w.*
89: 5 The heavens praise your *w,*
119: 27 then I will meditate on your *w.*
Joel 2:30 I will show *w* in the heavens
Ac 2:11 we hear them declaring the *w*
2:19 I will show *w* in the heaven above
5:12 many miraculous signs and *w*
2Co 12:12 that mark an apostle—signs, *w*
2Th 2: 9 and *w,* and in every sort
Heb 2: 4 also testified to it by signs, *w*

WOOD
Isa 44:19 Shall I bow down to a block of *w?*"
1Co 3:12 costly stones, *w,* hay or straw,

WOOL
Pr 31:13 She selects *w* and flax
Isa 1:18 they shall be like *w.*
Da 7: 9 hair of his head was white like *w.*
Rev 1:14 and hair were white like *w,*

WORD (BYWORD WORDS)
Nu 30: 2 he must not break his *w*
Dt 8: 3 but on every *w* that comes
2Sa 22:31 the *w* of the LORD is flawless.
Ps 56: 4 In God, whose *w* I praise,
119: 9 By living according to your *w.*
119: 11 I have hidden your *w* in my heart
119:105 Your *w* is a lamp to my feet
Pr 12:25 but a kind *w* cheers him up.
15: 1 but a harsh *w* stirs up anger.
25:11 A *w* aptly spoken
30: 5 "Every *w* of God is flawless;
Isa 55:11 so is my *w* that goes out
Jer 23:29 "Is not my *w* like fire," declares
Mt 4: 4 but on every *w* that comes
12:36 for every careless *w* they have
15: 6 Thus you nullify the *w* of God
Mk 4:14 parable? The farmer sows the *w.*
Jn 1: 1 was the *W,* and the *W* was
1:14 The *W* became flesh and made his
17:17 them by the truth; your *w* is truth.
Ac 6: 4 and the ministry of the *w.*"
2Co 2:17 we do not peddle the *w* of God
4: 2 nor do we distort the *w* of God.
Eph 6:17 of the Spirit, which is the *w* of God.
Php 2:16 as you hold out the *w* of life—
Col 3:16 Let the *w* of Christ dwell
2Ti 2:15 and who correctly handles the *w*
Heb 4:12 For the *w* of God is living
Jas 1:22 Do not merely listen to the *w,*
2Pe 1:19 And we have the *w* of the prophets

WORDS (WORD)
Dt 11:18 Fix these *w* of mine in your hearts
Ps 12: 6 the *w* of the LORD are flawless,
119:103 How sweet are your *w* to my taste,
119:130 The unfolding of your *w* gives light;
Ps 119:160 All your *w* are true;
Pr 2: 1 My son, if you accept my *w*
10:19 When *w* are many, sin is not absent
16:24 Pleasant *w* are a honeycomb,
30: 6 Do not add to his *w,*
Ecc 12:11 The *w* of the wise are like goads,
Jer 15:16 When your *w* came, I ate them;
Mt 24:35 but my *w* will never pass away.
Lk 6:47 and hears my *w* and puts them
Jn 6:68 You have the *w* of eternal life.
15: 7 in me and my *w* remain in you,
1Co 2:13 but in *w* taught by the Spirit,
14:19 rather speak five intelligible *w*
Rev 22:19 And if anyone takes *w* away

WORK (WORKED WORKER WORKERS WORKING WORKMAN WORKMANSHIP WORKS)
Ge 2: 2 day he rested from all his *w.*
Ex 23:12 "Six days do your *w,*
Nu 8:11 ready to do the *w* of the LORD.
Dt 5:14 On it you shall not do any *w,*
Ps 19: 1 the skies proclaim the *w*
Ecc 5:19 his lot and be happy in his *w*—
Jer 48:10 lax in doing the LORD's *w!*
Mt 20: 1 to hire men to *w* in his vineyard.
Jn 6:27 Do not *w* for food that spoils,
9: 4 we must do the *w* of him who sent
Ac 13: 2 for the *w* to which I have called
1Co 3:13 test the quality of each man's *w.*
4:12 We *w* hard with our own hands.
Eph 4:16 up in love, as each part does its *w.*
Php 1: 6 that he who began a good *w*
2:12 continue to *w* out your salvation
Col 3:23 Whatever you do, *w* at it
1Th 4:11 and to *w* with your hands,
5:12 to respect those who *w* hard
2Th 3:10 If a man will not *w,* he shall not eat
2Ti 3:17 equipped for every good *w.*
Heb 6:10 he will not forget your *w*
2Jn :11 him shares in his wicked *w.*
3Jn : 8 men so that we may *w* together

WORKED (WORK)
1Co 15:10 No, I *w* harder than all of them—
2Th 3: 8 On the contrary, we *w* night

WORKER (WORK)
Lk 10: 7 for the *w* deserves his wages.
1Ti 5:18 and "The *w* deserves his wages."

WORKERS (WORK)
Mt 9:37 is plentiful but the *w* are few.
1Co 3: 9 For we are God's fellow *w;*

WORKING (WORK)
Col 3:23 as *w* for the Lord, not for men,

WORKMAN (WORK)
2Ti 2:15 a *w* who does not need

WORKMANSHIP* (WORK)
Eph 2:10 For we are God's *w,* created

WORKS (WORK)
Ps 66: 5 how awesome his *w* in man's behalf
145: 6 of the power of your awesome *w,*
Pr 8:22 As the first of his *w,*
31:31 let her *w* bring her praise
Ro 4: 2 in fact, Abraham was justified by *w*
8:28 in all things God *w* for the good
Eph 2: 9 not by *w,* so that no one can boast.
4:12 to prepare God's people for *w*

WORLD (WORLDLY)
Ps 9: 8 He will judge the *w*
50:12 for the *w* is mine, and all that is in it
96:13 He will judge the *w*
Pr 8:23 before the *w* began.
Isa 13:11 I will punish the *w* for its evil,
Zep 1:18 the whole *w* will be consumed,
Mt 5:14 "You are the light of the *w.*
16:26 for a man if he gains the whole *w,*
Mk 16:15 into all the *w* and preach the good
Jn 1:29 who takes away the sin of the *w!*
3:16 so loved the *w* that he gave his one
8:12 he said, "I am the light of the *w.*
15:19 As it is, you do not belong to the *w,*
16:33 In this *w* you will have trouble.
17: 5 had with you before the *w* began.
17:14 not of the *w* any more than I am
18:36 "My kingdom is not of this *w.*
Ac 17:24 "The God who made the *w*
Ro 3:19 and the whole *w* held accountable

Ro 10:18 their words to the ends of the *w*."
1Co 1:27 things of the *w* to shame the strong.
3:19 the wisdom of this *w* is foolishness
6: 2 that the saints will judge the *w*?
2Co 5:19 that God was reconciling the *w*
10: 3 For though we live in the *w*,
1Ti 6: 7 For we brought nothing into the *w*,
Heb 11:38 the *w* was not worthy of them.
Jas 2: 5 poor in the eyes of the *w* to be rich
4: 4 with the *w* is hatred toward God?
1Pe 1:20 before the creation of the *w*,
1Jn 2: 2 but also for the sins of the whole *w*.
2:15 not love the *w* or anything in the *w*.
5: 4 born of God overcomes the *w*.
Rev 13: 8 slain from the creation of the *w*.

WORLDLY (WORLD)
1Co 3: 1 address you as spiritual but as *w*—
Tit 2:12 to ungodliness and *w* passions,

WORM
Mk 9:48 " 'their *w* does not die,

WORRY (WORRYING)
Mt 6:25 I tell you, do not *w* about your life,
10:19 do not *w* about what to say

WORRYING (WORRY)
Mt 6:27 of you by *w* can add a single hour

WORSHIP (WORSHIPED WORSHIPS)
Jos 22:27 that we will *w* the LORD
2Ki 17:36 arm, is the one you must *w*.
1Ch 16:29 *w* the LORD in the splendor
Ps 95: 6 Come, let us bow down in *w*,
100: 2 *w* the LORD with gladness;
Zec 14:17 up to Jerusalem to *w* the King,
Mt 2: 2 and have come to *w* him."
4: 9 "if you will bow down and *w* me."
Jn 4:24 and his worshipers must *w* in spirit
Ro 12: 1 to God—this is your spiritual act of *w*.
Heb 10: 1 perfect those who draw near to *w*.

WORSHIPED (WORSHIP)
2Ch 29:30 and bowed their heads and *w*.
Mt 28: 9 clasped his feet and *w* him.

WORSHIPS (WORSHIP)
Isa 44:15 But he also fashions a god and *w* it;

WORTH (WORTHY)
Job 28:13 Man does not comprehend its *w*;
Pr 31:10 She is *w* far more than rubies.
Mt 10:31 are *w* more than many sparrows.
Ro 8:18 sufferings are not *w* comparing
1Pe 1: 7 of greater *w* than gold,
3: 4 which is of great *w* in God's sight.

WORTHLESS
Pr 11: 4 Wealth is *w* in the day of wrath,
Jas 1:26 himself and his religion is *w*.

WORTHY (WORTH)
1Ch 16:25 For great is the LORD and most *w*
Mt 10:37 more than me is not *w* of me;
Lk 15:19 I am no longer *w* to be called your
Eph 4: 1 to live a life *w* of the calling you
Php 1:27 in a manner *w* of the gospel
Col 1:10 in order that you may live a life *w*
1Ti 3: 8 are to be men *w* of respect, sincere,
Heb 3: 3 Jesus has been found *w*
3Jn : 6 on their way in a manner *w* of God.
Rev 5: 2 "Who is *w* to break the seals

WOUND (WOUNDS)
1Co 8:12 and *w* their weak conscience,

WOUNDS (WOUND)
Pr 27: 6 *w* from a friend can be trusted
Isa 53: 5 and by his *w* we are healed.
Zec 13: 6 'What are these *w* on your body?'
1Pe 2:24 by his *w* you have been healed.

WRAPS
Ps 104: 2 He *w* himself in light

WRATH
2Ch 36:16 scoffed at his prophets until the *w*
Ps 2: 5 and terrifies them in his *w*, saying,
76:10 Surely your *w* against men brings
Pr 15: 1 A gentle answer turns away *w*,
Isa 13:13 at the *w* of the LORD Almighty,
51:17 the cup of his *w*,
Jer 25:15 filled with the wine of my *w*
Eze 5:13 my *w* against them will subside,
20: 8 So I said I would pour out my *w*
Am 1: 3 I will not turn back ⌞my *w*⌟.
Na 1: 2 maintains his *w* against his enemies
Zep 1:15 That day will be a day of *w*,
Jn 3:36 for God's *w* remains on him."
Ro 1:18 The *w* of God is being revealed
2: 5 you are storing up *w*
5: 9 saved from God's *w* through him!
9:22 choosing to show his *w*
1Th 5: 9 God did not appoint us to suffer *w*
Rev 6:16 and from the *w* of the Lamb!
19:15 the fury of the *w* of God Almighty.

WRESTLED
Ge 32:24 and a man *w* with him till daybreak

WRITE (WRITER WRITING WRITTEN WROTE)
Dt 6: 9 *W* them on the doorframes
10: 2 I will *w* on the tablets the words
Pr 7: 3 *w* them on the tablet of your heart.
Jer 31:33 and *w* it on their hearts.
Heb 8:10 and *w* them on their hearts.
Rev 3:12 I will also *w* on him my new name.

WRITER* (WRITE)
Ps 45: 1 my tongue is the pen of a skillful *w*.

WRITING (WRITE)
1Co 14:37 him acknowledge that what I am *w*

WRITTEN (WRITE)
Dt 28:58 which are *w* in this book,
Jos 1: 8 careful to do everything *w* in it.
23: 6 to obey all that is *w* in the Book
Ps 40: 7 it is *w* about me in the scroll.
Da 12: 1 everyone whose name is found *w*
Mal 3:16 A scroll of remembrance was *w*
Lk 10:20 but rejoice that your names are *w*
24:44 must be fulfilled that is *w* about me
Jn 20:31 these are *w* that you may believe
21:25 for the books that would be *w*.
Ro 2:15 of the law are *w* on their hearts,
1Co 4: 6 "Do not go beyond what is *w*."
10:11 as examples and were *w* down
2Co 3: 3 *w* not with ink but with the Spirit
Col 2:14 having canceled the *w* code,
Heb 10: 7 it is *w* about me in the scroll—
12:23 whose names are *w* in heaven.
Rev 21:27 but only those whose names are *w*

WRONG (WRONGDOING WRONGED WRONGS)
Ex 23: 2 Do not follow the crowd in doing *w*
Nu 5: 7 must make full restitution for his *w*,
Dt 32: 4 A faithful God who does no *w*,
Job 34:12 unthinkable that God would do *w*,
Ps 5: 5 you hate all who do *w*.
Gal 2:11 to his face, because he was clearly in the *w*.
1Th 5:15 that nobody pays back *w* for *w*,

WRONGDOING (WRONG)
Job 1:22 sin by charging God with *w*.
1Jn 5:17 All *w* is sin, and there is sin that

WRONGED (WRONG)
1Co 6: 7 not rather be *w*? Why not rather

WRONGS (WRONG)
Pr 10:12 but love covers over all *w*.
1Co 13: 5 angered, it keeps no record of *w*.

WROTE (WRITE)
Ex 34:28 And he *w* on the tablets the words
Jn 5:46 for he *w* about me.
8: 8 down and *w* on the ground.

XERXES
King of Persia, husband of Esther. Deposed Vashti; replaced her with Esther (Est 1–2). Sealed Haman's edict to annihilate the Jews (Est 3). Received Esther without having called her (Est 5:1–8). Honored Mordecai (Est 6). Hanged Haman (Est 7). Issued edict allowing Jews to defend themselves (Est 8). Exalted Mordecai (Est 8:1–2, 15; 9:4; 10).

YEAR (YEARS)
Ex 34:23 Three times a *y* all your men are
Lev 16:34 to be made once a *y* for all the sins
25: 4 But in the seventh *y* the land is
25:11 The fiftieth *y* shall be a jubilee
Heb 10: 1 repeated endlessly *y* after *y*,

YEARS (YEAR)
Ge 1:14 to mark seasons and days and *y*,
Ex 12:40 lived in Egypt was 430 *y*.
16:35 The Israelites ate manna forty *y*,
Job 36:26 of his *y* is past finding out.
Ps 90: 4 For a thousand *y* in your sight
90:10 The length of our days is seventy *y*
Pr 3: 2 they will prolong your life many *y*
Lk 3:23 Jesus himself was about thirty *y* old
2Pe 3: 8 the Lord a day is like a thousand *y*,
Rev 20: 2 and bound him for a thousand *y*.

YEAST
Ex 12:15 are to eat bread made without *y*.
Mt 16: 6 guard against the *y* of the Pharisees
1Co 5: 6 you know that a little *y* works

YESTERDAY
Heb 13: 8 Jesus Christ is the same *y*

YOKE (YOKED)
1Ki 12: 4 and the heavy *y* he put on us,
Mt 11:29 Take my *y* upon you and learn
Gal 5: 1 be burdened again by a *y*

YOKED (YOKE)
2Co 6:14 Do not be *y* together

YOUNG (YOUNGER YOUTH)
2Ch 10:14 he followed the advice of the *y* men
Ps 37:25 I was *y* and now I am old,
119: 9 How can a *y* man keep his way
Pr 20:29 The glory of *y* men is their strength
Isa 40:11 he gently leads those that have *y*.
Joel 2:28 your *y* men will see visions.
Ac 2:17 your *y* men will see visions,
7:58 at the feet of a *y* man named Saul.
1Ti 4:12 down on you because you are *y*,
Tit 2: 6 encourage the *y* men
1Pe 5: 5 *Y* men, in the same way be
1Jn 2:13 I write to you, *y* men,

YOUNGER (YOUNG)
1Ti 5: 1 Treat *y* men as brothers, older
Tit 2: 4 Then they can train the *y* women

YOUTH (YOUNG)
Ps 103: 5 so that your *y* is renewed like
Ecc 12: 1 Creator in the days of your *y*,
2Ti 2:22 Flee the evil desires of *y*,

ZACCHAEUS
Lk 19: 2 A man was there by the name of *Z*;

ZEAL (ZEALOUS)
Ps 69: 9 for *z* for your house consumes me,
Pr 19: 2 to have *z* without knowledge,
Isa 59:17 and wrapped himself in *z*
Jn 2:17 "*Z* for your house will consume me
Ro 10: 2 their *z* is not based on knowledge.
12:11 Never be lacking in *z*,

ZEALOUS (ZEAL)
Nu 25:13 he was *z* for the honor of his God
Pr 23:17 always be *z* for the fear
Eze 39:25 and I will be *z* for my holy name.
Gal 4:18 fine to be *z*, provided the purpose is

ZEBULUN
Son of Jacob by Leah (Ge 30:20; 35:23; 1Ch 2:1). Tribe of blessed (Ge 49:13; Dt 33:18–19), numbered (Nu 1:31; 26:27), allotted land (Jos 19:10–16; Eze 48:26), failed to fully possess (Jdg 1:30), supported Deborah (Jdg 4:6–10; 5:14, 18), David (1Ch 12:33), 12,000 from (Rev 7:8).

ZECHARIAH
1. Son of Jeroboam II; king of Israel (2Ki 15:8–12).
2. Post-exilic prophet who encouraged rebuilding of temple (Ezr 5:1; 6:14; Zec 1:1).
3. Father of John the Baptist (Lk 1:13; 3:2).

ZEDEKIAH
1. False prophet (1Ki 22:11–24; 2Ch 18:10–23).
2. Mattaniah, son of Josiah (1Ch 3:15), made king of Judah by Nebuchadnezzar (2Ki 24:17–25:7; 2Ch 36:10–14; Jer 37–39; 52:1–11).

ZEPHANIAH
Prophet; descendant of Hezekiah (Zep 1:1).

ZERUBBABEL
Descendant of David (1Ch 3:19; Mt 1:3). Led return from exile (Ezr 2:2; Ne 7:7). Governor of Israel; helped rebuild altar and temple (Ezr 3; Hag 1–2; Zec 4).

ZILPAH

Servant of Leah, mother of Jacob's sons Gad and Asher (Ge 30:9–12; 35:26, 46:16–18).

ZIMRI

King of Israel (1Ki 16:9–20).

ZIMRI

King of Israel (1Ki 16:9–20).

ZION

2Sa 5: 7 David captured the fortress of *Z,*
Ps 2: 6 King on *Z,* my holy hill."
9:11 to the LORD, enthroned in *Z;*
74: 2 Mount *Z,* where you dwelt.
87: 2 the LORD loves the gates of *Z*
102: 13 and have compassion on *Z,*
137: 3 "Sing us one of the songs of *Z!*"
Isa 2: 3 The law will go out from *Z,*
28:16 "See, I lay a stone in *Z,*
51:11 They will enter *Z* with singing;
52: 8 When the LORD returns to *Z,*
Jer 50: 5 They will ask the way to *Z*
Joel 3:21 The LORD dwells in *Z!*
Am 6: 1 to you who are complacent in *Z,*
Mic 4: 2 The law will go out from *Z,*
Zec 9: 9 Rejoice greatly, O Daughter of *Z!*
Ro 9:33 I lay in *Z* a stone that causes men
11:26 "The deliverer will come from *Z;*
Heb 12:22 But you have come to Mount *Z,*
Rev 14: 1 standing on Mount *Z,*

ZIPPORAH*

Daughter of Reuel; wife of Moses (Ex 2:21–22; 4:20–26; 18:1–6).

ZOPHAR

One of Job's friends (Job 11; 20).

Index to Color Maps

The Index to Color Maps will lead you to place-names found on the color maps in the back of this Bible. References are to the map number and the margin markings.

Notes

Notes

The Living Insights Study Bible

Project management and editorial by *Dirk R. Buursma, Sherry Harney, Kevin Harney*

Interior design, time lines and charts by *Sharon Wright, Belmont, MI*

Interior typesetting by *Auto-Graphics, Inc., Pomona, CA*

Interior proofreading by *Peachtree Editorial and Proofreading Service, Peachtree City, GA*

Cover design by *Rick Devon, Grand Rapids, MI*

Literary agency by *Sealy M. Yates, Orange, CA*

Printed by *Quebecor Printing Kingsport, Kingsport TN*

Map 1: **WORLD OF THE PATRIARCHS**

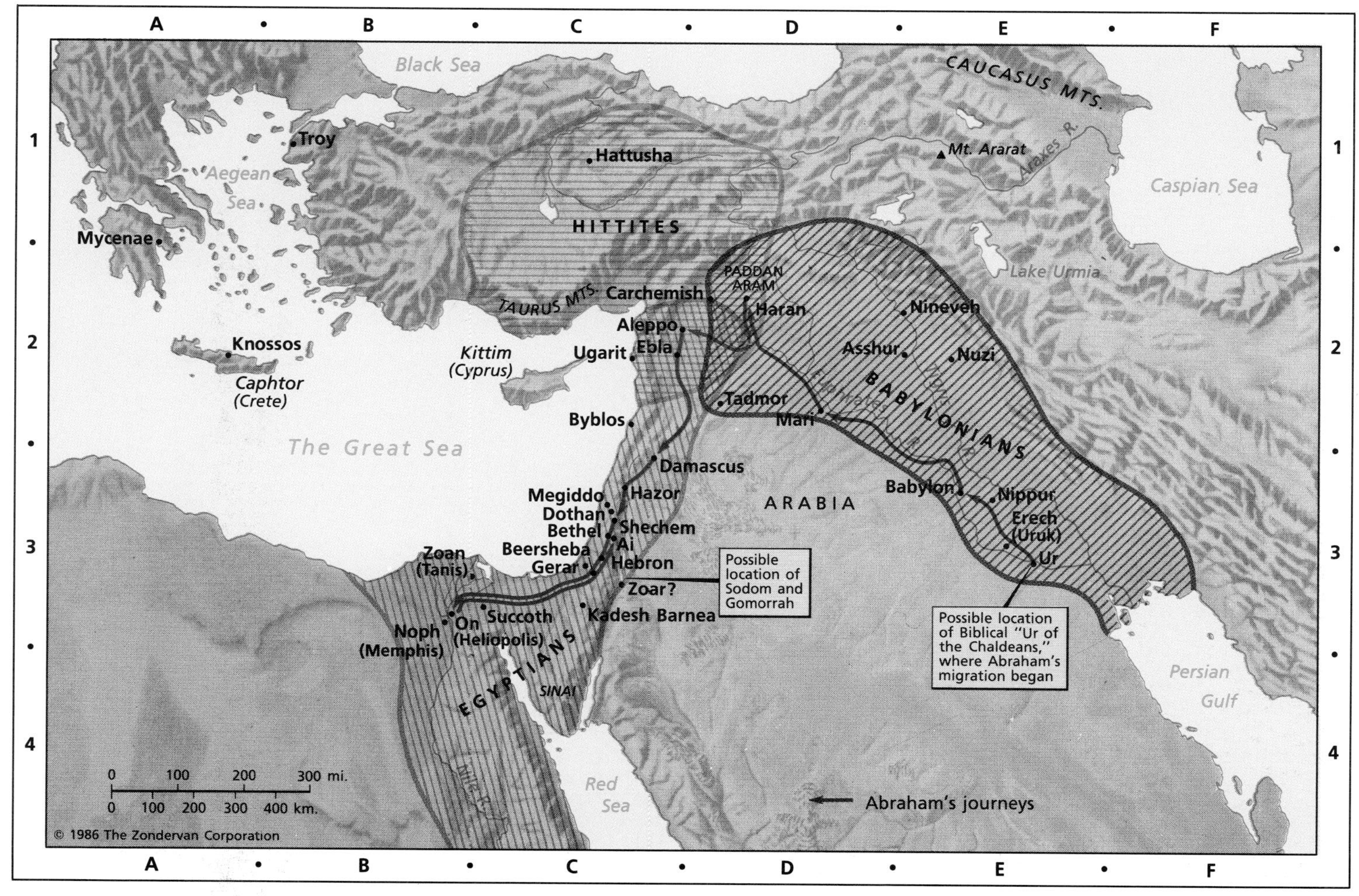

Map 2: **PALESTINE AND SINAI**

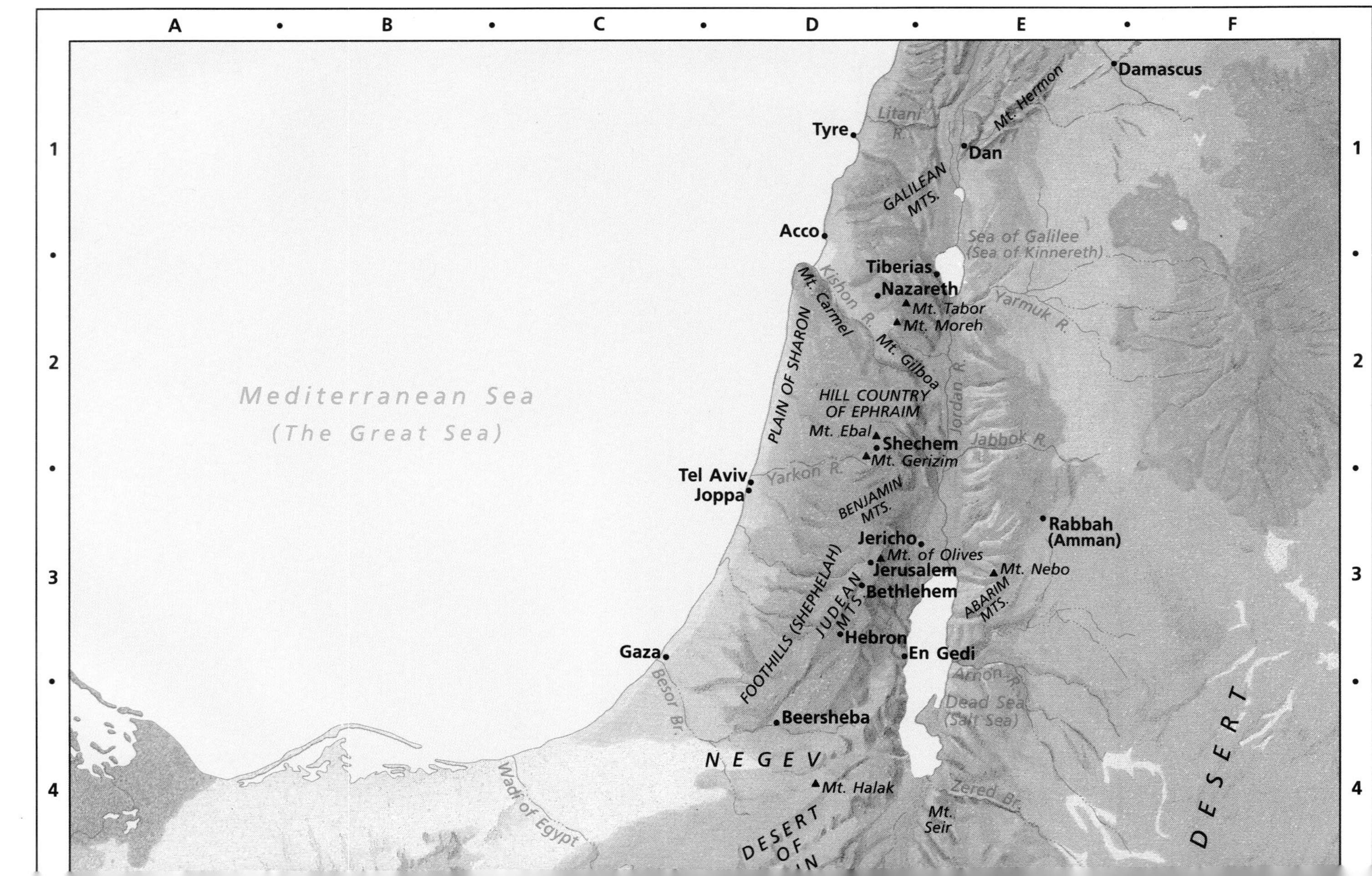

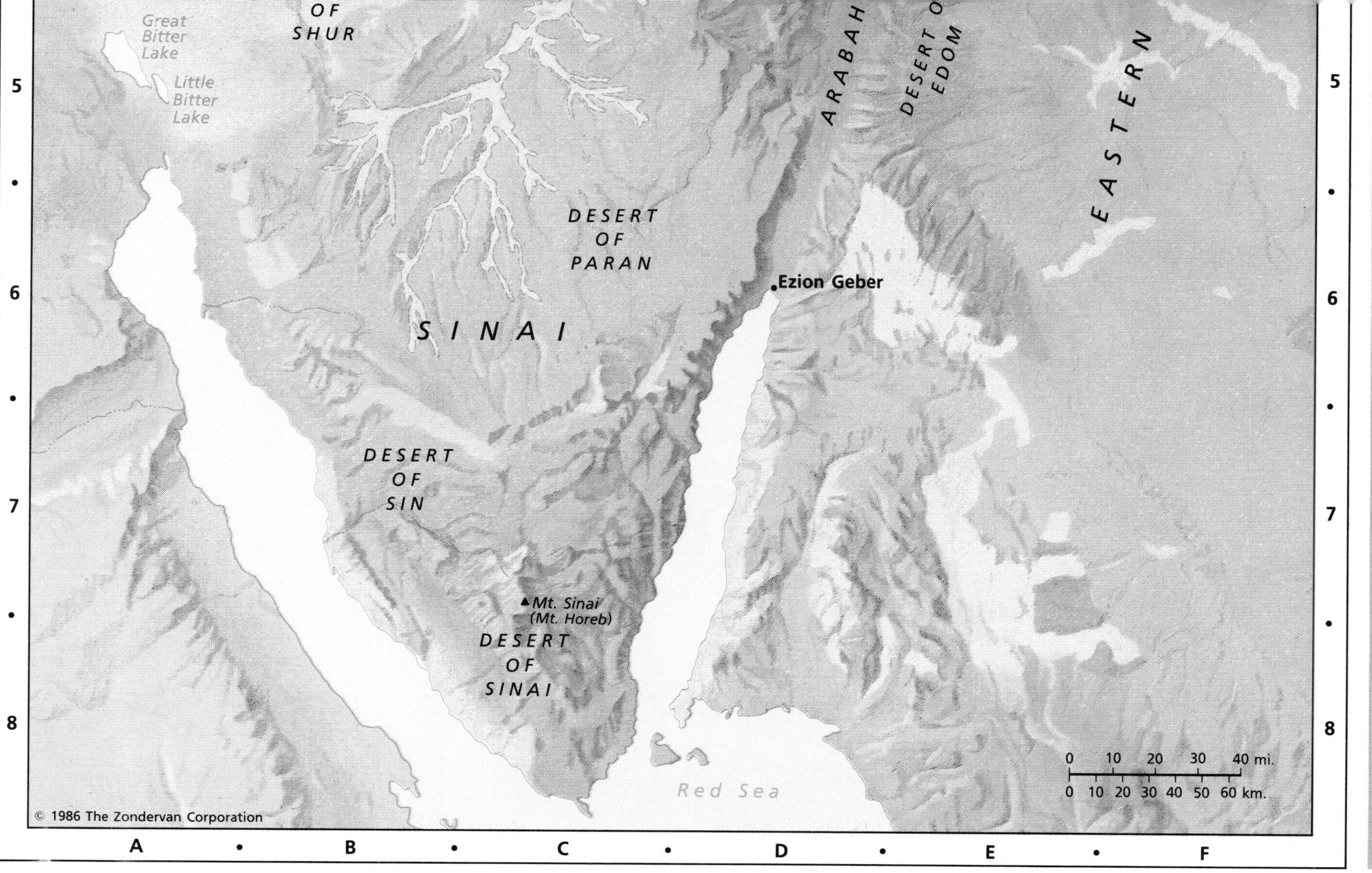
OF
SHUR
Great
Bitter
Lake
Little
Bitter
Lake
ARABAH
DESERT O
EDOM
EASTERN
DESERT
OF
PARAN
Ezion Geber
SINAI
DESERT
OF
SIN
Mt. Sinai
(Mt. Horeb)
DESERT
OF
SINAI
Red Sea
0 10 20 30 40 mi.
0 10 20 30 40 50 60 km.
© 1986 The Zondervan Corporation
5
6
7
8
A
B
C
D
E
F

Map 3: **EXODUS AND CONQUEST OF CANAAN**

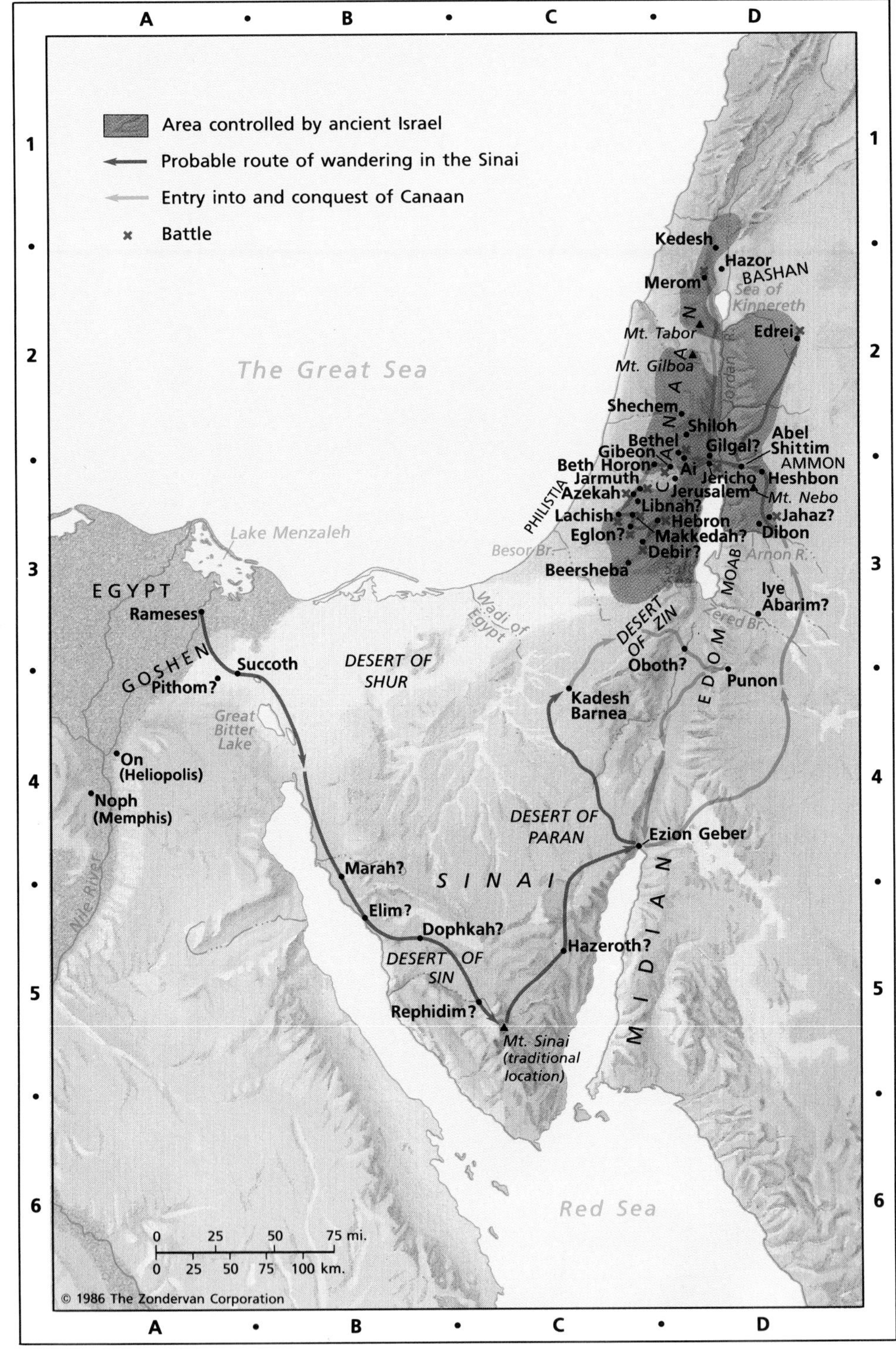

A
B
C
D
1
2
3
4
5
6
Area controlled by ancient Israel
Probable route of wandering in the Sinai
Entry into and conquest of Canaan
Battle
The Great Sea
Kedesh
Hazor
BASHAN
Merom
Sea of Kinnereth
CANAAN
Mt. Tabor
Edrei
Mt. Gilboa
Jordan
Shechem
Shiloh
Bethel
Gilgal?
Abel Shittim
Gibeon
AMMON
Beth Horon
Ai
Jarmuth
Jericho
Heshbon
PHILISTIA
Azekah
Jerusalem
Mt. Nebo
Libnah?
Lachish
Hebron
Jahaz?
Eglon?
Makkedah?
Dibon
Lake Menzaleh
Besor Br.
Debir?
Arnon R.
Beersheba
MOAB
EGYPT
Iye Abarim?
Rameses
Wadi of Egypt
Zered Br.
DESERT OF ZIN
GOSHEN
Succoth
DESERT OF SHUR
Oboth?
EDOM
Punon
Pithom?
Kadesh Barnea
Great Bitter Lake
On (Heliopolis)
Noph (Memphis)
DESERT OF PARAN
Ezion Geber
Marah?
SINAI
Nile River
Elim?
Dophkah?
Hazeroth?
DESERT OF SIN
MIDIAN
Rephidim?
Mt. Sinai (traditional location)
Red Sea
0 25 50 75 mi.
0 25 50 75 100 km.

Map 4: **LAND OF THE TWELVE TRIBES**

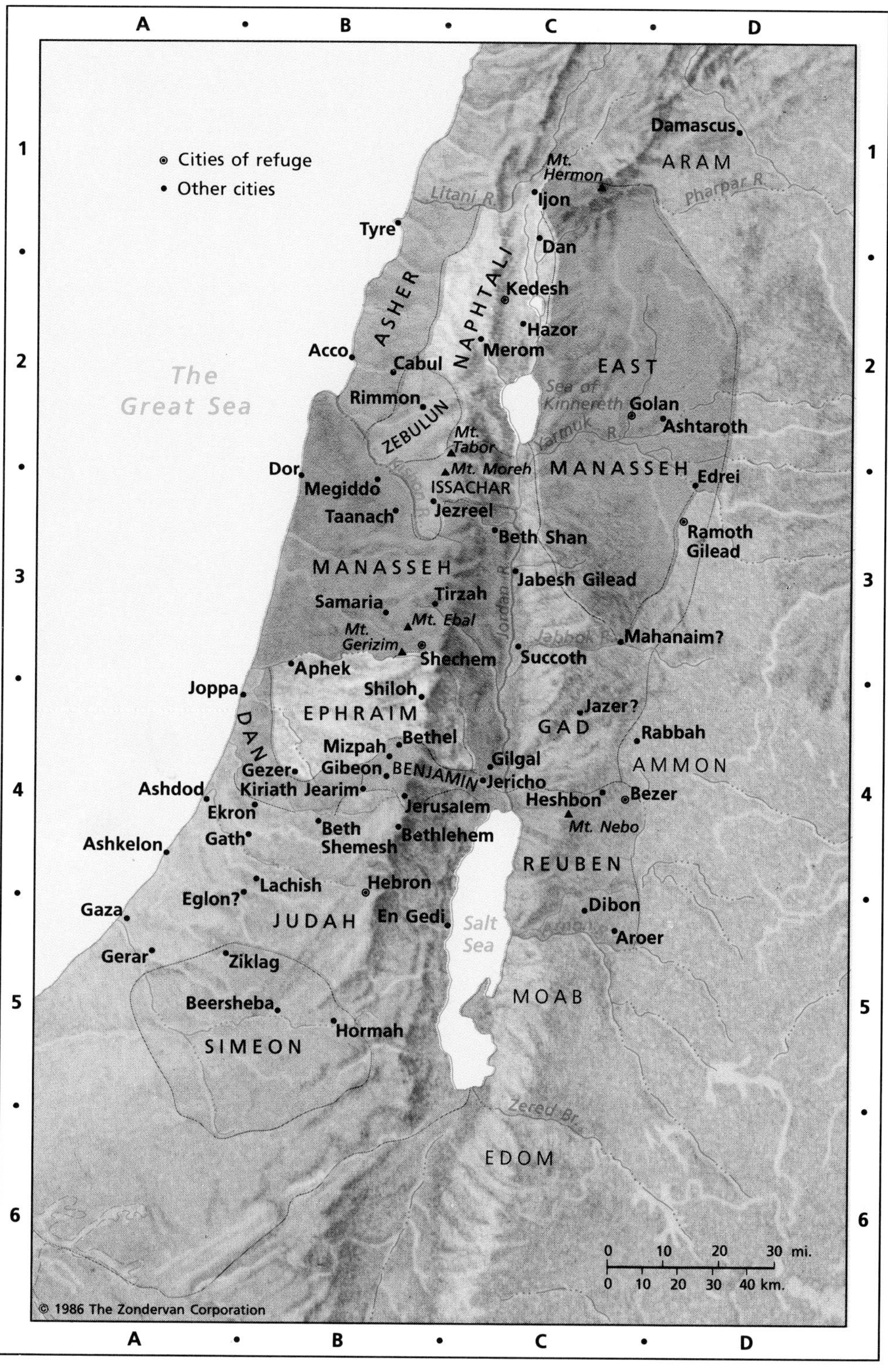

Map 5: KINGDOM OF DAVID AND SOLOMON

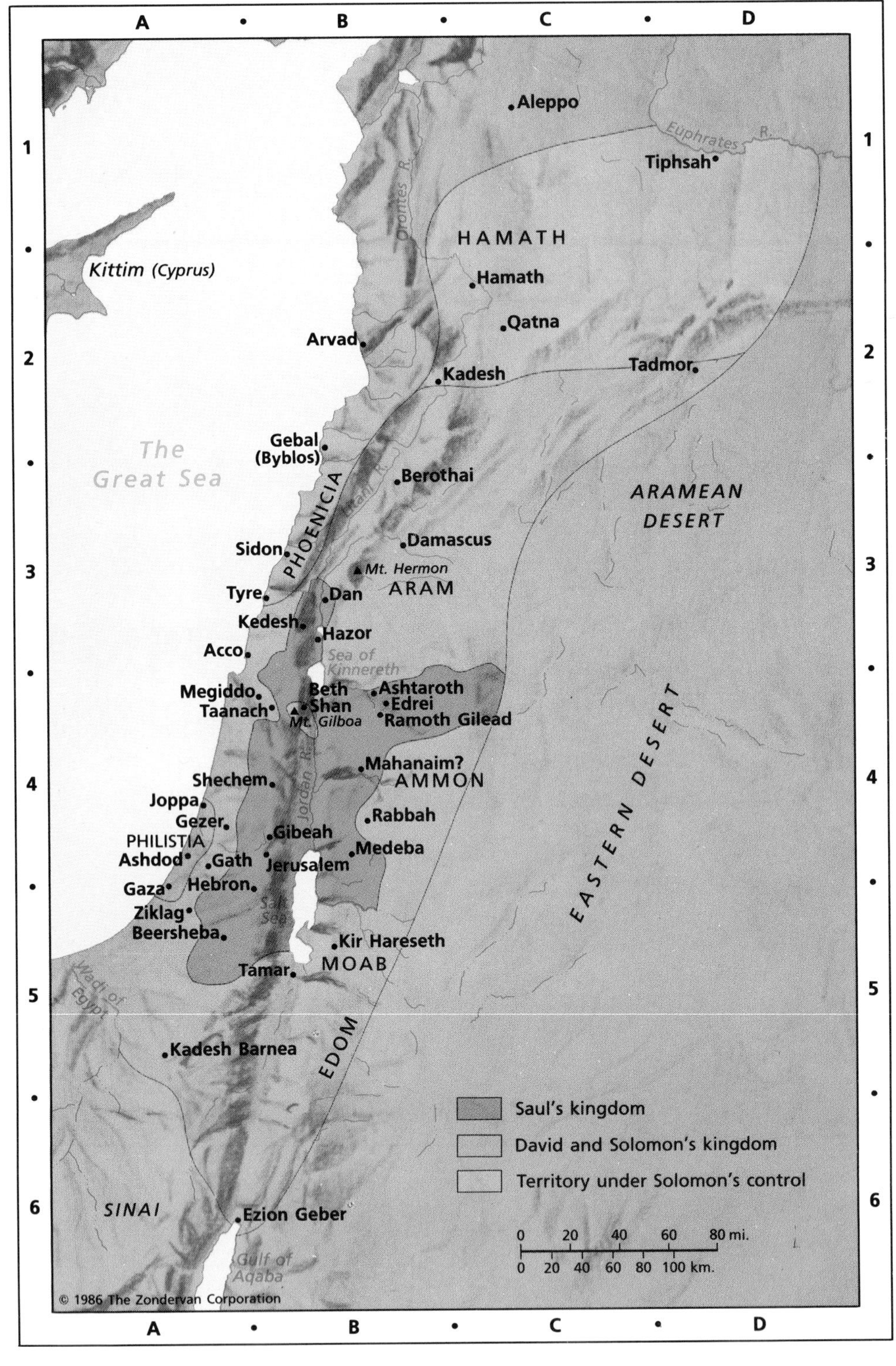
A
B
C
D
1
2
3
4
5
6
Aleppo
Euphrates R.
Tiphsah
Orontes R.
HAMATH
Hamath
Kittim (Cyprus)
Qatna
Arvad
Tadmor
Kadesh
The Great Sea
Gebal (Byblos)
Berothai
PHOENICIA
ARAMEAN DESERT
Damascus
Sidon
Mt. Hermon
Tyre
Dan
ARAM
Kedesh
Hazor
Acco
Sea of Kinnereth
Megiddo
Beth Shan
Ashtaroth
Taanach
Edrei
Mt. Gilboa
Ramoth Gilead
Mahanaim?
Jordan R.
Shechem
AMMON
EASTERN DESERT
Joppa
Gezer
Rabbah
Gibeah
PHILISTIA
Medeba
Ashdod
Gath
Jerusalem
Gaza
Hebron
Salt Sea
Ziklag
Beersheba
Kir Hareseth
Tamar
MOAB
Wadi of Egypt
EDOM
Kadesh Barnea
Saul's kingdom
David and Solomon's kingdom
Territory under Solomon's control
SINAI
Ezion Geber
0 20 40 60 80 mi.
0 20 40 60 80 100 km.
Gulf of Aqaba
© 1986 The Zondervan Corporation

Map 6: **PROPHETS IN ISRAEL AND JUDAH**

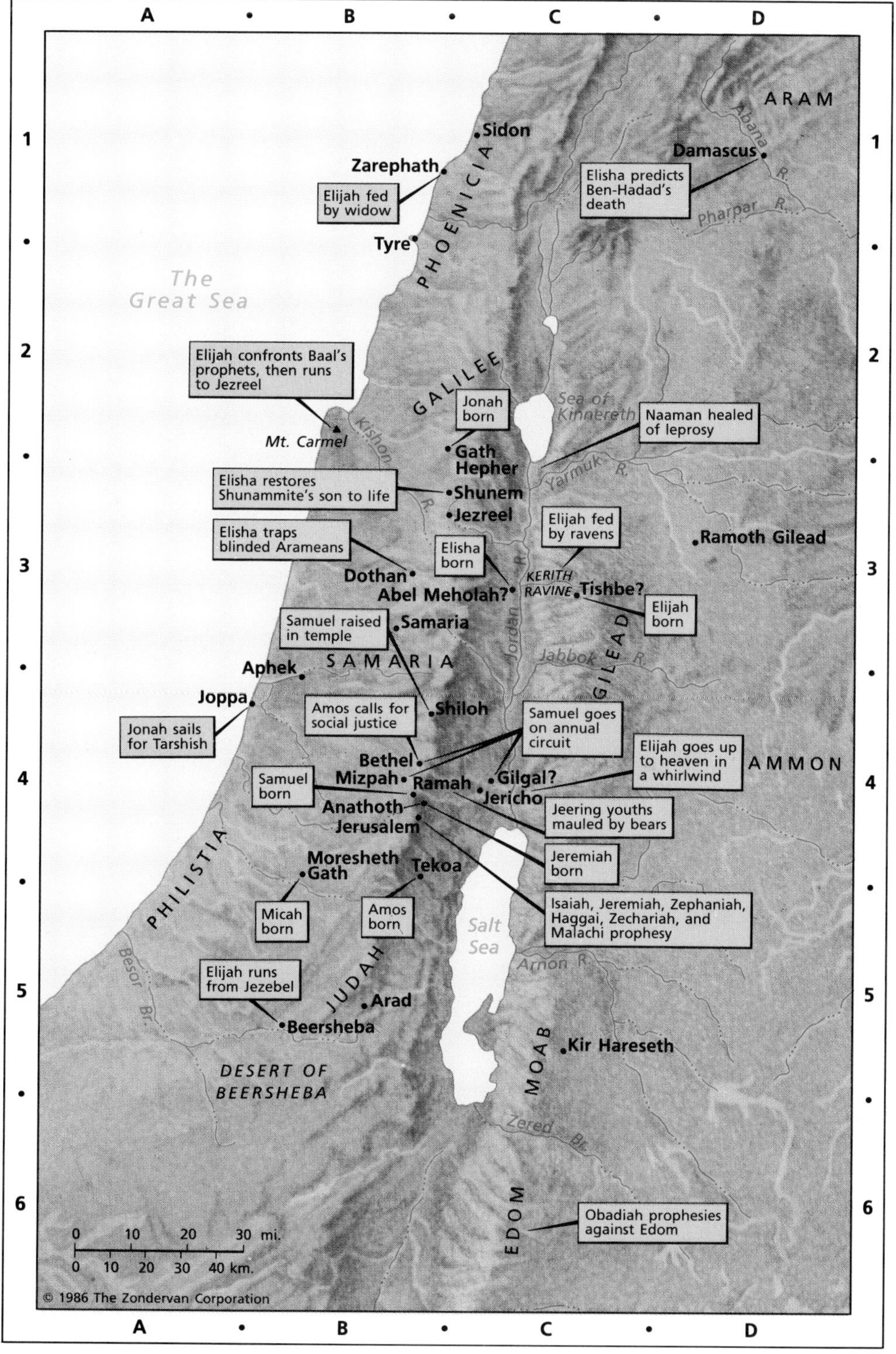

A
B
C
D
1
2
3
4
5
6
ARAM
Sidon
Damascus
Zarephath
Elijah fed by widow
Elisha predicts Ben-Hadad's death
Abana R.
Pharpar R.
PHOENICIA
Tyre
The Great Sea
Elijah confronts Baal's prophets, then runs to Jezreel
GALILEE
Jonah born
Sea of Kinnereth
Naaman healed of leprosy
Mt. Carmel
Kishon R.
Gath Hepher
Yarmuk R.
Elisha restores Shunammite's son to life
Shunem
Jezreel
Elijah fed by ravens
Elisha traps blinded Arameans
Elisha born
Ramoth Gilead
Dothan
KERITH RAVINE
Abel Meholah?
Tishbe?
Elijah born
Samuel raised in temple
Samaria
Jordan R.
SAMARIA
GILEAD
Jabbok R.
Aphek
Joppa
Jonah sails for Tarshish
Amos calls for social justice
Shiloh
Samuel goes on annual circuit
Elijah goes up to heaven in a whirlwind
AMMON
Bethel
Samuel born
Mizpah
Ramah
Gilgal?
Jericho
Anathoth
Jeering youths mauled by bears
Jerusalem
Jeremiah born
PHILISTIA
Moresheth Gath
Tekoa
Isaiah, Jeremiah, Zephaniah, Haggai, Zechariah, and Malachi prophesy
Micah born
Amos born
Salt Sea
Besor Br.
Arnon R.
Elijah runs from Jezebel
JUDAH
Arad
Beersheba
MOAB
Kir Hareseth
DESERT OF BEERSHEBA
Zered Br.
EDOM
Obadiah prophesies against Edom
0 10 20 30 mi.
0 10 20 30 40 km.

Map 7: ASSYRIAN AND BABYLONIAN EMPIRES

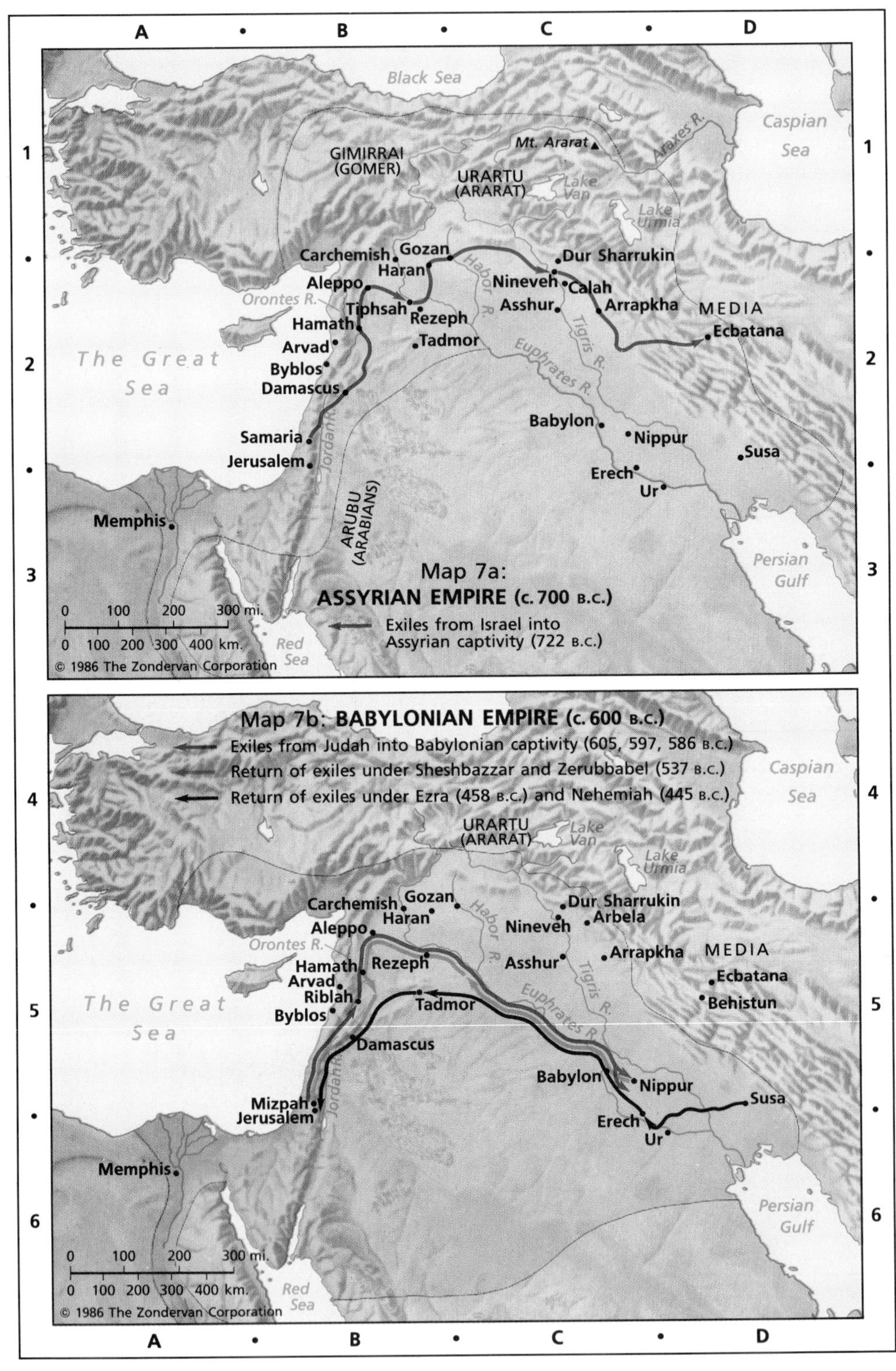

Map 8: **JERUSALEM IN JESUS' TIME**

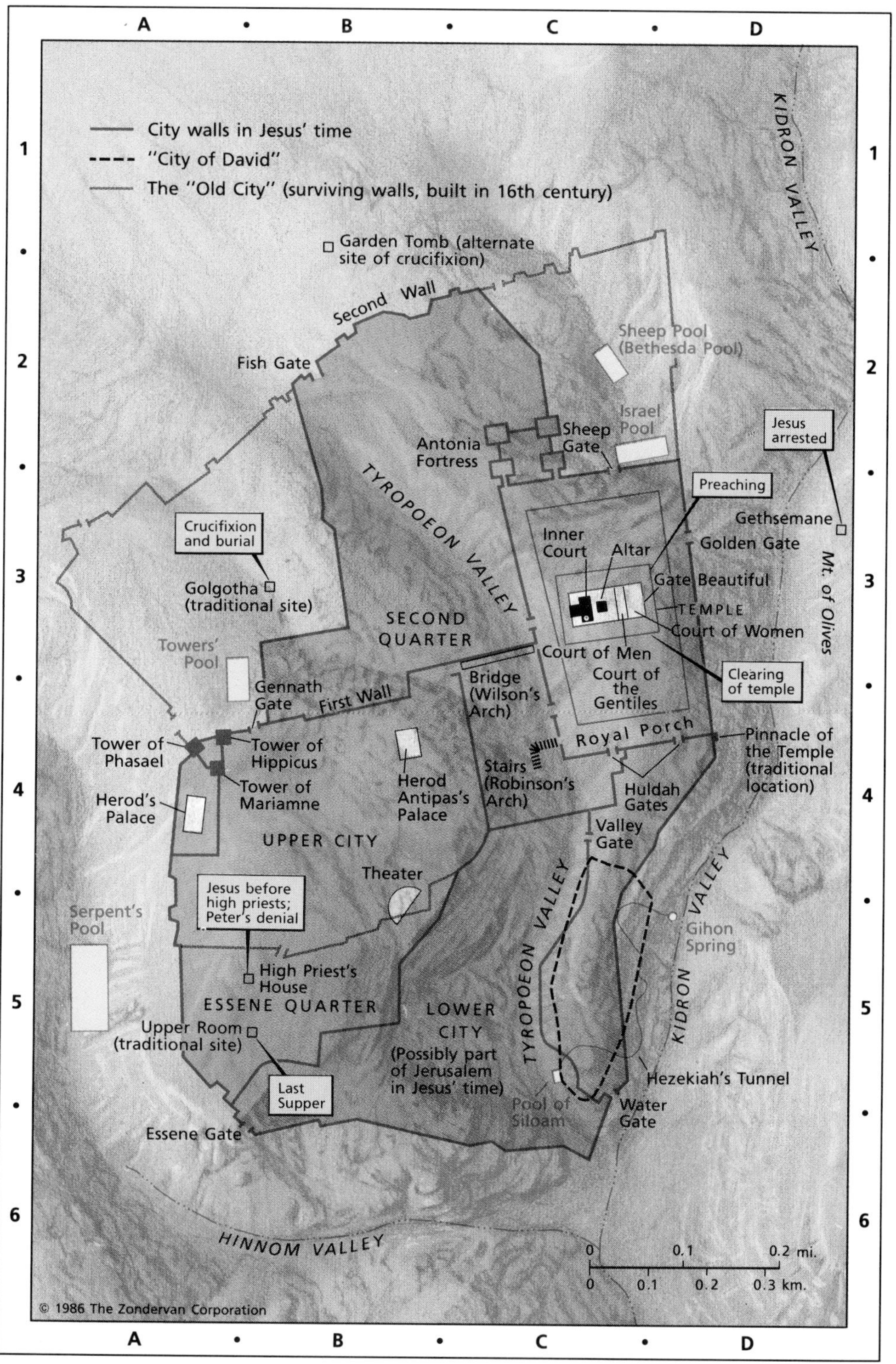
A
B
C
D
1
2
3
4
5
6
City walls in Jesus' time
"City of David"
The "Old City" (surviving walls, built in 16th century)
KIDRON VALLEY
Garden Tomb (alternate site of crucifixion)
Second Wall
Sheep Pool (Bethesda Pool)
Fish Gate
Israel Pool
Jesus arrested
Antonia Fortress
Sheep Gate
TYROPOEON VALLEY
Preaching
Gethsemane
Crucifixion and burial
Inner Court
Altar
Golden Gate
Mt. of Olives
Golgotha (traditional site)
Gate Beautiful
TEMPLE
SECOND QUARTER
Court of Women
Towers' Pool
Court of Men
Court of the Gentiles
Clearing of temple
Gennath Gate
First Wall
Bridge (Wilson's Arch)
Royal Porch
Pinnacle of the Temple (traditional location)
Tower of Phasael
Tower of Hippicus
Stairs (Robinson's Arch)
Tower of Mariamne
Herod Antipas's Palace
Huldah Gates
Herod's Palace
Valley Gate
UPPER CITY
Theater
Jesus before high priests; Peter's denial
Serpent's Pool
Gihon Spring
High Priest's House
ESSENE QUARTER
LOWER CITY (Possibly part of Jerusalem in Jesus' time)
TYROPOEON VALLEY
KIDRON VALLEY
Upper Room (traditional site)
Last Supper
Hezekiah's Tunnel
Pool of Siloam
Water Gate
Essene Gate
HINNOM VALLEY
0 0.1 0.2 mi.
0 0.1 0.2 0.3 km.

Map 9: **JESUS' MINISTRY**

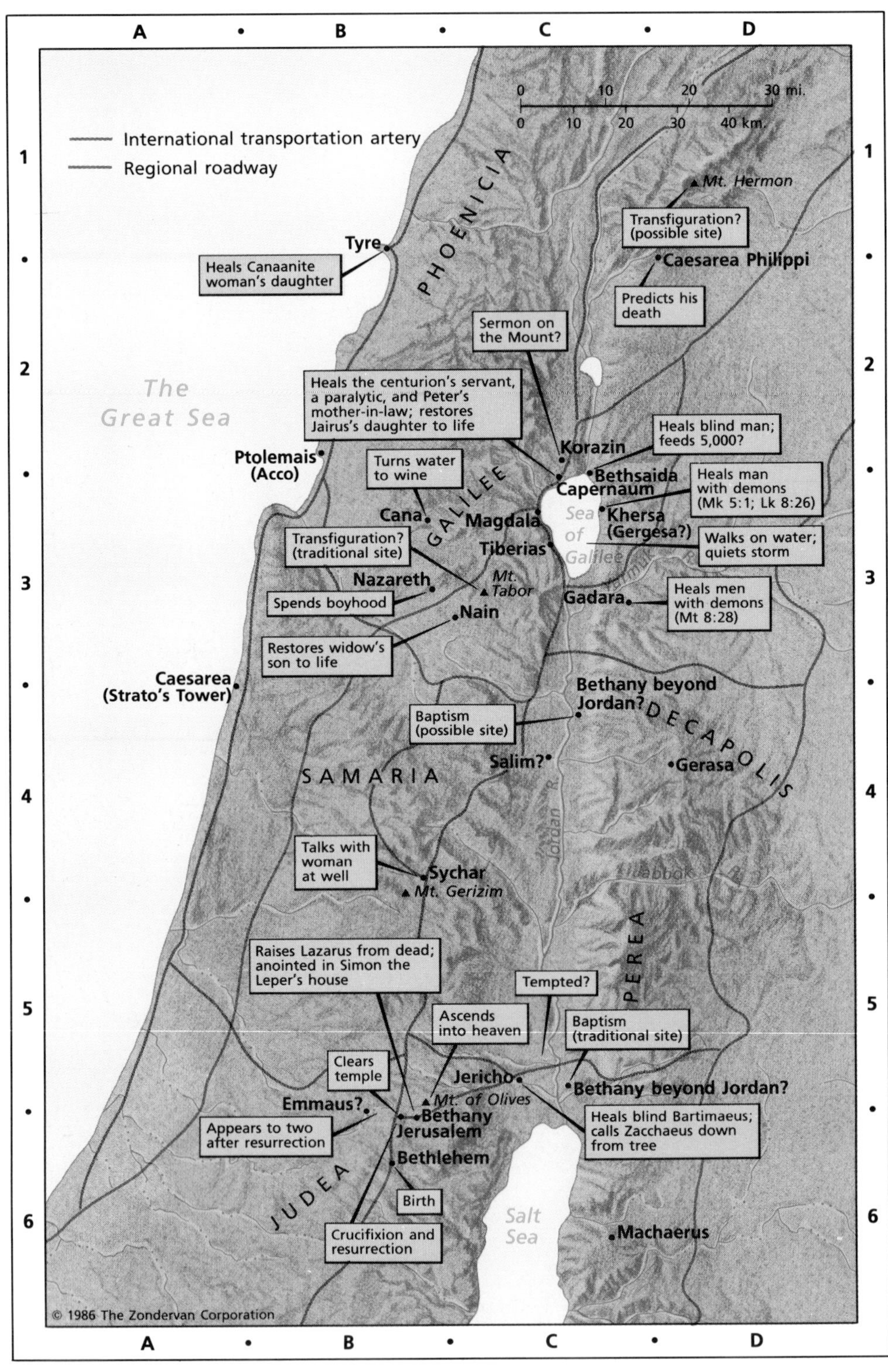

A • B • C • D
1 • 2 • 3 • 4 • 5 • 6 •
0 10 20 30 mi.
0 10 20 30 40 km.
International transportation artery
Regional roadway
PHOENICIA
Mt. Hermon
Transfiguration? (possible site)
Caesarea Philippi
Predicts his death
Tyre
Heals Canaanite woman's daughter
Sermon on the Mount?
The Great Sea
Heals the centurion's servant, a paralytic, and Peter's mother-in-law; restores Jairus's daughter to life
Heals blind man; feeds 5,000?
Korazin
Ptolemais (Acco)
Turns water to wine
Bethsaida
Capernaum
Heals man with demons (Mk 5:1; Lk 8:26)
GALILEE
Cana
Magdala
Sea of Galilee
Khersa (Gergesa?)
Transfiguration? (traditional site)
Tiberias
Walks on water; quiets storm
Nazareth
Mt. Tabor
Spends boyhood
Gadara
Heals men with demons (Mt 8:28)
Nain
Restores widow's son to life
Caesarea (Strato's Tower)
Bethany beyond Jordan?
DECAPOLIS
Baptism (possible site)
Salim?
Gerasa
SAMARIA
Jordan R.
Talks with woman at well
Sychar
Mt. Gerizim
PEREA
Raises Lazarus from dead; anointed in Simon the Leper's house
Tempted?
Ascends into heaven
Baptism (traditional site)
Clears temple
Jericho
Bethany beyond Jordan?
Emmaus?
Mt. of Olives
Appears to two after resurrection
Bethany
Jerusalem
Heals blind Bartimaeus; calls Zacchaeus down from tree
Bethlehem
JUDEA
Birth
Salt Sea
Machaerus
Crucifixion and resurrection

Map 10: **APOSTLES' EARLY TRAVELS**

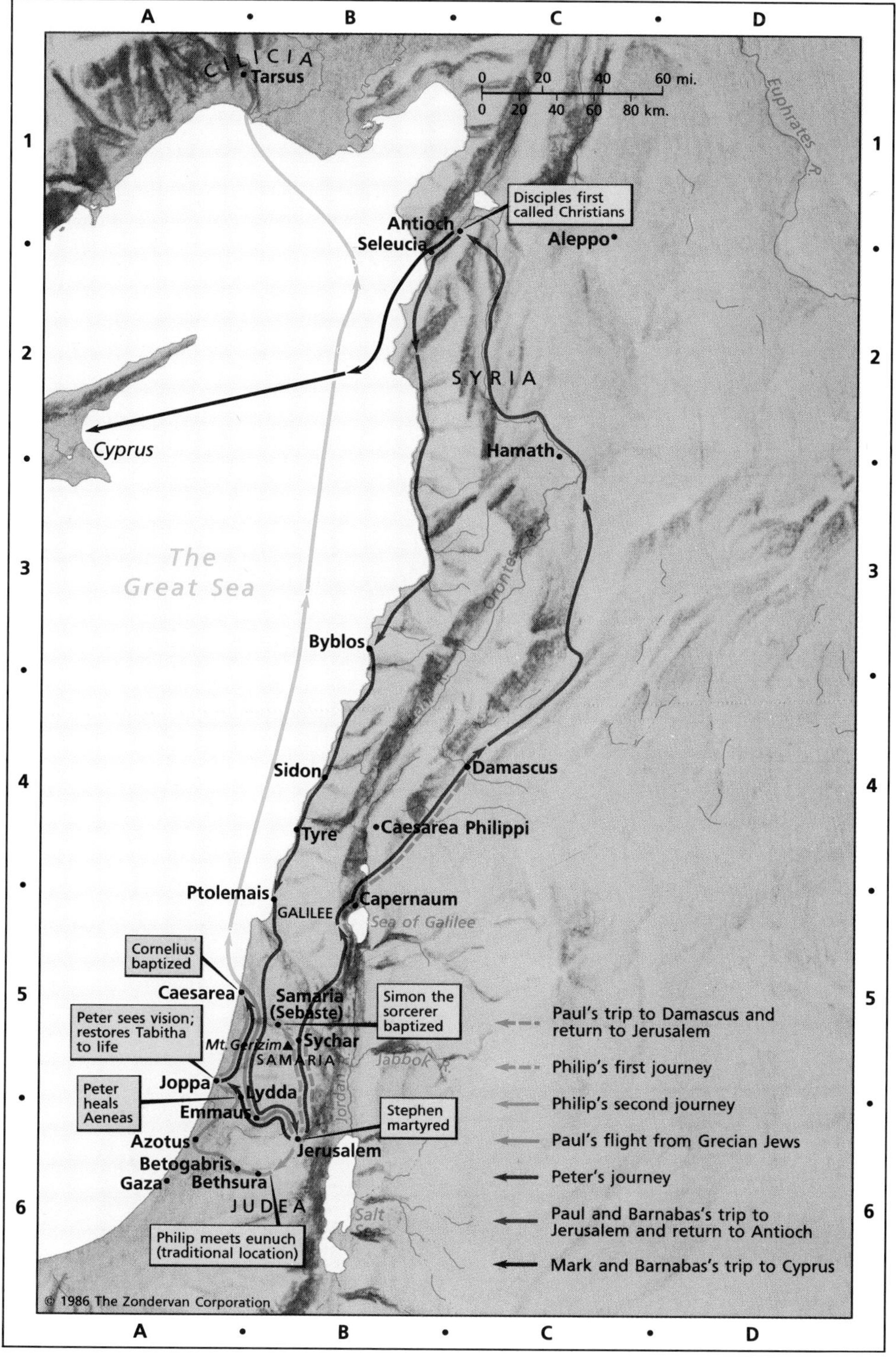

A B C D
1 2 3 4 5 6
CILICIA
Tarsus
0 20 40 60 mi.
0 20 40 60 80 km.
Euphrates R.
Disciples first called Christians
Antioch
Seleucia
Aleppo
SYRIA
Cyprus
Hamath
The Great Sea
Orontes R.
Byblos
Sidon
Damascus
Tyre
Caesarea Philippi
Ptolemais
Capernaum
GALILEE
Sea of Galilee
Cornelius baptized
Caesarea
Samaria (Sebaste)
Simon the sorcerer baptized
Peter sees vision; restores Tabitha to life
Mt. Gerizim
Sychar
SAMARIA
Jabbok
Joppa
Lydda
Peter heals Aeneas
Emmaus
Jordan
Stephen martyred
Azotus
Jerusalem
Betogabris
Gaza
Bethsura
JUDEA
Salt Sea
Philip meets eunuch (traditional location)
Paul's trip to Damascus and return to Jerusalem
Philip's first journey
Philip's second journey
Paul's flight from Grecian Jews
Peter's journey
Paul and Barnabas's trip to Jerusalem and return to Antioch
Mark and Barnabas's trip to Cyprus

Map 11: **PAUL'S MISSIONARY JOURNEYS**

A
B
C
D
1
2
3
4
5
6
GERMANIA
GALLIA
DALMATIA
Adriatic Sea
ITALY
Corsica
Rome
Forum of Appius
Three Taverns
Puteoli
Sardinia
MACED
Berea
Tyrrhenian Sea
EPIRUS
Rhegium
Ionian Sea
Sicily
Syracuse
NUMIDIA
Malta
AFRICA
The
TRIPOLITANIA
First Missionary Journey (A.D. 46–48)
Second Missionary Journey (A.D. 49–52)
Third Missionary Journey (A.D. 53–57)
Trip to Rome (A.D. 59–60)
© 1986 The Zondervan Corporation

E
F
G
H
1
2
3
4
5
6
DACIA
MOESIA
THRACE
Black Sea
BITHYNIA AND PONTUS
GALATIA
CAPPADOCIA
COMMAGENE
LYCAONIA
CILICIA
Philippi
Neapolis
Amphipolis
Apollonia
Samothrace
Thessalonica
Mt. Olympus
Troas
Assos
Mitylene
Aegean Sea
MYSIA
Pergamum
Thyatira
ASIA
Sardis
Philadelphia
Kios
Smyrna
LYDIA
Delphi
Corinth
Athens
Samos
Ephesus
PHRYGIA
Laodicea
Colosse
Pisidian Antioch
Iconium
Lystra
Derbe
Tarsus
Issus
Euphrates R.
Cenchrea
Sparta
Miletus
Patmos
Cos
Cnidus
PISIDIA
Attalia
PAMPHYLIA
Perga
LYCIA
Patara
Myra
Rhodes
Antioch
Aleppo
Seleucia
SYRIA
Cyprus
Salamis
Paphos
Phoenix
Crete
Lasea
Salmone
Fair Havens
Sidon
PHOENICIA
ABILENE
Damascus
Tyre
Ptolemais
Caesarea
Jordan R.
JUDEA
Jerusalem
Salt Sea
ARABIA
Great Sea
CYRENAICA
EGYPT
Nile R.
Red Sea
0
100
200 mi.
0
100
200
300 km.

Map 12: THE WORLD TODAY

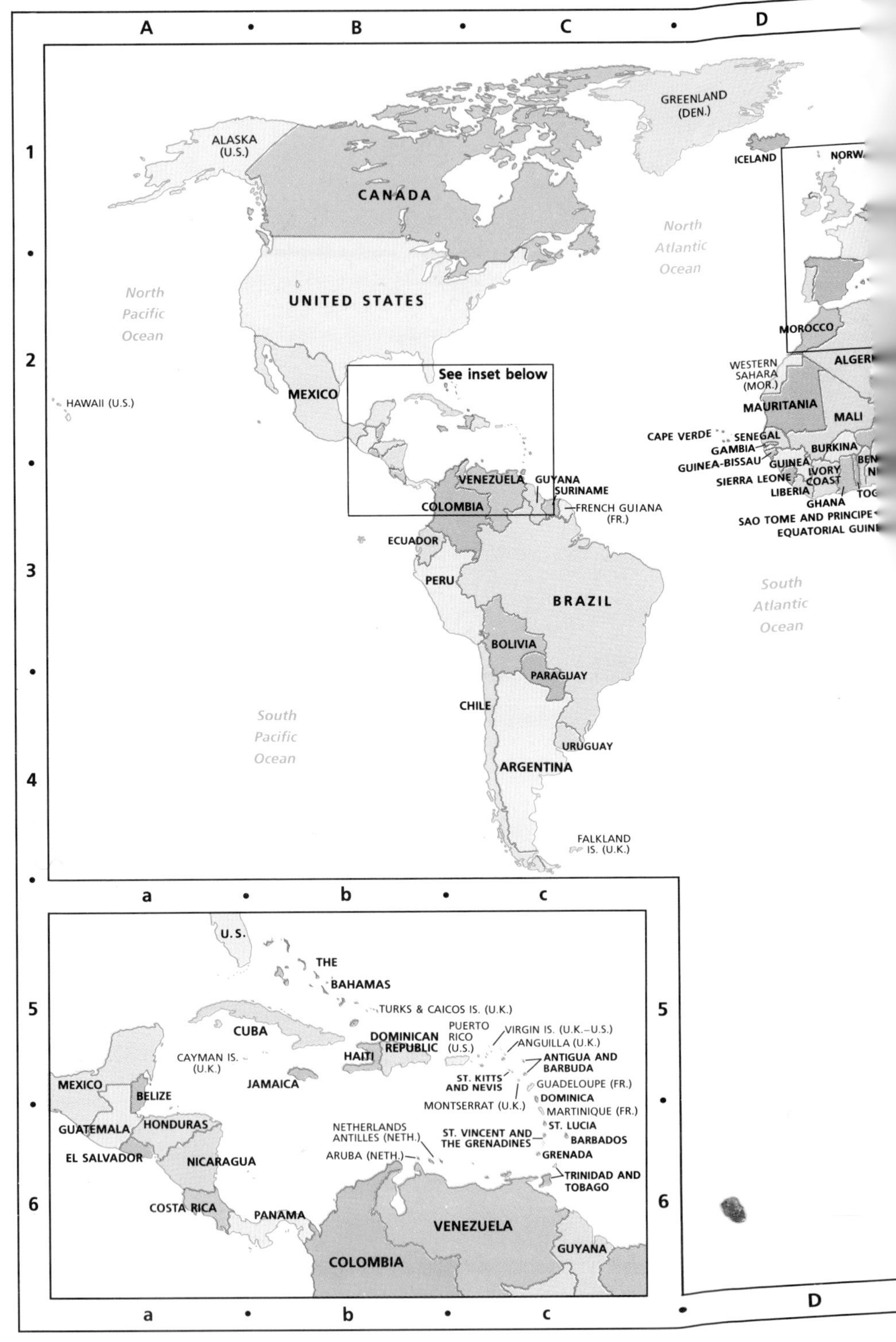

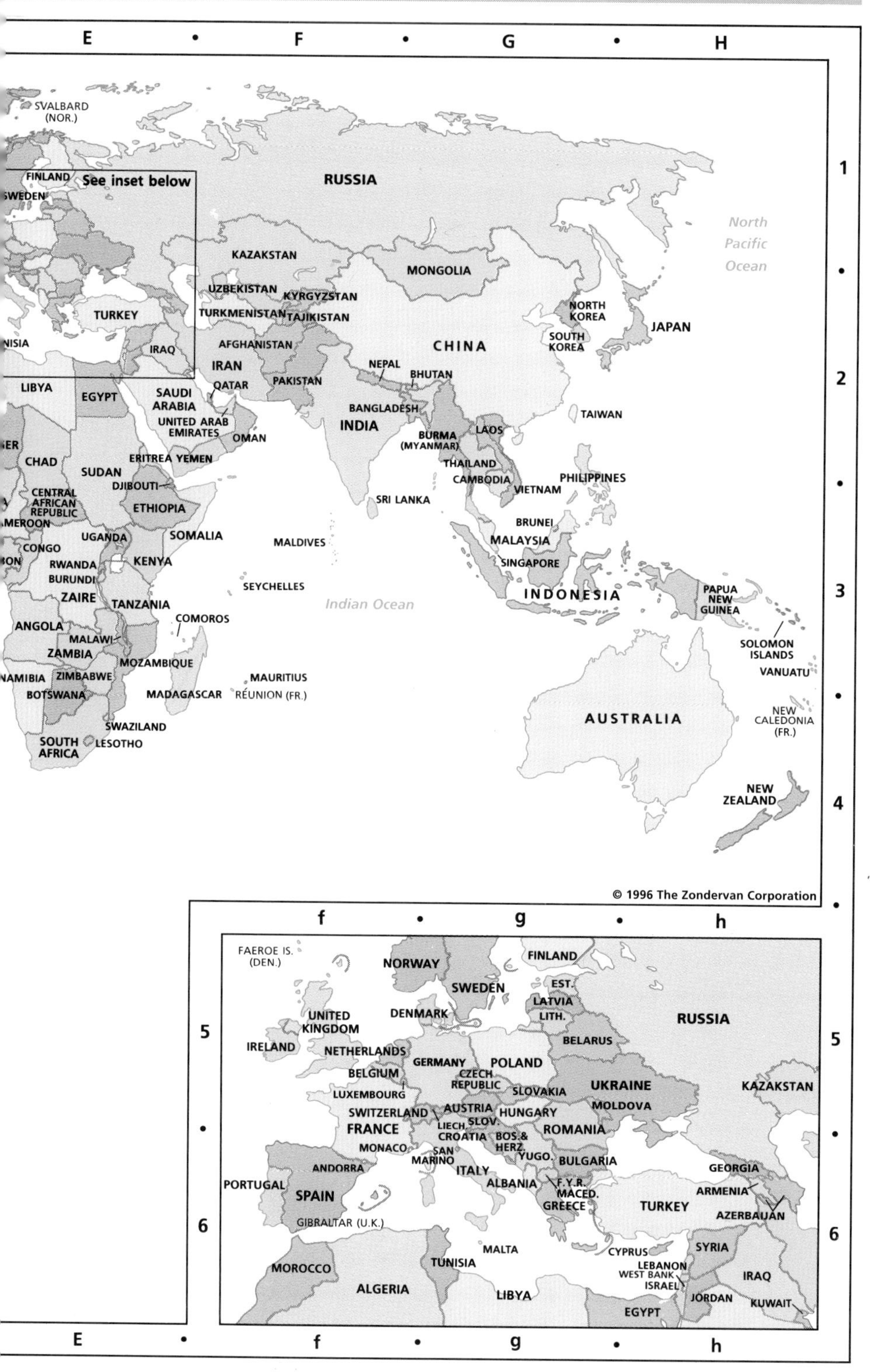

E
F
G
H
1
2
3
4
5
6
f
g
h
SVALBARD (NOR.)
FINLAND
See inset below
SWEDEN
RUSSIA
KAZAKSTAN
MONGOLIA
UZBEKISTAN
KYRGYZSTAN
TURKMENISTAN
TAJIKISTAN
TURKEY
NORTH KOREA
SOUTH KOREA
JAPAN
North Pacific Ocean
AFGHANISTAN
IRAQ
IRAN
CHINA
NEPAL
BHUTAN
PAKISTAN
LIBYA
EGYPT
SAUDI ARABIA
QATAR
BANGLADESH
INDIA
TAIWAN
UNITED ARAB EMIRATES
OMAN
BURMA (MYANMAR)
LAOS
CHAD
SUDAN
ERITREA
YEMEN
THAILAND
CAMBODIA
VIETNAM
PHILIPPINES
DJIBOUTI
CENTRAL AFRICAN REPUBLIC
ETHIOPIA
SRI LANKA
BRUNEI
CONGO
UGANDA
SOMALIA
MALDIVES
MALAYSIA
RWANDA
KENYA
SINGAPORE
BURUNDI
ZAIRE
TANZANIA
SEYCHELLES
Indian Ocean
INDONESIA
PAPUA NEW GUINEA
ANGOLA
COMOROS
MALAWI
ZAMBIA
SOLOMON ISLANDS
MOZAMBIQUE
ZIMBABWE
MAURITIUS
VANUATU
BOTSWANA
MADAGASCAR
RÉUNION (FR.)
AUSTRALIA
NEW CALEDONIA (FR.)
SWAZILAND
SOUTH AFRICA
LESOTHO
NEW ZEALAND
© 1996 The Zondervan Corporation
FAEROE IS. (DEN.)
NORWAY
FINLAND
SWEDEN
EST.
LATVIA
LITH.
UNITED KINGDOM
DENMARK
RUSSIA
IRELAND
BELARUS
NETHERLANDS
GERMANY
POLAND
BELGIUM
CZECH REPUBLIC
UKRAINE
KAZAKSTAN
LUXEMBOURG
SLOVAKIA
SWITZERLAND
AUSTRIA
MOLDOVA
HUNGARY
LIECH.
SLOV.
FRANCE
CROATIA
BOS.& HERZ.
ROMANIA
MONACO
SAN MARINO
YUGO.
BULGARIA
ANDORRA
ITALY
GEORGIA
PORTUGAL
ALBANIA
F.Y.R. MACED.
ARMENIA
SPAIN
GREECE
TURKEY
AZERBAIJAN
GIBRALTAR (U.K.)
MALTA
CYPRUS
SYRIA
TUNISIA
LEBANON
MOROCCO
WEST BANK
IRAQ
ISRAEL
ALGERIA
LIBYA
JORDAN
KUWAIT
EGYPT

Map 13: **ROMAN EMPIRE**

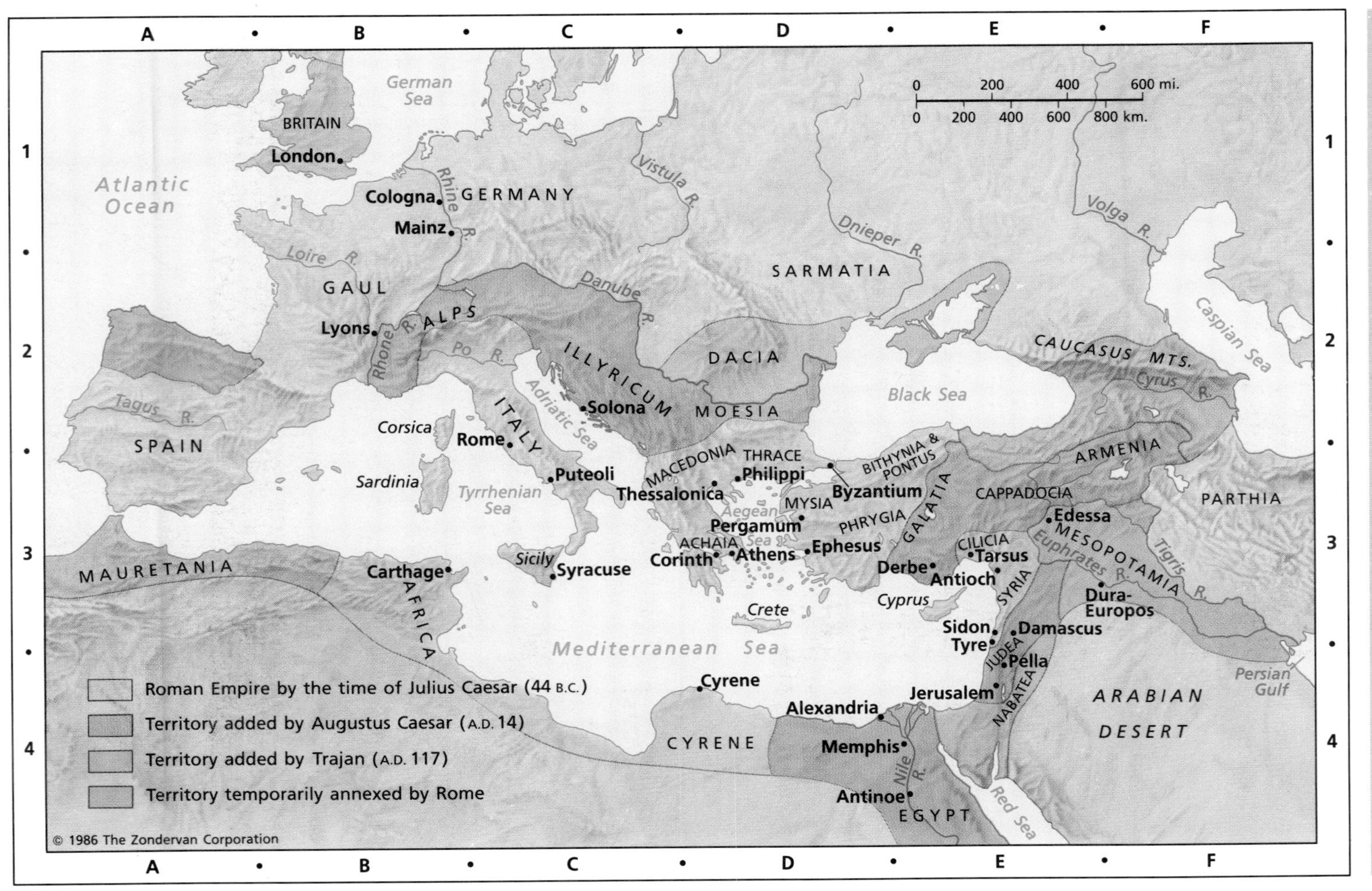